AN ETYMOLOGICAL DICTIONARY

OF THE

ENGLISH LANGUAGE

AN

ETYMOLOGICAL DICTIONARY

OF THE

ENGLISH LANGUAGE

BY THE

REV. WALTER W. SKEAT, Litt.D., D.C.L., LL.D., Ph.D., F.B.A.

ELRINGTON AND BOSWORTH PROFESSOR OF ANGLO-SAXON IN THE UNIVERSITY OF CAMBRIDGE
AND FELLOW OF CHRIST'S COLLEGE

NEW EDITION REVISED AND ENLARGED

'Step after step the ladder is ascended.'
GEORGE HERBERT, *Jacula Prudentum.*

'Labour with what zeal we will,
Something still remains undone.'
LONGFELLOW, *Birds of Passage.*

OXFORD
AT THE CLARENDON PRESS

Oxford University Press, Walton Street, Oxford OX2 6DP

OXFORD LONDON GLASGOW
NEW YORK TORONTO MELBOURNE WELLINGTON
IBADAN NAIROBI DAR ES SALAAM LUSAKA CAPE TOWN
KUALA LUMPUR SINGAPORE JAKARTA HONG KONG TOKYO
DELHI BOMBAY CALCUTTA MADRAS KARACHI

ISBN 0 19 863104 9

Impression of 1978
First Edition 1879–1882

Printed in Great Britain
at the University Press, Oxford
by Vivian Ridler
Printer to the University

CONTENTS.

PREFACE TO THE NEW AND REVISED EDITION

It is now more than a quarter of a century since the first edition of the present work was published. It was hardly possible for me to ascertain, at that date, that the time of its publication was not a very favourable one; it would, perhaps, have been better to have deferred its appearance for a few years, owing to the great advances that were being made, just at that period, in the methods of comparative philology. The whole system of estimating the vowel-sounds has since been completely reconsidered, and the history of their phonetic values, in particular, is now regarded in a very different light.

The chief writers on philology of that period, notably Curtius, Fick, Schleicher, and Vaniček agreed in the view, now known to be erroneous, that the primitive Indogermanic language had but three short primary vowels, viz. *a*, *i*, and *u*. This strange theory (for such we should now consider it) arose from the fact that the short primary vowels really were reduced to these three both in Gothic, which was justly regarded as being, *upon the whole*, the most primitive of the Teutonic (or Germanic) languages, and in Sanskrit, which was likewise known to possess many characteristics of extreme antiquity. But it is now recognized that more than half of the Indogermanic languages retain a primitive *e*, whilst just half of them retain a primitive *o*; so that the number of primary short vowels was really five, viz. *a*, *e*, *i*, *o*, *u*. The primitive form corresponding to the Gk. -τε, L. -*que*, Skt. *cha*, signifying 'and,' must have been **que*, rather than **qua*, because the Skt. *ch* is a palatal sound, due to the palatal vowel *e*, which once followed it. In other words, the Skt. *cha* was once **che*.

The advance due to the following up of this discovery (for it was nothing less) has been very considerable. The whole subject has been thoroughly revised, and the results are fully exhibited in the Comparative Grammar of the Indogermanic Languages by Karl Brugmann; as well as in the special German, Dutch, and Danish Etymological Dictionaries by Kluge, Franck, and Falk and Torp respectively. It is needless to add that the same correct principles have been adopted in the New English Dictionary.

Owing to the large number of corrections which the use of the newer method renders imperative, I took the opportunity, in 1901, of printing an entirely new edition of my Concise Etymological Dictionary, first issued in 1882, and partially corrected in four later editions; the result being that the edition of 1901 entirely supersedes all that preceded it.

The time has now arrived when it has become absolutely necessary, in the same way, to reprint my larger Dictionary also. Alterations have now been made, more or less, in almost every article except such as are of the simplest character.

Not only have the methods of comparative philology been greatly improved, but many valuable works on special subjects have appeared in recent years, as, for example, those by Kluge, Franck, Falk, Prellwitz, Bréal, Walde, Uhlenbeck, Godefroy, Hatzfeld, and others; not one of these was available in 1879-82. Above all, I have been much assisted by the admirable articles in the New English Dictionary, from the beginning of A down to Ph. For the latter part of the alphabet, I have mainly consulted the Century Dictionary, the editors of which, by the way, of course had access to the second edition of the present work.

The number of words dealt with has been considerably increased, and (exclusive of cross-references and the like) stands approximately thus :—A, 882 ; B, 865 ; C, 1434 ; D, 845 ; E, 575 ; F, 639 ; G, 518 ; H, 517 ; I, 724 ; J, 145 ; K, 108 ; L, 527 ; M, 782 ; N, 242 ; O, 376 ; P, 1231 ; Q, 104 ; R, 648 ; S, 1555 ; T, 821 ; U, 92 ; V, 265 ; W, 319 ; X, 2 ; Y, 45 ; Z, 25. The greatest number of these begins with S ; after which follow, in order, C, P, A, B, D, T, M, I, R, F, E, L, G, H, O, W, V, N, J, K, Q, U, Y, Z, X. Total number, 14,286.

I beg leave to refer the reader, for further information, to the former Prefaces here reprinted, the Brief Notes at p. xviii, the List of Books consulted, and the Key to the General Plan.

I am under obligation to a large number of correspondents and friends. In particular, I desire to mention the names of the Rev. A. L. Mayhew, of Oxford, who gave me so much assistance when revising my Concise Dictionary, and of P. Giles, M.A., of Emmanuel College, Cambridge, University Reader in Comparative Philology. My second daughter, Clara L. Skeat, has verified nearly all the references given in the third edition, and has in many ways rendered me efficient help.

CAMBRIDGE, *April 30*, 1909.

PREFACE TO THE FIRST EDITION

THE present work was undertaken with the intention of furnishing students with materials for a more scientific study of English etymology than is commonly to be found in previous works upon the subject. It is not intended to be always authoritative, nor are the conclusions arrived at to be accepted as final. It is rather intended as a guide to future writers, showing them in some cases what ought certainly to be accepted, and in other cases, it may be, what to avoid. The idea of it arose out of my own wants. I could find no single book containing the facts about a given word which it most concerns a student to know, whilst, at the same time, there exist numerous books containing information too important to be omitted. Thus Richardson's Dictionary is an admirable store-house of quotations illustrating such words as are of no great antiquity in the language, and his selected examples are the more valuable from the fact that he in general adds the exact reference[1]. Todd's Johnson likewise contains numerous well-chosen quotations, but perhaps no greater mistake was ever made than that of citing from authors like 'Dryden' or 'Addison' at large, without the slightest hint as to the whereabouts of the context. But in both of these works the etymology is commonly of the poorest description ; and it would probably be difficult to find a worse philologist than Richardson, who adopted many suggestions from Horne Tooke without inquiry, and was capable of saying that *hod* is 'perhaps *hoved*, *hov'd*, *hod*, past part. of *heafan* to heave.' It is easily ascertained that the AS. for *heave* is *hebban*, and that, being a strong verb, its past participle did not originally end in *-ed*.

It would be tedious to mention the numerous other books which help to throw such light on the *history* of words as is necessary for the right investigation of their etymology. The great defect of most of them is that they do not carry back that history far enough, and are very weak in the highly important Middle-English period. But the publications of the Camden Society, of the Early English

---

[1] I have verified a large number of these. Where I could not conveniently do so, I have added '(R.)' in parentheses at the end of the reference. I found, to my surprise, that the references to Chaucer are often utterly wrong, the numbers being frequently misprinted.

Text Society, and of many other printing clubs, have lately materially advanced our knowledge, and have rendered possible such excellent books of reference as are exemplified in Stratmann's Old English Dictionary and in the still more admirable but (as yet) incomplete 'Wörterbuch' by Eduard Mätzner. In particular, the study of phonetics, as applied to Early English pronunciation by Mr. Ellis and Mr. Sweet, and carefully carried out by nearly all students of Early English in Germany, has almost revolutionized the study of etymology as hitherto pursued in England. We can no longer consent to disregard vowel-sounds as if they formed no essential part of the word, which seems to have been the old doctrine; indeed, the idea is by no means yet discarded even by those who ought to know better.

On the other hand, we have, in Eduard Müller's Etymologisches Wörterbuch der Englischen Sprache[1], an excellent collection of etymologies and cognate words, but without any illustrations of the use or history of words, or any indication of the period when they first came into use. We have also Webster's Dictionary, with the etymologies as revised by Dr. Mahn, a very useful and comprehensive volume; but the plan of the work does not allow of much explanation of a purely philological character.

It is many years since a new and comprehensive dictionary was first planned by the Philological Society, and we have now good hope that, under the able editorship of Dr. Murray, some portion of this great work may ere long see the light. For the illustration of the *history* of words, this will be all-important, and the etymologies will, I believe, be briefly but sufficiently indicated. It was chiefly with the hope of assisting in this national work, that, many years ago, I began collecting materials and making notes upon points relating to etymology. The result of such work, in a modified form, and with very large additions, is here offered to the reader. My object has been to clear the way for the improvement of the etymologies by a previous discussion of all the more important words, executed on a plan so far differing from that which will be adopted by Dr. Murray as not to interfere with his labours, but rather, as far as possible, to assist them. It will, accordingly, be found that I have studied brevity by refraining from any detailed account of the *changes of meaning* of words, except where absolutely necessary for purely etymological purposes. The numerous very curious and highly interesting examples of words which, especially in later times, took up new meanings will not, in general, be found here; and the definitions of words are only given in a very brief and bald manner, only the more usual senses being indicated. On the other hand, I have sometimes permitted myself to indulge in comments, discussions, and even suggestions and speculations, which would be out of place in a dictionary of the usual character. Some of these, where the results are right, will, I hope, save much future discussion and investigation; whilst others, where the results prove to be wrong, can be avoided and rejected. In one respect I have attempted considerably more than is usually done by the writers of works upon English etymology. I have endeavoured, where possible, to trace back words to their Aryan roots, by availing myself of the latest works upon comparative philology. In doing this, I have especially endeavoured to link one word with another, and the reader will find a perfect network of cross-references enabling him to collect all the forms of any given word of which various forms exist; so that many of the principal words in the Aryan languages can be thus traced. Instead of considering English as an isolated language, as is sometimes actually done, I endeavour, in every case, to exhibit its relation to cognate tongues; and as, by this process, considerable light is thrown upon English by Latin and Greek, so also, at the same time, considerable light is thrown upon Latin and Greek by Anglo-Saxon and Icelandic. Thus, whilst under the word *bite* will be found

---

[1] It is surprising that this book is not better known. If the writers of *some* of the current 'Etymological' Dictionaries had taken E. Müller for their guide, they might have doubled their accuracy and halved their labour.

a mention of the cognate Latin *findere*, conversely, under the word *fissure*, is given a cross-reference to *bite*. In both cases, reference is also made to the root BHID; and, by referring to this root (no. 240, on p. 738), some further account of it will be found, with further examples of allied words. It is only by thus comparing all the Aryan languages together, and by considering them as one harmonious whole, that we can get a clear conception of the original forms; a conception which must precede all theory as to how those forms came to be invented[1]. Another great advantage of the comparative method is that, though the present work is nominally one on *English* etymology, it is equally explicit, as far as it has occasion to deal with them, with regard to the related words in other languages; and may be taken as a guide to the etymology of many of the leading words in Latin and Greek, and to all the more important words in the various Scandinavian and Teutonic tongues.

I have chiefly been guided throughout by the results of my own experience. Much use of many dictionaries has shown me the exact points where an inquirer is often baffled, and I have especially addressed myself to the task of solving difficulties and passing beyond obstacles. Not inconsiderable has been the trouble of verifying references. A few examples will put this in a clear light.

Richardson has numerous references (to take a single case) to the Romaunt of the Rose. He probably used some edition in which the lines are not numbered; at any rate, he never gives an exact reference to it. The few references to it in Tyrwhitt's Glossary and in Stratmann do not help us very greatly. To find a particular word in this poem of 7,700 lines is often troublesome; but, in every case where I *wanted* the quotation, I have found and noted it. I can recall several half-hours spent in this particular work.

Another not very hopeful book in which to find one's place, is the Faerie Queene. References to this are usually given to the book and canto, and of these one or other is (in Richardson) occasionally incorrect; in every case, I have added the number of the stanza.

One very remarkable fact about Richardson's dictionary is that, in many cases, references are given only to obscure and late authors, when all the while the word occurs in Shakespeare. By keeping Dr. Schmidt's comprehensive Shakespeare Lexicon[2] always open before me, this fault has been easily remedied.

To pass on to matters more purely etymological. I have constantly been troubled with the vagueness and inaccuracy of words quoted, in various books, as specimens of Old English or foreign languages. The spelling of 'Anglo-Saxon' in some books is often simply outrageous. Accents are put in or left out at pleasure; impossible combinations of letters are given; the number of syllables is disregarded; and grammatical terminations have to take their chance. Words taken from Ettmüller are spelt with *ä* and *œ*; words taken from Bosworth are spelt with *æ* and *æ*[3], without any hint that the *ä* and *œ* of the former answer to *æ* and *é* in the latter. I do not wish to give examples of these things; they are so abundant that they may easily be found by the curious. In many cases, writers of 'etymological' dictionaries do not trouble to learn even the alphabets of the languages cited from, or the most elementary grammatical facts. I have met with supposed Welsh words spelt with a *v*, with Swedish words spelt with *æ*, with Danish infinitives ending in *-a*[4], with Icelandic infinitives in *-an*, and so on; the only languages correctly spelt being Latin and Greek, and commonly French and German. It is clearly assumed, and probably with safety, that most readers will not detect misspellings beyond this limited range.

---

[1] I refrain from discussing theories of language in this work, contenting myself with providing materials for aiding in such discussion.

[2] To save time, I have seldom verified Dr. Schmidt's references, believing them to be, in general, correct. I have seldom so trusted *any other* book.

[3] *Sic*; printers often make *æ* do duty for *é*. I suspect that *é* is seldom provided for.

[4] Todd's Johnson, s. v. *Boll*, has 'Su. Goth. *bulna*, Dan. *bulner*.' Here *bulna* is the Swedish infinitive, whilst *bulner* is the first person of the present tense. Similar jumbles abound.

But this was not a matter which troubled me long. At a very early stage of my studies, I perceived clearly enough, that the spelling given by some authorities is not necessarily to be taken as the true one ; and it was then easy to make allowances for possible errors, and to refer to some book with reasonable spellings, such as E. Müller, or Mahn's Webster, or Wedgwood. A little research revealed far more curious pieces of information than the citing of words in impossible or mistaken spellings. Statements abound which it is difficult to account for except on the supposition that it must once have been usual to *manufacture* words for the *express purpose* of deriving others from them. To take an example, I open Todd's Johnson at random, and find that under *bolster* is cited 'Gothic *bolster*, a heap of hay.' Now the fragments of Gothic that have reached us are very precious but very insufficient, and they certainly contain no such word as *bolster*. Neither is *bolster* a Gothic spelling. *Holster* is represented in Gothic by *hulistr*, so that *bolster* might, possibly, be *bulistr*. In any case, as the word certainly does not occur, it can only be a pure invention, due to some blunder ; the explanation 'a heap of hay' is a happy and graphic touch, regarded in the light of a fiction, but is out of place in a work of reference.

A mistake of this nature would not greatly matter if such instances were rare ; but the extraordinary part of the matter is that they are extremely common, owing probably to the trust reposed by former writers in such etymologists as Skinner and Junius, men who did good work in their day, but whose statements require careful verification in this nineteenth century. What Skinner was capable of, I have shown in my introduction to the reprint of Ray's Glossary published for the English Dialect Society. It is sufficient to say that the net result is this ; that words cited in etymological dictionaries (with very few exceptions) cannot be accepted without verification. Not only do we find puzzling misspellings, but we find actual fictions ; words are said to be 'Anglo-Saxon' that are not to be found in the existing texts ; 'Gothic' words are constructed for the mere purpose of 'etymology ;' Icelandic words have meanings assigned to them which are incredible or misleading ; and so on of the rest.

Another source of trouble is that, when real words are cited, they are wrongly explained. Thus, in Todd's Johnson, we find a derivation of *bond* from AS. '*bond*, bound.' Now *bond* is not strictly Anglo-Saxon, but an Early English form, signifying 'a band,' and is not a past participle at all ; the AS. for 'bound' being *gebunden*. The error is easily traced ; Dr. Bosworth cites '*bond*, bound, ligatus' from Somner's Dictionary, whence it was also copied into Lye's Dictionary in the form: '*bond*, ligatus, obligatus, *bound*.' Where Somner found it, is a mystery indeed, as it is absurd on the face of it. We should take a man to be a very poor German scholar who imagined that *band*, in German, is a past participle ; but when the same mistake is made by Somner, we find that it is copied by Lye, copied by Bosworth (who, however, marks it as Somner's), copied into Todd's Johnson, amplified by Richardson into the misleading statement that '*bond* is the past tense [1] and past participle of the verb to *bind*,' and has doubtless been copied by numerous other writers who have wished to come at their etymologies with the least trouble to themselves. It is precisely this continual reproduction of errors which so disgraces many English works, and renders investigation so difficult.

But when I had grasped the facts that spellings are often false, that words can be invented, and that explanations are often wrong, I found that worse remained behind. The science of philology is comparatively modern, so that our earlier writers had no means of ascertaining principles that are now well established, and, instead of proceeding by rule, had to go blindly by guesswork, thus sowing crops of errors which have sprung up and multiplied till it requires very careful investigation

---

[1] *Bond* is a form of the *past tense* in Middle English, and indeed the sb. *bond* is itself derived from the 'second grade' found in the AS. pt. t. *band* ; but *bond* is certainly not 'the past participle.'

to enable a modern writer to avoid all the pitfalls prepared for him by the false suggestions which he meets with at every turn. Many derivations that have been long current and are even generally accepted will not be found in this volume, for the plain reason that I have found them to be false; I think I may at any rate believe myself to be profoundly versed in most of the old fables of this character, and I shall only say, briefly, that the reader need not assume me to be ignorant of them because I do not mention them. The most extraordinary fact about comparative philology is that, whilst its principles are well understood by numerous students in Germany and America, they are far from being well known in England, so that it is easy to meet even with classical scholars who have no notion what ‘Grimm’s law’ really means, and who are entirely at a loss to understand why the English *care* has no connexion with the Latin *cura*, nor the English *whole* with the Greek ὅλος, nor the French *charité* with the Greek χάρις. Yet for the understanding of these things nothing more is needed than a knowledge of the relative values of the letters of the English, Latin, and Greek alphabets. A knowledge of these alphabets is strangely neglected at our public schools; whereas a few hours carefully devoted to each would save scholars from innumerable blunders, and a boy of sixteen who understood them would be far more than a match, in matters of etymology, for a man of fifty who did not. In particular, some knowledge of the vowel-sounds is essential. Modern philology will, in future, turn more and more upon phonetics; and the truth now confined to a very few will at last become general, that the vowel is commonly the very life, the most essential part of the word, and that, just as pre-scientific etymologists frequently went wrong because they considered the consonants as being of small consequence and the vowels of none at all, the scientific student of the present day may hope to go right, if he considers the consonants as being of great consequence and the vowels as all-important.

The foregoing remarks are, I think, sufficient to show my reasons for undertaking the work, and the nature of some of the difficulties which I have endeavoured to encounter or remove. I now proceed to state explicitly what the reader may expect to find.

Each article begins with a word, the etymology of which is to be sought. When there are one or more words *with the same spelling*, a number is added, for the sake of distinction in the case of future reference. This is a great convenience when such words are cited in the ‘List of Aryan Roots’ and in the various indexes at the end of the volume, besides saving trouble in making cross-references.

After the word comes a brief definition, merely as a mark whereby to identify the word.

Next follows an exact statement of the actual (or probable) language whence the word is taken, with an account of the channel or channels through which it reached us. Thus the word ‘Canopy’ is marked ‘(F.—Ital.—L.—Gk.),’ to be read as ‘French, from Italian, from Latin, from Greek;’ that is to say, the word is ultimately Greek, whence it was borrowed, first by Latin, secondly by Italian (from the Latin), thirdly by French (from the Italian), and lastly by English (from French). The endeavour to distinguish the exact history of each word in this manner conduces greatly to care and attention, and does much to render the etymology correct. I am not aware that any attempt of the kind has previously been made, except very partially; the usual method, of offering a heap of more or less related words in one confused jumble, is much to be deprecated, and is often misleading [1].

After the exact statement of the source, follow a few quotations. These are intended to indicate the period at which the word was borrowed, or else the usual Middle-English forms. When the word is not a very old one, I have given one or two of the earliest quotations which I have been able to find, though I have here preferred quotations from well-known authors to somewhat earlier ones from

[1] In Webster’s dictionary, the etymology of *canopy* is well and sufficiently given, but many articles are very confused. Thus *Course* is derived from ‘ F. *cours*, *course*, Prov. *cors*, *corsa*, Ital. *corso*, *corsa*, Span. and Port. *curso*, Lat. *cursus*,’ &c. Here the Latin form should have followed the French. With the Prov., Ital., Span., and Port. forms we have absolutely nothing to do.

more obscure writers. These quotations are intended to exemplify the history of the *form* of the word, and are frequently of great chronological utility; though it is commonly sufficient to indicate the period of the world's first use within half a century. By way of example, I may observe that *canon* is not derived from F. *canon*, but appears in King Ælfred, and was taken immediately from the Latin. I give the reference under *Canon*, to Ælfred's translation of Beda, b. iv. c. 24, adding 'Bosworth' at the end. This means that I took the reference from Bosworth's Dictionary, and had not, at the moment, the means of verifying the quotation (I now find it is quite correct, occurring on p. 598 of Smith's edition, at l. 13). When no indication of the authority for the quotation is given, it commonly means that I have verified it myself; except in the case of Shakespeare, where I have usually trusted to Dr. Schmidt.

A chief feature of the present work, and one which has entailed enormous labour, is that, whenever I cite old forms or foreign words, from which any given English word is derived or with which it is connected, I have actually verified the spellings and significations of these words by help of the dictionaries of which a list is given in the 'Key to the General Plan' immediately preceding the letter *A*. I have done this in order to avoid two common errors; (1) that of misspelling the words cited [1], and (2) that of misinterpreting them. The exact source or edition whence every word is copied is, in every case, precisely indicated, it being understood that, when no author is specified, the word is taken from the book mentioned in the 'Key.' Thus every statement made may be easily verified, and I can assure those who have had no experience in such investigations that this is no small matter. I have frequently found that some authors manipulate the meanings of words to suit their own convenience, when not tied down in this manner; and, not wishing to commit the like mistake, which approaches too nearly to dishonesty to be wittingly indulged in, I have endeavoured by this means to remove the temptation of being led to swerve from the truth in this particular. Yet it may easily be that fancy has sometimes led me astray in places where there is room for some speculation, and I must therefore beg the reader, whenever he has any doubts, to verify the statements for himself (as, in general, he easily may), and he will then see the nature of the premises from which the conclusions have been drawn. In many instances it will be found that the meanings are given, for the sake of brevity, less fully than they might have been, and that the arguments for a particular view are often far stronger than they are represented to be.

The materials collected by the Philological Society will doubtless decide many debatable points, and will definitely confirm or refute, in many cases, the results here arrived at. It is, perhaps, proper to point out that French words are more often cited from Cotgrave than in their modern forms. Very few good words have been borrowed by us from French at a late period, so that modern French is not of much use to an English etymologist. In particular, I have intentionally disregarded the modern French accentuation. To derive our word *recreation* from the F. *récréation* gives a false impression; for it was certainly borrowed from French before the accents were added.

In the case of verbs and substantives (or other mutually related words), considerable pains have been taken to ascertain and to point out whether the verb has been formed from the substantive, or whether, conversely, the substantive is derived from the verb. This often makes a good deal of difference to the etymology. Thus, when Richardson derives the adj. *full* from the verb to *fill*, he reverses the fact, and shows that he was entirely innocent of any knowledge of the relative value of the Anglo-Saxon vowels. Similar mistakes are common even in treating of Greek and Latin. Thus, when Richardson says that the Latin *laborare* is ' of uncertain etymology,' he must have meant the remark to apply to the sb. *labor*. The etymology of *laborare* is obvious, viz. from that substantive.

---

[1] With all this care, mistakes creep in; see the Errata. But I feel sure that they are not very numerous.

The numerous cross-references will enable the student, in many cases, to trace back words to the Aryan root, and will frequently lead to additional information. Whenever a word has a 'doublet,' i. e. appears in a varying form, a note is made of the fact at the end of the article ; and a complete list of these will be found in the Appendix.

The Appendix contains a list of Prefixes, a general account of Suffixes, a List of Aryan Roots, and Lists of Homonyms and Doublets. Besides these, I have attempted to give lists showing the Distribution of the Sources of English. As these lists are far more comprehensive than any which I have been able to find in other books, and are subdivided into classes in a much stricter manner than has ever yet been attempted, I may crave some indulgence for the errors in them.

From the nature of the work, I have been unable to obtain much assistance in it. The mechanical process of preparing the copy for press, and the subsequent revision of proofs, have entailed upon me no inconsiderable amount of labour ; and the constant shifting from one language to another has required patience and attention. The result is that a few annoying oversights have occasionally crept in, due mostly to a brief lack of attention on the part of eye or brain. In again going over the whole work for the purpose of making an epitome of it, I have noticed some of these errors, and a list of them is given in the Errata. Other errors have been kindly pointed out to me, which are also noted in the Addenda ; and I beg leave to thank those who have rendered me such good service. I may also remark that letters have reached me which cannot be turned to any good account, and it is sometimes surprising that a few correspondents should be so eager to manifest their entire ignorance of all philological principles. Such cases are, however, exceptional, and I am very anxious to receive, and to make use of, all reasonable suggestions. The experience gained in writing the first 'part' of the book, from A—D, proved of much service ; and I believe that errors are fewer near the end than near the beginning. Whereas I was at first inclined to trust too much to Brachet's Etymological French Dictionary, I now believe that Scheler is a better guide, and that I might have consulted Littré even more frequently than I have done. Near the beginning of the work, I had no copy of Littré of my own, nor of Palsgrave, nor of some other very useful books ; but experience soon showed what books were most necessary to be added to my very limited collection. In the study of English etymology, it often happens that instantaneous reference to some rather unexpected source is almost an absolute necessity, and it is somewhat difficult to make provision for such a call within the space of one small room. This is the real reason why some references to what may, to some students, be very familiar works, have been taken at second-hand. I have merely made the best use I could of the materials nearest at hand. But for this, the work would have been more often interrupted, and time would have been wasted which could ill be spared.

It is also proper to state that with many articles I am not satisfied. Those that presented no difficulty, and took up but little time, are probably the best and most certain. In very difficult cases, my usual rule has been not to spend more than three hours over one word. During that time, I made the best I could of it, and then let it go [1]. I hope it may be understood that my object in making this and other similar statements regarding my difficulties is merely to enable the reader to consult the book with the greater safety, and to enable him to form his own opinion as to how far it is to be trusted. My honest opinion is that those whose philological knowledge is but small may safely accept the results here given, since they may else do worse ; whilst advanced students will receive them with that caution which so difficult a study soon renders habitual.

One remark concerning the printing of the book is worth making. It is common for writers to

---

[1 This refers to the first preparation of the copy for the first edition. There has been much verification and further research since then.]

throw the blame of errors upon the printers, and there is in this a certain amount of truth in some instances. But illegible writing should also receive its fair portion of blame; and it is only just to place the fact on record, that I have frequently received from the press a first rough proof of a sheet of this work, abounding in words taken from a great many languages, in which not a single *printer's* error occurred of any kind whatever; and many others in which the errors were very trivial and unimportant, and seldom extended to the actual spelling.

I am particularly obliged to those who have kindly given me hints or corrections; Mr. Sweet's account of the word *left*, and his correction for the word *bless*, have been very acceptable, and I much regret that his extremely valuable collection of the *earliest* English vocabularies and other records is not yet published, as it will certainly yield valuable information. I am also indebted for some useful hints to Professor Cowell, and to the late Mr. Henry Nicol, whose knowledge of early French phonology was almost unrivalled. Also to Dr. Stratmann, and the Rev. A. L. Mayhew, of Oxford, for several corrections; to Professor Potwin, of Hudson, Ohio; to Dr. J. N. Grönland, of Stockholm, for some notes upon Swedish; to Dr. Murray, the Rev. O. W. Tancock, and the Rev. D. Silvan Evans, for various notes; and to several other correspondents who have kindly taken a practical interest in the work.

In some portions of the Appendix I have received very acceptable assistance. The preparation of the lists showing the Distribution of Words was entirely the work of others; I have done little more than revise them. For the word-lists from A—Literature, I am indebted to Miss Mantle, of Girton College; and for the lists from Litharge—Reduplicate, to A. P. Allsopp, Esq., of Trinity College, Cambridge. The rest was prepared by my eldest daughter, who also prepared the numerous examples of English words given in the List of Aryan Roots, and the List of Doublets. To Miss F. Whitehead I am indebted for the List of Homonyms.

To all the above-named and to other well-wishers I express my sincere thanks.

But I cannot take leave of a work which has closely occupied my time during the past four years without expressing the hope that it may prove of service, not only to students of comparative philology and of early English, but to all who are interested in the origin, history, and development of the noble language which is the common inheritance of all English-speaking peoples. It is to be expected that, owing to the increased attention which of late years has been given to the study of languages, many of the conclusions at which I have arrived may require important modification or even entire change; but I nevertheless trust that the use of this volume may tend, on the whole, to the suppression of such guesswork as entirely ignores all rules. I trust that it may, at the same time, tend to strengthen the belief that, as in all other studies, true results are only to be obtained by reasonable inferences from careful observations, and that the laws which regulate the development of language, though frequently complicated by the interference of one word with another, often present the most surprising examples of regularity. The speech of man is, in fact, influenced by physical laws, or in other words, by the working of divine power. It is therefore possible to pursue the study of language in a spirit of reverence similar to that in which we study what are called the works of nature; and by aid of that spirit we may gladly perceive a new meaning in the sublime line of our poet Coleridge, that

' Earth, with her thousand voices, praises God.'

CAMBRIDGE, *Sept.* 29, 1881.

PREFACE TO THE SECOND EDITION

In a work which, like the present undertaking, covers so much ground and deals with so many languages, it is very difficult to secure complete accuracy; it can, perhaps, at best be only aimed at. Several errors have been detected by myself, and kind friends have pointed out others. New facts are continually being brought to light; for the science of philology is, at this time, still rapidly progressive. Fortunately, everything tends in the direction of closer accuracy and greater certainty, and we may hope that the number of doubtful points will steadily diminish.

In particular, I am obliged to Mr. H. Wedgwood for his publication entitled 'Contested Etymologies in the Dictionary of the Rev. W. W. Skeat; London, Trübner and Co., 1882.' I have carefully read this book, and have taken from it several useful hints. In reconsidering the etymologies of the words which he treats, I have, in some cases, adopted his views either wholly or in part. In a few instances, he does not really contest what I have said, but notices something that I have left unsaid. For example, I omitted to state that he was the first person to point out the etymology of *wanion*; unfortunately, I did not observe his article on the subject, and had to rediscover the etymology for myself, with the same result. Hence the number of points on which we differ is now considerably reduced; and I think a further reduction might have been made if he could have seen his way, in like manner, to adopting views from me. I think that some of the etymologies of which he treats cannot fairly be said to be 'contested'; for there are cases in which he is opposed, not only to myself, but to every one else. Thus, with regard to the word *avoid*, he would have us derive the F. *vuide* (or *vide*), empty, from OHG. *wît* rather than from the Lat. *uiduus*; to which I would reply that, in a matter of *French* etymology, most scholars are quite content to accept the etymology given by Littré, Scheler, and Diez, in a case wherein they are all agreed and see no difficulty in the matter[1].

The List of Errata and Addenda, as given in the first edition, has been almost entirely rewritten. Most of the Errata (especially where they arose from misprints) have been corrected in the body of the work; and I am particularly obliged to Mr. C. E. Doble for several minute corrections, and for his kindness in closely regarding the accentuation of Greek words. The number of Additional Words in the present Addenda is about *two hundred*, whereas the list of Additional Words in the first edition is little more than *fifty*. I am much obliged to Mr. Charles Sweet for suggesting several useful additions, and especially for sending me some explanations of several legal terms, such as *assart, barrator, escrow, essoin*, and the like. I think that some of the best etymologies in the volume may be found in these additional articles, and I hope the reader will kindly remember to consult this supplement, commencing at p. 777, before concluding that he has seen all that I have to say upon any word he may be seeking for. Of course this supplement remains incomplete; there are literally no bounds to the English language.

I also gladly take the opportunity of gratefully acknowledging the assistance of the Rev. A. L. Mayhew, who not only sent me a large number of suggestions, but has much assisted me by reading the proof-sheets of the Addenda. I also beg leave to thank here the numerous correspondents who have kindly corrected individual words.

[¹ But *both* solutions are now rejected.]

I have also made some use of the curious book on Folk-Etymology by the Rev. A. S. Palmer, which is full of erudition and contains a large number of most useful and exact references. The author is not quite sound as to the quantity of the Anglo-Saxon vowels, and has, in some instances, attempted to connect words that are really unrelated ; thus, under *Hatter*, he connects AS. *hát*, hot, with Goth. *hatis*, hate. In many places I think the plan of his book has led him into multiplying unduly the number of 'corruptions'; so that caution is needful in consulting the book.

At the time of writing this, we are anxiously expecting the issue of the first part of Dr. Murray's great and comprehensive English Dictionary, founded on the materials collected by the Philological Society ; and I suppose it is hardly necessary to add that, if any of my results as to the etymology of such words as he has discussed are found not to agree with his, I at once submit to his careful induction from better materials and to the results of the assistance his work has received from many scholars. I have already had the benefit of some kindly assistance from him, as for example, in the case of the words *adjust, admiral, agnail, allay, alloy, almanack,* and *almond*.

Every day's experience helps to show how great and how difficult is the task of presenting results in a form such as modern scientific criticism will accept. Every slip is a lesson in humility, showing how much remains to be learnt. At the same time, I cannot close these few words of preface without hearty thanks to the many students, in many parts of the world, who have cheered me with kindly words and have found my endeavours helpful.

CAMBRIDGE, *December* 21, 1883.

PREFACE TO THE THIRD EDITION

IN this Third Edition a few changes have been made in cases where the etymology previously given was certainly wrong. More might have been made if the spare time at my disposal had sufficed for making a more careful revision of the work.

CAMBRIDGE, *November* 18, 1897.

BRIEF NOTES UPON THE LANGUAGES CITED IN THE DICTIONARY

ENGLISH. Words marked (E.) are pure English, and form the true basis of the language. They can commonly be traced back for about a thousand years, but their true origin is altogether pre-historic and of great antiquity. Many of them, such as *father*, *mother*, &c., have corresponding cognate forms in Sanskrit, Greek, and Latin. These forms are collateral, and the true method of comparison is by placing them side by side. Thus *father* is no more 'derived' from the Sanskrit *pitā* than the Skt. *pitā* is 'derived' from the English *father*. Both are descended from a common Indo-germanic type, and that is all. Sometimes Sanskrit is said to be an 'elder sister' to English; the word 'elder' would be better omitted. Sanskrit has doubtless suffered less change, but even twin sisters are not always precisely alike, and, in the course of many years, one may come to look younger than the other. The symbol **+** is particularly used to call attention to collateral descent, as distinct from borrowing or derivation. English forms belonging to the 'Middle-English' period are marked 'ME.' This period extends, roughly speaking, from about 1200 to 1460, both these dates being arbitrarily chosen. Middle-English consisted of three dialects, Northern, Midland, and Southern; the dialect depends upon the author cited. The spellings of the 'ME.' words are usually given in the actual forms found in the editions referred to, not always in the theoretical forms as given by Stratmann, though these are, etymologically, more correct. Those who possess Stratmann's Dictionary will do well to consult it.

Words belonging to English of an earlier date than about 1150 or 1200 are marked 'AS.', i.e. Anglo-Saxon. Some have asked why they have not been marked as 'OE.', i.e. Oldest English. Against this, there are two reasons. The first is, that 'OE.' would be read as 'Old English,' and this term has been used so vaguely, and has so often been made to include 'ME.' as well, that it has ceased to be distinctive, and has become comparatively useless. The second and more important reason is that, unfortunately, Oldest English and Anglo-Saxon are not coextensive. The former consisted, in all probability, of three main dialects, but the remains of two of these are very scanty. Of Old Northern, we have little left beyond the Northumbrian versions of the Gospels and the glosses in the Durham Ritual: of Old Midland (or Mercian) we possess the Rushworth gloss to St. Matthew's Gospel, the important 'Corpus Glossary,' and the glosses to the 'Vespasian Psalter' (see Sweet's Oldest English Texts); but of Old Southern, or, strictly, of the old dialect of Wessex, the remains are fairly abundant, and these are commonly called Anglo-Saxon. It is therefore proper to use 'AS.' to denote this definite dialect, which, after all, represents only the speech of a particular *portion* of England. The term is well established and may therefore be kept; else it is not a particularly happy one, since the Wessex dialect was distinct from the Northern or Anglian dialect, and 'Anglo-Saxon' must, for philological purposes, be taken to mean Old English in which Anglian is not necessarily included. Our modern English is mainly Mercian.

Anglo-Saxon cannot be properly understood without some knowledge of its phonology, and English etymology cannot be fairly made out without some notion of the gradations of the Anglo-Saxon vowel-system. For these things, the student must consult Sweet's Anglo-Saxon Reader and the Grammars by Sievers and Wright. Only a few brief hints can be given here.

SHORT VOWELS: *a, æ, e, i, o, u, y*.

LONG VOWELS: *ā, ǣ, ē, ī, ō, ū, ȳ*.

DIPHTHONGS: *ēa*, answering to Goth. *au*; *ēo*, Goth. *iu*; also (in early MSS.) *ie* and *īe*.

BREAKINGS. The vowel *a* commonly becomes *ea* when preceded by *g, c*, or *sc*, or when followed by *l, r, h*, succeeded by a consonant, or by *x*. Similarly *e* or *i* may become *eo*. The most usual vowel-change is that produced by the occurrence of *i* (which often disappeared afterwards) in the following syllable. This 'mutation' changes the vowels in row (1) below to the corresponding vowels in row (2) below.

(1) *a, e, u, ea, eo, ā, ō, ū, ēa, ēo*.

(2) *e, i, y, ie,y, ie,y, ǣ, ē, ȳ, īe,ȳ, īe,ȳ*.

These two rows should be learnt by heart, as a knowledge of them is required at almost every turn. Note that *ā* usually arises from an original Idg. (Indo-germanic) *oi* or *ai*; *ēo* from Idg. *eu*; and *ēa* from an Idg. *ou* or *au*.

Modern E. *th* is represented by AS. þ or ð, used indifferently in the MSS.; see note to **Th** (p. 638).

Strong verbs are of great importance, and originated many derivatives; these derivatives can be compared with the form of the past tense singular, of the past tense plural, or of the past participle, as well as with that of the infinitive mood. It is therefore necessary to ascertain all these leading forms or 'gradations.' Ex.: *bindan*, to bind; pt. t. s. *band*, pl. *bundon*, pp. *bunden*. The sb. *band* or *bond* exhibits the same 'grade' as the pt. t. s.; whilst the sb. *bund-le* exhibits that of the pp.

Examples of the 'principal parts' of the seven Strong Conjugations are these.

1. *Scīnan*, to shine; pt. t. *scān*, pl. *scinon*, pp. *scinen*. Base SKEI.
2. *Bēodan*, to bid; pt. t. *bēad*, pl. *budon*, pp. *boden*. Base BEUD = √ BHEUDH.
3. *Bindan*, to bind; pt. t. *band*, pl. *bundon*; pp. *bunden*. Base BEND = √ BHENDH.
4. *Beran*, to bear; pt. t. *bær*, pl. *bǣron*, pp. *boren*. Base BER = √ BHER.
5. *Metan*, to mete; pt. t. *mæt*, pl. *mǣton*; pp. *meten*. Base MET = √ MED.
6. *Faran*, to fare; pt. t. *fōr*, pl. *fōron*, pp. *faren*. Base FAR = POR, from √ PER.
7. *Feallan*, to fall; pt. t. *fēoll*, pl. *fēollon*; pp. *feallen*. Base FAL = √ SPHAL.

Strong verbs are often attended by secondary or causal verbs; other secondary verbs are formed from substantives. Many of these ended originally in *-jan*; the *j* of this suffix often disappears, causing gemination of the preceding consonant. Thus we have *þeccan*, to thatch (for **þac-jan*); *biddan*, to pray (for **bed-jan*); *secgan*, to say (for **sag-jan*); *sellan*, to give, sell (for **sal-jan*); *dyppan*, to dip (for **dup-jan*); *settan*, to set (for **sat-jan*). With a few exceptions, these are weak verbs, with pt. t. in *-ode*, *-de* (*-te*), and pp. in *-od*, *-d* (*-t*).

Authorities: Grein, Ettmüller, Somner, Bosworth, Leo, Clark Hall, Sweet, Wright's Vocabularies, Napier's Glosses; also the grammars by Sievers and Wright, and Mayhew's Old English Phonology. For many particulars concerning the 'native element' in English, see my Principles of English Etymology, Series I.

OLD LOW GERMAN. Denoted by 'OLowG.' This is a term which I have employed for want of a better. It is meant to include a not very large class of words, the *precise* origin of which is wrapped in some obscurity. If not precisely English, they come very near it. The chief difficulty about them is that the time of their introduction into English is uncertain. Either they belong to Old Friesian, and were introduced by the Friesians who came over to England with the Saxons, or to some form of Old Dutch or Old Saxon, and may have been introduced from Holland, possibly even in the fourteenth century, when it was not uncommon for Flemings to come here; or indeed, directly, from Hamburg and the other Hanseatic towns. Some of them may yet be found in Anglo-Saxon. I call them Old Low German because they clearly belong to some Old Low German dialect; and I put them in a class together in order to call attention to them, in the hope that their early history may receive further elucidation.

DUTCH. The introduction into English of Dutch words is somewhat important, yet seems to have received but little attention. I am convinced that the influence of Dutch upon English has been much underrated, and a closer attention to this question might throw some light even upon English history. I think I may take the credit of being the first to point this out with sufficient distinctness. History tells us that our relations with the Netherlands have often been rather close. We read of Flemish mercenary soldiers being employed by the Normans, and of Flemish settlements in Wales, 'where (says old Fabyan, I know not with what truth) they remayned a longe whyle, but after, they sprad all Englande ouer.' We may recall the alliance between Edward III and the free towns of Flanders; and the importation by Edward of Flemish weavers. The wool used by the cloth-workers of the Low Countries grew on the backs of English sheep; and other close relations between us and our nearly related neighbours grew out of the brewing-trade, the invention of printing, and the reformation of religion. Caxton spent thirty years in Flanders (where the first English book was printed), and translated the Low German version of Reynard the Fox. Tyndale settled at Antwerp to print his New Testament, and was strangled at Vilvorde. But there was a still closer contact in the time of Elizabeth. Very instructive is Gascoigne's poem on the Fruits of War, where he describes his experiences in Holland; and every one knows that Zutphen saw the death of the beloved Sir Philip Sidney. As to the introduction of cant words from Holland, see Beaumont and Fletcher's play entitled 'The Beggar's Bush.' After Antwerp had been captured by the Duke of Parma, 'a third of the merchants and manufacturers of the ruined city,' says Mr. Green, 'are said to have found a refuge on the banks of the Thames.' All this cannot but have affected our language, and it ought to be accepted, as tolerably certain, that during the fourteenth, fifteenth, and sixteenth centuries, particularly the last, several Dutch and Low German words were introduced into England; and it would be curious to enquire whether, during the same period, several English words did not, in like manner, find currency in the Netherlands. The words which I have collected, as being presumably Dutch, are deserving of special attention.

For the pronunciation of Dutch, see Sweet's Handbook of Phonetics. It is to be noted that the English *oo* in *boor* exactly represents the Dutch *oe* in *boer* (the same word). Also, that the Dutch *sch* is very different from the German sound, and is Englished by *sc* or *sk*, as in *landscape*, formerly *landskip*. The audacity with which English has turned the Dutch *ui* in *bruin* (brown) into *broo-in* is an amazing instance of the influence of spelling upon speech. *V* and *z* are common, where English has *f* and *s*. The symbol *ij* is used for double *i*, and was formerly written *y*; it is now pronounced like E. *i* in *wine*. The standard Old Low German *th* appears as *d*; thus, whilst *thatch* is English, *deck* is Dutch. *Ol* appears as *ou*, as in *oud*, old, *goud*, gold, *houden*, to hold. *D* between two vowels sometimes disappears, as in *weer* (for **weder*), a wether. The language abounds with frequentative verbs in *-eren* and *-elen*, and with diminutive substantives in *-je* (also *-tje*, *-pje*, *-etje*), a suffix which has been substituted for the obsolete diminutive suffix *-ken*.

Authorities: Oudemans, Kilian, Hexham, Sewel, Ten Kate, Calisch; dictionary printed by Tauchnitz.

For some account of the Dutch element in English, see my Principles of English Etymology, Series I, ch. xxiv.

OLD FRIESIC. Closely allied to Anglo-Saxon; some English words are rather Friesian than Saxon.

Authorities: Richthofen; also (for modern North Friesic) Outzen; (for modern East Friesic) Koolman.

OLD SAXON. The old dialect of Westphalia, and closely allied to Old Dutch. Authority: Heyne.

LOW GERMAN. This name is here especially given to an excellent vocabulary of a Low German dialect, in the work commonly known as the Bremen Wörterbuch. Other authorities: Lübben, Berghaus, Woeste, &c.

SCANDINAVIAN. By this name I denote the Old Norse, introduced into England by the Danes and Northmen who, in the early period of our history, came over to England in great numbers. Often driven back, they continually returned, and on many occasions made good their footing and remained here. Their language is now best represented by Icelandic, owing to the curious fact that, ever since the first colonisation of Iceland by the Northmen about A.D. 874, the language of the settlers has been preserved with but slight changes. Hence, instead of its appearing strange that English words should be borrowed from Icelandic, it must be remembered that this name represents, for philological purposes, the language of those Northmen, who, settling in England, became ancestors of some of the very best men amongst us; and as they settled chiefly in Northumbria and East Anglia, parts of England not strictly represented by Anglo-Saxon, 'Icelandic' or 'Old Norse' (as it is also called) has come to be, it may almost be said, English of the English. In some cases, I derive 'Scandinavian' words from Swedish, Danish, or Norwegian; but no more is meant by this than that the Swedish, Danish, or Norwegian words are the best representatives of the 'Old Norse' that I could find. The number of words actually borrowed from what (in the modern sense) is strictly Swedish or strictly Danish is but small, and they have been duly noted.

Icelandic. Vowels, as in Anglo-Saxon, are both short and long, the long vowels being here marked with a mark of length, as *ā*, *ē*, &c. To the usual vowels are added *ö*, and the diphthongs *au*, *ey*, *ei*; also *æ*, which is written both for *æ* and *œ*, strictly of different origin; also *ja*, *jā*, *jö*, *jō*, *jū*. Among the consonants are *ð*, the voiced *th* (as in E. *thou*), and *þ*, the voiceless *th* (as in E. *thin*). *D* was at one time written both for *d* and *ð*. *Þ*, *æ*, and *ö* come at the end of the alphabet. There is now no *w*. The AS. *w* and *hw* appear as *v* and *hv*. The most usual vowel-change is that which is caused by the occurrence of *i* (expressed or understood) in the following syllable; this changes the vowels in row (1) below into the corresponding vowels in row (2) below.

(1)   *a*,   *e*,   *o*,   *u*,   *au*,   *ā*,   *ō*,   *ū*,   *jō*,   *jū*.
(2)   *e*,   *i*,   *y*,   *y*,   *ey*,   *æ*,   *æ*,   *ȳ*,   *ȳ*,   *ȳ*.

Assimilation is common; thus *dd* stands for *ðd*, or for Goth. *zd* (= AS. *rd*); *kk*, for *nk*; *ll*, for *lr* or *lþ*; *nn*, for *nþ*, *nd*, or *nr*; *tt*, for *dt*, *ht*, *kt*, *nt*, *ndt*, *tþ*. Initial *sk* should be particularly noticed, as many E. words beginning with *sc* or *sk* are of Scand. origin; the AS. *sc* being represented by E. *sh*. Very remarkable is the loss of *v* in initial *vr* = AS. *wr*; the same loss occurring in modern English. Infinitives end in *-a* or *-ja*; verbs in *-ja*, with very few exceptions, are weak, with pp. ending in *-ð*, *-ðr*, *-t*, *-tr*, &c.; whereas strong verbs have the pp. in *-inn*.

I subjoin examples of the 'principal parts' of the seven Strong Conjugations.

1. *Skína*, to shine; pt. t. s. *skein*, pl. *skinu*; pp. *skininn*.

2. *Bjōda*, to bid; pt. t. s. *bauð*, pl. *buðu*; pp. *boðinn*.

3. *Binda*, to bind; pt. t. s. *batt* [for *band], pl. *bundu*; pp. *bundinn*.

4. *Bera*, to bear; pt. t. s. *bar*, pl. *bāru*; pp. *borinn*.

5. *Meta*, to value [mete out]; pt. t. s. *mat*, pl. *mātu*; pp. *metinn*.

6. *Fara*, to fare; pt. t. s. *fōr*, pl. *fōru*; pp. *farinn*.

7. *Falla*, to fall; pt. t. s. *fĕll*, pl. *fĕllu*; pp. *fallinn*.

Authorities: Cleasby and Vigfusson, Egilsson, Möbius, Noreen; also (for Norwegian), Aasen, Ross.

Swedish. To the usual vowels add å, ä, ö, which are placed at the end of the alphabet. Diphthongs do not occur, except in foreign words. *Qv* occurs where English has *qu*. The Old Swedish *w* (= AS. *w*) is now *v*. The Icelandic and AS. initial þ (= *th*) is replaced by *t*, as in Danish, not by *d*, as in Dutch; and our language bears some traces of this peculiarity, as, e. g. in the word *hustings* (for *husthings*), and again in the word *tight* or *taut* (Icel. *þéttr*).

Assimilation occurs in some words, as in *finna* (for *finda), to find, *dricka* (for *drinka), to drink; but it is less common than in Icelandic.

Infinitives end in -*a*; past participles of strong verbs in -*en*; weak verbs make the p. t. in -*ade*, -*de*, or -*te*, and the pp. in -*ad*, -*d*, or -*t*.

Authorities: Ihre (Middle Swedish, also called Suio-Gothic, with explanations in Latin); Widegren; Öman; Björkman; Tauchnitz dictionary; Rietz (Swedish dialects, a valuable book, written in Swedish).

For some account of the Scandinavian element in English, see my Principles of English Etymology, Series I, ch. xxiii.

Danish. To the usual vowels add æ and ö, which are placed at the end of the alphabet. The symbol ö is also written and printed as *o* with a slanting stroke drawn through it; thus ø. *Qv* is used by Ferrall where English has *qu*; but is replaced by *kv* in Larsen, and in Aasen's Norwegian dictionary. *V* is used where English has *w*. The Icelandic and AS. initial þ (*th*) is replaced by *t*, as in Swedish; not by *d*, as in Dutch. Assimilation occurs in some words, as in *drikke*, to drink, but is still less common than in Swedish. Thus the Icel. *finna*, Swed. *finna*, to find, is *finde* in Danish. *Mand* (for *mann), a man, is a remarkable form. We should particularly notice that final *k*, *t*, *p*, and *f* sometimes becomes *g*, *d*, *b*, and *v* respectively; as in *bog*, a book, *rag-e*, to rake, *tag-e*, to take; *ged*, a goat, *bid-e*, to bite, *græd-e*, to weep (Lowland Scotch *greet*); *reb*, a rope, *grib-e*, to grip or gripe, *knib-e*, to nip; *liv*, life, *kniv*, knife, *viv*, wife. Infinitives end in -*e*; the past participles of strong verbs once ended in -*en*, but these old forms are not common, being replaced by later forms in -*et* or -*t*, throughout the active voice.

Authorities: Ferrall and Repp's Dictionary; Larsen's Dictionary; Molbech (dialects); Kalkar (Middle Danish); Falk and Torp (etymological).

Norwegian. Closely allied to Danish.

Authority: Aasen's Dictionary of Norwegian dialects (written in Danish), with Ross's supplement.

GOTHIC. The Gothic alphabet, chiefly borrowed from Greek, has been variously transliterated into Roman characters. I have followed the system used in my Mœso-Gothic Dictionary, which I still prefer. It is the same as that used by Massmann, except that I put *w* for his *v*, *kw* for his *kv*, and *hw* for his *hv*, thus turning all his *v*'s into *w*'s, as every true Englishman ought to do. Stamm has the same system as Massmann, with the addition of þ for *th* (needless), and *q* for *kw*, which is not pleasant to the eye; so that he writes *qaþ* for *kwath* (i. e. quoth). *J* corresponds to the E. *y*. One peculiarity of Gothic must be particularly noted. As the alphabet was partly imitated from Greek, its author used *gg* and *gk* (like Gk. γγ, γκ) to represent *ng* and *nk*; as in *tuggo*, tongue, *drigkan*, to drink. The Gothic vowel-system is particularly simple and clear, and deserving of special attention, as being the best standard with which to compare the vowel-systems of other Teutonic languages. The primary vowels are *a*, *i*, *u*, always short, and *ē*, *ō*, always long. Original Germanic *ĕ* usually appears as *i* (or as *ai* before *r*, *h*, *hw*), and Germanic *ŏ* as *u* (or as *au* before *r*, *h*); thus AS. *etan*, to eat, is Goth. *itan*; AS. *beran*, to bear, is Goth. *bairan*; AS. *geoc*, a yoke, is Goth. *juk*; and AS. *word*, a word, is Goth. *waurd*. The diphthongs are *ai*, *au*, *ei*, and *iu*; the two former being distinguished, theoretically, into *ai* and *ái*, *au* and *áu*.

I subjoin examples of the 'principal parts' of the seven Strong Conjugations.

1. *Skeinan*, to shine; pt. t. s. *skain*, pl. (1 p.) *skinum*; pp. *skinans*.

2. *Biudan*, to bid; pt. t. s. *bauth*, pl. *budum*; pp. *budans*.

3. *Bindan*, to bind; pt. t. s. *band*, pl. *bundum*; pp. *bundans*.

4. *Bairan*, to bear; pt. t. s. *bar*, pl. *bērum*; pp. *baurans*.

5. *Mitan*, to mete; pt. t. s. *mat*, pl. *mētum*; pp. *mitans*.

6. *Faran*, to fare; pt. t. s. *fōr*, pl. *fōrum*; pp. *farans*.

7. *Haldan*, to hold; pt. t. s. *haihald*, pl. *haihaldum*; pp. *haldans*.

OLD HIGH GERMAN. Some remarks upon Old High German are given in the next paragraph (concerning **German**), but I shall here subjoin, for comparison, examples of the 'principal parts' of the OHG. Strong Verbs.

1. *Scīnan*, to shine; pt. t. s. *scein*, pl. *scinun*; pp. *giscinan*.

2. *Biotan*, to bid, offer; pt. t. s. *bōt*, pl. *butun*; pp. *gibotan*.

3. *Bintan*, to bind; pt. t. s. *bant*, pl. *buntun*; pp. *gibuntan*.

4. *Beran*, to bear; pt. t. s. *bar*, pl. *bārun*; pp. *giboran*.

5. *Mezzan*, to mete; pt. t. s. *maz*, pl. *māzun*; pp. *gimezzan*.

6. *Faran*, to go; pt. t. s. *fuor*, pl. *fuorun*; pp. *gifaran*.

7. *Fallan*, to fall; pt. t. s. *fial*, pl. *fiallun*; pp. *gifallan*.

If we now compare all the examples of the vowel-gradations as exhibited in the principal parts of the strong verbs, as seen in Anglo-Saxon, Icelandic, Gothic, and Old High German, respectively, it becomes easy to compile a list of the comparative values of their vowels and diphthongs. In the following table, the first column exhibits the (theoretical) values of the original Teutonic vowels, the second column the Gothic, and so on. Lines 1, 2, 3 are due to the *first* conjugation, by omitting the gradation of the pt. t. plural; lines 4, 5, 6 are similarly due to the *second* conjugation; lines 7, 8, 9 to the *third*; 10, 11, 12, to the *fourth*; 13, 14, to the first two grades of the *fifth*; and 15, 16, to the first two grades of the *sixth*. Line 17 is due to comparing the past tense plurals in conjugations 4 and 5. Line 18 depends upon such instances as that of the AS. *blōwan*, to bloom as a flower, in which the *ō* is an original Indo-germanic long vowel, as shown by the cognate Latin *flōrēre*, to flourish.

TABLE OF THE USUAL EQUIVALENCE OF VOWEL-SOUNDS.

	TEUT.	GOTH.	ICEL.	OHG.	AS.	GK.	LAT.	IDG.
1.	(EI) Ī	ei	ī	ī	ī	ει	ī	EI
2.	AI	ai	ei	ei	ā	οι	œ, ū, ī	OI
3.	I	i	i	i	i	ι	i	I
4.	EU	iu	jō	io	ēo	εν	ū	EU
5.	AU	au	au	ō	ēa	ον	au, ō	OU
6.	O (U)	u, au	o	o	o (u)	ν	u	U
7.	(EN), IN	in	in	in	in	εν	en, in	EN
8.	AN	an	*an	an	an	ον	on	ON
9.	UN	un	un	un	un	αν, α	en	ṇ
10.	ER	air	er	er	er (eor)	ερ	er	ER
11.	AR	ar	ar	ar	ær (ear)	ορ	or	OR
12.	OR (UR)	aur	or	or	or (ur)	αρ, ρα	or	ṛ
13.	E	i	e	e	e	ε	e	E
14.	A	a	a	a	æ, a	ο	o (u)	O
15.	A	a	a	a	a (æ, ea)	α	a	A
16.	Ō	ō	ō	uo	ō	ā, η	ā	Ā
17.	Ǣ	ē	ā	ā	ǣ	η	ē	Ē
18.	Ō	ō	ō	uo	.ō	ω	ō	Ō

It will be noticed that Greek and Latin equivalents are given in the above scheme. Corresponding to the 'gradations' in the six Teutonic conjugations of strong verbs we may note similar examples in Greek; viz. as follows.

1. πείθω; perf. t. πέ-ποιθα; 2 aorist ἔ-πιθον.

2. ἐ-λεύσομαι; perf. t. εἰ-λή-λουθα; 2 aorist ἤ-λυθον.

3. τενῶ, future tense; τόνος, sb.; perf. pass. τέταμαι.

4. δέρκομαι; perf. t. δέ-δορκα; 2 aorist ἔ-δρακον.

5. πέτομαι; ποτή, sb. Cf. L. sequi, v., socius, sb.

6. ἄγω; whence στρατ-ηγός, sb. Cf. L. agere; whence ambāges, sb.

It is interesting to note that the E. words *ear, hear, berry*, are the same as Goth. *ausō, hausjan, basi*, showing that in such words the E. *r* is due to original *s*.

Authorities for Gothic: Gabelentz and Löbe, Diefenbach, Schulze, Massmann, Stamm, Uhlenbeck.

For examples of English words cognate with Greek and Latin, see my Primer of Classical and English Philology.

For an account of the phonology of Gothic, see Prof. Wright's Primer of the Gothic language.

GERMAN. Properly called High-German, to distinguish it from the other Teutonic dialects, which belong to Low-German. This, of all Teutonic languages, is the furthest removed from English, and the one from which fewest words are directly borrowed, though there is a very general popular notion (due to the utter want of philological training so common amongst us) that the contrary is the case. A knowledge of German is often the sole idea by which an Englishman regulates his 'derivations' of Teutonic words; and he is better pleased if he can find the German equivalent of an English word than by any *true* account of the same word, however clearly expressed. Yet it is well established, by Grimm's law of sound-shiftings, that the German and English consonantal systems are very different. Owing to the replacement of the Old High German *þ* by the Mod. G. *b*, and other changes, English and German now approach each other more nearly than Grimm's law suggests; but we may still observe the following very striking differences in the dental consonants.

English. *d   t   th.*

German. *t   z (ss)   d.*

These changes are best remembered by help of the words *day, tooth, foot, thorn*, German *tag, zahn, fuss, dorn*; and the further comparison of these with the other Teutonic forms is not a little instructive.

Teutonic type	DAGOZ	TANTH	FŌT	THORNOZ, THORNUZ.
Anglo-Saxon	*dæg*	*tóð*	*fōt*	*þorn.*
Old Friesic	*dei*	*toth*	*fōt*	*thorn.*
Old Saxon	*dag*	*tand*	*fōt*	*thorn.*
Low German	*dag*	*tän*	*foot*	*dorn.*
Dutch	*dag*	*tand*	*voet*	*doorn.*
Icelandic	*dag-r*	*tönn*	*fōt-r*	*þorn.*
Swedish	*dag*	*tand*	*fot*	*törne.*
Danish	*dag*	*tand*	*fod*	*tjörn.*
Gothic	*dag-s*	*tunthu-s*	*fōtu-s*	*thaurnu-s.*
German	*tag*	*zahn*	*fuss*	*dorn.*

The number of words in English that are borrowed directly from German is quite insignificant, and they are nearly all of late introduction. It is more to the purpose to remember that there are, nevertheless, a considerable number of German words that were borrowed *indirectly*, viz. through the French.

Authorities: Schade, Kluge, Flügel, E. Müller. There is a good MHG. Dictionary by Lexer, another by Benecke, Müller, and Zarncke; and many more. For an account of the phonology, see Prof. Wright's Old High German Primer, and his German Grammar.

FRENCH. The influence of French upon English is too well known to require comment. But the method of derivation of French words from Latin or German is often very difficult, and requires the greatest care. There are numerous French words in quite common use, such as *aise*, ease, *trancher*, to cut, which have never yet been clearly solved; and the solution of many others is highly doubtful. Latin words often undergo the most curious transformations, as may be seen by consulting Brachet's or Darmesteter's or Schwan's Historical

Grammar. What are called 'learned' words, such as *mobile*, which is merely a Latin word with a French ending, present no difficulty; but the 'popular' words in use since the first formation of the language, are distinguished by three peculiarities: (1) the continuance of the tonic accent, (2) the suppression of the short vowel, (3) the loss of the medial consonant. The last two peculiarities tend to disguise the origin, and require much attention. Thus, in the Latin *bonitātem*, the short vowel *i*, near the middle of the word, is suppressed; whence F. *bonté*, E. *bounty*. And again, in the Latin *ligāre*, to bind, the medial consonant *g*, standing between two vowels, is lost, producing the F. *lier*, whence E. *liable*.

The result is a great tendency to compression, of which an extraordinary but well-known example is the Late Latin *ætāticum*, reduced to *edage* by the suppression of the short vowel *i*, and again to *eage*, *aage* by the loss of the medial consonant *d*; hence F. *âge*, E. *age*.

One other peculiarity is too important to be passed over. With rare exceptions, the substantives (as in all the Romance languages) are formed from the *accusative* case of the Latin, so that it is commonly a mere absurdity to cite the Latin nominative, when the form of the accusative is absolutely necessary to show how the French word arose. On this account, the form of the accusative is usually given, as in the case of *caution*, from L. *cautiōnem*, and in numberless other instances.

French may be considered as being a wholly unoriginal language, founded on debased Latin; but it must at the same time be remembered that, as history teaches us, a certain part of the language is necessarily of Celtic origin, and another part is necessarily Frankish, that is, Old High German. It has also borrowed words freely from Old Low German dialects, from Scandinavian (due to the Normans), and in later times, from Italian, Spanish, &c., and even from English and many entirely foreign languages.

Authorities: Cotgrave, Palsgrave, Littré, Scheler, Diez, Hatzfeld, Brachet, Burguy, Roquefort, Bartsch, &c. See also my Principles of English Etymology, Series II; especially chapter vi, for the phonology of Anglo-French, and chapters x and xi for the phonology of Central (or Parisian) French.

OTHER ROMANCE LANGUAGES. The other Romance languages, i. e. languages of Latin origin, are Italian, Spanish, Portuguese, Provençal, Romansch, and Wallachian. English contains words borrowed from the first four of these, but there is not much in them that needs special remark. The Italian and Spanish forms are often useful for comparison with (and consequent restoration of) the crushed and abbreviated Old French forms. Italian is remarkable for assimilation, as in *ammirare* (for *admirare*), to admire, *ditto* (for *dicto*), a saying, whence E. *ditto*. Spanish, on the other hand, dislikes assimilation, and carefully avoids double consonants; the only consonants that can be doubled are *c*, *n*, *r*, besides *ll*, which is sounded as E. *l* followed by *y* consonant, and is not considered as a double letter. The Spanish *ñ* is sounded as E. *n* followed by *y* consonant, and occurs in *dueña*, Englished as *duenna*. Spanish is also remarkable as containing many Arabic (Moorish) words, some of which have found their way into English. The Italian infinitives commonly end in *-are*, *-ere*, *-ire*, with corresponding past participles in *-ato*, *-uto*, *-ito*. Spanish infinitives commonly end in *-ar*, *-er*, *-ir*, with corresponding past participles in *-ado*, *-ido*, *-ido*. In all the Romance languages, substantives are most commonly formed, as in French, from the Latin accusative. See further in my Principles of English Etymology, Series II; ch. xiv (on the Italian element); ch. xv (on the Spanish element); and ch. xvi (on the Portuguese element).

CELTIC. Words of Celtic origin are marked '(C.)'. This was formerly a particularly slippery subject to deal with, for want of definite information as to its older forms in a conveniently accessible arrangement; but the contribution by Whitley Stokes to the 4th edition of Fick's Vergleichende Wörterbuch is now of great assistance, and Macbain's Etymological Dictionary of Gaelic is also very useful. That English has borrowed a few words from Celtic cannot be doubted, but we must take care not to multiply the number of these unduly. Again, 'Celtic' is merely a general term, and in itself means nothing definite, just as 'Teutonic' and 'Romance' are general terms. To prove that a word is Celtic, we must first show that the word is borrowed from one of the Celtic languages, as Irish, Gaelic, Welsh, Cornish, or Breton, or that it is of a form which, by the help of these languages, can be fairly presumed to have existed in the Celtic of an early period. The chief difficulty lies in the fact that Welsh, Irish, Cornish, and Gaelic have all borrowed English words at various periods, and Gaelic has certainly also borrowed some words from Scandinavian, as history tells us must have been the case. We gain, however, some assistance by comparing all the languages of this class together, and again, by comparing them with Latin, Greek, Sanskrit, &c., since the Celtic consonants often agree with these, and at the same time differ from Teutonic. Thus the word *bard* is Celtic, since it only appears in Welsh, Irish, and Gaelic; and again, the word *down* (2), a fortified hill, is Celtic, because it may be compared with the AS. *tūn*, a Celtic *d* answering to AS. *t.* On the other hand, the W. *hofio,* to hover, is nothing but the common ME. *hoven,* to tarry, to hover, which appears to be of native E. origin. The Lectures on Welsh Philology by Prof. Sir John Rhys give a clear and satisfactory account of the values of Irish and Welsh letters as compared with other Indo-germanic languages.

Some Celtic words have come to us through French, for which assistance is commonly to be had from Breton. A few words in other Teutonic languages besides English are probably of Celtic origin.

RUSSIAN. This language belongs to the Slavonic branch of the Aryan languages, and, though the words borrowed from it are very few, it is frequently of assistance in comparative philology, as exhibiting a modern form of language allied to the Old Church Slavonic. My principal business here is to explain the system of transliteration which I have adopted, as it is one which I made out for my own convenience, with the object of avoiding the use of diacritical marks. The following is the Russian alphabet, with the Roman letters which I use to represent it. It is sufficient to give the small letters only.

Russian Letters:	а	б	в	г	д	е	ж	з	и	і	к	л	м	н	о	п	р	с	т	у	ф	х	ц	ч	ш
Roman Letters:	a	b	v	g	d	e(é)	j	z	i	i	k	l	m	n	o	p	r	s	t	u	f	kh	ts	ch	sh

Russian Letters:	щ	ъ	ы	ь	ѣ	э	ю	я	ѳ	ѵ
Roman Letters:	shch	'	ui	(e)	ie	é	iu	ia	ph	y

This transliteration is not the best possible, but it will suffice to enable any one to verify the words cited in this work by comparing them with a Russian dictionary. It is necessary to add one or two remarks.

The symbol ъ only occurs at the end of a word or syllable, and only when that word or syllable ends in a consonant; it is not sounded, but throws a greater stress upon the consonant, much as if it were doubled; I denote it therefore merely by an apostrophe. The symbol ь most commonly occurs at the end of a word or syllable, and may be treated, in general, as a mute letter, like the final *e* in French. э only occurs at the beginning of words, and is not common. е may be represented by *e* at the beginning of a word, or otherwise by *é*, if necessary, since it cannot then be confused with э. It is to be particularly noted that *j* is to have its *French* value, not the English; seeing that ж has just the sound of the French *j*, it is here so written. и and i are distinguished by the way in which they occur; ie can be written *iĕ*, to distinguish it from *ie* = ѣ. ѳ, which is rare, can be written *ph*, to distinguish it from ф, or *f*; the sound is all one. By *kh*, Russ. х, I mean the German guttural *ch*, which comes very near to the sound of the letter; but the combinations *ts, ch, sh, shch* are all as in English. ы, or *ui*, somewhat resembles the French *oui*. The combinations *ie, iu, ia,* are to be read with *i* as English *y*, i. e. *yea, you, yaa.* ѵ, or *y*, pronounced as E. *ee*, is of slight consequence, being rare. I do not recommend the scheme for general use, but only give it as the one which I have used.

The Russian and Slavonic consonants agree with Sanskrit, Greek, and Latin rather than with Teutonic. The same may be said of Lithuanian, which is a very well preserved language, and often of great use in comparative philology. The infinitive mood of Russian regular verbs ends in *-ate, -iate, -iete, -ite, -ote, -ute,* all with final mute *e*; that of some irregular verbs in *-che,* or *-ti.* In Lithuanian, the characteristic suffix of the infinitive is *-ti.*

The best authority is the Comparative Etymological Dictionary of the Slavonic Languages by F. Miklosich.

SANSKRIT. In transliterating Sanskrit words, I follow the scheme given in Benfey's Dictionary, with slight modifications. For श, I print *ç*, as in Benfey and Uhlenbeck, instead of *ś*, as in Monier Williams's Grammar. There is this advantage about the symbol *ç*, viz. that it reminds the student that this sibilant is due to an original *k*. I also follow Uhlenbeck in printing *ṛ* (instead of *ṛi,* as in Benfey) for ऋ; but retain *sh* for ष, which Uhlenbeck denotes by *ṣ*. I also follow him in writing *ñ* for ञ (Benfey's *ṅ*). He also employs *c* and *ch* for Benfey's *ch* and *chh*; but I have not adopted these two changes.

Thus the complete alphabet is represented by *a, ā, i, ī, u, ū, ṛ, ṝ, ḷ, ē, ai, ō, au;* gutturals, *k, kh, g, gh, ṅ;* palatals, *ch, chh, j, jh, ñ;* cerebrals, *ṭ, ṭh, ḍ, ḍh, ṇ;* dentals, *t, th, d, dh, n;* labials, *p, ph, b, bh, m;* semivowels, *y, r, l, v;* sibilants, *ç, sh, s;* aspirate, *h.* Add the nasal symbol *ṁ,* and the final aspirate, *ḥ.*

It is sometimes objected that the symbols *ch, chh,* are rather clumsy, especially when occurring as *chchh*; but as they are perfectly definite and cannot be mistaken, the mere appearance to the eye cannot much matter. Some write *c* and *ch,* and consequently *cch* instead of *chchh*; but what is gained in appearance is lost in distinctness; since च is certainly our *ch,* whilst *c* gives the notion of E. *c* in *can.*

The scientific order in which the letters of the Sanskrit alphabet is arranged should be observed.

There are a few points about the values of the Sanskrit letters too important to be omitted. The following short notes will be found useful.

The Skt. ŗ is a sonant, and is perfectly distinct from r.   Thus ŗch, to shine, is distinct from rich, to leave. Other languages sometimes preserve a better form than Skt.; thus the √ AG, to drive, gives Lat. ag-ere, Gk. ἄγ-ειν, and (by regular change from g to k) Icelandic ak-a; but the Skt. is aj, a weakened form in which the g has been palatalised.

The chief difficulty in comparing the values of the consonants in different Indo-germanic languages lies in dealing with the guttural sounds.   It has been ascertained that there are actually *three* distinct sets of gutturals, distinguished by difference of treatment in some of the languages belonging to the family.   They are called by Brugmann the *palatals*, the *pure velars*, and the *labio-velars*; and by others the *palatal, middle,* and *labialised velar* gutturals.   I distinguish the first set by the symbols GH, G, K; the second, by G(w)H, G(w), Q; and the third, by GwH, Gw, Qw.

It is not a little remarkable that, in Greek, Latin, and Celtic (all of which keep the original *k*-sound in the word for 'hundred,' as Greek ἑκατόν, L. *centum*, Welsh *cant*) the middle gutturals are treated exactly like the palatals; whilst, on the contrary, in Sanskrit, Persian, Lithuanian, and Slavonic (all of which have an *s*-sound in the same word, as Skt. *çatam*, Pers. *sad*, Lith. *szimtas*, Russ. *sto*) the middle gutturals are treated like the labialised velars. Teutonic belongs to the former set, and goes with Greek, Latin, and Celtic.   We may roughly characterise the two sets as Western and Eastern respectively.

Dental Series.   The easiest series to deal with is that of the dentals; so it will be taken first.   It will be noticed that the Germanic languages *shift* an original DH, D, or T to D, T, and TH respectively.   This is called 'consonantal sound-shifting,' or simply 'sound-shifting'; otherwise known as 'Grimm's Law.'

Labial Series.   In the same way, the Germanic languages shift an original BH, B, or P, to B, P, F respectively; by the same Law.   The following table exhibits the results.

USUAL CORRESPONDENCES OF DENTAL AND LABIAL SOUNDS.

IDG.	SKT.	SLAV.	LITH.	GK.	LAT.	IRISH.	GOTH.	AS.	TEUT.
DH	dh	d	d	θ	f (d, b)	d	d	d	D
D	d	d	d	δ	d, l	d	t	t	T
T	t	t	t	τ	t	t, th	th [d]	þ [d]	TH
BH	bh	b	b	φ	f, h (b)	b (m)	b	b	B
B	b	b	b	β	b	b	p	p	P
P	p	p	p	π	p	...	f [b]	f	F

The Skt. *dh* answers to Lat. *f* initially; the *d, b* only occur medially.   The Irish *th* is an aspirated *t*, not the E. *th*.   The AS. þ is only a symbol for the sound of *th*, as in E. *thorn*.   The appearance of L. *l* for *d* is remarkable; thus L. *lingua* represents an older *dingua*; and as L. *d* corresponds to AS. *t*, it is cognate with E. *tongue*.   The Skt. *bh* corresponds to L. *f* or *h* initially; medially, to *b*.   The Gothic [b] and Gothic and AS. [d] within square brackets are due to what is known as 'Verner's Law'; the *th* became *d*, and the *f* became *b* whenever the vowel next preceding these consonants did *not*, according to the original Indo-germanic system of accentuation, bear the principal accent of the word.   See Wright's Gothic Primer, § 119.

Guttural Series.   The usual correspondence of guttural sounds in the principal Indo-germanic languages is here given.   It has been explained above that there are three sets of gutturals.   Observe the identity of treatment in the second and third sets of rows to the left of the dark line, and in the first and second sets to the right of it.

IDG.	SKT.	SLAV.	LITH.	GK.	LAT.	IRISH.	GOTH.	AS.	TEUT.
GH	h	z	ž	χ	h, g	g	g	g	G
G	j	z	ž	γ	g	g	k	c	K
K	ç	s	sz	κ	c	c	h [g]	h [g]	H
G(w)H	gh, h	g, ž, z	g	χ	h, g	g	g	g	G
G(w)	g, j	g, ž, z	g	γ	g	g	k	c	K
Q	k, ch	k, č, c	k	κ	c	c	h [g]	h [g]	H
GwH	gh, h	g, ž, z	g	φ, θ, χ	f, gu, u, g	g	g	g	Gw
Gw	g, j	g, ž, z	g	β, δ, γ	gu, u, g	b	kw, k	cw, c	Q
Qw	k, ch	k, č, c	k	π, τ, κ	qu, c	c	hw, h [g]	hw, h [g]	Hw

Authorities: Benfey, Macdonell, Uhlenbeck, for Sanskrit; Prellwitz, Vaniček, Liddell and Scott, for Greek; Walde, Bréal, Vaniček, Lewis and Short, for Latin; Miklosich, for Slavonic; and for comparative philology, Brugmann, Fick, Stokes-Fick, Uhlenbeck, Kluge, Franck, and others. Cf. Giles, Manual of Comparative Philology, 2nd ed., 1901.

NON-ARYAN LANGUAGES: HEBREW. The Hebrew words in English are not very numerous, whilst at the same time they are tolerably well known, and the corresponding Hebrew words can, in general, be easily found. I have therefore contented myself with denoting the alphabet *beth, gimel, daleth,* &c. by *b, g, d, h, v, z, kh, t, y, k, l, m, n, s, ', p, ts, q, r, sh* or *s, t.* This gives the same symbol for *samech* and *sin,* but this difficulty is avoided by making a note of the few instances in which *samech* occurs; in other cases, *sin* is meant. So also with *teth* and *tau*; unless the contrary is said, *tau* is meant. This might have been avoided, had the words been more numerous, by the use of *ş* and *ţ* for *samech* and *teth.* I put *kh* for *cheth,* to denote that the sound is guttural, not E. *ch.* I denote *ayin* by the mark '. The other letters can be readily understood. The vowels are denoted by *a, e, i, o, u, ā, ē, ī, ō, ū.*

ARABIC. The Arabic alphabet is important, being also used for Persian, Turkish, Hindustani, and Malay. But as the letters are variously transliterated in various works, it seemed to be the simplest plan to use the spellings given in Richardson's Arabic and Persian Dictionary (with very slight modifications), or in Marsden's Malay Dictionary; and, in order to prevent any mistake, to give, in every instance, the *number of the page* in Richardson or Marsden, or the *number of the column* in Palmer's Persian Dictionary; so that, if in any instance, it is desired to verify the word cited, it can readily be done. Richardson's system is rather vague, as he uses *t* to represent ت and ط (and also the occasional ة); also *s* to represent ث س and ص; also *h* for ح and ه; *z* for ز ذ ض and ظ; *k* for ق and ك; and he denotes *ayin* by the Arabic character. I have got rid of one ambiguity by using *q* (instead of *k*) for ق; and for *ayin* I have put the mark ', as in Palmer's Persian Dictionary. In other cases, the reader can easily tell which *t, s, h,* or *z* is meant, if it happens to be an *initial* letter (when it is the most important), by observing the *number* of the page (or column) given in the reference to Richardson's or Palmer's Dictionary. Thus in Richardson's Dictionary, pp. 349-477 contain ت; pp. 960-981 contain ط; pp. 477-487 contain ث; pp. 795-868 contain س; pp. 924-948 contain ص; pp. 548-588 contain ح; pp. 1660-1700 contain ه; pp. 705-712 contain ذ; pp. 764-794 contain ز; pp. 949-960 contain ض; and pp. 981-984 contain ظ. In Palmer's Dictionary, the same letters are distinguished as *t* (coll. 121-159); *ţ* (coll. 408-416); *ṡ* (coll. 160, 161); *s* (coll. 331-371); *ş* (coll. 396-405); *ḥ* (coll. 191-207); *h* (coll. 692-712); *ż* (coll. 283-287); *z* (coll. 314-330); *ẓ* (coll. 405-408); and *ẓ̈* (coll. 416-418). Palmer gives the complete alphabet in the form *a* [*ā, i,* &c.], *b, p, t, ṡ, j, ch, ḥ, kh, d, ż, r, z, zh, s, sh, ş, ẓ, ţ, ẓ̈, ', gh, f, ḳ* [which I have written as *q*], *k, g, l, m, n, w, h, y.* It deserves to be added that Turkish has an additional letter *sāghir nūn,* which I denote by *ñ,* occurring in the word *yeñi,* which helps to form the E. word *janisary.*

In words derived from Hindi, Hindustani, Chinese, &c., I give the page of the dictionary where the word may be found, or a reference to some authority. See, in particular, the List of Books referred to, at p. xxx.

CANONS FOR ETYMOLOGY

In the course of the work, I have been led to adopt the following canons, which merely express well-known principles, and are nothing new. Still, in the form of definite statements, they are worth giving.

1. Before attempting an etymology, ascertain the earliest form and use of the word; and observe chronology.

2. Observe history and geography; borrowings are due to actual contact.

3. Observe phonetic laws, especially those which regulate the mutual relation of consonants in the various Indogermanic languages, at the same time comparing the vowel-sounds.

4. In comparing two words, A and B, belonging to the same language, of which A contains the lesser number of syllables, A must be taken to be the more original word, unless we have evidence of contraction or other corruption.

5. In comparing two words, A and B, belonging to the same language and consisting of the same number of syllables, the older form can usually be distinguished by observing the sound of the principal vowel.

6. Strong verbs, in the Teutonic languages, and the so-called 'irregular verbs' in Latin, are commonly to be considered as primary, other related forms being taken from them.

7. The whole of a word, and not a portion only, ought to be reasonably accounted for; and, in tracing changes of form, any infringement of phonetic laws is to be regarded with suspicion.

8. Mere resemblances of form and apparent connexion in sense between languages which have different phonetic laws or no necessary connexion are commonly a delusion, and are not to be regarded.

9. When words in two different languages are more nearly alike than the ordinary phonetic laws would allow, there is a strong probability that one language has borrowed the word from the other. Truly cognate words ought not to be *too much* alike.

10. It is useless to offer an explanation of an English word which will not *also* explain all the cognate forms.

These principles, and other similar ones well known to comparative philologists, I have tried to observe. Where I have not done so, there is a chance of a mistake. Corrections can only be made by a more strict observance of the above canons.

A few examples will make the matter clearer.

1. The word *surloin* or *sirloin* is often said to be derived from the fact that the *loin* was knighted as *Sir Loin* by Charles II, or (according to Richardson) by James I. Chronology makes short work of this statement; the word being in use long before James I was born. It is one of those unscrupulous inventions with which English 'etymology' abounds, and which many people admire because they are 'so clever.' The number of those who literally prefer a story about a word to a more prosaic account of it, is only too large.

As to the necessity for ascertaining the oldest form and use of a word, there cannot be two opinions. Yet this primary and all-important rule is continually disregarded, and men are found to rush into 'etymologies' without the slightest attempt at investigation or any knowledge of the history of the language, and think nothing of deriving words which exist in Anglo-Saxon from German or Italian. They merely 'think it over,' and take up with the first fancy that comes to hand, which they expect to be 'obvious' to others because they were themselves incapable of doing better; which is a poor argument indeed. It would be easy to cite some specimens which I have noted, but it is hardly necessary[1]. I will rather relate my experience, viz. that I have frequently set out to find the etymology of a word without any preconceived ideas about it, and usually found that, by the time its earliest use and sense had been fairly traced, the etymology presented itself unasked.

2. The history of a nation generally accounts for the constituent parts of its language. When an early English word is compared with Hebrew or Coptic, as used to be done in the *old* editions of Webster's dictionary, history is set at defiance; and it was a good deed to clear the later editions of all such rubbish. As to geography, there must always be an intelligible geographical contact between races that are supposed to have borrowed words from one another; and this is particularly true of olden times, when travelling was less common. Old French did not borrow words from Portugal, nor did Old English borrow words from Prussia, much less from Finnish or Esthonian or Coptic, &c., &c. Yet there are people who still remain persuaded that *Whitsunday* is derived, of all things, from the German *Pfingsten*.

3. Few delusions are more common than the comparison of L. *cūra* with E. *care*, of Gk. ὅλος with

---

[1] I cite a few of these in my Principles of English Etymology, Series II, ch. xxv—'On some False Etymologies.'

E. *whole*, and of Gk. χάρις with E. *charity*. I dare say I myself believed in these things for many years, owing to that utter want of any approach to any philological training, for which England in general has long been so remarkable. Yet a very slight (but honest) attempt at understanding the English, the Latin, and the Greek alphabets soon shows these notions to be untenable. The E. *care*, AS. *cearu*, meant originally sorrow, which is only a secondary meaning of the Latin word; it never meant, originally, attention or painstaking. But this is not the point at present under consideration. Phonetically, the AS. *c* and the L. *c*, when used initially, do not correspond; for where Latin writes *c* at the beginning of a word, AS. has *h*, as in L. *cēl-āre*, related to AS. *hel-an*, to hide. Again, the AS. *ea*, before *r* following, stands for original *a*, *cearu*, answering to an older *caru*. But the L. *cūra*, Old Latin *coira*, is spelt with a long *ū*, originally a diphthong, which cannot answer exactly to an original *a*. It remains that these words both contain the letter *r* in common, which is not denied; but this is a slight ground for the supposed equivalence of words of which the primary senses were different. The fact of the equivalence of L. *c* to AS. *h*, is commonly known as being due to Grimm's law. The popular notions about 'Grimm's law' are extremely vague. Many imagine that Grimm *made* the law not many years ago, since which time Latin and Anglo-Saxon have been bound to obey it. But the word *law* is then strangely misapprehended; it is only a law in the sense of *an observed fact*. Latin and Anglo-Saxon were thus differentiated in times preceding the earliest record of the latter, and the difference might have been observed in the eighth century if any one had had the wits to observe it. When the difference has once been perceived, and all other AS. and Latin equivalent words are seen to follow it, we cannot consent to *establish an exception* to the rule in order to compare a single (supposed) pair of words which do not agree in the vowel-sound, and did not originally mean the same thing.

As to the Gk. ὅλος, the aspirate (as usual) represents an original *s*, so that ὅλος answers to Skt. *sarva-*, all, L. *saluus*, safe, unhurt. But the AS. *hāl* (which is the old spelling of *whole*) has for its initial letter an *h*, answering to Gk. κ. As to χάρις, the initial letter is χ, a guttural sound answering to Lat. *h* or *f*, and it is, in fact, allied to L. *hortārī*. But in *charity*, the *ch* is French, due to a peculiar pronunciation of the Latin *c*, and the F. *charité* is of course due to the L. acc. *cāritātem*, whence also Ital. *caritate* or *carità*, Span. *caridad*, all from L. *cārus*, with long *a*. When we put χάρις and *cārus* side by side, we find that the initial letters are different, that the vowels are different, and that, just as in the case of *cearu* and *cūra*, the sole resemblance is, that they both contain the letter *r*! It is not worth while to pursue the subject further. Those who are confirmed in their prejudices and have no guide but the ear (which they neglect to train), will remain of the same opinion still; but some beginners may perhaps take heed, and if they do, will see matters in a new light. To all who have acquired any philological knowledge, these things are wearisome.

4. Suppose we take two Latin words such as *cāritās* and *cārus*. The former has a stem *cār-i-tāt-*; the latter has a stem *cār-o-*, which may very easily turn into *cār-i-*. We are perfectly confident that the adjective came first into existence, and that the sb. was made out of it by adding a suffix; and this we can tell by a glance at the words, by the very form of them. It is a rule in all Indogermanic languages that words started from monosyllabic roots or bases, and were built up by supplying new suffixes at the end; and, the greater the number of suffixes, the later the formation. When apparent exceptions to this law present themselves, they require especial attention; but as long as the law is followed, it is all in the natural course of things. Simple as this canon seems, it is frequently not observed; the consequence being that a word A is said to be derived from B, whereas B is its own offspring. The result is a reasoning in a circle, as it is called; we go round and round, but there is no progress upward and backward, which is the direction in which we should travel. Thus Richardson derives *chine* from 'F. *echine*,' and this from 'F. *echiner*, to chine, divide, or break the back of (Cotgrave), probably from the AS. *cinan*, to chine, chink, or rive.' From the absurdity of deriving the 'F. *echiner*' from the 'AS. *cinan*' he might have been saved at the outset, by remembering that, instead of *echine* being derived from the verb *echiner*, it is obvious that *echiner*, to break the back of, is derived from *echine*, the back, as Cotgrave certainly meant us to understand; see *eschine*, *eschiner* in Cotgrave's Dictionary. Putting *eschine* and *eschiner* side by side, the shorter form is the more original.

5. This canon, requiring us to compare vowel-sounds, is a little more difficult, but it is extremely important. In many dictionaries it is utterly neglected, whereas the information to be obtained from vowels is often extremely certain; and few things are more beautifully regular than the occasionally complex, yet often decisive manner in which, especially in the Teutonic languages, one vowel-sound is educed from another. The very fact that the AS. *ē* is a modification of *ō* tells us at once that *fēdan*, to feed, is a derivation of *fōd*, food; and that to derive *food* from *feed* is simply impossible. In the same way the vowel *e* in the verb to *set* owes its very existence to the vowel *a* in the past tense of the verb to *sit*; and so on in countless instances.

The other canons require no particular comment.

BOOKS REFERRED TO IN THE DICTIONARY

The following is a list of the principal books referred to in the Dictionary, with a statement, in most instances, of the editions which I have actually used.

The abbreviation 'E.E.T.S.' signifies the Early English Text Society; and 'E.D.S.,' the English Dialect Society.

The date within square brackets at the end of a notice refers to the probable date of *composition* of a poem or other work; or to its first appearance in print.

Aasen; see Norwegian.

Abbott's Shakespearian Grammar. Third Edition, 1870.

Acosta, Joseph d', The Naturall and Morall Historie of the East and West Indies; tr. by E. G[rimstone]; London, 1604. 4to.

Ady, T., Discovery of Witches. 1661.

Ælfred, King, tr. of Boethius, De Consolatione Philosophiae, ed. S. Fox, 1864. [ab. 880–900.]
—— tr. of Beda's Ecclesiastical History, ed. Whelock, 1644.
—— tr. of Beda's Ecclesiastical History, ed. J. Smith, 1722. *Also* ed. T. Miller, E.E.T.S., 1890, 1898.
—— tr. of Gregory's Pastoral Care, ed. Sweet; E.E.T.S., 1871.
—— Version of the history of the world by Orosius; ed. J. Bosworth, London, 1859. [ab. 880–900.] *Also* ed. Sweet, E.E.T.S., 1883.

Ælfred's Metres; see Grein.

Ælfric, Lives of Saints; ed. W. W. Skeat; 2 vols.; E.E.T.S., 1881–1900.

Ælfric on the Old Testament; see Grein, Bibliothek der A. Prosa.

Ælfric's Glossary, pr. in Wright's Vocabularies; see Wright, T. [ab. 975.] *Also*, in Somner's Anglo-Saxon Dictionary.

Ælfric's Grammar; ed. J. Zupitza, Berlin, 1880. [ab. 975.]

Ælfric's Homilies; ed. Thorpe (Ælfric Society). [ab. 975.]

Alexander and Dindimus; ed. Skeat. E.E.T.S., extra series, 1878. [ab. 1350.]

Alexander, The Wars of; ed. W. W. Skeat. E.E.T.S., 1886.

Algonkin.—Cuoq; Lexique de la langue Algonquine. Montreal, 1886.

Alisaunder, Kyng; see Weber's Metrical Romances. [after 1300.]

Alliterative Poems; ed. Morris; E.E.T.S., 1864; reprinted, 1869. [ab. 1360.]

Altenglische Dichtungen des MS. Harl. 2253; ed. Dr. K. Böddeker. Berlin, 1878. 8vo.

Altenglische Legenden; ed. Dr. Carl Horstmann. Paderborn, 1875.

Altmark, dialect of; see Low German dialects.

Amadas, Sir; see Robson.

Ancren Riwle; ed. Jas. Morton. Camden Soc., 1873. [ab. 1230.]

Anglia; Zeitschrift für Englische Philologie; herausg. von R. P. Wülcker. Halle a / S. 1878 and following years.

Anglo-French.—A Rough List of English Words found in Anglo-French; by the Rev. W. W. Skeat. (Phil. Soc. Transactions, 1883.) Reprinted, with many additions, in Notes on Eng. Etymology, by W. W. Skeat, 1901; pp. 353–470.
—— Annals of Burton; pr. in Annales Monastici, ed. Luard (Record Series), 1864, pp. 446–453. [1258.]
—— Edw. Conf. = Life of Edward the Confessor, ed. Luard (Record Series), 1858. [12th century.]
—— French Chronicle of London, ed. Aungier (Camden Soc.), London, 1844. [ab. 1350.]
—— Geoffrey Gaimar's Chronicle, ed. T. Wright (Caxton Soc.), 1850. [ab. 1150.]
—— Havelok.—Lai d'Havelok; pr. in the same vol. as the preceding. [12th century.]
—— Langtoft's Chronicle, ed. T. Wright (Record Series), 2 vols. London, 1866–8. [ab. 1307.]
—— Laws of William I; pr. in Ancient Laws and Institutes of England, ed. B. Thorpe; vol. i. p. 466.
—— Liber Albus, ed. H. T. Riley (Record Series), 1859. [Before 1419.]
—— Liber Custumarum, pr. in Munimenta Gildhalliæ, vol. ii; ed. H. T. Riley (Record Series), 1860. [1270 to 1400.]
—— St. Nicholas, by Maistre Wace; ed. Delius; Bonn, 1850. [12th century.]

Anglo-French.—Philippe de Thaun, Bestiary and Livre des Creatures; pr. in Wright's Popular Treatises on Science, 1841. [12th century.]
—— Political Songs of England, ed. T. Wright (Camden Soc.), London, 1839.
—— Royal Wills, ed. J. Nichols; 1780. *See* Nichols, J.
—— Statutes of the Realm, pr. by command of Geo. III in 1810. First Volume.
—— Vie de St. Auban, ed. R. Atkinson; London, 1876.
—— Year-Books of Edward I, ed. A. J. Horwood (Record Series). Vols. 1 to 3. Dates: vol. i, 1292–3; vol. ii, 1302–3; vol. iii, 1304–5.
    A much fuller list of A.F. works is given in Notes on Eng. Etymology (as above).

Anglo-Saxon.—Ettmüller, L., Lexicon Anglo-Saxonicum; Quedlinburg and Leipzig, 1851. See also Bosworth, Grein, Leo, Loth, Lye, March, Somner, Sweet, Wright.

Anglo-Saxon and Early English Psalter; ed. J. Stevenson. Surtees Soc., 1843–7. 2 vols.

Anglo-Saxon Chronicle; ed. B. Thorpe; 2 vols. 1861. (Rolls Series.)
—— ed. C. Plummer and J. Earle. Oxford, 1892–9. 2 vols.

Anglo-Saxon Glosses; see Voc.; and see O.E. Texts.

Anglo-Saxon Gospels. The Gospel of St. Matthew, in Anglo-Saxon and Northumbrian Versions, ed. W. W. Skeat, Cambridge, 1887.—St. Mark, 1871.—St. Luke, 1874.—St. John, 1878.

Annual Register; commenced in 1758. London. 8vo.

Anstey, C.; The New Bath Guide. (First ed. in 1766.)

Antiquarian Repertory; a Miscellany. London, 1775–84. 4to. 4 vols.

Anturs of Arthur; see Robson. [ab. 1440.]

Arabic.—A Dictionary, Persian, Arabic, and English. By J. Richardson; new edition, by F. Johnson. London, 1829.

Arber.—English Reprints, ed. E. Arber; various dates.

Arber, E., An English Garner, vols. i to vii; 1877–1883.

Arnold's Chronicle; reprinted from the First Edition, with the additions included in the Second. London, 1811. [1502.]

Ascham, Roger; Toxophilus, ed. Arber, 1868. [1545.]
—— The Scholemaster, ed. Arber, 1870. [1570.]

Ash, J., Dictionary of the English Language; 2 vols., 1775.

Assumption of Mary; see Horn.

Atkinson, Rev. J. C., Glossary of the Cleveland Dialect. London, 1868.

Austin, T.; Two fifteenth-century Cookery Books (ab. 1430 and 1450). E.E.T.S., 1888.

Australian English; A Dictionary of Australasian Words, Phrases, and Usages; by Prof. E. E. Morris. London, 1898.

A. V. = Authorized Version; see Bible.

Avowing of Arthur; see Robson.

Awdelay's Fraternity of Vagabonds, ed. Viles and Furnivall; E.E.T.S., 1869; see Harman's Caveat. [1560–1565.]

Awntyrs of Arthure; see Scottish Alliterative Poems, and Three Metrical Romances.

Ayenbite of Inwyt, or Remorse of Conscience, by Dan Michel of Northgate; ed. R. Morris, E.E.T.S., 1866. [1340.]

Babees Book; ed. F. J. Furnivall, E.E.T.S., 1868. [15th cent.]

Bacon, Lord, Advancement of Learning, ed. W. Aldis Wright; Clarendon Press, Oxford, 1869. [1605.] An early edition by G. Wats, Oxford; 1640, folio.
—— Essays; ed. S. W. Singer, London, 1857. Also (including Colours of Good and Evil), ed. W. Aldis Wright, London, 1871. [1597.]

Bacon, Lord, Life of Henry VII, ed. J. R. Lumby, 1876. [1621.]
—— Natural History, or Sylva Sylvarum, Fifth Ed., 1639. [1627.]
Bailey, N., Universal Etymological English Dictionary, Seventh Edition, 1735.
—— English Dictionary, Vol. ii, Second Edition, 1731.
Bale, John, Kynge Johan, a Play; Camden Soc., 1838. [ab. 1552.]
Barbour's Bruce; ed. W. W. Skeat, E.E.T.S., 1870-1877. [1375.]
Barclay's Ship of Fools, ed. Jamieson; Edinburgh, 1874. 2 vols. [1509.]
Bardsley's Surnames.—Our English Surnames, by C. W. Bardsley; London, n. d. Third edition, 1884.
Baret, John, Alvearie or Quadruple Dictionary, London, 1580.
Barnes, R., Workes of, pr. by John Day; see Tyndall.
Bartsch, K., Chrestomathie Provençale; Elberfeld, 1875.
—— Chrestomathie de l'Ancien Français; Leipzig, 1875.
—— La Langue et la Littérature Françaises . . . précédés d'une Grammaire de l'Ancien Français, par A. Horning. Paris, 1887.
Basilicon Doron, by King James I; repr. in A Miscellany, ed. H. Morley; London, 1888. [1603.]
Basque.—Larramendi, M. de, Diccionario trilingue Castellano, Bascuence, y Latin. San Sebastian, 1853.
Bavarian.—Bayerisches Wörterbuch, von J. A. Schmeller, Four Parts, Stuttgart, 1827-1837.
Beaumont and Fletcher, Works of; ed. G. Darley. 2 vols. 1859. [1606-1616.]
Beckmann, J., History of Inventions; tr. by W. Johnston. New ed., London, 1846. 2 vols.
Becon, T., Works; ed. Rev. J. Ayre, M.A. Parker Soc. 1843-4. First collected ed. 1563-4.
Beda; see Ælfred.
—— De Temporibus Rationum; see Wright, T.
Be Dómes Dæge, ed. J. R. Lumby, E.E.T.S., 1876.
Beket, Thomas, Life of; by Robert of Gloucester; ed. W. H. Black. Percy Soc. 1845. [ab. 1300.]
Benfey; see Sanskrit.
Beowulf; ed. B. Thorpe, Oxford and London, 1855. Ed. Grein, 1857. Ed. A. J. Wyatt, 1894.
Berghaus, H.; see Low German dialects (Saxon).
Berners; see Froissart.
Beryn, The Tale of, ed. F. J. Furnivall; Chaucer Society, 1876.
Bestiary; see Old English Miscellany. [ab. 1250-1300.]
Beves of Hamtoun, ed. Turnbull, Edinburgh, 1838 (cited by Stratmann.) [ab. 1320-1330?] Also, ed. Prof. E. Kölbing. E.E.T.S., extra series, 1885-6, 1894.
Bevis.—Der Anglonormannische Boeve de Haumtone; ed. A. Stimming. 1899.
Bewick, T.; History of Quadrupeds. (First ed., 1790.)
Bible, English; Authorized Version, 1611.
—— Imprinted at London by Jhon Day, 1551.
Biblesworth (for Bibbesworth), Walter de, the treatise of; pr. in Wright's Vocabularies, First Series, pp. 142-174. [ab. 1300.]
Biblia Sacra Vulgatæ Editionis. Auctoritate edita. Parisiis, 1872.
Birch, W. de Gray; Cartularium Saxonicum (Charters relating to Anglo-Saxon History). London, 1885-93. 3 vols. 8vo.
Black Book of the Admiralty; ed. Sir T. Twiss. Vols. 1-4. 1871-6. (Rolls Series.)
Blackstone's Commentaries (cited in Richardson, and Todd's Johnson). [1764-1768.]
Blickling Homilies; ed. R. Morris, E.E.T.S., 1874-6. [10th cent.]
Blount's Law Dictionary.—Nomo-λεξikon; a Law-Dictionary, by Tho. Blount. Second Edition. London, 1691
Blount, T., Glossographia., 1674.
Body and Soul, the Debate of the; printed in the Latin Poems of Walter Mapes, ed. T. Wright; Camden Soc., London, 1841. (See also the reprint in Mätzner's Altenglische Sprachproben, pp. 90-103.) [13th century.]
Boethius, Chaucer's translation of, ed. R. Morris, E.E.T.S., 1878. [ab. 1380.] And see Ælfred and Chaucer.
Bohn's Lowndes.—The Bibliographer's Manual of English Literature, by W. T. Lowndes; New Edition, by H. G. Bohn, 1857.
Boke of St. Albans; first printed in 1486. [Fac-simile reprint, 1881.] Contains a Book on Hawking, a Book on Hunting (by Dame Julians Barnes), and a Book on Coat-Armour.
Book of Quintessence; ed. F. J. Furnivall. E.E.T.S. 1866. [1460-70.]
Borde, Andrew, The Fyrst Boke of the Introduction of Knowledge, &c. [1547.] Also, A Dyetary of Helth. [1542.] Ed. F. J. Furnivall, E.E.T.S., extra series, 1870.
—— Breviarie of Health. (First ed. 1547.)
Boswell, J., Life of Johnson; ed. J. W. Croker, 1876. [1791.]

Bosworth and Toller.—An Anglo-Saxon Dictionary based on the MS. collections of the late J. Bosworth, D.D.; edited and enlarged by T. Northcote Toller. M.A. Oxford, 1882, &c.
Boutell's Heraldry; ed. S. T. Aveling. London, 1873.
Boyle, Robert, Works. First ed. 1744; 5 vols. (Cited by Richardson.)
Bozon.—Les Contes Moralisés de N. Bozon; ed. Miss L. Toulmin Smith and P. Meyer; Paris, 1889. (Anglo-French.)
Brachet, A., Etymological French Dictionary, tr. by G. W. Kitchin, 1873.
—— Historical Grammar of the French Language; enlarged by P. Toynbee, M.A. Oxford, 1896. 8vo.
Brand, John, M.A.—Observations on Popular Antiquities. Arranged and revised, with additions, by H. Ellis. Republished, in Bohn's Antiquarian Library, post 8vo, 1848. 3 vols.
Bray.—See French dialects.
Brazil.—Historia Naturalis Brasiliæ; by Piso, Marcgraf, and de Laet. Amsterdam, 1648.
Brazilian.—Cf. Vocabulario Rioplatense razonado, por D. D. Granada. Montevideo, 1890.
Brazilian Language, The; by A. Cavalcanti, Rio Janeiro, 1883.
Bréal; see Latin.
Bremen Wörterbuch.—Versuch eines bremisch-niedersächsischen Wörterbuchs, herausgegeben von der bremischen deutschen Gesellschaft, 5 vols. Bremen, 1767.
Brende, J., tr. of Quintius Curtius, 1561 (cited by Richardson).
Breton.—Dictionnaire Breton-Français, par J.F.M.M.A. Le Gonidec; Angoulême, 1821.
Breton, Nicholas (1545?-1626?); Works, ed. Grosart (Chertsey Library), 1877.
Britten and Holland.—A Dictionary of English Plant-names; by J. Britten and R. Holland. E.D.S. 1886.
Britton; the French Text, with an E. translation, introduction and notes; by F. M. Nichols, M.A. Oxford, 1865. 2 vols. 8vo. (Anglo-French.)
Brockett, J. T., A Glossary of North Country Words, Third Edition. 2 vols. Newcastle, 1846.
Browne, Sir Thomas, Works of, ed. S. Wilkin, 4 vols., 1852. (In Bohn's Standard Library.) [1640-1680.]
Browne, W., Britannia's Pastorals, see English Poets. [1613-1616.]
Bruce: see Barbour.
Brugmann.—Elements of the Comparative Grammar of the Indo-Germanic Languages. Vol. i, tr. by Joseph Wright, Ph.D. London, 1888. Vols. 2-4, with Index; tr. by R. S. Conway and W. H. D. Rouse. London, 1891-5.
Brugmann, K.; Grundriss der vergleichenden Grammatik der indogermanischen Sprachen. Strassburg, 1886-1900. 5 vols.
Brugmann, K., and B. Delbrück; Grundriss der vergleichenden Grammatik der indogermanischen Sprachen. Zweite Bearbeitung. Vol. I. Strassburg, 1897.
Brunne, Robert of, Handlyng Synne; ed. F. J. Furnivall; Roxburghe Club, 1862. [1303.]
Buffon's Natural History abridged. London, 1792. 2 vols.
Bullein's Dialogue against the Fever Pestilence; ed. M. and A. H. Bullen. E.E.T.S., extra series, 1888. [1578.]
Bullinger, H., Works; ed. Rev. T. Harding. Parker Soc., 1849-52. 4 vols. 8vo.
Burguy's Glossaire.—In tome iii. of Grammaire de la Langue D'Oïl, par G. F. Burguy; 2me édition, Berlin and Paris, 1870.
Burke, Select Works, ed. E. J. Payne, vol. i, 1876. [1774-1776.]
Burne, Charlotte S., Shropshire Folk-lore. London, 1883.
Burnet, Bp., History of his own time. London, 1724-34, folio. 2 vols. (Several editions. Cited by Richardson.)
Burns, R., Poems, Songs, and Letters, the Globe Edition, 1868. [1786-1796.]
Burton, Robert, Anatomy of Melancholy (cited in Richardson, and Todd's Johnson). [1621.]
Bury Wills, ed. S. Tymms, Camden Soc. 1850. [15th cent.]
Butler, Jos., Bp. of Durham; The Analogy of Religion. (Works, in 1807.)
Butler's Poems (including Hudibras), ed. Robert Bell. 3 vols. London, 1855. [Hudibras, 1663-1678.]
—— Hudibras; parts 1 and 2; ed. A. Milnes. London, 1881.
Byron, Poems, Dramas, &c. 8 vols. London: J. Murray, 1853.
Cædmon, ed. B. Thorpe. Published by the Society of Antiquaries, London, 1832.
Campbell, T., Poetical Works of. A new ed. London, 1853.
Carey, H., Chrononhotonthologos; repr. in Burlesque Plays, ed. H. Morley. London, 1885.
Caribbean.—Dictionnaire Caraïbe-François; par le R. P. Raymond Breton. Auxerre, 1665.

Castle off Loue. An Early English Translation of an Old French Poem, by Robert Grosseteste, bp. of Lincoln; ed. R. F. Weymouth. (Published for the Philological Society.) [1370?]

Catholicon Anglicum; ed. S. J. Herrtage; E.E.T.S. 1881. [1483.]

Cavendish, G., Life of Thomas Wolsey, Cardinal; ed. F. S. Ellis. London, 1893 (Kelmscott Press). Written in 1557.

Caxton, W., tr. of Reynard the Fox, ed. Arber, 1878. [1481.]

Caxton's Blanchardyn and Eglantine; ed. Dr. Leon Kellner. E.E.T.S., extra series. 1890. [ab. 1489.]

—— Dictes and Sayengis of Philosophirs, by Lord Rivers; pr. by Caxton in 1477. [Fac-simile edition.]

—— Eneydos; ed. W. T. Culley and F. J. Furnivall. E.E.T.S., extra series. 1890. [1490.]

—— Godeffroy of Boloyne; ed. Mary N. Colvin, Ph.D. E.E.T.S., extra series. 1893. [1481.]

—— The Golden Legend; pr. in 1483. Reprint by F. S. Ellis and W. Morris. London, 1892. 3 vols.

—— The Recuyell of the Historyes of Troye. Exact reprint by H. O. Sommer, Ph.D. London, 1894. 2 vols. [ab. 1474.]

Centlivre, Mrs. S.; Plays. 1761. 12mo. 3 vols.

Century Dictionary of the English Language, The. New York and London, 1889-91. In six vols.

Chalmers; see English Poets.

Chambers's Etymological Dictionary of the English Language, ed. J. Donald, 1871.

Chambers, R.; The Book of Days, A Miscellany of Popular Antiquities. 2 vols. London and Edinburgh, 1864.

Chanson de Roland, La; Texte, &c., par L. Gautier. Tours, 1881. (Early 11th cent.)

Chapman, George, Plays, ed. R. H. Shepherd, 1874. [1598-1634.]

—— Translation of Homer, ed. R. H. Shepherd, 1875. (In this edition the lines are not numbered; a far better edition is that by Hooper.) [1598.]

Chaucer.—The Workes of Geffray Chaucer. (First collected Edition by W. Thynne, 1532.) Facsimile reproduction. Oxford (1904). Second ed. 1542. Third ed. (ab. 1550.)

—— Chaucers Woorkes, with diuers Addicions; newlie prynted by Jhon Kyngston, 1561. [Fourth ed., by J. Stowe.] Contains the first edition of the Court of Love; also the Testament of Love.

—— The Complete Works of Geoffrey Chaucer. Ed. by the Rev. W. W. Skeat, Litt.D. Oxford, 1894. Six vols. 8vo.

—— Chaucer Society, publications of the.

—— Canterbury Tales: Six-text edition, ed. F. J. Furnivall. (Chaucer Society.)

—— ed. Tyrwhitt.—A reprint of Tyrwhitt's edition of the Canterbury Tales, with his notes and glossary; to which were added (by the publisher) reprints of Chaucer's Minor Poems, &c. London, E. Moxon, 1855; first printed, 1843. [1369-1400.]

—— tr. of Boethius; ed. Morris, E.E.T.S., extra series, 1868. [ab. 1380.]

—— Treatise on the Astrolabe; ed. Skeat, Chaucer Society and E.E.T.S., extra series, 1872. [1391.]

Chaucer's Dream. A late poem, not by Chaucer; printed by Moxon with Chaucer's Works. [15th cent.]

Chaucerian and Other Pieces. Ed. by the Rev. W. W. Skeat, Litt.D. Oxford, 1897.

Chester Whitsun Plays; ed. T. Wright. Shakespeare Soc. nos. 17 and 35; 1843 and 1847.

Chinese.—A Syllabic Dictionary of the Chinese Language. By S. W. Williams. Shanghai, 1874.

—— Chinese-English Dictionary of the Amoy vernacular. By the Rev. C. Douglas, 1873.

Christ's Own Complaint; see Political, Religious, and Love Poems.

Churchill's Collection of Voyages and Travels. London, 1704, folio. 4 vols. (Another ed. 1732.)

Clare, John; Poems. Second edition, London, 1820. Another ed. 1821. 2 vols.

Clarendon, Earl of. History of the Rebellion and Civil Wars in England. Oxford, 1826. 8vo. 8 vols. (Many other editions.)

Clavigero's History of Mexico; tr. by C. Cullen. London, 1787. 4to. 2 vols.

Cockayne, O., Leechdoms, Wortcunning, and Starcraft of Early England. (Record Series.) 1864-1866. 3 vols.

—— The Shrine. London, 1864. (Contains several pieces in Anglo-Saxon.)

Cockeram, H.—The English Dictionarie. By H. C. Gent. 7th ed. London, 1642. 8vo. (First ed. 1632.)

Codex Diplomaticus; see Kemble.

Coles, E., an English Dictionary, 1684.

Collins, W.; Poems. See English Poets.

Complaynte of Scotlande. Re-edited by James A. H. Murray, E.E.T.S., extra series, 1872, 1873. [1549.]

Congreve, W., Plays; see Wycherley. [Died 1729.]

Cookery Books; see Austin.

Cooper, T., Thesaurus Linguæ Romanæ et Britannicæ, 1565.

Cooper's Report on Rymer's Fœdera. Appendix A (first vol.). Appendix B. C. D. (second vol.). App. B contains the AS. Glosses to Prudentius.

Coptic.—Lexicon Linguæ Copticæ. By A. Peyron. Turin, 1835.

Corblet; see French dialects (Picard).

Cornish.—Lexicon Cornu-Britannicum; by R. Williams. Llandovery and London, 1865.

Coryat, T.—Coryat's Crudities hastily gobled vp, &c. London, 1611. 4to.

Cotgrave.—A French and English Dictionary, composed by Mr. Randle Cotgrave; with another in English and French; ed. J. Howell. London, pr. by Wm. Hunt, in Pye-corner, 1660.

Cotton, C., Poems; see English Poets.

Court of Love; a late poem first printed with Chaucer's Works, 1561. [15th or 16th cent.] See Chaucerian Pieces.

Coventry Mysteries, ed. J. O. Halliwell. Shakespeare Society, 1841. [ab. 1460.]

Cowel, Dr., The Interpreter of Words and Terms. Augmented and improved. London, 1701.

Cowley, A., Works of, London, 1688. [1633-1667.] And see English Poets.

Cowley's Prose Works; ed. Rev. J. R. Lumby. Cambridge, 1887. (For Poems, see English Poets.)

Cowper, W., the Poetical Works of; ed. R. A. Wilmott. London, 1866. [1782-1799.]

Cranmer, T., Works. Parker Soc. 1844-6. 2 vols.

Cursor Mundi: ed. Dr. R. Morris, E.E.T.S., Parts i-vi, 1874-92. [ab. 1300.]

Curtius, G., Greek Etymology; tr. by Wilkins and England. 2 vols. 1876.

Dähnert; see Low German dialects (Pomeranian).

Dampier's Voyages, an. 1681 (cited by Richardson). A New Voyage, 1699; 2 vols.

Daniel, S., Civil Wars; see English Poets. [1595.]

Danish.—Molbech, C., Dansk Ordbog; Kiöbenhavn, 1859.

—— Ferrall og Repps dansk-engelske Ordbog, gjennemseet og rettet af W. Mariboe; Kjöbenhavn, 1861. (When 'Dan.' alone is cited, this book or the next is meant.)

—— A Dictionary of the Dano-Norwegian and English Languages, by A. Larsen. 3rd ed. Copenhagen, 1897.

—— A New Practical and Easy method of Learning the Danish Language; by H. Lund. Second Edition, London, 1860.

Danish, Middle.—Ordbog til det ældre Danske Sprog (1300-1700) af Otto Kalkar. Kœbenhavn. 1881-1907. (In 4 vols.)

Danish dialects.—Det Danske Folkesprog i Sönderjylland [South Jutland]; ved Johannes Kok. København, 1863-7. 2 vols.

—— Bidrag til en Ordbog over Jyske Almuesmål; af H. F. Feilberg. Kjöbenhavn, 1886—. Vol. 1; A-H. Vol. 2; I-P. Parts 24-31; R-St.

—— Dansk Dialect-Lexicon; ved C. Molbech. Kiöbenhavn, 1841.

—— Etymological Dictionary; see Falk.

Davenant, Sir W., Poems; see English Poets.

Davies, J., Antiquæ.. Wallicæ et Latinæ Dictionarium Duplex. A Welsh-Latin Dict. London, 1632. Fol.

Davies, T. Lewis O., M.A.; A Supplementary English Glossary. London, 1881. 8vo.

De Bo; see Flemish.

Decorde; see French dialects (Bray).

Degrevant, Sir; see Thornton Romances.

Dekker, T., The Dramatic Works of. London, 1873. 4 vols. 8vo.

—— The Seven Deadly Sins of London (1606); ed. Arber, 1879.

—— Five Plays; ed. E. Rhys. London, 1887. (Mermaid Series.)

Delfortrie; see Flemish.

Denham, Sir John; see English Poets.

Derby, Earl of, Expeditions to Prussia and the Holy Land in 1390-1 and 1392-3; ed. Lucy Toulmin Smith. Camden Soc. 1894.

Derham, W., Physico-Theology. First ed. 1713; best ed. 1798. 8vo. 2 vols.

Destruction of Troy; see Gest Hystoriale.

Devic, M., Dictionnaire étymologique de tous les mots d'origine Orientale; in the Supplement to Littré's French Dictionary.

D'Hombres; see French dialects (Languedoc).

Dictes of the Philosophirs; see Caxton.

Dictionary of the Bible, ed. W. Smith. Concise edition, by W. Aldis Wright, 1865.

Dictionary of National Biography. London, 1885–. 8vo.

Diez, F., Etymologisches Wörterbuch der Romanischen Sprachen. Fourth Edition. Bonn, 1878.

Digby Mysteries.—Ancient Mysteries from the Digby MSS.; Edinburgh, 1835 (cited by Stratmann). [ab. 1430?] *Also*, The Digby Plays, ed. F. J. Furnivall. E.E.T.S., extra series. 1896.

Dodsley, Robert. A Select Collection of Old English Plays, originally published by R. D. Fourth Edition. By W. Carew Hazlitt. London, 1874–6. 8vo. 15 vols. [16th cent.]

Donne, J., Poems; see English Poets.

Douglas, Gavin, Works of; ed. J. Small. 4 vols. Edinburgh, 1874. [1501–1513.]

Drama, The Ancient British; (containing many of the plays in Dodsley's Collection). London, 1810. royal 8vo. 3 vols.

—— The Modern British; containing plays by Beaumont and Fletcher, Mrs. Centlivre, Congreve, Dryden, Farquhar, Fielding, Foote, Ford, Garrick, Jonson, Lillo, Massinger, Otway, Steele, Vanbrugh, Wycherley, Young, &c. London, 1811. royal 8vo. 5 vols.

Drant, T.; translations from Horace. Satires, 1566; Art of Poetry, Epistles, and Satires, 1567.

Drayton.—Poems of Michael Drayton; see English Poets.

Drummond, W., Poems; see English Poets.

Dryden, J., Poetical Works, London, 1851. [Died 1701.]

—— The Works of; ed. W. Scott. London, 1808. 18 vols. 8vo.

—— tr. of Virgil; reprint by F. Warne and Co.; n. d.

Du Bois; see French dialects (Norman).

Ducange.—Glossarium Mediæ et Infimæ Latinitatis, conditum a Carolo du Fresne Domino Du Cange . . cum Supplementis . . . Editio Nova . . a L. Favre. Niort et Londres. 1884–7. In ten vols.

—— Lexicon Manuale ad Scriptores Mediæ et Infimæ Latinitatis, ex glossariis C. D. D. Ducangii et aliorum in compendium accuratissime redactum. Par W.-H. Maigne D'Arnis. Publié par M. L'Abbé Migne. Paris, 1866. (A compendium in one volume.)

Duméril; see French dialects (Norman).

Dunbar, W., Poems; ed. J. Small and W. Gregor. In 5 parts. Scottish Text Soc. 1883–93.

Durham Ritual.—Rituale Ecclesiæ Dunelmensis. Ed. J. Stevenson. Surtees Soc. 1840. (I give a large number of corrections in my Collation with the MS.; in Phil. Soc. Trans. 1877–9; pp. 49*–72*.)

Dutch.—A Large Dictionary, English and Dutch, by W. Sewel. Fifth Edition. Amsterdam, 1754.

—— A large Netherdutch and English Dictionarie, by H. Hexham. Rotterdam, 1658.

—— Kilian, C., Old Dutch Dictionary. Utrecht, 1777.

—— Oudemans, A. C., Old Dutch Dictionary, 7 parts, 1869–80.

—— Ten Kate, L., Aenleiding tot de Kennisse van het verhevene Deel der Nederduitsche Sprake. 2 vols. Amsterdam, 1723.

—— A New Pocket-Dictionary of the English and Dutch Languages. Leipzig; C. Tauchnitz. (When only 'Du.' is cited, this book or the next is meant.)

—— Nederlandsch-Engelsch en Engelsch-Nederlandsch Woordenboek; door I. M. Calisch. Tiel, 1875. 2 vols.

—— Etymological Dictionary; see Franck.

Dutch dialect.—Wörterbuch der Groningeschen Mundart; by H. Molema. Norden and Leipzig, 1888.

Du Wes, An Introductorie for to lerne to rede, to pronounce, and to speke French trewly; by Giles Du Wes. Printed together with Palsgrave's French Dictionary. See Palsgrave.

Dyer, J., Poems; see English Poets.

E.D.D.—English Dialect Dictionary, ed. Prof. Wright. Oxford, 1898–1905. 6 vols.

Earl of Derby's Accounts; see Derby.

Earle, J.; Handbook to the Land Charters and other Saxonic Documents. Oxford. 1888.

—— Micro-cosmographie; 1628. (In Arber's Reprints.)

—— Two Saxon Chronicles; see Anglo-Saxon Chronicle.

Earliest English Prose Psalter; ed. Dr. K. D. Buelbring. E.E.T.S. 1891.

Early English Homilies; ed. Dr. Richard Morris; E.E.T.S., First Series, 1867; Second Series, 1873. [13th century.]

Early English Poems and Lives of Saints; ed. F. J. Furnivall. Phil. Soc. 1862.

Early English Popular Poetry.—Remains of the Early Popular

Poetry of England; by W. Carew Hazlitt. London, 1864–6. 4 vols.

Early English Psalter.—Anglo-Saxon and Early English Psalter, ed. J. Stevenson. 2 vols. (Surtees Society.) 1843–1847.

Early E. Wills.—The Fifty Earliest English Wills; ed. F. J. Furnivall. E.E.T.S. 1882. [1387–1454.]

Eastwood and Wright's Bible Wordbook.—A Glossary of Old English Bible Words, by J. Eastwood and W. Aldis Wright. London, 1866.

Eden, R., The First Three English Books on America; ed. E. Arber. Birmingham, 1885. [1511?–1555.]

Edmondston, T., Glossary of the Shetland and Orkney Dialect. Phil. Soc. 1866.

E.D.S. = English Dialect Society, publications of the. (Including Ray's Collections, Pegge's Kenticisms and Derbicisms, Whitby Glossary, Mid-Yorkshire Glossary, Holderness Glossary, Glossaries of words in use in Cheshire, Cumberland, Hants, Lancs., Leics., Lincs., Northumberland, Somersets., Surrey, Swaledale, Warwicks., Wilts., Worcs., &c., Bird-names, Plant-names, Old Farming Words, Turner's Names of Plants, Fitzherbert's Husbandry, Tusser's Husbandry, &c.)

E.E.T.S.—Early English Text Society's publications. See Ælfred, Ælfric, Alexander, Alliterative Poems, Ayenbite, Barbour, Be Dómes Dæge, Blickling Homilies, Bullein, Catholicon, Caxton, Chaucer, Complaint of Scotland, Cursor Mundi, Early English Homilies, Ellis, English Gilds, Fisher, Floriz, Gawayn, Genesis, Gregory, Hali Meidenhad, Havelok, Joseph, King Horn, Knight of la Tour, Lancelot, Legends of the Holy Rood, Levins, Lyndesay, Morte Arthure, Myrc, Myrour of Our Lady, Old Eng. Miscellany, Palladius, Partenay, Piers Plowman, Political, St. Juliana, Seinte Marharete, Troybook, Will. of Palerne, &c.

Egilsson; see Icelandic.

Eglamour, Sir; see Thornton Romances.

Ellis, A. J., Early English Pronunciation, E.E.T.S., extra series, 1867, 1869, 1871, 1874, 1889.

Ellis, Sir H.; Original Letters illustrative of English History. Three Series. London, 1824–46. cr. 8vo. 11 vols.

Elyot, Sir T., The Castel of Helthe; ed. 1539. [1533.]

—— The Gouernor. (Black-letter Edition; no title-page.) [1531.]

—— The Boke named The Gouernour; from the first ed. of 1531; ed. H. H. S. Croft, M.A. London, 1883. 2 vols.

Emaré, Romance of; see Ritson.

—— ed. Edith Rickert, Ph.D. E.E.T.S. 1906.

Engelmann and Dozy, Glossaire des mots Espagnols et Portugais tirés de l'Arabe. Second Edition, Paris, 1869.

Englische Studien. Heilbronn; from 1877 onwards.

English Cyclopædia, conducted by Charles Knight. 22 vols., with Three Supplements and Index.

English Dialect Society's publications. (References to these are marked E.D.S.) See E.D.S. and E.D.D. above.

English Garner, An; ed. E. Arber. Birmingham, 1877–83. Vols. 1–7.

English Gilds, ed. Toulmin Smith. E.E.T.S., 1870. [1389–1450.]

English Poets, from Chaucer to Cowper, ed. A. Chalmers. London, 1810. 21 vols.

Epinal Glossary; see O.E. Texts.

Etheredge, Sir G., Works of; ed. A. W. Verity. London, 1888. 8vo.

Ettmüller; see Anglo-Saxon.

Evans, A. B. and S.; Leicestershire Words. E.D.S. 1881.

Evelyn, John, Diary of; ed. W. Bray. (Reprint by F. Warne; n. d.) [1620–1706.]

—— Parallel of Ancient and Modern Architecture. 1669.

—— Sylva. First ed. 1664. 4to. (Many editions.)

Excerpta Historica. London, 1831. 8vo.

Exeter Book.—Codex Exoniensis; a Collection of AS. Poetry. Ed. B. Thorpe. London, 1842. (And see Grein.)

Exmoor Scolding and Courtship; E.D.S. 1879.

Fabyan's Chronicles of England and France, ed. Henry Ellis. London, 1811. 4to. [1516.]

Faire Em., a play; see Shakespeare Apocrypha.

Fairfax, tr. of Tasso; ed. R. A. Willmott, 1858. (Modernized and spoilt in the editing.) [1600.]

Fairholt, F. W., Costume in England. 3rd ed.; by the Hon. H. A. Dillon, F.S.A. London, 1885. 8vo. 2 vols.

Falconer's Shipwreck; see English Poets.

Falk, H. og A. Torp; Etymologisk Ordbog over det Norske og det Danske Sprog. Kristiania, 1903–6. 2 vols.

Farquhar, G., Plays; see Drama, The Modern British; also in the Mermaid Series; and see Wycherley.

Feilberg; see Danish dialects.

Ferrex and Porrex; see Sackville; and Drama, Ancient British.

Ferumbras, Sir; ed. S. J. Herrtage. E.E.T.S., extra series, 1879.

Fick, A., Vergleichendes Wörterbuch der Indogermanischen Sprachen, sprachgeschichtlich angeordnet. Third Edition. 3 vols. Göttingen, 1874. And see Stokes-Fick.

Fisher, Bp. J., English Works of; ed. J. E. B. Mayor. E. E. T. S., extra series. 1876. [Died 1535.]

Fitzherbert, Book of Husbandry; ed. W. W. Skeat. E. D. S. 1882. [1534.] (Written by John F., not by Sir Anthony, as stated in the Preface.)

Flemish.—Mémoire sur les Analogies des Langues Flamande, Allemande, et Anglaise; par E.-J. Delfortrie. Bruxelles, 1858.

—— West-Flemish Dictionary; by L.—L. De Bo. Gent, 1892.

Fletcher, John, Plays; see Beaumont.

—— Phineas, Poems of; see English Poets. [1633.]

Florio; see Italian.

Floriz and Blancheflour; ed. J. R. Lumby. E. E. T. S., 1866. [End of 13th cent.]

Flower and the Leaf; see Chaucerian Pieces.

Flügel; see German.

Foote, Sam., Dramatic Works of. London, n. d. 2 vols. And see Drama, Modern British, vol. v.

Forby.—The Vocabulary of East Anglia, by the late Rev. Robert Forby. 2 vols. London, 1830.

Ford, John, Plays; ed. W. Gifford. London, 1827. 8vo. 2 vols.

Foxe, John, Acts and Monuments of these latter and perillous Dayes, touching Matters of the Church, &c.; first ed. in 1563, folio. Generally known as Foxe's Book of Martyrs.

Frampton, J., Ioyfull Newes out of the newe founde worlde. 1577. London. 4to. Tr. from the Spanish of Monardes.

Franck, Dr. J.; Etymologisch Woordenboek der Nederlandsche Taal. 's-Gravenhage, 1892.

French; see Bartsch, Brachet, Burguy, Cotgrave, Roquefort, Schwan, Vie de Seint Auban. (When only ' F.' is cited, the reference is either to Hatzfeld, or to Hamilton and Legros.) 'MF.' refers to Cotgrave.

—— Dictionnaire International Français-Anglais, par MM. H. Hamilton et E. Legros. Paris, 1872.

—— Dictionnaire Général de la Langue Française; par MM. A. Hatzfeld, A. Darmesteter, et A. Thomas. Paris (undated; commenced in 1871). 2 vols. (Referred to as ' Hatzfeld '.)

—— Littré, É., Dictionnaire de la Langue Française. 4 vols.; with supplement (see Devic). Paris, 1877.

—— Scheler, A., Dictionnaire d'Étymologie Française; par A. Scheler. Nouvelle édition. Bruxelles et Londres, 1873.

French, Old.—Dictionnaire de L'Ancienne Langue Française et de tous ses Dialectes du IXᵉ au XVᵉ siècle; par F. Godefroy. Paris, 1881-1902. 10 vols. (with Supplement).

French dialects.—Berry: Vocabulaire du Berry; par un amateur du vieux Langage. Paris, 1842.

—— Bourgogne: Vocabulaire . . du dialecte . . de la Province de Bourgogne; par Mignard. Paris, 1870.

—— Bray: Dictionnaire du Patois du Pays de Bray; par l'Abbé J.-E. Decorde. Paris, 1852.

—— Gascon: Dictionnaire Gascon-Français; par C. Moncaut. Paris, 1863.

—— Haut-Maine: Vocabulaire du Haut-Maine; par C. R. de M[ontesson]. Paris, 1859.

—— Ille-et-Vilaine: Glossaire Patois du département d'Ille-et-Vilaine; par Ad. Orain. Paris, 1886.

—— Languedoc: Dictionnaire du patois du Bas-Limousin (Corrèze) et des environs de Tulle; par M. Nic. Béronie. Tulle, n. d.

—— : Dictionnaire Languedocien-Français par M. D'Hombres et G. Charvet. Alais, 1884.

—— Lyons: Dictionnaire du Patois Forézien; par L.-P. Graz. Lyon, 1863.

—— : Dictionnaire étymologique du patois Lyonnais; par N. du Puitspelu. Lyon, 1887-90.

—— la Meuse: Glossaire abrégé du Patois de la Meuse; par H. Labourasse. Arcis-sur-l'Aube, 1887.

—— Norman: Glossaire du Patois Normand; par M. Louis du Bois. Caen, 1856.

—— : Glossaire du Normand; par le Héricher. Paris (no date). 2 vols.

—— : Glossaire du Patois Normand; par MM. Édélestand et Alfred Duméril. Caen, 1849.

—— : Dictionnaire de Patois Normand; par Henri Moisy. Caen 1887.

—— : Glossaire comparatif Anglo-Normand; par Henri Moisy. Caen, 1895.

—— : Dictionnaire du Patois Normand en usage dans le département de l'Eure; par MM. Robin, Le Prevost, A. Passy, et de Blosseville. Évreux, 1879.

French dialects.—Guernsey: Dictionnaire Franco-Normand; ou recueil des Mots particuliers au dialecte de Guernesey; par G. Métivier. London, 1870.

—— Picard: Glossaire Étymologique et Comparatif du Patois Picard, ancien et moderne; par l'Abbé Jules Corblet. Paris, 1851.

—— Rouchi: Dictionnaire Rouchi-Français; par G. A. I. Hécart. (Troisième édition.) Valenciennes, 1834.

—— Verdun.—Dictionnaire du langage populaire Verduno-Chalonnais (Saône-et-Loire); par F. Fertiault. Paris, 1896.

—— Walloon: Dictionnaire de la langue Wallonne; par Grandgagnage. Liège, 1847.

—— : Dictionnaire Wallon-Français; par L. Remacle. Deuxième édition. Liège, 1843. 2 vols.

—— : Dictionnaire du Wallon du Mons; par J. Sigart. (Deuxième édition.) Paris, 1870.

Friesic.—Altfriesisches Wörterbuch, von K. von Richthofen; Göttingen, 1840.

—— Glossarium der friesischen Sprache, besonders in nordfriesischer Mundart, von N. Outzen. Kopenhagen, 1837.

—— Koolman, J., ten Doorkaat, Wörterbuch der Ostfriesischen Sprache. Norden, 1879-84. 3 vols.

Frith: see Tyndall.

Froissart, tr. by Lord Berners. (Cited by Richardson.) [1523-25.]

Fryer, John. A New Account of East India, &c. London, 1698. fol.

Fuller, T., A Pisgah Light of Palestine. (Reprint.) London, 1869. 8vo. [1650.]

—— The Church History of Britain. (First ed. 1655-6.)

—— The History of the Worthies of England. (First ed. 1662.)

—— Holy and Profane State. New edition. London, 1841. 8vo. [1642.]

Gaelic.—A Dictionary of the Gaelic Language, by Macleod and Dewar; Glasgow, 1839.

—— An Etymological Dictionary of the Gaelic Language. By A. Macbain, M.A. Inverness, 1896.

Gallée; see Low German, Old; under Low German dialects.

Gamelyn, the Tale of. In Wright's edition of Chaucer's Canterbury Tales. Also ed. W. W. Skeat. 2nd ed. Oxford, 1893. [14th cent.]

Gamester, The Compleat. London, 1674. 12mo. And London, 1680.

Gammer Gurton's Needle; see Drama, Ancient British, vol. i.

Garcilasso de la Vega; Royal Commentaries of Peru; tr. by Sir P. Rycaut. London, 1688. fol.

Garlande, John de, Dictionarius; pr. in Wright's Vocabularies, First Series, pp. 120-138. [13th cent.]

Garrick, D., Plays; see Drama, Modern British.

Gascoigne, G., Works of; ed. W. C. Hazlitt, 1869. [Died 1577.]

Gawayn and the Green Knight; an alliterative Romance-Poem, ed. Dr. Richard Morris, E.E.T.S., 1864; reprinted, 1869. [ab. 1360.]

Gay, J., Poems of; see English Poets. [Died 1732.]

Gazophylacium Anglicanum. London, 1689. 8vo.

Generydes, A Romance; ed. W. Aldis Wright. E.E.T.S., 1873 and 1878. [ab. 1440.]

Genesis and Exodus, The Story of; ed. Dr. Richard Morris, E.E.T.S., 1865. [1250-1300?]

Gentleman's Magazine. London, 1731-1858. 8vo. 205 vols.

Gerarde, J.; The Herbal, or general History of Plants. (First ed. in 1597.)

German.—Altdeutsches Wörterbuch; von Oskar Schade. (2nd ed.) Halle a. S. 1872-82.

—— Dictionary, by Flügel; ed. Feiling, Heimann, and Oxenford. London, 1861. (When only ' G.' is cited, this book is meant.)

—— F. L. K. Weigand, Deutsches Wörterbuch. Third ed. 2 vols. Giessen, 1878.

—— F. Kluge, Etymologisches Wörterbuch der deutschen Sprache. (Fifth ed.) Strassburg, 1894.

German dialects.—Thüringer Sprachschatz; von Dr. L. Hertel. Weimar, 1895. (Central Germany.)

—— Westerwald: Westerwäldisches Idiotikon; von K. C. L. Schmidt. Hadamar und Herborn, 1800. (Nassau.)

Gest Hystoriale of the Destruction of Troy; an alliterative Romance, ed. G. A. Panton and D. Donaldson, E.E.T.S., 1869 and 1874. [ab. 1390.]

Gesta Romanorum, English Version of; ed. S. J. Herrtage, E.E.T.S., extra series, 1879. [15th cent.]

Gibbon, E.; The History of the Decline and Fall of the Roman Empire. Illustrated Edition. London, n. d. 2 vols.

Gifford, G., A Dialogue of Witches and Witchcraft. London, 1603; ed. T. Wright, Percy Soc., 1842.

Glossary of Architecture. Oxford, 1840.

Glossary to Prudentius ; see Cooper.

Glossographia Anglicana Nova. London, 1719. 8vo.

Godefroy ; see French, Old.

Golden Booke (cited by Richardson). This is the Life of Marcus Aurelius, tr. by Lord Berners ; of which I have a black-letter copy, without a title-page. [First ed. 1534.]

Golding, Arthur, tr. of Ovid's Metamorphoses. London, 1603. (First complete ed. in 1567.)

Goldsmith, O., Works of ; ed. P. Cunningham. London, 1855. 8vo. 4 vols.

Gosson, Stephen, The Schoole of Abuse ; ed. E. Arber, 1868. [1579.]

Gothic.—A Mœso-Gothic Glossary ; by W. W. Skeat. London, 1868.

—— Ulfilas ; Text, Grammatik und Wörterbuch ; ed. Dr. M. Heyne. (7th ed.) Paderborn, 1878.

—— Etymological Dictionary ; see Uhlenbeck.

Gower, John, The Complete Works of (English, French, and Latin) ; ed. G. C. Macaulay, M.A. Oxford, 1899-1902. 8vo. 4 vols.

Gower's Confessio Amantis ; ed. Dr. Reinhold Pauli. London, 1857. 3 vols. [1393.]

Granada ; see Brazilian.

Gray, T., Poems of ; see English Poets.

Greek.—Liddell and Scott's Greek-English Lexicon, 1849.

—— Etymological Dictionary ; see Prellwitz.

Greene, R.—The Dramatic and Poetical Works of Rob. Greene and Geo. Peele ; ed. Rev. A. Dyce. London, 1883. 8vo.

Gregor, Rev. W., The Dialect of Banffshire. Phil. Soc., 1866.

Gregory's Pastoral Care, King Alfred's West-Saxon Version of ; ed. H. Sweet, M.A. E.E.T.S., 1871-2.

Grein, C. W. M., Bibliothek der Angelsächsischen Poesie. Göttingen, 1857, 1858. 2 vols.

—— Sprachschatz der Angelsächsischen Dichter. Cassel and Göttingen, 1861. 2 vols. (A concordance to Anglo-Saxon poetry.)

—— Bibliothek der Angelsächsischen Prosa, 1872. (Contains the Pentateuch, Joshua, Judges, Job, in Anglo-Saxon.)

Grey, Life of Lord ; ed. Sir P. de M. Grey Egerton. Camden Soc., 1847.

Grimm, J., Deutsche Grammatik. In 4 parts. Second edition. Göttingen, 1822-37. (With a Register (Index) by K. G. Andresen, 1865.)

Grindal, E., Remains ; ed. Rev. W. Nicholson, M.A. Parker Soc., 1843.

Grose, F., A Classical Dictionary of the Vulgar Tongue. [Slang Dictionary.] London, 1785. 8vo.

—— A Provincial Glossary. London, 1790. 8vo. (First ed. in 1787.)

Guillim, John, A Display of Heraldry. 4th ed. London, 1660.

Guthlac.—The Anglo-Saxon version of the Life of St. Guthlac ; ed. C. W. Goodwin, M.A. London, 1848.

Guy of Warwick ; ed. Prof. J. Zupitza. E.E.T.S., 1883, 1887, 1891.

Hakluyt, R., The Principal Navigations, Voiages, &c. of the English Nation. London, 1588, 1589, 1600. fol. 3 vols. in 2.

Haldeman, S. S., Affixes of English Words. Philadelphia, 1865.

Hales, J. W., Longer English Poems. London, 1872.

Hali Meidenhad, an Alliterative Homily of the 12th century ; ed. O. Cockayne, M.A. E.E.T.S., 1866. [ab. 1220.]

Hall, Fitzedward, Modern English. London, 1873. 8vo.

—— on English Adjectives in -able, with special reference to Reliable. London, 1877. 8vo.

Hall, J. (Bp.), Satires in Six Books. Oxford, 1753. [1597, 1598.]

—— Contemplations on the Old and New Testaments. Reprint. 1860. [1612-15.]

Halle, Edw. ; Hall's Chronicle ; reprinted. London, 1809. royal 4to. [1548, 1550.]

Halliwell, J. O., A Dictionary of Archaic and Provincial Words. Fifth edition. London, 1865. 2 vols.

Hamilton ; see French.

Hampole, Richard Rolle de, English Prose Treatises ; ed. Geo. G. Perry, M.A. E.E.T.S., 1866. [ab. 1340.]

—— Pricke of Conscience ; a Northumbrian Poem ; ed. R. Morris (Philological Society), London, 1863. [1340.]

—— The Psalter ; with a translation and exposition in English by R. Rolle of Hampole ; ed. Rev. H. R. Bramley. Oxford, 1884.

Hardyng's Chronicle ; ed. H. Ellis. London, 1812. royal 4to. [1543.]

Harington, Sir J., tr. of Ariosto ; see English Poets.

Harman's Caveat ; printed with the Fraternitye of Vacabondes, by John Awdeley ; ed. E. Viles and F. J. Furnivall. E.E.T.S., extra series, 1869. [1567.]

Harrison, W., A Description of England (Second and Third Books); ed. F. J. Furnivall. (New Shakspere Society), 1878. [1577.]

Hatton Correspondence (1601-1704) ; ed. E. M. Thompson. (Camden Soc.) 1878. 2 vols.

Havelok the Dane ; ed. W. W. Skeat and Sir F. Madden. E.E.T.S., extra series, 1868. [ab. 1280.]

Hawes, Stephen, The Pastime of Pleasure ; reprinted from the edition of 1555 ; ed. T. Wright. Percy Soc., 1845.

Hawkesworth, J., An Account of the Voyages .. by Commodore Byron, Capt. Wallis, Capt. Carteret, and Capt. Cook. London, 1773. 4to. 3 vols.

Haydn's Dictionary of Dates ; Thirteenth Edition, by B. Vincent. London, 1868.

Hazlitt ; see Early English Popular Poetry ; and see Gascoigne.

Hazlitt, W. C. ; reprint of Dodsley's Collection of Old Plays. 1874-76. 15 vols. [16th cent.]

Hearne, Th. ; see his glossary to Rob. of Gloucester.

Hebrew.—Lexicon Hebraicum et Chaldaicum ; edidit E. F. Leopold. Lipsiæ, 1872.

—— Hebräisches und Chaldäisches Handwörterbuch über das Alte Testament ; von W. Gesenius. Leipzig, 1883. (Ninth edition.)

Hécart ; see French dialects (Rouchi).

Héliand ; see Old Saxon.

Henry VII, The Statutes of ; in exact facsimile, from the very rare original, printed by Caxton in 1489 ; ed. J. Rae. London, 1869.

Henrysoun, R., Complaint and Testament of Creseide ; pr. with Chaucer's Works. [15th cent.] See Chaucerian Pieces ; also Ancient Scottish Poems, Edinburgh, 1770 ; and Sibbald's Scottish Poetry.

Henslow, G. ; see Medical Works.

Herbert, George, Poems of ; ed. R. A. Willmott. London, 1859. [Died 1633.]

Herbert, Sir T., Travels. Third edition. London, 1665.

Héricher, le ; see French dialects (Norman).

Herrick, R., Poetical Works of ; ed. W. Carew Hazlitt. London, 1869. 2 vols. 8vo.

Hertel, L. ; see German dialects (Thüringen).

Hexham ; see Dutch.

Heyne, M. See Old Saxon and Gothic.

Heywood, T., The Dramatic Works of. London, 1874. 6 vols.

Hickes, G., Linguarum veterum Septentrionalium Thesaurus. Oxford, 1703-5. 3 vols.

Higden.—Polychronicon Ranulphi Higden, with Trevisa's translation. (Rolls Series.) Vols. i and ii ed. by Churchill Babington, B.D. Vols. iii-ix by the Rev. J. Rawson Lumby, 1865-86. See Trevisa.

Hindi, Hindustani.—Bate, J. D., A Dictionary of the Hindee Language. Benares, 1875.

—— Fallon, S. W., Hindustani and English Dictionary. Benares, 1879.

—— Forbes, D., Hindustani Dictionary. London, 1848. New edition, 1859.

Hist. Nat. Brasiliæ ; see Brazil.

Hoccleve, T., Minor Poems ; ed. F. J. Furnivall. E. E. T. S., extra series, 1892.

—— Letter of Cupid ; see Chaucerian Pieces. [1402.]

—— Regement of Princes ; ed. F. J. Furnivall. E. E. T. S., 1897. [1412.]

—— To the Lordes and Knightes of the Garter ; see Chaucerian Pieces.

Hole, C., A Brief Biographical Dictionary, 1865.

Holinshed, Ralph, Chronicles of England, Scotland, and Ireland. London, 1807-8. 4to. 6 vols. (Reprint ; first ed., 1577-87.)

Holland, Philemon, tr. of Pliny's Natural History. London, 1634. fol. 2 vols.

—— tr. of Ammianus Marcellinus ; 1609. (Cited by Richardson.)

—— tr. of Plutarch's Morals ; 1603. (Cited by Richardson.)

Holland, Sir R., The Buke of the Howlat ; see Scottish Alliterative Poems.

Homilies appointed to be read in Churches. (Reprint.) S.P.C.K., London, 1852.

Hone, Wm., Every-Day Book. London, 1825-7. 8vo. 2 vols.

Hooker, R., The Laws of Ecclesiastical Polity. Eight Bookes. (First ed. in 1594.)

Horn.—Kyng Horn, Floriz and Blancheflour, &c. ; ed. Rev. J. Rawson Lumby. E.E.T.S., 1866.

Horn, Paul ; see Persian.

Horne Tooke ; see Tooke.

Horstmann, Dr. C., Altenglische Legenden. Paderborn, 1875.

—— Neue Folge. Heilbronn, 1881.

—— Sammlung Altenglischer Legenden. Heilbronn, 1878.

Howard, Sir R., The Committee ; a play (1665) ; see Drama, mod. British ; vol. 3.

Howell, J., Epistolæ Ho-Elianæ, Familiar Letters. Fifth edition, 4 vols. in one. 1678.

Howell, J., Instructions for Forreine Travell (1642); ed. Arber, 1868.

Huloet, R., Abecedarium Anglo-Latinum. London, 1552.

Hungarian.—Dankovsky, G., Magyricæ Linguæ Lexicon. Presburg, 1833.

Icelandic.—An Icelandic-English Dictionary, based on the MS. collections of the late R. Cleasby; by G. Vigfusson. Oxford, 1874. With an Appendix containing a list of words etymologically connected with Icelandic, by W. W. Skeat, 1876.

—— Egilsson, S., Lexicon Poeticum antiquæ Linguæ Septentrionalis. Hafniæ, 1860.

—— Möbius, T., Altnordisches Glossar. Leipzig, 1866.

Ihre; see Swedish.

Irish.—An Irish-English Dictionary, by E. O'Reilly; with a supplement by J. O'Donovan. Dublin, 1864.

—— Irische Texte mit Wörterbuch; von E. Windisch. Leipzig, 1880. (Old Irish.)

Isidore, St., Works of; in Migne's Cursus Patrologicus.

Isumbras, Romance of; see Thornton Romances.

Italian.—Florio, John. A Worlde of Wordes, or most copious and exact Dictionarie in Italian and English. London, 1598. (First edition.)

—— Florio, J. Queen Anna's New Worlde of Wordes, or Dictionarie of the Italian and English tongues. London, 1611.

—— Italian and English Dictionary, by J. Florio; and English and Italian Dictionary, by G. Torriano; ed. J. D[avies], M.D. London, 1688.

—— Italian-English and English-Italian Dictionary, by Jos. Baretti. Eighth edition. London, 1831. 2 vols.

—— Italian and English Dictionary, by F. C. Meadows; Fifteenth edition. London, 1857. [When 'Ital.' is cited without further notice, this book is meant.]

Iwain (or Ywaine) and Gawin; see Ritson.

Jackson, Georgina F., Shropshire Word-book. London, 1879–81.

Jago, R., Poems of; see English Poets.

Jamieson's Scottish Dictionary. A new edition, ed. J. Longmuir and D. Donaldson. Paisley, 1879–87. 4to. 4 vols. and Supplement.

Johns, Rev. C. A., Flowers of the Field. Fourth edition. London, S.P.C.K., n. d.

Johnson's Dictionary of the English Language; ed. by the Rev. H. J. Todd. London, 1827. 4to. 3 vols.

Johnson, Dr. Sam., A Journey to the Western Islands of Scotland, 1775. Included (as a Tour to the Hebrides) in Boswell's Life of Johnson, ed. Right Hon. J. W. Croker, new ed., 1876.

Johnson, S., the Rambler. (Cited by Richardson.) [1750–2; 2 vols. 1767 and 1779; 4 vols.] And see Boswell.

Jonson, Ben, Works of; ed. W. Gifford. (Reprint.) London, 1860. [Died 1637.]

—— Every Man in his Humour; ed. H. B. Wheatley, 1877. [ab. 1598.]

Joseph of Arimathie, or the Holy Grail; ed. W. W. Skeat. E.E.T.S., 1871. [ab. 1350.]

Joye, G., The Exposicion of Daniel the Prophete. London, 1550 (two editions). 16mo. (First pr. at Geneva, 1545.)

Juliana, St.; ed. Cockayne and Brock. E.E.T.S., 1872. [Early 13th cent.]

Kalkar; see Danish, Middle.

Kemble, J. M., Codex Diplomaticus Ævi Saxonici. English Historical Soc. 1839–48. 5 vols.

—— Salomon and Saturn. Ælfric Soc., 1848.

Kersey, J., English Dictionary. 1715.

Kilian; see Dutch.

King Horn; ed. J. R. Lumby. E.E.T.S., 1866. [Before 1300.]

King, W., Poems of; see English Poets.

King of Tars; see Ritson.

Kingis Quair, The; by King James I of Scotland; ed. Rev. W. W. Skeat. S.T.S., 1884.

Kluge; see German.

Knight of la Tour-Landry, The Book of the; ed. T. Wright. E.E.T.S., 1868. [ab. 1440.]

Knox, J., The Works of; ed. D. Laing. Edinburgh, 1846–56. 8vo. 6 vols.

Koch, C. F., Historische Grammatik der Englischen Sprache. Weimar, 1863; Cassel and Göttingen, 1865, 1869. 3 vols.

Kok; see Danish dialects.

Koolman; see Friesic.

Körting, G., Lateinisch-Romanisches Wörterbuch. Second edition. Paderborn, 1901.

Kotzebue, Otto von, A New Voyage round the World. London, 1830. 2 vols. 12mo.

La Belle Dame sans Merci; see Chaucerian Pieces.

Labourasse; see French dialects, la Meuse.

Lady Alimony; in Dodsley's Old Plays, vol. 14.

Lai le Freine; see Weber.

Laing, D., Select Remains of the Ancient Popular Poetry of Scotland. New ed. by J. Small. Edinburgh, 1885. 8vo.

Lancelot of the Laik; ed. W. W. Skeat. E.E.T.S., 1865. [15th century.]

Lanfrank's Science of Cirurgie; ed. R. v. Fleischhacker, Ph.D. Part I; text. E.E.T.S., 1894. [Ab. 1400.]

Langtoft.—Peter Langtoft's Chronicle, as illustrated and improved by Robert of Brunne; ed. Thomas Hearne, M.A. Oxford, 1725. 2 vols. Reprinted, London, 1810. [ab. 1338.]

Languedoc; see French dialects.

Larramendi; see Basque.

Larsen; see Danish.

Latimer, H., Seven Sermons before Edward VI; ed. E. Arber, 1869. [1549.]

Latin.—A Latin-English Dictionary, by J. T. White and J. E. Riddle. Fifth edition. London, 1876.

—— A Latin Dictionary, by C. T. Lewis and C. Short. Oxford, 1880.

—— Dictionnaire étymologique latin, par MM. Bréal et A. Bailly. Paris, 1885.

—— Lateinisches etymologisches Wörterbuch, von Dr. Alois Walde. Heidelberg, 1906.

Laws of Ina; see Thorpe, Ancient Laws.

Layamon's Brut; ed. Sir F. Madden. (Society of Antiquaries.) 1847. 3 vols. [ab. 1200.]

Lee, F. G., Glossary of Liturgical and Ecclesiastical Terms. London, 1877. 8vo.

Leechdoms, &c.; see Cockayne.

Legend of St. Catherine; The Life of St. Catherine, ed. Dr. Einenkel. E.E.T.S., 1884.

Legend of St. Christopher; see Early E. Poems.

Legendary, The Early South-English, or Lives of Saints; ed. Dr. C. Horstmann. E.E.T.S., 1887.

Legends of the Holy Rood; ed. Dr. Richard Morris. E.E.T.S., 1871.

Legends of the Saints in the Scottish Dialect; ed. W. M. Metcalfe. Parts I–V. S.T.S., 1887–95.

Le Gonidec; see Breton.

Leo, H., Angelsächsisches Glossar; Halle, 1872.

Leslie's History of Scotland, tr. by Father J. Dalrymple; ed. Rev. Father E. G. Cody, O.S.B. S.T.S., 1884–95. In 4 parts.

Levins, Manipulus Vocabulorum; ed. H. B. Wheatley. E.E.T.S., 1867. [1570.]

Lewis, or Lewis and Short; see Latin.

Lex Salica, the ten texts; ed. J. H. Hessels; with notes on the Frankish words by Prof. H. Kern. London, 1880. 4to.

Libell of Englische Policye; ed. R. Pauli. Leipzig, 1878. [1436.]

Liber Albus; ed. H. T. Riley, vol. i. Rolls Series, 1859.

Liber Cure Cocorum; ed. R. Morris. Phil. Soc., 1862.

Liber Custumarum; ed. H. T. Riley. In two parts. Rolls Series, 1860.

Liber Scintillarum; ed. E. Rhodes, B.A. E.E.T.S., 1889.

Liddell and Scott; see Greek.

Liden, E., Studien zur altindischen und vergleichenden Sprachgeschichte. Upsala, 1897.

Lindisfarne MS.; see Anglo-Saxon Gospels.

Lithuanian.—Wörterbuch der Littauischen Sprache, von G. H. F. Nesselmann. Königsberg, 1851.

Littré; see French.

Locke, J., An Essay concerning the human Understanding. First complete ed., 1694. (Many editions.)

Longfellow, H. W., Poems of. London, 1855.

Loth, J., Etymologische angelsæchsisch-englische Grammatik. Elberfeld, 1870.

Low German.—See Bremen Wörterbuch; and see below.

Low German dialects.—Altmark: Wörterbuch der altmärkischplattdeutschen Mundart; von J. F. Danneil. Salzwedel, 1859. (N. of Prussian Saxony.)

—— Bremen: see under Bremen.

—— Göttingen: Wörterbuch der niederdeutschen Mundart der Fürstenthümer Göttingen und Grubenhagen; von G. Schambach. Hannover, 1858.

—— Hamburg: Idioticon Hamburgense; by Mich. Richey. Hamburgi, 1743.

—— Kurhessen: Idiotikon von Kurhessen; von Dr. A. F. C. Vilmar. Marburg, 1868.

—— Pomeranian: Platt-deutsches Wörterbuch nach der alten und neuen Pommerschen und Rügischen Mundart; von J. C. Dähnert. Stralsund, 1781.

—— Saxon: Der Sprachschatz der Sassen; von Dr. H. Berghaus.

Vol. 1, A–H. Vol. 2, I–N. Vol. 3 (unfinished), O–Paddeln. Brandenburg, 1880.

Low German dialects.—Strassburg: Wörterbuch der Strassburger Mundart; von C. Schmidt. Strassburg, 1896.

—— Westphalian: Wörterbuch der Westfälischen Mundart; von F. Woeste. Norden und Leipzig, 1882.

—— **Middle Low German.** Mittelniederdeutsches Handwörterbuch, von A. Lübben. Norden und Leipzig, 1888.

—— **Old Low German.**—Vorstudien zu einem Altniederdeutschen Wörterbuche, von J. H. Gallée. Leiden, 1903.

Low Latin.—See Ducange.

Lowndes; see Bohn's Lowndes.

Lübben; see Low German, Middle.

Lybeaus Disconus; see Ritson.

Lydgate, J., The Storie of Thebes; printed at the end of Chaucer's Woorkes, with diuers Addicions. London, 1561. [ab. 1430.]

—— Assembly (or Banquet) of Gods; ed. Prof. O. L. Triggs, M.A. E.E.T.S., 1896.

—— Complaint of the Black Knight, The Flour of Curtesye, &c.; see Chaucerian Pieces.

—— Fall of Princes; entitled (by Pynson, in 1494) The Boke called de John Bochas descriuinge the Falle of Princis, &c. London; pr. by J. Wayland. 1558.

—— Sege of Troye; pr. with the title—The Auncient Historie . . . of the warres betwixte the Grecians and the Troyans, &c.; . . . newly imprinted, 1555. [First pr. by Pynson, 1513, fol.]

—— Temple of Glass; ed. Dr. J. Schick. E.E.T.S.; extra series, 1891.

—— Minor Poems; ed. J. O. Halliwell. Percy Soc., 1840.

Lye, E., and O. Manning; Dictionarium Saxonico-et-Gothico-Latinum. London, 1772. 2 vols.

Lyly, J., Euphues; ed. E. Arber, 1868. [1579, 1580.]

Lyly, or Lilly, Dramatic Works of; ed. F. W. Fairholt. London, 1856. 2 vols.

Lyndesay, Sir D., Works of. E.E.T.S., 1865, 1866, 1868. [1552, &c.]

Lyte's Dodoens, A Niewe Herball, or Historie of Plantes, translated [from Rembert Dodoens] by Hy. Lyte. First ed., 1578, fol. Also 1586, 4to; 1595, 4to.

Macbain; see Gaelic.

Macdonell; see Sanskrit.

Macklin, C., Love à la Mode; see Drama, Modern British. [1760.]

Mahn, K. A. F., Etymologische Untersuchungen, &c. Berlin, 1863.

Malay.—Marsden, W.; A Dictionary of the Malayan Language. London, 1812.

—— Pijnappel, J., Maleisch-Hollandsch Woordenboek. Amsterdam, 1875.

—— The Malayan Words in English; by C. P. G. Scott. New Haven, Ct., U.S.A., 1897.

Malayalim.—Bailey, Rev. B., A Dictionary of Malayalim and English; Cottayam, 1846. Another by Rev. H. Gundert; Mangalore, 1871–2.

Malory, Sir T., Le Morte Darthur; pr. by Caxton. Exact reprint by H. O. Sommer, Ph.D. London, 1889–91. 2 vols. [1485.]

—— Morte Darthur. The Globe Edition, London, 1868. [1469.] And see Morte Arthure.

Mandeville; see Maundeville.

Manlove, E., The Liberties and Customes of the Lead Mines, &c.; a poem. E.D.S., Ser. B, Gloss. VIII, 1874. [1653.]

Manwood, J., Treatise and Discourse of the Lawes of the Forest. (First ed., London, 1744.)

Mapes, Walter, The Latin Poems attributed to; ed. T. Wright. Camden Soc., 1841.

March, F. A., A Comparative Grammar of the Anglo-Saxon Language. London, 1870.

Marco Polo.—The Book of Ser Marco Polo, newly translated and ed. by Col. H. Yule, C.B. London, 1871. 2 vols.

Marharete; see Seinte.

Marie de France; Die Lais der Marie de France, herausgegeben von K. Warnke. Halle, 1885. (In Norman French.)

Marlowe's Works; ed. Lt.-Col. F. Cunningham. London, 1870. [Died 1593.]

Marsden; see Malay.

Marsh, G. P., Lectures on the English Language; ed. Dr. W. Smith. London, 1862. [The Student's Manual of the English Language.]

Marston, J., Works of; ed. J. O. Halliwell. London, 1856. 3 vols. 8vo.

Mason, W., Poems of; see English Poets.

Massinger.—The Plays of Philip Massinger; ed. Lt.-Col. F. Cunningham. London, 1868. [Died 1640.]

Mather, I., Remarkable Providences, &c. With pref. by G. Offor. London, 1856. (Orig. edition, 1684.)

Mätzner.—Englische Grammatik, von E. Mätzner. 3 parts. Berlin, 1860–5.

—— Altenglische Sprachproben, nebst einem Wörterbuche; ed. E. Mätzner. Erster Band, Sprachproben; Berlin, 1867–9. Zweiter Band [unfinished]; Berlin, 1872–6.

Maundeville.—The Voiage and Travaile of Sir John Maundeville, Knt.; London, E. Lumley, 1839; reprinted by J. O. Halliwell in 1866. [1356.]

Meadows; see Italian and Spanish.

Medical Works of the Fourteenth Century; by the Rev. Prof. G. Henslow, M.A., F.L.S. London, 1899. 8vo.

Merlin, The Romance of; ed. H. B. Wheatley. E.E.T.S., 1865–99.

Metcalfe; see Legends of the Saints.

Métivier; see French dialects (Guernsey).

Metres of Boethius; pr. with Ælfred, tr. of Boethius, q. v.; and by Grein.

Metrical Homilies; Eng. Met. Homilies, ed. J. Small, M.A. Edinburgh, 1862.

Mexican.—Clavigero's History of Mexico; tr. from the Italian by C. Cullen. London, 1787. 2 vols.

—— Dictionnaire de la langue Nahuatl ou Mexicaine; par Rémi Siméon. Paris, 1885.

—— Grammaire de la langue Nahuatl ou Mexicaine; ed. Rémi Siméon. Paris, 1875. [Written by Olmos in 1547.]

Middleton, T., Plays; ed. H. Ellis. 2 vols. 1887–90. (Mermaid Series.)

Miklosich; see Slavonic.

Milton.—The Poetical Works of John Milton, with a life of the author, and Verbal Index by C. Dexter Cleveland. New edition, London, 1865. [Died 1674.]

—— Areopagitica; ed. J. W. Hales. Oxford, 1874. [1644.]

Minot, L., poems of; pr. in Political Poems and Songs relating to English History, vol. i.; ed. T. Wright (Rolls Series). London, 1859. [1352.] Also ed. J. Hall; Oxford, 1887.

Minsheu, J., The Guide into the Tongues. Second edition. London, 1627. And see Spanish.

Mirror for Magistrates, in five parts; ed. Jos. Hazlewood. London, 1815. 4to. 3 vols. [First ed. 1559.]

Möbius; see Icelandic.

Molbech; see Danish dialects.

Molema, H.; see Dutch dialect.

Möller; see Swedish dialects.

Moncaut; see French dialects (Gascon).

Mone, B., Quellen und Forschungen zur Geschichte der teutschen Literatur und Sprache. Leipzig, 1830. 8vo.

Monk of Evesham, The Revelation to the. Reprint by E. Arber; no. 18. [1482.]

Monlau, Dr. E. P. F.; Diccionario Etimológico de la Lengua Castellana. Segunda edicion. Madrid, 1881.

Montgomerie, A., The Poems of; ed. J. Cranstoun, LL.D. S.T.S., 1885–7.

Moore, T., Poetical Works of. London, 1854.

More, Sir T., Works of; printed in 1557. [Died 1535.]

—— tr. of Sir T. More's Utopia, by R. Robinson, 1551; Second edition, 1556; ed. E. Arber, 1869. [1551.]

Morris, E. E.; see Australian.

Morris, R., Historical Outlines of English Accidence. London, 1872.

Morte Arthure (an alliterative poem); ed. E. Brock. E.E.T.S. Reprint, 1871. [ab. 1440.] The First edition, by the Rev. G. G. Perry, appeared in 1865. And see Malory.

Moryson, Fynes, An Itinerary. London, 1617. fol.

Müller, E., Etymologisches Wörterbuch der englischen Sprache. In two parts. Second edition. Cöthen, 1879.

Müller, F. Max, Lectures on the Science of Language. Eighth edition. London, 1875. 2 vols.

—— Selected Essays. London, 1881. 2 vols.

Murphy, A., Plays; see Drama, Modern British. [1756–76.]

Murray, [Sir] J. A. H.; see Complaynte.

Myrc's Duties of a Parish Priest; ed. E. Peacock. E.E.T.S., 1868. [ab. 1420.]

Myrour of Our Lady; ed. J. H. Blunt. E.E.T.S., extra series, 1873. [1530.]

Napier's Glosses; Old English Glosses, ed. A. S. Napier, M.A., Ph.D. Oxford, 1900.

Nares, R.; A Glossary to the Works of English Authors, particularly Shakespeare and his contemporaries. New edition, by Halliwell and Wright. London, 1859. 2 vols.

Naval Accounts and Inventories; ed. M. Oppenheim. Pr. for the Navy Records Soc., 1896. [1485–8 and 1495–7.]

N.E.D.—A New English Dictionary on Historical Principles; ed. [Sir] J. A. H. Murray, H. Bradley, and W. A. Craigie. 1884–. A–Piper; Q–Rib.

Neckam, A., De Utensilibus; pr. in Wright's Vocabularies, First Series, pp. 96–119. [12th cent.]

Nesselmann; see Lithuanian.

Neuman; see Spanish.

Newton's Birds; A Dictionary of Birds, by Prof. A. Newton. London, 1893-6.

Nichols, J., A Collection of all the Wills, now known to be extant, of the kings and queens of England, to that of Henry VII. exclusive. London, 1780. (Cited as 'Royal Wills'.)

Nicolas; see Testamenta Vetusta.

Noreen, Altisländische und altnorwegische Grammatik, von A. Noreen. (2nd ed.) Halle, 1892.

Norman; see French dialects.

North, R., Examen. London, 1740. (Cited at second-hand.)

North, Sir T., tr. of Plutarch, 1612.

Northumberland Household Book; see Antiquarian Repertory.

Norwegian.—Aasen, Ivar; Norsk Ordbog med Dansk Forklaring. Christiania, 1873.

———— Norsk Ordbog, af H. Ross. Christiania, 1895.

Notes on English Etymology, by the Rev. W. W. Skeat, Litt.D. Oxford, 1901.

Notes and Queries (published weekly). First Series, 1850-5; second, 1856-61; third, 1862-67; fourth, 1868-73; fifth, 1874-9; &c.

Nottingham Records; Records of the Borough of Nottingham; ed. W. H. Stevenson. London, 1882-1900. 5 vols. [Vol. 1; 1155-1399.]

Occleve; see Hoccleve.

Octavian, the Emperor; ed. J. O. Halliwell. Percy Soc., 1844.

Octovian; see Weber.

O. E. Texts.—The Oldest English Texts; ed. H. Sweet, M.A. E.E.T.S. London, 1885.

Ogilvie, The Imperial Dictionary of the English Language, by J. Ogilvie, LL.D. New ed., by C. Annandale. London, 1883. 8vo. 4 vols.

O'Hara; Midas, a play; see Drama, Mod. British. [1764.]

Old English Homilies; see Early English Homilies.

Old English Miscellany; ed. Dr. R. Morris. E.E.T.S., 1872.

Old English Plays; see Dodsley.

Old Saxon.—Héliand; mit ausführlichem Glossar herausgegeben; von M. Heyne. Paderborn, 1866.

———— Kleinere altniederdeutsche Denkmäler; mit ausführlichem Glossar herausgegeben; von M. Heyne. Paderborn, 1866.

Oliphant, T. L. K., Old and Middle English. London, 1878.

Öman; Swedish-English Dictionary, 1897.

Ordinances and Regulations, &c.; A Collection of Ordinances and Regulations for the Government of the Royal Household, made in divers Reigns. 1790. 4to. (Cited in Halliwell's Dict.; see p. 956.)

O'Reilly; see Irish.

Original Letters, &c.; see Ellis.

Ormulum; ed. R. M. White. Oxford, 1852. 2 vols. [1220-50.]

Orosius; see Ælfred.

Otway, T., The Works of. London, 1768. 3 vols.

Oudemans; see Dutch.

Outzen; see Friesic.

Owl and Nightingale, ed. Thos. Wright; Percy Soc., 1843. Re-ed. by Dr. F. H. Stratmann; Krefeld, 1868. [ab. 1300.]

Oxford Helps to the Study of the Bible.—Helps to the Study of the Bible. Oxford, n. d.

Palladius on Husbandrie; in English; ed. B. Lodge. E.E.T.S., 1872, 1877. [ab. 1420.]

Palmer, E. H.; see Persian.

Palmer, Rev. A. Smythe, Folk-etymology. London, 1882. 8vo.

———— Leaves from a Word-hunter's Notebook. London, 1876.

Palmer, Rev. W., Origines Liturgicæ. Oxford, 1832. 8vo. 2 vols.

Palsgrave.—Lesclaircissement de la Langue Francoyse, par Maistre Jehan Palsgrave, 1530. Together with An Introductorie for to lerne to speke French trewly; by G. Du Wes. [Reprint, Paris, 1852.]

Pardonere and Tapster; introducing the Tale of Beryn. See Beryn.

Parker Society Publications. (The excellent Index has been of much service.)

Parlement of the Thre Ages, The; also Winnere and Wastoure; ed. I. Gollancz, M.A. Roxburge Club, 1897.

Parliament Rolls; Parliamentorum Rotuli. (Edw. I—Hen. VII.) 1765. fol. 6 vols.

Partenay, Romance of; ed. W. W. Skeat, E.E.T.S., 1866. [ab. 1500-20.]

Paston Letters; ed. J. Gairdner. London, 1872-5. 3 vols. [1422-1509.]

Peacham, H., The Gentleman's Exercise. London, 1634. 4to.

Peacock, E., A Glossary of Words used in the Wapentakes of Manley and Corringham, Lincolnshire. E.D.S., 1877.

Peele, G.; see Greene.

Pegge, S., LL.D., An Alphabet of Kenticisms; printed in Series C, Part III, of the E.D.S. publications, ed. W. W. Skeat, 1876.

———— Anonymiana. London, 1809. 8vo.

——- Derbicisms; ed. W. W. Skeat. E.D.S. 1896.

Pegge, S., Jun., Curialia, or an Historical Account of some Branches of the Royal Household. London, 1782. 4to.

Pepys, S., Memoirs of, comprising his Diary, &c.; ed. Richard Lord Braybrooke. (Reprint.) London, F. Warne, n. d. [1659-69.]

Perceval, Sir; see Thornton Romances. [ab. 1440.]

Percy Folio MS.; ed. J. W. Hales and F. J. Furnivall. London, 1867-8. 3 vols.

Percy, T.; Reliques of Ancient English Poetry; reprint, ed. R. A. Willmott. London, 1857.

Persian.—A Concise Dictionary of the Persian Language; by E. H. Palmer. London, 1876.

———— A Dictionary, Persian, Arabic, and English. By J. Richardson; new edition, by F. Johnson. London, 1829.

———— Grundriss der neupersischen Etymologie; von Paul Horn. Strassburg, 1893.

———— Vullers, J. A., Lexicon Persico-Latinum. Bonn, 1855-67. 2 vols.

———— **Old.**—Die altpersischen Keilinschriften. By F. Spiegel. Leipzig, 1862.

Peruvian.—Vocabulario de la lengua de Peru; by D. Gonçalez. La Ciudad de los Reyes. [Lima?] 1608.

Phaer, T., and Twyne, T.; tr. of Virgil's Æneid. London, 1583. 4to. (The first edition.)

Philip de Thaun; see Wright, T., Popular Treatises.

Philips, J., Cider, and other Poems; see English Poets.

Phillips, E., The New World of Words. London, 1706. fol.

Phil. Soc.—Transactions of the Philological Society.

Picard.—Glossaire du Patois Picard, par l'Abbé Jules Corblet. Paris, 1851.

Pierce the Ploughman's Crede, about 1394 A.D.; ed. W. W. Skeat. E.E.T.S., 1867. [1394.]

Piers Plowman. The Vision of William concerning Piers the Plowman; ed. W. W. Skeat. A-text (earliest version); B-text (second version); C-text (latest version). E.E.T.S., 1867, 1869, 1873. Notes and Glossary, 1877-84. [1362-1400.]

Pilgrim's Sea Voyage; ed. F. J. Furnivall (with the Stacions of Rome). E.E.T.S., 1867.

Pineda; see Spanish.

Pistyll of Susan; see Scottish Alliterative Poems.

Poems and Lives of Saints; ed. F. J. Furnivall. Phil. Soc. Berlin, 1862. [ab. 1300.]

Polish.—Nouveau Dictionnaire Portatif Francais-Polonais et Polonais-Français; par J. A. E. Schmidt. Leipzig, 1847.

Political Poems and Songs relating to English History; ed. Thos. Wright. (Rolls Series.) 1851-61. 2 vols.

Political, Religious, and Love Poems; ed. F. J. Furnivall. E.E.T.S., 1866.

Political Songs; ed. T. Wright. Camden Soc., 1839. [1264-1327.]

Pope, A., Works of; ed. H. F. Cary. London, 1849. [Died 1744.]

———— Concordance to the Works of; by E. Abbott. London, 1875.

Portuguese.—Novo Diccionario Portatil das linguas Portugueza e Ingleza, resumido do diccionario de Vieyra; nova edição por J. P. Aillaud. Paris, 1857. 2 vols.

———— A Grammar of the Portuguese Language; by A. Vieyra. Twelfth edition. London, 1858.

Prellwitz, Dr. W., Etymologisches Wörterbuch der Griechischen Sprache. (2nd ed.) Göttingen, 1905.

Prescott, W. H., History of the Conquest of Peru. 7th ed. London, 1854. 8vo.

———— History of the Conquest of Mexico. 7th ed. London, 1854. 8vo.

Pricke of Conscience; see Hampole.

Prior, R. C. A., On the Popular Names of British Plants. Third edition. London, 1879.

Prior, M., Poems of; see English Poets. [Died 1721.]

Prompt. Parv. = Promptorium Parvulorum sive Clericorum Dictionarius Anglo-Latinus Princeps, auctore fratre Galfrido Grammatico dicto, circa A. D. MCCCCXL. Ed. A. Way, Camden Soc., 1843, 1853, and 1865. [1440.]

Provençal.—Lexique Roman, by M. Raynouard. Paris, 1836. 5 vols.

———— Dictionnaire Provençal-Français. Par F. Mistral. Aix-en-Provence, n. d. 2 vols.

Proverbs of Hendyng ; see Altenglische Dichtungen.

Prynne, W., Histriomastix. London, 1633. 4to.

—— The Soveraigne Power of Parliaments. London, 1643. 4to.

Puitspelu ; see French dialects (Lyonnais).

Purchas, S., His Pilgrimage.... Third ed., 1617. fol.

Puttenham, G., The Arte of English Poesie, 1589. In Arber's Reprints. London, 1869.

Queene Elizabethes Achademy, &c. ; ed. F. J. Furnivall. E.E.T.S., extra series, 1869.

Ramsay's Poems (cited by Jamieson).

Ratis Raving ; ed. Rev. J. R. Lumby, M.A. E.E.T.S., 1870.

Rauf Coilyear ; see Scottish Allit. Poems.

Ray, John ; A Collection of English Words not generally used. Ed. W. W. Skeat. E.D.S., 1874. [1674-91.]

Raynouard ; see Provençal.

Red Book of the Exchequer ; ed. W. D. Selby. (Rolls Series.)

Reliquiæ Antiquæ ; ed. Wright and Halliwell. 1841-3. 2 vols.

Remacle ; see French dialects (Walloon).

Return from Parnassus ; ed. E. Arber. 1870. [1606.]

Reynard the Fox.—Willems Gedicht van den vos Reinaerde ; ed. E. Martin. Paderborn, 1874. 8vo.

Rhys, J., Lectures in Welsh Philology. London, 1877.

Richard Coer de Lion ; see Weber.

Richardson ; see Arabic ; and see Persian.

Richardson, C., A Dictionary of the English Language. London, 1863. 4to. 2 vols.

Richard the Redeles ; printed with the C-text of Piers the Plowman, pp. 469-521. See Preface iv, in the same volume, pp. ciii-cxxiv.

Richey ; see Low German dialects (Hamburg).

Richthofen ; see Friesic.

Rietz ; see Swedish.

Riley.—Liber Albus : The White Book of the city of London ; tr. by H. T. Riley, M.A. London, 1861.

Riley's Memorials of London. London, 1868.

Ritson's Metrical Romances.—Ancient Engleish (sic) Metrical Romanceës (sic) ; ed. by Joseph Ritson. London, 1802. 3 vols. Vol. i contains Ywaine and Gawin ; Launfal. Vol. ii contains Lybeaus Disconus ; King Horn ; King of Tars ; Emare ; Sir Orpheo ; Chronicle of England. Vol. iii contains Le bone Florence ; Erle of Tolous ; Squyre of Lowe Degre ; Knight of Curtesy.

Robert of Brunne, Handlyng Synne ; ed. F. J. Furnivall (Roxburghe Club), 1862. [1303.] And see Langtoft.

Robert of Gloucester's Chronicle ; ed. T. Hearne. Oxford, 1724. 2 vols. Reprinted, London, 1810. [ab. 1298.]

—— ed. W. Aldis Wright. (Rolls Series.) 1887. 2 vols.

Robin ; see French dialects (Norman).

Robinson, F. K., A Glossary of Words used in the neighbourhood of Whitby. E.D.S., 1875-6.

Robson, J.—Three Early English Metrical Romances ; ed. J. R. Camden Soc., 1842.

Rochester, Earl of ; see English Poets.

Rock, D., The Church of our Fathers. London, 1849-52. 3 vols.

Roland ; see Chanson.

Rolland's Court of Venus ; ed. Rev. W. Gregor. S.T.S., 1883-4.

Romance of Partenay ; ed. Rev. W. W. Skeat. E.E.T.S., 1866.

Roman de la Rose ; ed. M. Méon. Paris, 1813. 4 vols.

Romania (for Romance Philology) ; ed. P. Meyer and G. Paris. From 1872.

Romaunsch.—Rætoromanisches Wörterbuch, Surselvisch-Deutsch ; von P. B. Carigiet. Bonn and Chur, 1882.

Romaunt of the Rose.—An English translation of the French Roman de La Rose ; Part A, ll. 1-1705, by Chaucer. Part B, in Northern dialect. Part C, from l. 5811 to end.

Roquefort, J. B. B., Glossaire de la Langue Romane. Paris, 1808. 2 vols. With Supplement, 1820.

Roy, W., Rede Me and be not Wrothe ; ed. E. Arber, 1871. [1528.]

Royal Wills ; see Nichols, J.

Rule of St. Benet.—Die Winteney-Version der Regula S. Benedicti ; von Dr. M. M. A. Schröer. Halle a. S., 1888.

Rushworth MS. ; see Anglo-Saxon Gospels.

Russell, J., Book of Nurture ; see Babees Book.

Russian.—New parallel Dictionaries of the Russian, French, German, and English Languages, in four parts ; ed. Ch. Ph. Reiff. First Part, Russian-English ; Fourth Part, English-Russian. Third edition. Carlsruhe, St. Petersburg, Leipzig, and Paris, 1876.

Sackville, Th., Works of ; ed. R. W. Sackville-West. London, 1859. 8vo.

St. Benet, Rule of ; ed. Schröer. Halle a. S., 1888.

St. Brandan ; ed. T. Wright. Percy Soc., 1844.

St. Catherine ; see Legend.

St. Christopher ; see Legend.

St. Cuthbert ; ed. Rev. J. T. Fowler. Surtees Soc., 1889-91. [1450.]

St. Erkenwald ; see Horstmann, Altengl. Legenden, Neue Folge.

St. Juliana ; ed. Cockayne and Brock. E.E.T.S., 1872. [1200-50?]

St. Margaret ; see Seinte.

St. Veronica ; ed. C. W. Goodwin. 1851. (With St. Andrew.)

Salomon and Saturn.—Anglo-Saxon Dialogues of Salomon and Saturn ; ed. J. M. Kemble. (Ælfric Society), 1845, 1847, 1848.

Sandys, G., A Relation of a Journey an. dom. 1610. Third edition. 1632.

Sanskrit.—Sanskrit-English Dictionary ; by T. Benfey, 1866. [When 'Skt.' only is cited, this book is meant.]

Sanskrit Dictionary ; by Böhtlingk and Roth, 7 parts. St. Petersburg, 1855-75.

Sanskrit-English Dictionary ; by A. A. Macdonell, M.A., Ph.D. London, 1893.

Schade ; see German.

Schambach ; see Low German dialects (Göttingen).

Scheler ; see French.

Schleicher, A., Indogermanische Chrestomathie. Weimar, 1869.

Schmeller ; see Bavarian Dictionary.

Schmid, Dr. R., Die Gesetze der Angelsachsen. Leipzig, 1858.

Schmidt, A. ; see Shakespeare.

Schwan, Dr. E., Grammatik des Altfranzösischen. 3rd ed. Leipzig, 1898.

Scott.—The Select Poetry of Sir Walter Scott, Bart. 6 vols. Edinburgh, 1849. Waverley Novels ; Edinburgh, 1854-63. 25 vols. [Died 1832.]

Scott, C. P. G. ; see Malay.

Scottish Alliterative Poems ; ed. F. J. Amours. Part I. S.T.S., 1891-2.

Seinte Marharete ; ed. O. Cockayne. E.E.T.S., 1866. [1200-50.]

Selden, J., Table-talk ; ed. E. Arber. London, 1868. [1689.]

Selden's Notes on Drayton ; see Drayton, in English Poets, vol. iv.

Select Charters, &c. By W. Stubbs, M.A. Oxford.

Seven Sages.—The Seven Sages, in English Verse ; ed. Thos. Wright. London (Percy Society), 1845. [ab. 1420.]

—— The Seuyn Sages (another copy). Printed in vol. iii of Weber's Metrical Romances. See Weber.

Sewel ; see Dutch.

Shadwell, T., Dramatic Works. London, 1720. 12mo. 4 vols.

Shakespeare.—The Globe Edition ; ed. by W. G. Clark and W. Aldis Wright. Cambridge and London, 1864. [Died 1616.]

—— Shakespeare Lexicon ; by A. Schmidt. Berlin and London, 1875.

Shakespeare Apocrypha ; ed. C. F. Tucker Brooke. Oxford, 1908.

Shakespeare's Plutarch ; being a selection from North's Plutarch. By W. W. Skeat. London, 1875.

Sharp, T., A Dissertation on Pageants. Coventry, 1825. 4to.

Shelley, P. B., Poetical Works. London, 1840.

Shenstone ; see English Poets.

Sheridan, R. B., Works. London, 1875. 8vo.

Sherwood, index to Cotgrave's F. Dict. ; see French.

Shirley, J., Dramatic Works and Poems ; ed. A. Dyce. London, 1833. 8vo. 6 vols.

Shoreham, W., Poems of ; ed. T. Wright. Percy Soc., 1849. Also ed. Dr. M. Konrath. E.E.T.S., extra series, 1902-3.

Shrine, The ; see Cockayne.

Sidney, Sir P., Apology for Poetrie ; ed. E. Arber, 1868. [1595.]

Sievers, E., Angelsächsische Grammatik. 3rd ed. Halle, 1898.

Sigart ; see French dialects (Walloon).

Sinonima Bartolomei ; ed. J. L. G. Mowat. Oxford, 1882. 4to.

Sir Bevis, &c. ; see Bevis, &c.

Skeat, W. W., Notes on English Etymology. Oxford, 1901.

—— Principles of English Etymology. Series I, 2nd ed. Series II. Oxford, 1891-2.

Skelton's Poetical Works ; ed. Rev. A. Dyce. London, 1843. 2 vols. [Died 1529.]

Skinner, S., Etymologicon Linguæ Anglicanæ. London, 1671. [The chief source of the etymologies in Johnson's Dictionary.]

Slang Dictionary ; London, 1874.

Slavonic.—Etymologisches Wörterbuch der Slavischen Sprachen, von Franz Miklosich. Wien, 1886. 8vo.

Smith, Capt. John, Works ; ed. Arber. Birmingham, 1884. [1608-31.]

Smith, W.—A Concise Bible Dictionary ; ed. by Wm. Smith, B.D. London, 1865.

Smith, Toulmin, English Gilds. E.E.T.S., 1870. [1389-1450.]

Somervile, W. ; see English Poets.

Somner, W., Dictionarium Saxonico-Latino-Anglicum. Oxford, 1659.

Songs and Carols ; ed. T. Wright. London, 1847. [ab. 1470.]

South-English Legendary ; ed. C. Horstmann. E.E.T.S., 1887.

Sowdone of Babylone; ed. Dr. Hausknecht. E.E.T.S., extra series, 1881.

Spanish.—Minsheu, J., A Dictionary in Spanish and English. London, 1623.

—— Pineda, P., A New Dictionary, Spanish and English, and English and Spanish. London, 1740. fol.

—— Spanish and English Dictionary; by F. C. Meadows. Eighth edition. London, 1856.

—— Spanish and English Dictionary, originally compiled by Neuman and Baretti; by M. Seoane, M.D. New edition. London, 1862. 2 vols. And see Monlau.

Specimens of Early English, Part I, A.D. 1150-1300; by the Rev. R. Morris, LL.D. 2nd ed. Oxford, 1885.

—— Part II, A.D. 1298-1393; by Dr. Morris and the Rev. W. W. Skeat. New edition, revised for the third time. Oxford, 1894.

Specimens of English Literature, A.D. 1394-1579; by the Rev. W. W. Skeat. Oxford, 1871. Fifth edition, 1890.

Specimens of Lyric Poetry written in England in the reign of Edward I; ed. T. Wright. (Percy Society), 1842.

Spectator, The; ed. H. Morley, n. d. [1711-14.]

Spelman, J., Psalterium Davidis Latino-Saxonicum vetus. London, 1640. [A Latin Psalter, with A. S. glosses.]

Spenser.—The Complete Works of Edmund Spenser. The Globe Edition, ed. by R. Morris, with memoir by J. W. Hales. London, 1869. [Shep. Kal., 1579; Fairy Queen, 1590-6.]

Spiegel, F.; see Persian, Old.

Spurrell; see Welsh.

Squyre of Low Degree; see Ritson.

Stacions of Rome, &c.; ed. F. J. Furnivall. E.E.T.S., 1867.

Stanford Dictionary (The) of Anglicised Words and Phrases; ed. C. A. M. Fennell, D.Litt. Cambridge, 1892.

Stanyhurst, R., tr. of Virgil's Æneid, books i-iv, 1582; ed. E. Arber, 1880. [1582.]

Statutes of Henry VII. In exact facsimile; ed. J. Rae. London, 1869. [Pr. by Caxton in 1489.]

Statutes of the Realm; vol. i. Pr. by command of Geo. III in 1810. fol.

Stedman, Capt. J. G., Narrative . . . of Surinam. London, 1796. 4to. 2 vols.

Sterne, L., Works of. London, 1802. 7 vols. [Died 1768.]

Stokes-Fick, Vergleichendes Wörterbuch der indog. Sprachen, von August Fick. 4th ed. Part 2 (by Whitley Stokes). Göttingen, 1894.

Stow, J., A Survey of London, written in the year 1598. New edition, by W. J. Thoms. London, 1842.

Stratmann.—A Middle-English Dictionary, by F. H. Stratmann. New ed., by H. Bradley. Oxford, 1891.

Streitberg, Dr. W., Urgermanische Grammatik. Heidelberg, 1896.

Strutt, J., Manners, &c., of the Inhabitants of England. London, 1774-6. 4to. 3 vols.

—— The Sports and Pastimes, &c. (Reprint.) London, 1876.

S.T.S.—Scottish Text Society.

Surrey, Lord; see Tottel. *Also*, ed. R. Bell. London, n. d.

Swainson, Rev. C., Provincial Names of British Birds. E.D.S., 1885.

Swedish.—Pocket-dictionary of the English and Swedish languages. Leipzig, C. Tauchnitz, n. d. And see Öman.

—— Ihre, J., Glossarium Suiogothicum. 2 vols., folio. Upsal. 1769.

—— Svenskt och Engelskt Lexicon, af G. Widegren. Stockholm, 1788.

Swedish dialects.—Ordbok öfver Halländska Landskaps-Målet, samlad af F. Möller. Lund, 1858. (South Sweden.)

—— Svenskt Dialekt-Lexicon; Ordbok öfver Svenska allmoge-språket, af J. E. Rietz. Lund, 1867.

Sweet, H., An Anglo-Saxon Reader. Oxford, 1876. 7th ed. 1894.

—— A History of English Sounds. Oxford, 1888. 8vo. And see Ælfred and Oldest English Texts.

Swift, Jonathan; see English Poets.

Swinburne, H., Travels through Spain in 1775 and 1776. London, 1779.

Tatar.—Courteille, P. de, Dictionnaire Turk-Oriental. Paris, 1870.

Tatler.—The Tatler and Guardian; complete in one volume. [Reprint.] London, 1877. [1709-13.]

Taylor, Bp. Jeremy; A Course of Sermons. London, 1828. 8vo. 2 vols.

Taylor, I., Words and Places. Third edition. London, 1873.

Ten Kate; see Dutch.

Tennyson, Alfred Lord, Works of. London, 1892. 8vo.

Testamenta Eboracensia. Surtees Soc., 1836, 1855. 2 vols.

Testamenta Vetusta; ed. Sir N. H. Nicolas. London, 1826. Royal 8vo. 2 vols.

Testament of Love; by Th. Usk. See Chaucerian Pieces. [ab. 1387.]

Thomson, Jas.; see English Poets.

Thornton Romances; ed. J. O. Halliwell. (Contains the romances of Perceval, Isumbras, Eglamour, and Degrevant.) Camden Soc. London, 1844. [ab. 1440.]

Thorpe, B., Ancient Laws and Institutes of England. London, 1840. 2 vols.

—— Codex Exoniensis. A Collection of A. S. Poetry; ed. by B. Thorpe. London, 1842.

—— Diplomatarium Ævi Saxonici. A Collection of English Charters, from A. D. 605 to the reign of William the Conqueror. London, 1865.

—— Liber Psalmorum; cum paraphrasi Anglo-Saxonica. Oxford, 1835. 8vo.

Three Early English Metrical Romances; see Robson.

Thurneysen, R., Keltoromanisches. (On Celtic Etymologies in Diez.) Halle, 1884.

Thwaites, E., Heptateuchus, Liber Job, et Evangelium Nicodemi, Anglo-Saxonice, &c. London, 1698. (See Grein.)

Toller; see Bosworth.

Tooke, John Horne, Diversions of Purley; ed. R. Taylor, 1857.

Torrent of Portugal; ed. Halliwell, London, 1842; re-ed. E. Adam, Ph.D. E.E.T.S., 1887.

Torriano; see Italian.

Tottel's Miscellany. Songs and Sonettes by Henry Howard, Earl of Surrey, Sir Thomas Wyatt, the elder, &c.; ed. E. Arber. London, 1870. [First printed in 1557.]

Tourneur, Cyril, The Plays and Poems of; ed. J. Churton Collins. London, 1878. 8vo. 2 vols.

Towneley Mysteries; printed for the Surtees Society. London, 1836. [ab. 1450.] *Also* ed. G. England and A. W. Pollard. E.E.T.S., extra series, 1897.

Toynbee; see Brachet.

Trench, R. C., English Past and Present. Fourth edition. London, 1859. Ninth edition, 1875.

—— On the Study of Words. Twentieth edition; ed. Rev. A. L. Mayhew. London, 1888.

—— A Select Glossary. Fourth edition. London, 1873.

Trevisa, John of, tr. of Higden's Polychronicon; printed in the edition of Higden's Polychronicon in the Rolls Series. [1387.] See Higden.

Tristan; ed. F. Michel. Londres, 1835. 2 vols.

Tristrem, Sir; ed. G. B. McNeill. S.T.S., 1885-6.

Troy-book; see Gest Historiale.

Turbervile's Poems; see English Poets. [Died 1594?]

Turkish.—Zenker, J. T., Dictionnaire Turc-Arabe-Persan. 2 vols. Leipzig, 1866-76.

Turner, W., The Names of Herbes; ed. J. Britten. E.D.S., 1881. [1548.]

Tusser, T., Fiue hundred Pointes of Good Husbandrie; the edition of 1580, collated with those of 1573 and 1577; ed. W. Payne and S. J. Herrtage. E.D.S. London, 1878.

Two Fifteenth-century Cookery Books; ed. T. Austin. E.E.T.S., 1888.

Two Noble Kinsmen; by Shakespeare (?) and Fletcher; ed. Skeat. Cambridge, 1875.

Tyndall.—The Whole Workes of W. Tyndall, John Frith, and Doctor Barnes, pr. by John Daye, 1572. [Tyndall died in 1536.]

Udall, N., Roister Doister (a play); ed. E. Arber, 1869. [ab. 1553.]

—— tr. of the Paraphrase of Erasmus vpon the newe Testamente. London, 1548-9.

—— tr. of the Apophthegmes of Erasmus. Boston, 1877. [1532.]

Uhlenbeck, Dr. C. C., Etymologisches Wörterbuch der altindischen Sprache. Amsterdam, 1898-9.

—— Etymologisches Wörterbuch der Gotischen Sprache. 2nd ed. Amsterdam, 1900.

Unton Inventories; ed. J. G. Nichols. Berkshire Ashmolean Society. 1841. sm. 4to.

Utopia; see More.

Vanbrugh's Plays; see Wycherley.

Vaniček, A., Griechisch-Lateinisches Etymologisches Wörterbuch. Leipzig, 1877. 2 vols.

Vespasian Psalter. (A Latin Psalter with an Old Mercian Gloss; in O.E. Texts, q.v.)

Vie de Saint Gile, La; ed. G. Paris. Paris, 1881.

Vie de Seint Auban; a poem in Norman French; ed. R. Atkinson. London, 1876.

Vieyra; see Portuguese.

Vigfusson; see Icelandic.

Voc.—Anglo-Saxon and Old English Vocabularies, by T. Wright. 2nd ed.; ed. R. P. Wülcker. London, 1884. 2 vols.

Vulgate, the; see Biblia.

Vullers; see Persian.

Wadington, Wm. of, Manuel des Pechiez; ed. F. J. Furnivall, 1862.

Walde, Dr. A., Lateinisches Etymologisches Wörterbuch. Heidelberg, 1906.

Wallace.—The Wallace, by Henry the Minstrel; ed. J. Jamieson, D.D. Edinburgh, 1820. *Also*, ed. J. Moir. S.T.S., 1884-9. [ab. 1460.]

Wallachian.—Walachisch-deutsches Wörterbuch; von A. Isser. Kronstadt, 1850. (The same as Roumanian.)

—— Dictionnaire d'étymologie Daco-Romane; par A. de Cihac. Frankfort, 1870.

Waller, E., Poems; ed. R. Bell. London, n. d. And see English Poets.

Walloon; see French dialects.

Wanley, H., Catalogue of A. S. MSS.; pr. in vol. iii of Hickes's Thesaurus; see Hickes.

Warburton, W., The Divine Legation of Moses demonstrated. (First ed. 1737-8. Cited by Richardson.)

Warner, W., Albion's England; see English Poets.

Wars of Alexander; see Alexander.

Warton, T., History of English Poetry. London, 1840. 8vo. 3 vols. Also ed. W. C. Hazlitt, London, 1871. 8vo. 4 vols.

Way; see Prompt. Parv.

Webbe, E., Travels; ed. E. Arber. 1868. [1590.]

Weber's Metrical Romances. 3 vols. London, 1810. Vol. i contains King Alisaunder; Sir Cleges; Lai le Freine. Vol. ii contains Richard Coer de Lion; Ipomydon; Amis and Amiloun. Vol. iii contains Seuyn Sages; Octouian; Sir Amadas; Hunting of the Hare.

Webster, J., Works of; ed. A. Dyce; new edition. London, 1857. [1607-61.]

Webster, N., International Dictionary of the English Language; ed. N. Porter. Springfield, Mass., 1898.

Wedgwood, H., A Dictionary of English Etymology. Second edition, London, 1872. Third edition, London, 1878.

—— Contested Etymologies in the Dictionary of the Rev. W. W. Skeat. London, 1882.

Weigand; see German.

Welsh.—A Dictionary of the Welsh Language, by W. Spurrell. Second edition. Carmarthen, 1859.

Whitby Glossary; see E.D.S.

Whitehead, W., Poems; see English Poets.

Wiat, Sir T.; see Tottel's Miscellany.

Widegren; see Swedish.

William of Palerne; ed. W. W. Skeat. E.E.T.S., extra series, 1867. [ab. 1360.]

William of Shoreham, The Religious Poems of; ed. Thos. Wright. (Percy Society.) 1849. [ab. 1325?]. And see Shoreham.

Williams; see Cornish.

Wills and Inventories . . of the Northern Counties. Surtees Soc., 1835.

Wilson, H. H., A Glossary of Judicial and Revenue Terms, from various Indian languages London, 1855.

Windisch; see Irish.

Winner and Wastoure; see Parlement.

Winzet's [Winyet's] Works; ed. Rev. J. K. Hewison. S.T.S., 1887-8, 1890-1.

Woeste; see Low German dialects (Westphalian).

Worcester, J. E., A Dictionary of the English Language. London (1859).

Wordsworth, W., Poetical Works. London, 1854.

Wotton, Sir H., Reliquiæ Wottonianæ. 4th ed. London, 1685. [First ed. 1651.]

Wright, T., Homes of Other Days. London, 1871.

—— Popular Treatises on Science. London, 1841. Contains Ælfric's tr. of Beda, De Temporibus Rationum; Philip de Thaun, Livre des Créatures and Bestiary; and M. E. Fragment on Popular Science.

—— Specimens of Lyric Poetry (temp. Edw. I). Percy Soc., 1842.

—— Vocabularies. (First Series.) Liverpool, 1857. (Second Series.) Liverpool, 1873. And see Voc.

Wülcker's Glossaries; see Voc.

Wulfstan; ed. A. Napier. Part I. Berlin, 1883.

Wyatt, Sir T.; see Tottel's Miscellany.

Wycherley, Congreve, Vanbrugh, and Farquhar, Dramatic Works of. London, 1840. 8vo.

Wyclif, English Works of, hitherto unprinted; ed. F. D. Matthew. E.E.T.S., 1880.

—— Select English Works of John Wyclif; ed. T. Arnold. Oxford, 1869-71. 3 vols. [Died 1384.]

—— The Holy Bible, in the earliest English Versions made by John Wycliffe and his followers; ed. Rev. J. Forshall and Sir F. Madden. Oxford, 1850. 4 vols. (With a Glossary.) [ab. 1382-8.]

Wycliffite Glossary.—A Glossary to the Wycliffite Versions of the Bible (above). (Sometimes met with separately.)

Wyntown, Andrew of, The Orygynale Cronykil of Scotland; ed. D. Laing. Edinburgh, 1872-9. 3 vols.

York Plays; ed. Lucy Toulmin Smith. Oxford, 1885. 8vo.

York Wills.—Wills and Inventories . . . of the counties of York, Westmoreland, and Lancashire; ed. Rev. J. Raine. Surtees Soc., 1853.

Young, E, The Complaint, or Night Thoughts. London, 1817. [Died 1765.] And see English Poets.

Yule, Col. H., and A. C. Burnell; Hobson-Jobson; being a Glossary of Anglo-Indian Colloquial Words and Phrases. London, 1886. 8vo.

Zambaldi, F., Vocabolario Etimologico Italiano. Città di Castello, 1889.

Zenker; see Turkish.

KEY TO THE GENERAL PLAN OF THE ETYMOLOGICAL
· DICTIONARY

Each article is arranged, as far as seemed advisable, according to a uniform scheme, and the following details will explain the nature of the information to be found in this work.

§ 1. **The words selected.** The Word-list contains all the primary words of most frequent occurrence in modern literature; and, when their derivatives are included, supplies a tolerably complete vocabulary of the language. I have been largely guided in the choice by the work known as the Student's English Dictionary, by John Ogilvie, as edited by Charles Annandale (1895). A few unusual words have been included on account of their occurrence in familiar passages of standard authors.

§ 2. **The Definitions.** These are given in the briefest possible form, chiefly for the purpose of identifying the word and showing the part of speech.

§ 3. **The Language.** The language to which each word belongs is distinctly marked in every case by means of letters within marks of parenthesis immediately following the definition. In the case of words derived from French, a note is (in general) also made as to whether the French word is of Latin, Celtic, German, or Scandinavian origin. The symbol ' — ' signifies ' derived from.' Thus the remark '(F.—L.)' signifies 'a word introduced into English from *French*, the French word itself being of *Latin* origin.' The letters used are to be read as follows.

Arab. = Arabic. **AF.** = Anglo-French. **C.** = Celtic, *used as a general term for* Irish, Gaelic, Welsh, Breton, Cornish, &c. **E.** = English. **F.** = French. **G.** = German. **Gk.** = Greek. **L.** *or* **Lat.** = Latin. **Scand.** = Scandinavian, *used as a general term for* Icelandic, Swedish, Danish, &c. **Skt.** = Sanskrit. **W.** = Welsh.

For other abbreviations, see § 8 below.

§ 4. **The History.** Next follows a brief account of the history of the word, showing (approximately) the time of its introduction into the language; or, if a native word, the Middle-English form or forms of it, with a few quotations and references. This is an important feature of the work, and (I believe) to some extent a new one. In attempting thus, as it were, to *date* each word, I must premise that I often cite Shakespeare in preference to a slightly *earlier* writer whose writings are less familiar; that an attempt has nevertheless been made to indicate the date within (at least) a century; and lastly, that in some cases I may have failed to do this, owing to imperfect information or knowledge. In general, sufficient is said, in a very brief space, to *establish* the earlier uses of each word, so as to clear the way for a correct notion of its origin.

§ 5. **The References.** A large number of the references are from Richardson's Dictionary, denoted by the symbol '(R.).' Some from Todd's Johnson, sometimes cited merely as 'Todd.' Many from Stratmann's Old English Dictionary, or the still better (but unfinished) work by Mätzner; these are all 'ME.,' i.e. Middle-English forms. Many others are due to my own reading. I have, in very many instances, given *exact* references, often at the expenditure of much time and trouble. Thus Richardson cites ' The Romaunt of the Rose' at large, but I have given, in almost every case, the exact number of the line. Similarly, he cites the Fairy Queen merely by the *book* and *canto*, omitting the *stanza*. Inexact quotations are comparatively valueless, as they cannot be verified, and may be false.

For a complete list of authorities, with dates, see p. xxx (above).

§ 6. **The Etymology.** Except in a few cases where the etymology is verbally described, the account of it begins with the symbol **—**, which is always to be read as '**directly derived from**,' or '**borrowed from**,' wherever it occurs. A succession of these symbols occurs whenever the etymology is traced back through another language. The order is always backward, from old to still older forms.

§ 7. **Cognate Forms.** Cognate forms are frequently introduced by way of *further illustration*, though they form, strictly speaking, no part of the direct history of the etymology. But they frequently throw so much light upon the word that it has always been usual to cite them; though no error is more common than to mistake a word that is merely *cognate* with, or *allied* to, the English one for the *very original* of it! For example, many people will quote the German word *acker* as if it *accounted for*, or is the *original* of the English *acre*, whereas it is (like the Lat. *ager*, or the Icelandic *akr*) merely a parallel form. It is remarkable that many beginners are accustomed to cite German words in particular (probably as being the only continental-Teutonic idiom with which they are acquainted) in order to account for English words; the fact being that no Teutonic language has contributed so little to our own tongue, which is, in the main, a *Low*-German dialect as distinguished from that *High*-German one to which the specific name 'German' is commonly applied. In order to guard the learner from this error of confusing *cognate* words with such as are immediately concerned with the etymology, the symbol **+** is used to mark off such words. This symbol is, in every case, to be read as '**not derived from, but cognate with.**' The symbol has, in fact, its usual algebraical value, i. e. *plus*, or *additional*; and indicates **additional information to be obtained from the comparison of cognate forms.**

§ 8. **Symbols and Etymological References.** The symbols used are such as to furnish, *in every case*, an exact reference to some authority. Thus the symbol 'Ital.' does not mean *merely* Italian, but that the word has actually been verified by myself (and may be verified by any one else) as occurring in Meadows's Italian Dictionary. This is an important point, as it is common to cite foreign words at random, without the slightest hint as to where they may be found; a habit which leads to false spellings and even to gross blunders. And, in order that the student may the more easily verify these words (as well as to curb myself from citing words of unusual occurrence), I have expressly preferred to use common and cheap dictionaries, or such as came most readily to hand, except where I refer *by name* to such excellent books as Rietz's Svenskt Dialekt-Lexicon. The following is a list of these symbols, with their exact significations.

AS.—Anglo-Saxon, or Wessex English in its earliest form. The references are to Grein, Bosworth, or Lye, as cited; or to some AS. work, as cited. All these words are *authorized*, unless the given form is marked by an asterisk preceding it, to denote that it is theoretical.

Bret.—Breton; as in Le Gonidec's Dictionary, ed. 1821.

Corn.—Cornish; as in Williams's Dictionary, ed. 1865.

Dan.—Danish; as in Ferrall and Repp's Dictionary, ed. 1861, or in Larsen (1897).

Du.—Dutch; as in the Tauchnitz stereotyped edition, or in Calisch (1875).

E.—Modern English; see Webster's English Dictionary, ed. Goodrich and Porter; or the Century Dictionary; and see **N.E.D.**

ME.—Middle English; i. e. English from about A.D. 1200 to about A.D. 1500. See § 5 above.

F.—French, as in the Dict. by Hamilton and Legros. The reference 'Cot.' is to Cotgrave's French Dictionary, ed. 1660; also denoted by **MF.** (Middle French). Wherever **OF.** (= Old French) occurs, the reference is to Burguy's Glossaire, unless the contrary be expressly stated, in which case it is (in general) to Godefroy, or to Roquefort.

Gael.—Gaelic; as in Macleod and Dewar's Dictionary, ed. 1839.

G.—German; as in Flügel's Dictionary, ed. 1861.

Gk.—Greek; as in Liddell and Scott's Lexicon, ed. 1849.

Goth.—Moeso-Gothic; as in Stamm's Ulfilas, ed. 1878.

Heb.—Hebrew; as in Leopold's small Hebrew Dictionary, ed. 1872; or in Gesenius (1883).

Icel.—Icelandic; as in Cleasby and Vigfusson's Icelandic Dictionary, ed. 1874.

Ir. or **Irish.**—Irish; as in O'Reilly's Dictionary, ed. 1864.

Ital.—Italian; as in Meadows's Dictionary, ed. 1857.

L. or **Lat.**—Latin; as in Lewis and Short's Dictionary, ed. 1880.

Low Lat.—Low Latin; as in Ducange, ed. Favre; 1884.

ME.—Middle-English; see the line following **E.** above.

MHG.—Middle High German; as in Wackernagel's Wörterbuch, ed. 1861; or Schade; see **OHG.** below.

N.E.D.—A New English Dictionary, on Historical Principles; Oxford, 1888–.

OF.—Old French; as in Godefroy, or in Burguy's Glossaire, ed. 1870.

OHG.—Old High German; chiefly from Schade, 2nd ed., 1872–82.

Pers.—Persian; as in Palmer's Persian Dictionary, ed. 1876.

Port.—Portuguese; as in Vieyra's Dictionary, ed. 1857.

Prov.—Provençal; as in Raynouard's Lexique Roman (so called).

Russ.—Russian; as in Reiff's Dict. of Russian, German, English, and French, ed. 1876.

Skt.—Sanskrit; as in Benfey's Dictionary, ed. 1866.

Span.—Spanish; as in Meadows's Dictionary, ed. 1856; or in Neuman, 1862.

Swed.—Swedish; as in the Tauchnitz stereotyped edition; or in Öman, 1897; or Widegren, 1788.

W.—Welsh; as in Spurrell's Dictionary, ed. 1861.

For a complete list of authorities, see p. xxx.   The above includes only such as have been used too frequently to admit of special reference to them by name.

Other abbreviations.—Such abbreviations as ' adj.' = adjective, ' pl.' = plural, and the like, will be readily understood.   I may particularly mention the following.   Cf. = confer, i. e. compare.   pt. t. = past tense. pp. = past participle.   q. v. = quod vide, i. e. which see.   s. v. = sub verbo, i. e. under the word in question. tr. = translation, *or* translated.   b. (*or* bk.) = book.   c. (*or* ch., *or* cap.) = chapter; *sometimes* = canto.   l. = line s. = section.   st. = stanza.   A. V. = Authorized Version of the Bible (1611).

§ 9. **The Roots.**   In some cases, the words have been traced back to their original Indogermanic roots. This has only been attempted, for the most part, in cases where the subject scarcely admits of a doubt; it being unadvisable to hazard too many guesses, in the present state of our knowledge.   The root is denoted by the symbol ✔, to be read as 'root.'   I have here most often referred to Brugmann, Uhlenbeck, Prellwitz, or Kluge.

§ 10. **Derivatives.**   The symbol ' **Der.**,' i. e. Derivatives, is used to introduce forms derived from the primary word, or from the same source.   For an account of the various suffixes, see Morris's Historical Outlines of English Accidence, and Haldemann's Affixes to English Words; or, for the purpose of comparative philology, consult Brugmann.

§ 11. **Cross-references.**   These frequently afford additional information, and are mostly introduced to save repetition of an explanation.

CORRIGENDA

BAROUCHE, l. 1.   *For* (G.—Ital.) *read* (G.—Ital.—L.)

DEFINE, l. 7.   Insert a comma after *dē*.

EDUCATE, l. 1.   *Insert a comma after* to cultivate.

FLOTSAM, l. 1.   *For* (AF.—E.) *and* L.) *read* (AF.—E. *and* L.)

JAUNT; at the end of l. 5.   *For* id. *read* Rom.

TRACE (1), l. 9.   For **trăctiare* read **tractiāre*.

WARE (1); at the end.   *For* **Weir** (1) and **Worth** *read* **Weir** and **Worth** (1).

*** For some other corrections see the Supplement; pp. 777-780.

A, the indef. article; see **An.**

A-, prefix, has at least twelve different values in English. **α.** Representative words are (1) adown; (2) afoot; (3) along; (4) arise; (5) achieve; (6) avert; (7) amend; (8) alas; (9) abyss; (10) ado; (11) aware; (12) avast. **β.** The full form of these values may be represented by *of-, on-, and-, ā-, ad-, ab-, ex-, he-, an-, at-, ge-, houd.* **γ.** This may be illustrated by means of the examples given; cf. (1) AS. *ofdūne*; (2) *on foot*; (3) AS. *andlang*; (4) AS. *ā-risan*; (5) verb from F. *à chef*, L. *ad caput*; (6) L. *āuertere*, for *abuertere*; (7) F. *amender*, from L. *ēmendāre*, for *exmendāre*; (8) F. *hélas*, where *hé* is interjectional; (9) Gk. ἄβυσσος, for ἄν-βυσσος; (10) for *at do*, i.e. to do; (11) for ME. *ywar*, AS. *gewær*; (12) *avast*, Dutch *houd vast*, hold fast. These prefixes are discussed at greater length under the headings **Of, On, Along, Arise, Ad-, Ab-** (1), **Ex-, Alas, Un-** (1), **At, Aware, Avast**; each being given in its proper place in the Dictionary. ¶ Prefix *a* (5) really has two values: (*a*) French, as in *avalanche*; (*b*) Latin, as in *astringent*; but the source is the same, viz. L. *ad.* Similarly, prefix *a* (6) really has two values; (*a*) French, as in ME. *a-soilen*, now spelt *assoil*; (*b*) Latin, as in *avert, avocation*; the source being L. *ab.* ☞ In words discussed below, the prefix has its number assigned in accordance with the above scheme, where necessary.

AARDVARK, the S. African ground-hog. (Cape Du.) Lit. 'earth-hog.' From Du. *aard-*, for *aarde*, earth; and *vark*, for *varken*, a hog. See **Earth** and **Farrow.**

AB-, prefix. (L.) L. *ab*, short form *a-*; sometimes extended to *abs-*. Cognate with Skt. *apa*, away, from; Gk. ἀπό; Goth. *af*; AS. *of*; G. *ab*; see **Of.** Hence numerous compounds, as *ab-use, a-vert, abs-tract*, &c. In French, it becomes *a-* or *av-*; see **Assoil, Advantage.**

ABACK, backwards. (E.) ME. *abak*; as in 'And worthi to be put *abak*;' Gower, C. A. i. 295 (bk. iii. 481). For *on bak*, as in 'Sir Thopas drough *on bak* ful fast;' Chaucer, C. T., B 2017, in the Harleian MS., where other MSS. have *a*ʰ*ak*.—AS. *onbæc*; Matt. iv. 10. Thus the prefix is *a-* (2); for *on*. See **On** and **Back.**

ABACUS, a calculating frame; upper member of the capital of a column. (L.—Gk.) See Trevisa, tr. of Higden, vii. 69. L. *abacus.*—Gk. ἄβαξ (gen. ἄβακος), a slab for reckoning on.

ABAFT, on the aft, behind. (E.) **α.** From the prefix *a-* (2), for *on*, and *-baft*, which is contracted from *bi-aft*, i.e. by aft. Thus *abaft* is for *on by aft*, i.e. in that which lies towards the after part. **β.** *-baft* is ME. *baft*, Allit. Poems, C. 148; the fuller form is *biaft*, with which cf. 'He let *biaften* the more del'=he left behind the greater part; Genesis and Exodus, 3377. ME. *biaften* is from AS. *beæftan*, compounded of *be*, by, and *æftan*, behind; Grein, i. 53. See **By** and **Aft.**

ABANDON, to forsake, give up. (F.—Low L.—OHG.) ME. *abandounen.* 'Bot thai, that can thame *abandoune* Till ded'= but they, that gave themselves up to death; Barbour's Bruce, ed. Skeat, xvii. 642.—F. *abandonner*, to give up.—F. *à bandon*, at liberty, at one's disposal; orig. 'in the power of;' discussed in Brachet, Etym. F. Dict.—F. *à*, prep., and *bandon*, control, jurisdiction.—L. *ad*, to; and Low L. *bandum*, a feudal term (also spelt *bannum*) signifying an order, decree; see **Ban.** ¶ The F. *à bandon* is lit. 'by proclamation,' and thus has the double sense (1) 'under control,' and (2) 'at one's discretion, by permission.' The former is obsolete in modern English; but occurs frequently in ME. See Glossary to the Bruce; and cf. 'habben *abandun*,' to have at one's will, O. Eng. Homilies, ed. Morris, i. 189, l. 24. **Der.** *abandon-ed*, lit. given up; *abandon-ment.*

ABASE, to bring low. (F.—L.) Shak. has 'abase our sight so low;' 2 Hen. VI, i. 2. 15. Cf. 'So to *abesse* his realte;' Gower, C. A. i. 111 (bk. i. 2063). From *a-* (5), for F. *a-*, L. *ad*, and **Base**; in imitation of OF. *abaissier, abessier*, MF. *abaisser, abbaisser*, 'to debase, abase, abate, humble;' Cotgrave.—Late L. *abassāre*, to lower.—L. *ad*, to; and Late L. *bassāre*, to lower, from Late L. *bassus*, low. See **Base. Der.** *abase-ment*, A. V., Ecclus. xx. 11. ¶ It is extremely probable that some confusion has taken place between this word and to *abash*; for in Middle E. (in the Northern dialect) we find *abaist* with the sense of *abashed* or dismayed. See examples under *abasen* in Mätzner's Wörterbuch; and see N. E. D.

ABASH, to confuse with shame. (F.) ME. *abaschen, abaischen, abaissen, abasen,* &c. 'I *abasshe*, or am amased of any thynge;' Palsgrave. 'Thei weren *abaischid* with a greet stonying;' Wyclif, Mk. v.

42. 'He was *abasched* and agast;' K. Alisaunder, ed. Weber, l. 224.—OF. *esbaïss-*, stem of pres. part. of *esbair*, to astonish (see note below); mod. F. *ébahir.*—OF. *es-* (L. *ex*, out, extremely); and *bair, bahir*, to express astonishment, an imitative verb formed from the interjection *bah!* of astonishment. Cf. prov. E. *bo, boh*, interj., a sudden cry to cause fright; Gk. βοάειν, L. *boāre*, to shout out. ¶ The final *-sh* is to be thus accounted for. French verbs in *-ir* are of two forms, those which (like *venir*) follow the Latin inflexions, and those which (like *fleurir*) sometimes add *-iss-* to the root. See Brachet's Hist. French Grammar, ed. Toynbee, § 581. This *-iss-* is imitated from the L. *-esc-, -isc-*, seen in 'inchoative' verbs, such as *flor-esco, trem-isco*, and appears in many parts of the French verb, which is conjugated to a great degree as if its infinitive were **fleurissir* instead of *fleurir.* **β.** An excellent example is seen in *óbeir*, to obey, which would similarly have, as it were, a secondary form **óbeissir*; and, corresponding to these forms, we have in English not only *to obey*, but the obsolete form *obeysche, obesche*, as in 'the wynd and the see *obeschen* to hym;' Wyclif, Mk. iv. 40. **γ.** Easier examples appear in E. *abolish, banish, cherish, demolish, embellish, establish, finish, flourish, furbish, furnish, garnish, languish, nourish, polish, punish*, all from French verbs in *-ir.* **δ.** We also have examples like *admonish, diminish, replenish*, evidently from French sources, in which the termination is due to analogy; these are discussed in their proper places. ¶ It is probable that the word to *abash* has been to some extent confused with to *abase.* See **Abase. Der.** *bash-ful* (for *abash-ful*); *abash-ment.*

ABATE, to beat down. (F.—L.) ME. *abaten.* 'To *abate* the bost of that breme duke;' Will. of Palerne, 1141. 'Thow ... *abatest* alle tyrannè;' K. Alisaunder, ed. Weber, l. 7499.—OF. *abatre*, to beat down.—Late L. *abbattere*; see Brachet.—L. *ad*, to; and *battere*, popular form of *battuere*, to beat. **Der.** *abate-ment*, Hamlet, iv. 7. 121; *abat-is* (below), and F. *abatt-oir*, a public slaughter-house. ¶ Often contracted to *bate*, q. v.

ABATIS, ABATTIS, a military defence made of felled trees. (F.—L.) Spelt *abatis* in Todd's Johnson.—F. *abatis*; OF. *abateis* (Hatzfeld).—OF. *abatre*, to beat down (above).

ABBESS, fem. of abbot. (F.—L.—Gk.—Syriac.) ME. *abbesse*, Rob. of Glouc. p. 370, l. 7624; Early E. Poems, ed. Furnivall, p. 70, l. 165.—AF. *abbesse*; earlier OF. *abaesse*; see *abbesse* in Hatzfeld.—L. *abbātissa*, fem. in *-issa* from *abbāt-*, stem of *abbas*, an abbot. See **Abbot.**

ABBEY, a religious house. (F.—L.—Gk.—Syriac.) ME. *abbeye, abbaye.* 'Abbeye*, abbatia' [*misprinted* abbacia]; Prompt. Parv. Spelt *abbei* in the Metrical Life of St. Dunstan, l. 39.—AF. *abbeie, abeie*, f.; OF. *abeie, abaie*; Bartsch's Chrestomathie.—Late L. *abbātia.*—Late L. *abbāt-*, stem of *abbas.* See **Abbot.**

ABBOT, the father (or head) of an abbey. (L.—Gk.—Syriac.) ME. *abbot, abbod.* 'Abbott*, abbas;' Prompt. Parv. Spelt *abbod*, Ancren Riwle, p. 314. AS. *abbod, abbad*; Ælfric's homily on the Old Test. begins with the words 'Ælfric *abbod.*'—L. *abbātem, abbādem*, acc. of *abbās*, father.—Late Gr. ἀββᾶς (gen. ἀββάτ-ος, ἀββάδ-ος); see Ducange.—Syriac *abbā*, father; see Romans, viii. 15; Galat. iv. 6. ¶ The restoration of the *t* (for *d* in AS.) was due to a knowledge of the L. form; cf. OF. *abez* (= *abets*, pl.), Chanson de Roland, 2955.

ABBREVIATE, to shorten. (L.) Fabyan has *abreuyatyd* in the sense of abridged; Henry III., an. 26, ed. 1811, p. 333. Elyot has 'an *abbreuiate*, called of the Grekes and Latines *epitoma*;' The Governor, b. iii. c. 25.—L. *abbreuiāre* (pp. *abbreuiātus*), to shorten, in Rom. ix. 28 (Vulgate).—L. *ad*, to; and *breuis*, short. See **Brief** and **Abridge. Der.** *abbreviat-ion, -or.* **Doublet**, *abridge.* ¶ Here *adbreuiāre* would at once become *abbreuiāre*; cf. Ital. *abbonare*, to improve, *abbassare*, to lower, *abbellare*, to embellish, where the prefix is plainly *ad.* ☞ The formation of verbs in *-ate* in English is curious; a good example is *create*, equivalent to L. *creāre*; but it does not follow that *crea*' was necessarily formed from the pp. *creātus.* Such verbs in *-ate* can be formed *directly* from L. verbs in *-āre*, by mere analogy with others. All that was necessary was to initiate such a habit of formation. This habit began with words like *advocate*, which was originally a pp. used as a sb., and, secondarily, was used as a verb by the common English habit of creating verbs from sbs.

ABDICATE, lit. to renounce. (L.) In Levins, A. D. 1570; and used by Bishop Hall, in his Contemplations, N.T., b. iv. cont. 6.

§ 2. — L. *abdicāt-us*, pp. of *abdicāre* (see note to **Abbreviate**). — L. *ab*, from ; and *dicāre*, to proclaim. *Dicāre* is allied to *dicere*, to say ; see **Diction**. Der. *abdicat-ion*.

ABDOMEN, the lower part of the belly. (L.) Defined as 'the fat which is about the belly ;' Coles, ed. 1684. Der. *abdomin-al*.

ABDUCE, to lead away. (L.) Not old, and not usual. Used by Sir T. Browne, Vulg. Errors, b. iii. c. 20. § 4 ; where some edd. have *adduce*. More common is the derivative *abduction*, used by Blackstone, Comment. b. iv. c. 15, and a common law-term. — L. *abdūcere*, to lead away. — L. *ab*, from, away ; and *dūcere*, to lead. See **Duke**. Der. *abduct*, *abduct-ion*, *abduct-or* ; cf. the pp. *abductus*.

ABED, in bed. (E.) Shakespeare has *abed*, As You Like It, ii. 2. 6, and elsewhere ; ME. *a-bedde*, Chaucer, Troil. i. 915. The prefix *a-* stands for *on*. ' Thu restest the *on bædde*' = thou restest thee abed ; Layamon, ii. 372.

ABELE, the white poplar. (Du.—F.—L.) In Kersey (1708). Du. *abeel*. — OF. *abel*, *aubel* (*aubel* in Godefroy). — Late L. *albellum*, acc. of *albellus*, white poplar ; Duc. — L. *alb-us*, white. See **Alb**.

ABERRATION, a wandering. (L.) In Blount's Gloss., ed. 1674. — L. *aberrātiōnem*, acc. of *aberrātio*. — L. *aberrāre*, to wander from. — L. *ab*, away ; and *errāre*, to wander. See **Err**.

ABET, to incite. (F.—Scand.) Used by Shak. Com. of Errors, ii. 2. 172. ME. *abetten*, Sir Ferumbras, l. 5816 (ab. 1380). [Cf. ME. *abet*, sb., meaning 'instigation ;' Chaucer, Troilus, ii. 357.] — OF. *abeter*, to deceive, also to incite (Godefroy) ; AF. and OF. *abet*, instigation, deceit. — OF. *a-* < L. *ad*, to ; and *beter*, to bait. Cf. ' Nus ours, quant il est bien *betes*' = No bear, when he is well baited ; Rom. Rose, 10168. OF. *beter* is from Icel. *beita*, to bait, chase with dogs, set dogs on ; lit. 'to make to bite ;' causal verb from *bīta*, to bite. See **Bait** ; and see **Bet**. Der. *abetment*, AF. *abettement* ; *abett-or*, Shak. Lucrece, 886.

ABEYANCE, expectation, suspension. (F.—L.) A law term ; used by Littleton, and in Blackstone's Commentaries ; see Cowel's Law Dict., and Todd's Johnson. — A.F. *abéiance*, as in the phrase 'droit *en abéiance*,' a right in abeyance, or which is suspended ; OF. *abeance*, expectation ; see Godefroy. — F. prefix *a-* (< L. *ad*) ; and *beance*, expectation (Godefroy) ; allied to OF. *béant*, gaping, pres. pt. of obs. verb *béer* (mod. F. *bayer*), to gape, to expect anxiously. — L. *ad* ; and *badāre*, to gape, to open the mouth, used by Isidore of Seville ; see Brachet, s.v. *bayer*. The word *badāre* is probably imitative.

ABHOR, to shrink from with terror. (L.) Shak. has it frequently. It occurs in Lord Surrey's translation of Virgil, b. ii. l. 16 ; cf. ' quanquam animus meminisse *horret* ;' Aen. ii. 12. Caxton has *abhorryng*, Troy Book, leaf 20, l. 11. — L. *abhorrēre*, to shrink from. — L. *ab*, from ; and *horrēre*, to bristle (with fear). See **Horrid**. Der. *abhorr-ent*, *abhorr-ence*.

ABIDE (1), to wait for. (E.) ME. *abiden*, Chaucer, C. T., E 757, 1106 ; and in common use. AS. *ābīdan*, Grein, i. 12. — AS. prefix *ā-* ; and *bīdan*, to bide. Cf. Goth. *usbeidan*, to expect. See **Bide**. Der. *abid-ing* ; *abode*, formed by gradation, from the 2nd grade *bād*.

ABIDE (2), to suffer for a thing. (E.) *a.* We find in Shak. 'lest thou *abide* it deare ;' Mids. Nt. Dream, iii. 2. 175 ; where the first quarto has *aby*. The latter is correct ; the verb in the phrase 'to *abide* it' being a mere corruption, due to confusion with *abide* (1). *β.* The ME. form is *abyen*, as in 'That thou shalt with this launcegay *Abyen* it ful soure ;' Chaucer, C. T., B 2011 (l. 13751). This verb *abyen* is also spelt *abuggen* and *abiggen*, and is common in Middle E. ; see examples in Mätzner and Stratmann. Its pt. tense is *aboughte*, and we still preserve it, in a reversed form, in the modern *to buy off*. *γ.* Hence ' lest thou *abide* it dear ' signifies 'lest thou have to *buy* it *off* dearly,' i. e. lest thou have to *pay* dearly *for* it. — AS. *ābycgan*, to pay for. ' Gif frīman wið frīes mannes wíf geligeð, his wergelde *ābicge*' = If a free man lie with a freeman's wife, let him pay for it with his wergeld ; Laws of King Æthelbirht, 31 ; in Thorpe's Ancient Laws, i. 10. — AS. *ā-*, prefix ; and AS. *bycgan*, to buy. See **Buy**.

ABIGAIL, a waiting-woman. (Heb.) See T. L. O. Davies, Suppl. Glossary. From the character *Abigail* in Beaumont and Fletcher's Scornful Woman. See 1 Sam. xxv.

ABILITY ; see **Able**.

ABJECT, mean ; lit. cast away. (L.) Shak. has it several times, and once the subst. *abjécts* ; Rich. III, i. 1. 106. It was formerly used also as a verb. ' Almightie God *abiected* Saul, that he shulde no more reigne ouer Israhel ;' Sir T. Elyot, The Governour, b. ii. c. i. § 3. — L. *abiectus*, cast away, pp. of *abicere*, to cast away. — L. *ab*, from, away ; and *iacere*, to cast. Cf. **Jet** (1). Der. *abject-ly*, *abject-ion*, *abject-ness*, *abjects* (pl. sb.).

ABJURE, to forswear. (L.) Sir T. More has *abiure*, Works, p. 214 b. Cotgrave has '*abjurer*, to abjure, forswear, deny with an oath.' — L. *abiūrāre*, to deny. — L. *ab*, from ; and *iūrāre*, to swear, from *iūs* (gen. *iūris*), law, right. ☞ In several words of this kind, it is almost impossible to say whether they were derived from Lat.

immediately, or through the French. It makes no ultimate difference. Der. *abjur-at-ion*.

ABLATIVE, taking away. (F.—L.) ME. *ablatyfe*, Reliq. Ant. ii. 14, l. 19. — F. *ablatif*, 'the ablative case,' Cot. — L. *ablātiuus*, the name of a case. — L. *ab*, from ; and *lātum*, to bear, used as active supine of *fero*, but from a different root. *Lātum* is from an older form *tlātum*, supine of *tollere*, to lift, take away. Co-radicate words are *tolerate* and the ME. *thole*, to endure. See **Tolerate**. ¶ ' We learn from a fragment of Cæsar's work, *De Analogiâ*, that he was the inventor of the term *ablative* in Latin. The word never occurs before ;' Max Müller, Lectures, i. 118 (8th edit.).

ABLAZE, on fire. (E.) For *on blaze*, i. e. in a blaze. ' Al *on blase* ;' Gower, C. A. ii. 244 (bk. v. 3510). The AS. and ME. *on* commonly has the sense of *in*. See **Abed** and **Blaze**.

ABLE, having power ; skilful. (F.—L.) ME. *able*, Chaucer, Prol. 584. — OF. *able* (Godefroy), able ; F. *habile*, ' able, . . active ;' Cot. — L. *habilis*, easy to handle, active. — L. *habēre*, to have, to hold. *β.* The spelling *hable* is also found, as, e. g. in Sir Thomas More, Dialogue concerning Heresies, b. iii. c. 16 ; Works, p. 245 a ; *habilitie*, R. Ascham, The Schoolmaster, ed. 1570, leaf 19 (ed. Arber, p. 63). Der. *abl-y*, *abil-i-ty* (from L. acc. *habilitātem*, from *habilitās*).

ABLUTION, a washing. (F.—L.) Used by Bp. Taylor (R.) ME. *ablucioun*, Chaucer, C. T., G 856. — F. *ablution*. — L. acc. *ablūtiōnem*. — L. *abluere*, to wash away. — L. *ab*, away ; and *luere*, to wash. Cf. L. *lauāre*, to wash ; see **Lave**.

ABNEGATE, to deny. (L.) Used by Dr. Johnson, s. v. *abjure*. Minsheu (1627) has *abnegation*. — L. *abnegāt-us*, pp. of *abnegāre*, to deny. — L. *ab*, from, away ; and *negāre*, to deny. See **Negation**. Der. *abnegat-ion*.

ABNORMAL, irregular. (F.—L.—Gk.) Modern ; and very corrupt (N. E. D.). Made by popular etymology, as if from L. *ab*, from, and *norma*, rule (see **Normal**) ; but really from F. *anormal* (Hatzfeld). — Med. L. *anormālis*, by-form of *anormalus* (Duc.), a corruption of *anōmalus* (whence F. *anomal*). — Gk. ἀνώμαλος, uneven ; see **Anomaly**. ¶ An anomalous word.

ABOARD, on board. (E.) For *on board*. ' And stood *on borde* baroun and knyght To help kyng Rychard for to fyght ;' Richard Coer de Lion, 2543 ; in Weber, Met. Romances.

ABODE, a dwelling. (E.) The ME. *abood* almost always has the sense of 'delay' or 'abiding ;' see Chaucer, C. T. 967 (A 965). Also North E. *abād*, Barbour's Bruce, i. 142. A verbal sb. from *abide*, with the same stem-vowel as *ābād*, the pt. t. of that verb. See **Abide** (1). For the modern sense, see John, xiv. 23.

ABOLISH, to annul. (F.—L.) Caxton has the pp. *abolysshed*, Eneydos, ch. xxvi (p. 92, l. 32). Hall, Henry VIII, an. 28. § 8, has the unnecessary spelling *abholish*, just as *abominate* was once written *abhominate*. — F. *aboliss-*, from inf. *abolir* ; (for the ending *-sh* see remarks on *Abash*.) — L. *abolesc-ere*, inceptive form of *abolēre*, to annul. ¶ The etymology of *abolēre* is not clear ; Fick (ii. 47) compares it with Gk. ἀπόλλυναι, to destroy ; see Prellwitz, s. v. ὄλεθρος. Bréal derives *ab-olēre* from *ab* and **olēre* as in *ad-olēre*, as if it meant 'to check the growth.' See **Adolescent**. Der. *abol-it-ion*, *abol-it-ion-ist*.

ABOMINATE, to hate. (L.) The verb is in Levins, A. D. 1570 ; spelt *abhominate*, p. 41, l. 30 [not noted in N. E. D. before 1644]. Wyclif has *abhominable*, Titus i. 16 ; *abhominable*, Gower, C. A. i. 263 ; iii. 204 (bk. ii. 3107 ; bk. vii. 3337). — L. *abōmināt-us*, pp. of *abōmināri*, to dislike ; lit. to turn away from a thing that is of ill omen ; (for the ending *-ate*, see note to **Abbreviate**.) — L. *ab*, from ; and *ōmin-*, for *ōmen*, a portent. See **Omen**. Der. *abomin-able*, *abomin-at-ion*.

ABORIGINES, indigenous inhabitants. (L.) ' Calling them *aborigines* and αὐτόχθονες ;' Selden's notes to Drayton's Polyolbion, song 8, note 2. — L. *aborigines*, the ancestors of the Romans, the nation which, previous to historical record, drove out the Siculi (Lewis and Short). Coined from L. *ab origine*, where *origine* is the abl. of L. *origo* ; see **Origin**. Cf. Virgil, Æn. i. 642. Der. *aborigin-al*.

ABORTION, an untimely birth. (L.) *Abortion* occurs in Minsheu, ed. 1627 ; and in Hakewill's Apology, p. 317 (R.) Shak. has *abortive*, L. L. L. i. 1. 104. — L. acc. *abortiōnem*, from *abortio* ; cf. *abortus*, pp. of *aboriri*, to fail. — L. *ab*, from, away ; and *oriri*, to arise, grow. See **Orient**. From the same stem, *abort-ive*, *-ly*, *-ness*.

ABOUND, to overflow, to be plentiful. (F.—L.) ME. *abounden*, Wyclif, 2 Cor. ix. 8. Also spelt *habounden*, as in Chaucer's tr. of Boethius, b. ii. pr. 4, l. 62. — OF. (and F.) *abonder*. — L. *abundāre*, to overflow. — L. *ab* ; and *undāre*, to flow in waves, from *unda*, a wave. See **Undulate**. Der. *abund-ance*, q.v. ; *abund-ant* (*habundant* in Ch. C. T., E 59) ; *abund-ant-ly*.

ABOUT, around, concerning. (E.) ME. *abuten*, Ormulum, 4087 ; later, *abouten*, *aboute*. AS. *ābūtan* ; as in ' *ābūtan* þone munt' = around the mountain, Exod. xix. 12. *a.* Here the prefix *ā-* is short for *an-*, another form of *on*; and we accordingly find also the form *onbūtan*, Genesis ii. 11. [A commoner AS. form was *ymbūtan*, but here the prefix is different, viz. *ymb*, about, corresponding to G. *um*.] β. The word *būtan* is itself a compound of *be*, by, and *ūtan*, outward. Thus the wo.d is resolved into *on-be-ūtan*, on (that which is) by (the) outside. γ. Again *ūtan*, outward, outside, is an adverb formed from the prep. *ūt*, out. See **On, By,** and **Out.** The words *abaft* and *above* have been similarly resolved into *on-by-aft* and *on-by-ove(r)*. See **Abaft, Above.** ¶ Similar forms are found in Old Friesic, where *abefta* is deducible from *an-bi-efta*; *abuppa* (above), from *an-bi-uppa*; and *abūta* (about), from *an-bi-ūta*.

ABOVE, over. (E.) ME. *abufen*, Ormulum, 6438; later, *aboven*, *above*. AS. *ābūfan*, AS. Chron. an. 1090. — AS. *an*, on; *be*, by; and *ufan*, upward; the full form *be-ufan* actually occurs in the Laws of Æthelstan, iv. 4; in Thorpe, i. 224. See **About.** The word *ufan* is equivalent to the cognate G. *oben*, which is allied to E. *over*. See **On, By,** and **Over.** Cf. Du. *boven*, above.

ABRADE, to scrape off. (L.) In Bailey, vol. ii. ed. 1731 (an earlier notice in N.E.D. under 1677). — L. *abrādere*, to scrape off, pp. *abrāsus*. — L. *ab*, off; and *rādere*, to scrape. See **Rase.** Der. *abrase*, pp. in Ben Jonson, Cynthia's Revels, Act v. sc. 3, descr. of Apheleia; *abras-ion*, in Blount's Gloss., ed. 1674.

ABREAST, side by side. (E.) In Shak. Hen. V, iv. 6. 17. The prefix is for *an*, ME. form of *on*; cf. *abed*, *asleep*, &c.

ABRIDGE, to shorten. (F.—L.) ME. *abrege*, Hampole, Pricke of Conscience, 4571; also *abregge*, Chaucer, C. T. 3001 (A 2999). — OF. *abrevier* (Godefroy); also *abregier*, *abrigier*. — L. *abbreuiāre*, to shorten. Der. *abridɡe-ment*, Lucrece, 1198. **Doublet,** *abbreviate*, q.v.

ABROACH, TO SET, to broach. (Hybrid; E. and F.) ME. *sette abroche*, Gower, C. A. ii. 183; (bk. v. 1677). For *setten on broche*; cf. the phrase 'to set on fire.' From E. *on*; and OF. *broche*, a spit, spigot. See **Broach.** *Sɪt abroach* is a translation of AF. *mis abroche*, Liber Custumarum, p. 304.

ABROAD, spread out. (E.) ME. *abrood*, Chaucer, C. T., F 441; *abrod*, Rob. of Glouc. p. 542, l. 11228. For *on brood*, or *on brod*. 'The bavme thurghe his brayn all *on brod* ran;' Destruction of Troy, 8780. ME. *brod*, *brood* is the mod. E. *broad*. See **Broad.**

ABROGATE, to repeal. (L.) In Shak. L. L. L. iv. 2. 55. Earlier, in Hall, Ed. IV, an. 9. § 23. — L. *abrogāt-us*, pp. of *abrogāre*, to repeal a law; (for the ending -*ate*, see note on **Abbreviate**.) — L. *ab*, off, away; and *rogāre*, to ask, to propose a law. See **Rogation.** Der. *abrogat-ion*, from F. *abrogation*, Cot.

ABRUPT, broken off, short, rough. (L.) Shak. 1 Hen. VI, ii. 3. 30. — L. *abruptus*, broken off, pp. of *abrumpere*, to break off. — L. *ab*; and *rumpere*, to break. See **Rupture.** Der. *abrupt-ly*, *abrupt-ness*; *abrupt*, sb., as in Milton, P. L. ii. 409.

ABS-, prefix; sometimes used instead of *ab* before *c* and *t*; as in *abscond*, *abs-tain*. — L. *abs-*, prefix. Cf. Gk. ἄψ, allied to ἀπό, from.

ABSCESS, a sore. (L.) In Kersey, ed. 1715. — L. *abscessus*, a going away, a gathering of humours into one. — L. *abscēdere*, to go away; pp. *abscessus*. — L. *abs*, away; *cēdere*, to go. See **Cede.**

ABSCIND, to cut off. (L.) Bp. Taylor has the sb. *abscission*, Sermons, series ii. s. 13. § 12. The verb occurs in Johnson's Rambler, no. 90. § 9. — L. *abscindere*, to cut off. — L. *ab*, off; and *scindere*, to cut. *Scindere* is allied to Gk. σχίζειν, Skt. *chhid*, to cut; see **Schism.** Der. *absciss-a*, from the L. fem. pp.; *absciss-ion*, from the pp. *abscissus*.

ABSCOND, to hide from, go into hiding. (L.) In Blackstone, Comment. b. iv. c. 24. — L. *abscondere*, to hide. — L. *abs*, away; and *condere*, to lay up, to hide, which is from L. *con-* = *cum*, together, and -*dere*, to put; from the weak grade (*dhə*) of √DHĒ, to put, place; Brugm. i. § 589. See **Do.**

ABSENT, being away. (F.—L.) In Wyclif, Philip. i. 27; where it is taken directly from L.; but the later examples represent F. *absent*. — L. *absentem*, acc. case of *absens*, absent, pres. pt. of *abesse*, to be away. — L. *ab*, away, and **sens*, being, which is a better division of the word than *abs-ens*; cf. *præ-sens*, present. See **Present.** Der. *absence*, in Chaucer, C. T., A 1239, from F. *absence*, L. *absentia*; *absent*, v., *absent-er*, *absent-ee*, *absent-ly*.

ABSOLUTE, unrestrained, complete. (L.) Chaucer has *absolut*; tr. of Boethius, b. iii. pr. 10, l. 20. — L. *absolūtus*, pp. of *absoluere*, to set free. See **Absolve.**

ABSOLVE, to set free. (L.) In Shak. Henry VIII, iii. 1. 50. The sb. *absoluciun* is in the Ancren Riwle, p. 346. [The ME. form of the verb was *assoile*, taken from the OF.] — L. *absoluere*, to set free. — L. *ab*; and *soluere*, to loosen. See **Solve.** Der. *absolute*, from the pp. *absolūtus*; whence *absolut-ion*, *absolut-ory*.

ABSORB, to suck up, imbibe. (L.) Sir T. More has *absorpt* as a past participle, Works, p. 267 c. Caxton has *absorbed*, Eneydos, ch. xxvii. (p. 104, l. 31). — L. *absorbēre*, to suck up. — L. *ab*, off, away; and *sorbēre*, to suck up. + Gk. ῥοφέειν, to sup up. Brugm. ii. § 801.

Der. *absorb-able*, *absorb-ent*; also *absorpt-ion*, *absorpt-ive*; cf. the pp. *absorptus*.

ABSTAIN, to refrain from. (F.—L.) ME. *absteynen*; Wyclif, 1 Tim. iv. 3. The sb. *abstinence* occurs in the Ancren Riwle, p. 340. From *abstien-*, tonic stem of MF. *abstenir*, variant used in place of OF. *astenir*, to abstain; cf. mod. F. *abstenir*. — L. *abstinēre*, to abstain. — L. *abs*, from; and *tenēre*, to hold. See **Tenable.** Der. *abstin-ent*, *abstin-ence*, from L. *abstin-ēre*; and *abstent-ion*; cf. the pp. *abstent-us*.

ABSTEMIOUS, temperate. (L.) In Shak. Temp. iv. 53. The suffix -*ous* is formed on a F. model. — L. *abstēmius*, temperate, refraining from strong drink. — L. *abs*, from; and **tēmum*, strong drink, a word only preserved in its derivatives *tēmētum*, strong drink, and *tēmulentus*, drunken. Cf. Skt. *tam*, to be breathless, originally, to choke; *tāmyati*, he is exhausted, is beside himself. Der. *abstemiousness*, *abstemious-ly*.

ABSTENTION; see under **Abstain.**

ABSTRACT, a summary; as a verb, to separate, draw away from. (L.) Shak. has the sb. *abstract*, All's Well, iv. 3. 99. The pp. *abstracted* is in Milton, P. L. ix. 463. A still older form is *abstracte* used as a pp., in the later translation of Higden, Polychron. vol. i. p. 21, lower text (ab. 1450), l. 9; misdated 1387 in N.E.D. — L. *abstractus*, withdrawn, separated, pp. of *abstrahere*, to draw away. — L. *abs*, from; and *trahere*, to draw. See **Trace, Tract.** Der. *abstract-ed*, *abstract-ion*, *abstract-ive*.

ABSTRUSE, difficult, out of the way. (L.) In Minsheu, ed. 1627; and Milton, P. L. viii. 40. — L. *abstrūsus*, concealed, difficult, pp. of *abstrūdere*, to thrust aside, to conceal — L. *abs*, away; and *trūdere*, to thrust. Cf. **Intrude**; and see **Threaten.** Der. *abstruse-ly*, *abstruse-ness*.

ABSURD, ridiculous. (L.) In Shak. 1 Hen. VI, v. 4. 137. — L. *absurdus*, contrary to reason, inharmonious. — L. *ab*, away; and *surdus*, indistinct, harsh-sounding; also, deaf. Perhaps *absurdus* was, originally, a mere intensive of *surdus*, in the sense of harsh-sounding. See **Surd.** Der. *absurd-ity*, F. *absurdite*, Cot.; *absurd-ness*.

ABUNDANCE, plenty. (F.—L.) ME. *aboundance*, Wyclif, Luke xii. 15. — OF. *abondance*. — L. *abundantia*, plenty. — L. *abundant-*, stem of the pres. pt. of *abundāre*, to abound. See **Abound.**

ABUSE, to use amiss. (F.—L.) ME. *abusen*; the pp. *abuseɪ*, spelt *abwsyt*, occurs in the Scottish romance of Lancelot of the Laik, l. 1207. 'I *abuse* or misse order a thing;' Palsgrave. Chaucer has the sb. *abusion*, Troilus, iv. 990. — OF. *abuʃer*, to use amiss. — L. *abūsus*, pp. of *abūti*, to abuse, mis-use. — L. *ab*, from (here, amiss); and *ūtī*, to use. See **Use.** Der. *abus-ive*, F. *abusif*, Cot.; *abus-iveness*.

ABUT, to project towards, to border on, be close upon. (F.—G.) Shak. speaks of England and France as being 'two mighty monarchies Whose high, upreared, and *abutting* fronts The perilous narrow ocean parts asunder;' Prol. to Hen. V, l. 21. 'The southe hede therof *abuttyth* vppon the wey;' Bury Wills, p. 52; an. 1479. — OF. *abouter* (Godefroy), to fix bounds, to abut upon, also spelt *abuter*; mod. F. *abouter*, to join end to end. — OF. *a*, prefix < L. *ad*, to, at; and *bout*, an end, allied to F. *bouter*, OF. *bouter*, *buter*, to push, thrust, but, also to place; see **Butt** (1). Der. *abut-ment*, which is that which bears the 'thrust' of an arch; cf. *bu'tress*, a support; but see **Buttress.**

ABY, to pay for; see **Abide.**

ABYSS, a bottomless gulf. (L.—Gk.) Very frequent in Milton, P. L. i. 21, &c. Spenser has *abysse*, Teares of the Muses, l. 260. — L. *abyssus*, a bottomless gulf, borrowed from Gk. — Gk. ἄβυσσος, bottomless. — Gk. ἀ-, negative prefix; and βυσσός, depth, akin to βυθός and βάθος, depth; and βαθύς, deep. Cf. **Bathos.** Der. *abys-m*, Temp. i. 2. 50; *abys-m-al*. ¶ The etymology of *abysm* is traced by Brachet, s.v. *abîme*. It is from OF. *abisme*; from a Late L. **abyssimus*, a superlative form, denoting the lowest depth.

ACACIA, a kind of tree. (Gk.) 'The Egyptian thorne *acacia*;' Holland, tr. of Pliny, bk. xiii. c. 9. Described by Dioscorides as a useful astringent thorn, yielding a white transparent gum; a description which applies to the gum-arabic trees of Egypt. — L. *acacia*, borrowed from Gk. — Gk. ἀκακία, the thorny Egyptian acacia. — Gk. ἀκίς, a point, thorn. See **Acute.** Brugm. ii. § 52. 4.

ACADEMY, a school, a society. (F.—L.—Gk.) Shak. has *academe*, L. L. L. i. 1. 13; pl. *academes*, iv. 3. 303; and Milton speaks of 'the olive grove of *Academe*, Plato's retirement;' P. R. iv. 244. [This form is more directly from the Latin.] Greene has *académy*, Friar Bacon, sc. ii. 37. Burton says 'affliction is a school or *academy*;' Anat. of Melancholy, p. 717 (Todd's Johnson). — F. *académie*. — L. *academia*, borrowed from Gk. — Gk. ἀκαδήμεια, a gymnasium near Athens where Plato taught, so named from the hero Akadēmus. Der. *academ-ic*, *academ-ic-al*, *academ-ic-ian*.

ACAJOU, the cashew-nut; see **Cashew-nut.**

ACANTHUS, a plant famous in Greece for its elegant leaves. (L.—Gk.) In Milton, P. L. iv. 696. — L. *acanthus*. — Gk. ἄκανθος, the plant brank-ursine. — Gk. ἄκανθα, a thorn, prickle. — Gk. ἀκ-, in ἀκίς, a point, barb. See **Acute.**

ACATALECTIC, not catalectic. (Gk.) Formed with Gk. prefix ἀ-, not, from **Catalectic**, q. v.

ACCEDE, to come to terms, agree to. (L.) The verb is rare in early use; but the sb. *access* is common in Shak. and Milton. In ME. we have *accesse* in the sense of a sudden accession of fever or ague, a fever-fit; as in Lydgate's Complaint of the Black Knight, l. 136; Chaucer, Troil. ii. 1315. This is a French use of the word. — L. *accēdere*, to come towards, assent to; also spelt *adcēdere*; pp. *accessus.* — L. *ad*, to; and *cēdere*, to come, go, yield. See **Cede.** **Der.** *access, access-ary, access-ible, acce·s-or-y*; all from the pp. *accessus.*

ACCELERATE, to hasten. (L.) 'To *accelerate* and spede his iorney;' Hall, Hen. VI, an. 31, l. 29. — L. *accelerāre*, to hasten; (for the ending -*ate*, see note on **Abbreviate.**) — L. *ac-* (= *ad*); and *celerāre*, to hasten, from *celer*, quick. See **Celerity.** **Der.** *accelerat-ion, accelerat-ive, -or.*

ACCENT, a tone. (F. — L.) Shak. L. L. L. iv. 2. 124; and in Sidney, Apol. for Poetrie, ed. Arber, p. 71, l. 2. — F. *accent*, Cot. — L. *accentum*, acc. of *accentus*, an accent. — L. *ac-*, for *ad*, to; and *cantus*, a singing, from *canere*, to sing (pp. *cantus*). See **Canorous.** **Der.** *accent-u-al, accent-u-ate, accent-u-at-ion.*

ACCEPT, to receive. (F. — L.) ME. *accepten*, Wyclif, Rom. iv. 6. — F. *accepter.* — L. *acceptāre*, to receive; a frequentative form. — L. *accept-us*, pp. of *accipere*, to receive. — L. *ac-*, for *ad*, to; and *capere*, to take. See **Capable.** **Der.** *accept-able, accept-able-ness, accept-at-ion, accept-ance, accept-er.*

ACCESS, ACCESSARY; see **Accede.**

ACCIDENT, a chance event. (F. — L.) In Chaucer, C. T. 8483 (E607). — F. *accident.* — L. *accident-*, stem of *accidens*, happening, pres. pt. of *accidere*, to happen. — L. *ac-*, for *ad*; and *cadere*, to fall. See **Chance.** **Der.** *acci·ent-al*; also *accidence* (French; from L. *accident-ia*).

ACCLAIM, to shout at. (L.) In Milton four times, but only as a sb.; P. L. ii. 520; iii. 397; x. 455; P. R. ii. 235. The word *acclaiming* is used by Bishop Hall, Contemplations, N. T., b. v. c. 25. § 4. [The word is formed on a French model (cf. *claim* from OF. *claimer*), but from the Latin.] — L. *acclāmāre*, to cry out at. — L. *ac-*, for *ad*, at; and *clāmāre*, to cry out, exclaim. See **Claim.** **Der.** *acclam-a·ion*; cf. *acclāmāt-us*, pp. of L. *acclāmāre.*

ACCLIMATIZE, to adapt to a new climate. (F. — L. — Gk.) Modern. Formed with suffix -*ize* (F. -*iser*, Gk. -ιζειν) from F. *acclimat-er*, to adapt to a climate. — F. *a-* (L. *ad*), to; and *climat*, a climate; see **Climate.**

ACCLIVITY, an upward slope. (L.) Used by Ray, On the Creation (R.) — L. acc. *accliuitātem*, from nom. *accliuitās*, a steepness; whence *acclivity* is formed in imitation of a F. model: the suffix -*ty* answers to F. -*té*, from L. -*tātem.* — L. *ac-*, for *ad*, to; and -*cliuitās*, a slope, a word which does not occur except in compounds; from L. *cliuus*, a hill, sloping ground; properly, sloping. From √KLEI, to lean, slope; whence also L. *inclināre*, to incline, Gk. κλίνειν, to lean, and E. *lean*. See **Lean (1), Incline, Declivity.**

ACCOLADE, the dubbing of a knight. (F. — Ital. — L.) '*Accollade*, a clipping about the neck, which was formerly the way of dubbing knights;' Phillips (1658). — F. *accollade* (Cot.), an embrace round the neck; then a salutation, light tap with a sword in dubbing a knight. — Ital. *accollata*, fem. of pp. of *accollare*, to embrace about the neck (Florio). — L. *ac-*, for *ad*, to, about; and *collum*, the neck; see **Collar.**

ACCOMMODATE, to adapt, suit, provide with. (L.) Shak. Lear, iv. 6. 81. Spelt *accomodate* in Palsgrave. — L. *accommodāre*, to fit, adapt; (for the ending -*ate*, see note on **Abbreviate.**) — L. *ac-*, for *ad*, to; and *commodāre*, to fit, from *commodus*, fit, commodious. See **Commodious** and **Mode.** **Der.** *accommod-at-ion, accommod-at-ing.*

ACCOMPANY, to attend. (F. — L.) Caxton has the pt. t. *acompanyed* in his Troy-book, leaf 104, l. 11. — OF. *acompaigner*, to associate with. — F. *a*, for L. *ad*, to, beside; and OF. *compaignier, compaigner, cumpagner*, to associate with, from *compaing*, a companion. See **Company.** **Der.** *accompani-ment.*

ACCOMPLICE, an associate, esp. in crime. (F. — L.) Shak. 1 Hen. VI, v. 2. 9. An extension (by prefixing either F. *a* or L. *ac-* = *ad*, or the E. indef. article) of the older form *complice*, which occurs in Baret (1580). — F. *complice*, 'a complice, confederate, companion in a lewd action;' Cot. — L. acc. *complicem*, from nom. *complex*, an accomplice, lit. interwoven. — L. *com-*, for *cum*, together; and *plicāre*, to fold. See **Complex.**

ACCOMPLISH, to complete. (F. — L.) ME. *accomplicen*, in Chaucer's Tale of Melibeus (B 2322). — OF. *acomplis-*, a stem of *acomplir*, to complete; (for the ending -*ish*, see note to **Abash.**) — L. *ad*, to; and *complēre*, to fulfil, complete. See **Complete.** **Der.** *accomplish-able, accomplish-ed, accomplish-ment.*

ACCOMPT, an archaic form of **Account**, q. v.

ACCORD, to grant; to agree. (F. — L.) ME. *acorden*, to agree;

Chaucer, C. T., B 2137; and still earlier, viz. in Rob. of Glouc. p. 209, l. 6319; K. Alisaunder, ed. Weber, l. 148. — OF. *acorder*, to agree. — Late L. *accordāre*, to agree, used in much the same way as L. *concordāre*, and similarly formed. — L. *ac-*, for *ad*, to, i. e. in agreement with; and *cord-*, stem of *cor*, the heart. Cf. E. *concord, discord.* The L. *cor* is cognate with E. **Heart**, q. v. **Der.** *accord*, sb., Chaucer, C. T., C 25; *accord-ance, accord-ing, according-ly, accord-ant, accord-ant-ly*; also *accord-ion*, from its pleasing sound; invented in 1829.

ACCOST, to address. (F. — L.) Shak. Tw. Nt. i. 3. 52, which see. Spenser has *accoste*, i. e. border upon; F. Q. v. 11. 42. — F. *accoster*, 'to accoast, or join side to side;' Cot. — Late L. *accostāre*, which occurs in the Acta Sanctorum, iii. Apr. 523 (Brachet). — L. *ac-*, for *ad*; and *costa*, a rib; so that *accostāre* means to join side to side, in accordance with Cotgrave's explanation. See **Coast.**

ACCOUNT, to reckon, value. (F. — L.) ME. *acompten, acounten.* In Gower, C. A. iii. 298 (bk. viii. 701), we find *acompteth* written, but it rhymes with *surmounteth*. The pl. sb. *acountes*, i. e. accounts, occurs in Rob. of Brunne, tr. of Langtoft, p. 135. — OF. *aconter* or *acompter* (Godefroy); the two forms being still preserved in F. *compter* and *conter*, which are doublets. — F. *a*, prefix, for L. *ad*; and *conter*, or *compter*, to count, from L. *computāre*, to compute, count. See **Count.** **Der.** *account*, sb., *account-able, account-able-ness, account-ant.*

ACCOUTRE, to equip. (F. — L.?) Shak. has *accoutred*, Jul. Cæs. i. 2. 105. — MF. *accoutrer, accoustrer.* Cotgrave gives both forms, and explains *accoustrer* by 'to cloath, dress, apparell, attire, array, deck, trim.' Marked by Brachet 'origin unknown.' β. But a likely guess is that which connects it with the OF. *costre, coustre*, nom. case of OF. *costor, coustor* (Godefroy), the sacristan of a church. One of the sacristan's duties was to have charge of the sacred vestments, whence the notion of dressing may have arisen. The OF. *costre* represents the Late L. *custor*, just as OF. *costor* represents the acc. *custōrem*. Ducange (ed. Favre) quotes the Late L. *custor*, glossed by *ædituus*; and it is a variant of L. *custōs*, which was also used in the same sense of 'sacristan.' See **Custody.** ¶ Cf. G. *küster*, a sacristan, vestry-keeper; from the same Late L. *custor.* **Der.** *accoutrement*, Merry Wives, iv. 2. 5.

ACCREDIT, to give credit to. (F. — L.) Not in early use; added by Todd to Johnson's Dict. In Cowper, Letter 43 (R.) — F. *accréditer*, to accredit; formed from F. *à*, to, and the sb. *crédit*, credit. See **Credit, Creed.**

ACCRETION, an increase. (L.) In Sir T. Browne, Vulgar Errors, b. ii. c. 1. § 13. — L. acc. *accrētiōnem*, from nom. *accrētio*; cf. L. *accrēt-us*, pp. of *accrescere*, to grow, increase. — L. *ac-* for *ad*, to; and *crescere*, to grow. See **Crescent.** **Der.** *accret-ive*; and see *accrue.*

ACCRUE, to grow to, to come to in the way of increase. (F. — L.) Spenser, F. Q. iv. 6. 18, has both *decrewed*, decreased, and *accrewed*, increased or gathered. Holinshed, Chron. iii. 1135, has 'new *accrewes* of soldiers,' where *accrew* is a sb. — MF. *accruë*, f., 'a growth, increase, augmentation;' Cot. Orig. fem. of MF. '*accreu*, growne, increased, enlarged, augmented, amplified;' Cot. [The E. word must have been borrowed from the sb., and turned into a verb.] — MF. *accroistre* (Cotgrave), now *accroître*, to increase, enlarge; of which *accreu* (*accru*) is the pp. — L. *accrescere*, to enlarge. — L. *ac-*, for *ad*, to; and *crescere*, to grow. See above. ¶ The AF. *acru*, accrued, pp., occurs in the Year-books of Edw. I, iii. 415. **Der.** *crew*, q. v.

ACCUMULATE, to amass. (L.) In Othello, iii. 3. 370; Hall has *accumulated*; Hen. VII, an. 16. § 1. — L. *accumulāt-us*, pp. of *accumulāre*, to amass; (for the ending -*ate*, see note to **Abbreviate.**) — L. *ac-*, for *ad*, to; and *cumulāre*, to heap up, from *cumulus*, a heap. See **Cumulate.** **Der.** *accumulat-ion, accumulat-ive, -or.*

ACCURATE, exact. (L.) In Sherwood's index to Cotgrave. Used by Bishop Taylor, Artificial Handsomeness, p. 19; Todd. — L. *accūrātus*, studied; pp. of *accūrāre*, to take pains with. — L. *ac-*, for *ad*; and *cūrāre*, to take care, from *cūra*, care. See **Cure.** **Der.** *accurate-ness, accurate-ly*; also *accur-acy*, answering (nearly) to L. *accūrātio.*

ACCURSED, cursed, wicked. (E.) The spelling with a double *c* is false, and due to the frequency of the use of *ac-* = L. *ad* as a prefix. ME. *acorsien, acursien.* 'Ye schule . . . *acursi* alle fiʒtinge;' Owl and Nightingale, 1703; *acorce*, Rob. of Glouc. p. 296, l. 5993. — AS. *ā-*, intens. prefix; and *cursian*, to curse. See **Curse.**

ACCUSE, to lay to one's charge. (F. — L.) Chaucer has *accused, accusinge*, and *accusors*, all in the same passage; see his tr. of Boethius, b. i. pr. 4, ll. 80–84. The pt. t. *acusede* is in the Life of Beket, l. 369. — OF. *acuser*, F. *accuser.* — L. *accūsāre*, to criminate, lay to one's charge. — L. *ac-*, for *ad*, to; and *caussa*, a suit at law, a cause. See **Cause.** **Der.** *accus-able, accus-at-ion, accus-at-ory, accus-er, accus-at-ive* (the name of the case expressing the *subject* governed by a transitive verb).

ACCUSTOM, to render familiar. (F. — L.) 'He was euer *accustomed*;' Hall, Hen. V, an. 5. § 6. [The sb. *acustomaunce*, custom, occurs in Chaucer's Hous of Fame, l. 28.] — OF. *acostumer* (F. *ac-*

coutumer), to accustom. — F. prefix *a*, for L. *ad*; and OF. *costume, coustume, costome*, a custom, Late L. *costūma*, custom, from L. *consuētūdinem* (> *costudne, costumne*), acc. of *consuētūdo*, custom. See **Custom.**

ACE, the 'one' of cards or dice. (F. — L. — Gk.) ME. *as*, Chaucer, C. T. 14579 (B 3851). — OF. *as*, an ace. — L. *ās*, a unit. — Gk. *ἄς*, said to be the Tarentine form of Gk. *εἶς*, one.

ACEPHALOUS, without a head. (Gk.) In Bailey's Dict., ed. 1731. — Gk. *ἀκέφαλ-ος*, without a head; with suffix -*ous*. — Gk. *ἀ-*, privative; and *κεφαλή*, the head.

ACERBITY, bitterness. (F. — L.) Used by Bacon, On Amending the Laws; Works, vol. ii. p. 542 (R.) — F. *acerbité*, 'acerbitie, sharpnesse, sourenesse;' Cot. — L. *acerbitātem*, acc. of *acerbitās*, bitterness. — L. *acerbus*, bitter. — L. *acer*, sharp, acrid. See **Acrid.**

ACETOUS, of the nature of vinegar, sour. (F. — L.) Used by Boyle; quoted in Johnson. — F. *acéteux*, 'sourish;' Cot. — Late L. *acetōsus*, vinegar-like. — L. *acētum*, vinegar. — L. *acēre*, to be sour; cf. *acidus*, sour. See **Acid. Der.** (from L. *acēt-um*) acet-ic, acet-ate.

ACHE, to throb with pain; as a sb., a severe pain. (E.) The spelling *ache* is non-phonetic, and chiefly due to the attempt to connect it with the Gk. *ἄχος*, which is wholly unconnected with it. In old authors the spelling *ake* is common both for the verb and the sb. Strictly, *ake* represented the verb only, whilst *ache* (pronounced nearly as mod. E. *archer*) represented the form of the sb. in the Southern and Midland dialects of Middle English. Hence Shak. has 'When your head did but *ake*,' K. John, iv. 1. 41; and 'Fill all thy bones with *ach-es*, make thee roar,' Temp. i. 2. 370. The sb. form is really obsolete, and the verbal form is used both for sb. and verb. Cf. '*Ake*, or *ache*, or *akynge*, dolor;' Prompt. Parv. β. The ME. *aken*, to ache, was a *strong* verb, forming its past tense as *ook, ok*, pl. *ooke, oke, oken*. 'She saide her hede *oke*' [better spelt *ook*, pron. *awk*]; The Knight of La Tour, ed. Wright, p. 8. 'Thauh alle my fyngres *oken*;' P. Plowman, C. xx. 159. From AS. *acan* (pt. t. *ōc*), strong verb, to ache; from the same root as L. *ag-ere*, to drive; see **Agent.** Cf. Icel. *aka* (pt. t. *ōk*), to drive. ¶ The ME. *ache*, sb., a pain, is regularly formed from AS. *œce*, sb., a pain; which is derived from the strong verb *acan*.

ACHIEVE, to accomplish. (F. — L.) ME. *acheuen = acheven*. Chaucer has '*acheued* and performed;' tr. of Boethius, b. i. pr. 4, l. 141. — OF. *achever*, to accomplish. Formed from the phrase *venir a chef* or *venir a chief*, to come to the end or arrive at one's object. — Late L. *ad caput uenire*, to come to a head (Brachet). See **Chief. Der.** *achievement*, Hen. V, iii. 5. 60; also *hatchment*, q. v.

ACHROMATIC, colourless. (Gk.) Modern and scientific. Formed with suffix -*ic* from Gk. *ἀχρώματ-ος*, colourless. — Gk. *ἀ-*, privative; and *χρώματ-*, stem of *χρῶμα*, colour. See **Chromatic.**

ACID, sour, sharp. (L.) Bacon speaks of 'a cold and *acide* Iuyce;' Nat. Hist. § 644. — L. *acidus*, sour. — √AK, to pierce; cf. Skt. *aç*, to pervade; E. to *egg* on. See **Egg,** verb. **Der.** *acid-ity, acid-ify, acid-ul-ate* (from L. *acid-ul-us*, subacid), *acid-ul-at-ed, acid-ul-ous.*

ACKNOWLEDGE, to confess, own the knowledge of. (E.) Common in Shakespeare; cf. ME. *knowlechen*, to acknowledge. α. The prefixed *a-* is due to the curious fact that there was a ME. verb *aknowen* with the same sense; ex. 'To mee wold shee neuer *aknow* That any man for any meede Neighed her body,' Merline, 901, in Percy Folio MS., i. 450. This *aknowen* is the AS. *oncnāwan*, to perceive. Hence the prefixed *a-* stands for AS. *on*. β. The verb *knowlechen* is common; as e. g. in Wyclif; 'he *knouelechide* and denyede not, and he *knoulechide* for I am not Christ;' John, i. 20. It appears early in the thirteenth century, in Hali Meidenhad, p. 9; Legend of St. Katharine, l. 1352. And hence was formed the sb. *knowleche*, now spelt *knowledge*. See **Knowledge. Der.** *acknowledg-ment*, a hybrid form, with F. suffix; in Hen. V, iv. 8. 124.

ACME, the highest point. (Gk.) Altogether a Greek word, and written in Gk. characters by Ben Jonson, Discoveries, sect. headed *Scriptorum Catalogus.* — Gk. *ἀκμή*, edge. — √AK, to pierce.

ACOLYTE, a servitor. (F. — Late L. — Gk.) ME. *acolite*, Polit. Songs, ed. Wright, p. 329; AF. *acolyte.* Cotgrave has '*Acolyte, Accolite*, he that ministers to the priest while he sacrifices or saies mass.' — Late L. *acolythus*, borrowed from Gk. — Gk. *ἀκόλουθος*, a follower. — Gk. *ἀ-*, with (akin to Skt. *sa-*, with); and *κέλευθος*, a road, way (with gradation of *ευ* to *ου*); so that *ἀκόλουθος* meant originally 'a travelling companion.' The Gk. *κέλευθος* is cognate with L. *callis*, a path; see Prellwitz.

ACONITE, monk's hood; poison. (F. — L. — Gk.) Occurs in Ben Jonson, Sejanus, Act iii. sc. 3, l. 29. [It may have been borrowed from the Latin, or through the French.] — F. *aconit, aconitum*, 'a most venemous herb, of two principall kinds, viz. Libbards-bane and Wolf-bane;' Cot. — L. *aconītum.* — Gk. *ἀκόνιτον*, a plant like monk's-hood; Pliny, Nat. Hist. bk. xxvii. c. 3. ¶ Pliny says it is so called because

it grew *ἐν ἀκόναις*, on 'steep sharp rocks' (Liddell and Scott). — Gk. *ἀκόνη*, a whetstone, hone. — √AK, to pierce; Prellwitz.

ACORN, the fruit of the oak. (E.) Chaucer speaks of '*acornes* of okes;' tr. of Boethius, b. ii. met. 5, l. 6. AS. *æcern, æcirn*; pl. *æcernu*, which occurs in the AS. version of Gen. xliii. 11, where the exact meaning is not clear, though it is applied to some kind of fruit. Lit. 'fruit of the field;' from AS. *æcer*, a field; see **Acre.** + Icel. *akarn*, an acorn; Dan. *agern*; Goth. *akrana*-, fruit, in the comp. *akrana-laus*, fruitless. ¶ The suffix -*ern* has been changed to -*orn*, from a notion that *æcern* meant an *oak-corn*; but it is remarkable that *acorn* is related, etymologically, neither to *oak* nor to *corn*. β. If it be remembered that *acre* should rather be spelt *acer* or *aker* (the latter is common in ME.), and that *acorn* should rather be *acern* or *akern*, it will be seen that *akern* is derived from *aker* much in the same way as *silvern* from *silver*, or *wooden* from *wood*. γ. The cognate languages help here. The Icel. *akarn* is derived from *akr*, a field, not from *eik*, oak. Danish has *agern*, an acorn, from *ager*, a field; Goth. *akrana-*, fruit, is from *akrs*, a field. δ. Thus the original sense of the AS. neut. pl. *æcirnu* or *æcernu* was simply 'fruits of the field,' understanding 'field' in the sense of wild open country; cf. Gk. *ἀγρός*, a field, the country, and *ἄγριος*, wild. ε. Hence Chaucer's expression 'acornes of okes' is correct, not tautological.

ACOTYLEDON, without a seed-lobe. (Gk.) From Gk. *ἀ-*, negative prefix; and **Cotyledon,** q. v.

ACOUSTIC, relating to sound. (Gk.) In Coles's Dict., ed. 1684. — Gk. *ἀκουστικός*, relating to hearing (or sound). — Gk. *ἀκούειν*, to hear. **Der.** *acoustic-al, acoustic-s.*

ACQUAINT, to render known, to make aware. (F. — L.) ME. *aqueynten*, earlier *acoin en, akointen*. '*Aqueyntyn*, or to make knowleche, *notifico*;' Prompt. Parv. 'Wel *akointed* mid ou' = well acquainted with you; Ancren Riwle, p. 218. — OF. *acointer, acointier*, to acquaint with, to advise. — Late L. *adcognitāre*, to make known; see Brachet. — L. *adcognitum, accognitum*, pp. of *accognoscere*, to recognise (Tertullian). — L. *ad*, to; and *cognitus*, known, pp. of *cognoscere*, to know, which is compounded of *co-*, for *cum*, with, and *gnoscere* (commonly spelt *noscere*), to know, cognate with E. *know*. See **Quaint** and **Know. Der.** *acquaint-ance*, in Chaucer, C. T., A 245; *acquaintance-ship.*

ACQUIESCE, to rest satisfied. (L.) Used by Ben Jonson, New Inn, Act iv. sc. 3 (Lady F.) — L. *acquiescere*, to rest, repose in. — L. *ac-*, for *ad*; and *quiescere*, to rest, from *quiēs*, rest. See **Quiet. Der.** *acquiescence, acquiesc-ent.*

ACQUIRE, to get, obtain. (L.) Used by Hall, Hen. VIII, an. 37. § 18. — L. *acquīrere*, to obtain. — L. *ac-*, for *ad*; and *quærere*, to seek. See **Query. Der.** *acquir-able, acquire-ment*; also *acquisit-ion* (Temp. iv. 1. 13), *acquisit-ive, acquisit-ive-ness*; cf. *acquīsitus*, pp. of *acquirere.*

ACQUIT, to set at rest, set free, &c. (F. — L.) ME. *acwiten, aquyten*, to set free, perform a promise. 'Uorto *acwiten* ut his fere' = to release his companion, Ancren Riwle, p. 394; 'wan it *aquited* be' = when it shall be repaid; Rob. of Glouc. p. 565, l. 11881. — OF. *aquiter*, to settle a claim. — Late L. *acquiētāre*, to settle a claim; see Brachet. — L. *ac-*, for *ad*; and *quiētāre*, a verb formed from L. *quiētus*, discharged, free. See **Quit. Der.** *acquitt-al, acquitt-ance.*

ACRE, a field. (E.) ME. *aker*. The pl. *akres* occurs in Rob. of Brunne's tr. of P. Langtoft, ed. Hearne, p. 115. AS. *æcer*, a field.+ OFries. *ekker*; OSax. *akkar*; Du. *akker*; Icel. *akr*; Swed. *åker*; Dan. *ager*; Goth. *akrs*; OHG. *achar*, G. *acker*. + L. *ager*; Gk. *ἀγρός*; Skt. *ajra-s*. Teut. type *akroz*; Idg. type *agros*. Brugm. i. § 175. Perhaps originally 'a chase' or hunting-ground; cf. Gk. *ἄγρα*, the chase); later sense 'a pasture;' from √AG, to drive; L. *ag-ere*, Gk. *ἄγ-ειν*, Skt. *aj*, to drive. See **Act.** ¶ The spelling *acre* is AF.; see Year-books of Edw. I. **Der.** *acre-age.*

ACRID, bitter, pungent, tart. (L.) Not in early use. Bacon has *acrimony*, Nat. Hist. sect. 639. There is no good authority for the form *acrid*, which has been made (apparently in imitation of *acid*) by adding -*d* to *acri-*, stem of L. *ācer*, sharp; from √AK, to pierce. **Der.** *acrid-ness; acri-mony, acri-moni-ous*, from L. *ācrimōnia*, sharpness. Co-radicate words are *acid, acerbity*, and many others.

ACROBAT, a tumbler. (F. — Gk.) Modern. Borrowed from F. *acrobate.* — Gk. *ἀκρόβατος*, lit. walking on tip-toe. — Gk. *ἀκρο-ν*, a point, tip, of *ἄκρος*, pointed; and *βατός*, verbal adj. of *βαίνειν*, to walk, which is cognate with E. *come*. See **Acrid** and **Come. Der.** *acrobat-ic.*

ACROPOLIS, a citadel. (Gk.) Borrowed from Gk. *ἀκρόπολις*, a citadel, lit. the upper city. — Gk. *ἄκρο-s*, pointed, highest, upper; and *π.λις*, a city. For *ἄκρος*, see **Acrid.** For *πόλις*, see **Police.**

ACROSS, cross-wise. (E. and Scand.) Surrey, in his Complaint of Absence, l. 22, has 'armes *acrosse*.' Formed from the common prefix *a* (short for *an*, a later form of AS. *on*), and *cross*; so that *across* is for *on-cross*, like *abed* for *on bed*. Thus the prefix is English; but *cross* is Scand. See **Cross.**

ACROSTIC, a short poem in which the letters beginning the lines spell a word. (Gk.) Better *acrostich*; cf. *distich*. Ben Jonson has *Acrostichs*; Underwoods, lxi. 39. From Gk. ἀκροστιχίς, an acrostic. ‒ Gk. ἄκρο-s, pointed, also first; and στίχος, a row, order, line. ‒ √AK, to pierce; and *stigh, weak grade of √STEIGH, to climb, march, whence Gk. verb στείχειν, to march in order. See **Acrid** and **Stirrup**.

ACT, a deed. (F. ‒ L.) ME. *act*, pl. *actes*. The pl. *actes* occurs in Chaucer's Pardoner's Tale, C. T. 12508 (C 574). ‒ F. *acte*. ‒ L. *ac/a*, pl. of *actum*, an act, thing done, neut. of pp. *actus*, done. ‒ L. *agere*, to do, lit. to drive. + Gk. ἄγειν, to drive; Icel. *aka*, to drive; Skt. *aj*, to drive. ‒ √AG, to drive; Brugm. i. § 175. Der. *act*, verb, whence *act-ing*; also *act-ion*, *act-ion-able*, *act-ive*, *act-iv-ity*, *act-or*, *act-r-ess*; also *act-ual* (L. *actuālis*), *act-ual-ity*; also *act-uary* (L. *actuārius*); also *act-u-ate* (from Late L. *actuāre*, to perform, put in action). From the same root are *exac!*, *react*, and a large number of other words, such as *acre*, &c. See **Agent**.

ACTINIC, pertaining to the sun-rays. (Gk.) Modern. From Gk. ἀκτῖν-, stem of ἀκτίς, a ray; with suffix -*ic*. So also *actin-ism*, *actino-meter*.

ACUMEN, keenness of perception. (L.) It occurs in Selden's Table-Talk, art. Liturgy. Borrowed from L. *acūmen*, sharpness. ‒ √AK, to pierce; whence the verb *ac-u-ere*, to sharpen, *ac-ū-men*, sharpness, *ac-u-s*, a needle, with added *u*. Brugm. i. § 177. Der. *acumin-a ed*, i. e. pointed, from the stem *acūmin-*.

ACUTE, sharp. (L.) Shak. L. L. L. iii. 67. ‒ L. *acūtus*, sharp; properly pp. of verb *acuere*, to sharpen. From the stem *ac-u-*; from √AK, to pierce. See **Acumen**. Der. *acute-ly*, *acute-ness*.

AD-, prefix; corresponding to L. *ad*, to, cognate with E. *at*. See **At**. ¶ The L. *ad* often changes its last letter by assimilation; becoming *ac-* before *c*, *af-* before *f*, *ag-* before *g*, *al-* before *l*, *an-* before *n*, *ap-* before *p*, *ar-* before *r*, *as-* before *s*, *at-* before *t*. Ex. *ac-cord*, *af-fect*, *ag-gregate*, *al-lude*, *an-nex*, *ap-pear*, *ar-rest*, *as-sist*, *at-test*.

ADAGE, a saying, proverb. (F. ‒ L.) Used by Hall, Edw. IV, an. 9. § 17; and in Macb. i. 7. 45. ‒ F. *adage*, 'an adage, proverb, old-said saw, witty saying;' Cot. ‒ L. *adagium*, a proverb. ‒ L. *ad*, to; and *-agium*, a saying, related to the verb *āio*, I say.

ADAGIO, slowly; in music. (Ital.) Ital. *ad agio*, at leisure; lit. ' at ease.'

ADAMANT, a diamond. (F. ‒ L. ‒ Gk.) *Adamaunt* in Wyclif, Ezek. iii. 9; *adamant*, Chaucer, C. T. 1992 (A 1990). [It first occurs in the phrase ' *adamantines* stan;' Hali Meidenhad, p. 37. The sense in Mid.E. is both 'diamond' and 'magnet.'] ‒ OF. *adamant* (a 'learned' form). ‒ L. *adamanta*, acc. of *adamas*, a very hard stone or metal. ‒ Gk. ἀδάμας, gen. ἀδάμαντος, a very hard metal, lit. 'unconquerable.' ‒ Gk. ἀ-, privative; and δαμάειν, to conquer, tame, cognate with E. *tame*. See **Tame**. Der. *adamant-ine*, Jer. xvii. 1; from L. *adamantinus*, Gk. ἀδαμάντινος. Doublet, *diamond*.

ADAPT, to fit, make suitable. (L.) In Ben Jonson's Discoveries; § cxxviii. 4. ‒ L. *adaptāre*, to fit to. ‒ L. *ad*, to; and *aptāre*, to fit, from *apt-us*, fit. See **Apt**. Der. *adapt-able*, *adapt-at-ion* (F. *adaptation*, Cot.); *adapt-abil-ity*.

ADD, to put together, sum up. (L.) ME. *adden*. Wyclif has *addide*, Luke, xix. 11. Chaucer has *added*, Prol. to C. T. 501 (A 499). ‒ L. *addere*, to add. ‒ L. *ad*, to; and *-dere*, to put, place; see **Abscond**. Der. *add-endum*, pl. *add-enda*, neut. of *add-endus*, fut. part. pass. of L. *addere*; also *addit-ion*, Antony, v. 2. 164; *addit-ion-al*; cf. the pp. *addit-us*.

ADDER, a viper. (E.) ME. *addere*, P. Plowman, B. xviii. 352; and again, in P. Plowman, C. xxi. 381, we find 'in persone of *an addere*,' where other MSS. have *a naddere* and *a neddere*. The word *addere* is identical with *naddere*, and the two forms are used interchangeably in ME. [There are several similar instances of the loss of initial *n* in English, as in the case of *auger*, *umpire*, *orange*, &c.; see note on N.] AS. *nǣdre*, *nǣddre*, an adder, snake; Grein, ii. 275. + Du. *adder*, a viper, OS. *nādra*; G. *natter*, OHG. *nātara*. Teut. type *nǣdrōn-*, fem.; Sievers, § 276. Allied (by gradation) to Icel. *naðr*, Goth. *nadrs*, masc. Also to Oir. *nathir*, W. *neidr*, a snake; and perhaps to L. *nātrix*, a water-snake. See Stokes-Fick, p. 189. ¶ Wholly unconnected with AS. *āttor*, *ātor*, poison.

ADDICT, to give oneself up to. (L.) *Addicted* occurs in Grafton's Chronicles, Hen. VII, an. 5 (R.). ‒ L. *addict-us*, pp. of *addicere*, to adjudge, assign. ‒ L. *ad*, to; and *dīcere*, to say, proclaim. See **Diction**. Der. *addict-ed-ness*.

ADDLE, ADDLED, rotten, unproductive; unsound. (E.) Shak. has 'an *addle* egg;' Troilus, i. 2. 145. Here *addle* was afterwards lengthened to *addled*, which occurs in Cowper, Pairing-time Anticipated. We find *ade eye*, i. e. 'addle egg,' in The Owl and Nightingale, 133. Here *adel* is due to an attributive use of the ME. sb. *adel*, filth; so that *adel-ey* was lit. ' filth-egg,' = Late L. *ōvum ūrīnæ*, urine-egg, mistaken form of L. *ōuum ūrīnum*, wind-egg; which was due to Gk. οὔριον ᾠον, wind-egg, unproductive egg. ME. *adel* orig. meant

' mud,' or ' filth;' from AS. *adela*, mud (Grein). Cf. Low G. *adel*, a puddle. See N.E.D.

ADDRESS, to direct oneself to. (F. ‒ L.) ME. *adressen*. ' And therupon him hath *adresced*;' Gower, C. A. ii. 295 (bk. v. 5021). ‒ F. *adresser*, to address. ‒ F. *a-*, for L. *ad*; and *dresser*, to direct, dress. See **Dress**. Der. *address*, sb., Samson Agonistes, 731.

ADDUCE, to bring forward, cite. (L.) Bp. Taylor has *adduction* and *adductive*; Of the Real Presence, § 11. 37; cf. L. *adduct-us*, pp. of *addūcere*, to lead to. ‒ L. *ad*, to; and *dūcere*, to lead. See **Duke**. Der. *adduc-ible*; also *adduc-tion*, *adduct-ive*.

ADEPT, a proficient. (L.) ' *Adepts*, or *Adeptists*, the obtaining sons of art, who are said to have found out the grand elixir, commonly called the philosopher's stone;' Kersey's Dict. ed. 1715. ‒ L. *adeptus*, one who has attained proficiency; properly pp. of *adipisci*, to attain, reach to. ‒ L. *ad*, to; and *apisci*, to reach. The form *ap-isci* is related to *apere*, to fasten, join, whence *aptus*, fit. See **Apt**.

ADEQUATE, equal to, sufficient. (L.) It occurs in Coles's Dict. (1684); and in Johnson's Rambler, No. 17. § 3. ‒ L. *adaequātus*, made equal to, pp. of *adaequāre*, to make equal to. ‒ L. *ad*, to; and *aequāre*, to make equal, from *aequus*, equal. See **Equal**. Der. *adequate-ly*, *adequacy*.

ADHERE, to stick fast to. (L.) The phrase *be adherand to* occurs in The Test. of Love, bk. i. c. 9. 103; and Sir T. More has *adherentes*, Works, p. 222 d. ‒ L. *adhaerēre*, to stick to. ‒ L. *ad*, to; and *haerēre*, to stick, pp. *haesus*. ‒ √GHAIS, to stick; whence also Lith. *gaisz-ti*, to linger. Brugm. i. § 627 (1). Der. *adher-ence*, *adher-ent*; also *adhes-ive*, *adhes-ion*, from pp. *adhaesus*.

ADIEU, farewell. (F. ‒ L.) Written *a dieu*, Gower, C. A. i. 251 (bk. ii. 2739). ‒ F. *à dieu*, (I commit you) to God. ‒ L. *ad deum*, to God.

ADIPOSE, fatty. (L.) Bailey (1735) has *adipous*. ‒ Late L. *adipōsus*, fatty. ‒ L. *adip-*, stem of *adeps*, sb., fat.

ADIT, access to a mine. (L.) In Blount's Gloss. (1681). ‒ L. *adit-us*, approach. ‒ L. *aditum*, supine of *adire*, to go to. ‒ L. *ad*, to; and *īre*, to go.

ADJACENT, near to. (L.) It occurs in Lydgate's Siege of Thebes, pt. 1 (R.); see Chaucer's Works, ed. 1561, fol. 360 back, col. 1: '*Adiacent* vnto this countree.' ‒ L. *adiacent-*, base of *adiacens*, pres. pt. of *adiacēre*, to lie near. ‒ L. *ad*, to, near; and *iacēre*, to lie. *iacēre* is allied to *iacere*, to throw. See **Jet** (1). Der. *adjacenc-y*.

ADJECT, to add to. (L.) Unusual. Fuller has *adjecting*; General Worthies, c. 24. [The derivative *adjective* (F. *adjectif*) is common as a grammatical term, and occurs in P. Plowman, C. iv. 338.] ‒ L. *adiectus*, pp. of *adicere*, to lay or put near. ‒ L. *ad*, near; and *iacere*, to throw, put. See **Jet**. Der. *adject-ion*, *adject-ive*, *-iv-al*.

ADJOIN, to lie next to. (F. ‒ L.) Occurs in Sir T. More's Works, p. 40 b. ME. *aioynen*; the pp. *aioynet* occurs in The Destruction of Troy, 1135. ‒ OF. *ajoin-*, a stem of *ajoindre*, to adjoin. ‒ L. *adiungere*, to join to; pp. *adiunctus*. ‒ L. *ad*, to; and *iungere*, to join. See **Join**. Der. *adjunct*, *adjunct-ive*; both from pp. *adiunctus*.

ADJOURN, to postpone till another day. (F. ‒ L.) ME. *aiornen* (*ajornen*), to fix a day, Rob. of Brunne's tr. of P. Langtoft, p. 309. ‒ OF. *ajorner*, *ajurner*, properly to draw near to day, to dawn; cf. Late L. *adiornāre*, to appoint a day, to adjourn (Ducange). ‒ OF. *a-*, for L. *ad*; and Late L. *jurnus* (Ital. *giorno*), a day, from L. *diurnus*, adj., daily, a derivative of *diēs*, a day. See *jour* in Brachet; and see **Journey**, **Journal**. Der. *adjourn-ment*.

ADJUDGE, to decide with respect to, assign (F. ‒ L.) ME. *adiugen* (= *adjugen*), or better *aiugen* (= *ajugen*); Fabyan, an. 1211-12, p. 319; Grafton, Hen. II, an. 9 (R.). Chaucer has *aiuged*, tr. of Boethius, bk. i. pr. 4, l. 72. ‒ OF. *ajuger*, to decide. ‒ OF. *a-*, for L. *ad*; and *juger*, to judge. See **Judge**. ¶ Since the F. *juger* is from the L. *iudicāre*, this word has its doublet in *adjudicate*.

ADJUDICATE, to adjudge. (L.) See above. Der. *adjudicat-ion*. which occurs in Blount's Law Dict., ed. 1691.

ADJUNCT, an attendant; Shak. L. L. L. iv. 3. 314. See **Adjoin**.

ADJURE, to charge on oath. (L.) It occurs in the Bible of 1539, 1 Sam. xiv. 28. Chaucer, Pers. Tale, De Ira (I 603), has 'thilke horrible swering of *adiuracion* and coniuracion.' ‒ L. *adiūrāre*, to swear to; in Late L. to put to an oath. ‒ L. *ad*, to; and *iūrāre*, to swear. See **Abjure**. Der. *adjurat-ion*.

ADJUST, to settle, make right. (F. ‒ L.) In Cotgrave; who has ' *ajuster*, to adjust, place justly;' as if from L. *ad*, to, and *iustus*, exact. See **Just**. But this use was due to a misunderstanding of MF. *adjouster*, 'to adjoine or put unto, also, as *ajuster*;' Cot. ‒ OF. *ajoster*, *ajuster*, *ajouster* (mod. F. *ajouter*), to arrange, lit. to put side by side. ‒ Late L. *adiuxtāre*, to put side by side, arrange. ‒ L. *ad*, to, by; and *iuxtā*, near to. See **Joust**. Der. *adjust-able*; *adjust-ment*.

ADJUTANT, lit. assistant. (L.) Richardson cites a passage from Shaw's translation of Bacon, Of Julius Cæsar. *Adjutors* occurs in Drayton's Barons' Wars, bk. iv. st. 11; and '*Adjuting* to his companee' in Ben Jonson, King's Entertainment at Welbeck. ‒ L. *adiūt-*

antem, acc. of *adiūtans*, assisting, pres. pt. of *adiūtāre*, to assist; frequentative form of *adiuuāre*, to assist. — L. *ad*, to; and *iuuāre*, to assist, pp. *iūtus*. See **Aid**. Der. *adjutanc-y*; and (from the vb. *adiūtāre*) *adjut-or*, *adjute*.

ADMINISTER, to minister to. (F. — L.) *Administred* occurs in The Testament of Love, bk. i. 8. 81; and *administracion* in the same, bk. ii. 10. 43. ME. *aministren*, Chaucer, tr. of Boethius, b. iv. pr. 6. 62. — OF. *aministrer*. — L. *administrāre*, to minister to. — L. *ad*, to; and *ministrāre*, to minister. See **Minister**. Der. *administrat-ion*, *administrat-ive*, *administrat-or*; all from L. *administrāre*.

ADMIRAL, the commander of a fleet. (F. — Arabic.) See Trench's Select Glossary, which shows that the term was often applied to the leading vessel in a fleet, called in North's Plutarch the 'admiral-galley,' i. e. galley of the admiral. Thus Milton speaks of 'the mast Of some great *ammiral*;' P. L. i. 294. ME. *admiral*, *admirel*, *admirail* (Layamon, iii. 103), also *amiral*, *amirail*. Rob. of Glouc. has *amirail*, p. 4:9, l. 8460. — OF. *amirail*, *amiral*; also found as *amiré*. — Arabic *amir*, a prince, an 'emir;' see Rich. Dict., p. 171. The suffix *-al* (as if from L. *-ālis*) was really due to the frequent use of the Arab. *al* in phrases, such as *amir-u'l umarā*, prince of princes (Rich. Dict.), *amir-al-bahr*, prince of the sea, &c., see N.E.D. And see **Emir**. Popular etymology confused the *am-* with F. *am-* from L. *adm-*, and thus produced forms with *adm-*; it also turned the Arab. *al* into Late L. *-ald-us*, OF. *-ald*, *-aud*. In King Horn, l. 89, *admirald* rhymes with *bald*, bold; and in numerous passages in ME., *amiral* or *amirail* means no more than 'prince,' or 'chief.' Der. *admiral-ty*.

ADMIRE, to wonder at. (F. — L.) Shak. has '*admir'd* disorder;' Macb. iii. 4. 110. — F. *admirer*, 'to wonder, admire, marvel at;' Cot. — L. *admirāri*, to wonder at. — L. *ad*, at; and *mīrāri*, to wonder. *Mīrāri* is from the adj. *mī-rus*, wonderful; from √SMEI, to smile at; whence also Gk. μειδιειν, to smile, Skt. *smi*, to smile, *smera*, smiling, and E. *smirk* and *smile*; Brugm. i. § 389; Prellwitz. See **Smile**. Der. *admir-able*, *admir-at-ion*, *admir-er*, *admir-ing-ly*.

ADMIT, to permit to enter. (L.) Fabyan has *admytted*, *admyssyon*; Hen. III, an. 1260-1, p. 347; cf. Palsgrave, p. 417. — L. *admittere*, lit. to send to. — L. *ad*, to; and *mittere*, to send, pp. *missus*. See **Missile**. Der. *admitt-ance*, *admitt-able*; also *admiss-ion*, *admiss-ible*, *admiss-ibil-ity*, from pp. *admissus*.

ADMONISH, to warn. (F. — L.) ME. *amonesten*, so that *admonish* has taken the place of the older form *amonest*. 'I *amoneste*, or warne;' Wyclif, 1 Cor. iv. 14 (earlier text). 'This figure *amonesteth* thee;' Chaucer, tr. of Boethius, b. v. met. 5. l. 14. 'He *amonesteth* [advises] pees;' Chaucer, Tale of Melibeus (B 2484). The sb. *amonestement* is in an Old Eng. Miscellany, ed. Morris, p. 28. — OF. *amonester* (F. *admonester*), 'to admonish,' Cot. — Late L. *admonestāre*, a new formation from L. *admonēre*, to advise. — L. *ad*, to; and *monēre*, to advise. See **Monition**. Der. *admonit-ion*, *admonit-ive*, *admonit-ory*; cf. the pp. *admonitus*.

A-DO, to-do, trouble. (E.) ME. *at do*, to do. 'We have othere thinges *at do*;' Towneley Mysteries (Surtees Soc.), p. 181; and again, 'With that prynce . . . Must we have *at do*;' id. p. 237. In course of time the phrase *at do* was shortened to *ado*, in one word, and regarded as a substantive. '*Ado*, or grete bysynesse, *sollicitudo*;' Prompt. Parv. p. 7. ¶ The prep. *at* is found thus prefixed to other infinitives, as *at ga*, to go; Seuyn Sages, ed. Weber, 3017; 'That es *at say*,' that is to say; Halliwell's Dict. s. v. *at*. See Matzner, Engl. Gram. ii. 2. 58. This idiom was properly peculiar to Northern English, and is of Scandinavian origin; for the sign of the infinitive is *at* in Icelandic, and *att* in Swedish.

ADOBE, an unburnt brick dried in the sun. (Span.) Modern. — Span. *adobe*, an unbaked brick; Minsheu (1623) has : *adobe de barro*, mortar, clay. — Span. *adobar*, 'to mend, to botch, to daube;' Minsheu. — Span. *a*, for L. *ad*; and *-dober* = OF. *douber* to dub. See **Dub**.

ADOLESCENT, growing up. (L.) Rich. quotes *adolescence* from Howell, bk. iii. letter 9 (dated 1647); and *adolescencie* occurs in Sir T. Elyot's Governour, b. ii. c. 4. § 1. — L. *adolescentem*, acc. of *adolescens*, pres. pt. of *adolescere*, to grow up. — L. *ad*, to, up; and **olescere*, to grow, the inceptive form of **olēre*, to grow; which is allied to *alere*, to nourish. — √AL, to nourish; whence also Icel. *ala*, to produce, nourish, and Goth. *alan*, to nourish. See **Aliment**. Der. *adolescence*; and see *adult*.

ADOPT, to choose or take to oneself. (L.) *Adopt* occurs in Hall, Hen. VII, an. 7. § 6; and Othello, i. 3. 191. The sb. *adopcioun* is in Wyclif, Romans, viii. 15; and in the Ayenbite of Inwyt, pp. 101, 102, 146. — L. *adoptāre*, to adopt, choose. — L. *ad*, to; and *optāre*, to wish. See **Option**. Der. *adopt-ive*, *adopt-ion*.

ADORE, to worship. (L.) See Levins, Manip. Vocabulorum, p. 174; *adored* is in Surrey's Virgil, tr. of Æn. ii. 700; l. 922 of the E. version. [The ME. *adouren* in The Legends of the Holy Rood, p. 163, was probably taken from the OF. *aourer*, with an insertion of *d*.] — L. *adōrāre*, lit. to pray to. — L. *ad*, to; and *ōrāre*, to pray, from *ōs*,

gen. *ōris*, the mouth; cf. Skt. *āsya-*, the mouth. See **Oral**. Der. *ador-at-ion*, *ador-er*, *ador-able*, *ador-able-ness*, *ador-ing-ly*.

ADORN, to deck. (L.) Chaucer has *adorneth*, Troilus, iii. 2. — L. *adornāre*, to deck. — L. *ad*, to, on; and *ornāre*, to deck. See **Ornament**. Der. *adorn-ing*, *adorn-ment*.

ADOWN, downwards. (E.) ME. *adune*, Havelok, 2735; very common. AS. *of-dūne*, lit. off the down or hill. — AS. *of*, off, from; and *dūne*, dat. of *dūn*, a down, hill. See **Down**; and **A-** (1), prefix.

ADRIFT, floating at random. (E.) In Milton, P. L. xi. 832. For *on drift*; as *afloat* for *on float*, *ashore* for *on shore*. See **Afloat** and **Drift**.

ADROIT, dexterous. (F. — L.) Used by Evelyn, The State of France (R.); Butler, Hudibras, iii. 1. 365. — F. *adroit*, 'handsome, nimble, wheem, ready or quick about;' Cotgrave. — F. *à droit*, lit. rightfully, rightly; from *à*, to, towards (L. *ad*); and *droit*, right. The F. *droit* is from L. *directum*, right, justice (in Late L.), neut. of *directus*, direct. See **Direct**. Der. *adroit-ly*, *adroit-ness*.

ADSCITITIOUS; see **Ascititious**.

ADULATION, flattery. (F. — L.) In Shak. Henry V, iv. 1. 271. ME. *adulacioun*, Lydgate, Ballad of Good Counsel, 61. — F. *adulation*, 'adulation, flattery, fawning,' &c.; Cotgrave. — L. *adūlātiōnem*, acc. of *adūlātio*, flattery. — L. *adūlāri*, to flatter, fawn, pp. *adūlātus*. Hence also *adulation*, *adulator*.

ADULT, one grown up. (L.; or F. — L.) Spelt *adulte* in Sir T. Elyot, the Governour, b. ii. c. 1. § 2. [Perhaps through the French, as Cotgrave has '*Adulte*, grown to full age.'] — L. *adultus*, grown up, pp. of *adolescere*, to grow up. See **Adolescent**.

ADULTERATE, to corrupt. (L.) Sir T. More, Works, p.636 h, has *adulterate* as a past participle; Shak. has it both as adj. and verb; Hamlet, i. v. 42; K. John, iii. 1. 56. — L. *adulterāt-us*, pp. of *adulterāre*, to commit adultery, to corrupt, falsify; cf. L. *adulter*, an adulterer, a debaser of money. β. L. *ad-ulterāre* was orig. 'to change;' from L. prefix *ad*, and *alterāre*, to alter; see **Alter**. (Bréal.) Der. *adulterat-ion*; also (from L. *adulterium*) the words *adulter-y*, Winter's Tale, iii. 2. 15; *adulter-er*, *adulter-ess*; and (from L. *adulter*) *adulter-ous*, *adulter-ine*. The AF. *adulterie* occurs in the Year-books of Edw. I, 1292-3, p. 183.

ADUMBRATE, to shadow forth. (L.) *Adumbrations* occurs in Sir T. Elyot, The Governour, book iii. c. 26. § 2. — L. *adumbrāre*, to cast shadow over. — L. *ad*, to, towards, over; and *umbrāre*, to cast a shadow, from *umbra*, a shadow. Der. *adumbrant* (from pres. pt. *adumbrans*), *adumbrat-ion*.

ADVANCE, to go forward. (F. — L.) [The modern spelling is not good; the inserted *d* is due to the odd mistake of supposing that, in the old form *avance*, the prefix is *a-* and represents the L. *ad*. The truth is, that the prefix is *av-*, and represents the L. *ab*. The inserted *d* came in about A.D. 1500, and is found in the Works of Sir T. More, who has *aduauncing*, p. 1369 g. The older spelling is invariably without the *d*.] ME. *avancen*, *avauncen*. Chaucer has '*avaunsed* and forthered,' tr. of Boethius, b. ii. pr. 4, l. 48. The word is common, and occurs in the Ancren Riwle, p. 156. — OF. *avancer* (F. *avancer*), to go before. — OF. and F. *avant*, before. — Late L. *ab ante*, also written *abante*, before (Brachet). — L. *ab*, from; *ante*, before. See **Ante-**, and **Van**. Der. *advance-ment*, ME. *auauncement*, Rob. of Glouc. p. 312, l. 6388; and see below.

ADVANTAGE, profit. (F. — L.) Properly a state of forwardness or advance. [The *d* is a mistaken insertion, as in *advance* (see above); and the ME. form is *avantage* or *avauntage*.] '*Avantage*, proventus, emolumentum;' Prompt. Parv. p. 17. Hampole has *avantage*, Pricke of Conscience, l. 1012; and it is common. — OF. and F. *avantage*, formed with suffix *-age* from prep. *avant*, before. See **Advance**. Der. *advantage-ous*, *advantage-ous-ness*.

ADVENT, approach. (L.) ME. *aduent*, Rob. of Glouc. p. 463, l. 9510; Ancren Riwle, p. 70. — L. *aduentus*, a coming to, approach. — L. *aduent-us*, pp. of *aduenire*, to come to. — L. *ad*, to; and *uenire*, to come, cognate with E. *come*. See **Come**. Der. *advent-ū-al*, *advent-it-i-ous*; *adventure* (below).

ADVENTURE, an accident, enterprise. (F. — L.) [The older spelling is *aventure*, the F. prefix *a-* having been afterwards replaced by the corresponding L. prefix *ad-*.] Sir T. More, Works, p. 761 e, has *adventure* as a verb. The old form *aventure* is often cut down to *auntre*. Rob. of Glouc. has the sb. *aunter* at p. 65 (l. 1482). The sb. *auenture*, i. e. occurrence, is in the Ancren Riwle, p. 340. — OF. *aventure*, fem., an adventure. — Late L. *aduentūra*, fem. sb., analogous to L. sbs. in *-tūra*; see Roby's Lat. Gram., 3rd ed., pt. i. § 893. Formed as if from L. *aduentūr-us*, fut. part. of *aduenire*, to come to, happen. — L. *ad*, to; and *uenire*, to come, cognate with E. *come*. See **Come**. Der. *adventure*, vb., *adventur-er*, *adventur-ous*, *adventur-ous-ness*; also *per-adventure*.

ADVERB, a part of speech. (F. — L.) In Ben Jonson, Eng. Grammar, ch. xxi; and in Palsgrave, p. 798. Used to qualify a verb;

and adapted from F. *adverbe* (in Sherwood's index to Cotgrave).−L. *aduerbium.*−L. *ad*, to; and *uerbum*, a verb, a word. See **Verb. Der.** *adverb-ial, adverb-ial-ly.*

ADVERSE, opposed to. (F.−L.) ME. *aduerse.* Gower has 'Whan he fortune fint [finds] *aduerse*;' C. A. ii. 116 (bk. iv. 3403). *Aduersite*, i.e. adversity, occurs in the Ancren Riwle, p. 194. Chaucer has *aduersarie*, an adversary, C. T. 14596 (B 3868).−OF. *advers*, generally *avers*, adverse to.−L. *aduersus*, turned towards, contrary, opposed to; pp. of *aduertere*, to turn towards.−L. *ad*, to; and *uertere*, to turn. See **Verse. Der.** *advers-ary, advers-at-ive, adverse-ness, advers-ity.* See below.

ADVERT, to turn to, regard. (L.) *Aduert* occurs in Lydgate, Beware of Doubleness, l. 45; and in The Court of Love, l. 150, written after A.D. 1500.−L. *aduertere*, to turn towards; see above. **Der.** *advert-ent, advertence, advert-enc-y.*

ADVERTISE, to inform, warn. (F.−L.) Fabyan has *aduertysed*, Hist. c. 84. § 2.−MF. *advertiss-*, lengthened stem of *advertir* (OF. *avertir*). Cotgrave has 'Advertir, to inform, certifie, advertise, warn, admonish.'−Late L. *aduertire*, used in place of L. *aduertere*, to turn towards, advert to. See **Advert.** [Thus *advertise* is really a doublet of *advert.*] **Der.** *advertis-er, advertis-ing*; also *advertise-ment*, in Caxton, Troy-book, leaf 122, l. 8, from MF. *advertissement*, which see in Cotgrave.

ADVICE, counsel. (F.−L.) Sir T. More, Works, p. 11 a, has *aduisedly.* Fabyan has *aduyce*, Hen. III, an. 46. § 5. Cotgrave has 'Advis, m., advise, opinion, counsell, sentence, judgment,' &c. β. But in ME. and OF. there is generally no *d.* Rob. of Glouc. has *auys*, p. 144 (l. 3042).−OF. *avis*, an opinion; really a compounded word, standing for *a vis*, lit. according to my opinion, or 'as it seems' to me; which would correspond to a L. form *ad uīsum.*−L. *ad*, according to; and *uīsum*, that which has seemed best, pp. neuter of *uidēre*, to see; from √WEID, to know. See **Wit. Der.** *advise* (MF. *adviser*); *advis-able, advis-able-ness, advis-ed, advis-ed-ness, advis-er.* See below.

ADVISE, to counsel. (F.−L.) The form *advise* is from MF. *adviser*, a form given by Cotgrave, and explained to mean 'to *advise*, marke, heed, consider of,' &c. β. But in ME., as in OF., the usual form is without the *d*; *avised* occurs in Gower, C. A. i. 5 (prol. 65). The pt. t. *avisede* occurs in Rob. of Glouc. p. 558 (l. 11694); and the sb. *auys* (i.e. advice) in the same, p. 144 (l. 3042).−OF. *aviser*, to have an opinion.−OF. *avis*, opinion; see above.

ADVOCATE, one called on to plead. (L.) 'Be myn *aduócat* in that heyè place;' Chaucer, Sec. Nun's Ta., G 68.−L. *aduocātus*, a common forensic term for a pleader, advocate, one 'called to' the bar. [Cf. also MF. *aduocat*, 'an aduocate,' Cot.]−L. *ad*, to; *uocātus*, called, pp. of *uocāre*, to call. See **Voice. Der.** *advocate*, verb; *advocate-ship*; *advocac-y* (MF. *advocat-ie*, which see in Cotgrave); also *advowee, advowson*, for which see below.

ADVOWSON, the right of presentation to a benefice. (F.−L.) Occurs in the Statute of Westminster, an. 13 Edw. I, c. 5; see Blount's Law Dictionary. From AF. *advoeson*, older form *avoeson*, Stat. of Realm, i. 293; and see Godefroy. The sense is patronage, and the corresponding term in Law L. is *aduocātio* (see Blount), because the patron was called *aduocātus*, or in OF. *avoué*, MF. *advoué* (Cotgrave), now spelt *avowee* and *advowee* in English. Hence *advowson* is derived from L. *aduocātiōnem*, acc. of *aduocātio*, and *advowee* is derived from L. *aduocātus.* See **Advocate.**

ADZE, a cooper's axe. (E.) ME. *adse*; the pl. *adses* occurs in Palladius on Husbandrie, bk. i. l. 1161; *adese*, Wyclif, Isaiah xliv. 13. AS. *adesa*, an axe or hatchet; Ælfric's Glossary, Voc. 141. 29; Beda, Hist. Eccl. iv. 3; Grein, p. 1.

ÆDILE, a magistrate in Rome, a municipal officer. (L.) In Shak. Cor. iii. 1. 173.−L. *ædilis*, a magistrate who had the charge of temples, &c.−L. *ædes, aedēs*, a building. See **Edify.**

ÆGIS, a shield. (L.−Gk.) First used by Rowe in 1704 (N.E.D.). −L. *ægis, aegis.*−Gk. αἰγίς, the shield of Zeus or Pallas.

AERIAL, airy, high, lofty. (L.−Gk.) Milton has *aërial*, also written *aëreal*, P.L. iii. 445, v. 548, vii. 442; also *aëry*, P.L. i. 430, 775. Formed, apparently in imitation of *ethereal* (P. L. i. 45, 285, &c.), from L. *aërius*, dwelling in the air.−L. *aër*, the air.−Gk. ἀήρ, air. See **Air. Der.** From the same L. sb. we have *aër-ate, aër-ify.* ¶ From Gk. ἀήρ we have the Gk. prefix ἀερο-, relative to air, appearing in English as *aero-.* Hence *aero-lite*, an air-stone, from Gk. λίθος. a stone; *aero-naut*, F. *aéronaute*, a sailer or sailor in the air, from Gk. ναύτης (L. *nauta*) a sailor, which is from Gk. ναῦς, a ship; *aero-static*, for which see **Static,** &c.; *aer-ate.*

ÆRUGINOUS, rusty, as copper. (L.) In Phillips (1658).− L. *æruginōsus*, rusty.−L. *ærūgo* (gen. *ærūgin-is*), verdigris.−L. *ær-*, from *æs, aes*, brass (L. *ae*, rather than *æ*).

AERY, lit. an eagle's nest; also, a brood of eagles or hawks. (F.) 'And like an eagle o'er his *aery* (orig. *ayerie*) towers;' K. John, v. 2. 149. 'There is an *aery* (orig. *ayrie*) of young children;' Hamlet, ii.

2. 354. From Med. L. *aeria, aria*, Latinised form of F. *aire*; Cotgrave has '*Aire*, m. an airie or nest of hawkes.' Cf. Late L. *ārea*, a nest of a bird of prey; of which we find an example in Ducange. 'Aues rapaces ... exspectant se inuicem aliquando prope *nidum* suum consuetum, qui a quibusdam *area* dicitur;' Fridericus II, de Venat. lib. ii. c. 3. β. The word *aire* is marked as masculine in Cotgrave, whereas F. *aire*, L. *ārea*, in the ordinary sense of 'floor,' is feminine. It is probable that the Late L. *ārea* is quite a distinct word from the classical L. *ārea*; and some derive F. *aire* from L. *ātrium*, a hall, a court, or from *agrum*, acc. of *ager*, a field. See Körting, § 828. The OF. *aire* was both m. and f.; the former would correspond to L. *ātrium*, the latter to *ātria*, pl. taken as fem. sing. The mod. F. *airer*, to make a nest, represents OF. *aairier, adairier*; see Godefroy. ¶ The E. word was sometimes connected with ME. *ey*, an egg, as if the word meant an *egg-ery*; hence it came to be spelt *eyrie* or *eyry*, and to be misinterpreted accordingly.

ÆSTHETIC, tasteful, refined; relating to perception. (Gk.) Modern. Formed from Gk. αἰσθητικός, perceptive.−Gk. αἰσθέσθαι, to perceive.−√AW; see Brugmann, ii. § 841. ¶ The word was really introduced from German, the G. word being formed from Greek. 'His *Vorschule der Ästhetik* (Introduction to Æsthetics);' Carlyle, Essay on Richter, in Edinb. Rev., June, 1827, p. 183; Essays, i. 8 (pop. edition). Cf. Baumgarten's *Æsthetica*, 1750. **Der.** *æsthetic-s, æsthetic-al.*

AFAR, at a distance. (E.) For *on far* or *of far.* Either expression would become *o far*, and then *a-far*; and both are found; but, by analogy, the former corresponds better with the modern use; cf. *abed, asleep*, &c. Stratmann gives *of feor*, O. E. Homilies, i. 247; *a fer*, Gower, C. A. i. 314 (bk. iii. 1039); *on ferum*, Gawain, 1575; *o ferrum*, Minot, vii. 70. See **Far.** ¶ Apparently, *of feor* became *ofer*, and was refashioned as *on fer*, which became *a fer.*

AFFABLE, easy to be addressed. (F.−L.) Milton has *affable*, P. L. vii. 41; viii. 648.−F. *affable*, 'affable, gentle, curteous, gracious in words, of a friendly conversation, easily spoken to by, willingly giving ear to others;' Cot.−L. *affabilis*, easy to be spoken to.−L. *af-*, for *ad*, to; and *fāri*, to speak. See **Fable. Der.** *affabl-y, affabil-ity*, in Sir T. Elyot, The Governour, bk. i. c. 3. § 3 (F. *affabilité* = L. *affābilitātem*, acc. of *affābilitās*).

AFFAIR, business. (F.−L.) ME. *affere, afere, effer*; the pl. *afferes* is in P. Plowman, C. vii. 152. Commonest in Northern English; spelt *effer* in Barbour's Bruce, vii. 30.−OF. *afaire, afeire* (and properly so written with one *f*), business; merely the phrase *a faire*, to do, used as a substantive, like *ado* in English for *at do*; see **Ado.** OF. *faire* = L. *facere*; see below.

AFFECT, to act upon. (F.−L.) In Shak. it means to love, to like; Gent. of Ver. iii. 1. 82; Antony, i. 3. 71, &c. The sb. *affection* (formerly *affeccioun*) is in much earlier use, and common in Chaucer. −MF. *affecter*, 'to affect, fancy;' Cot.−L. *affectāre*, to apply oneself to; frequentative form of *afficere*, to aim at, treat.−L. *af-*, for *ad*; and *facere*, to do, act. See **Fact. Der.** *affect-ed, affect-ed-ness, affect-ing, affect-at-ion, affect-ion, affect-ion-ate, affect-ion-ate-ly.* Of these, *affectation* occurs in Ben Jonson, Discoveries, sect. cxx. headed *Periodi*, &c. Also *dis-affect.*

AFFEER, to assess, confirm. (F.−L.) Rare; but it occurs in Macbeth, iv. 3. 34; 'the title is *affeer'd.*' Blount, in his Law Dictionary, explains *Affeerers* as 'those that are appointed in court-leets upon oath, to *settle and moderate the fines* of such as have committed faults arbitrarily punishable.' β. Blount first suggests an impossible derivation from F. *affier*, but afterwards adds the right one, saying, 'I find in the Customary of Normandy, cap. 20, this word *affeurer*, which the Latin interpreter expresseth by *taxare*, that is, to set the price of a thing, which etymology seems to me the best.'− AF. *aferer*, OF. *afeurer*, to fix the price of things officially; Godefroy (s. v. *aforer*).−Late L. *afforāre*, to fix the price of a thing; Ducange. −L. *af-*, for *ad*; and *forum*, or *forus*, both of which are used synonymously in Late L. in the sense of 'price;' the OF. form of the sb. being *fuer* or *feur*, which see in Godefroy. The classical L. is *forum*, meaning 'a market-place,' also 'an assize;' and is also (rarely) written *forus.* Allied to L. *forēs*, and E. *door*; Brugmann, i. § 360. See **Door.** ☞ The change from L. *o* to AF. and E. *ee* is clearly seen in L. *bovem*, OF. *buef*, AF. *béf*, E. *beef.* The Late L. equivalent of *affeerer* is *afforātor.*

AFFIANCE, trust, marriage-contract. (F.−L.) [The verb *affy* is perhaps obsolete. It means to trust, confide, Titus Andron. i. 1. 47; also to betroth, Tam. of Shrew, iv. 4. 49.] Both *affie* and *affiance* occur in Rob. of Brunne's tr. of P. Langtoft, pp. 87, 155. 1. The verb is from OF. *affier*, to trust in, also spelt *afier*; which is from *a-*, for L. *ad*, and *fier*, formed from Late L. *fidāre*, a late form from L. *fidus*, faithful, allied to *fides*, faith, and *fidere*, to trust. 2. The sb. is from OF. *afiance*, which is compounded of *a-*, for L. *ad*, and *fiance*, formed from Late L. *fidantia*, a pledge, security; which is from the same *fidāre*, pres. pt. *fidans*, of which the stem is *fidant-*. Thus both are allied to L. *fidere*, to trust. See **Faith**. Der. *affiance*, verb; *affianc-ed*.

AFFIDAVIT, an oath. (L.) Properly the Late L. *affīdāvit* = he made oath, 3 p. s. perf. of *affidāre*, to make oath, pledge. − L. *af-*, for *ad*; and Late L. *fidāre*, to pledge, from *fīdus*, faithful. See above.

AFFILIATION, assignment of a child to its father. (F. − L.) The verb *affiliate* seems to be later than the sb., and the sb. does not appear to be in early use, though the corresponding terms in French and Latin may long have been in use in the law courts. − F. *affiliation*, explained by Cotgrave as ' adoption, or an adopting.' − Law L. *affiliātiōnem*, acc. of *affiliātio*, ' an assigning a son to ;' Ducange. − Late L. *affiliāre*, to adopt; cf. the pp. *affiliātus*. − L. *af-*, for *ad*, to; and *filius*, a son. See **Filial**.

AFFINITY, nearness of kin, connexion. (F. − L.) Fabyan has *affynite*, c. 134 ; *affynyte* is in Rob. of Brunne, Handling Synne, l. 7379. − F. *affinité*, ' affinity, kindred, allyance, nearness ;' Cot. − L. *affinitātem*, acc. of *affinitās*, nearness. − L. *affinis*, near, bordering upon. − L. *af-*, for *ad*, near; and *finis*, a boundary. See **Final**.

AFFIRM, to assert strongly. (F. − L.) ME. *affermen* ; Chaucer has *affermed* ; C. T. 2351 (A 2349). It occurs earlier, in Rob. of Brunne's tr. of P. Langtoft, p. 316. − OF. *afermer*, to fix, secure. − OF. *a-*, for L. *ad*; and L. *firmāre*, to make firm, from *firmus*, firm. See **Firm**. ¶ The word has been assimilated to L. spelling, but was not taken immediately from L. Der. *affirm-able*, *affirm-at-ion*, *affirm-at-ive*, *affirm-at-ive-ly*.

AFFIX, to fasten, join on to. (F. − L.) ' To *affyxe* the desyres ;' Caxton, Golden Legend ; The Ascension, § 6. [Not from L. directly, but from French, the spelling being afterwards accommodated to L.] ME. *affichen*. Gower has ' Ther wol thei al here love *affiche*,' rhyming with *riche* ; C. A. ii. 211 (bk. v. 2520). Wyclif has *afficchede* (printed *affitchede*), 4 Kings, xviii. 16. − OF. *aficher*, to fix to. − OF. *a-*, for L. *ad*; and *ficher*, to fix, from Late L. **figicāre* (an unauthenticated form) developed from L. *figere*, to fix. See **Fix**. Der. *affix*, sb.

AFFLICT, to harass. (L.) Sir T. More has *afflicteth*, Works, p. 1080 g. [The pp. *aflyght* occurs in Octovian, l. 191; and the pt. t. *aflihte* in Gower, C. A. i. 327 (bk. iii. 1422); these are from OF. *aflit* (fem. *aflite*), pp. of *aflire*, to afflict. The sb. *affliction* occurs early, in Rob. of Brunne's tr. of Langtoft, p. 202.] − L. *afflictus*, pp. of *affligere*, to strike to the ground. − L. *af-*, for *ad*, to, i. e. to the ground; and *fligere*, to dash, strike, pp. *flictus*. From the same root are *con-flict*, *in-flict*, *pro-flig-ate*. Der. *afflict-ion* (L. acc. *afflict-iōnem*, from pp *afflictus*) ; also *afflict-ive*.

AFFLUENCE, profusion, wealth. (F. − L.) It occurs in Wotton's Reliquiæ, art. A Parallel ; and in his Life of Buckingham in the same collection (R.). Also in Caxton's Eneydos, ch. vi. p. 26. − F. *affluence*, ' affluence, plenty, store, flowing, fulness, abundance ;' Cot. − L. *affluentia*, abundance. − L. *affluere*, to flow to, abound. − L. *af-*, for *ad*; and *fluere*, to flow. See **Fluent**. Der. *affluent* (from L. *affluentem*, acc. of *affluens*, pres. pt. of *affluere*) ; *afflux*, given by Cotgrave as being also a French word (from L. *affluxus*, pp. of *affluere*).

AFFORD, to supply, produce. (E.) This word should have but one *f*. The double *f* is due to a supposed analogy with words that begin with *aff-* in Latin, where *aff-* is for *adf-*; but the word is not Latin, and the prefix is not *ad-*. Besides this, the pronunciation has been changed at the end. Rightly, it should be *aforth*, but the *th* has changed as in other words ; cf. *murther*, now *murder*, *further*, provincially *furder*. From ME. *aforthen*, to afford, suffice, provide. ' And here and there, as that my litell witte *Aforthe* may [i. e. may suffice], I thinke translate it ;' Hoccleve, Regement of Princes, l. 2113. ' And thereof was Peres proude, and put hem to werke, And yaf hem mete as he myghte *aforth* [i. e. could afford or provide], and mesurable huyre ' [hire] ; P. Plowman, B. vi. 200. **β**. In this word, as in *aware*, q. v., the prefix *a-* is substituted for the AS. prefix *ge-*, which in ME. became *ye-*, later *y-* or *i-*, and *iforth* easily passed into *aforth*, owing to the atonic nature of the syllable. We find the forms *yeforthian* and *iforthien* in the 12th century. Ex. ' thenne he iseýe thet he ne mahte na mare *yeforthian*' = when he saw that he could *afford* no more ; Old Eng. Homilies, ed. Morris, 1st series, p. 31 ; ' do thine elmesse of thon thet thu maht *ifor/hien* ' = in thine alms of that which thou mayest *afford*, id. p. 37. − AS. *ge-forðian* (where the *ge-* is a mere prefix that is often dropped), or *forðian*, to further, promote, accomplish, provide, afford. ' Hwilc man swa haued behāten to faren to Rome, and he ne muge hit *forðian* ' = whatever man has promised [vowed] to go to Rome, and may not *accomplish* it ; AS. Chron. ed. Thorpe, an. 675, later interpolation ; see footnote on p. 58. ' þa wæs *geforðad* þin fægere weorc ' = then was *accomplished* thy fair work (Grein) ; ' hæfde *geforðod*, þæt hē his frēan gehēt ' = had *performed* that which he promised his lord ; Grein, i. 401. − AS. *ge-*, prefix (of slight value) ; and *forðian*, to promote, forward, produce, cause to come forth, from AS. *forð*, forth, forward. See **Forth**.

AFFRAY, to frighten ; **AFRAID**, frightened. (F. − L. and Teut.) Shak. has the verb, Romeo, iii. 5. 33. It occurs early. Rob. of Brunne, in his translation of P. Langtoft, p. 174, has ' it *affraied* the Sarazins ' = it frightened the Sarazens ; and ' ther-of had many *affray* ' = thereof many had terror, where *affray* is a sb. − OF. *effreier*, *effraier*, *esfreer*, to frighten. − Late L. *ex-fridāre*, to break the king's peace, to cause an affray or fray ; hence, to disturb, frighten. − L. *ex*, intensive prefix ; and OHG. *fridu* (G. *friede*), peace. See Romania, 1878, vii. 121. Der. *affray*, sb., also shortened to *fray* ; *afraid*, orig. *affrayed*, pp. of *affray*.

AFFREIGHTMENT, the act of hiring a ship for the transportation of goods. (F. − L. and G.) Still in use. Blount gives *affrettamentum*, with a reference to Pat. 11 Hen. IV. par. 1. m. 12, which represents an OF. *affretement*, the same word as mod. F. *affrétement*, the hiring of a ship (Littré). Formed with suffix *-ment* from OF. *affreter* (mod. F. *affréter*), to hire a ship (Littré). − L. *af-*, for *ad*, prefix ; and F. *fret*, ' the fraught or fraight of a ship, also the hire that's paid for a ship, or for the fraught thereof ;' Cotgrave. This *fret* is of G. origin ; see further under **Fraught**, **Freight**.

AFFRIGHT, to frighten. (E.) The double *f* is modern, and a mistake. The prefix is AS. *ā-*. A transitive verb in Shak. Mids. Nt. Dream, v. 142, &c. A late formation ; from ME. *afright*, which was really a pp., and was lengthened to *affright-ed* by mistake, as in Othello, v. 2. 99. Cf. ME. *afright*, in Chaucer, Nun's Priest's Tale, l. 75. AS. *āfyrht* (contracted form of *āfyrht-ed*), pp. of *āfyrhtan*, to terrify ; Grein, i. 19. Cf. ' þā weardas wǣron *āfyrhte*,' the guards were *affright* (frightened) ; Matt. xxviii. 4. − AS. *ā-*, prefix, with intensive force ; and *fyrhtan*, to terrify, from AS. *fyrhto*, fright, terror. See **Fright**. Der. *affright-ed-ly*.

AFFRONT, to insult, lit. to stand front to front. (F. − L.) The double *f* was originally a single one, the prefix being the F. *a*. ME. *afronten*, *afrounten*, to insult. ' That *afrontede* me foule ' = who foully insulted me ; P. Plowman, C. xxiii. 5. The inf. *afrounti* occurs in the Ayenbite of Inwyt, p. 229. − OF. *afronter*, to confront, oppose face to face ; also, to slap in the face. − OF. *a*, to, against; and *front*, the front ; so that *a front* answers to L. *ad frontem* ; cf. Late L. *affrontāre*, to strike against. − L. *ad*; and *frontem*, acc. case of *frons*, the forehead. See **Front**. Der. *affront*, sb.

AFFY, to trust in ; see **Affiance**.

AFLOAT, for *on float*. (E.) ' Now er alle *on flote* ' = now are all afloat ; Rob. of Brunne's tr. of P. Langtoft, p. 169. So also *on flot*, afloat, in Barbour's Bruce, ed. Skeat, xiv. 359.

AFOOT, for *on foot*. (E.) ' The way-ferande frekez *on fote* and on hors ' = the wayfaring men, *afoot* and on horse ; Allit. Poems, ed. Morris, B. 79. We still say ' to go *on foot*.'

AFORE, before, in front ; for *on fore*. (E.) ME. *afore*, *aforn*. ' As it is *afore* seid,' Book of Quinte Essence, ed. Furnivall, p. 12 ; *aforn*, Rom. Rose, 3952. AS. *onforan*, adv. in front, Grein, ii. 344. There is also an AS. form *ætforan*, prep., Grein, i. 61. See **Fore**. Der. *afore-said*, *afore-hand*, *afore-time*.

AFRAID; for *affrayed*, pp. of *affray* ; see **Affray**.

AFREET, **AFRIT**, an evil demon. (Arab.) In Southey, Thalaba, bk. xii. st. 19. − Arab. *'ifrit*, a giant, demon, spectre ; Rich. Dict. p. 1016.

AFRESH, anew. (E.) Sir T. More, Works, p. 1390 c ; Shak. Tam. Shrew, i. 1. 143. Either for *on fresh* or *of fresh*. Perhaps the latter, by analogy with *anew*, q. v.

AFT, **AFTER**, behind. (E.) Comparison with *abaft* shows that *aft* is shortened from AS. *æftan*, adv., behind. *After* answers to AS. *æfter*, both prep. and adv. ; Grein, i. 53, 54. + Icel. *aptan* (pron. *af an*), adv. and prep. behind ; *aptr*, *aftr*, *aptan*, backwards ; *aftr*, back, in composition ; Dan. and Swed. *efter*, prep. and adv. behind, after ; Du. *achter*, prep. and adv. behind ; OHG. *aftar*, prep. and adv. behind. ¶ In English, there has, no doubt, been a feeling that *after* was formed from *aft* ; but we can only compare the AS. forms *æ'tor* and *æftan*. **β**. Of these, *æftan* is cognate with Goth. *aftana*, from behind, from *afta*, behind ; and *af-ta* is from Goth. *af*, off, away, with an orig. superl. suffix *-ta* (Idg. *-to*), as in Gk. πρῶ-το-s, first. **γ**. *After* is a comparative form, to be divided as *af-ter*. The *-ter* is the suffix which appears in the Gk. comparative form ἀπω-τέρ-ω, further off. The positive form *af-* corresponds to Skt. *apa*, Gk. ἀπό, L. *ab*, Goth. *af*, AS. *of*, E. *of* and *off*. See **Of**. Der. *after-crop*, *after-most* (q.v.), *after-noon*, *after-piece*, *after-ward*, *after-wards* (q.v.), *ab-aft* (q.v.).

AFTERMATH, a second crop of mown grass. (E.) In Holland, tr. of Pliny, b. xvii. c. 8. *Math* = AS. *mǣð*, a mowing ; Kemble, Cod. Dipl. ii. 400; allied to **Mow** and to **Mead** (2), q. v. Cf. G. *mahd*, a mowing ; *nachmahd*, aftermath.

AFTERMOST, hindmost. (E.) ' The suffix *-most* in such words as *utmost* is a double superlative ending, and not the word *most* ;' Morris, Outlines of Eng. Accidence, p. 110. ME. *eftemeste*, Early Eng. Homilies, ed. Morris, ii. 23. AS. *æftemest*, *æftemyst*, last, used by Ælfric and Alfred (Bosworth). **+**Goth. *aftumists*, the last; also *aftuma*, the last, which is a shorter form, showing that *aftum-ists* is formed regularly by the use of the suffix *-ists* (E. *-est*). ¶ The division of *aftuma* is into *af* and *-tu-ma* (see explanation of *aft*), where *af* is the Goth. *af*, E. *of*, and *-tu-ma* is the same as the L. *-tu-mus* in OL. *op-tu-mus*, best, and the Skt. *-ta-ma-*, a double superl. termination. Thus *aftermost* is for *aftemest*, i.e. *af-'e-m-est*, superl. of *af* = *of*, *off*. See **Aft**.

AFTERWARD, AFTERWARDS, subsequently. (E.) ME. *afterward*, Ormulum, 14793; *efter-ward*, Ayenbite of Inwyt, p. 24. The adverbial suffix *-s*, ME. *-es* (originally a gen. sing. suffix) was added at a later time. Shakespeare has both forms; and the earliest example of the lengthened form occurs about A.D. 1300, in the form *afterwardes*; St. Brandan, l. 10 (N. E. D.). AS. *æfterweard*, adj. behind, Grein, i. 55.—AS. *æfter*, behind; and *weard*, answering to E. *-ward*, towards. See **After** and **Towards**.

AGA, AGHA, a chief officer; in Turkey. (Turk.) 'Ianizaries ... commanded by their *Aga*;' Sandys, Travels, 1632, p. 48.—Turk. *aghā*, master.

AGAIN, a second time; **AGAINST**, in opposition to. (E.) ME. (North.) *ogain*, *again*; (South.) *ayein*, *ayen*, *aye*, *onyain*, generally written with *3* for *y*, and very common both as an adverb and preposition. Also in the (North.) forms *ogaines*, *againes*; (South.) *ayaines*, *ayens*, *onyænes*, generally written with *3* for *y*. β. At a later period an excrescent *t* (common after *s*) was added to the latter, as in *whilst* from the older form *whiles*, or in the provincial Eng. *wunst* for *once*; and in *betwix-t*, *amongs-t*. *Ayenst* occurs in Maundeville's Travels, p. 220; and *ayeynest* in Chaucer's Boethius, bk. i. pr. 3. 51 (MS. Addit. 10340); it is hardly older than A.D. 1350. γ. The final *-es* in *ayaines* is the adverbial suffix *-es*, originally marking a gen. singular. The form *ayeines* occurs in Old Eng. Homilies, ed. Morris, i. 7; *onyænes* is in the Ormulum, l. 249; it is hardly older than A.D. 1200, though the word *tō-gegnes* or *tōgēnes* is common at an early period. AS. *ongegn*, *ongēan*, against, again, prep. and adv. Grein, ii. 344.**+**OSax. *angegin*, prep. and adv. again, against; Icel. *ī gegn*, against; Dan. *igen*, adv. again; Swed. *igen*, adv. again; OHG. *ingagene*, *ingegine* (mod. G. *entgegen*, where the *t* appears to be merely excrescent). ¶ Hence the prefix is plainly the AS. and mod. E. *on*, generally used in the sense of *in*. The simple form *gēan* occurs in Cædmon, ed. Thorpe, p. 62, l. 5 (ed. Grein, 1009); 'he him *gēan* þingade' = he addressed him *again*, or *in return*; cf. Icel. *gegn*, G. *gegen*, contrary to. AS. *ongēan* seems thus to mean 'in opposition to.' The orig. sense seems to have been 'in a direct line with;' hence, over against, opposite; cf. prov. E. *gain*, direct, straight, Icel. *gegn*, direct (said of a path); the orig. Teut. type being apparently **gaginoz*, adj. Cf. Gk. κιχάνω, **κίχημι*, I light upon, I meet with. ¶ The prefix *again-* is very common in Mid. Eng., and enters into numerous compounds in which it frequently answers to L. *re-* or *red-*; ex. *ayenbite* = again-biting, i.e. re-morse; *ayenbuyen*, = buy back, i.e. *red-eem*. Nearly all these compounds are obsolete. The chief remaining one is ME. *ay-in-seien*, now shortened to *gain-say*.

AGALLOCHUM; see **Aloes-wood**, under **Aloe**.

AGAPE, on the gape. (E.) In Milton, P. L. v. 357; for *on gape*; cf. '*on* the broad grin.' See **Abed**; and see **Gape**.

AGARIC, a kind of fungus. (F.—L.—Gk.) Turner has *agarike*; Names of Herbes, p. 9.—F. *agaric*, 'agarick, a white and soft mushrome;' Cot.—L. *agaricum*.—Gk. ἀγαρικόν, a tree-fungus.

AGATE, a kind of stone. (F.—L.—Gk.) Shak. L. L. L. ii. 236. [Perhaps confused with *gagate* or *gagates*, i.e. jet, in Middle English; see Spec. of Eng., ed. Morris and Skeat, sect. xviii. A. 30, and *gagate* in Halliwell.]—MF. *agate*, spelt *agathe* in Cotgrave.—L. *achātes*, an agate (see Gower, C. A. iii. 130, bk. vii. 1362); borrowed from Gk. ἀχάτης, an agate; which, according to Pliny, 37. 10, was so called because first found near the river *Achates* in Sicily. For the ME. *gagate*, see **Jet**.

AGE, period of time, maturity of life. (F.—L.) 'A gode clerk wele in *age*;' Rob. of Brunne, tr. of P. Langtoft, p. 114.—OF. *aage*, *age*; fuller form, *edage* (11th century).—Late L. **ætāticum*, a form which is not found, but the ending *-āticum* is very common; for the changes, see *âge* in Brachet.—L. *ætātem*, acc. of *ætās*, age; which is a contraction from an older form *æuitās*, formed by suffixing *-tās* to the stem *æui-*; from *æuum*, life, period, age.**+**Gk. αἰών, (for αἰϝών), a period; Goth. *aiws*, a period, time, age; Skt. *āyus*, life. Brugm. ii. § 112. Der. *age*, v.; *ag-ed*. (See Max Müller, Lectures, i. 337, ii. 274. 8th ed.) And see **Aye**.

AGENT, one who performs or does, a factor. (L.) Shak. Macb. iii. 2. 53.—L. *agentem*, acc. of *agens*, pres. pt. of *agere*, to do, drive, conduct; pp. *actus*.**+**Gk. ἄγειν, to conduct; Icel. *aka*, to drive; Skt. *aj*, to drive — √AG, to drive, conduct. See Brugm. i. 175. Der. *agency*, from Late L. *agentia*, a faculty of doing, cf. F. *agencer*, to arrange, which see in Brachet; also (from L. pp. *actus*) *act*, *act-ion*, &c. See **Act**. Also, from the same root, *ag-ile*, *ag-ility*; see **Agile**.

Also, from the same root, *ag-itate*, *ag-itation*, *ag-itator*; see **Agitate**. Also, from the same root, *ag-ony*, *ant-ag-onist*; see **Agony**. Also *amb-ig-uous*, q. v.; as well as *co-ag-ulate*, *co-g-ent*, *co-g-itate*, *counter-act*, *en-act*, *essay*, *ex-act*, *examine*, *ex-ig-ent*, *prod-ig-al*, *trans-act*.

AGGLOMERATE, to mass together. (L.) In Coles's Dict. (1684). Used by Thomson, Autumn, 766.—L. *agglomerātus*, pp. of *agglomerāre*, to form into a mass, to wind into a ball.—L. *ad*, to, together (which becomes *ag-* before *g*); and *glomerāre*, to wind into a ball, from *glomer-*, decl. stem of *glomus*, a clue of thread (for winding), a thick bush, orig. a mass; related to L. *globus*, a globe, a ball. See **Globe**. Der. *agglomeration*.

AGGLUTINATE, to glue together. (L.) *Agglutinated* occurs in Sir T. Browne, Vulgar Errors, b. ii. c. 1. § 14.—L. *agglūtinātus*, pp. of *agglūtināre*, to glue together.—L. *ad* (> *ag-* before *g*); *glūtināre*, to fasten with glue, from *glūten* (decl. stem *glūtin-*), glue. See **Glue**. Der. *agglutinat-ion*, *agglutinat-ive*.

AGGRANDISE, to make great. (F.—L.) Young has *aggrandize*, Night Thoughts, Nt. 6, l. 111.—F. *aggrandiss-*, extended stem of *aggrandir*, which Cotgrave explains by 'to greaten, augment, enlarge,' &c. The older form of the verb was *agrandir*, with one *g*, as in mod. F.; the double *g* is due to analogy with L. words beginning with *agg-*.—OF. *a*, to (for L. *ad*); and *grandir*, L. *grandire*, to increase, from *grandis*, great. See **Grand**. Der. *aggrandise-ment*, in Blount's Gloss.

AGGRAVATE, lit. to make heavy, to burden. (L.) Shak. Rich. II, i. 1. 43. Spelt *agravate* in Palsgrave, p. 418.—L. *aggrauātus*, pp. of *aggrauāre*, to add to a load.—L. *ad* (> *ag-* before *g*); *grauāre*, to load, make heavy, from *grauis*, heavy. See **Grave**. Der. *aggravat-ion*. ¶ Nearly a doublet of *aggrieve*.

AGGREGATE, to collect together. (L.) *Aggregate* occurs in Sir T. Elyot, The Governour, b. iii. c. 23. § 7. [ME. has the form *aggreggen*, from the F. *agréger* (which see in Brachet); it occurs in Chaucer's Melibeus (B 2477).]—L. *aggregāt-us*, pp. of *aggregāre*, to collect into a flock.—L. *ad* (> *ag-* before *g*); *gregāre*, to collect a flock, from *grex* (stem *greg-*), a flock. See **Gregarious**. Der. *aggregate*, pp. as adj. or sb.; *aggregate-ly*, *aggregat-ion*.

AGGRESS, to attack. (F.—L.) Prior has '*aggressing* France;' Ode to Qu. Anne, st. 14.—F. *aggresser*, 'to assail, assault, set on;' Cot.—Late L. *aggressāre*.—L. *aggressus*, pp. of *aggredior*, I assail.—L. *ad* (> *ag-* before *g*); *gradior*, I walk, go, from *gradus*, a step. See **Grade**. Der. *aggress-ion*, *aggress-ive*, *aggress-ive-ness*, *aggress-or*.

AGGRIEVE, to bear heavily upon. (F.—L.) ME. *agreuen*; whence *agreued*, Chaucer, C. T. 2059 (A 2057); Rob. of Brunne, tr. of Langtoft, p. 323.—OF. *agrever*, to overwhelm.—OF. *a*, to; and *grever*, to burden, injure.—L. *ad*, to; *grauāre*, to weigh down, from *grauis*, heavy. See **Grave**. ¶ *Aggrieve* is thus nearly a doublet of *aggravate*.

AGHAST, struck with horror. (E.) Misspelt, and often misinterpreted. Rightly spelt *agast*. [Appearing as *agazed* in Shak. 1 Hen. VI, i. 1. 126, 'All the whole army stood *agazed* on him;' evidently with the notion that it is connected with *gaze*.] Shakespeare did not write this line, as he rightly has *gasted* for 'frightened' in Lear, ii. 1. 57; a word which is often now misspelt *ghasted*. 1. ME. *agasten*, to terrify, of which the pp. is both *agasted* and *agast*; and examples of the latter are numerous. See Mätzner, Altenglische Sprachproben (Wörterbuch), ii. 41. In Wyclif's Bible, Luke xxiv. 37, we have 'Thei, troublid and *agast*,' where one MS. has *agasted*. 'He was abasched and *agast*;' K. Alisaunder, ed. Weber, l. 224. 'So sore *agast* was Emelye;' Chaucer, C. T. 2343 (A 2341). 'What may hit be That me *agasteth* in my dreme?' Leg. of Good Wom. Dido, 248. 'The deouel schal ʒet *agesten* ham' = the devil shall yet terrify them; Ancren Riwle, p. 212. 2. The simple form *gasten* also occurs. '*Gaste* crowen from his corn' = to frighten crows from his corn; P. Plowman, A. vii. 129.—AS. intensive prefix *ā-*; and *gǣstan*, to terrify, hence, to frighten by torture, torment; 'hie gǣston godes cempan gāre and līgē' = they tortured God's champions with spear and flame; Juliana, 17; Grein, i. 374. The vowel-change in AS. *gǣstan*, EE. *gesten*, later *gasten*, is just parallel to that in AS. *lǣstan*, EE. *lesten*, mod. E. *last*. The final *t* in the base *gǣs-t* answers to Idg. *-d-*, which appears to be an addition to the root. B. Hence the root is an AS. *gǣs-*, answering to Goth. *gais-*, to terrify, which appears in the compound *us-gaisjan*, to make afraid. See Brugmann, i. § 816 (2); and see **Ghastly**. ¶ With the form *agazed* compare: 'the were so sore *agased*' = they were so sorely terrified; Chester Plays, ed. T. Wright, ii. 85.

AGILE, active. (F.—L.) Shak. has *agile* once; Romeo, iii. 1. 171.—F. *agile*, which Cotgrave explains by 'nimble, agile, active,' &c.—L. *agilis*, nimble, lit. moveable, easily driven about; formed with suffix *-ilis* from *agere*, to drive.—√AG, to drive. See **Agent**. Der. *agil-ity*, from F. *agilité* (Cotgrave); from L. *agilitātem*, acc. of *agilitās*.

AGIO, difference of value in exchanging money. (Ital.) In Bailey, vol. ii (1731). — Ital. *agio*, ease, convenience.

AGISTMENT, the pasturage of cattle by agreement. (F. — L.) See Halliwell; Blount gives a reference for the word, anno 6 Hen. VI. cap. 5, and instances the verb to *agist* and the sbs. *agistor, agistage.* All the terms are Law French. The F. verb *agister* occurs in the Year-Books of Edw. I, vol. iii. 231; *agistement* in the same, iii. 23; and *agistours*, pl. in the Statutes of the Realm, vol. i. p. 161, an. 1311. The sbs. are from the vb. *agister*, lit. to assign a resting-place or lodging. — F. *a* (L. *ad*), to; and OF. *giste*, 'a bed, couch, lodging, place to lie on or to rest in,' Cotgrave. This OF. *giste* = mod. E. *joist*; see **Joist.**

AGITATE, to stir violently. (L.) Shak. has *agitation*, Macb. v. 1. 12. *Agitate* is used by Cotgrave to translate F. *agiter.* — L. *agitātus*, pp. of *agitāre*, to agitate; which is the frequentative of *agere*, to drive. See **Agent.** Der. *agitat-ion, agitat-or.*

AGLET, a tag of a lace; a spangle. (F. — L.) Spenser has *aygulet*, F. Q. ii. 3. 26. Sir T. More *aglet*, Works, p. 675 h. '*Agglot*, or an *aglet* to lace wyth-alle;' Prompt. Parv. — F. *aiguillette*, a point (Cotgrave), dimin. of *aiguille*, a needle; formed by adding the dimin. fem. suffix *-ette.* — Late L. *acūcula*, for *acicula*, dimin. of L. *acus*, a needle. — √AK, to pierce. See **Acid, Acme.**

AGNAIL, a corn on the foot (obsolete); a 'hang-nail.' (E.) Much turns on the definition. In Ash's Dictionary, we find it to be 'the disease called a witlow (*sic*)'; but in Todd's Johnson it is 'a disease of the nails; a whitlow; an inflammation round the nails;' without any citation or authority. The latter definition proves that the definer was thinking of the provincial E. *hangnails*, more correctly *angnails*, explained by Halliwell to be 'small pieces of partially separated skin about the roots of the finger-nails;' an explanation due to a perverted meaning (by popular etymology) of AS. *angnægl*, of which the orig. sense seems to have been a corn on the foot, a compressed, painful, round-headed excrescence fixed in the flesh like an iron nail; see E. D. D. and N. E. D., s. v. *agnail.* Cf. A. S. Leechdoms, ii. 81, § 34. β. The old word *agnail* really meant a swelling or a corn. It means 'a corn' in Rider's Dictionary, A.D. 1640 (Webster); especially used of a corn on the foot. Palsgrave has '*agnayle* upon ones too;' and in MS. Med. Linc. fol. 300 is a receipt 'for *agnayls* one [on] mans fete or womans' (Halliwell). The fuller form is *angnail*; see E. D. D. γ. The sense was much perverted; partly (perhaps) by confusion with MF. *angonailles*, which Cotgrave explains by 'botches, pockie bumps, or sores;' partly by comparison with late Gk. παρωνυχία, late L. *paronychia* (Pliny, xxi. 20), as if the reference were to a sore beside the finger-nail; but chiefly by losing sight of the original sense of 'iron nail' or 'spike.' The etymology is from AS. *ang-*, painful, compressed, as in *ang-sum*, narrow, hard; and *nægl*, an (iron) nail, spike. See **Anger, Anguish,** and **Nail.** E. Müller cites, as cognate words, OHG. *ungnagel*, prov. G. *anneglen, einneglen*, O. Fries. *ongneil, ogneil.*

AGNATE, allied; as sb., a kinsman. (L.) '*Agnation*, kindred;' Phillips (1658). — L. *agnāt-us*, allied; pp. of *agnasci = ad-gnasci.* — L. *ad*, to; *nasci*, earlier form *gnasci*, to be born. See **Natal.**

AGNOSTIC, one who disclaims knowledge of what is behind material phenomena. (Gk.) First used in 1869 (N. E. D.). From Gk. ἀ-, negative prefix; and **Gnostic.**

AGO, AGONE, past, past. (E.) [Distinct from *ygo*, the old pp. of *go*.] ME. *ago, agon, agoon*; common, and used by Chaucer, C. T., A 1782. This is the pp. of the verb *agōn*, to go away, pass by. Thus we find 'þis worldes wele al *agoth*' = this world's wealth all passes away; Reliquiæ Antiquæ, i. 160. — AS. *āgān*, to pass away (not uncommon); Grein, i. 20. — AS. *ā-*, prefix, away; and *gān*, to go. See **Go.** Cf. G. *ergehen*, to come to pass; Goth. *us-gaggan*, to go forth.

AGOG, in eagerness; hence, eager. (F.) Well known as occurring in Cowper's John Gilpin; 'all *agog*,' i.e. all eager. *Gog* signifies eagerness, desire; and is so used by Beaumont and Fletcher: 'you have put me into such a *gog* of going, I would not stay for all the world;' Wit Without Money, iii. 1; near the end. To 'set *agog*' is to put in eagerness, to make one eager or anxious to do a thing. *A-gog*, for *on gog*, is an adaptation of the F. phrase *en gogues* (Littré), lit. 'in mirth.' Cotgrave has *estre en ses gogues*, 'to be frolick, ... in a veine of mirth.' Cf. Norm. dial. *en gogue*, mirthful, *goguer*, to be mirthful (Moisy). The origin of OF. *gogue*, mirth, diversion, is unknown. (Perhaps cf. Breton *gôgé*, trickery, raillery.)

AGONY, great pain. (F. — L. — Gk.) The use of *agonie* by Gower, C. A. i. 74 (bk. i. 968) shows that the word was not derived *directly* from Gk., but from French. Wyclif employs *agonye* in Luke xxii. 43, where the Vulgate has 'factus in *agonia*.' — F. *agonie* (Cotgrave). — L. *agōnia*, borrowed from Gk. ἀγωνία, agony; orig. a contest, wrestling, struggle. — Gk. ἀγών, (1) an assembly, (2) an arena for combatants, (3) a contest, wrestle. — Gk. ἄγειν, to drive, lead. —

√AG, to drive. See **Agent.** Der. *agonise*, from F. *agoniser*, 'to grieve extreamly, to be much perplexed' (Cotgrave); whence *agonising, agonis-ing-ly*; *Agonistes*, directly from Gk. ἀγωνιστής, a champion. Also *ant-agon-ist, ant-agon-istic, ant-agon-ism.*

AGOUTI, a rodent animal, of the guinea-pig family. (F. — Span. — Brazil.) Spelt *agouty* in Bailey, vol. ii. (1731). — F. *agouti.* — Span. *aguti.* — Brazil. *acuti, aguti*; Hist. Nat. Brasiliæ, ii. 224.

AGRAFFE, a kind of clasp. (F. — OHG.) In Scott, Ivanhoe, ch. 8. — F. *agrafe*, also *agraphe* (Cot.), a hook, clasp; *agrafer*, to clasp. The verb is from F. *a*, for L. *ad*, to; and MHG. *krapfe*, OHG. *crapo, chrapfo*, a hook, which is allied to E. *cramp.*

AGRARIAN, pertaining to land. (L.) 'The *Agrarian* Law;' Phillips (1658). — L. *agrāri-us*, pertaining to land; with suffix *-an* (L. *-ānus*). — L. *agr-*, for *ager*, field; with suffix *-ārius.* See **Acre.**

AGREE, to accord. (F. — L.) ME. *agreën*, to assent. 'That ... Ye wolde somtyme freendly on me see And thanne *agreën* that I may ben he;' Chaucer, Troilus, iii. 131. Chaucer also has *agreeably*, graciously, tr. of Boethius, bk. ii. pr. 4. 92, whence mod. E. *agreeably.* — OF. *agreer*, to receive favourably; a verb made up from the phrase *à gre.* — OF. *à gre*, favourably, according to one's pleasure; composed of prep. *à*, according to (L. *ad*), and *gre*, also *gret, greit*, pleasure, from L. neuter *grātum*, an obligation, favour; from *grātus*, pleasing. See **Grateful.** Der. *agree-able* (F.), *agree-able-ness, agree-ment*; also *dis-agree, dis-agree-able, dis-agree-ment.*

AGRICULTURE, the art of cultivating fields. (L.) Used by Sir T. Browne, Vulg. Errors, bk. vi. c. 3. § 7. — L. *agricultūra* (Cicero). — L. *agrī*, gen. of *ager*, a field; *cultūra*, culture. *Ager* is cognate with E. *acre*; *cultūra* is from L. *colere*, to till, pp. *cult-us.* See **Acre** and **Culture.** Der. *agricultur-al, agricultur-ist.*

AGRIMONY, a plant. (F. — L. — Gk.) ME. *agremoine, egremoine*, Chaucer, C. T. 16268 (G 800). — MF. *agrimoine, aigremoine*, 'agrimony, or egrimony;' Cot. — Late L. *agrimōnia*, corruption of L. *argemōnia*, a plant, Pliny, xxv. 9 (Lewis). We also find L. *argemōnē*, Pliny, xxvi. 9, answering to a Gk. ἀργεμώνη.

AGROUND, on the ground. (E.) For *on ground.* 'On *grounde* and on lofte,' i.e. aground and aloft; Piers Plowman, A. i. 88; the B-text reads '*agrounde* and aloft,' i. 90.

AGUE, a fever-fit. (F. — L.) ME. *agu, ague.* Spelt *agu* in Rich. Coer de Lion, ed. Weber, l. 3046. 'Brennyng *agues*,' P. Plowman, B. xx. 83. '*Agwe*, sekenes, *acuta, querquera*;' Prompt. Parv. p. 8. 'A fever terciane Or an *agu*;' Chaucer, C. T. 14965 (B 4149). — OF. *ague*, sharp, acute, fem. of *agu* (mod. F. *aigu*). — L. *acūta*, fem. of *acūtus*, acute. The explanation is found in Ducange, who speaks of 'febris *acūta*,' a violent fever; the Prompt. Parv. gives L. *acūta* as the equivalent of ME. *agwe.* √AK, to be sharp. See **Acute.**

AH! an interjection. (F. — L.) Not in AS. 'He bleynte and cryde *a*! As though he stongen were unto the herte,' Chaucer, C. T. 1080 (A 1078). In the 12th century we find *a wah* or *a wey*, i.e. ah! woe! See Old Eng. Homilies, ed. Morris, i. 25, 29. — OF. *a*, interjection. — L. *ah*, interjection. + Gr. ἄ, int.; Skt. *ā*, int.; Icel. *æ, ai*, int.; OHG. *ā*, int.; Lithuanian *à, à à*, int. See **Fick,** i. 4. We also find ME. *a ha!* as in Towneley Myst. p. 214. This is formed by combining *a* with *ha!* Mätzner remarks that *a ha!* in Mid. English denotes satisfaction or irony. See **Ha!**

AHEAD, in front. (E.) Prob. for *on head*, where *on* signifies *in*, as common in ME.; cf. *afoot, abed, &c.* Used by Milton, on the Doctrine of Divorce (R.); and Dryden, Æn., bk. v. l. 206. See **Head.**

AHOY, interj. esp. used in hailing a boat. (E.) The prefixed *a-* is here a mere interjectional addition, to give the word more force; and *hoy!* is a natural exclamation, which occurs in P. Plowman, C. ix. 123; where the B-text has *how!* and the A-text has *hey!* Cf. mod. E. *hi!*

AI, a three-toed sloth. (Brazil.) Brazil. *ai*, a kind of sloth; Hist. Nat. Brasiliæ, ii. 221. Named from its cry.

AID, to help. (F. — L.) Palsgrave has 'I *ayde* or helpe;' p. 419. — OF. *aider*, to aid. — L. *adiūtāre*, to aid, in Late L. *aiūtāre*, afterwards shortened to *aitāre*; see Brachet. *Adiūtāre* is the frequent. form of *adiuuāre*, to assist. — L. *ad*, to; and *iuuāre*, to help, pp. *iūtus.* Cf. Brugm. ii. § 583. See **Adjutant.** Der. *aid*, sb.; also F. *aide-de-camp*, lit. one who aids in the field. From the same root, *adjutant.*

AIGRETTE, a tuft of feathers (orig. those of the egret); a spray of gems. (F. — OHG.) '*Aigrettes* by Omrahs worn, Wrought of rare gems;' Scott, Vision of Don Roderick, ii. 31. — F. *aigrette*, the lesser white heron; see **Egret.**

AIL, to feel pain; to give pain. (E.) ME. *eilen*, rarely *ailen.* 'What *eyleth* thee?' Chaucer, C. T., A 1081. Spelt *eȝlen*, Ormulum, 4767. AS. *eglan*, to trouble, pain; Grein, i. 222. From AS. *egle*, troublesome, hostile. + Goth. *agljan*, only in the comp. *us-agljan*, to distress, to weary out, Luke, xviii. 5; from *aglus*, difficult, hard; cf. *aglō*, anguish; *aglitha*, tribulation. From a stem *ag-*, with 1dg. adj. suffix *-lu-*; see Brugmann, ii. § 107. The stem *ag-* appears in Icel. *ag-i*, mod. E. *awe*, and in AS. *eg-esa*, awe, terror, distress, *eg-sian*, to frighten; also in Goth. *ag-is*, fright, *af-ag-jan*, to terrify; also in Gk. ἄχ-ος, distress, pain. See **Awe**. Der. *ail-ment*, in Kersey, a hybrid compound, with F. suffix.

AIM, to endeavour after. (F.—L.) ME. *amen, aimen, eimen*, to guess at, to estimate, to intend. 'No mon vpon mold might *ayme* the number;' Will. of Palerne, 1596, 3819, 3875. Wyclif has *eymeth*, Levit. xxvii. 8. 'Gessyn or *amyn*, estimo, arbitror;' Prompt. Parv. p. 190. 'I *ayme*, I mente or gesse to hyt a thynge;' Palsgrave. 'After the mesure and *eymyng* [L. æstimationem] of the synne;' Wycl. Levit. v. 18; cf. xxvii. 2, 8.—OF. *aesmer*, to estimate; prob. confused with *esmer* (without *a-*, prefix). [Cotgrave has '*esmer*, to aime, or levell at; to make an offer to strike, to purpose, determine, intend;' also '*esme*, an *aime*, or levell taken; also, a purpose, intention, determination.'] The *s* was dropped in English before *m* just as in *blame*, from OF. *blasmer*, *emerald* from OF. *esmeralde*, *ammell* (i.e. *en-amel*) from OF. *esmail* (translated by Cotgrave, 'ammell or enammell'), &c. The OF. *esmer* = L. *æstimāre*, but OF. *aesmer* = L. *adæstimāre*; yet they may have been confused. There was also a form *eesmer*, by-form of *aesmer*. See examples in Godefroy.—L. *ad*-; and *æstimāre*, to estimate. See **Estimate**. Der. *aim*, sb., *aim-less*.

AIR (1), the atmosphere, &c. (F.—L.—Gk.) ME. *air, eir*. Spelt *ayr* in Mandeville's Travels, p. 312; *eyre* in Chaucer, C. T., G 767 (Can. Yeom. Tale).—F. *air*, · ·L. *āër*, air.—Gk. ἀήρ, air, mist; allied to ἄημι, I blow; see Prellwitz. Cf. Skt. *vā*, to blow, and E. *wind*, q.v. Der. *air*, verb, *air-y*, *air-less*, *air-gun*, &c.

AIR (2), demeanour; tune; an affected manner. (F.—L.—Gk.) As in the phrase 'to give oneself *airs*,' &c. 'His very *air*;' Shak. Wint. Tale, v. 1. 128.—F. *air*, mien, tune (see Cot.). Affected by Ital. *aria*, 'a looke, . . . a tune;' Florio.—L. *āeria*, fem. of *āerius*, adj. formed from *āër*.—Gk. ἀήρ, air. See **Air** (1).

AIRT, a point of the compass. (Gael.) In Burns, I love my Jean, l. 1; ME. *art*, Blind Harry, Wallace, i. 309.—Gael. *aird*, a quarter or point of the compass. Cf. O. Irish *aird*, a point, limit. Some compare Gk. ἀρδις, a point.

AISLE, the wing of a church. (F.—L.) Spelt *aisle* in Gray's Elegy and by Addison; see Richardson. Spelt *ele* in 1370; *eill* in 1410; also *ile*, *isle*.—F. *aile*, a wing.—L. *āla*, a wing; the long *a* being due to contraction. It is no doubt contracted from *axla or *acslā, whence the dimin. *axilla*, a wing; see Cicero, Orat. 45. 153; Brugm. i. § 490. The proper meaning of *acslā is rather 'shoulder-blade' or 'shoulder;' cf. G. *achsel*. It is a diminutive of L. *axis*, a word borrowed by us from that language. See **Axis** and **Axle**. (Max Müller quotes the passage from Cicero; see his Lectures, ii. 309, 8th ed.) ¶ The word *aisle* was confused with Late L. *ascella*, a form of *axilla*; with F. *isle* (L. *insula*), to which word it owes its present pronunciation; and even with E. *alley*; see N.E.D. The spelling is a cross between *aile* and *isle*.

AIT, a small island. (E.) ME. *eit, æit*; Layamon, 1117, 23873. From *ēget, by-form of *ȳget*, AF. form of AS. *iggað, igeoð*, an island, from AS. *īg*, O. Merc. *ēg*, island; see **Eyot** and **Island**. The form *ȳget* occurs in Kemble, Cod. Dipl. v. 17, l. 30.

AITCH-BONE, the rump-bone. (Hybrid; F.—L. *and* E.) Miss Baker, in her Northamp. Gloss., gives '*aitch-bone*, the extreme end of a rump of beef, cut obliquely.' It also appears as *edge-bone* (Webster), *ice-bone* (Forby), *nache-bone* (Carr's Craven Glossary). All the forms are corruptions of *nache-bone*, i.e. rump-bone. The *nache* is 'the point of the rump;' Old Country Words, E.D.S., p. 97. We find *nache* also in Fitzherbert's Husbandry (Glossary); and *nach* in G. Markham's Husbandry (Of Oxen). The earliest example I have found is *hach-boon*, Book of St. Albans, leaf f 3, back, l. 8; A.D. 1486. —OF. *nache*, sing. of *naches*, the buttocks (Godefroy).—L. *naticās*, acc. of *naticæ*, buttocks; not in Ducange, but cited by Roquefort. Dimin. of L. *natēs*, pl. of *natis*, the rump. Allied to Gk. νῶτον, the back. ¶ Dr. Murray draws my attention to the fact that Mr. Nicol obtained this etymology (independently) in 1878; see Minutes of Meetings of Phil. Soc. Feb. 1, 1878.

AJAR, on the turn; only used of a door or window. (E.) A corruption of *a-char*, which again stands for *on char*, i.e. on the turn; from ME. *char*, a turn.

'Quhairby the day was dawin, weil I knew; . . .
Ane schot-wyndo vnschet a lytill *on char*,
Persawit the mornyng bla, wan, and har.'

G. Douglas, tr. of Virgil; Prol. to Book vii. 129.

It means 'I undid a shot-window, a little *ajar*.' The ME. *char* was earlier spelt *cherre*, as in the Ancren Riwle, pp. 36, 408; it is not uncommon; see Stratmann.—AS. *on cerre, on cyrre*, on the turn; where *cerre* is the dat. case of *cerr*, a turn, turning, time, period; cf. AS. *cerran, cirran, cyrran*, to turn; Grein, i. 156, 161, 180.+OHG. *cherren* (G. *kehren*), to turn.

AKIMBO, in a bent position. (Scand.?) In the Tale of Beryn, ed. Furnivall, oddly spelt in *kenebowe*; 'The host . . set his hond *in kenebowe*;' l. 1838 (l. 1105 in Urry). Cotgrave, s.v. *Arcade*, has 'to set his hands

a-kenbow.' Dryden uses *kimbo* as an adj. in the sense of 'bent,' 'curved.' 'The *kimbo* handles seem with bears-foot carved;' Virgil, Ecl. 3. **a.** It is clear that *in kenebowe*, lit. in a sharp curve, is a corruption, because *kene* in ME. is not used to denote 'sharp' in such a context. Also *in* is here a translation of the older form *on*, of which *a* is a shortened form (through the intermediate form *an*). **β.** Cf. prov. E. *a-kingbow*, akimbow, in E. D. D., s.v. *kingbow*, which suggests that it arose from Icel. *i keng*, 'into a crook;' with the E. *bow* needlessly added. Here *keng* is the acc. of *kengr*, a crook, twist, kink. Cf. Icel. *kengboginn*, bent into a crook. See **Kink**.

AKIN, of kin. (E.) For *of kin*; 'near *of kin*' and 'near *akin*' are equivalent expressions. *A-* for *of* occurs in **Adown**, q.v.

ALABASTER, a kind of soft marble. (F.—L.—Gk.) '*Alabaster*, a stone;' Prompt. Parv. p. 8. Wyclif has 'a boxe of *alabastre*' in Mark xiv. 3, borrowed from the Vulgate word *alabastrum*.—OF. *alabastre* (F. *albâtre*).—L. *alabastrum*, alabaster.—Gk. ἀλάβαστρος, ἀλάβαστρον, alabaster, more properly written ἀλάβαστος. Said to be derived from *Alabastron*, the name of a town in Egypt; see Pliny, Nat. Hist. 36. 8, 37. 10. Another suggestion is to derive the Gk. forms from Arab. *al-basrah*; where *basrah* means 'whitish stones, earth out of which they dig stones, also the city of Bassora;' Rich. Dict. p. 275. (Zeitschrift der deutschen Morgenländischen Gesellschaft, xxv. 528.)

ALACK, interjection. (E.) Very common in Shakespeare; Temp. i. 2. 151; L. L. L. ii. 186, &c. From ME. *a*, ah! interjection; and *lak*, signifying loss, failure, defect, misfortune. 'God in the gospel grymly repreueth Alle that *lakken* any lyf, and *lakkes* han hem-selue' = God grimly reproves all that blame anybody, and have faults themselves; P. Plowman, B. x. 262. Thus *alack* would mean 'ah! failure' or 'ah! a loss;' and *alackaday* would stand for 'ah! lack on (the) day,' i.e. ah! a loss to-day! It is almost always used to express failure. Cf. *alack the day!* Shak. Pass. Pilgrim, 227. In modern English *lack* seldom has this sense, but merely expresses 'want.'

ALACRITY, briskness. (L.) Sir T. More has *alacritie*, Works, p. 75 b. [The word must have been borrowed *directly* from the Latin, the termination being determined by analogy with such words as *bounty* (from OF. *bonte, bontet*, L. acc. *bonitātem*). This we know because the MF. form was *alaigreté*, which see in Cotgrave; the form *alacrité* being modern.]—L. acc. *alacritātem*, from nom. *alacritās*, briskness.—L. *alacer*, brisk. Perhaps from √EL, to drive, Fick, i. 500; he compares Gk. ἐλαύνειν, ἐλάειν, to drive. ¶ The Ital. *allegro* is likewise from L. *alacer*.

ALARM, a call to arms. (F.—Ital.—L.) ME. *alarme*, used interjectionally, to call men to arms. '*Alarme! Alarme!* quath that lord;' P. Plowman, C. xxiii. 92.—F. *alarme*, a call to arms. Cotgrave gives '*Alarme*, an alarum.' Brachet says that the word *alarme* was first introduced into French in the 16th century, but this must be a mistake, as it occurs in the Glossary to Bartsch's Crestomathie, and came to England before 1400. The form, however, is not French, as the OF. form was *as armes*; and we actually find *as armes* in Alisaunder, ed. Weber, 3674. It was obviously borrowed from Italian, and may have become generally known in the crusades.—Ital. *all'arme*, to arms! a contracted form of *alle arme*, where *alle* stands for *a le*, lit. 'to the,' and *arme* is the pl. of *arma*, a weapon, not now used in the singular. The corresponding Latin words would be *ad illa arma*, but it is remarkable that the L. pl. *arma* is neuter, whilst the Ital. pl. *arme* is feminine. Ducange, however, notes a Late L. sing. *arma*, of the feminine gender; and thus Ital. *all'arme* answers to Late L. *ad illās armās*. See **Arms**. Der. *alarm-ist*. ¶ *Alarm* is a doublet of *alarum*, q.v.

ALARUM, a call to arms; a loud sound. (F.—Ital.—L.) ME. *alarom*; mention is made of a 'loude *alarom*' in Allit. Poems, ed. Morris, B. 1207. The *o* is no real part of the word, but due to the strong trilling of the preceding *r*. Similarly in Havelok the Dane, the word *arm* is twice written *arum*, ll. 1982, 2408; *harm* is written *harum*, and *corn* is written *koren*. Thus *alarom* is really the word *alarm*, which see above.

ALAS, an interjection, expressing sorrow. (F.—L.) ME. *alas, allas*. Occurs in Rob. of Glouc. p. 125, l. 2670; Havelok, l. 1878.—OF. *alas*, interjection. [The mod. F. has only *hélas*, formed with interj. *hé* in place of the interj. *a*, the second member *las* being often used as an interjection in OF. without either prefix.]—OF. *a*, ah! and *las!* wretched (that I am)! Cf. Ital. *ahi lasso* (or *lassa*), ah! wretched (that I am)!—L. *ah!* interj. and *lassus*, fatigued, miserable. See Brugm. i. § 197, where he supposes *lassus* to stand for *lad-tus, and compares it with Goth. *lats*, which is the E. *late*. See **Late**.

ALB, a white priestly vestment. (F.—L.) ME. *albe*, Rob. of Brunne's tr. of Langtoft, p. 319; and in O. Eng. Homilies, ed. Morris, ii. 163.—OF. *albe*, an alb.—Late L. *alba*, an alb; fem. of L. *albus*, white. Cf. Gk. ἀλφός, a white rash; OHG. *elbiz*, a swan; see Brugm. i. § 481. Cf. *album*, *albumen*.

ALBACORE, a kind of tunny. (Port. – Arab.?) 'The fish which is called *albacore*;' Hakluyt, Voy. ii. pt. 2. p. 100. – Port. *albacor, albacora* (Span. *albacora*). Said to be of Arab. origin (N. E. D.).

ALBATROSS, a large sea-bird. (Port. – Span. – Arab. – Gk.) The word occurs in Hawkesworth's Voyages, A.D. 1773 (Todd's Johnson). 'The name *albatross* is a word apparently corrupted by Dampier [died 1712] from the Portuguese *alcatraz*, which was applied by the early navigators of that nation to cormorants and other sea-birds;' Eng. Cyclopædia. [Dampier, Voy. i. 531, has *algatrosses*; N. E. D.] And Drayton has *alcatraz*, in his poem named The Owl. – Portuguese *alcatraz*, a sea fowl; Span. *alcatraz*, a pelican. Variant of Port. *alcatruz*, a bucket, Span. *alcaduz*, M. Span. *alcaduz* (Minsheu), a bucket on a water-wheel. – Arab. *al-qādūs*, the same (Dozy). [Similarly, Arab. *saqqā*, a water-carrier, a pelican, because it carries water in its pouch (Devic; supp. to Littré).] Finally, Arab. *qādūs* is from Gk. κάδος, a jar, cask.

ALBEIT, although it may be. (E.) ME. *al be it*, Cursor Mundi, 4978. From ME. *al*, in the sense 'although;' *be*, subj. mood, pres. t.: and *it*.

ALBINO, a human being with skin and hair abnormally white, and pink eyes. (Span. – L.) Applied to some negroes by the Portuguese (1777; N. E. D.); but the word is rather Spanish. – Span. *albino*, 'born with very white hair and a white skin;' Pineda. – L. *alb-us*, white; with suffix -*inus*. See **Alb.**

ALBUM, a white book. (L.) L. *album*, a tablet, neuter of *albus*, white. See **Alb.**

ALBUMEN, white of eggs. (L.) Merely borrowed from L. *albūmen ōui*, the white of an egg, rarely used. More commonly *album ōui*. From L. *albus*, white (whence *albū-men*, lit. whiteness). See **A'b.** Der. *albumin-ous*.

ALCAYDE, a judge. See **Cadi.**

ALCHEMY, the science of transmutation of metals. (F. – Arab. – Gk.) Chaucer has *alkamistre*, an alchemist; C. T., G 1204. The usual ME. forms of the word are *alkenamye* and *alconomye*; P. Plowman, A. xi. 157; Gower, C.A. ii. 89 (bk. iv. 2612); where the mistaken suffix -*onomye* is imitated from that of *astr-onomye*. – OF. *alchemie, arquemie*; see *arquemie* in Roquefort. – Arab. *al-kīmīā*; in Freytag, iv. 75 b, Rich. Dict. p. 1224; a word from no Arabic root, but composed of the Arabic def. article *al*, prefixed to the late Gk. χημεία, i.e. 'transmutation' of gold and silver, occurring about A.D. 300 (N. E. D.). – Late Gk. χημεία, transmutation of metals, alchemy, chemistry, a word of uncertain origin, which was confused with Gk. χυμεία, a mingling, from Gk. χέειν, to pour (root χευ), cognate with *fundere*. See **Chemist.** See N. E. D.; and Devic.

ALCOHOL, pure spirit. (Low L. – Arabic.) From Low L. *alcohol*, the original signification of which is a fine, impalpable powder. 'If the same salt shall be reduced into *alcohol*, as the chymists speak, or an impalpable powder, the particles and intercepted spaces will be extremely lessened;' Boyle (in Todd's Johnson). – Arab. *alkohl*, compounded of *al*, the definite article, and *kohl*, the (very fine) powder of antimony, used to paint the eyebrows with; from *kahala*, to stain the eyes; cf. Heb. *kākhal* (the same), Gesenius, p. 376. And see T. L. O. Davies, Supplementary Glossary. See Richardson's Dict. p. 1173; cf. *kuhl*, collyrium; Palmer's Pers. Dict. col. 484. The extension of meaning from 'fine powder' to 'rectified spirit' is European, not Arabic. Der. *alcohol-ic, alcohol-ize*.

ALCORAN; see **KORAN.** (*Al* is the Arabic def. article.)

ALCOVE, a recess, an arbour. (F. – Span. – Arabic.) 'The Ladies stood within the *alcove*;' Burnet, Hist. of His Own Time, an. 1688 (R.) – F. *alcôve*, a word introduced in the 16th century from Spanish. – Span. *alcoba*, a recess in a room; 'a close room for a bed;' Minsheu (1623). – Arab. *al*, def. article, and *qobbah*, a vaulted space or tent; Freytag, iii. 388 a; *qubbah*, a vault, arch, dome; Palmer's Pers. Dict. col. 467. See *Alcova* in Diez, whose explanation is quite satisfactory. ¶ Not to be confused with E. *cove*.

ALDER, a kind of tree. (E.) Chaucer has *alder*, C. T. 2923 (Kn. Ta. 2063). '*Aldyr-tre* or oryelle tre, *alnus*;' Prompt. Parv. p. 9. [The letter *d* is, however, excrescent, as in *alder-first* for *aller-first*, i.e. first of all; or as in *alder-liefest*, used by Shakespeare for *aller-liefest*. Hence the older form is *aller*.] 'Coupet de aunne, of *allerne*;' Wright's Vocabularies, i. 171; 13th century. – AS. *alr*, an alder-tree = L. *alnus*; Ælfric's Glossary, Nomina Arborum; also *alor, aler*.+Du. *els*, alder; *elzen*, aldern; *elzen-boom*, alder tree; Icel. *ölr*, an alder; Swed. *al*; Dan. *elle, el*; OHG. *elira, erila, erla*; MHG. *erle*; G. *erle*; prov. G. *eller, else*; Span. *aliso* (from Gothic). Teut. types **aluz-, *aliz-*. Allied to L. *alnus*; Lithuanian *alksnis* (with excrescent *k*), an alder-tree; Church-Slavonic *jelikha*, an alder-tree; Russian *olékha*. Perhaps allied to **Elm.**

ALDER-, prefix, of all. (E.) As in *alder-liefest*, dearest of all, 2 Hen. VI, i. 1. 28. For ME. *aller, alre*, O. Merc. *alra*, AS. *ealra*, gen. pl. of *al, eal*, all; see **All.**

ALDERMAN, a chief officer in the corporation of a town. (E.) ME. *aldermon, alderman*. 'Princeps, *aldermon*;' Wright's Vocabularies, 538; 12th century. Spelt *aldermon* in Layamon, i. 60. – O. Merc. and Northumbrian *aldormon*, used to explain *centurio* in Mark, xv. 39, and occurring in many other passages in the Northumbrian glosses; West-Saxon *ealdor-man*, a chief. See Turner's Hist. of the Anglo-Saxons, bk. viii. c. 7. – AS. *ealdor, aldor*, a chief (Grein, i. 241); and *man*, a man. Allied to O. Fries. *aldirmon*, a chief; *alder*, a parent; G. *eltern*, parents; L. *al-tor*, a bringer up, from *alere*, to nourish. E. *old* is from the same root; see **Old.**

ALE, a kind of beer. (E.) ME. *ale*, Reliquiæ Antiquæ, i. 177; Layamon, ii. 604. AS. *ealu*, Grein, i. 244 (gen. *aloþ*); stem **alut*.+Icel. *öl*; Swed. *öl*; Dan. *öl*; Lithuanian *alus*, a kind of beer; Church-Slavonic *olu*, beer. ¶ See Fick, iii. 57. [The nature of the connexion with Gaelic and Irish *ol*, drink, is not clear.] Der. *brid-al*, i.e. *bride-ale*; *ale-stake* (Chaucer), *ale-house*, *ale-wife*, *ale-conner* (see **Con**).

ALEMBIC, a vessel formerly used for distilling. (F. – Span. – Arab. – Gk.) Also *limbeck*, as in Shak. Macb. i. 7. 67, but that is a docked form. Chaucer has the pl. *alembykes*, C. T., G 794. – F. *alambique*, 'a limbeck, a stillatory;' Cot. – Span. *alambique*. – Arab. *al-anbīq*; where *al* is the definite article, and *anbīq* (pron. *ambiq*) is 'a still,' adapted from the Greek. – Gk. ἄμβιξ-, stem of ἄμβιξ, a cup, goblet, used by Dioscorides to mean the cap of a still.

ALERT, on the watch. (F. – Ital. – L.) *Alertness*, Spectator, no. 566. 'The prince, finding his rutters [knights] *alert*, as the Italians say,' &c.; Sir R. Williams, Actions of the Low Countries, 1618, p. 27 (R.). – F. *alerte*, formerly *allerte*, and in Montaigne and Rabelais *à l'erte, à l'herte*, on the watch; originally a military term, borrowed from Italian in the 16th century (Brachet). – Ital. *all'erta*, on the watch; properly in the phrase *stare all'erta*, to be on one's guard. – Ital. *alla* (for *a la*), at the, on the; and *erta*, fem. of adj. *erto*, erect. – L. *ad*, prep., at; *illam*, fem. accus. of *ille*, he; and *ērectam*, fem. accus. of *ērectus*, erect. See **Erect.** ¶ The phrase 'on the alert' contains a reduplication; it means 'on-the-at-the-erect.' Der. *alert-ness*.

ALGEBRA, calculation by symbols. (Low L. – Arab.) It occurs in Ben Jonson, The Alchemist, i. 1. 38. Brachet (s.v. *algèbre*) terms *algebra* a medieval scientific Latin form; and Prof. De Morgan, in Notes and Queries, 3 S. ii. 319, cites a Latin poem of the 13th century in which 'computation' is oddly called 'ludus *algebræ almucgrabalæque*.' β. This phrase is a corruption of Arab. *al jabr wa al moqābalah*, lit. the putting-together-of-parts and the equation, to which the nearest equivalent English phrase is 'restoration and reduction.' γ. In Palmer's Pers. Dictionary, col. 165, we find 'Arabic *jabr*, power, violence; restoration, setting a bone; reducing fractions to integers in Arithmetic; *aljabr wa'lmuqābalah*, algebra.' – Arab. *jabara*, to set or re-unite a bone, to bind together, to consolidate. *Muqābalah* is lit. 'comparison;' from the root *qabala*, he approached; Rich. Dict., pp. 494, 1114, 1465. Der. *algebra-ic, algebra-ic-al, algebra-ist*.

ALGUAZIL, a police-officer. (Span. – Arab.) In Beaum. and Fletcher, Span. Curate, v. 2. – Span. *alguacil*, a police-officer; spelt *alguazil* in Minsheu's Dict., 1623. – Arab. *al*, def. art., the; and *wazir*, a vizier, officer, lieutenant. Cf. Port. *alvasil*. See **Vizier.**

ALGUM, the name of a tree; sandal-wood. (Heb. – Skt.) Called *algum* in 2 Chron. ii. 8, ix. 10, 11; corrupted to *almug* in 1 Kings, x. 11, 12. – Heb. *algummīm*; or (transposed) *almugīm*. A foreign word in Hebrew, and borrowed from some Indo-germanic source, being found in Sanskrit as *valguka*, sandal-wood. 'This *valguka*, which points back to a more original form *valgu* [for the syllable -*ka* is a suffix], might easily have been corrupted by Phenician and Jewish sailors into *algum*, a form, as we know, still further corrupted, at least in one passage of the Old Testament, into *almug*. Sandal-wood is found indigenous in India only, and there chiefly on the coast of Malabar;' Max Müller, Lectures, i. 232, 8th ed.

ALIAS, otherwise. (L.) Law Latin; *aliās*, otherwise; from *alius*, another. From the same root as E. *else*. See **Alien** and **Else.**

ALIBI, in another place. (L.) Law Latin *alibi*, in another place, elsewhere. – L. *ali-us*, another; for the suffix, cf. L. *i-bi*, there, *u-bi*, where. See above.

ALIEN, strange; a stranger. (F. – L.) We find 'an *aliene* knyght;' K. Alisaunder, ed. Weber, l. 3919. Wyclif has *alyens*, i.e. strangers, Matt. xvii. 24; also 'an *alien* womman,' Ecclus. xi. 36. '*Aliens* suld sone fond our heritage to wynne;' Rob. of Brunne, tr. of Langtoft, p. 141. – OF. *alien, allien*, a stranger (Roquefort). – L. *aliēnus*, a stranger; or as adj., strange. – L. *alius*, another (stem *ali-*; whence *ali-ēnus* is formed).+Gk. ἄλλος, another; Goth. *aljis* (stem *aljo-*), other; Old Irish *aile*, another. Brugm. i. § 175. See **Else.** Der. *alien-able, alien-ate, alien-at-ion*; cf. *al-ter, al-ter-nate, al-ter-c-at-ion*.

ALIGHT, (1) to descend from; (2) to light upon. (E.) **1.** ME. *alighten, alihten*, particularly used of getting off a horse. 'Heo letten alle tha horsmen i than wude *alihten*' = they caused all the horsemen to alight in the wood; Layamon, iii. 58, 59. **2.** Also ME. *alighten*, *alihten*; as in 'ur louerd an erthe *alighte* her' = our Lord alighted here upon earth; Rob. of Glouc., p.1.468,1.9589. **β**. The two senses of the word seem at first to show that the prefix *a-* has not the same force in both cases; but both go back to AS. *ālīhtan*, to get down, in Ælfric's Grammar, De Quarta Conj. § iii; where we find '*Dissilio*, of ālīhte;' so that the prefix is the AS. intensive prefix *ā-*; see **A-** (4). The simple form *lihtan*, to alight (from horseback), occurs in the Death of Byrhtnoth, ed. Grein, l. 23. [The radical sense of *lihtan* is to render light, to remove a burden from.] — O. Merc. *liht*, Northumbrian *lēht*, West-Saxon *lēoht*, light (i.e. unheavy); see AS. Gospels, Matt. xi. 30. See **Light** (3).

ALIGN; see **Aline**.

ALIKE, similar. (E.) ME. *alike, alyke*, adj. and adv. '*Alyke* or euynlyke, *equalis*; *alyke*, or lyke yn lykenes, *similis*;' Prompt. Parv. p. 10. Also *olike*, Gen. and Exodus, ed. Morris, l. 2024. **a**. The forms *alike, olike*, are short for *anlike, onlike*; the adverbial form retains the final *e*, but the adj. is properly without it. **β**. The adj. form *anlik* is also written *anlich*, as in 'thet is him *anlich*' = that is like him; Ayenbite of Inwyt, p. 186. **γ**. The prefix is therefore *a-* or *o-*, short for *an-* or *on-*, and corresponding to AS. *on-*. — AS. *onlic*, adj. like, Grein, ii. 348; also written *anlīc*, Grein, i. 8. — AS. *on*, prep. on, upon; and *lic*, like. Cf. also Icel. *ā-likr*, the form cognate with AS. *on-līc*; which was doubtless confused with it (N. E. D.). ¶ The fullest form appears in the Gothic adv. *analeikō*, in like manner. See **Like** and **On**.

ALIMENT, food. (F.—L.) Milton has *alimental*, P. L. v. 424; Bacon has 'medicine and *aliment*,' Nat. Hist. sect. 66. — F. *aliment*, 'food, sustenance, nourishment;' Cot. — L. *alimentum*, food; formed with suffix *-mentum* from *alere*, to nourish. [This suffix is due to a combination of the Idg. suffixes *-men* and *-to*, on which see Brugmann.] — L. *alere*, to nourish. + Goth. *alan*, to nourish; Icel. *ala*, to nourish, support. Cf. Old Irish *altram*, nourishment. — √AL, to nourish. See Brugm. i. § 490. **Der.** *aliment-al, aliment-ary, aliment-at-ion*; cf. also *alimony* (from L. *alimōnia*, sustenance, which from stem *ali-*, with suffixes *-mōn-* and *-jā*). ¶ From the same root *al-* we have also *adolescent, ad-ult, old, elder, alder*; also *altitude, alto, coalesce, exalt, haughty, hautbois, proletarian*.

ALINE, ALIGN, to range in a line. (F.—L.) First used in 1693 (N. E. D.). From F. *aligner*, to range in a line. — F. *à ligne*, into line. — L. *ad*, to; *linea*, a line. See **Line**. ¶ *Aline* is the better spelling for the E. word.

ALIQUOT, proportionate. (F.—L.) Borrowed from F. *aliquote*, as in *partie aliquote*, a proportional part. = Late L. *aliquota*, fem. of *aliquotus*, an adj. made from L. *aliquot*, indef. indecl. numeral, 'several;' which is from *ali-us*, other, some, and *quot*, how many.

ALIVE, in life. (E.) A contraction of the ME. phrase *on liue*, in life, where *on* signifies *in*, and *liue* or *lyue* (*livè, lyvè*) is the dat. case of *lyf*, life. 'Yf he haue wyt and his *on lyue*' = if he has wit, and is *alive*; Seven Sages, ed. Wright, l. 56. — AS. *on life*, alive, Grein, ii. 184: where *on* is the preposition, and *life* is dat. case of *lif*, life. See **On** and **Life**.

ALKALI, a salt. (Arabic.) Chaucer has *alkaly*, C. T., G 810. — Arab. *al qali*; where *al* is the def. article, and *qali* is the name given to the 'calcined ashes' of the plant glass-wort (*Salicornia*), which abounds in soda. ¶ By some, *qali* is derived from the Ar. verb *qalay*, to fry, hence, to calcine (Rich. Dict. p. 1146); Palmer's Pers. Dict. gives '*qali*, alkali; and '*qaliyah*, a fricassee, curry;' col. 474. **Der.** *alkali-ne, alkal-escent, alkal-oid, alkali-fy*.

ALL, every one of. (E.) ME. *al*, in the singular, and *alle* (disyllabic) in the plural; the mod. E. is the latter, with the loss of final *e*. Chaucer has *al a*, i.e. the whole of, in the phrase '*al a* companye,' C. T., G 996; also *at al*, i.e. wholly, C. T., C 633. The plural *alle* is very common. — AS. *eal*, sing., *ealle*, plural; but the mod. E. follows the O. Merc. form *alle*; see Matt. v. 15 (Rushworth gloss). + Icel. *allr*, sing., *allir*, pl.; Swed. *all*, pl. *alle*; Dan. *al*, pl. *alle*; Du. *al, alle*; OHG. *al, aller*; Goth. *alls, allai*. Teut. type *alnoz. Allied to Irish and Gael. *uile*, all, every, whole; from Idg. type *oljos; Stokes-Fick, p. 52. Brugmann (ii. § 66) takes Teut. *alnoz as from Teut. *alan- (Goth. *alan*), to grow up, to increase; allied to L. *al-ere*, to nourish. As if *all* = full, complete. ¶ When *all* is used as a prefix, it was formerly spelt with only one *l*, a habit still preserved in a few words. The AS. form of the prefix is *eal-*, O. Merc. *al-*, Icel. *al-*, Gothic *ala-*. Hence *al-mighty, al-most, al-one, al-so, al-though, al-together, al-ways*; and ME. *al-gates*, i.e. always. This prefix is now written *all* in later formations, as *all-powerful*, &c. In *all-hallows*, i.e. all saints, the double *l* is correct, as denoting the plural. ☞ In the phrase *all to-brake*, Judges, ix. 53, there is an ambiguity. The proper spelling, in earlier English, would be *al tobrak*, where *al* is an adverb, signifying 'utterly,' and *tobrak* the 3 p. s. pt. t. of the verb *tobreken*, to break in pieces; so that *al tobrak* mean 'utterly brake in pieces.' The verb *tobreken* is common; as '*Al* is *to-broken* thilke regioun;' Chaucer, C. T., A 2757 (Harl. MS.). **β**. There was a large number of similar verbs, such as *tobresten*, to burst in twain,

tocleouen, to cleave in twain, *todelen*, to divide in twain, &c.; see Stratmann's OE. Dict. pp. 611–616. **γ**. Again, *al* was used before other prefixes besides *to*; as 'he was *al* awondred;' Will. of Palerne, l. 872; and again '*al* biweped for wo;' id. 661. **δ**. But about A.D. 1500, this idiom became misunderstood, so that the *to* was often joined to *al* (misspelt *all*, producing a form *all-to*, which was used as an intensive prefix to verbs, yet written apart from them, as in 'we be fallen into the dirt, and be *all-to* dirtied;' Latimer, Remains, p. 397. See the article on *all to* in Eastwood and Wright's Bible Wordbook. **B**. The gen. pl. of AS. *eal* was *ealra*, in later English written *aller*, and sometimes *alder*, with an inserted excrescent *d*. Hence Shakespeare's *alderliefest* is for *allerliefest*, i.e. dearest of all; 2 Hen. VI, i. 1. 28. See **Almighty, Almost, Alone, Already, Also, Although, Altogether, Always, As, Withal**; also **Hallowmass**.

ALLAY, to assuage. (E.) The history of this word proves that the orig. E. verb has been confused with four other verbs of Romance origin; for the full history, see N. E. D. The orig. source is seen in ME. *aleyen, alaien*, to put down; as in 'unbileue, þat is aiware *aleid*,' unbelief, that is everywhere put down; OE. Homilies, ii. 11. The stem of ME. *aleyen* is due to AS. *āleg-*, stem of the 2nd and 3rd persons sing. pres. of AS. *ālecgan*, to put down, which also produced ME. *aleggen*, to lay aside. — AS. *ā-*, prefix; and *lecgan*, to lay; see **A-** (4) and **Lay** (1). ¶ But confused with ME. *aleggen*, to alleviate, which is really no more than a (French) doublet of (the Latin) *alleviate*, q. v. Cf. '*Aleggyn*, or to softe, or relese peyne, *allevio*;' Prompt. Parv. p. 9. And further confused with an obs. vb. *aleye*, to allege, and with old forms of E. *alloy*.

ALLEGE, to affirm. (F.—L.) ME. *aleggen, alegen*, to affirm. '*Aleggyn* awtowrs, allego;' Prompt. Parv. p. 9. 'Thei wol *alleggen* also, and by the gospel preuen;' P. Plowman, B. xi. 88. In form, the ME. *alegen* answers to AF. *alegier, aligier* = OF. *esligier*, 'to clear' at law (see Godefroy); from AF. *a-* = OF. *es-* (L. *ex-*), and *ligier*, to contend, from L. *lītigāre*, to contend, to litigate; see **Litigate**. **β**. This AF. *alegier* was Latinised (wrongly) as *adlēgiāre* (Ducange), and was treated as if allied to MF. *alleguer*, 'to alleadge, to urge, or produce reasons;' Cot.; from L. *allēgāre*, to send, despatch; also to bring forward, mention. — L. *al-*, for *ad*; and *lēgāre*, to send, appoint; from *lēg-*, stem of *lex*, law. See **Legal**. ¶ The MF. *alleguer* (if uninfluenced by the AF. *alegier*) would have produced an E. form *alleague*. **Der.** *alleg-at-ion*, from F. *allégation*, L. acc. *allēgātiōnem* (correctly).

ALLEGIANCE, the duty of a subject to his lord. (F.—OHG.) Fabyan has *allegeaunce*, cap. 207. § 5. The older form is with one *l*. 'Of *alegeaunce* now lerneth a lesson other tweyne;' Richard the Redeles, i. 9. Spelt *alegeawns* in Wyntown, vii. 8. 14. Formed by prefixing *a-* (= F. *a-*, L. *ad-*) to the word *legeaunce*, borrowed from the OF. *ligeance, ligance*, homage. Of these forms, *ligance* was due to an imaginary connexion with L. *ligāre*, to bind; but *ligeance* was derived from OF. *lige*, liege; with suffix *-ance* (= L. *-antia*). Of Germanic origin; see **Liege**.

ALLEGORY, a kind of parable. (L.—Gk.) The pl. *allegories* occurs in Tyndal's Prol. to Leviticus, and Sir T. More's Works, p. 1041 a. ME. *allegorie*, Wyclif, Gal. iv. 24 (earlier version). [Cf. MF. *allegorie*, an allegory; Cot.] — L. *allēgoria*, borrowed from Greek, in the Vulgate version of Galat. iv. 24. — Gk. ἀλληγορία, a description of one thing under the image of another; cf. ἀλληγορεῖν, to speak so as to imply something else. — Gk. ἀλλο-, stem of ἄλλος, another; and ἀγορ-, as in ἀγορεύειν, to speak, ἀγορά, a public assembly, allied to ἀγείρειν, to assemble. The prefix ἀ appears to answer to Skt. *sa*, together, and -γείρειν implies a base γερ-, with which L. *grex*, a flock, is connected; Brugmann, i. § 633. **Der.** *allegor-ic, allegor-ic-al, allegor-ic-al-ly, allegor-ise, allegor-ist*.

ALLEGRO, lively, brisk. (Ital.—L.) In Milton's *L'Allegro*, *l'* = *lo*, the Ital. def. article, from L. *ille*, he (acc. *illum*). The Ital. *allegro*, brisk, is from L. *alēcrum*, substituted for *alacrem*, acc. of *alacer*, brisk. See **Alacrity**. **Der.** *allegr-etto*.

ALLELUIA, ALLELUJAH, an expression of praise. (L.—Gk.—Heb.) L. *allelūia*; Rev. xix. 6. — Gk. ἀλληλούϊα; Rev. xix. 6. Better *hallelujah*. — Heb. *halelū jāh*, praise ye Jehovah. — Heb. *halelū*, praise ye, from *hālal*, to shine, which in one 'voice' signifies 'praise;' and *jāh*, Jah, Jehovah.

ALLEVIATE, to lighten. (L.) Used by Bp. Hall, Balm of Gilead, c. 1. § 2. Formed as if from *alleviātus*, pp. of Late L. *alleviāre*, to alleviate; see note on **Abbreviate**. — L. *allevāre*, to lighten, which passed into the occasional form *alleviāre*, as in Isaiah, ix. 1 (Vulgate). — L. *al-*, for *ad*; and *leuāre*, to lift up, to lighten, from *leus*, light, cognate with Gk. ἐλαχύς, small. **Der.** *alleviat-ion*.

ALLEY, a walk. (F.—L.) ME. *aley, alley*. 'So longe aboute the *aleyes* he he goon;' Chaucer, C. T. 10198 (E 2324). — OF. *alee*, a gallery; a participial substantive. — OF. *alee*, pp. fem. of *aler*, to go; mod. F. *aller*. ¶ The etymology of F. *aller*, much and long discussed, remains unknown. The Prov. equivalent is *anar*, allied to Ital. *andare*, to go.

ALLIANCE, ALLIES. See **Ally**.

ALLIGATION, a rule in arithmetic. (L.) Phillips (ed. 1658) has '*Alligation*, a binding unto.' The verb *alligate*, to bind together, is hardly in use; Rich. shows that it occurs in Hale's Origin of Mankind (1677), pp. 305, 334. The sb. is formed, with suffix -*tion* (F. -*tion*, L. acc. -*tiōnem*) from L. *alligāre*, to bind together. − L. *al*-, for *ad*; and *ligāre*, to bind. See **Ligament**.

ALLIGATOR, a crocodile. (Span. − L.) Properly it merely means 'the lizard.' In Shak. Romeo, v. 1. 43. A mere corruption from the Spanish. Called 'a monstrous *legarto* or crocodile' by J. Hortop in 1591; Eng. Garner, ed. Arber, v. 314. [The F. *alligator* is borrowed from English.] − Span. *el lagarto*, the lizard, a name esp. given to the American crocodile, or *cayman*. 'In Hawkins's Voyage, he speaks of these under the name of *alagartoes*;' Wedgwood. − L. *ille*, he (whence Ital. *il*, Span. *el*, the); and *lacertus* (more commonly *lacerta*), a lizard. See **Lizard**.

ALLITERATION, repetition of initial letters. (L.) The well-known line 'For apt *alliteration's* artful aid' occurs in Churchill's Prophecy of Famine; l. 86. The stem *alliterat*- is formed as if from the pp. of a L. verb **allitterāre*, which, however, did not exist. This verb is put together as if from L. *ad litteram*, i. e. according to the letter. Thus the word is a mere modern invention. See **Letter**. Der. A verb, to *alliterate* (found in 1816), and an adj., *alliterat-ive* (found in 1764), have been invented to match the sb.

ALLOCATE, to place or set aside. (L.) Burke, On the Popery Laws, uses *allocate* in the sense of 'to set aside,' by way of maintenance for children. [On the suffix -*ate*, see **Abbreviate**.] − Late L. *allocātus*, pp. of *allocāre*, to allot; see Ducange. − L. *al*-, for *ad*; and *locāre*, to place, from *locus*, a place. See **Locus**. Der. *allocat-ion*. ¶ *Allocate* is a doublet of *allow*, to assign. See **Allow** (1).

ALLOCUTION, an address. (L.) Spelt *adlocution* by Sir G. Wheler in 1689 (R.). Borrowed from Latin; with F. suffix -*ion* < L. acc. ending -*iōnem*. − L. *allocūtio*, *adlocūtio*, an address. − L. *ad*, to; and *locūtio*, a speaking, allied to *locūtus*, pp. of *loquī*, to speak; see **Loquacious**.

ALLODIAL, not held of a superior; used of land. (L. − Teut.) Englished from Late L. *allōdiālis*, an adj. connected with the sb. *allōdium*. 'The writers on this subject define *allōdium* to be every man's own land, which he possesseth merely in his own right, without owing any rent or service to any superior;' Blackstone, Comment. b. ii. c. 7. **α.** The word *allōdium* is 'Merovingian Latin;' Brachet (s. v. *alleu*). It is also spelt *alaudum*, *alaudium*, *alōdium*, *alōdum*, *alōdis* (Lex Salica), and means a free inheritance, as distinguished from *beneficium*, a grant for the owner's life-time only. **β.** The word appears as *alleu* in French, which Brachet derives from O. Frankish *alōd* (see Schade), meaning 'entire property,' or 'entirely one's property;' where *al*- is related to E. *all*, and *ōd* signifies 'property' or 'wealth.' This O. Frank. *ōd* is cognate with OHG. *ōt*, AS. *ēad*, Icel. *auðr*, wealth; originally 'a thing granted,' as it is derived from a strong verb of which the Teut. type is **audan*-, to grant, represented by AS. *ēadan* (pt. t. *ēod*), to grant. Cf. Goth. *auda-hafts*, blessed.

ALLOPATHY, an employment of medicines to produce an effect different to those produced by disease; as opposed to *homœopathy*, q. v. (Gk.) Modern. Formed from Gk. ἄλλο-, for ἄλλος, another; and -πάθεια, allied to πάθος, suffering, from παθεῖν, πάσχειν, to suffer. See **Pathos**. Der. *allopath-ic*, *allopath-ist*.

ALLOT, to assign a portion or lot to. (Hybrid; AF. − L. *and* E.) A hybrid compound; formed by prefixing the AF. or OF. *a*- (for L. *ad*) to the English word *lot*. AF. *aloter*, Year-book of Edw. I (1304-5), p. 337. Cotgrave gives MF. '*Allotir*, to divide or part, to allot;' also '*Allotement*, a parting, dividing; an allotting, or laying out, unto every one his part.' [It is likely that the F. word was borrowed from the English in this case.] Shak. not only has *allot*, but even *allottery*, As You Like It, i. 1. 77; and *allotted* occurs much earlier, viz. in Lord Surrey's translation of the 2nd bk. of the Æneid, l. 554 (or l. 722 of the E. version). See **Lot**. Der. *allot-ment*, *allott-ery*.

ALLOW (1), to assign, grant as a portion or allowance. (F. − L.) **1.** Properly distinct from *allow* in the sense of 'to approve of,' 'to praise,' which is the common sense in old writers; see Luke, xi. 48. Shakespeare has both verbs, and the senses run into one another so that it is not always easy to distinguish between them in every case; indeed, they were often confused, which produced new senses; see N. E. D. Perhaps a good instance is in the Merch. of Ven. iv. 1. 303, 'the law *allows* it,' i.e. assigns it to you. **2.** This verb is rare in early use, and Shakespeare is an early authority for it when it was becoming very common. − F. *allouer*, formerly *alouer*, 'to let out to hire, to appoint or set down a proportion for expence, or for any other employment;' Cot. − Law L. *allocāre*, to admit a thing as proved, to place, to use, expend, consume; see Ducange. [Blount, in his Law

Dict., gives *allocation* as a term used in the exchequer to signify 'an allowance made upon an account.'] See **Allocate**. Der. *allow-able*, *allow-able-ness*, *allow-abl-y*, *allow-ance*. Doublet, *allocate*.

ALLOW (2), to praise, highly approve of. (F. − L.) Sometimes confused with the preceding; now nearly obsolete, though common in early authors, and in earlier use than the former. See Luke, xi. 48. ME. *alouen*. Chaucer rhymes 'I *allow* the' = I praise thee, with the sb. *youthè*, youth; C. T. 10988 (F 676). − OF. *alouer*, later *allouer*, 'to allow, advow [i. e. advocate], to approve, like well of;' Cot. − L. *allaudāre*, *adlaudāre*, to applaud. − L. *ad*, to; and *laudāre*, to praise. See **Laud**.

ALLOY, a due proportion in mixing metals. (F. − L.) [The verb to *alloy* is made from the substantive, which was formerly spelt *alay* or *allay*, though wholly unconnected with the verb *allay*, to assuage.] ME. sb. *alay*; Chaucer has the pl. *alayes*, C.T. 9043 (E 1167). The sing. *alay* is in P. Plowman, B. xv. 342; the pp. *alayed*, alloyed, is in P. Plowman, C. xviii. 79. − AF. and OF. *alai*, *alei*, admixture or combination (of metals); a sb. due to the v. *aleier*, to combine. − L. *alligāre*, to combine or join together. − L. *al*-, for *ad*, to; and *ligāre*, to bind. See **Ligament**. In later Central F., the forms *alei*, *aleier*, became *aloi*, *aloier*, and were then confused with the phrase *à loi*, from L. *ad lēgem*, according to law; and this false etymology was commonly accepted. The form *alay*, sb., occurs in the Statutes of the Realm, i. 140 (A.D. 1300). Cf. Span. and Port. *ligar*, to tie, bind, to allay or alloy; from L. *ligāre*.

ALLUDE, to hint at. (L.) Used by Sir T. More, Works, p. 860 a. − L. *allūdere*, to laugh at, allude to. − L. *al*-, for *ad*; and *lūdere*, to play, pp. *lūsus*. See **Ludicrous**. Der. *allus-ion*, *allus-ive*, *allus-ive-ly*; from pp. *allūsus*.

ALLURE, to tempt by a bait. (F. − L. *and* G.) Sir T. More has *alewre*, Works, p. 1276 c [marked 1274]. − AF. *alurer* (Wright's Vocab. i. 151), OF. *aleurrer*, to entice to a lure (Godefroy). From F. *à leurre*, to the lure or bait; a word of Germanic origin. See **Lure**. Der. *allure-ment*.

ALLUSION, ALLUSIVE. See **Allude**.

ALLUVIAL, washed down; applied to soil. (L.) Not in early use; the sb. now used in connexion with it is *alluvium*, prop. the neuter of the L. adj *alluuius*, alluvial. In older works the sb. is *alluvion*, as in Blackstone, Comment. b. ii. c. 16, and in three other quotations in Richardson. − MF. and F. *alluvion*, a washing up, an inundation; Cot. − L. *alluuiōnem*, acc. case of *alluuio*, a washing up of earth, an alluvial formation. − L. *al*-, for *ad*, to, in addition; and *luere*, to wash. From the same root, *ab-lu-tion*, *di-luv-ial*.

ALLY, to bind together. (F. − L.) ME. *alien*, with one *l*. 'Alied to the emperour;' Rob. of Glouc. p. 65, l. 1499. [The sb. *aliance*, alliance, occurs at p. 89, l. 1985. It is spelt *alliaunce* in Gower, C. A. i. 199 (bk. ii. 1184).] − OF. *alier*, to bind to. − OF. *a*, to; and *lier*, to bind. − L. *ad*; and *ligāre*, to bind. See **Ligament**. Der. *ally*, sb., one bound, pl. *allies*; *alli-ance*. From the same root, *allig-ation*, q. v.

ALMANAC, ALMANACK, a calendar. (F. − Late L.) Spelt *almanac* by Blackstone, Comment. b. iii. c. 22; *almenak* in Chaucer. On the Astrolabe, prol. l. 67. − F. *almanach*, 'an almanack, or prognostication;' Cot. − Late L. *almanach*, *almanac*. The form *almanac* occurs in Roger Bacon, Opus Majus, xv (A.D. 1267). The origin of the word is wholly unknown; Dozy decides that it is *not* Arabic, as is often said; and the Gk. and L. origins sometimes assigned to it have to be manipulated and misspelt in order to suit the case; see N. E. D.

ALMIGHTY, all-powerful. (E.) In very early use. O. Merc. *almæhtig*; AS. *ealmihtig*, Grein, i. 244; *ælmihtig*, id. 57. See **Might**. On the spelling with one *l*, see **All**. Der. *almighti-ness*.

ALMOND, a kind of fruit. (F. − L. − Gk.) 'As for *almonds*, they are of the nature of nuts;' Holland's Pliny, bk. xv. c. 22. Wyclif has *almaundis*, almonds, Gen. xliii. 11; *almaunder*, an almond-tree, Eccles. xii. 5 (where the Vulgate has *amygdalus*). [The *l* is an inserted letter, owing to confusion of initial *a* with the Arab. def. art. *al* in the Span. forms.] − OF. *almandre*, *almande*; also *amandele*, *amendele* (nearer to the Latin). Cf. Span. *almendra*. Cotgrave has '*Amande*, an almond.' − L. *amygdala*, *amygdalum*, an almond; whence (as traced by Brachet) the forms **amygdala*, **amy'dala*, **amyndala* (with excrescent *n* before *d*), and next OF. *amendele*, *amende*, later *amande*. − Gk. ἀμυγδάλη, ἀμύγδαλον, an almond. Origin unknown.

ALMONER, a distributer of alms. (F. − L. − Gk.) Spelt *almoygners* by Sir T. More, Works, p. 235 h. ME. *aumoner*, Cursor Mundi, 15219. − OF. *almosnier*, *aumosnier*, a distributer of alms; forms in which the *s* was soon dropped, as in F. *aumône* from OF. *almosne*, alms. − OF. *almosne*, alms; with the suffix -*ier* of the agent. − Folk-L. **alimosina*, for L. *eleëmosyna*; see **Alms**.

ALMOST, nearly. (E.) Chaucer has *almost*, C. T. 9275 (E 1401). Also ME. *almast*, *almest*; the latter is especially common. 'He is *almost* dead;' Layamon, ii. 387 (later text). AS. *ealmæst*, *ælmæst*; thus in the AS. Chron. an. 1091, we have 'seo scipfyrde . . . *ælmæst*

earmlīce forfōr' = the fleet for the most part (or nearly all of it) miserably perished. — AS. *eal-*, prefix, completely; and *mǣst*, the most. ¶ The sense is, accordingly, 'quite the greatest part,' or in other words 'nearly all.' Hence it came to mean 'nearly,' in a more general use and sense. For the spelling with one *l*, see **All**.

ALMS, relief given to the poor. (L. – Gk.) ME. *almesse*, later *almes*. Wyclif has *almes*, Luke, xi. 41. For *almesse*, see OE. Homilies, ii. 29, l. 35. Still earlier, we have the AS. forms *ælmæsse* and *ælmesse*, a word of three syllables. [Thus *ælmæs-se* first became *almes-se*; and then, dropping the final syllable (*-se*), appeared as *almes*, in two syllables; still later, it became *alms*. The AS. *ælmæsse* is from the Folk-L. **alimosina* (whence OF. *almosne*, Ital. *limosina*); for the eccles. Latin *eleemosyna*, borrowed from Greek (hence being that the word has been reduced from *six* syllables to one.] — Gk. ἐλεημοσύνη, compassion, and hence, alms. — Gk. ἐλεήμων, pitiful. — Gk. ἐλεεῖν, to pity; from ἔλεος, pity. **Der.** *alms-house*. From the same root, *almoner*, q. v. ¶ The word *alms* is properly singular; hence the expression 'asked *an alms*;' Acts, iii. 3.

ALMUG, the name of a tree; see **Algum**.

ALOE, the name of a plant. (L. – Gk.) '*Aloe* is an herbe which hath the resemblance of the sea-onion,' &c.; Holland's Pliny, bk. xxvii. c. 4. Cotgrave has '*Aloes*, the herb aloes, sea-houseleeke, sea-aigreen; also, the bitter juyce thereof congealed, and used in purgations.' In like manner we still speak of 'bitter *aloes*;' and Wyclif has *aloes*, John, xix. 39, where the Vulgate has *aloës*, really the gen. case of the L. *aloë*, used by Pliny, and borrowed from the Gk. ἀλόη, the name of the plant, used by Plutarch, and in John, xix. 39; where the AS. version has *alewan*. ¶ **Der.** *aloes-wood*; a name given to a totally different plant, the *agallochum*, because one kind (the *Aquilaria Agallocha*, natural order of *Thymeleaceæ*) yields a bitter secretion. The word *agallochum* is of Skt. origin; cf. Skt. *aguru*, aloes-wood; whence also Heb. masc. pl. *ahālim*, *ahālōth*, aloes-wood or 'lign-aloes,' Numb. xxiv. 6. See *Aloes* and *Eaglewood* in Yule.

ALOFT, in the air. (Scand.) 1. For *on lofte*. In P. Plowman, B. i. 90, we find 'agrounde and *aloft*;' but in the same poem, A. i. 88, the reading is 'on grounde and on *lofte*.' 2. *On lofte* signifies 'in the air,' i. e. on high. The AS. prep. *on* frequently means 'in;' and is here used to translate the Icel. *á*, which is really the same word. 3. The phrase is, strictly, Scandinavian, viz. Icel. *á lopt*, aloft, in the air (the Icel. *-pt* being sounded like the E. *-ft*, to which it answers). The Icel. *lopt* = AS. *lyft*, the air; whence ME. *lift*, the air, still preserved in prov. E. and used by Burns in his Winter Night, l. 4. Cf. G. *luft*, the air; Goth. *luftus*, the air. See **Loft, Lift**.

ALONE, quite by oneself. (E.) ME. *al one*, written apart, and even with a word intervening between them. Ex. '*al himself one*' = himself alone; Will. of Palerne, 3316. [The *al* is also frequently omitted. Ex. 'left was he *one*,' he was left alone, id. 211.] The ME. *al* is mod. E. *all*; but the spelling with one *l* is correct. See **All** and **One**. Cf. Du. *all-een*, G. *all-ein*, alone. ¶ The word *one* was (in late ME.) pronounced *own*, rhyming with *bone*; and was frequently spelt *oon*. The ME. *one* was disyllabic (pron. *awn-y*, later *own*), the *e* representing AS. *-a* in the word *āna*, a secondary form from AS. *ān*, one; see examples of *āna* in the sense of 'alone' in Grein, i. 31, 32. The pronunciation as *own* is retained in *al-one*, *at-one*, *on-ly*. **Der.** *lone* (with loss of *a-*); *lonely*.

ALONG (1), lengthwise of. (E.) [The prefix here is very unusual, as the *a-* in this case arose from the AS. *and-*; see **A-** (3), prefix; and see **Answer**.] ME. *along*, Allit. Poems, ed. Morris, B. 769; earlier *anlong*, Layamon, i. 7. AS. *andlang*, along, prep. governing a genitive; '*andlang þæs wēstenes*' = along the waste, Joshua, viii. 16. + O. Fries. *ondlinga*, prep. with gen. case; as in '*ondlinga thes reggis*' = along the back (Richthofen); G. *entlang*, prep. with gen. or dat. when preceding its substantive. β. The AS. prefix *and-* is cognate with O. Fries. *ond-*, OHG. *ant-* (G. *ent-*), Goth. *and-*, *and-*, L. *ante*, Gk. ἀντί, Skt. *anti*, over against, close to. The 2nd syllable is the AS. adj. *lang*, long. The sense is 'over against in length.' See **Anti-** and **Long**.

ALONG (2), in the phr. *along of* or *along on*. (E.) This is not quite the same word as *along* (1), but differs in the prefix. We find 'It's all *'long on* you,' Prol. to the Return to Parnassus (1606). Chaucer has: '*wheron* it was *long*;' C. T. 16398 (G 930); and again: 'Som seide it was *long on* the fyr-making,' id. 16390. Gower has: 'How al is *on* miself *along*;' C. A. ii. 22 (bk. iv. 624). Here *along* is a corruption of *ilong*, and *long* is *ilong* without the initial *i*. This prefix *i-* is the usual ME. form of the AS. prefix *ge-*, and *along* answers, accordingly, to AS. *gelang*, as pointed out by Todd in his ed. of Johnson's Dict. Moreover, the very form *ilong* (used with *on*) occurs in Layamon, 15502. — AS. *gelang*, *gelong*, as in *on ðām gelong*, along of that, because of that, Ælfred, tr. of Orosius, bk. iv. c. 10, § 9. — AS. *ge-*, prefix; and *lang*, long. ¶ Precisely the same corruption of the prefix occurs in **Aware**, q. v.

ALOOF, away, at a distance. (E. and Du.) 1. Spelt *aloofe* in Surrey's Virgil, bk. iv, l. 90 of E. version; *aloufe* in Sir T. More's Works, p. 759 g. The latter says, 'But surely this anker lyeth too farre *aloufe* fro thys shyppe, and hath neuer a cable to fasten her to it.' This suggests a nautical origin for the phrase. 2. The diphthong *ou* signifies the *ou* in *soup*, pronounced like the Du. *oe*, so that *louf* at once suggests Du. *loef*, and as many nautical terms are borrowed from that language, we may the more readily accept this. Cf. E. *sloop* from Du. *sloep*. 3. The prefix *a-* stands for *on*, by analogy with a large number of other words, such as *abed*, *afoot*, *asleep*, *aground*; so that *aloof* is for *on loof*, and had originally the same sense as the equivalent Du. phrase *te loef*, i. e. to windward. Compare also *loef houden*, to keep the luff or weather-gage; *de loef afwinnen*, to gain the luff, &c. So too, Danish *holde luven*, to keep the luff or the wind; *have luven*, to have the weather-gage; *tage luven fra en*, to take the luff from one, to get to windward of one. Our phrase 'to hold aloof' is equivalent to the Du. *loef houden* (Dan. *holde luven*), and signifies lit. 'to keep to the windward.' ¶ The tendency of the ship being to drift on to the leeward vessel or rock, the steersman can only *hold aloof* (i. e. keep or remain so) by keeping the head of the ship *away*. Hence to *hold aloof* came to signify, generally, to keep away from, or not to approach. The quotation from Sir T. More furnishes a good example. He is speaking of a ship which has drifted to leeward of its anchorage, so that the said place of anchorage lies 'too farre aloufe,' i. e. too much *to windward*; so that the ship cannot easily return to it. Similar phrases occur in Swedish; so that the term is of Scandinavian as well as of Dutch use; but it came to us from the Dutch more immediately. See further under **Luff**.

ALOUD, loudly. (E.) Chiefly in the phrase 'to cry aloud.' ME. *aloude*, P. Plowm. C. vii. 23. By analogy with *abed*, *asleep*, *afoot*, &c., the prefix must be *on*; and *loude* is the adj. *loud*, used as a sb.; cf. *alow*, *ahigh*. See **Loud**.

ALP, a high mountain. (L.) Milton has *alp*, P. L. ii. 620; Samson, 628. ME. *Alpes*, Trevisa, tr. of Higden, i. 173. We generally say 'the Alps.' Milton merely borrowed from Latin. — L. *Alpes*, pl. the Alps; said to be of Celtic origin. 'Gallorum lingua alti montes *Alpes* uocantur;' Servius, ad Verg. Georg. iii. 474; cited by Curtius, i. 364. β. Even granting it to be Celtic, it may still be true that L. *Alpes* is connected with L. *albus*, white, spelt *alpus* in the Sabine form, with reference to the snowy tops of such mountains. See Stokes-Fick, p. 21. **Der.** *alp-ine*.

ALPACA, the Peruvian sheep. (Span. – Peruvian.) Borrowed by us from Span. *alpaca*, a Span. rendering of the Peruvian name; made by prefixing *al-* (for Arab. *al*, def. article) to the native Peruvian name *paco*.

ALPHABET, the letters of a language. (Late L. – Gk. – Phœnician.) Used by Shak. Titus And. iii. 2. 44. — Late L. *alphabetum*. — Gk. ἄλφα, βῆτα, the names of α and β (*a* and *b*), the first two letters of the Gk. alphabet. From Phœnician names represented by Heb. *āleph*, an ox, also the name of the first letter of the Hebrew alphabet; and *bēth*, a house, also the name of the second letter of the same. **Der.** *alphabet-ic*, *alphabet-ic-al*, *alphabet-ic-al-ly*.

ALREADY, quite ready; hence, sooner than expected. (E.) Rich. shows that Udal (on Luke, c. i. v. 13) uses '*already* looked for' in the modern sense; but Gower, Prol. to C. A. i. 18 (l. 424) has *al redy* [badly spelt *all ready* in Richardson] as separate words. *Al* as an adverb, with the sense of 'quite,' is common in Mid. English. [So *al clene* = quite entirely, wholly, Rob. of Glouc. p. 407 (l. 8419); see Mätzner's Altengl. Wörterbuch, p. 57.] The spelling with one *l* is correct; see **All**. And see **Ready**.

ALSO, in like manner. (E.) Formerly frequently written *al so*, separately; where *al* is an adverb, meaning 'entirely;' see **Already**, and **All**. — OMerc. *al swā*, AS. *eal swā*, *ealswā*, just so, likewise, Matt. xxi. 30, where the later Hatton MS. has *allswa*. See **So**. ¶ *As* is a contracted form of *also*; see **As**.

ALTAR, a place for sacrifices. (L.) [Frequently written *auter* in Mid. Eng., from the O. French *auter*; so spelt in Wyclif, Acts, xvii. 23, Gen. viii. 20.] Rob. of Brunne, p. 79, has the spelling *altere*; it occurs much earlier, in the Ormulum, l. 1061. AS. *altar*; dat. *altare*, Matt. v. 24. — L. *altāre*, an altar, a high place. — L. *altus*, high. See **Altitude**.

ALTER, to make otherwise. (L.) *Altered* occurs in Tyndall's Works, ed. 1572, p. 456, col. 1; and in Chaucer, Troil. iii. 1778. [Perhaps through the F. *alterer*, given by Cotgrave, and explained by 'to alter, change, vary;' but it may have been taken directly from Late L.] — Late L. *alterāre*, to make otherwise, to change; Ducange. — L. *alter*, other. — L. *al-*, of the same source with *alius*, another, and Gk. ἄλλος, other; with suffix *-ter* (as in *u-ter*, *neu-ter*), an old comparative ending answering to E. *-ther*, Gk. *-τερο-*, Skt. *-tara-*, Idg. *-tero-*. See **Alien**. **Der.** *alter-able*, *alter-at-ion*, *alter-at-ive*.

ALTERCATION, a dispute. (F. – L.) ME. *altercacioun*; Chaucer, C. T. 9347 (E 1473). — OF. *altercation*, for which see Littré.

It is also given by Cotgrave, and explained by 'altercation, brabling, brawling,' &c. – L. altercātiōnem, acc. of altercātio, a dispute. – L. altercāri, to dispute. – L. alter, another; from the notion of speaking alternately. See above, and see below.

ALTERNATE, adj. by turns. (L.) Milton has alternate, P. L. v. 657; and even coins altern, P. L. vii. 348. – L. alternātus, pp. of alternāre, to do by turns. – L. alternus, alternate, reciprocal. – L. alter, another; with suffix -no- (Brugm. ii. § 66). See **Alter.** Der. alterna-ion, alternat-ive; also the vb. to alternate (Levins).

ALTHOUGH, however. (E.) ME. al thagh, al thah, al though; Mandeville's Travels, p. 266; Allit. Poems, ed. Morris, A. 878. From al, adverb, in the sense of 'even;' and though. β. We even find al used alone with the sense 'although,' as in 'Al telle I noght as now his observances;' Chaucer, C. T. 2266 (A 2264). γ. On the spelling with one l, see **All.** And see **Though.**

ALTITUDE, height. (F. – L.) It occurs frequently near the end of Chaucer's Treatise on the Astrolabe, to translate L. altitūdo. – OF. (and F.) altitude. – L. altitūdo, height. – L. altus, high. Altus was originally the pp. of al-ere, to nourish, and meant 'well nourished;' hence, grown up, tall, high.

ALTO, a high voice. (Ital. – L.) Modern. – Ital. alto, high. – L. altus, high. Der. alto-relievo, high relief; Ital. alto rilievo; see **Relief.**

ALTOGETHER, completely. (E.) Used by Sir T. More, Works, p. 914 b. ME. al togedere, Ancren Riwle, p. 320. Formed by prefixing ME. al, adv. 'wholly,' to together. See **All** and **Together.**

ALTRUISM, regard for others. (F. – Ital. – L.; with Gk. suffix.) F. altruisme, a word due to A. Comte (d. 1857). Coined (with the Greek suffix -ism) from Ital. altrui, another, others. – Ital. altrui; from altro, nom. sing. masc.; altra, nom. sing. fem.; altri, nom. pl.; which, when preceded by any preposition, is changed into altrui for both genders and numbers (Meadows). – L. alteri huic, to this other; where alteri is the dat. of alter, another. See **Alter.** Der. altru-ist-ic, adj.

ALUM, a mineral salt. (F. – L.) ME. alum, Allit. Poems, ed. Morris, B. 1035; alom, Mandeville's Travels, p. 99; and used by Chaucer, C. T. 16281 (G 813). – OF. alum (mod. F. alun), alum; Roquefort. – L. alūmen, alum, used by Vitruvius and others; of unknown origin. Der. alumin-a, alumin-ous, alumin-ium; all directly from L. alumin-, the stem of alumen.

ALVEOLAR, pertaining to the sockets of the teeth. (L.) Modern. – L. alueolus, a small channel; dimin. of alueus, a cavity, a channel.

ALWAY, ALWAYS, for ever. (E.) Chaucer has alway, always, Prol. 275; sometimes written al way. 1. In O. Eng. Misc., ed. Morris, p. 148, l. 54, we find alne way, where alne is the acc. case masc., AS. ealne. The usual AS. form is ealne weg, where both words are in the acc. sing.; Grein, ii. 655. This form became successively alne way, al way, and alway. 2. In Hali Meidenhad, p. 27, l. 22, we find alles weis, where both words are in the gen. sing. This occasional use of the gen. sing., and the common habit of using the gen. sing. suffix -es as an adverbial suffix, have produced the second form always. Both forms are thus accounted for. See **All** and **Way.**

AM, the first pers. sing. pres. of the verb to be. (E.) O. Northumbrian am, O. Merc. eam, AS. eom, I am. The full form of the word is shown by the Idg. type *es-mi, whence also Skt. asmi, Gk. εἰμί, Goth. im, Icel. em, I am; compounded of the √ES, to be, and the suffix -mi, perhaps related to E. me. See further under **Are.**

AMADAVAT, a bird; see Avadavat.

AMADOU, a tinder prepared from a fungus. (F. – Prov. – L.) Modern. – F. amadou. – Prov. amadou, O. Prov. amador, lit. 'a lover;' also tinder, from its catching fire quickly. – L. amātōrem, acc. of amātor, a lover; from amāre, to love (Hatzfeld; Mistral).

AMAIN, with full power. (E.) Used by Turberville, To his Absent Friend, st. 7. As in other words, such as abed, afoot, aground, asleep, the prefix is the AS. on, later an, latest a, signifying 'in' or 'with,' prefixed to the dat. case of the sb. The usual AS. phrase is, however, not on mægene, but ealle mægene, with all strength; Grein, ii. 217. See **On,** and **Main,** sb. strength.

AMALGAM, a compound of mercury with another metal, a mixture. (F. – Gk.) [The restriction in sense to a mixture containing mercury is perhaps unoriginal; it is probable that the word properly meant 'a pasty mixture,' and at last 'a mixture of a metal with mercury.'] Chaucer has amalgaming, C.T., G 771. – F. amalgame, which Cotgrave explains by 'a mixture, or incorporation of quicksilver with other metals;' Late L. amalgama. β. Generally taken to be a perversion (perhaps with prefixed a-, for Arab. al, def. art.) of L. malagma, a mollifying poultice or plaster. – Gk. μάλαγμα, an emollient; also a poultice, plaster, or any soft material. – Gk. μαλάσσειν, to soften (for *μαλάκ-yειν). – Gk. μαλακός, soft; cf. **Mallow.** Der. amalgam-ate, amalgam-at-ion.

AMANUENSIS, one who writes to dictation. (L.) In Burton's Anat. of Melancholy; Dem. to the Reader; ed. 1827, i. 17. Bor-

rowed from L. āmanuensis, a scribe who writes to dictation, used by Suetonius. – L. ā manū, by hand; with suffix -ensis, signifying 'belonging to,' as in castrensis, belonging to the camp, from castra, a camp. See **Manual.**

AMARANTH, an everlasting flower. (L. – Gk.) An error for amarant; perhaps by confusion with -anthus, Gk. ἄνθος, a flower. Milton has amarant, P.L. iii. 352; and amarantine, P. L. xi. 78. The pl. amaraunz (with z = ts) is in Allit. Poems, ed. Morris, B. 1470; in which case it is not from the Gk. directly, but from L. amarantus. – Gk. ἀμάραντος, unfading; or, as sb., the unfading flower, amaranth. [Cf. Gk. ἀμαράντινος, made of amaranth.] – Gk. ἀ-, privative; and μαραίνειν (for *μαράν-γειν), to wither. – √MER, to grind down. Der. amaranth-ine. Perhaps allied to **Mar.**

AMASS, to heap up. (F. – L. – Gk.) Used by Surrey, on Eccles. c. 3; l. 3 from end. – F. amasser, 'to pile, heap, gather;' Cot. – F. à masse, to a mass; so that amasser is 'to put into a mass.' – L. ad, to; and massam, acc. of massa, a mass. [Curtius remarks concerning this word (ii. 326) that the Latin ss in the middle of a word answers to Gk. ζ.] – Gk. μᾶζα, μάζα, a barley-cake; lit. a kneaded lump. – Gk. μάσσειν (base μαγ-), to knead. Cf. μαγ-ίς, a cake. See **Mass** (1).

AMATORY, loving. (L.) Milton has amatorious, Answer to Eikon Basilike; amatory is used by Bp. Bramhall (died 1663) in a work against Hobbes (Todd). – L. amātōrius, loving. – L. amātor, a lover (acc. amātōrem, whence the F. amateur, now used in English). – L. amāre, to love, with suffix -tor denoting the agent. Der. from the same L. verb, ama-teur (above), amat-ive, amat-ive-ness. Amatory is practically a doublet of **Amorous,** q. v.

AMAZE, to astound. (E.) Formerly written amase. The word amased, meaning 'bewildered, infatuated,' occurs three times in the Ancren Riwle, pp. 270, 284, 288. AS. āmasian, pp. āmasod; Wulfstan's Hom. p. 137, l. 23. The prefix is the intensive AS. ā; thus to amase is 'to confound utterly.' We also find the compound form bimased, Ancren Riwle, p. 270. See **Maze.** Der. amaz-ed, amaz-ed-ness, amaz-ing, amaz-ing-ly, amaze-ment.

AMAZON, a female warrior. (Gk.) They were said to cut off the right breast in order to use the bow more efficiently; a story due to a popular etymology of a foreign word. Shak. has Amazon, Mids. N. D. ii. 1. 70; and Amazonian, Cor. ii. 2. 95. – Gk. ἀμαζών, pl. ἀμαζόνες, one of a warlike nation of women in Scythia. Explained as if from Gk. ἀ-, privative; and μαζός, the breast. Der. Amazon-ian.

AMBASSADOR, a messenger. (F. – Ital. – Late L. – C.) Udal, on Math. c. 28, v. 19, has ambassadour. Also written embassadour; Chaucer, Troil. iv. 145. Chaucer has embassadrye, an embassy, C. T. 4653 (B 233). – F. ambassadeur, 'embassadour;' Cot. – F. ambassade, an embassy. a. Of this word Brachet says: 'not found in French before the 14th century, and shown to be foreign by its ending -ade (unknown in OF., which has -ée for -ade).' Hatzfeld derives it from Ital. ambasciata; cf. Late L. ambassiāta (Ducange). From Late L. ambaxiāre, ambactiāre [to relate, announce], formed from ambactia, a very common term in the Salic Law, meaning 'a mission, embassy.' – Late L. ambactus, a servant, especially one who is sent on a message; used once by Cæsar, de Bello Gallico, vi. 15. β. This is expressly said, by Festus, to be a word of Gaulish origin; and it is now accepted as Celtic, with the lit. sense of 'one driven about,' a slave; a pp. formation from the prefix embi, or ambi, about; and the Celtic root ag-, to drive, cognate with L. agere, to drive. The verb appears in O. Irish as imm-agim, I drive about, I send about; and the derived sb. is represented in Welsh by amaeth, a husbandman. See Brugmann, ii. § 79; Stokes-Fick, p. 34. ¶ The OHG. ambaht, a servant, whence G. amt, is merely borrowed from Celtic (Kluge). Der. ambassadr-ess. See **Embassy.**

AMBER, a fossil resin; ambergris. (F. – Span. – Arab.) The resin is named from its resemblance to ambergris, a waxlike substance due to the sperm-whale, also called amber in early writers. – ME. aumbre, Prompt. Parv. 1. In Holland's Pliny, b. xxxvii. c. 3, the word means the fossil amber. 2. When Beaumont and Fletcher use the word amber'd in the sense of 'scented' (Custom of the Country, iii. 2. 6), they must refer to ambergris. – F. ambre, 'amber;' Cot. – Span. ambar. – Arab. 'amber, ambergris, a perfume; Palmer's Pers. Dict. col. 433; 'ambar, ambergris, a rich perfume and cordial; Rich. Dict. p. 1031. ¶ Ambergris is the same word, with addition of F. gris, signifying 'gray.' In Milton, P. R. ii. 344, it is called gris amber. The F. gris is a word of German origin, from OHG. gris, gray, used of the hair; cf. G. greis, hoary.

AMBI-, AMB-, prefix. (L.) L. ambi-, about; cf. Gk. ἀμφί, on both sides, whence E. amphi-, prefix. Related to L. ambo, Gk. ἄμφω, both. Cf. AS. ymb, Irish im, about; Skt. abhi, towards.

AMBIDEXTROUS, using both hands. (L.) Sir T. Browne, Vulg. Errors, b. iv. c. 5, § 10, has 'ambidexterous, or right-handed on both sides.' He also uses ambidexters as a plural sb. – L. ambidexter, using both hands equally; not used in classical Latin, and only given by Ducange with a metaphorical sense, viz. as applied to one who is equally ready to deal with spiritual and temporal business. ─ L. *ambi-*, generally shortened to *amb-*; and *dexter*, the right hand. See **Ambi-** and **Dexterous**.

AMBIENT, going about. (L.) Used by Milton, P. L. vi. 481. ─ L. *ambient-*, going about. ─ L. *amb-* (shortened form of *ambi-*), about; and *iens*, going, pres. pt. of *īre*, to go. 1. On the prefix see **Ambi-**. 2. The verb *īre* is from √ EI, to go; cf. Skt. and Zend *i*, to go.

AMBIGUOUS, doubtful. (L.) Sir T. Elyot has *ambiguous*, The Governour, bk. iii. c. 4, § 4. The sb. *ambiguite* (printed *anbiguite*) occurs in the Tale of Beryn, ed. Furnivall, 2577. [The adj. is formed with the suffix *-ous*, which properly represents the F. *-eux*, and L. *-ōsus*, but is also frequently used in place of L. *-us* merely; cf. *pious, sonorous*, &c., from L. *pius, sonōrus*.] ─ L. *ambiguus*, doubtful; lit. driving about. ─ L. *ambigere*, to drive about, go round about. ─ L. *amb-* = *ambi-*, about; and *agere*, to drive. On the prefix, see **Ambi-**. And see **Agent**. Der. *ambiguous-ly*; also *ambigu-it-y*, from L. acc. *ambiguitātem*, nom. *ambiguitās*, doubt.

AMBITION, seeking for preferment. (F. ─ L.) Spelt *ambition* by Sir T. Elyot, The Governour, b. iii. c. 16. § 1; *ambicioun* in Wyclif, Acts, xxv. 23 (earlier version). *Ambicion* also occurs in the Ayenbite of Inwyt, pp. 17, 22. ─ F. *ambition*, given by Cotgrave. ─ L. *ambitiōnem*, acc. of *ambitio*, a going round; esp. used of the canvassing for votes at Rome. ─ L. *ambīre*, supine *ambītum*, to go round, solicit. [Note that L. *ambītio* and *ambitus* retain the short *i* of the supine *ĭtum* of *īre*, the simple verb.] ─ L. *ambi-*, *amb-*, prefix, about; and *īre*, to go. See **Ambi-** and **Ambient**. Der. *ambiti-ous*, *ambiti-ous-ly*.

AMBLE, to go at a pace between a walk and a trot. (F. ─ L.) We find 'fat palfray *amblant*,' i.e. ambling; King Alisaunder, ed. Weber, l. 3462; and see Gower, C. A. i. 210 (bk. ii. 1506). Chaucer has 'wel *ambling*,' C. T. 8265 (E 388); and 'it gooth an *ambel*' = it goes at an easy pace, said of a horse, C. T. 13815 (B 2075); and he calls a lady's horse an *ambler*, Prol. to C. T. 471 (A 469). ─ O.F. *ambler*, to go at an easy pace. ─ L. *ambulāre*, to walk. See **Ambulation**. Der. *ambl-er*, *pre-amble*.

AMBROSIA, food of the gods. (Gk.) In Milton, P. L. v. 57; he frequently uses the adj. *ambrosial*. ─ Gk. ἀμβροσία, the food of the gods; fem. of adj. ἀμβρόσιος. ─ Gk. ἀμβρόσιος, a lengthened form (with suffix *-yo*) of ἄμβροτ-ος, immortal. ─ Gk. ἄ-μβροτος, where ἀ- is the negative prefix, and μβροτός is for *μροτός, lit. 'dead,' earlier form of the word which was afterwards spelt βροτός. See **Mortal**. ¶ The Gk. ἄμβροτος has its exact counterpart in Skt. *a-mṛta-s*, immortal, used in the neuter to denote the beverage of the gods. Southey misspells this word *amreeta*; see his Curse of Kehama, canto xxiv. 9, and note on 'the *amreeta*, or drink of immortality.' Der. *ambrosi-al*, *ambrosi-an*.

AMBRY, AUMBRY, a cupboard. (F. ─ L.) **a.** Nares remarks that *ambry* is a corruption of *almonry*, but this remark only applies to a particular street in Westminster so called. The word in the sense of 'cupboard' has a different origin. **β.** The word is now almost obsolete, except provincially; it is spelt *aumbrie* by Tusser, Five Hundred Points, E. D. S., § 75. 2 (p. 167). ME. *awmery*, *awmebry*, Prompt. Parv. Earlier *almary*, P. Plowman, C. xvii. 88. Clearly a corruption of F. *armarie*, a repository for arms (Burguy), which easily passed into *almarie* (as in Roman de Rou, 4565), *a'm'rie*, and thence into *ambry*, with the usual excrescent *b* after *m*. The OF. *armarie* became later *armaire*, *armoire*; Cotgrave gives both these forms, and explains them by 'a cupboard, ambrie, little press; any hole, box contrived in, or against, a wall,' &c. Hence *ambry* is a doublet of *armory*; and both are to be referred to Late L. *armāria*, a chest or cupboard, esp. a bookcase. Another form is *armārium*, esp. used to denote a repository for *arms*, which is plainly the original sense. ─ L. *arma*, arms. See **Arms**. ¶ It is remarkable that, as the *ambry* in a church was sometimes used as a place of deposit for *alms*, it was popularly connected with *alms* instead of *arms*, and looked upon as convertible with *almonry*.

AMBULATION, walking about. (L.) Used by Sir T. Browne, Vulg. Errors, b. iii. c. 1. § 4; but uncommon. Of the adj. *ambulatory* Rich. gives five examples, one from Bp. Taylor's Great Exemplar, pt. iii. s. 13. Formed with F. suffix *-tion*, but really directly from Latin. ─ L. acc. *ambulātiōnem*, from nom. *ambulātio*, a walking about; from *ambulāre*, to walk about. ─ L. *amb-*, about (see **Ambi-**); and *-ulāre*, allied to Gk. ἀλ-άομαι, I wander, roam; ἄλ-η, a wandering (Prellwitz). Der. *ambula-tory* (from L. *ambulāre*, with suffix *-tōr-ius*). From the same root, *amble*, *per-ambulate*, *pre-amble*. See **Amble**. Also F. *ambul-ance*, a movable hospital, now adopted into English.

AMBUSCADE, an ambush. (Span. ─ Late L.) Often spelt *ambuscado* by Ben Jonson, Every Man in his Humour, ed. Wheatley, ii. 4. 16, and the note. Dryden has *ambuscade*, tr. of Æneid, vi. 698; Richardson, by a misprint, attributes the word to Spenser. ─ Span. *emboscada*, an ambuscade. ─ Span. *emboscado*, placed in ambush, pp. of *emboscar*, to set in ambush. ─ Late L. *imboscāre*; see **Ambush**.

AMBUSH, a hiding in a wood. (F. ─ Late L.) In Shakespeare,

Meas. for Meas. i. 3. 41. A corruption of an older *embush* or *enbush*, which was originally a *verb*, signifying 'to set in ambush.' Rob. of Brunne, in his tr. of P. Langtoft, has *enbussement*, p. 187, *bussement*, p. 242; also the pp. *enbussed*, set in ambush, p. 187, as well as the shortened form *bussed* on the same page. In all these cases, *ss* stands for *sh*, as in Rob. of Gloucester. Gower has *embuisshed*, *embuisschement*, C. A. i. 260, iii. 208 (bk. ii. 3007, bk. vii. 3476). ─ OF. *embuscher*, *embuissier*, to set in ambush. ─ Late L. *imboscāre*, to set in ambush, lit. 'to set in a bush,' still preserved in Ital. *imboscare*. ─ L. *in-*, in (which becomes *im-* before *b*); and Late L. *boscus*, a bush, wood, thicket, whence OF. *bos*, mod. F. *bois*. See **Bush**. Der. *ambush-ment*; and see above.

AMEER, a commander; see **Emir**.

AMELIORATE, to better. (F. ─ L.) Not in early use. Formed with suffix *-ate*; on which see **Abbreviate**. ─ MF. *ameliorer*, to better, improve; see Cotgrave. ─ F. prefix *a-* = L. *ad*; and MF. *meliorer*, to make better, also given by Cotgrave. ─ L. *ad*, to; and Late L. *meliōrāre*, to make better (Ducange), from *melior*, better. See **Meliorate**. Der. *ameliorat-ion*.

AMEN, so be it. (L. ─ Gk. ─ Heb.) Used in the Vulgate version of Matt. vi. 13, &c. ─ Gk. ἀμήν, verily. ─ Heb. *āmēn*, adv. verily, so be it; from adj. *āmēn*, firm, true, faithful; from vb. *āman*, to sustain, support, found, fix, orig. 'to be firm.'

AMENABLE, easy to lead. (F. ─ L.) Spelt *amesnable* by Spenser, View of the State of Ireland (R.); but the *s* is superfluous; printed *ameanable* in the Globe edition, p. 622, col. 2, l. 1. Formed, with the common F. suffix *-able*, from the F. verb. ─ F. *amener*, 'to bring or lead unto;' Cot. Burguy gives the OF. spellings as *amener* and *amenier*. ─ F. *a-*, prefix (L. *ad*); and F. *mener*, to conduct, to drive, Late L. *mināre*, to conduct, to lead from place to place; also, to expel, drive out, chase away; Ducange. The Late L. *mināre* is from L. *mināri*, to threaten, from L. *minæ*, threats. See **Menace**. Der. *amen-abl-y*. From the same root, *de-mean* (1), q. v.

AMEND, to free from faults. (F. ─ L.) ME. *amenden*, to better, repair; Chaucer, C. T. 10511 (F 197); Ancren Riwle, p. 420. Hence *amendement*, Gower, C. A. ii. 373 (bk. v. 7153). ─ OF. *amender* (mod. F. *amender*), to amend, better. ─ L. *ēmendāre*, to free from fault, correct. [For the unusual change from *e* to *a*, see Brachet's Hist. Grammar, sect. 685. xi.] ─ L. *ē* = *ex*, out, away from; and *mendum*, or *menda*, a blemish, fault. On the prefix *ex*, see **Ex-**. Der. *amend-able*, *amend-ment*; also *amends*, q. v. And see **Mend**.

AMENDS, reparation. (F. ─ L.) ME. pl. *amendes*, *amendis*, common in the phr. *to maken amendes*, to make amends; Will. of Palerne, 3919; Ayenbite of Inwyt, pp. 113, 148. ─ AF. *amendes*, Liber Custumarum, p. 223; pl. of OF. *amende*, reparation, satisfaction, a penalty by way of recompense. ─ OF. *amender*, to amend. See **Amend**.

AMENITY, pleasantness. (F. ─ L.) The adj. *amen*, pleasant, occurs in Lancelot of the Laik, ed. Skeat, l. 999; spelt *amene* in a quotation from Lydgate in Halliwell. Sir T. Browne has *amenity*, Vulg. Errors, b. vii. c. 6. § 3. ─ MF. *amenité*, 'amenity, pleasantness;' Cot. ─ L. acc. *amoenitātem*, from nom. *amoenitās*, pleasantness. ─ L. *amoenus*, pleasant; allied to *amāre*, to love. See **Amorous**.

AMERCE, to fine. (F. ─ L.) ME. *amercien*, *amercen*, to fine, mulct. 'And thowgh ye mowe *amercy* hem, late [let] mercy be tax-oure;' P. Plowman, B. vi. 40. '*Amercyn* in a corte or lete, *amercio*;' Prompt. Parv. p. 11. ─ AF. *amercier*, to fine; not used in OF.; see Year-books of Edw. I, 1338-9, p. 5. The Late L. form is *amerciāre*, to fine (Ducange); observe the citation of *amercio* above. Due to the OF. phrase *a merci*, at the mercy of (the court); whence *estre a merci*, to be at the mercy of, and *estre amercié*, to be at the mercy of, to be fined; and hence *amercier*, actively, to fine; see Britton. ─ L. *ad mercēdem*, orig. 'for a reward;' but L. *mercēs* had acquired many other senses; as, hire, wages; also reward, in the sense of punishment; also detriment, cost, trouble, pains. In late times, it acquired also the sense of 'mercy, pity,' as noted by Ducange, s. v. *Merces*. See further under **Mercy**. ¶ The etymology has been confused by Blount, in his Law Dictionary, s. v. *Amerciament*, and by other writers, who have supposed the F. *merci* to be connected with L. *misericordia* (with which it has no connexion whatever), and who have strained their definitions and explanations accordingly. Der. *amerce-ment*, *amercia-ment*; the latter being a Latinised form.

AMETHYST, a precious stone. (L. ─ Gk.) 'As for the *amethyst*, as well as the herb as the stone of that name, they who think that both the one and the other is (*sic*) so called because they withstand drunkennesse, miscount themselves, and are deceived;' Holland, tr.of Plutarch's Morals, p. 560. Boyle, Works, vol. i. p. 513, uses the adj. *amethystine*. ─ L. *amethystus*, used by Pliny, 37. 9. [Note: directly from the Latin, the F. form being *ametiste* in Cotgrave. However, the form *amatiste*, from the Old French, is found in the 13th century; OE. Miscellany, ed. Morris, p. 98, l. 171.] ─ Gk. ἀμέθυστος, sb. a remedy against drunkenness; an amethyst, from its supposed virtue in that way. — Gk. ἀμέθυστος, adj. not drunken. — Gk. ἀ-, privative; and μεθύειν, to be drunken, from μέθυ, strong drink, wine, cognate with E. mead. See Mead (1). Der. ame hyst-ine.

AMIABLE, friendly; worthy of love. (F. — L.) 'She was so amiable and tree;' Rom. Rose, 1226. 'The amiable tonge is the tree of lyf;' Chaucer, Pers. Tale, De Ira (I 629). — OF. amiable, friendly; also lovable, by confusion with aimable (L. amābilis). — L. amicābilis, friendly, amicable. — L. amīcā-re, to make friendly; with suffix -bili-, used in forming adjectives from verbs. — L. amicus, a friend; prop. an adj., friendly, loving. — L. amāre, to love. See **Amorous**. Der. amiable-ness, amiabl-y; and abil-i-ty, formed by analogy with amicability, &c. Amicabili y and aminability are doublets.

AMICABLE, friendly. (L.) In Levins, ed. 1570. Used by Bp. Taylor, Peacemaker (...); he uses amicableness in the same work. [Formed with suffix -ble as if French, but really from Latin.] — L. amicābilis, friendly; whence the OF. amiable. Thus amicable and amiable are doublets. See **Amiable**. Der. amicabl-y, amicable-ness.

AMICE (1), a rectangular piece of white linen, variously worn by priests. (F. — L.) ME. amyse, Wyclif, Isa. xxii. 17 (where the Latin has amictum); also amyte, Wyclif, Heb. i. 12 (earlier version). — OF. amis, amit (Burguy). — L. amictus, a covering (amit being from the acc. amictum). — L. amictus, pp. of amicire, to throw round. — L. am- (amb-), around; and iacere, to cast. Cf. MF. amict, 'an amict, or amice;' part of a massing priest's habit;' Cot.

AMICE (2), a hood for pilgrims, &c. (F. — Span. — Teut.?) 'Came forth, with pilgrim steps, in amice gray;' Milton, P. R. iv. 427. Confused with amice (1), but really from OF. aumuce (F. aumusse), 'an ornament of furre worne by canons,' Cot.; also 'a furred hood;' see Fairholt's Glossary, s. v. almuce. — Span. almucio, 'an ornament of furrs, worn by canons,' Pineda; where al is the Arab. def. article. — G. mütse, a cap (cf. Lowl. Sc. mutch). ¶ But some think that G. mütse is from Late L. almucia. Cf. Ital. mozzetta, a rochet (Torriano); Port. murça, 'a garment lined with fur worn by canons.'

AMID, AMIDST, in the middle of. (E.) Amidst is common in Milton, P. L. i. 791; &c. He also uses amid. Shak. also has both forms. α. Amidst is not found in earlier English, and the final t is merely excrescent (as often after s), as in whilst, amongst, from the older forms whiles, amonges. β. The ME. forms are amiddes, P. Plowman, B. xiii. 82; in middes, Pricke of Conscience, 2938; amidde, Ayenbite of Inwyt, p. 143; on midden, OE. Homilies, i. 87. γ. Of these, the correct type is the earliest, viz. on midden; whence on-midde, a-midde were formed by the usual loss of final n, and the change of on to a, as in abed, afoot, a le p. δ. The form amiddes was produced by adding the adverbial suffix -s, properly the sign of a gen. case, but commonly used to form adverbs. — AS. on middan, in the middle; see examples in Grein, ii. 249, s. v. mi e. Here on is the prep. (mod. E. on), used, as often elsewhere, with the sense of 'in;' and middan is the dat. case of midde, sb. the middle, orig. the nom. fem. of the adj. mid or midd, middle, cognate with L. medius. See **Middle**.

AMISS, adv. wrongly. (Scand.) α. In later authors awkwardly used as a sb.; thus 'urge not my amiss;' Shak. Sonn. 151. But properly an adverb, as in 'That he ne dooth or seith somtyme amis;' Chaucer, C. T. 11092 (F 780). The mistake was due to the fact that misse was, without a-, meant 'an error' in early times, as will appear. β. Ami s stands for ME. on misse, lit. in error, where on (from AS. on) has the usual sense of 'in,' and passes into the form a-, as in so many other cases; cf. abed, afoot, asleep. γ. ME. amis or on misse may have been taken immediately from the Icel. phrase ā mis, amiss; from Icel. ā (= AS. on) and mis, adv., wrongly. Or we may explain misse as the dat. case from nom. misse, a disyllabic word, not used as a sb. in AS., but borrowed from the Icel. missa, a loss; also used with the notion of 'error' in composition, as in Icel. mis-taka, to take in error, whence E. mistake. The ME. misse hence acquired the sense of 'guilt,' 'offence,' as in 'to mende my misse,' to repair my error; Will. of Palerne, 532. See **Miss**.

AMITY, friendship. (F. — L.) Udal, Pref. to St. Marke (near the end), has amytie. Skelton has amyte, Why Come Ye Nat to Courte, 371. — F. amitié, explained by Cotgrave to mean 'amity, friendship,' &c.; OF. amiste, amisted [= Span. amistad, Ital. amistà (for amistate)]. — Late L. *amicitātem, acc. of *amicitās, friendship, a vulgar form, not recorded by Ducange, but formed by analogy with mendicitās from mendicus, antiquitās from antiquus. — L. amicus, friendly. — L. amāre, to love. See **Amiable, Amorous**. ¶ It is impossible to derive the old Romance forms from L. amicitia.

AMMONIA, an alkali. (L. — Gk. — Egypt.) A modern word, adopted as a contraction of sal ammoniac, L. sal ammōniacum, rock-salt; common in old chemical treatises, and still more so in treatises on alchemy. [Chaucer speaks of sal armoniak, C. T., G 798, 824; but this is a false form.] — Gk. ἀμμωνιακόν, sal ammoniac, rock-salt; Dioscorides. — Gk. ἀμμωνιάς, Libyan. — Gk. ἄμμων, the Libyan Zeus-

Ammon; known to be an Egyptian word; Herodotus, ii. 42; and Smith, Dict. of the Bible, s. v. Amon. It is said that sal ammoniac was first obtained near the temple of Jupiter Ammon.

AMMONITE, a kind of fossil shell. (Gk. — Egypt.) Modern; first in 1758. Formed by adding the suffix -ite to the name Ammon. The fossil is sometimes called by the L. name of cornu Ammonis, the horn of Ammon, because it much resembles a closely twisted ram's horn, and was fancifully likened to the horns of Jupiter Ammon, who was represented as a man with the horns of a ram. See above.

AMMUNITION, store for defence. (F. — L.) Used by Bacon, Advice to Sir G. Villiers (R.); and by Milton, Samson, 1277. From MF. ammunition, a soldiers' corruption of munition, 'victuals for an army,' Cot.; due to substituting l'amunition for la munition (Littré). — L. acc. mūnitiōnem, from mūnitio, a defence, a defending. — L. mūnire, to defend. See **Munition**.

AMNESTY, a pardon of offenders; lit. a forgetting of offences. (F. — L. — Gk.) Used in the L. form amnestia by Howell, b. iii. letter 6 (1647). Barrow has amnesty, vol. iii. serm. 41. — F. amnestie, which Cotgrave explains by 'forgetfulness of things past.' — L. amnēstia, a Latinised form of the Gk. word. [Ducange gives amnescia, but this is an error; for t is constantly mistaken for c in MSS., and frequently so printed.] — Gk. ἀμνηστία, a forgetfulness, esp. of wrong; hence, an amnesty. — Gk. ἄμνηστος, forgotten, unremembered. — Gk. ἀ-, privative; and μνάομαι, I remember; from a stem mnā, by gradation from a root men; cf. L. me-min-i, I remember. — √MEN, to think; cf. Skt. man, to think.

AMONG, AMONGST, amidst. (E.) α. The form amongst, like amidst, is not very old, and has assumed an additional final t, such as is often added after s; cf. whilst, amidst, from the older forms whiles, amiddes. Amongist occurs in Torrent of Portugal, l. 2027 [2127]; but I suppose it does not occur earlier than the fifteenth century. β. The usual form is amonges, as in P. Plowman, B. v. 129; amonge is also common, id. v. 169. Earlier, the commonest form is among, Ancren Riwle, p. 158. γ. Amonges is formed by adding the usual adverbial suffix -es, properly a genitive form, and amonge by adding the adverbial suffix -e, also common, properly a dative form. — AS. onmang, prep. among, Levit. xxiv. 10; the forms on gemang (John, iv. 31) and gemang (Mark, iii. 3) also occur, the last of the three being commonest. δ. Thus the prefix is AS. on, and the full form onmang, used as a preposition. Like most prepositions, it originated with a substantive, viz. AS. (ge)mang, a crowd, assembly, lit. a mixture; so that on mang(e) or on gemang(e) meant 'in a crowd.' Allied to AS. mengan, mængan, to mix; Grein, ii. 231. See **Mingle**.

AMOROUS, full of love. (F. — L.) Gower has amorous, C. A. i. 89 (bk. i. 1414); it also occurs in the Romaunt of the Rose, 83. — OF. amoros, mod. F. amoureux. — Late L. amōrōsus, full of love; Ducange. Formed with the common L. suffix -ōsus from amōr-, stem of amor, love. — L. amāre, to love. Der. amorous-ly, amorous-ness. Also F. amour, love (now used in Eng.), from L. amōrem, acc. case of amor, love.

AMORPHOUS, formless. (Gk.) In Bailey (1731). Formed from Gk. ἀ-, privative; and Gk. μορφή, shape, form.

AMORT, inanimate, spiritless. (F. — L.) 'What, all amort?' Shak. 1 Hen. VI, iii. 2. 124. From F. à la mort, to the death; turned into E. all amort, as if amort were the F. à mort. — L. a, to; illam, acc. fem. of ille, he; mortem, acc. of mors, death. See **Mortal**.

AMOUNT, to mount up to. (F. — L.) ME. amounten, to mount up, come up to, esp. in reckoning. Chaucer, C. T. 3899, 4989 (A 3901, B 569); Rob. of Glouc. p. 497, l. 10214. Amuntet, ascends, Old Eng. Miscellany, ed. Morris, p. 28. — OF. amonter, to amount to. — OF. a mont, towards or to a mountain, to a large heap. [The adv. amont is also common, in the sense of 'uphill,' 'upward,' and is formed by joining a with mont.] — L. ad montem, lit. to a mountain; where montem is the acc. case of mons, a mountain. See **Mount, Mountain**. Der. amount, sb.

AMPERSAND, a corruption of 'and per se, and,' the old way of spelling and naming the character & ; i.e. '& by itself = and.' (Hybrid; E., L., and E.) Common in E. dialects. So, in ME., we have A per se, A by itself; Henrysoun, Test. of Creseide, 78.

AMPHI-, prefix. (Gk.) The strict sense is 'on both sides.' — Gk. ἀμφί, on both sides; also, around. + L. ambi, amb-, on both sides, around; see **Ambi-**, where other cognate forms are given. Der. amph'i-bious, amphi-brach, amphi-theatre.

AMPHIBIOUS, living both on land and in water. (Gk.) In Sir T. Browne's Vulg. Errors, bk. iii. c. 13. § 8. From amphibi-a, pl., amphibious animals; with suffix -ous. — Gk. ἀμφίβιος, living a double life, i.e. both on land and water. — Gk. ἀμφί, here used in the sense of 'double;' and βίος, life. See **Amphi-** and **Biology**.

AMPHIBRACH, a foot in prosody. (Gk.) Puttenham has amphibrachus; Eng. Poesie, bk. ii. c. 13 (14). A name given, in prosody, to a foot composed of a short syllable on each side of a long one (◡–◡). — Gk. ἀμφίβραχυς, the same. — Gk. ἀμφί, on both sides;

and βραχύς, short; cognate with L. *breuis*, short, whence E. *brief*. See **Amphi-** and **Brief**.

AMPHISBÆNA, a fabled serpent, with a head at each end, and able to proceed in either direction. (L.—Gk.) In Milton, P. L. x. 524.—L. *amphisbæna*.—Gk. ἀμφίσβαινα.—Gk. ἀμφίς, both ways; and βαίνειν, to go.

AMPHITHEATRE, an oval theatre. (Gk.) Puttenham has the pl. *amphitheaters*; Eng. Poesie, bk. i. c. 17. From Gk. ἀμφιθέατρον, a theatre with seats all round the arena. [Properly neuter from ἀμφιθέατρος, i.e. seeing all round.]—Gk. ἀμφί, on both sides; and θέατρον, a theatre, place for seeing shows, from Gk. θεάομαι, I see.

AMPHORA, a two-handled jar. (L.—Gk.) 'A glas clepid *amphora*;' Book of Quinte Essence, ab. 1465, ed. Furnivall, p. 5. l. 4.—L. *amphora*.—Gk. ἀμφορεύς, short for ἀμφιφορεύς, a two-handled jar.—Gk. ἀμφί, on both sides; φορεύς, a bearer, from φέρειν, to bear. See **Amphi-** and **Bear** (1).

AMPLE, full, large. (F.—L.) Used by Hall, Hen. VIII, an. 31. § 23; Shak. K. Lear, i. 1. 82. [Fox and Udal use the obsolete derivative *ampliate*, and Burnet has *ampliation*; from L. *ampliāre*, to augment.]—F. *ample*, which Cotgrave explains by 'full, ample, wide, large,' &c.—L. *amplus*, large, spacious. Bréal derives L. *amplus* from *am-*, *amb-*, prefix, 'about;' and *-plus*, as in *du-plus*, double (Gk. δι-πλός). See **Ambi-** and **Double**. **Der.** *ampli-tude*; *ampli-fy*, K. Lear, v. 3. 206 (F. *amplifier*, from L. *amplificāre*); *ampli-fic-at-ion*; see *amplifier* and *amplification* in Cotgrave. Also *ampl-y*, *ample-ness*.

AMPUTATE, to cut off round about, prune. (L.) Sir T. Browne has *amputat on*, Vulg. Errors, b. iv. c. 5. § 1. On the suffix *-ate*, see **Abbreviate**.—L. *amputāre*, to cut off round about, pp. *amputātus*.—L. *am-*, short for *amb-*, *ambi-*, round about (see **Ambi-**); and L. *putāre*, to cleanse, also to lop or prune trees, from L. *putus*, pure, clean; from the same root as **Pure**, q.v. **Der.** *amputat-ion*.

AMUCK, AMOK, a term applied to mad rage. (Malay.) Only in phr. 'to run amuck,' where *am ck* is all one word; yet Dryden has 'runs *an* Indian *muck*,' Hind and Panther, iii. 1188. To run *amuck* = to run about in a mad rage.—Malay *āmuq*, 'rushing in a state of frenzy to the commission of indiscriminate murder;' Marsden, Malay Dict.

AMULET, a charm against evil. (F.—L.) Used by Sir T. Browne, Vulg. Errors, b. ii. c. 5, part 3.—F. *amulette*, 'a counter-charm;' Cot.—L. *amulētum*, a talisman, esp. one hung round the neck (Pliny). The suggestion that this is a word of Arabic origin is now commonly abandoned.

AMUSE, to engage, divert. (F.—L.) Milton has *amus'd*, P.L. vi. 581, 623; and see Cowley, To the Royal Soc., l. 20.—F. *amuser*, 'to amuse, to make to muse or think of; wonder or gaze at; to put into a dump; to stay, hold, or delay from going forward by discourse, questions, or any other *amusements*;' Cot.—F. *a-*, prefix (L. *ad*), at; and OF. *muser*, to stare, gaze fixedly, like a simpleton, whence E. *muse*, verb, used by Chaucer, C. T., B 1033. See **Muse**, v. **Der.** *amus-ing*, *amus-ing-ly*, *amuse-ment*; also *amus-ive*, used in Thomson's Seasons, Spring, 216.

AMYGDALOID, almond-shaped. (Gk.) See **Almond**.

AN, A, the indef. article. (E.) The final *n* is occasionally preserved before a consonant in Layamon's Brut, which begins with the words '*An* preost wes on leoden,' where the later text has '*A* prest was in londe.' This shows that the loss of *n* before a consonant was taking place about A. D. 1200.—AS. *ān*, often used as the indef. article; see examples in Grein, i. 30; but properly having the sense of 'one,' being the very word from which mod. E. *one* is derived. *An* and *a* represent the unstressed forms of *one*. See **One**.

AN-, A-, negative prefix. (Gk.) Gk. ἀν-, ἀ-, negative prefix. Cognate with the Skt. *an-*, *a-*, L. *in-*, G. and E. *un-*, OIrish *an-*, all negative prefixes. Brugm. i. § 432. See **Un-**. The form *an-* occurs in several words in English, e.g. *an-archy*, *an-ecdote*, *an-eroid*, *an-odyne*, *an-omaly*, *an-onymous*. The form *a-* is still commoner; e.g. *a-byss*, *a-chromatic*, *a-maranth*, *a-sylum*, *a-symptote*, *a-tom*.

AN, if. (E.) See **And**.

ANA-, AN-, prefix. (Gk.) It appears as *an-* in *an-eurism*, a kind of tumour. The usual form is *ana-*, as in *ana-logy*, *ana-baptist*. From Gk. ἀνά, upon, on, up; also back, again; it has the same form *ana* in Gothic, and is cognate with E. *on*. See **On**.

ANA, ANNA, the sixteenth part of a rupee. (Hindustani.) Hind. *āna* (written *ānā* in Skt.), the sixteenth of a rupee, commonly, but incorrectly, written *anna*. Also used as a measure, to express a sixteenth part of a thing; H. H. Wilson, Gloss. of Indian Terms, p. 24. Given as *ānā*; Forbes, Hind. Dict.

ANABAPTIST, one who baptises again. (Gk.) Used by Sir T. More, Works, p. 656 g. Formed by prefixing the Gk. ἀνά, again, to *baptist*. See **Ana-** and **Baptist**. So also *ana-baptism*. ¶ The sect of *Anabaptists* arose in Germany about 1521 (Haydn).

ANACHRONISM, an error in chronology. (Gk.) Used by Walpole; Anecd. of Painting, vol. i. c. 2. § 32. From Gk. ἀναχρονισμός, an anachronism.—Gk. ἀναχρονίζειν, to refer to a wrong time.—Gk.

ἀνά, up, sometimes used in composition in the sense of 'backwards;' and χρόνος, time. See **Ana-** and **Chronic**.

ANACONDA, a large serpent. (Cingalese.) Now used of a S. American boa, but previously applied to a large snake in Ceylon; see the account in Yule; whose etymology, however, is incorrect. The true Sinhalese (Cingalese) word is *henakandayā*, a name at first applied to the whip-snake, and transferred to some large serpents by mistake. From *hena*, 'lightning,' and *kanda*, 'stem;' with suffix *-yā*. See N. and Q., 8 S. xii. 123; 9 S. viii. 80.

ANÆMIA, bloodlessness. (L.—Gk.) Modern. A Latinised form of Gk. ἀναιμία, want of blood.—Gk. ἀν-, negative prefix; and αἷμα, blood.

ANÆSTHETIC, adj., rendering persons insensible to pain. (Gk.) Modern. Formed by prefixing the Gk. ἀν-, cognate with E. *un-*, negative prefix, to Gk. αἰσθητικός, perceptive, full of perception. See **Æsthetics**. Also used as a sb.

ANAGRAM, a change in a word due to transposition of letters. (F.—L.—Gk.) Ben Jonson, in his Masque of Hymen, speaks of 'IUNO, whose great name Is UNIO in the *anagram*.'—F. *anagramme* (Cotgrave).—L. *anagramma*, borrowed from Gk.—Gk. ἀνάγραμμα, an anagram.—Gk. ἀνά, up, which is also used in a *distributive* sense; and γράμμα, a written character, letter, from Gk. γράφειν, to write, originally to cut, scratch marks; allied to E. *carve*. See **Graphic**. **Der.** *anagramm-at-ic-al*, *anagramm-at-ic-al-ly*, *anagramm-at-ist*. ¶ *Examples of anagrams*. Gk. Ἀρσινόη, Arsinoe, transposed to ἴον Ἥρας, Hera's violet. L. *Galenus*, Galen, transposed to *angelus*, an angel. E. *John Bunyan*, who transposed his name to *Nu hony in a B*!

ANALOGY, proportion, correspondence. (F.—L.—Gk.) Tyndal has *analogie*, Works, p. 473; so in Elyot, The Governour, b. ii. c. 4. § 2.—F. *analogie*; Cot.—L. *analogia*.—Gk. ἀναλογία, equality of ratios, correspondence, analogy.—Gk. ἀνά, up, upon, throughout; and *-λογία*, made by adding the suffix *-yā* (= Gk. *-ια*) to the stem of λόγ-ος, a word, a statement, account, proportion, from the second grade (λογ-) of Gk. λέγ-ειν, to speak. See **Logic**. **Der.** *analog-ic-al*, *analog-ic-al-ly*, *analog-ise*, *analog-ism*, *analog-ist*, *analog-ous*; also *analogue* (F. *analogue*, prop. an adj. signifying *analogous*, from Gk. adj. ἀνάλογος, proportionate, conformable).

ANALYSE, to resolve into parts. (F.—Gk.) Sir T. Browne, Hydriotaphia, c. 3. § 18, says, 'what the sun compoundeth, fire *analyzeth*, not transmuteth.' Ben Jonson has *analytic*, Poetaster, A. v. sc. 1. 134. *Analysis* occurs in Kirke's Argument to Spenser's Shep. Kal. § 2. Cotgrave gives no related word in French, and perhaps the F. *analyser* is later. Most likely the word *analytic* was borrowed directly from the Gk. ἀναλυτικός, and the verb to *analyse* may easily have been formed directly from the F. sb. *analyse*, or Late L. *analysis*, i. e. Gk. ἀνάλυσις, a loosening, resolving.—Gk. ἀναλύειν, to loosen, undo, resolve.—Gk. ἀνα, back; and λύειν, to loosen. See **Lose**. **Der.** *analys-t*; also (from *analytic*) *analytic-al*, *analytic-al-ly*.

ANANAS, the pine-apple. (Port.—Brazil.) Thomson has *anána*, with wrong form and accent; Summer, 685.—Port. *ananás*; Vieyra, p. 284 (Span. *ananas*, Pineda).—Guarani *anānā*, the name of the fruit; that of the plant is *nānā*; in La Plata, both fruit and plant are called *ananá* (Granada). ¶ The Peruv. name was *achupalla*.

ANAPEST, ANAPÆST, the name of a foot in prosody. (L.—Gk.) In Puttenham, Eng. Poesie, bk. ii. c. 13 (14).—L. *anapæstus*.—Gk. ἀνάπαιστος, struck back, rebounding; because the foot is the *reverse* of a dactyl.—Gk. ἀναπαίειν, to strike back or again.—Gk. ἀνά, and παίειν, to strike. ¶ An anapest is marked ∪ ∪ −, the reverse of the dactyl, or − ∪ ∪.

ANARCHY, want of government in a state. (F.—L.—Gk.) Milton has *anarch*, P. L. ii. 988; and *anarchy*, P. L. ii. 896.—F. *anarchie*, 'an anarchy, a commonwealth without a head or governour;' Cot.—L. *anarchia*.—Gk. ἀναρχία, a being ἄναρχος, without head or chief; from Gk. ἀν- (E. *un-*) and ἀρχός, a ruler, from Gk. ἄρχειν, to rule, to be the first. See **Arch-**. **Der.** *anarch-ic*, *anarch-ic-al*, *anarch-ism*, *anarch-ist*.

ANATHEMA, a curse. (L.—Gk.) Bacon, Essay on Goodness, refers to *anathema* as used by St. Paul.—L. *anathema*, in the Vulgate version of Rom. ix. 3.—Gk. ἀνάθεμα, lit. a thing devoted; hence, a thing devoted to evil, accursed.—Gk. ἀνατίθημι, I devote.—Gk. ἀνά, up; and τίθημι, I lay, place, put. Cf. **Theme**. **Der.** *anathemat-ise* (from stem ἀναθεματ- of sb. ἀνάθεμα) in Sir T. Herbert's Travels, ed. 1665, p. 348: from MF. *anathematiser*, Cot.

ANATOMY, the art of dissection. (F.—L.—Gk.) *Anatomy*, in old writers, commonly means 'a skeleton,' as being a thing on which anatomy has been performed; see Shak. Com. Errors, v. 238. Gascoigne has a poem on The *Anatomye* of a Lover.—F. *anatomie*, 'anatomy; a section of, and looking into, all parts of the body; also, an anatomy, or carkass cut up;' Cot.—L. *anatomia*.—Gk. ἀνατομία, of which a more classical form is ἀνατομή, dissection.—Gk. ἀνατέμνειν, to cut up, cut open.—Gk. ἀνά, up; and τέμνειν (second grade τομ-), to cut. See **Tome**. **Der.** *anatom-ic-al*, *anatom-ise*, *anatom-ist*.

ANCESTOR, a predecessor, forefather. (F.—L.) ME. *ancessour, ancestre, auncestre.* Chaucer has *auncestres,* C. T. 6742 (D 1160). *Ancestree,* Rob. of Brunne's tr. of Langtoft, p. 9; *accessoure,* id. p. 177; from OF. *ancestre,* nom. and *ancessour,* acc., of the same sb. β. Thus OF. *ancestre* represents L. *an'tecessor,* nom.; and OF. *ancessour* is from *antecessōrem,* acc. case of *anteces or,* a fore-goer. — L. *ante,* before; and *cēdere,* pp. *cessus,* to go. See Cede. Der. *ancestr-al, ancestr-y, ancestr-ess.*

ANCHOR, a hooked iron instrument for holding a ship in its place. (L.—Gk.) ME. *anker,* Havelok, 521. AS. *ancor,* Grein, i. 3. — L. *ancora;* sometimes illspelt *anchora,* which is imitated in the mod. E. form. — Gk. ἄγκυρα, an anchor; Max Müller, Lectures, i. 108, note; 8th ed. Orig. a bent hook, and allied to Gk. ἀγκών, a bend; also to Skt. *añch,* to bend. From √ANQ, to bend, curve; Brugm. i. § 633. See Angle, a hook. Der. *anchor,* verb, *anchor-age.*

ANCHORET, ANCHORITE, a recluse, hermit. (F.—Late L.—Gk.) The former is the better spelling. ME. has the form *ancre,* which is rather common, and used by Wyclif, Langland, and others; esp. in the phrase *Ancren Riwle,* i. e. the rule of (female) anchorets, the title of a work written early in the 13th century. Shak. has *anchor,* Hamlet, iii. 2. 229. This ME. word is modified from AS. *ancra,* or *ancer,* a hermit. β. The AS. *ancer-lif,* i. e. 'hermit-life,' is used to translate the L. *uīta anachōrētica* in Beda's Eccl. Hist. iv. 28; and the word *ancer* is no native word, but a mere adaptation of Late L. *anachōrēta,* a hermit, recluse. γ. The more modern form *anchoret,* which occurs in Burton's Anat. of Melan., pt. i. s. 2. m. 2. subs. 6. § 3, is from the French. — MF. *anachorete,* m. 'the hermit called an ankrosse [corruption of *ankress,* a female *anker* or anchoret] or anchorite;' Cot. — Late L. *anachōrēta,* a recluse. — Gk. ἀναχωρητής, a recluse, lit. one who has retired from the world. — Gk. ἀναχωρεῖν, to retire. — Gk. ἀνά, back; and χωρέειν, χωρεῖν, to withdraw, make room, from χῶρος, space, room; related to χωρίς, asunder, apart, and to χῆρος, bereft. The form of the root is GHE, GHŌ. See Prellwitz.

ANCHOVY, a small fish. (Span.) Formerly written *anchove.* Shak. has *anchoues,* 1 Hen. IV, ii. 4. 588 (qu. of 1596). Burton, Anatomy of Melancholy, speaks of 'sausages, *anchoues,* tobacco, caveare;' p. 106, ed. 1827. — Span. (and Port.) *anchova.* ¶ Remoter origin uncertain. Mahn (in Webster) says 'a word of Iberian origin, lit. a dried or pickled fish, from Biscayan *antzua, anchua, anchuva,* dry.' I find the Basque forms *anchóa, ánchua, ánchova,* signifying 'anchovy,' in the Dict. François-Basque by M.-H.-L. Fabre. Again, in the Diccionaria Trilingue del padre Manuel de Larramendi, in Spanish, Basque, and Latin, I find: 'Seco, aplicado á los pechos de la muger, *antzua, antzutua,* L. *siccus,*' i. e. dry, applied to a woman's breasts; Basque *antzua, antzutua,* L. *siccus.* Perhaps Mahn's suggestion is correct.

ANCIENT (1), old. (F.—L.) Skelton has *aunciently,* Works, ed. Dyce, i. 7. The ME. form is *auncyen,* Mandeville, p. 93; thus the final *t* is excrescent, as in *tyrant.* — OF. *ancien* (mod. F. *ancien*), old; cognate with Ital. *anziano,* Span. *anciano.* — Late L. *antiānus,* old; Ducange. Formed, with L. suffix *-ānus,* from L. *ante,* before. See Ante-. Der. *ancient-ly, ancient-ness.*

ANCIENT (2), a banner, standard-bearer. (F.—L.) In Shak. 1 Hen. IV, iv. 2. 34; cf. Oth. i. 1. 33. The form of the word is due to confusion with *ancient* (1), but it really represents the MF. *enseigne,* m. 'an ensigne, auncient, standard-bearer,' Cot.; closely related to MF. *enseigne,* f., an ensign, standard. This explains the twofold sense. See Ensign.

ANCILLARY, subservient. (L.) In Blackstone, Comment. iii. 7. § 19. — L. *ancillār-is,* belonging to a maid-servant. — L. *ancilla,* a maid, dimin. of *ancula,* a fem. dimin. of early L. *ancus* (f. *anca*), a servant.

ANCLE; see Ankle.

AND, copulative conjunction. (E.) Common from the earliest times. AS. *and,* also written *ond;* by-form, *end.*+O. Fries. *ande, and, an; end, en;* Du. *en;* Icel. *enda,* if, even if, moreover (rather differently used, but the same word or closely related); OHG. *anti, enti, inti, unti;* mod. G. *und.* Teut. types, **andi,* conj., **anda,* prep.; see N.E.D. The latter is the same as the AS. prefix *and-* (occurring in *along* and *answer*) and the Gothic prefix *and-,* which answer to the Gk. ἄντα, over against, and are clearly related to the L. *ante,* before, Gk. ἀντί, over against, Skt. *anti,* a Vedic form, equivalent to Gk. ἀντί, over against; (see *antika,* vicinity, in Benfey's Skt. Dict. p. 28.) This sense of 'over against' is fairly well preserved in G. *entgegen,* and in the AS. *andswarian,* E. *an-swer;* and from this sense to its use as a copulative conjunction is an easy step. See Answer. 2. The use of *and* to mean 'if' arose from a peculiar use of the conjunction, and is prob. independent of Icel. *enda,* if, but parallel in development. It occurs in Havelok; as: '*And* thou wile my conseyl tro, Ful wel shal ich with the do;' i. e. if you will trust my counsel, I will do very well by you; l. 2862. 3. In order to differentiate the senses, i. e. to mark off the two meanings of *and* more readily, it became at last usual to drop the final *d* when the word was used in the sense of 'if;'

a use very common in Skakespeare. Thus Shakespeare's *an* is nothing but another use of the common word *and.* When the force of *an* grew misty, it was reduplicated by the addition of 'if;' so that *an if,* really meaning 'if-if,' is of common occurrence. Neither is there anything remarkable in the use of *and if* as another spelling of *an if;* and it has been preserved in this form in a well-known passage in the Bible: 'But *and if,*' Matt. xxiv. 48. **4.** If the Skt. *anti* is allied to *anta-s,* 'end,' there is an etymological connexion with *end.* See End.

ANDANTE, slow, slowly. (Ital.) A musical term. Borrowed from Ital. *andante,* adj. going; sb. a moderate movement. It is properly the pres. part. of the verb *andare,* to go; which is of unknown origin.

ANDIRON, a kitchen fire-dog. (F.—L.?) The ME. forms are numerous, as *anderne, aunderne, aundirne, aundire, awndyern,* &c. In the Prompt. Parv. p. 19, we have '*Awnderne, awndyryn, awndyrn,* andena, ipoporgium.' In Wright's Vocabularies, vol. i. p. 171, we have *Aundyrne·,* les chenes;' and at p. 197, '*Awndyren,* andena.' [It is clear that the ending -*iron* is a corruption, upon English soil, in order to give the word some sort of sense.] The form *aundyre* comes very near to the original French. — OF. *andier* (mod. F. *landier,* i. e. *l'andier,* the article being prefixed as in *lierre,* ivy, from L. *hedera*), a fire-dog. ¶ The remoter origin is obscure; but it may be noted that the Late L. forms are numerous, viz. *andasium,* a fire-dog, prop for supporting the logs, and, with the same sense, *andedus, andena* (quoted above in the extract from the Prompt. Parv.), *anderius.* The F. form corresponds with the last of these; with *andena* cf. OF. *andein* and the mod. Burgundian *andain,* an andiron (Mignard). The form *andasium* corresponds to Span. *andas,* a frame or bier on which to carry a person; cf. Portuguese *andas,* 'a bier, or rather, the two poles belonging to it,' Vieyra; also Port. *andor,* 'a bier to carry images in a procession, a sort of sedan;' id. Possibly related to L. *amitem,* acc. of *ames,* a pole, esp. a pole for bearing a litter (Lewis). See Körting, § 595. **2.** No certain origin of this word has been given. We may, however, easily see that the E. *iron* formed, originally, no part of it. We can guess, perhaps, how it came to be added, viz. by confusion with the AS. *brand-īsen,* lit. 'a brand-iron,' which had the same meaning, and became, at a later time, not only *brondiron* but *brondyre.*

ANECDOTE, a story in private life. (F.—L.—Gk.) Used by Sterne, Serm. 5. § 24. '*Anecdots,* treatises or pieces that never were published;' Glossographia Anglicana Nova, ed. 1719. — F. *anecdo e,* f., not in Cotgrave. — Gk. ἀνέκδοτα, neut. pl. (used as fem. sing.), from ἀνέκδοτος, unpublished; so that our word means properly 'an unpublished story,' 'a piece of gossip among friends.' — Gk. ἀν- (E. *un-*); and ἔκδοτος, given out, from ἐκ, out, and δίδωμι, I give; from the same root as E. **Donation,** q. v. Der. *anecdot-al, anecdot-ic-al.*

ANEMONE, the name of a flower. (Gk.) In Thomson, Spring, 536. It means the 'wind-flower;' in Greek ἀνεμώνη, the accent in E. being now placed on *e* instead of *o.* — Gk. ἄνεμος, the wind. From the same root as **Animate,** q. v. Cf. *anemo-meter,* an instrument for measuring the wind s velocity.

ANENT, regarding, near to, beside. (E.) Nearly obsolete, except in Northern English. ME. *anent, anende, anendes, anentis,* &c. [The forms *anendes, anentis,* were made by adding the suffix -*es,* -*is,* orig. the sign of a gen. case, but frequently used as an adverbial suffix; for *anentes,* see Cursor Mundi, l. 26957.] *Anent* is a contraction of *anefe t,* or *onefent,* which occurs in the Ancren Riwle, p. 164, as another reading for *anonde.* In this form, the *t* is excrescent, as commonly after *n* (cf. *tyrant, ancient*), and the true form is *anefen* or *onefen.* — AS. *on-efen,* prep. near; sometimes written *on-emn,* by contraction; Grein, i. 218, 225. — AS. *on,* prep. in, and *efen,* even, equal; so that *on-efen* meant originally 'on an equality with,' or 'even with.' See Even. ¶ The cognate G. *neben,* beside, is similarly derived from G. *in,* in, and *eben,* even; and, to complete the analogy, was sometimes spelt *nebent.* See Mätzner, Wörterbuch; Stratmann, s. v. *anefen;* Koch, Engl. Gramm. v. ii. p. 389.

ANEROID, dry; without liquid mercury; applied to a barometer. (Gk.) Modern. — Gk. ἀ-, privative; νηρό-s, wet; and εἶδ-os, form. Gk. νηρός is from νάειν, to flow.

ANEURISM, ANEURYSM, a morbid dilatation of the coats of an artery. (Gk.) Formed as if from *aneurisma,* false form of *aneurysma,* a Latinised form of Gk. ἀνεύρυσμα, a widening. — Gk. ἀν-, for ἀνά, up; and εὐρύνειν, to widen, from εὐρύς, wide.+Skt. *uru-s,* large, wide. Cf. MF. *aneurisme* in Cotgrave.

ANEW, newly. (E.) A shortening of ME. *of-newe,* used by Chaucer, C. T., E 938. Cf. *adown* for AS. *ofdūne.* Here *f* is the AS. *of,* prep., and *newe* is our mod. E. *new;* the final -*e* being an adverbial suffix, as usual.

ANGEL, a divine messenger. (F.—L.—Gk.) [In very early use. AS. *angel, engel,* an angel; Grein, i. 227; borrowed from L. *angelu.*] But the modern pronunciation is due to the OF. *angele,* from L. acc. *angelum.* — Gk. ἄγγελος, lit. a messenger; hence, an angel. Cf. ἄγγαρος, a mounted courier, which is an old Persian word; also Skt.

aṅgira-s, a messenger from the gods to men (Macdonell). **Der.** *angel-ic*, *angel-ic-al*, *angel-ic-al-ly*; also *angelic-a*, a plant.

ANGER, hot displeasure due to a sense of injury. (Scand.) In ME. the word is more passive in its use, and denotes 'affliction,' 'trouble,' 'sore vexation.' ' If he thole here *anger* and wa ' = if he suffer here affliction and woe; Hampole's Pricke of Conscience, 3517. ‒Icel. *angr*, grief, sorrow; Dan. *anger*, compunction, regret; Swed. *ånger*, compunction, regret. +Lat. *angor*, a strangling, bodily torture; also mental torture, anguish; from *angere*, to strangle. Cf. AS. *ange*, oppressed, sad; Gk. ἄγχειν, to strangle; Skt. *aṁhas*, pain; all from √ANGH, to choke, oppress. See Brugm. i. § 178. **Der.** *angr-ily*; from the same root, *anguish*, *anxious*; also *quinsy*, q. v.; and L. *anxina*.

ANGINA, severe suffering. (L.) Borrowed from L. *angīna*, quinsy, lit. 'a choking,' from *angere*, to strangle. See above.

ANGLE (1), a bend, a corner. (F.‒L.) Chaucer has *angles*, C.T., F 230; also *angle*, as a term of astrology (L. *angulus*), id. 263. ‒ OF. *angle* (mod. F. *angle*), an angle. ‒ L. *angulum*, acc. of *angulus*, an angle. Cf. Gk. ἀγκύλος, crooked. From the same root as the next word. **Der.** *angul-ar*, *angul-ar-ly*, *angul-ar-i-ty*; all from the L. *angul-āris*, adj., from *angulus*.

ANGLE (2), a fishing-hook. (E.) In very early use. AS. *angel*, a fish-hook, Matt. xvii. 27; spelt *ongul* in the Northumbrian version. +Icel. *öngull*, Dan. *angel*, a fishing-hook; G. *angel*, dimin. of OHG. *ango*, a prickle, fish-hook. Cf. L. *uncus*, a hook, Gk. ὄγκος; ἀγκών, a bend; ἄγκυρα, a bent hook, whence E. *anchor*; Skt. *añch*, to bend. ‒ √ANQ, to bend, curve; Fick, i. 6. From the same root comes the word above; also **Anchor**, q. v. **Der.** *angle*, vb., *angl-er*, *angl-ing*.

ANGRY, i. e. *anger-y*; Chaucer, C.T. 12893 (C 959); see **Anger**.

ANGUISH, oppression; great pain. (F.‒L.) ME. *anguis*, *anguise*, *angoise*, &c. Spelt *anguys* in Pricke of Conscience, 2240; *anguisse*, Rob. of Glouc. p. 177, l. 3687; *anguise*, Ancren Riwle, p. 178. ‒OF. *anguisse*, *angois e*, mod. F. *angoi se*, f., anguish. ‒ L. *angustia*, narrowness, poverty, perplexity. ‒ L. *angustus*, narrow. ‒ L. *angere*, to stifle, choke, strangle. +Gk. ἄγχειν, to strangle. ‒ √ANGH, to choke. See **Anger**, from the same root.

AN-HUNGERED, very hungry. (E.) In Matt. xii. 1. It is a variant of *a-hungred*, and this, of *afyngred*; see P. Plowman, B. x. 59. All from AS. *of-hyngred*, very hungry, pp. of *of-hyngrian*, to be very hungry. ‒AS. *of-*, very; and *hyngrian*, to hunger, from *hungor*, hunger. See **Of**, **Off**, and **Hunger**.

ANHYDROUS, waterless. (Gk.) Modern. ‒ Gk. ἄνυδρος, waterless. ‒ Gk. ἀν-, neg. prefix; and ὕδωρ, water; with suffix *-ous* added. See **Hydra**.

ANILE, old-woman-like. (L.) Used by Walpole, Catalogue of Engravers; Sterne, Serm. 21. § 19, has *anility*. Not in early use. ‒ L. *anīlis*, like an old woman. ‒ L. *anus*, an old woman. Cf. OHG. *ana*, a grandmother.

ANILINE, a liquid which furnishes a number of dyes. (F.‒ Span.‒ Arab.‒ Pers.‒ Skt.) Modern. Formed with suffix *-ine* (F. *-ine*, L. *-īnus*) from *anil*, a shrub from which the W. Indian indigo is made. '*Anil* . . is a kind of thing to dye blue withal;' Eng. Garner, ed. Arber, vi. 18 (ab. 1586). ‒ F. *anil*, anil. ‒ Span. *añil*, 'azure, skie colour;' Minsheu, p. 25, l. 12. ‒ Arab. *an-nil*, for *al nil*; where *al* is the def. art., and *nil* is borrowed from Pers. *nil*, the indigo plant. ‒ Skt. *nīlī*, the indigo plant; from *nīla-s*, blue. See **Lilac, Nylghau**.

ANIMADVERT, to criticise, censure. (L.) Lit. 'to turn the mind to.' In Glossographia Anglicana Nova, ed. 1719. ‒ L. *anim-aduertere*, to turn the mind to, pp. *animaduersus*. ‒ L. *anim-us*, the mind; *ad*, to; and *uertere*, to turn. For roots, see **Animate** and **Verse**. **Der.** *animadvers-ion*, in Ben Jonson's Discoveries, sect. 123.

ANIMAL, a living creature. (L.) In Hamlet, ii. 2. 320; used as an adj., Chaucer, C. T., A 2749. ‒ L. *animal*, a breathing creature. ‒ L. *anima*, breath. See below. **Der.** *animal-ism*, *animal-cule*.

ANIMATE, to endue with life. (L.) Used by Hall, Edw. IV, an. 8. § 5. ‒ L. *animātus*, pp. of *animāre*, to give life to. ‒ L. *anima*, breath, life. ‒ √AN, to breathe; which appears not only in the Skt. *an*, to breathe, blow, live; Gk. ἄνεμος, wind; but also in Goth. *us-anan*, to breathe out, expire, Mark xv. 37, 39; and in Icel. *anda*, to breathe, *önd*, breath, whence Lowland Scotch *aynd*, breath. **Der.** *animat-ed*, *animat-ion*.

ANIMOSITY, vehemence of passion, hostility. (F.‒L.) Bp. Hall, Letter of Apology, has the pl. *animosities*; so in Bacon, Adv. of Learning, ii. xxiii. 48. ‒ F. *animosité*, 'animosity, stoutness;' Cot. ‒ L. acc. *animōsitātem*, from nom. *animōsitās*, ardour, vehemence. ‒ L. *animōsus*, full of spirit. ‒ L. *animus*, mind, courage. +Gk. ἄνεμος, breath, wind. ‒ √AN, to breathe. See **Animate**. ¶ The L. *animus* is now used as an E. word.

ANISE, a medicinal herb. (F.‒L.‒Gk.) In Matt. xxiii. 23, the Wycliffite versions have both *anese* and *anete*. In Wright's Lyric Poetry,

p. 26, we find *anys*; and in Wright's Vocabularies, i. 227, is: ' Hoc anisium, *anys*.' ‒ F. *anis*, anise; see Cotgrave. ‒ L. *anisum*, also *anēthum* (whence Wyclif's *anete*). ‒ Gk. ἄνισον, ἄνησον, usually ἄνηθον, anise, dill. Perhaps named from its scent; cf. ἄν-εμος, a breath of air (Prellwitz). **Der.** *aniseed* (for *anise-seed*).

ANKER, a liquid measure of 8 to 10 gallons. (Du.‒ Late L.) Mentioned in Bailey's Dict., vol. ii. ed. 1731, as in use at Amsterdam. ‒Du. *anker*, the same; cf. Swed. *ankare*; G. *anker*. Probably from Late L. *anceria*, a keg, a small vat.

ANKLE, the joint between leg and foot. (E.) ME. *ancle*, Chaucer, C. T. 1662 (A 1660). [Also *anclowe*, Ellis's Specimens, i. 279. AS. *anclēow*, ankle, Ælfric's Gloss., Voc. 160. 21; which is the origin of ME. *anclowe*.] But the mod. E. form answers to OFries. *ankel*; Dan. and Swed. *ankel*; Icel. *ökkla* (for *önkla*); Du. *enkel*; OHG. *anchala*, *anchla*, *enchila*, the ankle; mod. G. *enkel*. [On the other hand, the AS. *anclēow* answers to OFries. *anklef*, Du. *enklaauw*. The Du. *klaauw* means 'claw,' and the AS. *clēow* seems to point to the same word, but these endings are probably mere adaptations in the respective languages, to give the words a more obvious etymology.] β. The word is clearly a diminutive, formed with suffix *-el* from a stem *ank-*. Indeed, the OHG. has the shorter form *ancha*, meaning leg, ankle. The root is the same as that of Skt. *anguli-s*, a finger, *anga-m*, a limb. **Der.** *ankle-join'*, *ankl-et* (ornament for the ankle).

ANNA; see **Ana**.

ANNALS, a relation of events year by year. (F.‒L.) In Shak. Cor. v. 6. 114. Grafton speaks of 'short notes in maner of *annales*;' Ep. to Sir W. Cecil. ‒ F. *annales*, s. pl. fem. 'annales, annual chronicles;' Cot. ‒ L. *annālēs*, pl. adj.; for *libri annālēs*, yearly books or chronicles; from nom. sing. *ann-ālis*, yearly. ‒ L. *annus*, a year. Prob. allied to Goth. *athn*, n., a year; Brugm. ii. § 66. Perhaps from √AT, to move on; cf. Skt. *at*, to go, wander. **Der.** *annal-ist*.

ANNATES, first-fruits paid to the pope. (F.‒L.) 'These cardinals . . have the *Annat* of Benefices to support their greatne s;' Howell, Famil. Letters, 1678, vol. i. let. 38 (Sept., 1621). ‒ F. *annate*, 'the first-fruits of a benefice; the profit of a whole year after the remove, or death, of the incumbent;' Cot. ‒ Late L. *annāta*; Duc. ‒ L. *annus*, a year.

ANNEAL, to temper by heat. ((1) E.; (2) F.‒L.) Two distinct words seem to have been confused. 1. The word was originally applied to metals, in which case it was English, and denoted rather the fusing of metals than the tempering process by gradual cooling. This is the ME. *anelen*, to inflame, kindle, heat, melt, burn. Gower, C. A. iii. 96 (bk. vii. 337), speaks of a meteoric stone, which the fire 'hath *aneled* [melted] Lich unto slym, which is congealed.' Wyclif, Isa. xvi. 7 has '*anelid* tyil' as a translation of L. *cocti la'eris*. It also means simply 'to burn' or 'inflame.' Thus, in OE. Homilies, ed. Morris, i. 219, the word *seraphim* is explained to mean 'birninde other *anhelend*' [better spelt *anelend*] = burning or kindling; and again, at p. 97, it is said that the Holy Ghost '*onealde* eorthlichen monnan heortan' = inflamed earthly men's hearts. ‒AS. *onǣlan*, to burn, kindle, Grein, ii. 339; a compound verb. ‒ AS. *on*, prefix (answering to mod. E. prep. *on*); and *ǣlan*, to burn, Grein, i. 55. Cf. Icel. *eldr*, Swed. *eld*, Dan. *ild*, fire; corresponding to AS. *ǣled*, fire, a derivative of *ǣlan*, to burn. 2. But in the fifteenth century, a similar word was introduced from the French, having particular reference to the fixing of colours upon glass by means of heat. This is the late ME. *anelen*, to enamel glass. Thus Palsgrave has 'I *aneel* a potte of erthe or suche lyke with a coloure, *je plomme*.' [The word was also applied to the enamelling of metal, and is perhaps meant in the entry in the Prompt. Parv. at p. 11; '*Anelyn* or *enelyn* metalle, or other lyke.'] The initial *a-* is either the French prefix *a-* (L. *ad*), or may have been merely due to the influence of the native word. ‒OF. *neeler*, to enamel; orig. to paint in black upon gold or silver. ‒ Late L. *nigellāre*, to blacken ‒ L. *nigellus*, blackish; dimin. of *niger*, black. See Diez, s. v. *niello*. ¶ There is yet a *third* word not unlike these two, which appears in 'unaneled,' i.e. not having received extreme unction: Hamlet. i. 5 77. This is from AS. *onelan*, to put oil upon; from AS. *on*, prefix, and *ele*, oil; see **Oil**.

ANNEX, to fasten or unite to. (F.‒L.) The pp. *annexed* occur in the Romaunt of the Rose, 4811. ‒ F. *annexer*, 'to annex, knit, linke, joyn;' Cot. ‒ L. *annexus*, pp. of *annectere*, to knit or bind to. ‒ L. *ad*, to (> *an-* before *n*); and *nectere*, to bind. **Der.** *annex-at-ion*.

ANNIHILATE, to reduce to nothing. (L.) Hall, Edw. IV, an. 1, has *adnihilate*; Bacon, Nat. Hist. sect. 100, has *annihila'ed*. Formed with suffix *-ate*, on which see **Abbreviate**. ‒ L. *annihilātus*, pp. of *annihilāre*, to reduce to nothing. ‒ L. *ad*, to (> *an-* before *n*); and *nihil*, *nihilum*, nothing. **Der.** *annihila'-ion*.

ANNIVERSARY, the annual commemoration of an event. (L.) Fabyan, an. 1368-9, speaks of 'an *annyuersarye* yerely to be kept.' The pl. *anniuersaries* occurs in the Ancren Riwle, p. 22. It is properly an adjective, and so used by Bp. Hall, On the Obser. of Christ's Nativity, where he speaks of an '*anniversary* memorial.' — L. *anniuersārius*, returning yearly. — L. *anni-*, for *anno-*, from *annus*, a year; and *uertere*, to turn, pp. *uersus*. See **Annals** and **Verse**.

ANNOTATE, to make notes upon. (L.) Richardson remarks that the verb is very rare; Foxe uses *annotations* in his Life of Tyndal, in Tyndal's Works (1572), fol. B i, last line. Formed with the suffix *-ate*, on which see **Abbreviate**. — L. *annotātus*, pp. of *annotāre*, to make notes. — L. *ad*, to (> *an-* before *n*); and *notāre*, to mark, from *nota*, a mark. See **Note**. Der. *annotat-or*, *annotat-ion*.

ANNOUNCE, to make known to. (F. — L.) In Cotgrave. Milton has *announc't*, P. R. iv. 504. [Chaucer has *annunciat*, C. T. 14021 (B 3205); but this is directly from L. pp. *annunciātus*.] — F. *annoncer*, 'to announce;' Cot. — L. *annunciāre*, *annuntiāre*, to announce; pp. *annuntiātus*. — L. *ad* (> *an-* before *n*); and *nuntiāre*, to report, give a message, from *nuntius*, a messenger. See **Nuncio**. Der. *announce-ment*; and, directly from L., *annunciate*; also *annunciat-ion*.

ANNOY, to hurt, vex, trouble. (F. — L.) ME. *anoien*, *anuien* (with one *n*, correctly), to vex, trouble. See King Alisaunder, ed. Weber, ll. 876, 1287, 4158; Chaucer (Glossary). [The sb. *anoi*, *anoy* was also in very common use; see Romaunt of the Rose, 4404; Ayenbite of Inwyt, p. 267, &c.; but is now obsolete, and its place to some extent supplied by *annoyance* and the F. *ennui*.] — OF. *anoier*, *anuier*, to annoy, trouble; from the OF. sb. *anoi*, *anui* (mod. F. *ennui*), annoyance, vexation, chagrin; cognate with mod. Prov. *enodi*, Span. *enojo*, OVenetian *inodio*. — L. *in odiō*, lit. in hatred, which was used in the phrase *in odiō habui*, lit. I had in hatred, i. e. I was sick and tired of, occurring in the Glosses of Cassel, temp. Charles the Great; see Brachet and Diez. Other phrases were L. *in odiō esse* and *in odiō uenīre*, both meaning to incur hatred, and used by Cicero; see Att. ii. 21. 2. *Odiō* is the abl. of *odium*, hatred. See the account in Diez. See **Odium** and **Noisome**. Der. *annoy-ance* (Chaucer); from OF. *anoiance*, a derivative of vb. *anoier*.

ANNUAL, yearly. (F. — L.) ME. *annuel*, an anniversary mass for the dead, is a special use of the word; see P. Plowman's Crede, l. 414; Chaucer, C. T., G 1012, on which see my note, or that to Tyrwhitt's Chaucer, C. T. 16480. — F. *annuel*, annual, yearly; Cot. — L. *annuālis*, yearly; formed with suffix *-ālis* from stem *annu-*. — L. *annus*, a year. See **Annal**. ¶ It will be observed that the spelling was changed from *annuel* to *annual* to bring it nearer to the Latin; but the word really came to us through French. Der. *annual-ly*. From the same source: *annu-i-ty*, ME. *annuitee*, Hoccleve, de Regim. Princ. 821, from AF. *annuité* (unknown in OF.; but see Year-books of Edw. I, 1304–5, p. 179); and the more modern *annu-it-ant*.

ANNUL, to nullify, abolish. (F. — L.) The pp. *anulled* occurs in T. Usk, Test. of Love, iii. 2. 81. — AF. *annuller*, Stat. Realm, i. 367 (1361); OF. *anuller*, MF. *annuller*, given by Cotgrave. — L. *annullāre*, to annul. — L. *ad* (> *an-* before *n*); and L. *nullus*, none, a contraction from *ne ullus*, not any. See **Null**. Der. *annul-ment*.

ANNULAR, like a ring. (L.) Ray, On the Creation, p. 2, has both *annular* and *annulary* (R.). — L. *annulāris*, like a ring; formed with suffix *-āris* from stem *annul-* (for *annulo-*). — L. *annulus*, a ring; earlier form *ānulus*, dimin. of *ānus*, a rounding, a circular form, an iron ring (Lewis). Cf. OIrish *ānne*, a little ring; Stokes-Fick, p. 16. Also Skt. *akna-s*, bent; *añch*, to bend. From the same source (L. *annulus*) we have *annul-at-ed*, *annul-et*, *annul-ose*.

ANNUNCIATION, ANNUNCIATE; see **Announce**.

ANODYNE, a drug to allay pain. (L. — Gk.) Used by Bp. Taylor, Epistle Dedicatory to Serm. to the Irish Parl., 1661 (R.). Also in Pope, Moral Essays, ii. 111. Cotgrave gives '*remedes anodins*, medicines which, by procuring sleep, take from a patient all sence of pain.' But the spelling *anodyne* is Latin. — Late L. *anōdynus*, a drug relieving pain; Ducange. — Gk. *ἀνώδυνος*, adj. free from pain; whence *φάρμακον ἀνώδυνον*, a drug to relieve pain. — Gk. *ἀν-*, negative prefix; and *ὀδύνη*, pain. Curtius, i. 300, refers *ὀδύνη* to the verb *ἔδ-ειν*, to eat, as if it were 'a gnawing;' rightly. See **Eat**.

ANOINT, to smear with ointment. (F. — L.) Wyclif has *anoyntidist*, Acts, iv. 27, from ME. verb *anointen* or *anoynten*; see Prompt. Parv. p. 12. Chaucer has *anoint* as a past participle, Prol. 199. It is clear that *anoint* was orig. a past-participial form, but was afterwards lengthened into *anointed*, thus suggesting the infin. *anointen*. Both forms, *anoynt* and *anoynted*, occur in the Wycliffite Bible, Gen. l. 3; Numb. vi. 15. All the forms are also written with initial *e*, viz. *enoint*, *enointed*, *enointen*. — OF. *enoint*, anointed, pp. of *enoindre*, to anoint. — OF. *en-* (L. *in-*), upon, on); and *oindre*, to smear, anoint, from L. *ungere*, to smear, pp. *unctus*. See **Ointment, Unction**.

ANOMALY, deviation from rule. (Gk.) Used by Sir T. Browne, Vulg. Errors, b. iii. c. 15. § 5. Cotgrave's French Dict. gives only the adj. *anomal*, inequal; so that the sb. was taken from L. *anōmalia*, or directly from the Gk. — Gk. *ἀνωμαλία*, irregularity, unevenness. — Gk. *ἀνώμαλος*, uneven. — Gk. *ἀν-*, negative prefix, and *ὁμαλός*, even. The Gk. *ὁμαλός* is formed with suffix *-αλ-* from *ὁμ-*, base of *ὁμός*,

one and the same, joint, common; closely related to E. *same*. See **Same**. Der. *anomal-ous*.

ANON, immediately. (E.) In early use. ME. *anon*, *anoon*, *onan*, *anan*. Rob. of Glouc. has *anon*, p. 6; l. 134. The earliest ME. forms are *anon*, Ancren Riwle, p. 14; *anan*, Ormulum, 225. The *a* is convertible with *o* in either syllable; but in the latter syllable the vowel was *long*. — AS. *on ān*, lit. in one moment (answering to MHG. *in ein*), but in AS. generally signifying 'once for all;' see examples in Grein, i. 31, sect. 8. — AS. *on* (mod. E. *on*), often used with the sense of '*in*;' and AS. *ān*, old form of '*one*.' See **On** and **One**.

ANONYMOUS, nameless. (Gk.) In Phillips' Dict. (1658). Formed directly from Gk., by substituting *-ous* for Gk. suffix *-os*, just as it is often substituted for the L. suffix *-us*. — Gk. *ἀνώνυμος*, nameless. — Gk. *ἀν-*, neg. prefix; and *ὄνομα*, Æolic *ὄνυμα*, a name. See **Onomatopœia**. Der. *anonymous-ly*.

ANOTHER, i.e. one another. (E.) Merely the words *an* and *other* written together. In Mid. Eng. they were written apart. 'Hauelok thouthe al *an other*,' Havelok thought quite *another* thing; Havelok, 1395. See **An** and **Other**.

ANSERINE, goose-like. (L.) Not in early use; first in 1839 (N. E. D.). — L. *anserinus*, belonging to a goose. — L. *anser*, a goose, cognate with E. *goose*. See **Goose**.

ANSWER, to reply to. (E.) The verb is from the sb. The lit. sense is 'to make a (sworn) reply in opposition to,' orig. used, no doubt, in trials by law. ME. *andswerien*, Layamon, ii. 518. AS. *andswarian*, *andswerian*, to reply to; from *andswaru*, sb., a reply. — AS. *and-*, in opposition to, cognate with Gk. *ἀντί* (see **Anti-**); and *swar-*, base of *swerian*, to swear; see **Swear**. Der. *answer-able*, *answer-abl-y*. ¶ The prefix *ant-* in G. *antworten*, to answer, is cognate with the AS. prefix *and-* in the E. word.

ANT, a small insect; the emmet. (E.) *Ant* is a contraction from AS. *ǣmette* (L. *formica*), an emmet; Ælf. Gloss., Nomina Insectorum; so that *ant* and *emmet* are doublets. The form *ǣmette* became, by the ordinary phonetic changes in English, *amette*, *amte*, *ante*, *ant*; of these *amte* occurs in Wyclif, Prov. vi. 6. ¶ Examples of the change of *m* to *n* before *t* occur in *Hants* as a shortened form of *Hamptonshire* (see Mätzner, Engl. Gram. i. 123); also in E. *aunt* from L. *amita*. See **Emmet**. Der. *ant-hill*, *-eater*.

ANTAGONIST, an opponent. (Late L. — Gk.) Ben Jonson has *antagonistic*, Magnetic Lady, iii. 4 (Compass, 10th speech); Milton has *antagonist*, P. L. ii. 509. — Late L. *antagōnista* (or directly from the Gk.). — Gk. *ἀνταγωνιστής*, an adversary, opponent. — Gk. *ἀνταγωνίζομαι*, I struggle against. — Gk. *ἀντ-*, for *ἀντί*, against; and *ἀγωνίζομαι*, I struggle, from *ἀγών*, a struggle. See **Agony**. Der. *antagonist-ic*, *antagonist-ic-al-ly*; also *antagonism*, from Gk. *ἀνταγώνισμα*, a struggle with another.

ANTARCTIC, southern; opposite to the arctic. (F. — L. — Gk.) Marlowe, Faustus, i. 3. 3; Milton, P. L. ix. 79. ME. *antartik*, Chaucer, Astrolabe, ii. 25. 7. — OF. *antartique*; Cotgrave has '*Antartique*, the circle in the sphere called the South, or *Antartick* pole.' — L. *antarcticus*, southern. — Gk. *ἀνταρκτικός*, southern. — Gk. *ἀντ-* for *ἀντί*, against; and *ἀρκτικός*, arctic, northern. See **Arctic**.

ANTE-, prefix, before. (L.) Occurs in words taken from Latin, e.g. *ante-cedent*, *ante-date*, *ante-diluvian*, &c. — L. *ante*, before; of which an older form seems to have been *anti*, as in *anti-cipāre*; Brugm. i. § 84. The prefix *anti-* is cognate; see **Anti-**, prefix.

ANTECEDENT, going before. (L.) Used by Sir T. More, Works, p. 1115, last line. Used as a (Latin) logical term by T. Usk, Test. of Love, ii. 5. 12. — L. *antecēdentem*, acc. case of *antecēdens*, going before. — L. *ante*, before; and *cēdens*, going, pres. pt. of *cēdere*, to go; see **Cede**. Der. *antecedent-ly*; also *antecedence* (with F. suffix *-ence*). And see **Ancestor**.

ANTEDATE, to date before. (L.) Used by Massinger in the sense of 'anticipate;' Duke of Milan, i. 3 (Sforza, speech 9). Formed by prefixing L. *ante*, before, to *date*, q. v.

ANTEDILUVIAN, before the flood. (L.) Used by Sir T. Browne, Vulg. Errors, bk. vii. c. 3. § 2. A coined word; from L. *ante*, before, and *diluui-um*, a deluge; with adj. suffix *-an*. See **Deluge**.

ANTELOPE, a deer-like quadruped. (F. — L. — Gk.) In Spenser, F.Q. i. 6. 26. Pl. *antelopis*, Lydgate, Minor Poems, p. 6, l. 1. — OF. *antelop* (Godefroy; Hatzfeld). — Late L. *antalopus*. — Late Gk. *ἀνθάλοψ*, stem of *ἀνθάλωψ* (gen. *ἀνθάλοπος*), used by Eustathius (flor. circa 330), Hexaëm., p. 36 (Webster's Dict.). The 'antelope' was orig. a fabulous and nondescript animal; so that the orig. meaning of *ἀνθάλωψ* is not known; neither do we know whence Eustathius took it. See N. E. D. ¶ Mod. F. *antilope* (from E.); AF. *antelope* (1415), Riley, Mem. of London, p. 613.

ANTENNÆ, the feelers of insects. (L.) Modern and scientific; see N. E. D. Borrowed from L. *antennæ*, pl. of *antenna*, properly 'the yard of a sail.' Remoter origin uncertain.

ANTEPENULTIMA, the last syllable but two. (L.) Used

in prosody; sometimes shortened to *antepenult.* — L. *antepēnultima,* also *antepaenultima,* fem. adj. (with *syllaba* understood), the last syllable but two. — L. *ante,* before; and *paenultima,* fem. adj., the last syllable but one: from *paene,* almost, and *ultima,* fem. of *ultimus,* last. See **Ultimate.** Der. *antepenultim-ate.*

ANTERIOR, before, more in front. (L.) Sir T. Browne, Vulg. Errors, b. iii. c. 15. § 3, has *anteriour* (better *anterior*); Cotgrave has *anterior,* s.v. *Anterieur.* The word is borrowed directly from L. *anterior,* more in front, compar. adj. from *ante,* before. See **Ante-.**

ANTHEM, a musical composition, sung responsively. (L. — Gk.) In very early use. ME. *antem, antym;* cf. '*antym,* antiphona;' Prompt. Parv. p. 12. Chaucer has *antem,* C.T., B 1850. *Antem* is a contraction from an older form *antefn;* 'biginneth thesne *antefne'* = begin this anthem, Ancren Riwle, p. 34. AS. *antefn,* an anthem; AS. tr. of Beda, Eccl. Hist. i. 25, ed. Smith; spelt *ontemn,* ed. Miller. This AS. *antefn* is a mere reduction from the Latin. — Late L. *antiphōna,* an anthem; see Ducange. This form arose from considering the Gk. neut. pl. to be a fem. sing. — Gk. ἀντίφωνα, pl. of ἀντίφωνον, an anthem; properly neut. of adj. ἀντίφωνος, sounding in response to. Aristotle has ἀντίφωνον, 'an accord in the octave;' so that ἀντίφωνα meant 'musical accords.' [Thus there is no need for the assertion that the *anthem* was named from its being sung by choristers alternately, half the choir on one side responding to the half on the other side.] — Gk. ἀντί, over against; and φωνή, voice. *Anthem* is a doublet of *antiphon,* q.v.

ANTHER, the part of the stamen of a flower which contains the pollen. (F. — L. — Gk.) Phillips (1706) has: '*Anthera,* the yellow seeds in the middle of a rose.' — MF. *anthere,* 'the yellow tuft in the middle of a rose;' Cot. Adapted from L. *anthēra,* a medicine composed of flowers (Lewis). Borrowed from Gk. ἀνθηρά, fem. of ἀνθηρός, adj. flowery, blooming. — Gk. ἀνθεῖν, to bloom; ἄνθος, a young bud or sprout. The Gk. ἄνθος is cognate with Skt. *andhas,* n., herb, sacrificial food. See Prellwitz.

ANTHOLOGY, a collection of choice poems. (Gk.) Several Gk. collections of poems were so called; hence the extension of the name. Sir T. Browne, Vulg. Errors, b. iv. c. 9. § 2, refers to 'the Greek *Anthology.*' — Gk. ἀνθολογία, a flower-gathering, a collection of choice poems. — Gk. ἀνθολόγος, adj. flower-gathering. — Gk. ἄνθο-, for ἄνθος, a flower; and λέγειν, to collect. See **Anther** and **Legend.**

ANTHRACITE, a kind of hard coal. (Gk.) Modern; first in 1812. Suggested by Gk. ἀνθρακίτης, adj. resembling coals; formed with suffix -ιτης, expressing resemblance, from ἀνθρακ-, stem of Gk. ἄνθραξ, coal, charcoal, also a carbuncle, precious stone. Cf. L. *anthracītis,* a kind of carbuncle, Pliny, bk. xxxvii. c. 7 (see Holland's translation).

ANTHROPOLOGY, the natural history of man. (Gk.) '*Anthropology,* a speaking or discoursing of men;' Blount's Gloss. — Gk. ἄνθρωπο-, for ἄνθρωπος, a man; and -λογία, a discourse, from λέγ-ειν, to speak. Der. (from *anthropo-*), *anthropo-id,* from Gk. εἶδ-ος, form; *anthropo-morph'ic,* from Gk. μορφ-ή, form. And see below.

ANTHROPOPHAGI, cannibals. (L. — Gk.) Used by Shak. Oth. i. 3. 144. Lit. 'men-eaters.' A Latinised plural of Gk. ἀνθρωποφάγος, adj. man-eating. — Gk. ἄνθρωπο-ς, a man; and φαγεῖν, to eat. The form ἄνθρωπος is of doubtful origin; φαγεῖν is from √BHAG, to distribute (as a portion); cf. Skt. *bhaksh,* to eat, devour. Brugm. i. § 183. Der. *anthropophag-y.*

ANTI-, ANT-, prefix, against. (Gk.) Occurs in words taken from Gk., as *antidote, antipathy,* &c. In *anticipate,* the prefix is for the L. *ante.* In *ant-agonist, ant-arctic,* it is shortened to *ant-.* — Gk. ἀντί, against, over against. + Skt. *anti,* over against; a Vedic form and perhaps allied to Skt. *anta-s,* end, boundary, also proximity, cognate with E. *end,* q.v. ¶ This Gk. prefix is cognate with the AS. *and-,* appearing in mod. E. *along* and *answer,* q.v. Also with Goth. *and-;* and with G. *an'-,* as seen in *antworten,* to answer.

ANTIC, fanciful, odd; as sb., a trick. (Ital. — L.) Orig. an adjective, and used with the sense of 'grotesque.' Hall, Henry VIII, an. 12. § 12, has: 'a fountayne . . ingrayled with *anticke* woorkes.' Florio has: '*Grottesca,* a kinde of rugged vnpolished painters worke, *anticke* worke.' Cotgrave gives, s.v. *Antique,* 'taillé à antiques, cut with *anticks,* or with *antick*-works;' but this usage is from Italian. — Ital. *antico,* 'ancient, anticke, old;' Florio. — L. *antiquus,* old. See **Antique** (which is the F. form).

ANTICHRIST, the great opponent of Christ. (L. — Gk.) L. *Antichristus.* — Gk. ἀντίχριστος; 1 John, ii. 18. From Gk. ἀντί, against; and χρίστος, Christ. See **Anti-** and **Christ.** Der. *antichrist-ian.*

ANTICIPATE, to take before the time, forestall. (L.) Used by Hall, Henry VI, an. 38. § 4; Shak. Oth. ii. 1. 76. Formed with suffix -*ate* (on which see **Abbreviate**), from L. *anticipāre,* to take beforehand, prevent; pp. *anticipātus.* — L. *anti-,* old form of *ante,* beforehand; and *capere,* to take. See **Ante-** and **Capable.** Der. *anticipat-ion, anticipat-ory.*

ANTICLIMAX, the opposite of a climax. (Gk.) Compounded of **Anti-,** against; and **Climax.**

ANTIDOTE, a medicine given as a remedy. (F. — L. — Gk.) Used by Shak. Macb. v. 3. 43. — F. *antidote,* m., given by Cotgrave. — L. *antidotum,* neut. (and *antidotus,* fem.), an antidote, remedy. — Gk. ἀντίδοτος, adj. given as a remedy; whence, as sb., ἀντίδοτον, neut., an antidote, and δοτός, fem., the same (Liddell and Scott). — Gk. ἀντί, against; and δοτός, given, from weak grade δο- allied to δίδωμι, I give; with suffix -τος. See **Anti-** and **Dose.** Der. *antidot-al, antidot-ic-al.*

ANTIMONY, the name of a metal. (Late L. — Arab.) In Sir T. Herbert's Travels, ed. 1665, p. 317; first known in 1477 (N. E. D.). Englished from Late L. *antimōnium* (11th cent.); Ducange. Origin uncertain; but Devic traces it to Arab. *ithmid, uthmud,* 'a stone from which antimony is prepared;' Rich. Dict., p. 21, col. 1. Der. *antimon-ial.*

ANTINOMIAN, one who denies the obligation of moral law. (Gk.) Tillotson, vol. ii. ser. 50, speaks of 'the *Antinomian* doctrine.' Milton, Doctrine and Discipline of Divorce, b. ii. c. 3, uses the sb. *antinomie.* The suffix -*an* is adjectival, from L. -*ānus.* The word is from Gk. ἀντινομία, an ambiguity in the law, explained as if from Gk. ἀντί, against, and νόμος, law, which is from the verb νέμειν, to deal out, also to pasture. See **Anti-** and **Nomad.**

ANTIPATHY, a feeling against another. (L. — Gk.) Used by Bacon, Nat. Hist. sect. 479. Fuller has *antipathetical,* Worthies of Lincolnshire. Either from F. *antipathie,* explained as 'antipathy' by Cotgrave; or directly from L. *antipathia* (Pliny). — Gk. ἀντιπάθεια, an antipathy, lit. 'a suffering against.' — Gk. ἀντί, against; and παθεῖν, to suffer. See **Anti-** and **Pathos.** Der. *antipath-et-ic, antipath-et-ic-al.*

ANTIPHON, an anthem. (L. — Gk.) Milton has the pl. *antiphonies,* Areopagitica, ed. Hales, p. 12. The book containing the *antiphons* was called an *antiphoner,* a word used by Chaucer, C. T., B 1709. — Late L. *antiphōna,* representing a fem. sing. instead of a neut. plural. — Gk. ἀντίφωνα, pl. of ἀντίφωνον, an anthem; properly neut. of adj. ἀντίφωνος, sounding in response to; but Aristotle used ἀντίφωνον to mean 'an accord in the octave,' whence the sense of concord. — Gk. ἀντί, contrary, over against (see **Anti-**); and φωνή, voice, allied to φημί, I speak, say. See **Phonetic.** *Antiphon* is a doublet of *anthem,* q. v.

ANTIPHRASIS, the use of words in a sense opposed to their meaning. (L. — Gk.) In Puttenham, Eng. Poesie, bk. iii. c. 18; p. 201, sidenote, ed. Arber. — Late L. *antiphrasis.* — Gk. ἀντίφρασις, lit. a contradiction; also the use of words in a sense opposed to their literal meaning. — Gk. ἀντιφράζειν, to express by negation (in sarcasm). — Gk. ἀντί, against, contrary; and φράζειν, to speak. See **Anti-** and **Phrase.** Der. *antiphras-t-ic-al.*

ANTIPODES, men whose feet are opposite to ours. (L. — Gk.) Shak. Mid. Nt. Dr. iii. 2. 55; Holland's tr. of Pliny, b. ii. c. 65. Also in Trevisa, tr. of Higden, ii. 205. — L. *antipodes;* a borrowed word. — Gk. ἀντίποδες, pl., men with feet opposite to us; from nom. sing. ἀντίπους, opposite to another; and πούς, a foot, cognate with E. *foot.* See **Anti-** and **Foot.** Der. *antipod-al.*

ANTIQUE, old. (F. — L.) Shak. has 'the *antique* world;' As You Like It, ii. 3. 57. — F. *antique;* Cot. — Lat. *antiquus,* old; also written *anticus,* and formed with suffix -*cus* from *anti,* old form of *ante,* before, just as L. *posticus,* behind, is formed from *post,* after. Brugm. ii. § 86. See **Ante-.** Der. *antiqu-it-y* (Hamlet, iv. 5. 104), *antiqu-ate, antiqu-at-ed, antiqu-ar-y, antiqu-ar-i-an, antiqu-ar-i-an-ism.* ¶ *Antique* is a doublet of *antic,* which follows the Italian spelling. See **Antic.**

ANTISEPTIC, counteracting putrefaction. (Gk.) Modern. Formed from Gk. ἀντί, against; and σηπτικ-ός, putrefying, from σηπτ-ός, decayed, rotten, verbal adj. from σήπειν, to make rotten.

ANTISTROPHE, a kind of choral song. (L. — Gk.) In Milton, Introd. to Samson. — L. *antistrophē.* — Gk. ἀντιστροφή, a return of a chorus, answering to a preceding στροφή, or *strophe.* — Gk. ἀντί, over against; and στροφή, a verse or stanza, lit. 'a turning,' from the movement of the chorus; from the verb στρέφειν, to turn. See **Anti-** and **Strophe.**

ANTITHESIS, a contrast, opposition. (Gk.) Used by Bp. Taylor, Dissuasive from Popery, bk. i. pt. ii. s. 1 (R.). — Gk. ἀντίθεσις, an opposition, a setting opposite. — Gk. ἀντί, over against; and θέσις, a setting, placing, from θε-, weak grade allied to τίθημι, I place. See **Anti-** and **Thesis.** Der. *antithet-ic, antithet-ic-al, antithet-ic-al-ly;* from Gk. ἀντιθετικός, adj.

ANTITYPE, that which answers to the type. (Gk.) Bp. Taylor, Of the Real Presence, s. 12. § 28, speaks of 'type and *antitype.*' The word is due to the occurrence of the Gk. ἀντίτυπον (A. V. 'figure') in 1 Pet. iii. 21, and the pl. ἀντίτυπα (A. V. 'figures') in Heb. ix. 24. This sb. ἀντίτυπον is the neut. of adj. ἀντίτυπος, formed according to a model, responding as an impression to a blow given to a stamp. — Gk. ἀντί, over against; and τύπος, a blow, also a stamp, pattern, type, allied to τύπτειν, to strike. See **Anti-** and **Type.** Der. *antityp-ic-al.*

ANTLER, the branch of a stag's horn. (F. − L.) Like most terms of the chase, this is of F. origin. The oldest E. form is *auntelere,* occurring in Twety's treatise on Hunting, pr. in Reliquiæ Antiquæ, i. 151. − OF. *antoillier* (Dict. de Trévoux), an antler.−Folk-L. acc. **ant(e)-oculārem (rāmum)*, branch placed before the eye; cf. G. *augen-sprosse,* a brow-antler (lit. eye-sprout).−L. *ante,* before; and *oculus,* the eye. See Hatzfeld, s.v. *andouillier* (the mod. F. form); and see Romania, iv. 349.

ANUS, the lower orifice of the bowels. (L.) In Phillips' Dict. (1706). Borrowed from L. *ānus.*

ANVIL, an iron block on which smiths hammer their work into shape. (E.) *Anvil* is for *anvild* or *anvilt,* a final *d* (for *t*) having dropped off. We find *anvelde* in Palsgrave (1530). In Wright's Vocabularies, i. 180, is the entry '*anfeld,* incus.' In Chaucer's Book of the Duchess, 1165, we find *anvel'.*−AS. *anfilte,* explained by L. *incus,* Ælf. Glos., Voc. 141. 23; OMerc. *onfilti,* Corpus Gloss. 1072 (Sweet).−AS. *on-,* prefix, often written *an-,* answering to mod. E. *on;* and (probably) *fieltan (see below), causal of **fealtan,* to infix, reduplicating verb cognate with OHG. **falzan,* MHG. *valzen,* to infix, inlay, whence G. *falz,* a groove. ¶ Some derive it from *on* and *fealdan,* to fold; however, the OHG. *anafalz,* an anvil, is not derived from *ana,* on, and *faldan,* to fold, but from *ana* and the MHG. *valzen* (above), which is allied to L. *pellere,* to drive. Cf. L. *incūs,* an anvil, from *in,* on, and *cūdere,* to strike; and note the AS. gloss: '*Cudo, percutio,* anfilte,' Voc. 217. 5; which authorises the form *fieltan (*filtan*) as postulated above. See **Felt.** ¶ In Napier's glosses, 11. 67, we find *anfealte onsmeðre,* showing the by-form *anfealt,* fem. sb., an anvil, with the same gradation as the OHG. *anafalz,* and strongly confirming the above etymology. See Kluge, s.v. *Falz;* Schade, p. 1322.

ANXIOUS, distressed, oppressed, much troubled. (L.) In Milton, P. L. viii. 185. Sir T. More, Works, p. 197 e, has *anxyete.* [The sb. was perhaps taken from F. *anxieté,* given by Cotgrave, and explained by 'anxietie;' but the adj. must have been taken directly from Latin, with the change of *-us* into *-ous* as in other cases, e. g. *pious, amphibious, barbarous.*]−L. *anxius,* anxious, distressed.−L. *angere,* to choke, strangle. +Gk. ἄγχειν, to strangle.−√ANGH, to choke, oppress; Brugm. i. § 178. Der. *anxious-ly, anxious-ness;* also *anxi-e-ty,* from F. *anxieté,* L. acc. *anxietātem.* From the same root we have *anger, anguish,* L. *angina,* and even *quinsy.*

ANY, indef. pronoun; some one. (E.) An indeterminate derivative of *one.* The ME. forms are numerous, as *æniȝ, æni, ani, oni. eni,* &c.; *ænig* is in OE. Homilies, i. 219. AS. *ænig,* formed with suffix *-ig* (cf. *greed-y* from AS. *grǣd-ig*) from the numeral *ān,* one.+Du. *eenig,* any; from *een,* one. Cf. G. *einiger,* any one; from *ein,* one. See **One.** Der. *any-thing, any-wise.*

AORIST, a name for two of the past tenses of a Greek verb. (Gk.) In Phillips (1658).−Gk. ἀόριστος, lit. 'indefinite.'−Gk. ἀ-, neg. prefix; and ὁρίζειν, to define, limit; see **Horizon.**

AORTA, the great artery rising up from the left ventricle of the heart. (Late L.−Gk.) In Burton, Anat. of Melancholy, i. 1. 2. 3; ed. 1827, p. 26. Late L. *aorta;* borrowed directly from Gk. ἀορτή, the aorta.−Gk. ἀείρειν, to raise up; pass. ἀείρεσθαι, to rise up. See Prellwitz, p. 4.

APACE, at a great pace. (Hybrid; E. and F.) Marlow has 'gallop *apace;*' Edw. II, A. iv. sc. 3, l. 12. At an earlier period the word was written as two words, *a pas,* as in Chaucer, C. T., F 388: 'And forth she walketh esily *a pas.*' [It is also to be remarked that the phrase has partly changed its meaning. In Chaucer, both here and in other passages, it means 'at a foot-pace,' and was originally used of men or horses when proceeding at no great speed.] The phrase is composed of *a,* for *on,* i. e. at; and the ME. *pas,* mod. E. *pace,* a word of F. origin. See **A-** (2) and **Pace.**

APART, aside. (F.−L.) T. Usk speaks of the 'fyve sondrye wittes, eueriche *apart* to his own doing;' Testament of Love, iii. 6. 51. The phrase is borrowed from the F. *à part,* which Cotgrave gives, and explains by '*apart,* alone, singly.'−L. *ad partem,* to the one part or side, apart.−L. *ad,* to; and *partem,* acc. case of *pars,* a part. See **Part.**

APARTMENT, a separate room. (F.−Ital.−L.) In Dryden, tr. of Virgil, Æn. ii. 675.−F. *appartement.*−Ital. *appartamento,* a separation, Florio; an apartment, Torriano.−Ital. *appartare,* to withdraw apart, id.; also (formerly) *apartare.*−Ital. *a parte,* apart. See above.

APATHY, want of feeling. (F.−L.−Gk.) In Holland's Plutarch, p. 62, we have the pl. *apathies;* he seems to use it as if it were a new word in English. Pope has *apathy,* Essay on Man, ii. 101.−F. *apathie* (Hatzfeld).−L. *apathīa* (Gellius).−Gk. ἀπάθεια, apathy, insensibility. −Gk. ἀ-, neg. prefix; and παθεῖν, to suffer. See **Pathos.** Der. *apath-et-ic.*

APE, a kind of monkey. (E.) ME. *ape,* King Alisaunder, ed. Weber, 4344; Ancren Riwle, p. 248. AS. *apa,* Ælf. Glos., Nomina Ferarum. +Du. *aap;* Icel. *api;* Swed. *apa;* G. *affe;* Teut. type **apon-,* m. Prob. borrowed from a non-Teut. source. ¶ ORuss. *opica* (Miklosich), is borrowed from Teut. Der. *ap-ish, ap-ish-ly, ap-ish-ness.*

APEPSIA, lack of digestion. (Gk.) Phillips (1658) has *apepsie.* −Gk. ἀπεψία, indigestion.−Gk. ἀ-, neg. prefix; and πέπτειν, to digest, allied to Gk. πεπ-τός, cooked, and πέσσειν, to cook. See **Cook.**

APERIENT, a purgative. (L.) The word signifies, literally, 'opening.' Used by Bacon, Nat. Hist. sect. 961.−L. *aperient-,* stem of *aperiens,* pres. pt. of *aperire,* to open. (Perhaps from *ap-,* old form of *ab-,* away; and *-uer-* = Lith. *wer-* in *werti,* to move (to or fro); whence Lith. *at-werti,* to open. See Brugm. i. § 361.) From same source, *aperture,* L. *apertūra,* from *aperire* (pp. *apert-us*).

APEX, the summit, top. (L.) Used by Ben Jonson, King James's Entertainment; description of a Flamen.−L. *apex,* summit. Origin uncertain.

APH-, prefix. See **Apo-,** prefix.

APHÆRESIS, the taking away of a letter or syllable from the beginning of a word. (L.−Gk.) In Cotgrave, s. v. *Aphairese.*−Late L. *aphæresis.*−Gk. ἀφαίρεσις, a taking away.−Gk. ἀφαιρεῖν, to take away.−Gk. ἀπό, from (> ἀφ- before an aspirate); and αἱρεῖν, to take. See **Heresy.**

APHELION, the point in a planet's orbit furthest from the sun. (Gk.) Scientific. Spelt *aphelium* in Blount's Gloss. (1681). Coined from Gk. ἀφ-, for ἀπό, from; and ἥλιος, the sun. See **Solar.**

APHIS, one of a family of minute and destructive insects. (Gk.?) A name due to Linnæus; with pl. *aphides.* Of unknown etymology; but probably the pl. *aphides* represents Gk. ἀφειδεῖς, pl. of ἀφειδής, 'unsparing,' hence voracious; from which a sing. *aphis* was evolved. From Gk. ἀ-, neg. prefix; and φείδομαι, I spare.

APHORISM, a definition, brief saying. (F.−Gk.) *Aphorisms* is in Bacon, Adv. of Learning, i. 5. 4; spelt *aphorismes,* Sir T. Elyot, Castel of Helth, b. iii. c. 1; p. 54. Perhaps mediately, through the French. Cf. '*Aphorisme,* m., aphorisme or generall rule in physick;' Cot.−Gk. ἀφορισμός, a definition, a short pithy sentence.−Gk. ἀφορίζειν, to define, mark off.−Gk. ἀπό, from, off (> ἀφ- before an aspirate); and ὁρίζειν, to divide, limit; from ὅρος, a boundary. See **Horizon.** Der. *aphoris-t-ic, aphoris-t-ic-al, aphoris-t-ic-al-ly.*

APIARY, a place for keeping bees. (L.) Used by Evelyn; Diary, July 13, 1654. Formed, with suffix *-y* for *-ium,* from L. *apiārium,* a place for bees, neut. of *apiārius,* of or belonging to bees. The masc. *apiārius* means 'a keeper of bees.'−L. *apis,* a bee.

APIECE, in a separate share. (Hybrid; E. and F.) Often written *a-piece;* Shak. Merry Wives, i. 1. 160. For *a piece* (two words); meaning 'for one piece.' Here *a* is the indef. article. See **Piece.**

APO-, prefix, off. (Gk.) Gk. ἀπό, off, from. Cognate with E. *of, off.* See **Of, Off.** Der. *apo-calypse,* &c.; see below. ¶ Since ἀπό becomes ἀφ- before an aspirate, it appears also in *aph-æresis, aph-(h)elion,* and *aph-orism.*

APOCALYPSE, a revelation. (L.−Gk.) A name given to the last book of the Bible. ME. *apocalips,* used by Wyclif.−L. *apocalypsis,* Rev. i. 1 (Vulgate version), Rev. i. 1; lit. 'an uncovering.'−Gk. ἀποκαλύπτειν, to uncover.−Gk. ἀπό, off (cognate with E. *off*); and καλύπτειν, to cover. Cf. Gk. καλύβη, a hut, cabin, cell, cover; καλιά, a cot. Allied to **Calyx** and **Cell.** Der. *apocalyp-t-ic, apocalyp-t-ic-al.*

APOCOPE, a cutting off of a letter or syllable at the end of a word. (L.−Gk.) In Palsgrave, p. 402, l. 1. A grammatical term; L. *apocopē,* borrowed from Gk. ἀποκοπή, a cutting off.−Gk. ἀπό, off (see **Apo-**); and κόπτειν, to hew, cut. Brugm. i. § 645.

APOCRYPHA, certain books of the Old Testament. (Gk.) 'The other [bookes] folowynge, which are called *apocripha* (because they were wont to be reade, not openly and in common, but as it were in secrete and aparte) are neytherfounde in the Hebrue nor in the Chalde;' Bible, 1539; Pref. to Apocrypha. The word means 'things hidden;' hence, unauthentic.−Gk. ἀπόκρυφα, things hidden, neut. pl. of ἀπόκρυφος, hidden.−Gk. ἀποκρύπτειν, to hide away.−Gk. ἀπό, off, away (see **Apo-**); and κρύπτειν, to hide. See **Crypt.** Der. *apocryph-al.*

APOGEE, the point in the moon's orbit furthest from the earth. (F.−L.−Gk.) Scientific. *Apoge* in Cockeram (1624). F. *apogée* (Cot.).−Late L. *apogæum.*−Gk. ἀπόγαιον, neut. of ἀπόγαιος, adj., away from earth.−Gk. ἀπό, away; and γῆ, earth.

APOLOGUE, a fable, story. (F.−L.−Gk.) In Minsheu, ed. 1627. Used by Bp. Taylor, vol. i. ser. 25. § 9.−F. *apologue,* m., which Cotgrave explains by 'a pretty and significant fable or tale, wherein bruit beasts, or dumb things, are famed to speak.'−L. *apologum,* acc. of *apologus.*−Gk. ἀπόλογος, a story, fable.−Gk. ἀπό, off; and λογ-, second grade of λέγειν, to speak. See **Apo-** and **Logic.**

APOLOGY, a defence, excuse. (L.−Gk.) Sir T. More, Works, p. 932 a, speaks of 'the booke that is called mine *apology.*' [He probably Englished it from the L. *apologia*, used by St. Jerome, rather than from the Gk. immediately.]—Gk. ἀπολογία, a speech made in one's defence.—Gk. ἀπό, off (see **Apo-**); and λέγειν, to speak; see **Logic**. Der. *apolog-ise*, *apolog-ist*; *apolog-et-ic* (Gk. ἀπολογητικός, fit for a defence), *apologet-ic-al*, *apolog-et-ic-al-ly*. And see above.

APOPHTHEGM, APOTHEGM, a terse saying. (Gk.) Bacon wrote a collection of *apophthegms*, so entitled. Udall's tr. of Erasmus' *Apophthegmes* is dated 1542. The word is sometimes shortened to *apothegm*.—Gk. ἀπόφθεγμα, a thing uttered; also, a terse saying, apophthegm.—Gk. ἀποφθέγγομαι, I speak out my mind plainly.—Gk. ἀπό, off, out (see **Apo-**); and φθέγγομαι, I cry out, cry aloud, utter. From the same root are *di-phthong*, *mono-phthong*.

APOPLEXY, a sudden deprivation of motion by a shock to the system. (F.—Late L.—Gk.) Chaucer, in l. 21 of The Nun's Priest's Tale, has the form *poplexye*; like his *potecarie* for *apothecary*.—F. *apoplexie* (Cot.).—Late L. *apoplexia*, also spelt *poplexia*; see the latter in Ducange.—Gk. ἀποπληξία, stupor, apoplexy.—Gk. ἀποπλήσσειν, to cripple by a stroke.—Gk. ἀπό, off (see **Apo-**); and πλήσσειν, to strike. See **Plague**. Der. *apoplec-t-ic*.

APOSTASY, APOSTACY, a desertion of one's principles or line of conduct. (F.—Late L.—Gk.) In rather early use. ME. *apostasie*, Wyclif's Works, ii. 51.—F. *apostasie*, 'an apostasie;' Cot.—Late L. *apostasia*; Ducange.—Gk. ἀποστασία, a later form of ἀπόστασις, a defection, revolt, lit. 'a standing away from.'—Gk. ἀπό, off, from (see **Apo-**); and στάσις, a standing, from στα-, base allied to ἵστημι. I place, set. See **Statics**. And see below.

APOSTATE, one who renounces his belief. (F.—Late L.—Gk.) The sb. *apostate* occurs in the Ayenbite of Inwyt, p. 19, and is often spelt *apostata* (the Late L. form), as in P. Plowman, B. i. 104, and indeed very much later, viz. in Massinger's Virgin Martyr, A. iv. sc. 3. l. 62.—OF. *apostate*, later *apostat*, as given by Cotgrave, and explained 'an apostata.'—Late L. *apostata* (also a common form in English).—Gk. ἀποστάτης, a deserter, apostate.—Gk. ἀπό; and στα-, base allied to ἔστην; I placed myself, ἵστημι, I place, set; see above. Der. *apostat-ise*. ¶ The L. form *apostata* occurs even in AS.

APOSTEME, an abscess; now **Imposthume**, q.v.

APOSTLE, one sent to preach the gospel; especially applied to the earliest disciples of Christ. (L.—Gk.) Wyclif has *apostle*, Rom. i. 1. The initial *a* was often dropped in ME., as in *posteles*, P. Plowman, B. vi. 151. The earlier writers use *apostel*, as in OE. Homilies, i. 117. The AS. form was *apostol*, Matt. x. 2.—L. *apostolus*.—Gk. ἀπόστολος, an apostle; Matt. x. 2, &c. Lit. 'one who is sent away.'—Gk. ἀποστέλλειν, to send away.—Gk. ἀπό (see **Apo-**); and στέλλειν, to send. See **Stole**. Der. *apostle-ship*; also *apostol-ic*, *apostol-ic-al*, *apostol-ic-al-ly*, *apostol-ate*; from L. *apostolus*.

APOSTROPHE, a mark showing that a word is contracted; also an address to the dead or absent. (L.—Gk.) Ben Jonson, Engl. Gram. b. ii. c. 1, calls the mark an *apostrophus*; Shak. *apostropha*, L. L. L. iv. 2. 123. These are Latinised forms; the usual L. form is *apostrophē*. Palsgrave has: 'the fygure called *Apostrophe*;' p. xix. l. 2.—Gk. ἀποστροφή, a turning away; ἀπόστροφος, the mark called an apostrophe; [from which the mod. E. form should have been *apostroph*.] Ἀποστροφή also signifies a figure in rhetoric, in which the orator turns away from the rest to address one only, or from all present to address the absent.—Gk. ἀπό, away (see **Apo-**); and στρέφειν, to turn. See **Strophe**. Der. *apostroph-ise*.

APOTHECARY, a seller of drugs. (F.—Late L.—Gk.) Lit. 'the keeper of a store-house or repository.' ME. *apothecarie*, Chaucer, C. T., Prol. 425; sometimes shortened to *pothecarie* or *potecarie*, id., C 852.—OF. *apotecaire*.—Late L. *apothecarius*, *apotecarius*; Wright's Vocabularies, i. 129.—L. *apotheca*, a storehouse.—Gk. ἀποθήκη, a storehouse, in which anything is laid up or put away.—Gk. ἀπό, away (see **Apo-**); and τί-θη-μι, I place, put. See **Thesis**.

APOTHEGM. See **Apophthegm**.

APOTHEOSIS, deification. (L.—Gk.) Quotations (without references) from South and Garth occur in Todd's Johnson. Bacon has it, Adv. of Learning, i. vii. 1.—L. *apotheōsis*.—Gk. ἀποθέωσις, deification.—Gk. ἀποθεόω, I deify; lit. 'set aside as a god.'—Gk. ἀπό (see **Apo-**); and θέος, a god. See **Theism**.

APPAL, to terrify, dismay. (F.—L.) The present sense is modern. The ME. *appallen* meant 'to become pale,' or 'to make pale' or 'feeble.' Thus Palsgrave has: 'I *appale* ones colour, Ie *appalis*;' and 'I *appalle*, as drinke clothe or wyne, whan it leseth his colour or ale whan it hath stande longe, Ie *appalys*.' Chaucer has *appalled*, made pale, C. T., F 365 (10679). Gower has 'myn hed *appalleth*,' my head becomes pale, C. A. ii. 107; bk. iv. 3160.—OF. *apallir*, *apalir*, *appalir*, to wax pale; also, to make pale (Cot.).—OF. *a-*, prefix; *pale*, *palle*, pale.—L. *ad*, to: and *pallidus*, pale. See **Pale** (2), **Pall** (2).

APPANAGE, APANAGE, provision for a dependent; esp. used of lands set apart as a provision for younger sons. (F.—L.) A French law term. Cotgrave gives 'Appanage, Appennage, the portion

of a younger brother in France; the lands, dukedomes, counties, or countries assigned by the king unto his younger sons, or brethren, for their entertainment; also, any portion of land or money delivered unto a sonne, daughter, or kinsman, in lieu of his future right of succession to the whole, which he renounces upon the receit thereof; or, the lands and lordships given by a father unto his younger sonne, and to his heires for ever, a child's part.' [Mod. F. *apanage*, which in feudal law meant any pension or alimentation; Brachet. The Late L. forms *apānagium*, *appānagium* are merely Latinised from the French.] β. Formed with F. suffix *-age* (L. *-āticum*), from OF. *apaner*, to nourish, lit. to supply with bread, written *apānāre* in Late L.; Ducange.—L. *ap-* (for *ad*), to, for; and *pān-is*, bread. See **Pantry**.

APPARATUS, preparation, provision, gear. (L.) Used by Hale, Origin of Mankind, p. 366. Borrowed from L. *apparātus*, preparation; cf. *apparātus*, pp. of *apparāre*, to prepare for.—L. *ad*, to, for (>*ap-* before *p*); and *parāre*, to make ready. See **Prepare**.

APPAREL, to clothe, dress. (F.—L.) The ME. *aparailen*, to make ready, occurs in An Old Eng. Miscellany, ed. Morris, p. 26. [The sb. is ME. *apparel*, *appareil*; Wyclif, 1 Macc. ix. 35, 52; 2 Macc. xii. 14.=OF. *aparail*, *apareil*, apparel, dress.]—OF. *aparailler*, to dress, to apparel.—OF. *a-*, prefix (L. *ad*); and *pareiller*, *parailler*, to assort, to put like things together with like, to arrange, from *pareil*, *parail*, like, similar; mod. F. *pareil*. β. The adj. *pareil* is from Late L. *pariculum*, acc. of *pariculus*, like, similar, found in old medieval documents: 'hoc sunt *pariculas* cosas,' Lex Salica; Brachet.—L. *pari-*, stem of *pār*, equal; with suffixes *-cu-* and *-lo-*, both diminutive. See **Par, Pair, Peer**. Der. *apparel*, sb.

APPARENT, APPARITION; see **Appear**.

APPEAL, to call upon, have recourse to. (F.—L.) ME. *appelen*, *apelen*. Gower, C. A. iii. 192, has *appele* as a verb, and *appeel* as a sb. (bk. vii. 3171, 3175). The sb. *apel*, appeal, occurs in Rob. of Glouc., p. 473, l. 9705.—OF. *apeler*, to invoke, call upon, accuse; spelt with one *p* because the prefix was *a*, the OF. form of L. *ad*.—L. *appellāre*, to address, call upon; also spelt *adpellāre*; a secondary form from L. *appellere*, *adpellere*, to drive to, bring to, incline towards.—L. *ad*, to; and *pellere*, to drive. See **Impel**. Der. *appeal*, sb., *appeal-able*; *appell-ant*, MF. *appell-ant*, pres. pt. of *appeller*; and (from L. *appellāre*) *appell-ate*, *appell-at-ion*, *appell-at-ive*.

APPEAR, to become visible, come forth visibly. (F.—L.) ME. *apperen*, *aperen*; spelt *appiere*, P. Plowman, B. iii. 113; pt. t. *aperede*, O. Eng. Misc., ed. Morris, p. 27.—OF. *aper-*, tonic stem (as in pres. subj. *apere*) of *aparoir*, to appear.—L. *appārēre*, to appear.—L. *ad*, to (which becomes *ap-* before *p*); and *pārēre*, to appear, come in sight, which is also written *parrēre*. Der. *appear-ance*; and (from L. *appārēre*) *appar-ent*, *appar-ent-ly*, *appar-ent-ness*, *appar-it-ion*, *appar-it-or*. The phrase *heir apparaunt* = heir apparent, is in Gower, C. A. i. 203 (bk. ii. 1320).

APPEASE, to pacify, quiet. (F.—L.) ME. *apaisen*, *apesen*, *appesen*. 'Cacus *apaysede* the wratthes of Evander;' Chaucer, tr. of Boethius, b. iv. met. 7, l. 36. Gower has *appesed*, C. A. i. 341 (bk. iii. 1849).—AF. *apeser*, *apeiser*, OF. *apeser*, mod. F. *apaiser*, to pacify, bring to a peace.—OF. *a peis*, *a pais*, to a peace.—L. *ad pācem*, to a peace.—L. *ad*, to; and *pācem*, acc. of *pax*, peace. See **Peace** and **Pacify**. Der. *appeas-able*.

APPELLANT, &c.; see **Appeal**.

APPEND, to add afterwards. (F.—L.) Now used in the sense 'to hang one thing on to another;' from F. *appendre*, the same.—L. *appendere*, to suspend on.—L. *ap-*, for *ad*, to; and *pendere*, to hang. β. But formerly intransitive, and lit. 'to hang on to something else,' to depend upon, belong to; the ME. *appenden*, *apenden* always has this intransitive sense. 'Telle me to whom, madame, that tresore *appendeth*,' i.e. belongs; P. Plowman, B. i. 45.—OF. *apendre*, to depend on, belong to, be attached to, lit. 'hang on to.'—Late L. *appendere*, for L. *appendēre*, to hang to or upon.—L. *ap-*, for *ad*, to; and *pendēre*, to hang. See **Pendant**. Der. *append-age* (F.), *append-ix* (L.).

APPERTAIN, to belong to. (F.—L.) ME. *apertenen*, *aperteinen*; Chaucer, C. T., G 785; tr. of Boethius, b. iii. pr. 4. 25.—OF. *apartein-*, a stem of the verb *apartenir* (mod. F. *appartenir*), to pertain to.—OF. *a*, prefix (L. *ad*); and OF. *partenir*, to pertain, from L. *pertinēre*, to pertain, a compound of L. *per*, through, thoroughly, and *tenēre*, to hold. See **Pertain**. Der. *appurten-ance* (OF. *apurtenaunse*, *apartenance*), *appurten-ant*.

APPETITE, strong natural desire for a thing. (F.—L.) ME. *appetyt*, Chaucer, C. T., B 3390; Maundevile's Travels, p. 157.—OF. *appetit*.—L. *appetītus*, an appetite, lit. 'a flying upon,' or 'assault upon.'—L. *appetere*, to fly to, to attack.—L. *ad-*, to (>*ap-* before *p*); and *petere*, to fly, rush swiftly, seek swiftly.—√PET, to fall, fly. Cf. Gk. πέτ-ομαι, I fly; Brugm. i. § 116. See **Petition**. Der. *appet-ise*; Milton *appet-ence*, desire, P. L. xi. 619.

APPLAUD, to praise by clapping hands. (L.) Shak. Macb. v. 3. 53. Directly from L. *applaudere*, pp. *applausus*. The L. *applau-*

dere means 'to clap the hands together.'—L. *ad*, to, together (>*ap*- before *p*); and *plaudere*, to strike, clap, also spelt *plōdere* (whence E. *ex-plode*). See **Explode**. Der. *applause*, Shak. Cor. i. 9. 64; *a,p'us-ive*, from L. pp. *a plausus*.

APPLE, the fruit of the apple-tree. (E.) The *apple* of the eye (Deut. xxxii. 10) is properly the pupil (see N. E. D.); but was sometimes used of its round shape; see Catholicon Anglicum, p. 11, note 5. ME. *appel, appil*; spelt *appell* in the Ormulum, 8118. AS. *æpl, æppel*; Grein, i. 58. OFries. *appel*. **+** Du. *appel*, apple, ball, eye-ball; Icel. *epli*; Swed. *äple, äpple*; Dan. *æble*; OHG. *aphol, aphul*, G. *apfel*; Irish *abhal*, Gael. *ubhal*, W. *afal*, Bret. *aval*. Cf. also Russ. *jabloko*, Lithuanian *obolys*, &c. Origin unknown. Some connect it with Abella in Campania; cf. Verg. Æn. vii. 740. This is not satisfactory.

APPLY, to fix the mind on; to appropriate to. (F.—L.) ME. *applyen*. 'Applyyn, applico, oppono;' Prompt. Parv. p. 13. It occurs in the Wycl. Bible, Numb. xvi. 5, &c.—OF. *aplier* (s. v. *aploier*, Godefroy).—L. *applicāre*, to join to, attach; turn or direct towards, apply to; pp. *applicātus*.—L. *ad*, to (>*ap*- before *p*); and *plicāre*, to fold or lay together, twine together. See **Ply**. Der. *appli-able, appli-ance*; and (from L. *applicāre*), *applica-ble, applic-ant, applic-at-ion*.

APPOGGIATURA, a grace-note or passing tone prefixed as a support to an essential note of a melody. (Ital.—L. and Gk.) Modern; in music.—Ital. *appoggiatura*, lit. a support.—Ital. *appoggiare*, to lean upon.—L. *ap*-, for *ad*, to, upon; *poggio*, a place to lean on.—L. *ad*, to; *podium*, an elevated place, balcony, from Gk. πόδιον, lit. 'little foot,' a footstool, gallery to sit in, &c.; from Gk. ποδ-, as in πόδ-α, acc. of πούς, foot. See **Foot** and **Pew**.

APPOINT, to fix, settle, equip. (F.—L.) ME. *appointen, apointen*; 'apointed in the newe mone;' Gower, C. A. ii. 265 (bk. v. 4115).—OF. *apointer*, to prepare, arrange, settle, fix.—Late L. *appunctāre*, to repair, appoint, settle a dispute; Ducange.—L. *ad*-, to (>*ap*- before *p*); and Late L. *punctāre*, to mark by a prick, from *punc'us*, pp. of *pungere*, to prick, pt. t. *pupugi*; the orig. L. root *pug*- being preserved in the reduplicated perfect tense. See **Point**. ¶ In some senses, OF. *apointer* was from the phrase *a point*, L. *ad punctum*. Der. *appoint-ment*; Merry Wives, ii. 2. 272.

APPORTION, to portion out. (F.—L.) Used by Bp. Taylor, Of Repentance, c. 3. s. 6 (R.)—F. *apportioner*, 'to apportion, to give a portion, or child's part;' Cot. Formed by prefixing F. *a*- (which in later times was written *ap*- before *p*, in imitation of the L. prefix *ap*-, the form taken by *ad*- before *p*) to the F. verb *portionner*, 'to apportion, part, share, deal,' Cot.; from F. *portion*, a portion, from L. *portiōnem*, acc. of *portio*, a portion, share. See **Portion**. Der. *apportion-ment*.

APPOSITE, suitable. (L.) [The ME. verb *apposen* was used in the special sense of 'to put questions to,' 'to examine by questions;' but this was really another form of *op'osen*, 'to argue against,' and is preserved as *pose*; see **Pose** (2).] Bacon speaks of 'ready and *apposite* answers;' Life of Henry VII, ed. Lumby, p. 111, l. 22.—L. *appositus*, adj. suitable; orig. pp. of *appōnere*, to place or put to, join, annex to.—L. *a d*, to (>*ap*- before *p*); and *pōnere*, to place, put. See **Position**. Der. *apposite-ly, apposite-ness, apposit-ion*.

APPRAISE, to set a price on, to value. (F.—L.) Sometimes spelt *apprize*, as in Bp. Hall's Account of Himself, quoted by Richardson. The ME. forms (with one *p*) *apreisen, apraisen*, signify to value, to esteem highly, as in 'Hur enparel was *a'raysut* with princes of my3te' = her apparel was highly prized by mighty princes; Anturs of Arthur, st. 29. In P. Plowman, B. v. 334, the simple verb *prei ed* occurs with the sense of 'appraised.'—OF. *a*, prefix (L. *ad*); and *preiser, prei ier, prisier*, to appreciate, value, set a price on; the compound being suggested by OF. *aprisier*, to appraise, appreciate (Godefroy). The verb *preiser* is from OF. *preis*, a price, value, L. *pretium*, a price. See **Price**. ¶ The E. words *price* and *praise* being doublets, the words *apprize*, in the sense of to 'value,' and *appraise* are also doublets. To *apprize* in the sense 'to inform' is a different word; see **Apprize**. Der. *a praiser, appraise-ment*. And see below.

APPRECIATE, to set a just value on. (L.) Richardson gives a quotation from Bp. Hall containing the sb. *appreciation*. Fuller has it also; Pisgah Sight, b. ii. c. 12. § 47. Gibbon uses *appreciate*, Rom. Empire, c. 44. § 5 (from end). Formed from L. *appretiātus*, pp. of *appretiāre*, to value at a price. [The spelling with *c* instead of *t* is due to the fact that the sb. *appreciation* seems to have been in earlier use than the verb, and was borrowed directly from F. *appreciation*, which Cotgrave explains by 'a praising or prizing; a rating, valuation, or estimation of.'] The L. *appretiāre* is a made up word, from L. *ad* (becoming *ap*- before *p*) and *pretium*, a price. See **Price**; and see **Appraise** above. Der. *appreciat-ion; apprecia-ble, apprecia-bly*.

APPREHEND, to lay hold of, to understand; to fear. (L.) Hall, Henry IV, an. 1. § 12, has *apprehended* in the sense of attached, taken prisoner.—L. *apprehendere*, to lay hold of, seize.—L. *ad*, to (becoming

ap- before *p*); and *prehendere*, to seize, pp. *prehensus*. See **Prehensile**. Der. *apprehens-ion, apprehens-ible, apprehens-ive, apprehens-ive-ness*; from L. pp. *apprehensus*. And see below.

APPRENTICE, a learner of a trade. (F.—L.) 'Apparailled hym as *apprentice*;' P. Plowman, B. ii. 214, in MS. W.; see the footnote; other MSS. read *a prentice* in this passage. [The forms *apprentice* and *prentice* were used indifferently in ME., and can be so used still; the syllable *a*- was easily confused with the indef. article.]—OF. *aprentis*, nom. case of *aprentif*; see Supp. to Godefroy, p. 156. The forms *aprentis, aprentif* represent Folk-L. types *apprenditīvus*, nom., and *apprenditīvum*, acc.; from a Late L. *apprenditus*, used as a new pp. of L. *apprendere*, short form of *apprehendere*, to lay hold of. See **Apprehend**. See F. *apprenti* in Hatzfeld; cf. Gascon *aprentis*, Span. and Port. *aprendiz*. Der. *apprentice-ship*.

APPRIZE, APPRISE, to inform, teach. (F.—L.) 'You must be extremely well *apprized*, that,' &c.; Spectator, no. 518 (1712). Formed from MF. *apprendre* (Palsgrave, p. 606, s. v. *lerne*), pp. *appris*, 'taught, instructed,' Cot.; by analogy with *comprise, surprise*, from F. *comprendre, surprendre*. From Late L. *apprendere*, to learn; contr. form of *apprehendere*, to apprehend, lay hold of. See **Apprehend**.

APPROACH, to draw near to. (F.—L.) ME. *approchen, aprochen*; Allit. Poems, ed. Morris, B. 8; Chaucer, tr. of Boethius, b. i. pr. 1, l. 31.—OF. *aprochier*, to approach, draw near to.—L. *appropiāre*, to draw near to; in the Vulgate version of Exod. iii. 5.—L. *ad*, to (becoming *ap*- before *p*); and *propius*, comp. of *prope*, near, which appears again in E. *prop-inquity*. Der. *approach-able*.

APPROBATION; see **Approve**.

APPROPRIATE, adj. fit, suitable; v. to take to oneself as one's own. (L.) The sb. *apropriacioun* is in Gower, C. A. i. 240; bk. ii. 2396. The pp. *appropriated* is in the Bible of 1539, 3rd Esdras, c. 6 (Richardson). Tyndal, Works, p. 66, col. 1, has *appropriate* as an adjective, adopted from L. pp. *appropr.ātus*. [This is how most of our verbs in -*ate* were formed; first came the pp. form in -*ate*, used as an adj., from L. pp. in -*ātus*; also used with the sense of a pp., which at once suggested a verb in -*ate*.]—L. *appropriātus*, pp. of *appropriāre*, to make one's own.—L. *ad*, to (becoming *ap*- before *p*); and *proprius*, one's own; whence E. **Proper**, q. v. Der. *appropriate-ly, appropriate-ness, appropriat-ion*.

APPROVE, to commend; sometimes, to prove. (F.—L.) ME. *approuen, appreuen* (with *u* for *v*). Chaucer has 'approued in counseilling;' C. T., B 2345.—OF. *aprover*, to approve of (Godefroy); mod. F. *approuver*.—L. *approbāre*, to commend; pp. *approbātus*.—L. *ad*, to (becoming *ap*- before *p*); and *probāre*, to test, try; to approve, esteem as good, from *probus*, good. See **Prove**. Der. *approv-ing-ly, approv-able, approv-al*; also *a probat-ion*, ME. *approbac-ion* (Gower, C. A. ii. 86; bk. iv. 2519), from L. *approbātio*.

APPROXIMATE, adj. near to; v. to bring or come near to. (L.) Sir T. Browne, Vulg. Errors, b. iii. c. 21. § 9, has *approximate* as an adjective; hence was formed the verb; see note on **Appropriate**.—L. *approximātus*, pp. of *approximāre*, to draw near to.—L. *ad*, to (becoming *ap*- before *p*); and *proximus*, very near, superlative adj. formed from *prope*, near. See **Approach**. Der. *approximate-ly, approximat-ion*.

APPURTENANCE, in P. Plowman, B. ii. 103 (MS. W); see **Appertain**.

APRICOT, a kind of plum. (F.—Port.—Arab.—Gk.—L.) [Formerly spelt *apricock*, Shak. Mids. Nt. Dr. iii. 1. 169; Rich. II, iii. 4. 29; from the Port. *albricoque*, an apricot.] Cotgrave has *abricot*, of which *apricot* is a corruption. We also find *abricot* in Phillips' Dict., 1658.—F *abricot*, which Cotgrave explains by 'the abricot, or apricote plum.'—Port. *albricoque*, an apricot; the F. word having been introduced from Portuguese; see Brachet. Cf. Span. *albaricoque*, Ital. *albercocca*. β. These words are traced, in Webster and Littré, back to the Arabic *al-barqūq* (Rich. Dict. p. 263), where *al* is the Arabic def. article, and the word *barqūq* is no true Arabic word, but a corruption of the Mid. Gk. πραικόκιον, Dioscorides, i. 165 (see Sophocles' Lexicon); pl. πραικόκια, borrowed from the L. *præcoqua*, apricots, neut. pl. of *præcoquus*, another form of *præcox*, lit. precocious, early-ripe. [They were also called *armenia*, i.e. Armenian fruit.] They were considered as a kind of peach (peaches were cal'ed *persica* in Latin) which ripened sooner than other peaches; and hence the name. 'Maturescunt æstate *præcocia* intra triginta annos reperta et primo denariis singulis uenundata;' Pliny, Nat. Hist. xv. 12; which Holland translates: 'the abricocts are ready to be eaten in summer; these have not bin known full 30 yeares, and at their first comming up, were sold for Roman deniers apeece.' 'Vilia maternis fueramus *præcoqua* ramis Nunc in adoptiuis *persica* cara sumus;' Martial, 13. 46. The L. *præcox*, early-ripe, is from *præ*, beforehand, and *coquere*, to ripen, to cook. See **Precocious**. ¶ The word thus came to us in a very roundabout way, viz. from L. to Gk.; then to Arab.; then to Port.; then to French, whence we borrowed *apricot*, having previously borrowed the older form *apricock* from the Portuguese directly.

APRIL, the name of the fourth month. (F.–L.) ME. *Aprille, April*; Chaucer, C. T. Prol. 1; also *Aueril* [*Averil*], Rob. of Glouc. p. 506; l. 10410. This older form is French; the word was afterwards conformed to Latin spelling.–OF. *Avril.*–L. *Aprīlis*, April; *said* to be so called because the earth then opens to produce new fruits.–L. *aperire*, to open. See **Aperient.**

APRON, a cloth worn in front to protect the dress. (F.–L.) In the Bible of 1539, Gen. iii. 7. Formerly spelt *napron* or *naprun*, so that an initial *n* has been lost. 'Napron or barm-clothe, *limas*;' Prompt. Parv. p. 351. 'Hir *napron* feir and white i-wassh;' Prol. to Tale of Beryn, l. 33.–OF. *naperon*, a large cloth (Roquefort); *naperon, napron*, a napkin (Godefroy). Formed with suffix -*r*- (appearing in OF. *nape-r-ie*, a place for keeping cloths), and suffix -*on* (answering to Ital. -*one*), from OF. *nape*, a cloth; mod. F. *nappe*, a cloth, table-cloth.–L. *mappa*, a cloth; with change of *m* to *n*, as in L. *matta*, F. *natte*, L. *mespilum*, F. *nefle*. See **Map.** ¶ On the loss of *n* in *napron*, see remarks prefixed to the letter N.

APROPOS, to the purpose. (F.–L.) Mere French; viz. *à propos*, to the purpose, lit. with reference to what is proposed.–L. *ad prōpositum*, to the purpose.–L. *ad*, to; and *prōpositum*, a thing proposed, neut. of *prōpositus*, proposed, pp. of *prōpōnere*, to propose. See **Propose** and **Purpose.**

APSE, an arched recess at the E. end of a church. (L.–Gk.) Modern and architectural; a corruption of *apsis*, which has been longer in use in astronomy, in which it is applied to the turning-points of a planet's orbit, when it is nearest to or farthest from the sun. The astronomical term is also now often written *apse.*–L. *apsis*, gen. written *absis*, a bow, turn; pl. *apsides.*–Gk. ἁψίς, ἀψίς, a fastening, felloe of a wheel, curve, bow, arch, vault.–Gk. ἅπτειν, to fasten, bind.

APT, fit, liable, ready. (L.) 'Flowring today, tomorowe *apt* to faile;' Lord Surrey, Frailtie of Beautie. First used in 1398 (N. E. D.) –L. *aptus*, fit, fitted; properly pp. of obsolete verb *apere*, to fasten, join together, but used in L. as the pp. of *apiscī*, to reach, seize, get. Der. *apt-ly, apt-ness, apt-i-tude*; also *ad-apt*, q. v., *ad-ept*, q. v.

APTERYX, a New Zealand bird; the kiwi. (Gk.) Lit. 'wingless;' because it has only rudimentary wings.–Gk. ἀ-, neg. prefix; and πτέρυξ, a wing, from πτ-, weak grade of πέτ-ομαι, I fly.

AQUATIC, pertaining to water. (L.) Used by Ray, On the Creation. Spelt *aquatyque*, Caxton, Eneydos, c. xxiv, p. 90, l. 2. Holland has *aquaticall*, Plutarch, p. 692 (R.). [Sir T. Browne has *aqueous*, Vulgar Errors, bk. ii. c. 1. § 6. Cotgrave has *aqueduct*, both as F. and E.]–L. *aquāticus*, pertaining to water.–L. *aqua*, water.+ Goth. *ahwa*, water; OHG. *aha*, MHG. *ahe*, water (obsolete); AS. *ēa*, a stream; Icel. *ā*, Dan. *aa*, Swed. *å*, stream. From L. *aqua* are also derived *aqua-fortis*, i.e. strong water, by the addition of *fortis*, strong; *aquā-rium, Aquā-rius, aque-ous; aque-duct*, from *aquæ*, gen. of *aqua*, water, and *ductus*, a duct.

AQUILINE, pertaining to or like an eagle. (L.; or F.–L.) 'His nose was *aquiline*;' Dryden, Palamon and Arcite, l. 1350. Perhaps from L. direct; but Cotgrave gives F. *aquilin*, of an eagle, like an eagle, with the example 'nez *aquilin*, a hawkenose, a nose like an eagle.'–L. *aquilinus*, belonging to an eagle.–L. *aquila*, an eagle. See **Eagle.**

ARABESQUE, Arabic, applied to designs. (F.–Ital.–Arab.) In Swinburne's Travels through Spain, lett. 31, qu. in Todd's Johnson, we find 'interwoven with the *arabesque* foliages.'–F. *Arabesque*, which Cotgrave explains by 'Arabian-like; also sb. f., *rebesk*-worke, a small and curious flourishing;' where *rebesk* is a corruption of the very word in question.–Ital. *Arabesco*, Arabian.–Arab. *'arab*, Arabia; Rich. Dict., p. 1000. The ending -*esco* in Italian answers to E. -*ish*. Der. From the name of the same country we have also *Arab, Arab-ian, Arab-ic.*

ARABLE, fit for tillage. (F.–L.) North speaks of '*arable* land;' Plutarch, p. 189 (R.). 'Land *arable*;' Tusser, Januaries Husbandrie, st. 52.–F. *arable*, explained by Cotgrave as 'earable, ploughable, tillable.'–L. *arābilis*, that can be ploughed.–L. *arāre*, to plough. See **Ear** (3).

ARAUCARIA, a genus of coniferous trees. (S. America.) So called from *Arauco*, the name of a province to the S. of Chili.

ARBALEST, another form of **Arblast,** q.v.

ARBITER, an umpire, judge of a dispute. (L.) In Milton, P. L. ii. 909. 'As *arbiter* of war and peace;' Ben Jonson, The Gipsies (Captain). [Some derivatives, borrowed from the French, are in much earlier use, viz. the fem. form *arbytres* (i.e. arbitress), Ayenbite of Inwyt, p. 154; *arbitrour*, Wyclif, 3 Esdras, viii. 26; *arbitrè, arbitree* (L. *arbitrium*, choice), Chaucer, tr. of Boethius, b. v. pr. 3. l. 12; *arbitracion*, Chaucer's Tale of Melibeus (B 2943); *arbitratour*, Hall, Henry VI, an. 4; *arbitrement*, Shak. Tw. Nt. iii. 4. 286.]–L. *arbiter*, a witness, judge, umpire; lit. 'one who comes to look on.' β. This curious word is compounded of *ar-* and -*biter*. Here *ar-* is a dialectal variation of L. *ad*, to, as in *ar-cessere* (Corssen, Ausspr. i. 2. 239);

and -*biter* means 'a comer,' from the weak grade of *bētere* (also *baetere* and *bitere*), to come, used by Pacuvius and Plautus. The root of *bētere* is perhaps *g(w)ē-* (cf. Lettish *gai-ta*, a going); see Brugm. i. §§ 587 (7), 663. Der. *arbitr-ess*; see also below.

ARBITRARY, depending on the will; despotic. (L.) In Milton, P. L. ii. 334.–L. *arbitrārius*, arbitrary, uncertain; lit. 'what is done by arbitration,' with reference to the discretion of the umpire.– L. *arbitrāre*, to act as umpire.–L. *arbitro-*, stem of *arbiter*, an umpire. See further under **Arbiter.** Der. *arbitrari-ly, arbitrari-ness*; and see below.

ARBITRATE, to act as umpire. (L.) Shak. Macb. v. 4. 20. He also has *arbitrator*, Troilus, iv. 5. 225; which appears as *arbitratour* (F. *arbitrateur*, Cotgrave) in Hall, Henry VI, an. 4; Chaucer has *arbitracioun* (F. *arbitration*), Tale of Melibeus, C. T., B 2943. Formed with suffix -*ate* (see **App opriate**) from L. *arbitrār-*, to act as arbiter, to be umpire (above). Der. *arbitrat-or, arbitrat-ion*; also *arbitra-ment* (F., from L. *arbitrāre*). And see above.

ARBLAST, ARBALEST, a steel cross-bow. (F.–L. and Gk.) Obsolete. ME. *arblaste*, dat., Rob. of Glouc. p. 377, l. 7735; AS. Chron. (MS. D.), an. 1079.–AF *arblast*, OF. *arbaleste* (F. *arbalète*). –L. *arcuballista*, a 'ballista' furnished with a bow.–L. *arcu-*, for *arcus*, a bow; and *ballista*, a machine for throwing stones, from Gk. βάλλ-ειν, to throw, with suffix -*ista*, Gk. -ιστης.

ARBOREOUS, belonging to trees. (L.) Used by Sir T. Browne, Vulg. Errors, b. ii. c 6, § 20. [Milton has *arborets*, i.e. groves (L. *arborētum*, a place planted with trees), P. L. ix. 437; and the same word occurs in Spenser, F. Q. iii. 6. 12; but we now use the L. *arborētum* in full.]–L. *arboreus*, of or belonging to trees, with the change of -*us* into -*ous*, as in *pious, strenuous.*–L. *arbor*, a tree. Der. (from the same source) *arbor-et, arbor-etum, arbor-escent*; also *arbori-culture, arbori-cultur-ist.*

ARBOUR, a bower made of branches of trees. (F.–L.; but altered.) Milton has *arbour*, P. L. v. 378, ix. 216; *arbours*, iv. 626. Shak. refers to an *arbor* within an orchard; 2 Hen. IV, v. 3. 2. In Sidney's Arcadia, bk. i, is described 'a fine close *arbor*, [made] of trees whose branches so lovingly interbraced one the other.' In Sir T. More's Works, p. 177 e, we read of 'sitting in an *arber*,' which was in 'the gardine.' α. There is no doubt that this word is, however, a later form of *herber*, or *erber*, a small lawn or herb-garden, which lost its initial *h* quite regularly; it is the ME. *herbere, erbere*, a garden of herbs or flowers, OF. *herbier*, L. *herbārium.* β. This latter word, being of F. origin, had the initial *h* weak, and sometimes silent, so that it was also spelt *erbare*, as in the Prompt. Parv. p. 140, where we find '*Erbare*, herbarium, viridarium, viridale.' Cf. 'Herbes he tok in an *herb r*;' K. Alisaunder, ed. Weber, 331. 'I entred in that *erber* grene;' Allit. Poems, A 38. And see P. Plowman, B. xvi. 13-15. γ. This occasioned a loss of *h* in *herbere*, and at the same time suggested a connexion with L. *arbor*, a tree; the result being further forced on by the fact that the ME. *herbere* was used not only to signify 'a garden of herbs,' but also 'a garden of fruit-trees' or orchard. δ. The L. *herbārium* is from *herba*, a herb. See **Herb.** ¶ See this explained in the Romance of Thomas of Erceldoune, ed. J. A. H. Murray, note to l. 177; and see N. E. D. Mr. Way, in his note to the Prompt. Parv., p. 140, is incorrect as to the certainty of *arbour* being a corruption of *harbour*, with which it has no connexion.

ARC, a segment of a circle. (F.–L.) Chaucer has *ark*, Man of Law's Prologue, l. 2; and frequently in his Treatise on the Astrolabe. In the latter, pt. ii. sect. 9, l. 2, it is also spelt *arch*, with *ch* for *k*; see **Arch** (1); cf. *ditch, dyke.*–OF. *arc*, an arc.–L. *arcum*, acc. of *arcus*, an arc, a bow. See **Arrow.** Der. *arc-ade*, q.v.; and see **Arch, Archer.**

ARCADE, a walk arched over. (F.–Ital.–L.) Pope has *arcades*, Moral Essays, Ep. iv. 35.–F. *arcade*, which Cotgrave explains by 'an arch, an half circle.'–Ital. *arcata*, lit. arched; fem. of pp. of *arcare*, to bend, arch.–Ital. *arco*, a bow.–L. *arcum*, acc. of *arcus*, a bow. See **Arc.** (See Hatzfeld, Etym. Dict. pref. p. 22.)

ARCANA: see Ark.

ARCH (1), a construction of stone or wood, &c., in a curved or vaulted form. (F.–L.) 'Arch yn a walle, arcus;' Prompt. Parv. p. 14 'An *arche* of marbel;' Trevisa, tr. of Higden, i. 215.–OF. *arche*, fem. sb. an arch, arcade (Godefroy).–Late L. *arca*, an ark, chest; but also improperly used with the sense of 'arch,' by confusion with L. *arcus*, a bow (Ducange). See **Arc.** ¶ Hence the *Court of Arches*, 'originally held in the arches of Bow Church–St. Mary *de Arcubus*–the crypt of which was used by Wren to support the present superstructure;' I. Taylor, Words and Places. And see Todd's Johnson. Der. *arch-ing, arch-ed.*

ARCH (2), chief; in later use, clever, cunning, roguish, waggish, sly. (L.–Gk.) 'Dogget . . . spoke his request with so *arch* a leer;' Tatler, no. 193 (1710). 'The most *arch* act of piteous massacre;' Rich. III, iv. 3. 2. 'An heretic, an *arch* one,' i.e. an arch-heretic;

Hen. VIII, iii. 2. 102. ' Byends . . . a very **arch** fellow, a downright hypocrite;' Bunyan, Pilg. Progress (Greatheart, in part ii). This curious adj. arose solely out of the use of the prefix *arch-*, which came to be used as a separate word. See **Arch-.** Der. *arch-ly*, *arch-ness*.

ARCH-, chief; almost solely used as a prefix. (L.—Gk.) Shak. has ' my worthy *arch* and patron,' Lear, ii. 1. 61 ; whence the use of *arch*, adj., as above. In *arch-bishop*, we have a word in very early use; AS. *erce-bisceop*, *arce-bisceop* (Bosworth). β. Thus *arch-* is to be rightly regarded as descended from AS. *arce-*, *ærce-*, *erce-*, which was borrowed from L. *archi-* (in *archi-episcopus*), and this again from Gk. ἀρχι- in ἀρχιεπίσκοπος, an archbishop.—Gk. ἀρχός, chief; ἄρχειν, to be first; cf. ἀρχή, beginning. ¶ The form of the prefix being once fixed, it was used for other words; it occurs also in OF., as in OF. *arche-diacre*, archdeacon. Der. *arch-bishop*, *arch-deacon*, *arch-duke*, *arch-duchy*, &c. ☞ In the word *arch-angel*, the *ch* remained hard (as *k*) in the Romance languages, on account of the *a* following; cf. Ital. *arcangelo*, Span. *arcangel*.

ARCHÆOLOGY, the science of antiquities. (Gk.) See *archaiology* in Todd's Johnson. Made up from Gk. ἀρχαῖο-s, ancient, and suffix *-logy* (Gk. -λογία), from Gk. λόγος, discourse; cf. λογ-, second grade of λέγειν, to speak. See **Archaic.** Der. *archæolog-ist*.

ARCHAIC, old, antique, primitive. (Gk.) Spelt *archaick*; added by Todd to Johnson's Dict. (1827). From Gk. ἀρχαϊκός, primitive, antique.—Gk. ἀρχαῖος, old, ancient, lit. ' from the beginning.'—Gk. ἀρχή, beginning.

ARCHAISM, an antiquated phrase. (Gk.) In Todd's Johnson, with a quotation dated 1643. From Gk. ἀρχαϊσμός, an archaism.—Gk. ἀρχαΐζειν, to speak antiquatedly.—Gk. ἀρχαῖος, old.—Gk. ἀρχή, beginning. See above.

ARCHER, a bowman. (F.—L.) In early use. Used by Rob. of Glouc., p. 199 (l. 4096); and still earlier, in King Alisaunder, ed. Weber, l. 6344.—AF. *archer*, Gaimar, 2814; OF. *archier*, an archer. —Late L. *arcārius*. Formed with L. suffix *-ārius* from L. *arc-us*, a bow. See **Arc.** Der. *arch-er-y*.

ARCHETYPE, the original type. (F.—Late L.—Gk.) Used by Bp. Hall, The Peacemaker, s. 23.—F. *archetype*, ' a principall type, figure, forme; the chief pattern, mould, modell, example, or sample, whereby a thing is framed;' Cot.—L. *archetypum*, the original pattern. —Gk. ἀρχέτυπον, a pattern, model; neut. of ἀρχέτυπος, stamped as a model.—Gk. ἀρχε-, another form of ἀρχι-, prefix (see **Archi-**); and τυπ-, as in τύπτειν, to beat, stamp. See **Type.** Der. *archetyp-al*.

ARCHI-, chief; used as a prefix. (L.—Gk.) The older E. form is *arch-*, which (as explained under **Arch-**) was a modification of AS. *arce-*, from L. *archi-*. The form *archi-* is of later use, and borrowed from the L. directly.—Gk. ἀρχι-, prefix. See **Arch-.** Der. *archi-episcopal*, *archi-episcopy*, *archi-diaconal*. ¶ In the word *arch-angel*, the final *i* of the prefix is dropped before the vowel following. In the word *arche-type*, the prefix takes the form *arche-*; see **Archetype.** The same prefix also forms part of the words *archi-mandrite*, *archi-pelago*, *archi-tect*, *archi-trave*, which see below.

ARCHIMANDRITE, the superior of a monastery or convent, in the Greek Church. (L.—Gk.) ' Archimandrite, an abbot, prior, or chief of an hermitage;' Blount's Gloss., ed. 1674.—Late L. *archimandrīta*, a chief or principal of monks, an abbot; Apollinaris Sidonius, Ep. 8. 14 (Lewis).—Late Gk. ἀρχιμανδρίτης, the same.— Gk. ἀρχι-, chief (see **Archi-**); μάνδρα, an enclosed space, fold, (in late Gk.) a monastery; see **Madrigal.**

ARCHIPELAGO, chief sea, i.e. Ægean Sea. (Ital.—Gk.) ' Archipelagus, or Archipelago;' Phillips (1706).—Ital. *arcipelago*, modified to *archipelago* by the substitution of the more familiar Gk. prefix *archi-* (see **Archi-**) for the Ital. form *arci-*.—Gk. ἀρχι-, prefix, signifying ' chief;' and πέλαγος, a sea. ¶ The Ital. *arcipelago* occurs as early as 1268; see N. E. D.

ARCHITECT, a designer of buildings. (F.—L.—Gk.) Lit. ' a chief builder.' Used by Shak. Tit. Andr. v. 3. 122; Milton, P. L. i. 732.—F. *architecte*, an architect; Cotgrave.—L. *architectus*, a form in use as well as *architectōn*, which is the older and more correct one, and borrowed from Gk.—Gk. ἀρχιτέκτων, a chief builder or chief artificer.—Gk. ἀρχι-, chief (see **Archi-**); and τέκτων, a builder, closely allied to τέχνα, art. See **Technical, Texture.** Der. *architect-ure*, *architect-ur-al*.

ARCHITRAVE, the part of an entablature resting immediately on the column. (F.—Ital.—Hybrid of Gk. and L.) Used by Milton, P. L. i. 715; and by Ben Jonson, The New Inn, iii. 2 (Lovel). Evelyn, On Architecture, remarks: ' the Greeks named that *epistilium* which we from a mungril compound of two languages (ἀρχή-*trabs*, or rather from *arcus* and *trabs*) called *architrave*.' His second derivation is wrong; the first is nearly right. His observation that it is ' a mungril compound ' is just. Lit. it means ' chief beam.'—F. *architrave*, ' the architrave (of pillars, or stonework); the reason-peece or master-beam (in buildings of timber);' Cot.—Ital. *architrave* (Torriano); *arcotrave*

(Florio), chief beam.—Gk. ἀρχι-, prefix, chief, adopted into L. as *archi-*; and L. acc. *trabem*, a beam, from the nom. *trabs*, a beam. Cf. Gk. τράφηξ. a spear-shaft, a beam.

ARCHIVES, s. pl. (1) the place where public records are kept; (2) the public records. (F.—L.—Gk.) The former is the true sense. The sing. is rare, but Holland has ' *archive* or register;' Plutarch, p. 116 (R.).—F. *archives*, *archifs*, ' a place wherein all the records, &c. [are] kept in chests and boxes;' Cot.—L. *archīuum* (*archivum*), also *archīum*, the archives.—Gk. ἀρχεῖον, a public building, residence of the magistrates.—Gk. ἀρχή, a beginning, a magistracy.

ARCTIC, northern. (F.—L.—Gk.) In Marlowe's Edw. II, A. i. sc. 1, l. 16. Milton has *arctick*, P. L. ii. 710. Chaucer has *artik*, Astrolabe, i. 14. 6.—F. *arctique*, northern, northerly; Cot.—L. *arcticus*, northern.—Gk. ἀρκτικός, near ' the bear,' northern.—Gk. ἄρκτος, a bear; esp. the Great Bear, a constellation situate not far from the northern pole of the heavens. + L. *ursus*, a bear; Irish *art*, W. *arth*; Skt. *ṛksha-*; Pers. *khirs*, a bear. See Brugm. i. § 920. Allied to **Ursine.** Der. *ant-arctic*, q. v.

ARDENT, burning, fiery. (F.—L.) Chaucer has ' the most *ardaunt* love of his wyf;' tr. of Boethius, b. iii. met. 12. l. 10. The spelling has, at a later time, been conformed to Latin.—OF. *ardant*, burning, pres. pt. of *ardoir*, to burn.—L. *ardēre*, to burn. Allied to *āridus*, dry (Bréal); see **Arid.** Der. *ardent-ly*, *ardenc-y*; *ardour*, Tempest, iv. 56 (OF. *ardor*, L. acc. *ardōrem*, from nom. *ardor*, a burning).

ARDUOUS, difficult to perform. (L.) In Pope, Essay on Criticism, l. 95. Not in early use. Formed by change of L. *-us* into *-ous*, by analogy with *pious*, &c.—L. *arduus*, steep, difficult, high. + Irish, Gaelic, Cornish, and Manx *ard*, high, lofty; Icel. *ǫrðugr*, erect. Brugm. i. § 360. Der. *arduous-ly*, *arduous-ness*.

ARE, the pres. pl. of the verb substantive. (Northern E.) The whole of the present tense of the verb substantive is from the same root, viz. ES, to be. I here discuss each person separately. The singular is I *am*, thou *art*, he *is*; pl. we, ye, they *are*.

AM is found in the Northumbrian glosses of the Gospels, Luke, xxii. 33, and frequently elsewhere. The Wessex form is *eom*. These stand for *es-m*, the *s* having been assimilated to *m*, and then dropped. Here *es* is the root, and *-m* is short for *-mi*; the Idg. type being **es-mi*. [The Northumbrian retains this *-mi* in other instances, as in *geseo-m*, I see, Mark, viii. 24; *dōa-m*, I do, Mark, xi. 33; *beo-m*, I be, Mark, ix. 19.] β. The original Idg. type **esmi* is further represented by the Skt. *as-mi*, Zend *ah-mi*, Gk. εἰ-μί, L. *s-u-m* (for **es-(u)-mi*), Lithuan. *es-mi*, Goth. *i-m*, Icel. *e-m*, Swed. *är* (for *es*, dropping the suffix), Dan. *er*, OIrish *a-m*. It is the only word in English in which the old suffix *-mi* appears. See Brugm. ii. § 976.

ART. This is the OMerc. *earð*, *erð*; cf. ONorthumbrian *arð* (Luke, iv. 34), and the AS. (Wessex) *eart* (with *t* due to the *-t* in *sceal-t*, shalt, &c.). The Icel. form is *er-t*, OIcel. *es-t*; and E. and Icel. are the only languages which have this *-t*. β. The orig. Idg. types were **es-i*, **es-si*; cf. Skt. *as-ī*, Zend *a-hi*, Doric Gk. ἐσ-σί (Attic εἶ), L. *ēs*, Lithuan. *es-si*, Goth. *i-s* (or *is*), Swed. *är*, Dan. *er*. See Brugm. ii. § 984.

IS. This is the same in Northumbrian and Wessex, viz. *is*, as at present. β. The orig. Idg. type was **es-'i*; cf. Skt. *as-ti*, Zend *ash-ti*, Gk. ἐσ-τί, L. *es-t*, Lith. *es-ti*, Goth. *is-t*, Icel. *er*, Swed. *är*, Dan. *er*, G. *is-t*. The English form has lost the suffix, preserving only *is*, as a weakened form of √ES. So also OIrish *is*.

ARE. This is the OMerc. *earun*, ONorthumbrian *aron* (Matt. v. 14) as distinguished from AS. (Wessex) *sindon*; but the forms *sindon* and *sint* are also found in Northumbrian. All three persons are alike in Old English; but the Icel. has *er-um*, *er-uð*, *er-u*. β. The gen. Idg. type of the 3rd pers. plu. was **es-enti*; whence Skt. *s-anti*, Gk. εἰσ-ίν, L. *s-unt*. Goth. *s-ind*, G. *s-ind*, Icel. *er-u* (for **es-u*), Swed. *är-e* (for **äs-e*), Dan. *er-e* (for **es-e*), ONorthumb. *ar-on* (for **as-on*), ME. *ar-en*, later *are*, AS. *s-ind(on)*. In the AS. *s-indon*, the *-on* is a later suffix, peculiar to English. γ. Thus E. *are* is short for *aren*, and stands for the **es-en* of the primitive **es-enti*, whilst the AS. *sind* stands for the **s-ent* of the same primitive form. See Brugm. ii. § 1017.

The √ES, to be, appears in Skt. *as*, to be, Gk. ἐσ- of Doric ἐσ-σι, L. *es-se*, to be, G. *s-ein*, to be, and in various parts of the verb in various languages, but chiefly in the present tense. ¶ For other parts of the verb, see **Be, Was.**

AREA, a large space. (L.) Used by Dryden, Ded. to Span. Fryar (R.).—L. *ārea*, an open space, piece of level ground.

ARECA, a genus of palms, of which one species produces the areca-nut, which the natives roll up with a little lime in the leaves of the betel, and chew. (Port.—Canarese.) Port. *areca*. From the Karnāta (Canarese) *aḍike*, areca-nut; Wilson, Indian Terms, p. 7. Cf. Malayālam *aḍekka*, Tamil *aḍaikāy*; from *aḍai*, denoting close arrangement of the cluster, and *kāv*, nut, fruit. The accent is on the initial *a* in all the languages; see N. E. D. The cerebral *ḍ* has been replaced by *r*.

AREFACTION, a drying, making dry. (L.) Used by Bacon,

Adv. of Learning, b. ii. 8. 3 ; ed. Wright, p. 124, l. 14. A coined word, from L. *ārefacere*, to make dry. – L. *ārē-re*, to be dry (cf. *āridus*, dry) ; and *facere*, to make. See **Arid**. **Der.** By adding *-fy* (F. *-fier*) to make, to the stem *are-*, dry, the verb *arefy* has also been made ; it is used by Bacon, Nat. Hist. sect. 294.

ARENA, a space for disputants or combatants. (L.) It occurs in Hakewill, Apologie (1630), p. 396. 'The *arena* or pit ;' Gibbon, Hist. c. lxxi. § 10. – L. *arēna*, sand ; hence, a sanded space for gladiators in the amphitheatre. Older form *harēna* ; cf. Sabine *fasēna*, sand. **Der.** *arena-ce-ous*, i.e. sandy.

AREOPAGUS, Mars' hill ; the supreme court at Athens. (L. – Gk.) From L. *arēopagus*, which occurs in the Vulgate version of Acts, xvii. 22, where the A. V. has 'Mars' hill.' – Gk. Ἀρειόπαγος, a form which occurs in no good author (Liddell and Scott) ; more commonly Ἄρειος πάγος, which is the form used in Acts, xvii. 22. – Gk. Ἄρειος, of or belonging to Ἄρης, the Gk. god of war ; and πάγος, a rock, mountain peak, hill. **Der.** *Areopag-ite*, *Areopag-it-ic-a* (Milton's treatise).

ARÊTE, a sharp ascending ridge of a rock. (F. – L.) Chiefly with reference to French Switzerland. – F. *arête* ; OF. *areste*. – L. *arista*, an ear of corn, fishbone or spine ; hence (in F.) a ridge, sharp edge. See **Arris**.

ARGENT, white, in heraldry ; silvery. (F. – L.) In Marlowe, Massacre at Paris, i. 6. 2 ; as an heraldic term, much earlier. – F. *argent*, silver ; also, 'argent in blason ;' Cot. – L. *argentum*, silver ; of which the old Oscan form was *aragetom* ; connected with *argilla*, white clay. Cf. Gk. ἄργυρος, silver ; connected with ἀργός, white ; Skt. *arjuna*-s, white ; OIrish *argat*, W. *ariant*, silver. – √ARG, to shine. Brugm. i. §§ 529, 604. **Der.** *argent-ine* (F. *argentin*, Cotgrave ; Late L. *argentīnus*).

ARGILLACEOUS, clayey. (L.) In Bailey (1731). – L. *argillāceus*, clayey ; with *-ous* for *-us*. – L. *argilla*, white clay. + Gk. ἄργιλος, white clay. – √ARG, to shine. See **Argent**.

ARGONAUT, one who sailed in the ship Argo. (L. – Gk.) In Spenser, F. Q. iv. 1. 23 ; and see Trevisa, tr. of Higden, ii. 405. L. *argonauta*, one who sailed in the Argo. – Gk. Ἀργοναύτης, an Argonaut. – Gk. Ἀργώ, the name of Jason's ship (meaning 'the swift ;' from ἀργός, swift) ; and ναύτης, a ship-man, sailor, from ναῦς, a ship. **Der.** *Argonaut-ic*.

ARGOSY, a merchant-vessel. (Dalmatian.) In Shak. Mer. of Ven. i. 1. 9 ; on which Clark and Wright note : '*Argosy* denotes a large vessel, gen. a merchant-ship, more rarely a ship of war. The word has been supposed to be a corruption of *Ragosie*, "a ship of Ragusa ;"' and this is correct. β. The etymology of this word has been set at rest by Mr. Tancock, in N. and Q. 6. S. iv. 490. See The Present State of the Ottoman Empire, by Sir Paul Ricaut, 1675, c. 14, p. 119 ; Lewis Roberts's Marchants Map of Commerce, 1638, c. 237, where he speaks of the great ships 'vulgarly called *Argoses*, properly *Rhaguses* ;' and especially the earlier quotation about '*Ragusyes*, Hulks, Caravels, and other foreign rich laden ships,' in The Petty Navy Royal, by Dr. John Dee, 1577, pr. in Arber's English Garner, ii. 67. See also Wedgwood (Contested Etymologies) ; Palmer (Folk-Etymology). [The OF. *argousin* is unrelated ; see Palmer, Brachet.] Ragusa is a port in Dalmatia, on the E. coast of the Gulf of Venice.

ARGUE, to make clear, prove by argument. (F. – L.) 'Aristotle and other moo to *argue* I taughte ;' P. Plowman, B. x. 174. – OF. *arguer*. – Late L. *argūtāre* (L. *argūtāri*), frequentative of *arguere*, to prove, make clear ; cf. *argūtus*, clear. Perhaps allied to Gk. ἀργός, white, bright. See **Argent**. **Der.** *argu-ment*, Chaucer, C. T. 11198 (F 886) ; *argument-at-ion*, *argument-at-ive*, *argument-at-ive-ly*, *argument-at-ive-ness*.

ARID, dry, parched. (L.) Not in early use ; Rich. quotes from Swift's Battle of the Books, and Cowper's Homer's Iliad, bk. xii. *Aridity* is in Phillips (1658). It was probably taken immediately from L. *āridus*, dry. – L. *ārēre*, to be dry. Cf. Skt. *āsa*-s, dust. **Der.** *arid-it-y*, *arid-ness* ; and see **Arefaction**, **Ashes**.

ARIGHT, in the right way. (E.) We find in Layamon, l. 17631, 'ær he mihte fusen *a riht*,' i.e. ere he might proceed aright. The *a* is (as usual) for *an*, ME. form of AS. *on*, often used in the sense of 'in.' Thus *aright* is for 'on right,' i.e. in right ; *right* being a substantive. Cf. *abed*, *asleep*, *afoot*, &c. See **Right**.

ARISE, to rise up. (E.) ME. *arisen*, Old Eng. Homilies, i. 49 ; very common. AS. *ārisan*, to arise ; Grein, i. 38. – AS. *ā-*, and *risan*, to rise. ¶ Cf. Goth. *ur-reisan*, to arise, Matt. viii. 15, where *ur-* is the prefix which commonly appears in Gothic as *us-*, but becomes *ur-* before a following *r*. But we cannot equate the AS. prefix *ā-* to Goth. *us*, which is related to G. *ur-*, *er-*, AS. *or-*. See **Rise**.

ARISTOCRACY, a government of the best men ; a government by a privileged order ; the nobility. (Gk.) In Ben Jonson, The Fox, iv. 1 (Lady P.). Holland speaks of 'an *aristocracy*, or regiment [i.e. government] of wise and noble senate ;' Plutarch, p. 276 (R.). Cf.

F. *aristocratie*, 'an *aristocracy* ; the government of nobles, or of some few of the greatest men in a state ;' Cot. [But the word may have been taken directly from Gk.] – Gk. ἀριστοκρατία, the rule of the best-born or nobles. – Gk. ἀριστο-, for ἄριστος, best ; and κρατεῖν, to be strong, to rule, govern. β. The Gk. ἄριστος, best, is a superlative from a form ἀρ-, proper, good, which appears in ἀρ-ετή, excellence. The Gk. κρατεῖν, to be strong, is from κρατύς, strong, cognate with E. *hard*. See **Arm** (1) and **Hard**. **Der.** *aristo crat-ic*, *aristocrat-ic-al*, *aristocrat-ic-al-ly*, and even *aristocrat* (not a very good form) ; all from the Gk. stem ἀριστοκρατ-.

ARITHMETIC, the science of numbers. (F. – L. – Gk.) [In ME. we find the OF. form *arsmetike*, Genesis and Exodus, ed. Morris, 792 ; further altered to *arsmetrik*, Chaucer, C. T. 1900 (A. 1898) ; these are from OF. *arismetique* (see Hatzfeld) ; adapted from Prov. *arismetica*, from L. *arithmētica*. At a later period the word was conformed to the Gk.] We find *arithmetick* in Holland's Pliny (concerning Pamphilius), b. xxxv. c. 10 (ii. 537) ; and in Shak. Troil. i. 2. 123. – F. *arithmétique*, explained as 'arithmetick' by Cotgrave. – L. *arithmētica*. – Gk. ἀριθμητική, the science of numbers, fem. of ἀριθμητικός, belonging to numbers. – Gk. ἀριθμέ-ειν, to number. – Gk. ἀριθμός, number, reckoning. See Prellwitz. ¶ The ME. *arsmetrik* was popularly supposed to represent L. *ars metrica*, metrical art ! **Der.** *arithmetic-al*, *arithmetic-al-ly*, *arithmetic-ian*.

ARK, a chest, or box ; a large floating vessel. (L.) In very early use as a Bible word. In the AS. version of Gen. vi. 15, it is spelt *arc*. cf. Goth. *arka*, Icel. *örk* (from Latin). – L. *arca*, Gen. vi. 15 (Vulgate) ; cf. L. *arcēre*, to keep. + Gk. ἀρκεῖν, to keep off, suffice ; ἄρκιος, safe, certain. **Der.** *arcana*, L. neut. pl., things kept secret, secrets ; from L. *arcānus*, hidden, from *arcēre*, to keep, enclose.

ARM (1), sb., the limb extending from the shoulder to the hand. (E.) ME. *arm*, Layamon, iii. 207 ; also *earm*, *ærm*. O. Northumbrian *arm*, Luke i. 51 ; AS. *earm*, Grein i. 248. + Du. *arm* ; Icel. *armr* ; Dan. and Swed. *arm* ; Goth. *arms* ; G. *arm*. Cf. also L. *armus*, the shoulder ; *artus*, a limb ; Gk. ἁρμός, joint, shoulder ; Russ. *ramo*, shoulder ; Pers. *arm*, upper arm ; Skt. *īrma*-s, arm ; cf. Gk. ἄρθρον, a joint, limb. All from √AR, to fit, join ; expressive of the articulation of the limb, and its motion from the joint. See Curtius, i. 424 ; Prellwitz, p. 29 ; Brugm. i. § 524. **Der.** *arm-let*, *arm-ful*, *arm-less*, *arm-pit*. From the same root are *ar-istocracy*, *ar-ithmetic*, *ar-ticle*, *ar-t*, q.v.

ARM (2), vb., to furnish with weapons. (F. – L.) ME. *armen*, to arm ; Rob. of Glouc. p. 63 (l. 1446) ; Layamon, l. 15313. – OF. *armer*, to arm. – L. *armāre*, to furnish with weapons. – L. *arma*, weapons. See **Arms**. **Der.** *arma-da*, *arma-dillo*, *arma-ment*, *armour*, *army* ; all from L. *armā-re* ; see these words. *Armistice* is from L. *arma*, s. pl. ; see below.

ARMADA, an 'armed' fleet ; a large fleet. (Span. – L.) Well known in the time of Elizabeth. Camden speaks of the 'great *armada* ;' Elizabeth, an. 1588. Often ill written *armado*, as in Shak. K. John, iii. 4. 2. – Span. *armada*, a fleet ; fem. of *armado*, armed, pp. of *armar*, to arm, equip. – L. *armāre*, to arm. See **Arm** (2). Doublet, *army*, q.v.

ARMADILLO, an animal with a bony shell. (Span. – L.) 'A beast called by the Spaniards *armadilla* ;' Hakluyt, Voy. iii. 650. A Brazilian quadruped ; lit. 'the little armed one,' because of its protecting shell. – Span. *armadillo*, dimin. with suffix *-illo*, from *armado*, armed, pp. of *armar*, to arm. – L. *armāre*, to arm. See **Arm** (2).

ARMAMENT, armed forces ; equipment. (L.) In Pope's Iliad, xx. 152. Direct from L. *armāmentum*, gen. used in pl. *armāmenta*, tackling. – L. *armāre*, to arm ; with suffix *-mentum*. See **Arm** (2).

ARMATURE, formerly used in the sense of armour, now chiefly of a 'protector' for a magnet. (F. – L.) '*Armature*, armour ; also, skill in arms ;' Bailey (1735). – F. *armature* (Hatzfeld). – L. *armātūra* ; see **Armour**. Doublet, *armour*.

ARMISTICE, a short cessation of hostilities. (F. – L.) In Glossographia Anglica Nova (1707) ; and in Smollet's Hist. of England, an. 1748. – F. *armistice*, a cessation of hostilities. – Late L. *armistitium*, a coined word, not in the dictionaries ; but the right form for producing F. *armistice*, Ital. *armistizio*, and Span. *armisticio* ; cf. L. *solstitium*, whence E. *solstice*. – L. *armi-*, for *arma*, arms, weapons ; and *-stitium*, for *-statium* (as in *sol-stit*ium) from *statum*, supine of *stāre*, to stand, cognate with E. *stand*. See **Arms** and **Stand**.

ARMOUR, defensive arms or dress. (F. – L.) ME. *armour*, corrupt form of the earlier *armure*. Pl. *armures*, K. Alisaunder, 937. Rob. of Glouc. has *armure*, p. 397 (l. 8195). – OF. *armure*, *armeüre*. – L. *armātūra*, armour ; from *armāre*, to arm. See **Arm** (2). **Der.** *armour-er*, *armour-y* ; also *armorial* (F. *armorial*, belonging to arms ; Cotgrave). Doublet, *armature*.

ARMS, sb. pl., weapons. (F. – L.) ME. *armes*, Havelok, 2925 ; Ancren Riwle, p. 60. – OF. *armes*, pl. ; sing. *arme*. – L. *arma*, neut.

pl., arms, weapons, lit. 'fittings,' equipments. Cf. Gk. ἄρμενα, the tackling of a ship, tools of a workman. ─√AR, to fit, join. See **Arm** (1). Der. *arm* (1), verb; also *arm-i-stice*, q. v.

ARMY, a large armed body of men. (F. ─ L.) In Chaucer's C. T. Prol. 60, many MSS. read *armee*, but the word is very rare at so early a time. It is spelt *army* in Fabyan's Chron. c. 42. ─ OF. *armee*, fem. of *arme*, pp. of *armer*, to arm. ─ L. *armāre*, to arm, of which the fem. pp. is *armāta*, whence Span. *armada*. **Doublet,** *armada*, q. v.

ARNICA, a medicine prepared from *Arnica montana*, or Mountain Tobacco. (L. ─ Gk.?) Mod. L. *arnica*; of uncertain origin. First used in 1753 (N. E. D.); cf. F. *arnica*, also *arnique* (1752). Supposed to be a corruption of L. *ptarmica*, Gk. πταρμική, a plant that caused sneezing : from πτάρνυμαι, I sneeze (Hatzfeld).

AROINT THEE! begone! (E.) '*Aroint* thee, witch!' Macbeth, i. 3. 6. Usually explained by 'avaunt!' The lit. sense seems to be 'make room,' or 'get out of the way.' The prefix is the AS. *ge-*, as in **Aware**, q. v. Prov. E. *roynt ta* (North), *rynt thee, roynt thee*, get out of the way (Cheshire); *rynt you, witch*, get out of the way, witch (Ray). AS. *rȳm ðū, gerȳm ðū*, make thou room; see Luke, xiv. 9; from *rȳman*, or *gerȳman*, to make room; from *rūm*, adj. roomy, wide. See E. D. D., s. v. *roint, rim, rime*; E. Dial. Gram. § 178.

AROMA, a sweet smell. (L. ─ Gk.) The sb. is modern in the sense of 'scent;' but ME. *aromat* (from OF. *aromat*, F. *aromate*) was in early use, meaning 'spice;' see Ancren Riwle, p. 376, where the pl. is *aromaz* (= *aromats*). The adj. *aromatic* is found rather early. Maundevile has '*aromatyk* thinges;' c. xvi. p. 174. ─ Late L. *arōma*, borrowed from Gk. ─ Gk. ἄρωμα, a spice, a sweet herb. Der. *aroma-t-ic, aroma-t-ise*, from the Gk. stem ἀρωματ-.

AROUND, prep. and adv., on all sides of, on every side. (Hybrid; E. and F.) Spenser has *arownd*, F. Q. i. 10. 54. ME. *around*, Life of Beket, ed. Black, l. 2052. The prefix is the E. *a-*, in its commonest use as short for *an*, the ME. form of AS. prep. *on*; so that *a-round* is for *on round*, i. e. in a round or circle. *Round* is from OF. *roond, rond*, L. *rotundus*. Cf. *abed, asleep*. See **Round**.

AROUSE, to rouse up. (Hybrid; E. and Scand.) In Shak. 2 Hen. VI, iv. 1. 3. The prefix is a needless addition; no doubt meant to be intensive, and imitated from that in *arise*, which is from the AS. *ā-*; see **Arise**. And see **Rouse**.

ARPEGGIO, the employment of notes of a chord in rapid succession instead of simultaneously. (Ital. ─ Teut.) In Bailey (1735). ─ Ital. *arpeggiare*, to play upon the harp. ─ Ital. *arpa*, a harp; a word of Teut. origin. See **Harp**.

ARQUEBUS, HARQUEBUS, a kind of gun. (F. ─ MDu.) Used by Nicholas Breton, an Elizabethan poet, in A Farewell to Town (R.). Spelt *hargabushe*, Tottell's Misc., ed. Arber, p. 173 (1557). ─ F. *arquebuse*, 'an harquebuse, caleever, or hand-gun;' Cot. He also gives the spelling *harquebuse*; cf. Walloon *harkibuse*, in Dict. de la langue Wallonne, by Grandgagnage, i. 266, 278, qu. by Diez, who traces the word. [A corrupt form; cf. Ital. *archibuso* (Torriano), variant of *archibugio*, 'a harquebuse,' Florio; also written *arcobugio* (id.). The Ital. form is doubly corrupt, being due to a popular etymology from *arco*, a bow, and *bugio*, a hole (referring to the barrel).] ─ MDu. **hakebusse, haeckbusse*, 'an arquebusse,' Hexham; Du. *haak-buss.* ─ MDu. *hake, haeck*, Du. *haak*, a hook, clasp, and MDu. *busse*, Du. *bus*, a gun-barrel, gun; exactly parallel to G. *hakenbüchse*, an arquebuse, from *haken*, a hook, and *büchse*, a gun-barrel, gun. β. The word means 'gun with a hook,' alluding to the hook which was cast with the piece, by which it was fastened to the 'carriage;' but the name was afterwards applied to other kinds of portable fire-arms, so that the original kind was renamed *arquebuse à croc*, arquebus with a hook, as in Cotgrave. Other E. forms were *hackbush* and *hackbut*. See **Hackbut**: also **Hook** and **Bush** (2).

ARRACK, an ardent spirit used in the East. (F. ─ Arab.) Better spelt *arak* or *arac*, as in Sir T. Herbert's Travels, ed. 1665, pp. 45, 241, 328. ─ OF. *arack* (Supp. to Godefroy); A. D. 1519. ─ Arab. *'araq*, juice, the more literal signification being 'sweat;' in allusion to its production by distillation. In Palmer's Pers. Dict. col. 425, is the entry: 'Arab. *'araq*, juice, essence, sweat; distilled spirit.' ─ Arab. *'araqa*, he sweated. See *Arrack* in Yule. ¶ Sometimes shortened to **Rack**.

ARRAIGN, to call to account, put on one's trial. (F. ─ L.) ME. *arainen, areinen, arenen* (with one *r*). 'He *arayned* hym ful runyschly, what raysoun he hade,' &c.; Allit. Poems, ed. Morris, C. 191. ─ AF. *aresner, arener, arreiner*; OF. *araisnier, arainier, araignier*, to speak to, discourse with; also, to cite, arraign. ─ OF. *a-*, prefix (L. *ad*); and *raisnier, resnier, rainier*, to reason, speak, plead, from *raison, reson*, reason, advice, account; from L. acc. *ratiōnem*, from nom. *ratio*, reason. See **Reason**. ¶ The Late L. form of *arraign* is *arratiōn-āre*; similarly the Late L. *dērationāre*, to reason out, decide, produced the now obsolete *darraign*, to decide, esp. used of deciding by

combat or fighting out a quarrel ; see Chaucer, Kn. Ta. 773 ; C. T., A 1631. Der. *arraign-ment*.

ARRANGE, to range, set in a rank. (F. ─ OHG.) ME. *arayn-gen*, as in 'he *araynged* his men;' Berners, Froissart, c. 325 ; orig. spelt with one *r*. ─ OF. *arengier*, to put into a rank, arrange. ─ OF. *a-*, prefix (L. *ad*, to): and *rengier, renger*, to range, put in a rank (F. *ranger*, Littré); from OF. *renc*, mod. F. *rang*, a rank, file, orig. a ring or circle of people; from OHG. *hrinc*, mod. G. *ring*, a ring, esp. a ring or circle of people; cognate with E. *ring*. See **Rank**, **Ring**. Der. *arrangement*.

ARRANT, knavish, mischievous, notoriously bad. (F. ─ L.) *Arrant* is a later spelling of *errant*, and was first used in the phrase *theef erraunt*, a roving outlaw or notorious robber, which occurs in Chaucer : 'an outlawe or a *theef erraunt*;' C. T. 17173 (H 224). Hence it was extended to other ill-doers, with the sense of 'notorious,' or 'out-and-out.' 'An *erraunt* usurer;' P. Plowman, C. vii. 307; '*errant* traytours,' Orig. Letters, ed. Ellis, ii. 105 (A. D. 1539); '*errant* theues' and '*erraunt* theefe;' Lever, Sermons (1550), ed. Arber, p. 66. In Holinshed's (really Stanihurst's) Desc. of Ireland, repr. 1808, p. 68, we find: '[they] gad and range from house to house like *arrant* knights of the round table;' where 'arrant knights' = knights errant; cf. 'knight *erraunt*' in Malory's Morte Arthur, bk. iv. c. 25, l. 23. Chapman, in Byron's Tragedy, A. v. sc. 1 (Byron) has : 'As this extravagant and *errant* rogue.' ─ OF. *errant*, pres. pt. of *errer, eirer*, to wander. ─ Late L. *iterāre*, to travel. ─ L. *iter*, a journey. ¶ It sometimes represents the pres. pt. of L. *errāre*, to wander. See **Errant, Err**.

ARRAS, tapestry. (F. ─ L. ─ C.) In Shak. Haml. iv. 1. 9. 'Riche *Aresse* or tapestrie;' Elyot, The Governor, bk. iii. c. 2. § 3. The AF. *arras* occurs in 1376, Royal Wills, p. 72; and in 1392, id. p. 132; cf. 'peces of *arras*,' in 1447, id. p. 283. So named from *Arras*, in Artois, N. of France, where it was first made. ─ L. **Atrabates*, for *Atrebates*, a people of Artois; Cæsar, B. G., ii. 4. Of Celtic origin. ─ Celtic **atreb-*, whence W. *athref*, a domain, district. ─ Celt. prefix *ad-* (OIrish *ad-*), at (cognate with L. *ad*, E. *at*); and O Welsh *treb*, W. *tref*, a house. Stokes-Fick, pp. 10, 137.

ARRAY, to set in order, get ready. (F. ─ L. and Scand.) ME. *arraien, araien*, to array; Chaucer, Kn. Ta. 1188 (A 2046); Rob. of Glouc. p. 36 (l. 841, note). ─ AF. *arayer*, OF. *araier, aroier* (areër in Godefroy), to array, prepare, arrange. ─ Romanic type **arrēdāre* (= Ital. *arrēdare*), to array, prepare, prepare. β. Formed by prefixing *ar-* (imitation of the L. prefix *ar-*, the form assumed by *ad*, to, before a following *r*) to the Low G. *rēde*, ready (Bremen Wört. iii. 452), OFries. *rēde*, ready; cf. AS. *rǣde*, OHG. *reiti*, ready. See further under **Ready**. ¶ Note also Scottish *graithe*, to make ready, *graith*, ready, *graith*, apparatus, words directly borrowed from Icel. *greiða*, to equip, *greiðr*, ready, and *greiði*, arrangement; in which *g-* (= *ge-*) is a prefix. Hence to *array*, to *graithe*, and to make *ready*, are three equivalent expressions containing the same root. Der. *array*, sb.; the same root occurs in *curry*, vb.; see **Curry** (1).

ARREARS, debts unpaid and still due. (F. ─ L.) The ME. *arere* is mostly an adverb, signifying backward, in the rear; e. g. 'Somme tyme *aside*, and somme tyme *arrere*' = sometimes on one side, and sometimes backward; P. Plowman, B. v. 354. It is more commonly spelt *arere* (with one *r*), or a *rere* (in two words), id. C. vii. 405. ─ OF. *arere, ariere* (*arrere* in Godefroy), backward. ─ L. *ad*, towards; and *retro*, behind. [Similarly OF. *deriere* (mod. F. *derrière*) is from L. *dē*, from, and *retro*, backward; and we ourselves use the word *rear* still.] See **Rear**; and see *arrière* in Hatzfeld. ¶ What we now express by *arrears* is expressed in ME. by *arrerages* or *arerages*, a sb. pl. formed from ME. *arere* by the addition of the F. suffix *-age*. For examples of *arrerages*, see N. E. D.; and cf. P. Plowman, C. xii. 297. The mod. E. *arrear*, sb., arose from the ME. phrase *in arere*, by dropping *in*.

ARREST, to stop, to seize. (F. ─ L.) ME. *arresten*, or commonly *aresten*; Chaucer, Prol. 829 (A 827). ─ OF. *arester*, to stay (mod. F. *arrêter*). ─ L. *ad*, to (which becomes a in OF.); and *restāre*, to stay, remain, stop, compounded of *re-*, back, and *stāre*, to stand, remain, cognate with E. *stand*. See **Re-** and **Stand**; and see **Rest** (2).

ARRIS, a ridge, the edge formed by the angular contact of two plane (or curved) surfaces. (F. ─ L.) 'Burford stone . . carries a finer *arris* than that at Heddington;' Plot's Oxfordsh. (1677), p. 75. ─ OF. *areste*: F. *arête*. See **Arête**.

ARRIVE, to come to a place, reach it. (F. ─ L.) Gen. followed by *at* in modern E.; but see Milton, P. L. ii. 409; Shak. Jul. Cæs. i. 2. 110. ME. *aryuen, ariuen* (*u* for *v*); Rob. of Glouc. p. 18, l. 415. ─ OF. *ariver, arriver*. ─ Late L. **adrīpāre*, to come to the shore, spelt *arripāre* in a 9th cent. text, and *arribāre* in an 11th cent. chartulary; Brachet. See the note also in Brachet, showing that it was originally a seaman's term. ─ L. *ad rīpam*, towards the shore. ─ L. *ad*, to; and *rīpa*, shore, bank. The orig. sense of L. *rīpa* was 'a rift, a break;'

cf. Gk. ἐρίπνη, a broken cliff; Icel. *rifa*, whence E. *rive*. See **Rive**. D r. *arriv-al*, spelt *arivaile* in Gower, C. A. ii. 4; bk. iv. 94.

ARROGATE, to lay claim to, assume. (L.) Used by Barnes, Works, p. 371, col. 1. The sb. *arrogance* is much older; Chaucer, C. T. 6694 (D 1112); so is the adj. *arrogant*, C. T. Persones Tale, De Superbia (I 396). Formed with suff. -*ate* (see **Abbreviate**) from L. *arrogāre*, to ask of, to adopt, attribute to, add to; pp. *arrogātus*. — L. *ad*, to (>*ar*- before *r*); and *rogāre*, to ask. See **Rogation**. Der. *arrogat-ion*; also (from L. *arrogā-re*, pres. pt. acc. *arrogant-em*) *arrogant, arrogan-ly, arrogance, arrogance-v*.

ARROW, a missile shot from a bow. (E.) ME. *arewe, arwe* (with one *r*); Chaucer, Prol. 107; Ancren Riwle, pp. 60, 62. AS. *arewe*, AS. Chron. an. 1083 (Laud MS.); older form *arwe*, Thorpe's Anc. Laws, ii. 212, § 28. Teut. type **arhwōn-*, weak fem. Another form is *earh*, Grein, i. 248; Teut. type **arhwom*, neut.+Icel. *ör*, an arrow, pl. *örvar*; Teut. type **arhwā*, strong fem. Cf. also Goth. *arhwazna*, f., an arrow, a dart, Eph. vi. 16; allied to L. *arcus*, a bow; Brugm. i. § 241 (b). Der. *arrow-y, arrow-root*. See **Arc**.

ARROW-ROOT, a farinaceous substance, made from the tubers of the *Maranta Arundinacea*, and other plants. (E.) From *arrow* and *root*. 'The E. name of this preparation is derived from the use to which the Indians of S. America were accustomed to apply the juice extracted from another species of *Maranta*—the *Maranta galanga*, which was employed as an antidote to the poison in which the arrows of hostile tribes were dipped;' Eng. Cyclopædia, Arts and Sciences, s. v. *Arrow-root*. Observe the L. name, 'Maranta *arundinacea*.' ¶ The account in N. E. D. is similar, with a reference to Sir Hans Sloane, Catal. Plant. Jamaica, 122.

ARSE, the buttocks. (E.) ME. *ars, ers*; P. Plowman, B. v. 175, and footnote. AS. *ærs, ears*; Bosworth.+Du. *aars*; Icel. *ars*, Swed. and Dan. *ars*; MHG. *ars*; mod. G. *arsch*. Teut. type **ursoz*.+Gk. ὄρρος, the rump; Idg. type **orsos* (Prellwitz).

ARSENAL, a magazine for naval stores, &c. (Ital.—Span.—Arab.) Holland speaks of 'that very place where now the *arsenall* and shipdocks are;' Livy, p. 106; and see Ben Jonson, The Fox, iv. 1 (Sir P.); Milton, P. R. iv. 270. [Rather from Ital. than from F. *arcenal*, which Cotgrave, following the F. spelling, explains by 'an *Arcenall*.'] — MItal. *arsenale*, 'a storehouse for munition' (Florio); cf. Ital. *arzana*, an arsenal, *darsena*, a wet dock. — MSpan. *ataraçana*, 'a dock where ships are made or amended; a storehouse for munition,' Minsheu; Span. *atarazana, atarazanal*. [The varying forms are due to the word being foreign, viz. Arabic. The final -*l* is merely formative, and no part of the original word. The Span. *atarazana* (with *a*- for Arab. *al*, the, def. art.) and Ital. *darsena* are the best forms.] — Arab. *dār aç-çinā'ah*, house of construction. — Arab. *dār*, house; *aç-*, for *al*, the; *çinā'ah*, art, trade, construction. See Devic; and Rich. Dict. 646, 943. The two words together signify 'a house of art or construction,' 'a place for making things.' Mr. Wedgwood says: 'Ibn Khaldoun quotes an order of the Caliph Abdalmelic to build at Tunis a *dārcinā'a* for the construction of everything necessary for the equipment and armament of vessels. Pedro de Alcala translates *atarazana* by the Arab. *dār a-cinā'a*; see Engelmann and Dozy.'

ARSENIC, a poisonous mineral. (Gk.—Arab.—Pers.) Chaucer speaks of *arsenik*, C. T., G 798. It was one of the four 'spirits' in alchemy. — L. *arsenicum*. — Gk. ἀρσενικόν, orpiment, yellow arsenic, a name occurring in Dioscorides, 5. 121. [This Gk. word lit. means 'male;' in allusion to the extraordinary alchemical fancy that some metals were of different sexes. *Gold*, e. g. also called *Sol*, the sun, was masculine, whilst *silver*, also called *luna*, the moon, was feminine. But these fables arose out of popular etymology, the Gk. name being really borrowed.] — Arab. *az-zernikh*; from *az-*, for *al*, the, def. art., and *zernikh*, orpiment, borrowed from Pers. *zerni*, orpiment, yellow arsenic, which is from Pers. *zar*, gold. See Devic, p. 4; Rich. Dict., p. 774. And see **Gold**. Der. *arsenic-al*.

ARSIS, the place of a stressed syllable in English verse. (Gk.) The sense has varied; see N. E. D. '*Arsis*, a raising or lifting up;' Phillips (1706). — Gk. ἄρσις, a raising. — Gk. αἴρειν, to raise.

ARSON, the crime of burning houses. (F.—L.) Old Law French; see Blackstone's Comment. b. iv. c. 16. — OF. *arson, arsun*, incendiarism; Late L. acc. type **arsiōn-em*. — L. *ardēre*, to burn; pp. *arsus*. See **Ardent**.

ART (1), 2 p. s. pres. of the verb substantive. (E.) OMerc. *eardð*, *erð*; ONorthumbrian *arð*, later *art*; AS. *eart*. The *ar*- stands for *es*-, from √ES, to be; and the -*t*, ONorthumb. -*ð*, is a suffix. See further under **Are**.

ART (2), skill, contrivance, method. (F.—L.) ME. *art*; Rob. of Brunne, tr. of P. Langtoft, p. 336; and in Floriz and Blauncheflur, ed. Lumby, l. 521. — OF. *art*, skill. — L. acc. *artem*; from nom. *ars*, skill. Perhaps from √AR, to fit (Bréal). See **Article**. Der. *art-ful*, *art-ful-ness, art-ist, art-ist-ic, art-ist-ic-al, art-ist-ic-al-ly, art-less, art-less-ly, art-less-ness*; also *art-ifice, art-illery, art-isan*, which see.

ARTERY, a tube or pipe conveying blood from the heart. (L.—Gk.) Shak. L. L. L. iv. 3. 306. ME. *arterie*, Lanfrank, Cirurgie, ii. 5; p. 162, l. 17. — L. *artēria*, the windpipe; also, an artery. [The F. form is *artere*, which is shorter than the E., and consequently the E. word is not from French.] — Gk. ἀρτηρία, an artery; but orig. the windpipe. Perhaps connected with ἀορτή, the aorta (Prellwitz). See **Aorta**. Der. *arteri-al, arteri-al-ise*.

ARTESIAN, adj., applied to a well. (F.—L.—C.) These wells are made by boring till the water is found; and the adj. is properly applied to such as are produced by boring through an impermeable stratum, in such a way that the water, when found, overflows at the outlet. Englished from F. *Artésien*, of or belonging to *Artois*, a province in the N. of France, where the wells were in use in the eighteenth century and earlier. *Artois* is from L. *Atrebatensem*, acc. of *Atrebatensis*, adj. formed from *Atrebat-es*; see further under **Arras**. See Eng. Cycl. s. v. *Artesian well*.

ARTHRITIS, pain in the joints, gout. (Gk.) In Kersey (1708). — Gk. ἀρθρῖτις. — Gk. ἄρθρον, a joint; allied to L. *artus*, a joint; see **Article**.

ARTICHOKE, an esculent plant; *Cynara Scolymus*. (Ital.—Span.—Arab.) 'A *artochocke*, cynara;' Levins, 159. 5. Holland has the odd spelling *artichoux* for the plural; Pliny, b. xx. c. 23. [He seems to have been thinking of F. *choux*, cabbage.] The pl. *artichokes* occurs in 1537, in the Privy Purse Expenses of the Princess Mary, ed. Madden, p. 33. — Ital. *articiocco*, an artichoke (Diez); cf. F. *artichaut*, spelt *artichault* by Cotgrave, and explained by him as 'an artichock.' A corrupt form. Florio gives the spellings *archiciocco, archicioffo*; also *carciocco, carcioffo*. — MSpan. *alcarchofa* (Minsheu); whence Span. *alcachofa*, Port. *alcachofra*. — Arab. *al harshaf*, an artichoke; Rich. Pers. Dict. p. 562. ¶ The pretended Arab. *ar'ḍi shaukī*, cited by Diez, is a mere modern corruption from Italian.

ARTICLE, a small item; a part of speech. (F.—L.) ME. *article*, Ayenbite of Inwyt, pp. 11, 12. — F. *article*, 'an article; a head, principall clause, title or point of a matter; .. also, a joint or knuckle;' Cot. — L. *articulum*, acc. of *articulus*, a joint, knuckle, member of a sentence, an article in grammar; the lit. sense being 'a little joint.' Formed, by help of suffixes -*cu-lo*-, from L. *artus*, a joint, a limb. — √AR, to fit; Prellwitz (s. v. ἀραρίσκω). See Max Müller, Lect. i. 104 (8th ed.). See **Arm**. Der. *article*, verb. And see below.

ARTICULATE, adj., jointed, fitted; also, distinct, clear. (L.) Speech is *articulate* when distinctly divided into joints, i. e. into words and syllables; not jumbled together. — L. *articulātus*, distinct, articulate; pp. of *articulāre*, to supply with joints, or divide by joints, chiefly applied to articulate speaking. — L. *articulus*, a little joint (above). Der. *articulate*, verb; *articulate-ly, articulat-ion*.

ARTIFICE, a contrivance. (F.—L.) Gower has *artificiers*, C. A. iii. 142; bk. vii. 1691. Shak. has *artificer*, K. John, iv. 2. 201; and *artificial*, Romeo, i. 1. 146. *Artifice* is in Milton, P. L. ix. 39. — F. *artifice*, skill, cunning, workmanship; Cot. — L. *artificium*, a craft, handicraft. — L. *artific-*, stem of *artifex*, a workman. — L. *arti-*, for *ars*, art; and *facere*, to make, the stem *fac*- being altered to *fic*- in compounds. See **Art** and **Fact**. Der. *artifici-al, artifici-al-ly*; also *artific-er*.

ARTILLERY, gunnery; great weapons of war. (F.—L.) Milton, P. L. ii. 715; Shak. K. John, ii. 403. Chaucer, C. T., B 2523, in his Tale of Melibeus, speaks of 'castelles, and other maner edifices, and armure, and *artelleries*.' — OF. *artillerie*, machines or equipment of war; see quotation in Roquefort s. v. *artillement*. The word was used to include crossbows, bows, &c., before the invention of gunpowder. — OF. *artiller*, to fortify, equip; Roquefort. — Late L. **artillāre*, to make machines; a verb inferred from the word *artillātor*, a maker of machines, given by Ducange. — L. *art-*, stem of *ars*, art. See **Art**. We also find Late L. *artilliātor*, answering to an older form **articulātor*, from Late L. *articula, articulum*, art, artifice, derivatives of *ars*, art (not from *artus*, a joint); see Ducange. Der. *artiller-ist*.

ARTISAN, a workman. (F.—Ital.—L.) In Blount's Gloss., ed. 1674; and in Marlowe, Faustus, i. 1. 53. — F. *artisan*, an artisan, mechanic. — Ital. *artigiano*, a workman; whence it was introduced into F. in the 16th century; Brachet. β. This corresponds, according to Diez, to a late L. form **artītiānus* (not found), formed in its turn from L. *artītus*, cunning, artful (see Ducange), which is from *arti-*, decl. stem of *ars*, art. See **Art**. ¶ Rabelais has *artizan* (Hatzfeld); if here the *z* = *ts*, the F. word may have been taken immediately from L., and not through Italian.

ARUM, the cuckoo-pint, or wake-robin. (L.—Gk.) In Turner, Names of Herbes, 1548 (E.D.S.), p.15. — L. *arum, aron*. — Gk. ἄρον, arum.

AS, adverb and conjunction. (E.) ME. *as, als, alse, also, alswa*; and *al so, al swa*, written separately. That these are all one and the same word has been proved by Sir F. Madden, in remarks upon Havelok, and is a familiar fact to all who are acquainted with Middle English. In other words, *as* is a contracted form of *also*. β. The successive spellings are: AS. *eal swā*, Grein, i. 239; *al swa*, Layamon, l. 70; *al* *so*, Seven Sages, 569, ed. Weber; *alse*, P. Plowman, A. v. 144; *als*, id. B. v. 230 (where *als* means 'also'); *als* manye *as* = *as* many as, Mandeville's Travels, p. 209. The AS. *eal swā* means both 'just so' and 'just as.' See **Also**.

ASAFŒTIDA, ASSAFŒTIDA, a medicinal gum. (Hybrid; Pers. and L.) Spelt *azafedida*, Arnold's Chron. (1502), ed. 1811, p. 234. A juice made chiefly from the *Ferula Narthex*, an umbelliferous plant, growing in Persia. The Persian name is *āzā*, 'mastic,' Rich. Dict. p. 65. The L. *fœtida*, stinking, refers to its offensive smell. See **Fetid**.

ASBESTOS, a fibrous mineral. (Gk.) In Holland's Pliny, b. xxxvii. c. 10; ii. 624. Written *asbeston*, Trevisa, tr. of Higden, i. 187. So called because it is incombustible. ━ Gk. ἄσβεστος, incombustible; lit. 'unquenchable.' ━ Gk. ἀ-, negative prefix; and -σβεστός, quenchable, from σβέννυμι, I quench, extinguish. See Brugm. i. § 653, and Prellwitz, as to this curious verb. Der. *asbest-ine*, adj.

ASCEND, to climb, mount up. (L.) Chaucer has *ascensioun* and *ascended*, C. T. 14861, 14863 (B 4045, 4047). [There is a F. sb. *ascension*, but the OF. *ascendre* is rare and obsolete; the E. verb was probably suggested by the Vulgate.] ━ L. *ascendere*, to climb up to, ascend; pp. *ascensus*. ━ L. *ad-*, to (reduced to *a-* before *sc*); and *scandere*, to climb. See **Scan**. Der. *ascendent*, Chaucer, Prol. 417, from L. pres. pt.; also *ascendant*, as in Drayton, Legend of T. Cromwell, l. 399, from F. pres. pt.; *ascendenc-y*; *ascens-ion*, cf. L. pp. *ascensus*; *ascent* (Shak.), coined to pair off with *descent*, the latter being a true F. word.

ASCERTAIN, to make certain, determine. (F. ━ L.) The *s* is an idle addition to the word, and should never have been inserted. Yet the spelling *ascertayn* occurs in Fabyan, c. 177, § 6. Bale has *assartened*; Image, pt. i. ME. *acertainen*; 'For now I am *acértainéd* throughly;' Flower and Leaf, 568. ━ OF. *acertainer*, variant of *acertener* (Godefroy). Cotgrave has '*acertener*, to certifie, *ascertaine*, assure.' β. *Acertener* is a coined word, made up of F. prefix *a-* (L. *ad*), and the adj. *certain*, certain, sure. See **Certain**. Der. *ascertain-able*.

ASCETIC, adj. often used as sb., one who is rigidly self-denying in religious observances; a strict hermit. (Gk.) Gibbon speaks of 'the *ascetics*;' Hist. c. 37, § 2. In the Life of Bp. Burnet, c. 13, we find: 'he entered into such an *ascetic* course.' The adjective was 'applied by the Greek fathers to those who *exercised* themselves in, who employed themselves in, who devoted themselves to, the contemplation of divine things: and for that purpose, separated themselves from all intercourse with the world;' Richardson. ━ Gk. ἀσκητικός, industrious, lit. given to exercise; applied to hermits, who strictly exercised themselves in religious devotion. ━ Gk. ἀσκητής, one who exercises an art, esp. applied to an athlete. ━ Gk. ἀσκεῖν, to work, adorn, practise, exercise; also, to mortify the body, in Ecclesiastical writers. Root unknown. Der. *ascetic-ism*.

ASCIDIAN, a term applied to some tunicate molluscs; and to pitcher-shaped leafy appendages, in botany. (Gk.) Modern; lit. 'pitcher-like.' ━ Gk. ἀσκίδιον, dimin. of ἀσκός, a leathern bag, wine-skin.

ASCITITIOUS, ADSCITITIOUS, supplemental, additional. (L.) Little used. '*Adscititious*, added, borrowed;' Kersey's Dict. 'Homer has been reckoned an *ascititious* name, from some accident of his life;' Pope, qu. in Todd's Johnson. Coined, as if from L. **ascītītius* (not used), from *ascītus*, received, derived from others, not innate; pp. of *asciscere*, to take in, admit, receive from without, also written *adsciscere*. ━ L. *ad*, to; and *sciscere*, to learn, find out, accept, which is formed from *sci-re*, to know, by the addition of the ending *-scere*, common in forming 'inchoative' or 'inceptive' verbs in Latin. See **Science**.

ASCRIBE, to attribute, impute. (L.) It occurs in the Lamentation of Mary Magdeleine, l. 254; a poem later than Chaucer, but sometimes printed with his works. ━ L. *ascribere*, to write down to one's account; pp. *ascriptus*. ━ L. *ad*, to (which becomes *a-* before *sc*); and *scribere*, to write. See **Scribe**. Der. *ascrib-able*, *ascript-ion*.

ASH, the name of a tree. (E.) ME. *asch*, *esch*, *assch*; Chaucer, C. T. 2924 (A 2922). '*Esche*, tre, *fraxinus*;' Prompt. Parv. p. 143. AS. *æsc*, Grein, i. 58. ╋ Du. *asch*; Icel. *askr*; Dan. and Swed. *ask*; OHG. *asc*; MHG. *asch*; G. *esche*. Teut. type **askiz*. Cf. Russ. *iasene*, Lith. *úsis*, ash. Der. *ash-en*, adj.

ASHAMED, pp. as adj., affected by shame. (E.) ME. *aschamed*, often written *a-schamed*. 'Aschamyd, or made ashamyd, *verecundatus*;' Prompt. Parv. p. 15. But we also find ME. *ofschamed*, ashamed; Shoreham's Poems, p. 160; *of-chamed*, Owl and Nightingale, l. 932. Hence, in this instance, we may consider the prefix *a-* as equivalent to *of-*, as it is in the case of the word *adown*, q. v. This would point back to the AS. form *ofsceamod*, which occurs in Ælfric, Lives of Saints, 2. 178. β. Or it may represent AS. *āsceamod*, with prefix *ā-*; whilst *sceamod* is the pp. of *sceamian*, to shame, from *sceamu*, shame. See **Shame**.

ASHES, the dust or relics of what is burnt. (E.) The pl. of *ash*, which is little used. ME. *asche*, *axe*, *aske*, a disyllabic word, the usual pl. being *aschen*, *axen*, *asken*, but in Northern and Midland E. *askes*,

axes. See *asken*, in the (Southern) Ancren Riwle, p. 214; and *askes* in Hampole's Pricke of Conscience, 424. AS. *æsce*, *axe*, *asce*; pl. *æscan*, *axan*, Grein, i. 10, 11, 58. ╋ Du. *asch*; Icel. *aska*; Swed. *aska*; Dan. *aske*; Goth. *azgō*, sing., *asgōn*, pl.; Luke, x. 13; OHG. *asga*, *asca*; MHG. *asche*, *esche*; G. *asche*. Teut. types **askōn-*, **azgōn-*, fem.; perhaps for **as(t)kōn-*, **az(d)gōn-*; and allied to Gk. ἄζ-ειν, to dry up, parch, L. *ār-ēre*, to be dry, Skt. *āsa-s*, ashes, dust (Macdonell). Der. *ash-y*; *Ash-Wednesday*, so called from the sprinkling of ashes on the heads of penitents, the L. name being *diēs cinerum*.

ASHLAR, ASHLER, a facing made of squared stones. (F. ━ L.) 'In countries where stone is scarce, *ashler* principally consists of thin slabs of stone used to face the brick and rubble walls of buildings;' Eng. Cycl. s. v. *Ashler*. Again, *Ashlering* is used in masonry to signify 'the act of bedding in mortar the *ashler* above described;' id. It is also used in carpentry 'to signify the short upright pieces of wood placed in the roof of a house to cut off the acute angle between the joists of the floor and the rafters; almost all the garrets in London are built in this way;' id. β. The clue to understanding the word is to remember that the use of wood preceded that of stone. From OF. *aiseler*, Livre des Rois, iii. 6 (see *aisselier* in Hatzfeld), a crosspiece used to bind together two pieces of timber; extended from OF. *aiselle*, *aiselle* (*aisselle* in Cotgrave), f., 'a little boord, or shingle of wood;' Cotgrave. ━ L. *axilla*, dimin. of *axis*, an axis, also a board, a plank. See **Axis**. ¶ The thin square slabs of stone were likened to the wooden shingles that preceded them. The Scot. spellings are *estler*, *aislair*. Jamieson quotes 'houses biggit a' with *estler* stane' = houses all built with squared stone, from Ramsay's Poems, i. 60. And again, he quotes from Abp. Hamilton's Catechism, fol. 5 a: 'A mason can nocht hew ane euin *aislair* without directioun of his rewill' = cannot hew a straight ashlar without drawing a line with his rule to guide him.

ASHORE, on shore. (E.) Shak. has *on shore*, Temp. v. 219, where we might say *ashore*. Thus *a-* is short for *an*, ME. form of *on*. So also in *a-bed*, *a-sleep*, &c.

ASIDE, to one side, on one side. (E.) For *on side*. Wyclif has *asydis-hond* in Gal. ii. 2, but *on sidis hond* in Mark, iv. 34 (earlier version), 'he expounyde to his disciplis alle thingis *on sidis hond*, or by hem-self.' See above.

ASININE; see **Ass**.

ASK, to seek an answer, to request. (E.) ME. *asken*, *aschen*, *axien*, &c. *Asken* is in Ancren Riwle, p. 338. *Axien* in Layamon, i. 307. AS. *āscian*, *āhsian*, *ācsian*, Grein, i. 14, 24, 40. The form *ācsian* is not uncommon; whence mod. prov. E. *ax*, as a variant of *ask*. The AS. *āscian* produced ME. *ashen*, now lost; the surviving form *ask* was orig. Northern. ╋ Du. *eischen*, to demand, require; Swed. *äska*, to ask, demand; Dan. *æske*, to demand; OHG. *ei-scōn*, *eisgōn*; MHG. *eischen*; mod. G. *heischen*, to ask. Teut. types **aiskōn*, **aiskōjan*. All related to Skt. *ichchhā*, a wish, desire, *ēshana-*, a wish, *ēsh*, to search; Gk. ἰότης, wish, will; Lith. *jëszkóti*, Russ. *iskate*, to seek. The root is seen in Skt. *ish*, to desire, wish; from √EIS, to seek, wish; Brugm. i. § 619, ii. § 676; Prellwitz. ¶ The Icel. *æskja* does not mean 'to ask,' but 'to wish;' and is not related to *ask*, but to *wish*; see **Wish**.

ASKANCE, obliquely. (Ital. ━ L. ?) Sir T. Wyatt, in his Satire Of the Meane and Sure Estate, l. 52, says: 'For, as she lookt *a scance*, Under a stole she spied two stemyng eyes;' &c. We also find *a scanche*, explained by *de travers*, *en lorgnant*, i. e. obliquely; Palsgrave's French Dict. p. 831. Origin uncertain; but perhaps related to Ital. *scansare*, 'to go aslope or *a-sconce* or askew, to go sidelin;' Florio. This verb is derived from Ital. *s-* (for L. *ex*), and (according to Diez) L. *campsāre*, to turn round a place, bend round it; cf. Gk. κάμπτειν, to bend. Paretti's Ital. Dict. (1831) has *di scancio*, adv. slanting, aslope; *scancio*, adj. oblique; but this appears in Torriano (1688) as *schiancio*, 'athwart;' apparently from a Teut. source allied to E. *slant*.

ASKEW, awry. (OLow G.) 'But he on it lookt scornefully *askew*;' Spenser, F. Q. iii. 10. 29. As usual, the prefix *a-* stands for *an*, ME. form of *on*, and *askew* means 'on the skew.' Hexham explains MDu. *scheef* by 'askew, awry.' See **Skew**.

ASLANT, on the slant, obliquely. (Scand.) *A-slonte* occurs in the Prompt. Parv. p. 6, as equivalent to *acyde* (aside) and to the L. *obliquē*, obliquely. It stands for *on slonte*, on the slant, a form which occurs in the Anturs of Arthur, st. xlviii. 6; cf. *abed*, *afoot*, *asleep*. It appears as *o slante* in the Morte Arthure, ed. Brock, 2254. Cf. Swed. dial. adj. *slant*, slippery (Rietz). See **Slant**.

ASLEEP, in a sleep. (E.) For 'on sleep;' *a-* being short for *an*, ME. form of *on*. 'David .. fell *on sleep*;' Acts, xiii. 36. See **Sleep**.

ASLOPE, on a slope, slopingly. (E.) For 'on slope,' as in many other instances; see above. In the Romaunt of the Rose, l. 4464, *a slope* occurs in the sense of 'awry.' See **Slope**.

ASP, ASPIC, a venomous serpent. (F. ━ L. ━ Gk.) Shak. has *aspick*, Antony, v. 2. 296, 354; and Palsgrave has *aspycke*. Gower speaks of 'A serpent, which that *aspidis* Is cleped;' C. A. i. 57; bk. i. 463. The form *aspic* is French; Cotgrave gives: '*Aspic*, the serpent called an *aspe*.' The form *asp* is also French; see Brachet, who notes, s. v. *aspic*, that there was an OF. form *aspe*, which existed as a doublet of the Provençal *aspic*; both of them being from L. acc. *aspidem*, from nom. *aspis*. The false form in Gower is due to his supposing that, as *aspides* is the nom. pl., it would follow that *aspidis* would be the nom. singular. — Gk. ἀσπίς, gen. ἀσπίδος, an asp. ¶ Hatzfeld gives the Prov. form as *aspit*, which might easily be misread *aspic*. The mod. Prov. form is *aspit*, from L. acc. *aspidem*.

ASPARAGUS, a garden vegetable. (L. — Gk. — Pers.?) Formerly written *sperage*; Holland's Pliny, bk. xix. c. 8; ii. 27 c. Also *sparage* or *sparagus*; thus Cotgrave explains F. *asperge* by ' the herb *sparage* or *sparagus*.' But these are mere corruptions of the L. word. — L. *asparagus*. — Gk. ἀσπάραγος, Attic ἀσφάραγος, asparagus. Curtius, ii. 110, compares it with the Zend *ǫparegha*, a prong, and the Lith. *spurgas*, a shoot, sprout, and thinks it was a word borrowed from the Persian. If so, the orig. sense was 'sprout.' Brugm. i. § 525.

ASPECT, view, appearance, look. (L.) In old authors, often *aspéct*: 'In thin *aspéct* ben alle liche;' Gower, C. A. i. 143; bk. i. 3009. Chaucer, Treatise on the Astrolabe, pt. ii. 4. 31, uses *aspectes* in the old astrological sense, of the ' aspects ' of planets. [Probably from L. directly. Whilst known in English in the 14th century, the F. *aspect* does not seem to be older than the 15th; see Littré.] — L. *aspectus*, look. — L. *aspectus*, pp. of *aspicere*, to behold, see. — L. *ad*, to, at (> *a*- before *sp*); and *specere*, to look, cognate with E. *spy*. See **Spy**.

ASPEN, ASP, a kind of poplar, with tremulous leaves. (E.) The form *aspen* (more usual) is properly adjectival, like *gold-en, wood-en*, and the sb. is *asp*. The tree is still called the *asp* in Herefordshire, and in the S. and W. of England it is called *aps*. The phrase 'lyk an *aspen* leef,' in Chaucer, C. T. 7249 (D 1667), is correct, as *aspen* is there an adjective. ME. *asp, aspe, espe*. Chaucer has *asp*, C. T. 2923 (A 2921). '*Aspe* tre, *Espe* tre;' Prompt. Parv. pp. 15, 143. AS. *æspe*, also *æps*; Bosworth. + Du. *esp*, sb., *espen*, adj.; Icel. *ösp*; Dan. and Swed. *asp*; G. *espe, äspe* (OHG. *aspa*; MHG. *aspe*). See Fick, iii. 29, who adds Lettish *apsa*, Lithuanian *apuszis*; Polish and Russ. *osina*. Origin unknown.

ASPERITY, roughness, harshness. (F. — L.) *Asperite*, Sir T. More, Works, p. 1218 c. Chaucer has *asprenesse*, tr. of Boethius, b. iv. pr. 4, l. 106. The contracted OF. form *asprete* occurs in Ancren Riwle, p. 354, as an E. word. — OF. *asperiteí*, later *asperité*, roughness. — L. acc. *asperitātem*; nom. *asperitās*, roughness. — L. *asper*, rough. See Brugm. i. § 760.

ASPERSE, to cast calumny upon. (L.) Milton, P. L. ix. 296. Formed from L. *aspersus*, the pp. of *aspergere*, to besprinkle; also, to bespatter. — L. *ad*, to (> *a*- before *sp*); and *spargere*, to sprinkle, scatter. See **Sparse**. Der. *aspers-ion*, Tempest, iv. 1. 18.

ASPHALT, ASPHALTUM, a bituminous substance. (Late L. — Gk.) 'Blazing cressets fed With naphtha and *asphaltus*;' Milton, P. L. i. 728,729. *Aspalt* occurs in Mandeville's Travels, p. 100, and *aspaltoun* in Allit. Poems, ed. Morris, B. 1038. — Late L. *asphaltum*; Higden, Polychron. i. 116. — Gk. ἄσφαλτος, ἄσφαλτον, asphalt, bitumen. Of foreign origin. Der. *asphalt-ic*; Milton, P. L. i. 411.

ASPHODEL, a plant of the lily kind. (Gk.) In Milton, P. L. ix. 1040. — Gk. ἀσφόδελος, a plant of the lily kind. In English, the word has been corrupted into *daffodil*; see **Daffodil**.

ASPHYXIA, suspended animation, suffocation. (Gk.) In Kersey, ed. 1708. — Gk. ἀσφυξία, a stopping of the pulse; cf. ἄσφυκτος, without pulsation. — Gk. ἀ-, privative; and σφύζειν, to throb, pulsate; cf. σφυγμός, pulsation; σφ. *pochen*, to throb. Der. *asphyxi-ate*.

ASPIRE, to pant after, to aim at eagerly. (F. — L.) Generally followed by *to* or *unto*. 'If we shal . . desyrously a *pyre* vnto that countreye of heauen with all our whole heartes;' Udal, 1 Peter, c. 3. vv. 21, 22. — F. *aspirer*, 'to breathe, . . also to desire, covet, aime at, aspire unto;' Cot. — L. *aspirāre*, to breathe towards, to seek to attain. — L. *ad*, to, towards (> *a*- before *sp*); and *spirāre*, to breathe, blow. Cf. E. *spirit*. Der. *aspir-ing, aspir-ing-ly, aspir-ant, aspir-ate* (vb.), to pronounce with a full breathing, *aspirate*, sb., *aspirat-ion*.

ASS, a well-known quadruped of the genus *Equus*; a dolt. (C. — L. — Semitic.) ME. *asse*; Ancren Riwle, p. 32. AS. *assa*, Grein, i. 10. The origin of the word is uncertain; and the extent to which one language has borrowed it from another is not clear; the Icel. *asni*, e. g., is merely the L. *asinus* contracted. The AS. *assa* was probably borrowed from OIrish *assan* (Stokes, p. 24); and this from L. *asinus*. The Celtic languages have W. *asyn*, Corn. *asen*, Bret. *azen*, Irish and Gael. *asal*, Manx *essyl* (Williams); all probably from Latin. Cf. Du. *ezel*, an ass, also, a dolt, blockhead, G. *esel*, Dan. *esel, æsel*, Goth. *asilus*, Lith. *asilas*, Polish *osiel*, Icel. *asni*, Swed. *åsna*; all from L. *asinus* or *asellus*. Cf. also Gk. ὄνος, an ass. Most likely the word is of Semitic origin; cf. Arab. *a'ān*, Heb. *āthōn*, she-ass. Der. *asin-ine*, from Latin.

ASSAFŒTIDA: see **Asafœtida**.

ASSAGAI, ASSEGAI. (Port. — Moorish.) Spelt *azaguay* in Sir T. Herbert, Travels (1665), p. 23. A word (like *fetish*) introduced

into Africa by the Portuguese. — Port. *azagaia*, a dart, javelin. For *az-zaghāyah*; from *az-*, for *al*, the Arab. def. article, and Berber *zaghāyah*, the native name of a Berber weapon adopted by the Moors (whence F. *zagaie*); see Devic. See **Lancegay**.

ASSAIL, to leap or spring upon, to attack. (F. — L.) In early use. ME. *assailen, asailen*; Ancren Riwle, pp. 246, 252, 362. — OF. *assaillir, asaillir* (Chanson de Roland), to attack; cf. L. *assilīre*. — OF. *a-*, prefix (L. *ad*, > *as-* before s); and *saillir, sallir*, to leap, rush forward, from L. *salire*, to leap, rush forth. See **Salient**. Der. *assail-able, assail-ant*; also *assault* (OF. *asalt* (Littré), from L. *ad*, to, and *saltus*, a leap; from *saltus*, pp. of *salire*, to leap); whence *assault*, verb.

ASSART, the offence of grubbing up trees, and so destroying the coverts of a forest. (F. — L.) See Blount, Nomo-Lexicon; Manwood, Forest Laws, &c. The word is due to AF. *assartir* (Britton), F. *essarter*, ' to make glades in a wood, to grub up, or clear a ground of bushes, shrubs, thorns, &c.; ' Cot. — Late L. *exsartāre*, to grub up, occurring an. 1233 (Ducange); also spelt *exartāre*. — L. *ex*, out, thoroughly; and Late L. *sartāre*, to grub up, occurring an. 1202 (Ducange). *Sartāre* (= *sartitare*) is the frequentative of L. *sarrīre, sarīre*, to weed, grub up weeds (whence also *sar-culum*, a hoe); see *essart* in Diez. Cf. Gk. σαίρειν, to sweep, σάρος, a besom. The L. pl. *exsarta*, weeded lands, occurs in Liber Custumarum, p. 660.

ASSASSIN, a secret murderer. (F. — Arabic.) Milton has *assassin-like*, P. L. xi. 219; and *assassinated*, Sams. Agon. 1109. — F. *assassin*, given by Cotgrave, who also gives *assassiner*, to slay, kill, and *assassinat*, sb., a murther. ['*Assassin*, which is *assacis* in Joinville, in the 13th cent., and in late L. *hassessin*, is the name of a well-known sect in Palestine which flourished in the 13th century, the *Haschischin*, drinkers of *haschisch*, an intoxicating drink, a decoction of hemp. The Scheik Haschischin, known by the name of the Old Man of the Mountain, roused his followers' spirits by help of this drink, and sent them to stab his enemies, esp. the leading Crusaders;' Brachet. See the whole account.] — Arab. *hashīsh*, an intoxicating preparation of *Cannabis indica*; Palmer's Pers. Dict. col. 199; Rich. Dict. p. 569; whence the adj. *hashīshī, hashāshī*; pl. *hashāshīn*, i.e. 'hashish-eaters;' so that *assassin* is a pl. form (Devic). Der. *assassin-ate, assassin-at-ion*, Macb. i. 7. 2.

ASSAULT; see under **Assail**.

ASSAY, sb., examination, test, trial; chiefly used of the trial of metal or of weights. (F. — L.) In the sense of 'attempt' it is generally spelt *essay* in mod. E.; see Acts, ix. 26, xvi. 7; Heb. xi. 29. Chaucer uses *assay* to denote the 'trial of an experiment;' C. T., G 1249, 1338. Gower uses *assay* for 'an attempt,' C. A. i. 68; bk. i. 791. [The form *assay* came in through the use of the OF. verb *asaier* as another spelling of *essaier*, to judge of a thing, derived from the sb. *essai*, a trial.] — OF. *essai*, a trial. — L. *exagium*, a weighing, a trial of exact weight. See **Essay**, a better spelling. Cf. *amend* = *emend*. Der. *assay*, verb; *assay-er*.

ASSEMBLE, to bring together, collect. (F. — L.) ME. *assemblen, asemblen*; Will. of Palerne, 1120, 1288. Chaucer has ' to *asemble* moneye;' tr. of Boethius, b. iii. pr. 8. l. 5. The sb. *asemblaye*, assembly, is in K. Alisaunder, ed. Weber, l. 3473. — OF. *assembler, asemblɛr*, to assemble, approach, come together, often with the sense of ' to engage in battle,' as frequently in Barbour's Bruce. — Late L. *assimulāre*, to collect, bring together into one place; different from classical L. *assimulāre*, to pretend, feign. — L. *ad*, to; and *simul*, together; so that Late L. *assimulāre* is 'to bring together;' the L. *ad* becoming *as-* before *s*, as usual. [The class. L. *assimulāre* is from *ad*, to, and *similis*, like; and *similis* is from the same source as *simul*.] β. The L. *simul* and *similis* are from the same source as E. *same*, Gk. ἅμα, at the same time, Skt. *sam*, with, together with. See **Similar**. Der. *assembl-y, assembl-age*. From the same source are *similar, simulate, assimilate*.

ASSENT, to comply, agree, yield. (F. — L.) ME. *assenten*; Chaucer, C. T., 4761, 8052 (B 342, E 176). 'They *assentyn*, by on *assent*,' i. e. they assent with one consent; K. Alisaunder, ed. Weber, l. 1480. — OF. *assentir*, to consent, acquiesce. — L. *assentīre*, to assent to, approve, consent. — L. *ad*, to (> *as-* before s); and *sentīre*, to feel; pp. *sensus*. See **Sense**. Der. *assent*, sb., in early use; Hampole, Pricke of Conscience, 8391; *assent-at-ion*.

ASSERT, to affirm, declare positively. (L.) In Milton, P. L. i. 25. Sir T. More has *assertation*, Works, p. 141 e; and *assercion*, p. 473 e. The E. word is formed from the L. pp. *assertus*. — L. *asserere*, to add to, take to one's self, claim, assert. — L. *ad*, to (> *as-* before s); and *serere*, to join or bind together, connect, to range in a row. See **Series**. Der. *assert-ion, -ive*.

ASSESS, to fix a rate or tax. (F. — L.) 'I will make such satisfaction, as it shall please you to assess it at;' North's Plutarch, p. 12; repr. in ' Shakespeare's Plutarch,' ed. Skeat, p. 289. Hall has *assessement*, Hen. VIII, an. 24 (end). — OF. *assesser* (Godefroy). — Late L. *assessāre*; cf. Law L. *assessor*, one whose duty it was to assess, i. e. to adjust and fix the amount of, the public taxes; 'qui tributa peræquat vel imponit;' Ducange. [The title of *assessor* was also given to a judge's assistant, in accordance with the etymological meaning, viz. 'one who sits beside' another.] — L. *assessus*, pp. of *assidēre*, to sit beside, to be assessor to a judge. — L. *ad*, to, near (> *as-* before *s*); and *sedēre*, to sit, cognate with E. *sit*. See **Sit**. Der. *assess-ment*; *assessor* (above). And see *assize*.

ASSETS, effects of a deceased or insolvent debtor, &c. (F. — L.) So called because sufficient 'to discharge that burden, which is cast upon the heir, in satisfying the testator's debts or legacies;' Blount's Law Dict. In early use in a different form. 'And if it sufficith not for *aseth*;' P. Plowman, C. xx. 203, where another reading is *assetz*, B. xvii. 237; see my note on the passage, Notes to P. Plowman, p. 390. In the Romaunt of the Rose, 5600, the E. *asseth* is used to translate the F. *assez*. β. The final *-ts* is an orthographical device for representing the sound of OF. *z*, which was sounded as *ts*; cf. F. *avez* with L. *habētis*, shortened to 'abet's, and cf. F. *assez* with L. *ad satis*, shortened to *a' sat's*. — L. *ad satis*, up to what is enough; from *ad*, to, and *satis*, enough. See **Satisfy, Satiate**. ¶ It will be observed that *assets* was originally an adverb, then used adjectively, and lastly a substantive. It is, etymologically, in the *singular*, like *alms, riches, eaves*, &c.; but it was treated as a plural, and in modern use has a sing. *asset*.

ASSEVERATE, to declare seriously, affirm. (L.) Bp. Jewell has *asseveration*, Defence of the Apology, p. 61. The verb to *assever* was sometimes used. The verb *asseverate* is formed, like others in *-ate*, from the pp. of the L. verb. — L. *asseuērātus*, pp. of *asseuērāre*, to speak in earnest. — L. *ad*, to (> *as-* before *s*); and *seuērus*, adj., earnest, serious. See **Severe**. Der. *asseverat-ion*.

ASSIBILATION, pronunciation with a hissing sound. (L.) Modern. Formed from the L. vb. *assibilāre*; from *as-* (for *ad*), to, and *sibilāre*, to hiss; see **Sibilant**.

ASSIDUOUS, constant in application, diligent. (L.) In Milton, P. L. xi. 310. Dryden has '*assiduous* care;' tr. of Virgil, Georg. iii. 463. Englished by putting *-ous* for L. *-us*, as in *abstemious*, &c. — L. *assiduus*, sitting down to, applying closely to, constant, unremitted. — L. *assidēre*, to sit at or near. — L. *ad*, to, near (> *as-* before *s*); and *sedēre*, to sit, cognate with E. *sit*. See **Sit**. Der. *assiduous-ly, assiduous-ness*; also *assidu-i-ty*, from L. acc. *assiduitā'em*, nom. *assiduitās*, formed from the adj. *assiduus*.

ASSIGN, to mark out to one, to allot, &c. (F. — L.) ME. *assignen, asignen*; Rob. of Glouc. p. 502, l. 10321. — OF. *assigner*, to assign. — L. *assignāre*, to affix a seal to, to appoint, ascribe, attribute, consign. — L. *ad*, to (> *as-* before *s*); and *signāre*, to mark. — L. *signum*, a mark. See **Sign**. Der. *assign-able, assign-at-ion, assign-er, assign-ment* (spelt *assignement*, Gower, C. A. ii. 373, bk. v. 7154); *assign-ee* (from Law French *assigné*, pp. of *assigner*).

ASSIMILATE, to make similar to, to become similar to. (L.) Bacon has *assimilating* and *assimilateth*; Nat. Hist. sect. 899. Sir T. Browne has *assimilable* and *assimilation*; Vulg. Errors, bk. vii. c. 19. § last; bk. iii. c. 21. § 9. Formed, like other verbs in *-ate*, from the pp. of the L. verb. — L. *assimilāre*, also *assimulāre*, to make like. — L. *ad*, to (> *as-* before *s*); and *similis*, like. See **Similar**. Der. *assimil-at-ion, assimilat-ive*. And see *assemble*.

ASSIST, to stand by, to help. (F. — L.) 'Be at our hand, and frendly vs *assist*;' Surrey, Virgil, Æn. bk. iv. l. 772. — F. *assister*, to assist, help, defend; Cot. — L. *assistere*, to step to, approach, stand at, stand by, assist. — L. *ad*, to (> *as-* before *s*); and *sistere*, to place, to stand, from *stāre*, to stand, which is cognate with E. *stand*. See **Stand**. Der. *assist-ant*, adj., Hamlet, i. 3. 3; sb., id. ii. 2. 166; *assist-ance*, Macbeth, iii. 1. 124.

ASSIZE, (1) a session of a court of justice; (2) a fixed quantity or dimension. (F. — L.) In mod. E. mostly in the pl. *assizes*; the use in the second sense is almost obsolete, but in ME. we read of 'the *assise* of bread,' &c. It is still, however, preserved in the contracted form *size*; cf. *sizings*. See **Size**. ME. *assise*, in both senses. (1) 'For to loke domes and *asise*;' Rob. of Glouc. p. 53, l. 1230. (2) 'To don trewleche the *assys* to the sellere and to the byggere [buyer];' Eng. Guilds, ed. T. Smith, p. 359. [We also find ME. verb *assisen*, to appoint; Gower, C. A. i. 181; bk. ii. 636. But the verb is derived from the sb.] — OF. *asise, assise*, sitting at table; also, a tax, impost; see Godefroy. Orig. the pp. fem. of the OF. verb *asseoir*, to sit at table, also to place, provide. — L. *assidēre*, to sit at or near, to act as assessor to a judge (in Late L., to impose a tax); pp. *assessus*. — L. *ad*, to, near (> *as-* before *s*); and *sedēre*, to sit, cognate with E. *sit*. See **Sit**. Der. *assize*, verb, to assess; *assiz-er*. And see *assess*.

ASSOCIATE, a companion. (L.) Properly a past participle. Cf. 'yf he intend to be *associate* with me in blisse;' Udal, S. Mark, viii. 34; where we should now rather use *associated*. A mere sb. in Shak. Hamlet, iv. 3. 47. — L. *associātus*, joined with in company; pp. of *associāre*, to join, unite. — L. *ad*, to (> *as-* before *s*); and *sociāre*, to join, associate, from *socius*, a companion, lit. a follower, from *sequī*, to

follow; cf. *toga*, cloak, from *tegere*, to cover, *procus*, a wooer, from *precāri*, to pray. See **Sequence**. Der. *associate*, verb; *associat-ion*.

ASSOIL, to absolve, acquit. (F. — L.) In Spenser, F. Q. i. 10. 52, ii. 5. 19, &c. Lowland Sc. *assoilyie*, often miswritten *assoilzie* (with *z* for ʒ=*y*). ME. *assoilen*, P. Plowman, B. prol. 70, 3. 40, &c.; and the pp. *asoiled* in OEng. Miscellany, ed. Morris, p. 32, l. 4. We find Anglo-French *assoile*, pres. sing. subj. Liber Custumarum, 199; but the pp. is spelt *assolz*, Polit. Songs, ed. Wright, p. 275. — OF. *assoile, asoile*, pres. s. subj. of *assoudre* (Godefroy); the same as *absouldre*, 'to absolve,' Cot. — L. *absoluere*, to absolve. See **Absolve**, of which *assoil* is merely a doublet. ¶ Especially common in the pres. subj. or imperative, as in the phrase 'God *assoil* you,' and the like; hence the form.

ASSONANT, adj., applied to a (certain) resemblance of sounds. (Span. — L.) [Chiefly used in prosody, esp. in discussing Spanish poetry, in which *assonance*, or a correspondence of *vowel-sounds only*, is a marked feature. Thus the words *beholding, rosebud, boldly*, are said to be *assonant*, all having the accented vowel *o* in common in the penultimate syllable. So, in Spanish, are the words *crueles, tienes, fuerte, teme*.] — Span. *assonante*, 'an assonant, in Span. verse;' Pineda (1740); now spelt *asonante*. — L. *assonantem*, acc. of *assonans*, sounding like. *Assonans* is the pres. pt. of *assonāre*, to respond to. — L. *ad*, to (> *as-* before *s*); and *sonāre*, to sound, from *sonus*, sound. See **Sound**. Der. *assonance*.

ASSORT, to sort, dispose, arrange; to be companion with. (F. — L.) Not much used formerly. — F. *assortir*, 'to sort, assort, suit, match, equall;' Cot.; occurring as early as 1457 (Hatzfeld); cf. Late L. *assortāre*. — F. prefix *as-*, imitated from L. *as-* (the form assumed by *ad*, to, before *s*); and sb. *sorte*, 'sort, manner, form, fashion, kind;' Cot. Thus *assortir* is to put together things of like kind. The sb. *sorte* (like Ital. *sorta*, a sort, kind, species) represents a Folk-L. **sorta*, from L. *sort-*, stem of *sors*, a lot. See **Sort**. Der. *assort-ment* (cf. F. *assortiment*).

ASSUAGE, to soften, allay, abate, subside. (F. — L.) ME. *assuagen, asuagen, aswagen*. 'His wr,ath forto *asuage*;' Rob. of Brunne, tr. of Langtoft, p. 300. — OF. *assouagier, asoagier*, to soft n, appease, assuage, console; a word of which the Provençal forms are *assuaviar, asuaviar*. Formed (as if from a L. verb **assuāuiāre*, to sweeten) from the OF. prefix *a-* (L. *ad*), and L. *suāuis*, sweet. See **Suave**. Der. *assuage-ment*.

ASSUASIVE, softening, soothing. (L.) Pope, in his Ode on St. Cecilia's day, l. 25, has the line: 'Music her soft, *assuasive* voice applies;' and the word has been used also by Johnson and Warton in a similar way; see Todd's Johnson. This queer word seems to have been meant to be connected with the verb to *assuage*, and to have been confused with *persuasive* at the same time. It is a mistaken formation, as if from a non-existent L. **assuādēre*, from *ad* and *suādēre*. See **Persuasive**.

ASSUME, to take to one's self, to appropriate; take for granted. (L.) The derived sb. *assumption* was in use in the 13th century as applied to the Assumption of the Virgin Mary. It is spelt *assumciun* in the Ancren Riwle, p. 412. The use of the verb is later. It is used by Hall, Hen. VII, an. 2. § 5; and in Hamlet, i. 2. 244. — L. *assūmere*, to take to one's self; pp. *assumptus*. — L. *ad*, to (> *as-* before *s*); and *sūmere*, to take. β. The L. *sūmere* is a compound verb, from some prefix connected with *sub*, and *emere*, to take, buy. See Brugm. i. § 240. The same root occurs in **Redeem**. Der. *assum-ing, assumpt-ion, assumpt-ive, assumpt-ive-ly*.

ASSURE, to make sure, insure, make confident. (F. — L.) Chaucer has '*assureth* vs,' C. T. 7969 (E 93), and *assurance*, C. T. 4761 (B 431). — OF. *aseürer, asseürer*, to make secure, assure, warrant. — OF. prefix *a-* (L. *ad*, to); and adj. *seür*, secure, from L. *sēcūrus*, secure, sure. See **Sure**. Der. *assur-ed, assur-ed-ly, assur-ed-ness, assur-ance*.

ASTER, the name of a genus of flowers. (L. — Gk.) In Kersey (1708). A botanical name, from L. *aster*, Gk. ἀστήρ, a star; from the star-like shape of the flowers. See **Asterisk, Asterism, Asteroid**.

ASTERISK, a little star used in printing, thus *. (L. — Gk.) Spelt *asterisque* in Blount's Gloss., ed. 1674. — L. *asteriscus*. — Gk. ἀστερίσκος, a little star, also an asterisk *, used for distinguishing fine passages in MSS. (Liddell and Scott). Formed, with dimin. suffix *-ισκος*, from ἀστερ-, base of ἀστήρ, a star, a word cognate with E. *star*. See **Star**. ☞ An *asterisk* is sometimes called a *star*.

ASTERISM, a constellation, a cluster of stars. (Gk.) In Drayton, Barons' Wars, b. vi. st. 31. A coined word, made by adding the Gk. suffix *-ισμος* (E. *-ism*) to the stem ἀστέρ- of the Gk. ἀστήρ, a star.

ASTERN, on the stern, behind. (E.) Sir F. Drake, in The World Encompassed, 1578, has: 'Having left this strait a stern.' It stands for *on stern*; see *abed, afoot, asleep*, and other words in which the prefix *a-* stands for *an*, ME. form of *on*.

ASTEROID, a term applied to the minor planets situate between the orbits of Mars and Jupiter. (Gk.) Modern, and astronomical. Properly an adj., signifying 'star-like,' or 'star-shaped.' — Gk. ἀστερο-ειδής, star-like. — Gk. ἀστερο-, for ἀστήρ, a star (cognate with E. **Star**, q. v.); and εἶδ-ος, form, figure. Der. asteroid-al.

ASTHMA, a difficulty in breathing. (Gk.) In Phillips (1658). — Gk. ἄσθμα, short-drawn breath, panting. — Gk. ἀάζειν, to breathe out, breathe through the mouth; allied to ἄημι, I blow.+Goth. waian, to blow; Skt. vā, to blow. See **Wind**. Der. asthmat-ic, asthmat-ic-al, from Gk. adj. ἀσθματικός.

ASTIR, on the stir. (E.) For on stir. 'The host wes all on steir' = the army was all astir; Barbour's Bruce, ed. Skeat, vii. 344. 'Var on steir,' i. e. they were on the move, id. xix. 577. See **Stir**.

ASTONISH, to astound, amaze. (F. — L.) The addition of the suffix -ish (as in extinguish) is due to analogy. Rich. quotes 'Be astonyshed, O ye heauens,' from the Bible of 1539, Jerem. ii. 12; and 'astonishment hathe taken me,' from the Geneva Bible, 1540-57, Jerem. viii. 21. Palsgrave has : 'I astonisshe, I amase one, Iestonne.' 2. The suffix -ish is here added to the ME. aston-, for astonen, as in : 'uour strokes of thondre, that astoneth thane zeneyere,' four strokes of thunder that astound the sinner; Ayenbite of Inwyt, p. 130. The same ME. astonen was the origin of mod. E. astound. See further under **Astound**. Der. astonish-ment, astonish-ing.

ASTOUND, to astonish, amaze. (F. — L.) Astound and astonish are both deducible from the ME. astonen, also found as astonien (whence a later form to astony). Astonish occurs in Shakespeare, and as early as in Palsgrave (1530). Astound is in Milton, Comus, 210, and astounded in the same, P. L. i. 281. It is remarkable that Milton also uses both astonish'd, P. L. i. 266, and astonied, P. L. ix. 890. Cf. 'Astonynge or astonynge, Stupefactio;' also 'Astonynn, or brese werkys, quatio, quasso;' Prompt. Parv. p. 16. 'Hit astonieth yit my thought;' Chaucer, Ho. of Fame, 1174. 'The folc that stod theraboute ful adoun for drede, And leye [misprinted seye] ther as hi were astoned and as hi were dede;' St. Margarete, 291, 292. 'Yif he be slowe and astoned and lache, he liveth a an asse;' Chaucer, tr. of Boethius, b. iv. pr. 3. l. 82. β. The form astound probably arose from ME. astoned, pp. of astonen; for which see under **Astonish**. — OF. estoner (mod. F. étonner), to amaze. — Late L. type *extonāre, to thunder out. — L. ex, out; and tonāre, to thunder. Cf. L. attonāre, to thunder at, astound; with prefix at- for L. ad, at. See **Ex-**, prefix, and **Thunder**. ¶ The word may have been influenced by the native verb to stun. See **Stun**.

ASTRAL, belonging to the stars; starry. (L. — Gk.) Seldom used. Rich. quotes from Boyle's Works, vol. v. p. 161. — L. astrālis, belonging to the stars. — L. astrum, a star. — Gk. ἄστρον, a star.

ASTRAY, out of the right way. (E. and F.) 'His poeple goth aboute astray;' Gower, C. A. iii. 175; bk. vii. 2679. 'They go a straye and speake lyes;' Bible, 1539, Ps. lviii. 3. For on stray (cf. abed, asleep). 'Mony a steid Fleand on stray;' Barbour's Bruce, 13. 195. See **Stray**.

ASTRICTION, a binding or constriction. (L.) It occurs in Bacon, Nat. Hist. sect. 342; and astringe in the same, sect. 714. The verb to astrict is in Hall, Hen. VI, an. 37. — L. acc. astrictiōnem, from nom. astrictio, a drawing together, contracting; cf. astrictus, pp. of astringere, to bind or draw closely together. See **Astringe**.

ASTRIDE, on the stride. (E.) In Butler, Hudibras, pt. i. c. ii. l. 390. For on stride, like afoot for on foot.

ASTRINGE, to draw closely together. (L.) In Bacon (see **Astriction**); now almost obsolete; we should say 'acts as an astringent.' Astringent is in Holland's Pliny, bk. xxiv. c. 13. § 2. — L. astringere, pp. astrictus, to bind or draw closely together. — L. ad, to, closely (> a- before st); and stringere, to bind closely. See **Stringent**. Der. astring-ent, astring-enc-y; astric/ion, q. v.

ASTROLOGY, the knowledge of the stars. (F. — L. — Gk.) Orig. practical astronomy; later, astromancy, a pretended and exploded science. In Chaucer, Treat. on the Astrolabe, Prol. l. 70 (or 75). — F. astrologie. — L. astrologia, used to denote 'astronomy' also. — Gk. ἀστρολογία, astronomy. — Gk. ἀστρο-, for ἄστρον, a star, cognate with E. **Star**, q. v.; and λέγειν, to speak about, whence -λογία, allied to λόγος, a discourse. Der. astrolog-ic-al, astrolog-ic-al-ly, astrolog-er.

ASTRONOMY, the science of the stars. (F. — L. — Gk.) In early use. ME. astronomie, Layamon, ii. 598. — OF. astronomie. — L. astronomia. — Gk. ἀστρονομία. — Gk. ἀστρο-, for ἄστρον, a star, cognate with E. **Star**, q. v.; and νέμειν, to distribute, dispense, whence -νομία, allied to νόμος, law. See **Nomad**. Der. astronom-ic-al, astronom-ic-al-ly, astronom-er.

ASTUTE, crafty, sagacious. (L.) In Blount's Gloss., ed. 1674. [Cotgrave has MF. astut, 'astute, crafty.'] — L. astūtus, crafty, cunning. — L. astus, craft, craftiness. Der. astute-ly, astute-ness.

ASUNDER, apart. (E.) For on sunder, a form which occurs in Genesis and Exodus, ed. Morris, l. 3909; in l. 116, we have the form

o sunder. AS. onsundran, adv. 'And lædde hi sylfe onsundran' = and led them apart by themselves; Mark, ix. 2. See **Sunder**.

ASYLUM, a place of refuge. (L. — Gk.) 'A sanctuarie . . . asylum;' Holland's Livy, p. 7. — L. asylum, a sanctuary, place of refuge. — Gk. ἄσυλον, an asylum; neut. of adj. ἄσυλος, safe from violence, unharmed. — Gk. ἀ-, negative prefix; and σύλη, a right of seizure, συλάω, I despoil an enemy.

ASYMPTOTE, a line which, though continually approaching a curve, never meets it within a finite distance. (Gk.) Geometrical. In Phillips, ed. 1706. Barrow, in his Math. Lectures, lect. 9, has 'asymptotical lines.' — Gk. ἀσύμπτωτος, not falling together. — Gk. ἀ-, negative prefix; σύν, together (> συμ before π); and πτωτός, falling, apt to fall, a derivative of πίπτειν, to fall (perf. tense πέ-πτωκα). The Gk. πίπτειν (Dor. aorist ἔ-πετ-ον), is from √PET, to fly, to fall. Cf. L. im-pet-us. Brugm. i. § 116. Der. asymptot-ic-al.

AT, prep. denoting nearness. (E.) In earliest use. AS. æt, Grein, i. 59.+Icel. at; Dan. ad; Swed. åt; Goth. at; OHG. az (obsolete); L. ad, which enters largely into English. See **Ad-**.

ATABAL, a kettle-drum. (Span. — Arab.) In Dryden, Don Sebastian, Act i. sc. 1. Cf. 'attabalies, which are a kind of drummes;' Hakluyt, Voy. iii. 480. — Span. atabal, a kettle-drum. — Arab. at-, for al, the; ṭabl, a drum. See **Tabour**.

ATAGHAN. See **Yataghan**.

ATAXY, ATAXIA, irregularity of the animal functions. (Gk.) Ataxia in Kersey (1708). — Gk. ἀταξία, want of order. — Gk. ἀ-, neg. prefix; and τάξις, order, from τάσσειν, to arrange. See **Tactics**.

ATHEISM, disbelief in the existence of God. (Gk.) Bacon has an essay 'Of Atheism.' Milton has atheist, P. L. i. 495; and atheous, P. R. i. 487. All are coined words from the Gk. ἄθεος, denying the gods, a word introduced into Latin by Cicero in the form atheos. — Gk. ἀ-, neg. prefix; and θεός, a god. See **Theism**. Der. atheous, athe-ism, athe-ist, athe-ist-ic, athe-ist-ic-al.

ATHIRST, very thirsty. (E.) Athirst, now an adj., is properly a pp.; and the prefix a- was originally of-. The ME. forms are ofthurst, ofthyrst, corrupted sometimes to athurst, and sometimes to afurst. See P. Plowman, B. x. 59; also King Horn, ed. Lumby, 1120, Ancren Riwle, p. 240, where the form is ofthurst. This form is contracted from ofthursted = made exceedingly thirsty. AS. ofþyrsted, very thirsty, Grein, ii. 321; pp. of ofþyrstan. — AS. of-, intensive prefix, signifying 'very;' and þyrstan, to thirst; Grein, ii. 614. See **Thirst**.

ATHLETE, a contender for victory in a contest; a vigorous person. (Gk.) Bacon speaks of the 'art of activity, which is called athletic;' Adv. of Learning, II. 10. 1; ed. Wright, p. 133. We should now say athletics. The L. form athleta occurs in 1528 (N.E.D.). — L. athlēta. — Gk. ἀθλητής, a combatant, contender in athletic games. — Gk. ἀθλεῖν, to contend. — Gk. ἆθλος, a contest, contracted from ἄεθλος; ἆθλον, the prize of a contest, contracted from ἄεθλον. See **Wed**. Der. athlet-ic, athlet-ics.

ATHWART, across. (E. and Scand.) Orig. an adverb, as in Shak. Meas. i. 3. 30; later a prep., as in L. L. L. iv. 3. 135. Athirt, across, occurs in the Romance of Partenay, ed. Skeat, l. 169. It stands for on thirt, on thwert; see **Thwart**.

ATLAS, a collection of maps. (Gk.) Named after Atlas, a Greek demi-god who was said to bear the world on his shoulders, and whose figure used to be given on the title-page of atlases. Cf. Shak. 3 Hen. VI, v. 1. 36. Ἄτλας (gen. Ἄτλαντος) probably means 'bearer' or 'sustainer,' from the √TEL, to bear, sustain, which appears in Gk. τλῆναι, to endure, L. tollere, to lift, and tolerare, to endure; see Prellwitz. See **Tolerate**. Der. Atlantes, in arch., figures of men used instead of columns or pilasters (Phillips, ed. 1706), from the Gk. form for the pl. of Atlas; also Atlant-ic, the name of the ocean (Milton, Comus, 97), with reference to Mount Atlas, in the N.W. of Africa.

ATMOSPHERE, the sphere of air round the earth. (Gk.) In Phillips (1658); and in Pope's Dunciad, iv. 423. A coined word; from Gk. ἀτμο- for ἀτμός, vapour; and σφαῖρα, a sphere. See **Sphere**. Der. atmospher-ic, atmospher-ic-al.

ATOLL, a group of coral islands forming a ring. (Maldive Islands.) 'We derive the expression from the Maldive Islands . . where the form of the word is atolu. It is prob. connected with the Singhalese prep. ätul, inside;' Yule.

ATOM, a very small particle. (F. — L. — Gk.) Cudworth, in his Intellectual System, p. 26, speaks of atoms, atomists, and 'atomical physiology.' Milton has atom, P. L. viii. 18. — F. atome, a mote in the sun; Cotgrave. — L. atomum, acc. of atomus, an atom. — Gk. ἄτομος, sb. fem., an indivisible particle; ἄτομος, adj., indivisible. — Gk. ἀ-, neg. prefix; and τομ-, 2nd grade of τέμνειν, to cut, divide. See **Tome**. Der. atom-ic, atom-ic-al, atom-ist.

ATOMY (1), an atom. (L. — Gk.) Shak. has : 'it is as easy to count atomies,' As You Like It, iii. 2. 245. From L. atomi, pl. of atomus, an atom; by adding the E. pl. suffix -es. See **Atom**.

ATOMY (2), a skeleton. (F. — L. — Gk.) Short for anatomy, which was resolved into *an atomy*; 2 Hen. IV, v. 4. 33. And see E. D. D. See **Anatomy**.

ATONE, to set at one; to reconcile. (E.) Made up of the two words *at* and *one*; so that *atone* means to 'set at one.' **α**. The interesting point is that an old pronunciation of *one* is here preserved; and there are at least two other similar instances, viz. in *alone* (ME. *al oon*), and *on-ly* (ME. *oon-ly*). **β**. The use of *atone* arose from the frequent use of ME. *at oon* (also written *at on*) in the phrases 'be at oon' = to agree, and 'set at oon,' i.e. to set at one, to make to agree, to reconcile. Examples are: 'Hii made certein couenaunt that hii were al *at on*' = were all agreed; Rob. of Glouc. p. 113 (l. 2451). 'Sone they were *at one*, with wille *at on* assent' = they were soon agreed, with will in one concord; Rob. of Brunne, tr. of P. Langtoft, p. 220. 'If gentil men, or othere of hir contree Were wrothe, she wolde bringen hem *atoon*;' Chaucer, C. T., E 437, where the two words are run into one in the Ellesmere MS., as printed. They are similarly run together in a much earlier passage: '*Aton* he was wiþ þe king;' King Horn, ed. Lumby, 925. **γ**. Particularly note the following from Tyndal: 'Where thou seest bate or strife betwen person and person, . . leaue nothing vnsought, to set them *at one*;' Works, p. 193, col. 2. 'One God, one Mediatour, that is to say, aduocate, intercessor, or an *atone-maker*, between God and man;' Works, p. 158. 'One mediatour Christ, . . and by that word vnderstand an *atonemaker*, a peacemaker;' id. p. 431 (Remarks on the Testament of M. W. Tracie). 'Hauyng more regarde to their olde variaunce then their newe *attonement*;' Sir T. More, Works, p. 41 c (written in 1513, pr. in 1557). See also the same, p. 40 f (qu. in Richardson). 'And like as he made the Jewes and the Gentiles *at one* betwene themselfes, euen so he made them bothe *at one* with God, that there should be nothing to breake the *attonement*, but that the thynges in heauen and the thinges in earth, should be ioined together as it wer into *one* body;' Udal, Eph. ii. 16. '*Attonement*, a louing againe after a breache or falling out;' Baret, Alvearie, s. v. 'So beene they both *at one*;' Spenser, F. Q. ii. 1. 29. See also Shak. Rich. II, i. 1. 202; Oth. iv. 1. 244; Ant. ii. 2. 102; Cymb. i. 4. 42; Timon, v. 4. 58; As You Like It, v. 4. 116; Cor. iv. 6. 72; also *atonement*, Merry Wives, i. 1. 33; 2 Hen. IV, iv. 1. 221; Rich. III, i. 3. 36. Also Ben Jonson, Epicœne, Act iv. sc. 2 (Truewit to La Foole); Massinger, Duke of Milan, Act iv. sc. 3 (Pescara); Milton, P. L. iii. 234. Bp. Hall says: 'Ye . . set such discord 'twixt agreeing parts Which never can be *set at one-ment* more;' Sat. iii. 7. And Dryden: 'If not *atton'd*, yet seemingly at peace;' Aurungzebe, Act iii. The word *atonement* came into use soon after A.D. 1500. **δ**. The simple verb *onen*, to unite, pp. *oned*, occurs in Chaucer, C. T. 7550 (B 1968). N.B. This E. idiom was perhaps translated from AF. 'Il ne peusent *estre a un*,' they could not be *at one*, could not agree; Le Livre de Reis de Angleterre (Rolls Series), p. 220. ¶ It is to be added that the phrase *at once* was for a long period written as *one* word, spelt *atones*, or quite as often *attones*, *attonis*, or *attonys*. See examples in Gloss. to Specimens of English from 1394 to 1579, ed. Skeat. By introducing the sound of *w* into once (*wunce*), we have again made *at once* into two words. Der. *atone-ment*.

ATRABILIOUS, melancholy. (L.) Kersey (1708) has: '*Atra bilis*, black choler;' a L. translation of Gk. μελαγχολία, black bile. — L. *ātra bīli-s*, black bile; with suffix *-ous*.

ATROCITY, extreme cruelty. (F. — L.) The adj. *atrocious*, an ill-formed word, apparently founded on the F. adj. *atroce*, heinous, is not known before 1669. It occurs in Thomson's Liberty, iii. 305. But *atrocity* is much older, and occurs, spelt *atrocyte*, in Sir T. More's Works, p. 1294 f (N.E.D.). — F. *atrocité*, 'atrocity, great cruelty;' Cotgrave. — L. acc. *atrōcitātem*, from nom. *atrocitās*, cruelty. — L. *atrōci-*, from *atrox*, cruel; more lit. horrible, frightful. Root unknown; cf. *āter*, black, dark, malicious. From the same source, *atroci-ous*, *atroci-ous-ly*, *atroci-ous-ness*.

ATROPHY, a wasting away of the body. (F. — L. — Gk.) Medical. It means lit. 'want of nourishment.' Milton has: 'pining *atrophy*;' P. L. xi. 486. Holland writes of 'no benefit or nutriment of meat, which they call in Greek *atropha*;' Pliny, bk. xxii. c. 25; ii. 143 c. — F. *atrophie*; Cot. — L. *atrophia*. — Gk. ἀτροφία, want of food, hunger, atrophy. — Gk. ἀ-, neg. prefix; and τρέφειν, to nourish (perf. t. τέτροφ-α); allied to Gk. θρέμμα, a nursling.

ATTACH, to take and hold fast; to apprehend. (F. — Teut.) ME. *attachen*, to take prisoner, arrest, much in use as a law term. '*Attache* tho tyrauntz,' apprehend those cruel men; P. Plowman, B. ii. 199. — OF. *atachier*, F. *attacher*, to attach, fasten; cf. F. *détacher*, to detach, unfasten, which is obviously from the same root. **β**. As Diez remarks, the root is to be found in the word which appears in English as *tack*, with the signification of 'peg' or 'small nail;' that to *attach* is to fasten with a tack or nail, whilst to *detach* is to unfasten what has been but loosely held together by such a nail. The prefix is the OF. prep. *a*, to = L. *ad*; and *-tacher* is probably from the Low G.

takk, or EFries. *takke*; see **Tack**. Der. *attach-able*, *attach-ment*, *attach-é* (F. pp.). Doublet, *attack*.

ATTACK, to assault. (F. — Ital. — Teut.) Rich. remarks that it is not an old word in the language. The verb occurs in Milton, Sams. Agonistes, 1113. — F. *attaquer*, explained by Cotgrave as 'to assault, or set on;' he does not use the work *attack*. *Attaquer* was borrowed from Ital. *attaccare*, 'to fasten, to ioyne; *attaccar battaglia*, to ioyne battell;' Florio. — L. *ad*, to (>*at-* before *t*); and Low G. *takk*, a tine, pointed thing; see **Tack** and **Attach**. Hence *attack* and *attach* are doublets. Der. *attack*, sb.

ATTAIN, to reach to, obtain. (F. — L.) ME. *attainen*, *atteinen*; 'they wenen to *ateine* to thilke good that they desiren;' Chaucer, tr. of Boethius, b. iv. pr. 2. l. 192. — OF. *ateign-*, pres. stem of *ateindre*, *ataindre*, to reach to, attain; also to punish, accuse, convict (*ataindre* in Godefroy). — Folk-L. **attangere*; for L. *attingere*, to touch upon, to attain. — L. *ad*, to (>*at-* before *t*); and *tangere*, to touch. See **Tangent**. Der. *attain-able*, *attain-able-ness*, *attain-ment*; also *attainder*, from a substantival use of OF. infin. *ateindre* (above), in the sense 'to convict.' Also *attaint* (below).

ATTAINT, to convict. (F. — L.) The similarity in sound between *attaint* and *taint* has led, probably, to some false law; see the remarks about it in Blount's Law Dictionary. But etymologically, and without regard to imported senses, to *attaint* is to convict, and *attainder* is conviction. As a fact, *attaint* is a verb that has been made out of a past participle, viz. the pp. of the verb to *attain*, used in a technical sense in law. The Prompt. Parv. has: '*Atteyntyn*, convinco;' p. 16. Palsgrave even has 'I *atteynt*, I hyt or touche a thyng,' i.e. *attain* it. In the 14th century, we find ME. *atteynt*, *atteint*, *ateynt* in the sense of 'convicted,' and the verb *atteyn* in the sense of 'convict.' 'And justise of the lond of falsnes was *atteynt*' = and the justice administered in the land was convicted of falseness; Rob. of Brunne, tr. of Langtoft, p. 246. 'To reprove tham at the last day, And to *atteyn* tham,' i.e. to convict them; Hampole, Prick of Conscience, 5331. Cf. P. Plowman, C. xxiii. 162. — OF. *ateint*, *ataint*, pp. of *ateindre*, to attain (above). ¶ The sense was affected by confusion with *taint* (N.E.D.).

ATTAR OF ROSES, perfumed oil of roses. (Arabic.) Often called, less correctly, 'otto of roses.' Byron has '*atar-gul*, ottar of roses;' note to Bryde of Abydos, i. 10. From Arab. *'itr*, perfume; from *'atira*, he smelt sweetly. See Richardson's Arab. Dict. p. 1014; and *otto* in Yule.

ATTEMPER, to temper, qualify. (F. — L.) Now little used. ME. *attempren*, *attempren*. '*Atempreth* the lusty houres of the firste somer sesoun;' Chaucer, tr. of Boethius, b. i. met. 2. — OF. *atemprer* (F. *attremper*), to modify. — OF. *a*, to (L. *ad*); and *temprer*, to temper, from L. *temperāre*, to moderate, control. See **Temper**.

ATTEMPT, to try, endeavour. (F. — L.) 'For to *attempt* his fansie by request;' Surrey, tr. of Æneid, bk. iv. l. 142. [Not in Gower, C. A. i. 287.] — OF. *atempter*, to undertake; Roquefort. The simple verb *tempter* was also spelt *tenter*, *tanter*; Burguy. Hence *atempter* is a Latinised form of an older *atenter*, which appears as *attenter* in the Supp. to Godefroy. — L. *attentāre*, often *attemptāre*, to attempt. — L. *ad* (becoming *at-* before *t*); and *tentāre*, to try, endeavour; so that '*attempt*' is to 'try at.' See **Tempt**. Der. *attempt*, sb.

ATTEND, to wait upon, to heed. (F. — L.) 'The Carthage lords did on the quene *attend*;' Surrey, Virgil, Æn. b. iv. l. 171. The sbs. *attencioun* and *attendance* occur in Chaucer, tr. of Boethius, b. ii. pr. 1, l. 2; C. T. 6515 (D 933). — OF. *atendre*, to wait. — L. *attendere*, pp. *attentus*, to stretch towards, think upon, give heed to. — L. *at-*, for *a*, to; and *tendere*, to stretch. See **Tend** (1). Der. *attend-ance*, *attend-ant*; and, from L. pp. *attentus*, we have *attent*, adj. (2 Chron. vi. 40, vii. 15); cf. *attent-ion*, *attent-ive*, *attent-ive-ly*, *attent-ive-ness*.

ATTENUATE, to make thin. (L.) It occurs in Elyot, Castel of Health, bk. ii. c. 7. § 6; Bacon, Nat. Hist. sect. 299. Formed, like other words in *-ate*, from a past participle. — L. *attenuātus*, thin, pp. of *attenuāre*, to make thin. — L. *ad-* (>*at-* before *t*); and *tenuāre*, to make thin, from *tenuis*, thin. See **Thin**. Der. *attenuat-ion*.

ATTEST, to bear witness to. (L.) In Shak. Hen. V, iii. 1. 22. — L. *attestārī*, to bear witness to; pp. *attestātus*. — L. *ad* (>*at-* before *t*); and *testārī*, to be witness, from *testis*, a witness. See **Testify**. Der. *attest-at-ion*.

ATTIC, a low-built top story of a house, or a room in the same. (F. — L. — Gk.) 'A term in architecture, comprehending the whole of a plain or decorated parapet wall, terminating the upper part of the façade of an edifice;' Eng. Cyclopædia, s. v. '*Attick*, in arch., a kind of order, after the manner of the city of Athens; in our buildings, a small order placed upon another that is much greater;' Kersey's Dict., ed. 1708. — F. *attique*, upper part of a building; so called as belonging to the Attic order of architecture. — L. *Atticus*. — Gk. Ἀττικός, Attic, Athenian.

ATTIRE, apparel, dress; vb., to adorn, dress. (F.) In early use. **α.** The sb. is ME. *atyr, atir* (with one *t*), and is derived from the verb. 'Mid his fourti cnihtes and hire hors and hire *atyr*' = with his forty knights and their horses and their apparel; Layamon, l. 3275 (later text). In William of Palerne, l. 1725, it is spelt *tyr*; in l. 1147, it is *atir*. **β.** The verb is ME. *atyren, atiren* (mostly with one *t*). 'Hii . . . newe knightes made And armede and *atired* hem' = they made new knights and armed and equipped them; Rob. of Glouc. p. 547, l. 11370. The sb. appears as *atir, atyr* in AF. (Godefroy), but not, apparently, in continental French. **γ.** From OF. *atirier, atierer* (*atirer* in Godefroy), to arrange, set in order, equip, adorn. – OF. *a* (from L. *ad*, to) and *tiere, tire* (*tire* in Godefroy), f., a row, rank, order; cognate with OProv. *tiera*, a row (Bartsch). Whether this is the same word as mod. E. *tier*, is doubtful; and the remoter origin of this OF. *tiere* still remains undecided. See **Tier**. Diez would connect it with OHG. *ziarī*, G. *zier*, ornament; see Diez, ed. 1878, p. 687; Körting, § 9464. ¶ As the prefix *a-* was unaccented, it was often thrown off in English, as in the well-known text: 'she painted her face, and *tired* her head;' 2 Kings, ix. 30. The sb. *tire*, a head-dress, is common in the Bible (Isaiah, iii. 18; Ezek. xxiv. 17, 23; Judith, x. 3, xvi. 8). See **Tire** (2) and (3).

ATTITUDE, position, posture. (Ital. – L.) ''Tis the business of a painter in his choice of *attitudes* to foresee the effect and harmony of the lights and shadows;' Dryden, Dufresnoy, sect. 4. This, being a word connected with the painter's art, came from Italy. – Ital. *attitudine*, aptness, skill, attitude. – L. *aptitūdinem*, acc. of *aptitūdo*, aptitude. See **Apt**. ¶ Ital. assimilates *pt* into *tt*. Der. *attitud-in-al, attitud-in-ise*. Doublet, *aptitude*.

ATTORNEY, an agent appointed to act in the 'turn' of another. (F. – L. and Gk.) ME. *attourné, aturneye*, '*Aturneye*, suffectus, atturnatus;' Prompt. Parv. p. 17. '*Attourneis* in cuntre thei geten silver for noht;' Polit. Songs, p. 339. – OF. *atorné*, pp. of *atorner*, to direct, turn, prepare, arrange or ordain. – OF. *a*, to (L. *ad*) and *torner*, to turn, from *tornāre*, to turn, esp. to turn in a lathe (of Gk. origin). See **Turn**. Der. *attorney-ship*.

ATTRACT, to draw to, allure. (L.) Used by Grafton, Rich. III, an. 2. Shak. has *attract*, Tw. Nt. ii. 4. 89; *attraction*, Timon, iv. 3. 439; *attractive*, Haml. iii. 2. 117. Formed, like *convict*, from a past participle. – L. *attractus*, pp. of *attrahere*, to draw to, attract. – L. *ad* (>*at-* before *t*); and *trahere*, to draw. See **Trace** (1). Der. *attract-able, attract-ib-il-it-y, attract-ion, attract-ive, attract-ive-ly, attract-ive-ness*.

ATTRIBUTE, a quality ascribed to a person or thing; as vb., to assign, ascribe. (L.) Formed, like *attract*, from a past participle. The sb. is in Shak. Merch. iv. 1. 191; the verb in Sir T. More, Works, p. 1121 d. – L. *attribūtus*, pp. of *attribuere*, to assign. – L. *ad*, to (>*at-* before *t*); and *tribuere*, to give, bestow. See **Tribute**. Der. *at'tribut-able, attribu'-tion, attribut-ive*.

ATTRITION, a wearing by friction. (F. – L.) Formerly in use in a theological sense, as expressing sorrow for sin without shrift; after shrift, such sorrow became *contrition*; see Tyndal, Works, p. 148, col. 2; Chaucer, Troil. i. 557. [Perhaps from Latin directly.] – F. *attrition*, 'a rubbing, fretting, wearing;' Cotgrave. – L. acc. *attrītiōnem*, from nom. *attrītio*, a rubbing, wearing away; allied to L. *attrītus*, rubbed away, pp. of *atterere*. – L. *ad* (> *at-* before *t*); and *terere*, to rub. See **Trite**.

ATTUNE, to make to harmonise, put in tune. (Hybrid; L. and Gk.) A coined word. In Spenser, F. Q. i. 12. 7. Made by prefixing L. *ad* (which in composition becomes *at-* before *t*) to the sb. *tune*, so that *attune* is to 'bring to a like tune or tone.' See **Tune**.

AUBURN, reddish brown. (F. – L.) ME. *auburne, awburne*. '*Awburne* coloure, *citrinus*;' Prompt. Parv. p. 17. Thus the old sense was 'citron-coloured' or light yellow. The modern meaning was probably due to some confusion in the popular mind with the word *brown*; indeed Hall, in his Satires, bk. iii. Sat. 5, speaks of '*abron* locks,' which perhaps suggested this. – OF. *alborne, auborne*, blond (Godefroy). [Cf. Ital. *alburno*, of which one of the old meanings is 'that whitish colour of women's hair called an *aburn* colour.'] – Late L. *alburnus*, whitish, light-coloured; Ducange. Cf. L. *alburnum*, the sap-wood, or inner bark of trees (Pliny). – L. *albus*, white. See **Alb**.

AUCTION, a public sale to the highest bidder. (L.) A 'sale by *auction*' is a sale by 'increase of price,' till the article is knocked down to the highest bidder. *Auction* occurs in Kersey (1708); and in Pope, Moral Essays, iii. 119. – L. *auctiōnem*, acc. of *auctio*, a sale by auction, lit. an 'increase;' allied to L. *auctus*, pp. of *augēre*, to increase. See **Eke**. Der. *auction-eer*.

AUDACIOUS, bold, impudent. (F. – L.) Ben Jonson has '*audacious* ornaments;' The Silent Woman, A. ii. sc. 3. Bacon has *audacitie*, Nat. Hist. sect. 943. – F. *audacieux*, 'bold, stout, hardy, .. audacious,' &c.; Cot. Formed as if from a L. form *audāciōsus*, which again is from L. *audāci-*, from *audax*, bold, daring. – L. *audēre*,

to be bold, to dare. Der. *audacious-ly, audacious-ness*; also *audacity*, from L. acc. *audācitātem*, nom. *audāci:ās*, boldness.

AUDIENCE, hearing, an assembly of listeners. (F. – L.) In Chaucer, C. T. 5093 (B 673); and tr. of Boethius, b. ii. pr. 7, l. 80. Sir T. More has *audible*, Works, p. 1259 c. – F. *audience*, 'an audience or hearing;' Cot. – L. *audientia*, attention, hearing. – L. *audīre*, pp. *audītus*, to hear. For *auiz-dīre*; cf. Gk. αἰσθέσθαι, to perceive (for *ἀϝισ-θέσθαι*); Brugm. i. § 240. Der. From L. *audīre*, to hear, we have also *audi-ble, audi-ble-ness, audi-bly*. From the pp. *audītus*, we have *audit* (Kersey, 1708, cf. L. *auditus*, sb., a hearing); cf. also *audit-or* (spelt *auditour* in Gower, C. A. ii. 191, bk. v. 1919), *audit-or-y, audit-or-ship*.

AUGER, a centre-bit, a tool for boring holes. (E.) 'An *augoure*, *terebrum*;' Levins, 222. 38. A corruption of *nauger*. Like *adder*, and some other words, it has lost an initial *n*. It is spelt *nauger* in Wright's Vol. of Vocabularies, 1st Series, p. 170. In Halliwell's Dict. we find: '*Navegor*, an auger, a carpenter's tool.' This word occurs in an inventory dated A.D. 1301, and in Nominale MS.' AS. *nafugār, nafogār*, an auger, 'foratorium uel terebellum;' Wright's Voc. 408. 39; early spelling *nabogār*, id. 44. 11. It means, literally, a nave-piercer, being used for boring the hole in the centre of a wheel for the axle to pass through. – AS. *nafu, nabu*, the nave of a wheel (see **Nave** (1)); and *gār*, a piercer, that which *gores* (see **Gore** (3)). + Du. *avegaar* (for *navegaar*); Icel. *nafarr*; Swed. *nafvare*; OHG. *nabagēr*. Cf. Du. *naafboor*, an auger, from *naaf*, nave, and *boren*, to bore.

AUGHT, a whit, anything. (E.) Very variously spelt in ME., which has *awiht, eawiht, eawt, ewt, aht, aght, aught, ouht, ought, out, oht, oght*. 'Yif he *awiht* delan wule' = if he will give aught; O. Eng. Homilies, i. 103. AS. *āwiht*, aught, Grein, i. 48; lit. 'e'er a whit,' or 'anything whatever.' – AS. *ā*, ever; and *wiht*, a wight, creature, thing, whit. See **Aye** and **Whit**.

AUGMENT, to increase. (F. – L.) 'My sorowes to *augment*;' Remedie of Love (15th cent.), anon. poem in old editions of Chaucer's Works, st. 13; and see Rom. Rose, 5597. – F. *augmenter*, 'to augment, increase;' Cot. – L. *augmentāre*, to enlarge, pp. *augmentātus*. – L. *augmentum*, an increase, augment. – L. *aug-ēre*, to increase; with suffix *-mentum*. See **Auction**. Der. *augment-able, augment-at-ion, augment-at-ive*. The sb. *augment* is (etymologically) more original than the verb.

AUGUR, a soothsayer, a diviner by the flight and cries of birds. (L.) Gower has *augurre*, C. A. ii. 82; bk. iv. 2404. Chaucer has *augurie*, Troil. v. 380. – L. *augur*, a priest at Rome, who foretold events, and interpreted the will of the gods from the flight and singing of birds. Hence it is usual to derive *augur* from *auis*, a bird. If it be right, the etym. is from *aui-*, for *auis*, a bird, and *-gur*, telling, '*gur* being connected with *garrire, garrulus*, and the Skt. *gar* or *gṛ*, to shout;' Max Müller, Lect. on Science of Lang. ii. 266 (8th ed.). Cf. L. *au-ceps*, a bird-catcher. Der. *augur-y* (OF. *augurie*, L. *augur-ium*), *augur-al, augur-ship*; also *in-augurate*, q.v. And see **Auspice**.

AUGUST, adj., venerable. (L.) Dryden, Virgil, Æn. i. 825, has: '*August* in visage, and serenely bright.' – L. *augustus*, honoured, venerable. Cf. Skt. *ōjas*, strength; Brugm. i. § 213. Allied to **Auction**. Der. *August*, the 8th month, named after *Augustus* (i.e. the honoured) Cæsar; *August-an, august-ly, august-ness*.

AUK, a sea-bird. (Scand.) Given by Edmondston as an Orkney word, and by Ray as Northern. – Swed. *alka*, an auk: Icel. *alka, ālka*: Dan. *alke* (see Falk and Torp). Hence L. *alca*, a Latinised form.

AUNT, a father's or mother's sister. (F. – L.) ME. *aunte*, Rob. of Glouc. p. 37, l. 871. – OF. *ante, aunte* (mod. Norman *ante*, corrupted to *tante* in mod. F.). – L. *amita*, a father's sister. Cf. Icel. *amma*, a grandmother, OHG. *amma*, mother, mamma; the mod. G. *amme* means 'nurse.' ¶ For the change of *m* to *n* before *t*, see **Ant**.

AUREATE, golden. (L.) Formerly *aureat*, a word first used by Lydgate, as in A Balade in Commendation of Our Lady, l. 13; and common in some of the older Scotch poets. 'The *aureat* fanys,' the golden streamers; G. Douglas, Prol. to Æn. bk. xii. l. 47. – Late L. *aureātus*, golden; a corrupted form due to confusion with *aureus*, golden, adj. The correct form is L. *aurātus*, gilded, pp. of *aurāre*, to gild, a verb not in use. – L. *aurum*, gold; old form, *ausum*. Cf. Lith. *auksas*, gold. Der. From L. *aurum* we have *aur-elia* (Ital. *aurelia*), the gold-coloured chrysalis of an insect; *aur-e-ola, aur-e-ole*, the halo of golden glory in paintings (spelt *auriole* in Hali Meidenhad, p. 23, from L. *corōna aureola*, Exod. xxv. 25, Vulgate); *aur-ic*, golden; *aur-i-ferous*, gold-producing, from L. *ferre*, to produce, cognate with E. *bear*; also *or* (3), *oriflamme, oriole, dory*.

AURICULAR, told in the ear, secret. (L.) Well known in the phrase '*auricular* confession.' Udal speaks of it, Reuel. of St. John, c. 21. vv. 21-27; and Grafton, K. John, an. 14; cf. Shak. K. Lear, i. 2. 99. – Late L. *auriculāris*, in the phr. *auriculāris confessio*, secret confession. — L. *auricula*, the lobe of the ear ; double dimin. from the stem *auri-* of L. *auris*, the ear. See **Ear** (1). Der. From L. *auricula* we have *auricle*, the outer ear ; pl. *auricles,* two ear-like cavities of the heart ; *auricula*, the ' bear's ear,' a kind of primrose, named from the shape of its leaves, Thomson, Spring, 536 ; *auricul-ar, auricul-ar-ly, auricul-ate.* From L. *auris* we have *auri-form, aur-ist.*

AUROCHS, the European bison. (G.) Properly the name of an extinct wild ox. — G. *aurochs* ; MHG. *ûrohse.* — MHG. *ûr,* cognate with AS. *ûr,* an aurochs (whence L. *ûrus*) ; and OHG. *ohso,* G. *ochse,* cognate with E. **Ox.**

AURORA, the dawn. (L.) In Shak. Romeo, i. 1. 142. — L. *aurôra,* the dawn, the goddess of the dawn ; which stands for an older form **âusôsa.*+Gk. ἠώς, Æolic αὔως, Attic ἕως, dawn, for pre-historic *αὔσως ; Skt. *ushâs,* dawn. Brugmann, i. § 930. See **East.** Cf. *Aurora-borealis,* i. e. northern dawn or dawn-like halo ; from L. *Boreas,* the North wind.

AUSCULTATION, a listening. (L.) First used in 1634 (N. E. D.) ; now chiefly medical, applied to the use of the stetho-scope. — L. *auscultâtiônem,* acc. of *auscultâtio,* a listening ; from *auscul-târe,* to listen. — L. **aus-,* base of *auris* (for *ausis), the ear ; and *-cultâre,* as in *oc-cultâre,* to hide ; see **Occult.** See **Auricular** and **Ear** (1).

AUSPICE, a prognostic, prosperous lead, favour, patronage. (F. — L.) Used by Dryden in the sense of ' patronage ;' Annus Mirabilis, st. 288 ; and see ' The Auspices ' in Introd. to Ben Jonson's Masque of Hymen. Shak. has *auspicious,* Temp. i. 2. 182 ; v. 314. — F. *auspice,* ' a sign, token . . . of things by the flight of birds ; also, fortune, lucke, or a luckie beginning of matters ;' Cot. — L. *auspicium,* a watching of birds for the purpose of augury. A contraction of **auispicium.* — L. *aui-,* stem of *auis,* a bird ; and *spicere, specere,* to spy, look into, cognate with E. *spy.* See **Aviary** and **Species.** Der. pl. *auspices* ; and (from L. *auspicium*), *auspici-ous, auspici-ous-ly, aus-pici-ous-ness.*

AUSTERE, harsh, rough, severe. (F. — L. — Gk.) In early use. ' He was fulle *austere* ;' Rob. of Brunne, tr. of Langtoft, p. 54. — OF. *austere,* which Cotgrave explains by ' austere, severe, stern,' &c. — L. *austêrus,* harsh, tart, sour to the taste ; also, severe, rigorous. — Gk. αὐστηρός, making the tongue dry, harsh. — Gk. αὖος, dry, withered, parched, sere ; αὔειν, Attic αὔειν, to parch, dry. See **Sere.** Der. *austere-ly, austere-ness, auster-i-ty.*

AUSTRAL, southern. (L. ; or F. — L.) The use of L. *Auster* for the South wind occurs in Chaucer, tr. of Boethius, b. ii. met. 3, l. 9. The adj. *australe* is in Cockeram (1642) ; ME. *austral* (N.E.D.). [Perhaps directly from Latin.] — F. *australe,* southerly ; Cot. — L. *Austrâlis,* southerly. — L. *Auster,* the South wind. It probably meant ' burning.' See **Aurora.** Der. *Austral-ia, Austral-ian, Austral-asia* (from *Asia*), *Austral-asian.*

AUTHENTIC, original, genuine. (F. — L. — Gk.) In early use. ME. *autentik, autentique, auctentyke.* Spelt *auctentyke* in Hampole, Pricke of Conscience, 7116. — OF. *autentique, auctentique,* later *au-thentique,* which is the form in Cotgrave, who explains it by ' authen-tick, authenticall, of good authority ;' the E. and F. words having been alike modified by reference to the original Greek. — L. *authen-ticus,* original, written by the author's own hand. — Gk. αὐθεντικός, authentic, vouched for, warranted. — Gk. αὐθέντης, one who does things with his own hand ; the same as αὐτο-έντης, a murderer (Sophocles). — Gk. αὐτο-s, himself, which became αὐθ- before an as-pirate ; and ἐντ-, connected (by gradation) with L. *sont-,* stem of *sons,* guilty, and with E. *sin* ; see **Sin.** Der. *authentic-al, authentic-al-ly, authentic-ate, authentic-at-ion, authentic-i-ty.* Cf. *effendi.*

AUTHOR, the originator of a book or work. (F. — L.) ME. *autor, autour, auctor, auctour* ; Chaucer, C. T. 9017 (E 1141). The pl. *autors* is in K. Alisaunder, ed. Weber, 4519. For the spelling *authour,* see Rom. Rose, l. 7. — OF. *auteur, auctor, auctour* (Supp. to Godefroy, p. 241). — L. *auctôrem,* acc. of *auctor,* an originator, lit. ' one who makes a thing to grow.' — L. *augêre,* pp. *auct-us,* to make to grow. See **Auction.** Der. *author-ess, author-ship, author-i-ty, author-i-tat-ive, author-i-tat-ive-ly, author-ise* (spelt *auctorize* in Gower, C. A. iii. 134, bk. vii. 1480) ; *author-is-at-ion.* ¶ The form *authour,* for *autour,* was at first a mere scribal variant ; but this newer spelling affected the pronunciation, and at last established the present sound.

AUTOBIOGRAPHY, a life of a man written by himself. (Gk.) Modern. Made by prefixing *auto-,* from Gk. αὐτο-, stem of αὐτός, self, to *biography,* q. v. Der. *autobiograph-ic, -graph-ic-al, -graph-er.*

AUTOCRACY, self-derived power, absolute and despotic govern-ment by one man. (Gk.) Spelt *autocrasie* in Phillips (1658) ; *autoc-rasy* in South's Sermons, vol. viii. ser. 10 (R.) ; see Todd. — Gk. αὐ-τοκράτεια, absolute government. — Gk. αὐτο-, stem of αὐτός, self ; and -κράτεια (in compounds), from κρατέειν, to rule, which is from κρατύς, strong, cognate with E. **Hard.** Der. *autocrat* (Gk. αὐτοκρατής), *auto-crat-ic-al.*

AUTO-DA-FE, a judgment of the Inquisition ; also, the execution of such judgment, when the decree or sentence is read to the victims. (Port. — L.) Lit. ' act of faith.' — Port. *auto,* action, decree ; *da,* for *de a,* of the ; *fe,* faith. [The Span. form is *auto de fé*: without the Span. art. *la* = Port. art. *a.*] — L. *actum,* acc. of *actus,* act, deed ; *dê,* pre-position ; *illa,* fem. of *ille,* he ; *fidem,* acc. of *fides,* faith. See **Act** and **Faith.** Worcester's Dict. has the following note : ' as the details of an *auto-da-fe* were first made familiar to the English public in an account of the Inquisition at Goa (a Port. colony in the E. Indies), published in the 17th [18th] century, the Port. form of the phrase has generally prevailed in E. literature.' Haydn, Dict. of Dates, has : ' 20 persons perish at an *auto-da-fe,* at Goa, A.D. 1717 ; Malagrida, a Jesuit, burnt at Lisbon, 1761.'

AUTOGRAPH, something in one's own handwriting. (F. — L. — Gk.) Used by Anthony à Wood to denote an original MS. ; see the quotation in Richardson from his Athenæ Oxonienses. — Spelt *auto-graphum* in Kersey (1708). — F. *autographe,* ' written with his own hand ;' Cot. — L. *autographus,* adj. ; *autographum,* sb. — Gk. αὐτόγρα-φος, written with one's own hand ; αὐτόγραφον, an original. — Gk. αὐτο-, stem of αὐτός, self ; and γράφειν, to write. Der. *autograph-ic, auto-graph-y.*

AUTOMATON, a self-moving machine. (Gk.) In Beaum. and Fletcher, Bloody Brother, iv. 1 (Latorch) ; and in Boyle's Works, vol. v. p. 251. Browne, in his Vulg. Errors, b. v. c. 18, § 1, uses the adj. *automatous.* — Gk. αὐτόματον, neut. of αὐτόματος, self-moving. — Gk. αὐτο-, stem of αὐτός, self ; and -ματος, allied to Skt. *matás,* thought, considered, known, pp. of *man,* to think ; see Benfey, s. v. *man.* — √MEN, to think. Brugm. i. § 387. See **Mind.** Der. pl. *automatons* or *automata* ; *automat-ic, automat-ic-al, automat-ic-al-ly.*

AUTONOMY, self-government. (Gk.) In Cockeram (1623). — Gk. αὐτονομία, independence. — Gk. αὐτόνομος, free, living by one's own laws. — Gk. αὐτο-, stem of αὐτός, self ; and νομ-, 2nd grade of νέμομαι, I sway, middle voice of νέμω, I distribute. See **Nomad.** Der. *autonom-ous,* from Gk. αὐτόνομος.

AUTOPSY, personal inspection. (Gk.) Used by Ray, On the Creation ; and by Cudworth, Intellectual System, p. 160 (R.) — Gk. αὐτοψία, a seeing with one's own eyes. — Gk. αὐτο-, stem of αὐτός, self ; and ὄψις, sight. See **Optic.** Der. *autoptic-al* (Phillips, 1658).

AUTUMN, the harvest time of the year. (F. — L.) Spelt *autompne* in Chaucer, tr. of Boethius, b. i. met. 2, l. 17. — OF. *autompne* (Hatz-feld). — L. *autumnum,* acc. of *autumnus, auctumnus,* autumn. By some connected with *augêre* (pp. *auctus*), to increase, as being the season of produce. Der. *autumn-al.*

AUXILIARY, adj., helping ; sb., a helper. (L.) Holland, Livy, p. 433, speaks of ' *auxiliarie* or aid souldiers lightly armed.' — L. *auxi-liârius, auxiliâris,* assisting, aiding. — L. *auxilium,* help, assistance. — L. *augêre,* to increase. See **Auction.**

AVADAVAT, a finch-like E. Indian bird. (Arab. *and* Pers.) ' A corruption of *amaduvad,* the name by which the bird is known to Anglo-Indians, and under which it was figured, in 1735, by Albin, Suppl. Nat. Hist. Birds, pl. 77, p. 72. Jerdon (Birds of India, ii. 361) says that Blyth has shown that this word took its origin from the city of *Ahmedabad,* whence the bird used to be imported into Europe in numbers.' — A. Newton, in N. and Q. 6 S. ii. 198. Ahmedābād is near the Gulf of Cambay, on the W. coast of Hindostan ; and its name is derived from *Ahmed,* a proper name, and the Pers. *âbâd,* city. *Ahmed* is from Arab. *aḥmad,* very laudable, Rich. Dict. p. 33 ; from the root *ḥamada,* he praised ; see **Mohammedan.** For Pers. *âbâd,* see Horn, § 4.

AVAIL, to be of value or use. (F. — L.) ME. *auailen* (*u* for *v*). '*Avaylyn* or profytyn ;' Prompt. Parv. p. 17. Spelt *auail,* Cursor Mundi, l. 90. Hampole has *availes,* Pricke of Conscience, l. 3587. The compound verb was not used in the French of the continent ; it was made by prefixing the OF. *a* (= L. *ad,* to) to the OF. *vail,* 1 p. pr. s. of *valoir,* to be of use, from L. *ualêre,* to be strong. Der. *avail-able, avail-abl-y.* The simple form appears in *valiant,* q. v.

AVALANCHE, a fall of snow. (F. — L.) Modern. In Cole-ridge's Hymn in the Vale of Chamouni, and in Byron's Manfred, Act i. sc. 2. l. 77. — F. *avalanche,* a descent of snow into the valley ; given by Cotgrave in the form *avallanche,* ' a great falling or sinking down, as of earth, &c.' — F. *avaler,* which in mod. F. means ' to swallow,' but Cotgrave also gives, s. v. *avaller,* the senses ' to let, put, cast, lay, fell down, to let fall down.' — F. *aval,* downward ; common in OF. as opposed to *amont,* upward (L. *ad montem,* towards the hill). — OF. *a val,* from L. *ad uallem,* towards the valley ; hence, downward. See **Valley.**

AVARICE, greediness after wealth. (F. — L.) ME. *auarice* (*u* as *v*) ; used by Chaucer, tr. of Boethius, b. ii. pr. 5, l. 11 ; Wyclif, 1 Kings, viii. 3. — OF. *avarice, auarice.* — L. *auâritia, auarice.* — L. *auârus,* greedy ; cf. L. *auidus,* greedy. — L. *auêre,* to wish, desire. Cf. Skt. *av,* to be pleased, to desire. Der. *avarici-ous, avarici-ous-ly, avarici-ous-ness.*

AVAST, hold fast, stop. (Dutch *or* Span.) '*Avast*, stop, hold, or stay;' Kersey (1708). It occurs in Poor Jack, a sea-song by C. Dibdin, died A.D. 1814. 1. Perhaps from Du. *hou vast*, hold fast. *Hou*, short for *houd*, is the imp. s. of *houden*, cognate with E. *hold*. *Vast* is cognate with E. *fast*. 2. Otherwise it may be from Span. *abasto*, 'as much as need, enough, sufficiently,' Minsheu; the Span. *b* being taken as an E. *v*. Pineda, in his Eng.-Span. vocabulary, has: '*Avast*, basta.' Cf. Port. *abasta*, it is enough; mod. Prov. *abasto* (sea-term), it is enough (Mistral); Ital. *basta*, it is enough.

AVATAR, the descent of a Hindu deity in an incarnate form. (Sanskrit.) Modern. 'The Irish *Avatar*;' a poem by Byron. An English modification of Skt. *avatāra-s*, m., descent. — Skt. *ava*, down; and *tṛ, tar*, to pass over.

AVAUNT, begone! (F. — L.) In Shak. Mer. Wives, i. 3. 90, &c.; Skelton, against Garnesche, iv. 112. — AF. *avaunt*, OF. *avant*, forward! on! — L. *ab ante*. See **Advance.**

AVE, hail! (L.) As mostly used, it is short for *Avē, Maria*, i.e. hail, Mary! alluding to St. Luke, i. 28, where the Vulgate version has: '*Ave gratia plena*.' Spenser Englishes the phrase by *Ave-Mary*, F. Q. i. 1. 35. Cf. Chaucer, ABC, 104. — L. *auē*! hail! imp. sing. of *auēre*, to fare well.

AVENGE, to take vengeance for an injury. (F. — L.) 'This sinne of ire . . . is wikked wil *to be auenged* by word or by dede;' Chaucer, Pers. Tale, De Ira (I 535). — OF. *avengier*, to avenge (Burguy). — OF. *a*, prefix (L. *ad*, to); and *vengier*, to revenge, take vengeance, from L. *uindicāre*, to lay claim to; also, to punish, revenge. See **Vindicate.**

AVENS, name of a flower. (F.) AF. *avence*, explained by *harefot*, hare-foot; Voc. 555. 6. Also OF. *avence*; med. L. *avencia*, *avantia*. Origin unknown.

AVENUE, an approach, esp. an alley shaded by trees forming the approach to a house. (F. — L.) Spelt *advenue* in Holland's Livy, p. 413, but *avenue* at p. 657 (R.). — F. *avenue*, also spelt *advenue* by Cotgrave, and explained by 'an access, passage, or entry unto a place.' It is the fem. pp. of the verb *avenir* or *advenir* (Cotgrave), used in the Latin sense of 'to come to.' — L. *aduenire*, to come to. — L. *ad*; and *uenire*, to come, cognate with E. *come*, q.v.

AVER, to affirm to be true. (F. — L.) In Shak. Cymb. v. 5. 203. — F. *averer*, 'to aver, avouch, verifie, witness;' Cotgrave. — Late L. *āuērāre*, *aduērāre*, to prove a thing to be true;' Ducange. A coined word, from L. *ad*, prep. to, and *uērum*, truth, a true thing, neut. of *uērus*, true. See **Verity.** Der. *aver-ment*; in Blackstone, Comment. b. iv. c. 26.

AVERAGE, a medial or equalised estimate of a series or number of things; an arithmetical mean. (F.) See the N. E. D. for the numerous senses at different dates. Thus it meant (1) a duty, tax, impost; (2) an extra charge on goods above the freight; (3) expense or loss to owners, due to damage at sea; (4) the mode of incidence of such loss, estimated proportionally; (5) the distribution of the aggregate inequalities of a number of things, with a view to equalise them, a medial estimate; (6) the arithmetical mean thus obtained. β. It first occurs, with the sense of duty, tax, or custom, in Arnold's Chron. (1502), p. 180 : 'And ouer that alle manere of grauntis . . . of your custumes or subsidyes or *auerage*.' And, in sense 2, in the same, p. 112 : 'And ouer that to pai or doo pay all maner *auerays*;' with a somewhat different spelling. γ. The spelling *average* seems to be English only, and substituted for *avaries*, a pl. formed from F. *avarie* (below); and perhaps Arnold's spelling *auerays* points back to the same form. — F. *avarie*, damage, injury to goods, extraordinary expenses for goods (see Hatzfeld); Cot. has *avaris* (for *avaries*, pl.?), 'decay of wares or merchandise; . . the charges of the carriage . . thereof.' Cognate forms are Span. *averia*, *haberia*, 'the custom paid for goods that are exported' (Pineda); Port. *avaria*; Ital. *avaria*, 'an account made by the crew of a ship of the loss they have had at sea' (Baretti); Late L. *avaria*, *averia*. Orig. a Mediterranean maritime term, signifying 'duty charged on goods' (G. P. Marsh, in N. E. D.). Origin unknown; but perhaps from MSpan. *averes*, *haveres*, 'goods, wealth, substance' (Minsheu), *haberes*, 'substance, wealth, or riches' (Pineda); which is from the infin. *aver*, to have, spelt *haber* (Pineda), used substantively, like F. *avoir*, and Ital. *hauere*, 'to have, also wealth, riches, goods' (Florio). ¶ Not from Arab. *'awār*, damage, which is merely borrowed from Ital. *avaria*, in a late sense. N.B. The form *average* may very well have been due to confusion with another E. word *average*, now usually represented by *arriage* in the phrase 'arriage and carriage,' the sense of which was some kind of service due by tenants to the feudal superior, and derived from OF. *average*, an ill-coined term due, apparently, to OF. *ovre*, work (L. *opera*), and confused with *aver*, which meant property or cattle. See the whole account in N.E.D., where this difficult word is fully discussed.

AVERT, to turn aside. (L.) 'I *averte*, I tourne away a thyng;' Palsgrave, French Dict. (1530). — L. *āuertere*, to turn away. — L. *ā*, short form of *ab*, *abs*, away, from; and *uertere*, to turn. See **Verse.** Der. (From L. *auersus*, pp. of *auertere*) *averse*, Milton, P. L. ii. 763, *averse-ly*, *averse-ness*, *avers-ion*. ¶ The F. *avertir* = L. *aduertere*, and is therefore a different word.

AVIARY, a place for keeping birds. (L.) 'For *aviaries*, I like them not;' Bacon, Essay 46; Of Gardens. — L. *auiārium*, a place for birds; neut. of adj. *auiārius*, belonging to birds. — L. *aui-*, stem of *auis*, a bird. Cf. Gk. ἀετός, αἰετός (for *αἰϝετός), an eagle; Brugm. i. § 205 (3).

AVIDITY, greediness, eagerness. (F. — L.) In Phillips (1658). The pl. *aviditles* is in Boyle's Works, ii. 317. — F. *avidité*, 'greedinesse, covetousnesse, extreame lust, ardent affection, eager desire;' Cotgrave (who has not 'avidity' as an English word). — L. acc. *auiditātem*, from nom. *auiditās*, eagerness. — L. *auidus*, greedy, desirous. — L. *auēre*, to crave. See **Avarice.**

AVOCATION, pursuit, employment, business. (L.) 'Avocation, a calling away;' Phillips (1658). Used by Dryden (Todd's Johnson); also in Boyle, Occas. Reflections, s. 2. med. 6. Not found in French, but formed with the common F. suffix -*tion* (L. acc. -*tiōnem*), from L. *āuocātio*, a calling away of the attention, a diverting of the thoughts; hence, a diversion, amusement. It is in this sense that Boyle uses it. He says : 'In the time of health, visits, businesses, cards, and I know not how many other *avocations*, which they justly stile *diversions*, do succeed one another so thick, that in the day there is no time left for the distracted person to converse with his own thoughts.' Dryden (in Todd's Johnson) speaks of the '*avocations* of business.' — L. *āuocāre*, to call away; pp. *āuocātus*. — L. *ā*, for *ab*, away; and *uocāre*, to call. See **Vocal.** β. The word has gradually changed its meaning from 'diversions' to '*necessary* employments,' by confusion with OF. *avocation*, *advocation*, which sometimes meant a profession (Godefroy), and is derived from L. *aduocātio*, with prefix *ad-*.

AVOCET, AVOSET, a wading bird. (F. — Ital.) In a tr. of Buffon, 1792; ii. 120. — F. *avocette*. — Ital. *avosetta*, 'a fowle like a storke;' Florio. Prof. Newton (Dict. of Birds) says it is Ferrarese, and by some is considered to be a derivative of L. *auis*, a bird (unlikely). The Ital. word is also spelt *avoserta* (Florio).

AVOID, to get out of the way of, to shun. (F. — L.) ME. *auoiden* (*u* for *v*), *auoyden*. '*Auoyden*, evacuo, devacuo; *avoydyd*, evacuatus;' Promp. Parv. p. 19. In ME. it is generally transitive, meaning (1) to empty, (2) to remove, (3) to go away from; but also intransitive, meaning (1) to go away, (2) to flee, escape. Of these, the true original sense is 'to empty,' as in '*avoyd* thou thi trenchere' = empty your plate, Babees Book, p. 23. In Eccles. xiii. 6 (xiii. 5 in A. V.) the Vulgate version has: 'Si habes, conuiuet tecum, et euacuabit te;' where the A. V. has: 'If thou have anythng, he will live with thee, yea, *he will make thee bare*;' but Wyclif has : 'He shal lyue with thee and *auoide thee out*,' equivalent to the modern slang expression 'he will clean you out.' β. It is obvious that the word is closely connected with the adj. *void*, empty, as stated in F. Müller. Often used like the F. *éviter*, with which it cannot, etymologically, have any connexion; though it gradually acquired a similar sense. Thus Cotgrave gives : '*Eviter*, to avoid, eschew, shun, shrink from.' And Shak., though he has '*avoid* the house' (Cor. iv. 5. 25), and 'how may I *avoid* [get rid of] the wife I chose' (Troil. ii. 265), often uses it in the sense of 'shun' (Merry Wives, ii. 2. 289, &c.). In Palsgrave's French Dict., we have : 'Never have to do with hym, if thou mayst *avoyde* hym (*escheuer* or *euiter*).' γ. Chaucer uses only the simple form *voiden*, and in senses that are all connected with the adj. *void*. δ. The prefix *a*- (in AF. *avoider*, Godefroy) is a corruption of OF. *es*- (L. *ex*, out), as in *abash*, q. v.; this prefix was extremely common in OF., and Godefroy gives the forms *esvuidier*, *esveudier*, *evuider*, to empty out; compounded of *es*-, prefix, and *vuidier*, *voidier*, to empty, make void, from OF. *vuit*, *vuide* (F. *vide*), empty. See **Void.** Der. *avoid-able*, *avoid-ançe*. ¶ In a word, *avoid* = *evoid*; just as *amend* = *emend*.

AVOIRDUPOIS, a particular way of estimating weights, viz. by a pound of 16 oz. (F. — L.) Shak. uses *avoirdupois* (spelt *haber-de-pois* in old edd.) in 2 Hen. IV, ii. 4. 277 simply with the sense of 'weight.' His use of *de* (for *du*) is correct; we find *avoir de pois*, lit. 'goods of weight,' in the Statutes of the Realm, i. 159 (1311); *aver de poys* in the same, 156 (1309); *avoir de peise* in Early E. Poems, ed. Furnivall, p. 154, st. 11 (ab. 1308). From AF. *aveir de peis*, 'goods of weight,' i.e. heavy articles. — L. *habēre*, to have, whence F. *avoir*, to have, also as sb., wealth, goods; *dē*, of; and L. *pensum*, that which is weighed out, from *pensus*, pp. of *pendere*, to weigh. The spelling *pois* is correct; the word is misspelt *poids* in mod. F. from a false notion of a connexion with L. *pondus*, weight; see **Poise.**

AVOUCH, to declare, confess. (F. — L.) ME. *avouchen*, Gower, C. A. i. 295, in Pauli's edition; but the right reading is *vouche*; bk. iii. 486. Sometimes in the sense 'to make good,' 'maintain,' or 'answer for it,' as in Macb. iii. 1. 120. Grafton has *avouchment* in the sense of 'maintenance,' K. John, an. 14. Cf. ME. *vouchen*, used by Chaucer in the phrase *vouchen sauf*, to vouchsafe, C. T. 11355, 11885 (F 1043, 1581). — OF. *avochier*, to call upon (Godefroy); a more 'learned' form of the popular OF. *ovoer, avouer*, representing L. *ad-uocāre*, to call to, or summon (a witness). — L. *ad*, to; and *uocāre*, to call. See **Avow** (1) and **Vouchsafe**. Doublets, *advocate, avow* (1).

AVOW (1), to acknowledge, affirm, vouch for, declare oneself. (F.—L.) ME. *avouen, avowen*, Gower, iii. 191; bk. vii. 3163*; Chaucer, C. T., G 642. 'I avowe, I warrant or make good;' Palsgrave. Shak. Troil. i. 3. 271. — OF. *avoer, avouer*. — L. *aduocāre*, to call upon; Late L. to call on as patron or client, to acknowledge, recognise. — L. *ad*, to; *vocāre*, to call. See **Avouch, Advocate**. Der. *avow-ry*.

AVOW (2), to bind with a vow, to vow. (F.—L.) Obsolete; but easily confused with *avow* (1); the sb. *avow, vow*, occurs in 'I make mine *avow*,' Sir W. Scott, Fair Maid of Perth, iii. 45 (N. E. D.); ch. 25 (near the end). 'I *avowe*, I make God a vowe;' Palsgrave. ME. *avowen*, Chaucer, Anelida, 355. — OF. *avouer*. — OF. *a* (for L. *ad*, to); and *vouer*, from Late L. *votāre*, to vow, from L. *uōtum*, a vow. See **Vow**.

AVULSION, a forcible tearing away. (L.) In Phillips (1658). — L. *auulsiōn-em*, acc. of *āuulsio*, a tearing away; cf. L. *auuls-us*, pp. of *āuellere*, to pluck away. — L. *ā*, from; and *uellere*, to pluck.

AWAIT, to wait for. (F.—OHG.) In early use. ME. *awaiten*, to wait for; also, to lie in wait for. 'Me *awaiteth* ou' = people lie in wait for you; Ancren Riwle, p. 174. — OF. *awaitier*, an older and Northern form of OF. *agaiter*, to lie in wait for, watch for (Godefroy). — OF. prefix *a-* (L. *ad*); and OF. *waitier, gaitier* (mod. F. *guetter*) to watch, from OHG. *wahtēn*, to watch (mod. G. *wachten*). This is a denominative verb from the sb. *wahta*, a watch, whence OF. *waite*, a sentinel, preserved in the E. *wait*, as used in the phrase 'the Christmas *waits*.' See **Wait**.

AWAKE, to rouse from sleep; to cease sleeping. (E.) In ME. we find both *awaken*, strong verb, answering to mod. E. *awake*, strong verb; and *awaken*, a weak verb, which accounts for the pt. t. and pp. *awaked* as used by Shakespeare (Timon, ii. 2. 21) and others. 'Thæ awoc Brutus' = then Brutus awoke, Layamon, i. 53. Two AS. verbs are here confused; *āwacian*, weak verb, and *onwǣcnan*, with a weak pres. t., but strong pt. t. *onwōc*, pp. *onwacen*. The prefix is AS. *ā-* or *on-*. See **Wake**. Cf. G. *erwachen*, OHG. *irwachēn*, weak verb, to awake. Der. *awake*, adj., as used in Milton, 'ere well *awake*,' P. L. i. 334. This was originally a past participle, viz. the ME. *awake*, short for *awaken*, AS. *onwacen*, pp. of *onwǣcnan* (above). And see below.

AWAKEN, to awake. (E.) Strictly speaking, this is an intransitive verb only, and never used transitively till after 1500; it is thus distinguished from *awake*, which was used in both senses; and it is slightly different in origin. ME. *awakenen, awaknen*. 'I *awakned* therewith;' P. Plowman, B. xa. 478. — AS. *āwacnan, āwacnian*, to awake; Grein, i. 46, 47; also *onwacnian*, id. ii. 353; easily confused with *onwǣcnan*, which was a strong verb. In the suffix, the former *n* is formative, and conspicuous in both Mœso-Gothic and Scandinavian, in which languages it is used to form verbs that are intransitive or reflexive. Thus the verb *awaken* is essentially intransitive, and should be so used; but the ME. suffix *-n-en, -ne* was easily confused with the late transitive suffix *-en* in such words as *strengthen*.

AWARD, to adjudge, determine, grant, assign. (F.—OLow G.) 'This I *awarde*' = thus I decide, Chaucer, C. T. 12136 (C 202). — AF. *awarder*, OF. *eswarder, esgarder*, to examine, to adjudge after examination; see *esgarder* in Godefroy. — OF. prefix *es-*, from L. *ex*, out; and OF. *warder*, old spelling of *garder*, to observe, regard, guard. [The word is thus a hybrid; for, while the prefix is Latin, the rest is OLow G.] From OLow G. **wardēn* (OSax. *wardōn*, G. *warten*), to regard, look at, guard. See **Ward**. Der. *award*, sb., Chaucer, C. T., I 483.

AWARE, adj., informed of, in a watchful state. (E.) In this particular word, the prefix *a-* has an unusual origin; it is a corruption of ME. prefix *i-*, or *y-*, which again is a reduction of AS. *ge-*. The spelling *aware* occurs in Early E. Poems, ed. Furnivall, p. 16, l. 9, but is very rare, the usual spelling being *iwar, ywar*, or *iwer*; see Layamon, ll. 7261, 7581; Ancren Riwle, p. 104; Owl and Nightingale, l. 147; P. Plowman, B. i. 42; Rob. of Glouc. p. 168, l. 3503; Ayenbite of Inwyt, p. 100. AS. *gewær*, aware; AS. Chron. 914 (MS. D.), 1095 (Laud MS.); in which the addition of AS. *ge-* as a prefix makes no appreciable difference. *Gewær* is thus equivalent to *wær*, aware, cautious, Grein, ii. 649; where we find 'wes thu *wær*' = be thou aware. Cf. also G. *gewahr werden*, to be aware; where *gewahr* is from OHG. *giwar*, *gawar*, from the prefix *gi-* (AS. *ge-*) and *war*, cognate with AS. *wær*. See **Wary**.

AWAY, out of the way, absent. (E.) The proper sense is 'on the way,' though now often used as if it meant '*off* (or out of) the way.' To 'go away' meant 'to go on one's way.' ME. *awei, owei*, O. Eng. Homilies, ed. Morris, i. 21; spelt *oway* in Hampole, Pricke of Conscience, 2269. — AS. *onweg*, away, Grein, ii. 354; from AS.

on, on, and *weg*, way. See **Way**. It was sometimes spelt *āweg*, Grein, i. 47; but the prefix *ā-* is probably the same as *on*.

AWE, fear. (Scand.) ME. *aȝe, aȝhe, awe*, properly a disyllabic word; Ormulum, 7185. [Another form is ME. *eȝe, eghe, eye*, also disyllabic, Ormulum, 4481; from AS. *ege*. We also meet with AS. *ōga*, fear, dread. Both words occur in the same passage: 'And bēo eōwer *ege* and *ōga* ofer ealle nītenu' = and let the fear of you and the dread of you be over all animals, Gen. ix. 2. Both can be referred to a common base *ag-*, to dread.] — Icel. *agi*, awe, terror; Dan. *ave*, check, control, restraint; *ave*, to control. + OHG. *egiso*, terror; Goth. *agis*, fear, anguish. Further related to Irish *eagal*, fear, terror; Gk. ἄχος, anguish, affliction. Brugm. i. § 124 (3). Der. *aw-ful, aw-ful-ly, aw-ful-ness*. ¶ The final *e* in *awe*, now quite unnecessary, records the fact that the word was once disyllabic.

AWKWARD, clumsy. (Hybrid; Scand. *and* E.) **α.** The modern sense of 'clumsy' is seldom found in old authors; though it means this or something very near it in 'ridiculous and *awkward* action;' Shak. Troil. i. 3. 149. We also find: ''tis no sinister nor no *awkward* claim,' Hen. V, ii. 4. 85; and again, 'by *awkward* wind,' i.e. by an adverse wind, 2 Hen. VI, iii. 2. 83; and again, '*awkward* casualties,' i.e. adverse chances, Per. v. 1. 94. **β.** In tracing the word backwards, its use as an adjective disappears; it was, originally, an adverb, like *forward, backward, onward*. Its sense was 'transversely,' 'sideways,' especially used with regard to a back-handed stroke with a sword. 'As he glaid by, *aukwart* he couth hym ta' = as he glided by, he took him a back-handed stroke; Wallace, iii. 175. 'The world thai all *awkeward* sett' = they turn the world topsy-turvy, Hampole, Pricke of Conscience, 1541. **γ.** The suffix *-ward*, as in *onward, forward*, means 'in the direction of,' 'towards,' like the cognate L. *uersus*. The prefix *awk* is the ME. *awk, auk*, adj., signifying 'contrary,' hence 'wrong.' '*Awke* or angry, contrarius, bilosus, perversus. *Awke* or wronge, sinister. *Awkely* or wrawely [angrily], perverse, contrarie, bilose;' Prompt. Parv. p. 18. Palsgrave has: 'auke stroke, *revers*.' *Auk* is a contraction of Icel. *öfug-*, like *hawk* from AS. *hafoc*. — Icel. *öfigr, öfugr, afigr*, often contracted to *öfgu, öfgir* in old writers, adj. turning the wrong way, back foremost; as in '*öfgum* vápnum,' with the butt-end of a weapon; 'við hendi *öfgri*,' with the back of the hand; see examples in Cleasby and Vigfusson. Cf. the expression *afu-lic geflit*, gloss to L. *peruersa certamina*, in Prol. to St. Matthew, p. 2, l. 12 (Lindisfarne MS.). **δ.** Here *öf-* stands for *af*, from; and *-ug-* is a suffix. Cognate forms appear in Swed. *afvig*, cross, wrong, O. Sax. *aðuh*, perverse, evil (from *af*, from, and suffix *-uh*); in OHG. *apuh*, MHG. *ebich*, turned away, perverse, evil (from OHG. *ap* = G. *ab*, off, from, and suffix *-uh*, or from OHG. *apa*, off, and suffix *-h*, cognate with L. *que*). Thus the sense of *awk* is 'turned away;' from Icel. *af*, cognate with E. *of, off*, Gk. ἀπο. Cf. Skt. *apāka-s*, adj., coming from afar; from *apa*, off. Der. *awk-ward-ly, awkward-ness*.

AWL, a pointed instrument for piercing holes in leather. (E.) Spelt *aule* in Shak. Jul. Cæsar, i. 1. 25; Exod. xxi. 6 (1611). ME. *an alle*; Wyclif, Exod. xxi. 6; later version, *a nal*. Also *el*, Ancren Riwle, p. 324. AS. *æl, al*; dat. *æle*, Exod. xxi. 6; *ale*, Levit. xxv. 10. + Icel. *alr*, an awl; OHG. *ala*, G. *ahle*; Du. *aal*. Teut. types **aloz, alā*. Cf. Skt. *ārā*, an awl. ¶ Distinct from ME. *aule*, flesh-hook, Ancren Riwle, 212; AS. *awel*, grappling-hook, trident, Voc. 7. 6; *awul*, Voc. 127. 10. (W. A. Craigie, Phil. Soc. Trans. 1906; p. 261).

AWN, a beard of corn or grass. (Scand.) ME. *awn*. 'Hec arista, a *nawn*, i.e. an *awn*;' Wright's Vocabularies, i. 233. An older (13th-century) form *agune* appears at p. 155 of the same volume. [AS. *ægnan*, pl., awns; Corpus Glos.; whence prov. E. *ain*, awn.] — Icel. *ögn*, chaff, a husk; Dan. *avne*, chaff; Swed. *agn*, pl. *agnar*, husks. + Goth. *ahana*, chaff; Luke, iii. 17; OHG. *agana*, MHG. *agene, agen*, chaff. Cf. Gk. ἄχνη, pl., chaff; OL. *agna*, a straw. Brugm. i. § 729. ¶ Finnish *akana*, awn, is borrowed from O. Teutonic (Streitberg). In some parts of England (e.g. Essex) beards of barley are called *ails*; here *ail* is from AS. *egl*, a beard of corn, a prickle, mote, Luke, vi. 41, 42; which is allied to **Ear** (2).

AWNING, a cover spread out, usually of canvas, to defend those under it from the sun. (OF. ? or Low G.?) The earliest quotation is dated 1630, from Capt. Smith's Works, ed. Arber, p. 957: 'Wee did hang an *awning* (which is an old saile) to . . trees to shadow us from the sunne;' N. E. D. It also occurs in Sir T. Herbert's Travels, p. 7, in Todd's Johnson: 'Our ship became sulphureous, no decks, no *awnings*, nor invention possible, being able to refresh us.' Four editions of this work appeared, viz. in 1634, 1638, 1665, and 1667; in the ed. of 1665, the ref. is to p. 8. The proper sense seems to be 'a sail or tarpauling spread above the deck of a ship, to keep off the heat of the sun.' Origin doubtful; perhaps suggested by OF. *auvan, auvant*, mod. F. *auvent*, which Cotgrave explains by 'a penthouse of cloth before a shop-window.' Cf. Prov. *anvan*, Late L. *antevanna, anvanna, avanna*; which seems to be from L. *ante*, before, and *uannus*, f., a fan. Or from Low G. *havenung*, a shelter (Brem. Wört., p. 607); also spelt *havening* (Berghaus); cf. Dan. *havne*, to put into harbour, from *havn*, a haven. See prov. E. *haun*, a haven (E. D. D.). So also Lübben gives Low G. *havenen*, to seek a haven, and *haveninge*, a haven; but the connexion is not made out.

AWORK, at work. (E.) Used by Shak., only in the phr. 'to set *a-work*;' 2 Hen. IV, iv. 3. 124; Troil. v. 10. 38; Haml. ii. 2. 510; K. Lear, iii. 5. 8. Also in Chaucer: 'I sette hem so *a werke*, by my fay;' C. T. 5797 (D 215). Here *a* probably stands for *an*, ME form of AS. *on*; as in so many other instances. Cf. *abed*, *asleep*, &c. The phrase 'he fell *on sleep*' is similar in construction. See **Work.**

AWRY, obliquely, distortedly, sideways. (E.) In Shak. Tam. Shr. iv. 1. 150. ME. *awrie* (better *awry*), Romaunt of the Rose, 291. *Awry* is properly an adverb, and compounded of *on* and *wry*; cf. *abed*, *asleep*, &c. 'Owthir all evin, or *on wry*' = either all even or awry; Barbour's Bruce, 4. 705. β. The lit. sense is 'on the twist;' and thus *wry* is, in this phrase, a sb., though no instance of its use as a sb. occurs elsewhere. We may conclude that it is the adj. *wry* (cf. 'wry nose,' ' wry neck') used substantively to form the phrase. See **Wry.**

AXE, AX, an implement for cutting trees. (E.) ME. *ax*, *eax*, *ex*; also *axe*, *exe*. Spelt *ax*, Havelok, 1894; Layamon, i. 196. AS. *eax*, *æx*; older forms *acus*, *æcus* (Sweet). In Luke, iii. 9, the AS. version has *æx*, where the Northumbrian glosses have the fuller forms *acasa*, *acase*.+Icel. *öx*, *öxi*; Swed. *yxa*; Dan. *öxe*; Goth. *akwisi*; OHG. *acchus*, MHG. *ackes*, mod. G. *axt* (with excrescent *t*); OSax. *acus*, Du. *aaks*. Cf. also L. *ascia* (for *acsia*?), an axe, mattock, trowel; Gk. *ἀξίνη*, an axe. Brugmann, i. § 992.

AXIL, the upper angle between a leaf or petiole and the stem. (L.) First in 1794 (N. E. D.).−L. *axilla*, lit. armpit; dimin. of **acsla* > *āla*, a wing; see **Aisle.** Der. *axill-ary*.

AXIOM, a self-evident truth. (L.−Gk.) In Burton, Anat. of Melan. ed. 1827, i. 316; and in Locke, On the Human Understanding, bk. iv. c. 7. Spelt *axiomaes*, pl., Lyly, Euphues, ed. Arber, p. 100.− L. *axiōma*.− Gk. *ἀξίωμα*, gen. *ἀξιώματος*, worth, quality, resolve, decision; *in science*, that which is assumed as the basis of demonstration, an assumption.− Gk. *ἀξιόω*, I deem worthy, esteem.− Gk. *ἄξιος*, worthy, lit. 'weighing as much as.'− Gk. *ἄγειν*, to lead, drive, also 'to weigh as much.' − √AG, to drive. See **Agent.** Der. From the stem *ἀξιωματ-*, *axiomat-ic*, *-ic-al*, *-ic-al-ly*.

AXIS, the axle on which a body revolves. (L.) In Pope, Essay on Man, iii. 313. Also in Complaint of Scotland, ed. Murray, c. vi; p. 48, l. 27. [In earlier writers, the word used is generally *axle*, or *axletree*, as in Marlowe's Faustus, A. ii. sc. 2.]−L. *axis*, an axletree, axis.+Gk. *ἄξων*, an axle; Skt. *aksha-s*, an axle, wheel, cart. Cf. also OHG. *ahsa*, G. *achse*, an axle; AS. *eax*, an axle, Grein, i. 250; Du. *as*; Russ. *os'*; Lith. *aszis*. [Curtius, i. 479, considers the Gk. stem *ἀξ-* as a secondary form from *ἀγ-*, to drive. Benfey likewise connects Skt. *aksha-s* with Skt. *aj*, to drive.] − √AG, to drive. Der. *axi-al*. ☞ *Axle* is the diminutive form; see **Axle.**

AXLE, the axis on which a wheel turns. (Scand.) ME. *axel*, *exel*, which is common in the compound *axeltree*; the latter is in Gower, C. A. i. 320 (bk. iii. 1209), and see Prompt. Parv. p. 20. [The simple word *axel* generally means 'shoulder' in early writers. 'He hit berð on his *eaxlun*' = he bears it on his shoulders; OE. Homilies, ed. Morris, i. 245. 'On his *exle*' = on his shoulder; Layamon, i. 96. This is an allied native word; from AS. *eaxl*, the shoulder, Grein, i. 250.]−Icel. *öxull*, an axis; Swed. and Dan. *axel*, axle, axle-tree. The Icel. *öxull*, m., answers to Teut. type **ahsuloz*, m., dimin. of **ahsā*, f., as in AS. *eax*, f., axis; see **Axis.** Cf. W. *echel*, axle. β. Cf. Icel. *öxl*, shoulder-joint, AS. *eaxl*, f., shoulder, G. *achsel*, f., Teut. type **ahsulā*, f.; from base **ahs-*, as in **ahsā* (above). The explanation is, no doubt, that the shoulder-joint is the axis on which the arm turns. Der. *ax'e-tree*, Icel. *öxul-trē*; where *tree* has the meaning of 'block,' or 'piece of wood.'

AXOLOTL, a Mexican batrachian reptile. (Mex.) From Mex. *axolotl*, lit. 'servant of the water.'−Mex. *a-*, for *atl*, water; and *xolotl*, a servant. From a story in Mex. mythology; see my Notes on Etymology, p. 333.

AY! interjection of surprise. (E.) Distinct from *aye*, yes; see below. ME. *ey*, interjection. 'Why ryse ye so rathe? *ey!* ben'-dic'te;' Chaucer, C. T. 3766 (A 3768); cf. l. 10165 (E 2291). A natural exclamation. ¶ The phrase 'ay me!' is certainly French, viz. the OF. *aymi*, ah! for me; Burguy. Cf. Ital. *ahimè*, alas for me! Span. *ay di mi!* alas for me! Gk. *οἴμοι*, woe's me! See also **Ah!**

AY, AYE, yea, yes. (E.) In Shak. frequently; Temp. i. 2. 268, &c.; always spelt *I* in old editions. The use of *ay*, *aye*, or *I* with the above sense is not found in early authors. We may conclude that *aye* is a peculiar use of *aye*, ever; used affirmatively. See **Aye.** Perhaps influenced by **Yea.** ¶ Or it may be a peculiar use of the pers. pron. *I*, as the old edd. indicate.

AYAH, a native waiting-maid, in India. (Port. − L.) The spelling answers more nearly to the Span. *aya*, a governess, fem. of *ayo*, a tutor, but the word was certainly introduced into India by the Portuguese; the final *h* is an E. addition. − Port. *aia*, a nurse, governess; fem. of *aio*, a tutor of a young nobleman. Origin uncertain; Diez imagines it to be of Germanic origin; Wackernagel (with greater probability) suggests L. *auia*, by-form of *aua*, a grandmother, allied to *auus*, a grandfather. See **Uncle.** Minsheu's Span. Dict. (1623) has *aya*, 'a nurse, schoolmistresse.'

AYE, adv., ever, always. (Scand.) The phr. 'for *ay*' occurs in Iwain and Gawain, l. 1510; in Ritson's Met. Romances, vol. i. We also find '*ay* withouten ende,' Li Beaus Disconus, l. 531, in Ritson's M. R., vol. ii. [Also '*a* buten ende,' Ancren Riwle, p. 396; where *a* = AS. *ā*.]−Icel. *ei*, ever.✚AS. *ā*, aye, ever, always; Grein, i. 11; used in various phrases, as *ā forð*, *ā on worlda forð*, *ā tō worulde*, &c. It also appears in the longer forms *āwa*, *āwo*, Grein, i. 46, of which *ā* is merely a contraction. It is an adverbial use of a substantive which meant 'a long time,' as shown by Goth. *aiw*, ever, an adverb formed from the sb. *aiws*, time, an age, a long period, eternity, Luke, i. 70. Cf. L. *æuum*, an age; Gk. *αἰών*, an age, *αἰεί*, *ἀεί*, ever, always, aye; Skt. *ēva-s*, course, conduct. See **Age.**

AYE-AYE, a squirrel-like nocturnal animal. (F. − Malagasy.) F. *aye-aye*; Supp. to Littré.− Malagasy *ai'ay*; supposed to be named from its cry; Richardson's Malag. Dict.

AZALEA, a genus of shrubby plants. (Gk.) From Gk. *ἀζαλέα*, fem. of *ἀζαλέος*, dry, parched; perhaps from growing in dry places. − Gk. *ἄζ-ειν*, to dry up.

AZIMUTH, an arc of the horizon intercepted between the meridian of the place and a vertical circle passing through any celestial body. (Arabic.) Briefly, *azimuthal* circles are great circles passing through the *zenith*; whereas circles of declination pass through the *poles*. 'These same strykes [strokes] or diuisiouns ben cleped [called] *Azimuthz*; and they deuyden the Orisonte of thyn astrolabie in 24 deuisiouns;' Chaucer, tr. on Astrolabe, ed. Skeat, pt. i. sect. 19. Properly, *azimuth* is a *plural* form, being equivalent to Arabic *assamūt*, i.e. ways, or points (or quarters) of the horizon; from *al samt*, sing., the way, or point (or quarter) of the horizon, or the arc from a particular point in the horizon to the zenith; cf. Arab. '*samt*, a road, way, quarter, direction;' Palmer's Pers. Dict. col. 360. Cf. *samt*, 'travelling, a way, tract, quarter;' *samtu'r'ras*, the zenith; *as-samt*, the azimuth;' Rich. Dict. p. 848. From the same Arabic word is derived the E. *zenith*. See **Zenith.**

AZOTE, nitrogen. (F. − Gk.) The name given by Lavoisier (d. 1794) to nitrogen gas; because destructive to animal life.−F. *azote* (an ill-coined word; Littré).− Gk. *ἀ-*, negative prefix; and *ζωτ-*, as in *ζωτικός*, fit for preserving life.− Gk. *ζω-ή*, life; *ζάω*, I live. From the same root we have Gk. *βίος*, life, L. *uiuere*, to live; also E. *quick*, *vivid*, *vital*, &c.; as also *zoo-logy*. See **Zoology.**

AZURE, adj., of a bright blue colour. (F.−Arab.−Pers.) ME. *asur*, Joseph of Arimathie, ed. Skeat, ll. 195, 198. 'Clad in *asure*;' Chaucer, Queen Anelida, l. 330. − AF. *asur*; OF. *azur*, azure; a corrupted form. [So also Ital. *azzurro*, Span. *azul*, *azur*, Port. *azul*.]− Late L. *asur*, *azurum*; also *lazur*, an azure-coloured stone, known also as *lapis lazuli*; also, the colour itself.− Arab. *lājward*, lapis lazuli, azure; Palmer's Pers. Dict. col. 509.− Pers. *lājward*, 'lapis lazuli, a blue colour;' Rich. Dict. p. 1251. So called from the mines of Lajward, situate in Turkestan; see Marco Polo's Travels, ed. Yule. The initial *l* was no doubt dropped, because it was supposed to be the def. article (F. *l'*, Span. *el*, Ital. *il*, Arab. *al*). So Diez and Devic.

B

BAA, to bleat like a sheep. (E.) Chapman uses *baaing* in his tr. of Homer, Iliad, bk. iv. l. 463; see quotation in Richardson s. v. *bleat*. Shak. has the verb to *ba*, Cor. ii. 1. 12, and the sb. *baa*, Two Gent. i. 1. 98. An imitative word, and may be considered as English. Cf. G. *bä*, the bleating of sheep. Der. *baa*, s.

BABBLE, to gossip, prate. (E.) ME. *babelen*, to prate; Ancren Riwle, p. 100 (ab. 1230); to mumble, say repeatedly, P. Plowman, B. v. 8. Though not recorded in A.-S. MSS., it may be considered as an English word; cf. EFries. *babbelen*, *babbeln*, to babble. ✚ Du. *babbelen*, to chatter; Dan. *bable*, to babble; Icel. *babbla*; G. *pappeln*; also *bappeln*, *bappern*, to babble; Grimm's Dict. β. The suffix *-le* is frequentative, and the verb means 'to keep on saying *ba ba*,' syllables imitative of the efforts of a child to speak. Cf. F. *babiller*, to chatter. Der. *babble*, sb., *babble-ment*, *babbl-ing*, *babbl-er*, A. V. Acts, xvii. 18. Palsgrave has 'Babler, babillart.'

BABE, an infant; (formerly) a doll. (E.) ME. *babe*, Gower, C. A.

i. 290; bk. iii. 320; *bab*, Towneley Myst. p. 149; the full form being *baban*, Ancren Riwle, p. 234 (ab. 1230); and even Levins has: '*Babbon*, pupus,' 163. 12. Probably formed from the infantine sound *ba*, rath r than borrowed from Celtic. The similar forms in Celtic, viz. Welsh, Gael., Irish, Corn. *baban* are all late, and some may even have been borrowed from English. Cf. Mid. Swed. and Swed. dial. *babe*, little one. Cf. *babble* (above). *Baby* is a diminutive form; like *la sie* from *lass*. **Der.** *bab-y*, *baby-ish*, *baby-hood*.

BABIRUSA, BABIROUSSA, a kind of wild hog. (Malay.) 'The *Babiroussa*, or Indian hog;' tr. of Buffon (1792). — Malay *babi rūsa*, hog like a deer; from *rūsa*, deer, and *babī*, hog (Yule).

BABOON, a large ape. (F. *or* Late L.) Probably borrowed, in its present form, from F. *babouin*, OF. *babouin* (H.). The form *bavian* in the Two Noble Kinsmen, iii. 5, is from Du. *baviaan*. Other spellings, *babion*, *babian*, may be modifications of ME. *babewin*; Mandeville's Travels, ed. Halliwell, p. 210; Prompt. Parv. p. 20; cf. Chaucer, H.F. 1189. The last is either from OF. *babouin* or represents the Late L. *babewynus*. 'In an English inventory of 1295, in Ducange, we read—" Imago B. V. . . . cum pede quadrato stante super quatuor paruos *babewynos*;" and the verb *bebuinare* signified, in the 13th century, to paint grotesque figures in MSS.;' Brachet. Remoter origin uncertain; but Hatzfeld regards *babouin* as formed from F. *baboue*, MF. *babou*; Cot. has *faire la babou*, 'to make a mow at,' to grimace. Cf. mod. Prov. *babau*, a bugbear. Allied to F. *babine*, 'the lip of a beast,' Cot. Prob. of Germ. origin; from *bab*, or *ba ba*, the root of *babble*. See **Babe, Babble;** of imitative origin.

BACCHANAL, a worshipper of Bacchus. (L. — Gk.) Properly, an adjective. 'Unto whom [Bacchus] we yearely celebrated the feast *bacchanal*;' Nicolls, Thucydides, p. 50 (R.) 'The Egyptian *Bacchanals*,' i. e. revels, Shak. Ant. ii. 7. 110. 'The tipsy *Bacchanals*,' i. e. revellers, Mids. Nt. Dr. v. 48. — L. *Bacchānālis*, adj., devoted to Bacchus. — L. *Bacchus*, the god of wine. — Gk. Βάκχος, the god of wine. Also named Ἴακχος, and said to be so named from the shouting of worshippers at his festival. — Gk. ἰάχειν, to shout; a verb apparently formed by onomatopœia, to express an interjectional ἰαχ! Cf. **Echo.** **Der.** *Bacchanal-ian*.

BACHELOR, a young knight, a young unmarried man. (F.— Late L.) ME. *bacheler*, Chaucer, Prol. 80; Rob. of Glouc. (1297) pp. 77, 228, 453. — OF. *bacheler*. — Late L. *baccalāris*, allied to *baccalārius*, a farm-servant. Etym. unknown, and much disputed. For conjectures, see Diez, s. v. *baccalare*; Godefroy, s. v. *bachelle*; Körting, § 1134. Not from Celtic type *bekkos*, small (Thurneysen).

BACILLUS, a genus of microscopic vegetable or anisms. (L.) First in 1883; pl. *bacilli.* — Late L. *bacillus*, a little rod (from the shape); dimin. of *baculus*, variant of *baculum*, a stick. See **Bacterium.**

BACK, a part of the body. (E.) ME. *bak*, Ch. Book Duch. 957. AS. *bæc* (in common use). +OSax. and Icel. *bak.* Teut. type *bak-om*, neut. β. ME. derivatives are: *bacbon*, backbone; *bacbiten*, to backbite (P. Plowman, B. ii. 80); *bacward*, backward (Layamon, ii. 578). **Der.** *back-bite*, *back-bit-er*, *back-bit-ing*, *back-bone*, *back-side*, *back-slide*, *back-slid-er*, *back-slid-ing*, *back-ward*, *back-wards*, *back-ward-ness*.

BACKGAMMON, a kind of game. (E.) Spelt *baggammon* in Howell's Letters, vol. ii. letter 68, dated Nov. 30, 1635. A quotation from Swift in Johnson's Dict. has the spelling *backgammon.* It is *backgammon* in Butler's Hudibras, c. iii. pt. 2, l. 1062. The game seems to have been much the same as that formerly called 'tables.' β. The etym. given by Strutt (Sports and Pastimes, b. iv. c. 2. § 16) is probably correct. 'The words are perfectly Saxon, as *bæc*, and *gamen*, that is, Back-Game; because the pieces are sometimes taken up and obliged to go *back*, i. e. re-enter.' See **Back** and **Gammon** (2). Cf. Du. *verkeeren*, to turn, change; *verkeerd*, reverse; *verkeer-bord*, a backgammon-board.

BACON, swine's flesh, cured for eating. (F.—OHG.) ME. *bacoun*, *bacon*, Chaucer, C. T. 5799 (D 217). — OF. *bacon.* — Low L. acc. *bacōnem*, from nom. *baco*; from a Teutonic source. — OHG. *bahho*, *bacho*, MHG. *bache*, hinder part or piece, ham, bacon. Teut. type *bakon-*, m.; allied to Teut. *bakom*, the back; see **Back.**

BACTERIUM, a genus of microscopic vegetable organisms, a disease-germ. (L.—Gk.) Pl. *bacteria.* First in 1847. — L. *bactē-rium*; L. form of Gk. βακτήριον, a little rod (from the shape); dimin. of βάκτρον, a stick. Allied to L. *baculum*, a stick. See **Bacillus.**

BAD, evil, wicked. (E.) ME. *badde*, Ch. C. T., A 3155; Chaucer also has *badder*, i. e. worse, C. T. 10538 (F 224). Not in use much earlier in English. Rob. of Glouc. (in 1297) has *badde*, evil, p. 108, l. 17; and we find *never on badde*, not one bad, King Alis. 2118; this is perhaps the earliest instance. [The Pers. *bad*, wicked, has a remarkable resemblance to the Eng. word, but was unknown to Rob. of Glouc. The Pehlevi form *vat* (Horn, § 187) shows that the words are unrelated.] Most scholars now believe the word to be

English. Zupitza explains the ME. *badde* as shortened from AS. *bæddel*, an hermaphrodite, used contemptuously, like its derivative *bædling*, an effeminate fellow; whence prov. E. *badling*, a worthless person. Sarrasin refers it to AS. *bǣded*, constrained, *gebǣded*, oppressed (cf. *mad*, from AS. (*ge*)*mǣded*); allied to Lith. *bėda*, ill-luck, sorrow. **Der.** *bad-ly*, *bad-ness*.

BADGE, a mark of distinction. (F.) It occurs in Spenser, F. Q. i. l. 2. The Prompt. Parv. has: 'Bage, or bagge, or badge, of armys, *banidium*.' — AF. *bage*, Royal Wills, p. 68 (A. D. 1376); OF. *bage*, a badge (Godefroy), A.D. 1465; cf. Late L. *bagea*, *bagia*, 'signum, insigne quoddam;' Ducange. Of unknown origin.

BADGER, the name of an animal. (F.) Formerly *bageard*, as in Sir T. More, Works, p. 1183 g; but the final *d* is there excrescent. In ME., the animal had three familiar names, viz. the *brock*, the *gray*, and the *bawson*, but was not called the *badger* till the 16th century; cf. 'a *bauson* or a *badger*;' Fitzherbert's Husbandry, § 71. β. The name is a sort of nickname, the true sense being the animal marked with a *badge*, in allusion to the white mark on its face; so also *bauson* is from the OF. *bausan*, pie-bald (N. E. D.).

BADINAGE, jesting talk. (F.—Prov.—L.) In Coles's Dict. (1684); also in Phillips, ed. 1658.—F. *badinage*, jesting talk.—F. *badiner*, to jest.—F. *badin*, sportive, orig. foolish, silly, 'gaping.'— Prov. *badar*, to gape.—Late L. *badāre*, to gape (Isidore). Probably an imitative word; from the syllable *ba*, denoting the opening of the mouth. Cf. *babble*, q. v.

BAFFLE, to foil, disgrace. (F.—MHG.) See Spenser, F. Q. v. 3. 37. The history of the word is recorded by Hall, Chron. Hen. VIII, anno 5. Richardson and N. E. D. quote the passage to show that to *baffull* is 'a great reproche among the Scottes, and is used when a man is openly periured, and then they make of hym an image paynted reuersed, with hys heles vpwarde, with his name, wonderyng, cryenge, and blowing out of [i. e. at] hym with hornes, in the moost despitefull manner they can.' The word is here confused with Lowland Scotch *bauchle*, to treat contemptuously; see the poem of Wallace, ed. Jamieson, viii. 724. For change of *ch* to *ff*, cf. *tough*, *rough*, &c. β. *Bauchle* is a verb, formed by suffix *-le*, from adj. *bauch*, weak, poor, jaded, &c. This was probably borrowed from Icel. *bāgr*, uneasy, poor, or the related sb. *bāgr*, a struggle; from which is formed, in Icelandic, the vb. *bægja*, to push, or metaphorically, to treat harshly. Fick (iii. 198) connects this Icel. *bāgr*, a struggle, with MHG. *bāgen*, OHG. *fāgan*, to strive, to brawl. γ. But the E. *baffle* seems to be more directly derived from F. *beffler*, to deceive, mock (Cot.), or F. *bafouer*, MF. *baffouer*, 'to baffle, revile, disgrace;' which are allied to Ital. *beffare*, 'to flout, scoffe' (Florio), from *beffa*, a scoff; and to Norman F. *baffer*, to slap in the face, Prov. *bafa*, a scoff. Prob. from MHG. *beffen*, to scold; cf. G. *baffen*, Du. *baffen*, to bark, yelp; of imitative origin, like Du. *paf*, a pop, a box on the ear. Cf. further Prov. E. *baff*, a blow, a suppressed bark (of a dog); *baff*, to strike; *baff*, adj., useless, worthless; *baffle*, to annoy; &c.

BAG, a flexible case. (Scand.) ME. *bagge*, P. Plowman, B. prol. 41; Ancren Riwle, p. 168 (ab. 1230). — Icel. *baggi*, a bag; Norw. and MSwed. *bagge*. Remoter origin unknown. **Der.** *bag*, vb., *bag-gy*, *bag-pipe* (Chaucer, C. T. 567, A 565), *bag-piper*.

BAGATELLE, a trifle; a game. (F.—Ital.—Teut.) 'Trifles and *bagatels*;' Howell, vol. ii. letter 21, dated Aug. 1, 1633. — F. *baga-t-lle*, a trifle; introduced in the 16th cent. from Ital. *bagatella*, a trifle (Brachet). Diez thinks it is from the same root as *baggage*. *Bagatella* he takes to be the dimin. of Parmesan *bagata*, a little property; and this to be formed from the Lombard *baga*, a wine-skin, allied to E. *bag.* See **Baggage** (1), **Bag.**

BAGGAGE (1), travellers' luggage. (F.—Scand.) ME. *baggage*, *bagage*; occurring in Lydgate's Hors, Sheep, and Goose, l. 109; in Chaucer's Dream, by an anonymous author, l. 1555; and in Hall, Chron. Rich. III, an. 3. § 4 from end. — OF. *bagage*, a collection of bundles, from OF. *bague*, a bundle. — Norw. *bagge*, Icel. *baggi*, a bag; see **Bag.** And cf. Lombard *baga*, a wine-skin, a bag.

BAGGAGE (2), a worthless woman. (F. — Scand.) A peculiar use of the word above (see N. E. D.); but probably influenced by F. *bagasse*. Cotgrave explains *bagasse* by 'a baggage, quean, jyll, punke, flirt.' Burguy gives the forms *baiasse*, *bajasse*, *bagasse*, a chambermaid, light woman. Cf. Ital. *bagascia*, a worthless woman. β. Etym. doubtful, but probably derived, like *baggage* (1), from OF. *bague*, a bundle.

BAIL (1), security; to secure. (F.—L.) Shak. has both sb. and verb; Meas. iii. 2. 77, 85. **a.** *Bail* as a verb is from the AF. *bailler*, introduced as a law-term, occurring in the Statutes of the Realm, p. 132 (1299). — OF. *bailler*, to keep in custody. — L. *bāiulāre*, to carry about or take charge of a child. — L. *bāiulus*, a porter, a carrier. Root *bad-*; cf. Gk. βαστάζειν, to carry. Brugm. i. § 759. β. *Bail* as a substantive is the OF. *bail*, safe keeping, security; whence 'to be *bail*.' This is the verbal sb. from OF. *bailler*.

BAIL (2), a bucket. (F. — Late L.) See **Bale** (3).

BAILIFF, a deputy, one entrusted with control. (F.—L.) Chaucer has *bailif*; Prol. 603; also in Polit. Songs, ed. Wright, p. 149, l. 16 (temp. Edw. II).—OF. *baillif*; AF. *baillif*, Stat. of Realm, p. 27 (1275).—Late L. *bāiulivum*, acc.—L. *bāiulāre*. See **Bail** (1).

BAILIWICK, the jurisdiction of a bailiff. (F. and E.) Fabyan speaks of ' the offyce of *ballywycke*;' Rich. II, p. 528, ed. 1811. A hybrid word; from OF. *baillie*, government; and ME. *wike*, AS. *wice*, an office, duty, function; see **Bail** (1). 2. Also used to denote the district under his jurisdiction; apparently from AS. *wic*, an abode; see **Wick** (2).

BAILS, small cross-bars used in the game of cricket. (F. — L.?) The history of the word is obscure. Roquefort gives OF. *bailles*, in the sense of barricade, palisade, with a quotation from Froissart : ' Il fit charpenter des *bailles* et les asseoir au travers de la rue ;' which I suppose to mean, he caused sticks to be cut and set across the street. Godefroy says that ' in the arrondissement of Vervains and of Avesnes, *bail* is the name of a horizontal piece of wood fixed upon two stakes.' Perhaps from L. acc. *baculum*, a stick, rod (*baille< bacula*, pl. form), used in many senses.

BAIRN, a child. (E.) ME. *barn*, P. Plowman, A. ii. 3. AS. *bearn*, Grein, i. 103.+Icel. *barn*, a child; Swed. and Dan. *barn*; Goth. *barn*. Teut. type *bar-nom*, neut. sb.; lit. ' that which is born ;' from *bar*, 2nd grade of *beran*, to bear, with suffix *-no-*. See **Bear** (1).

BAIT, to make to bite, to feed. (Scand.) ME. *baiten*, to feed, Chaucer, Troilus, i. 192. ' And shoten on him, so don on bere Dogges, that wolden him to-tere, Thanne men doth the bere *beyte* = and rushed upon him like dogs at a bear, that would tear him in twain, when people cause the bear to be baited ; Havelok, 1838. To *bait* a bear is to make the dogs bite him. To *bait* a horse is to make him eat.—Icel. *beita*, to make to bite, the causal of Icel. *bita* (pt. t. *beit*), to bite; Swed. *beta*, to pasture; Dan. *bede*. See **Bite**. **Der.** *bait*, sb., i. e. an enticement to bite.

BAIZE, a coarse woollen stuff. (F.—L.) Spelt *bays*, Arnold's Chron. (1502), ed. 1811, p. 235. An error for *bayes*, which is a plural form ; viz. the pl. fem. of the MF. *baye*.—MF. '*baye*, a lie, fib, . . . a cozening trick, or tale; also, a berry; also, the cloth called *bayes*,' &c.; Cotgrave (who here confuses three distinct words); cf. F. *bai*, bay-coloured. β. That the *-ze* is no part of the original word, and that the word is closely connected with *bay*, i. e. bay-coloured, reddish brown, is clear by comparison. Cf. Du. *baai*, baize ; Swed. *boi*, bays, baize (Tauchnitz); Dan. *bai*, baize. Also Span. *bayo*, bay, *bayeta*, baize; Port. *baio*, bay, *baeta*, baize; Ital. *baio*, bay, chesnut-coloured; *bajetta*, baize. See **Bay** (1).

BAKE, to cook by heat. (E.) ME. *baken*, Chaucer, Prol. 384. AS. *bacan*, pt. t. *bōc*, pp. *bacen* ; Levit. xxvi. 26 ; Exod. xii. 39.+Du. *bakken* ; Icel. *baka* ; Swed. *baka* ; Dan. *bage* ; OHG. *pachan*, MHG. *bachen*, G. *backen*. Allied to Gk. φώγειν, to roast ; see Brugm. i. § 165.—√BHOG, to roast. ¶ Not connected with Skt. *pach*, which is allied to E. *cook*, q.v. **Der.** *bak-er*, *bak-ing*, *bak-er-y*, *bake-house*.

BAKSHISH, BACKSHEESH, a present, small gratuity. (Pers.) Pers. *bakhshish*, a present, gratuity, drink-money; Rich. Dict. p. 247 ; also *bakhshish*, id., and in Palmer, Pers. Dict. col. 72. Cf. Pers. *baksh*, part, share, *bakhshīdan*, to give. bestow; *bakhshah*, *bakhshi*, a portion. From Zend *bakhsh*, to distribute ; Horn, § 186. Cf. Skt. *bhaj*, to divide ; Fick, i. 381.

BALANCE, a weighing-machine. (F.—L.) Shak. has *balance*, Mids. Nt. Dr. v. 324; the pl. form used by him is also *balance*, Merch. iv. 1. 255. ME. *balance*, Ayenbite of Inwyt, pp. 30, 91 (1340). —F. *balance*, fem. ' a ballance, a pair of weights or ballances ;' Cot. —L. type *bilancia* ; from L. acc. *bilancem*, nom. *bilanx*, having two scales ; see Brachet.—L. *bi-*, double (for *bis*, twice) ; and *lanx*, a platter, dish, scale of a balance. See Fick, i. 748. **Der.** *balance*, verb.

BALAS-RUBY, a variety of ruby, of a pale rose-red colour. (F.—Low L.—Arab.—Pers.) Formerly also *balais, balays*; spelt *baleys* in the Expeditions of Henry, Earl of Derby (Camden Soc. 1894), p. 287, l. 25. Palsgrave has ' balays, a precious stone, *balé*.' Cotgrave explains MF. *balay* as ' a balleis ruby.'—F. *balais*, a balas-ruby (Littré); OF. *balais, balai* (id.); MF. *balay, balé*, as above.— Low L. *balascius, balascus, balasius, balassus, balagius*, a balas-ruby (Ducange). Cf. Ital. *balascio*, Span. *balax*.—Arab. *balakhsh*, a ruby (given by Devic, Supp. to Littré, q.v.)—Pers. *badakhshī*, a ruby ; so called because found at *Badakhsh*, or *Badakhshān*, ' the name of a country between India and Khurāsān from whence they bring rubies ;' Rich. Dict. p. 249. Badakhshan lies to the N. of the river Amoo (Oxus), and to the E. of a line drawn from Samarcand to Cabul ; see Black's Atlas. The change from *d* to *l* is precisely the change found in L. *lacrima* for **dacrima*. Cf. Malagasy with *Madagascar*.

BALCONY, a platform outside a window. (Ital.—Teut.) Milton has *balcones* (*sic*) as a plural ; Areopagitica (1644), ed. Hales,

p. 24. ' The penult is long with Sherburne (1618-1702), and with Jenyns (1704-87), and in Cowper's John Gilpin ; Swift has it short ; see Richardson ;' Hales.—Ital. *balcone*, an outjutting corner of a house, also spelt *balco* (Florio). Ital. *palco* or *palcone*, a stage, scaffold, also occurs. β. Hence Diez well suggests a derivation from OHG. *balcho, palcho*, a scaffold, cognate with Eng. *balk*, a beam, rafter. See **Balk** (1). The term. *-one* is the usual Ital. augmentative suffix ; cf. *ballcon*.

BALD, deprived of hair. (C.) ME. *balled, ballid*, a disyllable ; P. Plowman, B. xx. 183. Chaucer has : ' His heed was *balled*, that schoon as any glas ;' Prol. 198. The final *-d* thus stands for *-ed*, like the *-ed* in *spotted*, and serves to form an adj. from a sb. ' The original meaning seems to have been (1) shining (2) white, as a *bald*-faced stag ;' note in Morris's Glossary. A *bald-faced* stag is one with a white streak on its face ; cf. Welsh *bal*, adj , having a white streak on the forehead, said of a horse ; *bali*, whiteness in the forehead of a horse. Cf. also Gk. φαλακρός, bald-headed ; φαλαρός, having a spot of white, said of a dog, φαλιός, white, φαληρός, shining.—Gael. and Irish *bal* or *ball*, a spot, mark, speckle (whence the adj. *ballach*, spotted, speckled) ; Bret. *bal*, a white mark on an animal's face ; cf. Welsh *bali*, whiteness in a horse's forehead. β. Cf. also Lith. *baltas*, white, *balti*, to be white ; Gk. φαλιός, white (as above) ; Skt. *bhāla-m*, lustre. See Prellwitz, and Stokes-Fick, p. 164. ¶ We also find MDan. and Dan. dial. *bældet*, bald, Swed. dial. *bälloter*, *bället*, bald. **Der.** *bald-ness* (ME. *ballednesse* or *ballidnesse*, Wyclif, Levit. xiii. 42) ; *bald-head-ed*.

BALDACHIN (with *bal-* as in *bald* or as in *balcony*, and *ch* as *k*), a canopy over an altar, throne, &c. (F.—Ital.—Arab.) Orig. the name of the stuff employed.—F. *baldaquin*.—Ital. *baldacchino*, a canopy, tester ; orig. hangings or tapestry made at Bagdad.—Ital. *Baldacco*, Bagdad.—Arab. *Baghdād*, Bagdad.

BALDERDASH, poor stuff. (Scand. ?) Generally used now to signify weak talk, poor poetry, &c. But it was formerly used also of adulterated or thin potations, or of frothy water ; and, as a verb, to adulterate drink so as to weaken it. ' It is against my freehold, my inheritance, . . To drink such *balderdash*, or bonny-clabber ;' Ben Jonson, New Inn, Act i ; see the whole passage. ' Mine is such a drench of *balderdash* ;' Beaum. and Fletcher, Woman's Prize, iv. 5. ' What have you filled us here, *balderdash* ?' Chapman, May-day, iii. 4. ' Can wine or brandy receive any sanction by being *balderdashed* with two or three sorts of simple waters?' Mandeville, on Hypochond. Dis. 1730, p. 279 (Todd's Johnson). β. To *dash* is, in one sense, to mix wine with water (see N.E.D.), and this accounts for the latter part of the word. *Dash* is Scandinavian ; and we may therefore look to Scandinavian for the other part of the word. We find Dan. *balder*, noise, clatter ; Norw. *bjaldra*, to speak indistinctly (Ross) ; Icel. *baldrast, ballrast*, to make a clatter. The Dan. *daske* is to slap, to flap ; and *dask* is a slap, a dash. Hence *balderdash* may have been compounded (like *slap-dash*) to express a hasty or unmeaning noise, a confused sound ; secondarily, a ' hodge-podge,' as in Halliwell ; and generally, any mixture. Cf. prov. E. *balder*, to use coarse language ; *balderdash*, filthy talk, weak drink ; see E. D. D. (Uncertain.)

BALDRIC, BALDRICK, a girdle, belt. (F.—MHG.—L.) ME. *baudrik, bawdrik*, Chaucer, Prol. 116 ; *bawderyke*, Prompt. Parv. p. 27 ; also *baudry* (ab. 1300), King Alis. 4698. An *l* appears in Palsgrave's *baldrike* ; and Shak. has *baldrick*, Much Ado, i. 1. 244.— OF. **baldric*, not found ; cf. OF. *baldred, baldrei*, given by Godefroy ; and cf. Low L. *baldringus* in Ducange.—MHG. *balderich*, a girdle (Schade) ; formed with suffixes *-er* and *-ik*, from *bald-*, for OHG. *balz, palz*, a belt.—L. *balteus*, a belt. See **Belt**.

BALE (1), a package. (F.—MHG.) ' *Bale* of spycery, or other lyke, *bulga* ;' Prompt. Parv. p. 22. Also spelt *balle*, as in ' a *balle* bokrom,' a bale of buckram, Arnold's Chron. ed. 1811, p. 206. Cf. AF. *bale*, a bale, Stat. Realm, i. 218 (ab. 1284).—OF. and MF. *bale*, a ball ; also, a pack, as of merchandise ; Cot.—Low L. *bala*, a round bundle, package. Merely an adaptation of MHG. *balle*, a ball, sphere, round body. See **Ball** (2).

BALE (2), evil. (E.) Shak. has *baile* (1st folio), Cor. i. 1. 167 ; and *baleful*, Romeo, ii. 3. 8. ME. *bale*, Havelok, 327 (and very common) ; *balu*, Layamon, 1455, 2597. AS. *balu, bealu, bealo*, Grein, i. 101.+OSax. *balu*, Icel. *böl*, misfortune ; OHG. *balo*, destruction ; lost in mod. G. The gen. of OMerc. *balu* (neut.) is *balwes* ; and the Teut. type is **bal-wom*, neuter ; orig. neuter of Teut. **balwoz*, adj., evil (like L. *malum* from *malus*). Cf. Goth. *balwawesei*, wickedness. Allied to Russ. *bole*, pain, sorrow, OCh. Slav. *boli*, sickness. **Der.** *bale-ful, bale-ful-ly*.

BALE (3), to empty water out of a ship. (F. — Late L.) Not in ME. A better spelling is *bail*. We find : ' having freed our ship thereof [of water] with *baling* ;' Hackluyt's Voyages, v. ii. pt. ii. p. 109. It means to empty by means of *bails*, i. e. buckets.—F. *baille* (naut.), a bucket; whence also Du. *balie*, a tub. — Late L. *bacula, dimin. of *baca, bacca*, a vessel for water, also a small boat (whence also Du. *bak*, a bowl, pail); see **Basin**. Körting, § 1136.

BALE-FIRE, a blazing fire; esp. of a funeral pyre. (E.) From *bale* and *fire*. ME. *bale* meant 'a blazing fire,' or burning pile; also, a funeral pyre. 'In a *bale* of fijr;' P. Plowman's Crede, 667. AS. *bǽl*, fire, Béowulf, 2323; *bǽl-fýr*, id. 3144.+Icel. *bāl*, a great fire; cf. Gk. φαλός, shining, bright, Lith. *baltas*, white; Skt. *bhāla-m*, lustre. ¶ Distinct from *Baal*, which is Semitic.

BALK (1), a beam; a ridge, a division of land. (E.) Not much in use except in prov. E.; common in old authors. ME. *balke*. '*Balke* in a howse, *trabs*;' '*Balke* of a londe eryd, *porca*;' Prompt. Parv. p. 22; *balkes*, rafters, Chaucer, C. T. 3626; '*baulke* of lond, *separaison*;' Palsgrave. AS. *balca*, a heap; in the phr. 'on *balcan lecgan*'=to lay in heaps, Boeth. xvi. 2; which explains Shak. '*balked*,' laid in heaps, 1 Hen. IV, i. 1. 61.+OSaxon *balko*, a beam, Heliand, l. 1708; Du. *balk*, a beam, rafter, bar; Icel. *bālkr*, a partition; Swed. *balk*, a beam, partition; G. *balken*, a beam, rafter; OHG. *balcho*. Teut. type **balkon-*; a bar, weak masc. β. Further allied to Icel. *bjālki*, Swed. *bjälke*, Dan. *bjælke*, a beam, Teut. type **belkon-*; and to AS. *bolca*, a plank for a ship's gang-way, Teut. type **bolkon-*. Perhaps further allied to Gk. φάλαγξ, a round bar of wood. See **Phalanx**.

BALK (2), to hinder. (E.) Shak. has *balked*, Tw. Nt. iii. 2. 26. '*Balkyn* or ouerskyppyn, *omitto*;' Prompt. Parv. And again, '*Balkyn*, or to make a balke yn a londe, *porco*;' Prompt. Parv. p. 22. A *balk* also means a bar, a beam, see above; and to *balk* means to bar one's way, hence to foil; cf. Icel. *bālkr*, a beam of wood, also a piece of wood laid across a door; also, a fence. Hence the vb. is derived from **Balk** (1).

BALL (1), a dance. (F. — Late L.) Used by Dryden, tr. of Lucretius, b. ii. l. 29. Chapman and Shirley wrote a play called *The Ball*, licensed in 1632. — F. *bal*, a dance; from OF. *baler* (Lewis). Prob. suggested by Gk. βαλλίζειν, to dance; which is possibly connected with Gk. βάλλειν, to throw. See **Ballet, Ballad**.

BALL (2), a spherical body. (Scand.) ME. *balle*, King Alisaunder, 6481; Layamon, ii. 307, 616. — Icel. *böllr*, a ball, globe, gen. *ballar*; Swed. *bāll*, Dan. *bold*. Teut. type *balluz.+MHG. *balle*, OHG. *pallo*, a ball, sphere. Perhaps allied to L. *follis*, an inflated ball. From the same source, *ball-oon, ball-ot*.

BALLAD, a sort of song. (F. — Prov. — Low L.) ME. *balade*, Ch., L. G. W. 270; Gower, C. A. i. 134. — OF. *balade*, F. *ballade*, of which Brachet says that it 'came, in the 14th century, from the Provençal *balada*.' *Balada* seems to have meant a dancing song, and is clearly derived from Late L. (and Ital.) *ballāre*, to dance. See **Ball** (1). ¶ In some authors the form *ballat* or *ballet* occurs; in this case, the word follows the Ital. spelling *ballata*, 'a dancing song,' from Ital. *ballare*, to dance. See *ballats* and *ballatry* in Milton's Areopagitica; ed. Hales, pp. 8, 24.

BALLAST, a load to steady a ship. (Dutch — Scand. ?) *Ballasting* occurs in Cymbeline, iii. 6. 78; *balast or ballast* in Hacklyyt's Voyages, i. 594; ii. pt. ii. 173; Palsgrave (1530) has *balast*. — Du. *ballast*, ballast; *ballasten*, to ballast. (Many of our sea-terms are Dutch.) Cf. also Dan. *ballast*, ballast; *ballaste*, to ballast; also spelt *baglast, baglaste*; Swed. *barlast*; MDan. *barlast*. B. The latter syllable is, as all agree, the Du., Dan., and Swed. *last*, a burden, a word also used in English in the phr. 'a *last* of herrings;' see **Last** (4). The former syllable is disputed; but perhaps we may rely upon the Swed. and MDan. form *bar-last*, i. e. 'bare (mere) load;' whence *ballast* by assimilation. In this view, the first syllable is cognate with E. *bare*. [The Dan. *bag* means 'behind, at the back, in the rear;' and we may conclude that *baglast* was so called because stowed more in the after part of the ship than in front, so as to tilt up the bows; see **Back**. But this form was probably due to popular etymology.] C. Another etymology is given in the Wörterbuch der Ostfriesischen Sprache, by J. ten D. Koolman. The EFriesic word is also *ballast*, and may be explained as compounded of *bal* (the same word with E. *bale*, evil), and *last*, a load. In this case *ballast* = bale-load, i. e. useless load, unprofitable lading. This view is possible, yet not convincing; it does not account for the MDan. *barlast*, which is prob. the oldest and most correct form. And it is not clear that EFries. *bal* can mean 'useless'; it is rather 'evil' or 'harmful.'

BALLET, a sort of dance. (F. — Ital. — Late L.) First used by Dryden, Essay on Dram. Poesie (1668); ed. T. Arnold, p. 61. — F. *ballet*, a little dance. — Ital. *balletto*, dimin. of *ballo*, a dance. — Ital. *ballare*, to dance. See **Ball** (1).

BALLOON, a large spherical bag. (F. — OHG.) Formerly *balowne, baloon*: see quotations in Richardson from Burton, Anat. of Melancholy, pt. ii. sec. 2, m. 4, and Eastward Ho, Act i. sc. 1. In both instances it means a ball used in a game resembling football; and this

form was borrowed from the Ital. *ballone*, 'a great ball, a ballone, a footeball,' Florio; augment. of *balla*, a ball. The modern E. word is from F. *ballon*, augment. of F. *balle*, a ball. See **Ball** (2). ☞ The game of *baloon* is better known by the Italian name *pallone*, which Diez says is from the OHG. form *palla, pallo*, an earlier form of G. *ball*, a ball.

BALLOT, a mode of voting, for which little balls were used; also, to vote by ballot. (Ital. — OHG.) 'They would never take their *balls* to *ballot* [vote] against him;' North's Plutarch, p. 927 (R.) — Ital. *ballotta*, a little ball used in voting; whence *ballottare*, 'to cast lots with bullets, as they vse in Venice;' Florio. *Ballotta* is a dimin. of *balla*, a ball. [Hence also F. *ballotter*, to cast lots (Cotgrave); *ballote, balotte*, a little ball used in voting (Cotgrave), a word used by Montaigne (Brachet).] See **Ball** (2).

BALM, an aromatic plant. (F. — L. — Gk. — Arab.) The spelling has been modified so as to bring it nearer to *balsam*; the spelling *balm* occurs in Chapman's Homer, Iliad, b. xvi. 624, but the ME. form is *baume* or *bawme*; Chaucer, Ho. of Fame, 1686; spelt *bame*, Ancren Riwle (ab. 1230), p. 164; spelt *balsme*, Gower, C. A. iii. 315. The derivative *enbawmen* occurs in P. Plowman, B. xvii. 70. — OF. *basme*. — L. *balsamum*. — Gk. βάλσαμον, the fragrant resin of the balsam-tree; cf. βάλσαμος, a balsam-tree. Of Semitic origin; from Arab. *bashām*, the name of a fragrant shrub; Rich. Dict. p. 273; cf. Heb. *bāsām*, balsam; see Gesenius. Der. *balm-y*. Doublet, *balsam*.

BALSAM, an aromatic plant (Timon, iii. 5. 110). See **Balm**.

BALUSTER, a rail of a staircase, a small column. (F. — Ital. — L. — Gk.) Evelyn (Of Architecture) speaks of 'rails and *balusters*;' Dryden has *ballustred*, i. e. provided with balusters, Art of Poetry, canto i. l. 54; Mason has *balustrade*, English Garden, b. ii. 351. — F. *balustre*; Cotgrave has: '*Balustres*, ballisters, little, round, and short pillars, ranked on the outside of cloisters, terraces;' &c. He also has: '*Balustre, Balauste*, the blossome, or flower of the wild pomgranet tree.' — Ital. *balaustro*, a baluster, small pillar; so called from a fancied similarity in form to that of the calyx of the pomegranate flower. — Ital. *balausto, balausta, balaustra*, the flower of the wild pomegranate tree. — L. *balaustium*. — Gk. βαλαύστιον, the flower of the wild pomegranate; Dioscorides.

BALUSTRADE, a row of balusters. (F. — Ital. — L. — Gk.) In Evelyn's Diary, Nov. 19, 1644. Borrowed from F. *balustrade*. — Ital. *balaustrata*, furnished with balusters, as if pp. of a verb *balaustrare*, to furnish with balusters. See **Baluster**.

BAMBOO, a sort of woody Indian reed. (Malay — Canarese.) 'They raise their houses upon arches or posts of *bamboos*, that be large reeds;' Sir T. Herbert, Travels (1665), p. 378. — Malay *bambū*, the name of the plant; Marsden's Malay Dict., p. 47; but not original. H. H. Wilson thinks it is from the Canarese *banbu*. See *bamboo* in Yule.

BAMBOOZLE, to trick, cajole. (F.? — Ital.?) The quotations point to the original sense as being to cajole by confusing the senses, to confuse, to obfuscate. It occurs in Arbuthnot, Hist. of John Bull, part iii. ch. 6, who talks of 'a sort of fellows that they call banterers and bamboozlers, that play such tricks.' In the Tatler, no. 31 (1709), is the remark: 'But, sir, I perceive this is to you all *bamboozling*,' i. e. unintelligible trickery; and in no. 230, *bambʹozle* is noted as a new word. The word to *bam*, i. e. to cheat, is, apparently, a contraction of it, and not the original. 'The statement that it is a Gipsy word wants proof;' N.E.D. But it may well have been suggested by F. *bambocher*, 'to be on the lark, to play pranks;' Hamilton. — F. *bamboche*, 'a puppet . . . spree, pranks;' id. — Ital. *bamboccio*, a child, simpleton; augment. of *bambo*, 'a foolish fellow,' Florio; which is prob. of imitative origin. Cf. E. *babble*, and Gk. βαμβαίνειν, to stammer.

BAN, a proclamation; pl. **BANNS**. (E.) ME. *ban*, Rob. of Glouc. p. 188, l. 3881. Cf. ME. *bannien, bannen*. to prohibit, curse; Layamon, i. 344; Gower, C. A. ii. 96; bk. iv. 2834. [Though the Low L. *bannum* and OF. *ban* are found (both being derived from the OHG. strong vb. *bannan*, or *pannan*, to summon) the word may well be E., the G. word being cognate; the influence of OF. *ban* was only partial.] AS. *gebann*, a proclamation, in Ælfric's Hom. i. 30. Cf. 'þa hēt se cyng *ābannan* ūt ealne þēodscipe'=then the king commanded to order out (assemble) all the population; AS. Chron. A.D. 1006.+Du. *ban*, excommunication; *bannen*, to exile; Icel. and Swed. *bann*, a ban; *banna*, to chide; Dan. *band*, a ban; *bande*, to curse. All from a Teut. strong verb **bannan-* (conj. 7), to proclaim. β. Brugmann (i. § 559) connects *ban* with L. *fāma, fāri*, from √BHĀ, to speak. Cf. Skt. *bhan*, to speak, related to *bhāsh*, to speak; Gk. φημί, I say. See **Bandit, Banish, Abandon**. ¶ Hence pl. *banns*, spelt *banes* in Sir T. More, Works, p. 434 g; cf. '*Bane* of mariage,' Prompt. Parv.

BANANA, the plantain tree, of the genus *Musa*. (Port. — W. African.) Noticed by Dampier in 1686; Voyages, i. 316 (Yule).

The pl. *bananas* occurs as early as 1599 in J. Davis, Voyages (Hakluyt Soc.), p. 138. Borrowed from Port. (or Span.) *banana*, the fruit of the plantain or banana-tree; the tree itself is called in Spanish *banano*. The name is said by early Port. writers to have come from Guinea; see Yule. So also in Voyages (1745), ii. 336.

BAND (1), also **BOND**, a fastening, ligature. (Scand.) ME. *bond, band,* Prompt. Parv. p. 43; Ormulum, 19821.—Icel. *band;* Swed. *band;* Dan. *baand.*+OFriesic *band;* Du. *band,* a bond, tie; G. *band;* OHG. *pant.* Teut. type **bandom,* neut.; from *band,* 2nd grade of *bind-an-,* to bind. Further allied to AS. *bend,* Goth. *bandi,* a band. Also to Skt. *bandha-s,* a binding, tie, fetter; from Skt. *bhand,* to bind. See **Bind.** But orig. unconnected with *bondage,* q.v. Der. *band-age, band-box.* N.B. The *band-box* was orig. made for the *bands* or ruffs of the 17th cent.; see Fairholt, Gloss., p. 26, l. 1.

BAND (2), a company of men. (F.—G.) Not found in this sense in ME. Shak. has: 'the sergeant of the *band*;' Com. of Errors, iv. 3. 30; also *banding* as a pres. pt., 1 Hen. VI, iii. 1. 81.— F. 'bande, a band; also, a band, a company of souldiers, a troop, or crue;' Cot. [whence mod. G. *bande,* a gang, set.]—G. *band,* a band, tie; cf. Low L. *banda,* a gang. Allied to Low L. *bandum,* a banner. See further under **Banner.** Der. *band,* vb.; *band-ed, band-ing, band-master;* and see *bandy.*

BANDANNA, a silk handkerchief with white spots. (Hind.—Skt.) 'Waving his yellow *bandanna*;' Thackeray, Newcomes, ch. 4.—Hind. *bāndhnū,* 'a mode of dyeing, in which the cloth is tied in various places, to prevent the parts tied from receiving the dye . . . a kind of silk cloth;' Forbes. Cf. Hind. *bāndhnā,* to tie, bind.—Skt. *bandh,* to bind.

BANDICOOT, a large Indian rat. (Telugu.) Telugu *pandi-kokku,* lit. pig-rat (Yule).—Tel. *pandi,* hog; *kokku,* rat (Brown).

BANDIT, a robber; prop. an outlaw. (Ital.—Teut.) *Bandite* occurs in Comus, l. 426, and *banditto* in Shak. 2 Hen. VI, iv. 1. 135. Borrowed from Ital. *bandito,* outlawed, pp. of *bandire,* to proscribe. —Low L. *bandire,* to proclaim; formed (with excrescent *d*) from *bannire,* with the same sense.—Low L. *bannum,* a proclamation; of Teut. origin. See **Ban, Banish.**

BANDOG, a large dog, held in a band or tied up. (Scand. *and* E.) For *band-dog.* Sir T. More, Works, p. 586 c, has *bandedogges.* Prompt. Parv. p. 43, has 'Bondogge, or bonde dogge, *Molosus*;' and Way, in a note, quotes 'A bande doge, *Molosus*;' Cath. Angl. So also: 'Hic molosus, a *banddogge,*' Wright's Vocab. i. 187; also spelt *bonddoge,* id. p. 251. 'A bandogge, *canis catenarius*'=a *chained* dog;' Levins, Manip. Vocab. col. 157. Hexham has: '*een bandt-hondt,* a banndogge.' See **Band** (1) and **Dog.**

BANDOLEER, BANDOLIER, a shoulder-belt; now used for cartridges. (F.—Span.—Teut.) 'Six musketts with *bandileares*;' Unton Invent. (1596); p. 3. From MF. *bandouillere,* 'a musketiers *bandoleer,*' Cot.; F. *bandoulière.*—Span. *bandolera,* a bandoleer; from *banda,* a sash, band. Of Teut. origin; see **Band** (1).

BANDY, to beat to and fro, to contend. (F.—G.) Shak. has *bandy,* to contend, Tit. And. i. 312; but the older sense is to beat to and fro, as in Romeo, ii. 5. 14. It was a term used at tennis, and was formerly also spelt *band,* as in 'To *band* the ball;' G. Turbervile, To his Friend P., Of Courting and Tenys (ab. 1570?). The chief difficulty is to account for the final *-y,* though we have a similar suffix in *parley.* One sense of *bandy* was a particular stroke at tennis, perhaps from MF. *bandé,* lit. 'struck.'—MF. 'bander, to bind, fasten with strings; also, to *bandie,* at tennis;' Cotgrave. He also gives: 'Iouer à *bander* et à racler contre, to *bandy* against, at tennis; and, by metaphor, to pursue with all insolency, rigour, extremity.' Also: 'Se *bander* contre, to *bandie* or oppose himselfe against, with his whole power; or to ioine in league with others against.' Also: 'Ils se *bandent* à faire un entreprise, they are plot[t]ing a conspiracy together.' β. The word is therefore the same as that which appears as *band,* in the phrase 'to *band* together.' The F. *bander* is derived from *bande, sb.;* from the G. *band,* a band, tie; see **Band** (2).

BANDY-LEGGED, crook-legged. (F. and E.) Swift (in 1727) has: 'Your *bandy* leg, or crooked nose;' Furniture of a Woman's Mind, l. 22. The prefix *bandy* is merely borrowed from the MF. *bandé,* bent, spoken of a bow. *Bandé* is the pp. of F. *bander,* explained by Cotgrave as 'to bend a bow; also, to bind, . . . tie with bands.' He has here inverted the order; the right sense is (1) to *string* a bow; and (2) to bend it in stringing it.—G. *band,* a band.— G. *band,* 2nd grade of *binden,* to bind. See **Bind.** ¶ Observe that *bande* is the F. equivalent of *bent,* because *bend* is also derived from *bind.* See **Bend.**

BANE, harm, destruction. (E.) ME. *bane,* Chaucer, C. T. 1099 (A 1097). AS. *bana,* a murderer.+Icel. *bani,* death, a slayer; Dan. and Swed. *bane,* death. Teut. type **banon-,* masc. Cf. Goth. *banja,* a wound. Perhaps allied to OIrish *ben-im,* I strike, Bret. *ben-a,* to cut, Stokes-Fick, p. 167. Der. *bane-ful, bane-ful-ly.*

BANG (1), to beat violently. (Scand.) Shak. has *bang'd,* Tw. Night, iii. 2. 24.—Icel. *banga,* Dan. *banke,* to beat; cf. Icel. *bang,* a hammering; Dan. *bank,* a beating. Note also MSwed. *bængel,* G. *bengel,* a cudgel (lit. 'bang-er'); MDan. *bange,* to make a noise, *bang,* noise, uproar.

BANG (2), **BHANG,** a narcotic drug. (Port.—Hind.—Skt.) Formerly *bangue* (see Yule). — Port. *bangue;* cf. 'they call it in Portuguese *banga*;' Capt. Knox (A.D. 1681), in Arber's Eng. Garner, i. 402.—Hind. *bhāng,* hemp (*Cannabis sativus*); Forbes; cf. Pers. *bang,* an inebriating draught, hashish; Palmer's Pers. Dict. col. 93.—Skt. *bhaṅgā,* hemp; the drug being made from the wild hemp.

BANGLE, a kind of bracelet. (Hind.) 'The ankles and wrists ornamented with large rings or *bangles*;' Archæologia, vol. viii. p. 256, an. 1787 (Davies). From Hindustani *bangrī,* fem. 'a bracelet, an ornament for the wrist; corruptly, a bangle;' Wilson, Gloss. of Indian Terms, p. 59; Forbes, p. 88.

BANIAN, a tree; see **Banyan.**

BANISH, to outlaw, proscribe. (F.—OHG.) ME. *banishen,* Chaucer, Kn. Tale, 1727 (A 1725).—OF. *ban-ir, bann-ir* (with suffix *-ish* due to the *-iss-* which occurs in conjugating a F. verb of that form; answering to the L. inchoative suffix *-isc-, -esc-*).—Low L. *bannire,* to proscribe; from a Teutonic source.—OHG. *bannan, pannan,* to summon; a strong verb. See **Ban.** Der. *banish-ment.*

BANISTERS, staircase railings. (F.—Ital.—L.—Gk.) 'Thumping the *banisters* all the way;' Sheridan, The Rivals, ii. 1 (Fag). A corruption of *balusters;* see **Baluster.**

BANJO, a six-stringed musical instrument. (Ital.—Gk.) A negro corruption of *bandore,* which occurs in Minsheu's Dict. (1627). Again, *bandore* is for *bandora,* described in Queene Elizabethes Achademy, ed. Furnivall, p. 111; Chappell's Popular Music, i. 224, ii. 776. Also written *pandore:* 'The cythron, the *pandore,* and the theorbo strike;' Drayton, Polyolbion, song 4.—Ital. *pandora, pandura,* 'a musical instrument with three strings, a kit, a croude, a rebecke;' Florio.— Gk. πανδοῦρα, πανδουρίς, also φάνδουρα, a musical instrument with three strings (Liddell and Scott). Not a true Gk. word; Chappell says the Greeks borrowed it from the ancient Egyptians. ¶ *Mandolin,* q.v., is from the same source.

BANK (1), a mound of earth. (Scand.) ME. *banke,* P. Plowman, B. v. 521; *bankes* in Ormulum, 9210.—OScand. **banke,* orig. form of Icel. *bakki,* ridge, eminence, bank of a river; cf. Jutland *banke* (Feilberg), Dan. *bakke,* Swed. *backe,* bank; whence also Norman F. *banque,* a bank. Teut. stem **bankon-,* m.+OHG. *panch,* a bank; also, a bench. Note also AS. *hō-banca,* lit. 'heel-bench,' as a gloss to *sponda*; Voc. 280. 12. Oldest sense ridge or shelf; hence bench, table. See **Bench.**

BANK (2), a place for depositing money. (F.—Ital.—G.) *Bank* is in Udall, on Luke, c. xix. 23.—F. *banque,* a money-changer's table or bench; Cot.—Ital. *banca,* f., a bench; also *banco,* m. 'a bench, a marchants banke,' Florio.—MHG. *banc,* a bench, table. See **Bench;** and see above. Der. *bank-er,* q.v.; *bank-rupt,* q.v.; *bank-rupt-cy.*

BANKER, a money-changer. (F.; with E. suffix.) *Banker* occurs in Sir T. More, Works, p. 1385 h. It is formed from *bank,* with E. suffix *-er.* Cf. F. *banquier,* 'a banker;' Cot.

BANKRUPT, one unable to pay just debts. (F.—Ital.) ME. *bankeroupte,* Sir T. More, Works, p. 881 f. An earlier sense was 'bankruptcy;' N. E. D. The word has been modified by a knowledge of its relation to the L. *ruptus,* but was originally French rather than Latin. The true French word, too, was *banqueroutier* (Cotgrave), formed from *banqueroute,* f., which properly meant 'a breaking or becoming bankrupt;' i.e. bankruptcy. The latter was introduced into French in the 16th cent. from Ital. *banca rotta* (Brachet).—Ital. *banca,* a bank, bench; *rotta,* broken.—MHG. *banc,* a bench; and L. *rupta,* f. of *ruptus,* broken, pp. of *rumpere,* to break. See **Bank** (2), and **Bench;** also **Rupture.** ¶ The usual account, that a bankrupt person had his bench (i.e. money-table) broken, is unauthorized and needless. Cf. Late L. *ruptus,* a bankrupt (A.D. 1334) in Ducange. It was the *man* that was 'broken.'

BANNER, a flag, ensign. (F.—Teut.) ME. *banere,* Ancren Riwle (1230), p. 300; AF. *banere,* Stat. Realm, i. 185 (1322).—OF. *banere, baniere;* cf. Prov. *bandiera.*—Low L. type **bandāria,* f. (the form *bandēria* occurs), a banner.—Low L. *bandum,* a standard; with suffix *-āria.* From a Teut. (Langobardic) source: 'uexillum, quod *bandum* appellant;' Paulus, De gestis Langob. i. 20; cf. Goth. *bandwa, banduō,* a sign, token.—Teut. **band,* 2nd grade of **bindan-,* to bind. See **Bind.**

BANNERET, a knight of a higher class, under the rank of a baron. (F.—Teut.) AF. *baneret,* Le Prince Noir, l. 193 (ab. 1386); F. *banneret,* which Cotgrave explains as 'a Banneret, or Knight banneret, a title, the priviledge whereof was to have a *banner* of his own for his people to march and serve under,' &c. Spelt *banret* by Stanihurst, in Holinshed's Desc. of Ireland, ed. 1808; vi. 57. From a

Lat. type *banerātus*, i.e. provided with a banner. — OF. *banere*, a banner : see above.

BANNOCK, a kind of flat cake. (C. — L. ?) Lowland Sc. *bannock*; AS. *bannuc*; Napier, OE. Glosses. — Gael. *bonnach*, a cake. Prob. not a Celtic word, but due to L. *pānicium*, a baked cake. — L. *pānis*, bread. Cf. **Pantry.**

BANNS, a proclamation of marriage. (E.) The plural of **Ban,** q.v.

BANQUET, a feast. (F. — Ital. — G.) *Banquet,* vb., occurs in Hall's Chron. Henry V, an. 2 (1809), p. 57. The more usual old form is *banket*; as in Fisher's Works, ed. Mayor (E. E. T. S.), p. 294. — F. *banquet,* which Cotgrave explains as 'a banket; also a feast,' &c. The word has reference to the table on which the feast is spread. — Ital. *banchetto,* dimin. of *banco,* orig. a bench. (Florio has *banchettare,* 'to banquet.') — MHG. *banc,* a bench, a table. See **Bank** (1), **Bench.**

BANSHEE, a female spirit supposed to warn families of a death. (Irish.) 'In certain places the death of people is supposed to be foretold by the cries and shrieks of *benshi,* or the Fairies wife ;' Pennant, Tour in Scotland, 1769, p. 205 (Jamieson). — Gael. *beanshith,* a banshee ; lit. fairy-woman (Macleod, p. 627) ; from Irish *bean sidhe,* OIr. *ben side,* 'woman of the fairies;' see Macbain, p. 293. The Gael. and Ir. *bean* = OIrish *ben,* is cognate with E. *quean.* Windisch has OIr. *ban-side*; where *ban-* is for *ben* (in composition) ; and *side* is a pl. form, meaning 'fairies.'

BANTAM, a kind of fowl. (Java.) The *bantam* fowl is said to have been brought from Bantam, the name of a place in Java, at the western extremity of the island.

BANTER, to mock or jeer at; mockery. (E. ?) 'When wit hath any mixture of raillery, it is but calling it *banter,* and the work is done. This polite word of theirs was first borrowed from the bullies in White Friars, then fell among the footmen, and at last retired to the pedants ; but if this *bantering,* as they call it, be so despicable a thing,' &c.; Swift, Tale of a Tub ; Author's Apology. *Banterer* occurs A. D. 1709, in the Tatler, no. 12. Origin unknown ; apparently slang. Davies (Supplem. Gloss.) gives an earlier quotation : 'Occasions given to all men to talk what they please, especially the *banterers* of Oxford (a set of scholars so called, some M.A.), who make it their employment to talk as a venture, lye, and prate what nonsense they please ;' A. Wood, Life, Sept. 6, 1678. Prob. picked up from some E. dialect ; cf. prov. E. *bant,* vigour ; *bant,* to conquer, haggle ; *banter,* to cheapen, haggle, tease, taunt (E. D. D.) Perhaps we may compare Schmeller's Bavarian Dict. (col. 248) : '*bündeln* (pron. *banteln*), used jocularly or ironically, to be busy about a bandage (called *bantl*), fig. to intrigue ;' see the whole article.

BANTLING, an infant, a brat. (G.) Occurs in Drayton's Pastorals, ecl. 7, st. 17 ; where Cupid is called the 'wanton *bantling'* of Venus. Apparently confused with *band,* as if for *band-ling,* one wrapped in swaddling-bands ; but really an adaptation of G. *bänkling* (with the same sense as Low G. *bankert*), an illegitimate child ; from G. *bank,* a bench ; i.e. 'a child begotten on a bench, not in the marriage-bed;' see *Bankert* in Brem. Wörterbuch. And see **Bastard.**

BANYAN, a kind of tree. (Port. — Skt.) Sir T. Herbert, in describing the religion of 'the Bannyans' of India, proceeds to speak of 'the *bannyan* trees,' which were esteemed as sacred ; ed. 1665, p. 51 ; see also p. 123. The *bannyans* were merchants, and the *bannyan-trees* (an English, not a native, term) were used as a sort of market-place, and are (I am told) still so used. At first applied to a particular tree ; see Yule. — Port. *banian,* a trader. — Gujarātī *vānnio,* one of the trading caste (H. H. Wilson, p. 541). — Skt. *vaṇij, baṇij,* a merchant (Benfey, p. 625).

BAOBAB, a kind of large tree. (W. African.) In Arber's Eng. Garner, i. 441. The native name ; in Senegal.

BAPTIZE, v. to christen by dipping. (F. — L. — Gk.) Formerly *baptise* was the commoner form ; it occurs in Rob. of Glouc., p. 86 ; l. 1918. [The sb. *baptiste* occurs in the Ancren Riwle, p. 160; and *baptisme* in Gower, C. A. i. 189 ; bk. ii. 899.] — OF. *baptiser.* — L. *baptizāre.* — Gk. βαπτίζειν ; from βάπτειν, to dip. From a root GwEBH ; whence also Icel. *kwefja,* to dip, quench. Brugm. i. § 677 ; Prellwitz. Der. *baptist* (Gk. βαπτιστής, a dipper) ; *baptism* (Gk. βάπτισμα, a dipping) ; and *baptist-er-y.*

BAR, a rail, a stiff rod. (F.) ME. *barre,* Chaucer, C. T., A 1075; Havelok, 1794. — OF. *barre.* — Late L. *barra,* a bar (of unknown origin; whence also Port., Span., and Ital. *barra*). A connexion with Bret. *barr,* a branch, seems possible. Cf. Stokes-Fick, pp. 172–3. Der. *barricade,* q.v., *barrier,* q.v.; *barrister,* q.v.; prob. *barrel,* q.v.; and see *embarrass.*

BARB (1), the hook on the point of an arrow. (F. — L.) Merely an adaptation of the L. *barba,* a beard. Cotgrave has : '*Barbelé,* bearded ; also, full of snags, snips, jags, notches ; whence *flesche barbelée,* a bearded or *barbed* arrow.' — F. *barbe.* — L. *barba,* the beard. See **Barbel, Barber,** and **Beard.**

BARB (2), a Barbary horse. (F. — Barbary). So in Glossographia Anglicana ; 1719. Cotgrave has : '*Barbe,* a Barbery horse.' Named from the country.

BARBAROUS, uncivilized. (L. — Gk.) ME. *barbar, barbarik,* a barbarian ; Wyclif's earlier version, Col. iii. 11, 1 Cor. xiv. 11. Afterwards *barbarous,* in closer imitation of the Latin. — L. *barbarus.* — Gk. βάρβαρος, foreign ; cf. L. *balbus,* stammering. β. The name was applied by Greeks to foreigners to express the strange sound of their language ; see Curtius, i. 362 ; Fick, i. 684. Der. *barbar-ian, barbar-ic, barbar-it-y, barbar-ise, barbar-ism, barbar-ous-ness.*

BARBECUE, a frame-work of sticks supported on posts ; orig. used for sleeping on or for meat meant to be smoke-dried. (Span. — Hayti.) Hence the verb *barbecue,* to smoke-dry, to broil. 'They .. *barbacue* their game and fish in the smoke ;' Stedman, Surinam, i. 406. — Span. *barbacoa,* a scaffold raised above the ground ; Pineda. — Hayti *barbacoa,* a raised wooden framework ; Notes on E. Etym. p. 347.

BARBED, accoutred ; said of a horse. (F. — Scand. ?) Shak. has : '*barbed* steeds ;' Rich. III, i. 1. 10. Also spelt *barded,* the older form ; it occurs in Berners' tr. of Froissart, vol. i. c. 41. Cotgrave has : '*Bardé,* m. *-ée,* f. barbed, or trapped as a great horse.' — F. *barde,* horse-armour ; but explained in Cot. as 'a long saddle for an ass or moyle' [mule]. Referred by Diez to Icel. *barð,* a brim of a helmet; also, the beak or armed prow of a ship of war ; from which sense it might have been transferred so as to be used of horses furnished with spiked plates on their foreheads. Cf. also Icel. *barði,* a shield. β. But Devic refers F. *barde,* pack-saddle, Span. *albarda,* to Arab. *barda'at,* a pack-saddle. However, this may be a different word. See Körting. § 1237. (Uncertain.)

BARBEL, a kind of fish. (F. — L.) '*Barbylle* fysche, barbell fisshe, barbyllus ;' Prompt. Parv. p. 24. — OF. *barbel,* F. *barbeau.* Cotgrave has both forms, and defines *barbeau* as 'the river barbell . . . also, a little beard.' — L. acc. *barbellum,* from *barbellus,* dimin. of *barbus,* a barbel ; cf. *barbula,* a little beard, dimin. of *barba,* a beard. ¶ The fish is so called because it is furnished, near the mouth, with four barbels or beard-like appendages (Webster). See **Barb** (1).

BARBER, one who shaves the beard. (F. — L.) ME. *barbour,* Chaucer, C. T., A 2025 (Kn. Ta.) — OF. *barbeor, barbier,* a barber. — F. *barbe,* the beard, with suffix of agent. — L. *barba,* the beard ; which is cognate with E. *beard* ; Brugm. i. § 972. See **Beard.** β. ME. and AF. *barbour,* OF. *barbeor,* answer to a L. type *barbātōrem,* acc. ; OF. *barbier* to Late L. type *barbārium,* acc.

BARBERRY, BERBERRY, a shrub. (F. — L.) Cotgrave has : '*Berberis,* the barbarie-tree.' The Eng. word is borrowed from French, which accounts for the loss of final *s.* The ME. *barbaryn* (Prompt. Parv.) is adjectival. — Late L. *berberis,* the name of the shrub, also spelt *barbaris,* as in Prompt. Parv. Origin wholly unknown ; the Arab. *barbāris* (often cited) is not a true Arab. word. The name *barbaryn-tre* (Prompt. Parv.) answers to OF. *barbarin,* 'foreign ;' and an ultimate derivation from Gk. βαρβαρικός or βάρβαρος, foreign, does not seem impossible. The Span. *berberis,* Ital. *berberi,* afford no help. Mandeville has *barbarynes* (to translate F. *berberis*) ; c. ii. p. 14. 'Berberi, fructus, *berberynes* ;' Wright, Voc. 568. 4. ¶ This is an excellent example of *accommodated spelling* ; the change of the two final syllables into *berry* makes them significant ; but the word cannot claim three *r*'s.

BARBICAN, an outwork of a fort. (F. — Arab. *and* Pers.) ME. *barbican,* King Alisaunder, ed. Weber, l. 1591 ; Gawain and the Grene Knight, ed. Morris, l. 793. John de Garlande has 'antemuralia, *barbycons* ;' and 'propugnacula, Gallice *barbaquenne* ;' Wright's Voc. i. pp. 130, 131. — OF. *barbacan*; also *barbecan, barbicant, barbechant* ; 'Antemuralia, *barbechant*;' also 'Les creneaux ou *barbicants* ;' Godefroy. Cf. Low L. *barbacana,* an outwork ; a word of unknown origin. [Not AS.] ¶ Brachet says that it was adopted from Arabic *barbakkhaneh,* a rampart, a word which is not in Richardson's Arab. and Pers. Dict., and which appears to have been coined for the occasion. Diez derives it from Pers. *bālā-khānah,* upper chamber, which is far from satisfactory. For conjectures, see Devic, and Körting, § 1168. β. L. *barba cāna,* 'gray beard,' is exactly the mod. Prov. *barbocano,* a barbican ; and this may very well be a 'popular etymology,' due to trying to make sense of the Eastern name *bāb-khānah,* 'gate-house,' a term written on a barbican at Cawnpore ; see Yule's account. If this be right, the derivation is from Arab. *bāb,* a gate, and Pers. *khānah,* a house.

BARCAROLLE, a boatman's song. (F. — Ital. — Late L.) In Moore, National Airs, no. 10, l. 17. — F. *barcarolle.* — Venetian *barcarola* ; fem. of *barcarolo,* a waterman (Baretti), Ital. *barcaruolo.* — Ital. *barca,* a boat ; see **Bark** (1).

BARD (1), a poet. (C.) *Bard* occurs in Sir R. Holland's Houlate, ll. 795, 822, 825. Selden speaks of '*bardish* impostures;' On Drayton's Polyolbion ; Introduction. Borrowed from the Celtic ; Irish *bard,* Gael. *bard,* a poet ; so too W. *bardd,* Corn. *bardh,* Bret. *barz.* β.

Celtic type *bardos, which probably meant 'speaker;' cf. Gk. φράζειν (for φράδ-γειν), to speak. **Der.** bard-ic.

BARD (2), armour for a horse; see **Barbed.**

BARE, naked. (E.) ME. bar, bare, Owl and Nightingale, 547. AS. bær, bare, Grein, i. 77. **+** Icel. berr, bare, naked; OHG. par (G. bar), bare; Du. baar. Teut. type *bazoz; allied to Lith. basas, barefooted; OSlav. bosŭ, Russ. bosoi, barefooted. Idg. type *bhosos. **Der.** bare-ness, bare-faced, bare-headed, bare-footed.

BARGAIN, to chaffer. (F.) ME. bargayn, sb., Chaucer, Prol. 282; Robert of Brunne, tr. of Langtoft, p. 270. **–** OF. bargaigner, to chaffer. **–** Late L. barcāniāre, to change about, shift, shuffle. Origin uncertain; Diez and Burguy refer the Late L. form, without hesitation, to Late L. barca, a barque or boat for merchandise, but fail to explain the latter portion of the word. See below.

BARGE, a sort of boat. (F. – Late L.) ME. barge, Chaucer, Prol. 410; Robert of Brunne, tr. of Langtoft, p. 169. **–** OF. barge. **–** Late L. barga, apparently a variant of barca, for which see **Bark** (1). **β.** Diez derives barge from a Late Lat. type *barica, a supposed dimin. from L. bāris, a flat Egyptian row-boat (Propertius). **–** Gk. βᾶρις, a flat Egyptian row-boat; perhaps of Egyptian origin; Mahn cites a Coptic bari, a small boat. given by Peyron. See below.

BARK (1), **BARQUE,** a sort of ship. (F. – Ital. – Late L.) These are probably varieties of the same word as the above. Hackluyt has 'small barkes,' Voyages, vol. ii. part i. p. 227; and Fabyan's Chronicles, ed. 1811, p. 286, has 'smalle caruyles [caravels] and barkys;' clearly borrowed from F. barque. Cotgrave has 'Barque, a barke, little ship, great boat.' **–** Ital. barca, 'a boat, a lighter;' Florio. **–** Late L. barca, a small ship or boat (Paulinus Nolanus, ab. 400). **¶** Thurneysen thinks that L. barca may be of Celtic origin, from OIrish barc; but the borrowing was more probably in the other direction.

BARK (2), the rind of a tree. (Scand.) ME. barke, P. Plowman, B. xi. 251; bark, Legends of Holy Rood, p. 68. **–** Swed. bark, rind; Dan. bark; Icel. börkr (stem bark-).**+**MDu. borcke, barcke,' the bark of a tree, or a crust,' Hexham; Low G. borke. Teut. type *barkuz.

BARK (3), to yelp as a dog. (E.) ME. berke, Will. of Palerne. ed. Skeat, l. 35; the pp. borken is in Ch., tr. of Boethius, b. i. pr. 5, l. 1. AS. beorcan, Grein, i. 106; strong verb, pt. t. bearc, pp. borcen; cf. Icel. weak verb berkja, to bark, to bluster. **β.** Prob. of imitative origin; and somewhat similar to AS. brecan, to break, to crack, to snap, used of a sudden noise; cf. the cognate L. fragor, a crash. We find AS. brecan in the sense of 'to roar,' Grein, i. 137; cf. Icel. braka, to creak as timber does. See **Break.** Similarly Skt. barh, to roar as an elephant; Swed. bräka, to bleat.

BARLEY, a kind of grain. (E.) ME. barlich, barli, Wycl. Exod. ix. 31; barliȝ, Ormulum, 15551. AS. bærlic, AS. Chron., an. 1124; 'to bærlice crofte,' to the barley-croft; Cod. Dipl. vi. 79, an. 966. Bær- may be compared with Icel. barr, n., barley, and is allied to AS. bere, cognate with Goth. *baris, only found in the adj. bariz-eins, made of barley. The suffix -lic signifies 'like;' so that barley orig. meant 'of the bear-kind,' where bear is the Lowl. Scotch form of AS. bere, m. The AS. bær-, bere, are further allied to L. far, corn; and even to Skt. brashin̄o, food, Servian brashno, meal; see Miklosich, p. 19, col. 1, s. v. borshino; Uhlenbeck, Goth. Wört.; Brugm. i. § 180. See **Farina.**

BARM (1), yeast. (E.) ME. berm, Chaucer, C. T. 16281 (G 813). AS. beorma, m., Luke, xiii. 21. **+** Swed. bärma; Dan. bärme, dregs, lees; G. bärme, yeast. Teut. type *bermon-; cf. L. fermentum, yeast; from fervēre, to boil. See **Ferment.**

BARM (2), the lap. (E.) Nearly obsolete; ME. barm, barme, Prompt. Parv. p. 25. AS. bearm, m., the lap, bosom; Grein, i. 103.**+** Icel. barmr; Swed. and Dan. barm; Goth. barms; OHG. barm, parm. Teut. type *barmoz, m.; from bar, 2nd grade of ber-an-, to bear; whence also Finnish parmas, barm. See **Bear.**

BARN, a place for storing grain. (E.) ME. berne, Chaucer, C. T. 12996 (B 1256). AS. bern, Luke, iii. 17; a contracted form of ber-ern, which occurs in the Old Northumbrian version of the same passage; which glosses L. 'aream' by 'ber-ern vel bere-flor.' A compound word; from AS. bere, barley, and ern, ærn, a house or place for storing, which enters into many other compounds; see Grein, i. 228. The form ærn stands, by metathesis, for *ran(n), and is cognate with Icel. rann, Goth. razn, Teut. type *raznom, n. a house, abode. See **Ransack, Barton, Barley.** **Der.** barn-door.

BARNACLE (1), a species of goose. (F. – Late L.) 'A barnacle, bird, chelonalops;' Levins, 6. 2. Dimin. of ME. bernake; 'bernakes, foules liche to wylde gees;' Trevisa, tr. of Higden, i. 335; where Caxton's version has bernacles. **–** MF. bernaque, 'the fowle called a barnacle;' Cot. **–** Late L. bernāca, in Giraldus Cambrensis (ab. 1175). Ducange has 'Bernacæ, aves aucis palustribus similes,' with by-forms bernecelæ, bernechæ, bernestæ, and bernichæ. **β.** The history of the word is very obscure; but see the account in Max Müller's Lectures

on the Science of Language, 8th ed. ii. 602. His theory is that the birds were Irish ones, i.e. aves Hibernicæ or Hiberniculæ; that the first syllable was dropped, as in Low L. bernagium for hybernagium, &c.; and that the word was afterwards applied to the shell-fish from which the barnacle-goose was imagined to be produced. See **Barnacle** (2).

BARNACLE (2), a sort of small shell-fish. (F. – Late L.) Spelt bernacles by Sir T. Browne, Vulg. Errors, bk. iii. c. 28. § 17. The same word as the above, according to an extraordinary popular belief. Hence it would appear to be beside the question to explain the word as from the L. pernācula, dimin. of perna; see this discussed in Max Müller, Lect. on the Science of Language, 8th ed. ii. 584. [Cf. Lat. perna, used by Pliny, Nat. Hist. 32. 55: 'Appellantur et pernæ concharum generis, circa Pontias insulas frequentissimæ. Stant velut suillo crure longe in arena defixæ, hiantesque, qua limpitudo est, pedali non minus spatio, cibum venantur.' From Gk. πέρνα, lit. a ham.] **β.** The Gael. and Irish bairneach, a limpet, W. brenig, are perhaps from ME. bernake (Macbain). But Stokes (p. 162) derives these from a form barenn (?), a rock.

BARNACLES, spectacles; orig. irons put on the noses of horses to keep them quiet. (F.) 'Barnacles, an instrument set on the nose of unruly horses,' Baret; and see Levins. Hence the more modern jocular use in the sense of spectacles; first in 1571 (N. E. D.) Barnacle (which occurs in Trevisa, tr. of Higden, i. 353) has a dimin. of ME. bernak, explained by L. 'chāmus' in Prompt. Parv. **–** OF. bernac, gloss to cāmum, in A. Neckam (ab. 1200); Wright, Voc. i. 100, l. 3. Origin unknown. See the word discussed in Max Müller, Lect. on the Science of Language, 8th ed. ii. 583; but the solution there offered is untenable. See notes in the Eng. Dial. Dict.

BAROMETER, an instrument for measuring the weight of the air. (Gk.) Not in early use. Due to Boyle, in 1665 (N. E. D.) It occurs also in Glanvill, Ess. 3 (R.) Boyle (in 1665) has barometrical; Works, vol. ii. p. 798; and so Johnson, Rambler, no. 117. Coined from the Gk. **–** Gk. βαρο-, for βάρος, weight; and μέτρον, a measure. The Gk. βαρύς, heavy, is allied to L. grauis, heavy; Curtius, i. 77; Brugm. i. § 665. See **Grave** and **Metre.** **Der.** barometr-ic-al.

BARON, a title of dignity. (F. – L.) ME. baron, Rob. of Glouc. p. 125, l. 2669 (see Koch, Eng. Gram. iii. 154); barun, Old Eng. Homilies, ed. Morris, ii. 35. **–** F. baron (AF. barun, Vie de St. Auban, ed. Atkinson, l. 134, and note to l. 301). **β.** The final -on is the accus. suffix, and the nom. form is OF. ber; both ber and baron meaning, originally, merely 'man' or 'husband.' Diez quotes from Raynouard the OProvençal phrase—'lo bar non es creat per la femna, mas la femna per lo baro' = the man was not created for the woman, but the woman for the man. **–** Late L. bāro (gen. bārōnis), a man; the same word as L. bāro, a simpleton (Cicero). Körting says that sufficient proof of this identification is given by Settegast, in Roman. Forschungen, i. 240. Hence also Prov. bar (acc. baró); Span. varon, Port. varãon, a man. **Der.** baron-age, baron-y, baron-et, baron-et-cy.

BAROUCHE, a sort of carriage. (G. – Ital.) The word is not properly French; but G. barutsche modified so as to present a French appearance. The German word is borrowed from Ital. baroccio, commonly (and more correctly) spelt biroccio, a chariot. **β.** Originally, biroccio meant a two-wheeled car, from L. birotus, two-wheeled; with the ending modified so as to resemble Ital. carroccio, a carriage. from carro, a car. **–** L. bi-, double; and rota, a wheel; see **Rotary.** **¶** The F. form is brouette, a dimin. of *beroue, standing for L. birotum.

BARRACKS, soldiers' lodgings. (F. – Ital.) A modern word; Rich. quotes from Swift's Letters and Blackstone, Comment. bk. i. c. 13. The earliest quotation in N. E. D. is dated 1685; but it occurs at least seven years earlier. 'Monmouth writes from Ostend in 1678: "Many men ill . . . which they attribute to . . . damp lodging of men in the Barraques;"' Sir S. D. Scott, The British Army, iii. 399. **–** F. baraque, a barrack, spelt barraque in Supp. to Godefroy; introduced in the 16th century from Ital. baracca, f., a tent (Brachet), which Torriano (1688) explains as 'a shed made of boards.' Diez derives baracca from Ital. barra, a bar. See **Bar.**

BARRATOR, one who excites to quarrels and suits-at-law. (F.) Spelt barrator, barater, in Blount's Nomo-Lexicon; baratowre in Prompt. Parv. p. 115; see Way's note. The pl. barratours, deceivers, is in the F. text of Mandeville, Trav. p. 160, note f. From ME. barat, fraud, Ayenbite of Inwyt, pp. 39, 61, 82; barete, strife, R. Manning, tr. of Langtoft. p. 274; baret, Ancren Riwle, p. 172. The AF. pl. barettours occurs in the Stat. of the Realm, i. 364, an. 1361; and AF. barat, deceit, in Life of Edw. Confessor, ed. Luard, l. 36. **–** F. barat, 'cheating, deceit, guile, also a barter;' Cotgrave. See **Barter.** But the sense has certainly been influenced by Icel. barátta, strife.

BARREL, a wooden cask. (F.) ME. barel, Chaucer, C. T., B 3083 (ed. Tyrw. 13899). Spelt barell, King Alisaunder, ed. Weber, l. 28. **–** OF. baril, a barrel. **β.** Brachet says 'origin unknown;' Diez and Scheler suppose the derivation to be from OF. barre, a bar;

as if the barrel were looked upon as composed of *bars* or staves. [The Celtic forms are borrowed from English.] Cf. **Barricade.**

BARREN, sterile. (F.) ME. *bareyn,* Chaucer, C. T., A 1977; *barain,* Ancren Riwle, p. 158. — OF. *baraine, baraigne, brehaigne* (F. *bréhaigne,* all fem. forms), barren. ¶ Etym. unknown; the usual guess is, from Breton *brec'han,* sterile; but this is merely borrowed from French (Thurneysen).

BARRICADE, a hastily made fortification; also, as a verb, to fortify hastily. (F. — Span.) 'The bridge, the further end whereof was *barricaded* with barrells;' Hackluyt, Voyages, vol. ii. pt. ii. p. 142. — F. *barricade,* f., in Cotgrave *barriquade,* which he explains as 'a barricado, a defence of barrels, timber, pales, earth, or stones, heaped up, or closed together,' &c. β. The F. verb was *barriquer,* formed directly from *barrique,* a large barrel. But the F. sb. is clearly a mere borrowing from the Span. *barricada,* f., wrongly Englished as *barricado;* and this (supposed) Span. form appears in English also; e. g. 'they . . . *baricadoed* up their way;' Hackluyt, Voyages, iii. 568. The Span. *barricada* is formed as a pp. from a vb. *barricare,* which is from *barrica,* a barrel. Probably from Span. *barra,* a bar. See **Bar;** and cf. **Barrel.**

BARRIER, a boundary. (F. — Late L.) ME. *barrere,* in Lydgate, Siege of Thebes, pt. iii. l. 223; *barere* in E. E. Allit. Poems, B 1239. — OF. *barrere,* Godefroy (s. v. *bassein*); F. *barrière,* a barrier. — OF. *barrer,* to bar up. — OF. *barre,* a bar. See **Bar.**

BARRISTER, one who pleads at the bar. (F.; with E. suffix.) In Holland, Plutarch, p. 138. First found as *barrester* ab. 1545 (N. E. D.). Formed from the sb. *bar,* with suffixes *-ist-* and *-er;* or, more probably, from ME. *barre* with suffix *-ster.* Spelman cites a 16th cent. L. *barrasterius,* prob. from E. See **Bar.**

BARROW (1), a burial-mound. (E.) Sherwood, in his index to Cotgrave, has: 'A *barrow,* a hillock, *monceau de terre.*' ME. *bergh* (v. r. *berwe*), a hill, P. Plowman, C. viii. 227. 'Hul vel *beoruh,*' i. e. a hill or barrow, Wright's Vocab. i. 92. — AS. *beorge* (OMerc. *berge*), dat. of *beorh, beorg,* (1) a hill, (2) a grave-mound; Grein, i. 106. ✚ OSax., Du., G. *berg,* a hill. Teut. type *bergoz,* m. Further allied to Skt. *brhant-,* great, Pers. *burz,* high, Irish *brí,* W. *bre,* a hill; and to **Borough.**

BARROW (2), a wheelbarrow. (E.) ME. *barow, barowe,* Prompt. Parv. pp. 25, 105; *barewe,* Beket, l. 899 (ab. 1300). AS. *bearwe,* in comp. *meox-bearwe,* manure-barrow; Voc. 336. 8. — AS. *bar-* (*bær*), 2nd grade of the verb *beran,* to bear, carry; so that the signification is 'a vehicle.' Cf. EFries. *barfe,* a barrow; Low G. *barve* (Berghaus). See **Bear, Beir.**

BARTER, to traffic. (F. — C.?) ME. *bartryn,* to chaffer; Prompt. Parv. — OF. *bareter, barater;* Cotgrave has '*Barater,* to cheat, couzen, beguile . . . also, to truck, scourse, barter, exchange;' and Godefroy records the contracted form 'on *barta,*' with the sense 'barter,' in 1373. — OF. sb. *barat,* which Cotgrave explains by 'cheating, deceit; also a barter, &c.' Prob. of Celtic origin; cf. OIrish *mrath, brath,* treachery, W. *brad,* treachery, Gael. *brath,* betrayal; Irish and Gael. *bradach,* thievish; Stokes-Fick, p. 220. β. The suggestion of Diez, connecting *barat* with the Gk. πράσσειν, to do, is valueless. [Another meaning of *baret* in ME. is 'strife;' from Icel. *barátta,* strife.]

BARTISAN, a battlemented parapet. (F. — Teut.) A mistaken form due to Sir W. Scott. In Marmion, vi. 2. 21; &c. Due to ME. *bretasing;* the Catholicon Anglicum has: '*Bretasynge,* propugnaculum.' This is the mod. E. *brattic-ing;* see **Brattice.**

BARTON, a courtyard, manor; used in provincial English and in place-names and surnames. (E.) A compound word; from AS. *bere-tūn,* which occurs as a gloss for L. *aream* in the Lindisfarne MS., Matt. iii. 12. From AS. *bere,* barley; and *tūn,* a town, enclosure. See **Barley, Barn,** and **Town.**

BARYTES, older form of *baryta,* protoxide of barium, a heavy earth. (Gk.) Modern. So named from its weight. — Gk. βαρύτης, weight. — Gk. βαρύ-s, heavy; cognate with L. *grauis.* See **Grave.** Der. *baryt-a,* protoxide of barium, *barytes* being then used to mean sulphate of barium; *bari-um,* a newer coinage from Gk. βαρύs (N. E. D.).

BARYTONE, a grave tone, a deep tone; used of a male voice. (Ital. — Gk.) Also spelt *baritone.* An Italian musical term. — Ital. *baritono,* a baritone. — Gk. βαρύ-s, heavy (hence deep); and τόνοs, tone. See above; and see **Grave** and **Tone.**

BASALT, a kind of rock. (L.) Formerly *basaltes,* as in Holland's Pliny (1634), b. xxxvi. c. 7. — L. *basaltes,* a dark and very hard species of marble in Ethiopia; an African word. Pliny, Nat. Hist. 36. 7; cf. Strabo, 17, p. 818 (Lewis).

BASE (1), low, humble. (F. — L.) ME. *bass,* Gower, C. A. i. 98 (bk. i. l. 1678); *base,* Sir T. More, Works, p. 361 d. — F. *bas,* m., *basse,* fem. — Late L. *bassus.* β. Diez regards *bassus* as a genuine Latin word, meaning 'stout, fat' rather than 'short, low;' he says, and truly, that *Bassus* was a L. personal name at an early period. Der. *base-ness,*

base-minded, &c.; *a-base, a-base-ment; de-base; base-ment* (F. *sou-basse-ment,* Ital. *bassamento,* lit. *abasement*). And see **Bass** (1).

BASE (2), a foundation. (F. — L. — Gk.) ME. *bas, baas;* Chaucer, on the Astrolabie, ed. Skeat, ii. 41. 2; ii. 43. 2. — F. *base.* — L. *basis.* — Gk. βάσις, a going, a pedestal. For *βά-τις;* cf. Skt. *ga-ti-s,* a going. From Gk. βα-, allied to βαν- in βαίνειν (for *βάν-yειν), to go; from the same root as E. *come.* See **Come.** Der. *base-less, base-line.* Doublet, *basis.*

BASEMENT, lowest floor of a building. (F. — Ital. — L.) Appears in F. as *soubassement,* formerly *sousbassement;* a word made in the 16th cent., from *sous,* under, and *bassement,* borrowed from Ital. *bassamento,* of which the lit. sense is 'abasement' (Brachet, Torriano). Thus it belongs to the adj. *base,* not to the sb. See **Base** (1).

BASENET, a light helmet; see **Basnet.**

BASHAW, the same as **Pasha,** which see. (Pers.) Marlowe has *basso,* 1 Tamerlane, iii. 1. 1. Cf. F. *bachat,* 'a Bassa, a chief commander under the great Turk;' Cot.

BASHFUL, shy. (F. *and* E.) In Tempest, iii. 1. 81. From the verb *to bash* (Nares, ed. 1876), to be ashamed, which is short for *abash;* with the suffix *-ful.* See **Abash.**

BASIL (1), a kind of plant. (F. — L. — Gk.) '*Basil,* herb, *basilica;*' Levins, 124. 7. Spelt *basill* in Cotgrave. It is short for *basilic,* the last syllable being dropped. — F. *basilic,* 'the herb basill;' Cot. — L. *basilicum,* neut. of *basilicus,* royal. — Gk. βασιλικόs, royal; from Gk. βασιλεύs, a king. ¶ The G. name *königskraut,* i. e. king's wort, records the same notion.

BASIL (2), a bevelled edge; see **Bezel.**

BASIL (3), the hide of a sheep tanned. (F. — Span. — Arab.) Halliwell gives *basill lether,* mentioned in the Brit. Bibliographer, by Sir E. Bridges (1810), ii. 399. The form is corrupt, *l* being put for *n;* Johnson observes that a better spelling is *basen.* The Anglo-French form is *bazene, bazeyne,* Liber Custumarum, pp. 83, 84; also *bazain, bazein,* Gloss. to Liber Albus. — OF. *basanne,* given by Palsgrave as the equivalent of a 'schepskynne towed,' i. e. a tawed sheep-skin; *bazane,* Cotgrave; mod. F. *basane,* f. — Span. *badana,* a dressed sheep-skin. — Arab. *bitanat,* the [inner] lining of a garment; Rich. Dict. p. 276; because basil-leather was used for lining leathern garments. — Arab. root *batana,* to cover, hide (Freytag). Cf. Arab. *batn,* the belly, interior part, Rich. Dict. p. 277; Heb. *beten* (spelt with *teth*), the belly. See Littré; also Devic, Supplement to Littré; and Engelmann.

BASILICA, a palace, a large hall. (L. — Gk.) L. *basilica* (sc. *domus,* house), royal, fem. of *basilicus,* royal. — Gk. βασιλική (sc. στοά), a public building with colonnades, a church; fem. of βασιλικόs, royal. — Gk. βασιλεύs, a king. See below.

BASILISK, a kind of lizard or snake. (L. — Gk.) 'The serpent called a *basiliske;*' Holland's Pliny, bk. viii. c. 21. Also in E. E. Psalter (ab. 1300), Ps. xc. (xci.) 13. — L. *basiliscus;* same ref. — Gk. βασιλίσκοs, royal; from a white spot, resembling a crown, on the head (Pliny). — Gk. βασιλεύs, a king; of doubtful origin.

BASIN, a hollow circular vessel. (F. — Late L.) ME. *bacin, basin;* Seven Sages, ed. Weber, l. 2242; (used in the sense of helmet) King Alisaunder, l. 2333. — OF. *bacin* (F. *bassin,* m.); alluded to by Gregory of Tours, who cites it as a word of rustic use; '*pateræ quas vulgo bacchinon* vocant.' Romanic type *baccinum* (whence also Ital. *bacino,* Span. *bacin*); from Late L. *bacca,* a water-vessel (Isidore). Hence also Du. *bak,* a tray, trough, Dan. *bakke,* a tray. Der. *basn-et,* q.v.

BASIS, a foundation. (L. — Gk.) In Shak. Macb. iv. 3. 32; Beaum. and Fletcher, Valentinian, iv. 4. See **Base** (2).

BASK, to lie exposed to warmth. (Scand.) ME. *baske.* Palsgrave has — 'I *baske,* I bathe in water or any lycour.' β. It is certainly formed, like *busk,* from an Old Scand. source, the *-sk* being reflexive. The only question is whether it means 'to *bake* oneself' or 'to *bathe* oneself.' All evidence shows that it is certainly the latter. γ. Chaucer uses *bathe hire,* i. e. bathe herself, in the sense of *bask;* Nonne Prestes Tale, l. 447; and see Gower, C. A. i. 290 (bk. iii. ll. 312–15); and the quotation above. δ. The derivation is then from an OScand. *baðask* (for *baða sik*), to bathe oneself, now represented by Icel. *baðast,* to bathe oneself, with the common change of final *-sk* to *-st.* For loss of ð, cf. *or* for *other.* See **Bath,** and **Busk.**

BASKET, a vessel made of flexible materials. (F.) ME. *basket;* Chaucer, C. T., 12379 (C. 445). Sometimes said to be Celtic; but W. *basged,* a basket, Corn. *basced,* Irish *basceid,* Gael. *bascaid,* are merely borrowed from English; and the oft-quoted Celto-L. *bascauda* (Martial, Juvenal) gave rise to OF. *bachoe, bachoue,* a basket (Godefroy, Cotgrave), which greatly differs in form. β. Certainly French; the AF. form *basket* (with the characteristic AF. pl. *baskes*) appears in A. Neckam (ab. 1200); see Wright's Voc. i. 98, 6; 111, 2. The suffix *-et* is also usually French. But no such word has been recorded in O. French of the continent; unless we may consider the OF. *baste,* a basket, noted by Godefroy, to be allied to it. γ. The

AF. word may have been suggested by E. *bast*; cf. prov. E. *bass*, bast, also a mat, hassock, basket made of matting; *bastik*, a basket.

BASNET, BASSENET, BASSINET, a kind of light helmet. (F. – Late L.) Spelt *bassenet* in Halliwell, who gives several examples; *basenet* in Spenser, F. Q. vi. 1. 31. ME. *basinet*, Rich. Cuer de Lion, 403; *bacynet*, id. 5266; *basnet*, King Alisaunder, 2234. – OF. *bacinet* (Burguy, Roquefort); spelt *bassinet* in Cot., who explains it by 'a small bason, also a head-peece.' Dimin. of OF. *bacin*, a basin; see **Basin**.

BASS (1), the lowest part in a musical composition. (F. – L.) Shak. has *base*, generally printed *bass*; Tam. of Shrew, iii. 1. 46. Cotgrave has : '*Basse, contre*, the base part in music.' Sherwood has : 'The base in musick, *basse, basse-contre*.' – F. *basse*, fem. of *bas*, low ; cf. Ital. *basso*, which has influenced the spelling, but not the sound. See **Base** (1).   Der. *bass-relief* (Ital. *bassorilievo*).

BASS (2), **BARSE**; names of a fish. (E.) These are, radically, the same word. We make little real difference in sound between words like *pass* and *parse*. 'A *barse*, fishe, *tincha*;' Levins, 33. 13. ME. *bace*, a fish; Prompt. Parv. p. 20; see Way's note. AS. *bærs*, lupus vel scardo; Voc. 180. 26.+Du. *baars*, a perch; G. *bars, barsch*, a perch. Orig. applied to the perch, and named from its prickles. From **bars*, 2nd grade of Teut. root **bers*, whence also **Bristle**, q.v. Cf. Skt. *bhṛṣṭi-*, pointed.

BASSOON, a deep-toned musical instrument. (F. – L.) Not in early use. In Bailey's Dict., ed. 1735. Borrowed from F. *basson*, a bassoon; formed, with augmentative suffix *-on*, from *basse*, bass. See **Bass** (1), **Base** (1).

BAST, the inner bark of the lime-tree, or matting made of it. (E.) ME. *bast*; 'Hec tilia, *baste-tre*,' Vocab. 647. 11. AS. *bæst*, a lime-tree ; Vocab. 51. 2. Cf. Icel., Swed., Dan., Du., G. *bast*, bast. ☞ Sometimes corrupted to *bass*; see **Basket**.

BASTARD, a child of parents not married; illegitimate, false. (F. – Late L.) 'William *bastard*,' i.e. William the Conqueror; Rob. of Glouc. p. 295 (l. 5970). – OF. *bastard, bastart*, of which the etymology has been much disputed. β. The ending *-ard* is common in OF. (and even in English, cf. *cow-ard, drunk-ard*, the E. suffix having been borrowed from French). This suffix is certainly OHG., viz. the OHG. *-hart*, hard, first used as a suffix in proper names, such as *Regin-hart* (whence E. *reynard*), *Eber-hart* (whence E. *Everard*). In French words this suffix assumed first an intensive, and secondly, a sinister sense ; see examples in Pref. to Brachet's Etym. F. Dict. sect. 196. γ. It is now ascertained that OF. *bastard* meant 'a son of a *bast*' (not of a bed), where *bast* is the mod. F. *bât*, a pack-saddle, from Late L. *bastum*, a pack-saddle. See Ducange, who quotes : '*Sagma*, sella quam vulgus *bastum* vocat, super quo componuntur sarcinæ.' Brachet refers to M. G. Paris, Histoire poétique de Charlemagne, p. 441, for further information. The phrase *fils de bast*, 'pack-saddle child,' was quite common ; see *Bast* in Godefroy. Cf. 'thei [though] he were *abast* ibore,' i.e. born on bast ; Rob. of Glouc. p. 516 (l. 10629). ¶ The word was very widely spread after the time of William I, on account of his exploits, and found its way into nearly all the Celtic dialects, and into Icelandic. Scheler quotes OF. *coitr-art*, a bastard, lit. 'son of a *coitre* or quilt,' and G. *bank-art*, 'son of a bench;' see **Bantling**.

BASTE (1), vb., to beat, strike. (Scand.) We find 'basting and bear-baiting;' Hudibras, pt. ii. c. 1, l. 36. Also 'he has *basted* me;' Ben Jonson, Every Man, iv. 4. – Swed. dial. *basta*, to strike, to beat (Rietz, p. 25, col. 2); cf. *basta*, a beating (ibid.); MDan. *bastig*, adj., beating, striking; perhaps an extension from Swed. *basa*, to strike, beat, flog. Cf. Dan. *baske*, prov. E. *bash*, to beat.

BASTE (2), to pour fat over meat. (F. – Late L.) It occurs in Palsgrave, p. 442 ; in Gammer Gurton's Needle, i. 1 ; and in Shak., Com. Errors, ii. 2. 59. 'To baste, *linire*;' Levins, 36. 22. It appears to be only a particular use of OF. *bastir*, to build ; for in Du Wez, Supp. to Palsgrave, p. 938, we find these entries : 'To buylde, *baatir* (sic ; for *bastir*); 'To cast butter upon rost, *bastir*.' See **Bastile**.

BASTE (3), to sew slightly. (F. – OHG.) ME. *basten, bastyn*; Prompt. Parv. p. 26; Rom. of the Rose, l. 104. – OF. *bastir*, F. *bâtir*, to baste, which is distinct (according to Littré and Hatzfeld) from *bâtir*, to build. – MHG. *bestan* (for **bastjan*), to bind. – OHG. *bast*, the inner bark of the lime-tree. So also Dan. *baste*, to tie, to bind with bast; to pinion; from Dan. *bast*, bast. See **Bast**.

BASTILE, a fortress. (F. – Prov. – Late L.) Chiefly used of the *bastile* in Paris. – OF. *bastille*, a building. – Prov. *bastida*, the same, with change of suffix (Hatzfeld). – Late Lat. *bastire*, to build ; whence OF. *bastir*, to build. Usually referred to the same root as **Baton**, q.v.

BASTINADO, a sound beating ; to beat. (Span. – Late L.) Shak. has *bastinado* as a sb. ; K. John, ii. 463. – Span. *bastonada*, a beating with a stick. – Span. *baston*, a stick, staff, baton. See **Baton**.

BASTION, part of a fortification. (F. – Ital. – Prov. – Late L.)

In Howell, bk. i. letter 42 ; and in Goldsmith, Citizen of the World (R.) – F. *bastion*, introduced in the 16th century from Ital. *bastione* (Brachet) ; which is the augmentative of Ital. *bastia*, a building, fort, rampart. – Prov. *bastia, bastida*, the same. – Late L. *bastire*, to build. See **Bastile**.

BAT (1), a short cudgel. (E.) ME. *ba'te*, Prompt. Parv. p. 26; *botte*, Ancren Riwle, p. 366; Layamon, 21593. AS. *batt* ; in Napier's Glosses. Cf. Irish *bata, bat*, a staff. Prob. allied to **Batter** (1). Der. *bat-let* (with dimin. suffix *-let = -el-et*), a small bat for beating washed clothes; Shak., As You Like It, ii. 4. 49. Also *bat*, verb; Prompt. Parv.

BAT (2), a winged mammal. (Scand.) Corrupted from ME. *bakke*. The Prompt. Parv. has '*Bakke*, flyinge best [beast], *vespertilio*.' Wyclif (in some MSS.) has *backe*, Levit. xi. 19. – Dan. *bakke*, only used in the comp. *aftenbakke*, evening-bat. For change of *k* to *t*, cf. *apricot* for *apricock*. β. There is also an older form *blakke*, seen in Icel. *leðrblaka* = a 'leather-flapper,' a bat. – Icel. *blaka*, to flutter, flap. The equivalence of the forms is clearly shown by MSwed. *natt-backa*, lit. 'night-bat;' as compared with Swed. dial. *natt-blakka* and *natt-batta*. The form *blak*, a bat, occurs even in ME., viz. in Rob. Brunne, Handl. Synne, l. 11863, but is recorded neither by Stratmann nor in the N. E. D. Cf. also MDan. *natbakka*, a bat. ¶ The AS. word is *hrēremūs*, whence prov. Eng. *reremouse, rearmouse*.

BATCH, a quantity of bread. (E.) A *batch* is what is baked at once; hence, generally, a quantity, a collection. ME. *bacche*; '*bahche*, or bakynge, or *batche*, pistura;' Prompt. Parv. p. 21. Here *batche* is a later substitution for an older *bacche*, due to an AS. form **bæcce*; clearly a derivative of AS. *bac-an*, to bake. See **Bake**.

BATE (1), to abate, diminish. (F. – L.) Shak. has *bate*, to beat down, diminish, remit, &c. ; in many passages. We find too : '*Batyn*, or abaten of weyte or mesure, *subtraho*;' Prompt. Parv. p. 26. ME. *bate*, R. Brunne, tr. of Langtoft, p. 338. Merely a contraction of *abate*, borrowed from OF. *abatre*, to beat down. See **Abate**.

BATE (2), strife. (F. – L.) Shak. has 'breeds no *bate*;' 2 Hen. IV, ii. 4. 271 ; also *bate-breeding*, Ven. and Adonis, 655. '*Batyn*, or make debate, *jurgor*;' Prompt. Parv. p. 26. ME. *bat, bate*, Cov. Myst. p. 12 ; Gawain and the Grene Knight, l. 1461. It is agreed that *bate* is a mere contraction of the common old word *debate*, used in precisely the same sense ; borrowed from the OF. *debat*, strife ; a derivative of *battre*, to beat. See **Batter** (1).

BATH, a place for washing in. (E.) ME. *baþ*, Ormulum, 18044. AS. *bæð* (Grein). + Icel. *bað*; OHG. *bad, pad*; MSwed. *bad* (Ihre) ; Du., Dan. *bad*. Teut. type **ba-ðom*, neut. The OHG. appears to have a still older source in the OHG. vb. **bājan, bāhen*, to warm (G. *bähen*, to foment).

BATHE, to use a bath. (E.) The AS. *baðian*, to bathe, is a derivative from *bæð*, a bath ; not *vice versâ*. Der. *bask*.

BATHOS, lit. depth. (Gk.) Ludicrously applied to a descent from the elevated to the mean in poetry or oratory. See the allusion, in a note to Appendix I to Pope's Dunciad, to A Treatise of the *Bathos*, or Art of Sinking in Poetry. – Gk. βάθος, depth ; cf. Gk. βαθύς, deep.

BATON, BATOON, a cudgel. (F. – Late L.) Spelt *battoon* in Sir T. Herbert's Travels, ed. 1665, p. 149; *batune* in Phillips' Dict., ed. 1658; *battoone* in Davenant, Long Vacation in London, l. 9. – F. *bâton*, a cudgel. – OF. *baston*. – Late L. acc. *bastōnem*, from *basto*, a stick; of unknown origin. Diez suggests a connexion with Gk. βαστάζειν, to support. **Doublet**, *batten* (2).

BATTALION, a body of armed men. (F. – Ital. – Late L.) Milton has it ; P. L. i. 569. – F. *bataillon*, introduced, says Brachet, in the 16th cent. from Ital. *battaglione*; which was formed from Ital. *battaglia*, a battle, by adding the augment. suffix *-one*. See **Battle**.

BATTEN (1), to grow fat ; to fatten. (Scand.) Shak. has *batten*, to feed gluttonously (intransitive), Hamlet, iii. 4. 67 ; but Milton has '*battening* our flocks,' Lycidas, l. 29. Strictly, it is intransitive. – Icel. *batna*, to grow better, recover ; as distinguished from *bæta*, trans., to improve, make better.+Goth. *gabatnan*, to profit, avail, Mark, vii. 11, intrans.; as distinguished from *bōtjan*, trans., to avail, Mark, viii. 36. Both Icel. *batna* and Goth. *gabatnan* are formed from the Teut. base BAT, good, preserved in the E. *better* and *best*. See **Better**. ¶ Cf. also Du. *baten*, to yield profit; *baat*, profit.

BATTEN (2), a wooden rod. (F. – Late L.) '*Batten*, a scantling of wood, 2, 3, or 4 in. [or 7] broad, seldom above 1 thick, and the length unlimited;' Moxon ; in Todd's Johnson. Hence, to *batten down*, to fasten down with *battens*. A mere variant of *batton* or *baton*. See **Baton**.

BATTER (1), to beat. (F. – L.) ME. *bateren, batren*, P. Plowman, B. iii. 198; formed with frequentative suffix *-er* from a base *bat-*. – F. *battre*, to beat. – L. *battere*, a popular form of *battuere*, to beat. See **Battle**. Der. *batter* (2), *batter-y*, *batter-ing-ram*.

BATTER (2), a compound of eggs, flour, and milk. (F. – L.)

ME. *batowre*, Prompt. Parv., p. 27 ; *bature*, Catholicon. — OF. *bature*, a beating. — OF. *battre*, to beat. See above. So called from being *beaten* up together ; Wedgwood. So, too, Span. *batido*, batter, is the pp. of *batir*, to beat.

BATTERY, a beating ; a place for cannon ; a number of cannon in position. (F. — L.) See Twelfth Night, iv. 1. 36 ; Hen. V, iii. 3. 7. Cotgrave has : ' *Baterie* (also *Batterie*), a beating ; a battery ; a platform for battery.' — F. *battre*, to beat. See **Batter** (1). ¶ The AF. *baterie* (legal term) occurs in the Stat. of the Realm, i. 48 (an. 1278).

BATTLE, a combat. (F. — L.) ME. *bataille*, *bataile*, Chaucer, Leg. of Good Wom. 1631 ; King Horn, 574. — OF. *bataille*, meaning both (1) a fight, (2) a battalion. — Folk-L. *bat ālia*, neut. pl. (turned into a fem. sing.), fights ; Late L. *battuālia*, neut. pl. of adj. *battuālis*, fighting. — L. *battuere*, to beat. **Der.** *battal-ion*, q. v.

BATTLEDOOR, a bat with a thin handle. (South F. — L.) ' *Batyldoure*, a wasshynge betylle,' i. e. a bat for beating clothes whilst being washed, Prompt. Parv. p. 27. **a.** A corrupted form ; borrowed from the Provençal (South French) *batedor*, meaning exactly a washing-beetle, a bat for clothes ; cf. Span. *batidor*, the same. [The English held Bordeaux till 1451.] Once imported into English, the first two syllables were easily corrupted into *battle*, a dimin. of *ba'*, leaving *-door* meaningless. Cf. *crayfish*. Note prov. E. *batling-stone*, a stone on which wet linen was beaten to cleanse it ; *battling-stick* or *batlet*, a battledoor for washing. **β.** Formed from Prov. *batre*, Span. *batir*, to beat ; the suffix *-dor* in Span. and Prov. answers to the L. acc. suffix *-tōrem*, as in *amā-tōrem*, acc. of *amā-tor*, a lover. See **Batter** (1).

BATTLEMENT, a parapet for fortification. (F.) ME. *batel-ment*, Allit. Poems, ed. Morris, B. 1459. ' *Batylment* of a walle, *propugnaculum* ;' Promp. Parv. p. 27. As if from an OF. *ba'aillement*, formed from the verb *batailler*, *bateillier*, to fortify, to furnish with battlements, called in OF. *batailles*, a peculiar use of the pl. of *bataille*. a battle (Godefroy) ; see **Battle**. Thus ' mur bataillé,' an embattled wall, occurs in the Rom. de la Rose, l. 131 ; cf. Chaucer's translation, l. 139. But probably confused with a later OF. *batillement* (Godefroy), a redoubt, formed from OF. *bastiller*, to fortify. See **Battle** and **Bastile** ; and see **Embattle**.

BAUBLE (1), a fool's mace. (F.) This seems to be the same as *bauble*, a plaything. Palsgrave has : ' *Bable* for a foole, *marotte*.' ' As he that with his *babil* pleide ;' Gower, C. A. iii. 224 : bk. vii. 3955. — OF. *baubel*, *babel*, a child's plaything (Godefroy) ; perhaps connected with MItal. *babbola*, a toy (Florio), and with L. *babulus*, a fool. Cf. E. **Babble**. **β.** Prob. a distinct word from ME. *babulle*, *bable*, ' Librilla, pegma,' in Prompt. Parv. p. 20. As to this *bable*, see Way's note in Prompt. Parv., showing that *librilla* means a stick with a thong, for weighing meat, or for use as a sling ; and *pegma* means a stick with a weight suspended from it, for inflicting blows with. Perhaps so called from the wagging or swinging motion with which it was employed ; from the verb ' *bablyn*, or *babelyn*, or *waveryn*, *librillo* ;' Prompt. Parv. p. 20. We also find, at the same reference, ' *babelynge*, or *wauerynge*, *vacillacio*, *librillacio*.' Were this verb still in use, we might equate it to prov. E. *bobble*, to bob up and down, formed, as many frequentatives are, by adding the suffix *-le*. It is prob. imitative. See **Bob**.

BAUBLE (2), a plaything. (F.) Shak. has *bauble* in the sense of a trifle, a useless plaything, Tam. Shrew, iv. 3. 82. — OF. *baubel*, a plaything (Godefroy) ; also spelt *babel*. See **Bauble** (1) above.

BAVIN, a faggot. (F.) Prov. E. *bavin*, a faggot, brushwood ; hence, as adj., soon kindled and burnt out, 1 Hen. IV, iii. 2. 61. ' *Bauen*, great fagottes ;' Palsgrave (1530). — OF. *baffe*, a faggot, bundle (Godefroy, Roquefort). Remoter origin unknown.

BAWD, a lewd person. (F. — G.) ME. *baude*, Chaucer, C. T. 6936 (D 1354). But it is a contracted form ; the full form being *bawdstrot*, P. Plowm. A. iii. 42 (another MS. has *bawde*). — OF. *baldestrot*, *baudestrot*, found only in the later form *baudetrot*, as a gloss to L. *pronuba*, a bride-woman. — OHG. *bald*, bold, gay, lively (cognate with E. *bold*) ; and MHG. *strotzen*, to strut about, to be puffed up (cognate with E. *strut*). See **Bold**. **Der.** *bawd-y*, *bawd-i-ness* ; *baud-r-y* [distinct from OF. *bauderie*, *balderie*, vivacity] ; see below.

BAWDY, lewd. (F. — G.) Merely formed as an adj. from *bawd* ; see above. ¶ But the ME. *baudy*, dirty, used of clothes, in Chaucer and P. Plowman, is a different word, and may be of Celtic origin. Cf. W. *bawaidd*, dirty ; *baw*, dirt. The two words, having something of the same meaning, were easily assimilated in form.

BAWL, to shout. (Scand.) Sir T. More has ' yalping [yelping] and balling ;' Works, p. 1254 c. Cf. ' Baffynge or *bawlynge* of howndys ;' Prompt. Parv. p. 20. — Swed. *böla*, to low ; MDan. *bole*, to low ; mod. Icel. *baula*, to low ; Icel. *baul*, a cow. Of imitative origin. ✛ Low G. *bölen*, to bawl (Berghaus).

BAY (1), a reddish brown. (F. — L.) ME. *bay* ; ' a stede *bay*,' a bay horse ; Chaucer, C. T. 2159 (A 2157). — OF. *bai*. — L. *badius*, bay-coloured, in Varro. Cf. Gael. and Irish *buidhe*, OIrish *buide*, yellow. **Der.** *bay-ard* (a bay-horse) ; *baize*, q.v.

BAY (2), a kind of laurel-tree ; prop. a berry-tree. (F. — L.) ' The roiall lawrel is a very tal and big tree, with leaues also as large in proportion, and the *baies* or berries (*baccæ*) that it beareth are nothing [not at all] sharp, biting, and vnpleasant in tast ;' Holland's Pliny, b. xv. c. 30. ' *Bay*, frute, *bacca* ;' Prompt. Parv. — F. *baie*, a berry. — L. *bāca* (less correctly *bacca*), a berry. ¶ Cf. AF. ' *bayes de lorer* = *bacce lauri* ;' Alphita.

BAY (3), an inlet of the sea. (F. — L.) *Bay* occurs in Surrey, tr. of the Æneid, bk. ii. 31 ; ME. *baye*, Trevisa, tr. of Higden, i. 57. — F. *baie*, an inlet. — L. *baia*, in Isidore of Seville ; see Brachet and Ducange. **Der.** *bay-salt*.

BAY (4), an opening in a wall, esp. the space between two columns ; a division in a barn. (F. — L.) In Meas. for Meas. ii. 1. 255. ' Heye houses withinne the halle. . . . So brod bilde in a *bay* ;' Allit. Poems, B. 1392. — F. *baie* (for *baée*) ; AF. *baee*, a gap in a wall, P. de Thaun, Livre des Creatures, 38 ; pp. fem. of OF. *baer*, MF. *bayer*, to gape. Cf. Ital. *badare*, ' to delay, to gape idly,' Florio. — Late L. *badāre*, to gape. Sometimes confused with **Bay** (3).

BAY (5), to bark as a dog. (F. — L.) ' The dogge wolde *bay* ;' Berners' Froissart, vol. ii. c. 171. ' Braches *bayed*,' hounds bayed ; Gawain and Grene Knight, 1142. [Also common in the derived form ; ME. *abayen*, K. Alisaunder, 3882 ; from OF. *abaier*, MF. ' *abbayer*, to bark or bay at ;' Cot. ; F. *aboyer*.] — OF. *a* (L. *ad*), and *baier*, to yelp (Godefroy) ; cf. MItal. *baiare*, ' to barke,' Florio ; answering to a Late L. type *badiāre*, (Hatzfeld), prob. from *badāre*, to gape. See **Bay** (4).

BAY (6), in phr. *at bay*. (F. — L.) ' He folowed the chace of an hert, and . . . broughte hym to a *bay* ;' Fabyan, Chron. c. 127. Here ' to a *bay*' is really a corruption of ' to *abay* ;' cf. ' Wher hy hym myghte, so hound *abaye*, . . . bygile ' = where they might, like a hound at bay, beguile him ; King Alisaunder, ed. Weber, 3882 ; see also *abay* in N. E. D. ; and see further below. — OF. *abai*, pl. *abais* ; F. *abois*, *abbois*. Cotgrave says—' a stag is said *rendre les abbois* when, weary of running, he turns upon the hounds, and holds them at, or puts them to, *a bay*.' The same is also expressed by the phrase *être aux abois* ; see *aboi* in Brachet. The original sense of OF. *abai* is the bark of a dog. Cotgrave has ' *Abbay*, the barking or baying of dogs ;' ' *Abbois*, barkings, bayings ;' for the OF. *abai*, *abaier*, see *aboi*, *aboyer* in Littré. See **Bay** (5), to bark.

BAYADERE, a Hindoo dancing-girl. (F. — Port. — Late L.) Spelt *balliadera* (1598) ; *bayadere* (1826). — F. *bayadère*. — Port. *baila-deira*, a dancing girl. — Port. *bailar*, to dance. See **Ball** (2).

BAYARD, a horse ; orig. a bay horse. (F. — L.) See **Bay** (1).

BAYONET, a dagger at the end of a gun. (F.) Used by Burke ; Select Works, ed. E. J. Payne, i. 111, l. 15. Introduced in the 17th century, from F. *baionnette*, formerly *bayonette*, which at first meant a short flat dagger. So called from Bayonne, in France, where such daggers were first made ; see *bayonette* in Cotgrave, and see Hatzfeld. The bayonet was used at Killiecrankie in 1689, and at Marsaglia by the French, in 1693. See Haydn, Dict. of Dates.

BAY-WINDOW, a window within a recess. (Hybrid ; F. *and* Scand.) ' Within a *bay-window* ;' Court of Love, 1058 ; ' With *bay-windowes* ;' Assembly of Ladies, 163. From **Bay** (4) and **Window**. The modern *bow-window*, i.e. window with a curved or bowed outline, is an independent word.

BAZAAR, a market. (Pers.) Spelt *buzzar* by Sir T. Herbert, in his Travels, where he speaks of ' the great *buzzar* or market ;' ed. 1665, p. 41. — Pers. *bāzār*, a market. See Palmer's Pers. Dict. col. 65 ; Horn, § 166.

BDELLIUM, a precious substance. (L. — Gk. — Skt. ?) In Gen. ii. 12, it is joined with ' gold ' and ' onyx-stone ;' in Numb. xi. 7, manna is likened to it in colour. In Holland's Pliny, xii. 9, it is the gum of a tree, or the palm-tree that yields it, *Borassus flabelliformis* (Lewis) ; and Pliny also calls it *maldacon*. — L. *bdellium*. — Gk. βδέλλιον ; also βδέλλα. Other forms are βδολχόν, μάδελκον (whence L. *maldacon*) ; which Lassen derives from a supposed Skt. *madālaka*, from Skt. *mada-s*, m., musk. The Gk. βδολχόν corresponds to the Heb. *bĕdōlakh*, which see in Gesenius, Heb. Lex. 8th ed., p. 93.

BE-, *prefix*. (E.) AS. *be-*, prefix ; in very common use. It sometimes implies ' to make,' as in *be-foul*, to make foul. ' It sometimes serves to locate the act, and sometimes intensifies ;' Affixes of English Words, by S. S. Haldeman, p. 49. *Behead* means to deprive of the head ; *beset*, to set upon, attack ; *besiege*, to sit by or around, to invest with an army ; *bemire*, to cover with mire. Cf. *becalm*, *bedim*, *bedeck*, *bedrop* ; also *become*, *befall*, i. e. to come upon, to fall upon. Also used as a prefix of prepositions ; as in *before*, *between*. *Beside* = by the side of. *Below* = by low, on the lower side of ; so also *beneath*, on the nether side of. The AS. *be-* or *bi-* (ME. *be-*, *bi-*) is a weak or unstressed form of the prep. *bi*, E. *by*. See **By**.

BE, to exist. (E.) ME. *been*, Prompt. Parv. 30. AS. *bēon*, to be (*pass.im*).+Du. *ben*, I am; G. *bin*, I am; Irish *bu*, was; Russian *buite*, to be; *bu-du*, I shall be; L. *fore*, pt. t. *fui*; Gk. φύειν, aor. ἔφυν; Skt. *bhū*, to be.—√BHEU, to exist. See also **Are, Was**.

BEACH, a shore; esp. of the sea. (E.) Orig. a ridge of shingle, or shingle. Not found in early authors. 'The pibbles on the hungry beach;' Cor. v. 3. 58. 'A barre of *beach* or peeble-stones;' Hackluyt, Voyages, i. 355. Etym. doubtful, but perhaps the same as prov. E. *bache*, a river, also a sandbank or ridge by a river (E. D. D.); ME. *bache*. From AS. *bæce*, dat. of *bæc*, a valley; cf. 'of þam diopan *bæce*;' Birch, Cart. Sax. iii. 344, 646; to þam *bæce*, id. iii. 52; tō gīsles *bæce*, id. ii. 167. **Der.** *beach*, verb; *beach-y*, 2 Hen. IV, iii. 1. 50.

BEACON, a sign, signal. (E.) ME. *bekene*, P. Plowman, B. xvii. 262. AS. *bēacen*, a sign, signal, standard (Grein); also spelt *bēcn*.+OSax. *bōkan*; MHG. *bouchen*; OHG. *pouhhan*, a sign. Teut. type **bauknom*, neut. See **Beck, Beckon**.

BEAD, a perforated ball, used for counting prayers. (E.) The old sense is 'a prayer;' and the *bead* was so called because used for counting prayers; and not *vice versâ*. ME. *bede*, a bead; Chaucer, Prol. 159. 'Thanne he hauede his *bede* seyd'=when he had said his *prayer*; Havelok, 1385. AS. *bed-*, in comp., a prayer; gen. used in the form *gebed* (cf. G. *gebet*), Grein, i. 376.+Du. *bede*, an entreaty, request; *gebed*, a prayer; G. *bitte*, a request; *gebet*, a prayer, request. These are derived words from the verb; viz. AS. *biddan*, Du. *bidden*, OHG. *pit an* (G. *bitten*), to pray. Cf. Goth. *bida*, a prayer; *bidjan*, to pray. See **Bid** (1). **Der.** *bead-roll*, spelt *beadroule* in Tyndal's Works, p. 102, col. 2, ed. 1572; *beads-man*, Two Gent. of Verona, i. 1. 18.

BEADLE, properly, one who proclaims. (F. – Teut.) ME. *bedel*, P. Plowman, B. ii. 109; *bedele*, Cursor Mundi, 11006.—OF. *bedel*, a herald; F. *bedeau*, 'a beadle,' Cot.—MHG. *bütel*, OHG. *butil*, a proclaimer; but Latinised as *bidellus* (E. *bedell*), as if from OHG. *bitel*, one who a-ks.—OHG. *but-*, weak grade of *biotan*, to proclaim, cognate with AS. *bēodan*, whence AS. *bydel*, a herald; see **Bid** (2).

BEAGLE, a small dog, for hunting hares. (F. – L.?) ME. *begele*; Hall's Chron. Hen. VI, an. 28. § 3; *begle*, Squire of Low Degree, 771. Of uncertain origin. The index to Cotgrave has '*Beagle*, petite chienne.' Cf. '*Begle*, canicula;' Levins, 53, 43. It would seem to be an AF. fem. sb. Dr. Murray compares it with OF. *beegueule*, a noisy importunate person, lit. 'open mouth;' Late L. *baḍāta g la*; see **Bay** (4).

BEAK, a bill, point. (F. – C.) ME. *beke*, Chaucer, Leg. of Good Wom , 148; *bec*, Bestiary, 58 (ab. 1220).—F. *bec*.—Low L. *beccus*, quoted by Suetonius as of Gaulish origin (Brachet); and Thurneysen suggests a connexion with Irish *bacc*, W. *bach*, a crook, a hook.

BEAKER, a sort of cup. (Scand. – L. – Gk.) ME. *byker*, *biker*; Prompt. Parv. p. 35. Way notes that the word occurs as early as A.D. 1348.—Icel. *bikarr*, a cup.+Du. *beker*; G. *becher*; Ital. *bicchiere*. β. It appears in Late L. as *bicārium*, a wine-cup; a word formed from Gk. βῖκος, an earthen wine-vessel, whence also the dimin. forms βικίον, βικίδιον. γ. The Gk. βῖκος is of Eastern origin (Liddell). **Doublet**, *pitcher*.

BEAM (1), a piece of timber. (E.) ME. *beem*, *bem*, *beam*; Ch. C. T., B 4362 (l. 15178); Layamon, 2848. AS. *bēam*, a tree; Grein, p. 105.+OHG. *boum*, G. *baum*, a tree; Du. *boom*. Cf. also Icel. *baðmr*, a tree; Goth. *bagms*, a tree.

BEAM (2), a ray of light. (E.) A particular use of the word above. The 'pillar of fire' mentioned in Exodus is called in AS. poetry *byrnende bēam*, the burning beam; Grein, p. 105. **Der.** *beam-y*, *beam-less*.

BEAN, a kind of plant. (E.) ME. *bene*, Chaucer, C. T. 3770 (A 3772). AS. *bēan* (Lye, Bosworth).+Du. *boon*; Icel. *baun*; OHG. *pōna*; G. *bohne*. Teut. type **baunā*, fem.

BEAR (1), to carry. (E.) ME. *beren*, *bere*, P. Plowman, B. ii. 80. AS. *beran* (Grein).+Goth. *bairan*; OHG. *beran*; cognate with L. *ferre*; Gk. φέρειν; Skt. *bhṛ*, to bear; OIrish *ber-im*, I bear; Russ. *brate*, to take, carry; Pers. *burdan*, to bear.—√BHER, to carry. **Der.** *bear-able*, *bear-er*, *bear-ing*; *barrow* (2), *bier*, *birth*, *bore* (3), *burden* (1); and cf. *berth*.

BEAR (2), an animal. (E.) ME. *bere*, Chaucer, C. T., A 1640. AS. *bera*, ursus (Grein).+Du. *beer*; Icel. *bera*, *björn*; OHG. *pero*, *bero*, G. *bär*. Teut. type **beron-*, masc. Further allied to Russ. *ber-* in *ber-loga*, a bear's lair or den; Skt. *bhallas* (for **bhar-las*), a bear. Named from its colour. Cf. Lith. *bēras*, brown (Kluge).

BEARD, hair on the chin. (E.) ME. *berde*, *berd*; Chaucer, Prol. 332. AS. *beard*, Grein, i. 102.+Du. *baard*; G. *bart*. Teut. type **bardoz*, m. Allied to Russ. *boroda*; Lith. *barzda*; L. *barba*, the beard; from Idg. type **bhardhā*, fem. Brugm. i. § 972. **Der.** *beard-ed*, *beard-less*.

BEAST, an animal. (F. – L.) ME. *beste*, Chaucer, C. T. 1978 (A 1976); *beaste*, Old Eng. Homilies, i. 277.—OF. *beste* (F. *bête*).—L. *bestia*, an animal. **Der.** *beast-like*, *beast-ly*, ME. *beestli*, Wyclif, 1 Cor. xv. 44, to tr. L. *animāle*; *beast-li-ness*, *best-i-al* (L. *bestiālis*), *best-i-al-i-ty*, *best-i-al-ise*.

BEAT, to strike. (E.) ME. *beten*, *bete*, P. Plowman, B. xiv. 19. AS. *bēatan*, to beat; Grein, i. 106.+Icel. *bauta*, to beat; OHG. *pōzan*, MHG. *bōzen*, to beat. Teut. type **bautan-*. **Der.** *beat*, sb., *beat-er*, *beetle* (2). ¶ The resemblance to F. *battre*, L. *batuere*, is accidental.

BEATIFY, to make blessed. (F. – L.) Bp. Taylor has '*beatified* spirits;' vol. i. ser. 8.—MF. *beatifier*, 'to beatifie; to make blessed, sacred, or happy;' Cot.—L. *beātificāre*, to make happy.—L. *beāti-*, for *beātus*, happy; and *facere*, to make, the stem *fac-* becoming *fic-* in composition. *Beātus* is a pp. of *beāre*, to make happy, to bless. **Der.** *beatific*, Milton, P. L. i. 684, *beatific-al*, *beatific-al-ly*, *beatific-at-ion*.

BEATITUDE, happiness. (F. – L.) Used by Ben Jonson, Eupheme, ix. 137; Milton, P. L. iii. 62.—MF. *beatitude*, 'beatitude, happiness;' Cot.—L. *beātitūdinem*, acc. from nom. *beātitūdo*, happiness.—L. *beātus*, happy.—L. *beāre*, to bless. See **Beatify**.

BEAU, a fine, dressy man. (F. – L.) Sir Cloudesley Shovel is represented on his tomb 'by the figure of a *beau*;' Spectator, no. 26; cf. ME. *beau*, adj., as in *beau sir*, Ch., H. Fame, 643.—F. *beau*, comely (Cotgrave); OF. *bel*.—L. *bellum*, acc. of *bellus*, fine, fair; supposed to be a contracted form of **benlus*, dimin. of **benus*, related by gradation to *bonus*, good; cf. L. *bene*, well. See **Bounty**. **Der.** From the F. fem. form *belle* (L. *bella*) we have E. *belle*.

BEAUTY, fairness. (F. – L.) ME. *beauté*, Chaucer, C. T. 2387 (A 2385).—OF. *biaute*, *beltet*.—Late L. acc. *bellitātem*; from nom. *bellitās*, fairness.—L. *belli-*, for *bellus*, fair, with suffix *-tāt-*, signifying state or condition. See **Beau**. **Der.** *beaute-ous* (*bewteous* in Sir T. More, Works, p. 2 g), *beaute-ous-ly*, *beaute-ous-ness*, *beauti-ful*, Shak. Sonnet 106, *beauti-ful-ly*, *beauti-fy*.

BEAVER (1), an animal. (E.) ME. *bever*, in comp. *bever-hat*, Chaucer, Prol. 272. AS. *befer*, gloss to *fiber*; Ælfric's Gloss. (Nomina Ferarum).+Du. *bever*; Icel. *björr*; Dan. *bæver*; Swed. *bäfver*; G. *biber*; Russian *bobr'*; Lith. *bebrus*; L. *fiber*. Cf. Skt. *babhru-s*, (1) brown, (2) a large ichneumon. Teut. type **bebruz*, m.; Idg. type **bhebhrus*, reduplicated derivative of **bhru-s*, brown, tawny. Brugm. i. § 566. See **Brown**.

BEAVER (2), the lower (movable) part of a helmet. (F.) Shak. has *beaver*, Hamlet, i. 2. 230. Spelt *baviere* before 1490 (N. E. D.).—F. *bavière*, meaning 'the *bever* of an helmet;' and, primarily, a child's 'bib, mocket, or mocketer, to put before the bosome of a slavering child;' Cot. Thus, the lower part of the helmet was named from a fancied resemblance to a child's bib.—F. *baver*, to foam, froth, slaver; Cot.—F. *bave*, foam, froth, slaver, drivell; Cot. Perhaps imitative; from the movement of the lips; cf. Bret. *babouz*, slaver. ¶ The derivation from Ital. *bevere*, to drink, is quite unfounded. The spelling *beaver* is due to confusion with '*beaver* hat.'

BEAVER (3), **BEVER**, a potation, short intermediate repast. (F. – L.) '*Arete*. What, at your *bever*, gallants?' Ben Jonson, Cynthia's Revels, Act iv. ME. *beuer* (= *bever*), 'drinkinge tyme, Biberrium;' Prompt. Parv.—AF. *beivre*, a drink, Gaimar's Chron. l. 5868; pl. *beveres*, id. l. 5994. Merely the substantival use of OF. *bevre*, to drink.—L. *bibere*, to drink. See **Beverage**. For similar examples of infin. moods as sbs., cf. *leisure*, *pleasure*, *attainder*, *remainder*. ¶ Quite distinct from *beaver* (2). It is still in use; Clare speaks of 'the *bevering* hour,' in his Harvest Morning, st. 7.

BECALM, to make calm. (Hybrid; E. *and* F.) *Becalmed* is in Hackluyt's Voyages, vol. ii. pt. 2. p. 168; and in Mirror for Magistrates, p. 196 (R.) Formed by prefixing E. *be-* to *calm*, a word of F. origin. See **Be-** and **Calm**.

BECAUSE, for the reason that. (Hybrid; E. *and* F.) Formerly written *bi cause*, P. Plowman, B. iii. 99; also *be cause* and *by cause*. *Be*, *bi*, and *by* are all early forms of the prep. *by*. *Cause* is of F. origin. See **By** and **Cause**.

BECHANCE, to befall, happen. (Hybrid; E. *and* F.) In Shak. Merch. i. 1. 38. From *be-*, prefix, q. v., and *chance*, q. v.

BECK (1), a nod or sign; and, as a vb. to make a sign. (E.) The ME. *bek*, sb., is not common in early writers; *beck* occurs in Surrey's tr. of Virgil, Æneid, iv. 346; and *bek* in Wyclif, Job, xxvi. 11 (1st version). It is clearly formed from the verb, which is older, and occurs in Chaucer, C. T. 12330 (C 396). The verb, again, is not an original word, but was suggested by the *bek-* of ME. *beknen*, to beckon; cf. '*beknynge*, or a *bek*;' Prompt. Parv. See **Beckon**.

BECK (2), a stream. (Scand.) ME. *bek*, Prompt. Parv. p. 29; Legends of Holy Rood, p. 82, l. 742. [Not E., but Scandinavian.]—Icel. *bekkr*, a stream, brook; Swed. *bäck*, a brook; Dan. *bæk*. Teut. type **bakkiz*, m.; allied to Teut. type **bakiz*, whence Du. *beek*, G. *bach*.

BECKON, to make a sign. (E.) ME. *becnen*, Ormulum, 223. AS. *bēcnian*, *bēacnian* (also *biecnan*), to signify by a sign.—AS. *bēacen*, a sign, with the addition of the suffix *-ian*, used to form verbs from sbs. See **Beacon** and **Beck**.

BECOME, to attain to a state; to suit. (E.) ME. *becumen, bicumen*; as, 'and *bicomen* hise men' = and became his servants, Havelok, l. 2257; 'it *bicumeth* him swithe wel' = it becomes (suits) him very well, O. Eng. Bestiary, ed. Morris, l. 738. See the large collection of examples in Mätzner, p. 224, s. v. *bicumen*. AS. *becuman*, to arrive, happen, turn out, befal (whence the sense of 'suit' was later developed), Grein, i. 81; *bicuman*, i. 113. + Goth. *bikwiman*, to come upon one, to befal; 1 Thes. v. 3; OHG. *piqueman*, MHG. *bekomen*, to happen, befal, reach, &c.; whence mod. G. *bequem*, fit, apt, suitable, convenient. β. A compound of prefix *be-*, and AS. *cuman*, to come. See **Come**. Der. *becom-ing, becom-ing-ly.*

BED, a couch to sleep on. (E.) ME. *bed*, Chaucer, Prol. 295 (A 293). AS. *bed, bedd*.+Du. *bed*; Goth. *badi*, a bed; OHG. *petti*, G. *bett*, a bed. Teut. type *badjom*, n. Der. *bed*, verb; *bedd-ing*, Ch., C. T., A 1616; *bed-ridden*, q.v.; *bed-stead*, q.v., *bed-chamber* (Shak. Cymb. i. 6. 196), *bed-clothes* (All's Well, iv. 3. 287), *bed-fellow* (Temp. ii. 2. 42), *bed-hangings* (2 Hen. IV, ii. 1. 158), *bed-presser* (1 Hen. IV, ii 4. 268), *bed-right* (Temp. iv. 96), *bed-room* (Mids. Nt. Dr. ii. 2. 51), *bed-time* (Mids. Nt. Dr. v. 34), *bed-work* (Troil. i. 3. 205).

BEDABBLE, BEDAUB, BEDAZZLE. From the E. prefix *be-*, and *dabble, daub, dazzle*, q.v. Shak. has *bedabbled*, Mids. Nt. Dr. iii. 2. 443; *bedaubed*, Rom. iii. 2. 55; *bedazzled*, Tam. Shrew, iv. 5. 46.

BEDELL; see remarks upon **Beadle** (above).

BEDEW, to cover with dew. (E.) Spenser has *bedewd*, F. Q. i. 12. 16. It occurs in the Ayenbite of Inwyt: '*bedeaweth* the herte;' p. 116. From *be-*, prefix; and *dew*, q.v.

BEDIGHT, to array. (E.) 'That derely were *bydy3th*;' Sir Degrevant, 648. From *be-*, prefix, q.v.; and *dight*, q.v.

BEDIM, to make dim. (E.) In Shak. Temp. v. 1. 41. From *be-*, prefix, q.v.; and *dim*, q.v.

BEDIZEN, to deck out. (E.) Not in early use. The quotations in Richardson and N. E. D. show that the earlier word was the simple form *dizen*, from which *bedizen* was formed by help of the common prefix *be-*, like *bedeck* from *deck*. See **Dizen**.

BEDLAM, a hospital for lunatics. (Place-name; Heb.) A corruption of *Bethlehem*. 'Bethlehem hospital, so called from having been originally [in 1247] the hospital of St. Mary of Bethlehem, [a hospital for lunatics in 1402, and] a royal foundation for the reception of lunatics, incorporated by Henry VIII in 1547;' Haydn, Dict. of Dates. ME. *bedlem*, as in the phrase 'in *bedlem* and in babiloyne' = in Bethlehem and Babylon; P. Plowman, B. v. 534; according to three MSS., where other MSS. read *bethleem*. Cf. Cursor Mundi, 11561. The literal sense is 'house of bread.' Der. *bedlam-ite.*

BEDOUIN, a wandering Arab. (F. – Arab.) Modern; yet we find a ME. *bedoyne*, Mandeville, ch. 5, p. 35. Borrowed from F. *bédouin*, properly a pl. form, answering to Arab. *badawin*, pl. of *badawiy*, wild, rude, wandering, as the Arabs in the desert. – Arab. *badw*, a desert; also, departing for the desert, leading a wandering life. – Arab. root *badawa*, he went into the desert; see Rich. Dict., pp. 251, 252: and Devic.

BEDRIDDEN, confined to one's bed. (E.) ME. *bedreden*, used in the plural; P. Plowman, A. viii. 85; *bedrede*, sing. Chaucer, C. T. 7351 (D 1769). AS. *bedrida, bedreda*, glossed by *paraliticus*; Voc. 162. 7, 541. 29, and see Ælfric's Hom. i. 472. – AS. *bed*, a bed, and *rida*, a knight, a rider; thus the sense is a bed-rider, a term for a disabled man. The AS. *rid-a*, a rider, is from *rid-*, weak grade of *ridan*, to ride. The ME. form was shortened to *bedred, bedrid*; after which *-den* was added, under the impression that the form ought to represent a pp. We find the sing. *bedreden* as early as in Hampole, Prick of Consc. 808. β. There is a term of similar import, spelt *bedderedig* in the Bremen Wörterbuch, i. 65; from Low-G. *bedde*, a bed, and *redig*, riding. We find also ME. *bedlawer* for 'one who lies in bed,' which is said, in the Prompt. Parv. p. 28, to be a synonym for *bedridden*. See Prompt. Parv. p. 28, note 4.

BEDSTEAD, the frame of a bed. (E.) ME. *bedstede*, Prompt. Parv. p. 28. – AS. *bed*, a bed; and *stede*, a place, stead, station. So called from its firmness and stability; cf. ME. *stede-fast*, i. e. steadfast. See **Bed** and **Stead**.

BEE, an insect. (E.) ME. *bee*, pl. *bees* and *been*, both of which occur in Chaucer, C. T. 10518, 10296 (F 204, E 2422). AS. *béo, bí*, Grein, p. 109; early form, *bío*.+Du. *bij*; OHG. *pía*. Cf. G. *biene*, Irish *beach*, a bee.

BEECH, a kind of tree. (E.) ME. *beech*, Chaucer, C. T. 2925 (A. 2923). AS. *béce*, gloss to *fágus*, Voc. 268. 36. Earlier *bóece*; Sweet, O. E. Texts. Cf. AS. *béc-tréow*, beech-tree; Napier's Glosses, 23. 30; also the adj. *bécen*, E. *beechen*, as in '*Fáginus*, *bécen*,' Voc. 137. 22. The AS. *béce*, weak fem., represents a Teut. type *bók-jōn* (with mutation of *ō* to *ē*); allied to Teut. type *bók-ā*, str. fem., whence AS. *bóc*, a beech-tree; see **Book**. Further allied to Du.

beuk; G. *buche* (OHG. *puohha*); L. *fágus*; Gk. φηγός. These forms point to an orig. Idg. type *bhāgos*, meaning a tree with esculent fruit; cf. Gk. φαγεῖν, to eat. Der. *beech-en*, adj. (= AS. *bécen*).

BEEF, an ox; the flesh of an ox. (F. – L.) ME. *beof*, Polit. Songs, p. 334, l. 235 (temp. Edw. II); *beef*, Chaucer, C. T. 7335 (D 1753). – AF. *bef*, an ox, Year-books of Edw. I, 1292–3, p. 245; OF. *boef, buef*. – L. acc. *bouem*, an ox; nom. *bós*; an Oscan form + Gael. *bó*, a cow; AS. *cú*, a cow. Thus the word *beef* is co-radicate with *cow*. See **Cow**. Der. *beef-eater*, q. v.

BEEF-EATER, a yeoman of the guard. (Hybrid; F. *and* E.) 'Pensioners and *beefeaters*' [of Charles II.], Argument against a Standing Army, ed. 1697, p. 16; qu. in N. and Q. 5 S. viii. 398. Also in The Spectator, no. 625 (1714); and as early as 1610, in Histriomastix, iii. 1. 99. An *eater* of *beef*; but why this designation was given them is not recorded. ¶ In Todd's Johnson is the following notable passage. 'From *beef* and *ea'*, because the commons eat *beef* when on waiting. Mr. Steevens derives it thus. *Beefeater* may come from *beaufetier*, one who attends at the side-board, which was anciently placed in a *beaufet*. The business of the beefeaters was, and perhaps is still, to attend the king at meals. This derivation is corroborated by the circumstance of the beefeaters having a hasp suspended to their belts for the reception of keys.' This extraordinary guess has met with extraordinary favour, having been quoted in Mrs. Markham's History of England, and thus taught to young children. It is also quoted in Max Müller's Lectures, 8th ed. ii. 582, but with the substitution of *buffetier* for *beaufetier*, and *buffet* is explained as 'a table near the door of the dining-hall.' There is not the faintest tittle of evidence for the derivation beyond the 'hasp suspended to their belts.' I do not find *beaufetier* or *buffetier*, but I find in Cotgrave that *buffeteurs de vin* were 'such carmen or boatmen as steal wine out of the vessels they have in charge, and afterwards fill them up with water.' Mr. Steevens does not tell us what a *beaufet* is, nor how a sideboard was 'anciently placed in' it. On this point, see **Buffet**, sb. When the F. *buffetier* can be found, with the sense of 'waiter at a side-board' in reasonably old French, or when the E. *beefeater* can be found spelt differently from its present spelling in a book *earlier than the time of Mr. Steevens*, it will be sufficient time to discuss the question further. Meanwhile, we may note that Ben Jonson uses *eater* in the sense of 'servant,' as in 'Where are all my *eaters*?' Silent Woman, iii. 2. Also, that the expression 'powderbeef lubber' occurs in the sense of 'man-servant,' where *powder-beef* certainly means *salt-beef*; see 'Powder, to salt,' in Nares. A rich man is spoken of as having 'confidence of [in] so many *powdrebeefe* lubbers as he fedde at home;' Chaloner, translation of Prayse of Follie, 2nd edit. 1577, G v. (1st ed. in 1549). See Notes and Queries, 5 S. viii. 57; 6 S. vi. 491. Cf. *bread-winner*, a sb. of similar formation; and particularly, AS. *hláf-ǽ a*, a domestic servant, lit. 'loaf-eater;' so that the idea is very old. Also *pie-crust-eater*, in Dekker's Shoemaker's Holiday, in Works (1873), i. 62; *beef-eating slaves*, Eng. Garner, ed. Arber, i. 339 (1681); and see Tatler, no. 148.

BEER, a kind of drink. (E.) ME. *bere*, Prompt. Parv. p. 31; *ber*, King Horn, ed. Lumby, l. 1112. AS. *béor*, beer, Grein, i. 112. +Du. *bier*; Icel. *bjórr*; G. *bier* (OHG. *bior*). Origin unknown.

BEESTINGS; see **Biestings**.

BEET, a plant. (L.) ME. *bete*, in a vol. of Vocabularies, ed. T. Wright, p. 190. AS. *béte*, gen. *bétan*, fem. sb., in Cockayne's Leechdoms; but certainly borrowed from L. *béta*, used by Pliny.

BEETLE (1), an insect. (E.) Prov. E. *bittle*. ME. *bityl*, Prompt. Parv. p. 37. AS. *bitela, bitula*; as in 'Mordiculus, *bitela*,' Voc. 122. 8; 'Blattis, *bitulum*,' Sweet, O. E. Texts. – AS. *bit-*, weak grade of *bitan*, to bite; with suffix *-el* of the agent. Thus *beetle* means 'the biting insect;' cf. 'Mordiculus, *bitela*,' showing that the word was understood in that sense. See **Bite** and **Bitter**.

BEETLE (2), a heavy mallet. (E.) ME. *bytyl*, Prompt. Parv. p. 34; *bettles*, pl. Ancren Riwle, p. 188. AS. *býtel, býtl*; Judges, iv. 21; answering to OWessex *bietel*, OMerc. *bétel*; cf. Low G. *bötel*. Teut. type *bautiloz*, 'a beater,' from *bautan-* (AS. *béatan*), to beat; with regular mutation. See **Beat**. Der. *beetle-headed*, Tam. Shrew, iv. 1. 161, i.e. with a head like a log, like a *blockhead*, dull.

BEETLE (3), to jut out and hang over. (E.) 'The summit of the cliff That *beetles* o'er his base into the sea;' Hamlet, i. 4. 71. Apparently coined by Shakespeare. By whomsoever coined, the idea was adopted from the ME. *bitelbrowed*, beetle-browed, having prominent brows, as in P. Plowman, B. v. 190; also spelt *bitterbrowed*, id., footnote. The reference seems to be to the *beetle* (N.E.D.). Cf. F. *sourcils de hanneton* (Hatzfeld); cf. *beetle-browed*, which is really the older expression.

BEFALL, to happen. (E.) ME. *befallen, bifallen*, in common use; Havelok, 2981. AS. *befeallan*, Grein, i. 83.+OSax. *bifallan*

OFries. *bifalla*; Du. *bevallen*, to please: OHG. *bifallan*. From *be-*, prefix, and *fall*; see **Be-** and **Fall**. ¶ This is one of the original verbs on which so many others beginning with *be-* were modelled.

BEFOOL, to make a fool of. (E. *and* F.) ME. *befolen*, Gower, C. A. iii. 236 (b. vii. 4293). — E. prefix *be-*, and ME. *fol*, a fool; see **Fool**.

BEFORE, prep., in front of; adv., in front. (E.) ME. *bifore*, *before*, *biforen*, *beforen*; in common use; spelt *biforen*, Layamon, iii. 131. AS. *beforan*, *biforan*, prep. and adv., Grein, i. 83, 84, 115. — AS. *be-*, *bi-*, prefix, see **Be-** or **By**; and *foran*, before, prep. and adv., Grein, i. 315. AS. *foran* is a longer form (-*an* being a suffix) from *fore*, prep. and adv., before, for; Grein, i. 321. See **Fore**, **For**. Cf. OSax. *biforan*, before; MHG. *bevor*, *bevore*; OHG. *bifora*, before. See below.

BEFOREHAND, previously. (E.) In early use as an adverb. ME. *biuorenhond*, Ancren Riwle, p. 212; from ME. *biuoren*, before, and *hond*, hand. See **Before** and **Hand**.

BEG, to ask for alms. (F.) Cf. ME. *beggar*, *beggere*, a beggar. In the Ancren Riwle, p. 168, we read: ' Hit is *beggares* rihte uorte [*for to*] beren bagge on bac.' The word is French, or rather Anglo-French. The AF. *begger*, to beg, occurs in Peter Langtoft, ed. Wright, i. 248. It was evolved from the sb. *beggare*, found in the Ancren Riwle, as above; or from the equivalent OF. *begard*, *begart*, a name given to an order of lay brothers in the Low Countries in the 13th century; and it was soon adopted by many who were mere idle mendicants. The masc. form *Begard* seems to have imitated that of the female order of *Beguines*; the suffix -*ard*, -*art*, being masculine, as in *dot-ard*. See the examples of *Begger* in the Rom. of the Rose, C. 7256, 7282, and the note. See **Beguine**. ¶ The derivative *beguigner* likewise meant to beg; Britton, i. 22. § 15 (vol. i. p. 93). Der. (from *beggar*), *beg*, verb; also *beggar-ly*, *beggar-li-ness*, *beggar-y*.

BEGET, to generate, produce. (E.) ME. *bigiten*, *begeten*, (1) to obtain, acquire; (2) to beget. ' To *biȝiten* mine rihte ' = to obtain my right; Layamon, i. 405. ' Thus wes Marlin *biȝeten* ' = thus was Merlin begotten; Layamon, ii. 237. AS. *begitan*, *bigitan*, to acquire; Grein, i. 86, 115. — AS. *be-*, *bi-*, prefix; and *gitan*, to get. The Southern form would have been *beyet*; see **Get**. So too OSax. *bigetan*, to seize, get; and Goth. *bigitan*, to find. Der. *begett-er*.

BEGIN, to commence. (E.) ME. *beginnen*, *biginnen*, in common use. AS. *beginnan*, Grein, i. 86 (though the form *onginnan* with the same signification, is far more common). From the prefix *be-*, and AS. *ginnan*, to begin. Cf. Du. and G. *beginnen*, to begin. See **Gin (1)**. Der. *beginn-er*, *beginn-ing*.

BEGONE, pp. beset. (E.) In phr. *woe-begone*, i.e. affected or oppressed with woe, beset with grief. ' The orig. phrase was *him was wo begon*, i. e. to him woe had closed round; but already in Chaucer we find the later construction in *He was wo begon*;' N.E.D. *Wel bigon* occurs in the Rom. of the Rose, l. 580, apparently in the sense of ' glad;' lit. well surrounded or beset. It is the pp. of ME. *begon*, to beset; cf. ' wo þe bigo,' woe come upon thee, Reliq. Antiq. ii. 273. — AS. *bigān*, *begān*, orig. to go about, Grein, i. 115. From prefix *be-*, *bi-*, and AS. *gān*, to go. Cf. Du. *begaan*, concerned, affected. ☞ In the phrase ' begone!' we really use *two* words; it should be written ' be gone!' See **Go**.

BEGONIA, a plant. (F.) Named by Plumier, a French botanist (1646-1704), after Michel *Begon*, a French promoter of botany (1638-1710). See N. E. D.

BEGUILE, to deceive, amuse. (Hybrid; E. *and* F.) ME. *bigilen*, to beguile, Ancren Riwle, p. 330. — E. prefix *be-* (AS. *be-*, *bi-*); and ME. *gylen*, *gilen*, to deceive. ' As theigh he *gyled* were ' = as if he were beguiled; Will. of Palerne, 689. — OF. *guiler*, to deceive. — OF. *guile*, guile, deceit. See **Guile**. Der. *beguil-ing*, *beguil-ing-ly*, *beguil-er*.

BEGUINE, one of a class of religious devotees. (F.) The word is rather French than English; and, though we find a Low-Latin form *beguinus*, it was chiefly used as a feminine noun, viz. F. *béguine*, Low L. *beghina*. The *béguines* belonged to a religious order in Flanders, who, without taking regular vows of obedience, lived a somewhat similar life to that of the begging friars, and dwelt together in houses called *béguinages*. They were ' first established at Liège, and afterwards at Nivelle, in 1207, some say 1226. The *Grand Beguinage* of Bruges was the most extensive;' Haydn, Dict. of Dates. β. Another set of ' religious ' were called *Begardi*; and it has been clearly ascertained that both names were derived from the surname (or nickname) of a certain *Lambert Bègue* or *le Bègue* (the stammerer), a priest of Liège, who founded the order of Beguines in the 12th century. See Ducange, who quotes an annal of 1180, s.v. *Beghardi*. Cf. Walloon *bégui*, to stammer, in the dialect of Namur; Picard *béguer*; equivalent to F. *bégayer*. With the fem. form *Beguine* cf. *hero-ine*; with the masc. form *Beghard*, *Begard*, cf. *reyn-ard*. See also **Beggar** and **Biggen**.

BEGUM, in the E. Indies, a lady of the highest rank. (Pers. — Turk. *and* Arab.) Rich. Pers. Dict. p. 284, gives Pers. *begum*, a queen, lady of rank; also queen-mother, respectable matron; spelt *bigam* at p. 310. ' Queen mother ' seems to be the orig. sense, as Devic thinks that the word is compounded of Turk. *beg* or *bey*, a bey, governor, and Arab. *um* or *umm*, mother; hence ' governor's mother.' The Arab. *umm*, mother, is in Rich. Dict. p. 162. And see **Bey**. Yule (p. 59) explains it from Eastern Turki *bigam*, a fem. formation from *beg*. ¶ Another derivative of *bey* is the title *beglerbeg*, given to the governor of a province; see Massinger, Renegado, iii. 4. In Sandys' Travels (1632), we read of ' the *Beglerbegs*, the name signifying a lord of lords;' p. 47. This explanation is correct; *beglēr* or *beylēr* signifying lords, and *beg* or *bey*, a lord. See **Bey**.

BEHALF, interest, benefit. (E.) In ME., only in the phrase *in*, *on* (or *vppon*) *bihalue*, or *behalue*. Chaucer has: ' on my *bihalue* ' (*u = v*), Troil. and Cress. ii. 1458. So also: ' in themperours *bihelue* ' = on the emperor's behalf; Seven Sages, ed. Weber, 325. Here *on my bihalue* is a substitution for the AS. *on healfe*, on the side of (see exx. in Grein, i. 53), blended with a second common phrase *be healfe*, by the side of (same ref.). β. The AS. *healf*, lit. half, is constantly used in the sense of ' side;' and even now the best paraphrase of ' in my behalf ' is ' on my side.' That this explanation is correct can easily be traced by the examples in Mätzner's Old Eng. Dict., which shows that *bihalven* was in common use as a prep. and adv. before the sb. *behalf* came into use at all. See Layamon, vol. i. p. 349; ii. 58; iii. 65, 114, &c. The prefix *be-* is the unstressed form of the prep. *by*. See **Half**.

BEHAVE, to conduct oneself. (E.) Shak. has *behave*, refl., to conduct oneself, 2 Hen. VI, iv. 3. 5; and intr. but not refl., Oth. iv. 2. 108. Rare in early authors, but the phr. ' to lerne hur to *behave hur* among men ' = to teach her to behave herself amongst men, occurs in Le Bone Florence of Rome, l. 1567, in Ritson's Metrical Romances, vol. iii. It is a mere compound of the verb *to have* with the AS. and ME. prefix *be-*. [There was an AS. *behæbban*, to detain; but *behave* was formed independently of it.] ¶ E. *behave oneself* answers to G. *sich behaben*.

BEHAVIOUR, conduct. (E., with F. suffix.) Spelt *behavoure*, Levins, 222. 45. Formed, abnormally, from the verb *to behave*, q. v. The curious suffix is best accounted for by supposing a confusion with the Tudor E. *havour*, *haviour*, due to AF. *aveir*, F. *avoir*, used substantively, a word which not only meant ' wealth ' or ' possessions,' but also ' ability;' see Cotgrave. And see *Haviour* in Croft's Gloss. to Elyot's Governour. It must be remembered (1) that *behaviour* was often shortened to *haviour*, as in Shakespeare; and (2) that *havings*, at least in Lowland Scotch, had the double meaning of (*a*) possessions, and (*b*) carriage, behaviour. See Jamieson's Scot. Dict.

BEHEAD, to cut off the head. (E.) ME. *bihefden*, *biheafden*, *bihafden*. ' Heo us wulle *bihafdi* ' = they will behead us, Layamon, iii. 45. Later, spelt *biheden*; ' he *bihedide* Joon,' he beheaded John; Wyclif, Matt. xiv. 10. AS. *behēafdian*, to behead; Matt. xiv. 10. — AS. *be-*, prefix, lit. ' by,' with a privative force; and *hēafod*, head. See **Head**. Cf. Du. *onthoofden*, G. *enthaupten*, to behead.

BEHEMOTH, a hippopotamus. (Heb. — Egypt.) See Job, xl. 15. — Heb. *behēmōth*, apparently a plural, signifying ' beasts;' but here used to denote ' great beast;' as if from sing. *behēmāh*, a beast. But it is thought that this is merely a Heb. popular etymology; and that the word is really adapted from the Egypt. *p-ehe-mau*, ' water-ox,' a hippopotamus; see Gesenius, 8th ed. p. 94.

BEHEST, a command. (E.) ME. *beheste*, *biheste*, commonly used in the sense of ' a promise;' Chaucer, C. T. 4461 (B 41); and connected with the verb *bihote*, *behote*, to promise, Chaucer, C. T. 1856 (A 1854). From *be-*, prefix, and *hest*. Cf. AS. *behǣs*, a vow, *behāt*, a promise, *behātan*, to promise. ' He fela behǣsa behēt,' he made many promises; AS. Chron., anno 1093. The final *t* is excrescent. See **Hest**.

BEHIND, after. (E.) ME. *behinde*, *bihinde*, *bihinden*, after, at the back of, afterwards; Chaucer, C. T. 4847 (B 427). AS. *behindan*, adv. and prep., afterwards, after, Grein, i. 87. From AS. prefix *be-*; and *hindan*, adv., behind, at the back, Grein, ii. 76. Cf. OSax. *bihindan*, adv., behind; Heliand, l. 3660. See **Hind**. Der. *behind-hand*, not in early use; made in imitation of *before-hand*, q. v. It occurs in Shak. Winter's Tale, v. 1. 151.

BEHOLD, to see, watch, observe. (E.) ME. *biholden*, *beholden*, *biholde*, *beholde*, to see, observe, to bind by obligation; in common use. [The last sense appears only in the pp. *beholden*; ' *beholdyn*, or *bowndyn*, *obligor*, *teneor*;' Prompt. Parv. p. 28. Shak. wrongly has *beholding* for the pp. *beholden*, as in Merry Wives, i. 1. 283.] AS. *behealdan*, to hold, possess, guard, observe, see; Grein, i. 87. + OFries. *bihalda*, to keep; OSax. *bihaldan*, to keep; Du. *behouden*, to preserve, keep; G. *behalten*, to keep. From AS. prefix *be-*, and *healdan*, to hold. See **Be-** and **Hold**. [Cf. L. *tueor*, I see, keep; E. *guard*, as compared with *regard*, &c.] Der. *behold-er* ; also pp. *behold-en*, corrupted to *behold-ing*.

BEHOOF, advantage. (E.) Almost invariably found in ME. in the dat. case *behoue*, *bihoue* [*u* written for *v*], with the prep. *to* preceding it ; as in '*to* ancren *bihoue*,' for the use of anchoresses, Ancren Riwle, p. 90. AS. *behōf*, advantage, in Napier's Glosses ; also in the comp. *behōflic* ; see *bihōflic is*, gloss to L. *oportet* in Luke, xviii. 1, in the Lindisfarne MS. (Northumbrian dialect). Cf. OFries. *behōf*, *bihōf*.+Du. *behoef*, commonly in the phr. *ten behoeve van*, for the advantage of ; Swed. *behof*, want, need ; Dan. *behov*, need ; G. *behuf*, behoof. β. The *be-* is a prefix ; cf. Swed. *höfvas*, to beseem. All from Teut. type *hōf*, second grade of *haf-*, as in Goth. *haf-jan*, AS. *hebban*, to heave ; see **Heave**. From the √KAP, to hold, contain ; cf. L. *capax*, containing, *capere*, to seize, orig. to contain, hold, grasp. See Brugm. i. § 635. γ. The development of ideas is accordingly (1) to seize, hold fast, retain, (2) to fit for one's use, to make serviceable. Der. *behove* (below).

BEHOVE, to become, befit. (E.) ME. *bihoven*, *behoven* (written *bihouen*, *behouen* in MSS.) ; commonly as impers. verb, *bihoveth*, *behoveth*, Chaucer, Troil. iv. 1004 ; pt. t. *bihouede*, Ancren Riwle, p. 394. AS. *bihōfian*, *behōfian*, to need, be necessary ; Grein, i. 87, 116. Cf. OFries. *bihovia*, to behove.+Du. *behoeven*, to be necessary, to behove ; Swed. *behöfva* ; Dan. *behöve*. β. The forms of these verbs show that they are derivatives from the sb. (above). Also, the *be-* is a mere prefix. The simple verb appears only in the Icel. *hæfa*, to behove ; Swed. *höfvas*, to beseem. See **Behoof**.

BELABOUR, to ply vigorously, beat soundly. (Hybrid ; E. *and* F.–L.) 'He .. *belaboured* Jubellius with a cudgel ;' North's Plutarch, p. 964.–E. prefix *be-*, q. v. ; and *labour*, q. v.

BELAY, to fasten a rope. (Du.) To *belay* is to fasten a rope by *laying* it round and round a couple of pins. This use was prob. suggested by Du. *beleggen*, to cover, to overlay, to border, to lace, garnish with fringe, &c. ; and, as a naut. term, to belay. From prefix *be-* (the same as E. prefix *be-*), and *leggen*, to lay, place, cognate with E. *lay*. See **Lay** (1). ¶ There was also a native E. word to *belay*, a compound of *be-* and *lay*, but it meant 'to besiege' or 'beleaguer' a castle ; see Spenser, Sonnet 14. See **Beleaguer**.

BELCH, to eructate. (E.) ME. *belken*, *belke*, Towneley Myst. p. 314. The sb. *bolke* is found, in the dat. case, in P. Plowman, B. v. 397 ; and the vb. *bolken*, Prompt. Parv. p. 43. AS. *bealcan*, Ps. xviii. 2 ; commoner in the derived form *bealcettan*, Ps. xliv. 1 ; Ps. cxviii. 171 ; also *bælcan*, *belcettan* (Grein). Cf. Du. *balken*, to bray, Du. *bulken*, Low G. *bolken*, to low, bellow, roar ; Hamburg *bölcken*, to low ; *opbölcken* to belch up (Richey). Allied to **Bellow**.

BELDAM, an old woman. (F.–L.) Ironically used for *beldame*, i. e. fair lady, in which sense it occurs in Spenser, F. Q. iii. 2. 43. Cf. '*beldame*, *meregrant* ;' Palsgrave.–F. *belle*, fair ; *dame*, lady.–L. *bella*, fair ; *domina*, lady. Hence *beldam* is a doublet of *belladonna*.

BELEAGUER, to besiege. (Du.) 'In defence of *beleaguer*'d truth ;' Milton, Areop. ed. Hales, p. 46. We also find the verb *to beleague* ; as in 'beseiging and *beleaguing* of cities ;' Holland's Plutarch, p. 319 (R.) ; but this is a less correct form.–Du. *belegeren*, to besiege ; from prefix *be-* (as in E.), and *leger*, a bed, a camp, army in encampment ; which is from *leggen*, to lay, place, cognate with E. *lay*. [Thus the true E. word is *belay* ; see Note to *belay*. The Du. *leger* is E. *lair*.]+G. *belagern*, to besiege ; *lager*, a camp ; *legen*, to lay ; Swed. *belägra*, to besiege ; *läger*, a camp ; *lägga*, to lay. See **Lair**, **Lay** (1).

BELEMNITE, a kind of fossil. (Gk.) In Sir T. Browne, Vulg. Errors, b. ii. c. 5. s. 10. So called because shaped like the head of a dart.–Gk. βελεμνίτης, a kind of stone, belemnite.–Gk. βέλεμνον, a dart, missile.–Gk. βάλλειν, to cast, throw ; also to fall.+Skt. *gal*, to drop, distil, fall ; Brugm. i. § 653.

BELFRY, properly, a guard-tower. (F.–G.) Owing to a corruption, the word is now only used for 'a tower for *bells*.' Spelt *belfroy*, Caxton, Godefroy of Boloyne, ch. 153 (p. 227, l. 12). Corrupted from ME. *berfray*, Allit. Poems, ed. Morris, B. 1187 ; *berfrey*, King Alisaunder, ed. Weber, 2777.–ONorth F. *berfrei*, *berfreit* ; OF. *berfroi*, *berfroit* (also *belefroi*) ; cf. Guernsey *belfré* (Métivier).–MHG. *bercfrit*, *berchfrit*, a protecting tower.–MHG. *berc*, protection (from *bergen*, to protect) ; and MHG. *fride*, OHG. *fridu* (G. *friede*), a place of security (allied to OHG. *frī*, cognate with E. *free*). β. The mod. G. *friede* means only 'peace,' but OHG. *fridu* meant also 'a place of security,' and even 'a tower ;' so that *bercfrit* meant 'a protecting tower' or 'guard-tower.' ¶ The term was first applied to the towers upon wheels, so much used in the siege of towns. Even the OF. *bierfrois* is used with the sense of 'belfry ;' as in 'campanile, quod *bierfrois* dicitur ;' (dated 1226) ; in Pertz, Monumenta Germaniae, Legg. ii. 257.

BELIE, to tell lies about. (E.) Much Ado, iv. 1. 148. 'To *belye* the truth ;' Tyndal, Works, p. 105, l. 2. ME. *bilien*, *biliȝen* ; the

pp. *bilowen* occurs in P. Plowman, B. ii. 22, and in the Ancren Riwle, p. 68.–AS. *be-*, prefix ; and *lēogan*, to lie. See **Lie** (2).

BELIEVE, to have faith in. (E.) ME. *beleve*, Ayenbite of Inwyt, p. 151 ; EE. *bileflde*, pt. t. of *bilefen*, Layamon, 2856*. The prefix is AS. *be-* or *bi-*, substituted for the earlier prefix *ge-*.–OMerc. *gelēfan*, AS. *ge-lȳfan*, *gelīfan* (Grein, i. 424), to believe.+Goth. *galaubjan*, to believe, to esteem as valuable ; from *galaubs*, valuable, allied to Goth. *liubs*, dear, equivalent to AS. *lēof*. Eng. *lief* : OHG. *galaupjan*, to believe ; whence G. *glauben*. See **Lief**. Here AS. *lēof* represents a Teut. type *leub-oz* ; and from the 2nd grade (*laub*) we have the verb *laubjan-* ; which gives (by mutation) the AS. *-liefan*, *-lȳfan*, OMerc. *-lēfan*. Der. *belief* (ME. *bileue*, O. Eng. Homilies, i. 187), *believ-able*, *believ-er*.

BELL, a hollow metallic vessel for making a loud noise. (E.) ME. *belle*, a bell ; Prompt. Parv. p. 30 ; Layamon, 29441. AS. *belle*; Voc. 198. 8. Cf. EFries. *belle*, a bell, Du. *bel*.–AS. *bellan*, to bellow, make a loud sound (Grein). From Idg. √BHELS, to resound ; whence also Skt. *bhash*, to bark, Lith. *balsas*, voice, G. *bellen*, to bark (Uhlenbeck). See **Bellow**.

BELLADONNA, deadly nightshade. (Ital.–L.) Various reasons have been given for the name ; perhaps due to the use of it by ladies to give expression to the eyes, the pupils of which it expands. –Ital. *bella donna*, a fair lady.–L. *bella domina*, a fair lady. *Bella* is the fem. of *bellus*, handsome ; see **Beau**. *Domina* is the fem. of *dominus*, a lord ; see **Don**, sb. Doublet, *beldam*.

BELLE, a fair lady. (F.–L.) In Pope, Rape of the Lock, i. 8 ; Fletcher, Beggar's Bush, iv. 4.–F. *belle*, fem. of *beau*, fair, goodly. See **Beldam** and **Beau**.

BELLIGERENT, carrying on war. (L.) For *belligerant*. In Sterne, Tristram Shandy, vol. vi. c. 31.–L. *belligerant-*, stem of *belligerans*, waging war.–L. *belli-*, for *bello-*, stem of *bellum*, war ; and *gerere*, to carry.–(1) L. *bellum* stands for OL. *duellum* ; see **Duel**. (2) L. *gerere*, pp. *gestus*, appears in E. *jest* ; see **Jest**.

BELLOW, to make a loud noise. (E.) Gower uses *belwinge* with reference to the noise made by a bull ; C. A. iii. 203 (b. vii. 3322). From ME. *belwen*. 'As loude as *belweth* wind in helle ;' Chaucer, Ho. of Fame, iii. 713. We also find ME. *bellen* ; as in '*bellyng* as a bole' [bull], Will. of Palerne, 1891 ; from AS. *bellan*, to make a loud noise, Grein, i. 89.+OHG. *pellan*, *bellan*, to make a loud noise. Of imitative origin. β. The suffix *-ow* is due to the *g* in the derived AS. form *bylgean*, to bellow, Martyr. 17 Jan. (in Cockayne's Shrine, p. 52) ; cf. Icel. *belja*, to bellow. And see **Bell**.

BELLOWS, an implement for blowing. (Scand.) ME. *below*, a bag, used in the special sense of 'bellows.' The pl. *belowes* was also used in the same sense. '*Belowe*, or *belows*, follis ;' Prompt. Parv. p. 30. The numerous examples in Mätzner, s.v. *bali*, show that *bellows* is the pl. of *below*, a bag, from Icel. *belgr*, a bag. Another ME. form is *beli*, *bely*, bellows, as in Ch. C. T., I 351 ; where Tyrwhitt reads *belous*. This ME. *beli* is from AS. *bælig*, a bag. Cf. G. *blasebalg* = a blow-bag, a pair of bellows. See **Belly**.

BELLY, the lower part of the human trunk. (E.) ME. *bely*, pl. *belies* ; also *bali*, pl. *balies* ; P. Plowman, B. prol. 41, A. prol. 41. AS. *bælg*, *belig*, a bag, used, e. g. in the comp. *bēan-bælgas*, husks or shells of beans, Luke xv. 16 (Lindisfarne text) ; *þā beligas*, the bags, Matt. ix. 17 (Rushworth text).+Du. *balg*, the belly ; Swed. *bälg*, belly, bellows ; Dan. *bælg*, shell, husk, belly ; Icel. *belgr*, a bag ; Goth. *balgs*, a bag. Teut. type *balgiz*, m. From *balg*, 2nd grade of the Teut. root *belg-*, as in AS. *belg-an*, orig. 'to swell out.' Cf. Irish *bolg*, bag, belly ; *bolgaim*, I swell ; W. *bol*, belly. From √BHELGH, to swell. ¶ *Bellows* is from the pl. of the cognate Scand. form.

BELONG, to pertain to. (E.) ME. *belongen*, Gower, C. A. i. 12, 121, ii. 351 (prol. 259, i. 2345, v. 6624) ; Ayenbite of Inwyt, ed. Morris, p. 12, l. 15. Not found in AS., which has only the simple verb *langian*, to long after, to crave for ; Grein, ii. 157. But cf. Du. *belangen*, to concern ; *wat belangt*, as far as concerns, as for ; *belangende*, concerning ; EFries. *belangen*, to reach, attain to. See **Long** (1).

BELOVED, much loved. (E.) ME. *beloved*, Gower, C. A. i. 106 (i. 1920). It is the pp. of ME. *bilufien*, *biluvien*, to love greatly ; spelt *biluuien* in Layamon, i. 39.–AS. prefix *be-*, *bi-*, here used intensively ; and AS. *lufian*, to love. See **Love**. ¶ The ME. *biluuen* also means 'to please ;' O. Eng. Homilies, i. 257 ; cf. Du. *believen*, to please.

BELOW, beneath. (E.) ME. *bilooghe*, adv., beneath, Allit. Poems, ed. Morris, B. 116. Compounded of prep. *bi*, *be*, by ; and *loogh*, *low*, low. See **Low** (1).

BELT, a girdle. (L.) ME. *belt* ; Chaucer, C. T. 3927 (A 3929). AS. *belt*, Voc. 192. 15 ; cf. Icel. *belti* ; Irish and Gaelic *balt*, a belt, a border. All from L. *balteus*, a belt.

BELTANE, the first of May ; old May-day. (C.) 'At *Beltane* ;' Peblis to the Play (ab. 1550).–Gael. *bealltuinn*, May-day ; Irish *bealteine*, OIrish *bel-tene* (Windisch). Lit. 'blaze-kindling ;' from an old custom. Celtic type *belo-te(p)niā; where belo- is allied to AS. bǣl, a blaze, and -te(p)niā is from *tepnos, type of OIrish ten, fire. β. The AS. bǣl is further allied to Lith. bal-tas, white, Gk. φάλ-ιος, bright, Skt. bhāla(m), lustre. The OIrish ten is allied to L. tep-ēre, to be warm. 'Two need-fires were lighted on Beltane among the Gael, between which they drove their cattle for purification and good luck;' Macbain. See Stokes-Fick, pp. 125, 164.

BELVEDERE, BELVIDERE, a prospect-tower. (F. – Ital. – L.) 'Palaces and belvederes;' Webster, Devil's Law-case, i. i. 9. – F. belvédère (Hatzfeld). – Ital. belvedere, 'a place of a faire prospect;' Florio. – L. bellus, fair; uidēre, to see.

BEMOAN, to moan for, sorrow for. (E.) The latter vowel has been changed, as in moan. ME. bimenen, to bemoan; O. E. Homilies, i. 13. AS. bimǣnan; Grein, i. 117. – AS. bi-, prefix; and mǣnan, to moan. See **Moan.**

BENCH, a long seat or table. (E.) ME. benche, Chaucer, C. T., 7355 (D 1773). AS. benc (Grein).+Du. bank, a bench, form, pew, shelf; also, a bank for money; Icel. bekkr (for *benkr), a bench; Swed. bänk, Dan. bænk, a bench, form, pew; G. bank, a bench; a bank for money; Pomeran. benk. Teut. type *bankiz. See **Bank,** of which bench is a doublet. Der. bench-er.

BEND (1), to bow, curve. (E.) ME. benden, bende; 'bende bowys, tendo,' Prompt. Parv. p. 30. AS. bendan, to bend; Grein, i. 90; allied to AS. bend, a bond (Teut. type *bandiz). From band, 2nd grade of AS. bindan, to bind. See **Bind.**+Icel. benda; Swed. bända, to stretch, to strain. ¶ Bend means to strain a bow by fastening the band or string. The vowel e is a mutation of a; so that bendan is for *bandjan. Cf. bend = a band; Gower, C. A. iii. 11; bk. vi. 296; F. bander un arc, to bend a bow, to string it.

BEND (2), a slanting band, in heraldry; one of the nine ordinaries. (F. – G.) Spelt bende in Book of St. Albans (1486), pt. ii, leaf e 1. Perhaps orig. E. (see above), but modified by OF. bende, which was a modification of bande. The Anglo-French bende, in the heraldic sense, occurs in Langtoft's Chron. ii. 434. Cotgrave gives bende, the same as bande; and assigns 'a bend in armory' as being one meaning of bande; see **Band** (2). The ME. bende also meant a fillet; see Cath. Anglicum, p. 27, note 7.

BENEATH, below. (E.) ME. benethe, Gower, C. A. i. 35; prol. 931; bineoðen, Ancren Riwle, p. 390. AS. beneoðan, prep., below; Grein, i. 91.+Du. beneden, adv. and prep. From AS. prefix be-, by; and neoðan, adv., below; Grein, ii. 290. Here -an is an adverbial suffix, and neoð- = niðer, adv., below; and niðera, nether, lower. See **Nether.**

BENEDICTION, blessing. (F. – L.) Shak. has both benediction and benison; the former is really a 'learned' or Latin form, and the latter was in earlier use in English. See **Benison.** Caxton has benediction, Golden Legend, St. Nicholas, § 7.

BENEFACTOR, a doer of good to another. (L.) Benefactor in North's Plutarch, p. 735; benefactour in Tyndal's Works, p. 216, col. 1; but the word was not French. – L. benefactor, a doer of good. – L. bene, well; and factor, a doer, from facere, pp. factus, to do. Der. benefact-ion, benefact-ress.

BENEFICE, a church preferment. (F. – L.) ME. benefice, Chaucer, Prol. 291. – F. benefice (Cot.) – Late L. beneficium, a grant of an estate; L. beneficium, a kindness, lit. well-doing. – L. benefacere, to benefit. – L. bene, well; and facere, to do. See Beneficium in Ducange. From L. benefacere we have also benefic-ence, benefic-ent, benefic-i-al, benefic-i-al-ly, benefic-i-ary; and see benefit.

BENEFIT, a favour. (F. – L.) Rich. quotes from Elyot's Governour, bk. ii. c. 8. § 2 : 'And that vertue [benevolence] . . is called than beneficence; and the deed, vulgarly named a good tourne, may be called a benefite.' ME. bienfet, which occurs with the sense of 'good action' in P. Plowman, B. v. 621; Gower, C. A. iii. 187; bk. vii. 3029. – OF. bienfait (F. bienfait), a benefit. – L. benefactum, a kindness conferred. – L. bene, well; and factum, done, pp. of facere, to do. ¶ The word has been modified so as to make it more like Latin, with the odd result that bene- is Latin, and -fit (for -fait) is French ! The spelling benefet occurs in Wyclif's Bible, Ecclus. xxix. 9.

BENEVOLENCE, an act of kindness, charity. (F. – L.) In Hoccleve, Orison to the Virgin, l. 10. 'He reysed therby notable summes of money, the whiche way of the leuyinge of this money was after named a benyuolence;' Fabyan, Edw. IV, an. 1475. – F. benevolence, 'a well-willing, or good will; a favour, kindnesse, benevolence;' Cot. – L. beneuolentia, kindness. – L. beneuolus, kind; also spelt beniuolus; cf. uolent-, stem of uolens, willing. – L. beni-, from benus, by-form of bonus, good; and uolo, I wish. See **Voluntary.** Der. From the same source, benevolent, benevolent-ly.

BENIGHTED, overtaken by nightfall. (E.) In Dryden's Eleonora, l. 57. Pp. of the verb benight. 'Now jealousie no more benights her face;' Davenant, Gondibert, bk. iii. c. 5. st. 16. Coined by prefixing the verbal prefix be- to the sb. night.

BENIGN, affable, kind. (F. – L.) Chaucer has benigne, C. T. 4599 (B 179). – OF. benigne (F. bénin). – L. benignus, kind, a contracted form of *benigenus; from beni-, for benus, by-form of bonus, good; and -genus, born (as in indigenus), from the verb genere, old form of gignere, to beget : from √GEN, to beget. Der. benign-ly, benign-ant, benign-ant-ly, benign-i-ty.

BENISON, blessing. (F. – L.) Shak. has benison, Macb. ii. 4. 40; Chaucer has it also, C. T. 9239 (E 1365). Spelt beneysun, Havelok, 1723. – OF. beneison, beneiçon (Godefroy). – L. acc. benedictiōnem, from nom. benedictio; cf. benedictus, pp. of benedicere, (1) to use words of good omen, (2) to bless. – L. bene, well; and dicere, to speak. Doublet, benediction.

BENT-GRASS, a coarse kind of grass. (E.) 'Hoc gramen, bent;' Wright's Vocabularies, i. 191. AS. beonet, as in Beonet-lēah, mod. E. Bent-ley, in Kemble's Index. Cf. prov. E. bennet (E. D. D.) EFries. bente.+OHG. binuz, pinuz, MHG. binez, binz, G. binse, bent-grass, coarse grass growing in wet places. Teut. type *binut.

BENUMB, to make numb. (E.) Written benum by Turberville; Pyndara's Answere, st. 40. Benum is properly not an infin., but a past part. of the verb benim; and hence Gower has : 'But altogedre him is benome The pouer bothe of hond and fot' = he is deprived of the power; C. A. iii. 2 ; bk. vi. 36. And Palsgrave has : 'benombe of ones lymbes;' p. 3 ˙. Lit. 'taken away;' from AS. be-, bi-, prefix, 'away;' and numen, pp. of niman, to take. See **Numb.**

BENZOIN, a resinous substance. (F. – Span.+Ital. – Arab.) Spelt benzoine in Lingua, iv. 3, in Old Plays, ed. Hazlitt, ix. 419 (1607). Called also gum benzoin, and (by a singular popular etymology) gum Benjamin. Phillips (1706) calls it 'benjamin or benzoin.' – F. benjoin, 'the aromaticall gumme, called benjamin or benzoin;' Cotgrave. The n seems to be a F. addition; Cotgrave also notes that benjoin François meant 'the hearbe maisterwort, or false pellitory of Spain;' showing that benjoin was not a F. word, but Spanish. – Span. benjui, 'benjamin or benzoin, gum-resin;' Neuman. – Ital. bengivi (Torriano); also benzoino. Shown by Engelmann and Dozy (and approved by Devic) to be a corruption (dropping the first syllable) of the Arab. name for benzoin, which was lubān jāwi, lit. Javanese frankincense. Perhaps lu- was confused with the Ital. def. art. lo. The Arab. lubān means frankincense, benzoin; Rich. Dict. p. 1256; whilst jāwī means belonging to Java, Javanese. Benzoin really comes from Sumatra, but Devic says that the Arabs regarded Java as a name for that island also; and it is called 'Java minor' by Marco Polo. With Arab. lubān, cf. Heb. levōnāh, frankincense, from the root lāvan, to be white (whence Gk. λίβανος).

BEQUEATH, to dispose of property by will. (E.) ME. byquethe, Chaucer, C. T. 2770 (A 2768). AS. be-cweðan, bi-cweðan, to say, declare, affirm; Grein, i. 82, 113. From prefix be- or bi-, and AS. cweðan, to say. See **Quoth.**

BEQUEST, a bequeathing; a thing bequeathed. (E.) ME. biqueste, Rob. of Brunne, tr. of Langtoft, p. 86; but very rare. The usual form is biquide, byquide, bequide (trisyllabic), as in Rob. of Glouc., pp. 381, 384, ll. 7826, 7887; which is from prefix be-, and AS. cwide, a saying, opinion, declaration, Grein, i. 176; cf. AS. bicweðan, to declare. See **Bequeath.** β. But biqueste is a by-form of biquiste (P. Plowman, C. ix. 94); formed with added -t, -te, from AS. be-, prefix, and cwiss (in ge-cwis), a saying. This sb. cwiss represents a Teut. type *kwessiz, Idg. *g(w)ettis, formed (with suffix -ti-) from Idg. base *g(w)et, whence AS. cweð-an, to say (Sievers, A. S. Gr. § 232) ; and becwiss is thus a regular derivative of becweðan, to bequeath.

BEREAVE, to deprive of. (E.) ME. bireue, bereue (u for v), Chaucer, C. T. 7653 (D 2071). AS. birēafian, berēafian; Grein, i. 92, 118. – AS. be-, prefix; and rēafian, to rob. See **Reave.** Der. bereft, short for bireued (u for v), the pp. of bireuen; bereave-ment.

BERGAMOT, a variety of pear. (F. – Ital. – Turk.) F. bergamotte, in Cotgrave, explained as 'a yellow peare, with a hard rind, good for perry; also, the delicate Italian small peare, called the Bergamotte peare.' – Ital. bergamotta, bergamot pear, 'a kind of excellent pears, come out of Turky;' Torriano. – Turk. beg-armūdi, 'prince's pear.' – Turk. beg, a prince; armūd, a pear. ¶ Another bergamot, the name of an essence, is from the Ital. place-name, Bergamo, in Lombardy.

BERGOMASK, rustic. (Ital.) 'A bergomask dance;' Shak. Mid. Nt. Dr. v. 360. Explained by Nares as a rustic dance by the clownish people of Bergamo. More correctly Bergamask. – Ital. bergamasca, 'a kind of dance;' Baretti. – Ital. Bergamo (in Lombardy).

BERRY, a small round or ovate fruit. (E.) ME. berye, berie (with one r), Chaucer, prol. 207. AS. berige, berge, Deut. xxiii. 24; where the stem of the word is ber-, for bes-, which is for bas-.+Du. bes, bezie, a berry; Icel. ber; Swed. bär, Dan. bær; G. beere, OHG. peri; Goth. basi, a berry. Cf. Skt. bhas, to eat; the sense seems to have been 'edible fruit.' Der. goose-berry, &c.

BERTH, a secure position. (E.) It is applied (1) to convenient sea-room, or the place where a ship lies when at anchor or at a wharf; (2) to a place in a ship to stow things in, or to sleep in; (3) to a comfortable official position. β. The orig. sense was perhaps 'suitable position;' cf. prov. E. *berth*, a good foothold, a secure grasp. Better spelt *burth* (but cf. E. *stern* from AS. *styrne*, &c.); formed with suffix *-th* (as in *bir-th*, *dear-th*) from AS. *byr-*, as in *ge-byrian*, to suit, *ge-byr-e*, opportunity, *ende-byrd*, arrangement, order. From Teut. **bur-*, weak grade of *ber-an*, to bear. Cognate with EFries. *bort*, good time or position, Du. *beurt*, Norw. *byrt*, Swed. *börd*, a course, turn; Low G. *bört*, as in *in der bört liggen*, to lie in a good berth (as a ship). Cf. G. *gebühren*, to suit: &c.

BERYL, a precious stone. (L. – Gk. – Skt.) In the Bible (A.V.), Rev. xxi. 20. Spelt *beril* in An Old English Miscellany, ed. Morris, p. 98, l. 174. – L. *bēryllus*, a beryl. – Gk. βήρυλλος; cf. Arab. *billaur* or *ballūr*, crystal; a word given in Palmer's Pers. Dict. col. 91. – Skt. *vaidūrya* (Prakrit *velūriya*), orig. beryl, brought from Vidūra in S. India. See Yule, and Max Müller, Selected Essays 1881, ii. 352; Böhtlingk, Dict. p. 1392.

BESANT, BEZANT, a golden circular figure, in heraldry. (F. – L. – Gk.) Intended to represent a golden coin of Byzantium. ME. *besant*, Gower, C. A. ii. 191; bk. v. 1930; Wycliffe, Matt. xxv. 24. – AF. *besant*, Roll of Caerlaverock, p. 27; MF. and F. *besant*, 'an ancient gold coin;' Cot. – Late L. *byzantium*, acc. of *byzantius*, a besant, coin of Byzantium. – L. *Byzantium*. – Gk. Βυζάντιον, the old name of Constantinople.

BESEECH, to ask. (E.) ME. *biseche, beseche*, Gower, C. A. i. 115; bk. i. 2174; but also *biseke, beseke, biseken*, Chaucer, Knightes Tale, l. 60. From the prefix *be-*, and ME. *sechen, seken* to seek (*seken* being, usually, the Northern form, and *sechen* Southern). Cf. Du. *bezoeken*, G. *besuchen*, to visit; Swed. *besöka*, Dan. *besöge*, to visit, go to see. See **Seek**.

BESEEM, to be becoming. (E.) ME. *bisemen, besemen*. '*Becemyn*, decet;' Prompt. Parv. p. 27. 'Wel *bisemeð* þe' = it well beseems thee; St. Juliana, p. 55. From the prefix *be-*, *bi-*; and the ME. *semen*, to seem. See **Seem**.

BESET, to set about, surround, perplex. (E.) ME. *bisetten, besetten*, especially used of surrounding crowns, &c. with precious stones. 'With gold and riche stones *Beset*;' Gower, C. A. i. 127; bk. i. 2537. *Biset*, i. e. surrounded, Ancren Riwle, p. 378. AS. *bisettan*, to surround; Grein, i. 119.＋Du. *bezetten*, to occupy, invest (a town); Dan. *besætte*, to fill, occupy; Swed. *besätta*, to beset, plant, hedge about, people, garrison (a fort); Goth. *bisatjan*, to set round (a thing); G. *besetzen*, to occupy, garrison, trim, beset. From prefix *be-*, *bi-*, and AS. *settan*, to set. See **Be-** and **Set**.

BESHREW, to imprecate a curse on. (E.) ME. *bischrewen*; Chaucer, C. T. 6426, 6427 (D 844, 845). Wyclif uses *beshrewith* to translate L. *deprauat*, Prov. x. 9; A. V. 'perverteth.' Formed by prefixing *be-* to the sb. *shrew*; cf. *bestow*. See **Be-** and **Shrew**.

BESIDE, prep., by the side of; **BESIDES**, adv., moreover. (E.) ME. *biside, bisiden, bisides*, all three forms being used both as prep. and adverb. 'His daungers him *bisydes*;' Chaucer, C. T. prol. 402. '*Bisides* Scotlonde' = towards Scotland, said of the Roman wall built as a defence against the Scots; Layamon, ii. 6. AS. *be sidan*, used as two distinct words; where *be* means 'by,' and *sidan* is the dat. sing. of *side*, a side. ¶ The more correct form is *be-side*; *besides* is a later development, due to the habit of using the suffix *-es* to form adverbs; the use of *besides* as a *preposition* is, strictly, incorrect, but is as old as the 13th century.

BESIEGE, to lay siege to. (Hybrid; E. *and* F.) ME. *bisegen, besegen*. 'To *bisegi* þis castel;' Rob. of Glouc. p. 399; l. 8242. Formed by prefixing *be-* or *bi-* to the ME. verb *segen*, formed from the ME. sb. *sege*, a siege. See **Be-** and **Siege**. Der. *besieg-er*.

BESOM, a broom. (E.) ME. *besum*; as in 'Hæc scopa, a *besum*;' Wright's Vocabularies, i. 235, 276. Also *besme, besowme*, Prompt. Parv. p. 33. AS. *besma*; Luke, xi. 25; Mat. xii. 44.＋MDu. *bessem*, Oudemans; Du. *bezem*, a broom; OHG. *pësamo*, MHG. *bëseme*, G. *besen*, a broom, a rod. Teut. type **bes-mon-*, m.

BESOT, to make sottish. (E.) Shak. has *besotted*, infatuated, Troil. ii. 2. 143. From verbal prefix *be-*, and *sot*, q. v.

BESPEAK, to speak to; to order or engage for a future time. (E.) Shak. has *bespoke*, Errors, iii. 2. 176. ME. *bispeken*. 'And *byspekith* al his deth;' King Alisaunder, ed. Weber, 94. AS. *besprecan*, to speak to, tell, complain, accuse; Orosius, i. 10; ed. Sweet, p. 48, l. 18. [For the dropping of *r*, see **Speak**.] – AS. *be-*, prefix; and *sprecan*, to speak. Cf. OHG. *bisprächa*, detraction.

BEST: see **Better**.

BESTEAD (1), to assist, avail. (E.) 'How little you *bested*, Or fill the fixed mind;' Milton, Il Penseroso, 3. A late formation; from AS. and ME. *be-*, and *stead*, a verb due to *stead*, sb., a place; see Shak. Temp. i. 2. 165. See **Stead**.

BESTEAD (2), situated, beset. (Scand.) A verb only used in the past participle. '*Bestead*, or wytheholdyn yn wele or wo, *detentus*;' Prompt. Parv. p. 33. ME. *bistad, bestad*, pp. of a verb *bisteden, besteden*, to situate, to place under certain circumstances. Spelt *bistaðet* in St. Marherete, p. 3. Of Scand. origin. Cf. especially Dan. *bestede*, to place, to inter, to bury; with pp. *bestedt*, used as our E. *bestead*, as in *være ilde bestedt*, to be ill bestead, to be badly off; *være bestedt i Nöd*, to be in distress, to be badly off. Similarly is used Icel. *staddr*, circumstanced, the pp. of *steðja*, to stop, fix, appoint; also Swed. *stadd*, circumstanced; *vara stadd i fara*, to be in danger; whence ME. *bestad*, Cursor Mundi, 5254; 'sore *bestad*,' Spenser, F. Q. vi. 1. 4. The Icel. *steðja* is from *staðr*, a place. See **Be-** and **Stead**.

BESTIAL, beast-like. (F. – L.) In Rom. of the Rose, 6716. – F. *bestial*. – L. *bestiālis*, beast-like. – L. *bestia*, a beast. See **Beast**.

BESTOW, to place, locate, &c. (E.) ME. *bistowen, bestowen*, to place, occupy, employ, give in marriage; Chaucer, Troilus, i. 967; C. T. 3979, 5695 (A 3981, D 113). From the prefix *be-*, and ME. *stowe*, a place; hence it means 'to put into a place.' See **Be-** and **Stow**. Der. *bestow-er, bestow-al*.

BESTREW, to strew over. (E.) In Temp. iv. 1. 20; ME. *bistrewen*, Old Eng. Homilies, p. 5. – AS. *be-* or *bi-*, prefix; and *streowian*, to strew. See **Strew**.

BESTRIDE, to stride over. (E.) In Shak. Cor. iv. 5. 124. ME. *bistriden*, Layamon, iii. 118. AS. *bestrīdan*; Ælfric, Hom. ii. 136. – AS. *be-*, prefix; and *strīdan*, to stride. See **Stride**.

BET, a wager; to wager. (F. – Scand.) Shak. has it both as sb. and verb; Hen. V, ii. 1. 99; Haml. v. 2. 170. It is a mere contraction of *abet*, formerly used both as a sb. and a verb. See **Abet**. Phillips (1706) has: '*Abet*, to encourage, egg, or set on; to maintain, uphold, or back.' Cf. 'The meede of thy mischalenge and *abet*;' Spenser, F. Q. iv. 3. 11. The verb occurs as early as in Ascham, Toxophilus, 1545, ed. Arber, p. 19: 'ready to laye and *bet* with [against] him.'

BETAKE, to enter on, take to. (Hybrid; E. *and* Scand.) ME. *bitaken*, which was chiefly used in the sense of 'to entrust, deliver, hand over to.' 'Heo sculleð eow þat lond *bitaken*' = they shall give you the land;' Layamon, i. 266. Hence 'to commit:' as in: 'Ich *bitake* min soule God' = I commit my soul to God; Rob. of Glouc. p. 475; l. 9772. From AS. prefix *be-* or *bi-*; and ME. *taken*, which is a Scand. word, from Icel. *taka*, to take, deliver. No doubt the sense was influenced by the (really different) AS. *betǣcan*, to assign, Grein, i. 95. See **Be-**, **Take**, and **Teach**.

BETEEM, to think fit, grant, permit. (E.) In the sense of 'grant;' Shak. M.N.D. i. 1. 131; of 'permit,' Hamlet, i. 2. 141. From an AS. form **beteman, **betiman*, to befit, to suit; cf. Friesic *bytema* (Hettema), to befit, Low G. *betemen* (Lübben). From E. prefix *be-*, and AS. **teman*, OSax. *teman*, EFries. *temen*, G. *ziemen*, to suit.

BETEL, a species of pepper. (Port. – Malayālam.) Mentioned in 1681; see Arber's Eng. Garner, i. 414; and in 1585 (N. E. D.). – Port. *betel, betele*. – Malayāl. *vettila*, i. e. *veru + ila*, 'simple or mere leaf' (Yule). ¶ Used of the leaf (*ila*) which is chewed with the dried areca-nut.

BETHINK, to think on, call to mind. (E.) ME. *bithenchen, bithenken, bithinken*; Layamon, ii. 531. AS. *biþencan*, to consider, think about; Grein, i. 121.＋Du. *be-*, prefix; and *þencan*, to think; see **Think**.＋Du. and G. *bedenken*, to consider; Dan. *betænke*, to consider; Swed. *betänka*, to consider.

BETIDE, to happen to, befall. (E.) ME. *bitiden*, Ancren Riwle, p. 278.＋AS. prefix *bi-* or *be-*, and ME. *tiden*, to happen; which is from AS. *tidan*, to happen (Bosworth), from *tid*, a tide, time, hour. See **Tide**.

BETIMES, in good time. (E.) Formerly *betime*; the final *s* is due to the habit of adding *s* or *-es* to form adverbs; cf. *whiles* from *while*, afterwards lengthened to *whilst*; *besides* from *beside*; &c. 'Bi so thow go *bityme*' = provided that thou go betimes; P. Plowman, B. v. 647. – AS. *be* or *bi*, by; and *tima*, time. See **Time**.

BETOKEN, to signify. (E.) ME. *bitacnen, bitocnen, bitokenen*; Ormulum, 1717. Just as in the case of *believe*, q. v., the prefix *be-* has been substituted for the original prefix *ge-*. AS. *getácnian*, to betoken, signify; Grein, i. 462. – AS. *ge-*, prefix; and *tácn*, a token; Grein, i. 506. See **Token**. ¶ Observe that the final *-en* is for *-n*, where the *n* is a real part of the word, not the ME. infinitive ending. Cf. Du. *beteeken-en*, Dan. *betegn-e*, Swed. *beteckn-a*, G. *bezeichn-en*, to denote.

BETONY, a plant. (F. – Late L.) Spelt *betayne*, Voc. 568. 13; *betony*, id. 711. 19; the AF. form was *beteine*, id. 554. 13. – OF. *betoine* (Supp. to Godefroy). – Late L. *betonia*, Voc. 711. 19; for *vettonica, betonica*, a plant discovered by a Spanish tribe named *Vettones*; Pliny, bk. xxv. c. 8.

BETRAY, to act as traitor. (E. *and* F.) ME. *bitraien, betraien*, Chaucer, Troil. v. 1247. It appears early, e. g. in Rob. of Glouc.

p. 454, l. 9325; in King Horn, ed. Lumby, 1271; and in O. Eng. Misc., ed. Morris, p. 40, l. 104. From the E. prefix *be-*; and the ME. *traien*, to betray, of F. origin. [This hybrid compound may have been suggested by *bewray*, q. v.] β. The ME. *traien* is from OF. *traïr* (F. *trahir*); which is from L. *trādere*, to deliver. See **Tradition**. Der. *betray-er*, *betray-al*.

BETROTH, to affiance. (E.) ME. *bitreuthien*, to betroth; occurs thrice in Shoreham's Poems, ed. Wright (Percy Society), pp. 66, 70. Subsequently assimilated to **Troth**. Made by prefixing the verbal prefix *bi-* or *be-* to the sb. *treuthe*, or *treowthe*; which is from AS. *trēowð*, troth, truth; Grein, ii. 552. See **Troth, Truth**. Der. *betroth-al*, *betroth-ment*.

BETTER, BEST. (E.) 1. The ME. forms are, for the comparative, both *bet* (Chaucer, prol. 242) and *bettre* (Chaucer, prol. 256). The former is commonly adverbial, like L. *melius*; the latter adjectival, L. *melior*. AS. *bet*, adv.; *betera*, adj.; Grein, i. 95.╋Goth. *batiza*, adj., better; from a base BAT, good. 2. Again, *best* is short for AS. *betst* (Grein, i. 96), which is an obvious contraction of *bet-ist*.╋ Goth. *batista*, best; from the same base BAT. Some compare it with Skt. *bhadra-s*, excellent; *bhand*, to be fortunate, **or** to make fortunate; but wrongly (Uhlenbeck). ¶ The Gothic forms have been given above, as being the clearest. The other forms of *better* are: Du. *beter*, adj. and adv.; Icel. *betri*, adj., *betr*, adv.; Dan. *bedre*; Swed. *bättre*; G. *besser*. Other forms of *best* are: Du. and G. *best*; Icel. *beztr*, adj., *bezt*, adv.; Dan. *bedst*; Swed. *bäst*. See also **Batten** (1), **Boot** (1).

BETWEEN, in the middle of. (E.) ME. *bituene*, Rob. of Glouc. p. 371, l. 7654; Gower, C. A. i. 9; prol. 189; AS. *be-twēonan*, earlier *be-twēonum*, Grein, i. 96. — AS. *be*, prep., by; and *twēonum*, dat. pl. of *twēon*, double, twain, as in ' *bi* sǣm *twēonum*,' between two seas; Grein, ii. 557. β. *Twēon* is an adj. allied to AS. *twā*, two; and *twēonum* answers to Goth. *tweihnaim*, dat. pl. of *tweihnai*, two each. Cf. L. *bīni*; also G. *zwischen*, between, from *zwei*, two. See **Two**.

BETWIXT, between. (E.) Formed (with excrescent *t*) from ME. *betwixe*, *bitwixe*, Chaucer, C. T., A 2132. AS. *betweox*, *betweohs*, *betweoh*, Grein, i. 96. From *be*, by; and *twih, answering to *tweih-* in Goth. *tweih-nai*, two each; allied to AS. *twā*, two. A similar word is OFriesic *bitwischa*, for *bitwiska*, between; from *bi*, by, and *twisk*, *twiska*, between, which is allied to *twa*, two. Cf. G. *zwischen*, between, from OHG. *zwisc*, *zwiski*, two-fold; allied to OHG. *zwis*, twice and G. *zwei*, two. See **Two**.

BEVEL, sloping; to slope, slant. (F.) Shak. has : ' I may be straight, though they themselves be *bevel*,' i. e. crooked; Sonnet 121. Cotgrave has : ' *Buveau*, m. a kind of squire [carpenter's rule] or squire-like instrument, having moveable and compasse branches; or, the one branch compasse and the other straight : some call it a *bevell*.' Now, as F. *-eau* stands for OF. *-el*, it is clear that E. *bevel* represents an OF. *buvel, or more probably *bevel, which is not, however, to be found; though *béveau*, *buveau* occur in Hatzfeld, s.v. *biveau*. Godefroy cites a verb *bever*, ' biaiser,' to slope. We find, too, the Span. *baivel*, a bevel, accented on the *e*. The etym. of the OF. word is unknown.

BEVER, a potation; see **Beaver** (3) above.

BEVERAGE, drink. (F.—L.) Shak. has *beverage*, Winter's Tale, i. 2. 346; and see Mandeville's Travels, ch. xii. p. 141. Cotgrave has : ' *Bruvage*, *Breuvage*, drinke, beverage.' — OF. *bevrage*, drink (Supp. to Godefroy) ; with which cf. OF. *beverie*, the action of drinking. — OF. *bevre*, *boivre* (see *beivre* in Supp. to Godefroy), to drink; with OF. suffix *-age*, equiv. to L. *-āticum*. — L. *bibere*, to drink. ¶ Cf. Ital. *beveraggio*, drink; Span. *brebage*, drink.

BEVY, a company, esp. of ladies. (F.—L.) Spenser has : ' this *bevie* of Ladies bright ; ' Shep. Kal. April, 118. On which E. K. has the note : ' *Bevie* ; a beavie of ladyes is spoken figuratively for a company or troupe ; the terme is taken of larkes. For they say a *bevie* of larkes, even as a covey of partridge, or an eye of pheasaunts.' Spelt *beue* (= *bevè*) in Skelton, Garl. of Laurel, 771 ; and in the Book of St. Albans (1486), leaf f6 : ' A *beuy* of Ladies, A *beuy* of Roos (roes), A *beuy* of Quaylis.' — F. *bevée*, which Mr. Wedgwood cites, and explains as ' a brood, flock, of quails, larks, roebucks, thence applied to a company of ladies generally ; ' cf. ' *Bevee des heyrouns*, a bevy of herons ; ' Wright's Vocab. i. 151. Florio's Ital. Dict. has : ' *Beva*, a beanie ' [bevy] ; and mod. Ital. *beva* means ' a drink.' β. Origin uncertain ; but the Ital. points to the original sense as being a company for drinking, from OF. *bevre*, Ital. *bevere*, to drink. Cf. Ital. *beverare*, to water cattle (Torriano). See **Beverage**.

BEWAIL, to wail for, lament. (E. *and* Scand.) ME. *biweilen*, *bewailen* ; K. Alisaunder, ed. Weber, 4395. From the prefix *be-* ; and ME. *wailen*, to wail, of Scand. origin. See **Wail**.

BEWARE, to be wary, to be cautious. (E.) This is now written as *one* word, and considered as a verb ; yet it is nothing but the two words *be ware* run together ; the word *ware* being here an adjective,

viz. the ME. *war*, for which the longer term *wary* has been substituted in mod. E. ' *Be war* therfor ' = therefore be wary, Chaucer, C. T. 4539 (B 119). ' A ha ! felawes ! *beth ware* of swiche a Iape ! ' = aha ! sirs, beware (lit. be ye wary) of such a jest ; Chaucer, C. T., 13369 (B 1629). The latter phrase cannot be mistaken ; since *beth* is the imperative plural of the verb. So also : ' Whi nolden hii *be war* ? ' Polit. Songs, p. 217. Cf. AS. *wær*, adj., wary, cautious. See **Wary**.

BEWILDER, to perplex. (E.) Dryden has the pp. *bewilder'd*; tr. of Lucretius, bk. ii. l. 11. Made by prefixing *be-* to the prov. Eng. *wildern*, a wilderness, shortened to *wilder* by the influence of the longer form *wilderness*, which would naturally be supposed as compounded of *wilder-* and *-ness*, whereas it is rather compounded of *wildern-* and *-ness*, and should, etymologically, be spelt with double *n*. For examples of *wildern*, a wilderness, see Halliwell's Dictionary, and Layamon's Brut, l. 1238. β. Thus *bewilder* (for *bewildern*) is ' to lead into a wilderness,' which is just the way in which it was first used. Dryden has : ' *Bewilder'd* in the *maze* of life' (as above) ; and Addison, Cato, i. 1. 49, has : ' Puzzled in *mazes*, . . . Lost and *be-wildered* in the fruitless search.' γ. There is thus no reason for supposing it other than a purely native word, though other languages possess words somewhat similar. Cf. Du. *verwilderen*, to grow wild, *verwilderd*, uncultivated ; Dan. *forvilde*, to lead astray, bewilder, perplex ; passive *forvildes*, to go astray, lose one's way ; Swed. *förvilla*, to puzzle, confound ; Icel. *villr*, bewildered, astray ; *villa*, to bewilder. ¶ The Scandinavian words show that the peculiar sense of E. *bewilder* has a trace of Scandinavian influence. See **Wilderness**. Der. *bewilder-ment* (modern).

BEWITCH, to charm with witchcraft. (E.) ME. *biwicchen*, *bewicchen* ; spelt *biwicched* (unusual) in Layamon, ii. 597, where the later MS. has *iwicched*. From prefix *be-* or *bi-* ; and AS. *wiccian*, to be a witch, to use witchcraft, in Thorpe's Ancient Laws of England, ii. 274, sect. 39, from AS. *wicce*, f., a witch. See **Witch**. Der. *be-witch-ment*, *bewitch-er-y*.

BEWRAY, to disclose ; properly, to accuse. (E.) In A. V. Matt. xxvi. 73 ; and, for numerous examples, see Eastwood and Wright's Bible Wordbook. ME. *bewraien*, *biwreyen* ; Chaucer has *biwreye*, to disclose, reveal, C. T. 6530 (D 948), and also the simple verb *wreye* in the same sense, C. T. 3503. — Prefix *be-*, and AS. *wrēgan* (for *wrōg-ian), to accuse ; ' *agunnon hine wrēgan*,' they began to accuse him, Luke, xxiii. 2. So also OFries. *biwrōgia*, to accuse. Cf. Icel. *rægja* (orig. *vrægja*), to slander, defame ; Swed. *röja*, to discover, betray ; Goth. *wrōhjan*, to accuse ; G. *rügen*, to censure. These are denom. verbs, formed from a sb. which appears as Goth. *wrōhs*, an accusation ; Icel. *rōg*, a slander ; cf. G. *rüge*, censure. Fick, iii. 310. Perhaps allied to AS. *wearg*, a criminal, Goth. *gawargjan*, to condemn.

BEY, a governor. (Turkish.) ' The *By* . . . in their language a Duke ; ' Hakluyt, Voy. ii. pt. i. p. 168. — Turk. *bēg* (pron. nearly as E. *bay*), a lord, a prince ; Rich. Dict., p. 310. Cf. Persian ' *baig*, a lord ; a Mogul title ; ' Palmer's Pers. Dict. col. 102.

BEYOND, on the farther side of. (E.) ME. *beyonde*, *biyonde*, *beyeonden* ; Maundeville's Travels, pp. 1, 142, 314. AS. *begeondan*, Matt. iv. 25. — AS. *be-*, and *geond*, *giond*, prep., across, beyond ; with adv. suffix *-an*. See *geond* in Grein, i. 497 ; and cf. AS. *be-geonan*, beyond ; Sweet, O. E. Texts, p. 535. And see **Yon, Yonder**.

BEZEL, the sloping edge of a chisel ; the sloping facets of a cut gem ; the part of a ring in which the stone is set, and which holds it in. (F.—L. ?) Also spelt *basil*. It occurs in Cotgrave's Dict., who explains F. *biseau* by ' a *bezle*, *bezling*, or scuing [i. e. skewing] ; such a slopenesse, or slope forme, as is in the point of an iron leaver, chizle, &c.' The E. *basil* is generally used of the sloping edge to which a chisel is ground ; the application to the ring relates to the sloping edge or rim of metal round the stone. The F. *biseau* had an older spelling *bisel* (noted by Roquefort), from which E. *bezel* and *basil* are corruptions. — OF. *bisel*, which Roquefort explains by ' en pente ; angle imperceptible ; ' the true sense being, apparently, ' a sloping edge ; ' cf. Span. *bisel* (accented on *e*), a basil, bezel ; the edge of a looking-glass, or crystal plate. [Looking-glasses sometimes have a slanted border, so as to be thin at the edge.] β. Origin unknown ; perhaps (as Diez remarks) it contains the L. *bis*, double. Körting, § 1356, Supp., suggests *biais-el ; see **Bias**.

BEZIQUE, a game at cards. (F.—Pers. ?) Spelt *bazique* in Macmillan's Mag., Dec. 1861, p. 138. An error for F. *besigue*, also spelt *bésy* (Littré). The former is prob. from Pers. *bāzichah*, sport, a game ; the latter may be Pers. *bāzī*, play. — Pers. *bāzīdan*, to play. Cf. Pers. *bāzīgar*, a juggler, which perhaps suggested the form *be-sigue*. (Doubtful.)

BEZOAR, a kind of stone. (F.—Port.—Arab.—Pers.) *Bezoar-stone* is in Ben Jonson, Every Man out of his Humour, v. 4.— MF. *bezoar*, 16th cent. spelling of F. *bézoard*, according to Brachet. Cotgrave has : ' *Bezoard*, a Beazar stone.' — Port. *bezoar* ; see Brachet, who remarks that the word was introduced from India by the Portuguese; and cf. Span. *bezaar* in Pineda. — Arab. *bādzahr* (with *b* for *p*). — Pers. *pād-zahr*, the bezoar-stone, also called *zahr-dārū*; Palmer's Pers. Dict. coll. 105, 328. So called because it was a supposed antidote against poison. — Pers. *pād*, expelling; and *zahr*, poison; Rich. Dict. pp. 228, 315, 790. And see Yule; and Horn, § 273.

BEZONIAN, a beggarly fellow. (F.—Ital.) In 2 Hen. IV, v. 3. 118. Formerly *bisonian*; formed with suffix -(*i*)*an* from F. *bisogne*, spelt *bisongne* in Cotgrave, 'a filthie knave . . . bisonian.' — Ital. *bisogni*, pl., 'new-levied souldiers such as come . . . needy to the wars;' Torriano. — Ital. *bisogno*, want; of doubtful origin.

BI-, prefix. (L.) Generally Latin; in *bias*, it is F., but still from L. — L. *bi-*, prefix = *dui-*; cf. L. *bellum* for *duellum*. — L. *duo*, two. Cf. Gk. δι-, prefix, from δύω, two; Skt. *dvi-*, prefix, from *dva*, two; AS. *twi-*, prefix, from *twā*, two. See Fick, i. 625. See **Two.** In L. *bi-nī*, two each, *bi-* is for *bis*, twice. ☞ In ME. the prefix *bi-* occurs as another spelling of the prefix *be-*; see **Be-.**

BIAS, an inclination to one side, a slope. (F.—L.) Spelt *biais* in Holland's Pliny, bk. xxvii. c. 4 (on the Aloe, l. 2.) — F. *biais*, a slant, a slope. — L. acc. *bifacem*, used by Isidore of Seville in the sense of squinting, of one who looks sidelong. ¶ This is not wholly satisfactory; but see P. Toynbee, Hist. Gr. § 273.

BIB, a cloth on an infant's breast. (L.) Used by Beaum. and Fletcher, The Captain, iii. 5. It must have meant a cloth for *imbibing* moisture, borrowed, half jocularly, from the ME. *bibben*, to tipple, imbibe, used by Chaucer, C. T. 4160 (A 4162): 'This miller hath so wisly *bibbed* ale.' This, again, must have been borrowed directly from L. *bibere*, to drink, and may be imagined to have been also used jocularly by those familiar with a little monkish Latin. Hence *wine-bibber*, Luke, vii. 34, where the Vulgate has *bibens uinum*. +Skt. *pibāmi*, I drink; OIrish *ibim*, for **pibim*, I drink. Der. from the same source; *bibb-er*, *bib-ul-ous*.

BIBLE, the sacred book. (F.—L.—Gk.—Egypt.) ME. *bible*, *byble*; Chaucer, Ho. of Fame, iii. 244; P. Plowman, B. x. 318. — F. *bible*. — Late L. *biblia*, fem. sing.; for L. *biblia*, neut. pl. — Gk. βιβλία, a collection of writings, pl. of βιβλίον, a little book; dimin. of βίβλος, a book. — Gk. βύβλος, the Egyptian papyrus, whence paper was first made; hence a book. Of Egypt. origin; cf. **Paper.** Der. *bibl-ic-al*.

BIBLIOGRAPHY, the description of books. (Gk.) Modern. From Gk. βιβλίο-, for βιβλίον, a book; and γράφειν, to write. See **Bible.** Der. *bibliograph-ic-al*; and from the same source, *bibliograph-er*.

BIBLIOLATRY, book-worship. (Gk.) Used by Byrom, Upon the Bp. of Gloucester's Doctrine of Grace (R.) From Gk. βιβλίο-, for βιβλίον, a book; and λατρεία, service; see **Idolatry.**

BIBLIOMANIA, a passion for books. (Gk.) Modern. From Gk. βιβλίο-, for βιβλίον, a book; and E. *mania*, also of Gk. origin; see **Mania.** Der. *bibliomania-c*.

BICE, a pale blue colour; *green bice* is a pale green. (F.) The true sense is 'grayish.' Borrowed from F. *bis*, fem. *bise*, which Cotgrave explains as 'brown, duskie, blackish.' He gives too: 'Roche *bise*, a hard, and *blewish* rocke, or quarrey, of stone.' Cf. F. *bis blanc*, whitey-brown; OF. *azur bis*, grayish blue; *vert bis*, grayish green. Spelt *byse* in Skelton, Garlande of Laurell, l. 1158. The word is found also in Italian as *bigio*, grayish. Origin unknown; see Diez.

BICKER, to skirmish. (E. or F.) ME. *bikere*, P. Plowman, B. xx. 78; *biker*, sb., a skirmish, Rob. of Glouc. p. 538; l. 11147; but it is most commonly a verb. Apparently formed, with frequentative suffix -*er*, from the verb *biken*, to thrust with a pointed weapon, King Alisaunder, 2337; which may be a variant of ME. *beken*, to peck; from OF. *bequer*, to strike with the beak (see **Beak**), or from AS. *becca*, a pickaxe. Cf. Du. *bikken*, to notch a mill-stone; EFries. *bikkern*, to hack, gnaw, from Du. *bikken*, to hack, *bikke*, a pickaxe.

BICYCLE, a two-wheeled velocipede. (Hybrid; L. *and* Gk.) A hybrid substitute for *two-wheel*; in use since 1868. Coined from **Bi-** and **Cycle.**

BID (1), to pray. (E.) [*Bid*, to pray, is nearly obsolete; but used in what is really a reduplicated phrase, viz. 'a bidding prayer.' To 'bid beads' was, originally, to 'pray prayers.' See **Bead.**] ME. *bidden*, to pray, P. Plowman, B. vii. 81. AS. *biddan*, to pray (in common use) of conj. 5; pt. t. *bæd*, pp. *beden*.+Du. *bidden*, to pray; OHG. *pittan*, G. *bitten*, to pray, request. These are strong verbs, and so are Icel. *biðja*, Swed. *bedja*, Dan. *bede*, to pray, beg, and Goth. *bidjan*, to pray, ask, notwithstanding the weak form of the infinitive. Teut. type **bedjan-*. ¶ It has been suggested that the Teut. **bedjan-* (2nd grade **bad*) was a new strong verb substituted for **beidan-* (2nd grade **baid*), from the Idg. root BHEIDH, to which we may refer Gk. πείθειν, and L. *fides*, but not *bid* (2). Brugm. i. § 589; ii. § 890. See **Bide.**

BID (2), to command. (E.) [Closely connected as this word

appears to be with E. *bid*, to pray, it is certainly from a different root, and can be traced more easily. It has been assimilated to *bid* in spelling, but should rather have taken the form *bede*.] ME. *bede*, Chaucer, C. T. 8236 (E 360). AS. *bēodan*, to command (common) of conj. 2; pt. t. *bēad*, pp. *boden*.+Du. *bieden*, to offer; Icel. *bjóða*; G. *bieten*; Goth. *biudan*, only in comp. *ana-biudan*, to command, *faur-biudan*, to forbid. Allied to Skt. *bodhaya*, to cause to know, inform, causal of *budh*, to awake, understand; Gk. πεύθομαι, πυνθάνομαι, I enquire, learn, understand. Teut. type **beudan-*; from the root BHEUDH, to awake, observe; Fick, i. 162; Brugm. i. § 213. ¶ Confused in E. with *bid* (1). Der. *bidd-er*, *bidd-ing*.

BIDE, to await, wait. (E.) ME. *bide*, P. Plowman, B. xviii. 307. AS. *bīdan*, Grein, i. 122; of conj. 1; pt. t. *bād*, pp. *biden*.+Du. *beiden*; Icel. *bíða*; Swed. *bida*; Dan. *bie*; Goth. *beidan*; OHG. *bītan* (prov. G. *beiten*). Teut. type **beidan-*; from the root BHEIDH; cf. L. *fīd-ere*, to trust. Brugm. i. § 202. See also **Abide.**

BIENNIAL, lasting two years. (L.) 'The Duke is there but *biennial*;' Howell, Letters, vol. i. let. 41 (1621). — L. *biennālis*, the same as *biennis*, adj., for two years. [The second *i* in *biennial* is due to confusion with the sb. *biennium*, a space of two years.] — L. *bi-*, two, double; and *annālis*, lasting for a year, which becomes -*ennālis* in composition. — L. *annus*, a year. See **Annual.** Der. *biennial-ly*.

BIER, a frame on which a dead body is borne. (E.) ME. *beere*, Prompt. Parv. p. 32; *bære*, Layamon, 19481. AS. *bǣr*, Grein, i. 78. — AS. *bǣr-*, 3rd grade of *beran*, to bear.+Du. *baar*; OHG. *bāra* (G. *bahre*); allied to Icel. *barar*, fem. pl.; and to L. *fer-e-trum*; Gk. φέρετρον. See **Bear** (1). The present spelling is due to F. *bière*, a bier.

BIESTINGS, BEESTINGS, the first milk given by a cow after calving. (E.) Very common in provincial English, in a great number of differing forms, such as *biskins*, *bistins*, &c. AS. *bysting*, *bȳst* (for **biest*), thick milk; from AS. *bēost*, first milk after calving. We find, in Voc. 127. 35, and 129. 2, '*byst*, *bysting*, *þicce meolc*' = biest, biestings, thick milk.+Du. *biest*, biestings; G. *biestmilch*, biestings. All from a Teut. base **beust-*.

BIFFIN, a large rosy winter apple. (F.—L.; *with* E. *suffix*.) Prov. E. *beefin*; Suffolk. I have also heard them called *beefing apples* (correctly). 'As red as a *beefen* from her own orchard;' Godwin, Caleb Williams (1794), p. 63. *Beefing* refers to the beef-like colour. From *beef*; with suffix -*ing* (N. E. D.). See **Beef.**

BIFURCATED, two-pronged. (L.) Pennant, British Zoology, has 'a large *bifurcated* tooth;' Richardson. Sir T. Browne, Vulg. Errors, b. ii. c. 6. § 2, has the sb. *bifurcation*. — Late L. *bifurcātus*, pp. of *bifurcāri*, to part in two directions. — L. *bifurcus*, two-pronged. — L. *bi-*, double; and *furca*, a fork, prong. See **Fork.**

BIG, large. (Scand.) ME. *big*, Chaucer, Prol. 546; Havelok, 1774; *bigg*, 'rich, well-furnished,' Prick of Conscience, ed. Morris, 1460; see also Minot's Poems, Edward at La Hogue, l. 83. Being used by Minot and Hampole, it was probably at first a Northern word, and of Scandinavian origin; cf. Ægelric *Bigga*, Kemble, C. D., vi. 191. β. Allied to prov. E. *bug*, fine, *bog*, boastful; so that the base is *byg-*, mutated from *bug-*, weak grade of Teut. **beugan-*, to bow or bend; see **Bow** (1); from the notion of swelling out. Cf. Norw. *bugge*, a strong man (prov. E. a *big bug*); Dan. *bugne*, to bulge; also Swed. dial. *bogt*, (1) a bend, (2) strength.

BIGAMY, a double marriage. (F.—L. *and* Gk.) 'Bigamie is . . twice-wifing;' Genesis and Exodus, ed. Morris, i. 449. — F. *bigamie*. — L. *bigamia*. 'Bigamy (*bigamia*), . . is used for an impediment to be a clerk, Anno 4 Edw. I. 5;' Blount's Law Dictionary. A hybrid compound; from L. prefix *bi-*, twice, q. v., and Gk. -γαμία, from γάμος, marriage; imitated from Gk. διγαμία, a double marriage, which is from Gk. δι-, twice, and a form -γαμία, derived from γάμος, marriage. The Gk. γάμος, marriage, is from γα-, weak grade of √GEN, to beget. Brugm. i. § 437 (2). Der. *bigam-ist*.

BIGGIN, BIGGEN, a night-cap. (F.) In Shak. 2 Hen. IV, iv. 5. 27. — MF. *beguin*, 'a biggin for a child;' Cot. He also gives *beguiner*, to put on a biggin. Palsgrave has: '*Biggayne*, a woman that lyveth chaste;' and '*Byggen*, for a chyldes heed;' for both words he gives F. *beguine*. Doubtless named from a resemblance to the caps worn by the nuns called *Béguines*, who, as Cotgrave remarks, 'commonly be all old, or well in years.' See **Beguine.** ¶ *Biggin* also occurs as a spelling of *piggin*.

BIGHT, a coil of a rope; a bay. (E.) ME. *byght*, a bend; Gawain and the Grene Knight, l. 1349. AS. *byht*, as in *wæteres byht*, a bight (bay) of water; Grein, i. 151. Cf. Dan. and Swed. *bugt*, used in both senses, viz. (1) the bight of a rope; and (2) a bay; also G. *bucht*, a bay. β. The AS. *byht* (for **buhtiz*) is from AS. *bug-*, weakest grade of *būg-an*, to bend; with mutation of *u* to *y*. See **Bow** (1).

BIGOT, an obstinate devotee to a particular creed, a hypocrite. (F.) In Blount's Gloss. (1656) we find: '*Bigot*, an hypocrite, &c.:' as in Cotgrave. — F. *bigot*, which Cotgrave explains thus: 'An old Norman word (signifying as much as *de par Dieu*, or our for God's sake [he means *by God*] and signifying) an hypocrite, or one that seemeth much more holy than he is; also, a scrupulous or superstitious fellow.' **α.** The word occurs in Wace's Roman du Rou, ii. 71, where we find: 'Mult ont Franceis Normanz laidiz E de mesaiz e de mediz, Sovent lor dient reproviers, E claiment *bigoz* e draschiers,' i. e. the French have much insulted the Normans, both with evil deeds and evil words, and often speak reproaches of them, and call them *bigots* and dreg-drinkers (Diez); see *Drachier* in Godefroy. Roquefort quotes further from the Roman du Rou, fol. 228, in which the word occurs again: 'Sovent dient, Sire, por coi Ne tolez la terre as *bigos*;' i. e. they often said, Sire, wherefore do you not take away the land from these barbarians? **β.** The origin of the word is unknown. The old supposition that it is a corruption of *by God*, which is an *English* phrase, is mere 'popular etymology,' and inconsistent with the facts. *Bigot* occurs already in the 12th century, 'in the romance of Girart de Roussillon, as the proper name of some people, apparently of the south of Gaul;' N. E. D. It is not, however, a corruption of *Visigoth*, as has been absurdly suggested. ' Hue le Bigot' occurs in Wace, Roman de Rou, l. 8571. Mr. Wedgwood's guess that it arose in the 13th century is disproved at once by the fact that Wace died before A.D. 1200. **γ.** At the same time, it is very likely that this old term of derision may have been confused with the term *beguin*, which was especially used of religious devotees. See **Beguin.** And it is a fact that the name was applied to some of these orders; some *Beguttæ* of the order of St. Augustine are mentioned in a charter of A.D. 1518; and in another document, given by Ducange, we find: ' *Beghardus* et *Beguina* et *Begutta* sunt viri et mulieres tertii ordinis;' and again *Biguttæ* are mentioned, in a charter of A.D. 1499. This transference of the nickname to members of these religious orders explains the modern use of the term. Der. *bigot-ry.*

BIJOU, a trinket, jewel. (F.–C.) Modern; and mere French.– F. *bijou.* Perhaps of Celtic origin; cf. Breton *bizou* (Corn. *bisou*), a ring with a stone.– Bret. *biz,* W. *bys,* a finger; Stokes-Fick, p. 175.

BILATERAL, having two sides. (L.) From L. *bi-,* double· and *laterālis,* adj., lateral.– L. *later-,* decl. stem of *latus,* a side.

BILBERRY, a whortleberry. (Scand. *and* E.) ' As blue as *bilberry*;' Shak. Merry Wives, v. 5. 49. This form is due to the Jutland *byllebær* (Feilberg), Dan. *böllebær,* the bilberry; where *bær* is a berry. Cf. MDan. *bölle,* a boss, protuberance (Kalkar); perhaps allied to **Boil** (2); from **bul-,* weak grade of Teut. **beul-,* to swell; cf. Goth. *uf-bauljan,* to swell up. We also find Swed. dial. *böljon, böljan, bölen,* pl. bilberries. ¶ In the North of England we find *bleaberry* or *blaeberry,* i. e. a berry of a dark, livid colour; cf. our phrase 'to beat black and *blue.*' *Blae* is the Icel. *blár,* dark, livid, Dan. *blaa,* Swed. *blå,* dark-blue; whence Icel. *blåber,* Dan. *blaabær,* Swed. *blåbär,* a blaeberry. See **Blue.** Hence both *bil-* and *blae-* are Scandinavian; but *-berry* is English.

BILBO, a sword; **BILBOES,** fetters. (Span.) Shak. has both *bilbo,* Merry Wives, i. 1. 165, and *bilboes,* Hamlet, v. 2. 6. Both words are derived from Bilboa or Bilbao in Spain, 'which was famous, as early as the time of Pliny, for the manufacture of iron and steel.' Several *bilboes* (fetters) were found among the spoils of the Spanish Armada, and are still to be seen in the Tower of London. See note by Clark and Wright to Hamlet, v. 2. 6.

BILE (1), a secretion from the liver. (F.–L.) In Kersey's Dict., ed. 1708.– F. *bile,* which Cotgrave explains by 'choller, gall,' &c.– L. *bilis,* bile, anger. L. *bilis* is for **bislis*; Brugm. i. § 877; cf. W. *bustl,* Bret. *bestl,* bile; Stokes-Fick, p. 175. Der. *bili-ar-y, bili-ous.*

BILE (2), a boil; Shak. Cor. i. 4. 31. (E.) ME. *byle,* Prompt. Parv. See **Boil** (2).

BILGE, the belly of a ship or cask. (F.–C.) It means the protuberant part of a cask or of a ship's bottom, i. e. the belly, and is merely another form of *bulge,* adapted from OF. *boulge,* mod. F. *bouge,* which still means 'bilge' of a cask, &c. **β.** Hence the vb. *to bilge,* said of a ship, which begins to leak; but it occurs still earlier in a transitive sense, to stave in a ship's bottom. This verb *to bilge* is also written *to bulge*; see examples in Richardson, s. v. *bulge*; and Kersey's Dict., s. v. *bilged.* **γ.** Bilge-water is water which enters a ship when lying on her *bilge,* and becomes offensive. See **Bulge.**

BILL (1), a chopper; a halberd; sword. (E.) ME. *bil,* sword, halberd, Layamon, i. 74; ' *Bylle* of a mattoke, *ligo, marra*;' Prompt. Parv. p. 36. AS. *bil, bill,* a sword, axe, Grein, i. 116.+ OSax. *bil,* OHG. *bill,* n. Teut. type **biljom,* neut. Cf. G. *bille,* fem. a pick-axe. Cf. Skt. *bil, bhil,* to break, to divide, Benfey, p. 633; which is probably related to Skt. *bhid,* to cleave. See **Bite.**

BILL (2), a bird's beak. (E.) ME. *bile,* Owl and Nightingale, 79. AS. *bile*; Voc. 318. 13. Teut. type **biliz?* Allied to **Bill** (1).

BILL (3), a writing, account. (F.–L.) ME. *bille,* a letter, writing; Chaucer, C. T. 9811 (E 1937).–AF. *bille,* Polit. Songs, p. 231, l. 11; found in F. in the dimin. *billet.*– Late L. *billa,* a writing, with dimin. *billēta; bullēta* is also found, with the same meaning,

and is the dimin. of L. *bulla.* **β.** It is certain that *billa* is a corruption of L. *bulla,* meaning 'a writing,' 'a schedule' in medieval times; but esp. and properly 'a sealed writing;' from the classical L. *bulla,* a stud, knob; later, a round seal. See **Bull** (2), **Bullet, Bulletin.**

BILLET (1), a note, ticket. (F.–L.) Shak. has the vb. *to billet,* to direct to one's quarters by means of a ticket; to quarter; Cor. iv. 3. 48. Spelt *bylet,* Prompt. Parv.– AF. *billette,* f., Stat. Realm, i. 338 (1353); cf. F. *billet,* m.; dimin. of AF. *bille,* a ticket, note, writing. See **Bill** (3). We sometimes use *bille'-doux* for ' love-letter;' see Pope, Rape of the Lock, i. 118, 138. It is mere French, and means, literally, 'sweet letter;' from F. *billet,* letter, and *doux* (L. *dulcis*), sweet.

BILLET (2), a log of wood, block. (F.) In Shak. Measure, iv. 3. 58. Spelt *bylet,* Prompt. Parv.– F. *billette,* 'a billet of wood; also, a little bowle;' Cot. Cf. F. *billot,* 'a billet, block, or log of wood;' id. Dimin. of F. *bille,* a log of wood; in Cotgrave, 'a young stock of a tree to graft on.' This F. *bille* corresponds to Med. L. *billa, billus,* a branch, trunk of a tree; of unknown origin.

BILLIARDS, a game with balls. (F.) Shak. has *billiards,* Ant. and Cleop. ii. 5. 3.– F. *billard, billart,* 'a short and thick truncheon, or cudgell, . . a *billard,* or the stick wherewith we touch the ball at *billyards*;' Cot. He also has: '*Biller,* to play at billyards;' and '*bille,* a small bowl or billyard ball; also, a young stock of a tree to graft on;' but these *may* be two distinct words. Formed, by suffix *-ard,* from F. *bille,* signifying a 'billyard ball,' as explained by Cotgrave, and answering to Ital. *biglia,* 'a billiard ball' (Baretti); which Diez derives from MHG. *bickel,* a pick-axe, also a die to play with; which is doubtful. Korting, § 1367.

BILLION, a million of millions. (F.–L.) From F. *billion,* 'a million of millions;' Cot. A coined word, to express 'a double million;' from L. *bi-,* double; and *-illion,* the latter part of the word *million.* So also *trillion,* to express 'a treble million,' or a million times a billion. ¶ The mod. F. *billion* now means 'a thousand millions.'

BILLOW, a wave. (Scand.) Not in very early use. It occurs in Gascoigne's Jocasta, Act iii. chorus, l. 24.– Icel. *bylgja,* a billow; Swed. *bölja*; Dan. *bölge.*+MHG. *bulge,* a billow, also a bag; OHG. *pulga.* The Icel. *bylgja* has mutation of *u* to *y*; and is derived from *bulg-,* weak stem of the root which appears in AS. *belgan,* to swell, esp. to swell with anger; a *billow* means 'a swell,' 'a swelling wave.' Cf. Prov. G. (Hamburg) *bulgen,* a billow (Richey). From √BHELGH, to swell; see **Belly.** Der. *billow-y.*

BIN, a chest for wine, corn, &c. (C.) ME. *binne, bynne,* Chaucer, C. T. 595 (A 593). AS. *binn,* a manger, Luke, ii. 7, 16.+Du. *ben,* a basket; G. *benne,* a sort of basket. Said to be ultimately of Celtic origin; cf. F. *banne,* a tilt of a cart, from L. *benna,* a car of osier, body of a cart, noticed by Festus as a word of Gaulish origin. And cf. W. *ben,* a cart. Celtic type **bennā*: Stokes-Fick, p. 168. ¶ Sometimes confused with *bing,* which is a distinct word.

BINARY, twofold. (L.) In Holland's Plutarch, p. 665.– L. *binārius,* consisting of two things.– L. *bini,* two each.– L. *bi-,* double, for *bis,* twice. See **Bi-,** prefix.

BIND, to fasten, tie. (E.) ME. *binden,* Chaucer, C. T. 4082. AS. *bindan,* pt. t. *band,* pp. *bunden*; Grein, i. 117.+Du. *binden*; Icel. and Swed. *binda*; Dan. *binde*; OHG. *pintan,* G. *binden*; Goth. *bindan.* Teut. type **bindan-,* for **bendan-*; cf. Skt. *bandh,* to bind; √BHENDH. Brugm. i. § 124. Der. *bind-ing, binder, book-binder, bind-weed*; also *bundle, bend.*

BING, a heap of corn; provincial. (Scand.) Surrey has ' *bing* of corn' for 'heap of corn,' in his translation of Virgil, Book iv. l. 529. – Icel. *bingr,* a heap; Swed. *binge,* a heap. Allied to **Bunk.** ¶ Distinct from E. *bin,* though sometimes confused with it. Dan. *bing* came to mean 'bin.' See **Bin.**

BINNACLE, a box for a ship's compass. (MSpan.–L.) Modern; a singular corruption of the older form *bittacle,* due to confusion with *bin,* a chest. Only the form *bittacle* appears in Todd's Johnson, as copied from Kersey's Dict., viz. 'a frame of timber in the steerage of a ship where the compass is placed.' Spelt *bittakle* in Phillips (1658).–MSpan. *bitacula* (Minsheu); Port. *bitacola*; Span. *bitacora.* Cf. F. *habitacle,* a binnacle; prop. an abode.– L. *habitāculum,* a little dwelling, whence the Port. and Span. are derived by loss of the initial syllable.– L. *habitāre,* to dwell; frequentative of *habēre,* to have. See **Habit.** ¶ The 'habitaculum' seems to have been originally a sheltered place for the steersman. The earliest E. quotation has the spelling *bitakle*; Naval Accounts for 1485, ed. A. Oppenheim, p. 56.

BINOCULAR, suited for two eyes; having two eyes. (L.) 'Most animals are *binocular*;' Derham, Phys. Theol. (1713), bk. viii. c. 3, note *a.* Coined from *bin-* for L. *bini,* two each; and *oculus,* an eye. See **Binary** and **Ocular.**

BINOMIAL, consisting of two 'terms' or parts. (L.) Mathematical. — Late L. *binōmi-us*, for L. *binōminis*, having two names. — L. *bi-*, prefix, double ; and *nōmen*, a name, denomination. It should rather have been *binominal*.

BIOGRAPHY, an account of a life. (Gk.) In Johnson's Rambler, no. 60. Langhorne, in the Life of Plutarch, has *biographer* and *biographical*. — Late Gk. βιογραφία, a writing of lives ; Duc. — Gk. βίο-, for βίος, life ; and γράφειν, to write. Gk. βίος is allied to E. *quick*, living ; see **Quick**. And see **Carve**. Der. *biograph-er*, *bio-graph-ic-al*.

BIOLOGY, the science of life. (Gk.) Modern. Lit. a 'discourse on life.' — Gk. βίο-, for βίος, life ; and -λογία, from λόγος, a discourse. See above ; and see **Logic**. Der. *biolog-ic-al*.

BIPARTITE, divided in two parts. (L.) Used by Cudworth, Intellectual System ; Pref. p. 1. — L. *bipartitus*, pp. of *bipartīre*, to divide into two parts. — L. *bi-*, double ; and *partire*, to divide, from *part-*, stem of *pars*, a part. See **Bi-** and **Part**.

BIPED, two-footed ; an animal with two feet. (L.) 'A ... biped beast ;' Byrom, an Epistle. Also in Sir T. Browne's Vulg. Errors, b. iii. c. 4. s. 8. The adj. is sometimes *bipedal*. — L. *biped-*, stem of *bipēs*, having two feet ; from *bi-*, double, and *pēs*, a foot. ¶ So too Gk. δίπους, two-footed, from δι-, double, and πούς, a foot. See **Bi-** and **Foot**, with which *pēs* is cognate.

BIRCH, a tree. (E.) In North of England, *birk* ; which is Scandinavian. ME. *birche*, Chaucer, C. T. 2921. AS. *birce*, wk. f. (Bosworth) ; also *beorc*, str. f.+Du. *berk* ; Icel. *björk* ; Swed. *björk* ; Dan. *birk* ; G. *birke*. Teut. types *berkjōn-*, f. ; and *berkā*, f. Cf. Lith. *beržas* ; Russ. *bereza* ; Skt. *bhūrja-s*, a kind of birch, the leaves or bark of which were used for writing on (Benfey). Allied to Skt. *bhrāj*, to shine ; with reference to the whiteness of the bark. Cf. L. *fraxinus*, ash. See **Bright**. Der. *birch-en*, adj. ; cf. *gold-en*.

BIRD, a feathered flying animal. (E.) ME. *brid* ; very rarely *byrde*, which has been formed from *brid* by shifting the letter *r* ; pl. *briddes*, Chaucer, C. T. 2931 (A 2929). AS. *brid*, *bridd*, a bird ; but especially the *young* of birds ; as in *earnes brid*, the young one of an eagle, Grein, i. 142. The manner in which it is used in early writers suggests the idea that it was considered as 'a thing bred ;' but it can hardly be connected with AS. *brēdan*, to breed, as the Teut. type would be *bridjoz* or *bredjoz*. Der. *bird-bolt*, *bird-cage*, *bird-call*, *bird-catcher*, *bird-lime*, *bird's-eye*, &c.

BIRETTA, a clerical cap. (Ital. — L. — Gk.) Spelt *berretta* in Hall's Sat. iv. 7. 52, ed. 1598. — Ital. *berretta* (Baretti) ; *beretta* (Torriano), a cap ; cf. Late L. *birrētum*, orig. a scarlet cap. — Late L. *birrus*, *burrus*, reddish ; see **Bureau**.

BIRTH, a being born. (Scand.) ME. *birthe*, Chaucer, C. T. 4612 (B 192). Of Scand. origin. — OIcel. *byrð*, fem., quoted by Noreen, Gr. § 327 (cognate with Dan. *byrd*) ; the usual Icel. form is *burðr*, m. Teut. type *burðiz*, f. ; from *bur-*, weak grade of *beran-* (AS. *beran*), to bear. Cf. also AS. *ge-byrd* ; OHG. *kapurt*, G. *geburt* ; Goth. *gabaurths*, a birth ; Skt. *bhrtis*, f., nourishment ; Irish *breith*, birth.— √BHER, to bear. Der. *birth-day*, *-place*, *-mark*, *-right*.

BISCUIT, a kind of cake, baked hard. (F. — L.) In Shak., As You Like It, ii. 7. 39. 'Byscute brede, bis coctus ;' Prompt. Parv. — F. *biscuit*, 'a bisket, bisket-bread ;' Cot. — F. *bis*, twice ; and *cuit*, cooked ; because formerly prepared by being twice baked. (*Cuit* is the pp. of *cuire*, to cook.) — L. *bis coctus*, where *coctus* is the pp. of *coquere*, to cook. See **Cook**.

BISECT, to divide into two equal parts. (L.) In Barrow's Math. Lectures, Lect. 15. Coined from L. *bi-*, twice, and *sectum*, supine of *secāre*, to cut. See **Bi-** and **Section**. Der. *bisect-ion*.

BISHOP, an ecclesiastical overseer. (L. — Gk.) ME. *bisshop*, Chaucer, C. T., B 253. AS. *biscop*, in common use ; borrowed from L. *episcopus*. — Gk. ἐπίσκοπος, an overseer, overlooker. — Gk. ἐπί, upon ; and σκοπός, that watches, from σκοπ-, and 2nd grade of σκεπ-, as in σκέπ-τομαι, I spy, overlook. Brugm. i. § 1000. Der. *bishop-ric* : where *-ric* is AS. *rīce*, dominion, Grein, ii. 376 ; cf. G. *reich*, a kingdom ; and see **Rich**.

BISMUTH, a reddish-white metal. (G.) In Kersey's Dict., ed. 1708. Coles (1684) has *Bismutum* or *Wismuth*. Spelt *wisemute*, Harrison's Hist. of England, bk. ii. ch. 11 ; ed. Furnivall, p. 76. It is chiefly found at Schneeburg in Saxony. The F. *bismuth*, like the E. word, is borrowed from German ; and this word is one of the *very few* German words in English. — G. *bismuth*, bismuth ; more commonly *wismut*, also spelt *wissmut*, *wissmuth* ; of these, *wissmut* first occurs, in Georg Agricola (died in 1555), who also has the L. form *bisemūtum* (Weigand). Origin unknown.

BISON, a large quadruped. (F. or L. — Gk. — Teut.) In Minsheu, ed. 1627. Also in Cotgrave, q.v. Either from F. *bison* (Cot.) or from L. *bison* (Pliny). — Gk. βίσων, the wild bull, bison ; Pausanias, ed. Bekker, 10. 13 (about A. D. 160). Borrowed from Teutonic ; cf. AS. *wesend*, a wild ox, Bosworth ; Icel. *visundr*, the bison-ox ; OHG. *wisunt*, G. *wisent*, a bison. ¶ The word is Teutonic rather than

Greek, and only borrowed by the latter. See OHG. *wisunt* in Schade.

BISSEXTILE, a name for leap-year. (L.) In Holland's Pliny, bk. xviii. c. 25. — Late L. *bissextīlis annus*, the bissextile year, leap-year. — L. *bissextus*, in phr. *bissextus diēs*, an intercalary day, so called because the intercalated day (formerly an extra day after Feb. 24) was likewise called the sixth day before the calends of March (March 1) ; so that there were two days of the same name. — L. *bis*, twice ; and *sex*, six.

BISSON, purblind. (E.) Shak. has *bisson*, Cor. ii. 1. 70 ; and, in the sense of ' blinding,' Hamlet, ii. 2. 529. ME. *bisen*, *bisne*, purblind, blind ; Genesis and Exodus, ed. Morris, ll. 472, 2822. OE. *bisene*, pl., blind, Matt. ix. 27, in the Northumb. version, as a gloss upon L. *caeci*. β. Perhaps derived from the prefix *bi-*, *be-*, with a privative sense, as in E. *be-head*, and the AS. sb. *sīen*, *sȳn*, *sīn*, power of seeing, sight, allied to Goth. *siuns*, OSax. *siun*, Icel. *sjōn*, *sȳn*, Dan. *syn*, sight ; so that *bi-sēne* might mean ' sightless.'

BISTRE, a dark brown colour. (F. — G.?) ' *Bister*, *Bistre*, a colour made of the soot of chimneys boiled ;' Bailey's Dict., vol. ii. ed. 1731. — F. *bistre* ; of uncertain origin. Perhaps from G. *biester*, meaning (1) bistre, (2) dark, dismal, gloomy (in prov. G.) ; Flügel. It seems reasonable to connect these. Cf. also Du. *bijster*, confused, troubled, at a loss ; Pomeran. *biister*, bewildered, dark. [Dan. *bister*, grim, fierce, Swed. *bister*, fierce, angry, grim, Icel. *bistr*, angry, knitting the brows, may be unrelated.]

BIT (1), a small piece, a mouthful. (E.) ME. *bite*, in phr. *bite brædess* = a bit of bread, Ormulum, 8640. AS. *bita*, weak m., a bit, a morsel, John, xiii. 27 ; from AS. *bit-*, weak grade of *bitan*, to bite.+ Du. *beet*, a bite, also, a bit, morsel ; Icel. *biti*, a bit ; Swed. *bit* ; Dan. *bid* ; G. *bissen*, a bit. Teut. type *biton-*, m. See **Bite**.

BIT (2), a curb for a horse. (E.) ME. *bitt*, *bytt*. ' *Bytt* of a brydyile, *lupatum* ;' Prompt. Parv. p. 37. AS. *bite*, strong m., a bite. Teut. type *bitiz*, m. ; closely allied to the preceding. Cf. AS. *bitol*, dimin., as a gloss to *frænum* in Ps. xxxi. 12 (Spelman).+Du. *gebit* ; Icel. *bitill* (dimin.) ; Swed. *bett* ; Dan. *bid* ; G. *gebiss*. Compare these forms with those in the article above.

BITCH, a female dog. (E.) ME. *biche*, *bicche*, Wright's Vocab. i. 187. AS. *bicce* (Bosworth).+Icel. *bikkja* ; MDan. *bikke* ; allied to Icel. *grey-baka*, a bitch (Noreen).

BITE, to cleave, chiefly with the teeth. (E.) ME. *bite*, *biten*, pt. t. *bot*, *boot*, P. Plowman, B. v. 84. AS. *bītan* ; pt. t. *bāt*, pp. *biten*. Grein, i. 123.+Du. *bijten*, to bite ; Icel. *bíta* ; Swed. *bita* ; Dan. *bide* ; OHG. *pīzan* ; G. *beissen* ; Goth. *beitan*. Teut. type *beitan-*, pt. t. *bait*, pp. *bitanoz*. Allied to L. *findere*, pt. t. *fīdī*, to cleave ; Skt. *bhid*, to break, divide, cleave. — √BHEID, to cleave. Der. *bite*, sb. ; *bit*, *bit-er*, *bit-ing* ; *bitt-er*, q. v. ; *bait*, q. v.

BITTER, obnoxious to the taste. (E.) ME. *biter*, Ayenbite of Inwyt, p. 82. AS. *biter*, *bitor*, *bitter*, Grein, i. 120.+Du. *bitter* ; Icel. *bitr* ; Swed. and Dan. *bitter* ; OHG. *pittar* (G. *bitter*) ; Goth. *baitrs* (rather an exceptional form). β. The word orig. meant ' sharp' or ' biting ;' and is derived from AS. *bit-*, weak grade of *bītan*, to bite. Goth. *baitrs* is from *bait-*, second grade of *bītan*. See **Bite**. Der. *bitter-ly*, *bitter-ness*, *bitter-s* ; also *bitter-sweet*, Prompt. Parv. p. 37.

BITTERN, a bird of the heron tribe. (F. — Late L.) ME. *bitore*, *bytoure*, Chaucer, C. T. 6554 (D 972). — F. *butor*, 'a bittor ;' Cot. ; whence Low L. *butorius*, a bittern. Prob. named from its cry ; cf. L. *būtīre*, *būbere*, to cry like a bittern ; whence also L. *būtio*, said to mean a bittern, though it is a variant of *būteo*, a buzzard. See **Boom** (1). β. The mod. L. name *botaurus* is due to a fanciful derivation from L. *bōs taurus* ; *taurus* being used by Pliny, b. x. c. 42, for a bird that bellows like an ox, which is supposed to be the bittern. ¶ On the suffixed *-n* see Mätzner, i. 177 ; and see **Marten**. We actually find *viserne* for *visor* ; Three Met. Romances, ed. Robson, p. 15.

BITTS, a naval term. (Scand.) The *bitts* are two strong posts standing up on deck to which cables are fastened. [The F. term is *bittes*, but this may have been taken from English.] The word is properly Scand., and the E. form contracted ; in fact, the oldest form is *beetes* (1593) ; in Arber's Eng. Garner, v. 509. Prob. suggested by Swed. *beting*, a bitt (naut. term) ; cf. *betingsbult*, a bitt-bolt ; Dan. *beding*, a slip, bitts ; *bedingsbolt*, a bitt-bolt ; *bedingsknæ*, a bitt-knee ; &c. [It has found its way into Du. and G. ; cf. Du. *beting*, *betinghout*, a bitt ; G. *bäting*, a bitt ; *bätingholzer*, bitts.] β. The word probably arose from the use of a noose or tether for pasturing horses, or, in other words, for *baiting* them. Cf. Swed. *beta*, to pasture a horse ; whence *betingsbult*, as if a pin for tethering a horse while at pasture. Cf. Icel. *beiting*, grazing ; *beita*, to graze cattle, also, to yoke horses to a vehicle. See **Bait**. ¶ The word *bait* is Scand., showing that the Du. and G. words are borrowed. The E. word, on the other hand, may be native ; cf. AS. *ge-bǣte*, a bridle, *bǣtan*, to rein in; *bēting*, a rope for fastening; all from *bāt-*, mutation of *bāt-*, 2nd stem of *bītan*, to bite.

BITUMEN, mineral pitch. (L.) Milton has *bituminous*; P. L. x. 562. [Shak. has the pp. *bitumed*, Peric. iii. 1. 72. — F. *bitume* (Cotgrave).] — L. *bitūmen*, gen. *bitūmin-is*, mineral pitch; used by Virgil, Geor. iii. 451. Der. *bitumin-ous*, *bitumin-ate*.

BIVALVE, a shell or seed-vessel with two valves. (F. — L.) In Johnson's Dict. — F. *bivalve*, bivalve; both. adj. and sb. — L. *bi-*, double; and *ualua*, the leaf of a folding-door; gen. used in the pl. *ualuæ*, folding-doors. See **Valve**.

BIVOUAC, a watch, guard; especially, an encampment for the night without tents. (F. — G.) Oddly spelt '*biouac* or *bihovac*,' in Phillips, ed. 1706. Borrowed from F. *bivouac*, also spelt *bihouac*, *biouac*, in Richelieu (1680); see Hatzfeld. — G. *beiwache*, a guard, a keeping watch; introduced into F. at the time of the Thirty Years' War, 1618–1648 (Brachet). — G. *bei*, by, near; and *wachen*, to watch; words cognate with E. *by* and *watch* respectively. β. Or rather, from the Swiss *beiwacht* (in Stalder, ed. 1812, ii. 426), a term 'used in Aargau and Zurich to denote the patrol of citizens (*Schaar-wache*) added (*bei-gegeben*) to assist the ordinary town-watch by night at any time of special commotion. This remaining of a large body of men under arms all night explains the original sense of *bivouac*;' N. E. D. Cf. Diez, s. v. *bivac*, p. 525.

BIZARRE, odd, strange. (F. — Span.) In Dryden, Pref. to Maiden Queen. Merely borrowed from F. *bizarre*, strange, capricious. 'It originally meant valiant, intrepid; then angry, headlong; lastly strange, capricious;' Brachet. — Span. *bizarro*, valiant, gallant, high-spirited. In Mahn's Webster, the word is said to be 'of Basque-Iberian origin;' i. e. from Basque *bizarra*, a beard. The transference of sense would be like that in Span. *hombre de bigote*, a man of spirit, usually referred to *bigote*, a moustache. But this is certainly risky. ¶ Hatzfeld notes that F. *bizarre* was also spelt *bigearre* (see Cotgrave), and that its sense was influenced by F. *bigarrer*, to diversify. See Körting, § 1446.

BLAB, to tell tales. (E.) Often a sb.; Milton has: 'avoided as a *blab*;' Sams. Agon. 495; but also *blabbing*; Comus, 138. ME. *blabbe*, a tell-tale; see Prompt. Parv. p. 37, and Chaucer, Troil. iii. 300 (v. r. *labbe*). The verb more often occurs in early authors in the form *blabber*, ME. *blaberen*; see Prompt. Parv. p. 37. 'I *blaber*, as a chylde dothe or [ere] he can speke;' Palsgrave. 'I *blaberde*;' P. Plowman, A. v. 8. All are (like *babble*) imitative verbs, and may be considered as E. Similar are Dan. *blabbre*, to babble, to gabble; an Old Norse form *blabbra* is cited by Rietz; Swed. dial. *bladdra*, *blaffra*, to prattle, Rietz; G. *plappern*, to blab, babble, prate; Gael. *blabaran*, a stammerer, stutterer; *blabhdach*, babbling, garrulous; *plabair*, a babbler; MDu. *labben*, to babble; Dan. dial. *blaffre*, to babble. See **Bleb**, **Blob**, **Blubber**.

BLACK, swarthy, dark. (E.) ME. *blak*, Chaucer, C. T. 2132 (A 2130). AS. *blac*, *blæc*, black, Grein, i. 124. Cf. AS. *blæc*, Icel. *blek*, ink; Dan. *blæk*, sb., ink; Swed. *bläck*, ink, *bläcka*, to smear with ink; Swed. dial. *blaga*, to smear with smut (Rietz). So also OHG. *blach*, ink. ¶ Origin obscure; connexion with Du. *blaken*, to burn, scorch, is uncertain; so also that with L. *flagrāre*, Gk. φλέγειν. Connexion with *bleak* is probable; see N. E. D., and Noreen, Gr. § 149 (2); and OHG. *blah* in Schade. Der. *black*, sb.; *black-ly*, *black-ish*, *black-ness*, *black-en*; also *blackamoor* (spelt *blackmoor* in Beaum. and Fletcher, Mons. Thomas, v. 2), *black-ball*, *black-berry*, *black-bird*, *black-cock*, *black-friar*, *black-guard*, q.v., *black-ing*, *black-lead*, *black-letter*, *black-mail*, *black-rod*, *black-smith*, *black-thorn*, &c.

BLACKGUARD, a term of reproach. (Hybrid; E. and F.) From *black* and *guard*, q.v. A name given to scullions, turnspits, and the lowest kitchen menials, from the dirty work done by them. In the Accounts of St. Margaret, Westminster, p. 10, under the date 1532, we find: 'item, received for iiij. torches of the *black guard*, viijd.;' see Brand's Popular Antiquities, ed. Ellis, ii. 316. In Like Will to Like (1568), pr. in Dodsley's Old Plays, ed. Hazlitt, iii. 323, we find: 'Thou art served as Harry Hangman, captain of the *black guard*.' 'They are taken for no better than rakehells, or the devil's *blacke guarde*;' Stanihurst, Descr. of Ireland, ed. 1808, vi. 68. 'A lamentable case, that the devil's *black guard* should be God's soldiers;' Fuller, Holy War, bk. i. c. 12. 'Close unto the front of the chariot marcheth all the sort of weavers and embroiders; next unto whom goeth the *black guard* and kitchenry;' Holland, Ammianus, p. 12. 'A lousy slave, that within this twenty years rode with the *black guard* in the Duke's carriage, 'mongst spits and dripping-pans;' Webster, The White Devil, A. i. See Trench's Select Glossary.

BLADDER, a vesicle in animals. (E.) ME. *bladdre*, Chaucer, C. T. 15907 (G 439). AS. *blēdre*, f., a blister; Orosius, i. 7; *blēddre*, a bladder, A. S. Leechdoms, i. 360. Teut. type *blǣ-drōn-*, f., from the verbal root *blǣ-*, to blow out, and suffix *-drōn-* cognate with

Gk. -τρᾱ, -τρον. + Icel. *blaðra*, a bladder, a watery swelling; Swed. *bläddra*, a bubble, blister, bladder; Dan. *blære*, a bladder, blister; Du. *blaar*, a bladder, blister; cf. Du. *blaas*, a bladder, bubble, lit. a thing blown, from *blazen*, to blow; OHG. *blātara* (G. *blatter*), a bladder. Cf. AS. *blāwan*, to blow; L. *flāre*, to blow. See **Blow** (1). Der. *bladder-y*.

BLADE, a leaf; flat part of a sword. (E.) ME. *blade* (of a sword), Chaucer, Prol. 620 (A 618). AS. *blæd*, n., a leaf; Grein, i. 125. + Icel. *blað*, a leaf; Swed., Dan., and Du. *blad*, a leaf, blade; OHG. *plat*, G. *blatt*. β. Teut. type *bla-dom*, neut., with the sense of 'full blown,' 'flourishing;' a pp. form (with suffix *-dó-* = Idg. *-tó-*) from the weak grade of √BHLŌ. See **Blow** (2).

BLAEBERRY, BLEABERRY, a bilberry. (Scand. and E.) 'A *blabery*;' Catholicon Angl. (1483). From North E. *blae*, livid, dark; and *berry*. The form *blae* is from Icel. *blā-r*, livid; see under **Blue**. Cf. Icel. *blāber*, a blaeberry; Swed. *blåbär*; Dan. *blaabær*.

BLAIN, a pustule. (E.) ME. *blein*, *bleyn*; Promp. Parv. p. 39; Wyclif, Job, ii. 7. AS. *blegen*, a boil, pustule; Liber Medicinalis, i. 58, in A. S. Leechdoms, ii. 128. + Du. *blein*; Dan. *blegn*, a blain, pimple.

BLAME, to censure. (F. — L. — Gk.) ME. *blame*, Chaucer, C. T., E 76; *blamen*, Ancren Riwle, p. 64. — OF. *blasmer*, to blame. — L. *blasphēmāre*, used in the sense 'to blame' by Gregory of Tours (Brachet). — Gk. βλασφημεῖν, to speak ill. *Blame* is a doublet of *blaspheme*; see **Blaspheme**. Der. *blam-able*, *blam-abl-y*, *blam-able-ness*; *blame*, sb.; *blame-less*, *blame-less-ly*, *blame-less-ness*.

BLANCH (1), vb., to whiten. (F. — OHG.) Sir T. Elyot has *blanched*, whitened; Castle of Helth, bk. ii. c. 7 (Of Wallnuttes); and see Prompt. Parv. From ME. *blanche*, white, Gower, C. A. iii. 9; bk. vi. 239. — F. *blanchir*, to whiten, from *blanc*, white. See **Blank**.

BLANCH (2), vb., to blench. (E.) Sometimes used for *blench*. See **Blench**.

BLAND, gentle, mild, affable. (L.) [The ME. verb *blanden*, to flatter (Shoreham's Poems, p. 59), is obsolete; we now use *blandish*.] The adj. *bland* is in Milton, P. L. v. 5; taken rather from L. directly than from F., which only used the verb; see Cotgrave. — L. *blandus*, caressing, agreeable, pleasing. Brugm. i. § 413 (9). Der. *bland-ly*, *bland-ness*; also *blandish*, q.v.

BLANDISH, to flatter. (F. — L.) In rather early use. ME. *blandisen*, to flatter; Chaucer, tr. of Boethius, bk. ii. pr. 1, l. 20. — OF. *blandir*, to flatter, pres. part. *blandis-ant* (whence also the sb. *blandissement*). — L. *blandīrī*, to caress. — L. *blandus*, gentle. See **Bland**. Der. *blandish-ment*.

BLANK, void; orig. pale. (F. — OHG.) Milton has 'the *blanc* moon;' P. L. x. 656. ME. *blanke*, Prompt. Parv. — F. *blanc*, white. — OHG. *blanch*, *planch*, shining. Nasalised from OHG. *blah*, shining; cf. Gk. φλόγ-εος, flaming, shining, from φλέγ-ειν, to shine. See **Blink**. Der. *blank-ness*; also *blanch*, q.v.; and *blank-et*, q.v.

BLANKET, a coarse woollen cover. (F. — OHG.) Originally of a white colour. ME. *blanket*, as in 'whit *blanket*,' Life of Beket, ed. W. H. Black, l. 1167; and see Prompt. Parv. p. 38. — AF. *blanket* (F. *blanchet*), Stat. Realm, i. 381 (1363); formed by adding the dimin. suffix *-et* to F. *blanc*, white. — OHG. *blanch planch* white. See **Blank**. Der. *blanket-ing*.

BLARE, to roar, make a loud noise. (E.) Generally used of a trumpet; 'the trumpet *blared*;' or, 'the trumpet's *blare*.' Cf. ME. *blorien*, *bloren*, to weep; prov. E. *blare*, to make a loud noise (bleat, bray). Of imitative origin. Cf. Du. *blaren*, Low G. *blarren*, to bleat; MHG. *blēren* (G. *plärren*), to bleat, to blubber. Cf. MDu. *blaser*, a trumpeter; Oudemans. See further under **Blaze** (2).

BLASON; see **Blazon** (1) and (2).

BLASPHEME, to speak injuriously. (L. — Gk.) Shak. has *blaspheme*, Meas. i. 4. 38. ME. *blasfemen*; Wyclif, Mark, ii. 7. — L. *blasphēmāre*. — Gk. βλασφημεῖν, to speak ill of. — Gk. βλάσφημος, adj., evil-speaking. β. The first syllable is supposed to be for *βλαβες-*, i.e. hurtful, allied to βλάβ-η, hurt; the latter syllables are due to φημί, I say. *Blaspheme* is a doublet of *blame*. See **Blame** and **Fame**. Der. *blasphem-y* (ME. *blasphemie*, Ancren Riwle, p. 198; a F. form of L. *blasphēmia*, from Gk. βλασφημία); *blasphem-er*, *blasphem-ous*, *blasphem-ous-ly*. Brugm. i. § 744.

BLAST, a blowing. (E.) ME. *blast*, Chaucer, Troilus, ii. 1387; King Alisaunder, ed. Weber, 2571. AS. *blǣst*, m., a blowing, Grein, i. 126; (distinct from *blǣt*, a blaze, a flame). + Icel. *blāstr*, a breath, blast of a trumpet; OHG. *blāst*. Formed with Idg. suffix *-to-* from the Teut. base of **Blaze** (2). So also Swed. *blåst*, wind, from *blås-a*, to blow. Cf. OMerc. *blǣs-bælg*, bellows; Corp. Glos. 910. Der. *blast*, vb.

BLATANT, noisy, roaring. (E.) Best known from Spenser's '*blatant* beast;' F. Q. vi. 12 (heading); also *blattant*, id. vi. 1. 7. The suffix *-ant* is a fanciful imitation of the pres. part. suffix in French. Cf. prov. E. *blate*, to bellow, to roar; *blate*, noise (E. D. D.). Of imitative origin. Cf. *bleat*; and Gk. παφλάζειν (base φλαδ-), to bluster, splutter.

BLAY, a bleak (small fish). (E.) Cotgrave has F. *able*, 'a blay, or bleak, fish.' AS. *blǣge.*+Du. *blei*; G. *bleihe.* Allied to **Bleak** (2).

BLAZE (1), a flame; to flame. (E.) ME. *blase*, a flame, P. Plowman, B. xvii. 212; *blasen*, to blaze, id. B. xvii. 232. AS. *blǣse, blase*, a torch, John, xviii. 3; also a flame; in comp. *bǣl-blǣse*, a bright light, Grein, i. 77. Teut. type **blason-*, f. We also find AS. *blǣs*; 'facula, *blǣs*,' Mone, Quellen, 402. 61. Cf. MHG. *blas*, a torch; also G. *blässe*, Icel. *blesi*, Swed. *bläs*, a 'blaze' or white mark on a horse (or in E., on a tree). See Notes on E. Etym., p. 9.

BLAZE (2), to spread far and wide; to proclaim. (Scand.) 'Began to blaze abroad the matter;' Mark, i. 45. ME. *blasen*, used by Chaucer to express the loud sounding of a trumpet; Ho. of Fame, iii. 711.—Icel. *blāsa*, to blow, to blow a trumpet, to sound an alarm; Swed. *blå.a*, to blow, to sound; Dan. *bläse*, to blow a trumpet; Du. *blazen*, to blow, to blow a trumpet; G. *blasen*. Teut. type **blēsan-*; as also in Goth. *uf-blēsan*, to puff up. Extended from **blǣ-*, as in G. *blähen*, to puff up, and in AS. *blā-wan*, to blow. See **Blow** (1), **Blast.** Cf. **Blazon** (1) and **Blare.**

BLAZON (1), a proclamation; to proclaim. (Scand.) Shak. has *blason*, a proclamation, Hamlet, i. 5. 21; a trumpeting forth, Sonnet 106; also, to trumpet forth, to praise, Romeo, ii. 6. 26. This word is a corruption of *blaze*, in the sense of to blaze abroad, to proclaim. The final *n* is due to confusion with *blazon* in the purely heraldic sense; see below. ¶ *Blazon*, to proclaim, from ME. *blasen*, is from a Scand. source, see **Blaze** (2); whilst the heraldic word is French, but from a Teutonic source; see below.

BLAZON (2), to pourtray armorial bearings; an heraldic term. (F.—Teut.?) ME. *blason, blasoun*, a shield; Gawain and Grene Knight, l. 828.—F. *blason*, 'a coat of arms; in the 11th century a buckler, a shield; then a shield with a coat of arms of a knight painted on it; lastly, towards the fifteenth century, the coats of arms themselves;' Brachet (who gives it as of Teutonic origin). β. [Burguy remarks that the Provençal *blezō* had at an early period the sense of glory, fame; just as the Span. *blason* means honour, glory, as well as blazonry; cf. Span. *blasonar*, to blazon, also, to boast, brag of.] But the earliest sense, both in F. and E., is simply 'shield;' and the reference may be to its brightness or to bright marks on it: cf. Icel. *blesi*, Swed. *bläs*, a 'blaze' or white mark on a horse. There is thus, perhaps, a connexion with **Blaze** (1). Körting, § 1460. ¶ Notice '*blasyn*, or dyscry armys, *describo*;' and '*blasynge* of armys, *descripcio*;' Prompt. Parv. p. 38. Shields probably bore distinctive marks of some kind or other at a very early period. Der. *blazon-ry*.

BLEABERRY, a bilberry; see **Blaeberry.**

BLEACH, vb., to whiten. (E.) ME. *blechen*, to bleach, Ancren Riwle, p. 324, l. 1. AS. *blǣcan*; Ælfred, tr. of Beda, ed. Smith, i. 1. l. 20.—AS. *blāc*; see **Bleak** (1).+Icel. *bleikja*; Dan. *blege*; Swed. *bleka*; Du. *bleeken*; G. *bleichen*. Teut. type **blaikjan-*. From the adj. *bleak*, wan, pale (below). Der. *bleach-er, bleach-er-y, bleach-ing.*

BLEAK (1), pale, exposed. (Scand.) ME. *bleyke*, 'pallidus;' Prompt. Parv. p. 39; *bleik*, Havelok, 470.+Icel. *bleikr*, pale, wan; Dan. *bleg*; Swed. *blek*, pale, wan.+AS. *blāc*; Du. *bleek*, pale; OHG. *pleih*, pale; G. *bleich.* Teut. type **blaikoz*; from **blaik*, 2nd grade of **bleikan-* (AS. *blican*), to shine. Cf. Slavonic base **blig-*, as in *blisk-*, for **blig-sk-*, to shine; Miklosich. Der. *bleak*, sb., see below; *bleach*, q.v.

BLEAK (2), a kind of fish. (Scand.) Spelt *bleek* about A.D. 1613; Eng. Garner, ed. Arber, i. 157; *bleke* in Palsgrave (1530). Named from its *bleak* or pale colour. See above. Cf. Low G. *bleken*, a bleak. Cf. **Blay.**

BLEAR ONE'S EYE, to deceive. (E.) This is closely connected with *blear-eyed.* Shak. has ' *bleared thine eye* ' = dimmed thine eye, deceived; Tam. Shrew, v. 1. 120. So too in Chaucer, and in P. Plowman, B. prol. 74. β. The sense of *blear* here is to 'dim,' as with weeping. See **Blear-eyed.**

BLEAR-EYED, dim-sighted. (E.) ME. '*blereyed*, lippus;' Prompt. Parv. p. 39; *blere-nyed*, P. Plowman, B. xvii. 324. Cognate with Low G. *bleer-oged*, having weak and inflamed eyes, variant of *blarr-oged*, the same; from *blarren* (Pomeran. *blaren*), to blubber. See **Blare.**

BLEAT, to make a noise like a sheep. (E.) ME. *bleten*, used also of a kid; Wyclif, Tobit, ii. 21. AS. *blǣtan*, to bleat, said of a sheep, Ælfric's Gram., ed. Zupitza, p. 129; OMerc. *blētan*, Corp. Glos. 282.+Du. *blaten*, to bleat; OHG. *plāzan*, to bleat. Teut. type **blǣtan-*. Cf. Russ. *blejate*, to bleat; L. *flēre*, to weep.

BLEB, a small bubble or blister. (E.) We also find the form *blob*, in the same sense. Rich. quotes *blebs* from More, Songs of the Soul, conclusion. Jamieson gives: ' *Brukis, bylis, blobbis*, and blisteris;' qu. from Roul's Cursing, Gl. Compl. p. 330. The more usual form is *blubber*, ME. *blober*; ' *blober* upon water, *bouteillis*,'

Palsgrave. ' *Blobure, blobyr*, burbulium, Prompt. Parv. p. 40. ' At his mouthe a *blubber* stode of fome ' [foam]; Test. of Creseide, by R. Henrysoun, l. 192 (Thynne's edition). β. By comparing *blobber*, or *blubber*, with *bubble*, having the same meaning, we see the probability that they are imitative, from the action of forming a bubble with the lips. See also **Blubber, Blab, Blob.**

BLEED, to lose blood. (E.) ME. *blede*, P. Plowman, B. xix. 103. AS. *blēdan*, to bleed (Grein).—AS. *blōd*, blood. See **Blood.** ¶ The change of vowel is regular; the AS. *ē* is the mutation of *ō*. Cf. *feet, geese*, from *foot, goose*; also *deem* from *doom.*

BLEMISH, a stain; to stain. (F.—Scand. ?) ME. *blemisshen*; Prompt. Parv. ' I *blemysshe*, I hynder or hurte the beautye of a person;' Palsgrave.—OF. *blesmir, blemir*, pres. part. *blemis-ant*, to wound, soil, stain; with suffix *-ish*, as usual in E. verbs from F. verbs in *-ir*.—OF. *blesme, bleme*, wan, pale. Origin uncertain; if the *s* in *blesme* is unoriginal, it may be (as Diez says) from Icel. *blāmi*, a bluish or livid colour.—Icel. *blār*, livid, bluish; cognate with E. *blue*. The orig. sense, in that case, may have been to render livid, to beat black and blue. See **Blue.** ¶ The Icel. *blāmi* is in the Supp. to Vigfusson; Aasen gives Norw. *blaame*, a bluish colour, and Kalkar has MDan. *blām*, the mark of a bruise, p. 230.

BLENCH, to shrink from, start from, flinch. (E.) [Sometimes spelt *blanch* in old authors; though a different word from *blanch*, to whiten.] ME. *blenche*, to turn aside, P. Plowman, B. v. 589. AS. *blencan*, to deceive; Grein, i. 127.+Icel. *blekkja* (for **blenkja*), to impose upon. Origin doubtful; but apparently a causal form of *blink*; thus to *blench* meant originally to ' make to blink,' to impose upon; but it was confused with *blink*, as if it meant to wink, and hence to flinch. See **Blink.** ¶ Cf. *drench*, the causal of *drink.*

BLEND, to mix together. (Scand.) ME. *blenden*, Towneley Mysteries, p. 225; pp. *blent*, Sir Gawain and the Grene Knight, l. 1610. From the stem of the pres. t. (1 p. *blend*, 3 p. *blendr*) of Icel. *blanda*, to mix; Swed. *blanda*; Dan. *blande.*+Goth. *blandan sik*, to mix oneself with, communicate with; OHG. *plantan, blantan*, to mix. β. The Goth. *blandan* is a str. vb. of the 7th conjugation. ¶ The AS. *blendan* means to make blind, Grein, i. 127. See **Blind.**

BLESS, orig. to consecrate. (E.) ME. *blessen*, Chaucer, C. T., E 553, 1240; *bletseien*, Layamon, 32157. AS. *blētsian*, to bless (Grein); *blēdsian*, Vespasian Psalter, iii. 9, v. 13; ONorthumb. *bloedsia*, Matt. xxiii. 39, Jo. viii. 48; Durham Ritual, p. 117. These forms point to a Teut. type **blōdisōn*, to redden with blood, from *blōd*, blood. See **Blood.** ' In heathen time it was no doubt primarily used in the sense of consecrating the altar by sprinkling it with the blood of the sacrifice;' H. Sweet, in Anglia, iii. 1. 156 (whose solution I here give). This is generally accepted. Der. *bless-ing, bless-ed, blessed-ness.*

BLIGHT, to blast; mildew. (E.) The history of the word is very obscure; as a verb, *blight* occurs in The Spectator, no. 457. Cotgrave has: ' *Brulure*, blight, brant-corn (an herb);' where ' blight' means ' smut in wheat;' though it seems to be confused with the herb named *blite*. β. The word has not been traced, and can only be guessed at. Perhaps it answers to an AS. **blīht*, OMerc. **bleht*, and so to Icel. *blettr*, a spot, stain; just as E. *right* answers to AS. *riht*, OMerc. *reht*, and Icel. *rēttr* (for **rettr*). If so, we may refer it to √BHLEG, Gk. φλέγ-ειν, to burn; just as *light* is from √REG. ¶ Comparison with AS. *blecða*, in Sweet's O. E. Texts, p. 548, is not quite safe, because *blecða* is a gloss to L. *uitiligo*; and though this L. word is by Sweet translated by ' blight,' the proper sense of it is a tetter, or cutaneous eruption (Lewis).

BLIND, deprived of sight. (E.) ME. *blind, blynd*, Prompt. Parv. p. 40. AS. *blind*, Grein, i. 128.+Du. *blind*; Icel. *blindr*; Swed. and Dan. *blind*; OHG. *plint*, G. *blind*. Teut. type **blindoz*; from an Idg. base **bhlendh-*; whence also Lith. *blęsti-s*, to become dim (as the sun). Brugm. i. § 493. Der. *blind-fold.*

BLINDFOLD, to make blind. (E.) From ME. verb *blind-folden*, Tyndale's tr. of Lu. xxii. 64. This ME. *blindfolden* is a corruption of *blindfelden*, to blindfold, whence *blyndefelde*, used by Palsgrave; and, again, *blindfelden* (with excrescent *d*) is for an earlier form *blindfellen*, Ancren Riwle, p. 106.—AS. *blind*, blind; and *fyllan*, to fell, to strike. Thus it meant ' to strike blind.' See **Fell** (1). ¶ The popular form had reference to *folding* a bandage over the eyes.

BLINDMAN'S BUFF. (E.) ' To play at *blindman-buff*;' Randolph, Works, p. 394 (1651), ed. Hazlitt (cited by Palmer). It is mentioned earlier, in the Prol. to The Return from Parnassus (1606). And, in 1598, Florio explains Ital. *minda* by ' a play called hoodman blind, blind hob, or *blindman buffe*.' Here *buff* is the F. *buffe*, 'a buffet, blow, cuffe, box, whirret on the eare,' &c.; Cotgrave. From OF. *bufe* (a word widely spread); see further under **Buff** (2). The explanation is given by Wedgwood as follows:—'In West Flanders *buf* is a thump; *buffen*, to thump, *buf spelen*, a game which is essentially blindman's buff without the bandaging of the eyes. One player is made the butt of all the others, whose aim is to strike him on the back without his catching them. When he catches the boy who gave him the last buffet, he is released and the other takes his place. See De Bo, West-Flemish Dict.' See also Koolman, East-Frisian Dict., who quotes the phrase *dat geid up'n blinden buf*, that is done (lit. goes) at hap-hazard (lit. at blind buff). And see *buf* in Diez.

BLINK, to wink, glance; a glance. (Scand.) Shak. has 'a *blinking* idiot;' M. of Ven. ii. 9. 54; also 'to *blink* (look) through;' Mid. Nt. Dr. v. 178. Probably of Scand. origin; cf. Norw. *blinka*, to blink with the eyes, *blink*, a glimpse; MDan. *blinköjet*, with blinking eyes (Kalkar). ME. *blenken*, commonly 'to shine, to glance;' Gawain and the Grene Knight, ed. Morris, 799, 2315. The AS. *blencan* meant 'to deceive' (perhaps 'to cause to blink'). Allied to AS. *blanc*, white (as in *blanca*, a white horse); see **Blank**. Cf. also Du. *blinken*, Low G. *blænken*, to shine.

BLISS, happiness. (E.) ME. *blis*, Chaucer, C. T. Group B, 33. AS. *blis*, *bliss* (Grein); a contraction from AS. *bliðs* or *bliðs*, happiness, Grein, i. 130. — AS. *bliðe*, happy. See **Blithe.**+OSax. *blizza*, *blid-sea*, happiness. Teut. type *bliðsiā, f., for *blið-tiā; the suffix being -tiā, as in L. *læti-tia*. The sense was influenced by *bless*, which is unrelated. Der. *bliss-ful, bliss-ful-ly, bliss-ful-ness.*

BLITE, a plant-name. (L. — Gk.) In Turner's Herbal (1551). — L. *blitum*. — Gk. βλίτον, a kind of pot-herb.

BLISTER, a little bladder on the skin. (F. — Teut.) ME. *blister*, in The Flower and The Leaf, wrongly ascribed to Chaucer, l. 408. Also *blester*, as in Cursor Mundi, 6011. — OF. *blestre*, 'tumeur;' Godefroy. Of Teut. origin; from Icel. *blástr* (dat. *blæstri*), the blast of a trumpet, the blowing of a bellows; also, a swelling, mortification (in a medical sense). So also Norw. *blaaster*, a blast, a kind of tumour; cf. Swed. *blåsa*, a bladder, a blister. The root appears in Du. *blazen*, Icel. *blása*, Swed. *blåsa*, to blow. See **Blast, Blaze** (2). Der. *blister*, verb.

BLITHE, adj., happy. (E.) ME. *blithe*, Chaucer, Prol. 846; Havelok, 651. AS. *bliðe*, sweet, happy; Grein, i. 130.+Icel. *bliðr*; Swed., Dan. *blid*; Du. *blijde*; OSax. *bliði*, bright (said of the sky), glad, happy; Goth. *bleiths*, merciful, kind; OHG. *blidi*, glad. Teut. types *bleithoz, *bleithjoz. Der. *blithe-ly, blithe-ness, blithe-some, blithe-some-ness.*

BLOAT, to swell. (Scand.) Not in early authors. The history of the word is obscure. 'The *bloat* king' in Hamlet, iii. 4. 182, is an editorial alteration of 'the *blowt* king;' it means 'effeminate' rather than *bloated*. We find 'bloat him up with praise' in the Prol. to Dryden's Circe, l. 25; but it is not certain that the word is correctly used. However, *bloated* is now taken to mean 'puffed out,' 'swollen,' perhaps owing to a fancied connexion with *blow*; but the ME. form was *blout*, soft (hence puffy, swollen), Havelok, 1910. β. The word is connected with the Icel. *blotna*, to become soft, to lose courage; *blautr*, soft, effeminate, imbecile; cf. Swed. *blöt*, soft, pulpy; also Swed. *blöta*, to steep, macerate, sop; Dan. *blöd*, soft, mellow. [These words are not to be confused with Du. *bloot*, naked, G. *bloss*.] The Swedish also has the phrases *lägga i blot*, to lay in a sop, to soak; *blötna*, to soften, melt, relent; *blotfisk*, a soaked fish. The last is connected with E. *bloater*. See **Bloater**. γ. Further allied to Icel. *blaudr*, soft; AS. *bleáþ*, G. *blöde*, weak. Cf. Gk. φλυδ-άω, I become soft or flabby. See **Fluid**.

BLOATER, a prepared herring. (Scand.) 'I have more smoke in my mouth than Would *blote* a hundred herrings;' Beaum. and Fletcher, Isl. Princess, ii. 5. 'Why, you stink like so many *bloat-herrings*, newly taken out of the chimney;' Ben Jonson, Masque of Augurs, 17th speech. There can be hardly a doubt that Mr. Wedgwood's suggestion is correct. He compares Swed. *blöt-fisk*, soaked fish, from *blota*, to soak, steep. Cf. also Icel. *blautr fiskr*, fresh fish, as opposed to *harðr fiskr*, hard, or dried fish; whereon Mr. Vigfusson notes that the Swedish usage is different, *blötfisk* meaning 'soaked fish.' Thus a *bloater* is a cured fish, a prepared fish. They were formerly 'steeped for a time in brine before smoking;' N. E. D. See **Bloat**.

BLOB, a bubble (Levins); see **Bleb**.

BLOCK, a large piece of wood. (F. — G.) ME. *blok*, Legends of the Holy Rood, ed. Morris, p. 141, l. 314. [W. *ploc*, a block; Gael. *ploc*, a round mass, large clod, bludgeon with a large head, block, stump of a tree; Irish *ploc*, a plug, bung; are all borrowed from E.; Macbain.] — F. *bloc*, 'a gross, great, or generality; the whole of, or a heap of divers wares hudled together; also, a block or log;' Cotgrave. — MHG. *bloch*, a block. The word is widely spread; we find Du. *blok*, Dan. *blok*, Swed. *block*, OFries. *block*. Perhaps related to *balk* (Kluge). Der. *block-ade, block-house, block-head, block-tin.*

BLOND, fair of complexion. (F.) In Evelyn's Diary, July 25, 1683. Caxton has *blounde* (N. E. D.). Not in Johnson. *Blonde-lace* is a fine kind of silken lace, formerly of the colour of raw silk; a

blonde is a beautiful girl of light complexion. — F. '*blond*, m., *blonde*, f., light yellow, straw-coloured, flaxen; also, in hawkes or stags, bright tawney, or deer-coloured;' Cot. Origin unknown. β. Referred by Diez to Icel. *blandinn*, mixed; cf. AS. *blonden-feax*, with hair of mingled colour, gray-haired. But the Late L. form is *blundus* (whence also Span. *blondo*, Ital. *biondo*), prob. of Teut. origin, and allied to Skt. *bradh-na-s*, reddish, pale yellow (Kluge). Cf. OSlav. *bronŭ*, white.

BLOOD, gore. (E.) ME. *blod*, *blood*, Chaucer, C. T. 1548 (A 1546). AS. *blód* (Grein).+Du. *bloed*; Icel. *blóð*; Swed. *blod*; Goth. *blóth*; OHG. *pluot*; G. *blut*. Teut. type *blō-dóm*, neut. Doubtfully referred to the root of **Blow** (2), *blood* being considered as the symbol of flourishing life; cf. L. *florēre*, to flourish; see Curtius, i. 375. Der. *blood-hound, blood-shed, blood-stone, blood-y, blood-i-ly, blood-i-ness*; also *bleed*, q.v.

BLOOM, a flower, blossom. (Scand.) ME. *blome*, Havelok, 63; but not found in AS. — Icel. *blóm*, n., *blómi*, m., a blossom, flower; Swed. *blomma*; Dan. *blomme*. Cf. OSax. *blómo* (Heliand); Du. *bloem*; OHG. *bluomo*, m., *bluoma* (G. *blume*), f.; Goth. *blóma*, a flower. Teut. type *blō-mon-*, m., from *blō-*, to blow, flourish; cf. L. *flō-s*, a flower, *flō-rēre*, to flourish. The E. form of the root is *blow*; see **Blow** (2). ¶ The truly E. word is *blossom*, q.v.; the corresponding AS. *blóma*, 'a bloom,' is mod. E. *bloom*, but only in the secondary sense of 'a mass of hammered iron.'

BLOSSOM, a bud, small flower. (E.) ME. *blosme*, *blossum*; Prompt. Parv. p. 41. But the older form is *blostme*, Owl and Nightingale, 437; so that a *t* has been dropped. AS. *blóstma* [misprinted *bōstma*], Grein, i. 131.+Du. *bloesem*, a blossom; cf. MHG. *bluost*, a blossom. β. Formed, by adding the suffixes -*t* and -*ma*, to the base *blós*- (cf. L. *flor-ēre*, for *flōs-ēre*); extended from *blō*- in AS. *blówan*, to flourish, bloom. ¶ When the Idg. suffix -*mon*- (>AS. -*ma*, Icel. -*mi*) alone is added, we have the Icel. *blómi*, E. *bloom*. When the suffix -*t* alone is added, we have the MHG. *bluost*. See **Blow**, to flourish; and, see **Bloom**.

BLOT (1), a spot, to spot. (F. — Teut.) ME. *blot*, *blotte*, sb., *blotten*, vb. '*Blotte* vpon a boke, *oblitum*: *Blottyn* bokys, *oblitero*;' Prompt. Parv. p. 41. — MF. *blotter*, 'to blot, stain, blemish, defile;' Cot. Apparently from MF. *blotte*, also *bloutre*, 'a clod, or clot of earth;' Cot. The same as OF. *bloustre*, *blotte*, *bloutre*, a clot of earth turned up by the plough-share, Roquefort; see *bloste* in Godefroy. See **Blotch**.

BLOT (2), at backgammon. (Du.) A *blot* at backgammon is an exposed piece. The expression 'made a *blot*,' with reference to the game of *tables*, occurs in Dryden, Wild Gallant, i. 3. It corresponds, as Mr. Wedgwood well points out, to the Dan. *blot*, bare, naked; cf. the phrase *give sig blot*, to lay oneself open, to commit or expose oneself. Cf. Swed. *blott*, naked; *blotta*, to lay oneself open. — Du. *bloot*, naked; *blootstellen*, to expose. Calisch, in his Du. Dict., has: 'ik kan niet spelen zonder mij *bloot* te geven (at chess, draughts, &c.), I cannot play without unguarding myself.' The word is Dutch; from which the Dan. and Swed. forms were perhaps borrowed; the cognate G. word is *bloss*; which see in Kluge.

BLOTCH, a pustule, a blot. (F. — Teut.) The sense 'pustule' is the older. Drayton has: 'their *blotch'd* and blister'd bodies;' Moses, bk. ii. 328. — OF. *bloche*, 'tumeur;' Godefroy, s. v. *bloste*, also *bloustre*. Prob. of Teut. origin; cf. MDu. *bluyster*, a blister; Hexham. See Diez.

BLOUSE, a loose outer garment. (F.) Modern. — F. *blouse*, a smock-frock. Of unknown origin.

BLOW (1), to puff. (E.) ME. *blowen*; in Northern writers, *blaw*; very common; Chaucer, Prol. 567 (A 565). AS. *bláwan*, Grein.+OHG. *bláhan*, G. *blähen*, to puff up, to swell.+L. *flāre*, to blow. — √BHLĒ, to blow; Brugmann, ii. § 664. ¶ The number of connected words in various languages is large. In English we have *bladder, blast, blaze* (to proclaim), *blazon, blare* (of a trumpet), *blister*, &c.; also *flatulent, inflate*.

BLOW (2), to bloom, flourish as a flower. (E.) ME. *blowe*, Rob. of Glouc. ed Hearne, p. 352, l. 7232. AS. *blówan*, to bloom, Grein, i. 131.+Du. *bloeijen*, to bloom; OHG. *bluojan* (G. *blühen*). Cf. L. *flōrēre*, Fick, iii. 222; thus *flourish* is co-radicate with *blow*. See **Bloom, Blossom, Blood, Blade**. From the same root BHLŌ, to flourish; are *flourish, flour, flower*.

BLOW (3), a stroke, hit. (E.) ME. *blowe*; 'blowe on the cheke, *jouee*; *blowe* with ones fyst, *sufflet*;' Palsgrave. The AS. form does not appear; but we find MDu. *blauwen*, pt. t. *blau*, to strike, Kilian; and Du. *blouwen*, to dress flax. [The MDu. word is native and genuine, as the strong pt. t. *blau*, i. e. struck, occurs in a quotation given by Oudemans.]+G. *bläuen*, to beat with a beetle; cf. *bläuel*, a beetle; OHG. *bliuwen*, to beat; Goth. *bliggwan*, to beat. Teut. type *bliuwan-*, or *bleuwan-*, to strike. The history of the word is obscure. Almost the earliest quotation is 'He gat a *blaw*,' Wallace,

i. 348 (ab. 1470). It looks as if the Du. word had been borrowed, and made to coincide in form with **Blow** (1).

BLUBBER, a bubble; fat; to bubble or swell up; to weep copiously. (E.) Of imitative origin; thus (1) *blubber*, ME. *blober*, a bubble, spelt *blobure* in Prompt. Parv., is an extension of *bleb* or *blob*, a blister; see extracts s. v. *bleb*. (2) The fat of the whale consists of bladder-like cells filled with oil. (3) A *blubber-lipped* person is one with swollen lips; also spelt *blobber-lipped*, and in the Digby Mysteries, p. 107 (ed. Furnivall, p. 90), *blabyrlypped*; so that it was probably more or less confused with *blabber*, q. v. (4) To *blubber*, to weep, is ME. *bloberen*. Palsgrave has: ' I *blober*, I wepe, je pleure.' But the older meaning is to *bubble*, as in : 'The borne [bourn] *blubred* therinne, as hit *boyled* hade ;' Gawain and the Green Knight, l. 2174. Cf. EFries. *blubber*, a bubble, a blob of fat; *blubbern*, to bubble. See **Bleb, Blob.**

BLUDGEON, a thick cudgel. (F. ?) Rarely used; but given in Johnson's Dictionary. It has a short history; the N. E. D. says it occurs in Bailey's Dict., ed. 1730; but it is not in ed. 1731. The Corn. *blogon* (with *g* as *j*), a bludgeon, occurs in the Corn. miracle-play De Origine Mundi, l. 2709 (14th cent.?); see Phil. Soc. Trans. 1869, p. 148; prob. taken from E. It is prob. of F. origin. Godefroy has *bloquet, bloichet*, as dimin. of *bloc*, a block of wood. This suggests a form *blochon as a possible source, likewise from *bloc.*

BLUE, a colour. (F.—OHG.) ME. *blew, bleu*; Chaucer, C. T., F 644; Rom. Rose, 1578.—AF. *blu, bleu, blew*; OF. *bleu*, blue.— OHG. *blāo*, blue, livid; G. *blau.*+Icel. *blár*, Swed. *blå*, Dan. *blaa*, livid [whence ME. *blo*, livid, P. Plowm. B. iii. 97]; also AS. *blāw* (O. E. Texts, p. 588). Teut. type *blǣwoz. Cognate with L. *flāuus*, yellow. With the sense 'livid' compare the phr. 'to *beat* black and *blue.*' See Notes on E. Etym., p. 11. **Der.** *blu-ish, blue-bell, blue-bottle.*

BLUFF (1), downright, rude. (Dutch?) Not in early authors. Rich. cites 'a remarkable *bluffness* of face' from The World, no. 88; and the phrase 'a *bluff* point,' i. e. a steep headland, now shortened to 'a *bluff*,' from Cook's Voyages, bk. iv. c. 6. β. Origin uncertain; but a sailor's word, and prob. corrupted from Dutch. Cf. MDu. *blaf*, flat, broad; *blaffaert*, one having a flat broad face; also, a boaster, a libertine; Oudemans. And Mr. Wedgwood quotes from Kilian the phrases '*blaf aensight*, facies plana et ampla; *blaf van voorhooft*, fronto,' i. e. having a broad forehead, though Hexham says 'the flat of a forehead.' γ. If the MDu. *blaffaert*, having a flat broad face, is the same word as when it has the sense of 'boaster,' we can tell the root. The mod. Du. *blaffer*, a boaster, signifies literally a barker, yelper, noisy fellow; from *blaffen*, to bark, to yelp. See below.

BLUFF (2), to impose upon by a boastful demeanour, to cow by bragging. (Low G.) Modern; and partly a cant word. Perhaps the same as '*bluffe*, to blind-fold,' in Ray's N. Country Words (1691). Cf. Low G. *bluffen*, to bluff; *verbluffen*, to confuse; Bremen Wört. (1767); EFries. *bluffen*, to bellow, also to bluff; allied to MDu. *blaffen*, to mock (Hexham); EFries. *blaffen*, to bark, yelp. Of imitative origin. See **Bluff** (1).

BLUNDER, to flounder, to act stupidly. (Scand.) ME. *blondren*, to pore over a thing, as in 'we *blondren* euer and pouren in the fyr,' Chaucer, C. T. 16138 (G 670). '*Blondrynge* and hasty ;' Trevisa, ii. 169. ' I *blonder*, je perturbe;' Palsgrave's F. Dict.—Norw. *blundra*, to close the eyes. Formed, with frequentative suffix *-ra* (for *-era*), from Icel. *blunda*, to doze, slumber; so that it meant 'to keep dozing,' to be sleepy and stupid. Cf. Swed. *blunda*, to shut the eyes; Dan. *blunde*, to nap; Jutland *blunde*, to doze, to blink. We find also Icel. *blundr*, Dan. and Swed. *blund*, a doze, a nap. The sense of 'confusion' suggests a relationship to **Blend, Blind.**

BLUNDERBUSS, a short gun. (Hybrid; F.—L. *and* Du.) Used by Pope, Dunciad, iii. 150. For *blanterbuss*; see quot. (dated 1617) for ' harquesbusse, *plantier-busse*, alias *blanter-busse*, and mus-quettoon ;' Sir D. Scott, The Brit. Army, i. 405. This is from Du. *planten*, as in *het geschut planten*, 'to plant ordnance,' Hexham; and Du. *bus* (below). *Planten* is from F. *planter*, L. *plantāre*; see **Plant.** β. But doubtless confused with Du. *donderbus*, a blunderbuss; which should rather have been turned into *thunderbuss.*—Du. *donder*, thunder; and *bus*, a gun, orig. a box, a gun-barrel; cf. G. *donnerbüchse*, a blunderbuss; from *donner*, thunder, and *büchse*, a box, gun-barrel, gun. Thus it meant ' *thunder-box* ;' see **Thunder** and **Box** (1). See Palmer, Folk-Etymology.

BLUNT, not sharp. (E.) ME. *blunt* (of edge), Prompt. Parv. p. 41; ' *blont*, nat sharpe ;' Palsgrave's F. Dict. ' Unnwis mann iss *blunnt* and blind ;' Ormulum, 16954. Cf. also ' *Blunderer*, or *blunt warkere* [worker], hebefactor, hebeficus ;' Prompt. Parv. Origin unknown; but perhaps for *blund, from the weak grade allied to Goth. *blandan*, to mix; which see in Uhlenbeck. Allied, perhaps, to Icel. *blunda*, to doze; so that the orig. sense is 'sleepy, dull.' See **Blunder, Blend, Blind. Der.** *blunt-ly, blunt-ness.*

BLUR, to stain; a stain. (Scand.) Shak. has both sb. and verb; Lucrece, 222, 522. Levins has both: ' A *blirre*, deceptio;' and ' to *blirre*, fallere.' *Blur* is (1) to dim; (2) metaphorically, to delude. Of uncertain origin; cf. Swed. dial. *blura*, to blink, partially close the eyes; Swed. dial. *blira*, to blink; *blirra fojr augu*, to quiver (be dim) before the eyes, as in a haze caused by heat; Bavar. *plerr*, a mist before the eyes. Distinct from *blear*, but perhaps confused with it.

BLURT, to utter rashly. (E.) Shak. has *blurt at*, to deride, Per. iv. 3. 34. We commonly say 'to *blurt* out,' to utter suddenly and inconsiderately. The Scot. form is *blirt*, meaning ' to make a noise in weeping,' esp. in the phr. to *blirt* and *greet*, i. e. to burst out crying; Jamieson. This shows that it is of imitative origin, and allied to *blare*, to make a loud noise. Cf. Swed. dial. *blurra*, to speak fast and confusedly. See 'Bloryyn or wepyn, or bleren, *ploro, fleo*,' in Prompt. Parv. p. 40. The orig. sense of *blurt* is to blow violently. See **Blare, Bluster.**

BLUSH, to grow red in the face. (E.) ME. *bluschen, blusshen*, to glow; ' *blusshit* the sun,' the sun shone out; Destruction of Troy, ed. Panton and Donaldson, l. 4665. AS. *blyscan*, only found in the gloss: ' Rutilare, *blyscan*,' Mone, Quellen, p. 355; cf. *āblisian* (= *ā-blysian*), to blush, Levit. xxvi. 41. Allied to Du. *blozen*, to blush; Hamburg *blüsen*, to blush (Richey); Dan. *blusse*, to blaze, flame, burn in the face; Swed. *blossa*, to blaze. β. All these are verbs formed from a sb., viz. AS. *blys*, in comp. *bǣl-blys* (a fire-blaze (whence *blysige*, a torch); Du. *blos*, a blush; Dan. *blus*, a blaze, a torch; Swed. *bloss*, a torch. All from **blus-*, weak grade of a Teut. root *bleus, to glow. Hence also Low G. *bleustern*, to glow.

BLUSTER, to blow noisily; to swagger. (E.) Shak. has *blustering*, tempestuous, said of weather, Lucrece, 115. Palsgrave has: ' I bluster, Ie soufle ;' and ' This wynde *blustereth.*' It was doubtless associated with *blast*, but is probably a native word, as *blusterous, blusterly*, &c., are found in many dialects. Cf. EFries. *blüstern*, to be tempestuous (esp. of wind); *blüster, blüser*, a breeze; *blüsen*, to blow hard; *blüse*, a wind; Hamburg *bleuster*, a roaring fire (Richey). Of imitative origin; cf. **Blurt.**

BOA, a large snake. (L.) A term borrowed from Latin. In Cockeram's Dict., pt. iii. (1623). The pl. *boæ* occurs in Pliny, Nat. Hist. viii. 14, where it means serpents of immense size. Prob. allied to L. *bōs*, an ox, in allusion to the size of the reptile.

BOAR, a quadruped. (E.) ME. *bore, boor*, P. Plowman, B. xi. 333. AS. *bār*, Ælfric's Glossary, Nomina Ferarum. + Du. *beer*; OHG. *pēr*, MHG. *bēr*, a boar. Teut. type *bairoz, m.

BOARD (1), a table, a plank. (E.) ME. *bord*, a table, Chaucer, C. T., E 3. AS. *bord*, a board, the side of a ship, a shield (Grein).+ Du. *bord*, board, shelf; Icel. *borð*, plank, side of a ship; Goth. *-baurd*, in comp. *fōtu-baurd*, foot-board, footstool. Allied to AS. *bred*, Du. *berd*, G. *brett*, a board. Teut. types *bard-om, n. ; *bred-om, n. ¶ In the phrases ' star-*board*,' ' lar-*board*,' ' over *board*,' and perhaps in ' on *board*,' the sense of ' side of a ship ' is intended; but it is merely a different use of the same word; and not derived from F. *bord*, although this has reinforced the E. usage. The F. *bord* itself is of Teut. origin. We also find *bord* in Gaelic, Irish, Welsh, and Cornish; all borrowed from E. **Der.** *board*, to live at table; *board-ing-house, board-ing-school* ; also *board-ing*, a covering of boards.

BOARD (2), vb., to go on board a ship; also to accost. (F.— Teut.) Though the sb. *board* is E., the verb is borrowed from F., and does not appear in ME. It is common in Shak. in both senses; *bord*, to accost, is in Spenser, F. Q. ii. 2. 5, ii. 4. 24, &c.; see *boord* in Nares. 'At length herself *bordeth* Æneas thus ;' Surrey, tr. of Æneid, iv. 304 (l. 395 of the E. version). ' I *borde* a shyppe or suche lyke, *Jaborde vne nauire*,' Palsgrave. Short for *abord*, which occurs in Cotgrave.—F. *aborder*, ' to approach, accoast, abboord, boord, or lay aboord ;' Cot.—F. *a*, to (< L. *ad*); and *bord*, edge, brim, side of a ship, from Icel. *borð*, Du. *boord*, board, side of a ship; see **Board** (1).

BOAST, a vaunt. (F.—Scand.) ME. *bost*, vain-glory; Will. of Palerne, ed. Skeat, 1141. The oldest sense is, ' clamour, noise.' 'Now ariseth cry and *boost* ;' King Alisaunder, 5290. [The phonology shows (see N. E. D.) that *boast* represents AF. *bost*].—AF. *bost*, a boast; Wright's Vocab. i. 161, l. 12; as is more clearly shown in MS. Gg. 1. 1, fol. 287, back, col. 1, in the Camb. Univ. Library. Of Scand. origin; from a Norw. base *baust-*, represented by Norw. *bausta*, to act with violence (Ross). Cf. Swed. *bausten*, bold and reckless (id.) ; *baus*, proud, blustering (id.) ; allied to Norw. *baust*, boastfully, *bausa*, to bounce out, &c.; further allied to EFries. *büsen*, to be boisterous; see **Boisterous. Der.** *boast-er, boast-ful, boast-ful-ly, boast-ful-ness, boast-ing, boast-ing-ly.*

BOAT, a small ship. (E.) ME. *boot*, Wyclif, Mark, iv. 1. AS. *bāt*, Grein, p. 76. Teut. type *baitoz, m. A word peculiar to E. ; whence Icel. *bátr*, Swed. *båt*, Du. *boot*, are directly or indirectly borrowed. **Der.** *boat-swain* (below).

BOAT-SWAIN, an officer in a ship who has charge of the sails, rigging, &c. (E. *and* Scand.) The earliest quotation in the N. E. D. gives the spelling *bote-swayn* (ab. 1450). But it occurs as *bāt-swegen* in late AS., in the Leofric Missal, fol. 1, back; see Earle, A. S. Charters, p. 254, l. 5. Here *bāt* is the AS. form of *boat*; but *swegen* represents ONorse **sweinn*, Icel. *sveinn*, a servant, a lad; the AS. cognate form being *swān*. See **Swain.**

BOB, to jerk about, to knock. (E.) 'Against her lips I *bob*;' Mids. Nt. Dr. ii. 1. 49; 'beaten, *bobbed*, and thumped;' Rich. III, v. 3. 334. *Bobet*, a cuff, a blow, occurs in the Prompt. Parv. Usually assumed to be of imitative origin. Cf. Swed. dial. *bobba*, to knock against. ¶ 'A *bob* of cherys,' i.e. a cluster of cherries, Towneley Mysteries, p. 118, may be explained from Gael. *babag*, a cluster; or from the verb *bob*, to move like a thing hanging down.

BOBBIN, a wooden pin on which thread is wound; round tape. (F.) Holland has 'spindles or *bobins*;' Plutarch, p. 994.—F. '*bobine*, a quil for a spinning wheele; also, a skane or hanke of gold or silver thread;' Cot. Origin unknown.

BOBOLINK, an American singing bird. (Imitative.) At first called *Bob Lincoln*, or *Bob o'Lincoln*; see N. E. D. A free imitation of the bird's cry.

BODE, to foreshow, announce. (E.) ME. *boden*, Gower, C. A. i. 153; bk. i. 3282. *bodien*, Layamon, 23290. AS. *bodian*, to announce, Grein, i. 131.—AS. *bod*, a message, Grein; cf. *boda*, a messenger, id. Cf. Icel. *boða*, to announce; *boð*, a bid. From AS. *bod-*, weak grade of AS. *bēodan*, to command, *bid*. See **Bid** (2).

BODICE, stays for women. (E.) *Bodice* is a corruption of *bodies*, like *pence* for *pennies*; it was orig. used as a pl. Hence, in Johnson's Life of Pope: 'he was invested in *bodice* made of stiff canvass;' ed. 1854; iii. 46. Marston has 'a pair of *bodies* to a woman's petticote;' Malcontent, iii. 1. And Mr. Wedgwood quotes, from Sherwood's Dictionary (appended to Cotgrave, edd. 1632, 1660): 'A woman's *bodies*, or a pair of *bodies*; corset, corpset.' See **Body.**

BODKIN, orig. a small dagger. (F.?—Du.?) ME. *boydekin* (trisyllable), a dagger; Chaucer, C. T., B 3892, 3897. In Chaucer, C. T., A 3960, MS. Cm. has *boytekyn*. Origin unknown. I merely suggest that it may come from an OF. form **boitequin* (AF. **beitequin*). Cf. MDu. *beytelken*, 'a small beetle,' Hexham. For the MDu. *beytel* also meant 'a punce to engrave with,' Hexham; the same as mod. Du. *beitel*, a chisel; so that *beytelken* also meant 'a small chisel' or 'small punch.' See *beitel* in Franck. Cf. Low G. *bötel*, a kind of chisel, Berghaus; Norw. *beitel*, a chisel.

BODY, the material frame of man or any animal. (E.) ME. *bodi*, Owl and Nightingale, 73; Layamon, 4908. AS. *bodig*, body.+OHG. *potah*; MHG. *botech*. Of unknown origin. ¶ The Gael. *bodhaig* is unrelated (Macbain). Der. *bodi-ly*, *bodi-less*, *bodice*.

BOER, a Dutch colonist in S. Africa. (Du.) Du. *boer*, cognate with E. *boor*; see **Boor.**

BOG, a piece of soft ground; a quagmire. (C.) 'A great *bog* or marish;' North's Plutarch, p. 480. Also in Dunbar, Of James Dog, l. 15 (1505). 'Nouther busk ne *bog*;' Henrysoun, Wolf and Wedder, l. 77.—Irish *bogach*, a morass; lit. softish; *-ach* being the adjectival termination, so that *bogach* is formed from *bog*, soft, tender, penetrable; OIrish *bocc*, soft. Gael. *bogan*, a quagmire; cf. Gael. *bog*, soft, moist, tender. From Celtic type **bukkos*, soft; for **bugnos*, allied to Skt. *bhug-nas*, bent, pp. of *bhuj*, to bow, bend. From the weak grade **bhug* of √BHEUG or BHEUGH. See **Bow** (1). See Stokes-Fick, p. 180.

BOGGARD, BOGGART, a spectre. (C.; *with F. suffix.*) Levins has: 'A *boggarde*, spectrum.' From *bog*, variant of **Bug** (1); with suffix *-art*, *-ard* (F. *-ard* as in OF. *bastard*). See below.

BOGGLE, to start aside, swerve for fear. (C.?) Shak. has it, All's Well, v. 3. 232. Origin unknown; but there is a presumption that it is connected with Prov. Eng. *boggle*, a ghost, Scotch *bogle*, a spectre; from the notion of scaring or terrifying, and then, passively, of being scared. Cf. W. *bwg*, a goblin; *bwgwl*, a threat; *bwgwth*, to scare; *bygylu*, to threaten; *bygylus*, intimidating, scaring. Cf. *bug* in *bug-bear*. See **Bug** (1).

BOHEA, a kind of tea. (Chinese.) In Somervile, The Incurious Bencher, l. 28; Pope, Rape of the Lock, l. 620. So named from the *Bohea* hills. 'The *Bou-y tcha* (Bohea tea) takes its name from a mountain called *Bou-y*, situated in the province of Fo-kien;' Engl. Cycl. s. v. *Tea*. Also called *Wu-i* Hills, or *Bu-i* in the Fo-kien dialect. Cf. *bû-i-tê*, Bohea tea; Douglas, Dict. of Amoy dialect. *Fo-kien* is Fukian in Black's Atlas, on the S. E. coast of China.

BOIL (1), vb., to bubble up. (F.—L.) ME. *boile*, *boilen*; also '*boyle*, *buyle*, to break forth or boil, Exod. xvi. 20, Hab. iii. 16;' Wyclif's Bible (Glossary).—OF. *boillir*, to boil.—L. *bullire*, to bubble. ‒L. *bulla*, a bubble. See **Bull** (2). Der. *boil-er*.

BOIL (2), a small tumour. (E.) Spelt *byle* in Shak. Cor. i. 4. 31 (1623). ME. *bile*, *byle*, *buile*, P. Plowman, B. xx. 83. AS. *bȳl*, Voc.

245. 15; pl. *bȳlas*, Voc. 199. 25. Cf. Du. *buil*, a boil; G. *beule*, MHG. *biule*, OHG. *būlla*. All from Teut. base **bul-*, weakened grade of Teut. root **beul-*, to swell; whence also Goth. *uf-bauljan*, to puff up, Icel. *beyla*, a hump. Orig. sense 'a swelling.'

BOISTEROUS, wild, unruly, rough. (F.—Scand.) Shak. has *boisterous*, frequently. But it is an extended form. ME. *boistous*, Chaucer, C. T. 17160 (H 211); also *boystows* = rudis; Prompt. Parv. p. 42. The forms are numerous, and the senses various; see N.E.D. Just as E. *cloister* is from L. *claustrum*, so the AF. *boist-* is from Norw. *baust-*; for which see under **Boast.** From the weaker grade *bū t-* we have EFries. *büsterig*, boisterous (as wind), *büster*, a storm, from *būsen*, to be noisy or stormy; Jutland *busten*, harsh.

BOLD, daring. (E.) ME. *bold*, *bald*; P. Plowman, A. iv. 94; B. iv. 107. AS. *beald*, *bald*, Grein, i. 101; also *balþ-* (in comp.; O. E. Texts, p. 293).+Icel. *ballr*; MDu. *bald* (Oudemans), whence Du. *bout*; Goth. *balths*, bold, in derived adv. *balthaba*, boldly; OHG. *pald*. Teut. type **balthoz*. Der. *bold-ly*, *bold-ness*; also *bawd*, q. v.

BOLE, the stem of a tree. (Scand.) ME. *bole*, Allit. Poems, ed. Morris, B. 622.—Icel. *bolr*, *bulr*, the trunk of a tree; Swed. *bål*, a trunk, body; Dan. *bul*, trunk, stump, log; G. *bohle*, a plank, board. Prob. allied to Gk. φάλ-αγξ, a log, trunk (Kluge). See **Balk** (1). Der. *bul-wark*.

BOLERO, a lively Spanish dance. (Span.—L.?) 'She mingles in the gay *bolero*;' Byron, orig. draught of Song to Inez; Childe Harold, c. 1 (notes).—Span. *bolero*, a lively dance; also, the dancer of it. Applied as an adj. to a child who runs from school; and prob. allied to *bola*, a bowl, the game of bowls; cf. *escurrir la bola*, to run away.—L. *bulla*, a bubble, a ball; see **Bowl** (1).

BOLLED, swollen. (Scand.) In the A. V.; Exod. ix. 31. Pp. of ME. *bollen*, to swell; which occurs in *bolleþ*, P. Plowman, A. v. 99; and in the sb. *bolling*, swelling, P. Plowman, B. vi. 218, A. vii. 204. A more usual form of the pp. is *bolned*, whence the various readings *bolniþ*, *bolnyth*, for *bolleþ*, in the first passage.—Dan. *bulne*, to swell; Swed. *bulna*, to swell; Icel. *bólgna*; inchoative forms from *bolg-*, weak grade of Teut. **belgan-*, to swell, whence Icel. *belgja*, to inflate. Cf. AS. *belg-an* (pp. *bolgen*), to swell with anger. See **Bellows, Billow.**

BOLSTER, a sort of pillow. (E.) ME. *bolster*, Prompt. Parv. p. 43. AS. *bolster*; Grein.+Icel. *bolstr*; OHG. *polstar* (Stratmann, Schade). In Dutch, *bolster* is both a pillow, and a shell or husk. β. The suffix may be compared with that in *hol-ster*; see it discussed in Koch, Engl. Grammatik, iii. 46. Teut. type **bul-stroz*, from Teut. **bul-*, weak grade of **beul-*, to puff up; see **Boil** (2). See Franck.

BOLT, a stout pin, of iron, &c.; an arrow for a cross-bow. (E.) ME. *bolt*, a straight rod, Chaucer, C. T. 3264. AS. *bolt*, a cross-bow bolt; cf. '*Catapultas*, speru, boltas;' Voc. 508. 14 (Late L. *catapulta* meant a bolt as well as a catapult).+MDu. *bolt*, a bolt for shooting, a kind of arrow (Oudemans), whence Du. *bout*, a bolt, in all senses; OHG. *polz*, whence G. *bolzen*, a bolt; MSwed. *bult*. Teut. type **boltoz*, m. Origin unknown.

BOLT, BOULT, to sift meal. (F.—L.—Gk.) Shak. has *bolt*, Winter's Tale, iv. 4. 375; also *bolter*, a sieve, 1 Henry IV, iii. 3. 81. ME. *bulted* (written *bulltedd*) occurs in the Ormulum, l. 992. Palsgrave has: 'I *boulte* meale in a *boulter*, Ie bulte.'—OF. *buleter* (Supp. to Godefroy); later *bulter* (Palsgrave); to boult meal (Cotgrave); mod. F. *bluter*. β. In OF. we also find *buletel*, a sieve (Supp. to Godefroy), also spelt *buretel* (Littré), showing that *buleter* is a corruption of **bureter*; cf. Ital. *burattello*, a bolter; see proofs in Burguy and Brachet. **Bureter* meant 'to sift through a kind of cloth;' Florio has Ital. *burattino*, 'a kinde of stuffe called Burato; also a boulter; *buratto*, a boulter or sieve.' γ. The OF. **bureter* is thus derivable from OF. (and F.) *bure*, a coarse woollen cloth; Late L. *burra* (the same).—L. *burrus*, reddish (from its colour).—Gk. πυρρός, reddish.—Gk. πῦρ, fire. See **Bureau.**

BOLUS, a large pill. (L.—Gk.) In Phillips, ed. 1706; and Coles (1684). Phillips also explains it as a clod of earth, lump of metal, &c.—Late L. *bōlus* (not L. *bolus*), which is merely a Latinised form of Gk. βῶλος, a clod, lump of earth, a lump (generally). ¶ Cotgrave has *bolus* as a F. word.

BOMB, a shell for cannon. (F.—Span.—L.—Gk.) In Kersey's Dict., ed. 1708; and in Evelyn's Diary, Mar. 16, 1687. In older writers, it is called a *bumbard* or *bombard*. See **Bombard.**—F. *bombe*, a bomb.—Span. *bomba*; Minsheu (1623) has '*bomba de fuego*, a ball of wilde-fire.'—L. *bombus*, a humming noise.—Gk. βόμβος, a humming or buzzing noise; perhaps onomatopoetic. See **Boom** (1).

BOMBARD, to attack with bombs. (F.—L.—Gk.) 'To *Bombard* or *Bomb*, to shoot bombs into a place;' also '*Bombard*, a kind of great gun;' Kersey's Dict. ed. 1715. In older authors, it is a sb., meaning a cannon or great gun (as in Caxton, tr. of Reynard, c. 25), and, jocularly, a large drinking vessel; see Shak. Temp. ii. 2.

21. — F. *bombarde*, 'a bumbard, or murthering piece;' Cot. — Late L. *bombarda*, orig. a kind of catapult. — L. *bombus*, a humming noise (above). ¶ Cf. ME. *bombard*, a trumpet; Gower, C. A. iii. 358; bk. viii. 2482. Der. *bombard-ment*, *bombard-ier*, q. v.

BOMBARDIER. (F. — L. — Gk.) Cotgrave has: '*Bombardier*, a bumbardier, or gunner that useth to discharge murthering peeces· and more generally, any gunner.' See **Bombard.**

BOMBAST, originally, cotton-wadding; hence padding, affected language. (F. — L. — Gk.) '*Bombast*, the cotton-plant growing in Asia; also, a sort of cotton or fustian; also, affected language;' Kersey's Dict. (1708). 'White *Bumbast* [cotton] cloth;' Hakluyt, Voy. ii. pt. 1. 222. — OF. *bombace*, cotton (Godefroy); with added *t*. — Late L. *bombācem*, acc. of *bombax*, cotton; a corruption of L. *bombyx*. — Gk. βόμβυξ, silk, cotton; orig. a silkworm. Cf. 'to talk *fustian*.' Der. *bombast-ic*; and see below.

BOMBAZINE, BOMBASINE, a fabric, of silk and worsted. (F. — L. — Gk.) Borrowed from F. *bombasin*, which Cotgrave explains by 'the stuffe *bumbasine*, or any kind of stuffe that's made of cotton, or of cotton and linnen.' — Late L. *bombācinus*, made of the stuff called '*bombax*.' — Late L. *bombax*, cotton; a corruption of L. *bombyx*, a silk-worm, silk, fine cotton. — Gk. βόμβυξ, a silk-worm, silk, cotton. See above.

BOND, a tie. (Scand.) In Chaucer, C. T. 3096 (A 3094), where it rhymes with *hond* = hand. A mere variation of *band*; just as Chaucer has *lond*, *hond*, for *land*, *hand*. See **Band** (1). Der. *bond-ed*, *bonds-man*; but not (in the first instance) *bond-man*, nor *bond-age*; see **Bondage.**

BONDAGE, tenure of a cottar; service of a cottar; servitude. (F. — Scand.) ME. *bondage*, servitude, Rob. of Brunne, tr. of Langtoft, p. 71. — AF. *bondage*, explained by Roquefort as 'vilaine tenue,' i.e. a tenure of a lower character = Low L. *bondagium*, as in 'de toto tenemento, quod de ipso tenet in *bondagio*;' Monast. Anglic. 2 par. fol. 609 a, qu. in Blount's Nomo-lexicon. A holder under this tenure was called a *bondman*, or in earlier times *bonde* [AF. *bunde*, as in Statutes of the Realm, i. 211], AS. *bonda*, which merely meant a boor, a householder. β. That the word *bondage* has been connected from early times with the word *bond*, and the verb to *bind*, is certain; hence its sinister sense of 'servitude.' γ. It is equally certain that this etymology is wholly false, the AS. *bonda* having been borrowed from Icel. *bóndi*, a husbandman, a short form of *búandi*, a tiller of the soil; from Icel. *búa*, to till; so that AS. *bonda* is allied in sense and origin to E. *boor*. See **Boor.**

BONE, a separate part of the skeleton. (E.) ME. *boon*, Chaucer, Prol. 546. AS. *bān*, Grein. + Du. *been*; Icel. *bein*; Swed. *ben*; Dan. *been*; OHG. *pein*, *bein*. Teut. type **bainom*, neut. Der. *bon-y*; *bon-fire*, q. v.

BONFIRE, a fire to celebrate festivals, &c. (E.) Fabyan (continued) has: 'they sang Te Deum, and made *bonefires*;' Queene Marie, an. 1555. Several other quotations in R. show the same spelling. β. The origin, from *bone* and *fire*, is certain, but was obscured by the regular shortening of the stressed vowel, as in *knowledge*, *Monday*, &c.; whence arose numerous futile guesses. γ. The Lowland Scotch is *banefire*, in Acts of James VI (Jamieson); and the Catholicon Anglicum (1483) has: 'A *banefire*, ignis ossium.' This makes it 'bone-fire,' as being the only form that agrees with the evidence; and this explanation leaves the whole word native English, instead of making it a clumsy hybrid. ¶ Note the following passage. 'The English nuns at Lisbon do pretend that they have both the arms of Thomas Becket; and yet Pope Paul the Third . . . pitifully complains of the cruelty of K. Hen. 8 for causing all the bones of Becket to be burnt, and the ashes scattered in the winds; . . . and how his arms should escape that *bone-fire* is very strange;' The Romish Horseleech, 1674, p. 82. See also my Notes on E. Etymology, p. 13. It is remarkable that the Picard equivalent of *bonfire* is *fu d'os* (Corblet). Cf. *bonefire* in E. D. D.

BONITO, a fish of the tunny kind. (Span. *or* Port. — L.) Described in Eng. Garner, ed. Arber, v. 133 (ab. 1565). 'A *bonitoe*-fish;' Minsheu (1627). — Span. *bonito*, 'a fish called a tunnie;' Minsheu's Span. Dict. (1623); whence, probably, Arab. *baynîs*, 'the fish called bonito;' Rich. Dict. p. 312. [Here the final *s* of *baynîs* is not the usual *s*, but the 4th letter of the alphabet which, according to Palmer, is properly sounded as E. *th* in *both*.] β. Yule says the name is Portuguese; from Port. *bonito*, fine. The Span. *bonito* also means 'fine;' dimin. of Span. *bueno*, good. — L. *bonum*, acc. of *bonus*, good; see **Bounty.** ¶ The Arab. name is adapted from Spanish or Portuguese.

BONNET, a cap. (F. — Low L. — Hind. ?) 'Lynnen *bonnettes* vpon their heades;' Bible, 1551, Ezek. xliv. 18; and so in A. V. ME. *bonet*; written *bonat* in Barbour, Bruce, ix. 506 (but rhyming with *set*). — OF. *bonet*, bonnet, the name of a stuff, of which caps were made (stressed on the *latter* syllable); F. *bonnet*, a cap; Cot.

[Brachet says it was originally the name of a stuff; 'there were *robes de bonnet*; the phrase *chapel de bonnet* [cap of stuff] is several times found; this was abridged into *un bonnet*.' Cf. E. 'a beaver' for 'a beaver hat.'] — Low L. *bonnēta*, the name of a stuff, mentioned A. D. 1300. Origin unknown. Perhaps of Indian origin; cf. Hind. *banāt*, woollen cloth, broad cloth (Forbes).

BONNY, handsome, fair; blithe. (F. — L. ?) Shak. has 'blithe and *bonny*;' Much Ado, ii. 3. 69; also, 'the *bonny* beast;' 2 Hen. VI, v. 2. 12. Levins has: '*Bonye*, scitus, facetus,' 102. 32. A comparison of the word with such others as *bellibone*, *bonibell*, *bonilasse* (all in Spenser, Shep. Kal. August), suggests a connexion with F. *bonne*, fair, fem. of *bon*, good; from L. *bonus*, good. The ME. *bonie* (in King Alisaunder, l. 3903) is less easily connected with OF. *bone*, fem. of *bon*; but the suffix is prob. E. *-y* (AS. *-ig*). Cf. *jolly*, in which F. final *-i* is written as E. *-y*. Der. *bonni-ly*. See **Bounty.**

BONZE, a Japanese priest. (Port. — Japanese — Chinese.) Spelt *bonzee* in Sir T. Herbert's Travels, pp. 393, 394 (directly from Jap. *bonzi*). — Port. *bonzo*, a bonze. — Japan. *bonzi* or *bonzô*. — Chin. *fan seng*, 'a religious person;' Yule. (Sir T. Wade also regards it as the Japan. form of *fan seng*.)

BOOBY, a stupid fellow. (Span. — L.) In Beaum. and Fletcher, Hum. Lieutenant, iii. 7. 9. In Sir T. Herbert's Travels, ed. 1665, p. 11, we find: 'At which time some *boobyes* pearcht upon the yard-arm of our ship, and suffered our men to take them, an animal so very simple as becomes a proverb.' [The F. *boubie*, in the Supplement to the Dict. de l'Académie, is only used of the bird, and may have been borrowed from English. The name probably arose among the Spanish sailors.] — Span. *bobo*, a blockhead, dolt; a word in very common use, with numerous derivatives, such as *bobon*, a great blockhead, *bobote*, a simpleton, &c.; cf. Port. *bobo*, a mimic, buffoon. [Related to F. *baube*, stuttering (Cotgrave), and to OF. *baubi*, foolish, orig. pp. of *baubir*, to mock at.] — L. *balbus*, stammering, lisping, inarticulate. [Cf. Span. *bobear*, to talk foolishly, *bobada*, silly speech.] + Gk. βάρβαρος, lit. inarticulate. See **Barbarous.**

BOOK, a volume; a written composition. (E.) ME. *book*, Chaucer, C. T., B 190. AS. *bōc*, Grein, i. 134. + Du. *boek*; Icel. *bók*; Swed. *bok*; Dan. *bog*; OHG. *buoh*, MHG. *buoch*, G. *buch*. β. A peculiar use of AS. *bōc*, a beech-tree (Grein, i. 134); because the original books were written on beechen boards or bark. The Icel. *bókstafr* properly meant 'a beech-twig,' but afterwards 'a letter.' So, in German, we have OHG. *puocha*, *buocha*, MHG. *buoche*, a beech-tree, as compared with OHG. *buoh*, MHG. *buoch*, a book. The mod. G. forms are *buche*, beech; *buch*, a book. Cf. Goth. *bōka*, a letter; pl. *bōkōs*, a writing. AS. *bōc*, a 'charter,' occurs A. D. 808 (O.E. Texts). See **Beech.** Der. *book-ish*, *book-keeping*, *book-case*, *book-worm*.

BOOM (1), vb., to hum, buzz. (E.) ME. *bommen*, to hum. 'I *bomme* as a bombyll bee [i.e. bumble-bee] dothe or any flye;' Palsgrave. Not recorded in A.S.; cf. Du. *bommen*, to give out a hollow sound, to sound like an empty barrel. The MDu. *bommen* meant 'to sound a drum or tabor;' and MDu. *bom* meant 'a tabor,' Oudemans. Allied to *bump*, to make a noise like a bittern, which is the Welsh form; see **Bump** (2). ¶ That the word begins with *b* both in O. Low G. and in Latin (which has the form *bombus*, a humming), is due to the fact that it is imitative. See **Bomb.**

BOOM (2), a beam or pole. (Dutch.) *Boom* occurs in Kersey (1708); and in North's Examen (R.) — Du. *boom*, a beam, pole, tree. + E. *beam*. See **Beam.** Many of our sea-terms are Dutch. Der. *jib-boom*, *spanker-boom*.

BOOMERANG, an Australian missile weapon. (Australian.) See quotations in E. E. Morris, Austral English. Given as the native name at Port Jackson in 1827; derived from *buma*, to strike (with suffix *-arang*), by J. Fraser, Aborigines of New S. Wales, p. 69.

BOON, a petition, favour. (Scand.) ME. *bone*, *boone*, Chaucer, C. T. 2271 (A 2269); and in the Ancren Riwle, p. 28. — Icel. *bón*, a petition; Dan. and Swed. *bön*, a petition. + AS. *bēn*, a petition; whence *bene* in Wordsworth. [Note that the vowel shows the word to be Scandinavian in form, not A. S.] Teut. type **bōniz*, f. β. Fick connects it with the root *ban*, appearing in our E. *ban*; iii. 201. See **Ban.** γ. The sense of 'favour' is somewhat late, and points to a confusion with F. *bon*, L. *bonus*, good. δ. In the phrase 'a *boon* companion,' the word is wholly of the F. *bon*.

BOOR, a peasant, tiller of the soil. (Dutch.) In Shak. Merry Wives, iv. 5. 1; and Beaum. and Fletcher, Beggars' Bush, iii. 1. — Du. *boer* (pronounced *boor*), a peasant, lit. 'a tiller of the soil;' see the quotations in R., esp. the quotation from Sir W. Temple. — Du. *bouwen*, to till. β. In Mid. Eng. the term is very rare, but it is found, spelt *boueer*, in Lydgate, Chorle and Bird, st. 51; and it forms a part of the word *neigh-bour*, showing that it was once an English word as well as a Dutch one. Cf. AS. *gebūr* (rare, but found in the Laws of Ine, § 6), a tiller of the soil; AS. *būan*, to till, cultivate; OHG. *būwan*, to cultivate (whence G. *bauer*, a peasant, a boor); Goth.

bauan, to cultivate; all closely related to the word *be*. From √BHEU, to dwell; Fick, i. 161; Benfey, s.v. *bhū*; Streitberg, § 90. See Be. Der. *boor-ish, boor-ish-ly, boor-ish-ness*.

BOOT (1), a covering for the leg and foot. (F., – Late L.) Chaucer has *botes*, Prol. 203, 275. – OF. *bote, botte*, a boot. – Late L. *botta*, a boot; also spelt *bota*; cf. Span. and Port. *bota*. [In Eng. the word is even extended to mean the luggage-box of a coach; cf. F. *botte* (5) in Littré, and see N.E.D.] The old boots were often large and ample, covering the whole of the lower part of the leg. ¶ A connexion between *boot* and *butt* is sometimes assumed, but they are now known to be distinct; *boot* = Late L. *botta*; *butt* = Late L. *butta*.

BOOT (2), advantage, profit. (E.) Chiefly preserved in the adj. *bootless*, profitless. ME. *bote, boote*, common in early authors; the phr. *to bote* is in Langtoft, p. 163, &c. AS. *bōt*, Grein, i. 135; whence AS. *bētan*, to amend, help. + Du. *boete*, penitence; *boeten*, to mend, kindle, atone for; Icel. *bōt (bati)*, advantage, cure, *bæta*, to mend, improve; Dan. *bod*, amendment, *bøde*, to mend; Swed. *bot*, remedy, cure, *bōta*, to fine, mulct; Goth. *bōta*, profit, *bōtjan*, to profit; OHG. *puoza, buoza*, G. *busse*, atonement, G. *büssen*, to atone for. (In all these the sb. is older than the verb.) Teut. type *bōtā*, fem.; from *bōt-*, second grade of *bat-*; cf. Icel. *bati*, advantage; and see Better. Der. *boot-less, boot-less-ly, boot-less-ness*. ¶ The phrase *to boot* means 'in addition,' lit. 'for an advantage;' it is not a verb, as Bailey oddly supposes; and, in fact, the allied verb takes the form *to beet*, still used in Scotland in the sense of 'to mend a fire' (AS. *bētan*, to help, to kindle).

BOOTH, a slight building. (Scand.) ME. *bothe*, in comp. *tol-bothe*, a toll-house, Wyclif, St. Matt. ix. 9; also *boþe*, which seems to occur first in the Ormulum, l. 15817. – MDan. *bōth* (Kalkar); Jutland *bod* (locally pronounced *buwəd*), Feilberg; Dan. *bod*; cf. Icel. *būð*, a booth, shop; Swed. *bod*. + G. *bude*, a booth, stall. Teut. type *bū-thā*, fem.; from *bū-*, to dwell, as in Icel. *bū-a*; see Boor. β. Further related to Irish and Gael. *both, bothan*, a hut, W. *bôd*, a residence; Lith. *buta, buttas*, a house. [But W. *bwth*, a booth, Gael. *buth*, a shop, are from E.] Cf. Skt. *bhavana-m*, a house, a place to be in, from *bhū*, to dwell, be.

BOOTY, prey, spoil. (F. – Low G.) Not in very early use. One of the earlier examples is in Hall's Chron. Henry VIII, an. 14. § 49, where it is spelt *botie*. Palsgrave has *boty*, to translate F. *butin*. Caxton has both *botye* and *butyn* in his Boke of Chesse, bk. ii. ch. 4; 'Alle the *butyn* and gayne,' Troy-book, lf. 277, back. Formed (with loss of *n*, as in *haughty*) from F. *butin*, 'a booty, prey, or spoyle taken;' Cot. [The E. *oo* is due to the influence of *boot* (2).] – MDu. *büte*, Du. *buit*, booty, spoil, prize; *buit maken*, to get booty, take in war; cf. Icel. *bȳti*, Swed. *byte*, Dan. *bytte*, exchange, barter, booty, spoil. Allied to Celtic *boudi-*, as in Irish *buaid*, victory, W. *budd*, gain, profit. Stokes-Fick, p. 175. [The G. *beute*, booty, is merely borrowed from Low G., as shown by its unaltered form.] ¶ Cotgrave's explanation of *butiner* as 'to prey, get booty, make spoil of, to *bootehale*,' clearly shows how the Eng. spelling was affected by confusion with *boot*, advantage, profit.

BORAGE, a plant with rough leaves. (F. – Arab.) ME. *borage*, Liber Cure Cocorum, ed. Morris, p. 47; also *bourage*, as in Cotgrave, who gives: '*Bourroche, Bourrache*, bourage.' – F. *bourrache*; OF. *borrace* (Hatzfeld); cf. Late L. *borrāgo*, a name supposed to refer to its rough leaves, as if from Late L. *borra, burra*, rough hair, whence F. *bourre*, Ital. *borra*. But now (as in Hatzfeld) thought to be from (unauthorised) Arab. *abū rashh*, a sudorific plant; from *abū*, a father (hence, producing), and *rashh*, sweating, as in Rich. Dict., p. 734. Cf. Span. *borraja*, 'bourage;' Minsheu. (Littré; who thinks the Low L. *borrāgo* to be taken from the F.)

BORAX, biborate of soda; of a whitish colour. (Low L. – Arab. – Pers.) Cotgrave gives *borax, borrais*, and *boras* as the French spellings, with the sense 'borax, or green earth; a hard and shining minerall.' *Borax* is a Low Latin spelling; Ducange also gives the form *boracum*. The latter is the more correct form, and taken directly from the Arabic. – Arab. *būrāq* (better *būraq*), borax; Rich. Arab. Dict. p. 295. – Pers. *būrah*, borax (Vullers). See Devic.

BORDER, an edge. (F. – Low L. – Teut.) ME. *bordure*, Chaucer, tr. of Boethius, bk. i. pr. 1, l. 22. – F. *bordure* (Cotgrave); OF. *bordeüre* (Supp. to Godefroy); cf. Span. *bordadura*. – Low L. *bordā-tūra*, an edging. – Low L. *bordāre* (Ital. *bordare*, Span. *bordar*, F. *border*), to edge. – Du. *boord*, border, edge, brim, bank; which is cognate with AS. *bord* in some of its senses. See Board. Der. *border*, vb.; *border-er*.

BORE (1), to perforate. (E.) ME. *borien*, Ayenbite of Inwyt, p. 66. AS. *borian*, Bosworth, with a ref. to Ælfric's Glossary; he also quotes 'wyrm þe boraþ treow,' a worm that perforates wood. + Du. *boren*, to bore, pierce; Icel. *bora*; Swed. *borra*; Dan. *bore*; OHG. *porōn* (G. *bohren*). Teut. Type *borōn*, to perforate; from *boroz*, sb., a bore, gimlet, as seen in AS. *bor*, Icel. *borr*, Swed. *borr*,

Dan. *bor*, a bore, gimlet. + L. *forāre*, to bore; Gk. φαρ-, in φάρ-αγξ, a ravine, φάρ-υγξ, the pharynx, gullet; Brugm. i. § 510. – √BHER, to cut. Thus *bore* is co-radicate with *perforate* and *pharynx*. Der. *bor-er*.

BORE (2), to worry, vex. (E.) Merely a metaphorical use of *bore*, to perforate. Shak. has it in the sense, to overreach, trip up: 'at this instant He *bores* me with some trick;' Hen. VIII, i. 1. 128. Cf. 'Baffled and *bored*;' Beaum. and Fletcher, Span. Curate, iv. 5.

BORE (3), a tidal surge in a river. (Scand.) Used by Burke, On a Regicide Peace, letters 3 and 4 (R.). An old prov. E. word, of Scand. origin. ME. *se-bare*, sea-billow, surge; E. Metr. Hom., ed. Small, p. 135, l. 24. – Icel. *bára*, a billow caused by wind; Norw. *baara*, a billow, swell in the sea; Du. *baar*, a billow, also a bier; EFries. *bār*; Low G. *bare*. Lit. 'a thing borne along;' all from Teut. *bār-*, 3rd grade of *beran-*, to bear. See Bier. Doublet, *bier*.

BOREAS, the north wind. (L. – Gk.) In Shak. Troil. i. 3. 38. – L. *Boreas*, the north wind. – Gk. Βορέας, Βορρᾶς, the north wind. β. Perhaps it meant, originally, the 'mountain-wind;' cf. Ital. *tramontana*, mountain-wind. Cf. OSlav. and Russ. *gora*, Skt. *giri-s*, a mountain; Curtius, i. 434. Der. *borea-l*.

BOROUGH, a town. (E.) ME. *burgh, borgh*, P. Plowman, B. vi. 308; also *borwe*, in the sense 'a place of shelter' (cf. E. *burrow*), Will. of Palerne, l. 1889; *burȝe, burie, borwe, borewe*, Layamon, 2168, 3553, 9888. AS. *burh, burg*, Grein, i. 147; forming *byrig* in the gen. and dat. sing., whence the mod. E. *bury* in the sense 'town.' + Du. *burg*; Icel. *borg*, a fort, castle; Swed. and Dan. *borg*, a fort, castle; Goth. *baurgs*, a town; OHG. *purc* (G. *burg*), a castle. β. Teut. type *burgs*, f.; from *burg-*, weak grade of *bergan-*, AS. *beorgan*, to defend, protect, Grein, i. 107; Goth. *bairgan*, to hide, preserve, keep. – √BHERGH, to protect. Benfey (p. 635) suggests a connexion with Skt. *brhan*, large. See below; and see Burgess, Barrow (1).

BORROW, to receive money on trust. (E.) ME. *borwen*, Chaucer, C. T. 4525 (B 105). AS. *borgian*, to borrow, Matt. v. 42 (by usual change of AS. *g* to ME. *w*); the lit. meaning being 'to give a pledge.' – AS. *borg*, a pledge, more frequently spelt *borh* in the nom. case; common in the AS. laws. + Du. *borg*, a pledge, bail, security; MHG. and G. *borg*, security. (Merely a borrowed word in Icelandic, and perhaps also in Swed. and Danish.) From *borg-* = *burg-*, weak grade of *bergan-*, to protect; cf. AS. *borgen*, pp. of AS. *beorgan*, to protect, secure. See Borough. Der. *borrow-er*.

BOSH, nonsense; foolish talk. (Turkish.) From Turk. *bosh*, empty, worthless; introduced by Jas. Morier, in his novel of Ayesha, 1834; where he explains *bosh* by 'nothing.'

BOSKY, bushy. (Late L.) In Milton, Comus, 313. From Late L. *boscus*, a bush; see Bush.

BOSOM, a part of the body. (E.) ME. *bosom*, Chaucer, C. T. 7575 (D 1993). AS. *bōsm*, Grein, i. 134. + Du. *boezem*; OHG. *puosam*; G. *busen*. Origin unknown. The Teut. type is *bōs-moz*, m., from Idg. root *bhas*. Hence it may mean 'swelling,' from Skt. root *bhas*, to puff, swell, whence *bhas-trā*, bag, sack, pouch; see *babhasti* (2) in Uhlenbeck.

BOSS, a knob. (F. – OHG.) ME. 'bos(se) of a bocler' (buckler); Chaucer, C. T. 3266. – F. *bosse*, a hump; OF. *boce*; cf. Prov. *bossa*; Ital. *bozza*, a swelling. β. It has been supposed that (just as E. *bump* means (1) to strike, and (2) a hump, a swelling, with other similar instances) the root of the word is to be found in the OHG. *bōzan*, to strike, beat; cognate with E. *beat*. See Beat, and see further under Botch (2). Doublet, *botch* (2).

BOTANY, the science that treats of plants. (F. – Gk.) 'Botanical, belonging to herbs;' Coles (1682). The sb. *botany* is formed by analogy, being derived from the F. adj. *botanique*, a form which appears in Cotgrave, and is explained by 'herball, of, or belonging to herbs, or skill in herbs.' The mod. F. *botanique* is both adj. and sb. Thus *botany* is short for 'botanic science.' – Gk. βοτανικός, botanical, adj., formed from βοτάνη, a herb, plant. – Gk. βόσκειν, to feed (stem βο-); cf. βοτόν, a grazing animal. Der. *botanic, botanic-al, botanic-al-ly, botan-ist, botan-ise*.

BOTARGO, a cake made of the roe of the sea-mullet. (Ital. – Arab.) 'Sturgeon, mullit, caviare, and *buttargo*;' Capt. Smith, Works, ed. Arber, p. 240 (1614-15). – Ital. *botargo*, 'a kind of salt meate made of fish vsed in Italy in Lent;' Florio. – Arab. *butarkhah*, the same (Devic). The Arab. word is thought to be composed of the Coptic indef. art. *bu*, and the Gk. τάριχος, dried fish (Journal des Savants, Jan. 1848, p. 45).

BOTCH (1), to patch; a patch. (E.) Wyclif has *bocchyn*, to mend, 2 Chron. xxxiv. 10. Prob. a native word, but not found in A.S. Oudemans gives a parallel form *botsen* (mod. Du. *botsen*), to strike; with its variant *butsen*, meaning both (1) to strike or beat, and (2) to repair. The notion of repairing in a rough manner follows from that of fastening by beating. So also MDu. *butsen*, *botsen*, ' to push or to smite ; ' *botsen*, *boetsen*, ' to clout or patch ; ' Hexham. Der. *botch-er*, *botch-y*.

BOTCH (2), a swelling. (F. – G.) Used by Milton, '*botches* and blains ; ' P. L. xii. 180. The Prompt. Parv. has : '*Bohche, botche, sore*; *ulcus*.' Here *tch* is for *cch* or *ch*. The spelling *bocches* is in P. Plowman, B. xx. 83. – O. North F. *boche*, a botch, a boil ; Norm. dial. *boche* (Moisy) ; Picard *boche* ; for OF. *boce*, a swelling ; thus *botch* is a doublet of *boss*. See **Boss**. ¶ Oudemans gives *butse* as M. Du. for a boil, or a swelling, with the excellent example in an old proverb : ' Naar den val de *butse*' = as is the tumble, so is the *botch*.

BOTH, two together. (Scand.) Not formed from AS. *bā þā*, lit. ' both the,' but borrowed from the Scandinavian ; cf. Lowland Scotch *baith* ; spelt *baþe* and *beþe* in Havelok, 1680, 2543. – Icel. *bāðir* (*bā-ðir*), adj. pron. dual ; neut. *bæði, bāði* ; Swed. *bāda* ; Dan. *baade* ; cf. G. *beide*, both. **β.** AS. has only the shorter form *bā*, both ; cognate with Goth. *bai*, both ; cf. -*bo* in L. *am-bo* ; -*φω* in Gk. *ἄμ-φω* ; and -*bhāu* in Skt. *u-bhāu*, both. See Fick, i. 18. **γ.** The Icel. -*ðir* is for *þeir*, they, the ; so that *bo-th* (= *bo the*) was orig. *two* words ; cf. Goth. *ba þō skipa*, both the ships ; Luke, v. 7. See Noreen, Gr. § 122. For numerous examples of various forms of the word, see Koch, Engl. Gram. ii. 197.

BOTHER, to harass ; an embarrassment. (E. ?) There is no proof that the word is of any great antiquity in English. It first occurs in the writings of Irishmen, viz. T. Sheridan, Swift, and Sterne (N. E. D.). It may be a mere variant of *pother*, which is, at any rate, an older word. See further under **Pother**.

BOTS, BOTTS, small worms found in the intestines of horses. (E. ?) Shak. has *bots*, 1 Hen. IV, ii. 1. 11. Fitzherbert has *bottes* (Husbandry, § 102) ; whence Gael. *botus*, a belly-worm, is borrowed. The Sc form is *bats*, pl. Cf. WFlem. *botse*, a thick worm (De Bo).

BOTTLE (1), a hollow vessel. (F. – Late L.) ME. *botel*; Chaucer, C. T. 7513 (D 1931). – OF. *boteille, botele* (Supp. to Godefroy) ; cf. AF. *butuille*, a bottle (note to Vie de Seint Auban, ed. Atkinson, l. 677). – Late L. *buticula, butticula*, double dimin. of Late L. *buttis, butta*, a cask, butt. See **Butt** (2).

BOTTLE (2), a bundle of hay. (F. – OHG.) ME. *botel*, Chaucer, C. T. 16963 (H 14). – OF. *botel*; cf. '*botelle*, botte de foin ou de paille ; ' Roquefort. A dimin. of F. *botte*, a bundle of hay, &c. – OHG. *bōzo, pōzo*, a bundle of flax. – OHG. *bōzan, pōzan*, to beat, cognate with E. *beat* ; perhaps from the beating of flax. See **Beat**.

BOTTOM, the lower part, foundation. (E.) ME. *botym, botum, botun, bottome* ; also *bothome* ; see Prompt. Parv. p. 45 ; *bothem*, Gawain and the Grene Knight, ed. Morris, l. 2145. AS. *botm*, Grein, p. 133. + Du. *bodem* ; Icel. *botn* ; Swed. *botten* ; Dan. *bund* ; OHG. *podam* (G. *boden*). + L. *fundus* ; Gk. *πυθμήν* ; Skt. (Vedic) *budhna-s*, depth, ground ; Benfey, p. 634 ; Fick, iii. 214 ; Brugm. i. §§ 103, 704. **β.** The word appears also in Celtic ; cf. Irish *bonn*, the sole of the foot ; Gaelic *bonn*, sole, foundation, bottom ; W. *bon*, stem, base, stock. Der. *bottom-less, bottom-ry*. From the same root, *fund-ament*.

BOUDOIR, a small private room, esp. for a lady. (F.) Modern, and mere French. – F. *boudoir*, lit. a place to sulk in. – F. *bouder*, to sulk. Root uncertain ; but perhaps from the same source as E. *pout*, verb. Cf. Limousin *fa las boudos*, to pout ; *fa de pots*, to grimace (Mistral).

BOUGH, a branch of a tree. (E.) ME. *bough*, Chaucer, C. T. 1982 (A 1980). AS. *bōg, bōh*, Grein, i. 134. [The sense is peculiar to English ; the original sense of AS. *bōg* was ' an arm ; ' esp. the ' shoulder of an animal.'] + Icel. *bōgr*, the shoulder of an animal ; Dan. *boug, bov*, the shoulder of a quadruped ; also, the bow of a ship ; Swed. *bog*, shoulder, bow of a ship ; OHG. *puac, buog* (G. *bug*), the shoulder of an animal ; bow of a ship. + Gk. *πῆχυς*, the fore-arm ; Skt. *bāhus*, the arm. Teut. type *bōguz* ; Idg. type *bhāghus*. Brugm. i. § 184. See **Bow** (4).

BOUGHT, s., the bight of a rope, &c. ; see **Bout, Bight**.

BOULDER, a large round stone. (Scand.) Marked by Jamieson as a Perthshire word ; chiefly used in Scotland and the N. of England. ME. *bulder-ston*, Havelok, 1790. Mr. Wedgwood says : ' Swed. dial. *bullersten*, the larger kind of pebbles, in contrast to *klappersteen*, the small ones. From Swed. *bullra*, E. dial. *bolder*, to make a loud noise, to thunder.' *Klappersteen* means ' a stone that *claps* or rattles.' See his article ; and see Rietz. **β.** But I may add that the excrescent *d* occurs in Danish ; cf. Dan. *buldre*, to roar, to rattle ; *bulder*, crash, uproar, turmoil. (Danish puts *ld* for *ll*, as in *falde*, to fall.) So also E. Fries. *bullern*, to rumble ; *buller-wagen*, a waggon that rumbles through the streets ; Du. *bulderen*, to roar (as cannon). All these verbs are frequentative ; from *bull-* (as in MHG. *bullen*, to roar), weak grade of Teut. *bellan-*, to roar. See **Bell, Bellow, Bull** (1).

BOULEVARD, a promenade, with rows of trees. (F. – Teut.) Well known in Paris ; orig. a promenade laid out on a demolished fortification. – MF. *boulevard, bouleverd, boulever*, ' a bulwark ; ' Cot. – Du. *bolwerk*; see **Bulwark**.

BOULT, to sift meal ; see **Bolt** (2).

BOUNCE, to jump up quickly. (E.) ME. *bunsen, bounsen*, to strike suddenly, beat ; Ancren Riwle, p. 188. So also Low G. *bunsen*, to beat, knock, esp. used of knocking at a door ; Bremen Wörterbuch, i. 164 ; Du. *bonzen*, to bounce, throw ; Norw. *bunsa*, to bounce up (Ross). **β.** The word is clearly connected with *bounce*, a blow, bump, used also as an interjection, as in 2 Hen. IV, iii. 2. 304. Cf. Du. *bons*, a bounce, thump ; Swed. dial. *bums*, immediately (Rietz) ; G. *bumps*, bounce, as in *bumps ging die Thür* = bounce went the door ; Icel. *bops*, bump ! imitating the sound of a fall. The word is probably imitative, and intended to represent the sound of a blow. See **Bump** (1).

BOUND (1), to leap. (F. – L. – Gk.) Shak. has *bound*, All's Well, ii. 3. 314. – F. *bondir*, to bound, rebound, &c. ; but orig. to resound, make a loud resounding noise ; see Brachet. – L. *bombitāre*, to resound, hum, buzz ; whence Folk-L. *bombitīre*. – L. *bombus*, a humming sound. – Gk. *βόμβος*, a humming sound. See **Boom** (1).

BOUND (2), a boundary, limit. (F. – C. ?) ME. *bounde*, Chaucer, C. T. 7922 (E 46) ; earliest form *bunne*, Layamon, 1313. – OF. *bonne*, a limit, boundary, also spelt *bonde* ; AF. *bounde* ; also sometimes spelt *bodne* (which see in Burguy and in the Supp. to Godefroy). – Late L. *bodina, bonna*, a bound, limit. Origin uncertain ; some suggest a Celtic origin ; from Bret. *bôden*, a clump of trees (which might mark a boundary) ; cf. Bret. *bôd*, a tuft. The Late L. *bonna* answers well to Bret. *bonn*, a boundary, occurring in the compound *men-bonn*, a boundary-stone ; but this would separate *bodina* from *bonna* (yet the OF. *bodne* meant ' boundary-stone ; ' Godefroy, Supp.). The suggestion of Thurneysen (p. 91) does not help us. ¶ We may note that *bound* is a doublet of *bourn*, a boundary. See **Bourn** (1). Der. *bound*, vb., *bound-ary, bound-less*.

BOUND (3), ready to go. (Scand.) In the particular phrase ' the ship is *bound* for Cadiz,' the word *bound* means ' ready to go ; ' formed, by excrescent *d*, from ME. *boun*, ready to go. ' She was *boun* to go ; ' Chaucer, C. T. 11807 (F 1503). ' The maister schipman made him *boun* And gert him out ; ' Gower, C. A. iii. 322 ; bk. viii. 1407. ' Whan he sauh that Roberd . . . to wend was alle *bone* ; ' Langtoft, p. 99. – Icel. *būinn*, prepared, ready, pp. of vb. *būa*, to till, to get ready ; Norw. *buen* ; from the same root as **Boor**, q. v.

BOUNDEN, pp., as in ' *bounden* duty.' (E.) The old pp. of the verb to *bind*. See **Bind**.

BOUNTY, goodness, liberality. (F. – L.) Chaucer has *bountee*, C. T., B 1647, E 157, 415. – OF. *bonté, bonteit*, goodness. – L. acc. *bonitātem*, from nom. *bonitās*, goodness. – L. *bonus*, good ; Old L. *duonus*, good ; perhaps allied to Vedic Skt. *duvas*, honour ; Brugmann, ii. § 67. Der. *bounti-ful, bounti-ful-ness, bounte-ous, bounte-ous-ness*.

BOUQUET, a nosegay. (F. – Late L.) In Todd's Johnson (1831). Mere French. – F. *bouquet*, ' a nosegay or posie of flowers ; ' Cotgrave. – OF. (Norm. and Picard) *bosquet*, properly ' a little wood ' (Supp. to Godefroy) ; the dimin. of OF. *bos*, F. *bois*, a wood ; Brachet quotes from Mme. de Sévigné, who uses *bouquet* in the old sense. – Late L. *boscum, buscum*, acc. of *boscus, buscus*, a wood. See **Bush**. ¶ The lit. sense of ' little bush ' makes sense still.

BOURD, a jest ; to jest ; *obsolete*. (F.) Used by Holinshed, Drayton, &c. ; see Nares. ME. *bourde, boorde*. ' *Boorde*, or game, *ludus, jocus* ; ' Prompt. Parv. p. 44. The verb is used by Chaucer, C. T. 12712 (C 778). – OF. *bourde*, a game ; *bourder*, to play. Of unknown origin. Diez took OF. *bourder* to be a contraction of OF. *bohorder*, to tourney, joust with lances, hence to amuse oneself ; but this is no longer accepted.

BOURGEON ; see **Burgeon**.

BOURN (1), a boundary. (F.) Well known from Shak. Hamlet, iii. 1. 79 ; K. Lear, iv. 6. 57. – F. ' *borne*, a bound, limit, meere, march ; the end or furthest compass of a thing ; ' Cot. From OF. *bodne*, a bourn, limit, bound, boundary (Supp. to Godefroy). Thus *bourn* is a doublet of *bound*. See **Bound** (2).

BOURN, BURN (2), a stream. (E.) ' Come o'er the *bourn*, Bessy, to me ; ' K. Lear, iii. 6. 27. ME. *bourne*, P. Plowman, prol. l. 8. AS. *burna*, a stream, fountain ; Grein, i. 149. + Du. *bron*, a spring ; Icel. *brunnr*, a spring, fountain, well ; Swed. *brunn*, a well ; Dan. *brönd* ; Goth. *brunna*, a spring, well ; OHG. *prunno* (G. *brunnen*), a spring, well. Some think the Goth. *brunna* is from *brinnan*, to burn ; see Uhlenbeck, and Stokes-Fick, p. 172. The connexion is seen in the comparison of a bubbling well to boiling water ; and is remarkably exemplified in the words *well* and *torrent*, q. v. See **Burn**.

BOUSE, BOOSE, BOUZE, BOOZE, to drink deeply. (Dutch.) ME. *bousen*, Satire on Kildare, l. 45 ; in E. E. Poems, ed. Furnivall, p. 154. Spenser has : ' a *bouzing*-can ' = a drinking vessel ; F. Q. i. 4. 22. Cotgrave uses *bouse* to translate F. *boire*. – ODu. *būsen*, MDu. *buisen, buysen*, to drink deeply ; Oudemans. Cf. MDu. *buize, buyse*, a drinking-vessel with two handles (Oudemans) ; clearly the same word as the modern Du. *buis*, a tube, pipe, conduit, channel. Cf. also OF. *buse*, *buise*, a conduit; G. *bausen*, to bouse.

BOUT, a spell (of work), &c.; properly, a turn, turning, bending. (Low G.) Formerly *bought*; Milton has *bout*, L'Allegro, 139; Spenser has *bought*, F. Q. i. 1. 15; i. 11. 11. Palsgrave (1530) has: '*Bought* of the arme.' Levins has: '*Bought*, plica, ambages,' 217. 31. — Low G. *bugt*, a bend, turn; also, a gulf, bay, *bight* (as a naut. term); Norw. *bugt*, EFries. *bugt*, *bucht*, a turn; cf. Icel. *bugða*, a bend, a serpent's coil (the sense in which Spenser uses *bought*). All from Teut. **bug-*, weaker grade of **būgan-*, to bow. See **Bow** (1) and **Bight**. ¶ Wedgwood suggests the possibility that 'in the expressions of a *drinking-bout*, a *bout* of fair or foul weather,' we have to do with a different word. Cotgrave gives: '*par boutées*, by fits, or pushes, not all at once, eftsoons, now and then;' which just answers to E. *by bouts*. As *boutée* is merely the fem. pp. of *bouter*, to thrust, to *butt*, it would seem that such a *bout* is a *butt*, i.e. a thrust. Cf. Span. *bote*, a thrust, Ital. *botta*, 'a blowe, a stroake, a time,' Florio. Wedgwood further remarks that 'the Du. *bot* or *botte*, a stroke or blow (ictus, impulsus—Kilian), as well as the nasalised *bonte*, is used in the dialect of West Flanders exactly as E. *bout*. *Een bot regen*, *eene botte wind*, *vorst*: a bout of rain, wind, frost. *Bij botten*; by bouts or intervals. *Eene botte*, or *bonte goed*, *nat*, *droog*, *weder*: a bout of good, wet, dry weather. *De kinkhoest is bij bonten*: the chincough comes in fits;' see De Bo, West Flem. Dict. So also Koolman, in his East Fries. Dict., gives the form *bot*, as in *elk bot went't rägend*, every time that it rains. But this is accidental, and only accounts for a form *bot*, not *bout* (which means a turn).

BOW (1), vb., to bend. (E.) ME. *bugen*, *buwen*, *bogen*, *bowen*. '*Bowyn*, flecto, curvo;' Prompt. Parv. p. 46. Very common. AS. *būgan*, to bend (gen. intransitive), Grein, i. 149.+Du. *buigen*, to bend (both trans. and intrans.). Teut. **būgan-*, to bow; also **beugan-*, as in Goth. *biugan* (tr. and intr.); OHG. *piogan*, G. *beugen*. Allied to L. *fugere*, to turn to flight, give way; Gk. φεύγειν, to flee; Skt. *bhuj*, to bend.—√BHEUGH, to bend, to turn aside. Also in the form BHEUG; Brugm. i. §§ 658, 701. Der. *bow* (a weapon), *bow-man*, *bow-yer* (=*bow-er*, bow-maker), *bow-string*, *bow-window*, &c.; also *bight*, *bought*, *bout*.

BOW (2), a bend. (E.) 'From the *bowe* [bend] of the ryuer of Humber anon to the ryuer of Teyse' [Tees]; Trevisa, tr. of Higden, ii. 87. From the verb above.

BOW (3), a weapon to shoot with. (E.) Chaucer has *bowe*, Prol. 108. AS. *boga*; Grein, i. 132.+Du. *boog*; Icel. *bogi*; Swed. *båge*; Dan. *bue*; OHG. *pogo*, *bogo*; G. *bogen*. Teut. type **bug-on-*, m.; from **bug-*, weak grade of **beugan-*, to bend; see **Bow** (1). Der. *bow-yer* (Palsgrave, and Prompt. Parv.).

BOW (4), as a naut. term, the 'bow' of a ship. (Scand.) In Kersey (1658); and see quotation under **Bowline**.—Icel. *bōgr*; Dan. *bov*, Swed. *bog*; the 'shoulder' of a ship; the same word as the *bough*, or 'arm' of a tree. So also MDu. *boech*, Low G. *boog*. See **Bough**. ¶ *Not* from **Bow** (1). Der. *bow-line*, *bow-sprit*.

BOWEL, intestine. (F.—L.) ME. *bouele*, Gower, C. A. ii. 265; bk. v. 4137.—OF. *boele*, f., Godefroy; and *boel*, m., Godef. Supp., mod. F. *boyau*.—L. *botellum*, acc. of *botellus*, a sausage, also, intestine; dimin. of *botulus*, a sausage.

BOWER, an arbour. (E.) ME. *bour*, Chaucer, C. T. 3367. AS. *būr*, a chamber; often, a lady's apartment; Grein, i. 150.+Icel. *būr*, a chamber, also, a larder, pantry, store-room; Swed. *bur*, a cage; Dan. *buur*, a cage; MHG. *būr*, a house, a chamber, a cage (see quotation in E. Müller). β. The orig. sense is a dwelling-place, a place to be in; from AS. *būan*, to dwell. Teut. types *bū-rom, n., *bū-roz, m. See **Boor**. Der. *bower-y*; *bur-ly*, q.v.; *byre*, q.v.

BOWIE-KNIFE, a large knife, esp. in America. (Personal name.) Mentioned by Dickens, in 1842; Amer. Notes, ed. 1850, p. 32. Named from Col. Jas. Bowie.

BOWL (1), a round ball of wood for a game. (F.—L.) The Prompt. Parv. has: '*Bowle*, bolus;' p. 46; and again: '*Bowlyn*, or pley wythe *bowlys*, bolo.' Spelt *boule* in Lydgate and Hoccleve. The spelling with *ou* points to the old sound of *ou* (as in *soup*), and shows that, in *this* sense, the word is French.—F. '*boule*, a bowle, to play with;' Cot.—L. *bulla*, a bubble, a stud; later, a metal ball affixed to a papal *bull*, &c. See **Bowl** (2), **Bull** (2), and **Boil** (1). Der. *bowl*, vb.; *bowl-er*, *bowl-ing-green*.

BOWL (2), a drinking-vessel. (E.) The spelling has been assimilated to that of *Bowl*, a ball to play with; but the word is English. ME. *bolle*, P. Plowman, B. v. 369; pl. *bollen*, Layamon, ii. 406. AS. *bolla*, a bowl; Grein, i. 132.+Icel. *bolli*, a bowl; OHG. *bolla*, MHG. *bolle*, a bowl. β. Teut. type *bullon, for **bul-non-*, m.; from **bul-*, weak grade of **beul-*, to swell; cf. Goth. *uf-bauljan*, to puff up. Called *bowl* from its rounded shape. See **Bolster**.

BOWLDER; see **Boulder**.

BOWLINE, naut. term. (E.) Often wrongly defined; see

N. E. D. So called because it fastens the weather-edge of a square sail to the ship's *bow*; but the word is now usually wrongly pronounced, and associated with *bow* (1). So also in the case of *bowsprit*. ME. *boulyne*, Rob. of Brunne, in notes to Layamon, iii. 395. 'Hale the *bowelyne*!' Pilgrim's Sea Voyage, ed. Furnivall, l. 25. From *bow* (4) and *line*; cf. Norw. and Swed. *boglina*, bowline, from *bog*, bow of a ship; Du. *boeglijn*, from *boeg*, bow of a ship. See **Bow** (4) and **Line**.

BOW-WINDOW, a bowed window. (E.) At one time discredited in literature, because it was often asserted to be an incorrect form of *bay-window*, a word used by Shak. Yet it is a distinct word, and not a mere corruption of it. (1) A *bay-window* is a window forming a recess in the room; see **Bay** (3). (2) A *bow-window* is a specific kind of bay-window, viz. one of semi-circular form. The etymology is from *bow* (2), a bend.

BOX (1), the name of a tree. (L.—Gk.) ME. *box-tree*, Chaucer, C. T. 1304 (A 1302). AS. *box*, Cockayne's Leechdoms, iii. 315. (Not a native word.)—L. *buxus*, a box-tree.—Gk. πύξος, the box-tree. See below.

BOX (2), a case to put things in, a chest. (L.—Gk.) ME. *box*, Chaucer, C. T. 4392 (A 4390). AS. *box*; Matt. xxvii. 7. (Not a native word.)—L. *buxum*, anything made of box-wood; Late L. *buxis*, a box.—L. *buxus*, box-tree; from Gk. πύξος (above); cf. Gk. πυξίς, a case of box-wood. See **Box** (1). Thus *box* is closely allied to *pyx*, q.v. ¶ Hence flow a great many meanings in English; such as (1) a chest; (2) a *box* at the theatre; (3) a shooting-*box*; (4) a Christmas *box*; (5) a seat in the front of a coach (with a box under it formerly); &c. N.B. The orig. Christmas-box was an actual box of earthen-ware, in which apprentices collected pence from customers at Christmas; it was then broken to get at the contents; Brand, Pop. Antiq. ed. Ellis, i. 494.

BOX (3), (L.—Gk.) In the phr. 'to *box* the compass,' the word is applied to going round the compass-box, naming all the points in order. From **Box** (2).

BOX (4), to fight with fists; a blow. (E.) '*Box*, or buffet; alapa,' Prompt. Parv. p. 46; 'many a blody *box*;' Chaucer, Good Women, 1388. The vb. is from the sb., which seems to have been imitative of the sound of a blow. Cf. Low G. *baaks*, a beating, a blow; *baaksen*, to strike. Also NFries. *bakke*, Silt *bokke*, a blow (Outzen); MHG. *buc*, a blow; EFries. *bāken*, *bōken*, Du. *beuken*, Low G. *boken* (Lübben), to beat; WFlem. *bokken*, to hit hard. [Du. and G. *boxen* are from E.] Der. *box-er*.

BOY, a youngster. (E.) ME. *boy*, Havelok, 1899; sometimes used in a derogatory sense, like *knave*. Not in AS.; but preserved in East Friesic *boi*, *boy*, a boy; Koolman, p. 215. Cf. Du. *boef*, a knave, a villain; MDu. *boef*, a boy, youngling (Oudemans); Icel. *bōfi*, a knave, a rogue.+MHG. *buobe* (G. *bube*); Bavarian *bueb*, *bua*, *bui*, a boy. Cf. AS. *Bōfa*, a personal name; Pomeran. *bowe*, a boy. Der. *boy-ish*, *boy-ish-ly*, *boy-ish-ness*, *boy-hood*. ¶ The Gael. *boban*, a term of affection for a boy, *bobug*, a fellow, a boy, a term of affection or familiarity, are words that have no relation here, but belong to E. *babe*. See **Babe**.

BOYCOTT, to combine with others in refusing to have dealings with a certain person. (E.) From the treatment accorded to Capt. *Boycott*, of Lough Mask House, co. Mayo, Ireland, in Dec. 1880.

BRABBLE, to quarrel; a quarrel. (E.) Shak. has *brabble*, a quarrel, Tw. Nt. v. 68; and *brabbler*, a quarrelsome fellow, K. John, v. 2. 162. An imitative word, like *babble*, *blab*. Cf. Du. *brabbelen*, to confound, to stammer; whence *brabbelaar*, a stammerer, *brabbeltaal*, nonsensical discourse; *brabbeling*, stammering, confusion. Compare **Blab**, and **Babble**. Der. *brabbl-er*.

BRACE, that which holds firmly, a clasp, cramp; to hold firmly. (F.—L.—Gk.) 'A drum is ready *brac'd*;' K. John, v. 2. 169. '*Brace* of a balke, uncus;' Prompt. Parv.—OF. *brace*, *brasse*, fem., originally the two arms (Bartsch); then a measure of five feet, formed by the extended arms; see Godefroy and Cotgrave.—L. *brāchia*, pl. of *brāchium*, the arm; treated as a fem. sing.—Gk. βραχίων, the arm. See below. Der. *brace*, vb., to tighten, orig. to hold fast; *brace-let*, *em-brace*.

BRACELET, an ornament for the wrist or arm. (F.—L.—Gk.) 'I spie a *bracelet* bounde about mine arme;' Gascoigne, Dan Bartholomewe's Dolorous Discourses, l. 237 (p. 117).—F. *bracelet* (Cot.); dimin. of OF. *bracel*, an armlet (Godefroy).—L. *brāchiāle*, an armlet (see Brachet, s. v. *bracelet*).—L. *brāchium*, the arm.—Gk. βραχίων, the arm. Cf. Irish *brac*, W. *braich*, Bret. *bréach*, the arm; from L.

BRACH, a kind of hunting-dog. (F.—G.) Shak. has *brach*, Lear, iii. 6. 72, &c. ME. *brache*, Gawain and the Grene Knight, ed. Morris, l. 1142; shortened from AF. *brachet* (Supp. to Godefroy); OF. *braquet*. Dimin. of OF. *brac* (acc. *bracon*; see Littré), a hunting-dog, hound.—OHG. *bracco*, MHG. *bracke* (G. *bracke*), a dog who hunts by the scent. β. The origin of OHG. *bracco* is unknown;

some take it to be from the root seen in L. *frāgrāre*, to emit an odour; but this is only a guess. **γ.** There is a remarkable similarity in sound and sense to ME. *rache*, a kind of dog; cf. Icel. *rakki*, a dog, a lapdog; MSwed. *racka*, a bitch, which can hardly be disconnected from MSwed. *racka*, to run; but the resemblance seems to be accidental.

BRACK, BRACKISH, somewhat salt, said of water. (Dutch.) 'Water . . . so salt and *brackish* as no man can drink it;' North's Plutarch, p. 471 (R.); cf. *brackishness* in the same work, p. 610. Gawain Douglas (ed. Small, ii. 237) has *brake* = brackish, to translate *salsos*, Æneid v. 237.—Du. *brak*, brackish, briny; no doubt the same word that Kilian spells *brack*, and explains as 'fit to be thrown away;' Oudemans, i. 802. According to Franck, it may well be a later spelling of MDu. *wrack*; Hexham has: '*wrack*, or *brack*, brack, or saltish;' also '*wracke*, shipwrack;' and cf. Du. *wraken*, to reject, blame.—Du. *wrak*, orig. 2nd grade of *wreken*, to wreak, orig. to drive. See **Wreck, Wreak.** [So also Du. *wrang*, sour, is allied to *wringen*, to wring; Franck.] **Der.** *brackish-ness*.

BRACKEN, fern. (E.) ME. *braken*, Allit. Poems, ed. Morris, B. 1675. 'A *brakan*, filix; a *brakanbuske*, filicarium;' Cath. Angl. AS. *braccan*, pl.; Kemble, C. D. v. 277; Cockayne, Leechdoms, iii. 315. Cf. Swed. dial. *bräkne* (Rietz); Swed. *bräken*, fern; Dan. *bregne*, fern. Cf. also Icel. *burkni*, fern. ¶ Compare the shorter form *brake*, often used as synonymous with fern; thus, in the Prompt. Parv. p. 47, we have '*Brake*, herbe, or ferme (*sic*) *for* ferne), *Filix*;' also '*Brakebushe*, or *fernebrake*, *Filicetum, filicarium*;' and see Way's note. See also **Brake** (2).

BRACKET, a kind of corbel, a support consisting of two pieces of wood or iron joined at an angle; &c. (F.—Span.—C.) A technical word. Earliest spelling *bragget*. Baret (1580) has: 'a *bragget* or staie cut out of stone or timber . . to beare up the sommer [beam] or other part.' Coles (1684) has: '*brackets, braggets*, pieces supporting the ship's gallery.' Minsheu (1627) has: '*bragget*, a corbell.' Cotgrave has: '*Brague*, a kind of mortaise, or joining of peeces together;' and '*Braguette*,' a cod-piece,' i.e. the front part of a pair of breeches. —Span. *bragueta*, the same; also, 'a projecting mould in architecture.' Cf. MF. *bragues*, breeches; Span. *bragas*, breeches; from the notion of a fork.—L. *brācæ*, breeches; said to be of Celtic origin. Cf. OF. *bracon*, branch or fork of a tree, also a bracket, support, joist; allied to MItal. *bragoni*, 'great breeches;' Florio.

BRACKISH; see **Brack** (above).

BRACT, a small leaf or scale on a flower-stalk. (L.) A modern botanical term.—L. *bractea*, a thin plate or leaf of metal. **Der.** *bractea-l*, immediately from the L. form.

BRAD, a thin, long nail. (Scand.) ME. *brod*, spelt *brode* in Prompt. Parv. p. 53, where it is explained as 'a hedlese nayle.'—Icel. *broddr*, a spike; Swed. *brodd*, a frost-nail; Dan. *brodde*, a frost-nail. +AS. *brord*, a spike or spire or blade of grass, which see in Bosworth; and the second *r* in *brord* stands for an older *z*. Teut. type **brozdoz*, a spike. Further allied to O. Irish *brot*, Irish and Gael. *brod*, W. *brath*, a sting. (Stokes-Fick, p. 173.) And see **Broider.**

BRAE, a steep bank, lit. 'brow' of a hill. (Scand.) 'Ye banks and *braes* o' bonie Doon;' Burns, Songs. 'Under ane *bra*;' Barbour, Bruce, iv. 372.—Icel. *brá*, f., an eye-lid; whence the sense 'brow,' and brow of a hill.+OSax. *brāwa*, *brāha*, f., OHG. *brāwa*, f., AS. *augenbraue*, eye-brow. Cf. also AS. *brēw*, *brēaw*, m., eye-lid; MDu. *brauwen*, eye-brows, *brauwe*, 'the edge of any thing;' Hexham. Distinct from **Brow** (1), q.v.

BRAG, to boast. (Scand.) [The sb. *braggart* in Shak. (Much Ado, v. 1. 91, 189, &c.) = F. '*bragard*, gay, gallant, . . . braggard;' Cotgrave. But the older form is *braggere*, P. Plowman, A. vii. 142 (B. vi. 156), and the vb. to *brag* is to be regarded rather as Scand. than French.]—MDan. *brage*, to crack, also to speak great words (Kalkar); Norw. *braka*, to snap, also to prate, chatter (Ross); Icel. *braka*, to creak. Cf. Jutland *brag*, a noise (Feilberg); AS. *gebræc*, a crash, noise. From Teut. **brak-*, 2nd stem of **brekan-*, to break; cf. L. *frag-or*, noise. Hence also MF. *braguer*, to flaunt, brag; Cot. So also to *crack* is 'to boast;' Jamieson's Scot. Dict. See **Break** and **Bray** (2). **Der.** *bragg-er*, *bragg-art*, *bragg-adocio* (a word coined by Spenser; see F. Q. ii. 3).

BRAGGET, a kind of mead. (Welsh.) ME. *bragat*, *braget*, Chaucer, C. T. 3261.—W. *bragot*, a kind of mead; Corn. *bregaud*, *bragot*, a liquor made of ale, honey, and spices; receipts for making it are given in Wright's Prov. E. Dict.; Irish *bracat*, malt liquor. **β.** From W. *brag*, malt; Gael. *braich*, malt, lit. fermented grain; Irish *braich*, OIrish *mraich*, malt. See Stokes-Fick, p. 220. ¶ The Lowland Scottish *bragwort* is a corrupt form, due to an attempt to explain the Welsh suffix *-ot*.

BRAHMIN, BRAHMAN, a person of the upper caste among Hindoos. (Skt.) Spelt *brachman* in Ben Jonson, The Fortunate Isles. But the word appears early in Middle English. 'We were

in *Bragmanie* bred,' we were born in Brahman-land; Romance of Alexander and Dindimus, 175. In the Latin original, the men are called *Bragmanni*, i.e. Brahmans. The country is called 'Bramande;' King Alisaunder, ed. Weber, 5916.—Skt. *brāhman-*, base of *brahmā*, m., a brahman, holy man; cf. also Skt. *brahman-*, base of *brahma*, n., 1. a prayer; 2. the practice of austere devotion. . . . 7. the brahmanical caste; 8. the divine cause and essence of the world, the unknown god.

BRAID (1), to weave, entwine. (E.) ME. *breiden*, *braiden*. '*Breyde* lacys, *necto, torqueo*;' Prompt. Parv. p. 49. AS. *bregdan*, *brēdan*, to brandish, weave; Grein, i. 138.+Icel. *bregða*, to brandish, turn about, change, braid, start, cease, &c.; EFries. *breiden*, to knit; OHG. *brettan*, MHG. *bretten*, to draw, weave, braid. Teut. type **bregdan-*, pt. t. **bragd*. **Der.** *broided*, q.v.

BRAID (2), full of deceit. (E.) In All's Well, iv. 2. 73, *braid* is used in the sense of *braided*, i.e. full of *braids* or tricks. From ME. *braid*, trick, deceit; AS. *brægd*, deceit. From Teut. **bragd*, 2nd grade of **bregdan-* (above).

BRAIL, a kind of ligature. (F.—C.) 'Hale in the *brayles*;' Reliq. Antiq. i. 2; l. 33. A *brail* was a thong of leather to tie up a hawk's wing. Used as a nautical term, *brails* are small ropes fastened to the edges of sails, to assist in furling them. Borrowed from OF. *braiel*, a cincture, orig. a cincture for fastening up breeches.—Late L. *brācāle*, a breech-girdle.—L. *brācæ*, breeches. See **Breeches.**

BRAIN, the convoluted mass of nervous substance within the skull. (E.) ME. *brayne*, Prompt. Parv. p. 47; *brain*, Layamon, 1468. AS. *brægen*, *bregen* (Bosworth). + Du. *brein*; OFries. *brein*; Low G. *brägen*. Some connect it with Gk. βρεχμός, βρέγμα, the upper part of the head; see Prellwitz. **Der.** *brain-pan*, AS. *brægenpanne*, in Napier's Glosses; *brainless*.

BRAISE, to stew in a closed pan. (F.—Scand.) First in 1797. Properly, to stew with a charcoal fire above and below.—F. *braiser*; from *braise*, live cinders; see **Breeze** (3).

BRAKE (1), a machine for breaking hemp; a name for various mechanical contrivances. (MDu.) ME. *brake*, explained by 'pinsella, vibra, rastellum;' Prompt. Parv. p. 47, note 3. Cf. 'bowes of *brake*,' cross-bows worked with a winch, P. Plowman, C. xxi. 293. One of the meanings is 'a contrivance for confining refractory horses;' connecting it at once with MDu. *brake*, a clog or fetter for the neck; *braecke*, 'a brake to beate flax,' Hexham; *braake*, an instrument for holding by the nose (Oudemans). Cf. Low G. *brake*, an instrument for breaking flax; *braken*, to break flax; Bremen Wörterbuch, i. 132. Thus the word is MDu., from which source also comes the F. '*braquer*, to brake hempe;' Cotgrave. Comparison of Du. *braak*, a breach, breaking, with Du. *vlasbraak*, a flax-brake, shows that *braken*, to break flax, is from *brak*, 2nd grade of Du. *breken*, to break. See **Break.**

BRAKE (2), a bush, thicket; esp. of fern. (E.) Shak. has 'hawthorn-*brake*;' M. Nt. Dr. iii. 1. 4, and 77. '*Brakebushe* or *fernebrake*, filicetum;' Prompt. Parv. AS. *brac* (?), f. (?); we find *fearnbraca*, acc. pl. (?), in Birch, Cart. Saxon. ii. 295. Cf. EFries. *brāk*, thick bush, underwood.+Low G. '*Brake*, weidenbusch' = willow-bush, in the Bremen Wörterbuch, i. 131. The notion seems to be allied to that of 'broken' ground, with the over-growth that springs from it. Cf. OHG. *brācha*, MHG. *brāche*, land broken up, but unsown. It may then be referred to the prolific √BHREG, to break. See **Break, Brook.** See also **Bracken.**

BRAMBLE, a rough prickly shrub. (E.) ME. *brembil*, Wyclif, Ecclus. xliii. 21. AS. *brēmel*, *brembel*; Gloss. to Cockayne's Leechdoms, vol. iii. The second *b* is excrescent, and the vowel has been shortened. Teut. type **brǣmiloz*, m., dimin. of Teut. type **brǣmoz*, m., whence mod. E. *broom*. Cf. Du. *braam*, a blackberry; *braambosch*, a bramble-bush; Swed. *brom-bär*, a blackberry; Dan. *brambær*, a blackberry; G. *brombeere*, a blackberry; *brombeerstrauch*, a bramblebush. Here G. *bröm-* answers to OHG. *brāma*, f., a bramble; Teut. type **brǣmōn-*; closely allied to the type above. And see **Broom.**

BRAN, the husk of a grain of wheat. (F.—C.) ME. *bran*, Wright's Vocab. i. 201; *bren*, Chaucer, C. T., A 4053.—OF. *bran*, *bren*.—Bret. *brenn*, bran. So in Thurneysen; and Stokes-Fick, p. 172; cf. MItal. *brenna*, 'branne,' Florio; also Norm. dial. *bran*, bran (Duméril). ¶ W. *bran*, Irish *bran*, are from E.; but the Bret. word may be of true Celtic origin.

BRANCH, a bough of a tree. (F.—Late L.) ME. *branche*, Rob. of Glouc., p. 193, l. 3985.—F. *branche*, a branch.—Late L. *branca*, the claw of a bird or paw of a beast of prey. ¶ See Diez, who suggests that the Late L. *branca* is probably a very old word in vulgar Latin, as shown by the Ital. derivatives *brancare*, to grip, *brancicare*, to grope; and by the Wallachian form *brâncă*, a forefoot; cf. also MSpan. *branca*, a paw (Minsheu); OProv. *branca*, branch; Walloon *branke*, a branch. **Der.** *branch*, vb., *branch-let*, *branch-y*, *branch-less*.

BRAND, a burning piece of wood; a mark made by fire; a sword. (E.) ME. *brond*, burning wood, Chaucer, C. T., A 2338; a sword,

Will. of Palerne, l. 1244. AS. *brand, brond*, a burning, a sword; Grein, i. 135.+Icel. *brandr*, a fire-brand, a sword-blade (from its flashing); Du. *brand*, a burning, fuel (cf. MDu. *brand*, a sword; Oudemans); Swed. and Dan. *brand*, a fire-brand, fire; OHG. *brant*, a brand, a sword. [The sense is (1) a burning; (2) a fire-brand; (3) a sword-blade, from its brightness.] β. From Teut. **brann*, 2nd grade of **brennan-*, to burn. See **Burn.**

BRAND- or **BRANT-**, as a prefix. (Scand.) In *brant-fox*, a kind of Swedish fox, for which the Swedish name is *brandrüf*. Also in *brentgoose* or *brandgoose*, Swed. *brandgås*. The names were probably at first conferred from some notion of redness or brownness, or the colour of burnt wood, &c. The word seems to be the same as **Brand**, q. v. β. The redstart (i. e. red-tail) is sometimes called the *brantail*, i. e. the burnt tail; where the colour meant is of course *red*. γ. The prefix is probably of Scandinavian origin. See **Brindled.**

BRANDISH, to shake a sword, &c. (F.—Scand.) In Shak. Macb. i. 2. 17; &c. ME. *braundisen*, to brandish a sword; Will. of Palerne, 3294, 2322.—F. *brandir* (pres. pt. *brandissant*), to cast or hurl with violence, to shake, to brandish; Cot.—AF. *brand*, a sword, properly a Norman F. form; it occurs in Vie de St. Auban, ed. Atkinson, ll. 1234, 1303, 1499, 1838. Of Scandinavian origin; from Icel. *brandr*; see **Brand.** β. The more usual OF. *brant* answers to the OHG. form.

BRANDY, an ardent spirit. (Dutch.) Formerly called *brandy-wine, brand-wine*, from the former of which *brandy* was formed by dropping the last syllable. *Brand-wine* occurs in Beaum. and Fletcher, Beggar's Bush, iii. 1.—Du. *brandewijn*, brandy; lit. burnt wine; sometimes written *brandtwijn*.—Du. *brandt, gebrandt* (full form *gebrandet*), burnt; and *wijn*, wine. β. The Dutch *branden*, lit. to burn, also means to distil, whence Du. *brander*, a distiller, *branderij*, a distillery; hence the sense is really 'distilled wine,' brandy having been originally obtained from wine by distillation.

BRANKS, an iron instrument used for the punishment of scolds, fastened in the mouth. (E.) Described in Jamieson's Dict.; hence the Lowland Sc. *brank* means to bridle, restrain. From the E. *branks* were borrowed Gael. *brangus, brangas* (formerly spelt *brancas*), an instrument used for punishing petty offenders, a sort of pillory; Gael. *brang*, a horse's halter; Irish *brancas*, a halter. The form *brank* is probably due to a Celtic pron. of the E. word, of which the original form must have been *prang* (pl. *prangs*); whence both mod. E. *prong* and mod. E. *pang*, which see.+Du. *pranger*, pinchers, barnacle, iron collar; G. *pranger*, a pillory. β. The root appears in Du. *prangen*, to pinch; cf. Goth. *ana-praggan*, to harass, worry (with *gg* sounded as *ng*). ¶ For the Gaelic *br*<E. *pr* in some cases, cf. Gael. *brodail*, proud, from E. *proud* (Macbain); and see **Brass.**

BRAN-NEW, new from the fire. (E.) A corruption of *brand-new*, which occurs in Ross's Helenore, in Jamieson and Richardson. The variation *brent-new* occurs in Burns's Tam O'Shanter: 'Nae cotillon *brent-new* frae France.' Kilian gives Mid. Dutch *brandnieuw*, and we still find Du. *vonkelnieuw*, lit. spark-new, from *vonkel*, a spark of fire. 'The *brand* is the fire, and *brand-new*, equivalent to *fire-new* (Shak.), is that which is fresh and bright, as being newly come from the forge and fire;' Trench, English Past and Present, Lect. viii. See **Brand.**

BRANT-, prefix; see **Brand-.**

BRASIER, BRAZIER, a pan to hold coals. (F.—Scand.) The former spelling is better; see Johnson's Dict. [Evidently formed from F. *braise*, live coals, embers. Cotgrave gives *braisier*, but only in the same sense as mod. F. *braise*.]—F. *braisier*, a vessel for receiving *braise* when quenched (Littré).—F. *braise*, live coals.—Swed. *brasa*, fire; Norw. *bras*, flame. See **Brass** and **Braze** (1).

BRASS, a mixed metal. (E.) ME. *bras*, Prompt. Parv. p. 47; Chaucer, Prol. 366. AS. *bræs*, Ælfric's Grammar, ed. Zupitza, p. 15.+Icel. *bras*, solder (cited by Wedgwood, but not in Cleasby and Vigfusson's Dictionary). Cf. Gael. *práis*, brass, pot-metal; Irish *pras*, brass; W. *pres*, brass; all borrowed words. Perhaps allied to Icel. *brasa*, to harden by fire; Swed. *brasa*, to flame; Dan. *brase*, to fry; Norw. *brasa*, to flame, also to solder. Cf. Swed. *brasa*, fire. Der. *brass-y, braz-en* (ME. *brasen*, P. Plowman, C. xxi. 293 = AS. *bræsen*, Ælf. Gram., as above), *braz-ier*; also *braze* (2), verb, q. v.; and cf. *brasier* (above).

BRASSART, the piece of armour on the upper part of the arm. (F.—L.—Gk.) Also *brassard.*—F. *brassart* (Cot.); *brassard* (Littré); also *brassal* (Cot.). Formed with suffix *-ard* (*-art*) from F. *bras*, arm. —L. *brāchium*, arm.—Gk. βραχίων, arm.

BRAT (1), a cloak, rough mantle. (C.) Usually a rag, clout, also, a child's apron or pinafore. Chaucer has *brat* for a coarse cloak, a ragged mantle, C. T. 16349 (ed. Tyrwhitt); some MSS. have *bak*, meaning a cloth to cover the back, as in P. Plowman.—Gael. *brat*, a mantle, cloak, apron, rag; *brat-speilidh*, a swaddling-cloth; Irish *brat*, a cloak, mantle, veil; *bratog*, a rag; OIrish *brat*, a rough cloak; cf.

W. *brethyn*, woollen cloth. (W. *brat* is from E.) See Stokes-Fick, p. 182. ¶ The O. Northumbrian *bratt*, a cloak, a gloss to *pallium* in Matt. v. 40, was borrowed from the Celtic.

BRAT (2), a child; esp. 'a beggar's *brat*.' (C.?) In Shak. Com. Errors, iv. 4. 39. Perhaps 'a rag;' and the same as **Brat** (1).

BRATTICE, a fence of boards in a mine. (F.—Teut.?) ME. *bretage, bretasce, brutaske* (with numerous other spellings), a parapet, battlement, outwork, &c.; Rob. of Glouc. l. 11095. '*Betrax, bretasce, bretays* of a walle, *propugnaculum*;' Prompt. Parv. p. 50. — OF. *bretesche*, a small wooden outwork, &c.; Prov. *bertresca*, Ital. *bertesca*. A difficult word; prob. formed from G. *brett*, a plank. Körting, § 1564. See **Board** (1).

BRAVADO, a vain boast. (Span.) It occurs in Burton, Anat. of Melancholy, To the Reader; ed. 1845, p. 35 (see Todd). An E. substitution for *bravada.*—Span. *bravada*, a bravado, boast, vain ostentation.—Span. *bravo*, brave, valiant; also, fierce; cognate with F. *brave*. See **Brave.**

BRAVE, showy, valiant. (F.—Ital.) Shak. has *brave*, valiant, splendid; *brave*, vb., to defy, make fine; *brave*, sb., defiance; *bravery*, display of valour, finery; see Schmidt's Shak. Lexicon.—F. 'brave, brave, gay, fine, .. proud, braggard, ... valiant, hardy,' &c.; Cot. —Ital. *bravo*, brave, fine, also a boaster (Florio). Cf. Span. and Port. *bravo*; Prov. *brau*. Of unknown origin; for unsatisfactory suggestions, see Körting, § 1226. The Lowland Scottish form is *braw*. Der. *brav-ery*; also *bravo, bravado*, which see below and above.

BRAVO, a daring villain, a bandit. (Ital.) 'No *bravoes* here profess the bloody trade;' Gay, Trivia, bk. iii. l. 151.—Ital. *bravo*, brave, valiant; as a sb., a cut-throat, villain; whence also the F. *brave*. See **Brave.** β. The word *bravo!* well done! is the same word, used in the vocative case.

BRAWL (1), to quarrel, roar. (E.?) ME. *brawle*, to quarrel. '*Brawler*, litigator; *brawlyn*, litigo, jurgo;' Prompt. Parv. p. 48. *Braulyng*, P. Plowman, B. xv. 233. Apparently a native word, of imitative origin; cf. prov. G. (Kurhessen) *brallen*, to cry out lustily; Du. *brallen*, to brag, boast; Dan. *bralle*, to jabber, chatter; G. *prahlen*, to boast, brag, bluster; EFries. *pralen*, to talk loudly, boast; NFries. *prale* (the same). Even G. *brüllen*, to roar, bellow, is of a similar character. Der. *brawl-er, brawl-ing.*

BRAWL (2), a sort of dance. (F.—Scand.) In Shak. Love's La. Lo. iii. 9, we have 'a French *brawl*.' Sir T. Elyot mentions 'the *braule*;' The Governour, bk. i. c. 22. § 4; see the dance described in the note in Croft's ed., i. 242. It is a corruption of the F. *branle*, MF. *bransle*, explained by Cot. as 'a totter, swing, shake, shocke, &c.; also a *brawle* or daunce, wherein many men and women, holding by the hands, sometimes in a ring, and otherwhiles at length, move all together.'—F. *bransler*, to totter, shake, reel, stagger, waver, tremble (Cot.); now spelt *branler*. Contracted from OF. *brandeler*, to shake, agitate; and Cotgrave gives *brandiller*, to wag, shake, swing, totter; as well as *brandif*, brandishing, shaking, flourishing, lively. All from OF. *brandir*, to totter, tremble (Godefroy); a neuter use of *brandir*, tc shake, brandish. Körting, § 1545. See **Brandish.**

BRAWN, muscle; boar's flesh. (F.—OHG.) ME. *braun*, muscle, Chaucer, Prol. 546; *braun*, boar's flesh, P. Plowman, B. xiii. 63, 91. —OF. *braon*, a slice of flesh (Provençal *bradon*).—OHG. *brāto, prāto, brāton*, acc. of MHG. *brāte*, a piece of flesh (for roasting).—OHG. *prātan* (G. *braten*), to roast, broil.+AS. *brǣdan*, to roast. Teut. root **brǣd-*. ¶ The restriction of the word to the flesh of the boar is accidental; the original sense is merely 'muscle,' as seen in the derived adj. Der. *brawn-y*, muscular; Shak. Venus, 625. Cf. **Breath.**

BRAY (1), to bruise, pound. (F.—Teut.) ME. *brayen, brayin*; '*brayyn*, or stampyn in a mortere, *tero*;' Prompt. Parv. p. 47. —OF. *breier* (F. *broyer*); Roquefort.—OSax. *brekan*, to break; cognate with AS. *brecan*, to break. See **Break.**

BRAY (2), to make a loud noise, as an ass. (F.—C.) ME. *brayen, brayin*; '*brayen* in sownde, *barrio*;' Prompt. Parv. p. 47. Palsgrave has: 'I *brayye* as deere doth, or any other beest, Ie *brays*.'—OF. *braire.*—Low L. *bragīre*, to bray, *bragāre*, to cry as a child, squall. From a Celtic root; cf. Gael. *bragh*, a burst, explosion; cognate with L. *frag-or*, noise, crash; and thus related to L. *frangere* and E. *break* (Thurneysen, p. 92). See **Break.**

BRAZE (1), to harden. (F.—Scand.) Shak. has *brazed*, hardened, Hamlet, iii. 4. 37; Lear, i. 1. 11. Generally explained to mean 'hardened like brass;' but it may mean simply 'hardened.' Cotgrave says that 'braser l'argent' is to re-pass silver a little over hot embers (*sur la braise*).—OF. *braser*, to burn, pass through fire (Godefroy); F. *braser*, to solder; Roquefort has: '*Braser*, souder le fer.'—Icel. *brasa*, to harden by fire; Norw. *brasa*, to solder; Dan. *brase*, to fry; Jutland *brase*, to roast. See **Brass**, and see below.

BRAZE (2), to ornament with brass. (E.) Used by Chapman, Homer's Odys. xv. 113. In this sense, the verb is a mere derivative of the sb. *brass.* We find: 'aero, *ic brasige*;' Ælfric's Gr., ed. Zupitza, p. 215, l. 17.

BREACH, a fracture. (E.) ME. *breche,* a fracture, Gower, C. A. ii. 138; bk. v. 332. AS. *brece,* which appears in the compound *hlāf-gebrece,* a fragment of a loaf, bit of bread; Grein, ii. 80. The more usual form is AS. *brice = bryce,* breaking; in the phr. 'on hlāfes *brice,'* in the breaking of bread, Luke xxiv. 35; where *bryce* represents a Teut. type **brukiz,* from the weak grade of **brekan-,* to break (AS. *brecan*). Cf. OFries. *breke,* a breaking (a common word); EFries. *brek,* a breaking. ¶ ME. *breche* is also partly from OF. *breche* (F. *brèche*), a fracture. — G. *brechen,* to break. See **Break.**

BREAD, food made from grain. (E.) ME. *breed, bred,* Chaucer, Prol. 343. AS. *brēad,* Grein, i. 140.+Du. *brood;* Icel. *brauð;* Swed. and Dan. *bröd;* OHG. *prōt* (G. *brod*). β. Not found in Gothic. The orig. name for 'bread' was *loaf* (AS. *hlāf*); the sense of *bread* was orig. 'a fragment,' bit, or broken piece; cf. ONorthumb. *brēad,* a bit, morsel, John xiii. 27; pl. *brēadru,* 'frusta pānis,' in the Blickling Glosses. Teut. type **braudos,* neut. (-os-stem). Cf. L. *fru-s-tum,* a fragment.

BREADTH, wideness. (E.) This is a modern form. It occurs in Lord Berners' tr. of Froissart, spelt *bredethe,* vol. i. c. 131 (R.). β. In older authors the form is *brede,* as in Chaucer, C. T. 1972 (A 1970). AS. *brǣdu;* Grein, i. 137. γ. Other languages agree with the *old,* not with the *modern* form; cf. Goth. *braidei,* Icel. *breidd,* G. *breite;* all from Teut. **braidoz,* broad. The Dutch is *breedte.* See **Broad.**

BREAK, to fracture, snap. (E.) ME. *breke,* Chaucer, Prol. 551. AS. *brecan;* Grein, i. 137.+Du. *breken;* Goth. *brikan;* OHG. *prechan* (G. *brechen*).+L. *frangere,* to break. Teut. type **brekan-,* strong vb.; pt. t. **brak,* pp. **brokanoz.* From the 2nd grade we have Icel. *braka,* to creak; Swed. *braka,* to crack. Idg. √BHREG, to break with a noise. ¶ The original sense is 'to break with a snap;' cf. L. *fragor,* a crash; Gael. *bragh,* a burst, explosion. Der. *breach,* q. v.; *break-age, break-er, break-fast, break-water, brake* (1).

BREAM, a fish. (F. — OHG.) ME. *breem,* Chaucer, Prol. 350. — OF. *bresme* (F. *brême*). — MHG. *brahsem,* G. *brassen,* a bream (Kluge). +Du. *brasem,* a bream. Perhaps related to MHG. *breh-en,* to glitter. ¶ E. *brasse,* a kind of perch, is not from Du. or Low G., but from AS. *bærs;* see **Bass** (2).

BREAST, the upper part of the front of the body. (E.) ME. *brest,* Chaucer, Prol. 115. AS. *brēost;* Grein, i. 141.+Icel. *brjóst;* Swed. *bröst;* Dan. *bryst;* Teut. type **breustom,* n.+Goth. *brusts,* pl.; G. *brust;* Du. *borst;* Teut. stem **brust-* (with weak grade). Origin unknown. Der. *breast,* verb; *breast-plate, breast-work; bressomer.*

BREATH, air respired. (E.) ME. *breeth, breth;* dat. case *breethe, brethe,* Chaucer, Prol. 5. AS. *brǣð,* breath, odour; Genesis, viii. 21.+ OHG. *prādam;* G. *brodem, broden, brodel,* steam, vapour, exhalation; Flügel's G. Dict. *Breath* may have been likened to steam; prob. from the Teut. root **brǣ-,* to heat; see **Brawn** and **Brood.** Further relations uncertain. Der. *breathe, breath-less.*

BREECH, the hinder part of the body. (E.) ME. *brech, breech,* properly the breeches or breeks, or covering of the breech; in Chaucer, C. T. 12882 (C 948), the word *breech* means the breeches, not the breech. Thus the present word is a mere development of AS. *brēc,* the breeches, pl. of *brōc.* Phillips (1658) notes: '*Breetch* (a term in Gunnery) the aftermost part of a gun.' See **Breeches.**

BREECHES, BREEKS, a garment for the thighs. (E.) ME. '*breche,* or *breke,* braccæ, *plur.*;' Prompt. Parv. p. 48; and see Way's note. *Breeches* is a double plural, the form *breek* being itself plural; as *feet* from *foot,* so is *breek* from *brook.* AS. *brōc,* sing., *brēc,* plural (Bosworth).+Du. *broek,* a pair of breeches; Icel. *brók,* pl. *brœkr,* breeches; MHG. *bruoch,* breeches. All from a Teut. base **brōk-* (pl. **brōkiz*). Cf. L. *brācæ,* clothing for the legs, said to be of Celtic origin; prob. from Celtic **brāg-n-,* and cognate with the Teut. form. See **Brogues.**

BREED, to produce, engender. (E.) ME. *breden,* P. Plowman, B. xi. 339. AS. *brēdan,* to nourish, cherish, keep warm (= L. *fouēre*), in a gloss; Voc. 403. 39. Ælfric, Hom. ii. 10, has: 'hī *brēdað* heora *brōd,'* they nourish their brood. — AS. *brōd,* a brood (with mutation of *ō* to *ē*).+Du. *broeden,* to hatch, from *broed,* a brood; G. *brüten,* to hatch, from *brut,* a brood. See **Brood.** Der. *breed-er, breed-ing.*

BREEZE (1), a gadfly. (E.) Well known in Shak. Troil. i. 3. 48; Ant. and Cleop. iii. 10. 14. Cotgrave has: 'Oestre *Iunonique,* a gadbee, horse-fly, dun-fly, brimsey, brizze.' ME. *brese;* Prompt. Parv. p. 49. AS. *briosa;* Voc. 7. 20; 49. 42. ¶ The form *brimsey* is a distinct word; from Norw. *brims,* Dan. *brems,* a gadfly; cf. MDu. *bremme, bremse,* G. *bremse,* OHG. *bremo;* all from Teut. **brem-,* as in OHG. *breman-* (pt. t. *bram*), to hum, cognate with L. *fremere,* to murmur.+Skt. *bhramara-s,* a large black bee; from Skt. *bhram,* to whirl, applied originally to 'the flying about and humming of insects;' Benfey, p. 670. See Fick, i. 702.

BREEZE (2), a strong wind. (F.) Brachet says that the F. *brise,*

a breeze, was introduced into French from English towards the end of the 17th century. This can hardly be the case. The quotations in N.E.D. show that the E. word was at first spelt *brize* or *brise,* as in Hakluyt's Voyages, iii. 661; and in Sir F. Drake's The Worlde Encompassed. The earliest is ab. 1565, in Arber's Eng. Garner, v. 121: 'the *brise* .. which is the north-east wind.' This shows that the E. word was borrowed from French, since *brize* is a French spelling. β. Again, Cotgrave notes that *brize* is used by Rabelais (died 1553) instead of *bise* or *bize,* signifying the north wind.+Span. *brisa,* the N. E. wind; Port. *briza,* the N. E. wind; Ital. *brezza,* a cold wind. Remoter origin unknown. Der. *breez-y.*

BREEZE (3), cinders. (F. — Scand.) *Breeze* is a name given, in London, to ashes and cinders used instead of coal for brick-burning. In Ash's Dict. 1775. Also spelt *braize* (N.E.D.). — MF. *breze* (Cot.); F. *braise,* live cinders. — Swed. *brasa,* fire; see **Brasier.**

BRENT-GOOSE, the same as **BRANT-GOOSE;** see **Brand-.**

BRESSOMER, for **BREAST-SUMMER,** a 'summer' or beam extending horizontally over a wide opening, to support a wall above. (Hybrid; E. *and* F. — Late L. — Gk.) Cotgrave has: '*Contre-frontail,* the brow-piece, or upmost post of a door; a haunse, or *breast-summer.'* See **Breast** and **Summer** (2).

BREVE, a short note, in music. (F. — L.) [As a fact, it is now a *long* note; and, the old long note being now disused, has become the longest note now used.] Formerly also *brief;* Florio has: '*breue,* a briefe in musike.' — MF. *brief* (F. *bref*), brief, short. — L. *breuis,* short. *Breve* is a doublet of *brief,* q. v. Der. From the L. *breuis* we also have *brev-et,* lit. a short document, which passed into English from F. *brevet,* which Cotgrave explains by 'a briefe, note, breviate, little writing,' &c. Also *brev-i-ar-y, brev-i-er, brev-i-ty; semi-breve.* See **Brief.**

BREW, to concoct. (E.) ME. *brew,* pt. t., P. Plowman, B. v. 219; *brewe,* infin., Seven Sages, ed. Wright, l. 1490. AS. *brēowan;* of which the pp. *gebrowen* occurs in Ælfred's Orosius, ed. Sweet, p. 20, l. 19.+Du. *brouwen;* OHG. *briuwan* (G. *brauen*); Icel. *brugga;* Swed. *brygga;* Dan. *brygge.* [Cf. L. *dēfrutum,* new wine fermented or boiled down; Thracian βρῦτον, a kind of beer.] — √BHREU, to decoct. Brugm. i. §§ 373, 727. Der. *brew-er, brew-house, brew-er-y.*

BREWIS, BROWIS, pottage; see **Brose.**

BRIAR, BRIER, a prickly shrub. (E.) ME. *brere,* Chaucer, C. T. 9699 (E 1825). OMerc. *brēr,* Grein, i. 140; AS. *brǣmbel-brēr,* Voc. 269. 38. ¶ ME. *brere* has become *briar* just as ME. *frere* has become *friar.* Der. *briar-y.*

BRIAR-ROOT, for pipes. (Hybrid; F. *and* E.) The root is that of the white heath; and *briar* is here a popular corruption of F. *bruyère,* heath. See N.E.D.

BRIBE, an undue present, for corrupt purposes. (F.) ME. *bribe, brybe;* Chaucer. C. T. 6960 (D 1378). — OF. *bribe,* a present, gift, but esp. 'a peece, lumpe, or cantill of bread, given unto a begger;' Cot. [Cf. *bribours,* i. e. vagabonds, rascals, spoilers of the dead, P. Plowman, C. xxiii. 248.] Allied to OF. *briber,* to beg; Span. *briba,* idleness, *bribar,* to loiter about; Ital. *birba,* fraud; *birbante,* a vagabond. Origin unknown; not Celtic (Thurneysen). Der. *bribe,* verb; *brib-er, brib-er-y.*

BRICK, a lump of baked clay. (F. — O. Low G.) In Fabyan's Chron. Edw. IV, an. 1476–7; and in the Bible of 1551, Exod. cap. v. Spelt *brique,* Nicoll's Thucydides, p. 64 (R.). — F. *brique,* a brick; also a fragment, a bit, as in prov. F. *brique de pain,* a bit of bread (Brachet). — MDu. *brick, bricke,* a bit, fragment, piece; whence also Walloon *briquet,* a large slice of bread. — Du. *breken,* to break, cognate with E. *break.* See **Break.** Der. *brick-bat,* q. v.; *brick-kiln, brick-lay-er.*

BRICKBAT, a piece of a broken brick. (F. *and* E.) Used by Bacon; see Todd's Johnson. From *brick* and *bat.* Here *bat* is a rough lump; it is merely the ordinary word *bat* peculiarly used. See **Bat.**

BRIDE, a woman newly married. (E.) ME. *bride, bryde,* Prompt. Parv. p. 50. Older spelling, *brude;* Layamon, l. 294. AS. *brȳd;* Grein, i. 147.+Du. *bruid;* Icel. *brúðr;* Swed. and Dan. *brud;* Goth. *bruths;* OHG. *prūt* (G. *braut*). Teutonic type **brūdiz,* f. Perhaps from an Idg. type **mrū-ti-,* bespoken, promised; cf. Zend. *mraomi,* Skt. *bravīmi,* I speak; Uhlenbeck, s.v. *brúths;* Brugm. i. §§ 387, 401; and cf. Celtic root **mrū,* I say; Stokes-Fick, p. 221. Der. *brid-al,* q. v., *bride-groom,* q. v.

BRIDAL, a wedding; lit. a bride-ale, or bride-feast. (E.) ME. *bridale, bruydale,* P. Plowman, B. ii. 43; *bridale,* Ormulum, 14003. Composed of *bride* and *ale;* the latter being a common name for a feast. (There were leet-ales, scot-ales, church-ales, clerk-ales, bid-ales, and bride-ales. See Brand's Pop. Antiquities.) The comp. *brȳd-ealo* occurs in the A. S. Chron. (MS. D.), under the date 1076. ¶ It is spelt *bride-ale* in Ben Jonson, Silent Woman, ii. 4; but *bridall* in Shak. Oth. iii. 4. 151. See **Bride** and **Ale.**

BRIDEGROOM, a man newly married. (E.) Tyndal has *bridegrome*; John, iii. 29. But the form is corrupt, due to confusion of *grome*, a groom, with *gome*, a man. In older authors, the spelling is without the *r*; we find *bredgome* in the Ayenbite of Inwyt, ed. Morris, p. 233, written A.D. 1340; so that the change took place between that time and A.D. 1525. AS. *brȳd-guma*; Grein, i. 147.+Du. *bruidegom*; Icel. *brūðgumi*; Swed. *brudgum*; Dan. *brudgom*; OHG. *brūtigomo* (G. *bräutigam*). β. The latter part of the word appears also in Goth. *guma*, a man, cognate with L. *homo*, a man. See **Bride, Homage.**

BRIDGE, a structure built across a river. (E.) ME. *brigge*, Chaucer, C. T. 3920 (A 3922); *brig*, Minot's Poems, vii. 78; *brugge*, Allit. Poems, ed. Morris, B. 1187; *brugg*, Rob. of Glouc. p. 401 (l. 8285). AS. *brycg*, *bricg* (acc. *bricge*); Grein, i. 145 ;+Icel. *bryggja*, Swed. *brygga*, Dan. *brygge*, a pier; Du. *brug*; OHG. *prucca*, G. *brücke*. Teut. type *brugja*, fem. Further allied to Icel. *brū*, a bridge; Dan. *bro*, a bridge, pavement; MSwed. *bro*, a bridge, a paved way. Perhaps allied to Russ. *brevno*, a beam, joist. Stokes-Fick, p. 184.

BRIDLE, a restraint for horses. (E.) ME. *bridel*, Ancren Riwle, p. 74. AS. *brīdel*, Grein, i. 142; for an earlier *brigdel*; cf. AS. *brigdils*, a bridle, O. E. Texts, p. 44, l. 127. The stem is *bregd-il-s-*, from *bregd-an*, to pull, to twitch; see **Braid.** Parallel to G. *züg-el*, from *zieh-en*, to draw.+Du. *breidel*; OHG. *priddel*, *bridel*, *brittil*; MHG. *britel*; cf. F. *bride* being borrowed from this MHG. *bridel*. ¶ Similarly, the OHG. *brittil* is from OHG. *brettan*, cognate with AS. *bregdan*, to pull, weave, braid.

BRIEF (1), short. (F.—L.) Spelt *brief* in Barnes' Works, p. 347, col. 1, last line. In older English we find *bref, breef*, P. Plowman, C. xxiii. 327; with the dimin. *breuet* (*brevet*), sb., P. Plowman, C. i. 72.—OF. *brief* (so spelt in Cotgrave); mod. F. *bref*.—L. *breuis*, short. +Gk. βραχύς, short. Der. *brief-ly*. And see below.

BRIEF (2), a letter, &c. (F.—L.) Cotgrave has: '*Brief*, m. a writ, or *brief*; a short mandamus, injunction, commission, &c.' From the adj. above. Der. *brief-less*.

BRIER; see **Briar.**

BRIG, a ship; see **Brigantine.**

BRIGADE, a body of troops. (F.—Ital.) Milton has *brigads*, P. L. ii. 532.—F. '*brigade*, a troop, crue, or company;' Cot.—Ital. *brigata*, a troop, band, company.—Ital. *brigare*, to quarrel, fight. See **Brigand.** Der. *brigad-ier*.

BRIGAND, a robber, pirate. (F.—Ital.) ME. *bregaund*, Morte Arthure, 2096. Borrowed from F. *brigand*, an armed foot-soldier, which see in Cotgrave; who also gives '*Brigander*, to rob;' and '*Brigandage*, a robbing, theeverie.'—Ital. *brigante*, a busybody, intriguer; and, in a bad sense, a robber, pirate.—Ital. *brigante*, pres. part. of the verb *brigare*, to strive after.—Ital. *briga*, strife, quarrel, trouble, business; which see in Diez. ¶ No connexion with W. *brigant*, a highlander, from *brig*, a hill-top. Der. *brigand-age*; and see below.

BRIGANDINE, a kind of armour. (F.—Ital.) *Brigandine*, a kind of coat of mail, occurs in Jerem. xlvi. 4, li. 3, A.V.; see Wright's Bible Word-book.—F. *brigandine*, 'a fashion of ancient armour, consisting of many jointed and skale plates;' Cot. So called because worn by *brigands* or robbers; see **Brigand.** ¶ The Ital. form is *brigantina*, a coat of mail.

BRIGANTINE, BRIG, a two-masted ship. (F.—Ital.) *Brig* is merely short for *brigantine*. Cotgrave has the latter, to translate the F. *brigantin*, which he describes.—F. *brigantin*.—Ital. *brigantino*, a pirate-ship.—Ital. *brigante*, an industrious, intriguing man; also, a robber, brigand. See **Brigand.**

BRIGHT, clear, shining. (E.) ME. *bright*, Chaucer, C. T. 1064 (A 1062). AS. *berht, beorht* (in common use).+OS. *berht, beraht* (Heliand); Goth. *bairhts*; Icel. *bjartr*; OHG. *përaht*, MHG. *bërht*, shining. Teut. type *berh-toz*, shining. Cf. W. *berth*, fair; Gk. φορκ-ός, white; Skt. *bhargas*, light. Der. *bright-ly, bright-ness, bright-en.*

BRILL, a fish; *Rhombus vulgaris*. (E.) Spelt *prylle* and *brell* in 1481-90 (N.E.D.). Of unknown origin; but Kalkar, in his M. Dan. Dict., s.v. *butte*, cites the G. pl. *pfellen* or *pfrillen*, showing that the Low G. form was prob. *prille*. Cf. Bavar. *pfrille*, a very small fish (Schmeller). Other E. forms were *pearl, perl*. Kalkar gives *prille-mad*, dainty meat, allied to *prille*, to poke, apparently with reference to its firmness; cf. Low G. *prall*, firm and fleshy, as e.g., a man's calf. The *prill* may have been named from the firmness of the flesh. ¶ Quite distinct from the Cornish *brilli*, mackerel; where *bril-* stands for *brithel*, a mackerel, formed by the dimin. suffix *-el* from Corn. *brith*, streaked, variegated, pied, speckled. [So in Irish and Gaelic, *breac* means both 'spotted' and 'a trout;' and in Manx, *brack* means both 'trout' and 'mackerel.']

BRILLIANT, shining. (F.—L.—Gk.—Skt.) Not in early use. Dryden has *brilliant*, sb., meaning 'a gem;' Character of a Good Parson, last line but one.—F. *brillant*, glittering, pres. pt. of *briller*,

to glitter, sparkle.—Late L. *beryllāre* (an unauthorised form), to sparkle like a precious stone or beryl (Brachet).—Late L. *berillus, beryllus*, a gem, an eye-glass; see Diefenbach, Glossarium Latino-Germanicum; cf. *berillus*, an eye-glass, *brillum*, an eye-glass, in Ducange. ¶ This etymology is rendered certain by the fact that the G. *brille*, spectacles, is clearly a corruption of *beryllus*, a beryl; see Max Müller, Lectures on the Science of Language, ii. 583; 8th ed. 1875. See **Beryl.**

BRIM, edge, margin. (E.) ME. *brim, brym, brimme*, margin of a river, lake, or sea; Allit. Poems, ed. Morris, A. 1011, B. 365. AS. *brymme* (for *brimme*?), a brim, border, margin. [The AS. *brim*, surf, sea, is prob. a different word.] Allied to Swed. *bräm*, border, edge; MDan. *bræmme, bremme* (Kalkar); Dan. *bræm*; MDu. *breme*; G. *gebräme*, border, *verbrämen*, to border. Cf. Icel. *barmr*, brim. Perhaps related to **Barm** (2). Cf. **Brink.** Der. *brim-ful, brimm-er.*

BRIMSTONE, sulphur. (E.) Lit. 'burn-stone.' ME. *brimston, brymston; bremstoon, brimstoon*, Chaucer, Prol. 631 (A 629); also *brenstoon*, Wyclif, Gen. xix. 24; Deut. xxix. 23; cf. Icel. *brennisteinn*, brimstone.—ME. *bren-*, burning (from the vb. *brennen*, to burn); and *stoon*, a stone. β. So also the Icel. *brennisteinn* is from Icel. *brenna*, to burn, and *steinn*, a stone. See **Burn** and **Stone.**

BRINDLED, BRINDED, streaked, spotted. (Scand.) Shak. has 'brinded cat;' Macb. iv. 1. 1; *brindled* being an extended quasi-diminutive form. ME. *brended*; as in 'a grete brended flye,' in the Book of St. Albans, ed. 1496, p. 28; see N.E.D. Formed from *brend*, the pp. of *brennen*, to burn, the sense being 'branded.' Cf. prov. E. *branded*, brindled; also Icel. *brönd-*, in the comp. *bröndóttr*, brindled, said of a cow, Cleasby and Vigfusson's Dict. App. p. 772. We also find Icel. *brand-krosóttr*, brindled-brown with a white cross on the forehead; *brandr*, a brand, flame, firebrand, sword; *brenna*, to burn. ¶ Thus *brinded* is little more than another form of *branded*; the letter *i* appears again in Brimstone, q.v. And see **Brand** and **Burn.**

BRINE, pickle, salt water. (E.) ME. *brine, bryne*, Prompt. Parv. p. 51. AS. *brȳne* (for *brine*), salt liquor, Ælf. Gloss.; Voc. 128. 40. +MDu. *brijn, brijne*, pickle, sea-water (Oudemans); whence Du. *brijn*, brine, pickle. Der. *brin-y.*

BRING, to fetch. (E.) ME. *bringen* (common); pt. t. *broughte*. AS. *bringan*, pp. *brungen* (rare), Grein, i. 143; *brengan*, pt. t. *bröhte*, pp. *bröht*; the former being the strong and original form. +Du. *brengen*; Goth. *briggan* (with *gg* sounded as *ng*), pt. t. *brähta*; OHG. *pringan* (G. *bringen*). Teut. type *brangjan-*, pt. t. *branχ-ta*> *bräh-ta* (whence AS. *brengan*); from a strong type *brengan-* (whence AS. *bringan*).

BRINK, margin; but properly, a slope. (Scand.) ME. *brink*, edge of a pit, Chaucer, C. T. 9275 (E 1401); *brenk*, a shore, Wyclif, John, xxi. 4. 'Bi the se-*brinke*;' King Horn, 141.—ONorse *brenka*, Icel. *brekka*, a slope, also a crest of a hill, a hill; allied to Low G. *brink*, sward at the edge of a field; a grassy hill (Lübben); Westphal. *brink*, edge of a hill. Cf. **Brim.**

BRIONY; a variant of **Bryony,** q. v.

BRISK, nimble, lively, smart, trim. (F.—Ital.) Not in early authors; used by Shak. and Milton. Apparently the same as Lowl. Sc. *bruisk*, brisk (ab. 1560); N.E.D.—F. *brusque*, 'brisk, lively, quick, rash, harsh;' Cot.—Ital. *brusco*, tart, harsh. See **Brusque.** Der. *brisk-ly, brisk-ness.* **Doublet,** *brusque.*

BRISKET, part of the breast-piece of meat. (F.—Scand.) Ben Jonson has *brisket-bone*; Sad Shepherd, i. 2: 'The *brisket-bone*, upon the spoon Of which a little gristle grows.' ME. *brusket*, Voc. 704. 8. —OF. *brischet*, a form given by Brachet, s. v. *brechet*, but *bruschet* in Littré; however, Cotgrave has: '*Brichet*, m. the brisket, or breast-piece;' also '*Bruchet*, m. the craw-bone, or merry-thought of a bird;' F. *brechet*. [Bret. *bruched*, the breast, is from OF. *bruchet*.] The Guernsey *bruquet* (Métivier) gives *bruskot* as the oldest type, as in ME.—Dan. *brusk*, Swed. *brosk*, MSwed. *bryske* (Ihre, s. v. *brusk*), Icel. *brjösk*, gristle; cf. Norw. *brjosk*, gristle, *brjoskutt*, gristly. See Ben Jonson (as above). So Kluge, s.v. *brausche*; but the connexion with *brausche* is dark. With Dan. *brus-k* cf. AS. *brȳsan*, to bruise, hence, to crush. See **Bruise.**

BRISTLE, a stiff hair. (E.) ME. *bristle, berstle*, Chaucer, Prol. 556. AS. *byrst*, a bristle, Herbarium, 52; in A.S. Leechdoms, i. 156; with dimin. suffix *-el*.+Du. *borstel*, a bristle. Cf. Icel. *burst*, a bristle; Swed. *borst*, a bristle; G. *borste*, a bristle. The AS. *byrst*, fem., and Icel. *burst*, answer to Teut. types from the base *burs-t-*; from Teut. *burs-*, weak grade of *bers-*= Idg. *bhers-*, to bristle; cf. Skt. *sahasra-bhṛshti*, having a thousand points; Benfey, p. 666. Cf. Stokes-Fick, p. 172-3. Der. *bristle*, verb; *bristl-y, bristl-i-ness.*

BRITTLE, fragile. (E.) ME. *britel, brotel, brutel*; Chaucer has *brotel*, Leg. of Good Women, Lucr. 206. Answering to an AS. type *brytel* = Teut. *brut-iloz*, adj.; from *brut-*, weak grade of AS. *brēotan*, to break; Grein, i. 142.+Icel. *brjóta*, to break, destroy; Swed. *bryta*, Dan. *bryde*, to break. So that the sense was 'fragile.' ¶ Cf. the form *brickle*, used by Spenser, F. Q. iv. 10. 39, obviously from AS. *brecan*, to break; the L. *fragilis* (E. *fragile*, *frail*) being from the same root as *brickle*.

BRITZKA, BRITSKA, a kind of open carriage. (Polish.) First in 1832.—Pol. *bryczka* (with *cz* = E. *ch*), 'a light long travelling wagon;' dimin. of *bryka*, a goods-wagon (N.E.D.).

BROACH, to tap liquor. (F.—L.) The ME. phrase is *setten on broche*, to set a-broach, to tap, Babees Boke, ed. Furnivall, p. 266. Imitated from the F. *mettre en broche*, to tap a barrel, viz. by piercing it; cf. F. 'brocher', to broach, to spit;' Cot.—F. 'broche', a broach, spit;' Cot. See **Brooch, Abroach**.

BROAD, adj., wide. (E.) ME. *brod*, *brood*, Chaucer, Prol. 155. AS. *brād*, Grein, i. 136.+Du. *breed*; Icel. *breiðr*; Swed. and Dan. *bred*; Goth. *braids*; OHG. *preit* (G. *breit*). Teut. type *braidoz*. Der. *broad-ly*, *broad-ness*, *broad-en*, *broad-side*; also *breadth*, q. v.

BROCADE, a variegated silk stuff. (Span.—L.) 'Brocado, a cloth of gold or silver;' Blount. A '*brocade* waistcoat' is mentioned in the Spectator, no. 15.—Span. *brocado*, sb., brocade; also pp., brocaded, embroidered with gold; which explains the use of *brocade* as an adjective. *Brocado* is properly the pp. of a verb *brocar*, which no doubt meant ' to embroider,' answering to F. *brocher*, which Cotgrave explains by ' to broach, to spit; also, to stitch grossely, to set or sowe with great stitches,' der. from F. *broche*, explained by 'a broach, or spit; also, a great stitch.' [The Span. *broca*, a reel for silk, a drill, has lost the required sense.] See **Brooch**. Der. *brocade*, verb; *brocad-ed*.

BROCCOLI, BROCOLI, a vegetable resembling cauliflower. (Ital.—L.) Pope has *brocoli*, Horace's Sat., ii. 2. 138. Properly, the word is plural, and means ' sprouts.'—Ital. *broccoli*, sprouts, pl. of *broccolo*, a sprout; dimin. from *brocco*, a skewer, also, a shoot, stalk. *Brocco* is allied to F. *broche*, a spit, also a brooch. See **Brooch**.

BROCHURE, a pamphlet. (F.—L.) Mere French. F. *brochure*, a few printed leaves stitched together.—F. *brocher*, to stitch. See **Brocade**.

BROCK, a badger. (C.) Used by Ben Jonson, The Fox, i. 1; Sad Shepherd, Act ii. sc. 1. ME. *brock*, P. Plowman, B. vi. 31; cf. Prompt. Parv. p. 53. AS. *broc*, a badger (Bosworth), but the word is of slight authority, and borrowed from Celtic.—W. *broch*; Corn. *broch*; Bret. *broch*; Irish, Gaelic, and Manx *broc*, a badger. β. It is most probable, as Mr. Wedgwood suggests, that the animal was named from his white-streaked face; just as a trout is, in Gaelic, called *breac*, i. e. spotted, and a mackerel is, in Cornish, called *brithill*, i.e. variegated; see note under **Brill**. If so, cf. Gk. φορκός, white, gray; and E. *gray*, a badger. Hence also Gael. *brocach*, speckled in the face, grayish, as a badger; *brucach*, spotted, freckled, speckled, particularly in the face. See Stokes-Fick, p. 185.

BROCKET, a red deer two years old. (F.—L.) 'The hert .. the secunde yere [is] a *broket*;' Reliq. Antiquæ, i. 151. A corruption of F. *brocart*. Cotgrave has: '*Brocart*, m. a two year old deere; which if it be a red deere, we call a *brocket*; if a fallow, a *pricket*; also a kinde of swift stagge, which hath but one small branch growing out of the stemme of his horne.' So named from having but one tine to his horn.—F. *broche*, 'a broach, spit;' also, a tusk of a wild boar; hence, a tine of a stag's horn; see Cotgrave. See **Brooch**.

BROGUES, stout, coarse shoes. (C.—E.) In Shak. Cymb. iv. 2. 214.—Gael. and Irish *brog*, a shoe; MIrish *brócc*.—AS. *bróc*, breeches; or from Icel. *brók*. (Not really Celtic.) See **Breeches**.

BROIDER, to adorn with needlework. (F.—Teut.) In the Bible, A. V., Ezek. xvi. 10. This form of the word was due to confusion with the totally different word *to braid*, a variant of *braid*, due to AS. *brogden*, pp. of *bregdan*; see **Braid**. And note that AS. *brogden* regularly became *brouden* in ME., but was altered to *broiden* by confusion with *braid* (ME. *breiden*). In 1 Tim. ii. 19, *broidered* is actually used with the sense of *braided*! See *Broider* in Eastwood and Wright's Bible Wordbook. An older spelling of *broider* is *broder*; thus we find ' a spoyle of dyuerse coloures with *brodered* workes' in the Bible of 1551, Judges, v. 30. It is also spelt *broudered* or *browdered*; Henrysoun, Test. of Cresseid, 417.—F. 'border', to imbroyder,' Cotgrave [a word wholly distinct from *border*, also in Cotgrave with the explanation 'to border, gard, welt,' &c.]. The same as OF. *brosder*, *brouder*, to embroider (Godefroy, and Supp.); cf. Late L. *brosdus*, *brusdus*, embroidered work (Ducange). Apparently from Teut. *brozd-*, a point, whence AS. *brord*, Icel. *broddr*, a spike. See **Brad**.

BROIL (1), to fry, roast over hot coals. (F.—Teut.?) ME. *broilen*. '*Brolyyn*, or *broylyn*, ustulo, ustillo, torreo;' Prompt. Parv. p. 53. See Chaucer, Prol. 385. [Cf. also *brulen*, E. E. Prose Psalter, cxx. (cxxi.) 5; before 1350.]—AF. *broiller* (Bozon); OF. *bruillir*, to broil, intrans. (in Godefroy). Of unknown origin; cf. OF. *bruir*, to roast; perhaps from MHG. *brüejen*, to scald; see **Brood**.

BROIL (2), a disturbance, tumult. (F.) Occurs in Shak. 1 Hen. VI, i. 1. 53; iii. 1. 92. Spelt *breull* in Berners, tr. of Froissart, vol. ii. c. 140.—F. *brouiller*, explained by Cotgrave by ' to jumble, trouble,

disorder, confound, marre by mingling together; to huddle, tumble, shuffle things ill-favouredly; to make a troublesome hotch-potch; to make a hurry, or great hurbyburly.' Allied to Ital. *brogliare*, to disturb, *broglio*, confusion; whence E. *imbroglio*. Of unknown origin.

BROKER, an agent, a middle-man in transactions of trade. (F.—L.) ME. *broker*, *brocour*, P. Plowman, B. v. 130, 248. We also find *brocage* = commission on a sale, P. Plowman, B. ii. 87. The oath of the *brokers* in London is given in Liber Albus, ed. Riley, p. 315. Their business was ' to bring the buyer and seller together, and lawfully witness the bargain between them;' for which they were allowed a commission on the sale, called a *brocage*, or, in later times, *brokerage*. The ME. *brocour* also meant a retail-dealer, cf. P. Plowman, C. vii. 95, and answers to AF. *brocour*, a broker, Liber Albus, p. 400; and to ONorth F. *brokeor*, accus. of *brokiere*, which Godefroy (s. v. *brocheor*) explains by ' celui qui vend du vin *au broc*,' i. e. by the jugful.—Late L. *broccātor*, one who broaches wine.—Late L. *broccāre*, to broach.—Late L. *brocca*, *broca*, a pointed stick, a spike. See **Broach, Brooch**. Hence also AF. *abrocour*, a broker, Stat. Realm, i. 103 (1285); Late L. *abrocārius*, Liber Albus, p. 269. And cf. Walloon *abroki*, to set abroach.

BROMINE, a non-metallic chemical element. (Gk.) Modern; since 1826. Named from its ill odour. Formed, with the suffix *-ine*, from Gk. βρῶμ-ος, a stink.

BRONCHIAL, relating to the *bronchiæ* or *bronchia*. (Gk.) The *bronchiæ* are the ramifications of the windpipe, passing into the lungs. *Bronchiæ* is in use; but the more correct form is *bronchia*, neut. plural.—Gk. βρόγχια, neut. pl., the bronchia, or ramifications of the windpipe.—Gk. βρόγχος, the windpipe, trachea. Cf. Gk. βράγχια, neut. pl., the gills of fishes; βράγχος, a gill, also, a sore throat, and (as an adjective) hoarse.

BRONCHITIS, inflammation of the bronchial membrane. (L.—Gk.) A coined L. form *bronchītis*, made from Gk. βρόγχος, the windpipe. See above.

BRONZE, an alloy of copper with tin, &c. (F.—Ital.—L.) Not in early use. In Pope, Dunciad, ii. 10; iii. 169. F. *bronze*, introd. in 16th cent. from Ital. *bronzo* (Brachet).—Ital. *bronzo*, bronze; *bronzino*, made of bronze (*z* = *dz*). It has been shown, by M. Berthelot (Introduction à la Chimie des Anciens, pp. 275-9), that the Ital. *bronzino* = L. *Brundusinum*, i.e. belonging to *Brundusium* (Brindisi), in S. Italy, where bronze mirrors were made. Pliny has *æs Brundusinum*, Nat. Hist. xxxiii. 9, xxxiv. 17 (Athenæum, Dec. 30, 1893). See Notes on E. Etym., p. 18.

BROOCH, an ornament fastened with a pin. (F.—L.) So named from its being fastened with a pin. ME. *broche*, a pin, peg, spit, Prompt. Parv. p. 52; also a jewel, ornament, id.; cf. Chaucer, Prol. 160; Ancren Riwle, p. 420.—OF. *broche*, F. *broche*, a spit; also the tusk of a boar (Cotgrave).—Late L. *brocca*, a pointed stick; *broca*, a tooth, sharp point; from L. *broccus*, projecting, like teeth (Plautus). See **Broach**.

BROOD, progeny, offspring, young; a family. (E.) ME. *brōd*, Owl and Nightingale, 518, 1631; Rob. of Glouc. p. 70; l. 1595. AS. *brōd*, a brood (rare); 'hī brēdaŏ heora brōd,' they nourish their brood; Ælfric, Hom. ii. 10.+Du. *broed*, a brood, hatch; MHG. *bruot*, that which is hatched, also heat; whence G. *brut*, a brood. Teut. stem *brō-ð-. β. The primary meaning is that which is hatched, or produced by means of warmth; from the verbal base *brō-, preserved in G. brü-hen, to scald (orig. to heat), Du. broe-ien, to brood, to hatch. This base *brō- is related by gradation to *brē-(brǣ-), to roast; for which see **Brawn**. Der. *brood*, vb.; *breed*, q. v.

BROOK (1), to endure, put up with. (E.) ME. *brouke*, which almost invariably had the sense of ' to use,' or ' to enjoy;' Chaucer, C. T. 10182 (E 2308), P. Plowman, B. xi. 117; Havelok, 1743. AS. *brūcan*, to use, enjoy, Grein, i. 144.+Du. *gebruiken*, to use; Icel. *brūka*, to use; Goth. *brukjan*, to make use of; OHG. *prūhhan* (G. *brauchen*), to use, enjoy. Allied to L. *frui*, to enjoy; cf. L. *frūges*, *fructus*, fruit; Skt. *bhuj*, to eat and drink, to enjoy, which probably stands for an older form *bhruj*; Benfey, p. 656.—√BHREUG, to enjoy, use. Brugmann, i. § 111. *Brook* is co-radicate with *fruit*, q. v.

BROOK (2), a small stream. (E.) ME. *brook*, Chaucer, C. T. 3920 (A. 3922). AS. *brōc*, *brooc*, Grein, i. 144.+Du. *broek*, a marsh, a pool; Low G. *brook*, low land, broken up by marshes; OHG. *pruoch* (G. *bruch*), a marsh, bog. β. Even in prov. Eng. we find: '*Brooks*, low, marshy, or moory ground;' Pegge's Kenticisms (E. D. S.); at Cambridge, we have *Brook-lands*, i. e. low-lying, marshy ground. The G. *bruch* also means ' rupture;' and the notion in *brook* is that of *broken* ground or of water *breaking* up or forcing its way to the surface; from Teut. *brōk-, a variant (by gradation) of *brek-, the root of *break*, q. v. Der. *brook-let*.

BROOK-LIME, a plant. (E.) ME. *brok-lemke*, Med. Wks. of the fourteenth century, ed. Henslow, p. 29, l. 2.—AS. *brōc*, a brook; and *hleomoc*, brook-lime. Cf. Low G. *lömek*, *lömke*, brook-lime (Schambach).

BROOM, the name of a plant; a besom. (E.) ME. *brom, broom,* the plant; Wyclif, Jerem. xvii. 6. AS. *brōm,* broom, Gloss. to Cockayne's Leechdoms.+Du. *brem,* broom, furze; Low G. *braam,* broom; G. *brom-,* in *brom-beere,* a bramble-berry. Teut. type **bræmoz.* B. The confusion in old names of plants is very great; *broom* and *bramble* are closely related, the latter being, etymologically, the diminutive of *broom;* cf. Du. *braam-bosch,* a bramble-bush. See **Bramble.**

BROSE, BREWIS, a kind of broth or pottage. (F.—MHG.) *Brose* is a later form of *browis* or *brewis,* for which see Nares and Richardson. In Prompt. Parv. we find: '*Browesse, browes,* Adipatum;' and see Way's note, where *browyce* is cited from Lydgate.—OF. *brouez, broez,* nom. case of *brouet, broet,* soup made with broth of meat (see Supp. to Godefroy); dimin. of OF. *bro* (Hatzfeld, s.v. *brouet*), also spelt *breu,* pottage (Roquefort), Late L. *brodum,* gravy, broth.— MHG. *brod,* broth; cognate with E. *broth.* ¶ It is no doubt because *brewis* sounded like a plural, and because it has been confused with *broth,* that in prov. Eng. (e.g. Cambs.) *broth* is often alluded to as 'they' or 'them.' See **Broth** and **Brew.**

BROTH, a kind of soup. (E.) ME. *broth,* Rob. of Glouc. p. 528, l. 10857. AS. *broð* (to translate L. *iūs*), Bosworth.+Icel. *broð;* OHG. *prod, brod.* Teut. type **broðōm,* n.; from **bro-, *bru-,* weak grade of **breu-,* as in AS. *brēowan,* to brew. And see Stokes-Fick, p. 172. See **Brew** and **Brose.**

BROTHEL, a house of ill fame. (E.; *confused with* F.—Teut.) [Originally quite distinct from ME. *bordel* (= Ital. *bordello*).] The quotations from Bale (Votaries, pt. ii), and Dryden (Mac Flecknoe, l. 70) in Richardson, show that the old term was *brothel-house* (as in Much Ado, i. 1. 256), i.e. a house for brothels or prostitutes; for the ME. *brothel* was a *person,* not a *place.* Thus Gower speaks of 'A *brothel,* which Micheas hihte' = a *brothel,* whose name was Micheas; C. A. iii. 173 (bk. vii. 2595); and see P. Plowman, Crede, 772. Cf. 'A *brothelrie,* lenocinium;' Levins, 103, 34. We also find ME. *brethel,* a wretch, *bretheling,* a beggarly fellow. From the same root are the AS. *ábroðen,* degenerate, base; and the past tense *ábruðon,* they failed, A. S. Chron. an. 1004. The last forms are from AS. *broð-, bruð-,* weak grade of *-brēoðan,* to ruin, destroy, occurring in the comp. *ābrēoðan,* with the same sense. Thus *broth-el* orig. meant 'a lost' creature; like L. *perditus.* β. But, of course, a confusion between *brothel-house* and the ME. *bordel,* used in the same sense, was inevitable. Chaucer has *bordel* in his Persones Tale, § 885; and Wyclif even has *bordelhous,* Ezek. xvi. 24, showing that the confusion was already then completed; though he also has *bordelrie* = a brothel, in Num. xxv. 8, which is a French form.—OF. *bordel,* a hut; dimin. of *borde,* a hut, cot, shed made of boards; Cot.—MDu. (and Du.) *bord,* a plank. See **Board.**

BROTHER, a son of the same parents. (E.) ME. *brother,* Chaucer, Prol. 529. AS. *brōðor,* Grein, p. 144.+Du. *broeder;* Icel. *brōðir;* Goth. *brōthar;* Swed. *broder;* Dan. *broder;* OHG. *pruoder* (G. *bruder*).+Gael. and Irish *brathair;* W. *brawd,* pl. *brodyr;* Russian *brat';* L. *frāter;* Gk. φράτηρ; Church-Slavonic *bratru;* Zend *brāta;* Pers. *birādar;* Skt. *bhrātṛ;* Teut. type **brōther;* Idg. type **bhrāter.* Brugmann, i. § 555. **Der.** *brother-hood, brother-like, brother-ly.*

BROUGHAM, a kind of carriage. (Personal name.) Date 1839. Named after the first Lord Brougham, born 1778.

BROW, the eye-brow; edge of a hill. (E.) ME. *browe,* Prompt. Parv. p. 53. AS. *brū,* pl. *brūa,* Grein, i. 144.+Icel. *brún,* eye-brow; Dan. *bryn;* Lith. *bruwis;* Russian *brove;* Gk. ὀφρύς, eye-brow; Pers. *abrū;* Skt. *bhrū,* eye-brow. ¶ Quite a distinct word from AS. *bræw,* Du. *braauw* (in comp. *wenk-braauw,* an eye-brow), G. *braue.* **Der.** *brow-beat,* to beat by frowning; Holland's Plutarch, p. 107.

BROWN, the name of a darkish colour. (E.) ME. *broun,* Chaucer, Prol. 207. AS. *brūn,* Grein, i. 145.+Du. *bruin,* brown, bay; Icel. *brūnn;* Swed. *brun;* Dan. *bruun;* G. *braun;* Lith. *brunas.* Cf. Gk. φρῦνος, a toad; Skt. *ba-bhru(s),* tawny. Brugmann, i. § 109. **Der.** *brown-ish, brun-ette, burn-et, burn-ish.* **Doublet,** *bruin.*

BROWZE, to nibble; said of cattle. (F.—MHG.) Occurs in Shak. Wint. Tale, iii. 3. 69; Antony, i. 4. 66; Cymb. iii. 6. 38; spelt *brouze* in Spenser, Shep. Kal. May, 179; *brouse,* Fitzherbert, Husb., § 131.—MF. *brouser,* 'to *brouze,* knap, nibble off leaves, buds, &c.' A by-form of MF. *brouster,* also *brouter,* explained by Cotgrave by 'to *brouze,* to nip, or nibble off the sprigs, buds, barke, &c. of plants;' a sense still retained in prov. Eng. *brut* (Kent, Surrey), which keeps the *t* whilst dropping the *s.*—MF. 'broust, a sprig, tendrell, bud, a yong branch or shoot;' Cot.—MHG. *broz,* a bud (Graff, iii. 369); Bavarian *bross, brosst,* a bud (Schmeller).—OHG. *broz-, bruz-,* weak grade of *briozan,* to break, also, to break into bud; which is cognate with AS. *brēotan,* to break; see **Brittle.**

BRUIN, a bear. (Dutch.) In the old epic poem of Reynard the Fox, the bear is named 'brown,' from his colour; the Dutch version spells it *bruin,* which is the Dutch form of the word 'brown.' The proper pronunciation of the word involves a peculiar diphthong approaching the broad romic (əu); but we always pronounce it *broo-in,* disregarding the Dutch pronunciation. See **Brown.**

BRUISE, to pound, crush, injure. (E.; *partly* F.) ME. *brusen,* Joseph of Arimathie, ed. Skeat, l. 501; but more commonly spelt *brissen* or *brisen,* Wyclif's Bible, Deut. ix. 3; also *brosen,* id. Numbers, xxii. 25. In the S. Eng. Legendary, 295. 58, we find the pt. t. *to-bruysde,* representing AS. *tō-brysde,* pt. of *tō-brȳsan;* which shows that E. *bruise* represents AS. *brȳsan,* to bruise, occurring in Be Domes Dæge, ed. Lumby, l. 49; cf. Matt. xxi. 44. β. But it seems to have been confused with OF. *bruiser, bruser, brisier,* to break; forms which Diez would separate; but wrongly, as Mätzner says. See *brisier* in Supp. to Godefroy. Of uncertain origin; cf. OIrish *briss-im,* I break, allied to AS. *berstan,* to burst.

BRUIT, a rumour; to announce noisily. (F.—L.) Occurs in Shak. Macb. v. 7. 22. 'The kinge herde the *bruyt,*' Caxton, Hist. of Troye, leaf 112, l. 6.—F. *bruit,* a bruit, a great sound or noise, a rumbling, clamor,' &c.; Cot.—F. *bruire,* to make a noise, roar. Scheler derives F. *bruire* from L. *rūgīre,* to roar; the prefixed *b* may have been due to imitative alteration; cf. G. *brüllen,* to roar. And F. *bruit* = Late L. *brūgītus,* a clamour (Ducange); cf. L. *rugītus,* a roaring.

BRUNETTE, a girl with a dark complexion. (F.—G.) Mere French; but it occurs in the Spectator, No. 396. [The older E. equivalent is 'nut-brown,' as in the Ballad of The Nut-brown Maid.] —F. *brunette,* explained by Cotgrave as 'a nut-browne girle.'—F. *brunet,* masc. adj., *brunette,* fem. adj., brownish; Cot. Formed, with dimin. suffix *-et,* from F. *brun,* brown.—MHG. *brūn,* brown; cognate with E. *brown,* q. v.

BRUNT, the shock of an onset. (Scand.) Chiefly used in the phr. *brunt of battle,* the shock of battle, as in Shak. Cor. ii. 2. 104. However, Butler has: 'the heavy *brunt* of cannon-ball;' Hudibras, pt. i. c. 2, l. 872. ME. *brunt, bront.* '*Brunt,* insultus;' Prompt. Parv. p. 54. The oldest sense is 'smart blow,' as in E. E. Allit. Poems, A. 174. Partly imitative; cf. *dint,* prov. E. *dunt,* a blow, thump. Partly suggested by MDan. *brund,* heat, lust, Norw. *brund,* lust, heat (of animals in pairing-time). Allied to Icel. *bruna,* to advance with the speed of fire, said of a standard in the heat of battle, of ships advancing under full sail, &c.; Icel. *bruni,* burning, heat, passion, from *brenna,* to burn; cognate with E. *burn.* See **Burn.**

BRUSH, an implement for cleaning clothes; cf. *brushwood,* underwood. (F.—Teut.?) ME. *brusshe,* in the phrase 'wyped it with a *brusshe;*' P. Plowman, B. xiii. 460; also: '*Brusche,* bruscus,' i.e. brush-wood, Prompt. Parv.—OF. *broce, brosse,* brushwood, small wood; F. *brosse,* a bush, bushy ground, brush (Cotgrave); cf. Ital. *brusca* 'ling or heath to make brushes with:' Florio.—Late L. *bruscia,* a thicket. Derived by Diez from OHG. *bursta,* G. *borste,* a bristle; but perhaps influenced by Celtic (Thurneysen, p. 51). Cf. F. *broussailles,* brush-wood, and note the double sense of E. *broom.* **Der.** *brush-wood.*

BRUSQUE, rough in manner. (F.—Ital.) Spelt *brusk* by Sir Henry Wotton, d. 1639 (R.). He speaks of giving 'a *brusk* welcome' = a rough one; Reliq. Wotton., p. 582.—F. *brusque,* rude; introduced in 16th cent. from Ital. *brusco* (Brachet).—Ital. *brusco,* sharp, tart, sour, applied to fruits and wine. β. Of unknown origin; Diez suggests a corruption of OHG. *bruttisc,* brutish, brutal, which is unconvincing. Ferrari (says Diez) derives it from the L. *labruscus,* the Ital. dropping the first syllable. This is ingenious; the L. *labruscus* was an adj. applied to a wild vine and wild grape. ¶ The notion of connecting *brisk* with *brusque* appears in Cotgrave; it seems to be right; see **Brisk.**

BRUTE, a dumb animal. (F.—L.) Shak. has *brute* as an adj., Hamlet, iii. 2. 110; and other quotations in Richardson show that it was at first an adj., as in the phr. 'a *brute* beast.' Cf. 'alle *brute* beestis;' Book of Quinte Essence, ed. Furnivall, p. 11 (ab. 1460—70). —F. *brut,* masc., *brute,* fem. adj., in Cotgrave, signifying 'foul, ragged, shapeless,' &c.—L. *brūtus,* stupid. **Der.** *brut-al, brut-al-i-ty, brut-al-ise, brut-ish, brut-ish-ness.*

BRYONY, a kind of plant. (L.—Gk.) In Levins; also in Ben Jonson, Masques; The Vision of Delight.—L. *bryōnia.*—Gk. βρυωνία, also βρυώνη.—Gk. βρύειν, to teem, swell, grow luxuriantly.

BUBBLE, a small bladder of water. (E.) Shak. has the sb., As You Like It, ii. 7. 152; also as a vb., 'to rise in bubbles,' Macb. iv. 1. 11. Spelt *boble,* Castel of Helth, leaf 84, back. Not found much earlier in English. Cf. EFries. *bubbel,* a bubble. [Palsgrave has: '*Burble* in the water, *bubette,*' and the same form occurs in the Prompt. Parv. p. 56; but this is probably a somewhat different word, and from a different source; cf. Du. *borrel,* a bubble.]+Swed. *bubbla,* a bubble; Dan. *boble,* a bubble; to bubble; Du. *bobbel,* a bubble; *bobbelen,* to bubble; Low G. *bubbel,* sb.; *bubbeln,* vb. β. The form of the word is clearly a diminutive; and it is to be regarded as the dimin. of a form *bob* or *bub*, of imitative origin ; cf. prov. E. *bob*, a knob ; parallel to *blob*, a bubble.   See **Blob, Bleb.**

BUCCANIER, a pirate. (F.—West-Indian.) Modern. Borrowed from F. *boucanier*, a buccanier, pirate.—F. *boucaner*, to smoke-dry ; or, according to Cotgrave, 'to broyle or scorch on a woodden gridiron.'—F. *boucan*, 'a woodden gridiron, whereon the cannibals broile pieces of men, and other flesh ;' Cot. **β.** The word *boucan* is said to be a F. spelling of a Tupi (Brazilian) word, and to mean 'a frame on which meat is smoke-dried.' Mr. Wedgwood says : 'The natives of Florida, says Laudonnière (Hist. de la Floride, Pref. A.D. 1586, in Marsh), "mangent leurs viandes rosties sur les charbons et *boucanées*, c'est à dire quasi cuictes à la fumée." In Hakluyt's translation, "dressed in the smoake, which in their language they call *boucaned*;" Voyages, iii. 307. Hence those who established themselves in the islands for the purpose of smoking meat were called *buccaniers.*' Mr. Trumbull says :—'Jean de Lery (*Voyage fait en la Terre du Brésil*, 1578, p. 153) describes the construction and use, by the Tupinambas, of "the great wooden grilles, called in their language *boucan*, garnished with meats . . . drying slowly over fire."'

BUCK (1), a male deer, goat, &c. (E.) ME. *bukke*, Chaucer, C. T. 3387. AS. *bucca*, a he-goat, Levit. iv. 23. **+** Du. *bok*, a he-goat ; Icel. *bukkr* ; Swed. *bock*, a buck, a he-goat ; Dan. *buk*, a he-goat, ram, buck ; OHG. *poch* (G. *bock*), a buck, he-goat, battering-ram. Cf. also W. *bwch*, a buck ; *bwch gafr*, a he-goat ; Gael. *boc*, a buck, he-goat ; Irish *boc*, a he-goat. Brugmann, i. § 800. The Celtic type is *bukkos ; Stokes-Fick, p. 179.

BUCK (2), to wash linen, to steep clothes in lye. (E.) Shak. has *buck-basket*, a basket for washing linen, Merry Wives, iii. 3. 2. ME. *bouken*, to wash linen ; P. Plowman, B. xiv. 19 ; as if from an AS. *būcian, not found ; but regularly formed from AS. *būc*, a pitcher (prov. E. *bouk*, a pail, tub). The ME. *bouken* had the special sense of 'to steep in lye,' to buck-wash ; so also Swed. *byka*, Dan. *byge*, MDu. *buiken*, G. *beuchen*, OF. *buer*, to buck-wash. See **Bucket. Der.** *buck-basket.*

BUCKET, a kind of pail. (E.) ME. *boket*, Chaucer, Kn. Tale, 675 (A 1533) ; AF. *boket* (Bozon) ; cf. Guernsey *bouquet* (Métivier). Formed with AF. dimin. suffix *-et* from AS. *būc*, a pitcher, glossed by 'lagena,' and occurring also in Judges, vii. 20 (Bosworth). Cf. Irish *buicead*, a bucket, Gael. *bucaid*, a bucket ; both borrowed from E.

BUCKLE, a kind of fastening ; to fasten. (F.—L.) The sb. *bokeling* occurs in Chaucer, C. T. 2505 (A 2503).—OF. *bocle* (F. *boucle*), the boss of a shield, a ring ; from the latter of which senses 'buckle' has been evolved.—Late L. *buccula*, meaning (1) a part of the helmet covering the cheek, a visor ; (2) a shield ; (3) a boss of a shield ; (4) a buckle. The original sense of L. *buccula* was the cheek : dimin. of *bucca*, the cheek.

BUCKLER, a kind of shield. (F.—L.) Chaucer has *bokeler*, Prol. 112 ; the pl. *boceleris* occurs in King Alisaunder, ed. Weber, 1190.—OF. *bucler* (F. *bouclier*) ; so named from the *bocle*, *bucle*, or boss in the centre. See **Buckle.**

BUCKRAM, a coarse cloth. (F.) ME. *bokeram*, cloth ; Prompt. Parv. p. 42 ; also in 1326 (N. and Q. 8 S. i. 128.)—OF. *boucaran* (F. *bougran*), a coarse kind of cloth (Roquefort) ; *boquerant* (Hatzfeld) ; Late L. *boquerannus*, buckram ; also (in Italy) Late L. *būchirānus*, for Ital. *buchirano*, late Ital. *bucherame*. Origin uncertain ; perhaps from Bokhara, in Tartary (Hatzfeld).

BUCKWHEAT, the name of a plant. (E.) In Coles's Dict. (1684) ; Turner, Names of Herbes, p. 35, E.D.S. (1548). The *Polygonum fagopyrum*. The word *buckwheat* means *beech-wheat*, so called from the resemblance in shape between its seeds and the mast of the beech-tree. The same resemblance is hinted at in the term *fagopyrum*, from L. *fāgus*, the beech-tree. The form *buck* for *beech* is E. Anglian, from AS. *bōc*, beech. See Tusser's Husbandry. **+** Du. *boekweit* ; G. *buchweizen*. See **Beech, Book.**

BUCOLIC, pastoral. (L.—Gk.) Elyot has *bucolickes* ; the Governour, bk. i. c. 10 § 8. Skelton has 'bucolycall relations ;' Garlande of Laurell, l. 327.—L. *būcolicus*, pastoral.—Gk. βουκολικός.—Gk. βουκόλος, a cow-herd.—Gk. βου-, for βοῦς, an ox ; κολ-, second grade of κελ-, in κέλλειν, to drive. **+** OIrish and Gael. *buachaill*, W. *bugail*, cow-herd ; Stokes-Fick, p. 178.

BUD, a germ ; to sprout. (E.) The Prompt. Parv., p. 54, has : 'Budde of a tre, Gemma,' and : 'Buddun as trees, Gemmo.' The word does not appear earlier in ME. ; but may have been an E. word. The corresponding AS. form is *budda, m., or *budde, f. ; the latter exactly answers to MHG. *butte*, prov. G. (Strassburg) *butt*, Bavar. *butte*, mod. G. *hage-butte*, fruit of the dog-rose, taken as the type of a bud from its shape and bright colour. Hence Du. *bot*, a bud, eye, shoot ; *botten*, to bud, sprout out ; OF. *boton*, a button, a bud ; AF. *boton*, a hip (Vocab. 556. 7) ; Norm. dial. *bout*, a bud, *bouter*, to bud (Robin) ; the F. words being of Teutonic origin. Cf. also Swed. dial. *bodda opp*, to become leafy (as trees or bushes), *boddoter*, full of

leaves. See Notes on E. Etymology, pp. 20, 476. See **Button** and **Butt** (1).

BUDGE (1), to stir, move from one's place. (F.—L.) Shak. has *budge*, to stir, Haml. iii. 4. 18.—F. *bouger*, to stir ; cf. Prov. *bolegar*, to disturb oneself ; answering to Ital. *bulicare*, to bubble up. Formed, as a frequentative, from L. *bullīre*, to boil. See **Boil. β.** This derivation is made clearer by the facts that the Span. *bullir* means not only 'to boil,' but 'to be busy, to bestir oneself,' also 'to move from place to place ;' whilst the deriv. adj. *bullicioso* means 'brisk, active, busy.' So also Port. *bulir*, to move, stir, be active ; *bulicoso*, restless.

BUDGE (2), a kind of fur. (F.) Milton has : 'those *budge* doctors of the Stoic fur ;' Comus, 707 ; alluding to the lambskin fur worn by some who took degrees, and still worn at Cambridge by bachelors of arts. Halliwell has : '*budge*, lambskin with the wool dressed outwards ; often worn on the edges of capes, as gowns of bachelors of arts are still made. See Fairholt's Pageants, i. 66 ; Strutt, ii. 102 ; Thynne's Debate, p. 32 ; Pierce Penniless, p. 11.' Cotgrave has : 'Agnelin, lambs-fur, *budge*.' Palsgrave has *bouge furre*. Cf. AF. *boge*, fur ; Stat. Realm, i. 380 (1363). Apparently from OF. *boge*, (Burguy), *bouge*, a bag made of skin. Another sense of *budge* is 'a bag or sack ;' and a third, 'a kind of water-cask ;' Halliwell. These ideas are connected by the idea of 'skin of an animal ;' which served for a bag, a water-skin, or for ornamental purposes. When *budge* has the sense of 'bag,' its dimin. is *budget*. See further under **Budget,** below. **¶** The connexion is not quite certain. Dr. Murray suggests OF. *bochet, bouchet*, a young kid.

BUDGET, a leathern bag. (F.—C.) Shak. has *budget* (old edd. *bowget*), Wint. Tale, iv. 3. 20. Palsgrave has *bougette*.—F. 'bougette, a little coffer, or trunk of wood, covered with leather ; . . . also, a little male, pouch, or *budget*;' Cot. A dimin. of F. 'bouge, a budget, wallet, or great pouch ;' id. ; cf. OF. *boulge* (Roquefort).—L. *bulga*, a little (skin) bag ; according to Festus, a word of Gaulish origin (Brachet).—OIrish *bolg, bolc*, a bag ; W. *bol*, the belly. Allied to **Belly.**

BUFF (1), in **Blindman's buff.** (F.—Teut.) Formerly *blindman-buff*, a game ; in which boys used to *buffet* one (who was blinded) on the back, without being caught, if possible. From OF. *bufe*, F. *buffe*, a buffet, blow.—Low G. *buff, puf*, a blow (Lübben) ; EFries. *buf, buff*, a blow. See **Buffet** (1).

BUFF (2), the skin of a buffalo ; a pale yellow colour. (F.—L.—Gk.) *Buff* is a contraction of *buffe*, or *buffle*, from F. *buffle*, a buffalo. '*Buff*, a sort of thick tanned leather ;' Kersey. '*Buff, Buffle*, or *Buffalo*, a wild beast like an ox ;' id. 'The term was applied to the skin of the buffalo dressed soft, buff-leather, and then to the yellowish colour of leather so dressed ;' Wedgwood. See **Buffalo.**

BUFFALO, a kind of wild ox. (Port. *or* Ital.—L.—Gk.) The pl. *buffollos* occurs in Sir T. Herbert's Travels, ed. 1665, p. 43. The sing. *buffalo* is in Ben Jonson, Discoveries, Of the magnitude of any fable ; § 133. Borrowed from Port. *bufalo*, or Ital. *buffalo* ; in early books of travel. [But the term was not really new in English ; the Tudor Eng. already had the form *buffle*, borrowed from the French. Cotgrave has : '*Buffle*, m. the buffe, *buffle*, bugle, or wild oxe ; also, the skin or neck of a buffe.']—L. *būfalus*, used by Fortunatus, a secondary form of *būbalus*, a buffalo.—Gk. βούβαλος, a buffalo ; Polyb. xii. 3, 5. Not a true Gk. word ; apparently suggested by Skt. *gavala-s*, a buffalo (Macdonell) ; which is allied to Skt. *gāus*, a cow, and to Gk. βοῦς, E. *cow*. See **Cow** (1).

BUFFER (1), a foolish fellow. (F.) Jamieson has '*buffer*, a foolish fellow.' The ME. *buffer* means 'a stutterer.' 'The tunge of *bufferes* [Lat. balborum] swiftli shal speke and pleynly ;' Wycl., Isaiah, xxxii. 4. Lydgate has *buffard*, a foolish fellow ; Minor Poems, p. 32. From ME. *buffen*, to stammer.—OF. *buffer*, to puff out the cheeks, &c. See **Buffet** (1), **Buffoon. β.** The word is, no doubt, partly imitative ; to represent indistinct talk ; cf. **Babble.**

BUFFER (2), a cushion, with springs, used to deaden concussion. (F.) *Buffer* is lit. a striker ; from ME. *buffen*, to strike ; prov. Eng. *buff*, to strike, used by Ben Jonson (see Nares).—OF. *bufer*, *buffer*, to strike. See **Buffet** (1).

BUFFET (1), a blow ; to strike. (F.) ME. *buffet, boffet*, a blow ; esp. a blow on the cheek or face ; Wycl., John, xix. 3. Also *buffeten*, *bofeten*, translated by L. *colaphizo*, Prompt. Parv. p. 41. Also *bufetung*, a buffeting, Old Eng. Homilies, i. 207.—OF. *bufet*, a blow, esp. on the cheek.—OF. *bufe*, a blow, esp. on the cheek ; *bufer, buffer*, to strike ; also, to puff out the cheeks.—Low G. *buff, puf*, a blow (Lübben) ; of imitative origin ; like EFries. *buf, buff, puf*, a blow, Du. *bof*, G. *puff*, MHG. *buf, puf*. From the sound ; see **Buff** (1).

BUFFET (2), a side-board. (F.) Used by Pope, Moral Essays (Ep. to Boyle), l. 153 ; Sat. ii. 5.—F. '*buffet*, a court cupboord, or high-standing cupboord ; also, a cupboord of plate ;' Cot. Origin unknown.

BUFFOON, a jester. (F.) Holland speaks of '*buffoons*, pleasants, and gesters;' tr. of Plutarch, p. 487. Pronounced *búffon*, Ben Jonson, Every Man, ii. 3. 8. For the suffix, cf. *ball-oon.* – F. *bouffon*, which Cotgrave explains as 'a buffoon, jester, sycophant,' &c. – F. *bouffer*, to puff. Cf. Span. *bufa*, a scoffing, laughing at; equiv. to Ital. *buffa*, a trick, jest; which is connected with Ital. *buffare*, to joke, jest; orig. to puff out the cheeks, in allusion to the grimacing of jesters, which was a principal part of their business. Of imitative origin. See **Buffer** (1). Der. *buffoon-ery.*

BUG (1), **BUGBEAR**, a terrifying spectre. (C.) Fairfax speaks of children being frightened by 'strange *bug-beares*;' tr. of Tasso, Gier. Lib. bk. xiii. st. 18. Here *bug-bear* means a spectre in the shape of a bear. The word *bug* was used alone, as in Shak. Tam. Shrew, i. 2. 211; and Wyclif has *bugge* in the sense of 'scare-crow,' L. *formido*, Baruch, vi. 69. Shak. himself also has *bugbear*, Troil. iv. 2. 34. – W. *bwg*, a hobgoblin, spectre; *bwgan*, a spectre; Gael. (and Irish) *bocan*, a spectre, apparition, terrifying object. β. Probably connected further with Lithuanian *baugùs*, terrific, frightful, *bugti*, to frighten, which Fick further connects with L. *fuga*, flight, *fugāre*, to put to flight, and Skt. *bhuj*, to bow, bend, turn aside, cognate with E. *bow*, to bend. See **Bow** (1). Brugmann, i. § 701. And see below.

BUG (2), an insect. (E.) Apparently a particular application of the Tudor-English *bug*, an apparition, scarecrow, object of terror; as if equivalent to 'disgusting creature.' But rather, a modification, due to association with *bug* (1), of AS. *budda*, a beetle; cf. AS. *scearn-budda*, a dung-beetle, Voc. 543. 10, prov. E. *sharn-bug* (Kent).

BUGABOO, a spectre. (C.) In Lloyd's Chit-chat (R.). It is the word *bug*, with the addition of W. *bw*, an interjection of threatening, Gael. *bo*, an interjection used to frighten children, our 'boh!'

BUGLE (1), a wild ox; a horn. (F. – L.) *Bugle* in the sense of 'horn' is an abbreviation of *bugle-horn*, used by Chaucer, C. T. 11565 (F 1253). It means the horn of the *bugle*, or wild ox. Halliwell has: '*Bugle*, a buffalo; see King Alisaunder, ed. Weber, 5112; Maundeville's Travels, p. 269; Topsell's Beasts, p. 54; Holinshed, Hist. of Scotland, p. 16.' Perhaps *bugle* was confused with *buffle* or *buffalo* (see **Buffalo**), but etymologically it is a different word. – OF. *bugle*, a wild ox (whence, by the way, F. *beugler*, to bellow). – L. *būculum*, acc. of *būculus*, a bullock, young ox (Columella); a dimin. of L. *bōs*, cognate with E. *cow*. See **Cow**.

BUGLE (2), a kind of ornament. (F. – L.?) 'A gyrdle .. Embost with *buegle*;' Spenser, Shep. Kal. Feb. 66. *Bugles* are tube-shaped glass beads, or fine glass pipes, sewn on to a woman's dress by way of ornament. [Mr. Wedgwood quotes from Muratori, showing that some sort of ornaments, called in Low Latin *bugoli*, were worn in the hair by the ladies of Piacenza in A.D. 1388. These were pads, to support the hair, and have nothing to do with the present word.] From a fancied resemblance to a *bugle-horn*; see N.E.D., s.v. *bugle*, a horn, where a quotation is given dated 1615, in which *bugle* seems to mean 'a tube.' Cf. '*Bugle*, a little blacke horne;' Cockeram (1623).

BUGLE (3), a plant; *Aiuga reptans*. (F. – Late L.) ME. *bugle*, Medical Werkes of 14th Cent., ed. Henslow, p. 172. – F. *bugle*. – Late L. *būgula* (Hatzfeld); cf. L. *būgillo*, (perhaps) bugle. ¶ We find AF. *bucle* as a plant-name, Wright's Voc. i. 162 (spelt *bugle* in MS. Camb. Gg. 1. 1); this suggests Late L. *būcula*, 'pascua,' in Ducange; as if 'pasture-flower.'

BUGLOSS, a plant. (F. – L. – Gk.) Mentioned in Sir T. Elyot's Castle of Helth, b. iii. ch. 12; p. 70. – F. *buglosse.* – L. *būglōssa*; also *būglōssus.* – Gk. βούγλωσσος, ox-tongue; from the shape and roughness of the leaves. – Gk. βοῦ-ς, ox; γλῶσσ-α, tongue. See **Cow** (1).

BUILD, to construct a house. (E.) ME. *bulden*, Layamon, 2656; *bilden*, Coventry Mysteries, p. 20; also *buylden*, P. Plowman, B. xii. 228; and *belden*, P. Plowman, Crede, 706. The spellings *bielde*, *beelde*, in Wyclif's Bible, Gen. xi. 8, 3 Kings, xi. 7, show that the ME. vowel was long; and, in fact, *ui* is the regular representative (in Southern E. of the 13th c.) of AS. *ȳ*. The vowel was again shortened by the influence of the final dentals in *builded* and *built*, pt. t. and pp. – Late AS. *byldan*, lengthened to *bȳldan* in Norman pronunciation (cf. E. *mild* from AS. *mild*, &c.). – AS. *bold*, a dwelling; with regular mutation from *o* (Teut. *u*) to *y*. 'Pē wes bold gebyld,' for thee was a dwelling built; The Grave (in Thorpe, Analecta, p. 142). Sievers shows that *bold* is for *bol-þ-*, altered form of *boþ-l* >*botl*, a dwelling; from Teut. *bu-þlo-* (*bu-þro-*); from Teut. *bu-*, weaker grade of *bū-* in *būan*, to dwell, and Idg. suffix *-tro*. Closely allied to **Booth**, q.v. ¶ The vowel was still long in the 16th century. We find *beelde* rhyming with *feelde* (field) in Higgins, Mirror for Magistrates, Severus, st. 21.

BULB, a round root, &c. (F. – L. – Gk.) Not in early use. In Holland's Plutarch, p. 577; and *bulbous* is in Holland's Pliny, bk. xix. c. 4; vol. ii. p. 13; also *bulbes* in the same, p. 18 (last line). – F. *bulbe.* – L. *bulbus.* – Gk. βολβός, a bulbous root, an onion. Der. *bulb*, verb; *bulb-ed*, *bulb-ous.*

BULBUL, a nightingale. (Pers.) In Byron, Bride of Abydos,

i. 10. – Pers. *bulbul*, a bird with a melodious voice, resembling the nightingale. Of imitative origin: *bul-bul.*

BULGE, to swell out. (F. – C.) This word, in the sense of 'to swell out,' is rare except in modern writers. The earlier sense was to stave in the *bulge* (or *bilge*), i.e. the bottom of a ship. Blount has: '*Bulged* (or *Bilged*), a Sea-Term: a ship is said to be *bulged* when she strikes on a rock, anchor, or the like,' &c. From E. *bulge*, (1) a wallet, obs.; (2) a hump, obs.; (3) a protuberance; (4) the bottom of a ship's hull. – OF. *boulge*, *bouge*, f., a budget, wallet, Cot.; m. a swelling, boss, belly, Cot. – L. *bulga*, a skin-bag (Gaulish). See **Budget** and **Belly**. Der. *bilge*, sb., *bilge-water.* ¶ The F. change of gender raises a difficulty; but see Scheler.

BULK (1), magnitude, size. (Scand.) ME. *bolke*, a heap, Prompt. Parv. p. 43. – Icel. *būlki*, a heap (earlier *bulki*, Noreen, § 196); *būlkast*, to be bulky; Dan. *bulk*, a lump, clod; *bulket*, lumpy; Swed. dial. *bullk*, a knob, bunch; *bullkug*, bunchy, protuberant (Rietz); MSwed. *bolk*, a heap (Ihre); Norw. *bulk*, a boss. β. The Swed. dial. words are connected with Swed. dial. *buljna*, to bulge; Swed. *bulna*, to swell. The original idea in *bulk* is 'a swelling;' cf. the adj. *bulky*. See **Bolled**. Der. *bulk-y*, *bulk-i-ness.*

BULK (2), the trunk of the body. (Du.) Used by Shak. Hamlet, ii. 1. 95. – MDu. *bulcke*, thorax; Kilian. (Prob. confused with Icel. *būkr*, the trunk of the body; Swed. *buk*, the belly; Dan. *bug*, the belly; Du. *buik*, G. *bauch*, the belly.) Perhaps allied to **Bulk** (1).

BULK (3), a stall of a shop, a projecting frame for the display of goods. (Scand.) In Shak. Cor. ii. 1. 226; Oth. v. 1. 1. Halliwell has: '*Bulk*, the stall of a shop;' with references. He also notes that the Lincolnshire *bulkar* means (1) a beam; and (2) the front of a butcher's shop where meat is laid. – Dan. dial. *bulk*, a half-wall, a partition; MDan. *bulk*, a balk (Kalkar); NFries. *bulk*, balk. A form, with the weak grade (*u*), parallel to E. *balk*, Icel. *bālkr*, a beam, rafter, also a partition. The native E. word *balk* generally means a rafter, and does not give the right vowel. Florio translates the Ital. *balco* or *balcone* (from OHG. *balcho*) as 'the bulk or stall of a shop.'

BULK-HEAD, a partition in a ship made with boards, forming apartments. (Scand. *and* E.) Nautical. Spelt *bulke-hedde* in 1496; Naval Accounts, ed. Oppenheim, p. 168. Had it been of native origin, the form would have been *balk-head*, from *balk*, a beam. The change of vowel points to the MDan. *bulk* (above).

BULL (1), a male bovine quadruped. (E.) ME. *bole*, *bule*, Chaucer, C. T. 2141 (A 2139); *bule*, Ormulum, 990. Not found in AS., though occurring in the Ormulum, and in Layamon in comp. *bule-hude*, bull-hide; yet the dimin. *bulluc*, a bull-ock, little bull, really occurs (Bosworth); and AS. *Bulan*, as if from a noun *bula*, occurs in place-names (Kemble's Index). Cf. EFries. *bulle.* + MDu. *bolle*, a bull (Kilian); Du. *bul*; Icel. *boli*, a bull; Westphal. and G. *bulle*; Lith. *bullus*. Prob. 'the bellower;' from **bul-*, weak grade of AS. *bellan*, to bellow. Cf. MHG. *bullen*, to roar. See **Bellow**. Der. *bull-dog*, *bull-finch*, &c.; dimin. *bull-ock*, AS. *bulluc.*

BULL (2), a papal edict. (L.) In early use. ME. *bulle*, a papal bull; P. Plowman, B. prol. 69; Rob. of Glouc. p. 473; l. 9719. – L. *bulla*, a stud, knob; later, a leaden seal, such as was affixed to an edict; hence the name was transferred to the edict itself. See **Bowl** (1). Der. From the same source: *bull-et*, q. v., *bull-et-in*, q. v. ¶ The use of *bull* in the sense of 'blunder' is a different word; from OF. *boler*, *bouler*, to deceive (Godefroy).

BULLACE, wild plum. (F. – L.) Bacon has the pl. *bullises*; Essay on Gardens. '*Bolas* frute, pepulum;' and '*Bolas* tre, pepulus;' Prompt. Parv. p. 42; *bolás* (accented on *a*), Rom. Rose, 1377. – OF. *belóce*, *blosse*, a bullace (Supp. to Godefroy); also written *pelosse* (pl. *pelosses*) in Cotgrave. – Romanic type **pilottja*, for Late L. **pilottea*, lit. 'pellet-like.' – Late L. *pilota*, a pellet, ball. – L. *pila*, a ball. See **Pellet**, and **Pill** (1). Notes on E. Etym. p. 23. β. The OF. *beloce*, *belloce*, 'espèce de prunes,' is given by Roquefort; and Cotgrave has: '*Bellocier*, a bullace-tree, or wilde plum-tree.' Cf. Breton *bolos* (from OF. *beloce*), also *polos* (from OF. **peloce*, *plosse*; Gael. *bulaistear*, from ME. *bolas-tre*, a bullace-tree. Also Walloon *bilok*, *bulok*, a bullace; from North F. Puitspelu (on the pâtois of Lyons) has: '*Pelossi*, *pelosse*, OF. *beloce*, Suisse *belossa*, Norm. *beloche*, Jura *pelosse*, *pelousse*,' all meaning 'bullace.'

BULLET, a ball for a gun. (F. – L.) In Shak. K. John, ii. 227, 412. – F. *boulet*, 'a bullet;' Cot. A dimin. of F. *boule*, a ball. – L. *bulla*, a stud, knob; a bubble. See **Bull** (2).

BULLETIN, a brief public announcement. (F. – Ital. – L.) Burke speaks of 'the pithy and sententious brevity of these *bulletins*;' Appeal from the New to the Old Whigs (R.) – F. *bulletin*, 'a bill, ticket, a billet in a lottery;' Cot. – Ital. *bulletino*, a safe conduct, pass, ticket. Formed, with the dimin. suffix *-ino*, from *bulletta*, a passport, a lottery-ticket; which again is formed, with the dimin. suffix *-etta*, from *bulla*, a seal, a pope's letter. – L. *bulla*, a seal; later, a pope's letter. See **Bull** (2).

BULLION, uncoined metal. (F. – L.) Spelt *bolion* in Arnold's Chron., ed. 1811, p. 229 ; *bollyon* in 1586, in Orig. Letters, ed. Ellis, ii. 305. – F. *bouillon*, a boiling ; also a certain measure or weight (Godefroy, and Supp.). – Late L. *bulliōnem*, acc. of *bullio*, a mass of gold or silver ; also written *bulliōna*. – L. *bullīre*, to boil ; see **Boil** (1). For the history, see N. E. D. ¶ The mod. F. word is *billon* ; which Littré derives from F. *bille*, a log ; and F. *billon* seems to have been confused to some extent with the E. word.

BULLY, a noisy rough fellow ; to bluster. (Du.) Shak. has *bully* for 'a brisk dashing fellow ;' Merry Wives, i. 3. 6, 11, &c. ; Schmidt. Also *bully-rook* in a similar sense, Merry Wives, i. 3. 2 ; ii. 1. 200. But the earliest sense was 'sweet-heart ;' see N.E.D. Cf. Hen. V, iv. 1. 48. Apparently from Du. *boel*, a lover ; borrowed from G. – MHG. *buole*, a lover ; G. *buhle*. The later sense was a swaggering gallant ; lastly, a tyrannical coward who intimidates the weak. Perhaps influenced by Du. *bul*, a bull, also a clown, insolent fellow ; Du. *bulderen*, Low G. *bullern*, to bluster.

BULRUSH, a tall rush. (E.) ME. *bolroysche*, Voc. 786. 40 ; *bulrysche*, Prompt. Parv., p. 244, col. 2. Perhaps from its stout stem ; cf. Shetland *bulwand*, a bulrush. – Dan. *bul*, stem, trunk ; and E. *rush*. See **Bole** and **Rush** (2) ; also **Bulwark** (below). β. Or *bull* may mean 'large,' with reference to a bull ; cf. *bull-daisy*, &c. (Britten.)

BULWARK, a rampart. (Scand.) In Shak. Hamlet, iii. 4. 38. 'Fagottes for *bolewerckes* :' Excerpta Historica, p. 52 (anno 1419) ; nearly the earliest quotation known. ' Barbycans and also *bulworkes* huge ;' Lydgate, Siege of Troy, b. ii. ch. 11 ; ed. 1555, fol. F 5, col. 2. – MDan. *bulvirke*, a bulwark ; Swed. *bolverk*. Cf. Du. *bolwerk*, whence G. *bollwerk*. Corrupted in F. to *boulevarde*, from the Du. or G. form. Kilian explains *bol-werck*, or *block-werck* by 'propugnaculum, agger, vallum ;' showing that *bol* is equivalent to *block*, i.e. a log of wood. [The Dan. *bulværk* is commonly said to have been borrowed from Du. ; but Kalkar gives MDan. *bulvirke* as known in 1461, and the Scand. languages explain the word better ; the Du. *bol* is not commonly used for ' log,' nor is G. *böhle* anything more than 'a board, plank.'] β. From Dan. *bul*, a stem, stump, log of a tree ; MDan. *virke*, work ; cf. Icel. *bulr*, *bolr*, the bole or trunk of a tree, and *virki*, work. γ. Thus the word stands for *bole-work*, and means a fort made of the stumps of felled trees. See **Bole**. ¶ The G. *bollwerk*, as formerly used in the sense of 'mangonel,' is a different word ; from MHG. *boln*, to throw ; see Kluge.

BUM, buttocks. (E.) Used by Shak. Mids. Nt. Dr. ii. 1. 53. A word probably meaning 'protuberance,' and connected with such words as *bump*, a swelling, *bumb*, a pimple (Florio, s. v. *quosi*).

BUM-BAILIFF, an under bailiff. (E. *and* F.) In Shak. Twelfth Nt. iii. 4. 194. Blackstone (bk. i. c. 9) says it is a corruption of *bound-bailiff*, which is a guess ; for there is no such word. β. Todd quotes from a Tract at the end of Fulke's Defence of the English translations of the Bible, 1583, p. 33 : 'These quarrels .. are more meet for the *bum-courts* than for the schools of divinity. In this saying, if the term of bumcourts seem too light, I yield unto the censure of grave and godly men.' He also quotes the expression ' constables, tithing-men, bailiffs, *bumme* or shoulder-marshals ' from Gayton's Notes on Don Quixote, bk. ii. c. 2. He accordingly suggests that the term arose from the bailiff or pursuer catching a man ' by the hinder part of his garment ;' and he is probably right.

BUMBLE-BEE, a bee that hums. (E.) The verb *bumble* is a frequentative of *boom*. Cf. MDu. *bommelen*, to buzz, hum (Oudemans) ; Bremen *bummeln*, to sound ; EFries. *bummen*, to resound ; Du. *bommen*, to sound hollow (like an empty barrel). See **Boom** (1) and **Bump** (2). ☞ As both *boom* and *hum* signify 'to buzz,' the insect is called, indifferently, a *bumble-bee* or a *humble-bee*.

BUMBOAT, a boat used for taking out provisions to a ship. (E.) From *bum* and *boat* ; for the orig. sense was a scavenger's boat, employed to remove 'filth' from ships lying in the Thames, as prescribed by the Trinity House Bye Laws of 1685. See N. E. D.

BUMP (1), to thump, beat ; a blow, bunch, knob. (E.) Cotgrave has : '*Adot*, a blow, *bumpe*, or thump ;' also : '*Baculer*, to *bump* .. with a bat.' Shak. has *bump*, a knob, Rom. i. 3. 53. Of imitative origin ; cf. MDan. *bumpe*, to strike with the fist. So also W. *pwmp*, a round mass, a lump ; *pwmpio*, to thump, bang. ¶ In this case, and some other similar ones, the original word is the verb, signifying ' to strike ;' next, the sb. signifying ' blow ;' and lastly, the visible effect of the blow, the ' bump' raised by it. Allied to **Bunch**, q.v.

BUMP (2), to make a noise like a bittern. (E.) 'And as a bittour *bumps* within a reed :' Dryden, Wife of Bath's Tale, l. 194 ; where Chaucer has *bumbleth*, C. T. 6554 (D 972). Imitative ; a variant of **Boom** (1) ; and cf. **Bumblebee**. So also W. *bwmp*, a hollow sound ; *aderyn y bwmp*, a bittern ; Gk. βόμβος, a humming, buzzing.

BUMPER, a full glass, esp. when drunk as a toast. (E.) Dryden has *bumpers* in his Epistle to Sir G. Etherege, l. 46. Apparently

suggested by *bump*, a swelling, with the notion of *fulness*, so that a *bumper* generally means 'a glass filled to the brim.' Cf. *thumping*, with the sense of ' large.'

BUMPKIN, a thick-headed fellow. (Du.) Used by Dryden, who talks of ' the country *bumpkin*,' Juvenal, Sat. 3, l. 295. The index to Cotgrave says that the F. for *bumkin* is *chicambault* ; and Cot. has : ' *Chicambault*, m. The luffe-block, a long and thick piece of wood, whereunto the fore-saile and sprit-saile are fastened, when a ship goes by the wind.' I think it probable that *bumkin* (then pronounced nearly as *boomkin*) is the dimin. of *boom*, formed by adding to *boom* (a Dutch word) the Dutch dimin. ending *-ken* ; so that the form *boomken*, explained by Hexham as ' a little tree,' might also signify 'a small boom,' or ' luff-block ;' and metaphorically, a blockhead, a wooden-pated fellow ; perhaps originally a piece of nautical slang. The Dutch suffix *-ken* is hardly used now, but was once in use freely, particularly in Brabant ; see Ten Kate, ii. 73 ; it answers exactly to the E. suffix *-kin*, which took its place.

BUN, a sort of cake. (F. – Scand.) Skelton has *bun* in the sense of a kind of loaf given to horses ; ed. Dyce, i. 15. ME. *bunne*, Prompt. Parv. – O. prov. F. *bugne*, a name given at Lyons to a kind of fritters (Burguy, Puitspelu) ; a variation of F. *bigne*, a swelling rising from a blow (Burguy). β. These F. words are represented by the mod. F. dimin. *beignet*, a fritter ; the connexion is established by Cotgrave, who gives the dimin. forms as *bugnet* and *bignet*, with this explanation : ' *Bignets*, little round loaves, or lumps made of fine meale, oile, or butter, and raisons ; buns, Lenten loaves ; also, flat fritters made like small pancakes.' So also Minsheu's Span. Dict. has : ' *buñuelos*, pancakes, cobloaves, buns.' And Torriano has Ital. ' *bugna*, *bugno*, *bugnone*, any round knob or bunch, a bile or blain.' The word probably came to us from the S. of France ; cf. Prov. *bougno*, a swelling, *bougneto*, also *buegno*, a fritter. See Notes on E. Etymol. p. 25. γ. Perhaps of Scandinavian origin ; see **Bunion**.

BUNCH, a knob, a cluster. (E.?) ME. *bunche*, Debate of the Body and Soul, Vernon MS., l. 344 ; where the copy printed in Mätzner has *bulche*, l. 370. From ME. *bunchen*, to beat ; P. Plowman, A. prol. 71 ; B. prol. 74. Of imitative origin ; a parallel formation to **Bump** ; cf. Low G. *bunk*, a bone that sticks out, a bump ; Du. *bonk*, a mass of flesh. And cf. **Bunk, Bungle**. β. The notion of ' bunching out' is due to ' striking,' as in other cases, the swelling being caused by the blow ; see **Bump** (1). Cf. Du. *bonken*, to beat, belabour. Der. *bunch-y*.

BUNDLE, something bound up, a package. (E.) ME. *bundel* (ill-spelt *bundelia*), Prompt. Parv. p. 55. A dimin., by adding suffix *-el*, of *bund*, a bundle, a thing bound up ; the plural *bunda*, bundles, occurs as a gloss of L. *fasciculos* in the Lind. MS. in Matt. xiii. 30. + Du. *bondel*, a bundle ; G. *bündel*, a dimin. of *bund*, a bundle, bunch, truss. From *bund-*, weak grade of AS. *bindan*, to bind. See **Bind**.

BUNG, a plug for a hole in a cask. (Du. – L.) ME. *bunge*, Prompt. Parv. p. 55. ' *Bung* of a tonne or pype, *bondel* ;' Palsgrave. – MDu. *bonge*, ' the bung of a barrill,' Hexham ; a dialectal variant of MDu. **bonde*, whence MDu. *bonne*, a bung, stopple, for which Oudemans gives two quotations ; hence mod. Du. *bom*, a bung (Franck). Hence also F. *bonde*, of which Palsgrave has the dimin. *bondel*, cited above. Cotgrave explains *bonde* by ' a bung or stopple ; also, a sluice, a floodgate.' β. This MDu. **bonde* (preserved in F. *bonde*) is cognate with Alsatian *bunde*, Swiss *punt* (see Weigand, s. v. *Spund*, ii. 785). – L. *puncta*, an orifice ; orig. fem. of *punctus*, pp. of *pungere*, to prick. Cf. W. *bwng*, an orifice, also a bung ; from E. *bung*, which also means 'bung-hole.' See G. **Spund**, a bung, orifice, in Kluge ; in which the *s* (from F. *es-*, L. *ex*) was prefixed.

BUNGALOW, a Bengal thatched house. (Hind.) Spelt *bunglo*, Murphy, The Upholsterer, ii. 3 (1758). In Rich. Pers. Dict., p. 293, we find : ' Pers. *bangalah*, of or belonging to Bengal ; a bungalow.' From the name *Bengal*. Forbes gives Hind. *banglā*, m. a kind of thatched house (p. 88) ; Wilson gives the Bengáli form as *bānglā* (p. 59).

BUNGLE, to mend clumsily. (Scand.) Shak. has *bungle*, Hen. V, ii. 2. 115 ; Sir T. More has *bungler*, Works, p. 1089 c. Prob. from *bung-*, weak grade of an old Teut. str. vb. **bing-an-*, to strike, pt. t. **bang* ; cf. MDu. *bing-el*, 'a cudgill,' Hexham ; prov. E. *bang*, a strong pole, and *bang*, to beat ; G. *bengel*, a cudgel ; see EFries. *bingeln* in Koolman. β. This is rendered probable by comparison with Swed. dial. *bangla*, to work ineffectually (Rietz) ; Norw. *bunka*, to work by fits and starts (Ross). Ihre gives MSwed. *bunga*, to strike, and Rietz gives *bonka* and *bunka* as variants of Swed. dial. *banka*, to strike. See **Bang**. Der. *bungl-er*.

BUNION, a painful swelling on the foot. (Ital. – Teut.) Not in early use. Rich. quotes *bunians* from Rowe's Imitations of Horace, bk. iii. ode 9 ; written, perhaps, about A. D. 1718 ; the footnote (in Eng. Poets, ix. 472) says that it was ' Jacob's term for his corns,' so that we owe the word to J. Tonson, the book-seller, who may very well have known the Ital. form. – Ital. *bugnone*, *bugno*, any round knob or bunch, a boil or blain; cf. OF. *bugne, bune, buigne*, a swelling (Burguy); F. *bigne*, a bump, knob, rising, or swelling after a knock (Cotgrave).—Icel. *bunga*, an elevation, convexity; Norw. *bunga*, a round swelling, a bump (Ross); OHG. *bungo*, a lump (cited by Diez). Allied to Skt. *bahu-s*, thick, Gk. παχύς; Brugmann, Kurze Vergl. Gram. § 194. β. The prov. Eng. *bunny*, a swelling after a blow, in Forby's East-Anglian Dialect, is from the OF. *bugne*. See **Bun**. ¶ The Ital. *bugnone* is from Ital. *bugno*, the same as the OF. *bugne*; with the addition of the Ital. augmentative suffix -*one*.

BUNK, a wooden case or box, serving for a seat by day and a bed by night; one of a series of berths arranged in tiers. (Scand.) A nautical term; and to be compared with the MSwed. *bunke*, which Ihre defines as 'tabulatum navis, quo cæli injuriæ defenduntur a vectoribus et mercibus.' He adds a quotation, viz. 'Gretter giorde sier grof under *bunka*' = Gretter made for himself a bed under the boarding or planking [if that be the right rendering of 'sub tabulato']. The ordinary sense of MSwed. *bunke* is a pile, a heap, orig. something prominent; Icel. *bunki*; allied to E. *bunch*. Cf. M Dan. *bunke*, room for cargo.

BUNT, the belly or hollow of a sail; a nautical term. (Scand.— MHG.) '*Bunt*, the hollowness allowed in making sails;' Coles (1684). Also in Kersey's Dict. a. Wedgwood explains it from Dan. *bundt*, Swed. *bunt*, a bundle, a bunch; and so Webster; cf. EFries. *bund, bunt*, a bundle, packing. If so, the root is the verb to *bind*. Cf. Norw. *bunta*, to pack, pack tight (Ross). From MHG. *bunt*, a bundle.—OHG. *bunt-*, weak grade of *bintan*, to bind. β. But the sense agrees better with that of a different Scand. word, answering to E. *bow*, a bend; cf. Dan. *bug*, a belly; *bug paa Seil*, a bunt; *buggaarding*, a bunt-line; *bug-line*, bowline; *bug-spryd*, bowsprit; *bugne*, to bend; *de bugnende Seil*, the bellying sails or canvas; Swed. *buk på ett segel*, the bunt of a sail; *bugning*, flexure.

BUNTING (1), the name of a bird. (Scand. ?) ME. *bunting, bunting*; also *buntyle*, badly written for *buntel*. '*Buntynge*, byrde, *pratellus*;' Prompt. Parv. p. 56. 'A *bounting*;' Lyric Poems, ed. Wright, p. 40. 'Hic pratellus, a *buntyle*;' Wright's Vocab. i. 221. Cf. Lowland Scotch *buntlin*, a bunting. Origin unknown. As the bird has 'a clumsy figure' (Newton), we may compare Lowl. Sc. *buntin*, short and thick, plump, prov. E. *bunty*, short and stout; perhaps from Norw. *bunta*, stout and compact (Ross).

BUNTING (2), a thin woollen stuff, of which ships' flags are made. (E.?) In Johnson's Dict.; and first found in 1742 (N.E.D.). [The suggestion of a connexion with High G. *bunt*, variegated, is unlikely, though the word is now found in Dutch as *bont*.] Mr. Wedgwood says: 'To *bunt* in Somerset is to bolt meal, whence *bunting*, bolting-cloth, the loose open cloth used for sifting flour, and now more generally known as the material of which flags are made.' And he has noted that F. *étamine* means (1) a bolting-cloth, (2) bunting. The E. D. D. has *bunt*, to sift, to bolt, and *bunting*, a kind of cloth of which sieves are made (which seems decisive). The verb *bunt*, to bolt flour, is ME. *bonten*, to sift, and occurs in the Ayenbite of Inwyt, p. 93.

BUOY, a floating piece of wood fastened down. (Du.—L.) It occurs (spelt *bwoy*) in Hakluyt's Voyages, vol. iii. p. 411. Spelt *boy* in Palsgrave. Borrowed, as many sea-terms are, from the Dutch.—Du. *boei*, a buoy; also, a shackle, fetter. [The same word as OF. *boie, buie*, a fetter; Godefroy.]—Late L. *boia*, a fetter, a clog. ['Raynouard, Lex. Rom. ii. 232, quotes "jubet compedibus constringi, quos rustica lingua *boias* vocat." Plautus has it in a pun, Capt. iv. 2. 109, ". . Boius est; *boiam* terit;"' note to Vie de Seint Auban, l. 680, ed. Atkinson; q. v.]—L. *boiæ*, pl. a collar for the neck, orig. made of leather. Sometimes derived from L. *bōs*, an ox, and said to have meant 'a collar made of leather;' like Gk. βοεύς, βόειος from βοῦς. ¶ A *buoy* is so called because chained to its place, like a clog chained to a prisoner's leg. Cf. 'In presoune, fetterit with *boyis*, sittand;' Barbour's Bruce, ed. Skeat, x. 763. The mod. F. *bouée*, a buoy, is a modification of MF. *boyée*, 'a boy,' in Palsgrave, and means 'chained down,' being the f. pp. of a verb *boier*, to chain. Der. *buoy-ant* (Span. *boyante*); *buoy-anc-y*.

BUR, BURDOCK; see **Burr**.

BURBOT, a fish of the genus *Lota*. (F.—L.—Gk.) The pl. *borbottus* occurs in Reliq. Antiquæ, i. 85 (ab. 1475).—F. *bourbotte* (also *barbote*). —F. *bourbetter*, 'to wallow in mud;' Cot.—F. *bourbe*, mud.—Late L. *borba*, mud (Ducange).—Gk. βόρβορος, mud.

BURDEN (1), **BURTHEN**, a load carried. (E.) ME. *birþene*, Havelok, 807; altered to *birden* by Norman influence; spelt *birdin* in Cursor Mundi, 6830 (Cotton MS.). AS. *byrðen*, a load (Grein). +OSax. *burðinnia*. Teut. type *burthinnja*, extension of *bur-th-* with suffix -*innja*. Allied to Icel. *byrðr, byrði*; Swed. *börda*; Dan. *byrde*; Goth. *baurthei*; OHG. *burdi, burdin*; MHG. and G. *bürde*. All from Teut. *bur-*, weak grade of *ber-an-*, to bear; with varying suffixes. Further allied to Gk. φόρτος, a burden.—√BHER, to bear. See **Bear**. Der. *burden-some*.

BURDEN (2), the refrain of a song. (F.—Late L.) The same word as *bourdon*, the drone of a bagpipe or the bass in music. ME. *burdoun*,

Chaucer, Prol. 673.—F. *bourdon*, 'a drone or dorre-bee; also, the humming or buzzing of bees; also, the drone of a bagpipe;' Cot.— Late L. *burdōnem*, acc. of *burdo*, a drone or non-working bee, which is probably an imitative word, from the buzzing sound made by the insect; *bur-* being another form of *buzz*, q. v.; cf. Lowl. Sc. *birr*, to whiz. ¶ The ME. *bourdon* also means a pilgrim's staff, which is another meaning of the F. *bourdon*. The Late L. *burdo* also means (1) an ass, mule, (2) a long organ-pipe. Diez thinks the 'organ-pipe' was so named from resembling a 'staff,' which he derives from *burdo* in the sense of 'mule.' But *burdo*, an ass, may be a distinct word.

BURDOCK; see **Burr**.

BUREAU, an office for business. (F.—L.—Gk. ?) Used by Swift and Burke; see Richardson.—F. *bureau*, a desk, writing-table, so called because covered with baize. Cotgrave has: '*Bureau*, a thick and course cloath, of a brown russet or darke-mingled colour; also, the table that's within a court of audit or of audience (belike, because it is usually covered with a carpet of that cloth); also the court itself.' And see Brachet, who quotes from Boileau, *vêtu de simple bureau*.— OF. *burel*, coarse woollen stuff, russet-coloured.—OF. *buire* (F. *bure*), reddish-brown.—L. *burrus*, fiery-red (Fick, ii. 154).—Gk. πυρρός, flame-coloured.—Gk. πῦρ, fire. See **Fire**. ¶ Chaucer has '*borel* men,' i.e. men roughly clad, men of small account (C.T. B 3145); where *borel* is from the OF. *burel* above. Der. *bureau-cracy*; see **Aristocracy**.

BURGANET, BURGONET, a helmet. (F.—Late L.) See Shak. Ant. and Cleop. i. 5. 24.—F. *bourguignotte*, 'a *Burganet*, Hufkin, or Spanish Murrion' [morion, helmet]; Cot. So called because first used by the Burgundians.—F. *Bourgogne*, Burgundy.—Late L. *Burgundia*; cf. '*Bourguignon*, a Burgonian, one of Burgundy;' Cot. β. So, in Spanish, we have *borgoñota*, a sort of helmet; *a la Burgoñota*, after the Burgundy fashion; *Borgoña*, Burgundy wine. And, in Italian, *borgognone, borgognotta*, a burganet, helmet.

BURGEON, a bud; to bud. (F.—Teut.) ME. *borioune* (printed *borjoune*), a bud; Arthur and Merlin, p. 65 (Halliwell's Dict.); *burion* (printed *burjon*), Cursor Mundi, 10735. '*Gramino*, to *borioune* (printed *borionne*) or kyrnell;' Prompt. Parv. p. 276, note 3.—F. *bourgeon*, a young bud; Cot.; OF. *borion* = *borjon* (Hatzfeld). β. Diez cites a shorter form in the Languedoc *boure*, a bud, the eye of a shoot (mod. Prov. *bourro, bouro*, a bud); and he supposes the word to have been formed from the MHG. *buren*, OHG. *purjan*, to raise, push up. If so, we are at once led to MHG. *bor*, OHG. *por*, an elevation, whence is formed the word *in-por*, upwards, in common use as G. *empor*; cf. G. *empörung*, an insurrection, i.e. a breaking forth. Allied to Du. *beuren*, to lift up. From Teut. *bur-*, weak grade of *beran-*, to bear.

BURGESS, a citizen. (F.—MHG.) ME. *burgeys*, Chaucer, Prol. 369; Havelok, 1328; pl. *burgeises*, Ancren Riwle, p. 168.—OF. *burgeis*, a citizen.—Late L. *burgensis*, adj., belonging to a city.—Late L. *burgus*, a small fort (Vegetius).—MHG. *burc*, a fort (G. *burg*); cognate with E. *borough*. See **Borough**.

BURGHER, a citizen. (Du.) In Gascoigne, Fruites of Warre, st. 14.—Du. *burger*, a citizen.—Du. *burg*, a city; cognate with E. *borough*. See **Borough**.

BURGLAR, a housebreaker, thief. (AF.—E.) Dogberry misuses *burglary*, Much Ado, iv. 2. 52. Florio [ed. 1680, *not in* ed. 1611] interprets Ital. *grancelli* by 'roguing beggars, *bourglairs*.' *Burglar* is an AF. law term; spelt *burgler* in Fitzherbert's Graunde Abridgement, 268 b; *burglour* in a tr. of Fitzherbert's New Bk. Justyces, 125 b. The Late L. forms are *burgulator, burglator, burgator*, all with the sense of house-breaker. All are founded on AS. *burh*, a borough, whence ME. *burgh-breche*, 'breach of a borough.' See N.E.D. Der. *burglar-y*, *burglar-i-ous*.

BURGOMASTER, a chief magistrate of a town. (Du.) In 1 Hen. IV, ii. 1. 84. 'Euery of the foresayd cities sent one of their *burgomasters* vnto the towne of Hage in Holland;' Hakluyt, Voyages, i. 157.—Du. *burgemeester*, a burgomaster; whence it has been corrupted by assimilating *burge-* to *burgo-*, for Late L. *burgus*, a town (Latinised form of *borough* or *burgh*), whilst *meester* is spelt in the E. fashion.—Du. *burg*, a borough, cognate with E. *borough*, q. v.; and *meester*, a master (OF. *meistre*), for which see **Master**.

BURGONET, a helmet; see **Burganet**.

BURIAL, a grave, the act of burying. (E.) ME. *buriel*, a grave; Trevisa, ii. 27; *biriel*, a tomb, Wycl. Matt. xxvii. 60. But the form is corrupt; the older Eng. has *buriels*, which is a *singular*, not a *plural* substantive, in spite of its apparent plural form. '*Beryels*, sepulchrum;' Wright's Vocab. i. 178. 'An *buryels*,' i.e. a tomb; Rob. of Glouc., p. 204; l. 4184. AS. *byrgels*, a sepulchre; Gen. xxiii. 9; the commoner form being *byrgen*, Gen. xxiii. 3. Formed, with suffix -*els*, from AS. *byrg-an*, to bury. See **Bury**. ¶ Other examples of the suffix -*els* or -*else* occur in AS.; e.g. *fetels*, a bag, Josh. ix. 4; *rædelse*, a riddle, Numb. xii. 8. The suffix -*al* in E. *buri-al* is due to association with *funer-al*, &c.

BURIN, an engraver's tool. (F. — Ital. — G.) In Bailey, vol. ii. (1731). Borrowed from F. *burin*; a word borrowed from Ital. *borino* (Brachet). Probably formed from MHG. *boren* (OHG. *porōn*, G. *bohren*), to bore; cognate with E. *bore*. See **Bore** (1).

BURKE, to murder by suffocation, to stifle. (E.) From the name of *Burke*, an Irishman who committed murders by suffocation; executed at Edinburgh, Jan. 28, 1829. The name *Burke* (L. *de Burgo*) is due to an AF. pronunciation of AS. *burh*, a borough.

BURL, to pick knots and loose threads from cloth; in cloth-making. (F. — Late L.) To *burl* is to pick off *burls* or knots in cloth, the word being properly a sb. Halliwell has: '*Burle*, a knot, or bump; see Topsell's Hist. Beasts, p. 250 [220, ed. 1658]. Also, to take away the knots or impure parts from wool or cloth. "*Desquamare vestes*, to burle clothe;" Elyot. Cf. Herrick's Works, ii. 15.' ME. *burle*, a knot in cloth; see Prompt. Parv. p. 56. — OF. *bourle*, a tuft of wool, dimin. of *bourre* (Godefroy); cf. Prov. F. *bouril*, *bourril*, a flock or end of thread which disfigures cloth, cited by Mr. Wedgwood as a Languedoc word; spelt *bourri*, *bourril* in Mistral. — F. *bourre*, expl. by Cotgrave as 'flocks, or locks of wool, hair, &c. serving to stuff saddles, balls, and such like things.' — Late L. *burra*, a woollen pad (Ducange); cf. L. *burræ*, trifles; Late L. *reburrus*, rough.

BURLESQUE, comic, ironical. (F. — Ital. — L.) Dryden speaks of 'the dull *burlesque*;' Art of Poetry, canto i. l. 81. It is properly an adjective, as in Blount's Gloss. — F. *burlesque*, introd. in 16th cent. from the Ital. (Brachet). — Ital. *burlesco*, ludicrous. — Ital. *burla*, a trick, waggery, fun, banter. β. Diez suggests that *burla* is a dimin. from L. *burra*, used by Ausonius in the sense of a jest, though the proper sense is rough hair. This supposition seems to explain also the Span. *borla*, a tassel, tuft, as compared with Span. *borra*, goat's hair. See **Burl.**

BURLY, large, corpulent, huge. (E.) ME. *burely*, Perceval, 269; *borlic*, large, ample, Bestiary, 605; *burliche*, Morte Arthur, ed. Brock, 586, 2190. The same as Shetland *boorly*, stout; Prov. E. *bowerly*, comely, well made, stout. Cf. 'great and *bowerly* images,' in Udall's tr. of Erasmus' Apophthegmes (1542), p. 184 b. This shows clearly that the AS. form must have been *būr-līc*, in which the *u* was shortened before *rl*, as in mod. E. *Dunstan*, AS. *Dūn-stān*. Thus the orig. sense was 'suitable for a bower' or lady's chamber; hence handsome, goodly, &c. Cf. ME. *burmaiden*, a 'bower-maid.' (Athenæum, Mar. 24, 1894, p. 250; Notes on E. Etym. p. 26.) See **Bower.**

BURN (1), to set on fire. (E.) ME. *bernen*, Ancren Riwle, p. 306; allied to *brennen*, Chaucer, C. T. 2333 (A 2331). There are two types. α. intrans. AS. *byrnan*, to burn; Grein, i. 153; also *beornan*, p. 109; a strong verb, pt. t. *bearn*, *bran*, pp. *bornen*.+OIcel. *brinna*; Goth. *brinnan*; Teut. type *brenn-an-*; cf. AS. *bryn-e*, flame. β. trans. AS. *bærnan*, weak verb (Grein, i. 77).+Icel. *brenna*, Dan. *brænde*, Swed. *bränna*; G. *brennen*; Teut. type *brannjan-*, causal of the former.

BURN (2), a brook. See **Bourn** (2).

BURNET, a plant. (F. — OHG.) A name given chiefly to the *Poterium Sanguisorba* and *Sanguisorba officinalis*; see E.D.S. Plant-Names, and Prior. Prior says the name was given to the *Poterium* because of its brown flowers. The flowers of the *Sanguisorba* are of a deep purple-brown colour. The word occurs in MS. Sloane 2457, fol. 6 (see Halliwell) as synonymous with *pimpernel*, but Mr. Britten remarks that the *poterium* is meant. It also occurs in Late L. as *burneta*, Reliq. Antiq. i. 37, so that it is doubtless French. Cf. ME. *burnet*, dark brown; O. E. Hom. ii. 163. Also AF. *burnete*, burnet (Alphita). — OF. *brunete*, given by Godefroy as the name of a plant now unknown; but it is clearly our *burnet*. Also spelt *brunette*, and the same word with OF. *brunette*, also *burnette*, a kind of dark brown cloth, also a brunette. See further under **Brunette.**

BURNISH, to polish. (F. — OHG.) Shak. has *burnished*, Merch. Ven. ii. 1. 2; ME. *burnist*, Gawain and Grene Knight, ed. Morris, 212; cf. *burned*, Chaucer, C. T. 1985 (A 1983). — OF. *burnir*, *brunir*, to embrown, to polish; pres. pt. *burnis-ant* (whence the E. suffix *-ish*). — OHG. *brūnen* (<*brunjan*), to embrown, also to make bright, to polish. — OHG. *brūn*, brown; cognate with AS. *brūn*, brown. See **Brown.** Der. *burnish-er.*

BURNOUSE, an upper cloak worn by Arabs. (F. — Arab.) In G. Eliot, Daniel Deronda, ch. xi. Dryden describes Almeyda as having 'her face veiled with a *barnus*;' Don Sebastian, A. i. — F. *burnous.* — Arab. *burnus*, a kind of high-crowned cap, worn formerly in Barbary and Spain; whence Span. *albornoz*, a kind of cloak with a hood; Rich. Dict. p. 265; Devic.

BURR, BUR, a rough envelope of the seeds of plants, as in the *burdock.* (E.) ME. *burre*, tr. by 'lappa, glis;' Prompt. Parv. p. 56; cf. *borre*, a hoarseness or roughness in the throat, P. Plowman, C. xx. 306. In Cockayne's A. S. Leechdoms, iii. 316, we find: '*Burr*, pl. *burres*, burr, burrs, *Arctium lappa*;' Gl. Rawlinson, c. 607; Gl. Sloane, 5.' NFriesic *burre*, *borre*, a burr. + Swed. *borre*, a sea-

hedgehog, sea-urchin; *kardborre*, a burdock; Dan. *borre*, burdock. From Teut. base *burz-*, for *burs-*, weak grade of Teut. root *bers-*, to bristle. See **Bristle.** Der. *burr* (or perhaps of imitative origin); a roughness in the throat, hoarseness; *bur-dock.*

BURROW, a shelter for rabbits. (E.) ME. *borwgh*, a den, cave, lurking-place; 'Fast byside the *borwgh* there the barn was inne' = close beside the *burrow* where the child was; William of Palerne, l. 9. In the Prompt. Parv. p. 56, we find: '*Burwhe*, burwth [*burwch*?] *burwe*, *burrowe*, town; *burgus*.' Thus *burrow* is a mere variation of *borough.* β. The provincial Eng. *burrow*, a shelter, is the same word; from *burg-*, weak grade of AS. *beorgan*, to protect. See **Borough.** Der. *burrow*, verb.

BURSAR, a purse-keeper, treasurer. (Late L. — Gk.) Wood, in his Athenæ Oxonienses, says that Hales was '*bursar* of his college' (R.). The pl. *bursers* is in Harrison, Descr. of England, b. ii. ch. 3; ed. Furnivall, p. 82. — Late L. *bursārius*, a treasurer. — Late L. *bursa*, a purse, with suffix *-ārius*, denoting the agent. — Gk. βύρσα, a hide, skin; of which purses were made. See **Purse.** Der. *bursar-ship.*

BURST, to break asunder, break forth. (E.) ME. *bersten*, *bresten*, Chaucer, C. T. 1982 (A 1980); P. Plowman, A. vii. 165. AS. *berstan*, pt. t. *bærst*, pp. *borsten*; Grein, i. 92.+Du. *bersten*, to burst asunder; Icel. *bresta*; Swed. *brista*; Dan. *briste*; OHG. *prëstan*, MHG. *bresten* (G. *bersten*).+Gael. *bris*, to break; Irish *brisaim*, OIrish *briss-im*, I break. Teut. type *brest-an-*, pt. t. *brast.*

BURTHEN; see **Burden** (1).

BURY (1), to hide in the ground, to inter. (E.) ME. *buryen*, P. Plowman, B. xi. 66. AS. *byrgan*, *byrigan*, Grein, i. 152; from *burg-*, weak grade of AS. *beorgan*, to protect, to hide; for which see **Borough.** Der. *buri-al*, q. v.

BURY (2), a town; as in *Canterbury.* (E.) A variant of *borough*, due to the peculiar declension of AS. *burh*, which changes to the form *byrig* in the dat. sing., after the prep. *æt*, at. See **Borough.**

BUS, a shortened form of *omnibus* (ab. 1832). (L.) The pl. *omnibússes*, with the third syllable more stressed than at present, was shortened to '*busses*;' whence the sing. *buss* or *bus.* See **Omnibus.**

BUSH (1), a thicket. (Late L.) α A *Bush* answers to an AS. *bysc*, whence *Warde-busc*, *wiði-busce*, Birch, Cart. Sax. iii. 638, i. 35; cf. *Bissey*, *Bussey*, old forms of Bushey, Herts. ME. *bush*, Chaucer, C. T. 1519 (A 1517); *busch*, *busk*, P. Plowman, B. xi. 336; *busk*, Will. of Palerne, 3069; Gen. and Exodus, 2779. β. The form *busk* is of Scand. origin; cf. Dan. *busk*, a bush, shrub; Swed. *buske*, a bush. Cf. also Du. *bosch*, a wood, forest; OHG. *busc* (G. *busch*). All from Late L. *boscus*, a bush; a word of unknown origin; whence also Ital. *bosco*, F. *bois.* *Boscus* occurs in the Laws of Cnut, De Foresta, § 28. Der. *bush-y*, *bush-i-ness.*

BUSH (2), the metal box in which an axle of a machine works. (Dutch — L. — Gk.) Technical. Miss Jackson (Shropsh. Word-book) quotes 'one paire of *bushes*' from an inventory of 1625. — MDu. *busse*; Du. *bus*, a box; here the equivalent of the E. *box*, which is similarly used. — Late L. *buxis*, a box. — Gk. πυξίς, a box. — Gk. πύξος, box-wood, box-tree. See **Box** (1). Doublet, *pyx.*

BUSHEL, a measure. (F. — L. — Gk.) ME. *bushel*, Chaucer, C. T. 4091 (A 4093); Polit. Songs, ed. Wright, p. 331, l. 165, p. 341, l. 393 (ab. 1330). — AF. *bussel*; Britton, i. 189; OF. *boissel*; Burguy, s. v. *boiste*; Godefroy, Supp. — Late L. *boissellus*, *buscellus*, a bushel; also spelt *bustellus.* — Late L. *buxida* (>OF. *boiste*, F. *boite*), the acc. case of *buxis*, a box. — Gk. πυξίς, a box. See above.

BUSK (1), to get oneself ready. (Scand.) ME. *buske*, *busken*, P. Plowman, B. ix. 133; Cursor Mundi, 11585. — Icel. *būask*, to get oneself ready; see Cleasby and Vigfusson's Icel. Dict. pp. 87, col. 1, and 88, col. 1; Dasent, Burnt Njál, pref. xvi, note. It stands for *būa-sk*, where *būa* is to prepare, and *-sk* is for *sik* (cf. G. *sich*), oneself. The neut. sense of *būa* is to live, dwell; from √BHEU, to be. See **Boor,** and cf. **Bask.**

BUSK (2), a support for a woman's stays. (F.) *Busk* now means a piece of whalebone or stiffening for the front of a pair of stays; but was originally applied to the *whole* of the stays. — MF. *busque*; Cotgrave has: '*Busque*, . . . a buske, or buste;' mod. F. *busc.* Of uncertain origin; cf. also MF. *buc*, 'a buske, plated body, or other quilted thing, worn to make, or keep, the body straight;' Cot. Cf. F. *busc* in Supp. to Godefroy.

BUSKIN, a kind of legging. (F. — Ital. — L. — Gk.) Shak. has *buskin'd*, Mids. Nt. Dr. ii. 1. 71. Cotgrave has: '*Brodequin*, a buskin.' Palsgrave has: '*Buskyng*, brodequin;' and (at p. 907, col. 3), we find: 'The *buskyns*, *les brousequins*' among the articles of women's attire. — OF. *bousequin*, occurring in 1483 (Godefroy, Supp., s. v. *brodequin*), also *brousequin*, *brosequin*, *brosquin* (id.). [The form *brodequin* may have arisen from confusion with F. *broder*, OF. *brosder* (Hatzfeld).] Origin disputed; but *not* from Dutch, the MDu. *broseken* (Sewel) having been borrowed from F. (Franck). Perhaps from MItal. *borzacchino*, pl. *borzacchini*, 'buskins, fine bootes.' Florio; who also gives *borzachinetti*, 'little buskins, little cheuerell [i.e. kid] purses.' The last sense suggests a possible derivation from MItal. *borza*, variant of *borsa*, a purse, a bag (F. *bourse*); see **Purse**. Hence we might also derive Span. *borcegui*, a buskin, the *n* reappearing in *borceguin-ero*, a buskin-maker. ¶ The Ital. *borsa* (like MF. *bourse*) may have had the sense of leather case; cf. Gk. βύρσα, a hide. Cf. 'i. tunicam de *buskyns*, et i. togam viridem;' York Wills (1471); iii. 188.

BUSS (1), a kiss; to kiss. (E.) Used by Shak. K. John, iii. 4. 35. The sb. *busse* is in Spenser, F. Q. iii. 10. 46. *Buss* is of imitative origin; cf. Lith. *bucz-oti*, to kiss; Bavarian *bussen*, to kiss; Schmeller. Webster refers to Luther as an authority for *bus* in the sense of a kiss; cf. Swed. dial. *pussa*, to kiss; *puss*, a kiss (Rietz). Also Span. *buz*, a kiss; Gael. *bus*, W. *bus*, mouth, lip, snout. ¶ In ME., the form is *bass*. Cf. 'Thus they kiss and *bass*;' Calisto and Meliboea, in Old Plays, ed. Hazlitt, i. 74; *basse*, a kiss, Court of Love, l. 797; 'I *basse* or kysse a person;' Palsgrave. This is from F. *baiser*, to kiss; or from L. *bāsiāre*, to kiss, *bāsium*, a kiss.

BUSS (2), a herring-boat. (F.) In Rob. of Brunne, tr. of Langtoft, pp. 149, 153, 158, 169.—OF. *busse*, *buse*, *buce*, a sort of barge; cf. also Du. *buis*, a herring-boat; Late L. *bussa*, a kind of a larger boat. In the A.S. Chron. an. 1066, we find *butse-carlas*, barge-men. The origin of the word is unknown.

BUST, the upper part of the human figure. (F.—Ital.) Used by Cotgrave; who explains *buste* by 'a bust, the ... quilted body of a doublet; also, the whole bulk or body of a man from his face to his middle.'—F. *buste*, introduced in 16th century from Ital. (Brachet). —Ital. *busto*, bust, human body, stays; cf. *bustino*, bodice, corset, slight stays.—Late L. *bustum*, the trunk of the body, the body without the head. β. Etym. uncertain. Diez connects it with Late L. *busta*, a small box, from L. acc. *buxida*; see **Box** (2). Compare the E. names *chest* and *trunk*. Others connect it with Late L. *busta*, or *busca*, a log of wood, OF. *busche*, F. *bûche*, allied to Late L. *boscus*; for which see **Bush** (1). See Körting, §§ 1602, 1666.

BUSTARD, a kind of bird. (F.—L.) 'A *bustard*, buteo, picus;' Levins, 30. 12. Used by Cotgrave, who has: '*Bistarde*, a bustard.' Spelt *bustarde*, Book of St. Alban's, fol. d 3, back. [Sherwood's Eng. and Fr. Dictionary, appended to Cotgrave, has: 'A *bustard*, or bistard, *outarde*, *houtarde*, *oustarde*, *houstarde*, *hostarde*;' whence *houstarde* has been copied into Todd's Johnson as *boustarde*!] We thus see that it is a corruption of OF. *bistarde*, possibly due to confusion with the OF. variant *oustarde*.—L. *auis tarda*, a slow bird. Pliny has: 'proximæ iis sunt, quas Hispania *aues tardas* appellat, Græcia ὠτίδας;' Nat. Hist. x. 22. β. Thus *bistarde* is for *avis-tarde* with the *a* dropped; so in Portuguese the bird is called both *abetarda* and *betarda*. The mod. F. has made *avis tarda* into *outarde*; cf. the form *oustarde* quoted above; also Prov. *austarda*, Span. *avutarda*, Ital. *ottarda*. ¶ Thus Diez, who is clearly right. At the same time, the L. *avis tarda* is an absurd name, as the bird is very swift. It looks like a popular perversion of Gk. ὠτίδ-, stem of ὠτίς (above), which is a true Gk. word.

BUSTLE (1), to stir about quickly, to scurry. (Scand.) Shak. has *bustle*, to be active, Rich. III, i. 1. 152. '*Bustelyng* forth as bestes,' wandering blindly like beasts; Piers Plowman, A. vi. 4. A frequentative; cf. Icel. *bustla*, to splash about as a fish.—Norw. *busta*, to be violent; *būsa*, to rush forward headlong (Ross). Cf. EFries. *būsen*, to be noisy or violent; Swed. *busa på en*, to rush upon one. Also Low G. *buus*, bounce! *büstern*, to wander about; *er büstert wat herum*, he bustles about (Bremen); Swed. *bösta*, to bustle, work (Björkman); Low G. (Kurhessen) *bosseln*, *busseln*, to bustle about (Vilmar).

BUSTLE (2), a pad beneath a woman's skirt. (Scand.) Probably from *buskle*, vb., in its earliest sense 'to prepare, equip;' so that the sense is 'equipment.' Cf. *busk*, to attire, accoutre, dress, of which it is the frequentative. The N.E.D. quotes—'*Buskel* thyself [prepare thyself] and make thee bowne' [ready]; Bradford, Wks., p. 445.

BUSY, active. (E.) ME. *bisy*, Chaucer, Prol. 321. AS. *bisig*, *bysig*, busy, Grein, i. 153; cf. *bisgu*, *bysgu*, labour, *bisgian*, to employ, fatigue.+Du. *bezig*, busy, active; *bezigheid*, business, occupation; *bezigen*, to use, employ; Low G. *besich* (Lübben); EFries. *bäsig*, busy. Cf. Norw. *base*, to toil (Larsen). Der. *busi-ness*, *busy-body*. ¶ We find ONorthumb. *bisignesse*, solicitude, anxiety, in the Lindisfarne MS.; Table of Contents of St. Matthew, no. xx; ed. Skeat, p. 17, l. 10. The AS. form is *bisig* rather than *bysig*.

BUT, adv., prep. and conj., except. (E.) ME. *bute*, Havelok, 85; *būten*, Layamon, l. 23. AS. *būtan*, conj. except: prep. besides, without; contr. from *be-ūtan*, Grein, i. 150. The full form *biūtan* is frequently found in the Heliand, e.g. in l. 2188; and even *biūtan that*, unless, l. 2775. β. *Be*=by; *ūtan*=outward, outside; *būtan*= 'by the outside,' and so 'beyond,' 'except.' The form *ūtan* is adverbial; from *ūt*, out.+Du. *buiten*, except. ¶ All the uses of *but*

are from the same source; the distinction attempted by Horne Tooke is unfounded. The form *be* for *by* is also seen in the word *be-yond*, a word of similar formation. See further under **Out**.

BUT (2), to strike; a but-end; a cask. See **Butt** (1) and **Butt** (2).

BUTCHER, a slaughterer of animals. (F.—OHG.) ME. *bocher*, P. Plowman, B. prol. 218; King Alisaunder, ed. Weber, l. 2832.— OF. *bocher*, originally one who kills he-goats.—OF. *boc* (F. *bouc*), a he-goat.—OHG. *bok* (G. *bock*), a he-goat; allied to E. *buck*. See **Buck**. Der. *butcher*, verb; *butcher-y*.

BUTLER, one who attends to bottles. (F.—Late L.) ME. *boteler*, *botler*, Wyclif, Gen. xl. 1, 2; *boteler* (3 syll.), Chaucer, C.T. 15140 (B 4324).—AF. *butuiller*, a butler, Vie de St. Auban, ed. Atkinson, l. 677; and see note.—AF. *butuille*, a bottle; OF. *boteille*. See **Bottle**. Der. *buttery*, a corrupted word; q. v.

BUTT (1), a push, a thrust; to thrust. (F.—O. Low G.) [The senses of the sb. may be referred back to the verb, just as the F. *bout* depends on *bouter* (Brachet).] ME. *butten*, to push, strike, Ormulum, l. 2810; Havelok, 1916, 2322.—OF. *boter*, to push, butt, thrust, strike; of which the AF. form was *buter*, Vie de Saint Auban, 534.—OFrankish **botan*, corresponding to MDu. *booten*, to beat, MHG. *bōzen*, to strike, beat; cognate with AS. *bēatan*. See **Beat**. Der. In the sense of 'a butt to shoot at,' or 'a rising ground, a knoll,' we have borrowed the F. *butte*, which see in Cotgrave and Hatzfeld. Cf. F. *but*, a mark; *buter*, to strike; from the same root as before.

BUTT (2), a large barrel. (F.—Late L.) In Levins, 195. 13. 'A *Butte* of Malmesey;' Sir T. More, Hist. Rich. III. § 4. Not E. [The AS. *byt* (Voc. 123. 29), occurring in the pl. *bytta* in Matt. ix. 17, and the dat. sing. *bytte*, Psalm xxxii. 7, produced an ME. *bitte*, for which see *bit* (3), sb., in N.E.D.; cf. Icel. *bytta*, a pail, a small tub.] Our modern word is really French.—OF. *boute*; F. *botte*, which Cotgrave explains as 'the vessel which we call a *butt*.' Cf. also OF. *bote*, in the Supp. to Godefroy.—Late L. *butis*, *buttis*, a cask. See **Bottle**.

BUTT (3), a thick end, as of a gun. (E.) Prob. an E. word, though not found early; see **Buttock**. ME. *but*; 'the *but* of his spere;' Malory, Morte Arthur, bk. x. ch. 2; leaf 208, l. 25. Cf. EFries. *but*, NFries. *butt*, thick, stumpy. Also Icel. *buttr*, short, *būtr*, a log; Dan. *but*, Swed. *butt*, stumpy, surly; Low G. *butt*, stump, *butt*, a thick end; Du. *bot*, blunt, dull; prov. G. *butzig*, stumpy; Swed. *but*, MHG. *butze*, a lump, clod.

BUTT (4), a kind of flat fish. (E.) ME. *butte*, Havelok, 759. EFries. *but*. Allied to Swed. *butta*, a turbot; MDan. *butte*, Low G. *butt*, Du. *bot*, a butt, flounder. Prob. allied to **Butt** (3).

BUTTER, a substance obtained from milk by churning. (L.— Gk.) ME. *botere*, Wyclif, Gen. xviii. 8; *butere*, Havelok, 643. AS. *butere* (Bosworth); a borrowed word.—L. *būtyrum*.—Gk. βούτυρον; as if from βοῦ-, for βοῦς, an ox, and τυρός, cheese; but it is perhaps of Scythian origin; cf. Herodotus, iv. 2. ¶ The similarity of E. *butter* to G. *butter* is simply due to the word being borrowed, not native. Der. *butter-cup*; also *butter-fly*, q. v.

BUTTERFLY, an insect. (Hybrid; Gk. *and* E.) AS. *buttorflēoge*, in Ælfric's Glossary, ed. Somner, Nomina Insectorum.—AS. *buter-*, butter; and *flēoge*, a fly.+Du. *botervlieg*; G. *butterfliege*, a butterfly; cf. *butter-vogel* (butter-fowl, i.e. butter-bird), a large white moth. β. It has amused many to devise guesses to explain the name. Kilian gives a M. Du. name of the insect as *boter-schijte*, showing that its excrement was regarded as resembling butter; and this guess is better than others in so far as it rests on some evidence. It was also a popular belief that butterflies stole milk and cream; cf. G. *molken-dieb*, milk-thief, butterfly, and see *Schmetterling* in Kluge.

BUTTERY, a place for provisions, esp. liquors. (F.—Late L.) Shak. has *buttery*, Tam. Shrew, Ind. i. 102; 'bring your hand to the *buttery-bar*, and let it drink;' Tw. Night, i. 3. 74. [The principal thing given out at the *buttery-bar* was (and is) beer; the *buttery-bar* is a small ledge on the top of the half-door (or *buttery-hatch*) on which to rest tankards. But as *butter* was (and is) also kept in *butteries*, the word was easily corrupted into its present form.] β. It is, however, from ME. *boterye* (Prompt. Parv.), shortened from ME. *botelerie*, i.e. a *butlery*, or place for *bottles*. In Rob. of Glouc. p. 191, we read that 'Bedwer the boteler' (i.e. Bedivere the butler) took some men to serve in 'the *botelery*.' So, too, we find: 'Hec botelaria, *botelary*;' Voc. 670. 16.—OF. *boteillerie* (Supp. to Godefroy); F. *bouteillerie*, 'a cupboard, or table to set bottles on; also, a cupboord or house to keep bottles in;' Cotgrave.—OF. *boteille*, a bottle. See **Bottle**.

BUTTOCK, the rump. (E.) Chaucer has *buttok*, C.T. 3801 (A 3803). It is also spelt *bottoke*, and *botok*; Voc. 677. 17; 750. 7. It is a dimin. of *butt*, an end; with the E. suffix -*ock*, properly expressing diminution, as in *bull-ock*. See **Butt** (3).

BUTTON, a small round knob. (F.—O. Low G.?) ME. *boton*, P. Plowman, B. xv. 121; *botoun*, Polit. Songs, ed. Wright, p. 239 (ab. 1325); corrupted to *bothum*, a bud, Romaunt of the Rose, l. 1721.—OF. *boton*, a bud, a button; F. *bouton*, 'a button, a bud;'

Cot.—OF. *boter*, F. *bouter*, 'to thrust, push forward; also, to bud;' Cot. See **Butt** (1). ¶ But I suspect that OF. *bouter*, to bud, may have been different in origin from OF. *boter*, *bouter*, to thrust; and may have been suggested by MHG. *butte*; for which see **Bud**.

BUTTRESS, a support; in architecture. (F.—Low G.) Bale uses *butrasse* to mean a support; Apology, p. 155. ME. *boteras*, Prompt. Parv.; whence *boterased*, buttressed, P. Plowman, B. v. 598. Orig. a pl. form, as if for *boterets.—OF. *bouterez* (with *z*=*ts*), pl. of *bouteret*, a prop, support (Godefroy).—OF. *bouter*, to thrust, push; see **Butt** (1). Cotgrave also has: '*Boutant*, m. a buttress, or shorepost,' from the same verb. **Der.** *buttress*, vb.

BUTTY, a companion or partner in any work. (F.—Low G.) This is a prov. E. word, used in several dialects (Halliwell). A *butty-gang* is 'a gang of men to whom a portion of the work in the construction of railways, &c., is let, the proceeds of the work being *equally divided amongst them*, something extra being allowed to the head man;' Ogilvie's Dict. I make a note here that the etymology is clearly pointed out in Palsgrave, who gives: '*Boty-felowe*, *parsonner*,' for which read *parsonnier*, i. e. partner. Just below he has: '*Boty*, that man [*read* men] of warre take, *butin*.' Hence *boty-felowe* is *booty-fellow*, a partner or sharer in booty taken, and *butty-gang* is a gang of men who share equally. The shortening of the vowel *oo* to *u* is familiar to us in the words *blood*, *flood*; the use of *butty* for *butty-fellow* easily followed, when the etymology was lost sight of. See **Booty**.

BUXOM, healthy; formerly, good-humoured, gracious; orig. obedient. (E.) Shak. has *buxom*, lively, brisk, Hen. V, iii. 6. 27. Gower has *boxom*, *buxom*, obedient, C.A. ii. 221 (bk. v. l. 2807). In the Ancren Riwle, p. 356, it is spelt *buhsum*.—AS. *būgan*, to bow, bend, whence a stem *būh-* (for *būg-*); with the suffix *-sum*, like, as in E. *win-some*, i. e. joy-like, joyous; see March's A. S. Grammar, sect. 229. The actual word *būhsum* does not appear in A.S. (as far as we know), but is common in Early English, occurring in O.E. Homilies i. 57 (ab. 1175); and there is no doubt about the etymology. Hence the original sense is 'pliable, obedient.'+Du. *buigzaam*, flexible, tractable, submissive; similarly formed from *buigen*, to bow, bend; G. *biegsam*, flexible; from *biegen*, to bend. See **Bow** (1).

BUY, to purchase. (E.) ME. *biggen*, *biggen*, *beyen*, *byen*; also (S. Western) *buyen*, E. Eng. Poems, ed. Furnivall, p. 120, l. 6; whence the mod. E. spelling. The stem *buy-* is from *byg-*, a stem occurring in the 3 p.s. present and in the imper. sing. of the A.S. verb. See Sweet, N. E. Gr. § 1293. The ME. infin. is commonly *buggen*, as in the Ancren Riwle, p. 362. AS. *bycgan*, to buy, Grein, i 151.+Goth. *bugjan*, to buy; OSax. *buggean*. Root unknown. **Der.** ME. *abyen*, whence *abide* (2). **Der.** *buy-er*.

BUZZ, to hum. (E.) Shak. has *buzz*, to hum, Merch. Ven. iii. 2. 182; also *buzz*, a whisper, K. Lear, i. 4. 348. Sir T. More speaks of the *buzzyng* of bees; Works, p. 208 g. It is a directly imitative word; and much the same as the Lowland Sc. *birr*, to make a whirring noise, used by Douglas, and occurring in Burns, Tam Samson's Elegy, st. 7. Cf. also Sc. *bysse*, to hiss like hot iron in water (Douglas's Virgil), and *bizz*, to hiss, Ferguson's Poems, ii. 16. So also Ital. *buzzicare*, to whisper, buzz, hum.

BUZZARD, an inferior kind of falcon. (F.—L.) Spelt *bosarde* in the Romaunt of the Rose, l. 4033; also *busard*, K. Alisaunder, l. 3049.—OF. *busard*, 'a buzzard;' Cotgrave.—OF. *buse*, a buzzard, with suffix *-ard*; on which see N.E.D. β. The OF. *buse* (Supp. to Godefroy) represents a Low L. type *butia, representing L. *buteo*, used by Pliny for a sparrow-hawk. Cf. Gascon *busoc*, a buzzard (Moncaut); mod. Prov. *buso*, *busac*, Limousin *busard* (Mistral). ¶ The *buzzard* still retains its old Latin name; the common buzzard is *Buteo vulgaris*.

BY, beside, near; by means of, &c. (E.) ME. *bi*, AS. *bī*, *big*; Grein, i. 121, 122. [The form *big* even appears in composition, as in *big-leofa*, sustenance, something to live by; but the usual form in composition is *be*, as in *beset*.]+OFries. and OSax. *bi*; Du. *bij*; OHG. *bī*, *pī*; MHG. *bī*; G. *bei*; Goth. *bi*. Related to L. *am-bi-*, Gk. ἀμφί, Skt. *a-bhi*. **Der.** *by-name*, *by-word*, *by-way*. (But not *by-law*, q. v.) From *by*, prep. (as in *by twos*) came the phr. *by and by*, in order, hence, directly, soon, in due course; also *bye*, as in cricket.

BY-LAW, a law affecting a township. (Scand.) Often explained as being derived from the prep. *by*, as if the law were 'a subordinate law;' a definition which suits late usages of the word, and probably expresses a common mistake. Bacon has: '*bylaws*, or ordinances of corporations;' Hen. VII, p. 215 (R.), or ed. Lumby, p. 196, l. 10. β. Blount, in his Law Dict., shows that the word was formerly written *birlaw* or *burlaw*; and Jamieson, s. v. *burlaw*, shows that a *birlaw-court* was one in which every proprietor of a freedom had a vote, and was got up amongst neighbours. 'Laws of *burlaw* ar maid and determined be consent of neichtbors;' Skene (in Jamieson). There were also *burlaw-men*, whose name was corrupted into *barley-*

men.—Icel. *bæ-r*, *bȳ-r*, a village (gen. *bæjar*, *bȳjar*, whence *bir-*); cf. *bæjar-lög*, a town-law (Icel. Dict. s. v. *bær*); MSwed. *bylag*; from *by*, a village, and *lag*, law; Dan. *bylov*, municipal law; from *by*, a town, and *lov*, law. γ. The Icel. *bær* or *bȳr*, a town, village, is allied to *būa*, to dwell, co-radicate with AS. *būan*, to till, cultivate, whence E. *bower*. See **Bower**. ¶ The prefix *by-* in this word is identical with the suffix *-by* so common in Eng. place-names, esp. in Yorkshire and Lincolnshire, such as Whitby, Grimsby, Scrooby, Derby. The ME. *bi*, a town, occurs in the Cursor Mundi, ed. Morris, pp. 1210, 1216.

BYRE, a cow-house. (E.) It is Lowland Scotch and North. E. Jamieson quotes 'of bern [barn] or of *byre*,' from Gawain and Golagros, i. 3. The word is explained by AS. *bȳre*, a hut; Voc. 32. 11; 185. 15. This is a derivative (with mutation of *ū* to *ȳ*) from AS. *būr*, a bower. The allied E. *bower* came to be restricted to the sense of a 'lady's chamber' in most ME. writers. See **Bower**.

C

CAB (1), an abbreviation of *cabriolet*, q. v. (F.—Ital.—L.)

CAB (2), a Hebrew measure; 2 Kings, vi. 25. (Heb.) From Heb. *qab*, the 18th part of an *ephah*. The lit. sense is 'hollow' or 'concave;' Concise Dict. of the Bible; s. v. *Weights*. Cf. Heb. *qābab*, to form in the shape of a vault. See **Alcove**.

CABAL, a party of conspirators; also, a plot. (F.—Late L.—Heb.) Ben Jonson uses it to mean 'a secret:' 'The measuring of the temple; a *cabal* Found out but lately;' Staple of News, iii. 1. Bp. Bull, vol. i. ser. 3, speaks of the 'ancient *cabala* or tradition;' here he uses the Hebrew form. Dryden has: 'When each, by curs'd *cabals* of women, strove To draw th' indulgent king to partial love;' Aurengzebe, i. 1. 19. He also uses *caballing*, i. e. conspiring, as a present participle; Art of Poetry, canto iv. l. 972.—F. *cabale*, 'the Jewes Caball, or a hidden science of divine mysteries which, the Rabbies affirm, was revealed and delivered together with the [divine] law;' Cotgrave.—Late L. *cabbala*.—Heb. *qabbālāh*, reception, mysterious doctrine received; from the verb *qābal*, to take or receive; (in Piel) *qibbēl*, to adopt a doctrine. ¶ The cabinet of 1671 was called the *cabal*, because the initial letters of the names of its members formed the word, viz. Clifford, Arlington, Buckingham, Ashley, Lauderdale; but the word was in use earlier, and this was a mere coincidence. **Der.** *cab-l*, verb; *cabal-ist*, a mystic, *cabal-ist-ic*.

CABBAGE (1), a vegetable with a large head. (F.—L.) In Shak. Merry Wives, i. 1. 124. Spelt *cabages* in Ben Jonson, The Fox, ii. 1; *cabbages* in Holland's Pliny, bk. xix. c. 4. ME. *cabog-*, *cab che*; Two Cookery-Books, ed. Austin, pp. 6, 69.—F. (Picard) *caboche*, lit. 'great head;' cf. Picard *cabus*, F. '*choux cabus*, a cabbidge;' Cot. He also gives '*Cabusser*, to cabbidge; to grow to a head.' Formed, with an augmentative suffix, from L. *cap-ut*, a head; cf. Ital. *capocchia*, head of a nail, *capoccia*, a large head; also *capuccio*, a little head. See **Capital** (1).

CABBAGE (2), to steal. (F.—Prov.—Late L.—L.) In Johnson's Dict.—F. *cabasser*, to put into a basket; see Cot.—F. *cabas*, a basket. So also Norman F. *cabasser*, to steal, from *cabas*, deceit; and see Supp. to Godefroy.—Prov. *cabas*.—Late L. *cabātium*, a basket (Ducange; an. 1243).—L. type *capāceum, for L. *capācem*, containing; see **Capacious**. So Hatzfeld.

CABER, a pole, spar. (C.—L.) 'A *cabyr* or a spar;' Douglas, tr. of Virgil (cf. Æn. xii. 293).—Gael. *cabar*.—L. type *caprio, a rafter; Late L. *capro*; see **Chevron**. (Macbain.)

CABIN, a little room, a hut. (F.—Prov.—Late L.) ME. *caban*, *cabane*. '*Caban*, lytylle howse;' Prompt. Parv. p. 57. 'Creptest into a *caban*;' P. Plowman, A. iii. 184.—F. *cabane*.—Prov. *cabana*.—Late L. *capanna*, a hut (Isidore). ¶ The W. *caban* is from ME. *cabane*. **Der.** *cabin-et*, from the French.

CABLE, a strong rope. (F.—L.) In early use. ME. *cable*, *cabel*, *kabel*; pl. *kablen*, Layamon, i. 57; where the later text has *cables*.—OF. *cable* (F. *câble*), given in Cotgrave; but it must have been in early use, having found its way into Swedish, Danish, &c.—Late L. *caplum*, a cable, in Isidore of Seville; also spelt *capulum*. Lit. a strong (holding) rope; a halter (for cattle).—L. *capere*, to take hold of; cf. L. *capulus*, a handle, haft, hilt of a sword. See **Capable**.

CABOOSE, the cook's cabin on board ship. (Dutch.) First given by Falconer, in 1769. Sometimes spelt *camboose*, which is from the F. form *cambuse*. Like many sea-terms, it is Dutch.—MDu. *kabuys*, 'the cooking, or kitchin-roome in a ship;' Hexham (1658); Du. *kombuis*, a cook's room, caboose; or 'the chimney in a ship,' Sewel. Hence also Dan. *kabys*, Swed. *kabysa*, a caboose. Of unknown origin; perhaps short for *kaban-huys, 'cabin-house;' from MDu. *kaban*, a cabin, and *huys*, a house. This would also give *cambuse*.

CABRIOLET, a one-horse carriage, better known by the abbreviation *cab*. (F. – L.) Mere French. – F. *cabriolet*, a cab; dimin. of *cabriole*, a caper, a leap of a goat; named from the supposed lightness of the carriage. The older spelling of *cabriole* is *capriole*, used by Montaigne (Brachet). – Ital. *capriola*, a caper, the leap of a kid. – Ital. *caprio*, the wild-goat. – L. *caprum*, acc. of *caper*, a goat; cf. L. *caprea*, a kind of wild she-goat. See **Caper**. ¶ '*Cabriolets* were, in honour of his Majesty's birthday, introduced to the public [of London] this morning;' Gent. Maga. 1823, April 23; p. 463. George IV (b. Aug. 12) kept his birthday on St. George's day.

CACAO, the name of a tree. (Span. – Mexican.) In Blount's Gloss., ed. 1674, we find: '*Chocolate*, a kind of compound drink, which we have from the Indians; the principal ingredient is a fruit called *cacao*, which is about the bigness of a great black fig. See a Treatise of it, printed by Jo. Okes, 1640.' '[They] lade backe againe the *cacao*;' Hakluyt, Voy. iii. 457 (at bottom). – Span. *cacao*. – Mexican *cacauatl*, the name of the tree whence chocolate is made. See Notes on E. Etym., p. 331. ¶ The cacao-tree, *Theobroma cacao*, is a totally different tree from the cocoa-nut tree, though the accidental similarity of the names has caused great confusion. See **Cocoa**.

CACHALOT, a genus of whales, having teeth in the lower jaw. (F.) Spelt *cachelot* in 1747. – F. *cachalot* (the same). Supposed to be connected with Gascon *cachaou*, a large tooth (Moncaut). Mistral compares the ending *-alot* with mod. Prov. *alot*, a kind of tunny. ¶ Körting, § 2022, gives a different etymology, ultimately from L. *catulus*, a whelp.

CACHINNATION, loud laughter. (L.) In Bishop Gauden's Anti-Baal-Berith, 1661, p. 68 (Todd's Johnson). And in Cockeram (1623). Borrowed from Latin, with the F. suffix *-tion*. – L. *cachinnātiōnem*, acc. of *cachinnātio*, loud laughter. – L. *cachinnāre*, to laugh aloud; an imitative word. The Gk. form is καχάζειν. See **Cackle**.

CACHUCHA, a lively Spanish dance. (Span.) Span. *cachucha*; whence F. *cachucha* in Hatzfeld.

CACIQUE, CAZIQUE, a W. Indian prince or chief. (Span. – W. Indian.) A name given to a chief of some W. Indian tribes. In Minsheu, ed. 1627. First in R. Eden, Books on America, ed. Arber, p. 223 (1555). – Span. *cacique*, 'an Indian prince;' Minsheu, Span. Dict. (1623). From the old language of Hayti; see Notes on E. Etym., p. 346.

CACK, to go to stool. (L.) ME. *cakken*. '*Cakken*, or fyystyn, *caco*;' Prompt. Parv. p. 58. Found also in Dutch and Danish, but all are borrowed from the Latin. – L. *cacāre*.+Gk. κακκᾶν; which is from the sb. κάκκη, dung. Cf. W. *cach*, OIrish *cacc*, Skt. *çakam*, dung.

CACKLE, to make a noise like a goose. (E.) In early use. 'The hen . . . ne con buten *kakelen*,' the hen can only cackle; Ancren Riwle, p. 66. A frequentative of a primitive *cakken*; 'the goose may *cakke*' (pr. *calke*); Polit. Poems, ed. Furnivall, p. 16. See Notes on E. Etym. +Du. *kakelen*, to chatter, gabble; Swed. *kackla*, to cackle, gaggle; Dan. *kagle*; G. *gackeln, gakeln, gackern*, to cackle, gaggle, chatter. β. The termination *-le* has a frequentative force. The stem *cack-* (i. e. *kak*) is imitative, like *quack*; cf. *gag-* in prov. E. *gaggle*, to cackle, and *gob-* or *gab-* in *gobble*, to make a noise like a turkey, and *gabble*. Cf. AS. *ceahhetan*, to laugh loudly, Beda, v. 12; G. *kichern*, to giggle. From the Teutonic base KAK, to laugh, cackle; Fick, iii. 39. ¶ Observe the three varieties of this imitative root, viz. (1) KAK, as in *cackle*; (2) KIK, as in the nasalised *chink* in *chin-cough*, i. e. *kink*-cough or *chink*-cough; and (3) KUK, as in *cough* and *chuckle*. All refer to convulsive movements of the throat.

CACOETHES, an ill habit. (L. – Gk.) Chiefly in the phrase *cacoëthes scribendi* (Juvenal, Sat. vii. 52); cited by Addison, Spectator, no. 582. – L. *cacoēthes*. – Gk. κακόηθες, an evil habit, neut. of κακοήθης, ill-disposed. – Gk. κακό-, for κακός, evil; and ἦθος, character, habit; see **Ethic**.

CACOPHONY, a harsh, disagreeable sound. (Gk.) '*Cacophonies* of all kinds;' Pope, To Swift, April 2, 1733 (R.) – Gk. κακοφωνία, a disagreeable sound. – Gk. κακόφωνος, harsh. – Gk. κακό-, for κακός, bad; and φων-ή, sound, voice. Der. *cacophonous*; from the Gk. adj. κακόφωνος directly.

CACTUS, a prickly plant. (L. – Gk.) In Topsell, Fourfooted Beasts (1607), p. 102. – L. *cactus*. – Gk. κάκτος, a prickly plant found in Sicily.

CAD, a low fellow. (F. – Gascon. – Late L. – L.) Short for Sc. *cadie*, an errand boy; also, a low fellow; Burns, Author's Earnest Cry and Prayer, st. 19. See Jamieson; and Notes on E. Etym.; also *caddie* in E. D. D., which shows that *caddie* is for *cadet*. See **Cadet**.

CADAVEROUS, corpse-like. (L.) In Hammond's Works, vol. iv. p. 529; Sir T. Browne, Rel. Medici, i. § 38. – L. *cadāuerōsus*, corpse-like. – L. *cadāuer*, a corpse. – L. *cadere*, to fall, fall as a dead man. ¶ Similarly, Gk. πτῶμα, a corpse, is connected with πίπτειν, to fall. See **Cadence**.

CADDIS, a kind of worsted lace or tape. (F.) In Winter's Tale, iv. 4. 208. ME. *cadas*, 'bombicinium;' Prompt. Parv. – AF. *cadace*, Langtoft's Chron., ii. 428; MF. *cadarce*, 'the coursest part of silke, whereof sleave is made;' Cot.; also OF. *cadis* (Froissart, in Godefroy). Cf. Span. *cadarzo*, coarse, entangled silk; Port. *cadarço*, a coarse silk. Origin unknown; perhaps Eastern. Der. *caddis-worm*; perhaps from the appearance of the case of the larva.

CADDY, a small box for holding tea. (Malay.) 'The key of the *caddy*;' Letter from Cowper to Lady Hesketh, Jan. 19, 1793. The sense has somewhat changed, and the spelling also. It properly means 'a packet of tea of a certain weight,' and the better spelling is *catty*. 'An original package of tea, less than a half-chest, is called in the trade a "box," "caddy," or "catty." This latter is a Malay word; " *kātī*, a catty or weight, equal to 1⅓ lb. avoirdupois." In many dictionaries, catty is described as the Chinese pound;' R. W. W., in Notes and Queries, 3 S. x. 323. At the same reference I myself gave the following information. 'The following curious passage in a lately-published work is worth notice. "The standard currency of Borneo is brass guns. This is not a figure of speech, nor do I mean small pistols, or blunderbusses, but real cannon, five to ten feet long, and heavy in proportion. The metal is estimated at so much a *picul*, and articles are bought and sold, and change given, by means of this awkward coinage. The *picul* contains 100 *catties*, each of which weighs about 1⅓ English pounds. There is one advantage about this currency; it is not easily stolen."–F. Boyle, Adventures among the Dyaks, p. 100. To the word *catties* the author subjoins a footnote as follows: "Tea purchased in small quantities is frequently enclosed in boxes containing one *catty*. I offer a diffident suggestion that this may possibly be the derivation of our familiar tea-caddy." I may add that the use of this weight is not confined to Borneo; it is used also in China, and is (as I am informed) the only weight in use in Japan.'–Malay *kātī*, a catty, or weight of which one hundred make a *pikul* of 133⅓ pounds avoirdupois, and therefore equal to 21⅓ oz. or 1⅓ pound; it contains 16 *tāil*; Marsden's Malay Dict. p. 253. See **Catty**.

CADE, a barrel or cask. (L. – Gk. – Heb.) 'A *cade* of herrings; 2 Hen. VI, iv. 2. 36. '*Cade* of herynge, or othyr lyke, *cada, lacista*;' Prompt. Parv. p. 57. – L. *cadus*, a barrel, wine-vessel, cask; cf. F. *cade*, app. a late word. – Gk. κάδος, a pail, jar, cask, wine-vessel. – Heb. *kad*, a pail (Prellwitz).

CADENCE, a falling; a fall of the voice. (F. – Ital. – L.) 'The golden *cadence* of poesy;' Shak. L. L. L. iv. 2. 126. 'In ryme, or elles in *cadence*;' Chaucer, Ho. of Fame, ii. 115. – F. *cadence*, 'a cadence, a just falling, round going, of words;' Cot. – Ital. *cadenza*. – Late L. *cadentia*, a falling. – L. *cadere* (pres. part. *cadens*, gen. *cadentis*), to fall.+Skt. *çad*, to fall. Der. from the same source; *cadent*, K. Lear, i. 4. 307; *cadenza*, Ital. form of F. *cadence*. Doublet, *chance*, q. v.

CADET, a younger son, young military student. (F. – Gascon. – Late L. – L.) 'The *cadet* of an antient and noble family;' Wood's Athenæ Oxonienses (R.). 'The *cadet* of a very ancient family;' Tatler, no. 256 [not 265]. – F. *cadet*, 'a younger brother among gentlemen;' a Poitou word; Cot. The Gascon form is *capdet* (Hatzfeld), corresponding to Prov. *capdel*, formed from Late L. *capitellum*, 'a little head.' The eldest son was called *caput*, the 'head' of the family; the second, the *capitellum*, or 'lesser head.' – L. *caput*, the head. See **Capital**. Der. *cad*, q. v.; *cadet-ship*.

CADGER, an itinerant dealer, a hawker. (F. ?) Henrysoun has *cadgear*, Moral Fables, p. 66 (N.E.D.) From ME. *caggen*, to bind, to fasten, to carry a pack, to hawk; see Stratmann, N. E. D., and E. D. D. Prob. from ME. *cachen*, to seize, fasten; see **Catch**.

CADI, a judge. (Arab.) 'The graunde *Cady*;' E. Webbe, Travels (1590), ed. Arber, p. 33. – Arab. *qāḍī, qāzi*, a cadi or cazi, a judge, civil, criminal, and ecclesiastic; Rich. Dict. p. 1109; Palmer, p. 464. The third letter is ض, which Devic transliterates by *ḍ*. β. Hence was formed (by prefixing the Arab. article *al*, and inserting *l*) the Span. *alcalde*, a judge, which appears occasionally in E. literature; it is spelt *alcade* in An Eng. Garner, vi. 14 (ab. 1586). The inserted *l*, says Devic, arose from an emphatic pronunciation of the Arabic ض.

CADMIUM, a blueish white metal. (L. – Gk.) From *cadmia*. – Gk. καδμία, καδμεία, calamine, cadmia; lit. 'Cadmean earth.' Cadmea was the citadel of the Bœotian Thebes.

CADUCEUS, the herald's wand of Mercury. (L. – Gk.) In Shak. Troil. ii. 3. 14. – L. *cādūceus*; also *cādūceum*, orig. neut. adj. (sc. *sceptrum*). – Gk. (Doric) καρύκιον, (Attic) κηρύκειον, a herald's wand, as borne by Hermes. – Gk. κηρυκ-, for κῆρυξ, a herald.+Skt. *kāru-s*, a singer; cf. L. *car-men*, a song.

CADUCOUS, falling early, said of leaves or flowers. (L.) Fisher even uses the adj. *caduke*, i. e. transitory; Seven Psalms, Ps. cii. p. 196 (E. E. T. S.); which is also in an E. version of Palladius on

Husbandry, bk. xii. st. 20. — L. *cadūc-us*, easily falling; with suffix *-ous*. — L. *cadere*, to fall. See **Cadence**.

CÆSURA, a pause in a verse. (L.) In Phillips (1678). — L. *cæsūra*, a pause in a verse; lit. a cutting off. — L. *cæsus*, pp. of *cædere*, to cut.

CAFTAN, a Turkish garment. (Turk.) 'A *caftan* or a close coat;' Hakluyt, Voy. i. 497 (1598). — Turk. *qaftān*, a dress.

CAGE, an enclosure for keeping birds and animals. (F. – L.) In early use. 'Ase untowe brid ine *cage* ' = like an untrained bird in a cage; Ancren Riwle, p. 102. — OF. *cage* (F. *cage*), a cage. — Late L. *cavea*, for L. *cauea*, a hollow place, den, cave, cage for birds. [See the letter-changes explained in Schwan]. — L. *cauus*, hollow. See **Cave**.

CAIMAN, the same as **Cayman**, q. v.

CAÏQUE, a kind of boat. (F. – Turk.) 'Many a light caïque;' Byron, Childe Harold, c. ii. st. 81. — F. *caïque*. — Turk. *qāïq*, a boat.

CAIRN, a pile of stones. (C.) In Scott, Lady of the Lake, c. v. st. 14, where it rhymes with 'stern.' Spelt *cairne*, Montgomerie, Flyting, l. 401. Particularly used of a pile of stones raised on the top of a hill, or set up as a landmark; applied by us to a pile raised by artificial means. It seems to have come to us from the Gaelic in particular. β. The form *carn* (a rock) is common to Gaelic, Irish, Welsh, Manx, Cornish, and Breton; the sense is, in general, 'a pile of stones,' and it was chiefly used of a pile of stones raised over a grave. Cf. Gk. κραναός, rocky. **Der.** *cairn-gorm*, a yellow gem; from *Cairn-gorm* (blue cairn), in the Scot. Highlands. See **Crag**.

CAISSON, a large chest or case. (F. – Prov. – L.) In Bailey (1721). — F. *caisson*, augmentative of *caisse*, a case. — Prov. *caissa*. — L. *capsa*; see **Case** (2).

CAITIFF, a mean fellow, wretch. (F. – L.) It formerly meant 'a captive.' ME. *caitif*, a captive, a miserable wretch. ' *Caytif* to cruel king Agámemnon ' = captive to the cruel king A.; Chaucer, Troil. iii. 382. — ONorth. F. *caitif*, a captive, a poor or wretched man; OF. *chaitif*, now spelt *chétif*, which see in Hatzfeld. — Late L. acc. *captivum*, from L. *captiuus*, a captive, prisoner; but used in Late L. in the sense of 'mean,' or 'poor-looking.' — L. *captus*, pp. of *capere*, to take, seize. See **Capable**. **Doublet**, *captive*.

CAJOLE, to allure, coax, deceive by flattery. (F.) In Burnet, Hist. Reformation, an. 1522; and in Pepys, Diary, Mar. 17, 1662–3. — F. *cajoler*, MF. *cageoler*, 'to prattle or jangle, like a jay in a cage; to babble or prate much, to little purpose;' Cot. Prob. of imitative origin; cf. F. *caqueter*, 'to prattle;' Cot. **Der.** *cajol-er*, *cajol-er-y*.

CAJUPUT, CAJEPUT (with *j* as *y*), a tree yielding an oil. (Malay.) 'On hinges oil'd with *cajeput*;' Hood, Ode to Mr. Malthus (l. 9 from end). — Malay *kāyu pūtih*, lit. 'white wood.' — Malay *kāyu*, wood; *pūtih*, white.

CAKE, a small mass of dough baked, &c. (Scand.) In prov. E. *cake* means 'a small round loaf;' see Chaucer, C. T. 4092 (A 4094). In early use. Spelt *cake* in Hali Meidenhad, ed. Cockayne, p. 37, last line. — Icel. and Swed. *kaka*, a cake; found in MSwedish; see Ihre; Dan. *kage*; NFries. *kāk*, *kāg*. Teut. stem **kakōn-*, fem.; from Teut. base **kak-* of which the strong grade is **kōk-*, whence prov. E. *cookie*, Du. *koek*, a cake, dumpling, G. *kuchen*, a cake, tart.

CALABASH, a vessel made of the shell of a dried gourd. (F. – Span. – Arab. – Pers.) '*Calabash*, a species of cucurbita;' Ash's Dict. 1775. '*Calabashes*, or Gourd-shells;' Dampier, A New Voyage, i. 153. In Arber's Eng. Garner, vii. 359 (1689). — F. *calebasse*. Cotgrave has: ' *Callabasse*, a great gourd; also, a bottle made thereof.' — Span. *calabaza*, a pumpion, calabash; cf. Span. *calabaza vinatera*, a bottle-gourd for wine. — Arab.-Pers. *kharbuz*, a melon, a cucumber; lit. 'ass-gourd,' i. e. coarse gourd. — Pers. *khar*, ass (hence, coarse); *buzah*, odoriferous fruit. Cf. Skt. *khara-s*, an ass; Pers. *bū*, odour. See Richardson's Arab. Dict. ed. 1829, pp. 603, 270. **Der.** *calabash-tree*, a tree whence dried shells of fruit are procured.

CALAMANCO, a woollen stuff. (Late L.) Florio (1598) explains Ital. *tesserino* by 'calimanco.' We also find Du. *kalamink*, F. *calmande*, MF. *calamande*, G. *kalmank* (Weigand), mod. Span. *calamaco*. From Late L.; see the forms in Ducange, s. v. *camelaucum*. Of unknown origin.

CALAMINT, a herb. (F. – L. – Gk.) ME. *calament* (N.E.D.); also *calamynt*, Prompt. Parv. — MF. *calament*. — Late L. *calamentum*, Voc. 557. 17; also *calamintha*. — Gk. καλαμίνθη, calamint.

CALAMITY, a great misfortune. (F. – L.) In Shak. K. John, iii. 4. 60. And earlier, in Calvin, Four Godly Sermons, ser. 2. — F. *calamité*, calamity; Cot. — L. *calamitātem*, from nom. *calamitās*, a calamity, misfortune. Cf. *in-columis*, unharmed. **Der.** *calamit-ous*.

CALASH, a sort of travelling carriage. (F. – G. – Slavonic.) 'From ladies hurried in *caleches*;' Hudibras, pt. iii. c. 2. 871. — F. *calèche*, a barouche, carriage. — G. *kalesche*, a calash. — Polish *kolaska*, a small carriage, dimin. of *kolasa*, a carriage. Cf. Russ. *koliaska*, calash, carriage. So called from being furnished with wheels; from

Russ. *kolo*, a wheel. From Idg. **qol*, 2nd grade of √QEL, to drive; see **Pole** (2). Brugmann, i. § 652. β. The same word *calash* also came to mean (1) the hood of a carriage, and (2) a hood for a lady's head, of similar shape.

CALCAREOUS, like or containing chalk or lime. (L.) Better spelt *calcarious*, as in a quotation from Swinburne, Spain, Let. 29, in Richardson. — L. *calcāri-us*, pertaining to lime; with suffix *-ous*. — L. *calc-*, stem of *calx*, lime. See **Calx**. **Der.** (from *calc-*) *calc-ium*, a chemical element, the basis of lime.

CALCEOLARIA, a flower; a genus of *Scrophulariaceæ*. (L.) Coined from L. *calceolus*, a small shoe, dimin. of *calceus*, a shoe. — L. *calc-*, stem of *calx*, the heel. So called because the flower has some resemblance to a broad-toed slipper.

CALCINE, to reduce to a *calx* or chalky powder by heat. (F. – L.) Chaucer has *calcening*, C. T., Group G, 771. Better spelt *calcining*; we find *calcinacioun* in C. T., G 804. [Perhaps from Latin directly.] — F. *calciner*, 'to calcinate, burne to dust by fire any metall or minerall;' Cot. — Late L. *calcināre*, to reduce to a calx; common in medieval treatises on alchemy. — L. *calc-*, stem of *calx*, stone, lime; used in alchemy of the remains of minerals after being subjected to great heat. See **Calx**. **Der.** *calcin-at-ion*, from the Late L. vb.

CALCULATE, to reckon. (L.) In Shak. 2 Hen. VI, iv. 1. 34. This is a Latin form, from the L. pp. *calculātus*. [The older form is the ME. *calculen*; see Chaucer, C. T. 11596 (F 1284). — F. *calculer*, to reckon.] — L. *calculāre*, to reckon by help of small pebbles; pp. *calculātus*. — L. *calculus*, a pebble; dimin. of *calx* (stem *calc-*), a stone; whence also E. *chalk*. See **Calx**. **Der.** *calcula-ble*, *calculat-ion*, *calculat-ive*, *calculat-or*; also *calculus*, from the L. sb.

CALDRON, CAULDRON, a large kettle. (F. – L.) ME. *caldron*; Gower, C. A. ii. 266; bk. v. 4141. But more commonly *caudron*; Seven Sages, ed. Wright, l. 1231; Legends of the Holy Rood, ed. Morris, p. 60. — North F. (Picard) *cauderon*, for OF. *chauderon*; mod. F. *chaudron*. The OF. word *caldaru*, a cauldron, occurs in the very old Glossaire de Cassel; Bartsch, Chrestomathie Française, col. 2, l. 19. Cf. Ital. *calderone*, a vessel for hot water. Formed, with an augmentative suffix *-on* (Ital. *-one*) from L. *caldār-*, as in *caldāria*, a hot bath, also a caldron (1 Sam. ii. 14, Vulgate); cf. L. *caldārium*, a cauldron, properly neuter of *caldārius*, adj., that serves for heating; *caldāria* being the feminine. — L. *caldus*, hot; contracted form of *calidus*, hot. — L. *calēre*, to be hot. See **Caloric**, **Chaldron**. ¶ The Span. form *calderon* gave name to the great Spanish author.

CALEFACTION, a making warm. (L.) In Cockeram (1642). — L. acc. *calefactiōn-em*; nom. *calefactio*, a making warm. — L. *calefacere*, to warm (pp. *calefactus*). — L. *cale-* (as in *calēre*, to glow); and *facere*, to make; cf. L. *calidus*, hot. See **Caldron**. **Der.** (from *calefact-us*), *calefact-or*, *-or-y*.

CALENDAR, an almanac. (L.) In early use; spelt *kalender* in Layamon, i. 308. — L. *calendārium*, an account-book of interest kept by money-changers, so called because interest became due on the *calends* (or first day) of each month; in later times, a calendar. — L. *calendæ*, sb. pl., a name given to the first day of each month. The origin of the name is obscure; but it is agreed that the verbal root is the old verb *calāre*, to proclaim. See Bréal. It is cognate with Gk. καλεῖν, to summon. — √KAL, to shout; see Prellwitz. Allied to **Hale** (2).

CALENDER (1), a machine for pressing and smoothing cloth. (F. – Late L. – Gk.) Best known from the occurrence of the word in Cowper's John Gilpin, where it is applied to a 'calender-er,' or person who calenders cloth, and where a more correct form would be *calendrer*. In Bailey's Dict., ed. 1731, vol. ii, I find: 'To *calender*, to press, smooth, and set a gloss upon linnen, &c.; also the engine itself.' β. The word is French. The verb appears in Cotgrave, who has: '*Calendrer*, to sleeke, smooth, plane, or polish linnen cloth, &c.' The F. sb. (from which the verb was formed) is *calandre*; of which Godefroy's Supp. gives an example in 1483. — Late L. *celendra*, explained in Ducange by: 'instrumentum quo poliuntur panni; [French] *calandre*.' γ. This Late L. *celendra* is, probably, a corruption of L. *cylindrus*, a cylinder, roller; the name being given to the machine because a roller was contained in it, and (probably later) sometimes two rollers in contact. — Gk. κύλινδρος, a cylinder. See **Cylinder**. **Der.** *calender*, verb; *calendr-er*, or *calend-er*, sb.

CALENDER (2), a kind of wandering monk. (F. – Pers.) 'In the habit of *kalenders* or friars;' Sir T. Herbert, Trav. (1665), p. 63. — F. *calender*. — Pers. *qalandar*, a kind of Muhammadan monk, who abandons everything and retires from the world; Rich. Dict. p. 1145.

CALENDS, the first day of the month in the Roman calendar; see **Calendar**. (L.) In early use. AS. *calend*; Grein, i. 154.

CALENTURE, a feverous madness. (F. – Span. – L.) In Massinger, Fatal Dowry, iii. 1 (Charalois). — F. *calenture*. — Span. *calentura*. — L. *calent-*, stem of pr. pt. of *calēre*, to be hot. See **Caldron**.

CALF, the young of the cow, &c. (E.) ME. *kalf, calf;* sometimes *kelf.* Spelt *kelf* in Ancren Riwle, p. 136; the pl. *calveren* is in Maundeville's Travels, p. 105. AS. *cealf:* pl. *cealfas, calfru,* or *calferu;* Grein, i. 158.+Du. *kalf;* Icel. *kālfr;* Swed. *kalf;* Dan. *kalv;* Goth. *kalbō;* G. *kalb.* β. Probably related to Skt. *garbha-s,* a fœtus, embryo; see Brugmann, i. § 656. Der. *calve,* q. v. ¶ The *calf* of the leg, Icel. *kālfi* (whence also Ir. and Gael. *calpa*) is closely related; being likened to the fœtus. Cf. Gaulish L. *galba,* greatbellied; and Swed. *ben-kalf,* calf of the leg, from *ben,* leg. See notes on E. Etym.; and see **Cave in.**

CALIBER, CALIBRE, the size of the bore of a gun. (F.—Ital. —Arab.) The form *calibre* is closer to the French, and more usual. *Caliber* occurs in Reid's Inquiry, c. 6. s. 19 (R.) Neither form appears to be old; *calibre* occurs in 1567 and 1588 (N.E.D.). We also find the spellings *caliver* and *caliper* in Kersey's Dict. ed. 1715.—F. *calibre,* occurring in 1478, is said to have been introduced from Ital. *calibro;* Hatzfeld. Cotgrave has: '*Calibre,* a quality, state, or degree;' also: '*Qualibre,* the bore of a gun, or size of the bore, &c. *Il n'est pas de mon qualibre,* he is not of my quality, ranke, or humour, he is not a fit companion for me.'—Ital. *calibro, colibro,* 'an instrument that gunners vse, to measure the heighth of any piece or bullet; also, the heighth or bore of any piece;' Florio (ed. 1611). β. Of uncertain origin. Mahn suggests L. *quā librā,* of what weight, applied to the bore of a gun as determined by the weight (and consequent size) of the bullet. See **Librate.** γ. Diez suggests a more likely origin, viz. Arab. *kālib,* a form, mould, model; cf. Pers. *kālab,* a mould from which anything is made; Rich. Dict. pp. 1110, 1111. So Devic. Der. *calipers,* q. v.; also *caliver,* q. v.

CALICO, cotton-cloth. (East Indian.) Spelt *callico* in Drayton, Edw. IV to Mrs. Shore; *callicoe* in Robinson Crusoe, ed. J. W. Clark, 1866, p. 124; pl. *callicoes,* Spectator, no. 292. Hakluyt speaks of *Calicut cloth* (N.E.D.). Named from *Calicut,* on the Malabar coast, whence it was first imported.

CALIF, CALIPH, a title assumed by the successors of Mahomet. (F.—Arab.) Spelt *caliphe* in Gower, C.A. i. 245; b. ii. 2549; *califfe,* Maundeville's Trav. p. 36.—F. *calife,* a successor of the prophet.— Arab. *khalīfah,* lit. a successor; Richardson, p. 626.—Arab. *khalafa,* to succeed; id. p. 622, s. v. *khilāfat,* succeeding. Der. *caliph-ship, caliph-ate.*

CALIGRAPHY, CALLIGRAPHY, good hand-writing. (Gk.) Wood, in his Athenæ Oxonienses, uses the word when referring to the works of Peter Bales (not Bale, as in Richardson). Spelt *calligraphy;* Prideaux, Connection, pt. i. b. v. s. 5; *kalligraphy,* Ben Jonson, Magnetic Lady, iii. 4.—Gk. καλλιγραφία, beautiful writing.—Gk. καλλι-, for κάλλ-ος, beauty, from καλός, beautiful, fair; and γράφειν, to write. For Gk. γράφειν, see **Carve.**

CALIPASH, the upper shell or carapace of a turtle. (F.—Span.) 'The *calapatch* and *calapee,* i. e. the back and breast shells' [of a turtle]; Arber's Eng. Garner, vii. 358. Prob. a variant of *Carapace,* q. v.

CALIPEE, the lower shell of the turtle; see above. Only known in English; apparently coined to match *calipash;* ending perhaps suggested by *cap-a-pee,* in which *pee* means ' foot.' Spelt *callapee* by W. Dampier, A New Voyage, i. 106.

CALIPERS, compasses of a certain kind. (F.—Ital.—Arab.) Compasses for measuring the diameter of cylindrical bodies are called *calipers;* a contraction of *caliber-compasses.* See *Callipers* in Kersey's Dict. ed. 1715. From *caliber,* the size of a bore; q. v.

CALISTHENICS, CALLISTHENICS, graceful exercises. (Gk.) Modern. A coined word.—Gk. καλλισθενής, adorned with strength.—Gk. καλλι-, for κάλλ-ος, beauty, from καλός, beautiful, fair; and σθένος, strength, allied to Icel. *stinnr,* AS. *stið,* stiff, strong (Prellwitz). Der. *calisthenic,* adj.

CALIVER, a sort of musket. (F.—Ital.—Arab.) In Shak. 1 Hen. IV, iv. 2. 21. The name was given from some peculiarity in the size of the bore. It is a mere corruption of *caliber,* q. v. '*Caliver* or *Caliper,* the bigness, or rather the diameter of a piece of ordinance or any other firearms at the bore or mouth;' Kersey's Dict. ed. 1715.

CALK, CAULK, to stop up the seams of a ship. (F.—L.) The sb. *calkers* occurs in the A.V. Ezek. xxvii. 9; the marg. note has: 'strengtheners, or stoppers of chinks.' The ME. *cauken* signifies 'to tread;' P. Plowman, C. xv. 162; xiv. 171. The spelling with *l* was probably adopted to assimilate the word more closely to the orig. Lat.—OF. *cauquer,* to tread; also, to tent a wound, i. e. to insert a roll of lint in it, to prevent its healing too quickly; Cotgrave.—L. *calcāre,* to tread, trample, press grapes, tread down, tread in, press close. (The notion in *calk* is that of forcing in by great pressure.)— L. *calx* (stem *calc-*), the heel.

CALKIN, the turned down end of a horse-shoe. (F.—L.) The pl. *calkins* occurs in The Two Noble Kinsmen, v. 4. 55. '*Cawkons* of horse-shone;' Relig. Antiquæ, i. 83.—OF. *calcain,* the heel; Godefroy.—L. *calcāneum,* the heel.—L. *calc-,* for *calx,* heel; with suffix *-āneum.*

CALL, to cry aloud. (Scand.) ME. *callen,* Havelok, 2899. AS. *ceallian,* to call, Grein, i. 158; OMerc. *callian,* as in *hilde-calla,* a herald, lit. a ' war-caller,' Grein, ii. 73. Borrowed from Icel. and Swed. *kalla,* to call. Cf. Dan. *kalde,* to call; Du. *kallen,* to talk, chatter; OHG. *challōn,* MHG. *kallen.* Teut. type *kallōn or *kallōjan,* weak verb; cf. W. *galw,* to call, Russ. *golos',* voice, sound. See Brugm. i. § 639; Benfey, p. 270; Fick, i. 72. Der. *call-er; call-ing,* sb., an occupation, that to which one is called.

CALLET, CALLAT, a worthless woman. (F.—Low L.— Low G.) In Oth. iv. 2. 121. Origin doubtful; but it fairly answers to F. *caillette,* a gossip, chatterer; 'personne qui a du babil et point de consistance,' Supp. to Godefroy. Lit. 'little quail;' dimin. of *caille,* a quail, also a woman. Littré gives *caille coiffée,* femme galante. See **Quail.**

CALLIGRAPHY; see **Caligraphy.**

CALLIPERS; see **Calipers.**

CALLISTHENICS; see **Calisthenics.**

CALLOUS, hard, indurated. (F.—L.) *Callous* occurs in Holland's Pliny, bk. xvi. c. 31; and *callosity* in the same, bk. xvi. c. 7.— F. *calleux,* 'hard, or thick-skinned, by much labouring;' Cot.—L. *callōsus,* hard or thick-skinned, callous.—L. *callus, callum,* hard skin; *callēre,* to have a hard skin. Der. *callos-ity* (from L. acc. *callōsitātem,* hardness of skin); also *callous-ly, callous-ness.*

CALLOW, unfledged, said of young birds; also bald. (L.) See Milton, P. L. vii. 420. ME. *calu, calugh, calewe.* ' *Calugh* was his heuede [head];' King Alisaunder, 5950. AS. *calu,* bald; Grein, i. 155.+Du. *kaal,* bald, bare, naked, leafless; Swed. *kal,* bald, bare; G. *kahl;* cf. MDu. *kaluwe.* Teut. type *kalwoz;* an early borrowing from L. *caluus,* bald. Brugmann, i. § 529 (3).

CALM, tranquil, quiet; as sb., repose. (F.—Late L.—Gk.) ME. *calm,* Gower, C. A. iii. 230; b. vii. 4113.—F. *calme,* 'calm, still;' Cot. He does not give it as a substantive, but in mod. F. it is both adj. and sb., and the sb. *calme* is found as early as 1529 (Hatzfeld), as if borrowed from Ital. *calma.* β. The *l* is no real part of the word, though appearing in Ital., Span., and Portuguese; it seems to have been inserted, as Diez suggests, through the influence of the L. *calor,* heat, the notions of ' heat ' and ' rest ' being easily brought together. γ. The mod. Provençal *chaume* signifies ' the time when the flocks rest;' cf. F. *chômer,* formerly *chaumer,* to rest, to be without work; see *chômer* in Hatzfeld. δ. Derived from Late L. *cauma,* the heat of the sun (Job, xxx. 30; Vulgate); on which Maigne D'Arnis remarks, in his epitome of Ducange, that it answers to the Languedoc *caumas* or *calimas,* excessive heat.—Gk. καῦμα, great heat. —Gk. καίειν, to burn. See Korting, § 2032. Der. *calm-ly, calm-ness.*

CALOMEL, a preparation of mercury. (Gk.) Explained in Chambers's Dict. as ' the *white* sublimate of mercury, got by the application of heat to a mixture of mercury and corrosive sublimate, which is *black.*' The sense is ' a fair product from a black substance ;' and the word is coined from καλο-, for Gk. καλός, fair, and μέλ-ας, black, for which see **Melancholy.** ¶ The etymology seems certain; but the reasons for it are unsatisfactory. See Littré and Hatzfeld.

CALORIC, the supposed principle of heat. (F.—L.) A modern word, but now obsolescent; formed from the L. *calor,* heat, by the addition of the suffix *-ic.* The F. form is *calorique* (an. 1792), and we borrowed it from them in that form; but it comes to the same thing. See **Caldron.**

CALORIFIC, having the power to heat. (L.) Boyle speaks of '*calorifick* agents;' Works, vol. ii. p. 594.—L. *calōrificus,* making hot, heating.—L. *calōri-,* for *calor,* heat; and *-fic-us,* a suffix due to the verb *facere,* to make. Der. *calorific-at-ion.*

CALOYER, a Greek monk. (F.—Ital.—Gk.) ' How name ye yon lone *caloyer* ?' Byron, The Giaour, l. 786.—F. *caloyer* (Hatzfeld). —Ital. *caloiero* (N.E.D.)—mod. Gk. καλόγηρος, venerable.—Gk. καλό-, for καλός, fair; and -γηρος, aged, allied to γῆρας, old age.

CALTHROP, CALTRAP, a star-thistle, a ball with spikes for annoying cavalry. (L. *and* Teut.) *Calthrop* is gen. used to denote a ball stuck with four spikes, so arranged that one of them points upwards while the other three rest on the ground. ' Caltrappe, *chaussetrappe;*' Palsgrave. ' *Tribulus marinus,* calketrappe, sea-þistel;' Reliq. Antiq. i. 37. ME. *kalketrappe,* P. Plowman, C. xxi. 296. AS. *calcetreppe,* star-thistle, A. S. Leechdoms, iii. 316; cf. *calcatrippe,* Voc. 298. 30. The most likely solution of this difficult word is to derive it from L. *calci-,* decl. stem of *calx,* the heel, and a Latinised form of the Teutonic word *trap.* Florio gives MItal. *calcatrippa,* star-thistle, where *calca-* is plainly supposed to be allied to *calcāre,* to tread, the form of the Ital. word being slightly altered in order to suggest this sense. See further under **Calk** and **Trap.** Hatzfeld derives F. *chausse-* (in F. *chausse-trape*) from L. *calceāre,* to shoe, from *calceus,* a shoe; but this also goes back to L. *calx.* It either meant ' heel-trap,' or ' trap whereon one treads.' See my note to P. Plowman, C. xxi. 296; also Catholicon Anglicum, p. 52, note 3.

CALUMET, a kind of pipe for tobacco. (F. – L. – Gk.) 'Smoked the *calumet*, the Peace-pipe;' Longfellow, Song of Hiawatha, c. 1. – Norman F. *calumet*, the stem of a herb, a pipe (Littré); a dimin. form, allied to OF. *chalemel*, F. *chalumeau*, 'the stem of an herbe, also a wheaten or oaten straw, or a pipe made thereof;' Cot. These words, like E. *shawm*, are from L. *calamus*; see **Shawm**.

CALUMNY, slander, false accusation. (F. – L.) Shak. has *calumny*, Meas. ii. 4. 159; also *calumniate*, Troil. iii. 3. 174; and *calumnious*, All's Well, i. 3. 61. – F. *calomnie*, 'a calumnie;' Cot. – L. *calumnia*, false accusation. – L. *calui*, *caluere*, to deceive. Der. *calumni-ous*, *calumni-ous-ly*; also *calumniate* (from L. *calumniātus*, pp. of *calumniārī*, to slander); whence *calumniat-or*, *calumniat-ion*. Doublet, *challenge*, q. v.

CALVE, to produce a calf. (E.) ME. *caluen* (*u* for *v*); 'the cow *caluyde*;' Wyclif, Job, xxi. 10. AS. *cealfian*, Ælfric, Hom. ii. 300. – AS. *cealf*, a calf. See **Calf**. The verb appears in the Du. *kalven*, Dan. *kalve*, Swed. *kalfva*, G. *kalben*, to calve; all derivatives from the sb. And see **Cave in.**

CALX, the substance left after a metal has been subjected to great heat. (L.) In Kersey's Dict. ed. 1715. A word used in the old treatises on alchemy; now nearly superseded by the term *oxide*. Cf. 'With the *calce* of egg-shells;' Ben Jonson, Alchemist, A. ii. (Face). Merely borrowed from Latin. – L. *calx*, stone, limestone, lime (stem *calc-*). Cf. Gk. χάλιξ, rubble. Der. *calc-ine*, q. v.; *calc-areous*, q. v.; *calc-ium*; *calc-ul-us*; *cal-cul-ate*, q. v.

CALYX, the outer envelope in which the flower is enclosed while yet in the bud. (L. – Gk.) A botanical term. '*Calyx*, the cup of the flower in any plant;' Kersey's Dict. ed. 1715; showing that he confused it (as usual) with L. *calix*, a cup; for which see **Chalice**. – L. *calyx*, a case or covering, bud, calyx of a flower. – Gk. κάλυξ, a case, covering, calyx of a flower.＋Skt. *kalikā*, a bud. – √KĔL, to cover, hide, conceal (L. *cēl-āre*); from which come, in English, the words *helm* (2), *hell*, *hole*, and *helmet*.

CAM, a projecting part of a wheel, cog. (Du.) A technical term; fully explained in Webster's Dict. and in N.E.D. – Du. *kam*, a comb, also a cog; see Calisch and Kilian. Cf. Low G. *kamm*, Dan. *kam*, a comb, ridge; hence a ridge on a wheel; Dan. *kamhjul*, a cog-wheel; G. *kamm*, a comb, a cog of a wheel. See **Comb**.

CAMBRIC, a kind of fine white linen. (Flanders.) In Shak. Wint. Tale, iv. 4. 208. Cotgrave gives: '*Cambray*, *ou Toile de Cambray*, cambricke.' From *Kamerijk* (F. *Cambray*), a town in Flanders, where it was first made. Sewel has: '*Kameriks-doek*, chambric, lawn.'

CAMEL, the name of a quadruped. (F. – L. – Gk. – Heb.) Spelt *camaille* in Chaucer, C. T. 9072 (E 1196). The pl. *camelis* is in King Alisaunder, 854. The ME. forms are *camel*, *cameil*, *camail*, *chamel*, *chamail*, &c. [The form *camel*, in the Old Northumbrian glosses of S. Mark, i. 6, is directly from L. *camēlus*.] – OF. *chamel*, ONorth. F. *camel*. – L. *camēlus*. – Gk. κάμηλος. – Heb. *gāmāl*.＋Arab. *jamal*; Palmer's Pers. Dict., col. 173. Der. *camelo-pard*, q. v.

CAMELLIA, a genus of plants. (Personal name.) The *Camellia Japonica* is sometimes called the 'Japan rose.' The name was given by Linnæus (died 1778), in honour of George Joseph Kamel (or Camellus), a Moravian Jesuit, who travelled in Asia and wrote a history of plants of the island of Luzon; Encycl. Brit. 9th ed.

CAMELOPARD, the giraffe. (L. – Heb. *and* Gk.) Spelt *camelopardalis* and *camelopardus* in Kersey's Dict. ed. 1715, and in Bailey, vol. ii. ed. 1731. Shortened to resemble F. *camélopard*, the giraffe. – L. *camēlopardālis*. – Gk. καμηλοπάρδαλις, a giraffe. – Gk. κάμηλο-, for κάμηλος, a camel; πάρδαλις, a pard. See **Camel** and **Pard**.

CAMEO, a precious stone, carved in relief. (Ital.) The word occurs as *cameo* in Darwin's Botanical Garden, canto ii. 310. [The F. spelling *camaieu* is sometimes found in Eng. books, and occurs in Bailey's Dict. vol. ii. ed. 1731. The extraordinary form *kaadmau* occurs in Matthew Paris, vi. 387 (Rec. Ser.).] – Ital. *cammeo*, a cameo; Late L. *cammæus*, a cameo; also spelt *camahutus*; cf. F. *camaieu*. β. Etym. unknown; see the discussion of it in Diez, s. v. *cammeo*; and in Mahn, Etymologische Untersuchungen, Berlin, 1863, p. 73. Mahn suggests that *cammæus* is an adj. from *camma*, a Late L. version of a G. *＊camme*, a form due to G. pronunciation of OF. *game*, a gem (Lat. *gemma*), for which Roquefort gives a quotation. In the same way *camahutus* might be due to a German form of the same F. *game* and to F. *haute*, high. But the Span. is *camafeo*. See Körting, § 2359; Schade, OHG. Dict. p. 1341.

CAMERA, a box, chamber, &c. (L. – Gk.) Chiefly used as an abbreviation of L. *camera obscūra*, i. e. dark chamber, the name of what was once an optical toy, but now of great service in photography. See **Chamber**, of which it is the orig. form. Der. *camerated*, from a L. form *camerātus*, formed into chambers; a term in architecture.

CAMLET, a sort of cloth. (F. – Arab.) *Camlet* is short for *camelot*, which occurs in Sir T. Browne's Vulg. Errors, bk. v. c. 15. § 3. – F. *camelot*, which Cotgrave explains by 'chamlet, also Lisle grogram.' It seems to have been popularly understood as being made of *camel's* hair. Cf. 'For *camelot*, the camel ful of hare' [hair]; King James I, King's Quair, st. 157. But it doubtless represents the Arab. *khamlat*, *khamelat*, explained as 'camelot, silk and camel's hair; also, all silk or velvet;' Rich. Dict. p. 628. Cf. *khaml*, 'the skirts or laps of a garment, a carpet with a long pile, a cushion on a saddle;' ibid. It thus appears that camel's hair was sometimes used for making it, so that confusion may easy. See Marco Polo, ed. Yule, i. 248.

CAMOMILE; see **Chamomile**.

CAMP, the ground occupied by an army; the army itself. (F. – L.) Common in Shakespeare. Also used as a verb; All's Well, iii. 4. 14; and in the Bible of 1561, Exod. xix. 2. The proper sense is 'the field' which is occupied by the army; as in 'the gate of the camp was open;' North's Plutarch, Life of M. Brutus; see Shakespeare's Plutarch, ed. Skeat, p. 147; cf. Antony and Cleopatra, iv. 8. 33. [Perhaps taken directly from Latin.] – F. *camp*, 'a camp; an hoast, or army lodged; a field;' Cot. – L. *campus*, a field. See Brugm. i. § 563. Der. *camp*, verb, *en-camp-ment*, *camp-estr-al*, q. v., *camp-aign*, q. v. ¶ It is remarkable that *camp* in Middle English never has the modern sense, but is only used in the sense of 'fight' or 'battle.' Cf. 'alle the kene mene [men] of *kampe*,' i. e. all the keen fighting-men; Allit. Morte Arthure, 3702; cf. l. 3671. And see Layamon, i. 180, 185, 336; ii. 162. This is the AS. *camp*, a battle; *camp-sted*, a battle-ground. Allied words are the Du., Dan. and Swed. *kamp*, Icel. *kapp*, G. *kampf*, all signifying 'battle.' Teut. type *＊kampoz*. Notwithstanding the wide spread of the word in this sense, it is certainly non-Teutonic, and borrowed from L. *campus*, in Late L. 'a battle.' See also **Champion** and **Campaign**.

CAMPAGNOL, the short-tailed field-mouse. (F. – L.) Modern; from F. *campagne*, country; see below. And see **Vole**.

CAMPAIGN, a large field; the period during which an army keeps the field. (F. – Ital. – L.) The word occurs in Burnet, Hist. of his Own Time, an. 1666. And see *Campaign* in Blount's Gloss. – MF. *campaigne*, an open field given in Cotgrave as a variation of *campagne*, which he explains by 'a plaine field, large plain.' – Ital. *campagna*, a field, a campaign. – L. *campānia*, a plain, preserved in the name *Campania*, formerly given to the level country near Naples. – L. *campus*, a field. See **Camp**. Der. *campaign-er*. ¶ Shak. uses *champaign* (old edd. *champion*), K. Lear, i. 1. 65, for 'a large tract of land.' This is from the OF. *champagne*, the standard form; the form *campagne* having been borrowed (as above).

CAMPANIFORM, bell-shaped. (Late L.) '*Campaniformis*, a term apply'd by herbalists, to any flower that is shap'd like a bell;' Kersey's Dict. ed. 1715. From Late L. *campāna*, a bell; and L. *forma*, form. Der. From the same Late L. *campāna* are Ital. *campanile*, a bell-tower; also *campan-ul-a*, *campan-ul-ate*, *campan-o-logy*.

CAMPESTRAL, growing in fields. (L.) Modern, and rare. The form *campestrian* is in Bailey's Dict. vol. ii. ed. 1731. Formed from L. *campestr-is*, growing in a field, or belonging to a field, by adding the suffix *-al*. – L. *campus*, a field. See **Camp**.

CAMPHOR, a whitish crystalline substance, mostly obtained from some kinds of laurel. (F. – Late L. – Arab. – Malay.) Spelt *camphire* in the Song of Solomon, i. 14 (A. V.); and *camfor* in 1392-3 in the Earl of Derby's Expeditions, ed. Lucy T. Smith, p. 164. Massinger speaks of *camphire-balls*; The Guardian, iii. 1. – F. *camphre*, 'the gumme tearmed camphire;' Cot. [The *i* seems to have been inserted to make the word easier to pronounce in English.] – Late L. *camphora*, camphor; to the form of which the mod. E. *camphor* has been assimilated. β. A word of Eastern origin. Cf. Skt. *karpūra-m*, camphor (Benfey, p. 164); Arabic *kāfūr*, camphor, Palmer's Pers. Dict. col. 480. γ. All from Malay *kāpūr*, lit. chalk; the full form being *Barūs kāpūr*, i. e. chalk of Barous, a place on the W. coast of Sumatra; see J. Pijnappel's Malay-Dutch Dict. p. 74. '*Kāpūr bārus*, the camphor of Sumatra and Java, called also native camphor, as distinguished from that of Japan or *kāpūr tohōri*, which undergoes a process before it is brought to our shops; Marsden, Malay Dict. p. 249; where we also find '*kāpūr*, lime.'

CAMPION, a flower of the genus *Lychnis*. (F. – L.) First in 1576. Lyte describes the *rose campion*, and the *white campion*; tr. of Dodoens, bk. ii. ch. 9 and ch. 10. Origin uncertain; but prob. a variant of North F. *campagne*, as *champion* is of *champaign*. Tusser has 'the *champion* or open countrie' in the title to his book on Husbandry (1580). Thus *campion* = field flower. – L. *camp-us*, a plain.

CAN (1), I am able. (E.) α. The AS. *cunnan*, to know, to know how to do, to be able, forms its present tense thus: *ic can* (or *cann*), þu *canst* (or *const*), *he can* (or *cann*); plural, for all persons, *cunnon*. The Mœso-Goth. *kunnan*, to know, forms its present tense thus : *ik kann*, *thu kant*, *is kann*; pl. *weis kunnum*, *jus kunnuth*, *eis kunnun*. β. The verb is one of those which (like the Gk. οἶδα, I know) use as a present tense what is really an old preterite form, from which again a second *weak* preterite is formed. The same peculiarity is common to all the cognate Teutonic verbs, viz. Du. *kunnen*, to be able; Icel. *kunna*, to know, to be able; Swed. *kunna*, to know, to be able; Dan. *kunde*, to know, to be able; OHG. *chunnan*, MHG. *kunnen*, G. *können*, to be able. γ. The past tense is **Could**. Here the *l* is inserted in modern English by analogy with *would* and *should*, in which the *l* is radical. The ME. form was *coudè*, a dissyllable; the AS. form is *cúðe*. The lengthened *u* occasioned loss of *n*; *cúðe* stands for *cunðe (pronounced *koonthè*, with *oo* as in *foot*, and *th* as in *breathe*). The loss of the *n* has obscured the relation to *can*. The *n* reappears in Gothic, where the past tense is *kuntha*; cf. Du. *konde*, I could; Icel. *kunna* (for *kunda*, by assimilation); Swed. and Dan. *kunde*; OHG. *konda*, G. *konnte*. Whence it appears that the English alone has lost the *n*. γ. The past participle is **Couth**. This is only preserved, in mod. Eng., in the form *uncouth*, of which the original sense was 'unknown.' The AS. form is *cúð*, for *cunð, the *n* being preserved in the Goth. *kunths*, known. See **Uncouth**. Allied to *ken* (Icel. *kenna*) and *know* (AS. *cnáwan*). The Idg. form of the root is GEN; Brugmann, i. § 600. See **Know** and **Ken**.

CAN (2), a drinking-vessel. (E.) ME. *canne*. 'There weren set sixe stonun *cannes*;' Wyclif, John, ii. 6. AS. *canne*, as a gloss to L. *cráter*; Ælf. Gloss. ed. Somner, p. 60; Voc. 122. 32.+Du. *kan*, a pot, mug; Icel. *kanna*, a can, tankard, mug; also, a measure; Swed. *kanna*, a tankard, a measure of about 3 quarts; Dan. *kande*; OHG. *chann*, MHG. and G. *kanne*, a can, tankard, mug, jug, pot. ¶ It thus appears to be a true Teutonic word; Teut. type *kannōn, f. Some think that it was borrowed from L. *canna*, Gk. κάννη, a reed; but the sense is hardly close enough; whilst *cantharus* differs in form. **Der.** *cannikin*, dimin.; spelt *canykyn*, Barclay, Ship of Fools, ii. 261; *canakin*, Oth. ii. 3. 71.

CANAL, a conduit for water. (F.—L.) 'The walls, the woods, and long *canáls* reply;' Pope, Rape of the Lock, iii. 100. And in Bacon, Nat. Hist. §§ 30, 138.—F. *canal*, 'a channell, kennell, furrow, gutter;' Cot.—L. *canālis*, a channel, trench, canal, conduit; also, a splint, reed-pipe. ¶ Perhaps the accent on the latter syllable in E. was partly due to a familiarity with Du. *kanaal*, itself borrowed from French. See also **Channel**, **Kennel**.

CANARY, a bird; a wine; a dance. (Span.—L.) The dance is mentioned in Shak. All's Well, ii. 1. 77; so is the wine, Merry Wives, iii. 2. 89. Gascoigne speaks of ' Canara birds;' Complaint of Philomene, l. 33. All are named from the Canaries or Canary Islands. These take their name from *Canaria*, which is the largest island of the group. ' *Grand Canary* is almost as broad as long, the diameter being about fifty miles;' Sir T. Herbert, Travels, ed. 1665, p. 3.—Span. (*Gran*) *Canaria*.—L. *Canāria* (*insula*), isle abounding in large dogs (Pliny, vi. 32).—L. *canária*, fem. of *canárius*, pertaining to dogs.—L. *can-is*, a dog; see **Canine**.

CANCEL, to obliterate. (F.—L.) Originally, to obliterate a deed by drawing lines over it in the form of lattice-work (L. *cancelli*); afterwards, to obliterate in any way. Spelt *cancell* in the Mirrour for Magistrates, p. 632 (R.).—F. *canceler*, 'to cancell, cross, raze;' Cot.—Law L. *cancellāre*, to draw lines across a deed.—L. *cancellus*, a grating; gen. in pl. *cancelli*, railings, lattice-work; dimin. of *cancer*, pl. *cancri*, in the sense of 'lattice-work.' **Der.** *cancell-at-ed*, marked with cross-lines, from L. pp. *cancellātus*; from the same source, *chancel*, *chancery*, *chancellor*, which see.

CANCER, a crab, a corroding tumour. (L.) The tumour was named from the notion that the swollen veins round it were like a crab's limbs (Galen). *Cancer* occurs as the name of a zodiacal sign in Chaucer, Merchant's Tale, l. 643.—L. *cancer*, a crab; gen. *cancri*. +Gk. καρκίνος, a crab; Skt. *karkaṭa-s*, a crab; also the sign Cancer of the zodiac. β. So named from its hard shell; cf. Skt. *karkara-s*, hard. Brugmann, i. § 464. **Der.** *cancer-ous*, *cancri-form*, *cancer-ate*, *cancer-at-ion*; and see **Canker**.

CANDELABRUM; see under **Candle**.

CANDID, lit. white; fair; sincere. (F.—L.) Dryden uses *candid* to mean 'white;' tr. of Ovid, Metam. xv. l. 60. Camden has *candidly*; Elizabeth, an. 1598 (R.). Shak. has *candidatus* for *candidate*; Titus Andron. i. 185. Ben Jonson has *candor*, Epigram 123.—F. *candide*, 'white, fair, bright, orient, &c.; also, upright, sincere, innocent;' Cot.—L. *candidus*, lit. shining, bright.—L. *candēre*, to shine, be bright. —L. *candere, to set on fire; only in *ac-cendere*, *in-cendere*.+Skt. *chand*, to shine.—√SQEND, to shine. Brugm. i. §§ 456, 818 (2). **Der.** *candidate*, q. v.; *candour*, lit. brightness, from F. *candeur*, which from L. *candōrem*, acc. case of *candor*, brightness; also *candid-ly*, *candid-ness*. From L. *candēre* we also have *candle*, *incense*, *incendiary*, which see.

CANDIDATE, one who offers himself to be elected to an office. (L.) Shak. has: ' Be *candidatus* then and put it on;' Titus, i. 185; where the allusion is to the *white robe* worn by a candidate for office among the Romans.—L. *candidātus*, white-robed; a candidate for an office.—L. *candidus*, white. See **Candid**.

CANDLE, a kind of artificial light. (L.) In very early use. AS. *candel*, a candle, Grein, i. 155.—L. *candēla*, a candle, taper.—L. *candēre*, to glow.—L. *candere, to set on fire; see further under **Candid**. **Der.** *Candle-mas* (Feb. 2), A.S. Chron., an. 1014, with which cf. *Christ-mas*, q.v.; *candle-stick* (Trevisa, i. 223), AS. *candel-sticca*, Birch, Cart. Saxon., iii. 366; *candēlabrum*, a L. word, from L. *candēla*; also *chandel-ier*, q. v.; *chandl-er*, q. v.; *cannel-coal*, q. v.

CANDOUR; see under **Candid**.

CANDY, crystallised sugar; *as a verb*, to sugar, to crystallise. (F.—Ital.—Arab.—Skt.) In old authors, it is usually a verb. Shak. has both sb. and verb, 1 Hen. IV, i. 3. 251; Hamlet, iii. 2. 65; Temp. ii. 1. 279. The comp. *sugar-candy* is the oldest form; see Liber Cure Cocorum, p. 7.—F. *sucre candi*, sugar-candy; whence *se candir*, 'to candie, or grow candide, as sugar after boyling;' Cotgrave. [Here Cotgrave should rather have written *candied*; there is no connexion with L. *candidus*, white, as he easily might have imagined.]—Ital. *candire*, to candy; *candi*, candy; *zucchero candi*, sugar-candy.—Arabic and Persian *qand*, sugar, sugar-candy; Richardson's Arab. Dict. p. 1149; Arab. *qandat*, sugar-candy, id.; *qandi*, sugared, made of sugar; id. p. 1150.—Skt. *khaṇḍa-s*, a piece, part; also, powdered sugar (Macdonell); cf. *khaṇḍava-s*, a kind of sweetmeat.

CANDYTUFT, a plant, of the genus Iberis. (Hybrid.) First in Evelyn (1664). From *Candy* and *tuft*; where *Candy* refers to the island of *Candia* (or Crete), whence the plant came; and see **Tuft**.

CANE, a reed, a stick. (F.—L.—Gk.) ME. *cane*, *canne*. 'Reedes, that ben *cannes*;' Maundeville, p. 189; see also pp. 190, 199. ' *Cane*, canna;' Wright's Vocab. i. 191.—F. *canne*, a cane.—L. *canna*, a cane, reed.—Gk. κάννα, κάννη, a cane, reed. β. Perhaps *cane* is an Oriental word ultimately; cf. Heb. *qāneh*, a reed; Arab. *qanāh*, a cane; Richardson's Dict. p. 1148. If so, the L. and Gk. words are both borrowed ones. **Der.** *cane*, verb; *can-y*, Milton, P. L. iii. 439; *canister*, q. v.; also *cann-on*, q. v.; *can-on*, q. v.

CANINE, pertaining to a dog. (L.) In the Spectator, no. 209; and in Cockeram (1623).—L. *caninus*, canine.—L. *canis*, a dog; cognate with E. *hound*. See **Hound**.

CANISTER, a case, or box, often of tin. (L.—Gk.) Originally, a basket made of reed or cane. Spelt *cannisters* in Dryden's Virgil, bk. i. 981, to translate ' Cereremque *canistris* Expediunt;' Æn. i. 701. —L. *canistrum*, a basket made of twisted reed.—Gk. κάναστρον, a wicker-basket; properly, a basket of reed.—Gk. κάνη, a rarer form of κάννα, κάννη, a reed, cane. See **Cane**.

CANKER, something that corrodes. (F.—L.) ' *Canker*, sekeness, *cancer*;' Prompt. Parv. p. 60; it occurs very early, in Ancren Riwle, p. 330, where it is spelt *cancre*, as in ONorth. F. [AS. *cancer*, Leechdoms, ii. 110.]—ONorth. F. *cancre* (F. *chancre*).—L. *cancrum*, acc. of *cancer*, a crab, a cancer. See **Cancer**. **Der.** *canker-ous*, *canker-worm* (A. V.).

CANNEL-COAL, a coal that burns brightly. (L. *and* E.) First in 1538 (N.E.D.). Provincial Eng. *cannel*, a candle, and *coal*. ' *Cannle*, a candle; *cannle-coal*, or *kennle-coal*, so called because it burns without smoke like a candle;' F. K. Robinson, Whitby Glossary. And see E. D. D.

CANNIBAL, one who eats human-flesh. (Span.—W. Indian.) A corrupt form; it should rather be *caribal*. ' The Caribes I learned to be man-eaters or *canibals*, and great enemies to the islanders of Trinidad;' Hakluyt, Voyages, vol. iii. p. 576; a passage imitated in Robinson Crusoe, ed. J. W. Clark, 1866, p. 126. See Shak. Oth. i. 3. 143.—Span. *canibal*, a cannibal, savage; a variant of *Caribal*, a Carib, a form used by Columbus; see Trench, Study of Words. β. This word being ill understood, the spelling *canibal* prevailed in Spanish, from the notion that the cannibals had appetites *like a dog*; cf. Span. *canino*, canine, voracious, greedy. As the word *canibal* was unmeaning in English, a second *n* was introduced to make the first vowel short, either owing to stress, or from some notion that it ought to be shortened. γ. The word *Canibal* occurs in the following quotation from Herrera's Descripcion de las Indias Occidentales, vol. i. p. 11. col. 1, given in Todd's Johnson. ' Las Islas qui estan desde la Isla de San Juan de Porto rico al oriente de ella, para los costa de Tierra-Firme, se llamaron los *Canibales* por los muchos *Caribes*, comedores de carne humana, que truvo en ellas, i segun se interpreta en su lengua *Canibal*, quiere decir "hombre valiente," porque por tales eran tenidos de los otros Indios.' I. e. ' the islands lying next to the island of San Juan de Porto-rico [now called Porto Rico] to the East of it, and extending towards the coast of the continent [of South America] are called *Canibales* because of the many *Caribs*, eaters of human flesh, that are found in them, and according to the interpretation of their language *Canibal* is as much as to say "valiant man," because they were held to be such by the other Indians.' This hardly sufficiently recognises the fact that *Canibal* and *Carib* (as well as *Caliban*) are mere variants of one and the same word; but we learn that the West Indian word *Carib* meant, in the language of the natives, 'a valiant man.' Other testimony is to the same effect; and it is well ascertained that *cannibal* is equivalent to Carib or Caribbean, and that the native sense of the word is 'a valiant man,' widely different from that which Europeans have given it. The familiar expression 'king of the cannibal islands' really means 'king of the Caribbean islands.' **Der.** *cannibal-ism.*

CANNON (1), a large gun. (F.—Ital.—L.—Gk.) Frequent in Shak.; K. John, ii. 210, &c. And in Hakluyt, Voyages, vol. iii. p. 217.—F. *canon*, 'a law, rule, decree, ordnance, canon of the law; . . . also, the gunne tearmed a *cannon*; also, the barrell of any gunne,' &c.; Cot.—Ital. *cannone*, 'a canon or piece or ordnance, the barrell of any gun, . . a canon, a rule;' Florio. Thus *cannon* is a doublet of *canon*, q. v. See Trench, Study of Words. β. The spelling with two *n*'s may have been adopted to create a distinction between the two uses of the word, the present word taking the double *n* of Ital. *cannone*. The sense 'gun-barrel' is older than that of 'gun,' and the Ital. *cannone* is the augmentative of Ital. *canna*, a pipe, a cane.—L. *canna*; see **Cane**. **Der.** *cannon-ade*, *cannon-eer*.

CANNON (2), a particular stroke at billiards. (F.—Span.) A perversion of *carrom* or *carom*, shortened form of *carambole*; see Hoyle's Games, Billiards, law 9 (1779).—F. *carambole*, the red ball at billiards; cf. F. *caramboler*, (1) to touch the red ball, (2) to touch two other balls with one's own.—Span. *carambola*, a manner of playing at billiards, a device, trick. Origin unknown.

CANOE, a boat made of a trunk of a tree, &c. (Span.—W. Indian.) Formerly *canoa*, as spelt in Hakluyt's Voyages, iii. 646.—Span. *canoa*, an Indian boat. It is ascertained to be a native West Indian term for 'boat;' and properly, a word belonging to the old language of Hayti. See R. Eden, Books on America, ed. Arber, p. 66; Notes on E. Etym. p. 346. Spelt *canaoa* by R. Breton, in his Dict. Caraïbe-François (1665).

CANON (1), a rule, ordinance. (L.—Gk.) ME. *canon*, *canoun*; Chaucer, Treatise on the Astrolabe, ed. Skeat, prol. 68; C. T., Group C, 890. AS. *canon*; Beda, Eccl. Hist. (A. S. version), iv. 24; Bosworth.—L. *canon*, a rule.—Gk. κανών, a straight rod, a rule in the sense of 'carpenter's rule;' also, a rule or model, a standard of right.—Gk. κάννη, a rarer form of κάννη, a (straight) cane, reed. See **Cane**. **Der.** *canon* (2), one who lives according to a canon, q. v.; *canon-ic*, *canon-ic-al*, *canon-ic-al-ly*, *canon-ist*, *canon-ic-ity*, *canon-ise* (Gower, C. A. i. 254; b. ii. 2821), *canon-is-at-ion*, *canon-ry*. **Doublet**, *cannon* (1), q. v.

CANON (2), a dignitary of the church. (F.—L.—Gk.) ME. *canun*, Layamon, ii. 598, l. 24289; *canoun*, id. (later text), l. 24288. —ONorthF. *canonie* (Littré, s. v. *chanoine*); the pl. *canunies* occurs in the Chanson du Roland, 2956.—Late L. *canonicum*, acc. of *canonicus*, adj., one on the church-roll or list, and so in receipt of church-funds.—L. *canon*, the church-roll or list. See Hatch, Bampton Lectures, p. 202. See **Canon** (1). N.B. The Span. *cañon*, a deep ravine, lit. a tube, is the same word as F. *canon*; see **Cannon** (1).

CANOPY, a covering overhead. (F.—Ital.—L.—Gk.) Should be *conopy*; but the spelling *canopè* occurs in Italian, whence it found its way into French as *canapé*, a form cited by Diez, and thence into English; the proper OF. form is *conopé*. In Shak. Sonn. 125. In Bible of 1551, Judith, xiii. 9; retained in the A. V. Spelt *canopè* in Wyclif. Cf. MF. *conopée*, 'a canopy, a tent, or pavilion;' Cot.—L. *cōnōpēum*, used in Judith, xiii. 10 (Vulgate).—Gk. κωνωπεῖον, an Egyptian bed with musquito-curtains.—Gk. κώνωπ-, stem of κώνωψ, a gnat, mosquito; lit. 'cone-faced,' or a creature with a cone-shaped head, from the shape of its head.—Gk. κῶν-ος, a cone; and ὤψ, face, appearance, from Gk. √ ΟΠ, to see = Idg. √ OQ, to see. See **Cone** and **Optic**. **Der.** *canopy*, verb.

CANOROUS, tuneful. (L.) In Sir T. Browne, Vulg. Errors, b. vii. c. 14. § 5.—L. *canōrus*, singing, musical.—L. *canere*, to sing. See **Cant** (1).

CANT (1), to sing in a whining way; to talk hypocritically. (L.) Applied at first, probably, to the whining tone of beggars, with some allusion to chanting; used derisively. 'Drinking, lying, cogging, canting;' Ford, The Sun's Darling, Act i. sc. 1. 'A rogue, A very *canter* I, sir, one that maunds Upon the pad;' Ben Jonson, Staple of News, Act ii.—L. *cantāre*, to sing (whence Picard and Walloon *canter*, to sing); frequentative of *canere*, to sing; from the same root as E. *hen*, q. v.—√KAN, to sound. Brugmann, i. § 181. **Der.** *cant*, sb.; *cant-er*. From the same source, *can-orous*, q. v.; *cant-icle*, q. v.; *cant-o*, q. v. ¶ 'What was it, prose or ryme, metre or verse? I trowe it was *cantum*, for I herde you synge;' Caxton, Reynard the Fox, c. 27; ed. Arber, p. 63. In Harman's Caveat, p. 84, to *cante*, i. e. to speak, is given as a cant word. Cf. Walloon *canter*, to sing (Sigart); and see *Cant* in the E. D. D. **Der.** *cant-er*, *cant-ing*; also *cant-ata*, Ital. *cantata*, a poetical composition set to music; from the fem. of the pp. of L. *cantāre*, to sing.

CANT (2), an edge, corner; *as verb*, to tilt or incline. (Dutch—L.—Gk.) The sb. is nearly obsolete; we find 'in a *cant*' = 'in a

corner,' in Ben Jonson, Coronation Entertainment; Works, ed. Gifford, vi. 445 (Nares); see the description of Irene in the same, ed. 1860, p. 531. The verb means 'to turn upon an edge,' hence, to tilt, incline; said of a cask. The verb is derived from the sb.—Du. *kant*, a border, edge, side, brink, margin, corner.+Dan. and Swed. *kant*, a border, edge, margin; cf. Dan. *kantre*, to cant, upset, capsize; G. *kante*, a corner. All from Late L. *cantus*, a corner; which is prob. from L. *canthus* (pronounced as *cantus*) < Gk. κάνθος, the corner of the eye, felloe of a wheel. Körting, § 1851. **Der.** *cant-een*, q. v.; *de-cant-er*.

CANTEEN, a vessel for liquors used by soldiers. (F.—Ital.—L.—Gk.) First in 1744 (N.E.D.). The spelling is phonetic, imitating the F. *i* by the mod. E. *ee*.—F. *cantine*, a canteen; introduced from Ital. in the 17th century; Hatzfeld.—Ital. *cantina*, a cellar, cave, grotto, cavern; cf. Ital. *cantinetta*, a small cellar, ice-pail, cooler.—Ital. *canto*, a side, part, corner, angle; whence *cantina* as a diminutive, i. e. 'a little corner.'—Late L. *cantus*, a corner. See **Cant** (2).

CANTER, an easy gallop. (E. place-name.) An abbreviation for *Canterbury gallop*, a name given to an easy gallop; from the ambling pace at which pilgrims rode to Canterbury. 'In Sampson's Fair Maid of Clifton (1633), he who personates the hobby-horse speaks of his smooth ambles and *Canterbury paces*;' Todd's Johnson. 'Boileau's Pegasus has all his paces. The Pegasus of Pope, like a Kentish post-horse, is always on the *Canterbury*;' Dennis on the Prelim. to the Dunciad (Nares). We also have 'Canterbury bells.' **Der.** *canter*, verb.

CANTICLE, a little song. (L.) 'And wrot an *canticle*,' said of Moses; Genesis and Exodus, ed. Morris, l. 4124.—L. *canticulum*, a little song; dimin. of L. *canticum*, a song.—L. *cantus*, a song; cf. *cantus*, pp. of *canere*, to sing. See **Cant** (1).

CANTILEVER, a kind of bracket, projecting from a wall to support a balcony or the like. (F.) Pineda's Span. Dict., s. v. *can*, a dog, adds: 'in architecture, the end of timber or stone jutting out of a wall, on which in old buildings the beams used to rest, called *cantilevers*.' Possibly from *cantle*, a corner, and *lever*. The support could be obtained by letting one end of a lever into a *cantle* (projection or nook) in a wall, and the other into a notch in a horizontal beam above. The MDu. *kanteel-hout*, 'a roofe-beame,' in Hexham (lit. *cantle*-wood) is parallel. See below.

CANTLE, a small piece. (F.—L.—Gk.) In Shak. 1 Hen. IV, iii. 1. 100. ME. *cantel*, Chaucer, C. T., 3010 (A 3008).—ONorthF. *cantel* (mod. F. *chanteau*), a piece, corner, bit; see Littré, s. v. *chanteau*. The same as Late L. *cantellus*, a piece; formed with dimin. suffix -*ellus* from Late L. *cantus*, a corner. See **Cant** (2).

CANTO, a division of a poem. (Ital.—L.) Shak. has *cantons*, Tw. Nt. i. 5. 289, which is a difficult form to account for. The more correct form *cantion* (directly from L. *cantio*, a ballad) occurs near the beginning of the Glosse to Spenser's Shep. Kal., October.—Ital. *canto*, a singing, chant, section of a poem.—L. acc. *cantum*, a song. See **Canticle**.

CANTON, a small division of a country. (F.—Ital.—L.—Gk.) Sir T. Browne uses *cantons* for 'corners;' Religio Medici, pt. i. s. 15. In Heraldry, a *canton* is a small division in the corner of a shield; so used in Ben Jonson, Staple of News, A. iv. (Piedmantle). And see Cotgrave.—F. *canton*, 'a corner or crosseway, in a street; also, a *canton*, or hundred;' Cot. [Cf. Span. *canton*, a corner, part of an escutcheon, canton.]—Ital. *cantone*, a nook, angle; also, a corporation, township (Torriano).—Late L. *cantōnum*, *canto*, a region, province. Origin doubtful; the heraldic *canton*, F. *canton*, Ital. *cantone*, is from Ital. *canto*, an edge. See **Cant** (2). **Der.** *canton*, verb; *canton-al*, *canton-ment*. Cf. *se cantonner*, 'to sever themselves from the rest of their fellowes;' Cotgrave.

CANVAS, a coarse hempen cloth. (F.—L.—Gk.) ME. *canevas*; a trisyllable in Chaucer, C. T. 16407 (G 939).—ONorthF. *canevas*. —Late L. *canabācius*, hempen cloth, canvas.—L. *cannabis*, hemp.—Gk. κάνναβις, hemp, cognate with E. *hemp*, q. v. ¶ It is supposed that the Greek word was borrowed from the East; Curtius, i. 173. Cf. Pers. *kanab*, hemp; Rich. Dict. p. 1208; Skt. *çana-m*, hemp. **Der.** *canvass*, verb; q. v.

CANVASS, to discuss, solicit votes. (F.—L.—Gk.) In Shak. 'to take to task;' 1 Hen. VI, i. 3. 36. Spelt *kanvas* in Palsgrave. Merely derived from the sb. *canvas*, the orig. meaning being 'to sift through canvas.' Similarly, Cotgrave explains the MF. *canabasser* by 'to *canvas*, or curiously to examine, search or sift out the depth of a matter.' See above.

CANZONET, a little song. (Ital.—L.) In Shak. L. L. L. iv. 2. 124. —Ital. *canzonetta*, a little song; dimin. of *canzone*, a hymn; cf. *canzona*, a song, ballad.—L. *cantiōnem*, acc. of *cantio*, a song; whence also F. *chanson*, a song, used by Shak. Hamlet, ii. 2. 438.—L. *cantāre*, to sing; frequentative of *canere*, to sing. See **Cant** (1).

CAOUTCHOUC, india rubber. (F.—Caribbean.) Modern.

Borrowed from F. *caoutchouc,* from a Caribbean word which is spelt *cauchuc* in the Cyclop. Metropolitana, q. v. This word, used at Quito, belongs to the idiom of the Indians of the province of Mainas, and signifies 'juice of a tree.' La Condamine calls it *cahuchu.* See Notes on E. Etym. pp. 30, 31.

CAP, a covering for the head; a cover. (Late L.) In early use. AS. *cæppe,* as a gloss to Late L. *planēta,* a chasuble; Ælfric's Glossary; Voc. 124. 31.—Late L. *cappa,* a cape, a cope; see *capparius* in Ducange. [The words *cap, cape, cope* were all the same originally.] This Late L. *cappa,* a cap, occurs in a document of the year 660 (Diez); and is spelt *cappa* by Isidore of Seville, 19. 31. 3, who says: '*Cappa, quia capitis ornamentum est;*' a popular etymology. But the true origin is unknown. Perhaps the derivation from L. *capere, to contain,* suggested by Papias, may be right. See **Cape, Cope.** ¶ For *cap-a-pie, cap-a-pee,* i. e. from head to foot (from F. *cap,* head, *a,* to, and OF. *pie,* AF. *pee,* foot) see **Cape** (2).

CAPABLE, having ability. (F.—L.) In Shak. Troil. iii. 3. 310. —F. *capable,* 'capable, sufficient;' Cot.—Late L. *capābilis,* lit. comprehensible, a word used in the Arian controversy. β. The meaning afterwards shifted to 'able to hold,' one of the senses assigned by Cotgrave to F. *capable.* This would be due to the influence of L. *capax,* capacious, the word to which *capābilis* was probably indebted for its second *a* and its irregular formation from *capere.*—L. *capere,* to hold, contain.—√QAP, to hold; Brugm. i. § 635. **Der.** *capabil-ity.* See **Heave.**

CAPACIOUS, able to hold or contain. (L.) Used by Sir W. Ralegh, Hist. of the World, bk. i. c. 6. Shak. expresses the same idea by *capable.* Ill formed, as if from a F. *capacieux* or L. *capāciōsus;* but there are no such words, and the real source is the declensional stem *capāci-* of the L. adj. *capax,* able to contain.—L. *capere,* to contain, hold; cognate with E. *heave,* q. v. **Der.** *capacious-ly, capacious-ness;* and (from L. *capax,* gen. *capāci-s*) *capaci-t-ate, capaci-ty.* From the L. *capere* we also have *cap-able, cat-er.* Also *conceive, deceive, receive, &c.* Also *captious, captivate, captive, captor, capture; anticipate, emancipate, participate; acceptable, conception, deception, except, intercept, precept, receipt, receptacle, susceptible; incipient, recipient; occupy; prince, principal;* and all words nearly related to these.

CAPARISON, the trappings of a horse. (F.—Span.—Late L.) In Shak. Cor. i. 9. 12.—MF. *caparasson,* 'a caparison;' Cot.—Span. *caparazon,* a caparison, a cover for a saddle or coach; formed as an augmentative from Med. L. *caparo,* a cowl (cf. E. *chaperon*).—Late L. *cāpa,* a cloak, cape. See **Cape** (1). **Der.** *caparison,* verb; Rich. III, v. 3. 289.

CAPE (1), a covering for the shoulders. (F.—Span.—Late L.) In Shak. Tam. Shrew, iv. 3. 140. [ME. *cape,* in Layamon, ii. 122, is the modern *cope.*]—MF. *cape,* 'a short and sleevelesse cloake;' Cot. —Span. *capa,* a cape, cloak.—Late L. *cāpa,* for which see Ducange; see also **Cap** and **Cope.** Baret, s. v. *Cape,* has: '*a Spanishe cape.*' ¶ The word, being an ecclesiastical one, has spread widely; from the Late L. *cāpa* are derived not only OF. *cape,* but also Prov., Span., and Port. *capa,* Icel. *kápa* (whence E. *cope*), Swed. *kåpa,* Dan. *kaabe.* **Der.** *cap-arison,* q. v.; and see *chapel, chaperon, chaplet.*

CAPE (2), a headland. (F.—Ital.—L.) In Shak. Oth. ii. 1. 1; Chaucer, Prol. 408.—F. *cap,* 'a promontory, cape;' Cot.—Ital. *capo,* a head; a headland, cape.—L. *caput,* a head. ¶ In the phr. *cap-à-piè,* i. e. head to foot, the *cap*' is the F. *cap* here spoken of.

CAPER (1), to dance about. (Ital.—L.) In Shak. Temp. v. 238. The word was merely shortened from the older form *capreoll,* used by Sir P. Sidney in his translation of Ps. 114, quoted by Richardson: 'Hillocks, why *capreold* ye, as wanton by their dammes We *capreoll* see the lusty lambs?'—Ital. *capriolare,* to caper, leap about as goats or kids.—Ital. *capriola,* 'a caper in dancing;' Florio; from Ital. *capra,* a she-goat.—L. *capra,* a she-goat; *caper* (stem *capro-*), a he-goat. Cf. Gk. κάπρος, a boar; Curtius, i. 174.╋AS. *hœfer,* a he-goat; Icel. *hafr.* **Der.** *caper,* sb.; *capriole,* q. v., and cf. *cabriolet, cab.*

CAPER (2), the flower-bud of the caper-bush, used for pickling. (F.—L.—Gk.) There is a quibble on the word in Shak. Tw. Nt. i. 3. 129. Sir T. Elyot has *capers;* Castel of Helth, b. ii. c. 7. —MF. *capre, cappre,* a caper, Cot.; mod. F. *câpre.*—L. *capparis.*—Gk. κάππαρις, the caper-plant; also its fruit. Perhaps Eastern; cf. Arab. *kabar,* capers; Richardson's Arab. Dict. p. 1167.

CAPERCAILZIE, a species of grouse. (Gael.) The *z* is here no *z,* but a modern printer's way of representing the old ʒ, much better represented by *y;* thus the word is really *capercailyie.* [Similarly *Menzies* stands for *Menyies,* and *Dalziel* for *Dalyiel.*] 'The *capercalʒe,* . . horse of the forest;' J. Dalrymple, tr. of Leslie's Hist. Scot. p. 39. See Newton, Dict. of Birds; and the article on the *capercali, capercally,* or *capercailyie,* in the Engl. Cycl., div. Nat. History.—Gael. *capull-coille,* the great cock of the wood; more literally, the horse of the wood.—Gael. *capull,* a horse, from L. *caballus* (cf. E. *cavalier*); and *coille* or *coill,* a wood, a forest, cognate with E. **Holt.**

CAPIBARA, a large rodent quadruped. (Brazil.) The native name in Brazil. '*Capy-bara . . . Porcus est fluviatilis;*' Hist. Nat. Brasiliæ, 1648; vol. ii. p. 230. See **Cavy.**

CAPILLARY, relating to or like hair. (L.) '*Capillary* filaments;' Derham, Physico-Theology, b. iv. c. 12 (R.); and in Blount (1656).—L. *capillāris,* relating to hair.—L. *capillus,* hair; but esp. the hair of the head; from the same source as L. *caput,* the head; the base *cap-* being common to both words (Bréal).

CAPITAL (1), relating to the head; chief. (F.—L.) '*Eddren capitalen*' = veins in the head, where *capitalen* is used as a pl. adj.; Ancren Riwle, p. 258.—F. *capital,* 'chiefe, capitall;' Cotgrave (and in early use).—L. *capitālis,* relating to the head.—L. *caput* (stem *capit-*), the head. Allied to Skt. *kapāla*(*m*), skull; AS. *hafela,* head. Brugm. i. § 641. **Der.** *capital,* sb., which see below. And see **Capitol.**

CAPITAL (2), wealth, stock of money. (F.—L.) Not in early use; later than 1600 (N. E. D.).—F. *capital,* 'wealth, worth, a stocke, a man's principal, or chiefe substance;' Cotgrave.—Late L. *capitāle,* wealth, stock; properly neuter of adj. *capitālis,* chief; see above. **Der.** *capital-ist, capital-ise.* See **Cattle.**

CAPITAL (3), the head of a pillar. (Late L., *or* F.—L.) 'The pilers . . With harlas and *capitale*' = with fillet and capital; Land of Cokayne, l. 69.—Late L. *capitellum,* the head of a column or pillar; a dimin. from L. *caput* (stem *capit-*), a head. Or from ONorthF. *capitel* (Picard *capiteau,* F. *chapiteau*); the same. **Doublets,** *chapiter, chapter.*

CAPITATION, a tax on every head. (F.—L.) In Sir T. Browne, Vulg. Errors, bk. vii. c. 11. § 1.—F. *capitation,* 'head-silver, pole-money; a subsidy, tax, or tribute paid by the pole' [i.e. poll]; Cot.—Late L. *capitātiōnem,* acc. of *capitātio,* a capitation-tax.—L. *caput* (stem *capit-*), a head.

CAPITOL, the temple of Jupiter, at Rome. (L.) The temple was situate on the Mons Capitolinus, named from the *Capitōlium,* or temple of Jupiter, whence E. *capitol* is derived. In Shak. Cor. i. 1. 49, &c. 'The temple is said to have been called the Capitolium, because a human head (*caput*) was discovered in digging the foundations;' Smith's Classical Dictionary. For whatever reason, the etymology seems to be from the L. *caput,* gen. *capit-is* (above).

CAPITULAR, relating to a cathedral chapter. (L.) Properly an adj., but gen. used as a sb., meaning 'the body of the statutes of a chapter.' 'The *capitular* of Charles the Great joyns dicing and drunkenness together;' Bp. Taylor, Rule of Conscience, bk. iv. c. 1 (R.).—Late L. *capitulāris,* relating to a *capitulum,* in its various senses; whence neut. *capitulāre,* a writing divided into chapters; *capitulāre institūtum,* a monastic rule; and sb. *capitulārium,* a book of decrees, whence the E. *capitulary,* a more correct form, as a sb., than *capitular.* —Late L. *capitulum,* a chapter of a book; a cathedral chapter; dimin. from L. *caput,* the head. See **Chapter.**

CAPITULATE, to submit upon certain conditions. (L.) See Trench, Select Glossary. It properly means, to arrange conditions, and esp. of surrender; as in 'to *capitulate* and conferre wyth them touchynge the estate of the cytie, the beste that they could, so that their parsones [persons] might be saued;' Nicolls, tr. of Thucydides, p. 219 (R.). See Shak. Cor. v. 3. 82.—Late L. *capitulātus,* pp. of *capitulāre,* to divide into chapters, hence, to propose terms.—Late L. *capitulum,* a chapter (above). **Der.** *capitulat-ion.*

CAPON, a young cock castrated. (L.—Gk.) In very early use. AS. *capun,* as a gloss to 'gallinaceus;' Ælfric's Glossary, ed. Somner, *Nomina Avium.*—L. *capōnem,* acc. of *capo,* a capon.—Gk. κάπων, a capon.

CAPOTE, a long cloak or mantle. (F.—Late L.) 'In our rough *capote;*' Byron, Siege of Corinth, l. 10.—F. *capote,* f.; from *capot,* m., a mantle.—F. *cape,* a cape; see **Cape** (1).

CAPRICE, a whim, sudden leap of the mind. (F.—Ital.—L.) The word is now always spelt like the F. *caprice,* but we often find, in earlier writers, the Italian form. Thus Shak. has *capriccio,* All's Well, ii. 3. 310; and Butler has the pl. *capriches* to rhyme with *witches;* Hudibras, pt. ii. c. 1. l. 18.—F. *caprice,* 'humour, caprichio, giddy thought;' Cot.—Ital. *capriccio,* a caprice, whim; whence the word was introduced into French in the 16th century (Brachet). β. Derived by Diez from Ital. *caprio,* a goat, as if it were 'a frisk of a kid;' but this is not quite sure. Cf. *capriole* (below), which seems to be an analogous formation. Körting, § 1891. See **Caper** (1).

CAPRICORN, the name of a zodiacal sign. (L.) Lit. 'a horned goat.' In Chaucer, Treatise on the Astrolabe, pt. i. sect. 17. —L. *capricornus,* in the Norman-French treatise of P. de Thaun, in Pop. Treatises on Science, ed. Wright, l. 196.—L. *capri-,* for *capro-,* stem of *caper,* a goat; and *cornu,* a horn. See **Caper** (1) and **Horn.**

CAPRIOLE, a peculiar frisk of a horse. (F.—Ital.—L.) Not common. Merely F. *capriole,* 'a caper in dancing; also the *capriole,* sault, or goats leap, done by a horse;' Cot.—Ital. *capriola,* the leap of a kid.—L. *capra,* a she-goat. See **Caper** (1).

CAPSICUM, a genus of tropical plants, with hot pungent capsules and seeds. (L.) ' The Indian *capsicum*; ' Bradley, Fam. Dict. II. s. v. *sallet* (1725); N.E.D. A coined word, and incorrect. Prob. formed from L. *capsa*, a case ; with reference to the capsules.

CAPSIZE, to upset, overturn. (Span.?—L.) First in Dibdin (1788). *Perhaps* a nautical corruption of Span. *capuzar*, to sink ; as in *capuzar un bajel*, to sink a ship by the head ; or of mod. Prov. *cabussado*, the act of diving, an upset (Mistral); apparently derivatives of L. *caput*, the head. (A guess.)

CAPSTAN, a machine for winding up a cable. (Prov.—L.) ME. *capstan*, Allit. Poems, B. 418. ' The weighing of anchors by the *capstan* is also new ; ' Ralegh, Essays (in Todd s Johnson).—Prov. *cabestan* (whence MF. *cabestan*, ' the capstane of a ship ;' Cot.); cognate with Span. *cabrestante*, a capstan, engine to raise weights ; also spelt *cabestrante*.—L. *capistrāre*, to fasten with a halter, muzzle, tie up ; pres. part. *capistrans* (stem *capistrant-*), whence the Span. *cabestrante*. Cf. also Span. *cabestrage*, cattle-drivers' money, also a halter, answering to Low L. *capistragium*, money for halters.—L. *capistrum* (Span. *cabestro*), a halter.—L. *capere*, to hold. See **Capacious.** ¶ Sometimes derived from *cabra*, a goat, engine to cast stones, and *estante*, explained by ' standing,' i. e. upright ; but the conjecture (though adopted by Körting) is untenable and needless ; the shifting of *r* appears plainly in Port. *cabresto*, a halter, also (as a nautical term) cables belonging to the bowsprit, allied to *cabrestante*, capstan. So also Prov. *cabestran* (as well as *cabestan*), from *cabestre*, a halter. See N. E. D.

CAPSULE, a seed-vessel of a plant. (F.—L.) ' The little cases or *capsules* which contain the seed ; ' Derham, Physico-Theology, bk. x. note 1 (R.). Sir T. Browne has *capsulary* ; Vulg. Errors, b. iii. c. 27. § 3.—F. *capsule*, 'a little chest or coffer ; ' Cot.—L. *capsula*, a small chest ; dimin. of *capsa*, a chest, repository. See **Case** (2). Der. *capsul-ar*, *capsul-ar-y*.

CAPTAIN, a head officer. (F.—L.) ME. *capitain*, *capitein*, *captain*. Spelt *capitein*, Gower, C. A. i. 360 (iii. 2421); *capitain*, Chaucer, C. T., H 230.—OF. *capitaine* (14th cent., Supp. to Godefroy).—Late L. *cap tāneus*, *capitānus*, a leader of soldiers, captain ; formed, by help of suffix *-āneus*, *-ānus*, from stem *capit-* of L. *caput*, the head ; Der. *captain-cy*. Doublet, *chieftain*, q. v.

CAPTIOUS, critical, disposed to cavil. (F.—L.) ' They . . . moued unto Him this *capcious* question ; why (quoth they) do Johns disciples and the Phariseis ofttimes fast, and thy disciples not fast at alle ? ' Udal, on S. Mark, cap. ii. v. 18.—F. *captieux*, ' captious, cavilling, too curious ; ' Cot.—L. *captiōsus*, sophistical, critical.—L. *captio*, a taking, sophistical argument ; allied to *capt-us*, pp. of *capere*, to hold. See **Capacious.** Der. *captious-ness*.

CAPTIVE, a prisoner. (F.—L.) In Hakluyt, Voyages, i. 149 ; as a verb, to capture, in Sir T. More's Works, p. 279 c. Generally expressed by its doublet *caitiff* in Middle-English.—F. *captif* (f. *captive*).—L. *captiuus*, a captive.—L. *captus*, pp. of *capere*, to hold, take, catch, seize.—✓QAP, to hold. See **Caitiff.** Der. *captiv-i-ty*, *captiv-ate*, *captiv-at-ing* ; and from L. *capt-*, *capt-or*, *capt-ure*, *capt-ious*.

CAPUCHIN, a hooded friar ; a hood. (F.—Ital.—Late L.) Order established in 1525-8. Cotgrave has *capicin* in his explanation of F. *capucin*, but this is, no doubt, a misprint, since the spelling *capucine* occurs twice immediately below.—MF. *capuchin* (F. *capucin*), ' a capicin [*read* capucin] frier ; of S. Frances order ; weares neither shirt, nor breeches ; ' Cot. [He also has : ' *Capuchon*, a capuche, a monk's cowle, or hood ; also, the hood of a cloake.']—Ital. *cappucino*, a capuchin monk, small cowl ; the monk being named from the ' small cowl ' which he wore. Dimin. of Ital. *cappuccio*, a cowl, hood worn over the head.—Ital. *cappa*, a cape. See **Cape** (1), **Cap.** ¶ The form is *capuchin* both in Picard (Corblet) and in Walloon (Sigart).

CAPYBARA ; see Capibara (above).

CAR, a wheeled vehicle. (F.—C.) In Shak. Sonnet 7, &c. He also has *carman*, Meas. ii. 1. 269. ME. *carre*, Maundeville's Travels, p. 130.—ONorthF. *carre* in Ducange, s. v. *Marcellum.*—Late L. *carra* ; allied to *carrus*, a kind of four-wheeled carriage, which Cæsar first saw in Gaul ; a Celtic word.—Bret. *karr*, a chariot ; W. *car*, a raft, frame, drag ; OGael. *càr*, a cart, car, or raft for carrying things on ; Irish *carr*, a cart, dray, waggon. [Whence also G. *karre*, a cart, barrow.] β. Allied to L. *currus*, a chariot, and *currere*, to run ; the L. and Celt. *c* being the same letter etymologically. Brugm. i. § 516 ; Stokes-Fick, p. 72. Der. There are numerous derivatives ; see *career*, *cargo*, *cark*, *carry*, *cart*, *charge*, *chariot*.

CARABINE ; see **Carbine.**

CARACAL, a feline quadruped resembling a lynx. (F.—Turk.) In a tr. of Buffon (1792), i. 195.—F. *caracal.*—Turk. *qara(h)*, black ; *qulaq*, ear. Named from its black ears.

CARACOLE, a half-turn made by a horseman. (F.—Span.) ' *Caracol*, with horsemen, is an oblique *piste*, or tread, traced out in semi-rounds, changing from one hand to another, without observing a regular ground ;' Bailey's Dict. ed. 2 (1731); vol. ii. Also in Blount (165).—F. *caracol*, 'a snail ; whence, *faire le caracol*, [for] souldiers to cast themselves into a round or ring ;' Cot. Mod. F. *caracole*, a gambol ; introduced from Span. in the 16th cent. (Brachet).—Span. *caracol*, a snail, a winding stair-case, a wheeling about ; *caracol marino*, a periwinkle. Applied to a snail-shell from its spiral shape. β. Perhaps Celtic. Cf. Gael. *carach*, meandering, whirling, circling, winding, turning ; *car*, a twist, turn, revolution ; Irish *car*, a twist, turn, *cor*, circular motion. Körting, § 1918.

CARAFE, a glass water-bottle. (F.—Span.—Arab.) Modern.— F. *carafe.*—Span. *garrafa*, a cooler, vessel to cool wines in.—Arab. *ghirāf*, draughts of water ; Arab. root *gharafa*, to draw water. (So Dozy and Devic ; some identify it with *carboy* ; see **Carboy.**)

CARAPACE, the upper shell of a tortoise. (F.—Span.) Modern. —F. *carapace.*—Span. *carapacho* (Hatzfeld). But the Span. Dict. has only *carapuza*, variant of *caperuza*, a hood.

CARAT, a certain light weight. (F.—Ital.—Arab.—Gk.) Generally a weight of 4 grains. In Shak. Com. Err. iv. 1. 28.—F. *carat*, 'a carrat ; among goldsmiths and mintmen is the third part of an ounce, among jewellers or stone-cutters, but the 19 part ;' Cot.—Ital. *carato*. [Cf. O. Port. *quirate*, a small weight, a carat ; cited by Diez.]—Arab. *qirrāt*, a carat, the 24th part of an ounce, 4 barley-corns ; also, a bean or pea-shell, a pod, husk ; Richardson's Arab. Dict. p. 1122.— Gk. κεράτιον, the fruit of the locust tree ; also (like L. *siliqua*), a weight, the carat ; the lit. sense being ' a little horn.'—Gk. κέρας, (stem κερατ-), a horn ; allied to E. **Horn.** ¶ The locust-tree, carobtree, or St. John's-bread-tree is the *Ceratonia siliqua* ; ' The seeds, which are nearly of the weight of a *carat*, have been thought to have been the origin of that ancient money-weight ;' Engl. Cycl., div. Nat. Hist. s. v. *Ceratonia* ; a name which preserves the two former syllables of the Gk. κεράτ-ιον. See **Carob**, which is, however, unrelated.

CARAVAN, a company of traders or travellers. (F.—Pers.) In Milton, P. L. vii. 428. Spelt *carouan* in Hakluyt, Voy. ii. pt. 1. 203. —F. *caravane*, ' a convoy of souldiers, for the safety of merchants that travell by land ;' Cot.—Pers. *karwān*, a caravan ; Richardson's Arab. Dict. p. 1182.

CARAVANSARY, an inn for travellers. (Pers.) Occurs in the Spectator, no. 289.—Pers. *karwān-sarāy*, a public building for caravans ; Richardson's Arab. Dict. p. 1182.—Pers. *karwān*, a caravan ; and *sarāy*, a palace, public edifice, inn ; id. p. 821 (Horn, § 727).

CARAVEL, CARVEL, a kind of ship. (F.—Ital.—Gk.) R. Eden, Three Books on America, ed. Arber, p. 45, has : ' A *Carauel* or *Caruel*, a kynde of shyppes.'—F. *caravelle*, ' a carvell ;' Cot.—Ital. *caravella*, ' a kynde of ship called a caravell ;' Florio. Dimin. from Gk. κάραβος, a kind of light ship (Liddell). Cf. also Span. *carabela*, dimin. of *caraba*, f., formerly *carabo*, m., in Minsheu ; from Late L. *carabus* ; from Gk. κάραβος, as before.

CARAWAY, CARRAWAY, an umbelliferous plant. (Span. —Arab.) ME. *carawey*, E. of Derby's Expeditions, ed. L. T. Smith, p. 19, l. 7 (1390). Spelt *caroway* in Cotgrave, s. v. *carvi.*—Span. *alcarahueya*, a caraway ; where *al* is merely the Arab. def. article.— Arab. *karwiyā-a*, *karawiyā-a*, *karawiyā-a*, carraway-seeds or plant ; Richardson's Arab. Dict. p. 1183. Cf. Gk. κάρον, κάρος, cumin ; L. *careum*, MItal. *caro*, F. *carvi* (i.e. caraway) ; Liddell and Scott. ¶ The Arabic word may be ultimately derived from the Greek one ; it is so with *carat*.

CARBINE, a short light musket. (F.) Also spelt *carabine* or *carabin* ; and, in Tudor English, it means (not a gun, but) a man armed with a carbine, a musketeer. In this sense, the pl. *carbines* is in Knolles' Hist. of Turks, 1186, K (Nares) ; and *carbine* in Beaum. and Fletcher, Wit without Money, v. 1.—F. *carabin*, m., ' a carbine, or curbeene ; an arquebuzier, armed with a murrian and breast-plate and serving on horse-back ;' Cot. [Mod.F. *carabine*, fem., introduced from Ital. *carabina*, a small gun, in the 16th century (Brachet), is derived from *carabin* as used by Cotgrave.] Corrupted from OF. *calabr en*, *calabrin*, a carbineer, a sort of light-armed soldier ; Roquefort, Ducange. β. Of uncertain origin ; Ducange derives it from Late L. *Calabrinus*, a Calabrian ; from Calabria in SE. Italy. γ. Diez derives OF. *calabrin* from Prov. *calabre*, a war-engine used in besieging towns.—Late L. *chadabula*, a war-engine for throwing stones ; whence *calabre* is derived by the change of *d* into *l* (as in OLatin *dingua*, whence L. *lingua*) and by the common change of final *-la* to *-re*.—Gk. καταβολή, overthrow, destruction.—Gk. καταβάλλειν, to throw down, strike down, esp. used of striking down with missiles.— Gk. κατά, down ; βάλλειν, to cast. But the unborrowed OF. form corresponding to Prov. *calabre* is *chaable*, derived immediately from *cha la bula*. Körting, § 2004. Der. *carbin-eer*.

CARBON, charcoal. (F.—L.) A modern chemical word.—F. *carbone* ; first in 1787.—L. acc. *carbōnem*, from nom. *carbo*, a coal. Der. *carbon-i-fer-ous*, *carbon-ac-e-ous*, *carbon-ic*, *carbon-ise* ; and see below.

CARBOLIC, in *carbolic acid*, an alcohol containing carbon. (L.) A coined word; from *carb-*, for *carbon*, with the suffix *-ol-* of *alcoh-ol*; and the suffix *-ic*.

CARBONADO, broiled meat. (Span. – L.) Properly 'a rasher.' Cotgrave, s. v. *carbonade*, explains it by ' a carbonadoe, a rasher on the coales.' Used by Shak. Cor. iv. 5. 199. – Span. *carbonada*, meat broiled on a gridiron; as if a fem. pp. from a verb **carbonar*, to broil. – Span. *carbon*, charcoal, coal. – L. acc. *carbōnem*, coal (above). Der. *carbonado*, verb.; K. Lear, ii. 2. 41.

CARBOY, a large globular bottle of glass, protected by basket-work. (Pers.) Modern; in Webster, Worcester, and Brande. – Pers. *qarābah*, a large flagon; Rich. Dict. p. 1121, which is perhaps of Arab. origin. Cf. Pers. and Arab. *qirbah*, a water-skin, water-bottle, Rich. Dict. p. 1123; Palmer's Dict. col. 469; and Yule.

CARBUNCLE, a gem, a boil; a live coal. (L.) ME. *carbuncle*, Gower, C. A. i. 57; bk. i. 466. [Also *charbucle*, Havelok, 2145; from OF. *charboucle*.] The sense is, properly, 'a glowing coal;' hence 'an inflamed sore, or boil;' 'a bright glowing gem.' – L. *carbunculus*, 1. a small coal; 2. a gem; 3. a boil. For **carbōni-c-ul-us*, double dimin. from L. *carbo* (stem *carbōn-*), a coal, sometimes, a live coal. See **Carbon.** Der. *carbuncul-ar, carbuncl-ed.*

CARBURET, a compound containing carbon. (L.) Coined from *carb-*, shortened form of *carbon*; see **Carbon.**

CARCAJOU, the American wolverene. (F. – N. Amer. Indian.) F. *carcajou*; supposed to be of N. American Indian origin.

CARCANET, a collar of jewels. (F. – G.) In Shak. Com. Errors, iii. 1. 4. Formed as a dim., with suffix *-et*, from F. *carcan*, 'a carkanet, or collar of gold, &c.;' Cot.; OF. *carcan, carchant,* a collar, esp. of jewels; Supp. to Godefroy. – OHG. *querca*, the throat; cf. Icel. *kverka-*, in composition, the throat, *kverk,* s. f., the angle under the chin. So also OFris. *kwerka, querka,* to choke, throttle; and cf. Lith. *gerkle,* the throat. Brugm. i. § 653. ¶ The dimin. form *carcan-et* does not appear in OFrench, as we should expect.

CARCASE, CARCASS, a dead body. (F. – Ital.) [ME. *carcays, carkeys.* Spelt *carcays* in Hampole, Pricke of Conscience, 874. '*Carkeys,* corpus, cadaver;' Prompt. Parv. p. 62. AF. *carcois.* – Late L. *carcosium.*] The mod.E. form is from MF. *carquasse,* in Cotgrave, who explains it by 'a carkasse, or dead corps.' Mod.F. *carcasse,* introduced from Ital. in the 16th cent. (Brachet). – Ital. *carcassa,* a kind of bomb, a shell (a carcase being a shell); cf. Port. *carcassa,* a carcase. Of unknown origin. The suggestions in Diez are unsatisfactory.

CARD (1), a piece of pasteboard. (F. – Ital. – Gk.) Used by Shak. in the sense of *chart*; Macb. i. 3. 17; also a *playing-card,* Tam. Shrew, ii. 407. In the latter sense it is in Sir T. Elyot, The Governour, bk. i. c. 26; and in the Paston Letters, iii. 314 (ab. 1484). A corruption of *carte*; cf. *chart.* – F. *carte,* 'a paper, a card;' Cot. – Ital. *carta.* – L. (late) *carta,* earlier *charta,* paper, a piece of paper. – Gk. χάρτη, also χάρτης, a leaf of papyrus. **Doublet,** *chart,* q. v. Der. *card-board.*

CARD (2), an instrument for combing wool; *as verb,* to comb wool. (F. – L.) The sb. is the original word, but is rare. ME. *carde,* sb.; *carden,* vb. '*Carde,* wommanys instrument, *cardus, discerpiculum*;' Prompt. Parv. p. 62. '*Cardyn* wolle, *carpo*;' ibid. The pp. *carded* occurs in P. Plowman, B. x. 18. – F. *carde*; Cotgrave gives the pl. '*cardes,* cards for wooll.' He also gives '*Carder de laine,* to card wooll.' – Late L. *cardus,* L. *carduus,* a thistle, used for carding wool.

CARDAMOM, a kind of spice. (L. – Gk.) R. Eden, Three Books on America (ed. Arber), at p. 15, l. 5, has: 'spyces .. as ginger, . . cardamome,' &c. – L. *cardamōmum.* – Gk. καρδάμωμον. – Gk. κάρδαμ-ον, cress; and ἄμωμον, an Indian spice-plant. (Short for *cardamamōmum,* like *idolatry* for *idololatry.*)

CARDIAC, pertaining to the heart. (F. – L. – Gk.) Holland speaks of 'the *cardiacke* passion,' i.e. palpitation of the heart; tr. of Pliny, bk. xxiii. c. 1 (vol. ii. p. 153). – F. *cardiaque.* – L. *cardiacus.* – Gk. καρδιακός, adj. from καρδία, heart; see **Heart.**

CARDINAL, adj., principal, chief; sb., a dignitary of the church. (L.) As adj. we find '*cardinale* vertues;' P. Plowman, B. xix. 313. The sb. is much older in E., and occurs in Layamon, iii. 182. – L. *cardinālis,* principal, chief, cardinal; orig. 'relating to the hinge of a door.' – L. *cardin-,* stem of *cardo,* a hinge.

CARDOON, a plant like an artichoke. (F. – Prov. – L.) In Cotgrave, to translate F. *cardon.* – Prov. *cardon* (Hatzfeld); Gascon *cardoun* (Moncaut). Formed, with augmentative suffix, from Med. L. *card-us,* for L. *carduus,* a thistle.

CARE, anxiety, heedfulness. (E.) ME. *care,* Layamon, iii. 145. The usual sense is ' anxiety, sorrow.' AS. *caru, cearu,* sorrow, care, Grein, i. 158; whence AS. *cearian,* to care for. + OSax. *kara,* sorrow; *karōn,* to sorrow, lament; Goth. *kara,* sorrow; *karōn,* to sorrow; OHG. *chara,* lament; OHG. *charōn,* to lament. Teut. type, **karā,* fem., sorrow. Der. *care-ful, care-ful-ly, care-ful-ness, care-less, care-*

less-ly, care-less-ness; also *char-y,* q. v. ¶ Wholly unconnected with L. *cūra,* with which it is often confounded.

CAREEN, to lay a ship on her side. (F. – L.) ' A crazy rotten vessel, . . . as it were new *careened*;' Sir T. Herbert, Travels, 1665, p. 244. Used absolutely, as in 'we *careen'd* at the Marias;' in Dampier, Voyages, vol. ii. c. 13 (R.). Cook uses it with an accusative case, as 'in order to *careen* her;' First Voyage, b. ii. c. 6 (R.). It was once written *carine.* 'To lie aside until *carined*;' Otia Sacra (Poems, 1648), p. 162; Todd's Johnson. Lit. 'to clean the keel.' – MF. *carine,* 'the keele of a ship;' Cot.; also spelt *carène.* – L. *carina,* the keel of a ship; also, a nut-shell. From √ KAR, implying 'hardness;' cf. Gk. κάρυον, a nut, kernel; Skt. *karaka-s,* a cocoa-nut (Curtius). See **Cancer.** Der. *careen-age.*

CAREER, a race, race-course. (F. – Late L. – C.) Shak. Much Ado, ii. 3. 250. – F. *carriere,* 'an highway, rode, or streete (Languedoc); also, a *careere* on horsebacke; and, more generally, any exercise or place for exercise on horse-backe; as an horse-race, or a place for horses to run in; and their course, running, or full speed therein;' Cot. – Late L. *carrāria (via),* a road for cars. – Late L. *carra,* a car; see **Car.**

CARESS, to fondle, embrace. (F. – Ital. – L.) The sb. is in Milton, P. L. viii. 56. The verb is in Burnet, Own Time, an. 1671 (R.). – F. *caresse,* 's. f. a cheering, cherishing;' and *caresser,* 'to cherish, hug, make much of;' Cot. The sb. is the original, and introduced from Ital. in the 16th cent. (Brachet). – Ital. *carezza,* a caress, endearment, fondness. – Late L. *cāritia,* dearness, value. – L. *cārus,* dear, worthy, beloved. Cf. Irish *cara,* a friend; *caraim,* I love; W. *caru,* to love. From the same root, *charity,* q. v.

CARFAX, a place where four ways meet. (F. – L.) I enter this because of the well-known example of *carf:x* at Oxford, which has puzzled many. ME. *carfoukes,* a place where four streets met; it occurs in this sense in the Romance of Partenay, ed. Skeat, l. 1819, where the French original has *carrefourg.* The form *carfax* occurs in the Prompt. Parv. p. 62, col. 2, l. 1, as the Eng. of L. *quadrivium*; *quarfoxe* is in Caxton's Golden Legend, St. Nicholas, § 12. – AF. *carfeux,* Liber Albus, p. 465; OF. *carrefourgs,* pl. of *carrefourg*; cf. 'compitum, *carfourc*;' Catholicon Abbreviatum (1497). – Late L. *quadrifurcum,* acc. of *quadrifurcus,* adj., four-forked. – L. *quadri-,* from *quatuor,* four; and *furca,* a fork. See **Four** and **Fork.**

CARGO, a freight. (Span. – Late L. – C.) 'With a good *cargo* of Latin and Greek;' Spectator, no. 494. – Span. *cargo,* also *carga,* a burthen, freight, load; cf. Span. *cargare,* to load, freight. – Late L. *carricāre,* to load, lade. See **Charge.** ¶ Perhaps a Gascon form; as Gasc. *cargo,* f. = Span. *carga.*

CARIBOU, the N. American reindeer. (F. – American Indian). From Canadian F. *caribou*; of Amer. Indian origin.

CARICATURE, an exaggerated drawing. (Ital. – Late L. – C.) 'Those burlesque pictures, which the Italians call *caracatura's*;' Spectator no. 537. – Ital. *caricatura,* a satirical picture; so called from being overloaded or 'overcharged' with exaggeration. – Ital. *caricare,* to load, burden, charge, blame. – Late L. *carricāre,* to load a car. See **Cargo.** Der. *caricature,* verb; *caricatur-ist.*

CARIES, rottenness of a bone. (L.) Modern and medical. Merely L. *cariēs,* rottenness. Cf. Gk. κηραίνειν, to harm. Der. *cari-ous.*

CARILLON, a set of bells, or the melody played upon them. (F. – L.) In Rees, Cyclopædia (1803, 1819). – F. *carillon,* a chime; OF. *careignon, quarreignon, quarignon* (Godefroy). – Late L. type **quatriniōnem,* from nom. **quatrinio,* orig. a chime on four bells; like Prov. *trinho,* from Late L. *trinio,* a chime on three bells (Hatzfeld). From L. *quattuor,* four; see **Four.** (See *trinion* in Ducange.)

CARK, solicitude, anxiety. (F. – L. – C.) In Spenser, F. Q. i. 1. 44. ME. *cark* (spelt *carke*), Monk of Evesham, ed. Arber, p. 78, l. 12; Cursor Mundi, l. 20790 (Northern dialect; another MS. has *charge*); Gamelyn, l. 760. – [Somner gives AS. *carc,* care, but it is wholly unauthorised; the word being really French.] The true solution of this word (first given by myself in 1882) is to be found in the Anglo-French word *kark,* a burden, weight, cargo, which is nothing but the Norman form of F. *charge,* as is also evident from the Cursor Mundi, ll. 20790, 23994, 24233. This form *kark* occurs in the Liber Albus, ed. H. T. Riley, p. 224; and is corroborated by the occurrence of the verb *sorkarker* for *sorcharger* in the Statutes of the Realm, vol. i. p. 26, A.D. 1275; so also *descarkere,* to unload, Lib. Albus (Gloss.). Hence *cark* meant, originally, a weight, load; but came to be used particularly of 'a load of care.' The W. *carc,* anxiety, solicitude, is the E. word borrowed; cf. Bret. *karg,* a load, burden (from French); though the ultimate root is Celtic. The Late L. *carcāre,* to load, occurs in the Liber Albus (iii. 380). *Cark* is thus a doublet of *charge*; see **Charge.** Cotgrave gives F. *charge,* sb., 'a load, burthen, fardle, also a charge, hinderance, or cause of extraordinary expence;' &c. I may add that we even find *kark* or *karke,* a load, in English; for in Arnold's Chron.,

1502 (ed. 1811), p. 99, we find mention of 'a *karke* of peper' and a '*kark* of gynger.' **Der.** *cark*, verb, spelt *carke* in Palsgrave, whence the phr. '*cark-ing* care ;' in the Cursor Mundi, we find '*carkid* (also *charked*) wit care,' ll. 23994, 24870.

CARLINE, usually *carline thistle*, a kind of thistle. (F. – Late L. – G.) In Lyte, tr. of Dodoens, bk. iv. c. 67 ; he says : 'now they call it *Carlina* or *Carolina*, bicause of Charlemaine emperor of the Romanes, vnto whom an angell first shewed this thistle, as they say, when his armie was striken with the pestilence.' (So also in Ducange).—F. *carline*.—L. *Carolina*, fem. of *Carolīnus*, pertaining to *Carolus*. — G. *Karl*, name of the emperor.

CARMINATIVE, expelling wind from the body. (F. – L.) In the Tatler, no. 224, § 8 (Sept. 14, 1710).—F. *carminatif*, 'wind-voiding ;' Cot. – L. *carmināt-us*, pp. of *carmināre*, to card wool ; hence, to expel. – L. *carmin-*, stem of *carmen*, a card for wool. – L. *carere*, to card. ¶ *Not* from L. *carmen*, a song ; see Notes on E. Etym., p. 31.

CARMINE, a crimson colour, obtained from the cochineal insect originally. (Span. – Arab. – Skt.) ' *Carmine*, a red colour, very vivid, made of the cochineal mastique ;' Bailey's Dict. vol. ii ; 2nd ed. 1731. – F. *carmin* (Hatzfeld) ; or from Span. *carmin*, carmine, a contracted form of Span. *carmesin*, crimson, carmine.—Span. *carmesi*, adj., crimson ; sb. cochineal powder. – Arab. *qirmizī*, crimson ; *qirmiz*, crimson ; *qirmiz i firengī*, cochineal ; Palmer's Pers. Dict. col. 470. – Skt. *kṛmi(s)*, a worm, the cochineal insect. Brugm. i. § 418. See **Crimson.**

CARNAGE, slaughter. (F. – L.) In Holland's Plutarch, p. 371 (R.) ; Milton, P. L. x. 268. – F. *carnage*, 'flesh-time, the season wherein it is lawfull to eate flesh (Picardy) ; also, a slaughter, butcherie ;' Cot. – Late L. *carnāticum*, a kind of tribute of animals ; cf. *carnātum*, the time when it is lawful to eat flesh (whence the notion of a great slaughter of animals easily arose). – L. *caro* (stem *carn-*), flesh. Brugm. i. § 515.

CARNAL, fleshly. (L.) See Coventry Mysteries, p. 194 ; Sir T. More's Works, p. 1 d ; Sir T. Elyot, the Governour, bk. iii. c. 18 ; Henry's Wallace, b. xi. l. 1348. – L. *carnālis*, fleshly, carnal. – L. *carn-*, base of *caro*, flesh (above). **Der.** *carnal-ly, carnal-ist, carnal-i-ty* ; and see *carnage, carnation, carnival, carnivorous*, also *incarnation, carrion*.

CARNATION (1), flesh colour, pink. (F. – L.) See Hen. V, ii. 3. 35 ; Wint. Ta. iv. 4. 82. – F. *carnation*, carnation colour ; omitted by Cotgrave, but noted in Supp. to Godefroy. Cf. Ital. *carnagione*, 'the hew of ones skin and flesh, also fleshinesse' (Florio). – L. *carnātiōnem*, acc. of *carnātio*, fleshiness. – L. *carn-*, base of *caro*, flesh. See **Carnal.**

CARNATION (2), the name of a flower. (F. – L.) The orig. name seems to have been *coronation*, as in Spenser, Sheph. Cal., April, 138 ; from the flowers being ' dented or toothed like to a littall crownet ' (Lyte). See the account in N.E.D. It was then contracted to *cornation*, and confused with *carnation*. See **Coronation** and **Carnation** (1).

CARNELIAN, another form of **Cornelian,** q. v.

CARNIVAL, the feast held just before Lent. (F. – Ital. – L.) The spelling is a mistaken one ; it should rather be *carnaval, carneval*, or *carnoval*. ' Our *carnivals* and Shrove-Tuesdays ;' Hobbes, Of the kingdom of darkness, c. 45 (R.). ' The *carnival* of Venice ;' Addison, On Italy, Venice (R.). It is rightly spelt *carnaval* in Blount's Glossographia, ed. 1674. – F. *carnaval* ; Cot. Introduced from Ital. in the 16th cent. (Brachet). – Ital. *carnovale, carnevale*, orig. the eve of Ash Wednesday ; later, the last three days before Lent. – Late L. *carnelevāmen, carnelevārium, carnilevāria*, a removal of meat, Shrovetide ; also spelt *carnelevāle* in a document dated 1130, in Carpenter's supplement to Ducange. Afterwards shortened from *carnelevāle* to *carnevāle*, a change promoted by a popular etymology which resolved the word into Ital. *carne*, flesh, and *vale*, farewell, as if the sense were 'farewell ! O flesh.' [Not 'farewell *to* flesh,' as Lord Byron attempts to explain it.] – L. *carne-m*, acc. of *caro*, flesh and *levāre*, to remove, whence *-levār-ium*, a removal, taking away, *-levāle*, i. e. removing, taking away, and *levāmen* ; the latter being the true L. form, with a difference of sense. See **Carnal** and **Lever.** ¶ As *carnelevāmen* might also mean ' solace of the flesh,' the word was often completely misunderstood and misapplied ; and the sense was altered from 'a time of fasting' to 'a time of feasting.' Hence the word is often wrongly explained ; see N.E.D.

CARNIVOROUS, flesh-eating. (L.) In Ray, On the Creation, pt. i. Also in Blount's Gloss., ed. 1674. – L. *carniuor-us*, feeding on flesh ; with suffix *-ous*. – L. *carni-*, declensional stem of *caro*, flesh ; and *uorāre*, to devour. See **Carnal** and **Voracious.**

CAROB-TREE, the locust-tree. (F. – Arab.) 'A *carobe* tree ;' Turner, Names of Herbes, s. v. *Siliqua* (1548). – MF. *carobe, carrobe*, 'the carob ; also a small weight (among mintmen and goldsmiths) making but the 24 part of an ounce ;' Cot. – Arab. *kharrūb*, Pers. *kharnūb*, bean-pods ; see Richardson's Arab. Dict. p. 608. Cf. **Carat.**

CAROCHE, a kind of coach. (F. – Ital. – Late L. – C.) Obsolete ; but the present sense of *carriage* was brought about by confusion with it. ' The great *caroch*,' Ben Jonson, Devil is an Ass, iv. 1 (Lady T.). Stow, in his Annals, 1615 ; p. 857, says that the 'ordinary use of *caroches*' began about A. D. 1605 ; Dekker, in his Seven Deadly Sinnes, 1606, ed. Arber, p. 20, mentions 'the Grand Signiors *Caroach*.' – F. *carroche*, 'a caroache ;' Cot. ; given as a variant of *carosse* or *carozze*, 'a carosse or coarach ;' Cot. *Caroche* is a Walloon form (Sigart). – Ital. *carroccia, carrozza*, 'a caroce, a coche, a chariot ;' Florio. Extended from Ital. *carro*, 'a cart, chariot,' Florio. – L. *carrus*, a car ; which is of Celtic origin. See **Car.**

CAROL, a kind of song ; orig. a dance. (F. – L. – Gk.) 'Faire is *carole* of maide gent ;' King Alisaunder, l. 1845. – OF. *carole*, orig. a sort of dance ; later *carolle*, 'a sort of dance wherein many dance together ; also, a *carroll*, or Christmas song ;' Cot. Godefroy (s. v. *carole*) cites Swiss Rom. *coraula*, a round dance ; also, a dance-song. – L. *choraula*, by-form of *choraulēs* (Gk. χοραύλης), a flute-player, who accompanied with a flute the chorus-dance. – Gk. χορ-ός, a chorus, round-dance ; and αὐλός, a flute, from ἄημι, I blow. See **Chorus.** So Körting, § 2145.

CAROTID, related to the two great arteries of the neck. (Gk.) ' The *carotid*, vertebral, and splenick arteries ;' Ray, On the Creation (Todd). ' *Carotid Arteries*, certain arteries belonging to the brain ; so called because, when stopt, they immediately incline the person to sleep ;' Kersey's Dict. ed. 1715 – Gk. καρωτίδες, s. pl. the two great arteries of the neck ; with respect to which the ancients believed that compression of them would cause drowsiness. – Gk. καρόω, I plunge into heavy sleep, I stupefy. – Gk. κάρος, heavy sleep, torpor.

CAROUSE, a drinking-bout. (F. – G.) Orig. an adverb meaning 'completely,' or 'all out,' i. e. 'to the bottom,' used of drinking. Whence the phrase, 'to quaff *carouse*,' to drink deeply. 'Robin, here's a *carouse* to good king Edward's self ;' George a Greene, Old Plays, iii. 51 (Nares) ; see Peele's Works, ed. Dyce, p. 267. ' The tippling sottes at midnight which *to quaffe carowse* do use, Wil hate thee if at any time to pledge them thou refuse ;' Drant's Horace, ep. to Lollius (See Horat. Epist. i. 18. 91. Drant died A.D. 1578.) ' He in that forrest did death's cup *carowse*,' i. e. drink up ; Mirror for Magistrates, p. 646. ' Then drink they all around, both men and women ; and sometimes they *carowse* for the victory very filthily and drunkenly ;' Hakluyt, Voyages, i. 96. Also spelt *garouse*. 'Some of our captains *garoused* of his wine till they were reasonably pliant ;' also, 'And are themselves . . . the greatest *garousers* and drunkards of the world ;' Raleigh, Discovery of Guiana ; Hakluyt Soc., p. 64 ; cf. Hakluyt, Voy. iii. 648, where the form is *karousers*. – F. *carous*, 'a carousse of drinke ;' Cotgrave. He also gives : '*Carousser*, to quaffe, swill, *carousse* it.' – G. *garaus*, adv., also used as a sb. to mean ' finishing stroke ;' as in 'einer Sache den *garaus* machen, to put an end to a thing ;' Flügel's Dict. The G. *garaus* signifies literally 'right out,' and was specially used of emptying a bumper to any one's health, a custom which became so notorious that the word made its way not only into French and English, but even into Spanish ; cf. Span. *caraos*, 'drinking a full bumper to one's health ;' Meadows. – G. *gar*, adv. completely (OHG. *karo*, allied to E. *yare*, which see) ; and *aus*, prep. out, cognate with E. *out*. ¶ Similarly, the phr. *allaus* was sometimes used, from the G. *all aus*, i. e. all out, in exactly the same connexion ; and this phrase likewise found its way into French. Cotgrave gives : '*Alluz*, all out ; or a carouse fully drunk up.' It even found its way into English. Thus Beaum. and Fletcher : 'Why, give's some wine then, this will fit us all ; Here's to you still, my captain's friend ! *All out !*' Beggar's Bush, Act ii. sc. 3. **Der.** *carouse*, verb ; also *carous-al*, in one sense of it, but not always ; see below.

CAROUSAL, a drinking-bout ; **Carousel,** a pageant. (1. F. – G. ; 2. F. – Ital.) 1. The form *carousal* is now generally understood as being a mere derivative of the verb *to carouse*, and would be so used. 2. But in old authors we find *carousél* (generally so accented and spelt) used to mean a sort of pageant in which some form of chariot-race formed a principal part. ' This game, these *carousels* Ascanius taught, And, building Alba, to the Latins brought ;' Dryden's Virgil, Æn. v. 777, where the Latin text (v. 596) has *certamina*. And see the long quotation from Dryden's pref. to Albian and Albanius in Richardson. – F. *carrousel*, a tilt, carousel, tilting-match. – Ital. *carosello* (variant *garosello*), a festival, a tournament. The form *carosello* is not given in Baretti, but is cited by Diez and Torriano. Torriano gives *caroselle* or *caleselle*, which he explains by ' a kind of sport or game used in Italy at Shrovetide.' Diez connects *carosello* with Ital. *carrozza* (s.v. *carriera*) ; see **Caroche.** So Körting, § 1973.

CARP (1), a fresh-water fish. (F. – Late L. – Teut. ?) ' *Carpe, fysche, carpus*.' Prompt. Parv. p. 62. – F. *carpe*. – Late L. *carpa* ; which occurs as early as the fifth century, being found in Cassiodorus, lib. xii. ep. 4 : ' Destinet *carpam* Danubius ;' quoted by Brachet.

Hence also Span. *carpa*, Ital. *carpione*. β. But prob. of Teut. origin, being found in most Teut. languages; cf. Du. *karper*; Icel. *karfi* (?); Dan. *karpe*; Swed. *karp*; G. *karpfen*; OHG. *charpho*. Whence also Russ. *karp'*, Lith. *karpa*.

CARP (2), to cavil at. (Scand.) In Shak. Much Ado, iii. 1. 71; K. Lear, i. 4. 222. **α.** There can be little doubt that the peculiar use of *carp*, in a bad sense, is due to its supposed connexion with the L. *carpere*, to pluck, to calumniate. At the same time, it is equally certain that the ME. *carpen* is frequently used, as noted by Trench in his Select Glossary, without any such sinister sense. Very frequently, it merely means 'to say,' as in to *karpe the sothe*, to tell the truth; Will. of Palerne, 503, 655, 2804. It occurs rather early. 'Hwen thou art on eise, *carpe* toward Ihesu, and seie thise wordes' = when thou art at ease, speak to Jesus, and say these words; Old Eng. Homilies, ed. Morris, i. 287. β. The word is Scandinavian, and had originally somewhat of a sinister sense, but rather significant of 'boasting' or 'prattling' than implying any malicious intent, a use of the word which is remarkably *absent* from Middle English; see the 26 examples of it in Mätzner's Wörterbuch. – Icel. *karpa*, to boast, brag; Swed. dial. *karpa*, to brag, boast, clatter, wrangle, rant; more frequently spelt *garpa* (Rietz); cf. *garper*, a contentious man, a prattler, great talker. **γ.** We may also note Swed. dial. *karper*, brisk, eager, industrious (Rietz); Icel. *garpr*, a warlike man, a bravo, a virago; MSwed. *garp*, a warlike, active man; also, a boaster (Ihre). **Der.** *carp-er*.

CARPEL, the cell of a pistil or fruit. (F. – Gk.) First used by Lindley in 1835. – F. *carpelle*; a dimin. form coined from Gk. καρπ-ός, fruit. See **Harvest**.

CARPENTER, a maker of wooden articles. (F. – L. – C.) In early use. ME. *carpenter*, Chaucer, C. T. 3189; Rob. of Glouc. p. 537, l. 11103; Legends of the Holy Rood, ed. Morris, p. 30, l. 155. – ONorthF. *carpentier* (mod. F. *charpentier*), a worker in timber. – Late L. *carpentārius*, a carpenter. – Late L. *carpentāre*, to work in timber; with especial reference to the making of carriages. – L. *carpentum*, a carriage, chariot, used by Livy; a word (like *car*) of Celtic origin. Cf. Gael. and Irish *carbad*, OIrish *carpat*, a carriage, chariot, litter, bier; W. *cerbyd*, a chariot; OBret. *cerpit*. Stokes-Fick, p. 71. Probably allied to L. *corbis*, a basket, with reference to 'the basket character of the body of these chariots;' Macbain. **Der.** *carpentr-y*.

CARPET, a thick covering for floors. (F. – L.) 'A *carpet*, tapes, -etis;' Levins (A.D. 1570). 'A ladyes *carpet*;' Hall, Edw. IV, an. xiv. § 6. 'A *carpet*,' an. 1284; J. E. T. Rogers, Hist. of Prices, ii. 536; N. and Q. 7 S. iii. 152. – OF. *carpite*, a carpet, sort of cloth; Supp. to Godefroy. – Late L. *carpita*, a kind of thick cloth or anything made of such cloth; allied to Late L. *carpia*, lint; cf. mod. F. *charpie*, lint. – L. *carpere*, to pluck, pull in pieces (lint being made from rags pulled to pieces, and carpet (probably) from shreds); also to crop, gather. Cf. Gk. καρπός, what is gathered, fruit; also E. *harvest*, q. v. Brugm. i. § 631.

CARPUS, the wrist. (L. – Gk.) In Phillips (1706). – L. *carpus*. – Gk. καρπός, the wrist; allied to E. *whirl*. See **Whirl**.

CARRACK, a ship of burden. (F.) In Shak. Oth. i. 2. 50. ME. *caracke*, Squyr of Low Degre, l. 819. [We also find *carryk* (Voc. 570. 35), which comes nearer to Late L. *carrica*, a ship of burden.] – OF. *carraque* (Roquefort); spelt *carrake* by Froissart (Godefroy, Supp. p. 427). – Late L. *carraca*, a ship of burden; also spelt *carrica*. β. Etym. unknown; but perhaps connected with *carricāre*, to lade a car. – L. *carrus*, a car. See **Car**. ¶ The Du. *kraak*, a carrack, is merely borrowed from F. (Franck).

CARRIOLE, a small open car for one person. (F. – Ital. – L. – C.) Modern. – F. *cariole*. – Ital. *carriola*, also *carriuola*, 'a wheele-barrow, . . a kinde of chair couered, vsed in Italie for to carrie men vp and downe by porters;' Florio. – Ital. *carro*, 'a cart;' Florio. – L. *carrus*, a car; see **Car**.

CARRION, putrefying flesh, a carcase. (F. – L.) In early use. ME. *caroigne*, *careyne*, a carcase; Chaucer, C. T. 2015 (A 2013); spelt *charoine*, Ancren Riwle, p. 84. – OF. *caroigne*, *charoigne*, a carcase; mod. Norm. dial. *carogne*. – Late L. *carōnia*, a carcase. – L. *caro*, flesh. See **Carnal**.

CARRONADE, a sort of cannon. (Scotland.) So called from *Carron*, in Stirlingshire, Scotland, where there are some celebrated iron works. 'The articles [there] manufactured are machinery, agricultural implements, cannon, *carronades*, which take their name from this place, &c.;' Engl. Cycl. s.v. *Stirlingshire*.

CARROT, an edible root. (F. – L. – Gk.) 'A *carote*, pastinaca;' Levins (A.D. 1570). 'Their savoury parsnip next, and *carrot*, pleasing food;' Drayton's Polyolbion, s. 20, l. 49. – MF. *carote*, *carrote*, the carrot, Cot.; mod. F. *carotte*. – L. *carōta*, used by Apicius. (Apicius is probably an assumed name, and the date of the author's treatise uncertain.) – Gk. καρωτόν, a carrot (Liddell). – Gk. κάρα, a head; cf. κεφαλωτόν, headed, said of garlic, &c. **Der.** *carrot-y*.

CARROUSEL; see under **Carousal** (2).

CARRY, to convey on a car. (F. – Late L. – C.) ME. *carien*, with one *r*; Chaucer, Ho. of Fame, iii. 190. – ONorthF. *carier*, to carry, transport in a car, Picard *carrier* (Late L. *carricāre*). – OF. *car*, a cart, car (L. *carrus*). See **Car**. **Der.** *carri-age*, formerly *cariage*, with one *r*, Prompt. Parv. p. 62; see Trench, Select Glossary. ¶ A modern sense of *carriage*, viz. vehicle, is prob. partly due to association with **Caroche**, q. v.

CART, a two-wheeled vehicle. (Scand.) In early use. ME. *karte*, *carte*; Ormulum, 54. Chaucer has *carter*, C. T. 7122 (D 1540). [AS. *cræt*, by the common metathesis of *r*; pl. *cratu*, chariots, A. S. version of Gen. l. 9. Cf. 'veredus, *cræte-hors*,' i.e. cart-horse; Ælf. Gloss.; Voc. 108. 24.] From Icel. *kartr*, a cart; whence, probably, Picard *carti*, a cart. ¶ The W. *cart*, Gael. and Irish *cairt*, are from E. **Der.** *cart*, v.; *cart-age*, *cart-er*.

CARTE, a paper, a card, bill of fare. (F. – L. – Gk.) Modern, and mere French. Compare the phrase *carte blanche*. 'Carte blanche, a blank paper, seldom used but in this phrase, to send one a carte blanche, signed, to fill up with what conditions he pleases;' Bailey's Dict. vol. ii. ed. 1731. – F. *carte*, a card. See further under **Card** (1), of which *carte* is a doublet. **Der.** *cart-el* (F. *cartel*, from Ital. *cartello*), the dimin. form; *cart-oon* (F. *carton*, from Ital. *cartone*), the augmentative form; also *cartridge*, *cartulary*, which see. *Cartel* is spelt *chartel* in Ben Jonson, Every Man in his Humour, i. 5. *Cartoon* is spelt *carton* in the Spectator, no. 226. For *cartouche*, see **Cartridge**.

CARTILAGE, gristle. (F. – L.) In Boyle's Works, vi. 735, and in Blount's Gloss.; Ray has the adj. *cartilagineous* (sic), On the Creation, pt. i. (R.) – F. *cartilage*, gristle; Cot. – L. *cartilāginem*, acc. of *cartilāgo*, gristle; of unknown origin. (Perhaps cf. E. *hard*.) **Der.** *cartilag-in-ous*.

CARTOON; see under **Carte**.

CARTRIDGE, CARTOUCHE, a paper case for the charge of a gun. (F. – Ital. – L. – Gk.) *Cartridge* is a corruption of *cartrage*, a form which appears in Dryden's Annus Mirabilis, st. 149 (altered to *cartridge* in the Clar. Press ed. of Selections from Dryden). A still older form was *cartage*, itself a corruption of *cartouche*, the true F. form. Cf. 'their *cartrage* or ca[r]*touche* boxes;' Dampier, A New Voyage (1699); i. 231. – F. *cartouche*, 'the cornet of paper whereinto Apothecaries and Grocers put the parcels they retail; also, a *cartouch*, or full charge for a pistoll, put up within a little paper, to be the readier for use;' Cot. 2. A tablet for an ornament, or to receive an inscription, formed like a scroll, was also called a *cartouche*, in architecture; and Cot. also gives: '*Cartoche*, [the same] as *Cartouche*; also, a *cartridge* or roll, in architecture.' This shows that the corrupt form *cartridge* (apparently made up, by popular etymology, from the F. *carte*, a card, and the E. *ridge*, used for edge or projection) was then already in use. – Ital. *cartoccio*, a roll of paper, a cartridge. – Ital. *carta*, paper. – L. *charta* (Late L. *carta*), paper. – Gk. χάρτη, χάρτης, a leaf of papyrus. See **Carte, Card**.

CARTULARY, a register-book of a monastery. (Late L. – Gk.) 'I may, by this one, show my reader the form of all those *cartularies*, by which such devout Saxon princes endowed their sacred structures;' Weever, Anc. Fun. Mon., xiv. 99 (in Todd's Johnson). Also in Bailey's Dict. vol. ii. ed. 1731. – Late L. *cartulārium*, also *chartulārium*, a register. – Late L. *chartula*, a document; dimin. of L. *charta*, a paper, charter (above). See **Charter**.

CARUCATE, a measure of land. (L. – C.) It varied according to the soil; properly, as much as could be tilled with one plough (and a team of 8 oxen) in a year. Englished from Late L. *carūcāta*, *carrūcāta*, in Domesday Book; a fem. pp. from *carrūcāre*, to plough. – Late L. *carrūca*, a plough; L. *carrūca*, a four-wheeled travelling coach; (later, a wheel-plough, in the Salic Law). – L. *carrus*, a car; see **Car**.

CARVE, to cut. (E.) ME. *kerven*, *keruen* (*u* for *v*); Layamon, i. 250. AS. *ceorfan*, Grein, i. 159. + Du. *kerven*; G. *kerben*, to notch, jag, indent. Teut. type *kerfan*, pt. t. *karf*, pt. pl. *kurbum*, pp. *korbanoz*. From the 2nd stem are Dan. *karva*, Swed. *karfva*, to notch. β. The word is co-radicate with Gk. γράφειν. See **Graphic**. Brugmann, i. § 791. **Der.** *carv-er*.

CARVEL; the same as **Caravel**, q.v.

CARYATIDES, female figures in architecture, used instead of columns as supporters. (Gk.) In Kersey's Dict. ed. 1715. Sometimes written *Caryātes*, which is the Latin form, being the pl. of adj. *Caryātis*, i.e. belonging to the village of Caryæ in Laconia. *Caryātides* is the Gk. form, signifying the same thing. – Gk. Καρυάτιδες, s. pl., women of Caryæ.

CASCADE, a waterfall. (F. – Ital. – L.) Not given in Cotgrave. Used by Addison, in describing the Teverone (Todd's Johnson); and in Anson's Voyages, bk. ii. c. 1. 'Artificial *cascades*;' Evelyn, Diary, Oct. 8, 1641. – F. *cascade*, introduced from Ital. in the 16th century, according to Brachet; but perhaps later. – Ital. *cascata*, a waterfall;

formed as a regular fem. pp. from *cascare*, to fall; which is formed from L. *cāsāre*, to totter, to be about to fall, by help of the suffix -*ic*-, so that *cascare* is for *cāsicāre. β. L. *cāsāre* is a secondary verb; from *cāsum*, supine of *cadere*, to fall. See **Chance**.

CASE (1), that which happens; an event, &c. (F.—L.) In early use. ME. *cas*, seldom *case*; it often means 'circumstance,' as in Rob. of Glouc. p. 9, l. 205; also 'chance,' id. p. 528, l. 10871. —OF. *cas*, mod.F. *cas*.—L. *cāsum*, acc. of *cāsus*, a fall, accident, case.—L. *cāsus*, pp. of *cadere*, to fall. See **Chance**. Der. *casu-al*, *casu-al-ty*, *casu-ist*, *casu-ist-ic*, *casu-ist-ic-al*, *casu-ist-ry*; all from the declensional stem *cāsu-* of L. *cāsus*. *Casual* occurs in Chaucer, Tro. and Cress. iv. 419. *Casuist* is in Blount's Gloss., ed. 1674.

CASE (2), a receptacle, cover. (F.—L.) ME. *cass*, *kace*; spelt *cass*, Barbour, Bruce, xx. 304. '*Kace*, or *casse* for pynnys, capcella;' Prompt. Parv. p. 269.—ONorthF. *casse*, 'a box, case, or chest;' Cot. (mod.F. *châsse*).—L. *capsa*, a receptacle, chest, box, cover.—L. *capere*, to receive, contain, hold. See **Capable**. Der. *case*, verb; *cash*, q.v.; also *en-case*, *casement*. Doublet, *chase* (3), q.v.

CASEMATE, a bomb-proof chamber. (F.—Ital.) Originally, a bomb-proof chamber, furnished with embrazures; later, an embrazure. '*Casemate*, a loop-hole in a fortified wall to shoot out at; or, in fortification, a place in a ditch, out of which to plague the assailants;' Blount's Gloss., ed. 1674. 'Secure your *casamates*;' Ben Jonson, Staple of News, i. 1.—F. *casemate*, 'a casemate, a loop, or loop-hole, in a fortified wall;' Cot.—Ital. *casamatta*, 'a casamat, or a slaughter-house, and is a place built low vnder the wall or bulwarcke, not arriuing vnto the height of the ditch, seruing to skoure the ditch, annoying the enemie when he entreth into the ditch to skale the wall;' Florio.—Ital. *casa*, a house; and *matta*, fem. of adj. *matto*, mad, foolish, but also used nearly in the sense of E. 'dummy;' whilst the Sicilian *mattu*, according to Diez, means dim, dark. Hence the sense is dummy-chamber, or dark chamber. Cf. Ital. *carromatto*, 'a block carriage, sometimes used to spare field-carriages;' Torriano. —L. *casa*, a cottage; and Late L. *mattus*, sad, foolish, dull, lit. check-mated, for the origin of which see **Checkmate**. See Körting, §§ 1979, 5996. And see **Casino**.

CASEMENT, a frame of a window. (F.—L.) A *casement* is a small part of an old-fashioned window, opening by hinges, the rest of the window being fixed; also applied to the whole window. It occurs in Shak. Merry Wives, i. 4. 2. We also find '*casement*, a concave moulding,' in Halliwell's Dict.; cf. Gwilt's Architecture, § 2531. β. In the latter case, the word is equivalent to *enchasement*, from the verb to *enchase*; cf. the verb to *chase*, in the sense 'to engrave, adorn,' which is short for *enchase*. Observe, too, that *enchase* is a doublet of *encase*; see **Enchase**. γ. The difference is merely one of dialect; ONorthF. *casse* being the same as OF. *chasse*, mod.F. *châsse*; from L. *capsa*; see **Case** (2); and, just as *casement* in the sense of 'moulding' is connected with *enchase*, so *casement* in the sense of window, or rather 'window-frame,' is connected with *encase*. δ. In other words, *casement* is short for *encasement*; and was formed from the MF. *encasser*, 'to case, or inchest, to make up in, or put up into, a case or chest;' Cot. Cf. MF. *enchassiller*, 'to set in, to enclose, compass, bind, hold in with a wooden frame;' id. Also *enchasser en or*, 'to enchace, or set in gold;' also '*enchassement*, an enchacing or enchacement;' and '*enchasseure*, an enchacement, an enchacing, or setting in;' id. ε. Godefroy has OF. *enchassement*, *enchacement*, a frame; and the ONorthF. form of *enchassement* would have been *encassement*, from which *casement* followed easily by the loss of the prefix. Similarly, Shak. has *case* for *encase*, Com. Err. ii. 1. 85. Both *case* and the suffix -*ment* are of L. origin. See **Encase** and **Case** (2). ¶ The Ital. *casamento*, a large house, is quite a different word. Observe a similar loss of the first syllable in *fence*, for *defence*, *censer* for *incenser*, &c.

CASERN, a lodging for soldiers, barrack. (F.—Prov.—L.) Phillips (1706) has *casern*, a lodgment raised between the rampart and houses of a fortified town, for the soldiers.—F. *caserne*.—Prov. *cazerna*. Perhaps from L. *quaterna*, a lodging or watch-house for four soldiers.—L. *quattuor*, four; see **Four**. See Körting, § 7647; and Hatzfeld.

CASH (1), coin or money. (F.—Ital.—L.) So in Shak. Hen. V, ii. 1. 120. But the original sense is 'a chest,' or 'a till,' i.e. the box in which the ready money was kept; afterwards transferred to the money itself. 'So as this bank is properly a general *cash* [i.e. till, money-box], where every man lodges his money;' Sir W. Temple, On the United Provinces, c. 2 (R.). And see the quotation from Cotgrave below.—F. *casse*, 'a box, case, or chest, to carry or keep weares [wares] in; also, a merchant's *cash* or counter;' &c.—Ital. *cassa*, 'a chest . . . a merchant's *rash* or counter;' Florio.—L. *capsa*, a chest. Thus *cash* is a doublet of **Case** (2), q.v. Der. *cash-ier*, sb.; but see *cashier*, vb., below.

CASH (2), a coin of low value in India and China. (Tamil—Skt.) Spelt *cash* (1699), Dampier, Voy. II. 1. 4. 72 (N.E.D.).—Tamil

kāsu, a small coin, money.—Skt. *karsha-s*, a weight, abt. 180 grains Troy. See Yule, and H. H. Wilson's Glossary.

CASHEW-NUT, the nut of a W. and E. Indian tree. (F.—Brazil.) In Dampier's Voyages, iii. 68 (1703). *Cashew* is an E. form of *acajou*.—F. *acajou*.—Brazil. *acaju* (Yule, s.v. *Cashew*) or *acaiú*, in the Hist. Nat. Brasiliæ (1648), vol. ii. p. 94; which is the fruit of the tree named *acaiaba* (F. *acajaba*).

CASHIER, v., to dismiss from service. (Du.—F.—L.) [Quite unconnected with *cashier*, sb., which is simply formed from *cash*.] In Shak. Merry Wives, i. 3. 6. [Occasionally also written *cash*; from F. *casser*, directly. 'He *cashed* the old souldiers and supplied their roumes with yong beginners;' Golding, Justine, fol. 63 (R.). And the pp. *cashed*, for *cashiered*, occurs in a Letter of The Earl of Leicester, dated 1585; Nares, ed. Wright and Halliwell. Also spelt *cass*. 'But when the Lacedæmonians saw their armies *cassed*;' North's Plutarch, 180 E; quoted in Nares, s.v. *casse*, q.v.]—Du. *casséren*, 'to casheere;' Hexham.—F. *casser*, 'to breake, burst, . . . quash asunder, also to *casse*, *casseere*, discharge;' Cot.—L. *quassāre*, to shatter, frequentative of *quatere*, to shake (which in Late L. annexed the senses of L. *cassāre*, to bring to nothing, to annul, discharge; used by Sidonius and Cassiodorus; from L. *cassus*, empty, void; of uncertain origin). Körting, §§ 1988, 7645. ¶ It is easy to explain the suffix. The form *casseere* has been already quoted from Cotgrave; this is really the Du. *casseren*, to cast off, break, discard. This Du. *cass-eren* is nothing but the F. *casser* with the Du. suffix -*eren*, used in forming Du. verbs from Romance ones. So also G. -*iren*, as in *isoliren*, to isolate, from F. *isoler*.

CASHMERE, a soft wool. (India.) Esp. applied to a rich kind of soft woollen shawl; so called from the country of Cashmere, which lies close under the Himalayan Mountains, on the S. side of them. Also a name given to the stuff of which they are made, and to imitations of it. See **Cassimere**.

CASINO, a public room for music or dancing. (Ital.—L.) Modern. —Ital. *casino*, a summer-house, country-box; dimin. of *casa*, a house. —L. *casa*, a cottage.

CASK, a barrel or tub for wine, &c. (Span.—L.) 'The *caske* will haue a taste for evermore With that wherewith it seasoned was before;' Mirror for Magistrates, p. 193 (R.).—Span. *casco*, a skull, sherd, coat (of an onion); a cask; helmet; casque; cf. Span. *cascara*, peel, rind, hull; Port. *casca*, rind. See **Casque**, of which *cask* is a doublet. ¶ Imported from Spain, together with the wine.

CASKET, a little chest or coffer. (F.—L.) In Shak. Mer. of Ven. i. 2. 100. Earlier; 'the two shyrtys that wer in my *casket*;' Paston Letters, iii. 7 (1471); and as early as 1467. It looks like a dimin. of *cask*, in the sense of 'chest;' as in 'A jewel, locked into the wofullest *cask*;' 2 Hen. VI, iii. 2. 409; but this *cask* is not found before 1593. The form is anomalous, and must be regarded as a corrupt substitution for F. *cassette*, 'a small casket, chest, cabinet,' &c.; Cot. A dimin. form.—F. *casse*, a box, case, or chest.—L. *capsa*, a chest. See **Case** (2). ¶ The objection in N.E.D. that F. *cassette* dates from the 16th century is founded on a mistake. See Supp. to Godefroy, who gives the form *quacete* in 1348; much earlier than examples of E. *casket*.

CASQUE, a helmet. (F.—Span.—L.) In Shak. Rich. II, i. 3. 81. —F. *casque*, 'the head-piece tearmed a casque, or casket;' Cot.— Span. *casco*, 'a caske or burganet, a tile-shard;' Minsheu. The Span. has also *cascara*, peel, rind, shell (cf. Port. *casca*, bark, rind of trees); and these words, with numerous others, appear to be all derivatives from the very common Span. verb *cascar*, to burst, break open, crush; formed (as if from L. *quass-ic-āre) from an extension of L. *quassāre*, which also gives F. *casser*, to break. See **Quash**. Doublet, *cask*, q.v.

CASSATION, abrogation. (F.—L.) In Cotgrave.—F. *cassation*, 'a cassation, a quashing, cassing, breaking;' Cot.—Late L. acc. *cassātiōnem*.—Late L. *cassāre*, for L. *quassāre*, to quash; see **Quash**.

CASSAVA, a plant; also called mandioc. (Hayti.) In Eden's First Three Books on America, ed. Arber, pp. 159, 168, 175, 215, the Hayti name is given as *cazabbi*. In the tr. of Acosta by E. G., bk. iv. c. 17, it is *caçavi*.

CASSIA, a species of laurel. (L.—Gk.—Heb.) Exod. xxx. 24; Psalm xlv. 8 (A.V.), where the Vulgate has *casia*.—L. *casia*, *cassia*.— Gk. κασία, a spice of the nature of cinnamon.—Heb. *qetsī'ōth*, in Ps. xlv. 8, a pl. form from a fem. *qetsī'ōh*, cassia-bark; from the root *qātsa'*, to cut away; because the bark is cut or peeled off. See Gesenius.

CASSIMERE, a twilled cloth of fine wool. (India.) Also spelt *kerseymere* in Webster. These terms are nothing but corruptions of **Cashmere**, q.v.; and distinct from **Kersey**, q.v. *Cashmere* is spelt *Cassimer* in Herbert's Travels, 1665, p. 70.

CASSINO, a game at cards; the same word as **Casino**.

CASSOCK, a kind of vestment. (F.—Ital.—L.) Sometimes 'a military cloak;' All's Well, iv. 3. 192.—F. *casaque*, 'a cassock, long coat;' Cot.—Ital. *casacca*, 'a great coat, surtout. Apparently formed from Ital. *casa*, properly 'a house;' hence 'a covering,' used in a half jocular sense. Cf. Ital. *casaccia*, a large ugly old house. Indeed, Florio gives *casacca* as meaning ' an habitation or dwelling; also, a cassocke or long coate;' as if from L. *casa*, a cottage. See **Casino**. And see **Chasuble**, a word of similar origin; which renders this account of *cassock* probable. Cf. Körting, § 1978.

CASSOLET, CASSOLETTE, a vessel in which perfumes are burnt. (F.—Span.—Arab.) ' In *cassolets* and silver urns;' Moore, Lalla Rookh, Tale I, pt. 2, l. 67.—F. *cassolette*.—Span. *cazoleta*, a pan; dimin. of *cazuela*, an earthen pan; from *cazo*, a sauce-pan, an iron ladle (Hatzfeld).—Arab. *kās*, a cup, a bowl; *kāsa(h)*, a cup, plate, saucer (Devic).

CASSOWARY, a bird like an ostrich. (Malay.) ' *Cassowary* or *Emeu*, a large fowl, with feathers resembling camel's hair;' Kersey's Dict. ed. 1715. First in 1611; N. E. D.—Malay *kasuwāri*; also *suwāri*; C. P. G. Scott, p. 125. ' The cassowary is a bird which was first brought into Europe by the Dutch, from Java, in the East Indies, in which part of the world it is only to be found;' Eng. tr. of Buffon's Nat. Hist., ii. 9; London, 1792.

CAST, to throw. (Scand.) In early use, and one of the most characteristic of the Scand. words in English. ME. *casten, kesten*; St. Marharete, ed. Cockayne, pp. 4, 7; Havelok, ll. 1784, 2101.—Icel. *kasta*, to throw; Swed. *kasta*; Dan. *kaste*. β. The orig. sense was probably to 'throw into a heap,' or 'heap up;' cf. Swed. dial. *kas*, Icel. *köstr, kös*, a pile, heap; L. *con-gerere*, to heap together, pp. *con-gestus*. **Der.** *cast*, sb.; *cast-er, cast-ing, cast-away, out-cast*. Also *castor*, as in *pepper-castor*; a variant of *caster*.

CASTANETS, instruments composed of two small, concave shells of ivory or hard wood, loosely fastened together by a ribbon passing over the thumb, and made to snap together by beating one of them with the middle finger. (F.—Span.—L.—Gk.) In Blount's Gloss., ed. 1674. Spelt *castanietas* in Dryden, Ind. Emperor, iv. 3.—F. *castagnettes*, pl., 'finger-knackers, wherewith players make a pretty noise in some kind of daunces;' Cot.—Span. *castañetas*, castanets; pl. of *castañeta*; so called (according to Pineda and Monlau) because the castanet is shaped like a piece of the shell of a chestnut. (Some think the sound of the castanet resembled the cracking of roasted chestnuts.)—Span. *castaña*, a chestnut.—L. *castanea*, the chestnut-tree.—Gk. κάστανον, a chestnut; see **Chestnut**.

CASTE, a breed, race. (Port.—L.) ' Of two *castes*;' Hakluyt, Voy. iii. 659. Sir T. Herbert, speaking of men of various occupations in India, says: 'These never marry out of their own *casts*;' Travels, ed. 1665, p. 53. ' Four *casts* or sorts of men;' Lord's Discovery of the Banians [of India], 1630, p. 3 (Todd). Chiefly used in speaking of classes of men in India.—Port. *casta*, a race, stock; a name given by the Portuguese to classes of men in India.—Port. *casta*, adj. fem., chaste, pure, in allusion to purity of breed; from masc. *casto*.—L. *castum*, acc. of *castus*, chaste. See **Chaste**.

CASTIGATE, to chastise, chasten. (L.) In Shak. Timon, iv. 3. 240.—L. *castigātus*, pp. of *castigāre*, to chasten. The lit. sense is 'to keep chaste' or 'keep pure.'—L. *castus*, chaste, pure. See **Chaste**. **Der.** *castigat-ion, castigat-or*. **Doublet**, *chastise*.

CASTLE, a fortified house. (L.; *also* F.—L.) In very early use. AS. *castel*, used to render L. *castellum* in Matt. xxi. 2.—L. *castellum*, dimin. of *castrum*, a camp, fortified place. 2. ME. *castel*; Chaucer, C. T., 11159 (F 847).—ONorthF. *castel* (OF. *chastel*, F. *château*), a fort.—L. *castellum*, a fort. Brugmann, i. § 754. **Der.** *castell-a'-ed, castell-an*.

CASTOR, a beaver; a hat. (L.—Gk.) ' *Castor*, the beaver; or a fine sort of hat made of its fur;' Kersey's Dict. 1715. In Drayton's Polyolbion, s. vi. l. 4. Mere Latin.—L. *castor*.—Gk. κάστωρ, a beaver. β. Of Eastern origin. Cf. Skt. *kastūrī*, musk; Pers. *khaz*, a beaver. **Der.** *castor-oil*, q. v.

CASTOR-OIL, a medicinal oil. (L.—Gk.; *and* F.—L.—Gk.) Named from some confusion with *castoreum*. ' *Castoreum*, a medicine made of the liquor contained in the little bags that are next the beaver's groin;' Kersey's Dict. ed. 1715. See above. ¶ But really a vegetable production. The castor-oil plant, or *palma-Christi*, is *Ricinus communis*.

CASTRATE, to geld, to cut so as to render imperfect. (L.) ' Ye *castrate* [mortify] the desires of the flesh;' Martin, Marriage of Priests, 1554, Y i, b (Todd's Johnson). See also the Spectator, no. 179.—L. *castrātus*, pp. of *castrāre*. Cf. Skt. *çastri*, a knife; Gk. κεάζειν, to cleave (Prellwitz). **Der.** *castrat-ion*.

CASUAL, CASUIST; see **Case** (1).

CAT, a domestic animal. (E.) ME. *kat, cat*, Ancren Riwle, p. 102; AS. *cat, catt*, Wright's Vocab. i. 23, 78. + Du. *kat*; Icel. *köttr*; Dan. *kat*; Swed. *katt*; G. *kater, katze*. + W. *cath*; Irish and Gael. *cat*; Bret. *kaz*; Late L. *cātus*. + Russian *kot', koshka*. + Arab. *qitt*; Richardson's Dict. p. 1136; Turkish *kedi*. β. Origin and history of the spread of the word alike obscure. **Der.** *cat-call*; *cat-kin*, q. v.; *kitt-en*, q.v.; *cat-er-waul*, q. v.; also *caterpillar*, q. v.

CATA-, prefix; generally ' down.' (Gk.) Gk. κατα-, prefix; Gk. κατά, prep., down, downward; hence, in composition, also 'thoroughly,' or 'completely.' **Der.** *cata-clysm*, *cata-comb*, &c.

CATACLYSM, a deluge. (Gk.) In Hale, Origin of Mankind, p. 217 (R.). And in Blount's Gloss. ed. 1674.—Gk. κατακλυσμός, a dashing over, a flood, deluge.—Gk. κατακλύζειν, to dash over, to deluge.—Gk. κατά, downward; and κλύζειν, to wash or dash (said of waves). Cf. L. *cluere*, to cleanse; Goth. *hlūtrs*, pure.—√KLEU to wash; see Prellwitz; Brugm. i. § 490.

CATACOMB, a grotto for burial. (F.—Ital.—Late L.) In Addison's Italy, on Naples; and in the Tatler, no. 129. And in Kersey's Dict., 1715.—F. *catacombe*.—Ital. *catacomba*, a sepulchral vault.—Late L. *catacumba*, chiefly applied to the Catacombs at Rome; where *catacumba* is a nom. evolved out of an older *catacumbas*, an unexplained place-name. Cf. 'In loco qui dicitur *catacumbas*;' St. Gregory. See early references in N. E. D. ' On þære stōwe *catacumbe*;' The Shrine, ed. Cockayne, p. 55.

CATAFALQUE, a stage or platform, chiefly used at funerals. (F.—Ital.) Evelyn has the Ital. form *catafalco*, Diary, Oct. 8, 1641.—F. *catafalque*.—Ital. *catafalco*; of unknown origin. See **Scaffold**.

CATALEPSY, a sudden seizure. (Gk.) Spelt *catalepsis* in Kersey, ed. 1715; *catalepsie* in Phillips, ed. 1658. A medical term.—Gk. κατάληψις, a grasping, seizing.—Gk. κατά, down; and λαμβάνειν, to seize.

CATALOGUE, a list set down in order. (F.—Late L.—Gk.) In Shak. All's Well, i. 3. 149.—F. *catalogue*, 'a catalogue, list, rowl, register,' &c.; Cot.—Late L. *catalogus*.—Gk. κατάλογος, a counting up, enrolment.—Gk. κατά, down, fully; and λογ-, second grade of λέγειν, to say, tell. See **Logic**.

CATAMARAN, a sort of raft made of logs. (Tamil.) ' They call them *catamarans*;' Dampier, A New Voyage (1699), i. 143. Given as a Deccan word in Forbes' Hindustani Dict. ed. 1859, p. 280; ' *katmaran*, a raft, a float, commonly called a catamaran. The word is originally Tamul, and signifies in that language *tied logs*.'—Tamil *kaṭṭu*, binding; *maram*, wood (Yule); see H. H. Wilson, pp. 270, 331.

CATAPLASM, a kind of poultice. (F.—Late L.—Gk.) In Hamlet, iv. 7. 144.—F. *cataplasme*, 'a cataplasme, or poultis; a soft, or moyst plaister;' Cot.—L. *cataplasma*.—Gk. κατάπλασμα, a plaster, poultice.—Gk. καταπλάσσειν, to spread over.—Gk. κατά, down, over; and πλάσσειν, to mould, bring into shape. See **Plaster**.

CATAPULT, a machine for throwing stones. (Late L.—Gk.) In Holland's Pliny, bk. vii. c. 56 (R.).—Late L. *catapulta*, a war-engine for throwing stones.—Gk. καταπέλτης, the same.—Gk. κατά, down; and πάλλειν, to brandish, swing, also, to hurl a missile.

CATARACT, a waterfall. (L.—Gk.) In King Lear, iii. 2. 2. ME. *cateracte* (rare), Towneley Mysteries, pp. 29, 32.—L. *cataracta*, in Gen. vii. 11 (Vulgate).—Gk. καταρράκτης, as sb., a waterfall; as adj., broken, rushing down. β. Wedgwood derives this from Gk. καταράσσειν, to dash down, fall down headlong; but this is not quite clear. Littré takes the same view. γ. Others connect it with καταρρήγνυμι (root Ϝραγ), I break down; of which the aorist pass. κατερράγην was esp. used of waterfalls or storms, in the sense of ' rushing down.' The latter verb is a comp. from κατά, down, and ῥήγνυμι, I break.

CATARRH, a fluid discharge from the mucous membrane; a cold. (Gk.) In Shak. Troilus, v. 1. 22. Spelt *catarre*, Sir T. Elyot, Castel of Helth, b. ii. c. 17.—Late L. *catarrhus*, a Latinised form from the Gk. κατάρροος, a catarrh, lit. a flowing down.—Gk. κατά, down; and ῥέω, I flow. See **Rheum**.

CATASTROPHE, an upset, great calamity, end. (Gk.) In Shak. L. L. L. iv. 1. 77.—Gk. καταστροφή, an overthrowing, sudden turn.—Gk. κατά, down, over; and στρέφειν, to turn. See **Strophe**.

CATCH, to lay hold of, seize. (F.—L.) ME. *cachen, cacchen*, in very common and early use. In Layamon, iii. 266.—ONorthF. *cachier*, a (Picard) variant of OF. *chacier*, to chase. [Cf. Ital. *cacciare*, to hunt, chase; Span. *cazar*, to chase, hunt.]—Late L. *captiāre*, an assumed late form of *captāre*, to catch; the sb. *captia*, a chase, is given in Ducange.—L. *captāre*, to try to catch, chase; a frequentative form from L. *capere*, to take, lay hold of, hold, contain. See **Capacious**. ¶ The ME. pt. t. *cauȝte* (E. *caught*) imitated *lauȝte*, pt. t. of ME. *lacchen*, to catch. **Der.** *catch-word, catch-penny, catch-poll*. **Doublet**, *chase*.

CATCHPOLE, a sheriff's officer. (F.—L.) ME. *cachepol*, Old Eng. Homilies, ed. Morris, i. 97, l. 30; Late L. *chassipullus*, lit. ' chase-fowl.'—ONorthF. *cachier*, to catch (above); and OF. *pol, poul*, fowl, cock; Span. *pollo*, fowl, chick. See **Poult**.

CATCHUP, CATSUP, the same as **Ketchup**, q. v.

CATE, a dainty; see **Cates**.

CATECHISE, to instruct by questions. (L.—Gk.) Used of oral instruction, because it means 'to din into one's ears.' In Shak. Much Ado, iv. 1. 79.—Late L. *catechizāre*, to catechise; an ecclesiastical word.—Gk. κατηχίζειν, to catechise, to instruct; a lengthened form of κατηχέειν, to din into one's ears, impress upon one; lit. 'to din down.'—Gk. κατ-ά, down; and ἠχεῖν, to sound, ἦχος, a ringing in the ears. See **Echo**. Der. *catechis-er*; *catechism* (Late L. *catē-chismus*); *catechist* (Gk. κατηχιστής); *catechist-ic*, *catechist-ic-al*; *catechet-ic* (from Gk. κατηχητής, an instructor), *catechet-ic-al*, *catechet-ic-al-ly*; *catechumen* (Gk. κατηχούμενος, one who is being instructed).

CATECHU, an astringent extract from the wood of several species of acacia, &c. (Malay.) See Yule.—Malay *kāchu*. Also called *cachou* (F. *cachou*) and *cutch*; Canarese *kāchu*, Tamil *kāshu*.

CATEGORY, a leading class or order. (Gk.) 'The distribution of things into certain tribes, which we call *categories* or predicaments;' Bacon, Adv. of Learning, bk. ii. sect. xiv. subject 7.—Gk. κατηγορία, an accusation; but in logic, a predicament, class.—Gk. κατηγορεῖν, to accuse.—Gk. κατά, down, against; and *ἀγορεῖν, with the sense of ἀγορεύειν, to declaim, to address an assembly, from ἀγορά, an assembly. Cf. Gk. ἀγείρειν (for *ἀγέρ-γειν), to assemble; allied to L. *grex*, a flock. See **Gregarious**. Brugm. i. § 633. Der. *categor-ic-al*, *categor-ic-al-ly*.

CATENARY, belonging to a chain. (L.) Chiefly in the math. phr. a *catenary* curve, which is the curve in which a chain hangs when supported only at the ends. Formed from L. *catēn-a*, a chain, with suffix *-ārius*. See **Chain**.

CATER, to buy provisions, provide food. (F.—L.) Originally a sb. and used as we now use the word *caterer*, wherein the ending *-er* of the agent is unnecessarily reduplicated. So used by Sir T. Wyat, Satire i. l. 26. To *cater* means 'to act as a *cater*,' i. e. a buyer. The old spelling of the sb. is *catour*. 'I am oure *catour*, and bere oure aller purs' = I am *the* buyer for us, and bear the purse for us all; Gamelyn, l. 321. '*Catour* of a gentylmans house, *despensier*;' Palsgrave. β. Again, *catour* is a shortened form of *acatour*, by loss of initial *a*. *Acatour* is formed (by adding the OF. suffix *-our* of the agent) from ONorthF. *acater* (OF. *achater*, F. *acheter*), to buy. [Cf. *acat*, *achat*, a buying, a purchase; a word used by Chaucer, Prol. 571.] —Late L. *accaptāre*, to purchase, in a charter of A.D. 1000 (Brachet, s. v. *acheter*). A frequentative of *accipere*, to receive, but sometimes 'to buy.'—L. *ad*, to (> *ac-* before *c*); and *capere*, to take. See **Capacious**. Der. *cater-er*; see above.

CATERAN, a Highland soldier or robber. (Gaelic.) In Waverley, c. xv, Sir W. Scott defines *caterans* as being 'robbers from the Highlands;' see also Jamieson.—Late L. *caterānus*, due to Gael. *ceathairne*, yeomanry, lit. 'common people.' From Gael. *ceatharn*, Irish *cethern*, OIrish *ceithern*, a troop; allied to L. *caterua*, a troop; Macbain. See **Kern**.

CATER-COUSIN, a remote relation, good friend. (F.—L.) We find '*Cater-cousin*, quatre-cousin, remote relation, misapplied by Gobbo to persons who peaceably feed together;' Merch. Ven. ii. 2. 139;' Schmidt, Shak. Lexicon. '*Quater-cosins*, fourth or last cosins, good friends;' Coles (1684). But the form *quater-cousin* (with the explanation) seems to have been invented by Skinner (1671); and turns out to be baseless. It is more probable that *cater* is from *cater*, to provide food (as above); and that *cater-cousins* are cousins who feed (or are *catered* for) together. So N. E. D. And so Nares, who has: '*Cater-cousins*, friends so familiar that they eat together.' See **Cater** and **Cousin**.

CATERPILLAR, a kind of grub. (F.) In Shak. Rich. II, ii. 3. 166. Used also by Sir Jo. Cheeke, Hurt of Sedition (R.) Spelt *catyrpel*, Prompt. Parv. p. 63; to which the suffix *-ar* or *-er* of the agent was afterwards added; so as to assimilate it to *piller*, i.e. one who *pills*, or robs or spoils. Palsgrave has: '*caterpyllar worme*, *chattepeleuse*.' The ME. *catyrpel* is a corruption of ONorthF. *catepelose*; cf. *chatepelose* in Godefroy; and Norm. dial. *carpleuse*, *catepleuse*, a caterpillar (Robin). Cotgrave has: '*Chatepeleuse*, a corne-devouring mite, or weevell.' β. A fanciful name, meaning literally 'hairy she-cat,' applied primarily to the hairy caterpillar.—OF. *chate*, a she-cat, fem. of *chat* (Cotgrave); and *pelose*, orig. equivalent to Ital. *peloso*, hairy, from L. *pilōsus*, hairy, which again is from L. *pilus*, a hair. See **Cat** and **Pile** (4).

CATERWAUL, to cry as a cat. (E.) ME. *caterwawen*. Chaucer has 'gon a *caterwawed*' = go a-caterwauling (the pp. *-ed* being used with the force of the *-ing* of the (so-called) verbal substantive, by an idiom explained in my note on *blakeberyed* in Chaucer); C. T., 5936 (D 354). Formed from *cat*, and the verb *waw*, to make a noise like a cat, with the addition of *-l* to give the verb a frequentative force. 'Where cats do *waule*;' Return from Parnassus, v. 4. Cf. Low G. *katterwaulen*, to caterwaul (Schambach). The word *waw* is imitative; cf. *wail*, q. v.

CATES, provisions. (F.—L.) In Baret's Alveary, 1580, we find: 'A *Cater*, a steward, a manciple, a provider of *cates*, . . . *qui emit opsonia*.' Again: 'the *Cater* buyeth very dere *cates*;' Horman's Vulgaria. Thus the *cates* were the provisions bought by the *cater*, or, as we now say, the *caterer*, and were thence so called. *Cate* is

a shortened form of *acate*, sb.; just as *cater* is of *acater* or *acatour*; see Chaucer, Prol. 568 (Camb. MS.). See further under **Cater**. We may note that Ben Jonson uses the full form *acates*, Staple of News, Act ii, sc. 1, l. 16; Sad Shepherd, Act i, sc. 2, l. 40. Shak. has *cates*, Tam. Shrew., ii. 1. 190.

CATGUT, the dried and twisted intestines (chiefly of sheep) used for the strings of violins, &c. (E.) Lit. 'gut of a cat;' though it is not known that such were used. 'Tunes played upon *cat's guts*;' Middleton, Women beware Women, iii. 2. Cf. Du. *kattedarm*, cat-gut; from *darm*, gut. See Notes on E. Etymology.

CATHARTIC, purgative, lit. cleansing. (Gk.) *Cathartical* and *catharticks* occur in Blount's Gloss., ed. 1674. '*Cathartics* or purgatives of the soul,' Spectator, no. 507.—Gk. καθαρτικός, purgative. — Gk. καθαίρειν, fut. καθαρ-ῶ, to cleanse, purify.—Gk. καθαρός, clean, pure. Der. *cathartic*, sb.; *cathartic-al*.

CATHEDRAL, a church with a bishop's throne. (L.—Gk.) Properly an adj., being an abbreviation for *cathedral church*. 'In the *cathedral church* of Westminster;' 2 Hen. VI, i. 2. 37. 'Chyrche *cathedral*;' Rob. of Glouc., p. 282, l. 5715.—Late L. *cathedrālis*, adj.; whence *cathedrālis ecclēsia*, a cathedral church.—L. *cathedra*, a raised seat; with adj. suffix *-ālis*.—Gk. καθέδρα, a seat, bench, pulpit.— Gk. κατά, down (> καθ- before an aspirate), and ἕδρα, a seat, chair; cf. ἕδος, a seat.—Gk. ἕζομαι (root ἑδ), I sit. The Gk. root *hed* is cognate with E. *sit*. See **Sit**.

CATHOLIC, universal. (F.—L.—Gk.) Spelt *catholyke*; Sir T. Elyot, The Governour, bk. iii. c. 23. § 2.—F. *catholique*, 'catholick, universall;' Cot.—L. *catholicus*, used by Tertullian, adv. Marc. ii. 17. —Gk. καθολικός, universal, general; formed with suffix *-ικ-* from Gk. καθόλ-ου, adv., on the whole, in general.—Gk. καθ' ὅλου, where καθ' is for κατά (on account of the following aspirate), and ὅλου is the gen. case of ὅλος, whole, governed by the prep. κατά, according to; lit. 'according to the whole,' or 'on the whole.' The Gk. ὅλος is cognate with Skt. *sarva-s*, all. Der. *catholic-i-ty*, *catholic-ism*.

CATKIN, a loose spike of flowers resembling a cat's tail. (Du.) Used in botany; and borrowed by Lyte from Dutch; see Lyte, tr. of Dodoens, b. vi. c. 58: '*catkens* of Hasell.' Cotgrave has: '*Chattons*, the *catkins*, cat-tailes, aglet-like blowings, or bloomings of nut-trees, &c.' Called *kattekens* in MDutch; see *katten*, *kattekens*, the blossom of the spikes of nuts and hazels, Oudemans; *katteken*, a young cat, Hexham.—MDu. *katte*, cat; with dim. suffix *-ken*. See **Cat**.

CATOPTRIC, relating to optical reflexion. (Gk.) A scientific term; spelt *catoptrick* in Phillips (1658). Bailey has '*catoptrical* telescope' for reflecting telescope; vol. ii. ed. 1731.—Gk. κατοπτρικός, reflexive.—Gk. κάτοπτρον, a mirror.—Gk. κατ-ά, downward, inward; and ὄπ-το-μαι, I see; with suffix *-τρον*, of the instrument. See **Optics**. Der. *catopt-trics*, sb. pl.

CATTLE, live stock; collectively. (F.—L.) In early use. Properly 'capital,' or 'chattel,' i.e. property, without necessary reference to live stock. The ME. words *catel* and *chatel* are mere variants of one another, and alike mean 'property.' Spelt *catel*, Havelok, 225; Layamon, iii. 232, later text. Spelt *chatel*, Old Eng. Homilies, i. 271; *chetel*, Ancren Riwle, p. 224.—ONorthF. *catel*, OF. *chatel*.— Late L. *capitāle*, also *captāle*, capital, property, goods; neut. sb. formed from adj. *capitālis*. [Whence Late L. *uīuum capitāle*, i. e. live stock, cattle. *Capitāle* also meant the 'capital' or principal of a debt.]—L. *capitālis*, excellent, capital; lit. belonging to the head.— L. *caput* (decl. stem *capit-*), the head; see **Capital** (2). ¶ Hence it appears that *capital* is the Latin form, and *cattle*, *chattel* are the North and Central French forms, of the same word. From *chattel* is formed a pl. *chattels*, in more common use than the singular.

CATTY, a weight; see under **Caddy**.

CAUCUS, a name applied to a private meeting of the representatives of a political party. (American Indian?) We first hear of a *caucus-club* in 1763. The origin of the name is obscure; but Dr. Trumbull (Proc. Amer. Philol. Association, 1872) shows the probability of its being an adaptation of an Algonkin word meaning to speak, counsel, incite; whence *kaw-kaw-asu*, a counsellor. 'Their elders, called *cawcawwassoughes*'' Capt. Smith's Works, ed. Arber, p. 347; cf. p. 377.

CAUDAL, belonging to the tail. (L.) 'The *caudal* fin;' Pennant's Zoology, The Cuvier Ray (R.) Cf. '*caudate* stars,' i.e. tailed stars, comets; Fairfax's Tasso, xiv. 44. Formed by suffix *-al* (as if from a L. *caudālis*), from L. *caud-a*, a tail.

CAUDLE, a warm drink for the sick. (F.—L.) In Shak. L. L. L. iv. 3. 174. 'A *caudel*, *potio*;' Levins, col. 56 (A.D. 1570). But found much earlier, viz. in Rob. of Glouc. p. 561, l. 11767.— ONorthF. *caudel*, OF. *chaudel*, a sort of warm drink.—OF. *chaud*, formerly *chald*, hot; with adj. suffix *-el*, properly dimin., as in L. *-ellus*.—Late L. *caldus*, hot, a contr. form of *calidus*; Quinctilian, i. 6. 19.

CAUL, a net, covering, esp. for the head. (F.) ME. *calle*, *kalle*.

'Reticula, a lytell nette or *kalle*;' Prompt. Parv. p. 270, note 1. Chaucer, C. T. 6600 (D 1018). And see Polit. Songs, ed. Wright, p. 258 (1327).—OF. *cale*, 'a kinde of little cap;' Cot. Of unknown origin. Cf. '*kelle*, reticulum;' Prompt. Parv. p. 270.

CAULDRON; see **Caldron**.

CAULIFLOWER, a variety of the cabbage. (F.—L.) Spelt *collyflory* in Cotgrave, who gives: '*Chou*, the herb cole, or coleworts. *Choux fleuris, fleurs, et floris*, the collyflory, or Cypres colewort.' Thus the word is made up of the ONorthF. *col* (OF. *chol*), whence *colly*; and *flory*, for OF. *flori*, pp. of OF. *florir* (F. *fleurir*), to flourish; the sense being 'flowered cabbage.' **1.** The ONorthF. *col* (OF. *chol*, in Supp. to Godefroy) is from L. *caulem*, acc. of *caulis*, a cabbage, orig. the stalk or stem of a plant, cognate with Gk. καυλός, a stalk, stem, cabbage; see **Cole**. [From the L. *caulis* was thus formed OF. *chol*, whence mod. F. *chou*, a cabbage. The corruption of *col* to *colly* was probably due to an attempt to bring the word nearer to the original L. *caulis*, an attempt which has been fully carried out in the modern spelling *cauli-*.] **2.** The F. *floris* or *fleuris* is the pl. of *fleuri*, the pp. of the verb *fleurir*, to flourish; from L. *flōrēre*, to flourish. See **Flourish**. We have also modified this element so as to substitute the sb. *fleur* (E. *flower*) for the pp. pl. of the verb. The spelling *colliflower* occurs in Sir T. Herbert's Travels, 1665, p. 400.

CAULK; see **Calk**.

CAUSE, that which produces an effect. (F.—L.) In early use. So spelt in the Ancren Riwle, p. 316.—OF. and F. *cause*.—L. *causa*, a cause; better spelt *caussa*. Der. *caus-al, caus-al-i-ty, caus-at-ion, caus-at-ive, cause-less*. And see *ac-cuse, ex-cuse, re-cus-ant*.

CAUSEWAY, a raised way, a paved way. (F.—L.) A compound word; formerly *causey-way*; the word *way* being added to ME. *causé, causie*; later *causey*, as in Milton, P. L. x. 415; and in Berners' tr. of Froissart, vol. i. c. 413 (R.) Still earlier, *cawsè* occurs in Barbour's Bruce, ed. Skeat, xviii. 128, 140; spelt *cawsee*, xviii. 146.—ONorthF. *caucié*, OF. *chaucié* (mod. F. *chaussée*, Prov. *causada*, Span. *calzada*).—Late L. *calciāta*, short for *calciāta uia*, a causeway.—Late L. *calciātus*, pp. of *calciāre*, to make a roadway by treading it down; from L. *calcāre*, to tread.—L. *calx* (stem *calc-*), the heel. See **Caulk**.

CAUSTIC, burning, corrosive, severe. (L.—Gk.) Properly an adjective; often used as a sb., as in 'your hottest *causticks*;' Ben Jonson, Elegy on Lady Pawlet, l. 54.—L. *causticus*, burning.—Gk. καυστικός, burning.—Gk. καίειν, fut. καύσ-ω, to burn. Der. *caustic*, sb.; *caustic-i-ty*; and see *cauterise*.

CAUTERISE, to burn with caustic. (F.—Late L.—Gk.) The pp. *cauterized* is in Holland's Pliny, bk. xxxvi. c. 7.—MF. *cauterizer*, 'to cauterize, seare, burne;' Cotgrave.—Late L. *cautērizāre*, also found as *caūteriāre*, to cauterise, sear.—Gk. καυτηριάζειν, to sear.—Gk. καυτήριον, καυτήρ, a branding-iron.—Gk. καίειν, to burn (above). Der. *cauteris-at-ion, cauteris-m*; also *cautery* (from Gk. καυτήριον).

CAUTION, carefulness, heed. (F.—L.) ME. *caucion*, Rob. of Glouc. p. 506, l. 10418. Spelt *kaucyon*, K. Alisaunder, 2811.—OF. *caution*.—L. *cautiōnem*, acc. of *cautio*, a security; occurring in Luke, xvi. 6 (Vulgate) where Wyclif has *caucioun*; cf. *cautus*, pp. of *cauēre*, to take heed. Allied to Skt. *kavi-s*, wise. And see **Show**. Brugm. i. § 635. Der. *caution-ar-y*; also *cautious* (expanded from L. *cautus*, heedful), *cautious-ly, cautious-ness*; and see *caveat*.

CAVALCADE, a train of men on horseback. (F.—Ital.—L.) In Dryden, Palamon and Arcite, l. 1817.—F. *cavalcade*, 'a riding of horse;' Cotgrave. Introduced from Ital. in the 16th century.—Ital. *cavalcata*, a troop of horsemen.—Ital. *cavalcare* (pp. *cavalcato*, fem. pp. *cavalcata*), to ride.—Ital. *cavallo*, a horse.—L. *caballus*, a horse. Cf. Gk. καβάλλης, a horse, nag; also W. *ceffyl*, a horse, Gael. *capull*, a mare, Icel. *kapall*, a nag; all from Latin. See below.

CAVALIER, a knight, horseman. (F.—Ital.—L.) In Shak. Hen. V, iii. chor. 24.—F. *cavalier*, 'a horseman, cavalier;' Cotgrave.—Ital. *cavaliere*, a horseman.—L. *caballārium*, acc. of *caballārius*, the same.—L. *caballus*, a horse (above). Der. *cavalier*, adj.; *cavalier-ly*. **Doublet**, *chevalier*, q. v.

CAVALRY, a troop of horse. (F.—Ital.—L.) Spelt *cavallerie* in Holland's Ammianus, p. 181 (R.)—MF. *cavallerie*, in Cotgrave, who explains it by 'horsemanship, also, horsemen.'—Ital. *cavalleria*, knighthood; also cavalry.—Ital. *cavaliere*, a chevalier, knight (above). **Doublet**, *chivalry*, q. v.

CAVE, a hollow place, den. (F.—L.) In early use; see Genesis and Exodus, ed. Morris, 1137.—OF. *cave*, a cave; Folk-L. *cava*.—L. *cauus*, hollow. Cf. Gk. κύαρ, a cavity, a hollow.—√KEU, to swell, to hollow out. Der. *cav-i-ty*; *cav-ern* (L. *cauerna*), *cavern-ous*. From the same root, *con-cave, ex-cav-ate*; *cage*, q. v.

CAVE IN, (E.) First noted, as a literary phrase, in America, in 1796; but borrowed from prov. E. *calve*, or *calve in*, found in many dialects, esp. in Linc. and East Anglia; see E. D. D. Influenced by association with *cave*, as if the ground were hollow. Wedgwood

shows that *cave* is here a corruption of *calve* (the pronunciation of *cave* being formerly much the same as that of the modern pronunciation of *calve*). 'Properly to *calve in*, as it is still pronounced in Lincolnshire. It is said of a steep bank of earth at which men are digging, when a portion of the wall of earth separates and falls in upon them, the falling portion being compared to a cow dropping her calf.' He then cites 'the rock *calved* in upon him;' N. and Q. 4 S. xii. 166; also 'Tak heed, lads, there's a *cauf* a-comin';' Peacock's Linc. Gloss. E. D. S. s. v. *cauf*. He suggests that the word was introduced by Dutch navvies (which is unnecessary, as it may well be native), and adds: 'This explanation of the expression is rendered certain by the W. Flanders *inkalven*, used in exactly the same sense. *De gracht kalft in*, the ditch caves in.—De Bo, W. Flem. Dict.' But the phrase also occurs in E. Friesic; and Koolman cites *kalfen*, to calve as a cow, also to fall in, as in *de slotskante kalfd in*, the brink of the ditch caves in; and further, *kalferen* in E. Friesic means (1) to cave in, (2) to skip like a calf. Cf. Du. *uit-kalven*, to fall or shoot out, said of the sides of a cutting or the like. In Northamptonsh., when the earth is expected to fall, it is commonly said, 'we shall have a *calf*;' E. D. D., s. v. *Calve*. See **Calf**.

CAVEAT, a notice given, a caution. (L.) 'And gave him also a special *caveat*;' Bacon's life of Hen. VII, ed. Lumby, p. 85. From the L. *caueat*, let him beware.—L. *cauēre*, to beware, take heed. See **Caution**.

CAVIARE, the roe of the sturgeon, pressed and salted; as a relish. (F.—Ital.) In Shak. Hamlet, ii. 2. 457; see the article on it in Nares.—F. *caviar*, formerly also spelt *cavial* (Hatzfeld).—Ital. *caviaro*, in Florio, who explains it by 'a kinde of salt meate made of the roes of fishes, vsed in Italie;' also spelt *caviale*. Of unknown origin; the Turk. *khāvyār*, given as the equivalent of E. *caviare* in Redhouse's Eng.-Turkish Dictionary, is borrowed from Italian. [It is made in Russia; but the Russian name is *ikra*.]

CAVIL, to raise empty objections. (F.—L.) Spelt *cauyll* (*u* for *v*), in Udal, on St. Mark, c. 2. vv. 6-12; *cauil*, Levins, 126. 47. The sb. *cavillation* occurs early; spelt *cauillacioun* (*u* for *v*), Chaucer, C. T. 7718 (D 2136).—MF. *caviller*, 'to cavill, wrangle, reason crossely;' Cot.—L. *cauillāri*, to banter.—L. *cauilla* a jeering, cavilling. Der. *cavill-er*.

CAVY, CAVEY, a rodent quadruped. (F.—Carib.) 'The long-nosed *cavy*;' Stedman's Surinam, ii. 153.—F. *cavié* (Littré); a modification of *cabiai*, the Caribbean name in French Guiana (N. E. D.); allied to Brazil. *capibara*, q.v. Cf. *cavia cobaya*, a kind of rabbit; Hist. Brasiliæ, p. 224.

CAW, to make a noise like a crow. (E.) Shak. Mid. Nt. Dr. iii. 2. 22. The word is merely imitative, and may be classed as English. Cf. Du. *kaauw*, a jackdaw, Dan. *kaa*, Swed. *kaja*, a jackdaw; all from imitation of the cry of the bird. See **Chough**.

CAYENNE, the name of a pepper. (Brazil.) *Cayenne* is a later spelling, due to a popular etymology; early spellings are *cayán, kián, chian*, &c. ''Tis Chian pepper indeed;' Garrick, A Peep behind the Curtain, A. i (1767). From the Tupi (Brazilian) *kyýnha*; N. E. D.

CAYMAN, CAIMAN, an American alligator. (Caribbean.) 'Lezards or *Caymans*;' E. G., tr. of Acosta (1604), bk. iii. c. 15, p. 165. (There are three islands called *Cayman* to the S. of Cuba.) Span. *cayman, caiman*; F. *caiman*.—Galibi (Mainland Carib) *cayman*, in Martini's Dict.; Carib. *acáyouman*, Dict. F.-Carib by P. R. Breton (1661), p. 13, col. 1. Not *acayoúman*, as in Littré.

CEASE, to give over, stop, end. (F.—L.) ME. *cessen*, P. Plowman, B. vi. 181; vii. 117; iv. 1.—F. *cesser*.—L. *cessāre*, to loiter, go slowly, cease; frequent. of *cēdere* (pp. *cessus*), to go away, yield, give place. See **Cede**. Der. *cease-less, cease-less-ly*; also *cessat-ion* (from L. *cessātiōnem*, acc. of *cessātio*, a tarrying; cf. *cessātus*, pp. of *cessāre*).

CEDAR, a large fine tree. (L.—Gk.) In very early use. AS. *ceder-bēam*, a cedar-tree; Ælfric's Homilies, ed. Thorpe, ii. 578.—L. *cedrus*.—Gk. κέδρος. Der. *cedar-n*; Milton, Comus, 990.

CEDE, to give up, to yield. (L.) A late word, in the transitive use; not in Pope's poems. It occurs in Drummond's Travels (1754), p. 256 (Todd). [Probably directly from the L. rather than from F. *céder*.]—L. *cēdere*, pp. *cessus*, to yield. Der. *cess-ion*. ¶ From the L. *cēdere* we have many derivatives; such as *cease, accede, concede, exceed, intercede, precede, proceed, recede, secede, succeed*, and their derivatives. Also *antecedent, decease, abscess, ancestor, predecessor*, &c.

CEDILLA, a mark under the letter *c* (ç), to indicate that it has the sound of *s, z*, or *th*, not *k*. (Span.—Ital.—Gk.) In Minsheu, Span. Gram. (1623), p. 6. The symbol was derived from the sign for z.—Span. *çedilla* (Pineda).—Ital. *zediglia* (Diez).—Gk. ζῆτα, z.

CEIL, CIEL, to line the inner roof of a room. (F.—L.) Older form *syle*. 'And the greater house he *syled* with fyre-tree;' Bible, 1551, 2 Chron. iii. 5 (R.) Also spelt *seile* (Minsheu); and *ciel*, as in most modern Bibles. ME. *ceelen*; as in '*Ceelyn* wythe syllure, *celo*;' Prompt. Parv. p. 65; and see p. 452. The sb. is *seeling* in North's

Plutarch, p. 36; and *ceeling* in Milton, P. L. xi. 743 (R.) See *cieled*, *cieling* in the Bible Wordbook, by Eastwood and Wright. β. The verb to *ciel*, *seile*, or *syle* is closely connected with the sbs. *celure* or *selure*, and *syle* or *cyll*, a canopy, as in : 'The chammer was hanged of [with] red and of blew, and in it was a *cyll* of state of cloth of gold;' Fyancells of Margaret, dau. of K. Hen. VII, to Jas. of Scotland (R.) The verb *to syle* meant to canopy, to hang with canopies, as in : 'All the tente within was *syled* wyth clothe of gold and blewe veluet;' Hall, Hen. VIII, an. 5, § 30. γ. The word was afterwards extended so as to include the notion of covering with side-hangings, and even to that of providing with wainscoting. Cotgrave has : '*Plancher*, a boorded floor; also, a seeling of boords.' It seems to be connected with the idea of canopy, and with L. *caelum*, used in the sense of *cieling* in the 13th century; Way's note to Prompt. Parv. p. 65.—MF. *ciel*, pl. *ciels*, which Cotgrave explains by : 'a canopy for . . a bed; also, the canopie that is carried over a prince as he walks in state; also, the inner roofe [i. e. ceiling] of a room of state.' [This word is precisely the same as the F. *ciel*, heaven, pl. *cieux*: though there is a difference of usage. The Ital. *cielo* also means (1) heaven, (2) a canopy, (3) a cieling; see Florio; and Minsheu explains Span. *cielo* as 'the heaven, the skie, the tester of a bed.']—L. *caelum*, heaven, a vault; a 'genuine Lat. word, not to be written with *oe*;' Curtius, i. 193. ¶ The derivation appears to be tolerably certain, but many efforts have been made to render it confused. The word has no connexion with E. *sill*; nor with E. *seal*; nor with F. *siller*, to *seel* up the eyes of a hawk (from L. *cilium*, an eyelid); nor with L. *cēlāre*, to hide; nor with AS. *þil*, a plank. Yet all these have been needlessly mixed up with it by various writers. It has, however, certainly been influenced by the L. *cælare*, to emboss, which is the word intended by the entry 'celo' in the Prompt. Parvulorum; and it was confused with the sb. *celure* (*selure*, *syllure*), from a F. form due to the Late L. *cælātūra*, a vaulted roof, a derivative of that verb. And perhaps, in Late L., *cælāre* was meant to be a derivative of *cælum*. See *cælum* in Ducange, misspelt *cœlum* in the latest edition (1883). The other words are not at all to be considered. **Der.** *ceil-ing*.

CELANDINE, a plant; swallow-wort. (F.—Late L.—Gk.) Orig. the *greater* celandine. It occurs in Cotgrave. It is spelt *cellandyne* in Palsgrave. But Gower has *celidoine*, C. A. iii. 131, bk. vii. l. 1370.—F. *celidoine*, 'the herbe *celandine*, tetter-wort, swallow-wort;' also spelt *chelidoine* by Cotgrave.—Late L. *chelidonium* (the botanical name).—Gk. χελιδόνιον, swallow-wort; neut. from χελιδόνιος, adj., relating to swallows.—Gk. χελιδών (stem χελιδον-), a swallow. ¶ The *n* before *d* is intrusive, like *n* before *g* in *messenger*, for *messager*.

CELEBRATE, to render famous, honour. (L.) In Shak. Temp. iv. 84. Chaucer has the adj. *celebrable*, noted, in his tr. of Boethius, b. iii. pr. 9. 48; b. iv. met. 7. 20.—L. *celebrātus*, pp. of *celebrāre*, to frequent; also, to solemnise, honour.—L. *celeber*, frequented, populous; also written *celebris*. **Der.** *celebrat-ion*; *celebri-ty* (from L. *celebri-tās*, sb., from the adj. *celebris*).

CELERITY, quickness, speed. (F.—L.) In Shak. Meas. v. 399.—F. *celerité*, 'celerity, speedinesse;' Cotgrave.—L. *celeritātem*, acc. of *celeritās*, speed.—L. *celer*, quick. ✛ Gk. κέλης, a runner.—✓QEL, to drive; Brugm. i. § 633; cf. Skt. *kal*, to drive, urge on.

CELERY, a vegetable; regarded as a kind of parsley. (F.—Ital.—L.—Gk.) In Kersey's Dict., ed. 1715.—F. *céleri*, introduced from prov. Ital. *seleri*, a Piedmontese word (Brachet); where *r* must stand for an older *n*; cf. MItal. *seleni*, pl. of *seleno*, parsley (Florio).—L. *selinon*, parsley.—Gk. σέλινον, a kind of parsley. See **Parsley**. ¶ Wild celery was formerly called *smallage* (for *small ache*); from F. *ache*, representing *apia*, pl. form of L. *apium*, parsley. The form *seleno* is Venetian (Diez); mod. Ital. *sedano*.

CELESTIAL, heavenly. (F.—L.) In Shak. Temp. ii. 2. 122; and in Gower, C. A. iii. 301, b. viii. 780.—OF. *celestiel*, 'celestiall, heavenly;' Cot. Formed with suffix -*el* (as if from a L. form in -*ālis*), from *caelesti*-, the declensional stem of L. *caelestis*, heavenly.—L. *caelum*, heaven. See **Ceil**.

CELIBATE, pertaining to a single life. (L.) Now sometimes as sb., 'one who is single;' formerly an adj. 'pertaining to a single life.' And, when first used, a sb. signifying 'the single state,' which is the true sense. Bp. Taylor speaks of 'the purities of *cœlibate*,' i. e. of a single life; Rule of Conscience, bk. iii. c. 4 (R.)—L. *caelibātus*, sb. celibacy.—L. *caelebs* (stem *caelib*-), adj. single, unmarried. **Der.** *celibac-y* (as if for *caelibātia*).

CELL, a small room, small dwelling-place. (L.) In early use. ME. *celle*, Ancren Riwle, p. 152.—L. *cella*, a cell, small room, hut. Cf. Gk. καλιά, a hut; L. *cēlāre*, to hide; and E. *hel-m*; see **Helm** (2).—✓KEL, to hide. **Der.** -*cell-ul-ar*; also *cell-ar* (ME. *celer*, Wyclif, Luke, xii. 24, from OF. *celier*, L. *cellārium*), *cell-ar-age*.

CELT (1), a name orig. given to the Gauls. (C.) From L. pl. *Celtæ*, Celts. The word prob. means 'warriors;' cf. Lith. *kalti*, to strike, L. *per-cellere*, to strike through, AS. *hild*, Icel. *hildr*, war (Rhys).

CELT (2), a primitive chisel or axe. (Late L.) Not used before 1700; and due to Late L. *celtis*, the assumed nom. of the abl. *celte* (with a chisel) in the Vulgate version of Job, xix. 24. But this reading seems to be due to some error, and no such word is known in good Latin. Cf. *celtem*, glossed *chisel*; Wright's Vocab. i. 118.

CEMENT, a strong kind of mortar, or glue. (F.—L.) In Shak. Cor. iv. 6. 85; and Tyndal's Works (1572), p. 6, col. 2. Chaucer has *cementinge*, C. T., 16285 (G 817).—OF. *cement*, 'cement;' Cotgrave.—L. *caementum*, a rough stone, rubble, chippings of stone; apparently for *caedmentum*.—L. *caedere*, to cut. Brugm. i. § 587. **Der.** *cement*, vb. ; *cement-at-ion*.

CEMETERY, a burial-ground. (L.—Gk.) In Bp. Taylor's Holy Dying, s. 8. § 6 (R.) Spelt *cemitory*, Will of Hen. VI; Royal Wills, p. 298.—Late L. *cœmētērium*.—Gk. κοιμητήριον, a sleeping-room, sleeping-place, cemetery.—Gk. κοιμάω, I lull to sleep; in pass., to fall asleep, sleep. The lit. sense is 'I put to bed,' the verb being the causal from κεῖμαι, I lie down.

CENOBITE, CŒNOBITE, a monk who lives socially. (L.—Gk.) 'The monks were divided into two classes, the *cœnobites*, who lived under a common, and regular, discipline; and the *anachorets* [anchorites], who indulged their unsocial independent fanaticism;' Gibbon, History, c. 37. § 13. Bp. Taylor has the adj. *cœnobitic*; Lib. of Prophesying, s. 5 (R.)—L. *cœnobita*, a member of a (social) fraternity; used by St. Jerome.—L. *cœnobium*, a convent, monastery (St. Jerome).—Gk. κοινόβιον, a convent; neut. of adj. κοινόβιος, living socially.—Gk. κοινο-, for κοινός, common; and βίος, life.

CENOTAPH, an empty memorial tomb. (F.—L.—Gk.) 'An honorarie tomb, which the Greeks call *cenotaphium*;' Holland's Suetonius, p. 153 (R.) Dryden has *cenotaph*, tr. of Ovid, Metam. bk. xii. l. 3.—MF. *cenotaphe*; Cotgrave.—L. *cenotaphium*.—Gk. κενοτάφιον, an empty tomb.—Gk. κενο-, for κενός, empty; and τάφ-ος, a tomb.

CENSER, a vase for burning incense in. (F.—L.) Chaucer has *sencer*, and pres. pt. *sensing*, C. T. 3342, 3343 (A 3340, 3341). In P. Plowman, C. xxii. 86, the word *sense* occurs (in some MSS. *cense*), with the meaning 'incense.' The word is a familiar contraction for 'incenser,' and is taken from the French.—OF. *censier*, *senser* (Godefroy); shortened from OF. *encensier*, F. *encensoir*, 'a censer, or perfuming-pan;' Cot.—Late L. *incensārium*, *incensōrium*, a censer.—Late L. *incensum*, incense, lit. 'that which is burnt.'—L. *incensus*, pp. of *incendere*, to kindle, burn.—L. *in*, in, upon; and *candere*, to burn; cf. *candēre*, to glow. See **Candle**.

CENSOR, one who revises or censures. (L.) In Shak. Cor. ii. 3. 252; and North's Plutarch, Life of Paulus Æmilius, ed. 1631, p. 265 (Rich. says p. 221).—L. *censor*, a taxer, valuer, assessor, censor, critic.—L. *censēre*, to give an opinion or account, to tax, appraise. Cf. Skt. *çaṁs*, to praise, report, say; Benfey, p. 924. **Der.** *censor-i-al*, *censor-ship*, *censor-i-ous*, *censor-i-ous-ly*, *censor-i-ous-ness*. From L. *censēre* are also derived *census* (L. *census*, a register); and *censure* (L. *censūra*, an opinion), used by Shak. As You Like It, iv. 1. 7; whence *censure*, verb, *censur-a-ble*, *censur-a-ble-ness*, *censur-a-bl-y*.

CENT, a hundred, as in 'per cent.' (L.) In America, the hundredth part of a dollar. Gascoigne has 'por cento,' Steel Glas, l. 783; an odd phrase, since *por* is Spanish and *cento* Italian. The phrase *per cent* stands for L. *per centum*, i. e. 'for a hundred;' from L. *per*, for, and *centum*, a hundred, cognate with AS. *hund*, a hundred. See **Hundred**. **Der.** *cent-age*, in phr. *per centage*; and see *centenary*, *centennial*, *centesimal*, *centigrade*, *centipede*, *centuple*, *centurion*, *century*.

CENTAUR, a monster, half man, half horse. (L.—Gk.) Spelt *Centauros* in Chaucer, C. T., Group B, 3289; where he is translating from Boethius, who wrote: 'Ille *Centauros* domuit superbos;' De Cons. Phil. lib. iv. met. 7. And see Mid. Nt. Dream, v. 44.—L. *Centaurus*.—Gk. Κένταυρος, a Centaur; which some compare with Skt. *gandharvas*, a demi-god. **Der.** *centaur-y*, q. v.

CENTAURY, the name of a plant. (F.—L.—Gk.) ME. *centaurie*, Chaucer, C. T. 14969 (B 4153); *centorye* (Alphita).—AF. *centorye*, id.—L. *centaurēa*, *centaurēum*, centaury.—Gk. κενταύρειον, centaury; neut. of Κενταύρειος, belonging to the Centaurs; said to be named from the Centaur Chiron.

CENTENARY, relating to a hundred. (L.) 'Centenary, that which contains a hundred years, or a hundred pound weight;' Blount's Gloss., 1674. Often used for *centennial*, but by mistake.—L. *centēnārius*, relating to a hundred, containing a hundred (of whatever kind).—L. *centēnus*, a hundred (used distributively).—L. *centum*, a hundred. See **Cent**. **Der.** *cen-tenari-an*.

CENTENNIAL, happening once in a century. (L.) Modern. 'On her *centennial* day;' Mason, Palinodia. x. (R.) A coined word, made in imitation of *biennial*, &c., from L. *cent-um*, a hundred, and *annus*, a year; with change of *a* to *e* as in *biennial*.

CENTESIMAL, hundredth. (L.) Modern; in phr. '*centesimal part*,' &c. — L. *centēsim-us*, hundredth, with suffix -*al* (L. -*ālis*). — L. *centum*, a hundred. See **Cent.**

CENTIGRADE, having one hundred degrees. (L.) Chiefly used of the '*centigrade* thermometer,' invented by Celsius, who died A.D. 1744. — L. *centi-*, for *centum*, a hundred; and *grad-us*, a degree.

CENTIPEDE, CENTIPED, with a hundred feet. (F. — L.) Used as sb., 'an insect with a hundred (i.e. numerous) feet.' In Bailey's Dict., ed. 1731, vol. ii. — F. *centipède*. — L. *centipeda*, a many-footed insect. — L. *centi-*, for *centum*, a hundred; and *pēs* (stem *ped-*), a foot. See **Cent** and **Foot.**

CENTO, 'a composition formed by joining scraps from other authors;' Johnson. (L.) In Camden's Remains, 1614, p. 14. — L. *cento*, a patch-work garment, a cento. Cf. Gk. κέντρων, patch-work, Skt. *kanthā*, a patched cloth.

CENTRE, CENTER, the middle point, middle. (F. — L. — Gk.) Chaucer has the pl. *centres*, C. T. 11589 (F 1277). — F. *centre*. — L. *centrum*. — Gk. κέντρον, a spike, prick, goad, centre. — Gk. κεντέω, I prick, goad on. Cf. W. *cethr*, a spike. Der. *centr-al*, *centr-al-ly*, *centr-al-ise*, *centr-al-is-at-ion*, *centr-ic-al*, *centr-ic-al-ly*.

CENTRIFUGAL, flying from the centre. (L.) Maclaurin, in his Philosophical Discoveries of Newton, bk. ii. c. 1, uses both *centrifugal* and *centripetal*. — L. *centri-*, for *centro-*, stem of *centrum*, the centre; and *fug-ere*, to fly from. See **Centre** and **Fugitive.**

CENTRIPETAL, tending to a centre. (L.) See above. — L. *centri-*, from *centrum*, a centre; and *pet-ere*, to seek, fly to.

CENTUPLE, hundred-fold. (F. — L.) In Massinger, Unnatural Combat, Act i. sc. 1 (near the end), we have : 'I wish his strength were *centuple*, his skill equal,' &c. — F. *centuple* (Hatzfeld). — Late L. *centuplum*, acc. of *centuplus* (Luke, viii. 8). — L. *centu-*, for *centum*, a hundred; and suffix -*plus*, for which see **Double.** And see **Cent.**

CENTURION, a captain of a hundred. (L.) In Wyclif, Matt. viii. 8, where the Vulgate version has *centurio*. — L. *centurio*, a centurion; the *n* being added to assimilate the word to others in -*ion* (from French). — L. *centuria* (below).

CENTURY, a sum of a hundred; a hundred years. (F. — L.) In Shak. Cymb. iv. 2. 391. — F. *centurie*, 'a century, or hundred of;' Cot. — L. *centuria*, a body of a hundred men, &c. — L. *centum*, a hundred. See **Cent.**

CEPHALIC, relating to the head. (F. — L. — Gk.) '*Cephalique*, belonging to, or good for the head;' Blount's Gloss., 1674. — MF. *cephalique*, of, or belonging to the head;' Cot. — L. *cephalic-us*, relating to the head. — Gk. κεφαλικός, for the head. — Gk. κεφαλ-ή, the head; with suffix -ι-κ-ος. Brugm. i. § 740.

CERAMIC, relating to pottery. (Gk.) Modern. Not in Todd's Johnson. — Gk. κεραμικ-ός, adj. — Gk. κέραμ-ος, potter's earth. Cf. κεράννυμι (fut. κεράσω), I mix.

CERE, to cover with wax. (L.) Chiefly used of dipping linen cloth in melted wax, to be used as a shroud. The shroud was called a *cerecloth* or *cerement.* The former was often written *searcloth*, wrongly. 'Then was the bodye bowelled [i.e. disembowelled], embawmed [enbalmed], and *cered*,' i.e. shrouded in cerecloth; Hall, Hen. VIII, an. 5; with reference to King James IV of Scotland. 'To *ceare*, cærare;' Levins, 209. 33. 'She *sered* that body with specery, With wyrgin waxe;' Squire of Lowe Degree, l. 687. 'A bag of a *cerecloth*;' Wyatt, To the King, 7 Jan. 1540. Shak. has *cerecloth*, Merch. ii. 7. 51; *cerements*, Hamlet, i. 4. 48. — L. *cerāre*, to wax. — L. *cēra*, wax; whence W. *cwyr*, Corn. *coir*, Irish and Gael. *ceir*, wax.✚ Gk. κηρός, wax; Curtius, i. 183. Der. *cere-cloth*, *cere-ment.*

CEREAL, relating to corn. (L.) Relating to Ceres, the goddess of corn and tillage. '*Cereal*, pertaining to Ceres or bread-corn, to sustenance or food;' Bailey's Dict. ed. 1731, vol. ii. Sir T. Browne has '*cerealious* grains;' Misc. Tracts (1686), vol. i. p. 16. — L. *cereālis*, relating to corn. — L. *Ceres*, the goddess of corn and produce. Der. *cereals*, s. pl.

CEREBRAL, relating to the brain. (F. — L.) Modern; not in Johnson, but added by Todd. — F. *cérébral*; coined by suffixing -*al* to stem of L. *cerebr-um*, the brain. The former part of *cerebrum* (for *ceres-rom*) is allied to Gk. κάρα, the head; cf. Skt. *çira-s*, Pers. *sar*, the head; also ME. *hernes*, brains, Havelok, l. 1808; Lowland Scotch *hairns* or *harns*, brains. Brugm. i. §§ 619, 875.

CERECLOTH, CEREMENT, waxed cloth; see **Cere.**

CEREMONY, an outward rite. (F. — L.) ME. *ceremonie*, Chaucer, C. T. 10829 (F 515). — OF. *ceremonie*, 'a ceremony, a rite;' Cot. — L. *caerimōnia*, a ceremony; also *cērimōnia.* Cf. Skt. *karman*, action, work, a religious action, a rite. Der. *ceremoni-al*, *ceremoni-al-ly*, *ceremoni-ous*, *ceremoni-ous-ly*, *ceremoni-ous-ness.*

CERIPH, the same as **Serif,** q.v.

CERTAIN, sure, settled, fixed. (F. — L.) ME. *certein*, *certeyn*;

Chaucer, C. T. 3494; Rob. of Glouc. p. 52, l. 1207. — OF. *certein*, *certain.* — L. *cert-us*, determined; with suffix -*ānus* (F. -*ain*). β. Closely connected with L. *cernere*, to sift, discriminate; Gk. κρίνειν, to separate, decide, κριτός, select; Irish *ceart*, right; Prellwitz. Der. *certain-ly*, *certain-ty*; also *certi-fy*, q. v.

CERTIFY, to assure, make certain. (F. — L.) ME. *certifien*, Hampole, Pr. of Conscience, 6546; Gower, C. A. i. 192; b. ii. 963. — OF. *certefier*, *certifier.* — Late L. *certificāre*, pp. *certificātus*, to certify. — L. *certi-*, for *certus*, certain; and *facere*, to make, where *fac-* becomes *fic-* in forming derivatives. See **Certain** and **Fact.** Der. *certificate*, Arnold's Chron., p. 230; *certificat-ion* (cf. L. pp. *certificātus*).

CERULEAN, azure, blue. (L.) Spenser has '*cærule* stream;' tr. of Virgil's Gnat, l. 163. The term. -*an* seems to be a later E. addition. We also find : '*Cæruleous*, of a blue, azure colour, like the sky;' Bailey's Dict. vol. ii (1731). — L. *caeruleus*, *caerulus*, blue, bluish; also sea-green. β. Probably *caerulus* is for **caelulus*, i.e. sky-coloured; from L. *caelum*, the sky; Brugm. i. § 483 b; see **Celestial.**

CERUSE, white lead. (F. — L. — Gk.) In Chaucer, C. T. prol. 630. — OF. *ceruse* (Supp. to Godefroy); 'ceruse, or white lead;' Cot. — L. *cērussa*, white lead; connected with L. *cēra*, wax; but representing Gk. **κηροῦσσα*, contracted from **κηρόεσσα*, fem. of **κηρόεις*, waxy. — Gk. κηρός, wax. See **Cere.**

CERVICAL, belonging to the neck. (F. — L.) In Kersey's Dict., 2nd ed. 1715. — F. *cervical*, 'belonging to the nape;' Cot. — L. *ceruix* (stem *ceruīc-*), the neck, with suffix -*al*; cf. L. *ceruīcāl*, a bolster.

CERVINE, relating to a hart. (L.) '*Cervine*, belonging to an hart, of the colour of an hart, tawny;' Blount's Glossographia, 1674. — L. *ceruīnus*, belonging to a hart. — L. *ceruus*, a hart; see **Hart.**

CESS, an assessment, levy; also measure. (F. — L.) Spelt *cesse* by Spenser, View of the State of Ireland, Globe ed. p. 643, col. 2. He also has *cessors*, id. p. 648, col. 1. Cf. 'out of all *cesse*,' i.e. measure; 1 Hen. IV, ii. 1. 8. These are mere abbreviations of *assess* and *assessors.* See **Assess.**

CESSATION, discontinuance. (F. — L.) 'Withowte *cessacion*;' Coventry Myst. p. 107. — F. *cessation*, 'cessation, ceasing;' Cotgrave. — L. *cessātiōnem*, acc. of *cessātio*, a ceasing. See **Cease.**

CESSION, a yielding up. (F. — L.) 'By the *cession* of Maestricht;' Sir W. Temple, To the Lord Treasurer, Sept. 1678 (R.) ME. *cessyone*; Prompt. Parv. — F. *cession*, 'yeelding up;' Cot. — L. *cessiōnem*, acc. of *cessio*, a ceding; cf. L. *cessus*, pp. of *cēdere*, to cede. See **Cede.**

CESS-POOL, a pool for drains to drain into. (Hybrid; L. *and* E.) Also spelt *sess-pool*; both forms are in Halliwell, and in Webster. In Brockett's Glossary of North-Country Words, ed. 1846, we find : '*Sesspool*, an excavation in the ground for receiving foul water. I do not find the word in any dictionary, though it is in use by architects; see Laing's Custom-house Plans. *Sus-pool* occurs in Forster on Atmospheric Phenomena.' *Cess-pool* occurs in 1782, in Phil. Soc. Trans. lxxii. 364 (N. E. D.). β. Origin uncertain; N. E. D. suggests *secesspool*; from L. *sēcessus*, 'the draught,' Matt. xv. 17 (Vulgate); cf. *sēcessus*, 'latrina;' Ducange. Cf. Ital. *cesso*, a privy (Torriano), from the same L. *sēcessus*, which is formed from *sēcess-um*, supine of *sēcēdere*, lit. to secede, hence, to retire; see **Secede.** γ. But rather, for *recess-pool*, as the following quotation suggests :— 'I have, in my yard, what you usually see in most farmers' yards, two *recesses* or *pools*, as reservoirs of dung and water;' Museum Rusticum (1764); ii. 73.

CESURA; see **CÆSURA.**

CETACEOUS, of the whale kind. (L. — Gk.) '*Cetaceous* fishes;' Ray, On the Creation, pt. i. A coined word, from L. *cētus*, a large fish, a whale. — Gk. κῆτος, a sea-monster, large fish.

CH

CHABLIS, a white wine. (F.) From *Chablis*, 12 mi. E. of Auxerre, dep. Yonne, France. Mentioned in Oldham, Paraphrase of Horace, bk. i. ode 31 (ab. 1678).

CHAFE, to warm by friction, to vex. (F. — L.) The orig. sense was simply 'to warm;' secondly, to inflame, fret, vex; and, intransitively, to rage; see Schmidt, Shak. Lex. ME. *chaufen*, to warm. 'Charcole to *chaufen* the knyȝte,' Anturs of Arthur, st. 35. 'He . . . was *chaufid* with win' (incaluisset mero); Wyclif, Esther, i. 10. — OF. *chaufer* (F. *chauffer*), to warm; cf. Prov. *calfar*, to warm; answering to Folk-L. **calefāre* (Hatzfeld); for L. *calefacere*, to make warm. — L. *cale-*, from *calēre*, to glow; and *facere*, to make. See **Caldron.** Der. *chafe-wax*, *chaff-wax*, an officer who prepared wax for sealing documents; also *chaf-er*, *chaf-ing-dish*, both in Palsgrave.

CHAFER, COCK-CHAFER, a kind of beetle. (E.) In

Trevisa, tr. of Higden, ii. 211 (where the text has *harnettes*, and the Lat. has *scarabæi*), MS. *a* has *cheaffers*, and Caxton has *chauers*. AS. *cefer* (O. Eng. Texts, ed. Sweet); also *ceafor*. ' Bruchus, ceafor;' Ælfric's Gloss. (De Nominibus Insectorum). And again, *ceafar* is a gloss to *bruchus* in Ps. civ. 34 (Vulgate), where the A. V. has ' caterpillars;' Ps. cv. 34. [The AS. *cea-* becomes *cha-*, as in AS. *cealc*, E. *chalk*.]+Du. *kever*; G. *käfer*. Prob. from Teut. *kaf, 2nd grade of Teut. **kef-*, to gnaw; see **Jowl**.

CHAFF, the husk of grain. (E.) ME. *chaf*, Layamon, iii. 172; *caf*, *chaf*, Cursor Mundi, 25248. AS. *ceaf* (later version *chæf*), Luke, iii. 17.+Du. *kaf*; Low G. *kaff*. ¶ The vulgar English ' to *chaff*' is a mere corruption of the verb to *chafe*, q. v. The spelling *chaff* keeps up an old pronunciation of the verb. So also *chaff-wax*, for *chafe-wax*.

CHAFFER, to buy, to haggle, bargain. (E.) The verb is formed from the sb., which originally meant ' a bargaining.' The verb is ME. *chaffare*, Chaucer, C. T. 4559 (B 139). The sb. is ME. *chaffare*, Gower, C. A. ii. 278 (b. v. 4522); and this is a later form of the older *chapfare*, occurring in the Ayenbite of Inwyt, ed. Morris, pp. 35, 44, 45. β. *Chapfare* is a compound of *chap* and *fare*, i.e. of AS. *cēap*, a bargain, a price, Gen. xli. 56; and AS. *faru*, a journey (Grein), afterwards used in the sense of ' procedure, business.' Thus the word meant ' a price-business.' See **Cheap, Chapman,** and **Fare**.

CHAFFINCH, the name of a bird. (E.) ' *Chaffinch*, a bird so called because it delights in chaff;' Kersey's Dict. 2nd ed. 1715. This is quite correct; the word is simply compounded of *chaff* and *finch*. It often ' frequents our barndoors and homesteads;' Eng. Cycl. s.v. *Chaffinch*. Spelt *cafinche*, Levins, 134. 42; *chaffinch*, Baret (1580); *caffynche*, Prompt. Parv.

CHAGRIN, vexation, ill-humour. (F.) ' *Chagrin*, care, melancholy;' Coles' Dict. (1684). In Pope, Rape of the Lock, c. iv. l. 77. —F. *chagrin*, ' carke, melancholy, care, thought;' Cotgrave. Origin unknown; Hatzfeld. β. Diez, however, connects it with F. *chagrin*, answering to E. *shagreen*, a rough substance sometimes used for rasping wood; hence taken as the type of corroding care. [Cf. Ital. ' *limare*, to file; to fret or gnaw;' Florio.] Diez also cites the Genoese *sagrina*, to gnaw; *sagrinâse*, to consume oneself with anger. See **Shagreen**, which is spelt *chagrin* in Bailey's Dict. vol. ii. ed. 1731. From Turk. *saghri*, shagreen; given as ' Pers.' in Rich. Dict., p. 833. See Körting, § 8265. ¶ In North's Examen, 1740, p. 394, he tells us that certain plotters ' take into familiarity thoughts which, before, had made their skin run into a *chagrin*.'

CHAIN, a series of links. (F.—L.) In early use. ME. *chaine*, *cheine*; Chaucer, C. T. 2990 (A 2988); Wyclif, Acts, xii. 6.—OF. *chaëne*, *chaine*.—L. *catēna* (by the loss of *t*). Der. *chain*, verb, *chign-on* (=*chain-on*); and see *catenary*.

CHAIR, a movable seat. (F.—L.—Gk.) ME. *chaiere*, *chaere*, *chaier*, *chaire*; spelt *chaiere*, Gower, C. A. ii. 201 (b. v. 2214); *chaere*, King Horn, ed. Lumby, l. 1261; Rob. of Glouc. p. 321, l. 6559.—OF. *chaiere*, *chaere*, a chair (F. *chaire*, a pulpit, modified to *chaise*, a chair).—L. *cathedra*, a raised seat, bishop's throne (by loss of *th*, and change of *dr* to *r*; see Brachet).—Gk. καθέδρα, a seat, chair, pulpit. See **Cathedral**. Der. *chaise*, q.v.; and note that *cathedral* is properly an adj., belonging to the sb. *chair*.

CHAISE, a light carriage. (F.—L.—Gk.) In Cook's Voyages, vol. ii. bk. ii. c. 10. ' *Chaise*, a kind of light open chariot with one horse;' Kersey's Dict. ed. 1715.—F. *chaise*, a Parisian corruption of F. *chaire*, orig. a seat, pulpit. ' They of Parys . . saye . . *chaize* for *chayre*;' Palsgrave, p. 34. Thus *chaise* is a doublet of *chair*; for the change of sense, cf. *sedan-chair*. See **Chair**. Der. *chay*, a chaise; as if *chaise* were plural; Foote, The Maid of Bath, A. i. Sc. 1. l. 13.

CHALCEDONY, a variety of quartz. (L.—Gk.) [ME. *calsydoyne*, Allit. Poems, ed. Morris, A. 1003; with reference to Rev. xxi. 19. Also *calcydone*, An Old Eng. Misc., ed. Morris, p. 98, l. 171. These are French forms, but our mod. E. word is from the Latin.]— L. *chalcēdonius*, in Rev. xxi. 19 (Vulgate).—Gk. χαλκηδών, Rev. xxi. 19. Of doubtful origin; see Schade, O. H. G. Dict., p. 1363.

CHALDRON, a coal-measure; 36 bushels. (F.—L.) Spelt *chaldron* in Phillips, 1658; *chaldron* and *chalder* in Coles, 1684.—F. *chaudron*, a caldron; with restored *l*. β. The word merely expresses a vessel of a large size, and hence, a capacious measure. From OF. *chaldron* (mod. F. *chaudron*). See **Caldron**.

CHALET, a Swiss hut. (F.—L.) In Byron, Manfred, A. i. sc. 2 (near the end).—F. *chalet* (a Swiss word). Prob. from Late L. *casaletta, dimin. of *casella*, a little house (Ducange). This is a dimin. of L. *casa*, a cottage. Cf. **Casino**.

CHALICE, a cup; a communion-cup. (F.—L.) ' And stele the *chalice*;' Chaucer, Pers. Tale, De Luxuria (I 879). Spelt *calice* in O. Eng. Homilies, 2nd Ser. p. 91; and *caliz* in Havelok, l. 187. [We also find AS. *calic*, Matt. xxvi. 28; taken directly from the Latin.]— OF. *chalice* (Marie de France, Yonec, 192); usually *calice*.—L. *calicem*, acc. of *calix*, a cup, goblet (stem *calic-*).+Gk. κύλιξ, a drinking-cup;

Skt. *kalaça-s*, a cup, water-pot. Allied to *calyx*, but not the same word. Der. *chalic-ed*; Cymb. ii. 3. 24.

CHALK, carbonate of lime. (L.) ME. *chalk*, Chaucer, C. T. Group G, 1222. AS. *cealc*, Orosius, vi. 32.—L. *calx* (stem *calc-*), lime. [The G. *kalk*, Du. and Swed. *kalk* are all borrowed from Latin.] See **Calx**. Der. *chalk-y*, *chalk-i-ness*.

CHALLENGE, a claim; a defiance. (F.—L.) ME. *chalenge*, *calenge*; often in the sense of ' a claim.' ' *Chalaunge*, or *cleyme*, *vendicacio*;' Prompt. Parv. p. 68. It also means ' accusation;' Wyclif, Gen. xliii. 18; Cursor Mundi, 6714. [The verb, though derived from the sb., was really in earlier use *in* English; as in ' to *calangy* . . the kinedom'=to claim the kingdom; Rob. of Glouc. p. 451, l. 9247; and in ' hwar of *kalenges* tu me'=for what do you reprove me; Ancren Riwle, p. 54. Cf. Exod. xxii. 9 (A.V.).]—AF. *chalenge*, OF. *chalonge*, *calonge*, *calenge*, a dispute; properly ' an accusation.' —L. *calumnia*, a false accusation.—L. *caluī*, *caluere*, to deceive. Der. *chal'enge*, verb. Doublet, *calumny*, q.v.

CHALYBEATE, water containing iron. (L.—Gk.) Properly an adj. signifying ' belonging to steel,' as explained in Kersey's Dict. 2nd ed. 1715; he adds that ' chalybeate medicines are medicines prepared with steel.' ' *Chalybeate*, of the quality of steel;' Phillips (1658). A coined word, formed from L. *chalybs* (stem *chalyb-*), steel.—Gk. χάλυψ (stem χάλυβ-), steel; so called from the Gk. Χάλυβες, the nation of the Chalybes in Pontus, who prepared it. Milton has: ' *Chalybean*-tempered steel;' Sams. Agonistes, l. 133.

CHAMADE, a summons to a parley. (F.—Port.—L.) Not common. In the phr. ' to beat a *chamade*;' i.e. on the drum. First in 1684.—F. *chamade*.—Port. *chamada*, a parley; from *chamar*, to summon, call.—L. *clāmāre*, to call.

CHAMBER, a room, a hall. (F.—L.—Gk.) The *b* is excrescent. In early use. ME. *chaumbre*, *chambre*, *c'amber*; ' i *chaumbre*'=in the chamber, O. Eng. Homilies, i. 285.—OF. *chambre*; cf. Prov. *cambra*. —L. *camera*, a chamber, a vault; older spelling *camara*.—Gk. καμάρα, a vault, covered wagon. Cf. Skt. *kmar*, to be crooked.—√KAM, to cover over; cf. Icel. *hamr*, a covering, Goth. *af-hamōn*, to unclothe. Der. *chamber-ed*, *chamber-ing* (Rom. xiii. 13); also *chamber-lain*, q.v.

CHAMBERLAIN, one who has the care of rooms. (F.—L.—Gk.; with G. *suffix*.) ME. *chaumberlein*, Floriz and Blauncheflur, ed. Lumby, l. 18. [The form *chaumberling* in the Ancren Riwle, p. 410, is an accommodation, yet comes nearer the O.H.G. form.]— OF. *chamberlenc*, later *chamberlain*; a hybrid word, made up from OF. *chambre*, a chamber, and the termination of the OHG. *chamerling*, MHG. *kemerlinc*. β. This OHG. word is composed of OHG. *chamera*, a chamber, merely borrowed from L. *camera*; and the suffix *-ling* or *-linc*, answering to the E. suffix *-ling* in *hireling*. Der. *chamber-lain-ship*.

CHAMELEON, a kind of lizard. (L.—Gk.) In Shak. Two Gent. of Ver. ii. 1. 178. ME. *camelion*, Gower, C. A. i. 133; b. i. 2698.—L. *chamæleōn*.—Gk. χαμαιλέων, a chameleon, lit. ground-lion or earth-lion, i.e. dwarf lion.—Gk. χαμαί, on the ground (a word related to L. *humī*, on the ground, and to L. *humilis*, humble); and λέων, a lion. The prefix χαμαι-, when used of plants, signifies ' creeping;' also ' low,' or ' dwarf;' see **Chamomile**. And see **Humble** and **Lion**.

CHAMFER, a slight furrow cut in wood or stone, for ornament; a bevelling off of a square edge. (F.—L.) The former use is perhaps obsolete. Holland, tr. of Pliny, bk. xv. c. 18 (p. 442 i) has ' a white rift or *chamfre*.'—F. *chanfrein*; MF. *chanfrain*, ' a chanfering, or a channell, furrow;' Cot.—OF. *chanfraindre*, to bevel off; in the pp. *chanfraint* (Godefroy).—OF. *chant*, an edge, corner (Supp. to Godefroy, and Hatzfeld); and OF. *fraindre*, to break; hence ' to remove the corner or edge.'—Late L. *canthum*, acc. of *canthus*, the corner of the eye (Gk. κάνθος); and L. *frangere*, to break. See **Cant** (2); and see *Chanfrein* in Scheler. Der. *chamfer*, vb.

CHAMOIS, a kind of goat. (F.—G.) See Deut. xiv. 5, where it translates the Heb. *zemer*.—F. *chamois*, ' a wilde goat, or shamois; also, the skin thereof dressed, and called ordinarily Shamois leather;' Cot. A word of Swiss origin (Brachet); cf. Ital. *camoscio* (Baretti), *camoceia*, *camozza*, ' a chamoy or chamoise,' Florio; Romaunsch *camutsch* (Carigiet). Corrupted from some dialectal pronunciation of MHG. *gamz*, or *gamuz, a chamois (mod. G. *gemse*). Körting, § 4148.

CHAMOMILE, CAMOMILE, a kind of plant. (F.—Late L.— Gk.) In Shak. 1 Hen. IV, ii. 4. 441. ME. *camamyle*; Prompt. Parv. —AF. *camamille* (Alphita).—Late L. *camomilla*.—Gk. χαμαίμηλον, lit. earth-apple; so called from the apple-like scent of its flower; Pliny, xxii. 21.—Gk. χαμαί, on the earth (answering to L. *humī*, whence *humilis*, humble); and μῆλον, an apple, L. *mālum*. See **Humble**; and see **Chameleon**.

CHAMP, to eat noisily. (E.) ' The palfrey . . on the fomy bit of golde with teeth he *champes*;' Phaer's Virgil, bk. iv. 146. The older form is *cham* for *chamm*, and the *p* is merely excrescent. ' It must be *chammed*,' i.e. chewed till soft; Sir T. More, Works, p. 241 h. 'Chamming or drinking;' Tyndal's Works, p. 316, col. 2. Palsgrave has both *chamme* and *champe*. Prob. of imitative origin; cf. Swed. dial. *kämsa*, to chew with difficulty, champ (Rietz); Norw. *k,amsa*, to chew. Note also Gk. γαμφαί, jaws; Skt. *jambha-s*, a jaw, tooth.

CHAMPAGNE, a kind of wine. (F.—L.) So named from *Champagne* in France. which, lit., signifies 'a plain;' see below.

CHAMPAIGN, open country. (F.—L.) In Shak. King Lear, i. 1. 65; Deut. xi. 30 (A. V.); also spelt *champion* (corruptly), Spenser, F. Q. vi. 4. 26; but *champain*, id. vii. 6. 54.—F. *champaigne*, Picard *campaigne*, 'a plaine field;' Cot.—L. *campānia*, a plain. For the rest, see **Campaign**, of which it is a doublet.

CHAMPION, a warrior, fighting man. (F.—L.) In very early use. Spelt *champiun*, Ancren Riwle, p. 236.—OF. *champiun*, *champion*, North F. *campion*, a champion.—Late L. *campiōnem*, acc. of *campio*, a champion, combatant in a duel.—Late L. *campus*, a duel, battle, war, combat; a peculiar use of L. *campus*, a field, esp. a field of battle. See **Camp**. ¶ We still have *Champion* and *Campion* as proper names; we also have *Kemp*, from AS. *cempa*, a champion. Der. *champion-hip*.

CHAMPAK, a tree. (Hind.—Skt.) 'The *champak* odours fail;' Shelley, Lines to an Indian Air, 11.—Hind. *champak*.—Skt. *champaka-s*, a tree, the Michelia champaca of Linnæus (Benfey).

CHANCE, what befals, an event. (F.—L.) ME. *chaunce*. 'That swych a *chaunce* myght hym befalle;' Rob. of Brunne, Handlyng Synne, l. 5632 (A.D. 1303).—OF. *chaance* (Roquefort); more commonly *cheance*, chance.—Late L. *cadentia*, that which falls out, esp. that which falls out favourably, as used in dice-playing (Brachet). —L. *cadens* (stem *cadent-*), falling, pres. part. of *cadere*, to fall. See **Cadence**, of which *chance* is a doublet. Der. *chance*, verb (1 Cor. xv. 37); *mis-chance*, *chance-comer*, &c.

CHANCEL, the east end of a church. (F.—L.) So called, because formerly fenced off by a latticed screen. ME. *chancell*, *chanser*; Barbour's Bruce, ed. Skeat, v. 348, 356.—OF. *chancel*, an enclosure; esp. one defended by a screen of lattice-work.—Late L. *cancellus*, a latticed window; a screen of lattice-work; a chancel; L. *cancellus*, grating; chiefly used in pl. *cancelli*, lattice-work. See further under **Cancel**. Der. *chancell-or*, q.v.; *chance-ry* (for *chancel-ry*), q. v.

CHANCELLOR, a director of chancery. (F.—L.) In early use. ME. *chaunceler*, *chaunseler*; spelt *chaunselere*, King Alisaunder, l. 1810.—OF. *chancelier*, North F. *cancelier*.—Late L. *cancellārius*, a chancellor; orig. an officer who had care of records, and who stood near the screen of lattice-work or of cross-bars which fenced off the judgment-seat; whence his name.—L. *cancellus*, a grating; pl. *cancelli*, lattice-work. See **Chancel** and **Cancel**. ¶ For a full account, see *cancellārius* in Ducange. Der. *chancery*, q.v.

CHANCERY, a high court of judicature. (F.—L.) ME. *chancerye*, P. Plowman, B. prol. 93. An older and fuller spelling is *chancelerie* or *chancellerie*, as in Gower, C. A. ii. 191, b. v. 1921; Life of Beket, ed. Black, 359. [Hence *chancery* is short for *chancelry*.] —OF. *chancelerie* (Supp. to Godefroy), 'a chancery court, the chancery, seale office, or court of every parliament;' Cot.—Late L. *cancellāria*, orig. a place where public records were kept; the record-room of a chancellor.—Late L. *cancellārius*, a chancellor (above).

CHANDLER, a candle-seller; **CHANDELIER**, a candle-holder. (F.—L.) Doublets; i.e. two forms of one word, made different in appearance in order to denote different things. The former is the older *sense*, and came at last to mean 'dealer;' whence *corn-chandler*, a dealer in corn; see N. E. D. See *Candelere* in Prompt. Parv. p. 60, explained by (1) L. *candelārius*, a candle-maker, and by (2) L. *candelābra*, a candle-holder; also 'Chawndelere, cērārius,' id. p. 71; *chaundeler*, a chandler; Eng. Gilds, p. 18; *chandler*, Levins.—OF. *chandelier*, a chandler, a candlestick.—Late L. *candelārius*, a chandler; *candelārium*, for *candelāria*, a candle-stick.—L. *candēla*, a candle. See **Candle**.

CHANGE, to alter, make different. (F.—L.) ME. *chaungen*, *changen*. The pt. t. *changede* occurs in the later text of Layamon's Brut, l. 3791. *Chaungen*, Ancren Riwle, p. 6.—OF. *changier*, to change; later, *changer*.—Late L. *cambiāre*, to change, in the Lex Salica.—L. *cambire*, to exchange; Charisius. Cf. Late L. *cambium*, an exchange. Remoter origin unknown; cf. Körting, § 1777; Stokes-Fick, p. 79. Der. *change*, sb., *change-able*, *change-abl-y*, *change-able-ness*, *change-ful*, *change-less*; *change-ling* (a hybrid word, with E. suffix), Mids. Nt. Dream, ii. 1. 230.

CHANNEL, the bed of a stream. (F.—L.) ME. *chanel*, *canel*, *chanelle*. 'Canel, or chanelle, canalis;' Prompt. Parv. p. 60. *Chanel*, Trevisa, i. 133, 135; *canel*, Wyclif's Works, ed. Arnold, ii. 335.—OF. *chanel*, North F. *canel*, a canal; see Supp. to Godefroy.—L. *canālem*, acc. of *canālis*, a canal. See **Canal**, of which it is a doublet. Also **Kennel** (2).

CHANT, to intone, recite in song. (F.—L.) ME. *chaunten*,

chanter, Chaucer, C. T. 9724 (E 1850).—OF. (and mod. F.) *chanter*, to sing.—L. *cantāre*, to sing; frequentative of *canere*, to sing. See **Cant** (1), of which it is a doublet; and see **Hen**. Der. *chant-er*, in early use = ME. *chauntour*, Trevisa, ii. 349; *chant-ry* = ME. *chaunterie*, Chaucer, C. T. prol. 510; *chant-i-cleer*, i.e. clear-singing = ME. *chaunte-cleer*; Chaucer, Nun's Pres. Tale, l. 29.

CHAOS, a confused mass. (L.—Gk.) See *Chaos* in Trench, Select Glossary. In Shak. Romeo, i. 1. 185; Spenser, F. Q. iv. 9. 23.—L. *chaos*.—Gk. χάος, empty space, chaos, abyss; lit. 'a cleft.'—Gk. √ΧΑ, to gape; whence χάσκειν, to gape. See **Chasm**. Der. *chao-t-ic*, a coined adj., arbitrarily formed; in Bailey's Dict. vol. ii (1731).

CHAP (1), to cleave, crack. (E.) ME. *chappen*, to cut; hence, intransitively, to gape open like a wound made by a cut. See Jer. xiv. 4 (A. V.) 'Anon her hedes wer off *chappyd* = at once their heads were chopped off; Rich. Cuer de Lion, ed. Weber, 4550. Cf. EFries. *kappen*, to cut; NFries. *kappe*, to cut, lop. Not found in AS. ✛ MDu. *kappen*, to chop, cut, hew, mince; Low G. *kappen*, to cut off; Swed. *kappa*, to cut; Dan. *kappe*, to cut. Cf. **Chop**. Der. *chap*, a cleft; cf. 'it cureth clifts and *chaps*;' Holland, tr. of Pliny, bk. xxiii. c. 4 (p. 161 d).

CHAP (2), a fellow; **CHAPMAN**, a merchant. (E.) *Chap* is merely a familiar abbreviation of *chapman*, orig. a merchant, later a pedlar, higgler; explained by Kersey (1715) as 'a buyer, a customer.' See 2 Chron. ix. 14. ME. *chapman*, a merchant, Chaucer, Man of Law's Tale, l. 2; P. Plowman, B. v. 34, 233, 331. AS. *cēapman*, a merchant; spelt *ciepe-mon*, Laws of Ine, sect. 25; Ancient Laws, ed. Thorpe, i. 118.—AS. *cēap*, trade; and *mann*, a man; Grein, i. 159. Cf. Icel. *kaupmaðr*, G. *kaufmann*, a merchant. See **Cheap**.

CHAPE, a metal plate protecting the point of a scabbard, &c. (F.—Late L.) 'Chape of a schethe;' Prompt. Parv.—F. *chape*, 'a cope, also the chape, or locket of a scabbard;' Cot.—Late L. *cāpa*, a cope, cape; hence a cover, chape. See **Cape** (1).

CHAPEL, a sanctuary; an oratory; a lesser church. (F.—L.) ME. *chapele*, *chapelle*; Layamon's Brut, l. 26140 (later text); St. Marherete, p. 20.—OF. *chapele*, F. *chapelle*.—Late L. *cappella*, 'which from the 7th cent. has had the sense of a chapel; orig. a [cappella, less correctly] capella was the sanctuary in which was preserved the *cāpa* or cope of St. Martin, and thence it was expanded to mean any sanctuary containing relics;' Brachet.—Late L. *cappa*, *cāpa*, a cope; a hooded cloak, in Isidore of Seville. See **Cape, Cap**. Der. *chapel-ry*; *chapl-ain* = ME. *chapelein* (fem. *chapeleyne*, Chaucer, C. T. prol. 164), from Late L. *cappellānus*; *chapl-ain-cy*. ¶ The *pp* appears in Ital. *cappella*, and is required by the F. form, since L. *pp* > F. *p*, but L. *p* > F. *v*. In Late Latin, *cappa*, a cap, and *cāpa*, a cape, were soon confused.

CHAPERON, lit. a kind of hood or cap. (F.—L.) Chiefly used in the secondary sense of 'protector,' esp. one who protects a young lady. Modern; first in 1720; though ME. *chaperon* occurs, with the sense of 'hood.' 'To chaperon, an affected word, of very recent introduction into our language, to denote a gentleman attending a lady in a publick assembly;' Todd's Johnson. Seldom now applied to a gentleman.—F. *chaperon*, 'a hood, or French hood for a woman; also, any hood, bonnet, or letice cap;' Cot. An augmentative form from F. *chape*, a cope. See **Chaplet**.

CHAPITER, the capital of a column. (F.—L.) See Exod. xxxvi. 38; 1 Kings, vii. 16; Amos, ix. 1; Zeph. ii. 14 (A.V.) 'The *chapiter* of the piller;' Holinshed's Chron. p. 1006, col. 2. 'Capitulum, chapytur;' Voc. 670. 4.—OF. *chapitre*, usually a chapter of a book, but representing L. *capitulum*, which also means 'a chapiter' (Vitruvius). Dimin. from L. *caput* (stem *capit-*), the head.

CHAPLAIN; see under **Chapel**.

CHAPLET, a garland, wreath; rosary. (F.—L.) ME. *chapelet*, a garland, wreath; Gower, C. A. ii. 370; b. v. 7066.—OF. *chapelet*, a little head-dress, a wreath. 'The *chapelet de roses*, a chaplet of roses placed on the statues of the Virgin (shortly called a *rosaire*, or rosary), came later to mean a sort of chain, intended for counting prayers, made of threaded beads, which at first were made to resemble the roses in the Madonna's chaplets;' Brachet.—OF. *chapel*, a head-dress, hat; with dimin. suffix *-et*.—OF. *chape*, a cope, hooded cloak; with dimin. suffix *-l* (for *-el*).—Late L. *cāpa*, a hooded cloak. See **Cape** (1).

CHAPMAN; see under **Chap** (2).

CHAPS, CHOPS, the jaws. (E.) In Shak. Macb. i. 2. 22. The sing. appears in the compounds *chapfallen*, i.e. with shrunken jaw, or dropped jaw, Hamlet, v. 1. 212; *chapless*, without the (lower) jaw. Hamlet, v. 1. 97. Of disputed origin; but the double form, and the late appearance of the sb., show that it is a mere derivative of the verb *chap*, *chop*, to cut, hack. Cf. prov. E. *chap*, to mash; *chapper*, an instrument for mashing potatoes; *chop*, to break small, pulverise, *chop*, sb., food for horses, of chopped hay, &c. See **Chap** (1). ¶ Possibly suggested by prov. E. *chaff*, *chaft*, the jaw; which is from

Icel. *kjaptr* (pron. *kjaftr*), Swed. *käft*, the jaw; but this supposition is not necessary.

CHAPTER, a division of a book; a synod or corporation of the clergy of a cathedral church. (F.—L.) Short for *chapiter*, q.v. ME. *chapitre*, in very early use. The pl. *cheapitres*, in the sense of chapters of a book, occurs in the Ancren Riwle, p. 14. The comp. *chapitre-hous* (spelt *chaptire-hous*) occurs in Piers Ploughman's Crede, ed. Skeat, l. 199; and (spelt *chapitelhous*) in P. Plowman, B. v. 174; the sense being 'chapter-house.'—OF. *chapitre* (mod. F. *chapitre*), a variant of an older form *chapitle*; Brachet.—L. *capitulum*, a chapter of a book, section; in late L., a synod. A dimin. (with suffix *-ul-*) of L. *caput* (stem *capit-*), the head.

CHAR (1), to turn to charcoal. (E.) In Boyle's Works, v. ii. p. 141, we read: 'His profession .. did put him upon finding a way of *charring* sea-coal, wherein it is in about three hours .. brought to *charcoal*; of which having .. made him take out some pieces, .. I found them upon breaking to appear well *charr'd*' (R.) First found in 1679, in Plot's Staffordsh., p. 128 (ed. 1686): 'They have a way of *charring* it [coal], if I may so speak without a solecisme, in all particulars the same as they doe wood.' It thus appears to be a back-formation from *char-coal*, which is in much earlier use; see **Charcoal**.

CHAR (2), a turn of work. (E.) Also *chare*; 'and does the meanest *chares*;' Ant. and Cleop. iv. 15. 75; cf. v. 2. 231. Also *chewre*, as in: 'Here's two *chewres* chew'd,' i.e. two jobs done, Beaumont and Fletcher, Love's Cure, iii. 2. Also *chore*, a prov. E. form which is also a modern Americanism. Cf. mod. E. 'to go *a-charing*;' and see my note to The Two Noble Kinsmen, iii. 2. 21; and see Nares. ME. *cherr, chearr, cher, char*; of which Mätzner gives abundant examples. It means: (1) a time or turn; Ancren Riwle, p. 408; (2) a turning about, Bestiary, 643 (in Old Eng. Misc. ed. Morris); (3) a movement; Body and Soule, 158 (in Mätzner's Sprachproben); (4) a piece or turn of work, Polit. Songs, ed. Wright, p. 341; Towneley Myst. p. 106. AS. *cierr, cyrr*, a turn, space of time, period; Grein, i. 180; whence *cierran, cyrran*, to turn; id. AS. *cierr* (also *cerr*) answers to a Teut. type *karriz*, *karziz*. Hence it is difficult to connect it with Du. *keer*, a turn, time, circuit, or with G. *kehren*, to turn, which seem to be from an unrelated stem *kair-*; see Franck. **Der.** *char-woman*.

CHAR (3), a kind of fish. (C.) The belly is of a *red* colour; whence its name. 'Chare, a kind of fish;' Kersey's Dict. 2nd ed., 1715. '*Chare*, a kinde of fish, which breeds most peculiarly in Winandermere in Lancashire;' Phillips, World of Words, ed. 1658. [The W. name is *torgoch*, i.e. red-bellied; from *tor*, belly, and *coch*, red.] Of Celtic origin; cf. (obsolete) Gael. *ceara*, red, blood-coloured, from *cear*, blood; Irish *cear*, sb., blood, adj. red, ruddy. (Doubtful).

CHARACTER, an engraved mark, sign, letter. (L.—Gk.) In Shak. Meas. iv. 2. 208; and, as a verb, As You Like It, iii. 2. 6. [Shak. also has *charact*, Meas. v. 56; which answers to the common ME. *caract, carect*, Wyclif, Rev. xx. 4; from OF. *caracte*, recorded in Godefroy as a variant of *characte*. This is merely a clipped form of the same word.]—L. *character*, a sign or mark engraven.—Gk. χαρακτήρ, an engraved or stamped mark.—Gk. χαράσσειν (= χαράκ-γειν), to furrow, to scratch, engrave. Brugmann, i. § 605 (3). **Der.** *character-ise, character-ist-ic, character-ist-ic-al-ly*.

CHARADE, a sort of riddle. (F.—Prov.) Modern; and borrowed from F. *charade*, a word introduced into French from Provençal in the 18th century; Brachet. Hatzfeld gives the Prov. form as *charrado*, orig. 'talk;' from the verb *charra*, to talk. Cf. Languedoc *charado*, grumbling, from *chara*, to grumble (D'Hombres). Cf. also Span. *charrada*, 'a speech or action of a clown;' from Span. (and Port.) *charro*, a churl, peasant. See also Körting, § 1919.

CHARCOAL, the solid residue obtained from the imperfect combustion of wood, &c. (E.) ME. *charcole*, Gawain and Gr. Knt., 76,875; and Prompt. Parv. β. The mod. vb. *char*, to burn partially, is evolved from the comp. *char-coal*; but this is not against a prob. derivation of the comp. from the old verb *char*, to turn; as no other origin seems possible. For the sense, cf. 'Then Nestor broiled them on the *cole-turn'd* wood;' Chapman's Odyssey, b. iii. 621. And: 'Though the whole world *turn* to coal;' G. Herbert's Poems; Vertue. ME. *cherren*, to turn, represents AS. *cierran*, to turn; see **Char** (2). And see **Coal**. ¶ The spelling *charecole* occurs ab. 1400, in Henslow's Med. Werkes, p. 135. 20.

CHARGE, lit. to load, burden. (F.—L.—C.) ME. *chargen*, to load, to impose a command. 'The folk of the contree taken camayles [camels], ... and *chargen* hem,' i.e. lade them; Maundeville's Travels, p. 301. '*Chargede* thre hondred ssipes;' Rob. of Glouc. p. 13, l. 294.—OF. (and F.) *charger*, to load.—Late L. *carricāre*, to load a car, used by St. Jerome; later, *carcāre* (Brachet).—L. *carrus*, a car. See **Car**. **Der.** *charge*, sb.; *charge-able, charge-able-*

ness, charge-abl-y, charg-er (that which bears a load, a dish, Mat. xiv. 8; also a horse for making an onset). See **Charge, Charger** in the Bible Word-book. Also *cark, cargo*.

CHARIOT, a sort of carriage. (F.—L.—C.) In Shak. Hen. V, iii. 5. 54; and in Trevisa, tr. of Higden, ii. 341. Cf. ME. *charett*, Maundeville's Travels, p. 241. And in Exod. xiv. 6, the A.V. of 1611 has *charet*.—F. *chariot*, 'a chariot, or waggon;' also *charette*, 'a chariot, or waggon;' Cot. Extended from OF. *char*, a car.—L. *carrus*, a car. See **Car**. **Der.** *chariot-eer*.

CHARITY, love, almsgiving. (F.—L.) In early use. ME. *charité*, Old Eng. Homilies, ed. Morris, i. 57, l. 41.—OF. *charitet, chariteit*.—L. *cāritātem*, acc. of *cāritās*, dearness.—L. *cārus*, dear. See **Caress**. **Der.** *charit-able, charit-abl-y, charit-able-ness*. ¶ The Gk. χάρις, favour, is wholly unconnected with this word.

CHARLATAN, a pretender, a quack. (F.—Ital.) 'Quacks and charlatans;' Tatler, no. 240; and in Sir T. Browne, Vulg. Errors, i. 3. § 11.—F. *charlatan*, 'a mountebank, a cousening drug-seller, .. a tatler, babler, foolish prater;' Cot. Introduced from Ital. in the 16th century; Brachet.—Ital. *ciarlatano*, 'a mountibanke, pratler, babler;' Florio.—Ital. *ciarlare*, to prattle.—Ital. *ciarla*, 'a tittle-tattle;' Florio. An onomatopœic word; cf. E. *chirp*. **Der.** *charlatan-ry, charlatan-ism*.

CHARLOCK, a kind of wild mustard. (E.) Provincial E. *kerlock*, corrupted to *kedlock, kellock*, &c. ME. *carlok*. 'Carlok, herbe, eruca;' Prompt. Parv. p. 62; and see Wright's Vocab. i. 265. AS. *cerlic*, Gloss. to Cockayne's Leechdoms, vol. iii; also *cyrlic*. Of unknown origin.

CHARM (1), a song, a spell. (F.—L.) ME. *charme*; King Alisaunder, ed. Weber, l. 81; *charmen*, verb; id. l. 342.—OF. *charme*, an enchantment.—L. *carmen*, a song. Cf. Gk. κῆρυξ, a herald. Brugm. i. § 633. **Der.** *charm*, verb; *charm-ing, charm-ing-ly; charm-er*.

CHARM (2), a blended noise of voices. (E.) 'With *charm* of earliest birds;' Milton, P. L. iv. 642. Earlier *cherme*; Palsgrave, p. 617. ME. *chirm*; AS. *cirm*, Matt. xxv. 6 (Rushworth MS.); Corpus Gloss. 925. Of imitative origin; cf. Irish and Gael. *gairm*, W. *garm*, an outcry. See **Slogan**.

CHARNEL, containing carcases. (F.—L.) Milton has: '*charnel* vaults and sepulchres;' Comus, 471. Usually in comp. *charnel-house* (Macb. iii. 4. 71), where *charnel* is properly an adj.; but we also find ME. *charnel* as a sb., in the sense of 'charnel-house.' 'Undre the cloystre of the chirche .. is the *charnel* of the Innocentes, where here [their] bones ly3n' [lie]; Maundeville's Trav. p. 70.—OF. *charnel*, adj. carnal; *charnel*, sb. a cemetery.—L. *carnālis*, carnal; Late L. *carnāle*, a grave-yard. See **Carnal**.

CHARQUI, jerked beef; see **Jerked Beef**.

CHART, a paper, card, map. (L.—Gk.) Richardson quotes from Skelton, Garl. of Laurell, l. 503, for this word; but the word is hardly so old; *chart* in that passage is a misreading for *charter*; see Dyce's edition. However 'charts and maps' is in North's Plutarch (1580), p. 307 (R.); and 'figures and *chartis*,' i.e. drawings and maps, occurs in Elyot's Governour (1531), bk. i. ch. 8. § 3.—F. *charte*, a paper, card; Cot.—L. *charta*, a paper.—Gk. χάρτη, χάρτης, a sheet of paper. See **Card** (1). **Der.** *chart-er*, q.v.; also *chart-ist, chart-ism*, words much in use A.D. 1838 and 1848.

CHARTER, a document granting privileges. (F.—L.—Gk.) In early use. ME. *chartre*; see Rob. of Glouc. p. 277, l. 5603; also *cartre*, id. p. 77, l. 1736. *Chartre* in Havelok, l. 676.—OF. *chartre, cartre*, a charter.—Late L. *chartula*, dimin. of *charta* (above).

CHARTULARY, a set of charters. (Late L.—Gk.) The pl. *chartularies* is in Wood, Athen. Oxonienses, ii. 697 (1691).—Late L. *chartulārium*, a collection of charters.—Late L. *chartula* (above).

CHARWOMAN; see under **Char** (1).

CHARY, careful, cautious. (E.) See Nares. ME. *chari*, full of care; hence (sometimes) sad. 'For turtle ledeth chari3 lif' = for the turtle leads a mournful life; Ormulum, l. 1274. (Not often used.) AS. *cearig*, full of care, sad; Grein, i. 158.—AS. *cearu, caru*, care; id.+G. *karg*, sparing; OHG. *charag*, from *chara*, care; MDu. *karigh*, niggardly; EFries. *karig*, sparing. ¶ Thus *chary* is the adj. of *care*, and partakes of its double sense, viz. (1) sorrow, (2) heedfulness; the former of these being the older sense. See **Care**. **Der.** *chari-ly, chari-ness*.

CHASE (1), to hunt after, pursue. (F.—L.) ME. *chasen, chacen*; Will. of Palerne, 1207; Maundeville's Trav. p. 3.—OF. *chacier*, Picard *cachir*, to chase. *Chase* is a doublet of *catch*; see further under **Catch**. **Der.** *chase*, sb.

CHASE (2), to enchase, emboss. (F.—L.) 'A cuppe, *chased* with rosys;' Fifty E. E. Wills, ed. Furnivall, p. 110. 16. *Chase* is short for *enchase*, q.v.

CHASE (3), a printer's frame for type. (F.—L.) Merely a doublet of *case*.—F. *châsse*, a shrine.—L. *capsa*, a box, case. See **Case** (2).

CHASE (4), the cavity of a gun-barrel; a groove. (F. – L.) 'Chase of a gun, the whole bore;' Todd's Johnson. – F. chas, a needle's eye; orig. an enclosure. – Late L. capsum, n. an enclosure; parallel form to capsa, f. a case. See Case (2).

CHASM, a yawning gulf. (L. – Gk.) 'The chasms of thought;' Spectator, no. 471. – L. chasma, an opening. – Gk. χάσμα, an opening, yawning; cf. χάσκειν, to gape. See Chaos.

CHASTE, clean, pure, modest. (F. – L.) In early use. Chaste and chasteté (chastity) both occur at p. 368 of the Ancren Riwle. – OF. chaste, caste. – L. castus, chaste, pure. + Skt. çishṭa-s, disciplined; pp. of çās, to teach, govern, punish. Brugmann, i. § 193. Der. chaste-ness, chaste-ly; chast-i-ty; also chast-en, chast-ise; see below. And see caste.

CHASTEN, to make pure, to correct. (F. – L.) ME. chastien, chasten, often written chasty in the infinitive (Southern dialect). [The final -en may have been suggested by the free use of the old disyllabic form chasty.] – OF. chastier, castier, to chasten, castigate. – L. castigāre, to castigate, make pure. – L. castus, chaste. Der. chasten-ing; also chast-ise. Doublet, castigate, q. v.; and see chastise.

CHASTISE, to castigate, punish. (F. – L.) ME. chastisen. 'To chastysen shrewes;' Chaucer, tr. of Boethius, bk. iv. pr. 4. 59. 'God hath me chastyst;' An Old Eng. Miscellany, p. 222. An extension of ME. chastien, to chasten, by the addition of the ME. suffix -isen, L. -īzāre. See Chasten. Der. chastise-ment, Ayenb. of Inwyt, p. 17; formed from chastise in imitation of ME. chastiement (Ancren Riwle, p. 72), chastiment (Cursor Mundi, 26004), which is a derivative of ME. chastien, to chasten.

CHASUBLE, an upper priestly vestment. (F. – L.) ME. chesible, P. Plowman, B. vi. 12. – F. chasuble, which Cotgrave explains as 'a chasuble.' [The ME. chesible points to an OF. chasible.] – Late L. *casupula, later casubla, casubula, Ducange; also casibula; dimin. forms equivalent to Late L. casula, used by Isidore of Seville to mean 'a mantle,' and explained by Ducange to mean 'a chasuble.' The L. casula means properly a little cottage or house; being a dimin. of casa, a house, cottage. Cf. Ital. casipola, casupola, a little house.

CHAT, CHATTER, to talk, talk idly. (E.) The form chat (though really nearer the primitive) is rare in Middle English, and came into modern use only as a familiar abbreviation of ME. chateren (with one t). It first occurs in the York Mysteries, xxxiii. 3 (ab. 1440). ME. chateren, cheateren, to chatter; with a dimin. form chiteren, in very early use. 'Sparuwe is a cheaterinde brid, cheatereð euer ant chirmeð' = the sparrow is a chattering bird; it ever chatters and chirps; Ancren Riwle, p. 152. 'As eny swalwe chitering in a berne' [barn]; Chaucer, C. T. 3258 (Harl. MS.). The word is imitative, and the ending -er (ME. -eren) has a frequentative force. The form chatter is parallel to EFries. kwattern, Du. kwetteren, to chatter, to warble; and chiteren to Scot. quhitter, to twitter, Dan. kvidre, Swed. qvittra, to chirp. Der. chatter-er, chatter-ing; chatt-y.

CHATEAU, a castle. (F. – L.) 'Fine chateaux in air;' Cowper, Sonnet to W. Hayley (1793). – Mod. F. château; OF. chastel. – L. castellum. A doublet of Castle, q. v.

CHATELAINE. (F. – L.) A derivative of F. château is châtelaine, used instead of chaîne châtelaine, a chain to which keys, &c. are suspended, orig. a chain to which a castellan's keys were fastened (Hatzfeld). Here châtelaine is fem. of châtelain, adj.; from Late L. castellānus, adj. – L. castellum, a castle.

CHATTELS, goods, property. (F. – L.) Used also in the singular in old authors. ME. chatel (with one t), a mere variant of ME. catel, cattle, goods, property. 'Aihwer with chatel mon mai luue cheape' = everywhere with chattels may one buy love; Old Eng. Homilies, i. 271. See further under Cattle, its doublet.

CHATTER; see Chat.

CHAW, verb, to chew; see Chew.

CHAWDRON, entrails of a beast. (F. – L.) In Macb. iv. 1. 33. The r is intrusive, and due to confusion with F. chaudron, a caldron. ME. chaudoun, a dish containing entrails; see N.E.D. – OF. chaudun, also caudun, caldun (Godefroy). – Late L. *caldūnum, variant of caldūna, entrails. [Cf. G. kaldaunen, entrails.] Probably from L. caldus, for calidus, warm (F. chaud). See Caldron.

CHAWS, s. pl., another spelling of jaws; in the A. V. of the Bible, Ezek. xxix. 4; xxxviii. 4. So also in Udal's Erasmus, John, fol. 73; Holland's Pliny, b. xxiii. c. 2 (end). A by-form of jaw, due to association with the verb to chew or chaw. See Jaw.

CHEAP, at a low price. (E.) Never used as an adj. in the earlier periods. The ME. chep, cheap, ceep was a sb., signifying 'barter,' or price.' Hence the expression god chep or good cheap, a good price; used to mean cheap, in imitation of the F. phr. bon marché. 'Tricolonius .... Makth the corn good chep or dere;' Gower, C. A. ii. 168, 169; b. v. 1239. A similar phrase is so liht cheap,' i. e. so small a price; Ancren Riwle, p. 398. We have the simple sb. in the phrase 'hire cheap wes the wrse,' i.e. her value was the worse [less];

Layamon, i. 17. AS. cēap, price; Grein, i. 159; whence the verb cēapian, to cheapen, to buy. + Du. koop, a bargain, purchase; goedkoop, cheap, lit. 'good cheap;' koopen, to buy; Icel. kaup, a bargain, illt kaup, a bad bargain; gott kaup, a good bargain; kaupa, to buy; Swed. köp, a bargain, price, purchase; köpa, to buy; Dan. kiöb, a purchase; kiöbe, to buy; Goth. kaupōn, to traffic, trade, Lu. xix. 13; OHG. choufōn, MHG. koufen, G. kaufen, to buy; G. kauf, a purchase. ¶ Curtius (i. 174) holds that all these words, however widely spread in the Teutonic tongues, must be borrowed from Latin; so that OHG. choufo, a huckster, is merely the L. caupo, a huckster. But this is now held to be unlikely (Kluge, Franck). Der. cheap-ly, cheap-ness, cheap-en; also chap-man, q. v.

CHEAT, to defraud, deceive. (F. – L.) The verb is formed from the ME. chete, an escheat; to cheat was to seize upon a thing as escheated. The want of scruple on the part of the escheator, and the feelings with which his proceedings were regarded, may be readily imagined. The verb, in the modern sense, first occurs in Shakespeare, who uses it several times, esp. with the prep. of, with relation to the thing of which the speaker is defrauded. 'We are merely cheated of our lives;' Temp. i. 1. 59; 'hath cheated me of the island,' id. iii. 2. 49; 'cheats the poor maid of that;' K. John, ii. 572; 'cheated of feature;' Rich. III, i. 1. 19. In Merry Wives, i. 3. 77, Shak. uses cheaters in the very sense of 'escheators,' but he probably rather intended a quibble than was conscious of the etymology. β. The ME. chete, as a contraction of achete, variant of eschete, was in rather early use. 'Chete for the lorde, caducum, confiscarium, fisca;' Prompt. Parv. p. 73. 'The kynge ... seide .. I lese many chetes,' i. e. I lose many escheats; P. Plowman, B. iv. 175, where some MSS. have escheates. Hence were formed the verb cheten, to confiscate, and the sb. cheting, confiscation. 'Chetyn, confiscor, fisco;' Prompt. Parv. p. 73. 'Chetynge, confiscacio;' id. For further information see Escheat, of which cheat is a doublet. The intermediate form appears in 'Achetyn, confiscor;' Prompt. Parv. p. 6. ¶ See further remarks on the word in Trench's Select Glossary. He gives a clear example of the serious use of cheater with the sense of escheatour. We also find a description of some rogues called cheatours in Awdelay's Fraternitye of Vacabonds, ed. Furnivall, pp. 7, 8; but there is nothing to connect these with the cant word chete, a thing, of which so many examples occur in Harman's Caveat, and which Mr. Wedgwood guesses to be the origin of our word cheat. On the contrary, the word cheat seems to have descended in the world; see the extract from Greene's Michel Mumchance, his Discoverie of the Art of Cheating, quoted in Todd's Johnson, where he says that gamesters call themselves cheaters; 'borrowing the term from our lawyers, with whom all such casuals as fall to the lord at the holding of his leets, as waifes, straies, and such like, be called chetes, and are accustomably said to be escheated to the lord's use.'

CHECK, a sudden stop, a repulse. (F. – Arab. – Pers.) ME. chek, found (perhaps for the first time, but in a transferred sense) in Rob. of Brunne's tr. of Peter Langtoft. He has: 'for they did that chek' = because they occasioned that delay, p. 151; see also pp. 100, 225. Chaucer has chek as an interjection, meaning 'check!' as used in the game of chess: 'Therwith Fortune seyde "chek here!"' And "mate" in myd poynt of the chekkere,' i.e. thereupon Fortune said 'check! here!' and 'mate' in the middle of the chessboard; Book of the Duchesse, 658. β. The word was clearly taken from the game of chess, according to the received opinion. [The game is mentioned earlier, in the Romance of King Alisaunder, ed. Weber, l. 2096.] The orig. sense of the interj. check! was 'king!' i.e. mind your king, your king is in danger. – OF. eschec, eschac, which Cotgrave explains by 'a check at chess-play;' pl. esches, the game of chess. [The initial e is dropped in English, as in stable from OF. estable, and in chess, q.v.] – Arab. shāg, lit. 'king;' which is merely an Arab. pron. of Pers. shāh (Devic). – Pers. shāh, a king, the principal piece in the game of chess; Palmer's Pers. Dict. col. 374; whence also shāh māt, check-mate, from shāh, the king, and māt, he is dead, id. col. 518; the sense of check-mate being 'the king is dead.' Der. check, verb; check-mate; check-er, q.v.; chess, q.v.; exchequer, q.v.; cheque, for check. ¶ The Arab. pron. of the Pers. word gave rise to Late L. scaccus; whence Ital. scacco; Span. jaque; Port. xaque, check! (also shah); Icel. skák, G. schach; &c. The game was denoted by the pl.; Late L. scacci, Ital. scacchi, F. échecs, OF. esches. See Chess.

CHECKER, CHEQUER, to mark with squares. (F. – Arab. – Pers.) The term checky in heraldry means that the shield is marked out into squares like a chess-board. To checker in like manner is 'to mark out like a chessboard;' hence, to mark with cross-lines; and, generally, to variegate. The verb is derived from the ME. chekker, cheker, or chekere, a chess-board; used by Rob. of Glouc. p. 192, l. 3965; Chaucer, Book of the Duchesse, 660. The word is still used in the plural form The Checkers, not uncommon as the name of an inn; see below. — OF. *eschekier*, a chess-board; also an exchequer. — Late L. *scaccārium*, orig. a chess-board; from *scacci*, chess. See **Check**, and **Exchequer**.

CHECKERS, CHEQUERS, the game of draughts. (F. — Arab. — Pers.) Sometimes so called, because played on a *checkered* board, or chessboard. As the sign of an inn, we find mention of the 'Cheker of the hope,' i.e. the chequers on [or with] the hoop, in the Prologue to the Tale of Beryn, l. 14; and Canning, in his Needy Knife-grinder, makes mention of 'The Chequers.' See Larwood, Hist. of Sign-boards, p. 488; and see above.

CHECKMATE; see **Check**.

CHEEK, the side of the face. (E.) ME. *cheke*; also *cheoke*, as spelt in the Ancren Riwle, pp. 70, 106, 156. OMerc. *cēce* (O. E. Texts); AS. *cēace*, the cheek; of which the pl. *cēacan* occurs as a gloss to *maxillās*, Ps. xxxi. 12. We also find the Northumb. and Midland forms *ceica, ceke*, as glosses to *maxillā* in Matt. v. 39.+Du. *kaak*, the jaw, the cheek; Swed. *käk*, jaw, *käkben*, cheek-bone, MSwed. and OFries. *keke*; NFries. *keek*; EFries. *kake*. Teut. type **kĕkŏn-*, f.

CHEEP, to twitter shrilly, like young birds or mice. (E.) Levins (1570) has: 'To *cheepe*, pipilare.' Of imitative origin; cf. *pipe*.

CHEER, mien; entertainment. (F. — L. — Gk.?) ME. *chere*, commonly meaning 'the face;' hence, mien, look, demeanour; cf. the phr. 'be of good *cheer*,' and 'look *cheerful*.' 'With glad *chere*' = with pleasant mien; Hali Meidenhad, ed. Cockayne, p. 33. 'Maketh drupie *chere*' = makes drooping cheer, looks sad; Ancren Riwle, p. 88. — OF. *chere, chiere*, the face, look. — Late L. *cara*, a face, countenance, used by Corippus, a 6th-cent. poet, in his Paneg. ad Justinum (Brachet). Cf. Span. and Port. *cara*, face (not Ital.). Relationship to Gk. *κάρα*, head, is doubtful. **Der.** *cheer-ful, cheer-ful-ly, cheer-ful-ness; cheer-less, cheer-less-ness; cheer-y, cheer-i-ness*.

CHEESE, the curd of milk, coagulated. (L.) ME. *chese*, Havelok, 643; O. Eng. Homilies, ed. Morris, i. 53. OMerc. *cēse*, AS. *cȳse* (for earlier *cīese< *cēasi, with *i*-mutation); prehistoric OE. *cāsi-< *cāsioz. The pl. *cēsas* (*cȳsas* in some MSS.) occurs in the Laws of Ine, sect. 70; in Thorpe's Ancient Laws, i. 146. — L. *cāseus*, cheese; whence also Irish *cais*, Gael. *caise*, W. *caws*, Corn. *caus, cês*; Du. *kaas*, G. *käse*. **Der.** *chees-y*.

CHEETAH, CHEETA, a leopard used for the chase. (Hind. — Skt.) Spelt *chittah* in 1781; Phil. Trans., lxxi. 2 (N.E.D.). — Hind. *chītā*, m. a leopard or panther (Forbes). — Skt. *chitraka(s)*, m. the cheeta (Benfey). — Skt. *chitra(s)*, spotted, variegated; orig. visible. — Skt. *chit*, to perceive. Cf. **Chintz**.

CHEMISE, a lady's shift. (F. — Late L.) 'Hire *chemise* smal and hwit;' Reliquiæ Antiquæ, ed. Halliwell and Wright, i. 129; also in O. Eng. Homilies, ed. Morris, 2nd Ser. p. 162. — F. *chemise*. — Late L. *camisia*, a shirt, a thin dress; whence also OIrish *caimmse*, shirt; Arab. *qamīs*, shirt. Of unknown origin; hardly from Teutonic, but rather of classical origin, and allied to *Chamber*; cf. AS. *ham*, a shirt (O. E. Texts), G. *hemd*; Goth. *af-hamōn*, to unclothe. **Der.** *chemis-e'te*.

CHEMIST, CHYMIST, a modern 'alchemist.' (F. — L. — Gk.) The double spelling (*chemist, chymist*) is due to the double spelling *alchemy, alchymy*. 'Alchymist (alchymista) one that useth or is skilled in that art, a chymist;' Blount's Glossographia, 1681. *Chymist* is merely short for *alchymist*, and *chemist* for *alchemist*; see quotations in Trench's Select Glossary. 'For she a *chymist* was and Nature's secrets knew And from amongst the lead she antimony drew;' Drayton's Polyolbion, s. 26, l. 374. [Antimony was a substance used in alchemy.] Dropping the *al-*, which is the Arabic article, we have reverted to the Gk. *χημεία*, chemistry. Cf. Span. *quimista*, for *alquimista*. See further under **Alchemy**. **Der.** *chemistry*; and, from the same source, *chem-ic, chem-ic-al*.

CHEQUE. A modern spelling of *check*, from a connexion (which is real) with the word *exchequer*. For the etymology, see **Check**.

CHEQUER, CHEQUERS; see **Checker, Checkers**.

CHERISH, to fondle, take care of. (F. — L.) ME. *cherischen, chericen*; whence the sb. *cherissing*, cherishing, P. Plowman, B. iv. 117. Spelt *cherisch*, Allit. Poems, ed. Morris, B. 128. — OF. *cheris-*, stem of pres. pt. of *cherir* (mod. F. *chérir*, pres. pt. *chériss-ant*), to hold dear, cherish. — OF. (and F.) *cher*, dear. — L. *cārus*, dear. See **Caress**.

CHEROOT, a kind of cigar. (Tamil.) Spelt *cheroot* in 1759 (Yule). — Tamil *shuruṭṭu*, a roll (of tobacco).

CHERRY, a well-known stone-fruit. (F. — L. — Gk.) ME. *chery, chiri* (with one *r*). 'Ripe *chiries* manye;' P. Plowman, B. vi. 296; A. vii. 281. *Cheri* or *chiri* was a mistake for *cheris* or *chiris*, the final *s* being mistaken for the pl. inflection; the same error occurs in several other words, notably in *pea* as shortened from *pease* (L. *pīsum*). *Cherise* is a NorthF. modification of OF. *cerise*; representing a Folk-L. *ceresia, *ceresea. — L. *cerasus*, a cherry-tree; whence also the AS. *cyrs*. [We find the entry 'Cerasus, *cyrs-treow*,' in Ælfric's

Glossary, Nomina Arborum.] — Gk. *κέρασος*, a cherry-tree; see Curtius, i. 181, who ignores the usual story that the tree came from *Cerasos*, a city in Pontus; cf. Pliny, bk. xv. c. 25. Prellwitz connects *κέρασος* with *κράνεια*, a cornel-tree, and L. *cornus*; see **Cornel**.

CHERT, a kind of quartz, also called *horn-stone*. (E.?) 'Flint is most commonly found in form of nodules; but 'tis sometimes found in thin stratæ, when 'tis called *chert*;' Woodward, qu. in Todd's Johnson (no reference). Woodward the geologist died A.D. 1728. First in Plot's Staffordshire (1679); 'beds of *chirts*' p. 124 (1686). The word was probably taken up from provincial English. 'Churty, [of] rocky soil; mineral; Kent;' Halliwell's Dict. 'Chirt, sb. (Durh. Derb. Nott.) a hard, flinty, stratified white or black substance;' E. D. D. Of unknown origin. Cf. Swed. dial. *kart*, a pebble; Irish *ceart*, a pebble.

CHERUB, a celestial spirit. (Heb.) 'And he stegh ouer *Cherubin*, and flegh thar ' = and He ascended over the cherubim, and flew there; Metrical English Psalter (ab. A.D. 1300), Ps. xviii. 11, where the Vulgate has: 'et ascendit super *cherubim*.' The Heb. pl. is *cherubim*, but our Bibles wrongly have *cherubims* in many passages. The usual ME. form was *cherubin*, sing., as in Chaucer, Prol. 624; with pl. *cherubins*. — Heb. *k'rūb, k'rūv*, pl. *k'rūvīm* (the initial letter being *kaph*), a mystic figure. Origin unknown; see *Cherub* in Smith's Concise Dict. of the Bible. ¶ Discussed by Cheyne, Isaiah (1881), ii. 272, who connects Heb. *k'rūv* with the Assyrian *kirubu*, a synonym for the steer-god [winged human-headed bull], the winged guardian at the entrance of the Assyrian palaces. Of non-Semitic, perhaps Accadian origin; see Encycl. Brit. s. v. *Babylon*. — A. L. M. **Der.** *cherub-ic*.

CHERVIL, the name of a plant. (L. — Gk.) ME. *cheruelle*. The pl. *cheruelles* is in P. Plowman, B. vi. 296. AS. *cærfille*. The entry 'cerefolium, *cærfille*' is in Ælfric's Glossary (Nomina Herbarum). — L. *chærephylla*, pl. of *chærephyllum* (Columella); cf. *cærefolium* (Pliny, 19. 8. 54). — Gk. *χαιρέφυλλον*, chervil; lit. 'pleasant leaf.' — Gk. *χαίρ-ειν*, to rejoice; and *φύλλον*, a leaf. The Gk. *χαίρειν* is from √GHER, whence also E. *yearn*; and *φύλλον* is cognate with L. *folium*. See **Yearn** (1) and **Foliage**.

CHESS, the game of the kings. (F. — Arab. — Pers.) ME. *ches*, King Alisaunder, ed. Weber, l. 2096; Chaucer, Book of the Duchesse, l. 652. Equivalent to *checks*, i.e. 'kings.' Grammatically, *chess* is the pl. of *check*. — OF. *esches*, chess, pl. of *eschec*, check! lit. 'a king' (*c* being dropped before final *s*; Godefroy, iii. 380). See further under **Check**.

CHEST, a box; upper part of the trunk of the body. (L. — Gk.) ME. *cheste, chiste*. Spelt *chiste*, Havelok, 222; also *kiste*, Havelok, 2018. Also found without the final *e*, in the forms *chest, chist, kist*. AS. *cest* (O. E. Texts); *cyste*, as a tr. of Lat. *loculum* in Luke vii. 14. The Northumb. gloss has *ceiste*; the later AS. version has *cheste*. — L. *cista*, a chest, box. — Gk. *κίστη*, a chest, a box. ¶ The G. *kiste*, Du. *kist*, &c. are all borrowed forms.

CHESTNUT, CHESNUT, the name of a tree. (F. — L. — Gk.) *Chesnut* is short for *chestnut*, and the latter is short for *chesten-nut*. The tree is properly *chesten* simply, the fruit being the *chesten-nut*. ME. *chestein, chesten, chastein, castany*, &c. 'Medlers, ploumes, peres, *chesteynes*;' Rom. of the Rose, 1375. 'Grete forestes of *chesteynes*;' Maundeville's Trav. p. 307; *chasteyn*, Chaucer, C. T. 2924 (A 2922). — OF. *chastaigne* (F. *châtaigne*). — L. *castanea*, the chestnut-tree. — Gk. *κάστανον*, a chestnut; gen. in pl. *κάστανα*, chestnuts; also called *κάρυα Κασταναῖα*, from *Κάστανα* [Castana] or *Κασθαναία*, the name of a city in Pontus where they abounded. Or from Armen. *kaskeni*, a chestnut-tree; from *kask*, a chestnut (Kluge); in which case the place was named from the tree.

CHEVAL-DE-FRISE, an obstruction with spikes. (F.) Gen. in pl. *chevaux-de-frise*. First in 1688. The word is a military term, and mere French. — F. *cheval de Frise*, lit. a horse of Friesland, a jocular name for the contrivance; employed by Frisians in the 17th century. The form 'Chevaux de Frise' is given in Kersey's Dict. 1715. See below.

CHEVALIER, a knight, cavalier. (F. — L.) A doublet of *cavalier*. In Shak. K. John, ii. 287. — F. *chevalier*, a horseman; Cotgrave. — F. *cheval*, a horse. — L. *caballus*, a horse, nag. See **Cavalier**, and **Chivalry**.

CHEVERIL, kid leather. (F. — L.) 'Cheveril, roebuck-leather, symbol of flexibility, Tw. Nt. iii. 1. 13; Hen. VIII. ii. 3. 32; Romeo, ii. 4. 87;' Schmidt, Shak. Lex. 'Cheuerell lether, cheuerotin;' Palsgrave. AF. *cheverel, cheverel*; Liber Custumarum, 83, 306. — OF. *chevrel* (F. *chevreau*), a kid; cf. *char de chevrel*, kid-skin, in Supp. to Godefroy. Dimin. of OF. *chevre*, F. *chèvre*, fem., a goat, kid. — L. *capram*, acc. of *capra*, a she-goat. See **Caper** (1).

CHEVIN, CHEVEN, the fish usually called a chub. (F. — L.) The Book of St. Albans (1486) mentions the *cheuen*; fol. f 7, back. — F. *chevanne* (Hatzfeld); (MF. *cheviniau*, Cot.); OF. *chevesne*, *chevinel, chevenel* (Godefroy). Of uncertain form; but clearly connected with F. *chef*, head; from its broad blunt head; cf. L. *capito*, the name of a similar fish; also Ital. *cavedine*, 'the chieven,' Torriano. See **Chief**.

CHEVRON, an honourable ordinary in heraldry, in the shape of a reversed V. (F.—L.) ME. *cheueron*, Book of St. Albans, pt. ii. fol. f 1, back. Usually said to represent two rafters of the roof of a house; I think it must, in heraldry, rather have had reference to the (gable-like) peak of a saddle, as there is nothing highly honourable in a house-roof.—OF. *chevron*, 'a kid, a chevron of timber in building, a rafter, or sparre;' Cot. Augmentative form of OF. *chevre*, 'a she-goat,' id.—L. *capra*, a she-goat; see **Caper** (1). In the same way the L. *capreolus* meant a prop or support of timber.

CHEW, CHAW, to bruise with the teeth. (E.) Spelt *chawe* in Levins. ME. *chewen*; Chaucer, C. T. 3690; Ormulum, l. 1241. AS. *cēowan*, Levit. xi. 3; pt. t. *cēaw*, pp. *cowen*. +Du. *kaauwen*, to chew, masticate, OHG. *kiuwan*, MHG. *kiuwen*, G. *kauen*, to chew. Teut. type **kewwan-*. Cf. Russ. *jevate*, to chew. See Brugmann, i. § 312.

CHIBOUK, a Turkish pipe, for smoking. (F.—Turk.) Spelt *chibouque*, Byron, Corsair, ii. 2; Bride of Abydos, i. 8.—F. *chibouque*.— Turk. *chibūq*, a stick, tube, pipe; Devic (Supp. to Littré); *chybūk*, *chubūk*, a pipe; Zenker's Turk. Dict. p. 349.

CHICANERY, mean deception. (F.) We formerly find also *chicane*, both as sb. and verb. 'That spirit of *chicane* and injustice;' Burnet, Hist. of Own Time, an. 1696. 'Many who choose to *chicane*;' Burke, on Economical Reform. Of F. origin. Cotgrave has: '*Chicanerie*, wrangling, pettifogging;' also '*Chicaner*, to wrangle, or pettifog it.' β. Brachet says: 'Before being used for sharp practice in lawsuits, it meant a dispute in games, particularly in the game of the mall; and, originally, it meant the game of the mall: in this sense *chicane* represents a form **zicanum*, which is from the medieval Gk. τζυκάνιον, a word of Byzantine origin.' γ. This Late Gk. word is apparently borrowed from Pers. *chaugān*, a club used in the game of 'polo;' Palmer's Pers. Dict. col. 189; Rich. Dict. p. 545, col. 2. ¶ Diez supposes the word to be connected with OF. *chic*, little (cf. '*de chic à chic*, from little to little' in Cotgrave); and derives it from L. *ciccum*, that which is of little worth, whence mod. F. *chiche*, niggardly. See an article on *Chic* in N. and Q. 5 S. viii. 261; and see **Chigo**. Devic declares in favour of the Pers. origin.

CHICKEN, the young of the fowl. (E.) The form *chick* is a mere abbreviation of *chicken*, not the older form. ME. *chiken*, sing. '*Chekyn*, pullus;' Prompt. Parv. p. 74. The pl. *chiknes* is in Chaucer, Prol. 382 (A 380). AS. *cicen*; of which the pl. *cicenu*, chickens, occurs in Matt. xxiii. 37. This form is from an earlier **ciucin*. + Du. *kieken, kuiken*, a chicken; Low G. *küken*; cf. G. *küchlein*, a chicken, Icel. *kjúklingr*, Swed. *kyckling*; related to **Cock**, which is from the weak grade **kuk-*; see **Cock** (1). Sievers, 2nd ed. § 165; Noreen, §§ 143, 252. Der. *chick-ling*, dimin. (cf. Icel. *kjúklingr*); *chicken-hearted, chicken-pox*; *chick-weed* (Levins).

CHICORY, a plant; succory. (F.—L.—Gk.) Not in very early use. Formerly *cicorie*; 'cykorie or suckorie;' Castel of Helth, b. ii. c 8; fol. 23.—F. *chichorée, cichorée*, 'succorie;' Cot.—L. *cichorium*, succory.—Gk. κιχώριον; also κιχώρη; also neut. pl. κιχόρια, κιχορεία, succory. The form *succory* is more corrupt. See **Succory**.

CHIDE, to scold; also, to quarrel. (E.) ME. *chiden*; in Old Eng. Homilies, i. 113. AS. *cīdan*, to chide, brawl, Exod. xxi. 18; Luke, iv. 35, where the pt. t. *cidde* occurs. ¶ There do not seem to be cognate forms. The verb is weak; the pt. t. *chode* (Gen. xxxi. 36) is a new formation, by analogy with *rode*.

CHIEF, adj. head, principal; sb. a leader. (F.—L.) Properly a sb., but early used as an adj. ME. *chef, chief*. Rob. of Glouc. has *chef*, sb., p. 212, l. 4316; *chef*, adj., p. 231, l. 4758.—OF. *chef, chief*, the head.—L. type **capum* (cf. Ital. *capo*).—L. *caput*, the head. Der. *chief-ly*; *chief-tain*, q. v.; also *ker-chief*, q. v.; cf. *cape* (2), *capital*, &c.

CHIEFTAIN, a head man; leader. (F.—L.) A doublet of *captain*. In early use. ME. *cheuetein, chiftain*, &c. Spelt *cheuetein*, Layamon, i. 251 (later text).—OF. *chevetain*; also *chevetaine*, a chieftain.—Late Latin *capitānus, capitāneus*, a captain.—L. *caput* (stem *capit-*), the head. See above; and see **Captain**. Der. *chieftain-ship*.

CHIFFONIER, an ornamental cupboard. (F.) Modern; first in 1806. Lit. 'a place to put rags in.'—F. *chiffonnier*, a rag-picker; also, a piece of furniture, a chiffonier (Hamilton and Legros).—F. *chiffon*, a rag; an augmentative form (with suffix -*on*) from *chiffe*, a rag, a piece of flimsy stuff; explained by Cotgrave as 'a clout, old ragge, over-worn or off-cast piece of stuffe.' (Origin unknown. Cf. Körting, § 2133.)

CHIGNON, an arrangement of hair in a large coil at the back of the head. (F.—L.) First in 1783.—F. *chignon*, properly the

back of the neck, lit. a little chain, from the projections of the vertebrae (Littré); variant of F. *chaînon*, der. from *chaîne*, chain, with suffix -*on*; see **Chain**. See Cotgrave, s. v. *chainon*.

CHIGO, CHIGOE, a kind of small flea; also called *jigger*. (Span.—L.—Gk.) In the W. Indies and S. America. Prob. a negro corruption of Span. *chico*, small; since the F. name *chique* is also deducible from the same form.—L. *ciccum*, acc. of *ciccus*, the thin membrane round the grains of a pomegranate, something worthless, a trifle.—Gk. κίκκος, a fruit-husk.

CHILBLAIN, a blain caused by cold. (E.) Lit. 'chill-blain,' i.e. cold-sore, sore caused by cold. In Holland's Pliny, ii. 76, l. 6 (b. xx. c. 22). See **Chill** and **Blain**.

CHILD, a son or daughter, a descendant. (E.) ME. *child*, very early; also *cild*. Spelt *child*, Layamon, i. 13; *cild*, O. Eng. Homilies, i. 227. AS. *cild*; Grein, i. 160. Teut. type **kilthom*, n. Allied to Goth. *kilthei*, the womb, *in-kilthō*, a pregnant woman. ¶ Distinct from Du. and G. *kind*, a child. But Skt. *jathara-* (for **jalthara-*) may be related; so also Dan. *kuld*, Swed. *kull*, a litter (of animals). Cf. **Kilt**. Der. *child-ish, child-ish-ness, child-like, child-less*; *child-bed*; *child-hood* = AS. *cild-hád*, Grein, i. 160.

CHILIAD, the number 1000. (Gk.) Used by H. More to mean 'a period of a thousand years;' Defence of Moral Cabbala, c. 2 (R.).— Gk. χιλιάς (stem χιλιαδ-), a thousand, in the aggregate.—Gk. χίλιοι, pl. a thousand; Lesbian χέλλιοι, which is an older form (see Prellwitz).

CHILL, a sudden coldness; cold. (E.) Properly a sb. '*Chil*, cold, *algidus*,' and 'To *chil* with cold, *algere*' occur in Levins, col. 123, ll. 46, 28. Earlier than this, it is commonly a sb. only; but the pp. *child* (i.e. chilled) occurs in P. Plowman, C. xviii. 49. ME. *chil* sb., Trevisa, i. 51; but more commonly *chele*, O. Eng. Homilies, i. 33; Layamon, iii. 237. AS. *cele*, great cold; O. E. Texts; Grein, i. 157. Also *ciele*; 'Frigus, *ciele*,' Voc. 495. 28. Teut. type **kaliz*; from **kalan-*, to be cold, as in AS. *calan*, Icel. *kala*, to freeze. See **Cool**. Cf. also Du. *kil*, chilly; *killen*, to be chilled; L. *gelu*, frost; *gelidus*, cold. Der. *chill-y, chill-ness, chill-i-ness, chil-blain*; and see *gelid*.

CHILLI, red pepper. (Span.—Mex.) Spelt *chili* in Thackeray, Vanity Fair, c. iii.—Span. *chile*, red pepper.—Mex. *chilli*, red pepper. ¶ Not from *Chili*, in S. America.

CHIME, a harmonious sound. (F.—L.—Gk.) Palsgrave has: '*chyme* of belles.' The word has lost a *b*; it stands for *chimbe*. ME. *chimbe, chymbe*. 'His *chymbe-belle* [i.e. chime-bell] he doth rynge;' K. Alisaunder, ed. Weber, 1852. The true old sense is 'cymbal.' In the Cursor Mundi, ed. Morris, l. 12193, the Trin. MS. has: 'As a *chymbe* or a brasen belle' (with evident reference to 1 Cor. xiii. 1); where the Göttingen MS. has *chime*, and the Cotton MS. has *chim*. *Chimbe* or *chymbe* is from OF. *chimble* or *chymble*, a dialectic form of OF. *cimble, cymble*, or from a form without the *l*; Godefroy gives both *cymble* and *cymbe* with the sense of 'cymbal;' also *chinbe* (for *chimbe*) with the same sense.—L. *cymbalum*, a cymbal.—Gk. κύμβαλον, a cymbal. See further under **Cymbal**. ¶ Perhaps the ME. *chyme-belle* was a popular form for *chymbale*, a variant of *cymbale* in Cotgrave; yet we actually find a Late L. *cimba*, a dinner-bell, in the Chronicle of Abingdon, ed. Stevenson; doubtless from L. *cymbalum*. Der. *chime*, verb.

CHIMÆRA, CHIMERA, a fabulous monster. (L.—Gk.) In Milton, P. L. ii. 628. Spelt *chimera* in Trevisa, tr. of Higden, ii. 371.—L. *chimæra*, a monster.—Gk. χίμαιρα, a she-goat; also, a monster, with lion's head, serpent's tail, and *goat's* body; Iliad, vi. 181.—Gk. χίμαρος, a he-goat.+Icel. *gymbr*, a ewe-lamb of a year old; whence prov. Eng. *gimmer* or *gimmer-lamb*; Curtius, i. 249. Der. *chimer-ic-al, chimer-ic-al-ly*.

CHIMER, CHIMERE, a long loose robe. (F.—Span.) Variously used; Barbour has *chemer, chemeir*, of a bishop's coat-armour; Bruce, xvi. 580. Dryden has 'a slight *cymar*,' of a woman's robe; Cymon, 100.—F. *chamarre*, 'a loose and light gowne;' Cot. —Span. *chamarra, zamarra*, a shepherd's dress, of sheepskin. Of unknown origin (*not* Basque). The Sardinian *acciamarra* (in Diez), if for **al-ciamarra*, suggests an Arabic origin.

CHIMNEY, a fire-place, a flue. (F.—L.—Gk.) Formerly, 'a fire-place;' see Shak. Cymb. ii. 4. 80. 'A chambre with a *chymneye*;' P. Plowman, B. x. 98.—AF. *chimenee*, Liber Albus, p. 333; OF. *cheminée*, 'a chimney;' Cotgrave.—Late L. *camināta*, lit. 'provided with a chimney;' hence 'a room with a chimney;' and, later, the chimney itself.—L. *caminus*, a hearth, furnace, forge, stove, flue.— Gk. κάμινος, an oven, furnace. Perhaps allied to καμάρα, a vaulted chamber; see **Chamber**. Der. *chimney-piece, chimney-shaft*.

CHIMPANZEE, a kind of ape. (African.) In a translation of Buffon's Nat. Hist., published in London in 1792, vol. i. p. 324, there is a mention of 'the orang-outangs, which he [M. de la Brosse] calls *quimpeazes*.' [La Broess has *quimpezé*.] From the native name in Angola, W. Africa; see N. E. D. The Bantu form is *kampenzi*;

N. and Q., 9 S. viii. 341. I am informed that the Fantee name of the animal is *akatsia* or *akatshia*.

CHIN, part of the lower jaw. (E.) ME. *chin*, Layamon, i. 348; l. 8148. AS. *cin*; we find 'mentum, *cin*' in Ælfric's Gloss. ed. Somner, p. 70, col. 2.+Du. *kin*; Icel. *kinn*, the cheek; Dan. *kind*; Swed. *kind*, the cheek, *kindbåge*, cheekbone, but also jawbone; Goth. *kinnus*, the cheek; Matt. v. 39; O. H. G. *chinni*, G. *kinn*, the cheek.+L. *gena*, the cheek; Gk. γένυς, the chin, the jaw; Skt. *hanu-s*, the jaw; OIrish *gin*, mouth; W. *gên*, jaw, chin.

CHINA, porcelain-ware. (China.) Shak. has 'china dishes;' Meas. ii. 1. 97; see Pope, Moral Essays, ii. 268; Rape of the Lock, ii. 106. 'China, or China-ware, a fine sort of earthen ware made in those parts' [i. e. in China]; Kersey's Dict. ed. 1715. Named from the country. **Der.** *Chinese*, a native of China. Milton, P. L. iii. 438, has the pl. *Chineses*, correctly. The final *-se* has come to be regarded as a plural; and we now say *Chinese* in the plural. Hence, as a 'singular' development, the phrase 'that heathen *Chinee*.' Cf. *cherry*, *pea*, *sherry*, s*h*ay (for *chaise*), &c.

CHINCHILLA, a small rodent quadruped. (Span.–L.) 'Chin-chilles, like squirrels;' E. G., tr. of Acosta, bk. iv. c. 38.–Span. *chin-chilla*; dimin. of *chinche*, a bug, from an erroneous notion that it had a fetid smell.–L. *cimicem*, acc. of *cimex*, a bug.

CHINCHONA. See **Cinchona** below.

CHINCOUGH, the whooping-cough. (E.) 'No, it shall ne'er be said in our country Thou diedst o' the *chin-cough*;' Beaum. and Fletcher; Bonduca, i. 2. It stands for *chink-cough*, a form found in W. Yorkshire; prov. Eng. and Scot. *kink-cough* or *kink-host*, where *host* means 'a cough.' Cf. Scot. *kink*, to labour for breath in a severe fit of coughing; Jamieson. It is an E. word, as shown by 'cincung, cachinnatio' in a Glossary, pr. in Wright's Vocab. i. 50, col. 2; which shows that *kink* was also used of a loud fit of laughter. *Kink* is a nasalised form of a root *kik-, appearing in G. *keich-en*, to gasp, pant. Cf. Du. *kinkhoest*, the chincough, whooping-cough; M. Du. *kiechhoest*, *kickhoest*, the same (Kilian); Swed. *kikhosta*, the chincough; *kik-na*, to gasp, to pant; Dan. *kighoste*, the whooping-cough. See **Chink** (2).

CHINE, the spine, backbone. (F.–O. H. G.) 'Me byhynde, at my *chyne*, Smotest me with thy spere;' K. Alisaunder, l. 3977.–OF. *eschine* (mod. F. *échine*), the spine.–OHG. *skina*, a needle, a prickle (>G. *schiene*, a splint); see Diez. β. A similar change (or rather extension) of meaning is seen in the L. *spina*, a thorn, spine, back-bone. Körting, § 8783. Cf. **Shin**.

CHINK (1), a cleft, crevice, split. (E.) 'May shine through every *chinke*;' Ben Jonson; Ode to James, Earl of Desmond, l. 16. And see Mids. Nt. Dr. iii. 1. 66. Formed, with an added *k*, probably expressive of diminution (as in prov. E. *chin-kie*, the chin), from the base of ME. *chine*, a chink; cf. prov. Eng. *chine*, a rift in a cliff (Isle of Wight). 'In the *chyne* of a ston-wal;' Wyclif, Song of Solomon, ii. 14.–AS. *cinu*, a chink, crack; Ælfric's Hom. ii. 154.– AS. *cin-*, weak grade of *cinan*, to split, crack (intransitively), to chap; 'eal *tōcinen*,' i. e. chapped all over, Ælfric's Hom. i. 336.+Du. *keen*, a cleft; also, a germ; MDu. *kene*, a split, rift; *kenen*, to shoot up, as a plant, bud. Cf. G. *keimen*, to germinate; *keim*, a bud. β. The notion is that a *chine* signified originally a crack in the ground caused by the germination of seeds; and the connexion is clear between the AS. *cinu*, a rift, cleft, crack, and the Goth. *keinan*, to spring up as a plant, Mark, iv. 27; *uskeinan*, to spring up, Luke, viii. 8; *uskeian*, to produce, Luke, viii. 6. Teut. root *kei-, whence also AS. *ci-ð*, a germ, shoot. See **Chit** (2).

CHINK (2), to jingle; a jingling sound; money. (E.) In Shak. *chinks* means 'money,' jocularly; Romeo, i. 5. 119. Cf. 'he *chinks* his purse;' Pope, Dunciad, ii. 197. An imitative word, of which *jingle* may be said to be the frequentative. See **Jingle**. Cf. EFries. *kinken*, to ring (a strong verb). A similar word is **Clink**, q. v.

CHINTZ, parti-coloured cotton cloth. (Hind.–Skt.) In Pope, Moral Essays, i. 248; ii. 170. Formerly *chints*, pl. of *chint* (N. E. D.). 'Two new pieces of *chints*;' W. Dampier, New Voy. i. 517.–Hind. *chhint*, spotted cotton cloth; cf. *chhintā*, a spot; *chhintnā*, to sprinkle. More elementary forms appear in *chhit*, chintz, also, a spot; *chhitki*, a small spot, speck; *chhitnā*, to scatter, sprinkle. Chintz is accordingly so named from the variegated patterns which appear upon it. For the above words, see Duncan Forbes, Hindustani-Eng. Dict. p. 120. The simpler form *chhit* appears in Du. *sits*, G. *zitz*, chintz; and is derived from Skt. *chitra-s*, spotted, orig. visible, clear; from *chit*, to perceive. See **Cheeta**.

CHIP, to chop a little at a time. (E.) The dimin. of *chop*. ME. *chippen*, *chyppen*. 'I *chyppe* breed, je chappelle du payn; I *chyppe* wodde, je coepelle;' Palsgrave. The sb. *chip* is a derivative from the verb, yet it happens to occur rather earlier; ME. *chippe*, a chip, Chaucer, C. T. 3746 (A 3748); spelt *chip*, Rob. of Brunne's tr. of Langtoft, p. 91. For the change of vowel from *chop* (older form *chap*),

---

cf. *clink* with *clank*, *click* with *clack*. Lye cites *for-cyppud* (presumably for *for-cippod*) from a gloss to Canticum Ezechiæ, where another gloss (in Sweet, O. E. Texts, p. 402, last line) has *forcorfen* as a gloss to *praecisa*. EFries. *kippen*, to cut. β. Cf. G. *kippen*, to clip money; Low G. *kippen*, to cut away; MDu. *kippen*, to hatch chickens (i.e. to chip eggs) Hexham; MSwed. *kippa*, as a variant of MSwed. *kappa*, to chop; Ihre (s. v. *kappa*). See **Chop**. **Der.** *chip*, sb.

CHIROGRAPHY, handwriting. (Gk.) '*Chirograph* (chiro-graphum), a sign manual, a bill of ones hand, an obligation or hand-writing;' Blount's Glossographia, ed. 1674. [The term *chirography* is, however, rather formed directly from the Gk. than from the Late L. *chirographum*, a contract, indenture, or deed.]–Gk. χειρογραφεῖν, to write with the hand.–Gk. χειρο-, for χείρ, the hand; and γράφειν, to write. The Gk. χείρ is cognate with O. Lat. *hir*, the hand; cf. Skt. *hṛ*, to seize; Curtius, i. 247. **Der.** *chirograph-er*, *chirograph-ic*, *chirograph-ist*; from the same Gk. χειρο- we have also *chiro-logy*, *chiro-mancy*, *chiro-podist*; also *chir-urgeon*, q. v.

CHIRP, to make a noise as a bird. (E.) Sometimes extended to *chirrup*, by the trilling of the *r*. ME. *chirpen*, whence the sb. *chirp-inge*. '*Chyrpynge*, or claterynge, chirkinge or chaterynge of byrdys, garritus;' Prompt. Parv. p. 76. 'To *churpe*, *pipilare*;' Levins, p. 191. This ME. *chirpen* is a mere variant of ME. *chirken*. Chaucer has: 'And *chirketh* as a sparwe;' C. T. 7386 (D 1804). We also find the form *chirmen*. 'Sparuwe cheatereð euer ant *chirmeð*' = the sparrow ever chatters and chirms; Ancren Riwle, p. 152. β. These forms, *chir-p*, *chir-k*, *chir-m*, are connected with the form *chir-*, or rather *kir*, which is an imitative word, intended to express the continual chatter-ing and chirping of birds; cf. Du. *kirren*, to coo.

CHIRURGEON, a surgeon. (F.–L.–Gk.) Now always written *surgeon*, q. v. Shak. has *chirurgeon-ly*, surgeon-like, Temp. ii. 1. 140. ME. *cirurgian*, Rob. of Glouc. p. 566; l. 11925.–OF. *cirurgien*; F. *chirurgien*, 'a surgeon;' Cotgrave.–OF. *cirurgie*; F. *chirurgie*, surgery.–Late L. *chirurgia*.–Gk. χειρουργία, a working with the hands, handicraft, art; esp. the art of surgery (to which it is now restricted). –Gk. χειρο-, for χείρ, the hand; and ἔργειν, to work, cognate with E. *work*, q. v. On Gk. χείρ, see **Chirography**. From the same source we have *chirurg-ic*, *chirurg-ic-al*, words now superseded by *surgical*. ¶ The vowel *u* is due to Gk. ου, and this again to the coalescence of o and ε.

CHISEL, a sharp cutting tool. (F.–L.) ME. *chisel*, *chysel*; Prompt. Parv. p. 76; Shoreham's Poems, p. 137. Other spellings are *scheselle*, *sceselle*, in Wright's Vocab. i. 276.–AF. *chisel*, A. Neckam, in Wrt. Vocab. i. 118, l. 8; ONorthF. *chisel*, OF. *cisel*, mod. F. *ciseau*. Cotgrave gives the verb *ciseler*, 'to carve, or grave with a chisell; also, to clip or cut with sizars.'–Late L. *cisellum*, acc. of *cisellus*, forceps (Ducange); but lit. 'a cutting instrument;' cf. Ital. *cesello*, chisel, answering to L. type *caesellum*; also L. *cis-ōrium*, a cutting instrument.–L. *-cis-um*, for *caes-um*, supine of *caedere*, to cut (cf. E. *con-cise*, *pre-cise*). See **Caesura**. And see **Scissors**. **Der.** *chisel*, verb.

CHIT (1), young of a beast, whelp, cub; also a child, brat. (E.) 'There hadde diches the yrchoun, and nurshede out litle *chittes*;' Wyclif, Isa. xxxiv. 15, where the Vulgate has: 'ibi habuit foueam ericius, et enutriuit *catulos*;' so that *chit* here means 'the young one' of a hedgehog. In modern times associated with **Chit** (2), as when applied to 'a slip' of a girl, and the like. Another form of *kit*, whence *kitten*. Cf. E. *kit-ling*. Icel. *ket-lingr*, a kitten; prov. E. *chit*, a cat (E. D. D.). See **Kitten**.

CHIT (2), a shoot or sprout. (E.) Halliwell gives: '*Chit*, to germinate; the first sprouts of anything are called *chits*.' Holland, tr. of Pliny, bk. xiii. ch. 4, has 'the root or *chit* beginneth first to put forth.' Apparently a later substitute for ME. *chithe*, from AS. *ciþ*, a germ, sprig, sprout; Grein, i. 161. Cf. Goth. *uskeian*, to produce as a shoot, from a Teut. root *kei-, to sprout, whence *ki-thoz*, m., as in AS. *ciþ*, OSax. *kið*, OHG. *kidi*, Bavarian *keid* (Schmeller), a young shoot. See **Chink** (1).

CHITTERLINGS, small intestines. (E.) Levins (1570) has *chitterling*, *chyttering*, 'omasum.' See E. D. D. Cf. Low G. *küt*, G. *kuttel*, entrails; Du. *kuit*, spawn.

CHIVALRY, knighthood. (F.–L.) ME. *chivalrie*, *chivalerye*. In K. Alisaunder, l. 1496, we have 'with al his faire *chivalrie*' = with all his fair company of knights; such being commonly the older meaning.–OF. *chevalerie*, horsemanship, knighthood.–OF. *cheval*, a horse.–L. *caballus*, a horse. See **Cavalry**. **Der.** *chivalr-ic*, *chivalr-ous* (ME. *chivalerous*, Gower, C. A. i. 89), *chivalr-ous-ly*.

CHIVE, a small onion. (F.–L.) Palsgrave has: '*Chyve*, an herbe, ciue.'–Norm. dial. *chive* (Moisy); F. *cive*, 'a scallion, or unset leek;' Cot.–L. *cæpa*, an onion.

CHLORINE, a pale green gas. (Gk.) Modern. Named from its colour. The gas was discovered in 1774; the name was conferred on it by Sir H. Davy in 1810; Engl. Cyclopædia. From Gk. χλωρός, pale green; cf. Gk. χλόη, verdure, grass; χλόος, green colour; Skt. *hari-*, green, yellow. Allied to **Yellow**, q. v. Der. *chlor-ic, chlor-ide, chlor-ite*; also *chloro-form*, where the latter element has reference to *formic* acid, an acid originally obtained from red ants; from L. *formica*, an ant.

CHOCOLATE, a paste made from cacao. (Span.—Mexican.) First in E. G., tr. of Acosta, 1604, p. 271 (bk. iv. c. 22); also in Pope, Rape of the Lock, ii. 135; Spectator, no. 54. R. also quotes from Dampier's Voyages, an. 1682 [ed. 1699, i. 60] about the Spaniards making chocolate from the cacao-nut. Todd says that it was also called *chocolata* at first, and termed 'an Indian drink;' for which he refers to Anthony Wood's Athenæ Oxonienses, ed. 1692, vol. ii. col. 416.—Span. *chocolate*, chocolate.—Mexican *chocolatl*, chocolate (Siméon). Wholly unconnected with the word *cacao*, of which the Mex. name is *cacauatl*. Prescott confuses them.

CHOICE, a selection. (F.—Teut.) Not English, so that the connexion with the verb to *choose* is but remote. ME. *chois, choys*, Rob. of Glouc. p. 111, l. 17; l. 2415.—OF. *chois*, choice.—OF. *choisir*, to choose; ONorthF. *coisir*. β. Of Teut. origin.—Goth. *kausjan*, to prove, test; causal of *kiusan*, to choose. See **Choose**.

CHOIR, a band of singers; part of a church. (F.—L.—Gk.) Also spelt *quire*. The *choir* of a church is so called because the *choir* of singers usually sat there. In the former sense, we find the spellings *queir, quer*; Barbour's Bruce, xx. 293 (l. 287 in Pinkerton's edition). We also find 'Queere, *chorus*;' Prompt. Parv. p. 420. *Quire* is in Shak. Hen. VIII, iv. 1. 90; but it is altered to *choir* in modern reprints. The spellings *quere, quire* resemble those of *frere, frier* (friar); *choir* is pedantic, and our prayer-books have *quire* still.—OF. *cuer* (Littré); MF. *choeur*, 'the quire of a church; also, a round, ring, or troop of singers;' Cotgrave.—L. *chorum*, acc. of *chorus*, a band of singers.—Gk. χορός, a dance in a ring, a band of dancers and singers; see Prellwitz. **Doublet**, *chorus*; whence *chor-al, chor-al-ly, chor-i-ster*. See **Chorus**.

CHOKE, to throttle, strangle. (E.) 'Thus doth S. Ambrose *choke* our sophisters;' Frith's Works, p. 130, col. 1. 'Chekenyd or qwerkenyd, *chowked* or querkened, *suffocatus, strangulatus*;' Prompt. Parv., p. 72. The form *cheke*, to choke, occurs in Rob. of Brunne, Handling Synne, l. 3192; see Stratmann, s. v. *cheoken*, p. 114. [Cf. *chese* as another form of *choose*.] An E. word; Somner gives 'aceocod, suffocatus,' but without a reference; yet *ā-cēocod* occurs in Ælfric, Hom. i. 216. We also find AS. *ā-cēocung*, to translate L. *rūminatio*, which the glossator hardly seems to have understood; see Voc. 179. 1. Thus the AS. form was *cēocian*, whence ME. *chēken*, regularly; also (by change of *cēo-* to *ceō-*, as in the case of E. *choose*) an ME. *chōken*, later *choken* (with short *o*, as in *chock-ful*) and subsequent regular lengthening. The Teut. base is **keuk*. Perhaps *chuck-le* and Icel. *kok*, 'the gullet,' may be related. Der. *choke-ful*.

CHOLER, the bile; anger. (F.—L.—Gk.) The *h* is a 16th century insertion, due to a knowledge of the source of the word. ME. *colere*, bile; Gower, C. A. iii. 100; bk. vii. l. 459. The adj. *colerik* is in Chaucer's Prol. 587.—OF. *colere*, which in Cotgrave is also written *cholere*, and explained by 'choler, anger, . . also the complexion or humour tearmed choler.'—L. *cholera*, bile; also, *cholera*, or a bilious complaint (Pliny).—Gk. χολέρα, cholera; χολή, bile; χόλος, bile, also wrath, anger. The Gk. χολή is cognate with L. *fel*, and E. *gall*. See **Gall** (1). Der. *choler-ic*. **Doublet**, *cholera*, as shown.

CHOOSE, to pick out, select. (E.) ME. *cheosen, chesen, chusen*; of which *chesen* is the most usual. Spelt *chus* in the imperative, St. Marharete, l. 103; *cheosen*, Layamon, ii. 210. AS. *cēosan* (pt. t. *cēas*), later form *cēosan*, to choose; Grein, i. 160. AS. *cēosan* gave ME. *chēsen* regularly; the E. *choose* is from *cēosan* (with *eō* for *ēo*).+Du. *kiezen*; G. *kiesen*; Icel. *kjósa*; Goth. *kiusan*, to choose, also to prove, test. Teut. type **keusan-*, pt. t. **kaus*. Further allied to L. *gus-tare*, to taste; Gk. γεύομαι, I taste; Skt. *jush*, to relish, enjoy—√GEUS, to choose, taste. Brugmann, i. § 602. From the same root, *choice*, q. v.; also *gust* (2), *dis-gust*.

CHOP (1), to cut suddenly, strike off. (E.) ME. *choppen*, to cut up, strike off. 'Thei *choppen* alle the body in smale peces;' Maundeville's Travels, p. 201. The imperative *chop* occurs in P. Plowman, A. iii. 253. A later form of **Chap** (1), q. v. Der. *chop*, sb.; *chopp-er*.

CHOP (2), to barter, exchange. (E.) A variant of *chap*, to barter; due to the fact that *chap*, to cut, was also pronounced as *chop*. Further, this verb to *chap* seems to have been made out of *chap-man*, sb., a merchant. See **Chapman**. Hence also the phr. 'to *chop* and change;' we say also, 'the wind *chops*,' i.e. changes, veers.

CHOPINE, a high-heeled shoe. (F.—Span.—L.) In Hamlet, ii. 2. 447. An error for *chapine*.—MF. *chopine, chappin*; Cotgrave has 'chappins, choppins, a kinde of high slippers for low women;' OF. *chapin*, Godefroy.—Span. *chapin*, a clog with a cork sole; and see

chapin in Minsheu.—Span. *chapa*, the same as E. *chape*; see **Chape**. See Notes on Eng. Etym., p. 36.

CHOPS, the jaws, cheeks; see **Chaps**.

CHORD, a string of a musical instrument. (L.—Gk.) The same word as *cord*, which spelling is generally reserved for the sense 'a thin rope.' Milton has *chords*, P. L. xi. 561. In old edd. of Shak., it is spelt *cord*.—L. *chorda*.—Gk. χορδή, the string of a musical instrument. See further under **Cord**.

CHORUS, a company of singers. (L.—Gk.) In Milton, P. L. vii. 275.—L. *chorus*.—Gk. χορός. See further under **Choir**.

CHOUGH, a bird of the crow family. (E.) ME. *chough*, in Chaucer, Parl. Foules, 345. 'The crowes and the *choughes*;' Maundeville, p. 59. The pl. *choghen* occurs about 1305, in E. E. Poems, ed. Furnivall, p. 76, l. 185. Not found in AS., which has the form *ceō*; we find 'Gracculus vel monedula, *ceo*;' Ælf. Gloss., Nomina Avium; and in O. E. Texts we find the strange forms *ciae, chyae*. The various names imitate its cry; somewhat similar are NFries. *kauke*, a chough; Du. *kaauw*, a chough, jackdaw; Dan. *kaa*, a jackdaw; Swed. *kaja*, a jackdaw. We also find AF. *chouwe*, a chough, in Wright's Vocab. i. 145, l. 16; and even OF. *choe, choue, kauwe* (Godefroy).

CHOUSE, to cheat; orig. a cheat. (Ital.—Turkish.) Now a slang word; but its history is known. It was orig. a sb. Ben Jonson has *chiaus* in the sense of 'a Turk,' with the implied sense of 'a cheat.' In his Alchemist, Act i. sc. 1, Dapper says: 'What do you think of me, That I am a *chiaus*? *Face*. What's that? *Dapper*. The Turk was [i.e. who was] here: As one would say, do you think I am a Turk?' The allusion is to a Turkish *chiaus*, or interpreter, who, in 1609, defrauded some Turkish merchants resident in England of £4000; a fraud which was notorious at the time. See Richardson, Trench's Select Glossary, and Gifford's Ben Jonson, iv. 27. Gifford copied the story (without acknowledgment) from W. R. Chetwood, Memoirs of Ben Jonson, 1756; p. 15 (N. & Q. 9 S. v. 25). The pl. *chouses* occurs in Ford's Lady's Trial, ii. 2; and the pp. *chous'd* in Butler's Hudibras, pt. ii. c. 3. l. 1010 (ed. Bell, ii. 53).—Ital. *ciaus*, an officer of the great Turk (Florio, 1611).—Turk. *chāwush*, explained as meaning 'a sergeant, a lictor; any officer that precedes a magistrate or other great man; a herald, a pursuivant, a messenger; the head of a caravan;' Richardson's Pers. Dict. p. 534.

CHRISM, holy unction, holy oil. (F.—L.—Gk.) 'Anoynted with the holye *crisme*;' Sir T. More, Works, p. 377 c. It occurs also in Gen. and Exodus, ed. Morris, l. 2458. Hence *chrisome-child*, a child wearing a *chrisome-cloth*, or cloth with which a child, after baptism and holy unction, was covered. [The *o* is merely inserted for facility of pronunciation.] The spelling *crisme* or *chrisme* is due to a knowledge of the Greek source. It was formerly also spelt *creme* or *creyme*, as in William of Shoreham's Poems, De Baptismo, l. 144 (in Spec. of Eng., ed. Morris and Skeat).—OF. *cresme, chresme*, explained by Cotgrave as 'the crisome, or oyle wherewith a baptised child is annointed.'—Late L. *chrisma*, sacred oil.—Gk. χρῖσμα, an unguent. —Gk. χρίω, I graze, rub, besmear, anoint. Der. *chrism-al*; *chrisome-cloth, chrisome-child*.

CHRIST, the anointed one. (L.—Gk.) L. *Christus*.—Gk. Χριστός, anointed.—Gk. χρίω, I rub, anoint. See **Chrism**. Hence AS. *crist*, Christ; AS. *cristen*, a Christian (Boethius, cap. i), afterwards altered to *Christian* to agree with L. *Christiānus*; also AS. *cristnian*, to christen, where the suffix *-ian* is active, so that the word is equivalent to *cristen-ian*, i.e. to make a Christian; also AS. *cristen-dōm, cristenan-dōm*, Christendom, Christianity, the Christian world; Boethius, cap. i. These words were introduced in very early times, and were always spelt without any *h* after the *c*. The *h* is now inserted, to agree with the Greek. Der. *Christ-ian* (formerly *cristen*, as explained above); *Christen-dom* (i. e. Christian-dom, as shown); *Christian-like, Christian-ly, Christian-ity, Christian-ise*; *christen* (AS. *cristnian*, explained above); *Christ-mas*, for which see below. The mod. E. long *ī* is due to F. influence.

CHRISTMAS, the birth-day of Christ. (Hybrid; Gk. *and* L.) ME. *cristesmesse*, Ayenbite of Inwyt, p. 213; *cristenmas*, Gawain, l. 985; *cristemasse*, Chaucer, C. T., Group B, l. 126. AS. *cristes mæsse*, Chron. an. 1021 (MS. D). From AS. *crist*, i.e. Christ; and AS. *mæsse* (ME. *messe*), a mass, festival. See **Mass** (2). Der. *Christmas-box*; see **Box** (2).

CHROMATIC, lit. relating to colours. (Gk.) Holland has the expression 'never yet to this day did the tragedy use *chromatick* music nor rhyme;' Plutarch, p. 1022. And Dryden speaks of 'the third part of painting, which is *chromatique* or colouring;' Parallel bet. Poetry and Painting (near the end).—Gk. χρωματικός, suited for colour.—Gk. χρωματ-, stem of χρῶμα, colour; closely related to Gk. χρώς, skin, covering, χροιά, surface; and allied to χρίειν, to rub over. Der. *chromatics*.

CHROME, the same as **Chromium**, a metal. (Gk.) Its compounds are remarkable for the beauty of their colours; hence the name, given in 1797 (N. E. D.). The word is coined from Gk. χρῶμα, colour. See above. **Der.** chrom-ic.

CHRONICLE, a record of the times. (F. – L. – Gk.) ME. cronicle (always without h after c); Trevisa, ii. 77; Prompt. Parv. p. 104. The pp. cronyculd, i.e. chronicled, occurs in Sir Eglamour, 1339. The sb. cronicler also occurs, Prompt. Parv. – AF. cronicle, Gaimar, 954; with unoriginal l; we also find ME. cronique or cronike, a word frequently used by Gower in his C. A., ll. 101, 817, &c. – OF. cronique, pl. croniques, 'chronicles, annals;' Cotgrave. – Late L. chronica, a catalogue, description (Ducange); a sing. sb., formed (mistakenly) from the Gk. plural. – Gk. χρονικά, sb. pl. annals. – Gk. χρονικός, relating to time (mod. E. chronic). – Gk. χρόνος, time. **Der.** chronicl-er; from the same source, chron-ic, chron-ic-al; also chrono-logy, chrono-meter, for which see below.

CHRONOLOGY, the science of dates. (Gk.) Raleigh speaks of 'a chronological table;' Hist. of the World, b. ii. c. 22. s. 11. Either from F. chronologie (Cotgrave), or directly from the Gk. χρονολογία, chronology. – Gk. χρονο-, for χρόνος, time; and -λογία, from λόγος, discourse, from λέγειν, to speak. **Der.** chronolog-ic, chronolog-ic-al, chronolog-ic-al-ly, chronolog-er, chronolog-ist.

CHRONOMETER, an instrument for measuring time. (Gk.) 'Chronometrum or Chronoscopium perpendiculum, a pendulum to measure time with;' Kersey's Dict. 2nd ed. 1715. – Gk. χρόνο-, stem of χρόνος, time; and μέτρον, a measure.

CHRYSALIS, a form taken by some insects. (Gk.) Given in Bailey's Dict., vol. ii. ed. 1731. – Gk. χρυσαλλίς, the gold-coloured sheath of butter-flies, a chrysalis; called in Late L. aurēlia (from aurum, gold). – Gk. χρυσ-ός, gold. Prob. of Semitic origin; cf. Heb. hārūts, gold. The pl. is properly chrysalides.

CHRYSANTHEMUM, a flower. (L. – Gk.) In Lyte's Dodoens, bk. ii. c. 30. – L. chrȳsanthemum. – Gk. χρυσάνθεμον, a marigold. – Gk. χρυσ-ός, gold; ἄνθεμον, a bloom, from ἀνθεῖν, to bloom, related to ἄνθος, a flower, a bud.

CHRYSOLITE, a stone of a yellow colour. (F. – L. – Gk.) ME. crysolyt, Allit. Poems, ed. Morris, A. 1009; with ref. to Rev. xxi. 20. – OF. crisolit. – L. chrysolithus (Vulgate). – Gk. χρυσόλιθος, Rev. xxi. 20; lit. 'a gold stone.' – Gk. χρυσό-, for χρυσός, gold; and λίθος, a stone.

CHRYSOPRASE, a kind of stone. (L. – Gk.) ME. crysopase [sic], Allit. Poems, ed. Morris, A. 1013; crisopace [sic], An Old Eng. Miscellany, ed. Morris, p. 98, l. 174; with ref. to Rev. xxi. 20. – L. chrȳsoprasus (Vulgate). – Gk. χρυσόπρασος, Rev. xxi. 20; a precious stone of a yellow-green colour, and named, with reference to its colour, from Gk. χρυσό-s, gold, and πράσον, a leek.

CHUB, a small but fat fish. (E.) 'A chubbe, bruscum;' Levins, Manip. Vocab. col. 181, l. 29. [Sometimes said to be named from its large head, but it is rather its body which is thick and fat. Besides, the resemblance to AS. cop, which signifies 'top, summit' rather than 'head,' is but slight.] **β.** Not to be separated from the adj. chubby, i.e. fat; nor (perhaps) from the ME. chuffy, fat and fleshy; see Prompt. Parv. p. 77, note 1. Marston even speaks of a 'chub-faced fop;' Antonio's Revenge, A. iv. sc. 1. **γ.** The word is, doubtless, English, though the characteristic ch has not been explained. The prov. E. chub, a log of wood (E. D. D.), may be compared with prov. Swed. (and Dan.) kubb, a block, log of a tree; Icel. tré-kumbr, tré-kubbr, a log of a tree, a chump; Norw. kubbe, a log. These words are further allied to prov. Swed. kabba, kubba, to lop, Norw. kubba, to lop. Even more remarkable are Swed. dial. kubbug, chubby, fat, plump; Norw. kubben, stumpy. See **Chump.** ¶ The word chub does not appear to have been in early use; we commonly find the fish described as 'the chevin,' which is a French term. Cotgrave gives 'Cheviniau, a chevin,' a word apparently derived from chef, the head, and properly applied rather to the 'bull-head' or 'miller's-thumb,' by which names Florio explains the Ital. capitone, derived from L. capito, large-headed, from L. caput, the head. **Der.** chubb-y (see explanation above); chubb-i-ness.

CHUCK (1), to strike gently; to toss. (F. – O. Low Ger.) We use the phrase 'to chuck under the chin.' Sherwood, in his Index to Cotgrave, writes 'a chocke under the chinne.' Chuck, to toss, was also formerly chock, as shown by a quotation from Turberville's Epitaph on Master Win Drowned (R., s. v. Chock). Imitative; but prob. suggested by F. choquer, 'to give a shock;' Cotgrave. – Du. schokken, to jolt, shake; schok, a shock, bounce, jolt; allied to E. shock and shake. See **Shock.** **Der.** chuck-farthing, i.e. toss-farthing; Sterne, Tristr. Shandy, c. 10.

CHUCK (2), to cluck as a hen. (E.) A variant of cluck. Chaucer has chuk for the sound made by a cock, when he had found a grain of corn; C. T. 15180 (B 4364). The word is clearly imitative, like **Cluck.** **Der.** chuck-le, in the sense of 'cluck;' also in the sense 'to fondle;' both of which senses appear in Dryden, as cited by Todd. Cf. Norw. kukla, to chuckle, to cluck as a hen (Ross).

CHUCK (3), a chicken; Shak. L. L. L. v. 1, 117, &c. (E.) Merely a variant of chicken, q. v. Cf. Icel. kjūklingr, a chicken.

CHUCKLE, to laugh in the throat. (E.) 'Chuckle, to laugh by fits;' Kersey's Dict. ed. 1715. The suffix -le gives it a frequentative force. The sense now refers to suppressed laughter; as if related to choke more immediately than to chuck. See **Choke, Chuck** (2).

CHUM, a familiar companion. (F. – L.) The N. E. D. quotes ' my chum Mr. Hody' from Creech, Dedication to tr. of Theocritus, in 1684. This is the earliest instance. Origin uncertain. [Some say it is a 'corruption' of chamber-fellow, which seems incredible; and the Bremen Wörterb. identifies it with Low G. kumpaan, (often shortened to kump), a familiar companion (from French), which does not seem to be possible.] Cf. prov. E. chummy, a chimney-sweep (which is from chimney); E. D. D. Surely for chimney-fellow, i.e. fireside companion (chimney = fireplace). Cf. Brand, Pop. Antiq. ii. 452; i. 232; and see Phil. Soc. Trans., 1902, p. 656.

CHUMP, a log of wood. (E.) 'Chump, a thick and short log, or block of wood;' Phillips, ed. 1706. A late formation; prob. affected by chop, clump, &c. Common in dialects. Cf. Norw. kump, a round eminence, a lump (Ross); also Icel. kumbr, as seen in tré-kumbr, a tree-chump, a log. Cf. Icel. kumbr, equivalent to kubbr, a chopping; from kubba, to chop. See **Chub.** **Der.** chump-end, i.e. thick end.

CHURCH, the Lord's house. (Gk.) In very early use. ME. chirche, chireche, cherche; also (in Northern dialects), kirk, kirke. 'Chireche is holi godes hus, . . . and is cleped on boc kiriaka i. dominicalis;' the church is God's holy house, and is called in the book kiriaka, i.e. dominical; O. Eng. Hom. ii. 23. AS. cirice, circe; the pl. ciricean occurs in Gregory's Liber Pastoralis, tr. by Ælfred; ed. Sweet, p. 5; and see O. E. Texts. Cf. OSax. kerika, kirika; Du. kerk; Dan. kirke; Swed. kyrka; Icel. kirkja; OHG. chiricha, MHG. kirche, G. kirche. **β.** But all these are borrowed from Gk. κυριακόν, a church; neut. of adj. κυριακός, belonging to the Lord, from Gk. κύριος, the Lord; or (rather) from Gk. κυριακά, pl., treated as a fem. sing. (as in other cases). Κύριος orig. signified 'mighty;' from Gk. κῦρος, might, strength. Cf. Skt. çūra-s, a hero; Zend çura, strong. Brugm. i. § 474. ¶ The etym. has been doubted, on account of the rareness of the Gk. word κυριακόν; but see the discussion in N. E. D.; and consider the high probability that the word must be Greek. **Der.** church-man; church-warden (see warden); church-yard (see yard).

CHURL, a countryman, clown. (E.) ME. cherl, cheorl; spelt cherl, Ormulum, 14788. AS. ceorl, a churl; also 'husband,' as in John, iv. 18. ✛ Du. kerel, a clown, fellow; Dan. and Swed. karl, a man; Icel. karl, a male, man (whence Scot. carle, a fellow); OHG. charal, G. karl, a man, a male (whence Charles). Teut. type *kariloz; whence Finnish karilas, an old man; Streitberg, § 97. Cf. Gk. γέρ-ων, an old man. **Der.** churl-i h, churl-ish-ly.

CHURN, a vessel for making butter. (E.) ME. chirne, chyrne. 'Chyrne, vesselle, cimbia, cumbia. Chyrne botyr, cumo;' Prompt. Parv. p. 76. AS. cyrin; earlier form cirin (printed cirm), Corpus Gloss., l. 1866. 'Sinum, cyrin;' Voc. 280, 32. ✛ Icel. kirna, a churn; Swed. kärna, M. Swed. kerna, Dan. kierne, a churn. Further relations doubtful. **Der.** churn, verb; cf. Swed. kärna, M. Swed. kerna, Dan. kierne, Du. kernen, to churn.

CHUTNEY, CHUTNY, a kind of hot relish. (Hind.) In Thackeray, Vanity Fair, c. lix. § 6. – Hind. chaṭni (Forbes, Yule).

CHYLE, juice, milky fluid. (F. – L. – Gk.) A white fluid, due to a mixture of food with intestinal juices; a medical term. In Sherwood's Index to Cotgrave we have: 'the Chylus, chyle, chile;' so that it was at first called by the Latin name, which was afterwards shortened to the F. form chyle (given by Cotgrave), for convenience. Both F. chyle and L. chȳlus are from the Gk. χυλός, juice, moisture. – Gk. χέω (for χέϝ-ω), I pour. – √GHEU, to pour; whence also E. gush, q. v. **Der.** chyl-ous, chyl-ac-e-ous.

CHYME, juice, liquid pulp. (L. – Gk.) 'Chymus, any kind of juice, esp. that of meat after the second digestion;' Kersey's Dict., 2nd ed. 1715. Afterwards shortened to chyme, for convenience; chȳmus being the L. form. – Gk. χυμός, juice, liquid, chyme. – Gk. χέω, I pour. See **Chyle.** **Der.** chym-ous.

CHYMIST, CHYMISTRY; see **Chemist.**

CI–CZ

CICATRICE, the scar of a wound. (F. – L.) In Shak. Haml. iv. 3. 62. – F. cicatrice, 'a cicatrice, a skarre;' Cot. – L. cicātricem, acc. of cicātrix, a scar. **Der.** cicatrise, verb; from MF. cicatrizer, 'to cicatrize;' Cot.

CICERONE, a guide who explains. (Ital.—L.) Used by Shenstone, died 1763 (Todd). First found in 1726.—Ital. *cicerone*, a guide, lit. a Cicero.—L. *Cicerōnem*, acc. of *Cicero*, the celebrated orator. **Der.** From the same name, *Ciceron-ian*.

CID, a title of Ruy Diaz, the national hero of Spain. (Span.—Arab.) Span. *Cid.*—Arab. *sayyid*, a lord, prince; Rich. Dict. p. 864.

CIDER, a drink made from apples. (F.—L.—Gk.—Heb.) There is no reason why it should have been restricted to apples, as it merely means 'strong drink.' ME. *sicer, cyder, syder*. In Chaucer, C. T., Group B, 3245, some MSS. have *ciser*, others *siser*, *sythir*, *cyder*; the allusion is to Judges, xiii. 7: 'cave ne uinum bibas, nec siceram.' *Sicer* is here the L. form, and *cider* the F. form.—F. *cidre*, cider; OF. *sisre, sisdre, cisdre* (Supp. to Godefroy, s. v. *Cidre*).—L. *sicera*, strong drink.—Gk. σίκερα, strong drink.—Heb. *shēkār*, strong drink.—Heb. *shākar*, to be intoxicated. Cf. Arab. *sukr, sakr*, drunkenness; Rich. Dict. p. 838. ¶ L. *sicera* became *sis'ra*; whence OF. *sisre*, later *sisdre*, with excrescent *d*; later *ci'dre* (with loss of *s*). The Wallachian *tzighir*, cider, preserves the guttural.

CIELING, CIEL; see **Ceil**.

CIGAR, a small roll of tobacco. (Span.) 'Give me a *cigar*!' Byron, The Island, c. ii. st. 19. Spelt *segar* in Twiss's Travels through Spain, A.D. 1773 (Todd).—Span. *cigarro*, a cigar. Commonly supposed to be derived from *cigarra*, a grass-hopper; from a fanciful resemblance to the insect's body. (Monlau.)

CILIARY, pertaining to the eyelids or eyelashes. (L.) In Johnson's Dict., with a quotation from Ray. Formed as if from L. **ciliāris*, adj.; from *cilium*, the eyelid.

CIMETER; see **Scimetar**.

CINCHONA, Peruvian bark. (Spanish.) Named by Linnæus, in 1742, after the countess of Chinchon, wife of the governor of Peru, cured by it A.D. 1638. Hence the name should have been *Chinchona*. *Chinchon* is a small town in New Castile (Pineda); and lies to the E.S.E. of Madrid. ¶ Distinct from *quinine*, q.v.

CINCTURE, a girdle, belt. (L.) In Milton, P. L. ix. 1117. [Not in Shakespeare, though sometimes inserted in K. John, iv. 3. 155.]—L. *cinctūra*, a girdle.—L. *cingere*, pp. *cinctus*, to gird.

CINDER, the refuse of a burnt coal. (E.) ME. *sinder, sindyr, cyndir, cyndry*. '*Syndyr* of smythys colys, *casma*;' Prompt. Parv. p. 456; '*Cyndyr* of the smythys fyre, *casuma*;' id. p. 78. AS. *sinder*, scoria, dross of iron; cf. '*Scorium, sinder*;' Wright's Vocab. i. 86; 'scoria, *sinder*;' O. E. Texts, p. 95, l. 1808. NFries. *sinder*, slag. +Icel. *sindr*, slag or dross from a forge; Dan. *sinder, sinner*, a spark of ignited iron; also, a cinder; Swed. *sinder*, slag, dross; G. *sinter*, dross of iron, scale. [The Icel. verb *sindra*, to glow or throw out sparks, is a derivative from *sindr*, not vice versâ; and therefore does not help forward the etymology.] ¶ The spelling *cinder* has superseded *sinder*, through confusion with the F. *cendre* (with excrescent *d*), which is a wholly unconnected word, from the L. acc. *cinerem*, accus. of *cinis*, dust. The F. *cendre* would have given us *cender*, just as F. *genre* has given us *gender*. See below. The correct spelling *sinder* (in use from the 8th century to the 16th) is not likely to be restored. **Der.** *cinder-y*.

CINERARY, relating to the ashes of the dead. (L.) Not in Johnson. Modern; seldom used except in the expression 'cinerary urn,' i.e. an urn for enclosing the ashes of the dead. [The word is wholly unconnected with *cinder* (see above), and never used with reference to common cinders.]—L. *cinerārius*, relating to the ashes of the dead.—L. *cinis* (decl. stem *ciner-*), dust or ashes of the dead. +Gk. κόνις, dust. Brugm. i. § 84. **Der.** *cinerar-ia*, a flower; so named from the ash-coloured down on the leaves.

CINNABAR, CINOPER, red sulphuret of mercury. (L.—Gk.—Pers.) Spelt *cynoper*; Wyclif, Jerem. xxii. 14. 'Cinnaber or Cinoper (cinnabaris), vermillion, or red lead, is either natural or artificial;' Blount's Gloss., ed. 1674.—Late L. *cinnabaris*, the Latinised name.—Gk. κιννάβαρι, cinnabar, vermilion; a dye called 'dragon's blood' (Liddell and Scott). Of oriental origin. Cf. Pers. *zinjarf, zingifrah, zinjafr*, red lead, vermilion, cinnabar; Richardson's Dict. p. 784. ¶ Distinct from *sinople*, q. v.

CINNAMON, the name of a spice. (L.—Gk.—Heb.) In the Bible, Exod. xxx. 23, where the Vulgate has *cinnamōmum*. Also in Rev. xviii. 13, where the Gk. has κινάμωμον. Both are from the Heb. *qinnāmōn*, cinnamon; a word of non-Semitic origin; cf. Malay *kāyu mānis*, sweet wood, cinnamon; from *kāyu*, wood, *mānis*, sweet (Gesenius). ¶ In ME., *cinnamon* was called *canel*, from the OF. *canelle*, which Cotgrave explains by 'our modern cannell or cannamon;' where 'cannamon' is a misprint for 'cinnamon.' This *canelle* is a dimin. of OF. *cane*, cane. See **Cane**.

CINQUE, the number five. (F.—L.) Formerly used in diceplay. See *cinq* in Chaucer, C. T., Group C, l. 653.—F. *cinq*.—L. *quinque*, five; cognate with E. *five*, q. v. **Der.** *cinque-foil* (see *foil*); *cinque-pace*, Much Ado, ii. 1. 77; see Nares.

CIPHER, the figure o in arithmetic. (F.—Span.—Arab.) ME. *siphre*, Richard the Redeles, ed. Skeat, iv. 53.—OF. *cifre* (mod. F. *chiffre*, which see in Brachet).—Span. *cifra*, denoting 'nothing.'—Arab. *ṣifr*, a cipher; Palmer's Pers. Dict. col. 402 (the initial letter being *sād*); lit. 'an empty thing;' from Arab. *ṣifr*, adj. empty.—Arab. root *safara*, to be empty; Rich. Dict. p. 937. (A translation of Skt. *çūnyam*, a cipher, neut. of *çūnya*-, empty.) *Cipher* is a doublet of *zero*, q. v. **Der.** *cipher*, verb; *de-cipher*, from L. *dē*, in the verbal sense of *un*-; cf. MF. *dechiffrer*, 'to decypher;' Cot.

CIRCENSIAN; see under **Circus**.

CIRCLE, a ring, in various senses. (F.—L.) In very early use. 'Feower *circulas*;' i.e. four circles, A. S. Chron. A. D. 1104; where *circulas* is the pl. of AS. *circul*. [The spelling *circle* is due to the influence of AF. and F. *cercle*.]—L. *circulus*, a circle, small ring, dimin. of *circus*, a circle, a ring; cognate with E. *ring*, q. v.+Gk. κρίκος, κίρκος, a ring; AS. *hring*, a ring, circle. See **Ring** (1). **Der.** *circle*, verb; *circl-et*, *circul-ar*, *circul-ar-ly*, *circul-ar-i-ty*, *circul-ate*, *circul-at-ion*, *circul-at-or*, *circul-at-or-y*; and see *circuit*, *circum-*, *circus*.

CIRCUIT, a revolving, revolution, orbit. (F.—L.) Spelt *circuite*, Golden Boke, c. 36 (R.); *circuit*, Chaucer, C. T., 1889 (A 1887).—F. *circuit*, 'a circuit, compasse, going about;' Cot.—L. *circuitus*, a going about.—L. *circum*, around (see **Circum-**); and *īre*, to go.—√ EI, to go; cf. Skt. *i*, to go. **Der.** *circuit-ous*, *circuit-ous-ly*.

CIRCUM-, prefix, around, round about. (L.) Found in ME. *circum-stance*, Ancren Riwle, p. 316; and in other words.—L. *circum*, around, about. Orig. the accus. of *circus*, a circle. See **Circus, Circle**. For compounds, see below.

CIRCUMAMBIENT, going round about. (L.) In Blount's Gloss. (1681). Sir T. Browne has *circumambiency*, Vulg. Errors, b. ii. c. 1. § 13.—L. *circum*, around; and *ambientem*, acc. of *ambiens*, surrounding. See **Ambient**.

CIRCUMAMBULATE, to walk round. (L.) In Blount's Gloss. (1674).—L. *circum*, around; and *ambulātus*, pp. of *ambulāre*, to walk. See **Ambulation**.

CIRCUMCISE, to cut around. (L.) 'Circumcised he was;' Gen. and Exodus, ed. Morris, 1200. The ME. also used the form *circumcide*, Wyclif, Gen. xvii. 11; Josh. v. 2. The latter is, strictly, the more correct form.—L. *circumcīdere*, to cut around; pp. *circumcīsus*.—L. *circum*, around; and *cædere* (pt. t. *ce-cid-i*), to cut. See **Cæsura**. **Der.** *circumcis-ion*; from the pp. stem.

CIRCUMFERENCE, the boundary of a circle. (L.) 'The cercle and the *circumference*;' Gower, C. A. iii. 90; b. vii. 188.—L. *circumferentia*, the boundary of a circle; by substituting the F. suffix -ce for the L. -tia.—L. *circumferent-*, stem of *circumferens*, pres. pt. of *circumferre*, to carry round.—L. *circum*, around; and *ferre*, to carry, bear, cognate with E. *bear*, q. v. **Der.** *circumferenti-al*.

CIRCUMFLEX, lit. a bending round. (L.) 'Accent circonflex, a *circumflex* accent;' Sherwood's Index to Cotgrave. Cotgrave himself explains the F. *accent circonflex* by 'the bowed accent.'—L. *syllaba circumflexa*, a syllable marked with a circumflex.—L. *circumflexus*, pp. of *circumflectere*, to bend round.—L. *circum*, around; and *flectere*, to bend. See **Flexible**. **Der.** From the same source, *circumflect*, vb.

CIRCUMFLUENT, flowing around. (L.) In Pope's tr. of the Odyssey, i. 230. [Milton has *circumfluous*, P. L. vii. 270; from L. adj. *circumfluus*, flowing around.]—L. *circumfluent-*, stem of *circumfluens*, pres. pt. of *circumfluere*, to flow round.—L. *circum*, around; and *fluere*, to flow. See **Fluid**.

CIRCUMFUSE, to pour around. (L.) Ben Jonson has 'circumfused light,' in An Elegy on Lady Jane Pawlet; and see Milton, P. L. vi. 778.—L. *circumfūsus*, pp. of *circumfundere*, to pour around (the L. pp. being made, as often, into an E. infinitive mood).—L. *circum*, around; and *fundere*, to pour. See **Fuse** (1).

CIRCUMJACENT, lying round or near. (L.) In Sir T. Browne, Vulg. Errors, b. ii. c. 1. § 3.—L. *circumiacent-*, stem of *circumiacens*, pres. pt. of *circumiacēre*, to lie near or round.—L. *circum*, around; and *iacēre*, to lie, properly 'to lie where thrown,' a secondary verb formed from *iacere*, to throw. See **Jet** (1).

CIRCUMLOCUTION, round-about speech. (L.) In Udal, prol. to Ephesians, fol. 125; and Wilson's Arte of Rhetorique, p. 178 (R.).—L. *circumlocūtiōnem*, acc. of *circumlocūtio*, a periphrasis. Cf. L. *circumlocūtus*, pp. of *circumloqui*, to speak in a round-about way.—L. *circum*, around; and *loqui*, to speak. See **Loquacious**. **Der.** *circumlocut-or-y*.

CIRCUMNAVIGATE, to sail round. (L.) In Fuller's Worthies of Suffolk (R.)—L. *circumnāuigāre*, pp. *-gātus*, to sail round.—L. *circum*, around; and *nāuigāre*, to sail, from *nāui-s*, a ship. See **Navigable**. **Der.** *circumnavigat-or*, *-ion*.

CIRCUMSCRIBE, to draw a line round. (L.) Sir T. More has *circumscribed*, Works, p. 121 h. Chaucer has the form *circumscrive*, Troil. and Cres. v. 1865.—L. *circumscribere*, pp. *-scriptus*, to write or draw around, to confine, limit.—L. *circum*, around; and *scribere*, to write. See **Scribe**. Der. *circumscript-ion*.

CIRCUMSPECT, prudent, wise. (L.) 'Ful *circumspecte* and wise;' Lydgate, Minor Poems, p. 15. Sir T. Elyot has *circumspection*, The Governour, b. i. c. 24.—L. *circumspectus*, prudent; orig. the pp. of *circumspicere*, to look around.—L. *circum*, around; and *specere*, to look. See **Spy**. Der. *circumspect-ly*, *-ness*, *-ion*.

CIRCUMSTANCE, detail, event. (F.—L.) In early use. ME. *circumstaunce*, Ancren Riwle, p. 316.—AF. *circumstance*, Will. Wadington, l. 10359.—L. *circumstantia*, lit. 'a standing around,' a surrounding; also, a circumstance, attribute, quality. (But the L. word was assimilated to F.; the F. form is *circonstance*.)—L. *circumstant-*, stem of *circumstans*, pres. pt. of *circumstāre*, to stand round, surround.—L. *circum*, around; and *stāre*, to stand, cognate with E. *stand*. See **Stand**. Der. *circumstant-i-al*, *-i-al-ly*, *-i-ate*.

CIRCUMVALLATION, a continuous rampart. (L.) 'The lines of *circumvallation*;' Evelyn's Diary, Aug. 3, 1641; Tatler, no. 175. Formed from a L. acc.*circumuallātiōnem*, from a supposed sb. *circumuallātio*, regularly formed from the verb *circumuallāre* (pp. *-uallātus*), to surround with a rampart.—L. *circum*, around; and *uallāre*, to make a rampart, from *uallum*, a rampart; whence also E. *wall*. See **Wall**.

CIRCUMVENT, to delude, deceive. (L.) 'I was thereby *circumuented*;' Barnes' Works, p. 222; col. 2. Formed, like verbs in *-ate*, from the pp. of the L. verb.—L. *circumuentus*, pp. of *circumuenire*, to come round, surround, encompass, deceive, delude.—L. *circum*, around; and *uenire*, to come, cognate with E. *come*, q. v. Der. *circumvent-ion*, *-ive*.

CIRCUMVOLVE, to surround. (L.) 'All these [spheres] *circumvolve* one another like pearls or onyons;' Herbert's Travels, 1665, p. 345.—L. *circumuoluere*, to surround; lit. to roll round.—L. *circum*, around; and *uoluere*, to roll. See **Revolve**, and **Volute**. Der. *circumvolut-ion*, like pp. *uolūtus*.

CIRCUS, a circular theatre. (L.) '*Circus*, a circle, or rundle, a ring; also a sort of large building, rais'd by the ancient Romans, for shews, games, &c.;' Kersey's Dict. 2nd ed. 1715. Also in Dryden, tr. of Ovid's Art of Love, b. i. l. 159.—L. *circus*, a place for games, lit. a ring, circle.+Gk. κρίκος, κίρκος, a ring; AS. *hring*, a ring. See **Ring**, **Circle**. Der. *circ-le*, q. v.; also *circensian*, with reference to games held in the *Circus maximus* at Rome, from *circ-ensis*, adj.

CIRRUS, a tuft of hair; fleecy cloud; tendril. (L.) In Kersey's Dict. 2nd ed. 1715; explained as 'a tuft or lock of hair curled;' he also explains *cirri* as having the sense of tendrils, but without using the term 'tendril.' Blount's Gloss., ed. 1674, has the adj. *cirrous*, 'belonging to curled hair.'—L. *cirrus*, curled hair. Der. *cirr-ous*.

CISSOID, a certain curve of the second order. (Gk.) Lit. 'ivy-like;' because the cusp resembles the re-entrant angles of an ivy-leaf.—Gk. κισσοειδ-ής, ivy-like.—Gk. κισσό-ς, ivy; and εἶδ-ος, form.

CIST, a chest, a sort of tomb. (L.—Gk.) Sometimes used in modern works on antiquities, to describe a kind of stone tomb. The true E. word is *chest*, which is a doublet of *cist*.—L. *cista*, a chest.—Gk. κίστη, a chest. See **Chest**; and see below.

CISTERN, a reservoir for water. (F.—L.—Gk.) ME. *cisterne*; Maundeville's Trav. pp. 47, 106; Wyclif, Gen. xxxvii. 24, Deut. vi. 11.—OF. *cisterne*.—L. *cisterna*, a reservoir for water; extended from L. *cista*, a chest, box; see above. Cf. *cav-ern*.

CISTUS, a flower; the rock-rose. (L.—Gk.) Spelt *cisthus* in Turner's Names of Herbes (1548).—L. *cistus*.—Gk. κίστος, κίσθος.

CIT, short for 'citizen,' q. v. (F.—L.) Used by Dryden, Prologue to Albion and Albanius, l. 43; Pope, Sat. of Donne, iv. 144.

CITADEL, a fortress in a city. (F.—Ital.—L.) In Milton, P. L. i. 773; Shak. Oth. ii. 1. 94. 211.—F. *citadelle*, 'a citadell, strong fort;' Cot.—Ital. *cittadella*, a small town; dimin. of *cittade*, *cittate* (mod. Ital. *città*) a city.—L. *cīuitātem*, acc. of *cīuitās*, a city.—L. *ciui-*, for *ciuis*, a citizen; with suffix *-tās*. See **City**.

CITE, to summon, to quote. (F.—L.) The sb. *citation* (ME. *citacion*) is in early use, and occurs in Rob. of Glouc. p. 473; l. 9718. The pp. *cited* is in Sir T. More, Works, p. 254 f.—F. *citer*, 'to cite, summon, . . . to alledge as a text;' Cot.—L. *citāre*, pp. *citātus*, to cause to move, excite, summon; frequentative of *ciēre*, *cire*, to rouse, excite.+Gk. κίω, I go; κίνυμαι, I hasten. Der. *citat-ion*; also *ex-cite*, *in-cite*, *re-cite*.

CITHERN, **CITTERN**, a sort of guitar. (L.—Gk.) Spelt *cithern*, 1 Macc. iv. 54 (A. V.); *cittern*, Shak. L. L. L. v. 2. 614. The same as ME. *gyterne*, P. Plowman, B. xiii. 233; from OF. *guiterne*. The *n* is merely excrescent, as in ME. *gyter-ne*. It is even found in AS. in the form *cytere*, as a gloss to L. *cithara* in Ps. lvi. 11; Spelman's A. S. Psalter.—L. *cithara*.—Gk. κιθάρα, a kind of lyre or lute. Doublet, *guitar*, q. v.

CITIZEN, an inhabitant of a city. (F.—L.) ME. *citesein*, *citizein*, *citesain*. 'A Roman *citeseyn*;' Wyclif, Acts, xxii. 28; *citezein*, Chaucer, Ho. of Fame, ii. 422. The forms *citesein*, *citezein* are Anglo-French;

the introduction of *s* or *z* was perhaps suggested by *denizen*. The AF. pl. *citezeins* occurs in Liber Albus, p. 268. Hence *citizen* stands for the AF. *citizein*.—OF. *citeain* (cf. mod. F. *citoyen*), formed from sb. *cite*, a city, by help of the suffix *-ain* < L. *-ānus*.—OF. *cite*, F. *cité* a city. See **City**.

CITRON, the name of a fruit. (F.—L.—Gk.) In Milton, P. L. v. 22. Palsgrave has: '*Citron* frute, *citron*; Citron tree, *citronnier*;' p. 205. [Cf. ME. *citir*, Prompt. Parv. p. 78, directly from L. *citrus*.]—F. *citron*, 'a citron, pome-citron;' Cot.—Late L. *citrōnem*, acc. of *citro*, a citron; an augmentative form.—L. *citrus*, an orange-tree, citron-tree; whence Gk. κίτρον, a citron. Apparently a variant of L. *cedrus*, a cedar, and thence transferred to denote an African tree (*citrus*) with wood fragrant like that of the cedar; and finally to the citron-tree.—Gk. κέδρος, a cedar; see **Cedar**. Brugmann, i. § 764. Der. *citr-ine*, Chaucer, C. T., 2169 (A 2167); *citr-ic*; *citr-in-at-ion*, id., C. T. 16284 (G 816). ¶ *Sitron-ade*, a conserve of citrons, occurs in the Earl of Derby's Expeditions (C.S.), p. 228; an. 1393.

CITY, a state, town, community. (F.—L.) In early use. ME. *cité*, Ancren Riwle, p. 228.—OF. *cite*, F. *cité*, a city.—Late L. *cīu'tātem*, an abbreviated form of L. *cīuitātem*, acc. of *cīuitās*, a community, orig. the quality of citizenship.—L. *cīui-s*, a citizen. β. Closely related to Goth. *heiwa-*, a house; see Brugm. i. § 609. See **Hind** (2). Der. *citizen*, q. v., *citadel*, q. v.; and see *civic*, *civil*.

CIVE, **CHIVE**, a sort of garlic or leek. (F.—L.) '*Chives*, or *Cives*, a small sort of onion;' also '*Cives*, a sort of wild leeks, whose leaves are us'd for sallet-furniture;' Kersey's Dict. ed. 1715. The pl. of *cive*.—F. *cive*, 'a scallion, or unset leek;' Cot.—L. *caepa*, *cēpa*, *cēpe*, an onion. ¶ The form *chive* represents an ONorthF. *chive*.

CIVET, a perfume obtained from the civet-cat. (F.—Late Gk.—Arab.) In Shak. Much Ado, iii. 2. 50; As You Like It, iii. 2. 66, 69.—F. *civette*, 'civet, also the beast that breeds it, a civet-cat;' Cot. Cf. Ital. *zibetto*; from the medieval Gk. ζαπέτιον.—Arab. *zabād*, as in Palmer's Pers. Dict. col. 317; or *zubād*, as in Rich. Dict. p. 767. (The initial letter is *zain*.)

CIVIC, belonging to a citizen. (L.) 'A *civick* chaplet;' Holland's Pliny, b. xvi. c. 4.—L. *cīuicus*, belonging to a citizen.—L. *ciuis*, a citizen. See **City**.

CIVIL, relating to a community. (L.) '*Ciuile* warre;' Udal, Matt. c. 10, fol. 66; *ciuilytye* is in Sir T. More's Works, p. 951 h.—L. *cīuilis*, belonging to citizens.—L. *cīuis*, a citizen. Der. *civil-ly*, *civil-i-ty*; *civil-ise*, Dryden, Stanzas on Oliver Cromwell, st. 17; *civil-is-at-ion*; *civil-i-an*, Wyclif's Works, ed. Arnold, i. 32, l. 22. And see **City**.

CLACHAN, a small village with a church. (Gael.) In Leslie's Hist. of Scotland (1595), i. 14, l. 22 (S.T.S.).—Gael. *clachan*, (1) a circle of stones; (2) a small rude church; (3) a small village with a church. So also Irish *clachan*, a hamlet, from OIrish *cloch*, a stone.

CLACK, to make a sudden, sharp noise. (E.) ME. *clacken*, *clakken*. 'Thi bile [bill of an owl] is stif and scharp and hoked . . Tharmid [therewith] thu *clackes* oft and longe;' Owl and Nightingale, ll. 79-81. Of AS. origin, though only represented by the pt. t. *cleacode*, with the sense 'he hurried;' Ælfric, Saints' Lives, xxiii. 493. EFries. *klakken*.+Du. *klak*, a crack; *klakken*, to clack, to crack (cf. Du. *klakkebos*, a cracker, a popgun); Icel. *klaka*, to twitter as a swallow, to chatter as a pie, to wrangle; MHG. *klac*, a crack, break, noise; cf. also F. *claquer*. β. Evidently a variant of **Crack**, q.v.; cf. also Swed. *knaka*, to crack, make a noise. Note the analogies; as *clink* : *clank* : : *click* : *clack*; and again, as *clack* : *crack* : : κλάζειν : κράζειν. Cf. *clap*, *clatter*; also Gk. γλάζειν, to sing aloud, Irish *glag-an*, the clapper of a mill.

CLAD, a form of the pp. of the verb to **Clothe**, q. v.

CLAIM, to call out for, demand. (F.—L.) ME. *clamen*, *claimen*, *cleimen*, to call for; Will. of Palerne, 4481; P. Plowman, B. xviii. 327.—OF. *claim-*, accented stem of *clamer* (*claimer*) to call for, cry out.—L. *clāmāre*, to call out; a secondary verb, formed from the base *cal-* appearing in L. *calāre*, to cry out, publish, and in the Gk. καλεῖν, to convoke, summon. Similarly, in Greek, we have κλῆσις, a call, κλητεύω, I summon.—✓KAL, to make a noise, cry out; whence also Irish *cailech*, W. *ceiliog*, a cock; Stokes-Fick, p. 73. Der. *claim-able*, *claim-ant*; and, from the same source, *clam-our*, *clam-or-ous*, &c.; see *clamour*.

CLAM (1), to adhere, as a viscous substance. (E.) Dryden has: 'A chilling sweat, a damp of jealousy Hangs on my brows, and *clams* upon my limbs;' Amphitryon, Act iii (R.) [This word is not to be confused with *clem*, to pinch, starve, as in Richardson. See *clam* and *clem* distinguished in Atkinson's Cleveland Glossary; and see **Clamp**.] The verb is due to confusion of ME. *clam*, sticky (see **Clammy**) with ME. *clemen*, AS. *clǣman*, to smear, from AS. *clām*, clay (also a plaster), Exod. ii. 14; cf. prov. Eng. *cloam*, earthenware, *clomer*, a potter. The AS. *clām* corresponds to a West Germanic form *klai-moz*, m., from a Teutonic root *klei*, which is also the base of *clay*. See **Clay**.

CLAM (2), a kind of clamp or vice. (E.) Closely allied to *clamp*.

AS. *clamm, clomm*, a bond, fetter; Grein, i. 161. Hence applied to various bivalve shell-fish, which shut tightly together.

CLAMBER, to climb with hands and feet. (Scand.) In Shak. Cor. ii. 1. 226. The *b* is sometimes absent, giving a form *clamer*. The form *clamer'd up* occurs in Harrington's *Orlando*, b. xix. st. 20 (R.); also in Palsgrave's Dict.; for quotation, see **Clasp.** ME. *clameren*; '*clameryn*, repto;' Prompt. Parv. p. 79; but we find *clambrede up* in Altenglische Legenden, ed. Horstmann, 1875; p. 194, l. 400 (about 1300). [Another ME. *clambren* meant 'to mass closely together;' see examples in Mätzner, e. g. Gawain and the Grene Knight, ll. 801, 1722; from Icel. *klambra*, to pinch closely together, to clamp, Dan. *klamre*, to grasp, grip firmly; cf. G. *klammern*, to clamp, clasp, fasten together.] β. But in the sense of 'climb,' *clamb-er* is a frequentative formed from *clamb*, pt. t. stem of AS. *climban*, to climb. Similar formations are Low G. (Bremen) *klempern*, to clamber, Low G. *klemmern* (Berghaus), NFries. *klemre*, to clamber. See **Climb.**

CLAMMY, moist and sticky, viscous. (E.) '*Clammy* as breed is, nat through baken;' Palsgrave. Earliest form *claymy* (see N. E. D.), perhaps from AS. *clām*, clay (prov. E. *cloam*); but confused with an adj. *clam*, sticky, with which cf. EFries. *klam*, Dan. *klam*, Westphal. *klamm*, clammy, moist. And see **Clam** (1), **Clamp.**

CLAMOUR, an outcry, calling out. (F. – L.) ME. *clamour*, Chaucer, C. T. 6471 (D 889). – OF. *clamur, clamour*. – L. *clāmōrem*, acc. of *clāmor*, an outcry. – L. *clāmāre*, to cry out. See **Claim.** Der. *clamor-ous, clamor-ous-ly, clamor-ous-ness.*

CLAMP, to fasten tightly; a clasp. (Du.) 'And they were ioyned close both beneth, and also aboue, with *clampes*;' Bible, ed. 1551, Exod. xxxvi. 29. '*Clamp*, in joyners work, a particular manner of letting boards one into another;' Kersey. [Not in early use, though the AS. *clom*, a bond, is a related word.] – Du. *klamp*, a clamp, cleat, heap; *klampen*, to clamp, grapple. Cf. Dan. *klampe*, to clamp, to cleat; *klamme*, a clamp, a cramp, cramp-iron; Swed. *klamp*, a cleat; Icel. *klömbr*, a smith's vice, a clamp; G. *klampe*, a clamp. β. All from Teut. **klamp*, 2nd grade of **klempan-, *klimpan-*, as seen in the MHG. *klimpfen*, to press tightly together. Related on the one hand, to E. *clip*, and on the other, to E. *cramp*; also to E. *climb* and *clamber*. γ. Compare also the form *clam*, signifying 'a bond,' represented by AS. *clom*, a bond, which occurs in the AS. Chron. an. 942. Hence, by vowel-change, Swed. *klämma*, to squeeze, wring, Dan. *klemme*, to pinch, Du. and G. *klemmen*, to pinch, prov. Eng. *clem*, to pinch with hunger.

CLAN, a tribe of families. (Gaelic.) Milton has *clans*, pl., P. L. ii. 901. And see Leslie, Hist. of Scotland, i. 56, l. 2 (S. T. S.). – Gael. *clann*, offspring, children, descendants. + Irish *cland, clann*, children, descendants; a tribe, clan; W. *plant*, children. ¶ Usually regarded as borrowed from L. *planta*, a sprout; but perhaps Celtic. See Macbain; and Stokes-Fick, p. 63. Der. *clann-ish, -ly, -ness; clan-ship, clans-man.*

CLANDESTINE, concealed, secret, sly. (F. – L.) Fuller speaks of a '*clandestine* marriage;' Holy State, b. iii. c. 22, maxim 2. – F. *clandestin*, 'clandestine, close;' Cot. – L. *clandestinus*, secret. Allied to *clam*, secretly; see Vaniček, p. 1093. From the weak grade of √KEL, to hide; see **Helm** (1). Der. *clandestine-ly.*

CLANG, to make a sharp, ringing sound. (L.) As sb., the sound of a trumpet; Shak. Tam. Shrew, i. 2. 207. We also find *clangor*, 3 Hen. VI, ii. 3. 18. The vb. *clang* occurs in 'the *clanging* horns;' Somervile, The Chase, ii. 187. – L. *clangere*, to make a loud sound, to resound; whence sb. *clangor*, a loud noise. + Gk. κλαγγή, a clang, twang, scream, loud noise; allied to κλάζειν (fut. κλάγξω), to clash, clang, make a din. An imitative word. See Fick, i. 534, 538, 540. Der. *clang-or*; and see *clank.*

CLANK, to make a ringing sound. (E.) 'He falls! his armour *clanks* against the ground;' Cowley, Davideis, b. iv. 590. 'What *clanks* were heard, in German skies afar;' Dryden, tr. of Virgil, Georg. bk. i. 638 (where the original has 'armorum *sonitum*,' l. 474). The word is prob. E., and related to *clink*; see E. D. D., and cf. *clack* with *click*. β. Otherwise, it was borrowed from Du. *klank*, a ringing sound; cf. Du. *klonk*, pt. t. of *klinken*, to clink. Cf. Pomer. *klank*, a ringing sound; and see **Clang.** The word is imitative; see **Clink.**

CLAP, to strike together rather noisily. (E.) Very common in Shak. L. L. L. v. 2. 107, &c.; and in Chaucer, C. T., 7163, 7166, (D 1581, 1584), &c. 'He ... *clapte* him on the crune' (crown of the head); Havelok, l. 1814. The AS. *clæpp-etan*, to palpitate, is a secondary form; Voc. 473. EFries. *klappen*. + Icel. *klappa*, to pat, stroke, clap the hands; Swed. *klappa*, to clap, knock, stroke, pat; Dan. *klappe*, to clap, pat, throb; Du. *klappen*, to clap, smack, prate, blab; MHG. *klaffen*, to clap, strike together, prate, babble. Cf. Gael. *clabar*, a mill-clapper, clack; *clabaire*, a loud talker (from E.). An imitative word, allied to *clatter*, q. v., and *clack*, q. v. Der. *clapp-er, clap-trap, clap-dish.*

CLARET, orig. a light red wine. (F. – L.) Properly a 'clear' or 'clarified' wine, but used rather vaguely. ME. *claret*; with a by-form *claré, clarry* (from L. *clārātum*). '*Claret*, wyne, *claretum*;' Prompt. Parv. p. 79. Spelt *clarett*, Allit. Morte Arthur, ed. Brock, l. 200; [also *claré*, Havelok, l. 1728; *clarré*, Chaucer, C. T., 1473 (A 1471).] – AF. *claret*, Charlemagne, l. 585; OF. *clairet, claret*; see Cotgrave; Late L. *clārētum*, a sweet mixed wine, clarified with honey, &c. – L. *clārus*, clear, clarified, bright. See **Clear.**

CLARIFY, to make clear and bright. (F. – L.) ME. *clarifien*, sometimes 'to glorify,' as in Wyclif, John, xii. 28, where the Vulgate has *clarifica*. – OF. *clarifier*, to make bright. – L. *clārificāre*, to make clear or bright, to render famous, glorify. – L. *clāri-*, for *clārus*, clear, bright, glorious; and *-ficāre*, to make, for *facere*, to make, in forming compounds. See **Clear** and **Fact.** Der. *clarifi-er, clarific-at-ion.* See below.

CLARION, a clear-sounding horn. (F. – L.) ME. *clarioun, claryoun*; Chaucer, Ho. of Fame, iii. 150. – OF. *claron, clairon* (Supp. to Godefroy); and prob. **clarion*; the mod. F. is *clairon*. – Late L. *clāriōnem*, acc. of *clāriō*, a clarion; so named from its clear ringing sound. – L. *clāri- = clāro-*, for *clārus*, clear. See **Clear.** Der. *clarion-et, clarin-ette*, dimin. forms.

CLARY, a labiate plant; wild sage. (Late L.) Turner, Names of Herbes (1548), explains *Orminum* as *clarie*, and gives the L. name as *sclarea*; which Lyte (tr. of Dodoens), bk. ii. c. 79, spells *scarlea*. The AS. form is *slarige, slarege*; see Cockayne's A. S. Leechdoms, iii. 345. From the Late L. *sclarea*, in Turner (as above); this form being supported by AS. *slarige*. Little is known as to this obscure word, which lost its initial *s* in E. Cf. Gk. σκληρός, dry.

CLASH, a loud noise; to make a loud noise. (E.) This seems to be an Eng. variant of *clack*; cf. EFries. *klatsen*, to crack a whip; and compare *smash* with *smack*; *crash* with *crack*; *hash* with *hack*. 'He let the speare fall, ... and the heed of the speare made a great *classhe* on the bright chapewe [hat] of steel;' Berners, tr. of Froissart, vol. ii. c. 186. See **Clack.** The word is imitative; cf. Dan. *klask*, a smack (Larsen). Also Low G. *klattsch* (Berghaus), Du. *klets*, G. *klatsch*, a clash; from the base *klat* in **Clatter,** q. v.

CLASP, to grasp firmly, fasten together. (E.) ME. *claspen, clapsen* (the *ps* and *sp* being convertible as in *wasp*; cf. prov. E. *waps*, a wasp). Spelt *clapsed, clapsud, clasped* in Chaucer, C. T. prol. 275 (Six-text print). 'I *clamer* [clamber] or *clymme* up upon a tree ... that I may *claspe* bytwene my legges and myn armes;' Palsgrave, s. v. *clamer*. The form *clap-s-en* is an extension of a base *clap-*, to embrace, of which we find traces in prov. E. *clep*, a clasp (E. D. D.), G. *klaf-ter*, a fathom, Lith. *glèb-ys*, an armful; cf. also AS. *clyppan*, to embrace, grasp, ME. *cluppen, clippen*, to embrace; and the form may have been influenced by that of *grasp*. Cf. also *clamp*, to hold tightly. See **Clip, Clamp;** and observe the connexion of *grasp* with *grab, grapple.*+Low G. and Pomeran. *klaspe*, a clamp. Der. *clasp-er, clasp-knife.*

CLASS, a rank or order, assembly. (F. – L.) Bp. Hall speaks of '*classes* and synods;' Episcopacy by Divine Right, s. 6 (R.). Blount has *classe*, Gloss. (1681); also in ed. 1656, s.v. *Classical*. Milton has *classick*, Poem on the New Forcers of Conscience, l. 7. – F. *classe*, 'a rank, order;' Cot. – L. *classem*, acc. of *classis*, a class, assembly of people, an army, fleet. – √KAL, to cry out, convoke, seen in L. *calāre, clā.nāre*; as explained above, s.v. **Claim.** ¶ Bréal regards *classis* as borrowed from Gk. κλῆσις, Dor. κλᾶσις; from the same root. Der. *class-ic, class-ic-al, class-ic-al-ly, class-ic-al-ness, class-ic-al-i-ty, class-ics*; also *class-i-fy, class-i-fic-at-ion* (for the ending *-ify* see **Clarify**).

CLATTER, to make repeated sounds; a rattling noise. (E.) As sb.; ME. *clater*, Towneley Mysteries, p. 190. As verb; ME. *clateren*, Chaucer, C. T., 2361 (A 2359). A frequentative of *clat-*, a by-form of *clak-* (E. *clack*); formed by adding the frequentative suffix *-er*; hence *clat-er-en*, to rattle. Found in AS. in the word *clatrung*, a clattering, a rattle, glossed by *crepitaculum* (Bosworth). Cf. also AS. *clador*, a rattle (O. E. Texts). EFries. *klattern*, to clatter. + Du. *klater*, a rattle; *klateren*, to rattle; Low G. *klätern*, to rattle. See **Clack, Clap.**

CLAUSE, a sentence, part of a writing. (F. – L.) In very early use. ME. *clause*, Chaucer, Tr. and Cres. ii. 728; Ancren Riwle, p. 46. – F. *clause*, 'a clause, period;' Cot. – L. *clausa*, fem. of pp. *clausus*, used in the phr. *ōrātiō clausa*, a flowing speech, an eloquent period; hence *clausa* was used alone to mean 'a period, a clause.' *Clausus* is the pp. of *claudere*, to shut, enclose, close.+OFries. *sklūta*, to shut. Brugm. i. § 795 g. See **Close,** and **Slot** (1). Doublet, *close*, adj.

CLAVICLE, the collar-bone. (F. – L.) Sir T. Browne has '*clavicles* or collar-bones;' Vulg. Errors, b. iii. c. 1. § 8. – F. *clavicules*, 'the kannel-bones, channel-bones, neck-bones, craw-bones, extending on each side from the bottome of the throat unto the top of the shoulder;' Cot. – L. *clāvicula*, lit. a small key, a tendril of a vine; dimin. of L. *clāuis*, a key, which is allied to Gk. κληίς, a key, κλείω, I shut; and to Irish *clo*, a nail, peg, W. *cloi*, to shut. Stokes-Fick, p. 103; Brugmann, i. § 633. Der. *clavicul-ar*; and see *clef, con-clave*; also *clav-ier*, the key-board of a piano or organ.

CLAW, the talon of a beast or bird. (E.) ME. *claw, clau, clow*; also *clee, cley* (from AS. *clēa*). ‘ *Claw,* or *cle* of a beste, *ungula*;’ Prompt. Parv. p. 80. ‘ Oxë gaþ o clofenn fot and shædeþþ [divides] hisë *clawwes*;’ Ormulum, 1224. AS. *clawu*, Voc. 307. 35; *clā*, Grein, i. 162; pl. *clawa, clawe*, as in ‘ clawe tōdǣlede,’ i.e. divided hoofs, Levit. xi. 3; also *clēa* (O.E. Texts); *clēo*, Grein, i. 163.+Du. *klaauw*, a paw, claw, clutch, talon, weeding-hook; *klaauwen*, to claw, scratch. [Cf. Icel. *klō*, a claw; *klā*, to scratch; Dan. *klo*, a claw; *klö*, to scratch; Swed. *klo*, a claw; *klå*, to scratch; G. *klaue*, a claw, talon.] β. *Claw* is related to *clew*, a ball of thread, q.v.; from a base *klau-*, 2nd grade of *kleu*, to draw together; cf. OHG. *kluwi*, forceps. See **Clew.**

CLAY, a tenacious earth. (E.) ME. *clai, clei, clay, cley*. ‘ What es man bot herth [earth] and *clay*;’ Hampole, Pricke of Conscience, l. 411. AS. *clǣg*, in Ælfric’s Gloss.; Voc. 146. 19.+Dan. *klæg, kleg*, clay; Du. *klei*; G. *klei.* β. Teut. type *klai-jā*, fem.; from *klai*, 2nd grade of Teut. root *klei*, to stick; cf. AS. *clām* (for *klai-moz*), earthenware; Gk. γλοι-ός, sticky matter. See **Cleave** (2) and **Glue.** Der. *clay-ey.*

CLAYMORE, a Scottish broadsword. (Gaelic.) Spelt *glaymore* by Dr. Johnson, Journey to the Western Islands (Todd); but better *claymore*, as in Jamieson’s Sc. Dict. — Gael. *claidheamh mor*, a broadsword, lit. ‘ sword-great;’ where the *dh* is no longer sounded, and the *mh* is *ñv*. The sound somewhat resembles that of *cli-* in *cli-ent*, followed by the sound of F. *env-* in *environ.* β. The Gael. *claidheamh*, a sword, is cognate with W. *cleddyf*, a sword, OIrish *claideb*; cf. also L. *clād-es*, slaughter, *per-cellere*, to strike. The Gael. *mor*, great, is cognate with W. *mawr*, great, Irish *mor*, Corn. *maur*, Breton *méur*, great, AS. *mǣre*, illustrious.

CLEAN, pure, free from stain. (E.) ME. *clenè, clǣnè* (disyllabic), Layamon, i. 376. AS. *clǣne, clēne*, clear, pure, chaste, bright; Grein, i. 162.+OSax. *clēni, cleini*; OFries. *klēn*; Du. *klein*, small; OHG. *chleini*, MHG. *kleine*, fine, excellent, small; mod. G. *klein*, small. β. The original sense seems to have been ‘ bright’ or ‘ shining’; cf. Irish *glé*, shining, pure, clean; Stokes-Fick, p. 119; Brugmann, § 196. Der. *clean-ness, clean-ly, clean-li-ness, cleanse* (AS. *clǣnsian*, Grein, i. 163).

CLEAR, loud, distinct, shrill, pure. (F.—L.) ME. *cler, cleer*. ‘ On morwe, whan the day was *clere*;’ King Alisaunder, ed. Weber, l. 1978; cf. Floriz and Blauncheflur, 280. — OF. *cler, cleir, clair*, pure, bright. — L. *clārus*, illustrious, clear, loud. β. Curtius remarks that the *r* belongs to the suffix, as in *mi-rus*, so that the word is *clā-rus.* It is probably related to *clāmāre*, to cry aloud; see **Claim.** Cf. Gk. κλη-τός, called, chosen; from καλεῖν, to call. Der. *clear*, verb; *clear-ness, clear-ance, clear-ing, clear-ly*; cf. *claret, clarify, clarion.*

CLEAT, a piece of iron used to strengthen the soles of shoes; a piece of wood or iron to fasten ropes to. (E.) The radical sense is ‘ clump,’ as applied to a firm and close mass. ME. *clete*, a wedge, also *clite*; Prompt. Parv. p. 81; (where *clote* is prob. an error for *clete*). As if from AS. *clēat* (whence *clȳte>clite*); from a Teut. type *klautoz*, m.; clearly seen in Du. *kloot*, a ball, G. *klosz*, a clod, lump, ball; the weak grade *klut-* appears in **Clot,** q.v.

CLEAVE (1), strong verb, to split asunder. (E.) The pt. t. is *clave*, Ps. lxxviii. 15 (A.V.), sometimes *clove*; the pp. is *cloven*, Acts, ii. 3, sometimes *cleft* (Micah, i. 4), but the latter is unoriginal. ME. *cleoven, cleven, kleven*. ‘ Ful wel kan ich *kleuen* shides;’ Havelok, l. 917. AS. *clēofan* (pt. t. *clēaf*, pp. *clofen*), Grein, i. 163.+Du. *klieven*; Icel. *kljūfa* (pt. t. *klauf*, pp. *klofinn*); Swed. *klyfva*; Dan. *klöve*; OHG. *chlioban*, G. *klieben.* Teut. type *kleuban-*, pt. t. *klaub*, pp. *kluŏanoz.* β. Perhaps related to Gk. γλύφειν, to hollow out, to engrave; L. *glūbere*, to peel. From √GLEUBH; Brugmann, i. § 762 (1). Der. *cleav-age, cleav-er*; also *cleft*, q.v. [But not *cliff*.]

CLEAVE (2), weak verb, to stick, adhere. (E.) The true pt. t. is *cleaved*, pp. *cleaved*; but by confusion with the word above, the pt. t. most in use is *clave*, Ruth, i. 14 (A. V.) Writers avoid using the pp., perhaps not knowing what it ought to be. However, we find pt. t. *cleaved* in Job, xxix. 10; and the pp. *cleaved*, Job, xxxi. 7. ME. *cleovien, clivien, clevien, cliven.* ‘ Al Egipte in his wil *cliueð*;’ Genesis and Exodus, ed. Morris, l. 2384. ‘ *Cleouieð* faste;’ Layamon, i. 83. AS. *clifian, cleofian*, Grein, i. 163; a weak verb, pt. t. *clifode*, pp. *clifod.* +Du. *kleven*, to adhere, cling; Swed. *klibba sig*, to stick to; OHG. *chleben*, G. *kleben*, to cleave to. All from Teut. base *klib-*, weak grade of Teut. strong verb *kleiban-*, pt. t. *klaib*, pp. *klibanoz.* Traces of the strong form appear in AS. *ōð-clifan*, to cleave to; cf. also OHG. *kliban*, MHG. *klīben*, to cling to, take root; Icel. *klīfa*, to climb, viz. by grasping the tree; Du. *klijf*, ivy. See **Climb.** ¶ Observe the complete separation between this word and the preceding one; all attempts to connect them are fanciful. But we may admit a connexion between E. *cleave* (2) and Gk. γλία, γλοία, L. *glūten*, glue. See **Clay** and **Glue.**

CLEEK, a large hook or crook, used by fishermen, and in playing golf. (E.) From *cleek*, verb, to clutch or grasp; a Northern form allied to ME. *clechen* (pt. t. *clahte*), to seize firmly, grasp with hands or claws; Stratmann, p. 121. AS. form (not found) *clǣc(e)an*, pt. t. *clǣhte.* Apparently from Teut. base *klai-, klei-*; see **Clay** and **Cleave** (2); and not related to **Clutch.**

CLEF, a key, in music. (F.—L.) Formerly also spelt *cliff.* ‘ Whom art had never taught *cliffs*, moods, or notes;’ Ford, Lover’s Melancholy, A. i. sc. 1. — F. *clef*, ‘ a key, . . . a *cliffe* in musick;’ Cot. — L. *clāuem*, acc. of *clāuis*, a key. See **Clavicle.**

CLEFT, CLIFT, a fissure, a crack. (Scand.) Spelt *clift*, Exod. xxxiii. 22 (A.V.); some copies have *cliffs* for *clifts*, Job, xxx. 6. ‘ *Clyff, clyft*, or ryfte, scissura, rima,’ Prompt. Parv. p. 81; *clifte* in Chaucer, tr. of Boethius, bk. 4. pr. 4, l. 198. And in Cursor Mundi, 19842. The form *cliff* is corrupt; the final *t* distinguishes the word from *cliff.* Apparently Scandinavian. — Icel. *kluft*, a cleft; Swed. *klyft*, a cave, den, hole; Dan. *klöft*, a cleft, chink, crack, crevice. β. The Icel. *kluft* is from the weak grade of *kljūfa*, to cleave, split. See **Cleave** (1). ¶ The mod. spelling *cleft* is due to the feeling that the word is connected with *cleave*, so that the word is now thoroughly English in form, though originally Scandinavian (unless there was an AS. *clyft*).

CLEMATIS, a kind of creeping plant. (Gk.) ‘ *Clema* or *Clematis*, a twig, a spray; a shoot, or young branch: among herbalists, it is more especially applied to several plants that are full of young twigs;’ Kersey’s Dict. 2nd ed. 1715. — Late L. *clēmatis*, which is merely the Gk. word in Latin letters. — Gk. κληματίς, brushwood, a creeping plant; dimin. from κλήματ-, stem of κλῆμα, a shoot or twig. — Gk. κλάειν, to break off, to lop or prune. Brugm. ii. § 661.

CLEMENT, mild, merciful. (F.—L.) Rare; in Cymb. v. 4. 18; and in Cath. Angl. (1483). — F. *clement*, ‘ clement, gentle, mild;’ Cot. — L. *clēmentem*, acc. of *clēmens*, mild. Der. *clement-ly, clemenc-y* (*clemencie*, Gascoigne, i. 52, The Recantation of a Lover, l. 9; from L. *clēmentia*, mildness).

CLENCH, to fasten; see **Clinch.**

CLEPSYDRA, a water-clock. (L.—Gk.) ‘ They measured the hours . . in glasses called *clepsydræ*;’ Sir T. Browne, Vulg. Errors, bk. v. c. 18, § 2. — L. *clepsydra.* — Gk. κλεψύδρα. — Gk. κλεψ-, for κλέπτειν, to steal; and ὕδωρ, water; from the constant flow of the water.

CLERESTORY. (F.—L.) ‘ And all with *clere-story* lyghtys;’ Arnold’s Chron. ed. 1811, p. li. ‘ Englasid glittering with many a *clere story*;’ Skelton, Garland of Laurel, 479. It might as well be spelt *clear story*, since *clere* is merely the old spelling of *clear.* The pl. *cleare stories* occurs in the Will of Hen. VI; Nichols, Royal Wills, p. 303. So called because it is a story furnished with windows, rather than because ‘ it rises *clear* above the adjoining parts of the building,’ as sometimes said. ‘ The *triforium*, or series of arches between the nave and *clerestory* are called *le blyndstoris* in the life of Bp. Cardmey;’ Oxford Gloss. p. 57; quoted in Bury Wills, ed. Tymms, note on p. 253. See **Clear** and **Story** (2).

CLERGY, the ministry, body of ministers. (F.—L.—Gk.) ME. *clergie*, frequently used in the sense of ‘ learning;’ [like F. *clergé*, from Late L. *clēricātus*, clerkship]; but also with the modern meaning, as: ‘ Of the *clergie* at London . . . a conseil he made;’ Rob. of Glouc. p. 563, l. 11812. — OF. *clergie*, formed as if from a Late L. *clēricia*, a form not given in Ducange. — Late L. *clēricus*, a clerk, clergyman. — Gk. κληρικός, belonging to the clergy, clerical. — Gk. κλῆρος, a lot, allotment, portion; in eccl. writers, the clergy, because the Lord is their inheritance, Deut. xviii. 2; cf. Gk. τῶν κλήρων, A.V. ‘ God’s heritage,’ in 1 Pet. v. 3; but more especially Acts i. 17, where the lit. sense is ‘ the lot of this ministry.’ Moisy has the mod. Norman *clergi*, the clergy. Der. *clergy-man.*

CLERK, a clergyman, a scholar. (F.—L.—Gk.) Orig. a clergyman; ME. *clerc, clerk*, Ancren Riwle, p. 318. AS. *clerc*, a priest, A.S. Chron. an. 963. Either from OF. *clerc*, or immediately from L. *clēricus*, by contraction. — Gk. κληρικός, belonging to the clergy, clerical, one of the clergy. See further above. Der. *clerk-ship*; and, from the L. *clēric-us*, we have *cleric, cleric-al.*

CLEVER, skilful, dexterous. (E.) Rare in early use. ‘ As *cleverly* as th’ ablest trap;’ Butler, Hudibras, pt. i. c. 1. l. 398 (first published A.D. 1663). It is not easier to find an earlier example. Sir T. Browne cites *clever* as a Norfolk word, in his Tract VIII (Works, ed. Wilkins, iv. 205); see my edition of Ray’s Collection of Eng. Dialectal Words, Eng. Dial. Soc. pp. xv, xvii. The Norfolk word is commonly pronounced ‘klav-ur,’ and is used in many various senses, such as ‘ handsome, good-looking, healthy, tall, dexterous, adroit’ (Nall); also, ‘ kind, liberal’ (Wilkin). β. Mr. Wedgwood ingeniously suggests a connexion with ME. *cliver* or *clivre*, a claw, Owl and Nightingale, ll. 78, 84, 270; in this case ‘ clever’ would have meant originally ‘ ready to seize’ or ‘ quick at seizing,’ and the connexion would be with Lowl.Scot. *clever* (to climb), and *cleave* (2), to adhere. In accordance with this, the word *cliver* once occurs (in the Bestiary, l. 221, pr. in An Old Eng. Miscellany, ed. Morris) as an adj. with the apparent sense of ‘ ready to seize,’ or ‘ expert with the claws;' cf. ME. *clivers*, claws, clutches, from AS. *clifer*, a claw. So also, in Dunbar, Fenyeit Freir, 86, we find : 'Scho was so *cleverous* of her cluik,' she was so skilful to seize in her clutch. The base *clif-* is the same as that of the AS. *clif-ian*, to cleave to; see **Cleave** (2). **+** EFries. *klüfer*, clever; Dan. dial. *klöver*, *klever* (Molbech); all for **klifer*, **kliver*; the Norw. *kliva*, to climb, becoming *klyve* in Danish. Kalkar has MDan. *klever*, sprightly, wily; so that the E. word may be of Scand. origin; cf. Dunbar's *clever-ous*. ¶ It is remarkable that *clever* practically took the place of ME. *deliver*, nimble, Chaucer, prol. 84. But the words are not connected. **Der.** *clever-ness*.

CLEW, CLUE, a ball of thread. (E.) The orig. sense is 'a mass' of thread; then a thread in a ball, then a guiding thread in a maze, or 'a clue to a mystery;' from the story of Theseus escaping from the Cretan Labyrinth by the help of a ball of thread. Thus Trevisa, ii. 385: '3f eny man wente thider yn withoute a *clewe* of threde, it were ful harde to fynde a way out.' Cf. 'a *clue* of threde;' Gower, C. A. ii. 306; b. v. 5343. AS. *cliewen*, *clȳwen*, a ball of thread; by loss of the final *n*. We find 'glomus, *clȳwen*;' Ælfric's Gloss., ed. Somner, Nomina Vasorum. And the dat. *cliwene* (*cliewene*) occurs in Gregory's Pastoral, sect. xxxv; ed. Sweet, p. 240.**+** Du. *kluwen*, a clew; whence *kluwenen*, to wind on clews (cf. E. to *clew* up a sail); OHG. *chliuwa*, *chliuwi*, *chliwe*, MHG. *kliuwe*, a ball, ball of thread; and cf. G. *knäuel* (for **kläuel*), a clew. Allied to L. *glu-ere*, to draw together, *glo-mus*, a clew; from √GLEU (Teut. **kleu-*), to draw together. Cf. Skt. *glau-*, a lump (Macdonell). See **Claw.** **Der.** *clew*, verb (Dutch).

CLICK, to make a quick, light sound. (E.) Rather oddly used by Ben Jonson : 'Hath more confirm'd us, than if heart'ning Jove Had, from his hundred statues, bid us strike, And, at the stroke, *click'd* all his marble thumbs;' Sejanus, ii. 2. EFries. *klikken*. An imitative word, derived, as expressing a slighter sound, from *clack*, by the thinning of *a* to *i*. This is clearly shown by the Du. *klikklak*, the clashing of swords, and *klikklakken*, to clash together, lit. 'to click-clack.' See **Clack,** and **Clink.**

CLIENT, one who depends on an adviser. (F.–L.) ME. *client*, Gower, C. A. i. 284, bk. iii. 160; P. Plowman, C. iv. 396.–F. *client*, 'a client or suitor;' Cot.–L. *clientem*, acc. of *cliens*, a client, a dependent on a patron. *Cliens* represents *cluens*, one who hears, i.e. one who listens to advice; pres. pt. of *cluere*, to hear, listen. The L. *cluere* is cognate with Gk. κλύειν, to hear, and Skt. *çru*, to hear.– √KLEU, to hear; whence also E. *loud*. Curtius, i. 185. See **Loud.** **Der.** *client-ship*.

CLIFF, a steep rock, headland. (E.) ME. *clif*, *clef*, *cleve*. Spelt *clif*, Layamon, i. 82, where the later text has *clef*; spelt *cleue*, id. i. 81 (later text). AS. *clif*, a rock, headland; Grein, i. 164.**+**Du. *klif*, a brow, cliff; Icel. *klif*, a cliff; also *kleif*, a ridge of cliffs. We also find G. *klippe*, Du. *klip*, a crag, Dan. *klippe*, Swed. *klippa*, a crag, rock. ¶ Cf. AS. *clif*, cliff, with *clifian*, to cleave to; Icel. *klif* with Icel. *klifa* (pt. t. *kleif*), to climb. The connexion is probable.

CLIMACTER, a critical time of life. (F.–Gk.) Used by Sir T. Browne, Vulg. Errors, b. iv. c. 12. § 18. Now only used in the derivative adj. *climacter-ic*, often turned into a sb. 'This Is the most certain *climacterical* year;' Massinger, The Old Law, Act i. sc. 1. 'In the year of his *climacteric*, sixty-three;' Sir T. Herbert, Trav. (1665), pp. 337-8.–MF. *climactere*, 'climatericall (*sic*); whence *l'an climactere*, the climatericall year; every 7th, or 9th, or the 63 yeare of a man's life, all very dangerous, but the last, most;' Cot. – Late L. *climactēr*, borrowed from Gk.– Gk. κλιμακτήρ, a step of a staircase or ladder, a dangerous period of life.– Gk. κλῖμαξ (stem κλίμακ-), a ladder, climax; with agential suffix *-τηρ*. See **Climax.** **Der.** *climacter-ic*.

CLIMATE, a region of the earth. (F.–Gk.) See *Climate* in Trench, Select Glossary. ME. *climat*; Chaucer's treatise on the Astrolabe, ii. § 39, l. 18; Maundeville, p. 162; Gower, C. A. i. 8; prol. 137.–OF. *climat* (F. *climat*), a climate.–Late L. *climat-*, stem of *clima*. – Gk. κλίμα, gen. κλίματος, a slope, a zone or region of the earth, climate.– Gk. κλίνειν, to lean, slope; cognate with E. *lean*. See **Lean** (1). **Der.** *climat-ic*, *climat-ic-al*, *climat-ise*. Doublet, *clime*.

CLIMAX, the highest degree. (Gk.) Puttenham has *clymax*; Arte of E. Poesie, iii. 19; ed. Arber, p. 217. '*Climax*, a ladder, the step of a ladder, a stile; in Rhetorick, a figure that proceeds by degrees from one thing to another;' Kersey's Dict. 2nd ed. 1715.–L. *climax*.– Gk. κλῖμαξ, a ladder, staircase; in rhetoric, a mounting by degrees to the highest pitch of expression, a climax.– Gk. κλίνειν, to lean, slope, incline; cognate with E. *lean*. See **Lean** (1).

CLIMB, to ascend by grasping. (E.) Very common. ME. *climben*, Layamon, i. 37; pt. t. 'he *clomb*,' Ancren Riwle, p. 354; 'the king . . . *clam*,' Rob. of Glouc. p. 333. AS. *climban*, pt. t. *clamb*, pl. *clumbon*; A.S. Chron. an. 1070. We find also the derivative *clymmian*, Grein, i. 164.**+**Du. *klimmen*; OHG. *chlimban*, MHG. *klimmen*, to climb. **β.** The original sense is 'to grasp firmly,' as in climbing

a tree; and the connexion is with Icel. *klīfa*, to climb, AS. *clifian*, to cleave to. Streitberg, § 203. See **Cleave** (2), and **Clamber.**

CLIME, a region of the earth. (Gk.) In Shak. Rich. II. i. 3. 285.–L. *clima*, a climate.–Gk. κλίμα, a climate. **Doublet,** *climate*. See **Climate.**

CLINCH, CLENCH, to rivet, fasten firmly. (E.) ME. *clenchen*. '*Clenchyn*, retundo, repando;' Prompt. Parv. p. 80. 'I *clenche* a nayle;' also 'I *clynche* nayles;' Palsgrave. 'The cros was brede, whon Crist for us theron was *cleynt*,' i.e. fastened; Legends of the Holy Rood, ed. Morris, p. 138. The pp. *cleynt* points to an infin. *clenchen*, just as the pp. *dreint* is from *drenchen*, to drown. We also find ME. *clenken*, to strike smartly, Allit. Morte Arthure, l. 2113. This is the causal of *clink*, a by-form of *cling*, and means 'to make to clink,' 'to make to stick fast (see below).**+**Du. *klinken*, to clink, to rivet, *klink*, a blow, rivet; Dan. *klinke*, a latch, rivet, *klinke*, to clinch, to rivet; Swed. *klinka*, a latch, also, to rivet; OHG. *chlankhan*, *clenkan*, MHG. *klenken*, to knot together, knit, tie; MHG. *klinke*, a bar, bolt, latch. Teut. type **klankjan-* (>**klenkan*, **klinkan*), causal of a type **klinkan-* (pt. t. **klank*), as seen in EFries. and Low G. *klinken*, *klingen*, to cling, to become drawn, to shrivel up. See **Cling.** Cf. ME. *clengen*, causal of *clingen* (Stratmann). **Der.** *clinch-er*.

CLING, to adhere closely. (E.) ME. *clingen*, to become stiff; also, to adhere together. 'In cloddres of blod his her was *clunge*,' i.e. his hair was matted; Legends of the Holy Rood, ed. Morris, p. 142. AS. *clingan* (pt. t. *clang*, pp. *clungen*), to shrivel up by contraction, to dry up; Grein, i. 164. Cf. Dan. *klynge*, to cluster, *klynge*, a cluster; Swed. *klänge*, a tendril, a clasper; OHG. *clunga*, a clew.

CLINICAL, relating to a bed. (F.–L.–Gk.) Sometimes *clinick* occurs, but it is rare; it means one lying in bed; 'the *clinick* or sick person;' Bp. Taylor, Sermons, Of the Office Ministerial; see too his Holy Dying, s. 6. c. 4.–F. *clinique*, 'one that is bedrid;' Cot.–L. *clinicus*, a bedrid person (St. Jerome); a physician that visits patients in bed (Martial). – Gk. κλινικός, belonging to a bed; a physician who visits patients in bed; ἡ κλινική, his art. – Gk. κλίνη, a bed.–Gk. κλίνειν, to slope, to lie down. See **Lean** (1).

CLINK, to tinkle, make a ringing noise. (E.) Intrans. : 'They herde a belle *clinke*;' Chaucer, C. T., 12598 (C 664). Also trans. : 'I shal *clinken* yow so mery a belle,' id. 12925 (B 1186). EFries. *klinken*; pt. t. *klunk* (orig. *klank*), pp. *klunken*, to clink.**+**Du. *klinken*, to sound, tinkle (pt. t. *klonk*; pp. *geklonken*); Dan. *klinge*, to sound, jingle, *klingre*, to jingle (frequentative); Swed. *klinga*, to ring, clink, tingle; Icel. *kling*, interj. ting! tang! *klingja*, to ring. *Clink* is the nasalized form of *click*, and the thinner form of *clunk*. As *click* : *clack* :: *clink* : *clank*. **Der.** *clink-er*.

CLINKER, a cinder, or hard slag. (Du.) '*Clinkers*, those bricks that by having much nitre or salt-petre in them (and lying next the fire in the clamp or kiln) by the violence of the fire, run and are glazed over;' Bailey's Dict. vol. ii. ed. 1731. Evelyn, in his Diary, Aug. 19, 1641, refers to the *clincars*, or sun-baked bricks, with which Amsterdam was paved. Not in early use, but borrowed from Dutch; however, the word simply means 'that which clinks,' from the sonorous nature of these hardened bricks, which tinkle on striking together.–MDu. *klinckaert*, 'a hard and sounding bricke,' Hexham; Du. *klinker*, that which sounds, a vowel, a hardened brick; from *klinken*, to clink; cf. Dan. *klinke*, a hard tile. See above.

CLINKER-BUILT, applied to boats in which over-lapping boards are clinched together with copper nails. (E.) From *clinker*, a clinch-nail; which is from *clink*, to fasten together by a blow, a Northern verb of which *clinch* is the usual form; see **Clinch.**

CLINQUANT, glittering. (F.–Du.) In Shak. Hen. VIII, i. 1. 19. Said of spangles; lit. 'tinkling.'–OF. *clinquant* (Godefroy); pres. pt. of *clinquer*, to clink.–Du. *klinken*, to clink; see **Clink.**

CLIP (1), to shear, to cut off. (Scand.) ME. *clippen*, to cut off, shear off; Ormulum, ll. 1189, 4106, 4142.–Icel. *klippa*, to clip, cut the hair; Swed. *klippa*, to clip, shear, cut; Dan. *klippe*, to clip, shear. Cf. also NFries. *klappe*, *kleppe*, to clip, shear; which suggests a connexion with *clap*; with reference to the clicking of the shears. **Der.** *clipp-er*, *clipp-ing*.

CLIP (2), to embrace, to grip. (E.) In Shak. Coriolanus, i. 6. 29. ME. *clippen*, Chaucer, C. T., E 2413; *cluppen*, Ancren Riwle, p. 424. AS. *clyppan*; Grein, i. 164. Teut. type **kluppjan-*; cf. OHG. *kluppa*, forceps, tongs; from the weak grade of the Teut. **klæp* = Idg. **gleb*, to embrace, as in Lith. *gleb-ys*, an armful, OHG. *kläfter*, a cord of wood.

CLIPPER, a fast horse, a fast ship. (Du.) Modern; modified from Du. *klepper*, a steed.–Du. *kleppen*, to clap; with reference to the noise of hoofs. See **Clap.** Cf. Notes on E. Etym. p. 38.

CLIQUE, a gang, set of persons. (F.–Du.) Modern. From F. *clique*, 'a set, coterie, clique, gang;' Hamilton and Legros, French Dict. And see Hatzfeld.–MF. *cliquer*, to click, clack, make a noise; Cot.–Du. *klikken*, to click, clash; also, to inform, tell; whence *klik-*

ker, a telltale. [It probably meant a noisy gang, a set of talkers; cf. F. *claqueur*, a clapper of hands.] The Du. word is cognate with E. *click*. See **Click**.

CLOAK, CLOKE, a loose upper garment. (F.—C.) *Cloke* in S. Matt. v. 40 (A. V.). ME. *cloke*, Chaucer, C. T. prol. 157; Layamon, ii. 122 (later text). — OF. *cloke*, *cloque*, also *cloche*; Godefroy, s. v. *cloche*. — Low L. *cloca*, a bell; also, a horseman's cape, because its shape resembled that of a bell; see Chaucer, Prol. 263. See further under **Clock**, which is its doublet.

CLOCK, a measurer of time. (F.—C.) ME. *clok*, *clokke*, Chaucer, C. T., 4434 (B 14). [Cf. AS. *clugga*, a bell (Lat. *campāna*), Ælfred's tr. of Beda, iv. 23 (Bosworth).] The *clock* was so named from its striking, and from the bell which gave the sound. 'A great clock put up at Canterbury, A.D. 1292;' Haydn, Dict. of Dates.— AF. *cloke*, a bell, Gaimar, l. 2728; ONorthF. *cloque*, OF. and F. *cloche*, a bell; cf. MDu. *klocke* (Du. *klok*), a bell.—Low L. *clocca*, a bell. **β.** The origin of the word is disputed, and some difficulty is caused by its being so widely spread; still, the Celtic languages give a clear etymology for it, which is satisfactory. Cf. Irish *clog*, a bell, a clock; *clogau*, a little bell; *clogaim*, I ring or sound as a bell; OIrish *cloc*, a bell; W. and Corn. *cloch*, a bell. **γ.** In other languages we find Low L. *clocca*, *cloca*, a bell (whence F. *cloche*), Du. *klok*, a bell, clock; Icel. *klukka*, old form *klocka*, a bell; Dan. *klokke*, a bell, clock; Swed. *klocka*, a bell, clock, bell-flower; Du. *klok*, a clock, orig. a bell; G. *glocke*, a bell, clock; all, apparently, of Celtic origin. Celtic types **klukkos*, **klukkā*; Stokes-Fick, p. 103. Cf. Gael. *clag*, a bell; Gk. κλάζειν, to clash. See **Clang**. **Der.** *clock-work*.

CLOD, a lump or mass of earth. (E.) A parallel form to *clot*, which has much the same meaning. 'Clodde, gleba;' Prompt. Parv. p. 83. Pl. *cloddes*, Palladius on Husbandry, bk. ii. st. 3; bk. xii. st. 2. [But, earlier than about A.D. 1400, the usual spelling is *clot*. 'The *clottis* therof ben gold,' Lat. glebæ illius aurum; Wyclif, Job, xxviii. 6.] But AS. *clod*- occurs in compounds, as in *clod-hamer*, a fieldfare; and *Clod*- in proper names; cf. W. Flem. *klodde*, a ball (as of tow), De Bo; Swed. dial. *klodd*, a lump of snow or clay. Teut. type **klu-do-*, from the weak grade of **kleu-*, to stick together. See **Clew, Cloud**. **Der.** *clod-hopper* (a hopper, or dancer, over clods); *clod-poll*, *clod-pate*. ¶ Irish and Gael. *clod* are borrowed from English.

CLOG, a hindrance, impediment. (Scand.) The verb *to clog* is from the sb., not *vice versâ*. The sense of 'wooden shoe' is merely an extension of the notion of block, clump, or clumsy mass. ME. *clogge*, as in : 'Clogge, truncus,' i.e. a block; Prompt. Parv., p. 83. 'Clogge, billot;' Palsgrave. The final hard *g* makes a Scand. origin probable. Cf. Norw. *klugu*, a hard knotty log of wood (Ross). ¶ The Lowl. Sc. *clag*, a clot, and *claggy*, covered with adhesive mire, were associated with *clog* to some extent in late uses, but are of different origin; they appear to be connected with *clay*. **Der.** *clog*, verb.

CLOISTER, a place of religious seclusion. (F.—L.) ME. *cloister*, *cloistre*; Chaucer, C. T. prol. 181.—AF. *cloister*, Langtoft, i. 96; OF. *cloistre* (mod. F. *cloître*).—L. *claustrum*, a cloister, lit. 'enclosure.' —L. *claudere*, pp. *clausus*, to shut in, enclose. See **Close** (1). **Der.** *cloistr-al*, *claustr-al*, *cloister-ed*.

CLOKE, old spelling of **Cloak**, q. v.

CLOSE (1), to shut in, shut, make close. (F.—L.) In early use. ME. *closen*; the pt. t. *closed*, enclosed, occurs in Havelok, l. 1310. The verb was formed from the pp. *clos* of the French verb, or from other parts of the verb in which the stem *clos*- occurred; cf. OF. *clos*, pp. of OF. *clore*, to enclose, shut in.—L. *claudere* (pp. *clausus*), to shut, shut in. See **Clause**.

CLOSE (2), adj., shut up, confined, narrow. (F.—L.) In Allit. Poems, ed. Morris, i. 183. Also as sb., ME. *clos*, *cloos*, *close*, an enclosed place; Rob. of Glouc. p. 7, l. 154.—OF. *clos*; see above. **Der.** *close-ly*, *close-ness*, *clos-ure*; *clos-et*, q. v.

CLOSET, a small room, recess. (F.—L.) 'The highere *closet* of hir hows,' Wyclif, Tobit, iii. 10; Chaucer, Troil. and Cres. ii. 1215. — OF. *closet*, in Godefroy, who gives : 'Closet, Clozet, s.m., petit clos, petit enclos.' A dimin. from OF. *clos*, an enclosed space, a close, by affixing the dimin. suffix *-et*. *Clos* was orig. the pp. of OF. *clore*, to shut, L. *claudere*; see above. **Der.** *closet*, verb.

CLOT, a mass of coagulated matter. (E.) Still in use, and now somewhat differentiated from *clod*, though in ME. the senses of the two words differed but little. ME. *clot*, *clotte*; 'a *clot* of eorthe' = a clod of earth, Ancren Riwle, p. 172. 'Stony *clottes*,' Trevisa, ii. 23, where the Lat. text has 'globos saxeos.' The orig. sense is 'lump.' AS. *clott*, *clot* (rare); 'Massa, of clyne *vel* clottum;' Haupt's Zeitschrift, ix. 488; '*massa*, clyne, clotte;' Napier's OE. Glosses.+MDu. *klot*, 'a clod of earth,' Hexham; allied to MDu. *kluyte*, 'a clod of earth,' id.; and to EFries. *klute*, *klüte*, a lump; G. *klotz*, a log. Teut. type **klut-to-*, from the weak grade of Teut. base **kleut-*. See **Cleat, Clout, Cluster, Clew**.

CLOTH, a garment, woven material. (E.) ME. *cloth*, *clath*: Ancren Riwle, p. 418; Layamon, ii. 318. AS. *clāð*, a cloth, a garment; Grein, i. 162.+Du. *kleed*, clothes, dress; G. *kleid*, a dress, garment. **β.** Origin unknown, but evidently a Teutonic word. The Icel. *klæði*, Swed. *kläde*, Dan. *klæde*, cloth, do not exactly correspond in form. **Der.** *cloth-es*, from AS. *clāðas*, the pl. of *clāð*; also *clothe*, verb, q. v.

CLOTHE, to cover with a cloth. (E.) ME. *clathen*, *clothen*, *cleðen*; Ormulum, 2710; Havelok, 1138. The pt. t. is both *clothede* and *cladde*, the pp. both *clothed* and *clad*. *Clad* occurs in the Romaunt of the Rose, l. 219; and is still in use. ONorthumb. *clāðen*, pt. t. *clāðde*, Matt. xxv. 36; which accounts for the form *clad*. Formed from AS. *clāð*, cloth; see above.+Du. *kleeden*, from *kleed*; so also G. *kleiden*, from *kleid*. The Icel. verb was *klæða*, pt. t. *klæddi*, pp. *klæddr*. **Der.** *cloth-i-er*, *cloth-ing*.

CLOUD, a mass of vapours. (E.) ME. *cloud*, *clowde*. 'Moni clustered *clowde* ' = many a clustered cloud, Allit. Poems, ed. Morris, B. 367. The spellings *cloyd*, *clowde*, *cloud*, *cloude*, *clod*, occur in the Cursor Mundi, 2580, 2872. Earlier examples are scarcely to be found in the same sense, but the word is identical with ME. *clūd*, a mass of rock, a hill. 'The hulle was biclosed mid *cludes* of stone ' = the hill was enclosed with masses of stone; Layamon i. 370, 371. **β.** In corroboration of this identification, we may observe (1) that the sense of 'mass of rock ' passed out of use as the newer application of the word came in ; (2) that *both* words are sometimes found with a plural in *-en* as well as in *-es*; and (3) the orig. sense was simply 'conglomeration' or 'cumulus.' Indeed, we find the expression 'clowdys of clay,' i.e. round masses of clay, Coventry Mysteries, p. 402. **γ.** From AS. *clūd*, properly 'a round mass,' used in AS. to mean 'a hill' or 'mass of rock,' but easily transferred to mean 'cloud' at a later period, because the essential idea was 'mass' or 'ball,' and not 'rock.' In Orosius, iii. 9. sect. 13 (ed. Sweet, p. 132. 10), we read of a city that was 'mid *clūdum* ymbweaxen,' i.e. fortified with masses of rock. **δ.** The AS. *clū-d* is connected with the root seen in *clew* (Teut. root **kleu*); the weaker grade appearing in *clo-d*. See **Clew, Clod**. **Der.** *cloudy*, *cloud-i-ly*, *cloud-i-ness*, *cloud-less*, *cloud-let* (diminutive).

CLOUGH, a hollow in a hill-side. (E.) 'A *clough*, or *clowgh*, is a kind of breach or valley downe a slope from the side of a hill, where commonly shragges, and trees doe grow. It is the termination of Colclough or rather Coldclough, and some other sirnames;' Verstegan, Restitution of Decayed Intelligence, c. 9. ME. *clow*, *clough*; 'Sende him to seche in clif and *clow*;' Cursor Mundi, Trin. MS., l. 17590. Also spelt *clew*, Allit. Morte Arthur, 1639; and (in Scottish) *cleuch*, Wallace, iv. 539. The corresponding AS. form would be **clōh*, not yet found; but the parallel OHG. *klāh* occurs in *Klāhuelde* (Foerstemann, ii. 371). These answer to Teut. **klanχo-*, from *klanχ-*, 2nd grade of a root **klenχ*, appearing in OHG. *cling-o*, a torrent, a gorge (Schade). Cf. Low G. *klang*, also *klinge*, a torrent (Schambach); *klinge*, a defile, *klingende beek*, a rushing stream (Berghaus). From the noise. (Academy, Aug. 31, and Sept. 7, 21, 1889.)

CLOUT, a patch, rag, piece of cloth. (E.) ME. *clout*, *clut*; Ancren Riwle, p. 256. AS. *clūt*; we find 'commissura, *clūt*;' i.e. patch; in Ælfric's Glossary, ed. Somner, Nomina Vasorum, p. 61. [Hence were borrowed W. *clwt*, Corn. *clut*, a piece, patch, clout; Irish and Gael. *clud*, a clout, patch, rag.] Orig. sense, 'mass, piece of stuff;' Teut. type **klūt-oz*, from Teut. root **kleut*, of which the weaker grade occurs in **Clot**. Closely allied to **Cleat**. **Der.** *clout*, verb.

CLOVE (1), a kind of spice. (F.—L.) 'There is another fruit that commeth out of India, like vnto pepper-cornes, and it is called *cloues*;' Holland's Pliny, bk. xii. c. 7. Cotgrave has : 'clou de girofle, a clove.' ME. *clowe*, *clowe*; the latter is in Prompt. Parv.; and Chaucer has *clowe gilofre*, C.T., 13692 (B 1952). In the 16th cent. it became *cloue* (= *clove*), prob. by the influence of Ital. *chiovo*, a clove, or by confusion with *clove* (2), which was an older word. — F. *clou*, a nail; whence *clou de girofle*, a clove, which resembled a nail. — L. *clāuum*, acc. of *clāuus*, a nail. See **Cloy**. **Der.** *clove-pink*. ¶ There is also a weight called a *clove* (= 7 pounds of wool); see **Clove** (3).

CLOVE (2), a bulb, or tuber. (E.) 'A bulb has the power of propagating itself by developing, in the axils of its scales, new bulbs, or what gardeners call *cloves*;' Lindley, Botany, bk. i. c. 2. sect. 2. ME. *clof*, *cloue*, *clowe*. 'Clowe of garlykke, cloue of garlek;' Prompt. Parv. 'A lekes *clof*;' Guy of Warwick, A 3644. AS. *clufu*, Leechdoms, ii. 336; also in the compounds *clufþung*, crowfoot, *Ranunculus sceleratus*, where *cluf* means 'tuber,' and *þung*, poison, from the acrid principle of the juices; and in *clufwyrt*, the buttercup, *Ranunculus acris*; see Gloss. in Cockayne's Leechdoms, iii. 319. [I suspect the *cluf-wyrt* is rather the *Ranunculus bulbosus*, or bulbous buttercup; at any rate *cluf-wyrt* means 'bulb-wort.'] The orig. sense of AS. *clufu* was one of the small bulbs which make up the whole bulb of garlic,

&c.; so named from its cleavage. From AS. *cluf-*, weak grade of *clēofan*, to cleave; see **Cleave** (1).

CLOVE (3), a denomination of weight. (F.—L.) A *clove* of cheese is about 8 lbs.; of wool, about 7 lbs.; Phillips (1706). The word appears in the Liber Custumarum, where it is spelt *clous*, pl., in Anglo-French (p. 63), and *clauos*, acc. pl., in Latin (p. 107). This gives the etymology, and shows that it is identical with *clove* (1); see note on **Clove** (1) above. Ducange has *clāvus lānæ*, a certain weight or quantity of wool, which he notes as being an Eng. use of the word. *Clāvus* seems to have meant 'lump' as well as 'nail.' Cf. Ital. *chiova*, 'a kind of great weight in Italy' (Torriano).

CLOVER, a kind of trefoil. (E.) ME. *claver*, *clover*; spelt *clauer*, Allit. Morte Arthure, ed. Brock, l. 3241. AS. *clāfre*, O. E. Texts, p. 47, l. 375; *clǣfre*, fem. (gen. *clǣfran*), Gloss. to Cockayne's Leechdoms, q.v.+Du. *klaver*, clover, trefoil; whence Swed. *klöfver*, Dan. *klöver*; cf. G. *klee*. β. The suggestion that it is derived from AS. *clēofan*, to cleave, because its leaf is three-cleft, is inconsistent with phonology and impossible.

CLOWN, a clumsy lout, rustic, buffoon. (Scand.) 'This lowtish *clown*;' Sidney's Arcadia, bk. i. (R.; s. v. *Low*). 'To brag upon his pipe the *clowne* begoon;' Turberville, Agaynst the Ielous Heads, st. 6. Not found much earlier. Of Scandinavian origin.—Icel. *klunni*, a clumsy, boorish fellow; cf. *klunnalegr*, clumsy; North Friesic *klönne*, a clown, bumkin (cited by Wedgwood); Swed. dial. *klunn*, a log; *kluns*, a hard knob, a clumsy fellow, Rietz; Dan. *klunt*, a log, a block; *kluntet*, blockish, clumsy, awkward. Cf. AS. *clyne*, a mass, lump, ball. β. It is probably connected with E. *clump*, q.v.; cf. Icel. *klumba*, a club; Dan. *klump*, a clump, *klumpfod*, a club-foot; Swed. *klump*, a lump, *klumpig*, clumsy. See **Clump**. Der. *clown-ish* (Levins), *-ly*, *-n*-s.

CLOY, to glut, satiate, stop up. (F.—L.) In Shak. Rich. II, i. 3. 296; also *cl-yment*, Tw. Nt. ii. 4. 102; *cloyless*, Ant. ii. 1. 25. '*Cloyed*, or *Accloyed*, among farriers, a term used when a horse is pricked with a nail in shooing;' Kersey's Dict. 2nd ed. 1715. Cotgrave has: '*Encloüer*, to naile, drive in a naile; *enclouer artillerie*, to *cloy* a piece of ordnance; to drive a naile or iron pin, into the touch-hole thereof;' also: '*Encloué*, nailed, fastened, pricked, *cloyed* with a nail;' also: '*Encloyer* (obsolete), to cloy, choak, or stop up.' Hence the etymology.—MF. *cloyer*, a by-form of *clouer* (as shown above); Cotgrave gives: '*Clouer*, to naile; to fasten, join, or set on with nailes.' The older form is *cloer* (Burguy).—OF. *clo*, later *clou*, a nail.—L. *clāuum*, acc. of *clāuus*, a nail. See **Clove** (1). Der. *cloy-less*. *Cloy* was frequently used as short for *ac-cloy* or *a-cloy*, where the prefix *a-* represented F. *en-*; see *encloyer* (above).

CLUB (1), a heavy stick, a cudgel. (Scand.) ME. *clubbe*, *clobbe*, Layamon, ii. 216, iii. 35; Havelok, l. 1927, 2289.—Icel. *klubba*, *klumba*, a club; Swed. *klubba*, a club; *klubb*, a block, a club; *klump*, a lump; Dan. *klub*, a club; *klump*, a clump, lump; *klumpfod*, a clubfoot; *klumpfodet*, club-footed. Cf. Dan. *klunt*, a log, a block. β. The close connexion of *club* with *clump* is apparent; in fact, the Icel. *klubba* stands for *klumba*, by the assimilation so common in that language (Noreen). See **Clump**. Der. *club-foot*, *club-footed*.

CLUB (2), an association of persons. (Scand.) Not in very early use. A good example is in the Dedication to Dryden's Medal, where he alludes to the Whigs, and asks them what right they have 'to meet, as you daily do, in factious *clubs*.' In Sherwood's Index to Cotgrave, A.D. 1660, we find: '*To clubbe*, mettre ou despendre à l'egual d'un autre.' The word is really the same as the last, but applied to a 'clump' of people. See Rietz, who gives the Swed. dial. *klubb*, as meaning 'a clump, lump, dumpling, a tightly packed heap of men, a knoll, a heavy inactive fellow.' So we speak of a *knot* of people, or a *clump* of trees. Der. *club*, verb.

CLUB (3), one of a suit at cards. (Scand.) α. The *name* is a translation of the Span. *bastos*, i.e. cudgels, clubs; which is the Span. name for the suit. Thus the word is the same as **Club** (1) and **Club** (2). β. The *figure* by which the *clubs* are denoted on a card is a trefoil; the F. name being *trèfle*, a trefoil, a club (at cards); cf. Dan. *klöver*, clover, a club (at cards); Du. *klaver*, clover, trefoil, a club (at cards).

CLUCK, to call, as a hen does. (E.) 'When she, poor hen, hath *cluck'd* thee to the wars;' Cor. v. 3. 163; where the old editions have *clock'd*. ME. *clokken*. '*Clokkyn* as hennys;' Prompt. Parv. p. 83. [Cf. 'He *chukketh*,' said of a cock; Chaucer, C. T., 15188 (B 4372).] AS. *cloccian*; Anglia, viii. 309, l. 26; cf. A.S. Leechdoms, ii. 220, l. 18. The mod. E. form may have been influenced by the Danish.+Du. *klokken*, to cluck; Dan. *klukke*, to cluck; *kluk*, a clucking; *klukhöne*, a clucking hen; G. *glucken*, to cluck; *gluckhenne*, a clucking-hen. Cf. L. *glocire*, to cluck. An imitative word; see **Clack**.

CLUE; see **Clew**.

CLUMP, a mass, block, cluster of trees. (E.) 'England, Scotland, Ireland, and our good confederates the United Provinces, be all in a *clump* together;' Bacon, Of a War with Spain (R.). The AS. pl. *clymppan*, lumps, occurs in AS. Leechdoms, iii. 134. Cf. also AS. *clymp-re*, a lump (Grein); EFries. *klump*, *klunt*, a lump.+Du. *klomp*, a lump, clog, wooden shoe; cf. *klont*, a clod, lump; Dan. *klump*, a clump, lump; *klumpe*, to clot; cf. *klunt*, a log, block; Swed. *klump*, a lump; *klumpig*, lumpy, clumsy; Icel. *klumba*, *klubba*, a club; G. *klump*, a lump, clod, pudding, dumpling; *klumpen*, a lump, mass, heap, cluster; cf. *klunker*, a clod of dirt. β. Besides these forms, we find Dan. *klimp*, a clod of earth; Swed. *klimp*, a clod, a lump, a dumpling; these are directly derived from the root preserved in the MHG. *klimpfen* (strong verb, pt. t. *klampf*), to draw together, press tightly together, cited by Fick, iii. 51. γ. From the same root we have E. *clamp*, to fasten together tightly; so that *clamp* and *clump* are variants from the same root. See **Clamp**; and see **Club** (1), a doublet of *clump*.

CLUMSY, shapeless, awkward, ungainly. (Scand.) 'Apt to be drawn, formed, or moulded ... even by *clumsy* fingers;' Ray, On the Creation, pt. ii. In Ray's Collection of Provincial Eng. Words we find: '*Clumps*, *Clumpst*, idle, lazy, unhandy, a word of common use in Lincolnshire; see Skinner. This is, I suppose, the same with our *clumzy*, in the South, signifying unhandy; *clumpst* with cold, i.e. benummed;' and again he has: '*Clussumed*, adj. "a *clussumed* hand," a clumsie hand; Cheshire.' α. All these forms are easily explained, being deducible from the ME. *clumsed*, benumbed. From this word were formed (1) *clussumed*, for *clumsed*, which again is for *clumsed*, by a change similar to that in *clasp* from ME. *clapsen*; (2) *clumpst*, by mere contraction; (3) *clumps*, by loss of final *t* in the last; and (4) *clumsy*, with *-y* for *-ed*, giving an adjectival form. β. The ME. *clumsed*, also spelt *clomsed*, is the pp. of the verb *clumsen* or *clomsen*, to benumb, also, to feel benumbed. It is passive in the phrase 'with *clumsid* hondis,' as a translation of 'dissolutis manibus;' Wyclif, Jerem. xlvii. 3; see also Isaiah, xxxv. 3. 'He is outher *clomsed* [stupefied] or wode' [mad]; Hampole, Pricke of Conscience, l. 1651. See further in my note to Piers the Plowman, C. xvi. 2,3, where the intransitive use of the verb occurs, in the sentence: 'when thow *clomsest* for colde' = when thou becomest numb with cold. γ. Of Scandinavian origin. Cf. Swed. dial. *klummsen*, benumbed with cold, with frozen hands; spelt also *klumsun*, *klåumsen*, *klomsen*, *klummshändt* (i.e. with benumbed hands), &c., Rietz, p. 332; who also gives *krumpen* (p. 354) with the very same sense, but answering in form to the E. *cramped*. In Icelandic, *klumsa* means 'lockjaw.' δ. It is easily seen that ME. *clumsen* is an extension of *clum-*, weak grade of the root *clam*, or *cram*, to pinch, whence also E. *clamp* and *cramp*. See **Clamp**, **Cramp**. So in Dutch we find *kleumsch*, chilly, numb with cold; from *kleumen*, to be benumbed with cold, which again is allied to *klemmen*, to pinch, clinch, oppress (Franck). Cf. prov. E. *clem*, to pinch with hunger; *clum*, benumbed; also Westphal. *verklummen*, benumbed; MDan. *klums*, sluggish (Kalkar).

CLUSTER, a bunch, mass, esp. of grapes. (E.) ME. *cluster*, *clustre*, *closter*; Wyclif, Deut. xxxii. 32, Numb. xiii. 25, Gen. xl. 10. AS. *clyster*, *cluster*; the pl. *clystru*, clusters, occurs in Gen. xl. 10.+Low G. *kluster*. *Cluster* represents a Teut. form *klus-tro-*, for *klut-tro-*, from the base *klut-* which appears in **Clot**; so that a *cluster* means a bunch of things adhering closely together, as e.g. in the case of a cluster of grapes or of bees. From Teut. root *kleut*, to mass together; see **Cleat**, **Clout**.

CLUTCH, a claw; to grip, lay hold of. (E.) The verb is ME. *clucchen*; 'to *clucche* or to *clawe*;' P. Plowman, B. xvii. 188. The sb. is ME. *cloche*, *clouche*, *cloke*; 'and in his *cloches* holde;' P. Plowman, B. prol. 154; 'his kene *clokes*;' Ancren Riwle, p. 130; cf. the Lowl. Scot. *cleuck*, *cluik*, *cluke*, *clook*, a claw or talon. The old sb. was superseded by the verbal form, which answers to AS. *clyccan*, to bend or crook the fingers; extant in the imp. s. *clyce* (see **Clitch** in N.E.D.), and in the pp. *geclyht*, written *gecliht* in the Liber Scintillarum, § xxv; p. 99, l. 2. Teut. type *kluk-jan-*, (perhaps) 'to bend a joint.'

CLUTTER (1), to coagulate, clot. (E.) 'The *cluttered* bloud;' Holland, Pliny, b. xxi. c. 25. ME. *cloteren*; the pp. *clotered*, also written *clothred*, occurs in Chaucer, C. T., 2747 (A 2745). The same as *clotter*, the frequentative form of *clot*; see **Clot**.

CLUTTER (2), a confused heap; to heap up. (E.) 'What a *clutter* there was with huge, over-grown pots, pans, and spits;' L'Estrange, in Rich. and Todd's Johnson. 'Which *clutters* not praises together;' Bacon, to K. Jas. I; Sir T. Matthew's Lett. ed. 1660, p. 32 (Todd). The same word as **Clutter** (1); the sense of 'mass' suggested that of 'confused heap;' whence, further, that of 'confused noise;' see below.

CLUTTER (3), a noise, a great din. (E.) Not common; Rich. quotes from King, and Todd from Swift; a mere variation of **Clatter**, q.v.; affected by **Clutter** (2). Ihre gives M. Swed. *kluttra*, to quarrel. Cf. EFries. *klöter*, a rattle.

CLYSTER, an injection into the bowels. (L. – Gk.) The pl. *clisters* is in Holland's Pliny, b. viii. c. 27; the verb *clysterize* in the same, b. xx. c. 5; and Massinger has: 'Thou stinking *clyster-pipe*;' Virgin Martyr, A. iv. sc. 1; cf. Shak. Oth. ii. 1. 178. – L. *clyster.* – Gk. κλυστήρ, a clyster, a syringe; κλύσμα, a liquid used for washing out, esp. a clyster, a drench. – Gk. κλύζειν, to wash. Cf. L. *cluere*, to purge, Goth. *hlūtrs*, pure. – √KLEU, to cleanse. Brugm. i. § 490.

CO-, prefix; a short form of *con-.* See **Con-.**

COACH, a close carriage. (F. – Hung.) In Shak. Merry Wives, ii. 2. 66. – F. *coche*, 'a coach;' Cot. – Hungarian *kotsi, kocsi*, a coach, travelling carriage; whence the word was introduced into many other languages. See Beckmann's Hist. of Inventions, tr. in 1846, i. 77; who says: 'Stephanus Broderithus says, speaking of 1526; ... "he speedily got into one of those light carriages, which (from the name of the place) we called *kotcze*."' The word was used in Hungary from the reign of king Matthias Corvinus, 1458–90; and the 'coach' was named from a Hungarian village named *Kocs*, between Raab and Buda; see N.E.D. The word *coche* first appears in E. in 1556.

COADJUTOR, assistant. (L.) Spelt *coadiutour*, Sir T. Elyot, Governour, b. ii. c. 10. § 5. – L. *co-*, for *con-*, which for *cum*, together; and *adiūtor*, an assistant, allied to *adiūtus*, pp. of *adiuuāre*, to assist. See **Adjutant.** Der. *coadjutr-ix, coadjutor-ship.*

COAGULATE, to curdle, congeal. (L.) Shak. has *coagulate* as pp. = curdled; '*coagulate* gore;' Hamlet, ii. 2. 484. – L. *coāgulātus*, pp. of *coāgulāre*, to curdle. – L. *coāgulum*, rennet, which causes things to curdle. – L. *co-* (for *con-* or *cum*, together), and *ag-ere*, to drive; (in Latin, the contracted form *cōgere* is the common form); with suffix *-ul-*, having a diminutive force; so that *co-ăg-ul-um* would mean 'that which drives together slightly.' – √AG, to drive. See **Agent.** Der. *coagulat-ion, coagul-able, coagul-ant.*

COAITA, the red-faced spider monkey. (Brazil.) Spelt *quata* in Stedman's Surinam, ii. 10. [Sometimes misspelt *coaiti.*] – Tupi (Brazilian) *coaii, cuatá, coaitá* (N.E.D.); spelt *couatta* in Breton, Dict. Caraibe François, 1665; p. 180. ¶ Distinct from *coati.*

COAL, charcoal, a combustible mineral. (E.) ME. *col*, Layamon, l. 2366. AS. *col*, coal; Grein, i. 166. + Du. *kool*; Icel. and Swed. *kol*; Dan. *kul*; OHG. *cholo*, MHG. *kol*, G. *kohle*. The Skt. *jval*, to blaze, burn, is probably from the same root; cf. also OIrish *gūal*, coal. Der. *coal-y, coal-fish, coal-heaver*, &c.; also *collier*, q.v.; also *collied*, i.e. blackened, dark, in Mid. Nt. Dr. i. 1. 145.

COALESCE, to grow together. (L.) Used by Newton (Todd); in Blount's Gloss., ed. 1656; also by Goodwin, Works, v. iii. pt. iii. p. 345 (R.). R. doubtless refers to the works of T. Goodwin, 5 vols., London, 1681–1703. – L. *coalescere*, to grow together. – L. *co-*, for *con-* or *cum*, together; and *alescere*, to grow, inceptive form of *alere*, to nourish. See **Aliment.** Der. *coalescence, coalescent*, from *coalescent-*, stem of the pres. part. of *coalescere*; also *coalition* (used by Burke) allied to L. *coalitus*, pp. of *coalescere.*

COARSE, rough, rude, gross. (F. – L.) In Shak. Henry VIII, iii. 2. 239. Also spelt *course, cowrse*; 'Yea, though the threeds [threads] be *cowrse*;' Gascoigne, Complaint of the Grene Knight, l. 25; cf. '*Course*, vilis, grossus;' Levins, 224. 39. **α.** The origin of *coarse* is by no means well ascertained; it seems most likely that it stands for *course*, and that *course* was used as a contracted form of *in course*, meaning 'in an ordinary manner,' and hence 'ordinary,' or 'common.' The phrase *in course* was also used for the modern *of course*; Meas. for Meas. iii. 1. 259. **β.** The examples in the N.E.D. bear out this view. The phrase 'Too *cors* bordecloþes,' i.e. two coarse tablecloths occurs as early as 1424; Early Eng. Wills, p. 56. See **Course.** Der. *coarse-ly, -ness.*

COAST, side, border, country. (F. – L.) ME. *coste.* 'Bi thyse Englissche *costes'* = throughout these English coasts or borders; William of Shoreham, De Baptismo, st. 9; about A.D. 1315. – F. *coste* (F. *côte*), a rib, slope of a hill, shore. – L. *costa*, a rib, side. Der. *coast*, v., *coast-er, coast-wise.* From the same source is *ac-cost*, q.v.; also *cutlet*, q.v., *costermonger*, q.v.

COAT, a garment, vesture. (F. – G.) ME. *cote, kote*; K. Alisaunder, ed. Weber, 2413. – OF. *cote* (F. *cotte*), a coat; Low L. *cota, cotta*, a garment, tunic; cf. Low L. *cottus*, a tunic. – MHG. *kutte, kotte, kotze*, OHG. *chozzo*, a coarse mantle; whence also G. *kutte*, a cowl. Cognate with OSax. *cot*, with the same sense. See Kluge. Der. *coat*, vb., *coat-ing.*

COATI, COATI-MONDI, a carnivorous mammal. (Brazil.) Described as *coati* or *coati-mondi* in a tr. of Buffon (1792); i. 183. The nose is long and flexible, and marked with white. – Tupi (Brazilian) *coati, cuati, cuatim*; from *cua*, a cincture, and *tim*, a nose (*tim* being nasal). The word *mondi* is said to mean 'solitary' (N.E.D.).

COAX, to entice, persuade. (E.) Formerly spelt *cokes.* 'They neither kisse nor *cokes* them;' Puttenham, Arte of Poesie, lib. i. c. 8; ed. Arber, p. 36. The word *cokes* as a sb. meant a simpleton, gull, dupe. 'Why, we will make a *cokes* of this wise master;' Ben Jonson,

The Devil is an Ass, ii. 1. 'Go, you're a brainless *cox*, a toy, a fop;' Beaum. and Fletcher, Wit at Sev. Weapons, iii. 1. History unknown. ¶ We may note that Cotgrave seems to have regarded it as equivalent to the F. *cocard.* He has: '*Cocard*, a nice doult, quaint goose, fond or saucie *cokes*, proud or forward meacock.' Under the spelling *coquart*, he gives 'undiscreetly bold, peart, *cocket*, jolly, cheerful.' Thus the F. *coquart* may have suggested *cocket*, and now answers to the school-slang *cocky*, i.e. like a fighting cock. We may also note OF. *coquebert, coquibus, coquidé*, all meaning 'foolish;' see Godefroy.

COB (1), a small round hard lump, or knob; a head. (E.) The senses are numerous; see E.D.D. and N.E.D. In the sense of small hard lump, the dimin. is *cobble*, as used in *cobble-stones.* As applied to a pony or horse, it seems to mean short and stout. ME. *cob*, a head, a person, esp. a great or leading person; the pl. *cobbes* is used by Hoccleve, De Regim. Principum, l. 2806. The verb to *cob* or *cop*, to excel, is allied to AS. *copp*, a top, summit. Cf. Du. *kop*, a head, pate, person, man; G. *kopf*, the head. Der. *cob-web*, q.v.; *cobb-le* (2), sb., q.v.

COB (2), to beat, strike. (E.) In sailor's language and provincial E. Cf. ME. *cobben*, to fight; Destr. of Troy, ll. 8285, 11025. Also prov. E. *cop*, to strike on the head; whence, probably, W. *cobio*, to strike; cf. W. *cob*, a bunch, a tuft; *cop*, a head, bunch. See **Cob** (1).

COBALT, a reddish-gray mineral. (G.) One of the few G. words in English; most of such words are names of minerals. Used by Woodward, who died A.D. 1728 (Todd). – G. *kobalt*, cobalt. **β.** The word is a nick-name given by the miners because it was poisonous and troublesome to them; it is merely another form of G. *kobold*, a demon, goblin; and *cobalt* itself is called *kobold* in provincial German; see Flügel's Dict. – MHG. *kobolt*, a demon, sprite; in which the former element *kob-* answers to AS. *cof-* in *cof-godas*, household gods, used to translate L. *penātes*; Voc. 189. 10; from AS. *cofa*, a chamber. See **Cove.** (So in Kluge.)

COBBLE (1), to patch up. (E.) 'He doth but cloute [patch] and *cobbill*;' Skelton, Why Come Ye Nat to Court, l. 524. The sb. *cobelere*, a cobbler, occurs in P. Plowman, B. v. 327. Origin doubtful; perhaps the same as prov. E. *cobble*, to beat; from **Cob** (2). Der. *cob'l-er.*

COBBLE (2), a small round lump. (E.) Chiefly used of round stones, commonly called *cobble-stones.* 'Hic rudus, a *cobylstone*;' Voc. 768. 38. A dimin. of *cob*, with the suffix *-le* (for *-el*). See **Cob** (1). Cf. Norw. *koppull*, a small round stone.

COBLE, a small fishing-boat. (C.) 'Cobles, or little fishing-boats;' Pennant, in Todd's Johnson. ME. *coble*, Scot. Legends of Saints, ed. Metcalfe, xl. (Ninian), l. 504. – W. *ceubal*, a ferry-boat, skiff. Cf. W. *ceubren*, a hollow tree; *ceufad*, a canoe. – W. *ceuo*, to excavate, hollow out; boats being orig. made of hollowed trees. Cf. Breton *kōbar, gōbar*, also *kōbal*, a coble, small boat; from the form *gōbar* is derived the F. *gabare*, MF. *gabarre*, 'a lighter;' Cot.

COBRA DE CAPELLO, a snake with a hood. (Port. – L.) In a tr. of Buffon (1792), ii. 277, it is called '*cobra de* [error for *de capello*, or hooded serpent.' – Port. *cobra*, snake; *de*, of, with; *capello*, a hood. – L. *colubra*, a snake; *dē*, of, with; *capellum*, acc. of Late L. *capellus*, dimin. of Late L. *capa*, a cape. See **Chaplet** and **Cape** (1).

COBWEB, a spider's web. (E.) ME. *copweb*, Trevisa, tr. of Higden, vii. 343; so also in Bacon, Nat. Hist. § 728; *copwebbe* in Palsgrave, and in the Golden Boke, c. 17. *Copweb* is a shortened form of *attercop-web*, from the ME. *attercop*, a spider. **β.** In Wyclif's Bible we find: 'The webbis of an *attercop*,' Isaiah, lix. 5; and: 'the web of *attercoppis*,' Job, viii. 14. The ME. *attercop* is from AS. *attorcoppe*, a spider, Voc. 121. 28; a word compounded of AS. *ātor*, poison (Bosworth), and *coppe*, which perhaps also meant 'spider;' cf. MDu. *kop, koppe*, 'a spider,' or a cob;' Hexham. The exact relation to *cob* (1) is obscure. Cf. Du. *spinnekop*, a spider; also, a spider's head; W Flem. *koppe, kobbe*, a spider (De Bo); Westphal. *kobbenwebbe*, a cobweb.

COCA, a shrub, the leaves of which afford a stimulant. (Span. – Peruv.) In E. G., tr. of Acosta (1604), bk. iv. c. 22; and J. Frampton, Joyfull Newes (1577), fol. 101, back. – Span. *coca.* – Peruv. *cuca*; of which form the Span. *coca* is a corruption (Garcilasso, Comment. of Peru, bk. viii. c. 15). Der. *coca-ine.*

COCHINEAL, a scarlet dye-stuff. (F. – Span. – L. – Gk.) *Cochineal* consists 'of the dried bodies of females of the *Coccus cacti*, an insect native in Mexico, Central America, &c., and found on several species of cactus;' Webster. [These insects have the appearance of berries, and were thought to be such; hence the name.] The word *cochineal* occurs in Beaum. and Fletcher, Beggar's Bush, i. 3. Cf. 'the berrie of *cochenile*;' Hakluyt's Voy. iii. 46, l. 10. – F. *chinille*. – Span. *cochinilla*, cochineal; cf. Ital. *coccinicla*, the same. – L. *coccineus, coccinus* (Isaiah, i. 18), of a scarlet colour. – L. *coccum*, a berry; also, 'kermes,' supposed by the ancients to be a berry. – Gk.

κόκκος, a kernel, a berry; esp. the *coccus īlicis*, or 'kermes-berry,' used to dye scarlet. ¶ Distinct from Span. *cochinilla*, a wood-louse, dimin. of *cochina*, a pig (Monlau).

COCK (1), the male of the domestic fowl. (E.) ME. *cok*; see Chaucer's Nun's Priest's Tale. AS. *cocc*, Matt. xxvi. 34, 74; and much earlier, in Ælfred, tr. of Gregory, ed. Sweet, c. 63, p. 459. Of imitative origin; from the bird's cry. 'Cryde anon *cok! cok!*'; Chaucer, C. T., B 4467. Cf. Skt. *kukkuṭa-*, a cock; Malay *kukuk*, crowing of cocks. ¶ So also OF. *coc* (F. *coq*). ─ Low Lat. *coccum*, an accus. form occurring in the Lex Salica, vii. 16, and of onomato-poetic origin (Brachet). ─ Gk. κόκκυ, the cry of the cuckoo; also the cry of the cock, since the phrase κοκκόβόας ὄρνις occurs to signify a cock; lit. it means 'the cock-voiced bird,' or the bird that cries *cock!* Cf. **Cuckoo**. Der. *cock-er-el*, a little cock, apparently a double diminutive, ME. *cokerel*, Prompt. Parv. p. 86; *cock-fight-ing*, sometimes contracted to *cock-ing*; *cock-er*, one who keeps fighting-cocks; *cock-pit*; *cock's-comb*, a plant; and see *cock-ade*, *cock-atrice*, *coxcomb*. ☞ The *cock*, or stop-cock of a barrel, is probably the same word; cf. G. *hahn*, a cock, also, a faucet, stop-cock. See **Cock** (3), and **Chicken**.

COCK (2), to stick up abruptly. (E.) We say to *cock* one's eye, one's hat; or, of a bird, that it *cocks* up its tail. '[She] spreads and *cocks* her tail;' A. Marvell, Rehearsal Transposed, i. 161 (N.E.D.) Apparently with reference to the posture of a cock's head when crow-ing; or to that of his crest or tail. See **Cock** (1). So also Gael. *coc*, to cock, as in *coc do bhoineid*, cock your bonnet; cf. Gael. *coc-shron*, a cock-nose; *coc-shronach*, cock-nosed. Der. *cock*, sb., in the phrase 'a *cock* of the eye,' &c.

COCK (3), part of the lock of a gun. (E.) 'Pistol's *cock* is up;' Hen. V, ii. i. 55. So named from its original shape; from the like-ness to the head and neck of a *cock*. Similarly, the G. name is *hahn*; as in the phrase *den Hahn spannen*, i. e. to cock (a gun).

COCK (4), a small pile of hay. (Scand.) 'A *cocke* of hay;' Tyn-dale's Works, p. 450. Cf. 'cockers of harnest folkes,' Rastall, Statutes; Vagabonds, &c. p. 474 (R.). And see P. Plowman, C. vi. 13, and my note upon it.─Dan. *kok*, a heap, pile; Dan. dial. *kok*, a haycock, *at kokke hòet*, to cock hay; cf. Icel. *kökkr*, a lump, a ball.

COCK (5), **COCKBOAT**, a small boat. (F.─L.─Gk.) The addition of *boat* is superfluous; see *cock* in K. Lear, iv. 6. 19.─OF. *coque*, also *cogue*, a kind of boat (Godefroy); cf. Ital. *cocca*, Span. *coca*, a boat. β. The word also appears in the form *cog* or *co˅ge*, as in Morte Arthure, ed. Brock, 476; Chaucer, Legend of Good Women, Ypsiphyle, 114. This is the Du. and Dan. *kog*, Icel. *kuggr*, a boat; the same word. γ. The word was very widely spread, and is perhaps to be referred, as suggested by Diez, to the L. *concha*, a shell; cf. also mod. F. *coche*, a boat, and *coque*, a shell.─Gk. κόγχη, a mussel, cockle-shell; κόγχος, a mussel, cockle, cockle-shell.+Skt. *çaṅkha-*, a conch-shell. See **Conch**; and see **Cockle** (1). ¶ But some regard the Du. and Scand. forms as Teutonic; from Teut. types **kukkon-*, **kuggon-*. It is probable that these types were confused with derivatives of *concha*. Cf. Körting, § 2283. Der. *cock-swain*, by the addition of *swain*, q.v.; now gen. spelt *coxswain*.

COCKADE, a knot of ribbon on a hat. (F.) 'Pert infidelity is wit's *cockade*;' Young's Nt. Thoughts, Nt. 7, l. 109 from end. The *a* was formerly sounded as *aa* in *baa*; and the word is, accordingly, a corruption of *cockard*.─F. *coquarde*, fem. of *coquard*, 'foolishly proud, saucy, presumptuous, malapert, undiscreetly peart, cocket, jolly, cheerful;' Cotgrave. He also gives: '*coquarde, bonnet à la coquarde*, a Spanish cap, . . . any bonnet or cap worne proudly.' Formed by suffix *-ard* from F. *coq*, a cock. See **Cock** (1).

COCKATOO, a kind of parrot. (Malay.) The pl. is spelt *cacatoes*, and the birds are said to be found in the Mauritius; Sir T. Herbert, Travels, p. 383 (Todd's Johnson); or ed. 1665, p. 403.─Malay *kakatūa*, a cockatoo; a word which is doubtless imitative, like our *cock*; see **Cock** (1). This Malay word is given at p. 84 of Pijnappel's Malay-Dutch Dictionary; he also gives the imitative words *kakak*, the cackling of hens, p. 75; and *kukuk*, the crowing of a cock, p. 94. So also '*kakatūa*, a bird of the parrot-kind;' Marsden's Malay Dict. p. 261. Cf. Skt. *kukkuṭa-*, a cock; so named from its cry. See **Cock**, **Cuckoo**.

COCKATRICE, a fabulous serpent hatched from a cock's egg. (F.─Late L.─L.) In Shak. Tw. Nt. iii. 4. 215. ME. *cocatryse*, *kokatrice*, Wyclif, Ps. xc. 13; Isa. xi. 8, xiv. 29.─OF. *cocatrice*, *cocatris*, an ichneumon, a crocodile; Godefroy. Cf. Span. *cocotriz*, a crocodile.─Late L. *cōcātricem*, acc. of *cōcātrix*, *caucātrix*, a croco-dile, basilisk, cockatrice. β. The form *cōcātrix* is a corruption of Late L. *calcātrix* (*caucātrix* in Ducange), lit. 'the treader,' or 'tracker out,' used to translate Gk. ἰχνεύμων.─L. *calcāre*, to tread; see **Caulk**, and see **Ichneumon**. The word being once corrupted, the fable that the animal was produced from a *cock's* egg was invented to account for it.

COCKER, to pamper, indulge children. (Scand.) 'A beardless boy, a *cockered* silken wanton;' K. John, v. 1. 70. 'Neuer had so *cockered* us, nor made us so wanton;' Sir T. More, Works, p. 337 d; see Eastwood and Wright's Bible Word-book. '*Cokeryn*, carifoveo;' Prompt. Parv. p. 85. β. Prob. of Scand. rather than of native origin. Orig. 'to cry *cok!*' as a cock does, repeatedly; the verb being fre-quentative in form. Hence to call chickens repeatedly, to be ever feeding them, to pet, pamper, &c. This is borne out by MDan. *kokre*, to call often, as a cock or hen does; Norweg. *kokla* (1), to cackle, (2), to cocker, pet; Norw. *kokra*, to utter monotonous cries, also to cocker; Norw. *kokrebarn*, a pet child; *kokren*, adj., cockering (Ross). So also MDu. *kokelen*, 'to cocker, foster,' Hexham; whence F. *coqueliner*, of which Cotgrave says: '*coqueliner un enfant*, to dandle, cocker, fondle, pamper, make a wanton of a child.' The W. *cocri*, to fondle, is from E. All from **Cock** (1).

COCK-EYED, squinting. (E.) See Halliwell. From **Cock** (2). q. v.

COCKLE (1), a sort of bivalve. (F.─L.─Gk.) In P. Plowman, C. x. 95, occurs the pl. *cockes*, with the sense of *cockles*, the reading in the Ilchester MS. being *cokeles*. Thus the ME. form is *cokel*, dimin. of *cok* or *cock* (F. *coque*), the orig. sense of which was 'shell.' The word was borrowed from the French *coquille*, a cockle-shell; cf. Ital. *cocchiglia*, Walloon *kokil* (Remacle).─Late L. type **coc-chylia*, by-form of *conchylia*, pl. of *conchylium*.─Gk. κογχύλιον, dimin. of κόγχη, a mussel, a cockle. See **Cock** (5). Without the nasal, we find also L. *cochlea*, a snail; cf. Gk. κοχλίας, a snail with a spiral shell; κόχλος, a fish with a spiral shell, also a bivalve, a cockle. See Körting, § 2283. ¶ The ME. *cockes* answers to the pl. of AS. *sǣ-cocc*, a sea-shell, cockle, and of OF. *coque*.

COCKLE (2), a weed among corn; darnel. (E.) ME. *cokkel*. 'Or springen [sprinkle, sow] *cokkel* in our clene corn;' Chaucer, C. T., 12923 (B 1183). AS. *coccel*, tares, translating Lat. *zizania*, Matt. xiii. 27; whence also Gael. *cogall*, tares, the herb cockle; *cogull*, the corn-cockle; Irish *cogal*.

COCKLE (3), to be uneven, pucker up. (Scand.) 'It made such a short *cockling* sea, . . that I never felt such uncertain jerks in a ship;' Dampier, Voyage, an. 1683 (R.). Of Scand. origin; cf. Norw. *koklutt*, lumpy, uneven, i.e. cockled up; from Norw. *kokle*, a little lump, dim. of *kok*, a lump. Cf. Swed. dial. *kokkel*, dimin. of *koka*, a clod.

COCKLOFT, an upper loft, garret. (Hybrid; E. and Scand.) '*Cocklofts* and garrets;' Dryden, tr. of Juvenal, Sat. iii. l. 329. From *cock* (1) and *loft*. '*Desvan de casa*, a garret or *cockloft*;' Min-sheu, Span. Dict. (1623). So in German we find *hahnbalken*, a roost, a cock-loft; and in Danish *hanebielkeloft*, lit. a cock-balk-loft; cf. prov. E. *hen-loft*. It meant originally a place in the rafters where cocks roosted, hence, a little room among the rafters; called also in Danish *loftkammer*, i.e. loft-chamber. See **Loft**. ¶ The W. *coeg-lofft*, a garret, is nothing but the E. *cockloft* borrowed.

COCKNEY, an effeminate person. (E.) ME. *cokenty*, in P. Plow-man, B. vi. 287; where it means 'an egg'; so also in the Tourna-ment of Tottenham in Percy's Reliques, last stanza. The ME. *cokeney* represents *coken-ey*, lit. 'egg of cocks,' from AS. *æg*, an egg, where *coken* is the gen. pl. of *cok*, a cock, as *clerken* is of *clerk*. This singular name was applied particularly to the small misshapen eggs occasionally laid by fowls; see prov. E. *cock's egg* (s.v. *cock*) in E.D.D. 'The small yolkless eggs which hens sometimes lay are called *cock's eggs*, generally in the firm persuasion that the name states a fact;' C. S. Burne, Shropshire Folk-Lore, p. 229. Cf. Harl. Miscell. iii. 531. Florio's Ital. Dict. (1598) has: '*Caccherelli*, cacklings of hens; also egs, as we say *cockanegs*.' Hence *cockney* was often a term of reproach, and meant a foolish or effeminate person, or a spoilt child; see *Cockncy* in Halliwell. The ME. spelling was *cokeney* or *cokenay*, which was trisyllabic. 'I sal been halde a daf, a *cokenay*; Unhardy is unsely, thus men sayth;' Chaucer, C. T. 4206 (A 4208). Der. *cockney-dom*, *cockney-ism*.

COCKROACH, a kind of beetle. (Span.) '*Cockroches*, a kind of insect;' Phillips, ed. 1706. Capt. J. Smith has *cacarootch*; Works, ed. Arber, p. 630 (1624). 'Called *cakreluce* in Surinam'; Stedman, i. 194 (1796). 'Without question, it is from the Portuguese *caroucha*, chafer, beetle, and was introduced into our language by sailors;' F. Hall, Modern English, 1873, p. 128. But a friend kindly points out that the E. word is borrowed, not from Port. *caroucha*, but from Span. *cucaracha*, 'a wood-louse, a kind of centi-pede, blatta or short-legged beetle, common aboard of American ships, a cockroach, *Blatta americana*, L.;' Neuman. I think the Port. *caroucha* is merely a clipped form of the same word, with loss of the first syllable. The etymology of *cucaracha* is obscure.

COCKSHUT TIME, twilight. (E.) In Shak. Rich. III, v. 3. 70. 'A fine *cockshoot* evening,' i.e. a fine evening for using cock-shoots; Middleton, The Widow, A. iii. sc. 1. A *cockshoot* (shortened to *cockshot* or *cockshut*) was a glade cut through a wood along which woodcocks might dart or 'shoot' and be caught in nets, esp. at twilight; see E.D.D. Palsgrave has: '*Cockesshote* to take wodcockes with, *uolee.*' Woodcocks were taken 'in *cockshoote tyme*, as yt is tearmed, which is the twylight, when yt ys no strange thinge to take a hundred or sixe score in one woodd in twenty-four houres;' A. Newton, Dict. of Birds, p. 1044. Prof. Newton adds that 'another MS. speaks of one wood having 13 cockshots.' From *cock, shoot*, and *time.* ¶ Often absurdly referred to the verb *to shut.* See Phil. Soc. Trans., 1904; p. 166.

COCO, wrongly **COCOA** (1), the cocoa-nut palm-tree. (Port.) 'Give me to drain the *cocoa's* milky bowl;' Thomson, Summer, l. 677. 'A fruit called *cocos*' [at Goa]; Hakluyt, Voy. ii. 2. 101. [Misspelt *cocoa* in Johnson's Dict.]—Port. (and Span.) *coco,* a bugbear; also, a cocoa-nut, cocoa-tree. 'Called *coco* by the Portuguese in India on account of the monkey-like face at the base of the nut, from *coco,* a bugbear, an ugly mask to frighten children; see De Barros, Asia, Dec. iii. bk. iii. c. 7;' Wedgwood. Cf. Port. *fazer coco,* to play at bo-peep; Span. *ser un coco,* to be an ugly-looking person; *cocar,* to make grimaces; also, *guarda el Coco,* i.e. see the bogy; Pineda. Of unknown origin.

COCOA (2), a corrupt form of **Cacao,** q. v.

COCOON, the case of a chrysalis. (F.—L.—Gk.) Spelt *cocon* in 1699 (N.E.D.).—F. *cocon,* a cocoon; formed by adding the suffix *-on* (gen. augmentative, but sometimes diminutive) to F. *coque,* a shell. From a by-form of L. *concha,* a shell.—Gk. κόγχη, a shell; see **Conch, Cock** (5). Der. *cocoon-ery.*

COCTION, a boiling, decoction. (L.) In Boyle's Works, vol. ii. p. 109 (R.). Formed from Latin, by analogy with F. words in *-tion.* —L. *coctiōnem,* acc. of *coctio,* a boiling, digestion; allied to *coctus,* pp. of *coquere,* to cook. See **Cook.**

COD (1), a kind of fish. (E.) In Shak. Othello, ii. 1. 156. '*Codde,* a fysshe, *cableau;*' Palsgrave; cf. '*Cabilaud,* the chevin;' and '*Cabillau,* fresh cod;' Cot. Spelt *cod,* Statutes of the Realm, i. 356 (A.D. 1357). β. I suppose that this word *cod* must be the same as the ME. *codde,* a bolster; though the resemblance of the fish to a bolster is but fanciful. It is obvious that Shakespeare knew nothing of the Linnæan name *gadus* (Gk. γάδος); nor is any connexion between *cod* and *gadus* possible. See **Cod** (2), and **Cuttle.** Der. *cod-ling,* q. v.

COD (2), a husk, shell, bag, bolster. (E.) Perhaps obsolete, except in prov. E. In Shak., in *cod-piece,* Gent. of Verona, ii. 7. 53; *peascod,* i.e. pea-shell, husk of a pea, Mids. Nt. Dr. iii. 1. 191. ME. *cod, codde;* '*codde* of frute, or pese-codde;' Prompt. Parv. p. 85. The pl. *coddis* translates Lat. *siliquis,* Wyclif, Luke. xv. 16. [*Cod* also means pillow, bolster; as in: 'A *cod,* hoc ceruical, hoc puluinar;' Cath. Ang.; in this sense it is of Scand. origin.] AS. *cod, codd,* a bag; translating Lat. *pera* in Mark, vi. 8. ✠ Icel. *koddi,* a pillow; *koðri,* the scrotum of animals; Swed. *kudde,* a cushion. Cf. Swed. dial. *kudde,* a pod; MDu. *kodde,* a club (Hexham), also 'coleus, testiculus;' Kilian; Jutland *kodde,* a pod, the scrotum. AS. *codd* answers to a Teut. type **kuddoz,* m.; Icel. *koddi* to **kuddon-,* a weak sb. ¶ The W. *cod,* a bag, pouch, was borrowed from English.

CODDLE, to treat as an invalid, to nurse overmuch, to render effeminate. (F.—L.) Another sense of *coddle* (still known in prov. E.) was to parboil, to stew fruit; thus Dampier says of the guava: 'It bakes as well as a pear, and it may be *coddled,* and it makes good pies;' A New Voyage, vol. i. c. 8. p. 222. In Beaumont and Fletcher's Philaster, A. V. sc. 4, l. 31, the phrase 'I'll have you *coddled*' alludes to 'Prince Pippin.' Apparently short for *caudle,* verb, i.e. to treat with *caudle;* see Shak. Timon, iv. 3. 226. See **Caudle.**

CODE, a digest of laws. (F.—L.) ME. *code;* as in 'Theodocius his *code;*' Trevisa, tr. of Higden, iii. 255. Pope has the pl. *codes,* Sat. vii. 96.—F. *code.*—L. *cōdicem,* acc. of *cōdex, caudex,* a trunk of a tree; hence, a wooden tablet for writing on, a set of tablets, a book. β. The orig. form was perhaps **scaudex,* connected with **scauda* (i.e. *cauda*), a tail, and the orig. sense a shoot or spray of a tree, thus connecting L. *cauda* with E. *scut,* the tail of a hare or rabbit. See **Scut.** Der. *cod-i-fy, cod-i-fic-at-ion;* also *cod-ic-il,* q. v.

CODICIL, a supplement to a will. (F.—L.) Used by Warburton, Divine Legation, bk. iv. note 22 (R.). It occurs as early as 1417-8. 'In this *codicill;*' Fifty E. Eng. Wills (E. E. T. S.), p. 40. —MF. *codicile,* 'a codicile;' Cot.—L. *cōdicillus,* a writing-tablet, a memorial, a codicil to a will.—L. *cōdic-,* stem of *cōdex,* a tablet, code; with addition of the dimin. suffix *-illus.* See **Code.**

CODLING (1), a young cod. (E.) ME. *codlyng.* 'Hic mullus, a *codlyng;*' Voc. 642. 16. '*Codlynge,* fysche, morus;' Prompt. Parv. p. 85. Formed from *cod* (1) by help of the dimin. suffix *-ling;* cf. *duck-ling.*

CODLING (2), **CODLIN,** a kind of apple. (C.; *with* E. *suffix.*) In Shak. Tw. Nt. i. 5. 167, it means an unripe apple. Bacon men-

tions *quadlins* among the July fruits; Essay 46, Of Gardens. *Quadling* is from ME. *querdling.* '*Querdlynge,* appulle, Duracenum;' Prompt. Parv. The suffix *-ling* is E.; but *querd-* may be Celtic; from Irish *cueirt, cuirt,* an apple-tree. ¶ The Irish *cueirt* is a very old word, as it was the name of Q in the Ogham alphabet. 'The names of the letters are taken from those of trees, as follows: B—*beith,* birch .. Q—*queirt,* apple:' J. R. Allen, Monumental Hist. of Early Brit. Church; p. 71; Rhys, Lect. on Welsh Philology, 2nd ed. p. 285.

COEFFICIENT, coöperating with; a math. term. (L.) R. quotes *coefficiency* from Glanvill, Vanity of Dogmatising, c. 12 (A.D. 1655).—L. *co-,* for *con,* i.e. *cum,* with; and *efficient-,* stem of *efficiens,* pres. part. of *efficere,* to cause, a verb compounded of prep. *ex,* out, and *facere,* to make. See **Efficient.** Der. *coefficienc-y.*

CŒNOBITE; see **Cenobite** (above).

COEQUAL; from **Co-,** q. v.; and **Equal,** q. v.

COERCE, to restrain, compel. (L.) Sir T. Elyot has *coertion,* The Gouernour, bk. i. c. 8. § 6. *Coerce* occurs in Butler, Sat. on Age of Ch. II., l. 162.—L. *coercēre,* to compel.—L. *co-,* for *con-,* which for *cum,* with; and *arcēre,* to enclose, confine, keep off. From the same root is the L. *arca,* a chest, whence E. *ark.* See **Ark.** Der. *coerc-i-ble, coerc-ive, coerc-ive-ly, coerc-ion.*

COEVAL, of the same age. (L.) In Blount's Gloss., ed. 1681. Formed by help of the adj. suffix *-al* (as in *equal*) from L. *coævu-us,* of the same age.—L. *co-,* for *con-,* i.e. *cum,* together with; and *æuum,* an age. See **Age.**

COFFEE, a decoction of berries of the coffee-tree. (Turk.—Arab.) 'A drink call'd *coffa;*' Bacon, Nat. Hist. s. 738. 'He [the Turk] hath a drink called *cauphe;*' Howell, bk. ii. lett. 55 (A.D. 1634). 'Their best drink is *coffa;*' Capt. J. Smith, Works, p. 856 (1603).—Turk. *qahveh,* coffee.—Arabic *qahweh,* coffee; Palmer's Pers. Dict. col. 476; also *qahwah* or *qahwa(t),* Rich. Dict. p. 1155.

COFFER, a chest for money. (F.—L.—Gk.) ME. *cofer, cofre* (with one *f*). 'But litel gold in *cofre;*' Chaucer, prol. 300. And see Rob. of Brunne, tr. of Langtoft, pp. 135, 224, 297.—OF. *cofre,* also *cofin,* a coffer. The learned form is *cofin;* the like popular change of *n* to *r* is seen in E. *order,* F. *ordre,* from L. *ordinem.* Thus *coffer* is a doublet of *coffin.* See **Coffin.** Der. *coffer-dam.*

COFFIN, a chest for enclosing a corpse. (F.—L.—Gk.) Originally any sort of case; it means a pie-crust in Shak. Tit. And. v. 2. 189. ME. *cofin, coffin.* The pl. *cofines* is in Rob. of Brunne, tr. of Langtoft, p. 135.—OF. *cofin,* a chest, case.—L. *cophinum,* acc. of *cophinus,* a basket.—Gk. κόφινος, a basket; Matt. xiv. 20, where the Vulgate version has *cophinos* and Wyclif has *cofyns.*

COG (1), a tooth on the rim of a wheel. (Scand.) ME. *cog, kog.* 'Scariaballum, *kog;*' Voc. p. 627. 'Hoc striabellum, a *cog* of a welle,' id. 725. 7. '*Cogge* of a mylle, *scarioballum;*' Prompt. Parv. p. 85. And see Owl and Nightingale, l. 86. [Gael. and Irish *cog,* a mill-cog: W. *cocos, cocs,* cogs of a wheel, are from E.] Of Scand. origin.—MDan. *kogge,* a cog; *kogge-hjul,* also *kagge-hjul,* a cog-wheel (Kalkar); Swed. *kugge;* MSwed. *kugg* (Ihre). Der. *cog-wheel.*

COG (2), to cheat, trick, delude. (Scand.) Obsolete. Common in Shak.; see Merry Wives, iii. 1. 123. 'To shake the bones and *cog* [cheat with] the craftie dice;' Turbervile, To his Friend P. Of Courting, l. 13. To *cog* dice was to control their fall, in a cheating way; see 'slyding, cogging, foysting;' Ascham, Toxophilus, ed. Arber, p. 54. Very likely, the little finger was used as a *cog,* being hitched against the die so as to direct it. The verb is almost certainly connected with the preceding sb.; cf. MDan. *kogge,* a cog, Norw. *kogga,* to dupe; Swed. *kugge,* a cog, *kugga,* to cheat. See **Cog** (1).

COGENT, powerful, convincing. (L.) In H. More, Immortality of the Soul, bk. i. c. 4.—L. *cōgent-,* stem of *cōgens,* pres. part. of *cōgere,* to compel.—L. *co-,* for *con,* which for *cum,* with; and *agere,* to drive. Brugm. i. § 968. See **Agent.** Der. *cogenc-y.*

COGITATE, to think, consider. (L.) Shak. has *cogitation,* Wint. Ta. i. 2. 271. But it also occurs very early, being spelt *cogitaciun* in the Ancren Riwle, p. 288.—L. *cōgitātus,* pp. of *cōgitāre,* to think. *Cōgitāre* is for **coagitāre,* i.e. to agitate together in the mind. —L. *co-,* for *con,* which for *cum,* with, together; and *agitāre,* to agitate, frequentative of *agere,* to drive. Brugm. i. § 968. See **Agitate, Agent.** Der. *cogitat-ion, cogitat-ive.*

COGNATE, of the same family, related, akin. (L.) In Howell's Letters, bk. iv. lett. 50. Bp. Taylor has *cognation,* Rule of Conscience, bk. ii. c. 2; and see *cognacioun* in Wyclif, Gen. xxiv. 4.—L. *cognātus,* allied by birth, akin.—L. *co-,* for *con,* which for *cum,* together; and *gnātus,* born, old form of *nātus,* pp. of *gnascī,* later *nascī,* to be born. See **Natal.**

COGNISANCE, knowledge, a badge. (F.—L.) We find *conisantes* in the sense of 'badges' (which is probably a scribal error for *conisances*) in P. Plowman's Crede, ed. Skeat, l. 185; also *conoiscance,* Gower, C. A. iii. 56; bk. vi. 1638. *Conisaunce* for 'knowledge' occurs in the Rom. of the Rose, 5559. – OF. *conoissance*, knowledge ; at a later time a *g* was inserted to agree more closely with the Latin ; see *cognoissance* in Cotgrave. – OF. *conoissant*, knowing, pres. pt. of OF. *conoistre*, to know. – L. *cognoscere*, to know. – L. *co-*, for *con*, i.e. *cum*, together ; and *gnoscere*, to know, cognate with E. *know*. See **Know**. Der. From the same F. verb we have *cognis-able*, *cognis-ant*. Here belongs *cognoscente*, pl. *-ti*, a connoisseur, Ital. *cognoscente*, from the pres. pt. stem of L. *cognoscere*.

COGNITION, perception. (L.) In Shak. Troil. v. 2. 63. Spelt *cognicion*, Sir T. More, Works, p. 4 a. – L. *cognitiōnem*, acc. of *cognitio*, a finding out, acquisition of knowledge ; cf. *cognitus*, pp. of *cognoscere*, to learn, know. – L. *co-*, for *con*, which for *cum*, together ; and *gnoscere*, to know, cognate with E. *know*. See **Know**.

COGNOMEN, a surname. (L.) Merely Latin, and not in early use. *Cognominal* occurs in Sir T. Browne, Vulg. Errors, bk. iii. c. 24. § 3. – L. *cognōmen*, a surname. – L. *co-*, for *con*, i.e. *cum*, together with ; and *nōmen*, a name, altered to *gnōmen* by confusion with *gnoscere*, to know, which is unrelated. See **Noun**.

COHABIT, to dwell together with. (L.) In Holland, Suetonius, p. 132. Barnes has *cohabitation*, Works, p. 322, col. 1. – L. *cohabitāre*, to dwell together. – L. *co-*, for *con*, i.e. *cum*, with ; and *habitāre*, to dwell. See **Habitation**, **Habit**. Der. *cohabit-at-ion*.

COHERE, to stick together. (L.) In Shak. Meas. ii. 1. 11. – L. *cohærēre*, to stick together. – L. *co-*, for *con*, i.e. *cum*, together ; and *hærēre*, to stick. Cf. Lithuanian *gaisz-ti*, to delay, tarry. See **Hesitate**. Der. *coher-ent*, *coher-ent-ly*, *coher-ence* ; also, like the pp. *cohæs-us*, we have *cohes-ion*, *cohes-ive*, *cohes-ive-ness*.

COHORT, a band of soldiers. (F. – L.) In Shak. K. Lear, i. 2. 162. – F. *cohorte*, ' a cohort, or company . . . of souldiers ;' Cot. – L. *cohortem*, acc. of *cohors*, a band of soldiers. The orig. sense of *cohors* was an enclosure, a sense still preserved in E. *court*, which is a doublet of *cohort* ; see Max Müller, Lectures, 8th ed. ii. 277. See **Court.**

COIF, a cap, cowl. (F. – MHG. – L.) ME. *coif*, *coife* ; Polit. Songs, ed. Wright, p. 329 ; Wyclif, Exod. xxviii. 40 ; xxix. 6. – OF. *coife* (Supp. to Godefroy) ; spelt *coiffe*, Cotgrave ; Low L. *cofia*, a cap ; also spelt *cuphia*, *cofea*. – MHG. *kuffe*, *kupfe*, OHG. *chuppa*, *chuppha*, a cap worn under the helmet ; Teut. stem **kupp-jōn-*. β. This word is a derivative of MHG. *kopf*, OHG. *chuph*, a cup, also the head. – L. *cuppa*, a cup. Körting, § 5339. See **Cup**. Der. *coiff-ure*.

COIGN, a corner. (F. – L.) In Shak. Macb. i. 6. 7. – F. *coing*, given by Cotgrave as another spelling of *coin*, a corner ; he also gives the dimin. *coignet*, a little corner. The spellings *coign*, *coing*, were convertible. – L. *cuneum*, acc. of *cuneus*, a wedge. See **Coin.**

COIL (1), to gather together. (F. – L.) ' *Coil'd* up in a cable ;' Beaum. and Fletcher, Knight of Malta, ii. 1. – OF. *coillir*, *cuillir*, *cueillir*, to collect ; whence also E. *cull*. – L. *colligere*, to collect. See **Cull, Collect.** Der. *coil*, sb.

COIL (2), a noise, bustle, confusion. (F. – L.) It occurs frequently in Shak. ; see Temp. i. 2. 207 ; Much Ado, iii. 3. 100. Orig. a collection ; hence, in prov. E., a hay-cock, heap of hay ; also (through the idea of a collected crowd) confusion, bustle, stir, noise, &c. ' This mortal *coil*,' the turmoil of life ; Hamlet, iii. 1. 67. All from **Coil** (1). See E.D.D. and N.E.D. [Gael. *coileid*, a stir, is from E.]

COIN, stamped money. (F. – L.) ME. *coin*, *coyn* ; Chaucer, C. T. 9044 (E. 1168). – OF. *coin*, a wedge, a stamp upon a coin, a coin ; so named from its being stamped by means of a wedge. – L. *cuneum*, acc. of *cuneus*, a wedge. A doublet of *coign*, a corner, q. v. Der. *coin*, verb ; *coin-age*, ME. *coyngnage*, Lydgate, Minor Poems, p. 49.

COINCIDE, to agree with, fall in with. (L.) In Wollaston, Relig. of Nature, s. 3 ; the word *coincident* is in Bp. Taylor, On Repentance, c. 7, s. 5. – L. *co-*, for *con*, i.e. *cum*, together with ; and *incidere*, to fall upon, from *in*, upon, and *cadere*, to fall. See **Cadence**. Der. *coincid-ent*, *coincid-ence*.

COIR, the prepared fibre of the husk of cocoa-nut, for making ropes. (Malayālam.) The true sense is ' rope.' ' Sowed together with *cayro*, which is threede made of the huske of cocoes ;' Hakluyt, Voy. ii. pt. 1. p. 251. – Malayālam *kāyar*, rope, cord ; from *kāyaṟu*, to be twisted (Yule) ; Tamil *kayaṟu*, rope (H. H. Wilson).

COISTREL, **COYSTRIL**, a mean paltry fellow. (F. – L.) In Shak. Tw. N. i. 3. 43 ; Per. iv. 6. 176. Used for *coustrel*, which was the older form. ' Coustrell, that wayteth on a speare, *cousteillier* ;' Palsgrave. From this evidence we may also infer that *coustrell* was an E. adaptation of the MF. word *cousteillier* or *coustillier*, probably formed by the dropping of the last syllable and insertion of *r* after *t* (as in *cart-r-idge*). – MF. *coustillier*, ' an esquire of the body, an armour-bearer unto a knight, the servant of a man-at-armes [which explains Palsgrave's definition] ; also a groom of a stable, a horse-keeper ;' Cotgrave. The use of the word in the sense of ' paltry fellow ' is precisely parallel to the similar use of *groom*, *lackey*, *hind*, &c. The

lit. sense is one who carries a poniard. – MF. *coustille*, ' a kind of long ponniard, used heretofore by esquires ;' Cot. Variant of OF. *coustel*, spelt *cousteau* in Cotgrave, ' a knife, or whittle, a sword, or any such cutting weapon.' The *s* is unoriginal ; the proper OF. spelling is *coutel* or *cotel*, also *cultel*. – L. *cultellus*, a knife ; see **Cutler**, **Cutlass**. The Late L. equivalent of *coistrel* is *cultellārius*, a soldier armed with a cutlass (Ducange).

COIT, another spelling of **Quoit**, q. v.

COITION, a meeting together, copulation. (L.) Used by Sir T. Browne of the meeting together of magnetised substances ; Vulgar Errors, bk. ii. c. 2. § 8. – L. acc. *coitiōnem*, a meeting together ; cf. L. *coitus*, pp. of *coīre*, to come together. – L. *co-* (for *cum*), together ; *īre*, to go, come.

COKE, charred coal. (Scand. ?) Not in early use. Plot, in his Staffordshire, ed. 1686, p. 128, says : ' The coal thus prepared they call *coaks*.' It may be identified with ME. *colke*, the core of an apple, the same as prov. E. *coke*, the core of an apple, also spelt *cowk*. ' *Coke*, pit-coal or sea-coal charred ;' Coles, Dict. ed. 1684. ' *Cowks*, or cinders ;' E. D. S., Gloss. B. 17. ' *Cowk*, the core : it's badly burnt lime, it's nought but *cowks* ;' Cumberl. Gloss., E. D. S. Of doubtful origin. Perhaps allied to MSwed. *kok*, *koka*, Swed. *koka*, a clod, clot ; Norw. *kōk*, a clod, lump (as of earth or snow).

COLANDER, a strainer. (Prov. – L.) ' A *colander* or strainer ;' Holland, Plutarch, p. 223. Also in Dryden, tr. of Virgil, Georg. ii. 328 ; see also his tr. of Ovid, Metam. bk. xii. l. 588. ' Colatorium, a *colyndore* ;' Voc. 574. 10. [Also spelt *cullender*.] A SFrench or Provençal word. – OProv. *colador (Span. *colador*), mod. Prov. *couladou* (for *couladour), a small basket used for straining wine from a cask (Mistral). – L. type *cōlātōrem, acc. of *cōlātor, a strainer ; by-form of L. *cōlātōrium*, a strainer. – L. *cōlāre*, to strain. – L. *cōlum*, a strainer, colander, sieve. The *n* is intrusive, as in *celandine*.

COLCHICUM, a genus of liliaceous plants. (L. – Gk.) Described as ' Mede Saffron ' in Lyte, tr. of Dodoens, bk. iii. c. 35. – L. *colchicum*. – Gk. Κολχικόν, meadow saffron ; neut. of Κολχικός, Colchian. – Gk. Κολχίς, Colchis ; a country to the E. of the Black Sea.

COLD, without heat, chilled. (E.) ME. *cold*, *cald*, *kald* ; Old Eng. Homilies, ed. Morris, i. 251, 283. OMerc. *cald* ; AS. *ceald* ; Matt. x. 42. ✛ Icel. *kaldr* ; Swed. *kall* ; Dan. *kold* ; Du. *koud* ; Goth. *kalds* ; G. *kalt*. Teut. type *kal-doz, cold ; from **kal-*, to be cold, as in Icel. *kal-a*, to freeze ; with suffix *-doz* = Gk. *-τός*. Cf. L. *gelidus* : and see **Cool**, **Chill.** Der. *cold-ly*, *cold-ish*, *cold-ness*.

COLE, **COLEWORT**, cabbage. (L.) For the syllable *-wort*, see **Wort**. ME. *col*, *caul* ; spelt *cool* in Palladius on Husbandry, bk. ii. st. 32. The comp. *kole-plantes* is in P. Plowman, B. vi. 288. AS. *cawel*, *cāul* ; see numerous examples in Gloss. to Cockayne's Leechdoms. Not an E. word. – L. *caulis*, a stalk, a cabbage. ✛ Gk. *καυλός*, a stalk ; lit. a hollow stem ; cf. L. *caulæ*, openings ; and prob. allied to E. *hollow*. See **Hollow.** ¶ The numerous related Teutonic words, including G. *kohl*, are all alike borrowed from the Latin. *Cole* is a variant of *kail*, q. v. ; cf. *cauliflower*, *colza*.

COLEOPTERA, an order of insects. (Gk.) A modern scientific term, to express that the insects are ' sheath-winged.' – Gk. κολεό-s, κολεό-ν, a sheath, scabbard ; and πτερ-όν, a wing. For κολεός, see Prellwitz. The Gk. πτερόν is from ✔ PET, to fly ; see **Feather**. Der. *coleopter-ous*.

COLIBRI, a humming-bird. (F. – Carib.) In Churchill's Collection of Voyages (1732), v. 650, we find : ' Very little birds, by the French called *colibris*, but by the English humming-birds.' This is in a description of Martinique, one of the French Caribbean islands. – F. *colibri* ; from Caribbean. See Notes on E. Etym., p. 349.

COLIC, a pain in the bowels. (F. – L. – Gk.) Also spelt *cholic* ; Shak. Cor. ii. 1. 83. Properly an adjective, as in ' *collick* paines ;' Holland, Pliny, bk. xxii. c. 25 (Of Millet). ME. *colyke* ; Prompt. Parv. – F. *colique*, adj. ' of the chollick,' Cotgrave ; also used as sb. and explained by ' the chollick, a painful windinesse in the stomach or entrailes.' – L. *colicus*, affected with colic. – Gk. κωλικός, better κολικός, suffering in the colon. – Gk. κῶλον, better κόλον, the colon, intestines. See **Colon** (2).

COLISEUM, a bad spelling of Colosseum ; see **Colossus.**

COLLABORATOR, a fellow-labourer. (L.) A modern word ; suggested by F. *collaborateur*, and formed on a Latin model. – L. *collabōrātor*, a modern coined word, formed by suffixing the ending *-tor* to *collabōrā-*, for *collabōrāre*, to work together with. – L. *col-*, for *con-* before *l*, which is for *cum*, together with ; and *labōrāre*, to labour, from the sb. *labor*. See **Labour.**

COLLAPSE, to shrink together, fall in. (L.) The sb. is in much later use than the verb, and is omitted in Todd's Johnson ; Richardson's three examples give only the pp. *collapsed*, as in ' *collapsed* state,' Mirrour for Magistrates, p. 588. This pp. is a translation into English of the L. *collapsus*, pp. of *collābi*, to fall together, fall in a heap. — L. *col-*, for *con-* before *l*, which is for *cum*, with ; and *lābī*, to glide down, lapse. See **Lapse.** Der. *collapse*, sb.

COLLAR, something worn round the neck. (F. — L.) ME. *coler*, later *coller* ; Rob. of Glouc. p. 223, l. 4577 ; P. Plowman, B. prol. 162, 169. — AF. *coler*, Royal Wills, p. 155 ; OF. *colier*, later *collier*, a collar ; see Cotgrave. — L. *collāre*, a band for the neck, collar. — L. *collum*, the neck ; cognate with Goth. *hals*, G. *hals*, AS. *heals*, the neck. Brugmann, i. § 662. Der. *collar-bone* ; from the same source is *coll-et* (F. *collet*), the part of a ring in which the stone is set, lit. a little neck. See **Collet.**

COLLATERAL, side by side, indirect. (L.) In Shak. All's Well, i. 1. 99. Also in P. Plowman, C. xvii. 136. — Late L. *collaterālis* ; Ducange. — L. *col-*, for *con*, i.e. *cum*, with ; and *laterālis*, lateral, from *later-*, decl. stem of *latus*, a side. See **Lateral.** Der. *collateral-ly*.

COLLATION, a comparison ; formerly, a conference. (F. — L.) The verb *collate*, used by Daniel in his Panegyric to the King, was hardly borrowed from Latin, but rather derived from the sb. *collation*, which was in very common use at an early period in several senses. See Chaucer, C. T., 8201 (E 325) ; tr. of Boethius, bk. iv. pr. 4. 49. The common ME. form was *collacion*. — OF. *collacion, collation*, a conference, discourse ; Godefroy. — L. *collātiōnem*, acc. of *collātio*, a bringing together, conferring ; cf. *collātum*, supine in use with the verb *conferre*, to bring together, but from a different root. — L. *col-*, for *con*, i.e. *cum*, together with ; and *lātum*, supine used with the verb *ferre*, to bring. The older form of *lātum* was *tlātum*, and it was connected with the verb *tollere*, to take, bear away ; so that the L. *tlātus* = Gk. τλητός, borne. — √TEL, to lift, sustain ; whence also E. *tolerate*, q. v. Der. *collate, collat-or*.

COLLEAGUE (1), a coadjutor, partner. (F. — L.) 'S. Paule gaue to Peter hys *colleague* ;' Frith, Works, p. 61, col. 1. — MF. *legue*, 'a colleague, fellow, or co-partener in office ;' Cot. — L. *collēga*, a partner in office. — L. *col-*, for *con*, i.e. *cum*, together with ; and *legere*, to choose. See **Legend, College, Collect.**

COLLEAGUE (2), verb, to join in an alliance. (F. — L.) In Hamlet, i. 2. 21. — OF. *colleguer, colliguer*, to colleague with. — L. *colligāre*, to bind together. — L. *col-*, for *con-* or *cum*, together ; *ligāre*, to bind. See **League** (1).

COLLECT, vb., to gather together. (F. — L.) In Shak. K. John, iv. 2. 142. [But the sb. *cóllect* is in early use, spelt *collecte* in the Ancren Riwle, p. 20. This is derived from Late L. *collecta*, a collection in money, an assembly for prayer ; used ecclesiastically to signify a collect ; on which see Trench, On the Study of Words. L. *collecta* is the fem. of the pp. *collectus*, gathered together.] — OF. *collecter*, to collect money ; Roquefort. — Late L. *collectāre*, to collect money. — L. *collecta*, a collection in money. — L. *collecta*, fem. of *collectus*, gathered together, pp. of *colligere*, to collect. — L. *col-*, for *con*, i.e. *cum*, together ; and *legere*, to gather, to read. See **Legend.** Der. *collect-ion, collect-ive, collect-ive-ly, collect-or, collect-or-ate, collect-or-ship.* From the same source are *college*, q.v., and *colleague* (1), q. v. Doublets, *cull*, q. v., *coil* (1), q. v.

COLLEEN, a girl. (Irish.) Modern. — Irish *cailín*, a girl ; dimin. of *caile*, a country-woman. The E. *colleen bawn* is from Irish *cailín bān*, a fair (lit. white) girl.

COLLEGE, an assembly, seminary. (F. — L.) Spelt *collage*, Skelton, Garland of Laurel, l. 403 ; *colledge* in Tyndal, Works, p. 359, col. 2. — MF. *college*, 'a colledge ;' Cot. — L. *collēgium*, a college, society of persons or colleagues. — L. *collēga*, a colleague. See **Colleague** (1). Der. *collegi-an, collegi-ate*, both from L. *collegi-um*.

COLLET, the part of the ring in which the stone is set. (F. — L.) Used by Cowley, Upon the Blessed Virgin, l. 11. It also means a collar. — F. *collet*, a collar, neck-piece. — F. *col*, the neck ; with suffix *-et*. — L. *collum*, the neck. See **Collar.**

COLLIDE, to dash together. (L.) Burton, Anat. of Melancholy, p. 274, uses both *collide* and *collision* (R.). — L. *collīdere*, pp. *collīsus*, to clash or strike together. — L. *col-*, for *con-*, i.e. *cum*, together ; and *lædere*, to strike, dash, injure, hurt. See **Lesion.** Der. *collis-ion*, allied to the pp. *collis-us*.

COLLIE, COLLY, a kind of shepherd's dog. (E.) 'Coaly, Coley, a cur dog ;' Brockett's Glossary of N. Eng. Words, 1825. 'Coley, a cur-dog ; North ;' Grose, Gloss. (1790). Shepherd-dogs 'in the N. of England are called *coally* dogs ;' Recreations in Nat. History, London, 1815. — Supposed to be the same word as *coaly*, black (like coal) ; from the coal-black hairs. Cf. prov. E. *colley*, soot, also to blacken ; and see below. Cf. *collied*, i.e. blackened, in Shak. Mid. Nt. Dr. i. 1.145 ; see **Colly** (1).

COLLIER, a worker in a coal-mine. (E.) ME. *colier, colʒer* ; spelt also *kolier, cholier*, William of Palerne, ed. Skeat, 2520, 2523. Formed from ME. *col*, coal, by help of the suffix *-er*, with the insertion of *i* for convenience of pronunciation, just as in *law-yer* for *law-er*,

---

bow-yer for *bow-er, saw-yer* for *saw-er*. Thus the strict spelling should, by analogy, have been *col-yer*. See further under **Coal.** Der. *collier-y*.

COLLIMATE, to adjust a telescope accurately. (L.) Cockeram has : '*Collimate*, to levell, or winke with one eye ;' he means ' to aim at.' — L. *collīmāt-us*, pp. of *collīmāre*, a false form, being a misreading for *collīneāre*, to direct in a straight line, to aim, in some editions of Cicero. Being mistaken for a real word, it was used by Kepler (1604). — L. *col-*, for *cum*, together, with ; *līneāre*, to make straight, from *līnea*, a straight line. See **Line.** Der. *collimat-ion*.

COLLOCATE, to place together. (L.) In Hall's Chron. Rich. III, an. 3. § 45. — L. *collocātus*, pp. of *collocāre*, to place together. — L. *col-*, for *con*, i.e. *cum*, together ; and *locāre*, to place, from *locus*, a place. See **Locus.** Der. *collocat-ion*. Doublet, *couch*, q. v.

COLLODION, a solution of gun-cotton. (Gk.) Modern. Named from its glue-like qualities. — Gk. κολλώδης, like glue, viscous. — Gk. κόλλα, glue ; and suffix *-ειδης*, like, from ειδος, appearance ; see **Idol.**

COLLOP, a slice of meat. (E.) '*Colloppe*, frixatura, carbonacium, carbonella ;' Prompt. Parv. p. 88. The pl. *coloppes* is in P. Plowman, B. vi. 287. But in the same, C. ix. 309, 4 MSS. out of 6 have the older spelling *colhoppes*. A compound word ; orig. *col-hoppe*, where *col-* is the ME. *col*, a coal. In Noreen's Altschwed. Lesebuch, p. 145, we have : '*kol-huppadher* . . , adj. roasted in the glow of the coals ; cf. Swed. *glöd-hoppad*.' The latter means 'roasted on the gledes or glowing coals ;' from *glöd*, a glede. Rietz has Swed. dial. *glö-hoppa, glöd-hyppja, glö-hyppe*, a cake baked on the gledes. We may conclude that ME. *col-hoppe* meant 'a thing baked or fried on the coals.' But the form *hoppe* requires further elucidation. See Notes on E. Etym., p. 44. A connexion with G. *hippe* (for *hüppe*, formerly *hyp*), a wafer, seems possible ; see Weigand.

COLLOQUY, conversation. (L.) Used by Wood, Athenæ Oxonienses (R.) 'In the midst of this divine *colloquy* ;' Spectator, no. 237. [Burton and others use the corrupt verb to *collogue*, now obsolete.] — L. *colloquium*, a speaking together. — L. *colloqui*, to confer, converse with. — L. *col-*, for *con-*, i.e. *cum*, together ; and *loqui*, to speak. See **Loquacious.** Der. *colloqui-al, colloqui-al-ism*.

COLLUDE, to act with others in a fraud. (L.) Not very common. It occurs in Milton's Tetrachordon (R.) ; and Cotgrave has F. *colluder*, 'to collude.' The sb. *collusion* is commoner ; it is spelt *collucyoun* in Skelton, Garland of Laurel, l. 1195 ; and *collusioun* in Chaucer, Lak of Stedfastnesse, l. 11. — L. *collūdere*, pp. *collūsus*, to play with, act in collusion with. — L. *col-*, for *con-*, i.e. *cum*, with ; and *lūdere*, to play. See **Ludicrous.** Der. *collus-ion, collus-ive, collus-ive-ly, collus-ive-ness* ; all like the pp. *collūs-us*.

COLLY (1), to blacken, darken. (E.) 'Brief as the lightning in the *collied* night ;' Mid. Nt. Dream, i. 1. 145. ME. *colwen* ; whence '*colwyd*, Carbonatus ;' Prompt. Parv. From AS. *col*, a coal ; so that the orig. sense was 'to begrime with coal-dust ;' see **Collie.**

COLLY (2), a kind of dog. (E.) See **Co'lie.**

COLOCYNTH, COLOQUINTIDA, the pulp of the fruit of a species of cucumber. (Gk.) *Coloquintida* is in Shak. Othello, i. 3. 355. '*Colocynthis*, a kind of wild gourd purging phlegm ;' Kersey's Dict. ed. 1715. *Coloquintida* stands for *colocynthida* (with hard *c* before *y*), and is the acc. case of *colocynthis* (iv [ii] Kings, iv. 39, Vulgate) ; this is the Latinised form of Gk. κολοκυνθίς, the plant *colocynth*, of which the acc. case is κολοκυνθίδα. The construction of new nominatives from old accusatives was a common habit in the middle ages. Besides κολοκυνθίς, we find also κολόκυνθος, κολοκύντη, a round gourd or pumpkin. β. Perhaps for κολο-κυνθίς, from κολο-, large, as in κολό-κυμα, great wave, and *-κυνθίς*, from κυείν, to be big (as with child) ; see Prellwitz.

COLON (1), a mark printed thus (:) to mark off a clause in a sentence. (Gk.) The word occurs in Blount's Glossographia, ed. 1674 ; and in Puttenham, Arte of E. Poesie, bk. ii. c. 5 ; ed. Arber, p. 88. The mark occurs much earlier, viz. in the first English book ever printed, Caxton's Recuyell of the Historyes of Troye, ab. 1474 ; leaf 250, back, l. 7. — Gk. κῶλον, a member, limb, clause ; the mark being so called as marking off a limb or clause of a sentence.

COLON (2), part of the intestines. (Gk.) It occurs in Massinger, Virgin-Martyr, iii. 3 (Hircius, speech 12) ; and in Coles's Dict. 1684. — Gk. κῶλον, a part of the intestines ; more correctly κόλον (Liddell and Scott). Der. *colic*, q. v.

COLONEL, the chief commander of a regiment. (F. — Ital. — L.) It occurs in Milton, Sonnet on When the Assault was intended to the City. Massinger has *colonelship*, New Way to pay Old Debts, Act iii. sc. 2. [Also spelt *coronel*, Holland's Pliny, bk. xxii. c. 23 ; which is the Spanish form of the word, due to substitution of *r* for *l*, a common linguistic change ; whence also the present pronunciation *curnel*. An early example is : 'Hee was *coronell* of the footemen, thowghe that tearme *in those dayes unuzed* ;' Life of Lord Grey

(Camden Soc.), p. 1; written in 1575, and referring to 1544.]—F. *colonel*, *colonnel*; Cotgrave has: '*Colonnel*, a colonell or coronell, the commander of a regiment.' Introduced from Ital. in the 16th century (Brachet).—Ital. *colonello*, a colonel; also a little column. The *colonel* was so called because he led the little column or company at the head of the regiment. 'La campagnie colonelle, ou la colonelle, est la première compagnie d'un regiment d'infanterie;' Dict. de Trevoux, cited by Wedgwood. The Ital. *colonello* is a dimin. of Ital. *colonna*, a column.—L. *columna*, a column. See **Column, Colonnade.** Der. *colonel-ship*, *colonel-cy*.

COLONNADE, a row of columns. (F.—Ital.—L.) Spelt *colonade* (wrongly) in Bailey's Dict. vol. ii. ed. 1731.—F. *colonnale* (not in Cotgrave).—Ital. *colonnata*, a range of columns.—Ital. *colonna*, a column.—L. *columna*, a column. See **Column.**

COLONY, a body of settlers. (F.—L.) The pl. *colonyes* is in Spenser, View of the State of Ireland, Globe ed. p. 614, col. 2; *colonye* in Wyclif, Acts xvi. 12.—F. *colonie*, 'a colony;' Cotgrave.—L. *colōnia*, a colony.—L. *colōnus*, a husbandman, colonist.—L. *colere*, to till, cultivate land. *Colere* is for *quelere; cf. L. *in-quilinus*, a sojourner; Brugm. i. § 121. Allied to Gk. πέλομαι, I am, Skt. *char*, to move. Der. *coloni-al*; also *colon-ise*, *colonis-at-ion*, *colon-ist*.

COLOPHON, an inscription at the end of a book, giving the name or date. (Gk.) Used by Warton, Hist. of Eng. Poetry, sect. 33, footnote 2.—Late L. *colophōn*, a Latinised form of the Gk. word.—Gk. κολοφών, a summit, top, pinnacle; hence, a finishing stroke. Allied to Gk. κολώνη, a hill, L. *cel-sus*, lofty, and E. *hol-m* and *hill*.

COLOPHONY, a dark-coloured resin obtained from distilling turpentine. (L.—Gk.) Spelt *colophōnia* in Coles's Dict. ed. 1684. L. *colophōnia*. Named from *Colophōn*, a city of Asia Minor.—Gk. κολοφών, a summit; see above.

COLOQUINTIDA; see **Colocynth.**

COLOSSUS, a gigantic statue. (L.—Gk.) In Shak. Jul. Cæs. i. 2. 136. Particularly used of the statue of Apollo at Rhodes.—L. *colossus*.—Gk. κολοσσός, a great statue. Lit. 'lofty;' allied to Gk. κολωνός, a hill, and to **Column.** Der. *coloss-al*; *coloss-eum*, also written *coliseum*, named from its magnitude (Gibbon).

COLOUR, a hue, tint, appearance. (F.—L.) ME. *colur*, *colour*. 'Rose red was his *colur*;' K. Horn, ed. Lumby, l. 16.—OF. *colur*, *colour* (F. *couleur*).—L. *colōrem*, acc. of *color*, colour, tint. Der. *colour*, verb, *colour-able*, *colour-ing*, *colour-less*.

COLPORTEUR, a hawker of wares. (F.—L.) Modern, and mere French. F. *colporteur*, one who carries things on his neck and shoulders.—F. *colporter*, to carry on the neck.—F. *col*, the neck; and *porter*, to carry.—L. *collum*, the neck; and *portāre*, to carry. See **Collar** and **Porter.** Der. *colport-age*.

COLT, a young animal, young horse. (E.) Applied in the A.V. (Gen. xxxii. 15, Zech. ix. 9) to the male young of the ass and camel. ME. *colt*, a young ass; O. Eng. Homilies, ed. Morris, i. 3, l. 8. AS. *colt*, a young camel, a young ass; Gen. xxxii. 15.+Swed. dial. *kullt*, a boy, lad; cf. Swed. *kull*, a brood, a hatch, Dan. *kuld*, a brood, Dan. dial. *koltring*, a lad. Der. *coltish*.

COLTER; see **Coulter.**

COLUMBINE, the name of a plant. (F.—L.) Lit. 'dove-like.' ME. *columbine*, Lyric Poems, ed. Wright, p. 26; Prompt. Parv. p. 88.—OF. *colombin*, dove-like; Cotgrave gives: '*Colombin*, the herbe colombine; also colombine or dove-colour, or the stuff whereof 'tis made.'—Late L. *columbīna*, as in 'Hec *columbīna*, a columbyne;' Voc. 710. 35.—L. *columbīnus*, dove-like; fem. *columbīna*.—L. *columba*, a dove; *columbus*, a male dove. Perhaps borrowed from Gk. κόλυμβος, a diver; cf. κολυμβίς, a diver, sea-bird. ¶ The calyx and corolla resemble doves.

COLUMN, a pillar, body of troops. (L.) Also applied to a perpendicular set of horizontal lines, as when we speak of a *column* of figures, or of printed matter. This seems to have been the earliest use in English. '*Columne* of a lefe of a boke, *columna*;' Prompt. Parv. p. 88.—L. *columna*, a column, pillar; allied to L. *columen*, a top, height, summit, *culmen*, the highest point. Cf. also *collis*, a hill, *celsus*, high. See **Colophon, Culminate.** (√QEL). Der. *column-ar*; also *colonnade*, q. v.

COLURE, one of two great circles on the celestial sphere at right angles to the equator and to each other. (L.—Gk.) So named because a part of them was always beneath the horizon in Greece; the word means clipped, lit. curtailed, docked. Used by Milton, P. L. ix. 66.—L. *colūrus*, curtailed; also, a coline.—Gk. κόλουρος, dock-tailed, stump-tailed, truncated; as sb., a colure.—Gk. κολ-, stem of κόλος, docked, clipped, stunted; and οὐρά, a tail.

COLZA OIL, a lamp-oil made from the seeds of a variety of cabbage. (F.—L. *and* Du.) See Webster and London; *colza* means 'cabbage-seed,' and should not be used of the cabbage itself.—F. *colza*, better spelt *colzat*, as in Richelet; borrowed from the Walloon *colza*, *golza*, Rouchi *colia*; see Remacle and Sigart.—Du. *koolzaad*,

rape-seed, cole seed, lit. cabbage-seed.—Du. *kool*, cabbage; *zaad*, seed (Littré). The Du. *kool* is not a Teut. word, but borrowed from L. *caulis*; Du. *zaad* is cognate with E. *seed*. See **Cole** and **Seed.**

COM-, a common prefix; the form assumed in composition by the L. prep. *cum*, with, when followed by *b, f, m*, or *p*. See **Con-.**

COMA, a deep sleep, trance, stupor. (Gk.) '*Coma*, or *Coma somnolentum*, a deep sleep;' Kersey's Dict. ed. 1715. Late L. *cōma*, a Latinised form of Gk. κῶμα, a deep sleep; perhaps allied to Gk. κοιμάω, I put to sleep. See **Cemetery.** Der. *comat-ose*, *comat-ous*; from κωματ-, stem of κῶμα, gen. κώματος.

COMB, a toothed instrument for cleansing hair. (E.) ME. *camb*, *comb*. Spelt *camb*, Ormulum, 6340. 'Hoc pecten, *combe*;' Wright's Vocab. i. 199. Spelt *komb*, Polit. Songs, ed. Wright, p. 327. A cock's crest is another sense of the same word. '*Combe*, or other lyke of byrdys;' Prompt. Parv. p. 88. It also means the crest of a hill, of a dyke, or of a wave; as in 'the dikes *comb*;' Genesis and Exodus, ed. Morris, 2564. In *honey-comb*, the parallel cells seem to have been likened to the arrangement of teeth in a comb. AS. *camb*, a comb, crest; *camb helmes*, the crest of a helmet; *camb on hætte*, or *on helme*, a crest on the hat or helmet; see the examples in Bosworth. +Du. *kam*, a comb, crest; Icel. *kambr*, a comb, crest, ridge; Dan. *kam*, a comb, ridge, cam on a wheel; Swed. *kam*, a comb, crest; OHG. *kamb*, *kambo*; MHG. *kamp*, G. *kamm*, a comb, crest, ridge, cog of a wheel. Teut. type *kamboz; Idg. type *gombhos. β. Perhaps named from the teeth in it; cf. Gk. γόμφος, a peg, γαμφή, a jaw; Skt. *jambha-s*, a tooth; Russ. *zub'*, a tooth. Allied to O. Church Slav. *zobati*, to eat. Brugmann, i. § 138. Der. *comb*, verb, *comb-er*.

COMB, COOMB, a dry measure; 4 bushels. (E.) '*Coomb* or *Comb*, a measure of corn containing four bushels;' Kersey's Dict. ed. 1715. 'A *coeme* (or *coome*) is halfe a quarter;' Tusser, Husbandrye, § 17, st. 7. AS. *cumb*, a liquid measure, in Bosworth; see Birch, Cart. Saxon. i. 380; Cockayne, Leechdoms, iii. 28.+Du. *kom*, a bowl; Low G. *kumm*, *kump*; G. *kumme*, *kumpf*, a bowl, deep dish. ¶ *Coomb* is the better form; *cumb* became *cūmb*; cf. *room* from AS. *rūm*.

COMBAT, to fight, contend, struggle against. (F.—L.) A verb in Shak. Much Ado, ii. 3. 170; a sb. in Merry Wives, i. 1. 165. He also has *combatant*, Rich. II, i. 3. 117.—OF. *combatre*, 'to combate, fight, bicker, battell;' Cot.—F. *com-*, from L. *com-*, for *cum*, with; and F. *battre*, from *battere, for L. *battuere*, to beat, strike, fight. See **Batter.** Der. *combat*, sb., *combat-ant* (F. *combatant*, pres. part. of *combatre*); *combat-ive*, *combat-ive-ness*.

COMBE, a hollow in a hill-side. (C.) Common in place-names, as Farncombe, Hascombe, Compton (for Combe-ton). These names prove the very early use of the word, but the word is not E.; it was in use in England beforehand, being borrowed from the Celtic inhabitants of Britain. AS. *cumb*; see Birch, Cart. Saxon. i. 290.—W. *cwm* [pron. *koom*], a hollow between two hills, a dale, dingle; occurring also in place-names, as in *Cwm lychan*, i.e. little combe; Corn. *cum*, a valley or dingle; more correctly, a valley opening downwards, from a narrow point; from Celtic type *kumbā, a valley.

COMBINE, to join two things together, unite. (L.) In Shak. K. John, v. 2. 37. ME. *combinen*, *combynen*. '*Combynyn*, or copulyn, *combino*, *copulo*;' Prompt. Parv. p. 88. Lydgate has the pp. *combyned*, Minor Poems, p. 61.—L. *combināre*, to combine, unite; lit. to join two things together, or to join by two and two.—L. *com-*, for *cum*, together; and *binus*, pl. *bini*, two and two. See **Binary.** Der. *combin-at-ion*, Hamlet, iii. 4. 60.

COMBUSTION, a burning, burning up. (F.—L.) In Shak. Macb. ii. 3. 63. Also *combustious*, adj., Venus and Adonis, 1162. Sir T. More has *combustib'e*, Works, p. 264 d. The astrological term *combust* was in early use; Chaucer, Troil. and Cress. iii. 717.—F. *combustion*, 'a combustion, burning, consuming with fire;' Cot.—L. *combustiōnem*, acc. of *combustio*, a burning; cf. *combustus*, pp. of *combūrere*, to burn up.—L. *comb-*, for *cum*, together, wholly; and *ūrere*, pp. *ustus*, to burn; the insertion of the *b* being perhaps due to association with *amb-ūrere*. Der. From the same source, *combustible*, *combust-ible-ness*.

COME, to move towards, draw near. (E.) ME. *cumen*, *comen*, to come; pt. t. *I cam* or *com*, *thu come*, *he cam* or *com*, *we*, *ye*, or *thei comen*; pp. *cumen*, *comen*, *come*; very common. AS. *cuman*, pt. t. *cwōm*, *cōm*, pp. *cumen*.+Du. *komen*; Icel. *koma*; Dan. *komme*; Swed. *komma*; Goth. *kwiman*; OHG. *queman*, MHG. *komen*, G. *kommen*.+L. *uenire* (for *guen-ire or *guem-ire)? Gk. βαίνειν, to come, go (where β is for *gw*); Skt. *gam*, to come, go.—√GwEM, to come, go. Brugm. i. § 431. Der. *come-ly*, q. v.

COMEDY, a humorous dramatic piece. (F.—L.—Gk.) Shak. has *comedy*, Merry Wives, iii. 5. 76; also *comedian*, Tw. Nt. i. 5. 194. Spelt *commedy*, it occurs in Trevisa, i. 315.—OF. *comedie*, 'a comedy, a play;' Cotgrave.—L. *cōmoedia*.—Gk. κωμῳδία, a comedy, ludicrous spectacle. − Gk. κωμῳδός, a comic actor. − Gk. κωμο-, for κῶμος, a banquet, a jovial festivity, festal procession ; and ἀοιδός, a singer, from ἀείδειν, to sing ; a comedy was originally a festive spectacle, with singing and dancing. For the latter part of the word, see **Ode**. **Der.** comedi-an. Closely related is the adj. comic, from L. cōmicus, Gk. κωμικός, belonging to comedy ; whence, later, comic-al (Levins).

COMELY, becoming, seemly, handsome. (E.) ME. cumlich, cumelich, comlich, comli, comeliche. Spelt comeliche, Will. of Palerne, ed. Skeat, 963, 987 ; comly, id. 294. Also used as an adv., id. 660 ; but in this sense comlyly also occurs ; Chaucer, Book of the Duchess, 848. The comparative was comloker, and the superl. comlokest or comliest. AS. cymlic, comely, Grein, i. 177 ; cymlice, adv. id. β. According to the account in the N. E. D. (from which I dissent), the AS. cymlic was formerly cȳmlīc (with ȳ), and was allied to AS. cyme (formerly cȳme ?), fine, beautiful ; which again is allied to OHG. cūmig, weak, tender, and to OHG. kūm, with difficulty (G. kaum). Thus the orig. sense was 'like what is weak or tender ; ' but the ȳ was shortened before ml, and the AS. cymlīc was associated with AS. cuman, to come, and so gained the sense of ' becoming,' pleasing, decorous. γ. But we find AS. cymlicor as early as in Beowulf, l. 38, where it practically means ' stronger ; ' and the other examples of AS. cymlīc point to a similar reference to beauty or strength. Moreover, we find MDu. komelick, ' apt, fit, or conveniable,' Hexham ; which is connected with komen, to come. Cf. also **Become**. I see no reason for connecting comely with OHG. cūmig ; but prefer to connect it with **Come**. See Phil. Soc. Trans. 1902, p. 658. **Der.** comeli-ness.

COMET, a star with a hair-like tail. (F. − L. − Gk.) ME. comete, Rob. of Glouc. pp. 416, 548. − OF. comete, ' a comet, or blazing star ; ' Cot. It occurs as early as the 12th century (Hatzfeld). − L. comēta, comētēs, a comet. − Gk. κομήτης, long-haired ; hence, a comet. − Gk. κόμη, the hair of the head ; cognate with L. coma, the same. **Der.** comet-ar-y. ☞ The L. comēta occurs frequently in the AS. Chron. an. 678, and later. But the later form was due to French influence ; cf. AF. comete, Gaimar, 1433.

COMFIT, a confect, a dry sweetmeat. (F. − L.) In Shak. 1 Hen. IV, iii. 1. 253. Spelt comfitte, Hall's Chron. Henry VIII, an. 13. Corrupted from confit, by the change of n to m before f. ME. confite, so spelt in Babees Book, ed. Furnivall, p. 121, l. 75 ; cf. ' Confectio, confyt,' Voc. 574. 36. − OF. confit, preserved, prepared, lit. ' steeped, confected, fully soaked ; ' Cotgrave. This word is the pp. of confire, ' to preserve, confect, soake ; ' id. − L. conficere, to put together, procure, supply, prepare, manufacture ; pp. confectus ; whence Late L. confectæ, fruits preserved with sugar (Ducange), OF. confite, f., a comfit, also confit, m. (the same) ; Godefroy. − L. con-, for cum, with, together ; and facere, to make. See **Fact**. Comfit is a doublet of confect, q. v. **Der.** comfit-ure ; see Chaucer, C. T., C 862.

COMFORT, to strengthen, encourage, cheer. (F. − L.) See Comfort in Trench, Select Glossary. Though the verb is the original of the sb., the latter seems to have been earlier introduced into English. The ME. verb is conforten, later comforten, by the change of n to m before f. It is used by Chaucer, Troil. and Cress. iv. 722, v. 234, 1395. [The sb. confort is in Chaucer, Prol. 775, 778 (A 773, 776); but occurs much earlier. It is spelt cunfort in O. Eng. Homilies, ed. Morris, i. 185 ; kunfort in Ancren Riwle, p. 14.] − OF. conforter, to comfort ; spelt cunforter in A. F. ; see Vie de St. Auban, ed. Atkinson, 59, 284. − Late L. confortāre, to strengthen, fortify ; Ducange. − L. con-, for cum, together ; and fortis, strong. See **Fort**. **Der.** comfort, sb. ; comfort-able, comfort-abl-y, comfort-less.

COMFREY, the name of a plant. (F. − L.) Spelt comfory, Book of St. Albans, fol. c 6, back, l. 1 ; confery in the 14th cent., Reliquiæ Antiquæ, i. 55 ; and in Henslow, Medical Werkes, 46. 10. (See also comfrey in Britten and Holland's Plant-Names.) − OF. cumfirie ; we find ' cumfiria, cumfirie, galloc,' in a vocab. of the 13th cent., Voc. 555. 4 ; also OF. cunfirie, confire in Godefroy. Here cumfirie is the OF. name ; galloc the AS. name, and cumfiria, the Late L. name ; the last appears to be merely the OF. name Latinised. We even find the F. form consire in Cotgrave, explained as ' the herbe comfrey ; ' but this may be an error for confire. [The mod. F. name is consoude (cf. Span. consuelda, Ital. consolida), derived from L. consolidāre, from its supposed healing powers.] β. The OF. cumfirie or cunfirie appears to be a corruption of L. conferua, comfrey, Pliny, xxvii. 8. [Another Late L. name was confirma ; we find ' confirma, galluc,' in the Durham Glossary, pr. in Cockayne's Leechdoms, iii. 301 ; and at p. 162 of vol. i. we learn that the plant was called confirma or galluc. Halliwell gives ' galloc, comfrey.' Perhaps the change from conferva or confirma to cumfirie was due to some confusion with F. confire (L. conficere), ' to preserve, confect, soake, or steep in ; ' Cotgrave.] γ. If this be right, the derivation is either from L. conferuēre, to heal, grow together, said of broken limbs (Celsus) ; or from L. confirmāre, to strengthen, from its healing

powers ; see Cockayne's Leechdoms, i. pref. p. liii, and cf. the Gk. name σύμφυτον.

COMIC, COMICAL ; see under **Comedy**.

COMITY, urbanity. (L.) Not very common. ' Comity, gentleness, courtesie, mildness ; ' Blount, Glossographia, ed. 1674. Not from F., but directly from L., the suffix -ity being employed by analogy with words ending in F. -ité, from L. -itātem. − L. cōmitātem, acc. of cōmitās, urbanity. − L. cōmis, friendly, courteous.

COMMA, a mark of punctuation, written thus (,). (L. − Gk.) ' The shortest pause . . they called comma ; ' Puttenham, Arte of E. Poesie, bk. iv. c. iv (v) ; ed. Arber, p. 88. In Hamlet, v. 2. 42. − L. comma, a separate clause of a sentence. − Gk. κόμμα, that which is struck, a stamp, a clause of a sentence, a comma that marks off the clause. − Gk. κόπ-τειν, to hew, strike.

COMMAND, to order, enjoin. (F. − L.) ME. commanden, comanden, Chaucer, C. T., B 4270 ; Cursor Mundi, 6809. − OF. commander, comander. − Late L. commandāre, a new compound, with the sense of L. mandāre, to command ; confused with and partly replacing L. commendāre, to commend, also (in Late L.) to command. − L. com-, for cum, together with ; mandāre, to put into the hands of, entrust, command. See **Mandate**. **Der.** command, sb. ; commander, -er-ship ; command-ing, -ing-ly ; command-ment (F. commandement), whence ME. commandement, in O. Eng. Misc., ed. Morris, p. 33, and command-e-ment, quadrisyllabic, in Spenser, F. Q. i. 3. 9 ; command-ant, (F. command-ant, pres. pt. of commander) ; also command-eer (Du. kommanderen, to force into military service, from F. commander). And see **Commodore**.

COMMEMORATE, to celebrate with solemnity. (L.) Cockeram (in 1642) has : ' Commemorate, to rehearse or make mention.' − L. commemorāt-us, pp. of commemorāre, to call to mind. − L. com-, for cum, together ; and memorāre, to mention, from memor, mindful. See **Memory**. **Der.** commemorat-ion, -ive.

COMMENCE, to begin. (F. − L.) In Shak. Macb. i. 3. 133. The contracted form comsen (for comencen) occurs frequently in ME. ; see P. Plowman, B. i. 161, iii. 103. The sb. commencement was in early use ; O. Eng. Miscellany, ed. Morris, p. 30. − OF. comencer, commencer, commencier (Supp. to Godefroy). [Rightly with one m ; cf. Ital. cominciare.] − L. com-, for cum, together ; initiāre, to begin, from initium, a beginning. See **Initiate**. **Der.** commence-ment.

COMMEND, to commit, entrust to, praise. (L.) ' It shal commende ; ' Wyclif, Isaiah x. 28 ; where the Vulgate has commendabit. − L. commendāre, to entrust, commit to. − L. com-, for cum, with ; and mandāre, to put into the hands of ; see **Command**. **Der.** commend-at-ion (see Rom. Rose, 4887), -able, -abl-y, -able-ness, -at-or-y.

COMMENSURATE, co-extensive, of equal extent. (L.) ' Commensurate, of the same or equal measure ; ' Glossographia Anglicana (1719). Sir T. Brown has it as a verb ; ' Yet can we not thus commensurate the sphere of Trismegistus ; ' Vulgar Errors, bk. vii. c. 3, end. − L. commensurātus, as if the pp. of *commensūrāre, to measure in comparison with. − L. com-, for cum, together ; mensūrāre, to measure, from mensūra, a measure ; see **Measure**. **Der.** commensurate, adj., -ly, -ness ; commensur-able, -abl-y, -abil-i-ty.

COMMENT, to make a note upon. (F. − L.) In As You Like It, ii. 1. 65. The pl. sb. commentes is in Sir T. More, Works, p. 152 c ; and in Sir T. Elyot, The Governour, bk. i. c. 14. § 10. − F. commenter, ' to comment, to write commentaries, to expound ; ' Cot. − Late L. commentāre, for L. commentāri, to reflect upon, consider, explain. − L. commentus, pp. of comminisci, to devise, invent, design. − L. com-, for cum, with ; and the base -min-, seen in me-min-i, a reduplicated perfect of an obsolete verb *men-ere, to call to mind ; with the inceptive deponent suffix -sci. √ MEN, to think ; cf. Skt. man, to think. Brugmann, i. § 431. See **Mental**. **Der.** comment, sb., comment-ar-y, comment-at-or.

COMMERCE, trade, traffic. (F. − L.) In Hamlet, iii. 1. 110. [Also formerly in use as a verb ; see Milton, Il Penseroso, l. 39.] − F. commerce, m., ' commerce, intercourse of traffick, familiarity ; ' Cot. − L. commercium, commerce, trade. − L. com-, for cum, with ; and merc-, for merx, goods, wares, merchandise, with suffix -i-um. See **Merchant**. **Der.** commerci-al, commerci-al-ly ; both from L. commerci-um.

COMMINATION, a threatening, denouncing. (F. − L.) ' The terrible comminacion and threate ; ' Sir T. More, Works, p. 897 f. − F. commination, ' a commination, an extreme or vehement threatning ; ' Cot. − L. comminātiōnem, acc. of comminātio, a threatening, menacing ; cf. comminātus, pp. of comminārī, to threaten. − L. com-, for cum, with ; and minārī, to threaten. See **Menace**. **Der.** commina-tor-y, from L. inf. comminārī.

COMMINGLE, to mix together. (Hybrid ; L. and E.) Also comingle ; Shak. has comingled or commingled, Hamlet, iii. 2. 74. An ill-coined word ; made by prefixing the L. co- or com- (for cum, with) to the E. word mingle. See **Mingle** ; and see **Commix**.

COMMINUTION, a reduction to small fragments. (L.) Bacon has *comminution*, Nat. Hist. § 799. Sir T. Browne has *comminuible*, Vulgar Errors, b. ii. c. 5. § 1. [The verb *comminute* is later, and due to the sb.; it occurs in Pennant's Zoology, The Gilt Head.] Formed on the model of F. sbs. in *-ion*, from L. *comminūtus*, pp. of *comminuere*, to break into small pieces; (easily imitated from L. *minūtionem*, acc. of *minūtio*, a diminishing, allied to *minūtus*, pp. of *minuere*, to make smaller). — L. *com-*, for *cum*, together; and *minuere*, to make smaller, diminish. See **Minute**. Der. *comminute*, verb.

COMMISERATION, a feeling of pity for, compassion. (F. — L.) In Shak. L. L. L. iv. 1. 64. We also find the verb *commiserate*; Drayton, Dudley to Lady Jane Grey, l. 98. Bacon has '*commiserable* persons;' Essay 33, Of Plantations. — F. *commiseration*, 'commiseration, compassion;' Cot. — L. *commiserātionem*, acc. of *commiserātio*, a part of an oration intended to excite pity (Cicero); cf. *commiserātus*, pp. of *commiserāri*, to endeavour to excite pity. — L. *com-*, for *cum*, with; and *miserāri*, to lament, pity, commiserate, from *miser*, wretched, deplorable. See **Miserable**. Der. from the same source, *commiserate*, verb.

COMMISSARY, an officer to whom something is entrusted. (L.) 'Specyall *commyssaries*;' Fabyan, ed. Ellis, p. 549. 'The emperor's *commisaries*' answere, made at the diett;' Burnet, Rec. pt. iii. b. v. no. 32 (R.) We also find *commisariship* in Foxe's Martyrs, p. 1117, an. 1544 (R.)—Late L. *commissārius*, one to whom anything is entrusted (F. *commissaire*); Ducange.—L. *commissus*, pp. of *committere*, to commit. See **Commit**. Der. *commisari-al*, *commisari-at*, *commissary-ship*.

COMMISSION, trust, authority, &c. (F.—L.) In Chaucer, Prol. 315.—F. *commission*, 'a commission, or delegation, a charge, mandate;' Cot.—L. *commissionem*, acc. of *commissio*, the commencement of a play or contest, perpetration; in Late L., a commission, mandate, charge (Ducange); cf. *commissus*, pp. of *committere*, to commit. See **Commit**. Der. *commission-er*.

COMMIT, to entrust to, consign, do. (L.) 'Thanne shul ye *committe* the kepyng of your persone to your trewe frendes that been approued and y-knowe;' Chaucer, Tale of Melibeus (Six-text), Group B, l. 2495.—L. *committere*, pp. *commissus*, to send out, begin, entrust, consign, commit.—L. *com-*, for *cum*, with; and *mittere*, to send. See **Missile**. Der. *commit-ment*, *committ-al*, *committ-ee*; also (like pp. *commissus*), *commissary*, q. v.; and *commission*, q. v.

COMMIX, to mix together. (Hybrid; L. *and* E.) 'Commyxt with moold and flynt;' Palladius on Husbandry, bk. ii. st. 21; cf. bk. iii. st. 3. A coined word; made by prefixing L. *com-* (for *cum*, with) to E. *mix*. See **Mix**, and **Commingle**. Der. *commixture*, which is, however, *not* a hybrid word, the sb. *mixture* being of L. origin, from L. *mixtūra* or *mistūra*, a mixing, mixture; it occurs in Shak. L. L. L. v. 2. 296. He also has *commixtion* (MF. *commistion*, Cot.: from L. *commistiōnem*, acc. of *commistio*, a mixing, mixture); but it occurs earlier, spelt *comyxtioun* in Trevisa, ii. 159; see Spec. of Eng. ed. Morris and Skeat, p. 241, l. 161.

COMMODIOUS, comfortable, useful, fit. (F.—L.) Spelt *commodiouse* in Palladius on Husbandry, bk. ii. st. 22. Englished from OF. *commodieux* (Godefroy).—Late L. *commodiōsus*, useful; Ducange. Formed with suffix *-ōsus* from *commodi-*, for L. *commodus*, convenient; lit. in good measure.—L. *com-*, for *cum*, together; and *modus*, measure. See **Mode**. Der. *commodious-ly*, *commodious-ness*; from the same source, *commod-ity*; also *commode*, which is the F. form of L. *commodus*.

COMMODORE, the commander of a squadron. (Du.—F.—L.) 'Commodore, a kind of admiral, or commander in chief of a squadron of ships at sea;' Kersey's Dict. ed. 1715. Applied to Anson, who died A.D. 1762; it occurs in Anson's Voyage, b. i. c. 1. First used in the time of Will. III., and spelt *commander* (N. E. D.)—Du. *commandeur*; 'den *Commandeur van een Stadt*, the Commandeur of a Towne;' (Hexham). This shows that E. *commandeur*, in the sense of 'commander,' is as early as 1658.—F. *commandeur*.—L. acc. type **commandātōrem*; from Late L. *commandāre*; see **Command**.

COMMON, public, general, usual, vulgar. (F.—L.) ME. *commun*, *comun*, *comoun*, *comon*, *comune*. Spelt *commun*, Rob. of Glouc. p. 541, l. 11215.—OF. *commun*.—L. *commūnis*, general.—L. *com-*, for *cum*, with; and *mūnis*, complaisant, obliging, ready to serve (Plautus). Cf. L. *mūnus*, service. (As if 'serving each other.') Cf. also Lith. *mainas*, Russ. *miena*, barter. Brugm. i. § 208. Der. *common-ly*, *common-ness*, *common-er*, *common-al-ty*, *common-place* (see *place*), *common-weal*, *common-wealth* (see *weal*, *wealth*); s. pl. *commons*. Also, from L. *commūnis*, we have *commun-ion*, *commun-ist*, *commun-i-ty*; and see *commune*.

COMMOTION, a violent movement. (F.—L.) Spelt *commocion*; Sir T. More, Works, p. 43 f.—F. *commotion*, 'a commotion, tumult, stirre;' Cot.—L. *commōtiōnem*, acc. of *commōtio*, a commotion. —L. *com-*, for *cum*, with; and *mōtio*, motion. See **Motion**.

COMMUNE, to converse, talk together. (F.—L.) ME. *comunen*. 'With suche hem liketh to *comune*;' Gower, C. A. i. 64; bk. i. l. 651. Also *communien*; spelt *communy*, Ayenbite of Inwyt, p. 102. 'Y ne shal nouʒt *commune* wyth;' Early E. Prose Psalter, Ps. cxl. (cxli.) 5; where the Vulgate has *non communicabo*.—OF. *communier*, to communicate.—L. *commūnicāre*, to communicate, pp. *commūnicātus*. —L. *commūnis*, common. See **Common**. ¶ Partly also from OF. *communer*, to have in common. Der. From the L. *communicāre* we also have *communicate*, a doublet of *commune*; *communicant* (pres. part. form); *communicat-ive*, *-ive-ness*, *-ion*, *-or-y*; *communica-ble*, *-bl-y*.

COMMUTE, to exchange. (L.) In Bp. Taylor, Liberty of Prophesying, s. 19 (R.) The sb. *commutation* is in Strype's Records, no. 23 (R.) The adj. *commutative* (F. *commutatif*) is in Sir T. Elyot, The Governour, b. iii. c. 1. § 3.—L. *commūtāre*, to exchange with.—L. *com-*, for *cum*, with; and *mūtāre*, to change, pp. *mūtātus*. See **Mutable**. Der. *commut-able*, *-abil-i-ty*, *-at-ion*, *-at-ive*, *-at-ive-ly*.

COMPACT (1), adj., fastened or put together, close, firm. (F.—L.) '*Compacte*, as I mought say, of the pure meale or floure;' Sir T. Elyot, The Governour, b. i. c. 14. § 5.—MF. *compacte*, 'compacted, well set, knit, trust [trussed], pight, or joined together;' Cot.—L. *compactus*, well set, joined together, pp. of *compingere*, to join or put together.—L. *com-*, for *cum*, with; and *pangere*, to fasten, plant, set, fix, pp. *pactus*. See **Pact**. Der. *compact*, verb; *compact-ly*, *-ed-ly*, *-ness*, *-ed-ness*; and see below.

COMPACT (2), sb., a bargain, agreement. (L.) In Shak. gen. accented *compáct*, As You Like It, v. 4. 5.—L. *compactum*, an agreement.—L. *compactus*, pp. of *compacisci*, to agree with.—L. *com-*, for *cum*, with; and *pacisci*, to covenant, make a bargain; formed from an old verb *pac-ere*, with inceptive suffix *-sc-ī*. See **Pact**.

COMPANY, an assembly, crew, troop. (F.—L.) ME. *companie*, *companye*, in early use; see An Old Eng. Miscellany, ed. Morris, p. 138, l. 709.—OF. *companie*, *compaignie*, *compagnie*, company, association (cf. OF. *compain*, a companion, associate; also OF. *compainon*, *companion*, a companion).—Late L. *compāniem*, acc. of *compāniēs*, a company, a taking of meals together; cf. Late L. *compānis*, victuals eaten along with bread.—L. *com-*, for *cum*, with; and *pānis*, bread. See **Pantry**. Der. *compani-on*; whence *companion-ship*, *-able*, *-abl-y*, *-less*; also *ac-company*, q. v.

COMPARE, to set things together, in order to examine points of likeness or difference. (F.—L.) In Shak. K. John, i. 79. Spelt *comper* in Barbour, Bruce, i. 403. [The sb. *comparison* is in early use; see Chaucer, C. T. Group E. 666, 817 (Clerk's Tale).]—OF. *comperer*; F. *comparer*; Cot.—L. *comparāre*, pp. *comparātus*, to couple together, to match, compare.—L. *compar*, like, equal.—L. *com-*, for *cum*, together; and *pār*, equal. See **Par**. ¶ Distinct from L. *comparāre*, to acquire, a derivative of *parāre*, to prepare; see *compare* in Spenser, F. Q. i. 4. 28. Der. *compar-able*, *comparat-ive*, *-ive-ly*; also *compar-ison*, from F. *comparaison* (Cotgrave), which from L. *comparātiōnem*, acc. of *comparātio*, a comparing.

COMPARTMENT, a separate division of an enclosed space. (F.—Ital.—L.) In Florio's Ital. Dict. (1598). 'In the midst was placed a large *compartment*;' Carew, A Masque at Whitehall, an. 1633 (R.)—F. *compartiment*, 'a compartement, . . . a partition;' Cot.—Ital. *compartimento*, 'a compartment, a partition;' Florio.—Ital. *compartire*, Late L. *compartīre*, to divide, partition; Ducange.—L. *com-*, for *cum*, with, together; and *partīre*, to divide, part, share, from L. *parti-*, declensional stem of *pars*, a part. See **Part**.

COMPASS, a circuit, circle, limit, range. (F.—L.) ME. *compas*, *cumpas*, of which a common meaning was 'a circle.' 'As the point in a *compas*' = like the centre within a circle; Gower, C. A. iii. 92; bk. vii. 229. 'In manere of *compas*' = like a circle; Chaucer, C. T., A 1889.—F. *compas*, 'a compasse, a circle, a round; also, a paire of compasses;' Cot.—Late L. *compassus*, a circle, circuit; cf. Late L. *compassāre*, to encompass, to measure a circumference.—L. *com-*, for *cum*, together; and *passus*, a pace, step, track, or in Late L. a passage, way, pass, route: whence the sb. *compassus*, a route that comes together, or joins itself, a circuit (?). See **Pace, Pass**. ¶ But there is much doubt as to the history of the senses of Late L. *compassus* and *compassāre*. Der. *compass*, verb, Gower, C. A. i. 173, bk. ii. 409; Polit. Songs, p. 202 (ab. 1308); (a pair of) *compass-es*, an instrument for drawing circles.

COMPASSION, pity, mercy. (F.—L.) ME. *compassioun*, Chaucer, C. T., B 659.—OF. *compassion*; which Cotgrave translates by 'compassion, pity, mercie.'—L. *compassiōnem*, acc. of *compassio*, sympathy; cf. *compassus*, pp. of *compati*, to suffer together with, to feel compassion.—L. *com-*, for *cum*, together with; and *pati*, to suffer. See **Passion**. Der. *compassion-ate* (Tit. Andron. ii. 3. 217; Rich. II, i. 3. 174); *compassion-ate-ly*, *-ate-ness*. Shak. has also the verb *to compassion*, Tit. Andron. iv. 1. 124. And see *compat-ible*.

COMPATIBLE (often followed by **WITH**), that can bear with, suitable with or to. (F.—L.) Formerly used without *with*;

'not repugnant, but *compatible* ;' Sir T. More, Works, p. 485 d. – F. *compatible*, 'compatible, concurrable; which can abide, or agree together ;' Cot. – Late L. *compatibilis*, used of a benefice which could be held together with another. – L. *compati-*, for *compati*, to suffer or endure together with ; with passive suffix *-bilis*. – L. *com-*, for *cum*, together with ; and *pati*, to suffer. See above. Der. *compatibl-y* ; *compati-bili-ty* (F. *compatibilité*, as if from a L. acc. *compatibilitātem*).

COMPATRIOT, of the same country. (F.–L.) 'One of our *compatriots* ;' Howell's Letters, b. i. s. 1. letter 15 (1619). – MF. *compatriote*, 'one's countryman ;' Cot. – Late L. *compatriota*, a compatriot (Lewis). – L. *com-*, for *cum*, together with ; and *patriota*, a native, from *patria*, one's native soil, fem. of the adj. *patrius*, paternal (the subst. *terra*, land, being understood) ; from L. *patri-*, declensional stem of *pater*, father. See **Patriot**. ¶ The L. *patriōta* is an imitation of the Gk. πατριώτης, a fellow-countryman ; from Gk. πατριά, a lineage, allied to πατήρ, father.

COMPEER, a fellow, equal, associate. (F.–L.) ME. *comper*. 'His freend and his *compeer* ;' Chaucer, C. T. prol. A 670 (672). – OF. **comper*, a word not found, but probably in use as an equivalent of the L. *compar* ; the OF. *per* (whence E. *peer*) is very common. – L. *compar*, equal ; also, an equal, a comrade. – L. *com-*, for *cum*, together with ; and *pār*, an equal, a peer. See **Peer**. ¶ The F. *compère*, a gossip, godfather, is quite a different word ; it stands for L. *com-pater*, i.e. a godfather.

COMPEL, to urge, drive on, oblige. (F.–L.) ME. *compellen* ; the pp. *compelled* occurs in Trevisa, i. 247 ; ii. 159 ; see Spec. of English, ed. Morris and Skeat, p. 241, l. 166. – AF. *compeller*, Stat. of the Realm, i. 375 (1362) ; OF. *compeller*. – L. *compellere*, to compel, lit. to drive together ; pp. *compulsus*. – L. *com-*, for *cum*, together ; and *pellere*, to drive. See **Pulsate**. Der. *compell-able* ; also *compuls-ion* (K. John, ii. 218) ; *compuls-ive*, *-ive-ly*, *-or-y*, *-or-i-ly*, all like the L. pp. *compulsus*.

COMPENDIOUS, brief, abbreviated. (F.–L.) In Sir T. Elyot, The Governour, b. ii. c. 2, last section. The adv. *compendiously* is in the Romaunt of the Rose, l. 2346. Adapted from OF. *compendieux* (Palsgrave, p. 308). – L. *compendiōsus*, reduced to a small compass, compendious. – L. *compendi-um*, an abbreviation, abridgement ; with suffix *-ōsus* ; the lit. sense of *compendium* is a saving, sparing from expense. – L. *com-*, for *cum*, with ; and *pendere*, to weigh, to esteem of value. See **Pension**. Der. *compendious-ly*. The L. *compendium* is also in use in English.

COMPENSATE, to reward, requite suitably. (L.) 'Who are apt . . . to think no truth can *compensate* the hazard of alterations ;' Stillingfleet, vol. ii. sermon 1 (R.) *Compensation* is in Shak. Temp. iv. 1. 2. [The ME. form was *compensen*, used by Gower, C. A. i. 365 (bk. iii. 2554), now obsolete : borrowed from F. *compenser*, from L. *compensāre*.] – L. *compensātus*, pp. of *compensāre*, to reckon or weigh one thing against another. – L. *com-*, for *cum*, together with ; and *pensāre*, to weigh, frequentative form of *pendere*, to weigh, pp. *pensus*. See **Pension**. Der. *compens-at-ion*, *compens-at-or-y*.

COMPETE, to vie with another, contend in rivalry. (L.) Little used till lately, though found as early as 1620 (N. E. D.) Coles (1684) has *competize* instead of it. Englished from L. *competere* (below). See **Petition**.

COMPETENT, fit, suitable, sufficient. (F.–L.) '*Competente* salarye ;' Gesta Romanorum, ed. Herrtage ; c. lxi. p. 257. Also in Shak. Hamlet, i. 1. 90. Cf. *competence*, 2 Hen. IV, v. 5. 70 ; *competency*, Cor. i. 1. 143. – F. *competent*, 'competent, sufficient, able, full, convenient ;' Cot. Properly pres. part. of the F. verb *competer*, 'to be sufficient for ;' id. – L. *competere*, to solicit, to be suitable or fit. – L. *com-*, for *cum*, with ; and *petere*, to fly to, seek. Der. *competent-ly*, *competence*, *competenc-y*.

COMPETITOR, one who competes with another, a rival. (L.) In Shak. Two Gent. ii. 6. 35. [*Competition* occurs in Bacon, Hist. of Henry VII, ed. Lumby, p. 8, l. 23. The verb to *compete* came into general use later.] – L. *competitor*, a fellow-candidate for an office. – L. *com-*, for *cum*, together with ; and *petitor*, a candidate ; cf. *peti-tus*, pp. of *petere*, to fall, fly towards, seek ; with suffix *-tor* of the agent. – √ PET, to fly, fall ; cf. Skt. *pat*, to fly, Gk. πέτομαι, I fly ; and see **Feather**, **Pen** (1). Der. From the same source, *competit-ive*, *competit-ion* ; and see *compete*, *competent*.

COMPILE, to get together, collect, compose. (F.–L.) 'As I finde in a bok *compiled* ;' Gower, C. A. iii. 48 ; bk. vi. 1382. – OF. *compiler*, of which Cotgrave gives the pp. *compilé*, which he explains by 'compiled, heaped together ;' but the word is quite distinct from *pile*, a pillar or heap. – L. *compilāre*, pp. *compilātus*, to plunder, pillage, rob ; so that the word had at first a sinister meaning. – L. *com-*, for *cum*, with ; and *pilāre*, only with the sense 'to thrust,' perhaps allied to L. *pīlum*, a javelin ; see **Pile** (3). [Not the same word as *pilāre*, to deprive of hair.] Der. *compil-er* ; also *compilation*, from F. *compilation*, which from L. *compilātiōnem*, acc. of *compilātiō*.

COMPLACENT, gratified ; lit. pleasing. (L.) *Complacence* is in Milton, P. L. iii. 276 ; viii. 433. *Complacent* first appears about 1767 : 'with *complacent* smile ;' Jago, Edgehill, bk. iv. l. 104. – L. *complacent-*, stem of *complacens*, pres. pt. of *complacēre*, to please. – L. *com-*, for *cum*, with ; and *placēre*, to please. See **Please**. Der. *complacent-ly*, *complacence*, *complacenc-y*. Doublet, *complaisant*, q. v.

COMPLAIN, to lament, express grief, accuse. (F.–L.) In Chaucer, C. T. 6340 (D 758) ; Troil. and Cress. iv. 1170. – OF. *complaign-*, a stem of *complaindre*, 'to plaine, complaine ;' Cot. – Late L. *complangere*, to bewail. – L. *com-*, for *cum*, with ; and *plangere*, to bewail. See **Plaint**. Der. *complain-ant* (for *complaignant*, F. pres. part.), *complaint* (F. past part.).

COMPLAISANT, pleasing, obliging. (F. – L.) Used by Cowley, on Echo, st. 2. – F. *complaisant*, 'obsequious, observant, soothing, and thereby pleasing ;' Cotgrave. Pres. pt. of verb *complaire*, to please. – L. *complacēre*, to please. *Complaisant* is a doublet of *complacent*, q. v. Der. *complaisance*, in Dryden, Kind Keeper, iv. 1.

COMPLEMENT, that which completes ; full number. (L.) 'The *complement* of the sentence following ;' Sir T. More, Works, p. 954 b. – L. *complēmentum*, that which serves to complete. Formed with suffix *-mentum* from the verb *complē-re*, to complete. See **Complete**. Der. *complement-al*, used by Prynne, Sovereign Power of Parliaments, pt. i. ; but in old books it is often another spelling of *complimental* ; see Shak. Troil. iii. 1. 42. ¶ *Complement* is a doublet of (Ital.) *compliment* ; the distinction in spelling is of late date. See *complement* in Schmidt, Shak. Lexicon. See **Compliment**.

COMPLETE, perfect, full, accomplished. (L.) The verb is formed from the adjective. 'The fourthe day *compleet* fro none to none ;' Chaucer, C. T. 9767 (E 1893). – L. *complētus*, pp. of *complēre*, to fulfil, fill up. – L. *com-*, for *cum*, with, together ; and *plēre*, to fill. See **Plenary**. Der. *complete*, verb ; *complete-ly*, *-ness*, *complet-ion* ; also *complement*, q. v. ; *complement*, q. v. *Complete*, verb, is a doublet of *comply*, q. v. ; and see *compline*.

COMPLEX, intricate, difficult. (L.) In Locke, Of Human Understanding, b. ii. c. 12. – L. *complexus*, entwined round, hence, intricate ; pp. of *complecti*, to embrace. – L. *com-*, for *cum*, together ; and *plectere*, to plait, allied to *plicāre*, to twine, whence E. *plait*. See **Plait**. Der. *complex-i-ty* ; and see *complex-ion*, *complic-ate*, *complic-ity*.

COMPLEXION, texture, outward appearance. (F.–L.) 'Of his *complexion* he was sanguin ;' Chaucer, C. T., A 333. – OF. (and mod. F.) *complexion*, complexion, appearance. – L. *complexiōnem*, acc. of *complexio*, a comprehending ; in Late L., a habit of the body, complexion ; cf. *complexus*, pp. of *complecti*, to embrace, twine around. – L. *com-*, for *cum*, with ; and *plectere*, to plait (above). Der. *complexion-ed*, *-al*.

COMPLIANCE, COMPLIANT ; see Comply.

COMPLICATE, to render complex. (L.) *Complicate* was originally used as an adj., as in : 'though they are *complicate* in fact, yet are they separate and distinct in right ;' Bacon, Of a War with Spain (R.) Milton has *complicated*, P. L. x. 523. – L. *complicātus*, pp. of *complicāre*, to plait together, entangle. – L. *com-*, for *cum*, together ; and *plicāre*, to fold. Cf. **Complex**. Der. *complic-at-ion* ; and see *complicity*.

COMPLICITY, the state of being an accomplice. (F.–L.) '*Complicity*, a consenting or partnership in evil ;' Blount's Glossographia, ed. 1674. [Not much used formerly ; but *complice*, i.e. accomplice, was common, though now less in use ; see Shak. Rich. II, ii. 3. 165.] – F. *complicité*, 'a conspiracy, a bad confederacy ;' Cot. – F. *complice*, 'a complice, confederate, companion in a lewd action ;' Cot. – L. *complicem*, acc. of *complex*, adj., confederate with, lit. interwoven. – L. *com-*, for *cum*, together, and *plicāre*, to fold. See **Accomplice** and **Plait**.

COMPLIMENT, compliance, courtesy. (F. – Ital. – Span. – L.) Often spelt *complement* in old edd. ; see Shak. Merry Wives, iv. 2. 5 ; Tw. Nt. iii. 1. 110 (where the First Folio has *complement* in both places) ; and editors systematically make the same alteration in other books. – F. *compliment*, introduced in the 16th cent. from Ital. (Brachet). – Ital. *complimento*, compliment, civility. Formed, by help of the suffix *-mento*, from the verb *compli-re*, to fill up, fulfil, suit. – MSpan. *complir*, to fit, to furnish. See **Comply**. ☞ *Complement* is the Lat. spelling of the same word. Der. *compliment*, verb ; *compliment-ar-y*. *Compliment* is also a doublet of *compliance* ; see **Comply**.

COMPLINE, the last church-service of the day. (F.–L.) ME. *complin*, Chaucer, C. T., 4169 (A 4171) ; Cursor Mundi, 25609. *Complin* is an adj. form (cf. *culver-in*, *flor-in*), as in *complin* song. The phr. *compling* (for *complin*) *song* is in Douglas's tr. of Virgil ; Prol. to bk. xiii. l. 35. The sb. is *complie*, or *cumplie*, Ancren Riwle, p. 24. – OF. *complie* (mod. F. *complies*, which is the plural of *complie*). – Late L. *complēta*, compline ; the fem. of L. *complētus*, complete.

See **Complete**. ¶ *Complēta* (sc. *hōra*) ; because it completed the 'hours' of the daily service.

COMPLOT, a conspiracy. See **Plot** (1).

COMPLY, to yield, assent, agree, accord. (Ital. – Span. – L.) In Shak. to *comply with* is to be courteous or formal; Hamlet, ii. 2. 390; v. 2. 195. Cf. Oth. i. 3. 264. Milton has *comply*, Sams. Agon. 1408; also *compliant*, P. L. iv. 332; *compliance*, P. L. viii. 603. [The word is closely connected with *compliment*, and may even have been formed by striking off the suffix of that word (see Skinner). It has no doubt been much influenced by *ply* and *pliant*, but is of quite a different origin. It is not of French, but of Italian origin.] – Ital. *complire*, to fill up, to fulfil, to suit; also 'to use or accomplish all complements;' Florio. – MSpan. *complir*, now *cumplir*, 'to fit, furnish, accomplish,' Minsheu; the true Ital. form being *compire*. – L. *complēre*, to fill up, complete. See **Complete**. ☞ Thus *comply* is really a doublet of *complete*. Der. *compli-ant*, *compli-ance*; false formations, imitating *pliant*, *appliance*.

COMPONENT, composing. (L.) Sometimes used as a sb., but generally as an adjective, with the sb. *part*. 'The *components* of judgments;' Digby, Of Man's Soul, c. 10, § 10 (A.D. 1645). – L. *compōnent-*, stem of *compōnens*, pres. part. of *compōnere*, to compose. See **Compound** (1).

COMPORT, to agree, suit, behave. (F. – L.) '*Comports* not with what is infinite;' Daniel, A Defence of Rhyme, § 8, ed. 1603 (R.) Spenser has *comportance*, i.e. behaviour, F.Q. ii. 1. 29. – F. *comporter*, 'to endure, beare, suffer;' Cotgrave. He also gives '*se comporter*, to carry, bear, behave, maintaine or sustaine himselfe.' – Late L. *comportāre*, to behave; L. *comportāre*, to carry or bring together. – L. *com-*, for *cum*, with; and *portāre*, to carry. See **Port** (1).

COMPOSE, to compound, make up, arrange, soothe. (F. – L. and Gk.) In Shak. Temp. iii. 1. 9; and somewhat earlier. '[He] *composed* and made a lampe;' Caxton, Troy-book, leaf 206, back. [Cf. ME. *compounen*, to compose; Chaucer's tr. of Boethius, bk. iii. met. 9. 6.] – F. *composer*, 'to compound, make, frame, dispose, order, digest;' Cot. – F. *com-*, from L. *com-*, for *cum*, with; and *poser*, to place, pose. See **Pose**. β. Not derived from L. *compōnere*, though used in the same sense, but from L. *com-* and *pausāre*, which is quite distinct from *pōnere*. Der. *compos-er*; *compos-ed*, *-ed-ly*, *-ed-ness*; *compos-ure*; and see below. And see **Compound** (1).

COMPOSITION, an agreement, a composing. (F. – L.) 'By forward and by *composicioun*;' Chaucer, C. T., A 848. – F. *composition*, 'a composition, making, framing,' &c.; Cot. – L. *compositiōnem*, acc. of *compositio*, a putting together; cf. *compositus*, pp. of *compōnere*, to put together, compose. See **Compound** (1). Der. Hence also *composit-or*, *composite*; *compost*.

COMPOST, a mixture, composition, manure. (F. – L.) '*Compostes* and confites' = condiments and comfits; Babees Boke, ed. Furnivall, p. 121, l. 75. Shak. has *compost*, Hamlet, iii. 4. 151; and *composture*, Timon, iv. 3. 444. – OF. *composte*, f., 'a condiment, or composition, . . . also pickle;' Cot. Also OF. *compost*, m. a mixture (Godefroy). – L. *compositus*, mixed, pp. of *compōnere*, to compose. See below. Thus *compost* is a doublet of *composite*; see above.

COMPOUND (1), to compose, mix, settle. (L.) The *d* is merely excrescent. ME. *componen*, *compounen*; *componeth* is in Gower, C. A. iii. 138; bk. vii. 1590. Chaucer has *compounen*, tr. of Boethius, bk. iii. met. 9. 6. – L. *compōnere*, to compose. – L. *com-*, for *cum*, together; and *pōnere*, to put, lay, a contraction of *po-sinere*, lit. 'to set behind;' whence the old pt. t. *posīuī*, Plautus, Pseudolus, v. 1. 35. See **Site**. Brugm. i. § 240. Der. *compound*, adj., short for *compoun-ed*, pp. of ME. *compounen* (above); whence *compound*, sb.; and see *compose*.

COMPOUND (2), the enclosure in which an Anglo-Indian house or factory stands. (Malay.) See the discussion and exx. in Yule. – Malay *kampong*, 'an enclosure, . . . a fenced village; a collection of buildings;' Marsden (1812).

COMPREHEND, to seize, grasp. (L.) ME. *comprehenden*, Chaucer, C. T. 10537 (F 223). – L. *comprehendere*, to grasp. – L. *com-*, for *cum*, with; and *prehendere*, to seize. β. *Prehendere* is compounded of L. *præ*, beforehand, and *hendere*, to seize, get, an obsolete verb cognate with Gk. χανδάνειν and with E. *get*. See **Prehensile**, **Get**. Der. *comprehens-ive*, *-ly*, *-ness*; *comprehens-ible*, *-ibl-y*, *-ible-ness*, *-ibil-i-ty*, *-ion*; all like *comprehens-us*, pp. of *comprehendere*. **Doublet**, *comprise*.

COMPRESS, to press together. (F. – L.) Used by Ralegh, Hist. of the World, b. i. c. 2. s. 7 (R.) Not in Shak. 'With his chekys *compressyd*;' Monk of Evesham, ed. Arber, p. 23. – OF. *compresser* (Godefroy); not in Cotgrave. [The sb. *compress* in the sense of 'bandage' is also French. Cotgrave gives : '*Compresse*, a boulster, pillow, or fold of linnen, to bind up, or lay on, a wound.'] – L. *com-pressāre*, to oppress; Tertullian. – L. *com-*, for *cum*, with; and *pressāre*,

to press; which from *pressus*, pp. of *premere*, to press. See **Press** (1). Der. *compress*, sb.; *compress-ible*, *-ibil-i-ty*, *-ion*, *-ive*.

COMPRISE, to comprehend. (F. – L.) 'The substance of the hole sentence is herin *comprised*;' Sir T. Elyot, The Governour, b. i. c. 13, § 10. The pt. t. *comprisit* occurs in The King's Quair, st. 28. – OF. (and F.) *compris*, also *comprins*. Burguy gives the form *compris* as well as *comprins*; but Cotgrave only gives the latter, which he explains by 'comprised, comprehended.' *Compris* is the shorter form of *comprins*, old pp. of F. *comprendre*, to comprehend. – L. *comprehendere*, to comprehend. Thus *comprise* is a doublet of *comprehend*, q.v. Der. *compris-al*.

COMPROMISE, a settlement by concessions. (F. – L.) Shak. has both sb. and verb; Merry Wives, i. 1. 33; Merch. i. 3. 79. Palsgrave has the sb. *compromyse*. – F. *compromis*, m., 'a compromise, mutuall promise of adversaries to refer their differences unto arbitrement;' Cot. Properly pp. of F. *compromettre*, 'to compromit, or put unto compromise;' Cot. – L. *comprōmittere*, to make a mutual promise. – L. *com-*, for *cum*, together; and *prōmittere*, to promise. See **Promise**. Der. *compromise*, verb (formerly also *compromit*).

COMPTROLLER, another spelling of *controller*; see **Control**.

COMPULSION, COMPULSIVE; see **Compel**.

COMPUNCTION, remorse. (F. – L.) 'Have ye *compunccioun*;' Wyclif, Ps. iv. 5; where the Vulgate version has *compungimini*. – OF. *compunction*, 'compunction, remorse;' Cot. – Late L. *compunctiōnem*, acc. of *compunctio* (Lewis); cf. L. *compunctus*, pp. of *compungī*, to feel remorse, pass. of *compungere*, to prick, sting. – L. *com-*, for *cum*, with; and *pungere*, to prick. See **Fungent**. Der. *compuncti-ous*.

COMPUTE, to calculate, reckon. (L.) Sir T. Browne has *computers*, Vulg. Errors, b. vi. c. 4. § 4; *computists*, id. b. vi. c. 8. § 17; *computable*, id. b. iv. c. 12. § 23. Shak. has *computation*, Com. Errors, ii. 2. 4; Milton, *compute*, P. L. iii. 580. – L. *computāre*, to compute. – L. *com-*, for *cum*, together; and *putāre*, to think, settle, adjust. β. The primary notion of *putāre* was to make clean, 'then to bring to cleanness, to make clear, and according to a genuinely Roman conception, to reckon, to think (cp. I *reckon*, a favourite expression with the Americans for I *suppose*);' Curtius, i. 349. – √PEU, to purify; see **Pure**. Der. *comput-at-ion*, *comput-able*. **Doublet**, *count* (2), q.v.

COMRADE, a companion. (F. – Span. – L.) In Shak. Hamlet, i. 3. 65. [Rather introduced by a blending of the Span. and F. forms than through the French only; the MF. *camerade* was only used, according to Cotgrave, to signify 'a chamberfull, a company that belongs to, or is ever lodged in, one chamber, tent, [or] cabin.' And the F. *camarade* was also taken from the Spanish; see Brachet. Besides, the spelling *camrado* occurs in Marmyon's Fine Companion, 1633; see Nares's Glossary, ed. Halliwell and Wright.] – Span. *camarada*, a company, society; also, a partner, comrade; [Minsheu has Span. *camarada*, 'a comerade or cabbin-mate souldier;'] *camaradas de navio*, ship-mates. – Span. *camara*, a chamber, cabin. – L. *camara*, *camera*, a chamber. See **Chamber**.

CON (1), to peruse, scan, observe closely. (E.) ME. *cunnien*, to test, examine. Of Jesus on the cross, when the vinegar was offered to him, it is said : 'he smeihte and *cunnede* therof' = he took a smack of it and *tasted* it, i.e. to see what it was like; Ancren Riwle, p. 114. – AS. *cunnian*, to test, try, examine into; Grein, i. 171. β. A secondary verb, formed from AS. *cunnan*, to know; it signifies accordingly 'to try to know;' and may be regarded as the desiderative of *to know*. See **Can**. Der. *ale-conner*, i.e. ale-tester (obsolete); *conn-ing-tower*, a tower for observation.

CON (2), used in the phrase *pro and con*; short for L. *contrā*, against; *prō* meaning 'for;' so that the phr. means 'for and against.'

CON-, a very common prefix; for *com-*, a form of L. *cum*, with. The form *con-* is used when the following letter is *c*, *d*, *g*, *j*, *n*, *q*, *s*, *t*, or *v*; and sometimes before *f*. Before *b*, *f*, *m*, *p*, the form is *com-*; before *l*, *col-*; before *r*, *cor-*. See **Com-**.

CONCATENATE, to link together. (L.) An unusual word; *concatenation* is in Bp. Beveridge's Sermons, vol i. ser. 38. 'Seek the consonancy and *concatenation* of truth;' Ben Jonson, Discoveries; section headed Notæ domini Sti. Albani, &c. – L. *concatēnātus*, pp. of *concatēnāre*, to chain together, connect. – L. *con-*, for *cum*, together; and *catēnāre*, to chain, from *catēna*, a chain. See **Chain**. Der. *concatenat-ion*.

CONCAVE, hollow, arched. (F. – L.) Shak. Jul. Cæs. i. 1. 52. – OF. *concave* (Hatzfeld). – L. *concauus*, hollow. – L. *con-*, for *cum*, with; and *cauus*, hollow. See **Cave**. Der. *concav-ity*.

CONCEAL, to hide, disguise. (F. – L.) ME. *concelen*, Gower, C. A. ii. 282; bk. v. 4635. – OF. *conceler* (Godefroy). – L. *concēlāre*, to conceal. – L. *con-*, for *cum*, together, wholly; and *cēlāre*, to hide. – √KEL, to hide, whence also *oc-cul-t*, *cell*, *domi-cile*, *cl-andestine*; cognate with Teutonic √HEL, whence E. *hell*, *hall*, *hole*, *hull*, *holster*, &c. Der. *conceal-ment*, *conceal-able*.

CONCEDE, to cede, grant, surrender. (L.) 'Which is not

conceded;' Sir T. Browne, Vulg. Errors, bk. i. c. 4. § 6. — L. concēdere, pp. concessus, to retire, yield, grant. — L. con-, for cum, together; wholly; and cēdere, to cede, grant. See **Cede.** Der. concess-ion, -ive, -or-y; like L. pp. concessus.

CONCEIT, a conception, idea, notion, vanity. (F. — L.) ME. conceipt, conceit, conseit, conseyt. 'Allas, conceytes wronge!' Chaucer, Troil. and Cress. iii. 804. Gower has conceite, C. A. i. 7; prol. 113. Formed, by analogy with deceit, as if from an OF. form *conceite, from L. concepta, f. [There is no OF. or AF. conceite, but Godefroy has deceite, and AF. deceyte is in the Statutes of the Realm, i. 34 (1275).] — L. concepta, fem. of conceptus, pp. of concipere, to conceive. See **Conceive.** Der. conceit-ed, -ed-ly, -ed-ness; cf. conception.

CONCEIVE, to be pregnant, take in, think. (F. — L.) ME. conceiuen, conceuen; with u for v. 'This preyere ... conceues [conceives, contains] alle the gode that a man schuld aske of God;' Wyclif's Works, ed. Arnold, iii. 442. — OF. conceiv-, a stem of concevur, concevoir, to conceive. — L. concipere, to conceive, pp. conceptus. — L. con-, for cum, together, wholly; and capere, to take, hold. See **Capable.** Der. conceiv-able, -abl-y, -able-ness; concept-ion, q. v.; conceit, q. v.

CONCENTRE, to tend or bring to a centre. (F. — L.) 'Two natures ... have been concentred into one hypostasis;' Bp. Taylor, vol. ii. ser. 1 (R.) Chaucer has concentrik; On the Astrolabe, i. 17. 3; i. 16. 6. Concentre is now supplanted by the (Latin) form concentrate. — F. concentrer, 'to joine in one center;' Cot. — F. con- (from L. con-, for cum, together); and centre, a centre. See **Centre.** Der. concentr-ic, concentrate (a coined word), concentrat-ive, -ion.

CONCEPTION, the act of conceiving; a notion. (F. — L.) ME. concepcion; Cursor Mundi, 220. — F. conception. — L. concept-iōnem, acc. of conceptio; cf. conceptus, pp. of concipere, to conceive. See **Conceive.**

CONCERN, to regard, belong to. (F. — L.) 'Such points as concerne our wealth;' Frith's Works, p. 46, col. 2. — F. concerner, 'to concerne, touch, import, appertaine, or belong to;' Cot. — L. concernere, to mix, mingle; in Late L. to refer to, regard; Ducange. — L. con-, for cum, together; and cernere, to separate, sift, decree, observe. L. cernere is cognate with Gk. κρίνειν, to separate, decide; Lith. skir-ti, to separate. — √SKER, to separate; Brugmann, ii. § 612. Der concern-ed, -ed-ly, -ed-ness, -ing, -ment.

CONCERT, to plan with others, arrange. (F. — Ital. — L.) [Often confused in old writers with consort, a word of different origin. Thus Spenser: 'For all that pleasing is to living eare Was there consorted in one harmonee;' F. Q. ii. 12. 70. See **Consort.**] 'Will any one persuade me that this was not ... a concerted affair?' Tatler, no. 171. — F. concerter, 'to consort, or agree together;' Cot. — Ital. concertare, 'to agree or tune together, accord together, to sing or play in consort;' Florio. β. Formed from L. concertāre, to dispute, contend, vie with, orig. a word of almost opposite meaning; but the Span. concertar meant to bargain, and (hence) to agree, covenant, come to terms; also, to settle, to harmonize, and even to tune musical instruments (see Minsheu and Neuman). Baretti (Ital. Dict., 1831) gives to concertare only the senses 'to concert, to contrive, to bring to pass;' with the sb. concerto, concert, harmony. γ. From L. con-, for cum, together; and certāre, to contend, vie with, orig. 'to decide by contest,' frequent. of cernere, to decide (Bréal). See **Concern.** Der. concert, sb., concerto (Ital.), concert-ina.

CONCESSION, CONCESSIVE; see **Concede.**

CONCH, a marine shell. (L. — Gk.) 'Adds orient pearls which from the conchs he drew;' Dryden, Ovid's Metam. x. 39 (Pygmaleon). — L. concha, a shell. — Gk. κόγχη (also κόγχος), a mussel, cockle-shell. +Skt. çankha-, a conch-shell. See **Cockle** (1). Der. conchi-ferous, shell-bearing, from L. ferre, to bear; concho-idal, conch-like, from Gk. εἶδος, appearance, form; concho-logy, from Gk. -λογία, from λέγειν, to speak; concho-log-ist. These forms with prefix concho- are from the Gk. κόγχο-s. Brugmann, i. § 631.

CONCILIATE, to win over. (L.) 'A philter or plant that conciliates affection;' Sir T. Browne, Vulgar Errors; bk. vii. c. 7. § 7. 'To conciliate amitie;' Joye, Exposition of Daniel, c. 11. — L. conciliātus, pp. of conciliāre, to conciliate, bring together, unite. — L. concilium, an assembly, union. See **Council.** Der. conciliat-ion, -or, -ory.

CONCINNITY, harmony, congruity, elegance of expression. (L.) Spelt concinnitie, meaning 'harmony;' Sir T. Elyot, The Governour, i. 20 (near the end). — L. acc. concinnitātem, skilful adjustment; from concinnus, skilfully adjusted. Der. concinnous, adj., from L. concinn-us, with suffix -ous.

CONCISE, cut short, brief. (F. — L.) Used by Drayton, Moses his Birth and Miracles, b. ii. 161. 'The concise style;' Ben Jonson, Discoveries; sect. headed De Stylo: Tacitus. [Perhaps taken directly from Latin.] — F. concis, m. concise, f. 'concise, briefe, short, succinct, compendious;' Cot. — L. concisus, brief; pp. of concidere, to hew in pieces, cut down, cut short, abridge. — L. con-, for cum, with; and cædere, to cut. See **Cæsura.** Der. concise-ly, -ness; also concis-ion (Philipp. iii. 2), from L. concisio, a cutting to pieces, dividing.

CONCLAVE, an assembly, esp. of cardinals. (F. — L.) In early use. ME. conclave, Gower, C. A., i. 254; bk. ii. 2812. — F. conclave, 'a conclave, closet,' &c.; Cot. — L. conclāve, a room, chamber; in Late L., the place of assembly of the cardinals, or the assembly itself. Orig. a locked up place. — L. con-, for cum, together; and clāuis, a key. See **Clef.**

CONCLUDE, to end, decide, infer. (L) 'And shortly to concluden al his wo;' Chaucer, C. T., 1360 (A 1358). — L. conclūdere, pp. conclūsus, to shut up, close, end. — L. con-, for cum, together; and claudere, to shut. See **Clause.** Der. conclus-ion, -ive, -ive-ly, -iveness; like pp. conclus-us.

CONCOCT, to digest, prepare, mature. (L.) 'Naturall heate concocteth or boyleth;' Sir T. Elyot, Castel of Helth, b. ii. ch. 1. — L. concoctus, pp. of concoquere, to boil together, digest. — L. con-, for cum, with; and coquere, to cook. See **Cook.** Der. concoct-ion, in Sir T. Elyot, Castel of Helth, b. iv. c. 1. § 1.

CONCOMITANT, accompanying. (L.) 'The waiting-maids Or the concomitants of it, are his patience,' &c.; Ben Jonson, New Inn, A. iv. sc. 3. 'Without any concomitant degree of duty or obedience;' Hammond, Works, iv. 657 (R.). Formed from concomitant-, stem of pres. part. of concomitāri, to accompany. The pp. concomitātus, accompanied, occurs in Plautus. — L. con-, for cum, together; and comitāri, to accompany, from comit-, stem of comes, a companion. See **Count** (1). Der. concomitant-ly; hence also concomitance (in Cotgrave), and concomitanc-y.

CONCORD, amity, union, unity of heart. (F. — L.) 'Concorde, concord;' Palsgrave's F. Dict. 1530; ME. concord, Chaucer, C. T. 9005 (E 1129). [The ME. verb concorden, to agree, is in Chaucer, Troil. and Cress. iii. 1752.] — F. concorde. — L. concordia. — L. concord-, stem of concors, concordant, agreeing. — L. con-, for cum, together; and cord-, stem of cor, the heart. See **Cordial,** and **Heart.** Der. concordant, q.v.; also concordat, q.v.

CONCORDANT, agreeing. (F. — L.) 'Concordant discords;' Mirror for Magistrates, p. 556 (R.). — F. concordant, pres. pt. of concorder, to agree. — L. concordāre, to agree. — L. concord-, stem of concors, agreeing. See above. Der. concord-ant-ly; concord-ance (AF. concordance, Bozon, p. 160).

CONCORDAT, a convention. (F. — L.) Borrowed from F. concordat, 'an accord, agreement, concordancy, act of agreement;' Cot. [Cf. Ital. concordato, a convention, esp. between the pope and French kings.] — Late L. concordātum, from the pp. of concordāre, to agree. See above.

CONCOURSE, an assembly. (F. — L.) 'Great concourse of people;' Fabyan, Chron. vol. i. c. 132. — F. concours; Hatzfeld; (omitted in Cot.). — L. concursus, a running together. — L. concursus, pp. of concurrere, to run together. See **Concur.**

CONCRETE, formed into one mass; used in opposition to abstract. (L.) 'Concrete or gathered into humour superfluous;' Sir T. Elyot, Castel of Helth, b. iv. (R.). — L. concrētus, grown together, compacted, thick, dense; pp. of concrescere, to grow together. — L. con-, for cum, together; and crescere, to grow. See **Crescent.** Der. concrete, sb.; concret-ion, -ive.

CONCUBINE, a paramour. (F. — L.) ME. concubine, Rob. of Glouc. p. 27; l. 630. — OF. (and F.) concubine. — L. concubina, a concubine. — L. con-, for cum, together; and cubāre, to lie. Cf. L. -cumbere (perf. -cubui), to bend, in the comp. incumbere, concumbere; and perhaps Gk. κυφός, bent. Der. concubin-age.

CONCUPISCENCE, lust, desire. (F. — L.) ME. concupiscence, Gower, C. A. iii. 267; bk. vii. 5223. — F. concupiscence. — L. concupiscentia, desire; Tertullian. — L. concupiscere, to long after; inceptive form of concupere, to long after. — L. con-, for cum, with, wholly; and cupere, to desire. See **Cupid.** Der. concupiscent, from L. concupiscent-, stem of pres. pt. of concupiscere.

CONCUR, to run together, unite, agree. (L.) In Douglas, tr. of Æneid, bk. x. l. 20; and in Shak. Tw. Nt. iii. 4. 73. — L. concurrere, to run together, unite, join. — L. con-, for cum, together; and currere, to run. See **Current.** Der. concurr-ent, -ly; concurr-ence (F. concurrence), from concurrent-, stem of concurrens, pres. part. of concurrere; also concourse, q. v.

CONCUSSION, a violent shock. (F. — L.) 'Their mutual concussion;' Bp. Taylor, On Orig. Sin, Deus Justificatus. Also in Caxton's Eneydos, heading to c. x. — F. concussion, 'concussion, . . a joulting, or knocking one against another;' Cot. — L. concussiōnem, acc. of concussio, a violent shaking; cf. concussus, pp. of concutere, to shake together. — L. con-, for cum, together; and quatere, to shake. See **Quash.** Der. concuss-ive, from L. pp. concussus.

CONDEMN, to pronounce to be guilty. (F. — L.) 'Ye shulden neuer han condempnyd innocentis;' Wyclif, Matt. xii. 7; where the Vulgate has 'nunquam condemnassetis innocentes.' And see Cursor

Mundi, l. 18176.—OF. *condemner*, *condempner* (Supp. to Godefroy).
—L. *condemnāre*, to condemn.—L. *con-*, for *cum*, with, wholly; and
damnāre, to condemn, damn. See **Damn.** Der. *condemn-able*; also
condemnat-ion, *-or-y*, like L. pp. *condemnātus*.

CONDENSE, to made dense, compress. (F.—L.) See Milton,
P. L. i. 429, vi. 353, ix. 636.—F. *condenser*, 'to thicken, or make
thick;' Cot.—L. *condensāre*, pp. *condensātus*, to make thick, press
together.—L. *con-*, for *cum*, together; and *densāre*, to thicken, from
densus, dense, thick. See **Dense.** Der. *condens-able*, *condens-ate*,
vb. (Cockeram), *-at-ion*, *-at-ive*.

CONDESCEND, to lower oneself, deign. (F.—L.) ME. *con-
descenden*; Chaucer, C. T. 10721 (F 407).—F. *condescendre*, 'to
condescend, vouchsafe, yield, grant unto;' Cot.—Late L. *con-
descendere*, to grant; Ducange.—L. *con-*, for *cum*, together; and
descendere, to descend. See **Descend.** Der. *condescend-ing*; *condescension*, Milton, P. L. viii. 649 (Late L. *condescensio*, indulgence,
condescension, from L. *con-* and *descensio*, a descent).

CONDIGN, well merited. (F.—L.) 'With a *condygne* [worthy]
pryce;' Fabyan, Chron. vol. i. c. 200. ME. *condigne*, Lydgate,
Minor Poems, p. 136.—F. *condigne*, 'condigne, well-worthy;' Cot.
—L. *condignus*, well-worthy.—L. *con-*, for *cum*, with, very; and
dignus, worthy. See **Dignity.** Der. *condign-ly*.

CONDIMENT, seasoning, sauce. (F.—L.) 'Rather for condiment . . . than any substantial nutriment;' Sir T. Browne, Vulg.
Errors, b. iii. c. 22. § 4.—F. *condiment*.—L. *condīmentum*, seasoning,
sauce, spice. Formed with suffix *-mentum* from the verb *condīre*, to
season, spice. Brugmann, i. § 656 (1).

CONDITION, a state, rank, proposal. (F.—L.) ME. *condicion*,
condition; in rather early use. See Hampole, Pricke of Conscience,
3955; Chaucer, C. T. 1433 (A 1431).—F. *condition*, OF. *condicion*.
—L. *conditiōnem*, acc. of *conditio*, *condicio*, a covenant, agreement,
condition. β. The usual reference of this word to the L. *condere*, to
put together, is wrong; the true L. spelling is *condicio*, from *con-*, for
cum, together, and the base *dic-* seen in *indicāre*, to point out; closely
related to *condicere*, to talk over, agree upon; which is from *con-*
(*cum*), together, and *dīcere*, to say, speak (Bréal). See **Diction.**
Der. *condi'tion-ed*, *-al*, *-al-ly*.

CONDOLE, to lament, grieve with. (L.) 'In doleful dittie to
condole the same;' Mirror for Magistrates, p. 783 (R.).—L. *con-
dolēre*, to grieve with.—L. *con-*, for *cum*, with; and *dolēre*, to grieve.
See **Doleful.** Der. *condol-ence*, *-ent*, *condole-ment*, *condol-at-or-y* (an
ill-formed word).

CONDONE, to forgive, pardon. (L.) 'Condone, or Condonate,
to give willingly, to forgive or pardon;' Blount's Glossographia, ed.
1674; 'Condone, to give;' (Cockeram), 1642.—L. *condōnāre*, to
remit; pp. *condōnātus*.—L. *con-*, for *cum*, together, wholly; and
dōnāre, to give. See **Donation.** Der. *condonat-ion*.

CONDOR, a large kind of vulture. (Span.—Peruvian.) '*Condor*, or *Contur*, in Peru in America, a strange and monstrous bird;'
Bailey's Dict. vol. ii. ed. 1731. Pl. *condores*; E.G., tr. of Acosta's
Hist. of the Indies, bk. iv. c. 37 (1604).—Span. *condor*, corrupted
from Peruvian *cuntur*. 'Garcilasso enumerates among the rapacious
birds those called *cuntur*, and corruptly by the Spanish *condor*;' and
again; 'many of the clusters of rocks [in Peru] . . are named after
them Cuntur Kahua, Cuntur Palti, and Cuntur Huacana, for example
—names which, in the language of the Incas, are said to signify the
Condor's Look-out, the Condor's Roost, and the Condor's Nest;'
Engl. Cycl. art. *Condor*; cf. Notes on Eng. Etym., p. 342.

CONDUCE, to lead or tend to, help towards. (L.) In the
Romance of Partenay, prol. 206. 'To *conduce* [conduct] me to my
ladies presence;' Wolsey to Henry VIII, an. 1527; in State Papers
(R.).—L. *condūcere*, to lead to, draw together towards.—L. *con-*, for
cum, together; and *dūcere*, to lead. See **Duke.** Der. *conduc-ible*,
ibl-y, *-ive*, *-ive-ly*, *-ive-ness*; and see *conduct*, *conduit*.

CONDUCT, escort, guidance, behaviour. (L.) Common in
Shak. both as sb. and verb. The orig. sense is 'escort;' see Merchant of Ven. iv. 1. 148.—Late L. *conductus*, defence, protection,
guard, escort, &c.; Ducange.—L. *conductus*, pp. of *condūcere*, to
bring together, lead to (above). Der. *conduct*, verb; *conduct-ible*,
-ibil-i-ty, *-ion*, *-ive*, *-or*, *-r-ess*. **Doublet,** *conduit*, q.v.

CONDUIT, a canal, water-course. (F.—L.) 'As water, whan
the *conduit* broken is;' Chaucer, Leg. of Good Women, Thisbe,
147.—OF. *conduit*, spelt *conduict* in Cotgrave, who explains it by
'a conduit.'—Late L. *conductus*, a defence, escort; also, a canal,
conduit; Ducange. See **Conduct.**

CONE, a solid pointed figure on a circular base. (F.—L.—Gk.)
In Milton, P. L. iv. 776.—MF. *cone*, 'a cone;' Cot.—L. *cōnus*.—Gk.
κῶνος, a cone, a peak, peg. ✛ Skt. *çāṇa(s)*, a whet-stone; cf. L. *cōs*,
a whet-stone. See **Hone.** Brugmann, i. § 401. Der. *con-ic*,
con-ics, *cono-id* (from Gk. κῶνο-, for κῶνος, and εἶδος, form); *coni-fer-
ous* (from L. *cōni-*, for *cōnus*, and *ferre*, to bear).

CONEY; see **Cony.**

CONFABULATE, to talk together. (L.) 'Confabulate, to
talke, to tell tales,' Cockeram; ed. 1642.—L. *confābulātus*, pp. of
dep. verb *confābulāri*, to talk together.—L. *con-*, for *cum*, together;
and *fābulāri*, to converse, from *fābula*, a discourse, a fable. See
Fable. Der. *confabulat-ion*.

CONFECT, to make up, esp. to make up into confections or
sweetmeats. (L.) 'Had tasted death in poison strong *confected*;'
Mirror for Magistrates, p. 858. Nearly obsolete. Gower has *confection*, C. A. iii. 23; bk. vi. 654; Chaucer has *confecture*, C. T.
12796 (C 862).—L. *confectus*, pp. of *conficere*, to make up, put
together. Cf. Late L. *confecta*, sweetmeats, comfits; Ducange.—L.
con-, for *cum*, together; and *facere*, to make. See **Fact.** Der. *confect*, sb., *confect-ion*, *-ion-er*, *-ion-er-y*; also *comfit*, q.v.

CONFEDERATE, leagued together; an associate. (L.) Orig.
used as a pp. 'Were *confederate* to his distruction;' Sir T. Elyot,
The Governour, b. iii. c. 8 (end). ME. *confederat*; Trevisa, tr. of
Higden, ii. 157.—L. *confœderātus*, united by a covenant, pp. of *con-
fœderāre*.—L. *con-*, for *cum*, together; and *fœderāre*, to league, from
fœder-, for *fœdes*, stem of *fœdus*, a league. See **Federal.** Der.
confederate, verb; *confederat-ion*, *confederac-y*.

CONFER, to bestow, consult. (L.) In Shak. Temp. i. 2. 126.
Palsgrave has *conferre*, p. 493.—L. *conferre*, to bring together, collect,
bestow.—L. *con-*, for *cum*, together; and *ferre*, to bring, cognate
with E. *bear*. See **Bear** (1). ¶ Not from F. Der. *confer-ence*,
from F. *conference*, 'a conference, a comparison;' Cot.

CONFESS, to acknowledge fully. (F.—L.) ME. *confessen*;
P. Plowman, B. xi. 76.—OF. *confesser*, to confess.—Late L. *confessāre*
(Ducange).—L. *confessus*, confessed, pp. of *confitēri*, to confess.—L.
con-, for *cum*, together, fully; and *fatēri*, to acknowledge; allied to
L. *fāri*, to speak, *fāma*, fame. Cf. Gk. φάτις, a speech. Brugmann,
i. § 195. See **Fame.** Der. *confess-ed-ly*, *-ion*, *-ion-al*, *-or*.

CONFIDE, to trust fully, rely. (L.) Shak. has *confident*, Merry
Wives, ii. 1. 194; *confidence*, Temp. i. 2. 97. Milton has *confide*,
P. L. xi. 235.—L. *confidere*, to trust fully.—L. *con-*, for *cum*, with,
fully; and *fidere*, to trust, allied to *fides*, faith. See **Faith.** Der.
confid-ent, from L. *confident-*, stem of *confidens*, pres. pt. of *confidere*;
confident-ly, *confidence*, *confident-ial*, *-ial-ly*; also *confidant*, *confidante*,
from F. *confidant*, masc., *confidante*, fem., 'a friend to whom one
trusts;' Cot.

CONFIGURATION, an external shape, aspect. (F.—L.)
'The *configuration* of parts;' Locke, Human Underst. b. ii. c. 21.—
F. *configuration*, 'a likenesse or resemblance of figures;' Cot.—L.
configūrātiōnem, acc. of *configūrātio*, a conformation; Tertullian;
cf. *configūrātus*, pp. of *configūrāre*, to fashion or put together.—L.
con-, for *cum*, together; and *figūrāre*, to fashion, from *figūra*, a form,
figure. See **Figure.**

CONFINE, to limit, bound, imprison. (F.—L.) [The sb. *confine* (Othello, i. 2. 27) is really formed from the English verb; but
the pl. *confines* in Romeo, iii. 1. 6, is from OF. *confines*, pl. f.
(Godefroy), from L. *confinia*, pl. of *confinium*, a border.] The old
sense of the verb was 'to border upon;' cf. 'his kingdom *confineth*
with the Red Sea;' Hackluyt's Voyages, v. ii. pt. ii. p. 10.—F. *con-
finer*, 'to confine, to abbut, or bound upon; . . to lay out bounds
unto; also, to confine, relegate;' Cot.—F. *confin*, adj., 'neer, neighbour, confining or adjoining unto;' id.—L. *confinis*, adj., bordering
upon.—L. *con-*, for *cum*, together; and *finis*, a boundary. See
Final. Der. *confine*, sb. (above); *confine-ment*.

CONFIRM, to make firm, assure. (F.—L.) ME. *confermen*,
rarely *confirmen*; see Rob. of Glouc. pp. 324, 446, 522, 534; ll.
6628, 9171, 10710, 11028.—OF. *confermer* (F. *confirmer*), to confirm.
—L. *confirmāre*, to strengthen, pp. *confirmātus*.—L. *con-*, for *cum*,
together, wholly; and *firmāre*, to make firm, from *firmus*, firm.
See **Firm.** Der. *confirm-able*, *-at-ion*, *-at-ive*, *-at-or-y*.

CONFISCATE, to adjudge to be forfeit. (L.) Orig. used as a
pp., Merch. of Ven. iv. 1. 332. 'Thou art banished from Rome,
and all thy goodes *confiscate*;' Lord Berners, tr. of Golden Book,
Letter iii. l. 23.—L. *confiscātus*, pp. of *confiscāre*, to lay by in a coffer
or chest, to confiscate, transfer to the prince's privy purse.—L. *con-*,
for *cum*, together; and *fiscus*, a basket, bag, purse, the imperial
treasury. See **Fiscal.** Der. *confiscat-ion*, *-or*, *-or-y*.

CONFLAGRATION, a great burning, fire. (F.—L.) Milton
has *conflagrant*, P. L. xii. 548. 'Fire . . . which is called a πύρωσις, a
combustion, or being farther broken out into flames, a *conflagration*;'
Hammond's Works, iv. 593 (R.). [First ed. pub. 1674, 2nd ed.
1684.] Also in Blount (1656).—F. *conflagration*, 'a conflagration,
a generall burning;' Cot.—L. *conflagrātiōnem*, acc. of *conflagrātio*,
a great burning; cf. *conflagrātus*, pp. of *conflagrāre*, to consume by
fire.—L. *con-*, for *cum*, together, wholly; and *flagrāre*, to burn. See
Flagrant.

CONFLATION, a blending or fusing of different things, sources, or readings. (L.) 'A *conflation* of them all;' Bacon, Nat. Hist., § 225. — L. acc. *conflātiōnem*, a casting in metal (hence, a blending); Jerem. li. 17 (Vulgate); cf. L. *conflātus*, pp. of *conflāre*, to blow together, to fuse. — L. *con*- (for *cum*), together; and *flāre*, to blow, cognate with E. *blow* (1).

CONFLICT, a fight, battle. (L.) [Perhaps from F. *conflict*, 'a conflict, skirmish;' Cot. Or immediately from Lat.] ME. *conflycte*, sb.; Prompt. Parv. Also *conflicten*, vb., later tr. of Higden, i. 139. The sb. also occurs in Sir T. Elyot, The Governour, b. 1. c. 1. § 2. Shak. has both sb. and vb.; L. L. L. iv. 3. 369; Lear, iii. 1. 11. — L. *conflictus*, a striking together, a fight; cf. L. *conflictāre*, to strike together, afflict, vex. *Conflictus* is the pp., and *conflictāre* the frequentative, of *confligere*, to strike together, to fight. — L. *con*-, for *cum*, together; and *fligere*, to strike. Der. *conflict*, verb.

CONFLUENT, flowing together. (L.) 'Where since these *confluent* floods;' Drayton, Polyolbion, s. 20. Shak. has *confluence*, Timon, i. 1. 42; *conflux*, Troil. i. 3. 7. G. Douglas has *confluence*, tr. of Virgil, bk. v. c. 11. l. 20. — L. *confluent*-, stem of *confluens*, pres. pt. of *confluere*, to flow together. — L. *con*-, for *cum*, together, and *fluere*, to flow. See **Fluent**. Der. *confluence*; also *conflux*, from *confluxus*, pp. of *confluere*.

CONFORM, to make like, to adapt. (F. — L.) ME. *conformen*, Chaucer, C. T. 8422 (E 546; Camb. MS.) — F. *conformer*, 'to conforme, fit with, fashion as;' Cot. — L. *conformāre*, pp. *conformātus*, to fashion as. — L. *con*-, for *cum*, together; and *formāre*, to form, fashion. See **Form**. Der. *conform-able, -abl-y, -at-ion, -er, -ist, -i-ty*.

CONFOUND, to pour together, confuse, destroy. (F. — L.) ME. *confounden*, Chaucer, Boethius, b. ii. pr. 6. l. 36. *Confund* occurs in the Cursor Mundi, 730. — OF. (and F.) *confondre*. — L. *confundere*, pp. *confūsus*, to pour out together, to mingle, perplex, overwhelm, confound. — L. *con*-, for *cum*, together; and *fundere*, to pour. See **Fuse** (1). Der. *confuse*, ME. *confus*, used as a pp. in Chaucer, C. T. 2232 (A 2230), OF. *confus*, from the L. pp. *confūsus*; *confus-ion, confus-ed-ly*. Thus *confound* is, practically, a doublet of *confuse*.

CONFRATERNITY, a brotherhood. (F. — L.) In Holland's Plutarch, p. 23 (R.). Coined by prefixing *con*- (L. *cum*, with) to the sb. *fraternity*. The form *confraternitās*, a brotherhood, occurs in Ducange. See **Fraternity**.

CONFRONT, to stand face to face, oppose. (F. — L.) In Titus Andron. iv. 4. 3. 'A noble knight, *confronting* both the hosts;' Mirror for Magistrates, p. 597 (R.). — F. *confronter*, 'to confront, or bring face to face;' Cot. Formed, with a change of meaning, from the Late L. *confrontāre*, to assign bounds to, *confrontāri*, to be contiguous to, to be near to. — L. *con*- (*cum*), together; and *front*-, stem of *frons*, forehead. See **Front, Affront**.

CONFUSE, CONFUSION; see **Confound**.

CONFUTE, to prove to be false, disprove, refute. (F. — L.) In Shak. Meas. v. 100. — F. *confuter*, 'to confute, convince, refell, disprove;' Cot. [Or perhaps borrowed immediately from Latin.] — L. *confūtāre*, to cool by mixing cold water with hot, to damp, repress, allay, refute, confute; pp. *confūtātus*. — L. *con*-, for *cum*, together; and the stem *fūt*-, seen in *fūtis*, a water-vessel, a vessel for pouring from; an extension of the base *fū*-, seen in *fū-di, fū-sus*, perf. and pp. of *fundere*, to pour. — √ GHEU, to pour. See **Fuse** (1), **Refute, Futile**. Der. *confut-at-ion, -able*.

CONGEAL, to solidify by cold. (F. — L.) 'Lich unto slime which is *congeled*;' Gower, C. A. iii. 96; bk. vii. 338. — OF. *congeler*, 'to congeale;' Cot. — L. *congelāre*, pp. *congelātus*, to cause to freeze together. — L. *con*-, for *cum*, together; and *gelāre*, to freeze, from *gelu*, frost. See **Gelid**. Der. *congeal-able, -ment*; also *congel-at-ion*, Gower, C. A. ii. 86, from F. *congelation* (Cot.), L. *congelātio*.

CONGEE, leave to depart, farewell. (F. — L.) Also *congé*. Spelt *congie* in Fabyan's Chron. c. 243; *congee* in Spenser, F. Q. iv. 6. 42. ME. *congeye*, P. Plowman, B. xiii. 202. Hence the verb to *congie*, Shak. All's Well, iv. 3. 100 'a word in use even in the 14th century;' we find 'to *congey* thee for euere,' i.e. to dismiss thee for ever; P. Plowman, B. iii. 173. — F. *congé*, 'leave, licence, . . discharge, dismission;' Cot.; OF. *congie, cunge, congiet* (Burguy); equivalent to Provençal *comjat*. — Late L. *commeātus*, leave, permission (8th century); a corruption of L. *commeātus*, a passage, travelling, leave of absence, furlough (Brachet). — L. *com*-, for *cum*, together; and *meātus*, a going, a course, from *meātus*, pp. of *meāre*, to go, pass. See **Permeate**.

CONGENER, allied in kin or nature. (L.) In Bailey, vol. ii. (1731). Merely L. *congener*, of the same kin. — L. *con*-, for *cum*, with; and *gener*-, for **genes*-, stem of *genus*, kin. See **Genus**.

CONGENIAL, kindred, sympathetic. (L.) In Dryden's Dedication of Juvenal, § 3; and in Pope, Dunciad, iv. 448. A coined word, made by prefixing L. *con*- (for *cum*, with) to *genial*, from L. *geniālis*. See **Genial**. Der. *congenial-ly, -i-ty*.

CONGENITAL, cognate, born with one. (L.) First found in 1796; made by suffixing *-al* to the now obsolete word *congenite* or *congenit*, of similar meaning, used by Bp. Taylor, Rule of Conscience, b. ii. c. 1, and by Boyle, Works, v. 513 (R.). — L. *congenitus*, born with. — L. *con*-, for *cum*, with; and *genitus*, born, pp. of *gignere*, to produce. — √ GEN, to produce. See **Generate**.

CONGER, a sea-eel. (F. — L. — Gk.) In Shak. 2 Hen. IV, ii. 4. 266. ME. *cungyr*, Rich. Coer de Lion, 3515. — F. *congre*, 'a congar;' Cot. — L. *congrum*, acc. of *congrus*, a sea-eel; cf. also L. *conger*, a sea-eel. — Gk. γόγγρος, the same.

CONGERIES, a mass of particles. (L.) In Glossographia Anglicana Nova, 1719 (after *congruous*). Merely L. *congeriēs*, a heap. — L. *congerere*, to heap up, bring together. — L. *con*-, for *cum*, together; and *gerere*, to carry, bring: see **Gerund**. See below.

CONGESTION, accumulation. (L.) Shak. has the verb *congest*, Compl. of a Lover, 258. 'By *congestion* of sand, earth, and such stuff;' Drayton, Polyolbion, Illustrations of s. 9. — F. *congestion* (Hatzfeld). — L. acc. *congestiōnem*, from *congestio*, a heaping together; cf. *congestus*, pp. of *congerere*, to bring together, heap up. See above. Der. *congest-ive*.

CONGLOBE, to form into a globe. (L.) Milton has *conglob'd*, P. L. vii. 239; *conglobing*, vii. 292. — L. *conglobāre*, pp. *conglobātus*, to gather into a globe, to conglobate. — L. *con*-, for *cum*, together; and *globus*, a globe, round mass. See **Globe**. Der. *conglobate, conglobat-ion*, like L. pp. *conglobātus*; similarly *conglobulate*, from L. *globulus*, a little globe, dimin. of *globus*.

CONGLOMERATE, gathered into a ball; to gather into a ball. (L.) Orig. used as a pp., as in Bacon's Nat. Hist. § 267. — L. *conglomerātus*, pp. of *conglomerāre*, to wind into a ball or clew, to heap together. — L. *con*-, for *cum*, together; and *glomerāre*, to form into a ball, from *glomer*-, for **glomes*-, stem of *glomus*, a clew of thread, a ball; allied to L. *globus*, a globe. See **Globe**. Der. *conglomerat-ion*.

CONGLUTINATE, to glue together. (L.) Orig. used as a pp., as in Sir T. Elyot, Castel of Helth, b. ii. c. 21. § 2. — L. *conglūtinātus*, pp. of *conglūtināre*, to glue together. — L. *con*-, for *cum*, together; and *glūtināre*, to glue, from *glūtin*-, decl. stem of *glūten*, glue. See **Glue**. Der. *conglutin-ant, conglutinat-ive, -ion*.

CONGOU, a kind of black tea. (Chinese.) '*Congou* tea;' Sheridan, School for Scandal, v. 1. In the Amoy dialect of Chinese, called *kang-hu tê*, where *kang-hu* is lit. 'work, labour;' i.e. tea on which labour has been expended (Douglas). The true Chinese is *kang-fu ch'a*, with the same sense.

CONGRATULATE, to wish all joy to. (L.) In Shak. L. L. L. v. 1. 93. — L. *congrātulātus*, pp. of *congrātulāri*, to wish much joy. — L. *con*-, for *cum*, with, very much; and *grātulāri*, to wish joy. a deponent verb formed, with suffix *-ul*-, from *grāt-us*, pleasing. See **Grateful**. Der. *congratulat-ion, -or-y*.

CONGREGATE, to gather together. (L.) In Shak. Merch. of Ven. i. 3. 50. Rich. quotes from the State Trials (Sir J. Oldcastle), showing that *congregated* was used A.D. 1413. — L. *congregātus*, pp. of *congregāre*, to assemble. — L. *con*-, for *cum*, together; and *gregāre*, to collect in flocks, from *greg*-, stem of *grex*, a flock. See **Gregarious**. Der. *congregat-ion, -al, -al-ist, -al-ism*.

CONGRESS, a meeting together, assembly. (L.) 'Their *congress* in the field great Jove withstands;' Dryden, tr. of Æneid, x. 616. — L. *congressus*, a meeting together; also an attack, engagement in the field (as above). — L. *congressus*, pp. of *congredī*, to meet together. — L. *con*-, for *cum*, together; and *gradi*, to step, walk, go, from *gradus*, a step. See **Grade**. Der. *congress-ive*.

CONGREVE, (1) a kind of rocket; (2) a friction-match. (Personal name.) Both invented by Sir W. Congreve, who died in 1828. Orig. a place-name.

CONGRUE, to agree, suit. (L.) In Shak. Hamlet, iv. 3. 66. Hence *congruent*, apt; L. L. L. i. 2. 14; v. 1. 97; also in Sir T. Elyot, The Governour, bk. i. c. 8. § 3. — L. *congruere*, to agree together, accord, suit, correspond; pres. part. *congruens* (stem *congruent*-), used as adj., fit. — L. *con*-, for *cum*, together; and *-gruere*, a verb which only occurs in the comp. *congruere* and *ingruere*, and is of uncertain meaning and origin. Der. *congru-ent, congru-ence, congru-i-ty* (ME. *congruite*, Gower, C. A. iii. 136; bk. vii. 1531); also *congruous* (from L. adj. *congruus*, suitable), *-ly, -ness*.

CONIC, CONIFEROUS; see **Cone**.

CONJECTURE, a guess, idea. (F. — L.) In Chaucer, C. T. 8281 (E 405). — F. *conjecture*, 'a conjecture, or ghesse;' Cot. — L. *coniectūra*, a guess; cf. *coniect-us*, pp. of *conicere* (= *conjicere*), to cast or throw together. — L. *con*-, for *cum*, together; and *iacere*, to cast, throw. See **Jet** (1). Der. *conjecture*, verb; *conjectur-al, -al-ly*.

CONJOIN, to join together, unite. (F. — L.) ME. *conioignen*; Chaucer, tr. of Boethius, b. iii. pr. 10, l. 149. [*Conioint* (*conjoint*) is in Gower, C. A. iii. 101; bk. vii. 502. *Coniuncioun* (*conjunction*) in Chaucer, On the Astrolabe, ed. Skeat, ii. 32. 1.] — OF. *conjoign-*, a stem of *conjoindre* (Burguy); still in use. — L. *coniungere*, pp. *coniunctus*, to join together, unite. — L. *con-*, for *cum*, together; and *iungere*, to join. See **Join**. Der. *conjoint* (pp. of F. *conjoindre*), *-ly*; also *conjunct*, *-ion*, *-ive*, *-ive-ly*, *-ure*, like L. pp. *coniunctus*.

CONJUGAL, relating to marriage. (F. — L.) In Milton, P. L. iv. 493. — F. *conjugal*, 'conjugall;' Cot. — L. *coniugālis*, relating to marriage (Tacitus). — L. *coniug-em*, acc. of *coniux*, a spouse. — L. *con-*, for *cum*, together; and *iug-*, as in *iugum*, a yoke. (√YEU, to join.) See **Join**, **Yoke**. Der. *conjugal-ly*, *-i-ty*.

CONJUGATION, the inflexion of a verb. (L.) [The verb to *conjugate* is really formed from the sb. *conjugation*; it occurs in Palsgrave, Introd. p. xxxiii.] *Coniugacyon* is in Skelton's Speke Parrot, l. 185; and in Palsgrave, p. 399. Formed, in imitation of F. words in *-ion*, from L. *coniugātio*, a conjugation; used in its grammatical sense by Priscian. The lit. sense is 'a binding together.' Cf. *coniugātus*, pp. of *coniugāre*, to unite, connect. — L. *con-* (*cum*), together; *iugāre*, to yoke, from *iugum*, a yoke. Der. *conjugate*, vb.; also *conjugate* as an adj., from pp. *coniugātus*. Cf. *conjunct-ion*.

CONJUNCTION; see under **Conjoin**.

CONJURE, to implore solemnly. (F. — L.) ME. *conjuren*, P. Plowman, B. xv. 14. — F. *conjurer*, 'to conjure, adjure; also, to conjure or exorcise a spirit;' Cot. — L. *coniūrāre*, to swear together, combine by oath; pp. *coniūrātus*. — L. *con-*, for *cum*, together; and *iūrāre*, to swear. See **Jury**. Der. *conjur-or*, *conjur-er*, *conjurat-ion*. ☞ The verb to *cónjure*, i.e. to juggle, is the same word, and refers to the invocation of spirits. Cf. 'Whiles he madè *cóniuryng*;' King Alisaunder, ed. Weber, l. 345.

CONNATE, born with us. (L.) 'Those *connate* principles born with us into the world;' South, Sermons, vol. ii. ser. 10 (R.). — L. *con-nātus*, pp. of *connascī*, to be born with (another). — L. *con-* (*cum*), with; and *nascī*, to be born. See **Cognate**.

CONNATURAL, of the same nature with another. (L.) In Milton, P. L. x. 246, xi. 529. A coined word, made by prefixing L. *con-* (for *cum*, together with) to the E. word *natural*, from L. *nātūrālis*, natural. Probably suggested by OF. *connaturel*, 'connaturall, natural to all alike;' Cot. See **Nature**.

CONNECT, to fasten together, join. (L.) First found in 1537. Used by Pope, Essay on Man, i. 280, iii. 23, iv. 349. Old writers also use *connex*, formed from the L. pp. — L. *connectere*, to fasten or tie together; pp. *connexus*. — L. *con-*, for *cum*, together; and *nectere*, to bind, tie, knit, join. Der. *connect-ed-ly*, *-or*, *-ive*; also *connex-ion* (like the pp. *connexus*), a word which is usually misspelt *connection*. Cotgrave has: 'Connexion, a connexion.'

CONNING-TOWER; see under **Con** (1).

CONNIVE, to wink at a fault. (F. — L.) In Shak. Winter's Tale, iv. 4. 692. — F. *conniver*, 'to winke at, suffer, tollerate;' Cot. — L. *conniuēre*, to close the eyes, overlook, connive at. — L. *con-*, for *cum*, together; and a form **niguere*, to wink, whence the perf. tense *connixi* and *nic-t-āre*, to wink with the eyes. ✛ Goth. *hneiwan*, to bow. Brugmann, i. § 664. Der. *conniv-ance*; better *connivence*, as in Cotgrave.

CONNOISSEUR, a critical judge. (F. — L.) Used by Swift, on Poetry. And in Bailey, vol. ii (1731). — F. *connaisseur*, formerly spelt *connoisseur*, a critical judge, a knowing one. — OF. *connoiss-* (F. *connaiss-*), a base used in conjugating the OF. verb *connoistre* (F. *connaître*), to know. — L. *cognoscere*, to know fully. — L. *co-*, for *cum*, together, fully; and *gnoscere*, to know, cognate with E. *know*. See **Know**. Der. *connoisseur-ship*.

CONNOTE, to imply, indicate. (L.) 'To *connote*, to make known together;' Glossographia Anglicana (1719). Sir T. More has *connotacyon*, Works, p. 417, col. 1. — Late L. *connotāre*, to mark in addition or along with. — L. *con-* (for *cum*), together; and *notāre*, to mark, from *nota*, a mark. See **Note**. Der. *connotat-ion*, like the pp. *connotāt-us*.

CONNUBIAL, matrimonial, nuptial. (L.) In Milton, P. L. iv. 743. — L. *connūbiālis*, relating to marriage. — L. *con-*, for *cum*, together; and *nūbere*, to cover, to veil, to marry. See **Nuptial**.

CONOID, cone-shaped; see **Cone**.

CONQUER, to subdue, vanquish. (F. — L.) In early use. ME. *conqueren*, *conquerien* or *conquery*. Spelt *conquery*, Rob. of Glouc. p. 200, l. 4115; oddly spelt *cuncweari* in Hali Meidenhad, ed. Cockayne, p. 33; about A.D. 1200. — OF. *conquerre*, *cunquerre*, to conquer. — L. *conquīrere*, pp. *conquīsītus*, to seek together, seek after, go in quest of; in Late Latin, to conquer; Ducange. — L. *con-*, for *cum*, together; and *quærere*, pp. *quæsītus*, to seek. See **Quest**, **Query**. Der. *conquer-able*, *-or*; *conquest* = ME. *conqueste*, Gower, C. A. i. 27 (prol. 709), (AF. *conqueste*, from Late L. *conquīsīta*, f. of pp. *conquīsītus*).

CONSANGUINEOUS, related by blood. (L.) In Shak. Tw. Nt. ii. 3. 82; also *consanguinity*, Troil. iv. 2. 103. — L. *consanguine-us*, related by blood; with suffix *-ous*. — L. *con-*, for *cum*, together; and *sanguineus*, bloody, relating to blood, from *sanguin-*, decl. stem of *sanguis*, blood. See **Sanguine**. Der. *consanguin-i-ty* (F. *consanguinité*, given by Cot.; from L. *consanguinitātem*, acc. of *consanguinitās*, relationship by blood).

CONSCIENCE, consciousness of good or bad. (F. — L.) In early use. Spelt *kunscience*, Ancren Riwle, p. 228; also *conscience*, p. 306. — OF. (and F.) *conscience*. — L. *conscientia*. — L. *con-*, for *cum*, together with; and *scientia*, knowledge. See **Science**. Der. *conscientious*, from F. *conscientieux*, 'conscientious,' Cot.; which is from Late L. *conscientiōsus*. Hence *conscientious-ly*, *-ness*. And see *conscious*, *conscionable*.

CONSCIONABLE, governed by conscience. (Coined from L.) 'Indeed if the minister's part be rightly discharged, it renders the people more *conscionable*, quiet and easy to be governed;' Milton, Reformation in England, bk. ii (R.). 'As uprightlie and as *conscionablie* as he may possible;' Holinshed, Ireland; Stanihurst to Sir H. Sidney. An ill-coined word (cf. *fashion-able*), used as a contraction of *conscien(ce)-able*; the regular formation from the verb *conscīre*, to be conscious, would have been *conscible* (cf. L. *scībilis*), but this would not have given the sense. Der. *conscionabl-y*. See above.

CONSCIOUS, aware. (L.) In Dryden, Theodore and Honoria, 202. Englished from L. *conscius*, aware, by substituting *-ous* for *-us*, as in *arduous*, *egregious*. — L. *conscīre*, to be aware of. — L. *con-*, for *cum*, together, fully; and *scīre*, to know. See **Conscience**.

CONSCRIPT, enrolled, registered. (L.) 'O fathers *conscripte*, O happie people;' Lord Berners, Golden Boke, Letter 11. § 7. In later times, used as a sb. — L. *conscriptus*, enrolled; pp. of *conscribere*, to write down together. — L. *con-*, for *cum*, together; and *scribere*, to write. See **Scribe**. Der. *conscript-ion*.

CONSECRATE, to render sacred. (L.) In Barnes, Works, p. 331, col. 1. ME. *consecrat*, i.e. consecrated, Chaucer, C. T. 14023 (B 3207). — L. *consecrātus*, pp. of *consecrāre*, to render sacred. — L. *con-*, for *cum*, with, wholly; and *sacrāre*, to consecrate, from *sacr(o)-*, stem of *sacer*, sacred. See **Sacred**. Der. *consecrat-or*, *-ion*.

CONSECUTIVE, following in order. (F. — L.) Not in early use. One of the earliest examples appears to be in Cotgrave (1611), who translates the F. *consecutif* (fem. *consecutive*) by 'consecutiue or consequent;' where *.consequent* is the older form. The Late L. *consecūtīvus* is not recorded. — L. *consecūt-*, stem of *consecūtus*, pp. of *consequī*, to follow. See **Consequent**. Der. *consecutive-ly*; also *consecut-ion*, like the pp. *consecūtus*.

CONSENT, to feel with, agree with, assent to. (F. — L.) ME. *consenten*; spelt *kunsenten* in Ancren Riwle, p. 272. — OF. (and F.) *consentir*. — L. *consentīre*, to accord, assent to. — L. *con-*, for *cum*, together; and *sentīre*, to feel, pp. *sensus*. See **Sense**. Der. *consent*, sb.; *consent-i-ent*, *-an-e-ous* (L. *consentāneus*, agreeable, suitable); *-aneous-ly*, *-ness*; also *consensus*, a L. word.

CONSEQUENT, following upon. (L.) Early used as a sb. 'Vengeance is the *consequent*;' Chaucer, Tale of Melibeus, B 2578. Properly an adj. — L. *consequent-*, stem of *consequens*, pres. part. of *consequī*, to follow. — L. *con-*, for *cum*, together; and *sequī*, to follow. See **Second**. Der. *consequent-ly*, *-i-al*, *-i-al-ly*; *consequence* (MF. *consequence*, Cot., from L. *consequentia*).

CONSERVE, to preserve, retain, pickle. (F. — L.) 'The poudre in which myn herte, ybrend [burnt], shal torne That preye I thee, thou take, and it *conserve*;' Chaucer, Troilus, v. 309; and see C. T. 15855 (G 387). — OF. and F. *conserver*, to preserve. — L. *conseruāre*. — L. *con-*, for *cum*, with, fully; and *seruāre*, to keep, serve. See **Serve**. Der. *conserve*, sb.; *conserv-er*, *-ant*, *-able*, *-at-ion*, *-at-ive*, *-at-ism*, *-at-or*, *-at-or-y*.

CONSIDER, to deliberate, think over, observe. (F. — L.) ME. *consideren*; Chaucer, C. T. 3023 (A 3021). — OF. *considerer*. — L. *consīderāre*, pp. *consīderātus*, to observe, consider, inspect, orig. to inspect the stars. — L. *con-*, together; and *sīder-*, for **sīdes-*, stem of *sīdus*, a star, a constellation. See **Sidereal**. Der. *consider-able*, *-abl-y*, *-able-ness*; *-ate*, *-ate-ly*, *-ate-ness*; *-at-ion*.

CONSIGN, to transfer, intrust, make over. (F. — L.) 'My father hath *consigned* and confirmed me with his assured testimonie;' Tyndal, Works, p. 457; where it seems to mean 'sealed.' It also meant 'to agree;' Hen. V, v. 2. 90. — F. *consigner*, 'to consigne, present, exhibit or deliver in hand;' Cot. — L. *consignāre*, to seal, attest, warrant, register, record, remark. — L. *con-*, for *cum*, with; and *signāre*, to mark, sign, from *signum*, a mark. See **Sign**. Der. *consign-er*, *-ee*, *-ment*.

CONSIST, to stand firm, subsist, to be made up of, to agree or coexist, depend on. (F. — L.) In Shak. Tw. Nt. ii. 3. 10. — F. *consister*, 'to consist, be, rest, reside, abide, to settle, stand still or at a stay;' Cot. — L. *consistere*, to stand together, remain, rest, consist, exist, depend on. — L. *con-*, for *cum*, together; and *sistere*, to make to stand, also to stand, the causal of *stāre*, to stand. See **Stand**.

Der. *consist-ent, -ent-ly, -ence, -enc-y*; also *consist-or-y*, from Late L. *consistōrium*, a place of assembly, an assembly; *consistori-al*.

CONSOLE (1), to comfort, cheer. (F.—L.) Shak. has only *consolate*, All's Well, iii. 2. 131. Dryden has *consol'd*, tr. of Juv. Sat. x. l. 191.—F. *consoler*, 'to comfort, cherish, solace;' Cot.—L. *con-sōlāri*, pp. *consōlātus*, to console.—L. *con-*, for *cum*, fully; and *sōlāri*, to solace. See **Solace**. **Der.** *consol-able, -at-ion, -at-or-y*.

CONSOLE (2), a kind of bracket or corbel, a supporting bracket. (F.—L.) In Phillips (1706).—F. *console*, 'a corbell, a bracket;' Cot. Also called *consolateur* (Cot.); and therefore from F. *consoler*, to comfort, solace, cherish; see **Console** (1). ¶ Perhaps influenced by L. *consolidāre*, to strengthen; but see Körting, §§ 2445, 2446.

CONSOLIDATE, to render solid, harden. (L.) Orig. used as a past participle. 'Wherby knowledge is ratified, and, as I mought saye, *consolidate*;' Sir T. Elyot, The Governour, b. iii. c. 26. § 1.—L. *consolidātus*, pp. of *consolidāre*, to render solid.—L. *con-*, for *cum*, with, wholly; and *solidāre*, to make solid, from *solidus*, solid, firm. See **Solid**. **Der.** *consolidat-ion*; also *consols* (first found in 1770), a familiar abbreviation for *consolidated annuities*.

CONSONANT, agreeable to, suitable. (F.—L.) 'A confourme [conformable] and *consonant* ordre;' Bale, Apologie, fol. 55 (R.). Shak. has *consonancy*, Hamlet, ii. 2. 295.—F. *consonant*, 'consonant, accordant, harmonious;' Cot.—L. *consonant-*, stem of *consonāns*, pres. pt. of *consonāre*, to sound together with; hence, to harmonise.—L. *con-*, for *cum*, together; and *sonāre*, to sound. See **Sound** (3). **Der.** *consonant*, sb. (Reliq. Antiq. ii. 174); *consonant-ly, consonance*.

CONSORT, a fellow, companion, mate, partner. (L.) In Milton, P. L. iv. 448. [Shak. has *consórt* in the sense of company, Two Gent. of Verona, iv. 1. 64; but this is not quite the same word, being from the verb to *consórt with*, itself a derivative of *cónsort*, sb. Note that *consort* was often written for *concert* in old authors, but the words are quite distinct, though confused by Richardson. The quotation from P. Plowman in Richardson is wrong; the right reading is not *consort*, but *confort*, i.e. comfort; P. Plowman, C. vi. 75.]—L. *consort-*, stem of *consors*, one who shares property with others, a brother or sister, in Late L. a neighbour, also a wife; it occurs in the fem. MF. sb. *consorte* in the last sense only.—L. *con-*, for *cum*, together; and *sort-*, stem of *sors*, a lot, a share. See **Sort**; and compare **Assort**. **Der.** *consórt*, verb, Shak., L. L. L. ii. 1. 178.

CONSPICUOUS, very visible. (L.) Frequent in Milton, P. L. ii. 258, &c. Adapted from L. *conspicuus*, visible, by the change of *-us* into *-ous*, as in *consanguineous*, *arduous*, &c.—L. *conspicere*, to see plainly.—L. *con-*, for *cum*, with, thoroughly; and *specere*, to look, see. See **Species**. **Der.** *conspicuous-ly, -ness*.

CONSPIRE, to plot, unite for evil. (F.—L.) In Gower, C. A. i. 81, 82; bk. i. 1173, 1206; Chaucer, C. T. 13495 (B 1755).—F. *conspirer*.—L. *conspirāre*, to blow together, to combine, agree, plot, conspire.—L. *con-*, for *cum*, together; and *spirāre*, to blow. See **Spirit**. **Der.** *conspir-at-or, conspir-ac-y* (Chaucer, C. T., B 3889).

CONSTABLE, an officer, peace-officer. (F.—L.) In early use. ME. *constable, conestable*; Havelok, l. 2286, 2366.—OF. *conestable* (F. *connétable*).—L. *comes stabulī*, lit. 'count of the stable,' a dignitary of the Roman empire, transferred to the Frankish courts. A document of the 8th [9th] century has: '*comes stabuli* quem corruptè *conestabulum* appellamus;' Brachet. [This document is the Chronicon Reginonis abbatis Prumiensis (who died in 915); anno 807.] See **Count** (1) and **Stable**. **Der.** *constable-ship*; *constabul-ar-y*, from Late L. *constabulāria*, the dignity of a *constabulus* or *conestabulus*.

CONSTANT, firm, steadfast, fixed. (F.—L.) *Constantly* is in Frith's Works, Life, p. 3. Chaucer has the adj. *constant*, C. T. 8923 (E 1047); and the sb. *constance*, C. T. 8544, 8876 (E 688, 1000).—F. *constant* (Cot.).—L. *constant-*, stem of *constans*, constant, firm; orig. pres. pt. of *constāre*, to stand together.—L. *con-*, for *cum*, together; and *stāre*, to stand, cognate with E. *stand*, q.v. **Der.** *constant-ly, constanc-y*.

CONSTELLATION, a cluster of stars. (F.—L.) ME. *constellacion*. In Gower, C. A. i. 21, 55 (prol. 532, and bk. i. 393).—OF. *constellacion*, F. *constellation*.—L. *constellātiōnem*, acc. of *constellātio*, a cluster of stars.—L. *con-*, for *cum*, together; and cf. *stellāt-us*, pp. of *stellāre*, to set with stars, from *stella*, a star, cognate with E. *star*, q.v.

CONSTERNATION, fright, terror, dismay. (F.—L.) Rich. quotes the word from Strype, Memorials of Edw. VI, an. 1551. It was not much used till later.—F. *consternation*, 'consternation, astonishment, dismay;' Cot.—L. *consternātiōnem*, acc. of *consternātio*, fright; cf. *consternātus*, pp. of *consternāre*, to frighten, collateral form to *consternere*, to bestrew, throw down.—L. *con-*, for *cum*, together, wholly; and *sternere*, to strew. See **Stratum**.

CONSTIPATE, to cram together, obstruct, render costive. (L.) Sir T. Elyot has *constipations*, Castel of Helth, b. iii. c. 7. The verb

is in the same, bk. ii. c. 5.—L. *constīpātus*, pp. of *constīpāre*, to make thick, join thickly together.—L. *con-*, for *cum*, together; and *stipāre*, to cram tightly, pack; perhaps connected with *stīpes*, a stem; see Curtius, i. 264. **Der.** *constipat-ion*; *costive*.

CONSTITUTE, to appoint, establish. (L.) Gower has the sb. *constitucion*, C. A. ii. 75; bk. iv. 2206. The verb is later; see Caxton, Eneydos, c. 28, Sign. Hij, back (p. 109, l. 9, E. E. T. S.); Bp. Taylor, Holy Living, c. iii. 1. 1.—L. *constitūtus*, pp. of *constituere*, to cause to stand together, establish.—L. *con-*, for *cum*, together; and *statuere*, to place, set, denominative verb from *status*, a position. See **State**. **Der.** *constitu-ent, constitu-enc-y*, from L. stem *constituent-*, pres. part. of *constituere*; also *constitut-ion* (F. *constitution*), whence *constitut-ion-al, -al-ly, -al-ist, -al-ism*; also *constitut-ive*.

CONSTRAIN, to compel, force. (F.—L.) ME. *constreinen*; Chaucer, tr. of Boethius, b. i. pr. 1. l. 9; C. T. 8676 (E 800).—OF. *constreign-*, a stem of *constreindre, constraindre*, to constrain (Godefroy), later form *contraindre*, as in Cotgrave.—L. *constringere*, to bind together, fetter.—L. *con-*, for *cum*, together; and *stringere*, pp. *strictus*, to draw tight. See **Strict, Stringent**. **Der.** *constrain-able, constrain-ed-ly*; *constraint* = ME. *constreint*, Gower, C. A. iii. 380, bk. viii. 3018 (Old F. pp. of *constreindre*); also *constrict, con-strict-ion, constrict-or*, from L. pp. *constrictus*; also *constringe, constring-ent*, from L. *constringere*.

CONSTRUE, to set in order, explain, translate. (L.) 'To construe this clause;' P. Plowman, B. iv. 150; cf. l. 145. [Adopted directly from Lat., not from F. *construire*.]—L. pp. *con-structus*, to heap together, to build, to construe a passage.—L. *con-*, for *cum*, together; and *struere*, to heap up, pile. See **Structure**. Doublet, *construct*, from L. pp. *constructus*; whence *construct-ion, construct-ive, -ive-ly*.

CONSUBSTANTIAL; see **Con-**, and **Substantial**.

CONSUETUDE, custom. (L.) In Wyclif, 1 Kings xx. 25; where the Vulgate has *consuētūdinem*.—L. *consuētūdo*, custom; see **Custom**.

CONSUL, a (Roman) chief magistrate. (L.) In Gower, C. A. iii. 138; bk. vii. 1598.—L. *consul*, a consul. Etym. doubtful, but allied to the verb *consulere*, to consult, deliberate. See **Consult**. **Der.** *consul-ar, -ate, -ship*.

CONSULT, to deliberate. (F.—L.) In Merry Wives, ii. 1. 111.—F. *consulter*, 'to consult, deliberate;' Cot.—L. *consultāre*, to consult; frequent. form of *consulere*, to consult, consider. Root uncertain; perhaps allied to *sedēre*, to sit; cf. *solium*, a seat (Bréal). **Der.** *consultat-ion*.

CONSUME, to waste wholly, devour, destroy. (L.) 'The lond be not *consumed* with myschef;' Wyclif, Gen. xli. 36; where the Vulgate has 'non *consumetur* terra inopia.'—L. *consūmere*, pp. *consumptus*, to consume, lit. to take together or wholly.—L. *con-*, for *cum*, together, wholly; and *sūmere*, to take. The L. *sūmere* is a compound of **sups*, allied to *sub*, under, up, and *emere*, to buy, take. Brugmann, i. § 240. See **Redeem**. **Der.** *consum-able*; also (like L. pp. *consumptus*) *consumpt-ion, -ive, -ive-ly, -ive-ness*.

CONSUMMATE, extreme, perfect. (L.) Properly a past part., as in Shak. Meas. for Meas. v. 383; and in Palsgrave, p. 495, col. 2, l. 18. Thence used as a verb, K. John, v. 7. 95.—L. *consummātus*, from *consummāre*, to bring into one sum, to perfect.—L. *con-*, for *cum*, together; and *summa*, a sum. See **Sum**. **Der.** *consummate*, verb; *consummate-ly, consummat-ion*.

CONSUMPTION, CONSUMPTIVE; see **Consume**.

CONTACT, a close touching, meeting. (L.) Dryden has *contáct*, Essay on Satire, 184.—L. *contactus*, a touching.—L. *contactus*, pp. of *contingere*, to touch closely.—L. *con-*, for *cum*, together; and *tangere*, to touch. See **Tact, Tangent**. And see below.

CONTAGION, transmission of disease by contact. (F.—L.) In Frith's Works, p. 115, col. 2. ME. *contagioun*, Chaucer, C. T. 15540 (G 72).—F. *contagion*, 'contagion, infection;' Cot.—L. *con-tāgiōnem*, acc. of *contāgio*, a touching, hence, contagion.—L. *con-*, for *cum*, with; and *tāg-*, 2nd grade of *tag-*, as in **tag-tus* (> *tac-tus*), pp. of *tangere*, to touch. See **Contact**. **Der.** *contagi-ous, -ous-ly, -ous-ness*. And see *contaminate, contiguous*.

CONTAIN, to comprise, include, hold in. (F.—L.) ME. *contenen, conteinen*; Rob. of Glouc. p. 547, l. 11373.—OF. *contien-*, a tonic stem of *contenir* (Supp. to Godefroy).—L. *continēre*, pp. *contentus*.—L. *con-*, for *cum*, together; and *tenēre*, to hold. See **Tenable**. **Der.** *contain-able*; also *content*, q.v.; *continent*, q.v.; *continue*, q.v.

CONTAMINATE, to pollute, corrupt, defile. (L.) In Shak. J. Cæs. iv. 3. 24. Used as a pp., spelt *contamynate*, in Hall, Chron., Hen. VII. an. xi. § 1.—L. *contāmināātus*, pp. of *contāmināre*, to defile.—L. *contāmin-*, stem of *contāmen-*, contagion, which stands for **contagmen*.—L. *con-*, for *cum*, together; and *tag-*, as in *tac-tus* (for **tag-tus*), pp. of *tangere*, to touch. See Max Müller, Lectures,

8th ed. ii. 309. See **Contact, Contagion.** Der. *contami-nat-ion.*

CONTANGO, the percentage which a buyer of stock pays to the seller to postpone transfer. (Span. ? – L. ?) Said to be an arbitrary or fortuitous formation from the verb to *continue.* But it answers in form to Span. *contengo,* 1 p. s. pr. of *contener,* 'to refrain, curb, restrain, repress, check the motion or progress of anything;' Neuman. – L. *continēre,* to contain; see **Contain.** Thus *contango* means 'I check progress,' i. e. 'I put it off.'

CONTEMN, to despise. (F. – L.) 'Vice to *contemne,* in vertue to rejoyce;' Lord Surrey, On the Death of Sir T. W., ii. 10. – F. *contemner* (Cot.). – L. *contemnere,* to despise, pp. *contemtus* or *contemptus.* – L. *con-,* for *cum,* with, wholly; and *temnere,* to despise (of uncertain origin). Der. *contempt,* from MF. *contempt,* which from L. *contemptus,* scorn, from the L. pp. *contemptus;* hence *contempt-ible, -ibly, -ible-ness; contemptu-ous, -ly, -ness.*

CONTEMPLATE, to consider attentively. (L.) [The sb. *contemplation* was in early use; spelt *contemplaciun* in Ancren Riwle, p. 142; and derived from OF. *contemplacion.*] Shak. has *contemplate,* 3 Hen. VI, ii. 5. 33. – L. *contemplātus,* pp. of *contemplāri,* to observe, consider, used orig. of the augurs who observed a *templum* in the sky. – L. *con-,* for *cum,* together; and *templum,* a space marked out in the sky for observation; also, a temple. See **Temple;** and compare **Consider,** a word of similar origin. Der. *contemplat-ion, -ive, -ive-ly, -ive-ness.*

CONTEMPORANEOUS, happening or being at the same time. (L.) 'The *contemporaneous* insurrections;' State Trials, Col. J. Penruddock, an. 1655 (R.). – L. *contemporāneus,* at the same time; with change of *-us* to *-ous,* as in *conspicuous,* q. v. – L. *con-,* for *cum,* together; and *tempor-,* for **tempos-,* stem of *tempus,* time. See **Temporal.** Der. *contemporaneous-ly, -ness.* Similarly is formed *contemporary,* from L. *con-* and *temporāriu͞,* temporary; cf. L. *contemporāre,* to be at the same time (Tertullian).

CONTEND, to strive, dispute, fight. (F. – L.) In Hamlet, iv. 1. 7. – F. *contendre* (by loss of the final *-re,* which was but slightly sounded); cf. **Vend.** – L. *contendere,* to stretch out, extend, exert, fight, contend. – L. *con-,* for *cum,* with, wholly; and *tendere,* to stretch. See **Tend** (1). Der. (like L. pp. *contentus*) *content-ion* (F. *contention*), *content-ious* (F. *contentieux), -ious-ly, -ious-ness.*

CONTENT, adj. satisfied. (F. – L.) In Shak. Temp. v. 144. – F. *content,* 'content, satisfied;' Cot. – L. *contentus,* content; pp. of *continēre,* to contain. See **Contain.** Der. *content,* verb, from F. *contenter,* which from Late L. *contentāre,* to satisfy, make content; also *content-ed, -ed-ly, -ed-ness;* also *content,* sb., that which is contained; and *content-s,* pl.

CONTEST, to call in question, dispute. (F. – L.) In Shak. Cor. iv. 5. 116. – F. *contester,* 'to contest, call or take to witnesse, make an earnest protestation or complaint unto; also, to brabble, argue, debate,' &c.; Cot. – L. *contestāri,* to call to witness. – L. *con-,* for *cum,* together; and *testāri,* to bear witness, from *testis,* a witness. See **Testify.** Der. *contest,* sb.; *contest-able.*

CONTEXT, a passage connected with part of a sentence quoted. (L.) See quotation in Richardson from Hammond, Works, ii. 182; and Phillips (1658). Also MF. *contexte,* 'a context,' &c.; Cot. – L. *contextus,* a joining together, connexion, order, construction. – L. pp. *contextus,* woven together; from *contexere,* to weave together. – L. *con-,* for *cum,* together; and *texere,* to weave. See **Text.** Der. *context-ure;* see *texture.*

CONTIGUOUS, adjoining, near. (L.) In Milton, P. L. vi. 828, vii. 273. Formed from L. *contiguus,* that may be touched, contiguous, with change of *-us* into *-ous,* as in *contemporaneous,* &c. – L. *con-* (*cum*), together; and *tig-,* weakened form of *tag-,* as in *tac-tus* (for **tag-tus*), pp. of *tangere,* to touch. See **Contingent.** Der. *contiguous-ly, -ness;* also *contigu-i-ty.*

CONTINENT, restraining, temperate, virtuous. (F. – L.) Spelt *contynent,* Wyclif, Titus, i. 8, where the Vulgate has *continentem.* – F. *continent,* 'continent, sober, moderate;' Cot. – L. *continentem,* acc. of *continens,* pres. pt. of *continēre,* to contain. See **Contain.** Der. *continent,* sb.; *continent-ly, continence, continenc-y.*

CONTINGENT, dependent on. (L.) *Contingent* occurs in T. Usk, Test. of Love, bk. i. c. 4. l. 56; bk. ii. c. 9. l. 147. He also has *contingence,* bk. ii. c. 9. l. 181. *Contingency* is in Dryden, Threnodia Augustalis, st. xviii. l. 494. – L. *contingent-,* stem of pres. pt. of *contingere,* to touch, relate to. – L. *con-,* for *cum,* together; and *tangere,* to touch. See **Tangent.** Der. *contingent-ly, contingence, contingenc-y.*

CONTINUE, to persist in, extend, prolong. (F. – L.) ME. *continuen,* whence ME. pres. part. *continuende,* Gower, C. A. ii. 18; bk. iv. 508. – F. *continuer;* Cot. – L. *continuāre,* to connect, unite, make continuous. – L. *continuus,* holding together, continuous. – L. *continēre,* to hold together, contain. See **Contain.** Der. *con-*

tinu-ed, continu-ed-ly, continu-ance (Gower, C. A. ii. 14; bk. iv. 368); also *continu-al, continu-al-ly,* words in early use, since we find *cuntinuelement* in the Ancren Riwle, p. 142; also *continuat-ion, -ive, -or,* from the L. pp. *continuātus;* and see below.

CONTINUOUS, holding together, uninterrupted. (L.) *Continuously* is in Cudworth's Intellectual System, p. 167 (R.). – L. *continuus,* holding together; with change of *-us* into *-ous,* as in *contemporaneous,* &c. – L. *continēre,* to hold together; see **Contain.** Der. *continuous-ly;* and, from the same source, *continu-i-ty.*

CONTORT, to writhe, twist about. (L.) 'In wreathes *contorted;*' Drayton, The Moon-calf, l. 81. – L. *contortus,* pp. of *contorquēre,* to turn round, brandish, hurl. – L. *con-,* for *cum,* together; and *torquēre,* to turn, twist. See **Torture.** Der. *contort-ion.*

CONTOUR, an outline. (F. – Ital. – L. and Gk.) In Phillips (1706). Borrowed from F. *contour;* Cotgrave explains 'le contour d'une ville' by 'the compasse, or whole round of territory or ground, lying next unto and about a towne.' – Ital. *contorno,* a circuit; from *contornare,* 'to encircle;' Florio. – L. *con-* (*cum*), together; and *tornāre,* to round off, to turn. See **Turn.**

CONTRA, prefix, against; from L. *contrā,* against. L. *contrā* was orig. the ablative fem. of an obsolete form **con-t(e)r-us,* a comparative form from *con-* (for *cum*), prep. together; cf. *extrā,* prep., from *exterus.*

CONTRABAND, against law, prohibited. (Span. – Ital. – L.) '*Contraband* wares of beauty;' Spectator, no. 33. Hakluyt has 'by *Contrabanda;*' Voy. ii. 1. 224, l. 24. – Span. *contrabando,* prohibited goods. – Ital. *contrabbando,* prohibited goods (whence also F. *contrebande*). – Ital. *contra,* against; and *bando,* a ban, proclamation. – L. *contrā,* against; and Late L. *bandum,* a ban, proclamation. See **Ban.** Der. *contraband-ist.*

CONTRACT (1) to draw together, shorten. (L.) In Shak. All's Well, v. 3. 51. Palsgrave has *contracte,* p. 497. – L. *contractus,* pp. of *contrahere,* to contract, lit. to draw together. – L. *con-,* for *cum,* together; and *trahere,* to draw. See **Trace.** Der. *contract-ed, -ed-ly, -ed-ness; contract-ible, -ible-ness, -ibil-i-ty; contract-ile, -il-i-ty, -ion;* and see *contract* (2).

CONTRACT (2) a bargain, agreement, bond. (F. – L.) In Shak. Temp. ii. 1. 151. – MF. *contract,* 'a contract, bargaine, agreement;' Cot. [Cf. F. *contracter,* 'to contract, bargaine;' id.] – L. *contractum,* acc. of *contractus,* a drawing together; also a compact, bargain. – L. *contractus,* drawn together. See **Contract** (1). Der. *contract,* verb, i.e. to make a contract (F. *contracter*); *contract-or.*

CONTRADICT, to reply to, oppose verbally. (L.) In the Mirror for Magistrates, p. 850. Sir T. More has *contradictory,* Works, p. 1109 e. T. Usk has *contradiccion,* Test. of Love, bk. ii. c. 11. l. 116; and *contradictorie,* bk. ii. c. 13. l. 129. – L. *contrādictus,* pp. of *contrādicere,* to speak against. – L. *contrā,* against; and *dicere,* to speak. See **Diction.** Der. *contradict-ion, contradict-or-y.*

CONTRADISTINGUISH, to distinguish by contrast. (Hybrid; L. *and* F.) Used by Bp. Hall, Episcopacy by Divine Right, pt. iii. s. 2 (R.). Made up of L. *contrā,* against; and *distinguish,* q. v. Der. *contradistinct-ion, -ive.*

CONTRALTO. In singing, the part next above the alto. (Ital. – L.) First found in 1769; *contrealt* in 1730. Ital. *contralto.* – Ital. *contra,* against (L. *contrā*); and *alto,* the high voice in singing, from Ital. *alto,* high; which from L. *altus,* high.

CONTRAPUNTAL, relating to counterpoint. (Ital. – L.) Modern. From MItal. *contrapunto* (Ital. *contrappunto*), counterpoint. – Ital. *contra* (L. *contrā*), over against; and *punto* (L. *punctum*), a point. See **Counterpoint.**

CONTRARY, opposite, contradictory. (F. – L.) Formerly accented *contráry.* ME. *contrarie.* In early use. In An Early Eng. Miscellany, ed. Morris, p. 30, l. 1. – AF. *contrarie,* Year-books of Edw. I., 1302–3, p. 363; OF. *contraire.* – L. *contrārius,* contrary. Formed from the prep. *contrā,* against. See **Contra.** Der. *contrari-ly, -ness, -e-ty, -wise.*

CONTRAST, to stand in opposition to, to appear by comparison. (F. – L.) The neuter sense of the verb is the orig. one in Latin; whence the act. sense 'to put in contrast with.' 'The figures of the groups ... must *contrast* each other by their several positions;' Dryden, A Parallel between Poetry and Painting (R.). p. 164 (ed. Yonge). – F. *contraster,* 'to strive, withstand, contend against;' Cot. – Late L. *contrastāre,* to stand opposed to, oppose. – L. *contrā,* against; and *stāre,* to stand. See **Stand.** Der. *contrast,* sb.

CONTRAVENE, to oppose, hinder. (F. – L.) 'Contravened the acts of parliament;' State Trials, John Ogilvie, an. 1615 (R.). – MF. *contrevenir,* 'to thwart;' Cot. [Cf. AF. *contrevenant,* contravening; Statutes of the Realm, i. 104 (1285).] – L. *contrāuenire,* to break a law; lit. to come against, oppose. – L. *contrā,* against; and *uenire,* to come, cognate with E. *come,* q. v. Der. *contravent-ion,* from the L. pp. *contrauentus.*

CONTRETEMPS, a mishap, a hitch. (F.—L.) In Thackeray, Vanity Fair, ch. 34 (near the end); and see the Stanford Dict.—F. *contre-temps,* a mishap, inopportune event.—L. *contrā,* against; and *tempus,* time, opportunity.

CONTRIBUTE, to pay a share of a thing. (L.) Accented *contribúte* in Milton, P. L. viii. 155. Shak. has *contribution,* Hen. VIII, i. 2. 95.—L. *contribūtus,* pp. of *contribuere,* to distribute, to contribute.—L. *con-,* for *cum,* together; and *tribuere,* to pay. See **Tribute.** Der. *contribut-ion, -ive, -ar-y, -or-y.*

CONTRITE, very penitent, lit. bruised thoroughly. (F.—L.) Chaucer has *contrite* and *contrition,* near the beginning of the Persones Tale (I 110, 133).—OF. (and F.) *contrit.*—L. *contrītus,* thoroughly bruised; in Late L., penitent; pp. of *conterere.*—L. *con-,* for *cum,* together; and *terere,* to rub, grind, bruise; see **Trite.** Der. *contrite-ly, contrit-ion.*

CONTRIVE, to hit upon, find out, plan. (F.—L. *and* Gk.) *Contrive* is a late and altered spelling; ME. *controuen, controeuen, contreuen* (where *u* is for *v*); 15th cent., *contreve, contryve;* 16th cent., *contrive.* Spelt *controue,* rhyming with *reproue (reprove),* in the Romaunt of the Rose, 7547; Gower, C. A. i. 216; bk. ii. 1708.—OF. *controver,* to find, to imagine, invent; 3 p. s. pr. *contreuve* (whence ME. *controeuen, contreuen*); see Godefroy. The pt. t. pl. *controuerent* occurs in st. 9 of La Vie de Saint Léger (Bartsch, Chrestomathie Française).—OF. *con-* (L. *con-,* for *cum*) with, wholly; and OF. *trover,* mod. F. *trouver,* to find. The OF. *trover* was formerly explained from L. *turbāre,* but was really formed from Late L. *tropāre;* for which see **Troubadour, Trover.** Der. *contriv-ance, contriv-er.* ¶ An old pronunciation of the *-treve* in *contreve* is preserved in *retrieve.*

CONTROL, restraint, command. (F.—L.) *Control* is short for *contre-rolle,* the old form of *counter-roll.* The sb. *conterroller,* i.e. *comptroller* or *controller,* occurs in P. Plowman, C. xii. 298; and see *Controller* in Blount's Law Dictionary.—OF. *contre-role, contre-rolle,* a duplicate register, used to verify the official or first roll; see *Contrôle* in Brachet; and see Godefroy (Supplement) and Cotgrave.—OF. *contre,* over against; and *role, rolle,* a roll, from *rotulum,* acc. of L. *rotulus.* See **Counter** and **Roll.** Der. *control,* verb; *controll-ab'e, control-ment;* also *controller* (sometimes spelt *comptroller,* but badly), P. Plowman, C. xii. 298; *controller-ship.*

CONTROVERSY, dispute, variance. (F.—L.) 'Controuersy and varyaunce;' Fabyan's Chron. K. John of France, an. 7; ed. Ellis, p. 505. ME. *controuersie,* Wyclif, Heb. vi. 16 (earlier text). [The verb *controvert* is a later formation, and of E. growth; there is no L. *contrōuertere.*]—AF. *controversye,* Langtoft's Chron., ed. Wright, i. 434 (1307).—L. *contrōuersia,* a quarrel, dispute.—L. *contrōuersus,* opposed, controverted.—L. *contrō-,* masc. or neut. form allied to fem. *contrā,* against; and *uersus,* turned, pp. of *uertere,* to turn. See **Contra** and **Verse.** Der. *controversi-al, -al-ly, -al-ist;* also *controvert* (see remark above), *controvert-ible, -ibl-y.*

CONTUMACY, pride, stubbornness. (F.—L.) In Fabyan's Chron. King John, an. 7; ed. Ellis, p. 316. Chaucer has *contumacie,* C. T., Pers. Tale, I 391. [The L. adj. *contumax,* contumacious, was adopted both into French and Middle-English without change, and may be seen in P. Plowman, C. xiv. 85, in Chaucer's Pers. Tale (De Superbia), and in Cotgrave.]—AF. *contumacie,* Year-books of Edw. I., 1302-3, p. 367.—L. *contumācia,* obstinacy, contumacy.—L. *contumax,* gen. *contumāci-s,* stubborn.—L. *con-* (*cum*), very, wholly; **tum-ax,* adj. formed from *tum-ēre,* to swell with pride. See **Tumid.** Der. *contumaci-ous, -ous-ly, -ous-ness;* and see below.

CONTUMELY, reproach. (F.—L.) 'Not to feare the contumelyes of the crosse;' Barnes, Works, p. 360, col. 1. ME. *contumelie,* Chaucer, C. T., Pers. Tale, I 556.—F. *contumelie,* 'contumely, reproach;' Cot.—L. *contumēlia,* misusage, insult, reproach. Prob. connected with L. *contumax;* see above. Der. *contumeli-ous, -ous-ly, -ous-ness.*

CONTUSE, to bruise severely, crush. (L.) Used by Bacon, Nat. Hist. § 574.—L. *contūsus,* pp. of *contundere,* to bruise severely.—L. *con-,* for *cum,* with, very much; and *tundere,* to beat, of which the base is *tud-;* cf. Skt. *tud,* to strike, sting (which has lost an initial *s*), Goth. *stautan,* to strike, smite.—√STEUD, to strike; Brugmann, i. § 818 (2). Der. *contus-ion.*

CONUNDRUM. (L. ?) 'I must have my crotchets! And my *conundrums!*' Ben Jonson, The Fox, Act v. sc. 7. It here means a conceit, device. 'I begin To have strange *conundrums* in my head;' Massinger, Bondman, Act ii. sc. 3. Again, in Ben Jonson's Masque, called News from the New World, Factor says: 'And I have hope to erect a staple for news ere long, whither all shall be brought, and thence again vented under the name of Staple News, and not trusted to your printed *conundrums* of the Serpent in Sussex, or the witches bidding the devil to dinner at Derby; news that, when a man sends them down to the shires where they are said to be done, were never

there to be found.' Here *conundrum* means a hoax or a *canard.* In Ram Alley, iii. 1. 2 (Hazlitt's Old Plays, x. 313) we find: 'We old men have our crotchets, our *conundrums,* Our figaries, quirks, and quibbles, As well as youth.' Also spelt *quonundrum, conuncrum, conimbrum.* Etymology unknown; but doubtless of Latin origin, originating in a university joke; attributed (in 1645) to Oxford; see N. E. D. Cf. *quillet,* as a corruption of *quidlibet.* It might thus be an old term of the schools, purposely perverted, such as **quo-nunc-rum;* like *quidnunckery,* found in 1804. For the later sense, see Spectator, no. 61, May 10, 1711.

CONVALESCE, to recover health, grow well. (L.) 'He found the queen somewhat *convalesced;*' Knox, Hist. Reformation, b. v. an. 1566.—L. *conualescere,* to begin to grow well; an inceptive form.—L. *con-,* for *cum,* together, wholly; and *-ualescere,* an inceptive form of *ualēre,* to be strong. See **Valiant.** Der. *convalesc-ent, convalesc-ence.*

CONVENE, to assemble. (F.—L.) 'Now *convened* against it;' Baker, Charles I, Jan. 19, 1648 (R.). It is properly a neuter verb, signifying 'to come together;' afterwards made active, in the sense 'to summon.'—F. *convenir,* 'to assemble, meet, or come together;' Cot.—L. *conuenīre,* pp. *conuentus,* to come together.—L. *con-,* for *cum,* together; and *uenīre,* to come, cognate with E. *come,* q. v. Der. *conven-er; conven-i-ent,* q. v.; also *convent,* q. v., *convent-ion,* q. v.

CONVENIENT, suitable, commodious. (L.) In early use. In Chaucer, tr. of Boethius, b. iii. pr. 11, l. 80.—L. *conuenient-,* stem of *conueniens,* suitable; orig. pres. pt. of *conuenīre,* to come together, to suit. See **Convene.** Der. *convenient-ly, convenience.*

CONVENT, a monastery or nunnery. (L.) [ME. *couent (u* for *v),* in Chaucer, C. T., B 1827, 1867; from OF. *covent;* still preserved in *Covent* Garden. *Convent* is the L. form.]—L. *conuentus,* an assembly.—L. *conuentus,* pp. of *conuenīre,* to come together; see **Convene.** Der. *conventu-al; convent-ic-le* (Levins).

CONVENTION, assembly, agreement. (F.—L.) 'Accordyng to his promes [promise] and *conuencion;*' Hall, Hen. VI, an. 18. § 4.—F. *convention,* 'a covenant, contract;' Cot.—L. *conuentiōnem,* acc. of *conuentio,* a meeting, a compact; cf. *conuentus,* pp. of *conuenīre,* to come together; see **Convene.** Der. *convention-al, -al-ly, -al-ism, -al-i-ty.*

CONVERGE, to verge together to a point. (L.) 'After they [the rays] have been made to *converge* by reflexion or refraction;' Newton, Optics (Todd).—L. *conuergere,* to incline together (Isidore).—L. *con-,* for *cum,* together; and *uergere,* to turn, bend, incline. See **Diverge,** and **Verge,** verb. Der. *converg-ent, -ence, -enc-y.*

CONVERSE, to associate with, talk. (F.—L.) ME. *conuersen* (with *u* for *v*); the pres. pt. *c·nuersand* occurs in the Northern poem by Hampole, entitled The Pricke of Conscience, l. 4198.—F. *converser;* Cotgrave gives: 'Converser avec, to converse, or be much conversant, associate, or keep much company with.'—L. *conuersāri,* to live with any one; orig. passive of *conuersāre,* to turn round, the frequentative form of *conuertere,* to turn round. See **Convert.** Der. *converse,* sb.; *convers-at-ion* (ME. *conuersacion,* Ayenbite of Inwyt, p. 96, from OF. *conversacion*); *conversation-al, -al-ist; convers-able, -ant;* also *conversazione,* the Ital. form of *conversation.*

CONVERT, to change, turn round. (F.—L.) ME. *conuerten* (with *u* for *v*); Hampole, Pricke of Conscience, 4502; Chaucer, C. T., B 435.—AF. and OF. *convertir.*—Folk-L. **convertīre,* for L. *conuertere,* to turn round, to change; pp. *conuersus.*—L. *con-,* for *cum,* together, wholly; and *uertere,* to turn. See **Verse.** Der. *convert,* verb; *convert-ible, -ibl-y, -ibil-i-ty;* also *converse,* adj., *-ly, convers-ion;* and see *converse* above.

CONVEX, roundly projecting; opposed to *concave.* (L.) In Milton, P. L. ii. 434, iii. 419.—L. *conuexus,* convex, arched, vaulted; properly the pp. of L. *conuehere,* to bring together, hence, to unite by an arch.—L. *con-,* for *cum,* together; and *uehere,* to carry. See **Vehicle.** Der. *convex-ly, -ed, -i-ty.*

CONVEY, to bring on the way, transmit, impart. (F.—L.) ME. *conueien* (with *u* for *v*), to accompany, convoy (a doublet of *convey*); Allit. Poems, ed. Morris, B. 678, 768.—AF. and ONorth F. *conueier,* answering to O. Central F. *convoier,* to convey, convoy, conduct, accompany, bring on the way.—Late L. *conuiāre,* to accompany on the way.—L. *con-,* for *cum,* together; and *uia,* a way, allied to *uehere* (above). See **Viaduct.** Der. *convey-able, -ance, -anc-er, -anc-ing.* Doublet, *convoy.*

CONVINCE, to convict, refute, persuade by argument. (L.) See *Convince* in Trench, Select Glossary. Palsgrave has *convynce,* p. 498. 'All reason did *convince;*' Gascoigne, The Fable of Philomela, st. 22.—L *conuincere,* pp. *conuictus,* to overcome by proof, demonstrate, refute.—L. *con-,* for *cum,* with, thoroughly; and *uincere,* to conquer. See **Victor.** Der. *convinc-ible, -ing-ly;* also (from L. pp. *conuictus*) *convict,* verb and sb.; *convict-ion, -ive.*

CONVIVIAL, festive. (L.) Shak. has the verb *convive,* to feast;

Troilus, iv. 5. 272. Sir T. Browne has *convival*, Vulg. Errors, b. iii. c. 25. § 15. The form *convivial* is used by Denham, Of Old Age, pt. iii. 47. — L. *conuiuiālis*, belonging to a feast. Formed, with suffix -*ālis*, from L. *conuīui-um*, a feast. — L. *conuīuere*, to live or feast with any one. — L. *con-*, for *cum*, with; and *uīuere*, to live. See **Victuals**. Der. *convivial-ly, -i-ty*.

CONVOKE, to call together. (L.) Used by Sir W. Temple, On the United Provinces, c. 2. Florio has Ital. *convocare*, 'to conuoke.' [The sb. *convocation* was in use much earlier, in Trevisa, tr. of Higden, vii. 111.] — L. *conuocāre*, pp. *conuocātus*, to call together. — L. *con-*, for *cum*, together; and *uocāre*, to call. See **Vocal**. Der. *convoc-at-ion*.

CONVOLVE, to writhe about. (L.) In Milton, P. L. vi. 328. — L. *conuoluere*, to roll or fold together; pp. *conuolūtus*. — L. *con-*, for *cum*, together; and *uoluere*, to roll. See **Voluble**. Der. *convolute, convolut-ed, -ion*; also *convolv-ul-us*, a twining plant, a pure L. word.

CONVOY, to conduct, bring on the way. (F. — L.) ME. *conuoien* (with *u* for *v*), another form of ME. *conueien*, to convey; common in Barbour's Bruce. 'Till *convoy* him till his cuntrè;' Bruce, v. 195. It is the Central F. form of *convey*. See **Convey**. Der. *convoy*, sb.

CONVULSE, to agitate violently. (L.) *Convulsion* is in Shak. Tempest, iv. 260. The verb *convulse* is later; Todd gives a quotation for it, dated A. D. 1681. — L. *conuulsus*, pp. of *conuellere*, to pluck up, dislocate, convulse. — L. *con-*, for *cum*, together, wholly; and *uellere*, to pluck. Der. *convuls-ion, -ive, -ive-ly, -ive-ness*.

CONY, CONEY, a rabbit. (F. — L.) ME. *coni, conni*; also *conig, coning, conyng*. 'Conies ther were also playinge;' Rom. of the Rose, 1404. '*Cony*, cuniculus,' Prompt. Parv. p. 90. 'Hic cuniculus, a *conyng*;' Vocab. 759. 25. — AF. *conil* (pl. *conis*), Stat. of the Realm, i. 380 (1363); *conyn* (*conin*), Lib. Custumarum, p. 305; OF. *connil*. — L. *cuniculum*, acc. of *cuniculus*, a rabbit. ¶ Du. *konijn*, Dan. *kanin*, G. *kanin-chen*, are all of L. origin. The E. word is from the OF. pl. *conis*, by dropping *s*.

COO, to make a noise as a dove. (E.) 'Coo, to make a noise as turtles and pigeons do;' Kersey's Dict. ed. 1715. 'Croo, or Crookel, to make a noise like a dove or pigeon;' id. A purely imitative word, formed from the sound. See **Cuckoo**.

COOK, to dress food; a dresser of food. (L.) ME. *coken*, to cook; P. Plowman, C. xvi. 60; *cook*, a cook, Chaucer. The verb seems, in English, to have been made from the sb., which occurs as AS. *cōc*, Grein, i. 167. The word so closely resembles the Latin that it must have been borrowed, and is not cognate. — L. *coquus*, a cook; from *coquere*, to cook. ✛Gk. πέσσειν, to cook; Skt. *pach*, to cook; Russ. *pech(e)*, to bake. — √PEQ; whence L. **pequere*, becoming **quequere* by assimilation, and finally *coquere*; Gk. **πέϙ-ιειν*, whence πέσσειν. See Brugmann, i. § 661. ¶ AS. *cōc* < Late L. *cōcus*, for *coquus*. Der. *cook-er-y* = ME. *cokerie*, Gower, C. A. ii. 83; bk. iv. 2433.

COOL, slightly cold. (E.) ME. *col, cole*; Rob. of Glouc. p. 131, l. 2775. AS. *cōl*, cool, Grein, i. 167.✛Du. *koel*. Teut. type **kōl-uz*; also, with mutation, Dan. *köl, kölig*, cool, chilly; G. *kühl*. From *kōl-*, 2nd grade of *kal-*, as in AS. *cal-an*, Icel. *kala*, to freeze (pt. t. *kōl*). See **Cold**. Der. *cool*, verb; *cool-ly, cool-ness, cool-er*; *chill*.

COOLIE, COOLY, an East Indian porter. (Hindustani.) The pl. *coolyes* occurs in Sir T. Herbert's Travels, ed. 1665, p. 78 (head-line). — Hind. *kūli*, a labourer, porter, cooley; Hindustani Dict. by D. Forbes, ed. 1859, p. 309. Prob. from *Koli*, a tribal name (Yule); though Wilson would derive it from Tamil *kūli*, daily hire or wages.

COOMB, a dry measure; see **Comb** (2).

COOP, a box or cage for birds, a tub, vat. (L.) Formerly, it also meant a basket. ME. *cupe*, a basket. 'Cupen he let fulle of flures' = he caused (men) to fill baskets with flowers; Floriz and Blancheflur, ed. Lumby, 435; see also ll. 438, 447, 452, 457. — L. *cūpa*, a tub, vat, butt, cask; whence also F. *cuve*. The L. *cūpa* is cognate with Skt. *kūpa-*, a pit, well, hollow; Curtius, i. 194. Cf. also Du. *kuip*, Icel. *kūpa*, a bowl; also from L. *cūpa*. See **Cup** and **Hive**. Der. *coop*, verb; *coop-er, coop-er-age*.

CO-OPERATE, to work together. (L.) Sir T. More has the pres. part. *coöperant* (a F. form), Works, p. 383 e. — Late L. *coöperātus*, pp. of *coöperārī*, to work together; Mark, xvi. 20 (Vulgate). — L. *co-*, for *com*, i. e. *cum*, together; and *operārī*, to work. See **Operate**. Der. *coöperat-or, coöperant* (pres. pt. of F. *coöperer*, to work together, from L. *coöperārī*), *coöperat-ion, -ive*.

CO-ORDINATE, of the same rank or order. (L.) 'Not subordinate, but *co-ordinate* parts;' Prynne, Treachery of Papists, pt. i. p. 41 (R.). — L. *co-*, for *com*, i. e. *cum*, together; and *ordinātus*, pp. of *ordināre*, to arrange. See **Ordain**. Der. *coördinat-ion*.

COOT, a sort of water-fowl. (E.) ME. *cote, coote*. 'Cote, mergus;' Voc. 641. 10. 'Coote, byrde, mergus, fullica;' Prompt. Parv. p. 95. Spelt *coote* in Wyclif, Levit. xi. 16.✛Du. *koet*, a coot; fem. β. From an AS. form **cōte*, not found. History unknown.

COPAIBA, a kind of balsam. (Port. — Brazil.) Spelt *copayba* in 1712 (N. E. D.) — Port. *copaiba* (Vieyra; Eng.-Port. Dict.). — Brazil. *copaiba*; Hist. Brasil. (1648); ii. 230. Cf. Span. *copayva* in Pineda. The suffix -*iba* means 'plant,' 'tree.'

COPAL, a resinous substance. (Span. — Mexican.) 'Copal, a kind of white and bright resin, brought from the West Indies;' Blount's Gloss. ed. 1674. 'Copall, or Suchicopal;' E. G., tr. of Acosta, b. iv. c. 29; also in Frampton, tr. of Monardes, fol. 2. It is a product of the *Rhus copallīnum*, a native of Mexico; Engl. Cyclopædia. — Span. *copal*, copal. — Mexican *copalli*, resin. 'The Mexican *copalli* is a generic name for resin;' Clavigero's Hist. of Mexico, tr. by C. Cullen, ed. 1787; vol. i. p. 33.

CO-PARCENER, a co-partner. (L. and F. — L.) From L. *co-*, for *com*, i. e. *cum*, with; and ME. *parcener*, a partner. We find Anglo-French *parcener, parcenere*, Year-books of Edw. I., 1292–3, p. 155; *parceners*, pl., id. 45; Stat. Realm, i. 49, an. 1278; Annals of Burton, pp. 471, 480. Also *parcenerie*, partnership, Year-books of Edw. I., 1292–3, p. 45. See **Partner**.

COPE, (1), a cap, hood, cloak, cape. (Late L.) ME. *cape, cope*. 'Hec capa, a *cope*;' Voc. 570. 16. And see Ancren Riwle, p. 56; Havelok, 429. Gower has: 'In kirtles and in *copes* riche;' and again: 'Under the *cope* of heven;' Conf. Amantis, ii. 46, 102; iii. 138. The phrase '*cope* of heaven' is still in use in poetry. However afterwards differentiated, the words *cope, cape* were the same originally. *Cope* represents an AS. **cāpe*, f.; cf. Icel. *kápa*, a cape; and cf. *pope* (from AS. *pāpa*). — Late L. *cāpa*, a cape. See **Cape**. Der. *cop-ing, cop-ing-stone*, i. e. capping-stone.

COPE (2), to vie with, match. (F. — L. — Gk.) In Shak. Hamlet, iii. 2. 60. ME. *coupen*, to strike, encounter; Destr. of Troy, l. 7231. — OF. *couper, coper*; see further under **Coppi2e**.

COPE (3), to buy. (Du.) ME. *copen*; Lydgate, London Lickpeny, st. 7, in Spec. of English, ed. Skeat, p. 25. A word introduced into England by Flemish and Dutch traders. — Du. *koopen*, to buy, purchase; orig. to bargain. Cognate with AS. *cēapian*, to cheapen, from AS. *cēap*, a bargain. See **Cheap**.

COPECK, a small Russian coin, worth less than ½*d*.; a hundredth part of a rouble (Russ.) Spelt *copec* in 1698 (N. E. D.). — Russ. *kopieika*, a copeck; dimin. of *kopeé*, a lance. So called from the figure of Ivan IV, holding a *lance* (1535). See **Rouble**.

COPING-STONE; see under **Cope** (1).

COPIOUS, ample, plentiful. (F. — L.) 'A *copyous* oost,' Wyclif, I Maccab. xvi. 5; where the Vulgate has 'exercitus copiosus.' — OF. *copieux*, fem. *copieuse*, 'copious, abundant;' Cot. — L. *cōpiōsus*, plentiful; formed with suffix -*ōsus* from L. *cōpi-a*, plenty. The L. *cōpia* stands for **co-opia*; from *co-* (for *com*, i. e. *cum*, together, exceedingly), and the stem *op-*, seen in *opēs*, riches, and in *in-opia*, want. See **Opulent**. Der. *copious-ly, -ness*; and see *copy*.

COPPER, a reddish metal. (Cyprus.) ME. *coper*, Chaucer, C. T. 16760 (G 1292). AS. *copor*. — Late L. *cuper*; L. *cuprum*, copper; a contraction for *cuprium æs*, i. e. Cyprian brass. See Max Müller, Lectures, 8th ed. ii. 257. — Gk. Κύπριος, Cyprian; from Κύπρος, Cyprus, a Greek island on the S. coast of Asia Minor, whence the Romans obtained copper; Pliny, xxxiv. 2. ¶ From the same source is G. *kupfer*, Du. *koper*, F. *cuivre*, copper. Der. *copper-y, copper-plate*; also *copperas*, q. v.

COPPERAS, sulphate of iron. (F. — L.) Formerly applied also to sulphate of *copper*, whence the name. ME. *coperose*. 'Coperose, vitriola;' Prompt. Parv. p. 91. — OF. *coperose*, the old spelling of *couperose*, which Cotgrave explains by 'copres,' i. e. copperas. Cf. Ital. *copparosa*, Span. *caparrosa*, copperas. β. Diez supposed these forms to be from L. *cuprī rosa*, lit. copper-rose, a supposition which he strengthened by the fact that the Greek name for copperas was χάλκανθος, lit. brass-flower. But this is prob. mere popular etymology; the Late L. *cuprōsa* seems to be an ordinary fem. adj. formation from L. *cupr-um*.

COPPICE, COPPY, COPSE, a wood of small growth. (F. — Gk.) *Coppy* (common in prov. Eng.) and *copse* are both corruptions of *coppice*. *Coppice* is used by Drayton, The Muses' Elysium, Nymph. 4. It should rather be spelt *copice*, with one *p*. — OF. *copeiz, copeis*, cut wood; Godefroy. Hence applied to brushwood or underwood, frequently cut for fuel, or to a wood kept under by cutting. [Cf. Late L. *copecia*, underwood, a coppice.] — OF. *coper*, to cut; F. *couper*. — OF. *cop*, formerly *colp*, a blow, stroke; F. *coup*; see *coup* in the Supp. to Godefroy. — Late L. *colpum*, acc. of *colpus*, a stroke; from L. *colap'us*, a blow. — Gk. κόλαφος, a blow; a word of uncertain origin. ¶ OF. *copeiz* represents a Late L. type **colpāticium*, from *colpāre*, to strike. *Coppy* arose from *coppice* being taken as *coppies*, pl.; and *copse* from reducing a supposed pl. **coppis* to *copse*.

COPROLITE, a roundish stone, supposed to consist of fossilised fæces (Gk.) Modern; in 1829. — Gk. κόπρο-, for κόπρος, dung; and λίθος, a stone.

COPULATE, to couple together. (L.) Used as a pp. by Bacon, Essay 39, Of Custom. — L. *cōpulātus*, joined; pp. of *cōpulāre*. — L. *cōpula*, a band, bond, link; see **Couple.** Der. *copulat-ion, copulat-ive*; and see *couple*.

COPY, an imitation of an original. (F. — L.) [The orig. signification was 'plenty;' and the present sense was due to the multiplication of an original by means of numerous copies.] ME. *copy, copie*. 'Copy of a thinge wretyn, copia;' Prompt. Parv. p. 92. 'Grete *copy* [i.e. abundance] and plente of castelles, of hors, of metal, and of hony;' Trevisa, i. 301. — F. *copie*, 'the copy of a writing; also store, plenty, abundance of;' Cot. — L. *cōpia*, plenty. See **Copious.** Der. *copy*, verb; *copi-er, copy-ist, -hold, -right*.

COQUETTE, a vain flirt. (F. — L. — Gk.) 'The coquet (*sic*) is in particular a great mistress of that part of oratory which is called action;' Spectator, no. 247. 'Affectations of *coquetry*;' id. no. 377. — F. *coquette*, 'a pratling or proud gossip;' Cot. The fem. form of *coquet*, the dimin. of *coq*, meaning 'a little cock,' hence vain as a cock, strutting about; like prov. E. *cocky*. Cf. '*coqueter*, to swagger or strowte it, like a cocke on his owne dung-hill;' Cot. — F. *coq*, a cock. See **Cock** (1). Der. *coquet-ry, coquett-ish, -ish-ly, -ish-ness*.

COR, a Hebrew measure of capacity. (Heb.) In Wyclif we have the pl. '*coris* of whete;' Luke, xvi. 7; where the Vulgate version has *coros*, and the Gk. has κόρους. — Heb. *kōr*, a measure, a round vessel; allied to *kārar*, to roll round.

CORACLE, a light round wicker boat. (Welsh.) See Southey, Madoc in Wales, c. xiii, and footnotes. In use in Wales and on the Severn. Cotgrave explains F. *carabe* as 'a corracle, or little round skiffe.' — W. *corwgl, cwrwgl*, a coracle; dimin. of W. *corwg*, a trunk, a carcase, *cwrwg*, a frame, carcase, boat. Cf. Gael. *curachan*, a coracle, dimin. of *curach*, a boat of wicker-work; Gael. and Irish *corrach*, OIrish *curach*, a boat. Stokes-Fick, p. 93.

CORACOID, beaked like a crow. (Gk.) '*Coracoides*, a process of the shoulder-blade;' Phillips (1706). Medical L. *coracoïdes*. — Gk. κορακοειδής, like a raven. — Gk. κορακο-, for κόραξ, a raven; and εἶδος, form.

CORAL, a secretion of certain zoophytes. (F. — L. — Gk.) Chaucer has *coral*, Prol. 158. — OF. *coral*; see *corail* in Hatzfeld. — L. *corallum*, coral; also spelt *corallium*. — Gk. κοράλλιον, coral. See Schade, OHG. Dict., p. 1374. Der. *corall-ine*; *coralli-ferous*, i.e. coral-bearing, from the L. suffix *-fer*, bearing, from *ferre*, to bear.

CORBAN, a gift. (Hebrew.) In Mark, vii. 11. — Heb. *qorbān*, an offering to God of any sort, whether bloody or bloodless, but particularly in fulfilment of a vow; Concise Dict. of the Bible. — Heb. *qārav*, to draw near, to offer. Cf. Arabic *qurbān*, a sacrifice, victim, oblation; Rich. Dict. p. 1123.

CORBEL, an architectural ornament. (F. — L.) Orig. an ornament in architecture, named from the idea of a projecting beak. Cotgrave translates F. *corbeau* by 'a raven; also, a *corbell* (in masonry);' and F. *mutules* by 'brackets, corbells, or shouldring pieces.' 'Corbell of a roffe' [roof]; Prompt. Parv. 'Chemyneis, *corbels*;' Arnold's Chron. (1502); ed. 1811, p. 138. [The OF. form of *corbeau* was *corbel*, but there were two distinct words of this form, viz. (1) a little raven, from L. *coruus*, a raven, and (2) a little basket.] — OF. *corbel*, old spelling of *corbeau*, a corbel; answering to mod. Ital. *corbella*, a corbel, a bracket, given in Torriano's Dict.; named from a fancied likeness to a raven's beak. — Folk-Lat. *corbellum*, for *corvellum*, acc. of *corvellus*, dimin. of L. *coruus*, a raven. Hatzfeld (s.v. *corbeau*) explains that the projecting corbel was orig. cut slantwise, so that its profile was beaklike. See **Corvette.** ¶ Another architectural ornament was a *corbeil* (wrongly, *corbel*), in the form of a basket; from F. *corbeille*, L. *corbicula*, a little basket; from L. *corbis*, a basket.

CORBY, a raven. (F. — L.) In Henryson; Dog, Wolf, and Sheip, l. 15. — OF. *corbin*, dimin. of *corb*, a raven (Godefroy). — L. *coruus*, a raven.

CORD, a small rope. (F. — L. — Gk.) ME. *corde, cord*; Cursor Mundi, 2247. — OF. (and F.) *corde*. — Late L. *corda*, a cord; L. *chorda*. — Gk. χορδή, the string of a musical instrument; orig. a string of gut. See **Chord.** Doublet, *chord*. Der. *cord*, verb; *cord-age* (F. *cordage*), *cord-on* (F. *cord-on*); also *cordelier* (F. *cordelier*, a twist of rope, also a Gray Friar, who used such a twist, from *cordeler*, to twist ropes, which from OF. *cordel*, dimin. of OF. *corde*); also *corduroy*, q.v.; *cord-illera* (Span.), a chain of hills.

CORDIAL, hearty, sincere. (F. — L.) Also used as a sb. 'For gold in phisik is a *cordial*;' Chaucer, C. T., Prol. 443 (or 445). — F. *cordial*, m. *cordiale*, f. 'cordiall, hearty;' Cot. '*Cordiale*, the herbe motherwort, good against the throbbing or excessive beating of the heart;' id. — L. *cordi-*, declensional stem of *cor*, the heart; with suffix *-ālis*. See **Heart.** Der. *cordial-ly, -i-ty*.

CORDUROY, a thick-ribbed or corded stuff. (F. — L.) Rees' Cyclop., (s.v. *Fustian*) speaks of 'the various cotton stuffs known by the names of *corduroy*,' &c. Already, in 1748, we find mention of 'Serges, *Duroys*, Druggets, Shalloons,' &c.; Defoe, Tour through Great Britain, i. 94 (4th ed.). In 1722, the London Gazette (no. 6089/4) mentions 'a grey *duroy* coat.' Hence it is probable that *corduroy* represents F. *corde du roi*; indeed, it was also called *king's-cord*; see N. E. D.

CORDWAINER, a shoemaker. (F. — *a town in* Spain.) 'A counterfeit earl of Warwick, a *cordwainer's* son;' Bacon, Life of Hen. VII, ed. Lumby, p. 177, l. 15. '*Cordwaner*, alutarius;' Prompt. Parv. p. 92. It orig. meant a worker in *cordewan* or *cordewane*, i.e. leather of Cordova; thus it is said of Chaucer's Sir Thopas that his shoon [shoes] were 'of *Cordewane*;' C. T., B 1922. — OF. *cordoanier*, a cordwainer. — OF. *cordoan, cordouan, cordewan*, Cordovan leather; Godefroy. — Late L. *cordoānum*, Cordovan leather; Ducange. — Late L. *Cordoa*, a spelling of Cordova, in Spain (Lat. *Corduba*), which became a Roman colony in B.C. 152. ¶ 'Gallice *corduan*; alio modo dicitur *cordubunum*, a Corduba, civitate Hispaniæ, ubi fiebat primo;' J. de Garlande, in Wright, Vocab. i. 125.

CORE, the hard central part of fruit, &c. (F. — L.) 'Core of frute, arula;' Prompt. Parv. p. 93. 'Take quynces ripe . . . but kest away the *core*;' Palladius on Husbandry, bk. xi. st. 73. — OF. *cor*, a horn; also horn (the substance); also a corn on the foot, a callosity; Cotgrave, and Supp. to Godefroy. — L. *cornū*, a horn, a horny excrescence. Hollyband (1580) has: '*Vn cor*, a core in the feete.' ¶ In the 16th century, associated with OF. *coer, cuer*, MF. *coeur* (F. *cœur*), and used with the sense of 'heart.' Hence Cotgrave has: '*Coeur*, a heart . . . also, the *core* of fruit; also, the *queer* of a church,' &c.; by further confusion with F. *chœur*.

CORIANDER, the name of a plant. (F. — L. — Gk.) See Exod. xvi. 31; Numb. xi. 7; where Wyclif has *coriandre*. — F. *coriandre*, 'the herb, or seed, coriander;' Cot. — L. *coriandrum*; Exod. xvi. 31 (Vulgate version); where the *d* is excrescent, as is so commonly the case after *n*. — Gk. κορίαννον, κορίανον, also κόριον, coriander. β. *Said* to be derived from Gk. κόρις, a bug, because the leaves have a strong and bug-like smell (Weigand); but prob. a foreign word.

CORK, the bark of the cork-tree. (Span. — L.) '*Corkbarke*, cortex; *Corktre*, suberies;' Prompt. Parv. p. 93. The earliest use of *corke* was in the sense of a cork shoe or slipper. In 1391, the Earl of Derby paid 3*s*. 'pro uno pare *corkes*,' for a pair of cork shoes; see Earl of Derby's Expeditions (Camden Soc.), p. 91, l. 19. The Acts of Edw. IV (in 1463–4, Act 2, c. 4) have: 'Botes, shoen, galoches, or *corkes*' (N. E. D.). Adapted from M.Span. *al-corque*, 'a corke shooe, a pantofle;' Minsheu. This seems to be an Arab. form allied to M.Span. (and Span.) *al-cornoque*, the cork-tree; where *al* is the Arab. def. article, and *corn-oque* is formed from L. *quern-us* (for **quercnus*), oaken, adj. from *quercus*, an oak; the tree being the *Quercus Suber*. ¶ But the *bark* of the tree was called, in Spanish, *corcho*; from L. *corticem*, acc. of *cortex*, bark. Hence E. *cork* is often derived from Span. *corcho*, though *k* from *ch* seems hardly possible. Der. *cork*, verb.

CORMORANT, a voracious sea-bird. (F. — L.) In Shak. Rich. II, ii. 1. 38. '*Cormerawnte*, coruus marinus, cormeraudus;' Prompt. Parv. p. 93. Chaucer has *cormeraunt*, Parl. Foules, l. 362. — OF. *cormarant*, prob. for **cormarenc*, as in Godefroy (Supp.); MF. *cormerant*, m., *cormerande*, f.; Palsgrave. — OF. *corp*, a crow; and OF. **marenc*, belonging to the sea, from L. *mare*, sea, with G. suffix *-ing*; cf. F. *flam-ant*, flamingo, OF. *flam-enc*, with the same suffix; see Hatzfeld, Introd. § 142. [Cf. also Port. *corvomarinho*, Span. *cuervo marino*, a cormorant, lit. sea-crow; L. *coruus marinus*, which occurs as an equivalent to *mergulus* (sea-fowl) in the Reichenau Glosses, of the 8th century.] ¶ Another name for the bird is *coq-marant*, 'sea-cock;' see Godefroy (Supp.). The late spelling with *o* may have been due to Bret. *morvran* (W. *morfran*), a cormorant. The Breton and W. words are derived from Bret. and W. *mór*, the sea, and *bran*, a crow, by the usual change of *b* into *v* or *f*.

CORN (1), grain. (E.) ME. *corn*, Layamon, i. 166. The pl. *cornes* is in Chaucer, C. T., B 3225. AS. *corn*, Grein, i. 166. + Du. *koren*; Icel., Dan., and Swed. *korn*; Goth. *kaurn*; G. *korn*. Teut. type **kurnom*, n.; Idg. type **gurnom*, corn; whence OSlav. *zrŭno*, Russ. *zerno*, corn. Cf. L. *grānum*, grain; and Skt. *jirṇa-*, 'worn down,' pp. of *jṛi*, to grow old. Doublet, *grain*. (✓GER.) Brugmann, i. § 628. See **Grain, Kernel.**

CORN (2), an excrescence on the toe or foot. (F. — L.) In Shak. Romeo, i. 5. 19. Spelt *coorne* in Prompt. Parv. — F. *corne*, 'a horn; . . a hard or horny swelling in the backepart of a horse;' Cot. Cf. OF. *cor* (F. *cor*), a horn, horny swelling. — L. *cornū*, horn, cognate with E. *horn*, q.v. Cf. prov. F. (Verdun) *corne*, a corn on the foot (Fertiault). Der. *corn-e-ous*, horny; from the same source are *cornea*, q.v., *cornel*, q.v., *corner*, q.v., *cornet*, q.v., *cornelian*, q.v.; also *corni-gerous*, horn-bearing, from L. *ger-ere*, to bear; *corni-c-ul-ate*, horn-shaped, horned, from L. *corniculātus*, horned; *cornu-copia*, q.v. See **Core.**

CORNEA, a horny membrane in the eye. (L.) L. *cornea*, fem. of *corneus*, horny; from *cornū*, a horn. See **Corn** (2).

CORNEL, a shrub; also called dogwood. (Du.–L.) '*Cornels* and bramble-berries gave the rest;' Dryden, Ovid's Metam. bk. i. l. 136. 'The cornell tree;' Lyte, tr. of Dodoens, bk. vi. c. 51. [Cf. also F. *cornille*, 'a cornell-berry;' Cotgrave; *cornillier*, 'the long cherry, wild cherry, or cornill-tree;' id. *Cornille* was also spelt *cornoalle* and *cornoille*; and *cornillier* was also *cornoaller* and *cornoiller*; id.]–MDu. *kornelle*, 'the fruit of the cornelle-tree,' Hexham; cf. MHG. *cornelbaum*, cornel-tree (Weigand).–Late L. *cornolium*, a cornel-tree.–L. *cornum*, a cornel-berry; *cornus*, a cornel-tree, so called from the hard, horny nature of the wood.–L. *cornū*, horn. Cf. Gk. κράνεια, κράνον, a cornel. See **Corn** (2).

CORNELIAN, a kind of chalcedony. (F.–L.) ME. *corneline*; Maundeville's Travels, c. xxvii. p. 275; Palsgrave has *cornalyn*, p. 208. Formerly spelt *corneline, cornaline*, as in Maundeville and Cotgrave.–F. *cornaline*, 'the cornix or cornaline, a flesh-coloured stone;' Cotgrave. Cf. Port. *cornelina*, the cornelian-stone; also Ital. *corniola*, (1) a cornel-berry, (2) a cornelian, prob. so named because its colour resembles that of the fruit of the cornel-tree (Schade).–Late L. *corniola*, cornel-berry; cf. *cornolium*, cornel.–L. *corneus*, adj. from *cornus*, a cornel. See above. β. From the Ital. *corniola*, a cornelian, came the G. *carniol*, a cornelian, and the E. *carneol*, explained by 'a precious stone' in Kersey's and Bailey's Dictionaries. The change from *corniol* to *carneol* points to a popular etymology from L. *carneus*, fleshy, in allusion to the flesh-like colour of the stone. And this etymology has even so far prevailed as to cause *cornelian* to be spelt *carnelian*.

CORNER, a horn-like projection, angle. (F.–L.) ME. *corner*; Gawayn and the Grene Knight, 1185.–AF. *cornere*, Liber Custumarum, p. 150; OF. *corniere*, 'a corner;' Cot.–Late L. *corněria*, a corner, angle; cf. Late L. *corneirus*, angular, placed at a corner.–Late L. *corna* (OF. *corne*), a corner, angle.–L. **corna*, for *cornua*, pl. of *cornū*, a horn, a projecting point; with change from n. pl. to fem. sing. (as often). See **Corn** (2). Der. *corner-ed*.

CORNET, a little horn; a sort of officer. (F.–L.) ME. *cornet*, a horn; Octovian Imperator, ll. 1070, 1190; in Weber's Met. Rom. iii. 202, 207. Also a horned head-dress, a flag or standard; and then a troop of horse (because accompanied by a *cornette* or standard), Shak. 1 Hen. VI, iv. 3. 25; lastly, an officer of such a troop.–F. *cornet*, a little horn, dimin. of F. *corne*, a horn; *cornette*, f., a horned head-dress, a flag, cornet. See above.

CORNICE, a moulding, moulded projection. (F.–Ital.–L.) In Milton, P. L. i. 716.–MF. *cornice*, also *corniche*, 'the cornish, or brow of a wall, piller, or other peece of building;' Cot.; mod.F. *corniche*.–Ital. *cornice*, 'the ledge wheron they hang tapestrie in any roome; also, an outietting peece or part of a house or wall;' Florio. Origin uncertain; by some identified with Late L. *corōnix*, a square frame.–Gk. κορωνίς, a wreath, the cornice of a building (?); literally an adj. signifying 'crooked;' and obviously related to L. *corōna*, a crown. ¶ But Ital. *cornice* rightly means a crow; from L. *cornicem*, acc. of *cornix*, a crow. Cf. **Corbel.**

CORNUCOPIA, the horn of plenty. (L.) Ben Jonson has *cornucopiæ*, Every Man, iii. 6. 24; rightly.–L. *cornū cōpiæ*, horn of plenty; from *cornū*, horn; and *cōpiæ*, gen. of *cōpia*, plenty. See **Corn** (2) and **Copious.**

COROLLA, the cup of a flower formed by the petals. (L.) A scientific term. Not in Johnson.–L. *corolla*, a little crown; dimin. of *corōna*, a crown. See **Crown.** And see below.

COROLLARY, an additional inference, or deduction. (L.) 'A *corolarie* or mede of coroune,' i.e. present of a crown or garland; Chaucer, tr. of Boethius, b. iii. pr. 10, l. 101.–L. *corollārium*, a present of a garland, a gratuity, additional gift; also an additional inference; prop. neuter of *corollārius*, belonging to a garland.–L. *corolla*, a garland; see above.

CORONACH, an outcry, a dirge. (Gael.) In Dunbar, Dance of the 7 Sins, l. 112; spelt *correnoch*.–Gael. *corranach*, a dirge; lit. 'howling together.'–Gael. *comh-* (=L. *cum*), together; *rànaich*, a howling, from *ràn*, to howl; which is from *ràn*, sb., an outcry. Cf. Irish *coranach*, a dirge.

CORONAL, a crown, garland. (F.–L.) In Drayton's Pastorals, Ecl. 3. Properly an adj., signifying 'of or belonging to a crown.'–F. *coronal*, 'coronall, crown-like;' Cot.–L. *corōnālis*, belonging to a crown.–L. *corōna*, a crown. See **Crown.**

CORONATION, a crowning. (L.) '*Corownynge* or *coronacion*;' Prompt. Parv. p. 93. [Not a F. word, but formed by analogy with F. words in *-tion*.]–Late L. *corōnātio*, a coined word, from L. *corōnāre*, to crown, pp. *corōnātus*.–L. *corōna*, a crown. See **Crown.**

CORONER, an officer appointed by the crown. (F.–L.) Also *crowner*. 'Coroners and bailiffs;' Stow, King Stephen, an. 1142. The word *coroner* occurs in a spurious charter of King Athelstan to Beverley, dated A.D. 925, but really of the 14th century; see Diplomatarium Ævi Saxon., ed. Thorpe, p. 181, last line.–AF. *coroner, coruner*, Statutes of the Realm, i. 28, 29 (1275).–OF. *corone*, a crown.–L. *corōna*, a crown. β. The AF. *coroner* was Latinised as *corōnārius*, i.e. a crown-officer. Thus *coroner* is 'a crown-er,' and the equivalent term *crowner* (Hamlet, v. 1. 4) is quite correct.

CORONET, a little crown. (F.–L.) 'With *coronettes* upon theyr heddes;' Fabyan, Chron. an. 1432. Formed as a dimin., by help of the suffix *-ete* (or *-ette*) from the OF. *corone*, a crown.–L. *corōna*, a crown. See **Crown.**

CORPORAL (1), a subordinate officer. (F.–L.) In Shak. Merry Wives, ii. 1. 128. First found in 1579.–MF. *corporel*, spelt *corporeau* in 1562 (Supp. to Godefroy).–Late L. *corporālis*, a captain, a leader of a troop (1405).–L. *corpor-*, for **corpos-*, stem of *corpus*, body. ¶ Another MF. (and F.) form was *caporal*, 'the corporall of a band of souldiers;' Cot.–Ital. *caporale*, a chief, a corporal; whence it was introduced into French in the 16th century (Brachet); cf. Late L. *caporālis*, a chief, a commander; Ducange. This form is corrupt, due to association with Ital. *capo*, the head (from L. *caput*); which could never have evolved the syllable *-or-*. Cf. also Ital. *capoparte*, 'a ringleader,' Florio; which may easily have suggested the change. Note Norm. dial. *corporal*, a corporal (Moisy). Der. *corporal-ship*.

CORPORAL (2), belonging to the body. (F.–L.) In Shak. Meas. iii. 1. 80. ME. *corporel*, Rom. Rose, 6757.–OF. *corporel, corporal*.–L. *corporālis*, bodily.–L. *corpor-*, for **corpos*, stem of *corpus*, the body; with suffix *-ālis*. See **Corps.** Brugmann, i. § 555. Der. From the same stem we have *corpor-ate, -ate-ly, -at-ion*; *-e-al* (from L. *corporeus*, belonging to the body), *-e-al-ly, -e-al-i-ty*; and see *corps, corpse, corpulent, corpuscle, corset, corslet.*

CORPS, CORPSE, CORSE, a body. (F.–L.) *Corps*, i.e. a body of men, is mod. French, and not in early use in English. *Corse* is a variant of *corpse*, formed by dropping *p*; it occurs in An Old Eng. Miscellany, ed. Morris, p. 28, l. 10. *Corpse* was also in early use; ME. *corps*, Chaucer, C. T., 2821 (A 2819); and is derived from late O.French, in which the *p* was sounded.–OF. *cors*, later (14th cent.) *corps*, the body.–L. *corpus*, the body. Der. *corp-ul-ent*, q.v.; *corpus-c-le*, q.v.; *corset, corslet.*

CORPULENT, stout, fat. (F.–L.) In Shak. 1 Hen. IV, ii. 4. 464. ME. *corpulent*, Gesta Roman., c. 65, p. 281, l. 4 (E. E. T. S.). –F. *corpulent*, 'corpulent, gross;' Cot.–L. *corpulentus*, fat.–L. *corpu-s*, the body; with suffixes *-l-* and *-ent-*. See **Corps.** Der. *corpulent-ly, corpulence.*

CORPUSCLE, a little body, an atom. (L.) A scientific term. In Derham, Physico-Theology, bk. i. c. 1. note 2 (R.).–L. *corpusculum*, an atom, particle; double dimin. from L. *corpus*, the body, with suffix *-cu-lo-*. See **Corps.** Der. *corpuscul-ar.*

CORRAL, an enclosure for animals, pen. (Span.–L.) Chiefly in Span. America and U. S.–Span. *corral*, a court, pen, enclosure.– Span. *corro*, a circle, a ring of people met to see a show. From the Span. *correre toros*, to hold a bull-fight; lit. to run bulls.–L. *currere*, to run. Doublet, *kraal*, q.v.

CORRECT, to put right, punish, reform. (L.) ME. *correcten*; Chaucer, C. T. 6242 (D 661).–L. *correct-us*, pp. of *corrigere*, to correct.–L. *cor-*, for *con-* (i.e. *cum*), with, thoroughly, before *r*; and *regere*, to rule, order. See **Regular.** Der. *correct*, adj. (also from L. *correct-us*); *-ly, -ness, -ion, -ion-al, -ive, -or*; also *corrig-ible, corrigenda* (L. *corrigenda*, things to be corrected, from *corrigendus*, fut. pass. part. of *corrigere*); *corregidor*, a Span. magistrate, lit. 'correcter;' from Span. *corregir*, to correct.

CORRELATE, to relate or refer mutually. (L.) In Johnson's Dictionary, where it is defined by 'to have a reciprocal relation, as father to son.' Cf. 'Spiritual things and spiritual men are *correlatives*, and cannot in reason be divorced;' Spelman, On Tythes, p. 141 (R.). These are mere coined words, made by prefixing *cor-*, for *con-* (i.e. *cum*, with) before *relate, relative*, &c. Ducange gives a Late L. *correlātio*, a mutual relation; and Cotgrave has MF. *correlatif*, explained by 'correlative.' See **Relate.** Der. *correlat-ive, correlat-ion.*

CORRESPOND, to answer mutually. (F.–L.) Shak. has *corresponding*, i.e. suitable; Cymb. iii. 3. 31; also *corresponsive*, fitting, Troil. prol. 18.–OF. (and F.) *correspondre* (Supp. to Godefroy).– Late L. *correspondēre*. These are coined words, made by prefixing *cor-* (for *con-*, i.e. *cum*, together) to OF. *respondre*, L. *respondēre*. Ducange gives a Late L. adv. *correspondenter*, 'at the same time.' See **Respond.** Der. *correspond-ing, -ing-ly, -ent, -ent-ly, -ence.*

CORRIDOR, a gallery. (F.–Ital.–L.) In Blount's Gloss. (1656); defined as in Cotgrave (below). 'The high wall and corridors that went round it [the amphitheatre] are almost intirely ruined;' Addison, On Italy (Todd's Johnson). Also used as a term in fortification.–F. *corridor*, 'a curtaine, in fortification;' Cot.–Ital. *corridore*, 'a runner, a swift horse; also a long terrase or gallerie;' Florio. — Ital. *correre*, to run; with suffix -*dore*, a less usual form of -*tore*, answering to L. acc. suffix -*tōrem*. — L. *currere*, to run. See **Current**.

CORRIE, a mountain dell or combe. (Gael.) 'Fleet foot on the *corrie*;' Scott, Lady of the Lake, iii. 16. — Gael. *coire*, a cauldron, kettle; also, a circular hollow among mountains. +W. *pair*, a cauldron; AS. *hwer*, a cauldron. See Notes on Eng. Etym., p. 46; Brugmann, i. § 123.

CORROBORATE, to confirm. (L.) 'Dothe *corroborate* the stomake;' Sir T. Elyot, Castel of Helth, bk. ii. c. 7 (Of Olyues). Properly a past part., as in 'except it be *corroborate* by custom;' Bacon, Essay 39, On Custom. — L. *corrōborātus*, pp. of *corrōborāre*, to strengthen. — L. *cor*-, for *con*- (i.e. *cum*, together, wholly) before *r*; and *rōborāre*, to strengthen, from *rōbor*-, stem of *rōbur*, strength. See **Robust**. Der. *corroborat-ive*, -*ion*, *corrobor-ant*.

CORRODE, to gnaw away. (F. — L.) In Sherwood's Index to Cotgrave; in Florio's Ital. Dict. (1598); and in Donne, To the Countess of Bedford. [*Corrosive* was rather a common word in the sense of 'a caustic;' and was frequently corrupted to *corsive* or *corsy*; see Spenser, F. Q. iv. 9. 14.] — F. *corroder*, to gnaw, bite; Cot. — L. *corrōdere*, pp. *corrōsus*, to gnaw to pieces. — L. *cor*-, for *con*- (i.e. *cum*, together, wholly) before *r*; and *rōdere*, to gnaw. See **Rodent**. Der. *corrod-ent*, -*ible*, -*ibil-i-ty*; also (from L. pp. *corrōsus*) *corros-ive*, -*ive-ly*, -*ive-ness*, -*ion*.

CORRODY, an allowance for maintenance. (Late L. — F. — Teut.) See *Corody*, *Corrody*, in Blount, Nomolexicon. AF. *corodie*, Stat. of the Realm, i. 256 (1327); Late L. *corrōdium*, earlier *corrēdium*. — AF. *conrei*, *conreit*, provision, corrody (Britton). See further under **Curry** (1).

CORRUGATE, to wrinkle greatly. (L.) In Bacon, Nat. Hist. § 964. — L. *corrūgātus*, pp. of *corrūgāre*, to wrinkle greatly. — L. *cor*-, for *con*- (i.e. *cum*, together, wholly) before *r*; and *rūgāre*, to wrinkle, from *rūga*, a wrinkle, fold, plait. Der. *corrugat-ion*.

CORRUPT, putrid, debased, defiled. (L.) In Chaucer, C. T. 4939 (B 519); Gower, C. A. i. 217, bk. ii. 1732. Wyclif has *corruptid*, 2 Cor. iv. 16. — L. *corruptus*, pp. of *corrumpere*, to corrupt, intensive of *rumpere*, to break. — L. *cor*-, for *con*- (i.e. *cum*, together, wholly); and *rumpere*, to break in pieces. See **Rupture**. ¶ We also find AF. *corupt*, Liber Albus, p. 465. Der. *corrupt*, vb.; *corrupt-ly*, -*ness*, -*er*; -*ible*, -*ibl-y*, -*ibil-i-ty*, -*ible-ness*; *corrupt-ion* = ME. *corrupcion*, Gower, C. A. i. 37 (prol. 986), from F. *corruption*; *corrupt-ive*.

CORSAIR, a pirate, a pirate-vessel. (F. — Ital. — L.) 'Corsair, a courser, or robber by sea;' Kersey's Dict. ed. 1715. — F. *corsaire*, 'a courser, pyrat;' Cot. — MItal. *corsaro*, 'a pirate, or rouer by sea;' Florio (s. v. *corsale*). — Late L. *cursārius*, a pirate. — L. *cursus*, a course. — L. *cursus*, pp. of *currere*, to run. See **Course, Current**. Doublet, *hussar*, q. v.

CORSE, a dead body. (F. — L.) ME. *cors*: 'Thanne wolen the freres for the *cors* fihte;' Polit. Songs, p. 331, l. 182 (1307-1327). — OF. *cors*. — L. *corpus*, a body. See **Corps**.

CORSET, a pair of stays. (F. — L.) 'A *corsette* of Ianyr' [Dejanira]; Trevisa, tr. of Higden, ii. 361. Cotgrave has: '*Corset*, a little body, also a paire of bodies [i.e. bodice] for a woman.' — OF. *cors*, a body; with dimin. suffix -*et*. See **Corps**.

CORSLET, CORSELET, a piece of body-armour. (F. — L.) *Corslet* in Shak. Cor. v. 4. 21. — F. *corselet*, which Cotgrave translates only by 'a little body;' but the special use of it easily follows. [The Ital. *corsaletto*, a cuirass, must have been modified from the F. *corselet* and OF. *cors*, a body, not from the Ital. *corpo*.] — OF. *cors*, a body; with dimin. suffixes -*el*- and -*et*. See **Corps**. Cf. Norm. dial. *corselet*, a corset (Moisy).

CORTEGE, a train of attendants. (F. — Ital. — L.) In Evelyn's Diary, 1 July, 1679. From F. *cortège*, a procession. — Ital. *corteggio*, a train, suit, retinue, company. — Ital. *corte*, a court; from the same L. source as E. *court*, q. v.

CORTES, the Span. national assembly. (Span. — L.) Lit. 'courts.' — Span. *cortes*, pl. of *corte*, a court. — L. acc. *cortem*, a court.

CORTEX, bark. (L.) Modern. L. *cortex* (stem *cortic*-), bark. Der. *cortic-al*; *cortic-ate*, *cortic-at-ed*, i.e. furnished with bark.

CORUNDUM, a crystallised mineral, like a ruby. (Tamil — Skt.) See Yule. — Tamil *kurundam*; cf. Hind. *kurand* (Forbes). — Skt. *kuruvinda(s)*, a ruby (Benfey).

CORUSCATE, to flash, glitter. (L.) Bacon has *coruscation*, Nat. Hist. § 121. — L. *coruscātus*, pp. of *coruscāre*, to glitter, vibrate; cf. *coruscus*, trembling, vibrating, glittering. Der. *corusc-ant*, -*at-ion*.

CORVÉE, forced labour. (F. — L.) In Ayenbite of Inwit, p. 38; where the pl. is printed *tornees*. — F. *corvée*, f. 'a drudging daies worke;' Cot. — Late L. *corrogāta* (sc. *opera*), requisitioned work; fem. pp. of *corrogāre*, to exact. — L. *cor*- (for *cum*), together, very; and *rogāre*, to ask. See **Rogation**.

CORVETTE, a sort of small frigate. (F. — Port. — L.) Known

in 1636; see Todd's Johnson. — F. *corvette*. — Port. *corveta*, a corvette; Brachet. This is the same as the Span. *corveta* or *corbeta*, a corvette. — L. *corbita*, a slow-sailing ship of burthen. — L. *corbis*, a basket. See **Corbel**.

CORYMB, a species of inflorescence. (F. — L. — Gk.) F. *corymbe*. — L. *corymbus*. — Gk. κόρυμβος, a head, cluster. Allied to Gk. κέρας, E. *horn*. Cf. Skt. *çṛiṅga(m)*, a horn.

COSHER, to feast, to pamper. (Irish.) In Shirley St. Patrick, v. 1. — Irish *coisir*, a feast.

COSMETIC, that which beautifies. (Gk.) 'This order of *cosmetick* philosophers;' Tatler, no. 34. — Gk. κοσμητικός, skilled in adorning; whence also F. *cosmétique*. — Gk. κοσμέω, I adorn, decorate. — Gk. κόσμος, order, ornament. See below.

COSMIC, relating to the world. (Gk.) Modern. From Gk. κοσμικός, relating to the world. — Gk. κόσμος, order; also, the world, universe. Der. *cosmic-al*, used by Sir T. Browne, Vulg. Errors, bk. iv. c. 13. § 2; *cosmic-al-ly*.

COSMOGONY, the theory of the origin of the universe. (Gk.) In Warburton, Divine Legation, b. iii. s. 3 (R.). — Gk. κοσμογονία, origin of the world. — Gk. κόσμο-s, stem of κόσμος, the world; and -γονια, a begetting, from -γον-, as in γέ-γον-α, perf. of γίγνομαι, I become, am produced; where γον- is the second grade of √GEN, to produce. Der. *cosmogon-ist*.

COSMOGRAPHY, description of the world. (Gk.) In Sir T. Elyot, The Governor, bk. i. c. 11. § 6; and in Bacon, Life of Henry VII, ed. Lumby, p. 171. — Gk. κοσμογραφία, description of the world. — Gk. κόσμο-s, world, universe; and γράφειν, to describe. Der. *cosmograph-er*, -*ic*, -*ic-al*.

COSMOLOGY, science of the universe. (Gk.) In Blount (1656). Formed as if from a Gk. *κοσμολογία; from κόσμο-s, the world, and λέγειν, to speak, tell of. Der. *cosmolog-ist*, -*ic-al*.

COSMOPOLITE, a citizen of the world. (Gk.) Used in Howell's Letters; b. i. s. 6, let. 60, § 1. — Gk. κοσμοπολίτης, a citizen of the world. — Gk. κόσμο-s, the world; and πολίτης, a citizen; see **Politic**. Der. *cosmopolit-an*.

COSSACK, a light-armed S. Russian soldier. (Russ. — Tartar.) Spelt *Cassacke* in Hakluyt, Voy. i. 388. — Russ. *kozak'*, *kazak'*, a Cossack; of Tartar origin. — Turkī *quzzāq*, a vagabond, a predatory horseman (Yule).

COSSET, a pet-lamb, a pet. (E.) Spenser has *cosset*, for *cosset-lamb*, a pet-lamb. Prob. for *cot-set*, lit. 'cot-sitter,' i.e. living in a cot, brought up within doors; cf. G. *haus-lamm*. AF. *coscet*, *cozet*, a cottar; AS. *cotsæta* (Latinised as *cotsetus*), by-form of *cot-setla*, a cottar; see Schmidt, Gloss. to AS. Laws. Cf. also G. *kossat*, a cottager (Weigand); Ital. *cassiccio*, a pet-lamb (Florio), from *casa*, a cottage. See Notes on Eng. Etym. p. 46. Der. *cosset*, vb., to pet. ¶ For *ts* > *ss*, cf. *boat-swain*, *bless*.

COST, to fetch a certain price. (Du. — F. — L.) ME. *costen*. In Chaucer, C. T. 1910 (A 1908); P. Plowman, B. prol. 203. — MDu. *kosten*, to cost. — OF. *coster*, *couster* (F. *coûter*), to cost. — L. *constāre*, to stand together, consist, last, cost. — L. *con*- (for *cum*), together; and *stāre*, to stand. See **Constant**. ¶ The OF. *coster* should have given a form *coast*. Der. *cost*, sb., -*ly*, -*li-ness*.

COSTAL, relating to the ribs. (L.) In Sir T. Browne, Vulg. Errors, b. iv. c. 10. § 5. Formed, with suffix -*al*, from L. *costa*, a rib. See **Coast**.

COSTERMONGER, an itinerant fruit-seller. (Hybrid; F. and E.) Formerly *costerd-monger* or *costard-monger*; the former spelling is in Drant's Horace, where it translates L. *pōmārius* in Sat. ii. 3. 227. It means *costard-seller*. 'Costard, a kind of apple. Costard-monger, a seller of apples, a fruiterer;' Kersey's Dict. ed. 1715. Much earlier, we find: 'Costard, appulle, quirianum;' Prompt. Parv. p. 94. 'Costardmongar, fruyctier,' i.e. fruiterer; Palsgrave. β. The etymology of *costard*, an apple, is uncertain; but the suffix -*ard* is properly OF., so that the word is presumably OF., and related to OF. *coste*, a rib, with reference to such apples as had prominent ribs. — L. *costa*, a rib. Cf. F. *fruit coʼelé*, ribbed fruit; Hamilton. γ. The word *monger* is E.; see **Ironmonger**. ¶ There is no reason for connecting *costard* with *custard*. The *custard-apple* mentioned in Dampier's Voyages, an. 1699 (R.) is quite a different fruit from the ME. *costard*.

COSTIVE, constipated. (F. — L.) 'But, trow, is he loose or costive of laughter?' Ben Jonson, The Penates. — OF. *costevé*, pp., constipated (Godefroy). — L. *constipātus*, pp. of *constipāre*, to constipate. See **Constipate**. Der. *costive-ness*.

COSTMARY, a plant. (F. — L. — Gk.) Lyte has *costmary*; tr. of Dodoens, bk. ii. c. 76. ME. *costmarye*, Two Cookery Books, ed. Austin, p. 110, l. 4. Compounded of *cost* and *Marye*; the latter referring to St. Mary the Virgin. *Cost* is F. *cost*, which Cotgrave explains by 'costmary, balsamine, alecoast.' — L. *costum*, n. — Gk. κόστος, an aromatic root (of a different odoriferous plant). This is of Eastern origin; cf. Skt. *kushṭha-*, Costus speciosus; Arab. *qust*, *costus*; Rich. Dict. p. 1130.

COSTUME, a customary dress. (F.—Ital.—L.) A modern word; added by Todd to Johnson's Dict. Richardson cites a quotation from Sir Joshua Reynolds, Dis. 12.—F. *costume*; a late form, borrowed from Italian.—Ital. *costume*; Late L. *costūma*, contracted from L. acc. *consuētūdinem*, custom. *Costume* is a doublet of *custom.* See **Custom.**

COSY, COZY, snug, comfortably sheltered. (Scand.) This word appears to have been introduced from Lowl. Scotch. We find: '*cosie* in a hoord,' Ramsay's Poems, i. 305 (Jamieson); and '*cozie* i' the neuk,' Burns, Holy Fair, st. 20. It seems to be from Norw. *kosa*, (*o* = *oo*), v., to refresh, whence *kosa seg*, to enjoy oneself; whence also *koseleg* = Dan. *hyggelig*, which Ferrall translates by 'comfortable, snug, cozy;' and *kosing*, refreshment, recreation (Aasen). Larsen gives Norw. *koselig*, 'snug, cosy.' Prob. allied to Swed. dial. *kasa*, to warm, *kasug*, warm.

COT, a small dwelling; **COTE,** an enclosure. (E.) 'A lutel *kot*;' Ancren Riwle, p. 362. *Cote*, in Havelok, ll. 737, 1141. 'Hec casa, casula, a *cote*,' Wright's Vocab. i. 273. AS. *cot, cote*, a cot, den; 'tō þeofa *cote*' = for a den of thieves, Matt. xxi. 13. 'In *cotte* ðīnum,' into thy chamber; Northumbrian gloss to Matt. vi. 6. [We also find AS. *cyte*, Grein, i. 181.]+Du. *kot*, a cot, cottage; Icel. *kot*, a cot, hut; G. *koth*, a cot (a provincial word); Flügel's Dict. [The W. *cwt*, a cot, was borrowed from English.] Der. *cott-age* (with F. suffix); *cott-ag-er*; *cott-ar, cott-er*; cf. also *sheep-cote, dove-cote,* &c. Also *cot-quean,* lit. a hussy (living in) a cot, Romeo, iv. 4. 6; see **Quean.**

COTERIE, a set, company. (F.—Teut.) Mere French. Cotgrave gives: '*Coterie*, company, society, association of people.' β. Marked by Brachet as being of unknown origin. Referred in Diez to F. *cote*, a quota, share, from L. *quotus*, how much. But Littré rightly connects it with OF. *coterie, cotterie*, servile tenure, *cottier*, a cottar, &c. A *coterie* (Low L. *coteria*) was a tenure of land by cottars who clubbed together.—Low L. *cota*, a cot; of Teutonic origin. See **Cot.**

COTILLON, COTILLION, a dance for eight persons. (F.—Teut.) It occurs in a note to v. 11 of Gray's Long Story.—F. *cotillon*, lit. a petticoat, as explained by Cotgrave. Formed with suffix *-ill-on* from F. *cotte*, a coat, frock. See **Coat.**

COTTON (1), a downy substance obtained from a certain plant. (F.—Span.—Arabic.) ME. *cotoun, cotune, cotin* (with one *t*). Spelt *cotoun* in Mandeville's Travels, ed. Halliwell, p. 212.—F. *coton* (spelt *cotton* in Cotgrave).—Span. *coton*, printed cotton, cloth made of cotton; Span. *algodon*, cotton, cotton-down (where *al* is the Arab. def. art.).—Arab. *qutn, qutun*, cotton; Richardson's Dict. p. 1138; Palmer's Pers. Dict. col. 472.

COTTON (2), to agree. (F.—Span.—Arab.) '*Cotton*, to succeed, to hit, to agree;' Kersey's Dict. ed. 1715. 'To *cotton* well' was orig. to form a good nap (to cloth, &c.). Thus Phillips (ed. 1706), s.v. *Cottum* (sic) has: 'in making Hats, to *cotton well* is when the wooll and other materials work well and imbody together.' From **Cotton** (1), above. Cf. prov. E. *cotton* (E.D.D.).

COTYLEDON, the seed-lobe of a plant. (Gk.) Introduced by Linnæus in a new sense. As an anatomical term, it occurs as early as 1545. See Phillips.—Gk. κοτυληδών, a cup-shaped hollow.—Gk. κοτύλη, a hollow, hollow vessel, small cup. Cf. Goth. *hēthjō*, a chamber (Uhlenbeck). Der. *cotyledon-ous.*

COUCH, to lay down, set, arrange. (F.—L.) ME. *couchen, cowchen*, to lay, place, set. 'Cowchyn, or leyne thinges togedyr, *colloco*;' Prompt. Parv. p. 96. Occurs frequently in Chaucer; see C. T. 2163 (A 2161).—OF. *coucher*, earlier *colcher*, to place.—L. *collocāre*, to place together.—L. *col-* for *con-* (i.e. *cum*, together) before *l*; and *locāre*, to place, from *locus*, a place. See **Locus.** Der. *couch*, sb., ME. *couche*, Gower, C. A. iii. 315, bk. viii. 1193; *couch-ant.* **Doublet,** *collocate.*

COUCHGRASS, a grass which is troublesome as a weed. (E.) Here *couch* is a variant of *quitch*, which is a palatalised form of *quick*, i.e. tenacious of life. See **Quick.**

COUGH, to make a violent effort of the lungs. (E.) ME. *coughen, cowhen*; Chaucer, C. T. 10082 (E 2208). AS. *cohhian; only found in the deriv. *cohhetan*, to make a noise. EFries. *kuchen.* +Du. *kugchen*, to cough; MHG. *kūchen*, G. *keuchen*, to pant, to gasp; WFlem. *kuffen*, to cough (De Bo). β. From an imitative root *keuh, weak grade *kuh, to gasp; see **Chin-cough.** Der. *cough*, sb.; *chin-cough.*

COUGUAR, COUGAR, the puma. (F.—Brazil.) Spelt *couguar* in a tr. of Buffon (1792), i. 193.—F. *couguar* (Buffon). From the Guarani name, given as *cuguacu-arana* in Hist. Brasil. (1648), ii. 235.

COULD, was able to; see **Can.**

COULTER, COLTER, the iron blade in front of a plough-share. (L.) ME. *culter, colter*; Chaucer, C. T. 3761 (A 3763). AS. *culter*, Ælf. Gloss. 8 (Bosworth); a borrowed word.—L. *culter*, a coulter, knife; lit. a striker; cf. L. *per-cellere*, to strike. **Der.** From the same source are *cutlass*, q.v.; and *cutler*, q.v.

COUNCIL, an assembly. (F.—L.) In Shak. L. L. L. v. 2. 789. Often confused with *counsel*, with which it had originally nothing to do; *council* can only be rightly used in the restricted sense of 'assembly for deliberation.' Misspelt *counsel* in the following quotation. 'They shall deliuer you vp to their *counsels*, and shall scourge you in their sinagoges or *counsel-houses*;' Tyndal, Works, p. 214, col. 2; cf. *conciliis* in the Vulgate version of Matt. x. 17.—AF. *councylle*, Langtoft's Chron. i. 488; F. *concile*, 'a councill, an assembly, session;' Cot.—L. *concilium*, an assembly called together.—L. *con-*, for *cum*, together; and *calāre*, to summon; see **Calends.** Der. *councill-or*, ME. *conseiller*, Gower, C. A. iii. 192; bk. vii. 3148.

COUNSEL, consultation, advice, plan. (F.—L.) Quite distinct from *council*, q.v. In early use. ME. *conseil, cunseil*; Havelok, 2862; Rob. of Glouc. p. 412; l. 8535.—AF. *cunseil*, Laws of Will. I, § 10; OF. *conseil*.—L. *consilium*, deliberation.—L. *consulere*, to consult. See **Consult.** Der. *counsel*, verb; *counsell-or.*

COUNT (1), a title of rank. (F.—L.) The orig. sense was 'companion.' Not in early use, being thrust aside by the E. word *earl*; but the fem. form occurs earlier, being spelt *cuntesse* in the AS. Chron. A.D. 1140. The derived word *counté*, a county, occurs in P. Plowman, B. ii. 85. Shak. has *county* in the sense of *count* frequently; Merch. of Ven. i. 2. 49.—AF. *counte*, Polit. Songs, p. 127; OF. *conte, comte*; Cotgrave gives '*Conte*, an earl,' and '*Comte*, a count, an earle.'—L. acc. *comitem*, a companion, a count; from nom. *comes*.—L. *com-*, for *cum*, together; and *it-um*, supine of *ire*, to go. Der. *count-ess, count-y.*

COUNT (2), to enumerate, compute, deem. (F.—L.) ME. *counten*; Allit. Poems, ed. Morris, B. 1731; also 1685.—AF. *counter, cunter*, Year-books of Edw. I, 1292–3, pp. 69, 157; OF. *cunter, conter*; F. *conter*.—L. *computāre*, to compute, reckon. Thus *count* is a doublet of *compute.* See **Compute.** Der. *count*, sb.; *count-er*, one who counts, anything used for counting, a board on which money is counted.

COUNTENANCE, appearance, face. (F.—L.) In early use. ME. *contenaunce, cuntenaunce, countenaunce*; P. Plowman, B. prol. 24; Cursor Mundi, 3368; *continaunce*, Polit. Songs, p. 216 (temp. Edw. I). —OF. *contenance*, which Cotgrave explains by 'the countenance, looke, cheere, visage, favour, gesture, posture, behaviour, carriage.' —L. *continentia*, which in Late L. meant 'gesture, behaviour, demeanour;' Ducange.—L. *continent-*, stem of pres. part. of *continēre*, to contain, preserve, maintain; hence, to comport oneself. See **Contain.** Der. *countenance*, vb.; *dis-countenance.*

COUNTER, in opposition (to), contrary. (F.—L.) 'This is *counter*;' Hamlet, iv. 5. 110; 'a hound that runs *counter*,' Com. Errors, iv. 2. 39. And very common as a prefix.—F. *contre*, against; common as a prefix.—L. *contrā*, against; common as a prefix. See **Contra.**

COUNTERACT, to act against. (Hybrid; F. *and* L.) *Counteraction* occurs in The Rambler, no. 93. Coined from *counter* and *act.* See **Counter** and **Act.** Der. *counteract-ion, -ive, -ive-ly.*

COUNTERBALANCE, sb., a balance against. (F.—L.) The sb. *counterbalance* is in Dryden, Annus Mirabilis (A.D. 1666), st. 12. From *counter* and *balance.* See **Counter** and **Balance.** Der. *counterbalance*, verb.

COUNTERFEIT, imitated, forged. (F.—L.) ME. *counterfeit, contrefet*, Gower, C. A. i. 70, 192; bk. i. 832; ii. 982.—OF. *contrefait*, pp. of *contrefaire*, to counterfeit, imitate; a word made up of *contre*, against, and *faire*, to make, do.—L. *contrā*, against; and *facere*, to make. See **Counter** and **Fact.** Der. *counterfeit*, vb.; ME. *counterfeten*; whence pp. *countrefeted*, Chaucer, C. T. 5166 (B 746). ☞ The same spelling *-feit* occurs in *forfeit*, q.v.

COUNTERMAND, to revoke a command given. (F.—L.) Used by Fabyan, Chron. c. 245, near end; Palsgrave has *contremaunde*, p. 497.—F. *contremander*, 'to countermand, to recall, or contradict, a former command;' Cot. Compounded of *contre*, against; and *mander*, to command.—L. *contrā*, against; and *mandāre*, to command. See **Mandate.** Der. *countermand*, sb.

COUNTERPANE (1), a coverlet for a bed. (F.—L.) A twice altered form, connected neither with *counter* nor with *pane*, but with *quilt* and *point.* The English altered the latter part of the word, and the French the former. The older E. form is *counterpoint*, as in Shak. Tam. Shrew, ii. 353. 'Bedsteads with silver feet, imbroidered coverlets, or *counterpoints* of purple silk;' North's Plutarch, p. 39. 'On which a tissue *counterpane* was cast;' Drayton, The Barons' Wars, b. vi. st. 43.—MF. *contrepoinct*, 'the back stitch or quilting-stitch; also a quilt, counterpoint, quilted covering;' Cot. β. Thus named, by a mistaken popular etymology, from a fancied connexion with OF. *contrepoincter*, 'to worke the back-stitch,' id.; which is from *contre*, against, and *pointe*, a bodkin. But Cotgrave also gives '*coutrepointer*, to quilt;' and this is a better form, pointing to the right origin. [In mod. F. we meet with the still more corrupt form *courtepointe*, a counterpane, which see in Hatzfeld.] γ. The right form is *coutepointe* (Supp. to Godefroy, p. 233), where *coute* is from L. *culcita*, the same as *culcitra*, a cushion, mattress, pillow, or quilt. —Late L. *culcita puncta*, a counterpane; lit. stitched quilt. 'Estque toral lecto quod supra ponitur alto Ornatus causa, quod dicunt *culcita puncta*;' Ducange. δ. Thus *coutepointe* has become *courtepointe* in mod. French, but also produced *contrepoincte* in Middle French, whence the E. derivative *counterpoint*, now changed to *counterpane*. See **Quilt**. The fem. pp. *puncta* is from the verb *pungere*, to prick; see **Point**. ¶ The AF. forms are *cutepoint*, *quilt poynt*, Royal Wills, pp. 36, 100 (1360, 1381); *coilte pointe*, Vie de St. Auban.

COUNTERPANE (2), the counterpart of a deed or writing. (F.—L.) 'Read, scribe; give me the *counterpane*;' Ben Jonson, Bart. Fair, Induction.—AF. *countrepan*, Britton, i. 237; *cuntrepan*, Wadington's Manuel des Peches, l. 10645.—F. *contre*, against; and *pan*, in the sense of 'a pane, piece, or pannell of a wall,' Cot.—L. *contrā*, against; *pannum*, acc. of *pannus*, a cloth, patch. See **Counter** and **Pane**.

COUNTERPART, a copy, duplicate. (F.—L.) In Shak. Sonnet 84. Merely compounded of *counter* and *part*.

COUNTERPOINT, the composing of music in parts. (F.—L.) 'The fresh descant, prychsonge [*read* prycksonge], *counterpoint*;' Bale on The Revel, 1550, Bb 8 (Todd's Johnson).—MF. *contrepoinct*, 'a ground or plain song, in musick;' Cot.—F. *contre*, against; and *poinct* (mod. F. *point*), a point. See **Counter** and **Point**. '*Counterpoint* in its literal and strict sense signifies *point against point*. In the infancy of harmony, musical notes or signs were simple points or dots, and in compositions in two or more parts were placed on staves, over, or against, each other;' Engl. Cycl. Div. Arts and Sciences, s. v.

COUNTERPOISE, the weight in the other scale. (F.—L.) In Shak. All's Well, ii. 3. 182.—F. *contrepois*, *contrepoids*. Cotgrave gives the former as the more usual spelling, and explains it by '*counterpois*, equall weight.' See **Counter** and **Poise**. Der. *counterpoise*, verb.

COUNTERSCARP, the exterior slope of a ditch. (F.—Ital.—L. *and* Teut.) The interior slope is called the *scarp*. The word is merely compounded of *counter* and *scarp*. 'Bulwarks and *counterscarps*;' Sir T. Herbert, Travels, ed. 1665, p. 64; and see Marlowe, II Tamb. iii. 2. 78. '*Contrescarpe*, a counterscarfe or countermure;' Cot.—Ital. *contrascarpa*.—Ital. *contra*, over against; and *scarpa*, a scarp. See **Counter** and **Scarp**.

COUNTERSIGN, to sign in addition, attest. (F.—L.) 'It was *countersigned* Melford;' Lord Clarendon's Diary, 1688–9; Todd's Johnson.—F. *contresigner*, 'to subsigne;' Cot.—F. *contre*, over against; and *signer*, to sign. See **Counter** and **Sign**. Der. *countersign*, sb. (from *counter* and *sign*, sb.); *countersign-at-ure*.

COUNTERTENOR, the highest adult male voice. (F.—Ital. —L.) It occurs in Cotgrave, who has: '*Contreteneur*, the countertenor part in musick.'—Ital. *contratenore*, a countertenor; Florio.—Ital. *contra*, against; and *tenore*, a tenor. See **Counter** and **Tenor**.

COUNTERVAIL, to avail against, equal. (F.—L.) In Shak. Romeo, ii. 6. 4. ME. *contrevailen*, Gower, C. A. i. 28; prol. 728.—OF. *contrevail-*, a stem of *contrevaloir*, to avail against; see Godefroy. —F. *contre*, against; and *valoir*, to avail.—L. *contrā*, against; and *ualēre*, to be strong, to avail. See **Valiant**. Der. *countervail*, sb.

COUNTESS; see under **Count**.

COUNTRY, a rural district, region. (F.—L.) In early use. ME. *contré*, *contree*; Layamon's Brut, i. 54.—OF. *contree*, country; with which cf. Ital. *contrada*.—Late L. *contrāta*, *contrāda*, country, region; an extension of L. *contrā*, over against. β. This extension of form was explained by Diez as a Germanism, viz. as an imitation of G. *gegend*, country, lit. 'that which is opposite to the view,' from *gegen*, against; but the imitation arose in the contrary way, the G. *gegend* (which is meaningless) having been suggested by the Late L. *contrāta*, which appears as Ital., Prov., and Roumansch *contrada*, as well as F. *contrée*. γ. *Contrāta* is regularly formed, as if a fem. pp. from a verb **contrāre*, to place opposite, from *contrā*, over against. Der. *country-dance*, *country-man*.

COUNTRY-DANCE, a dance of country-people. (F.—L. *and* OHG.) '*Heydeguies*, a *country daunce* or rownd;' E. K., Glosse to Spenser, Shep. Kal., June, l. 27. From **Country** and **Dance**. Hence (first used in 1626) the F. *contredanse* (as if from F. *contre*, against); but it is a mere perversion of the E. word (Hatzfeld).

COUNTY, an earldom, count's province, shire. (F.—L.) ME. *counté*, *countee*; P. Plowman, B. ii. 85. See **Count** (1).

COUPLE, a pair, two joined together. (F.—L.) ME. *couple*, Gower, C. A. iii. 241; bk. vii. 4437. The verb appears early, viz. in '*kupleð* boðe togederes'=couples both together; Ancren Riwle, p. 78.—OF. *cople*, later *couple*, a couple.—L. *cōpula*, a bond, band; contracted from **co-ap-ul-a*, where *-ul-* is a dimin. suffix.—L. *co-*, for *com*, i.e. *cum*, together; and OL. *apere*, to join, preserved in the pp. *aptus*. See **Apt**. Der. *couple*, verb, *coupl-ing*, *coupl-et*. Doublet, *copula*.

COUPON, one of a series of conjoined certificates or tickets. (F.—L.—Gk.) Modern.—F. *coupon*, lit. 'a piece cut off.'—F. *couper*, to cut, slash; from *coup*, sb., a blow.—Late L. *colpus*, for *colaphus*, a blow.—Gk. κόλαφος, a blow on the ear. See **Cope** (2).

COURAGE, valour, bravery. (F.—L.) ME. *courage*, *corage*; Chaucer, C. T. prol. 11, 22; King Alisaunder, 3559.—OF. *corage*, *courage*; formed with suffix *-age* (answering to L. *-āticum*) from L. *cor*, the heart. See **Cordial**, and **Heart**. Der. *courage-ous*, *-ly*, *-ness*.

COURIER, a runner. (F.—Ital.—L.) In Shak. Macb. i. 7. 23. —MF. *courier*, given in Cotgrave as equivalent to *courrier*, 'a post, or a poster.'—Ital. *corriere*, lit. 'runner.'—Ital. *correre*, to run.—L. *currere*, to run. See **Current**.

COURSE, a running, track, race. (F.—L.) ME. *course*, *cours*; Hampole, Pricke of Conscience, 4318; King Alisaunder, ed. Weber, l. 288.—OF. *cours*.—L. *cursum*, acc. of *cursus*, a course; from *cursus*, pp. of *currere*, to run. See **Current**. Der. *course*, verb; *cours-er*, spelt *corsour* in King Alisaunder, l. 4056; *cours-ing*.

COURT (1), a yard, enclosed space, tribunal, royal retinue, judicial assembly. (F.—L.) In early use. ME. *cort*, *court*, *curt*. 'Vnto the heye *curt* he yede'=he went to the high court; Havelok, 1685. It first occurs, spelt *curt*, in the AS. Chron. A. D. 1154. Spelt *courte*, P. Plowman, B. prol. 190.—OF. *cort*, *curt* (F. *cour*), a court, a yard, a tribunal.—L. acc. *cōrtem*, *cohortem* (nom. *cohors*), a hurdle, enclosure, cattle-yard; see Ovid, Fasti, iv. 704; also, a cohort.—L. *co-*, for *con-*, i. e. *cum*, together; and *hort-*, as in *hort-us*, a garden, cognate with Gk. χόρτος, a court-yard; and perhaps with **Yard** (1). Der. *court-e-ous*, q.v.; *court-es-an*, q.v.; *court-es-y*, q.v.; *court-i-er*, q.v.; *court-ly*, *-li-ness*, *-martial*, *-plaster*; also *court*, verb, q.v.

COURT (2), *verb*, to woo, seek favour. (F.—L.) In Shak. L. L. L. v. 2. 122. Orig. to practise arts in vogue at court. 'For he is practiz'd well in policie, And thereto doth his *courting* most applie;' Spenser, Mother Hubberd's Tale, 784; see the context. From the sb. *court*: see above. Der. *court-ship*.

COURT CARDS, pictured cards. A corruption of *coat cards*, also called *coated cards*; Fox, Martyrs, p. 919 (R.). 'Here's a trick of discarded cards of us! We were rank'd with *coats*, as long as old master lived;' Massinger, The Old Law, iii. 1. *Coat* referred to the dress of the king, queen, and knave; the king and queen suggested *court*. See Nares. See **Coat**.

COURTEOUS, of courtly manners. (F.—L.) ME. *cortais*, *cortois*, seldom *corteous*. Spelt *corteys*, Will. of Palerne, 194, 2704; *curteys*, 231; *curteyse*, 406, 601.—OF. *cortois*, *curtois*, *curteis*, courteous. —OF. *cort*, *curt*, a court; with suffix *-eis* < L. *-ensis*. See **Court**. Der. *courteous-ly*, *-ness*; also *courtes-y*, q. v.

COURTESAN, a prostitute. (F.—Ital.—L.) Spelt *courtezan*, Shak. K. Lear, iii. 2. 79.—F. *courtisane*, 'a lady or waiting-woman of the court;' also, a professed strumpet;' Cot.; fem. of *courtisan*, 'a courtier;' id.—Ital. *cortegiana*, *cortesana*, 'a curtezan;' Florio; fem. of *cortegiano*, 'a courtier;' id. The latter is for **cortesiano*, an extension of *cortese*, courteous.—Ital. *corte*, court. See **Court**, **Courteous**. ¶ The ME. *courtezane* occurs with the sense of 'courtier;' Paston Letters, let. 7.

COURTESY, politeness. (F.—L.) In early use. ME. *cortaisie*, *corteisie*, *curtesie*; spelt *kurteisie*, Ancren Riwle, p. 70.—OF. *curteisie*, courtesy.—OF. *corteis*, *curteis*, courteous. See **Courteous**.

COURTIER, one who frequents the court. (F.—L.) In Shak. Hamlet, i. 2. 117. ME. *courteour*, Gower, C. A. i. 89; bk. i. 1410. From AF. **cortei-er* = OF. *cortoi-er*, to live at court, Godefroy; with suffix *-our* < L. acc. suffix *-ātōrem*.—OF. *cort*, a court. See **Court**.

COUSIN, a near relative. (F.—L.) Formerly applied to a kinsman generally, not in the modern restricted way. ME. *cosin*, *cousin*; Rob. of Glouc. p. 91, l. 2019; Chaucer, C. T., A 1131; K. Horn, l. 1444; spelt *kosin*, Polit. Songs, p. 343, l. 429 (ab. 1310).— OF. *cosin*, *cousin*, a cousin.—Late L. *cosinus*, found in the 7th cent. in the St. Gall Vocabulary (Brachet). A contraction of L. *consobrīnus*, the child of a mother's sister, a cousin, relation; whence also Roumansch *cusrin*, a cousin; cf. Ital. *cugino*.—L. *con-*, for *cum*, together; and *sobrinus*, a cousin-german, by the mother's side. *Sobrinus* is for **swesr-inus*, belonging to a sister; from L. *soror* (for **swesōr*), a sister; cf. Skt. *svasṛ*, a sister. Brugmann, i. § 319. See **Sister**.

COUVADE, a custom of 'man child-bed' practised by some

primitive races. (F.—Ital.—L.) Modern.—F. *couvade*, a brood; *faire la couvade*, 'to sit cowring or skowking within doores;' Cot.— Ital. *covata*, 'a covie, a brood;' Florio.—Ital. *covata*, fem. of pp. of *covare*, to hatch.—L. *cubāre*, to lie down. **Doublet**, *covey*, q.v.

COVE, a nook, creek, a small bay. (E.) 'Within secret *coves* and noukes;' Holland, Ammianus, p. 77. ME. *coue* (= *cove*), a den; Cursor Mundi, l. 12341. AS. *cofa*, a chamber, Mercian gloss to Matt. vi. 6, xxiv. 26; a cave (L. *spelunca*), N. gloss to John, xi. 38. **+** Icel. *kofi*, a hut, shed, convent-cell; G. *koben*, a cabin, pig-sty. **β**. Remote origin uncertain; not to be confused with *cave*, nor *coop*, nor *cup*, nor *alcove*, with all of which it has been connected without reason. Cf. Brugmann, i. § 658 (a). **Der**. *cove*, verb, to over-arch. ☞ The obsolete verb *cove*, to brood (Richardson) is from quite another source, viz. Ital. *covare*, to brood; from L. *cubāre*; see **Covey**.

COVENANT, an agreement. (F.—L.) ME. *couenant*, *couenaunt*, *covenand* (with *u* for *v*); often contracted to *conand*, as in Barbour's Bruce. Spelt *couenaunt*, printed *covenaunt*, K. Alisaunder, ed. Weber, 2036.—OF. *convenant*, *covenant*; Godefroy. Formed as a pres. pt. from *convenir*, to agree, orig. to meet together, assemble.—L. *con-uenire*, to come together. See **Convene**. **Der**. *covenant*, verb; *covenant-er*.

COVER, to conceal, hide, spread over. (F.—L.) ME. *coueren*, *keueren*, *kiueren* (with *u* for *v*). Chaucer has *couered*, C. T. 6172 (D 590).—OF. *covrir*, *couvrir*, to cover; cf. Ital. *coprire*.—L. *coöperire*, to cover.—L. *co-*, for *com*- i.e. *cum*, together, wholly; and *operire*, to shut, hide, conceal. **β**. It is supposed that L. *operire*, to shut, is for **op-uerire*; cf. Lith. *aż-wer-iu*, I shut, Lith. *wartai*, doors; and Oscan acc. *veru*, a door. See Brugmann, i. § 350. **Der**. *cover-ing*, *cover-let*, q.v.; also *covert*, q.v.; *ker-chief*, q.v.; *cur-few*, q.v.

COVERLET, a covering for a bed. (F.—L.) ME. *coverlite*, *couerlite*; Wyclif, 4 Kings, viii. 15.—AF. *coverlit*, Royal Wills, p. 181 (1399); mod. F. *couvrelit*, a bed-covering (Littré).—OF. *covrir*, to cover; and F. *lit*, a bed, from L. *lectum*, acc. of *lectus*, a bed. ☞ Hence the word should rather be *coverlit*.

COVERT, a place of shelter. (F.—L.) In early use. 'No *couert* miȝt thei cacche' = they could find no shelter;' William of Palerne, 2217.—OF. *covert*, a covered place; pp. of *covrir*, to cover. See **Cover**. **Der**. *covert*, adj., *-ly*; *covert-ure* (Gower, C. A. i. 224).

COVET, to desire eagerly and unlawfully. (F.—L.) ME. *coueiten*, *coueten* (with *u* for *v*). 'Who so *coveyteth* al, al leseth,' who covets all, loses all; Rob. of Glouc. p. 306.—AF. *coveiter*, Lai d'Havelok, l. 695; (F. *convoiter*, with inserted *n*), to covet; cf. Ital. *cubitare* (for **cupitare*), to covet. **β**. Formed, as if from a L. **cupiditāre*, from acc. *cupiditā-tem*, eager desire: which is from *cupidus*, desirous of.—L. *cupere*, to desire. See **Cupid**. **Der**. *covetous* (AF. *cuveitus*, Edw. Confessor, l. 223; OF. *covoitus*, F. *convoiteux*); *-ly*, *-ness*. *Covetous* was in early use, and occurs, spelt *couetus*, in Floriz and Blancheflur, ed. Lumby, l. 355.

COVEY, a brood or hatch of birds. (F.—L.) 'Covey of pertry-chys,' i.e. partridges; Prompt. Parv. p. 96.—OF. *covee*, F. *couvée*, a covey of partridges; fem. form of the pp. of OF. *cover*, F. *couver*, to hatch, sit, brood.—L. *cubāre*, to lie down; cf. E. *incubate*. Cf. Gk. κύπτειν, to bend, κυφός, bent.

COVIN, secret agreement, fraud; a law-term. (F.—L.) The Anglo-French *covine* occurs in the Stat. of the Realm, i. 162, an. 1311. The ME. *covine*, *covin*, counsel, trick, sleight, is in Chaucer, C. T. 606 (A 604).—OF. *covin*, m., *covine*, f., counsel, intention (Godefroy). —Late L. *convenium*, a convention, pl. *convenia* (whence the OF. fem. form).—L. *conuenīre*, to come together; see **Covenant**, **Convene**. Thus *covin* = *convention*.

COW (1), the female of the bull. (E.) ME. *cu*, *cou*; pl. *ky*, *kie*, *kye*; also *kin*, *kuyn*, mod. E. *kine*, due to AS. *cȳna*, gen. pl. The pl. *ky* is in Cursor Mundi, 4564; *kin* in Will. of Palerne, 34, 480; *kyen* in Caxton, Godfrey of Boloyne, ch. 8, l. 15; *kie* in Golding's Ovid, fol. 26. AS. *cū*, pl. *cȳ*, formed by vowel-change; Grein, i. 172. Teut. stem **kū-*, whence also Icel. *kȳr*. Cf. also Du. *koe*, Swed. and Dan. *ko*, G. *kuh*; from Teut. stem **kō-*. Further allied to OIrish *bó*, Gael. *bó*, a cow; W. *buw*, a cow; L. *bōs*, gen. *bouis*, an ox; Gk. βοῦς, an ox; Pers. *gāw*, Skt. *gō-* (nom. *gāus*): Russ. *goviado*, oxen. Idg. stems **g(w)ōu-*, **g(w)ow-*. See **Beef**, **Kine**.

COW (2), to subdue, dishearten, terrify. (Scand.) 'It hath *cow'd* my better part of man;' Macb. v. 8. 18.—Icel. *kūga*, to cow, tyrannise over; *lāta kūgask*, to let oneself be cowed into submission; see Cleasby and Vigfusson; Dan. *kue*, to bow, coerce, subdue; Swed. *kufva*, to check, curb, suppress, subdue. See **Cuff** (1).

COWARD, a man without courage. (F.—L.) ME. *couard*, more often *coward*; spelt *coward* in King Alisaunder, ed. Weber, l. 2108. —AF. *coward*, a coward, Langtoft's Chron. i. 194; OF. *couart*, more usually *coart* (Supp. to Godefroy), a coward, poltroon; equivalent to Ital. *codardo*. **β**. Sometimes explained as an animal that drops his tail; cf. the heraldic expression *lion couard*, a lion with his tail between his legs. Mr. Wedgwood refers to the fact that a hare was called *couard* in the old terms of hunting; 'le *coward*, ou le *court cow*' = the hare, in Le Venery de Twety, in Reliquiæ Antiquæ, i. 153; and he thinks that the original sense was 'bob-tailed,' with reference to the hare in particular. To which may be added, that *Coart* is the name of the hare in the French version of Reynard the Fox. Or again, it may merely mean one who shows his tail, or who turns tail. **γ**. Whichever be right, there is no doubt that the word was formed by adding the suffix *-ard* (Ital. *-ardo*) to the OF. *coe*, a tail (Ital. *coda*).—OF. *coe*, a tail; with the suffix *-ard*, of Teutonic origin.—L. *cauda*, a tail; with OHG. suffix *-hart*, orig. 'hard.' See **Caudal**. **Der**. *coward*, adj., *-ly*, *-li-ness*, *-ice* = ME. *cowardis*, Gower, C. A. ii. 66 (OF. *coard-ise*).

COWER, to crouch, shrink down, squat. (Scand.) ME. *couren*. 'Couren in a cope;' Polit. Songs, p. 157 (temp. Edw. I). 'He koured low;' William of Palerne, l. 47; 'Ye . . . cowardli as caitifs *couren* here in meuwe' = ye cowardly cower here in a mew (or cage) like caitiffs; id. 3336.—Icel. *kūra*, to doze, lie quiet; Swed. *kura*, to doze, to roost, to settle to rest as birds do; Dan. *kure*, to lie quiet, rest; Swed. dial. *kura*, to sit hunched up. Cf. G. *kauern*, to cower.

COWL (1), a monk's hood, a cap, hood. (L.) ME. *cowle*. 'Cowle, munkys abyte [monk's habit], *cuculla*, *cucullus*;' Prompt. Parv. p. 97. [Another form *covel* occurs 5 times in Havelok, ll. 768, 858, 964, 1144, 2904, spelt *couel*, *cuuel*, *kouel*, and meaning 'a coat;' from AS. *cufle*, a cowl (Bosworth); the *f* passing into ME. *v*.] ME. *cowle* is from AS. *cugele*, *cugle*, *cūle*; the last of these occurs in Ælfric's Saints' Lives, c. xxxiii. l. 237. **β**. These words are all from Late L. *cuculla*, a frock, sometimes a hood; from L. *cucullus*, a hood.

COWL (2), a vessel carried on a pole. (F.—L.) The pole supporting the vessel was called a *cowl-staff*; see Merry Wives, iii. 3. 156. '*Coul*, a large wooden tub; formerly, any kind of cup or vessel;' Halliwell. ME. *cuuel* (= *cuvel*), as in *cuuel-staf*, a cowl-staff, Gen. and Exodus, l. 3710.—OF. *cuvel*, later *cuveau*, 'a little tub;' Cot. Dimin. of F. *cuve*, 'an open tub, a fat, or vat;' id.—L. *cūpa*, a vat, butt, large cask. **Der**. *cowl-staff*; see *staff*.

COWRY, a small shell used for money. (Hind.—Skt.) 'Cowries (the *Cypræa moneta*) are used as small coin in many parts of Southern Asia, and especially on the coast of Guinea in Africa;' Eng. Cycl., Arts and Sciences, s.v. *Cowry*. The word is Hindustani, and must therefore have been carried to the Guinea-coast by the English.— Hind. *kauṛī*, 'a small shell used as coin; money, fare, hire;' Forbes' Hind. Dict. p. 281.—Skt. *kaparda*, *kapardika*, a cowry. See Yule. H. H. Wilson, at p. 271, cites also Bengālī *kaṛi*, Guzerāthī *koṛi*.

COWSLIP, the name of a flower. (E.) In Milton, Comus, 898. Shak. has both *cowslip*, Temp. v. 1. 89; and *oxlip*, Mids. Nt. Dr. ii. 1. 250. ME. *cowslope*, *cowslop*; Prompt. Parv. p. 99. AS. *cū-slyppe*, *cūsloppe*; for the former form, see Cockayne's Leechdoms, Glossary; the entry 'britannica, *cūsloppe*' is in Ælfric's Glossary; Voc. 135. 26; cf. 361. 23. **β**. By the known laws of AS. grammar, the word must be divided as *cū-slyppe* or *cū-sloppe*, where *cū* means cow; cf. *cū-nille*, wild chervil (Leo). The word *ox-lip* was made to match it, and therefore stands for *ox-slip* or *ox-slop*; cf. prov. E. *bull-slop*, a large oxlip, E.D.D., p. 435. The word *slyppe* or *sloppe* means lit. a *slop*, i.e. a piece of dung. An examination of the AS. names of plants in Cockayne's Leechdoms will strengthen the belief that many of these names were of a very homely character. Cf. Icel. *kū-reki*, a primrose, lit. 'cow-leavings;' MDan. *kodriv*, marsh marigold, lit. 'cow-drift.' See **Slop**.

COXCOMB, a fool, a fop. (E.) In Shakespeare, it means (1) a fool's cap, Merry Wives, v. 5. 146; (2) the head, Tw. Nt. v. 179, 193, 195; (3) a fool, Com. Err. iii. 1. 32. 'Let the foole goe like a *cockescome* still;' Drant's Horace, Ep. bk. i. To Scæua. For *cock's comb*, i.e. cock's crest. See *cockescombe* in Minsheu (1627), who explains it. See **Cock** and **Comb**.

COXSWAIN, **COCKSWAIN**, the steersman of a boat. (Hybrid; F. *and* Scand.) The spelling *coxswain* is modern; *cock-swain* occurs in Drummond's Travels, p. 70 (Todd's Johnson); in Anson's Voyage, b. iii. c. 9; and in Cook's Voyage, vol. i. b. ii. c. 1 (R.). The word is compounded of *cock*, a boat, and *swain*; and means the person in command of a boat, not necessarily the steersman, though now commonly so used. See **Cock** (5) and **Swain**.

COY (1), modest, bashful, retired. (F.—L.) 'Coy, or sobyr, sobrius, modestus;' Prompt. Parv. p. 86.—OF. *coi*, earlier *quei*, *cooit* (Godefroy), still, quiet.—Folk-L. **quētum*; acc. of **quētus*, for L. *quiētus*, quiet, still.—L. *quiēt-*, stem of *quiēs*, rest. See **Quiet**. **Der**. *coy-ly*, *-ness*, *-ish*, *-ish-ness*. **Doublet**, *quiet*.

COY (2), a decoy for wild duck. (Du.—L.) See N.E.D. and E.D.D.—Du. *kooi*, a cage; MDu. *koye* (Hexham).—Late L. *cavea*, a cage. See **Cage**; of which *coy* is a doublet.

COYOTE, a prairie-wolf. (Span.—Mexican.) Span. *coyote.*—Mexican *coyotl*, the Mexican wolf; *Canis latrans.*

COZEN, to flatter, to beguile. (F.—L.) In Shak. Merry Wives, iv. 2. 180. 'When he had played the *cousining* mate with others . . . himselfe was beguiled;' Hakluyt, Voyages, i. 586. Here the spelling agrees with that of **Cousin**, q.v. *Cozen* is, in fact, merely a verb evolved out of *cousin.*—F. *cousiner*, 'to claime kindred for advantage, or particular ends; as he, who to save charges in travelling, goes from house to house, as *cosin* to the honour of every one;' Cot. So in mod. F., *cousiner* is 'to call cousin, to sponge, to live upon other people;' Hamilton and Legros. The change of meaning from 'sponge' to 'beguile' or 'cheat' was easy. Cf. OF. *cosin*, a dupe (Godefroy). **Der.** *cozen-age, cozen-er.*

CRAB (1), a common shell-fish. (E.) ME. *crabbe*, Old Eng. Homilies, ed. Morris, i. 51. AS. *crabba*, as a gloss to Lat. *cancer*; Ælfric's Gloss.; Voc. 180. 41.+Icel. *krabbi*; Swed. *krabba*; Dan. *krabbe*; Du. *krab*; G. *krabbe.* Allied to EFries. and Du. *krabben*, to scratch, to claw; also to G. *krebs*, Du. *kreeft*, crab. See **Crayfish.**

CRAB (2), a kind of apple. (E.) 'Mala maciana, wode-*crabbis*;' MS. Harl. 3388, qu. in Cockayne's Leechdoms, Glossary. '*Crabbe*, appulle or frute, macianum;' Prompt. Parv. p. 99. '*Crabbe*, tre, acerbus, macianus, arbutus;' id. Cf. prov. E. *scrab*, a crab-apple, E.D.D.; and Swed. dial. *skrabba*, fruit of the wild apple; also, anything poor or weak; cf. Swed. *skrabbig*, weakly.

CRABBED, peevish; cramped. (E.) 'The arwes [arrows] of thy *crabbed* eloquence;' Chaucer, C. T. 9079 (E 1203). Cf. Lowland Scotch *crab*, to provoke, in Jamieson; he cites the sentence 'thou hes *crabbit* and offendit God' from Abp. Hamiltoun's Catechisme, fol. 153 b. '*Crabbyd*, awke, or wrawe, ceronicus, bilosus, cancerinus;' Prompt. Parv. p. 99. β. From the same root as **Crab** (1), q.v. Cf. Du. *krabben*, to scratch; *kribben*, to quarrel, to be cross, to be peevish; *kribbig*, peevish, forward; evidently the equivalent of *crabbed* in the sense of peevish. γ. As regards the phrase 'to write a *crabbed* hand,' cf. Icel. *krab*, a crabbed hand, Icel. *krabba*, to scrawl, write a crabbed hand; Du. *krabbelen*, to scribble, scrawl, scrape, a dimin. form from *krabben*, to scratch. Thus *crabbed*, in both senses, is from the same root. It is remarkable that the Prompt. Parv. translates *crabbyd* by L. *cancerinus*, from *cancer*, a crab. **Der.** *crabbed-ly, -ness.*

CRACK, to split suddenly and noisily. (E.) ME. *craken, kraken*; Havelok, 1857. 'Speren *chrakeden*,' spears cracked; Layamon, iii. 94. AS. *cracian*, to crack (Bosworth). 'Sio eorþe eall *cracode*,' the earth all cracked; Psalm xlv. 3, ed. Thorpe. + Du. *kraken*, to crack, creak; *krakken*, to crack; *krak*, a crack; *krak*, crack!; G. *krachen*, to crack; *krach*, a crack; Gael. *crac*, a crack, fissure; *cnac*, to crack, break, crash (from E.). β. An imitative word, like *creak, croak, crash, gnash.* Cf. Skt. *garj*, to roar. **Der.** *crack*, sb., *crack-er*; *crack-le*, the frequentative form, signifying 'to crack often;' *crake*, to boast, an obsolescent word; also *crack-n-el*, q.v.

CRACKNEL, a kind of biscuit. (F.—Du.) '*Crakenelle*, brede, creputellus, fraginellus;' Prompt. Parv. p. 100. '*Crakenell*, cracquelin;' Palsgrave. A curious perversion of F. *craquelin*, which Cotgrave explains by 'cracknell;' the E. *crak-en-el* answering to F. *craq-el-in.*—Du. *krakeling*, a cracknel; formed with dim. suffix *-el* and the suffix *-ing* from *kraken*, to crack; from the crisp nature of the biscuit.

CRADLE, a child's crib; a frame. (E.) ME. *cradel*, Ancren Riwle, p. 260. AS. *cradol*; in comp. *cild-cradol*, child-cradle; Ælfric's Homilies, ed. Thorpe, ii. 76. [A true Teutonic word, not borrowed from Celtic. Irish *craidhal*, Gael. *creathall*, a cradle, a grate, are from English.] Allied to mod. G. *krätze*, a basket, given by Kluge; MHG. *kratte, kretze*, OHG. *cratto, crezzo*, a basket (Schade). On the other hand, Schade regards these G. words as derived from L. *crātes*, a hurdle; which seems unlikely.

CRAFT, skill, ability, trade. (E.) ME. *craft, creft*; Layamon, i. 120. AS. *cræft*, Grein, i. 167. + Du. *kracht*, power; Icel. *kraptr, kraftr*, craft, force; Swed. and Dan. *kraft*, power; G. *kraft*, power, energy. β. Formed with suffixed *-t* from Teutonic stem *kraf-*; cf. Icel. *kræfr*, strong, or daring. Perhaps allied to AS. *crafian*, to crave, demand; see **Crave.** **Der.** *craft-y, -i-ly, -i-ness, craft-s-man*; also *hand-i-craft*, q.v.

CRAG, a rock. (C.) ME. *crag*, pl. *cragges*; Hampole, Pricke of Conscience, 6393; Cursor Mundi, 9885.—W. *craig*, a rock, crag; allied to Gael. and Irish *creag*, a crag. Cf. W. *careg*, a stone; Bret. *karrek*, a rock in the sea, rock covered with breakers; Gael. and Irish *carraig*, a rock, cliff. From a base *kars*, to be rough or hard; Stokes-Fick, p. 72. **Der.** *cragg-y.*

CRAKE, CORNCRAKE, the name of a bird. (E.) So named from its cry, a kind of grating croak. Cf. ME. *craken*, to cry, shriek out. 'Thus they begyn to *crake*;' Pilgrims' Sea Voyage, l. 16; see Stacions of Rome, ed. Furnivall, E. E. T. S. 1867. An imitative

word, like *crack, creak*, and *croak*; and see **Crow.** ☞ The Gk. κρέξ, Lat. *crex*, also signifies a sort of land-rail, similarly named from its cry. **Der.** *corn-crake*, Holland The Howlat, l. 782; *night-crake*, Voc. 639. 40.

CRAM, to press close together. (E.) ME. *crammen.* 'Ful crammyd;' Wyclif, Hos. xiii. 6. AS. *crammian*, to stuff. The entry 'farcio, ic *crammige*' occurs in Ælfric's Grammar, De Quarta Conjugatione. The compound verb *undercrammian*, to fill underneath, occurs in Ælfric's Homilies, i. 430.[+Icel. *kremja*, to squeeze, bruise; Swed. *krama*, to squeeze, press; Dan. *kramme*, to crumple, crush.] From *cramm-*, 2nd grade of the AS. strong verb *crimm-an*, to crumble. Cf. OHG. *chrimman*, MHG. *krimmen*, to seize with the claws, G. *grimmen*, to grip, gripe. Allied to **Cramp.**

CRAMBO, a name of game; doggerel verse. (L.—Gk.) A popular variation of L. *crambē*, cabbage; esp. with reference to L. *crambē repetita*, cabbage served up again; hence, a tasteless repetition; see Juvenal, Sat. vii. 154.—Gk. κράμβη, cabbage.

CRAMP, a tight restraint, spasmodic contraction. (F.—Teut.) The verb to *cramp* is much later than the sb. in English use. ME. *crampe*, a cramp, spasm. '*Crampe*, spasmus;' Prompt. Parv. p. 100. 'I cacche the *crampe*;' P. Plowman, C. vii. 78.—F. *crampe*, 'the crampe;' Cot. Cf. F. *crampon*, 'a cramp-iron.'—Du. *kramp*, a cramp, spasm. From the 2nd grade of Teut. *kremtan-*, *krimtan-*, to draw together, as in OHG. *krimphan*, str. vb. Cf. E. *crimp, cramp, crump-le.* Also Swed. *kramp*, cramp; *krampa*, a cramp-iron, staple; MDan. *krampe*, cramp; *krampe*, a cramp or iron clasp; G. *krampf*, cramp; *krampen, krampfen*, to cramp; Icel. *krappr*, cramped, strait, narrow; *kreppa*, to cramp, to clench; where the *pp* stands for *mp*, by assimilation. 'Der. *cramp-fish*, the torpedo, causing a spasm; *cramp-iron*, a vice, clamp.

CRANBERRY, a kind of sour berry. (Low G.) For *crane-berry*; from some fanciful notion. Perhaps 'because its slender stalk has been compared to the long legs and neck of a crane' (Webster). Not in ME.; first in 1672; from Low G.—Low G. *kraanbere* (Berghaus); G. *kranbeere*, explained in Flügel's Dict. as 'a crane-berry, red bilberry.' And, most unequivocally, in Dan. *tranebær*, a cranberry, Swed. *tranbär*, a cranberry, where the word follows the peculiar forms exhibited in Dan. *trane*, Swed. *trana*, a crane. See **Crane**, and **Berry.**

CRANE, a long-legged wading bird. (E.) 'Crane, byrde, grus;' Prompt. Parv. p. 100. Spelt *cron*, Layamon, ii. 422. AS. *cran*; we find 'grus, *cran*' in Ælfric's Glossary, Nomina Avium. + Du. *kraan*; Swed. *trana* (for *krana*); Dan. *trane* (for *krane*); Icel. *trani* (for *krani*); G. *kran-ich*, a crane. + W. *garan*, a crane; Corn. and Bret. *garan*; Gk. γέρανος, a crane. Cf. also L. *grus*, a crane; Lith. *garnys*, a stork. β. The word is usually derived from the bird's cry; from √ GER, to call, cry out; cf. Gk. γηρύειν. β. It is to be noted, further, that, in the sense of a machine for raising weights, we have still the same word; see Arnold's Chronicle, 1502 (ed. 1811, p. 127). In this sense, we find Gk. γέρανος, Dan. and Swed. *kran*, Du. *kraan*, G. *krahn*; cf. Icel. *trana*, a framework for supporting timber. In English, *crane* also means a bent pipe, or siphon, from its likeness to the bird's neck; and cf. F. *grue*, 'a crane, also, the engine so called;' Cot. Brugmann, i. § 632. **Der.** *crane*, vb., to extend the neck (cf. Westphal. *kränen*, to make a long neck); *cran-berry.*

CRANIUM, the skull. (L.—Gk.) Medical. Borrowed from L. *crānium*, the skull.—Gk. κρανίον, the skull; allied to κάρα, κάρηνον, the head, and to L. *cerebrum*; cf. also Skt. *çiras*, the head. See Brugmann, i. §§ 508, 619. **Der.** *crani-al, cranio-log-y, cranio-log-ist, cranio-log-ic-al* (from Gk. λόγος, discourse, λέγειν, to speak).

CRANK (1), a bent arm, for turning an axis. (E.) Shak. has *crank*, a winding passage, Cor. i. 1. 141; also *crank*, to wind about, 1 Hen. IV, iii. 1. 98. Cf. Milton, L'Allegro, l. 27. 'Cranke of a welle;' Prompt. Parv. p. 100. AS. *cranc-*, in the comp. *cranc-stæf*; Anglia, ix. 263, l. 14. Cf. EFries. *krunken*, bent. From Teut. type *krank*, 2nd grade of *krenkan- (*krinkan-)*, pt. t. *krank*, pp. *krunkanoz.* Cf. AS. *crincan*, by-form of *cring-an*, to fall in battle, orig. 'to be bent up;' Du. *kronkel*, a rumple, wrinkle, i.e. little bend; *kronkelen*, to rumple, wrinkle, bend, turn, wind. Hence also **Crinkle**, which see. And see **Cringe.** **Der.** *crank*, to twist about, 1 Hen. IV, iii. 1. 98; *crank-le*, to twist about, as in Cotgrave, s.v. *serpeger.*

CRANK (2), liable to be upset, said of a boat. (E.) 'The Resolution was found to be very *crank*;' Cook, Voyage, vol. iii. b. i. c. 1. Allied to **Crank** (1). Cf. Du. *krank*, ill, poor; Walloon *krankier*, to turn aside, shift, *krankieu*, rickety (said of children), twisty (said of trees); also Du. *krengen*, to careen, to bend upon one side in sailing; Swed. *kränga*, to heave down, to heel; *krängning*, a careening, heeling over; Dan. *krænge*, to heave down; also, to lie along, to lurch; *krængning*, a lurch. See **Cringe.** **Der.** *crank-y, crank-ness.*

CRANK (3), lively, brisk. (E.) Obsolescent and provincial.

'Crank, brisk, jolly, merry;' Halliwell. 'He who was a little before bedred, and car.ed lyke a dead karkas on fower mennes shoulders, was now cranke and lustie;' Udal, on Mark, c. 2. v. 6. Ultimately, a very different use of crank (2), from the notion of turning quickly. Cf. Norw. kring, active, brisk, Dan. dial. kræng, dexterous, Icel. kringr, easy.

CRANNY, a rent, chink, crevice. (F.–L.) ME. crany, with one n; see Prompt. Parv. p. 100, where crayne or crany is translated by L. rima, a chink. 'Crany, cravasse;' Palsgrave. Formed by adding the E. dimin. suffix -y to F. cran, a notch; also spelt cren, as in Cotgrave; or from OF. crenee, a nook (Godefroy). Cf. Ital. crena, a notch (Florio); and perhaps L. crēna, a notch, used by Pliny, but of doubtful authority; see Körting, § 2591. **Der.** (from L. crēna) cren-ate, q.v., cren-ell-ate, q.v.

CRANTS, a garland, wreath. (MDu.–G.) In Hamlet, v. 1. 255. Lowland Scotch crance (Jamieson). The spelling krants is given by Kilian for the Du. word now spelt krans, a wreath, garland, chaplet; cf. Dan. krands, Swed. krans.–G. kranz, a wreath.

CRAPE, a thin crisp silk stuff. (F.–L.) 'A saint in crape;' Pope, Moral Essays, i. 136.–F. crêpe, spelt crespe in Cotgrave, who explains it by 'cipres, cobweb lawne.' OF. crespe, 'curled, frizzled, crisped, crispe;' id.–L. crispus, crisped, curled. See **Crisp**. Thus crape is a doublet of crisp.

CRAPULOUS, intemperate, sick with drunkenness. (L.–Gk.) In Bailey and Johnson. Charles Cotton has crapula; Night Quatrains, l. 72.–L. crāpulōsus, drunken.–L. crāpula, intoxication. –Gk. κραιπάλη, nausea, effect of a surfeit; prob. orig. 'giddiness.' Allied to κραιπνός, rapid, swift; Lith. kreip-ti, to turn, turn round.

CRARE, a kind of ship. (F.) Shak. has 'sluggish crare;' Cymb. iv. 2. 205 (old edd. care); see also craier in Halliwell; cray in Nares. ME. crayer, Allit. Morte Arthure, 738, 3666.–OF. craier, creer, a vessell of war (Godefroy); apparently a Norman word; Low L. craiera, creyera. Origin unknown.

CRASH, to break in pieces forcibly, to make a sudden grating noise. (Scand.?) Shak. has the sb. crash, Hamlet, ii. 2. 498. 'He shak't his head, and crash't his teeth for ire;' Fairfax, tr. of Tasso, bk. vii. st. 42. 'Craschyn, as tethe, fremo;' Prompt. Parv. p. 100; Allit. Morte Arthure, ed. Brock, l. 1109. A mere variant of craze, and both crash and craze are again variants of crack. Cf. clash, dash; of imitative origin. Perhaps suggested by Swed. krasa, to crackle; slå i kras, to dash to pieces; Dan. krase, to crackle; slaae i kras, to break to shivers. See **Craze**, **Crack**. **Der.** crash, sb.

CRASIS, the contraction of two vowels into a long vowel or diphthong. (Gk.) Grammatical. Borrowed from Gk. κρᾶσις, a mixing, blending.–Gk. κεράννυμι, I mix, blend. See **Crater**.

CRASS, thick, dense, gross. (L.) 'Of body somwhat crasse and corpulent;' Hall's Chron. Hen. VII, an. 21. § 5.–L. crassus, thick, dense, fat. D*e*r. crass-i-tude; cresset, q.v.

CRATCH, a manger, crib for cattle. (F.–OHG.) ME. cracche, crecche; used of the manger in which Christ was laid; Cursor Mundi, 11237; spelt crecche, Ancren Riwle, p. 260.–OF. creche (mod. F. crèche), a manger, crib. [The Provençal form is crepcha, and the Ital. is greppia; all are of OHG. origin.]–OHG. crippea (whence G. krippe), a crib; cf. OSax. kribbia, a crib; see the Heliand, ed. Heyne, l. 382. And see **Crib**. **Der.** cratch-cradle, i.e. crib-cradle; often unmeaningly turned into scratch-cradle.

CRATE, a wicker case for crockery. (MDu.) 'I have seen a horse carrying home the harvest on a crate;' Johnson, Journey to the Western Islands. Grose (1790) has: 'crates, panniers for glass or crockery.' And see E.D.D. Perhaps from MDu. kratte, Du. krat, a basket; cf. MDu. kretse, a wicker pannier (Hexham); OHG. cratto, a basket. β. Or, otherwise, from L. crātes, a hurdle; properly, of wicker-wo k. And see **Cart**, **Cradle**.

CRATER, the cup or opening of a volcano. (L.–Gk.) Used by Berkeley, to Arbuthnot, Description of Vesuvius, 1717 (Todd's Johnson). 'Crater, a cup or bowl, a goblet;' Bailey, vol. ii. (1731). –L. crātēr, a bowl; the crater of a volcano.–Gk. κρατήρ, a large bowl in which things were mixed together.–Gk. κεράννυμι, I mix; from the base κερ-. Cf. Skt. çrī, to mix.

CRAVAT, a kind of neckcloth. (F.–Austrian.) Spelt crabat in Hudibras, pt. i. c. 3. 1166: 'Canonical crabat of Smeck.' But this is a corrupted spelling. Dryden has: 'His sword-knot this, his crávat that designed;' Epilogue to the Man of Mode, l. 23.–F. cravate, meaning (1) a Croat, Croatian; and (2) a cravat. β. The history of the word is recorded by Ménage, who lived at the time of the first introduction of cravats into France, in the year 1636. He explains that the ornament was worn by the Croates (Croatians), who were more commonly termed Cravates; and he gives the date (1636) of its introduction into France, which was due to the dealings the French had at that time with Germany; it was in the time of the Thirty Years' War. See the passage quoted in Brachet, s.v. cravate;

and in Nares, s.v. crabat. γ. Brachet also explains, s.v. corvée, the insertion, for euphony, of the letter v, whereby Croate became Crovate or Cravate; a similar striking instance occurs in F. pouvoir, from L. potēre, for potesse. The word is, accordingly, of historic origin; from the name of Croatia, now a province of Austria. Cf. Cravatts, i.e. Croatians, which occurs in 1658; see Sir S. D. Scott, The British Army (1850), iii. 101; also N. and Q. 6 S. vi. 113. The name is of Slavonic origin; cf. Russ. Kroat', a Croatian.

CRAVE, to beg earnestly, beseech. (E.) ME. crauen (with u for v); Genesis and Exodus, ed. Morris, l. 1408. AS. crafian, to crave; A. S. Chron. an. 1070; ed. Thorpe, p. 344. Cf. Icel. krefja, to crave, demand; Swed. kräfva, to demand; Dan. kræve, to crave, demand, exact; also Icel. krafa, a craving, a demand. **Der.** crav-ing.

CRAVEN, one who is defeated, a recreant. (F.–L.) ME. crauant (with u for v); also spelt crauand, crauaund. 'Al ha cneowen ham crauant and ouercumen' = they all knew them to be craven and overcome; Legend of St. Katharine, 132. 'Haa! crauaunde knyghte!' = ha! craven knight; Morte Arthure, ed. Brock, l. 133. β. The termination in -en is a mistaken one, and makes the word look like a past participle. The word is really cravant, where -ant is the regular French form of the present participle.–OF. cravant, pres. part. of craver, by-form of crever, to burst, to break; and hence, to be overcome. [Cf. Span. quebrar, to fail, to be bankrupt, which is the same word.]–L. crepantem, acc. of pres. part. of crepāre, to burst. See further the uses of F. crever; thus, OF. le cuer me creve means 'my heart is breaking;' OF. crevé means 'dead;' and Walloon se krever de rire is denounced by Remacle as being not a polite phrase. See Phil. Soc. Trans. 1902, p. 659.

CRAW, the crop, or first stomach of fowls. (E.) ME. crawe; Wyclif, 4 Kings, vi. 25. 'Crawe, or crowpe of a byrde or other fowlys, gabus, vesicula;' Prompt. Parv. p. 101. [Allied to crag or craig, the neck.] As if from AS. *craga, the neck (not found); NFries. krage, neck, craw. Cf. Du. kraag, the neck, collar; G. kragen, a collar. Also (perhaps) Dan. kro, Swed. kröfva, craw.

CRAWFISH; see Crayfish.

CRAWL, to creep along. (Scand.) Spelt crall; Spenser, F. Q. iii. 3. 26. See Cursor Mundi, 6612. Cf. prov. E. craffle, croffl, to crawl.–Icel. krafla, to paw, to scrabble with the hands; krafla fram ūr, to crawl out of; Swed. krafla, to grope; Swed. dial. kralla, to creep on hands and feet; Dan. kravle, to crawl, creep. β. The orig. base is here Teut. *krab-, signifying 'to paw' or 'seize with the hands;' with the frequentative suffix -la; thus giving the sense of 'to grope,' to feel one's way as an infant does when crawling along. Cf. Low G. krabbeln, krawweln, kraulen, to crawl (Schambach).

CRAYFISH, **CRAWFISH**, a species of crab. (F.–OHG.) Spelt craijish in Holland, tr. of Pliny, bk. xxxii. c. 7 (p. 439 b). A mistaken accommodation of ME. crevis or creves, Wars of Alexander, 3864; spelt crevise, Babees Book, ed. Furnivall, p. 158; creveys, Prompt. Parv.–OF. crevisse, given by Roquefort as another spelling of OF. escrevisse, mod. F. écrevisse, a crayfish; Hatzfeld also cites the OF. form crevice.–OHG. crebiz, MHG. krebez, G. krebs, a crayfish, crab; allied to G. krabbe, a crab. See **Crab** (1). ☞ It follows that the etymological division of the word into syllables is as crayf-ish; and thus all connexion with fish disappears.

CRAYON, a pencil of coloured chalk. (F.–L.) In Evelyn's Diary, Sept. 30, 1644. Borrowed from F. crayon, explained by Cotgrave as 'dry-painting, or a painting in dry colours,' &c. Formed with suffix -on from F. craie, chalk.–L. crēta, chalk. See **Cretaceous**.

CRAZE, to break, weaken, derange. (Scand.) ME. crasen, to break, crack. 'I am right siker that the pot was crased,' i.e. cracked; Chaucer, C. T., 16402 (G 934). Allied to crash, but nearer to the original.–Swed. krasa, to crackle; slå i kras, to break in pieces. Ihre also cites Swed. gå i kras, to go to pieces; and the MSwed. kraslig, easily broken; so also Dan. krase, to crackle. ¶ The F. écraser is from the same source; the E. verb was (probably) not borrowed from the French, but directly from Scand.; but the adj. crazy may have been suggested by the F. pp. écrasé, broken. **Der.** craz-y, craz-i-ly, craz-i-ness. Cf. **Crash**.

CREAK, to make a sharp grating sound. (E.) ME. creken. 'He cryeth and he creketh;' Skelton, Colin Clout, l. 19. 'A crowe ... kreked;' Fabyan, Chron. vol. i. c. 213. An imitative word, like Crake and Crack. Cf. EFries. kraken, to creak; as in krakende wagens, creaking wains (Koolman); OHG. chregēn, krekēn, to creak; MDu. kreken, 'to creake,' Hexham; also Du. krekel, a cricket (from its cry).

CREAM, the oily substance which rises in milk. (F.–L.–Gk.) ME. creme, crayme. 'Cowe creme;' Babees Book, ed. Furnivall, p. 266; 'crayme of cowe;' id. 123. Also craym, creem, creyme, P. Plowm. A. vii. 269; B. vi. 284; C. ix. 306.–OF. cresme, F. crème, cream. Really the same word as OF. cresme (F. chrême), chrism.–L. chrisma.

—Gk. χρῖσμα; see **Chrism**. ¶ Derived in late times from L. *cremor*, by error; whence *cremor lactis*, and even *crema lactis* (Ducange); but the guess was a wrong one. **Der.** *cream*, verb; *cream-y, cream-i-ness*. **Doublet**, *chrism*.

CREASE (1), a wrinkle, small fold. (F.—L.) Richardson well remarks that 'this word so common in speech, is rare in writing.' He quotes an extract containing it from Swift, Thoughts on Various Subjects. Also: 'The *creses* here are excellent good; the proportion of the chin good;' Sir Gyles Goosecappe (1606), Act ii. sc. 1; a quotation which seems to refer to a portrait. Phillips (in 1706) has *crease*, a fold; and the word is noted by Skinner (1671). But the earliest spelling is *creast*. In Lyte's tr. of Dodoens, bk. vi. c. 40, a peach-stone is said to be 'ful of *creastes* [i.e. crests, ridges] and gutters.' Hence Phillips (in 1658) has '*Creast-tile*, a roof-tile, which is made to lay upon the ridge of a house ;' whence prov. E. *crease*, 'a ridge-tile;' E.D.D. Suggested by OF. *cresté*, crested; also, wrinkled or ruffled, in speaking of the surface of water; the form is Walloon, which has *kress*, a crest, a ridge, &c. (Remacle); cf. mod. Prov. *crest, creis*, a ridge. Thus *crease* is a doublet of *crest*; see **Crest**. Cf. Notes on E. Etym. p. 49. ¶ For the spelling *creast*, a crest, see Caxton, Morte Darthur, bk. v. c. 5. l. 66.

CREASE (2), **CREESE**, a Malay dagger. (Malay.) 'Four hundred young men, who were privately armed with *cryzes*;' Sir T. Herbert, Travels, ed. 1665; p. 68. — Malay *kris* or *kris*, 'a dagger, poignard, kris, or creese;' Marsden's Malay Dict., 1812, p. 258.

CREATE, to make, produce, form. (L.) Orig. a past part. 'Whan our lord hadde *creat* Adam ;' Chaucer, C. T., B 2293. 'Since Adam was *create* ;' Gascoigne, Dan Bartholomew, His Last Will, l. 3. Cf. K. John, iv. 1. 107.—L. *creātus*, pp. of *creāre*, to create, make. β. Related to Skt. *kṛ*, to make, causal *kārayāmi*, I cause to be performed. Brugmann, i. § 641. **Der.** *creat-ion, -ive, -or*; also *creat-ure* (OF. *creature*, L. *creātūra*), a sb. in early use, viz. in Hampole, Pricke of Conscience, l. 38, King Alisaunder, 6948.

CREED, a belief. (L.) ME. *crede*, Ancren Riwle, p. 20; and frequently *credo*, O. Eng. Homilies, ed. Morris, i. 75. An AS. form *creda* is given in Lye and Bosworth.—L. *crēdo*, I believe, the first word of the Latin version of the Apostles' and Nicene Creeds; from L. *crēdere*, to believe.✝OIrish *cretim*, I believe; Skt. *çraddadhāmi*, I believe; cf. *çraddhā*, faith; both from the base *çrat*. Brugmann, i. § 539. **Der.** From the L. *crēdere* we have also *cred-ence*, Gower, C. A. i. 249, bk. ii. 2677 (OF. *credence*, Late L. *crēdentia*, from the pres. part. *crēdent-*); *cred-ent, -ent-i-al*; *cred-i-ble* (Gower, C. A. i. 23), *cred-i-bil-i-ty, -i-ble-ness, -i-bl-y*; also *credit* (from L. pp. *crēditus*), *credit-able, -abl-y, -able-ness, -or*; also *credulous* (L. *crēdulus*, by change of *-us* into *-ous*), *-ly, -ness*; and *credul-i-ty* (F. *credulité*, Englished by *credulity* in Cotgrave, from L. acc. *crēdulitātem*, nom. *crēdulitās*).

CREEK, an inlet, cove, nook, bend. (MDu.?) Cf. Du. *kreek*, a creek; MDu. *krēke* (Franck); whence the Tudor E. *creke*, mod. E. *creek*, was probably derived. We also find ME. *cryke*, Chaucer, C. T. prol. 411; *krike* in Havelok, 708. — OF. *crique*, a creek, bay (Supp. to Godefroy). — Swed. dial. *krik*, a bend, nook, corner, creek, cove (Rietz); Icel. *kriki*, a crack, nook; cf. *handarkriki*, the arm-pit; Dan. dial. *krig*, a turn, bend, bending in. β. Possibly W. *crig*, a crack, *crigyll*, a ravine, creek, are from ME. The Swed. dial. *armkrik* also means the bend of the arm, elbow (Rietz); but the orig. form and sense are alike obscure. See **Crick**. **Der.** *creek-y*.

CREEL, a large wicker basket. (F.—L.) 'Crelle, baskett;' Prompt. Parv. The pl. *crelis* occurs in Wyntown, Chron. VIII. xxxviii. 51 (N.E.D.). Lowland Sc. *creil*.—OF. *creil* (Lacurne); given also in Ducange, s.v. *cleia*, to translate L. *crātes*, a hurdle.— Late L. **crāticulum*, neuter; just as F. *grille* is from Late L. *crāticula*. Dimin. of L. *crātes*, a hurdle. See Notes on E. Etym., p. 51.

CREEP, to crawl, as a snake, &c. (E.) ME. *crepen, creopen*; Ancren Riwle, p. 292. AS. *crēopan*, Grein, i. 169. ✝ Du. *kruipen*, to creep, crawl; Icel. *krjūpa*; Swed. *krypa*; Dan. *krybe*. Teut. type **kreupan-*, pt. t. **kraup*, pp. **krupanoz*. **Der.** *creep-er*.

CREESE, a Malay dagger; see **Crease** (2).

CREMATION, burning, esp. of the dead. (L.) Used by Sir T. Browne, Urn Burial, c. 1.—L. *cremātiōnem*, acc. of *cremātio*, a burning; cf. *cremātus*, pp. of *cremāre*, to burn.

CRENATE, notched, edged with leaves. (L.) A botanical term. Formed as if from L. **crēnātus*, notched (not used), from Late L. *crēna* (Ital. *crena*), a notch. See **Cranny**.

CRENELLATE, to furnish with a parapet, to fortify. (Late L.—F.—L.) See List of Royal Licences to *Crenellate*, or Fortify; Parker's Eng. Archæologist's Handbook, p. 233. — Late L. *crēnellāre*, whence F. *creneler*, 'to imbattle ;' Cotgrave. — Late L. *crenellus*, a parapet, battlement; [OF. *crenel*, later *creneau*, a battlement; dimin. of OF. *cren, cran*, a notch]; from Late L. *crēna*, a notch (above). See **Cranny**.

CREOLE, one born in the West Indies, but of European or foreign blood. (F.—Span.—L.) See the quotations in Todd's Johnson.

—F. *créole*.—Span. *criollo*, a native of America or the W. Indies; a corrupt word, made by the negroes; said to be a contraction of *criadillo*, the dimin. of *criado*, one educated, instructed, or bred up, pp. of *criar*, lit. to create, but commonly also to bring up, nurse, breed, educate, instruct. Hence the sense is 'a little nursling.'—L. *creāre*, to create. See **Create**. ¶ Cf. Span. *criadilla*, a worthless servant-maid, dimin. of *criada*, a servant-maid.

CREOSOTE, a liquid distilled from wood-tar. (Gk.) Discovered in 1832; so called because it has the quality of preserving flesh from corruption; lit. 'flesh-preserver.'—Gk. κρεο-, for κρέας, flesh (allied to L. *caro*, flesh); and σωτ-, shortened from σωτήρ, a preserver, from σώζειν, to save, preserve. (Incorrectly formed.)

CREPITATE, to crackle. (L.) Medical.—L. *crepitātus*, pp. of *crepitāre*, to crackle, rattle; frequentative of *crepāre*, to rattle. **Der.** *crepitat-ion*. See **Crevice**.

CREPUSCULAR, pertaining to twilight. (L.) First in 1668. —L. *crepuscul-um*, twilight; with suffix *-ar*. Allied to Sabine *creper*, dark (Varro).

CRESCENT, the increasing moon. (L.) Properly an adj. signifying 'increasing;' Hamlet, i. 3. 11.—L. *crescent-*, stem of *crescens*, pres. pt. of *crescere* (pp. *crētus*), to increase, to grow; an inchoative verb formed with suffix *-sc-*, allied to *cre-āre*, to create, make. See **Create**. **Der.** From the base of pp. *crēt-us* we have the derivatives *ac-cret-ion, con-crete*. The Ital. *crescendo*, increasing, a musical term, is equivalent to *crescent*. ¶ It must be added that the spelling *crescent* is an accommodated one. The word was formerly spelt *cressent* or *cressaunt*. We find '*Cressaunt*, lunula' in the Prompt. Parv. p. 102. This is not from the Latin immediately, but from OF. *creissaunt*, pres. part. of OF. *creistre*, to grow, from L. *crescere*. It comes to the same at last, but makes a difference chronologically. Cf. 'a *cressant*, or halfe moone, *croissant* ;' Sherwood's Index to Cotgrave; '*cressent*, the newe mone, *cressant* ;' Palsgrave.

CRESS, the name of several plants of the genus *Cruciferæ*. (E.) ME. *cresse, cres*; also spelt *kerse, kers, carse*, by shifting of the letter *r*, a common phenomenon in English; cf. mod. E. *bird* with ME. *brid*. 'Wisdom and witte now is nought worth a *carse*;' P. Plowman, B. x. 17, where 4 MSS. read *kerse*. '*Cresse*, herbe, nasturtium;' Prompt. Parv. p. 102. 'Anger gaynez [avails] the not a *cresse*;' Allit. Poems, ed. Morris, i. 343. ['Not worth a *cress*' or 'not worth a *kers*' was a common old proverb, now turned into the meaningless 'not worth a *curse*.'] AS. *cærse, cerse, cressæ*; see numerous references in Cockayne's Leechdoms, iii. 316. Cf. the entry 'nasturtium, *tūn-kerse*,' i.e. town-cress, in Ælfric's Glossary; Voc. 135. 36. ✝ Du. *kers*, cress; G. *kresse*, water-cresses; OHG. *cressa* (whence F. *cresson*, according to Hatzfeld). Teut. type **kras-jōn-* (Franck); from **kras*, 2nd grade of **kres-*, as in OHG. *cresan, chresan*, to creep. Hence the sense is 'creeper.'

CRESSET, an open lamp, placed on a beacon or carried on a pole. (F.—L.) '*Cresset*, crucibollum;' Prompt. Parv. p. 102. 'A lyht brennende in a *kressette*;' Gower, C. A. iii. 217; bk. vii. 3743. —OF. *cresset, craisset*, a cresset. β. A glance at a picture of a *cresset*, in Webster's Dict. or elsewhere, will show that it consisted, in fact, of an open iron cup at the top of a pole; and the cup was filled with burning grease or oil; whence the name.—OF. *craisse* (F. *graisse*), grease; Hatzfeld.—Folk L. **crassia*, grease; from L. *crassus*, thick, dense. So also Walloon *craché*, a cresset; from *crache*, grease. See **Grease, Crass**.

CREST, a tuft on a cock's head, plume, &c. (F.—L.) ME. *creste, crest*; Chaucer, C. T. 13834 (B 2096).—OF. *creste*, 'a crest, cop, combe, tuft;' Cot.—L. *crista*, a comb or tuft on a bird's head, a crest. **Der.** *crest*, verb, *crest-less*; *crest-fallen*, i.e. with fallen or sunken crest, dejected. Doublet, *crease* (1).

CRETACEOUS, chalky. (L.) It occurs in J. Philips, Cyder, bk. i. l. 54; first printed in 1708.—L. *crētāceus*, chalky; by change of *-us* to *-ous*, as in *credulous*, &c.—L. *crēta*, chalk; generally explained to mean Cretan earth, but this is hardly the *origin* of the word. See **Crayon**.

CRÉTIN, a deformed idiot, chiefly in the Swiss Alps. (F.—L.—Gk.) First in 1779.—F. *crétin*, which in Swiss patois means (1) Christian, (2) a Christian being, one who is not a brute animal merely.—L. acc. *Christiānum*; from *Christus*, Christ.—Gk. Χριστός; see **Christ**.

CRETONNE, a kind of stout unglazed cloth. (F.) Modern.— F. *cretonne*, a fabric orig. made at *Creton*, a village in Normandy (Hatzfeld).

CREVICE, a crack, cranny. (F.—L.) ME. *crevice*, but also *crevace*. Spelt *creuisse* (with *u* for *v*), Gawain and the Grene Knight, ed. Morris, 2183; *crevace*, Chaucer, Ho. of Fame, iii. 996.—AF. *crevace* (see quot. in Hatzfeld); MF. *crevasse*, 'a crevice, chink, rift, cleft;' Cot. (Late L. *crepātia*).—OF. (and F.) *crever*, 'to burst or break asunder, to chink, rive, cleave, or chawn;' id.—L.

crepāre, to crackle, rattle; also, to burst asunder; a word possibly of imitative origin. **Doublet**, *crevasse*.

CREW, a company of people. (F.—L.) Formerly *crue*; Gascoigne, The Fruits of Warre, st. 46; 'If she be one of Cressid's *crue*;' Turberville, His Love flitted from wonted Troth; st. 15. Common as a sea-term, 'a ship's crew.' First used in 1455, Parliament Rolls, v. 297; where 300 men are 'ordeigned for a *crue* over the ordinary charge' at Calais. The earliest sense was a reinforcement; later, a company sent on an expedition; and lastly, a company (generally). 'The Frensh kynge sent soone after into Scotlande a *crewe* of Frenshemen, to ayde suche enemyes as kyng Edwarde there had;' Fabyan's Chron. ed. Ellis, p. 444. *A crewe* is a corrupt substitution for *acrewe, accrewe*, or *accrue*, the obsolete sb. from which the verb to *accrue* is derived. Thus Holinshed (Chron. iii. 1135) has: 'The towne of Calis and the forts thereabouts were not supplied with anie new *accrewes* [reinforcements] of soldiors.' —OF. *acreue, accrue,* s. f. augmentation, reinforcement; Godefroy. —OF. *acreue,* fem. of pp. of *acroistre,* to augment (Supp. to Godefroy). —L. *accrescere,* to increase. —L. *ac-,* for *ad,* to, in addition; *crescere,* to grow. See **Accrue, Accretion.**

CREWEL, worsted yarn slackly twisted. (F.—Teut.) In King Lear, ii. 4. 7. Halliwell explains it by 'fine worsted, formerly much in use for fringe, garters, &c.' The Whitby Gloss. has '*creeals* or *crules,* coloured worsteds for ornamental needle-work, &c.' Palsgrave has: 'Caddas or crule, *sayette*.' The earliest mention of *crules* is in Test. Eboracensia, ii. 100 (an. 1444). Generally in the pl. *crewels,* prob. at first applied to the hanks or skeins, of which there were many, of different colours. —OF. *escrouelles (de laine),* portions of wool (Godefroy); dimin. of OF. *escroe, escroue,* a shred. See **Escrow.** See Phil. Soc. Trans. 1905; p. 251.

CRIB, a manger, rack, stall, cradle. (E.) ME. *crib, cribbe*; Ormulum, 3321; Cursor Mundi, 11237. AS. *crib, cryb*; Grein, i. 169. **+** OSax. *kribbia*; see **Cratch**; Du. *krib,* a crib, manger; OHG. *krippha,* MHG. *kripfe,* G. *krippe,* a crib, manger. Cf. also Icel. and Swed. *krubba,* Dan. *krybbe,* a crib. Perhaps allied to MHG. *krebe,* a basket; but distinct from Du. *korf,* G. *korb,* if these are from L. *corbis.* **Der.** *crib,* verb, to put into a crib, hence, to confine; also to hide away in a crib, hence, to purloin; from the latter sense is *crib-age,* in which the *crib* is the secret store of cards.

CRICK, a spasmodic affection of the neck. (E.) '*Crykke,* sekenesse, spasmus;' Prompt. Parv. p. 103. 'Those also that with a *cricke* or cramp have their necks drawne backward;' Holland, tr. of Pliny, b. xx. c. 5. Allied to prov. E. *crink,* a bend, a crick in the neck (E.D.D.); which answers to Norw. *krenk,* a twist, sprain; which again is allied to *crank* (1). See **Crinkle.**

CRICKET (1), a shrill-voiced insect. (F.—Du.) '*Crykette,* salamandra, crillus;' Prompt. Parv. p. 103. Spelt *crykett,* P. Plowman, C. xvi. 243. —OF. *crequet, criquet,* a cricket, Supp. to Godefroy; a diminutive form. —OF. *criquer,* 'to creake, rattle,' Cot.; a word of Germanic origin, being an attenuated form of F. *craquer,* 'to cracke, creake,' id. See **Creak, Crack.** The Germanic word is preserved in Du. *kriek,* a cricket, and in the E. *creak,* sometimes written *crick* (N.E.D.); also in the Du. *krikkrakken,* to crackle, and MDu. *kricken,* 'to creake or to crack,' Hexham. Cf. prov. E. *cracket, creaker,* a cricket.

CRICKET (2), a game with bat and ball. (F.—Du.) The word *cricket-ball* occurs in The Rambler, no. 30. Cotgrave translates the F. *crosse* as 'a crosier or bishop's staffe; also a *cricket-staffe,* or the crooked staff wherewith boies play at *cricket*.' The first mention of *cricket* is in 1598; it was a development of the older game of *club-ball,* which was played with a crooked stick, and was something like the modern *hockey*; see Engl. Cycl. Supplement to Arts and Sciences, col. 653. —OF. *criquet,* 'bâton servant de but au jeu de boule' (Godefroy); so that the *criquet* was practically the wicket. Godefroy has a quotation of 1478: 'Le suppliant arriva en ung lieu ou on jouoit a la boulle, pres d'une atache [vine-stake] ou *criquet*.'—MDu. *krick, kricke,* a crutch (Hexham). Cf. AS. *cricc, crycc,* a crutch, staff. See **Crutch. Der.** *cricket-er.*

CRICOID, adj., applied to the ring-shaped cartilage forming a part of the larynx. (Gk.) First in 1746. —Mod. L. *cricoides,* transcription of Gk. κρικοειδής, ring-shaped. —Gk. κρίκο-, for κρίκος or κίρκος, a ring; and εἶδος, form. See **Circus.**

CRIME, an offence against law, sin. (F.—L.) ME. *crime, cryme*; Chaucer, C. T., D 1307. —F. *crime,* 'a crime, fault;' Cot. —L. *crimen,* an accusation, charge, fault, offence. Generally connected with L. *cernere,* to sift, and the Gk. κρίνειν, to separate, decide, whence κρῖμα, κρίμα, a decision. **Der.** From the stem *crimin-* of L. *crimen,* we have *crimin-al, -al-ly, -al-i-ty, -ate, -at-ion, -at-or-y.*

CRIMP, to wrinkle, corrugate, make crisp. (E.) Often used in cookery, as 'to *crimp* a skate;' see N.E.D. The frequentative *crimple,* to rumple, wrinkle, occurs in the Prompt. Parv. p. 103. It

answers to an AS. **crempan,* EFries. *krempan,* causal derivative of **Cramp.** Or to AS. *crympan,* from the weak grade; cf. 'Calamistratis, *gecrymptum*;' Voc. 378. 26. Cf. Du. *krimpen,* to shrink, shrivel, diminish; Swed. *krympa,* to shrink, active and neuter; Dan. *krympe sig sammen,* to shrink oneself together; G. *krimpen,* to crumple, to shrink cloth. β. The orig. strong verb appears as EFries. and Du. *krimpen,* Swed. dial. *krimpa,* OHG. *krimfan*; Teut. type **krempan-* (*krimpan-*), to draw oneself together, to shrink up; pt. t. **kramp*; pp. **krumpanoz.* See **Cramp** and **Crumple. Der.** *crimp-le.*

CRIMSON, a deep red colour. (F.—Arab.—Skt.) ME. *crimosine,* Gascoigne, Steel Glass, l. 767; *crimosin,* Berners, tr. of Froissart, vol. ii. c. 157 (R.); spelt *crammysyn,* G. Douglas, Prol. to xii Book of Eneados, l. 15; *cremesin,* Caxton, Troy-book, leaf 74, l. 28. —OF. *cramoisin, cramoisi* (F. *cramoisi*); see Supp. to Godefroy; cf. Late L. *cramoisinus,* crimson. The correct L. form appears in the Late L. *carmesinus,* crimson (Span. *carmesi,* Ital. *chermisi*); so called from the *kermes* or cochineal insect with which it was dyed. —Arab. and Persian *qirmisī,* crimson; *qirmiz,* crimson; see Palmer's Pers. Dict. col. 470. —Skt. *kṛmi(s),* a worm, an insect. β. The colour was so called because produced by the cochineal-insect; see **Cochineal.** The Skt. *kṛmi(s)* is cognate with Irish *cruim* and W. *pryf,* a worm. *Carmine* is a doublet of *crimson*; see **Carmine.**

CRINGE, to bend, crouch, fawn. (E.) Used by Shak. in the sense of to distort one's face; Ant. and Cleop. iii. 13. 100; cf. *crinkle,* to wrinkle, which is related to *cringe.* ME. *crengen*; 'he *crengit*,' he cringed; Holland, The Houlate, l. 956. A causal derivative of AS. *cringan, crincgan, crincan,* to sink in battle, fall, succumb; Grein, i. 169; and see Sweet's A. S. Reader. Thus *cringe* is a causative of *cring,* and *cring* is a by-form of *crink,* with the sense of 'to bend' or 'to give way;' further related to *crank.* See **Crank** (2). Cf. EFries. *krengen,* to lay on its side, careen (a ship). **Der.** *crink-le,* q.v.

CRINGLE, a ring worked into the bolt-rope of a sail. (Low G.) '*Cringle,* a kind of wrethe or ring wrought into a rope for the convenience of fastening another rope to it;' Ash's Dict., ed. 1775. In Falconer's Shipwreck (1762), c. iii. l. 330. —Low G. *kringel,* a ring (Lübben); EFries. *kringel.* Allied to Icel. *kringla,* a circle, orb, disk (hence, simply a circle or ring); cf. *kringlöttr,* circular, *kringar,* pl., the pulleys of a drag-net. Cf. *kring,* adv., around, *kringja,* to encircle, surround; Swed. *kring,* prep., around about; Du. *kring,* a circle, circuit, orb, sphere. Allied to **Crinkle, Cringe,** and **Crank** (1).

CRINITE, hairy. (L.) 'How comate, crinite, caudate stars are framed;' Fairfax, tr. of Tasso, bk. xiv. st. 44. —L. *crīnītus,* having long hair. —L. *crini-,* for *crinis,* hair.

CRINKLE, to rumple slightly, wrinkle. (E.) 'Her face all bowsy, Comely *crynklyd*;' Skelton, Elynour Rummyng, l. 18. Cf. *crincled,* full of twists or turnings, Chaucer, Legend of Good Women, 2012. Formed by adding *-le,* the common frequentative termination, to the base *crinc-* of the AS. strong verb *crincan,* to give way, bend in, fall in a heap. See **Cringe.** Thus *crink-le* is to bend frequently, to make full of bends or turns. Cf. Dan. *krinkelgange,* meanderings (Larsen). Compare **Crimple.**

CRINOLINE, a lady's stiff skirt. (F.—L.) Formerly made of hair-cloth. —F. *crinoline,* (1) hair-cloth; (2) crinoline; an artificial word. —F. *crin,* hair, esp. horse-hair, from L. *crīnem,* acc. of *crinis,* hair; and *lin,* flax, hence, thread, from L. *linum,* flax. See **Crinite** and **Linen.**

CRIPPLE, one who has not the full use of his limbs. (E.) ME. *crupel, crepel, cripel*; see Cursor Mundi, 13106. An AS. word, but the traces of it are not very distinct; spelt *crypel* in the Lindisfarne MS., Luke, v. 24, as a gloss to *paralyticus.* Lit. 'a creeper.'—AS. *crup-* (with vowel-change from *u* to *y*), weak grade of *crēopan,* to creep; see **Creep.** The suffix *-el* (for *-ilo-*) denotes the agent. **+** Du. *kreupel,* adj. crippled, lame (cf. *kruipelings,* creepingly, by stealth), *kruipen,* to creep; OFrisian *kreppel,* a cripple; Icel. *kryppill,* also *kryplingr,* a cripple; Dan. *kröbling,* a cripple; cf. Dan. *krybe,* to creep; G. *krüppel,* a cripple; cf. MHG. *krūfen,* to creep. β. The suffix has the same active force as in AS. *byd-el,* i.e. one who proclaims. The AS. *crēopere,* lit. 'creeper,' likewise means a cripple; Ælfric's Saints' Lives, vi. 20. **Der.** *cripple,* verb.

CRISIS, a decisive point or moment. (Gk.) 'This hour's the very *crisis* of your fate;' Dryden, Spanish Friar (Todd's Johnson); and in Minsheu (1627). —Gk. κρίσις, a separating, discerning, decision, crisis. —Gk. κρίνειν, to decide, separate; allied to L. *cernere,* to sift. See **Critic.**

CRISP, wrinkled, curled. (L.) ME. *crisp,* Wyclif, Judith, xvi. 10. Also *crips,* by change of *sp* to *ps,* a phenomenon due to the more frequent converse change of *ʃs* into *sp,* as in *aspen, clasp,* which see. *Crips* is in Chaucer, Ho. of Fame, iii. 296. In very early use; the

AS. *crisp* occurs in the tr. of Beda, v. 2 (near the end).—L. *crispus*, curled; allied to W. *crych*, rumpled; see Brugmann, i. § 565 (3). Der. *crisp-ly*, *-ness*.

CRISTATE, crested. (L.) First in 1661.—L. *cristātus*, furnished with a crest.—L. *crista*, a crest. See **Crest**.

CRITIC, a judge, in literature or art. (L.—Gk.) In Shak. L. L. L. iii. 178.—L. *criticus*.—Gk. κριτικός, able to discern; cf. κριτής, a judge.—Gk. κρίνειν, to judge. See **Crisis**. Der. *critic-al* (Oth. ii. 1. 120); *-ise*, *-is-m*; *critique* (F. *critique*, from Gk. κριτικός). From the same source is *criterion*, Gk. κριτήριον, a test.

CROAK, to make a low hoarse sound. (E.) In Macbeth, i. 5. 40. Spenser has *croking*; Epithalamion, l. 349. From a theoretical AS. *crācian*, to croak; represented only by its derivative *crǣcetung*, a croaking; the expression *hrǣfena crǣcetung*, the croaking of ravens, occurs in the Life of St. Guthlac, cap. viii. ed. Goodwin, p. 48. β. Of imitative origin; allied to *crake*, *creak*, *crow*, which see. Cf. Swed. *krǎka*, a crow; L. *grāc-ulus*, a jackdaw. Der. *croak-er*.

CROCHET, lit. a little hook. (F.—Late L.) Modern. Applied to work done by means of a small hook.—F. *crochet*, a little crook or hook; dimin., with suffix *-et*, from F. *croche*, variant of *croc*, a crook. See **Crotchet**.

CROCK, a pitcher. (C.) ME. *crokke*, *crok*; the dat. case *crocke* occurs in the Ancren Riwle, p. 214. AS. *crocca*, as a gloss to *olla* in Ps. lix. 8; ed. Spelman. [OFries. *krocha*, a pitcher; Du. *kruik*; Icel. *krukka*; Swed. *kruka*; Dan. *krukke*; OHG. *chruac*, MHG. *kruoc*, G. *krug*.] Yet, notwithstanding the wide spread of the word, it was probably originally Celtic.—OIrish *crocan*, Irish *crogan*, Gael. *crog*, a pitcher, jar; W. *crochan*, a pot. + Gk. κρωσσός (for *κρωκ-γός), a pitcher. Der. *crock-er*, a potter, now obsolete, but occurring in Wyclif, Ps. ii. 9; also *crock-e-ry*, a collective sb., made in imitation of F. words in *-rie*; cf. *nunnery*, *spicery*.

CROCKET, an architectural ornament. (F.—Late L.) ME. *croket*, a roll of hair; R. Brunne, Handlyng Synne, l. 3208.—AF. *croket*, Wm. of Wadington, Manuel des Peches, l. 3305; NorthF. form of F. *crochet*; see **Crochet**. Doublets, *crochet*, *crotchet*, *croquet*.

CROCODILE, an alligator. (F.—L.—Gk.) In Hamlet, v. 1. 299.—F. *crocodile*, 'a crocodile;' Cot.—L. *crocodīlus*.—Gk. κροκόδειλος, a lizard (an Ionic form, Herod. ii. 69); hence, an alligator, from its resemblance to a lizard. Origin unknown. ☞ The ME. form was *cokedrill*, King Alisaunder, 5720; from the corrupt Late L. *cocodrillus*.

CROCUS, the name of a flower. (L.—Gk.) In Milton, P. L. iv. 701.—L. *crocus*.—Gk. κρόκος, the crocus; saffron. Cf. Skt. *kuṅkuma-*, saffron. β. Apparently of Semitic origin; cf. Heb. *karkōm*, saffron; Arab. *karkam* or *kurkum*, saffron; Richardson's Dict. p. 1181.

CROFT, a small field. (E.) ME. *croft*, P. Plowman, B. v. 581; vi. 33. AS. *croft*, a field; Kemble's Codex Diplomaticus, 1257; vol. vi. p. 79, l. 10. + Du. *kroft*, a hillock; MDu. *krochte*, *crocht*, a field on the downs, high and dry land; also MDu. *kroft*, *krocht*, high and dry land (Oudemans). [This is quite a different word from the MDu. *krochte*, when used in the sense of *crytt*; see **Crypt**.] ¶ The mod. Gael. *croit*, a croft, small piece of arable ground, is borrowed from E.

CROMLECH, a structure of large stones, in which a flat stone rests upon upright ones. (W.) Merely borrowed from Welsh.—W. *cromlech*, an incumbent flagstone; compounded of *crom*, bending, bowed (hence, laid across); and *llech*, a flat stone, flag-stone.

CRONE, an old woman. (F.—L.) In Chaucer, C. T. 4852 (B 432). Shortened from Picard *carone*, carrion, an old worn-out horse (Corblet); answering to F. *carogne*, a contemptuous term for a woman (Hatzfeld), *charogne*. carrion. See **Carrion**. β. Tusser has *crone* in the sense of 'an old ewe.'—MDu. *kronie*, *karonie*, an old sheep.—Picard *carone* (as above).

CRONY, an intimate associate. (Gk.?) 'Jack Cole, . . who was a great *chrony* of mine;' Pepys, Diary, May 30, 1665 (N.E.D.). Said by Skinner, in 1671, to be 'vox academica,' i.e. university slang; and Butler (Hudibras, pt. III. c. 2. l. 1269) rhymes *cronies* with *monies*. Perhaps for Gk. χρόνιος, a 'long-lasting' friend.—Gk. χρόνος, time; see **Chronicle**.

CROOK, a hook, bend, bent staff. (Scand.) ME. *crōk*; the pl. *crokes* is in the Ancren Riwle, p. 174.—Icel. *krókr*, a hook, bend, winding; Swed. *krok*, a hook, bend, angle; Dan. *krog*, a hook, crook; *kroge*, to crook, to hook; *kroget*, crooked. Prob. allied to OHG. *chracho*, a crook; from a base *krak*, 2nd grade *krōk*. Perhaps allied to *crank*, but without the nasal; cf. *crick*. ¶ The Gael. *crocan*, a crook, is from Scand. or E. Der. *crook*, verb; *crook-ed*, *-ed-ly*, *-ed-ness*; also *crock-et*, q.v.

CROON, to hum, to utter a low, deep sound. (MDu. or Low G.) Douglas has *croyn* (L. *mūgīre*), tr. of Virgil, bk. vi. § 4. l. 40.—MDu.

krōnen (Du. *kreunen*), to groan, murmur (see Franck); Low G. *krōnen* (Lübben). Of imitative origin.

CROP, the top of a plant, the craw of a bird. (E.) ME. *croppe*, *crop*. In Chaucer, prol. l. 7, 'the tendre *croppes*' means 'the tender upper shoots of plants.' To *crop off* is to take off the top; whence *crop* in the sense of what is reaped, a harvest. AS. *cropp*, *crop*; as a gloss to 'cima;' Voc. 149. 13. We find *cropp* as a gloss to *spica* (ear of corn), Luke, vi. 1; Northumbrian version. In Levit. i. 16, we have 'wurp þone *cropp*,' i.e. throw away the bird's crop. The orig. sense seems to have been that which sticks up or out, a protuberance, bunch. + Du. *krop*, a bird's crop; *kroppen*, to cram, to grow to a round head; G. *kropf*, a crop, craw; Icel. *kroppr*, a hunch or bump on the body; Swed. *kropp*, Dan. *krop*, the trunk of the body. Cf. Gk. βρέφος; Brugmann, i. § 421 (7). β. Also in the Celtic languages; W. *cropa*, the crop, or craw of a bird (from E.); Gael. and Irish *sgroban*, the crop of a bird. Der. *crop-full*, Milton, L'Allegro, 113; *crop*, verb; *crop out*, verb, i.e. to bunch out, stick out. Doublet, *croup* (2).

CROQUET, a game with mallets, balls, posts, and hoops. (F.—Late L.) Noticed in N. and Q. 3 S. iv. 349, 439, v. 494 (1863, 1864). Introduced into Ireland about 1835, and into England in 1852. Of F. origin.—NormanF. (dialect) *croquet*, variant of F. *crochet*, a crook (Moisy); also a hooked stick (Hatzfeld); used in some F. dialects with the sense of hockey-stick (N.E.D.). The N.E.D. refers to Dr. Prior's Notes on Croquet (1872). See **Crotchet**. Doublets, *crochet*, *crotchet*.

CRORE, ten millions (of rupees). (Hind.—Skt.) See Yule.—Hind. *kror*, *karor*, ten millions; Wilson, p. 297, col. 2. From the Prakrit form (*kroḍi*) of Skt. *koṭi*, highest point, ten millions.

CROSIER, a staff with a curved top. (F.—Late L.) 'Because a *crosier*-staff is best for such a *crooked* time;' Gascoigne, Flowers: Richard Courtop, &c., last line. Spelt *crocer*, *croser*, *croycer*, *croyser* in the MSS. of P. Plowman, C. vi. 113. Made by adding the F. suffix *-ier* to the sb. *croce*, also signifying a crosier or bishop's staff, P. Plowman, C. xi. 92. The 19th line of Chaucer's Freres Tale alludes to a bishop catching offenders 'with his *hook*.' Moreover, *crosier* (as now used) is practically short for *crosier-staff*, i.e. the staff carried by the 'crosier' or crook-bearer.—OF. *crossier*, one who carries a *crosse* (Godefroy).—OF. *crosse*, 'a crosier, a bishop's staff;' Cot.; spelt *croce* in the Chanson de Roland, 1670. Mod. F. *crosse*, a crosier.—Late L. type *croccea; cf. Late L. *crocia*, *crochia*, a curved stick, a bishop's staff (Ducange).—OF. *croc*, a crook, hook.—Late L. *croccum*, acc. of *croccus*, a hook. ¶ The usual derivation from *cross* is historically wrong; but, as ME. *croce*, a crook, and *cross* were easily confused, the mistake was often made. Still the fact remains, that the true shape of the *crosier* was with a hooked or curved top; the archbishop's staff alone bore a cross instead of a crook, and was of exceptional, not of regular form. See my note to P. Plowman, C. xi. 92. 'Many 19th century ecclesiastical antiquaries have erroneously transferred the name *crosier* to the cross borne before an archbishop;' N.E.D.

CROSS, the instrument of the Passion. (C.—L.) ME. *cros*, Layamon's Brut, iii. 261. AS. *cros*, as in *Normannes cros*, in Birch, Cart. Sax. iii. 367 (A.D. 963-984).—OIrish *cros*; in the glossary to Leabhar Breac, ed. Atkinson; [cf. Irish *cros*, a cross, a hindrance; *crosaim*, I cross, stop, hinder; *crosanach*, cross, perverse]; Gael. *crois*, a cross, W. *croes*. All from L. *crux*, a cross, orig. a gibbet. Der. *cross*, adj. transverse, perverse, *cross-ly*, *-ness*, *-bill*, *-bow*, &c.; *cross-ing*, *-wise*, *-let*; also *crusade*, q. v.

CROTCHET, a term in music; a whim. (F.—Late L.) ME. *crochet*; 'crochett of songe;' Prompt. Parv. The sense of 'whim' seems derived from that of 'tune' or 'air,' from the arrangement of *crotchets* composing the air. 'As a good harper stricken far in years Into whose cunning hands the gout doth fall, All his old *crotchets* in his brain he bears, But on his harp plays ill, or not at all;' Davies, Immortality of the Soul. § 32.—F. *crochet*, 'a small hooke . . . also, a quaver in musick;' Cotgrave; who also has: '*Crochue*, a quaver in Musicke, whence *il a des crochues en teste*, his head is full of crotchets.' Dimin. of F. *croc*, 'a grapple, or great hooke;' id.— Late L. *croccum*, acc. of *croccus*, a hook. Der. *crotchet-y*. Doublets, *croche*, *crochet*, *croquet*. Cf. *crosier*, *crouch*.

CROTON, the name of a genus of plants. (Gk.) Modern.—Gk. κρότων, a tick, which the seed of the croton resembles (Webster). Liddell and Scott give κρότων or κροτών, a dog-louse, tick; also, the palma Christi or thorn bearing the castor-berry (from the likeness of this to a tick) whence is produced *croton* and castor oil. The N.E.D. gives κροτών, a tick, also the castor-oil plant (*Ricinus communis*), taken in botany as the name of an allied genus.

CROUCH, to bend down, squat, cower. (F.—Late L.) ME. *crouchen*, to bend down, stoop; 'thei so lowe *crouchen*;' Piers the Plowman's Crede, ed. Skeat, 302; cf. l. 751.—OF. *crochir*, to become crooked; Godefroy; cf. OF. and F. *crochu*, crooked. = F. *croche, croc*, a hook. = Late L. *croccum*, acc. of *croccus*, a hook.

CROUP (1), an inflammatory affection of the larynx. (E.) Lowland Scotch *croup*, the disease; also *croup, crowp*, to croak, to cry with a hoarse voice, to speak hoarsely; Jamieson. Allied to *crope*, which is synonymous. 'The ropeen of the rauynis gart the crans *crope*' = the croaking of the ravens made the cranes *croup*; Complaint of Scotland, ch. vi. ed. Murray, p. 39. All of imitative origin; associated with *crow, croak*, and also with Sc. *roup*, AS. *hrópan*, to cry, call aloud; Grein, ii. 108; Icel. *hrópa*, to call out; Goth. *hróp-jan*, to call out; Du. *roepen*; G. *rufen*, to call.

CROUP (2), the hinder parts of a horse, back of a saddle. (F. = Teut.) 'This carter thakketh his hors upon the *croupe*;' Chaucer, C. T. 7141 (D 1559). = OF. (and F.) *croupe*, the crupper, hind part of a horse; older spellings were *crope, crupe*. 'The orig. sense is a protuberance, as in *croupe d'une montagne*, etc.' (Brachet). [Cf. E. *to crop out*.] = Icel. *kroppr*, a hunch or bump on the body; cf. *kryppa*, a hunch, hump. Thus *croup* is a doublet of **Crop**, q. v. Der. *croup-ier* (see Hatzfeld); also *crupper*, q. v.

CROW, to make a noise as a cock. (E.) ME. *crawen, crowen*; Wyclif, Lu. xxii. 34. AS. *cráwan*, to crow, pt. t. *créow*; Lu. xxii. 34, 60. + Du. *kraaijen*, to crow; hence, to proclaim, publish; G. *krähen*, to crow; both weak verbs. Cf. OSlav. *grajati*, Lith. *groti*, to crow. All of imitative origin. See Max Müller's Lectures, 8th ed. i. 416. Der. *crow*, a croaking bird, from AS. *cráwe*, which see in Ps. cxlvi. 10, ed. Spelman; and cf. OSax. *kráia*, Du. *kraai*, G. *krähe*, a crow; also *crow-bar*, a bar with a strong beak like a crow's; also *crow-foot*, a flower, called *crow-toe* in Milton, Lycidas, 143.

CROWD (1), to push, press, squeeze. (E.) ME. *crouden*, to push, Chaucer, C. T. 4716 (B 296). AS. *crúdan*, to crowd, press, push, pt. t. *créad*, pp. *croden*. Grein, i. 168. Cf. AS. *croda, gecrod*, a crowd, throng, id. 169. Also prov. E. (Norfolk) *crowd*, to push along in a wheelbarrow. + MDu. *kruyden*, Du. *kruijen*, to push along in a wheelbarrow, to drive. ¶ The form of the infin. was *crúdan*, not *créodan* (as in Grein); cf. MDu. *kruyden*, with *uy* = AS. *ú*. The 3 p. pres. sing. *crýdeþ* and the pt. t. *créad* occur. Der. *crowd*, sb.

CROWD (2), a fiddle, violin. (W.) Obsolete. 'The pipe, the tabor, and the trembling *croud*;' Spencer, Epithalamion, 131. ME. *crowde*, Wyclif, Luke, xv. 25, where the Vulgate has *chorum*; also spelt *crouth*, King of Tars, 485. = W. *crwth*, anything swelling out, a bulge, trunk, belly, crowd, violin, fiddle (Spurrell). + Gael. *cruit*, a harp, violin, cymbal; OIrish *crot*, a harp; Celtic type *krot-tā*; whence Late L. *chrotta*. See Macbain; and Rhys, Lect. on W. Philology, p. 114. Doublet, *rote* (2).

CROWN, a garland, diadem. (F. = L. = Gk.). ME. *corone, coroune*; also in the contracted form *crune, croun*, by loss of the former *o*. The contracted form is common at a very early period; *crune* occurs in Layamon, i. 181; Havelok, 1814. = AF. *coroune*; OF. *corone* (F. *couronne*), a crown. = L. *corōna*, a garland, wreath. = Gk. κορώνη, the curved end of a bow; κορωνίς, a wreath, garland; cf. κορωνός, curved, bent. Allied to Gk. κυρτός, bent, L. *curuus*; also to Gael. *cruinn*, round, circular; W. *crwn*, round, circular. See **Curve**. Der. *corolla, corollary, coron-al, coron-er, coron-et*, all from L. *corōna*. See these words. Also *crown*, vb.

CRUCIAL, in the manner of a cross; testing, as if by the cross. (F. = L.) 'Crucial incision, the cutting or lancing of an imposthume or swelling crosswise;' Phillips (1706). = F. *crucial*, 'cross-wise, cross-like;' Cot. Formed (as if from a L. *cruciālis*) from *cruci-*, declensional stem of *crux*, a cross. See **Cross**.

CRUCIBLE, a melting-pot. (Late L.) Spelt *crusible* in Sir T. Browne, Vulg. Errors, b. ii. c. 1; and Cotgrave translates F. *creuset* by 'crucible.' = Late L. *crucibulum, crucibolus*, a hanging lamp, also, a melting-pot, Ducange; and see the Theatrum Chemicum. Diefenbach's Supplement to Ducange gives: '*Crucibolus*, kruse, kruselin, krug, becher.' The suffix *-bulum, -bolus* answers to L. *-bulum* in *thūri-bulum*, a censer. β. The prefix *cruci-* points to the fact that the word was connected with L. *crux* (gen. *crucis*), a cross; and the original application was doubtless to a lamp with four nozzles, pointing four ways like the arms of a cross. I possess such a lamp, bought in Italy, and the pattern is common. In the N.E.D., it is explained as 'a lamp with crossed wicks, giving four flames;' but the wicks do not exactly cross. They point outwards from a common centre, and each flame is at the end of an arm.

CRUCIFY, to fix on the cross. (F. = L.) ME. *crucifien*, Wyclif, Mark, xv. 13. = OF. *crucifier*, 'to crucifie, to naile or put to death on a cross;' Cot. = L. *crucificāre*, for *crucifigere*, to fix on a cross; pp. *crucifixus*. = L. *cruci-*, declensional stem of *crux*, a cross; and *figere*, to fix. See **Cross** and **Fix**. Der. *crucifix*, which occurs early, in the Ancren Riwle, p. 16; *crucifix-ion*, allied to the L. pp. *crucifixus*. From L. *cruci-* are also formed *cruci-ferous*, cross-bearing, from the L. *ferre*, to bear; and *cruci-form*.

CRUDE, raw, unripe. (L.) The words *crude* and *cruditie* occur in Sir T. Elyot, Castel of Helth; bk. ii. c. 28; bk. iv. c. 1. Chaucer has *crude*, C. T. 16240 (G 772). = L. *crūdus*, raw; connected with E. *raw*. See **Raw**. Der. *crude-ly, -ness*; *crud-i-ty*; and see *cruel, crust, crystal*.

CRUEL, severe, hard-hearted. (F. = L.) ME. *cruel*, Rob. of Glouc. p. 417, l. 8615. = OF. *cruel*, harsh, severe. = L. *crūdēlis*, severe, hard-hearted. From the same root as *crude*. Der. *cruel-ly*; *cruel-ty*, from OF. *cruelte* (F. *cruauté*), from L. acc. *crudēlitātem*.

CRUET, a small pot or jar. (F. = Teut.) ME. *cruet*; 'waischingis of cuppis and cruetis;' Wyclif, Mark, vii. 4. And see Prompt. Parv., p. 105, and note; Catholicon Anglicum, p. 84, note 4. = AF. *cruet*, Royal Wills, p. 26 (1360); dimin. of OF. *crue, cruie*, an earthen pot (Godefroy). = Low L. *krūga*, a pitcher. = OHG. *kruog*, G. *krug*, a pitcher. Cf. Du. *kruik*, a pitcher, a jug.

CRUISE, to traverse the sea. (Du. = L.) 'A *cruise* to Manilla;' Dampier's Voyages, an. 1686. = Du. *kruisen*, to cross, crucify; also, to cruise, lit. to traverse backwards and forwards. = Du. *kruis*, a cross. = L. *crucem*, acc. of *crux*, a cross, with lengthening of *u*. Thus *cruise* merely shews to *cross*, to traverse. See **Cross**. Der. *cruis-er*.

CRUMB, a small morsel. (E.) The final *b* is excrescent. ME. *crume, crome, crumme, cromme*. Spelt *crume*, Ancren Riwle, p. 342. AS. *crúma*, Matt. xv. 27. + Du. *kruim*, crumb, pith; cf. Du. *kruimelen*, to crumble, *kruimel*, a small crumb; *kruimig, kruimelig*, crumby, or crummy; Dan. *krumme*, a crumb; G. *krume*, a crumb; cf. G. *krümelig*, crumbling; *krümeln*, to crumble. β. The *u* in *crúma* was long; cf. prov. E. *croom*, a crumb, and Du. *kruim*. Hence prov. E. *cream, creem*, to press, represents OE. *créman* = *crýman*, formed by mutation. Der. *crumm-y* or *crumb-y*, adj.; *crumb-le*, verb, cognate with Du. *kruimelen*, G. *krümeln*.

CRUMPET, a kind of bread-cake. (E.) In Todd's Johnson. Wyclif has '*crompid* cake,' to render L. *laganum* (Exod. xxix. 23); cf. prov. E. *crumpy* cake, crisp cake. For *crump-ed*, pp. of ME. *crumpen*, to curl up; whence E. *crumple* (below). Cf. G. *krümpen, krumpen*, to crumple, to curl up; *krumm*, crooked, curved; also AS. *crompeht*, wrinkled. ¶ Orig. a thin (curled up) cake, cooked on a griddle.

CRUMPLE, to wrinkle, rumple. (E.) ME. *cromplen*. 'My skinne is withered, and *crompled* together;' Bible, 1551, Job, vii. 5. '*Crompled* togyther;' Palsgrave, p. 309; with *om* for *um*. β. *Crumple* is allied to *cramp*; from the weak grade of the strong verb *krimpen* (in EFriesic), pp. *krump-en*. It signifies 'to cramp frequently,' 'to pinch often;' hence, to pinch or squeeze into many folds or plaits. Cf. AS. *crump*, crooked; O. E. Texts, p. 81, l. 1411. See **Cramp, Crimp**.

CRUNCH, to chew with violence, grind with violence and noise. (E.) Rare in books. Swift has *craunch*. 'She would *craunch* the wing of a lark, bones and all, between her teeth;' Voyage to Brobdingnag, ch. 3. An imitative word, and allied to *scrunch*. Cf. prov. E. *crinch, cranch*, to crunch; also Du. *schransen*, to eat heartily. ¶ A similar imitative word is '*Crunk*, to cry like a crane;' Kersey's Dict. ed. 1715. This is the Icel. *krúnka*, to cry like a raven, to croak.

CRUPPER, the hinder part of a horse. (F. = Teut.) ME. *croper*, King Alisaunder, l. 3421. Spelt *crouper* in Spenser, F. Q. iv. 4. 40. = AF. *cropere*, OF. *cropiere* (Supp. to Godefroy); MF. *croupiere*, as in 'croupiere de cheval, a horse-crupper;' Cot. = OF. *crope* (Supp. to Godefroy), F. *croupe*, the croup of a horse. See **Croup** (2).

CRURAL, belonging to the leg. (L.) 'Crural, belonging to the leggs, knees, or thighs;' Blount's Glossographia, ed. 1674. = L. *crūrālis*, belonging to the shin or leg. = L. *crūr-*, decl. stem of *crūs*, the shin, shank.

CRUSADE, an expedition for sake of the cross. (F. = Span. = L.) 'Baldwine archbishop of Canturburie preached the *croisad* there;' Harrison, Desc. of England (1577-87), bk. iii. ch. 4 (near the end). 'A pope of that name [Urban] did first institute the *croisado*;' Bacon, On an Holy War (R.). Spelt *croysado* in Blount's Glossographia, ed. 1674. '*Croisado* or *Crusade*;' Phillips, 1706. Hence the word is due to a blending of OF. *croisee*, a crusade (Roquefort) with the Prov. *crozada* and Span. *cruzada*. = F. *croisade*, 'an expedition of Christians . . . because every one of them wears the badge of the cross;' Cot. = Span. *cruzada* (with *u* changed to *oi*); Late L. *cruciāta*, a marking with the cross; orig. f. pp. of *cruciāre*, to cross. = L. *cruci-*, decl. stem of *crux*, a cross. See **Cross**. Der. *crusad-er*.

CRUSE, a small cup or pot. (Scand. or E.) See 1 Kings, xiv. 3; 2 Kings, ii. 20. ME. *cruse, crowse, crouse*. '*Crowse*, or *cruse*, potte, amula;' Prompt. Parv. p. 105. 'A *cruse* of this [honey] now putte in a wyne-stene;' Palladius on Husbandry, xi. 51. Spelt *cruce*, id. xi. 348. = Icel. *krús*, a pot, tankard; Swed. *krus*, a mug; Dan. *kruus*, a jug, mug. β. Or the word may be English; cf. NFries. *kröss*, EFries. *krōs*; also Du. *kroes*, a cup, pot, crucible; MHG. *krūse*, an earthen mug, G. *krause*.

CRUSH, to break in pieces, overwhelm. (F.—Teut.) 'Cruschyn or quaschyn, quasso;' Prompt. Parv. p. 106.—OF. cruisir, croissir, to crack, break. (Span. crujir, Ital. crosciare). From a Teut. type *krau-tjan, causal form from *kreustan-, Goth. kriustan, to gnash with the teeth. Cf. Swed. krysta, to squeeze; Dan. kryste, to squeeze, press; Icel. kreista, kreysta, to squeeze, pinch, press; also Swed. krossa, to crush. β. See Goth. kriustan, to gnash with the teeth, grind the teeth, Mk. ix. 18; whence Goth. krusts, gnashing of teeth, Matt. viii. 12.

CRUST, the rind of bread, or coating of a pie. (F.—L.) ME. crust, Polit. Songs, ed. Wright, p. 204; Prompt. Parv. p. 106.—OF. crouste; in Cot.—L. crusta, crust of bread. Cf. Irish cruaidh, hard; Gk. κρύος, frost. See Crystal. Der. crust, verb; crust-y [perhaps a perversion of curst, ill-tempered, which occurs as early as in Cursor Mundi, l. 19201] Beaum. and Fletcher, Bloody Brother, iii. 2. 23; crust-i-ly, -i-ness; -at-ed, -at-ion; also crust-acea, formed with L. suffix -āceus, neuter plural -ācea.

CRUTCH, a staff with a cross-piece. (E.) ME. crucche; Layamon's Brut, ii. 394. AS. crycc, a crutch, staff, in the AS. tr. of Beda, iv. 31.—Du. kruk, a crutch; Swed. krycka, Dan. krykke, a crutch; G. krücke, a crutch. β. The base is *kruk, weak grade of *kreuk (meaning unknown); perhaps allied to G. kriechen, OHG. kriochan, to creep, creep about; cf. cripple.

CRY, to call aloud, lament, bawl. (F.—L.) ME. crien, cryen; Rob. of Glouc. p. 401, l. 8282. The sb. cri is in Havelok, l. 270, and in Layamon, ii. 75.—OF. crier, to cry; of which fuller forms occur in Ital. gridare, Span. gritar, and Port. gritar.—L. quīritāre, to shriek, cry, lament; see Brachet. Lit. 'to implore the help of the Quirites' or Roman citizens (Varro). Der. cry, sb., cri-er.

CRYPT, an underground cell or chapel. (L.—Gk.) 'Caves under the ground, called cryptæ;' Homilies, Against Idolatry, pt. iii. See Cryptæ in Phillips (1706).—L. crypta, a cave underground, crypt.—Gk. κρύπτη, or κρυπτή, a vault, crypt; orig. fem. nom. of κρυπτός, adj. hidden, covered, concealed.—Gk. κρύπτειν, to hide, conceal. Doublet. grot.

CRYPTOGAMIA, a class of flowers in which fructification is concealed. (Gk.) A Linnæan name (1735). Made up from Gk. κρυπτο-, for κρυπτός, hidden, and γαμ-εῖν, to marry. See Crypt and Bigamy. Der. cryptogam-ic, -ous; cf. apo-cryph-al.

CRYSTAL, clear glass, a kind of transparent mineral. (F.—L.— Gk.) In its modern form, it is Latinised; but it was first introduced into English from the French. We find ME. cristal, Floriz and Blancheflur, ed. Lumby, 274.—OF. cristal, crystal.—L. crystallum, crystal; Ps. 147. 6 (Vulgate).—Gk. κρύσταλλος, clear ice, ice, rock-crystal.—Gk. κρυσταίνειν, to freeze.—Gk. κρύος, frost. Der. crystall-ine, -ise, -is-at-ion; also crystallo-graphy, from Gk. γράφειν, to describe.

CUB, a whelp, young animal. (Scand.?) In Shak. Merch. of Ven. ii. 1. 29. Palsgrave has 'Cubbe, a yong foxe.' Of uncertain origin; but prob. Scand. The Shetland coob, to bring forth young, is applied to the seal only; from Icel. kobbi, a young seal, Dan. kobbe. The Dan. kubbe means a block, stump, short log; so also Swed. kubb. The sense of 'lump' seems common to both words. Rietz (p. 361, col. 1) gives Swed. kibb, kubbe, kobbe, as playful names for a calf.

CUBE, a solid figure contained by six equal squares, a die. (F.— L.—Gk.) In Milton, P. L. vi. 552. The word occurs in Cotgrave, who gives the F. cube, with the explanation 'a cube, or figure in geometry, foursquare like a die.'—L. acc. cubum, a cube, die.—Gk. κύβος, a cube. Der. cube, verb; cub-ic, -ic-al, -ic-al-ly, -at-ure, cubi-form; cuboid, from Gk. κυβοειδής, resembling a cube, which from κύβο-, for κύβος, and εἶδ-ος, form, figure.

CUBEB, the spicy berry of a tropical plant. (F.—Span.—Arab.) Spelt quybybes, pl., in Mandeville, Trav. c. 5, p. 50; the Lat. text has cubeba. Spelt cububes, pl., in Sir T. Elyot, Castel of Helth, b. iii. c. 12. Mentioned, under the Anglo-French form cubibes, pl., in the Liber Albus, p. 230.—MF. cubebe, pl. cubebes, 'cubebs, an aromaticall and Indian fruit;' Cot.—Span. cubeba, fem. sing.—Arab. kabāba(t), pl. kabābah, cubeb, an aromatic; Rich. Dict. p. 1166. See also Devic, Supp. to Littré.

CUBIT, an old measure of length. (L.) ME. cubite, Wyclif, Matt. vi. 27.—L. cubitus, Matt. vi. 27; meaning lit. a bend, an elbow; hence, the length from the elbow to the middle finger's end. Cf. L. cubāre, to recline, lie down; see Covey.

CUCKOLD, a man whose wife is unfaithful. (F.—L.) ME. kokewold, kukwald, kukeweld, cokold. Spelt cokewold, Chaucer, C. T. 3154 (A 3152); P. Plowman, B. v. 159. 'Hic zelotopus, a kukwald,' Wright's Vocab. i. 217. Spelt kukeweld, Owl and Nightingale, 1542. β. The word seems to have been modified at the end by confusion with the ME. suffix -wold occurring in an-wold, power, dominion. Cf. cokolde in the Coventry Mysteries, p. 120.—OF. cucualt, coucual, a cuckold (Godefroy).—OF. cucu, F. coucou, a cuckoo; with the depreciatory suffix -ault, -al (from G. -wald); see Diez, Gram. ii. 346. The F. coucou also had the secondary sense of cuckold. [The

allusions to the comparison between a cuckold and a cuckoo are endless; see Shak. L. L. L. v. 2. 920.]—L. cuculum, acc. of cuculus, a cuckoo. See Cuckoo.

CUCKOO, a bird which cries cuckoo. (F.—L.) ME. coccou, cukkow, &c. 'Hic cuculus, a cocow, cucko;' Voc. 640. 32, 762. 33. —OF. cucu, F. coucou.—L. cuculum, acc. of cuculus, a cuckoo. ✠ Gk. κόκκυξ, a cuckoo, κόκκυ, the cry of a cuckoo; Skt. kōkila-, a cuckoo. All imitative words, from the sound kuku made by the bird; indeed, the OF. cucu need not be referred to the L. form, as it is itself imitative. See Cock, Cockatoo. Der. cuckold, q.v.

CUCUMBER, a creeping plant with edible fruit. (L.) ME. cucumer, later cucumber, with excrescent or inserted b. Spelt cucumer, Wyclif, Baruch, vi. 69.—L. cucumerem, acc. of cucumis, a cucumber. β. Perhaps so called because ripened by heat; cf. L. cucuma, a cooking-kettle, from L. coquere, to cook, bake, ripen. See Cook.

CUD, food chewed by ruminants. (E.) ME. cude, Ormulum, 1237. In Wyclif, Deut. xiv. 6, where the text has code, three MSS. have quide, which is a mere variant of the same word. AS. cudu, for cwudu, later form of cwidu; see AS. Leechdoms, vol. ii. pp. 54, 56, 66, where hwit cwudu means 'mastic;' called hwit cwidu (gen. cwidwes) at p. 182; hwit cudu, id. iii. 72. Teut. type *kwedwom, neuter. Cf. Skt. jatu-, resin; Icel. kwāδa, resin. Orig. sense 'glutinous substance.'

CUDBEAR, a purple or violet powder, used for dyeing. (E.) First in 1771. 'A name devised, from his own Christian name, by Dr. Cuthbert Gordon, who obtained a patent for this powder;' N.E.D. From AS. Cūδbeorht; compounded of cūδ, well known, and beorht, bright.

CUDDLE, to embrace closely, fondle. (E.) Rare in books. R. quotes: 'They cuddled close all night;' Somervile, Fab. 11. l. 9. 'Cudlyng of my cowe;' Burlesque Song, in Reliq. Antiquæ, i. 239. Probably a corruption of *couth-le, to be frequently familiar, a frequentative verb formed with the suffix -le from the ME. couth, well known, familiar; whence also prov. E. cootle, to fondle. We find kud for cuδ in Will. of Palerne, ed. Skeat, ll. 51, 114, 501, &c. See numerous examples of couth, familiar, loving, in Jamieson's Scottish Dict. This adj. couth was originally a pp. signifying known, well-known.—AS. cūδ, known, familiar; used as pp. of cunnan, to know; cf. Icel. kūδr, another form of kunnr, familiar; Goth. kunths, known, pp. of kunnan, to know. Compare further AS. cūδlæcan, to be friendly; Ælfric's Saints' Lives, xxv. 644.

CUDGEL, a thick stick. (E.) In Shak. Merry Wives, ii. 2. 292. ME. kuggel; Ancren Riwle, p. 292. AS. cycgel, a cudgel; in Gregory's Pastoral Care, ed. Sweet, c. 40, p. 297. Perhaps a 'knobbed' stick; and allied to Cog.

CUDWEED, a plant of the genus Gnaphalium. (E.) 'Cotton-weed or Cudweed, a sort of herb;' Kersey's Dict. ed. 1715. 'Cud-weed, the cotton-weed;' Halliwell. Turner, in his Names of Herbes (1548) explains Centunculus by chafweede, 'in Yorkeshyre cudweede.' 'The common name for the genus Gnaphalium; [so named from] the plant being administered to cattle that had lost their cud;' N.E.D. From Cud and Weed.

CUE (1), a tail, a billiard-rod. (F.—L.) The same word as queue, q. v. [An actor's cue is a different word; see below.] Ash's Dict. (1775) has 'Cue, the tail of a wig.'—OF. cue (Supp. to Godefroy), coe (Roquefort); mod. F. queue, a tail.—L. cōda, cauda, a tail. See Caudal. ¶ The F. queue also means a handle, stalk, billiard-cue. See Hatzfeld.

CUE (2), a direction for an actor's appearance. (F.—L.) In Shak. Merry Wives, iii. 3. 39. Sometimes written q or qu in the 16th century, and said to stand for quando, when. This is the more probable because cue or q was previously in use to denote the sum of half a farthing in college accounts, and signified quadrans. 'Cue, half a farthing;' Minsheu (1627). 'Cu, Cue, halfe a farthynge;' Prompt. Parv.; see Way's note. The sound of cue denotes the Anglicised pronunciation of the French name of the Latin letter. Hence also cue, an actor's part, and the phrase 'a merry cue.'

CUFF (1), to strike with the open hand. (Scand.) Taming of the Shrew, ii. 221. 'I cuffe one;' Palsgrave, p. 502.—Swed. kuffa, to thrust, push. Ihre translates it by 'verberibus insultare,' and says it is the E. cuff; adding that it is the frequentative (!) of the Swed. kufva, MSwed. kufwa, to subdue, suppress, cow; see Cow (2); but this is improbable. Berghaus has kuffen, to hit, cuff, and it is found also in Hamburgh and in Pomeranian (Richey, Dähnert); cf. Norw. kuffa, to cuff (Ross). De Bo gives WFlem. koove, koffe, (1) a coif, (2) a box on the ear; which seems to connect it with cuff (2). Der. cuff, sb.

CUFF (2), part of the sleeve. (L.?) Formerly it meant a glove or mitten; now used chiefly of the part of the sleeve which covers the hand but partially. ME. cuffe, coffe. 'Cuffe, glove or meteyne, or mitten, mitta;' Prompt. Parv. p. 106. The pl. coffes is in P. Plowman, B. vi. 62. The later use occurs in: 'Cuffe over ones hande, poignet;' Palsgrave. **β.** Origin uncertain; but probably the same word as *cuffie*, which occurs in the pl. *cuffian*, in Kemble's ed. of the A. S. Charters, no. 1290, vol. vi. 133, l. 20, where Leo supposes it to signify 'a covering for the head;' whence, perhaps, a covering for the hand. Cf. OHG. *chuppha*, MHG. *kupfe*, *kuppe*, *kuffe*, a coif. See **Coif**, and **Cuff** (1).

CUIRASS, a kind of breast-plate. (F. – Ital. – L.) Orig. made of leather, whence the name. In Milton, Samson, 132. Also in Chapman's tr. of the Iliad, bk. vii. l. 221. – MF. *cuirace*, *cuirasse* (now *cuirasse*), 'a cuirats (*sic*), armour for the breast and back;' Cot. [Introduced from Ital. in the 16th century (Brachet).] – Ital. *corazza*, a cuirass; Late L. *corātia*, *corācium*, a cuirass, breast-plate. Formed as if from an adj. **corācius*, for *coriāceus*, leathern. – L. *corium*, hide, leather; whence F. *cuir*. **Der.** *cuirass-ier*.

CUISSES, pl., armour for the thighs. (F. – L.) In Shak. 1 Hen. IV, iv. 1. 105. ME. *quyssewes*, Gawain and Grene Knight, 578. – OF. *cuissaux*, 'cuisses, armour for the thighs;' Cotgrave. – F. *cuisse*, the thigh. – L. *coxa*, the hip; see Brachet. Brugmann, i. § 609.

CULDEE, one of an old Celtic monkish fraternity. (C.) 'The pure *Culdees* Were Albyn's earliest priests of God;' Campbell, Reullura, l. 5. The note on the line says: 'The *Culdees* were the primitive clergy of Scotland, and apparently her only clergy from the 6th to the 11th century. They were of Irish origin, and their monastery on the island of Iona, or Icolmkill, was the seminary of Christianity in North Britain.' – OIrish *céle dé*, Irish *ceilede*, a servant of God, a Culdee. From OIrish *céle*, Ir. *ceile*, a spouse, also a servant; and *dé*, gen. of *dia*, God. See Rhys, Lect. on W. Philology, p. 412. Cf. Late L. *Culdei*, *Colidei*, Culdees; misspelt *colidei* as if from L. *colere Deum*, to worship God.

CULINARY, pertaining to the kitchen. (L.) 'Our *culinary* fire;' Boyle's Works, i. 523. – L. *culinārius*, belonging to a kitchen. – L. *culina*, a kitchen; cf. *coquina*, a kitchen, with similar suffix. *Culina* is for **coc-slīna*, from *coquere*, to cook; Giles, § 188.

CULL, to collect, gather. (F. – L.) ME. *cullen*. 'Cullyn owte, segrego, lego, separo;' Prompt. Parv. p. 107. – OF. *coillir*, *cuillir*, *cueillir*, to cull, collect. – L. *colligere*, to collect. See **Collect**, of which *cull* is a doublet.

CULLENDER, a strainer; see **Colander**.

CULLION, a mean wretch. (F. – L.) In Shak. Tam. Shrew, iv. 2. 20. A coarse word. – F. *couillon*, *couille*, Cotgrave; cf. Ital. *coglione*, *coglioni*, *coglionare*; Florio. – L. *cōleus*. From a like source (perhaps) is *cully*, a dupe, or to deceive.

CULLIS (1), a strong broth, boiled and strained. (F. – L.) ME. *colis*, Liber Cure Cocorum, p. 20. – OF. *coleïs*, *couleïs*, later *coulis*, 'a cullis,' Cot.; substantival use of *coleïs*, later *coulis*, adj. 'gliding,' Cot. – L. type **cōlāticius*; from *cōlāre*, to strain; see **Colander**.

CULLIS (2), in *port-cullis*. (F. – L.) The fem. form of the preceding; see **Portcullis**.

CULM, a stalk, stem. (L.) Botanical. '*Culmus*, the stem or stalk of corn or grass;' Kersey's Dict. ed. 1715. – L. *culmus*, a stalk; cf. *calamus*, a stalk, stem, cognate with E. *haulm*. See **Haulm**. **Der.** *culmi-f rous*, stalk-bearing; from L. *ferre*, to bear.

CULMINATE, to come to the highest point. (L.) See Milton, P. L. iii. 617. – Late L. *culmināt-us*, pp. of Late L. *culmināre* (Ducange), to come to the top. – L. *culmin-*, decl. stem of *culmen*, the highest point of a thing; of which an older form is *columen*, a top, summit. See **Column**. **Der.** *culminat-ion*.

CULPABLE, deserving of blame. (F. – L.) ME. *culpable*, *coulpable*, *coupable*. Spelt *culpable*, Rob. of Brunne, tr. of Langtoft, p. 302. Spelt *coupable*, P. Plowman, B. xvii. 300. – OF. *culpable*, *colpable*, F. *coupable*, culpable. – L. *culpābilis*, blameworthy. – L. *culpāre*, to blame; with suffix *-bilis*. – L. *culpa*, a fault, failure, mistake, error. **Der.** *culpabl-y*; *culpabil-i-ty*, from L. *culpābilis*; and see *culprit*.

CULPRIT, a criminal. (F. – L.) 'Then first the *culprit* answered to his name;' Dryden, Wife of Bath's Tale, 273. Not orig. a single word, but due to a fusion of AF. *cul-* (for *culpable*, i.e. guilty), and AF. *prist* or *prest* (i.e. ready to prove it), signifying that the clerk of the crown was ready to prove the indictment (N.E.D.).

CULTER, a plough-iron; see **Coulter**.

CULTIVATE, to till, improve, civilise. (L.) 'To *cultivate* . . . that friendship;' Milton, To the Grand Duke of Tuscany (R.). It occurs also in Blount's Glossographia, ed. 1656. – Late L. *cultīvātus*, pp. of *cultivāre*, to till, work at, used A. D. 1446; Ducange. [Hence also F. *cultiver*, Span. *cultivar*, Ital. *coltivare*.] – Late L. *cultivus*, cultivated; Ducange. Allied to L. *cultus*, tilled, pp. of *colere*, to till. Brugmann, i. § 121. See **Culture**. **Der.** *cultivat-ion*, *-or*.

CULTURE, cultivation. (F. – L.) 'The *culture* and profit of their myndes;' Sir T. More, Works, p. 14 d. ME. *culture*. – F. *culture*, 'culture, tillage, husbandry;' Cot. – L. *cultūra*, cultivation; allied to *cultus*, pp. of *colere*, to till. **Der.** *culture*, verb.

CULVER (1), a dove. (E.) Used by Spenser, F. Q. ii. 7. 34; Tears of the Muses, 246. Preserved in the name of the Culver Cliffs, near Sandown, Isle of Wight. Chaucer has *colver*, Leg. of Good Women, Philom. 92. AS. *culfre*, translating L. *columba*, Mark, i. 10. Thought to be an E. word, notwithstanding its superficial resemblance to L. *columba*. **Der.** *culver-tail*, an old word for *dove-tail*; see Blount's Glossographia, ed. 1674.

CULVER (2), another form of **Culverin**; see below.

CULVERIN, a sort of cannon. (F. – L.) In Shak. 1 Hen. IV, ii. 3. 56. Palsgrave has 'Culveryng, gonne, *culuerine*.' A corrupt form for **culverin*. – OF. *coulevrine* (Hatzfeld), MF. *couleuvrine*, 'a culverin, the piece of ordnance called so;' Cot. Fem. form of OF. *couleuvrin*, 'adder-like;' id. – OF. *couleuvre*, an adder; id. – L. *colubra*, fem. form of *coluber*, a serpent, adder; whence the adj. *colubrīnus*, snake-like, cunning, wily. ¶ It appears that this cannon was so called from its long, thin shape; some were similarly called *serpertina*; see Junius, quoted in Richardson. Other pieces of ordnance were called *falcons*.

CULVERT, an arched drain under a road. (Du.?) Not in Johnson. First used ab. 1770. Origin unknown. We might expect it to be Dutch, in connexion with making of canals, &c. But no such word is known in Dutch; though we might imagine a Du. **coul-vaart*, to express the sense, viz. from Du. *coul-*, as in *coul-age*, leakage, *coul-ant*, flowing (Calisch), and Du. *vaart*, a channel, canal, water-course, from *varen*, to go; see **Fare**. **β.** The Du. *coul-* is borrowed from F.; cf. MF. *coulouère*, 'a channel, gutter,' &c.; Cot. – F. *couler*, to flow, trickle. – L. *cōlāre*, to filter. – L. *cōlum*, a strainer. See **Colander**.

CUMBER, to encumber, hinder. (F. – Late L.) ME. *combren*, Chaucer, tr. of Boethius, bk. iii. met. 10. l. 6; Piers Plowman's Crede, 461, 765. The sb. *comburment* occurs in K. Alisaunder, ed. Weber, 472. – OF. *combrer*, to hinder; cf. mod. F. *encombre*, an impediment. – Late L. *cumbrus*, a heap, 'found in several Merovingian documents, e.g. in the Gesta Regum Francorum, c. 25;' Brachet. Ducange gives the pl. *combrī*, impediments. Of doubtful origin; some refer it to G. *kummer*, grief, oppression, prov. G. *kummer*, rubbish. Others, to L. *cumulus*, a heap, by change of *l* to *r*, not uncommon; with inserted *b*. See **Cumulate**. **Der.** *cumbr-ous* (i.e. *cumber-ous*), *-ly*, *-ness*; also *cumber-some*, by adding the E. suffix *-some*.

CUMIN, CUMMIN, the name of a plant. (L. – Gk. – Heb.) ME. *comin*, King Alisaunder, ed. Weber, 6797; also *cummin*, Wyclif, St. Matt. xxiii. 23. In the AS. translation we find the forms *cymyn*, *cymen*, and *cumin*, in the MSS. There is an OF. form *comin*; see Bartsch, Chrest. Franc. col. 275, l. 29. Cotgrave has: 'Commin, cummin.' Both OF. and AS. forms are from the L. *cuminum* or *cyminum* in Matt. xxiii. 23. – Gk. κύμινον. – Heb. *kammōn*, cummin. Cf. Arab. *kammūn*, cummin-seed; Rich. Dict. 1206, 1207.

CUMMERBUND, a waist-band, sash. (Hind. – Pers.) See examples in Yule. – Hind. *kamar-band*, a girdle, piece of cloth round the loins. – Pers. *kamar*, the waist, the loins; and *band*, a band.

CUMULATE, to heap together. (L.) 'All the extremes of worth and beauty that were *cumulated* in Camilla;' Shelton's Don Quixote, c. 33. The adj. *cumulative* is in Bacon, On Learning, by G. Wats, b. iii. c. 1. – L. *cumulātus*, pp. of *cumulāre*, to heap up. – L. *cumulus*, a heap. **Der.** *cumulat-ive*, *-ion*; also *ac-cumulate*, q. v.

CUNEATE, wedge-shaped. (L.) Modern; botanical. Formed with suffix *-ate*, corresponding to L. *-ātus*, from L. *cune-us*, a wedge. See **Coin**. **Der.** From the same source is *cunei-form*, i.e. wedge-shaped; a modern word.

CUNNING (1), skilful, knowing. (E.) ME. *cunning*, *conning*; Northern form *cunnand*, from Icel. *kunnandi*, pres. pt. of *kunna*, to know. Spelt *kunnynge*, P. Plowman, B. xi. 70. Really the pres. pt. of ME. *cunnen*, to know, in very common use; Ancren Riwle, p. 280. – AS. *cunnan*, to know. See **Can** (1). **Der.** *cunning-ly*.

CUNNING (2), knowledge, skill. (Scand.) ME. *cunninge*, Chaucer, Ho. of Fame, iii. 966. Suggested by Icel. *kunnandi*, knowledge, which is derived from *kunna*, to know, cognate with AS. *cunnan*, to know; see Grein, i. 171. ¶ The AS. *cunnung* signifies temptation, trial. See **Can** (1).

CUP, a drinking-vessel. (L.) ME. *cuppe*, Gen. and Exodus, ed. Morris, 2310. AS. *cuppe*, a cup. 'Caupus, vel obba, *cuppe*;' Ælfric's Gloss. ed. Somner; Nomina Vasorum. [Cf. Du. and Dan. *kop*, Swed. *kopp*, F. *coupe*, Span. *copa*, Ital. *coppa*, a cup; all alike borrowed from Latin.] – Late L. *cuppa*, a cup; variant of L. *cūpa*, a vat, butt, cask; in later times, a drinking-vessel; see Ducange. **+** Gk. κύπελλον, a cup, goblet; cf. κύπη, a hole, hollow; also Skt. *kūpa*, a pit, well, hollow. Brugmann, i. § 930 (4). **Der.** *cup*, verb; *cup-board*, q. v.; *cupping-glass*, Beaum. and Fletcher, Bloody Brother, iv. 2. See **Coop**.

CUPBOARD, a closet with shelves for cups. (Hybrid; L. *and* E.) ME. *cup-borde*, a table for holding cups. 'And couered mony a *cupborde* with clothes ful quite;' Allit. Poems, ed. Morris, ii. 1440; see the whole passage. And cf. Morte Arthure, ed. Brock, 206. Formed from *cup* and ME. *bord*, a table, esp. a table for meals and various vessels. See **Cup** and **Board**. ¶ The sense of the word has somewhat changed; it is possible that some may have taken it to mean *cup-hoard*, a place for keeping cups; but there was no such word, and such is *not* the true etymology.

CUPEL, a small, shallow, porous, cup-like vessel used in refining metals. (L.) Spelt *coppell* in Cotgrave, s. v. *coupelle*. — Late L. *cŭpella*, dimin. of *cŭpa*, a cask. See **Cupola**. Der. *cupell-ate, cupell-at-ion.*

CUPID, the god of love. (L.) In Shak. Merry Wives, ii. 2. 141. — L. nom. *cupido*, desire, passion, Cupid. — L. *cupere*, to desire. Cf. Skt. *kup*, to become excited. See **Covet**. Der. *cupid-i-ty*, q. v. And, from the same root, *con-cup-isc-ence.*

CUPIDITY, avarice, covetousness. (F. — L.) *Cupiditie*, in Hall's Chron. Hen. VII, an. 11. § 8. — F. *cupidité*, 'cupidity, lust, covetousness;' Cotgrave. — L. acc. *cupiditātem*, from nom. *cupiditās*, desire, covetousness. — L. *cupidus*, desirous. — L. *cupere*, to desire. See above.

CUPOLA, a sort of dome. (Ital. — L.) 'The ruined *Cupola*;' Sandys' Travels (1632), p. 264. '*Cupola*, or *Cuppola*, . . an high tower arched, having but little light;' Gazophylacium Anglicanum, ed. 1689. Spelt *cupolo* in Blount, Glossographia, edd. 1674, 1681; *cupola* in Kersey's Dict. ed. 1715. — Ital. *cupola*, a cupola, dome. — L. *cūpula*, a small cask, a little vault; dimin. of *cŭpa*, a cask, vat. See **Cup**.

CUPREOUS, coppery, like copper. (L.) '*Cupreous*, of or belonging to copper;' Blount, Glossographia, ed. 1674. — L. *cupre-us*, of copper; with suffix *-ous.* — L. *cuprum*, copper. See **Copper**.

CUR, a small dog. (E.) ME. *kur, curre.* In early use. 'The fule *kur* dogge,' i.e. the foul cur-dog, Ancren Riwle, p. 290. Cf. Piers Plowman's Crede, ed. Skeat, 644. + MDu. *korre*, a house-dog, watch-dog, Oudemans; Swed. dial. *kurre.* β. So named from his growling; cf. Icel. *kurra*, to murmur, grumble; Dan. *kurre*, to coo, whirr; Swed. *kurra*, to rumble, to croak; Low G. *kurren*, to snarl (Lübben); MDu. *korrepot*, a grumbler (Oudemans), equivalent to Du. *knorrepot*, a grumbler, from Du. *knorren*, to grumble, growl, snarl. The word is imitative, and the letter R is known to be 'the dog's letter,' Romeo, ii. 4. 222. Cf. ME. *hurren*, to make a harsh noise. 'R is the dog's letter, and *hurreth* in the sound;' Ben Jonson, Eng. Grammar. Der. (perhaps) *curmudgeon.*

CURAÇAO, CURAÇOA, a liqueur. (Span.) So named, apparently, because first made from Curaçao oranges. [The usual spelling, with *-oa*, is incorrect.] — Span. *Curaçao*, 'an island off the coast of Venezuela in South America;' Pineda.

CURASSOW, a gallinaceous bird, like a turkey. (Span.) In a tr. of Buffon (1792); ii. 52. A phonetic spelling of *Curaçao* (above); whence it came

CURARI, another spelling of **Wourali**, q.v.

CURATE, one who has cure of souls. (L.) ME. *curat*, Chaucer, C. T. prol. 219. — Late L. *cūrātus*, a priest, curate; cf. Late L. *cūrātus*, adj.; *cūrātum beneficium*, a benefice with cure of souls pertaining to it. Formed as a pp., from the sb. *cūra*, a cure. See **Cure**. Der. *curac-y.* From the L. pp. *cūrātus* we have also *curat-ive*; also (from *cūrāre*), the sb. *cura-tor*, a guardian.

CURB, to check, restrain, lit. to bend. (F. — L.) In Merch. of Ven. i. 2. 26. *Curbed* = bent. 'By crooked and *curbed* lines;' Holland, Plutarch, p. 678. ME. *courben*, to bend; used also intransitively, to bend oneself, bow down. 'Yet I *courbed* on my knees;' P. Plowman, B. ii. 1. Cf. 'Hir necke is schort, hir shuldres *courbe*,' i.e. bend; Gower, C. A. bk. i. 1687. Also ME. *corbe*, sb.; as in 'a strong bitte with a *corbe*;' Dictes of the Philosophers (1477); fol. 26, back. — OF. (and F.) *courber*, to bend, crook, bow. — L. *curuāre*, to bend. — L. *curuus*, bent, curved. See **Curve**. Der. *curb*, sb., *curb-stone, kerb-stone.*

CURD, the coagulated part of milk. (E.) ME. *curd*, more often *crud* or *crod*, by the shifting of *r* so common in English. 'A fewe *cruddes* and creem;' P. Plowman, B. vi. 284; spelt *croddes*, id. C. ix. 306. From AS. *crud-*, weak grade of *crūdan*, to crowd, to press together; whence also prov. E. *crowd-y*, a kind of oatmeal gruel. + Irish and Gael. *gruth*, curds. See Stokes-Fick, p. 119. See **Crowd** (1). Der. *curd-y, curd-le.*

CURE, care, attention. (F. — L.) ME. *cure*, Chaucer, C. T. prol. 305; King Alisaunder, 4016. — OF. *cure*, care. — L. *cūra*, care, attention, cure. Origin uncertain; the OLat. form was *coera* or *coira*, for *koizā*; Brugmann, i. 874. ¶ It is well to remember that *cure* is wholly unconnected with E. *care*; the similarity of sound and sense is accidental. In actual speech, *care* and *cure* are used in different ways. Der. *cure*, verb; *cur-able*; *cure-less*; also *curate*, q. v.; *curious*, q. v. And, from the same source, *ac-cur-ate*, q. v.

CURFEW, a fire-cover; the time for covering fires; the curfew-bell. (F. — L.) ME. *courfew, curfew, curfu.* 'Aboute *corfew-tyme*;' Chaucer, C. T., A 3645. '*Curfu, ignitegium*;' Prompt. Parv. p. 110. — AF. *coeverfu*, Statutes of the Realm, i. 102 (an. 1285); *curfeu*, Liber

Albus, p. 369; OF. *covre-feu*, later *couvre-feu*, in which latter form it is given by Roquefort, who explains it as a bell rung at a fixed hour as a signal for putting out fires. The history is well known; see *Curfew* in Eng. Cycl., div. Arts and Sciences. — OF. *covrir*, later *couvrir*, to cover; and F. *feu*, fire, which is from the L. *focum*, acc. of *focus*, hearth, fire. See **Cover** and **Focus**. Der. *curfew-bell.*

CURIOUS, inquisitive. (F. — L.) ME. *curious*, busy; Romaunt of the Rose, 1052. — OF. *curios*, careful, busy. — L. *cūriōsus*, careful. — L. *cūra*, attention. See **Cure**. Der. *curious-ly, -ness*; *curios-i-ty* (ME. *curiosité*, Gower, C. A. iii. 383, bk. viii. 3114); F. *curiosité*, Englished 'curiosity' by Cotgrave, from L. acc. *cūriōsitātem*. Bacon uses *curiosity* to mean 'elaborate work;' Essay 46, On Gardens.

CURL, to twist into ringlets; a ringlet. (Scand.) In English, the verb seems rather formed from the sb. than *vice versâ.* Gascoigne has: 'But *curle* their locks with bodkins and with braids;' Epil. to the Steel Glas, l. 1142; in Skeat, Spec. of English. Palsgrave has *curled*, p. 309. We find another form *crul*, due to the shifting of *r*; cf. *cress, curd.* Chaucer has: 'With lokkes *crulle*,' i.e. with curled or crisped locks; Prol. 81; from the adj. *crul*, curly. Not in AS.; but cf. EFries. *krulle, krull, krul*, a curl. β. The form *curl* is of Scand. origin; cf. Norw. *kurle, kurl*; Dan. dial. *kurle*, a twist in thread; Swed. dial. *kurla*, to curl. + Du. *krul*, a curl; *krullen*, to curl; MDu. *krol*, adj. curled; *krollen*, to curl, wrinkle, rumple; Dan. *krölle*, a curl; *krölle*, to curl; Swed. *krullig*, crisp; Swed. dial. *krulla*, to curl (Rietz); Norw. *kurle, krull*, a curl (Aasen); G. *krolle.* γ. The orig. sense is clearly to twist, or bend; it is allied to EFries. *krillen*, to bend, turn, wind; Low G. *krellen*, to turn; NFries. *krall*, closely twisted; suggesting a Teut. base *krellan-*, to wind, str. vb.; pt. t. *krall*, pp. *krullanoz* (Franck). Der. *curl-y, -ing.*

CURLEW, an aquatic wading bird. (F.) ME. *corlew, curlew, curlu.* Spelt *corlew*, P. Plowman, C. xvi. 243; *corlue*, id. B. xiv. 43; *curlu*, Early E. Psalter, Ps. 104 (105). 38. — OF. *courlieus*, a curlew (Godefroy); MF. *corlieu*, 'a curlue;' Cot. He also gives the F. spellings *corlis* and *courlis.* Cf. Ital. *chiurlo*, a curlew; Span. *chorlito*, a curlew, evidently a dimin. form from an older *chorlo.* β. An imitative word, from the bird's cry. Cf. Ital. *chiurlare*, to howl like the horn-owl, Meadows; also Swed. *kurla*, to coo (Widegren).

CURMUDGEON, a covetous, stingy fellow. (E. and F.?) Spelt *curmudgeon*, Ford, The Lady's Trial, A. v. sc. 1; *curmudgin*, Hudibras, pt. ii. c. 2, l. 497 (Richardson), altered to *curmudgeon* in Bell's edition, i. 220. First found in 1577, spelt *curmudgen*, in Stanyhurst's Descr. of Ireland (in Holinshed, p. 102). [Spelt *corne-mudgin* (or *cornmudgin*) by Holland, to translate the L. *frumentarius*, a corn-dealer; see Holland's tr. of Livy, pp. 150, 1104, as cited in Richardson. The latter passage speaks of fines paid by 'certain *cornmudgins* for hourding up and keeping in their graine.' This is a forced spelling, and only tells us that the first syllable is not really a derivative of *corn.*] The etymology is wholly unknown, but the form shows that at least the latter part of the word is of French origin. It has been suggested that *cur-* represents E. *cur*, a dog. Lowland Scotch has *murgeon*, to mock, to grumble; also *mudgeon*, a grimace; see E.D.D. Perhaps it meant 'grumbling cur.'

CURRANT, a Corinth raisin. (F. — L. — Gk.) In Shak. Wint. Tale, iv. 3. 40. Haydn gives 1533 as the date when currant-trees were brought to England; but the name was also given to the small dried grapes brought from the Levant and known in England at an earlier time. 'In Liber Cure Cocorum [p. 16] called *raysyns of corauns*, F. *raisins de Corinthe*, the small dried grapes of the Greek islands. Then applied to our own sour fruit of somewhat similar appearance;' Wedgwood. So also we find 'roysonys de coraunce;' Babees Book, ed. Furnivall, p. 211, last line. F. '*Raisins de Corinthe*, currants, or small raisins;' Cot. Thus *currant* is a corruption of F. *Corinthe*, Corinth. — L. *Corinthus.* — Gk. Κόρινθος. ¶ Referred to in 1390; 'pro j lb. *racemorum de corenc*, vj d.;' Earl of Derby's Expeditions, Camden Soc., p. 11, l. 22.

CURRENT, running, flowing. (F. — L.) ME. *corrant.* 'Lik to the *corrant* fire, that renneth Upon a corde, as thou hast sein, Whan it with poudre is so besein Of sulphre;' Gower, C. A. iii. 96; bk. vii. 352. Afterwards altered to *current*, to look more like Latin. — OF. *curant*, pres. pt. of OF. *curre* (more commonly *corre*), to run. — L. *currere*, to run. Prob. for *cursere*; and allied to *horse.* Brugmann, i. §§ 499, 516. See **Horse**. Der. *current*, sb.; *-ly, currenc-y*; *curricle*, q. v.; and from the same source are *cursive, cursory*, q. v. From the same root are *concur, incur, occur, recur*; *corridor, courier*; *course, concourse, discourse, intercourse*; *excursion, incursion*; *courser, precursor*; *corsair*, &c.

CURRICLE, a short course; a chaise. (L.) 'Upon a *curricle* in this world depends a *long course* of the next;' Sir T. Browne, Christ. Morals, vol. ii. p. 23 (R.). The sense of 'chaise' is late; see N.E.D. — L. *curriculum*, a running, a course; also, a light car (Cicero). Formed as a double diminutive, with suffixes *-cu-* and *-lo-*

from the stem *curri-*; cf. *parti-cu-la*, a particle. – L. *currere*, to run. See **Current. Doublet,** *curriculum*, which is the L. word, unchanged. Cf. *curule*.

CURRY (1), to dress leather. (F.–L. *and* Teut.) 'Thei *curry* kinges,' i.e. flatter kings, lit. dress them ; said ironically ; Piers Plowman's Crede, ed. Skeat, 365. 'Like as he wold *coraye* his maystres hors ;' Lydgate, Minor Poems, p. 53. The E. verb is accompanied by the ME. sb. *currie*, apparatus, preparation, armament ; K. Alisaunder, 5118. – OF. *conreer, correier*, to prepare, arrange, set in order ; earliest form *conreder* (Godefroy) ; later *couroier* ; whence the forms *conroyer, courroyer*, given by Cotgrave, and explained by ' to curry, tew, or dress leather.' – OF. *conrei*, later *conroy*, equipage, gear, preparation of all kinds ; earliest form *cunreid* (Godefroy). [Formed, like *array* (OF. *arroi*), by prefixing a Latin preposition to a Teutonic word ; see **Array.**] – OF. *con-*, prefix, from L. *con-* (for *cum*), together ; and the OF. *reid*, array, order. This word answers to Ital. *-redo*, order, seen in Ital. *arredo*, array. – Late L. *-rēdum, -rēdium*, seen in the derived *arrēdium, conrēdium*, equipment, furniture, apparatus, gear. β. This *-rēdium* is of Teut. origin ; cf. Swed. *reda*, order, sb., or, as verb, to set in order ; Dan. *rede*, order, sb., or as verb, to set in order ; Icel. *reiδi*, tackle ; also O. Low G. *rēde*, AS. *rǣde*, ready ; see **Ready.** The same root appears in *array* and *disarray* ; and in F. *désarroi, arroi, corroyer*. **Der.** *curri-er*. ☞ The phr. to *curry favour* is a corruption of ME. to *curry favel*, i.e. to rub down a fallow-coloured horse. *Favell* was a common old name for a horse ; and *curry favel* occurs in Hoccleve, De Regim. Principium, st. 755, l. 5282. See my note to P. Plowman, C. iii. 6.

CURRY (2), a kind of seasoned dish. (Tamil.) A general term for seasoned dishes in India, for which there are many recipes. See *Curry* in Yule. – Tamil *kari*, sauce, relish for rice. Yule adds that the Port. form *caril* is from the cognate Canarese *karil*.

CURSE, to imprecate evil upon. (E.) ME. *cursien, cursen, corsen*. 'This *cursed* crone ;' Chaucer, C. T. 4852 (B 432) ; 'this *cursed* dede ;' id. 4853 (B 433). The sb. is *curs*, Chaucer, C. T. Prol. 663. AS. *cursian*, A. S. Chron. an. 1137 ; where the compound pp. *forcursæd* also occurs. The AS. sb. is *curs* ; Liber Scintillarum, c. 56 ; p. 174, l. 6. β. Remoter origin unknown ; perhaps originally Scandinavian, and due to a particular use of Swed. *korsa*, Dan. *korse*, to make the sign of the cross, from Swed. and Dan. *kors*, a cross, a corruption of Icel. *kross*, a cross, and derived from OIrish *cros* ; see **Cross.** γ. The N.E.D. says there is no trace of any connexion ; but Norw. *kors*, *kross*, a cross, plague, worry, trouble, comes very near the sense of a curse ; so Du. *kruis*, tribulation ; *slechte kinderen hebben is een groot kruis*, it is a great *cross* to have bad children ; cf. Dan. dial. *korselig*, that which one dreads, or crosses oneself against ; as, *korseligt veir*, horrible weather, which comes near the sense of ' cursed weather.' The ultimate connexion seems to me possible. Indeed, Berghaus gives Low G. *krüütsigen*, to curse (lit. to cross). Note, further, that Windisch gives OIrish *cúrsaigim*, 'I reprehend.' **Der.** *ac-cursed, curs-ed, curs-er*.

CURSIVE, running, flowing. (L.) Modern. Not in Todd's Johnson. A mere translation of Late L. *cursīvus*, cursive, as applied to handwriting. – L. *cursus*, pp. of *currere*, to run. See **Current.**

CURSORY, running, hasty, superficial. (L.) The odd form *cursorary* (other edd. *cursenary, curselary*) is in Shak. Hen. V, v. 2. 77. ' He discoursed *cursorily* ;' Bp. Taylor, Great Exemplar, pt. iii. § 14 (R.). – Late L. *cursōrius*, chiefly used in the adv. *cursōriē*, hastily, quickly. – L. *cursōri-*, declensional stem of *cursor*, a runner. – L. *curs-us*, pp. of *currere*, to run. See **Current. Der.** *cursori-ly*.

CURT, short, concise. (L.) ' *Maestro del campo*, Peck ! his name is *curt* ;' Ben Jonson, The New Inn, iii. 1. – L. *curtus*, docked, clipped. Cf. Gk. καρτός, chopped. – √SKER, to shear, cut ; whence also E. *shear*, and Icel. *skarδr*, docked. See **Shear. Der.** *curt-ly, curt-ness ; curt-ail*, q. v.

CURTAIL, to cut short, abridge, dock. (F.–L.) α. *Curtail* is a corruption of an older *curtall*, and was orig. accented on the former syllable ; there is no pretence for saying that it is derived from the F. *court tailler*, to cut short, a phrase which does not appear to have been used ; though it is probable that both E. *tail* and F. *tailler* had some influence on the development of the word. The two instances in Shakespeare may suffice to show this. ' I, that am *cúr-tail'd* of this fair proportion ;' Rich. III, i. 1. 18. And again : ' When a Gentleman is dispos'd to sweare, it is not for any standers-by to *curtall* his oathes ;' Cymbeline, ii. 1. 12, according to the first folio ; altered to *curtail* in later editions. β. Cotgrave translates *accourcir* by ' to shorten, abridge, *curtall*, clip, or cut short ;' and this may help to show that the French for to *curtail* was not *court tailler* (!), but *accourcir*. γ. The verb was, in fact, derived from the adj. *curtall* or *curtal*, having a docked tail, occurring four times in Shakespeare, viz. Pilgr. 273 ; M. Wives, ii. 1. 114 ; Com. Err. iii. 2. 151 ; All's Well, ii. 3. 65. – MF. *courtault, courtaut* ; both forms are

given by Cotgrave, and explained by ' a curtall ;' or, as an adj., by ' curtall, being curtalled.' He also gives : ' *Double courtaut*, a strong curtall, or a horse of middle size between the ordinary curtall, and horse of service.' δ. The occurrence of the final *ll* in *curtall* shows that the word was taken into English before the old form *courtault* fell into disuse. Cf. Florio, who gives the Ital. ' *cortaldo*, a curtall, a horse without a taile ; *cortare*, to shorten, to curtall ; *corta*, short, briefe, curtald.' – OF. *court* (Ital. *corto*), short ; with suffix *-ault, -alt*, equivalent to Ital. *-aldo*, Late L. *-aldus*, of Germanic origin, as in *Regin-ald* ; from G. *walt*, O. Low G. *wald* (Icel. *vald*), power. See Hatzfeld's French Dict. pref. § 138. – L. *curtus*, docked. See **Curt.**

CURTAIN, a hanging cloth. (F.–L.) ME. *cortin, curtin* ; Chaucer, C. T. 6831 (D 1249). The pp. *cortined*, furnished with curtains, is in K. Alisaunder, ed. Weber, 1028. – OF. *cortine, curtine*, a curtain. – Late L. *cortina*, a small court, small enclosure, croft, rampart or ' curtain ' of a castle, hanging curtain round a small enclosure. See Exod. xxvi. 1 (Vulgate). – L. *cort-*, stem of *cōrs*, a court ; with suffix *-ina*, fem of *-inus*, adj. suffix. See **Court** (1). **Der.** *curtain*, verb.

CURTILAGE, a court-yard. (F.–L.) ' All the comedities (*sic*) wythyn the seid gardyn and *curtelage* ;' Bury Wills, ed. Tymms, p. 46 (A.D. 1467). – AF. *curtilage*, Stat. of the Realm, i. 221. Formed, with suffix *-age*, from OF. *cortil, courtil*, ' a back-yard ;' Cot. – Late L. *cortile*, an enclosure, small yard (Ducange). Dimin. of Late L. *cortis*, a court-yard, from L. *cōrs*. See **Court** (1).

CURTLEAXE, a corruption of *cutlass* ; see **Cutlass.**

CURTSEY, an obeisance ; see **Courtesy.**

CURULE, chiefly in the phr. *curule chair*, a chair used by the highest magistrates of Rome. (L.) Butler has ' *curule* wit ;' Hudibras, i. 1. 715. – L. *curūlis, currūlis*, applied to *equi*, horses, and to *sella*, the curule chair. – L. *currus*, a chariot ; see **Curricle.**

CURVE, adj. crooked ; sb. a bent line. (L.) Not in early use. The ME. form was *courbe*, whence E. *curb*, q. v. Blount's Glossographia, ed. 1674, has the adjectives *curvous* and *curvilineal*, and the sbs. *curvature* and *curvity*. ' This line thus *curve* ;' Congreve, An Impossible Thing, l. 137. – L. *curuus*, crooked, bent (base *cur-*). + Gk. κυρ-τός, bent. See **Crown. Der.** *curve*, verb ; *curvat-ure*, L. *cur-uātūra*, from *curuāre*, to bend ; *curvi-linear* ; also *curvet*, q. v. And see *curb*.

CURVET, to bound like a horse. (Ital. – L.) The verb is in Shak. As You Like It, iii. 2. 258 ; the sb. is in All's Well, ii. 3. 299. – Ital. *corvetta*, a curvet, leap, bound ; *corvettare*, to curvet, frisk. [The E. word was orig. *corvet*, thus Florio has : ' *Coruetta*, a coruet, a sault, a prancing or continuall dancing of a horse.'] – MItal. *corvare*, old spelling of *curvare*, ' to bow, to bende, to stoope, to crouch, to make crooked ;' Florio. Thus *to curvet* meant to crouch or bend slightly ; hence, to prance, frisk. – L. *curuāre*, to bend. – L. *curuus*, bent. See **Curve. Der.** *curvet*, sb. (Ital. *corvetta*).

CUSHAT, the ring-dove, wood-pigeon. (E.) ' *Cowshot*, palumbus ;' Nicholson's Glossarium Northanhymbricum, in Ray's Collection, ed. 1691, pp. 139–152. *Cowschote* ; Catholicon Angl. (1483). AS. *cúsceote*, a wild pigeon ; Voc. 260. 7 ; *cūscote*, E. E. Texts, p. 85. For *cū-scote*, where *scote* prob. means darter, lit. ' shooter,' from *scot-*, weak grade of *scēotan*, to shoot (cf. AS. *scēota*, a kind of trout) ; and perhaps *cū* refers to the *coo* of the bird. Cf. ' Coo, coo, come now,' &c. ; Song of the Cushat ; in T. Dyer, Folklore, p. 98.

CUSHION, a pillow, soft case for resting on. (F.–L.) The pl. *cuischuns* is in Wyclif, 1 Kings, v. 9. Spelt *quysshin*, Chaucer, Troil. and Cress. ii. 1229. – OF. *coissin*, a cushion (Supp. to Godefroy) ; later *coussin*, ' a cushion to sit on ;' Cot. [It is supposed that *coissin* was the true form ; perhaps it was influenced by OF. *coute*, a quilt.] – Late L. type *coxinum*, a support for the hip ; from *coxa*, hip, thigh (like L. *cubital*, elbow-cushion, from *cubitus*, elbow). Cf. Ital. *cuscino*, cushion, *coscia*, hip ; Span. *cojin*, cushion, *cuja*, hip. See *Romania*, 1892, p. 87. ¶ The AF. form *quissine* occurs in A. Neckam (Wright's Vocab. i. 100) ; cf. E. *cuisses*, q. v. ¶ The G. *kissen*, cushion, is borrowed from one of the Romance forms ; cf. Ital. *cucino*, *cuscino*, Span. *coxin*, Port. *coxim*.

CUSP, a point, tip. (L.) Not in early use. ' Full on his *cusp* his angry master sate, Conjoin'd with Saturn, baleful both to man ;' Dryden, The Duke of Guise, Act iv (R.). It was a term in astrology. ' No other planet hath so many dignities, Either by himself or in regard of the *cuspes* ;' Beaum. and Fletcher, Bloody Brother, iv. 2. – L. *cuspis*, a point ; gen. *cuspid-is*. **Der.** *cuspid-ate, cuspid-at-ed.*

CUSTARD, a composition of milk, eggs, &c. (F.–L.) In Shak. All's Well, ii. 5. 41 ; *custard-coffin*, the upper crust covering a custard ; Tam. Shrew, iv. 3. 82. The old *custard* was something widely different from what we now call by that name, and could be cut into squares with a knife. John Russell, in his Boke of Nurture, enumerates it amongst the ' Bake-metes ;' see Babees Boke, ed. Furnivall, p. 147, l. 492 ; p. 271, l. 1 ; p. 273, l. 21 ; and esp. the note on l. 492, at

p. 211. It was also spelt *custade*, id. p. 170, l. 802. β. And there can be no reasonable doubt that such is a better spelling, and that it is, moreover, a corruption of the ME. *crustade*, a general name for pies made with *crust*; see the recipe for *crustade ryal* quoted in the Babees Book, p. 211. [A still older spelling is *crustate*, Liber Cure Cocorum, ed. Morris, p. 40, derived immediately from L. *crustātus*.] ─OF. *croustade*, 'paté, tourte, chose qui en couvre une autre,' i.e. a pasty, tart, crust; Roquefort. Roquefort gives the Prov. form *crustado*. Cf. Ital. *crostata*, 'a kind of daintie pye;' Florio.─L. *crustātus*, pp. of *crustāre*, to encrust, from *crusta*, a crust. See **Crust.** **Der.** *custard-apple*, an apple like custard, having a soft pulp; Dampier, Voyage, an. 1699, iii. 33.

CUSTODY, keeping, care, confinement. (L.) Spelt *custodye*, Sir T. More, Works, p. 40.─L. *custōdia*, a keeping guard.─L. *custōd-*, stem of *custos*, a guardian; lit. 'a hider.'─√ KEUDH, to hide, conceal; whence also Gk. κεύθειν, to hide, and E. *hide.* See Brugmann, i. § 699. See **Hide** (1). **Der.** *custodi-al, custodi-an.*

CUSTOM, wont, usage. (F.─L.) ME. *custume, custome, costume*; Chaucer, C. T. 6264 (D 682). Spelt *cu·tume*, Old Eng. Homilies, ed. Morris, ii. 11, l. 11.─OF. *costume, custume*, custom (Late L. *costuma*, Chartulary of 705); mod. F. *costume.* From a Romanic type **costumne*, prob. for **costudne*, shortened from *consuētūdinem*, acc. of the classical L. *consuētūdo*, custom.─L. *consuētus*, pp. of *consuescere*, to accustom; inchoative form of L. **consuēre*, to be accustomed.─L. *con-*, for *cum*, together, greatly, very; and *suēre*, to be accustomed (Lucr. i. 60), more commonly used in the inchoative form *suescere*. β. *Suēre* appears to be derived from L. *suus*, one's own, as though it meant 'to make one's own,' or 'to have it one's own way.' ¶ Cf. F. *amertume*, for L. *amāritūdinem*; F. *enclume*, for L. *incūdinem.* **Der.** *custom-ar-y, -ar-i-ly, -ar-i-ness, -er*; *-house*; also *ac-custom*, q. v.

CUT, to make an incision. (Scand.) ME. *cutten, kitten*, a weak verb; pt. t. *kutte, kitte.* The form *cutte*, signifying 'he cut,' past tense, occurs in Layamon, i. 349; iii. 228; later text. These appear to be the earliest passages in which the word occurs. It answers to Late AS. form **cyttan* (for **cut-ian*); and is of Scand. origin. Cf. Swed. dial. *kuta, kåta, kvota*, to cut with a knife; *kuta, kytti*, a knife (Rietz); Icel. *kuti*, a little knife; Norw. *kyttel, kjutul*, a knife for barking trees (Aasen); MSwed. *kotta*, to cut with a knife (Ihre). All (possibly) due to OF. *cout-el*, a knife; see **Cutlass.** **Der.** *cut*, sb.; *cutt-ing, -er*; *cut-water*; *cut-purse.*

CUTCHERRY, a court-house, office. (Hind.) 'The prodigious labour of *cutcherry*;' Thackeray, Vanity Fair, ch. 57 (or ch. 22 of vol. ii).─Hind. *kachahrī*, 'a hall of justice, town-house, court, a public office for the receipt of revenue,' &c.; Forbes.

CUTICLE, the outermost thin skin. (L.) '*Cuticle*, the outermost thin skin;' Kersey's Dict. ed. 1715; and in Phillips (1658). The adj. *cuticular* is in Blount's Glossographia, ed. 1674.─L. *cutícula*, the skin; double dimin., with suffixes *-cu-la-*, from *cuti-*, declensional stem of *cutis*, the skin, hide. [Cf. *particle* from *part.*] The L. *cutis* is cognate with E. *hide.* See **Hide** (2). **Der.** *cuticul-ar*, from the L. *cutícula*; also *cut-an-e-ous*, from a barbarous Latin *cutāneus*, not given in Ducange, but existing also in the F. *cutané*, skinny, of the skin (Cotgrave), and in the Ital. and Span. *cutaneo.*

CUTLASS, a sort of sword. (F.─L.) The orig. sense was 'a little knife.' Spelt *coutelace*, in Dodsley's Old Plays, ed. Hazlitt, v. 189. Better spelt *cutlas*, with one *s.*─F. *coutelas*, 'a cutlelas, or courtelas, or short sword, for a man-at-arms;' Cot. Cf. Ital. *coltellaccio*, 'a curtelax, or knife;' Florio. [The Ital. suffix *-accio* (L. *-āceum*) is a general augmentative one, that can be added at pleasure to a sb.; thus from *libro*, a book, is formed *libraccio*, a large ugly book. So also Ital. *coltellaccio* means 'a large ugly knife.']─OF. *coutel, cultel* (Littré), whence F. *couteau*, a knife. Cf. Ital. *coltello*, a knife, dagger.─L. *cultellum*, acc. of *cultellus*, a knife; dimin. of *culter*, a ploughshare. See **Coulter.** ¶ The F. suffix *-as*, Ital. *-accio*, was suggested by the L. suffix *-āceus*; but was so little understood that it was confused with the F. *axe.* Hence the word was corrupted to *curtleaxe*, as in Shak. As You Like It, i. 3. 119: 'a gallant *curtleaxe* upon my thigh.' Yet a *curtleaxe* was a sort of sword!

CUTLER, a maker of knives. (F.─L.) ME. *coteler*; Geste Historyal of the Destruction of Troy, ed. Panton and Donaldson, l. 1597.─AF. *cotillere*, Liber Custumarum, p. 185; OF. *cotelier*; later *coutelier*, as in mod. F.─Late L. *cultellārius*, (1) a soldier armed with a knife; (2) a cutler. Formed with suffix *-ārius* from L. *cultell-*, base of *cultellus*, a knife, dimin. of *culter*, a ploughshare. See **Coulter.** **Der.** *cutler-y.*

CUTLET, a slice of meat. (F.─L.) Lit. 'a little rib.' '*Cutlets*, a dish made of the short ribs of a neck of mutton;' Kersey's Dict. ed. 1715.─F. *côtelette*, a cutlet; spelt *costelette* in Cotgrave, who explains it by 'a little rib, side, &c.' A double diminutive, formed with suffixes *-el-* and *-ette*, from OF. *coste*, a rib (Cotgrave).─L. *costa*, a rib. See **Coast.**

CUTTER, a swift sailing vessel. (Scand.) First in 1745; from the verb *to cut*, to speed (E.D.D.).─Norw. *kut-*, weak grade of *kūta* (pt. t. *kaut*), to run, to speed. See Phil. Soc. Trans. 1903, p. 145.

CUTTLE, CUTTLE-FISH, a sort of mollusc. (E.) Cotgrave translates the F. *cornet* by 'a sea-cut or *cuttle-fish*;' and the F. *seche* by 'the sound or *cuttle-fish.*' *Cuttle* occurs in Bacon, Nat. Hist. § 742. The Prompt. Parv. has both *cotul* and *codull.* Cf. prov. E. *cuddle, coodle.* Corrupted from *cuddle* by the influence of similar words in MDu. and H. German. The form *cuddle* is a legitimate and regular formation from AS. *cudele*, the name of the fish. 'Sepia, *cudele*, vel *wāse-scīte*;' Ælfric's Glossary, ed. Somner, Nomina Piscium. [The name *wāse-scīte* means ooze-shooter, dirt-shooter, from the animal's habit of discharging sepia.] + MDu. *kuttel-visch*, a cuttle-fish; Kilian. But this is rather a High-German form, and borrowed from the G. *kuttel-fisch*, a cuttle-fish. β. The remoter origin is obscure; the G. *kuttel-fisch* is in no way connected with the G. *kuttel*, bowels, entrails. γ. Perhaps it meant 'little bag,' from its shape, or its ink-bag; cf. Low G. *kudel*, a purse (Lübben), AS. *codd*, a bag. See **Cod** (2). See Phil. Soc. Trans. 1902, p. 661.

CYANOGEN, a compound radical (in chemistry), consisting of nitrogen and carbon. (Gk.) Named by Gay-Lussac (1815) from its occurring in Prussian blue; N.E.D.─Gk. κύανο-, for κύανος, a dark blue mineral; and *γεν-*, as *γέν-ος*, race, with the idea of 'producing.' **Der.** (from κύανος), *cyan-ide, cyan-ite, cyano-type.*

CYCLE, a circle, round of events. (F.─L.─Gk.) '*Cycle* and *epicycle*, orb in orb;' Milton, P. L. viii. 84. And in Sir T. Browne, Vulgar Errors, b. iv. c. 12. § 10. Older form *cikle*, Sir T. Elyot, The Governour, bk. i. c. 25. § 3.─F. *cycle*, 'a round, or circle;' Cotgrave. ─L. *cyclus*, merely a Latinised form of Gk. κύκλος, a circle, cycle. + Skt. *chakra-*, a wheel, disc, circle, astronomical figure. Allied to E. *wheel*; see **Wheel.** ¶ The word may have been borrowed immediately from Latin, or even from the Greek. **Der.** *cycl-ic, cycl-ic-al*; *cycloid*, from Gk. κυκλοειδής, circular (but technically used with a new sense), form κύκλο-, for κύκλος, and εἶδος, form, shape; *cycloid-al*; *cyclone*, a coined word of modern invention, from Gk. κυκλῶν, whirling round, pres. part. of κυκλόω, I whirl round, from Gk. κύκλος. [Hence the final *-e* in *cyclone* is mute, and merely indicates that the vowel *o* is long.] Also *cyclo-metry*, the measuring of circles; see **Metre.** Also *cyclo-pædia* or *cyclo-pedia*, from Gk. κυκλοπαιδία, which should rather (perhaps) be *encyclopedia*, from Gk. ἐγκυκλοπαιδεία, used for ἐγκύκλιος παιδεία, the circle of arts and sciences, lit. circular or complete instruction; der. from ἐγκύκλιος, circular, and παιδεία, instruction; which is from ἐν, in, κύκλος, a circle, and παῖς (gen. παιδός), a boy, child. Also *epi-cycle, bi-cycle, tri-cycle.*

CYCLAMEN, a flower; a genus of *Primulaceæ.* (L.─Gk.) Lyte (tr. of Dodoens, bk. iii. c. 11) has *cyclamen*, and *cylaminon.*─Late L. *cyclamen*, for L. *cyclamīnos, -on.*─Gk. κυκλάμινος, -ον, cyclamen; named from its bulbous roots; from Gk. κύκλος, a circle.

CYCLOPS, one of a race of one-eyed giants. (L.─Gk.) Douglas, tr. of Æneid, bk. iii. c. 10, has *Ciclopes*, for *Cyclopes*, pl. of Cyclops.─L. *Cyclops*, pl. *Cyclōpes*, Virgil, Æn. iii. 644.─Gk. κύκλωψ, a one-eyed giant; Homer, Od. ix. 106; pl. κύκλωπες. Lit. 'round-eyed.'─Gk. κύκλ(ο)-, for κύκλος, a circle; and ὤψ, an eye.

CYGNET, a young swan. (F.─L.─Gk.) Spelt *cignet* in old edd. of Shak. Tro. and Cress. i. 1. 58. Formed as a diminutive, with suffix *-t*, from OF. *cigne*, a swan; Cot. **1.** At first sight it seems to be from Lat. *cygnus*, a swan; earlier form *cycnus.*─Gk. κύκνος, a swan. **2.** But the oldest F. form appears as *cisne* (Littré); cf. Span. *cisne*, a swan; and these must be from Late L. *cicinus* (Diez), a by-form of *cucinus* (Brugmann, i. § 950), likewise from κύκνος (as before). β. The Gk. κύκνος is allied to Skt. *çakuna-s*, a large bird; L. *ciconia*, a stork. See Diez; 4th ed. p. 714.

CYLINDER, a roller-shaped body. (F.─L.─Gk.) *Cilinder* is in Minsheu, ed. 1627. [An older form *chilyndre* is in Chaucer, C. T. Group B, 1396, where Tyrwhitt reads *kalender*, C. T. 13136. It there means a cylindrically shaped portable sun-dial.]─MF. *cilindre*, later *cylindre*, the *y* being introduced to look more like the Latin; both forms are in Cotgrave.─L. *cylindrus*, a cylinder.─Gk. κύλινδρος, a cylinder, lit. a roller.─Gk. κυλίνδειν, to roll; an extension of κυλίειν, to roll. Cf. Church-Slav. *kolo*, a wheel. (√ QEL.) **Der.** *cylindr-ic, cylindr-ic-al.*

CYMBAL, a clashing musical instrument. (F.─L.─Gk.) ME. *cimbale, cymbale*; Wyclif, 2 Kings, vi. 5; Ps. cl. 5.─OF. *cimbale*, 'a cymball;' Cot. Later altered to *cymbale* (also in Cotgrave) to look more like the Latin.─L. *cymbalum*, a cymbal; also spelt *cymbalon.*─Gk. κύμβαλον, a cymbal; named from its hollow, cup-like shape.─Gk. κύμβος, κύμβη, anything hollow, a cup, basin. + Skt. *kumbha-s, kumbhi*, a pot, jar. The form of the root is KEUBH; Benfey, p. 196.

CYME, a species of inflorescence. (F.─L.─Gk.) Modern.─F. *cyme*; also *cime*, 'the toppe or knappe of a plant;' Cot.─L. *cyma.*─Gk. κῦμα, anything swollen, a wave, the young sprout of a cabbage (as in L.). — √ KEU, to swell; Gk. κύειν, to be pregnant. Doublet, *cyma* (L. *cȳma*), an ogee moulding of a cornice.

CYNIC, misanthropic; lit. dog-like. (L. — Gk.) In Shak. Jul. Cæs. iv. 3. 133. — L. *cynicus*, one of the sect of Cynics. — Gk. κυνικός, dog-like, cynical, a Cynic. — Gk. κυν-, stem of κύων, a dog. **+** L. *can-is*, a dog; Irish *cū* (gen. *con*), a dog; Skt. *çvan-*, a dog; Goth. *hunds*, a hound. See **Hound.** Der. *cynic-al, -al-ly, -ism*; and see *cynosure*.

CYNOSURE, a centre of attraction. (L. — Gk.) ‘The *cynosure* of neighbouring eyes;’ Milton, L’Allegro, 80. — L. *cynosura*, the constellation of the Lesser Bear, or rather, the stars composing the tail of it; the last of the three is the pole-star, whence the sense of ‘guiding-star,’ or centre of interest. — Gk. κυνόσουρα, a dog’s-tail; also, the Cynosure, another name for the Lesser Bear, or, more strictly, for the tail of it. — Gk. κυνός, dog’s, gen. case of κύων, a dog; and οὐρά, a tail. See **Cynic.**

CYPRESS (1), a kind of tree. (F. — L. — Gk.) ME. *cipres, cipresse, cupresse.* ‘Ase palme other ase *cipres*;’ Ayenbite of Inwyt, p. 131. Also called a *cipɪr-tre*. ‘Hec cipressus, a *cypyr-tre*;’ Wright’s Vocab. i. 228. — OF. *cypres*, later *cyprès*, explained by Cotgrave as ‘the Cyprus tree, or Cyprus wood.’ — L. *cyparissus*; also *cupressus*. — Gk. κυπάρισσος, the cypress. β. Prob. of Eastern origin; by some supposed to be the Heb. *gōpher*, gopher-wood, Gen. vi. 14; see Gesenius.

CYPRESS (2), **CYPRESS-LAWN**, a kind of lawn or crape. (F. — L. — Gk.) ‘A *cipresse* [or *cypress*] not a bosom Hideth my heart;’ Tw. Nt. iii. 1. 132. ‘*Cypress* black as e’er was crow;’ Wint. Tale, iv. 4. 221. See note on *cypress* in Ben Jonson, Every Man in his Humour, i. 3. 121, ed. Wheatley. β. Palsgrave explains F. *crespe* by ‘a cypres for a womans necke;’ and Cotgrave has: ‘ *Crespe*, cipres, cob-web lawn;’ which seems to show some confusion between *cypress* and *crape.* But in old wills they are kept distinct. Thus, in Testamenta Eboracensia, i. 240 (A.D. 1398), we find: ‘unum [velum] de *cypres*,’ a cypress veil; ‘ij. flameola de *cipres*,’ id. i. 289 (A.D. 1402); also ‘flameolam meam de *crispo*,’ my crape veil, i. 271 (1400); ‘flameolum de *krespe*,’ i. 382 (1415). γ. But the ME. *cipres* also meant (1) a cloth of gold or other valuable material; (2) a valuable satin (N.E.D.). It is probable that all these were alike named from the island of Cyprus, whence they were imported. — OF. *Cipre, Cypre*, Cyprus. — L. *Cyprum*, acc. of *Cyprus.* — Gk. Κύπρος, Cyprus.

CYST, a pouch (in animals) containing morbid matter. (L. — Gk.) Formerly written *cystis.* ‘*Cystis*, a bladder; also, the bag that contains the matter of an imposthume;’ Kersey’s Dict. ed. 1715. — Late L. *cystis*, merely a Latinised form of the Gk. word. — Gk. κύστις, the bladder, a bag, pouch. Der. *cyst-ic.*

CZAR, the emperor of Russia. (Russ. — Teut. — L.) ‘Two *czars* are one too many for a throne;’ Dryden, Hind and Panther, iii. 1278. — Russian *tsare* (with *e* mute), a king. OSlav. *cěsarĭ*; Miklosich, p. 28. Borrowed from Teutonic; cf. Goth. *kaisar.* — L. *Cæsar.* ¶ This has been disputed; but see Miklosich. Cf. Matt. xiii. 24, in Schleicher, Indogermanische Chrestomathie, p. 275; where OSlav. *cesarstvo* occurs for Russ. *tsarstvo*, kingdom; &c. Der. *czar-ina*, with Ital. suffix -*ina*, from G. -*in*, fem. suffix, as in *landgravine, margravine*, the Russ. form being *tsaritsa*; also *czarowitz*, from Russ. *tsarevich'*, the czar’s son.

D

DAB (1), to strike gently. (E.) ME. *dabben.* ‘The Flemmisshe hem *dabbeth* o the het bare ’ = the Flemings strike them on the bare head; Polit. Songs, ed. Wright, p. 192. The ME. sb. is *dabbe.* ‘Philot him gaf anothir *dabbe*’ = Philotas gave him another blow; K. Alisaunder, ed. Weber, l. 2306. Now generally associated with the notion of striking with something soft and moist, but the orig. sense is merely to *tap.* An E. word; of imitative origin. MDu. *dabben*, to pinch, to knead, to fumble, to dabble; Oudemans. Cf. Norw. *dabba*, to tap with the foot (Ross); prov. G. (Strassburg) *dabbe* = G. *tappen* (C. Schmidt); G. *tappen*, to grope, fumble; prov. G. *tapp, tappe*, fist, paw, blow, kick; Flügel’s Dict. ¶ From the G. *tappen* we have F. *taper*, and E. *tap.* Hence *dab* and *tap* are doublets. See **Tap.** Der. *dab*, sb. See **Dabble**, and **Dub.**

DAB (2), expert. (E.) The phrase ‘he is a *dab* hand at it’ means he is expert at it. Goldsmith has: ‘one writer excels at a plan; ... another is a *dab* at an index;’ The Bee, no. 1. A word of slang origin, and perhaps due to *dab*, vb. (above). It may have been to some extent confused with the adj. *dapper.* See **Dapper.** ¶ There is no evidence connecting it with *adept*, as some have guessed.

DAB (3), a fish. (E.) A small flat fish; ME. *dabbe*, Liber Albus, p. 375; pl. *dabys* (A.D. 1460), Antiquarian Repository, ii. 211. Prob. considered as a soft mass *dabbed* down. See **Dab** (1). And cf. prov. G. (Kurhessen) *dob*, soft, *dabberig*, soft (Vilmar).

DABBLE, to keep on dabbing. (E.) The frequentative of *dab*, with the usual suffixed -*le.* The word is used by Drayton, Polyolbion, s. 25, l. 97; see quotations in Richardson. Cf. ‘ *dabbled* in blood;’ Shak. Rich. III, i. 4. 54. **+** MDu. *dabbelen*, to pinch, to knead, to fumble, to dabble, splash about; formed by the frequentative suffix -*el*- from MDu. *dabben*, with a like sense; Oudemans. See **Dab** (1). Cf. Norw. *dabla*, to dabble in water (Ross); Icel. *dafla*, to dabble; WFlem. *dɐbbelen*, to fumble, handle.

DAB-CHICK, DOB-CHICK; see **Didapper.**

DACE, a small river-fish. (F. — O. Low G.) ‘*Dace* or *Dare*, a small river-fish;’ Kersey’s Dict. ed. 1715. Shak. has *dace*, 2 Hen. IV, iii. 2. 356. 1. Another name for the fish is the *dart.* 2. *Dare*, formerly pronounced *dahr* (daar), is simply the F. *dard* (=Late L. acc. *dardum*), and *dart* is due to the same source. Cf. ME. *dar*, Voc. 763. 36. 3. So also *dace*, formerly *darce* (Babees Book, ed. Furnivall, p. 174), answers to the OF. nom. *dars* or *darz*, a dart, javelin, for which Roquefort gives quotations, and Littré cites OF. *dars* with the sense of ‘dace.’ The AF. pl. *darces* occurs in Liber Custumarum, p. 279. This OF. *dars* is due to Late L. nom. *dardus*, a dart, javelin, of Low G. origin. ¶ From this OF. *dars* is also derived the Breton *darz*, a dace; cf. F. *dard*, ‘a dart, a javelin; ... also, a dace or dare fish;’ Cotgrave. **☞** So named from its quick motion. See **Dart.**

DACHSHUND, a badger-hound. (G.) From G. *dachshund*, badger-hound. See *dachs*, a badger, in Kluge.

DACOIT, a robber. (Hind.) See Dacoit in Yule. — Hind. *ḍakait*, a robber belonging to an armed gang (Forbes). — Hind. *ḍākā*, robbery by an armed gang (Forbes; H. H. Wilson). Der. *dacoit-y*, robbery.

DACTYL, the name of a foot, marked — ∪ ∪. (L. — Gk.) Puttenham, Arte of Poetrie, ed. Arber, p. 83, speaks of ‘the Greeke *dactilus*;’ this was in A.D. 1589. Dryden speaks of ‘spondees and *dactyls*’ in his Account prefixed to Annus Mirabilis. — L. *dactylus*, a dactyl. — Gk. δάκτυλος, a finger, a dactyl; from the *three* joints of the finger. See Trench, On the Study of Words, on the sense of *dactyl.* Der. *dactyl-ic.*

DAD, a father. (E.) In Shak. Tw. Nt. iv. 2. 140; K. John, ii. 467. A child’s word for father. So also EFries. *tatte*; W. *tad*, father; Corn. *tat*; Bret. *tad, tat*, father; Irish *daid*; Gael. *daidein*, papa (used by children); Gk. τάτα, father; used by youths to their elders; Skt. *tata-*, father; *tāta-*, dear one; a term of endearment, used by parents addressing their children, by teachers addressing their pupils, and by children addressing their parents. A familiar word, and widely spread. Der. *dadd-y*, a dimin. form.

DADO, the die, or square part in the middle of the pedestal of a column, between the base and the cornice; also, that part of an apartment between the plinth and the impost moulding. (Ital. — L.) So defined by Gwilt, in Webster; see also Gloss. of Architecture, Oxford, 1840. The word is somewhat old, and occurs in Phillips, ed. 1706. Like some other architectural terms, it is Italian. — Ital. *dado*, a die, cube, pedestal; Torriano (1688) has ‘*dado*, any kind of dye to play withall, any cube or square thing.’ The pl. *dadi*, dice, is in Florio, from a sing. *dado.* The same word as Span. *dado*, OF. *det*; further under **Die** (2), which is a doublet.

DAFFODIL, a flower of the amaryllis tribe. (F. — L. — Gk.) The *d* is no part of the word, but prefixed much in the same way as the *t* in *Ted*, for *Edward.* It is difficult to account for it; it is just possible that it is a contraction from E. *th’affodill*, used by Cotgrave. At any rate, the ME. form was *affodill.* ‘*Affodylle*, herbe, affodillus, albucea;’ Prompt. Parv. — OF. *asphodile*, more commonly *affrodile*, ‘th’ affodill, or asphodill flower;’ Cotgrave. Cf. ‘*aphrodille*, the affodill, or asphodill flower;’ id. [Here the French has an inserted *r*, which is no real part of the word, and is a mere corruption. It is clear that the E. word was borrowed from the French *before* this *r* was inserted. We have sure proof of this, in the fact that Cotgrave gives, not only the forms *asphrodille, asphrodile*, and *affrodille*, but also *asphodile*, ‘the daffadill.’ The last of these is the oldest.] — L. *asphodelus*, borrowed from the Greek. — Gk. ἀσφόδελος, asphodel. See **Asphodel.** Der. Corrupted forms are *daffadilly* and *daffadowndilly*, both used by Spenser, Shep. Kal. April, ll. 60, 140. ¶ See N.E.D.; and the article by Dr. Murray in Phil. Soc. Proceedings, Feb. 6, 1880.

DAFT, foolish. See **Deft**, below.

DAGGER, a dirk; short sword for stabbing. (F.) ME. *daggere*, Chaucer, C. T. prol. 113. [Connected with the ME. verb *daggen*, to pierce. ‘Derfe dynttys thay dalte with *daggande* sperys,’ i.e. they dealt severe blows with piercing spears; Allit. Morte Arthure, ed. Brock, l. 3749. Cf. MDu. *duggen*, to stab; Oudemans; MDu. *dag*, a dagger; id.] — F. *dague*, a dagger, of unknown origin; and certainly neither Celtic nor Germanic; Körting, § 2738. β. It might be better to take Late L. *daga* as the source; since OF. *dague* hardly occurs before 1397 (see Ducange). Cf. also Ital. and Span. *daga*, a dagger; Port. *adaga*. The Port. form suggests an Eastern origin; cf. Heb. *dākhāh*, to strike; or Arab. *dahw*, driving, thrusting.

DAGGLE, to moisten, wet with dew. (Scand.) So in Sir W. Scott. 'The warrior's very plume, I say, Was *daggled* by the dashing spray;' Lay of the Last Minstrel, i. 29. Pope uses it in the sense of to run through mud, lit. to become wet with dew; Prol. to Satires, l. 225. Palsgrave has: 'I *daggyll*, or I *dagge* a thing with myer;' p. 506. It is a frequentative verb, formed from the prov. Eng. *dag*, to sprinkle with water; see Atkinson's Cleveland Glossary. ─ Swed. *dagg*, dew; Icel. *dögg* (gen. *daggar*), dew. These sbs. are cognate with E. *dew*. See **Dew**. Cf. also Icel. *döggva*, Dan. *bedugge*, to bedew.

DAGUERROTYPE, a method of taking pictures by photography. (Hybrid; F. *and* Gk.) '*Daguerrotype process*, invented by Daguerre, and published A.D. 1838;' Haydn, Dict. of Dates. Formed from *Daguerre*, a French personal name (with o added as a connecting vowel), and E. *type*, a word of Gk. origin. See **Type**.

DAHABEEYAH, a large sailing-boat, used by travellers up the Nile. (Arab.) Lit. 'golden;' as being like a gilded state barge. ─ Arab. *ðahabiyah*, golden; from *ðahab*, gold; Rich. Dict. p. 712. (ð = *th* in *that*.)

DAHLIA, the name of a flower. (Swedish.) 'Discovered in Mexico by Humboldt in 1789, and sent to Prof. Cavanilles, of the Botanic Garden at Madrid, who [in 1791] named the genus in honour of the Swedish Professor *Dahl*;' Beckmann, Hist. of Inventions (1846); i. 517. *Dahl* is a Swedish personal name; the suffix *-ia* is botanical Latin.

DAINTY, a delicacy; pleasant to the taste. (F. ─ L.) ME. *deinté*, *deintee*, generally as a sb.; Ancren Riwle, p. 412. But Chaucer has: 'Ful many a *deynté* hors hadde he in stable;' C. T. prol. 168. This adjectival use is, however, a secondary one, and arose out of such phrases as 'to leten *deinté*' = to consider as pleasant (Ancren Riwle, p. 412), and 'to thinken *deyntee*,' with the same sense (P. Plowman, B. xi. 47). ─ OF. *daintie* (to be accented *daintié*), also *deintie*, *dainte* (*deintié*, *dainté*), joy, pleasure, also a tit-bit (Godefroy). ─ L. acc. *dignitātem*, dignity, worth. ─ L. *dignus*, worthy. See **Dignity**. ¶ Cotgrave gives the remarkable adj. *dain*, explained by 'dainty, fine, quaint, curious (an old word);' this is precisely the popular F. form of L. *dignus*, the learned form being *digne*. Cf. *disdain*, in which *-dain* again represents L. *dignus*. Der. *dainti-ly*, *dainti-ness*.

DAIRY, a place for keeping milk to be made into cheese. (Scand. and F.) ME. *daierie*, better *deyerye*, Chaucer, C. T. 597 (or 599). The Low L. form is *dayeria*, but this is merely the E. word written in a Latin fashion. α. The word is hybrid, being made by suffixing the F. *-erie* (L. *-āria*) to the ME. *deye*, a maid, a female-servant, esp. a dairymaid; late AS. *dæge*, Thorpe, Diplom. p. 641. Similarly formed words are *butte-ry* (= bottle-ry), *vin-t-ry*, *pan-t-ry*, *laund-ry*; see Morris, Hist. Outlines of Eng. Accidence, p. 233. β. The ME. *deye*, a maid, occurs in Chaucer, Nonne Pr. Tale, l. 26 (B 4036), and is of Scand. origin. ─ Icel. (ONorw.) *deigja*, a maid, esp. a dairy-maid; see note upon the word in Cleasby and Vigfusson; Swed. *deja*, a dairymaid. γ. However, the still older sense of the word was 'kneader of dough,' and it meant at first a woman employed in baking, a baker-woman. The same maid no doubt made the bread and attended to the dairy, as is frequently the case to this day in farm-houses. Teut. type *daig-jōn-, f., lit. 'dough-er;' from the Teut. type *daig-oz, as in the Icel. *deig*, Swed. *deg*, dough. The suffix *-jōn-* had an agential force; cf. Mœso-Gothic verbs in *-jan*. See further under **Dough**; and see **Lady**.

DAIS, a raised floor in a hall. (F. ─ L. ─ Gk.) Now used of the raised floor on which the high table in a hall stands. Properly, it was the table *itself* (L. *discus*). Later, it was used of a canopy over a seat of state or even of the seat of state itself. ME. *deis*, *deys*, sometimes *dais*, a high table; Chaucer, Kn. Tale, 1342 (A 2200); P. Plowman, B. vii. 17, on which see the note. ─ AF. *deis*, OF. *dois*, *dais*, a high table in a hall. The later sense appears in Cotgrave, who gives: '*Dais*, or *Daiz*, a cloth of estate, canopy, or heaven, that stands over the heads of princes thrones; also, the whole state, or seat of estate.' For examples of OF. *dois* in the sense of 'table,' see *deis* in Supp. to Godefroy. ─ L. *discum*, acc. of *discus*, a quoit, a plate, a platter; in late Latin, a table (Ducange). ─ Gk. δίσκος, a round plate, a quoit. See **Dish**, **Disc**.

DAISY, the name of a flower. (E.) Lit. *day's eye*, or *eye of day*, i.e. the sun; from the sun-like appearance of the flower. ME. *dayesye*; explained by Chaucer: 'The *dayesye*, or elles the *ye of day*,' Prol. to Legend of Good Women, 184. AS. *dægesēge*, a daisy, in MS. Cott. Faustina, A. x. fol. 115 b, printed in Cockayne's Leech-

doms, iii. 292. ─ AS. *dæges*, day's, gen. of *dæg*, a day; and *ēge*, Mercian form of AS. *ēage*, an eye. See **Day** and **Eye**. Der. *daisi-ed*.

DALE, a low place between hills, vale. (E.) ME. *dale*, Ormulum, 9203. AS. *dæl* (pl. *dalu*), a valley; Grein, i. 185. [As much Scand. as AS.; the commoner AS. word was *denu*, used to translate *uallis* in Lu. iii. 5; hence mod. E. *dean*, *dene*, *den*; see **Den**.] + Icel. *dalr*, a dale, valley; Dan. *dal*; Swed. *dal*; Du. *dal*; OFries. *del*; OSax. *dal*; Goth. *dal*; G. *thal*. Further allied to OSlav. *dolŭ*, Russ. *dol'*, a dale; cf. Gk. θόλος, a vault. Der. *dell*; see **Dell**.

DALLY, to trifle, to fool away time. (F. ─ Teut.) ME. *dalien*. 'Dysours *dalye*,' i.e. dicers play; K. Alisaunder, ed. Weber, 6991. 'To *daly* with derely your daynte wordez' = to play dearly with your dainty words; Gawayn and the Grene Knight, 1253. Also spelt *daylien*, id. 1114. ─ AF. *dalier*, to converse, chat, pass the time in social converse; see gloss. to N. Bozon, ed. P. Meyer; OF. *dallier*, to 'chaff,' jest at (Godefroy). Of Teut. origin; cf. Bavar. *dalen*, to speak and act as children (Schmeller); mod. G. *dahlen*, to trifle (which see in Kluge). See Notes on E. Etym. p. 56. Der. *dalliance*, ME. *daliaunce*, Gawain and Grene Knight, 1012; AF. *daliaunce*, Polit. Songs, p. 320.

DALMATIC, an ecclesiastical vestment. (F. ─ Dalmatia.) ME. *dalmatyk*, Wyntown, Chron. IX. vi. 153 (N.E.D.). ─ F. *dalmatique*, 'a fashion of a long white gown, .. spotted .. with purple, at first brought up by the Dalmatian, or Sclavonian priests; also a wide-sleeved vestment, worn .. by deacons;' Cot. ─ L. *dalmatica* (*uestis*); fem. of *Dalmaticus*, belonging to Dalmatia.

DAM (1), an earth-bank for restraining water. (E.) ME. *dam*, tr. by Lat. *agger*; Prompt. Parv. p. 113. No doubt an AS. word, being widely spread; but not recorded. We find, however, the derived verb *fordemman*, to stop up; AS. Psalter, ed. Spelman, Ps. lvii. 4; OFries. *dam*, *dom*, a dam; NFries. *dām*. + Du. *dam*, a dam, mole, bank; whence the verb *dammen*, to dam; Icel. *dammr*, a dam; *demma*, to dam; Dan. *dam*, a dam; *dæmme*, to dam; Swed. *damm*, sb.; *dämma*, verb; Goth. *dammjan*, verb, only used in the comp. *faur-dammjan*, to stop up; 2 Cor. xi. 10; MHG. *tam*, G. *damm*, a dike. β. Remoter origin uncertain; prob. allied to Gk. θωμός, a heap, θεμ-όω, I constrain. Observe that the E. sb. is older in form than the verb. Der. *dam*, vb.

DAM (2), a mother; chiefly applied to animals. (F. ─ L.) ME. *dam*, *damme*; Wyclif, Deut. xxii. 6; pl. *dammes*, id. Cf. the A. V. A mere variation of **Dame**, q. v.

DAMAGE, harm, injury, loss. (F. ─ L.) ME. *damage*, K. Alisaunder, 959. ─ OF. *damage*, *domage* (F. *dommage*), harm (Supp. to Godefroy); corresponding to the Prov. *damnatje*, *dampnatje*, in Bartsch, Chrestomathie Provençale, 85. 25; 100. 26; 141. 23; cf. F. *dame* < L. *domina*. ─ Late L. **damnāticum*, harm; not actually found; but cf. Late L. *damnāticus*, condemned to the mines. [The OF. *-age* answers to L. *-āticum*, by rule.] ─ L. *damnāt-us*, pp. of *damnāre*, to condemn. ─ L. *damnum*, loss. See **Damn**. Der. *damage*, verb; *damage-able*.

DAMASK, Damascus cloth, figured stuff. (Ital. ─ Syria.) ME. *damaske*. 'Clothes of ueluet, *damaske*, and of golde;' Lydgate, Storie of Thebes, pt. iii. l. 214; ed. 1561, fol. ccclxix, col. 2. ─ Ital. *damasco*; Late L. *Damascus*, cloth of Damascus (Ducange). ─ L. *Damascus*, proper name. ─ Gk. Δαμασκός. ─ Heb. *dmeseq*, damask; Heb. *Dammeseq*, Damascus, one of the oldest cities in the world, mentioned in Gen. xiv. 15. Der. Hence also *damask-rose*, Spenser, Shep. Kal. April, 60; Hakluyt's Voyages, vol. ii. pt. i. p. 165; *damask*, verb; *damaskine*, to inlay with gold (F. *damasquiner*); also *damson*, q. v.

DAME, a lady, mistress. (F. ─ L.) In early use. ME. *dame*, Ancren Riwle, p. 230. ─ OF. (and F.) *dame*, a lady. ─ L. *domina*, a lady; fem. form of *dominus*, a lord. See **Don** (2), and **Domina**. Der. *dam-s-el*, q. v. Doublet, *dam* (2).

DAMN, to condemn. (F. ─ L.) ME. *damnen*; commonly also *dampnen*, with excrescent *p*. '*Dampned* was he to deye in that prisoun;' Chaucer, C. T. 14725 (B 3605). ─ OF. *damner*; frequently *dampner*, with excrescent *p*. ─ L. *damnāre*, pp. *damnātus*, to condemn, fine. ─ L. *damnum*, loss, harm, fine, penalty. Brugmann, i. § 762. Der. *damn-able*, *-able-ness*, *-ation*, *-at-ion*, *-at-or-y*; and see *damage*.

DAMP, moisture, vapour. (E.) In Shak. Lucrece, 778. The verb appears as ME. *dampen*, to choke, suffocate, Allit. Poems, ed. Morris, ii. 989. Though not found earlier, it can hardly be other than an E. word; cf. EFries. *damp*, vapour. [It can hardly be Scandinavian, the Icel. *dampr* being a mod. word; see Cleasby and Vigfusson.] + Du. *damp*, vapour, steam, smoke; whence *dampen*, to steam; Dan. *damp*, vapour; whence *dampe*, to reek; G. *dampf*, vapour. Cf. Swed. *damb*, dust. From the 2nd grade of Teut. **dempan-, pt. t. **damp*, pp. **dumpanoz*; as seen in MHG. *dimpfen*, *timpfen*, str. verb, to reek. Cf. Swed. dial. *dimba*, str. verb, to reek. See **Dumps**. Der. *damp*, verb; *damp*, adj.; *-ly*, *-ness*.

DAMSEL, a young unmarried woman, girl. (F. ─ L.) ME. *damo-*

sel. 'And ladies, and *damoselis*;' K. Alisaunder, 171. — OF. *damoisele* (with many variations of spelling), a girl, damsel; fem. form of OF. *damoisel*, a young man, squire, page, retained in mod. F. in the form *damoiseau.* — Late L. *domicellus*, a page, which occurs in the Statutes of Cluni (Brachet). This is shortened from *domnicellus*, also *dominicellus*, a regular double diminutive from L. *dominus*, a lord; made by help of the suffixes -*c*- and -*el*-. See **Don** (2), and **Dominate.** ¶ For *dan* = sir (Chaucer), see **Dan.**

DAMSON, the Damascene plum. (F. — L. — Syria.) 'When *damsines* I gather;' Spenser, Shep. Kal. April, 152. Bacon has *dammasin*, Essay 46, Of Gardens; also 'the *damasin plumme*;' Nat. Hist. § 509. Lydgate has *damysyns*; Minor Poems, p. 15. — MF. *damaisine*, 'a Damascene, or Damson plum;' Cotgrave. — F. *Damas*, Damascus; with fem. suffix -*ine.* — L. *Damascus.* See **Damask.**

DAN, an honourable title; sir. (F. — L.) Spenser speaks of '*Dan* Chaucer;' F. Q. iv. 2. 32. Chaucer has '*dan* John;' C. T., B 3119. — OF. *dan*, acc., *dans*, nom., sir, lord. — L. *dominum*, acc. of *dominus*, lord. See **Don** (2). Der. *dam* (2), *dame*, *damsel.*

DANCE, to trip with measured steps. (F. — OHG.) ME. *dauncen*, *daunsen*; 'Maydens so *dauncen*,' K. Alisaunder, 5213. — OF. *danser*, *dancer* (F. *danser*), to dance. — OHG. *dansōn*, to draw, draw along, as in a round dance; a secondary verb from MHG. *dinsen*, OHG. *tinsen*, *thinsen*, to draw or drag forcibly, to trail along, draw a sword; cognate with Goth. *thinsan*, which only occurs in the compound *at-thinsan*, to draw towards one, John, vi. 44, xii. 32. β. Related to MHG. *denen*, OHG. *thenen*, to stretch, stretch out, draw, trail; Goth. *ufthanjan*, to stretch after; L. *tendere*, to stretch; see further under **Thin.** — √TEN, to stretch. Der. *danc-er*, *danc-ing.*

DANDELION, the name of a flower. (F. — L.) The word occurs in Cotgrave. The older spelling *dent-de-lyon* occurs in G. Douglas, Prol. to xii Book of Æneid, l. 119; see Skeat, Specimens of English. ME. *dent de lyoun*, Medical Werkes, ed. Henslow, p. 91, l. 12. — F. *dent de lion*, 'the herbe dandelyon;' Cot. [Cf. Span. *diente de leon*, dandelion.] β. The plant is named from its jagged leaves, the edges of which present rows of teeth. — L. *dentem*, acc. of *dens*, a tooth; *dē*, preposition, of; and *leōnem*, acc. of *leo*, a lion. See **Tooth**, and **Lion.**

DANDLE, to toss a child in one's arms, or fondle it in the lap. (Low G.) In Shak. Venus, 562; 2 Hen. VI, i. 3. 148. Palsgrave has: 'I *dandyll*, as a mother or nourryce doth a childe upon their lappe.' Another meaning was to play, trifle with. Thus we find: 'King Henries ambassadors into France having beene *dandled* [trifled with, cajoled] by the French during these delusive practises, returned without other fruite of their labours;' Speed, Hen. VII, b. ix. c. 20. s. 28 (R). Not known before the 16th century. β. In form, it is a frequentative verb, made by help of the suffix -*le* from an O. Low German base *dand-*, which appears in the WFlem. *dand-eren*, to bounce up and down, like an elastic ball (De Bo). γ. Cf. MItal. *dandolare*, *dondolare*, 'to dandle or dangle, to play the babie or gull;' Florio; *dandola*, *dondola*, 'a babie [doll], a puppie, .. a kinde of play at the ball; also, dandling or dangling;' id. This word is from the same Low G. root. Perhaps we may also compare MF. *dandiner*, to balance or sway the body, or to swagger (Supp. to Godefroy); and EFries. *dindannen*, to walk unsteadily, to sway from side to side (Koolman). And see prov. E. *dander*, to tremble, shake, saunter, trifle, in E.D.D.; MHG. *tant*, G. *tand*, a trifle, toy.

DANDRIFF, scurf on the head. (Scand. ?) Formerly *dandruff*; 'the *dandruffe* or unseemly scales within the haire of head or beard;' Holland's Pliny, b. xx. c. 8. A compound word; composed of *dander* and *hurf*. Of these, *dander* is a Yorksh. word, signifying a slight scurf on the skin (E.D.D.); and *hurf* or *urf* (at Whitby), or *huff* (EAnglia), with the sense of 'scurf,' is from Icel. *hrufa*, a scab. Thus the latter part of the word is of Scand. origin; perhaps the former was the same. See *Hurf* in E.D.D.; and Notes on E. Etym., p. 57.

DANDY, a fop, coxcomb. (Gk. ?) The N.E.D. says: 'In use on the Scottish border at the end of the 18th century; and about 1813–9 in vogue in London, for the "exquisite" or "swell" of the period. Perhaps the full form was *Jack-a-dandy*, which occurs from 1659, and in 18th c. had a sense which might easily pass into that of *dandy.*' *Jack o' Dandy* occurs in 1632, which suggests that *Dandy* was a variant of the name *Andrew* (as in Scotland). If so, the word is of Greek origin. — Gk. Ἀνδρέας; from ἀνδρεῖος, manly. — Gk. ἀνήρ (gen. ἀνδρός), a man. + Skt. *nara-s*, a man.

DANGER, penalty, risk, insecurity. (F. — L.) On the uses of this word in early writers, see Trench, Select Glossary, and Richardson; and consult Brachet, s.v. *danger.* ME. *daunger*, *daungere*; Rob. of Glouc. p. 78, l. 1751; Chaucer, C. T. Prol. 663 (or 665). Still earlier, in the Ancren Riwle, p. 356; 'ge þolieð ofte *daunger* of swuche oðerhwule þet muhte beon ower þrel' = ye sometimes put up with the arrogance of such an one as might be your thrall. —

OF. *dangier* (mod. F. *danger*), absolute power, irresponsible authority; hence, power to harm, as in Shak. Merch. of Venice, iv. 1. 180. The word was also spelt *dongier*, which rhymes with *alongier* in a poem of the 13th century cited in Bartsch, Chrestomathie Française, col. 362, l. 2; and this helps us out. β. According to Hatzfeld, this answers to a Late L. **domniārium*, a form not found, but an extension from *dominium*, power, for which see **Dominion.** At any rate, *dominium* is certainly the true source of the word, and was used (like OF. *dongier*) to denote the absolute authority of a feudal lord, which is the idea running through the old uses of F. and E. *danger.* γ. Brachet remarks: 'just as *dominus* had become *domnus* in Roman days, so *dominiārium* became *domniārium*, which consonified the *ia* (see the rule under *abréger* and Hist. Gram. p. 65), whence *domnjārium*, whence OF. *dongier*; for *m* = *n*, see *changer* [from *cambiāre*]; for -*ārium* = -*ier* see § 198.' A word similarly formed, and from the same source, is the E. *dungeon.* See **Dominion**, and **Dungeon.** Der. *danger-ous*, -*ous-ly*, -*ous-ness.*

DANGLE, to hang loosely, swing about. (Scand.) In Shak. Rich. II, iii. 4. 29. — Dan. *dangle*, to dangle, bob; Swed. dial. *dangla*, to swing, Rietz; who also cites NFriesic *dangeln* from Outzen's Dict. p. 44. Ihre gives MSwed. *dængla*, *dangla*; and Aasen has Norw. *dangla.* Another form appears in Swed. *dingla*, Icel. *dingla*, Dan. *dingle*, to dangle, swing about. β. The suffix -*le* is, as usual, frequentative; and the verb is the frequentative of *dang*, 2nd grade of *ding*, to strike, throw; so that the sense was to throw about often, to bob, to swing. See **Ding.** ¶ We even find Low G. *dungeln*, to dangle; from the weak grade *dung-.* Der. *dangl-er.*

DANK, moist, damp. (Scand.) In the Allit. Morte Arthure, ed. Brock, l. 313, we find 'the dewe that is *daunke*;' and in l. 3750, we have it as a *sb.* in the phrase 'one the *danke* of the dewe,' i.e. the moisture of the dew. And cf. 'Dropis as dew or a *danke* rayne;' Destruction of Troy, 2368. It also occurs as a *verb*, in Specimens of Lyric Poetry, ed. Wright; see Specimens of Early Eng. ed. Morris and Skeat, sect. IV d. l. 28: 'deawes *donketh* the dounes,' i.e. dews moisten the downs. — Swed. dial. *dank*, a moist place in a field, marshy piece of ground, Rietz; Icel. *dǫkk*, a pit, pool; where *dǫkk* stands for *dǫnk*, by the assimilation so common in Icelandic, from Teut. stem **dank-wō.* We also find Swed. dial. *dänka*, to moisten; Dan. dial. *dönke*, *dynke*, to sprinkle linen with water before ironing it; also MSwed. *dunkenhet*, moisture, Dan. dial. *dunkel*, moist; Norw. *dynka*, to wet. The forms prove the existence of an obs. Scand. verb **dinka*, to be wet, pt. t. **dank*, pp. **dunkinn.* See Notes on E. Etym., p. 57. Cf. **Damp.**

DAPPER, spruce, neat. (Du.) Orig. good, valiant; hence brave, fine, spruce. Spenser speaks of his '*dapper* ditties;' Shep. Kal. October, l. 13. 'Dapyr, or praty [pretty], *elegans*;' Prompt. Parv. — Du. *dapper*, valiant, brave, intrepid, bold. + OHG. *taphar*, heavy, weighty, (later) valiant; G. *tapfer*, brave. + Ch. Slav. *dobrŭ*, good; Russ. *dobrui*, good, excellent. See Brugmann, i. § 563.

DAPPLE, a spot on an animal. (Scand.) 'As many eyes upon his body as my gray mare hath *dapples*;' Sidney, Arcadia, b. ii. p. 271 (R). Hence the expression: 'His stede was al *dapple-gray*;' Chaucer, C. T. 13813 (B 2074). — Icel. *depill*, a spot, dot; a dog with spots over the eyes is also called *depill*; the orig. sense is a pond, a little pool, from Norw. *dape*, a pool, in Aasen; Cleasby and Vigfusson. Cf. Swed. dial. *depp*, a large pool of water. Also MDan. *duppe*, a puddle, a hole where water collects. Der. *dapple*, verb; 'Dapples the drowsy east with spots of grey;' Much Ado, v. 3. 27; and *dappled.* ¶ As Mr. Wedgwood well observes, 'the resemblance of *dapple-grey* to Icel. *apalgrār*, or apple-grey, Fr. *gris pommelé*, is accidental.' The latter phrase is equivalent to Chaucer's *pomely-grey*, C. T. prol. 616 (or 618). Still, association with *apple* may have changed *dep*- into *dap*-.

DARE (1), to be bold, to venture. (E.) α. The verb to *dare*, pt. t. *dared*, pp. *dared*, is the same word with the auxiliary verb to *dare*, pt. t. *durst*, pp. *durst.* But the latter keeps to the older forms; *dared* is much more modern than *durst*, and grew up by way of distinguishing, to some extent, the uses of the verb. β. The present tense, *I dare*, is really an old past tense, so that the third person is *he dare* (cf. *he shall*, *he can*); but the form *he dares* is now often used, and will probably displace the obsolescent *he dare*, though grammatically as incorrect as *he shalls*, or *he cans.* ME. *dar*, *der*, *dear*, I dare; see Stratmann's O. E. Dict. 'The pore *dar* plede,' i.e. the poor man dare plead; P. Plowman, B. xiv. 108. Past tense *dorste*, *durste.* 'For if he yaf, he *dorste* make avaunt' = for if he gave, he durst make the boast; Chaucer, C. T. prol. 227. AS. *ic dear* (for *dearr*), I dare; þu *dearst*, thou darest; *he dear(r)*, he dare or dares; *wē*, *gē*, or *hīg durran*, we, ye, or they dare. Past tense, *ic dorste*, I durst or dared; pl. *we durston*, we durst or dared. Infin. *durran*, to dare; Grein, i. 212. + Goth. *dars*, I dare; *daursta*, I durst; pp. *daursts*; infin. *daursan*, to dare; OHG. *tar*, I dare; *torsta*, I dared; *turran*, to dare.

[This verb is distinct from the OHG. *durfan*, to have need, now turned into *dürfen*, but with the sense of 'dare.' In like manner, the Du. *durven*, to dare, is related to Icel. þurfa, to have need, AS. þurfan, Goth. *þaurban*, to have need; and must be kept distinct. The verb requires some care and attention.] ╋ Gk. θαρσεῖν, to be bold; θρασύς, bold; Skt. *dhṛsh*, to dare. ╌ √DHERS, to be bold, to dare; Brugmann, i. § 502. ¶ AS. *dearr* < *darr* < *darz* = Goth. *dars*; cf. pt. t. *d·rs-te*. Der. *dar-ing*, *dar-ing-ly*.

DARE (2), a dace; see **Dace**.

DARK, obscure. (E.) ME. *dark*, *derk*, *deork*; see *deorc* in Stratmann. AS. *deorc*, Grein, i. 191; base *derk-*. The OHG. *tarchanjan*, to hide (answering to WGerm. *dark-n-jan*) is from the 2nd grade *dark-* of the same base. Cf. also OSax. *der-ne*, AS. *der-ne*, OHG. *t·r·i*, secret, dark. See **Darn** and **Tarnish**.

DARKLING, adv., in the dark. (E.) In Shak. Mid. Nt. Dream, ii. 2. 86; Lear, i. 4. 237; also in 'goth him-self *darkeling*;' Lord Rivers, Dictes and Sayings (Caxton), fol. 35, l. 7. Formed from *dark* by help of the adverbial suffix *-ling*, which occurs also in *flatling*, i.e. flatly, on the ground; see Halliwell's Dict. p. 360. It occurs also in *hedling*; 'heore hors *hedlyng* mette,' i.e. their horses met head to head, King Alisaunder, l. 2261. β. An example in older English is seen in the AS. *bæcling*, backwards, Grein, i. 76; and see Morris, Hist. Outlines of Eng. Accidence, sect. 322, Adv. Suffixes in *-long*, *-ling*.

DARKSOME, obscure. (E.) In Shak. Lucrece, 379. Palsgrave has *darkesome*, p. 309. Formed from *dark* by help of the suffix *-some* (AS. *sum*); cf. *ful-some*, *blithe-some*, *win-some*, &c.

DARLING, a little dear, a favourite. (E.) ME. *deorling*, *derling*, *durling*; spelt *deorling*, Ancren Riwle, p. 56. AS. *dēorling*, a favourite; Ælfred's tr. of Boethius, lib. iii. prosa 4. β. Formed from *dēor*, dear, by help of the suffix *-ling*, which stands for *-l-ing*, where *-l* and *-ing* are both suffixes expressing diminution. Cf. *duckl-ing*, *gos-l-ing*; see Morris, Hist. Outlines of Eng. Accidence, sect. 321. See **Dear**.

DARN, to mend, patch. (E.) 'For spinning, weaving, *derning*, and drawing up a rent;' Holland's Plutarch, p. 783 (R.). This *dern* seems to be merely a peculiar use of ME. *dernen*, to hide, conceal (prob. also to stop up a hole). Related to AS. *gedyrnan*, which not only meant 'to hide, conceal, keep secret,' but also 'to stop up a hole,' as shown by the gloss: 'oppilatum, *gedyrned*;' Voc. 461. 7; 494. 25. So also prov. E. *darn* (Aberdeen) means not only 'to hide,' but also 'to stop up a hole with straw;' E.D.D. So also Westphalian *stoppen* means (1) to stop up; (2) to darn a stocking; Notes on E. Etym., p. 57. β. AS. *gedyrnan* is from the adj. *dyrne*, *dierne* (Merc. *derne*), 'secret,' for Teut. *darn-jo-* (Sievers, AS. Gr. §§ 159, 299), whence also OHG. *tarni*, secret, dark; see under **Dark**.

DARNEL, a kind of weed, rye-grass. (F.─Scand. *and* L.) ME. *darnel*, *dernel*, Wyclif, Matt. xiii. 25, 29. Apparently a F. word. Mr. Wedgwood cites (from Grandgagnage) the Rouchi *darnelle*, *darnel* (given by Hécart); and compares it with Walloon *darnie*, *daurnise*, tipsy, stunned, giddy (also in Grandgagnage). β. The former syllable also appears as *dor-* in Lowl. Sc. *dornel*, darnel; and is explained by Swed. *dår-repe*, bearded darnel (Öman). This prefix prob. signifies 'stupefying;' cf. MDu. *door*, foolish (Oudemans), Swed. *dåra*, to infatuate, *dåre*, a fool, Dan. *daare*, a fool, G. *thor*, a fool; all of which are from a base *daur-*, for *dauz-*, *daus-*, the weak grade of which appears in AS. *dys-ig*, stupid; see **Dizzy**. γ. The latter syllable is from OF. *nelle*, *neele*, *nielle*, darnel (Godefroy). ─Late L. *nigella*, a plant, one kind of which has black seeds.─L. *nigellus*, blackish; dimin. of *niger*, black. See Notes on E. Etym., p. 59; Lyte, tr. of Dodoens, bk. i. c. 96, bk. iv. c. 45. At least three plants have been confused, gith, cockle, and darnel. In *Lolium temulentum*, *temulentum* is represented by *dar-*, and *lolium* by *-nel*. Cf. M.F. *yuraye*, 'darnell,' Cot.; from *yvre*, 'drunken;' id.

DART, a javelin. (F.─O. Low G.) ME. *dart*, Rob. of Brunne, tr. of Langtoft, p. 17⁸; Chaucer, C. T., A 1564.─OF. *da·t* (mod. F. *dard*), a dart; a word of O. Low G. origin. Cf. AS. *dar ð*, *darað*, or *dareð*, a dart; Swed. *dart*, a dagger, poniard; Icel. *darraðr*, a dart; cf. OHG. *tart*, a dart. β. Perhaps from the base *dar-* of AS. *derian*, to harm, injure. ¶ The Low L. *dardus* is evidently from an O. Low German source. Der. *dart*, verb, and see *dace*.

DASH, to throw with violence. (Scand.) Orig. to beat, as when we say that waves *dash* upon rocks. ME. *daschen*, *dasschen*. 'Into the cité he con *dassche*,' i.e. he rushed, King Alisaunder, 2837; and see Layamon, i. 62; l. 1469.─Dan. *daske*, to slap; Swed. *daska*, to beat, to drub; Swed. dial. *daska*, to slap with the open hand, as one slaps a child (Rietz).╋Low G. *daschen*, to thrash (Berghaus). β. A shorter form appears in Swed. dial. *diza*, to strike (Rietz). Der. *dash-ing*, i.e. striking; *dash-ing-ly*.

DASTARD, a cowardly fellow. (Scand.; with F. suffix.) 'Dastard or dullarde, *duribuctius*;' Prompt. Parv. p. 114. 'Dastarde,

estourdy, butarin;' Palsgrave. 1. The suffix is the usual F. *-ard*, as in *dull-ard*, *slugg-ard*; a suffix of Germanic origin, and related to Goth. *hardus*, hard. In many words it takes a bad sense; see Brachet, Introd. to Etym. Dict. sect. 196. 2. The stem *dast-* answers to E. *dazed*, and the *t* appears to be due to a past participial form. ─ Icel. *dæstr*, exhausted, breathless, pp. of *dæsa*, to groan, lose breath from exhaustion; closely related to Icel. *dasaðr*, exhausted, weary, pp. of *dasask*, to become exhausted, a reflexive verb standing for *dasa-sik*, to daze oneself. Another past participial form is Icel. *dasinn*, commonly shortened to *dasi*, a lazy fellow. Thus the word is to be divided *das-t-ard*, where *das-* is the base, *-t-* the past participial form, and *-ard* the suffix. The word actually occurs in MDutch without the *t*, viz. in MDu. *dasaert*, *daasaardt*, a fool (Oudemans); and an ME. *dasart*, a dullard, occurs once, in Minor Poems of the Vernon MS. (E.E.T.S.), p. 333. On the other hand, we find Swed. dial. *däst*, weary (Rietz). See further under **Daze**. ¶ The derivation from AS. *adastrigan*, to frighten, is absurd; I find no such word; it is recorded by Somner, but is an error for ONorthumb. *adustriga*, to curse; Matt. xxvi. 74. Der. *dastard-ly*, *-li-ness*.

DATE (1), an epoch, given point of time. (F.─L.) ME. *date*; Allit. Poems, ed. Morris, i. 505. 'Date, of scripture, *datum*;' Prompt. Parv. p. 114. ─ F. *date*, the date of letters or evidences; Cotgrave. ─ Late L. *data*, a date.─L. *data*, neut. pl. of *datus*, pp. of *dare*, to give. In classical Latin, the neut. *datum* was employed to mark the time and place of writing, as in the expression *datum Romæ*, given (i.e. written) at Rome. ╋ Gk. δί-δω-μι, I give; Gk. δωτήρ, a giver, δοτός, given; Skt. *da-dā-mi*, I give, from the root *dā*, to give; cf. *dātṛ*, a giver; Church Slav. *dati*, to give; Russ. *dari·e*, to give.─√ DŌ, to give. Der. From the L. *datus*, given, we have also neut. sing. *datum*, and neut. pl. *data*; also *dat-ive*. And see *dose*, *donation*.

DATE (2), the fruit of a palm. (F.─L.─Gk.─Semitic.) ME. *date*; Maundeville's Travels, ch. 5, p. 57. 'Date, frute, dactilus;' Prompt. Parv. p. 114.─AF. *date*, Liber Albus, p. 224; OF. *date* (Littré); later F. *datte*, badly written *dacte*, a date; both spellings are in Cotgrave.─L. *dactylus*, a date; also, a dactyl.─Gk. δάκτυλος, a date (no doubt assimilated to the Gk. word for 'finger;' but of Eastern origin). From Semitic; cf. Aramaic *diqlā*, a palm-tree; whence Heb. *Diqlah*, as a proper name, Gen. x. 27; also Arab. *daqal*, a kind of palm; Rich. Dict. p. 679.

DAUB, to smear over. (F.─L.) ME. *dauben*, to smear; used to translate L. *linire*, Wyclif, Ezek. xiii. 10, 11; and see note 3 in Prompt. Parv. p. 114.─OF. *dauber*, occurring in the sense of 'plaster.' Cf. AF. *daubours*, plasterers, Late L. *dealbātōrēs*, Liber Custumarum, pp. 52, 99. The earlier form of this OF. verb could only have been *dalber*, from L. *dealbāre*, to whitewash, plaster. [Cf. F. *aube* from L. *alba* (see **Alb**), and F. *dorer* from L. *deaurāre*.] β. This etymology of *dauber* is confirmed by Span. *jalbegar*, to whitewash, plaster, corresponding to a hypothetical L. derivative *dealbicāre*. γ. From L. *dē*, down; and *albāre*, to whiten, from *albus*, white. See **Alb**. ¶ The sense of the word has probably to some extent influenced that of *dab*, which is of Low G. origin. W. *dwb*, plaster, *dwbio*, to daub; Gael. *dob*, plaster, *dobair*, a plasterer; Irish *dob*, plaster, *do'aim*, I plaster, are all borrowed from E. *daub*.

DAUGHTER, a female child. (E.) ME. *doghter*, *doughter*, *douhter*, *dohter*, *dowter*, &c.; the pl. *dohtren* occurs in Layamon, i. 124, l. 2924; *dehtren* in O. Eng. Homilies, i. 247; *deȝter* in Allit. Poems, ed. Morris, ii. 270. AS. *dohtor*, pl. *dohtor*, *dohtra*, *dohtru*, and *dohter*; Grein, i. 195.╋ Du. *dochter*; Dan. *datter*, *dotter*; Swed. *dotter*; Icel. *dóttir*; Goth. *dauhtar*; OHG. *tohter*, G. *tochter*. Teut. type *dohtēr*; Idg. type *dhughǝtēr*; whence Lith. *duktē*, Russ. *doche*; Gk. θυγάτηρ, Pers. *dukhtar*, Skt. *duhitā*. β. Lassen's etymology from the Skt. *duh* (for *dhugh*), to milk─'the milker'─is not now generally accepted.

DAUNT, to frighten, discourage. (F.─L.) ME. *daunten*, K. Alisaunder, 1312.─AF. *danter* (Gaimar, 3201), *daunter* (Bozon); OF. *danter* (Roquefort); MF. *donter* (Cotgrave), (of which the last = mod. F. *dompter*), written for an older *domter*, to tame, subdue, daunt.─L. *domitāre*, to subdue; frequentative of *domāre*, to tame; which is cognate with E. *tame*. See **Tame**. Der. *dauntless*, *-lessness*.

DAUPHIN, eldest son of the king of France. (F.─L.─Gk.) Formerly spelt *Daulphin*, Fabyan, vol. ii. Car. VII. an. 16 (p. 560); also *Dolphine*, Hall, Edw. IV, an. 18. § 1.─OF. *daulphin*, for *dauphin*, a dolphin; also 'the Dolphin, or eldest son of France; called so of *Daulphiné*, a province given or (as some report it) sold in the year 1349 by Humbert earl thereof to Philippe de Valois, partly on condition, that for ever the French king's eldest son should hold it, during his father's life, of the empire;' Cotgrave. Brachet gives the date as 1343, and explains the name of the province by saying that the title of *Dauphin* was peculiar to SE. France. It first appears A.D. 1140. The origin of it is unknown, though it certainly represents the L. *delphīnus*. A doublet of *dolphin*; see **Dolphin**.

DAVIT, a spar used as a crane for hoisting a ship's anchor clear of the vessel; one of two supports for ship's boats. (Heb.) 'Davit, a short piece of timber, us'd to hale up the flook of the anchor, and to fasten it to the ship's bow;' Kersey's Dict. ed. 1715. Older spelling *David*, a Christian name of Heb. origin. Capt. Smith (Works, ed. Arber, p. 793, A.D. 1626) has: 'the block at the *Dauid's* ende.' So also F. *davier*, formerly *daviet*, from *Daviet*, dimin. of OF. *Davi*, David; as in '*davier de barbier*, the pinser wherewith he [the barber] draws or pulls out teeth;' Cotgrave. He also gives: '*Davier d'un pelican*, a certain instrument to pick a tooth withall; an iron hook, or cramp-iron for that purpose.' So also AF. *daviot*, a davit, Riley, Memorials of London, p. 370 (1373); E. *daviot*, Naval Accounts, p. 49 (1485).

DAW, a jackdaw, bird of the crow family. (E.) In Skelton, Ware the Hawk, l. 327. In l. 322 he uses the compound *daw-cocke*. The compound *ca-daw*, i.e. caw-daw, occurs in the Prompt. Parv. p. 57; on which see Way's Note. May be claimed as an E. word, being certainly of O. Low G. origin. β. A cognate word is traced by Schmeller, in his Bavarian Dict. col. 494. He says that the Vocabularius Theutonicus of 1482 gives the forms *dach* and *dula*; the latter of these answers to G. *dohle*, a jackdaw, and is a dimin. form, for an older *dāhele*, dimin. of *dāha*. This *dāha* is the O. Low G. form answering to OHG. *tāha*, MHG. *tāhe*, a daw; whence MHG. *tāhele*, later *dahle*, and now spelt *dohle*. γ. The word, like *chough*, is doubtless imitative; Schmeller gives *dah dah* as a cry used by hunters. By a change of the initial letter, we have the imitative E. word *caw*; and by uniting these words we have *caw-daw*, as above. Cf. also Ital. *taccola*, 'a chough, a rooke, a dawe; also a skould, a pratler; also a rayling or a skoulding;' Florio. This Ital. word is plainly derived from Old High German. **Der.** *jack-daw*.

DAWDLE, to waste time, to loiter. (Scand.) 'And *dawdle* over a dish of tea;' Boswell's Johnson, June 3, 1781. Of Scand. origin; cf. Norw. *daudall*, indolent (Ross); Swed. dial. *dödolger*, a slothful man (Rietz); Low G. *dödeln*, to dawdle (Berghaus); Pomeran. *deudeln*, to waste time. Allied to Norw. *daudleg*, faint, stupid, lifeless (lit. deadly); and to Icel. *dauði*, Swed. *död*, death. See **Death**.

DAWK, transport by relays of horses or bearers; a post. (Hind.) See Yule.━Hind. *ḍāk*, transport, the post (Forbes). Cf. Skt. *drāk*, quickly; *drā*, to run.

DAWN, to become day. (Scand.) ME. *dawnen*; but the more usual form is *dawen*. '*Dawyn*, idem est quod *Dayyn*, *dawnyn*, or *dayen*, auroro;' Prompt. Parv. p. 114. 'That in his bed ther *daweth* him no day;' Chaucer, C. T., A 1676; cf. l. 14600 (B 3872). We find *daiening*, *daigening*, *daning*, =dawning; Genesis and Exodus, 77, 1808, 3264. β. The *-n* is a suffix, often added to verbs to give them a neuter or passive signification; cf. Goth. *fullnan*, to become full, from *fulljan*, to fill; Goth. *gahailnan*, to become whole; and the like. The ME. word is to be divided as *daw-n-en*, from the older *dawen*; and the insertion of the *n* was suggested by Swed. and Dan. *dagning*, sb., a dawning, a dawn, as if from a verb *dagna*, from *dag*, a day. γ. ME. *dawen* is the AS. *dagian*, to dawn; Grein, i. 182; from the AS. *dæg*, day. So G. *tagen*, to dawn, from *tag*, day. See **Day**. **Der.** *dawn*, sb.

DAY, the time of light. (E.) ME. *day*, *dai*, *dæi*; spelt *dæi* in Layamon, ii. 2, l. 10246. AS. *dæg*, pl. *dagas*. + Du. *dag*; Dan. and Swed. *dag*; Icel. *dagr*; Goth. *dags*; G. *tag*. Teut. type *dagoz*, m.; allied to Lith. *dagas*, a hot season, *dagà*, harvest; OPruss. *dagis*, summer; Skt. *ni-dāgha-*, the hot season, *dāha-*, a burning, heat.━√DHEGH, to burn, as in Lith. *dèg-ti*, to burn, Skt. *dah*, to burn. Thus the orig. sense was 'hot time.' Brugmann, ii. § 60. ¶ Perhaps it is well to add that the L. *diēs*, Irish *dia*, W. *dydd*, meaning 'day,' are from quite a different root, and are wholly unrelated. **Der.** *dai-ly*, *day-book*, *-break*, *-spring*, *-star*, and other compounds. Also *daisy*, q.v.; *dawn*, q.v.

DAYWOMAN, dairy-woman. (Scand. *and* E.) In Shak. L. L. L. i. 2. 137. The addition of *woman* is needless. *Day* = ME. *deye*, a dairy-woman.━ONorw. *deigja*, a dairy-maid; see **Dairy**.

DAZE, to stupefy, render stupid. (Scand.) ME. *dasen*; the pp. *dased* (or *daswed*) is in Chaucer, Ho. of Fame, ii. 150; in the Pricke of Conscience, 6647; and in Allit. Poems, ed. Morris, i. 1085. The ME. *dasen* is also intransitive, in the sense to become stupefied; see N.E.D.━Icel. *dasa*, in the reflexive verb *dasask*, to daze oneself, to become weary and exhausted; Swed. *dasa*, to lie idle; Norw. *dasa*, to grow faint; *dæsa*, to grow faint, be exhausted by cold or wet; *dæst*, pp. faint, tired out; Dan. dial. *dase*, to be idle. Cf. Low G. *däsen*, *dösen*, to be listless; *in 'n däs' siin*, to be in a daze (Berghaus). ¶ Hence also OF. *daser*, to be dazed. **Der.** *das-t-ard*, q.v., and *dazzle*, q.v.

DAZZLE, to confuse the sight by strong light. (Scand.; with E. suffix.) In Shak. Hen. V, i. 2. 279; also intransitively, to be confused in one's sight, 3 Hen. VI, ii. 1. 25. 'I *dasyll*, as ones eyes

do for lokyng agaynst the sonne;' Palsgrave. The frequentative of *daze*, formed with the usual suffix *-le*; lit. 'to daze often.' See **Daze**.

DE-, *prefix*, (1) from L. prep. *dē*, down, from, away; also (2) occurring in French words, being the OF. *des-*, F. *dé-* in composition; in which case it = L. *dis-*. 'It is negative and oppositive in *destroy*, *desuetude*, *deform*, &c. It is intensive in *declare*, *desolate*, *desiccate*, &c.;' Morris, Hist. Outlines of Eng. Accidence; sect. 326.

DEACON, one of the third order of clergy. (L.━Gk.) ME. *deken*; Chaucer has the compound *erchedeken*, C. T. 6884 (D 1300). The pl. *dekenes* is in Wyclif, 1 Tim. iii. 8. AS. *deacon*, Exod. iv. 14.━L. *diāconus*, a deacon.━Gk. διάκονος (with *ā*), a servant; hence, a deacon. The Ionic form is διήκονος. 'From διά and *ἀ-κονος* (*a < ᵊn*); allied to ἐγ-κονέω, I am quick, ἐγ-κονίς, a maid-servant;' Prellwitz. **Der.** *deacon-ess*, where the suffix is of F. origin; *deacon-ship*, where the suffix is of AS. origin; *deacon-ry*, with F. suffix *-ry* (for *-rie*); also *diacon-ate*, *-al*, formed from L. *diācon-us* by help of the suffixes *-ate* and *-al*, of L. origin.

DEAD, deprived of life. (E.) ME. *deed*, *ded*; Chaucer, C. T. prol. 148. AS. *dēad*, dead, Grein, i. 189; [where *dēad* is described as an *adjective*, rather than as a past participle. And to this day we distinguish between *dead* and *died*, as in the phrases 'he is dead' and 'he has died;' we never say 'he has dead.' But see below.] + Du. *dood*; Dan. *död*; Swed. *död*; Icel. *dauðr*; Goth. *dauths*, dead. β. The termination *-ths* in Mœso-Gothic is the special mark of a weak past participle, and there can be no doubt that *dauths* was formed with this participial ending from the stem *dau-*, second grade of Teut. *deu-*, whence the Gothic *diwan*, to die. The Teut. type is *daudóz*, answering to Idg. *dhautós*, the change from *-tós* to *-dóz* being due to Verner's Law. And this *daudoz* is the pp. of Teut. *dau-jan*, to die, exactly preserved (with mutation of *au* to *ey*) in Icel. *deyja*, to die. Further allied to Russ. *davite*, to strangle. **Der.** *dead-ly* (ME. *deedli*, Wyclif, Heb. vii. 8); *dead-li-ness*; *dead-en*, *-ness*; and see **Death**.

DEAF, dull of hearing. (E.) ME. *deef*, *def*, *defe*; Chaucer, C. T., prol. 446 (or 448). AS. *dēaf*; Grein, i. 190;+Du. *doof*; Dan. *döv*; Swed. *döf*; Icel. *daufr*; Goth. *daubs*; G. *taub*. β. Teut. type *dauƀoz*; orig. 'obfuscated;' and allied to the G. *toben*, to bluster, rage, be delirious; also to the Gk. τῦφος, smoke, darkness, stupefaction, stupor; and to τυφλός, 'blind.' (√DHEUBH). **Der.** *deaf-ly*, *deaf-ness*, *def-en*.

DEAL (1), a share, division, a quantity. (E.) The sense of 'quantity' arose out of that of 'share' or 'portion.' ME. *deel*, *del*, Chaucer, C. T., A 1825; Kn. Tale, 967. AS. *dǣl*, a portion, share; Grein, i. 186. + Du. *deel*, a portion, share; Dan. *deel*, a part, portion; Swed. *del*, a part, share; Goth. *dails*, a part; OHG. *teil*; G. *theil*. Teut. type *dailiz*; allied to Lith. *dalis*, a share; OSlav. *dêlŭ*. Brugmann, i. § 279 (2). **Der.** *deal*, verb; whence *deal-er*, *-ing*, *-ings*; cf. *dole*.

DEAL (2), to divide, distribute; to traffic. (E.) ME. *delen*, Chaucer, C. T. prol. 247, where it has the sense of 'traffic.' AS. *dǣlan*, to divide; Grein, i. 186.+Du. *deelen*, to divide, share; Dan. *dele*; Swed. *dela*; Icel. *deila*; Goth. *dailjan*; OHG. *teilan*; G. *theilen*. Teut. type *dailjan-*, from *dailiz*, sb. The form of the verb shows that it is derived from the sb. See **Deal** (1).

DEAL (3), a thin plank of timber. (Du.) The word is not E., but Dutch. The earliest use of the word is in the Earl of Derby's Expeditions, 1390-3 (Camden Soc.), where find *deles*, boards, frequently; see p. 359, col. 2, s.v. *Wood*. 'A thousand *deal-board*; to make huts for the soldiers;' Clarendon, Civil War, ii. 675 (R.). In Florio (1598), we find: '*Doga*, a *deale boord* to make hogsheads with.'━Du. *deel*, fem., deal, board, plank, threshing-floor (distinct from *deel*, deal, part, which is neuter). In MDu. the word was disyllabic; Hexham gives *deele*, 'a planck, or a board' (distinct from *deel*, *deyl*, a part). + Low G. *dele*, a board (which in the Bremen Wörterbuch is wrongly connected with AS. *dǣl*); G. *diele*, board, plank; MHG. *dille*; OHG. *dilla*; AS. *þille*, E. *thill*. Thus *deal* (3) is the same word with **Thill**, q.v. ¶ The use of Du. *d* for Eng. *th* appears again in *drill* (1), q.v., and in *deck*.

DEAN, a dignitary in cathedral churches and colleges. (F.━L.) The orig. sense is 'a chief of ten.' ME. *den*, *deen*, *dene*, P. Plowman, B. xiii. 65; also found in the comp. pl. *suddenes*, equivalent to *subdenes*, i.e. sub-deans; P. Plowman, B. ii. 172.━OF. *deien* (Roquefort); mod.F. *doyen*.━L. *decānum*, acc. of *decānus*, one set over ten soldiers; later, one set over ten monks; hence, a dean.━L. *decem*, ten; cognate with E. *ten*. See **Decemvir** and **Ten**. **Der.** *dean-ery*, *dean-ship*; also *decan-al*, directly from L. *decān-us*.

DEAR, precious, costly, beloved. (E.) ME. *dere*, *deere*; spelt *deore* in Layamon, i. 7, l. 143. AS. *dēore*, *dýre*, Grein, i. 193, 215. + Du. *dier*; Dan. and Swed. *dyr*, dear, expensive; Icel. *dýrr*, dear, precious; OSax. *diuri*; OHG. *tiuri*, MHG. *tiure*, G. *theuer*, dear, beloved, sacred. Teut. type *deur-joz*. Root unknown. **Der.** *dear-ly*, *-ness*; also *dar-ling*, q.v., *dear-th*, q.v.

DEARTH, dearness, scarcity. (E.) ME. *derthe*, P. Plowman, B. vi. 330; Polit. Songs, ed. Wright, p. 342. Not found in AS., but regularly formed from AS. *dēore*, dear; cf. *heal-th*, *leng-th*, *warm-th*; see Morris, Hist. Outlines of Eng. Accidence, sect. 321. **+** Icel. *dȳrð*, value; hence, glory; OSax. *diuritha*, value; OHG. *tiurida*, value, honour. See above.

DEATH, the end of life. (E.) ME. *deeth*, *deth*, Chaucer, C. T., 964 (or 966). We also find the form *ded*, Havelok, 1687; a Scand. form still in use in Lincolnshire and elsewhere. AS. *dēað*, Grein, i. 189. **+** Du. *dood*; [Dan. *död*; Swed. *död*; Icel. *dauði*]; Goth. *dauthus*; G. *tod*. Teut. type *dau-thuz*. See **Dead** and **Die**. ¶ The ME. form *ded* is rather Scandinavian than AS.; cf. the Danish and Swedish forms.

DEBAR, to bar out from, hinder. (F.) In Shak. Sonnet 28. Earlier, in The Floure of Curtesie, st. 10, by Lydgate; pr. in Chaucer's Works, ed. 1561, fol. ccclviii, back. Made up by prefixing the OF. *des-* [=L. *dis-*] to the E. *bar*; see **Bar**. ¶ It agrees in sense neither with Late L. *dēbarrāre*, to take away a bar, nor with OF. *desbarrer*, to unbar (Cotgrave).

DEBARK, to land from a ship. (F.) 'Debark (not much used), to disembark;' Ash's Dict. 1775. — F. *débarquer*, to land; spelt *desbarquer* in Cotgrave. — F. *des-* (for L. *dis-*, away), and F. *barque*, a bark, ship. See **Bark** (1). Der. *debark-at-ion*, also spelt *debarc-at-ion*.

DEBASE, to degrade, lower, abase. (Hybrid.) In Shak. Rich. II, iii. 3. 127. A mere compound, from L. *dē-*, down, and *base*. See **Base**. Der. *debase-ment*, *debas-ing*, *-ing-ly*.

DEBATE, to argue, contend. (F. — L.) 'In which he wol *debate*;' Chaucer, C. T. 13797 (B 2058). The ME. sb. *debat* occurs in P. Plowman, C. xxii. 251. — OF. *debatre* (F. *débattre*), 'to debate, argue, discuss;' Cot. — L. *dē-*, down; and *battere*, popular form of L. *batuere*, to beat. See **Beat**, and **Batter**. Der. *debate*, sb., *debat-er*, *-able*.

DEBAUCH, to seduce, corrupt. (F. — L. *and* Teut.) Only the pp. *debauched* is in Shakespeare, and it is generally spelt *debosh'd*; Tempest, iii. 2. 29. — OF. *desbaucher* (mod. F. *débaucher*), 'to debosh, mar, corrupt, spoyle, viciate, seduce, mislead, make lewd, bring to disorder, draw from goodness;' Cot. — OF. *des-*, prefix, from L. *dis-*, away from; and OF. *bauche*, of rather uncertain meaning. Cotgrave has: '*bauche*, a rew [row], rank, lane, or course of stones or bricks in building.' See *Bauche* in Diez, who remarks that, according to Nicot, it means a plastering of a wall; according to Ménage, a workshop (apparently in order to suggest an impossible derivation from L. *apothēca*). β. The compounds are *esbaucher*, to rough-hew, frame (Cotgrave); *embaucher*, 'to imploy, occupy, use in business, put unto work' (id.); and *desbaucher*. Roquefort explains OF. *bauche* as a little house, to make it equivalent to Low L. *bugia*, a little house. Diez proposes to explain *débaucher* by 'to entice away from a workshop.' He suggests as the origin either Gael. *balc*, a balk, boundary, ridge of earth (which is mere English), or the Icel. *bálkr*, a balk, beam. γ. The latter of these suggestions may be nearly right; but it may be better to derive it from OSax. *balko*, a beam, or OHG. *balco*, *balcho*; the word *bauche* had clearly some connexion with building operations. At this rate, we should have *esbaucher*, to balk out, i. e. set up the frame of a building; *embaucher*, to balk in, to set to work on a building; *desbaucher*, to dis-balk, to take away the frame or the supports of a building before finished or to leave it incomplete. Cf. Körting, § 1183. And see OF. *desbaucher* in Supp. to Godefroy. See **Balk** (1). Der. *debauch*, sb.; *debauch-ee* (F. *débauché*, debauched); *debauch-er-y*.

DEBENTURE, an acknowledgment of a debt. (L.) Spelt *debentur* by Lord Bacon, in the old edition of his speech to King James, touching Purveyors. The passage is thus quoted by Richardson: 'Nay, farther, they are grown to that extremity, as is affirmed, though it be scarce credible, that they will take double poundage, once when the *debenture* [old ed. *debentur*] is made, and again the second time when the money is paid.' Blount, in his Law Dict., has: '*Debentur*, was, by a Rump-Act in 1649, ordained to be in the nature of a bond or bill, &c. The form of which *debentur*, as then used, you may see in Scobel's Rump-Acts, Anno 1649, cap. 63.' Also in the Paston Letters, i. 364; no. 264 (ab. 1455). — L. *dēbentur*, they are due; 'because these receipts began with the words *dēbentur mihi*;' Webster. — L. *dēbēre*, to be due. See **Debt**.

DEBILITATE, to weaken. (L.) The verb occurs in Sir T. Elyot, Castel of Helth, bk. i. c. 30; Shak. has *debile*, i. e. weak, Cor. i. 9. 48; and *debility*, As You Like It, ii. 3. 51; cf. MF. *debiliter*, 'to debilitate, weaken, enfeeble;' Cot. — L. *dēbilitātus*, pp. of *dēbilitāre*, to weaken. — L. *dēbilis*, weak. Prob. from L. *dē*, away, not; and *-bilis*, allied to Skt. *bala-* (for *dus-bala-*), feeble. Brugmann, i. § 553. Der. From the same source is *debility*, spelt *debilitie*, Sir T. Elyot, Castel of Helth, b. ii. c. 10; OF. *debilité*, from L. *dēbilitātem*, acc. of *dēbilitās*, weakness.

DEBONAIR, courteous, of good appearance. (F.—L.) In early use. ME. *debonere*, Rob. of Glouc. p. 167, l. 3481; Ancren Riwle, p. 186; also the sb. *debonairte*, O. Eng. Hom. i. 269, l. 15.— AF. *debonere*, *debonaire*, adj. affable, Life of Edw. Confessor, l. 238; compounded of *de bon aire*, lit. of a good mien. Here *de* is L. *dē*, of; *bon* is from L. *bonus*, good; and *aire* was a sb. (orig. masc.) signifying place, stock, race, a word of uncertain origin, but perhaps from L. *ārea*, an open space, or L. acc. *agrum*, field. Körting, § 828.

DEBOUCH, to march out of a narrow pass. (F.—L.) First in 1760. A modern military word (Todd). — F. *déboucher*, to uncork, to emerge. — F. *dé-*, for L. *dis-*, out, away; and *boucher*, to stop up the mouth; thus *déboucher* is lit. 'to unstop.' From F. *bouche*, the mouth; L. *bucca*, the cheek; also, the mouth.

DEBRIS, broken pieces, rubbish. (F.—L. *and* C.) First in 1708. Merely French.— F. *débris*, fragments.— OF. *debrisier*, to break in pieces (Godefroy).— OF. *de-*, for L. *dē*, down; and *brisier* (F. *briser*), to break, of Celtic origin; cf. Gael. *bris*, to break, Irish *bris-im*, I break.

DEBT, a sum of money due. (F.—L.) The introduction of the *b* (never really sounded) was due to a knowledge of the Latin form, and was a mistake. See Shak. L. L. L. v. 1. 23. ME. *dette*, Chaucer, C. T. Prol. 280 (or 282); P. Plowman, B. xx. 10. The pl. *dettes* and *dettur* (i. e. debtor) both occur on p. 126 of the Ancren Riwle. — OF. *dette*, a debt; Cot. has both *dette* and *debte.*— L. *dēbita*, a sum due; fem. of *dēbitus*, owed, pp. of *dēbēre*, to owe. β. *Dēbēre* is for *dēhibēre*, lit. to have away, i.e. to have on loan; from *dē*, down, away, and *habēre*, to have. See **Habit**. Der. *debt-or* (ME. *dettur*, OF. *deteur*, from L. *dēbitōrem*, acc. of *dēbitor*, a debtor). We also have *debit*, from L. *dēbitum*.

DEBUT, a first appearance in a play. (F.) Modern, and French. — F. *début*, a first stroke, a first cast or throw in a game at dice, first play in a game at bowls; verbal sb. from *débuter*. The MF. *desbuter* meant 'to repell, to put from the mark he aimed at;' Cot. The change of meaning is singular; the verb seems to have meant (1) to displace an opponent's bowl, and thence (2) to lead in the next bout (as is usual at bowls). See Notes on E. Etym., p. 63. — OF. *des-*, for L. *dis-*, apart; and *but*, an aim. See **Butt** (1).

DECADE, an aggregate of ten (F. — L. — Gk.) The pl. *decades* is in the title of 'The *Decades* of the newe worlde,' by R. Eden (1555). — F. *decade*, 'a decade, the tearme or number of ten years or months; also, a tenth, or the number of ten;' Cot.— L. *decadem*, acc. of *decas*. — Gk. δεκάδα, acc. of δεκάς, a company of ten.— Gk. δέκα, ten; cognate with E. **Ten**, q. v.

DECADENCE, a state of decay. (F.—L.) In Goldsmith, Citizen of the World, let. 40, § 1. Spelt *decadens*, Complaint of Scotland, ch. vii. p. 71, l. 10.— F. *décadence*, 'decay, ruin;' Cot.— Late L. *dēcadentia*, decay.— L. *dē*, down; and Late L. *cadentia*, a falling. See **Cadence**. Der. *decadenc-y*; and see *decay.*

DECAGON, a plane figure of ten sides. (Gk.) So named because it also has ten angles. A mathematical term; in Phillips' Dict. ed. 1658. Comp. of Gk. δέκα, ten; and γωνία, a corner, an angle, allied to γόνυ, the knee. See **Ten** and **Knee**.

DECAHEDRON, a solid figure having ten bases or sides. (Gk.) A mathematical term. Not in Kersey or Bailey. Comp. of Gk. δέκα, ten; and ἕδρα, a base, a seat (with aspirated ε), from ἕδ-ος, a seat; from the base *heδ*, cognate with E. *sit*. See **Ten** and **Sit**.

DECALOGUE, the ten commandments. (F. — L. — Gk.) Written *decaloge*; Barnes, Epitome of his Works, p. 368, col. 2. Earlier, in Wyclif, prologue to Romans; p. 299, l. 23.— F. *décalogue*; Cot.— L. *decalogus*.— Gk. δεκάλογος, the decalogue; comp. of Gk. δέκα, ten, and λόγος, a speech, discourse, from λέγειν, to speak.

DECAMP, to go from a camp, depart quickly. (F.—L.) Formerly *discamp*, as in Cotgrave. *Decamp* occurs in the Tatler, no. 11, and in Kersey's Dict. ed. 1715, who also gives *decampment.*—F. *décamper*; Cot. gives '*descamper*, to discampe, to raise or to remove a camp.'— L. *dis-*, away; and *campus*, a field, later a camp (Ducange). See **Camp**.

DECANAL; see under **Dean**.

DECANT, to pour out wine. (F. — L. *and* Gk.) 'Let it stand some three weeks or a month . . . Then *decant* from it the clear juyce;' Reliq. Wottonianæ, p. 454; from a letter written A. D. 1633. Kersey explains *decantation* as a chemical term, meaning 'a pouring off the clear part of any liquor, by stooping the vessel on one side.'—F. *décanter*, to decant (Span. *decantar*).—Med. L. *dēcanthāre*, to pour out (a word used by alchemists).— L. *dē*, down, from; and *canthus*, the 'lip' of a cup, a peculiar use of Gk. κάνθος, corner of the eye. See Hatzfeld, under *décanter* and *canthus*. Cf. Hamburg *kanten*, *upkanten*, to tilt a vessel (Richey). Der. *decant-er*.

DECAPITATE, to behead. (L.) Cotgrave has: '*Decapiter*, to *decapitate*, or behead.'— Late L. *dēcapitātus*, pp. of *dēcapitāre*, to behead; Ducange. — L. *dē*, down, off; and *capit*-, stem of *caput*, the head. **Der.** *decapitat-ion.*

DECASYLLABIC, having ten syllables. (Gk.) Modern. Coined from Gk. δέκα, ten; and συλλαβή, a syllable. See **Ten,** and **Syllable.**

DECAY, to fall into ruin. (F. — L.) Surrey uses the verb *decaie* actively, in the sense of 'wither;' The Constant Lover Lamenteth. The sb. *decas* (= L. *dēcāsus*) is in Gower, C. A. i. 32; prol. 837. — ONorth F. *decair* (pr. s. subj. *decaie*), OF. *dechaoir*, &c., to decay; cf. Span. *decaer.* — L. *dē*, down; and Folk L. *cadīre, cadēre*, for L. *cadere*, to fall. See **Cadence. Der.** From the same source is *decadence*, q. v.; *deciduous*, q. v.

DECEASE, death. (F. — L.) ME. *deces, deses*; spelt *decess* in Gower, C. A. iii. 243; bk. vii. l. 4516; *deses* in Rob. of Brunne, tr. of Langtoft, p. 126. — OF. *deces* (mod. F. *décès*), decease. — L. *dēcessum*, acc. of *dēcessus*, departure, death. — L. *dēcēdere*, to depart. — L. *dē*, from; and *cēdere*, to go. See **Cede. Der.** *decease*, verb.

DECEIVE, to beguile, cheat. (F. — L.) ME. *deceyuen* (with *u* for *v*); P. Plowman, C. xix. 123; Polit. Songs, p. 337, l. 300. The sb. *deceit* is in P. Plowman, C. i. 77. — OF. *deceveir, decevoir*; pr. s. subj. *deceive.* — L. *dēcipere*, pp. *dēceptus*, to take away, deceive. — L. *dē*, from; and *capere*, to take. **Der.** *deceiv-er, -able, -abl-y, -able-ness*; also *deceit* (through French from the L. pp. *dēceptus*), spelt *disseyte* in K. Alisaunder, 7705; *deceit-ful, -ful-ly, -ful-ness*; also (like L. *dēceptus*) *decept-ive, -ive-ly, -ive-ness*; *deception*, q. v.

DECEMBER, the twelfth month. (L.) In Chaucer, On the Astrolabe, pt. i. § 10. — L. *December*, the tenth month of the Roman year, as at first reckoned. — L. *decem*, ten. See **Ten.**

DECEMVIR, one of ten magistrates. (L.) In Holland's Livy, pp. 109, 127. — L. *decemuir*, one of the *decemuirī*, or ten men joined together in a commission. — L. *decem*, ten; and *uirī*, men, pl. of *uir*, a man, which is cognate with AS. *wer*, a man. **Der.** *decemvir-ate*, from L. *decemuirātus*, the office of a decemvir.

DECENNIAL, belonging to ten years. (L.) 'Decennial, belonging to or containing ten years;' Blount's Gloss. ed. 1674. — L. *decennālis*, of ten years; modified to go with *biennial.* — L. *decem*, ten; and *ann-us*, a year, changing to *enn-us* in composition. **Der.** From the same source is *dec-enn-ary*, which see in N.E.D.

DECENT, becoming, modest. (F. — L.) 'Cumlie and *decent*;' R. Ascham, Scholemaster, ed. Arber, p. 64. — MF. *decent*, 'decent, seemly;' Cot. — L. *decent*-, stem of *decens*, fitting, pres. pt. of *decēre*, to become, befit; cf. L. *decus*, honour, fame. See **Decorate. Der.** *decent-ly, decenc-y.*

DECEPTION, act of deceit. (F. — L.) In Berners' Froissart, ii. cap. 86; and Lydgate, Minor Poems, p. 76. — OF. *deception*, 'deception, deceit;' Cot. — L. acc. *dēcep'iōnem*, from nom. *dēceptio*; cf. *dēceptus*, pp. of *decipere*, to deceive. See **Deceive.**

DECIDE, to determine, settle. (F. — L.) 'And yit the cause is noght *decided*;' Gower, C. A. i. 15; prol. 334. — OF. *decider*, 'to decide;' Cot. — L. *dēcīdere*, pp. *dēcīsus*, lit. to cut off; also, to decide. — L. *dē*, from, off; and *cædere*, to cut. **Der.** *decid-able, -ed*; also *decis-ion, -ive, -ive-ly, -ive-ness*, like pp. *dēcīsus.*

DECIDUOUS, falling off, not permanent. (L.) In Blount's Glossographia, 1674. — L. *dēciduus*, that falls down; with (frequent) change of *-us* to *-ous.* — L. *dēcidere*, to fall down. — L. *dē*, down; and *cadere*, to fall. See **Cadence. Der.** *deciduous-ness.*

DECIMAL, relating to tens. (F. — L.) In Blount's Gloss. ed. 1674. — OF. *decimal*, 'tything, or belonging to tythe;' Cot. — Late L. *decimālis*, belonging to tithes. — L. *decima*, a tithe; fem. of *decimus*, tenth. — L. *decem*, ten; cognate with E. *ten.* See **Ten. Der.** *decimal-ly.*

DECIMATE, to kill every tenth man. (L.) Shak. has *decimation*, Tim. v. 4. 31. — L. *dēcimātus*, pp. of *decimāre*, to take by lot every tenth man, for punishment. — L. *decimus*, tenth. See above. **Der.** *decimat-or, -ion.*

DECIPHER, to uncipher, explain secret writing. (F. — L. and Arab.) In Shak. Mer. Wives, v. 2. 10. Imitated from MF. *dechiffrer*, 'to decypher;' Cot. From L. *dē*-, here in the sense of the verbal *un*-; and *cipher.* See **Cipher. Der.** *decipher-able.*

DECISION, DECISIVE; see Decide.

DECK (1), to cover, clothe, adorn. (MDu.) In Surrey's tr. of Æneid, bk. ii. l. 316; see Spec. of Eng. ed. Skeat, p. 208. Not in early use, and not English; the AS. *decan* and *gedecan* are mythical. — MDu. *decken*, to hide; Du. *dekken*, to cover; *dek*, a cover, a ship's deck. +Dan. *dække*, to cover; *dæk*, a deck; Swed. *täcka*, to cover; G. *decken*, to cover; AS. *þeccan*, to thatch. See **Thatch. Der.** *deck*, sb.; *deck-er, three-deck-er.* **Doublet,** *thatch.*

DECK (2), a pack of cards. (MDu.) In Shak. 3 Hen. VI, v. 1. 44. So called because the cards cover up or hide one another when piled up; cf. MDu. *decken*, 'to cover, to deck, or to hide' (Hexham). See above.

DECLAIM, to declare aloud, advocate loudly. (L.) Wilson has *declame*; Arte of Retoriqu*e*, p. 158 (R.). Skelton has *declamacyons*, Garlande of Laurell, 326. The reading *declamed* occurs in Chaucer, Troilus, ii. 1247; where old edd. have *declared*. [Not found in CF.] — L. *dēclāmāre*, to cry aloud, make a speech. — L. *dē*, down, here intensive; and *clāmāre*, to cry out. See **Claim. Der.** *declaim-er, -ant*; and (from L. pp. *dēclāmātus*) *declamat-ion, -or-y.*

DECLARE, to make clear, assert. (F. — L.) ME. *declaren*; Chaucer, Comp. of Mars, 163; Gower, C. A. i. 158; bk. i. l. 3436. — OF. *declairier* (Godefroy), later *declarer*, 'to declare, tell, relate;' Cot. — L. *dēclārāre*, pp. *dēclārātus*, to make clear, declare. — L. *dē*-, i. e. fully; and *clārus*, clear. See **Clear. Der.** *declarat-ion, -ive, -ive-ly; declarat-or-y, -or-i ly.*

DECLENSION, a declining downwards. (F. — L.) In Shak. Rich. III, iii. 7. 189; and (as a grammat. term) Merry Wives, iv. 1. 76. — OF. *declinaison*; see index to Cotgrave, which has: 'declension of a noune, *declinaison de nom.*' — L. acc. *dēclīnātiōnem*, from nom. *dēclīnātio*, declination, declension. Thus *declension* is a doublet of *declination*. See **Decline.**

DECLINE, to turn aside, avoid, refuse, fail. (F. — L.) ME. *declinen*; 'hem þat eschuen and declinen fro vices and taken the wey of vertu;' Chaucer, tr. of Boethius, b. iv. pr. 7; l. 31. — OF. *decliner*; Cot. — L. *dēclīnāre*, to bend aside from. — L. *dē*, from, away; and *-clīnāre*, to bend, incline, lean; allied to E. *lean.* See **Lean** (1). **Der.** *declinat-ion*, in Chaucer, C. T. 10097 (E 2223), from OF. *declination*, L. acc. *dēclīnā'iōnem*; see **Declension, Declivity.**

DECLIVITY, a descending surface, downward slope. (F. — L.) Opposed to *acclivity*, q.v. Given in Blount's Gloss. ed. 1674. — F. *déclivité.* — L. *dēclīuitātem*, acc. of *dēclīuitās*, a declivity. — L. *dēclīuis*, inclining downwards. — L. *dē*, down; and *clīuus*, a slope, a hill, from the same root as *-clīnare*, to bend, incline. See **Decline.**

DECOCT, to digest by heat. (L.) In Shak. Hen. V, iii. 5. 20; cf. 'slowe in *decoction*;' Sir T. Elyot, Castel of Helth, b. ii. ch. 18; *decoccioune*, Lydgate, Minor Poems, p. 82. — L. *dēcoctus*, pp. of *dēcoquere*, to boil down. — L. *dē*, down; and *coquere*, to cook. See **Cook. Der.** *decoct-ion, -ive.*

DECOLLATION, a beheading. (F. — L.) 'The feast of the *decollacion* of seynt John Baptist;' Fabyan, an. 1349-50; also in Trevisa, v. 49. — OF. *decollation*, 'a beheading: *decollation sainct Jean*, an holyday kept the 29 of August;' Cot. — Late L. *dēcollātiōnem*, acc. of *dēcollātio*; cf. *dēcollātus*, pp. of *dēcollāre*, to behead. — L. *dē*, away from; and *collum*, the neck. See **Collar. Der.** Hence the verb *decollate*, used by Burke, Introd. to On the Sublime.

DECOMPOSE, to resolve a compound into elements. (F. — L. and Gk.) Modern. First about 1751 (N.E.D.). Coined by prefixing L. *dē* to the hybrid word *compose.* See **Compose**; and see note below.

DECOMPOSITION, a decomposing or resolution. (F. — L.) Modern; first (in this sense) in 1731; Bailey, vol. ii. ed. 1731, has *decomposite, decomposition*, and *decompound.* All are coined words, made by prefixing the L. *dē* to *composite*, &c. See **Composite, Compound. Der.** *decompos-ite, -it-ion.* ¶ Etymologically distinct from *decompose*, but much confused with it.

DECORATE, to ornament, adorn. (L.) Hall has *decorated*, Edw. IV, an. 23. § 1. 'O noble prynces, in worshyp *decorate*;' Barclay, Ship of Fools, ed. Jamieson, ii. 16. And see Palsgrave, p. 509. [Hall also uses the short form *decore* (from OF. *decorer*); Hen. V, an. 2. § 19. The word *decorat* in Chaucer, tr. of Boethius, b. iii. pr. 4, is a proper name, L. *Decorātus.*] — L. *decorātus*, pp. of *decorāre*, to adorn. — L. *decor*-, for **decos*-, stem of *decus*, an ornament. See **Decorum. Der.** *decorat-ion, -ive, -or.*

DECORUM, decency of conduct. (L.) In Ascham, Scholemaster, ed. Arber, p. 139, l. 16. — L. *decōrum*, sb., seemliness, neut. of *decōrus*, seemly. — L. *decōr*-, stem of *decor*, seemliness; closely related to *decor*-, from *decus*, ornament, grace. — L. *decēre*, to befit; *decet*, it befits, seems. Cf. Gk. δοκέω, I am valued at, I am of opinion; δοκεῖ, it seems. **Der.** We also have *decorous* (which is from L. *decōrus*, seemly); *decorous-ly.* See **Decent.**

DECOY, to allure, entice. (Hybrid; L. *and* Du. — L.) A coined word. The word *decoy-duck*, i.e. duck for decoying wild ducks, occurs in Beaum. and Fletcher, Fair Maid, Act iv. sc. 2 (Clown); 'you are worse than simple widgeons, and will be drawn into the net by this *decoy-duck*, this tame cheater.' But Burton, Anat. Melan. ii. 2. 4, has: 'Fowling .. with .. *coy-ducks*.' Made by prefixing L. *dē*-, down, to prov. E. *coy*, a decoy, which was borrowed from Du. *kooi*, a cage, a decoy, MDu. *koye*, also *kouwe* (Hexham). This is not a true Du. word, but adapted from Late L. *cavea*, whence also F. and E. *cage*; see **Cage.** β. Perhaps the prefixing of *de-* was due to association with ME. *coyen*, to quiet; so that *de-coy* seemed to mean 'to quiet down.' (See Notes on E. Etym., p. 64.) Cf. *accoy*, Spenser, F. Q. iv. 8. 59; 'Coyyn, blandior;' Prompt. Parv. See **Coy. Der.** *decoy-duck, -bird.*

DECREASE, to grow less, diminish. (F.—L.) Both act. and neut. in Shak. Tam. Shrew, ii. 119; Sonn. 15. [Gower has the verb *discresen*, C. A. ii. 189; from Late L. *discrescere*.] 'Thanne begynneth the ryvere for to wane and to *decrece*;' Maundeville, p. 44.—AF. *decreiss-*, a stem of *decreistre* (Bestiary, 919); substituted for OF. *descreiss-*, *descroiss-*, a stem of *descroistre*, to decrease (Godefroy).—Late L. *discrescere*, for L. *dēcrescere*, to decrease (so that the AF. form was more correct than the OF. form).—L. *dis-*, for *dē-*, off, from, away; and *crescere*, to grow. See **Crescent**. Cf. Norm. dial. *décreitre*, to decrease (Moisy). **Der.** *decrease*, sb. (ME. *descres*, Gower, C. A. iii. 154; bk. vii. l. 2054; AF. *descrees*, Stat. Realm, i. 158; from OF. stem *descreiss-*, above); *decreas-ing-ly*; and see *decrement*.

DECREE, a decision, order, law. (F.—L.) In early use. ME. *decree*, *decre*, Rob. of Brunne, tr. of Langtoft, p. 122; Chaucer, C. T. 17328 (I 17).—OF. *decret*, a decree.—L. *dēcrētum*, a decree; neut. of *dēcrētus*, pp. of *dēcernere*, to decree, lit. to separate.—L. *dē*, away from, and *cernere*, to sift, separate, decide; cognate with Gk. κρίνειν, to separate, decide. See **Critic**. **Der.** *decree*, verb; also *decret-al*, q. v., *-ive*, *-or-y*, from pp. *dēcrētus*.

DECREMENT, a decrease. (L.) 'Twit me with the *decrements* of my pendants;' Ford, Fancies Chaste, A. i. sc. 2.—L. *dēcrēmentum*, a decrease. Formed with suffix *-mentum* from *dēcrē-*, occurring in *dēcrēui* and *dēcrētus*, perf. tense and pp. of *dēcrescere*, to decrease; see **Decrease**.

DECREPIT, broken down with age. (L.) In Spenser, F. Q. ii. 9. 55; Sir T. Elyot, Castel of Helth, b. i. ch. 2 (Ages); Henrysoun, Praise of Age, l. 2.—L. *dēcrepitus*, that makes no noise; hence creeping about noiselessly like an old man, aged, broken down.—L. *dē*, away; and *crepitus*, pp. of *crepāre*, to crackle. See **Crepitate**. **Der.** *decrepit-ude*; also *decrepit-ate*, *-at-ion*.

DECRETAL, a pope's decree. (L.) In Rob. of Brunne, tr. of Langtoft, p. 337; P. Plowman, B. v. 428.—Late L. *dēcrētāle*, a pope's decree; neut. of *dēcrētālis*, adj., containing a decree.—L. *dēcrētum*, a decree. See **Decree**.

DECRY, to cry down, condemn. (F.—L.) In Dryden, Prol. to Tyrannic Love, l. 4.—OF. *descrier*, 'to cry down, or call in, uncurrent or naughty coin; also, publiquely to discredit, disparage, disgrace;' Cot.—OF. *des-*, L. *dis-*, implying the reversal of an act, and here opposed to 'cry up;' and OF. *crier*, to cry. See **Cry**. **Der.** *decri-al*.

DECUPLE, tenfold. (F.—L.) Rare. In Blount's Gloss. ed. 1674.—MF. *décuple*, ten times as much; Cot. [Cf. Ital. *decuplo*, tenfold.] Formed from L. *decuplus* (Daniel, i. 20).—L. *decem*, ten; and suffix *-plus* as in *duplus*, double; see **Ten** and **Double**.

DECURRENT, extending downwards. (L.) As a botanical term.—L. *dēcurrent-*, stem of *dēcurrens*, pres. pt. of *dēcurrere*, to run down.—L. *dē*, down; and *currere*, to run. See **Current**. **Der.** *decurs-ive*, from *dēcursus*, pp. of *dēcurrere*.

DECUSSATE, to cross at an acute angle. (L.) 'Decussated, cut or divided after the form of the letter X, or of St. Andrew's Cross, which is called *crux decussata*;' Blount's Gloss. ed. 1674.—L. *decussātus*, pp. of *decussāre*, to cross, put in the form of an X.—L. *decussis*, a coin worth 10 as-es, and therefore marked with an X.—L. *dec-em*, ten; and *assi-*, declensional stem of *as*, an as, ace. See **Ten** and **Ace**. **Der.** *decussat-ion*.

DEDICATE, to consecrate, devote. (L.) Formerly used as a pp. signifying 'dedicated.' 'In chirche *dedicat*;' Chaucer, Pers. Tale, 2nd Part of Penitence (I 964).—L. *dēdicātus*, pp. of *dēdicāre*, to devote.—L. *dē*, down; and *dicāre*, to proclaim, devote, allied to *dicere*, to say, tell, appoint, orig. to point out.—√DEIK, to show. See **Token**. **Der.** *dedicat-ion*, *-or-y*.

DEDUCE, to draw from, infer. (L.) In Sir T. More, Works, p. 461; Tyndall, Works, p. 21, col. 2, l. 41; Palsgrave, p. 509.—L. *dēdūcere*, to lead or bring down.—L. *dē*, down; and *dūcere*, to lead. See **Duke**. **Der.** *deduc-ible*, *deduce-ment*; and see below.

DEDUCT, to draw from, subtract. (L.) 'For having yet, in his *deducted* spright, Some sparks remaining of that heavenly fyre;' where it means *deduced* or 'derived;' Spenser, Hymn of Love, 106. And in Palsgrave, p. 509.—L. *dēductus*, pp. of *dēdūcere*, to lead or bring down. See above. **Der.** *deduct-ion*, *-ive-ly*.

DEED, something done, act. (E.) ME. *deed*, *dede*; Chaucer, C. T. prol. 744 (or 742). OMerc. *dēd*; AS. *dǣd*, deed; Grein, i. 185. + Du. *daad*; Dan. *daad*; Swed. *dåd*; Icel. *dáð*; Goth. *ga-dēds*, a deed; cf. *missa-dēds*, a misdeed; OHG. *tāt*, G. *that*. Teut. type *dǣdiz; Idg. type *dhētis; from √DHĒ, to place, put, do. See **Do** (1). **Der.** *deed-less*, *mis-deed*.

DEEM, to judge, think, suppose. (E.) ME. *demen*, Chaucer, C. T. 1883 (A 1881). AS. *dēman*, to judge, deem. Here the long *ē* is the mutation of *ō*; the verb being derived from the sb. *dōm*, a doom, judgment. + Du. *doemen*, to doom; Dan. *dømme*; Swed. *döma*; Icel. *dæma*; Goth. *gadōmjan*; OHG. *tuomian*, MHG. *tuemen*, to honour, also to judge, doom. Teut. type *dōmjan. All from the sb.

See **Doom**. **Der.** *deem-ster*, a judge, ME. *demestre*, Cursor Mundi, 5586 (Fairfax MS.), used as a masc. sb.; but AS. *dēmestre* was a fem. form, from masc. *dēmere*, lit. 'deem-er.'

DEEP, extending far downwards, profound. (E.) ME. *deep*, P. Plowman, C. i. 17; spelt *depe*, id. B. prol. 15; *deop*, id. A. prol. 15. AS. *dēop*, Grein, i. 191.+Du. *diep*; Dan. *dyb*; Swed. *djup*; Icel. *djūpr*; Goth. *diups*; OHG. *tiuf*, G. *tief*. Teut. type *deupoz. Cf. Lith. *dubùs*, deep, W. *dwfn*, deep. Brugmann, i. § 566. From the same source as **Dip**, which see. **Der.** *deep-ly*, *-ness*, *-en*; also *depth*, q. v., which compare with Goth. *diupitha*, Icel. *dýpt* or *dýpð*, and Du. *diepte*, depth (the AS. form being *dēopnes*, i. e. deepness); *depth-less*.

DEER, a ruminant quadruped. (E.) Lit. a wild beast, and applied to all sorts of animals; cf. 'rats, and mice, and such small *deer*,' King Lear, iii. 4. 144. ME. *deer*, *der*, *deor*; spelt *der*, Ormulum, 1177. AS. *dēor*, a wild animal; Grein, i. 192.+Du. *dier*, an animal, beast; Dan. *dyr* (the same); Swed. *djur* (same); Icel. *dýr* (same); Goth. *dius*, a wild beast; Mark, i. 13; OHG. *tior*, G. *thier*. Teut. type *deuzom. Idg. type *dheusóm, prob. 'animal;' from *dheus, to breathe (Kluge). Brugmann, i. § 539 (2). **Der.** *deer-stalk-er*, *deer-stalk-ing* (for which see *Stalk*).

DEFACE, to disfigure. (F.—L.) ME. *defacen*, *desfacen*, Chaucer, Ho. of Fame, iii. 74; Gower, C. A. ii. 46; bk. iv. l. 1322.—OF. *desfacier*, MF. *desfacer*, 'to efface, deface, raze;' Cot.—OF. *des-*, prefix.<L. *dis-*, apart, away; and *face*, a face, from L. *faciēs*, a face. [Similarly, Ital. *sfacciare*, to deface (Florio), is from Ital. prefix *s-*<L. *dis*, and Ital. *faccia*, a face.] And see **Efface**. **Der.** *deface-ment*.

DEFALCATE, to lop off, abate, deduct. (L.) See Trench, Select Glossary. Used as a pp. by Sir T. Elyot: 'yet be nat these in any parte *defalcate* of their condigne praises;' The Governour, b. ii. c. 10.—Late L. *dēfalcāre* [also *diffalcāre*, with prefix *dif-* for *dis-*], to abate, deduct, take away.—L. *dē*, away; and Late L. *falcāre* (see *falcastrāre* in Ducange), to cut with a sickle, from *falc-*, stem of *falx*, a sickle; see **Falchion**. **Der.** *defalcat-ion*.

DEFAME, to destroy fame or reputation. (F.—L.) ME. *defame*, *diffame*, used convertibly, and the same word. Chaucer has both 'for his *defame*' and 'of his *diffame*;' Six-text, Ellesmere MS., Group B, 3738, Group E, 730; (C. T. 14466, 8606.) The verb *diffamen* is used by Rob. of Brunne, tr. of Langtoft, p. 321; and by Chaucer, Ho. of Fame, iii. 491.—OF. *defamer*, to take away one's reputation (Roquefort, who gives a quotation); also *desfamer*, *diffamer* (Godefroy).—L. *diffāmāre*, to spread abroad a report, esp. a bad report; hence, to slander.—L. *dif-*, for *dis-*, apart, away; and *fāma*, a report. See **Fame**. **Der.** *defam-at-ion*, *dıfam-at-or-y*.

DEFAULT, a failing, failure, defect, offence. (F.—L.) ME. *defaute*; the *l* was a later insertion, just as in *fault*. The pl. *defautes*, meaning 'faults,' is in the Ancren Riwle, p. 136; Gower has *defalte*, C. A. ii. 122; bk. iv. l. 3588.—OF. *deffaute*, *defaute*, fem., later *defaut*, *default*, masc., a default, fault, as in Cotgrave. Cf. AF. *defalte*, Year-books of Edw. I, 1392–3, p. 303.—OF. *def-*<L. *dif-*, for *dis-*, apart; and *faute*, oldest form *falte*, a fault (=Ital. *falta*, a failing), from Late L. *fallita*, a deficiency, fem. of *fallitus, a new pp. of L. *fallere*, to fail. See **Fault**. **Der.** *default*, verb; *default-er*.

DEFEASANCE, a rendering null and void. (F.—L.) A law term. 'Defeizance, a condition relating to a deed, ... which being performed, ... the deed is disabled and made void;' Blount's Law Dict. ed. 1691. Spenser has *defeasaunce* = defeat; F.Q. i. 12. 12.—AF. *defesaunce* (Godefroy), a rendering void.—OF. *defaisant*, *deffaisant*, *desfaisant*, pres. part. of *defaire*, *deffaire*, *desfaire* (Godefroy), to render void, lit. to undo.—OF. *des-*<L. *dis-*, apart, [with the force of E. verbal *un-*]; and *faire*, to do, from L. *facere*, to do. See **Defeat**. **Der.** From the like source, *defeas-ible*.

DEFEAT, to overthrow, frustrate a plan. (F.—L.) The *verb* is the original, as far as Eng. is concerned. ME. *defeiten*, to defeat. 'To ben *defet*,' to be wasted; Chaucer, Troil. v. 618. Also *defeted*, Chaucer, tr. of Boethius, b. ii. pr. 1. l. 7. Formed from the F. pp. —OF. *defait*, *desfait*, pp. of *defaire*, *desfaire*, to defeat, undo; see Cot. and Godefroy.—OF. *des-*<L. *dis-*, [with the force of E. verbal *un-*]; and *faire*, to do, from L. *facere*, to do. See **Feat, Fact, Forfeit**. **Der.** *defeat*, sb.; Hamlet, ii. 2. 598. And see above.

DEFECATE, to purify from dregs. (L.) Used as a pp. by Sir T. Elyot, Castel of Helth, b. ii. c. 21.—L. *dēfæcātus*, pp. of *dēfæcāre*, to cleanse from dregs.—L. *dē*, away, from; and *fæc-*, stem of *fæx*, sediment, dregs; of unknown origin. **Der.** *defecat-ion*.

DEFECT, an imperfection, want. (L.) [The instance from Chaucer in R. is wrong; for *defect* read *desert*. The ME. word of like meaning was *defaute*; see **Default**.] In Shak. Temp. iii. 1. 44.—L. *dēfectus*, a want.—L. *dēfectus*, pp. of *dēficere*, to fail; orig. a trans. verb, to undo, loosen.—L. *dē*, down, from; and *facere*, to do. See **Fact**. **Der.** *defect-ive*, *-ively*, *-ive-ness*; *-ion*; also (from L. *deficere*) *deficit*, i. e. it is wanting, 3 pers. sing. present; *deficient*, from the pres. part.; *deficienc-y*.

DEFENCE, a protection, guard. (F.—L.) ME. *defence*, K. Alisaunder, 2615.—OF. *defense*.—L. *dēfensa*, a defending; Tertullian —L. *dēfensus* (fem. *dēfensa*), pp. of *dēfendere*, to defend; see below. **Der.** *defence-less*, *-less-ly*, *-less-ness*; also (from pp. *dēfensus*), *defens-ive*, *-ive-ly*, *-ible*, *-ibl-y*, *-ibil-i-ty*. Also *fence*, q. v.

DEFEND, to ward off, protect. (F.—L.) In early use. ME. *defenden*; *defendyng* occurs as a sb. in K. Alisaunder, 676.—OF. *defendre*.—L. *dēfendere*, to defend.—L. *dē*, down; and (obsolete) *fendere*, to strike, occurring in the comp. *dē-fendere*, *of-fendere*. β. *Fendere* is allied to Gk. θείνειν, to strike, and Skt. *han*, to kill; from √ GHwEN, to strike. Brugmann, i. § 654. **Der.** *defend-er*, *defendant* (F. pres. pt.); also *defence*, q. v.; also *fence*, *fender*.

DEFER (1), to put off, delay. (F.—L.) 'Deferred vnto the yeares of discretion;' Tyndall, Works, p. 388, col. 1. ME. *differren*, Gower, C. A. i. 262; bk. ii. l. 3074. [A similar confusion between the prefixes *de-* and *dif-* occurs in *defame*, q. v.]—OF. *differer*, 'to defer, delay;' Cot.—L. *differre*, to bear different ways; also, to delay.—L. *dif-* < *dis-*, apart; and *ferre*, to bear. See **Bear** (1). Doublet, *differ*. ¶ Distinct from the following.

DEFER (2), to submit or lay before; to submit oneself. (F.—L.) 'Hereupon the commissioners . . . *deferred* the matter unto the earl of Northumberland;' Bacon, Life of Hen. VII, ed. Lumby, p. 65. The sb. *deference* occurs in Dryden, On Satire, § 12.—OF. *deferer*, 'to charge, accuse, appeach; *deferer à vn appel*, to admit, allow, or accept of, to give way unto an appeale;' Cot.—L. *dēferre*, to bring down, to bring a thing before one.—L. *dē-*, down; and *ferre*, to bear. See **Bear** (1). ¶ Distinct from the above. **Der.** *defer-ence*, *-enti-al*, *-enti-al-ly*.

DEFIANCE, DEFICIENT; see **Defy, Defect**.

DEFILE (1), to make foul, pollute. (Hybrid; L. *and* E.) A clumsy compound, with a L. prefix to an E. base. The *force* of the word is due to E. *foul*, but the *form* of the word was suggested by OF. *defouler*, to trample under foot; so that the ME. *defoulen*, to tread down, passed into (or gave way to) a later form *defile* (occasionally *defoil*). [We also had *befoul* and *befile*.] Both sources must be taken into account. **A.** We have (1) ME. *defoulen*, to tread down. Rob. of Glouc., describing how King Edmund seized the robber Liofa, says that he 'fram the bord hym drou, And *defouled* him vnder him mid hond and mid fote,' i.e., thrust him down; p. 277, l. 5620. Wyclif translates *conculcatum est* (A. V. 'was trodden down') by *was defoulid*; Luke, viii. 5. 'We *defoule* wiþ our fet þe fine gold schene,' as a translation of 'aurum pedibus *conculcamus*;' Alexander and Dindimus, ed. Skeat, 1027. This is the OF. *defouler*, 'to tread or trample on;' Cot. Derived from L. *dē-*, down; and Late L. *fullāre*, to full cloth; see **Fuller**. **B.** Again, we have (2) ME. *defoulen*, to defile, imitated from the former word, but with the sense of E. *foul* engrafted on it. Wyclif translates *coinquinat* (A. V. 'defileth') by *defoulith*; Matt. xv. 11. Later, we find *defoylyd*, Sir T. More, Works, p. 771 a; afterwards *defile*, Much Ado, iii. 3. 60. This change to *defile* was due to the influence of ME. *fylen*, the true E. word for 'to pollute,' correctly used as late as in Shak. Macb. iii. 1. 65 : 'have I *fil'd* my mind.' This is the AS. *fýlan*, to make foul, whence the comp. *āfýlan*, to pollute utterly, in Gregory's Pastoral, § 54, ed. Sweet, p. 421; also *befýlan*, to defile; Bosworth. The verb *fýlan* is regularly formed, by the usual mutation of *ū* to *ȳ*, from the adj. *fúl*, foul. See **Foul**. **Der.** *defilement*.

DEFILE (2), to pass along in a file. (F.—L.) 'Defile, to march or go off, file by file;' Kersey's Dict. ed. 1715. Hence 'Defile, or Defilee, a straight narrow lane, through which a company of soldiers can pass only in file;' id.—F. *défiler*, to file off, defile; an earlier sense was to unravel, said of thread.—F. *dé-* < OF. *des-*, L. *dis-*, apart; and *filer*, to spin threads, from *fil*, 'a thread, . . . also a file, ranke, order,' Cot.; from L. *filum*, a thread. See **File** (1). **Der.** *defile*, sb., formerly *defilee* (as above), from F. *défilé*, pp. of *défiler*.

DEFINE, to fix the bounds of, describe. (F.—L.) ME. *definen* 'I have *defyned* that blisfulnesse is þe sovereyn good;' Chaucer, tr. of Boethius, b. iii. pr. 2; l. 49. Cf. *diffinicioun*, Chaucer, C. T. 5607 (D 25). (The latter is a false form; for *definicioun*.)—OF. *definer*, Romanic variant of *definir*, 'to define, conclude, determine or discuss, precisely to express, fully to describe;' Cot.—L. *dēfinire*, to limit, settle, define.—L. *dē* down; and *finire*, to set a bound, from L. *fīnis*, a bound, end. See **Finish**. **Der.** *defin-able*, *-ite*, *-ite-ly*, *-ite-ness*, *-it-ion*, *-it-ive*, *-it-ive-ly*.

DEFLAGRATION, a rapid burning. (L.) In Phillips (1706). From L. acc. *deflāgrātiōnem*, a great burning.—L. *dēflāgrāre*, to burn down, consume by fire.—L. *dē*, fully; *flāgrāre*, to burn; see **Flagrant**.

DEFLECT, to turn aside, swerve aside. (L.) 'At some part of the Azores it [the needle] *deflecteth* not;' Sir T. Browne, Vulg. Errors, bk. ii. c. 2, § 13. 'Deflexure, a bowing or bending;' Blount's Gloss. ed. 1674.—L. *dēflectere*, to bend aside.—L. *dē*, down, away;

and *flectere*, to bend; pp. *flexus*. See **Flexible**. **Der.** *deflect-ion*, *deflex-ure*.

DEFLOUR, DEFLOWER, to deprive of flowers, to ravish. (F.—L.) ME. *dēflouren*; Gower, C. A. ii. 322; bk. v. l. 5812. Spelt *deflowre*, Spenser, F. Q. ii. 12. 75.—OF. *defleurer*, 'to defloure, to defile;' Cot.—Late L. *dēflōrāre*, to gather flowers, to ravish.—L. *dē*, from, away; and *flor-*, decl. stem of *flōs*, a flower. See **Flower**. ¶ Cf. also OF. *desflorir*, with the same sense (prefix *dis-*). Observe the use of *floures* in the sense of 'natural vigour' or 'bloom of youth;' Gower, C. A. ii. 267; bk. v. l. 4174. **Der.** *deflour-er*; also (from pp. *dēflōrātus*) *deflorate*, *deflorat-ion*.

DEFLUXION, a flow or discharge of humours. (L.) Medical. 'Defluxion of salt rheum;' Howell's Letters, b. i. sec. 2. let. 1.—L. acc. *dēfluxiōnem*, from nom. *dēfluxio*, a flowing down.—L. *dē*, down; and *fluxus*, pp. of *fluere*, to flow. See **Fluid**.

DEFORCE, to deprive by force. (F.—L.) Legal. 'Deforsour, one that overcomes and casts out by force. See the difference between a *deforsour* and a *disseisor*, in Cowel, on this word;' Blount's Gloss. ed. 1674.—OF. *deforcier*, *desforcier*, MF. *deforcer*, 'to disseise, dispossess, violently take, forcibly pluck from;' Cot. Cf. Late L. *difforciāre*, to take away by violence; Ducange.—OF. *de-*, for *des-* < L. *dis-*, apart, away; and *force*, power, from Late L. *fortia*, power, from L. *fortis*, strong. See **Force**. **Der.** *deforce-ment*; *defors-our* (obsolete).

DEFORM, to disfigure, misshape. (F.—L.) ME. *deformen*, *defformen*. The pp. *defformyd* is in Wyclif, 2 Cor. iii. 7. 'Deformed is the figure of my face;' The Testament of Creseide, l. 448.—OF. *difformer*, to deform (Godefroy); with *dif-* for *dis-*, in place of *de-*.—L. *dēformare*, to deform; *dēformis*, deformed, ugly.—L. *dē*, away; and *forma*, beauty, form. See **Form**. **Der.** *deform-i-ty*, ME. *deformité*, Court of Love, 1169; *deform-at-ion*.

DEFRAUD, to deprive by fraud. (F.—L.) ME. *defrauden*, Wyclif, Luke, xix. 8; P. Plowman, B. vii. 69.—OF. *defrauder*, 'to defraud;' Cot.—L. *dēfraudāre*, to deprive by fraud.—L. *dē*, away, from; and *fraud-*, stem of *fraus*, fraud. See **Fraud**.

DEFRAY, to pay costs. (F.—L. *and* G.) In Cotgrave; and see Spenser, F. Q. i. 5. 42.—MF. *defrayer*, 'to defray, to discharge, to furnish, or bear all the charges of,' Cot.; OF. *desfrayer* (Littré).—OF. *des-*, for L. *dis-*, away; and *frai*, sing. of *frais*, cost, expense, now used as a plural sb. Cotgrave also has the form *fraiz* (=*fraits*), the pl. of a form *frait*; and Hatzfeld cites OF. *fres*, pl. β. The OF. sing. *fre*, later *frait*, *frai*, is equivalent to Low L. *fredum*, a fine, composition, hence, a cost.—OHG. *fridu* (G. *friede*), peace; also, a fine for a breach of the peace. Körting, §§ 3943, 3968. **Der.** *defray-ment*.

DEFT, neat, dexterous. (E.) In Chapman, tr. of Homer's Iliad, b. i. l. 11 from end. The adv. *deftly* is commoner; Macb. iv. 1. 68. ME. *dafte*, *defte*, (1) becoming, mild, gentle, (2) innocent, whence the sense of 'foolish,' as in prov. E. *daft*; Ormulum, 2175, 4610; Bestiary, 37; cf. *dafftelike*, fittingly, becomingly, Orm. 1215. AS. *dæfte*, as seen in *ge-dæfte*, mild, gentle, meek, Matt. xxi. 5; *ge-dæftlice*, fitly, seasonably, Ælfred, tr. of Gregory's Past. Care, ed. Sweet, p. 97, l. 15; and see l. 17. Cf. also *dæftan*, and *ge-dæftan*, to prepare, Ælf. Hom. i. 212, 362. β. The *t* is merely a suffix, and disappears in prov. E. and ME. *daff*, *daffe*, a foolish person, P. Plowman, B. i. 138; formed from the base *daf-*, to fit, appearing in AS. *ge-daf-en*, fit (Grein), the pp. of a lost strong verb **dafan*, to fit, suit. Cf. Du. *deftig*, grave, respectable, genteel; Low G. *deftig*, fit, good, excellent; Goth. *ga-dōfs*, *ga-dōbs*, fitting, fit, from *ga-daban*, to happen, befall, to be fit. All from Teut. base **daƀ*, to suit; Fick, i. 633, iii. 144. Cf. also **Dapper**. Doublet, *daft*, in a sinister sense, as, 'dafte, doltishe,' in Levins. **Der.** *deft-ly*, as above; *deft-ness*.

DEFUNCT, deceased, dead. (L.) Lit. ♣ having fully performed the course of life.' Shak. has *defunct*, Cymb. iv. 2. 358; *defunction*, Hen. V, i. 2. 58; *defunctive*, Phœnix, l. 14.—L. *dēfunctus*, pp. of *dēfungī*, to perform fully.—L. *dē*, down, off, fully; and *fungī*, to perform. See **Function**. **Der.** *defunct-ive*, *-ion* (above).

DEFY, to renounce allegiance, challenge, brave. (F.—L.) In early use. ME. *defyen*, *deffien*; Chaucer, C. T. 15177 (B 4361). The sb. *defying* is in K. Alisaunder, 7275.—MF. *defier*, 'to defie, challenge;' Cot. Earlier spelling *deffier*, *desfier* (Godefroy), with the sense 'to renounce faith.'—Late L. *diffidāre*, to renounce faith, defy.—L. *dif-*, for *dis-*, apart; and *fidus*, faithful, *fidere*, to trust; allied to *fides*, trust, faith. See **Faith**. **Der.** *defi-ance*, ME. *defyaunce*, Lydgate, Minor Poems, p. 92; *defi-ance*.

DEGENERATE, having become base. (L.) Always an adj. in Shak.; see Rich. II, i. 1. 144; ii. 1. 262.—L. *dēgenerātus*, degenerated, pp. of *dēgenerāre*.—L. *dēgener*, adj. base, ignoble.—L. *dē*, down; and *gener-* (for **genes-*), stem of *genus*, race, kind, cognate with E. *kin*. See **Kin**. **Der.** *degenerate*, verb; *-ly*, *-ness*; *degenerat-ion*, *-ive*; *degenerac-y*.

DEGLUTITION, the act of swallowing. (F. – L.) 'Deglutition, a devouring or swallowing down;' Blount's Gloss. ed. 1674. – MF. deglutition; see F. déglutition in Hatzfeld. Coined from L. dē, down, and glūtīt-us, pp. of glūtīre, to swallow. See **Glut.**

DEGRADE, to lower in rank, debase. (F. – L.) In Sir T. More, Works, p. 624. 'That no man schulde be degraded;' Trevisa, v. 35. The pp. is spelt degradyt, Barbour, Bruce, i. 175. – OF. degrader, 'to degrade, or deprive of degree, office, estate, or dignity;' Cot. – Late L. dēgradāre, to deprive of rank. – L. dē, down, away; and gradus, rank. See **Grade.** Der. degrad-at-ion; and see degree.

DEGREE, rank, state, position, extent. (F. – L.) In early use. ME. degre, degree; Chaucer, C. T. 9901 (E 2027). The pl. degrez is in Hali Meidenhad, p. 23, l. 21. – OF. degre, degret, a degree, step, rank. Cf. Prov. degrat. 'This word answers to a type *dēgradus;' Brachet. – L. dē, down; and gradus, a step, grade. See **Degrade.**

DEHISCENT, gaping. (L.) A botanical term. – L. dēhiscent-, stem of dēhiscens, pres. pt. of dēhiscere, to gape open. – L. dē, down, fully; and hiscere, to yawn, gape, inceptive of hiāre, to yawn. See **Hiatus.** Der. dehiscence.

DEIFY, to account as a god. (F. – L.) ME. deifyen; 'that they may noght be deified;' Gower, C. A. ii. 153; bk. v. l. 776. – OF. deifier, 'to deifie;' Cot. – Late L. deificāre. – L. deificus, accounting as gods. – L. dei-, nom. deus, God; and facere, to make, which becomes fic- in composition. See **Deity.** Der. (from L. deificus) deific, deific-al; (like L. pp. deificātus) deificat-ion, Gower, C. A. ii. 158; bk. v. l. 934.

DEIGN, to condescend, think worthy. (F. – L.) ME. deignen, deinen; Gower, C. A. iii. 11; bk. vi. l. 293. Commonly used as a reflexive verb. 'Him ne deinede noȝt;' Rob. of Glouc. p. 557, l. 11645. 'Deineth hir herte reste;' Chaucer, Troil. iii. 1281. – AF. deigne, Edw. Confessor, 4489; pres. s. of OF. digner, Godefroy. – L. dignāri, to deem worthy. – L. dignus, worthy. See **Dignity, Dainty.** Der. dis-dain, q.v.

DEITY, the divinity. (F. – L.) ME. deité, Romaunt of the Rose, 5656; Chaucer, C. T. 11359 (F 1047). – OF. deité, a deity. – L. deitātem, acc. of deitās, deity. – L. dei-, nom. deus, god; cf. diuus, godlike. Allied to W. duw, God; Gael. and Ir. dia, God; Gk. δῖος, divine; Skt. deva-, a god; daiva-, divine. And see **Tuesday.** Der. From the same source, dei-fy, q.v.; also dei-form, dei-st, -sm.

DEJECT, to cast down. (L.) 'Christ deiected himself euen vnto the helles;' Udal, Ephes. c. 4. v. 9. – L. dēiectus, pp. of dēicere (dēiicere), to cast down. – L. dē, down; and iacere, to cast. See **Jet** (1). Der. deject-ed, -ed-ly, -ed-ness, -ion.

DELATE, to accuse (in Scots law); to report. (L.) 'If a minister be thus left at liberty to delate sinners from the pulpit;' Case of Jas. Thomson, in App. to Boswell's Johnson. – Late L. dēlātāre, to accuse; used as frequent. of dēferre, to defer. – L. dē, fully; and lāt-us, for tlātus, pp. of tollere, to take away. See **Delay.**

DELAY, vb., to put off, to linger. (F. – L.) In early use; the pp. delaied occurs in Rob. of Glouc. p. 513, l. 10563; the sb. delai is in Layamon, ii. 308. – OF. delayer, dilaier, given as variants of deleer in Godefroy. It answers in sense to L. dilatāre, to defer, delay, put off; which would properly give only OF. dileer. β. The L. dīlātāre is from dīlātus, deferred, put off. [The pp. dīlātus is used as a pp. of differre, though from a different root.] – L. dī-, for dis-, apart; and lātus, borne, carried, for tlātus, allied to L. tollere, to lift; cf. Gk. τλητός, enduring. – √TEL, to lift. ¶ Since dilātus is used as pp. of differre, the word delay is equivalent to defer; see **Defer** (1). The OF. spelling delaier (with ai) causes a difficulty. The AF. form deslaier occurs in the Liber Albus, p. 217. Cf. Gascon delaya, to delay (Moncaut). Der. delay, sb.; OF. delay, sb., from the verb. Note AF. delai, sb., delaier, vb., in the Statutes of the Realm, pp. 28, 38 (1275).

DELECTABLE, pleasing. (F. – L.) [The usual ME. word was delitable; see **Delight.** The quotations in Richardson are misleading; in the first and second of them, read delitable and delitably. The occurrence of dilectable in the Romaunt of the Rose, 1440, is due to Thynne's edition, and the occurrence of delectable in the only edition of Mandeville's Travels, c. 14, p. 155, is suspicious.] However, we find dilectable in Lydgate, Minor Poems, p. 22; delectable in Caxton's Golden Legend, St. Poul first Hermit, § 1; and in the Bible of 1551, 2 Sam. i. 26, where the A. V. has 'pleasant.' Also in Shak. Rich. II, ii. 3. 7. – OF. delectable, 'delectable;' Cot. (first found in 14th c.) – L. dēlectābilis, delightful. – L. dēlectāre, pp. dēlectātus, to delight. See **Delight.** Der. delectabl-y, delectable-ness, delect-at-ion.

DELEGATE, a chosen deputy. (L.) Cockeram (1642) has: 'Delegate, to assigne, to send in commission.' The sb. occurs in the State Trials, an. 1613, Countess of Essex (R.). – L. dēlēgātus, pp. of dēlēgāre, to send to a place, depute, appoint. – L. dē, from; and lēgāre, to send, depute, appoint, from lēg-, stem of lex, law. See **Legate, Legal.** Der. delegate, verb; delegat-ion.

DELETE, to erase, blot out. (L.) 'Studiously deleting the character of that sacrament;' T. Fuller, A Pisgah Sight, bk. iii. sect. 10. § 2. – L. dēlētus, pp. of dēlēre, to destroy. – L. dē, down, away; and -lēre, an unused verb closely related to linere, to daub, smear, erase. Cf. the pt. t. dēlēui with lēui, pt. t. of linere (Bréal).

DELETERIOUS, hurtful, noxious. (Gk.) Used by Sir T. Browne, Vulgar Errors, b. iii. c. 7, § 4. 'Tho' stored with deletery med'cines;' Butler, Hudibras, pt. i. c. 2, l. 317. – Late L. dēlētērius, noxious (with -ous for -us); merely Latinised from Gk. – Gk. δηλη-τήριος, noxious. – Gk. δηλητήρ, a destroyer. – Gk. δηλέομαι, I do a hurt, I harm, injure.

DELF, a kind of earthenware. (Du.) 'Delf, earthenware; counterfeit China, made at Delft;' Johnson. Named from Delft in Holland. 'Delft, S. Holland, a town founded about 1074; famous for Delft earthenware, first manufactured here about 1310. The sale of delft greatly declined after the introduction of potteries into Germany and England;' Haydn, Dict. of Dates. β. The -t is excrescent; the old name of the place was Delf; and it was named from the canal on which it stood. – WFlem. delf, a canal; De Bo. – WFlem. and Du. delven, to dig; see **Delve.** (Franck.)

DELIBERATE, carefully considered. (L.) 'Of a deliberate purpose;' Sir T. More, Works, p. 214 f. [There was an earlier ME. verb deliberen; 'For which he gan deliberen for the beste;' Chaucer, Troil. iv. 169.] – L. dēlīberātus, pp. of dēlīberāre, to consult. – L. dē, down, thoroughly; and lībrāre, to weigh, from libra, a balance. See **Librate.** Der. deliberate, verb; -ly, -ness; deliberat-ion (deliberacioun, Gower, C. A. iii. 352; bk. viii. l. 2302), -ive, -ive-ly.

DELICATE, alluring, dainty, nice, refined. (L.) ME. delicat, P. Plowman, C. ix. 279. Chaucer has delicat, C. T. 14389 (B 3661); delicacie, id. 14397 (B 3669). – L. dēlīcātus, luxurious; cf. dēlicia, luxury, pleasure; dēlicere, to amuse, allure, from dē, away, greatly, and lacere, to allure, entice. See **Delicious.** Der. delicate-ly, -ness, delicac-y.

DELICIOUS, very pleasing, delightful. (F. – L.) ME. deliciouse, King Alisaunder, 38; delicious, Gower, C. A. iii. 24; bk. vi. l. 671. – OF. delicieus (Godefroy). – Late L. dēlīciōsus, pleasant, choice. – L. dēlicia, pleasure, luxury. See **Delicate.** Der. delicious-ly, -ness.

DELIGHT, great pleasure; vb., to please. (F. – L.) A false spelling. ME. delit, sb.; deliten, verb. Of these, the sb. is found very early, in O. Eng. Homilies, i. 187, l. 17. The verb is in Chaucer, C. T. Group E, 997 (Cler. Tale). [In French, the verb appears to be the older.] – OF. deliter, earlier deleiter, to delight; whence delit, earlier deleit, sb. delight. – L. dēlectāre, to delight; frequentative of dēlicere, to allure. – L. dē, fully; and lacere, to allure. See **Delectable, Delicate.** Der. delight-ful, -ful-ly, -ful-ness, -some; all hybrid compounds, with E. suffixes.

DELINEATE, to draw, sketch out. (L.) Orig. a pp. 'Destinate to one age or time, drawne, as it were, and delineate in one table;' Bacon, On Learning, by G. Wats, b. ii. c. 8 (R.). So also in Edw. III., A. ii. sc. 2. l. 75. – L. dēlineātus, pp. of dēlineāre, to sketch in outline. – L. dē, down; and lineāre, to mark out, from linea, a line. See **Line.** Der. delineat-or, -ion.

DELINQUENT, failing in duty. (L.) Orig. a pres. part., used as adj. 'A delinquent person;' State Trials, an. 1640; Earl Strafford (R.). As sb. in Shak. Macb. iii. 6. 12. – L. dēlinquent-, stem of dēlinquens, omitting one's duty, pres. part. of dēlinquere, to omit. – L. dē, away, from; and linquere, to leave. Der. delinquenc-y.

DELIQUESCE, to melt, become liquid. (L.) A chemical term. – L. dēliquescere, to melt, become liquid. – L. dē, down, away; and liquescere, to become liquid, inceptive form of liquēre, to be wet. See **Liquid.** Der. deliquesc-ent, -ence.

DELIRIOUS, wandering in mind, insane. (L.) A coined word, made from the L. dēlirium, which was also adopted into English. 'Delirium this is call'd, which is mere dotage;' Ford, Lover's Melancholy, A. iii. sc. 3. The more correct form was delirous. We find in Blount's Gloss. ed. 1674: 'Delirium, dotage;' and 'Delirous, that doteth and swerveth from reason;' but in Kersey's Dict. ed. 1715, the latter word has become delirious. – L. dēlirium, madness; from dēlirus, one that goes out of the furrow in ploughing, hence, crazy, doting, mad. – L. dē, from; and līra, a furrow, allied to OHG. leisa, G. g-leis, a track, a rut. Der. delirious-ly, -ness.

DELIVER, to liberate, set free. (F. – L.) ME. deliueren, deliveren; King Alisaunder, 1319, 3197; Rob. of Glouc., pp. 382, 462; ll. 7836, 9502. – OF. delivrer, to set free. – Late L. dēliberāre, to set free. – L. dē, from; and liberāre, to free, from liber, free, which may be connected with libido, pleasure, libet, it pleases, and the E. lief. Brugmann, i. § 102. See **Lief.** Der. deliver-ance, -er, -y.

DELL, a dale, valley. (E.) ME. delle, Reliquiæ Antiquæ, ii. 7 (Stratmann); pl. dellun (=dellen), Anturs of Arthur, st. 4. AS. dell, n.; Cart. Saxon., ed. Birch, i. 547; ii. 71. + MDu. delle (Hexham);

EFries. *delle.* See Notes on E. Etym., p. 65. Teut. type **dal-jom.* A variant of *dale.* See **Dale.**

DELTA, the Greek name of the letter *d.* (Gk.—Phœnician.) [Hence *deltoid.* ' *Deltoides* (in anatomy) a triangular muscle which is inserted to the middle of the shoulder-bone, and is shaped like the Greek letter Δ;' Kersey, ed. 1715. *Deltoid* is the Gk. δελτοειδής, delta-shaped, triangular. — Gk. δέλτα; and εἶδος, appearance.] The Gk. δέλτα answers to, and was borrowed from, the Heb. *dāleth,* the Phœnician name of the fourth letter of the alphabet. The orig. sense of *daleth* was 'a door of a tent.'

DELUDE, to deceive, cajole. (L.) ME. *deluden.* 'That it *deludis* the wittes outwardly;' Henrysoun, Test. of Creseide, l. 509. — L. *dēlūdere,* to mock at, banter, deceive; pp. *dēlūsus.* — L. *dē,* fully; and *lūdere,* to play, jest. Der. *delus-ive, -ive-ly, -ive-ness, -ion, -or-y;* all from pp. *dēlūsus.*

DELUGE, a flood, inundation. (F.—L.) In Lenvoy de Chaucer a Skogan, l. 14. — OF. *deluge,* 'a deluge;' Cot. — L. *dīluuium,* a deluge. — L. *dīluere,* to wash away. — L. *dī,* for *dis-,* apart; and *luere,* to wash, allied to *lave.* See **Lave.**

DELVE, to dig with a spade. (E.) ME. *deluen* (with *u* for *v*), pt. t. *dalf;* Rob. of Glouc. pp. 131, 395; ll. 2772, 8134. AS. *delfan,* to dig; Grein, i. 187.+Du. *delven,* to dig; OHG. *bidelban,* MHG. *telben,* to dig. Allied to Russ. *dolbite,* to hollow out; OPruss. *dalp-tan,* a punch. Brugmann, i. §§ 493, 521 (2). Der. *delv-er.*

DEMAGOGUE, a leader of the people. (F.—Gk.) It occurs in the Eikon Basilike; and Milton, Ans. to Eikon Basilike, calls it a 'goblin word.' — F. *démagogue,* a word 'first hazarded by Bossuet [died A.D. 1704, 30 years after Milton], and counted so bold a novelty that for long [?] none ventured to follow him in its use;' Trench, Eng. Past and Present. Yet it had previously been employed by Oresme, in the 14th c. (Littré). — Gk. δημαγωγός, a popular leader. — Gk. δημ-, base of δῆμος, a country district, also the people; and ἀγωγός, leading, from ἄγειν, to lead, which is from √AG, to drive.

DEMAND, to ask, require. (F.—L.) In Shak. All's Well, ii. 1. 21; and in Caxton (N.E.D.). [But the sb. *demand* (ME. *demaunde*) was in early use, and occurs in Rob. of Glouc. p. 500, l. 10285; Chaucer, C. T. 4892 (B 472).] — OF. *demander,* to *dēmandāre,* to give in charge, entrust; in Late L., to demand (Ducange). — L. *dē,* down, wholly; and *mandāre,* to entrust, consign. See **Mandate.** Der. *demand,* sb.; *-able, -ant* (law French).

DEMARCATION, DEMARKATION, a marking off of bounds, a limit. (Span. — L. *and* MHG.) 'The speculative line of *demarcation;*' Burke, On the Fr. Revolution (R.). — Span. *demarcacion* (see N.E.D.); whence also F. *démarcation,* in the phr. *ligne de démarcation,* a line of demarcation. — L. *dē,* down; and Span. *marcar,* to mark, a word of Germanic origin. See **Mark.** ¶ It will be seen that the sb. *démarcation* is quite distinct from the F. verb *démarquer,* to dis-mark, i. e. to take away a mark. The prefix must be L. *dē-,* not L. *dis-,* or the word is reversed in meaning.

DEMEAN (1), to conduct; *refl.* to behave. (F.—L.) ME. *demainen, demeinen, demenen;* Chaucer, Ho. of Fame, ii. 451. — OF. *demener,* to conduct, treat, manage (Godefroy). — OF. *de-,* from L. *dē,* down, fully; and *mener,* to conduct, control, from Late L. *mināre,* to drive cattle, to lead from place to place; L. *mināre,* to urge, drive on; *minārī,* to threaten. See **Menace.** Der. *demean-our,* q. v.

DEMEAN (2), to debase, lower. (Hybrid; L. *and* E.) Perhaps suggested by **Demean** (1); but really formed, on the analogy of *debase,* from the L. prep. *dē,* down, and the E. *mean,* adj. base. See **Mean** (2).

DEMEANOUR, behaviour. (F.—L.) A coined word; ME. *demenure,* from *demenen,* to demean; see **Demean** (1). 'L for *leude,* D for *demenure;*' Remedie of Loue, st. 63; in Chaucer's Works, ed. 1561, fol. cccxxiiii. *Demeanyng* occurs in the same stanza, used as a sb. Cf. Spenser, F. Q. iv. 10. 49.

DEMENTED, mad. (L.) The pp. of the old verb *demente,* to madden. 'Which thus seke to *demente* the symple hartes of the people;' Bale, Apology, fol. 80. — L. *dēmentāre,* to drive out of one's mind (Acts, viii. 11); cf. *dementia,* madness. — L. *dē,* away from; and *ment-,* stem of *mens,* mind. See **Mental.**

DEMERIT, ill desert. (F.—L.) In Shak. Macb. iv. 3. 226; but also used in a *good* sense, i. e. merit, Cor. i. 1. 276. — OF. *demerite,* 'desert, merit, deserving; also (the contrary) a disservice, demerit, misdeed, ill carriage, ill deserving; in which sense it is most commonly used at this day;' Cot. — Late L. *dēmeritum,* a fault. — L. *dēmerēre,* to deserve (whence the *good* sense of the word). — L. *dē-,* down, fully; and *merēre, merērī,* to deserve. See **Merit.**

DEMESNE, orig. possession; also a manor-house, with lands. (F.—L.) Also written *demain,* and a doublet of *domain.* ME. *demein, demeyn,* a domain; Rob. of Brunne, tr. of Langtoft, p. 7; Chaucer, C. T. 14583 (B 3855). [The spelling *demesne* is false, due

probably to confusion with OF. *mesnee* or *maisnie,* a household; see *Demain* in Blount's Law Dict.] — AF. *demeine,* Laws of Will. I., § 17; *demene,* Year-books of Edw. I., 1292-3, p. 5; *demesne,* id., 1302-3, p. 19; OF. *demaine, demeine,* orig. an adj., specially belonging to; whence also E. *domain.* So also Cot. gives: '*Demain,* a demaine, the same as *Domain.*' See **Domain.**

DEMI-, a prefix, signifying 'half.' (F.—L.) OF. *demi,* m. *demie,* f. 'halfe, demy;' Cot. — L. *dimidium,* half. — L. *di-* = *dis-,* apart; and *medius,* middle. See **Medium, Medial.** Der. *demi-god, demi-semiquaver,* &c.; also *demy,* q. v.

DEMIJOHN, a glass vessel with a large body and small neck, enclosed in wickerwork. (F.) Spelt *dame-jeanne* in Falconer's Dict. of the Marine (1769). — F. *dame-jeanne* (Littré). Much disputed; and prob. *not* of Eastern origin. The F. form seems to be right as it stands; cf. Span. *dama-juana,* a demijohn. — F. *dame* (Span. *dama*), lady; and *Jeanne* (Span. *Juana*), Jane, Joan. See N.E.D.

DEMISE, transference, decease. (F.—L.) Shak. has the vb. *demise,* to bequeath; Rich. III, iv. 4. 247. For the sb., see Blount's Law Dict. — OF. *demise,* also *desmise,* fem. of *desmis,* 'displaced, deposed, ... dismissed, resigned;' Cot. This is the pp. of OF. *desmettre,* to displace, dismiss. — L. *dīmittere,* to send away, dismiss. — L. *dī-* = *dis-* (OF. *des-*), away, apart; and *mittere,* to send. See **Dismiss.** [The sense changed from 'resigned' to 'resigning.'] Der. *demise,* vb.

DEMOCRACY, popular government. (F.—L.—Gk.) Formerly written *democraty,* Milton, Areopagitica, ed. Hales, p. 4. — MF. *democratie,* 'a democratie, popular government;' Cot. — Med. L. *dēmocratia.* — Gk. δημοκρατία, popular government. — Gk. δημο-, for δῆμος, a country-district, also, the people; and κρατέω, I am strong, I rule, from κράτος, strength, allied to κρατύς, strong, which is cognate with E. *hard.* Der. *democrat, -ic, -ic-al, -ic-al-ly.*

DEMOLISH, to overthrow, destroy. (F.—L.) 'Were not the tailor's wife to be *demolish'd;*' Ben Jonson, The New Inn, A. iv. sc. 3. And in Ralegh, Hist. of the World, b. ii. c. 20. s. 2 (R.). — OF. *demoliss-,* inchoative form of the verb *demolir,* 'to demolish;' Cot. — L. *dēmōlīri,* pp. *dēmōlītus,* rarely *dēmōlīre,* to pull down, demolish. — L. *dē,* down; and *mōlīri,* to endeavour, throw, displace, from *mōles,* a heap, also labour, effort. See **Mole** (3). Der. *demolit-ion.*

DEMON, an evil spirit. (F.—L.—Gk.) In Shak. Hen. V, ii. 2. 121; and in Trevisa, tr. of Higden, iii. 279. The adj. *demoniak* is in Chaucer, C. T. 7874 (D 2292). — OF. *demon,* 'a devill, spirit, hobgoblin;' Cot. — L. *dæmon,* a demon, spirit. — Gk. δαίμων, a god, genius, spirit; also fate. Perhaps meaning 'distributer;' from δαίομαι, I impart (Prellwitz). Der. (from L. stem *dæmoni-*) *demoni-ac, -ac-al, -ac-al-ly;* also (from Gk. δαιμονο-) *demono-latry,* i. e. devil-worship, from Gk. λατρεία, service; also *demono-logy,* i. e. discourse about demons, from Gk. λόγος, discourse, which from λέγειν, to say.

DEMONSTRATE, to show, explain fully. (L.) In Shak. Hen. V, iv. 2. 54. Much earlier are ME. *demonstratif,* Chaucer, C. T. 7854 (D 2272); *demonstracioun,* Ch. tr. of Boethius, b. ii. pr. 4. l. 122; *demonstrable,* Rom. of Rose, 4688. — L. *dēmonstrātus,* pp. of *dēmonstrāre,* to show fully. — L. *dē,* down, fully; and *monstrāre,* to show. See **Monster.** Der. *demonstrat-ion;* also *demonstra-ble,* from L. *dēmonstrā-bilis;* *demonstrat-ive,* formerly *demonstratif* (see above), from MF. *demonstratif* (Cotgrave), which from L. *dēmonstrātiuus;* *demonstrative-ly, -ness.*

DEMORALISE, to corrupt in morals. (F.—L.) A late word. First in 1793. Todd cites a quotation, dated 1808. — F. *démoraliser,* to demoralise; Hamilton. — F. *dé-,* here = OF. *des-*<L. *dis-,* apart; and *moraliser,* 'to expound morally;' Cot. See **Moral.** Der. *demoralisat-ion.*

DEMOTIC, pertaining to the people. (Gk.) Modern. Not in Todd. — Gk. δημοτικός, pertaining to the people. Formed, with suffix *-ι-κο-,* from δημότης, a commoner. This is formed, with suffix *-της* (denoting the agent), from δημο-, for δῆμος, a country-district, also, the people. Cf. OIrish *dām,* a retinue.

DEMULCENT, soothing. (L.) Modern. The verb *demulce* is once used by Sir T. Elyot, The Governour, b. i. c. 20. § 1. — L. *dēmulcent-,* stem of pres. pt. of *dēmulcēre,* to stroke down, caress; hence, to soothe. — L. *dē,* down; and *mulcēre,* to stroke, allay. Cf. Skt. *mr̥ç,* to stroke.

DEMUR, to delay, hesitate, object. (F.—L.) 'If the parties *demurred* in our iudgement;' Sir T. More, Works, p. 215 h. ME. *demeoren* (eo = F. *eu*), Ancren Riwle, p. 242. — OF. *demeurer, demourer,* 'to abide, stay, tarry;' Cot. — L. *dēmorārī,* to retard, delay. — L. *dē,* from, fully; and *morārī,* to delay, from *mora,* hesitation, delay. Der. *demurr-er, -age.*

DEMURE, sober, staid, grave. (F.—L.) See Spenser, F. Q. ii. 1. 6. [And see Trench, Select Glossary, who points out that the word was once used in a thoroughly good sense.] *Demurely* occurs in La Belle Dame sans Merci, l. 246; and *demure* in Lydgate, Minor Poems, pp. 19, 29. Coined by prefixing *de* (for L. *dē-,* very) to ME.

mure, mature, calm, demure, which occurs in Polit. Rel. and Love Poems, ed. Furnivall, p. 107, l. 139; Sir J. Holland, The Howlat, l. 83; &c.—OF. *meur* (F. *mûr*), mature. See **Mature.** ¶ Palsgrave has: 'Sadly, *demeurement*; Soberly, sadly, *meurement*, p. 841. *Demeurement* = L. *dē mātūrā mente*.

DEMY, a certain size of paper. (F.—L.) A printer's term; another spelling of **Demi-**, q. v.

DEN, a cave, lair of a wild beast. (E.) ME. *den*; Will. of Palerne, 20. AS. *denn*, a cave, sleeping-place; L. 'cubile;' Grein, i. 187.+ MDu. *denne*, a den, cave; Kilian. ¶ Probably closely allied to ME. *dene*, a valley, AS. *denu*, a valley; Grein, i. 187; still preserved in place-names, as *Tenter-den, Rotting-dean*.

DENARY, relating to tens. (L.) Modern arithmetic employs ' the *denary* scale.' —L. *dēnārius*, containing ten. —L. pl. *dēni* (= *decni*), ten by ten. Formed on the base of *decem*, ten. See **Decimal.** Der. Hence *denier* (below).

DENDROID, resembling a tree. (Gk.) Modern. From Gk. δενδρο-, for δένδρον, a tree; and *-ειδης*, like, from εἶδος, form. The Gk. δένδρον appears to be a reduplicated form, connected with Gk. δρῦς, a tree, an oak, and E. *tree*; Curtius, i. 295. See **Tree.** Der. From the same source is *dendro-logy*, i.e. a discourse on trees, from λόγος, a discourse.

DENIAL, DENIER; see **Deny.**

DENIER, a (former) French coin, the twelfth part of a sou. (F.—L.) In Shak. Rich. III, i. 2. 252.—F. *denier*, 'the tenth part of an English penny;' Cot.—L. *dēnārium*, acc. of *dēnārius*, a Roman coin worth 10 as-es.—L. *dēn-i*, ten by ten, from L. *dec-em*, ten; and suffix *-ārius*. See **Denary.**

DENIZEN, a naturalized citizen, inhabitant. (F.—L.) Formerly *denisen*, Udal, Matt. c. 5. v. 5. [The verb to *denize* or *dennize* also occurs. ' The Irish language was free *dennized* [naturalized] in the English pale;' Holinshed, desc. of Ireland, c. 1.] ' In the Liber Albus of the City of London the F. *deinzein* [also *denzein, denszein*], the original of the E. word, is constantly opposed to *forein*, applied to traders *within* and *without* the privileges of the city franchise respectively. Ex. " Qe chescun qavera lowe ascun ou ascuns terres ou tenementz de *denszein* ou de *forein* deinz la fraunchise de la citee;" p. 448;' Wedgwood. β. Thus E. *denizen* is from AF. *deinzein*, a word formed by adding the suffix *-ein* = L. *-ānus* (cf. OF. *vilein* = L. *uillānus*) to the AF. *deinz*, within, which occurs in the above quotation, and is the word now spelt *dans*.—L. *dē intus*, from within; which became *d'einz, d'ens, dens*, and finally *dans*.—L. *dē*, from; and *intus*, within; see **Internal.** Der. *denizen*-ship.

DENOMINATE, to designate. (L.) 'Those places, which were *denominated* of angels and saints;' Hooker (in Todd).—L. *dēnōminātus*, pp. of *dēnōmināre*, to name.—L. *dē*, down; and *nōmināre*, to name, from *nōmin-*, stem of *nōmen*, a name. See **Noun, Name.** Der. *denominat-ion* (in Sir T. Elyot, Castel of Helth, b. i. c. 2. § 1; and in Usk, Test. of Love, bk. ii. c. 9, l. 162); *denominat-ion, -al, -alism*; *denominat-ive, -or*.

DENOTE, to mark, indicate, signify. (F.—L.) In Hamlet, i. 2. 83.—OF. *denoter*, ' to denote, shew;' Cot.—L. *dēnotāre*, to mark out. —L. *dē*, down; and *notāre*, to mark, from *nota*, a mark. See **Note.**

DENOUEMENT, the unravelling of the plot of a story. (F.—L.) ' The *denouement*, as a pedantic disciple of Bossu would call it, of this poem [The Rape of the Lock] is well conducted;' Dr. Warton, Ess. on Pope, i. 250 (Todd).—F. *dénouement*; formed with suffix *-ment* from the verb *dénouer*, to untie.—F. *dé*<L. *dis-*, apart; and *nouer*, to tie in a knot, from *noue*, a knot, which is from L. *nōdum*, acc. of *nōdus*, a knot. See **Node.**

DENOUNCE, to announce, threaten. (F.—L.) ME. *denounsen*. Wyclif has *we denounsiden* to translate *dēnunciābāmus*; 2 Thess. iii. 10. —OF. *denoncer*; Cot.—L. *dēnuntiāre*, to declare.—L. *dē*, down, fully; and *nuntiāre*, to announce, from *nuntius*, a messenger. See **Nuncio.** Der. *denounce-ment*; also (like L. pp. *dēnuntiātus*) *denunciat-or, -or-y*.

DENSE, close, compact. (L.) In Milton, P. L. ii. 948; Bacon, Nat. Hist. § 29.—L. *densus*, thick, close.+Gk. δασύς, thick. Brugmann, i. § 851. Der. *dense-ness, dens-i-ty*; also *con-dense*, q. v.

DENT, a mark of a blow. (E.) A variant of *dint*; the orig. sense was merely ' a blow.' ME. *dent, dint, dunt*. Spelt *dent* or *dint* indifferently in Will. of Palerne, 2757. 3750, 1234, 2784. See further under **Dint.** Der. *dent*, verb. ¶ Partly confused with *dent*, an indentation; from F. *dent*, a tooth (below).

DENTAL, belonging to the teeth. (L.) 'The Hebrews have assigned which letters are labial, which *dental*, and which guttural;' Bacon, Nat. Hist. § 198. Formed with suffix *-al* (= L. *-ālis*) from L. *dent-*, stem of *dens*, a tooth, cognate with E. *tooth*. See **Tooth.**

DENTATED, furnished with teeth. (L.) 'Dentated, having teeth;' Bailey, vol. ii.—L. *dentātus*, toothed; formed with suffix *-ātus*, a pp. form, from *dent-*, stem of *dens*, a tooth. See **Tooth.**

DENTICLE, a small tooth. (L.) In Chaucer's Astrolabe, pt. i. § 23. ' *Denticle*, a little tooth;' Blount's Gloss. ed. 1674.—L. *denti-cu-lus*, formed with dimin. suffixes *-cu-* and *-lu-s* from *denti-*, declensional stem of *dens*, a tooth. See **Tooth.** Der. *denticul-ate, -at-ion*.

DENTIFRICE, tooth-powder. (F.—L.) It occurs in Blount's Gloss. ed. 1674; Ben Jonson, Catiline, Act ii. (Sempronia); and in Holland's Pliny, b. xxviii. c. 11 (end).—MF. and F. *dentifrice* (Hatzfeld).—L. *dentifricium*, tooth-powder; Pliny.—L. *denti-*, for *dens*, a tooth; and *fricāre*, to rub. See **Tooth** and **Friction.**

DENTIST, one who attends to teeth. (L.) First about 1760; not in Johnson. Formed by adding the suffix *-ist* to L. *dent-*, stem of *dens*, a tooth; see **Tooth.** Der. *dentist*-ry.

DENTITION, cutting of teeth. (L.) In Blount's Gloss. ed. 1674.—L. *dentītiōnem*, acc. of *dentītio*, dentition.—L. *dentīre*, to cut teeth.—L. *denti-*, declensional stem of *dens*, a tooth. See **Tooth.**

DENUDE, to lay bare. (L.) Used by Cotgrave to explain F. *dénuer*.—L. *dēnūdāre*, to lay bare.—L. *dē*, down, fully; and *nūdāre*, to make bare, from *nūdus*, bare. See **Nude.**

DENUNCIATION, a denouncing. (L.) In Shak. Meas. i. 2. 152.—L. *dēnuntiātiōnem*, acc. of *dēnuntiātio*.—L. *dēnuntiāre, denunciāre*, to denounce. See **Denounce.**

DENY, to gainsay, refuse. (F.—L.) In early use. ME. *denien*; Rob. of Brunne, tr. of Langtoft, p. 249; Wyclif, Matt. xvi. 24, xxvi. 34.—OF. *denier*, earlier *deneier, denoier*, to deny.—L. *dēnegāre*, to deny.—L. *dē*, fully; and *negāre*, to deny, say no. See **Negation.** Der. *deni-al, -able*.

DEODAND, a thing (formerly) forfeited to the crown, for pious uses. (AF.—L.) See Blount's Nomolexicon. Lit. 'given to God.' —AF. *deodande*; Britton, bk. i. c. 2. § 14.—L. *Deō*, to God, dat. case of *Deus*, God; and *dandum*, to be given, from *dare*, to give.

DEODAR, an ornamental tree, a sub-species of cedar. (Hind.— Skt.) See Yule.—Hind. *dewdārū*, the name of a tree (Forbes); called *dewdār* in Kashmir (Yule).—Skt. *deva-dāru*, timber of the gods. —Skt. *deva-*, a deity (see **Tuesday**); and *dāru*, a kind of pine (see **Tree**).

DEPART, to separate, to part from, quit, die. (F.—L.) In early use. ME. *departen*; Floriz and Blauncheflur, ed. Lumby, l. 12; Chaucer, Troilus, v. 1073.—OF. *departir, despartir* (Godefroy).— OF. *des-* (L. *dis-*), asunder; and *partir*, to part, from L. *partire*, to part; which is from L. *parti-*, decl. stem of *pars*, a part. See **Part.** Der. *depart-ment, -ure*.

DEPEND, to hang, be connected with. (F.—L.) ME. *dependen*. ' The fatal chaunce Of life and death *dependeth* in balaunce;' Lydgate, Thebes, pt. iii. sect. headed The Wordes of the worthy Queene Iocasta, l. 33.—OF. *dependre*, ' to depend, rely, hang on;' Cot.—L. *dēpendēre*, to hang down, depend on.—L. *dē*, down; and *pendēre*, to hang. See **Pendant.** Der. *depend-ant* (F. pres. pt.), *depend-ent* (L. pres. pt.), *-ent-ly, -ence, -enc-y*.

DEPICT, to picture, represent. (L.) 'His armes are fairly depicted in his chamber;' Fuller, Worthies, Cambs. (R.). But *depict* was orig. a pp. 'I fond a lyknesse *depict* upon a wal;' Lydgate, Minor Poems, p. 177; cf. p. 259.—L. *dēpictus*, pp. of *dēpingere*, to depict.—L. *dē*, down, fully; and *pingere*, to paint. See **Paint.**

DEPILATORY, removing hair. (L.) ' The same *depilatory* effect;' Holland, Pliny, b. xxxii. c. 7, ed. 1634, p. 439 d. Formed, in imitation of MF. *depilatoire* (which Cotgrave explains by *depilatory*) from a Late L. form **dēpilātōrius*, not found, but formed regularly from L. *dēpilāre*, to remove hair.—L. *dē*, away; and *pilāre*, to pluck away hair, from *pilus*, a hair. See **Pile** (4).

DEPLETION, a lessening of the blood. (L.) ' *Depletion*, an emptying;' Blount's Gloss. 1674. Formed, in imitation of *repletion*, as if from a L. acc. **dēplētiōnem*, from nom. **dēplētio*. [Cf. L. *replētio, complētio*.] Cf. *dēplētus*, pp. of *dēplēre*, to empty.—L. *dē*, away, here used negatively; and *plēre*, to fill. See **Plenary.**

DEPLORE, to lament. (F.—L.; or L.) In Shak. Tw. Nt. iii. 1. 174. See Trench, Select Glossary. [Perhaps directly from Latin.] —MF. *deplorer*, ' to deplore;' Cot.—L. *dēplōrāre*, to lament over.— L. *dē*, fully; and *plōrāre*, to wail. Allied to E. *flood*. Brugmann, i. § 154. Der. *deplor-able, -abl-y, -able-ness*.

DEPLOY, to unfold, open out, extend. (F.—L.) A modern military term; not in Johnson, but see Todd, who rightly takes it to be a doublet of *display*.—F. *déployer*, to unroll; OF. *desployer*, to unfold;' Cot.—OF. *des-*<L. *dis-*, apart; and *ployer*, to fold, from L. *plicāre*, to fold. See **Ply.** Doublet, *display*.

DEPONENT, one who gives evidence. (L.) ' The sayde *deponent* sayeth;' Hall, Hen. VIII, an. 6. § 33. Palsgrave has: ' verbes *deponentes*,' i. e. deponent verbs, p. 403. We also find the verb to *depone.* ' And further, Sprot *deponeth*;' State Trials, Geo. Sprot, an. 1606 (R.).—L. *dēpōnent-*, stem of *dēpōnens*, pres. pt. of *dēpōnere*, to lay down, which in Late L. also meant ' to testify;' Ducange.—L. *dē*, down; and *pōnere*, to put, place. β. *Pōnere* is a contracted verb, standing for *posinere*, where *po-* is an old prep., and *sinere* means to allow, also to set, put. See **Position, Deposit**.

DEPOPULATE, to take away population. (L.) In Shak. Cor. iii. 1. 264.—L. *dēpopulātus*, pp. of *dēpopulāre*, to lay waste.—L. *dē*, fully; and *populāre*, to lay waste, in Late L. to deprive of people or inhabitants, from *populus*, a people. See **People**. Der. *depopulat-ion, -or*.

DEPORT, to carry away, remove, behave. (F.—L.) 'How a man may bee valued, and *deport* himselfe;' Bacon, Learning, by G. Wats, b. viii. c. 2. (R.) Milton has *deport* as sb., in the sense of *deportment*; P. L. ix. 389; xi. 666. [The peculiar uses of the word are French, not Latin.]—OF. *deporter*, 'to beare, suffer, endure; also, to spare, or exempt from; also to banish: *se deporter*, to cease, forbear, ... quiet himself, hold his hand; also to disport, play, recreate himself;' Cot.—L. *dēportāre*, to carry down, remove; with extended senses in Late Latin.—L. *dē*, down, away; and *portāre*, to carry. See **Port** (1). Der. *deportat-ion* (L. acc. *dēportātiōnem*, from nom. *dēportātio*, a carrying away); *deport-ment* (MF. *deporte-ment*; Cotgrave gives the pl. *deportemens*, which he explains by 'deportments, demeanor').

DEPOSE, to degrade, disseat from the throne. (F.—L. and Gk.) In early use. ME. *deposen*; King Alisaunder, ed. Weber, 7822; P. Plowman, B. xv. 514.—OF. *deposer*; Cot.—OF. *de-* < L. *dē-*, from, away; and *poser*, to place, from *pausāre*, to pause; in late L., to place; Ducange. β. *Pausāre*, to place, is derived from *pausa*, sb., a pause, from Gk. παῦσις, a pause; but *pōnere* and *pausāre* were much confused. See **Pose, Pause**. Der. *depos-able, -al*. ¶ Note that *depose* is not derived, like *deposit*, from L. *dēpōnere*, but is partly Gk. See below.

DEPOSIT, to lay down, intrust. (F.—L.) 'The fear is *deposited* in conscience;' Bp. Taylor, Rule of Conscience, b. ii. c. 1. rule 3 (R.). —MF. *depositer*, 'to lay down as a gage, to infeoffe upon trust, to commit unto the keeping or trust of;' Cot.—L. *dēpositum*, a thing laid down, neuter of pp. of *dēpōnere*. See **Deponent**. Der. *deposit, sb., -or; -ar-y*, King Lear, ii. 4. 254; -*or-y*.

DEPOSITION, a deposing, evidence. (F.—L.) Used by Cotgrave.—MF. *deposition*, 'the deposition of witnesses;' Cot.—L. acc. *dēpositiōnem*, from nom. *dēpositio*, a depositing, a deposition; cf. *dēpositus*, pp. of *dēpōnere*, to lay down; see above. ¶ Not derived from the verb to *depose*; see **Depose**.

DEPOT, a store, place of deposit. (F.—L.) Modern. In use in 1794; Todd's Johnson.—F. *dépôt*, a deposit, a magazine; Hamilton; OF. *depost*, 'a pledge, gage;' Cot.—L. *dēpositum*, a thing laid down, neut. of *dēpositus*, pp. of *dēpōnere*, to lay down. See **Deposit**, of which (when a sb.) *depot* is the doublet.

DEPRAVE, to make worse, corrupt. (F.—L.) ME. *deprauen* (with *u* for *v*), to defame; P. Plowman, C. iv. 225; see Trench, Select Gloss.—OF. *depraver*, 'to deprave, mar, viciate;' Cot.—L. *dēprāuāre*, pp. *dēprāuātus*, to make crooked, distort, vitiate.—L. *dē*, down, fully; and *prāuus*, crooked, misshapen, depraved. Der. *deprav-ed, -ed-ly, -ed-ness, -at-ion, -i-ty*.

DEPRECATE, to pray against. (L.) Occurs in the State Trials, an. 1589; the Earl of Arundel (R.); and in J. Earle, Microcosmography, § 64 (end).—L. *dēprecātus*, pp. of *dēprecārī*, to pray against, pray to remove.—L. *dē*, away; and *precārī*, to pray, from *prec-*, stem of *prex*, a prayer. See **Pray**. Der. *deprecat-ing-ly, -ion, -ive, -or-y*.

DEPRECIATE, to lower the value of. (L.) 'Undervalue and *depreciate*;' Cudworth, Intell. System, pref. to Reader (R.).—L. *dēpretiātus*, pp. of *dēpretiāre*, to depreciate.—L. *dē*, down; and *pretium*, price, value. See **Price**. Der. *depreciat-ion, -ive, -or-y*.

DEPREDATE, to plunder, rob, lay waste. (L.) The verb is rare. *Depredatours* occurs in Bacon, Nat. Hist. § 492; *depredation* in Burnet, Hist. Reformation, an. 1537.—L. *dēprædātus*, pp. of *dēprædārī*, to plunder, pillage.—L. *dē*, fully; and *prædārī*, to rob, from *præda*, prey, plunder. See **Prey**. Der. *depredat-ion, -or, -or-y*.

DEPRESS, to lower, let down. (L.) First used in an astrological sense; Lydgate has *depressed*, Siege of Thebes, pt. i. l. 228. So Chaucer uses *depressioun*; On the Astrolabe, ed. Skeat, ii. 25. 6.—L. *dēpressus*, pp. of *dēprimere*, to press down.—L. *dē*, down; and *premere*, to press. See **Press**. Der. *depress-ion, -ive, -or*.

DEPRIVE, to take away property. (F.—L.) ME. *depriuen*; Rob. of Brunne, tr. of Langtoft, p. 222; Allit. Poems, ed. Morris, i. 449.—OF. *depriver*.—Late L. *dēpriuāre*, to deprive one of office, degrade.—L. *dē*, down, fully; and *priuāre*, to deprive (of which the pp. *priuātus* means free from office, private), from *priuus*, single, peculiar. See **Private**. Der. *deprivat-ion*.

DEPTH, deepness. (E.) In the later text of Wyclif, Luke, v. 4; Gen. i. 2. The word is English, but the usual AS. word is *dēopnes*, i.e. deepness. + Icel. *dȳpt*, *dȳpð*; Du. *diepte*; Goth. *diupitha*. See **Deep**.

DEPUTE, to appoint as agent. (F.—L.) In Shak. Oth. iv. 1.

248. But *deputacion* is in Gower, C. A. iii. 178; bk. vii. l. 2750.— OF. *deputer*, 'to depute;' Cot.—L. *dēputāre*, to cut off, prune down; also to impute, to destine; in Late L. to select.—L. *dē*, down; and *putāre*, to cleanse, prune, arrange, estimate, think.—√ PEU, to cleanse. See **Pure**. Der. *deputat-ion*; also *deputy* (OF. *depute*; see Cotgrave).

DERANGE, to disarrange, disorder. (F.—L. and OHG.) In late use. Condemned as a Gallicism in 1795, but used by Burke (Todd).—F. *déranger*, to disarray; spelt *desranger* in Cotgrave.— OF. *des-* < L. *dis-*, apart, here used negatively; and OF. *ranger*, to rank, range, a word of Germanic origin. See **Range**. Der. *derange-ment*.

DERELICTION, complete abandonment. (L.) *Derelict*, in the sense of 'abandoned,' is also in use. *Dereliction* is in Hooker, Eccl. Polity, b. v. § 17.—L. acc. *dērelictiōnem*, from nom. *dērelictio*, complete neglect; cf. *dērelictus*, pp. of *dērelinquere*, to forsake utterly.— L. *dē*, fully; and *relinquere*, to leave. See **Relinquish**.

DERIDE, to laugh at, mock. (L.) In Spenser, F. Q. vi. 7. 32. —L. *dērīdēre*, pp. *dērīsus*, to mock.—L. *dē*, fully, very much; and *rīdēre*, to laugh. See **Risible**. Der. *derid-er*; also *deris-ion* (Caxton, Troy-book, leaf 95, l. 8), -*ive*, -*ive-ly*, from pp. *dērīsus*.

DERIVE, to draw from, make to flow from. (F.—L.) For the classical use of the word in English, see Trench, Select Gloss. ME. *deriuen* (with *u* for *v*), used as a neuter verb by Chaucer, C. T. 3008 (A 3036), but in the usual way in l. 3040 (A 3038).—OF. *deriver*, 'to derive, or draw from; also, to drain or dry up;' Cot.—L. *dēriuāre*, pp. *dēriuātus*, to drain, draw off water.—L. *dē*, away; and *rīuus*, a stream. See **Rival**. Der. *deriv-able, -abl-y, -at-ion, -at-ive, -at-ive-ly*.

DERM, the skin. (Gk.) 'Derma, the skin of a beast, or of a man's body;' Phillips, ed. 1706. Hence *derm*, for brevity.—Gk. δέρμα, the skin.—Gk. δέρειν, to skin, flay; cognate with E. *tear*.— √ DER, to burst, tear. See **Tear** (1). Der. *derm-al*; also *epi-dermis*, *pachy-derm*.

DEROGATE, to take away, detract. (L.) 'Any thinge ... that should *derogate*, minish, or hurt his glory and his name;' Sir T. More, Works, p. 1121 c.—L. *dērogātus*, pp. of *dērogāre*, to repeal a law, to detract from.—L. *dē*, away; and *rogāre*, to propose a law, to ask. See **Rogation**. Der. *derogat-ion, -or-y, -or-i-ly*.

DERRICK, a kind of crane for raising weights. (Du.) Applied to a sort of crane from its likeness to a gallows; and the term *derrick crane* had special reference to a once celebrated hangman of the name of *Derrick*, who was employed at Tyburn. He is mentioned in Blount's Gloss., ed. 1674, and Mr. Tancock sends me the following clear example. 'The theefe that dyes at Tyburne .. is not halfe so dangerous .. as the Politick Bankrupt. I would there were a *Derick* to hang vp him too;' T. Dekker, Seven Deadly Sins of London (1606); ed. Arber, p. 17. The name is Dutch; Sewel's Du. Dict. (p. 523) gives *Diederik*, *Dierryk*, and *Dirk* as varying forms of the same name. This name answers to the G. *Dietrich*, AS. *þeodric*, i.e. 'ruler of the people.' The AS. *þeod* is cognate with Goth. *thiuda*, people; see **Dutch**. The suffix -*ric* answers to Goth. -*reiks*, as in *Frithareiks*, Frederick; cp. Goth. *reiks*, adj., chief, mighty, hence rich; see **Rich**.

DERRING-DO, desperate courage. (E.) Spenser has: 'For ever, who in *derring-doe* were dreade,' &c.; Shep. Kal., Oct. 65. This extraordinary word is due to a total misconception of a phrase in Chaucer; he has imagined it to mean 'daring action.' But Chaucer has: 'In *durring don* that longeth to a knight;' Troil. v. 837; where *durring* is a sb., meaning 'daring;' and *don* is the infin., meaning 'to do.' Later authors have blindly adopted Spenser's error, in total ignorance of ME. grammar. See my Notes on E. Etym., p. 65.

DERVIS, DERVISH, a Persian monk, ascetic. (Pers.) 'The *Deruisse*, an order of begging friar;' Sir T. Herbert, Travels, ed. 1665, p. 324. 'An order of Monkes, who are called *Dervises*;' Sandys, Trav. (1532), p. 55.—Pers. *darvish*, poor, indigent; a dervish, monk; Palmer's Pers. Dict. col. 260. So called from their profession of extreme poverty. Cf. Zend *driɣu-*, poor (Horn).

DESCANT, a variation (in music), a disquisition. (F.—L.) 'Twenty doctours expounde one text xx. wayes, as children make *descant* upon playne song;' Tyndal's Works, p. 168; col. 1. Spelt *dyscant*, Squire of Low Degree, l. 790.—ONF. *descant*, for OF. *deschant*, 'descant of musick, also, a psalmody, recantation, or contrary song to the former;' Cot.—OF. *des-* < L. *dis-*, apart, separate; and ONF. *cant*, for OF. *chant*, a song; see Burguy, who gives *cant, canter* as variants of *chant, chanter*. From L. *cantus*, a song; *cantāre*, to sing. See **Chant**, and **Cant**. Der. *descant*, verb.

DESCEND, to climb down, go down. (F.—L.) ME. *descenden*, Rob. of Brunne, tr. of Langtoft, pp. 134, 243.—OF. *descendre*, 'to descend, go down;' Cot.—L. *dēscendere*, pp. *dēscensus*, to descend.

—L. *dē*, down; and *scandere*, to climb. See **Scan**. Der. *descendant* (OF. *descendant*, descending; Cot.); *descend-ent* (L. pres. pt. stem *descendent-*); *descens-ion*, *descens-ion-al*; *descent*, Gower, C. A. iii. 207; bk. vii. 3432 (OF. *descente*, a sudden fall; formed from *descendre* by analogy with the form *vente* from *vendre*, and the like).

DESCRIBE, to write down, trace out, give an account of. (L.) In Shak. Merch. of Ven. i. 2. 40. [But the ME. *descriuen* was in early use; see K. Alisaunder, 4553; Chaucer, C. T. 10354 (F 40). This was a French form, from OF. *descrivre*.]—L. *dēscribere*, pp. *dēscriptus*, to copy, draw out, write down.—L. *dē*, fully; and *scribere*, to write. See **Scribe**. Der. *describ-able*, *descript-ion* (Chaucer, C. T., Group A, 2053), *descript-ive*, *-ive-ly*.

DESCRY, to make out, espy. (F.—L.) In early use. ME. *descryen*, *discryen*. ' No couthe ther non so muche *discrye*' [badly spelt *discryghe*, but rhyming with *nygremauncye*], i.e. nor could any one discern so much; King Alisaunder, l. 138.—OF. *descrire*, a shorter spelling of *descrivre*, to describe; cf. mod. F. *décrire*.—L. *dēscribere*, to describe. See **Describe**. ¶ Thus the word is merely a doublet of *describe*; but it was not well understood, and we frequently find in our authors a tendency to confuse it with *decry*. Cf. ' *Descryynge*, Descripcio;' Prompt. Parv. p. 119.

DESECRATE, to profane. (L.) ' *Desecrated* and prophaned by human use;' Bp. Bull, vol. i. ser. 4 (R.).—L. *dēsecrātus*, pp. of *dēsecrāre*, to desecrate.—L. *dē*, away; and *sacrāre*, to make sacred, from *sacro-*, for *sacer*, sacred. See **Sacred**. Der. *desecrat-ion*, Bailey, vol. ii. (1727).

DESERT (1), a waste, wilderness. (F.—L.) Prop. an adj. with the sense ' waste,' but early used as a sb. ME. *desert*, K. Alisaunder, p. 199, l. 4772; Rob. of Glouc. p. 232, l. 4785; Wyclif, Luke, iii. 4.—OF. *desert*, a wilderness; also, as adj. deserted, waste.—L. *dēsertus*, waste, deserted; pp. of *dēserere*, to desert, abandon, lit. to unbind.—L. *dē*, in a negative sense; and *serere* (pp. *sertus*), to bind, join. See **Series**. Der. *desert*, verb; *desert-er*, *-ion*.

DESERT (2), merit. (F.—L.) ME. *deserte*, Rob. of Glouc. p. 253, l. 5059; Gower, C. A. i. 62; bk. i. 614.—OF. *deserte*, merit; lit. a thing deserved; pp. of *deservir*, to deserve. See **Deserve**.

DESERVE, to merit, earn by service. (F.—L.) ME. *deseruen* (with *u* for *v*), P. Plowman, C. iv. 303; Chaucer, C. T. 12150 (C 216).—OF. *deservir*.—L. *dēseruire*, to serve devotedly; in Late L. to deserve; Ducange.—L. *dē*, fully; and *seruire*, to serve, from *seruus*, a slave, servant. See **Serve**. Der. *deserv-ing*, *-ing-ly*, *-ed-ly*; also *desert* (2), q. v.

DESHABILLE, undress, careless dress. (F.—L.) So in Mrs. Centlivre, Busybody, A. i. sc. 1 (Miranda). But formerly quadrisyllabic (with final *-é*); Steele has *deshabilé*, Spectator, no. 49, § 3.—F. *déshabillé*, undress; orig. pp. of *déshabiller*, to undress.—F. *dés-*, OF. *des-*<L. *dis-*, apart, used as a negative prefix; and *habiller*, to dress. See **Habiliment**. ¶ Now usually *dishabille*.

DESICCATE, to dry up. (L.) In Bacon, Nat. Hist. § 727.—L. *dēsiccātus*, pp. of *dēsiccāre*, to dry up.—L. *dē*, thoroughly; and *siccāre*, to dry, from *siccus*, dry. See **Sack** (3), sb. dry wine. Der. *desiccat-ion*.

DESIDERATE, to desire. (L.) Orig. a pp., and so used in Bacon, On Learning, by G. Wats, b. iv. c. 2 (R.).—L. *dēsiderātus*, pp. of *dēsiderāre*, to desire. *Desiderate* is a doublet of *desire*, vb. See **Desire**. Der. *desideratum*, neut. of L. pp., with pl. *desiderata*.

DESIGN, to mark out, plan. (F.—L.) In Shak. Rich. II, ii. 1. 203. Also as sb., Meas. i. 4. 55.—OF. *designer*, ' to denote, signifie, . . . designe, prescribe;' Cot.—L. *dēsignāre*, pp. *dēsignātus*, to mark, denote.—L. *dē*, fully; and *signāre*, to mark, from *signum*, a mark, a sign. See **Sign**. Der. *design*, sb.; *-ed-ly*, *-er*; also *design-ate*, *-at-ion*, *-at-or* (like the L. pp. *dēsignātus*).

DESIRE, to long for, yearn after. (F.—L.) In early use. ME. *desyren*, *desiren*, K. Alisaunder, l. 15; P. Plowman, B. xv. 461. [The sb. *desyr* is in Chaucer, C. T. 1503 (A 1501).]—OF. *desirer*, formerly *desirrer* (Burguy).—L. *dēsiderāre*, to long for, esp. to regret, to miss. β. The orig. sense is obscure, perhaps ' to note the absence of the stars,' hence to miss, regret; but there can be little doubt that, like *consider*, it is derived from *sider-*, for **sides-*, stem of *sidus*, a star. See **Consider**. Der. *desire*, sb.; *desir-able*, *-abl-y*, *-able-ness*; *-abil-i-ty*; *-ous*, *-ous-ly*.

DESIST, to cease from, forbear. (F.—L.) In Shak. Ant. and Cleop. ii. 7. 86.—OF. *desister*, ' to desist, cease, forbear;' Cot.—L. *dēsistere*, to put away; also, to leave off, desist.—L. *dē*, away; and *sistere*, to put, place; causal form of *stāre*, to stand, which is cognate with E. *stand*. See **Stand**.

DESK, a sloping table, flat surface for writing on. (L.) In Shak. Haml. ii. 2. 136. Earlier, in Fabyan, vol. i. c. 201. § 3. ME. *deske*, Prompt. Parv. (A. D. 1440); pp. 120, 299.—Med. L. *desca*, a desk (Ducange). Cf. Ital. *desco*, ' a desk' (Florio); from L. *discum*, acc. of *discus*, a disc, table. See **Dish**.

DESOLATE, solitary. (L.) ME. *desolat*, Chaucer, C. T. 4551 (B 131).—L. *dēsōlātus*, forsaken; pp. of *dēsōlāre*.—L. *dē*, fully; and *sōlāre*, to make lonely, from *sōlus*, alone. See **Sole**, adj. Der. *desolate*, verb; *-ly*, *-ness*; *'ce olat-ion*.

DESPAIR, to be without hope. (F.—L.) ME. *dispeiren*, *disperen*. ' He was *despeyred*;' Chaucer, C. T. 11255 (F 943).—OF. *despeir-*, tonic stem of *desperer*, to despair.—L. *dēspērāre*, pp. *dēspērātus*, to have no hope.—L. *dē*, away; and *spērāre*, to hope, from *spēr-*, as in OL. *spēr-es*, pl. of *spēs*, hope. Der. *despair*, sb. ME. *despeir*, Chaucer, C. T., A 3474; *despair-ing-ly*; also (from L. pp. *dēspērātus*) *desperate*, Tempest, iii. 3. 104; *-ly*, *-ness*, *desperat-ion*; also *desperado*, a Spanish word = L. *dēspērātus*.

DESPATCH, **DISPATCH**, to send off quickly. (Span.—L.) The orig. sense was ' to dispatch business.' In Shak. K. John, i. 99; v. 7. 90; the sb. is also common, as in Cymb. iii. 7. 16. The spelling *dispatch* is very common, and is also more in accordance with E. analogy (N.E.D.). First in 1517 (spelt *dispached*); Palsgrave (1530) has *dispatche*, vb., p. 520.—Span. *despachar*, ' to dispatch, to ridde out of the way;' Minsheu. Cognate with Ital. *dispacciare*, to dispatch (Torriano); usually *spacciare*, ' to dispatch, hasten, speed' (Florio).—L. type **dis-pactiāre*; from *dis-*, intensive particle, and **pactiāre*, for Late L. *pactāre*, to make an agreement, from L. *pactum*, an agreement; see **Pact**. β. Confused by Johnson with F. *dépêcher*, OF. *depescher*, obs. E. *depeach* (N.E.D.). Here *pescher* answers to a Late L. *pedicāre*, as in *impedicāre*, to place obstacles in the way. Hence to *depeach* = to remove obstacles. *Pedicāre* is formed from L. *pedica*, a fetter; from *ped-*, stem of *pes*, a foot; see **Impeach**. ¶ *Dispatch* might have been from Ital., but Ital. generally has the shortened form; and *dispatch* seems to have been due to dealings with Spain (ab. 1517). Der. *despatch* or *dispatch*, sb.

DESPERATE, **DESPERADO**; see **Despair**.

DESPISE, to contemn. (F.—L.) ME. *despisen*, *dispisen*; K. Alisaunder, 2988; P. Plowman, B. xv. 531.—OF. *despis-*, stem of pres. pt., &c., of *despire*, to despise.—L. *despicere*, to look down on, scorn.—L. *dē*, down; and *specere*, to look. See **Spy**. Der. *despic-able* (from L. *despic-ere*), *-abl-y*; also *despite*, q.v.

DESPITE, spite, malice, hatred. (F.—L.) ME. *despit*, *dispit*; K. Alisaunder, 4720; Rob. of Glouc., p. 547; l. 11376.—OF. *despit*, ' despight, spight, anger;' Cot.—L. *despectus*, contempt.—L. *despectus*, pp. of *despicere*, to despise. See **Despise**. Der. *despite*, as prep.; *despite-ful*, *-ful-ly*, *-ful-ness*. Also ME. *dispitous*, Chaucer, C. T. 6343, D 761 (obsolete). Doublet, *spite*.

DESPOIL, to spoil utterly, plunder. (F.—L.) In early use. ME. *despoilen*, Ancren Riwle, p. 148.—OF. *despoiller* (mod. F. *dépouiller*), to despoil.—L. *despoliāre*, to plunder.—L. *dē*, fully; and *spoliāre*, to strip, rob, from *spolium*, spoil, booty. See **Spoil**.

DESPOND, to lose courage, despair. (L.) In Blount's Gloss., 1656. ' *Desponding* Peter, sinking in the waves;' Dryden, Britannia Rediviva, 258.—L. *despondēre*, (1) to promise fully, (2) to give up, lose.—L. *dē*, (1) fully, (2) away; and *spondēre*, to promise. See **Sponsor**. Der. *despond-ent* (pres. part.), *-ent-ly*, *-ence*, *-enc-y*.

DESPOT, a master, tyrant. (F.—L.—Gk.) Used by Cotgrave. Dryden has ' *despotick* power;' Sigismunda, 599.—OF. *despot*, MF. *despote*, ' a despote, the chief, or soveraign lord of a country;' Cot.—Late L. *despotum*, acc. of *despotus*.—Gk. δεσπότης, a master. β. The syllable δεσ- =*Idg. *dems*, ' of a house;' cf. Skt. *dam-pati-*, master of the house.' The syllable -ποτ- is related to Gk. πόσις, husband, Skt. *p.ti-*, lord, L. *potens*, powerful; see **Potent**. Brugmann, i. § 408. Der. *despo ic*, *-ic-al*, *-ic-al-ly*, *-ism*.

DESQUAMATION, a scaling off. (L.) A modern medical term; in Bailey (1735). Regularly allied to L. *desquāmātus*, pp. of *desquāmāre*, to scale off.—L. *dē*, away, off; and *squāma*, a scale.

DESSERT, a service of fruits after dinner. (F.—L.) ' *Dessert*, the last course at a feast, consisting of fruits, sweetmeats, &c.;' Blount's Gloss. ed. 1674.—F. *dessert*, ' the last course or service at table;' Cot.—F. *desservir*, ' to do one ill service; *desservir sus table*, to take away the table;' Cot.—OF. *des-* < L. *dis-*, apart, away; and F. *servir*, from L. *seruire*, to serve. See **Serve**.

DESTEMPER; see **Distemper**.

DESTINE, to ordain, appoint, doom. (F.—L.) In Shak. Meas. ii. 4. 138. The pp. *destaned* is in The Wars of Alexander, l. 518. [The sb. *destiny* is in early use; ME. *destinee*, Chaucer, C. T. 2325 (A 2323).—OF. *destiner*, ' to destinate, ordain;' Cot.—L. *destināre*, to destine.—L. *destina*, a support, prop.—L. *dē*, down; and **stanāre*, to cause to stand, set up, a derivative of *stāre*, to stand. Cf. Cretic σταυίω, I set. Brugmann, ii. § 603. See **Stand**. Der. *destin-ate*, *destin-at-ion* (like L. pp. *destinātus*); also *destiny* (ME. *destinee*, from OF. *destinee* < L. *destināta*, fem. of the same pp.).

DESTITUTE, forsaken, very poor. (L.) ' This fair lady, on this wys *destitut*;' Test. of Creseide, st. 14; Lydgate, Minor Poems, p. 34.—L. *destitūtus*, left alone, pp. of *destituere*, to set or place alone.—L. *dē*, off, away; and *statuere*, to place, from *status*, a position; cf. *status*, pp. of *stāre*, to stand; cognate with E. *stand*. See **Stand**. Der. *destitut-ion*.

DESTROY, to unbuild, overthrow. (F.—L.) In early use. The pp. *distryed* is in King Alisaunder, l. 130. ME. *destroien, destryen, destruyen*; the pt. t. *destrude* occurs in Rob. of Glouc., p. 242. Rob. of Brunne, tr. of Langtoft, has *destroied*, p. 8; *destruction*, p. 202.—OF. *destruire* (F. *détruire*, Ital. *distruggere*). —Folk-L. **destrŭgere* (pp. *destructus*), for L. *destruere* (pp. *destructus*), to pull down, unbuild.—L. *dē*, with sense of E. verbal *un-*; and *struere*, to build. See **Structure**. Der. *destroy-er*; also (like L. pp. *destructus*) *destruct-ion, -ible, -ibl-y, -ibil-i-ty, -ive, -ive-ly, -ive-ness*.

DESUETUDE, disuse. (L.) In Howell's Letters, i. 1. 35 (dated Aug. 1, 1621).—L. *dēsuetudo*, disuse.—L. *dēsuetus*, pp. of *dēsuescere*, to grow out of use.—L. *dē*, with negative force; and *suescere*, inceptive form of *suēre*, to be used. See **Custom**.

DESULTORY, jumping from one thing to another, random. (L.) 'Light, *desultory*, unbalanced minds;' Atterbury, vol. iii. ser. 9 (R.). Bp. Taylor has *desultorious*, Rule of Conscience, b. i. c. 2.— L. *dēsultorius*, belonging to a *dēsultor*; hence, inconstant, fickle. [Tertullian has *desultrix uirtus*, i.e. inconstant virtue.]—L. *dēsultor*, one who leaps down; one who leaps from horse to horse; an inconstant person; cf. *dēsultus*, pp. of *dēsilire*, to leap down.—L. *dē*, down; and *salire*, to leap. See **Saltation**. Der. *desultori-ly, -ness*.

DETACH, to unfasten, separate. (F.—L. and G.) Orig. a military term, and not in early use. '*Detach* (French mil. term), to send away a party of soldiers upon a particular expedition;' Kersey, ed. 1715.—F. *détacher*, lit. to unfasten.—F. *dé-*=OF. *des-*<L. *dis-*, apart; and *-tacher*, to fasten, only in the comp. *dé-tacher, at-tacher*. See **Attach**. Der. *detach-ment*.

DETAIL, a small part, minute account. (F.—L.) 'To offer wrong in *detaile*;' Holland's Plutarch, p. 306 (R.).—OF. *detail*, 'a peecemealing, also, retaile, small sale, or a selling by parcels;' Cot.—OF. *detailler*, 'to piecemeale, to cut into parcels;' Cot.—OF. *de-*=L. *dē-*, fully; and *tailler*, to cut. See **Tailor**. Der. *detail*, verb. ¶ The vb. is from the sb. in English; conversely in French.

DETAIN, to hold back, stop. (F.—L.) *Detaining* is in Sir T. More, Works, p. 386 e. From OF. *detien-*, a stem of OF. *detenir*, 'to detaine or withholde;' Cot.—L. *dētinēre*, to detain, keep back. —L. *dē*, from, away; and *tenēre*, to hold. See **Tenable**. Der. *detain-er, -ment*; *detent-ion*, q. v. Also *detent*, sb., a catch preventing motion of a machine.

DETECT, to expose, discover. (L.) Sir T. More has the pp. *detected*; Works, pp. 112 e, 219 c.—L. *dētectus*, pp. of *dētegere*, to uncover, expose.—L. *dē*, with sense of verbal *un-*; and *tegere*, to cover. See **Tegument**. Der. *detect-ion, -er, -or, -ive*.

DETENTION, a withholding. (F.—L.) In Shak. Tim. ii. 2. 39.—MF. *detention*, 'a detention, detaining;' Cot.—L. acc. *dētentiōnem*, from nom. *dētentio*; cf. *dētentus*, pp. of *dētinēre*, to detain. See **Detain**.

DETER, to frighten from, prevent. (L.) Milton has *deter*, P. L. ii. 449; *deterr'd*, ix. 696. It occurs earlier, in Lyly's Euphues, ed. Arber, p. 106.—L. *dēterrēre*, to frighten from.—L. *dē*, from; and *terrēre*, to frighten. See **Terror**. Der. *deterr-ent*.

DETERGE, to wipe off. (L.) '*Deterge*, to rub out;' Cockeram (1642).—L. *dētergere*, to wipe off.—L. *dē*, off, away; and *tergere*, pp. *tersus*, to wipe. Der. *deterg-ent*; also *deters-ive, -ion*, like pp. *deters-us*.

DETERIORATE, to make or grow worse. (L.) '*Deteriorated*, made worse, impaired;' Blount's Gloss. ed. 1674.—L. *dēteriorātus*, pp. of *dēteriorāre*, to make worse.—L. *dēterior*, worse. β. The word stands for *de-ter-ior*, in which the first syllable is the prep. *dē*, away, from; and *-ter-* and *-ior* are comparative suffixes; cf. *in-ter-ior*. Der. *deteriorat-ion*.

DETERMINE, to fix, bound, limit, end. (F.—L.) ME. *determinen*, Rom. of the Rose, 6631. Chaucer has *determinat*, C. T. 7041 (D 1459).—OF. *determiner*, 'to determine, conclude, resolve on, end, finish;' Cot.—L. *dētermināre*, pp. *dēterminātus*, to bound, limit, end.—L. *dē*, down, fully; and *termināre*, to bound, from *terminus*, a boundary. See **Term**. Der. *determin-able, -abl-y, -ate, -ate-ly, -at-ion, -at-ive*, like pp. *determinātus*; also *determin-ed, -ed-ly, -ant*.

DETEST, to hate intensely. (F.—L.) 'He *detesteth* and abhorreth the errours;' Sir T. More, Works, p. 422 a. Barnes has *detestable*, Works, p. 302, col. 2.—OF. *detester*, 'to detest, loath;' Cot.—L. *dētestārī*, to imprecate evil by calling the gods to witness, to execrate. —L. *dē*, down, fully; and *testārī*, to testify, from *testis*, a witness. See **Testify**. Der. *detest-able, -abl-y, -able-ness*; also *-at-ion* (like pp. *dētestātus*).

DETHRONE, to remove from a throne. (F.—L. and Gk.) In Speed's Chron. Rich. II, b. ix. c. 13 (R.).—OF. *desthroner*, 'to dis-thronize, or unthrone;' Cot.—OF. *des-*<L. *dis-*, apart; and OF. *throne*, a royal seat, from Late L. *thronus*, an episcopal seat, from Gk. θρόνος, a seat. See **Throne**. Der. *dethrone-ment*.

DETONATE, to explode. (L.) The verb is rather late. The sb. *detonation* is older, and in Kersey's Dict. ed. 1715.—L. *dētonātus*, pp. of *dētonāre*, to thunder down.—L. *dē*, down, fully; and *tonāre*, to thunder. See **Thunder**. Der. *detonat-ion*.

DETOUR, a winding way. (F.—L. and Gk.) Late; not in Johnson; N.E.D. gives a quotation, dated 1738.—F. *détour*, a circuit; verbal substantive from *détourner*, to turn aside, OF. *destourner* (Cot.).—OF. *des-*<L. *dis-*, apart; and *tourner*, to turn. See **Turn**.

DETRACTION, a taking away from one's credit. (L.) The verb *detract* is in Shak. Temp. ii. 2. 96, and is due to the older sb. The pres. pt. *detractinge* is in Barclay, Ship of Fools, ed. Jamieson; i. 17. Chaucer has *detractioun*, or *detraccion*, Pers. Tale, Six-text, Group I, l. 614. [So also in l. 493, the six MSS. have *detraccion*, not *detracting* as in Tyrwhitt.]—L. acc. *dētractiōnem*, lit. a taking away, from nom. *dētractio*; cf. *dētractus*, pp. of *dētrahere*, to take away, also, to detract, disparage.—L. *dē*, away; and *trahere*, to draw. See **Trait**. Der. *detract*, verb; *-or*.

DETRIMENT, loss, injury. (F.—L.) In Sir T. Elyot, Castel of Helth, b. ii. c. 3.—OF. *detriment*, 'detriment, loss;' Cot.—L. *dētrimentum*, loss, lit. a rubbing away.—L. *dētri-*, seen in *dētritus*, pp. of *dēterere*, to rub away; with suffix *-mentum*.—L. *dē*, away; and *terere*, to rub. See **Trite**. Der. *detriment-al*; also (like pp. *dētritus*) *detritus, detrit-ion*.

DETRUDE, to thrust down. (L.) 'And theim to cast and *detrude* sodaynly into continual captiuitie;' Hall, Rich. III, an. 3. (R.).—L. *dētrūdere*, pp. *dētrūsus*, to thrust down.—L. *dē*, down; and *trūdere*, to thrust. E. *thrust* is from the same root. Der. *detrus-ion*.

DEUCE (1), a two, at cards or dice. (F.—L.) In Shak. L. L. L. i. 2. 49. Spelt *dews*, Skelton, Bouge of Courte, l. 347.—F. *deux*, two.—L. *duōs*, acc. of *duo*, two; cognate with E. *two*. See **Two**.

DEUCE (2), an evil spirit, the devil. (F.—L.) 'Owe! *dewes*! all goes downe!' O! the deuce! all is lost;' York Plays, Play 1, l. 92. The orig. sense was exclamatory, signifying 'Oh! ill-luck!' because the *deuce*, or 'two,' was a losing throw at dice. Then it came to be equivalent to 'the devil!' It is really the same word as the preceding. See Academy, Jan. 30, 1892, p. 111; and see N.E.D. Cf. Low G. *de deus!* (Bremen Wört.).

DEUTERONOMY, the fifth book of the Pentateuch. (L.—Gk.) Spelt *Deutronomye* by Wyclif.—L. *Deuteronomium* (as in Deut. xvii. 18);' as if 'a repetition of the law.'—Gk. Δευτερονόμιον; from δεύτερο-s, second, and νόμος, law.

DEVASTATE, to lay waste. (L.) A late word; not in Johnson; but it occurs in Bailey, vol. ii. 1727 (though *not* in ed. 1731). *Devastation* is in Blount's Gloss. ed. 1674. Instead of *devastate*, the form *devast* was formerly used, and occurs in Ford, Perkin Warbeck, A. iv. sc. 1. l. 6.—L. *dēuastātus*, pp. of *dēuastāre*, to lay waste.—L. *dē*, fully; and *uastāre*, to waste, cognate with E. *waste*. See **Waste**. Der. *devastat-ion*.

DEVELOP, to unroll, unfold, open out. (F.—L. and Teut.) In Pope, Dunciad, iv. 269. The pp. *developed* is in Blount's Gloss. (1656).—F. *développer*, to unfold, spelt *desveloper* in Cotgrave.—OF. *des-*<L. *dis-*, apart; and *-veloper*, occurring in F. *envelopper*, formerly *enveloper*, to enwrap, wrap up. See **Envelope**. Der. *develop-ment*.

DEVEST, the old form of **Divest**. (F.—L.) OF. *desvestir* (Hatzfeld).—L. *dis-*, away; and *uestire*, to clothe. See **Divest**.

DEVIATE, to go out of the way. (L.) 'But Shadwell never *deviates* into sense;' Dryden, Macflecknoe, l. 20.—L. *dēuiātus*, pp. of *dēuiāre*, to go out of the way.—L. *dēuius*, out of the way.—L. *dē*, away from; *uia*, way. See **Devious**. Der. *deviat-ion*. ME. *deuiacioun*, T. Usk, Test. of Love, iii. 1. 6.

DEVICE, a plan, project, opinion. (F.—L.) ME. *deuise, deuys* (with *u* for *v*); Chaucer, C. T. 816 (or 818).—OF. *devis*, m., 'speech, talke, . . . a device;' *devise*, f., 'a device, poesie, embleme, . . . invention; also, a division, bound;' Cot.—Late L. *diuisum, diuisa*, a division of goods, bound, mark, device, judgment. See further under **Devise**.

DEVIL, an evil spirit. (L.—Gk.) ME. *deuil, deouel* (with *u* for *v*); spelt *deuel*, P. Plowman, B. ii. 102. AS. *dēoful, dēofol* (Grein, i. 191.—L. *diabolus*.—Gk. διάβολος, the slanderer, the devil. —Gk. διαβάλλειν, to slander, traduce, lit. to throw across.—Gk. διά, through, across; and βάλλειν, to throw, cast. See **Belemnite**. Der. *devil-ish, -ish-ly, -ish-ness, -ry*.

DEVIOUS, going out of the way. (L.) In Milton, P. L. iii. 489.—L. *dēuius*, going out of the way; with change of *-us* to E. *-ous*, as in numerous other cases.—L. *dē*, out of; and *uia*, a way. See **Viaduct**. Der. *devious-ly, -ness*; also *deviate*, q. v.

DEVISE, to imagine, contrive, bequeath. (F.—L.) In early use. ME. *deuisen* (with *u* for *v*), King Horn, ed. Lumby, 930; Gower,

C. A. i. 19, 31 ; prol. 464, 822. – OF. *deviser*, to distinguish, regulate, bequeath, talk. [Cf. Ital. *divisare*, to divide, describe, think.] – OF. *devise*, a division, project, order, condition. [Cf. Ital. *divisa*, a division, share, choice.] – Late L. *diuīsa*, a division of goods, portion of land, bound, decision, mark, device. – L. *diuīsa*, fem. of *diuīsus*, pp. of *diuīdere*, to divide. See **Divide**. Der. *devis-er, -or* ; *device*, q. v.

DEVOID, quite void, destitute. (F. – L.) ME. *deuoyd* (with *u* for *v*) ; Rom. of the Rose, 3723. The pp. *deuoided*, i. e. emptied out, occurs in the same, 2929 ; from ME. *deuoiden*, to empty. – OF. *desvuidier, desvoidier*, to empty out (mod. F. *dévider*). – OF. *des-* < L. *dis-*, apart ; and *voidier, vuidier*, to void, from OF. *voide, vuide*, f. (m. *vuit*), void. See **Void**.

DEVOIR, duty. (F. – L.) In early use. ME. *deuoir, deuer* (with *u* for *v*), Chaucer, C. T. 2600 (A 2598) ; P. Plowman, C. xvii. 5. – MF. *devoir*, OF. *deveir*, to owe ; also, as sb., duty. – L. *dēbēre*, to owe. See **Debt**.

DEVOLVE, to roll onward, transfer, be transferred. (L.) 'He did *devolve* and intrust the supreme authority . . . into the hands of those persons ; ' Clarendon, Civil War, vol. iii. p. 483 (R.). ME. *deuoluen*, Palladius, bk. xi. 497. – L. *dēuoluere*, to roll down, bring to. – L. *dē*, down ; and *uoluere*, to roll. See **Voluble**. Der. *devolution*, defined as ' a rolling downe ' in Cockeram ; cf. *deuolūt-us*, pp.

DEVOTE, to vow, consecrate to a purpose. (L.) Shak. always uses the pp. *devoted*, as in Oth. ii. 3. 321. [The sb. *devotion* was in quite early use ; it is spelt *deuociun* in the Ancren Riwle, p. 368, and was derived from Latin through the OF. *devotion*.] – L. *dēuōtus*, devoted ; pp. of *dēuouēre*, to devote. – L. *dē*, fully ; and *uouēre*, to vow. See **Vow**. Der. *devot-ed, -ed-ly, -ed-ness* ; *devot-ee* (a coined word, see Spectator, no. 354) ; *devot-ion, -ion-al, -ion-al-ly* ; and see *devout*.

DEVOUR, to consume, eat up. (F. – L.) ME. *deuouren* (with *u* for *v*) ; P. Plowman, C. iii. 140 ; Gower, C. A. i. 64 ; bk. i. l. 654. – OF. *devoure*, 1 p. s. pr. of *devorer*, to devour. – L. *dēuorāre*, to devour. – L. *aē*, fully ; and *uorāre*, to consume. See **Voracious**. Der. *devour-er*.

DEVOUT, devoted to religion. (F. – L.) In early use. ME. *deuot* (with *u* for *v*) ; Ancren Riwle, p. 376, l. 3. Spelt *devoute* in Gower, C. A. i. 64 ; bk. i. l. 669. – OF. *devot*, devoted ; see Godefroy. – L. *dēuōtus*, pp. devoted. See **Devote**.

DEW, damp, moisture. (E.) ME. *deu, dew* ; spelt *deau, dyau*, Ayenbite of Inwyt, 136, 144. The pl. *dewes* is in P. Plowman, C. xviii. 21. AS. *dēaw, dēw* ; cf. *dēaw*, P. Plowman, C. i. 190. + Du. *dauw* ; Icel. *dögg*, gen. sing. and nom. pl. *döggvar* ; cf. Dan. *dug*, Swed. *dagg* ; OHG. *tou, tau* ; G. *thau*. Teut. type **dauwo-*. β. Perhaps connected with Skt. *dhav, dhāv*, to run, flow (Fick) ; and Gk. θέειν (for **θέϝειν*), to run (Prellwitz). Der. *dew-y* ; also *dew-lap* (Mids. Nt. Dream, ii. 1. 50, iv. 1. 127) ; *dew-point* (modern).

DEXTER, on the right side, right. (L.) A heraldic term. In Shak. Troil. iv. 5. 128. He also has *dexterity*, Haml. i. 2. 157. Dryden has *dexterous*, Abs. and Achit. 904. – L. *dexter*, right, said of hand or side. + Gk. δεξιός, δεξίτερος, on the right ; Skt. *dakshiṇa-*, on the right, on the south (to a man looking eastward) ; OHG. *zëso*, on the right ; Goth. *taihswa*, the right hand ; Russ. *desnitsa*, the right hand ; W. *deheu*, right, southern ; Gael. and Irish *deas*, right, southern. β. The Skt. *dakshiṇa-* is from the Skt. *daksh*, to satisfy, suit, be strong ; cf. Skt. *daksha-*, clever, able. Brugmann, i. § 598. Der. *dexter-i-ty, -ous, -ous-ly, -ous-ness, dextr-al*.

DEY, a governor of Algiers, before the French conquest. (F. – Turk.) 'The *dey* deposed, 5 July, 1830 ; ' Haydn, Dict. of Dates. – F. *dey*. – Turk. *dāī*, a maternal uncle. ' Orig. a maternal uncle, then a friendly title formerly given to middle-aged or old people, esp. among the Janizaries ; and hence, in Algiers, consecrated at length to the commanding officer of that corps, who frequently became afterward pacha or regent of that province ; hence the European misnomer of *dey*, as applied to the latter ; ' Webster.

DHOW, DOW, a kind of ship, a slave-ship. (E. Indian ?) See *Dhow* in Yule ; *not* of Arab. origin. Given as *dāo* or *dāva* in Molesworth's Mārāthī Dict. Perhaps from Skt. *dhāv*, to run, flow ; *dhāvin*, running.

DI- (1), prefix ; ' apart.' (L.) L. *dī-*, shorter form of *dis-* ; see **Dis-**.

DI- (2), prefix, signifying ' twice ' or ' double.' (Gk.) Gk. δι-, for δίς, twice. + L. *bis, bi-*, twice ; Skt. *dvis, dvi-*, twice. Connected with Gk. δύω, L. *duo*, Skt. *dva*, E. *two*. See **Two**.

DIA-, a common prefix. (Gk.) From Gk. διά, through, also, between, apart ; closely related to δίς, twice, and δύο, two. Cf. L. *dis-*, apart. ' Both the prefixal and the prepositional use of διά are to be explained by the idea *between* ; ' Curtius, i. 296. See **Two**. ¶ This prefix forms no part of the words *diamond, dial*, or *diary*, as may be seen.

DIABETES, a disease accompanied with excessive discharge of urine. (Gk.) Medical. In Kersey, ed. 1715. The adj. *diabetical* is in Cockeram (1642). – Gk. διαβήτης, diabetes ; orig. a pair of compasses, a siphon. – Gk. διαβαίνειν, to stand with the legs apart (like compasses) ; also, to pass through (a siphon). – Gk. διά, apart ; and βαίνειν, to go, cognate with E. **Come**, q. v.

DIABOLIC, DIABOLICAL, devilish. (L. – Gk.) Spelt *diabolick*, Milton, P. L. ix. 95. – L. *diabolicus*, devilish. – Gk. διαβολικός, devilish. – Gk. διάβολος, the devil. See **Devil**.

DIACHYLON, an adhesive plaister. (F. – L. – Gk.) ' *Diachylon*, a plaister ; ' Phillips (1658). Spelt *diachilon* in W. Bullein, Dialogue against the Fever (1578), p. 48 (E.E.T.S.). – MF. *diaculon, diachylon* ; Cot. – Late L. *diachȳlon*, a medicament (Lewis). – Gk. διὰ χυλῶν, a medicine composed of juices ; from διά, by means of ; and χυλῶν, gen. pl. of χυλός, juice ; see **Chyle**. ¶ The Gk. διά, ' consisting of,' was formerly in much use as a prefix in medicinal remedies, as *dia-codium, dia-pente*, &c.

DIACONAL, pertaining to a deacon. (F. – L. – Gk.) From F. *diaconal*, which Cotgrave translates by ' diaconall.' – Late L. *diāconālis*, formed with suffix *-ālis* from L. *diācon-us*, a deacon. – Gk. διάκονος, a deacon. See **Deacon**. Similarly *diaconate* = F. *diaconat*, from L. *diācon-ātus*, deacon-ship.

DIACRITIC, distinguishing between. (Gk.) ' *Diacritick* points ; ' Wallis to Bp. Lloyd (1699), in Nicholson's Epist. Cor. i. 123 (Todd). – Gk. διακριτικός, fit for distinguishing. – Gk. διά, between ; and κρίνειν, to distinguish. See **Critic**. Der. *diacritic-al* ; used by Sir W. Jones, Pref. to Pers. Grammar.

DIADEM, a fillet on the head, a crown. (F. – L. – Gk.) In early use. ME. *diademe*, Chaucer, C. T. 10357, 10374 (F 43, 60) ; Becket, 2149 (marked 2049) ; cf. P. Plowman, B. iii. 286. – OF. *diademe* ; Cot. – L. *diadēma*. – Gk. διάδημα, a band, fillet. – Gk. διαδέω, I bind round. – Gk. διά, round, lit. apart ; and δέω, I bind. Cf. Skt. *dā*, to bind ; *dāman*, a garland. – √DE, to bind ; Brugmann, ii. § 707.

DIÆRESIS, a mark (¨) of separation. (L. – Gk.) In Kersey's Dict. ed. 1715. – L. *diæresis*. – Gk. διαίρεσις, a dividing. – Gk. διαιρέω, I take apart, divide. – Gk. δι-, for διά, apart ; and αἱρέω, I take. See **Heresy**.

DIAGNOSIS, a scientific determination of a disease. (Gk.) The adj. *diagnostic* was in earlier use than the sb. ; it occurs in Blount's Gloss. ed. 1674. – Gk. διάγνωσις, a distinguishing ; whence the adj. διαγνωστικός, able to distinguish. – Gk. διά, between ; and γνῶσις, enquiry, knowledge, from γι-γνώσκω, I know, cognate with E. *know*. See **Know**.

DIAGONAL, running across from corner to corner. (F. – L. – Gk.) In Blount's Gloss. ed. 1674 ; and in Cotgrave. – F. *diagonal*, ' diagonall ; ' Cot. – L. *diagōnālis*, formed with suffix *-ālis* from a stem *diagōn-*. – Gk. διαγών-ιος, diagonal. – Gk. διά, through, across, between ; and γωνία, a corner, angle. Der. *diagonal-ly*.

DIAGRAM, a sketch, figure, plan. (L. – Gk.) ' *Diagram*, a title of a book, a sentence or decree ; also, a figure in geometry ; and in music, it is called a proportion of measures, distinguished by certain notes ; ' Blount's Gloss. ed. 1674 ; *diagramme* in Cockeram (1642). – L. *diagramma*, a scale, gamut. – Gk. διάγραμμα, a figure, plan, gamut, list ; lit. that which is marked out by lines. – Gk. διαγράφειν, to mark out by lines, draw out, describe. – Gk. διά, through ; and γράφειν, to write.

DIAL, a clock-face, plate for showing the time of day. (L.) In Shak. Oth. iii. 4. 175. ME. *dyal, dial* ; Lydgate, Minor Poems, p. 245 ; Prompt. Parv. p. 120. – Med. L. *diālis*, relating to a day ; cf. Med. L. *diāle*, as much land as could be ploughed in a day. [The word *journal* has passed from an adjectival to a substantival sense in a similar manner.] – L. *diēs*, a day. See **Diary**. Der. *dial-ist, diall-ing*.

DIALECT, a variety of a language. (F. – L. – Gk.) In Shak. K. Lear, ii. 2. 115. – F. *dialecte*, ' a dialect, or propriety of language ; ' Cot. – L. *dialectos*, a manner of speaking. – Gk. διάλεκτος, discourse, speech, language, dialect of a district. – Gk. διαλέγομαι, I discourse ; from the act. form διαλέγω, I pick out, choose between. – Gk. διά, between ; and λέγειν, to choose, speak. ¶ From the same source is *dialogue*, q. v. Der. *dialect-ic, -ics, -ic-ian, -ic-al, -ic-al-ly*.

DIALOGUE, a discourse. (F. – L. – Gk.) In early use. ME. *dialoge*, Ancren Riwle, p. 230. – OF. *dialoge* (Hatzfeld), later *dialogue* (Cotgrave). – L. *dialogus*, a dialogue (Cicero). – Gk. διάλογος, a conversation. – Gk. διαλέγομαι, I discourse (above). Der. *dialog-ist, -ist-ic, -ist-ic-al*.

DIAMETER, the line measuring the breadth across or thickness through. (F. – L. – Gk.) ME. *diametre*, Chaucer, Astrolabe, pt. ii. § 38. 8. – OF. *diametre*, ' a diameter ; ' Cot. – L. *diametros*. – Gk. διάμετρος, f. a diagonal, a diameter. – Gk. διά, through ; and μετρεῖν, to measure. See **Metre**. Der. *diametr-ic-al, -ic-al-ly*.

DIAMOND, a hard precious stone. (F. – L. – Gk.) [A doublet of *adamant*, and used in the sense of *adamant* as late as in Milton,

P. L. vi. 364; see Trench, Select Glossary.] 'Have herte as hard as *diamaunt*;' Rom. of the Rose, 4385; spelt *diamant*, P. Plowman, B. ii. 13. —OF. *diamant*, 'a diamond, also, the load-stone, instead of *aymant*;' Cot. [Cf. Ital. and Span. *diamante*, G. and Du. *diamant*, a diamond.] β. Known to be a mere corruption of *adamant*, OF. *aimant* (Hatzfeld); hence Ital. and Span. *diamantino*, adamantine. See **Adamant**.

DIAPASON, a whole octave, harmony. (L.—Gk.) In Shak. Lucrece, 1132; also in Milton, Ode at a Solemn Music, l. 23; Dryden, Song for St. Cecilia's Day, l. 15. ME. *dyapason*, Trevisa, tr. of Higden, iii. 209.—L. *diapāsōn*, an octave, a concord of a note with its octave.—Gk. διαπασῶν, the concord of the first and last notes of an octave; a contracted form of the phrase διὰ πασῶν χορδῶν συμφωνία, a concord extending through all the notes; where διὰ means through, and πασῶν is the gen. pl. fem. of the adj. πᾶς, all (stem παντ-). The same stem appears in *pan-theism*, *panto-mime*, &c. See **Pantomime**.

DIAPER, figured linen cloth. (F.—L.—Gk.) 'In *dieper*, in damaske, or in lyne' [linen]; Spenser, Muiopotmos, 364. 'Covered in cloth of gold *diapred* weel;' Chaucer, C. T. 2160 (A 2158).—OF. *diapré*, 'diaperd or diapred, diversified with flourishes or sundry figures;' Cot. From the verb *diaprer*, 'to diaper, flourish, diversifie with flourishings.' β. In still earlier French we find *diaspre*, with the sense of 'fine silk cloth,' often described as *blanc* (white); see Godefroy.—Late L. *diasprus*, adj.; also used as a sb. (as in 'tunica de diaspra alba'); Ducange.—Late Byzantine Gk. δίασπρος, pure white; from διά, wholly, and ἄσπρος, white (see N.E.D.). ¶ Not the same as Ital. *diaspro*, a jasper. But cf. Prov. *diaspres*, diaper, costly cloth (Bartsch); also Late L. *asperī*, white money (Ducange).

DIAPHANOUS, transparent. (Gk.) '*Diaphanous*, clear as crystal, transparent;' Blount's Gloss. ed. 1674. Sir T. Browne has the sb. *diaphanity*; Vulg. Errors, b. ii. c. 1. § 18.—Gk. διαφανής, seen through, transparent; with -*ous* for -ης; cf. διαφαίνειν, to show through.—Gk. διά, through; and φαν-, base of φαίνειν, to show. See **Phantom**. Der. *diaphanous-ly*; from the same source, *diaphan-i-ty* or *diaphane-i-ty*.

DIAPHORETIC, causing perspiration. (Gk.) '*Diaphoretick*, that dissolveth, or sends forth humours;' Blount's Gloss. ed. 1674. —L. *diaphorēticus*, sudorific.—Gk. διαφορητικός, promoting perspiration.—Gk. διαφόρησις, perspiration.—Gk. διαφορεῖν, to carry off, throw off by perspiration.—Gk. διά, through; and φορεῖν, to carry, allied to φέρειν, to bear, cognate with E. *bear*. See **Bear** (1).

DIAPHRAGM, a dividing membrane, the midriff. (F.—L.—Gk.) The L. form *diaphragma* is in Beaum. and Fletcher, Mons. Thomas, iii. 1. '*Diaphragm*, . . . the midriff;' Blount's Gloss. ed. 1674.—F. *diaphragme*, 'the midriffe;' Cot.—L. *diaphragma*.—Gk. διάφραγμα, a partition-wall, the midriff; cf. διαφράγνυμι, I divide by a fence.—Gk. διά, between; and φράσσω, I fence in, enclose (fut. φράξω); allied to L. *farcīre*, to stuff. See **Farce**. Der. *diaphragmat-ic*, from διαφραγματ-, stem of διάφραγμα.

DIARRHŒA, looseness of the bowels. (L.—Gk.) In Kersey's Dict. ed. 1715; *diarrhea* in Cockeram (1642).—L. *diarrhœa*.—Gk. διάρροια, lit. a flowing through.—Gk. διαρρέειν, to flow through.—Gk. διά, through; and ῥέειν, to flow.—√ SREU, to flow. Brugmann, i. § 318. See **Stream**.

DIARY, a daily record. (L.) 'He must alwayes have a *diary* about him;' J. Howell, Instructions for Foreign Travel, sect. iii. § 4; ed. 1642.—L. *diārium*, a daily allowance for soldiers; also, a diary. —L. *diēs*, a day. Brugmann, i. § 223. Der. *diar-ist*; cf. *dial*.

DIASTOLE, a dilatation of the heart. (Gk.) In Kersey's Dict. ed. 1715; and in Spenser, Globe ed.; p. 709, col. 1, l. 20.—Gk. διαστολή, a drawing asunder; dilatation of the heart.—Gk. διαστέλλειν, to put aside.—Gk. διά, in the sense of 'apart;' and στέλλειν, to place.

DIATONIC, proceeding by tones. (Gk.) '*Diatonick Musick* keeps a mean temperature between *chromatic* and *enharmonic*, and may go for plain song;' Blount's Gloss. ed. 1674.—Gk. διατονικός, diatonic; we find also διάτονος (lit. on the stretch) used in the same sense.—Gk. διατείνειν, to stretch out.—Gk. διά, through; and τείνειν, to stretch.—√ TEN, to stretch. See **Tone**. Der. *diatonic-al-ly*.

DIATRIBE, an invective discourse. (L.—Gk.) '*Diatribe*, an auditory, or place where disputations or exercises are held;' Blount's Gloss. ed. 1674. Also 'a disputation;' Kersey, ed. 1715.—L. *diatriba*, a place for learned disputations, a school; an extension of the sense of the Gk. διατριβή, lit. a wearing away, a waste of time, a discussion, argument.—Gk. διατρίβειν, to rub away, waste, spend time, discuss.—Gk. διά, thoroughly; and τρίβειν, to rub (with long ι). Brugmann, ii. § 676.

DIB, to dab lightly, to make small holes in the ground. (E.) A lighter form of *dab*; see N.E.D. and E.D.D. Hence *dibber*, a dibble; Pegge, Kenticisms (E.D.S.). Cf. **Dab**.

DIBBER, DIBBLE, a tool used for setting plants. (E.) 'I'll not put The *dibble* in earth to set one slip of them;' Wint. Tale, iv. 4. 100. ME. *debylle*, a setting-stick; Cath. Anglicum, p. 92 (and note). From the stem *dab-*; see **Dab**. And see above.

DICE, the plural of *die*; see **Die** (2).

DICKER, half a score, esp. of hides. (L.) Once common; the acc. pl. *dicras* occurs in Domesday Book; see Blount's Nomolexicon. From AS. *dicor*, not recorded; but representing Late L. *dicora*.—L. *decūria*, a company or set of ten.—L. *decem*, ten; see **Ten**. ¶ So also F. *dacre*, Late L. *dacra*; Swed. *däcker*, 'a dicker;' Widegren.

DICOTYLEDON, a plant with two seed-lobes. (Gk.) In Bailey, vol. ii. (1727, 1731). A mod. botan. term; in common use. Coined from Gk. δι-, double (from δίς, twice); and Gk. κοτυληδών, a cup-shaped hollow or cavity.—Gk. κοτύλη, anything hollow, a cup. Cf. L. *catīnus*, a bowl; see **Kettle**. Der. *dicotyledon-ous*.

DICTATE, to command, tell what to write. (L.) 'Sylla could not skill of letters, and therefore knew not how to *dictate*;' Bacon, Adv. of Learning, ed. W. A. Wright, i. 7. 29; p. 66. Shak. has *dictator*; Cor. ii. 2. 93.—L. *dictātus*, pp. of *dictāre*, to dictate; cf. 'Sylla nesciuit literas, non potuit *dictare*,' quoted in Bacon, Essay xv. β. *Dictāre* is the frequentative of *dīcere*, to say; see **Diction**. Der. *dictat-ion*, -*or*, -*or-ship*, -*or-i-al*, -*or-i-al-ly*.

DICTION, manner of discourse. (F.—L.) In Shak. Haml. v. 2. 123.—F. *diction*, 'a diction, speech, or saying;' Cot.—L. acc. *dictiōnem*, from nom. *dictio*, a saying, speech; cf. *dict-*, pp. stem of *dīcere*, to say, also, to appoint; from the same root as *dicāre*, to tell, publish.+Gk. δείκνυμι, I show, point out; Skt. *diç*, to show, produce; Goth. *ga-teihan*, to tell, announce; G. *zeigen*, to point out.—√DEIK, to show, point out; Brugmann, i. § 207. Der. *diction-ary*; also *dictum* (neut. sing. of L. pp. *dictus*), pl. *dicta*; and see ditto. Hence also *bene-diction*, benison, *male-diction*, malison, *contra-diction*, &c. From the same root are *indicate*, *indict*, *index*, *avenge*, *judge*, *preach*, &c.

DID, pt. t. of *do*; see **Do**.

DIDACTIC, instructive. (Gk.) In Bp. Taylor, vol. iii. ser. 10; also in his Dissuasive from Popery, pt. i. s. 9 (R.).—Gk. διδακτικός, instructive; cf. 1 Tim. iii. 2.—Gk. διδάσκειν, to teach; where διδάσκειν = *δι-δακ-σκειν. + L. *doc-ēre*, to teach; cf. *disc-ere*, to learn. Allied to δοκεῖν, to think; δέκομαι, Ionic for δέχομαι, receive. (√DEK.) Brugmann, i. § 707. Der. *didactic-al*, -*al-ly*.

DIDAPPER, a diving bird, a dabchick. (E.) '*Doppar*, or *dy-doppar*, watyr-byrde, mergulus;' Prompt. Parv. p. 127. For *dive-dapper*. 'Like a *dive-dapper* peering through a wave;' Shak. Venus, 86. Compounded of *dive* (q. v.) and *dapper*, i. e. a diver, dipper, plunger, so that the sense of *dive* occurs twice in the word, according to a common principle of reduplication in language. [Cf. Derwentwater = white-water-water.] β. *Dapper* answers to AS. *doppa*; cf. *dop-chicken*, the Linc. word for the dab-chick (Halliwell); *doppers*, i. e. dippers or Anabaptists, used by Ben Jonson in his masque entitled News from the New World; and the form *doppar* cited from the Prompt. Parv. above. The AS. form *dūfe-doppa* actually occurs, to translate the L. *pelicanus* (Bosworth); where -*a* is an agential suffix, replaced (later) by -*er*; and *dop-* = *dup-*, weak grade of *deup-*, as seen in AS. *dēop*, deep. + L. Swed. *doppa*, to dip, plunge, immerge. Hence also *dap-chick*, for *dop-chick*, i. e. the diving bird, corrupted to *dab-chick* for ease of pronunciation. See **Dip, Deep**.

DIDDLE, to overreach. (E.) Also, to waste time by dawdling; see E.D.D. From the base *dyd-*, as in AS. *dyd-rian*, to delude; formed (by vowel-change of *u* to *y*) from *dud-*, weak grade allied to *dauth-*, as seen in *dēaδ*, death; cf. **Dawdle**. Cf. EFries. *dudjen*, *bedudjen*, to overreach, *dudden*, to be stupid, doze, dream; Norw. *dudda*, to hush to sleep (Ross); Dan. *dude*, darnel (because it stupefies); Larsen.

DIE (1), to lose life, perish. (Scand.) ME. *dien*, *dyen*, *diȝen*, *deȝen*, *deyen*. Spelt *deȝen* in Layamon, 31796. Late AS. *dēȝan*, Holy Rood-tree, ed. Napier (E.E.T.S., 1894), p. 14, l. 25; so that the word may be a native one, after all. [The ordinary AS. word is *steorfan* or *sweltan*; hence it is usual to regard *die* as Scandinavian.] —Icel. *deyja*, to die; Swed. *dö*; Dan. *döe*. + OSax. *dōian*; MHG. *touwen*, to die. Cf. also OFries. *deia*, *deja*, to kill; Goth. *af-daujan*, to harass, Matt. ix. 36. The Teut. base is *dau*; whence *dau-jan*, to die (Icel. *deyja*). Cf. Russ. *davite*, to strangle. See **Death, Dead**.

DIE (2), a small cube used for gaming. (F.—L.) The sing. *die* is in Shak. Wint. Tale, iv. 3. 27; he also uses the pl. *dice* (id. i. 2. 133). Earlier, the sing. is seldom found; but the ME. pl. *dys* is common; see Chaucer, C. T. 1240, 11002, 12557 (A 1238, F 690, C 623). Some MSS. spell the word *dees*, which is, etymologically, more correct.—OF. *det*, a die (Burguy), later *dé*, pl. *dez* (Cotgrave); cf. Prov. *dat*, a die (Brachet); also Ital. *dado*, pl. *dadi*, a die, cube, pedestal; Span. *dado*, pl. *dados*.—Late L. *datum*, a thing given or decreed; hence applied to a die for casting lots. Orig. neuter of *datus*, pp. of *dare*, to give, let go, give forth, thrust, throw. See Date (1). Der. *die*, a stamp, pl. *dies*; also *dice*, verb, ME. *dycen*, Prompt. Parv. p. 121. Doublet, *dado*.

DIET (1), a prescribed allowance of food. (F.—L.—Gk.) 'Of his *diete* mesurable was he;' Chaucer, C. T. 437 (A 435). Cf. 'And ʒif thow *diete* the thus,' i.e. diet thyself in this way; P. Plowman, B. vi. 270.—OF. *diete*, 'diet, or daily fare; also, a Diet, Parliament;' Cot.—Late L. *diēta*, *diæta*, a ration of food.—Gk. δίαιτα, mode of life; also, diet. Brugmann, i. § 650. Der. *diet-ary*, *-et-ic*.

DIET (2), an assembly, council. (F.—L.—Gk.) 'Thus would your Polish *Diet* disagree;' Dryden, Hind and Panther, ii. 407. It occurs also in Cotgrave.—OF. *diete*, 'diet; also, a Diet, Parliament;' Cot.—Late L. *diæta*, a public assembly; also, a ration of food, diet. β. The peculiar spelling *diæta* and the suffix *-ta* leave no doubt that this word is nothing but a peculiar use of the Gk. δίαιτα, mode of life, diet. In other words, this word is identical in *form* with Diet (1), q.v. γ. At the same time, the peculiar *sense* of the word undoubtedly arose from a popular etymology that connected it with the L. *diēs*, a day, esp. a set day, a day appointed for public business; whence, by extension, a meeting for business, an assembly. We even find *diæta* used to mean 'a day's journey;' and *diēta*, 'a day's work,' or 'a daily duty;' Ducange.

DIFFER, to be distinct, to disagree. (F.—L.) 'Dyuerse and *differinge* substaunces;' Chaucer, tr. of Boethius, b. v. pr. 5; l. 17. Ch. also has the sb. *difference*, id. b. v. pr. 6; l. 157.—OF. *differer* (Hatzfeld); F. *différer*, also with the sense of 'defer.'—L. *differre*, to carry apart, to differ; also, to defer.—L. *dif-* (for *dis-*), apart; and *ferre*, to bear, cognate with E. *bear*. See Bear (1). Der. *differ-ent* (OF. *different*, from L. pres. part. stem *different-*), *-ent-ly*, *-ent-i-al*; also *differ-ence* (OF. *difference*, from L. *differentia*). Doublet, *defer*.

DIFFICULTY, an obstacle, impediment, hard enterprise. (F.—L.) [The adj. *difficult* is in Shak. Oth. iii. 3. 82, but it is somewhat rare in early authors, and was merely developed from the sb. *difficulty*, which was a common word and in earlier use. The ME. word for 'difficult' was *difficile*, occurring in Sir T. Elyot, The Governour, b. i. c. 23. § 5.] ME. *difficultee*; Chaucer, C. T. 6854 (D 1272).—OF. *difficulté*; Cot.—L. *difficultātem*, acc. of *difficultās*, difficulty, an abbreviated form of **difficilitās*.—L. *difficilis*, hard.—L. *dif-*, = *dis-*, apart; and *facilis*, easy. See Facile, Faculty. Der. *difficult-ly*.

DIFFIDENT, distrustful, bashful. (L.) In Florio (1598), to translate Ital. *diffidente*; and Milton, P. L. viii. 562, ix. 293. Shak. has *diffidence*, K. John, i. 65.—L. *diffidentem*, acc. of *diffidens*, pres. pt. of *diffidere*, to distrust; cf. L. *diffidentia*, distrust.—L. *dif-* = *dis-*, apart, with negative force; and *fidere*, to trust, allied to *fidēs*, faith. See Faith. Der. *diffident-ly*, *diffidence*; see *diffidence* in Trench, Select Glossary.

DIFFRACT, to deflect and break up a beam of light. (L.) Scientific; not in Johnson.—L. *diffract-us*, pp. of *diffringere*, to break up.—L. *dif-*, for *dis-*, apart; and *frangere*, to break. See Fraction. Der. *diffract-ion*, *-ive*.

DIFFUSE, to shed abroad, pour around, spread, scatter. (L.) In Shak. Temp. iv. 1. 79. Chaucer has *diffusioun*, Troilus, iii. 296.—L. *diffūsus*, pp. of *diffundere*, to shed abroad.—L. *dif-* = *dis-*, apart; and *fundere*, to pour. See Fuse (1). Der. *diffuse*, adj., *-ly*, *-ness*, *diffus-ible*, *-ed*, *-ed-ly*, *-ed-ness*, *-ion*, *-ive*, *-ive-ly*, *-ive-ness*.

DIG, to turn up earth with a spade. (F.—Du.) ME. *diggen*. 'Dikeres and delueres *digged* up the balkes' = ditchers and delvers dug up the baulks;' P. Plowman, B. vi. 109, where, for *digged*, the earlier version (A. vii. 100) has *dikeden*. [Thus *diggen* is equivalent to *dikien*, to dig.]—F. *diguer*, to make a dike (15th cent.); Littré.—F. *digue*, 'a ditch;' Cot.—Du. *dijk*, a dike; cognate with AS. *dīc*, a dyke, or dike, a ditch. Cf. Swed. *dika*, to dig a ditch, from *dike*, a ditch; Dan. *dige*, to dig, from *dige*, a ditch. ¶ At first a weak verb; the strong pt. t. *dug* is of late invention, the true pt. t. being *digged*, which occurs 18 times in the A. V. of the Bible, whereas *dug* does not occur in it at all. Cf. *stuck*, late pt. t. of *stick*. See Dike. Der. *digg-er*, *digg-ings*.

DIGAMMA, a Greek letter representing the sound of E. *w*. (Gk.) '*Digamma*, the letter ϝ;' Cooper's Thesaurus (1565). Lit. 'double gamma;' from its shape (ϝ), which resembled that of a gamma (Γ) with a doubled horizontal bar.—Gk. δι-, double; and γαμμα, the letter *g*. See Di- (2), and Gamut.

DIGEST, to assimilate food, arrange. (L.) In Shak. L. L. L. v. 2. 289; Merch. iii. 5. 95. [But *digestion* is much earlier, viz. in Chaucer, C. T. 10661 (F 347); so also *digestive*, id. 14967 (B 4151); and *digestible*, id. 439.] ME. *digest*, used as a pp. = digested; Lydgate, Minor Poems, p. 195.—L. *digestus*, pp. of *dīgerere*, to carry apart, separate, dissolve, digest.—L. *dī-* = *dis-*, apart; and *gerere*, to

carry. See Jest. Der. *digest*, sb. (L. *dīgestum*), *-er*, *-ible*, *-ion*, *-ive*, *-ibil-i-ty*.

DIGHT, prepared, disposed, adorned. (L.) Nearly obsolete. 'The clouds in thousand liveries *dight*;' Milton, L'All. 62. *Dight* is here short for *dighted*, so that the infinitive also takes the form *dight*. 'And have a care you *dight* things handsomely;' Beaum. and Fletcher, Coxcomb, Act iv. sc. 3 (end). ME. *dihten*, *diʒten*, verb; the pp. *dight* is in Chaucer, C. T. 14447 (B 3719). AS. *dihtan*, to set in order, dispose, arrange, prescribe, appoint; Luke, xxii. 29.—L. *dictāre*, to dictate, prescribe. See Dictate. ¶ Similarly, the G. *dichten*, MHG. *tihten*, *dihten*, is borrowed from the same L. verb.

DIGIT, a finger, a figure in arithmetic. (L.) 'Computable by *digits*;' Sir T. Browne, Vulg. Errors, b. iv. c. 12. § 23.—L. *digitus*, a finger, a toe; the sense of 'figure' arose from counting on the fingers. ¶ Gk. δάκτυλος, a finger, seems to be unrelated. Der. *digit-al*, *-ate*, *-at-ed*, *-at-ion*.

DIGNIFY, to make worthy, exalt. (F.—L.) In Shak. Two Gent. ii. 4. 158.—OF. *dignifier*, to dignify (Godefroy); omitted in Cotgrave, but given in Sherwood's index to that work.—Late L. *dignificāre*, to think worthy, lit. to make worthy.—L. *digni-*, for *digno-*, for *dignus*, worthy; and *-ficāre*, a suffix due to *facere*, to make. See Dignity and Fact. Der. *dignifi-ed*.

DIGNITY, worth, rank. (F.—L.) In early use. ME. *dig-netee*, *dignitee*, Chaucer, C. T. 13386 (B 1646); spelt *dignete* in Hali Meidenhad, ed. Cockayne, p. 15, l. 3.—OF. *dignité*, *digniteit*.—L. *dignitātem*, acc. of *dignitās*, worth.—L. *dignus*, worthy; perhaps related to *decus*, esteem, and *decet*, it is fitting. Brugmann, i. § 762 (3). Der. *dignit-ar-y*. Doublet, *dainty*, q.v.

DIGRAPH, a double sign for a single sound. (Gk.) Modern. Made from Gk. δι-, double, and γράφειν, to write.

DIGRESS, to step aside, go from the subject. (L.) In Shak. Romeo, iii. 3. 127. [The sb. *digression* is much older, and occurs in Thynne's edition of Chaucer, Troilus, i. 143; the MSS. have *digressioun*.]—L. *digressus*, pp. of *dīgredī*, to go apart, step aside, digress.—L. *dī-* = *dis-*, apart; and *gradī*, to step; cf. *gradus*, a step. See Grade. Der. *digress-ion*, *-ion-al*, *-ive*, *-ive-ly*.

DIJUDICATE, to judge between two parties, to decide. (L.) Phillips (1658) has *dijudication*.—L. *diiūdicātus*, pp. of *diiūdicāre*, to decide.—L. *dī-*, apart; and *iūdicāre*, to judge. See Di- (1) and Judge.

DIKE, a trench, a ditch with its embankment, a bank. (E.) ME. *dik*, *dyk* (also *diche*, whence the mod. E. *ditch*). 'In a *dyke* falle' = fall in a ditch (where 2 MSS. have *diche*); P. Plowman, B. xi. 417. AS. *dīc*, a dike; 'hī dulfon āne mycle *dīc*' = they dug a great dike; AS. Chron. an. 1016. + Du. *dijk*; Icel. *dīki*; Dan. *dige*; Swed. *dike*; MHG. *tīch*, a marsh, canal; G. *teich*, a pond, tank; the mod. G. *deich*, a dike, being merely borrowed from Low G. Der. *dig*, q.v.

DILACERATE, to tear asunder. (L.) Used by Sir T. Browne, Vulg. Errors, b. iii. c. 6. § 3.—L. *dīlacerātus*, pp. of *dīlacerāre*, to tear apart.—L. *dī-* = *dis-*, apart; and *lacerāre*, to tear. See Lacerate. Der. *dilacerat-ion*.

DILAPIDATE, to pull down stone buildings, to ruin. (L.) In Levins, 41. 36. Used by Cotgrave, who translates F. *dilapider* by 'to dilapidate, ruin, or pull down stone buildings.'—L. *dīlapidātus*, pp. of *dīlapidāre*, to destroy, lit. to scatter like stones or pelt with stones; cf. Columella, x. 330.—L. *dī-* = *dis-*, apart; and *lapid-*, stem of *lapis*, a stone. See Lapidary. Der. *dilapidat-ion*.

DILATE, to spread out, enlarge, widen. (F.—L.) 'In dylating and declaring of hys conclusion;' Sir T. More, Works, p. 648 h. [Chaucer has the sb. *dilatacioun*, C. T. 4652 (B 232).]—OF. *dilater*, 'to dilate, widen, inlarge;' Cot.—L. *dīlātus*, spread abroad; used as pp. of *differre*, but from a different root.—L. *dī-* = *dis-*, apart; and *lātus*, carried, borne, for OLat. *tlātus* = Gk. τλητός, borne, endured. —√TEL, to lift; whence L. *tollere*. Der. *dilat-er*, *-able*, *-abil-i-ty*, *-ion*, *-or-y*, *-or-i-ness*; also *dilat-at-ion* (OF. *dilatation*, which see in Cotgrave).

DILEMMA, a perplexity, puzzling situation. (L.—Gk.) In Cockeram (1642); and in Shak. Mer. Wives, iv. 5. 87; All's Well, iii. 6. 80.—L. *dilemma*.—Gk. δίλημμα, a double proposition, an argument in which one is caught between (διαλαμβάνεται) two difficulties.—Gk. δι-, twice, double; and λῆμμα, an assumption, a premiss. See Di- (2) and Lemma.

DILETTANTE, a lover of the fine arts. (Ital.—L.) Modern. The pl. *dilettanti* occurs in Burke, On a Regicide Peace (Todd).— Ital. *dilettante*, pl. *dilettanti*, a lover of the fine arts; properly pres. pt. of *dilettare*, to delight, rejoice.—L. *dēlectāre*, to delight. See Delectable. Der. *dilettante-ism*.

DILIGENT, industrious. (F.—L.) Chaucer has *diligent*, C. T. 485 (A 483); and *diligence*, id. 8071 (E 195).—OF. *diligent*; Cot. —L. *dīligentem*, acc. of *dīligens*, careful, diligent, lit. loving; pres. part. of *dīligere*, to select, to love; lit. to choose between.—L. *dī-* =

dis-, apart, between; and *legere*, to choose, cognate with Gk. λέγειν, to choose, say. See **Legend**. Der. *diligent-ly, diligence*.

DILL, the name of a plant. (E.) ME. *dille, dylle*. 'Dylle, herbe, anetum;' Prompt. Parv. p. 121. AS. *dile*; 'myntan and *dile* and *cymyn*' = mint and dill and cummin; Matt. xxiii. 23.+ Du. *dille*; Dan. *dild*; Swed. *dill*; OHG. *tilli*, MHG. *tille*, G. *dill*.

DILUTE, to wash away, mix with water, weaken. (L.) 'Diluted, alayed, tempered, mingled with water, wet, imperfect;' Blount's Gloss. ed. 1674.—L. *dīlūtus*, pp. of *diluere*, to wash away, mix with water.—L. *di-* = *dis-*, apart; and *luere*, to wash, cognate with Gk. λούειν, to wash. Der. *dilute*, adj., *dilut-ion*; from the same source, *dilu-ent, diluv-ium*, *-ial, -ian*; and see *deluge*.

DIM, obscure, dusky, dark. (E.) ME. *dim, dimme*; 'though I loke *dymme*;' P. Plowman, B. x. 179. AS. *dim*, dark; Grein, i. 194. + Icel. *dimmr*, dim; MDan. *dim*; cf. Swed. *dimmig*, foggy; *dimma*, a fog, a mist, haze; MHG. *timmer*, *timber*, dark, dim. And cf. OIrish *deim*, dark; *deme*, darkness. Der. *dim-ly, dim-ness*.

DIME, a tithe; a tenth of a dollar. (F.—L.) ME. *dyme*, P. Plowman, B. xv. 526.—OF. *disme*, *dime*.—L. *decima*, sc. *pars*, a tenth part; fem. of *decimus*, tenth.—L. *decem*, ten; see **Ten**. Doublet, *tithe*.

DIMENSION, measurement, extent. (F.—L.) 'Without any *dimensions* at al;' Sir T. More, Works, p. 1111 g.—MF. *dimension*, 'a dimension, or measuring;' Cot.—L. acc. *dimensiōnem*, from nom. *dīmensio*, a measuring; cf. *dimensus*, pp. of *dīmētīrī*, to measure off a part of a thing, to measure out.—L. *dī-* = *dis-*, apart; and *metīrī*, to measure. See **Measure**.

DIMINISH, to lessen, take from. (F.—L.) 'To fantasy [fancy] that giving to the poore is a *diminishing* of our goods;' Latimer, Sixth Ser. on Lord's Prayer (R.). [Chaucer has *diminucion*, i.e. diminution, Troilus, iii. 1335.] A coined word, made by prefixing *di-* to the E. *minish*, in imitation of L. *diminuere*, to diminish, where the prefix *dī-* (= L. *dis-*, apart) is used intensively. See **Minish**, **Minute**. Der. *diminish-able*; like L. pp. *diminūtus* are *diminut-ion* (OF. *diminution*, L. acc. *diminutiōnem*), *diminut-ive, -ive-ly, -ive-ness*.

DIMISSORY, giving leave to depart. (L.) 'Without the bishop's *dimissory* letters presbyters might not go to another dioces;' Bp. Taylor, Episcopacy Asserted, s. 39 (R.).—L. *dīmissōrius*, giving leave to go before another judge.—L. *dimissus*, pp. of *dīmittere*, to send forth, send away, dismiss.—L. *dī-*, for *dis-*, away; and *mittere*, to send. See **Dismiss**.

DIMITY, a kind of stout white cotton cloth. (Ital.—L.—Gk.) 'Dimitty, a fine sort of fustian;' Kersey's Dict. ed. 1715. 'We do vse to buy many of their silke quilts, and of their *Scamato* and *Dimite*;' Hakluyt, Voy. ii. pt. 1. p. 115 (misnumbered 127).—Ital. *dimiti*, pl. of *dimito*, 'a kind of course cotton or flanell;' Florio.—Late L. *dimitum* (pl. *dimita*), silk woven with two threads.—Gk. δίμιτος, made with a double thread.—Gk. δί-, double; and μίτος, a thread of the woof. ¶ Mr. Wedgwood quotes from Muratori (in Ducange) a passage containing the words 'amita, dimita, et trimita,' explained to mean silks woven with *one*, *two*, or *three* threads respectively. The word thus passed from Gk. into Latin, and thence into Ital. *dimito*, which is duly recorded by Florio; and so into English.

DIMORPHOUS, of two forms. (Gk.) Modern.—Gk. δίμορφ-ος, of two forms; with suffix *-ous*.—Gk. δι-, double; μορφ-ή, form; see **Di-** (2) and **Morphia**.

DIMPLE, a small hollow. (E.) In Shak. Wint. Ta. ii. 3. 101. ME. *dympull*. 'Hir chyn full choise was .. with a *dympull*;' Destruction of Troy (E.E.T.S.), l. 3060. Apparently from a base **dump* (with mutation of *u* to *y*). It answers in form to G. *tümpel*, *dümpfel*, a pool; OHG. *tumphilo*. Cf. Dan. dial. *dump*, a hollow in a field; Du. *dompelen*, to dive. All perhaps allied to Swed. dial. *dimpa*, to fall down, to plunge, str. vb. (pt. t. *damp*, supine *dumpid*). If so, the orig. sense of *dimple* was 'deep pool;' thence, a hollow place. Cf. Lith. *dùbti*, to be hollow (pres. t. *dumb-u*). See **Dingle**.

DIN, a loud noise, clamour; to sound. (E.) The sb. is ME. *din*, *dene*, *dune*; spelt *dine*, Havelok, 1860; *dune*, Layamon, i. 43; l. 1009. AS. *dyn, dyne*, noise; Grein, i. 213; *dynnan*, to make a loud sound; id. + Icel. *dynr*, a din; *dynja*, to pour, rattle down, like hail or rain; Swed. *dån*, a din; *dåna*, to ring; Dan. *døn*, a rumble, booming; *døne*, to rumble, boom; Skt. *dhuni*-, roaring, a torrent; *dhvani-*, a sound, din; *dhvan*, to sound, roar, buzz.

DINE, to take dinner, eat. (F.—L.) ME. *dinen, dynen*; P. Plowman, B. v. 75; Rob. of Glouc. p. 558. [The sb. is *diner* (with one *n*), P. Plowman, B. xiii. 28; Rob. of Glouc. p. 561.]—OF. *disner*, mod. F. *dîner*, to dine.—Late L. **disjūnāre*, short for **disjējūnāre*, to break one's fast.—L. *dis-*, away; and *iēiūnāre*, to fast, from *iēiūnus*, fasting. See Romania, viii. 95; where it is explained that OF. *disner*, inf., answers to Late L. type **disjūnāre*, whilst the Late L. type **disjúno* (1 p. s. pr.) produced the OF. *desjeune*, F. *déjeune*, I breakfast. The difference in form is due to the difference

in accentuation. Somewhat similar is the formation of F. *aider* from L. *adiūtāre*. See **Aid**. Körting, § 3007. Der. *dinner* (ME. *diner*, from OF. *disner*, where the infin. is used as a sb.).

DING, to throw violently, beat, urge, ring. (E.) 'To *ding* (i.e. fling) the book a coit's distance from him;' Milton, Areopagitica, ed. Hales, p. 32. ME. *dingen*, pt. t. *dang, dong*, pp. *dungen*. 'Godrich stert up, and on him *dong*;' Havelok, 1147; *dungen*, id. 227. Though not found in AS., the word is probably E. rather than Scand.; for it is a *strong* verb, whereas the related Scand. verbs are but *weak*. Cf. Icel. *dengja*, to hammer; Dan. *dænge*, to bang; Swed. *dünga*, to bang, thump, beat. Cf. also MDan. *dinge*, to blunt an edge by beating on it; OHG. *tangol*, a hammer. Teut. type **dengan-*, pt. t. **dang*, pp. **dunganoz*. See **Dangle**, **Dung**.

DING-DONG, an imitation of the sound of a bell. (E.) In Shak. Temp. i. 2. 403. A reduplicated form, with varied vowel; from *dong*, an imitative word echoing a ringing sound.

DINGHY, **DINGEY**, a rowing-boat. (Bengali.) From Beng. *ḍiṇgī*, a boat, a wherry (H. H. Wilson); and see Yule.

DINGLE, a small dell, little valley. (E.) In Milton, Comus, 312. ME. *dingel*, a deep hollow, an abyss; 'deopre then eni sea-*dingle*,' deeper than any sea-pool; O. Eng. Homilies, ed. Morris, i. 263. [It thus answers in sense to what appears to have been the orig. sense of *dimple*; cf. the variant *dimble*. 'Within a gloomie *dimble* shee doth dwell, Downe in a pitt, ore-grown with brakes and briars;' Ben Jonson, Sad Shepherd, A. ii. sc. 2. 'And satyrs, that in slades and gloomy *dimbles* dwell;' Drayton, Poly-Olbion, s. 2. l. 190.] β. It is clearly related to ME. *dung*, a pool; 'so deop *dung* that ha druncneth therin,' so deep a pool that they are drowned therein; Seinte Marherete, ed. Cockayne, p. 15, l. 21. Cf. OHG. *tunc*, an underground cave; Lith. *deng-ti*, to cover. See **Dimple**.

DINGO, the native Australian dog. (New S. Wales.) New S. Wales *dingo*, written *teingo* in 1798 (Morris).

DINGY, soiled, dusky, dimmed. (E.) Very rare in books. 'Dingy, foul, dirty; *Somersetshire*;' Halliwell. So also 'dingy, dirty;' Pegge, Kenticisms (1736). This sense of 'dirty' is the original one. The word really means 'dung-y' or 'soiled with dung.' The *i* is due to an AS. *y*, which is the modification of *u*, by the usual rule; cf. *fill*, from *full*: whilst *ng* has taken the sound of *nj*. β. This change from *u* to *i* (for *y*) appears as early as the tenth century; we find 'stercoratio, *dingiung*' = a dunging; Ælfric's Vocab., pr. in Voc. 104. 8. γ. We can explain the change from *ng* to *nj*, by observing that there was an AS. weak f. *dyncge* as well as the str. f. *dung*. Cf. *mixendinegan*, acc., lit. mixen-dung; Anglia, vol. ix. p. 261, l. 9; also AS. *gedyngan*, weak vb., prov. E. *dinge*, to soil. And cf. *stingy*, from *sting*. See **Dung**. ¶ Cf. Swed. *dyngig*, dungy, from *dynga*, dung.

DINNER; see under **Dine**.

DINT, a blow, force. (E.) ME. *dint, dunt, dent*; spelt *dint*, Will. of Palerne, 1234, 2784; *dent*, id. 2757; *dunt*, Layamon, 8420. AS. *dynt*, a blow; Grein, i. 213. + Icel. *dyntr*, a dint; *dynta*, to dint; Swed. dial. *dunt*, a stroke; *dunta*, to strike, to shake. All from a Teut. base *dunt-*. See **Dent**.

DIOCESE, a bishop's province. (F.—L.—Gk.) ME. *diocyse*, Chaucer, C. T. 666 (A 664).—OF. *diocese*, 'a diocess;' Cot.—L. *diœcēsis*.—Gk. διοίκησις, housekeeping, administration, a province, a diocese.—Gk. διοικέω, I keep house, conduct, govern.—Gk. δι-= διά, through, throughout; and οἰκέω, I inhabit, from οἶκος, a house, an abode; cognate with L. *uīcus*, a village (whence E. *wick*, a town), and Skt. *veça-s*, a house. Der. *dioces-an*.

DIŒCIOUS, having male and female flowers on separate plants. (Gk.) Botanical. From mod. Latin *diœcia* (Linnæus, 1735); Gk. type **διοικία*, sb., from **δίοικος*, adj. having two houses.—Gk. δι-, double; and οἶκος, a house. See above.

DIOPTRICS, the science of the refraction of light. (Gk.) 'Dioptricks, a part of optics, which treats of the different refractions of the light, passing thro' transparent mediums;' Kersey's Dict. ed. 1715.—Gk. τὰ διοπτρικά, the science of dioptrics.—Gk. διοπτρικός, belonging to the use of the δίοπτρα, an optical instrument for taking heights, &c.—Gk. δι-ά, through; and ὀπ-, as in Ionic ὄπ-ωπ-α, I have seen, ὄψ-ομαι, I shall see; with agential suffix *-τρα*, f. Cf. ὀπτήρ, a spy. See **Optics**. Der. *dioptric, -al*.

DIORAMA, a scene seen through a small opening. (Gk.) Modern. A term applied to various optical exhibitions, and to the building in which they are shown; first shown in 1823. Coined from Gk. δι-=διά, through; and ὅραμα, a sight, thing seen, from ὁράω, I see; see **Wary**. Der. *dioram-ic*.

DIP, to plunge, immerge, dive for a short time. (E.) ME. *dippen*; Prick of Conscience, 8044. Also *duppen*, Trevisa, tr. of Higden, i. 117. AS. *dippan*, Exod. xii. 22; *dyppan*, Levit. iv. 17.+ Dan. *dyppe*, to dip, plunge, immerge. Teut. type **dup-jan*, causal form from the base **dup-*, weak grade of **deup-*, as seen in AS. *dēop*, deep. See **Deep**. The second grade is *daup-*, as seen in Goth. *daupjan*, to dip, immerse, baptise, Du. *doopen*, to baptise. Swed. *döpa*, to baptise, G. *taufen*, OHG. *toufan*, to baptise. See **Deep** and **Dive**. Der. *dip*, sb.; *dipp-er*.

DIPHTHERIA, a throat-disease, accompanied with the formation of a false membrane. (Gk.) First in 1857. Coined from Gk. διφθέρα, leather; from the leathery nature of the membrane formed. Allied to Gk. δεψεῖν, to make supple; (hence, to prepare leather). Cf. L. *depsere*, to knead, make supple, tan leather. Der. *diphther-it-ic*.

DIPHTHONG, a union of two vowel sounds in one syllable. (F.—L.—Gk.) Spelt *dipthong* in Ben Jonson, Eng. Grammar, ch. 5; and in Sherwood's Index to Cotgrave, which also gives the MF. *diphthongue*.—MF. *dipthongue*, 'diphthonge;' Palsgrave (1530).—L. acc. *diphthongum*, f.—Gk. δίφθογγος, with two sounds.—Gk. δι- = δίς, double; and φθογγός, voice, sound, from Gk. φθέγγομαι, I utter a sound, cry out. Cf. Lith. *speng-ti*, to resound.

DIPLOMA, a document conferring a privilege. (L.—Gk.) 'Diploma, a charter of a prince, letters patents, a writ or bull;' Blount's Gloss. ed. 1674.—L. *diplōma* (gen. *diplōmatis*), a document conferring a privilege.—Gk. δίπλωμα, lit. anything folded double; a license, diploma, which seems to have been originally folded double.—Gk. διπλόος, twofold, double.—Gk. δι- = δίς, double; and πλόος, with the sense of E. *-fold*, respecting which see **Double**. Der. *diplomat-ic* (from the stem *diplōmat-*), *-ic-al*, *-ic-al-ly*, *-ist*, *diplomac-y*.

DIPSOMANIA, a morbid thirst for stimulants. (Gk.) Modern. From Gk. διψο-, for δίψος, thirst; and μανία, mania.

DIPTERA, an order of insects with two wings. (Gk.) First in 1819. In Kersey's Dict. ed. 1715, we find 'Dipteron, in architecture, a building that has a double wing or isle' (*sic*). Coined from Gk. δι- = δίς, double; and πτερόν, a wing, from πτ-, weak grade of πετ-, as in πέτ-ομαι, I fly.—√ PET, to fly; see **Feather**.

DIPTYCH, a double-folding tablet. (L.—Gk.) First in 1622. 'Diptychs, folded tables, a pair of writing tables;' Kersey, ed. 1715. —Late L. *diptycha*, pl.—Gk. δίπτυχα, pl. a pair of tablets.—Gk. δίπτυχος, folded, doubled.—Gk. δι-, for δίς, double; and πτυχ-ή, a fold; cf. also πτυκτός, folded, from πτύσσειν, to fold.

DIRE, fearful, terrible. (L.) Shak. has *dire*, Rich. II, i. 3. 127; *direful*, Temp. i. 2. 26; *direness*, Macb. v. 5. 14.—L. *dirus*, dreadful, horrible. Perhaps allied to Gk. δεινός, frightful; cf. δειλός, frightened, cowardly; connected with δέος, fear, δείδειν, to fear. Der. *dire-ful*, *-ful-ly*, *-ness* (all hybrid compounds).

DIRECT, straight onward, outspoken, straight. (L.) ME. *directe*, Chaucer, On the Astrolabe, ed. Skeat, ii. 35. 11. [He also has the verb *directen*; see Troil. b. v. last stanza but one.]—L. *directus*, straight, pp. of *dirigere*, to straighten, direct.—L. *dī-*, for *dis-*, apart; and *regere*, to rule, control. See **Rector**, and **Right**. Der. *direct-ly*, *-ness*; also *direct*, vb., *-ion*, *-ive*, *-or*, *-or-ate*, *-or-y*, *-or-i-al*. Doublet, *dress*, q.v.; and see *dirge*.

DIRGE, a funeral song or hymn, lament. (L.) ME. *dirige*; 'placebo and *dirige*;' P. Plowman, C. iv. 467; and see Ancren Riwle, p. 22; Prompt. Parv. p. 121. [See note to the line in P. Pl., which explains that an antiphon in the office for the dead began with the words (from Psalm v. 8) '*dirige*, Dominus meus, in conspectu tuo uitam meam;' whence the name.]—L. *dirige* direct thou, imperative mood of *dirigere*, to direct. See **Direct**.

DIRK, a poniard, a dagger. (Du.?) 'With a drawn dirk and bended [cocked] pistol;' State Trials, Marquis of Argyle, an. 1661 (R.). First found in 1602, spelt *dork* (N.E.D.). Probably *dork* is the same word with Du. *dolk*, Swed. and Dan. *dolk*, G. *dolch*, a dagger, poniard. This is thought to be a word of Slavonic origin; cf. Polish *tulich*, a dagger. ¶ Irish *duirc*, a poniard, is borrowed from E.

DIRT, any foul substance, mud, dung. (Scand.) ME. *drit*, by the shifting of the letter *r* so common in English. '*Drit* and *donge* = dirt and dung; K. Alisaunder, ed. Weber, 4718; cf. Havelok, 682.—Icel. *drit*, dirt, excrement of birds; *drita*, to void excrement; cf. Swed. dial. *drita*, with same sense; Rietz. + Du. *drijten*, with same sense; cf. MDu. *drijt*, dirt (Kilian). ¶ In AS. we find only the verb *gedritan*; it is rare, but occurs in Cockayne's Leechdoms, i. 364. Der. *dirt-y*, *dirt-i-ly*, *dirt-i-ness*.

DIS-, prefix. (L.) 1. From L. *dis-*, apart; *dis* and *bis* are both forms from an older *duis*, which is from L. *duo*, two; cf. Goth. *twis-*, apart. Brugmann, i. § 279. Hence the sense is 'in two,' i.e. apart, away. 2. The Gk. form of the prefix is *di-*; see **Di- (2)**. 3. The L. *dis-* became *des-* in OF., mod. F. *dé-*; this appears in several words, as in *de-feat*, *de-fy*, &c., where the prefix must be carefully distinguished from that due to L. *dē*. 4. Again, in some cases, *dis-* is a late substitution for an older *des-*, which is the OF. *des-*; thus Chaucer has *desarmen* from the OF. *des-armer*, in the sense of *dis-arm*.

DISABLE, to make unable, disqualify. (L.; *and* F.—L.) In Spenser, F. Q. v. 4. 31; and see Trench, Select Glossary. Made by prefixing L. *dis-* to *able*. See **Dis-** and **Able**. Der. *disabil-i-ty*.

DISABUSE, to free from abuse, undeceive. (L.; *and* F.—L.) In Clarendon, Civil War, vol. i. pref. p. 21 (R.); and in Cotgrave, s.v. *des-abuser*. From L. *dis-* and *abuse*. See **Dis-** and **Abuse**.

DISADVANTAGE, want of advantage, injury. (F.—L.) In Shak. Cor. i. 6. 49. ME. *disauauntage*, Trevisa, tr. of Higden, ii. 57. —OF. *desavantage* (Hatzfeld).—OF. *des-* < L. *dis-*, apart; and OF. *avantage*. See **Dis-** and **Advantage**. Der. *disadvantage-ous*, *-ous-ly*.

DISAFFECT, to make unfriendly. (L.; *and* F.—L.) 'Disaffected to the king;' State Trials, Hy. Sherfield, an. 1632 (R.). From L. *dis-* and *affect*. See **Dis-** and **Affect**. Der. *disaffected-ly*, *-ness*, *-ion*.

DISAFFOREST, to deprive of the privilege of forest lands; to render common. (L.) 'There was much land *disafforested*;' Howell's Letters, b. iv. let. 16. § 4. From L. *dis-*, away; and Law L. *afforestāre*, to make into a forest, from *af-* (for *ad*) and *foresta*, a forest. See **Dis-** and **Forest**.

DISAGREE, to be at variance. (F.—L.) In Tyndal, Works, p. 133, col. 2.—OF. *desagreer* (Hatzfeld).—OF. *des-* < L. *dis-*, apart; and OF. *agreer*. See **Dis-** and **Agree**. Der. *disagree-able*, *-abl-y*, *-able-ness*, *-ment*. ¶ The adj. *disagreeable* was suggested by OF. *desagreable*.

DISALLOW, to refuse to allow. (F.—L.) ME. *desallowen*, to refuse to assent to, to dispraise, refuse, reject. 'Al that is humble he *desalloweth*;' Gower, C. A. i. 83; bk. i. 1237.—OF. *desalouer*, *desalower*, to blame (Godefroy).—OF. *des-* (L. *dis-*); and *alouer*, to approve of. See **Dis-** and **Allow (2)**. Der. *disallow-able*, *-ance*.

DISANNUL, to annul completely. (L.; *and* F.—L.) In Shak. Com. Err. i. 1. 145. From L. *dis-*, apart, here used intensively; and *annul*. See **Dis-** and **Annul**. Der. *disannul-ment*.

DISAPPEAR, to cease to appear, to vanish. (L.; *and* F.—L.) In Dryden, On the death of a very Young Gentleman, l. 23; and in Cockeram (1623). From L. *dis-*, apart, away; and *appear*. See **Dis-** and **Appear**. Der. *disappear-ance*.

DISAPPOINT, to frustrate what is appointed. (F.—L.) Shak. has *disappointed* in the sense of 'unfurnished,' or 'unready;' Hamlet, i. 5. 77. Ralegh has 'such *disappointment* of expectation;' Hist. of World, b. iv. c. 5. s. 11 (R.).—OF. *desapointer*, 'to disappoint or frustrate;' Cot.—OF. *des-* < L. *dis-*, apart, away; and OF. *apointer*, to appoint. See **Appoint**. Der. *disappoint-ment*.

DISAPPROVE, not to approve, to reject. (L.; *and* F.—L.) 'And *disapproves* that care;' Milton, Sonn. to Cyriack Skinner. From L. *dis-*, away; and *approve*. See **Dis-** and **Approve**. Der. *disapprov-al*; from the same L. source, *disapprob-at-ion*.

DISARM, to deprive of arms. (F.—L.) ME. *desarmen*, Chaucer, tr. of Boethius, b. i. met. 4; l. 11.—OF. *desarmer*, 'to disarme, or deprive of weapons;' Cot.—OF. *des-*, from L. *dis-*, apart, away; and *armer*, to arm. See **Dis-** and **Arms**. Der. *disarm-a-ment*, probably an error for *disarm-ment*; see 'desarmement, a disarming;' Cot.

DISARRANGE, to disorder. (L.; *and* F.—L.) Not in early use; the older word is *disarray*. 'The whole of the arrangement, or rather *disarrangement* of their military;' Burke, On the Army Estimates (R.). From L. *dis-*, apart, away; and *arrange*. Doubtless suggested by MF. *desarrenger*, 'to unranke, disorder, disarray;' Cot. See **Dis-** and **Arrange**. Der. *disarrange-ment*.

DISARRAY, a want of order. (F.—L. *and* Teut.) In early use. ME. *disaray*, also *disray*. Thus, in Chaucer, C. T. (Pers. Tale, Remed. Luxuriæ), Group I, 927, we find the readings *desray*, *disray*, and *disaray*, as being equivalent words; *disray* occurs yet earlier, in K. Alisaunder, ed. Weber, 4353.—AF. *desarrei*, OF. *desarroi*, later *desarray*, 'disorder, confusion, disarray;' Cot. There was also an AF. form *desray*, Stat. of the Realm, i. 246; OF. *desroi*, later *desroy*, 'disorder, disarray;' id.; see Godefroy. β. The former is from OF. *des-*, L. *dis-*, apart, away; and AF. *arrei*, OF. *arroi*, compounded of *ar-* (standing for L. *ad*, to) and AF. *rei*, OF. *roi*, order. In the latter, the syllable *ar-* is omitted. See **Dis-** and **Array**. Der. *disarray*, verb.

DISASTER, a calamity. (F.—L.) See Shak. Hamlet, i. 1. 118; All's Well, i. 1. 187.—MF. *desastre*, 'a disaster, misfortune, calamity;' Cot.—OF. *des-*, for L. *dis-*, with a sinister sense; and MF. *astre*, 'a star, a planet; also, destiny, fate, fortune, hap;' Cot., from L. *astrum*, a star; cf. '*astrum sinistrum*, infortunium;' Ducange. See **Astral**, **Aster**. ¶ The MF. *desastre* was suggested by Ital. *disastro* (Hatzfeld). Der. *disastr-ous*, *-ous-ly*.

DISAVOW, to disclaim, deny. (F.—L.) ME. *desavowen*; P. Plowman, C. iv. 322.—OF. *desavouer*, 'to disadvow, disallow;' Cot. —OF. *des-*, for L. *dis-*, apart; and OF. *avoer*, *avouer* (Godefroy), spelt *advouer* in Cotgrave, 'to advow, avouch.' See **Dis-** and **Avow**. Der. *disavow-al*.

DISBAND, to disperse a band. (F.—L. *and* Teut.) In Cotgrave. —OF. *desbander*, 'to loosen, unbind, unbend; also to casse [cashier] or *disband*;' Cot.—OF. *des-*, for L. *dis-*, apart; and OF. *bander*, to bend a bow, to band together. See **Dis-** and **Band** (2). Der. *disband-ment.*

DISBELIEVE, to refuse belief to. (L. *and* E.) In Kersey's Dict. ed. 1715; earlier, in Cudworth, Intellectual System, p. 18 (R.). From L. *dis-*, used negatively; and E. *believe.* See **Dis-** and **Believe.** Der. *disbeliev-er, disbelief.*

DISBURDEN, DISBURTHEN, to free from a burden. (L. *and* E.) In Shak. Rich. II, ii. 1. 229. From L. *dis-*, apart; and E. *burden* or *burthen.* See **Dis-** and **Burden.**

DISBURSE, to pay out of a purse. (F.—L. *and* Gk.) In Shak. Macb. i. 2. 61. Palsgrave has *disbourse*, p. 517.—OF. *desbourser*, of which Palsgrave gives the pp. *desboursé*, 'disbursed, laid out of a purse.'—OF. *des-*, from L. *dis-*, apart; and F. *bourse*, a purse. See **Dis-** and **Bursar.** Der. *disburse-ment.*

DISC, DISK, a round plate. (L.—Gk.) [In very early use in the form *dish*, q. v.] ' The *disk* of Phœbus, when he climbs on high Appears at first but as a bloodshot eye;' Dryden, tr. of Ovid, Metam. xv. 284.—L. *discus*, a quoit, a plate.—Gk. δίσκος, a quoit; from δικεῖν, to cast. Brugmann, i. § 744. Der. *disc-ous.* See **Desk, Dish.**

DISCARD, to throw away useless cards, to reject. (L.; *and* F.—L.—Gk.) In Spenser, F. Q. v. 5. 8. Sometimes spelt *decard*; see Richardson. From L. *dis-*, apart; and *card.* See **Dis-** and **Card.**

DISCERN, to distinguish, separate, judge. (F.—L.) ME. *discernen*; Chaucer, Troil. b. iii. l. 9.—OF. *discerner*; Cot.—L. *discernere*, to distinguish.—L. *dis-*, apart; and *cernere*, to separate, cognate with Gk. κρίνειν, to separate. See **Critic.** Der. *discern-er, -ible, -ibl-y, -ment;* see also *discreet, discriminate.*

DISCHARGE, to free from a charge, unload, acquit. (F.—L. *and* C.) In early use. ME. *deschargen*; K. Alisaunder, ed. Weber, 3868.—OF. *descharger*, 'to discharge, disburden;' Cot.—OF. *des-*, from L. *dis-*, apart, away; and *charger*, to charge, load. See **Dis-** and **Charge.** Der. *discharge*, sb., *discharg-er.*

DISCIPLE, a learner, follower. (F.—L.) In early use. In P. Plowman, B. xiii. 430. *Discepline* is in Ancren Riwle, p. 294.—OF. *disciple* (Supp. to Godefroy).—L. *discipulum*, acc. of *discipulus*, a learner.—L. *discere*, to learn; allied to *docēre*, to teach. See **Docile.** Der. *disciple-ship.* From the same source is *discipline*, from OF. *discipline*, L. *disciplina*; whence also *disciplin-able, -ar-i-an, -ar-y.*

DISCLAIM, to renounce claim to. (F.—L.) Cotgrave translates *desadvouer* by ' to disadvow, disclaime, refuse.'—AF. *desclamer*, Year-books of Edw. I., 1302-3, p. 83.—OF. *des-*, from L. *dis-*, apart, away; and F. *clamer*, from L. *clāmāre.* See **Dis-** and **Claim.** Der. *disclaim-er.*

DISCLOSE, to reveal, unclose, open. (F.—L.) ' And mihte of no man be *desclosed*;' Gower, C. A. ii. 262; bk. v. 4030.—OF. *desclos*, disclosed, pp. of *desclorre*, to unclose; Cotgrave gives ' secret *desclos*, disclosed, revealed.'—OF. *des-*, from L. *dis-*, apart, away; and OF. *clorre*, to shut in, from L. *claudere*, to shut. See **Dis-** and **Close.** Der. *disclos-ure.*

DISCOLOUR, to spoil the colour of. (F.—L.) Chaucer has *discoloured*, C. T. 16132 (G 664).—OF. *descolorer*, later *descoulourer*, as in Cot.—L. *dis-*, apart, away; and *colōrāre*, to colour, from *color-*, stem of *color*, colour. See **Dis-** and **Colour.**

DISCOMFIT, to defeat or put to the rout. (F.—L.) In Barbour's Bruce, xii. 459. [Chaucer has *disconfiture*, C. T. 1010 (A 1008).]—OF. *desconfit*, pp. of *desconfire*, 'to discomfit, vanquish, defeat;' Cot.; and see Godefroy. [The *n* before *f* easily passed into *m*, for convenience of pronunciation; the same change occurs in the word *comfort.*]—OF. *des-*, prefix; and *confire*, to preserve, make ready.—L. *dis-*, apart; and *conficere*, to finish, preserve. See **Dis-** and **Comfit.** Der. *discomfit-ure*, from OF. *desconfiture*; Cot.

DISCOMFORT, to deprive of comfort. (F.—L.) ME. *discomforten*; Rob. of Brunne, tr. of Langtoft, p. 70.—OF. *desconforter*; Cot. gives ' se desconforter, to be discomforted.'—OF. *des-*, prefix, from L. *dis-*, apart, away; and *conforter*, to comfort. See **Dis-** and **Comfort.**

DISCOMMEND, to dispraise. (L.; *and* F.—L.) In Frith's Works, p. 156, col. 2. From L. *dis-*, apart; and *commend.* See **Dis-** and **Commend.**

DISCOMMON, to deprive of the right of common. (L.; *and* F.—L.) ' Whiles thou *discommonest* thy neighbour's kyne;' Bp. Hall, b. v. sat. 3. l. 72. From L. *dis-*, apart; and *common.* See **Dis-** and **Common.**

DISCOMPOSE, to deprive of composure. (L.; *and* F.—L. *and* Gk.) Bacon has *discomposed* in the sense of 'removed from a position;' Hist. of Hen. VII, ed. Lumby, p. 217, l. 33.—L. *dis-*, apart; and *compose.* See **Dis-** and **Compose.** Der. *discompos-ure.*

DISCONCERT, to frustrate a plot, defeat, disturb. (F.—L.) In Bailey's Dict. ed. 1731, vol. ii.—MF. *disconcerter*, of which Cot.

gives the pp. ' *disconcerté*, disordered, confused, set awry.'—MF. *dis-* < L. *dis-*, apart; and *concerter*, to concert. See **Dis-** and **Concert.**

DISCONNECT, to separate. (L.) Occurs in Burke, On the French Revolution (R.).—L. *dis-*, apart; and **Connect**, q. v.

DISCONSOLATE, without consolation. (L.) ' And this Spinx awaped and amate Stoode al dismaied and *disconsolate*;' Lydgate, Storie of Thebes, pt. i. § 14.—Late L. *disconsōlātus*, comfortless.— L. *dis-*, apart; and *consōlātus*, pp. of *consōlāri*, to console. See **Dis-** and **Console.** Der. *disconsolate-ness.*

DISCONTENT, not content, dissatisfied. (L.; *and* F.—L.) ' That though I died *discontent* I lived and died a mayde;' Gascoigne, Complaint of Philomene, st. 69.—L. *dis-*, apart; and **Content**, q. v. Der. *discontent*, sb.; *discontent*, verb; *discontent-ed, -ed-ly, -ed-ness, -ment.*

DISCONTINUE, to give up, leave. (F.—L.) In Shak. Merch. of Ven. iii. 4. 75.—MF. *discontinuer*, 'to discontinue, surcease;' Cot.—L. *dis-*, apart, used negatively; and *continuāre*, to continue. See **Dis-** and **Continue.** Der. *discontinu-ance, -at-ion* (MF. *discontinuation*; Cotgrave).

DISCORD, want of concord. (F.—L.) ME. *descord, discord.* Spelt *descord* [not *discord*, as in Richardson] in Rob. of Glouc. p. 196; l. 4039.—OF. *descord* (Roquefort); later *discord*, Cot.; verbal sb. from OF. *descorder*, to quarrel, disagree; Godefroy.—L. *discordāre*, to be at variance.—L. *dis-*, apart; and *cord-*, stem of *cor*, the heart, cognate with E. **Heart**, q. v. Der. *discord-ant* (F. *discordant*, explained by Cotgrave to mean 'discordant, jarring,' pres. pt. of *discorder*); *discordant-ly, discordance, discordanc-y.* ¶ The special application of *discord* and *concord* to musical sounds is probably due in some measure to confusion with *chord.*

DISCOUNT, to make a deduction for ready money payment. (F.—L.) Formerly spelt *discompt.* ' All which the conqueror did *discompt*;' Butler, Hudibras, pt. ii. c. 3. l. 1105. ' *Discount*, to count, or reckon off;' Gazophylacium Anglic. ed. 1689.—OF. *desconter*, to relate; later *descompter*, ' to account back, or make a back reckoning;' Cot.—OF. *des-* < L. *dis-*, apart, away; and *conter, compter*, to count, from *computāre*, to compute, count. See **Dis-** and **Count** (2). Der. *discount*, sb.; *discount-able.*

DISCOUNTENANCE, to abash. (F.—L.) ' A great taxer of his people, and *discountenancer* of his nobility;' Bacon, Life of Hen. VII, ed. Lumby, p. 112. l. 20. ' Whom they . . . *discountenaunce*;' Spenser, Teares of the Muses, l. 340.—MF. *descontenancer*, to abash; see Cotgrave.—OF. *des-* < L. *dis-*, apart; and *contenance* the countenance. See **Dis-** and **Countenance.**

DISCOURAGE, to dishearten. (F.—L.) ' How th'erle of Chartres *discoraged* th'emperour;' Caxton, Godfrey of Bologne, ch. 132 (heading).—OF. *descourager*, ' to discourage, dishearten;' Cot.— OF. *des-* < L. *dis-*, apart; and *courage*, courage. See **Dis-** and **Courage.** Der. *discourage-ment.*

DISCOURSE, a discussion, conversation. (F.—L.) ME. *discours*, i. e. reason; Chaucer, tr. of Boethius, b. v. pr. 4. l. 134.—OF. *discours*, Cot.—L. *discursus*, a running about; also, conversation.— L. *discursus*, pp. of *discurrere*, to run about.—L. *dis-*, apart; and *currere*, to run. See **Dis-** and **Course.** Der. *discourse*, verb; also *discurs-ion, -ive* (like L. pp. *discursus*).

DISCOURTEOUS, uncourteous. (F.—L.) In Spenser, F. Q. vi. 3. 34.—OF. *discortois*, 'discourteous;' Cot.—OF. *dis-* = L. *dis-*, apart, here used negatively; and OF. *cortois, corteis*, courteous. See **Dis-** and **Courteous.** Der. *discourteous-ly;* from same source, *discourtes-y.*

DISCOVER, to uncover, lay bare, reveal, detect. (F.—L.) ME. *discoueren*, Rom. of the Rose, 4402.—OF. *descovrir*, MF. *descouvrir*, ' to discover;' Cot.—OF. *des-*, from L. *dis-*, apart, away; and *couvrir*, to cover; see **Dis-** and **Cover.** Der. *discover-er, -able, -y.*

DISCREDIT, want of credit. (L.; *and* F.—L.) As sb. in Shak. Wint. Tale, v. 2. 133; as vb. in Meas. iii. 2. 261. From L. *dis-*, apart, here used in a negative sense; and **Credit**, q. v. Der. *discredit*, verb; *discredit-able.*

DISCREET, wary, prudent. (F.—L.) ME. *discret*, P. Plowman, C. vi. 84; Chaucer, C. T. 520 (A 518).—OF. *discret*, 'discreet;' Cot.—L. *discrētus*, pp. of *discernere*, to discern. See **Discern.** Der. *discreet-ness; discret-ion* (Gower, C. A. iii. 156; bk. vii. 2116), *-ion-al, -ion-al-ly, -ion-ar-y, -ion-ar-i-ly;* also *discrete* (=L. *discrētus*, separate), *discret-ive, -ive-ly.*

DISCREPANT, differing. (F.—L.) In Sir T. More, Works, p. 262 h. ' *Discrepant* in figure;' Sir T. Elyot, The Governour, b. i. c. 17, l. 199 (in Spec. of Eng. ed. Skeat.)—MF. *discrepant*, 'discrepant, different;' Cot.—L. *discrepantem*, acc. of *discrepans*, pres. pt. of *discrepāre*, to differ in sound.—L. *dis-*, apart; and *crepāre*, to make a noise, crackle. See **Decrepit.** Der. *discrep-ance, -anc-y.*

DISCRIMINATE, to discern, distinguish. (L.) ' *Discriminate*, to divide, or put a difference betwixt;' Blount's Gloss. ed. 1674.—

L. *discrīminātus*, pp. of *discrīmināre*, to divide, separate.—L. *discrīmin-*, stem of *discrīmen*, a space between, separation.—L. *discernere* (pt. t. *discrē-uī*, pp. *discrē-tus*), to discern, separate. See **Discern.** Der. *discriminat-ion*, *-ive*, *-ive-ly*.

DISCURSIVE, desultory, digressive. (L.) Used by Ben Jonson, Hymenæi; The Barriers, l. 5. See **Discourse.**

DISCUSS, to examine critically, sift, debate. (L.) Chaucer, Ass. of Foules, 624, has the pp. *discussed*. Again, he has 'when that nyght was *discussed*,' i. e. driven away; tr. of Boethius, b. i. met. 3, where the L. has *discussa*.—L. *discussus*, pp. of *discutere*, to strike or shake asunder; in Late L., to discus — L. *dis-*, apart; and *quatere*, to shake. See **Quash.** Der. *discuss-ive*, *-ion*.

DISDAIN, scorn, dislike, haughtiness. (F.—L.) ME. *desdeyn*, *disdeyn*, *disdeigne*; Chaucer, C. T. 791 (A 789). Gower has *desdeigneth*, C. A. i. 84.—OF. *desdein*, *desdaing*, disdain.—OF. *desdegnier* (F. *dédaigner*), to disdain.—OF. *des-*, from L. *dis-*, apart, here used in a negative sense; and *degnier*, to deign, think worthy, from L. *dignārī*, to deem worthy, *dignus*, worthy. See **Deign.** Der. *disdain*, verb; *disdain-ful*, *-ful-ly*, *-ful-ness*.

DISEASE, want of ease, sickness. (F.) ME. *disese*, want of ease, grief, vexation; Chaucer, C. T. 10781, 14777 (F 467, B 3961). —OF. *desaise*, 'a sickness, a disease, being ill at ease;' Cot.—OF. *des-*, from L. *dis-*, apart; and *aise*, ease. See **Ease.** Der. *diseas-ed*.

DISEMBARK, to land cargo, to land from a ship. (F.) In Shak. Oth. ii. 1. 210.—MF. *desembarquer*, 'to disembarke, or unload a ship; also, to land, or go ashore out of a ship;' Cot.—OF. *des-*, from L. *dis-*, apart; and *embarquer*, to embark. See **Embark.** Der. *disembark-at-ion*.

DISEMBARRASS, to free from embarrassment. (F.) Used by Bp. Berkeley, To Mr. Thomas Prior, Ex. 7 (Feb. 6, 1726).—MF. *desembarrasser*, 'to unpester, disentangle;' Cot.—OF. *des-*, from L. *dis-*, apart; and *embarrasser*, to embarrass. See **Embarrass.**

DISEMBOGUE, to discharge at the mouth, said of a river, to loose, depart. (Span.—L.) The final *-gue* is an error for *-que*. 'He was inforced to *disemboque* at the mouth of the Amazones;' Hakluyt, Voy. iii. 636. 'My poniard Shall *disembogue* thy soul;' Massinger, Maid of Honour, Act ii. sc. 2.—Span. *desembocar*, to disembogue, flow into the sea.—Span. *des-*, from L. *dis-*, apart, away; and *embocar*, to enter the mouth, from Span. *em-*, from L. *im-*, for *in*, into, and *boca*, the mouth, from L. *bucca*, cheek, mouth.

DISEMBROIL, to free from broil or confusion. (L. and F.) In Dryden, Ovid, Met. i. 29.—L. *dis-*, apart; and F. *embrouiller*, 'to pester, intangle, incumber, intricate, confound;' Cot. See **Embroil.**

DISENCHANT, to free from enchantment. (F.—L.) 'Can all these *disenchant* me?' Massinger, Unnatural Combat, Act iv. sc. 1.—OF. *desenchanter*, 'to disinchant;' Cot.—OF. *des-*, from L. *dis-*, apart; and *enchanter*, to enchant. See **Enchant.** Der. *disenchant-ment*.

DISENCUMBER, to free, disburden. (F.) 'I have *disincumber'd* myself from rhyme;' Dryden, pref. to Antony and Cleopatra.—F. *désencombrer*; see Hatzfeld. From L. *dis-*, apart; and **Encumber**, q. v. Der. *disencumbr-ance*.

DISENGAGE, to free from engagement. (F.) In Kersey's Dict. ed. 1715; spelt *disingage* in Cotgrave.—MF. *desengager*, 'to disingage, ungage, redeem;' Cot.—OF. *des-*, from L. *dis-*, apart; and *engager*, to engage, pledge. See **Engage.** Der. *disengage-ment*.

DISENTHRAL, to free from thraldom. (L. and F. and E.) In Milton, Ps. iv. l. 4. From L. *dis-*, apart; and **Enthral**, q. v.

DISENTRANCE, to free from a trance. (L. and F.—L.) 'Ralpho, by this time *disentranc'd*;' Butler, Hudibras, pt. i. c. 3. l. 717. From L. *dis-*, apart; and **Entrance** (2), q. v.

DISFIGURE, to deprive of beauty, deform. (F.—L.) 'What list yow thus yourself to *disfigúre*?' Chaucer, Troil. ii. 223.—OF. *desfigurer*, 'to disfigure, deforme;' Cot.—OF. *des-*, from L. *dis-*, apart, away; and *figurer*, from L. *figūrāre*, to fashion, form; from *figūra*, figure. See **Figure.** Der. *disfigure-ment*.

DISFRANCHISE, to deprive of a franchise. (L. and F.) 'Sir Wylliam Fitzwilliam [was] *disfraunchysed*;' Fabyan, vol. ii. an. 1509, p. 695. From L. *dis-*, away; and **Franchise**, q. v. Der. *disfranchise-ment*.

DISGORGE, to vomit, give up prey. (F.—L.) In Shak. As You Like It, ii. 7. 69; and Caxton, Siege of Troy, leaf 224, l. 17.—OF. *desgorger*, 'to disgorge, vomit;' Cot.—OF. *des-*, from L. *dis-*, apart; and **Gorge**, q. v. Der. *disgorge-ment*.

DISGRACE, dishonour, lack of favour. (F.—L.) In Spenser, F. Q. v. 4. 23.—MF. *disgrace*, 'a disgrace, an ill fortune, hard luck;' Cot.—L. *dis-*, apart; and F. *grace*, from L. *grātia*, favour. See **Grace.** Der. *disgrace-ful*, *-ful-ly*, *-ful-ness*.

DISGUISE, to change the appearance of. (F.—L. and G.) ME. *disgysen*. 'He *disgysed* him anon;' K. Alisaunder, l. 121.—OF.

desguisier, MF. *desguiser*, 'to disguise, to counterfeit;' Cot.—OF. *des-*, from L. *dis-*, apart; and *guise*, 'guise, manner, fashion;' Cot. See **Guise.** Der. *disguis-er*, *-ment*; also *disguise*, sb.

DISGUST, to cause dislike. (F.—L.) In Cotgrave as a sb., to translate MF. *desappetit*.—MF. *desgouster*, 'to distaste, loath, dislike, abhor;' Cot.—OF. *des-*, from L. *dis-*, apart; and *gouster*, to taste, from L. *gustāre*, to taste; from *gustus*, a tasting. See **Gust** (2). Der. *disgust*, sb.; *-ing*, *-ing-ly*.

DISH, a platter. (L.—Gk.) In very early use. ME. *disch*, Ancren Riwle, p. 344. AS. *disc*, a dish; see Mark, vi. 25, where the Vulgate has *in disco*.—L. *discus*, a disc, quoit, platter.—Gk. δίσκος, a quoit. β. *Dish* is a doublet of *Disc*, q.v.; *desk* is a third form of the same word; and see *dais*.

DISHABILLE, another form of **Deshabille**, q.v.

DISHEARTEN, to discourage. (Hybrid; L. and E.) In Shak. Macb. ii. 3. 37. Coined from L. prefix *dis-*, apart; and E. *hearten*, to put in good heart. See **Heart.**

DISHEVEL, to disorder the hair. (F.—L.) 'With . . . heare [hair] *discheveled*;' Spenser, F. Q. ii. 1. 13. '*Dischevele*, save his cappe, he rood al bare;' Chaucer, C. T. 685 (A 683); where the form is that of a F. pp.—OF. *descheveler*, 'to dischevell: *une femme toute deschevelée*, discheveled, with all her haire disorderly falling about her eares;' Cot.—OF. *des-*, from L. *dis-*, apart; and OF. *chevel* (F. *cheveu*), a hair, from L. *capillum*, acc. of *capillus*, a hair. See **Capillary.**

DISHONEST, wanting in honesty. (F.—L.) In the Romaunt of the Rose, 3442. Cf. 'shame, that eschueth al *deshonestee*;' Chaucer, Pers. Tale, Remedium Gulæ (I 833).—OF. *deshonneste*, 'dishonest, leud, bad;' Cot.—OF. *des-*, from L. *dis-*, apart; and *honneste*, or *honeste*, honest, honourable. See **Honest.** Der. *dishonest-y*.

DISHONOUR, lack of honour, shame. (F.—L.) ME. *deshonour*, King Alisaunder, ed. Weber, 3869.—OF. *deshonneur*, 'dishonour, shame;' Cot.—OF. *des-*, from L. *dis-*, apart; and *honneur*, honour. See **Honour.** Der. *dishonour*, vb.; *dishonour-able*, *-abl-y*, *-er*.

DISINCLINE, to incline away from. (L.) '*Inclined* to the king, or but *disinclined* to them;' Clarendon, Civil War, vol. ii. p. 20 (R.). From L. *dis-*, apart, away; and **Incline**, q. v. Der. *disinclin-at-ion*, *-ed*.

DISINFECT, to free from infection. (L.) In Florio, to translate Ital. *smorbare*. Coined from L. *dis-*, apart; and **Infect**, q. v. Der. *disinfect-ant*.

DISINGENUOUS, not frank. (L.) *Disingenuous* is in Dryden, tr. of Ovid's Metam., Dedication, § 1. *Disingenuity* occurs in Clarendon, Civil War, vol. i. p. 321 (R.). Coined from L. *dis-*, apart; and **Ingenuous**, q. v. Der. *disingenu-ous-ly*, *-ous-ness*, *-i-ty*.

DISINHERIT, to deprive of heritage. (L. and F.—L.) In Shak. Rich. III, i. 1. 57. Earlier, in Berners, Froissart, vol. i. c. 69 (R.). [The ME. form was *desheriten*, Havelok, 2547; this is a better form, being from OF. *desheriter*, to disinherit; see Cotgrave.] Coined from L. *dis-*, apart; and **Inherit**, q. v. Der. *disinherit-ance*, in imitation of OF. *desheritance*.

DISINTER, to take out of a grave. (L. and F.—L.) 'Which a proper education might have *disinterred*, and have brought to light;' Spectator, no. 215. Coined from L. *dis-*, apart; and **Inter**, q. v. Der. *disinter-ment*.

DISINTERESTED, free from private interests, impartial. (F.—L.) A clumsy form; the old word was *disinteress'd*, which was mistaken for a verb, causing a second addition of the suffix *-ed*. 'Because all men are not wise and good and *disinteress'd*;' Bp. Taylor, Rule of Conscience, b. ii. c. 3 (R.). This *disinteress'd* is the pp. of an obsolete vb. *disinteress*, for which see N.E.D. '*Disinteressed* or *Disinterested*, void of self-interest;' Kersey's Dict. ed. 1715.—MF. *desinteressé*, 'discharged from, or that hath forgone or lost all interest in;' Cot. This is the pp. of *desinteresser*, 'to discharge, to rid from all interest in;' id.—OF. *des-*, from L. *dis-*, apart; and MF. *interessé*, 'interested or touched in;' id., from L. *interesse*, to import, concern, compounded of *inter*, amongst, and *esse*, to be. Der. *disinterested-ly*, *-ness*.

DISINTHRAL; see **Disenthral.**

DISJOIN, to separate. (F.—L.) 'They wolde not *disioyne* nor disceuer them from the crowne;' Berners, Froissart, vol. ii. c. 200 (R.).—OF. *desjoign-*, pres. stem of *desjoindre*, 'to disjoyne, disunite;' Cot.—L. *disiungere*, to separate.—L. *dis-*, apart; and *iungere*, to join. See **Join.** And see below.

DISJOINT, to put out of joint. (F.—L.) In Shak. Macb. iii. 2. 16.—OF. *desjoinct*, 'disjoyned, parted;' Cot. This is the pp. of OF. *desjoindre*, to disjoin; see above. Der. *disjoint-ed-ness*.

DISJUNCTION, a disjoining, disunion. (L.) In Shak. Wint. Ta. iv. 4. 540.—L. acc. *disiunctiōnem*, from *disiunctio*, a separation; cf. *disiunctus*, pp. of *disiungere*, to disjoin. See **Disjoin.** From the same source, *disjunct-ive*, *-ive-ly*.

DISK, another spelling of **Disc**, q. v.

DISLIKE, not to like, to disapprove of. (L. *and* E.) In Shak. Meas. i. 2. 18. [A hybrid compound; the old form was *mislike*.]—L. *dis-*, apart; and E. **Like**, q. v. Der. *dislike*, sb.

DISLOCATE, to put out of joint. (L.) In Shak. Lear, iv. 2. 65.—Late L. *dislocātus*, pp. of *dislocāre*, to remove from its place.—L. *dis-*, apart, away; and *locāre*, to place, from *locus*, a place. See **Locus**. Der. *dislocat-ion*.

DISLODGE, to move from a resting-place. (F.) 'Dislodged was out of mine herte;' Chaucer's Dream, 2125 (a poem not by Chaucer, but belonging to the 15th century).—OF. *desloger*, 'to dislodge, remove;' Cot.—OF. *des-*, from L. *dis-*, away; and *loger*, to lodge. See **Lodge**. Der. *dislodge-ment*.

DISLOYAL, not loyal. (F.—L.) In Shak. Macb. i. 2. 52. 'Disloyall Treason;' Spenser, F. Q. ii. 7. 22.—MF. *desloyal*, 'disloyall;' Cot.—OF. *des-*, from L. *dis-*, apart; and *loial*, loyal. See **Loyal**. Der. *disloyal-ly*, *disloyal-ty*.

DISMAL, gloomy, dreary, sad. (F.—L.) 'More fowle than *dismall* day;' Spenser, F. Q. ii. 7. 26. The oldest use of the word appears to be in the phrase 'in the dismal,' signifying 'at an unlucky time;' or lit. 'in the evil days.' It occurs in Chaucer, Book of the Duchess, 1206; where the knight, in describing with what perturbation of mind he told his tale of love to his lady, says: 'I not [know not] wel how that I began, Ful euel rehersen hit I can; And eek, as helpe me God withal, I trowe hit was *in the dismal*, That was the ten woundes of Egipte.' The sense is: 'I believe it was *in an unlucky time* similar to the days of the ten plagues of Egypt.' The same phrase—*in the dismal*—occurs in The Pistil of Swete Susan (Laing's Anc. Pop. Poet. of Scotland), l. 305; and in Polit. Songs, ed. Wright, p. 303, l. 477.' β. When the equivalence of *dis-mal* to 'evil days' was forgotten, the word *days* was (tautologically) added. Thus Lydgate has: 'Her *dismale daies*, and her fatal houres;' Storie of Thebes, pt. iii. (ed. 1561, fol. 370). See further in my note to Chaucer, Bk. Duch. 1206; Brand, Pop. Antiq., ed. Ellis, ii. 45; Trevisa, tr. of Higden, ii. 329.—AF. *dis mal*, explained as *les mal jours* (evil days) in MS. Glasgow Q. 9. 13, fol. 100, back; in a passage by Rauf de Linham dated 1256; the MS. is described by M. Paul Meyer in his notes on Glasgow MSS.—OF. *dis*, pl. of *di*, a day (cf. F. *Lun-di*); and *mal*, pl., evil.—L. *diēs malī*, evil days. See Notes on E. Etym., p. 69.

DISMANTLE, to deprive of furniture, &c. (F.—L.) In Cotgrave; and in Shak. Wint. Tale, iv. 4. 666. 'Lambert presently took care so to *dismantle* the castle [of Nottingham] that there should be no more use of it for a garrison;' Clarendon, Civil War, vol. iii. p. 192 (R.).—MF. *desmanteller*, 'to take a man's cloak off his back; also, to dismantle, raze, or beat down the wall of a fortress;' Cot.—OF. *des-*, L. *dis-*, apart, away; and *manteler*, 'to cloak, to cover with a cloak, to defend;' id., from MF. *mantel*, later *manteau*, a cloak. See **Mantle**.

DISMASK, to divest of a mask. (F.) In Shak. L. L. L. v. 2. 296.—MF. *desmasquer*, 'to unmaske;' Cot.—OF. *des-*, from L. *dis-*, away; and F. *masquer*, to mask. See **Mask**.

DISMAY, to terrify, discourage. (Hybrid; F.—L. and OHG.) In early use; in King Alisaunder, 2801.—OF. **desmayer*, a form not found [though Palsgrave has 'I dismaye, I put a person in fere or drede, *je desmaye*, and *je esmaye*; p. 519] but equivalent to Span. *desmayar*, to dismay, dishearten, also, to be discouraged, to lose heart (cf. Port. *desmaiar*, Ital. *smagare*). The OF. **desmayer* was supplanted in French by the verb *esmayer*, to dismay, terrify, strike powerless. These two verbs are formed in the same way, and only differ in the forms of the prefixes, which are equivalent respectively to the L. *dis-*, apart, and to L. *ex*, out. Both are hybrid words, formed, with L. prefixes, from the OHG. *magan* (G. *mögen*), to be able, to have might or power. β. Hence we have OF. *desmayer* and *esmayer*, to lose power, to faint, fail, be discouraged, in a neuter sense; afterwards used actively to signify to render powerless with terror, to astonish, astound, dismay, terrify. γ. The OHG. *magan* is the same word with AS. *magan*, and E. *may*; se **May** (1). δ. Cf. also Ital. *smagare*, formerly *dismagare*, to lose courage; Florio gives both spellings, and notes also the active sense 'to quell,' i.e. to dismay. Der. *di.may*, sb.

DISMEMBER, to tear limb from limb. (F.—L.) In early use. The pp. *demembred* (for *desmembred*) is in Rob. of Glouc. p. 559, l. 11727. 'Swereth nat so sinfully, in *dismembringe* of Crist;' Chaucer, Pers. Tale, De Ira (I 591).—OF. *desmembrer*, 'to dismember;' Cot.—OF. *des-*, from L. *dis-*, apart; and *membre*, a member, limb. See **Member**.

DISMISS, to send away, despatch. (L.) In Spenser, F. Q. vii. 7. 59. A coined word; first in the pp. *dismissed*, Caxton, Jason, p. 80 (N.E.D.); from L. *dis-*, away, and *missus*, pp. of *mittere*, to send. Suggested by OF. *desmettre*, 'to displace, . . . to dismiss;' Cot.

☞ The true L. form is *dīmittere*, without *s*. See **Missile**. Der. *dismiss-al*, *-ion*; and see *dimissory*.

DISMOUNT, to descend. (F.—L.) In Spenser, Shep. Kal. May, 315.—OF. *desmonter*, 'to dismount, . . . to descend;' Cot.—OF. *des-*, from L. *dis-*, away; and *monter*, to mount, ascend, from F. *mont*, a mountain. See **Mount**.

DISOBEY, to refuse obedience. (F.—L.) 'Bot therof woll I *disobeie*;' Gower, C. A. i. 86; bk. i. 1315. Occleve has *disobeye* and *disobeyed*, Letter of Cupid, stanzas 51 and 55; in Chaucer's Works, vii. 228.—OF. *desobeir*, 'to disobey;' Cot.—OF. *des-*, from L. *dis-*, apart; and *obeir*, to obey. See **Obey**. Similarly we have *disobedient*, *disobedience*; see **Obedient**.

DISOBLIGE, to refrain from obliging. (F.—L.) In Cotgrave.—OF. *desobliger*, 'to disoblige;' Cot.—OF. *des-*, from L. *dis-*, apart, away; and *obliger*, to oblige. See **Oblige**. Der. *disoblig-ing*.

DISORDER, want of order. (F.—L.) 'Such *disordre* and confusion;' Udal, Pref. to 1st Ep. to Corinthians; fol. 44. 'By *disorderyng* of the Frenchemen;' Berners, Froissart, vol. ii. c. 217 (R.). —OF. *desordre*, 'disorder;' Cot.—OF. *des-*, from L. *dis-*, apart; and *ordre*, order. See **Order**. Der. *disorder*, verb; *-ly*.

DISOWN, to refuse to own. (Hybrid; L. *and* E.) 'To *own* or *disown* books;' State Trials, Col. John Lilburn, an. 1649 (R.). A coined word, from L. *dis-*, apart; and E. **Own**, q. v.

DISPARAGE, to offer indignity, to lower in rank or estimation. (F.—L.) ME. *desparagen*, William of Palerne, 485; *disparage*, Chaucer, C. T. 4269 (A 4271).—OF. *desparager*, 'to disparage, to offer unto a man unworthy conditions;' Cot.—OF. *des-*, from L. *dis-*, apart; and OF. *parage*, lineage, rank; id.; from Late L. *parāticum*, corruptly *parāgium*, society, rank, equality of rank; formed with suffix *-āticum* from L. *par*, equal. See **Peer**. Der. *disparage-ment*.

DISPARITY, inequality. (F.—L.) 'But the *disparity* of years and strength;' Massinger, Unnatural Combat, Act i. sc. 1 (near the end).—F. *disparité* (Montaigne).—F. *dis-* (L. *dis-*), with negative force; and *parité*, equality; see **Parity**. Suggested by L. *dispar*, unequal, unlike. See **Par**.

DISPARK, to render unenclosed. (Hybrid; L. *and* E.) In Shak. Rich. II, iii. 1. 23. Coined from L. *dis-*, apart; and E. **Park**, q. v.

DISPASSIONATE, free from passion. (L.) 'Wise and *dispassionate* men;' Clarendon, Civil War, vol. iii. p. 745 (R.). Coined from L. *dis-*, apart; and E. **Passionate**, q. v. Der. *dispassionate-ly*.

DISPATCH; see **Despatch**.

DISPEL, to banish, drive away. (L.) In Milton, P. L. i. 530. 'His rays their poisonous vapours shall *dispel*;' Dryden, Art of Poetry, 1074 (near end of c. iv).—L. *dispellere*, to drive away, disperse.—L. *dis-*, apart, away; and *pellere*, to drive. See **Pulsate**.

DISPENSE, to weigh out, administer. (F.—L.) 'Despensinge and ordeyning medes to goode men;' Chaucer, tr. of Boethius, b. i. pr. 6, l. 212.—OF. *dispenser*, 'to dispense with, . . . to distribute;' Cot.—L. *dispensāre*, to weigh out, pay, dispense; frequentative form of *dispendere* (pp. *dispensus*), to weigh out, to dispense, distribute, spend.—L. *dis-*, apart; and *pendere*, to weigh; see **Spend**. Der. *dispens-able*, *-able-ness*, *-er*, *-ar-y*; also (like L. pp. *dispensātus*) *dispensat-ion* (ME. *dispensacioun*, Trevisa, tr. of Higden, iii. 469); *-ive*, *-or-y*.

DISPEOPLE, to empty of people. (F.—L.) 'Leaue the land *dispeopled* and desolate;' Sir T. More, Works, p. 1212 d.—OF. *despeupler*, 'to dispeople or unpeople;' Cot.—OF. *des-*, from L. *dis-*, apart; and *peupler*, to people, from *peuple*, people. See **People**.

DISPERSE, to scatter abroad. (L.) ME. *dispers*, orig. used as a pp. signifying 'scattered.' 'Dispers in alle londes oute;' Gower, C. A. ii. 185; bk. v. 1729. 'Dispers, as schep upon an hell;' id. iii. 175; bk. vii. 1258.—L. *dispersus*, pp. of *dispergere*, to scatter abroad.—L. *di-*, for *dis-*, apart; and *spargere*, to scatter. See **Sparse**. Der. *dispers-ive*, *-ion*.

DISPIRIT, to dishearten. (L.) 'Dispirit, to dishearten, or discourage;' Kersey's Dict. ed. 1715. Written for *dis-spirit*; coined from L. *dis-*, apart; and **Spirit**, q. v.

DISPLACE, to remove from its place. (F.—L.) In Spenser, F. Q. vi. 9. 42.—OF. *desplacer*, 'to displace, to put from a place;' Cot.—OF. *des-*, from L. *dis-*, away; and *pιacer*, to place, from *place*, a place. See **Place**. Der. *displace-ment*.

DISPLANT, to remove what is planted. (F.—L.) 'Adorio, You may perceive I seek not to *displant* you;' Massinger, The Guardian, Act i. sc. 1. And in Shak. Rom. iii. 3. 59.—OF. *desplanter*, 'to displant, or pluck up by the root, to unplant;' Cot.—OF. *des-*, from L. *dis-*, apart, away; and *planter*, to plant, from *plante*, a plant. See **Plant**.

DISPLAY, to unfold, exhibit. (F.—L.) 'Displayed his banere;' Rob. of Brunne, tr. of Langtoft, p. 23; Gower, C. A. i. 221; bk. ii. 1835.—AF. *despleier*, *desplayer*, OF. *desplier*, to unfold, exhibit, show. —OF. *des-*, from L. *dis-*, apart; and AF. *pleier*, OF. *plier*, *ploier*, to fold, from L. *plicāre*, to fold. See **Ply.** Der. *display*, sb. ; *display-er.* Doublets, *deploy*, q. v., *splay*, q. v.

DISPLEASE, to make not pleased, offend. (F. – L.) ME. *displesen*, Allit. Poems, ed. Morris, i. 455; Rom. of the Rose, 3101. – OF. *desplaisir*, to displease. – OF. *des-*, from L. *dis-*, apart, with negative force; and *plaisir*, to please. See **Please.** Der. *displeasure*, in Rob. of Brunne, tr. of Langtoft, p. 200.

DISPORT, to sport, make merry. (F. – L.) ME. *disporten*, to divert, amuse ; Chaucer, Troil. iii. 1133. [The sb. *disport*, i.e. sport, is in Chaucer, C. T. 777 (A 775).] – OF. *se desporter*, to amuse oneself, cease from labour (Godefroy) ; also *se deporter*, 'to cease, forbeare, leave off, give over, quiet himself, hold his hand ; also to disport, play, recreate himself' (Cotgrave). Cf. Late L. *disportus*, diversion ; Ducange. – OF. *des-*, from L. *dis-*, away, apart ; and *porter*, to carry ; whence *se desporter*, to carry or remove oneself from one's work, to give over work, to seek amusement ; from L. *portāre*, to carry. See **Port,** and **Sport.**

DISPOSE, to distribute, arrange, adapt. (F. – L. *and* Gk.) ME. *disposen*, to ordain ; Chaucer, Troil. iv. 964 ; Gower, C. A. i. 84; bk. i. 1253. – OF. *disposer*, 'to dispose, arrange, order ;' Cot. – OF. *dis-*, from L. *dis-*, apart; and OF. *poser*, to place, of Gk. origin. See **Pose.** Der. *dispos-er*, *-able*, *-al.*

DISPOSITION, an arrangement, natural tendency. (F. – L.) In Chaucer, C. T. 2366 (A 2364). – F. *disposition.* – L. acc. *dispositiōnem*, from nom. *dispositio*, a setting in order ; cf. *dispositus*, pp. of *dispōnere*, to set in various places. – L. *dis-*, apart ; and *pōnere*, to place. See **Position.**

DISPOSSESS, to deprive of possession. (F. – L.) In Shak. K. John, i. 1. 131. Earlier, in Bale, Votaries, part ii (R.). – OF. *despossesser* (Godefroy). Coined from L. *dis-*, apart, away ; and OF. stem *possess-*; see **Possess.** Der. *dispossess-ion*, *-or.*

DISPRAISE, to detract from one's praise. (F. – L.) 'Whan Prudence hadde herd hir housbonde auanten hym [*boast himself*] of his richesse and of his moneye, *dispreysynge* the power of hise aduersaries ;' Chaucer, C. T. Tale of Melibeus (B 2741) ; *dispraise*, Cursor Mundi, l. 27585. – OF. *despreis-*, a stem of *desprisier* (Supp. to Godefroy), to dispraise. – OF. *des-*, from L. *dis-*, apart ; and *prisier*, to praise. See **Praise.** Der. *dispraise*, sb.

DISPROPORTION, lack of proportion. (F. – L.) In Shak. Oth. iii. 3. 233. Also as a verb, Temp. v. 290 ; 3 Hen. VI, iii. 2. 160. – MF. *disproportion*, 'a disproportion, an inequality ;' Cot. – OF. *dis-*, from L. *dis-*, apart ; and *proportion*, proportion. See **Proportion.** Der. *disproportion*, verb ; *-able*, *-abl-y* ; *-al*, *-al-ly* ; *-ate*, *-ate-ly*, *-ate-ness.*

DISPROVE, to prove to be false. (F. – L.) 'Ye, forsoeth (quod she) and now I wol *disproue* thy first wayes ;' T. Usk ; Testament of Love, b. ii ; ch. iv. 135. – OF. *des-*, L. *dis-*, apart, away ; and **Prove,** q. v. *disproof.*

DISPUTE, to argue, debate. (F. – L.) ME. *disputen*, *desputen* ; 'byzylyche *desputede*' = they disputed busily, Ayenbite of Inwit, p. 79, last line ; P. Plowman, B. viii. 20. – OF. *desputer.* – L. *disputāre.* – L. *dis-*, apart, away ; and *putāre*, to think, orig. to make clean, clear up. – √PEU, to purify. See **Pure.** Der. *dispute*, sb., *disput-able*, *-abl-y*, *-able-ness*, *-ant*, *-er* ; *-at-ion*, *-at-i-ous*, *-at-i-ous-ly*, *-at-i-ous-ness*, *-at-ive*, like L. pp. *disputātus.*

DISQUALIFY, to deprive of qualification. (F. – L.) 'Are so *disqualify'd* by fate ;' Swift, on Poetry, A Rhapsody, 1733; l. 39. Coined from the L. prefix *dis-*, apart ; and **Qualify,** q. v. Der. *disqualific-at-ion.* See **Qualification.**

DISQUIET, to deprive of quiet, harass. (L.) '*Disquieted* consciences ;' Bale, Image, pt. i (R.). As sb., Much Ado, ii. 1. 268; as adj., Tam. of the Shrew, iv. 1. 171. Coined from L. prefix *dis-*, apart; and **Quiet,** q. v. Der. *disquiet-ude* (Tatler, no. 97, § 3).

DISQUISITION, a searching enquiry, investigation. (L.) 'On hypothetic dreams and visions Grounds everlasting *disquisitions* ;' Butler, Upon the Weakness of Man, ll. 199, 200. – L. *disquisītiōnem*, acc. of *disquisitio*, a search into ; cf. *disquisitus*, pp. of *disquirere*, to examine. – L. *dis-*, apart ; and *quaerere*, to seek. See **Query.**

DISREGARD, not to regard. (L. *and* F.) 'Among those churches which . . . you have *disregarded* ;' Milton, Animadversions upon the Remonstrant's Defence (R.). A coined word ; from L. *dis-*, apart, here used negatively ; and **Regard,** q. v. Der. *disregard*, sb. ; *-ful*, *-ful-ly.*

DISRELISH, to loathe. (L. *and* F. – L.) In Shak. Oth. ii. 1. 236. Coined from L. *dis-*, apart, in a negative sense ; and **Relish,** q. v.

DISREPUTE, want of repute. (L. *and* F. – L.) Phillips' Dict. (ed. 1706) has '*disreputation* or *disrepute*.' The pp. *disreputed* is used by Bp. Taylor, Great Exemplar, pt. i. s. 1 (R.). Coined from L. *dis-*, apart ; and **Repute,** q. v. Der. *disreput-able*, *-abl-y.*

DISRESPECT, not to respect. (L. *and* F. – L.) 'Let then the world thy calling *disrespect* ;' Donne, to Mr. Tilman ; l. 35. Coined

from L. *dis-*, apart ; and **Respect,** q. v. Der. *disrespect*, sb. ; *-ful*, *-ful-ly.*

DISROBE, to deprive of robes, divest. (L. *and* F.) In Spenser, F. Q. i. 8. 49. Coined from L. *dis-*, away ; and **Robe,** q. v.

DISRUPTION, a breaking asunder. (L.) In Sir T. Browne, Vulg. Errors, b. iii. c. 16. § 6. – L. acc. *disruptiōnem*, from nom. *disruptio*, commonly spelt *diruptio*, a breaking asunder ; cf. *disruptus*, pp. of *disrumpere*, *dirumpere*, to burst apart. – L. *dis-*, *di-*, apart ; and *rumpere*, to burst. See **Rupture.**

DISSATISFY, to displease. (L. *and* F. – L.) 'Very much *dissatisfied* and displeased ;' Camden, Queen Elizabeth, an. 1599. Coined from L. *dis-*, apart ; and **Satisfy,** q. v. Der. *dissatisfaction* ; see **Satisfaction.**

DISSECT, to cut apart, cut up. (L.) 'Slaughter is now *dissected* to the full ;' Drayton, Battle of Agincourt ; st. 37 from end. – L. *dissectus*, pp. of *dissecāre*, to cut asunder. – L. *dis-*, apart ; and *secāre*, to cut. See **Section.** Der. *dissect-ion*, from F. *dissection*, given in Cotgrave both as a F. and Eng. word ; *dissect-or.*

DISSEMBLE, to put a false semblance on, to disguise. (F. – L.) In Frith's Works, p. 51, col. 2. – OF. *des-*, apart ; and *sembler*, to seem, appear. Cf. MF. *dissimuler*, 'to dissemble ;' Cot. – L. *dis-*, apart ; and *simulāre*, to pretend ; cf. L. *dissimulāre*, to pretend that a thing is not. See **Simulate** ; also **Dissimulation.**

DISSEMINATE, to scatter abroad, propagate. (L.) In Blount's Gloss. ed. 1656. And in Bp. Taylor, Of Original Sin, c. vi. s. 1 (R.) ; the word *dissemination* occurs in the same passage. – L. *dissēminātus*, pp. of *dissēmināre*, to scatter seed. – L. *dis-*, apart ; and *sēmināre*, to sow, from *sēmin-*, decl. stem of *sēmen*, seed. See **Seminal.** Der. *disseminat-ion*, *-or.*

DISSENT, to think differently, differ in opinion. (L.) 'If I *dissente* and if I make affray ;' Lydgate, Minor Poems, p. 44. 'There they vary and *dissent* from them ;' Tyndal's Works, p. 445, col. 2. [The sb. *dissension*, ME. *dissencioun*, occurs in Chaucer, Tale of Melibeus (B 2881).] – L. *dissentīre*, to differ in opinion. – L. *dis-*, apart ; and *sentīre*, to feel, think. See **Sense.** Der. *dissent-er*, *-i-ent* ; also *dissens-ion*, like pp. *dissensus* ; cf. OF. *dissention*, 'dissention, strife ;' Cot.

DISSERTATION, a treatise. (L.) Used by Speed, Edw. VI, b. ix. c. 22 (R.). – L. acc. *dissertātiōnem*, from nom. *dissertātio*, a debate ; cf. *dissertātus*, pp. of *dissertāre*, to debate, frequentative from *disserere*, to set asunder, to discuss. – L. *dis-*, apart ; and *serere*, to join, bind. See **Series.** Der. *dissertation-al*; also *dissertat-or*, like pp. *dissertātus.*

DISSERVICE, an injury. (F. – L.) Used by Cotgrave to translate F. *desservice.* – OF. *des-*, L. *dis-*, apart ; and **Service,** q. v.

DISSEVER, to part in two, disunite. (F. – L.) ME. *disseueren* (with *u* for *v*) ; Allit. Morte Arthure, ed. Brock, 1575 ; 'So that I scholde noght *disseuere* ;' Gower, C. A. ii. 97 ; bk. iv. 2838. – OF. *dessever*, 'to dissever ;' Cot. – OF. *des-*, from L. *dis-*, apart ; and *severer*, to sever, from L. *sēparāre.* See **Sever.** Der. *dissever-ance.*

DISSIDENT, dissenting, not agreeing. (L.) 'Our life and manners be *dissident* from theirs ;' tr. of Sir T. More, Utopia, b. ii. c. 7, p. 130 (ed. Arber). – L. *dissident-*, stem of *dissidens*, pres. part. of *dissidēre*, to sit apart, be remote, disagree. – L. *dis-*, apart ; and L. *sedēre*, to sit, cognate with E. **Sit,** q. v.

DISSIMILAR, unlike. (F. – L.) '*Dissimular parts* are those parts of a man's body which are unlike in nature one to another ;' Blount's Gloss. ed. 1674. – MF. *dissimilaire*, used with ref. to 'such parts of the body as are of sundry substances ;' Cot. – OF. *des-*, from L. *dis-*, apart ; and MF. *similaire*, like. See **Similar.** Der. *dissimilar-i-ty*, and see below.

DISSIMILITUDE, an unlikeness, variety. (L. *and* F. – L.) 'When there is such a *dissimilitude* in nature ;' Barrow's Sermons, v. ii. ser. 10 (R.). – L. *dis-*, apart ; and **Similitude,** q. v. ; suggested by L. *dissimilitūdo*, unlikeness.

DISSIMULATION, a dissembling. (F. – L.) In Chaucer, C. T. 7705 (D 2123). – OF. *dissimulation* (Hatzfeld). – L. *dissimulātiōnem*, acc. of *dissimulātio*, a dissembling, like *dissimulātus*, pp. of *dissimulāre*, to dissemble. See **Dissemble.**

DISSIPATE, to disperse, squander. (L.) '*Dissipated* and resolued ;' Wilson, Arte of Rhetorique, p. 213 (R.). – L. *dissipātus*, pp. of *dissipāre*, to disperse. – L. *dis-*, apart ; and obs. *sipāre*, to throw, appearing also in the compound *insipāre*, to throw into ; cf. Skt. *kship*, to throw. Brugmann, i. § 761. Der. *dissipation* ; see Shak. Lear, i. 2. 161.

DISSOCIATE, to separate from a company. (L.) Orig. used as a pp. 'Whom I wil not suffre to be *dissociate* or disseuered from me ;' Udal, John, c. 14. § 1. – L. *dissociātus*, pp. of *dissociāre*, to dissolve a friendship. – L. *dis-*, apart ; and *sociāre*, to associate, from *socius*, a companion. See **Sociable.** Der. *dissociat-ion.*

DISSOLUTE, loose in morals. (L.) See Spenser, F. Q. i. 7. 51. ME. *dissolut*, Lydgate, Minor Poems, p. 245. – L. *dissolūtus*, loose, licentious; pp. of L. *dissoluere*, to dissolve; see below. **Der.** *dissolute-ly, -ness*; also *dissolut-ion*, given by Cotgrave both as a F. and E. word, from L. acc. *dissolūtiōnem*.

DISSOLVE, to loosen, melt, annul. (L.) ME. *dissoluen*; Wyclif, 2 Pet. iii. 10; id. Select Works, iii. 68. — L. *dissoluere*, to loosen. — L. *dis-*, apart; and *soluere*, to loose. See **Solve**. **Der.** *dissolvable, -ent*; from the same source, *dissolu-ble, -bility*; and see *dissolute* above.

DISSONANT, sounding harshly. (F. — L.) 'This saiyng, to all curtesie *dissonant*;' The Remedy of Love, st. 67; in Chaucer's Works, ed. 1561, fol. 324, col. 1. — OF. *dissonant*, 'dissonant;' Cot. — L. *dissonantem*, acc. of *dissonans*, pres. pt. of *dissonāre*, to be unlike in sound. — L. *dissonus*, discordant. — L. *dis-*, apart; and *sonus*, a sound. See **Sound**, sb. **Der.** *dissonance*.

DISSUADE, to persuade from. (F. — L.) In Shak. As You Like It, i. 2. 170. Earlier, in Bale's Eng. Votaries, pt. i. (R.). — MF. *dissuader*, 'to disswade, or dehort from;' Cot. — L. *dissuādēre*, to dissuade. — L. *dis-*, apart; and *suādēre*, to persuade, pp. *suāsus*. See **Suasion**. **Der.** *dissuas-ion, -ive, -ive-ly*, like pp. *dissuāsus*.

DISSYLLABLE, a word of two syllables. (F. — L. — Gk.) Spelt *dissyllabe* formerly; Ben Jonson has 'verbes *dissyllabes*,' i. e. dissyllabic verbs, Eng. Gram. ch. vii; and again 'nouns *dissyllabic*' in the same chapter. — MF. *dissyllabe*, 'of two syllables;' Cot. — L. *disyllabus*, of two syllables. — Gk. δισύλλαβος, of two syllables. — Gk. δι-, double; and συλλαβή, a syllable. See **Di-** and **Syllable**. **Der.** *dissyllab-ic*. ¶ The spelling with double *s* is unoriginal, but the error appeared first in the French; the *l* before the final *e* has been inserted to bring the spelling nearer to that of *syllable*. The spelling *dissyllable* is in Blount's Gloss. ed. 1674; and *dissillable* in Puttenham, Arte of Poesie (1589); ed. Arber, p. 128.

DISTAFF, a staff used in spinning. (E.) The *distaff* is a staff provided with flax to be spun off. Palsgrave has: 'I *dysyn* a *dystaffe*, I put the flaxe upon it to spynne.' ME. *distaf*, Chaucer, C. T. 3772 (A 3774). 'Hec colus, a *dysestafe*;' 15th cent. Vocabulary, in Voc. 794. 14. AS. *distæf*, rare; but we find 'Colus, *distæf*' in a Vocabulary of the 11th century, in Voc. 125. 21. β. The quotation from Palsgrave and the spelling *dysestafe* show that AS. *distæf* = *dis-stæf* or *dise-stæf*. The latter element is our E. **Staff**, q. v. γ. The former element is remarkably exemplified by the Platt-deutsch *diesse*, the bunch of flax on a distaff; Bremen Wörterbuch, i. 215, v. 284; also by the E. **Dizen**, q. v. Cf. Low G. *dise, disene*, a bunch of flax (Lübben), EFries. *dīssen*; MHG. *dehse*, a distaff.

DISTAIN, to sully, disgrace. (F. — L.) ME. *desteinen*. In Chaucer, Legend of G. Women, 255. 'Which with the blod was of his herte Thurghout *desteigned* ouer al;' Gower, C. A. i. 234; bk. ii. 2245. — OF. *desteign-*, a stem of *desteindre*, 'to distaine, to dead, or take away the colour of;' Cot. — OF. *des-*, from L. *dis-*, apart; and OF. *teindre*, from L. *tingere*, to tinge. See **Tinge**; and see **Stain**, which is an abbreviation of *distain* (like *sport* from *disport*).

DISTANT, remote, far. (F. — L.) In Chaucer, Astrolabe, pt. i. sect. 17, l. 32. — OF. *distant*, 'distant, different;' Cot. — L. *distantem*, acc. of *distans*, pres. pt. of *distāre*, to stand apart, be distant. — L. *di-*, for *dis-*, apart; and *stāre*, to stand, cognate with E. **Stand**, q. v. **Der.** *distance*, in Rob. of Glouc. pp. 511, 570, ll. 10533, 12018, from F. *distance*, L. *distantia*.

DISTASTE, to make unsavoury, disrelish. (L. *and* F. — L.) In Shak. Oth. iii. 3. 327. Coined from L. *dis-*, apart; and **Taste**, q. v. **Der.** *distaste*, sb. ; *-ful, -ful-ly, -ful-ness*.

DISTEMPER (1), to derange the temperament of the body or mind. (F. — L.) See Trench, Study of Words; there is an allusion to the Galenical doctrine of the four humours or temperaments. 'The fourthe is, whan .. the humours in his body ben *destempered*;' Chaucer, Pers. Tale, De Gula (I 826). 'That *distemperes* a mon in body and in soule;' Wyclif, Select Works, iii. 157. — OF. *destemprer*, only in the pp. *destempré, destrempé*, immoderate (Godefroy). — OF. *des-*, from L. *dis-*, apart; and OF. *temprer*, to temper (mod. F. *tremper*), from L. *temperāre*. See **Temper**. **Der.** *distemper*, sb., derangement.

DISTEMPER (2), a kind of painting, in which the colours are tempered, or mixed with thin watery glue. (F. — L.) In Kersey's Dict. ed. 1715. — OF. *destemprer*, later *destremper*, which Cotgrave explains by 'to soake, steepe, moisten, water, season, or lay in water; to soften or allay, by laying in water; to make fluid, liquid, or thin.' The word is from the same source as the above.

DISTEND, to stretch asunder, swell. (L.) In Milton, P. L. i. 572; xi. 880. — L. *distendere*, pp. *distensus*, to stretch asunder. — L. *dis-*, apart; and *tendere*, to stretch. — √ TEN, to stretch. See **Tend**. **Der.** *distens-ible, -ive, -ion*, like pp. *distensus*.

DISTICH, a couple of verses, a couplet. (L. — Gk.) Spelt *distichon* in Holland's Suetonius, p. 224 (R.); *distick* in the Spectator, no. 43, and in Blount's Gloss. ed. 1674; *distich* in Kersey's Dict. ed.

1715. — L. *distichus, distichon*. — Gk. δίστιχον, a couplet; neut. of δίστιχος, having two rows. — Gk. δι-, double; and στίχος, a row, rank, allied to στείχειν, to go, cognate with AS. *stīgan*, to ascend, whence E. *stirrup* and *stile*. — √ STEIGH, to go, march.

DISTIL, to fall in drops, flow slowly. (F. — L.) ME. *distillen*; 'That it malice non *distilleth*;' Gower, C. A. i. 5; prol. 62. — OF. *distiller*, 'to distill;' Cot. — L. *distillāre*, pp. *distillātus*, the same as *dēstillāre*, to drop or trickle down. — L. *dē*, down; and *stillāre*, to drop, from *stilla*, a drop. See **Still**, sb. and vb. **Der.** *distillat-ion, -or-y*, like L. pp. *dēstillātus*; also *distill-er, -er-y*.

DISTINCT, distinguished. (F. — L.) 'In other manere been *distinct* the speces of glotonye;' Chaucer, Pers. Tale, De Gula (I 828). — OF. *distinct*; Cot. — L. *distinctus*, pp. of *distinguere*, to distinguish. See below. **Der.** *distinct-ive, -ion*.

DISTINGUISH, to set apart, mark off. (F. — L.) In Shak. Macb. iii. 1. 96. [The reading in Chaucer's Boethius, bk. ii. pr. v. 47, is *distingwed*, not *distinguished*.] — OF. *distinguer*, to distinguish; the ending *-ish* seems to have been added by analogy, and cannot be accounted for in the usual way. — L. *distinguere*, to distinguish, mark with a prick; pp. *distinctus*. — L. *di-*, for *dis-*, apart; and *stinguere*, to prick, cognate with Gk. στίζειν, to prick, and E. *stick*, vb. Brugmann, i. § 666. See **Instigate, Stigma**. **Der.** *distinguish-able*; also *distinct*, q. v.

DISTORT, to twist aside, pervert. (L.) First used as a pp. Spenser, F. Q. v. 12. 36. — L. *distortus*, distorted, pp. of *distorquēre*. — L. *dis-*, apart; and *torquēre*, to twist. See **Torsion**. **Der.** *distort-ion*.

DISTRACT, to harass, confuse. (L.) [ME. *destrat*, distracted. 'Thou shalt ben so *destrat* by aspre thinges;' Chaucer, Boethius, bk. iii. pr. 8. This is a F. form.] But we find also *distract* as a pp. '*Distracte* were þei stithly' = they were greatly distracted; Allit. Destruction of Troy, 3219. As vb. in Shak. Oth. i. 3. 327; see Lover's Complaint, 231. — L. *distractus*, pp. of *distrahere*, to pull asunder, pull different ways. — L. *dis-*, apart; and *trahere*, to draw. See **Trace** (1). **Der.** *distract-ed-ly, -ion*. Also *distraught*, an E. modification of ME. *destrat* (above).

DISTRAIN, to restrain, seize goods for debt. (F. — L.) The pp. *destreined*, i. e. restrained, is in Chaucer, Boethius, bk. ii. pr. 6, l. 74. — OF. *destreign-*, pres. t. stem of *destraindre*, 'to straine, press, wring, vex extreamly; also, to straiten, restrain, or abridge of liberty;' Cot. — L. *distringere*, to pull asunder. — L. *di-*, for *dis-*, apart; and *stringere*, to touch, hurt, compress, strain. See **Strain**, verb. **Der.** *distrain-or*; *distraint*, from OF. *destrainte*, MF. *destraincte*, restraint, fem. form of pp. *destrainct* (Cotgrave); and see **Distress, District**.

DISTRESS, great pain, calamity. (F. — L.) In early use. ME. *destresse*, Rob. of Glouc. pp. 143, 442; ll. 3010, 9111. — OF. *destresse*, 'distress;' Cot.; older spellings *destreice, destrece*; Godefroy. *Destrece* is a verbal sb. from OF. *destrecier* (Godefroy), corresponding to a Late L. type *districtiāre*, to afflict, formed regularly from *districtus*, severe, pp. of *distringere*, to pull asunder, in Late L., to punish. See **Distrain**. **Der.** *distress*, vb., ME. *distresen*, Allit. Poems, ed. Morris, ii. 880; *distress-ful, -ful-ly*.

DISTRIBUTE, to allot, deal out. (L.) In Spenser, F. Q. i. 10. 39. 'Whan that is *distribute* to pouer indigent peple;' Lord Rivers, Dictes and Sayings (Caxton), fol. 5, l. 10. — L. *distribūtus*, pp. of *distribuere*, to distribute. — L. *dis-*, apart; and *tribuere*, to give, impart. See **Tribute**. **Der.** *distribut-able, -er, -ion, -ive*.

DISTRICT, a region. (F. — L.) In Cotgrave. 'District is that territory or circuit, wherein any one has power to *distrain*; as a manor is the lord's district;' Blount's Gloss. ed. 1674. — MF. *district*, 'a district, . . the territory within which a lord . . may judge . . the inhabitants;' Cot. — Late L. *districtus*, a district within which a lord may distrain (distringere potest); Ducange. — L. *districtus*, pp. of *distringere*. See **Distrain**.

DISTRUST, want of trust. (Hybrid; L. *and* E.) Udal has *distrust* both as sb. and vb.; On St. Matthew, capp. 5. 33, and 17. 19. Coined from L. *dis-*, apart; and E. **Trust**, q. v. **Der.** *distrust-ful, -ful-ly, -ful-ness*.

DISTURB, to disquiet, interrupt. (F. — L.) In early use. ME. *disturben, distourben*; spelt *disturben*, Ancren Riwle, p. 162; *distourben*, Rob. of Glouc. p. 436, l. 8985. — OF. *destourber*, 'to disturbe;' Cot. — L. *disturbāre*, to drive asunder, disturb. — L. *dis-*, apart; and *turbāre*, to disturb, trouble, from *turba*, a tumult, a crowd. See **Turbid**. **Der.** *disturb-ance*, used by Chaucer, Compl. of Mars, l. 107; *disturb-er*. ¶ Borrowed from French, the spelling being afterwards conformed to the Latin.

DISUNITE, to disjoin, sever. (L.) In Shak. Troil. ii. 3. 109. — L. *disūnitus*, pp. of *disūnīre*, to disjoin. — L. *dis-*, apart, here used negatively; and *ūnīre*, to unite, from *ūnus*, one. See **Unite, Unit**. From the same source, *disun-ion*.

DISUSE, to give up the use of. (L. *and* F. — L.) 'Disuse, to forbear the use of;' Kersey's Dict. ed. 1715; ' *Disusage* or *Disuse*, a disusing;' id. ME. *disusen* (with *v* for *u*). ' *Dysvsyn* or *mysse vsyn*;' Prompt. Parv. p. 123. Barbour has *diswsyt*, for *disusit*, pp.; Bruce, xix. 183. Coined from L. *dis-*, apart; and Use, q. v. **Der.** *disuse*, sb.; *disus-age*.

DISYLLABLE (so spelt in Kersey, ed. 1715); see **Dissyllable.**

DIT, to stop up. (E.) Barbour has *dittit*, stopped up; Bruce, vi. 168. AS. *dyttan*, to stop up. Teut. type **dut-jan-*; from Teut. **dut-*, as in AS. *dott*, a small lump, clot; Low G. *dutte*, a plug. See **Dot.**

DITCH, a dike, a trench. (E.) ME. *diche*, P. Plowman, C. xiv. 236, where one MS. has *dike*. *Diche* is merely a variant of *dike*, due to palatalisation, as in *diche* for AS. *dīce*, dat. case of *dīc*, a dike. See **Dike.** **Der.** *ditch*, verb, ME. *dichen*, Chaucer, C. T. 1890 (A 1888), from AS. *dīcian*; *ditcher*, ME. *diker*, P. Plowman, C. i. 224.

DITHYRAMB, a kind of ancient hymn. (L. – Gk.) ' *Dithyramb*, a kind of hymn or song in honour of Bacchus who was surnamed *Dithyrambus*; and the poets who composed such hymns were called *Dithyrambicks*;' Blount's Gloss. ed. 1674. – L. *dithyrambus*. – Gk. διθύραμβος, a hymn in honour of Bacchus; also, a name of Bacchus. Origin unknown.

DITTANY, the name of a plant. (F. – L. – Gk.) ' *Dictamnus* groweth in Candy, and . . . maye be named in Englishe righte *Dittany*, for some cal *Lepidium* also *Dittany*;' Turner, Names of Herbes (1548), p. 34 (E. D. S.). Also called *dittander* (Prior). ME. *detane*, *detany*, Voc. 710. 15, 786. 10. – OF. *ditain* (Godefroy); MF. *dictame*, ' the herb ditany, dittander;' Cot. Also AF. *ditaundere*, Wright's Vocab. i. 140, col. 1. – L. *dictamnum*, acc. of *dictamnum* or *dictamnus*. – Gk. δίκταμνον, δίκταμνος, also δίκταμον, δίκταμος, dittany; so named from mount Dictè in Crete, where it grew abundantly.

DITTO, the same as before. (Ital. – L.) ' *Ditto*, the aforesaid or the same;' Phillips' Dict. ed. 1706. – Ital. *ditto*, that which has been said, a word, saying. – L. *dictum*, a saying; neut. of *dictus*, pp. of *dicere*, to say. See **Diction.** ¶ It may be observed that the pp. of Ital. *dire*, to say, properly takes the form *detto*, not *ditto*.

DITTY, a sort of song. (F. – L.) ME. *ditè*, *ditee*; Chaucer, Boethius, bk. iii. pr. 1. l. 2; later *dittie*, Spenser, Colin Clout, 385; shortened to *ditt*, id. F. Q. ii. 6. 13. – OF. *ditié*, *dité*, a kind of poem; Godefroy. – L. *dictātum*, a thing dictated for writing, neut. of *dictātus*, pp. of *dictāre*, to dictate. See **Dictate.**

DIURETIC, tending to excite passage of urine. (F. – L. – Gk.) In Sir T. Browne, Vulg. Errors, b. ii. c. 5. § 2. ' *Diureticalnes*, diuretick quality;' Bailey; vol. ñ. ed. 1731. – MF. *diuretique*; see Cotgrave. – L. *diūrēticus*. – Gk. διουρητικός, promoting urine. – Gk. διουρέειν, to pass urine. – Gk. δι-, for διά, through; and οὖρον, urine. See **Urine.**

DIURNAL, daily. (L.) In Lydgate, Complaint of the Black Knight, l. 590. – L. *diurnālis*, daily. – L. *diurnus*, daily. – L. *diēs*, a day. A doublet of **Journal**, q. v.

DIVAN, a council-chamber, sofa. (Pers.) ' A *Diuan*, so they call the Court of Iustice;' Sandys, Trav. (1632); p. 62. In Milton, P. L. x. 457. – Pers. *dīvān*, ' a tribunal, a steward; a collection of odes arranged in alphabetical order of rhymes; the *Dīvān i Hāfiz* is the most celebrated;' Palmer's Pers. Dict., col. 282. In Richardson, p. 704, the Pers. form is given as *diwān*, the Arab. as *daywān*, explained as ' a royal court, the tribunal of justice or revenue, a council of state, a senate or divan,' &c.

DIVARICATE, to fork, diverge. (L.) ' With two fingers *divaricated*,' i.e. spread apart; Marvell, Works, ii. 114 (R.). Sir T. Browne has *divarication*, Vulg. Errors, b. vi. c. 11, § 4. – L. *diuāricāt-us*, pp. of *diuāricāre*, to spread apart. – L. *di-*, for *dis-*, apart; and *uāricāre*, to spread apart, straddle, from *uāricus*, straddling, formed with suffix *-cu-s* from *uāri-* (= *uāro-*), for *uārus*, bent apart, straddling, crooked. See **Divaricat-ion.**

DIVE, to plunge into water. (E.) ME. *diuen*, also *duuen* (with *u* for *v*); spelt *dyuen*, P. Plowman, B. xii. 163; *duuen*, Ancren Riwle, p. 282, l. 10. AS. *dȳfan*, to dive, Grein, i. 214; confused with the strong verb *dūfan* (pt. t. *dēaf*, pp. *dofen*), to dive, id. 213. + Icel. *dȳfa*, to dive, to dip. Teut. base **deub*, a secondary form allied to **deup*, as in E. *deep*. See **Deep, Dip.** **Der.** *div-er*, *div-ing-bell*, *di-dapper*, i.e. *dive-dapper*. See **Dove.**

DIVERGE, to part asunder, tend to spread apart. (L.) ' *Divergent* or *Diverging Rays*, in opticks, are those rays which, going from a point of a visible object, are dispersed, and continually depart one from another;' Phillips' Dict. ed. 1706. – L. *di-*, for *dis-*, apart; and *uergere*, to incline, verge, tend. See **Verge.** **Der.** *diverg-ent*, *-ence*.

DIVERSE, DIVERS, different, various. (F. – L.) ME. *diuers*, *diuerse* (with *u* for *v*). Spelt *diuers* in An Old Eng. Miscellany, ed. Morris, p. 35. ' *Diuersè* men *diuersè* thingès seiden;' Chaucer, C. T. 4631 (B 211). Spelt *divers* in the Bible, Mk. viii. 3, &c. – OF. *divers*, m. *diverse*, f. ' divers, differing, unlike, sundry, repugnant;' Cot. – L.

diuersus, various; orig. pp. of *diuertere*, to turn asunder, separate, divert. See **Divert.** **Der.** *diverse-ly*, *divers-i-ty*, from ME. and F. *diversité*, Chaucer, Troil. v. 1793; *divers-i-fy*, from F. *diversifier*, ' to vary, diversifie' (Cot.), from Late L. *diuersificāre*, which from L. *diuersi-* (for *diuersus*), and *-ficāre* (from *facere*), to make; *diversification*, from Late L. pp. *diuersificātus*.

DIVERT, to turn aside, amuse. (F. – L.) ' List nat onys asyde to *dyuerte*;' Lydgate, Storie of Thebes, pt. ii. l. 1130 (in Spec. of Eng. ed. Skeat, p. 30). – MF. *divertir*, ' to divert, avert, alter, withdraw;' Cot. – L. *diuertere*, pp. *diuersus*, to turn asunder, part, divert. – L. *di-*, for *dis-*, apart; and *uertere*, to turn. See **Verse.** **Der.** *divers-ion*, ' a turning aside, or driving another way, recreation, or pastime;' Phillips, ed. 1706. And see above; also **Divorce.**

DIVEST, to strip, deprive of. (L.) In Shak. K. Lear, i. 1. 50. – Late L. *diuestire*, a late equivalent of L. *dēuestīre*, to undress. – L. *di-*, for *dis-*, apart; and *uestīre*, to clothe, from *uestis*, clothing. See **Vest** and **Devest.**

DIVIDE, to part asunder. (L.) ME. *diuiden*, *dyuyden* (with *u* for *v*), Wyclif, Exod. xiv. 16; also *deuyden*, Chaucer, On the Astrolabe, pt. i. § 7. – L. *diuidere*, pp. *diuisus*, to divide. – L. *di-*, for *dis-*, apart; and **uidere*, a lost verb, prob. ' to part,' from the same root as L. *uid-ua*, a widow, and E. *wid-ow*, which see. **Der.** *divid-er*, *-end*; also (from pp. *diuīsus*) *divis-ible*, *-ibl-y*, *-ibil-i-ty*, *-ive*, *-or*, *-ion*, *-ion-al*.

DIVINE, godly, sacred. (F. – L.) ' A gret *deuyn* that cleped was Calkas;' Chaucer, Troil. i. 66. ' Thus was the halle ful of *divyninge*,' i.e. divining, guessing; id. C. T. 2523 (A 2521). – OF. *divin*, formerly also *devin* (Godefroy), signifying (1) divine, (2) a diviner, augur, theologian; whence *deviner*, to divine, predict, guess. – L. *diuīnus*, divine; from the same source as *diuus*, godly, and *deus*, God. See **Deity.** **Der.** *divine-ly*, *divin-i-ty* (ME. *diuinité*, Gower, C. A. iii. 88; bk. vii. 122; also *divine*, verb, *divin-er*, *-at-ion*.

DIVISION; see **Divide.**

DIVORCE, a dissolution of marriage. (F. – L.) ' The same lawe yeueth lybel of departicion because of *deuorse*;' T. Usk, Testament of Loue, b. iii. ch. 2. l. 14. The pl. *deuorses* is in P. Plowman, B. ii. 175. – OF. *divorce*, ' a divorce;' Cot. – L. *diuortium*, a separation, divorce. – L. *diuortere*, another form of *diuertere*, to turn asunder, separate. See **Divert.** **Der.** *divorce*, verb; *divorc-er*, *divorce-ment*.

DIVULGE, to publish, reveal. (F. – L.) In Shak. Merry Wives, iii. 2. 43. – F. *divulguer*, ' to divulge, publish;' Cot. – L. *diuulgāre*, to make common, publish abroad. – L. *di-*, for *dis-*, apart; and *uulgāre*, to make common, from *uulgus*, the common people. See **Vulgar.**

DIVULSION, a rending asunder. (L.) ' *Divulsion*, or separation of elements;' Holland's Plutarch, p. 669; also in Blount's Glossographia and Kersey. – L. *diuulsiōnem*, acc. of *diuulsio*, a plucking asunder; like *diuulsus*, pp. of *diuellere*, to pluck asunder. – L. *di-*, for *dis-*, apart; and *uellere*, to pluck. See **Convulse.**

DIZEN, to deck out. (E.) Used by Beaum. and Fletcher, in Monsieur Thomas, iv. 6. 3 and The Pilgrim, iv. 3. Palsgrave has : ' I *dysyn* a dystaffe, I put the flaxe upon it to spynne.' Thus to *dizen* was, originally, to furnish a distaff with flax; hence, generally, to clothe, deck out, &c. β. Evidently from AS. **dise*, for which see **Distaff.** **Der.** *be-dizen*, q. v.

DIZZY, giddy, confused. (E.) ME. *dysy*, Pricke of Conscience, 771; *dusie*, O. Eng. Homilies, i. 117; superl. *dusigest*, Ancren Riwle, p. 182. AS. *dysig*, foolish, silly; Grein, i. 214; cf. *dysigian*, to be foolish; id. β. From a Teut. base **dus-*, appearing also in OHG. *tus-ig*, dull, foolish; Low G. *düsig*, dizzy. Allied to **dūs-*, as seen in Du. *duiz-elen*, to grow dizzy. Perhaps also to **dwǽs-*, as in AS. *dwǽs*, Du. *dwaas*, foolish (see Franck); and to **Doze.** Teut. root **dwes* (**dwas*, **dwǽs*, **dus*). **Der.** *dizzi-ly*, *dizzi-ness*.

DO, pt. t. **DID**, pp. **DONE**, to perform. (E.) ME. *don*, pt. t. *dude*, *dide*, pp. *don*, *doon*, *idon*, *ydon*; see Stratmann's O. E. Dict. AS. *dōn*, pt. t. *dyde*, pp. *gedōn*; Grein, i. 199–202. + Du. *doen*, pt. t. *deed*, pp. *gedaan*; OSax. *dōn*, *duōn*, *duan*, *dōan*, pt. t. *deda*, pp. *giduan*; OFries. *dua*, pt. t. *dede*, pp. *gedān*; OHG. *tōn*, *tōan*, *tuan*, MHG. *tuon*, *duon*, G. *thun*. Teut. stem **dō-*. Allied to Gk. τίθημι, I set, put, place; Skt. *dhā*, to place, put; Lith. *dė-ti*, Slav. *dê-ti*, to put, to place. – ✓DHĒ, to place, set. Brugmann, i. § 129. **Der.** *do-ings*; *a-do*, q. v.; *don*, i.e. do on; *doff*, i.e. do off; *dup*, i.e. do up. From the same root, *doom*, q.v., *deem*, q.v.; also *deed*, q.v.

DOCILE, teachable, easily managed. (F. – L.) ' Be brief in what thou wouldst command, that so The *docile* mind might soon thy precepts know;' Ben Jonson, tr. of Horace, Ars Poet. (335, 336), where the Lat. text has ' animi *dociles*.' – F. *docile*, ' docible, teachable ;' Cot. – L. *docilis*, teachable. – L. *docēre*, to teach. **Der.** *docil-i-ty*. From the same root, *didactic*, q.v., *disciple*, q.v.; also *doctor*, *doctrine*, *document*, q.v.

DOCK (1), to cut short, curtail. (E.) ' His top was *dokked* lyk a preest biforn;' Chaucer, C. T. 592 (A 590). From *dock*, sb., the stump of a tail, stump, cut end; cf. ' *dokkyn*, or smytyn away the tayle;' Prompt. Parv. See prov. E. *dock*, the solid, fleshy part of an animal's tail (E.D.D.). Cf. Low G. *dokke*, a bunch, a stump, peg (Berghaus); G. *docke*, a rail, plug, peg (like prov. E. *dock*, peg of a top); MHG. *tocke*, OHG. *toccha*, a round stick; Icel. *dockr*, a short stumpy tail (Haldorsson); EFries. *dokke*, a bundle, bunch of flax, hank of yarn. We even find MF. *docquer*, from Low G.; Palsgrave has: 'I scutte, *Ie docque*;' p. 707. And cf. WFlem. *dokken*, to strike, knock; MHG. *tuc*, a blow, stroke. **Der.** *docket*.

DOCK (2), a kind of plant. (E.) ME. *dokke*; Chaucer, Troil. iv. 461. AS. *docce*, a dock; very common in Cockayne's ed. of A.S. Leechdoms; see Glossary in vol. iii.+MDu. *docke* (as in *docken bladeren*, dock-leaves, Hexham); MDan. *å-dokka*, water-dock (Kalkar). Cf. also Gael. *dogha*, a burdock; Irish *meacan-dogha*, the great common burdock, where *meacan* means a tap-rooted plant, as carrot, parsnip, &c. **Der.** *bur-dock*.

DOCK (3), a basin for ships. (Du.) In North's Plutarch, p. 536 (R.). [G. Douglas has: 'Let every barge do prent hyr-self a *dok*;' L. 'sulcumque sibi premat ipsa carina;' Aen. x. 296. This answers to Norw. *dokk*, a hollow, depression; and seems to be quite a different word.] Cotgrave explains F. *haute* as 'a dock, to mend or build ships in.'—MDu. *dokke*, a harbour; Kilian, Oudemans; whence also Dan. *dokke*, Swed. *docka*, G. *docke*, a dock. Mod. Du. *dok*. **Der.** *dock*, verb; *dock-yard*. ☞ The history of the word is very obscure. The ME. *dok* (in G. Douglas) also resembles prov. E. *doke*, a hollow, depression; Du. *deuk*, a dent.

DOCKET, a label, list, ticket, abstract. (E.) 'The *docket* doth but signify the king's pleasure for such a bill to be drawn;' State Trials, Abp. Laud, an. 1640 (R.). 'Mentioned in a *docquet*;' Clarendon, Civil War, v. ii. p. 426. *Docket* is explained as being an abstract in Blount, Nomolexicon (1691). Apparently allied to the verb *dock*, to clip, curtail, hence to make a brief abstract; cf. '*doket*, or *dockyd*;' Prompt. Parv. See **Dock** (1). ¶ *Docket* might well be a F. form (as *docquet), from MF. *docquer*, to dock; but no F. *docquet* is found. **Der.** *docket*, verb.

DOCTOR, a teacher, a physician. (F.—L.) 'A *doctour* of phisik;' Chaucer, C. T. Prol. 413 (A 411); spelt *doctor*, P. Plowman, C. xii. 96.—OF. *doctour*.—L. *doctōrem*, acc. of *doctor*, a teacher.—L. *docēre*, to teach; with agential suffix *-tor*. See **Docile**. **Der.** *doctor-ate*; and see *doctrine*, *document*.

DOCTRINE, teaching, learning. (F.—L.) In P. Plowman, C. xii. 225.—F. *doctrine*.—L. *doctrina*, learning.—L. *doctor*, a teacher; see above. **Der.** *doctrin-al*.

DOCUMENT, a paper adduced to prove a thing. (F.—L.) 'Thus louers with ther moral *documents*;' The Craft of Lovers, st. 1; in Chaucer's works, ed. 1561, fol. 341.—F. *document*, 'a document;' Cot.—L. *documentum*, a proof.—L. *docēre*, to teach, with suffix *-mentum*; see **Docile**. **Der.** *document-al*, *document-ar-y*.

DODDER, a kind of twining parasitic plant. (E.) ME. *doder*; Voc. 557. 11.+Dan. *dodder*; Swed. *dodra*; G. *dotter*, MHG. *toter*; OWestphal. *doder*, Mone, Quellen, p. 287, l. 44. Orig. meaning uncertain.

DODECAGON, a plane figure, having 12 equal sides and angles. (Gk.) In Phillips' Dict. ed. 1658. Coined from Gk. δώδεκα, twelve; and γωνία, an angle. β. The Greek δώδεκα is from δω-, i.e. δύο, two; and δέκα, ten. See **Decagon**.

DODECAHEDRON, a solid figure, with 12 equal pentagonal faces. (Gk.) Spelt *dodecaedron* in Kersey, ed. 1715. Coined from Gk. δώδεκα, twelve; and ἕδρα, a base. See above, and **Decahedron**.

DODGE, to go hither and thither, evade, quibble. (E.) 'Let there be some *dodging* casuist with more craft than sincerity;' Milton, Tenure of Kings and Magistrates (R.). Florio (1598) explains Ital. *arrouelare* by 'to wheele or turne about, to *dodge*.' In Gammer Gurton's Needle, we find: 'dost but *dodge*,' i.e. thou dost but quibble; Hazlitt's Old Plays, iii. 254 (cf. p. 193). Of uncertain origin. α. The base seems to be that which appears in the Lowland Scotch *dod*, to jog, North Eng. *dad*, to shake; whence the frequentative forms seen in North Eng. *daddle*, *doddle*, to walk unsteadily, *dodder*, to shake, tremble, totter, as also in *dadge*, or *dodge*, to walk in a slow clumsy manner; *doggle*, or *dodgel*, to totter in walking, &c. (E.D.D.). β. The orig. sense appears to be 'to move unsteadily,' or 'to shift from place to place.' But the history is very obscure.

DODO, a kind of large bird, now extinct. (Port.—E.?) In Herbert's Travels, ed. 1665, p. 403, is a drawing of a dodo; at p. 402 he speaks of 'the *dodo*, a bird the Dutch call *walgh-vogel* or *dod-eersen*,' which was then found in the Mauritius. In his second edition, 1638, he adds: 'a Portuguize name it is, and has reference to her simplenes.'—Port. *doudo*, silly, foolish. According to Diez, this Port. word was borrowed from late ME. *dold*, stupid; formed from AS. *dol*, dull, stupid. See **Dold** in N.E.D.; and cf. *dolt*. ¶ Similarly the *booby* was named, also by the Portuguese. See the long article

on the *dodo* in the Engl. Cyclopædia. *Walg-vogel* in Dutch means 'nauseous bird;' it seems that the sailors killed them so easily that they were surfeited of them.

DOE, the female of the buck. (C. ?) ME. *doo*; Wyclif, Prov. vi. 5. AS. *dā*, translating L. *dāma* in a copy of Ælfric's Glossary cited by Lye; cf. '*damma, vel dammula*, da;' Voc. 320. 35. Cf. Dan. *daa*, a deer (from AS. *dā*); *daa-hiort*, lit. doe-hart, a buck; *daa-hind*, lit. doe-hind, a doe. Also Swed. *dofhjort*, a buck; *dofhind*, a doe; OHG. *tāmo*, m., a buck. β. Perhaps all from L. *dāma*, a deer; but the E. form may be Celtic; cf. Irish *dam*, an ox, *dam allaid*, a stag; Stokes-Fick, p. 142.+Gk. δαμάλης, a young steer, Skt. *damyas*, a steer, from *dam*, to tame. See **Tame**.

DOFF, to take off clothes or a hat. (E.) 'And *doffing* his bright arms;' Spenser, F. Q. vi. 9. 36. '*Dof* bliue ¦is bere-skin'=doff quickly this bear-skin; William of Palerne, 2343. A contraction of *do off*, i.e. put off, just as *don* is of *do on*, and *dup* of *do up*. The expression is a very old one. 'þā hē him *of* dyde īsernbyrnan'=then he *did off* his iron breast-plate; Beowulf, ed. Grein, 671.

DOG, a domestic quadruped. (E.) ME. *dogge* (2 syllables); Ancren Riwle, p. 290. AS. *docga*, in a gloss; 'Canum (gen. pl.), *docgena*;' Cooper's Report on Rymer's Fœdera, App. B. p. 148; col. 1 (Record Series). Cf. AS. *Doggi-þorn*, Birch, Cart. Saxon. iii. 113; *Doggene-ford*, Kemble, Cod. Dipl. vi. 231. Hence were borrowed Du. *dog*, a mastiff; Swed. *dogg*, a mastiff; Dan. *dogge*, a bull-dog. Root unknown. **Der.** *dog*, verb, to track (Shak.); *doggish*, *-ish-ly*, *-ish-ness*; also *dogg-ed*, i. e. sullen (Shak. K. John, iv. 1. 129), *-ed-ly*, *-ed-ness*. Also *dog-brier*, *-cart*, *-day*, *-fish*, *-rose*, *-star*; *dog's-ear*.

DOG-CHEAP, very cheap. (E.) In Holinshed's Chron. Eng. (1587), p. 476: 'wool was *dog-cheape*.' From *dog* (above). Cf. *dog-tired*, *dog-lame*, &c.

DOGE, a duke of Venice. (Ital.—L.) In Blount's Gloss. ed. 1674; and in Evelyn's Diary (June, 1645).—Ital. *doge*, a doge, captain, general; a provincial form of *doce.—L. *ducem*, acc. of *dux*, a leader. See **Duke**.

DOGGER, a kind of fishing vessel. (E.) AF. *doggere*, in an Act of 31 Edw. III. stat. 3. cap. 1 (1356). [Hence, apparently, Du. *dogger* and Icel. *dugga* were borrowed.] Origin uncertain; perhaps named, in some way, from E. *dog*. Cf. MDu. *doggen*, *doggeren*, 'to dogg one, or, to follow one secretly;' Hexham. See Notes on E. Etym. p. 70.

DOGGEREL, wretched poetry. (E.) Orig. an adj., and spelt *dogerel*. 'This may wel be rime *dogerel*, quod he;' Chaucer, C. T. 13853 (B 2155). 'Amid my *dogrell* rime;' Gascoigne, Counsel to Withipoll, l. 12. Prob. from *dog*; cf. **Dog-cheap**.

DOGMA, a definite tenet. (Gk.) 'This *dogma* of the world's eternity;' Cudworth, Intellectual System, p. 251 (R.). Rich. also quotes the pl. *dogmata* from Glanvill, Pre-existence of Souls, c. 12.—Gk. δόγμα, that which seems good, an opinion; pl. δόγματα.—Gk. δοκέω, perf. pass. δέδογμαι, I am valued at, I am of opinion. Allied to L. *docēre*, to teach; see **Docile**. **Der.** *dogmat-ic*, *-ic-al*, *-ic-al-ly*, *-ise*, *-is-er*, *-ism*, *-ist*, all from the stem δόγματ-.

DOILY, a small napkin. (Personal name.) Also used as the name of a woollen stuff. 'We should be as weary of one set of acquaintance, though never so good, as we are of one suit, though never so fine; a fool, and a *doily* stuff, would now and then find days of grace, and be worn for variety;' Congreve, Way of the World; A. iii. sc. 3. 'The stores are very low, sir, some *doiley* petticoats and manteaus we have, and half a dozen pair of laced shoes;' Dryden, Kind Keeper, iv. 1. 'The famous *Doily* . . . who raised a fortune by finding out materials for stuffs,' &c.; Spectator, no. 283 (1712). Pegge says that 'Doyley kept a Linnen-drapers shop in the Strand, a little W. of Catharine Street.' Some say no. 346, Strand, at the E. corner of Wellington Street. The stuff was named after him. The name is of French origin; cf. Rich. Coer de Lion, ed. Weber, l. 1647.

DOIT, a small Dutch coin. (Du.—Scand.) In Shak. Temp. ii. 2. 33.—Du. *duit*, a doit.—Icel. *þveit*, a piece, bit, small coin.—Icel. *þveit, 2nd grade of *þvita, to cut, a lost verb cognate with AS. *þwitan*, to cut; see **Thwite**.

DOLE, a small portion. (E.) ME. *dole*, *dale*. Spelt *dole*, Ancren Riwle, pp. 10, 412; *dale*, Layamon, 19646, where the later text has *dole*. AS. *dāl*, ge-*dāl*, Grein, i. 390; a variant of AS. *dǣl*, a portion. Thus *dole* is a doublet of *deal* (1), q. v. ¶ The difference between *deal* and *dole* appears to be due to the suffix; *dāl* is from a type **dailo-*; and *deal* from a type **daili-*.

DOLEFUL, sad, miserable. (Hybrid; F. *and* E.) A hybrid word, made by suffixing the AS. *-ful* to ME. *doel*, *deol*, *duel*, *dol*, *del*, of French origin. 'A *deolful* ¦ing;' Layamon, 6901, later text. The sb. appears in Lowland Scotch as *dool*; spelt *deol* in King Horn, ed. Lumby, 1048; *dol* in O. Eng. Hom. i. 285, l. 4.—OF.

doel, duel, dol, mod. F. *deuil,* grief, mourning (Supp. to Godefroy, s. v. *dueil*); verbal sb. of OF. *doloir,* to grieve; cf. L. *cordolium,* grief at heart.—L. *dolēre,* to grieve. Der. doleful-ly, -ness. See con-dole, and *dolour.*

DOLL, a child's puppet. (Gk.) 'I'll carry you and your *doll* too, Miss Margery;' Garrick, Miss in her Teens, Act ii. (Fribble). The same word as *Doll,* pet name for *Dorothy;* cf. *Doll* Tearsheet in 2 Hen. IV. 'O capitulum lepidissimum, . . O little pretie *doll toll*;' Cooper's Thesaurus, 1565. So also Sc. *doroty,* a doll; from *Dorothy,* which is a name of Gk. origin. In Johnson's Dict.

DOLLAR, a silver coin. (Low G.–G.) In Shak. Macb. i. 2. 62. —Low G. *daler,* a dollar. Adapted and borrowed from G. *thaler,* a dollar. β. The G. *thaler* is an abbreviation of *Joachimsthaler,* a coin so called because first coined from silver obtained from mines in *Joachimsthal* (i. e. Joachim's dale) in Bohemia about A.D. 1518; they were sometimes called *Schlickenthaler,* because coined by the counts of Schlick. The G. *thal* is cognate with E. *dale.* Thus *dollar* = *dale-er.* See **Dale.** ¶ The Du. form is *daalder.*

DOLMAN, a kind of loose jacket. (F.–G.–Hung.–Turk.) 'Clothed with a robe of *dollymant* crimson;' Hakluyt, Voy. vol. ii. pt. 1. p. 113.—F. *dolman.*—G. *dolman, dolman.*—Hung. *dolmany.* —Turk. *dōlāmān, ḍōlāmah,* a kind of long robe.

DOLMEN, a monument of two (or more) upright stones, with a flat stone above them. (C.) The French name for a cromlech.—F. *dolmen.* [Explained as 'stone-table' by Legonidec; from Bret. *tōl, taol,* table (from L. *tābula*); and *men,* a stone.] But rather 'a stone with a hole beneath.'—Corn. *dolmēn, tolmēn;* from Corn. *doll, toll* (W. *twll,* a hole); and *mēn* (W. *maen*), a stone. See N.E.D.

DOLOMITE, a kind of rock. (F.) Named, in 1794, after M. *Dolomieu,* a French geologist (1750–1801).

DOLOUR, grief, sorrow. (F.–L.) In Shak. Two Gent. iii. 1. 240. ME. *dolour,* O. Eng. Miscellany, ed. Morris, p. 212.—OF. *dolour,* MF. *doleur,* 'grief, sorrow;' Cot.—L. *dolōrem,* acc. of *dolor,* grief.—L. *dolēre,* to grieve; see **Doleful.** Der. *dolor-ous,* used by Cotgrave to translate MF. *douloureux,* from L. adj. *dolorōsus.*

DOLPHIN, a kind of fish. (F.–L.–Gk.) In Spenser, F. Q. iv. 11. 23. ME. *dolphyne,* Allit. Morte Arthure, 2054. [ME. *delfyn,* King Alisaunder, 6576, is immediately from L. *delphinus.*]—OF. *daulphin,* older spelling of *dauphin;* Cot.—Folk-L. *dalfinum,* acc. of *dalfinus,* for L. *delphinus.*—Gk. δελφιν-, stem of δελφίς, a dolphin; supposed to mean 'belly-fish;' cf. Gk. δελφύς, womb. See Curtius, i. 81. Doublet, *dauphin.*

DOLT, a dull or stupid fellow. (E.) In Shak. Oth. v. 2. 163. ME. *dult,* blunt; '*dulte neiles,*' blunt nails, i. e. instruments of the Passion; O. Eng. Hom. i. 203; and see Ancren Riwle, p. 292, where for *dulte* another reading is *dulle.* The word is a mere extension of ME. *dul,* dull. Cf. Prov. E. *dold,* stupid, confused (Halliwell), so that the suffixed *-t* = *-d* = *-ed*; and *dolt* or *dult* is for *dulled,* i. e. blunted. See **Dull.** Der. *dolt-ish, -ish-ness;* *dodo.*

DOMAIN, territory, estate. (F.–L.) 'A *domaine* and inheritance;' Holland's Pliny, b. xiii. c. 3. l. 4.—MF. *domaine,* 'a demaine' (*sic*), Cot.; OF. *demaine,* a domain; also, power; Godefroy. —Late L. *dominicum,* neut. of *dominicus,* with the same sense as L *dominium,* lordship, private property.—L. *dominus,* a lord; see **Dominate.** Doublet, *demesne,* q. v.

DOME, a hemi-spherical roof. (F.–Ital.–L.) '*Dome,* a townhouse, guild-hall, state-house, meeting-house in a city, from that of Florence, which is so called. Also, a flat round loover, or open roof to a steeple, banqueting-house, &c. somewhat resembling the bell of a great watch;' Blount's Gloss. ed. 1674.—MF. *dome,* 'a town-house, guild-hall,' &c. (as above); also *dosme,* 'a flat-round loover,' &c. (as above); Cot. [The spelling *dosme* is false.]—Ital. *duomo, domo,* a cathedral church (house of God).—L. *domum,* acc. of *domus,* a house, a building. (√DEM.) See **Timber.** Körting, § 3089.

DOMESTIC, belonging to a house. (F.–L.) In Shak. Rich. III, ii. 4. 60.—F. *domestique,* 'domesticall, housall, of our houshold;' Cot.—L. *domesticus,* belonging to a household.—L. *domus,* a house. Der. *domestic-al-ly, -ate, -at-ion;* and see *domicile, dome.*

DOMICILE, a little house, abode. (F.–L.) 'One of the cells, or *domicils* of the understanding;' Bacon, on Learning, by G. Wats, i. 12 (R.).—OF. *domicile,* 'an house, mansion;' Cot.—L. *domicilium,* a habitation.—L. *domi-* (= *domo-*), for *domus,* a house; and *-cilium,* possibly allied to *cella,* a cell; see **Dome** and **Cell.** Der. *domicili-ar-y, -ate;* from L. *domicili-um.*

DOMINATE, to rule over. (L.) Shak. has *dominator,* L. L. L. i. 1. 222; Titus, ii. 3. 31. [The sb. *domination,* ME. *dominacion,* is in early use; see Chaucer, C. T. 12494 (C 560); from OF. *domination.*]—L. *dominatus,* pp. of *dominari,* to be lord.—L. *dominus,* lord. ✚Skt. *damana-s,* a horse-tamer; from *dam,* to tame; see **Tame.** Der. *dominat-ion* (F. *domination*), *-ive;* *domin-ant* (F. *dominant,* pres.

pt. of *dominer,* to govern); and see *domineer, dominical, dominion, domino, domain, demesne, don* (2).

DOMINEER, to play the master. (Du.–F.–L.) In Shak. Tam. Shrew, iii. 2. 226.—MDu. *domineren,* to feast luxuriously; Oudemans.—OF. *dominer,* 'to govern, rule . . . domineere,* to have soverainty;' Cot.—L. *dominari,* to be lord; see above. For the suffix, cf. *cash-ier.*

DOMINICAL, belonging to our Lord. (F.–L.) In Shak. L. L. L. v. 2. 44.—MF. *dominical;* Cot.—Late L. *dominicālis,* dominical.—L. *dominicus,* belonging to a lord.—L. *dominus,* a lord; see **Dominate.**

DOMINION, lordship. (F.–L.) 'To haue lordship or *dominion*;' Lydgate, Storie of Thebes, pt. ii; The Answer of King Ethiocles.—OF. *dominion.*—Late L. acc. *dominiōnem,* from nom. *dominio.*—L. *dominium,* lordship.—L. *dominus,* a lord; see **Dominate.**

DOMINO, a masquerade-garment. (Span.–L.) '*Domino,* a kind of hood worn by the canons of a cathedral church; also a mourning-vail for women;' Kersey, ed. 1715.—Span. *domino,* a masquerade-dress. Orig. a hood worn by a master.—Span. *domine,* a master, a teacher of Latin grammar.—L. *dominus,* a master; see **Dominate.** Der. *dominoes,* the name of a game; from the phrase *faire domino,* to complete (and win) the game; Hatzfeld.

DON (1), to put on clothes. (E.) 'Don his clothes;' Hamlet, iv. 5. 52. A contraction of *do on,* i. e. put on. 'Brutus hehte his beornes *don on* hure burnan' = Brutus bade his men do on their breast-plates; Layamon, 1700, 1701. See **Doff, Dup.**

DON (2), sir; a Spanish title. (Span.–L.) In Shak. Two Gent. i. 3. 39.—Span. *don,* lit. master, a Spanish title.—L. *dominus,* a master; see **Dominate.** ¶ The Span. fem. is *duenna,* q. v.; *donna* is Italian. The word itself is ultimately the same as the ME. *dan,* as in '*dan* John,' or '*dan* Thomas' or '*dan* Albon;' Chaucer, C. T. 13935 (B 3119). This form is from the OF. *dan,* acc. of *dans* = L. *dominus.*

DONATION, a gift. (F.–L.) In Shak. Temp. iv. 85.—F. *donation,* 'a donation, a present;' Cot.—L. acc. *dōnātiōnem,* from nom. *dōnātio.*—L. *dōnāre,* to give.—L. *dōnum,* a gift; cognate with Gk. δῶρον, a present, Skt. *dāna-m,* a gift; cf. Skt. *dā,* to give; OSlavon. *da-mĭ,* I give; Lith. *dů-mi,* I give. ✔DŌ, to give. Brugmann, i. § 167. Der. From the same source are *donat-ive, don-or, don-ee.* From the same root are *anecdote, antidote, condone, pardon, dose, dower;* also *date* (1), *dative, dado, die* (2), &c.

DONJON, the keep of a fortress; see **Dungeon.**

DONKEY, a familiar name for an ass. (E.) Common in mod. E., but rare in E. literature; orig. dialectal. 'A Donky, or a Dicky. An ass. Essex and Suff.;' Gent. Mag. 1793, pt. ii. p. 1083. It seems at first to have rhymed with *monkey,* as still in Somersets. α. The word is a double diminutive, formed with the suffixes *-k-* and *-y* (*-ey*), the full form of the double suffix appearing in the Lowland Scotch *lass-ickie,* a little-little lass; this double suffix is particularly common in the Banffshire dialect, which has *beastikie* from *beast, horsikie* from *horse,* &c., as explained in The Dialect of Banffshire, by the Rev. Walter Gregor, p. 5. β. The stem is *dun,* a familiar name for a horse, as used in the common phrase 'dun is in the mire;' as to which see Chaucer, C. T. Mancip. Prol. l. 5; Shak. Romeo, i. 4. 41. The name *dun* was given to a horse or ass in allusion to its colour; see **Dun.** ¶ Similarly was formed *dunnock,* ME. *donek,* a hedge-sparrow, with a single suffix *-ock.*

DOOM, a judgment, decision. (E.) ME. *dom;* Havelok, 2487; and common. AS. *dōm;* Grein, i. 196. ✚ Swed. and Dan. *dom;* Icel. *dōmr;* Goth. *doms;* OHG. *tuom,* judgment. Teut. type *dōmoz,* m. Allied to Gk. θέμις, law; and τί-θη-μι, I place, set. From ✔DHĒ, to place; cf. Skt. *dhā,* to place, set; L. *-dere,* as in con-*dere;* Lith. *dė-ti,* to place; OSlavon. *dě-ti,* to place. Brugmann, i. § 573. Der. *deem,* verb; q. v.; *doomsday,* q. v. Observe that the suffix *-dom* (AS. *-dōm*) is the same word as *doom.* See **Theme, Thesis.**

DOOMSDAY-BOOK, a survey of England made by William I. (E.) So called, popularly, as being a final authority. The etymology is obvious, viz. from AS. *dōmes dæg,* the day of judgment or decision; cf. ME. *domesday,* Chaucer, Ho. of Fame, iii. 194 (1284).

DOOR, an entrance-gate. (E.) ME. *dore,* Havelok, 1788. AS. *dor,* n., *duru,* f.; Grein, i. 212. ✚ Du. *deur;* Dan. *dor;* Swed. *dorr;* Icel. *dyrr;* Goth. *daur;* OHG. *tor,* G. *thor, thür.* Further allied to L. *fores,* pl.; Lith. *dùrys,* pl.; OIrish *dorus,* n.; W. *drws,* m.; Russ. *dver(e);* Gk. θύρα; Skt. *dvār,* a door, gate. Root uncertain. Brugmann, i. § 462. Der. *door-nail* (ME. *doreneail,* Will. of Palerne, 628); *door-pin* (ME. *dorepin, durepin,* Gen. and Exodus, 1078); *door-ward* (ME. *doreward, dureward,* Layamon, ii. 317).

DOR, an insect that flies with a great humming noise. (E.) ME. *dore;* 'Crabro, *dore*;' Voc. 576. 4. AS. *dora,* 'Atticus, *dora*;' Voc. 7. 30. Lit. 'buzzer;' cf. Swed. dial. *dorrä,* to buzz loudly; Dan. *dure,* to roar (Larsen).

DORMANT, sleeping. (F. – L.) 'His table-*dormant*;' Chaucer, C. T. 355 (A 353). – F. *dormant*, pres. pt. of *dormir*, to sleep. – L. *dormire*, to sleep; see **Dormitory**. Der. *dormanc-y*.

DORMER-WINDOW, an attic-window. (F. *and* E.) A *dormer* was a sleeping-room. 'Or to any shop, cellar, .. chamber, *dormer*;' Chapman, All Fools, Act iv. sc. 1 (Notary). – OF. *dormeor*, a dormitory (Godefroy). – L. *dormitorium* (below).

DORMITORY, a sleeping-chamber. (L.) 'The *dormitorie*-door;' Holinshed, Desc. of Ireland, c. 3. – L. *dormitorium*, a sleeping-chamber; neut. of *dormitorius*, adj. of or belonging to sleeping. – L. *dormitor*, a sleeper. – L. *dormire*, to sleep. Allied to Russ. *dremat(e)*, to sleep; also to Gk. δαρθάνειν, to sleep, Skt. *drā*, to sleep.

DORMOUSE, a kind of mouse. (F. – L.; *and* E.) 'Laye still lyke a *dormouse*, nothynge doynge;' Hall, Hen. VII, an 7. § 6. ME. *dormows*. 'Hic sorex, a *dorm:ws*;' Voc. 700. 20; and in Prompt. Parv. Lit. 'sleeping-mouse.' The prefix is *dorm* (as if *dorm-mouse*); from prov. E. *dorm*, to sleep. Cf. Icel., Norw., and Swed. dial. *dorma*, to doze. All, apparently, from F. *dormir*, to sleep; see above. ¶ Halliwell gives *dorrer*, a sleeper; but it has not been found.

DORNICK, a kind of cloth; obsolete. (Flem.) See Bury Wills, p. 135. Spelt *dornecl es* in Palsgrave. Named from Flem. *Dornick* (Hexham); better known as F. *Tournay* (L. *Tornacus*). See **Cambric**.

DORSAL, belonging to the back. (F. – L.) The term '*dorsal* fin' is used by Pennant, Zool., iii. 32 (1769). – F. *dorsal*, of or belonging to the back; Cot. – Late L. *dorsālis*, belonging to the back. – L. *dorsum*, the back.+ Irish *druimm*, W. *trum*, back, ridge.

DORY, a fish. See **John Dory**.

DOSE, a portion of medicine. (F. – Gk.) 'Without repeated *doses*;' Dryden's tr. of Virgil, Dedication. And used by Cotgrave. – MF. *dose*, 'a dose, the quantity of potion or medicine,' &c.; Cot. – Gk. δόσις, a giving, a portion given or prescribed. – Gk. base δο-, allied to δίδωμι, I give; cf. Skt. *dā*, to give. Der. *dose*, verb. See **Donation**.

DOT, a small mark, speck. (E.) Not in early use, and uncommon in old authors. It occurs in Johnson's Dict., and the phrase '*dotted* lines' occurs in Burke's Letters (Todd). Levins (1570) has: 'A *dot*, *obstructorium*.' Cotgrave has: '*Caillon*, a dot, clot, or congealed lump.' The only other early trace I can find of it is in Palsgrave, qu. by Halliwell, who uses *dot* in the sense of 'a small lump, or pat.' Cf. prov. Eng. *dot*, a small lump, a small child. AS. *dott*, only in the sense of 'the head of a boil;' A. S. Leechdoms, iii. 40. Cf. Du. *dot*, 'a little bundle of spoiled wool, thread, silk, or such like, which is good for nothing;' Sewel; or, 'a whirled knot, clue, pellet;' Calisch. Also Norw. *dott*, a tuft, bunch, wisp to stop a hole with; Low G. *dutte*, a plug. See **Dit**. β. The remoter origin is obscure; cf. Swed. dial. *dott*, a little heap, clump; EFriesic *dotte*, *dot*, a clump (Koolman); NFries. *dodd*, a clump (Outzen); Norw. *dott*, a tuft, a wisp, something to stop up a hole with; Norw. *dytte*, AS. *dyttan*, to stop up. Rietz (s. v. *dotta*, to stop up) cites Swed. dial. *dott*, something soft rolled up, to stop up a hole with. See **Dit**.

DOTAGE, childishness, foolishness. (E. *with* F. *suffix*.) ME. *dotage*, Allit. Poems, ed. Morris, B. 1425. From the verb *dote*, with F. suffix -*age*, answering to L. suffix -*āticum*. See **Dote**.

DOTARD, a foolish fellow. (E. *with* F. *suffix*.) In Chaucer, C. T. 5913 (D 331). From the verb *dote*; with F. suffix -*ard*, of OHG. origin. See **Dote**.

DOTE, to be foolish. (E.) In early use. ME. *dotien*, *doten*; Layamon, l. 3294; P. Plowman, A. i. 129; B. i. 138. An Old Low G. word. Cf. MDu. *doten*, to dote, mope, Oudemans; Du. *dutten*, to take a nap, to mope; *dut*, a nap, sleep, dotage; Icel. *dotta*, to nod with sleep; MHG. *tüzen*, to keep still, mope. ¶ The F. *radoter*, OF. *re-doter*, is of O. Low G. origin, with L. prefix *re*-. Der. *dot-age*, q. v.; *dot-ard*, q. v.; *dott-er-el*, a silly bird, Drayton's Polyolbion, s. 25 (near the end); and Prompt. Parv.

DOUBLE, two-fold. (F. – L.) ME. *double*, Ancren Riwle, p. 70. – OF. *doble*, later *double*. – L. *duplus*, double, lit. two-fold. – L. *du*-, for *duo*, two; and -*plus*, related to -πλος in Gk. δι-πλός, two-fold. See **Two**. Der. *double*, verb; *double-ness*; also *doublet*, q. v., *doubloon*, q. v.

DOUBLET, an inner garment. (F. – L.) In Shak. Temp. ii. 1. 102. ME. *dobbelet*, 'a garment, *bigera*;' Prompt. Parv.; see Way's note. – OF. *doublet*, 'a doublet, a jewell, or stone of two peeces joyned or glued together;' Cot. [Here *doublet* is probably used in a lapidary's sense, but the word is the same; see Godefroy, and cf. MF. *doublure*, lining for a garment.] – F. *double*, double; with dim. suffix -*et*; see **Double**.

DOUBLOON, a Spanish coin. (F. – Span. – L.) A Spanish word, given in Johnson's Dict. as *doublon*, which is the F. form. – Span. *doblon*, so called because it was the *double* of a pistole. – Span. *doblo*, double; with suffix -*on* (= Ital. -*one*.) – L. *duplus*; see **Double**.

DOUBT, to be uncertain. (F. – L.) ME. *douten*, commonly in the sense 'to fear;' Havelok, l. 708. – OF. *douter*, later *doubter*, as in Cotgrave, whence *b* was inserted into the E. word also. – L. *dubitāre*, to doubt, be of two minds; allied to *dubius*, doubtful; see **Dubious**. Der. *doubt*, sb.; -*er*, -*ful*, -*ful-ly*, -*ful-ness*, -*less*, -*less-ly*.

DOUCEUR, a small present. (F. – L.) A French word, used by Burke (Todd). – F. *douceur*, lit. sweetness. – L. *dulcōrem*, acc. of *dulcor*, sweetness. – L. *dulcis*, sweet; see **Dulcet**.

DOUCHE, a shower-bath. (F. – Ital. – L.) Modern, and a French word. – F. *douche*, a douche, a shower-bath, introduced from Ital. in the 16th cent. (Brachet). – Ital. *doccia*, a conduit, canal, water-pipe, spout. – Ital. *docciare*, to pour; formed as if from a Late L. **ductiāre*, a derivation of *ductus*, a leading, in Late L., a duct, canal; see **Duct**.

DOUGH, kneaded flour. (E.) ME. *dah*, *dagh*, *doӡ*, *dogh*, *dow*; spelt *doӡ*, Ayenbite of Inwyt, p. 205; see *daӡ* in Stratmann, p. 151. AS. *dāh*, gen. *dāges*, dough; A. S. Leechdoms, ii. 342, l. 18.+ Du. *deeg*; Dan. *deig*; Swed. *deg*; Icel. *deig*; Goth. *daigs*, a kneaded lump. G. *teig*. Teut. type **daig-oz*, m. β. The sense is 'a kneaded lump;' the root appears in Goth. *deigan*, *digan*, to knead, to form out of a plastic material, Rom. ix. 20; cognate with L. *fingere*, to form, shape, mould; also with Skt. *dih*, to smear. – √DHEIGH, to mould, to knead; whence also Gk. τεῖχος, a wall (orig. of earth); and cf. **Paradise**. Brugmann, i. § 604. Der. *dough-y*. And see **Figure, Fiction, Dairy, Lady**.

DOUGHTY, able, strong, valiant. (E.) ME. *duhti*, *dohti*, *douӡti*; Layamon, 14791; P. Plowman, B. v. 102. AS. *dohtig*, also *dyhtig*, valiant; Grein, i. 213. – AS. *dugan*, to be strong, to avail. Cf. Du. *deugen*, to be worth; Dan. *due*, to avail; whence *dygtig*, able, capable; Swed. *duga*, to avail; whence *dugtig*, able, fit; Icel. *duga*, to avail; whence *dygðugr*, doughty; Goth. *dugan*, to avail, suit; OHG. *tugan*, G. *taugen*, to be worth; whence G. *tüchtig*, able. ¶ The AS. *dugan* is prov. E. *dow*, to be worth something.

DOUSE, to plunge into water, immerse. (Scand.?) 'I have washed my feet in mire or ink, *douz'd* my carnal affections in all the vileness of the world;' Hammond, Works, iv. 515 (R.). 'He was very often used . . . to be *dowssed* [perfundebatur] in water lukewarme;' Holland, Suetonius, p. 75 (R.). 'To swing i' th' air, or *douce* in water;' Butler, Hudibras, pt. ii. c. 1. l. 502. Perhaps of Scand. origin; cf. Norw. *du a*, to fall or topple down, as with a blow (Aasen); *dus* (with *uu*), a push, a blow (id.). Cf. also MSwed. *dunsa*, to fall heavily (Ihre); Swed. dial. *dunsa*, to plump down, fall clumsily; *duns*, the noise of a falling body; Rietz. And see **Dowse** (1).

DOUT, to extinguish. (E.) In Shak. Hen. V, iv. 2. 11. *Dout* is for *do out*, i.e. put out. Cf. *doff*, *don*, *dup*, for *do off*, *do on*, *do up*.

DOVE, the name of a bird. (E.) ME. *doue*, *donue*, *douwe* (where *u* = *v*); P. Plowman, B. xv. 393. AS. *dūfe*, only found in the compound *dūfe-doppa*, used to translate L. *pelicānus* (Bosworth); the usual AS. word was *culfra*.+OSax. *dūba* (Heliand); Goth. *dubo*; G. *taube*. β. The sense is 'diver,' the form *dūfe* being from the verb *dūfan*, to dive, with the suffix -*e* denoting the fem. agent, as usual. And see **Dive** and **Columbine**. Der. *dove-cot*; also *dove-tail*, q. v.

DOVETAIL, to fasten boards together. (E.) '*Dovetaild* is a term among joyners,' &c.; Blount's Gloss. From *dove* and *tail*; from the shape of the fitted ends of the board (◁).

DOWAGER, a widow with a jointure. (F. – L.) In Shak. Mids. N. D. i. 1. 5, 157. Spelt *douagier* in Palsgrave; Epistle, p. i. – OF. *douagere*, sb. f. (Godefroy); from *douage*, a dower. Cf. 'To make her *dowage* [endowment] of so rich a jointure;' Merry Devil of Edmonton (R.). β. Again, the OF. *dou-age* is from the F. *douer*, to endow. – L. *dōtāre*, to endow. See **Dower**.

DOWDY, shabbily dressed; as sb., a slattern. (Scand.) 'Dido, a *dowdy*;' Shak. Romeo and Juliet, ii. 4. 43. From ME. *dowd*, an ill-dressed person; found as early as 1330 (N.E.D.); cf. prov. E. *dowd*, a woman's cap (E.D.D.).+Icel. *dūða*, to wrap up, swathe; *dūði*, swaddling clothes. Cf. **Duds**.

DOWEL, a plug for connecting two pieces of wood, &c. (Low G.) 'The quelis [wheels] ar ioyned with mani a *dowle*;' Cursor Mundi, 21270. – Low G. *dovel*, a plug (Lübben); cf. G. *döbel*, OHG. *tubili*, a dowel; EFries. *döfel*. Allied to Swed. *dubb*, a plug, peg. Perhaps influenced by F. *douille*, a socket.

DOWER, an endowment. (F. – L.) ME. *dower*, Chaucer, C. T. 8683 (E 807). – OF. *doaire*, later *douaire*. – Late L. *dōtārium*. – L. *dōtāre*, to endow. – L. *dōt*-, stem of *dōs* (gen. *dōtis*), a gift, dowry. +Gk. δώς, a gift. – √DŌ, to give; cf. Skt. *dā*, to give. Der. *dower-ed*, *dower-less*; *dowry* (for *dower-y*); and see *dowager*.

DOWLAS, a coarse kind of linen. (Brittany.) 'Britaine [Brittany] where . . *Doulas* and *Lockeram* is made;' Act 28 Hen. VIII. c. 4. § 1 (N.E.D.). And in Shak. 1 Hen. IV. iii. 3. 79. – Bret. *Daoulas*, SE. of Brest, in Brittany. See **Lockram**.

DOWLE, a filament of a feather. (F. – L. ?) In Shak. Temp. iii. 3. 65. ME. *doule*, Plowman's Tale, 1272. Perhaps from OF.

doulle, douille, somewhat soft. ━ L. *ductilis ;* see **Ductile.** [A guess ; see Notes on E. Etym.]

DOWN (1), soft plumage. (Scand.) In Gower, C. A. ii. 103, bk. iv. 3021. ━ Icel. *dúnn,* down ; Swed. *dun ;* Dan. *duun.* Cf. Lith. *dujė,* down. **Der.** *down-y ; eider-down.*

DOWN (2), a hill. (C.) ME. *dun, doun ;* Layamon, 27256 ; Ormulum, 14568. AS. *dún,* a hill ; Grein, i. 213. ━ Irish *dún,* a fortified hill, fort, town ; Gael. *dun,* a hill, mount, fort ; W. *din,* a hillfort. **β.** Cognate with AS. *tún,* a fort, enclosure, town ; the AS. *t* answering Celtic *d* by Grimm's law. See **Town. Der.** *a-down,* q. v. ; also *down* (3), q. v. Also, ' the *downs,*' a famous road-stead for ships, opposite the North Downs (Kent) ; ' in the *Downes ;*' Capt. J. Smith, Works, p. 90. Stokes-Fick, p. 150. Doublet, *dune.*

DOWN (3), *adv.* and *prep.* in a descending direction. (E. and C.) The prep. *down* is a mere corruption, by loss of the initial, of ME. *a-down,* which again is for AS. *of-dúne,* i. e. off or from the hill. The loss of the prefix is of early date ; *dun* (for *a-dune*) occurs in Layamon, 6864, in the phrase ' he *dun* læi ' = he lay down. It will be observed that this form *dun* was originally an adverb, not a preposition. See **Down** (2), and **Adown. Der.** *down-cast, -fall, -hearted, -hill, -right, -ward, -wards. Dunward* (downward) occurs in Layamon, 13106.

DOWSE (1), to strike in the face. (Scand.) ' *Dowse,* a blow on the chaps ;' Kersey, ed. 1715. ' *Dowse,* to give one a slap on the chaps ;' Bailey (1735). [Cf. ME. *duschen,* to strike ; ' such a dasande drede *dusched* to his heart ' = such a dazing dread struck to his heart ; Allit. Poems, ed. Morris, B. 1538. Of Scand. origin ; cf. Norwegian *dusa,* to strike with violence (also to topple down, as from a blow, Ross) ; Ger. dial. *dusen, tusen,* to strike, run against, cited by Rietz s.v. *dust ;* also MDu. *doesen,* to beat heavily, strike (Kilian) ; EFries. *dössen,* to strike (Koolman). **β.** The prov. G. (Altmark) *dussen* means ' to daze one by a blow on the head ' (Danneil) ; cf. Low G. *dussen,* to be dased by a blow on the head. Perhaps allied to **Dizzy** and **Doze.**

DOWSE (2), to plunge into water ; see **Douse.**

DOWSE (3), to extinguish. (E.) A cant term ; ' *dowse* the glim,' i. e. extinguish the light. Probably only a particular use of *dowse* (1), to strike. Possibly suggested by *dout,* to extinguish.

DOXOLOGY, an utterance of praise to God. (L. ─ Gk.) ' *Doxology,* a song of praise,' &c. ; Blount's Gloss. ed. 1674. ━ Late L. *doxologia.* ━ Gk. δοξολογία, an ascription of praise. ━ Gk. δοξολόγος, giving praise. ━ Gk. δοξο-, for δόξα, glory ; and -λόγος, speaking, from λέγειν, to speak. Δόξα meant originally ' a notion,' from δοκεῖν, to think, expect ; see **Dogma.**

DOXY, a disreputable sweetheart. (MDu.) A cant term. In Shak. Wint. Ta. iv. 3. 2. (Cf. EFries. *doktje,* dimin. of *dokke,* a doll.) Prob. from MDu. *docke,* a doll. Cf. OHG. *toccha,* a doll, also a term of endearment (G. *docke*).

DOZE, to sleep lightly, slumber. (Scand.) ' *Dosed* with his fumes, and heavy with his load, They found him snoring in his dark abode ;' Dryden, tr. of Virgil, Ecl. vi. 21. Here *dosed* means ' stupefied,' ' rendered drowsy.' ━ Swed. dial. *dusa,* to doze, slumber ; Rietz ; Dan. *döse,* to doze, mope. Cf. Icel. *dúsa,* to doze ; Low G. *dussen,* to be dizzy. From Teut. base *dus-,* whence also *dizzy ;* see **Dizzy.**

DOZEN, twelve. (F. ─ L.) ME. *dosain ;* K. Alisaunder, l. 657. ━ OF. *dosaine, dozaine ;* modF. *douzaine,* a dozen. ━ OF. *doze,* modF. *douze,* twelve ; with suffix -*aine* (< L. -*ēna,* as in *cent-ēna*). ━ L. *duodecim,* twelve. ━ L. *duo,* two, cognate with E. *two ;* and *decem,* ten, cognate with E. *ten.* See **Two** and **Ten.**

DRAB (1), a low, sluttish woman. (E.) In Shak. Macb. iv. 1. 31. Palsgrave has : ' *Drabbe,* a slutte.' [Cf. also Irish *drabog,* a slut, slattern, Gael. *drabag,* a slattern ; Gael. *drabach,* dirty, slovenly, *drabaire,* a dirty, slovenly man ; all from E.] Not found in AS. Cf. EFries. *drabbe,* puddle-water ; Du. *drabbe,* dregs, draff ; Low G. *drabbeln,* to slaver. Allied to **Draff. Der.** *drab,* verb ; Hamlet, ii. 1. 26.

DRAB (2), of a dull brown colour. (F. ─ Late L.) ' *Drab,* adj. (with clothiers), belonging to a gradation of plain colours betwixt a white and a dark brown ;' Ash's Dict. ed. 1775. He also gives : ' *Drab,* s. (in commerce) a strong kind of cloth, cloth double milled.' Bailey (1721) has : ' *Drap, Drab,* cloth.' It would appear that *drab* was applied to the colour of undyed cloth. ━ F. *drap,* cloth. ━ Late L. acc. *drappum,* from nom. *drappus,* in Charlemagne's Capitularies (Brachet). Cf. Lith. *drapanos,* white linen. See **Drape** and **Trap** (2).

DRACHM, a weight ; see **Dram.**

DRAFF, dregs, refuse, hogwash. (E.) ME. *draf,* Chaucer, C. T. 17346 (I 35) ; and earlier, in Layamon, 29256. Not found in AS. ; but may be considered an E. word. ╋ Du. *draf,* swill, hog's wash ; also *drab,* draff ; Icel. *draf,* draff, husks ; Swed. *draf,* grains ; Dan. *drav,* dregs, lees ; G. *träber,* pl. grains, husks. Cf. AS. *dróf,* turbid ; G. *trübe ;* Goth. *dróbjan,* to trouble ; Gk. τρέφειν, to thicken, curdle,

nourish. Allied to **Drab** (1), q. v. [Cf. Gael. and Irish *drabh,* draff ; from E.]

DRAFT, the act of drawing, a draught. (E.) A corruption of *draught,* by the usual change of *gh* to *f,* as in *laugh* (pron. *laaf*). See **Draught. Der.** *dra/t,* verb, *drafts-man.*

DRAG, to pull forcibly. (Scand.) ME. *draggen,* Prompt. Parv. A secondary weak verb, due to *draw.* ━ Swed. *dragga,* to search with a grapnel ; *dragg,* a grapnel ; cf. Dan. *drag,* a pull, tug, draught, haul. ━ Swed. *draga,* to draw ; Icel. *draga,* to draw, pull, carry ; Dan. *drage,* to draw, pull, drag. See **Draw.**

DRAGGLE, to make or become dirty by drawing along the ground. (E.) ' His *draggling* tail hung in the dirt ;' Hudibras, pt. i. c. 1. l. 1l28. The frequentative of *drag,* by addition of the usual suffix -*le ;* cf. *waggle* from *wag.* See **Drag.** Doublet, *drawl.*

DRAGOMAN, an interpreter. (F.─Ital.─Gk.─Arab.) Spelt *druggerman,* Pope, Sat. viii. 83. Sandys has *drogermen* as a pl. ; Travels (1632), p. 62. [Found very early, spelt *drogman,* in King Alisaunder, l. 3401 ; from F. *drogman.*] ━ F. *dragoman, drogman.* ━ Ital. *dragommanno,* an interpreter. A word of Eastern origin, introduced from Constantinople by the Crusaders, who had borrowed it from the mediæval Gk. δραγούμανος, an interpreter (Brachet). ━ Arab. *tarjumān* (formerly *targumān*), an interpreter, translator, dragoman ; Palmer's Pers. Dict. col. 131 ; Rich. Dict. p. 388. Cf. Chaldee *targūm,* a version, interpretation. See **Targum.**

DRAGON, a winged serpent. (F. ─ L. ─ Gk.) ME. *dragun ;* Old Eng. Miscellany, ed. Morris, p. 24, l. 759. ━ F. *dragon.* ━ L. acc. *dracōnem,* from nom. *draco.* ━ Gk. δράκων, a dragon ; lit. ' seeing one,' i. e. sharp-sighted one. ━ Gk. δρακ-, weak grade of δέρκομαι, I see. ━ √ DERK, to see ; cf. Skt. *dṛç,* to see. **Der.** *dragon-ish, -et* (dimin. form), -*fly ;* and see *dragoon.*

DRAGOON, a kind of light horseman. (F.─L.─Gk.) ' A captain of *dragoons ;*' Spectator, no. 261. ━ F. *dragon,* a dragoon, horse-soldier ; the same word with F. *dragon,* a dragon, though the reason for the name has been disputed. ━ L. acc. *dracōnem,* from nom. *draco,* a dragon. See **Dragon. Der.** *dragonn-ade,* a French word. ¶ Littré gives 1585 as the date of the first use of *dragoons,* and quotes the supposition of Voltaire, that they were so named from OF. *dragon,* in the sense of ' standard ;' but this is unsupported. The fact is rather, that they were so called because armed with firearms called *dragons ;* and this is strongly supported by the use of E. *dragoon* in the sense of a kind of carbine, as early as 1622 (N.E.D.). And these carbines were so called because they ' breathed fire,' like the fabulous dragons of old. The dragoons were at first infantry soldiers, till 1784.

DRAIN, to draw off gradually. (E.) In Shak. Macb. i. 3. 18. Not found in ME. AS. *dréhnigean, dréhnian, drénian ;* in the phr. ' ge *dréhnigeað* [var. read. *dréhniað, dréniað*] þone gnæt aweg,' i. e. ye drain away the gnat ; Matt. xxiii. 24. Also spelt *dréahnian,* A. S. Leechdoms, iii. 72 ; orig. sense, ' to become dry.' ━ AS. **dréag-* = Teut. **draug-,* 2nd grade of Teut. **dreugan-,* to be dry ; cf. Icel. *draug-r,* a dry log. See **Dry. Der.** *drain,* sb. ; *drain-age, drain-er.* See Notes on Eng. Etym., p. 73.

DRAKE, the male of the duck. (E.) ' As doth the whyte doke after hir *drake ;*' Chaucer, C. T. 3576 ; cf. Havelok, 1241. This ME. *drake* answers to AS. **draca,* not found, but of the same form as AS. *draca,* a dragon, though the latter is merely borrowed from the L. *draco* (see **Dragon**). **β.** We find a similar equivalence of form in the Low G. *drake,* (1) a drake ; (2) a kite (Bremen Wört.) ; Low G. *drake, draak,* (1) a kite ; (2) a drake ; (3) a meteor (Berghaus) ; MDan. *drage,* (1) a dragon ; (2) a drake (Kalkar). Cf. also Swed. *and,* a duck, *and-drake,* a drake (from Low G.) ; G. *enterich,* OHG. *anetrecho,* MHG. *antrache* (Schade), for **anut-trahho* (Kluge) ; prob. for *anut* (AS. *ened*) duck, and *trahho,* of unknown meaning, the same in form as *trahho,* a dragon. Ihre notes MSwed. *drake,* a dragon, a war-ship, *and-drake,* a drake. Levins (1570) has : ' *drake,* birde, anas ;' and ' *drake,* dragon, draco.' Cf. G. *drache, drachen,* a dragon, a kite. **γ.** The AS. **draca* is probably Teutonic. Perhaps connected with Icel. *draka* or *drāk,* a streak ; Swed. dial. *drakig ;* Dan. dial. *draget,* marked (on the back) with a white stripe.

DRAM, DRACHM, a small weight, small quantity. (F. ─ L. ─ Gk.) In Shak. Timon, v. 1. 154 ; Merch. of Ven. iv. 1. 6. ' *Drame,* wyghte [weight], drama, dragma ;' Prompt. Parv. ━ OF. *dragme* (Hatzfeld) ; MF. *drame, dragme, drachme,* ' a dram ; the eighth part of an ounce, or three scruples ; also, a handful of ;' Cot. ━ L. *drachma,* borrowed from Gk. δραχμή, a handful, a drachma, used both as a weight and a coin ; cf. δράγμα, as much as one can grasp. ━ Gk. δράσσομαι, I grasp. Brugmann, i. § 509.

DRAMA, a representation of actions. (L. ─ Gk.) Puttenham speaks of ' enterludes or poemes *drammaticke ;*' Arte of Poesie, lib. i. cap. 17 (heading). Cf. the phrase ' *dramatis* personæ ' commonly prefixed to old plays. ━ L. *drāma.* ━ Gk. δρᾶμα (stem δραματ-), a deed, act, drama. ━ Gk. δράω, I do, perform. ✛ Lithuanian *daraù*, I make, do. **Der.** (from stem *dramat-*), *dramat-ic*, *-ic-al*, *-ic-al-ly*, *-ise*, *-ist*; and see *drastic*.

DRAPE, to cover with cloth. (F.━Late L.) Formerly, to manufacture cloth; ‘that the clothier might *drape* accordingly as he might afford;’ Bacon, Hen. VII, ed. Lumby, p. 74.━F. *draper*, to make cloth; Cot.━F. *drap*, cloth; see **Drab** (2). **Der.** *drap-er*, occurring in P. Plowman, B. v. 255; *-er-y*.

DRASTIC, actively purgative, effective. (Gk.) ‘ *Drastica*, drastick remedies, i.e. such as operate speedily and effectually;’ Phillips’ Dict. ed. 1706.━Gk. δραστικός, drastic, effective; allied to δραστέος, verbal adj. of δράω, I effect; see **Drama**.

DRAUGHT, also **DRAFT,** a drawing. (E.) ‘A *draughte* of wyn;’ Chaucer, C. T. Prol. 398 (A 396); spelt *drahte*, Layamon, 29259. Not found in AS., but evidently derived from AS. *drag-an*, to draw, drag; see **Draw**. The suffixed *-t* appears also in *flight* from *fly*, *drift* from *drive*, &c. ✛ Du. *dragt*, a load, burden; from *dragen*, to carry; Dan. *dragt*, a load; Icel. *drāttr*, a pulling, a draught (of fishes); from *draga*, to draw. **Der.** *draught-house* (for *withdraught-house*, where *withdraught* = a retreat, place to which one withdraws); *draughts-man* or *drafts-man*; also *draughts*, a game in which alternate *draughts*, i.e. ‘moves,’ are made; Chaucer uses *draughtes*, in the sense of ‘ moves’ at the game of chess, in The Boke of the Duchesse, l. 653; cf. Tale of Beryn, ed. Furnivall, 1779, 1812.

DRAW, to pull along. (E.) ME. *drawen*, Layamon, i. 57; l. 1339. AS. *dragan* (pt. t. *drōh*); cf. *law* from the older *lagu*. The form *draw* dates from after A.D. 1200. ✛ Du. *dragen*; Icel. and Swed. *draga*, Dan. *drage*; Goth. *dragan*; G. *tragen*, to pull along, carry. Teut. type *dragan-*, pt.-t. *drōg*. **Der.** *draw-back*, *-bridge*, *-er*, *-ers*, *-ing*; *draw-ing-room* (short for *withdraw-ing-room*, which was used as late as 1627; see Pegge’s Curialia, pt. i. p. 66); *-well*; also *withdraw*, q.v.; *drawl*, q.v.; *draught*, q.v.; *dray*, q.v.; *dredge* (1), q.v.

DRAWL, to speak very slowly. (E.) In Shak. Merry Wives, ii. 1. 145. An extension of *draw*, with the suffix *-l*, giving a frequentative force. Thus *drawl* is a doublet of *draggle*, q.v. Cf. Du. *dralen*, to loiter, linger, delay; similarly formed from *dragen*, to carry, endure; Icel. *dralla* (< *drag-la*), to loiter.

DRAY, a low cart for heavy goods. (E.) The word *dray-load* occurs in State Trials, an. 1643 (R.); *dray-men* in Shak. Rich. II, i. 4. 32. ME. *dreye*, Trevisa, tr. of Higden, iii. 145. The form *dray* agrees with AS. *drage*, which occurs in AS. *dræge* or *dræg-net*, a draw-net, or dredge-net; Voc. 105. 4.✛Swed. *drög*, a sledge, dray. It means ‘that which is drawn along;’ see **Draw**.

DREAD, to fear, be afraid. (E.) ME. *dreden*, P. Plowman, B. xx. 153. AS. *drǣdan*, only found in the compounds on-*drǣdan*, ādrǣdan, ofdrǣdan; of which the first is common.✛OSax. *drādan*, only in the compound *andrādan* or *anddrādan*, to be afraid; OHG. *trātan*, only in the comp. *intrātan*, MHG. *entrāten*, to be afraid. Teut. type *drǣdan-*. Root unknown. **Der.** *dread*, sb.; *dread-ful*, *-ful-ly*, *-ful-ness*, *-less*, *-less-ly*, *-less-ness*, *-naught*.

DREAM (1), a vision. (E.) ME. *dream*, *dreem*, *drem*; Havelok, 1284. [Distinct from ME. *dream*, ‘sound,’ or ‘ music;’ as in ‘ mid te dredful *dreame* of þe englene bemen’ = with the dreadful sound of the angels’ trumpets, Ancren Riwle, p. 214; AS. *drēam*, (1) a sweet sound, music, harmony; (2) joy, glee.] The sense of ‘vision’ is not found in the earliest English, but the AS. form must, in this case also, have been *drēam*. ✛ OSax. *drōm*, a dream; OFries. *drām*, a dream; Du. *droom*; Icel. *draumr*; Dan. and Swed. *dröm*; G. *traum*. Kluge suggests comparison with G. *trug-bild*, a phantom. If so, the Teut. type was *draugmoz*, m.; from Teut. *draug*, second grade of *dreugan-* (OHG. *triogan*, G. *trügen*), to deceive. Cf. Icel. *draugr*, a ghost. Also OPers. *drauga* (Pers. *durūgh*), a deceit, lie; from the Idg. root *dhreugh*. Brugmann, i. §§ 681, 689. **Der.** *dream*, verb, q.v.; *dream-less*, *dream-y*.

DREAM (2), to see a vision. (E.) The verb is derived from the sb., not *vice versa*. Cf. G. *traümen*, to dream, from sb. *traum*.

DREARY, DREAR, gloomy, cheerless. (E.) *Drear* is a late poetical form, used by Milton (Il Pens. 119), Parnell and Cowper. It is quite unauthorised, and a false form. ME. *dreori*, *dreri*, *druri*; spelt *dreery*, *drery*, Chaucer, C. T. 8390 (E 514). AS. *drēorig*, sad, mournful; originally ‘ bloody,’ or ‘gory,’ as in Beowulf, ed. Grein, 1417, 2789. Formed, with suffix *-ig*, from AS. *drēor*, gore, blood; Grein, i. 205. And again, AS. *drēor* is from the verb *drēosan*, to fall, drip, whence also *drizzle*, q.v. ✛ Icel. *dreyrigr*, gory; from *dreyri*, gore; G. *traurig*, sad, orig. gory, from OHG. *trōr*, gore. All from Teut. str. vb. *dreusan-* (pt. t. *draus*, pp. *druzanoz*), to fall in drops. See **Drizzle, Drowse**. **Der.** *dreari-ness*, *-ly*.

DREDGE (1), a drag-net. (E.) Also spelt *drudge*. ‘ Drudger, one that fishes for oysters;’ Blount’s Gloss. ed. 1674. ‘ Dredgers, fishers for oisters;’ Kersey, ed. 1715; cf. MF. *drege* (prob. from E.), ‘ a kind of fish-net, forbidden to be used except for oysters;’ Cot.

The NorthE. form is *dreg* (see Supp. to Jamieson). It answers to an AS. form *drecg* or *drecge* (from *drag-jo-*); from AS. *drag-an*, to draw. See **Draw**. Cf. MDu. *dregge*, ‘a drag;’ Hexham. ¶ There is an AS. *dræg-net*, a draw-net, Voc. 105. 4; but this would give *dray-net*; see **Dray**.

DREDGE (2), to sprinkle flour on meat, &c. (F.━Late L.━Gk.) ‘ Burnt figs *dreg’d* [dredged] with meal and powdered sugar;’ Beaum. and Fletcher, Scornful Lady, Act ii. sc. 3. ‘ *Dredge* you a dish of plovers;’ id. Bloody Brother, Act ii. sc. 2. To *dredge* is to sprinkle as in sowing *dreg*, or mixed corn; thus Holland says that ‘ choler is a miscellane seed, as it were, and a *dredge*, made of all the passions of the mind;’ Plutarch, p. 108 (R.). ‘ Dredge or Dreg, oats and barley mingled together;’ Kersey, ed. 1715.━OF. *dragée*, *dragée aux chevaux*, ‘ provender of divers sorts of pulse mingled together; also the course grain called bolymong, French-wheat, Block-wheat, or Buck-wheat;’ Cot. Cotgrave also gives the older sense of *dragée* as ‘a kind of disgestive (*sic*) powder, usually prescribed unto weak stomachs after meat;’ this is the mod. F. *dragée*, a sugar-plum. β. Allied to Ital. *treggea*, a sugar-plum; and supposed (by Diez) to be derived from Late L. *tragēmata*. Diez quotes from Papias: ‘ collibia sunt apud Hebraeos, quae nos vocamus *tragēmata* vel vilia munuscula, ut cicer frixum,’ &c.━Gk. τραγήματα, dried fruits, pl. of τράγημα, something nice to eat.━Gk. τρώγειν 2nd aor. ἔ-τραγ-ον, to gnaw; also to eat dried fruits; allied to τρώγλη, a hole, a cave (cf. E. *trout*, troglodyte).

DREGS, lees, sediment. (Scand.) A pl. form, from sing. *dreg*. ‘ Fra fen, ful of *dreg* ’ = out of a fen full of mire; Northern Met. version of Ps. xxxix. 3. ‘ Dreggis and draffe;’ P. Plowman, B. xix. 397.━Icel. *dregg*, pl. *dreggjar*, dregs, lees; Swed. *drägg*, dregs, lees. β. The theoretical Teut. form is *drag-jōn-* (Noreen); allied to OPrussian *dragios*, dregs; cf. Gk. ταραχή, disorder, θράσσειν, to trouble, disturb. ¶ Not allied to G. *dreck*, dirt, for that is the Icel. *þrekkr*; nor yet to L. *fracēs*, dregs of oil (Brugm. i. § 417). **Der.** *dregg-y*, *-i-ness*.

DRENCH, to fill with drink or liquid. (E.) The causal of ‘ drink;’ the old sense is ‘ to make to drink.’ ME. *drenchen*, Havelok, 561, 583. AS. *drencan*, to drench, Grein, i. 202; causal of AS. *drincan*, to drink.✛Du. *drenken*, to water a horse; Icel. *drekkja*, to drown, swamp; Swed. *dränka*, to drown, to steep; G. *tränken*, to water, to soak. See **Drink**. **Der.** *drench*, sb.; AS. *drenc*.

DRESS, to make ready, deck. (F.━L.) ME. *dressen*; King Alisaunder, 479.━OF. *dresser*, *drescer*, to erect, set up, arrange, dress.━Late L. type *dīrectiāre*, not found; but formed from L. *directus*, direct, straight, hence just, right, upright. See **Direct**. **Der.** *dress*, sb.; *-ing*, *-ing-case*, *-y*; also *dress-er* (in Palsgrave), a table on which meat was dressed.

DRIBBLE, to let fall in small drops. (E.) The reading *dribling* in Shak. Meas. for Meas. i. 3. 2, may be an error for *dribbling*. *Dribble* is the frequentative of *drib*, which is a variant of *drip*. ‘ Lyke drunkardis that *dribbis*,’ i.e. drip, slaver; Skelton, Garland of Laurel, 641. Cf. Dan. dial. *drible*, *dreble*, to dribble, MDan. *drybe*, to drip; Jutland *dribble*, to dribble. See **Drip**. **Der.** *dribbl-er*; also *dribl-et*, formed with dimin. suffix *-et*. Kersey has ‘ *dribblet* (old word), a small portion, a little sum of money owing.’ ☞ Not the same word as *drivel*.

DRIFT, that which is driven. (E.) ‘ The dragoun drew him awaie [departed] with *drift* of his winges,’ i.e. driving, violent movement; Alisaunder, frag. A., ed. Skeat, 998. Cf. Cursor Mundi, 496. Formed with suffix *-t*, from *drif-*, weak grade of AS. *drīfan*, to drive. ✛Du. *drift*, a drove, flock, course, current, ardour; Icel. *drift*, *dript*, a snow-drift; Swed. *drift*, impulse, instinct; G. *trift*, a drove, herd, pasturage. See **Drive**. **Der.** *drift*, verb; *drift-less*, *-wood*.

DRILL (1), to bore holes, to train soldiers. (Du.) Cotgrave explains F. *trappan* as ‘a stone-cutter’s *drill*, wherewith he bores little holes in marble.’ Ben Jonson hints at the Dutch origin of the word in the sense of ‘to train soldiers.’ ‘ He that but saw thy curious captain’s *drill* Would think no more of Flushing or the Brill;’ Underwoods, lxii, l. 29.━MDu. *drillen*, or *trillen*, ‘ moītatare, nutare, vacillare, ultro citroque cursitare, gyros agere, gyrare, rotare, volvere, tornare, terebrare,’ Kilian; mod. Du. *drillen*, to drill, bore, to turn round, shake, brandish, to drill, form to arms, to run hither and thither, to go through the manual exercise. Sewel’s Dutch Dict. gives *drillen*, to drill, shake, brandish; *met den piek drillen*, to shake a pike; to exercise in the management of arms. β. The orig. sense is ‘ to turn round and round,’ whence (1) to turn men about or drill them, (2) to turn a pike about, or brandish it. Allied to MHG. *drellen*, to turn round (pp. *gedrollen*), and to Low G. *drall*, twisted tight. Teut. type *þrellan-* (pt. t. *þrall*), to twist; cf. AS. *þearl*, strict. **Der.** *drill*, sb.

DRILL (2), to sow corn in rows. (Low G.) We find an old word *drill* used in the sense of ‘ rill.’ ‘ So does a thirsty land drink up all the dew of heaven that wets its face, and the greater shower makes no torrent, nor digs so much as a little furrow, that the *drils* of the water might pass into rivers, or refresh their neighbour's weariness;' Bp. Taylor, vol. i. ser. 6 (R.). We also find the verb *drill*, to trickle. 'And water'd with cool rivulets, that *drill'd* Along the borders;' Sandys, Ecclesiastes, c. ii. **β**. This verb cannot be separated from *trill*, used in precisely the same sense; as in 'Few drops . . . adowne it *trild*,' i. e. trickled; Spenser F. Q. ii. 12. 78. In Chaucer, C. T. 13604 (Group B, 1864), Tyrwhitt prints *trilled* where the Ellesmere MS. has *trykled*; and it is clear that *trill* has the same sense. It seems to be really the same word as the above, but with a sense more common in Low G. The W. Flem. *indrillen* means 'to drill in,' to bury grain to a slight depth in the earth (De Bo); and Berghaus notes not only the Low G. verb *drillen*, but *drill-ploʒ* (drill-plough) as used in *drill-kultur*. *Trill* is properly the Scand. form. See **Trill** (2).

DRILLING, a twilled linen or cotton fabric. (G. – L.) A corruption of G. *drillich*, ticking, huckaback. And the G. word is a corruption from L. *trilīc-*, stem of *trilix*, having or consisting of three threads. – L. *tri-*, from *tres*, three; and *līcium*, a thrum, a thread.

DRINK, to suck in, swallow. (E.) ME. *drinken*; Chaucer, C. T. 135. AS. *drincan* (common). + Du. *drinken*; Icel. *drekka* (for *drenka = drinka*); Swed. *dricka*; Dan. *drikke*; Goth. *drigkan* (for *drinkan*); G. *trinken*. Teut. type **drenkan*, pt. t. **drank*, pp. **drunkanoz*. **Der.** *drink-able, -er, -offering*; and see *drunken*, *drunkard, drench, drown*.

DRIP, to fall in drops. (Scand.) 'Dryppe or drope, gutta, stilla, cadula;' Prompt. Parv. p. 132. 'Dryppyn or droppyn, stillo, gutto;' id. 'Dryppynge, or droppynge, stillacio;' id. *Drip* is a secondary weak verb, closely allied to the sb. *drop*, and is of Scand. origin. – Dan. *dryppe*, to drip; *dryp*, a drop; cf. Icel. *dreypa*, to let drop, from *draup*, 2nd grade of the strong verb *drjúpa*, to drip. The Dan. *dryppe* represents a Teut. type **drupjan*, from **drup-*, weak grade of **dreupan-* as seen in AS. *dréopan*, strong vb., pp. *dropen*; see *ā-dréopan* in Grein; OSax. *driopan*, to drip; pt. t. *drôp*; OHG. *triufan*, G. *triefen*, to drip, trickle; pt. t. *troff*. See **Drop**.

DRIVE, to urge on, push forward. (E.) ME. *driuen* (with *u = v*), Chaucer, C. T. 7122 (D 1540). AS. *drifan*, Grein, i. 206. + Du. *drijven*; Icel. *drifa*; Swed. *drifva*; Dan. *drive*; Goth. *dreiban*; OHG. *trîpan*, MHG. *trîben*, G. *treiben*. Teut. type **dreiban-* (pt. t. **draib*, pp. **dribanoz*). **Der.** *drive*, sb., *driv-er*; also *drif-t*, q.v.; *drove*, q.v.

DRIVEL, to slaver, speak foolishly. (E.) ME. *driuelen*, to slaver. 'Drynken and *dryuelen*;' P. Plowman, B. x. 41. 'Thei don but *dryuele* þeron;' id. x. 11 : where the C-text (xii. 9) has *dreuele*. This *drevelen* answers to AS. *dreflian*, to drivel or run at the nose; Voc. 161. 34. From the base *drab-*, whence also *Draff*. Cf. Low G. *drabbeln*, to slaver; Bremen Wörterbuch. Also Swed. *drafvel*, foolish talk; like E. *drivel*, sb. **Der.** *drivel*, sb., *drivell-ing*, *drivell-er*.

DRIZZLE, to rain slightly. (E.) 'These tears, that *drizzle* from mine eyes;' Marlowe, Edw. II, Act iii. sc. 4. l. 18. The old spelling is *drissel* or *drisel*. 'Through sletie *drisling* day;' Drant's Horace, b. ii. Sat. 2. *Dris-el* means 'to fall often,' and is the frequentative of ME. *dresen*, to fall, from AS. *dréosan*, to fall in drops; see **Dreary**. Cf. Dan. *drysse*, to fall in drops; Swed. dial. *drösla*.

DROLL, strange, odd, causing mirth. (F. – Du.) Shak. has *drollery*, Temp. iii. 3. 21; 2 Hen. IV, ii. 1. 156. The phr. 'to play the *drol*' is in Howell's Letters, b. i. s. 1. let. 18 (1620). – MF. *drole*, 'a boon companion, merry grig, pleasant wag;' Cot. Also cf. *droler*, 'to play the wag,' id.; *drolerie*, 'waggery, good roguery;' id. [The early use of *drollery* shows that we took the word from the French.] – Du. *drollig*, 'burlesk, odd;' Sewel. [The sb. *drol*, a droll fellow, is not noticed by Sewel.] – MDu. *drol*, 'a juglar;' Hexham. Cf. Low G. *drullig*, droll. Perhaps from the pp. stem *droll-*; for which see **Drill** (1). Korting, § 3115. **Der.** *droll-ish, droll-ery*.

DROMEDARY, a kind of camel. (F. – L. – Gk.) In early use. ME. *dromedarie*, King Alisaunder, 3407. – OF. *dromedaire*, 'a dromedary;' Cot. – Late L. *dromedārius*, better spelt *dromadārius*; Ducange. – L. *dromad-*, stem of *dromas*, a dromedary; with suffix *-ārius*. – Gk. δρομαδ-, stem of δρομάς, fast running, speedy. – Gk. δραμεῖν, to run; used as infin. aor. of τρέχειν, to run, but from a different root. + Skt. *dram*, to run; akin to *drā*, to run.

DRONE (1), to make a deep murmuring sound. (E.) 'He that *dronis* ay as ane bee;' Dunbar, Poems, xv. 8. [Cf. also ME. *drounen*; 'he *drouned* as a dragon, dredefull of noyes;' Alisaunder, frag. A., ed. Skeat, l. 985.] Not found in AS., but an imitative word. Similar words (but with a different vowel) are Swed. *dröna*, to low, bellow, drone; Dan. *dröne*, to peal, rumble; *drön*, a rumbling noise; Goth. *drunjus*, a sound, voice; Rom. x. 18; Icel. *drynja*, to roar. Allied to Gk. θρῆνος, a dirge; Skt. *dhran*, to sound. See below.

DRONE (2), a non-working bee. (E.) ME. *dran*, *drane*; pl. *dranes*, Piers Plowman's Crede, l. 726. AS. *drān* ; AS. Chron. an.

1127. 'Fucus, *drān*;' Voc. 121. 10; also *drǣn*, Voc. 318. 35. The AS. *drān* (like EFries. *drāne*) was prob. borrowed from OSax. *drān* (cognate with AS. *drǣn*). Cf. MHG. *treno*, a drone; cited by Fick and Curtius. + Gk. θρῶναξ, a Laconian drone-bee (Hesychius); Gk. ἀν-θρήνη, a wild bee. Teut. stems *dren-*, *drǣn-*; cf. *drun-* in the article above. **Der.** *dron-ish*.

DROOP, to sink, faint, fail. (Scand.) ME. *drupen*, *droupen*; Chaucer, C. T. 107. The pres. part. *drupand* is in the Cursor Mundi, l. 4457. – Icel. *drúpa*, to droop; allied to the strong verb *drjúpa*, to drip or drop. In mod. Icel., *drúpa* and *drjúpa* are confounded; but *drúpa* is a weak verb, and from the weak grade **drúp-*. For the sense, cf. 'I am ready to *drop*,' i.e. I droop. See **Drop**, and **Drip**.

DROP, sb. a small particle of liquid; *verb*, to let fall small particles of liquid. (E.) ME. *drope*, a drop; *dropien*, *droppen*, to let drop. The sb. is in Chaucer, C. T. 131; the verb in C. T. 16048 (G. 580); and the vb. is from the sb. AS. *dropa*, a drop; Grein, i. 207; *dropian*, to drop, Psalter, ed. Thorpe, xliv. 10; cf. also *dréopan*, to drop, drip, Grein, i. 205. + Du. *drop*, a drop; Icel. *dropi*, a drop; Swed. *droppe*, a drop; Dan. *draabe*, sb. a drop; vb. to drop; OHG. *tropfo*, G. *tropfen*, a drop; Low G. *druppen*, a drop. **β**. All from Teut. **drup-*, weak grade of Teut. **dreupan-*, to drop, as seen in AS. *dréopan*; see **Drip**. And see **Droop**. Cf. OIrish *drucht*, dew.

DROPSY, an unnatural collection of serous fluid in the body. (F. – L. – Gk.) ME. *dropesie*, a spelling found in Wyclif, Luke xiv. 2; where the earlier text has *ydropesie*. See further under **Hydropsy**. **Der.** *drops-ic-al*.

DROSHKY, DROSKY, a kind of carriage. (Russian.) Mere Russian. – Russ. *drojki*, a low four-wheeled carriage. [The *j* sounded as in French.] Given by Reiff. Dimin. of *drogi*, a waggon; which was orig. pl. of *droga*, a perch (of a carriage).

DROSS, dregs, scum, impure matter, refuse. (E.) ME. *dros*, Ancren Riwle, p. 284. AS. *drōs*, Voc. 353. 20; cf. AS. *drōsna*, answering to Lat. *fæx*, Ps. xxxix. 2, ed. Spelman. Cf. Du. *droesem*, dregs; G. *drusen*, pl., lees, dregs; OHG. *truosana*, husks of pressed grapes. And perhaps cf. AS. *dærstan*, dregs; Westphal. *drost*, dregs. **Der.** *dross-y, -i-ness*.

DROUGHT, dryness. (E.) ME. *drogte*, *drougte*; Chaucer, C. T. l. 2. In P. Plowman, B. vi. 290, we have *drought*, but in the earlier text (A. vii. 275) we find *drouhþe*. In the Ormulum, l. 8626, it is spelt *druhhþe*. AS. *drúgað*, dryness; Voc. 317. 24. – AS. *drúgian*, to dry; cf. *drýge*, dry; Grein, i. 207. So also Du. *droogte*, drought, from *droogen*, to dry. See **Dry**. ¶ The form *drouth* or *drough* occurs as late as in Spenser's Daphnaida, l. 333; and in Bacon's Nat. Hist. § 669; and is still found in prov. English. The same change from final *th* to final *t* has occurred in *height*, spelt *highth* in Milton's Paradise Lost. **Der.** *drought-y, -i-ness*.

DROVE, a number of driven cattle, a herd. (E.) ME. *drof*, *droue* (with *u = v*); 'wiþ [h]is *droue* of bestis;' Will. of Palerne, 181. – AS. *dráf*; AS. Chron. an. 1016. – AS. *dráf*, 2nd grade of *drifan*, to drive. See **Drive**. **Der.** *drov-er*.

DROWN, to be killed by being drenched in water; to kill by drenching in water. (Scand.) Orig. an *intransitive* or *passive* verb, as particularly denoted by the suffixed *-n*; cf. the Mœso-Goth. verbs in *-nan*, which are of a like character. 'Shall we give o'er and *drown*?' Tempest, i. 1. 42. 'Alle . . . *drowned* [perished] þerinne;' Allit. Poems, ed. Morris, B. 372. 'Alle þai *drowned*;' Cursor Mundi, 11793; where the Cotton MS. has: 'Al þai *drund*.' The form is M. Danish. – MDan. *drukne*, *drougne*, *droune*, *drone*, to sink, to be drowned (Kalkar). **β**. The *-nkn-* was preserved in ME. *druncnien*, later *druncnen*, *drunknen*; the spelling *druncuen* is in the Ormulum, 15398; *drunknen* is in Wyclif, Isa. lxiii. 6; cf. ONorthumb. *druncnia*, to be drowned, to sink; 'ongann *druncnia*' = began to sink; Matt. xiv. 30 (Lindisfarne MS.). Formed, with suffix *-ian*, from *druncen*, lit. drunken, pp. of *drincan*, to drink. **γ**. Similarly, we find Swed. *drunkna*, to be drowned, from *drucken*, drunken, pp. of *dricka*, to drink; and Dan. *drukne*, to be drowned, from *drukken*, drunken, old pp. of *drikke*, to drink. See **Drunken**. ¶ It may be added that this will appear more plainly from the Lindisfarne MS., Luke, xii. 45; where the Lat. *inebriari* is translated by '*druncgnia* vel *þætte se druncenig*,' i.e. to drown or that he may be drunken. Cf. the numerous forms (without *k*) of Jutland *drukne* (Feilberg). See Notes on E. Etym., p. 76.

DROWSE, DROWZE, to be sluggish. (E.) Formerly *drouse*; Milton, P. L. xi. 131; viii. 289; whence *drousie*, id. Il Penseroso, 83. Not found (as yet) in the Mid. Eng. period. AS. *drúsian*, to be sluggish; 'lagu *drúsade*' = the lake lay sluggish; Beowulf, ed. Grein, 1630. The base *drús-* is a weaker grade of Teut. **dreus-*, as seen in AS. *dréosan*, to mourn; Grein, i. 206, which is the same as AS. *dréosan*, to fall; id. **β**. So, too, OHG. *trúrēn*, to cast down the eyes, to mourn (mod. G. *trauern*), is related to OHG. *trúreg*, mournful, and to the E. *dreary*. See **Dreary**. Cf. Pomeran. *druse*, slumber. Der. *drowz-y* (*drowsy* in Palsgrave), *drowz-i-ness*.

DRUB, to beat. (Arab.) In Butler, Hudibras, pt. i. c. 3. l. 1042. He also has the sb. *drubs*, id. pt. iii. c. 3. l. 209. First introduced in connexion with the East, and applied to the punishment of the bastinado. Phillips (1706) has : '*Drub*, to beat the soles of the feet with the stick, a punishment used in Turkey.' Prob. from Arab. *ḍarb* (*zarb*), a beating with a stick ; from Arab. root *ḍaraba* (*zaraba*), he beat ; Rich. Dict. p. 952 (N.E.D.). β. Ihre (in 1769) quotes Swed. *drabba*, to beat ; with the conjecture of Spegel (1645–1714) that it is from Arab. *darab*, 'percutere, verberari facere.' Der. *drub*, sb. ; *drubb-ing*.

DRUDGE, to perform menial work. (E.) Shak. has the sb. *drudge*, Merch. of Ven. iii. 2. 103. ME. *druggen* ; Chaucer has 'to *drugge* and drawe ;' C. T. 1418 (A 1416). [Irish *drugaire*, a drudger, drudge, slave, and Irish *drugaireachd*, drudgery, slavery, are from E.] It answers to an AS. *drycgean*, not found, but regularly formed from *drug-*, weak grade of *drēogan*, to work, perform, endure (= Teut. *dreugan*-), Goth. *driugan*, LowlSc. *dree*). Cf. Icel. *drjūg-virkr*, one who works slowly but surely ; Norw. *drugga*, to go slowly, like one under a heavy burden (Ross). Der. *drudge*, sb. ; *drudg-er-y*.

DRUG, a medical ingredient. (F.) ME. *drogge*, *drugge* ; the pl. *drogges*, *drugges* is in Chaucer, Six-text, A 426 ; where the Harl. MS. has *dragges*, Prol. l. 428. [But *dragges* and *drogges* cannot be the same word ; the former is from OF. *dragée*, discussed s. v. **Dredge** (2), q. v. ; the latter is OF. *drogue*.]—OF. (and mod. F.) *drogue*, a drug ; cf. Ital., Span., and Port. *droga*, a drug. β. Remoter origin uncertain ; Diez derives it from Du. *droog*, dry ; and Sewel's Du. Dict. has : '*Droogen*, gedroogde kruyden en wortels, *druggs* ;' but he has prob. confused the F. with the Du. word. The word may be Eastern. Körting, § 3116, suggests a Slavonic origin, viz. OSlav. *drag*, Pol. *drogi*, costly. Der. *drugg-ist*.

DRUGGET, a coarse woollen cloth. (F.) 'And, coarsely clad in Norwich *drugget*, came ;' Dryden, Mac Flecknoe, l. 33.—MF. *droguet*, 'a kind of stuff that's half silk, half wooll ;' Cot. Cf. Span. *droguete*. A dimin., with suffix *-et*, from F. *drogue*, (1) a drug ; (2), trash, rubbish, stuff (Hamilton and Legros, French Dict.) ; i.e. in the latter sense. But it is probable that *drogue*, trash, is not the same word as *drogue*, a drug.

DRUID, a priest of the ancient Britons. (F.—L.—C.) 'The British *Druyds* ;' Howell, Foreign Travel, ed. 1642, sect. 10.—F. *Druide*, a Druid.—L. pl. *Druides* ; Cæsar, De Bello Gallico, vi. 13. Of Celtic origin. From OIrish *druid-*, as in *druid*, dat. and acc. of *drui*, a magician, sorcerer ; Irish *draoi*, *druidh*, an augur, magician ; Gael. *draoi*, *draoidh*, *druidh*, a magician, sorcerer. Origin undetermined ; the attempt to connect it with Irish and Gael. *darach*, *darag*, an oak, is by no means convincing. ¶ The AS. *drȳ*, a magician, is from British (W. *dryw*).

DRUM, a cylindrical musical instrument. (Du.) 'The *drummes* crie dub-a-dub ;' Gascoigne, Flowers ; ed. Hazlitt, vol. i. p. 83, l. 26. First found, spelt *drome*, in 1541 (N.E.D.). An imperfect adaptation of MDu. *tromme*, Du. *trom*, *trommel*, a drum ; *trommelen*, to drum. Cf. G. *trommel*, a drum ; esp. Strassburg *drum*, a drum (C. Schmidt) ; Dan. *drum*, a booming sound. Der. *drum*, verb ; *drum-head*, *drum-major*, *drum-stick*. See also **Thrum** (2).

DRUMBLE, to be sluggish. (Scand.) Shak. has : 'look how you *drumble* ;' Merry Wives, iii. 3. 156.—Norw. *drumla*, to be half asleep ; allied to *drumba*, *drumma*, to straggle, lag behind (as cattle) ; see Ross. Cf. Swed. *drumla*, to be clumsy, *drummel*, a blockhead (Öman).

DRUNKARD, one addicted to drinking. (E. ; with F. suffix.) In the A. V., Joel, i. 5 ; and in the Bible of 1551. Palgrave has *dronkarde*. Formed from the base *drunk-* of the pp. *drunken*, with the F. suffix *-ard*, of OHG. origin, used with an intensive force. This suffix is of the same origin with E. *hard* ; Brachet, Etym. French Dict. introd. § 196. ¶ The ME. word is *dronkelew*.

DRUNKEN, DRUNK, inebriated. (E.) ME. *dronken*, *drunken* ; Chaucer, C. T. 1264. AS. *druncen*, pp. of *drincan*, to drink, but often used as an adj. ; Grein, i. 207 ; see **Drink**. Der. *drunken-ness*.

DRUPE, a fleshy fruit containing a stone. (F.—L.—Gk.) A botanical term. Modern ; not in Todd's Johnson.—F. *drupe*, a drupe, stone-fruit.—L. *drūpa*, an over-ripe, wrinkled olive (Pliny).—Gk. δρύππα, an over-ripe olive ; perhaps a contraction from, or allied to, Gk. δρυπετής, ripened on the tree ; [a word which is frequently varied to δρυπετής, i.e. falling from the tree.]—Gk. δρῦς, a tree ; and πέσσειν, to cook, ripen. See **Tree** and **Cook**. Der. *drup-ac-e-ous*, with suffix =L. *-āceus*.

DRY, free from moisture. (E.) ME. *druȝe*, OEng. Hom. i. 87, l. 12 ; *druye*, *dryȝe*, Allit. Poems, ed. Morris, B. 385 and 412 ; *dreye*, Chaucer, C. T. 8775 (E 899). AS. *drȳge*, *drīge*, Grein, i. 207. Cf. Du. *droog*, dry ; G. *trocken*, dry. Also Icel. *draugr*, a dry log. All

from a Teut. root *dreug-*, to be dry ; cf. AS. *drēog-an*, to last, endure, &c. The orig. sense may have been lasting, hard. See **Drudge**. Der. *dry*, verb ; *-ly*, *-ness* ; *-goods*, *-nurse*, *-rot*, *-salter* ; see also *drought*.

DRYAD, a nymph of the woods. (L.—Gk.) Milton has *Dryad*, P. L. ix. 387 ; and the pl. *Dryades*, Comus, 964.—L. *Dryad-*, stem of *Dryas*, a Dryad.—Gk. δρυαδ-, stem of δρυάς, a nymph of the woods.—Gk. δρῦς, a tree ; cognate with E. **Tree**, q.v.

DUAL, consisting of two. (L.) 'This *dualité* . . . is founden in euery creature ;' T. Usk, Test of Love, b. ii. ch. 13. l. 30.—L. *duālis*, dual.—L. *duo*, two. See **Two**. Der. *dual-ism*, *dual-i-ty*.

DUAN, a canto. (Gaelic.) In Macpherson's Ossian ; and used by Burns (The Vision).—Gael. *duan*, a song, canto ; OIrish *dūan* ; see Macbain.

DUB, to confer knighthood by a stroke on the shoulder. (E.) ME. *dubben*, Havelok, 2042. AS. *dubban* ; '*dubbade* his sunu . . . to rīdere,' dubbed his son knight ; AS. Chron. an. 1086. β. A much-disputed word ; but, apparently, of Teut. origin ; if not native, it may be of Scand. origin. The statement (in N. E. D.) that there is no such Germanic verb as *dubban*, is hardly borne out. The Icel. *dubba* may be foreign ; but the Teut. forms *dib*, *dab*, *dob*, *dub*, expressive of light movements, cannot all be unoriginal. Cf. Norw. *dabba*, to tap with the foot (Ross) ; E. *dab* ; Swed. dial. *dabb*, a viscous clot ; E. a *dab* ; Norw. *dibba*, to nod the head, to trip lightly (Ross) ; Swed. dial. *dibb*, to touch lightly ; Dan. *dobbe*, a float (because it bobs) ; Swed. dial. *dobb*, *dubb*, a float, also (as a verb) to duck or bob under ; Norw. *dubba*, to nod (Aasen) ; EFries. *dubbe*, a blow, *dubben*, to strike ; Low G. *dobber*, a buoy ; G. *tupfen*, to dab. The OF. *adober*, to dub, is therefore correctly derived by Diez from a Teut. base *dub-*, to dab or tap. Cf. E. *dub-a-dub* (see **Drum**) ; evidently of imitative origin.

DUBIOUS, doubtful. (L.) In Milton, P. L. i. 104 ; and in Hall, Edw. IV, an. 9. § 14.—L. *dubiōsus*, doubtful.—L. *dubium*, doubt ; neut. of *dubius*, doubtful, moving in two directions ; formed from L. *duo*, two. See **Two**. Der. *dubious-ly*, *-ness*.

DUCAL, belonging to a duke. (F.—L.) F. *ducal*, Cot.—Late L. *ducālis*, adj.—L. *duc-*, stem of *dux*, a leader ; see **Duke**.

DUCAT, a coin. (F.—Ital.—L.) 'As fine as *ducat* in Venise ;' Chaucer, Ho. of Fame, iii. 258.—OF. *ducat*, 'the coyne termed a duckat, worth vi s. viii d. ;' Cot.—Ital. *ducato*, a ducat ; a duchy.—Late L. *ducātus*, a duchy. β. So called because first coined in the duchy of Apulia (about A.D. 1140) ; and, after 1284, they bore the legend 'sit tibi, Christe, datus, quem tu regis, iste *ducatus*.' See **Duchy**.

DUCHESS, the wife of a duke. (F.—L.) Chaucer wrote The Book of the *Duchesse*.—OF. *duchesse*, fem. of *duc*, a duke ; with suffix *-esse* = L. *-issa* = Gk. *-ισσα*. See **Duke**.

DUCHY, a dukedom. (F.—L.) ME. *duche* ; P. Plowman, C. iv. 245.—F. *duché*.—Late L. *ducātus* ; formed with suffix *-ātus* from *duc-*, stem of *dux*, a leader. See **Duke**.

DUCK (1), a bird. (E.) ME. *doke*, *duke* ; P. Plowman, B. v. 75 ; xvii. 62. The word *duk-e* means ' diver ;' the final *-e* = AS. m. *-a*, f. *-e*, a suffix denoting the agent, as in *hunt-a*, a hunter. AS. *dūce*, a duck ; see Cart. Saxon., ed. Birch, ii. 162, l. 3. See below. + Dan. *duk-and*, a diver (bird) ; from *duk-* = *dukke*, to dive, and and (= G. *ente*), a duck ; Swed. *dyk-fågel*, a diver (bird). See **Duck** (2). The short *u* is due to the following *k*, as in *suck*. Der. *duck-ling*, with double dimin. suffix *-l-* and *-ing* ; cf. *gos-ling*.

DUCK (2), to dive, bob the head down. (E.) ME. *duken*, *douken* ; the pres. pt. *doukand*, diving, occurs in The Wars of Alexander, l. 4090 ; and the pp. *duked* in the Cursor Mundi, 23203. It answers to an AS. *dūcan* (pt. t. *dēac*, pp. *docen*), not found. + Du. *duiken*, to stoop, dive ; Dan. *dukke*, to duck, plunge ; Swed. *dyka*, to dive ; G. *tauchen*, to dive. Der. *duck* (1).

DUCK (3), a pet, darling. (E.) 'O dainty *duck* !' Mids. N. D. v. 286. Apparently, a transferred sense of **Duck** (1).

DUCK (4), light canvas. (Du.) Strutt, Manners and Customs, iii. 129, quotes 'lampas *douck*' in a description of a tourney, as early as 2 Henry VIII (1510).—Du. *doek*, linen cloth, towel, canvas. + Dan. *dug*, cloth ; Swed. *duk* ; Icel. *dūkr*, cloth, table-cloth ; G. *tuch*, cloth ; OHG. *tuoh*, MHG. *tuoch*.

DUCT, a conduit-pipe. (L.) Still spelt *ductus* in 1715. ' *Ductus*, a leading, guiding ; a conduit-pipe ;' Kersey's Dict.—L. *ductus*, a leading ; cf. *ductus*, pp. of *dūcere*, to lead. See **Duke**.

DUCTILE, malleable. (F.—L.) 'Soft dispositions, which *ductile* be ;' Donne, To the Countess of Huntingdon, l. 27 ; and see Bacon, Nat. Hist. § 845.—F. *ductile*, 'easie to be hammered ;' Cot.—L. *ductilis*, easily led ; cf. *ductus*, pp. of *dūcere*, to lead. See **Duke**. Der. *ductil-i-ty*.

DUDE, a fop, exquisite. (Low G.) Modern.—G. *dude*, a foolish fellow (Grimm) ; shortened from Low G. *duden-dop*, *duden-kop*, a lazy fellow ; EFries. *dud-kop*, a drowsy fellow. Cf. EFries. *dudden*, to be drowzy ; see **Dawdle**.

DUDGEON (1), resentment. (F.?) 'When civil *dudgeon* first grew high;' Butler, Hudibras, pt. i. c. i. l. 1. The form *endugine* is also found; see additions to Nares. Origin wholly unknown; though the form would seem to be French.

DUDGEON (2), the haft of a dagger. (Unknown.) 'And on thy blade and *dudgeon* gouts of blood;' Macb. ii. 1. 46. See Clark and Wright, notes to Macbeth; Furness, notes to ditto. The evidence goes to show that some daggers were called *dudgeon-hafted*, which Gifford explains by saying that 'the wood was gouged out in crooked channels, like what is now, and perhaps was then, called snail-creeping;' note on Jonson's Works, v. 221. The root of the box-tree was also called *dudgeon*, apparently because it was curiously marked; 'the root [of box] .. is *dudgin* and ful of work;' Holland's Pliny, b. xvi. c. 16; where the context shows the sense to be 'crisped damask-wise' or 'full of waving.' β. In the earliest examples, the sense seems to be 'boxwood;' at any rate, it is a material used by a cutler. A cutler speaks of 'yuery [ivory], *dogeon*, horn, mapyll, and the toel that belongeth to my craft;' Arnold's Chron. (1502, repr. 1811), p. 245. In the York Wills, iii. 96 (Surtees Soc.), we find, in 1439, 'j dagger, cum manubrio de *dogeon*.' 'Ronnyn, as *dojoun* or masere;' Prompt. Parv. p. 436. The earliest is AF. *digeon*, in 1380; see Riley, Memorials of London, p. 439.

DUDS, rags, poor clothes. (Scand.) ME. '*dudde*, clothe, *amphibilus*;' Prompt. Parv. Related to Icel. *dúði*, swaddling clothes; *dúða*, to swathe, wrap up. Cf. **Dowdy**. See Notes on E. Etym., p. 78.

DUE, owed as a debt. (F.—L.) ME. *dewe*. 'A maner *dewe* dette' = a kind of debt due; P. Plowman, C. iv. 307. — OF. *deu*, masc. *deue*, fem. 'due;' Cot.; pp. from *devoir* (spelt *debvoir* in Cot.), to owe. — L. *debēre*, to owe. See **Debt**. Der. *du-ly* (ME. *dueliche*, Gower, C. A. iii. 245; bk. vii. 4570); also *du-ty*, q. v.

DUEL, a combat between two. (Ital.—L.) Formerly *duello*, Shak. Tw. Nt. iii. 4. 337.—Ital. *duello*, whence also F. *duel.*—L. *duellum*, lit. a combat between two.—L. *duo*, two. See **Two**. ¶ Cf. L. *bellum<duellum*; see **Belligerent**. Der. *dwell-er, -ist, -ing*.

DUENNA, an elderly lady acting as guardian. (Span.—L.) It occurs in Dryden's Span. Friar, i. 2; and Mrs. Centlivre's Busy Body, ii. 2.—Span. *dueña*, a married lady, duenna.—L. *domina*, a lady. ¶ Thus *duenna* is the same as *donna*, q. v.; or *dame*, q. v.

DUET, a piece of music for two. (Ital.) A musical term.—Ital. *duetto*; in Baretti, Ital. Dict.—Ital. *due*, two.—L. *duo*, two. See **Two**. For the suffix, cf. *quart-ette*, *quint-ette*.

DUFFEL, a kind of coarse woollen cloth. (Du.) 'And let it be of *duffil* gray;' Wordsworth, Alice Fell.—Du. *duffel*, duffel. So named from Duffel, a town not far from Antwerp.

DUFFER, a stupid person. (Scand.) Prob. the same as Lowl. Sc. *dowfart*, formed with the suffix *-art*(= *-ard*) from the adj. *dowf*, stupid, lit. 'deaf.'—Icel. *dauf-r*, deaf. See **Deaf**. Cf. WFlem. den *doofaard* (or *doovaard*) *spelen*, to pretend to be deaf (De Bo).

DUG, a teat. (E.) In Shak. Romeo, i. 3. 26. '*Tete*, pappe, or *dugge*;' Palsgrave. The exact original is not forthcoming; it can hardly be allied to Swed. *dägga*, Dan. *dægge*, to suckle, fondle; or to Goth. *daddjan*, to suckle. β. On the other hand, it corresponds to Skt. *duh* (for *dhugh*), to milk; whence *dōghā*, a milch cow, *dōha-s*, a milking.

DUGONG, a swimming mammal, sea-cow. (Malay.) Malay *dūyōng*, a sea-cow; Marsden's Malay Dict. p. 138.

DUKE, a leader. (F.—L.) ME. *duc*, *duk*; Layamon, l. 86.—OF. *duc*, acc. formed from a nom. *dux.*—L. *dux*, a leader; allied to *dūcere*, to lead.—✓DEUK, to pull, draw; Brugmann, i. § 592. Der. *duke-dom*; and see *duc-al*, *duch-ess*, *duch-y*, *duc-at*, *doge*. From L. *dūcere* we have *ad-duce*, *con-duce*, *de-duce*, *in-duce*, &c.; also *duct*, *con-duct*, *de-duct*, *in-duct*, &c.

DULCET, sweet. (F.—L.) In Shak. Mids. N. D. ii. 1. 151; and used by Cotgrave to translate OF. *doucet*. The spelling was refashioned after L. *dulcis*; cf. M. Ital. *dolcetto*, somewhat sweet (Florio). Formed, with dimin. suffix *-et* (with force of E. *-ish*), from OF. *dols*, sweet; see *dols* in Supp. to Godefroy.—L. *dulcis*, sweet. See **Douceur**; and see below.

DULCIMER, a musical instrument. (F.—Span.—L. and Gk.) In the Bible, A. V., Dan. iii. 5; and in Baret's Alvearie.—OF. *doulcemer* (Roquefort); cf. *doulcemele* in Godefroy.—Span. *dulcemele*, a dulcimer; so called from its sweet sound.—L. *dulce melos*, a sweet song; *dulce* is neut. of *dulcis* (see above); and *melos* = Gk. μέλος, for which see **Melody**.

DULL, stupid, foolish. (E.) ME. *dul*; Chaucer, C. T. 10593 (F 279). [Also as a verb; 'it *dulleth* me;' id. 16561 (G 1093).] In the Ancren Riwle we have '*dulle* neiles,' i.e. blunt nails, as a various reading of 'dulte neiles;' see **Dolt**. Dull also appears as ME. *dill*; answering to a Teut. type *dul-joz*. Closely allied to AS. *dol*, foolish, stupid; Grein, i. 194. Cf. Du. *dol*, G. *toll*, mad; answering to Teut. type *dul-oz*. All from Teut. **dul*, for **dwul*, weak grade of

*dwel-an-, as seen in A.S. *dwelan*, to err, to be stupid; see **Dwell**. Cf. also AS. *ge-dwol-god*, a false god; Irish and W. *dall*, blind. Brugmann, i. § 375 (6). Der. *dull*, verb; *dul-ly*, *-ness*; *dull-sighted*, *-witted*; also *dull-ard* (with suffix as in *drunk-ard*, q. v.); also *dol-t*, q. v.

DULSE, an edible species of seaweed. (C.) See Jamieson, E.D.D., and N.E.D. From Irish and Gael. *duileasg*, dulse. According to Macleod, it means 'water-leaf;' from Irish and Gael. *duille*, leaf, and *uisg(e)*, water.

DUMB, silent, unable to speak. (E.) ME. *domb*, *dumb*; Chaucer, C. T. 776 (A 774). AS. *dumb*, mute; Grein, i. 212.+Du. *dom*, dull, stupid; Icel. *dumbr*, dumb; Swed. *dumb*; Dan. *dum*, stupid; Goth. *dumbs*, dumb; OHG. *tump*, G. *dumm*, mute, stupid. β. The form *dumb*, with the orig. sense of 'stupid,' is prob. allied to Goth. *daubs*, deaf. See further under **Deaf**. Der. *dumb-ly*, *-ness*; *dumb-bell*, *-show*; also *dumm-y* (= *dumb-y*). ¶ The dumb-bell exercise was called 'a ringing of the dumb bells;' which explains the name. See Spectator, no. 115, § 7.

DUMP (1), an ill-shapen piece. (E.) '*Dump*, a clumsy medal of metal cast in moist sand: *East*;' Halliwell. Cf. the phr. 'I don't care a *dump*,' i.e. a piece, bit. Cf. '*Dubby*, dumpy, short and thick: *West*;' Halliwell. The dimin. of *dump* is *dump-ling*, q. v. Probably 'a thing thrown down in a mass'; see **Dump** (2). Der. *dump-y*.

DUMP (2), to strike, fling down. (Scand.?) Cf. ME. *dumpen*, to fall down plump; Allit. Poems, C. 362; *dump*, to beat, strike with the feet; to *dump about*, to move with short steps; Jamieson. Perhaps associated with Icel. *dumpa*, to thump; Swed. dial. *dumpa*, to make a noise, dance awkwardly; *dompa*, to fall down plump, to thump. Also cf. Du. *dompneus*, a great nose. The root-verb appears in Swed. dial. *dimpa*, to fall down plump, pt. t. *damp*, supine *dumpið* (Rietz). Cf. EFries. *dumpen*, to press down quickly, to duck under water.

DUMPLING, a kind of pudding. (E.) 'A Norfolk *dumpling*;' Massinger, A New Way to Pay, A. iii. sc. 2. A *dumpling* is properly a small solid ball of pudding; a dimin. of *dump*, with double dimin. suffix *-ling* (= *-l + -ing*). See **Dump** (1).

DUMPS, melancholy, sadness. (Scand.) 'As one in doleful *dumps*;' Chevy Chase, later version, l. 198. The sing. is *dump*, somewhat rare. 'He's in a deep *dump* now;' Beaum. and Fletcher, Humourous Lieut. A. iv. sc. 6. Palsgrave has: 'I *dumpe*, I fall in a *dumpe* or musynge upon thynges.' The most closely allied word is Swed. dial. *dumpin*, melancholy (Rietz); which is formed as a pp. from Swed. dial. *dimba*, to steam, reek; cf. Dan. *dump*, dull, low. β. Further allied to G. *dumpf*, damp, Du. *dompig*, damp, hazy, misty, Du. *dompen*, to quench, extinguish, and to E. *damp*. Also to EFries. *dump*, heavy, moist. Cf. the phr. 'to *damp* one's spirits.' See **Damp**. Der. *dump-ish*, *dump-ish-ly*, *dump-ish-ness*.

DUN (1), of a dull brown colour. (C.) '*Dunne* of hewe;' Rom. of Rose, 1213. AS. *dunn*, dark; whence *dunnian*, to be darkened; Alfred's Boeth. lib. i. met. 5.—Irish and Gael. *donn*, brown; W. *dwn*, dun, dusky, swarthy. Celtic type **donnos*. ¶ Hence, I suppose, the river-name *Don*. Der. *don-key*, *dun-lin*.

DUN (2), to urge for payment. (Scand.) 'I shall be *dunning* thee every day;' Lord Bacon, Apophthegms, no. 288. Cf. ME. *dunning*, a loud noise, Prompt. Parv. p. 135.—Icel. *duna*, to thunder, make a hollow noise; *dynja*, to rattle, make a din; *koma einum dyn fyrir dyrr*, to make a din before one's door, take one by surprise; Swed. *dåna*, to make a noise, to ring. β. These words are cognate with AS. *dynian*, to make a din; and *dun* is thus related to *din*. See **Din**. Der. *dun*, sb.

DUNCE, a stupid person. (Proper name.) A proper name; originally in the phrase 'a Duns man.' 'A *Duns man*;' Tyndall, Works, p. 88; 'a great *Duns man*, so great a preacher;' Barnes, Works, p. 232; cf. p. 272. The word was introduced by the Thomists, or disciples of Thomas Aquinas, in ridicule of the Scotists, or disciples of John Duns Scotus, schoolman, died A.D. 1308. The Scotch claim him as a native of *Dunse*, in Berwickshire. ¶ Not to be confused with John Scotus Erigena, died A.D. 875.

DUNE, a low sand-hill. (F.—Du.—C.) First in 1790.—F. *dune*. —MDu. *dune* (Du. *duin*); cognate with AS. *dūn*, a down, of Celtic origin. See **Down** (2).

DUNG, excrement. (E.) ME. *dung*, *dong*; Chaucer, C. T. 15024 (B 4208). AS. *dung* (dat. *dunge*), Luke, xiii. 8 (Hatton MS.); the older MSS. have *meoxe*.+OFries. *dung*; Swed. *dynga*, muck; Dan. *dynge*, a heap, hoard, mass; cf. *dynge*, to heap, to amass; G. *dung*, *dünger*. Remoter origin unknown; perhaps from the weak grade of **Ding**, to cast, throw down, q. v. Der. *dung*, vb.; *dung-cart*, *-heap*, *-hill*; also *ding-y*, q. v.

DUNGEON, a keep-tower, prison. (F.—L.) The same word as *donjon*, a keep-tower of a castle. 'Which of the castel was the chief *dongeoun*;' Chaucer, C. T. 1059 (A 1057); cf. P. Plowman, B. prol. 15. —OF. *donjon*, the keep-tower or chief tower of a castle; Prov. *dompnhon* (Brachet).—Late L. *domniōnem*, acc. of *domnio*, a donjon-tower. Contracted from Late L. *dominiōnem*, acc. of *dominio*, the same as *dominium*, a principal possession, domain, dominion ; so called because the chief tower. See further under **Dominion, Domain**.

DUNIWASSAL, a Highland gentleman, a yeoman. (C.) In Sir W. Scott's 'Bonnie Dundee.' — Gael. *duine uasal*, a gentleman. — Gael. *duine* (W. *dyn*), a man ; and *uasal* (W. *uchel*), nobly born, orig. 'exalted.' See Brugmann, i. § 219 (4).

DUNLIN, the red-back sandpiper. (E.) See Newton, Dict. of Birds, on its variation of plumage according to the season. A variant of *dun-ling*, lit. 'the little dun-coloured bird ;' see **Dun**. Cf. *dun-nock*, a local name for the hedge-sparrow ; and *don-key*.

DUODECIMO, a name applied to a book in sheets of 12 leaves. (L.) 'Duodecimo ; a book is said to be *in duodecimo*, or *in twelves*, when it consists of 12 leaves in a sheet ;' Kersey, ed. 1715. — L. *duodecimō*, abl. case of *duodecimus*, twelfth. — L. *duodecim*, twelve. — L. *duo*, two ; and *decem*, ten. See **Two** and **Ten**. From same source, *duodecim-al* ; *duodec-ennial* (see *decennial*) ; *dozen* ; and see below.

DUODENUM, the first of the small intestines. (L.) 'Duodenum, the first of the thin guts, about 12 fingers-breadth long ;' Kersey, ed. 1715. A late L. anatomical word, formed from L. *duodēnī*, twelve apiece, a distributive form of *duodecim*, twelve. So named from its length. See above.

DUP, to undo a door. (E.) In Hamlet, iv. 5. 53. Lit. to *do up*, i. e. lift up the latch ; and contracted from *do up*. See **Don, Doff**.

DUPE, a person easily deceived. (F.) A late word. In Pope, Dunciad, iv. 502. — F. *dupe*, a dupe. Origin uncertain. Webster and Littré say that it is the same as the OF. name for a hoopoe, because the bird is easily caught. Cotgrave has : '*Dupe*, f. a whoop, or hooper ; a bird that hath on her head a great crest, or tuft of feathers, and loves ordure so well, that she nestles in it.' This word *dupe* is probably (like *hoopoe*) onomatopoetic, and imitative of the bird's cry. ¶ Cf. Bret. *houperik*, (1) a hoopoe, (2) a dupe. We have similar ideas in *gull*, *goose*, and *booby*. **Der.** *dupe*, verb.

DUPLICATE, double, two-fold. (L.) 'Though the number were *duplicate* ;' Hall, Hen. VII, an. 6. § 7 ; Lydgate, Minor Poems, p. 162. — L. *duplicātus*, pp. of *duplicāre*, to double. — L. *duplic-*, stem of *duplex*, twofold. — L. *du-*, for *duo*, two ; and *plicāre*, to fold. See **Complex**.

DUPLICITY, falsehood. (F. — L.) Lit. doubleness. 'No false *duplicité* ;' Craft of Louers, st. 22 ; in Chaucer's Works, ed. 1561, fol. 341, back. — F. *duplicité*. — L. acc. *duplicitātem*, from nom. *duplicitās*, doubleness. — L. *duplici-*, decl. stem of *duplex*, twofold. See above.

DURANCE, captivity. (F. — L.) Fabyan has *duraunce* in the sense of 'endurance,' vol. i. c. 105. The sense 'imprisonment,' common in Shak. (Meas. iii. 1. 67, &c.), comes from that of long sufferance or long endurance of hardship. Cotgrave explains *durer* by 'to dure, last, continue, indure, abide, remaine, persist ; also to sustaine, brook, suffer.' — OF. *durance*, duration (Godefroy). — OF. *durer*, to last. See **Dure**.

DURATION, length of time. (F. — L.) ME. *duracioun*, Chaucer, Ho. Fame, 2114. — OF. *duration*. — Late L. *dūrātiōnem*, acc. of *dūrātio*. — L. *dūrāre*, to last. See **Dure**.

DURBAR, a hall of audience. (Pers.) In Sir T. Herbert's Travels, ed. 1665, p. 103. A Hindustani word, but borrowed from Persian. — Pers. *dar-bār*, a prince's court, levee ; Palmer's Dict. col. 255. Lit. 'door of admittance.' — Pers. *dar*, a door (= E. *door*), and *bār*, admittance ; id. col. 64. ¶ The word *bār* alone is also used in the sense of court, congress ; Rich. Pers. Dict. p. 230.

DURE, to last, endure. (F. — L.) Once in common use, now nearly obsolete. ME. *duren*, King Alisaunder, 3276. — OF. (and F.) *durer*, 'to dure, last ;' Cot. — L. *dūrāre*, to last. — L. *dūrus*, hard, lasting. +Irish *dur*, dull, hard, stupid, obstinate, firm, strong ; Gael. *dúr*, the same ; W. *dur*, steel. — Cf. Gk. δύναμις, force. **Der.** *dur-ing* (orig. pres. pt. of *dure*), *dur-able*, *-abl-y*, *-able-ness*, *-abil-i-ty* ; and see *duration*, *duress*, *durance*.

DURESS, hardship, constraint. (F. — L.) ME. *duresse* ; Rom. of the Rose, 3547 ; Will. of Palerne, 1114. — OF. *duresce*, hardship. — L. *dūritia*, hardness, harshness, severity. — L. *dūrus*, hard.

DURIAN, a fruit. (Malay.) Malay *durian*, a fruit with a prickly rind. — Malay *dūri*, a thorn, a prickle.

DUSK, dull, dark, dim. (Scand.) 'Duskede his yën two ;' Chaucer, C. T. 2808 (A 2806). ME. *dosc*, dark, dim ; O. Eng. Homilies, i. 259, l. 16. Also *deosc* ; 'This word is *deosk* ' = this is a dark saying ; Ancren Riwle, p. 148. Prob. a Northern form (as the *sk* has not become *sh*). Cf. AS. *dox* (for **dosc*), translating L. *flāuus* ; Voc. 239. 36. Cf. Swed. dial. *duska*, to drizzle ; *dusk*, a slight shower ; *duskug*, misty (Rietz) ; Norw. *dusk*, mist. See Notes on E. Etym., p. 80. Cf. Skt. *dhūsara-*, gray (like dust) ; see **Dust**. **Der.** *dusk*, sb., *dusk-y*, *dusk-i-ness*, *dusk-i-ly*.

DUST, fine powder. (E.) ME. *dust*, Ancren Riwle, p. 122. AS. *dūst*, Grein, i. 212.+Du. *duist*, meal-dust ; Icel. *dust*, dust ; Dan. *dyst*, fine flour, meal ; OHG. *tunst*, G. *dunst*, vapour, fine dust. All from

a Teut. base **dunst-* (for **dwuns-t*), the *n* being lost except in G. Cf. Skt. *dhvaṁs*, to fall to pieces (pp. *dhvas-ta-*) ; *dhūs-ara-*, dust-coloured. **Der.** *dust-er*, *dust-y*, *dust-i-ness*.

DUTCH, belonging to Holland. (G.) Applied in old authors to the Germans rather than to the Dutch, who were called *Hollanders* ; see Trench, Select Glossary. However, Shak. has it in the usual sense. All's Well, iv. i. 78. — G. *Deutsch*, lit. belonging to the people ; MHG. *diut-isk*. Here the suffix *-isk* = E. *-ish*, and the base *diut-* is cognate with Goth. *thiuda*, AS. *þēod*, a people, nation. Cf. Irish *tuath*, a people ; Oscan *touto*, a city. Brugmann, i. § 218. See **Teutonic**.

DUTY, obligatory service. (AF. — L.) Chaucer has *duetee* in the sense of 'due debt ;' C. T. 6934 (D 1352) ; cf. Gower, C. A. iii. 124 ; bk. vii. 1160. — AF. *dueté*, Liber Albus, p. 211. The word appears to be an AF. coinage, there being no corresponding form in French ; formed by analogy with words in *-ty* from the OF. *deu*, *du*. See **Due**. ¶ The F. word for *duty* is *devoir* (Span. *deber*, Ital. *dovere*), i. e. the infin. mood used as a sb. ; hence ME. *deuoir*, *deuer* (with *u* = *v*), Chaucer, C. T. 2600 (A 2598). **Der.** *dute-ous*, *-ly*, *-ness* ; *duti-ful*, *-ly*, *-ness*.

DWALE, deadly nightshade. (Scand.) So called because it causes stupefaction or dulness. ME. *dwale*, P. Plowman, C. xxiii. 379 ; on which see my note. — Dan. *dvale*, a trance, torpor, stupor, *dvale-drik*, a soporific, dwale-drink ; Swed. *dwala*, a trance. Cf. AS. *dwala*, an error, stupefaction. From **dwal*, 2nd grade of AS. **dwel-an*, to be torpid, to err ; see **Dwell**.

DWARF, a small deformed man. (E.) The final *f* is a substitution for a final guttural sound, written *g* or *gh* ; in Lybeaus Disconus, l. 403, we have the form *dwerk*. The pl. *dwerghes* is in Mandeville's Travels, ed. Halliwell, p. 205. AS. *dweorg*, *dwerg*, *dweorh*, a dwarf ; OMerc. *dwerg* ; OE. Texts.+Du. *dwerg* ; Icel. *dvergr* ; Swed. and Dan. *dverg* ; MHG. *twerc* (also *querch*), G. *zwerg*. Teut. type **dwerg-oz*. **Der.** *dwarf-ish*, *-ish-ness*.

DWELL, to delay, linger, abide. (Scand.) ME. *dwellen*, to delay, linger ; Chaucer, C. T. 2356 (A 2354) ; to which are allied ME. *dwelen*, to be torpid, and *dwelien*, to err ; see Stratmann. [AS. *dwellan* (only used in the active sense), to retard, cause to delay, also, to seduce, lead astray, Grein, i. 213, 394 ; to which is allied *dwelian*, to go astray, err, wander about. The orig. sense is to mislead, cause to err, whence the intransitive sense of to err, to wander aimlessly. Causal of AS. *dwelan* (pt. t. *dwal*, pp. *dwolen*), to be torpid or dull, to err, found only in the pp. *gedwolen* (Grein) ; cf. *ge-dwol-god*, false god, and *duala*, error, in the Northumb. version of S. Matt. xxiv. 24 ; and the Goth. *dwals*, foolish. See **Dull**.] β. But in the modern sense it is Scand. — Icel. *dvelja*, to dwell, delay, tarry, abide ; orig. to hinder ; cf. *dvöl*, a short stay ; Swed. *dväljas*, to dwell, lit. to delay oneself ; Dan. *dvæle*, to linger ; cf. *dvale*, a trance ; OHG. *twaljan*, MHG. *twellen*, to hinder, delay. See **Dwale**. Cf. Skt. *dhvṛ*, to bend aside, *dhūr-ta-*, fraudulent. Brugmann, i. § 338. **Der.** *dwell-er*, *dwell-ing*.

DWINDLE, to waste away. (E.) In Shak. Macb. i. 3. 23. The suffix *-le* is a somewhat late addition, and has rather a diminutive than the usual frequentative force. The *d* is excrescent, as common after *n* ; cf. *sound* from ME. *soun*. ME. *dwinen* ; Rom. of the Rose, 360 ; Gower, C. A. ii. 117 ; bk. iv. 3440. AS. *dwīnan*, to dwindle, languish ; Bosworth.+Icel. *dvina* ; Swed. *tvina*, to dwindle, pine away ; Du. *ver-dwijnen*, to vanish. All from a Teut. str. vb. **dweinan-*.

DYE, to colour. (E.) ME. *deyen*, *dyen* ; Chaucer, C. T. 11037 (F 725). Chaucer also has *deyer*, *dyer*, a dyer, C. T. prol. 364 (A 362). The sb. *dehe*, dye, colour, hue, occurs in O. Eng. Miscellany, ed. Morris, p. 193, l. 20. AS. *dēagian*, to dye ; from *dēah*, sb. f., a dye, colour ; of which the Teut. type is **daugā*, f. Remoter origin unknown. ¶ Not allied to L. *fūcus* (<Gk. φῦκος). **Der.** *dy-er*, *dye-ing*, *-stuffs*.

DYKE, a ditch, bank ; see **Dike**.

DYNAMIC, relating to force. (Gk.) 'Dynamicks, the science of mechanical powers ;' Todd. — Gk. δυναμικός, powerful. — Gk. δύναμις, power. — Gk. δύναμαι, I am strong. Cf. L. *dūrus*, hard, lasting ; see **Dure**. **Der.** *dynamic-s*, *-al*, *-al-ly* ; *dynam-ite*, because it explodes with great force ; *dynamo-meter* (i. e. measurer of force, from *metre*, q. v.) ; and see below.

DYNASTY, lordship, dominion. (F. — L. — Gk.) Applied to the continued lordship of a race of rulers. 'The account of the *dynasties* ;' Raleigh, Hist. of the World, b. ii. c. 2. s. 2 (R.). — F. *dynastie*. — Late L. *dynastia* ; Higden, ii. 260. — Gk. δυναστεία, lordship. — Gk. δυνάστης, a lord ; cf. δυνατός, strong, able. — Gk. δύναμαι, I am strong ; see above.

DYSENTERY, a disease of the entrails. (L. — Gk.) 'The *dysenterie* or bloody flix ;' Holland's Pliny, b. xxviii. c. 9. — L. *dysenteria* (Pliny). — Gk. δυσεντερία, a bowel-complaint. — Gk. δυσ-, prefix, with a bad sense (like E. *mis-*) ; and ἔντερον, pl. ἔντερα, the bowels, from Gk. ἐντός (= L. *intus*), within ; from Gk. ἐν (= L. *in*), in.

¶ The prefix δυσ- is cognate with Skt. *dus-, dur-*, Irish *do-*, Goth. *tus-, tuz-*, Icel. *tor-*, OHG. *zur-*, G. *zer-*.

DYSPEPSY, indigestion. (L. – Gk.) ' *Dyspepsia*, a difficulty of digestion;' Kersey's Dict. ed. 1715. – L. *dyspepsia.* – Gk. δυσπεψία. – Gk. δύσπεπτος, hard to digest. – Gk. δυσ-, prefix, hard (on which see **Dysentery**); and πέπτειν, to soften, cook, digest, cognate with L. *coquere*, whence E. *cook.* See **Cook. Der.** *dyspept-ic* (from δύσπεπτος).

E

E-, *prefix*, out. (L.) In *e-vade, e-vince, e-volve, e-bullient, e-dict,* &c. – L. *ē, ex*, out. See **Ex-**.

EACH, every one. (E.) ME. *eche, ech*; Chaucer, C. T. 793 (A 791); older form *elch*, Layamon, 9921. AS. *ǽlc*, each, Grein, i. 56. Usually considered as standing for *ā + ge + līc*, i.e. aye-like or ever-like. + Du. *elk*, each; OHG. *eogalih*; MHG. *iegelīch*, G. *jeglicher.* See **Aye.**

EAGER, sharp, keen, desirous. (F. – L.) ME. *egre*, Chaucer, C. T. 9075 (E 1199); Rob. of Glouc. p. 80, l. 1786. – AF. *egre*; F. *aigre*, keen. – L. *ācrem*, acc. of *ācer*, keen. – √AK, to pierce, sharpen. See **Acrid. Der.** *eager-ly, -ness*; also *vin-egar*, q. v.

EAGLE, a large bird. (F. – L.) ME. *egle*, Chaucer, C. T. 10437 (F 123). – AF. *egle*; OF. *aigle*, 'an eagle;' Cot. – L. *aquila*, an eagle; see **Aquiline. Der.** *eagl-et.*

EAGRE, a tidal wave or 'bore' in a river. (F.?) 'But like an *eagre* rode in triumph o'er the tide;' Dryden, Threnod. August. 135. Sir T. Brown has *agar*, Vulg. Errors, bk. vii. c. 13. § 8. The Latinized form *higra* occurs in Will. of Malmesbury, Gest. Pontific. p. 292; whence Drayton has *higre*, Polyolbion, song vii. l. 10. Of unknown origin; apparently French.

EAN, EANLING; see **Yean.**

EAR (1), the organ of hearing. (E.) ME. *ere*, Chaucer, C. T. 6218 (D 636). AS. *ēare*, Grein, i. 255. + Du. *oor*; Icel. *eyra*; Swed. *öra*; Dan. *öre*; G. *ohr*; MHG. *ōre*; OHG. *ōra*; Goth. *auso.* Teut. type *auzon-*. Cf. also L. *auris*; Gk. οὖς; Russ. *ucho*; Lith. *ausis*, OIrish *ō.* Brugm. i. § 213 (3). **Der.** *ear-ed, -ache, -ring, -shot*, &c.; also *ear-wig*, q. v. And from the same root, *auricular*, q. v.; *auscultation*, q. v.

EAR (2), a spike, or head, of corn. (E.) ME. *er*; the dat. *ere* occurs in King Alisaunder, 797; see *ear* in Stratmann. AS. *ēar*, pl. ears of corn; Northumb. *eher*, an ear, pl. *ehera*; Matt. xii. 1. + Du. *aar*; Icel., Dan., and Swed., *ax* (= *ahs*); Goth. *ahs*; OHG. *ahir*; MHG. *eher*; G. *ähre.* Teut. type *ahoz* (*ahiz*-); cognate with L. *acus* (gen. *acer-is*), chaff; cf. Gk. ἀκ-ίς, a point, a barb. – √AK, to pierce. Brugmann, i. § 182.

EAR (3), to plough. (E.) In Deut. xxi. 4; 1 Sam. viii. 12; Is. xxx. 24. ME. *erien*, P. Plowman, B. vi. 4, 5; also *eren*, Chaucer, C. T. 888 (A 886). AS. *erian, erigan*, to plough, Grein, i. 228. + Icel. *erja*; MHG. *eren, ern*; Goth. *arjan*; Irish *araim*, I plough; L. *arāre*; Lith. *arti*; Russ. *orat(e)*; Gk. ἀρόω, I plough. – √AR, to plough. ¶ 'In its application to ploughing the √AR (always retaining too its vowel *a*) is proper to all the European languages, as distinguished from the Oriental;' Curtius, i. 426. **Der.** *ear-ing.* See **Arable.**

EARL, the Eng. equivalent of count. (E.) ME. *erl*, Chaucer, C. T. 6739 (D 1157). AS. *eorl*, a warrior, hero; Grein, i. 260. + Icel. *jarl*, older form *earl*, a warrior, hero; also, as a title; OSax. *erl*, a man. Teut. type *erloz.* ONorse (runic) *erilaR.* **Der.** *earl-dom*, from ME. *eorldom*, Layamon, 11560; AS. Chron. an. 1053; where the suffix is the AS. *dōm* (= E. *doom*).

EARLY, in good time. (E.) ME. *erly*, adv. Chaucer, C. T. 33; *earlich*, adj. Ancren Riwle, p. 258. AS. *ǽrlice*, adv.; not much used, as the simple form *ǽr* was used instead. The Northumb. adv. *arlice* occurs in Mark, xvi. 2. – AS. *ǽr*, adv. sooner (Grein, i. 69), and *līc*, like; so that *early* = *ere-like.* See **Ere. Der.** *earli-ness.* ¶ It appears that the word was originally in use only as an adverb.

EARN, to gain by labour. (E.) ME. *ernien*, O. Eng. Homilies, i. 7. l. 28. AS. *earnian*, Grein, i. 249. + OHG. *arnōn*; cf. also G. *ernten*, to reap, from G. *ernte*, harvest. Teut. type *az(a)nōjan*, to get the fruits of labour; from the sb. *az(a)na*, Icel. *önn*, labour; cf. OHG. *aran*, Goth. *asan-s*, a harvest; also Goth. *asneis* (= AS. *esne*), a hireling, labourer, lit. harvest-man. Cf. Russ. *osēne*, harvest, autumn; OPrussian *assanis*, harvest. Brugmann, i. § 903 (c). ¶ As the form of the root is AS, it has nothing to do with AS. *erian*, to plough. **Der.** *earn-ings.*

EARNEST (1), eagerness, seriousness. (E.) Chiefly in the phrase ' *in earnest*.' Also frequently used as an adj., but the ME. *ernest* is commonly a sb.; see Chaucer, C. T. 1127, 1128, 3186. AS. *eornost*; *on eornest*, in earnest, Wulfstan, ed. Napier, p. 163; cf. AS. *eornost*,

sb.; a fight, Grein, i. 261; also *eorneste*, adj. and adv. id. 262. + Du. *ernst*, earnestness, zeal; OHG. *ernust*, a fight, MHG. *ernest*, G. *ernst*, sb. seriousness. Allied to Goth. *arn-iba*, safely; cf. Gk. ὄρνυμι, to excite. See Uhlenbeck, s. v. *arniba.* **Der.** *earnest*, adj., *earnest-ly, -ness.*

EARNEST (2), a pledge, security. (F. – L. – Gk. – Heb.) In 2 Cor. i. 22; v. 5; Eph. i. 14. [The *t* is excrescent, as commonly after *s*; cf. *whils-t, amongs-t* from ME. *whiles, amonges.*] ME. *ernes, eernes*; Wyclif, 2 Cor. i. 22; v. 5; Eph. i. 14. [Cf. prov. Eng. *arles-penny*, an earnest-penny, where *arles* = *arnes* = *ernes*; Ray. W. *ernes*, an earnest, pledge; from E.; Gael. *earlas*, an earnest, earnest-penny; from prov. E. *arles.*] β. This ME. *ernes* is a corruption (by association with sbs. in -*nes*) of the earlier form *erles*; 'on *erles* of the eche mede,' an earnest of the eternal reward; Hali Meidenhad (E. E. T. S.), p. 7; whence also prov. E. *arles.* γ. The ME. *erles* answers to an OF. **erles* (< L. **arrhulās*), dimin. of OF. *erres*, pl., signifying 'an earnest.' Cf. MF. *arrhes* (Cot.). This OF. *erres* occurs in Rom. Rose, 3418 (ed. Méon), where the E. version has 'ernest,' l. 3680. – L. *arrhās*, acc. of *arrhæ*, pl. of *arrha*, shorter form of *arrhabo*, a pledge. – Gk. ἀρραβών, a pledge. This is a modification of the Eastern word, viz. Heb. *'ērāvōn*, a pledge, Gen. xxxviii. 17. This word was introduced by the Phœnicians into both Greece and Italy.

EARTH, soil, dry land. (E.) ME. *eorþe, erþe, erthe*; Layamon, 27817; P. Plowman, B. vii. 2. AS. *eorðe*, Grein, i. 258. + Du. *aarde*; Icel. *jörð*; Dan. and Swed. *jord*; Goth. *airtha*; G. *erde.* β. Teut. types **erthā, *erthōn-*, f. Allied to Gk. ἔρα, the earth. **Der.** *earth*, verb, *earth-born, -en* (ME. *erthen, eorthen*, Ancren Riwle, p. 388), -*ling, -ly, -li-ness, -y*; also *earth-quake, -work*, &c.

EARWIG, the name of an insect. (E.) 'You suffer such *earwigs* to creep into your ears;' Chapman, Mons. D'Olive, last scene. So called because supposed to creep into the ear. AS. *ēar-wicga*; Voc. 350. 36. From *ēare*, ear; and *wicga*, an insect, a beetle, lit. 'runner,' for **weg-jon-*; from AS. *weg-an*, to carry, to move, allied to L. *ueh-ere*, to carry; see **Vehicle.** Sievers, AS. Gram., § 247 (b). See **Ear** (1).

EASE, quietness, rest. (F.) ME. *ese, eise*; Rob. of Glouc. p. 42, l. 977; Ancren Riwle, p. 108. – OF. *aise*, ease. Origin doubtful; but OF. *aisance* occurs in the sense of 'neighbourhood,' and may represent the L. *adiacentia*, 'things adjacent;' which may have suggested OF. *aisier*, to make convenient, to facilitate, and *aise*, convenience. See Körting, § 215. If so, Ital. *agio* is not allied. See **Adjacent. Der.** *ease*, verb, *eas-y, eas-i-ly, eas-i-ness*; also *ease-ment*, in Udal, on S. James, c. 5. v. 13; also *dis-ease*, q. v.

EASEL, a support for pictures while being painted. (Du.) ' *Easell*, a frame, upon which the artist placeth his cloth;' Phillips, ed. 1658. – Du. *ezel*, lit. a little ass, an ass. ' Easel, *die Ezel der Schilders*,' i. e. the painter's easel;' Sewel's Eng.-Du. Dict. 1754. + G. *esel*, an ass, easel. These are diminutives, with suffix -*el*, from the stem *as-*, an ass; see **Ass.** ¶ The word was borrowed from Holland rather than Germany.

EAST, the quarter of sun-rise. (E.) ME. *est*, Chaucer, C. T. 4913 (B 493). AS. *ēast*, adv. in the east, Grein, i. 255; common in compounds, as in East-Sexa = East Saxons, men of Essex; AS. Chron. A. D. 449; cf. *ēastan*, from the east, *ēasterne*, eastern, *ēaste-weard*, east-ward. + Du. *oost*; Icel. *austr*; Dan. *öst*; Swed. *östan*; MHG. *ōsten*, G. *osten*, the east; G. *ost*, east. + L. *aurōra* (= *ausōsa*), east, dawn; Gk. ἠώς, Æol. αὔως, Att. ἕως, dawn; Skt. *ushās*, dawn. Brugmann, i. § 218 (4). **Der.** *east-er-ly, east-er-n, east-ward*; also *Es-sex* (= East-Saxon); also *East-er*, q. v.

EASTER, a Christian festival. (E.) ME. *ester*; whence *ester-dei*, Easter day, Ancren Riwle, p. 412. AS. *ēastre*, f.; Luke, xxii. 1; *ēastor-* (in comp.), Grein, i. 256; pl. *ēastro, ēastron*, the Easter festival; Matt. xxvi. 2; Mark, xiv. 1. AS. *Ēastre, Ēostre*, the name of a goddess whose festivities were in April, whence April was called *Ēaster-mōnað*, Easter-month; Beda, De Temporum Ratione, c. xv. β. The name *Ēastre* is to be referred to the same root as *east*, with reference to the increasing light and warmth of the spring-season. She was, in fact, the dawn-goddess; cf. Lith. *auszra*, f., dawn; Skt. *usrā*, f., dawn. See **East.**

EAT, to devour. (E.) ME. *eten*, Chaucer, C. T. 4349 (A 4351). AS. *etan*; pt. t. *æt*, pp. *eten*; Grein, i. 228. + Du. *eten*; Icel. *eta*; Swed. *äta*; Goth. *itan*; OHG. *ezzan, ezan*; MHG. *ezzen*; G. *essen.* + Ir. and Gael. *ith*; W. *ysu*; L. *edere*; Gk. ἔδειν; Skt. *ad.* √ED, to eat, consume. **Der.** *eat-er, -able*; also *fret* (= *for-eat*), q. v.

EAVES, the clipt edge of a thatched roof. (E.) A sing. sb.; the pl. should be *eaveses.* Also prov. E. *oavis* (Essex). ME. *euese* (*u* = *v*); pl. *eueses*, which occurs in P. Plowman, B. xvii. 227. AS. *efes*, a clipt edge of thatch, eaves, in the Lambeth Psalter, Ps. ci. 8 (Bosworth); whence the verb *efesian*, to clip, shave, shear, in Levit. xix. 27. Cf. also *oefsung*, Corpus Gloss., 474. + Icel. *ups*, eaves; MSwed. *ops*; Swed. dial. *uffs*, eaves (Rietz); Goth. *ubizwa*, a porch; John, x. 23; OHG. *opasa*, MHG. *obse*, a porch, hall; also, eaves.

[The sense 'porch' is due to the projection of the eaves, forming a cover.] **β.** The Teut. type is *obeswā, f. Allied to OHG. *opa, oba,* MHG. *obe,* G. *oben,* above (cf. G. *ob-dach,* a shelter). See **Over.** ¶ The orig. sense was 'cover,' or 'shelter.' **Der.** *eaves-dropp-er,* one who stands under the drippings from the eaves, hence, a secret listener; Rich. III, v. 3. 221; ME. *euesdroppers,* pl., Lydgate, Banquet of Gods and Goddesses, st. 99. Cf. Swed. dial. *uffsa-drup,* droppings from the eaves (Rietz); Icel. *upsar-dropi.*

EBB, the reflux of the tide. (E.) ME. *ebbe,* Chaucer, C. T. 10573 (F 259). AS. *ebba,* ebb; Ælfred's Boethius, lib. ii. met. 8. Cf. AS. *ebbian,* to ebb; AS. Chron. an. 897.+Du. *eb, ebbe,* sb.; *ebben,* vb. [whence Dan. *ebbe,* sb. and vb.; Swed. *ebb,* sb.; *ebba,* vb.]. Perhaps the Teut. type is *af-jon-,* or *að-jon-,* with the sense of 'going off;' see **Off. Der.** *ebb-tide.*

EBONY, a hard wood. (F.‒L.‒Gk.‒Heb.) In Shak. L. L. L. iv. 3. 247. Spelt *ebene* in Holland's Pliny, b. xii. c. 4. [The adj. *ebon* is in Milton, L'All. 8; spelt *heben,* Spenser, F. Q. i. 7. 37.] ME. *eban,* 'tre;' Prompt. Parv.‒OF. *ebenus* (Hatzfeld); MF. *ebene,* 'the black wood, called heben or ibonie;' Cot.‒L. *hebenus, hebenum, ebenus, ebenum.*‒Gk. ἔβενος; also ἐβένη.‒Heb. *hovnīm,* pl. ebony wood; Ezek. xxvii. 15. Prob. a non-Semitic word.

EBRIETY, drunkenness. (F.‒L.) In Sir T. Browne, Vulg. Errors, b. ii. c. 6, part 7; bk. v. c. 23, part 16.‒F. *ébriété,* 'drunkenness;' Cot.‒L. acc. *ēbrietātem,* from nom. *ēbrietās.*‒L. *ēbrius,* drunken; of obscure origin. **Der.** from same source, *in-ebriate.*

EBULLITION, a boiling. (F.‒L.) In Sir T. Browne, Vulg. Errors, b. iv. c. 7, § 5.‒OF. *ebullition,* 'an ebullition, boyling;' Cot. ‒L. *ēbullītiōnem,* acc. of *ēbullitio;* a rare word; cf. *ēbullītus,* pp. of *ēbullīre,* to bubble up.‒L. *ē,* out; and *bullire,* to bubble, boil. See **Boil. Der.** From same verb, *ebulli-ent,* Young, Nt. Thoughts, viii. l. 98 from end.

ÉCARTÉ, a game at cards. (F.‒L. *and* Gk.) First in 1824. In Thackeray, Van. Fair, c. xxv. In this game, cards may be *discarded* and exchanged; hence the name.‒F. *écarté,* discarded; pp. of *écarter,* to discard.‒L. *ex,* out, away; and F. *carte,* Late L. *carta,* from Gk. χάρτη, a leaf of papyrus; hence a card. See **Card** (1).

ECCENTRIC, departing from the centre, odd. (F.‒L.‒Gk.) In Holland's Pliny, b. ii. c. 15.‒F. *eccentrique,* 'out of the center; fol eccentrique,* an unruly or irregular coxcomb;' Cot.‒Late L. *eccentricus,* coined from Gk. ἔκκεντρος, out of the centre.‒Gk. ἐκ, out; and κέντρον, centre. See **Centre. Der.** *eccentric,* sb. (Milton, P. L. iii. 575); *-al, -al-ly, -i-ty.*

ECCLESIASTIC, belonging to the church. (L.‒Gk.) Chaucer has *ecclesiast,* sb., C. T. 710 (A 708). Selden, on Drayton's Polyolbion, song 1, note 10, and song 8, note 21, has both *ecclesiastic* and *ecclesiastical.*‒Late L. *ecclesiasticus.*‒Gk. ἐκκλησιαστικός, belonging to the ἐκκλησία, i.e. assembly, church.‒Gk. ἔκκλητος, summoned.‒ Gk. ἐκκαλέω, I call forth, summon.‒Gk. ἐκ, out; and καλέω, I call. See **Hale** (2). **Der.** *ecclesiast-ic-al.*

ECHELON, a particular (diagonal) arrangement of troops. (F.‒ L.) First in 1796 (N. E. D.).‒F. *échelon,* a step or rung of a ladder; with reference to the successive ranks.‒F. *échelle,* a ladder.‒L. *scāla* (Hatzfeld). See **Scale** (3).

ECHINUS, a sea-urchin. (L.‒Gk.) Chaucer has the pl. *echines;* tr. of Boethius, bk. iii. met. 8.‒L. *echinus.*‒Gk. ἐχῖνος, a hedge-hog, a sea-urchin. + OHG. *igil,* G. *igel,* AS. *īl,* a hedgehog.

ECHO, a repeated sound. (L.‒Gk.) ME. *ecco,* Chaucer, C. T. 9065 (E 1189).‒L. *echō.*‒Gk. ἠχώ, a sound, echo; cf. ἦχος, ἠχή, a ringing in the ears, noise. **Der.** *echo,* verb; also *cat-ech-ise,* q. v.

ECLAIRCISSEMENT, a clearing up. (F.‒L.) In Dryden, Marriage à la Mode, v. 1.‒F. *éclaircissement,* a clearing up.‒F. *éclaircir,* to clear up.‒F. *é-,* OF. *es-*<L. *ex,* out, fully; and *clair,* clear, from L. *clārus.* See **Clear.**

ECLAT, a striking effect, applause. (F.‒L. *and* Low G.) First in 1674 (N. E. D.).‒F. *éclat,* splendour; lit. a bursting out.‒F. *éclater,* to burst forth; OF. *esclater,* to shine; *s'esclater,* to burst; Cot. Of G. origin, though the form is doubtful; perhaps from Late L. type *exclappitāre,* formed from L. *ex,* out, fully, and Low G. *klappen,* to clap, make a noise; see **Clap.** And see **Slate** (1).

ECLECTIC, lit. choosing out. (Gk.) 'Horace, who is . . . sometimes a Stoic, sometimes an *Eclectic;*' Dryden, Discourse on Satire; Poet. Works, ed. 1851, p. 374.‒Gk. ἐκλεκτικός, selecting; an Eclectic.‒Gk. ἐκλέγειν, to select.‒Gk. ἐκ, out; and λέγειν, to choose. **Der.** *eclectic-al, -al-ly, -ism;* see **Eclogue.**

ECLIPSE, a darkening of sun or moon. (F.‒L.‒Gk.) ME. *eclipse,* often written *clips;* P. Plowman, C. xxi. 140, and footnote.‒ OF. *eclipse,* 'an eclipse;' Cot.‒L. *eclipsis.*‒Gk. ἔκλειψις, a failure, esp. of the light of the sun.‒Gk. ἐκλείπειν, to leave out, quit, suffer eclipse.‒Gk. ἐκ, out; and λείπειν, to leave. Brugmann, i. § 463. **Der.** *ecliptic,* Gk. ἐκλειπτικός; see Chaucer, On the Astrolabe, prol. l. 67.

ECLOGUE, a pastoral poem. (L.‒Gk.) In Sidney's Arcadia,

---

b. iii (R.). 'They be not termed *Eclogues,* but *Æglogues;*' Spenser, Argument to Sheph. Kal.; cf. F. *églogue,* an eclogue.‒L. *ecloga,* a pastoral poem.‒Gk. ἐκλογή, a selection; esp. of poems.‒Gk. ἐκλέγειν, to select; see **Eclectic.** ¶ Note the modification of spelling, due to F. *églogue.*

ECONOMY, household management. (F.‒L.‒Gk.) Spelt *oeconomy* in Cotgrave.‒MF. *oeconomie,* 'oeconomy;' Cot.‒L. *œconomia.*‒Gk. οἰκονομία, management of a household. Cf. οἰκονομέω, I manage a household.‒Gk. οἰκο-, for οἶκος, a house, cognate with L. *uīcus;* and *nom-,* 2nd grade of νέμειν, to deal out, whence also E. *nomad,* q. v. **Der.** *econom-ic* (spelt *iconomique,* Gower, C. A. iii. 141, bk. vii. 1670); *-ic-al, -ic-al-ly, -ist, -ise.*

ECSTASY, enthusiasm. (F.‒L.‒Gk.) In Shak. Mer. Ven. iii. 2. 112.‒OF. *extasie* (Godefroy); cf. MF. *ecstase,* 'an extasie, swooning, trance;' Cot.‒Late L. *ecstasis,* a trance.‒Gk. ἔκστασις, displacement; also, a trance.‒Gk. ἐκ, out; and στάσις, a standing, condition, allied to ἵστημι, I place.‒√STA, to stand; see **Stand.** Cf. the phrase ἐξιστάναι φρενῶν, to drive (one) out of his wits. **Der.** *ecstatic* (Gk. ἐκστατικ-ός); *-al, -al-ly.*

ECUMENIC, ECUMENICAL, common to the world, general. (L.‒Gk.) 'Oecumenicall, or universall;' Foxe, Martyrs, p. 8 (R.).‒Late L. *œcūmenicus,* universal.‒Gk. οἰκουμενικός, universal.‒Gk. οἰκουμένη (sc. γῆ), the inhabited world; fem. of οἰκούμενος, pres. pt. pass. of οἰκέω, I inhabit.‒Gk. οἶκος, a house. Brugmann, i. § 611. See **Economy.**

ECZEMA, a skin disease. (Gk.) First in 1753 (N. E. D.).‒ Gk. ἔκζεμα, a pustule.‒Gk. ἐκζέειν, to boil over.‒Gk. ἐκ, out; ζέειν, to boil. See **Yeast.**

EDDY, a whirling current of water. (E.) In Shak. Lucrece, 1669. ME. *ydy* (=*idy*), The Houlate, st. 64. [Either from a lost AS. word with the prefix *ed-*=back; or perhaps modified from the Scandinavian by changing Icel. *ið-* to the corresponding AS. *ed-.*] Cf. Icel. *iða,* an eddy, whirl-pool; *iða,* to be restless, whirl about; Norw. *ida;* Swed. *iða, idå,* an eddy; Dan. dial. *ide* (Rietz). **β.** Formed from AS. *ed-,* back, again, = Icel. *ið-,* back. Cf. Goth. *id-,* back; OSaxon *idug-,* back; OHG. *it-, ita-,* back. Brugmann, i. § 574. Cf. *Iddy stone* (now *Eddystone*), Arber, Eng. Garner, iii. 394 (A.D. 1599).

EDGE, the border of a thing. (E.) ME. *egge;* Ancren Riwle, p. 60. AS. *ecg,* f. (gen. dat. acc. *ecge*), Grein, i. 216.+Du. *egge;* Icel. and Swed. *egg;* Dan. *eg;* G. *ecke.* Teut. type *agjā,* f. Cf. L. *aciēs,* Gk. ἀκίς, a point; Skt. *açri-,* an edge, corner, angle.‒√AK, to pierce; cf. Skt. *aç,* to pervade. **Der.** *edge-tool, -wise, -less, edg-ing;* *egg* (2), q. v.

EDIBLE, eatable. (L.) In Bacon, Nat. Hist. sect. 859.‒Late L. *edibilis,* eatable.‒L. *edere,* to eat. See **Eat.**

EDICT, a proclamation, command. (L.) In Shak. Cor. i. 1. 84; and in Caxton (N. E. D.).‒L. *ēdictum,* a thing proclaimed.‒L. *ēdictus,* pp. of *ēdīcere,* to proclaim.‒L. *ē,* forth; and *dīcere,* to speak. See **Diction.**

EDIFY, to build up, instruct. (F.‒L.) In Shak. Tw. Nt. v. 298. ME. *edifien,* P. Plowm. C. xxi. 42.‒OF. *edifier,* 'to edifie, build;' Cot.‒L. *ædificāre,* to build.‒L. *ædi-,* stem of *ædēs,* a building; and *-fic-,* for *fac-ere,* to make. **β.** The L. *ædēs* orig. meant 'a fire-place,' or 'hearth;' cf. Irish *aodh,* fire.‒√AIDH, to kindle. Brugmann, i. § 202. **Der.** *edify-ing, edific-at-ion; edifice,* from F. *édifice,* 'an edifice' (Cotgrave), which is from L. *ædificium,* a building; *edile,* or *ædile,* from L. *ædīlis,* a magistrate who had the care of public buildings; *edile-ship.*

EDITION, publication. (F.‒L.) In Shak. Merry Wi. ii. 1. 78. First in 1551.‒OF. *edicion* (Hatzfeld).‒L. *ēditiōnem,* acc. of *ēditio,* a publishing; cf. *ēditus,* pp. of *ēdere,* to publish, give out.‒L. *ē,* out; and *dare,* to give.‒√DA, to give. **Der.** from the same source, *editor* (L. *ēditor*), *-ial, -i-al-ly, -ship;* also *edit, editress,* coined words.

EDUCATE, to cultivate, train. (L.) In Shak. L. L. L. v. 1. 86; also *education,* As You Like It, i. 1. 22, 72.‒L. *ēducātus,* pp. of *ēducāre,* to bring out, educate; allied to *ēdūcere,* to bring out; see **Educe. Der.** *educat-or* (L. *ēducātor*), *-ion, -ion-al.*

EDUCE, to bring out. (L.) Not common. In Pope, Ess. on Man, ii. 175; and earlier, in Glanville's Essays, ess. 3 (R.).‒L. *ēdūcere,* pp. *ēductus,* to bring out.‒L. *ē,* out; and *dūcere,* to lead. See **Duct. Der.** *educ-ible; educt-ion,* like pp. *ēductus.*

EEL, a fish. (E.) ME. *el* (with long *e*); pl. *eles,* spelt *elys,* Barbour's Bruce, ii. 577. AS. *ǣl,* pl. *ǣlas;* Ælfric's Colloquy, in Thorpe's Analecta, p. 23.+Du. *aal;* Icel. *áll;* Dan. *aal;* Swed. *ål;* G. *aal.* Teut. type *ǣloz.* **Der.** *eel-pout;* AS. *ǣle-pūta,* a kind of fish.

EERY, timid; also strange, weird. (E.) 'I'd rove, and ne'er be *eerie,* O;' Burns; My Ain Kind Dearie, O. ME. *arȝ, arh, arȝe, erȝe,* timid; spelt *eri* in Cursor Mundi, l. 17685. AS. *earg, earh,* timid, cowardly. Cf. Icel. *argr, ragr;* G. *arg,* timid; Du. *erg,* bad.

EFFACE, to destroy the appearance of. (F.–L.) In Caxton, Golden Legend, Life of St. James the More, § 8; also in Cotgrave; and Pope, Moral Essays, i. 166.–F. *effacer,* 'to efface, deface, raze;' Cot. Lit. 'to erase a face or appearance.'–F. *ef-* = L. *ef-,* for *ex,* out; and F. *face,* a face. See **Face.** Der. *efface-ment.*

EFFECT, a result, consequence. (F.–L.) ME. *effect,* Chaucer, C. T. 321 (A 319).–AF. *effect,* Stat. Realm, i. 189; MF. *effect,* 'an effect, or work;' Cot.–L. *effectum,* acc. of *effectus,* an effect.–L. *effectus,* pp. of *efficere,* to effect.–L. *ef-* = *ec-* (*ex*), out; and *-ficere,* for *facere,* to make. See **Fact.** Der. *effectu-al* (from decl. stem *effectu-* of sb. *effectus*), *-al-ly, -ate; effect-ive* (from pp. *effectus*), *-ive-ly, -ive-ness;* from same source, *effic-ac-y,* q. v.; *effici-ent,* q. v.

EFFEMINATE, womanish. (L.) In Shak. Rich. III, iii. 7. 211; as a verb, Gower, C. A. iii. 236; bk. vii. 4304.–L. *effēminātus,* pp. of *effēmināre,* to make womanish.–L. *ef-* = *ec-* (*ex*); and *fēmina,* a woman. See **Feminine.** Der. *effeminate-ly, -ness, effeminac-y.*

EFFENDI, sir, master. (Turkish–Gk.) Turk. *ĕfendi,* sir (a title). –Mod. Gk. ἀφέντης, which is from Gk. αὐθέντης, a despotic master, ruler. See **Authentic.**

EFFERVESCE, to bubble or froth up. (L.) '*Effervescence,* a boiling over, . . . a violent ebullition;' Kersey's Dict. ed. 1715.–L. *efferuescere.*–L. *ef-* = *ec-* (*ex*); and *feruescere,* to begin to boil, inceptive of *feruēre,* to glow, boil. See **Fervent.** Der. *effervesc-ent, -ence.*

EFFETE, exhausted. (L.) In Burton, Anat. of Melancholy, iii. 4. 1. 5; p. 370 (R.).–L. *effētus, effœtus,* weakened by having brought forth young.–L. *ef-* = *ec-* (*ex*); and *fētus,* breeding. See **Fetus.**

EFFICACY, force, virtue. (L.) In Sir T. Elyot, Castle of Health, b. ii. c. 22. Englished from L. *efficācia,* power.–L. *efficāci-,* from *efficax,* efficacious.–L. *ef-* = *ec-* (*ex*); *-fic-,* from *facere,* to make; and suffix *-ax.* See **Effect.** Der. *efficaci-ous, -ous-ly, -ness.* ¶ The ME. word for efficacy was *efficace,* Ancren Riwle, p. 246; from F. *efficace* (Cotgrave).

EFFICIENT, causing an effect. (F.–L.) In Tyndal's Works, p. 335; col. 1 (end).–F. *efficient,* 'efficient;' Cot.–L. *efficientem,* acc. of *efficiens,* pres. pt. of *efficere.* See **Effect.** Der. *efficient-ly, efficience, efficienc-y;* also *co-efficient.*

EFFIGY, a likeness of a man's figure. (L.) Spelt *effigies* in Shak. As You Like It, ii. 7. 193.–L. *effigiēs,* an effigy, image.–L. *effig-,* base of *effingere,* to form.–L. *ef-* = *ec-* (*ex*); and *fingere,* to form. See **Feign.** ¶ Cf. L. *effigie,* 15th cent. (Hatzfeld).

EFFLORESCENCE, a flowering, eruption on the skin, formation of a powder. (F.–L.) In Sir T. Browne, Vulg. Errors, b. vi. c. 12. § 5.–F. *efflorescence;* Cot.–L. *efflorescentia,* a coined word from *efflorescere,* inceptive form of *efflorēre,* to blossom.–L. *ef-* = *ec-* (*ex*); and *florēre,* to blossom, from *flōr-,* stem of *flōs,* a flower. See **Flower.**

EFFLUENCE, a flowing out. (L.) In Holland's Plutarch, p. 1059; Milton, P. L. iii. 6. Coined from L. *effluent-,* stem of pres. pt. of *effluere,* to flow out.–L. *ef-* = *ec-* (*ex*); and *fluere,* pp. *fluxus,* to flow. See **Fluent.** Der. from the same verb, *efflu-ent; efflux* (from pp. *effluxus*); *effluvium* (L. *effluuium*).

EFFORT, an exertion of strength. (F.–L.) In Cotgrave; and in Caxton, Sons of Aymon, c. 24 (p. 527, l. 21).–F. *effort,* 'an effort, endeavour;' Cot. Verbal sb. from F. *efforcer,* or *s'efforcer,* 'to indeavour;' Cot.–F. *ef-* = L. *ef-* = *ec-* (*ex*); and *forcer,* to force, from *force,* sb. See **Force.**

EFFRONTERY, boldness, hardihood. (F.–L.) In Kersey's Dict. ed. 1715.–F. *effronterie,* 'impudency;' Cot.–OF. *effronté,* 'shameless;' Cot. Formed with prefix *ef-* = L. *ef-* = *ec-* (*ex*) from F. *front,* the forehead, front. See **Front, Affront, Confront.**

EFFULGENT, shining forth. (L.) The sb. *effulgence* is in Milton, P. L. iii. 388.–L. *effulgent-,* stem of *effulgens,* pres. pt. of *effulgēre,* to shine forth.–L. *ef-* = *ec-* (*ex*); and *fulgēre,* to shine. See **Fulgent.** Der. *effulgence.*

EFFUSE, to pour forth. (L.) In Shak. 1 Hen. VI, v. 4. 52. [The sb. *effusion* is in Occleve, Letter of Cupide, st. 61.]–L. *effūsus,* pp. of *effundere,* to pour forth.–L. *ef-* = *ec-* (*ex*); and *fundere,* to pour. See **Fuse.** Der. *effus-ion, -ive, -ive-ly, -ive-ness.*

EFT, a newt; of which it is a variant. See **Newt.**

EGG (1), the oval body from which chickens, &c. are hatched. (Scand.) ME. *egg,* pl. *egges, eggis* (from Norse); also *ay, ey,* pl. *eiren* (from AS.). The pl. *egges* is in P. Plowman, B. xi. 343. [Chaucer has *ey,* C. T. 16274 (G 806); cf. pl. *eiren* in Ancren Riwle, p. 66. AS. *æg,* Grein, i. 55; pl. *ægru* (whence *eire,* and the double pl. *eire-n*); Du. *ei.*]–Icel. *egg;* Dan. *æg;* Swed. *ägg.*+G. *ei.* Prob. allied to Irish *ugh;* Gael. *ubh;* W. *wy;* L. *ōuum;* Gk. ὠόν. See **Oval.** Brugmann, i. § 309 (2).

EGG (2), to instigate. (Scand.) ME. *eggen,* Ancren Riwle, p. 146. –Icel. *eggja,* to egg on, goad.–Icel. *egg,* an edge; see **Edge.**

EGLANTINE, sweetbriar, &c. (F.–L.) In Spenser, Sonnet 26. ME. *eglentine, eglentier,* Maundeville, Trav. c. ii. p. 14.–F. *églantine,* formerly *aiglantine;* another OF. form was *aiglantier,* given by

Cotgrave, and explained as 'an eglantine or sweetbrier tree.'–OF. *aiglant, aiglent,* the same, Godefroy; (whence *aiglant-ine, aiglant-ier*); for *aiglent-.*–Late L. **aculentus,* prickly (not recorded), formed (with suffix *-lentus*) from *acus,* a needle. Cf. L. *acu-leus,* a sting, prickle. See **Aglet.**

EGOTIST, a self-opinionated person. (L.) Both *egotist* and *egotism* occur in the Spectator, no. 562. They are coined words, from L. *ego,* I. See **I.** ¶ Also *ego-ism, ego-ist* (F. *egoïsme, egoïste*). *Ego-ist* is the right form; *egotist* seems to have been imitated from words like *dramat-ist,* where, however, the *t* is a part of the stem of the sb. Der. *egotist-ic, egotise.*

EGREGIOUS, excellent, select. (L.) In Shak. Cymb. v. 5. 211. –L. *ēgregi-us,* chosen out of the flock, excellent; with suffix *-ous.*– L. *ē grege,* out of the flock. See **Gregarious.** Der. *egregious-ly, -ness.*

EGRESS, a going out, departure. (L.) In Shak. Merry Wives, ii. 1. 225.–L. *ēgressus,* a going out.–L. *ēgressus,* pp. of *ēgredior,* I go out.–L. *ē,* out; and *gradior,* I go. See **Grade.**

EGRET, the lesser white heron. (F.–OHG.) In Levins and Huloet. The Anglo-French *egret* occurs in the Liber Albus, p. 467. –OF. *egrette, aigrette,* 'a fowl like a heron;' Cot. Dimin. of a form **aigre,* of which OF. *aigron,* a heron (Supp. to Godefroy) is an augmentative form. This *aigron* is the same as F. *héron,* OF. *hairon,* a heron. **Aigre* exactly answers to the OHG. *heigir, heiger,* a heron; and *egret* (for *hegr-et*) is merely the dimin. of the *her-* (= *hegr-*) in *her-on.* See **Heron.**

EH! interj. of surprise. (E.) ME. *ey;* Chaucer, C. T. 3766 (A 3768). AS. *ēa,* eh! Grein, i. 63, 250. Cf. F. *eh!* Du. *he!* G. *ei!* See **Ah!**

EIDER-DUCK, a kind of sea-duck. (Scand.) Not old; and not in Johnson. 'The *eider* bolster;' Darwin, Bot. Garden, c. iii. 388. *Duck* is an English addition. Adapted from Icel. *æðar,* gen. of *æðr,* an eider-duck; where *æ* is pronounced like E. *i* in *time.* Der. *eider-down* (wholly Scandinavian); from Icel. *æðar-dūn,* eider-down. See Norw. *ederdun* in Falk and Torp.

EIGHT, twice four. (E.) ME. *eightè* (with final *e*), Chaucer, C. T. 12705 (C 771). AS. *eahta,* Grein, i. 235.+Du. *acht;* Icel. *átta;* Dan. *otte;* Swed. *åtta;* Goth. *ahtau;* OHG. *ahta,* MHG. *æhte, āhte,* G. *acht.*+Irish *ocht;* Gael. *ochd;* W. *wyth;* Corn. *eath;* Bret. *eich, eiz;* L. *octo;* Gk. ὀκτώ; Pers. *hasht,* Zend *ashta,* Skt. *ashṭau.* Idg. type, **oktō(u).* Der. *eighth* (for *eight-th*) = AS. *eahtoða; eighty* (for *eight-ty*) = AS. *eahtatig; eighteen* (for *eight-teen*) = AS. *eahtaȳne;* also *eighthly, eight-i-eth, eighteen-th.*

EISEL, vinegar. (F.–L.) Spelt *esile,* Hamlet, v. 1. 299. ME. *eisil,* Ancren Riwle, p. 404.–OF. *aisil, eisil,* vinegar. From a L. type **acētillum.*–L. *acētum,* vinegar.

EISTEDDFOD, a congress of Welsh bards. (W.) First in 1822 (N. E. D.). But it is spelt *stethva* in Drayton, Polyolb. iv. 179.– W. *eisteddfod,* a sitting, session, congress.–W. *eistedd,* to sit.

EITHER, one of two. (E.) ME. *either, eyther, aither, ayther;* Chaucer, Parl. Foules, 125. AS. *æghþer,* Matt. ix. 17; a contracted form of *æghwæþer,* Grein, i. 65. Compounded of *ā* + *ge* + *hwæþer;* where *ā* = aye, ever, *ge* is a common prefix, and *hwæþer* is E. *whether;* March, A. S. Gram. sect. 136. Cf. Du. *ieder;* OHG. *ēowedar,* MHG. *ieweder,* G. *jeder* [without *-ge-*]. See **Aye** and **Whether.** ¶ ME. *eyther* was confused with ME. *outher,* E. *or;* see **Or** (1).

EJACULATE, to jerk out an utterance. (L.) The sb. *ejaculation* is in Sir T. Browne, Vulg. Errors, b. iii. c. 4. 5.–L. *ēiaculātus,* pp. of *ēiaculārī,* to cast out.–L. *ē,* out; and *iaculārī,* to cast, from *iaculum,* a missile, from *iacere,* to throw. See **Jet.** Der. *ejaculat-ion, -or-y;* and see below.

EJECT, to cast out. (L.) In Shak. Cor. iii. 1. 287.–L. *ēiectus,* pp. of *ēicere,* to cast out.–L. *ē,* out; and *iacere,* to cast. See above. Der. *eject-ment, -ion.*

EKE (1), to augment. (E.) ME. *eken,* Northern form; the Southern form is *echen;* 'these fooles, that her sorowes *eche;*' Chaucer, Troil. i. 705. OMerc. *ēcan,* to augment; AS. *īecan;* Grein, i. 229. Teut. type **aukjan-,* weak verb; allied to Icel. *auka;* Swed. *öka;* Dan. *öge;* Goth. *aukan* (neuter). Cf. L. *augēre,* to increase; Skt. *ōjas,* strength. Brugmann, i. § 539 (2). (√AWEGw); whence also *auction, augment.* Der. *eke,* conj.

EKE (2), also. (E.) ME. *ek, eek, eke;* Chaucer, C. T. 41. AS. *ēac,* Grein, i. 251.+Du. *ook;* Icel. *auk;* Swed. *och,* and; Dan. *og,* and; Goth. *auk.* All from the Teut. base **auk-,* Idg. **aug-.*

ELABORATE, laborious, produced with labour. (L.) 'The *elaborate* Muse;' Ben Jonson, tr. of Horace's Art of Poetry, l. 140. –L. *ēlabōrātus,* pp. of *ēlabōrāre,* to labour greatly.–L. *ē,* forth, fully; and *labōrāre,* to work, from *labōr-,* stem of *labor,* work. See **Labour.** Der. *elaborate,* verb; *-ly, -ness, elaborat-ion.*

ELAND, a S. African antelope. (Du.–G.–Lith.) Spelt *elan;* Hakluyt, Voy. iii. 104. From Du. *eland,* an elk.–G. *elend.*–Lith. *élnis,* an elk. Cf. W. *elain,* a hind; Russ. *oléne,* a stag. See **Elk.**

ELAPSE, to glide away. (L.) '*Elapsed*, gone or slipt away;' Phillips, ed. 1706.—L. *ēlapsus*, pp. of *ēlābi*, to glide away.—L. *ē*, away; and *lābi*, to glide. See **Lapse**. Der. *elapse*, sb.

ELASTIC, springing back. (Gk.) Pope has *elasticity*; Dunciad, i. 186. Phillips, ed. 1706, has *elasticity* and *elastick*. A scientific word, coined from a Gk. *ἐλαστικός, propulsive; from Gk. ἐλάω = ἐλαύνω, I drive (fut. ἐλάσ-ω). Allied to L. *alacer*. See **Alacrity**. Der. *elastic-i-ty*.

ELATE, lifted up, proud. (L.) ME. *elat*; Chaucer, C. T. 14173 (B 3357).—L. *ēlātus*, lifted up.—L. *ē*, out, up; and *lātus* = *tlātus*, connected with *tollere*, to lift.—√TEL, to lift. Der. *elated-ly*, *-ness*; *elat-ion*.

ELBOW, the bend of the arm. (E.) ME. *elbowe*; Chaucer, Good Women, prol. 179. AS. *elboga*; in Voc. 158. 8; *eln-boga*, tr. of Beda, bk. v. c. 3.+Du. *elleboog*; Icel. *alnbogi, ölnbogi, ölbogi, olbogi*; Dan. *albue*; OHG. *elinpogo*, MHG. *elenboge*, G. *ellenbogen*. β. Compounded of AS. *el* (= *eln* < *alin-*), cognate with Goth. *aleina*, a cubit [L. *ulna*, the elbow, Gk. ὠλένη, the elbow]; and *boga*, a bending, a bow. 1. Of these, the first set is allied to Skt. *aratni-*, the elbow; see **Ell**. 2. The AS. *boga* is from √BHEUG, to bend; see **Bow** (1). ¶ Cf. Swed. *armbåge*, the elbow, lit. arm-bow. Der. *elbow*, verb; *elbow-room*.

ELD, old age, antiquity. (E.) Nearly obsolete; but once common. In Shak. Merry Wives, iv. 4. 36; Meas. iii. 1. 36. ME. *elde*, Chaucer, C. T. 2449 (A 2447). OMerc. *ældu*, old age (O. E. Texts, p. 542), from OMerc. *ald*, old. Cf. AS. *yldo, yldu*, antiquity, old age; Grein, ii. 769; also *æld, ældu, eld*, id. i. 56, 222.+Icel. *elli*; Dan. *ælde*. Allied to Icel. *old*, an age; Goth. *alths*, an age. See **Old**.

ELDER (1), older. (E.) The use as a sb. is very old. ME. *elder, eldre*; 'tho londes that his *eldres* wonnen;' Rob. of Brunne, p. 144; cf. P. Plowman, C. x. 214. In AS., the same use occurs in the Blickling Homilies, p. 195: 'ure *yldran*,' our elders. OMerc. *ældra* (AS. *yldra*), elder, adj.; compar. of OMerc. *ald* (AS. *eald*), old. See **Old**. Der. *elder-ly, elder-ship*.

ELDER (2), the name of a tree. (E.) The *d* is excrescent; the right form is *eller*. ME. *eller*, P. Plowman, B. i. 68; cf. *ellerne treo*, id. A. i. 66. AS. *ellen, ellern*, Cockayne's Leechdoms, iii. 324; *ellærn*, Corpus Gloss. 1775.+Low G. *elloorn*; Bremen Wörterbuch, i. 303; also *ellern, elhorn, alhorn* (Lübben). ¶ Distinct from *alder*. There is nothing to connect it in form with G. *holunder*.

ELDEST, oldest. (E.) ME. *eldest, eldeste*. OMerc. *ældesta* (AS. *yldesta*), Grein, i. 239; formed by vowel-change from OMerc. *ald* (AS. *eald*), old. See **Old**.

ELECAMPANE, a plant. (F.—L.) In Holland, tr. of Pliny, b. xix. c. 5. § 7; spelt *elycampane*, Sir T. Elyot, Castel of Helth, b. iii. c. 12. Shortened from F. *enule-campane*, 'the hearbe called helicampanie;' Cot.—L. *inula campāna*; where *inula* is the L. name for elecampane in Pliny, as above. At the same time, the substitution of *ele-* for F. *enule* was due to AS. *eolone, eolene* (for *iluna*, a perversion of *inula*); Voc. 26. 23; 36. 11. Cf. *elena campāna*, Med. Works of 14th Cent., ed. Henslow, p. 115. β. *Campāna*, fem. of *campānus*, is a Late L. form, and perhaps means merely growing in the fields; cf. L. *campāneus*, of or pertaining to the fields (Lewis), though the proper L. word for this is *campestris*; see **Campestral**.

ELECT, chosen. (L.) In Shak. Rich. II, iv. 126; and used by Caxton (see Trevisa, tr. of Higden, iii. 99, l. 2).—L. *ēlectus*, pp. of *ēligere*, to choose out.—L. *ē*, out; and *legere*, to choose. See **Legend**. Der. *elect*, verb; *elect-ion* (OF. *election*), Rob. of Brunne, p. 208; *election-eer*; *elect-ive, -or, -or-al*; cf. also *eligible*, q.v.; *elegant*, q.v.; *elite*, q.v.

ELECTRIC, belonging to electricity. (L.—Gk.) Sir T. Browne speaks of '*electrick* bodies;' Vulg. Errors, b. ii. c. 4. Coined from L. *ēlectrum*, amber; from its electrical power when rubbed.—Gk. ἤλεκτρον, amber; also shining metal; allied to ἠλέκτωρ, gleaming. Der. *electric-al, electric-ian, electric-i-ty, electri-fy, electro-meter*; &c.

ELECTUARY, a kind of confection. (L.—Gk.) [ME. *letuarie*, Chaucer, prol. 428 (A 426).—OF. *letuaire, lectuaire* (Godefroy); MF. *electuaire*, 'an electuary; a medicinable composition made of choice drugs, and of substance between a syrrop and a conserve;' Cot.]—L. *ēlectuārium, ēlectārium*, an electuary, a medicine that dissolves in the mouth; perhaps for *e(c)lictārium*; from Gk. ἐκλεικτόν, an electuary.—Gk. ἐκλείχειν, to lick away. See **Lick**. ¶ The usual Lat. word is *ecligma*, Latinised from Gk. ἔκλειγμα, medicine that is licked away, from λείχειν, to lick.

ELEEMOSYNARY, relating to alms. (L.—Gk.) '*Eleemosinary*, an almner, or one that gives alms;' Blount's Gloss. ed. 1674. Also used as an adj.; Glanvill, Vanity of Dogmatizing, c. 16 (R.).—Late L. *eleēmosynārius*, an almoner.—Gk. ἐλεημοσύνη, alms. See **Alms**.

ELEGANT, choice, grateful, neat. (F.—L.) In Cotgrave, and in Milton, P. L. ix. 1018. Shak. has *elegancy*, L. L. L. iv. 2. 126. Caxton has '*elegaunt* and fayr;' Golden Legend, Moses, § 2.—MF.

elegant, 'elegant, eloquent;' Cot.—L. *ēlegantem*, acc. of *ēlegans*, tasteful, neat.—L. *ē*, out; and *leg-*, base of *legere*, to choose. See **Elect**. Der. *elegance, eleganc-y*.

ELEGY, a lament, funeral ode. (F.—L.—Gk.) 'An *Elegie*' is the title of a poem by Spenser.—MF. *elegie*, 'an elegy;' Cot.—L. *elegia*.—Gk. ἐλεγεία, an elegy, fem. sing.; but orig. τὰ ἐλεγεῖα, neut. pl., an elegiac poem; plur. of ἐλεγεῖον, a distich consisting of a hexameter and a pentameter.—Gk. ἔλεγος, a lament. Der. *elegi-ac*, *eleg-ist*.

ELEMENT, a first principle. (L.) In early use. 'The four *elementz*;' On Popular Science, l. 120; in Wright's Popular Treatises on Science, p. 134.—OF. *element* (Hatzfeld).—L. *elementum*, a first principle. Der. *element-al, -al-ly, -ar-y*.

ELEPHANT, the largest quadruped. (F.—L.—Gk.) ME. *olifaunt*, King Alisaunder, 5293; Lydgate has *elyphaunt*, Sege of Troye, bk. ii. c. 11. l. 142. [The AS. form *olfend* was used to mean 'a camel;' Mark, i. 6.]—OF. *olifant* (Roquefort); *elefant*, Philip de Thaun, Bestiary, l. 691; also *elephaunt*; Cot.—L. *elephantem*, acc. of *elephas*.—Gk. ἐλέφαντα, acc. of ἐλέφας. Of unknown origin; some compare Heb. *eleph*, an ox; see **Alphabet**. Or from the Semitic *el*, def. article, and Skt. *ibhas*, an elephant. Der. *elephant-ine*.

ELEVATE, to raise up. (L.) 'As many degrees as thy pool [pole] is *elevat*;' Chaucer, Astrolabe, pt. ii. c. 23.—L. *ēleuātus*, pp. of *ēleuāre*, to lift up.—L. *ē*, out, up; and *leuāre*, to make light, lift, from *leuis*, light. See **Levity**. Der. *elevat-ion, -or*.

ELEVEN, ten and one. (E.) ME. *enleuen* (with *u* = *v*), Layamon, 23364. AS. *endlufon*, Gen. xxxii. 22; older form *endleofan*, tr. of Beda, bk. v. c. 18; ONorthumb. *ællefne*, Luke, xxiv. 9. Cf. OFries. *andlova, elleva*.+Du. *elf*; Icel. *ellifu*; later *ellefu*; Dan. *elleve*; Swed. *elfva*; Goth. *ainlif*; OHG. *einlif*, G. *eilf, elf*. β. All from a Teut. base *ainlif*, which best appears in the Goth. *ain-lif*. 1. Here *ain* = AS. *ān* = one. 2. The suffix *-lif* is plainly cognate with the suffix *-lika* in Lithuanian *wénolika*, eleven, Fick, ii. 292. And it is probable that *-lika* means 'remaining;' cf. L. *linquere* (pt. t. *līquī*), to leave. Thus the sense is 'one remaining,' after *ten*. Brugmann, ii. § 175. Cf. **twelve**; and Lith. *try-lika*, thirteen. Der. *eleven-th*.

ELF, a little sprite. (E.) ME. *elf*, Chaucer, C. T. 6455 (D 873). AS. *ælf*, Grein, i. 56.+Icel. *álfr*; Dan. *alf*; Swed. *alf*; OHG. *alp*; G. *elf*, also *alp*, a nightmare, incubus. Der. *elfin*, adj. (= *elf-en*), Spenser, F. Q. ii. 10. 71; *elfin*, sb. (= *elf-en*, dimin. of *elf*), id., i. 10. 60; *elf-ish*, ME. *eluish*, Chaucer, C. T. 16219 (G 751); *elf-lock*. ¶ Probably *elfin*, sb. is merely a peculiar use of *elfin*, adj.; and this again stands for *elf-en*, with adj. suffix *-en*, as in *gold-en*; though prob. suggested by AS. *ælfen*, a female elf, whence ME. *elven*, an elf, Guy of Warwick, ed. Turnbull, 3862 (N. E. D.). Doublet, *oaf*.

ELICIT, to draw out, coax out. (L.) Orig. a pp. '*Elicite*, drawn out or allured;' Blount's Gloss. ed. 1674.—L. *ēlicitus*, pp. of *ēlicere*, to draw out.—L. *ē*, out; and *lacere*, to entice. See **Lace**.

ELIDE, to strike out. (L.) 'The strength of their arguments is *elided*;' Hooker, Eccl. Polity, b. iv. s. 4.—L. *ēlidere*, to strike out.—L. *ē*, out; and *lædere*, to dash, hurt. See **Lesion**. Der. *elision*, q.v., from pp. *ēlisus*.

ELIGIBLE, fit to be chosen. (F.—L.) In Cotgrave.—MF. *eligible*, 'eligible, to be elected;' Cot.—Late L. *ēligibilis*; formed with suffix *-bilis* from *ēligere*, to choose. See **Elect**. Der. *eligibl-y*, *eligible-ness*; also *eligibili-ty*, formed from *ēligibilis*.

ELIMINATE, to get rid of. (L.) '*Eliminate*, to put out or cast forth of doors; to publish abroad;' Blount's Gloss., ed. 1674.—L. *ēliminātus*, pp. of *ēlimināre*, lit. to put forth from the threshold.—L. *ē*, forth; and *limin-*, stem of *limen*, a threshold, allied to *limes*, a boundary; see **Limit**. Der. *eliminat-ion*.

ELISION, a striking out. (L.) In Bacon, Nat. Hist. § 124.—L. *ēlisionem*, acc. of *ēlisio*, a striking out; cf. *ēlisus*, pp. of *ēlidere*, to strike out. See **Elide**.

ÉLITE, a choice set (in society). (F.—L.) 'The *élite* of crowds;' Byron, Don Juan, bk. xiii. st. 80.—F. *élite*.—L. *electa*, f. of *electus*, chosen, pp. of *ēligere*, to choose out. See **Elect**.

ELIXIR, the philosopher's stone. (Arab.—Gk.) In Chaucer, C. T. 16331 (G 863).—Arab. *el iksīr*, the philosopher's stone; where *el* is the definite article; Palmer's Pers. Dict. col. 44. It also meant a sort of powder (Devic); from Gk. ξήρ-ιον, dry powder, or ξηρ-όν, dry (residuum).

ELK, a kind of large deer. (E.) 'Th' unwieldy *elk*;' Drayton, Noah's Flood. ME. *elke*, Book of St. Alban's, fol. D iii, back, l. 4; *elk*, K. James I, King's Quair, st. 156. An AF. pronunciation of AS. *elh*, an elk, Voc. 12. 30; *elch*, Voc. 51. 36. (So also *Burke* from AS. *burh*, &c.) Cf. Icel. *elgr*; Swed. *elg*, an elk; OHG. *elaho*, MHG. *elch*.+Russ. *oléne*, a stag (cf. Du. *eland*, an elk); L. *alces*; Gk. ἄλκη; Skt. *ṛshya-s*, Vedic *ṛçya-s*, a kind of antelope. (History obscure.)

ELL, a measure of length. (E.) ME. *elle, elne*; Prompt. Parv. p. 138. AS. *eln*, a cubit; see Matt. vi. 27, Lu. xii. 25 (Grein, i. 225);

eln-gemet, the measure of an ell (ibid.). **+** Du. *elle,* an ell; somewhat more than 3-4ths of a yard (Sewel); Icel. *alin,* the arm from the elbow to the tip of the middle-finger; an ell; Swed. *aln,* an ell; Dan. *alen,* an ell; Goth. *aleina,* a cubit; OHG. *elina,* MHG. *elne,* G. *elle,* an ell. **+** L. *ulna,* the elbow; also, a cubit; Gk. ὠλένη, the elbow. The Teut. type is **alinā,* f. Brugmann, i. § 159. β. *Ell=el-* in *el-bow;* see **Elbow.**

ELLIPSE, an oval figure. (L.–Gk.) 'Ellipsis, a defect; also, a certain crooked line coming of the byas-cutting of the cone or cylinder;' Blount's Gloss., ed. 1674.–L. *ellipsis,* a want, defect; also, an ellipse.–Gk. ἔλλειψις, a leaving behind, defect, an ellipse of a word; also the figure called an ellipse, so called because its plane forms with the base of the cone a less angle than that of the parabola (Liddell). –Gk. ἐλλείπειν, to leave in, to come short.–Gk. ἐλ-, for ἐν, in; and λείπειν, to leave, cognate with L. *linquere.* See **Eclipse.** Der. *elliptic-al,* from Gk. ἐλλειπτικός, adj. formed from ἔλλειψις.

ELM, a kind of tree. (E.) ME. *elm,* Chaucer, C. T. 2924 (A 2922). AS. *elm;* Gloss. to Cockayne's Saxon Leechdoms.**+**Icel. *álmr;* Dan. *alm, ælm;* Swed. *alm.***+**L. *ulmus;* whence G. *ulm,* Du. *olm.* Cf. Gael. *leamhan,* Mid. Irish *lem,* elm.

ELOCUTION, clear utterance. (L.) In Ben Jonson, Underwoods, xxxi. 56; and Hawes, Pastime of Pleasure, c. xi. l. 1.–L. *ēlocūtiōnem,* from nom. *ēlocūtio;* cf. *ēlocūtus,* pp. of *ēloquī,* to speak out.–L. *ē,* out; *loquī,* to speak. See **Eloquent.** Der. *elocution-ar-y, -ist.*

ELOIGN, ELOIN, to remove and keep at a distance, to withdraw. (F.–L.) 'Eloine, to remove, banish, or send a great way from;' Blount's Nomo-lexicon. Still in use as a law term. Spenser writes *esloyne,* F. Q. i. 4. 20.–OF. *esloignier,* MF. *esloigner* (mod. F. *éloigner*), 'to remove, banish, drive, set, put far away, keep aloof;' Cotgrave.–OF. *es-,* prefix; and *loing* (mod. F. *loin*), 'far, a great way off;' Cot.–L. *ex,* off, away; *longē,* adv. afar, from *longus,* adj. long, far. See **Ex-** and **Long;** also **Purloin.**

ELONGATE, to lengthen. (Late L.) Formerly 'to remove;' Sir T. Browne, Vulg. Errors, b. iv. c. 13, § 14.–Late L. *ēlongātus,* pp. of *ēlongāre,* to remove; a verb coined from L. *ē,* out, off, and *longus,* long. See **Long.** Der. *elongat-ion.*

ELOPE, to run away. (AF.–Scand.) Spelt *ellope,* Spenser, F. Q. v. 4. 9.–AF. *aloper,* to elope; Year-books of Edw. III, 1337-8, p. 587. The AF. prefix *a-* is prob. for OF. *es-* (< L. *ex,* away), as in *abash.* β. ME. *lopen,* to run (Cath. Angl.) is from Icel. *hlaupa,* to run, cognate with E. **Leap,** q.v. Cf. Du. *loopen,* to run, whence Du. *ontloopen,* to escape, with prefix *ont-*=G. *ent-,* as in *entlaufen,* to run away. Der. *elope-ment.*

ELOQUENT, gifted with good utterance. (F.–L.) ME. *eloquent,* Gower, C. A. iii. 85; bk. vii. 37; cf. *eloquence,* Chaucer, C. T. 10990 (F 678).–OF. *eloquent;* Cot.–L. *ēloquent,* stem of pres. pt. of *ēloquī,* to speak out.–L. *ē,* out; and *loquī,* to speak. See **Elocution.** Der. *eloquent-ly, eloquence.*

ELSE, otherwise. (E.) ME. *elles,* always an adverb; Chaucer, C. T. 13867 (B 2129). AS. *elles,* otherwise, Matt. vi. 1; an adverbial form, orig. gen. sing. from a stem **aljo-,* signifying 'other;' cf. AS. *eleland,* a foreign land, Grein, i. 223.**+**MSwed. *äljes,* otherwise (Ihre); whence mod. Swed. *eljest,* with excrescent *t;* MHG. *alles, elles,* otherwise, else, an adverb of genitival form. Cf. Goth. *aljis,* other; L. *alias,* otherwise, else, from *alius,* other. See **Alien.** Der. *else-where.*

ELUCIDATE, to make clear. (Late L.) 'Elucidate, to make bright, to manifest;' Blount's Gloss., ed. 1674.–Late L. *ēlūcidātus,* pp. of *ēlūcidāre;* compounded from L. *ē,* out, very, and *lūcidus,* bright. See **Lucid.** Der. *elucidat-ion, -or, -ive.*

ELUDE, to avoid slily. (L.) In Bp. Taylor, vol. i. ser. 5 (R.); and Milton, P. L. ix. 158.–L. *ēlūdere,* pp. *ēlūsus,* to mock, deceive. –L. *ē,* out; and *lūdere,* to play. See **Ludicrous.** Der. *elus-ive, -ive-ly, -ion, -or-y;* from pp. *ēlūsus.*

ELYSIUM, a heaven. (L.–Gk.) In Shak. Two Gent. ii. 7. 38. –L. *elysium.*–Gk. Ἠλύσιον, short for Ἠλύσιον πεδίον, the Elysian field; Homer, Od. 4. 563. Der. *Elysi-an.*

EM-, prefix. (F.–L.) F. *em-,* from L. *im-,* for *in;* before *b* and *p.* Hence *em-balm,* to anoint with balm; *em-bank,* to enclose with a bank, cast up a bank; *em-body,* to enclose in a body; &c.

EMACIATE, to make thin. (L.) In Sir T. Browne, Vulg. Errors, b. vii. c. 13, § 6.–L. *ēmaciātus,* pp. of *ēmaciāre,* to make thin.–L. *ē,* out, very; and *maci-,* base of *maci-ēs,* leanness; cf. *macer,* lean. See **Meagre.** Der. *emaciat-ion.*

EMANATE, to flow from. (L.) 'In all bodily emanations;' Bp. Hall, Contemplations, New Test., b. iv. cont. 7. § 19.–L. *ēmānātus,* pp. of *ēmānāre,* to flow out.–L. *ē,* out; and *mānāre,* to flow. *Mānāre*=**madnare,* from the base *mad-* in L. *madidus,* wet, *madēre,* to be moist. Cf. Skt. *mad,* to be wet, to get drunk. Brugmann, i. § 762 (2). Der. *emanat-ion, -ive.*

EMANCIPATE, to set free. (L.) In Blount's Gloss., ed. 1674.

–L. *ēmancipātus,* pp. of *ēmancipāre,* to set free.–L. *ē,* out; and *mancipāre,* to transfer property, from *mancip-,* stem of *manceps,* one who acquires property; lit. one who takes it in hand; from *man-,* base of *manus,* the hand; and *capere,* to take. See **Manual** and **Capable.** Der. *emancipat-or, -ion.*

EMASCULATE, to deprive of virility. (L.) 'Which have *emasculated* [become emasculate] or turned women;' Sir T. Browne, Vulg. Errors, b. iii. c. 17, § 2.–L. *ēmasculātus,* pp. of *ēmasculāre,* to castrate.–L. *ē,* out of, away; and *masculus,* male. See **Male.** Der. *emasculat-ion.*

EMBALM, to anoint with balm. (F.) In Shak. Timon, iv. 3. 30. Spelt *imbalm* in Cotgrave. ME. *embaumen;* Chaucer, Leg. Good Women, 676; cf. *bawmyt, bawlmyt,* embalmed, in Barbour's Bruce, xx. 286.–OF. *embaumer,* 'to imbalm;' Cot.–OF. *em-=en-*<L. *in;* and *baume,* balm. See **Balm.**

EMBANK, to cast up a mound. (Hybrid; F. *and* E.) Spelt *imbank* in Bailey's Dict., vol. ii. ed. 1731. Coined from F. *em-* (L. *im-=in*), and E. *bank.* See **Em-** and **Bank.** Der. *embank-ment.*

EMBARGO, a stoppage of ships. (Span.–Late L.) 'By laying an *embargo* upon all shipping in time of war;' Blackstone, Comment. b. i. c. 7.–Span. *embargo,* an embargo, seizure, arrest; cf. Span. *embargare,* to lay on an embargo, arrest; for Late L. type **imbarricāre,* to bar in.–L. *im-,* for *in;* in; and Late L. *barra,* a bar. Hence *embargo*=a putting of a bar in the way. See **Bar, Barricade, Embarrass.** Der. *embargo,* verb.

EMBARK, to put or go on board ship. (F.) In Hamlet, i. 3. 1. –OF. *embarquer,* 'to imbark;' Cot.–F. *em-*<L. *im-=in;* and F. *barque,* a bark. See **Bark** (1). Der. *embark-at-ion.*

EMBARRASS, to perplex. (F.–Span.–Late L.) 'I saw my friend a little *embarrassed;*' Spectator, no. 109, § 6.–F. *embarrasser,* 'to intricate, pester, intangle, perplex;' Cot.–Span. *embarazar,* to embarrass.–Span. *em-* (=L. *im-=in*); and *barra,* a bar. See **Bar, Embargo.** Der. *embarrass-ment.* ¶ The form *barras* may be compared with Prov. *barras, barrasso,* a large bar (Mistral); or with Span. *barras,* pl. bars. There was a game called *juego de barras* (Minsheu, Span. Dict.). Körting, § 1245.

EMBASSY, the mission of an ambassador. (F.–Late L.–C.) 1. Shak. has *embassy,* L. L. L. i. 1. 135; also *embassage,* Much Ado, i. 1. 282; and *embassade* (=OF. *embassade,* Cotgrave), 3 Hen. VI, iv. 3. 32. 2. Latimer has *ambassages,* Sermon on the Ploughers, l. 180 (in Skeat's Specimens). Chaucer has *embassadrye,* Six-text, B 233. 3. *Embassy* is a modification of OF. *ambassée.*–Low L. *ambasciāta,* sb. (whence also MF. *embassade*); orig. fem. of pp. of *ambasciāre,* to send on a mission, from *ambascia,* a mission (of Celtic origin). See further under **Ambassador.**

EMBATTLE (1), to furnish with battlements. (F.) ME. *embattelen, enbattelen;* Chaucer, C. T. 14866 (B 4050; Lansdowne MS.). –OF. *em-* or *en-* (=L. *im-=in*), prefix; and OF. *bastiller,* to embattle. See **Battlement.** ¶ 1. The simple verb *battailen* or *battalen* occurs early; the pp. *battailyt* or *battalit,* i. e. embattled, occurs in Barbour's Bruce, ii. 221, iv. 134; and the sb. *battalyng,* an embattlement, in the same, iv. 136. 2. Obviously, these words were accommodated to the spelling of ME. *battale* (better *bataille*), a battle; and from the first a confusion with *battle* has been common.

EMBATTLE (2), to range in order of battle. (F.–L.) In Shak. Hen. V, iv. 2. 14. ME. *embataillen;* Gower, C. A. i. 221; bk. ii. 1837.–OF. *embataillier,* the same (Godefroy). A coined word, from F. prefix *em-* (< L. *im-,* in); and OF. *bataille,* a battle, a battalion; see **Battle.**

EMBAY, to enclose in a bay. (F.) In Shak. Oth. ii. 1. 18. A coined word; from F. *em-* (< L. *im-=in*); and E. *bay,* of F. origin. See **Bay** (3).

EMBELLISH, to adorn. (F.–L.) ME. *embelisshen,* Chaucer, Good Women, 1737.–OF. *embeliss-,* stem of pres. pt. &c. of OF. *embellir,* 'to imbellish, beautifie;' Cot.–OF. *em-* (L. *im-=in*); and *bel,* fair, beautiful, from L. *bellus,* well-mannered, fine, handsome. See **Beauty.** ¶ For the suffix *-ish,* see **Abash.** Der. *embellish-ment.*

EMBER-DAYS, fast-days at four seasons of the year. (E.) A corruption of ME. *ymber.* 'The Wednesdai Gospel in *ymber* weke in Septembre monethe;' Wyclif's Works, ed. Arnold, ii. 203; cf. pp. 205, 207. 'Umbridawes' (another MS. *ymbri wikes*), i. e. ember-days (or ember-weeks); Ancren Riwle, p. 70. AS. *ymbren,* pl. *ymbrenu;* as in *þā fēower ymbrenu;* Wulfstan, ed. Napier, p. 136, l. 17. 1. 'On þære pentecostenes wucan tō þām *ymbrene*' = in Pentecost week according to the *ymbren,* i. e. in due course; rubric to Luke, viii. 40. 'On ælcum *ymbren-fæstene,*' = at every ember-fast; Ælfric's Homilies, ii. 608. 2. The orig. form of the word is *ymb-ryne,* and the orig. sense 'a running round,' 'circuit,' or 'course;' compounded of AS. *ymb, ymbe,* around, cognate with G. *um-,* L. *ambi-;* and *ryne,* a running, from *rinnan,* to run. See **Ambi-,** prefix, and **Run.** ¶ This is the best explanation; for numerous examples and references, see *ymbren* in AS. Dictionary. Ihre rightly distinguishes between MSwed. *ymberdagar*, borrowed from AS. and obsolete, and the Swed. *tamperdagar*, corrupted ⟨like G. *quatember*⟩ from L. *quattuor tempora*, the four seasons.

EMBER-GOOSE, the great northern diver. (Scand.) An Orkney word; see E. D. D. Spelt *imber-goose*, Scott, Pirate, c. xxi. − Norw. *imbre, ymmer*; Icel. *himbrin*.

EMBERS, ashes. (E.) The *b* is excrescent. The ME. forms are *emers, emmeres, eymers, eymbers*, equivalent to Lowland Scotch *ammeris*, used by G. Douglas to translate L. *fauillam* in Æneid, vi. 227. '*Eymbre, eymery*, hote aschys;' Prompt. Parv. AS. *ǣmergean*, pl. of *ǣmerge*, f., an ember; A. S. Leechdoms, iii. 30, l. 18.+Icel. *eimyrja*, embers; Dan. *emmer*, embers; Swed. *-mörja*, in comp. *ask-mörja*, ash-embers; OHG. *eimurja*, embers; Bavarian *aimern, emmern*, pl., Schmeller, i. 75. β. Teut. type *aim-uz-jōn-*, weak fem.; for the suffix, cf. Goth. *juk-uzi* (stem *juk-uz-jā*), allied to *juk*, a yoke. The base *aim-* may be compared with Icel. *eim-r*, vapour; prov. E. *ome* (< AS. *ām*), vapour; Dan. *em*, Swed. *imma*, steam.

EMBEZZLE, to steal slily, filch. (F.−L.) Formerly *embesyll* or *embesell*. 'I concele, I *embesyll* a thynge, I kepe a thynge secret; I *embesyll* a thyng, or put it out of the way, *Je substrays*; He that *embesylleth* a thyng intendeth to steale it if he can convaye [it] clenly;' Palsgrave's F. Dict. Spelt *embesile* in The Lament of Mary Magdalen, st. 39; pr. in Chaucer's Works, ed. 1561, fol. 319. The earliest spellings are *enbesel, imbesel*, and the sense is not only to filch, but also to destroy fraudulently, as in 'the sayd boke .. was *enbesyld*, or loste;' Fabyan, ed. Ellis, p. 293. − AF. *enbeseiller*, to make away with; Royal Wills, p. 155 (A. D. 1397); (also AF. *beseler, besiler*; Notes on E. Etym., p. 399). − OF. *en-* (< L. *in*); and OF. *besiller, besiler*, to maltreat, destroy, apparently from OF. *bes-* (Late L. *bis-*, used as a pejorative prefix). Cf. OF. *besil*, ill-treatment, torture; and see **Bezzle** in the N. E. D. ¶ Certainly influenced in the 16th cent., by a supposed etymology from *imbécill*, to weaken, an obs. verb formed from the adj. *imbecile*. Der. *embezzle-ment*.

EMBLAZON, to adorn with heraldic designs. (F.) Shak. has *emblaze*, 2 Hen. VI, iv. 10. 76. Spenser has *emblazon*, F. Q. iv. 10. 55. Formed from *blazon*, q.v., with F. prefix *em-*, from L. *in-=in*. Cf. MF. *blasonner*, 'to blaze arms;' Cot. Der. *emblazon-ment, emblazon-ry*.

EMBLEM, a device. (F.−L.−Gk.) In Shak. All's Well, ii. 1. 44. ME. *embleme*, Lydgate, Chorle and Byrde (beginning). − OF. *embleme*, 'an embleme;' Cot. − L. *emblēma*, a kind of ornament. − Gk. ἔμβλημα, a kind of movable ornament, a thing put on. − Gk. ἐμβάλλειν, to put in, lay on. − Gk. ἐμ-=ἐν, in; and βάλλειν, to cast, throw, put. See **Belemnite**. Der. *emblemat-ic*, from Gk. stem ἐμβληματ-; *-ic-al*.

EMBLEMENTS, the produce of sown lands, crops which a tenant may cut after the determination of his tenancy. (F.−L.) In Blount's Nomo-lexicon; and still in use. Formed with suffix *-ment* from OF. *emble-er, embla-er*, also *emblad-er*, the same word as mod. F. *emblav-er*, 'to sow the ground with corn;' Cotgrave. See *emblaer* in Godefroy, and *emblaver* in Littré. All these forms are from Late L. *imblādāre*, to sow with corn. − L. *im-*, for *in*, in, prefix; and Late L. *blādum* (F. *blé*), contraction of *ablādum* = L. *ablātum*, i. e. '(corn) carried away;' neut. of *ablātus*, taken away; which is from *ab*, from, away, and *lātus*, for *tlātus*, pp. of *tollere*, to take away. (√TEL.)

EMBODY, to invest with a body. (Hybrid; F. *and* E.) In Spenser, F. Q. iii. 3. 22. Formed from E. *body* with F. prefix *em-*, for L. *im-=in*. Der. *embodi-ment*.

EMBOLDEN, to make bold. (Hybrid; F. *and* E.) In Shak. Timon, iii. 5. 3. Formed from E. *bold* with F. prefix *em-*, for L. *im-=in*; and with E. suffix *-en*.

EMBOLISM, an insertion of days, &c. to make a period regular. (F.−Gk.) 'Embolism, the adding a day or more to a year;' Blount's Gloss., ed. 1674. ME. *embolisme*, Trevisa, tr. of Higden, iii. 259. − OF. *embolisme*, 'an addition, as of a day or more, unto a year;' Cot. − Gk. ἐμβολισμός, an intercalation. − Gk. ἐμ-=ἐν, in; and βάλλειν, to cast; cf. ἐμβολή, an insertion. See **Emblem**. Der. *embolism-al*.

EMBONPOINT, plumpness of person. (F.−L.) 'No more than what the French would call *Aimable Embonpoint*;' Congreve's Poems, Doris, st. 4. Mere French. − F. *embonpoint*, 'fulness, plumpness;' Cot. Put for *en bon point*, in good condition, in good case. − L. *in*, in; *bon-um*, neut. of *bonus*, good; *punctum*, point. See **In, Bounty**, and **Point**.

EMBOSOM, to shelter closely. (Hybrid; F. *and* E.) In Spenser, F. Q. ii. 4. 25. From F. prefix *em-=en*, for L. *in*; and E. *bosom*, q.v.

EMBOSS (1), to adorn with bosses or raised work. (F.) Chaucer has *embossed*; Good Women, l. 1200. Cf. King Lear, ii. 4. 227. − OF. *embosser*, 'to swell or arise in bunches;' Cot. − F. *em-*, from L. *im-=in*; and OF. *bosse*, a boss. See **Boss**.

EMBOSS (2), to enclose or shelter in a wood. (F.) In Shak. All's Well, iii. 6. 107. − MF. *embosquer*, to shroud in a wood; Cot. −

F. *em-*, from L. *im-=in*; and OF. *bosc*, a wood (Supp. to Godefroy). See **Bouquet**.

EMBOUCHURE, a mouth, of a river, &c. (F.−L.) Mere French; not in Johnson. − F. *embouchure*, a mouth, opening. − F. *emboucher*, to put to the mouth; *s'emboucher*, to discharge itself (as a river). − F. *em-*, from L. *im-=in*; and F. *bouche*, the mouth, from L. *bucca*. See **Debouch** and **Disembogue**.

EMBOWEL, to enclose deeply. (F.−L.) 'Deepe *emboweled* in the earth;' Spenser, F. Q. vi. 8. 15. [Often wrongly put for *disembowel*; Shak. Rich. III, v. 2. 10.] From F. *em-*, from L. *im-=in*; and *bowel*, of F. origin, q.v. Der. *embowel-ment*.

EMBOWER, to place in a bower. (Hybrid; F. *and* E.) Spenser has *embowering*, i.e. sheltering themselves; tr. of Virgil's Gnat, 225. Coined from F. *em-*, from L. *im-=in*; and E. *bower*.

EMBRACE, to take in the arms. (F.−L.) In early use. ME. *embracen*, to brace on to the arm (said of a shield), King Alisaunder, 6651; cf. Chaucer, C. T. 8288 (E 412). − OF. *embracer*, to embrace, seize (Godefroy). − OF. *em-*, for *en*, L. *in*; and *brace*, the two arms, from L. *brāchia*, pl. of *brāchium*. See **Brace**. Der. *embrace*, sb.

EMBRASURE, an aperture with slant sides. (F.) 'Embrasure, an inlargement made on the inside of a gate, door, &c. to give more light;' Phillips, Dict., ed. 1706. − F. *embrasure*, orig. 'the skuing, splaying, or chamfretting of a door or window;' Cotgrave. − MF. *embraser* (cf. mod. F. *ébraser*) 'to skue, or chamfret off the jaumbes of a door or window;' Cot. 1. The prefix is F. *em-=en*, from L. *in*. 2. The rest is MF. *braser*, 'to skue, or chamfret;' Cot.; of unknown origin.

EMBROCATION, a fomenting. (F.−Late L.−Gk.) Spelt *embrochation* in Holland's Pliny, b. xx. c. 14, § 1.−MF. *embrocation*, 'an embrochation, fomenting;' Cot. Cf. Late L. *embrocātus*, pp. of *embrocāre*, to pour into a vessel, &c.; cf. Ital. *embroccare*, to foment. − Gk. ἐμβροχή, a fomentation. − Gk. ἐμβρέχειν, to soak in, to foment. − Gk. ἐμ-=ἐν, in; and βρέχειν, to wet, soak.

EMBROIDER, to ornament with needlework. (F.) ME. *embrouden, embroyden*, Chaucer, C. T. 89 (Six-text). [This ME. form produced a later form *embroid*; the *-er* is a needless addition, due to the sb. *embroid-er-y*.] Cotgrave gives 'to *imbroyder*' as a translation of OF. *broder*. − AF. *enbroyder*, Stat. Realm, p. 380 (A. D. 1393); OF. prefix *em-=en-*, from L. *in*; and OF. *broder*, to embroider, or broider. See **Broider**. Der. *embroider-er, embroider-y* (rightly *embroid-ery*, from ME. *embroid*; spelt *embrouderie*, Gower, C. A. ii. 41; bk. iv. 1175); *embroiderie*, Merry Wives, v. 5. 75.

EMBROIL, to entangle in a broil. (F.) See Milton, P. L. ii. 908, 966; Daniel, Civil Wars, bk. v. st. 47.−F. *embrouiller*, 'to pester, intangle, incumber, intricate, confound;' Cot. − OF. *em-=en-*, from L. *in*; and F. *brouiller*, 'to jumble, &c.' See **Broil** (2). Cf. Norm. dial. *embroiller* (Moisy). Der. *embroil-ment*.

EMBRUE, variant of **Imbrue**, q. v.

EMBRYO, the rudiment of an organised being. (F.−Gk.) Formerly also *embryon*. 'Though yet an *embryon*;' Massinger, The Picture, Act ii. sc. 2.−MF. *embryon*; Cot. − Gk. ἔμβρυον, the embryo, fœtus. − Gk. ἐμ-=ἐν, in, within; and βρύον, neut. of βρύων, pres. pt. of βρύειν, to be full of a thing, swell with it.

EMENDATION, correction. (L.) In Bp. Taylor, Great Exemplar, p. 3, disc. 18 (R.); Webbe, Eng. Poetrie, ed. Arber, p. 95.− L. *ēmendātio*; allied to *ēmendātus*, pp. of *ēmendāre*, to amend, lit. to free from fault. − L. *ē*, out of, hence, free from; and *mendum*, a fault. See **Amend**. Der. *emenda-tor, -tor-y*; from L. *ēmendāre*.

EMERALD, a green precious stone. (F.−L.−Gk.−Skt.−Heb.) ME. *emeraude, emerade*; Allit. Poems, ed. Morris, i. 1005; King Alisaunder, 7030.−MF. *esmeraude*, 'an emerald;' Cot.; OF. *esmeralde, esmeraude, esmeragde* (Supp. to Godefroy).−L. *smaragdum*, acc. of *smaragdus*, an emerald. − Gk. σμάραγδος, a kind of emerald. Explained as a contracted form of *σμα-μάραγδος*; from Skt. *asmā*, a stone, and *marakata(m)*, emerald; as if 'emerald-stone.' Skt. *marakatam* is of Semitic origin.−Heb. *bāreqet*, an emerald.−Heb. *bāraq*, to flash.

EMERGE, to issue, rise from the sea, appear. (L.) In Bacon; Learning, by G. Wats, b. ii. c. 13. Milton has *emergent*, P. L. vii. 286.−L. *ēmergere*, to rise out. − L. *ē*, out; and *mergere*, to dip. See **Merge**. Der. *emerg-ent*, from *ēmergentem*, acc. of pres. pt.; *emergence, emergenc-y*; *emersion*, like pp. *ēmersus*.

EMERODS, hemorrhoids. (F.−L.−Gk.) In Bible, A. V., 1 Sam. v. 6; spelt *emorade*, Levins; *emeroudes*, Palsgrave. ME. *emeraudis*, pl., Reliq. Antiq. i. 190.−MF. *hemorrhoïde*, pl. *hemorrhoïdes*; Cot. See **Hemorrhoids**.

EMERY, a hard mineral. (F.−Ital.−Gk.) Formerly *emeril*. '*Emeril*, a hard and sharp stone,' &c.; Blount's Gloss., ed. 1674.− F. *émeri*; MF. *emeril*, Cot.; and, still earlier, *esmeril* (Brachet).−Ital. *smeriglio*, emery.−Gk. σμῆρις, also σμύρις, emery. Allied to E. *smear* (Prellwitz). See **Smear**.

EMETIC, causing vomit. (L.—Gk.) Spelt *emetique* in Blount's Gloss., ed. 1674.—L. *emeticus*, adj. causing vomit.—Gk. ἐμετικός, provoking sickness.—Gk. ἐμέω, I vomit.+L. *uomere*, to vomit. See **Vomit.**

EMEU, the same as **Emu**, which see.

EMIGRATE, to migrate from home. (L.) *Emigration* is in Blount's Gloss., ed. 1674; the verb is later.—L. *ēmigrātus*, pp. of *ēmigrāre*.—L. *ē*, away; and *migrāre*, to migrate. See **Migrate.** Der. *emigrat-ion*; also *emigrant*, from pres. pt. of L. vb.

EMINENT, excellent. (L.) In Shak. All's Well, i. 2. 43.—L. *ēminent-em*, acc. of *ēminens*, pres. pt. of *ēminēre*, to stand out, project, excel.—L. *ē*, out; and *minēre*, to jut, project; for which cf. *imminent, pro-minent.* Der. *eminence.*

EMIR, a commander. (Arabic.) The pl. *emers* is in Sandys, Travels (1632), p. 64, l. 7.—Arab. *amīr*, a nobleman, prince; Palmer's Pers. Dict. col. 51.—Arab. root *amara*, he commanded; Chaldee *amar*, Heb. *āmar*, he commanded, or told; Rich. Dict. p. 167. See **Admiral.**

EMIT, to send forth. (L.) In Blount's Gloss., ed. 1674.—L. *ēmittere*, pp. *ēmissus*, to send out.—L. *ē*, out; and *mittere*, to send. See **Missile.** Der. *emiss-ion*, Dryden, Hind and Panther, l. 647; *emissar-y*, Ben Jonson, Underwoods, Of Charis, viii. l. 17.

EMMET, an ant. (E.) ME. *emete*, pl. *emeten*, Beket, 2141; [also ME. *amte*, Wyclif, Prov. vi. 6; full form *amote*, Ayenbite of Inwyt, p. 141.] AS. *ǣmete*, tr. of L. *formica*; Voc. 121. 26.+G. *ameise*, an ant; OHG. *āmeiza*. Discussed in Kluge. ¶ The AS. *ǣmete* became *amete* (*amote*) and *emete* in ME. The former became *amte, ante*, E. *ant*; the latter became E. *emmet*, which is therefore a doublet of *ant*. See **Ant.**

EMMEW, variant of **Enew**, q. v.

EMOLLIENT, softening. (F.—L.) Also as a sb. 'Some outward *emollients*;' Bacon, Nat. Hist. sect. 59.—MF. *emollient*, 'softening, mollifying;' Cot.—L. *ēmollient-*, stem of pres. pt. of *ēmollīre*, to soften.—L. *ē*, out, much; and *mollīre*, to soften, from *mollis*, soft. See **Mollify.**

EMOLUMENT, gain, profit. (F.—L.) In Cotgrave; and in Holinshed, Descr. of Engl. c. 5 (R.).—OF. *emolument*, 'emolument, profit;' Cot.—L. *ēmolumentum*, profit, what is gained by labour.—L. *ē-molere*, to grind thoroughly.—L. *ē*, out, thoroughly; and *molere*, to grind. See **Molar.** The orig. sense of *ēmolumentum* may have been 'miller's toll;' Bréal.

EMOTION, agitation of mind. (L.) In Bp. Taylor, Rule of Conscience, b. iv. c. 1 (R.). Suggested by obs. verb *emmove* (Spenser, F. Q. iv. 8. 3).—L. *ēmouēre*, pp. *ēmōtus*, to move away.—L. *ē*, away; and *mouēre*, to move. See **Move.** Der. *emotion-al.*

EMPALE, to fix on a stake. (F.—L.) Also *impale*, meaning 'to encircle as with pales;' Troil. v. 7. 5.—MF. *empaler*, 'to impale, to spit on a stake;' Cot.—OF. *em-* = *en-*, for L. *in*; and MF. *pal*, 'a pale, stake;' id. See **Pale** (1). Der. *empale-ment.*

EMPANEL, to put on a list of jurors. (F.—L.) Also *empannel*; Holland, Livy, p. 475. Coined from F. *em-* = *en*, from L. *in*; and **Panel**, q. v. ¶ Better than *impannel*, Shak. Sonn. 46.

EMPEROR, a ruler. (F.—L.) In early use. ME. *emperour*, King Alisaunder, 2719.—OF. *empereor* (Burguy).—L. *imperātōrem*, acc. of *imperātor*, a commander.—L. *imperāre*, to command.—L. *im-* = *in*, on, over; and *parāre*, to make ready, order. See **Parade.** From same source, *empire*, q. v.; *empress*, q. v.

EMPHASIS, stress of voice. (L.—Gk.) Hamlet, v. 1. 278.—L. *emphasis.*—Gk. ἔμφασις, an appearing, declaration, significance, emphasis.—Gk. ἐμ- = ἐν, in; and φάσις, an appearance. See **Phase.** Der. *emphasise*; also *emphatic*, from Gk. adj. ἐμφατικός, expressive; *emphatic-al, -al-ly.*

EMPIRE, dominion. (F.—L.) In early use. ME. *empire*; King Alisaunder, 1588.—OF. *empire.*—L. *imperium*, command; allied to *imperāre*, to command. See **Emperor.**

EMPIRIC, a quack doctor. (F.—L.—Gk.) All's Well, ii. 1. 125.—MF. *empirique*, 'an empirick, a physician, &c.;' Cot.—L. *empiricus.*—Gk. ἐμπειρικός, experienced; also, an Empiric, the name of a set of physicians.—Gk. ἐμπειρία, experience; ἔμπειρος, experienced.—Gk. ἐμ- = ἐν, in; and πεῖρα, a trial, attempt; connected with πόρος, a way; and with E. *fare*. See **Fare.** Der. *empiric-al, -ism.*

EMPLOY, to occupy, use. (F.—L.) In Shak. L. L. L. iii. 152; and in Caxton, Golden Legend, Lyf of St. Audegonde, § 1.—OF. *employer*, 'to imploy;' Cot.—L. *implicāre*; in Late L., to employ; see **Implicate, Imply.** Der. *employ*, sb., *-er*; *-ment*, Hamlet, v. 1. 77. Doublets, *imply, implicate.*

EMPORIUM, a mart. (L.—Gk.) In Dryden, Annus Mirab., st. 302; Holinshed, Desc. of Ireland, p. 148.—L. *emporium.*—Gk. ἐμπόριον, a mart; neut. of ἐμπόριος, commercial.—Gk. ἐμπορία, commerce; ἔμπορος, a passenger, a merchant.—Gk. ἐμ- = ἐν, in; and πόρος, a way. πορεύεσθαι, to travel, fare. See **Fare.**

EMPOWER, to give power to. (F.—L.) 'You are *empowered*;' Dryden, Disc. on Satire, paragraph 10. Coined from F. *em-* = *en*, from L. *in*, upon; and **Power**, q. v.

EMPRESS, the feminine of *emperor*. (F.—L.) In very early use. [Spelt *emperice* in the AS. Chron. an. 1140]; *emperesse*, Gower, C. A. iii. 363; bk. viii. 2612.—OF. *emperesse* (Godefroy).—L. type **imperātōrissa*, fem. of L. *imperātor*. See **Emperor.**

EMPRISE, an enterprise. (F.—L.) ME. *emprise*, Chaucer, C. T., A 2540; Cursor Mundi, 9802.—OF. *emprise*; orig. fem. of *empris*, pp. of *emprendre*, to take in hand.—L. *im-*, for *in*, in; and *prehendere*, to take. See **Prehensile.**

EMPTY, void. (E.) The *p* is excrescent. ME. *empti, empty*; Ancren Riwle, p. 156; Chaucer, C. T. 3892 (A 3894). AS. *æmtig*, empty, Gen. i. 2; *emtig*, idle, Exod. v. 8. β. An adj. formed with suffix *-ig* (= mod. E. *-y*) from *æmta* or *æmetta*, leisure; Alfred's Boethius, Preface; also *emota* (Epinal Gloss. 680). Perhaps this represents a type **æ-mōt-jon-*, from *æ-*, privative prefix, and *mōt*, a meeting for business. Der. *empty*, vb.; *empti-ness.*

EMPYREAL, EMPYREAN, pertaining to elemental fire. (Gk.) Milton has *empyreal* as adj., P. L. ii. 430; *empyrean* as sb., id. 771. Both are properly adjectives, coined with suffixes *-al* and *-an* from the base *empyre-*, in Latin spelling *empyræ-*, in Gk. ἐμπυραι-, in Late Gk. ἐμπύραιος, adj., which is extended from Gk. ἔμπυρ-ος, exposed to fire.—Gk. ἐμ- = ἐν, in; and πῦρ, cognate with E. *fire*. See **Fire.** ¶ First used in the phr. *celum empireum*, Caxton, Golden Legend, Of the Ascencion, § 4; from the neuter of the adj.

EMU, EMEU, a large bird. (Port.) Formerly applied to the American ostrich.—Port. *ema*, an ostrich. Remoter origin unknown. ¶ There is no proof of its being Arabic; see Newton, Dict. of Birds.

EMULATE, to try to equal. (L.) Properly an adj., as in Hamlet, i. 1. 83.—L. *æmulātus*, pp. of *æmulāri*, to try to equal.—L. *æmulus*, striving to equal. Der. *emulat-ion* (OF. *emulation*, Cotgrave); *emulat-or, emulat-ive*; also *emulous*, in Shak. Troil. iv. 1. 28 (L. *æmulus*), *-ly.*

EMULSION, a milk-like mixture. (F.—L.) In Cotgrave.—MF. *emulsion*, 'an emulsion, any kind of seed brayed in water, and strained to the consistence of an almond milk;' Cot. Formed from L. *ēmulsus*, pp. of *ēmulgēre*, to milk out, drain.—L. *ē*, out; and *mulgēre*, to milk. See **Milk.**

EN-, prefix; from F. *en*, from L. *in*, in, on; sometimes used to give a causal force, as in *en-able, en-feeble*. It becomes *em-* before *b* and *p*, as in *embalm, employ*. In *enlighten, en-* has supplanted AS. *in-*.

ENABLE, to make able. (F.—L.) 'To a-certain you I woll my-self *enable*;' Remedie of Love, st. 28; pr. in Chaucer's Works, ed. 1561, fol. 322, back. Formed from F. prefix *en-*, from L. *in*; and **Able**, q. v.

ENACT, to perform, decree. (F.—L.) Rich. III, v. 4. 2; and *enacte* in Palsgrave. Formed from F. *en* = L. *in*; and **Act**, q. v. Der. *enact-ment, enact-ive.*

ENALLAGE, the substitution of one grammatical form for another; as, e.g., of sing. for plural. (L.—Gk.) First in 1583 (N. E. D.); not common.—L. *enallagē.*—Gk. ἐναλλαγή, change; allied to ἐναλλάσσειν, to change.—Gk. ἐν, in; and ἀλλάσσειν, to change, alter, from ἄλλος, other, different; see **Alien.**

ENAMEL, a glass-like coating. (F.—L. *and* OHG.) ME. *enamayl*, Assemblie of Ladies, st. 77; l. 534. Formed from F. prefix *en* < L. *in*, i.e. upon, above; and *amaile*, later *amel* or *ammel*, a corruption of OF. *esmail* (= Ital. *smalto*), enamel. Thus Cotgrave renders *esmail* by 'ammell, or enammell; made of glass and metals;' and Palsgrave has *enamell*, vb. and '*ammell*, esmail.' β. Of Germanic origin; cf. OHG. *smalzjan*, MHG. *smelzen*, to smelt; Du. *smelten*, to smelt. See **Smelt.** Cf. also O. Low G. *smalt*, butter (Lübben), G. *schmalz*, suet, butter; MItal. *smalto*, 'morter, also amell,' Florio. γ. From Low G. base *smalt-*, allied to OHG. *smelzan*, to melt, str. vb. (pt. t. *smalz*). Der. *enamel*, verb.

ENAMOUR, to inflame with love. (F.—L.) The pp. *enamoured* is in Rob. of Brunne, tr. of Langtoft, p. 254.—OF. *enamorer* (Burguy).—F. *en*, from L. *in*; and F. *amour*, love. See **Amour.**

ENCAMP, to form into a camp. (F.—L.) In Henry V, iii. 6. 180. Formed from F. *en*, in; and **Camp**, q. v. Der. *encamp-ment.*

ENCASE, to put into a case. (F.—L.) 'Round *encasing* The moat of glass;' Ph. Fletcher, Purple Island, c. v. st. 34.—F. *encaisser*, 'to put into a case or chest;' Cot.—F. *en*, from L. *in*; and MF. *caisse*, a case, chest. See **Case** (2).

ENCAUSTIC, burnt in. (F.—L.—Gk.) In Holland's Pliny, b. xxxv. c. 11, § 2.—F. *encaustique*, 'wrought with fire;' Cot.—L. *encausticus.*—Gk. ἐγκαυστικός, relating to burning in.—Gk. ἐγκαίω (fut. ἐγκαύσω), I burn in; from ἐγ = ἐν, in, and καίω, I burn. See **Calm, Ink.**

ENCEINTE, pregnant. (F.—L.) F. *enceinte*, fem. of *enceint*, pp. answering to L. *incinctus*, girt about, of which the fem. *incincta* is used of a pregnant woman in Isidore of Seville.—L. *incingere*, to

gird in, gird about; from *in*, and *cingere*, to gird. See **Cincture.**
Isidore explains *incincta* as ' ungirt ;' but the Late L. *praecincta* likewise means ' pregnant.' The reference seems to be to pressure
against the girdle.

ENCHAIN, to bind with chains. (F.—L.) In Shak. Lucr. 934.
ME. *encheynen*, T. Usk, Test. of Love, bk. ii. c. 6, l. 4.—OF.
enchainer, ' to enchain ;' Cot.—OF. *en*, from L. *in* ; and *chaine*, a
chain. See **Chain.**

ENCHANT, to charm by sorcery. (F.—L.) ME. *enchaunten* ;
P. Plowman, C. xviii. 288.—F. *enchanter*, ' to charm, inchant ;' Cot.
—L. *incantāre*, to repeat a chant.—L. *in* ; and *cantāre*, to sing,
chant. See **Chant.** Der. *enchant-er* ; *enchant-ment*, spelt *enchaunte-
ment* in Rob. of Glouc. p. 10, l. 226 ; *enchant-r-ess.*

ENCHASE, to emboss, adorn, enshrine, engrave. (F.—L.) Often
shortened to *chase*, but *enchase* is the better form. In Shak. 2 Hen. VI,
i. 2. 8.—MF. *enchasser* ; as ' *enchasser en or*, to enchace or set in gold ;'
Cot.—F. *en*, from L. *in* ; and MF. *chasse*, ' a shrine for a relick, also
that thing, or part of a thing, wherein any thing is *enchased*, and hence
la chasse d'un rasoir, the handle of a rasor ;' Cot. MF. *chasse* (F.
châsse) is a doublet of F. *caisse* ; from L. *capsa*, a box. See **Case** (2),
Chase (2), **Chase** (3).

ENCIRCLE, to enclose in a circle. (F.—L.) In Merry Wives,
iv. 4. 56.—F. *en*, from L. *in* ; and F. *circle*. See **Circle.**

ENCLINE, to lean towards. (F.—L.) Often *incline*, but *encline*
is more in accordance with etymology. ME. *enclinen* ; Chaucer,
Pers. Tale, Group I, 361.—OF. *encliner*, ' to incline ;' Cot.—L.
inclīnāre, to bend towards ; from *in*, towards, and *clīnāre*, to bend,
cognate with E. *lean*. See **Lean**, verb, and see below.

ENCLITIC, a word which leans its accent upon another.
(L.—Gk.) A grammatical term ; spelt *enclitick* in Kersey, ed.1715.—
L. *encliticus.*—Gk. ἐγκλιτικός, lit. enclining.—Gk. ἐγκλίνειν, to lean
towards, encline.—Gk. ἐγ- = ἐν, in, upon ; and κλίνειν, cognate with
E. *lean*. See **Lean** (1). And see above.

ENCLOSE, to close in, shut in. (F.—L.) ME. *enclosen*, Chaucer,
C. T. 8096 (E 220).—OF. *enclos*, pp. of *enclorre*, to close in ; from
en (from L. *in*), and *clorre* (L. *claudere*), to shut. See **Close.**

ENCOMIUM, commendation. (L.—Gk.) Spelt *encomion* in Ben
Jonson, Every Man in his Humour, A. iv. sc. 2. Latinised from Gk.
ἐγκώμιον, a laudatory ode ; neut. of ἐγκώμιος, laudatory, full of
revelry.—Gk. ἐγ- = ἐν, in ; and κῶμος, revelry. See **Comic.** Der.
encomi-ast (Gk. ἐγκωμιαστής, a praiser) ; *encomiast-ic.*

ENCOMPASS, to surround. (F.—L.) In Rich. III, i. 2. 204.
ME. *encumpassen*, Early E. Psalter, xvii. 6. Formed from F. *en*,
from L. *in* ; and *compass*. See **Compass.** Der. *encompass-ment*,
Hamlet, ii. 1. 10.

ENCORE, again. (F.—L.) Mere French ; cf. Ital. *ancora*, still,
again.—L. *hanc hōram*, for *in hanc hōram*, to this hour ; hence, still.
See **Hour.**

ENCOUNTER, to meet in combat. (F.—L.) ' Causes *encoun-
tringe* and flowing *togidere* ;' Chaucer, tr. of Boethius, b. v. pr. 1,
l. 59.—OF. *encontrer*, ' to encounter ;' Cot.—F. *en-*, from L. *in* ; and
contre, from L. *contrā*, against ; cf. Late L. *incontram*, against. See
Counter-. Der. *encounter*, sb.

ENCOURAGE, to embolden. (F.—L.) As You Like It, i. 2.
252 ; ME. *encoragen*, Lydgate, Minor Poems, p. 27.—OF. *encoragier*
(Godefroy) ; MF. *encourager*, ' to hearten ;' Cot.—F. *en*, from L. *in* ;
and *courage*. See **Courage.** Der. *encourage-ment*, Rich. III, v. 2. 6.

ENCRINITE, the stone lily, a fossil. (Gk.) Geological. Coined
from Gk. ἐν, in ; and κρίνον, a lily ; with suffix -*ite* (Gk. -ιτης).

ENCROACH, to trespass, intrude. (F.—L. *and* Teut.) ' *En-
croaching* tyranny ;' 2 Hen. VI, iv. 1. 96. ME. *encrochen*, Allit.
Morte Arthure, l. 1243. Lit. ' to catch in a hook' or 'to hook
away.'—OF. *encrochier*, to seize upon (Godefroy). Formed from F.
en, in ; and *croc*, a hook, just as F. *accrocher*, to hook up, is derived
from F. *à* (<L. *ad*), and the same word *croc*, of Germanic origin ; cf.
MDu. *kroke*, Icel. *krókr*, a crook. See **Crook.** Der. *encroach-er*,
encroach-ment, Sir T. Browne, Vulg. Errors, To Reader, § 1. ¶ It is
impossible to derive *encroach* from OF. *encrouer* ; it is a fuller form.

ENCUMBER, to impede, load. (F.—L.?) In early use. ME.
encumbren, encombren ; Rob. of Brunne, tr. of Langtoft, p. 117 ; P.
Plowman, C. ii. 192.—OF. *encombrer*, ' to cumber, incumber ;' Cot.
—Late L. *incumbrāre*, to obstruct.—L. *in*, in ; and Late L. *cumbrus*, an
obstacle. See **Cumber.** Der. *encumbr-ance.* ¶ The ME. sb. was
encombrement, King Alisaunder, 7825.

ENCYCLICAL, lit. circular. (L.—Gk.) ' An *encyclical* epistle ;'
Bp. Taylor, Dissuas. from Popery, pt. ii. b. ii. s. 2 (R.). Formed
(with Latinised spelling, and suffix -*cal*) from Gk. ἐγκύκλι-ος, circular
(said of a letter sent round), successive.—Gk. ἐγ- = ἐν, in ; and
κύκλος, a ring. See **Cycle.**

ENCYCLOPÆDIA, a comprehensive summary of science.
(L.—Gk.) In Elyot, Governour, bk. i. c. xiii. § 4. *Encyclopædie*

occurs in Sir T. Browne, Vulg. Errors, To the Reader. § 1 ; cf. F.
encyclopedie in Cotgrave. Latinised from a coined Gk. *ἐγκυκλοπαιδεία*,
a barbarism for ἐγκύκλιος παιδεία, the circle of arts and sciences ; here
ἐγκύκλιος is fem. of ἐγκύκλιος (see above) ; and παιδεία means ' instruction,' from παιδ-, stem of παῖς, a boy. See **Pedagogue.** Der.
encycloped-ic, encycloped-ist.

END, close, termination. (E.) ME. *endè* (with final *e*) ; Chaucer,
C. T. 4565 (B 145). AS. *ende* (Grein). ✛ Du. *einde* ; Icel. *endi* ;
Swed. *ände* ; Dan. *ende* ; Goth. *andeis* ; G. *ende*. Teut. type **and-joz.*
Cf. OIrish *ind*, Skt. *anta-*, end, limit. Der. *end*, verb ; *end-less* (AS.
endelēas), -*ly*, -*ness* ; *end-wise*, -*ing*. ¶ The prefixes *ante-* (L. *ante*),
anti- (Gk. ἀντί), and *an-* (in *an-swer*) are connected with this word.

ENDANGER, to place in danger. (F.—L.) In Shak. Two Gent.
v. 4. 133. Coined from F. *en*, from L. *in* ; and **Danger,** q.v.

ENDEAR, to make dear. (Hybrid ; F. *and* E.) Shak. has *en-
deared*, K. John, iv. 2. 228. Coined from F. *en*, from L. *in* ; and E.
Dear, q.v. Der. *endear-ment*, used by Drayton and Bp. Taylor (R.).

ENDEAVOUR, to attempt, try. (F.—L.) 1. The verb *to endeavour* grew out of the ME. phrase ' to do his *dever*,' i.e. to do his
duty ; cf. ' Do now your *devoir*' = do your duty, Chaucer, C. T.
2600 (A 2598) ; and again, ' And doth nought but his *dever*' = and
does nothing but his duty ; Will. of Palerne, 474. ' He sholde *en-
deuore hym* to seche hem ;' Caxton, Reynard, ed. Arber, p. 93. Shak.
has *endeavour* both as sb. and vb. ; Temp. ii. 1. 160 ; Much Ado, ii.
2. 31. 2. The prefix *en-* has a verbal and active force, as in *enamour,
encourage, encumber, enforce, engage*, words of similar formation.—F.
en-, from L. *in*, prefix ; and ME. *devoir, dever*, equivalent to OF.
devoir, debvoir, a duty. See **Devoir.** Der. *endeavour*, sb.

ENDECA-, incorrect form of **Hendeca-**; which see.

ENDEMIC, peculiar to a people or district. (Gk.) ' *Endemical,
Endemial*, or *Endemious Disease*, a distemper that affects a great many
in the same country ;' Kersey, ed. 1715.—Gk. ἐνδήμι-ος, ἔνδημ-ος,
native, belonging to a people.—Gk. ἐν, in ; and δῆμος, a people. See
Democracy. Der. also *endemi-al, endemic-al.*

ENDIVE, a plant. (F.—L.—Gk.—Semitic.) ' Endyve, herbe, *endivia* ;' Prompt. Parv.—F. *endive* (cf. Ital. *endivia*).—L. type **intibea*,
f. adj. ; from *intibus, intubus*, endive.—Late Gk. ἔντυβον. Supposed
to be of Semitic origin ; cf. Arab. *hindab*, endive, Rich. Dict., p. 1691.
Perhaps from *Hind*, India.

ENDOGEN, a plant that grows from within. (F.—Gk.) The F.
term *endogène* belongs to the natural system of De Candolle (1813).
—Gk. ἔνδο-, for ἔνδον, within, an extension from ἐν, in ; and γεν-, base
of γίγνομαι, I am born or produced, from √ GEN, to produce. See
Genus. Der. *endogen-ous.*

ENDORSE, to put on the back of. (F.—L.) Modified from
endosse, the older spelling, and (etymologically) more correct ; see
Spenser, F. Q. v. 11. 53, where it rhymes with *bosse* and *losse*. But in
Ben Jonson, Underwoods, lxxi, it rhymes with *horse*. Palsgrave has ' I
endosse ;' p. 534.—OF. *endosser*, ' to indorse ;' Cot.—F. *en*, upon ;
and *dos*, the back.—L. *in* ; and *dorsum*, the back. See **Dorsal.**

ENDOW, to give a dowry to. (F.—L.) In Spenser, F. Q. iii. 4.
21. Hoccleve has *endowed* ; Reg. of Princes, st. 569, l. 3982.—F. *en*,
from L. *in* ; and *douer*, ' to indue, endow ;' Cot. ; from L. *dōtāre*, to
give a dowry. See **Dowry.** Der. *endow-ment*, Rich. II, ii. 3. 139.

ENDUE (1), to endow. (F.—L.) Partly another spelling of
endow. ' Among so manye notable benefites wherewith God hath
alreadie liberally and plentifully *endued* us ;' Sir J. Cheke, The Hurt
of Sedition (R.). ' *Indwyn* (= *induen*), doto ;' Prompt. Parv.—OF.
endoer (later *endouer*), to endow ; Burguy. See **Endow.** ¶ Also
used in senses which confuse it with L. *induere*. See **Indue.**

ENDUE (2), to clothe. (L.) The vb. *endue*, to endow (cf. Gen.
xxx. 20), is unconnected with L. *induere*. But there is another verb
endue, to clothe, which is merely a corruption of *indue* (1) ; [just contrary to *indue* (2), which is a corruption of *enūue* (1) ; cf. ' I indue, *Ie
endoue* ;' Palsgrave.] Thus, in Ps. 132. 9, we have ' let thy priests be
clothed with righteousness ;' in the Vulgate, ' sacerdotes tui *induantur
iustitiam* ;' and hence the versicle in the Morning Prayer : ' *endue*
thy ministers with righteousness.' See **Indue** (2). ¶ A third form
endue, from F. *enduire*, L. *indūcere*, appears to be obsolete.

ENDURE, to last. (F.—L.) ME. *enduren*, Chaucer, C. T. 2398
(A 2396).—OF. *endurer* ; compounded of *en*, from L. *in* ; and *durer*,
L. *dūrāre*, to last. See **Dure.** Der. *endur-able, -abl-y, -ance.*

ENEMA, an injection, a clyster. (Gk.) In Bailey (1735).—Gk.
ἔνεμα, an injection.—Gk. ἐν, in ; and ἑ-, weak grade allied to ἵημι
(for **σί-ση-μι*), I send ; see Prellwitz.

ENEMY, a foe. (F.—L.) In early use. ME. *enemi*, King Horn,
ed. Lumby, 952.—OF. *enemi*.—L. *inimicus*, unfriendly.—L. *in-* (= E.
un-), not ; and *amicus*, a friend. See **Amicable.** Der. from same
source, *enmity*, q. v.

ENERGY, vigour. (F.—L.—Gk.) In Cotgrave.—MF. *energie*,
'energy, effectual operation ;' Cot.—Late L. *energia*.—Gk. ἐνέργεια,

action. – Gk. ἐνεργός, at work, active. – Gk. ἐν, in ; and ἔργον, cognate with E. *work*. See **Work**. Der. *energetic* (Gk. ἐνεργητικός, active); *-al, -al-ly*.

ENERVATE, to deprive of strength. (L.) 'For great empires . . . doe *enervate*,' &c.; Bacon, Essay 58. – L. *ēneruātus*, pp. of *ēner-uāre*, to deprive of nerves or sinews, to weaken. – L. *ē*, out of; and *neruus*, a nerve, sinew. See **Nerve**. Der. *enervat-ion*.

ENEW, to drive into the water. (F. – L.) Misprinted *emmew* in Shak., Meas. iii. 1. 91. 'Youre hawke hath *ennewed* the fowle into the Ryuer;' Book of St. Albans, fol. d. ij. – F. *en*, in (L. *in*); and AF. *ewe* (F. *eau*, L. *aqua*), water. Cf. OF. *enewer*, to soak in water (Godefroy).

ENFEEBLE, to make feeble. (F. – L.) In Shak. Cymb. v. 2. 4. Earlier, in Sir T. More, Works, p. 892 d. – OF. *enfeblir*, to enfeeble (Godefroy). – F. *en-*, from L. *in-*, prefix ; and AF. *feble*, feeble. See **Feeble**. Der. *enfeeble-ment*.

ENFEOFF, to invest with a fief. (F. – L. and OHG.) In 1 Hen. IV, iii. 2. 69. Formed by prefixing the F. *en* (< L. *in*) to the sb. *fief*. Cf. ME. *feffen*, to enfeoff, P. Plowman, B. ii. 78, 146 ; which answers to OF. *fieffer*, 'to infeoffe;' Cot. See **Fief**. ¶ The peculiar spelling is due to Old (legal) AF., and appears in the Law L. *infeoffāre*, and *feoffātor* (Ducange). Der. *enfeoff-ment*.

ENFILADE, a line or straight passage. (F. – L.) '*Enfilade*, a ribble-row of rooms; a long train of discourse ; *in the Art of War*, the situation of a post, that it can discover and scour all the length of a straight line;' Kersey, ed. 1715. He also has the verb. – F. *enfilade*, 'a suite of rooms, a long string of phrases, raking fire ;' Hamilton. – F. *enfiler*, to thread. – F. *en*, from L. *in* ; and *fil*, a thread, from L. *filum*, a thread. See **File** (1). Der. *enfilade*, verb.

ENFOLD, to enclose, embrace. (F. – L.; and E.) Formerly also *infold*, which is better, as being wholly English. Shak. has *infold*, Romeo, iii. 3. 73. From *en-*, prefix (or *in*, as prefix), and *fold*. See **Fold** (1).

ENFORCE, to give force to. (F. – L.) 'Thou most *enforce* thee;' Chaucer, C. T. 5922 (D 340). – OF. *enforcer*, to strengthen (Burguy). – F. *en*, from L. *in*, in ; and *force*. See **Force**. Der. *enforce-ment*, As You Like It, ii. 7. 118.

ENFRANCHISE, to render free. (F.) In L. L. L. iii. 121. – OF. *enfranchiss-*, stem of pres. pt. of *enfranchir*, to free (Godefroy). – F. *en* (from L. *in*), in; and the adj. *franc*, free. See **Franchise**. Cf. OF. *franchir*, 'to free, deliver;' Cot. Der. *enfranchise-ment*, K. John, iv. 2. 52.

ENGAGE, to bind by a pledge. (F. – L. and Teut.) In Othello, iii. 3. 462. – F. *engager*, 'to pawn, impledge, ingage ;' Cot. – F. *en* (from L. *in*), in ; and F. *gage*, a pledge. See **Gage** (1). Der. *engage-ment*, J. Cæs. ii. 1. 307; *engag-ing, -ing-ly*.

ENGENDER, to breed. (F. – L.) ME. *engendren* ; Chaucer, C. T. 6047 (D 465). – OF. *engendrer*, 'to ingender;' Cot. [The *d* is excrescent.] – L. *ingenerāre*, to produce, generate. – L. *in*; and *gene-rāre*, to breed ; formed from *gener-* (for **genes-*), stem of *genus*, a race, brood. See **Genus**; and see **Gender**.

ENGINE, a skilful contrivance. (F. – L.) In early use. ME. *engin*, a contrivance, Floriz, ed. Lumby, 755 ; often shortened to *gin*, *ginne*, id. 131. – OF. *engin*, 'an engine, toole;' Cot. – L. *ingenium*, genius; also, an invention. See **Ingenious**. Der. *engin-eer*, formerly (and properly) *engin-er*, Hamlet, iii. 4. 206; *engineer-ing*.

ENGLISH, (originally) of or belonging to the Angles. (E.) AS. *Englisc, Ænglisc* ; adj. formed by subjoining *-isc* (*-ish*) to **Angli-*, orig. stem of AS. *Engle*, pl., the Angles, one of the Teutonic tribes who settled in Britain in the fifth century. Cf. *England*, for AS. *Engla land*, 'land of the Angles.'

ENGRAILED, indented with curved lines; in heraldry. (F. – L. and Teut.) Spelt *engraylyt* in The Book of St. Albans, pt. ii. fol. f 1, bk. ; *engrelede* in Allit. Morte Arthure, 4183. – OF. *engresle*, pp. of *engresler*, to engrail ; F. *engrêler* (Hatzfeld). – F. *en*, in ; OF. *gresle*, F. *grêle*, hail ; because the edge or line seems as if indented or 'pitted' by the fall of hailstones. The OF. *gresle* is of doubtful origin, but may be Teut. ; cf. OHG. *grioz*, grit.

ENGRAIN, to dye of a fast colour. (F. – L.) ME. *engreynen*, to dye *in grain*, i.e. of a fast colour ; P. Plowman, B. ii. 15. Cf. MF. *engrainer*, to dye ; in Palsgrave, s. v. *grayne*, vb. Coined from F. *en*, from L. *in*, and OF. *graine*, 'the seed of herbs, &c., also grain, wherewith cloth is died *in grain* ; scarlet die, scarlet in graine ;' Cot. – Late L. *grāna*, the cochineal berry or insect ; a fem. sb. formed from *grāna*, pl. of L. *grānum*, grain. See **Grain**.

ENGRAVE, to cut with a graver. (Hybrid ; F. *and* E.) Spenser has the pp. *engraven*, F. Q. iv. 7. 46 ; so also Shak. Lucr. 203. A hybrid word ; coined from F. prefix *en* (from L. *in*), and E. *grave*. See **Grave** (1). Der. *engrav-er, engrav-ing*. ¶ 1. The retention of the strong pp. *engraven* shows that the main part of the word is English. 2. But the E. compound was obviously suggested by the OF. *engraver*,

'to engrave,' (Cot.) ; der. rom F. *en*, and OHG. *graban*, G. *graben*, to dig, engrave, cut, carve.

ENGROSS, to occupy wholly. (F. – L.) The legal sense 'to write in large letters' is the oldest one. '*Engrossed* was vp [*read* it] as it is knowe, And enrolled, onely for witnesse In your registers ;' Lydgate, Siege of Thebes, pt. ii., Knightly answer of Tideus, l. 56. Cf. Rich. III, iii. 6. 2. AF. *engrosser*, Stat. Realm, i. 379 (A.D. 1363). – AF. *en grosse* ; where *grosse* represents Late L. *grossa*, large writing (Ducange); cf. MF. *grossoyer*, 'to ingross, to write faire, or in great and fair letters ;' Cot. See **Gross**. β. The sense 'to buy up wholesale' was from the phr. *en gros*, i.e. in large. Der. *engross-ment*, 2 Hen. IV, iv. 5. 80.

ENGULF, to swallow up in a gulf. (F. – L. *and* Gk.) In Spenser, F. Q. iii. 2. 32. – MF. *engolfer*, 'to ingulfe;' Cot. – F. *en*, from L. *in* ; and *golfe*, a gulf. See **Gulf**.

ENHANCE, to advance, raise, augment. (F. – L.) ME. *enhansen*, P. Plowman, C. xii. 58. AF. *enhauncer*, to promote ; Liber Custumarum, p. 219 ; apparently a corruption of AF. *enhaucer*, to raise, id., p. 192 ; OF. *enhaucier*, to raise, exalt (Ital. *inalzare*). – L. *in*, in, up ; and Late L. *altiāre*, to lift, from *altus*, high ; see **Altitude**. ¶ Hardly from OProv. *enansar*, to further, advance ; 'si vostra valors m'enansa=if your worth advances me ;' Bartsch, Chrestomathie Prov. 147, 5. – OProv. *enans*, before, rather ; formed from L. *in ante*, just as the Prov. *avans* is from Lat. *ab ante*. See **Advance**. Der. *enhance-ment*.

ENIGMA, a riddle. (L. – Gk.) In Shak. L. L. L. iii. 72. – L. *ænigma* (stem *ænigmat-*). – Gk. αἴνιγμα (stem αἰνίγματ-), a dark saying, riddle. – Gk. αἰνίσσομαι, I speak in riddles. – Gk. αἶνος, a tale, story. Der. *enigmat-ic, -ic-al, -ic-al-ly, -ise*.

ENJOIN, to order, bid. (F. – L.) ME. *enioinen* (with *i=j*), P. Plowman, C. viii. 72. – OF. *enjoindre* (1 p.s. pres. *enjoin-s*), 'to injoine, ordaine ;' Cot. – L. *iniungere*, to enjoin. See **Injunction**, and **Join**.

ENJOY, to joy in. (F. – L.) ME. *enioien* (with *i=j*), Wyclif, Colos. iii. 15. – AF. *enjcier*, Stat. Realm, i. 310 (A.D. 1351). Formed from F. *en*, from L. *in* ; and *joie*, joy. See **Joy**. Der. *enjoy-ment*.

ENKINDLE, to kindle. (Hybrid ; F. *and* Scand.) In Shak. K. John, iv. 2. 163. Formed from F. *en*=L. *in* ; and **Kindle**, q. v.

ENLACE, to encircle as with a lace, enfold, entangle. (F. – L.) ME. *enlacen* ; Chaucer, tr. of Boethius, bk. i. met. 4. l. 15. – OF. (and F.) *enlacer*, 'to intangle ;' Cot. – F. *en* (from L. *in*), in ; and *lacer*, 'to lace, to bind ;' Cot., from Folk-L. **laciare*, for L. *laqueāre*, to ensnare, from *laqueus*, a noose. See **Lace**.

ENLARGE, to make large. (F. – L.) In Spenser, F. Q. v. 5. 55. ME. *enlargen*, Mandeville, Trav., ch. v, p. 45. – AF. *enlarger*, Stat. Realm, i. 398 (A.D. 1377). Formed from F. *en*, from L. *in* ; and **Large**, q. v. Der. *enlarge-ment*, Shak. L. L. L. iii. 5.

ENLIGHTEN, to give light to. (Hybrid ; F. *and* E.) In Shak. Sonnets, 152. From F. *en*, from L. *in* ; and E. **Lighten**, q. v. Imitated from AS. *inlihtan*, to illuminate ; Grein, ii. 142. Der. *enlighten-ment*.

ENLIST, to enroll. (F. – L. *and* G.) First in 1698. In Johnson's Dict., only under the word *List*. From F. *en*, from L. *in* ; and F. *liste*, a list. See **List** (2). Der. *enlist-ment*.

ENLIVEN, to put life into. (Hybrid ; F. *and* E.) 'Lo ! of themselves th' *enlivened* chessmen move ;' Cowley, Pind. Odes, Destiny, l. 3. From F. *en*, from L. *in* ; and E. *life*. See **Life**, **Live**.

ENMITY, hostility. (F. – L.) ME. *enmité* ; Prompt. Parv. p. 140; also *enemyté*, Wyclif, Select Works, iii. 301. – AF. *enemité*, Stat. Realm. i. 290 (A.D. 1340); OF. *enemistié* (Supp. to Godefroy); later *inimitié* (Cot.). – OF. *en-*, from L. *in-*, negative prefix ; and *amisté, amistet*, amity. See **Amity**.

ENNOBLE, to make noble. (F. – L.) In Spenser, F. Q. iii. 3. 4. 'He was *ennoblyd* ;' Caxton, Golden Legend, Lyf of St. Fraunceis, § 38. – OF. *ennoblir*, 'to ennoble ;' Cot. – F. *en*, from L. *in* ; and F. *noble*. See **Noble**.

ENNUI, annoyance. (F. – L.) In Todd's Johnson. – F. *ennui* ; formerly *enui*, also *anoi* (Burguy). See **Annoy**.

ENORMOUS, great beyond measure. (F. – L.) In King Lear, ii. 2. 176; Milton, P. L. i. 511. Rarely *enorm* (as in Fairfax's Tasso, bk. viii. st. 71), which is a more correct form, the *-ous* being added unnecessarily. – MF. *enorme*, 'huge, . . . enormous ;' Cot. – L. *ēnormis*, out of rule, huge. – L. *ē*, out of ; and *norma*, a rule. See **Normal**. Der. *enormous-ly*; from the same source, *enorm-i-ty*. MF. *enormité*, 'an enormity ;' Cot.

ENOUGH, sufficient. (E.) ME. *ȝenoh, inoh, inou, inow, enogh* ; pl. *inohe, inowe* ; see Stratmann. The pl. *ynowe* (*ynough* in Tyrwhitt) is in Chaucer, C. T. 10784 (F 470). AS. *genōh, genōg*, adj. ; pl. *genōge*, Grein, i. 438 ; allied to the impers. vb. *geneah*, it suffices, id. 435. + Goth. *ganōhs*, sufficient ; allied to the impers. verb *ganah*, it suffices, in which *ga-* is a mere prefix. Cf. Icel. *gnōgr*, Dan. *nok*, Swed. *nok*, Du. *genoeg*, G. *genug*, enough. Cf. also Skt. *naç*, to attain, reach, L. *nancisci*, to acquire (pp. *nac-tus*); Idg. base **nak*.

ENOUNCE, to state definitely, to pronounce. (F. – L.) In late use; first in 1805. Coined, after the analogy of *announce*, from F. *énoncer*, L. *ēnuntiāre*; see **Enunciate**. Doublet, *enunciate*.

ENQUIRE, to search into, ask. (F. – L.) [Properly *enquere*, but altered to *enquire* to make it look more like Latin; and often further altered to *inquire*, to make it look still more so.] ME. *enqueren*; Rob. of Glouc. pp. 373, 508; ll. 7675, 10469; in Chaucer, *enquere* (rhyming with *lere*), C. T. 5049 (B 629). – OF. *enquerre* (Burguy), later *enquerir* (Cot.). – L. *inquīrere*, to seek after, search into. – L. *in*; and *quærere*, to seek. See **Inquisition, Inquire**. Der. *enquir-y*, Meas. for Meas. v. 5 (1st folio ed.; altered to *inquiry* in the Globe Edition); *enquest*, now altered to *inquest*, but spelt *enqueste* in P. Plowman, C. xiv. 85, and derived from OF. *enqueste*, 'an inquest;' Cot. See **Inquest**.

ENRAGE, to put in a rage. (F. – L.) In Macbeth, iii. 4. 118. G. Douglas has the pp. *enragit*, tr. of Virgil, bk. xiii. c. v. l. 20. – OF. *enrager*, 'to rage, rave, storme;' whence *enragé*, 'enraged;' Cot. [Whence it appears that the verb was originally intransitive, and meant 'to get in a rage.']—F. *en*, from L. *in*; and F. *rage*. See **Rage**.

ENRAPTURE, to fill with rapture. (L.; *with* F. *prefix*.) 'Now the brow We gain *enraptured*;' Dyer, Ruins of Rome, l. 134 (1740). From **En-**, prefix, and **Rapture**.

ENRICH, to make rich. (F. – L.) 'The Lord hath *enrychide* me;' Wyclif, Gen. xxx. 20 (earlier version). – OF. *enrichir*, 'to enrich;' Cot. – F. *en*, from L. *in*; and F. *riche*, rich. See **Rich**. Der. *enrich-ment*.

ENROL, to insert in a roll. (F. – L.) 'And [is] enrolled;' Lydgate, Siege of Thebes; see quotation under **Engross**. – OF. *enroller*, 'to enroll, register;' Cot. – F. *en*, from L. *in*; and OF. *rolle*, a roll. See **Roll**. Der. *enrol-ment*, Holland's Livy, p. 1221 (R.).

ENSAMPLE, an example. (F. – L.) In the Bible, 1 Cor. x. 11. ME. *ensample*, Rob. of Glouc. p. 35, l. 819. – AF. *ensample*, a corrupt form of OF. *essemple, exemple*, or *example*; see **Example**. This form occurs in the Statutes of the Realm, i. 104 (A.D. 1285).

ENSCONCE, to shelter, or to take shelter in. (F. – L.) 'And therein so *ensconc'd* his secret evil;' Shak., Lucrece, l. 1515. From **En-**, prefix, and **Sconce** (1).

ENSHRINE, to put in a shrine. (Hybrid; F. *and* L.) In Spenser, Hymn on Beauty, l. 188. From F. *en*, from L. *in*; and **Shrine**, q. v.

ENSIGN, a flag. (F. – L.) In Shak. Rich. II, iv. 94. ME. *enseigne*, Chaucer, Rom. Rose, l. 1200. – OF. *enseigne*, Roman de la Rose, l. 1184; as in Cotgrave, who explains it by 'a signe, . . . also an ensigne, standard.'—Late L. *insignia*, orig. pl. of L. *insigne*, a standard; neut. of *insignis*, remarkable; see **Insignia**. Der. *ensign-cy, -ship*.

ENSILAGE, green fodder preserved in a pit; or the process of preserving it. (F. – Span. – L. – Gk.) First in 1881 (N. E. D.). – F. *ensilage*, ensilage. – F. *ensiler*, verb. – Span. *ensilar*, to preserve grain in a pit. – Span. *en*, from L. *in*, in; and *silo*, a pit. See **Silo**.

ENSLAVE, to make a slave of. (Hybrid.) In Milton, P. R. iii. 75. – F. *en*, from L. *in*; and **Slave**, q. v. Der. *enslave-ment*.

ENSNARE, to catch in a snare. (Hybrid; F. *and* E.) In Shak. Oth. ii. 1. 170. – F. *en*, from L. *in*; and **Snare**, q. v.

ENSUE, to follow after. (F. – L.) 'Dyuyne vengeaunce *ensyewed* sodaynly;' Caxton, Golden Legend, St. Stephen, § 6. – AF. *ensu-*, as in *ensuera*, 3 p. fut. of OF. *ensivre*, to follow; see Year-books of Edw. I, 1302–3, p. 49. – Late L. *insequere*, used for L. *insequī*, to follow upon; from *in*, upon, and *sequī*, to follow. See **Sue**.

ENSURE, to make sure. (F. – L.) In Chaucer, C. T. 12077 (C 143). Compounded from F. *en* (from L. *in*), and OF. *seūr*, sure. See **Assure**, and **Sure**. ¶ Generally spelt *insure*, which is a confusion of languages; whence *insur-ance*.

ENTABLATURE, part of a building surmounting the columns. (F. – L.) Spelt *intablature* in Cotgrave. – MF. *entablature*, 'an intablature;' Cot.; an equivalent term to *entablement*, the mod. F. form. The OF. *entablement* meant, more commonly, 'a pedestal' or 'base' of a column rather than the entablature above. Both sbs. are formed from Late L. *intabulāre*, orig. to construct an *intabulātum* or flooring. – L. *in*, upon; and Late L. *tabulāre*, due to L. *tabulātum*, board-work, a flooring. – L. *tabula*, a board, plank. See **Table**. ¶ Since *entablature* simply meant something laid flat or boardwise upon something else in the course of building, it could be applied to the part either below or above the columns.

ENTAIL, to bestow as a heritage. (F. – L.) In Shak. 3 Hen. VI, i. 1. 194, 235; as sb., All's Well, iv. 3. 313. 1. The legal sense is peculiar; it was originally 'to convert (an estate) into *fee tail* (Late L. *feudum talliātum*); to settle (land) on a number of persons in succession, so that it cannot be bequeathed at pleasure by any one possessor.' 'To *entayle land*, addicere, adoptare hæredes;' Levins. – F. *en*, from L. *in*, in, upon; and AF. *tailer*, F. *tailler*, orig. to cut, hence to impose a fee upon; from Late L. *tāleāre, talliāre*, to cut; see *Tail* in Blount's Nomolexicon. 2. The ME. *entailen* 'to cut or carve,' in an ornamental way; see Rom. of the Rose, 140; P. Plowman's Crede, ed. Skeat, ll. 167, 200. – OF. *entailler*, 'to intaile, grave, carve, cut in;' Cot. – F. *en*, from L. *in*; and *tailler*, to cut. See **Tally**. Der. *entail-ment*.

ENTANGLE, to ensnare, complicate. (Hybrid; F. *and* Scand.) In Spenser, Muiopotmos, 387; also in Levins. – F. *en*, from L. *in*; and **Tangle**, q. v. Der. *entangle-ment*, Spectator, no. 352.

ENTER, to go into. (F. – L.) ME. *entren*, Rob. of Glouc. p. 47, l. 1097; King Alisaunder, 5782. – OF. *entrer*, 'to enter;' Cot. – L. *intrāre*, to enter, go into. – L. *in*; and **trāre*, as in *pene-trāre*, to penetrate, go into; cf. Skt. *tara-*, a passage, *tṛ*, to cross, pass over; L. *trans*, across. See Brugmann, ii. § 579; and see **Term**. Der. *entr-ance*, Macb. i. 5. 40; *entr-y*, ME. *entree*, Chaucer, C. T. 1985 (A 1983), from OF. *entree*, orig. the fem. of the pp. of F. *entrer*.

ENTERIC, pertaining to the intestines. (Gk.) Chiefly in the phr. 'enteric fever.' – Gk. *ἐντερικός*, adj., from *ἔντερον*, an intestine. A comparative derivative from *ἐν*, prep., in. Cf. L. *interus*, inward; Skt. *antara-*, interior. See **Interior**.

ENTERPRISE, an undertaking. (F. – L.) Palsgrave has *enterprise*, sb., and *entreprise*, vb. The sb. is in La Belle Dame sans Merci, l. 515. Skelton has it as a verb; 'Chaucer, that nobly *enterprysyd*;' Garland of Laurell, l. 388. – OF. *entreprise* (Burguy), commonly *entreprise*, 'an enterprise;' Cot. – OF. *entrepris*, pp. of *entreprendre*, to undertake. – Late L. *interprendere*, to undertake. – L. *inter*, among; and *prendere*, short for *prehendere*, to take in hand, which is from L. *præ*, before, and (obsolete) *hendere*, to get, cognate with Gk. *χανδάνειν*, and E. *get*. See **Prehensile** and **Get**. Der. *enterpris-ing*. Cf. *emprise*.

ENTERTAIN, to admit, receive. (F. – L.) In Spenser, F. Q. i. 10. 32. – OF. *entretien-*, a stem of *entretenir*, 'to intertaine;' Cot. – Late L. *intertenēre*, to entertain. – L. *inter*, among; and *tenēre*, to hold. See **Tenable**. Der. *entertain-er, -ing; -ment*, Spenser, F. Q. i. 10. 37.

ENTHRAL, to enslave. (Hybrid; F. *and* Scand.) In Mids. Nt. Dream, i. 1. 136. From F. *en*, from L. *in*; and E. **Thrall**, q. v. Der. *enthralment*, Milton, P. L. xii. 171.

ENTHRONE, to set on a throne. (F. – L. *and* Gk.) Shak., Mer. Ven. iv. 1. 194. – MF. *enthroner*, 'to inthronise;' Cot. From F. *en*, in; and MF. *throne*, 'a throne;' id. β. Imitated from Late L. *inthronīsāre*, to enthrone, which is from Gk. *ἐνθρονίζειν*, to set on a throne; from Gk. *ἐν*, in, on; and *θρόνος*, a throne. See **Throne**. Der. *enthrone-ment*.

ENTHUSIASM, inspiration, zeal. (L. – Gk.) In Holland's Plutarch, pp. 932, 1092 (R.); and in Marston, The Fawne, A. ii. sc. 1. [Cf. MF. *enthusiasme*; Cot.]—Late L. *enthūsiasmus*. – Gk. *ἐνθουσιασμός*, inspiration. – Gk. *ἐνθουσιάζω*, I am inspired. – Gk. *ἔνθους*, contracted form of *ἔνθεος*, full of the god, inspired. – Gk. *ἐν*, within; and *θεός*, god. See **Theism**. Der. *enthusiast* (Gk. *ἐνθουσιαστής*); *-ic*, Dryden, Abs. and Achit. 530; *-ical, -ical-ly*.

ENTICE, to tempt, allure. (F. – L.) ME. *enticen, entisen*; Rob. of Glouc., p. 235; P. Plowman, C. viii. 91. – OF. *enticier, entichier*, to excite, entice (Godefroy). – L. type **intitiāre*, to kindle, to set on fire. – L. *in*, on; and **titius*, for *titio*, a firebrand. Cf. F. *attiser*, Ital. *attizzare*, to set on fire; from the same sb. Der. *entice-ment*, Chaucer, Pers. Tale, Group I, l. 967.

ENTIRE, whole, complete. (F. – L.) ME. *entyre*; the adv. *entyreliche*, entirely, is in P. Plowman, C. xi. 188. – OF. *entier*, 'intire;' Cot.; cf. Prov. *enteir*, Ital. *intero*. – L. *integrum*, acc. of *integer*, whole. See **Integer**. Der. *entire-ly, entire-ness*; also *entire-ty*, spelt *entierty* by Bacon (R.), from OF. *entiereté* (Cot.), from L. acc. *integritātem*; whence *entirety* and *integrity* are doublets.

ENTITLE, to give a title to. (F. – L.) In Shak. L. L. L. v. 2. 822. From F. *en*, from L. *in*; and *title*. See **Title**.

ENTITY, existence, real substance. (L.) In Blount's Gloss., ed. 1674. A coined word, with suffix *-ty*, from L. *enti-*, decl. stem of Late L. *ens*, a thing, a being, formed as if it were the pres. pt. of *esse*, to be. – √ES, to be. See **Essence**.

ENTOMB, to put in a tomb. (F. – L. *and* Gk.) In Spenser, F. Q. ii. 10. 46. – F. *entomber*, 'to intombe;' Cot. – F. *en*, from L. *in*, in; and F. *tombe*, a tomb. See **Tomb**. Der. *entomb-ment*.

ENTOMOLOGY, the science treating of insects. (F. – L. – Gk.) First in 1776. – F. *entymologie* (1764). – Mod. L. **entomologia*. – Gk. *ἔντομο-*, for *ἔντομον*, an insect; properly neut. of *ἔντομος*, cut into; so called from the very thin middle part; see **Insect**. The ending

-logy is from Gk. λέγειν, to discourse. β. The Gk. ἔντομος is from Gk. ἐν, in; and τομ-, second grade of τέμνειν, to cut. See **Tome.** Der. *entomolog-ist, entomolog-ic-al.*

ENTOZOON, a parasitic animal living within another. (Gk.) Modern and scientific. From Gk. ἐντό-, for ἐντός, within; and ζῷον, an animal. See **Zoology.**

ENTRAILS, the inward parts of an animal. (F.–L.) The sing. *entrail* is rare; but answers to ME. *entraile,* King Alisaunder, l. 3628.–OF. *entraile,* entrails; MF. *entrailles,* pl. 'the intrals, intestines;' Cot.–Late L. *intrālia,* also spelt (more correctly) *intrānea,* entrails. [For the change from *n* to *l,* cf. *Boulogne, Bologna,* from L. *Bononia.*] β. *Intrānea* is contracted from L. *interānea,* entrails, neut. pl. of *interāneus,* inward, an adj. formed from *inter,* within. See **Internal.** ¶ The OF. *entraile* was a fem. sing., made from a neut. pl.

ENTRANCE (1), ingress; see **Enter.**

ENTRANCE (2), to put into a trance. (F.–L.) In Shak. Per. iii. 2. 94. From F. *en,* from L. *in;* and E. *trance* = F. *transe.* See **Trance.** Der. *entrance-ment; dis-entrance.*

ENTRAP, to ensnare. (F.–L. *and* Teut.) In Spenser, F. Q. ii. 1. 4.–OF. *entraper,* 'to pester; .. also, to intrap;' Cot.–F. *en,* from L. *in;* and OF. *trape,* a trap, of G. origin. See **Trap** (1).

ENTREAT, to treat, to beg. (F.–L.) In Spenser, F. Q. i. 10. 7. Chaucer has *entreteden,* discussed, C. T., B 2466 (Tale of Melibeus).–AF. *entreter,* F. Chron. of London, p. 48; OF. *entraiter,* to treat of (Godefroy).–F. *en,* from L. *in;* and OF. *traiter,* to treat, from L. *tractāre,* to handle. See **Treat.** Der. *entreat-y,* K. John, v. 2. 125; *entreat-ment,* Hamlet, i. 3. 122.

ENTRENCH, to cut into, fortify with a trench. (F.) '*Entrenched* deepe with knife;' Spenser, F. Q. iii. 12. 20; 'In stronge *entrenchments;*' id. ii. 11. 6. A coined word; from F. *en,* from L. *in;* and E. *trench,* of F. origin. See **Trench.**

ENTRUST, to trust with. (Hybrid; F. *and* E.) By analogy with *enlist, enrol, enrapture, entrance, enthrone,* we have *entrust;* as in Sir T. Browne, Vulgar Errors, bk. iii. c. 11. § 5. But *intrust* was also usual, and is the form in Kersey's Dict. ed. 1715; see **Intrust.**

ENTWINE, ENTWIST, to twine or twist with. (Hybrid; F. *and* E.) Milton has *entwined,* P. L. iv. 174; Shak. has *entwist,* Mids. Nt. Dr. iv. 1. 48. Both are formed alike; from F. *en* (from L. *in*), and the E. words *twine* and *twist.* See **Twine, Twist.**

ENUCLEATE, to lay open, clearly explain. (L.) Lit. 'to get out the kernel.' In Cockeram (1642), misprinted *enuncleate;* Kersey, in 1658, has *enucleation.*–L. *ēnucleāt-us,* pp. of *ēnucleāre,* to get out a kernel.–L. *ē,* out; and *nucleus,* kernel. See **Nucleus.**

ENUMERATE, to number. (L.) *Enumerative* occurs in Bp. Taylor, Holy Dying, c. 5. s. 3, 10. *Enumeration* is in Phillips (1658).–L. *ēnumerātus,* pp. of *ēnumerāre,* to reckon up.–L. *ē,* out, fully; and *numerāre,* to number, from *numerus,* number. See **Number.** Der. *enumerat-ion, -ive.*

ENUNCIATE, to utter. (L.) *Enunciatyue* occurs in Sir T. Elyot, The Governour, b. iii. c. 25, § 5.–L. *ēnunciātus,* pp. of *ēnunciāre,* better *ēnuntiāre,* to utter.–L. *ē,* out, fully; and *nuntiāre,* to announce, from *nuntius,* a messenger. See **Announce, Nuncio.** Der. *enunciat-ion, -ive, -or-y.*

ENVELOP, to wrap in, enfold. (F.–Teut.?) Spelt *envelop* in Spenser, F. Q. ii. 12. 34. ME. *envolupen,* Chaucer, C. T. 12876 (C 942). –OF. *envoluper,* later *enveloper,* to wrap round, enfold.–F. *en,* from L. *in;* and OF. *voluper, voloper, vloper,* to wrap; from a base *volup-,* of uncertain origin, but perhaps Low German. β. This base resembles the ME. *wlappen,* to wrap up, which occurs at least twelve times in Wyclif's Bible, and seems to be another form of *wrappen,* to wrap. See Wyclif, Numb. iv. 5, 7; Matt. xxvii. 59; Luke, ii. 7, 12; John, xx. 7, &c. See **Wrap.** ¶ But the base *wlap-* is unknown outside English, and thus does not account for the Romanic form. Note Walloon *ewalpé,* to envelop (Remacle); Ital. *viluppo,* a bundle, *inviluppare,* to envelope; MItal. *goluppare,* to wrap (Florio). Cf. **Develop, Lap** (3). Der. *envelope, envelope-ment.*

ENVENOM, to put poison into. (F.–L.) ME. *enuenimen* (with *u* = *v*); whence *enuenimed,* King Alisaunder, 5436; *enueniming,* Chaucer, C. T. 9934 (E 2060).–OF. *envenimer,* 'to invenome;' Cot. –OF. *en,* from L. *in;* and *venim,* or *venin,* poison, from L. *uenēnum.* See **Venom.**

ENVIRON, to surround. (F.–L.) Spelt *enuyrowne* in Wyclif, 1 Tim. v. 13; pt. t. *enuyrounyde,* Matt. iv. 23; cf. Gower, C. A. iii. 97; bk. vii. 373.–OF. *environner,* 'to inviron, encompasse;' Cot.–OF. (and F.) *environ,* round about.–OF. *en,* from L. *in;* and *virer,* to turn, veer. See **Veer.** Der. *environ-ment;* also *environs,* from F. *environ.*

ENVOY, a messenger. (F.–L.) 1. An improper use of the word; it meant 'a message;' and the F. for 'messenger' was *envoyé.* 2. The *envoy* of a ballad is the 'sending' of it forth, and the word is then correctly used; the last stanza of Chaucer's Ballad to K. Richard is headed *L'envoye.*–OF. *envoy,* 'a message, a sending; also the envoy or conclusion of a ballet [*ballad*] or sonnet;' Cot. Also '*envoyé,* a special messenger;' id.–OF. *envoyer,* to send; formerly *enveier* (Supp. to Godefroy).–OF. *en veie, en voie,* on the way.–L. *in uiam,* on the way. Cf. Ital. *inviare,* to send. See **Voyage.** Der. *envoyship.*

ENVY, emulation, malicious grudging. (F.–L.) In early use. ME. *enuie* (with *u* = *v*), *enuye, envy;* Rob. of Glouc. pp. 122, 287; ll. 2603, 5824.–OF. *envie,* 'envy;' Cot.–L. *inuidia,* envy. See **Invidious.** Der. *envy,* verb, Wyclif, 1 Cor. xiii. 4; *envi-ous,* ME. *enuius,* Floriz, ed. Lumby, l. 356; *-ous-ly, -able.*

ENWRAP, to wrap in. (Hybrid; F. *and* E.) In Spenser, F. Q. ii. 3. 27; earlier, in Wyclif, 1 Kings, xv. 6; 4 Kings, ii. 8. Coined from F. *en,* from L. *in;* and E. **Wrap,** q. v.

EOCENE, belonging to the lowest division of the tertiary strata. (Gk.) First used by Lyell (1833).–Gk. ἠώ-s, dawn; and καινός, new, recent.

EPACT, a term in astronomy. (F.–Late L.–Gk.) In Holland's Plutarch, p. 1051.–MF. *epacte,* 'an addition, the epact;' Cot.– Late L. *epacta.*–Gk. ἐπακτή (for ἐπακτός ἡμέρα), late fem. of ἐπακτός, added, brought in.–Gk. ἐπάγειν, to bring to, bring in, supply.–Gk. ἐπ-, for ἐπί, to; and ἄγειν, to lead.–√ AG, to drive. See **Act.**

EPAULET, a shoulder-knot. (F.–L.–Gk.) Used by Burke (R.).–F. *épaulette,* dimin. from *épaule,* OF. *espaule,* and still earlier *espalle,* a shoulder.–L. *spatula,* a blade; in Late L. the shoulder; see the account of the letter-changes in Brachet. β. *Spatula* is a dimin. of *spatha,* a blade; borrowed from Gk. σπάθη, a broad blade. See **Spatula.**

EPERGNE, a central ornament for a dinner-table. (F.–Teut.) Also spelt *epargne* in 1779 (N. E. D.); which is more correct.–F. *épargne,* lit. 'economy.' It seems to have been applied to the épergne from the manner of its ornamentation; Cotgrave has: '*taillé d'espargne,* cut with sparing work, the incutting being filled with enamell, and the work set out, or appearing among it, in gold.'– F. *épargner,* MF. *espargner,* to spare, save (Ital. *sparagnare,* in Florio). Formed, as if from an OHG. **sparanjan* (not found); from OHG. *sparōn,* to save, spare, cognate with AS. *sparian.* See **Spare.** (Körting, § 8910.)

EPHAH, a Hebrew measure. (Heb.–Egyptian.) In Exod. xvi. 36, &c.–Heb. *êyphâh,* a measure; a word of Egyptian origin; Coptic *ōpi,* a measure; Gesenius, ed. 8. p. 36.

EPHEMERA, flies that live but a day. (Gk.) 'Certain flyes that are called *ephemera,* that live but a day;' Bacon, Nat. Hist. § 697. A neut. pl., afterwards used as a fem. sing.–Gk. ἐφήμερα, neut. pl. of adj. ἐφήμερος, lasting for a day.–Gk. ἐφ- = ἐπί, for; and ἡμέρα, a day, of uncertain origin. Der. *ephemer-al; ephemeris* (Gk. ἐφημερίς, a diary).

EPHOD, a part of the priest's habit. (Heb.) In Exod. xxviii. 4, &c.–Heb. *êphôd,* a vestment; from *âphad,* to put on, clothe.

EPI-, prefix. (Gk.) Gk. ἐπί, upon, to, besides; in *epi-cene, epi-cycle,* &c. It becomes ἐφ- before an aspirate, as in *eph-emeral;* and *ep-* before a vowel, as in *ep-och.* Cf. L. *ob,* to, as in *obuiam, obire;* Oscan *op;* Skt. *api,* moreover; in composition, near to. Brugmann, i. § 557 (2).

EPIC, narrative. (L.–Gk.) In Blount's Gloss., ed. 1674; and Spectator, no. 267.–L. *epicus.*–Gk. ἐπικός, epic, narrative.–Gk. ἔπος, a word, narrative, song; allied to L. *uox,* a voice. See **Voice.**

EPICENE, of common gender. (L.–Gk.) *Epicoene* is the name of one of Ben Jonson's plays.–L. *epicœnus,* borrowed from Gk. ἐπίκοινος, common.–Gk. ἐπί; and κοινός, common. See **Cenobite.**

EPICURE, a follower of Epicurus. (L.–Gk.) In Macb. v. 3. 8.–L. *Epicūrus.*–Gk. Ἐπίκουρος, proper name; lit. 'assistant.' Der. *epicur-e-an, -e-an-ism.*

EPICYCLE, a small circle with its centre on the circumference of a larger one. (F.–L.–Gk.) In Milton, P. L. viii. 84. Chaucer has *episicle;* Astrolabe, pt. ii. § 35.–F. *epicycle* (Cot.).–L. *epicyclus.*– Gk. ἐπίκυκλος, an epicycle.–Gk. ἐπί, upon; and κύκλος, a cycle, circle. See **Cycle.**

EPIDEMIC, affecting a people, general. (L.–Gk.) 'An epidemic disease;' Bacon, Henry VII, ed. Lumby, p. 13, l. 10. Formed with suffix *-ic* from L. *epidēm-us,* epidemic; cf. MF. *epidimique* (Cot.). –Gk. ἐπίδημος, among the people, general.–Gk. ἐπί, among; and δῆμος, the people. See **Endemic, Demagogue.** Der. *epidemic-al.*

EPIDERMIS, the cuticle, outer skin. (L.–Gk.) 'Within the *epidermis;*' Bacon, Nat. Hist. § 297.–L. *epidermis.*–Gk. ἐπιδερμίς, an upper skin; from ἐπί, upon, and δέρμα, skin. See **Derm.**

EPIGLOTTIS, a cartilage protecting the glottis. (Gk.) In Kersey, ed. 1715.–Gk. ἐπιγλωττίς, Attic form of ἐπιγλωσσίς, epiglottis. –Gk. ἐπί, near; and γλῶσσα, the tongue. See **Gloss** (2), **Glottis.**

EPIGRAM, a short poem. (F.–L.–Gk.) In Shak. Much Ado,

v. 4. 103.   Sir T. Elyot has the pl. *epigrammata*, in The Governour, bk. i. c. 13. § 7.—F. *epigramme*, 'an epigram;' Cot.—L. *epigramma* (stem *epigrammat*-).—Gk. ἐπίγραμμα, an inscription, epigram.—Gk. ἐπί, upon; and γράφειν, to write.   See **Graphic.**   Der. *epigrammat-ic, -ic-al, -ic-al-ly, -ise, -ist*.   And, from the same verb, *epigraph*.

EPILEPSY, a convulsive seizure. (F.—L.—Gk.)   In Shak. Oth. iv. 1. 51.—MF. *epilepsie*, 'the falling sickness;' Cot.—L. *epilepsia*.—Gk. ἐπιληψία, ἐπίληψις, a seizure, epilepsy.—Gk. ἐπιλαμβάνειν (fut. ἐπιλήψ-ομαι), to seize upon.—Gk. ἐπί, upon; and λαμβάνειν, to seize.   See **Cataleptic.**   Der. *epileptic*, Gk. ἐπιληπτικός, subject to epilepsy; K. Lear, ii. 2. 87.

EPILOGUE, a short concluding poem. (F.—L.—Gk.)   In Shak. Mids. Nt. Dr. v. 360, 362, 369.—F. *epilogue*, 'an epilogue;' Cot.—L. *epilogus*.—Gk. ἐπίλογος, a concluding speech.—Gk. ἐπί, upon; and λόγος, a speech, from λέγειν, to speak.

EPIPHANY, Twelfth Day. (F.—L.—Gk.)   In Cotgrave; and in Caxton, The Golden Legend, Fest of the *Epiphanie*; and in Lyric Poetry, ed. Wright, p. 96.—F. *epiphanie*, 'the epiphany;' Cot.—L. *epiphania*.—Gk. ἐπιφάνια, manifestation; originally neut. pl. of adj. ἐπιφάνιος, but equivalent to sb. ἐπιφάνεια, appearance, manifestation.—Gk. ἐπιφαίνειν (fut. ἐπιφαν-ῶ), to manifest, show forth.—Gk. ἐπί, to; and φαίνειν, to show.   See **Fancy.**

EPISCOPAL, belonging to a bishop. (F.—L.—Gk.)   In Cotgrave, 'Epyscopall iurisdiction;' Caxton, Acts of Hen. VII, fol. a 3, bk.—OF. *episcopal*, 'episcopall;' Cot.—L. *episcopālis*, adj. formed from *episcopus*, a bishop.—Gk. ἐπίσκοπος, an over-seer, bishop.   See **Bishop.**   Der. *episcopal-i-an*; from the same source, *episcopate* (L. *episcopātus*); *episcopac-y*.

EPISODE, a story introduced into another. (Gk.)   In the Spectator, no. 267.—Gk. ἐπεισόδ-ιον, orig. neut. of ἐπεισόδιος, episodic, adventitious.—Gk. ἐπί, besides; and εἰσόδιος, coming in; which is from εἰς, into, and ὁδός, a way.   Der. *episodi-al* (from ἐπεισόδι-ος); *episod-ic, -ic-al, -al-ly*.

EPISTLE, a letter. (F.—L.—Gk.)   In early use.   The pl. *epistlis* is in Wyclif, 2 Cor. x. 10.—OF. *epistle*, the early form whence *epistre* (Cotgrave) was formed by the change of *l* to *r* (as in *chapter* from L. *capitulum*); F. *épitre*.—L. *epistola* (whence also AS. *epistol*).—Gk. ἐπιστολή, a message, letter.—Gk. ἐπιστέλλειν, to send to; from ἐπί, to, and στέλλειν, to send, equip.   See **Stole.**   Der. *epistol-ic, -ar-y*; from L. *epistol-a*.

EPITAPH, an inscription on a tomb. (F.—L.—Gk.)   In Shak. Much Ado, iv. 1. 209; ME. *epitaphe, epitaffe*, Gower, C. A. iii. 326; bk. viii. 1531.—F. *épitaphe*; Cot.—L. *epitaphium*.—Gk. ἐπιτάφιος λόγος, a funeral oration; where ἐπιτάφιος signifies 'over a tomb,' funeral.—Gk. ἐπί, upon, over; and τάφος, a tomb.   See **Cenotaph.**

EPITHALAMIUM, a marriage song. (L.—Gk.)   See the *Epithalamion* by Spenser.—L. *epithalamium*.—Gk. ἐπιθαλάμιον, a bridal song; neut. of ἐπιθαλάμιος, belonging to a nuptial.—Gk. ἐπί, upon, for; and θάλαμος, a bed-room, bride-chamber.

EPITHET, an adjective expressing a quality. (L.—Gk.)   In Shak. Oth. i. 1. 14.—L. *epitheton*.—Gk. ἐπίθετον, an epithet; neut. of ἐπίθετος, added, annexed.—Gk. ἐπί, besides; and the base θε-, allied to τίθημι, I place, set.—√DHĒ, to place; see **Do.**   Der. *epithet-ic*.

EPITOME, an abridgment. (L.—Gk.)   In Shak. Cor. v. 3. 68; and in Frith's Works (1572), p. 97, col. 1 (written in 1529).—L. *epitomē*.—Gk. ἐπιτομή, a surface-incision; also, an abridgment.—Gk. ἐπί, upon; and τέμνειν, to cut.   See **Tome.**   Der. *epitom-ise, -ist*.

EPOCH, a fixed date. (L.—Gk.)   In Blount's Gloss., ed. 1674.—Late L. *epocha*; Ducange.—Gk. ἐποχή, a stop, check, hindrance, pause, epoch.—Gk. ἐπέχειν, to hold in, check.—Gk. ἐπ-=ἐπί, upon; and ἔχειν, to have, hold; cognate with Skt. *sah*, to bear, undergo, endure.—√SEGH, to hold, check; Brugmann, i. § 602.

EPODE, a kind of lyric poem. (F.—L.—Gk.)   In Ben Jonson, The Forest, x., last line.—OF. *epode*; Cot.—L. *epōdos*.—Gk. ἐπῳδός, something sung after, an epode.—Gk. ἐπ-=ἐπί, upon, on; and ἀείδειν, ᾄδειν, to sing.   See **Ode.**

EPONYMOUS, that gives (his) name to anything, esp. to a place. (Gk.)   Used by Grote in 1846.—Gk. ἐπώνυμος, given as a name, or giving a name.—Gk. ἐπί, upon; and ὄνομα (Æolic ὄνυμα), a name.   See **Name.**

EQUAL, on a par with, even, just. (L.)   Chaucer has both *equal* and *inequal* in his Treatise on the Astrolabe; *equally* is in the C. T. 7819 (D 2237).   [We find also ME. *egal*, from OF. *egal*.]—L. *æquālis*, equal; formed with suffix *-ālis* from *æquus*, equal, just.   Der. *equal-ly, -ise, -is-at-ion; -i-ty*, King Lear, i. 1. 5; and see *equation*, and *equity*.

EQUANIMITY, evenness of mind. (F.—L.)   In Butler, Hudibras, pt. i. c. 3. l. 1020.—MF. *équanimité* (Cot.).—L. *æquanimitātem*, acc. of *æquanimitās*, evenness of mind.—L. *æquanimis*, kind, mild; hence, calm.—L. *æqu-*, for *æquus*, equal; and *animus*, mind.   See **Equal** and **Animate.**

EQUATION, a statement of equality. (L.)   ME. *equacion*,

Chaucer, On the Astrolabe, prol. 71 (or 76).   Palsgrave has *equate*, vb.—L. *æquātiōnem*, acc. of *æquātio*, an equalising; cf. *æquātus*, pp. of *æquāre*, to equalise.—L. *æquus*, equal.   See **Equal.**   Der. *equat-or* (Late L. *æquātor*, from *æquāre*), Milton, P. L. iii. 617; *equa-ble* (L. *æquābilis*, from *æquāre*); *equa-bl-y*; *equa-bil-i-ty*, spelt *equabilitie* in Sir T. Elyot, Governour, b. iii. c. 21. § 2.   Also *ad-equate*.

EQUERRY, an officer who has charge of horses. (F.—OHG.)   Properly, it meant 'a stable,' and *equerry* really stands for *equerry-man*.   It occurs in The Tatler, no. 19. § 2.—F. *écurie*, formerly *escurie*, a stable, spelt *escuyrie* in Cotgrave; Low L. *scūria*, a stable; Ducange.—OHG. *skiura, scūra*, MHG. *schiure*, a shed (G. *scheuer*); lit. a cover, shelter.—√SQEU, to cover; see **Sky.** Brugmann, i. § 109.   ¶ The spelling *equerry* is due to an attempt to connect it with L. *equus*, a horse.   There is, however, a real ultimate connexion with *esquire*, q. v.

EQUESTRIAN, relating to horsemen. (L.)   'A certain *equestrian* order;' Spectator, no. 104. § 1.   Formed, with suffix *-an*, from L. *equestri-*, stem of *equester*, belonging to horsemen.—L. *eques*, a horseman.—L. *equus*, a horse.   See **Equine.**

EQUI-, prefix, equally. (L.)   L. *æqui-*, from *æquus*, equal; see **Equal.**   Hence *equi-angular, equi-distant, equi-lateral, equi-multiple*, all in Kersey, ed. 1715.   And see **Equilibrium, Equinox, Equipoise, Equipollent, Equivalent, Equivocal.**

EQUILIBRIUM, an even balancing. (L.)   In Kersey, ed. 1715.—L. *æquilibrium*, a level position (in balancing).—L. *æquilibris*, level, balancing equally.—L. *æqui-*, for *æquus*, equal; and *librāre*, to balance, from *libra*, a balance.   See **Equal** and **Librate.**

EQUINE, relating to horses. (L.)   First in 1778 (N. E. D.); not in Todd's Johnson.—L. *equinus*, relating to horses.—L. *equus*, a horse. +Gk. ἵππος (dialectally ἵκκος), a horse; Skt. *açva-*, 'a runner,' a horse; Pers. *asp*; OIrish *ech*; AS. *eoh*.   Idg. type **ekwos*.   Brugmann, i. § 116.

EQUINOX, the time of equal day and night. (F.—L.)   In Shak. Oth. ii. 3. 129.   Chaucer has the adj. *equinoxial*, C. T. 14862 (B 4046). —F. *équinoxe*, spelt *equinocce* in Cotgrave.—L. *æquinoctium*, the equinox, time of equal day and night.—L. *æqui-*, for *æquus*, equal; and *nocti-*, decl. stem of *nox*, night.   See **Equal** and **Night.**   Der. *equinocti-al*, from L. *æquinocti-um*.   ¶ Note that the suffix *-nox* is *not* the L. nom. *nox*, but comes from *-noctium*.

EQUIP, to fit out, furnish. (F.—Scand.)   In Cotgrave; and used by Dryden, tr. of Ovid, Ceyx, l. 67.   Baret (1580) has *esquippe*.   [The sb. *equipage* is earlier, in Spenser, Sheph. Kal., Oct. 114; whence *equipage* as a verb, F. Q. ii. 9. 17.]—MF. *equiper*, 'to equip, arm;' also spelt *esquiper*; Cot.; AF. *eskipper*, Black Book of the Admiralty, i. 20.—Icel. *skipa*, to arrange, set in order; prob. allied to Icel. *skip*, a ship.   See **Ship.**   Der. *equip-age* (MF. *equipage*); *equip-ment*.

EQUIPOISE, an equal weight. (F.—L.)   In the Rambler, no. 95 (R.).   Coined from *equi-*=F. *equi*=L. *æqui-*, and *poise*.   See **Equi-** and **Poise.**

EQUIPOLLENT, equally powerful. (F.—L.)   'Thou wilt to kinges be *equipolent*;' Lydgate, Ballad of Good Counsel, st. 3; in Chaucerian Pieces.—OF. *equipolent*; Cot.—L. *æquipollent-*, stem of *æquipollens*, of equal value.—L. *æqui-*, for *æquus*, equal; and *pollens*, pres. part. of *pollēre*, to be strong.

EQUITY, justice. (F.—L.)   In Shak. K. John, ii. 241; ME. *equité*, Gower, C. A. i. 271; bk. ii. 3327.—OF. *equité*, 'equity;' Cot.—L. *æquitātem*, acc. of *æquitās*, equity; from *æquus*, equal.   See **Equal.**   Der. *equit-able*, OF. *equitable* (Cot.); *-abl-y, -able-ness*.

EQUIVALENT, of equal worth. (F.—L.)   In Shak. Per. v. 1. 92.—MF. *equivalent*, 'equivalent;' Cot.—L. *æquiualent-*, stem of pres. part. of *æquiualēre*, to be equivalent.—L. *æqui-*, for *æquus*, equal; and *ualēre*, to be worth.   See **Equal** and **Value.**   Der. *equivalent-ly, equivalence*.

EQUIVOCAL, of doubtful sense. (L.)   In Shak. Oth. i. 3. 217.   Formed, with suffix *-al*, from L. *æquiuoc-us*, of doubtful sense. —L. *æqui-*, for *æquus*, equal (i. e. alternative); and *uoc-*, base of *uoc-āre*, to call.   See **Equi-** and **Voice.**   Der. *equivocal-ly, -ness*; hence also *equivoc-ate* (used by Cotgrave to translate MF. *equivoquer*), *equivoc-at-ion*.

ERA, an epoch, fixed date. (L.)   Spelt *æra* in Blount's Gloss., ed. 1674.—L. *æra*, an era; derived from a particular use of *æra*, in the sense of 'counters,' hence, 'an item of an account,' which is properly the pl. of *æs*, brass, money (Lewis).

ERADICATE, to root up. (L.)   Sir T. Browne has *eradication*, Vulg. Errors, b. ii. c. 6. s. 8; Cockeram (1642) has *eradicate*.—L. *ērādicātus*, pp. of *ērādicāre*, to root up.—L. *ē*, out; and *rādic-*, stem of *rādix*, a root.   See **Radical.**   Der. *eradicat-ion*.

ERASE, to scrape out, efface. (L.)   *Eras'd* is in Butler, Hudibras, pt. iii. c. 3. l. 214.—L. *ērāsus*, pp. of *ērādere*, to scratch out.—L. *ē*, out; and *rādere*, to scrape.   See **Rase.**   Der. *eras-er, -ion, -ure*; *erase-ment*.

ERE, before, sooner than. (E.)   ME. *er*, Chaucer, C. T. 1042 (A 1040).   AS. *ǣr*, soon, before; prep., conj., and adv.; Grein, i. 69.   [Cf. AS. *ǣr-lic*, mod. E. *early*.]+Du. *eer*, adv. sooner; OHG. *ēr*, G. *eher*, sooner; Goth. *airis*, sooner, comp. of *air*, adv. early, soon. ¶ Orig. a comparative form ; the positive being found in Goth. *air*, soon, Icel. *ār*, soon. Cf. Gk. ἦρι, early. See **Erst.**

ERECT, upright. (L.) ME. *erect*, Chaucer, C. T. 4429 (B 9).— L. *ērectus*, set up, upright ; pp. of *ērigere*, to set up. — L. *ē*, out, up ; and *regere*, to rule, set. See **Regal.** Der. *erect*, vb., *-ion.*

ERGOT, a diseased transformation of the seed of rye, &c., due to a fungus, and thought to resemble a cock's spur. (F.) First in 1683 (N. E. D.).—F. *ergot*, 'a cock's spur, spurred rye, ergot ;' Hamilton. Cotgrave has both *ergot* and *argot*, a cock's spur ; and OF. *argot* occurs in the 12th century (Littré). Origin unknown. Connexion with L. *argūtus*, bright, clear, seems not impossible ; cf. L. *argūtārī*, to stamp with the feet, as a fuller. Cotgrave has *argoter*, to fight with spurs.

ERMINE, an animal of the weasel tribe. (F.—OHG.) ME. *ermyne*, Rob. of Glouc., p. 191, l. 3949 ; *ermin*, Old Eng. Homilies, ed. Morris, 1st Ser. p. 181, l. 361.—OF. *ermine* (F. *hermine*), 'the hate-spot ermelin ;' Cot. [Cf. Span. *armiño*, Ital. *ermellino*, ermine ; Low L. *armelīnus*, ermine-fur.] AF. *hermine*, Langtoft, i. 172. —OHG. *harmin*, MHG. *hermin*, ermine-fur ; cf. mod. G. *ermelin.* β. The forms *hermīn*, *hermelin*, are extended from OHG. *harmo*, MHG. *harme*, an ermine, corresponding to Lithuanian *szarmû*, *szarmonys*, a weasel (Diez) ; cf. AS. *hearma*, the name of some quadruped, Voc. 118.43 ; MDu. *armelijn*, 'an hermin ;' Hexham. ¶ The derivation, suggested by Ducange, that *ermine* is for *mūs Armenius*, Armenian mouse, which *may* have been an equivalent term to *mūs Ponticus*, a Pontic mouse, which *may* have meant an ermine, is adopted by Littré.

ERODE, to eat away. (F.—L.) In Bacon, Nat. Hist. s. 983.— MF. *eroder*, 'to gnaw off, eat into ;' Cot.—L. *ērōdere*, pp. *ērōsus*, to gnaw off ; from *ē*, off, and *rōdere*, to gnaw. See **Rodent.** Der. *eros-ion*, *-ive* ; cf. L. *ērōsus.*

EROTIC, amorous. (Gk.) 'This *eroticall* love ;' Burton, Anat. of Melancholy, iii. 2. 1, 2 ; p. 442 (R.).—Gk. ἐρωτικός, relating to love.—Gk. ἐρωτι-, decl. stem of ἔρως, love ; allied to ἔραμαι, I love.

ERR, to stray. (F.—L.) ME. *erren*, Chaucer, Troilus, b. iv. 302. —OF. *errer*, 'to erre ;' Cot.—L. *errāre*, to wander ; which stands for an older form **ers-āre.* **+** Goth. *airz-jan*, to make to err ; a causal form ; OHG. *irran* (for *irrjan*), to make to err ; G. *irren*, to wander, go astray ; G. *irre*, astray. Brugmann, i. § 878. Der. *err-or*, q. v. ; *errant*, q. v. ; *erratum*, q. v.

ERRAND, a message. (E.) ME. *erende*, *erande*, sometimes *arende* (always with one *r*) ; Layamon, 10057. AS. *ǣrende*, a message, business ; Grein, i. 70. Cf. OSax. *ārundi* ; Icel. *eyrendi*, *örendi*, *erendi* ; Swed. *ärende* ; Dan. *ærende* ; OHG. *ārunti*, a message. Teut. types uncertain ; apparently **ǣrundjom*, n., **arundjom*, n. Fick (iii. 21, 30) separates this word from Goth. *airus*, Icel. *ārr*, a messenger, and connects it with AS. *earu*, Icel. *örr*, swift, ready, Skt. *arvant-*, a horse. ¶ The initial vowel-sound is still unexplained.

ERRANT, wandering. (F.—L.) 'Of *errant* knights ;' Spenser, F. Q. v. 6. 6.—OF. *errant*, 'errant, wandering ;' Cot. Pres. pt. of OF. *errer*, *eirer*, *edrer*, to wander.—Late L. *iterāre*, to travel ; from *iter*, a journey ; see **Itinerant.** ¶ But in some instances (see Troil. and Cress. i. 3. 9) *errant* represents the pres. pt. of F. *errer*, to err, from L. *errāre.* See **Err.** Der. *errant-ry.* Doublet, *arrant.*

ERRATUM, an error in writing or printing. (L.) Most common in the pl. *errāta* ; Blount's Gloss. ed. 1674.—L. *errātum*, pl. *errāta*, an error ; neut. of *errātus*, pp. of *errāre.* See **Err.** Der. *errat-ic*, from pp. *errātus* ; whence *errat-ic-al*, Sir T. Browne, Vulg. Errors, b. ii. c. 6. § 7, *-ic-al-ly.*

ERRONEOUS, faulty. (L.) '*Erronious* doctrine ;' Life of Dr. Barnes, ed. 1572, fol. Aaa. iiij.—L. *errōne-us*, wandering about ; with suffix *-ous.*—L. *errōne-*, decl. stem of *erro*, a vagrant. —L. *errāre.* See **Err.** Der. *erroneous-ly*, *-ness.*

ERROR, a fault, mistake. (F.—L.) ME. *errour*, Gower, C. A. i. 21 ; prol. 511.—OF. *errour.*—L. *errōrem*, acc. of *error*, a mistake, wandering.—L. *errāre.* See **Err.** ¶ The spelling *errour* was altered to *error* to be more like the Latin.

ERST, soonest, first. (E.) ME. *erst*, Chaucer, C. T. 778 (A 776). AS. *ǣrest*, adv. soonest, adj. first, Grein, i. 71 ; the superl. form of AS. *ǣr*, soon. See **Ere.**

ERUBESCENT, blushing. (L.) Rare ; in Bailey, vol. ii (1731). —L. *ērubescent-*, stem of pres. pt. of *ērubescere*, to grow red.—L. *ē*, out, very much ; and *rubescere*, to grow red, inceptive form of *rubēre*, to be red. See **Ruby.** Der. *erubescence*, from MF. *erubescence* (Cotgrave) ; from L. *erubescentia*, a blushing.

ERUCTATE, to belch out, reject wind. (L.) 'Ætna in times past hath *eructated* such huge gobbets of fire ;' Howell's Letters, b. i. s. 1. let. 27.—L. *ēructātus*, pp. of *ēructāre*, to belch out ; from *ē*, out, and *ructāre*, to belch. Allied to *ērūgere*, to belch (Festus), *rugire*, to bellow, and to Gk. ἐρεύγεσθαι, to spit out, ἤρυγον, I bellowed ; from the base REUG, to bellow. Brugmann, i. § 221. Der. *eructat-ion.*

ERUDITE, learned. (L.) 'A most *erudite* prince ;' Sir T. More,

Works, p. 645 b.—L. *ērudītus*, pp. of *ērudīre*, to free from rudeness, to cultivate, teach ; (orig. 'rough-hewn into shape,' said of a tree ; Bréal).—L. *ē*, out, from ; and *rudis*, rude. See **Rude.** Der. *erudite-ly*, *erudit-ion.*

ERUPTION, a bursting out. (L.) In Shak. Haml. i. 1. 69.— L. acc. *ēruptiōnem*, from nom. *ēruptio*, a breaking out.—L. *ē*, out ; and *ruptio*, a breaking, allied to *ruptus*, broken. See **Rupture.** Der. *erupt-ive.*

ERYNGO, the candied root of the sea-holly. (Ital.—L.—Gk.) In Shak. Merry Wives, v. 5. 23. An incorrect form ; from MItal. *eringio*, *erigne*, 'the weede sea-hollie, also, eringos rootes ;' Florio. —L. *ēryngion.*—Gk. ἠρύγγιον, dimin. of ἤρυγγος, an eryngo ; see Prellwitz.

ERYSIPELAS, a redness on the skin. (L.—Gk.) Spelt *erysipely* (from OF. *erysipele*) in Blount's Gloss., ed. 1674.—L. *erysipelas.*—Gk. ἐρυσίπελας (stem ἐρυσιπελατ-), a redness on the skin.—Gk. ἐρυσι-, allied to ἐρυθρός, red ; and πέλλα, skin. See **Red** and **Pell.** Der. *erysipelat-ous* (from the stem).

ESCALADE, a scaling of walls. (F.—Span.—L.) Florio has Ital. *scalada*, 'an escalado.' The Span. form *scalado* (which occurs in Bacon, Hist. Hen. VII, ed. Lumby, p. 165) has given way to the F. *escalade.*—F. *escalade*, 'a scalado, a scaling ;' Cot.—Span. *escalado*, properly *escalada*, an escalade ; these are the masc. and fem. forms of the pp. of the verb *escalar*, to scale, climb.—Span. *escala*, a ladder. — L. *scāla*, a ladder. See **Scale** (3).

ESCAPE, to flee away, evade. (F.—L.) ME. *escapen*, Chaucer, C. T. 14650 (B 3922).—ONorth F. *escaper*, AF. *escaper*, OF. *eschaper* (F. *échapper*), to escape ; lit. 'to slip out of one's cape,' and so to get away.—L. *ex cappā*, out of one's cape or cloak. See **Cape** (1). ¶ In Italian, we not only have *scappare*, to escape, but also *incappare*, to 'in-cape,' to fall into a snare, to invest with a cape or cope ; also *incappucciare*, to wrap up in a hood, to mask. Cf. Norm. dial. *écapper*, to escape (Moisy). Der. *escape-ment* ; *escap-ade*, from F. *escapade*, orig. an escape, from Ital. *scappata*, an escape, fem. of pp. of *scappare*, to escape. Hence, later, the sense of 'breaking away from restraint.'

ESCARPMENT, a smooth and steep decline. (F.—Ital.—Teut.) A military term ; F. *escarpement.* Formed from F. *escarpe*, a scarp ; with suffix *-ment* (L. *-mentum*). The verb is generally *scarp* rather than *escarp* ; see **Scarp.**

ESCHEAT, a forfeiture of property to the lord of the fee. (F.— L.) ME. *eschete*, *escheyte* ; 'I lese menye *escheytes*'=I (the king) lose many *escheats* ; P. Plowman, C. v. 169.—OF. *eschete*, that which falls to one, rent ; a f. pp. form from the verb *escheoir*, to fall to one's share (F. *échoir*).—Late L. *excadere*, to fall upon, meet (any one), to fall to one's share ; used A.D. 1229 (Ducange) ; from L. *ex*, out, and *cadere*, to fall. See **Chance.** Der. *escheat*, verb ; and see **Cheat.**

ESCHEW, to shun, avoid. (F.—OHG.) ME. *eschewen*, *eschiwen* ; P. Plowman, C. ix. 51.—AF. *eschuer*, Liber Albus, p. 369 ; OF. *eschiver*, MF. *escheuer*, 'to shun, eschew, avoid, bend from ;' Cot. and Godefroy.—OHG. *sciuhan*, MHG. *schiuhen* (G. *scheuen*), to frighten ; also, intr. to fear, shy at.—OHG. **scioh*, MHG. *schiech*, shy ; cognate with E. *shy.* Thus *eschew* and *shy* (verb) are doublets. See **Shy.**

ESCORT, a guide, guard. (F.—Ital.—L.) '*Escort*, a convoy ;' Bailey's Dict., vol. ii. ed. 1731.—MF. (and F.) *escorte*, 'a guide, convoy ;' Cot.—Ital. *scorta*, an escort, guide, convoy ; fem. of pp. of *scorgere*, to see, perceive, guide. Formed as if from L. **excorrigere*, a compound of *ex* and *corrigere*, to set right, correct ; see **Correct.** Der. *escort*, verb. ¶ Similarly Ital. *accorgere*, to find out, answers to a L. **ad-corrigere* ; see Diez.

ESCRITOIRE, a writing-desk, bureau. (F.—L.) 'Captain Gibbet has made bold . . . with your study and *escritoir* ;' Farquhar, Beaux Stratagem, A. v. sc. 4 (near end).—F. *escritoire*, now *écritoire.* — L. *scriptōrium*, place for writing.—L. *script-us*, pp. of *scrībere*, to write. See **Scribe.**

ESCROW, a deed delivered on condition. (F.—Teut.) A law term (Webster) ; the same word as ME. *scroue*, *scrow*, examples of which are given s. v. **Scroll**, q. v. It is the orig. word of which *scroll* is the diminutive. Cf. AF. *escrouwe*, Britton, ii. 71.

ESCUAGE, a pecuniary satisfaction in lieu of feudal service. (F. —L.) In Blackstone, Comment., b. ii. c. 3.—OF. *escuage* (Godefroy) ; cf. Littré, s. v. *écuage*, who quotes from Ducange, s. v. *scutāgium*, which is the Low L. form of the word. Formed with suffix *-age* from OF. *escu*, a shield ; because *escuage* was, at first, paid in lieu of service in the field. See **Squire** and **Escutcheon.**

ESCULENT, eatable. (L.) 'Or any *esculent*, as the learned call it ;' Massinger, New Way to Pay, Act iv. sc. 2.—L. *esculentus*, fit for eating.—L. *esca*, food ; with suffix *-u-lentus* (cf. *uin-o-lentus* from *uinum*). The L. *esca* is for **ed-sca* ; from L. *ed-ere*, to eat, cognate with E. *eat.* See **Eat.** Brugmann, i. § 753.

ESCUTCHEON, a painted shield. (F.—L.) Spelt *scutchion* in

Bacon, Essay 29 (ed. Wright, p. 129); *scuchin*, Spenser, F. Q. iii. 4. 16; *scochen*, Sir Degrevant, l. 1481 (Thornton, Rom.); *scochon*, Book of St. Alban's, pt. ii. fol. f 8, l. 7. ME. *escochon* (1480; N.E.D.); AF. *escuchon*, Royal Wills, p. 67 (1376). – O. North F. *escuchon*, OF. *escusson*, 'a scutcheon,' Cot.; answering to a Late L. type *scūtiōnem*, from a nom. *scūtio. The form depends upon L. *scūtum*, a shield, just as F. *escusson* does upon OF. *escu*, a shield. See **Esquire**. Cf. Ital. *scudone*, a great shield, from *scudo*, a shield; but note that the F. suffix -*on* has a dimin. force, while the Ital. -*one* is augmentative.

ESOPHAGUS, the food-passage, gullet. (L. – Gk.) Also *oesophagus*. '*Oesophagus*, the gullet;' Kersey, ed. 1715. Oesophagus is a Latinised form of Gk. οἰσοφάγος, the gullet; lit. 'conveyer of food.' – Gk. οἰσο-, allied to οἴσω, I shall carry, used as a future from a base οἰ-, to carry, which is allied to εἶμι, I shall go; and φαγ-, base of φαγεῖν, to eat.

ESOTERIC, inner, secret. (Gk.) 'Exoteric and *esoteric*;' Warburton, Divine Legation, b. ii. note Bb (R.). – Gk. ἐσωτερικός, inner (Lucian); a term expanded from Gk. ἐσώτερος, inner, a comparative form from ἔσω, within, an adv. from ἐς = εἰς, into, prep. ¶ A term used of those disciples of Pythagoras, &c. who were *scientifically taught*, as opposed to those who had more popular views, the *exoteric*. See **Exoteric**.

ESPALIER, lattice-work for training trees. (F. – Ital. – L. – Gk.) In Pope, Sat. ii. 147. '*Espaliers*, trees planted in a curious order against a frame;' Kersey, ed. 1715. – MF. *espallier*, 'an hedge-rowe of sundry fruit-trees set close together;' Cot. – Ital. *spalliera*, the back of a chair; an espalier (from its forming a back or support). – Ital. *spalla*, a shoulder, top, back. – L. *spatula*, a blade; in Late L. a shoulder. See **Epaulet**.

ESPECIAL, special, particular. (F. – L.) ME. *especial*, Chaucer, C. T., B 2356 (Six-text). – OF. *especial*. – L. *speciālis*, belonging to a particular kind. – L. *speciēs*, a kind. See **Species**. Der. *especial-ly*. ¶ Often shortened to *special*, as in Chaucer, C. T. 1019 (A 1017).

ESPLANADE, a level space. (F. – Ital. – L.) '*Esplanade*, properly the *glacis* or slope of the counterscarp; but it is now chiefly taken for the void space between the glacis of a citadel and the first houses of a town;' Phillips, ed. 1696. – MF. *esplanade*, 'a planing, levelling, evening of ways;' Cot. Formed from MF. *es-planer*, to level, in imitation of Ital. *spianata*, an esplanade, lit. a levelled way, from Ital. *spianare*, to level. – L. *explānāre*, to flatten out, explain. See **Explain**.

ESPOUSE, to give or take as spouse. (F. – L.) In Shak. Hen. V, ii. 1. 81. – OF. *espouser*, 'to espouse, wed;' Cot. – OF. *espouse*, 'a spouse, wife;' id. See **Spouse**. Der. *espous-er*; *espous-al*, ME. *espousaile*, Gower, C. A. ii. 322; bk. v. 5815; from OF. *espousailles*, answering to L. *sponsālia*, neut. pl., a betrothal, which is from *sponsālis*, adj. formed from *sponsa*, a betrothed one.

ESPY, to spy, catch sight of. (F. – OHG.) ME. *espyen*, *espien*, Chaucer, C. T. 4744 (B 324); often written *aspien*, as in P. Plowman, A. ii. 201. [It occurs as early as in Layamon; vol. ii. p. 404.] – OF. *espier*, to spy. – OHG. *spehōn*, MHG. *spehen* (mod. G. *spähen*), to watch, observe closely. ✛ L. *specere*, to look; Skt. *paç, spaç*, to spy, used to form some tenses of *dṛç*, to see. – √SPEK, to see. Brugmann, i. § 551. See **Species, Spy**. Cf. Norm. dial. *espier*, to spy. Der. *espion-age*, F. *espionnage*, from MF. *espion*, a spy (Cotgrave); which is from Ital. *spione*, a spy, and from the same OHG. verb. Also *espi-al*, ME. *espiaile*, Gower, C. A. iii. 56; bk. vi. 1643.

ESQUIRE, a shield-bearer, gentleman. (F. – L.) In Shak. Mer. Wives, i. 1. 4. Often shortened to *squire*, ME. *squyer*, Chaucer, C. T. prol. 79. – OF. *escuyer*, 'an esquire, or squire;' Cot. (Older form *escuier*; mod. F. *écuyer*.) – Late L. *scutārius*, prop. a shield-bearer. – L. *scūtum* (whence OF. *escut, escu*, mod. F. *écu*), a shield. – √SQEU, to cover, protect; see **Sky**.

ESSART, a variant of **Assart**, q.v.

ESSAY, an attempt. (F. – L.) See Bacon's *Essays*. [Commonly spelt *assay* in Mid. English; Barbour has *assay*, an assault, Bruce, ix. 604, an effort, ii. 371, and as a verb, ix. 353. See **Assay**.] – OF. *essai*, a trial. – L. *exagium*, weighing, a trial of weight; cf. *exāmen*, a weighing, a swarm. – L. *ex*, out; and *agere*, to drive, impel, move. Der. *essay*, verb, spelt *assay* in Shakespeare, and even later; *essay-ist*, Ben Jonson, Discoveries, Ingeniorum Discrimina, not. 6.

ESSENCE, a being, quality. (F. – L.) In Shak. Oth. iv. 1. 16. – F. *essence*, 'an essence;' Cot. – L. *essentia*, a being; formed from *essent*-, base of a pres. participial form from *esse*, to be. – √ES, to be; cf. Skt. *as*, to be. See **Is**. Der. *essent-i-al*, *essent-i-al-ly*; from the decl. stem *essenti*-.

ESSOIN, an excuse for not appearing in court. (F. – L. and Teut.) ME. *essoine*, Chaucer, Pers. Tale, Introd. § 10 (I 164). Spelt *essoigne* in AF., Stat. of Realm, i. 49, an. 1278; also *essoyne*, Year-books of Edw. I., i. 13; *assoyne*, ibid. – OF. *essoine* (also MF. *exoine*), 'an essoine, or excuse;' Cot. – OF. *essonier*, to excuse (Godefroy). – OF. *es*- (from

L. *ex*, away); and Late L. *sunnia*, excuse, in the Lex Salica, ed. Hessels and Kern, Gloss. col. 673. From OHG. *sunne* (for *sundjā*, Braune, xiv. 9), lawful excuse. Cf. Goth. *sunjōn*, to excuse oneself, *gasunjōn*, o justify; from *sunja*, truth. Cf. also Goth. *sunjis*, true, which is allied to Icel. *sannr*, AS. *sōð*, Skt. *satja(s)*, true. See further under **Sooth, Suttee.**

ESTABLISH, to make firm or sure. (F. – L.) ME. *establissen*, Chaucer, tr. of Boethius, b. i. pr. 4 (l. 65). – OF. *establiss*-, base of some parts of the verb *establir*, to establish. – L. *stabilīre*, to make firm. – L. *stabilis*, firm. See **Stable**, adj. Der. *establish-ment*, Spenser, F. Q. v. 11. 35. ¶ Sometimes *stablish*; A.V., James, v. 8.

ESTATE, state, condition, rank. (F. – L.) In early use. ME. *estat*, Hali Meidenhad, ed. Cockayne, p. 13, l. 13; Chaucer, C. T. 928 (A 926). – OF. *estat* (F. *état*). – L. *statum*, acc. of *status*, a condition. See **State**. ¶ *State* is a later spelling.

ESTEEM, to value. (F. – L.) 'Nothing *esteemed* of;' Spenser, p. 3, col. 2 (Globe ed.). Palsgrave has *esteme*. – OF. *estimer*, 'to esteem;' Cot. – L. *aestimāre*, older form *aestumāre*, to value. This stands for *ais-tumāre*, to be compared with Goth. *ais-tan*, to regard; and further related to AS. *ār*, G. *ehre*, honour. Brugmann, ii. § 692. See below; and see **Aim**.

ESTIMATE, valuation, worth. (L.) In Shak. Rich. II, ii. 3. 56. – L. sb. *aestimātus*, estimation; from *aestimātus*, pp. of *aestimāre*, to value. See **Esteem**. Der. *estimate*, verb, in Daniel, Civil Wars, b. iv. st. 3; also *estimation*, from MF. *estimation*, 'an estimation' (Cot.), which from L. acc. *aestimātiōnem*; also *estimable*, Merch. of Ven. i. 3. 167, from OF. *estimable*, from L. *aestimābilis*, worthy of esteem; whence *estimabl-y*.

ESTOP, to bar, impede, stop up. (F. – L.) See **Stop**.

ESTOVERS, supplies of various necessaries. (F. – L. ?) 'Common of *estovers*, i. e. necessaries, .. is a liberty of taking necessary wood,' &c.; Blackstone, Comment. b. ii. c. 2; b. iii. c. 8. [He erroneously derives it from *estoffer*, to stuff, which is a distinct word.] – OF. *estover*, provisions; see **Stover**. The Anglo-F. *estover*, sb., sustenance, occurs in the Year-books of Edw. I., i. 19, 21, 231.

ESTRANGE, to alienate, make strange. (F. – L.) In Shak. L. L. L. v. 2. 213. – OF. *estranger*, 'to estrange, alienate;' Cot. – OF. *estrange*, 'strange;' id. See **Strange**. Der. *estrange-ment*. ¶ The adj. *strange* was in much earlier use.

ESTREAT, a true copy of an original record. (F. – L.) In Blount; he refers us to Fitzherbert, Natura Brevium, foll. 57, 76. AF. *estrete*, Stat. of the Realm, i. 32, an. 1275. (In the Lib. Custumarum, p. 434, we have the L. gen. pl. *extractārum*.) β. The lit. sense is 'extract.' – OF. *estrete*, fem. of *estret*, also spelt *estrait*, pp. of *estraire*, to extract (Godefroy). – L. *extracta*, fem. of pp. of *extrahere*; see **Extract**. Der. *estreat*, vb, to extract a record, as a forfeited recognizance, and return to the court of exchequer for prosecution, also to levy fines under an estreat (Ogilvie). Doublet, *extract*.

ESTUARY, the mouth of a tidal river. (L.) 'From hence we double the Boulnesse, and come to an *estuarie*;' Holinshed, Descr. of Britain, c. 14 (R.). – L. *aestuārium*, a creek. – L. *aestuāre*, to surge, foam as the tide. – L. *aestus*, heat, surge, tide; from L. base *aid*-, to burn, with suffix -*tu*-. – √AIDH, to burn, glow; whence also Gk. αἴθειν, to glow. See **Ether**.

ESURIENT, hungry. (L.) Bailey, vol. ii (1731) has '*esurient*, hungering.' – L. *ēsurient-em*, acc. of *ēsuriens*, pres. pt. of *ēsurīre*, to be hungry; a desiderative verb, formed from *ēs-us*, pp. of *edere*, to eat. See **Eat**. ¶ Often with special reference to Juvenal, Sat. iii. 78.

ETCH, to engrave by help of acids. (Du. – G.) '*Etching*, a kind of graving upon copper with Aqua-fortis;' Blount's Gloss., ed. 1674. – Du. *etsen*, to etch (a borrowed word from German). – G. *ätzen*, to feed, bait, corrode, etch; a causal form, orig. signifying 'to make to eat;' Teut. type *at-jan*-, causal form of Teut. *et-an*- (pt. t. *at*), to eat. See **Eat**. Der. *etch-ing*.

ETERNAL, everlasting. (F. – L.) ME. *eternal*, Chaucer, C. T. 15502 (G 34); also written *eternel*. – OF. *eternel*. – L. *aeternālis*, formed with suffix -*ālis* from *aetern-us*, everlasting, contracted form of *aeuiternus*. Again, *aeui-ternus* is formed, with suffix -*ternus*, indicating quality, from *aeui*-, for *aeuo*-, from *aeuum*, age. See **Age**. Der. *eternal-ly*; from same source, *eterni-ty* = ME. *eternitee*, Chaucer, tr. of Boethius, b. v. pr. 6, l. 8, from F. *eternité*, which is from L. acc. *aeternitātem*; also *etern-ise*, from OF. *eterniser*, 'to eternize;' Cotgrave. ¶ The Middle English also had *eterne*, Chaucer, C. T. 1992 (A 1990): = L. *aeternus*.

ETHER, the clear upper air. (L. – Gk.) In Dryden, tr. of Ovid's Metamorph. b. i. l. 86. [Milton has *ethereal, ethereous*, P. L. i. 45, vi. 473.] – L. *aether*. – Gk. αἰθήρ, upper air; cf. Gk. αἴθρα, clear sky. – Gk. αἴθειν, to burn, glow. – √AIDH, to burn. Brugmann, i. § 202. Der. *ether-e-al*, -*e-ous*, -*e-al-ly*, -*e-al-ise*. And see **estuary**.

ETHIC, relating to custom. (L. – Gk.) Commonly used as *ethics*, sb. pl. 'I will never set politics against *ethics* ;' Bacon (in Todd's Johnson). ME. *ethik*, Trevisa, tr. of Higd⸗ , iii. 363. – L. *ēthicus*, moral, ethic. – Gk. ἠθικός, moral, ethic. – Gk. ἦθος, custom, moral nature ; cf. ἔθος, manner, custom. β. Allied to Goth. *sidus*, custom, manner ; G. *sitte*, custom ; Skt. *svadhā*, self-will, strength. And cf. L. *suētus*, accustomed. γ. The Skt. form is easily resolved into *sva*, one's own self (cf. L. *sē* = Gk. ἔ), and *dhā*, to set, place (Gk. θη-) ; so that Skt. *svadhā* is ' a placing of one's self,' hence, self-assertion, self-will, habit. See Prellwitz, and Goth. *sidus* in Uhlenbeck. Der. *ethic-al*, *-al-ly*, *ethic-s*.

ETHNIC, relating to a nation. (L. – Gk.) In Ben Jonson's Discoveries ; Veritas proprium hominis. Also in Levins. – L. *ethnicus*. – Gk. ἐθνικός, national. – Gk. ἔθνος, a nation. Der. *ethnic-al* ; *ethno-logy*, *-graphy* (modern words).

ETIOLATE, to blanch plants. (F. – L.) 'Cellery blanched or *etiolated* ;' E. Darwin, Botanic Garden, note to c. 1, l. 462. – F. *étiol-er*, to blanch ; with suffix *-ate*. For Norm. dial. *s'étieuler*, to grow into haulm or stalk, like an etiolated plant. – F. *éteule*, OF. *esteule*, a stalk. – Late L. *stupula*, for *stipula*, straw. See **Stubble.**

ETIQUETTE, ceremony. (F. – G.) First in 1750 ; and mere French. – F. *étiquette*, f., a label, ticket ; explained by Cotgrave as 'a token, billet, or ticket, delivered for the benefit or advantage of him that receives it ;' i.e. a form of introduction. Cf. MF. *etiquet*, m., 'a little note, ... esp. such as is *stuck up* on the gate of a court,' &c. ; Cot. – G. *stecken*, to stick, put, set, fix ; causal of G. *stechen*, to pierce. See **Stick,** verb. Doublet, *ticket.*

ETYMON, the true source of a word. (L. – Gk.) In Sir T. Herbert's Travels, ed. 1665, p. 242 ; and earlier, in Holinshed's Chron. of Scotland (R.). – L. *etymon*. – Gk. ἔτυμον, an etymon ; neut. of ἔτυμος, true, real, allied to ἐτεός, true ; and to AS. *sōð*, true. See **Sooth.** Der. *etymo-logy*, spelt *ethimologie* in The Remedie of Love, st. 60, pr. in Chaucer's Works, ed. 1561, fol. 323, back (derived from F. *etymologie*, in Cotgrave, L. *etymologia*, Gk. ἐτυμολογία) ; *etymo-log-ise*, spelt *ethimologise*, id. st. 62 ; *-logi-st* ; also *-logi-c-al*, *-logi-c-al-ly*.

EU-, *prefix*, well. (Gk.) From Gk. εὖ, well ; properly neut. of ἐύς, good, for an older form *Ϝεσύς, good ; allied to Skt. *vasu(s)*, good (Prellwitz).

EUCALYPTUS, a gum-tree. (L. – Gk.) First in 1809. Named by L'héritier in 1788 ; from the sort of cap which covers the flower before it opens. Lit. 'well-covered.' – L. *eucalyptus, representing a coined Gk. form *εὐ-κάλυπτος ; from εὖ, well, and καλυπτός, covered, from καλύπτειν, to cover. See **Eu-** (above).

EUCHARIST, the Lord's supper. (L. – Gk.) Shortened from *eucharistia*, explained as 'thankes-geuing' in Tyndale's Works, p. 467, col. 2. Spelt *eukaryst*, Lydgate, Assembly of Gods, l. 1425. Cotgrave has : '*Eucharistie*, the Eucharist.' – L. *eucharistia*. – Gk. εὐχαριστία, a giving of thanks, the Eucharist. – Gk. εὖ, well ; and χαρίζομαι, I show favour, from χάρις, favour, closely related to χαρά, joy, and χαίρειν, to rejoice. – √ GHER, to desire ; whence also E. *yearn*. See **Eu-** and **Yearn.** Der. *eucharist-ic*, *-ic-al.*

EULOGY, praise. (L. – Gk.) In Spenser, Tears of the Muses, l. 372. Shortened from Late L. *eulogium*, which was itself used at a later date, in the Tatler, no. 138. [Cf. MF. *euloge.*] A form due to confusing L. *elogium*, a maxim, inscription, with Gk. εὐλογία, praise, lit. good speaking. – Gk. εὖ, well ; and λέγειν, to speak. See **Eu-** and **Logic.** Der. *eulog-ise*, *-ist*, *-ist-ic-al*, *-ist-ic-al-ly.*

EUNUCH, one who is castrated. (L. – Gk.) In Shak. L. L. L. iii. 201. – L. *eunūchus* (Terence). – Gk. εὐνοῦχος, a eunuch, a chamberlain ; one who had charge of the sleeping apartments. – Gk. εὐνή, a couch, bed ; and ὄχ-, 2nd grade of ἔχειν, to have in charge, hold, keep.

EUPHEMISM, a softened expression. (Gk.) '*Euphemismus*, a figure in rhetorick, whereby a foul harsh word is chang'd into another that may give no offence ;' Kersey's Dict., ed. 1715. But spelt *euphemism* in Blount's Gloss., ed. 1674. – Gk. εὐφημισμός, a later word for εὐφημία, the use of words of good omen. – Gk. εὖ, well ; and φημί, I speak, from √ BHĀ, to speak. See **Eu-** and **Fame.** Der. *euphem-ist-ic.*

EUPHONY, a pleasing sound. (Gk.) *Euphony* in Blount's Gloss., ed. 1674. '*Euphonia*, a graceful sound ;' Kersey's Dict., ed. 1715. – Gk. εὐφωνία, euphony. – Gk. εὔφωνος, sweet-voiced. – Gk. εὖ, well ; and φωνή, voice, from √ BHĀ, to speak. See **Eu-** and **Fame.** Der. *euphon-ic*, *-ic-al*, *-i-ous*, *-i-ous-ly.*

EUPHORBIA, a plant, usually called spurge. (L. – Gk.) 'Iuba, king of Mauritania, found out the herb *Euphorbia*, which he so called after the name of his own Physitian *Euphorbus* ;' Holland, tr. of Pliny, bk. xxv. c. 7. § 6. – L. *Euphorbus*. – Gk. Εὔφορβος, the name of Juba's physician (as above) ; lit. 'well-fed.' – Gk. εὖ, well, and φέρβειν, to feed, nourish.

EUPHRASY, the plant eye-bright. (Gk.) In Milton, P. L.

xi. 414. [Cf. F. *euphraise*, eye-bright ; Cot.] The eye-bright was called *Euphrasia*, and was supposed to be beneficial to the eyes. – Gk. εὐφρασία, delight. – Gk. εὐφραίνειν, to delight, cheer ; cf. εὔφρων, cheerful. – Gk. εὖ, well ; and φρεν-, base of φρήν, the mind, orig. the midriff, heart.

EUPHUISM, affectation in speaking. (Gk.) So named from a book called *Euphues*, by John Lyly, first printed in 1579. – Gk. εὐφυής, well-grown, goodly, excellent. – Gk. εὖ, well ; and φυή, growth, from φύομαι, I grow ; from √ BHEU, to be. See **Eu-** and **Be.** Der. *eu-phu-ist*, *-ist-ic.*

EUROCLYDON, a tempestuous wind. (Gk.) In Acts, xxvii. 14. – Gk. εὐροκλύδων, apparently 'a storm from the East,' but there are various readings. As it stands, the word is from εὖρο-s, the S. E. wind (L. *Eurus*), and κλύδων, surge, from κλύζειν, to surge, dash as waves. ¶ Another reading is εὐρακύλων = Lat. *Euro-Aquilo* in the Vulgate ; from *Eur-us*, E. wind, and *Aquilo*, N. wind.

EUSTACHIAN, used with reference to certain anatomical structures or organs. (L. – Gk.) So named after a celebrated Ital. anatomist called *Eustachius*, who died in 1574. – L. *Eustachius.* Suggested by Gk. εὔσταχυς, rich in corn. – Gk. εὖ, well ; and στάχυς, an ear of corn, lit. 'prickle,' and allied to E. *sting.*

EUTHANASIA, easy death. (Gk.) '*Euthanasie*, a happy death ;' Blount's Gloss., ed. 1674. – Gk. εὐθανασία, an easy death ; cf. εὐθάνατος, dying well. – Gk. εὖ, well ; and θανεῖν, to die, on which see Prellwitz.

EVACUATE, to discharge. (L.) In Sir T. Elyot, Castel of Helth, b. iii. c. 6. – L. *ēuacuātus*, pp. of *ēuacuāre*, to discharge, empty out. – L. *ē*, out ; and *uacuus*, empty. See **Vacation.** Der. *evacuat-ion*, *-or.*

EVADE, to shun, escape from. (F. – L.) In Shak. Oth. i. 1. 13 ; cf. *evadit* in G. Douglas, Æn. bk. ii. c. 7. l. 102. – F. *évader*, 'to evade ;' Cot. – L. *ēuādere*, pp. *ēuāsus*, to escape, get away from. – L. *ē*, off ; and *uādere*, to go. See **Wade.** Der. *evas-ion*, q. v., like pp. *ēuāsus* ; also *evas-ive*, *-ive-ly*, *-ive-ness.*

EVANESCENT, fading away. (L.) In Bailey's Dict., vol. ii. ed. 1731. – L. *ēuānescent-*, stem of pres. pt. of *ēuānescere*, to vanish away. – L. *ē*, away ; and *uānescere*, to vanish, from *uānus*, vain. See **Vanish.** Der. *evanescence.*

EVANGELIST, a writer of a gospel. (F. – L. – Gk.) In early use. Spelt *ewangeliste*, O. Eng. Homilies, ed. Morris, i. 209. – OF. *evangeliste*, 'an evangelist ;' Cot. – L. *euangelista*. – Gk. εὐαγγελιστής. – Gk. εὐαγγελίζομαι, I bring good news ; cf. εὐαγγέλιον, good tidings, gospel. – Gk. εὖ, well ; and ἀγγελία, tidings, from ἄγγελος, a messenger. See **Eu-** and **Angel.** Der. (from Gk. εὐαγγέλ-ιον) *evangel-ic*, *-ic-al*, *-ic-al-ly*, *-ic-ism*, *-ise*, *-is-at-ion.*

EVAPORATE, to fly off in vapour. (L.) The sb. *euaporation* is in Sir T. Elyot, Castel of Helth, b. ii. c. 22. The verb is in Cotgrave, to translate F. *évaporer.* – L. *ēuaporātus*, pp. of *ēuaporāre*, to disperse in vapour. – L. *ē*, away ; and *uapor*, vapour. See **Vapour.** Der. *evaporat-ion*, *evapora-ble.*

EVASION, an excuse. (F. – L.) In Sir T. More, Works, p. 693 c. – OF. *evasion* (Hatzfeld). – L. *ēuāsiōnem*, acc. of *ēuāsio* (Judith, xiii. 20), an escape ; cf. *ēuāsus*, pp. of *ēuādere* ; see **Evade.**

EVE, EVEN, the latter part of the day. (E.) *Eve* is short for *even*, by loss of final *n* ; *evening* is from the same source, but is discussed below separately. ME. *eue*, *euen*, both in Chaucer, C. T. 4993, 9090 (B 573, E 1214) ; the form *eue* occurs even earlier, in Owl and Nightingale, l. 41 ; the full form appears as *efen*, Ormulum, 1105 ; *æfen*, Layamon, 26696. AS. *ǣfen*, *ēfen*, Grein, i. 64. + OSax. *āband* ; OFries. *āvend* ; OHG. *āband*, MHG. *ābent*, G. *abend*. β. Origin doubtful ; nor is it known whether these words are allied to Icel. *aptan*, Swed. *afton*, Dan. *aften*, evening. Cf. Brugmann, i. § 980. ¶ Not connected with *even*, adj. Der. *even-song*, Chaucer, C. T. 832 (A 830) ; *even-tide*, Ancren Riwle, p. 404, = AS. *ǣfen-tīd*, Grein ; also *even-ing*, q. v.

EVEN, equal, level. (E.) ME. *euen*, *euene* ; P. Plowman, C. xxiii. 270. AS. *efen*, *efn*, sometimes contracted to *emn*, Grein, i. 218. + Du. *even* ; Icel. *jafn* ; Dan. *jævn* ; Swed. *jämn* ; Goth. *ibns* ; OHG. *epan* ; G. *eben*. β. The Teut. type is *ebnoz. Root unknown ; perhaps related to E. *ebb*. Der. *even*, adv., *even-handed*, &c., *even-ly*, *even-ness.*

EVENING, eve, the latter end of the day. (E.) ME. *euening*, *euenynge*, Rob. of Glouc. p. 312 ; l. 6382. AS. *ǣfnung*, Gen. viii. 11 ; formed with suffix *-ung* (= mod. E. *-ing*) from *ǣfn-ian*, to grow towards evening ; from *ǣfen*, even. See **Eve.**

EVENT, circumstance, result. (L.) In Shak. L. L. L. i. 1. 245. – L. *ēuentus*, or *ēuentum*, an event. – L. *ēuentus*, pp. of *ēuenire*, to happen. – L. *ē*, out ; and *uenire*, to come. See **Come.** Der. *event-ful* ; also *event-u-al*, *-u-al-ly* (from *ēuentu-s*).

EVER, continually. (E.) ME. *euer*, *euere* (where *u* = *v*), Chaucer, C. T. 834 (A 832) ; *æfre*, Ormulum, 206. AS. *ǣfre*, Grein, 1. 64.

Unexplained; but prob. related to AS. *ā, āwa*, ever, Goth. *aiw*, ever; which are based upon the sb. which appears as Goth. *aiws*, L. *æuum*, Gk. *aiōn*, life. See **Aye**. Der. *ever-green, -lasting* (Wyclif, Rom. vi. 22, 23), *-lasting-ly, -lasting-ness*; *ever-more*; also *ever-y*, q. v.; *ever-y-where*, q. v.; *n-ever*, q. v.

EVERY, each one. (E.) Lit. 'ever-each.' ME. *eueri* (with *u=v*) short for *euerich*, Chaucer, C. T. 1853 (A 1851); other forms are *euere-ilc*, Havelok, 1330; *euere-il*, id. 218; *euer-ulc*, Layamon, 2378; *æuer-ælc, euer-ech*, id. 4599.—AS. *æfre*, ever; and *ælc*, each (Scotch *ilk*). See **Ever** and **Each**.

EVERYWHERE, in every place. (E.) It represents *two* old forms. 1. Spelt *euerihwar*, Ancren Riwle, p. 200; *eauer ihwer*, Legend of St. Katharine, 681. Compounded of *euer* (AS. *æfre*), and ME. *ihwar* (AS. *gehwǣr*, everywhere, Grein, i. 415). In this case the word is *not* compounded of *every* and *where*, but of *ever* and *ywhere*, where *ywhere* = AS. *gehwǣr*, a word formed by prefixing AS. *ge* to *hwǣr*, where. Similarly we find *aywhere* = everywhere (lit. aye-where) in Allit. Poems, ed. Morris, B. 228. 2. Commonly regarded as = *every-where*, which answers to ME. *euery where, euerilk quar*, Cursor Mundi, 5567.

EVICT, to evince, to dispossess. (L.) In Minsheu, ed. 1627. 'That this deliverance might be the better *evicted*,' i. e. evinced; Bp. Hall, Contemplations, b. iv. c. xix. sect. 25.—L. *ēuictus*, pp. of *ēuincere*. See **Evince**. Der. *evict-ion*.

EVIDENT, manifest. (F.—L.) Chaucer has *euidently* (with *u=v*), Treat. on the Astrolabe, pt. ii. sect. 23, *rubric*; and *euidences*, pl. sb., id. prol. l. 2.—OF. *evident*, 'evident;' Cot.—L. *ēuident-*, stem of *ēuidens*, visible, pres. pt. of *ēuidēre*, to see clearly.—L. *ē*, out, clearly; and *uidēre*, to see; see **Vision**. Der. *evident-ly, evidence* (OF. *evidence*).

EVIL, wicked, bad. (E.) ME. *euel* (with *u=v*), Ayenbite of Inwyt, p. 85; also *iuel*, Havelok, 114; *ifel*, Ormulum, 1742; *vuel* (for *uvel*), Ancren Riwle, p. 52. AS. *yfel*, Grein, ii. 768; whence also *yfel*, sb. an evil. ✛ Du. *euvel*; OHG. *upil*, G. *übel*; Goth. *ubils*. Teut. type **ubiloz*. Prob. related to Goth. *ufar*, AS. *ofer*, over, beyond, as going beyond bounds. Cf. also Icel. *ūfr*, unfriendly, OHG. *uppi*, hostile. See **Over**. ¶ The ME. *evel* is properly Kentish; cf. OFries. *evel*, evil. Der. *evil*, sb.; *evil-ly*; *evil-doer*, &c.

EVINCE, to prove beyond doubt. (L.) In Dryden, Hind and Panther, ii. 190, 233.—L. *ēuincere*, to overcome.—L. *ē*, fully; and *uincere*, to conquer. See **Victor**. ¶ Older word, *evict*, q. v.

EVISCERATE, to disembowel. (L.) In Burton, Anat. of Melanch. i. 2. 3. 14.—L. *ēuiscerātus*, pp. of *ēuiscerāre*, to disembowel. —L. *ē*, out; and *uiscera*, bowels; see **Viscera**. Der. *eviscerat-ion*.

EVOKE, to call out. (L.) It occurs in Cockeram's Dict. (1st ed. 1623); but was not in common use till later. [The sb. *evocation* is in Sir T. Browne, Vulg. Errors, pref. sect. 1; also in Cotgrave, to translate MF. *evocation*.]—L. *euocāre*, to call forth.—L. *ē*, out; and *uocāre*, to call; allied to *uox*, voice. See **Voice**. Der. *evocat-ion*, from MF. *evocation*.

EVOLVE, to disclose, develop. (L.) In Hale's Origin of Mankind (ed. 1677), p. 31.—L. *ēuoluere*, to unroll.—L. *ē*, out; and *uoluere*, to roll. See **Voluble**. Der. *evolution*, in Hale (as above), p. 259; *evolution-ar-y, -ist*.

EVULSION, a plucking out. (L.) In Sir T. Browne, Cyrus' Garden, c. 2, § 11.—L. *ēuulsiōnem*, acc. of *ēuulsio*; cf. *ēuulsus*, pp. of *ēuellere*, to pluck out; from *ē*, out, and *uellere*, to pluck. See **Convulse**.

EWE, a female sheep. (E.) ME. *ewe*; see Wyclif, Gen. xxi. 28. AS. *ewe*, Laws of Ine, § 55; also AS. *eowu*, Gen. xxxii. 14.✛Du. *ooi*; Icel. *ær*; MHG. *ouwe*. Cf. Goth. *awistr*, a sheepfold; John, x. 16. ✛Lithuanian *avis*, a sheep; Russ. *ovtsa*, a sheep; OIrish *oi*; L. *ouis*; Gk. *öis*; Skt. *avi-*, a sheep, ewe. Brugmann, i. § 158.

EWER, a water-jug. (F.—L.) In Shak. Tam. Shrew, ii. 350. ME. *ewer*, Rob. Manning's Hist. of England, ed. Furnivall, l. 11425 (Stratmann).—AF. *ewer*, Royal Wills, p. 27 (1360); OF. *aiguier*, a vessel for water (Godefroy).—L. *aquārium*, a vessel for water.—L. *aqua*, water (whence AF. *ewe*, OF. *aigue*, F. *eau*). See **Aquatic**.

EX-, prefix, signifying 'out' or 'thoroughly.' (L.) L. *ex*, out; cognate with Gk. *ἐξ* or *ἐκ*, out, and Russ. *iz*, out; Lithuan. *isz*. It becomes *ef-* before *f*, as in *ef-fuse*. It is shortened to *e-* before *b, g, l, m, n, r*, and *v*; as in *e-bullient, e-dit, e-gress, e-late, e-manate, e-normous, e-rode, e-vade*. The Gk. form appears in *ec-centric, ec-clesiastic, ec-lectic, ec-logue, ec-lipse, ec-stasy*. It takes the form *es-* in OF. and Spanish; cf. *es-cape, es-cheat, es-cort, es-planade*. In some words it becomes *s-*, as in Italian; see *s-cald, s-camper*.

EXACERBATE, to embitter. (L.) The sb. *exacerbation* is in Bacon, Nat. Hist. § 61.—L. *exacerbātus*, pp. of *exacerbāre*, to irritate; from *ex*, out, thoroughly, and *acerbus*, bitter. See **Acerbity**. Der. *exacerbat-ion*.

EXACT (1), precise, measured. (L.) In Hamlet, v. 2. 19.—L. *exactus*, pp. of *exigere*, to drive out, also to weigh out, measure.—L.

ex, out; and *agere*, to drive. See **Agent**. Der. *exact-ly, -ness*; and see below.

EXACT (2), to demand, require. (F.—L.) In Shak. Temp. i. 2. 99.—MF. *exacter*, 'to exact, extort;' Cot.—Late L. *exactāre*, intensive of L. *exigere* (pp. *exactus*), to exact, lit. to drive out; see above. Der. *exact-ion*, from MF. *exaction*, 'exaction;' Cot.

EXAGGERATE, to heap up, magnify. (L.) In Cotgrave, to translate MF. *exaggerer*.—L. *exaggerātus*, pp. of *exaggerāre*, to heap up, amplify.—L. *ex*; and *aggerāre*, to heap, from *agger*, a heap, which is from *ag-* (for *ad*, to, together, before *g*) and *gerere*, to carry. See **Jest**. Der. *exaggerat-ion* (MF. *exaggeration*, Cot.).

EXALT, to raise on high. (F.—L.) In Shak. K. Lear, v. 3. 67. Lydgate has: 'As he that lyst her name so hyghe *exalte*;' Siege of Troy, bk. i. c. 5 (fol. c 6, col. 2). [The sb. *exaltacion* is in Chaucer, C. T. 6284 (D 702); and *exaltat* (pp.), id. 6286.]—OF. *exalter*, 'to exalt;' Cot.—L. *exaltāre*, to exalt.—L. *ex*, out; and *altus*, high. See **Altitude**. Der. *exalt-at-ion* (OF. *exaltation*, Cot.); *-ed*, *-ed-ness*.

EXAMINE, to test, try. (F.—L.) ME. *examinen*, Chaucer, Tale of Melibeus (B 2310); Gower, C. A. ii. 11; bk. iv. 293.—OF. *examiner*; Cot.—L. *exāmināre*, to weigh carefully.—L. *exāmen* (stem *exāmin-*), the tongue of a balance; for **exāg-men*; cf. *exigere*, to weigh out.—L. *ex*, out; and *agere*, to drive. See **Agent** and **Exact** (1). Brugmann, i. § 768. Der. *examin-er*; *-at-ion* (OF. *examination*, Cot.).

EXAMPLE, a pattern, specimen. (F.—L.) In Shak. Meas. iii. 1. 191. [Earlier form *ensample*, q. v.]—OF. *essample, ensample* (Godefroy), also *example* (Supp.); later *exemple* (Cot.).—L. *exemplum*, a sample, pattern, specimen.—L. *eximere*, to take out; hence, to select a specimen; with suffix *-lum*, and inserted *-p-* (as in *exem-p-tus*).—L. *ex*, out; and *emere*, to take, procure, buy. Der. *exemplar, exemplify, exempt*. Doublets, *ensample, sample*.

EXARCH, (1) a governor under the Byzantine emperors; (2) a patriarch of the Eastern church. (L.—Gk.) First in 1588; cf. Gibbon, Decline Rom. Empire, c. xlv.—L. *exarchus*.—Gk. *ἔξαρχος*, a leader; from *ἐξάρχειν*, to lead.—Gk. *ἐξ*, out, especially; and *ἄρχειν*, to begin. See **Arch-**. Der. *exarch-ate* (Gibbon).

EXASPERATE, to provoke. (L.) In Shak. K. Lear, v. 1. 60. Properly a pp., as in Macb. iii. 6. 38.—L. *exasperātus*, pp. of *exasperāre*, to roughen, provoke.—L. *ex*, much; and *asper*, rough. See **Asperity**. Der. *exasperat-ion*, from MF. *exasperation*, Cot.

EXCAVATION, a hollowing out. (F.—L.) The sb. *excavation* is in Cotgrave, to translate MF. *excavation*; the verb *excavate* occurs in 1599.—MF. *excavation*.—L. *excauātiōnem*, acc. of *excauātio*, a hollowing out; cf. *excauātus*, pp. of *excauāre*, to hollow out.—L. *ex*, out : and *cauāre*, to make hollow, from *cauus*, hollow. See **Cave**. Der. *excavate*, suggested by the L. pp.; *excava-tor*.

EXCEED, to go beyond, excel. (F.—L.) ME. *exceden*; 'That he mesure nought *excede*;' Gower, C. A. iii. 157; bk. vii. 2155.—OF. *exceder*, 'to exceed;' Cot.—L. *excēdere*, pp. *excessus*, to go out; from *ex*, out, and *cēdere*, to go. See **Cede**. Der. *exceed-ing* (Othello, iii. 3. 258), *exceed-ing-ly* (id. 372); and see *excess*.

EXCEL, to surpass. (F.—L.) In Spenser, F. Q. v. 12. 35. [The sb. *excellence* and adj. *excellent* are older; see Chaucer, C. T. 11941, 11944 (C 7, 10).]—OF. *exceller*, 'to excell;' Cot.—L. *excellere*, to rise up; also, to surpass.—L. *ex*, out; and **cellere*, to rise up, whence *ante-cellere, percellere*, &c.; allied to *cel-sus*, high, orig. 'raised.' Cf. Lith. *kélti*, to raise; and see **Hill**. Brugm. i. § 633. Der. *excell-ent* (OF. pres. pt. *excellent*); *excell-ence* (OF. *excellence*, from L. *excellentia*); *excellenc-y*.

EXCEPT, to take out, exclude. (F.—L.) See the phrase 'except Cryst one' = except Christ alone, P. Plowman, C. xvii. 215. [The sb. *exception* is in Lydgate, Complaint of the Black Knight, st. 23.]—OF. *excepter*, 'to except;' Cot.—L. *exceptāre*, frequentative of *excipere*, to take out.—L. *ex*, out; and *capere*, to take. See **Capable**. Der. *except*, prep.; *except-ing*; *except-ion* (OF. *exception*, Cot.); *-ion-al, -ion-able, -ive, -or*.

EXCERPT, a selected passage. (L.) First in 1638. Both the verb *to excerpt* and the verb *to excerp* were in use. '*Excerp*, to pick out or choose;' Blount's Gloss., ed. 1674.—L. *excerptum*, an extract, neut. of *excerptus*, pp. of *excerpere*, to select.—L. *ex*, out; and *carpere*, to pluck, cull. See **Harvest**.

EXCESS, a going beyond, intemperance. (F.—L.) In Shak. L. L. L. v. 2. 73; Gower, C. A. ii. 276; bk. v. 4457.—OF. *exces*, 'superfluity, excess;' Cot.—L. *excessum*, acc. of *excessus*, a going out, deviation; from the pp. of *excēdere*; see **Excede**. Der. *excess-ive*, ME. *excessif*, Gower, C. A. iii. 177; bk. vii. 2722.—OF. *excessif*, 'excessive;' Cot.; *excess-ive-ly, -ive-ness*.

EXCHANGE, a reciprocal giving and receiving. (F.—L.) ME. *eschaunge*, sb.; 'The Lumbard made non *eschaunge*;' Gower, C. A. i. 10; prol. 207. The verb is later; it occurs in Spenser, F. Q. vii. 6. 6. The prefix *es-* was changed to *ex-* to make the word more like Latin.—OF. *eschange*, sb.; *eschanger*, vb., to exchange; Cot.—OF.

es- (< L. *ex-*), out, away ; and *change*, change. See **Change**. Der. *exchang-er, exchange-able.*

EXCHEQUER, a court ; formerly a court of revenue. (F. — Arab. — Pers.) ME. *eschekere*, a court of revenue, treasury ; Rob. of Brunne, tr. of Langtoft, p. 280. Spelt *cheker*, P. Plowman, B. prol. 93. — OF. *eschequier*, a chess-board ; hence the checkered cloth on which accounts were calculated by means of counters ; see Blount's Law Dict. and Camden's Britannia. [See also *eschiquier* in Cotgrave.] — OF. *eschec*, check (at chess) ; *eschecs, esches*, chess. See **Check, Checker, Chess.** ¶ The Low L. form is *scaccārium*, meaning (1) a chess-board, (2) exchequer ; from Low L. *scacci*, chess.

EXCISE (1), a duty or tax. (Du. — F. — L.) ' The townes of the *Lowe-Countreyes* doe cutt upon themselves an *excise* of all thinges,' &c. ; Spenser, State of Ireland, Globe ed. p. 669. ' *Excise*, from the Belg. *acciise*, tribute ; so called, perhaps, because it is assessed according to the verdict of the *assise* (!), or a number of men deputed to that office by the king ;' Gazophylacium Anglicanum, 1689. ' This tribute is paid in Spain, . . I suppose it is the same with the *excise* in England and the Low Countries ;' Bp. Taylor, Rule of Conscience, b. iii. c. 2. R. 9 (R). β. A misspelling of MDu. *aksiis* or *aksys*, spelt *accijs* in Hexham, and *aksys* in Sewel's Du. Dict., where it is explained to mean ' excise.' Cf. G. *accise*, excise. The E. spelling *accise* occurs in Howell's Familiar Letters. ' 'Twere cheap living here [in Amsterdam], were it not for the monstrous *accises* which are imposed upon all sorts of commodities ;' vol. i. let. vii., dated May 1, 1619. Again, the Du. *aksiis* (like G. *accise*) is from OF. *acceis*, a tax ; found in the 12th c. riming with OF. *defeis*, from Late L. *defensum* (N. E. D. ; no reference). — Late L. type *accensum*, a payment ; allied to Late L. *accensāre*, to tax. — L. *ac-* (for *ad*); to ; and *census*, a tax. See **Census.** ¶ For the sound-change, cf. Du. *spijs*, food, from Late L. *spensa* (for *dispensa*), a larder, a spence. **Der.** *excise-man.*

EXCISE (2), to cut out. (L.) The sb. *excis-ion* is earlier ; Caxton has : ' the same grete *excysion* ;' Eneyd. c. xxi. p. 76, l. 27. — F. *excision.* — L. *excīsiōnem*, acc. of *excisio*, a cutting out. This sb. and E. *excise*, vb., are allied to L. *excīs-us*, pp. of *excīdere*, to cut out. — L. *ex*, out ; and *caedere*, to cut ; see **Cæsura.**

EXCITE, to stir up, rouse, incite. (F. — L.) ME. *exciten*, Chaucer, C. T. 16212 (G 744). — OF. *exciter*, ' to excite ;' Cot. — L. *excitāre*, to call out ; frequentative of *exciēre*, to set in motion, call forth. — L. *ex*, out ; and *ciēre*, to summon ; see **Cite.** Der. *excit-er, -ing, -ing-ly ; -able, -abil-i-ty ; excit-at-ion* (OF. *excitation*, ' excitation ;' Cot.) ; *excit-at-ive* (OF. *excitatif* ; Cot.) ; *excite-ment* (Hamlet, iv. 4. 58).

EXCLAIM, to cry out. (F. — L.) Both verb and sb. in Shak. All's Well, i. 3. 123 ; Rich. II, i. 2. 2. — OF. *exclamer*, ' to exclaime ;' Cot. — L. *exclāmāre* ; from *ex*, out, and *clāmāre*, to cry aloud. See **Claim.** Der. *exclam-at-ion* (OF. *exclamation*, ' an exclamation ;' Cot.) ; *exclam-at-or-y.*

EXCLUDE, to shut out. (L.) In Henryson, Test. of Creseide, st. 19 ; and in Wyclif, Numb. xii. 15. — L. *exclūdere*, pp. *exclūsus*, to shut out. — L. *ex*, out ; and *claudere*, to shut ; see **Clause.** Der. *exclus-ion, -ive, -ive-ly, -ive-ness* ; like pp. *exclūsus.*

EXCOGITATE, to think out. (L.) In Sir T. Elyot, The Governour, b. i. c. 23. § 6. — L. *excōgitātus*, pp. of *excōgitāre*, to think out. — L. *ex*, out ; and *cōgitāre*, to think ; see **Cogitate.** Der. *excogitat-ion* ; in the same chap. of The Governour, § 2.

EXCOMMUNICATE, to put out of Christian communion. (L.) Properly a pp., as in Shak. K. John, iii. 1. 173, 223. — L. *excommūnicātus*, pp. of *excommūnicāre*, to put out of a community. — L. *ex*, out ; and *commūnicāre* ; see **Communicate.** Der. *excommunicat-ion* ; Much Ado, iii. 5. 69.

EXCORIATE, to take the skin from. (L.) The pl. sb. *excoriat-ions* is in Holland's Pliny, b. xxiii. c. 3. The verb is in Blount's Gloss., ed. 1674. — L. *excoriātus*, pp. of *excoriāre*, to strip off skin. — L. *ex*, off ; and *corium*, skin, hide. See **Cuirass.** Der. *excoriat-ion.*

EXCREMENT, animal discharge, dung. (L.) In Sir T. Elyot, Castel of Helth, b. ii. c. 11. See Spenser, F. Q. iv. 11. 35. — L. *excrēmentum*, refuse, ordure. — L. *excrē-tum*, supine of *excernere*, to sift out, separate ; with suffix *-mentum*. See **Excretion.** ¶ In Shak. L. L. L. v. 1. 109, *excrement* is from another L. sb. *excrēmentum*, a derivative of *excrescere*, to grow out ; see below. Der. *excrement-al, -it-ious.*

EXCRESCENCE, an outgrowth. (F. — L.) In Holland's Pliny, b. xxii. c. 23 ; and in Cotgrave. — OF. *excrescence*, ' an excrescence ;' Cot. — L. *excrescentia.* Allied to L. *excrescent-*, stem of pres. pt. of *excrescere*, to grow out. — L. *ex*, out ; and *crescere*, to grow ; see **Crescent.** Der. *excrescent*, from L. *excrescent-*, as above.

EXCRETION, a purging, discharge. (F. — L.) In Sir T. Browne, Vulg. Errors, b. iii. c. 13, § 1. — MF. *excretion*, ' the purging or voiding of the superfluities ;' Cot. — L. *excrēt-us*, pp. of *excernere*, to sift out, separate ; with F. suffix *-ion*, as if from a L. *excrētiōnem*. — L. *ex*, out ; and *cernere*, to sift, separate, cognate with Gk. κρίνειν. See

Crisis. Der. *excrete* (rare verb), *excret-ive, -or-y*, from the pp. *excrētus.*

EXCRUCIATE, to torture. (L.) In Levins. Properly a pp., as in Chapman's Odyssey, b. x. l. 332. — L. *excruciātus*, pp. of *excruciāre*, to torment greatly. — L. *ex*, out, very much ; and *cruciāre*, to torment on the cross, from *cruci-*, decl. stem of *crux*, a cross. See **Crucify.** Der. *excru-ciat-ion.*

EXCULPATE, to free from a charge. (L.) In Blount's Gloss., ed. 1674. — L. *exculpātus*, pp. of *exculpāre*, to clear of blame. — L. *ex*, out of ; and *culpa*, blame. See **Culpable.** Der. *exculpat-ion, -or-y.*

EXCURSION, an expedition. (L.) In Holland's tr. of Livy, p. 77 ; Pope, Essay on Criticism, l. 627. — L. *excursiōnem*, acc. of *excursio*, a running out ; cf. *excursus*, pp. of *excurrere*, to run out ; from *ex*, out, and *currere*, to run. See **Current.** Der. *excursion-ist* ; also *excurs-ive, -iv-ly, -ive-ness*, from pp. *excursus.*

EXCUSE, to free from obligation, release. (F. — L.) ME. *excusen* ; P. Plowman, C. viii. 298. — OF. *excuser.* — L. *excūsāre*, to release from a charge. — L. *ex*, from ; and *causa*, a charge, lit. a cause. See **Cause.** Der. *excuse*, sb. ; *excus-able*, Gower, C. A. i. 76 ; bk. i. 1029 ; *-at-or-y.*

EXEAT, a permission to go away. (L.) Also, in old plays, as a stage direction, in place of *exit.* — L. *exeat*, let him go out, from *exire*, to go out. See **Exit.**

EXECRATE, to curse. (L.) In Cotgrave, to translate F. *execrer.* [Shak. has *execrable*, Titus, v. 3. 177 ; *execration*, Troil. ii. 3. 7.] — L. *execrātus*, pp. of *execrārī*, better spelt *exsecrārī*, to curse greatly. — L. *ex*, much ; and *sacrāre*, to consecrate, also, to declare accursed, from *sacr-um*, neuter of *sacer*, sacred, also accursed. See **Sacred.** Der. *execra-ble, execrat-ion.*

EXECUTE, to perform. (F. — L.) ME. *executen*, Chaucer, C. T., A 1664. — OF. *executer* ; Cot. — L. *execūtus*, better spelt *exsecūtus*, pp. of *exsequī*, to pursue, follow out. — L. *ex*, out ; and *sequī*, to follow ; see **Sue.** Der. *execut-ion* (OF. *execution*), Chaucer, C. T. 8398 (E 522) ; *execut-ion-er*, Shak. Meas. iv. 2. 9 ; *execut-or*, P. Plowman, C. vii. 254 ; *execut-or-y, -rix, -ive, -ive-ly* ; and see *exequies.*

EXEGESIS, exposition, interpretation. (Gk.) Modern. — Gk. ἐξήγησις, interpretation. — Gk. ἐξηγεῖσθαι, to explain. — Gk. ἐξ, out, fully ; and ἡγεῖσθαι, to guide ; perhaps allied to E. *seek.* Brugmann, i. § 187. Der. *exeget-ic* (Gk. ἐξηγητικός), *exeget-ic-al, exeget-ic-al-ly.*

EXEMPLAR, pattern. (F. — L.) ' Tho nine crowned be very *exemplaire* Of all honour ;' The Flower and the Leaf, l. 502. — OF. *exemplaire*, ' a pattern, sample ;' Cot. — L. *exemplārium*, a late form of *exemplar*, a copy ; to which the modern E. *exemplar* is now conformed. — L. *exemplāris*, that serves as a copy. — L. *exemplum*, an example, sample. See **Example** ; and **Sampler.** Der. *exemplar-y* ; Hooker, Eccl. Polity, b. i. 3. 4. § 1.

EXEMPLIFY, to show by example. (F. — L.) A coined word ; in Holland's Livy, p. 109, who has ' to *exemplifie* and copie out,' where *exemplifie* and *copie out* are synonyms. Lydgate also has *exemplefye*, Siege of Troy, bk. v. c. 35. l. 20. — OF. **exemplifier* ; not found. — Late L. *exemplificāre*, to copy out ; Ducange. — L. *exemplum*, a copy ; and *-ficāre* (=*facere*), to make. See **Example.**

EXEMPT, freed, redeemed. (F. — L.) Shak. has *exempt*, adj., As You Like It, ii. 1. 15 ; verb, All's Well, ii. 1. 198. The pp. *exemted* occurs in 1467, in Eng. Gilds, ed. Toulmin Smith, p. 393, l. 12. — OF. *exempt*, ' exempt, freed,' Cot. ; *exempter*, ' to exempt, free ;' id. — L. *exempt-us*, pp. of *eximere*, to take out, deliver, free. See **Example.** Der. *exempt*, verb ; *-ion*, from OF. *exemption*, ' exemption ;' Cot.

EXEQUIES, funeral rites. (F. — L.) In Shak. 1 Hen. VI, iii. 2. 133. ' The *exequies* of Abner ;' Wyclif, 2 Sam. iii. 31. — AF. *exsequies*, Stat. Realm, i. 224 ; OF. *exeques*, ' funerals, or funerall solemnities ;' Cot. — L. *exequiās, exsequiās*, acc. pl. of *exsequiæ*, funeral obsequies, lit. ' processions' or ' followings.' — L. *ex*, out ; and *sequī*, to follow ; see **Sequence**, and **Execute.**

EXERCISE, bodily action, training. (F. — L.) ME. *exercise*, Chaucer, C. T. 9032 (E 1156). — OF. *exercice*, ' exercise ;' Cot. — L. *exercitium*, exercise. — L. *exercitus*, pp. of *exercēre*, to drive out of an enclosure, drive on, keep at work. — L. *ex*, out ; and *arcēre*, to enclose, keep off. See **Ark.** Der. *exercise*, verb.

EXERGUE, the small space beneath the base-line of a subject engraved on a coin, left for the date or engraver's name. (F. — Gk.) The final *ue* is not pronounced, the word being French. It occurs in Todd's Johnson, and in works on coins. — F. *exergue*, used by Voltaire, Mœurs, 173 (Littré). So called because lying ' out of the work,' not belonging to the subject. Cf. F. *hors d'œuvre.* — Gk. ἐξ, out of ; ἔργ-ον, work. See **Ex-** and **Work.**

EXERT, to thrust out, put into active use. (L.) ' The stars . . . *Exert* [thrust out] their heads ;' Dryden, tr. of Ovid, Metam. b. i. ll. 88, 89. — L. *exertus*, better spelt *exsertus*, thrust forth ; pp. of *exserere.* — L. *ex*, out ; and *serere*, to join, put together, put ; see **Series.** Der. *exert-ion.*

EXFOLIATE, to scale off. (L.) *Exfoliation* is in Burnet, Hist.

of Own Time, an. 1699. '*Exfoliate*, in surgery, to rise up in leaves or splinters, as a broken bone does;' Kersey's Dict., ed. 1715. – L. *exfoliātus*, pp. of *exfoliāre*, to strip off leaves. – L. *ex*, off; and *folium*, a leaf. See **Foliage. Der.** *exfoliat-ion.*

EXHALE, to breathe out, emit. (F. – L.) In Shak. Rich. III, i. 2. 58. – F. *exhaler*, 'to exhale;' Cot. – L. *exhālāre*, pp. *exhālātus*, to breathe out. – L. *ex*, out; and *hālāre*, to breathe. **Der.** *exhal-at-ion*, K. John, ii. 4. 153; ME. *exalacion*, Gower, C. A. iii. 95; bk. vii. 330.

EXHAUST, to drain out, tire out. (L.) In Shak. Timon, iv. 3. 119. Used as a pp. in Sir T. Elyot, The Governour, bk. ii. c. 6. § 6. – L. *exhaustus*, pp. of *exhaurīre*, to draw out, drink up. – L. *ex*, out; and *haurīre*, to draw, drain. **Der.** *exhaust-ed*, *-er*, *-ible*, *-ion*, *-ive*, *-less.*

EXHIBIT, to show. (L.) Shak. has *exhibit*, Merry Wives, ii. 1. 29; *exhibiter*, Hen. V, i. 1. 74; *exhibition*, K. Lear, i. 2. 25. – L. *exhibitus*, pp. of *exhibēre*, to hold forth, present. – L. *ex*, out; and *habēre*, to have, hold; see **Habit. Der.** *exhibit-er*, *-or*; *exhibit-ion* (OF. *exhibition*, Cot.), *-ion-er*, *-or-y.*

EXHILARATE, to make merry, cheer. (L. – Gk.; *with* L. *prefix*.) Milton has *exhilarating*, P. L. ix. 1047. – L. *exhilarātus*, pp. of *exhilarāre*, to gladden greatly. – L. *ex*, much; and *hilarāre*, to cheer, from *hilaris*, glad; see **Hilarious. Der.** *exhila-rat-ion*, Bacon, Nat. Hist. § 721.

EXHORT, to urge strongly. (F. – L.) ME. *exhorten*, Henryson, Compl. of Creseide, last stanza. – OF. *exhorter*. – L. *exhortārī*. – L. *ex*, greatly; and *hortārī*, to urge; see **Hortative. Der.** *exhort-at-ion*, Wyclif, 1 Tim. iv. 13; *exhort-at-ive*, Levins; *exhort-at-or-y.*

EXHUME, to disinter. (L.) First in 1783; even *exhumation* is not in Johnson, but was added by Todd, who omits the verb altogether. – Late L. *exhumāre*; Ducange (A.D. 1285). Coined from L. *ex*, out; and *humus*, the ground. In Pliny we find *inhumāre*, to bury. See **Humble. Der.** *exhum-at-ion.*

EXIGENT, exacting, pressing. (L.) Gen. used as a sb. = necessity; Jul. Cæsar, v. 1. 19. – L. *exigent-*, stem of pres. pt. of *exigere*, to exact; see **Exact** (2). **Der.** *exigence*, MF. *exigence*, 'exigence;' Cot.; *exigenc-y.*

EXIGUOUS, small, minute. (L.) Cockeram (1623) has *exiguity*; *exiguous* occurs in 1651 (N. E. D.). – L. *exigu-us*, small; with suffix *-ous* for *-us*, as in *ardu-ous*, &c. – L. *exigere*, to weigh strictly, weigh exactly. – L. *ex*, fully; and *agere*, to drive, move forcibly. See **Exact. Der.** *exigu-ity*, from L. acc. *exiguitātem.*

EXILE, banishment. (F. – L.) ME. *exile*, Rob. of Brunne, p. 131, l. 14; *exilen*, verb, to banish, Chaucer, C. T. 4967 (B 547). – OF. *exil*, 'an exile, banishment;' Cot. – L. *exilium*, better spelt *exsilium*, banishment; cf. *exsul*, a banished man, one driven from his native soil. Prob. from L. *ex*, out; and *sedēre*, to sit, with change of *d* to *l*; cf. *consul* (Bréal). **Der.** *exile*, verb (OF. *exiler*, Late L. *exiliāre*); *exile*, sb. (imitated from L. *exsul*, but of French form), Cymbeline, i. 1. 166.

EXIST, to continue to be. (L.) In Shak. K. Lear, i. 1. 114. – L. *existere*, better spelt *exsistere*, to come forth, arise, be. – L. *ex*; and *sistere*, to set, place, causal of *stāre*, to stand; see **Stand. Der.** *exist-ence* (OF., in Supp. to Godefroy), Rom. of the Rose, 5549.

EXIT, departure. (L.) In Shak. As You Like It, ii. 7. 141. – L. *exit-us*, departure; from *exīre*, to go out. β. *Exit* also occurs in old plays as a stage direction. – L. *exit*, he goes out, from *exīre*. – L. *ex*, out; and *īre*, to go. – √ EI, to go; cf. Skt. *i*, to go.

EXODUS, a departure. (L. – Gk.) 'Sēo ōðer bōc ys *Exodus* gehāten,' the second book is called Exodus; Ælfric on the Old Testament. – L. *exodus*. – Gk. ἔξοδος, a going out. – Gk. ἐξ, out, and ὁδός, a way, march; cf. Russ. *khod'*, a march. – √ SED, to go; cf. Skt. *ā-sad*, to approach, Russ. *khodite*, to go. (See Prellwitz.)

EXOGEN, a plant increasing outwardly. (Gk.) Modern and scientific. – Gk. ἔξω, outside (from ἐξ, out); and γεν-, root of γίγνομαι, I am born or produced. See **Endogen. Der.** *exogen-ous.*

EXONERATE, to relieve of a burden, acquit. (L.) In Cotgrave, to translate F. *descharger*. – L. *exonerātus*, pp. of *exonerāre*, to disburden. – L. *ex*, off; and *oner-*, for **ones-*, stem of *onus*, a load; see **Onerous. Der.** *exonerat-ion*, *-ive.*

EXORBITANT, extravagant. (F. – L.) 'To the *exorbitant* waste;' Massinger, The Guardian, i. 1. 30. Earlier, in Henrysoun, The Wolf and the Lamb, l. 46. – OF. *exorbitant*, 'exorbitant;' Cot. – L. *exorbitant-*, stem of pres. pt. of *exorbitāre*, to fly out of the track. – L. *ex*, out; and *orbita*, a track; see **Orbit. Der.** *exorbitant-ly*, *exorbitance.*

EXORCISE, to adjure, deliver from a devil. (L. – Gk.) Shak. has *exorciser*, Cymb. iv. 2. 276; the pl. sb. *exorcistis* = L. *exorcistæ* in Wyclif, Acts, xix. 13 (earlier text); Lydgate has *exorcismes*, Siege of Thebes, pt. iii (How the bishop Amphiorax fell doune into helle). – Late L. *exorcizāre*. – Gk. ἐξορκίζειν, to drive away by adjuration. – Gk. ἐξ, away; and ὁρκίζειν, to adjure, from ὅρκος, an oath. **Der.** *exorcis-er*, *exorcism* (Gk. ἐξορκισμός), *exorcist* (Gk. ἐξορκιστής).

EXORDIUM, a beginning. (L.) In Sir T. Elyot, The Governour,

bk. i. c. 14. § 8; Spectator, no. 303. The pl. *exordiums* is in Beaum. and Fletcher, Scornful Lady, i. 1. – L. *exordium*, a beginning, the warp of a web. – L. *exordīrī*, to begin, weave. – L. *ex*, from; and *ordīrī*, to begin, weave; akin to **Order**, q. v. **Der.** *exordi-al.*

EXOTERIC, external. (Gk.) First in 1662. Opposed to *esoteric*. – Gk. ἐξωτερικός, external. – Gk. ἐξωτέρω, more outward, comp. of adv. ἔξω, outward, from ἐξ, out. See **Esoteric.**

EXOTIC, foreign. (L. – Gk.) '*Exotic* and exquisite;' Ben Jonson, Cynthia's Revels, A. iii. sc. 3. '*Exotical* and forraine drugs;' Holland's Pliny, b. xxii. c. 24 (end). – L. *exōticus*, foreign. – Gk. ἐξωτικός, outward, foreign. – Gk. ἔξω, adv., outward; from ἐξ, out. **Der.** *exotic-al.*

EXPAND, to spread out. (L.) Milton has *expanded*, P. L. i. 225; *expanse*, id. ii. 1014. – L. *expandere*, pp. *expansus*, to spread out. – L. *ex*, out; and *pandere*, to spread, allied to *patēre*; see **Patent.** Brugmann, ii. § 69. **Der.** *expanse* (L. *expansus*); *expans-ible*, *-ibl-y*, *-ibil-i-ty*, *-ion*, *-ive*, *-ive-ly*, *-ive-ness.*

EXPATIATE, to range at large. (L.) In Milton, P. L. i. 774. – L. *expatiātus*, pp. of *expatiārī*, better spelt *exspatiārī*, to wander. – L. *ex*, out; and *spatiārī*, to roam, from *spatium*, space; see **Space. Der.** *expatiat-ion*, Bacon, On Learning, by G. Wats, b. ii. c. 2 and c. 13 (R.).

EXPATRIATE, to banish. (L.) Not in Johnson. In Burke, On the Policy of the Allies (R.). – Late L. *expatriātus*, pp. of *expatriāre*, to banish; cf. MF. *expatrié*, 'banished;' (Cot.). – L. *ex*, out of; and *patria*, one's native country, from *patri-*, decl. stem of *pater*, a father; see **Patriot. Der.** *expatriat-ion.*

EXPECT, to look for. (L.) Gower has *expectant*, C. A. i. 216; bk. ii. 1712. – L. *expectāre*, better *exspectāre*, to look for. – L. *ex*, out; and *spectāre*, to look; see **Spectacle. Der.** *expect-ant*, *-ance*, *-anc-y*; *expect-at-ion* (K. John, iv. 2. 7).

EXPECTORATE, to spit forth. (L.) In Holland's Pliny, b. xxiv. c. 16. – L. *expectorātus*, pp. of *expectorāre*, to expel from the breast. – L. *ex*, out of; and *pector-*, for **pectos-*, stem of *pectus*, the breast; see **Pectoral. Der.** *expectorat-ion*, *-ive*; *-ant* (from the L. pres. pt.).

EXPEDITE, to hasten. (L.) In Cotgrave, to translate OF. *expedier*; properly a pp., as in 'the profitable and *expedite* service of Julius;' Holland's tr. of Ammianus, p. 431 (R.). – L. *expedītus*, pp. of *expedīre*, to extricate the foot, release, make ready. – L. *ex*, out; and *ped-*, stem of *pēs*, the foot. See **Foot. Der.** *expedit-ion*, Macb. ii. 3. 116; *expedit-i-ous*, Temp. v. 315; *-i-ous-ly*; also (from the pres. part. of L. *expedīre*) *expedient*, Much Ado, v. 2. 85; *-ly*; *expedience*, Rich. II, ii. 1. 287.

EXPEL, to drive out. (L.) ME. *expellen*; Chaucer, C. T. 2753 (A 2751). – L. *expellere*, pp. *expulsus*, to drive out. – L. *ex*, out; and *pellere*, to drive; see **Pulsate. Der.** *expulse*, OF. *expulser* (Cot.), from L. *expulsāre*, frequent. of *expell.re*, 1 Hen. VI, iii. 3. 25; *expuls-ion*, OF. *expulsion*, Cymb. ii. 1. 65; *-ive.*

EXPEND, to employ, spend. (L.) In Hamlet, ii. 2. 23. [The sb. *expence* is in Gower, C. A. iii. 153; bk. vii. 2027.] – L. *expendere*, to weigh out, lay out. – L. *ex*, out; and *pendere*, to weigh; see **Poise. Der.** *expense*, from L. *expensa*, money spent, fem. of pp. *expensus*; *expens-ive*, *-ive-ly*, *-ive-ness*; also *expendit-ure*, from Late L. *expenditus*, a false form of the pp. *expensus*. **Doublet,** *spend.*

EXPERIENCE, knowledge due to trial. (F. – L.) ME. *experience*, Chaucer, C. T. 5583 (D 1). – OF. *experience*. – L. *experientia*, a proof, trial. – L. *experient-*, stem of pres. pt. of *experīrī* (pp. *expertus*), to try thoroughly. – L. *ex*; and **perīrī*, to go through, as in the pp. *perītus* and in the compounds *experīrī*, *comperīrī*; see **Peril. Der.** *experienc-ed*, Wint. Ta. i. 2. 392; *experi-ment* (MF. *experiment*, L. *experimentum*), All's Well, ii. 1. 157; *-ment-al*, *-ment-al-ly*, *-ment-al-ist*; and see **Expert.**

EXPERT, experienced. (F. – L.) ME. *expert*, Chaucer, C. T. 4424 (B 4). – OF. *expert*, 'expert;' Cot. – L. *expertus*, pp. of *experīrī*; see **Experience. Der.** *expert-ly*, *-ness.*

EXPIATE, to atone for. (L.) In Shak. Sonnet xxii. 4. – L. *expiātus*, pp. of *expiāre*, to atone for fully. – L. *ex*, fully; and *piāre*, to propitiate, from *pius*, devout. See **Pious. Der.** *expiat-or*, *-or-y*, *-ion* (OF. *expiation*, 'expiation,' Cot.); *expia-ble*, Levins, from *expiā-re.*

EXPIRE, to die, end. (F. – L.) In Spenser, F. Q. iii. 2. 44. – OF. *expirer*, 'to expire;' Cot. – L. *expirāre*, better *exspirāre*, to breathe out, die. – L. *ex*, out; and *spirāre*, to breathe. See **Spirit. Der.** *expir-at-ion*, L. L. L. v. 2. 814; *-at-or-y*, *-a-ble.*

EXPLAIN, to make plain, expound. (F. – L.) In Cotgrave and Milton, P. L. ii. 518. – MF. *explaner*, 'to expound, expresse, explain;' Cot. – L. *explānāre*, to flatten, spread out, explain. – L. *ex*, fully; and *plānāre*, to flatten, from *plānus*, flat. See **Plain. Der.** *explain-able*; also *explan-at-ion*, *-at-or-y*, like L. pp. *explānāt-us.*

EXPLETIVE, inserted, used by way of filling up. (L.) As adj., in Blount (1656); as sb., in Pope, Essay on Criticism, 346. – L.

explētiuus, filling up; cf. MF. *expletif* (Cotgrave). — L. *explētus*, pp. of *explēre*, to fill up. — L. *ex*, fully; and *plēre*, to fill. See **Plenary**. Der. *explet-or-y*, like pp. *explētus*.

EXPLICATE, to explain, unfold. (L.) In Levins; and Dryden, Religio Laici, l. 289. — L. *explicātus*, pp. of *explicāre*, to unfold. — L. *ex*, out; and *plicāre*, to fold, from *plica*, a fold. See **Ply**. Der. *explicat-ion*, -*ive*, -*or*, -*or-y*; also *explica-ble*, Levins (from *explicā-re*); and see **Explicit**.

EXPLICIT, unfolded, plain, clear. (L.) 'Explicite, unfolded, declared, ended;' Blount's Gloss., ed. 1674. — L. *explicitus*, old pp. of *explicāre*, to unfold; the later form being *explicātus*. See above. Der. *explicit-ly*, -*ness*; and see **Exploit**.

EXPLODE, to drive away noisily, to burst noisily. (F. — L.) The old sense is seen in Milton, P. L. xi. 669; cf. 'Priority is *exploded*;' Massinger, Emperor of the East, iii. 2. — MF. *exploder*, 'to explode, publickly to disgrace or drive out, by hissing, or clapping of hands;' Cot. — L. *explōdere*, pp. *explōsus*, to drive off the stage by clapping. — L. *ex*, away; and *plaudere*, to applaud. See **Applaud, Plausible**. Der. *explos-ion*, 'a casting off or rejecting, a hissing a thing out;' Blount's Gloss., ed. 1674; -*ive*, -*ive-ly*, -*ive-ness*; like pp. *explōsus*.

EXPLOIT, achievement. (F. — L.) ME. *espleit* = success; Gower, C. A. ii. 258; bk. v. 3924. 'Al the ianglynge [blame] . . . is rather cause of *esploite* than of any hindringe;' Test. of Love, b. i. c. 5. l. 19. — OF. *esploit*, revenue, profit, achievement (Godefroy); later *exploict*, 'an exploit, act;' Cot. — L. *explicitum*, a thing settled, ended, displayed; neut. of *explicitus*, pp. of *explicāre*. Cf. Late L. *explicta*, revenue, profit. See **Explicit**.

EXPLORE, to examine thoroughly. (F. — L.) In Cotgrave; and in Milton, P. L. ii. 632, 971. — MF. *explorer*, 'to explore;' Cot. — L. *explōrāre*, to search out, lit. 'to make to flow out.' — L. *ex*, out; and *plōrāre*, to make to flow, weep. Cf. *im-plore*, *de-plore*. Brugmann, i. § 154. Der. *explor-er*, -*at-ion* (MF. *exploration*, 'exploration,' Cot.), -*at-or-y*.

EXPLOSION, EXPLOSIVE; see **Explode**.

EXPONENT, indicating; also, an index. (L.) First in 1581; often mathematical. — L. *exponent-*, stem of pres. pt. of *expōnere*, to expound, indicate; see **Expound**. Der. *exponent-ial*.

EXPORT, to send goods out of a country. (L.) 'They *export* honour from a man;' Bacon, Essay 48, Of Followers. — L. *exportāre*, to carry away. — L. *ex*, away; and *portāre*, to carry; see **Port** (1). Der. *export*, sb.; *export-at-ion*, -*able*.

EXPOSE, to lay open to view. (F. — L. and Gk.) In Spenser, F. Q. iii. 1. 46. Used by Caxton (N. E. D.). — OF. *exposer*, 'to expose, lay out;' Cot. — OF. *ex* (= L. *ex*), out; and OF. *poser*, to set, place; see **Pose** (1). Der. *expos-ure*, Macb. ii. 3. 133; and see *expound*.

EXPOSITION, an explanation. (F. — L.) In Gower, C. A. i. 141; bk. i. 2932. — OF. *exposition*; Cot. — L. *expositiōnem*, acc. of *expositio*, a setting forth; cf. *expositus*, pp. of *expōnere*; see **Expound**. Der. *exposit-or*, -*or-y*; from pp. *expositus*.

EXPOSTULATE, to reason earnestly. (L.) 'Ast. I have no commission To *expostulate* the act;' Massinger, Maid of Honour, iii. 1. 3. — L. *expostulātus*, pp. of *expostulāre*, to demand urgently. — L. *ex*, fully; and *postulāre*, to demand. See **Postulate**. Der. *expostu-at-ion*, -*or*, -*or-y*.

EXPOUND, to explain. (F. — L.) The *d* is excrescent, but was suggested by the form of the F. infinitive. ME. *expounen*; Chaucer, C. T. 14162 (B 3346); *expounden*, Gower, C. A. i. 31; prol. 823. — OF. *espondre*, to explain (see Godefroy). — L. *expōnere*, to set forth, explain. — L. *ex*, out; and *pōnere*, to put, set; see **Position**. Der. *expound-er*; also *exposition*, q. v. ¶ The OF. prefix *es-* became *ex* in English, by analogy with other words beginning with *ex*.

EXPRESS, exactly stated. (F. — L.) 'Lo here *expres* of womman may ye finde;' Chaucer, C. T. 6301 (D 719). Hence ME. *expressen*, verb, id. 13406 (B 1666). — OF. *expres*, 'expresse, speciall;' Cot. — L. *expressus*, distinct, plain; pp. of *exprimere*, to press out. — L. *ex*, out; and *primere*, to press; see **Press**. Der. *express*, verb, *express-ible*, -*ive*; -*ion* (OF. *expression*, 'an expression;' Cot.), -*ion-less*.

EXPULSION, EXPULSIVE; see **Expel**.

EXPUNGE, to efface, blot out. (L.) Ben Jonson has *expunged*; Staple of News, v. 1. 27. 'Which our advanced judgements generally neglect to *expunge*;' Sir T. Browne, Vulg. Errors, b. i. c. 9. § 6. — L. *expungere*, to prick out, blot out. — L. *ex*, out; and *pungere*, to prick; see **Pungent**. ¶ No doubt popularly connected with *sponge*, with which it has no real connexion. Some authors use the form *expunct*, from the pp. *expunctus*. Der. *expunction*, Milton, Areopagitica, ed. Hales, p. 27, l. 28.

EXPURGATE, to purify. (L.) Milton has *expurge*; Areopagitica, ed. Hales, p. 10, l. 25. The sb. *expurgation* is in Sir T. Browne, Pref. to Vulg. Errors, paragraph 7. — L. *expurgātus*, pp. of *expurgāre*, to purge out. — L. *ex*, out; and *purgāre*; see **Purge**. Der. *expurgat-ion*, -*or*, -*or-y*.

EXQUISITE, sought out, excellent, nice. (L.) 'His facound toung, and termis *exquisyte*;' Henryson, Test. of Creseide, st. 39; l. 268. — L. *exquīsītus*, choice; pp. of *exquīrere*, to search out. — L. *ex*, out; and *quærere*, to seek; see **Query**. Der. *exquisite-ly*.

EXSEQUIES, the same as **Exequies**, q. v.

EXTANT, existing. (L.) In Hamlet, iii. 2. 273. — Late L. *extant-*, stem of *extans*, a bad spelling of L. *exstans*, pres. pt. of *exstāre*, to stand forth, exist. — L. *ex*, out; and *stāre*, to stand; see **Stand**.

EXTASY, EXTATIC; see **Ecstasy, Ecstatic**.

EXTEMPORE, on the spur of the moment. (L.) Shak. has *extempore*, Mids. Nt. Dr. i. 2. 70; *extemporal*, L. L. L. i. 2. 189; *extemporal-ly*, Ant. and Cleop. v. 2. 217. — L. *ex tempore*, at the moment; where *tempore* is the abl. case of *tempus*, time; see **Temporal**. Der. *extempor-al* (L. *extemporālis*), -*an-e-ous*, -*ise*, -*ar-y*.

EXTEND, to stretch out, enlarge. (L.) ME. *extenden*, Chaucer, C. T. 4881 (B 461). — L. *extendere*, pp. *extensus*, to stretch out (whence OF. *estendre*). — L. *ex*, out; and *tendere*, to stretch; see **Tend**. Der. *extent*, sb.; *extens-ion* (OF. *extension*, 'an extension;' Cot.); *extens-ible*, -*ibil-i-ty*, -*ive*, -*ive-ly*, -*ive-ness* (like pp. *extensus*).

EXTENUATE, to reduce, palliate. (L.) 'To *extenuate* or make thyn;' Sir T. Elyot, Castel of Helth, b. ii. c. 9. — L. *extenuātus*, pp. of *extenuāre*, to make thin, reduce. — L. *ex*, fully; and *tenuāre*, to make thin, from *tenuis*, thin; see **Tenuity**. Der. *extenuat-ion*, 1 Hen. IV, iii. 2. 22; -*or-y*.

EXTERIOR, outward. (F. — L.) Formerly *exteriour*; afterwards Latinised. 'The *exteriour* ayre;' Sir T. Elyot, Castel of Helth, b. ii. c. 24, l. 5. 'What more *exteriour* honour can you deuise;' Barnes, Works, p. 341, col. 2. — MF. *exterieur*, 'exteriour;' Cot. — L. *exteriōrem*, acc. of *exterior*, outward, comp. of *exter* or *exterus*, outward. — L. *ex*, out; with compar. suffix -*tero-*.

EXTERMINATE, to drive beyond bounds. (L.) In Cotgrave, to translate F. *exterminer*, whence was formed Shakespeare's *extermine*, As You Like It, iii. 5. 89. — L. *exterminātus*, pp. of *extermināre*, to drive beyond the boundaries. — L. *ex*, out, beyond; and *terminus*, a boundary; see **Term**. Der. *exterminat-ion* (OF. *extermination*, Cot.); -*or*, -*or-y*.

EXTERNAL, outward. (L.) In Shak. K. John, ii. 571. Formed, with suffix -*al*, from *extern*, Oth. i. 1. 63. — L. *extern-us*, outward, extended form from *exterus*; see **Exterior**. Der. *external-ly*.

EXTINGUISH, to quench. (L.) In Shak. Lucrece, 313. 1. A false formation, made by adding -*ish* to L. *extingu-ere*, by analogy with properly-formed verbs in -*ish*, such as *ban-ish*, *abol-ish*, which are of French origin. 2. The Lat. *extinguere* is a later spelling of *exstinguere*, pp. *extinctus* or *exstinctus*, to put out, quench, kill. — L. *ex*, out; and **stinguere*, prop. to prick, also to extinguish, quench; orig. 'to blunt,' as a weapon (Bréal). Cf. *di-stinguish*. ¶ The OF. word is *esteindre*, F. *éteindre*. Der. *extinguish-able*; also (from pp. *extinctus*) *extinct*, Hamlet, i. 3. 118; *extinct-ed*, Oth. ii. 1. 81; *extinct-ion* (MF. *extinction*, 'an extinction;' Cot.).

EXTIRPATE, to root out. (L.) Shak. has *extirpate*, Temp. i. 2. 125; and *extirp* (from MF. *extirper*), Meas. iii. 2. 110. — L. *extirpātus*, pp. of *extirpāre*, better spelt *exstirpāre*, to pluck up by the stem. — L. *ex*, out; and *stirp-s* or *stirp-es*, the stem of a tree. Der. *extirpat-ion*, from MF. *extirpation*, 'an extirpation, rooting out;' Cot.

EXTOL, to exalt, praise. (L.) 'And was to heaven *extold*;' Spenser, F. Q. vii. 7. 37. — L. *extollere*, to raise up. — L. *ex*, out; and *tollere*, to raise. See **Elate**. Der. *extol-ment*, Hamlet, v. 2. 121.

EXTORT, to force out by violence. (L.) In Spenser, F. Q. v. 2. 5. The sb. *extortion* is in Chaucer, C. T. 7021 (D 1439). — L. *extortus*, pp. of *extorquēre*, lit. to twist out. — L. *ex*, out; and *torquēre*, to twist; see **Torsion**. Der. *extort-ion* (OF. *extorsion*); -*ion-er*, -*ion-ate*, -*ion-ar-y*.

EXTRA, beyond what is necessary. (L.) The use as an adj. is modern. — L. *extrā*, beyond; for *exterā* = *ex exterā parte* = on the outside; where *exterā* is the abl. fem. of *exter*; see **Exterior**. Also used as a prefix, as in *extra-ordinary*, -*vagant*, &c.

EXTRACT, to draw out. (L.) In Shak. Meas. iii. 2. 50. Properly a pp., as in 'the very issue *extract* [= extracted] from that good;' Holland's Plutarch, p. 839; cf. p. 1045. — L. *extractus*, pp. of *extrahere*, to draw out. — L. *ex*, out; and *trahere*, to draw; see **Trace**. Der. *extract*, sb., *extract-ion* (OF. *extraction*, Cot.); *extract-ive*, -*or*, -*ible*.

EXTRADITION, a surrender of fugitives. (F. — L.) Modern; not in Todd. — F. *extradition* (1798). Coined from L. *ex*, out; and **Tradition**, q. v.

EXTRAMUNDANE, out of the world. (L.) In Kersey's Dict., ed. 1715. — Late L. *extrāmundānus*; coined from *extrā*, beyond, and *mund-us*, world; with suffix -*ānus*. See **Extra** and **Mundane**.

EXTRANEOUS, external, unessential. (L.) In Sir T. Browne, Vulg. Errors, b. ii. c. 7, part 9. — L. *extrāneus*, external; by change of -*us* to -*ous*, as in *arduous*, *egregious*, &c. An extension from L. *extrā*, beyond. See **Extra**. Cf. **Strange**. Der. *extraneous-ly*.

EXTRAORDINARY, beyond ordinary. (L.) In Shak. Mer.

Wives, iii. 3. 75.—L. *extraordinārius*, rare. From the phrase *extrā ordinem*, outside the (usual) order. See **Order**. Der. *extraordinari-ly*, 2 Hen. IV, i. 2. 235.

EXTRAVAGANT, excessive, profuse. (F.—L.) See Shak. Hamlet, i. 1. 154.—MF. *extravagant*, 'extravagant;' Cot.—Late L. *extrāvagant-*, stem of *extrāvagans*; formed from *extrā* and *uagans*, pres. pt. of *uagāri*, to wander. See **Vague**. Der. *extravagant-ly*; *extravagance* (MF. *extravagance*, 'an extravagancy,' Cot.); *extravaganc-y*, Tw. Nt. ii. 1. 12; *extravaganza* (Ital. *estravaganza*).

EXTRAVASATE. (L.) '*Extravasate*, in surgery, to go out of its proper vessels, as the blood and humours sometimes do;' Kersey's Dict., ed. 1715. Coined from L. *extrā*, beyond; and *uās*, a vessel; with suffix *-ate*. See **Vase**. Der. *extravasat-ion*.

EXTREME, last, greatest. (F.—L.) Palsgrave has *extreme*. Spenser has *extremest*; F. Q. ii. 10. 31.—OF. *extreme*, 'extreme;' Cot.—L. *extrēmus*, superl. of *exterus*, outward; see **Exterior**. Der. *extrem-i-ty*, ME. *extremité*, Gower, C. A. ii. 85; bk. iv. 2489; from OF. *extremité*, which is from L. acc. *extrēmitātem*.

EXTRICATE, to disentangle. (L.) 'Which should be *extricated*;' Bp. Taylor, Dissuasive from Popery, pt. ii. b. i. s. 11.—L. *extrīcātus*, pp. of *extrīcāre*, to disentangle.—L. *ex*, out of; and *tricæ*, trifles, impediments; see **Intricate**. Der. *extricat-ion*, *extrica-ble*.

EXTRINSIC, external. (F.—L.) A false spelling for *extrinsec*, by analogy with words ending in *-ic*. 'Astronomy exhibiteth the *extrinsique* parts of celestial bodies;' Bacon, On Learning, by G. Wats, b. ii. c. 4 (R.).—MF. *extrinseque*, 'extrinsecall, outward;' Cot.—L. *extrinsecus*, from without.—L. *extrin-* = *extrim*, adverbial form from *exter*, outward (see **Exterior**); and *secus*, beside; thus *extrin-secus* = on the outside. *Sec-us* is from the same root as L. *sec-undum*, according to, viz., from L. *sequī*, to follow; see **Second**. And cf. L. *interim*. Der. *extrinsic-al* (formerly *extrinsecal*, Bp. Taylor, Rule of Conscience, b. i. c. 2, rule 3, and in Cotgrave, as above); *extrinsic-al-ly*; and see *intrinsic*.

EXTRUDE, to push out. (L.) In Levins, ed. 1570; and in Blount's Gloss., ed. 1674.—L. *extrūdere*, pp. *extrūsus*, to thrust forth.—L. *ex*, out; and *trūdere*, to thrust; from the same root as **Threat**, q.v. Cf. *in-trude*. Der. *extrus-ion*, from pp. *extrūsus*.

EXUBERANT, rich, superabundant. (F.—L.) In Cotgrave; Kersey's Dict., ed. 1715; Thomson, Spring, 75.—MF. *exuberant*, 'exuberant;' Cot.—L. *exūberant-*, stem of pres. pt. of *exūberāre*, to be luxuriant.—L. *ex*, very; and *ūberāre*, to be fruitful, from *ūber*, fertile; allied to *ūber*, an udder, fertility, cognate with E. *udder*; see **Udder**. Der. *exuberance*, from MF. *exuberance*, 'exuberancy;' Cot.

EXUDE, to distil as sweat. (L.) In Johnson's Dict., and first in 1574. Another form is *exudate*, Sir T. Browne, Vulg. Errors, b. iii. c. 4. § 5; the sb. *exudation* is in the same author, Cyrus' Garden, c. 3. § 52.—L. *exūdāre*, better spelt *exsūdāre*, lit. to sweat out.—L. *ex*, out; and *sūdāre*, to sweat; see **Sweat**. Der. *exud-at-ion*.

EXULT, to leap for joy, be glad. (L.) Shak. has *exult*, Tw. Nt. ii. 5. 8; *exultation*, Wint. Ta. v. 3. 131.—L. *exultāre*, better spelt *exsultāre*, to leap up, exult, frequentative form of *exsilere* (pp. *exsultus*), to spring out.—L. *ex*, out; and *salīre*, to leap; see **Salient**. Der. *exult-ing-ly*, *-ant*, *-at-ion*.

EXUVIÆ, cast skins of animals. (L.) In Kersey's Dict., ed. 1715.—L. *exuuiæ*, things laid aside or put off.—L. *exuere*, to put off, strip. Cf. L. *ind-uuiæ*, clothes.

EYAS, a nestling, a young hawk. (F.—L.) For *nias* or *niais*; by substituting *an eyas* for *a nias*, or *a niais*. 'An hawke is calde *an eyas*,' &c.; Boke of St. Alban's, fol. B ij. 'Thou art *a niaise*;' Ben Jonson, The Devil is an Ass, Act i. sc. 3.—F. *niais*, a nestling; Cot. [He also gives *niard*, whence *faulcon niard*, 'a nias faulcon.'] Cf. Ital. *nidiace*, or *nidaso falcone*, 'an eyase hawk, a young hawk taken out of her nest;' Torriano. From Late L. type *nīdācem*, acc. of *nīdax*, an adj. formed from *nīdus*, a nest. See **Nest**.

EYE, the organ of sight. (E.) ME. *eye*, *eiȝe*, *eighe*; pl. *eyen*, *eiȝen*, *eighen*, as well as *eyes*, *eiȝes*; P. Plowman, A. v. 90, B. v. 109, 134. [Chaucer uses the form *yë*, pl. *yën*, though the scribes commonly write it *eye*, *eyen*, against the rime. The old sound of *ey* was that of *ei* in *eight*, followed by a glide; the final *e* was a separate syllable.] OMerc. *ēge*; AS. *ēage*, pl. *ēagan*, Grein, i. 254.+Du. *oog*; Icel. *auga*; Dan. *öie*; Swed. *öga*; Goth. *augō*; G. *auge* (OHG. *ouga*). Teut. type *augon-*. Usually compared with L. *oc-ul-us*, dimin. of an older *ocus*; Gk. ὄσσομαι (=ὀκ-ζομαι), I see; Lith. *akis*, an eye; Skt. *akshi*. Brugmann, i. § 681. Der. *eye*, verb, Temp. v. 238; *eye-ball*, K. John, iii. 4. 30; *eye-bright*, used to translate F. *euphraise* in Cotgrave; *eye-brow*, ME. *eȝe-brewe*, Polit. Songs, ed. Wright, p. 239, l. 8, from Icel. *auga-brún*, an eyebrow (see **Brow**); *eye-lash*; *eye-less*; *eye-lid*, spelt *ehe-lid* in O. Eng. Homilies, i. 265, l. 5; *eye-salve*, spelt *eȝhe-sallfe* in Ormulum, l. 1852; *eye-service*, A.V. Eph. vi. 6; *eye-sight*, spelt *eihsihðe*, Ancren Riwle, p. 58; *eye-sore*, Tam. Shrew, iii. 2. 103; *eye-tooth*; *eye-witness*, A. V. Luke, i. 2. Also *dais-y*, q.v., *wind-ow*, q.v.

EYELET-HOLE, a hole like a small eye. (F. and E.) For ME. *oilet*, Wyclif, Exod. xxvi. 5; with *hole* added. ME. *oilet* is from OF. *oeillet*. 'Oeillet, a little eye; also, an oilet-hole;' Cot. Dimin. of OF. *oeil*, from L. *oculum*, acc. of *oculus*, the eye; see **Eye**.

EYOT, a little island. (E.) Also spelt *ait*. 'Eyet, an islet;' Kersey, ed. 1715. 'Ait or eyght, a little island in a river;' id. Spelt *eyt* in a charter of Edw. Confessor, Kemble, Cod. Dipl. iv. 211; and *ÿget* in Cod. Dipl. v. 17, l. 30; with AF. substitution of *-et* for *-oð*. From AS. *īgoð*, also written *igeoð*; 'tō ānum *igeoðe* þe is Paðmas gecīged' = to an eyot that is called Patmos; Ælfric's Hom. ed. Thorpe, i. 58. The shorter AS. form is *īg*, still preserved in *Shepp-y* and in *island*. See **Island**. (See Notes on Eng. Etym., p. 87.)

EYRE, a journey, circuit. (F.—L.) ME. *eire*. 'The *eire* of justize wende aboute in the londe;' Rob. of Glouc., p. 517; l. 10647. 'Justices in eyre = judiciarii itinerantes;' Blount's Nomolexicon.—OF. *eire*, way; as in 'le *eire* des feluns perirat' = the way of the ungodly shall perish, Ps. i. 7 (in Bartsch, Chrestomathie Française, col. 41, l. 35).—OF. *eirer*, to journey, wander about.—Late L. *iterāre*, to journey (for L. *itinerāre*); from L. *iter*, a journey. See **Errant**.

EYRY, a nest; see **Aery**.

F

FABLE, a story, fiction. (F.—L.) ME. *fable*, Chaucer, C. T. 17342 (I 31).—F. *fable*.—L. *fābula*, a narrative.—L. *fāri*, to speak.+Gk. φημί, I say; Skt. *bhāsh*, to speak. See **Fate**. Der. *fable*, verb; also (from L. *fābula*) *fabul-ous*, Hen. VIII, i. 1. 36; *-ous-ly*, *-ise*, *-ist*.

FABRIC, a structure. (F.—L.) In Shak. Temp. iv. 151; and in Caxton, Golden Legend; St. Austin, § 14.—F. *fabrique*; Cot.—L. *fabrica*, a workshop, art, fabric.—L. *fabri-* for *fabro-*, stem of *faber*, a workman.—L. *fab-*, to fit; with suffix *-er* (stem *-ro*) of the agent. The base *fab*, answering to a root DHAB, appears in Lith. *dab-inù*, I clean, adorn; Russ. *dob-rui*, good; Goth. *ga-dab-ith*, it is fit. See **Dapper**. Doublet, *forge*, sb. q.v.

FABRICATE, to invent. (L.) In Cotgrave, to translate F. *fabriquer*.—L. *fabricātus*, pp. of *fabricāri*, to construct.—L. *fabrica* (above). Der. *fabricat-ion*, from F. *fabrication*, 'a fabrication;' Cot.

FABULOUS; see **Fable**.

FAÇADE, the face of a building. (F.—Ital.—L.) 'Facade, the outside or fore-front of a great building;' Kersey's Dict. ed. 1715. And in Blount's Gloss. (1656).—MF. *facade*, 'the forefront of a house;' Cot.—Ital. *facciata*, the front of a building.—Ital. *faccia*, the face.—Folk L. *facia*, for L. *faciēs*, the face; see **Face**.

FACE, the front, countenance. (F.—L.) ME. *face*, Chaucer, prol. 460; *faas*, K. Alisaunder, 5661.—F. *face*.—Folk L. *facia*, for L. *faciēs*, the face. Der. *face*, verb, Macb. i. 2. 20; *fac-et*, spelt *fascet*, Bacon, Ess. 55, Of Honour, from F. dimin. *facette*; *faç-ade*, q.v. ; *fac-ing*; *faci-al*, from L. *faci-ēs*; also *sur-face*.

FACETIOUS, witty. (F.—L.) In Cotgrave.—F. *facétieux*, 'facetious;' Cot.—MF. *facetie*, 'witty mirth;' id.—L. *facētia*, wit; commoner in the pl. *facētiæ*, which is also used in English.—L. *facētus*, elegant, courteous; orig. 'of fair appearance;' connected with Gk. φά-ος, light. Der. *facetious-ly*, *-ness*.

FACILE, easy to do, yielding. (F.—L.) In Shak. Oth. i. 3. 23. And in Sir T. Elyot, The Governour, bk. i. c. 14. § 2.—F. *facile*.—L. *facilis*, easily done, lit. do-able.—L. *fac-ere*, to do; with suffix *-ilis*. See **Fact**. Der. *facil-i-ty*, Oth. ii. 3. 84, from F. *facilité*, L. *facili-tātem*, acc. of *facilitās*; *facil-it-ate*, imitated (but with suffix *-ate*) from F. *faciliter*, 'to facilitate, make easie;' Cot. And see **Faculty**.

FAC-SIMILE, an exact copy. (L.) First in 1661 (N. E. D.). From L. *fac simile*, make (thou) like.—L. *fac*, imp. s. of *facere*, to make; and *simile*, neut. of *similis*, like. See **Fact** and **Simile**.

FACT, a deed, reality. (L.) Formerly used like mod. E. *deed*; Shak. Macb. iii. 6. 10; cf. '*fact* of arms,' Milton, P. L. ii. 124.—L. *factum*, a thing done; neut. of *factus*, pp. of *facere*, to do. Allied to Gk. τίθημι, I put, set, and E. *do*; see **Do**. Brugmann, i. §§ 129, 193. Der. *fact-or*, Cymb. i. 6. 188, from L. *factor*, an agent; *fact-or-ship*, *-or-age*, *-or-y*, *-or-i-al*; also *fact-ion*, q. v.; also *fact-it-i-ous*, q.v., *feasible*, q.v., *feature*, q.v. Doublet, *feat*, q.v. ¶ From the same root we have not only *fac-ile*, *fac-ulty*, *fac-totum*, *fash-ion*, *feat-ure*, but many others; e.g. *af-fair*, *af-fect*, *arti-fice*, *com-fit*, *con-fect*, *counter-feit*, *de-feat*, *de-fect*, *dif-fic-ult*, *ef-fect*, *for-feit*, *in-fect*, *manu-fact-ure*, *of-fice*, *per-fect*, *pro-fic-ient*, *re-fect-ion*, *sacri-fice*, *suf-fice*, *sur-feit*, &c.

FACTION, a party, sect. (F.—L.) In Shak. Haml. v. 2. 249.—F. *faction*, 'a faction or sect;' Cot.—L. *factiōnem*, acc. of *factio*, a doing, working for or against, faction; cf. *factus*, pp. of *facere*, to do; see **Fact**. Der. *facti-ous*, Rich. III, i. 3. 128; *-ous-ly*, *-ous-ness*.

FACTITIOUS, artificial. (L.). 'Artificial and *factitious* gemms;' Sir T. Browne, Vulg. Err. b. ii. c. 1, § 6.—L. *factītius*, better *factīcius*, artificial; with change of *-us* to *-ous*, as in *arduous*, *egregious*.—L. *factus*, pp. of *facere*, to make; see **Fact**. Der. *factitious-ly*.

FACTOTUM, a general agent. (L.) 'Factotum here, sir;' Ben Jonson, New Inn, ii. 2.—L. *fac tōtum*, do (thou) all.—L. *fac*, imp. s. of *facere*, to do; and *tōtum*, all; see **Fact** and **Total**.

FACULTY, facility to act. (F.—L.) ME. *faculté*, Chaucer, C. T. 244.—F. *faculté*; Cot.—L. *facultātem*, acc. of *facultās*, capability to do, contracted form of *facilitas*; see **Facile**. Brugmann, i. § 241 (b). Doublet, *facility*.

FAD, a whim, fancy, pet project. (F.—Prov.—L.) Adopted from prov. E.; see E. D. D. Merely a shortened form of F. *fadaise*, 'fiddle-faddle, twaddle, trifle;' Hamilton. Cot. has F. *fadeses*, pl. 'follies, toyes, gulleries;' and *fadas*, 'sottish.' Miege (1679) has 'fadle [i. e. faddle], *fadaises*;' showing the association.—Prov. *fadeza*, folly (Hatzfeld).—Prov. *fat* (Gascon *fad*), foolish.—L. *fatuum*, acc. of *fatuus*, foolish. Der. *faddle*, nonsense.

FADE, to wither. (F.—L.) Gower has *faded*, C. A. ii. 109; bk. iv. 3208. Cf. 'That weren pale and *fade*-hewed;' id. i. 111; bk. i. 2043. [Also written *vade*, Shak. Pass. Pilgrim, 131, 132; from MDu. *vadden*, to fade (from F.).]—OF. *fader*, vb.; from *fade*, adj. 'unsavoury, tastelesse; weak, faint, witlesse;' Cot.—L. *uapidum*, acc. of *uapidus*, vapid, tasteless. The change to initial *f* was prob. due to confusion with L. *fatuus*, stupid; Körting, § 3660. Der. *fade-less*.

FADGE, to turn out, succeed. (Scand.) 'How will this *fadge*?' Tw. Nt. ii. 2. 34. It occurs in other obsolete senses, such as to fit, to suit, agree; and, transitively, to fit up or piece together. It appears to be a palatalised form due to Norw. *faga*, to suit, accommodate oneself to, or Norw. *fagga*, to cobble up, to wrap up carelessly (Ross). From Teut. base *fag-*, whence also OSax. *fōgian*, AS. *fēgan*, to join, suit, G. *fügen*, to join, Du. *voegen* (see Kluge and Franck); and cf. OHG. *gi-fag*, content; Goth. *fulla-fah-jan*, to satisfy. The same base occurs in **Fair** (1).

FÆCES, dregs. (L.) 'I sent you of his *fæces* there calcined;' Ben Jonson, Alchemist, ii. 1.—L. *fæcēs*, dregs, pl. of *fæx* (stem *fæc-*); of unknown origin. Der. *fec-ul-ent*, in Kersey's Dict., from L. *fæculentus*.

FAG, to drudge. (E.) 'Fag, to fail, grow weary, faint;' also, 'to beat, to bang;' Ash's Dict. 1775. 'To *fag*, deficere;' Levins, 10. 21, ed. 1570. Of uncertain origin; but prob. a corruption of *flag*, to droop; see Todd. See **Flag** (1). See below.

FAG-END, a remnant. (E.) 'Fag, the fringe at the end of a piece of cloth, the fringe at the end of a rope;' Ash's Dict. ed. 1775. 'Fagg (a sea-term), the fringed end of a rope;' id. 'The *fag-end* of the world;' Massinger, Virgin Martyr, Act ii. sc. 3. Origin unknown. Perhaps for *flag-end*=loose end; see **Flag** (1), and **Fag**. Thus, in the Boke of St. Albans (1486), fol. B j, we find: 'The federis at the wynges next the body be calde the *flagg* or the *fagg* federis.'

FAGGOT, **FAGOT**, a bundle of sticks. (F.—Scand.) In Shak. Tit. And. iii. 1. 69; 1 Hen. VI, v. 4. 56. ME. *fagot*, Cursor Mundi, l. 3164.—F. *fagot*, 'a fagot, a bundle of sticks;' Cot. Cf. Ital. *fagotto*, *fangotto*, a bundle of sticks; which was prob. borrowed from French; the F. *fagot* being found before 1300. Formed, with dimin. suffix *-ot*, from Norw. *fagg*, a bundle (Ross). The Norw. *fagg* also means a short, clumsy person; and prov. E. *faggot* is likewise used as a depreciatory term, often applied to children and women; whilst we also find prov. E. *fadge* with the precise sense of 'bundle.' The Norw. *fagga*, vb., means to bundle together or to cobble up, and is prob. related to *faga*, to suit. See **Fadge**. β. I feel inclined to connect Ital. *fangotto* (if distinct from *fagotto*) with Icel. *fang*, an armful, as in *skiðar-fang*, *viðar-fang*, an armful of fuel; *fanga-hnappr*, a bundle of hay, an armful; from Icel. *fā*, to fetch, get, grasp; see **Fang**. ¶ The W. *ffagod* is borrowed from E. Der. *faggot*, verb.

FAHRENHEIT, the name of a kind of thermometer. (G.) From the name of a Prussian physicist (1686–1736), inventor of the mercurial thermometer. (N. E. D.)

FAIENCE, crockery, pottery. (F.—Ital.) The N. E. D. quotes 'Fayances or earthen-ware' from a book of rates dated 1714.—F. *faience*, crockery; so named from *Faenza* in Italy (near Ravenna), where much pottery was once made.

FAIL, to fall short, be baffled. (F.—L.) In early use. ME. *failen*, Layamon, 2938 (later text).—F. *faillir*, 'to faile;' Cot.—Folk L. *fallire*, for L. *fallere*, to beguile, elude; pass. *falli*, to err, be baffled. Perhaps allied to AS. *feallan*, to fall. See **Fall**. Brugmann, i. § 757. Der. *fail*, sb., Wint. Tale, ii. 3. 170; *fail-ing*; *fail-ure* (substituted for an earlier *failer*, from AF. *failer*; F. *faillir*, infin. mood used substantively, used by Burke, On the Sublime, pt. iv. § 24 (R.); and see *fallible*, *fallacy*, *false*, *fault*, *faucet*.

FAIN, glad, eager. (E.) ME. *fayn*, Chaucer, C. T. 2709 (A 2707); common. AS. *fægen*, glad; Grein, i. 269.+OSax. *fagan*, glad; Icel.

feginn, glad. Cf. AS. *gefēon* (pt. t. *gefeah*), to rejoice. From Teut. base **feh-*, as in AS. *gefēon* (for **ge-feh-an*); cf. Goth. *fah-ēths*, joy. Der. *fawn*, verb; q. v.

FAINT, weak, feeble. (F.—L.) In early use. ME. *feint*, *feynt*; King Alisaunder, 612; Gower, C. A. ii. 5; bk. iv. 118.—OF. *feint*, pp. of *feindre*, to feign; so that the orig. sense is 'feigned;' see Bartsch, Chrest. Française, p. 515, l. 3. See **Feign**. ¶ Cf. ME. *feintise*, signifying (1) faintness, (2) cowardice; Glos. to Will. of Palerne; P. Plowman, B. v. 5. Der. *faint-ly*, Shak. Oth. iv. 1. 113; *faint-ness*, Mids. Nt. Dr. iii. 2. 428; *faint-hearted*, 3 Hen. VI, i. 1. 183; *faint*, verb, Mids. Nt. Dr. ii. 2. 35.

FAIR (1), pleasing, beautiful. (E.) ME. *fair*, *fayr*, Chaucer, prol. 575 (A 573); *fager*, Ormulum, 6392. AS. *fæger*, Grein, i. 269.+Icel. *fagr*; Dan. Swed. *fager*; Goth. *fagrs*, fit; used to tr. Gk. εὔθετον in Lu. xiv. 35; OHG. *fagar*. Teut. type **fagroz*. Cf. Gk. πηγός, firm, strong. Brugmann, vol. i. §§ 200, 701. And see **Fadge**. Der. *fair-ly*, *fair-ness*.

FAIR (2), a festival, holiday, market. (F.—L.) ME. *feire*, *fayre*; Chaucer, C. T. 5803 (D 221).—OF. *feire*; F. *foire*.—L. *fēria*, a holiday; in Late L. a fair; commoner in the pl. *fēriæ*. *Fēriæ* is for **fēs-iæ*, feast-days; from the same root as **Feast** and **Festal**. Brugmann, vol. ii. § 66.

FAIRY, a supernatural being. (F.—L.) ME. *faerie*, *fairye*, *fairy*, 'enchantment;' P. Plowman, B. prol. 6; Chaucer, C. T. 6441 (D 859). [The modern use of the word is improper; the right word for the elf being *fay*. The mistake was made long ago; and fully established before Shakespeare's time.]—OF. *faerie*, enchantment.—OF. *fae* (F. *fée*), a fairy; see **Fay**. Der. *fairy*, adj.

FAITH, belief. (F.—L.) The final *-th* is analogous to the E. suffix *-th*, as seen in *truth*, *ruth*, *wealth*, *health*, and other similar sbs. β. ME. *feiþ*, *feith*, *feyth*; as well as *fey*. The earliest example of the spelling *feith* is in Genesis and Exodus, l. 2187 (ab. 1250). We find *fayth* in the Cursor Mundi, l. 3405; and *fai* occurs in the same poem, ll. 2354 (riming with *delay*), and l. 7562 (riming with *nai*).—OF. *fei*, *feid*, *feit*.—L. *fidem*, acc. of *fides*, faith.+Gk. πίστις, faith; πείθειν, to persuade; πέποιθα, I trust. (√BHEIDH.) Allied to **Bide**. Brugmann, i. § 202. ¶ The assumption that OF. *feit*, *feid* was at first pronounced as *feiþ*, *feið*, is needless. The AF. *fei* appears in Phil. de Thaun, L. des Creatures, l. 244 (before 1150); I believe the *-th* to be a purely E. addition. Der. *faith-ful*, *-ful-ly*, *-ful-ness*; *-less*, *-less-ly*, *-less-ness*. From the same root are *fid-el-i-ty*, *af-fi-ance*, *con-fide*, *de-fy*, *dif-fid-ent*, *per-fid-y*.

FAKIR, a religious mendicant; see **Faquir**.

FALCHION, a bent sword. (F.—Ital.—Late L.) In Shak. L. L. L. v. 2. 618. ME. *fauchon*, P. Plowman, C. xvii. 169; directly from F. *fauchon*, 'a faulchion;' Cot.—Ital. *falcione*, a scimetar.—Late L. *falciōnem*, acc. of *falcio*, a sickle-shaped sword.—L. *falci-*, decl. stem of *falx*, a sickle. Allied to *flec-tere*, to bend; Brugmann, i. § 529 (2). ¶ The word was really taken from the F. *fauchon*, and afterwards altered to *falchion* by the influence of the Ital. form. Der. from L. *falx* are also *falc-on*, *de-falc-ate*.

FALCON, a bird of prey. (F.—L.) ME. *faukon*, King Alisaunder, 567; *faucon*, Chaucer, C. T. 10725 (F 411).—AF. *faucon*, Stat. of the Realm, i. 293 (1340); OF. *faucon*, MF. *faulcon*, 'a faulkon;' Cot.—Late L. *falcōnem*, acc. of *falco*, a falcon; so called from the hooked shape of the claws. 'Falcones dicuntur, quorum digiti pollices in pedibus intro sunt curuati;' Festus, p. 88; qu. in White and Riddle. That is, *falco* is derived from *falc-*, stem of *falx*, a sickle; see above. The *l* in *falcon* was inserted in the 15th century. Der. *falcon-er*; *falcon-ry*, from MF. *faulconnerie* 'a faulconry;' Cot.

FALDSTOOL, a folding-stool. (F.—Low L.—OHG.) Now applied to a low desk at which the litany is said; but formerly to a folding-stool or portable seat. 'Faldstool, a stool placed at the S. side of the altar, at which the kings of England kneel at their coronation;' Blount's Gloss., ed. 1674. He also has: 'Faldistory, the episcopal seat within the chancel.' [Not E., but borrowed from F.]—OF. *faldestoel* (Godefroy).—Low L. *faldistolium*, also *faldistorium* (corruptly), a faldstool.—OHG. *faldan* (G. *falten*), to fold; and *stuol* (G. *stuhl*), a chair, seat, throne. See **Fold** and **Stool**. ¶ We also find AS. *fældestōl*, A. S. Leechdoms, vol. i. p. lxii. l. 3. But had the word been native, it would have been *fold-stool*. See **Fauteuil**.

FALL, to drop down. (E.) ME. *fallen*, Chaucer, C. T. 2664 (A 2662). OMerc. *fallan*, Matt. x. 29; the AS. form being *feallan*.+Du. *vallen*; Icel. *falla*; Dan. *falde* (with excrescent *d*); Swed. *falla*; G. *fallen*. Teut. type **fallan-*. Cf. Lith. *pùlti*, to fall; and perhaps L. *fallere*, to deceive, *falli*, to err. Brugmann, i. § 757. Der. *fall*, sb.; *be-fall*, vb.; and see *fell* (1), *fail*.

FALLACY, a deceptive appearance, error in argument. (F.—L.) In Shak. Errors, ii. 2. 188. Spelt *falacye*, Caxton, Reynard, c. 28; ed. Arber, p. 67, l. 10. A manipulated word, due to the addition of *-y* to ME. *fallace* or *fallas*, in order to bring it nearer to the L. form.

ME. *fallace, fallas*; once common; see P. Plowman, C. xii. 22, and the note; also Gower, C. A. ii. 85; bk. iv. 2509. ‒ F. *fallace*, 'a fallacy;' Cot. ‒ L. *fallācia*, deceit. ‒ L. *fallāc-*, stem of *fallax*, deceptive. ‒ L. *fallere*, to deceive; see **Fail**. Der. *fallacious*, Milton, P. L. ii. 568; *-ous-ly, -ous-ness*; see below.

FALLIBLE, liable to error. (L.) In Shak. Meas. iii. 1. 170; Lydgate, Siege of Troye, bk. i. c. 6; fol. D 6. Late L. *fallibilis*. ‒ L. *fallere*, to deceive, *fallī*, to err; see **Fail**. Der. *fallibl-y*; *fallibili-ty*.

FALLOW (1), untilled. (E.) The meaning 'untilled' is a mere development. The orig. sense was (1) ploughed land; (2) ploughed and harrowed land, left uncropped; and it was at first a sb. ME. *falwe*, ploughed land, Havelok, 2509. AS. *fælging*, fallow land (Corpus gloss. 1385). ‒ AS. *fealg-*, as in *fealg-a*, pl., harrows (for breaking clods); Epinal gloss. 713. Allied to EFries. *falgen*, Low G. *falgen*, to fallow land; OHG. *felga*, a harrow. Der. *fallow*, verb.

FALLOW (2), used with reference to colour; pale brownish, pallid. (E.) 'His hewe *falwe*;' Chaucer, C. T., A 1364. 'Falewe lockes;' fallow locks of hair; Layamon, 18449. OMerc. *falu*; AS. *fealu*, pale red, yellowish red; Grein, i. 286. + Du. *vaal*; Icel. *fölr*, pale; G. *fahl*, pale, also *falb*; Lith. *palvas*. Cf. also L. *pallidus*; Gk. πολιός, gray; Skt. *palita-*, gray. See **Pale**. Brugmann, i. § 375 (9). Hence *fallow deer*; Sir T. Elyot has: 'Dere redde and *falowe*;' Castel of Helth, bk. ii. c. 12.

FALSE, untrue, deceptive. (F. ‒ L.) ME. *fals*, Chaucer, C. T., A 1580; earlier, in O. Eng. Homilies, 1st Ser. p. 185, l. 16. ‒ OF. *fals* (F. *faux*). ‒ L. *falsus*, false; pp. of *fallere*, to deceive; see **Fail**. Der. *false-ly, -ness, -hood* (spelt *falshede* in Chaucer, C. T. 16519, G 1051); *fals-i-fy*, 1 Hen. IV, i. 2. 235; *-i-fic-at-ion, -i-fi-er, -i-ty*; also *falsetto*, from Ital. *falsetto*, treble; also *faucet*, q. v.

FALTER, to totter, stammer. (E.) ME. *falteren, faltren*. 'Thy limes *faltren* ay' = thy limbs ever tremble with weakness; Chaucer, C. T. 5192 (B 772). 'And nawþer *faltered* ne fel' = and he neither gave way nor fell; Gawayne and the Grene Knight, 430. The old sense of to 'stumble,' to 'miss one's footing,' occurs late; 'his legges hath *foltred*' = the horse's legs have given way; Sir T. Elyot, The Governour, b. i. c. 17 (in Spec. of Eng., ed. Skeat, p. 197, l. 78). Formed from a base *falt-*, with frequentative suffix *-er*. Of obscure origin. Perhaps connected with Icel. refl. verb *faltra-sk*, to be cumbered, to be puzzled.

FAME, report, renown. (F. ‒ L.) In early use; King Alisaunder, 6385. ‒ F. *fame*. ‒ L. *fāma*, report. ‒ L. *fārī*, to speak. See **Fate**. Der. *fam-ed*: *fam-ous*, Gower, C. A. ii. 366; bk. v. 7125; *fam-ous-ly*.

FAMILY, a household. (L.) In Shak. Oth. i. 1. 84. Spelt *famylye* in Caxton, Golden Legend; Moses, § 3 from end. ‒ L. *familia*, a household. ‒ L. *famulus*, a servant; Oscan *famel*, a servant (White); cf. Oscan *faamat*, he dwells. Der. *famili-ar* (from L. *familiāris*), also found in ME. in the form *famuler, familier* (from OF. *familier*), Chaucer, C. T. prol. 215; *famili-ar-i-ty, -ar-ise*.

FAMINE, severe hunger. (F. ‒ L.) ME. *famine, famyne*; Chaucer, C. T. 12385 (C 451). ‒ F. *famine*. ‒ Late L. **famina*, unrecorded, but evidently a barbarous derivative from L. *famēs*, hunger. Der. *fam-ish*, Merch. of Ven. ii. 2. 113; formed with suffix *-ish* by analogy with *langu-ish, demol-ish*, and the like, from the base *fam-* in OF. *a-fam-er*, later *affamer*, to famish. This base *fam-* is from L. *fam-ēs*, hunger (F. *faim*).

FAN, an instrument for blowing. (L.) Used by Chaucer to describe a quintain; C. T. 16991 (H 42). AS. *fann*; Matt. iii. 12. Not a native word, but borrowed from Late L. *vannus*, for L. *uannus*, a fan; whence also F. *van*. See **Van** (2). Brugmann, i. § 357. Der. *fan*, verb; *fann-er, fan-light, -palm*.

FANATIC, religiously insane. (F. ‒ L.) 'Fanatick Egypt;' Milton, P. L. i. 480. And in Minsheu (1627). ‒ F. *fanatique*, 'mad, frantick;' Cot. ‒ L. *fānāticus*, (1) belonging to a temple, (2) inspired by a divinity, filled with enthusiasm. ‒ L. *fānum*, a temple; see **Fane**. Der. *fanatic-al, -al-ly, -ism*. ¶ On this word see a passage in Fuller, Mixt Contemplations on these Times, § 50 (Trench).

FANCY, imagination, whim. (F. ‒ L. ‒ Gk.) In Shak. Temp. iv. 122; v. 59. A corruption of the fuller form *fantasy*, Merry Wives, v. 5. 55. ME. *fantasie*, Chaucer, C. T. 6098 (D 516). P. Plowman, A. prol. 36. ‒ OF. *fantasie*, 'the fancy, or fantasie;' Cot. ‒ Late L. *fantasia* or *phantasia*. ‒ Gk. φαντασία, a making visible, imagination. ‒ Gk. φαντάζειν, to make visible; extended from φαίνειν, to bring to light, shine; cf. φάος, light, φάε, he appeared. See **Phantom**. Der. *fancy*, verb; *fanci-ful*. Doublet, *fantasy* (obsolete); whence *fantastic* (Gk. φανταστικός), *-al, -al-ly*. From same root, *epi-phany*, q.v.

FANDANGO, a Spanish dance. (Span.) Dr. Pegge has a note on it in his Anonymiana, cent. viii. § 30 (1818). ‒ Span. *fandango*, 'a dance used in the West Indies;' Pineda. Source uncertain; said to be of negro origin. See Notes on Eng. Etym., p. 88.

FANE, a temple. (L.) In Shak. Cor. i. 10. 20. ‒ L. *fānum*, a temple; from an earlier form **fasnom*; cf. Oscan *fisnam*, a temple,

allied to L. *festus*, festive. See **Feast**. Brugmann, ii. § 66. Der. *fan-at-ic*, q. v.

FANFARE, a flourish of trumpets. (F. ‒ Span.) Spelt *famphar* in Montgomerie, Misc. Poems, xliii. 40 (c. 1605). ‒ F. *fanfare*, 'a sounding of trumpets;' Cot. ‒ Span. *fanfarria*, bluster, loud vaunting; a word of imitative origin. Der. *fanfar-on-ade*, from F. *fanfarronade*, which from Span. *fanfarronada*, bluster, boasting; from Span. *fanfarron*, blustering, *fanfarrear*, to hector, bluster, boast.

FANG, a tusk, claw, talon. (E.) In Shak. K. John, ii. 353. ME. *fang*, a capture; Wallace, xi. 1219. So also AS. *fang* = a taking; A. S. Chron. an. 1016. However, the sb. is derived from the verb. AS. **fōhan*, to seize, only in use in the contracted form *fōn*, of which the pt. t. is *fēng*, and the pp. *gefangen*; the pp. alone survived, whence an infin. mood *fang-(en)* was evolved in dialects. + Du. *vangen*, to catch; Icel. *fā*, to get, seize, pp. *fenginn*; *fang*, a catch of fish, &c.; Dan. *faae*, to get; Swed. *få*, to get, catch; *fång*, a catch; Goth. *fāhan*, to catch; G. *fangen*, to catch; *fang*, a catch, also, a fang, talon. β. All from a Teut. verb **fanhan-*, pt. t. **fefang*, pp. **fang-anoz*; allied to L. *pangere*, to fasten, fix. Brugmann, i. § 421.

FANTASY, FANTASTIC; see **Fancy**.

FANTIGUE, FANTEAGUE, a state of excitement, fit of ill humour. (F. ‒ L.) Spelt *fantique* in 1825. Perhaps suggested by the F. *fanatique*, 'in a frenzie;' Cot. ‒ L. *fānāticus*; see **Fanatic**. ¶ For the loss of the second syllable, cf. *frantic, frenzy*.

FAQUIR, FAKIR, a religious mendicant. (F. ‒ Arab.) 'Not there the *Fakir's* self will wait;' Byron, The Giaour, § 11. ‒ F. *faquir, fakir*. ‒ Arab. *faqīr*, one of a religious order of mendicants; lit. 'poor, indigent;' Rich. Dict., p. 1096. See *Fakeer* in Yule.

FAR, remote. (E.) ME. *fer*, Chaucer, C. T. 496 (A 494); *feor*, Layamon, 543. AS. *feor*; Grein, i. 289. + Du. *ver*; Icel. *fjarri*; Swed. *fjerran*, adv. afar; Dan. *fjern*, adj. and adv.; G. *fern*; Goth. *fairra*, adv. β. All allied to Gk. πέραν, beyond; Skt. *paras*, beyond; *para-*, far, distant. See **Far**. Der. *far-th-er, far-th-est*; see **Farther**.

FARCE, a kind of comedy. (F. ‒ L.) The orig. sense is 'stuffing;' hence, a jest inserted into comedies. 'These counterfaityng plaiers of *farces* and mummeries;' Lord Berners, Golden Book, c. 14. Hence Ben Jonson speaks of 'other men's jests, ... to *farce* their scenes withal;' Induction to Cynthia's Revels. ‒ F. *farce*, 'a fond and dissolute play; ... any stuffing in meats;' Cot. ‒ F. *farcer*, to stuff. ‒ L. *farcīre*, to stuff. + Gk. φράσσειν, to shut in. See **Force** (2). Der. *farc-ic-al*; and see *frequent*.

FARCY, a disease of horses, somewhat like glanders. (F. ‒ L.) '*Farsye*, a sore upon a beast or horse;' Huloet (1552). Also called *farcin*, and even *fashion* or *fashions*. ‒ F. *farcin*, 'the farsy in a horse;' Cot. ‒ L. *farcīminum*, a disease in horses and other animals. ‒ L. *farcī-re*, to cram, stuff (above). See Tam. Shrew, iii. 2. 53.

FARDEL, a pack, bundle. (F. ‒ Span. ‒ Arab.) In Shak. Hamlet, iii. 1. 76. ME. *fardel*, Rom. of the Rose, 5683; Cursor Mundi, 5004. ‒ OF. *fardel*, the true old form of *fardeau*, 'a fardle, burthen, truss, pack;' Cot. Cf. Low L. *fardellus*, a burden, pack, bundle. *Fard-el* is a dimin. of F. *farde*, a burden, still in use in the sense of 'bale of coffee.' ‒ Span. (and Port.) *fardel, fardo*, a pack, bundle. β. Origin uncertain; but prob. from Arabic. Devic (Supp. to Littré) cites Arab. *fardah*, a package.

FARE, to travel, speed. (E.) ME. *faren*, Chaucer, C. T. 10802 (F 488). AS. *faran*, Grein, i. 264. + Du. *varen*; Icel. and Swed. *fara*; Dan. *fare*; OHG. *faran*, G. *fahren*; Goth. *faran*, to go. Teut. type **faran-* (pt. t. **fōr*). + Gk. πορεύομαι, I travel, go; πόρος, a way through; περάω, I pass through; L. *ex-per-ior*, I pass through, experience; Skt. *pr̥*, to bring over. ‒ √ PER, to pass over or through. Der. *fare-well* = may you speed well, ME. *fare wel*, Chaucer, C. T. 2762; and see *far, fer-ry*; also *thorough-fare*, a passage through; *welfare*, successful journey or state. From the same root are *ex-per-ience, ex-per-iment, port* (1), q. v., *per-il*.

FARINA, ground corn. (L.) The adj. *farinaceous* is in Sir T. Browne, Vulg. Errors, b. iii. c. 15. § 2. The sb. occurs in 1707. ‒ L. *farina*, meal. ‒ L. *far*, a kind of grain, spelt; cognate with E. **Barley**, q. v. Brugmann, i. § 180. Der. *farin-ac-e-ous* (L. *farināceus*).

FARM, ground let for cultivation. (F. ‒ L.) ME. *ferme*, Chaucer, C. T. 253. 'He sette .. [h]is londes *to ferme*;' Rob. of Glouc., p. 378, l. 7773. [Cf. also AS. *feorm*, a feast, entertainment; Luke, xiv. 12, 16; also food, hospitality, property, use; see Grein, i. 293.] AF. *ferme*, Stat. Realm, i. 140 (1300). ‒ OF. *ferme*, a farm; *à ferme*, on lease. ‒ Late L. *firma*, a feast, a farm, a tribute; also, a lasting oath. ‒ L. *firmus*, firm, durable. See **Firm**. ¶ For the curious use of the word, see *firma* in Ducange. Der. *farm*, verb; *-er, -ing*.

FARRAGO, a confused mass. (L.) 'That collection, or *farago* of prophecies;' Howell's Letters, b. iii. let. 22 (1648). ‒ L. *farrāgo*, mixed fodder for cattle, a medley. ‒ L. *far*, spelt (gen. *farr-is*). See **Farina**.

FARRIER, a shoer of horses. (F. ‒ L.) Lit. 'a worker in iron.'

Spelt *ferrer* in Holland's Pliny, b. xxxiii. c. 11. Cotgrave has: 'mareschal ferrant, a *farrier.*'—OF. *ferrier*, a farrier (Godefroy).—L. *ferrārius*, a blacksmith, worker in iron.—L. *ferrum*, iron. See **Ferreous. Der.** *farrier-y.*

FARROW, to produce a litter of pigs. (E.) 'That thair sow *ferryit* wes thar'='that their sow had farrowed, lit. was farrowed; Barbour's Bruce, xvii. 701. Also *i-varȝed*, pp. (from infin. *varȝen*), Ayenb. of Inwyt, p. 61, l. 29. [Cf. Dan. *fare*, to farrow.] Formed, as a verb, from ME. *farh*, which means (not a litter, but) a single pig. The word is scarce, but the pl. *faren* occurs in King Alisaunder, 2411. AS. *fearh*, a pig; the pl. *fearas* occurs in Ælf. Gloss., ed. Somner, Nomina Ferarum, explained by 'suilli, vel porcelli, vel nefrendes.'+ Du. *varken* (dimin.), a pig; OHG. *farah*, a pig; whence G. dimin. *ferk-el*, a pig.+L. *porcus*, a pig. See **Pork.**

FARTHER, FARTHEST, more far, most far. (E.) In Shak. Ant. and Cleop. ii. 1. 31; iii. 2. 26. These forms are due to a mistake, and to confusion with *further, furthest*; see **Further.** Not found at all early; the ME. forms are *fer, ferre, ferrer*, and *ferrest.* 'Than walkede I *ferrer*;' P. Plowman's Crede, 207; 'The *ferrest* in his parisch;' Chaucer, C. T. 496 (A 494). *Ferther* first appears as an adv.; Cursor Mundi, 6831 (ab. 1300). *Ferthest* first appears as an adj.; P. Plowman, B. v. 239 (ab. 1377).

FARTHING, the fourth part of a penny. (E.) ME. *ferthing, ferthynge*; P. Plowman, B. iv. 54. AS. *fēorðing, fērþyng*, Matt. v. 26 (Royal and Hatton MSS.); older form *fēorðling* (Camb. MS.).—AS. *fēorð-a*, fourth; with dimin. suffix *-ing* or *-ling* (=*-l-ing*). Allied to AS. *fēower*, four. See **Four.**

FARTHINGALE, FARDINGALE, a hooped petticoat. (F.—Span.—L.) In Shak. Two Gent. ii. 7. 51; a corrupt form.— MF. *verdugalle*, 'a vardingall;' Cot. Also *vertugalle*, 'a vardingale;' *vertugadin*, 'a little vardingale;' id.—Span. *verdugado*, a fardingale; so called from its hoops, the literal sense being 'provided with hoops.' —Span. *verdugo*, a young shoot of a tree, a rod.—Span. *verde*, green.— L. *uiridis*, green. See **Verdant.** ¶ The derivation from 'virtue-guard' is a very clumsy invention or else a joke. The word was well understood; hence the term 'his *verdugo-ship*' in Ben Jonson, The Alchemist, iii. 2 (Face).

FASCINATE, to enchant. (L.) '*Fascination* is ever by the eye;' Bacon, Nat. Hist. § 944. 'To *fascinate* or bewitch;' id. Essay 9, Of Envy.—L. *fascinātus*, pp. of *fascināre*, to enchant.—L. *fascinum*, a spell. **Der.** *fascinat-ion.*

FASCINE, a bundle of rods. (F.—L.) First found ab. 1688; and still a new term in 1711; see Spectator, no. 165. '*Fascines*, faggots or bavins;' Kersey, ed. 1715.—F. *fascine*, 'a faggot;' Cot.—L. *fascina*, a bundle of sticks.—L. *fasci-s*, a bundle. **Der.** From the same source, *fascēs*, pl. of L. *fascis*; *fasci-c-ul-ate*; *fess.*

FASH, to trouble, annoy, vex. (F.—L.) Common in Northern dialects; see E. D. D.—MF. *fascher* (F. *fâcher*), to displease, vex; Cot.—Folk L. *fasticāre*, to show arrogance; from L. *fastus*, arrogance (Hatzfeld).

FASHION, the make or cut of a thing. (F.—L.) ME. *faciun*, Cursor Mundi, l. 22322; *fasoun*, Rom. of the Rose, 551; *fassoun*, Dunbar, Thistle and Rose, st. 12.—OF. *faceon, façon*, form, shape.— L. *factiōnem*, acc. of *factio*, a making. See **Faction. Doublet,** *faction.* **Der.** *fashion*, verb, *-able, -abl-y.*

FAST (1), firm, fixed. (E.) ME. *fast*, Chaucer, prol. 200, 290. *faste*, Chaucer, C. T. 721 (A 719). AS. *fæst*, Grein, i. 271.+Du. *vast*; Dan. and Swed. *fast*; Icel. *fastr*; OHG. *vast*; G. *fest.* Teut. type **fastoz.* Cf. Armenian *hast*, firm. Brugmann, ii. § 79. **Der.** *fast*, verb (below); *fast-en*, q. v.; *fast-ness*, q. v. ¶ The phrase '*fast* asleep' is Scandinavian; Icel. *sofa fast*, to be fast asleep; see **Fast** (3).

FAST (2), to abstain from food. (E.) ME. *fasten*, Wyclif, Matt. vi. 16. AS. *fæstan*, Matt. vi. 16.+Du. *vasten*; Dan. *faste*; Swed. and Icel. *fasta*; Goth. *fastan*; G. *fasten.* β. A very early derivative from Teutonic *fast-*, firm, in the sense to be firm, observe, be strict. See **Fast** (1). **Der.** *fast*, sb., *fast-er, fast-ing, fast-day.*

FAST (3), quick, speedy. (Scand.) Merely a peculiar use of *fast*, firm. Chaucer has *faste*=quickly; C. T. 16150 (G 682). The peculiar usage is Scandinavian, and arose in the adverb. Cf. Icel. *drekka fast*, to drink hard; *sofa fast*, to be fast asleep; *fylgja fast*, to follow fast; *fastr ī verkum*, hard at work; *leita fast eptir*, to urge, press hard after. The development is through the senses 'closely,' 'urgently.' See **Fast** (1).

FASTEN, to secure. (E.) ME. *fastnen, festnen*; Chaucer has *festne*, prol. 195. AS. *fæstnian*, to make firm or fast; Grein, i. 273. —AS. *fæst*, fast, firm. See **Fast** (1). **Der.** *fasten-ing.* ¶ Observe that *fasten* stands for *fastn-* in AS. *fæstn-ian*, so that the *-en* is truly formative, not a sign of the infin. mood or a late addition.

FASTIDIOUS, over-nice. (L.) Orig. in the sense of 'causing disgust,' or 'loathsome;' Sir T. Elyot, The Governour, b. i. c. 9; see Trench (Select Glossary).—L. *fastīdiōsus*, disdainful, disgusting.—L.

fastīdium, loathing; for **fastu-tīdium.*—L. *fastus*, arrogance; and *tædium*, disgust. See **Dare** and **Tedious.** ¶ 'Bréal conjectures (Zeitschrift, xx. 79), I think rightly, that L. *fastus* (for **farstus*) and *fastīdium* (for **fasti-tīdium*) belong to this root,' viz. DHERS, to dare; Curtius, i. 318. **Der.** *fastidious-ly, -ness.*

FASTNESS, a stronghold. (E.) ME. *festnes*, Metrical Psalter, xvii. 2. (Spec. of Eng., part ii. p. 25.) The same as ME. *fastnesse*, certainty, strength; Wyclif, Gen. xli. 32 (early version). AS. *fæstnes, fæstnis*, the firmament; Gen. i. 6.—AS. *fæst*, firm; with suffix *-nes.* See **Fast** (1).

FAT (1), stout, gross. (E.) ME. *fat*, Chaucer, prol. 200, 290. AS. *fæt, fætt*, orig. a pp., contracted from **fæted*, fatted, enriched; Grein, i. 273.+OHG. *feizit* (G. *feist*), pp. of a Teut. verb **faitjan-*, to make fat, formed from a Teut. adj. **faitoz*, fat, which is represented by Icel. *feitr*, fat (Swed. *fet*, Dan. *fed*). β. Related to Gk. πίων, πιαρός, fat; Skt. *pīvan*, fat. **Der.** *fat*, sb., *fatt-y, fatt-i-ness, fat-ness*, Rom. of the Rose, 2686; *fatt-en*, where the *-en* is a late addition, by analogy with *fasten*, &c., the true verb being to *fat*, as in Luke, xv. 23, Chaucer, C. T. 7462 (D 1880); *fatt-en-er, -en-ing*; *fat-ling* (=*fat-l-ing*), Matt. xxii. 4.

FAT (2), a vat. (North E.) Joel, ii. 24, iii. 13. See **Vat.**

FATE, destiny. (F.—L.) ME. *fate*, Chaucer, Troil. v. 1552.—OF. *fat*, fate; not common (Godefroy).—L. *fātum*, what is spoken, fate.—L. *fātus*, pp. of *fāri*, to speak. Allied to Gk. φημί (Doric φαμί), I say. (√BHA.) Brugmann, i. § 187. ¶ Perhaps E. *fate* was simply made from the common OF. *fatal* (whence ME. *fatal*, Chaucer, C. T. 4681, B 261) in order to render L. *fātum.* **Der.** *fat-al, -ed*; *fatal-i-ty, -ism*; *fay*, q. v.; *fairy*, q. v.

FATHER, a male parent. (E.) ME. *fader*, Chaucer, C. T. 8098 (E 222). [The spelling *fader* is almost universal in ME.; *father* occurs in the Bible of 1551, and is due to dialectal influence, which changed *-der* to *-ther.*] AS. *fæder*, Matt. vi. 9.+Du. *vader*; Dan. and Swed. *fader*; Icel. *faðir*; Goth. *fadar*; G. *vater.*+L. *pater*; Gk. πατήρ; Pers. *pidar*; Skt. *pitṛ*; Irish *athair.* Idg. type **pater-.* **Der.** *father*, verb; *father-hood, -less, -ly*; also *father-land*, imitated from the Dutch by I. D'Israeli; see his Curiosities of Literature, Hist. of New Words. But it occurs earlier, in 1623.

FATHOM, a measure of 6 feet. (E.) Properly, the breadth reached to by the extended arms. ME. *fadme*, Chaucer, C. T., A 2918; *ueðme*, Layamon, 27686. AS. *fæðm*, the space reached by the extended arms, a grasp, embrace; Grein, i. 268. + Du. *vadem*, a fathom; Icel. *faðmr*, a fathom; Dan. *favn*, an embrace, fathom; Swed. *famn*, embrace, bosom, arms; G. *faden* (OHG. *fadam*), a fathom, a thread. Cf. L. *patēre*, to lie open, extend; *patulus*, spreading. See **Patent. Der.** *fathom*, vb. (AS. *fæðman*, Grein); *fathom-able, -less.*

FATIGUE, weariness. (F.—L.) '*Fatigue*, weariness;' Blount's Gloss. ed. 1674. '*Fatigate*, to weary;' id. (obsolete).—OF. *fatigue*, 'weariness;' Cot.—OF. *fatiguer*, to weary; id.—L. *fatīgāre*, to weary (whence *fatigate*, in Shak. Cor. ii. 2. 121). Connected with L. *fessus*, wearied, *fatiscere*, to gape open (Bréal); and perhaps with OLat. *adfatim*, sufficiently. **Der.** *fatigue*, verb. ¶ In French, the sb. is from the verb; in E., the reverse.

FATUOUS, silly. (L.) In Donne, Devotions, ed. 1625, p. 25 (Todd).—L. *fatu-us*, silly, feeble; with suffix *-ous*, for L. *-us.* **Der.** *fatu-i-ty*; *in-fatu-ate.*

FAUCES, the upper part of the throat. (L.) L. pl. *fauces*; of uncertain origin; but prob. allied to Gk. χάος. See **Chaos.**

FAUCET, a spigot, vent. (F.—L.) In Wyclif, Job, xxxii. 19.— OF. (and F.) *fausset*, 'a faucet,' Cot.; also spelt *faulset*, id. Origin uncertain; but perhaps from OF. *faulser*, to falsify, to forge; whence '*faulser vn escu*, to pierce or strike through a shield, to make a breach into it;' id.—L. *falsāre*, to falsify.—L. *falsus*, false. See **False.** ¶ See OF. *falser*, to pierce; Supp. to Godefroy.

FAULT, a failing, defect. (F.—L.) ME. *faute*, with the sense 'lack,' Cursor Mundi, 4504.—OF. *faute*, a fault. The *l* is due to the insertion of *l* in the 15th century; thus we find 'for *faulte* of trust;' Lord Rivers, Dictes of Philosophers, pr. by Caxton, fol. 20 b, l. 4; and Cotgrave has: '*Faulte*, a fault.' [Cf. Span., Port., and Ital. *falta*, a defect, want.]—OF. *faute*, a fault.—Folk-L. **fallita*, a defect; fem. of **fallitus*, new pp. of L. *fallere*, to beguile; *fallī*, to err. See **Fail. Der.** *fault-y, -i-ly, -i-ness*; *fault-less, -less-ly, -less-ness.*

FAUN, a rural (Roman) deity. (L.) ME. *faun*, Chaucer, C. T. 2930 (A 2928).—L. *Faunus.* Perhaps from L. *fauere*, to be propitious; pp. *fautus.* See **Favour. Der.** *faun-a.*

FAUTEUIL, an arm-chair. (F.—Low L.—G.) Mod. F. *fauteuil*; MF. *fauldetueil* (Cot.).—Low L. *faldistolium.* See **Faldstool.**

FAVOUR, kindliness, grace. (F.—L.) ME. *fauour* (with *u=v*), King Alisaunder, 2844.—OF. *favour*, F. *faveur*, 'favour;' Cot.—L. *fauōrem*, acc. of *fauor*, favour.—L. *fauēre*, to befriend; orig. to venerate. **Der.** *favour*, verb; *favour-able*, P. Plowman, B. iii. 153; *-abl-y, -able-ness*; also *favour-ite*, Shak. Much Ado, iii. 1. 9, orig. feminine, from OF. *favorite*, fem. of *favorit* or *favori*, favoured (Cot.);

favour-it-iem. Also *favonian*, gentle; from *Fauōnius*, the west wind; from *fau-ēre*, to favour. Brugmann, i. § 664. ☞ On the phr. *curry favour*, see **Curry**.

FAWN (1), to cringe to, rejoice servilely over. (E.) ME. *faunen, fauhnen* ; P. Plowman, B. xv. 295 ; C. xviii. 31. AS. *fahnian, fagnian*, to rejoice ; variants of *fægenian*, to fawn ; from *fægen*, fain, glad.+Icel. *fagna*, to rejoice, be fain ; *fagna einum*, to welcome one, receive with good cheer. See **Fain**. Der. *fawn-er, -ing*.

FAWN (2), a young deer. (F.—L.) ME. *fawn*, Chaucer, Book of the Duchess, 429.—OF. *fan, faon*, 'a fawne,' Cot. ; earlier *feōn* (Supp. to Godefroy).—Late L. **fētōnem*, acc. of **fētō*, a young one (not found), an extension of L. *fœtus*, offspring. See **Fetus**.

FAY, a fairy. (F.—L.) See the 'Song by two *faies*' in Ben Jonson's Oberon.—F. *fée*, a fairy, elf ; cf. Port. *fada*, Ital. *fata*, a fay.—Late L. *fāta*, a fairy, 'in an inscription of Diocletian's time' (Brachet) ; lit. 'a fate, goddess of destiny.'—L. *fāta*, pl. of *fātum*, fate ; later used as f. sing. See **Fate**. Der. *fai-ry*, q. v.

FEALTY, true service. (F.—L.) ME. *feautè*, Rob. of Brunne, tr. of Langtoft, p. 3 ; *feutè*, King Alisaunder, 2911. [The spelling *fealty* is later in E., though a better form ; see *feaultè* in Cotgrave ; but AF. *fealtè* occurs in Gaimar, l. 3719.]—OF. *fealtè, feelteit*, fidelity.—L. *fidēlitātem*, acc. of *fidēlitās*. See **Fidelity**, of which *fealty* is a doublet.

FEAR, terror. (E.) ME. *fere*, P. Plowman, B. xiii. 162 ; better spelt *feer*. AS. *fǣr*, a sudden peril, danger, panic, fear ; Grein, i. 277. Orig. used of the danger of travelling.—AS. *fǣr-*, 3rd stem of *faran*, to go, travel.+Icel. *fár*, bale, harm, mischief ; OHG. *fāra, vār*, treason, danger, fright, whence G. *gefahr*, danger ; Du. *gevaar*, danger. Cf. also L. *periculum*, danger, *experior*, I go through, experience ; also Gk. πεῖρα, an attempt, from περάω, I go through. —√PER, to pass through, travel ; whence E. *fare*, verb. See **Fare** and **Peril**. Der. *fear*, verb, often used actively = to frighten, terrify, as in Shak. Tam. Shrew, i. 2. 211 ; *fear-ful, -ful-ly, -ful-ness* ; *-less, -less-ly, -less-ness*.

FEASIBLE, easy to be done. (F.—L.) ' 'Tis *feasible*;' Massinger, Emp. of the East, i. 2. 76. [Also *feasable*.]—MF. *faisible, faisable*, 'feasible, doable ;' Cot.—F. *fais-*, as in *fais-ant*, pres. pt. of *faire*, to do.—L. *facere*, to do. See **Fact**. Der. *feasibl-y, feasible-ness, feasibil-i-ty*.

FEAST, a festival, holiday. (F.—L.) ME. *feste* ; Ancren Riwle, p. 22.—OF. *feste* (F. *fête*).—Late L. *festa*, fem.—L. *festa*, lit. 'festivals ;' pl. of *festum*, a feast, orig. neuter of *festus*, joyful. Allied to **Fair** (2). Der. *feast*, verb ; see *festal, fête*.

FEAT, a deed well done. (F.—L.) ME. *feet, feite, faite* ; P. Plowman, B. i. 184.—AF. *fet*, Statutes of the Realm, i. 47 (1278) ; OF. (and F.) *fait*.—L. *factum*, a deed. See **Fact**, of which *feat* is a doublet ; and see *feature*.

FEATHER, a plume. (E.) ME. *fether*, Chaucer, C. T. 2146 (A 2144). AS. *feðer* ; Grein, i. 278.+Du. *veder* ; Dan. *fjæder* ; Swed. *fjäder* ; Icel. *fjöðr* ; G. *feder*. + L. *penna* (for **pet-sna*) ; Gk. πτερόν, a wing ; Skt. *patra-*, a feather. Teut. type *feðrō*, f. ; Idg. type *petrā*. —√PET, to fly, fall. See **Pen**. Der. *feather*, verb ; *feather-y*.

FEATURE, make, fashion, shape, face. (F.—L.) ME. *feture*, Chaucer, C. T. 17070 (H 121).—AF. *feture*, Havelok, 743 ; OF. *faiture*, fashion.—L. *factūra*, formation, work.—L. *facere*, to make. See **Fact, Feat**. Der. *featur-ed, feature-less*.

FEBRILE, relating to fever. (F.—L.) Used by Harvey (Todd's Johnson).—F. *febrile*.—L. **febrilis* (not in Lewis's Dict.), relating to fever.—L. *febris*, a fever. Der. *febrifuge* (F. *fébrifuge*, L. *febrifugia*) ; from L. *fugāre*, to put to flight.

FEBRUARY, the second month. (L.). Englished from L. *Februārius*, the month of expiation ; named from *februa*, neut. pl., a Roman festival of expiation celebrated on the 15th of this month.—L. *februum*, purification, a word of Sabine origin ; whence also *februāre*, to expiate.

FECKLESS, ineffective. (F.—L. ; *with* E. *suffix*.) Formerly *fectless*, and short for *effectless* ; see **Effect**. ' A *fectless* arrogant conceit of their greatnesse ;' K. James I., Basilikon Doron, § 17.

FECULENT, relating to fæces ; see **Fæces**.

FECUNDITY, fertility. (F.—L.) In Blount's Gloss., ed. 1674. ME. *fecundité*, Palladius on Husbandry, bk. i. st. 9, l. 57.—OF. *fecondité* (Cot.), with *o* altered to *u* to bring it nearer Latin.—L. *fēcunditātem*, acc. of *fēcunditās*, fruitfulness.—L. *fēcundus*, fruitful ; from the same source as **Fetus**, q. v.

FEDERAL, belonging to a covenant. (F.—L.) In Kersey's Dict., ed. 1715. [Wyclif has *federed* = bound by covenant, Prov. xvii. 9.]—F. *fédéral*. Formed as if from L. **fœderālis*, from *fœder-*, for **fœdes*, stem of *fœdus*, a treaty, covenant ; akin to L. *fides*, faith ; see **Fidelity**. Der. *feder-ate*, from L. *fœderātus*, pp. of *fœderāre*, to bind by treaty ; *federat-ive* ; also *con-federate*.

FEE, a grant of land, fief, payment. (F.—OHG. ?) ME. *fee*.

There are two words of this form ; (1) property, cattle, AS. *feoh, fēo*, which is obsolete ; and (2), fief, payment, which alone survives and is here considered. Rob. of Brunne, tr. of Langtoft, p. 63, has : 'vnto tham tuo he gaf Gryffyns *feez*,' i.e. estates, fiefs. Cf. 'Held .. Normundie *in fe* ;' i.e. by feudal homage ; id. p. 86.—AF. *fee* ; as in Liber Custumarum, p. 469 : 'come soun droit et soun *fee*,' as his right and his fee ; OF. *fé, fié, fiu, fieu, fief* (see *fief* in Supp. to Godefroy).—Late L. *fevum*, a fief (Ducange). Prob. from OHG. *fehu*, payment, wages, a particular use of *fehu*, property (G. *vieh*).+ Du. *vee*, Icel. *fé*, Dan. *fæ*, Swed. *fä*, Goth. *faihu* ; L. *pecus* ; Skt. *paçu-*, cattle. (√PEK.) Also cognate with AS. *feoh*, property (above). Doublet, *fief*. Der. *fee*, verb ; *fee-simple*, Chaucer, C. T. 321.

FEEBLE, weak. (F.—L.) ME. *feble*, Ancren Riwle, p. 54 ; Havelok, 323.—AF. *feble*, Stat. Realm, i. 273 ; OF. *foible*, oldest form *fleble* (Godefroy) ; cf. Ital. *fievole*, feeble, where *i* is for *l*, as usual in Italian.—L. *flēbilis*, mournful, tearful, doleful.—L. *flē-re*, to weep. Brugmann, ii. § 590. Der. *feebl-y, feeble-ness*. Doublet, *foible*.

FEED, to take food. (E.) ME. *feden* ; Chaucer, C. T. 146. AS. *fēdan* ; Grein, i. 284. [For *fōdian*, by vowel-change from *ō* to *ē*.] —AS. *fōd*, food. So also Du. *voeden*, Icel. *fœða*, Swed. *föda*, Dan. *føde*, Goth. *fōdjan*, OHG. *fuotan*. Teut. type **fōdjan-*. See **Food**. Der. *feed-er*.

FEEL, to perceive by the touch. (E.) ME. *felen*, Chaucer, C. T. 2807 (A 2805). AS. *fēlan*, Grein, i. 285.+Du. *voelen* ; G. *fühlen* ; OHG. *fuolan*. Teut. type **fōljan-* ; from **fōl-*, 2nd grade of Teut. base **fal-* ; whence Icel. *fal-ma*, to grope ; cf. AS. *fol-m*, palm of the hand, L. *pal-ma*. Allied to **Palm** (1). Der. *feel-er, -ing*.

FEEZE, FEAZE, PHEESE, to drive away. (E.) Properly to drive away, put to flight ; hence, to worry, fret, punish ; see Tam. Shrew, Ind. i. 1 ; Troilus, ii. 3. 215 ; gloss. to York Mysteries, and Stratmann. OMerc. *fēsian*, to drive away ; Wulfstan, ed. Napier, p. 162, l. 18 ; AS. *fýsian*.+Swed. *fösa*, to drive away ; Norw. *föysa*. Teut. type **faus-jan-*.

FEIGN, to pretend. (F.—L.) ME. *feignen, feynen, feinen*, Rob. of Glouc. p. 336, l. 6906.—F. *feindre*, to feign ; pres. pt. *feign-ant*.—L. *fingere*, to feign. See **Figure**. Der. *feign-ed-ly, -ed-ness* ; also *feint* (in Kersey, ed. 1715), from F. *feinte*, fem. of *feint*, pp. of *feindre* ; and see *faint, fiction*.

FELDSPAR, a kind of mineral. (G.) First in 1757 ; with the spelling *feldspath*. Corrupted from G. *feldspath*, lit. 'field-spar.'—G. *feld*, a field, cognate with E. *field* ; and *spath*, spar ; see **Field** and **Spar** (2).

FELICITY, happiness. (F.—L.) ME. *felicitee*, Chaucer, C. T. 7985 (E109).—OF. *felicité*.—L. *fēlicitātem*, acc. of *fēlicitās*, happiness. —L. *fēlici-*, decl. stem of *fēlix*, happy, fruitful ; from the same root as *feline* (below). Der. *felicit-ous, -ous-ly* ; also *felicit-ate*, a coined word first used as a pp., as in King Lear, i. 1. 76 ; *-at-ion*.

FELINE, pertaining to the cat. (L.) In Johnson's Dict. First used in 1681.—L. *fēlīnus*, feline.—L. *fēleˢ*, a cat ; prob. allied to L. *fēlāre*, to suckle, and to Gk. θῆλυς, female (see Bréal).

FELL (1), to cause to fall, cut down. (E.) ME. *fellen* ; ' it wolde *felle* an oke ;' Chaucer, C. T. 1704 (A 1702). OMerc. *fællan*, AS. *fyllan*, Grein, i. 360 ; formed, as a causal, by vowel-change, from OMerc. *fallan*, AS. *feallan*, to fall.+Du. *vellen*, causal of *vallen* ; Dan. *fælde*, caus. of *falde* ; Swed. *fälla*, caus. of *falla* ; Icel. *fella*, caus. of *falla* ; G. *fällen*, caus. of *fallen*. Teut. type **falljan-*. See **Fall**. Der. *fell-er*.

FELL (2), a skin. (E.) ME. *fel*, Wyclif, Job, ii. 4 (early version). AS. *fel, fell*, Grein, i. 278.+Du. *vel* ; Icel. *fell* (App. to Dict. p. 773) ; Goth. *-fill*, skin, in the comp. *thrutsfill*, leprosy ; MHG. *vel*.+L. *pellis* ; Gk. πέλλα. Der. *fell-monger*, a dealer in skins. Doublet, *pell*. Der. *fil-m*.

FELL (3), cruel, fierce. (F.—Late L.—L. ?) ME. *fel*, Chaucer, C. T. 7584 (D 2002).—OF. *fel*, cruel, furious (Godefroy) ; Walloon *fel*, cruel, furious ; Ital. *fello*, cruel.—Late L. *fello, felo*, a malefactor, felon. Perhaps from L. *fel*, gall ; cf. Du. dial. *fel*, sharp, biting, acrid (Molema). Closely connected with *felon* ; see **Felon**. Der. *fel-ly, fell-ness*.

FELL (4), a hill. (Scand.) ME. *fel*, Sir Gawain and the Green Knight, 723.—Icel. *fjall, fell*, a mountain ; Dan. *fjæld* ; Swed. *fjall*. β. Probably allied to G. *fels*, a rock (Kluge). Cf. Gk. πέλλα, a stone.

FELLAH, a peasant, tiller of the soil. (Arab.) First used in 1743 ; pl. *fellahin*.—Arab. *fellāḥ* (Devic), *fallāḥ* (Rich. Dict. p. 1098), a farmer, villager, peasant. — Arab. root *falaḥa*, to plough, till the ground.

FELLOE, rim of a wheel ; see **Felly**.

FELLOW, a partner, associate. (Scand.) ME. *felawe*, Chaucer, C. T. 397 (A 395) ; *fela3e*, King Horn, ed. Lumby, 996.—Icel. *félagi*, a partner in a 'félag.'—Icel. *félag*, companionship, association, lit. 'a laying together of property ;' as if 'fee-lay.'—Icel. *fé*, property, cognate with AS. *feoh*, cattle, property, L. *pecus* ; and *lag*, a laying together. See **Law**. Der. *fellow-ship*, spelt *feolauschipe* in the Ancren Riwle, p. 160.

FELLY, FELLOE, part of the rim of a wheel. (E.) In Shak. Hamlet, ii. 2. 517. ME. *felwe*, Prompt. Parv. p. 154. AS. *felge*, also *felg*, fem. sb., a felly. ‘For þām þe ǣlces spācan bið ōþer ende fæst on þǣre næfe, oþer on ðǣre selge’ = because the one end of each spoke is fixed in the nave, the other in the felly; Boethius, c. 39, sect. 7 (lib. iv. pr. 6).+Du. *velg*; MDu. *velge*; Dan. *fælge*; G. *felge*; cf. Low G. *falge*, a felly. β. So named from the pieces of the rim being put together; from Teut. verb **felhan-*, to fit together; found in this sense in OHG. *felahan*, to put together, also, to hide; allied to Goth. *filhan*, to hide, and Icel. *fela*, to hide, preserve. The AS. *fēolan* (for *feolhan) means to stick, to be joined to.

FELON, a wicked person. (F.—Late L.—L.?) ME. *felun*, Floriz, ed. Lumby, 247, 329; *felonie* (= felony), id. 331.—OF. *felon*, a traitor, wicked man.—Late L. *fellōnem, felōnem*, acc. of *fello, felo*, a traitor, rebel. See **Fell** (3). Der. *felon-y, -i-ous, -i-ous-ly, -i-ous-ness*.

FELSPAR, the same as **Feldspar**, q. v.

FELT, cloth made by matting wool together. (E.) ME. *felt*, Allit. Poems, ed. Morris, B. 1689. AS. *felt*, Voc. 120. 5.+Du. *vilt*; Low G., Swed., Dan. *filt*; G. *filz*. Prob. allied to G. *falzen*, to groove, to fit together. See **Anvil**. Der. *felt*, vb., *-er, -ing*. Also *filter*, q. v.

FELUCCA, a kind of small ship. (Ital.—Arab.) In use in the Mediterranean Sea. Spelt *felucco*; Sandys’ Travels (1632); p. 274. —Ital. *feluca*; cf. Span. *faluca*.—Arab. *fulk*, a ship; Rich. Dict. p. 1099. (See Devic.)

FEMALE, of the weaker sex. (F.—L.) An accommodated spelling, to make it look more like *male*. ME. *femele*, Gower, C. A. ii. 45, bk. iv. 1301; P. Plowman, B. xi. 331.—OF. *femelle*, ‘female;’ Cot.—L. *fēmella*, a young woman; dimin. of *fēmina*, a woman. See **Feminine**.

FEMININE, womanly. (F.—L.) In Shak. L. L. L. iv. 2. 83; Chaucer, Ho. of Fame, 1365.—OF. *feminin*, ‘feminine;’ Cot.—L. *fēminīnus.*—L. *fēmina*, a woman. β. Allied to L. *fēlāre*, to suckle; Gk. θῆλυς, female, θηλή, the breast; Skt. *dhātri*, a nurse. Brugmann, i. § 134. Der. (from L. *fēmina*), *female*, q. v.; also *ef-femin-ate*.

FEMORAL, belonging to the thigh. (L.) In Johnson’s Dict.— L. *femorālis*; formed from *femor-*, stem of *femur*, the thigh.

FEN, a morass, bog. (E.) ME. *fen*, King Alisaunder, 3965. AS. *fenn*, Grein, i. 281.+Du. *veen*; Icel. *fen*; Goth. *fani*, mud. Teut. type *fanjom, n. Cf. OPruss. *pannean*, a morass. Der. *fenn-y*.

FENCE, a guard, hedge. (F.—L.) Merely an abbreviation for *defence*. ‘Without weapon or *fense*’ = defence; Udall, on Luke, c. 10. v. 3. ME. *fenss*, in the sense of ‘parrying with a sword,’ Barbour, Bruce, xx. 384. Cf. ‘The place ... was barryd and *fensyd* for the same entent;’ Fabyan’s Chron. an. 1408-9. ‘*Fence*, or *defence*;’ Prompt. Parv. See **Defence**, and **Fend**. Der. *fence*, verb, (1) to enclose, (2) to practise fencing; *fenc-ing, -ible*.

FEND, to defend, ward off. (F.—L.) ME. *fenden*; the pt. t. *fended* occurs in P. Plowman, B. xix. 46, C. xxii. 46, where some MSS. read *defended*. *Fend* is a mere abbreviation of *defend*, q. v. Der. *fend-er*, (1), a metal guard for fire; (2) a buffer to deaden a blow.

FENIAN, one of an Irish brotherhood for promoting revolution. (Irish.) From OIrish *Féne*, one of the names of the ancient population of Ireland (Windisch); later confused with OIrish *Fiann*, f., the name of a body of warriors who defended Ireland in the time of Finn and others (Windisch).

FENNEL, a kind of fragrant plant. (L.) ME. *fenel*, older form *fenkil*; P. Plowman, A. v. 156 (and footnote). AS. *finol, finul, finugle, finule*; Cockayne’s AS. Leechdoms, iii. 326.—L. *faeniculum, fēniculum*, fennel. Formed, with dimin. suffixes *-cu-* and *-l-*, from L. *faeni-*, for *faeno-*, from *faenum*, hay.

FENUGREEK, a plant, cultivated for its seeds. (F.—L.) ME. *venecreke*, Book of St. Albans, leaf c 4, back.—F. *fenugrec*, ‘the herbe, or seed, fennigreeke;’ Cot.—L. *faenum Graecum*, lit. ‘Greek hay.’

FEOFF, to invest with a fief. (F.—OHG.) ME. *feffen, feoffen*; Chaucer, C. T. 9572 (E 1698); P. Plowman, B. ii. 78, 146; Rob. of Glouc. p. 368; l. 7585.—OF. *feoffer*, more commonly *fieffer* (Godefroy), to invest with a fief.—OF. *fief*, a fief; see **Fief**. Der. *feoffee*, from OF. pp. *feoffé*, one invested with a fief.

FEON, a barbed arrow-head; see **Pheon**.

FERACIOUS, fruitful. (L.) ‘Nurs’d on *feracious* Algidum;’ Thomson, Liberty, Part iii. 363. From L. *ferāci-*, decl. stem of *ferax*, fruitful.—L. *fer-re*, to bear; see **Bear** (1).

FERAL (1), deadly, funereal. (L.) In Burton, Anat. Melan. I. i. 2. 11, we have mention of ‘*feral* diseases.’—L. *fērāl-is*, funereal.

FERAL (2), wild, uncultivated. (L.) Not common; first in 1659. —L. *fer-a*, a wild beast; with suffix *-al* (F. *-al*, L. *-ālis*). See **Fierce**.

FERMENT, yeast, leaven, commotion. (L.) ‘The nation is in

too high a *ferment*;’ Dryden, pref. to Hind and Panther, l. 1. ME. *ferment*, Palladius on Husbandry, bk. xi. 524.—L. *fermentum*, leaven; for *ferui-mentum; see **Barm**.—L. *feruēre*, to boil, be agitated; see **Fervent**. Der. *ferment*, vb., Milton, Samson, 619; *ferment-at-ion*, Chaucer, C. T. 16285 (G 817); *ferment-able, -at-ive*.

FERN, a plant with feathery fronds. (E.) ME. *ferne*, Chaucer, C. T. 10568 (F 254). AS. *fearn*, Gloss. to Cockayne’s AS. Leechdoms.+Du. *varen*; G. *farnkraut* = feather-plant; Skt. *parṇa-*, a wing, feather, leaf, tree; the orig. sense being ‘feather;’ just as Gk. πτέρις, fern, is allied to πτερόν, a wing, feather. Brugmann, i. § 973. Cf. also Lith. *papartis*, Russ. *paparot(e)*, Irish *raith*, W. *rhedyn*, fern. Stokes-Fick, p. 226. Der. *fern-y*.

FEROCITY, fierceness. (F.—L.) In Minsheu, ed. 1627; *ferocious* is in Blount’s Gloss., ed. 1674. ME. *ferocyté*, Caxton, Hist. of Troye, leaf 97, l. 24.—F. *ferocité*, ‘fierceness;’ Cot.—L. *ferōcitātem*, acc. of *ferōcitās*, fierceness.—L. *ferōci-*, decl. stem of *ferox*, fierce.— L. *ferus*, wild. See **Fierce**. Der. *feroci-ous*, an ill-coined word, suggested by the OF. *feroce*, cruel; *-ly, -ness*.

FERREOUS, made of iron. (L.) In Sir T. Browne, Vulg. Errors, b. ii. c. 3. § 4.—L. *ferreus* (by change of *-us* to *-ous*, as in arduous, egregious).—L. *ferrum*, iron. Der. (from L. *ferrum*), *ferri-fer-ous*, where *-fer-* is from √BHER, to bear; also *farrier*, q. v.

FERRET (1), an animal of the weasel tribe. (F.—Late L.—L.) See Shak. Jul. Cæsar, i. 2. 186. ME. *forette, ferette*; Prompt. Parv. ME. (and AF.) *furet*, Nominale, ed. Skeat, 736-7.—OF. *furet*, ‘a ferret;’ Cot.—Late L. *fūrētus, fūrectus*, a ferret; cf. *fūrō* (gen. *fūrōnis*), a ferret, in Isidore (7th cent.). β. Said to be the same as Late L. *fūrō*, a thief; from L. *fūr*, a thief (Diez); cf. Ital. *furone*, a robber. Der. *ferret*, verb; = MF. *fureter*, ‘to ferret, search, hunt;’ Cot.

FERRET (2), a kind of silk tape. (Ital.—L.) ‘When perchmentiers [lacemakers] put in no *ferret-silke*;’ Gascoigne, Steel Glass, 1095. [Also called *floret-silk*, which is the French form; from MF. *fleuret*, ‘floret silk;’ Cot.] Corrupted from Ital. *fioretto*, pl. *fioretti*, ‘flowrets, flourishings, a kinde of course [coarse] silke called foret or ferret silke;’ Florio.—Ital. *fiore*, a flower; with dimin. suffix *-etto*.—L. *flōrem*, acc. of *flōs*, a flower. See **Flower**. ¶ Apparently named from its use in ornamentation. The OF. *fleuret* is, similarly, the dimin. of F. *fleur*, a flower. The Ital. change of *l* to *i* accounts for the E. form.

FERRUGINOUS, rusty. (L.) In Blount’s Gloss., ed. 1674.— L. *ferrūgin-us*, shorter form of *ferrūgineus*, rusty; with suffix *-ous*.— L. *ferrūgin-*, stem of *ferrūgo*, rust; formed from L. *ferrum*, iron, just as *ærūgo*, rust of brass, is from *æs* (gen. *ær-is*), brass. See **Ferreous**.

FERRULE, a metal ring at the end of a stick. (F.—L.) An accommodated spelling, due to confusion with L. *ferrum*, iron. Formerly *verril*. ‘*Verrel, Verril*, a little brass or iron ring at the small end of a cane;’ Kersey’s Dict. ed. 1715. And so spelt in Sherwood’s index to Cotgrave. Also *vyroll*; in Palsgrave.—OF. *virole*, ‘an iron ring put about the end of a staff,’ &c.; Cot.—Late L. *virola*, a ring to bind anything.—L. *uiriola*, a little bracelet.—L. *uiria*, a bracelet, armlet; only found in pl. *uiriæ*.—L. *uiēre*, to twist, bind round.

FERRY, to transport, carry across a river. (E.) Orig. used merely in the sense ‘to carry.’ ME. *ferien*, to convey; the pt. t. *ferede* is in Layamon, l. 237. From AS. *ferian*, to carry; Grein, i. 283. From AS. *faran*, to fare, go.+Icel. *ferja*, to carry, ferry, from *fara*, to go; Dan. *færge*, Swed. *färja*, to ferry; Goth. *farjan*, to travel by ship, sail, allied to *faran*, to go. See **Fare**. Der. *ferry*, sb. (cf. Icel. *ferja*, sb.); *-boat, -man*.

FERTILE, fruitful. (F.—L.) In Shak. Temp. i. 2. 338.—OF. *fertile*, ‘fertile;’ Cot.—L. *fertilis*, fruitful.—L. *ferre*, to bear; cognate with E. *bear*. See **Bear** (1). Der. *fertil-i-ty, -ise*.

FERULE, a rod (or bat) for punishing children. (L.) Formerly spelt *ferula*. ‘They would . . . awaken him with the clappe of a *ferula*;’ Holland, tr. of Suetonius; Claudius, c. 8. Also the giant-fennel, used as a rod. ‘There is not a plant in the world lighter . . . being easie to . . . carrie, the stem serves old men instead of staves;’ Holland, tr. of Pliny, bk. xiii. c. 22.—L. *ferula*, a rod; orig. the stem of the *ferula* or ‘giant-fennel.’ Perhaps from *ferre*, to carry; see above.

FERVENT, heated, ardent, zealous. (F.—L.) ME. *feruent* (with *u*=*v*). Chaucer has *feruently*, Troilus, iv. 1384.—OF. *fervent*, ‘fervent, hot;’ Cot.—L. *feruent-*, stem of pres. pt. of *feruēre*, to boil. Allied to OIrish *berb-aim*, I boil. Der. *fervent-ly, fervenc-y*; also *ferv-id*, Milton, P. L. v. 301, from L. *feruidus*, which is from *feruēre*; *-id-ly, -id-ness*; *ferv-our*, Wyclif, Deut. xxix. 20, from OF. *fervor, ferveur* < L. *feruōrem*, acc. of *feruor*, heat; also *fer-ment*, q. v., *ef-ferv-esce*, q. v.

FESCUE, a mote in the eye, a pointer used in reading. (F.—L.) ‘A *feskue* in her fist;’ Two Noble Kinsmen, A. ii. sc. 2 (3). Used for ‘the mote in the eye;’ Wyclif, Matt. vii. 3, but spelt *festu* (the ME. form); cf. P. Plowman, B. x. 278.—OF. *festu* (F. *fétu*), ‘a feskue;

a straw, rush, little stalk used for a fescue;' Cot. — Folk-L. *festūcum*; for L. *festūca*, a stalk, stem, straw.

FESS, a horizontal band, in heraldry. (F. — L.) Spelt *fesse* in Minsheu, and in Cotgrave, s. v. *face.* The pl. *feces* occurs about A.D. 1500; see Queen Elizabeth's Academy, &c., ed. Furnivall, p. 98, l. 113. Florio (1598) translates Ital. *fasce* by ' bundles . . . also *fesses* in armorie.' — OF. *fesse* (Roquefort), spelt *face* in Cotgrave, and *fasce* in mod. F. — L. *fascia*, a girth; allied to *fascis*, a bundle; see **Fascine.**

FESTAL, belonging to a feast. (F. — L.) In Johnson's Dict. Apparently unused in the 16th and 17th centuries; but it occurs ab. 1480 in English Gilds, ed. T. Smith, pp. 414–5, where we find ' the *festall daie*.' — OF. *festel*, *festal*; Godefroy. From L. *fest-um*, a feast; with suffix *-ālis*. See **Feast.**

FESTER, to rankle. (F. — L.) ME. *festeren.* ' So *festered* aren hus wondes' = so festered are his wounds; P. Plowman, C. xx. 83. — OF. *festrir*, to fester (Godefroy). — OF. *festre*, *feste*, *fistle*, a festered wound, ulcer. — L. *fistula*, a tube, a pipe, an ulcer, a running sore. The L. *fistula* is still in use as a medical term. Hence the sb. is older than the verb. Cf. ' The *fester* thrild his bodi thurgh;' Cursor Mundi, l. 11824; and Norm. dial. *fê're*, a whitlow (Moisy). See **Fistula.**

FESTIVAL, a feast-day. (F. — L.) Properly an adj. 'With drapets *festivall*;' Spenser, F. Q. ii. 9. 27. — OF. *festival*, festive; also, as sb. a festival; Roquefort. — Late L. *festivālis*; formed, with suffix *-ālis*, from L. *festīuus*; see below.

FESTIVE, festal. (L.) Modern; see Todd's Johnson. ' To *festive* mirth;' Thomson. Summer, 404. — L. *festīuus*, festive. — L. *festum*, a feast. See **Feast.** Der. *festive-ly*, *festiv-i-ty*.

FESTOON, an ornament, garland. (F. — Ital. — L.) ' The *festoons*, friezes, and the astragals;' Dryden, Art of Poetry, 56. — F. *feston*, a garland, festoon: cf. Span. *feston.* — Ital. *festone*, ' a garland, a crowne of flowers;' Florio. β. Usually derived from *festum*, a holiday, from the use of garlands as festive ornaments. See **Feast.** Der. *festoon*, verb.

FETCH, to bring. (E.) ME. *fecchen*, pt. t. *fette*, pp. *fet*; Chaucer, C. T. 821 (A 819), 7646 (D 2064). AS. *fecc(e)an*, to fetch; Gen. xviii. 4; Luke xii. 20. A later form of AS. *fetian*, *gefetian*, to fetch; Grein, i. 283, 398; pp. *fetod.* Allied to AS. *fæt*, a pace, step, journey; Grein, i. 273. Cf. Icel. *feta*, to find one's way; Icel. *fet.* a step, pace. Connected with L. *pēs* (gen. *ped-is*), foot, and with **Foot,** q. v. ¶ Cf. AS. *gefeccan*, OE. Texts, p. 178. See Anglia, vi. 177; Sievers, A. S. Gr. Der. *fetch*, used by Shak. to mean 'a stratagem;' Hamlet, ii. 1. 38.

FÊTE, a festival. (F. — L.) Modern. — F. *fête*; OF. *feste*, a feast. See **Feast.**

FETICH, FETISH, an object of superstitious dread. (F. — Port. — L.) ' *Fetisso*, which is a kind of God;' W. Dampier, A New Voyage (1699); v. ii. part 2. p. 105. Not in Johnson. — F. *fétiche.* — Port. *feitiço*, sorcery; also a name given by the Portuguese to the roughly made objects of superstitious dread in W. Africa. The orig. sense is ' artificial.' — L. *factitius*, artificial. See **Factitious.** Der. *fetich-ism.*

FETID, stinking. (F. — L.) In Bacon, Nat. Hist. § 481. — MF. *fetide*, ' stinking;' Cot. — L. *fētidus*, *fœtidus*, stinking. — L. *fœtēre*, to stink. Der. *fetid-ness.*

FETLOCK, the part of the leg (in a horse) where the tuft of hair grows behind the pastern-joint. (Scand.) Also the tuft itself; by confusion with *lock* (of hair). ' *Fetlock*, or *fetterlock*, the hair that grows behind on a horse's feet;' Kersey. The pl. is spelt *feetlakkes* in Rich. Coer de Lion, 5816; and *fitlokes* in Arthur and Merlin, 5902. Cf. Low G. *fitlock* (Lübben); MHG. *vizzeloch* (Kluge). Of Scand. origin; the latter syllable is prob. only a double suffix (*-l-ock*); but was understood as being our ' lock' of hair, viz. Icel. *lokkr*, AS. *locc.* β. In connexion with *fet-* we find Icel. *fet*, a pace, step, *feti*, a pacer, stepper (used of horses), *feta*, to step, the *fetlock* being employed in stepping; cf. Swed. *fjät*, Dan. *fied*, a foot-print, footstep, track. Further allied to Icel. *fótr*, a foot, and to G. *fessel*, Low G. *vettel* (Lübben), a pastern; and thus connected with both *foot* and *fetter*; see **Fetter, Fetch, Foot.**

FETTER, a shackle. (E.) Orig. a shackle for the *foot.* ME. *feter*, Chaucer, C. T. 1281 (A 1279). AS. *fetor*, *feter*, Grein, i. 283. + Du. *veter*, lace; orig. a fetter; Icel. *fjöturr*; Swed. *fjättrar*, pl. fetters; MSwed. *fjätter*, a fetter (Ihre); cf. L. *pedica*; also *com-pēs* (gen. *com-ped-is*), a fetter; Gk. πέδη, a fetter. All from Idg. *ped-*, Teut. *fet-*; allied to Teut. *fōt-*, as in E. *foot.* See **Foot.**

FETUS (incorrectly **FŒTUS**), offspring, the young in the womb. (L.) Modern; in Johnson's Dict. — L. *fētus*, a bringing forth, off-spring. — L. *fētus*, fruitful, that has brought forth. From an Idg. base *bhwē* (< *bhu-ē*), to produce; related to *fu-* in *fuī*, I was, and in *futurus*, future. Cf. Gk. ἐφύη, was; φύειν, to beget; φύεσθαι, to grow; φυτός, grown; Skt. *bhū*, to become, be; AS. *bēon*, to be. See **Be.** (√BHEU.) Brugmann, i. § 361, ii. § 587. Der. (from the same root) *fe-cundity*, q. v.; *fe-line*, q. v.; *fe-licity*, q. v.; also *ef-fete*, *fawn* (2).

FEUD (1), perpetual hostility, hatred. (F. — OHG.) In Shak. Troil. iv. 5. 132. Modified in spelling from earlier *fede*, *feid*, in some unexplained way; perhaps by the influence of the word *foe*; see N. E. D. *fede* (a Northern form), Wallace, i. 354; *feid*, Raul Coilyear, 969; Levins has: ' *Feade*, *odium*' (1570). — OF. *faide*, *feide*, *fede*, perpetual hostility (Godefroy). — OHG. *fēhida*, G. *fehde*, hatred, enmity: cognate with AS. *fǣhð*, enmity, from *fāh*, hostile. See **Foe.**

FEUD (2), a fief; **FEUDAL,** pertaining to a fief. (Low L. — F. — OHG.) In Blackstone's Commentaries, b. ii. c. 4; and see *Fee* in Blount's Law Dict. — Low L. *feudum*, a fief; a barbarous L. form allied to OF. *fiu*, also spelt *fief*; see further under **Fief.** (The intrusive *d* is unexplained.) Der. *feud-al*; *feud-al-ism*, *feud-at-or-y.*

FEUTER, to lay the spear in rest. (F. — Teut.) ' His speare he *feutred*;' Spenser, F. Q. iv. 4. 45. From ME. *feuter*, sb., a rest for a spear; Will. of Palerne, 3437 (cf. l. 3593). — MF. *feutre*, felt, a piece of felt, Cot.; OF. *feltre*, a rest for the lance (Godefroy). It was fitted with a pad, lined with felt; Late L. *filtrum.* See **Filter.** From the Teut. type *felt-oz*; see **Felt.**

FEUTERER, a dog-keeper. (F. — Low L. — C.) ' A yeoman-*feuterer*;' Ben Jonson, Every Man out of his Humour, ii. 1 (Carlo). See Nares. ME. *vewter* (for *vewtrier*); Gawain and Grene Knight, 1146; cf. Anglo-L. *veltrārius* (Blount, s. v. *Vautrier*); OF. *veltrier* (Godefroy). — OF. *veltre*, *veutre*, a boar-hound (Godefroy); F. *vautre* (Littré). — Late L. *vertragum*, acc. of *vertragus* (Ducange, s. v. *Canis veltris*); L. *uertagus* (Martial). Of Celtic origin. — C. *ver-*, intensive prefix; and *trag-*, to run; Stokes-Fick, pp. 136, 283.

FEVER, a kind of disease. (L.) ME. *feuer* (with *u* for *v*), P. Plowman, C. iv. 96; *fefre*, Ancren Riwle, p. 112. AS. *fēfor*, *fēfer*; Matt. viii. 15. — L. *febris*, a fever. Der. *fever-ous*, *-ish*, *-ish-ly*, *-ish-ness*; also *fever-few*, a plant, corrupted from AS. *fēfer-fuge*, borrowed from Late L. *febrifuga* = fever-dispelling, from L. *fugāre*, to put to flight; see Voc. 134. 1.

FEW, of small number. (E.) ME. *fewe*, Chaucer, C. T. 641 (A 639). AS. *fēa*, both sing. and pl.; *fēawe*, pl. only, Grein, i. 287. + Icel. *fār*; Dan. *faa*; Swed. *få*; Goth. *fawai*, pl. + L. *paucus*; Gk. παῦρος, small.

FEY, doomed to die. (E.) ' Till *fey* men died awa', man;' Burns, Battle of Sheriffmuir, l. 19. ME. *feye*, P. Plowman, C. xvi. 2. AS. *fǣge*, doomed to die. + Icel. *feigr*, destined to die; Du. *veeg*, about to die; OHG. *feigi*, doomed to die; whence G. *feige*, cowardly. Also Swed. *feg*, Dan. *feig*, cowardly.

FEZ, a red Turkish cap, without a brim. (F. — Morocco.) Borrowed by us from F. *fez*, the same; the word is also Turkish (Turk. *fes*). So called because made at Fez, in Morocco; see Devic, Supp. to Littré.

FIASCO, a failure, break-down in a performance. (Ital. — Late L.) From the Ital. phrase *far fiasco*, to make a bottle; also, to fail, to break down (reason for this unknown; perhaps it means that the empty bottle fails to please). Torriano, ed. 1688, has: ' *fiaschi*, bottles, flaggons; also, an interjection of admiration, as *papæ* in Latin.' Also Ital. *fiasca*, f., a flask, bottle. — Late L. *flasca*; see **Flask.**

FIAT, a decree. (L.) In Young's Night Thoughts, vi. 465; and Donne, The Storm, l. 72. — L. *fiat*, let it be done. — L. *fio*, I become; used as pass. of *facere*, to make; but really allied to *fu-ī*, I was. (√BHEU.) Brugmann, i. § 282 (2).

FIB, a fable. (Low L.?) In Pope, Ep. to Lady Shirley, l. 24. Cotgrave has: ' *Bourde*, a jeast, *fib*.' Allied to *fob*, *fub off* (Shak.). Cf. G. *foppen*, to banter (formerly to lie); Westphal. *foppen*, to deceive; *fip-ken*, a small lie, a fib (Woeste). Der. *fib*, vb.

FIBRE, a thread, threadlike substance. (F. — L.) Spelt *fiber* in Cotgrave. — F. *fibre*; pl. *fibres*, ' the fibers, threads, or strings of mus-cles;' Cot. — L. *fibra*, a fibre, thread. Der. *fibr-ous*, *fibr-ine*; also *fringe*, q. v.

FIBULA, a clasp, buckle. (L.) First in 1673. ' The *fibula*;' Words-worth, The Highland Broach, 17. — L. *fibula*, a clasp, buckle. — L. *figere*, by-form of *figere*, to fix; see **Fix.**

FICKLE, deceitful, inconstant. (E.) ME. *fikel*, P. Plowman, C. iii. 25. AS. *ficol*, found in a gloss, Voc. 69. 18; formed, with a com-mon adj. suffix *-ol*, from *fic-ian*, to deceive, in comp. *be-fician*, to deceive; cf. *fic*, fraud, *fācen*, deceit; allied to Icel. *feikn*, an evil, a portent, OSax. *fēkn*, deceit. Cf. Skt. *piçuna-s*, malignant; Brugmann, i. § 646. Der. *fickle-ness.*

FICTION, a falsehood, feigned story. (F. — L.) In Skelton, Colin Clout, l. 114. — F. *fiction*, ' a fiction;' Cot. — L. *fictiōnem*, acc. of *fictio*, a feigning. Cf. L. *fictus*, pp. of *fingere*, to feign. See **Feign, Figure.** Der. (from L. *fictus*) *fict-it-i-ous*, *-ile*; and see **Figment, Figure.**

FIDDLE, a stringed instrument, violin. (E.?) ME. *fithel*, P. Plow-man, B. xiii. 457; *fidel*, Chaucer, C. T. 298 (A 296). AS. *fiðele*, only in the deriv. *fiðelere*, a fiddler, in a copy of Ælfric's Glossary (Bos-worth); cf. Icel. *fiðla*, a fiddle, *fiðlari*, a fiddler; Dan. *fiddel*; Du. *vedel*; G. *fiedel* (OHG. *fidula*). β. Of uncertain origin, but perhaps Teutonic; whence Late L. *vidula*, *vitula*, a viol, fiddle. See **Viol.**

FIDELITY, faithfulness. (F.–L.) In Shak. Mer. Wives, iv. 2. 160. Fabyan has *fydelite*, Chron. pt. vii. c. 238; p. 277.–F. *fidelité*, 'fidelity;' Cot.–L. *fidēlitātem*, acc. of *fidēlitās*.–L. *fidēlis*, faithful. –L. *fides*, faith. See **Faith**.

FIDGET, to be restless, move uneasily. (Scand.) In Boswell's Life of Johnson (Todd's Johnson). A dimin. form of *fidge*. 'Fidge *about*, to be continually moving up and down;' Kersey, ed. 1715. *Fidge* is apparently a modification of the North E. *fick* or *fike*. 'Fike, *fyke, feik*, to be in a restless state;' Jamieson. ME. *fiken*, Prompt. Parv. p. 160; Bestiary, 656. 'The Sarezynes fledde, away gunne *fyke*' = the Saracins fled, and away did *hasten*; used in contempt; Rich. Coer de Lion, 4749.–MDan. *fige*, Dan. dial. *fige*, to desire, strive, hasten, hurry (see Kalkar and Molbech); cf. Norw. *figa*, more commonly *fika*, to fidget, make restless movements (Ross); Icel. *fika*, to climb up nimbly, as a spider; Swed. *fika, fikas*, to hunt after; and see *fika* in Rietz; Norw. *fika*, to strive, take trouble; *fika etter*, to pursue, hasten after (Aasen). Cf. G. dial. (Alsace) *ficken*, to itch, to fidget. Der. *fidget*, sb., *fidget-y, fidget-i-ness*.

FIDUCIAL, showing trust. (L.) Rare; see Rich. Dict. 'Fiduciary, a feoffee in trust;' Blount's Gloss., ed. 1674. Both words are from L. *fidūcia*, trust.–L. *fidere*, to trust. See **Faith**.

FIE, an interjection of disgust. (F.–L.) ME. *fy*, Chaucer, C. T. 4500 (B 80); 'fy for shame;' id. 14897 (B 4081); Will. of Palerne, 481.–F. *fi*.–L. *fī*, interj. Cf. also Icel. *fȳ, fei*; Dan. *fy*, also *fy skam dig*, fie for shame; Swed. *fy*, also *fy skam*, fie for shame. We find similar forms in the G. *pfui*, L. *phui, phy*, Skt. *phut*, natural expressions of disgust, due to the sound of blowing away.

FIEF, land held of a superior. (F.–Low L.–OHG.?) In Dryden, On Mrs. Killigrew, l. 98. The ME. vb. *feffen*, to enfeoff, is common; see Chaucer, C. T. 9572 (E 1698); P. Plowman, B. ii. 78, 146.–OF. *fief*, early form *fiu* (Chanson de Roland).–Low L. *fevum*, a fief (Ducange). Prob. from OHG. *fehu*, property; see **Fee**.

FIELD, an open space of land. (E.) ME. *feeld*, Chaucer, C. T. 888 (A 886). AS. *feld*; Grein.+Du. *veld*; G. *feld* (whence Dan. *felt*, Swed. *fält*). Teut. type **felþuz*. Allied to AS. *folde*, earth, land. Cf. Russ. *polé*, a field; Skt. *pṛthivī*, earth. Brugmann, i. § 502. Der. *field-day, field-marshal*, &c.

FIELDFARE, a bird of the thrush kind. (E.) ME. *feldefare*, Chaucer, Troil. iii. 861; *feldfare*, Will. of Palerne, 183. AS. *felde-fare*, Wright's Vocab. i. 63, l. 27; but really miswritten *feldeware*; see Voc. 287. 17. Lit. 'field-traveller;' from *faran*, to travel; see **Fare**. ¶ There is also an AS. *feala-for*, but this is the name of some much larger bird, and is a different word altogether; see Sweet, O. E. Texts, p. 88; Ep. gl. 807.

FIEND, an enemy. (E.) ME. *fend*, Chaucer, C. T. 7256 (D 1674); earlier *feond*, Layamon, l. 237. AS. *fēond, fiond*, an enemy, hater; properly the pres. pt. of *fēon*, contr. form of *fēogan*, to hate; Grein, i. 294, 295.+Du. *vijand*, an enemy; Dan. and Swed. *fiende*; Icel. *fjándi*, pres. pt. of *fjá*, to hate; Goth. *fijands*, pres. pt. of *fijan*, to hate; G. *feind*.–√PEI, to hate; Fick, i. 145; whence also *foe*, q. v. Cf. Skt. *piy*, to hate (Fick). ¶ Similarly, *friend* is a pres. pt. from Teut. base *frei-*, to love; see **Friend**. Der. *fiend-ish, fiend-ish-ness*.

FIERCE, violent, angry. (F.–L.) ME. *fiers*, Chaucer, C. T., A 1598; Rob. of Glouc. p. 188, l. 3910.–OF. *fers, fiers*, old nom. form of OF. *fer, fier*, fierce (F. *fier*, proud).–L. *fěrus*, wild, savage; cf. *fera*, a wild beast.+Gk. θήρ, a wild animal. Brugmann, i. § 319. Der. *fer-oc-i-ous*, q. v.

FIFE, a shrill pipe. (F.–OHG.–L.) In Shak. Oth. iii. 3. 352. –F. *fifre*, 'a fife;' Cot.–OHG. *pfifa, fifa*; G. *pfeife*, a pipe.– OHG. *pfīfen*, to blow, puff, blow a fife; cf. G. *pfiff*, a whistle, hissing. –Late L. *pipāre*, to pipe; L. *pipāre, pīpiāre*, to chirp. See **Pipe**.

FIG, the name of a fruit. (F.–Prov.–L.) The pl. *figes* occurs in the Ancren Riwle, p. 150, where also the fig-tree is called *figer*. [The AS. *fic* (Matt. vii. 16) is a somewhat different form, being taken directly from L. *ficus*.]–F. *figue*, due to the OProvençal form *figa*, a fig; cf. Span. *figo*.–Folk-L. **fica*, for L. *ficus*, a fig. Cf. OF. *fie*, a fig; immediately from Folk-L. **fica*. Der. *fig-wort*.

FIGHT, to contend in war. (E.) ME. *fihten, fehten*, Layamon, ll. 1359, 1580. OMerc. *fehtan*, AS. *feohtan*, Grein, i. 289; whence the sb. *fehte*, AS. *feohte*, a fight. + Du. *vechten*; OHG. *fehtan*; G. *fechten* (whence Dan. *fegte*, Swed. *fäkta*). Teut. type **fehtan-*, pt. t. **faht*. β. Possibly connected with L. *pectere*, to comb, to card, hence, to pull, rend, fight (Streitberg). Der. *fight*, sb., *fight-er, -ing*.

FIGMENT, a fiction. (L.) 'You heard no *figment*, sir;' B. Jonson, Every Man out of his Humour, iv. 4.–L. *figmentum*, a fiction; formed (with suffix *-mentum*) from the base *fig-* of *fi(n)gere*, to feign; pt. t. *fic-tus* (for **fig-tus*). See below; and see **Fiction, Feign**.

FIGURE, something made, an appearance, representation. (F.–L.) ME. *figure*, Chaucer, C. T. 7892 (E 16).–F. *figure*.–L. *figūra*, a figure, thing made.–L. *fig-*, base of *fi(n)gere*, to form, fashion, feign; pp. *fic-tus* (for **fig-tus*).+Skt. *dih*, to smear; Goth.

deigan, to fashion as a potter does; whence *daigs*, cognate with E. *dough*. –√DHEIGH, to smear, handle, form with the hands. See **Dough**. Brugmann, i. § 589. Der. *figure*, vb., *figur-ed, figure-head*; *figur-ate, -at-ive, -at-ive-ly*; from the same root, *feign, fiction, figment, ef-fig-y, dis-figure, trans-figure*; also *dike, dough, la-dy*.

FILAMENT, a slender thread. (F.–L.) In Cotgrave, to translate MF. *filamens*, 'filaments;' Cot.–F. *filament* (Hatzfeld).– Late L. *filāmentum*, a thread; formed (with suffix *-mentum*) from Late L. *filāre*, to wind thread.–L. *filum*, a thread; see **File** (1).

FILBERT, the fruit of the hazel. (F.–OHG.) Formerly spelt *philibert* or *philiberd*. 'The *Philibert* that loves the vale;' Peacham's Emblems, ed. 1612 (R.). Gower has: 'That Phillis in the same throwe Was shape into a nutte-tre . . . And, after Phillis, *philliberd* This tre was cleped in the yerd;' C. A. ii. 30. [This is an allusion to the story of Phyllis and Demophon in Ovid, and of course does not account for the word, as it takes no notice of the last syllable.] β. From AF. *filbert*, a filbert; of which the pl. *philbers* occurs in Britton, ed. Nichols, i. 371, note 5. Short for *noix de philbert*, as the name is still *noix de filbert* in Normandy (Moisy). From the proper name *Philibert*. Cotgrave has: '*Philibert*, a proper name for a man; and particularly the name of a certain Bourgonian [Burgundian] saint; whereof *chaine de S. Philibert*, a kind of counterfeit chain.' Perhaps the nut was also named after St. Philibert, whose name also thus appears in another connexion. '*Noix de Filebert*, aveline; saint F., qui avait beaucoup enrichi l'abbaye de Jumièges [near Rouen], y avait sans doute introduit de meilleures noisettes;' Duméril; Dict. du Patois Normand. St. Philibert's day is Aug. 22 (Old Style), just the nutting season. The name is Frankish.–OHG. *filu-bert*, i.e. very bright; from *filu* (G. *viel*), much, very; and *bert = berht*, bright, cognate with E. *bright*. See Hist. of Christian Names, by Miss Yonge, ii. 231; where, however, *fili-* is equated to *wille* (will) by a mistake. ¶ Similarly, a filbert is called in German *Lambertsnuss* as if for Lambert's nut (St. Lambert's day is Sept. 17); but (according to Weigand) the real orig. sense of *Lambertsnuss* was 'nut from Lombardy.'

FILCH, to steal, pilfer. (Scand.?) [Rob. of Brunne has *filchid*; tr. of Langtoft, p. 282; but this seems to be a different word.] *Filch* first appears in 1581, as a slang term; and its origin is quite uncertain. Perhaps allied to ME. *felen*, to conceal; Icel. *fela*, to hide; whence Icel. *fylgsni, fylksni*, a hiding-place. Cf. Goth. *fulhsni*, secrecy.

FILE (1), a string, line, list, order. (F.–L.) In Macbeth, iii. 1. 95.–OF. *file*, 'a file, rank, row;' Cot. Allied to *fil*, a thread.– Late L. *fila*, a string of things (see *fila, filāre* in Ducange).–L. *filum*, a thread. Der. *file*, verb; *fil-a-ment*, q. v.; *fil-i-gree*, q. v.; *fill-et*, q. v.; also *en-fil-ade*; also *de-file* (2).

FILE (2), a steel rasp. (E.) ME. *file*, Chaucer, C. T. 2510 (A 2508). OMerc. *fil*, Corpus gloss., 1234; AS. *fēol*, a file; Bosworth.+Du. *vijl*; OHG. *fihala, figala*; G. *feile*. Teut. type **fihalā < *finhalā*. Perhaps cf. Skt. *piç*, to adorn, form; but this is doubtful. Der. *file*, verb; *fil-ings*.

FILE (3), to defile. (E.) 'For Banquo's issue have I *filed* my mind;' Macb. iii. 1. 65. ME. *fylen*, Early E. Allit. Poems, B. 136. AS. *-fȳlan*, to render foul (in comp. *gefȳlan*); for **fūl-ian*.–AS. *fūl*, foul. See **Defile** (1) and **Foul**.

FILIAL, relating to a child. (L.) 'All *filial* reuerence;' Sir T. More, Works, p. 63 f. Formed as if from Late L. *filiālis*; cf. Late L. *filiāliter*, in a mode resembling that of a son.–L. *filius*, son; *filia*, daughter; orig. an infant; cf. L. *fēlāre*, to suck.–√DHEI, to suck; cf. Skt. *dhā*, to suck. Der. *filial-ly, fili-at-ion, of-fili-ate*.

FILIBUSTER, a pirate, freebooter. (Span.–F.–Du.) First in 1587; from Spanish.–Span. *filibuster*, a buccaneer, a freebooter. –F. *flibustier*, spelt *fribustier* in 1667 (Hatzfeld). Corrupted from Du. *vrijbuiter*, a freebooter.–Du. *vrijbuiten*, to rob, plunder.–Du. *frij*, free; *buit*, booty. See **Free** and **Booty**. ¶ The exact history is obscure; but, in any case, the word is of Du. origin.

FILIGREE, fine ornamental work. (F.–Ital.–L.) A corruption of *filigrain* or *filigrane*, the older form. 'A curious *filigrane* handkerchief . . . out of Spain;' Dr. Browne's Travels, ed. 1685 (Todd). 'Several *filigrain* curiosities;' Tatler, no. 245.–F. *filigrane* (cf. Span. *filigrana*).–Ital. *filigrana*, filigree-work, fine wrought work.–Ital. *filo*, a thread, row, *filare*, to spin; and *grano*, the grain or principal fibre of the material; so called because the chief texture of the material was wrought in gold or silver thread. From L. *filum*, thread; and *grānum*, grain. See **File** (1) and **Grain**.

FILL, to make full. (E.) ME. *fillen*, P. Plowman's Crede, ed. Skeat, 763; older form *fullen*, Ancren Riwle, p. 40. AS. *fyllan, fullian*, Grein, i. 356, 360; from AS. *ful*, full.+Du. *vullen*; Icel. *fylla*; Dan. *fylde*; Swed. *fylla*; Goth. *fulljan*; G. *füllen*. Teut. type **fulljan-*. See **Full**. Der. *fill*, sb., Chaucer, C. T. 2561 (A 2559); *fill-er*.

FILLET, a little band. (F.–L.) ME. *filet*, Chaucer, C. T. 3243;

Polit. Songs, ed. Wright, p. 154.—OF. *filet*, dimin. of *fil*, a thread. —L. *filum*, a thread. See **File** (1). Der. *fillet*, verb.

FILLIBEG, FILIBEG, a kilt. (Gaelic.) Used by Dr. Johnson, in his Tour to the Western Islands (Todd).—Gael. *feileadh-beag*, the kilt in its modern shape; Macleod.—Gael. *feileadh*, *feile*, a kilt, prob. from L. *uĕlum*, a veil (Macbain); and *beag*, little, small. Cf. W. *bach*, small. (The older kilt was larger.)

FILLIP, to strike with the finger-nail, when jerked from under the thumb. (E.) In Shak. 2 Hen. IV, i. 2. 255.—Another form of **Flip.** Halliwell has: '*Flip*, a slight sudden blow; also, to fillip, to jerk; *Somerset*. Lillie (Mother Bombie, v. 3, ed. 1632, sig. Dd. ii) seems to use the word *flip* in the sense to *fillip*.' Der. *fillip*, sb., spelt *fyllippe* in Palsgrave. See **Flippant.**

FILLS, used for *thills* (Shak.). See **Thill.**

FILLY, a female foal. (Scand.) Shak. has *filly foal*, Mids. N. Dr. ii. 1. 46. Merely the fem. form of *foal*, formed by suffixing Teut. *-jön*, f., which modifies the vowel.—Icel. *fylja*, a filly; *foli*, a foal; cf. Dan. *föl*, neut. a foal; *fole*, masc. a foal; Swed. *föl*, neut. a foal; *fåle*, masc.; G. *füllen*, a colt; OHG. *volo*, a foal. See **Foal.**

FILM, a thin skin. (E.) In Shak. Romeo, i. 4. 63. ME. *film*, *fylme*, Prompt. Parv. p. 160. AS. *filmen*, written *fylmen*, membrane, prepuce; Gen. xvii. 11; OFries. *filmene*, skin. For W. Teut. *filmin-jo-*; from *felmen-*, *felmon-*, as in AS. *æger-felma*, the skin of an egg. Extended from *fel-*, as in AS. *fel*, skin. See **Fell** (2). Der. *film-y*, *-i-ness*.

FILTER, to strain liquors; a strainer. (F.—Low L.—O. Low G.) The sb. is in Cotgrave, s. v. *feutre*. '*Filter*, or *Filtrate*, to strain through a bag, felt, brown paper, &c.;' also '*Filtrum* or *Feltrum*, a strainer; . . . a felt-hat;' Kersey, ed. 1715.—MF. *filtrer*, 'to straine through a felt;' Cot.—MF. (and F.) *filtre*, a filter (Hatzfeld). β. A modification (due to the influence of Ital. *filtro*) of the OF. *feltre* (F. *feutre*). Cf. F. *feutre*, 'a felt, also a filter, a peece of felt . . . to straine things through;' Cot.—Low L. *filtrum*, felt.—O. Low G. *filt* (=E. *felt*), preserved in Du. *vilt*, Low G. *filt*, felt; cf. G. *filz*. See **Felt.** Der. *filt-r-ate*, *filt-r-at-ion*.

FILTH, foul matter. (E.) ME. *filth*, *felth*, *fulthe*; Prompt. Parv. p. 160; Ancren Riwle, p. 128. AS. *fylð*, Matt. xxiii. 27, where the Hatton MS. has *felthe*. Formed, by vowel-change of *ū* to *ȳ*, from the adj. *fūl*, foul, the AS. *fylð* being the exact equivalent of OSax. *fūlitha*, filth; so also OHG. *fūlida*, filth, from *fūl*, *vūl*, foul. See **Foul.** Der. *filth-y*, *-i-ness*.

FIMBRIATED, edged with a narrow band. (L.) In heraldry. 'This cros *fimbriatit* or borderit;' Book of St. Alban's, pt. ii. fol. d 1. —L. *fimbriātus*, pp. of *fimbriāre*, to fringe.—L. *fimbria*, fringe; see **Fringe.**

FIN, a wing-like organ of a fish. (E.) ME. *finne*; the pl. pp. *finnede*=furnished with fins, occurs in Alexander and Dindimus, ed. Skeat, l. 298. AS. *finn*; Levit. xi. 9.+Du. *vin*; Low G. *finne*; Swed. *finn-*, in *finnfisk*, a finned fish; *fena*, a fin; Dan. *finne*.+L. *pinna*, a fin, in the comp. *pinniger*, having fins; Ovid, Metam. xiii. 963. ¶ The usual connexion asserted between L. *pinna* and *penna* is not certain; if it were, we might connect *fin* with *feather*. Der. *finn-y*.

FINAL, pertaining to the end. (F.—L.) ME. *final*, Gower, C. A. iii. 348; bk. viii. 2183.—OF. *final*, 'finall;' Cot.—L. *finālis*.—L. *finis*, the end. See **Finish.** Der. *final-ly*, *-i-ty*; also *fin-ale*, from Ital. *finale*, final, hence, an ending.

FINANCE, revenue. (F.—L.) ME. *fynaunce*, used by Lord Berners in the sense of 'ransom;' tr. of Froissart, i. 311 (N.E.D.). 'All the *finances* or revenues;' Bacon, The Office of Alienations (R.).—OF. *finance*, pl. *finances*, 'wealth, substance, revenue, . . . all extraordinary levies;' Cot.—Late L. *financia*, a payment.—Late L. *fināre*, to pay a fine or tax.—Late L. *finis*, a settled payment, a *final* arrangement; L. *finis*, the end. See **Fine** (2), and **Finish.** Der. *financ-i-al*, *-i-al-ly*, *-i-er*.

FINCH, the name of several small birds. (E.) ME. *finch*, Chaucer, C. T. 654 (A 652). AS. *finc*; Voc. 23. 13.+Du. *vink*; Dan. *finke*; Swed. *fink*; G. *fink*; OHG. *fincho*.+W. *pinc*, a chaffinch; also Gk. σπίγγος, σπίζα, a finch; prov. E. *spink*, a finch. Of imitative origin. Der. *chaf-finch*, q.v.; *bull-finch*, &c.

FIND, to meet with, light upon. (E.) ME. *finden*, Chaucer, Prol. 738 (A 736). AS. *findan*; Grein.+Du. *vinden*; Dan. *finde*; Swed. and Icel. *finna* (<*finþa*); Goth. *finthan*; OHG. *findan*; G. *finden*. Teut. type *fenthan-* (pt. t. *fanth*, pp. *funth-anoz*); Idg. base *pent*, whence OIrish *ēt-aim*, I find. Perhaps allied to L. *pet-ere*, to seek after, fly towards; from √PET, to fall, fly. Der. *find-er*.

FINE (1), exquisite, complete, thin. (F.—L.) ME. *fyn*, K. Alisaunder, 2657; superl. *finest*; P. Plowman, B. ii. 9.—OF. *fin*, 'witty, . . . perfect, exact, pure;' Cot.—Late L. *finus*, fine, pure, used of money; in place of L. *finitus*, well rounded (said of a sentence); orig. pp. of L. *finire*, to end, from *finis*, end. *Finus* **was a** back-formation from *finire*. Thus *fine* is related to *finite*; see

Finite. Der. *fine-ly*, *-ness*; *fin-er-y*, used by Burke (R.); *fin-esse* (F. *finesse*); *fin-ic-al*, a coined word, in Shak. K. Lear, ii. 2. 19; *-ic-al-ly*; also *re-fine*. ¶ The Du. *fijn*, G. *fein*, &c., are not Teutonic words, but borrowed from the Romance Languages (Diez).

FINE (2), a tax, forced payment. (Law L.) ME. *fine*, sb., Sir T. More, Works, p. 62 b; vb., Fabyan's Chron. an. 1440-1 (at the end).—Law L. *finis*, a fine; see *Fine* in Blount's Law Dict., and *finis* in Ducange. The lit. sense is 'a final payment' or composition, to settle a matter; from L. *finis*, end. See **Finance, Finish.** Der. *fine*, verb; *fin-able*; *fin-ance*, q. v.

FINGER, part of the hand. (E.) ME. *finger*, P. Plowman, C. iii. 12. AS. *finger*, Grein.+Du. *vinger*; Icel. *fingr*; Dan. and Swed. *finger*; Goth. *figgrs* (=*fingrs*); G. *finger*. Teut. type *fingroz*, masc. The Idg. type was probably *penkros*; the word *fist* may be related. Der. *finger*, verb; *finger-post*.

FINIAL, an ornament on a pinnacle. (L.) In Holland's tr. of Suetonius, p. 162; and tr. of Pliny, bk. xxxv. c. 12. Cf. 'every butterace fined [ended] with *finials*;' Will of Hen. VI.; Royal Wills, ed. Nichols, p. 302 (1448). A coined word, suggested by Late L. *finiles lapidēs*, terminal stones; *finiābilis*, terminal.—L. *finire*, to finish; see **Finish.**

FINICAL, spruce, foppish; see **Fine** (1).

FINISH, to end, terminate. (F.—L.) ME. *finischen*; the pp. *finischid* occurs in Will. of Palerne, l. 5398.—OF. *finiss-*, base of *finiss-ant*; pres. pt. of *finir*, to finish.—L. *finire*, to end.—L. *finis*, end, bound. Der. *finish*, sb., *finish-er*; also *fin-ite*, q. v., *fin-ial*, q. v., *fin-al*, q. v., *af-fin-ity*, *con-fine*, *de-fine*, *in-fin-ite*.

FINITE, limited. (L.) In Dryden, Hind and Panther, i. 105. First in 1493.—L. *finitus*, pp. of *finire*, to end; see **Finish.** Der. *finite-ly*, *-ness*; *in-finite*.

FIORD, FJORD, a long narrow arm of the sea. (Norw.) First in 1674.—Norw. *fiord*; Icel. *fjörðr*, a firth, frith, bay. Teut. type *ferthuz*. See **Frith** (2), **Ford.**

FIR, the name of a tree. (Scand.) ME. *firre*, Chaucer, C. T. 2923 (A 2921); answering to a mutated form allied to AS. *furh*, in the comp. *furh-wudu*, fir-wood, which occurs in Voc. 39. 34, but is of Scand. origin. Cf. Icel. *fyri-skógr* (written *fyri-skögr*), a fir-wood; from Icel. *fura*, a fir; also Dan. *fyr*, Swed. *fura*.+OLombardic *fereha*, 'æsculus;' G. *föhre*; W. *pyr*.+L. *quercus*, an oak; see Max Müller, Lect. on Lang. vol. ii.

FIRE, the heat and light of flame. (E.) ME. *fyr*, Chaucer, C. T. 1248 (A 1296); also *fur*, P. Plowman, C. iv. 125. AS. *fȳr*, Grein, i. 364.+Du. *vuur*; Icel. *fȳri*; Dan. and Swed. *fyr*; G. *feuer*; OHG. *fuir*. Teut. type *fū-ir*; cognate with Gk. πῦρ. β. The root seems to be √PŪ, to purify; cf. Skt. *pāvaka-* (from *pū*), purifying, also fire. See **Pure.** Der. *fire*, vb., *fier-y* (=*fir-y*), *fir-ing*; also numerous compounds, as *fire-arms*, *-brand*, *-damp*, *-fly*, *-lock*, *-man*, *-place*, *-plug*, *-proof*, *-ship*, &c.

FIRK, to conduct, drive, beat. (E.) To beat; in Shak. Hen. V, iv. 4. 29. Orig. sense, to conduct; AS. *fercian*, AS. Chron. an. 1009; also *færcian*. Prob. from AS. *fær*, a journey; *faran*, to go; see **Fare.**

FIRKIN, the fourth part of a barrel. (MDu.) In the Bible of 1551; John, ii. 6. 'Kilderkyn and *firken*;' Arnold's Chron. (1502); ed. 1811, p. 85. Spelt *ferdkyn* in 1413; Riley, Mem. of London, p. 597; and *ferdekyn* in 1423 (N.E.D.).—Du. *vierde*, fourth; with MDu. dimin. suffix *-ken* (= *-k-en*), formerly common, but now superseded by *-tje* or *-je*; see Sewel's Du. Grammar (in his Dict.), p. 37. Cf. MDu. *vierdevat*, a peck (Sewel); and see **Farthing** and **Kilderkin.** β. Du. *vierde* is from Du. *vier*, four; see **Four.**

FIRM (1), steadfast, fixed. (F.—L.) ME. *ferme*, P. Plowman, B. xvi. 238.—OF. *ferme*.—L. *firmus*. Cf. Skt. *dharman*, right, law, justice; *dhara-*, preserving; Skt. *dhṛ*, to maintain, carry, support. Der. *firm*, sb.; *-ly*, *-ness*; *-a-ment*, q.v.; also *af-firm*, *con-firm*, *in-firm*; also *farm*, q.v.; and see below.

FIRM (2), a partnership. (Span.—L.) '*Firm*, the name or names under which any house of trade is established;' Ash's Dict., 1775. This is the proper sense; it alludes to the signature of the house; and the word was used with the sense of 'signature' as early as 1574 (N.E.D.).—Span. *firma*, a sign manual, signature; from *firmar*, vb., to confirm.—L. *firmāre*, to confirm.—L. *firmus*, firm (above).

FIRMAMENT, the celestial sphere. (F.—L.) In early use. ME. *firmament*, King Alisaunder, 714.—OF. *firmament*; Cot.—L. *firmāmentum*, (1) a support, (2) the expanse of the sky; Genesis, i. 6. —L. *firmāre*, to strengthen; with suffix *-mentum*.—L. *firmus*, firm. See **Firm.**

FIRMAN, a mandate. (Persian.) In Herbert's Travels, ed. 1665, p. 221.—Pers. *fermān*, a mandate, order; Palmer's Pers. Dict., col. 452; OPers. *framāna* (Horn); cf. Skt. *pramāṇam*, a measure, scale, authority, decision; from *pra*=Pers. *far-*=Gk. πρό, before; and *mā*, to measure.

FIRST, foremost, chief. (E.) ME. *first*, *firste*, Chaucer, C. T. 4715 (B 295). AS. *fyrst*, Grein, i. 364. + Icel. *fyrstr*; Dan. *förste*, Swed. *första*; OHG. *furisto*, first. Teut. type **furistoz*, superl. from the base **fur-*, fore. See **Fore, Former.**

FIRTH, the same as **Frith,** q. v.

FISCAL, pertaining to the revenue. (F.—L.) In Minsheu, ed. 1627.—MF. *fiscal*, 'fiscall;' Cot.—Late L. *fiscālis*, adj.—L. *fiscus*, a basket of rushes, also, a purse. Der. *con-fisc-ate*, q. v.

FISH, an animal that lives in water, and breathes through gills. (E.) ME. *fish*, *fisch*; Chaucer, C. T. 10587 (F 273). AS. *fisc*; Grein. + Du. *visch*; Icel. *fiskr*; Dan. and Swed. *fisk*; G. *fisch*. + L. *piscis*.+Irish and Gael. *iasg*, OIrish *iasc* (with loss of initial *p*, as in Irish *athair*=L. *pater*). Root unknown. Der. *fish*, verb; *fish-er*, *-er-y*, *-er-man*, *-ing*, *-y*, *-i-ness*, *-monger* (see *monger*).

FISSURE, a cleft. (F.—L.) In Blount's Gloss., ed. 1674.—F. *fissure*, 'a cleft;' Cot.—L. *fissūra*, a cleft; cf. *fissus*, pp. of *findere* (base *fid*), to cleave. + Skt. *bhid*, to break, pierce, disjoin.—√BHEID, to cleave; whence also E. **Bite,** q. v. Der. (from same root), *fiss-ile*, easily cleft.

FIST, the clenched hand. (E.) ME. *fist*; also *fest*, Chaucer, C. T. 12736 (C 802); *fust*, P. Plowman, B. xvii. 166. AS. *fýst*; Grein, i. 365.+Du. *vuist*; G. *faust*; OHG. *fūst*. Teut. type **fūstiz*. If the orig. type was **funhstiz*, it may be identified with Russ. *piaste*, the fist, OSlav. *pęsti*; from an Idg. type **penq-sti-*. Brugmann, i. § 647 (6).

FISTULA, a deep, narrow abscess. (L.) In Levins, ed. 1570; and Minsheu, ed. 1627.—L. *fistula*, a pipe; from its pipe-like shape. Der. *fistul-ar*, *-ous*; also *fester*.

FIT (1), to suit; as adj., apt, suitable. (Scand.) ME. *fitten*, to arrange, set (men) in array; Morte Arthure, ed. Brock, 1989, 2455. The adj. is ME. *fit*, *fyt*. '*Fyt*, or mete [meet];' Prompt. Parv. p. 163.—Icel. *fitja*, to knit together; Norse dial. *fitja*, to draw a lace together in a noose, knit (Aasen); Swed. dial. *fittja*, to bind together (Rietz). Cf. G. *fitzen*, to bind into skeins, from *fitze*, a skein. From Icel. *fit*, a hem, also 'web' of a bird's foot; cf. MDan. *fidde*, to bind, Dan. *fid*, a skein. Note MDu. *vitten*, 'to accommodate, to fitt, or to serve' (Hexham). ¶ Influenced as to sense by ME. *fete*, well done; from F. *fait*, L. *factus*; see **Feat.** Der. *fit*, verb; *fitt-ing*, Spenser, F. Q. vii. 7. 43; *fit-ly*, *-ness*; *fitt-er*.

FIT (2), a part of a poem; a sudden attack of illness. (E.) ME. *fit*, a part of a poem, burst of song, P. Plowman, A. i. 139; and see Chaucer, C. T. 4228 (A 4230). AS. *fit*, a song; also, a struggle; Grein, i. 300. Apparently related to Icel. *fet*, a pace, step, foot (in poetry), part of a poem. Cf. Skt. *pada-*, a step, trace, a verse of a poem; connected with *pad*, *pād*, a foot. See **Fetch,** and **Foot.** Der. *fit-ful*, Macbeth, iii. 2. 23; *fit-ful-ly*, *fit-ful-ness*.

FITCH, old spelling of *vetch*, Isaiah, xxviii. 25; see **Vetch.**

FITCHET, FITCHEW, a polecat. (F.—MDu.) Spelt *fitchew*, King Lear, iv. 6. 124; Troil. v. 1. 67; and earlier, in P. Ploughm. Crede, l. 295. The pl. *ficheux* occurs in 1438, in Fifty Earliest E. Wills, ed. Furnivall, p. 110.—OF. *fichau* (Godefroy); Picard *ficheux* (Sigart); answering to MF. *fissau*, expl. by Cot. as 'a fitch or fulmart,' i.e. polecat.—MDu. *fisse*, a polecat; Kilian. So called from the smell. Cf. Du. *vies*, nasty, loathsome; Icel. *fisi-sveppr*, a name of a fungus; Icel. *fisa*, Dan. *fise*, to make a smell.

FITZ, son. (AF.—L.) The spelling with *t* is unnecessary, but was due to a wish to preserve the old sound of Norm. F. *z*, which was pronounced as *ts*. The usual old spelling is *fiz*; see Vie de S. Auban, ed. Atkinson (Glossary); the spellings *filtz*, *fitz*, *fiz* all occur in P. Plowman, B. vii. 162 (and footnote).—L. *filius*, a son. See **Filial.**

FIVE, the half of ten. (E.) ME. *fif*, Layamon, 1425. At a later period, the pl. form *fyue* or *fiue* (with *u*=*v*, and with final *e*) is more common; cf. Rob. of Glouc. p. 6, l. 135 *n*. AS. *fíf*; sometimes *fífe*, five; Grein, i. 300. [Here *í* stands for *in* or *im*, and the true form was once **fínf*; or (by the influence of *f*) **fímf*.] + Du. *vijf*; Dan. and Swed. *fem*; Icel. *fimm*; Goth. *fimf*; OHG. *fimf*, *finf*; G. *funf*. +W. *pump*; OIrish *coic*; Lith. *penki*; Armenian *hing*; L. *quinque*; Gk. πέμπε, πέντε; Skt. *pañcha*. Idg. type **penqe*. Brugmann, ii. § 169. Der. *fives*, *five-fold*; *fif-teen*=ME. *fiftene*=AS. *fíftýne*, see **Ten;** *fif-th*=ME. *fifte*=AS. *fífta*; *fif-ty*=AS. *fíftig*.

FIVES, a disease of horses, the strangles. (F.—Span.—Arab.) In Shak. Tam. Shrew, iii. 2. 54. For *vives*, which is short for *avives*.—F. *avives*, 'vives;' Hamilton.—Span. *avivas*, *abivas*, *adivas*, 'the vives;' Pineda.—Arab. *ad-dhiba*, the same disease.—Arab. *al*, the; *dhīb*, a wolf (which strangles). See Devic (in Littré).

FIX, to bind, fasten. (F.—L.) Originally a pp. as in Chaucer, C. T. 16247 (G 779). [We also find a ME. verb *fichen*, to fix, pierce; Morte Arthure, ed. Brock, ll. 2098, 4239; formed directly from OF. *ficher*; from Late L. **figicāre* (not found), a secondary form from L. *figere*.]—OF. *fixe*, 'fixed, setled;' Cot.—L. *fixus*, pp. of *figere*, to fix. Der. *fix-ed*, *-ed-ly*, *-ed-ness*; *-at-ion*, Gower, C. A. ii. 86; bk. iv. 2520; *-i-ty*, *-ture*, Merry Wives, iii. 3. 67; *-ure*, Troil. i. 3. 101.

FIZZ, to make a hissing sound. (Scand.) We also find *fizzle*, a frequentative form, in Ben Jonson, The Devil is an Ass, v. 3. 2. Cf. ME. *fyse*, a blowing, Voc. 679. 23; allied to *fiist*, Prompt. Parv. p. 163.—Icel. *físa*, Dan. *fise*, with the same sense as L. *pedere*. An imitative word. See **Fitchew.**

FLABBERGAST, to frighten, greatly astonish. (E.) First in 1772. A dialect word, and more correctly *flapper-gast*; see E. D. D. The etymology is obvious; viz. *to gast* (frighten away) with a *flapper*, i.e. a clapper for frightening birds (E. D. D.). Cf. *gaste crowen*, to frighten crows; P. Plowman, A. vii. 129; and '*flappe*, instrument to smyte wythe flyys' [flies]; Prompt. Parv. See **Aghast** and **Flap.**

FLABBY, soft and yielding, hanging loose. (E.) Not in early use. '*Flabbiness*, limberness, softness and moistness;' Bailey's Dict. vol. ii. ed. 1731. 'His *flabby* flanks;' Dryden, tr. of Virgil, Georg. iii. 780. A variant of *flappy*, i.e. inclined to flap about. Cf. Low G. *flabbe*, a hanging lip, *flabbsig*, flabby (Danneil); MDu. *flabbe*, a contemptuous name for the tongue, Oudemans; Swed. dial. *fläbb*, the hanging underlip of animals, *flabb*, an animal's snout, Rietz; Dan. *flab*, the chops. See **Flap.**

FLACCID, soft and weak. (F.—L.) '*Flaccid*, withered, feeble, weak, flaggy;' Blount's Gloss., ed. 1674.—F. *flaccide*, 'weak, flaggie;' Cot.—L. *flaccidus*, flaccid.—L. *flaccus*, flabby, loose-hanging. Der. *flaccid-ness*, *-i-ty*.

FLAG (1), to droop, grow weary. (E.) 'Slow and *flagging* wings;' 2 Hen. VI, iv. 1. 5. Partly of F. origin (see at end); but also partly imitative, and weakened from the form *flack*. '*Flack*, to hang loosely, to flap;' E. D. D. It is the same word as ME. *flakken*, to move to and fro, to palpitate, as in Gower, C. A. iii. 315; bk. viii. 1196: 'her herte [began] to *flacke* and bete.' [Hence the frequentative verb *flacker*, 'to flutter, quiver;' E. D. D.] From the E. base *flak*, to waver; appearing in AS. *flacor*, flying, roving (Grein). +Dan. *flagre*, to flicker, flutter; cf. Icel. *flakka*, to rove about; *flaka*, to flap (said of garments); Swed. *flacksa*, to flutter; MDu. *flakkeren*, to waver; G. *flackern*, to flutter. ¶ The special sense is from OF. *flaquir*, to flag, MF. *flaque*, 'weake, feeble, faint, flaggy;' Cot.; from L. *flaccus*, limp. Cf. also MDu. *flaggēren*, 'to flagge, or grow wearie;' Hexham. See **Flabby, Flap, Flicker.** Der. *flagg-y*, *flagg-i-ness*.

FLAG (2), an ensign. (E.) In Shak. K. John, ii. 207.—The E. *flag* occurs in Palsgrave (1530), and is the oldest Teut. form. From ME. *flakken*, to waver, flutter; see **Flag** (1). Cf. Dan. *flag*; Norw. and Swed. *flagg*, a flag; Du. *vlag*; G. *flagge*.

FLAG (3), a water-plant, reed. (E.) Wyclif has *flaggy*, filled with flags or reeds; Exod. ii. 3. The same word as *flag* (2); and named from its waving in the wind; see **Flag** (1). Cf. prov. E. *flag*, a long, narrow leaf; Dan. *flæg*, an iris.

FLAG (4), **FLAGSTONE,** a paving-stone. (Scand.) Properly 'a thin slice' of stone; applied formerly also to a slice of turf. '*Flags*, the surface of the earth, which they pare off to burn: *Norfolk*;' Ray's Gloss. of Southern Words, ed. 1691. ME. *flagge*, 'flagge of the erthe;' Prompt. Parv.—Icel. *flaga*, a flag or slab of stone; *flag*, the spot where a turf has been cut out. [These would regularly give an E. form *flaw*, as in North E. (see E. D. D.), but *flag* is an E. Anglian form, found also in South E.] Cf. Swed. dial. *flagtorf*, a cut turf (Möller).—Icel. *flak-*, appearing in *flakna*, to flake off, to split; *flagna*, to flake off. **Flag** (4) is closely allied to **Flake,** q. v.

FLAGELLATE, to scourge. (L.) *Flagellation* is in Blount's Gloss. ed. 1674.—L. *flagellātus*, pp. of *flagellāre*, to scourge.—L. *flagellum*, a scourge; dimin. of *flagrum*, a scourge. Der. *flagellat-ion*; *flagell-ant*, from L. *flagellant-*, base of pres. pt. of *flagellāre*; also *flail*, q. v.; and perhaps *flog*.

FLAGEOLET, a sort of flute. (F.—Prov.) Spelt *flagellate* in Hudibras, c. ii. pt. ii. l. 610.—MF. *flageolet*, 'a pipe, whistle, flute;' Cot. Dimin. (with suffix *-et*) of OF. *flageol*, with the same sense; id.—OProv. *flaujols*, a flageolet; as if from a Late L. type **flaviolus*. Of unknown origin; the *fl-* may have been suggested by L. *flāre*, to blow.

FLAGITIOUS, very wicked. (L.) 'Many *flagicious* actes;' Hall's Chron. Rich. III, an. 3. § 39. ME. *flagiciouse*; Wyclif has 'most *flagiciouse*' (Vulg. *flagitiosissime*); 2 Macc. vii. 34.—L. *flāgitiōsus*, shameful.—L. *flāgitium*, a disgraceful act; cf. *flāgitāre*, to act with violence, implore earnestly. Perhaps allied to **Flagrant.** Der. *flagitious-ly*, *-ness*.

FLAGON, a drinking vessel. (F.—Late L.) In Berners, tr. of Froissart, vol. ii. c. 187 (R.). Spelt *flagan* in Caxton's ed. of Malory, Morte Arthure, b. vii. c. 14; leaf 117, back, l. 7.—OF. *flacon*, older form *flascon*, 'a great leathern bottle;' Cot.—Late L. *flascōnem*, acc. of *flasco*, a large flask; augmentative of *flascus*, *flasca*, a flask. See **Flask.**

FLAGRANT, glaring, said of a fault. (F.—L.) In Minsheu, ed. 1627.—MF. *flagrant*, 'flagrant, burning;' Cot.—L. *flagrantem*, acc. of pres. pt. of *flagrāre*, to burn.+Gk. φλέγειν, to burn; Skt.

bhrāj, to shine brightly. — √BHLEG, to burn. Brugmann, i. § 539 (2). **Der.** *flagrant-ly, flagranc-y*; see *con-flagrat-ion*.

FLAIL, an instrument for threshing corn. (F. — L.) In P. Plowman, B. vi. 187. — OF. *flael* (F. *fléau*), a flail, scourge. — L. *flagellum*, a scourge; in Late L., a flail. See **Flagellate.** ¶ The Late AS. *fliȝel*, Du. *vlegel*, G. *flegel*, are merely borrowed from L. *flagellum*.

FLAKE, a strip, thin slice or piece. (Scand.) 'As *flakes* fallen in grete snowes;' Chaucer, Ho. of Fame, iii. 102. Of Scand. origin; MSwed. *flake*, a slice; the Norwegian dialects have preserved the word as *flak*, a slice, a piece torn off, an ice-floe (Aasen); cf. Icel. *flakna*, also *flagna*, to flake off, split; Swed. *flaga*, a flaw, crack, breach, flake; *flagna*, to peel off. Also Swed. dial. *flag, flak*, a thin slice; Dan. *snee-flage*, a snow-flake. Perhaps allied to *flay*. See **Flay, Flaw, Floe,** and **Flag** (4). **Der.** *flak-y, flak-i-ness*.

FLAMBEAU, a torch. (F. — L.) In Herbert's Travels, ed. 1665, p. 135; and in Dryden, tr. of Juv. Sat. iii. 450. — F. *flambeau*, 'a linke, or torch of wax;' Cot. This answers to an *OF. *flambel*, dimin. of OF. *flambe*, a flame (below).

FLAME, a blaze, warmth. (F. — L.) In Chaucer, C. T. 15983 (G. 515). OF. *flame, flamme*; whence a secondary form *flambe*. — L. *flamma*, a flame. L. *flamma = *flag-ma*, from the base *flag-*, to burn; see **Flagrant. Der.** *flame*, verb, *flam-ing*; *flambeau*, q. v.; *flamingo*, q. v. Also *flamboyant*, characterised by waving lines; from F. *flamboyant*, pres. pt. of *flamboyer*, to flame; from OF. *flambe*, flame.

FLAMEN, a priest of ancient Rome. (L.) In Mandeville's Travels, p. 141; spelt *flamyn*. — L. *flāmen*, a priest. ¶ Perhaps for *flag-men* = he who burns the sacrifice; see **Flame.**

FLAMINGO, a bright red bird. (Span. — Prov. — L.) In Sir T. Herbert's Travels, ed. 1665, p. 403; spelt *flamengo*, Hakluyt, iii. 520. — Span. *flamenco*, a flamingo. — Prov. *flamenc, flamen*, a flamingo; so called from the colour. — Prov. *flama*, a flame. — L. *flamma*; see **Flame.** ¶ The Prov. suffix *-enc* is an adaptation of the Teut. suffix *-ing*. The F. form for 'flamingo' is *flamant*, lit. 'flaming;' but it seems to have been confused with F. *Flamand*, a Fleming. Palsgrave has: 'Flemmyng, *Flammant*.'

FLANGE, a projecting rim. (F. — OHG.) A dialectal form connected with prov. E. *flange*, to project out; E. D. D. Again, *flange* is a corruption of prov. E. *flanch*, a projection; cf. *flanch* in heraldry, an ordinary on each side (or *flank*) of the shield. — OF. *flanche* (AF. *flanke*), fem. sb. allied to F. *flanc*, side. Cf. MF. *flanchere*, 'a flanker, side-peece;' Cot. See below.

FLANK, the side. (F. — OHG.) ME. *flank*, King Alisaunder, 3745. — OF. (and F.) *flanc*, side. Connected by Diez with L. *flaccus*, soft; which is unsatisfactory. Now thought to be of OHG. origin. — OHG. *hlanca*, MHG. *lanke*, the loin, side (with change of initial *hl* to *fl*); cf. MDu. 'de Lancke, the flanks;' Hexham. Allied to AS. *hlanc*, slender. See **Lank. Der.** *flank*, verb; *flange*, q. v.

FLANNEL, a woollen substance. (Welsh.) 'The Welsh *flannel*;' Merry Wives, v. 5. 172. Prov. E. *flannen*, a more correct form; cf. 'apparelled in *flanen*,' Sidney's Arcadia, II. ii. 1 (ab. 1586). Prob. from W. *gwlanen*, an article made with wool, from *gwlan*, wool. The W. *gwlan* is cognate with E. *wool*; Rhys, Lect. on W. Philology, p. 10. See **Wool.**

FLAP, to strike or beat with the wings, &c. (E.) ME. *flappen*, P. Plowman, B. vi. 187. Also *flap*, sb., a blow, stroke, id. B. xiii. 67. EFries. *flappen*. Not found in AS. + Du. *flappen*, to flap; *flap*, a stroke, blow, box on the ear. β. A variant of *flack*, to beat, ME. *flakken*, to palpitate; see **Flag** (1); of imitative origin. **Der.** *flap*, sb.; *flapp-er*.

FLARE, to burn brightly, blaze, glare. (Scand.) In Shak. Merry Wives, iv. 6. 62. 'His *flaring* beams;' Milton, Il Pens. 132. Apparently of Scand. origin. Cf. Norweg. *flara*, to blaze, flame, adorn with tinsel; *flar*, tinsel, show; Aasen. Ross shows that it stands for *fladra*, to blaze, to display, to make a show; allied to Swed. *fladdra*, to flutter, also to blaze, flame (Widegren); Low G. *fladdern*, G. *flattern*, to flutter, flicker. From a Teut. base *flad*, to waver; cf. the base *flak*, noticed under **Flag** (1).

FLASH, to blaze suddenly. (E.) In Shak. Timon, ii. 1. 32; used of suddenly breaking out, K. Lear, i. 3. 4. ME. *flaschen*, to dash; Trevisa, tr. of Higden, i. 63, ii. 369. Cf. Swed. dial. *flasa*, to burn violently, blaze. And cf. Icel. *flasa*, to rush; *flas*, a headlong rushing. **Der.** *flash*, sb.; *flash-y, flash-i-ly, flash-i-ness*. ☞ We find: 'Heo *vlaskeð* water þeron' = she dashes or casts water on it; Ancren Riwle, p. 314; which seems to be allied.

FLASK, a kind of bottle. (Late L.) In Shak. Romeo, iii. 3. 132. AS. *flasce*, whence by metathesis, the form *flacse*, written *flaxe*. [This change of *sc* to *cs* or *x* is common in AS.; as in *āscian = ācsian = āxian*; mod. E. to *ask* and prov. E. to *ax*.] See *flasce* in Voc. 240. 3; *flaxe*, id. 109. 5. 'Twā fatu, on folcisc *flaxan* gehātene' = two vessels, vulgarly called flasks; Gregory's Dialogues, ii. 18 (Bosworth); where the L. text has 'quæ vulgo *flascones* vocantur.' We find also Icel. *flaska*

(an old word); Dan. *flaske*; Swed. *flaska*; G. *flasche*; OHG. *flasca*. β. But it is improbable that the word is really Teutonic; it seems to be rather from Late L. *flasca*, a flask, of uncertain origin; the deriv. *flasco* occurs in Gregory (as above), ab. A.D. 600. Perhaps from L. *uasculum*, a little vessel (Diez). We also find W. *fflasg*, Gael. *flasg* (from E.). **Der.** *flagon*, q.v.

FLAT, level, smooth. (Scand.) ME. *flat*; 'sche fel .. *flat* to the grounde;' Will. of Palerne, 4414. — Icel. *flatr*, flat; Swed. *flat*; Dan. *flad*. ¶ The connexion with Gk. πλατύς, broad, has not been made out; Curtius, i. 346. And it must be rejected; see **Flawn. Der.** *flat*, sb.; *-ly, -ness*; *flatt-en* (coined by analogy with *length-en*, &c.); *flatt-ish, flat-wise*.

FLATTER, to coax, soothe. (F. — Scand.; or E.) ME. *flateren* (with one *t*); P. Plowman, B. xx. 109. Perhaps from (or at any rate influenced by) OF. *flater* (later *flatter*), 'to flatter, sooth, smooth; .. also to claw, stroke, clap gently;' Cot. But this would have only given a ME. form *flat-en*; so that the *-er-* is an E. addition. β. The OF. *flat-er* is from Icel. *flat-r*, flat; with the notion of making smooth. γ. But the base *flat-* may have been of imitative origin, like *flak-*, whence MSwed. *fleckra*, to flatter (Ihre); Swed. dial. *fleka*, to caress (Rietz). Cf. ME. *flakken*, to move to and fro, and G. *flach*, flat; and note ME. *flakeren* as a variant of *flateren*, Ancren Riwle, p. 222. ¶ The sb. *flattery* is from OF. *flaterie*, F. *flatterie*; which, indeed, may have suggested the suffix *-er-*.

FLATULENT, full of wind, windy. (F. — L.) In Minsheu; also in Holland's Plutarch, p. 577 (R.). — MF. *flatulent*, 'flatulent, windy;' Cot. — Late L. *flātulentus*; not in Ducange, but regularly formed from the base *flātu-*, by analogy with *temulentus*, drunken. — L. *flātus*, a blowing, a breath. — L. *flātus*, pp. of *flāre*, to blow; cognate with E. *blow*. See **Blow** (1). **Der.** *flatulent-ly, flatulence, flatulenc-y*.

FLAUNT, to display ostentatiously. (Scand.) Shak. has *flaunts*, s. pl. fine clothes, Winter's Ta. iv. 4. 23. 'Yeeld me thy *flanting* [showy] hood;' Turberville, To his Friend that refused him, st. 10. 'With . . . fethers *flaunt-a-flaunt*,' i.e. showily displayed; Gascoigne, Steel Glass, 1163. Prov. E. *flant, flaunt*, to gad about, esp. in finery; *flanty* or *flaunty*, giddy, flighty. Of Scand. origin. Cf. Norw. *flanta*, to gad about; from *flana*, to climb, to rove about, to gad about; *flana*, a gad-about, *flanen*, adj. obtrusive, forward (of children). So also Jutland *flanted*, adj., as *en flanted Tös*, a gad-about (flaunting) hussy, from a verb *flante* (Kok); Jutland *flante*, a giddy girl, *flantet*, foolish (Feilberg); Dan. *flane*, a giddy girl, *flane*, to flirt. Also Swed. dial. *flana*, to be unsteady, to be extravagantly hilarious, *flana*, a flirt; whence also Swed. dial. *flanka*, to be unsteady, waver, hang and wave about, ramble; and the adj. and adv. *flankt*, loosely, flutteringly (which = Gascoigne's *flaunt-a-flaunt*). Perhaps also allied to Bavarian *flandern*, to flutter, flaunt, Schmeller, i. 792. Cf. Gk. πλάνη, a wandering; see **Planet.**

FLAVOUR, the taste, scent. (F. — L.) Milton, Sams. Agon., 544, says of wine 'the *flavor* or the smell, Or taste that cheers the heart of Gods or men,' &c. He here seems to distinguish *flavour* from both *smell* and *taste*; but he may have meant the former. ME. *flavour* (= *flavor*); Early E. Allit. Poems, ed. Morris, A. 87. But Wyntown has *flewoure*, scent, Chron. ix. 26. 107; Henryson has *flewer*, Moral Fables, p. 66 (N. E. D.). The word must have been modified by the influence of *savour*. — OF. *fleur, fleiur, flaur*, smell. Cf. Ital. *fiatore*, a bad odour; answering to a Late L. acc. type *flātōr-em*. — L. *flātus*, pp. of *flāre*, to blow. (Körting, § 3825.)

FLAW, a crack, break. (Scand.) ME. *flawe*, used in the sense of 'flake;' '*flawes* of fyre' = flakes of fire; Allit. Morte Arthure, ed. Brock, 2556. — Swed. *flaga*, a flaw, crack, breach; also, a flake; Norw. *flaga*, a piece flaked off; a place (on a tree-stem) without bark (Ross); see **Flake.** Cf. prov. E. *flaw*, a flake (as of snow); also a gust of wind, like Du. *vlaag*. **Der.** *flaw-less*.

FLAWN, a kind of custard. (F. — OHG.) 'Fill ouen full of *flawnes*;' Tusser, Husb. § 90. st. 5. ME. *flaun*; 'Pastees and *flaunes*,' Havelok, 644. — F. *flan*, OF. *flaon*. Cotgrave gives *flans*, 'flawns, custards, egg-pies; also, round plates of metall;' and *flaons*, 'round plates of metall.' [Cf. Span. *flaon*, flawn, plate of metal; Ital. *fiadone*, 'a kind of flawne,' Florio; Low L. *flado, flato*, a flawn.] — OHG. *flado*, a broad flat cake, flawn; MHG. *vlade*; G. *fladen*, a kind of pan-cake. β. Cf. G. *kuh-fladen*, a piece of cow-dung; MDu. *vlade*, 'a flawne,' Hexham; ME. *flathe*, a flawn, Wright, Vocab. i. 127; a flat fish (Prompt. Parv.). Further allied to Gk. πλατύς, broad, πλάθανον, a dish in which cakes were baked, a platter. (See Scheler, Diez, Kluge.)

FLAX, the name of a plant. (E.) ME. *flax*, Chaucer, C. T. 678 (A 676). AS. *fleax*; Ælfric's Gloss., ed. Somner, Vestium Nomina, l. 10. + Du. *vlas*; G. *flachs*; OHG. *vlahs, flahs*. β. Cf. Goth. *flahta*, a plaiting of the hair; it is probable that *flax* is from the same root; see Curtius, i. 203. If so, the root is PLEK, to weave; whence also

Gk. πλέκειν, to weave, plait. **Der.** *flax-en,* where *-en* is an AS. adj. suffix.

FLAY, to strip off skin, slice off. (E.) Formerly spelt *flea;* see Rich. and Halliwell. ME. *flean,* pt. t. *flow,* pp. *flain;* Havelok, 2502. AS. *flēan* (in a gloss); Bosworth.+Icel. *flā,* pt. t. *flō,* pp. *fleginn.* Teut. type **flah-an-,* pt. t. **flōh,* to strike. Cognate with Lith. *plak-ù,* I strike; cf. L. *plāga,* a stroke. See **Plague.** Brugmann, i. § 569.

FLEA, a small insect. (E.) ME. *flee,* pl. *fleen;* Chaucer, C. T. 16966 (H 17). AS. *flēah* (O. E. Texts); spelt *fleo,* as a gloss to *pulex,* in Æl. Gloss.; Voc. 121. 38.+Du. *vloo;* Icel. *flō;* G. *floh.* Teut. base **flauh-* (or rather **þlauh-*); allied to the verb *to flee.* See **Flee.**

FLEAM, a kind of lancet. (F.—L.—Gk.) In Kersey's Dict., ed. 1715. Spelt *fleame* in Cotgrave, s. v. *deschaussoir.*—OF. *flieme,* F. *flamme,* 'a fleam;' Hamilton and Legros. [Cotgrave gives only the dimin. *flammette,* 'a kind of launcet.']—Late L. *flētoma,* a lancet (Voc. 400. 11); shortened from *flevotomum, phlebotomum,* a lancet.—Gk. φλεβοτόμον, a lancet.—Gk. φλεβό-, decl. stem of φλέψ, a vein; and τομ-, 2nd grade of τέμνειν, to cut. See **Phlebotomy.** ¶ This pardonable abbreviation of too long a word is countenanced by Du. *vlijm,* G. *fliete,* and MHG. *fliedeme,* all various corruptions of the same surgical word.

FLECK, a spot. (Scand.) ME. has only the verb *flekken,* to spot; Chaucer, C. T. 16033 (G 565).—Icel. *flekkr,* a spot; *flekka,* to stain, spot; Swed. *fläck,* a spot; *fläcka,* to spot; Du. *vlek,* sb.; *vlekken,* vb.; G. *fleck,* sb.; *flecken,* vb.; to spot, stain, put on a patch.

FLECTION, a bending; see **Flexible.**

FLEDGE, to acquire (or be furnished with) feathers. (E.) Shak. has *fledged,* Merch. Ven. iii. 1. 32. This pp. *fledged* is a substitution for an older adj. *fledge,* meaning 'ready to fly.' ME. *flegge,* 'ready to fly' (Stratmann), a Kentish form of ME. *flygge,* ready to fly; spelt *fligge* in the Prompt. Parv. p. 167 (and note). AS. **flycge,* found in comp. *unflycge;* as in 'inplumes, *unflicge;*' O. E. Glosses (Napier), 28. 13. + Du. *vlug,* MDu. *vlugge;* Low G. *flugge;* OHG. *flucchi.* Teut. type **flugjoz,* adj.; from **flug-,* weak grade of **fleugan-,* to fly. Cf. also Icel. *fleygr,* able to fly; Icel. *fleygja,* to make to fly, causal of *fljūga,* to fly. See **Fly** (1). **Der.** *fledge-ling.*

FLEE, to escape, run away. (E.) Not the same word as *fly.* ME. *fleen,* pt. t. *fleh, fleih;* Cursor Mundi, 2818. [We also find the pt. t. *fledde,* and pp. *fled;* Chaucer, C. T. 2932; Havelok, 1431.] AS. *flēon* (pt. t. *flēah*).+OSax. *fliohan,* G. *fliehen;* Icel. *flýja* (pt. t. *flō,* also *flýði*); Swed. *fly* (pt. t. *flydde*); Goth. *thliuhan.* Teut. type **thliuhan-* (pt. t. *thlauh*); so that *fl* was orig. *thl,* and there was at first *no* connexion with the verb to *fly,* which was at an early date confused with it. ¶ The pt. t. *fled,* ME. *fledde,* was due to Icel. *flýði,* Swed. *flydde* (above).

FLEECE, a sheep's coat of wool. (E.) Here *-ce* stands for *s,* as often. ME. *flees,* Prompt. Parv. p. 166; Wyclif, Gen. xxx. 35. AS. *flēos* (Bosw.); earlier *flius* (O. E. Texts); also (with mutation) *flȳs,* Ps. lxxi. 6 (ed. Spelman).+Du. *vlies;* G. *fliess;* MHG. *vlius;* cf. also G. *flaus,* a woollen coat, MHG. *vlūs,* a sheep-skin. Teut. types **fleusi-, *fleuso-, *flūso-;* possibly allied to L. *plū-ma.* See **Plume.** (See Kluge.)

FLEER, to mock, to grin. (Scand.) In Shak. L. L. L. v. 2. 109; Jul. Cæs. i. 3. 117. ME. *flerien,* Morte Arthure, ed. Brock, 1088, 2778. Of Scand. origin; cf. Norw. *flira,* to titter, giggle, laugh at nothing; Aasen. Dan. dial. *flire,* to jeer. Also Norw. *flisa,* to titter; Swed. *flissa,* to titter. β. Another variation of this verb is Swed. *flina,* to titter; Swed. dial. *flina,* to make a wry face (Rietz).

FLEET (1), a number of ships. (E.) ME. *flete,* Morte Arthure, ed. Brock, 1189; *fleote,* Layamon, 2155. AS. *flēot,* a ship, Grein, i. 304. [It seems afterwards to have been used collectively.]—AS. *flēotan,* to 'fleet,' i.e. to float, swim.+OSax. *fliotan,* Du. *vlieten,* to flow; G. *fliessen,* to flow; Icel. *fljōta,* Swed. *flyta,* to flow. Teut. type **fleutan-,* pt. t. **flaut,* pp. **flutanoz;* Idg. base **pleud,* as in Lith. *plūdis,* a float of a fishing-net. (√PLEU.) Cf. Gk. πλέειν, to sail; Skt. *plu, pru,* to swim, float, flow. β. Hence also the more usual AS. form *flota,* a ship, Grein, i. 305 (=ME. *flote,* Havelok, 738); which is cognate with Icel. *floti,* (1) a raft, (2) a fleet. See **Float** (4).

FLEET (2), a creek, bay. (E.) In the place-names *North-fleet, Fleet* Street, &c. Fleet Street was so named from the Fleet ditch; and *fleet* was a name given to any shallow creek, or stream or channel of water; see E. D. D. ME. *fleet,* Prompt. Parv. p. 166. AS. *flēot,* a bay of the sea, as in *sǣs flēot*=bay of the sea; tr. of Beda, i. 34. Cf. also AS. *flēote,* a stream. The orig. sense was 'that which flows;' and the deriv. is from the old verb *fleet,* to float, flow; see above. Cf. OFries. *flēt,* Icel. *fljōt,* a stream; Du. *vliet,* a rill, a brook.

FLEET (3), swift. (E.) In Shak. L. L. L. v. 2. 261. It does not seem to appear in ME., but the AS. form is *flēotig* (=fleet-y), Grein, i. 304. It is a derivative from the old verb to *fleet,* and =

fleeting; see **Fleet** (4). Cf. Icel. *fljōtr,* fleet, swift; from the verb *fljōta;* see **Fleet** (1). **Der.** *fleet-ly, -ness.*

FLEET (4), to move swiftly. (E.) 'As seasons *fleet;*' 2 Hen. VI, ii. 4. 4. From **Fleet** (3). **Der.** *fleet-ing, fleet-ing-ly.* ¶ Not the same word as *flit,* though allied to it; see **Flit.**

FLESH, the soft muscular covering of the bones of animals. (E.) ME. *flesch, fleisch;* Chaucer, C. T. 147. AS. *flǣsc,* Grein, i. 302.+Du. *vleesch;* G. *fleisch,* flesh; and (with short vowel) Icel. *flesk,* in the special sense of 'pork,' or 'bacon;' Dan. *flesk,* pork, bacon; Swed. *fläsk,* pork, bacon. Teut. type **flaiskos,* neut. See **Flesh,** verb, K. John, v. 1. 71; *flesh-ed;* *-less, -ly, -y, -i-ly, -i-ness.*

FLETCHER, an arrow-maker. (F.—C.) ME. *flecchour,* Destruction of Troy, l. 1593.—OF. *flechier,* a fletcher.—OF. *fleche* (F. *flèche*), an arrow.—OIrish *flesc,* a rod, a wand. Stokes-Fick, p. 287.

FLEUR-DE-LIS, flower of the lily. (F.—L.) ME. *floure-de-lice,* Minot's Poems (Spec. of Eng. ed. Morris and Skeat, p. 131, l. 25).—OF. *fleur de lis;* whence also E. *flower-de-luce,* Winter's Ta. iv. 4. 127. Here *lis* is from the old pl. form, because there were three *flowers-de-lis* on the royal shield; the OF. nom. sing. was *lil.*—L. *lilium,* a lily. See **Flower** and **Lily.**

FLEXIBLE, easily bent. (F.—L.) In Shak. Troil. i. 3. 50; and Hoccleve, De Regim. Princ., 3358.—F. *flexible,* 'flexible;' Cot. —L. *flexibilis,* easily bent.—L. *flexus,* pp. of *flectere,* to bend. **Der.** *flexible-ness, flexibil-y, flexibil-i-ty;* from L. *flexus* are also *flex-ion* (wrongly *flect-ion*), *-or, -ile, -ure;* from the same source, *circum-flex, de-flect, in-flex-ion* (wrongly *in-flect-ion*), *re-flect.*

FLICKER, to flutter, waver. (E.) ME. *flikeren,* to flutter; Chaucer, Troil. iv. 1221. AS. *flicerian,* Deut. xxxii. 11; also *flicorian,* Ælfric, Hom. ii. 156. β. Here *flicerian* is a frequentative form from the base *flic-,* an attenuated form of the base FLAK, to beat; the sense is 'to beat slightly and often.' γ. This is made clear by the occurrence of the stronger form *flaker* in the ME. *flakeren,* Ancren Riwle, p. 222; of which the later form *flacker* occurs in Coverdale's Bible, Ezek. x. 19: 'And the cherubins *flackered* with their wings.' See **Flag** (1). ¶ The Icel. *flökra,* to flutter=E. *flacker;* Du. *flikkeren,* to sparkle=E. *flicker.* Cf. Prov. Du. *flik,* a light blow (Molema).

FLIGHT (1), the act of flying. (E.) ME. *flight,* Chaucer, C. T. 190. AS. *flyht,* Grein, i. 306; allied to AS. *flyg-e,* flight. Teut. type **fluhtiz;* from **flug-,* weak grade of **fleugan-,* to fly. **Der.** *flight-y, -i-ness.* See **Fly** (1).

FLIGHT (2), the act of fleeing away. (E.) ME. *fliht,* Layamon, l. 21405; Ormulum, l. 19683.+OSax. and OHG. *flucht.* Teut. type **thluhtiz;* from **thluh-,* weak grade of **thliuhan-,* to flee; see **Flee.**

FLIMSY, weak, slight. (Scand. ?) 'Flimsy, limber, slight;' Phillips, ed. 1706. In Pope, Prol. to Satires, l. 94. Lit. 'like the skim on milk.' Formed by adding *-y* to Dan. dial. *flims, flems,* skim on milk; cf. EFries. *flēm, flim,* a film. These forms are allied to E. *film.* If the ending was *-sy* (as from EFries. *flīm*), cf. *tip-sy, bump-sy,* also *limp-sy,* given by Webster as the synonym of *flimsy* in the U. S. A. **Der.** *flimsi-ness.*

FLINCH, to shrink back. (F.—Teut. ?) In Shak. All's Well, ii. 1. 190.—OF. *flenchir, flainchir,* to turn aside, bend (given by Godefroy, s. v. *flechir*). Perhaps from OHG. **hlencan,* answering to G. *lenken,* to bend, turn. This G. *lenken* is from OHG. *hlanca,* the side (Kluge); see **Flank.** ¶ The initial *fl* would then be accounted for, as in *flank,* from OHG. *hl.* See **Link** (1).

FLING, to throw, dart, scatter about. (Scand.) The pt. t. *flang* =flung, occurs in King Alisaunder, 2749. Cf. Swed. *flänga,* to use violent action, to romp; *flänga med hästarna,* to ride horses too hard; *fläng,* sb., violent exercise, *i fläng,* at full speed (cf. E. *to take one's fling*); Swed. dial. *flänga,* to strip bark from trees, to hack, strike (Rietz); MSwed. *flenga,* to strike, beat with rods (Ihre); Dan. *flenge,* to slash; *i fleng,* indiscriminately. β. These forms presuppose a strong verb **fling-a,* which the E. form perhaps represents.

FLINT, a hard stone. (E.) ME. *flint,* Havelok, 2667. AS. *flint,* a rock; Numb. xx. 10. + Dan. *flint;* Swed. *flinta.* Cf. Gk. πλίνθος, a brick; Brugmann, ii. §§ 575, 704. **Der.** *flint-y, -i-ness.*

FLIP (1), to fillip, jerk lightly. (Scand.) First in 1616; see further under **Flippant.**

FLIP (2), a mixture of beer and spirit with sugar, heated. (E.) 'Eat biscuit, and drink *flip;*' Congreve, Love for Love, A. iii. sc. 4 (Ben). From *flip* (above), to beat up. Moisy (Dict. of Norman patois) spells it *philippe,* as if from F. *Philippe;* but it is borrowed from E.

FLIPPANT, pert, saucy. (Scand.) 'A most *flippant* tongue she had;' Chapman, All Fools, Act v. sc. 1, prose speech by Gostanzo. The suffix *-ant* is due to the Northern E. pres. pt. in *-and;* hence *flippant*=*flippand,* i. e. prattling, babbling. Or else *-ant* imitates the F. pres. part., as in *ramp-ant.* From the base *flip-,* weak grade allied to Icel. *fleipa*, to babble, prattle; Swed. dial. *flepa*, to talk nonsense (Rietz). Cf. *flip*, the lip. **Der.** *flippant-ness*, *flippanc-y*.

FLIRT, to trifle in wooing. (E.) In old authors 'to mock,' or 'scorn,' and often spelt *flurt*; see The Two Noble Kinsmen, ed. Skeat, i. 2. 18 (and the note). The oldest sense of *flirt* was 'to jerk lightly away;' see N. E. D. and E. D. D. We find EFries. *flirr*, *flirt*, a light blow; *flirtje*, a giddy girl. **Der.** *flirt*, sb.; *flirt-ation*.

FLIT, to remove from place to place. (Scand.) ME. *flitten*; P. Plowman, B. xi. 62; also *flutten*, Layamon, 30503. — Swed. *flytta*, to flit, remove; Dan. *flytte*. From **flut-*, weak grade of Icel. *fljóta* (Swed. *flyta*, Dan. *flyde*), to float, flow. See **Fleet** (1). Cf. Icel. *flýta*, to hasten; *flytja*, to carry, cause to flit; *flytjask* (reflexive), to flit, remove. **Der.** *flitt-ing*, Ps. lvi. 8 (P.-Bk. version). Also *flitter-mouse*, i. e. a bat; see **Flutter**.

FLITCH, a side of bacon. (E.) ME. *flicche*, P. Plowman, B. ix. 169. AS. *flicce*, str. n., to translate L. *succidia*; Bosworth. The pl. *fliccu* occurs in Diplom. Angl., ed. Thorpe, p. 158; gen. *flicca*, id. p. 460. Teut. type **flik-jom*, n. + Icel. *flikki*, a flitch: *flik*, a flap, tatter. β. The Swed. *flik* is a lappet, a lobe; Dan. *flik* is a patch; cf. G. *flick-* (in comp.), a patch. Perhaps allied to **Fleck**.

FLOAT, to swim on a liquid surface. (E.) ME. *floten*, *flotian*, *flotten*; [very rare, the usual form being *fleten* (AS. *fléotan*)]; see **Fleet** (4). 'A whal . . . by that bot *flotte* '=a whale floated by the boat; Allit. Poems, ed. Morris, C. 248. AS. *flotian*; as in 'an scip *flotigende*,' a ship floating; A. S. Chron., an. 1031. Cf. AS. *flota*, a ship (Grein); allied words to which are Icel. *floti*, a float, raft, whence *flotna*, to float to the top; Swed. *flotta*, a fleet, a raft, *flotta*, to cause to float; Du. *vlot*, a raft, whence *vlotten*, to cause to float, to float; G. *floss*, a raft, whence *flössen*, to float; see also **Fleet** (1). Teut. type **flutōjan-*, to float; from **flut-*, weak grade of **fleutan-*, to float, whence mod. E. *fleet*. See **Fleet** (1). ¶ Partly confused with F. *flotter* (OF. *floter*), to float; from the same Teut. base **flut-*. See **Flotilla**. **Der.** *float*, sb.; *float-er*, *-age*, *-ing*, *-at-ion*; also *flotsam*, q. v.

FLOCK (1), a company of birds or sheep. (E.) ME. *flok*; 'a flok of bryddis '=birds; King Alisaunder, 566. AS. *flocc*, m., Gen. xxxii. 8. + Icel. *flokkr*; Dan. *flok*; Swed. *flock*. **Der.** *flock*, verb.

FLOCK (2), a lock of wool. (F. — L.) In Shak. 1 Hen. IV, ii. 1. 7; ME. *flokkys*, pl.; Prompt. Parv. — MF. *floc*, *floc de laine*, 'a lock or flock of wool;' Cot. — L. *floccum*, acc. of *floccus*, a lock of wool. **Der.** *flock-y*; and (from L. *floccus*), *flocc-ose*, *flocc-ul-ent*; also *flock-bed*, &c. Brugmann, i. § 585 (1). ¶ Not to be confused with *flake*, with which it is unconnected.

FLOE, a flake of ice. (Dan.) Modern; common in accounts of Arctic Voyages. — Dan. *flage*, in the comp. *iis-flage*, an ice-floe; Norw. *isflak*, *isflök*, lit. 'ice-flake.' See **Flake**. ¶ Strictly, Dan. *flage* gives E. *flaw*; the sound was not exactly caught.

FLOG, to beat, whip. (L.?) A late word. It occurs in Cowper's Tirocinium, l. 329; and in Swift (Todd); also in Coles' Dict. ed. 1671, which gives: '*Flog* (cant word), to whip.' Perhaps a school-boy's abbreviation from the L. *flagellāre*, to whip, once a familiar word. See **Flagellate**. ¶ This is paralleled by the use of Low G. *flogger*, as a common variant of *flegel*, a flail; where *flegel* represents L. *flagellum*.

FLOOD, a great flow of water. (E.) ME. *flod*, P. Plowman, B. vi. 326. AS. *flōd*, Grein, i. 305. + Du. *vloed*; Icel. *flód*; Swed. and Dan. *flod*; Goth. *flōdus*, a river; G. *fluth*. Teut. type **flō-ðuz*, act of flowing, also a flood; from the Teut. base **flō(u)-*. From the notion of flowing; see **Flow**. Allied to Gk. πλω-τός, floating. Brugmann, i. § 154. **Der.** *flood*, verb; *flood-ing*, *flood-gate*.

FLOOR, a flat surface, platform. (E.) ME. *flor*, Allit. Poems, ed. Morris, B. 133. AS. *flōr*, Grein, i. 306. + Du. *vloer*; G. *flur*. Teut. type **flōruz*. Cognate with W. *llawr*; Bret. *leur*; Irish and Gael. *lár* (< *plár*); Celtic type **(p)lāros*; Stokes-Fick, p. 236. From Idg. **plā-*, to spread out; whence also L. *plā-nus*, plain. See **Plain**. **Der.** *floor-ing*.

FLOP, to flap or sway heavily. (E.) A dialectal form; see E. D. D. An imitative variety of *flap*, expressive of greater heaviness or clumsiness. Cf. prov. Du. *flóp*, the sound of a blow or fall (Molema); Low G. *flupps*, suddenly (Berghaus).

FLORAL, pertaining to flowers. (L.) Late. In Johnson's Dict. — L. *flōrālis*, belonging to Flora. — L. *Flōra*, goddess of flowers; mentioned in Shak. Wint. Ta. iv. 4. 2. — L. *flōr-*, stem of *flōs*, a flower; cf. *flōr-ēre*, to flourish. See **Flower**. **Der.** *flor-esc-ence* (from L. *flōrescere*, to blossom); *flor-et*; *flori-culture*, *-fer-ous*, *-form*, *flor-ist*; also *flor-id*, q. v., *florin*, q. v.

FLORID, abounding in flowers, red. (L.) In Milton, P. L. iv. 278. [Directly from Latin; the OF. *floride* means 'lively.']—L. *flōridus*, abounding with flowers. — L. *flōri-*, decl. stem of *flōs*, a flower. See **Flower**. **Der.** *florid-ly*, *-ness*.

FLORIN, a coin of Florence. (F. — Ital. — L.) ME. *florin*,

Chaucer, C. T. 12704 (c. 770). *Florins* were coined by Edw. III in 1337, and named after the coins of Florence, which were much esteemed. First in 1303; spelt *florens* (N. E. D.). — OF. *florin*, 'a florin;' Cot. — Ital. *fiorino* (= *florino*), a florin; so named because it bore a lily, the symbol of Florence. — Ital. *fiore*, a flower; with allusion to L. *Flōrentia* (Florence). — L. acc. *flōr-em*, a flower, *flōr-ēre*, to flourish. See **Flower**.

FLOSCULE, a floret of a composite flower. (L.) Botanical and scientific. — L. *flosculus*, a little flower; double dimin. of *flōs*, a flower. See **Flower**.

FLOSS, a downy substance, untwisted silken filaments. (F. — L.) What is now called *floss-silk* was formerly called *sleave-silk*; see Nares. The term *floss-silk* is modern (first in 1759). Cot. gives ' soye *flosche*, sleave silk;' whence the E. word seems to have been borrowed. [Cf. Ital. *floscio*, flaccid, soft, weak; whence *floscia seta*, 'raveling or sleave silke;' Florio. The Venetian form, according to Wedgwood, is *flosso*, which exactly agrees with the E. *floss*.] An adj. formation from OF. *flocher*, to form into 'flocks' or tufts. — OF. *floc*; see **Flock** (2).

FLOTILLA, a little fleet. (Span. — Teut.) Merely Spanish; Bailey gives only the form *flota*. — Span. *flotilla*, a little fleet; dimin. of *flota*, a fleet, cognate with OF. *flote*, a fleet of ships, but also a crowd of people, a group (OF. *flote de gens*); see Burguy. This OF. *flote*, a fem. form, is from a Teut. source. Cf. Du. *vloot*, a fleet, allied to Icel. *floti*, (1) a raft, (2) a fleet, AS. *flota*, a ship. From the Teut. base **flut-*; see **Float**, **Fleet** (1). (Körting, § 3861.)

FLOTSAM, goods lost in shipwreck, and left floating on the waves. (AF. — E.) *and* L.) In Blackstone's Comment. b. i. c. 8; spelt *flotson* in Blount's Law Dict., ed. 1691. Cotgrave has: ' a *flo*, floating; *choses a flo*, flotsens or flotzams.' This is an Old Law F. term, appearing as AF. *floteson*, Black Book of the Admiralty, ed. Twiss, i. 82; which answers to OF. *flotaison*, a flooding of fields, F. *flott-aison*, flotation, formed with suffix *-eson*, *-aison* (L. *-ātionem*) from the verb *flotter*, to float; which is of Teut. origin (above).

FLOUNCE (1), to plunge about. (Scand.) 'After his horse had *flounced* and floundered with his heeles;' Holland, tr. of Ammianus, p. 77 (R.). 'Alexander *flounced* . . . into the floudde;' Udall, tr. of Erasmus, Apophthegmes (1542), p. 183, b (N. E. D.). Of imitative origin; Cf. Swed. dial. *flunsa*, to dip, plunge, to fall into water with a plunge (Rietz); MSwed. *flunsa*, to plunge, particularly used of the dipping of a piece of bread into gravy (Ihre); Norw. *fluns*, violent and unusual treatment (Ross). See **Flounder** (1).

FLOUNCE (2), a plaited border on a dress. (F. — L.) 'To change a *flounce*;' Pope, Rape of the Lock, ii. 100. 'Farthingales and *flounces*,' Beaum. and Fletcher, Mons. Thomas, iii. 2. 3. Made, by change of *r* to *l*, from ME. *frounce*, a plait, wrinkle; P. Plowman, B. xiii. 318; Chaucer, tr. of Boethius, b. i. pr. 2, l. 20. We also have *frounced*=frizzled and curled, in Milton, Il Pens. 123; cf. Spenser, F. Q. i. 4. 14. — OF. *froncer*, *fronser*, 'to gather, plait, fold, wrinkle; *fronser le front*, to frown or knit the brows;' Cot. β. Perhaps from Late L. **frontiāre*, to wrinkle the forehead; not found, but regularly formed from *fronti-*, decl. stem of *frons*, the forehead. See **Front**, and **Frounce**. (Körting, § 4009.)

FLOUNDER (1), to flounce about. (Scand.) See quotation under **Flounce** (1); also in Beaum. and Fletcher, Woman's Prize, ii. 6. 30. Of imitative origin; from Norw. *flundra*, to sprawl, to flounder (Ross). Cf. Norw. *fluna*, to sprawl, struggle; Du. *flodderen*, to dangle, flap, splash through the mire; Swed. *fladdra*, to flutter.

FLOUNDER (2), the name of a fish. (F. — Scand.) *Flounder-like* occurs in Massinger, Renegado, Act iii. sc. 1 (Mustapha's 5th speech). *Flounder* is in Beaum. and Fletcher, Mons. Thomas, iii. 3; and in John Dennis, Secrets of Angling (ab. A.D. 1613), in Arber's Eng. Garner, i. 171. ME. *floundre*, Expeditions of Earl of Derby, 1390–3, Camden Soc.; p. 159, l. 25. — OF. *flondre* (Normandy). — Swed. *flundra*, a flounder; Dan. *flynder*; EFries. *flunder*; Icel. *flyðra*. Prob. allied to Norw. *flindra*, a thin chip or slice, EFries. *flidder*, a flat fish; G. *fladen*, a flat cake. See **Flawn**.

FLOUR, the finer part of meal. (F. — L.) 'Fyne *flowre* of whete;' Sir T. Elyot, Castel of Helth, b. ii. c. 11; also spelt *flower*, with which it is identical. ME. *flour of whete*, Early E. Psalter, Ps. 80. 17 (81. 16). — OF. *flour*, F. *fleur de farine*, 'flower, or the finest meal;' Cot. See **Flower**.

FLOURISH, to blossom, thrive. (F. — L.) ME. *florisshen*; Prompt. Parv. p. 167; Wyclif, Ps. lxxxix. 6. — OF. *floriss-*, base of pres. pt. of *florir*, to flourish. — Folk-L. **florire*, for L. *flōrēre*, to flower; cf. L. *flōrescere*, inceptive form of *flōrēre*, to flower, bloom. — L. *flōr-*, stem of *flōs*, a flower. See **Flower**. **Der.** *flourish*, sb., *-ing*.

FLOUT, to mock. (F.) A peculiar use of *flute*, used as a verb; Shak. Temp. iii. 2. 130. ME. *flouten*, to play the flute; *floute*, a flute, Chaucer, Ho. of Fame, 1223. From French; see **Flute**. Cf. MDu.

fluyten, to play the flute, also to jeer, to impose upon; now spelt *fluiten* (Oudemans); MDu. *fluyt* (Du. *fluit*), a flute. **Der.** *flout*, sb.

FLOW, to stream, glide. (E.) ME. *flowen* (not very common), Chaucer, Troil. iii. 1758. AS. *flōwan*, Grein, i. 306.+Du. *vloeijen*; Icel. *flōa*, to boil milk, to flood. Teut. base **flō-*; cognate with Gk. πλώ-ειν (for πλώϝ-ειν), to float. Further allied to Gk. πλέειν (for πλέϝ-ειν), to sail, L. *plu-ere*, to rain; and therefore distinct from L. *fluere*, to flow. See **Flood. Der.** *flow*, sb., -*ing*; also *flood*, q. v.

FLOWER, a bloom, blossom. (F.—L.) ME. *flour*, Chaucer, C. T. 4; Havelok, 2917.—OF. *flour*, *flor* (F. *fleur*).—L. *flōrem*, acc. of *flōs*, a flower; cf. *flō-rēre*, to bloom, cognate with E. *blow*, to bloom. See **Blow** (2). **Der.** *flower-y*, -*et*; also *flor-id*, -*al*, -*in*; *flos-cule*, *flourish*, q.v. Doublet, *flour*, q.v.

FLUCTUATE, to waver. (L.) In Milton, P. L. ix. 668; and in Blount's Gloss., 1656, 1681.—L. *fluctuātus*, pp. of *fluctuāre*, to float about.—L. *fluctus*, a wave.—L. *fluctus*, old pp. of *fluere*, to flow; see **Fluent. Der.** *fluctu-at-ion*.

FLUE (1), an air-passage, chimney-pipe. (F.—L.) Evelyn speaks of 'chimney *flues*;' Diary, Aug. 9, 1654. [Phaer (tr. of Virgil, x. 209) translates *concha*, the sea-shell trumpet of the Tritons, by 'wrinckly wreathed *flue*' (R.); but this is a misprint for *flute*.] Prob. from ME. *fluen*, to flow; as the pipe conducts the flow of the smoke; 'to flue, *fluere*;' Cath. Angl. (1483).—OF. *flue*, a flowing; *fluer*, to flow.—L. *fluere*, to flow. ¶ So also Du. *vloei-pijp*, a ventilating shaft, from Du. *vloeijen*, to flow, cognate with E. *flow*; see **Flow.** But L. *fluere* is quite distinct from E. *flow.*

FLUE (2), light floating down. (E.?) In Johnson's Dict., explained as 'soft down or fur.' Also called *fluff.* Prob. of E. origin. Perhaps a derivative of **flug-*, weak grade of the verb to *fly*; see **Fly** (1). We find the exact equivalent in Norw. *flu*, flue (Ross); EFries. *flūg*, *flog*, flue; Low G. *flog*, flue. Cf. G. *flug*, flight.

FLUENT, flowing, eloquent. (L.) Used in the sense of 'copious,' in Shak. Hen. V, iii. 7. 36.—L. *fluentem*, acc. of pres. pt. of *fluere*, to flow. Cf. Gk. φλύειν, to swell, overflow, ἀναφλύειν, to spout up; see Curtius, i. 375. **Der.** *fluent-ly*, *fluenc-y*; from same source, *flu-id*, q.v., *flu-or*, q.v., *flux*, q.v., *fluctuate*, q.v.; also *af-flu-ence*, *con-flux*, *de-flux-ion*, *ef-flux*, *in-flux*, *re-flux*, &c.

FLUID, liquid. (F.—L.) In Milton, P. L. vi. 349; Bacon, Nat. Hist., sect. 68.—OF. *fluide*; Cot.—L. *fluidus*, flowing, liquid.—L. *fluere*, to flow; see **Fluent. Der.** *fluid-i-ty*, -*ness*.

FLUKE (1), a flounder, kind of fish. (E.) ME. *fluke*, Morte Arthure, ed. Brock, 1088. AS. *flōc*, gloss to L. *platissa*, a plaice; Ælfric's Colloquy.+Icel. *flōki*, a kind of halibut. From **flōk*, 2nd grade of a Teut. base **flak-*, which appears in G. *flach*, flat.

FLUKE (2), part of an anchor. (E.) In Kersey's Dict., ed. 1715. 'Flouke of an anchor;' Phillips (1658). Also spelt *flook.* Apparently the same word as *fluke* (1), applied to the *flattened* end of the hook. Apparently distinct from G. *flunke*, the fluke of an anchor; and from Icel. *akkerisfleinn*, Dan. *ankerflig*, Swed. *ankarfly*, G. *ankerflügel*, the fluke of an anchor.

FLUMMERY, a light kind of food. (W.) 'Flummery, a wholesome jelly made of oatmeal;' Kersey's Dict., ed. 1715.—W. *llymru*, *llymruwd*, flummery, sour oatmeal boiled and jellied.—W. *llymus*, sharp, tart.

FLUNKEY, a footman. (F.—OHG.) In Burns, Twa Dogs, l. 54. Its origin is clearly due to F. *flanquer*, to flank; it seems to be put for *flanker.* 'Flanquer, to flanke, run along by the side of; to defend, support, or fence; to be at ones elbow for a help at need;' Cot. See **Flank.**

FLUOR, FLUOR-SPAR, a mineral. (L.) Latinised from G. *fluss*, a flowing, fusion; a term applied by G. Agricola (in 1546) to minerals used as fluxes in smelting. The L. *fluor* (lit. a flowing) was formerly in use as a term in alchemy and chemistry. 'Fluor, a flux, course, or stream;' Kersey's Dict., ed. 1715.—L. *fluere*, to flow; see **Fluent.**

FLURRY, agitation, hurry. (E.) 'The boat was overset by a sudden *flurry* [gust of wind] from the North;' Swift, Voyage to Lilliput; c. 1. And see Rich. Dict. From *flurr*, to whir (N. E. D.); prov. E. *flurr*, to ruffle, to disarrange (E. D. D.); of imitative origin. Cf. Norw. *flurutt*, rough, shaggy, disordered (Aasen); Swed. dial. *flur*, disordered hair, whim, caprice; *flurig*, disordered; Norw. *flura*, to be in disorder (Ross).

FLUSH (1), to flow swiftly. (E.) 'The swift recourse of *flushing* blood;' Spenser, F. Q. iv. 6. 29. G. Douglas uses *flusch* to signify 'a pool;' prol. to Æn. vii., l. 54; spelt *fluss* in Barbour, Bruce, xiii. 20. From *flush*, vb., to fly up quickly, like a startled bird; cf. *flusk*, to make a whirring or fluttering sound (E. D. D.). Apparently of imitative origin; cf. EFries. *flöstern*, *flustern*, to fly with a noise, to rustle (as wind); murmur (as water). [MDu. *fluysen*, 'to gush or breake out violently' (Hexham), Dan. dial. *fluse*, to gush out, are from OF. *fluir* (pres. pt. *fluiss-ant*), to flow; and may be independent.]

FLUSH (2), to blush, to redden. (E.) Perhaps the same word as the above, but much influenced by **Flash,** and perhaps by **Blush.** Shak. has *flushing*=redness; Hamlet, i. 2. 155. ME. *flushen*, to redden, as in 'flush for anger;' Rich. the Redeless, ed. Skeat, ii. 166. Cf. Swed. dial. *flossa*, to burn (Rietz); Norw. dial. *flosa*, passion, vehemence, eagerness; Aasen. And see **Fluster. Der.** *flush*, sb., *flush-ing.*

FLUSH (3), level, even. (E.) Perhaps from **Flush** (1); as an adj., it meant 'in full flow;' Dampier has: 'Small brooks . . . that run *flush* into the sea;' Voy. i. 393. Hence, even or level, like a stream when running full.

FLUSH (4), a term at cards; a hand containing a prescribed number of cards of the same suit is 'a flush.' (F.—L.) 'He facithe owte at a *flusshe*, with shewe, take all!' Skelton, Speke Parrot, l. 424. —F. *flux*, 'a flowing, . . a flux, . . also, a flush at cardes;' Cot.—L. *fluxus*, a flowing; from the pp. stem of *fluere*, to flow; see **Fluent** and **Flux.**

FLUSTER, to heat with drinking, confuse. (Scand.) See Shak. Oth. ii. 3. 60. Also *flowster* (Yks., Som.), E. D. D. Cf. Icel. *flaustra*, to be flustered; *flaustr*, sb., fluster, hurry. Allied to EFries. *flöstern*, *flustern*, to rustle (as wind). **Der.** *fluster*, sb.

FLUTE, a musical pipe. (F.) ME. *floiten*, *flouten*, to play the flute; Chaucer, C. T. 91. The sb. *flute* is in North's Plutarch, p. 763 (R.).—OF. *fleute*, *flaute*, *flehute*, *flahute* (Supp. to Godefroy); *fleute* (Cot.), a flute; *flauter*, to play the flute. Cf. mod. Prov. *flahuto*, *flavuto*, *flaguto*, a flute (Mistral). Prob. of imitative origin; the *fl-* may have been suggested by L. *flāre*, to blow, cognate with E. *blow*; see **Blow** (1). **Der.** *flageolet*, q. v.; and see *flout.*

FLUTTER, to flap the wings. (E.) ME. *floteren*, to fluctuate, float about; Chaucer, tr. of Boethius, b. iii. pr. 11, l. 156; Wyclif, Isa. xxix. 9. AS. *flotorian*, to float about (fluctibus ferri); Gloss. to Prudentius, p. 150, l. 1; cf. AS. *flot*, the sea; *flota*, a ship.—AS. *flot-* (Teut. **flut-*), weak grade of *fléotan*, to float. β. Thus the orig. sense was to fluctuate, hover on the waves; and the form of the word is due to **Float.** The word was afterwards applied to other vibratory motions, esp. to the flapping of wings; cf. Low G. *fluttern*, flutter, flit about, Bremen Wörterbuch, i. 431, which is closely allied to *flit*; cf. prov. E. *flittermouse*, a bat; also EFries. *fluttern*, to fly noisily; Norw. *flotra*, to swim with difficulty (Ross). See **Flit**, which is likewise a derivative of Teut. **flut-*.

FLUVIATILE, belonging to a river. (F.—L.) In Bailey's Dict., vol. ii (1731).—F. *fluviatile*.—L. *fluuiātilis*.—L. *fluuius*, a river.—L. *fluere*, to flow.

FLUX, a flowing, a disease. (F.—L.) ME. *flux*, P. Plowman, C. vii. 161; xxii. 46.—OF. *flux*, 'a flowing, flux;' Cot.—L. *fluxus*, a flowing; from the pp. of *fluere*, to flow; see **Fluent. Der.** *flux-ible*, -*at-ion*, -*ion*; and see *flush* (4).

FLY (1), to float or move in air. (E.) ME. *flegen*, *fleyen*, *fliʒen*; pt. t. *he flew*, Chaucer, C. T. 15423 (B 4607). AS. *fléogan*, pt. t. *fléah*; Grein, i. 303.+Du. *vliegen*; Icel. *fljúga*; Dan. *flyve*; Swed. *flyga*; G. *fliegen*. β. Teut. type **fleugan-*, pt. t. **flaug*; pp. **flug-anoz.* Cf. L. *plūma*, a feather, wing; see **Plume.** ¶ *Not* allied to *flee*, but early confused with it. **Der.** *fly*, sb. = AS. *fléoge* (Grein); *fly-boat*, *fly-blown*, -*catcher*, -*fishing*, -*leaf*, -*wheel*, -*ing-fish*, *fli-er*; also *flight* = AS. *flyht*, Grein, i. 306; *flight-y*, -*il-y*, -*i-ness.*

FLY (2), a vehicle. (E.) Applied in 1708 to a stage-coach, to express its swiftness of motion; this use is obsolete. Also the name of a light vehicle, introduced at Brighton in 1816, and at first drawn by men. 'A nouvelle kind of four-wheeled vehicles, drawn by a man and an assistant, are very accommodating to visitors. They are denominated Flys;' Wright's Brighton Ambulator (1818); where the date 1816 is given.

FOAL, the young of a mare. (E.) ME. *fole*, P. Plowman, B. xi. 335. AS. *fola*, Matt. xxi. 2.+Du. *veulen*; Icel. *foli*; Swed. *fåle*; Goth. *fula*; G. *fohlen.* Teut. type **fulon-*, m. Cognate with L. *pullus*, the young of an animal; Gk. πῶλος, a foal. **Der.** *filly*, q. v.

FOAM, froth, spume. (E.) ME. *fome*, Chaucer, C. T. 16032 (G 564). AS. *fām*, Grein, i. 267.+Prov. G. *faim*; OHG. *feim.* Teut. type **faimo-*. Cognate with Russ. *piena*, foam; Skt. *phēna*, foam; and prob. with L. *spūma* (<**spoima*), foam, and L. *pūm-ex*, pumice. Cf. **Spume.** `Der. *foam*, verb.

FOB (1), a pocket for a watch. (O. Low G.) In Hudibras, pt. iii. c. 1, l. 107. An O. Low G. word, not preserved otherwise than in the cognate prov. HG. (Prussian) *fuppe*, a pocket, which is cited in the Bremen Wörterbuch, i. 437. The dimin. *fob-ke*, a pocket, is recorded by Berghaus.

FOB (2), to cheat, deceive, take in. (Low G.) Also *to fob off*, to put off; Shak. Cor. i. 1. 97; and see E. D. D.—Low G. *foppen*, to befool (Berghaus); G. *foppen*, to jeer, banter.

FOCUS, a point where rays of light meet. (L.) In Kersey, ed.

1715. First in 1656. — L. *focus*, a hearth; hence technically used as a centre of fire. **Der.** *foc-al.*

FODDER, food for cattle. (E.) ME. *fodder*, Chaucer, C. T. 3866 (A 3868). AS. *fōdor, fōddor, fōddur*, Grein, i. 334; an extended form from *fōda*, food.+Du. *voeder*; Icel. *fōðr*; Dan. and Swed. *foder*; G. *futter*. Teut. type **fōðrom*, n. See **Food**. **Der.** *fodder*, verb.

FOE, an enemy. (E.) ME. *fo, foo*; Chaucer, C. T. 63. AS. *fāh, fāg, fā*; Grein, i. 266. Teut. type **faihoz*, m.; Idg. type **poiqos*, whence also Irish *oech*, a foe, with loss of *p*. From the weak grade **piq-* we have Gk. πικ-ρός, bitter, Lith. *pik-tas*, unkind. Brugmann, i. § 646. **Der.** *foe-man.*

FŒTUS; see **Fetus**.

FOG, a thick mist. (Scand.) In Shak. Mids. Nt. Dr. ii. 1. 90. See N. E. D., where it is shown that the earliest sense of *fog* was coarse or rank winter-grass; see Early Eng. Allit. Poems, B. 1683, where we read of Nebuchadnezzar, that '*fogge* was his mete.' It also meant 'moss;' and hence the adj. *foggy*, covered with rank grass, mossy, marshy, damp; whence *fog*, sb., damp, as a back-formation.—Norw. *fogg*, long-strawed, weak, scattered grass in a moist hollow (Ross). **Der.** *fogg-y, fogg-i-ness, fog-bank.*

FOIBLE, a weak point in character. (F.—L.) In Dryden, Marriage à la Mode, iii. 1.—F. *foible*, feeble; see **Feeble**.

FOIL (1), to disappoint, defeat. (F.—L.) In Spenser, F. Q. v. 11. 33, *foyle* = to cover with dirt, to trample under foot. So *yfoiled* = trampled under foot; King Alisaunder, 2712. Corrupted from OF. *fouler*, perhaps by the influence of ME. *fylen*, to render foul.—OF. *fouler*, 'to tread, stampe, or trample on, .. to hurt, press, oppress, foyle, overcharge extremely;' Cot.—Late L. *fullāre, folāre*, to full cloth.—L. *fullo*, a fuller. See **Fuller**. **Der.** *foil*, sb., a blunt sword, so called because it could only *foil* or check, not kill; (in wrestling, a throw not resulting in a flat fall, and so incomplete, was called a *foil*); see Much Ado, v. 2. 13; also *foil*, a defeat; 1 Hen. VI, v. 3. 23.

FOIL (2), a set-off, in the setting of a gem. (F.—L.) In Hamlet, v. 2. 266.—AF. *foille*, a leaf; Stat. Realm, i. 219; MF. *fueille*, 'a leaf;' ... also the foyle of precious stones;' Cot.—L. *folia*, pl. of *folium*, a leaf; afterwards used as a fem. sing.; see **Foliage**.

FOIN, to thrust or lunge with a sword. (F.—L.) Obsolete. In Chaucer, C. T. 1654; and in Shak. Merry Wives, ii. 3. 24. Lit. 'to thrust with an eel-spear.'—OF. *foine, foisne*, an eel-spear.—L. *fuscina*, a three-pronged spear, trident (Littré).

FOISON, plenty, abundance. (F.—L.) Obsolete; but in Shak. Temp. ii. 1. 163; Chaucer, C. T. 4924 (B 504).—OF. *foison*, 'abundance;' Cot.—Folk-L. *fusiōnem*, with short *u*; for L. *fūsiōnem*, acc. of *fūsio*, a pouring out, hence, profusion; allied to *fūsus*, pp. of *fundere*, to pour; see **Fuse** (1).

FOIST, to intrude surreptitiously, orig. to palm or put off. (MDu.) In Shak. Sonnet 123, l. 6. The sb. *foist* is a trick: 'Put not your *foists* upon me; I shall scent them;' Ben Jonson, The Fox, Act iii (last speech but 21). To *foist* was a term in dice-play, and meant to palm (or conceal in the fist), to introduce so as to fall as required; see Ascham, Toxophilus, ed. Arber, p. 54, and quotations in N. E. D.).—Du. *vuisten*, to take in the fist or hand (N. E. D.).—Du. *vuist*, the fist; cognate with E. **Fist**. Cf. Low G. *füstjen*, to take in the fist (Low G. *fuust*); spelt *vūsten* (and *vūst*) in Lübben.

FOLD (1), to double together, wrap up. (E.) ME. *folden*; P. Plowman, B. xvii. 145, 176. OMerc. *faldan*; AS. *fealdan*, Grein, i. 286.+Dan. *folde*; Swed. *fålla*; Icel. *falda*; Goth. *falthan*; G. *falten*. β. Teut. type **falthan-*. Allied to Gk. δι-πλάσιος, doubled; πλάσσειν (for **πλάτ-γειν*), to form, mould; Skt. *puṭa-*, a fold (Macdonell). See **Plaster**. **Der.** *fold*, sb., ME. *fold*, a plait; *-fold*, in composition, as in *two-fold*, &c.

FOLD (2). (E.) The word *fold*, used as a sb., in the sense of sheep-fold, is not in any way allied to the verb *to fold*. It occurs as AS. *fald*, in John, x. 1; but this is contracted from an older form *falod*, also spelt *falud, falæd* (Sweet, O. E. Texts). Allied words are Du. *vaalt*, Low G. *faal*, EFries. *folt*, fold, a dung-pit; Dan. *fold*, a sheep-pen (Franck).

FOLIAGE, a cluster of leaves. (F.—L.) 'Foliage, branching work in painting or tapestry; also leafiness;' Blount's Gloss., ed. 1674. A F. word, but modified by the L. *foli-um*, a leaf; cf. *foliation*, in Sir T. Browne, Cyrus Garden, c. 3. § 11; *foliate*, in Bacon, Nat. Hist. § 293.—MF. *fueillage*, 'branched work, in painting or tapestry;' Cot.—MF. *fueille*, a leaf.—L. *folia*, pl. of *folium*, a leaf; later used as a fem. sing.+Gk. φύλλον, a leaf. See Curtius, i. 380. **Der.** *foliag-ed*; also (from L. *folium*) *foli-ate, -at-ed, -at-ion, -fer-ous*: also *folio*, from the phr. *in folio*, where *foliō* is the ablative case.

FOLK, a crowd of people. (E.) ME. *folk*; Chaucer, C. T. 2830 (A 2828). AS. *folc*; Grein.+Icel. *fōlk*; Dan. and Swed. *folk*; Du. *volk*; G. *volk*. Teut. type **folkom*, neut. ¶ Lithuan. *pùlkas*, a crowd, Russ. *polk'*, an army, were prob. borrowed from Teutonic at a very early date. **Der.** *folk-lore.*

FOLLICLE, a gland, seed-vessel. (F.—L.) 'Follicle, a little bag, purse, or bladder;' Blount's Gloss., ed. 1674.—F. *follicule*, 'a little bag, powch, husk;' Cot.—L. *folliculus*, a little bag, dimin. of *follis*, a pair of bellows, kind of bag.

FOLLOW, to go after. (E.) ME. *folwen, folowen*, Chaucer, C. T. 3260; P. Plowman, B. vi. 2. [The *w* is due to the AS. *g*.] AS. *folgian*, John, x. 27. We also find AS. *fylcgan, fylgian, fyligan*; Grein, i. 360.+Du. *volgen*; Icel. *fylgja*; Dan. *fōlge*; Swed. *fōlja*; G. *folgen*. So also OFries. *folgia, fulia*; OSax. *folgōn*. β. We also find AS. *fulgangan* (pt. t. *ful-ēode*), with the same sense, but derived from AS. *ful*, full, and *gangan*, to go; and, in like manner, OHG. *follegān*. Hence it is probable that the original sense was 'to go (or be) in full numbers,' to go in a crowd, to accompany; and that it is a derivative of Teut. **fulloz*, full. See **Full**. Cf. AS. *fylstan*, to assist, *fultum*, assistance; both derivatives of AS. *full*, full. **Der.** *follow-ing, follow-er.*

FOLLY, foolishness. (F.—L.) ME. *folie* (with one *l*); Layamon, later text, 3024.—OF. *folie*, folly.—OF. *fol*, a fool; see **Fool**.

FOMENT, to bathe with warm water, heat, encourage. (F.—L.) 'Which bruit [rumour] was cunningly *fomented*;' Bacon, Life of Hen. VII, ed. Lumby, p. 22, l. 28.—MF. *fomenter*, 'to foment;' Cot.—L. *fōmentāre*.—L. *fōmentum*, contr. from **fouimentum*, a warm application, lotion.—L. *fouēre*, to warm; of unknown origin. **Der.** *foment-er, -at-ion.*

FOND, foolish. (E.) ME. *fond*, but more commonly *fonned*, Wyclif, Exod. xviii. 18. *Fonned* is the pp. of the verb *fonnen*, to act foolishly; thus *thou fonnist* = thou art foolish; Coventry Myst. p. 36. *Fonnen* is formed from the sb. *fon*, a fool; of which the fuller form *fonne* is in Chaucer, C. T. 4087 (A 4089). Prob. of Fries. origin, as the sb. answers to EFries. *fone, fōn*, a maid, girl, weakling, simpleton (Koolman). This form has a large number of variants, as OFries. *famne, fomne, fovne, fone*, and appears to be ultimately the same word as AS. *fæmne*, Icel. *feima*, a virgin. See Notes on E. Etym., p. 102. **Der.** *fond-ly, -ness*; also *fond-le*, frequentative verb, to caress, used by Swift and Gay; also *fond-ling* (with dimin. suffix *-ling = -l + -ing*), Shak. Venus and Adonis, 229.

FONT (1), a basin of water for baptism. (L.) In very early use. AS. *font, fant*, Ælfric's Hom. i. 422.—L. *fontem*, acc. of *fons*, a fount; see **Fount**.

FONT (2), **FOUNT**, an assortment of types. (F.—L.) 'Font, a cast or complete set of printing-letters;' Kersey, ed. 1715.—F. *fonte*, 'a casting of metals;' Cot.—F. *fondre*, to cast. See **Found** (2).

FOOD, provisions, what one eats. (E.) ME. *fode*, P. Plowman, B. iv. 271. AS. *fōda*, Ælf. Hom. ii. 396. Cf. Icel. *fæði, fæða*, food; Dan. *fōde*; Swed. *fōda*. [In English, the verb *fēdan*, to feed, is derived from the sb. *fōda*, food; not vice versa.] β. From AS. **fōd-*, strong grade of AS. **fad-*, corresponding to Gk. πατ- in πατ-έεσθαι, to feed. From the Idg. root **pā-*, to feed; whence L. *pā-nis*, bread, *pā-bulum*, food, and *pā-scere*, to feed. See **Pasture**. **Der.** *feed*, q. v.; *fodder*, q. v.

FOOL (1), a silly person, jester. (F.—L.) ME. *fol*; Layamon (later text), 1442.—OF. *fol* (F. *fou*), a fool.—L. *foll-em*, acc. of *follis*, a pair of bellows, wind-bag; pl. *follēs*, puffed cheeks; whence the term was easily transferred to a jester, as in Late L. *follis*, a fool. Perhaps allied to **Ball** (1). **Der.** *fool-ish, -er-y*; *-hardy* = ME. *folherdi*, Ancren Riwle, p. 62 (see *hardy*); *-hardi-ness*; *fools-cap*, paper so called from the water-mark of a fool's cap and bells used by old paper-makers; also *folly*, q. v.

FOOL (2), a dish of crushed fruit, &c. (F.—L.) From the sb. above; named like *trifle*. Florio has: 'Mantiglia, a kind of clouted creame, called a *foole* or a *trifle* in English.'

FOOT, the extremity of an animal below the ankle. (E.) ME. *fot*, *foot*; pl. *fet, feet*; Chaucer, C. T. 474, 475 (A 472-3). AS. *fōt*, pl. *fēt*, Grein.+Du. *voet*; Icel. *fōtr*; Dan. *fod*; Swed. *fot*; Goth. *fōtus*; G. *fuss*. Teut. type **fōt* (consonant stem), corresponding to Idg. type **pōd*, with the variants **pod*, **ped*. Cf. L. *pēs*, foot, gen. *ped-is*; Gk. πούς, gen. ποδ-ός; Skt. *pād*, foot (gen. *pad-as*). Cf. **Fetter, Fet'ock, Fetch**. Brugmann, i. § 578. **Der.** *foot*, verb; *foot-ball* (1424), *-boy, -bridge, -fall, -guard, -hold, -man, -mark, -pad, -passenger, -rot, -rule, -soldier, -sore, -stalk, -stall, -step*; also *foot-ing, -less*; also *fetter*, q. v. From the same source, *ped-al, -estal, -estrian, -icle, bi-ped, quadru-ped, exped-ite, im-pede, centi-pede*, &c.

FOOTY, paltry, insignificant. (E.) First in 1752; a variant of the older *foughty*, musty (N. E. D.). 'A mustie and *foughtie* taste in the wine;' Surflet, Countrie Farme, vi. 2. 731 (1600). From an AS. form **fūhtig*; answering to Du. *vochtig*, Dan. *fugtig*, Swed. *fuktig*, damp; from AS. *fūht*, damp, moist. Cf. G. *feucht*, damp. From Teut. base **feuk-*, as in Icel. *fjūka*, to drift as snow or dust (Franck).

FOP, a coxcomb, dandy. (E.) Shak. has *fops*, K. Lear, i. 2. 14; *fopped* (or *fobbed*) = befooled, Oth. iv. 2. 197; *foppish*, K. Lear, i. 4. 182; *foppery*, id. i. 2. 128. ME. *foppe*, a foolish fellow, Prompt.

Parv.; *fop*, Cov. Mysteries, p. 295; also *fobbe*, P. Plowman, C. iii. 193. (Not in AS.) Cf. EFries. *foppen*, to jeer, banter; Du. *foppen*, to cheat, mock, prate; *fopper*, a wag; *fopperij*, cheating (= E. *foppery*); Low G. *fopp*, a lout; *foppen*, to befool (Berghaus). Der. *fopp-ish*, *-ish-ness*, *-er-y*, *fop-ling*. Cf. *fob* (2).

FOR (1), in the place of. (E.) The use of *for* as a conj. is due to such phrases as AS. *for-þām-þe*, *for-þȳ* = on account of; the orig. use is prepositional. AS. *for*, for; also, before that; the same word as AS. *fore*, before that, for; Du. *voor*, for, before, from; Icel. *fyrir*, before, for; Dan. *for*, for; *för*, adv. before; Swed. *för*, before, for; G. *vor*, before; *für*, for; Goth. *faura*, before, for.+L. *prō*, before; Gk. πρό, related to παρά; Skt. *pra*, before, away. See **Fore**; and see below. Der. *for-as-much*, *for-ever*.

FOR- (2), only in composition. (E.) *For-*, as a prefix to verbs, has usually an intensive force, or preserves something of the sense of *from*, to which it is related. The forms are: AS. *for-*, Icel. *for-*, Dan. *for-*, Swed. *för-*, Du. and G. *ver-*, Goth. *fra-* (rarely *fair-*) Skt. *parā*. The Skt. *parā* is an old instrumental sing. of *para-*, far; perhaps the orig. sense was 'away;' see **From**. β. The derived verbs are *for-bear*, *for-bid*, *for-fend*, *for-go* (spelt *forego*), *for-get*, *for-give*, *for-lorn*, *for-sake*, *for-swear*. ¶ It is distinct from *fore-*, though ultimately related to it; see **Fore**.

FOR- (3), only in composition. (F. – L.) In *forclose* (misspelt *foreclose*) and *forfeit*, the prefix is French. See those words.

FORAGE, fodder, chiefly as obtained by pillage. (F. – Low L. – Teut.) ME. *forage*, Chaucer, C. T. 9296 (E. 1422). – OF. *fourage*, forage, pillage. – OF. *forrer*, to forage. – OF. *forre*, *fuerre* (F. *feurre*), fodder, straw. – Low L. *fodrum*, a Latinised form of Teut. **fōdrom*, the same as E. *fodder*; see **Fodder**. Der. *forage*, verb; *forag-er*; also *foray*, sometimes spelt *forray*, a Lowland Scotch form coined from ME. *forrier*, *forreyer*, a forager. – OF. *forrier*, a forager. – OF. *forrer*, to forage (above). *Forray* occurs in Barbour's Bruce both as sb. and verb; see bk. ii. l. 281, xv. 511.

FORAMINATED, having small perforations. (L.) Modern and scientific. – L. *forāmin-*, stem of *forāmen*, a hole bored. – L. *forāre*, cognate with E. **Bore**, q. v.

FORAY, FORRAY, a raid for foraging; see **Forage**.

FORBEAR (1), to hold away from, abstain from. (E.) ME. *forberen*, Chaucer, C. T. 887 (A 885). AS. *forberan*; Grein, i. 316. – AS. *for-*, prefix; and *beran*, to bear. See **For-** (2) and **Bear**. Der. *forbearing*; *-ance*, a hybrid word, with F. suffix, K. Lear, i. 2. 182.

FORBEAR (2), an ancestor. (E.) Orig. Lowl. Scotch. 'His *forbearis* . . of hale lynage;' Wallace, i. 21. Lit. *fore-beër*, one who is (or exists) previously; from *fore*, before; and the verb *to be*. In Montgomery's Poems (Sc. Text Soc.), p. 211, the pl. *forbe-ars* rhymes with *le-ars* (liars). Cf. G. *vorweser*, a predecessor; from *vor*, before, and *wesen*, to be.

FORBID, to bid away from, prohibit. (E.) ME. *forbeden*, Chaucer, C. T. 12577 (C 643). AS. *forbēodan*; Grein, i. 316. – AS. *for-*, prefix; and *bēodan*, to bid, command. See **For-** (2) and **Bid**. Cf. Du. *verbieden*; Goth. *faurbiudan*; Dan. *forbyde*; Swed. *förbjuda*; G. *verbieten*. Der. *forbidd-en*, pp.; *forbidd-ing*.

FORCE (1), strength, power. (F. – L.) ME. *force*, *fors*, Chaucer, C. T. 7094 (D 1512); Will. of Palerne, 1217. – OF. *force*. – Late L. *fortia*, strength. – L. *forti-s*, strong; older form *fortis*. Allied to Skt. *bṛhant-*, large, great; and to E. **Borough**. Brugmann, i. §§ 566, 756. Der. *force*, verb; *force-ful*, *-ful-ly*; *forc-ible*, *-ibl-y*, *-ible-ness*; *force-less*, *forc-ing*, *force-pump*. Also *fort*, *fort-i-tude*, *fort-ress*, &c.

FORCE (2), to stuff fowls, &c. (F. – L.) A corruption of *farce*. 'Farced, crammed, stuffed with a farce;' Kersey's Dict. ed. 1715. 'Farce, in cookery, a compound made of several meats and herbs;' id. ME. *farsen*. 'Farse the catte within als thu *farses* a gos' [goose]; Reliq. Antiquæ, i. 51. – F. *farcer*, to stuff; see **Farce**. Der. *force-meat*, a corruption of *farce-meat* or *farced-meat*.

FORCE (3), **FOSS**, a waterfall. (Scand.) A Northern word, as in Stock Gill *Force*, &c. – Dan. *fos*; Norw. *foss*; Icel. *foss*, formerly *fors*, a waterfall; Swed. *forsa*, *frusa*, to gush.

FORCEPS, pincers. (L.) In Kersey's Dict. ed. 1715. – L. *forceps*, gen. *forcipis*, pincers, tongs; so called because used for holding hot iron, &c. (Paulus Diaconus); for **formi-ceps*. – L. *formus*, hot; and stem *cip-*, from *capere*, to take, hold. Der. *forcip-at-ed*, forceps-like.

FORD, a passage, esp. through a river. (E.) ME. *ford*, also *forth*; see P. Plowman, B. v. 576, and footnote. AS. *ford*; Grein, i. 317.+G. *furt*, *furth*. Teut. type **furðuz*; allied to L. *port-us*, a harbour, OWelsh (*b*)*rit*, W. *rhyd*, a ford. Also to *frith* (2). Brugmann, i. § 514. β. Extended from the weak grade (**fər*) of AS. *faran*, to fare, go; see **Fare**. Der. *ford*, vb.; *-able*.

FORE, in front, coming first. (E.) The adj. use, as in *fore feet*, is uncommon; but we find *fore fet*=fore feet, in Will. of Palerne, 3284. The word is properly a prep. or adv., and in the former case

is a longer form of *for*. AS. *fore*, for, before, prep.; *fore*, *foran*, adv. See **For** (1).+OHG. *fora*; Goth. *faura*. Cf. Gk. πάρος, Skt. *puras*, in front, *purā*, formerly. Der. *for-m-er*, q. v.; *fore-m-ost*, q. v.; and used as a prefix in numerous compounds, for which see below. Also in *for-ward* (=*fore-ward*), q. v. ¶ The old comparative of *fore* is *fur-ther*, q. v.

FORE-ARM (1), the fore part of the arm. (E.) A comparatively modern expression; first found in 1741. Merely made up from *fore* and *arm*. See **Arm** (1).

FORE-ARM (2), to arm beforehand. (Hybrid; E. *and* F.) In Dryden, tr. of Virgil's Æneid, vi. 1233. From *fore* and the verb to *arm*; see **Arms**.

FOREBODE, to bode beforehand. (E.) In Butler, Hudibras, pt. ii. c. 3. 172; and Dryden, tr. of Virgil's Æneid, iii. 470. Compounded of *fore* and *bode*; see **Bode**. Cf. Icel. *fyrirboða*; Swed. *förebuda*. Der. *fore-bod-er*, *-ing*, *-ment*.

FORECAST, to contrive beforehand. (E. *and* Scand.) See Chaucer, C. T. 15223 (B 4407). Compounded of *fore* and *cast*; see **Cast**. Der. *forecast*, sb., *-er*.

FORECASTLE, the fore part of a ship. (Hybrid; E. *and* L.) 'Forecastle of a ship, that part where the foremast stands;' Kersey's Dict., ed. 1715. Also in Blount's Gloss., ed. 1674. ME. *forcastel*, Destruction of Troy, 5657. A short deck placed in front of a ship, above the upper deck, is so called, because it used in former times to be much elevated, for the accommodation of archers and crossbow-men. From *fore* and *castle*; see **Castle**. ¶ Commonly corrupted to *foc'sle* or *foxle*.

FORECLOSE, to preclude, exclude. (F. – L.) 'Foreclosed, barred, shut out, or excluded for ever;' Blount's Law Dict., ed. 1691; with a reference to 33 Hen. VIII. c. 39. It should rather be spelt *forclosed*. 'He *forclosed* me fro all my kynsmen;' Caxton, Four Sons of Aymon, ch. xii. p. 289, l. 11. – OF. *forclos*, pp. of *forclorre*, to exclude. – OF. *for-*, from L. *foris*, outside; and *clorre*<L. *claudere*, to shut. See **Forfeit** and **Close**. Der. *forclos-ure*.

FOREDATE, to date beforehand. (Hybrid; E. *and* F.) Merely a compound of *fore* and *date*. Todd gives an example from Milton, Reason of Church Government, b. ii. See **Date**.

FOREFATHER, an ancestor. (E.) The pl. *forfadres* is in P. Plowman, C. viii. 134, where two MSS. have *forme faderes*, a fuller form. The ME. *forme* is the superlative of *fore*; see **Former**. Cf. Du. *voorvader*; G. *vorvater*; Icel. *forfaðir*.

FOREFEND, to avert; see **Forfend**.

FORE-FINGER, the first of the four fingers. (E.) In Shak. All's Well, ii. 2. 24. ME. *forefynger*, Voc. p. 626, last line. From *fore* and *finger*. So also *fore-foot*; see under **Fore**.

FOREFRONT, the front part. (Hybrid; E. *and* F.) In the Bible (A.V.), 2 Sam. xi. 15. 'At a *foyr frount*;' Wallace, bk. ix. 831. See **Fore** and **Front**.

FOREGO (1), to relinquish; see **Forgo**.

FOREGO (2), to go before. (E.) Chiefly in the pres. part. *fore-going* and the pp. *foregone* = gone before, previous; Othello, iii. 3. 428. Cf. AS. *foregangan*, to go before; Grein, i. 321. Der. *forego-er*; see P. Plowman, B. ii. 187.

FOREGROUND, front part. (E.) Dryden speaks of 'the *fore-ground* of a picture;' see Todd's Johnson. From *fore* and *ground*. Cf. Du. *voorgrond*; G. *vorgrund*.

FOREHAND, preference, advantage. (E.) Used in several senses, and both as adj. and sb.; see Shak. Hen. V, iv. 1. 297; Troil. i. 3. 143; Much Ado, iv. 1. 51; 2 Hen. IV, iii. 2. 52. A difficult word; but the etymology is clearly from *fore* and *hand*. Der. *fore-hand-ed*; in the phr. 'a pretty *forehanded* fellow;' Beaum. and Fletcher, Scornful Lady, ii. 3 (last speech but 6).

FOREHEAD, the front part of the head above the eyes. (E.) ME. *forheed*; Chaucer, C. T. 154. Older form *forheued* (with *u*= *v*); spelt *vorheaued*, Ancren Riwle, p. 18. From *fore* and *head*. Cf. Du. *voorhoofd*; G. *vorhaupt*.

FOREIGN, out of doors, strange. (F. – L.) The insertion of the *g* is unmeaning. ME. *foreine*, *foreyne*, Chaucer, tr. of Boethius, b. ii. pr. 2, l. 18. – OF. *forain*, 'forraine, strange, alien;' Cot. – Folk-L. **forānus*, for Late L. *forāneus*, applied to a canon who is not in residence, or to a travelling pedlar. – L. *forās*, out of doors; adv. with an acc. pl. form, allied to L. pl. *forēs*, doors; also to L. *forum*, a market-place, and E. *door*. See **Door**. Der. *foreign-er*, Shak. K. John, iv. 2. 172.

FOREJUDGE (1), to judge beforehand. (Hybrid; E. *and* F.) In Levins. [The pp. *foriugyd*, cited from Fabyan, vol. ii. an. 1400 (R.), has the prefix *for-*, not *fore-*.] Spenser has *forejudgement*; Muiopotmos, l. 320. From *fore* and *judge*. Der. *forejudge-ment*.

FOREJUDGE (2), **FORJUDGE**, to deprive a man of a thing by the judgment of a court. (F. – L.) Still in use as a law-term, and quite distinct from the hybrid word *fore-judge*, to judge beforehand. Better spelt *forjudge*; indeed, Blount's Nomolexicon (1691) has: '*forjudged the court*, is when an officer of any court is banished or expelled the same.' The pp. *foriugit* is in the Kingis Quair, l. 21.─F. *forjuger*, 'to judge or condemn wrongfully, also to disinherite, deprive, dispossess of;' Cotgrave. ─OF. *for*-, prefix, out, outside; and *juger*, to judge. The OF. *for*- is short for *fors*<L. *foris*, outside. See **Foreclose**, and **Judge**.

FOREKNOW, to know beforehand. (E.) Shak. has *foreknowing*, Hamlet, i. 1. 134; also *foreknowledge*, Tw. Night, i. 5. 151. Chaucer has *forknowing*; tr. of Boethius, b. v. pr. 6, l. 194. From *fore* and *know*. **Der.** *foreknow-ledge*.

FORELAND, a headland, cape. (E.) In Milton, P. L. ix. 514. ME. *forlond*, Gawain and Grene Knight, l. 699. From *fore* and *land*. Cf. Dan. *forland*; Du. *voorland*; G. *vorland*; Icel. *forlendi*, the land between the sea and hills.

FORELOCK, the lock of hair on the forehead. (E.) In Milton, P. L. iv. 302; Spenser, son. 70. From *fore* and *lock*.

FOREMAN, a chief man, an overseer. (E.) The expression '*foreman* of the petty jury' occurs in The Spectator, no. 122; and in Baret (1580), G 620. From *fore* and *man*. Cf. Du. *voorman*, G. *vormann*, the leader of a file of men; Icel. *fyrirmaðr, formaðr*. Brugmann, i. § 518 (1).

FOREMOST, most in front. (E.) A double superlative, due to the fact that the old form was misunderstood. α. From the base *fore* was formed the AS. superlative adj. *forma*, in the sense of first; a word in common use; see Grein, i. 329. Hence the ME. *forme*, also meaning 'first;' see Stratmann. β. A double superlative *formest* was hence formed, as a by-form to the regular *fyrmest*; cf. '*þat fyrmeste bebod*,' the first commandment; Matt. xxii. 38. This became the ME. *formest*, both adj. and adv.; as in Will. of Palerne, 939. See examples in Stratmann. γ. Lastly, this was corrupted to *foremost*, by misdividing the word as *for-mest* instead of *form-est*. Spenser has *formost*, F. Q. v. 7. 35. See **Former**. ¶ The Mœso-Gothic also has *frumists*, a double superlative; the single superlative being *fruma*, cognate with Gk. πράμος, πρόμος, first, from πρό, before. Brugmann, i. § 518 (1).

FORENOON, the part of the day before noon. (Hybrid; E. and L.) In Shak. Cor. ii. 1. 78. From *fore* and *noon*; see **Noon**.

FORENSIC, legal, belonging to law-courts. (L.) '*Forensal*, pertaining to the common-place used in pleading or in the judgment-hall;' Blount's Gloss., ed. 1674. *Forens-ic* and *forens-al* are coined words, formed (with suffixes -*ic* and -*al*) from L. *forens-is*, of or belonging to the *forum* or market-place or place of public meeting.─ L. *forum*, a market-place, orig. a vestibule · connected with L. *forēs*, doors. See **Forum**.

FORE-ORDAIN, to ordain beforehand. (Hybrid; E. and F.) See 1 Pet. 1. 20 (A. V.). From *fore* and *ordain*.

FOREPART, front part. (Hybrid; E. and F.) In Acts, xxvii. 41; and in Levins. From *fore* and *part*.

FORERANK, front rank. (Hybrid; E. and F.) In Shak. Hen. V, v. 2. 97. From *fore* and *rank*.

FORERUN, to run before. (E.) In Shak. L. L. L. iv. 3. 380. From *fore* and *run*. Cf. Goth. *faurrinnan*, G. *vorrennen*. **Der.** *forerunn-er*, Heb. vi. 20 (A. V.); cf. Icel. *fyrir-rennari, forrennari*.

FORESEE, to see beforehand. (E.) In Shak. Troil. v. 3. 64. AS. *foreseon*; Grein, i. 322.─AS. *fore*, before; and *seon*, to see. +Du. *voorzien*; G. *vorsehen*. See **See**. **Der.** *foresight*, q. v.

FORESHIP, the front part of a ship. (E.) In Acts, xxvii. 30 (A. V.). AS. *forscip*; Voc. 166. 14. From *fore* and *ship*.+Du. *voorschip*.

FORESHORTEN, to shorten parts that stand forward in a picture. (E.) In Kersey's Dict., ed. 1715. From *fore* and *shorten*. **Der.** *foreshorten-ing*.

FORESHOW, FORESHEW, to show beforehand. (E.) In Shak. Cymb. v. 5. 473. From *fore* and *show*.

FORESIGHT, prescience. (E.) ME. *foresiht, forsyghte*; Prompt. Parv. p. 171. From *fore* and *sight*. See **Foresee**.

FOREST, a wood, a wooded tract of land. (F.─L.) ME. *forest*, King Alisaunder, 3581.─OF. *forest*, 'a forrest;' Cot.─Late L. *foresta*, a wood; *forestis*, an open space of ground over which rights of the chase were reserved. Medieval writers oppose the *forestis* or open wood to the walled-in wood or *parcus* (park). '*Forestis est ubi sunt feræ non inclusæ; parcus*, locus ubi sunt feræ inclusæ;' document quoted in Brachet, q. v.─L. *foris*, out of doors, abroad; whence *forestis*, lying open. Allied to L. *forēs*, doors; see **Foreign**. **Der.** *forest-er*, contracted to *forster*, Chaucer, C. T. 117; and to *foster*, Spenser, F.Q. iii. 1. 17.

FORESTALL, to anticipate in a transaction. (E.) ME. *forestallen, forstallen*; P. Plowman, B. iv. 56, where we find: '*forstalleth my feires*'=anticipates my sales in the fair. Thus to *forestall*, orig. used as a marketing term, was to buy up goods by intercepting them on the way. The object was, to sell again in the market at a higher

price; see Kersey's Dict. From AS. *forsteal*, sb., obstruction, interception; see gloss. to Schmidt, A. S. Laws. In the Laws of Henry I (Thorpe's A. S. Laws, i. 586) we read that '*forestel* est, si quis ex transverso incurrat, vel in via expectet et assalliat inimicum suum.'─ AS. *fore*, before; and *steal*, a stall, the occupying of a fixed position. See **Fore** and **Stall**.

FORETASTE, to taste beforehand. (Hybrid; E. and F.) In Milton, P. L. ix. 929. From *fore* and *taste*. **Der.** *foretaste*, sb.

FORETELL, to prophesy. (E.) ME. *foretellen*; P. Plowman, A. xi. 165. From *fore* and *tell*. **Der.** *foretell-er*.

FORETHOUGHT, a thinking beforehand, care. (E.) ME. *forthoght*, Cursor Mundi, l. 27661. [Shak. has the verb to *forethink*; Cymb. iii. 4. 171; from AS. *fore-þencan*.] From *fore* and *thought*.

FORETOKEN, a token beforehand. (E.) ME. *foretokne*; Gower, C. A. i. 137; bk. i. 2812; spelt *fortaken*, Ormulum, 16157. AS. *foretācen*; Grein, i. 322. + Du. *voorteeken*, a presage; G. *vorzeichen*. From *fore* and *token*; see **Token**. **Der.** *foretoken*, verb.

FORETOOTH, a front tooth. (E.) ME. *foretoþ*, pl. *foreteþ*; in Le Bone Florence, 1609, in Ritson's Metrical Romances, and in P. Plowman, C. xxi. 386. AS. *foreteð*, pl.; Voc. 157. 30. From *fore* and *tooth*.

FORETOP, the hair on the fore part of the head. (E.) ME. *fortop*, Treatises on Popular Science, ed. Wright, p. 137, l. 230. The simple form *top* or *toppe* is in P. Plowman, B. iii. 139. See **Top**. **Der.** *foretop-mast*.

FOREWARN, to warn beforehand. (E.) In Shak. Wint. Ta. iv. 4. 215. ME. *for-warnen*; Rob. of Brunne, tr. of Langtoft, p. 96, l. 15. From *fore* and *warn*; see **Warn**.

FORFEIT, a thing forfeited or lost by misdeed. (F.─L.) Properly a pp. as in 'So that your lif be noght *forsfet*;' Gower, C. A. i. 194; bk. ii. 1039. Hence ME. verb *forfeten*, P. Plowman, C. xxiii. 25; and the ME. sb. *forfeture, forsfaiture*, Gower, C. A. ii. 153; bk. v. 780.─OF. *forfait, forfet, forsfait*, a crime punishable by fine, a fine (Supp. to Godefroy; cf. AF. *forfeit*, Laws of Will. I., § 1); also pp. of *forfaire*, orig. *forsfaire*, to trespass, transgress.─Late L. *forisfactum*, a trespass, a fine; also pp. of *forisfacere*, to transgress, do amiss, lit. 'to act beyond.'─L. *foris facere*, lit. to do or act abroad or beyond.─ L. *foris*, out of doors; and *facere*, to do. See **Foreign**; and see **Fact**. **Der.** *forfeit*, vb., -*ure*, -*able*; and cf. *counter-feit*.

FORFEND, FOREFEND, to avert, forbid. (Hybrid; E. and F.) In Shak. Wint. Ta. iv. 4. 541. ME. *forfenden*, Wyclif, Job, xxxiv. 31. An extraordinary compound, due to E. *for*- (as in *for-bid*), and *fend*, a familiar abbreviation of *defend*, just as *fence* (still in use) is a familiar abbreviation of *defence*. See **For-** (2) and **Fence**. ¶ The spelling *forefend* is bad.

FORGE, a smith's workshop. (F.─L.) In Gower, C. A. i. 78; bk. i. 1087; hence ME. *forgen*, to forge, Chaucer, C. T. 11951 (C 17). ─OF. *forge*, a forge; whence *forgier*, to forge.─Folk-L. **faurga*< **favrega* (Schwan); for L. *fabrica*, a workshop, also a fabric. Cf. Span. *forja*, a forge, *forjar*, to forge; mod. Prov. *fabreja, faureja*, to forge (Mistral). Thus *forge* is a doublet of *fabric*. **Der.** *forge*, vb., *forg-er, -er-y*. See further under **Fabric**.

FORGET, to lose remembrance of, neglect. (E.) ME. *forgeten, forȝeten*; Chaucer, C. T. 1916 (A 1914). AS. *forgitan*; Grein, i. 324; also *forgetan* (E. E. Texts).─AS. *for*-, prefix; and *gitan*, to get. See **For-** (2) and **Get**. Cf. Du. *vergeten*; G. *vergessen*. **Der.** *forget-ful* (which has supplanted AS. *forgitol*); -*ful-ly*, -*ful-ness*, -*forget-me-not* (Palsgrave, p. 1024, l. 1).

FORGIVE, to give away, remit. (E.) ME. *forgiuen* (with *u*=*v*), *forȝiuen, forȝeuen*; Chaucer, C. T. 8402 (E 526). AS. *forgifan*; Grein, i. 323.─AS. *for*-, prefix; and *gifan*, to give. See **For-** (2) and **Give**. Cf. Du. *vergeven*; Swed. *förgifva*, to give away, forgive; G. *vergeben*; Goth. *fragiban*, to give, grant; Dan. *tilgive*, to forgive, pardon (with prefix *til* in place of *for*). **Der.** *forgiv-ing, forgive-ness*.

FORGO, FOREGO, to give up. (E.) The spelling *forego* is as absurd as it is general; it is due to confusion with *foregone*, in the sense of 'gone before,' from a verb *forego* of which the infinitive is little used. ME. *forgon*, Chaucer, C. T. 8047 (E 171). AS. *forgān*, to pass over; '*he forgǽð þæs hūses duru*'=he will pass over the door of the house; Exod. xii. 23.─AS. *for*-, prefix; and *gān*, to go. See **For-** (2) and **Go**.

FORJUDGE, a better spelling of **Forejudge** (2), q. v.

FORK, a pronged instrument. (L.) ME. *forke*; the pl. *forkis* is in King Alisaunder, 1191. Chaucer has 'a *forked* berd'=beard, C. T. 272 (A 270). AS. *forc*; Ælfric's Homilies, i. 430.─L. *furca*, a fork; of uncertain origin. **Der.** *fork*, vb., -*ed*, -*ed-ness*; -*y*, -*i-ness*; also *car-fax*, q.v. Brugmann, i. § 605 (3). ¶ The Du. *vork*, Icel. *forkr*, F. *fourche* (whence *fourch-ette*) are all from L. *furca*.

FORLORN, quite lost, desolate, wretched. (E.) ME. *forlorn*, used by Chaucer in an active sense=quite lost; C. T. 11861 (F 1557). It is the pp. of ME. *forleosen*, to lose entirely. AS. *forloren*, pp. of *forlēosan*, to destroy, lose utterly; Grein, i. 328. ‑ AS. *for-*, prefix; and *loren*, pp. of *lēosan*, to lose, whence ME. *lorn*, Chaucer, C. T. 3536. Cf. Dan. *forloren*, lost, used as an adj.; Swed. *förlorad*, pp. of *förlora*, to lose wholly; Du. *verloren*, pp. of *verliezen*, to lose; G. *verloren*, pp. of *verlieren*, to lose; Goth. *fraliusan*, to lose. See For- (2) and **Lose**. Der. *forlorn hope*, in North's Plutarch, p. 309 (R.), or p. 372, ed. 1631, a vanguard; a military phrase borrowed from MDu. *de verloren hoop* = the forlorn hope (of an army); Kilian. Cotgrave has: '*Perdu*, lost, forlorn, past hope of recovery. *Enfans perdus*, perdus, or the forlorne hope of a camp, are commonly gentlemen of companies.' For Du. *hoop*, see **Hope** (2).

FORM, figure, appearance, shape. (F.‑L.) ME. *forme*, King Alisaunder, 388; whence *formen*, *fourmen*, to form, id. 5687. ‑ OF. *forme*. ‑ L. *forma*, shape. ‑ √DHER, to hold, maintain; cf. Skt. *dʰṛ*, to bear, maintain, support; *dharman*, virtue, right, law, duty, character, resemblance. Brugmann, ii. § 72. Der. *form*, vb.; *form-al*, Sir T. More, Works, p. 125 f; *-al-ly*, *-al-ism*, *-al-ist*, *-al-i-ty*; *-at-ion*, *-at-ive*, cf. L. *formātus*, pp. of *formāre*, to form; *form-er*, sb.; *form-ul-a*, from L. *formula*, dimin. of *forma*; *-ul-ar-y*. Also *con-form*, *de-form*, *in-form*, *per-form*, *re-form*, *trans-form*, *uni-form*, &c. ¶ *Form*, a bench, is the same word. See F. *forme* in Cotgrave.

FORMER, more in front, past. (E.) First in latest text of AS. Gospels, Matt. xxi. 36 (ab. 1160). In Shak. Jul. Cæs. v. 1. 80. Spenser has *formerly*, F. Q. ii. 12. 67. *a*. The word is really of secondary formation, and due to the mistake of supposing the ME. *formest* (now *foremost*) to be a *single* superlative instead of a *double* one; see this explained under **Foremost**. *β*. Just as ME. *form-est* was formed from AS. *forma* by adding *-est* to the base *form-*, so *form-er* was made by adding *-er* to the same base; hence *form-er* is a comparative made from the old superlative *for-m-a*. Cf. L. *prī-m-us*, first. *γ*. We may therefore resolve *for-m-er* into *for-* (= *fore*), *-m-*, superlative suffix, and *-er*, comparative suffix. Der. *former-ly*.

FORMIC, pertaining to ants. (L.) First in 1671; chiefly used of '*formic acid*.' Short for **formic-ic*. ‑ L. *formīca*, an ant. Brugmann, i. § 413 (8). Der. *chloro-form*.

FORMIDABLE, causing fear. (F.‑L.) In Milton, P. L. ii. 649. Fisher has *formydable*; Works (E. E. T. S.); Ps. 38, p. 53, l. 27. ‑ F. *formidable*, 'fearfull;' Cot. ‑ L. *formīdābilis*, terrible. ‑ L. *formīdāre*, to dread; *formido*, fear. Der. *formidabl-y*, *formidable-ness*.

FORMULA, a prescribed form. (L.) In Kersey's Dict., ed. 1715. ‑ L. *formula*, dimin. of *forma*, a form; see **Form**. Der. *formul-ate*, *-ar-y*.

FORNICATE, to commit lewdness. (L.) The E. verb *fornicate* is of late use, appearing in the Works of Bp. Hall (R.); and first in 1552. It was certainly developed from the sbs. *fornication* and *fornicator*, both in early use. Chaucer has *fornicatioun*, C. T. 6886 (D 1302); and *fornicatour* is in P. Plowman, C. iii. 191 (footnote). These are, respectively, OF. *fornication* and *fornicateur*; Cot. ‑ L. *fornicātus*, pp. of *fornicāri*, to seek a brothel. ‑ L. *fornic-*, base of *fornix*, (1) a vault, an arch, (2) a brothel. Perhaps allied to **Furnace**; cf. OL. *fornus*, L. *furnus*, an oven (of vaulted shape). Der. *fornication*, *fornicat-or*, explained above.

FORSAKE, to give up, neglect. (E.) ME. *forsaken*, Chaucer, C. T. 14247 (B 3431). AS. *forsacan*, Ælfred's tr. of Orosius, i. 12. sect. 3. The orig. sense seems to be 'to contend strongly against,' to 'oppose.' ‑ AS. *for-*, intensive prefix; and *sacan*, to contend, Exod. ii. 13. *β*. This verb *sacan* is a strong verb, cognate with Goth. *sakan*, to strive, dispute; and is represented in E. by the derived sb. *sake*. Cf. Dan. *forsage*, to forsake; Swed. *försaka*; Du. *verzaken*. See For- (2) and **Sake**.

FORSOOTH, in truth, verily. (E.) ME. *for sothe* = for the truth, verily; P. Plowman, B. iv. 2. ‑ AS. *for*, for; and *sōðe*, dat. of *sōð*, truth. See **Sooth**.

FORSWEAR, to deny on oath, esp. falsely. (E.) ME. *forsweren*, Prompt. Parv. p. 173; earlier *forswerien*, O. Eng. Homilies, i. 13, l. 11. AS. *forswerian*; Grein, i. 332. ‑ AS. *for-*, prefix; and *swerian*, to swear. See For- (2) and **Swear**.

FORT, a stronghold. (F.‑L.) In Hamlet, i. 4. 28. ‑ OF. *fort*, 'a fort, hold;' Cot. ‑ Late L. *fortis* (*domus*), strong (house). ‑ L. *fortis*, strong. See **Force**. Der. *fort-al-ice*, q. v.; *fort-i-fy*, q. v.; *fort-i-tude*, q. v.; *fort-r-ess*, q. v. From L. *fortis* we have also Ital. *forte*, loud (in music), with its superl. *fortissimo*.

FORTALICE, a small outwork of a fort. (Late L.‑L.) Rare; see Jamieson's Scottish Dict. Cf. OF. *fortelesce*, a fortress; Span. *fortaleza*. ‑ Late L. *fortalitia*, *fortalitium*. See **Fortress**.

FORTIFY, to make strong. (F.‑L.) In Shak. K. John, iii. 4. 10. ‑ OF. *fortifier*, 'to fortifie, strengthen;' Cot. ‑ Late L. *fortificāre*. ‑ L. *forti-*, decl. stem of *fortis*, strong; and *fic-*, from *facere*, to make. See **Fort**, **Force**. Der. *fortifi-er*; *fortific-at-ion*, from Late L. pp. *fortificatus*.

FORTITUDE, strength. (F.‑L.) In Shak. Temp. i. 2. 154.

‑ F. *fortitude* (Littré). ‑ L. *fortitūdo*, strength; see '*spiritus fortitudinis*' in P. Plowman, B. xix. 284. ‑ L. *fortis*, strong. See **Fort**.

FORTH, forward, in advance. (E.) ME. *forth*, Chaucer, C. T. 858 (A 856). AS. *forð*, adv. (common); extended from *fore*, before. +Du. *voort*, forward; from *voor*, before; G. *fort*, MHG. *vort*; from *vor*, before. See **Fore**, **Further**. Der. *forth-coming*, Shak. Tam. Shrew, v. 1. 96. Also *forth-with*, in a poem of the 15th century called Chaucer's Dream, l. 1109, substituted for earlier *forth mid* = 'forth along with,' O. E. Hom. i. 117, l. 18; cf. also ME. *forthwithall*, Gower, C. A. iii. 262; bk. vii. 5064.

FORTNIGHT, a period of two weeks. (E.) ME. *fourtenight*, (trisyllable), Chaucer, C. T. 931 (A 929). Written *fourten niȝt*, Rob. of Glouc. p. 533, l. 17; l. 11010. From ME. *fourten* = fourteen; and *niȝt*, old pl. = nights. The AS. form was *fēowertýne niht*; Laws of Ine, § 55. *β*. Similarly, we have *sennight* = seven night; the phr. *seofon niht* (= a week) occurs in Cædmon, ed. Grein, l. 1349. It was usual to reckon by *nights* and *winters*, not by *days* and *years*; see Tacitus, Germania, c. xi. Der. *fortnight-ly*.

FORTRESS, a small fort. (F.‑L.) ME. *fortresse*, King Alisaunder, 2668. ‑ OF. *forteresce*, a variant of *fortelesce*, a small fort (Burguy). ‑ Late L. *fortalitia*, a small fort. ‑ Late L. *fortis*, sc. *domus*, a fort. ‑ L. *fortis*, strong; see **Fort**, **Fortalice**.

FORTUITOUS, depending on chance. (L.) In Blount's Gloss., ed. 1674. [The ME. *fortuit*, borrowed from OF. *fortuit*, occurs in Chaucer, tr. of Boethius, b. v. pr. 1. l. 58, in the Camb. MS.; see the footnote.] Englished, by change of *-us* to *-ous* (as in *arduous*, *strenuous*, &c.) from L. *fortuitus*, casual. ‑ L. *fortū-*, related to *forti-*, decl. stem of *fors*, chance (below). Der. *fortuitous-ly*, *-ness*.

FORTUNE, chance, hap. (F.‑L.) In Chaucer, C. T. 1254 (A 1252); Cursor Mundi, 23719. ‑ F. *fortune*. ‑ L. *fortūna*. ‑ L. *fortū-*, allied to *forti-*, decl. stem of *fors*, chance, orig. 'that which is produced;' from *for-*, weak grade of *fer-*, as in Latin *fer-re*, to bear; cf. E. *bear*. ‑ √BHER, to bear; see **Bear**. See Bréal. Der. *fortun-ate*, ME. *fortunat*, Chaucer, C. T. 14782 (B 3966), from L. pp. *fortūnātus*; *-ate-ly*, *-ate-ness*; *fortune-less*, *-hunter*, *-teller*; from the same source, *fortu-it-ous* (above).

FORTY, four times ten. (E.) ME. *fourty*, Chaucer, C. T. 16829 (G 1361). AS. *fēowertig*; Grein, i. 296. ‑ AS. *fēower*, four; and *-tig*, a suffix allied to *ten*; see **Four** and **Ten**. +Du. *veertig*; Icel. *fjörutíu*; Dan. *fyretyve*; Swed. *fyratio*; G. *viertig*; Goth. *fidwörtigjus*. The Goth. *tigjus* is the pl. of *tigus*, a decade; cf. Gk. δεκάς. Der. *forti-eth*, from AS. *fēowertigoða*.

FORUM, the Roman market-place. (L.) In Holland, tr. of Pliny, bk. xxii. c. 6. § 2. ‑ L. *forum*, a market-place, place for business; a forecourt; allied to *forēs*, doors; see **Door**. Der. *for-ensic*, q. v.

FORWARD, adj. towards the front. (E.) ME. *forward*, adj. and adv.; but rare, as the form *forthward* was preferred. *Forward*, adv. occurs in Chaucer, C. T. Six-text, Group B, 263, in the Camb. MS., where the other 5 MSS. have *forthward*. AS. *foreweard*, adj.; Grein, i. 322. ‑ AS. *fore*, before; and *-weard*, suffix; see **Toward**. Der. *forwards*, ME. *forwardes*, Maundeville, p. 61, where *-es* is an adv. suffix, orig. the sign of the gen. case (cf. Du. *voorwaarts*, G. *vorwärts*); *forward*, verb, Shak. 1 Hen. IV, i. 1. 33; *forward-ly*; *forward-ness*, Cymb. iv. 2. 342.

FOSSE, a ditch. (F.‑L.) In Holland, tr. of Suetonius, p. 185 (R.); ME. *fos*, Rob. of Glouc., l. 179. ‑ OF. *fosse*, 'any pit or hole;' Cot. ‑ L. *fossa*, a ditch. ‑ L. *fossa*, fem. of *fossus*, pp. of *fodere*, to dig. Brugmann, i. § 166. Der. *fossil*, q.v.

FOSSET, a spigot; the same as **Faucet**, q.v.

FOSSIL, petrified remains of an animal, obtained by digging. (F.‑L.) Formerly used in a more general sense; see Phillips' Dict., ed. 1706. ‑ OF. *fossile*, 'that may be digged;' Cot. ‑ L. *fossilis*, dug up. ‑ L. *fossus*, pp. of *fodere*, to dig; see **Fosse**. Der. *fossil-ise*, *fossili-ferous*.

FOSTER (1), to nourish. (E.) ME. *fostren*, Chaucer, C. T. 8098 (E 222). AS. *fōstrian*, in a gloss (Leo); cf. *fōstring*, sb., a disciple, Pref. to St. Luke, l. 2 (Lind. MS.). ‑ AS. *fōstor*, *fōstur*, nourishment; Leo, p. 23; Grein, i. 335; Teut. type **fōstrom*, for **fōd-trom*, neut.; allied to AS. *fōda*, food; see **Food**, **Fodder**. +Icel. *fóstr*, nursing; *fóstra*, to nurse, foster; Dan. *foster*, offspring; *fostre*, *opfostre*, to rear, bring up; Swed. *foster*, embryo; *fostra*, to foster. Der. *foster-er*; also (from AS. *fōstor*) *foster-brother*, *foster-child*, *foster-parent*.

FOSTER (2), a forester; see **Forest**.

FOTHER, a load, cartload; a heavy mass. (E.) See Chaucer, Prol. 530. AS. *fōðer*, n.; A. S. Chron. an. 852 (Laud MS.). +MDu. *voeder*, Du. *voer*; OHG. *fuodar*, G. *fuder*. Teut. type **fōþrom*, n. From **fōþ-*, strong grade of **faþ-*, tō grasp; see **Fathom**.

FOUL, dirty, unclean. (E.) ME. *foul*, P. Plowman, C. xix. 54. AS. *fūl*, Grein, i. 358. +Du. *vuil*; Icel. *fúll*; Dan. *fuul*; Swed. *ful*; Goth. *fūls*; G. *faul*. Teut. type **fū-loz*; cf. Icel. *-fúinn*, rotten; akin to **Putrid.** Brugmann, i. § 113. **Der.** *foul-ly, -ness, -mouth-ed*; also *foul*, vb.; *de-file*, q. v.

FOUMART, a polecat. (E.) Lowland Sc. *fowmart*; Jamieson. ME. *folmard*, Allit. Poems, ed. Morris, B. 534; also *fulmard, fulmard*, as in Stratmann, s. v. *ful* = foul. From AS. *fūl*, foul, stinking; and AS. *mearð*, a marten. Thus it means 'foul marten;' see **Foul** and **Marten.**

FOUND (1), to lay the foundation of. (F.—L.) ME. *founden*, Wyclif, Heb. i. 10; P. Plowman, B. i. 64.—OF. *fonder*, to found.—L. *fundāre*.—L. *fundus*, foundation, base, bottom; cognate with E. *bottom*; see **Bottom.** And see **Fund.** Der. *found-er*, ME. *foundour*, Rob. of Brunne, tr. of Langtoft, p. 109; *-r-ess*; *-at-ion*.

FOUND (2), to cast metals. (F.—L.) In Milton, P. L. vi. 518; and in Holland, tr. of Pliny, we find 'famous for mettal-*founding*,' b. xxxiv. c. 2; 'the excellent *founders* and imageurs of old time,' id. c. 8 (of Dædalus); 'the art of *founderie* or casting mettals for images;' id. c. 7.—OF. *fondre*, 'to melt, or cast, as metals;' Cot.—L. *fundere*, to pour, cast metals; see **Fuse** (1). Der. *found-er, found-r-y* (= *found-er-y*), *-ing*, *font* (2) or *fount*.

FOUNDER, to go to the bottom. (F.—L.) ME. *foundren*, said of a horse falling;' 'and *foundred* as he leep;' Chaucer, C. T. 2689 (A 2687).—OF. *fondrer*, chiefly in the comp. *afondrer* (obsolete) and *effondrer*, to fall in (still in use), as well as in the sb. *fondrière*, a place to founder in, a slough, bog; see *fond* in Burguy, and *fondrière* in Hatzfeld. The sense seems to have been 'to sink in,' and the deriv. is from F. *fond*, the bottom of anything.—L. *fundus*, the bottom; see **Found** (1). ¶ The form of the OF. verb should rather have been *fonder*; the *r* is intercalated, as in *chanvre* = *chanve*, hemp, from L. *cannabis*; and may have been due to the influence of OF. *fondre*, to melt; see **Found** (2). We have similar instances in E. *part-r-idge, t-r-easure, cart-r-idge*, &c.

FOUNDLING, a deserted child. (E.) ME. *fundeling*, Will. of Palerne, 481; *fundling*, King Horn, 228.—AS. *fund-*, weak grade of *findan*, to find; and *-ling* = *-l-ing*, double dimin. suffix.+Du. *vondeling*; similarly formed. See **Find.**

FOUNT (1), a spring, fountain. (F.—L.) In Shak. Meas. iv. 3. 102; and Lucrece, 850.—OF. *funt, font*, a fountain.—L. *fontem*, acc. of *fons*, a spring. Brugmann; Addenda to vol. iv. **Der.** *fountain*, Spenser, F. Q. ii. 12. 60, from OF. *funtaine* (F. *fontaine*), which from Late L. *fontāna*; *fountain-head*; and see *font* (1).

FOUR, twice two. (E.) ME. *feower, fower, feour, four*, Layamon, 25, 194, 1902, 2092, 25395. Chaucer adds a final *e*, and treats it as a pl. adj. 'With *foure whīe* bolës in the trays;' C. T. 2141 (A 2139). AS. *feōwer*, Grein, i. 296.+OFries. *fiower, fiuwer, fior*; Icel. *fjórir*; Dan. *fire*; Swed. *fyra*; Du. *vier*; Goth. *fidwor*; OHG. *fior*; G. *vier*.+ W. *pedwar*; Gael. *ceithir*; OIrish *cethir*; L. *quatuor*; Gk. τέτταρες, τέσσαρες; dial. πίσυρες; Russ. *chetvero*; Lith. *keturi*; Pers. *chehār*; Skt. *chatvāras*. Idg. type *qetwer-. **Der.** *four-fold, -foot-ed, -square*; also *four-th* (AS. *feōrþa*); *four-teen* (AS. *feōwertēne*); *four-teen-th*; also *for-ty*, q. v.

FOWL, a kind of bird. (E.) In ME. it signifies 'bird' generally. ME. *foul*, Chaucer, C. T. 190; earlier, *fuȝel, fowel*, Layamon, 2832. AS. *fugol*; Grein, i. 355.+Du. *vogel*; Icel. *fugl, fogl*; Dan. *fugl*; Swed. *fogel*; Goth. *fugls*; OHG. *fugal*; G. *vogel*. All from Teut. type *fugloz, m.; certainly for *flugloz*, by dissimilation; the form *fluglas*, pl., occurs in Matt. xiii. 32 (Rushworth gloss); *flugles*, gen., in the Erfurt glossary, 1085; and cf. *flugol*, adj., flying. Thus it is from *flug-*, weak grade of Teut. *fleugan-*, to fly. See **Fugleman** and **Fly.** Brugmann, i. § 491. **Der.** *fowl-er* = ME. *foulere*, Wyclif, Prov. vi. 5; *fowl-ing-piece*.

FOX, a cunning quadruped. (E.) ME. *fox*, also (Southern ME.) *vox*; P. Plowman, C. xxiii. 44; Owl and Nightingale, 817. AS. *fox*; Grein, i. 334.+Du. *vos*; G. *fuchs*. Teut. type *fuhs*, masc. We also find Icel. *fōa*, Goth. *fauhō*, fem., a vixen; Teut. type *fuhā*. Both from a base *fuh-*. A suggested connexion with Skt. *puchchha-*, 'tail,' is doubtful. **Der.** *fox-hound, fox-y*; also *fox-glove*, a flower = AS. *foxes glōfa*, Cockayne's A.S. Leechdoms, iii. 327 (cf. Norw. *revhandske* = foxglove, from *rev*, a fox, also Norw. *revbjölla* (fox-bell), a foxglove; and prov. E. *fox-fingers*, a fox-glove). And see *vix-en*.

FOY, a parting entertainment, given by (or to) a wayfarer. (Du.—F.—L.) 'Hoping .. to give you a frendly *foy*;' Howell, Letters, vol. ii. let. 12 (1634).—MDu. *foy* (Du. *fooi*), [a] 'banquet given by one at his parting from his friends;' Hexham. Prob. from F. *voie*, a way, journey; from L. *uia*, a way; as suggested by Kilian. ¶ But Franck derives it from F. *foi*, from L. acc. *fidem*; because Late L. *fides* occurs with the sense of 'payment.'

FRACAS, an uproar. (F.—Ital.—L.) Not in Johnson; borrowed from mod. F. *fracas*, a crash, din.—F. *fracasser*, to shatter; borrowed from Ital. in 15th cent. (Hatzfeld).—Ital. *fracassare*, to break in pieces; whence *fracasso*, a crash.—Ital. *fra-*, prefix, from *fra*, prep. amongst; short for L. *infrā*, within; and *cassare*, to break. Imitated (or trans-

lated) from L. *interrumpere*, to break in amongst, destroy (Diez). The vb. *cassare* is from L. *quassāre*, to shatter, intensive of *quatere*, to shake. See **Quash.**

FRACTION, a portion, fragment. (F.—L.) ME. *fraction, fraccion*; Chaucer, On the Astrolabe, ed. Skeat, prol. l. 51 (or 53). —OF. (and F.) *fraction*, 'a fraction, fracture;' Cot.—L. acc. *fractiōnem*, from nom. *fractio*, a breaking; cf. L. *fractus*, pp. of *frangere*, to break (base *frag-*), cognate with E. *break*; see **Break.** **Der.** *fraction-al*; also (from pp. *fractus*) *fract-ure*; also (from base *frag-*) *frag-ile*, q. v., *frag-ment*, q. v.; and (from *frangere*) *frang-ible*, q. v.

FRACTIOUS, peevish. (E.; *partly* F.—L.) Not found in early literature; it is given in Todd's Johnson, without a quotation. A prov. E. word, *fratchous, fratchious*, as if from the North. E. *fratch*, to squabble, quarrel, chide with another; see E. D. D. Cf. ME. *fracchen*, to creak as a cart; '*Fracchyn*, as newe cartys;' Prompt. Parv. p. 175. Of imitative origin. **β.** But it also occurs (in 1725) in the sense of 'refractory,' as if formed from *fraction*, in the (obsolete) sense of 'dissension;' see N. E. D. See **Fraction** (above).

FRACTURE, a breakage. (F.—L.) In Minsheu; and G. Herbert's Poems, Repentance, last line.—OF. *fracture*, 'a fracture, breach;' Cot.—L. *fractūra*, a breach.—L. *fract-us*, pp. of *frangere*, to break; see **Fraction.** **Der.** *fracture*, vb.

FRAGILE, frail. (F.—L.) In Shak. Timon, v. 1. 204.—F. *fragile*, 'fraile;' Cot.—L. *fragilis*, easily broken; from the base *frag-*, to break; see **Fraction.** **Der.** *fragil-i-ty*. **Doublet,** *frail*, q. v.

FRAGMENT, a piece broken off. (F.—L.) In Shak. Much Ado, i. 1. 288.—F. *fragment*, 'a fragment;' Cot.—L. *fragmentum*, a piece; formed with suffix *-mentum* from the base *frag-*, to break; see **Fraction.** **Der.** *fragment-ar-y, -al*.

FRAGRANT, sweet-smelling. (F.—L.) 'The *fragrant* odor;' Sir T. More, Works, p. 1366 c.—F. *fragrant*, 'fragrant;' Cot.—L. *fragrantem*, acc. of *fragrans*, pres. pt. of *fragrāre*, to emit an odour. Brugmann, i. § 665 (3). **Der.** *fragrant-ly, fragrance*.

FRAIL (1), easily broken. (F.—L.) ME. *freel, frele*, Wyclif, Rom. viii. 3. Chaucer has *freletee*, frailty; C. T. 12012 (C 78).— OF. *fraile*, 'fraile, brittle;' Cot.—L. *frag-lis*; see **Fragile.** **Der.** *frail-ty, -ness*.

FRAIL (2), a light basket for figs, &c. (F.—L.) Common in E. dialects; see E. D. D. ME. *fraiel*, Wyclif, Jerem. xxiv. 2.—OF. *freël*, also *fleël*, a basket, usually of rushes, for figs and grapes (Godefroy). The older form is *fleël*, whence *freël* by dissimilation.—L. *flagellum*, a whip; but also a vine-shoot, whence baskets for grapes could conveniently be made. **β.** Verified by observing that both *fleël* and *flagellum* had the peculiar sense of a certain measure of wax; thus Godefroy has ' quatre *fleaus* de chandele de cire;' and Ducange, s. v. *fleolum*, has 'unum *flagellum* ceræ, quorum sex debent ponderare libram.' Cf. Gk. φραγέλλιον, for *flagellum*, in John ii. 15. (Athenæum, Mar. 9, 1901).

FRAME, to form, construct. (E.) In Spenser, F. Q. iii. 8. 5. ME. *framien, fremien; fremen*, Havelok, 441. AS. *framian*, to be profitable, to avail; also *fremian, fremman*, to promote, effect, do; Grein, i. 339. Lit. 'to further.'—AS. *fram, from*, strong, excellent; lit. 'surpassing,' or 'forward.' Cf. AS. *fram*, prep. from, away; see **From.**+Icel. *fremja*, to further; from *framr*, adj. forward; *fram*, adv. forward; and closely related to *frá*, from. **β.** The AS. adj. *fram*, excellent, is cognate with Icel. *framr*, Du. *vroom*, G. *fromm*, good; see Kluge. **Der.** *frame*, sb. = ME. *frame*, a fabric (Prompt. Parv.), also *profit*, Ormulum, 961; cf. Icel. *frami*, advancement; also *fram-er*, *fram-ing, frame-work*.

FRAMPOLD, quarrelsome. (Low G.) Obsolete. In Shak. Merry Wives, ii. 2. 94. Spelt *frampald, frampard*, and explained as 'fretful, peevish, cross, forward' in Ray, Gloss. of South-Country Words. Allied to prov. E. *rantipole*, a romping child. **β.** The former part of the word is explained by EFries. *frante-pot, wrante-pot*, a peevish man; from EFries. *franten, wranten*, to be cross; MDu. *wranten*, to chide, Dan. *vrante*, to be peevish; Dan. *vranten*, peevish. Cf. also Dan. *vrampet*, warped; Low G. *wrampachtigh*, morose (Lübben); Low G. *frampe*, a coarse, violent man (Berghaus). More exactly, the root is supplied by MDu. *wrimpen*, 'to wring the mouth,' Hexham. Note also Lowl. Sc. *frample*, to disorder, and E. *frump*. **γ.** The second element, viz. *-old, -ald, -art, -(p)art*, may have arisen from EFries. *pot*, a pot (a term of contempt), confused with E. *poll*, the head.

FRANC, a French coin, worth about 10d. (F.—G.) ME. *frank*, Chaucer, C. T. 13117 (B 1377).—OF. (and F.) *franc*; see Cotgrave. Short for *Francorum Rex*, on a coin of 1360 (Hatzfeld); see **Frank.**

FRANCHISE, freedom. (F.—G.) ME. *franchise*, freedom; Chaucer, C. T. 9861 (E 1987); Beket, 1289. Hence the verb *franchisen, fraunchisen*, to render free, endow with the privileges of a free man; P. Plowman, C. iv. 114.—OF. *franchise*, privileged liberty.

—OF. *franchis-*, stem of parts of the verb *franchir*, to frank, render free.—OF. *franc*, free; see **Frank**.

FRANGIBLE, brittle. (L.) Rare; first in 1440. In Blount's Gloss., ed. 1674.—Late L. *frangibilis*, a coined word, from L. *frangere*, to break. See **Fraction**. Der. *frangibil-it-y*.

FRANION, a gay idle companion. (F.—L.) 'Franion, a gay idle fellow; see Heywood's Edw. IV, p. 45 [A. i. sc. 1];' Peele, i. 207 [Old Wives' Tale, near beginning.]' Halliwell. See further in Nares; also Dodsley's O. Plays, iv. 60, vi. 179. Apparently from OF. *fraignant*, one who infringes (law); orig. pres. pt. of OF. *fraindre*, *freindre*, to break; hence, to infringe.—L. *frangere*, to break. See **Fragile**. ¶ Perhaps somewhat confused with F. *fainéant*, an idle fellow, lit. 'one who does nothing.'

FRANK, free. (F.—OHG.) In Spenser, Shepherd's Kal. Nov. 203.—OF. *franc*, free; Low L. *francus*, free.—OHG. *franko*, a Frank, free man. The Franks were a Germanic people. Der. *frank*, vb., *-ly*, *-ness*; *frank-incense*, q. v.; *franchise*, q. v., *frank-lin*, q. v.

FRANKALMOIGN, the name of the tenure by which most church lands are held. (F.—OHG.; *and* L.—Gk.) In Blackstone, Comment., b. ii. c. 4. Spelt *frankalmoin* in Blount's Nomolexicon; lit. 'free alms.'—F. *franc*, free; and *almoine*, Anglo-F. variant of OF. *almosne*, mod. F. *aumône*, alms. See **Frank and Almoner**.

FRANKINCENSE, an odorous resin. (F.—OHG. *and* L.) In Holland's tr. of Pliny, b. xii. c. 14. ME. *frank encens*, Mandeville's Trav., p. 120.—OF. *franc encens*, pure incense. See *franc* in Cotgrave, who gives the example : ' *Terre franche*, mould, pure soyle, soyle of it selfe; a soyle without sand, gravell, or stones.' See **Frank** and **Incense**.

FRANKLIN, a freeholder. (F.—OHG.) ME. *frankeleyn*, Chaucer, C. T. 333 (A 331); shortened to *franklen*, P. Plowman, C. vi. 64.—AF. *fraunkelayn*, Langtoft, ii. 212; Low L. *francalānus*, *franchilānus*; Ducange.—Low L. *francus*, free; see **Frank**. β. The suffix is from OHG. *-linc*=G. and E. *-ling*, as in G. *fremd-ling*, a stranger, and E. *dar-ling*; precisely as in *chamber-lain*.

FRANTIC, full of rage or madness. (F.—L.—Gk.) ME. *frenetik*, contr. form *frentik*. Chaucer has *frenetyk*, Troilus, v. 206; *frentik* is in P. Plowman, C. xii. 6.—OF. *frenatique* (better *frenetique*), 'frantick;' Cot.—L. *phrenēticus*, *phrenīticus*, mad.—Gk. φρενητικός, rightly φρενιτικός, mad, suffering from φρενῖτις, or inflammation of the brain.—Gk. φρεν-, base of φρήν, the heart, mind, senses. See **Frensy**.

FRATERNAL, brotherly. (F.—L.) In Milton, P. L. xii. 26; Minsheu, ed. 1627; and in Palsgrave. Altered to the L. spelling.—OF. *fraternel*, 'fraternall;' Cot.—Late L. *frāternālis*, substituted for L. *frāternus*, brotherly.—L. *frāter*, cognate with E. *brother*; see **Brother**. Der. *fraternal-ly*; from the same source, *fraternity*, q. v.; *fratricide*, q. v.

FRATERNITY, brotherhood. (F.—L.) ME. *fraternitè*, Chaucer, C. T. 366 (A 364).—OF. *fraternité*.—L. *frāternitātem*, acc. of *frāternitās*.—L. *frāternus*, brotherly.—L. *frāter*, a brother; see above. Der. *fratern-ise*=OF. *fraterniser*, 'to fraternize,' Cot.; *-is-er*, *-is-at-ion* (from *frāternus*).

FRATRICIDE (1), a murderer of a brother. (F.—L.) In Minsheu, ed. 1627. This is the true sense; see below.—OF. *fratricide*, 'a murtherer of his own brother;' Cot.—L. *frātricīda*, a fratricide.—L. *frātri-*, decl. stem of *frāter*, a brother; and *-cīda*, a slayer, from *cædere* (pt. t. *ce-cīdi*), to slay. See **Fraternal and Cæsura**.

FRATRICIDE (2), murder of a brother. (L.) 'Fratricide, brother-slaughter;' Blount's Gloss., ed. 1674.—L. *frātricīdium*, a brother's murder.—L. *frātri-*; and *-cīdium*, a slaying; see above.

FRAUD, deceit. (F.—L.) ME. *fraude*; Chaucer, tr. of Boethius, b. i. pr. 4, l. 86.—OF. *fraude*, 'fraud, guile;' Cot.—L. *fraudem*, acc. of *fraus* (old form *frūs*), guile. Der. *fraud-ful*, *-ful-ly*, *-less*; *fraud-u-lent*, from MF. *fraudulent*, 'fraudulent,' Cot., from L. *fraudulentus*; *fraud-u-lent-ly*, *-u-lence*.

FRAUGHT, to lade a ship. (Friesic.) 'If after this command thou *fraught* the court;' Cymb. i. i. 126; 'The *fraughting* souls within her;' Temp. i. 2. 13. ME. *fraghten*, *fragten*, chiefly used in the pp. *fraught*, Will. of Palerne, 2732, Chaucer, C. T., B 171 (see my note on the line). [The form *freight* was also used; see **Freight**.] From EFries. *frachten* (in comp. *be-frachten*); Low G. *vrachten* (Lübben); Du. *be-vrachten*; and cf. Swed. *frakta*, Dan. *fragte*, to fraught or freight (from Friesic). From the sb. appearing as EFries. *fracht*, Low G. *vracht* (Lübben), Du. *vracht*, G. *fracht*, a load, cargo. See further under **Freight**.

FRAY (1), an affray. (F.—L.) 'There began a great *fraye* between som of the gromes and pages;' Berners, tr. of Froissart, v. i. c. 16 (R.). Short for *affray*, in the sense of 'brawl' or 'disturbance.' AF. *affray*, disturbance (Bozon). Formed, with prefix *a-* (F. *a-*, L. *ad*), from OF. *freier*, to rub (against); see **Fray** (3). Cf. Ital.

fregare, 'to rub, to chafe with one' (Florio); and Span. *refriega*, an affray, a skirmish.

FRAY (2), to terrify. (F.—L. *and* Teut.) In the Bible, Deut. xxviii. 26, Jer. vii. 33, Zech. i. 21. Short for *affray*, to terrify, whence the mod. E. *afraid*. See **Afraid, Affray**.

FRAY (3), to wear away by rubbing. (F.—L.) Ben Jonson, Sad Shepherd, i. 2. 13, has *frayings*, in the sense of peel rubbed off a stag's horn. 'A deer was said to *fray* her head, when she rubbed it against a tree to renew it;' Halliwell.—OF. *freier*, MF. *frayer*, 'to grate upon, rub,' Cot.—L. *fricāre*, to rub. See **Friction**.

FREAK (1), a whim, caprice. (E.) 'The fickle *freaks* . . . Of fortune false;' Spenser, F. Q. i. 4. 50. This use as a sb., though now common, is unknown in ME. in the same sense. Perhaps closely allied to the once common adj. *frek*, in the sense of eager, quick, vigorous. ' Es nan sa *frek*,' is none so eager; Cursor Mundi, 5198. And see *frec* in Stratmann. AS. *frec*, bold, rash; Grein, i. 338. + Icel. *frekr*, voracious, greedy; Swed. *fräck*, impudent, audacious; Dan. *fræk*, audacious; G. *frech*, saucy; OHG. *freh*, greedy. Cf. Goth. *faihufriks*, lit. fee-greedy, avaricious. (An obscure word.) Der. *freak-ish*, Pope, Wife of Bath, 91.

FREAK (2), to streak, variegate? (E.) 'The pansy *freak'd* with jet;' Milton, Lycidas, 144. Perhaps 'to streak whimsically;' from **Freak** (1). β. But cf. prov. E. *freck*, to mark with spots, to dapple; which is allied to **Freckle**.

FRECKLE, a small spot. (Scand.) Spelt *frekell* in Sir T. More, Works, p. 7 f. From a base *frek-*, whence *frek-el* and *frek-en* are diminutives. The latter is used by Chaucer, who has the pl. *freknes*, *fraknes*, C. T. 2171 (A 2169).—Icel. *freknur*, pl. freckles; Swed. *fräkne*, pl. *fräknar*, freckles; Dan. *fregne*, pl. *fregner*, freckles. Cf. **Fleck**. Der. *freckle*, vb., *freckl-ed*, *-y*.

FREE, at liberty. (E.) ME. *fre*, Chaucer, C. T. 5631 (D 49). AS. *frēo*; Grein, i. 344. + Du. *vrij*; Goth. *freis* (base *frijo-*); G. *frei*. β. Teut. type *frijoz*; closely connected with Skt. *priya-*, beloved, dear, agreeable; and E. **Friend**. Cf. also W. *rhydd*, for (*p*)*rydd*, free. Der. *free*, vb., *free-ly*, *-ness*; *freedom*=AS. *frēo-dōm*; *free-booter* (see **Booty**); *free-hold*, *-hold-er*; *free-man*=AS. *frēoman*; *free-mason*, *-mason-ry*; *free-stone* (a stone that can be freely cut), a tr. of F. *pierre franche*; *free-think-er*, *-will*. As to *freestone* see Notes on Eng. Etym., p. 105.

FREEBOOTER, a rover, pirate. (Du.) Bacon, in his Life of Hen. VII, ed. Lumby, p. 129, l. 28, says that Perkin Warbeck's men were chiefly 'strangers born, and most of them base people and *free-booters*.' These strangers were mostly Flemings; see p. 112, l. 11, &c. In a letter dated 1597, in the Sidney State Papers, ii. 78, is a mention of 'the *freebutters* of Flushenge;' Todd's Johnson.—Du. *vrijbuiter*, a freebooter.—Du. *vrijbuiten*, to rob, plunder.—Du. *vrijbuit*, plunder, lit. 'free booty.' The Du. *vrij* is cognate with E. *free*; and *buit* is allied to *booty*. See **Free** and **Booty**. Doublet, *filibuster*, q. v.

FREEZE, to harden with cold, to be very cold. (E.) ME. *freesen*, *fresen*; P. Plowman, C. xiii. 192. AS. *frēosan*, Grein, i. 347; pp. *froren*. + Icel. *frjōsa*; Swed. *frysa*; Dan. *fryse*; Du. *vriezen*; G. *frieren*; OHG. *freosan*. Teut. type *freusan-*. + L. *prūrīre*, to itch, orig. to burn; cf. *pruīna*, hoar-frost, *prūna*, a burning coal; Skt. *plōsha-*, a burning. From √PREUS, to burn; whence the Teutonic base FREUS, appearing in Goth. *frius*, frost, as well as in the words above. Der. *fros-t*, q. v., *frore*, q. v.

FREIGHT, a cargo. (F.—OHG.) ME. *freyte* (1463); 'freyght or huyr,' i. e. hire, Caxton, Golden Legend; St. Giles, § 3. *Freighted* occurs in North's Plutarch; see Shakespeare's Plutarch, ed. Skeat, p. 16, l. 3. Apparently an altered spelling of OF. *fret*, 'the freight of a ship, also the hire that's paid for a ship;' Cot.—OHG. *frēht*, earnings, hire (supposed to be the same word as G. *fracht*, a cargo). β. The OHG. *frēht* is thought to represent an OHG. type *fra-aihtiz*; from *fra-*, prefix (see **Fret** (1)), and *aihtiz* > AS. *æht*, acquisition, property, from *āgan*, to own. See **Own** (1). Der. *freight*, vb., *freight-age*.

FRENZY, madness, fury. (F.—L.—Gk.) ME. *frenesye* [not *frenseye* as in Tyrwhitt], Chaucer, Troil. i. 727; P. Plowman, C. xxiii. 85.—OF. *frenaisie* [better *frenesie*], 'frenzie;' Cot.—L. *phrenēsis*.—Late Gk. φρένησις, equivalent to Gk. φρενῖτις, inflammation of the brain.—Gk. φρεν-, base of φρήν, the midriff, heart, senses. Der. *frantic*, q. v.

FREQUENT, occurring often, familiar. (F.—L.) 'How *frequent* and famyliar a thynge;' Sir T. Elyot, Governour, b. iii. c. 7, § 2. 'Frequently in his mouthe;' id. b. i. c. 22.—MF. *frequent*, omitted by Cotgrave, but given in Sherwood's Index.—L. *frequentem*, acc. of *frequens*, crowded, crammed, frequent; pres. part. of a lost verb *frequēre*, to cram, closely allied to *farcire*, to cram, and from the same root. See **Farce**. Brugmann, ii. § 713. Der. *frequent-ly*, *-ness*, *frequenc-y*; also *frequent*, vb. < MF. *frequenter*, 'to frequent,' Cot. < L. *frequentāre*; *frequent-at-ion*, *-at-ive*.

FRESCO, a painting executed on plaster while fresh. (Ital. — OHG.) See *Fresco* in Kersey's Dict., ed. 1715. — Ital. *fresco*, cool, fresh. — OHG. *frisc* (G. *frisch*), fresh. See **Fresh.**

FRESH, new, recent, vigorous. (E.; *and* F. — OHG.) ME. *fresh*, *fresch*. 'Ful *freshe* and newe;' Chaucer, C. T. 367 (A 365). — OF. *fres*, *freis* (fem. *fresche*), fresh. — OHG. *frisc* (above). β. Also *fersch*, *fersh*; spelt *fersse* (= *fershe*), Rob. of Glouc. p. 397, l. 8187; also *uersc* (= *fersc*), O. Eng. Homilies, i. 175, l. 248; representing AS. *fersc*; 'ne *fersc* ne mersc' = neither fresh water nor marsh; Ancient Laws, ed. Thorpe, ii. 184, l. 8. + Icel. *ferskr*, fresh; Du. *versch*; G. *frisch*; OHG. *frisc*. γ. Teut. type *friskoz*. Allied to Lith. *prëskas*, sweet, unsoured, i.e. unleavened (applied to bread); Russ. *priesnuii*, fresh. Der. *fresh-ly*, *-ness*, *-en*, *-man*; also *fresh-et*, a small stream of flowing water, Milton, P. R. ii. 345. See **Frisk, Fresco.**

FRET (1), to eat away. (E.) ME. *freten*, a strong verb; Chaucer, C. T. 2070 (A 2068). AS. *fretan*, pt. t. *frœt*; Grein, i. 340. Contracted from *fra-etan*, as is clearly shown by the Gothic form; from Teut. *fra-*, intensive prefix, and *etan*, to eat. + Swed. *fräta*, to corrode; Du. *vreten* (*ver-eten*); G. *fressen* (*ver-essen*); Goth. *fraitan*, from *fra-*, intensive prefix, and *itan*, to eat. See **For** (2) and **Eat.** Der. *fret-ful*, Shak. 2 Hen. VI, iii. 2. 403; *-ful-ly*, *-ful-ness*; *frett-ing*. ¶ The strong pp. occurs in Levit. xiii. 55, in the form *fret*; contr. from the ME. strong pp. *freten*, *frete*; see Chaucer, C. T. 4895 (B 475).

FRET (2), to ornament, variegate. (F.) ME. *fretten*, to adorn with interlaced work, esp. with gold or silver embroidery. 'Fyoles *fretted* with flores and fleez of gold, phials [cups] adorned with flowers and fleeces of golde,' Allit. Poems, ed. Morris, B. 1476; cf. P. Plowman, A. ii. 11. — OF. *freter*, to adorn; from *frete*, an (interlaced) fret (in heraldry, F. *frette*). See **Fret** (3). ¶ It can hardly have been influenced by AS. *frætwan*, to adorn, as this would become ME. *fratwen*, *fratewen*; see Matt. xii. 44 (AS. version). Der. *fret-work.*

FRET (3), a kind of grating. (F. — L. *or* G.) A term in heraldry, meaning 'a bearing composed of bars crossed and interlaced.' See explanation in Minsheu, ed. 1627. Kersey, ed. 1715, has: 'in heraldry, a bearing wherein several lines run crossing one another.' — OF. *frete*, F. *frette*, a fret. Cotgrave gives '*fretté*, fretty, a term of blazon' [heraldry]. According to Diez, *frettes*, pl., means an iron grating. Roquefort gives: '*freter*, to cross, interlace.' Cf. Span. *fretes*, 'frets, narrow bands of a shield, a term in heraldry' (Meadows); from a sing. *frete*. β. Of doubtful origin. According to Diez, from a Late L. type *ferritta*; from L. *ferrum*, iron; cf. Ital. *ferriata*, a grate of iron (Florio). Another suggestion (also doubtful) is to derive it from OSax. *feter-*, in *feter-ōs*, pl., fetters, AS. *feter*, a fetter. See Körting, §§ 3700, 3715. Der. *frett-y.*

FRET (4), a stop on a musical instrument. (F. — L.) In Shak. Tam. Shrew, ii. 150. A *fret* was a stop such as is seen on a guitar, to regulate the fingering; formed by thin pieces of metal or wires running like bars across the neck of the instrument; see Levins. I take it to be a particular use of OF. *frete*, a ferrule; or 'the iron band or hoop that keeps a woodden toole from riving;' Cot. Cf. Ital. *ferretti*, little irons, tags for points (Florio). Perhaps the same word as the above; but this is doubtful.

FRIABLE, easily crumbled. (F. — L.) In Sir T. Browne, Vulg. Errors, b. iii. c. 23. § 5. — MF. *friable*, 'bruizeable, easie to be broken;' Cot. — L. *friābilis*, easily crumbled. — L. *friāre*, to rub, crumble. Der. *friable-ness*, *friabil-i-ty.*

FRIAR, a member of a religious order. (F. — L.) ME. *frere*, Chaucer, C. T. 208; Rob. of Glouc. p. 530, l. 10930. — OF. *frere*, *freire*. — L. *frātrem*, acc. of *frāter*, cognate with E. *brother*; see **Brother.** Der. *friar-y.*

FRIBBLE, to trifle. (Flem. — Du.) 'Than those who with the stars do *fribble*,' Butler, Hudibras, pt. ii. c. 3. l. 36; and see Spectator, no. 288. To *fribble away* is to waste foolishly and triflingly. — W. Flemish *fribbelen*, *wribbelen*, to rub between the finger and thumb (as a thread), to roll together by rubbing (De Bo); cf. Low G. *wribbeln*, to rub between the fingers, to rub away. (Hence, to twiddle, trifle.) Frequentative of Du. (and EFries.) *wrijven*, to rub, rub with the hand, rub away, grind (pt. t. *wreef*, pp. *gewreven*); G. *reiben*, to rub.

FRICASSEE, a dish made of fowls. (F. — L.?) 'A dish made by cutting chickens or other small things in pieces, and dressing them with strong sauce;' Todd's Johnson. 'Soups, and olios, *fricassees*, and ragouts;' Swift, Tale of a Tub, § 7; id. — F. *fricassee*, a fricassee; 'any meat fried in a panne,' Cot.; fem. pp. of *fricasser*, to fry, also, to squander money. Of unknown origin (Brachet). ¶ Perhaps a derivative of *frīgere*, to fry; with *c* inserted by a fancied connexion with *fricāre*, to rub; cf. Körting, § 3990. We once had *fricasy* in the sense of rubbing; as in '*fricasyes* or rubbings;' Sir T. Elyot, Castel of Helth, b. ii. c. 32.

FRICTION, rubbing, attrition. (F. — L.) 'Hard and vehement *friction*;' Holland, tr. of Pliny, b. xxviii. c. 4. — F. *friction*, 'a friction, or frication;' Cot. — L. *frictiōnem*, acc. of *frictio*, a rubbing. — L. *fric-tus*, usual pp. of *fricāre*, to rub; allied to *friāre*, to crumble. Der. *friction-wheel*; cf. *friable.*

FRIDAY, the sixth day of the week. (E.) ME. *Friday*, Chaucer, C. T. 1536 (A 1534). AS. *frīge-dæg*; rubric to S. Mark, xi. 11. — AS. *Frīge*, gen. case of *Frig*, the wife of Woden (considered as the goddess of love) and *dæg*, a day; see Grein, i. 349. — √PREI, to love; see **Friend.** Cf. Icel. *frjādagr*, Friday, OHG. *Frīatag*, *Frīgetag*, Friday. The Teut. type (of AS. *Frig*) is *frijā*, fem. of *frijoz*, dear, beloved, 'free;' Skt. *priyā*, wife, loved one. Brugmann, i. § 309 (2). See **Free, Friend.** ¶ AS. *Frīge dæg* was meant to translate L. *diēs Veneris.*

FRIEND, an intimate acquaintance. (E.) ME. *frend*, *freond*; Ormulum, 443, 1609, 17960. AS. *frēond*; Grein, i. 346. Orig. pres. pt. of *frēon*, *frēogan*, to love; so that the sense is 'loving;' id. 345. + Du. *vriend*, a friend; cf. *vrijen*, to court, woo; Icel. *frændi*, a kinsman, from *frjā*, to love; Dan. *frænde*, Swed. *frände*, a kinsman; Goth. *frijōnds*, a friend, pres. pt. of *frijōn*, to love; G. *freund*, a friend; OHG. *friunt*. — √PREI, to love; cf. Skt. *prī*, to love. Der. *friend-ly* (AS. adv. *frēondlīce*), *-li-ness*, *-less* (AS. *frēondleas*), *-less-ness*, *-ship* (AS. *frēondscipe*).

FRIEZE (1), a coarse woollen cloth. (F. — Du.) Palsgrave (1530) has: 'Fryse, roughe clothe, *drap frise*.' Cf. 'a gowne of grene *frese*,' in 1418; Fifty E. E. Wills, ed. Furnivall, p. 37, l. 1. 'Panni lanei de *Frise*;' Earl of Derby's Expeditions, 1390–3, p. 280, l. 25. 'Woven after the manner of deep, *frieze* rugges;' Holland's tr. of Pliny, b. viii. c. 48. — MF. *frise*, *frize*, 'frise;' Cot. He also gives *drap de frise* as an equivalent expression; lit. cloth of Friesland. — Du. *Vriesland*, Friesland; *Vries*, a Frieslander. ¶ The ME. *Frise*, meaning 'Friesland,' occurs in the Romaunt of the Rose, 1093. Similarly, the term 'cheval de Frise' means 'horse of Friesland,' because there first used in defensive warfare.

FRIEZE (2), part of the entablature of a column. (F. — L.) In Shak. Macb. i. 6. 6. — MF. *frize* '(in architecture) the broad and flat band, or member, that's next below the cornish [cornice], or between it and the architrave; called also by our workemen the *frize*;' Cot. Cf. Span. *friso*, a frieze, Ital. *fregio*, 'a fringe, lace, border, ornament, or garnishment;' Florio. Whether F. *frise* is from Ital. *fregio* is not clear. The source is L. *Phrygium* (*opus*), Phrygian work; cf. *Phrygiam chlamydem*, embroidered cloak, Æn. iii. 484.

FRIGATE, a large ship. (F. — Ital.) In Cotgrave; spelt *frigat* in Hakluyt, Voy. iii. 665 (last line). — MF. *fregate*, 'a frigate, a swift pinnace;' Cot. — Ital. *fregata*, 'a frigate, a spiall ship;' Florio. ¶ Of uncertain origin; Diez supposes it to stand for *fargata*, a supposed contracted form of *fabricāta*, i.e. constructed, from *fabricāre*, to build; but this explanation is not now accepted. Der. *frigat-oon* (Ital. *fregatone*), *frigate-bird.*

FRIGHT, terror. (E.) ME. *fryʒt*; Seven Sages, ed. Wright, 948. It stands for *fyrʒt*, by the shifting of *r* so common in English, as in *bride*, *bird*, *brimstone*, &c. ONorthumb. *fyrihto*, Matt. xxviii. 4; AS. *fyrhto*, *fyrhtu*, fright; Grein, i. 362. Cf. *fyrht*, timid; *āfyrhtan*, to terrify. + OSax. *forhta*, fright; Goth. *faurhtei*, fright; *faurhtjan*, to fear; G. *furcht*, OHG. *forhta*, *forohta*, *forahta*, fright; G. *fürchten*, to fear. Allied to OSax. *forʜt*, OHG. *foraht*, Goth. *faurhts*, timid, fearful. Der. *fright*, verb (later form *fright-en*); Shak. uses the form *fright* only; *fright-ful*, Rich. III, iv. 4. 169; *-ful-ly*, *-ful-ness.*

FRIGID, cold, chilly. (L.) 'The *frigid* region;' Chapman, The Ball, A. iv. sc. 2 (Lamount). *Frigidity* is in Sir T. Browne, Vulg. Errors, b. ii. c. 1. § 4. — L. *frigidus*, cold. — L. *frigēre*, to be cold. — L. *frīgus*, sb. cold. + Gk. ῥῖγος, cold; see Brugmann, i. § 875. Der. *frigid-ly*, *-ness*, *-i-ty.*

FRILL, a ruffle on a shirt. (Low G.) In Ash's Dict., ed. 1775. The N.E.D. quotes 'that can *fril* and paint herself' (1574); and 'their flaunting ruffes, their borowed *frilles*' (1591). Of Teutonic (prob. Low G.) origin; but insufficiently recorded. Represented by W.Flem. *frul*, *frulle*, a wrinkled plait, wrinkled fold in a small shred or band; De Bo cites '*frullen* round the bottom of a dress,' and 'sleeves with *frullen*.' Another trace of it occurs in Swed. dial. *fråll*, *fröll*, a wrinkled or curled strip, as on a woman's cap, whence *fryllig*, wrinkled. This points to a Teut. *frulle*, a frill, whence a verb *fryllan-*; so that the E. form *frill* appears to be verbal.

FRINGE, a border of loose threads. (F. — L.) Palsgrave has: 'Freng, *frenge*.' Chaucer has *frenges*, pl.; Ho. of Fame, iii. 228. — OF. *frenge*, *fringe* (Supp. to Godefroy); F. *frange*. Cot. has: '*Frange*, fringe.' The Wallachian form (according to Cihac) is *frimbie*, which stands for *fimbrie*, by a transposition of *r*, for greater ease of pronunciation; cf. F. *brebis* from L. *ueruēcem*. — L. *fimbria*, fringe; chiefly in the pl. *fimbriæ*, curled ends of threads, fibres. Brugmann, i. § 875. See **Fibre.** Der. *fringe*, verb, *fringed*, Tempest. i. 2. 408; *fring-y.*

FRIPPERY, worn out clothes, trifles. (F. — L.) 'Some *frippery* to hide nakedness;' Ford, Fancies Chaste and Noble, A. i. sc. 1 (R.).

Shak. has it in the sense of an old-clothes' shop; Temp. iv. 225.—MF. *friperie*, 'a friperie, broker's shop, street of brokers, or of fripiers;' Cot.—MF. *fripier*, 'a fripier, or broker; a mender or trimmer up of old garments, and a seller of them so mended;' id.—OF. *frepe* (also *ferpe*, *felpe*), frayed out fringe, rag, old clothes (Godefroy). Prob. from L. *fibra*, a fibre; Körting, § 3724.

FRISK, to skip about. (F.—OHG.) In Shak. Wint. Ta. i. 2. 67. A verb formed from the adj. *frisk*, which occurs in Cotgrave.—MF. *frisque*, 'friske, lively, jolly, blithe, brisk, fine, spruce, gay;' Cot.; OF. *frisque*, NorthF. variant of *frische*, lively, alert (Godefroy); cf. 'Fresshe, gorgeous, gay, *frisque*, Palsgrave, p. 313;' Walloon *frisquette*, a gay girl (Sigart).—OHG. *frisc*, G. *frisch*, fresh, brisk, lively; see **Fresh**. Cf. Norm. dial. *frisquet*, frisky (whence E. *frisky*); Moisy. Der. *frisk-y*, equivalent to the old adj. *frisk*; *frisk-i-ly*, *-i-ness*; *frisk-et*, a printer's term for a light frame often in motion.

FRITH (1), an enclosure, forest, wood. (E.) It occurs as a place-name in Chapel-le-*Frith*, Derbyshire, and is common in Kent in the names of woods; but is obsolescent. Drayton has: 'Both in the tufty *frith* and in the mossy fell,' Polyolbion, song 17. ME. *frith*, peace; Layamon, l. 2549; Rob. of Brunne, tr. of Langtoft, p. 90; also in the sense of enclosed land, enclosure, park for hunting, forest, wood; thus in Layamon, 1432, where the older MS. speaks of hunting in the king's *frith* [friðe], the later MS. speaks of hunting in the king's *park* [parc]. See numerous examples in Mätzner, and cf. AS. *fr.ð-geard*, an enclosed space, lit. 'peace-yard' or 'safety-yard,' for which see Thorpe, Anc. Laws, ii. 298; also MSwed. *fridgiärd*, an enclosure for animals (Ihre). AS. *frið*, peace; *freoðo*, *freoðu*, *friðu*, peace, security, asylum; Grein, i. 343, 347, 348.+Icel. *friðr*, peace, security, personal security; Dan. *fred*; Swed. *fred*, MSwed. *frid*. Cf. Du. *vrede*, peace, quiet; G. *friede*. Teut. type *friþuz*. From *fri-*, base of *fri-joz*, free; see **Free**. ¶ The ME. *frith* sometimes means 'wooded country;' this may be a different word; viz. from AS. *gefyrhðe* (Birch, Cart. Sax. iii. 120). Borrowed forms are W. *ffridd*, park, forest; Irish *frith*, a wild mountainous place; Gael. *frith*, a forest for deer.

FRITH (2), **FIRTH**, an estuary. (Scand.) ME. *firth*, Barbour's Bruce, xvi. 542, 547.—Icel. *fjörðr*, pl. *firðir*, a firth, bay; Dan. *fiord*; Swed. *fjärd*. Teut. type, *ferðuz*; Noreen, § 139. Allied to L. *portus*, a haven; see **Ford**. (*Not* connected with L. *fretum*.)

FRITILLARY, a genus of liliaceous plants. (L.) In Phillips, ed. 1706. Called *Frettellaria* in Bacon, Essay 46 (Of Gardens). So called because chequered markings on the corolla were associated with a *fritillus*, which (according to Gerarde) was by some supposed to mean a chessboard. Englished from Late L. *fritillāria*, coined from L. *fritillus*, a dice-box.

FRITTER (1), a kind of pancake. (F.—L.) Spelt *frytowre* in Prompt. Parv. Cotgrave has: '*Friteau*, a fritter.' But the E. word rather answers to OF. *friture*, a frying, a dish of fried fish. Both *friteau* and *friture* are related to OF. *frit*, fried.—L. *frictus*, fried, pp. of *frigere*, to fry. See **Fry** (1). Der. *fritter*, vb., to reduce to slices, waste.

FRITTER (2), a fragment. (F.—L.) 'One that makes *fritters* of English;' Merry Wives, v. 5. 151 [but this may belong to the word above]. Johnson has: '*Fritter*, a fragment, a small piece;' but his examples from Bacon and Butler are wrong, as the reading is *fitters* in both. Pope has the verb *fritter*, to break into fragments, twice; see Dunciad, i. 278, iv. 56.—OF. *freture*, *fraiture*, a fracture, a fragment (Godefroy).—L. *fractūra*, a breaking; from *fract-*, pp. stem of *frangere*, to break. See **Fracture, Break**.

FRIVOLOUS, trifling. (L.) In Shak. Tam. Shrew, v. 1. 28. Cotgrave translates F. *frivole* by 'frivolous, vain.'—L. *friuol-us*, silly, trifling; with change of L. *-us* to E. *-ous*, as in *abstemious*, *arduous*, &c. The orig. sense of *friuolus* seems to have been 'rubbed away;' also applied to refuse, broken sherds, &c. '*Friuola* sunt proprie uasa fictilia quassa;' Festus.—L. *friāre*, *fricāre*, to rub; see **Friction**. Der. *frivolous-ly*, *-ness*; also *frivol-i-ty*, from F. *frivolité*.

FRIZ, FRIZZ, to curl, render rough. (F.—Du.) More often used in the frequentative form *frizzle*. 'Mæcenas, if I meete with thee without my *frisled* top;' Drant, tr. of Horace, Epist. i. 1. 94 (Lat. text). 'Her haire *frized* short;' Pepys, Diary, Nov. 22, 1660.—MF. *frizer*, 'to frizle, crispe, curle;' Cot. β. The orig. sense perhaps was to roughen the nap of a cloth, to make it look like *frieze*. This is rendered probable by Span. *frisar*, to frizzle, to raise the nap on frieze; from Span. *frisa*, frieze.—OF. *frize*, 'the cloth called frise;' Cot. Cf. MDu. *viséren* [from F. *friser*], 'to frieze cloth;' Hexham. See **Frieze** (1). Der. *frizz-le*.

FRO, adv. from. (Scand.) ME. *fra*, *fro*, also used as a prep. Ormulum, 1265, 4820; Havelok, 318.—Icel. *frā*, from; also adv. as in the phrase *til ok frā* = to and fro, whence our phrase 'to and fro' is copied. Dan. *fra*.+AS. *from*; see **From**. Der. *fro-ward*, q.v. ¶ *Fro* is the doublet of *from*; but from a Scand. source.

FROCK, a monk's cowl, loose gown. (F.—Late L.—L.) In Shak. Hamlet, iii. 4. 164. ME. *frok*, of which the dat. *frokke* occurs in P. Plowman, B. v. 81.—OF. *froc*; whence '*froc de moine*, a monk's cowle or hood;' Cot.; Late L. *frocus*, a monk's frock; also spelt *floccus*, by the common change of *l* to *r*; see *floccus* in Ducange; and cf. Port. *froco*, a snow-flake, from L. *floccus*. Prob. so called because woollen (Diez); Körting, § 3847). See **Flock** (2). ¶ Otherwise in Brachet; viz. from OHG. *hroch* (G. *rock*), a coat.

FROG (1), a small amphibious animal. (E.) ME. *frogge*, Rob. of Glouc. p. 69, l. 1562; pl. *froggen*, O. E. Homilies, i. 51, l. 30. AS. *frocga* (pl. *frocgan*); and *frox* (pl. *froxas*); Ps. lxxvii. 50. Of these, *frox* =*frocs* =*frosc*, cognate with Icel. *froskr*, Du. *vorsch*, G. *frosch*. β. The ME. forms are various; we find *froke*, *frosche*, *frosh*, *froske*, and *frogge*, all in Prompt. Parv. p. 180.

FROG (2), a horny substance in a horse's foot. (E. ?) a. The *frog* of a horse's foot is shaped like a fork, and I suspect it to be a corruption of *fork*, q.v. Cf. F. *fourchette*, 'a fork; (vet.) a frush or frog;' Hamilton. β. On the other hand, it was certainly understood as being named after a *frog* (though it is hard to see why), because it was also called a *frush*, which much resembles *frosh*, a ME. form of *frog*; see **Frog** (1); though this might also be a substitute for F. *fourche*, a fork, and this for F. *fourchette*. 'Frush or frog, the tender part of a horse's hoof, next the heel;' Kersey's Dict., ed. 1715.

FROLIC, adj., sportive, gay, merry. (Du.) In Shak. Mids. Nt. Dr. v. 394. Gascoigne speaks of a '*frolicke* fauour' = a merry look; Fruites of Warre, st. 40. It seems to have been one of the rather numerous words imported from Dutch in the reign of Elizabeth.—MDu. *vrolick*, 'frolick, merrie,' Hexham; Du. *vrolijk*, frolic, merry, gay.+G. *fröhlich*, merry. β. Formed by help of the suffix *-ljk* (= E. *like*, *-ly*) from the base *vro-*, orig. an adj. with the sense of 'merry,' found in OSax. *frāh*, OFries. *frō*, and preserved in mod. G. *froh*, joyous, glad. γ. Perhaps allied to Icel. *frār*, swift, light-footed (Kluge). Der. *frolic*, verb, *frolic*, sb.; *frolic-some*, *-some-ness*.

FROM, prep., away, forth. (E.) ME. *from*; common. AS. *from*, *fram*.+Icel. *frā*, from; OHG. *fram*, adv. forth; prep. forth from; Goth. *fram*, prep. from. Cf. also Icel. *fram*, adv. forward (Swed. *fram*, Dan. *frem*); Goth. *framis*, adv. further. Doublet, *fro*; and see *frame*.

FROND, a leafy branch. (L.) Not in Johnson. Modern and scientific. First in 1785.—L. *frond-*, stem of *frons*, a leafy branch. Der. *frond-esc-ence*, *frondi-fer-ous* (from decl. stem *frondi-*, and *fer-re*, to bear).

FRONT, the forehead. (F.—L.) In early use. ME. *front*; used in the sense of 'forehead,' King Alisaunder, 6550.—OF. *front*, 'the forehead, brow;' Cot.—L. *frontem*, acc. of *frons*, the forehead. Der. *front*, verb, 2 Hen. IV, iv. 1. 25; *front-age*, *-less*; *front-al*, q.v., *front-ier*, q.v., *front-let*, q.v., *fronti-spiece*, q.v. Also *front-ed* (rare), Milton, P. L. ii. 532. Also *af-front*, *con-front*, *ef-front-ery*. Also *frounce*, *flounce*.

FRONTAL, a band worn on the forehead. (F.—L.) 'Which being applied in the manner of a *frontall* to the forehead;' Holland, tr. of Pliny, b. xx. c. 21. ME. *frountel*, Polit. Songs, p. 154.—OF. *frontal*, 'a frontlet, or forehead-band;' Cot.—L. *frontāle*, an ornament for a horse's forehead.—L. *front-*, stem of *frons*, the front. See **Front**.

FRONTIER, a part of a country bordering on another. (F.—L.) In Shak. Hamlet, iv. 4. 16; and Caxton, Hist. Troye, leaf 207 b, l. 9.—OF. *frontiere*, 'the frontier, marches, or border of a country;' Cot.—Late L. *frontēria*, *frontāria*, a frontier, border-land; formed with suffix *-āria*, fem. of *-ārius*, from *front-*, stem of *frons*. See **Front**.

FRONTISPIECE, a picture at the beginning of a book, front of a house. (F.—L.) A perverse spelling of *frontispice*, by confusion with *piece*; see Trench, Eng. Past and Present. In Minsheu, ed. 1627; and Milton, P. L. iii. 506.—F. *frontispice*, 'the frontispiece, or fore-front of a house;' Cot.—Late L. *frontispicium*, the front of a church; lit. 'front view.'—L. *fronti-*, decl. stem of *frons*, the front; and *specere*, to view, behold, see. See **Front**, and **Special** or **Spy**.

FRONTLET, a small band on the forehead. (F.—L.) In Shak. K. Lear, i. 4. 208; Exod. xiii. 16, Deut. vi. 8 (A. V.); and in Palsgrave.—OF. *frontelet*, dimin. of *frontel*, with suffix *-et*. 'A *frontlet*, also the part of a hedstall of a bridle, that commeth over the forehead;' Baret's Alvearie. See **Frontal**.

FRORE, frozen. (E.) In Milton, P. L. ii. 595. Short for *froren*, the old pp. of the verb 'to freeze.' See An O. Eng. Miscellany, ed. Morris, p. 151. AS. *froren*, *gefroren*, pp. of *frēosan*, to freeze.+Du. *gevroren*, pp. of *vriesen*, to freeze; G. *gefroren*, pp. of *frieren*. See **Freeze**.

FROST, the act or state of freezing. (E.) ME. *frost*; also *forst*, by the common shifting of *r*; Wyclif, Ps. lxxvii. 47. AS. *forst* (the usual form), Grein, i. 331.+Du. *vorst*; Icel., Dan., and Swed. *frost*; G. *frost*. Teut. types *frus-toz*, m., *frus-tom*, n.; from *frus-*, weak grade of *freusan-*, to freeze. See **Freeze.** Der. *frost*, verb, *frost-y*, *-i-ly*, *-i-ness*, *-bite*, *-bitt-en*, *-bound*, *-ing*, *-nail*, *-work*.

FROTH, foam upon liquids. (Scand.) ME. *frothe*, Prompt. Parv. p. 180. Chaucer has the verb *frothen*, C. T. 1661 (A 1659). — Icel. *froða*, *frauð*; Dan. *fraade*; [Swed. *fradga*]. β. From the weak grade (*fruth*) of the Teut. verb *freuthan-*, to froth up; seen in AS. *ā-frēoðan*, to froth up. Der. *froth-y*, *-i-ly*, *-i-ness*.

FROUNCE, to wrinkle, curl, plait. (F. — L.) The older form of *flounce*; see **Flounce** (2). Der. *frounce*, sb.

FROWARD, perverse. (Scand. *and* E.) ME. *froward*, but commonly *fraward*; Hampole, Pricke of Conscience, 87; Ormulum, 4672. This *fraward* is a Northern form of *from-ward*, due to substitution of the Scand. Eng. *fro* for the AS. *from*. From Icel. *frā*, fro; and E. *ward*; see **Fro.** Cf. AS. *fromweard*, only in the sense of 'about to depart' in Grein, i. 351; *froward* has the orig. sense of *from-ward*, i. e. averse, perverse. Cf. *wayward*; i. e. away-ward. And see **Toward.** Der. *froward-ly*, *-ness*, Spenser, F. Q. iii. 6. 20.

FROWN, to look sternly. (F. — Scand.) ME. *frounen*; Chaucer, C. T. 8232 (E 356). — OF. *frongnier*, whence F. *re-frongner*, 'to frown, lowre, look sternly, sullenly;' Cot. In mod. F., *se refrogner*, to frown. Cf. Ital. *infrigno*, wrinkled, frowning; Ital. dialectal (Lombardic) *frignare*, to whimper, to make a wry face. β. Of Teut. origin. From Teut. *frunjan-*, as seen in Swed. dial. *fryna*, to make a wry face (Rietz), Norw. *fröyna*, the same (Aasen). (Körting, § 3834.) Der. *frown*, sb.

FRUCTIFY, to make fruitful. (F. — L.) In Shak. L. L. L. iv. 2. 30; and in Chaucer, Lenvoy à Scogan, 48. — F. *fructifier*, 'to fructifie;' Cot. — L. *fructificāre*, to make fruitful. — L. *fructu-*, for *fructu-*, decl. stem of *fructus*, fruit; and *-ficāre*, suffix due to *facere*, to make. See **Fruit** and **Fact.** Der. *fructifica-tion*, from the same L. verb.

FRUGAL, thrifty. (F. — L.) In Shak. Much Ado, iv. 1. 130. — F. *frugal*, 'frugall;' Cot. — L. *frūgālis*, economical, lit. of or belonging to fruits. — L. *frūg-*, stem of *frux*, fruits of the earth; of which the dat. *frūgī* was used to signify useful, temperate, frugal. Allied to **Fruit.** Der. *frugal-ly*, *-ity*; also *frugi-fer-ous*, i. e. fruit-bearing, *frugi-vor-ous*, fruit-eating, from L. *frūgi-*, decl. stem of *frux*, combined with *fer-re*, to bear, *uor-āre*, to eat.

FRUIT, produce of the earth. (F. — L.) ME. *fruit*, *frut*; spelt *frut* in the Ancren Riwle, p. 150. — OF. *fruit* (Burguy). — L. *fructum*, acc. of *fructus*, fruit. — L. *fructus*, pp. of *frui*, to enjoy; cognate with E. *brook*, to endure. — √BHREUG, to enjoy; see **Brook** (1). Brugmann, i. § 111; ii. § 532. Der. *fruit-age*; *fruit-er-er* (for *fruit-er*, with suffix *-er* unnecessarily repeated), 2 Hen. IV, iii. 2. 36; *fruit-ful*, Tam. Shrew, i. 1. 3; *-ful-ly*, *-ful-ness*, *-less*, *-less-ly*, *-less-ness*; also *fruition*, q. v., *fructify*, q. v., *fructiferous*, *fructivorous*.

FRUITION, enjoyment. (F. — L.) In Shak. 1 Hen. VI, v. 5. 9. — OF. *fruition*, 'fruition, enjoying;' Cot. — Late L. *fruitiōnem*, acc. of *fruitio*; cf. *fruitus*, by-form of *fructus*, pp. of *frui*, to enjoy.

FRUMENTY, FURMENTY, FURMETY, food made of wheat boiled in milk. (F. — L.) Spelt *firmentie* in Gascoigne, Steel Glas, 1077; see Specimens of English, ed. Skeat, p. 322. Palsgrave has *furmenté*. Holland speaks of 'frumenty or spike corne;' tr. of Pliny, b. xviii. c. 23. — OF. *fromentee*, MF. *froumenté*, 'furmentie, wheat boyled;' Cot. Formed, with suffix *-ee* (L. *-āta*), from OF. *froment*, 'wheat;' id. — Late L. *frumentum*; for L. *frūmentum*, corn; formed (with suffix *-mentum*) from the base *frū-*, *frūg-*; see **Fruit, Frugal.**

FRUMP, a cross, ill-tempered person. (MDu.?) The older sense was a jeer or a sneer; then, ill humour; lastly, an ill-humoured person. 'Sweet widow, leave your *frumps*;' Beaum. and Fletcher, Scornful Lady, A. ii. sc. 3. Apparently from MDu. *wrump-*, *wromp-*, weak grade of *wrimpen*, 'to wring the mouth,' Hexham; Kilian makes it equivalent to *grijsen*, i. e. to frown. So also Low G. *frampe*, a coarse, violent man (Berghaus); *wrampach'ich*, morose (Lübben); from the 2nd grade *wramp*. The E. D. D. has also *frump*, an unseemly fold, *frumple*, to wrinkle. The base *wrimp-* is a variant of *wrink-*, as in *wrink-le*; cf. *wring.* Cf. **Frampold.**

FRUSH, to bruise, to batter. (F. — L.) In Shak. Troil. v. 6. 29. ME. *fruschen*, to crush; Wallace, iii. 197. — OF. *fruissier*, *froissier* (F. *froisser*), to break in pieces; L. type *frustiāre*. — L. *frustum*, a piece; see **Frustum.**

FRUSTRATE, to render vain. (L.) Formerly used as an adj., as in Sir T. Elyot, The Governour, b. iii. c. 10; and in Shak. Temp. iii. 3. 10. — L. *frustrātus*, pp. of *frustrāri*, to disappoint, render vain. — L. *frustrā*, in vain; properly fem. abl. of obsolete adj. *frustrus*, for *frud-trus*, originally meaning 'deceitful.' Allied to E. *fraud*. See **Fraud.** Der. *frustrat-ion*.

FRUSTUM, a piece of a cone or cylinder. (L.) The pl. *frustums* is used by Sir T. Browne, Cyrus' Garden; ch. iii. § 51. — L. *frustum*, a piece cut off, or broken off. Cf. Gk. θραυστός, broken, brittle;

θραῦσμα, a fragment; from θραύειν, to break in pieces. Brugmann, i. § 853. Der. *frust-ule*.

FRY (1), to dress food over a fire. (F. — L.) ME. *frien*; Chaucer, C. T. 6069 (D 487); P. Plowman, C. ix. 334. — OF. *frire*, 'to frie;' Cot. — L. *frigere*, to roast. + Gk. φρύγειν, to parch; Skt. *bhrajj*, to boil, fry. Der. *fry*, sb.

FRY (2), the spawn of fishes. (F. — L.) In Shak. All's Well, iv. 3. 250. ME. *fri*, *fry*; 'to the and to thi *fri* mi blissing graunt I' = to thee and to thy seed I grant my blessing; Towneley Mysteries, p. 24. AF. *fry*, *frie*, Liber Albus, pp. 507-8. — OF. *fri*, variant of OF. *froi* (F. *frai*), spawn (Supp. to Godefroy); cf. OF. *frier*, variant of OF. *froier*, to spawn (id.); Norm. dial. *frier*, to rub (Moisy). — L. *fricāre*, to rub. See F. *frai* in Hatzfeld.

FUCHSIA, the name of a flower. (G.) A coined name, first used in 1703 by C. Plumier, a French botanist; made by adding the L. suffix *-ia* to the surname of the German botanist Leonhard Fuchs (d. 1566), who published his De Historia Stirpium in 1542; see N. and Q. 7 S. xi. 326.

FUDDLE, to tipple, to render tipsy. (Low G.) Also found in the sense 'to waste time;' as, 'they *fuddle* away the day with riot and prophaneness;' Gent. Mag. xxvi. 431 (1756); see N. E. D. and E. D. D. A specialised sense of Low G. *fuddeln*, to work lazily (Brem. Wört.); also to go about in rags (Berghaus); cf. Low G. *fuddelke*, a slattern. From the sb. *fudden*, rags; EFries. *fudde*, a rag, a slut; Du. *vod*, a rag, a slut. Cf. Low G. *fuddig*, ragged, dirty; Du. *voddig*.

FUDGE, an interjection of contempt. (F.) In Goldsmith, Vicar of Wakefield (1766); also in Macklin, Love-à-la-Mode, A. ii. sc. 1 (Groom); 1760. — Picard *fuche*, *feuche*, an interjection of contempt (Corblet); Rouchi *fuche*, bah! (Hécart); Walloon *foge*, bah! (Grandgagnage); cf. Low G. *futsch*! begone! cited by Wedgwood from Danneil; see also Sanders, Ger. Dict. i. 525. Of onomatopoetic origin; cf. *pish*. The verb *to fudge* seems to have been influenced by *fadge*.

FUEL, materials for burning. (F. — L.) Also spelt *fewel*, *fewell*; Spenser, F. Q. i. 7. 36. Also *fwaill*, *fewell*; Barbour's Bruce, iv. 170. Here, as in Richard Coer de Lion, 1471, it seems to mean 'supplies.' AF. *fewaile*, Liber Albus, p. 337. — OF. *fouaille*, *fuaille*, fuel, fagots (Godefroy). — Late L. *focālia*, pl. of *focāle*, fuel. — L. *focus*, a hearth, fire-place. See **Focus.**

FUGITIVE, fleeing away, transitory. (F. — L.) Properly an adj., Shak. Antony, iii. 1. 7; also as a sb., id. iv. 9. 22; ME. *fugitif*, Chaucer, Ho. of Fame, 146. — OF. *fugitif*, 'fugitive;' Cot. — L. *fugitīuus*, fugitive. — L. *fugitum*, supine of *fugere*, to flee; cognate with E. *bow*, to bend. + Gk. φεύγειν, to flee; Skt. *bhuj*, to bend, turn aside. — √BHEUGH, to bow, to bend. Der. *fugitive-ly*, *-ness*. From the same source, *fug-ac-ious*, *fug-ac-i-ty*; *fugue*, q. v.; also *centri-fug-al*, *re-fuge*, *subter-fuge*.

FUGLEMAN, the leader of a file. (G.) Modern. Not in Todd's Johnson. Also written *flugelman*; as in Sydney Smith, Works, 1859, ii. 120 (N. E. D.). Borrowed from G. *flügelmann*, the leader of a wing or file. — G. *flügel*, a wing; cf. *flug*, flight, from the weak grade of *fliegen*, to fly; and *mann*, man. See **Fly** (1).

FUGUE, a musical composition. (F. — Ital. — L.) In Milton, P. L. xi. 563. — OF. (and F.) *fugue*, 'a chace or report of musick, like two or more parts in one;' Cot. — Ital. *fuga*, a flight, a fugue. — L. *fuga*, flight. See **Fugitive.** Der. *fugu-ist*.

FULCRUM, a point of support. (L.) 'Fulcrum, a stay or support;' Phillips, ed. 1706. — L. *fulcrum*, a support. — L. *fulcīre*, to prop.

FULFIL, to complete. (E.) ME. *fulfillen*; P. Plowman, B. vi. 36. AS. *fulfyllan*, which occurs in Ælfric's Grammar, ed. Zupitza, p. 153. Compounded of *ful*, full; and *fyllan*, to fill. See **Full** and **Fill.** Der. *fulfil-ler*, *fulfil-ment*.

FULGENT, shining, bright. (L.) In Minsheu, ed. 1627; Milton, P. L. x. 449; and York Mysteries, p. 514, l. 1. — L. *fulgent-* stem of pres. pt. of *fulgēre*, to shine. + Gk. φλέγειν, to burn, shine; Skt. *bhrāj*, to shine. Der. *fulgent-ly*, *fulgenc-y*; also *ef-fulg-ence*, *re-fulg-ent*.

FULIGINOUS, sooty. (L.) In Bacon, Nat. Hist. § 18 (R.). Either from MF. *fuligineux* (Cot.); or, more likely, immediately from L. *fūliginōsus*, sooty. — L. *fūligin-*, stem of *fūligo*, soot. From the same base as *fū-mus*, smoke; cf. Skt. *dhūli-*, dust. See **Fume.**

FULL (1), filled up, complete. (E.) ME. *ful*; P. Plowman, B. prol. 17. AS. *ful*; Grein, i. 355. + Du. *vol*; Icel. *fullr*; Dan. *fuld* (for *full*); Swed. *full*; Goth. *fulls*; G. *voll*. Teut. type *fulloz*; Idg. type *pelnos*. Cf. Lith. *pilnas*, full; Russ. *polnuii*, full; OIrish *lān* (< *plān*), W. *llawn*, full; Skt. *pūrna-*, Pers. *pur*; Gk. πλήρης; L. *plēnus*. Idg. root *plē* (weak form, *pal*), to fill. Brugmann, i. §§ 393, 461. Der. *full*, adv., *full-y*, *ful-ness*; *-blown*, *-faced*, *-hearted*, *-orbed*; *ful-fil* (= *full fill*), *ful-fil-ment*; also *fill*, by vowel-change, q. v. Also *ful-some*, q. v. And see **Plenary.**

FULL (2), to full cloth, to felt. (F. — L.) To *full* cloth is to felt the wool together; this is done by severe beating and pounding. The word occurs in Cotgrave; also as ME. *fullen*, P. Plowman, B. xv. 445. —OF. *fuler, fouler*; MF. *fouller*, 'to full, or thicken cloath in a mill;' Cot. Also spelt *fouler*, 'to trample on, press;' id. —Late L. *fullāre* (1) to cleanse clothes, (2) to full cloth. —L. *fullo*, a fuller. ¶ The orig. sense of L. *fullo* was probably a cleanser, or bleacher; then, as clothes were often washed by being trampled on or beaten, the sense of 'stamping' arose; and the verb to *full* is now chiefly used in this sense of stamping, pounding, or felting wool together. Der. *full-ing-mill*, mentioned by Strype, Annals, Edw. VI, an. 1553.

FULLER, a bleacher of cloth; a fuller of cloth. (L.) See note to **Full** (2) above. AS. *fullere*, Mark, ix. 3. Adapted from L. *fullo*, a fuller (above).

FULMAR, a sea-bird of the petrel kind. (Scand.) The name is used in the Hebrides (E. D. D.); and is of Scand. origin. Lit. 'foul mew;' from its disagreeable odour. —Icel. *fúl-*, for *fúll*, foul; and *már*, a mew. See **Foul** and **Mew** (2).

FULMINATE, to thunder, hurl lightning. (L.) In Minsheu, ed. 1627. Sir T. Browne has *fulminating*, Vulg. Errors, b. ii. c. 5. § 19. [Spenser has the short form *fulmine*, F. Q. iii. 2. 5 ; from OF. *fulminer*, 'to thunder, lighten;' Cot.]—L. *fulminātus*, pp. of *fulmināre*, to thunder, lighten. —L. *fulmin-*, for *fulmen*, lightning, a thunder-bolt (= **fulg-men*). —L. base *fulg-*, to shine; seen in *fulg-ēre*, to shine. See **Fulgent**. Der. *fulmin-at-ion*.

FULSOME, cloying, satiating, superabundant. (E.) ME. *fulsum*, abundant, Genesis and Exodus, 748, 2153; cf. Will. of Palerne, 4325. Chaucer has the sb. *fulsomnesse*, C. T. 10719 (F 405). Made up from ME. *ful* = AS. *ful*, full; and the suffix *-som* = AS. *-sum* (mod. E. *-some*). See **Full**. Der. *ful-some-ness*. ¶ *Not* from *foul*.

FULVOUS, FULVID, tawny. (L.) Rare. *Fulvid* is in Todd's Johnson. Borrowed, respectively, from L. *fuluus*, tawny, and Late L. *fuluidus*, somewhat tawny. Allied to **Yellow**. Brugmann, i. § 363.

FUMBLE, to grope about. (Du.) In old authors 'to bungle.' 'False *fumbling* fantasye;' Sir T. More, Works, p. 698 a; Shak. Antony, iv. 4. 14. The *b* is excrescent, and *fumble* stands for *fummle*. —Du. *fommelen*, 'to fumble, grabble;' Sewel; Low G. *fummeln*, to fumble. +M. Swed. (and Swed.) *fumla*, to fumble. Cf. Swed. *famla*, to grope; Dan. *famle*; Icel. *fálma*, to grope about. β. Prob. allied to AS. *folm*, the palm of the hand (Grein, i. 311), cognate with L. *palma*. See **Palm** (of the hand). Der. *fumbl-er*.

FUME, a smoke, vapour. (F. —L.) Sir T. Elyot speaks of '*fumes* in the stomake;' The Castel of Helth, b. ii. c. 17. ME. *fume*, Sowdone of Babylon, l. 681. —OF. *fum*, smoke (Burguy). —L. *fūmum*, acc. of *fūmus*, smoke. +Skt. *dhūma-*, smoke; Gk. θυμός, spirit, anger; cf. Skt. *dhū*, to shake, blow. Brugmann, i. § 106. Der. *fume*, verb (see Minsheu) ; *fumi-ferous* ; *fum-ig-ate*, q. v., *fum-i-tory*, q. v.

FUMIGATE, to expose to fumes. (L.) 'You must be bath'd and *fumigated* first;' Ben Jonson, The Alchemist, A. i. —L. *fūmigātus*, pp. of *fūmigāre*, to fumigate. —L. *fūm-*, base of *fūmus*, smoke; and *-ig-*, for *ag-*, base of *agere*, to drive; thus the sense is 'to drive smoke about.' See **Fume**. Der. *fumigat-ion*, from MF. *fumigation*, 'fumigation, smoaking;' Cot.

FUMITORY, a plant; earth-smoke. (F. —L.) In Shak. Hen. V, v. 2. 45; a corruption of the older form *fumiter*, K. Lear, iv. 4. 3; ME. *fumetere*, Chaucer, C. T. 14969 (B 4153). —OF. *fume-terre*, 'the herb fumitory;' Cot. This is an abbreviation for *fume de terre*, smoke of the earth, earth-smoke; so named from its abundance (Trevisa). —Late L. *fūmus terræ*. —L. *fūmus*, smoke; and *terra*, earth. See **Fume** and **Terrace**. The G. name is *erd-rauch*, earth-smoke; cf. W. *cwd y mwg*, lit. bag of smoke, fumitory.

FUN, merriment, sport. (Perhaps Scand.) Not found early. 'Rare compound of oddity, frolic, and *fun*;' Goldsmith, Retaliation, Post-script, l. 3. Probably from the prov. E. verb *to fun*, to cheat, to hoax; see E. D. D. This is ME. *fonnen*, to be foolish, dote; or, as act. vb., to deceive, befool; whence pp. *fonned* = mod. E. *fond*. See **Fond**; where the word is traced further back. Der. *funn-y, funn-i-ly*. ¶ Irish *fonn* is from E.

FUNAMBULIST, one who walks on a rope. (L.) Formerly *funambulo*, a rope-dancer; see Gloss. to Bacon, Adv. of Learning, ed. Wright; so that the word was suggested by Spanish; though *-ist* has been put for *-o*; cf. Span. *funambulo*, a walker on a rope. —L. *fūn-*, stem of *fūnis*, a rope; and **ambulus*, a walker, a coined sb. from *ambulāre*, to walk; see **Amble**.

FUNCTION, performance, duty, office. (F. —L.) Common in Shak.; see Meas. i. 2. 14; ii. 2. 39; &c. —MF. *function*, 'a function;' Cot. (F. *fonction*). —L. *functiōnem*, acc. of *functio*, performance; cf. *functus*, pp. of *fungi*, to perform; orig. to enjoy, have the use of. Cf. Skt. *bhunj*, to enjoy. Brugmann, ii. § 628. Der. *function-al, -ar-y*.

FUND, a store, supply, deposit. (F. —L.) '*Fund*, land or soil; also, a foundation or bottom;' Blount's Gloss., ed. 1674. And see Burnet, Hist. of his Own Time, an. 1698 (R). [It should rather have been *fond*, as in Eng. Garner, ed. Arber, vi. 387 (ab. 1677); but it has been

accommodated to the L. form.] —MF. *fond*, 'a bottom, floore, ground; . . . a merchant's stock;' Cot. —L. *fundus*, bottom, depth; cognate with E. *bottom*. See **Bottom**, and see **Found** (1). And see below.

FUNDAMENT, foundation, base. (F. —L.) ME. *foundement, fundement*; Chaucer, C. T. 7685 (D 2103); Wyclif, Luke, vi. 48. [Really F., and properly *fundement*, but altered to the L. spelling.]— OF. *fondement*, foundation. —L. *fundāmentum*, foundation. Formed, with suffix *-mentum*, from *fundā-re*, to found. See **Found** (1). Der. *fundament-al*, All's Well, iii. 1. 2.

FUNERAL, relating to a burial. (F. —L.) Properly an adj., as in 'To do th' office of *funeral* servyse;' Chaucer, C. T. 2914 (A 2912). —OF. *funeral*, adj. (Godefroy). —Late L. *funerālis*, belonging to a burial. —L. *fūner-*, for **fūnes-*, stem of *fūnus*, a burial; with suffix *-ālis*. Der. *funeral*, sb. ; *funer-e-al*, Pope, Dunciad, iii. 152, coined from L. *fūnere-us*, funereal, with suffix *-al*.

FUNGUS, a spongy plant. (L.) 'Mushromes, which be named *fungi*;' Holland, tr. of Pliny, bk. xxii. c. 23. —L. *fungus*, a fungus.+ Gk. σφόγγος, Attic form of σπόγγος, a sponge. Thus *fungus* is allied to *sponge*. See **Sponge**. Der. *fung-ous*, *-o-id*.

FUNICLE, a small cord, fibre. (L.) In Johnson's **Dict**. —L. *fūni-cu-lus*, double dimin. of *fūnis*, a rope. See **Funambulist**. Der. *funicul-ar*.

FUNNEL, an instrument for pouring in liquids into vessels. (Prov. —L.) In Ben Jonson, Discoveries, sect. headed *Præcipiendi modi*. And in Levins' Dict., ed. 1570. ME. *fonel*; Prompt. Parv. A Southern F. word, due to the Bourdeaux wine-trade. —Prov. *founil, enfounil, enfounilh*, a funnel; Mistral, p. 911 (whence also Span. *fonil*, Port. *funil*). —Late L. *fundibulum*, a funnel (Lewis); L. *infundibulum*. —L. *infundere*, to pour in. —L. *in*, in; and *fundere*, to pour. See **Fuse** (1).

FUR, short hair of animals. (F. —O. Low G.) [The orig. sense was 'casing.'] ME. *forre*; whence *forred* (or *furred*) *hodes* = furred hoods; P. Plowman, B. vi. 271. Also *furre*, Chaucer, Rom. Rose, 228. Spelt *for* in King Alisaunder, 3295. —OF. *forre, fuerre*, a sheath, case; (cf. Span. *forro*, lining of clothes, Ital. *fodero*, lining, fur, scabbard); whence the verb *forrer*, to line with fur; Chaucer translates F. *forrée* by *furred*; Rom. Rose, 408. β. From an O. Low G. source, preserved in Goth. *fōdr*, a scabbard, sheath (John, xviii. 11); and in Icel. *fóðr*, lining. The cognate German word is *futter*. Allied to Skt. *pātra(m)*, a receptacle; cf. Gk. πῶμα, a cover. From √PĀ, to protect. Brugmann, i. § 174. Der. *fur*, verb, *furr-ed, furr-y, furr-i-er* (Goldsmith, Animated Nature, b. iv. c. 3), *furr-i-er-y*.

FURBELOW, a flounce. (F.) In the Spectator, no. 15. —F. *farbala*, a flounce; which, according to Diez (who follows Hécart), is a Hainault word; the usual form is F., Span., Ital., and Port. *falbala*, a word traced back to 1692 (Hatzfeld); whence also E. *falbala*, as 'a *falbala* apron,' in C. Cibber, Careless Husband, A. i. sc. 1 (1704). Origin unknown. Hatzfeld gives the orig. sense as 'bande d'étoffe plissée;' and suggests a derivation from Ital. *faldella*, which Torriano (ed. 1688) explains as 'a plaiting, or puckering, also a kind of thick-gathered frock.' This Ital. word is the dimin. of *falda*, a fold; from OHG. *faldan*, to fold; see **Fold** (1). Cf. Norm. dial. *farbalas* (Moisy); Lyons dial. *farbella* (Puitspelu).

FURBISH, to polish, trim. (F. —OHG.) In Shak. Rich. II, i. 3. 76; Macb. i. 2. 32. ME. *furbishen*; Wyclif, Ezek. xxi. 9.—OF. *fourbiss-*, stem of pres. pt. of *fourbir*, 'to furbish, polish;' Cot. — OHG. **furbjan, furban*, MHG. *furben*, to purify, clean, rub bright.

FURCATE, forked. (L.) The sb. *furcation* occurs in Sir T. Browne, Vulg. Errors, b. iii. c. 9. § 4. —L. *furcātus*, forked. —L. *furca*, a fork. See **Fork**. Der. *furcat-ion*.

FURFURACEOUS, scurfy. (L.) Scarce; first in 1650. Merely L. *furfurāceus*, like bran. —L. *furfur*, bran.

FURIOUS, full of fury. (F. —L.) In Chaucer, Compl. of Mars, 123.—OF. *furieux*, 'furious;' Cot. —OF. *furie*; see **Fury**. Der. *furious-ly, -ness*.

FURL, to roll up a sail. (F. —Arab.) α. A contracted form of an older *furdle*. 'Nor to urge the thwart enclosure and *furdling* of flowers;' Sir T. Browne, Cyrus' Garden, c. iii. § 15; spelt *fardling* in Wilkin's edition. 'The colours *furdled* [furled] up, the drum is mute;' John Taylor's Works, ed. 1630; cited in Nares, ed. Halliwell. '*Farthel*, to furl;' Kersey, ed. 1715. β. *Furdle* and *farthel* are corruptions of *fardle*, to pack up (see Nares); from the sb. *fardel*, a package, burden. Note that *fardle* also means to *furl*; as in '*fardle* it [the main-sheet] to the yard;' Golding's Ovid, fol. 138, l. 3 (ed. 1603). See further under **Fardel**.

FURLONG, one-eighth of a mile. (E.) ME. *furlong, fourlong*; P. Plowman, B. v. 5; Chaucer, C. T. 11484 (F 1172). AS. *furlang*, Luke, xxiv. 13. The lit. sense is 'furrow-long,' or the length of a furrow. It thus came to mean the length of an 'acre,' which was originally a piece of land measuring 220 yards (40 poles) by 22 yards (4 poles). See *acre* in N. E. D. —AS. *furh*, a furrow; and *lang*, long. See **Furrow** and **Long**.

FURLOUGH, leave of absence. (Du.) Spelt *furlough* in Blount's Gloss., ed. 1674. The *gh* was once sounded as *f*, and the word was Dutch; hence Ben Jonson has 'Like a Low-Country *vorloffe*;' Staple of News, A. v. sc. 1. — Du. *verlof*, leave, furlough; cf. Dan. *forlov*, leave, furlough; Swed. *förlof*; G. *verlaub*, leave, permission. β. The Du. word stands for an older *verloof*; from *ver-*, prefix, and *-loof*, the equivalent of G. *-laub*, as seen in *er-laub-en*, to permit, and in AS. *léaf*, leave, permission; see **Leave** (2). γ. The prefix *ver-* = Dan. *for-* = E. *for-*; see **For-** (2).

FURMENTY, FURMETY; see **Frumenty.**

FURNACE, an oven. (F. — L.) ME. *forneis*, *fourneys*; Chaucer, C. T. 14169 (E 3353). — OF. *fornaise*, later *fournaise*, 'a furnace;' Cot. — L. *fornācem*, acc. of *fornax*, an oven. — L. *fornus*, *furnus*, an oven; with suffix *-āc-*; allied to L. *formus*, warm. Cf. Skt. *gharma-*, glow, warmth; see Brugmann, i. § 146.

FURNISH, to fit up, equip. (F. — OHG.) Common in Shak.; see Merch. of Ven. ii. 4. 9. — OF. *fournis-*, stem of pres. part. of *fournir*, 'to furnish;' Cot. Formerly spelt *fornir*, *furnir* (Burguy); which are corruptions of *formir*, *furmir*. The AF. *furmir* occurs in the Life of Edw. Confessor, l. 1443; the form *formir* occurs in Prov., and is also spelt *fromir*, which is the older spelling. — OHG. *frumjan*, to perform, provide, procure, furnish; allied to OHG. *fruma* (MHG. *vrum*, *vrume*), utility, profit, gain; cf. mod. G. *fromm*, good. From the same root as E. *former*; see **Former, Frame.** Der. *furnish-er*, *-ing*; also *furni-ture* (Spenser, F. Q. v. 3. 4), from F. *fourniture*, 'furniture;' Cot.

FURROW, a slight trench, wrinkle. (E.) ME. *forwe*, P. Plowman, B. vi. 106; older form *foruh*, Chaucer, tr. of Boethius, b. v. met. 5. l. 3. AS. *furh*, a furrow; Ælfric's Gloss., l. 17. The dat. pl. *furum* is in Ælfred, tr. of Boethius, v. 2; lib. i. met. 6. + Du. *voor*, a furrow; Icel. *for*, a drain; Dan. *fure*; OHG. *furh*, MHG. *vurch*, G. *furche*, a furrow. Cf. W. *rhych* (*p-rych*), a furrow; L. *porca*, a ridge between two furrows. Brugmann, i. § 514. Der. *furrow*, verb; *fur-long*, q. v.

FURTHER, comparative of *fore*. (E.) ME. *furðer*, Ancren Riwle, p. 228; *forþer*, *ferþer*; Chaucer, C. T. 36, 4115 (A 4117). AS. *furðra*, adj. m.; *furður*, *furðor*, further, adv. Grein, i. 358. + Du. *vorders*, adv., further; OFries. *fordera*, adj.; OHG. *fordaro*, G. *vorder*, adj. Teut. type *furtheroz* (i. e. *fur-ther-oz*), answering to Gk. πρό-τερ-ος, compar. of πρό. In this view, the comp. suffix is *-ther*, Gk. *-τερ-*. See below. Der. *further*, vb., AS. *fyrðran*, formed from *furðor* by mutation of *u* to *y*.

FURTHEST. (E.) Not in very early use. ME. *furthest*, adj., Gower, Conf. Amantis, i. 208; bk. i. l. 1966. Made as the superl. of *forth*; and due to regarding *further* as the compar. of the same. The true superl. of *fore* is *first*.

FURTIVE, thief-like, stealthy. (F. — L.) In Kersey, ed. 1715. — MF. *furtif*, m. *furtive*, f. 'filching, theevish;' Cot. — L. *furtiuus*, stolen, secret. — L. *furtum*, theft. — L. *fūrāri*, to steal. — L. *fūr*, a thief. + Gk. φώρ, a thief; connected with φέρειν, to bear, carry off. — √ BHER, to bear. See **Bear.** Der. *furtive-ly*.

FURY, rage, passion. (F. — L.) ME. *furie*, Chaucer, C. T. 11262 (F 950). — OF. *furie*, 'fury;' Cot. — L. *furia*, madness. — L. *furere*, to rage; cf. Skt. *bhuraṇya*, to be active. — √ BHEUR, to move about quickly (Uhlenbeck). Der. *furi-ous*, q. v., *-ous-ly*, *-ous-ness*. Also *furi-oso*, from Ital. *furioso*; and *fur-ore*, from Ital. *furore*.

FURZE, the whin or gorse. (E.) ME. *firse*, also *friise*, Wyclif, Isaiah, lv. 13, Mic. vii. 4. AS. *fyrs*, Ælfred's tr. of Boethius, lib. iii. met. 1; c. xxiii. Older form *fyres*, Voc. 269. 22.

FUSCOUS, brown, dingy. (L.) 'Sad and *fuscous* colours;' Burke, On the Sublime, s. 16. — L. *fuscus*, dark, dusky; with change of *-us* into *-ous*, as in *arduous*, *strenuous*.

FUSE (1), to melt by heat. (L.) In Johnson; but the verb is modern, and really due to the far older words (in E.), viz. *fus-ible*, Chaucer, C. T. 16324 (G 856), *fus-il*, i. e. capable of being melted, Milton, P. L. xi. 573; *fus-ion*, Sir T. Browne, Vulg. Errors, b. ii. c. 1. § 11; all founded upon L. *fūsus*. — L. *fūsus*, pp. of *fundere*, to pour, melt. + Gk. χέειν, for χέϝειν (base χεϝ-), to pour; Goth. *giutan*, to pour. All from √ GHEU, to pour; of which the extended form GHEUD (= Goth. GEUT) appears in Latin. Der. *fus-ible*, from OF. *fusible*, 'fusible' (Cot.), from Late L. *fūsibilis*, not recorded in Ducange; *fus-i-bili-ty*; *fus-ion*, from F. form of L. *fūsiōnem*, acc. of *fūsio*, a melting; *fus-il* (Milton, as above), from L. *fūsilis*, molten, fluid. ¶ From the same root are *found* (2), *con-found*, *con-fuse*, *dif-fuse*, *ef-fus-ion*, *in-fuse*, *pro-fus-ion*, *re-fund*, *suf-fuse*, *trans-fuse*; *fut-ile*; also *foison*; also *chyme*, *chyle*, *gush*, *gut*.

FUSE (2), **FUSEE** (1), a tube with combustible materials for discharging shells, &c. (F. — L.) Also spelt *fusee*. In Kersey's Dict., ed. 1715; we find: '*Fuse*, *Fusee*, a pipe filled with wild fire, and put into the touch-hole of a bomb.' 1. *Fuse* first occurs in 1644, and may have been taken directly from Ital. *fuso*, a spindle (with tow), also 'a shaft

or shank of anything;' (Torriano). — L. *fūsus*, a spindle. 2. *Fusee* first occurs in 1744, but is much earlier in French. — OF. *fusée*, a spindle-ful of tow, also a fusee (Godefroy). — Late L. *fūsāta*, a spindle-ful of tow; orig. fem. of pp. of *fūsāre*, to use a spindle. — L. *fūsus*, a spindle. See below.

FUSEE (2), a spindle in a watch. (F. — L.) '*Fusee* or *Fuzy* of a watch, that part about which the chain or string is wound;' Kersey, ed. 1715. — OF. *fusée*, 'a spoole-ful or spindle-ful of thread, yarn, &c.;' Cot. — Late L. *fūsāta*, a spindle-ful of thread; orig. fem. pp. of *fūsāre*, to use a spindle. — L. *fūsus*, a spindle. See above.

FUSIL (1), a light musket. (F. — L.) The name has been transferred from the steel or fire-lock to the gun itself. Hollyband's F. Dict. (1580) explains F. *fusil* by 'a *fusill* to strike fire in a tinder-boxe.' — F. *fusil*, 'a fire-steele for a tinder-box;' Cot.; the same word as Ital. *focile*, a steel for striking fire. — Late L. *focile*, a steel for kindling fire. — L. *focus*, a hearth. See **Focus.** Der. *fusil-ier*, *-eer*.

FUSIL (2), a spindle, in heraldry. (F. — L.) Explained in Blount's Gloss., ed. 1674. — OF. *fuisel*, *fusel*, a piece of wood, a spindle (Godefroy); he cites 'Hoc fusum, *fusel*' from the Glasgow glossary. — Late L. *fūsellus*, formed as a dimin. from *fūsus*, a spindle. See **Fusee** (2).

FUSIL (3), easily molten. (L.) See **Fuse** (1).

FUSS, haste, flurry. (E.) 'There's such a *fuss* and such a clatter about their devotion;' Farquhar, Sir H. Wildair, A. iii. sc. 1. A dialectal word, of imitative origin; cf. *fuss up*, to boil up, *fussock about*, to bustle about quickly, make a fuss; E.D.D. Related words are, probably, Norw. *fussa*, to complicate, to botch up, *fjussa*, to complicate by using bustling haste, *fjussa*, a bewildered ninny; *fjassa*, to bustle about, to fuss, to prate; *fjass*, a fuss (Ross); Swed. *fjäs*, Swed. dial. *fjas*, a fuss.

FUST (1), to become mouldy. (F. — L.) 'To *fust* in us unused;' Hamlet, iv. 4. 39. 'I mowld or *fust* as corne dothe, *je moisis*;' Palsgrave. Made from the form *fusty* (found in 1398), which is a lit. translation of OF. *fusté*, 'fusty, tasting of the cask, smelling of the vessel;' Cot. — OF. *fuste*, 'a cask,' Cot.; allied to *fust*, 'any staffe, stake, stocke, stump, trunke, or log.' [The cask was so named from its resemblance to the trunk of a tree.] — L. *fustem*, acc. of *fustis*, a thick knobbed stick, cudgel. Der. *fus-ty*, *fust-i-ness*; and see below.

FUST (2), the shaft of a column. (F. — L.) '*Fust*, the shaft, or body of a pillar;' Kersey's Dict., ed. 1715. — OF. *fust*, a stump, trunk; Cot. — L. *fustem*; as above. Der. *fust-ig-ate*, q. v.

FUSTIAN, a kind of coarse cloth. (F. — Ital. — Egypt.) In early use. ME. *fustane*. 'The mes-hakele of medeme *fustane*' = the mass-cloth [made] of common fustian; O. E. Homilies, ed. Morris, ii. 162. Also *fustian*, Chaucer, C. T. 75. — OF. *fustaine*; Supp. to Godefroy, Cot. — Ital. *fustagno*; Low L. *fustāneum*, *fustānium*. — Arab. *fustāt*, a suburb of Cairo, in Egypt; whence the stuff first came. The Arab. *fustāt* also means 'a tent made of goat's hair.' See Rich. Arab. Dict. p. 1090. ¶ Introduced into French in the middle ages, through Genoese commerce.

FUSTIGATE, to cudgel. (L.) '*Fustigating* him for his faults;' Fuller's Worthies, Westmorland (R.). 'Six *fustigations*;' Fox, Martyrs, p. 609 (R.). — Late L. *fustigāre*, to cudgel (White and Riddle). — L. *fust-*, base of *fustis*, a cudgel; and *-ig-*, weakened form from *agere*, to drive. See **Fust** (1). Der. *fustigat-ion*.

FUSTY, mouldy. (F. — L.) In Shak. Cor. i. 9. 7. See **Fust** (1).

FUTILE, trifling, vain. (F. — L.) Orig. signifying 'pouring forth,' esp. pouring forth vain talk, talkative. 'As for talkers and *futile* persons, they are commonly vain;' Bacon, Essay VI. — F. *futile*, 'light, vain;' Cot. — L. *fūtilis*, *futtilis*, that which easily pours forth; also, vain, empty, futile. Formed with suffix *-ilis* from the base *fud-*, to pour; cf. *ef-fūt-īre*, for *effudtīre*, to blab (Bréal). — √ GHEU, to pour; see **Fuse.** Der. *futile-ly*, *futil-i-ty*.

FUTTOCKS, certain timbers in a ship. (E.) '*Futtocks*, the compassing timbers in a ship, that make the breadth of it;' Kersey's Dict., ed. 1715. Called *foot-hooks* in Bailey. Explained as *foot-hooks* in 1644; *hook* referring to the bent shape of the timbers. Cf. '*Courbaston*, a crooked peece of timber tearmed a knee, or *futtock*;' Cot.

FUTURE, about to be. (F. — L.) ME. *futur*; Chaucer, C. T. 16343 (G 875). — OF. *futur*, m. *future*, f. 'future;' Cot. — L. *futūrus*, about to be; future part. from base *fu-*, to be; cf. *fu-ī*, I was. — √ BHEU, to be. See **Be.** Der. *futur-i-ty*, Shak. Oth. iii. 4. 117; *future-ly*, Two Noble Kinsmen, i. 1. 174 (Leopold Shakspere).

FUZZ-BALL, a spongy fungus. (E.) Spelt *fusseballe* in Minsheu, ed. 1627. A *fuzz-ball* is a light, spongy ball resembling (at first sight) a mushroom; also called *puff-ball*. Cf. prov. E. *fuzzy*, light and spongy; *fozy*, spongy; E.D.D. Of English origin. Cf. Du. *voos*, spongy; Norw. *fos*, spongy; Low G. *fussig*, loose, weak. Allied to L. *pūs-ula*, *pustula*, a pimple; Gk. φυσᾶειν, to blow. ¶ Also called *puckfiste*, as in Cotgrave (s. v. *vesse de loup*); but this is from *foist*.

FYLFOT, a peculiarly formed cross, each arm being bent at right angles, always in the same direction. (E.) Also called a *gamma-*

dion. See Fairholt, Dict. of Terms in Art ; and Boutell's Heraldry. Modern ; and due to a mistake. MS. Lansdowne 874, at leaf 190, has *fylfot,* meaning a space in a painted window, at the bottom, that *fills the foot.* This was erroneously connected (in 1842) with the 'gammadion,' as the cross was rightly named.

G

GABARDINE, GABERDINE, a coarse frock for men. (Span.—Teut.) In Shak. Merch. i. 3. 113 ; and in Du Wes, Supp. to Palsgrave, p. 907, col. 1 : 'the gabardine, *la gauardine.*'—Span. *gabardina,* a coarse frock. Cf. Ital. *gavardina* (Florio) ; and OF. *galvardine,* 'a gaberdine,' Cot. ; whence ME. *gawbardyne.* Prob. 'a pilgrim's frock ;' from MHG. *walfart* (G. *wallfahrt*), pilgrimage.— MHG. *wallen,* to wander ; *fart,* travel, from *faran,* to go ; see **Fare.**

GABBLE, to chatter, prattle. (E.) In Shak. Temp. i. 2. 356. Formed, as a frequentative, with suffix *-le,* from ME. *gabben,* to talk idly, once in common use ; see Chaucer, C. T. 15072 (B 4256) ; P. Plowman, B. iii. 179. Of imitative origin ; cf. *gaggle, jabber, gobble.* ¶ The ME. *gabben,* to mock, from OF. *gaber,* to mock, is from Icel. *gabba,* to mock, and is prob. of imitative origin. Cf. Icel. *gap,* 'gab, gibes ;' Norw. *gapa,* to clamour. See **Gape** ; and compare **Babble.** Der. *gabbl-er, gabbl-ing.*

GABION, a bottomless basket filled with earth, as a defence against the fire of an enemy. (F.—Ital.—L.) 'Gabions, great baskets 5 or 6 foot high, which being filled with earth, are placed upon batteries ;' Kersey's Dict., ed. 1715. Also found in Minsheu ; and in Marlowe, 2 Tamb. iii. 3. 56.—F. *gabion,* 'a gabion ;' Cot.—Ital. *gabbione,* a gabion, large cage ; augmentative form of *gabbia,* a cage. The Ital. *gabbia* also means 'the top of the maste of a ship where the shrouds are fastened' (Florio) ; the Span. *gavia* is used in the same sense. The Ital. *gabbia,* in the latter sense, is also spelt *gaggia,* which is allied to F. and E. *cage.* β. All from Late L. *cavea,* L. *cauea,* a hollow place, cage, den, coop.—L. *cauus,* hollow. See **Cage, Cave, Gaol.** Der. *gabionn-ade* (F. *gabionnade,* Cot. ; from Ital. *gabbionata,* an intrenchment formed of gabions).

GABLE, a peak of a house-top. (F.—Scand.) ME. *gable,* Chaucer, C. T. 3571 ; P. Plowman, B. iii. 49.—OF. *gable* (Godefroy) ; Norm. dial. *gable* ; cf. Late L. *gabulum,* a gable, front of a building ; Ducange.—Icel. *gafl,* Norw. and Dan. *gavl,* Swed. *gafvel,* a gable.+ AS. *geafel,* a fork ; Du. *gaffel,* G. *gabel,* a fork. Further allied to OIrish *gabul,* a fork, gallows ; W. *gafl,* the fork of the thighs. With a different gradation, we find Goth. *gibla,* pinnacle, G. *giebel,* Du. *gevel,* gable, OHG. *gebal,* head ; also Gk. κεφαλή (Idg. **ghebhalā*). See **Gaff.** Der. *gable-end.*

GABY, a simpleton. (Scand.) A dialectal word ; see E. D. D. Also in the form *gawby.* Prob. Scand. ; cf. MDan. *gabe,* also *gåbe* (Jutland), a fool (Kalkar) ; Dan. dial. *gabenar,* a simpleton (Dan. *nar* means 'fool'). Allied to Dan. *gabe,* to gape. Cf. also Icel. *gapi,* a rash, reckless man ; *gapamuðr* (lit. gape-mouthed), a gaping, heedless fellow ; Icel. *gapa,* to gape. See **Gape.**

GAD (1), a bar of steel, goad. (Scand.) 'A *gad* of steel ;' Titus Andron. iv. 1. 103. Also 'upon the *gad,*' i.e. upon the goad, suddenly ; K. Lear, i. 2. 26. '*Gadde* of steele, quarreau dacier ;' Palsgrave. ME. *gad,* a goad or whip ; 'bondemen with her *gaddes*' = husbandmen with their goads or whips ; Havelok, 1016.—Icel. *gaddr* (for **gazdr*), a spike, sting, hence a goad. + Goth. *gazds,* a rod ; Irish *gath,* a spear, sting ; L. *hasta,* a spear. ¶ Much influenced by *goad,* with which it is *not* etymologically connected. Der. *gad-fly,* i. e. sting-fly ; and see *gad* (2).

GAD (2), to ramble idly. (Scand.?) 'Where have you been *gadding* ?' Romeo, iv. 2. 16. '*Gadde* abrode, *vagari* ;' Levins, 7. 47. Perhaps the orig. sense was to run about like cattle stung by a gad-fly. Cf. *to have a gadfly,* to gad about (1591) ; in N. E. D.—Icel. *gadda,* to goad.—Icel. *gaddr,* a goad. See above. ¶ Or possibly a back-formation from ME. *gadeling,* a vagabond, for which see **Gather.**

GAFF, a light fishing-spear ; also, a sort of boom. (F.—Teut.) The *gaff* of a ship takes its name from the fork-shaped end which rests against the mast. '*Gaff,* an iron hook to pull great fishes into a ship ; also, an artificial spur for a cock ;' Kersey's Dict., ed. 1715. —OF. *gaffe,* 'an iron hook wherewith sea-men pull great fishes into their ships ;' Cot. ; and see Supp. to Godefroy. Cf. Span. and Port. *gafa,* a hook, gaff. β. Of Teut. origin.—Low G. *gaffel,* a two-pronged hayfork ; EFries. *gaffel,* a fork, a ship's gaff ; Du. *gaffel,* a pitchfork, a ship's gaff. Allied to G. *gabel,* a fork. See **Gable.** (Körting, § 4101.)

GAFFER, an old man, grandfather. (Hybrid ; *F. and E.*) 'And *gaffer* madman ;' Beaum. and Fletcher, The Captain, iii. 5. Similarly, *gammer* is a familiar name for an old woman, as in the old play of 'Gammer Gurton's Needle ;' in which '*gaffar* vicar' also occurs ; A. v. sc. 2. The words are corruptions of *gramfer* and *grammer,* which are the West of England forms of *grandfather* and *grandmother* ; see E. D. D.

GAG, to stop the mouth forcibly, to silence. (E.) In Shak. Tw. Nt. i. 5. 94 ; v. 384. ME. *gaggen,* to suffocate ; Prompt. Parv. Of imitative origin ; cf. *gaggle, guggle.* Of similar formation is the Irish *gagach,* stammering. See **Gaggle.** Der. *gag,* sb.

GAGE (1), a pledge. (F.—Teut.) ME. *gage,* King Alisaunder, 904.—F. *gage,* m., 'a gage, pawne, pledge ;' Cot. Cf. Late L. *uadium,* a pledge.—Teut. type **wadjom,* n., a pledge ; as in Goth. *wadi,* AS. *wedd,* a pledge. See **Wed,** and see **Wage.** From the same source are Ital. *gaggio,* Span. and Port. *gage,* a pledge (Hatzfeld). Der. *gage,* vb. ; *en-gage, dis-en-gage.*

GAGE (2), to gauge ; see **Gauge.**

GAGGLE, to cackle as geese. (E.) ME. *gaglen,* Rich. Redeles, iii. 101. An imitative word ; a frequentative from the base *gag-.* Cf. *cack-le, gabb-le ;* also Icel. *gagl,* a wild goose ; *gagg,* a fox's cry ; Lithuan. *gagéti,* to gaggle. Cf. **Guggle.**

GAIETY, mirth. (F.—Teut.) 'Those *gayities* how doth she slight ;' Habington, Castara, pt. iii. last poem, l. 2 ; the 1st ed. appeared in 1634.—OF. *gayeté,* 'mirth, glee ;' Cot.—OF. *gay,* 'merry ;' id. See **Gay.**

GAIN (1), profit, emolument. (F.—Teut.) First in 1496 ; Palsgrave has : 'Gayne or gettyng,' p. 224 ; and 'I *gayne,* I wynne,' p. 559.—OF. *gain,* m., F. *gagne,* f. sb. ; from OF. *gaigner,* F. *gagner,* to gain ; see **Gain** (2) below. ¶ It displaced ME. *gain,* advantage, which was of Scand. origin ; from Icel. *gagn,* gain, advantage ; Swed. *gagn,* Dan. *gavn.* Allied to the (obsolete) ME. verb *gainen,* to profit, be of use, avail, gen. used impersonally ; see Chaucer, C. T. 1178 (A 1176) ; this answers to Icel. and Swed. *gegna,* to encounter, to suit. Der. *gain-ful, gain-ful-ly, gain-ful-ness, gain-less, gain-ness.*

GAIN (2), to acquire, get, win. (F.—Teut.) Not in early use. 'Yea, though he *gaine* and cram his purse with crounes ;' Gascoigne, Fruites of Warre, st. 69. Again, he has just above, in st. 66 : 'To get a *gaine* by any trade or kinde.' See **Gain** (1). [This verb superseded the old use of the ME. *gainen,* to profit.] β. The etymology of F. *gagner,* OF. *gaigner* (Cotgrave), *gaagnier, gaaignier* (Burguy) = Ital. *guadagnare,* is from the OHG. *weidenēn* (for **weidin-jan*), to pasture, which was the orig. sense, and is still preserved in the F. sb. *gagnage,* pasturage, pasture-land.—OHG. *weida* (G. *weide*), pasturage, pasture-ground ; cf. MHG. *weiden,* to pasture, hunt. + Icel. *veiðr,* hunting, fishing, the chase ; *veiða,* to catch, to hunt ; AS. *wāð,* a hunt ; Grein, ii. 636. Cf. L. *uēnāri,* to hunt. Further allied to Skt. *vēti,* he follows after (Uhlenbeck).

GAINLY, suitable, gracious. (Scand.) Nearly obsolete, except in *ungainly,* now meaning 'awkward.' In Allit. Poems, ed. Morris, C. 83 ; B. 728. Formed, with suffix *-ly,* from Icel. *gegn,* ready, serviceable, kind, good. See **Ungainly.**

GAINSAY, to speak against. (Scand. *and* E.) In the A.V. Luke, xxi. 15. ME. *geinseien,* a rare word. 'That thei not ȝein-seye my sonde' = that they may not gainsay my message ; Cursor Mundi, 5769 (Trinity MS.). The Cotton MS. reads : 'þat þai noght *sai agains* mi sand.' β. The latter part of the word is E. *say,* q. v. The prefix is rather the Icel. *gegn,* against, than the AS. *gegn,* against, as occurring in the sb. *gegncwide,* a speech against anything. The latter is better known in the comp. *ongegn, ongēan,* signifying *again* or *against.* See **Again.** Der. *gainsay-er,* A.V. Titus, i. 9 ; *gainsay-ing,* A.V. Acts, x. 29.

GAIRISH, GARISH, gaudy ; see **Garish.**

GAIT, manner of walking. (Scand.) In Shak. Temp. iv. 102. A particular use of ME. *gate,* a way. 'And goth him forth, and in his *gate*' = and goes forth, and in his way ; Gower, C. A. iii. 196 ; bk. vii. 3314.—Icel. *gata,* a way, path, road ; Swed. *gata,* a street ; Dan. *gade,* a street. + Goth. *gatwō,* a street ; G. *gasse,* a street. See **Gate** (2).

GAITER, a covering for the ankle. (F.—Teut.) Modern. Not in Johnson's Dict.—F. *guêtre,* a gaiter ; formerly spelt *guestre.* 'Guestres, startups, high shooes, or gamashes for countrey folkes ;' Cot. Marked by Brachet as 'of unknown origin.' β. However, the form of the word shows it to be of Teutonic origin ; and prob. from the same source as MHG. *wester,* a child's chrisom-cloth (G. *wester-hemd*) and the Goth. *wasti,* clothing ; cf. Skt. *vastra,* a cloth, garment ; see **Vesture, Vest.** But see Körting, § 10014.

GALA, pomp, festivity. (F.—Ital.—OHG.) Chiefly in the comp. 'a gala-day' or 'a gala-dress.' Modern ; not in Johnson. Sheridan has : 'the annual *gala* of a race-ball ;' Sch. for Scandal, i. 2.—F. *gala,* borrowed from Ital. *gala,* ornament, finery, festive attire. Cf. Ital. *di gala,* merrily ; closely connected with Ital. *galante,* gay, lively.

See **Gallant**. Der. *gala-day* = F. *jour de gala*, Span. and Port. *dia de gala*.

GALAXY, the ' milky way ' in the sky ; a splendid assemblage. (F. – L. – Gk.) ' See yonder, lo, the *galaxye* Which men clepeth the milky wey ; ' Chaucer, Ho. of Fame, ii. 428. – OF. *galaxie*, ' the milky way ; ' Cot. – L. *galaxiam*, acc. of *galaxias*. – Gk. γαλαξίας, the milky way. – Gk. γαλακ-, for γαλακτ-, stem of γάλα, milk. Certainly allied to L. *lact*-, stem of *lac*, milk ; see **Lacteal**.

GALE (1), a strong wind. (Scand.) In Shak. Temp. v. 314. To be explained from Dan. *gal*, mad, furious ; the Norweg. *galen* is particularly used of storm and wind, as *ein galen storm*, *eit galet veer*, a furious storm (Aasen). We say, ' it blows a *gale*.' Cf. Icel. *gola*, a breeze, *fjall-gola*, a breeze from the fells. β. The Icel. *galinn*, furious, is from *gala*, to sing, enchant. Cf. F. *galerne*, a north-west wind.

GALE (2), a plant ; the bog-myrtle. (E.) ME. *gayle* ; Cath. Anglicum. AS. *gagel* ; AS. Leechdoms, iii. 6. +Du. *gagel*.

GALEATED, helmeted. (L.) Botanical. – L. *galeātus*, helmeted. – L. *galea*, a helmet.

GALINGALE, the pungent root of a plant. (F. – Span. – Arab. – Pers. – Chinese.) ME. *galingale*, Chaucer, C. T. 383 (A 381). – OF. *galingal* (Godefroy) ; the form *garingal* is more common, and the usual later F. form is *galangue*, as in Cotgrave. – Span. *galanga*, the same. – Arab. *khalanjān*, galingale ; Rich. Dict. p. 625. – Pers. *khūlanjān* ; id. p. 639. Said to be of Chinese origin ; see N. E. D. See Devic, Supp. to Littré ; Marco Polo, ed. Yule, ii. 181.

GALIOT, a small galley ; see **Galliot**.

GALL (1), bile, bitterness. (E.) ME. *galle* ; P. Plowman, B. xvi. 155. OMerc. *galla*, AS. *gealla* ; Matt. xxvii. 34. +Du. *gal* ; Icel. *gall* ; Swed. *galla* ; Dan. *galde* (with excrescent *d*) ; G. *galle*. +L. *fel* ; Gk. χολή. β. From the same root as E. *yellow* ; so that gall was named from its yellowish colour ; Prellwitz. Cf. Russ. *jelch(e)*, gall (*j* = *zh*) ; *jeltuii*, yellow. See **Yellow**. Der. *gall-bladder*.

GALL (2), to rub a sore place, to vex. (F. – L.) ' Let the *galled* jade wince ; ' Hamlet, iii. 2. 253. ME. *gallen*. ' The hors . . was . . . *galled* on the bak ; ' Gower, C. A. ii. 46 ; bk. iv. 1344. – OF. *galler*, ' to gall, fret, itch, rub ; ' Cot. – OF. *galle*, ' a galling, fretting, itching of the skin ; ' id. ; F. *gale*, a scab on fruit. – Late L. *galla*, a soft tumour, app. the same word as L. *galla*, a gall-nut ; see below. ¶ But also partly E. ; cf. AS. *gealla*, (1) gall, bile ; (2) a gall on a horse. So also Du. *gal*. Der. *gall*, sb., Chaucer, C. T. 6522 (D 940).

GALL (3), **GALL-NUT**, a vegetable excrescence produced by insects. (F. – L.) In Shak. ; ' Though ink be made of *gall* ; ' Cymb. i. 1. 101. ME. *galle*, Prompt. Parv. – OF. *galle*, ' the fruit called a gall ; ' Cot. – L. *galla*, an oak-apple, gall-nut.

GALLANT, gay, splendid, brave, courteous. (F. – OHG.) ' Good and *gallant* ship ; ' Shak. Temp. v. 237. ' Like young lusty *galantes* ; ' Berners, tr. of Froissart, vol. ii. c. 105 (R.). ME. *galaunt*, Polit. Poems, ed. Wright, i. 274. – OF. *gallant* ; Cotgrave gives ' *gallant homme*, a gallant, goodly fellow ; ' properly spelt *galant* (with one *l*), as in mod. F. β. *Galant* is the pres. part. of OF. *galer*, to rejoice ; Cotgrave has : ' *galler le bon temps*, to make merry, to pass the time pleasantly.' – OF. *gale*, show, mirth, festivity ; the same word as Ital., Span., and Port. *gala*, ornament, festive attire. γ. Of Teutonic origin ; and prob. from MHG. *wallen*, OHG. *wallōn*, to go on pilgrimage (Hatzfeld). Der. *gallant*, sb., whence also *gallant*, vb. ; *gallant-ly*, *gallant-ness* ; also *gallant-r-y* (Spectator, no. 4) from MF. *gallanterie*, ' gallantness,' Cot. Also see *gala*, *gala-oon*.

GALLEON, a large galley. (Span.) Cotgrave explains MF. *gallion* as ' a gallion, an armada, a great ship of warre ; ' but the word is Spanish. – Span. *galeon*, a galleon, Spanish armed ship of burden ; formed, with augmentative suffix *-on*, from Late L. *galea*, a galley. See **Galley**.

GALLERY, a balcony, long covered passage. (F. – Late L.) ' The long *galleries* ; ' Surrey, tr. of Virgil's Æneid, b. ii. l. 691. – OF. *gallerie*, *galerie*, ' a gallerie, or long roome to walke in ; ' Cot. – Late L. *galeria*, a long portico, gallery ; Ducange. β. Uncertain ; perhaps from Gk. καλόν, wood, timber (Körting).

GALLEY, a long, low-built ship. (F. – Late L.) In early use. ME. *galeie* ; King Horn, ed. Lumby, 185. – OF. *galie* (Godefroy) ; *gallée* (Cotgrave). – Late L. *galea*, a galley. Of unknown origin ; perhaps from Gk. καλόν, wood, also sometimes a ship (Körting). Der. *galley-slave* ; see *galle-on*, *galli-ot*.

GALLIARD, a lively dance. (F. – C. ?) In Shak. Tw. Nt. i. 3. 127, 137. ' Dansyng of *galyardes* ; ' Sir T. Elyot, Castel of Helth, bk. ii. c. 33. – F. *gaillarde*, fem. of *gaillard*, lively ; cf. *galop gaillard*, ' the galliard ; ' Cot. Span. *gallarda* [in which *ll* is pronounced as *ly*], a kind of lively Spanish dance ; Span. *gallardo*, pleasant, gay, lively. β. Of uncertain origin ; Diez rejects a connexion with *gala* and *gallant* (Span. *galante*) on account of the double

l and the F. form *gaillard*. The OF. *gaillard* meant ' valiant ' or ' bold ; ' perhaps of Celtic origin. Cf. Bret. *galloud*, power, *galloudek*, strong ; Corn. *galluodoc*, able ; Irish and Gael. *galach*, valiant, brave ; W. *gallu*, to be able. Cf. Lith. *galiu*, I am able (Thurneysen).

GALLIAS, a sort of galley. (F. – Ital. – Late L.) In Shak. Tam. Shrew, ii. 380. – OF. *galeace*, ' a galeass ; ' Cot. – Ital. *galeazza*, a heavy, low-built galley. – Ital. and Late L. *galea*, a galley. See **Galley**. ¶ On the termination *-ace*, see **Cutlass**.

GALLIGASKINS, large hose or trousers. (F. – Ital. – L.) α. Cotgrave has : ' *Garguesques*, a fashion of strait Venitians without cod-peeces.' Also : ' *Greguesques*, slops, gregs, gallogascoins, Venitians.' Also : ' *Gregues*, wide slops, *gregs*, gallogascoins, Venitians, great Gascon or Spanish hose.' Also : ' *Greguesque*, the same as *Gregeois*, Grecian, Greekish.' β. Here it is clear that *Garguesques* is a corruption of *Greguesques* ; that *Greguesque* originally meant Greekish ; and that *Gregues* (whence obs. E. *gregs*) is a mere contraction of *Greguesque*. γ. And further, *Greguesque* is borrowed from Ital. *Grechesco*, Greekish, a form given by Florio ; which is derived (with suffix *-esco* = E. *-ish*) from Ital. *Greco*, Greek. – L. *Græcus*, Greek. δ. Finally, it seems probable that *gallogascoin* is nothing but a derivative of Ital. *Grechesco*, a name given (as shown by the evidence) to a particular kind of hose or breeches originally worn at Venice. The corruption seems to have been due to a mistaken notion on the part of some of the wearers of *galligaskins*, that they came, not from Venice, but from Gascony. ¶ This suggestion is due to Wedgwood ; it would seem that *galligaskins* = *garisgascans* < *garguesquans* ; where the suffix *-an* is the same as in *Greci-an*, &c. The word was also influenced by E. *galley* ; they were thought to be ' like shipmen's hose ; ' N. E. D.

GALLIMAUFREY, a hodge-podge, a ragout. (F.) Robinson, in his tr. of More's Utopia, has : ' a tragycall comedye or *gallymal-freye* ; ' ed. Arber, p. 64. – F. *galimafrée* a hodge-podge ; spelt *calimafree* in the 14th cent. (Hatzfeld). Of unknown origin.

GALLINACEOUS, pertaining to a certain order of birds. (L.) Modern. Englished from L. *gallināceus*, belonging to poultry. Formed from L. *gallina*, a hen. – L. *gallus*, a cock.

GALLIOT, a small galley. (F. – Late L.) ME. *galiote*, Minot's Poems, Expedition of Edw. III to Brabant, l. 81 (Spec. of Eng. ed. Morris and Skeat, p. 129). – OF. *galiote*, ' a galliot ; ' Cot. – Late L. *galeota*, a small galley ; dimin. of *galea*, a galley. Cf. Ital. *galeotta*, a galliot. See **Galley**.

GALLIPOT, a small glazed earthen pot. (F. *and* E.) In Beaum. and Fletcher, Nice Valour, iii. 1. 43. Similarly earthen tiles were called *galley-tiles*. Wedgwood (ed. 1872) quotes from Stow : ' About the year 1570, I. Andries and I. Janson, potters, came from Antwerp and settled in Norwich, where they followed their trade, making *galley-tiles* and apothecaries vessels ' [gallipots]. Apparently so called because at first brought over in *galleys*. Cf. *galley-halfpenny*. See N. E. D. Phillips, ed. 1706, says that the *galley-men* came in *galleys* from Genoa, ' landed their goods at a place in Thames-street nam'd *galley-key*, and traded with their own silver small coin call'd *galley-halfpence*.' From **Galley** and **Pot**.

GALLON, a measure holding 4 quarts. (F.) ME. *galon*, *galun*, *galoun* ; P. Plowman, B. v. 224, 343 ; Chaucer, C. T. 16973 (H 24). Spelt *galun* in King Horn, ed. Lumby, 1123. – OF. *gallon*, *galon*, *jalon*, a gallon (Godefroy) ; Late L. *galōna* (also *galo*), an English measure for liquids ; Ducange. β. The suffix *-on* is augmentative ; and a shorter form appears in mod. F. *jale*, a bowl, which evidently stands for an older form *gale*, just as *jalon* is for *galon*. Thus the sense is ' a large bowl.' Of unknown origin.

GALLOON, a kind of lace or narrow ribbon. (F. – OHG.) The compound *galloon-laces* occurs in Beaum. and Fletcher, Philaster, v. 4. 46. Cotgrave has : ' *Galon*, galloon-lace.' – F. *galon*, as in Cotgrave (like E. *balloon* from F. *ballon*) ; cf. Span. *galon*, galloon, lace ; orig. any kind of finery for festive occasions. – OF. *gale*, Span. *gala*, parade, finery, court-dress ; the suffix *-on* being augmentative, as in *balloon*. See **Gallant**, **Gala**.

GALLOP, to ride very fast. (F. – Teut.) ' Styll he *galoped* forth right ; ' Berners, tr. of Froissart, vol. i. c. 140. We also find the form *walopen*, in the Romance of Partenay, ed. Skeat, 4827 (and note on p. 259) ; and the pres. pt. *walopande*, Morte Arthur, ed. Brock, 2827. – OF. *galoper*, to gallop ; of which an older form must have been *waloper*, as shown by the derivative *walopin* in Roquefort, spelt *galopin* in mod. F. The sb. *galop* also appears as *walop* in OFrench (Bartsch) ; and may be the original whence the verb was derived. The sense was perhaps ' Celtic running.' – OSax. *Walh*, a Celt ; and *hlōpan*, to run, to leap ; see **Walnut** and **Leap**. The Norw. *vallhopp*, a gallop (Aasen) ; lit. ' a bounding over a field,' or ' field-hop,' would account for the word even better ; but is merely an adaptation from Teutonic. Der. *gallop-ade*.

GALLOW, to terrify. (E.) In Shak. King Lear, iii. 2. 44. Prov. E. (Somerset.) *gally*. ME. *galwen*. AS. *gǣlwan*, in the comp.

āgælwan, to astonish ; ' þa wearð ic āgælwed ' = then was I astonished ; Ælfred, tr. of Boethius, c. xxxiv. § 5 ; lib. iii. pr. 10.

GALLOWAY, a nag, pony. (Scotland.) So called from *Galloway* in Scotland ; the word occurs in Drayton's Polyolbion, s. 3. l. 28. Cf. *Galloway-nag* in Shak. 2 Hen. IV, ii. 4. 205.

GALLOW-GLASS, GALLOGLASS, a heavy-armed foot-soldier. (Irish.) In Macbeth, i. 2. 13. — Irish *galloglach,* a servant, a heavy-armed soldier. — Irish *gall,* a foreigner, an Englishman ; *oglach,* a youth, servant, soldier (from *og,* OIrish *óac, óc,* young). It meant 'an English servitor ;' according to Spenser, View of Ireland, Globe ed. p. 640 ; but *gall* orig. referred to Danes (Windisch). (N. and Q. 6 S. x. 145.)

GALLOWS, a gibbet, an instrument for hanging criminals. (E.) ME. *galwes,* Chaucer, C. T. 6240 (D 658). AS. *galga, gealga,* a cross, gibbet, gallows ; Grein, i. 492. Hence was formed ME. *galwe,* by the usual change from *-ga* to *-we* (and later still to *-ow*) ; and it became usual to employ the word in the plural *galwes,* so that the mod. E. *gallows* is also, strictly speaking, a plural form. **+** Icel. *gálgi,* the gallows, a gibbet ; Dan. and Swed. *galge,* a gibbet ; Du. *galg* ; Goth. *galga,* a cross ; G. *galgen.* Teut. type **galgon-* ; cf. Lith. *žalga,* a pole (ž=zh).

GALOCHE, a kind of shoe or slipper. (F. — Late L. — Gk.) ME. *galoche,* Chaucer, C. T. 10869 (F 555) ; P. Plowman, B. xviii. 14. — F. *galoche,* 'a wooden shooe or patten, made all of a piece, without any latchet or tie of leather, and worne by the poor clowne in winter ;' Cot. — Late L. **galopia, *calopia,* formed from **calopus* = Gk. καλάπους (Hatzfeld) ; we find Late L. *calopedia,* a clog, wooden shoe (Brachet) ; also *calopodium* = Gk. καλοπόδιον, dimin. of καλόπους, καλάπους, a shoe-maker's last. — Gk. κᾱλο-, stem of κᾶλον, wood ; and πούς (gen. ποδ-ός), a foot, cognate with E. *foot.*

GALORE, abundantly, in plenty. (C.) First in 1675. Also spelt *gelore, gilore* in Jamieson, and *golore* in Todd's Johnson. 'Galloor, plenty, *North*;' Grose (1790). — Irish *goleor,* sufficiently ; where *go,* lit. 'to,' is a particle which, when prefixed to an adjective, renders it an adverb, and *leor,* adj., means sufficient ; Gael. *gu leor, gu leoir,* which is the same. Cf. Irish *lia,* more, allied to L. *plūs* (Stokes-Fick, p. 41).

GALT (1), **GAULT,** a series of beds of clay and marl. (Scand.) A modern geological term. Prov. E. *galt,* clay, brick-earth, *Suffolk* (Halliwell). Perhaps of Scand. origin. — Norw. *gald,* hard ground, a place where the ground is trampled hard by frequent treading, also a place where snow is trodden hard ; Icel. *gald,* hard snow, also spelt *galdr.* (Doubtful.)

GALT (2), a boar-pig. (Scand.) 'Growene as a *galte*;' Allit. Morte Arthure, 1101. — Icel. *göltr, galti,* a boar ; Swed. Dan. *galt,* a hog. Cf. OHG. *galza,* a sow ; (see Schade).

GALVANISM, a kind of electricity. (Ital.) Named from Luigi *Galvani,* of Bologna in Italy, inventor of the galvanic battery in A.D. 1791. Der. *galvani-c, galvani-se.*

GAMBADO, a kind of legging. (F. — Ital. — L.) 'Gambadoes, much worne in the west, whereby, while one rides on horseback, his leggs are in a coach, clean and warme ;' Fuller's Worthies, Cornwall (R.). An E. adaptation, simulating Spanish, of F. *gambade,* of which the usual sense is 'gambol ;' see **Gambol.**

GAMBESON, a military tunic, sometimes padded. (F. — Teut.) 'A band of Moorish knights gaily arrayed in *gambesons* of crimson silk ;' Longfellow, Outre-Mer (Ancient Spanish Ballads). ME. *gambisoun,* King Alisaunder, 5151. — OF. *gambison, gambeison, wambison* (Godefroy) ; cf. Late L. *wambasium.* So called from covering the belly. — OHG. *wamba,* belly ; see **Womb.**

GAMBIT, an opening at chess. (F. — Ital. — L.) F. *gambit.* — Ital. *gambetto,* a tripping up. — Ital. *gamba,* the leg ; see **Gambol.**

GAMBLE, to play for money. (E.) Comparatively a modern word. It occurs in Cowper, Tirocinium, 246 ; and Burns has *gambling,* Twa Dogs, 154. Formed, by suffix *-le* (which has a frequentative force), from the verb to *game,* the *b* being merely excrescent ; so that *gamble* = *gamm-le.* This form, *gamm-le* (Yorkshire, see E. D. D.) has taken the place of the ME. *gamenien* or *gamenen,* to play at games, to gamble, which occurs in King Alisaunder, ed. Weber, 5461. AS. *gamenian,* to play at a game, in the Liber Scintillarum, § 55 (p. 172). — AS. *gamen,* a game. See **Game.** Der. *gambl-er.*

GAMBOGE, a gum-resin, of a bright yellow colour. (Asiatic.) In Johnson's Dict. 'Brought from India by the Dutch, about A.D. 1600 ;' Haydn, Dict. of Dates. The word is a corruption of *Cambodia,* the name of the district where it is found. Cambodia is in the Annamese territory, not far from the gulf of Siam. 'The derivation' is given by Dampier in 1699; Supp. to Voy. round the World, vi. 105 ;' (N.E.D.)

GAMBOL, a frisk, caper. (F. — Ital. — L.) In Shak. Hamlet, v. 1. 209. Older spellings are *gambold,* Phaer, tr. of Virgil, Æn. vi.

(l. 643 of Lat. text) ; *gambawd,* or *gambaud,* Skelton, Ware the Hawk, 65 ; *gambolde, gambalde* in Palsgrave, s. v. *Fetche* ; *gambauld,* Udal, Flowers of Lat. Speaking, fol. 72 (R.). — OF. *gambade,* 'a gamboll ;' Cot. — Ital. *gambata,* a kick (Brachet). — Ital. *gamba,* the leg ; the same word as F. *jambe,* OF. *gambe.* — Late L. *gamba,* earlier spelling *camba* ; cf. acc. pl. *cambas,* glossed by AS. *homme* in A. S. Leechdoms, vol. i. p. lxxi ; 'the bend' of the leg. Cf. Gael. and W. *cam,* crooked, answering to OCelt. **kambos* (fem. **kambā*), bent, crooked ; Stokes-Fick, p. 78. ¶ The spelling with *l* seems to have been due to the confusion of the F. suffix *-ade* with F. suffix *-aude,* the latter of which stands for an older *-alde.* Hence *gambade* was first corrupted to *gambaude* (Skelton) ; then written *gambauld* (Udal) or *gambold* (Phaer) ; and lastly *gambol* (Shakespeare), with loss of final *d.* Der. *gambol,* vb., Mids. Nt. Dr. iii. 1. 168.

GAME, sport, amusement. (E.) In Shak. Mids. Nt. Dr. i. 1. 240. ME. *game,* Chaucer, C. T. 1808 (A 1806) ; older form *gamen,* spelt *gammyn* and *gamyn* in Barbour's Bruce, ed. Skeat, iii. 465, ix. 466, &c. AS. *gamen, gomen,* a game, sport ; Grein, i. 366. **+** OSax. *gaman* ; Icel. *gaman* ; Dan. *gammen,* mirth, merriment ; MSwed. *gamman,* joy (Ihre) ; OHG. *gaman,* MHG. *gamen,* joy. Root unknown. Der. *game,* vb., *gam-ing* ; *game-some,* ME. *gamsum* (= *gamen-sum*), Will. of Palerne, 4193 ; *game-ster* (Merry Wives, iii. 1. 37), where the suffix *-ster,* orig. feminine, has a sinister sense, Koch, Engl. Gram. iii. 47 ; also *game-cock, game-keeper.* Doublet, *gammon* (2).

GAMMER, an old dame ; lit. 'grandmother ;' see **Gaffer.**

GAMMON (1), the thigh of a hog, pickled and dried. (F. — L.) 'A *gammon* of bacon ;' 1 Hen. IV, ii. 1. 26. Older form *gambon,* Book of St. Alban's, fol. f 2, back, l. 9. — OF. *gambon* (Picard *gambon*), the old form of F. *jambon,* corresponding to OF. *gambe* for *jambe.* Cotgrave explains *jambon* by 'a gammon ;' and Florio explains Ital. *gambone* by 'a hanche [haunch], a gammon.' Formed, with suffix *-on,* from OF. *gambe,* a leg. See **Gambol.**

GAMMON (2), nonsense, orig. a jest. (E.) A slang word ; but really the ME. *gamen* preserved ; see **Backgammon** and **Game.** Cf. 'This *gamon* shall begin ;' Chester Plays, vi. 260. And Stanihurst has *gamening,* i. e. 'gambling ;' Virgil, ed. Arber, p. 153.

GAMUT, the musical scale. (Hybrid ; F. — Gk. *and* L.) In Shak. Tam. Shrew, iii. 1. 67, 71. A compound word, made up from OF. *game* or *gamme,* and *ut.* 1. Gower has *gamme* in the sense of 'a musical scale ;' C. A. iii. 90 ; bk. vii. 172. — OF. *game, gamme,* 'gamut, in musick ;' Cot. — Gk. γάμμα, the name of the third letter of the alphabet. Cf. Heb. *gimel,* the third letter of the alphabet, so named from its supposed resemblance to a camel, called in Hebrew *gāmāl* (Farrar, Chapters on Language, 136). Brachet says : 'Guy of Arezzo [born about A.D. 990] named the notes of the musical scale *a, b, c, d, e, f, g,* in which *a* was the low *la* on the violoncello ; then, to indicate one note below this *a,* he used the Gk. γ, which thus standing in front of the whole scale, has given its name to it.' 2. The word *ut* is Latin, and is the old name for the first note in singing, now called *do.* The same Guy of Arezzo is said to have named the notes after certain syllables of a monkish hymn to S. John, in a stanza written in sapphic metre. The lines are : '*Ut* queant laxis *resonare* fibris *Mira* gestorum *famuli* tuorum *Solve* polluti *labii* reatum *Sancte Iohannes* ;' the last term *si* being made from the initials of the final words.

GANDER, the male of the goose. (E.) ME. *gandre,* Mandeville's Travels, p. 216. AS. *gandra* ; Ælfric's Gram. De Tertia Declinatione, sect. xviii ; where it translates L. *anser.* Also spelt *ganra,* Voc. 131. 23. **+** Du. *gander* ; Low G. *ganner* (Berghaus). β. The *d* is excrescent, as in *thunder,* and as usual after *n* ; *gandra* stands for the older *gan-ra.* Teut. type **gan-ron-,* m. See further under **Gannet, Goose.**

GANG (1), a crew of persons. (Scand.) The word *gang* occurs in ME. in the sense of 'a going,' or 'a course.' The peculiar use of *gang* in the sense of a 'crew' is late, and is rather Scand. than E. In Skinner, ed. 1671. '*Gang,* a company, a crew ;' Kersey's Dict., ed. 1715. He adds that 'in sea-affairs, *gangs* are the several companies of mariners belonging to a ship.' But in the sense of a 'set' of things, it occurs as early as 1340 in Northern E. (N.E.D.). — Icel. *gangr,* a going ; also, collectively, a gang, as *músagangr,* a gang of mice, *þjófagangr,* a gang of thieves. Cf. Swed. *gång,* a going, a time ; Dan. *gang,* walk, gait ; AS. *gang,* a going, a procession ; Du. *gang,* course, pace, gait, tack, way, alley, passage ; Goth. *gaggs* (= *gangs*), a way, street. β. The ME. *gang,* a course, way, is from AS. *gang,* a journey (Bosworth) ; which is from AS. *gangan,* to go ; Grein, i. 367, 368. So also Icel. *gangr* is from Icel. *ganga,* to go. See **Gang** (2). Der. *gang-days,* from Icel. *gangdagar,* pl. ; *gang-week,* AS. *gang-wuce* ; *gang-way,* from AS. *gang-weg,* a way, road ; *gang-board,* a Dutch term, from Du. *gangboord,* a gangway.

GANG (2), to go. (Scand.) In Barbour's Bruce, ii. 276, iv. 193, x. 421. — Icel. *ganga,* to go. **+** AS. *gangan* ; OHG. *gangan* ; Goth.

gaggan (=*gangan*). Teut. type *ganggan-. Allied to Lith. *žengiù*, I stride; Skt. *jaṅghā*, the leg. Brugmann, i. § 609.

GANGLION, a tumour on a tendon. (L.—Gk.) Medical. In Kersey's Dict. ed. 1715.—L. *ganglion* (Vegetius).—Gk. γάγγλιον, a tumour near a tendon. **Der.** *ganglion-ic*.

GANGRENE, a mortification of the body, in its first stage. (F.—L.—Gk.) Shak. has the pp. *gangrened*, Cor. iii. 1. 307. The sb. is in Bacon, Nat. Hist., § 333; and in Cotgrave.—MF. *gangrene*, 'a gangreen, the rotting or mortifying of a member;' Cot.—L. *gangræna*. —Gk. γάγγραινα, an eating sore. A reduplicated form. Allied to γέρ-ων, an old man, Skt. *jaraya*, to consume, *jaras*, old age; see Prellwitz. **Der.** *gangrene*, vb.; *gangren-ous*.

GANNET, a sea-fowl, Solan goose. (E.) ME. *gante* (contracted from *ganet*); Prompt. Parv. p. 186; see Way's note. AS. *ganot*; 'ofer *ganotes* bæð' = over the sea-fowl's bath, i.e. over the sea; A. S. Chron. an. 975.+Du. *gent*, a gander; OHG. *ganazo*, MHG. *ganze*, a gander; Low G. *gante*. β. Formed with suffix -*ot* (-*et*), from the base *gan*-; for which see **Gander, Goose**.

GANTLET (1), a spelling of **Gauntlet**, q.v.

GANTLET (2), also **GANTLOPE**, a military punishment. (Swed.) In Skinner, ed. 1671. Formerly written *gantlope*, but corrupted to *gantlet* or *gauntlet* by confusion with *gauntlet*, a glove. 'To run the gantlope, a punishment used among souldiers;' Phillips' Dict., ed. 1658. Again, the *n* is inserted, being no part of the orig. word, which should be *gatlope*.—Swed. *gatlopp* (older form *gatulopp*), lit. 'a running down a lane,' because the offender has to run between two files of soldiers, who strike him as he passes. Widegren's Swed. Dict. (1788) has: '*löpa gatulopp*, to run the gantelope.'—Swed. *gata*, a street, lane; see **Gate** (2); and *lopp*, a course, career, running, from *löpa*, to run, cognate with E. **Leap**. ¶ Prob. due to the wars of Gustavus Adolphus (died 1632).

GAOL, JAIL, a cage, prison. (F.—L.) Spelt *gayole* in Fabyan's Chron. (1516), an. 1293; *gayhol* in An Old Eng. Miscellany, ed. Morris, p. 153, l. 219. The peculiar spelling *gaol* is due to the OF. *gaole* (Godefroy, s. v. *jaiole*), and has been preserved in Law French. Chaucer has *gayler*, C. T. 1476 (A 1474); whence *jailer* and *jail*.—AF. *gaole*, OF. *jaiole*, *gaole*, mod. F. *geôle*, a prison, cage for birds. 'In the 13th cent. people spoke of the *geôle d'un oiseau* as well as of the *geôle d'un prisonnier*;' Brachet. [But it must be remembered that the 13th cent. spelling was not *geôle*, but *gaole*.]—Late L. *gabiola*, a cage, in a charter of A.D. 1229, cited by Brachet. A dimin. of Late L. *gabia*, for *cavea*, a cage; Ducange.—L. *cauea*, a cage, coop, lit. a hollow place, cavity. —L. *cauus*, hollow. See **Cage, Cave**, and **Gabion**. **Der.** *gaol-er* or *jail-er*.

GAPE, to yawn, open the mouth for wonder. (Scand.) ME. *gapen*, P. Plowman, B. x. 41.—Icel. *gapa*, Swed. *gapa*, Dan. *gabe*, to gape. So also EFries., Du., Low G. *gapen*.+G. *gaffen*. Cf. Skt. *jabh, jambh*, to gape, yawn. **Der.** *gap-er*; and *gaby*, q.v. Also *gap*, sb., ME. *gappe* (dat.) in Chaucer, C. T. 1641 (A 1639); a word which is rather Scand. than E.; cf. Icel. and Swed. *gap*, a gap, breach, abyss, from *gapa*, vb.; Dan. *gab*, mouth, throat, gap, chasm, from *gabe*, vb.

GAR (1), **GARFISH**, a kind of pike. (E.) A fish with a long slender body and pointed head. ME. *garfysche*; Prompt. Parv. Prob. named from AS. *gār*, a spear, from its shape; see **Garlic**. Cf. Icel. *geirsil*, a kind of herring, Icel. *geirr*, a spear; and observe the names *pike* and *ged*.

GAR (2), to cause. (Scand.) Common in Lowland Scotch; and see P. Plowman, B. i. 121; v. 130; vi. 303.—OIcel. *gørua* (Noreen), Icel. *göra*; Dan. *gjøre*; Swed. *göra*, to cause, make, do; lit. 'to make ready.' —Icel. *görr*, ready; cognate with E. *yare*. See **Yare**. So also AS. *gierwan, gearwian*, to make ready, from *gearu*, ready, yare; see below.

GARB (1), dress, manner, fashion. (F.—Ital.—OHG.) Used by Shak. to mean 'form, manner, mode of doing a thing' (Schmidt); Hamlet, ii. 2. 390; K. Lear, ii. 2. 103.—MF. *garbe*, 'a garbe, comelinesse, handsomenesse, gracefulnesse, good fashion,' Cot.; (whence F. *galbe*, contour).—Ital. *garbo*, 'grace, handsomeness, garbe;' Florio. —OHG. *garwi, garawi*, preparation, getting ready, dress, gear; MHG. *gerwe, garwe*; allied to OHG. *garawen*, MHG. *gerwen*, to get ready.— OHG. *garo*, MHG. *gar, gare*, ready; cognate with E. *yare*. See **Gear**.

GARB (2), a sheaf. (F.—OHG.) In Minsheu, ed. 1627. ME. *garbe*, in A. Neckam; Wright's Vocab. i. 113. An heraldic term.— AF. and Picard *garbe* (F. *gerbe*), a sheaf.—OHG. *garba*, a sheaf (G. *garbe*). Lit. a handful, or 'what is grabbed.' Cf. E. *grab*, Swed. *grabba*, to grasp; Skt. *grah* (Vedic form *grabh*), to seize. See **Grab**. Brugm. i. § 531.

GARBAGE, offal, refuse. (F.) In Shak. Hamlet, i. 5. 57. 'The *garbage*, aluus, intestina;' Levins, 11. 13. Florio translates the Ital. *tara* by the tare, waste, or *garbish* of any marchandise or ware.' Palsgrave has: '*garbage* of a foule,' i.e. a fowl's entrails. It agrees in form with OF. *garbage, gerbage*, a tax paid in garbs or sheaves; and

is prob. similarly formed from OF. *garbe*, a handful, small bundle, Low L. *garba*, the same. See above.

GARBLE, to select for a purpose, to mutilate or corrupt an account. (F.—Ital.—Arab.—L.) The old sense was 'to pick out,' or 'sort,' so as to get the best of a collection of things. The statute 1 Rich. III, c. 11, was made 'for the remedie of the excessiue price and badnesse of bowstaues, which partly is growen because the merchants will not suffer any *garbeling* [or sorting] of them to be made.' There was an officer called the *Garbler of spices*, whose business was to visit the shops, examine the spices, and *garble*, or make clean the same; mentioned an. 21 Jacob. c. 1. See Blount's Nomolexicon, where it is further explained that '*garbling* of spice, drugs, &c. (1 Jacob. cap. 19) is nothing but to purifie it from the dross and dirt that is mixed with it.'—OF. *garbeller* (in Godefroy, entered by mistake under *gerbele*), usually *grabeller*, 'to garbell spices, also to examine precisely, sift neerly;' Cot. The same word as Span. *garbillar*, to sift, garble; Ital. *garbellare*, 'to garbel spices' (Torriano); and Low L. *garbellāre*, to sift, a word which occurs A. D. 1269 (Ducange). Cf. Span. *garbillo*, a coarse sieve, sifter.—Pers. *gharbīl*, a sieve; Arab. *ghirbāl*, a large sieve; Arab. *kirbāl*, a sieve; *gharbala, karbala*, to sift. Prob. not an Arabic word, but adapted from L. *crībellum*, dimin. of *crībrum*, a sieve; allied to L. *cernere*, to sift. Rich. Dict., pp. 1046, 1177, 1178. See **Riddle** (2).

GARBOIL, a disturbance, commotion. (F.—Ital.) In Shak. Antony, i. 3. 61; ii. 2. 67.—OF. *garbouil*, 'a garboile, hurliburly, great stirre;' Cot. Cf. Span. *garbullo*, a crowd, multitude.—Ital. *garbuglio*, 'a garboile, .. tumult, disorder;' Florio. β. Of uncertain origin. Referred by Diez to L. *garr-īre*, to prattle, chatter; in conjunction with *bullīre*, to boil, bubble, boil with rage. γ. The latter part of the word is thus well accounted for; see **Boil**. The former part is less sure, and seems to be more directly from the Ital. *gara*, strife, since Florio has '*garabullare*, to rave.' The source is probably imitative; see **Jar**, to creak.

GARDANT, in heraldry: looking full at the spectator. (F.— Teut.) Also *guardant*.—MF. *gardant*, pres. pt. of *garder*, 'to ward, watch, regard;' Cot. See **Guard**.

GARDEN, a yard, enclosure. (F.—Teut.) ME. *gardin*, Chaucer, C. T. 1053 (A 1051); King Alisaunder, ed. Weber, 1028.—AF., O. North F. (Norm. dial. and Picard) *gardin*; F. *jardin*.—OSax. *gardo*, a yard; cf. OHG. *gartin*, gen. and dat. of OHG. *garto*, a yard, garden (Diez). The stem *gartin*- was retained in compounds, such as OHG. *gartin-āri*, a gardener; and this prob. suggested a Late L. form *gard-īnum (with L. suffix -*īnum*), whence the OF. form. β. The OSax. *gardo* is cognate with AS. *geard*, whence E. *yard*; see **Yard**. The substitution of OHG. *t* (as in *gart*-) for Low G. *d* is regular. **Der.** *garden*, vb.; *garden-ing, garden-er*.

GARFISH, a kind of pike. See **Gar** (1).

GARGLE, to rinse the throat. (F.—Late L.—Gk.) In Cotgrave. Modified from F. *gargouiller*, just as the ME. *gargyll* (a gargoyle) is from F. *gargouille*.—F. *gargouiller*, 'to gargle, or gargarize;' Cot. —F. *gargouille*; for which see **Gargoyle**. ☞ The ME. *gargarise*, used by Sir T. Elyot, Castel of Helth, b. iv. c. 10, is from MF. *gargarizer*, to gargle (Cot.), borrowed (through L. *gargarizāre*) from Gk. γαργαρίζειν, to gargle. From an imitative base, viz. Gk. γαργ-; cf. Gk. γαργαρεών, the uvula. Hence also Ital. *garg-agliare*, to murmur, *garg-atta*, the throat (see below). **Der.** *gargle*, sb.

GARGOYLE, in architecture, a projecting spout. (F.—Late L. —Gk.) ME. *gargoyle*, also spelt *gargyll*. The spelling *gargoyle* is in Lydgate's Siege of Troy, bk. ii. c. 11 (fol. F 5, back, col. 1); we read of '*gargylles* of gold fiersly faced with spoutes running' in Hall's Chron. Henry VIII, an. 19.—F. *gargouille*, 'the weesle or weason [weazand] of the throat; also, the mouth of a spout, a gutter;' Cot. Cf. Span. *gargola*, a gargoyle. β. We find, in Ital., not only *gargatta, gargozza*, the throat, windpipe, but also *gorgozza*, the throat, gullet, dimin. of *gorga*, the throat. Thus *garg-ouille* is from the imitative Gk. base γαργ- (see above), just as Ital. *gorga* and E. *gorge* are from the parallel L. base *gurg*-; see **Gorge**. (Körting, §§ 4169, 4401.)

GARISH, glaring, staring, showy. (Scand.) 'The *garish* sun;' Romeo, iii. 2. 25. 'Day's *garish* eye;' Milton, Il Penseroso, 141. Chaucer uses the form *gauren*, to stare; C. T. 5332 (B 912); with which cf. '*gaurish* in colour,' Ascham, Scholemaster, ed. Arber, p. 54. Perhaps from Norw. *gagra*, to bend the head backwards (Ross); from *gag*, adj., bent backwards. From the attitude adopted in staring or gazing fixedly. The change *ag* > *au* is regular.

GARLAND, a wreath. (F.—Teut.?) In early use. ME. *gerlond*, Chaucer, C. T. 668 (A 666). The form *gerlaundesche* occurs in Hali Meidenhad, ed. Cockayne, p. 23.—OF. *garlande*, 'a garland;' Cot. [The mod. F. *guirlande* is borrowed from Ital. *ghirlanda*.] Cf. Span. *guirnalda*, Ital. *ghirlanda*, a garland. β. Of uncertain origin; see the discussion of the word in Diez. It seems as if formed with a suffix -*ande* from a MHG. *wierel-en, a supposed frequentative of *wieren*, to adorn; from OHG. *wiara*, MHG. *wiere*, gold wire, fine ornament. (Körting, § 10389.) Cf. E. *wire*. **Der.** *garland*, vb.

GARLIC, a plant of the genus *Allium*. (E.) Lit. 'spear-plant;' from the shape of the leaves. ME. *garleek*, Chaucer, C. T. 636 (A 634). AS. *gārlēac*, used to translate L. *allium* in Ælfric's Glossary, Nomina Herbarum. ‒ AS. *gār*, a spear; and *lēac*, a leek, plant. ╉ Icel. *geirlaukr* (similarly formed). See **Gar** (1), **Gore**, and **Leek**. ¶ The W. *garlleg* is borrowed from E.

GARMENT, a robe, coat. (F. ‒ Teut.) A corruption of ME. *garnement*, P. Plowman, C. x. 119. ‒ OF. *garnement*, *garniment*, a robe, lit. a defence; formed (with suffix *-ment* = L. *-mentum*) from OF. *garnir*, to protect, garnish, adorn. See **Garnish**.

GARNER, a granary, store for grain. (F. ‒ L.) ME. *gerner*; Chaucer, C. T. 595 (A 593). ‒ OF. *gernier*, a variant of *grenier*, a granary (Supp. to Godefroy). ‒ L. *grānārium*, a granary. **Doublet**, *granary*, q. v. **Der.** *garner*, verb.

GARNET, a kind of precious stone. (F. ‒ L.) 'And gode *garnettes* bytwene;' Romance of Emare, ed. Ritson, l. 156; so also *garnettes*, pl., in Lydgate, Chorle and Bird, st. 34. A corruption of *granat*, a form also used in E., and found in Cotgrave. ‒ OF. *grenat* [also *granat*], 'a precious stone called a granat, or garnet;' Cot. Cf. Span. *granate*, Ital. *granato*, a garnet. ‒ Late L. *grānātus*, a garnet. 'So called from its resemblance in colour and shape to the grains or seeds of the pomegranate;' Webster. ‒ L. *grānātus*, having many grains or seeds; *grānātum* (for *mālum grānātum*), a pomegranate. ‒ L. *grānum*, a grain; see **Grain**.

GARNISH, to embellish, decorate. (F. ‒ Teut.) In Spenser, Verses addressed to Lord Ch. Howard, l. 2; Prompt. Parv. p. 188. Also spelt *warnish* in ME.; the pp. *warnished* is in Will. of Palerne, l. 1083. ‒ OF. *garnis-*, *warnis-*, stem of pres. pt. of *garnir*, *guarnir*, older form *warnir*, to avert, defend, fortify, garnish (Godefroy). ‒ OHG. **warnōjan*, OHG. *warnōn*, to guard against; cf. OHG. *warna*, foresight, care. See **Ware**. **Der.** *garnish*, sb., *garnish-ment*, *garnish-er*; also *garniture* (Cotgrave), from F. *garniture*, 'garniture, garnishment' (Cot.), Low L. *garnitūra*, from Low L. *garnīre*, to adorn, which is merely the F. word Latinised; also *garnish-ee* = 'the party in whose hands another man's money is attached' (Kersey's Dict., ed. 1715), barbarously formed on the model of a F. pass. part. as opposed to *garnish-er* considered as an agent; also *garment*, q. v., and *garrison*, q. v.

GARRET, a room at the top of a house. (F. ‒ OHG.) ME. *garite* (with one *r*), Prompt. Parv. p. 187; P. Plowman's Creed, ed. Skeat, 214. It properly means 'a place of look out,' or 'watch-tower.' ‒ OF. *garite*, a place of refuge, place of look-out, watch-tower (F. *guérite*). ‒ OF. *garir*, older spelling *warir*, to preserve, save, keep. ‒ OHG. *warjan*, to defend; cf. AS. *werian*, to defend. Allied to **Weir**, q. v.

GARRISON, a supply of soldiers for defending a fort. (F. ‒ Teut.) 1. ME. *garnison*, provision, in La Belle Dame sans Mercy, l. 175; Barbour's Bruce, ed. Skeat, xvii. 294 (footnote), where another spelling is *warnyson*, and other reading is *varnysing*. ‒ OF. *garnison*, store, provision, supply (Norm. dial. *garnison*, Moisy). ‒ OF. *garnis-ant*, pres. part. of *garnir*, to supply, garnish; see **Garnish**. Thus *garnison* is allied to *garniture*. 2. But it was supplanted by ME. *garison* or *warison*, defence, safety; from OF. *garis-*, pres. pt. stem of *garir*, to defend; see **Garret**.

GARROTE, GARROTTE, a method of effecting strangulation. (Span. ‒ C.) 'Garrotte, a machine for strangling criminals, used in Spain. Many attempts to strangle were made by thieves called *garrotters*, in the winter of 1862-63. An act was passed in 1863 to punish these acts by flogging;' Haydn, Dict. of Dates. [See *garrot* and *garroter* in Cotgrave.] ‒ Span. *garrote*, a cudgel, tying a rope tight, strangling by means of an iron collar; Minsheu says, 'a cudgel to wind [twist] a cord.' Formed, with dimin. suffix *-ote*, from Span. *garra*, a claw, a talon, clutch, whence also the phrase *echarle a uno la garra*, to grasp, imprison; Minsheu has '*garra*, a paw of a beast;' cf. Prov. *garra*, leg (Mistral). Of Celtic origin; connected with Breton *gar*, *garr*, W. and Corn. *gar*, the shank of the leg (Diez); Celtic type **garris*, Stokes-Fick, p. 107. See **Garter**. **Der.** *garrotte*, verb; *garrott-er*. (Körting, § 4160.)

GARRULOUS, talkative. (L.) 1. Milton has *garrulity*, Sams. Agonistes, 491; and it occurs in Cotgrave, to translate F. *garrulité*, from L. acc. *garrulitātem*, talkativeness. 2. The adj. *garrulous* occurs in Chapman's Homer, Comment. on Iliad, b. iii; note 2. It is borrowed from L. directly, by change of *-us* to *-ous*, as in *ardu-ous*, *strenu-ous*, &c. ‒ L. *garrulus*, talkative. Formed, with suffix *-(u)lu-*, from *garr-īre*, to prattle. ‒ √ GAR, to shout, call; whence also W. *gar-m*, an outcry, Irish *gairm*. Brugmann, i. § 638. **Der.** *garrulous-ness*; also *garrul-i-ty*, as above.

GARTER, a band round the leg, for fastening the hose. (F. ‒ C.) 'Eek ther be knightes old of the *garter*;' The Flower and the Leaf

(15th cent.), l. 519. Hoccleve has a poem addressed to 'Knightes of the Garter.' The order was instituted by Edw. III, ab. 1344. ‒ AF. *garter*, Stat. of the Realm, i. 380 (an. 1363); OF. *gartier*, in dialects of N. France (Hécart), Walloon *gartier* (Sigart), spelt *jartier* in Cotgrave, and explained by him as 'a garter;' mod. F. *jarretière*. Closely connected with OF. *garet* (Godefroy), mod. F. *jarret*, the ham of the leg. ‒ Bret. *gar*, *garr*, the shank of the leg; cf. W. *gar*, the shank; see **Garrote**. **Der.** *garter*, verb, All's Well, ii. 3. 265.

GARTH, a yard, enclosure, fence. (Scand.) Northern; the pl. *garthis* is in Hampole, Psalm xxxvi. 2. ‒ Icel. *garðr*, a yard. ╉ AS. *geard*, a yard; see **Yard**.

GAS, an aeriform fluid. (Dutch.) The term is known to have been a pure invention. The Belgian chemist Van Helmont (died A.D. 1644) invented two corresponding terms, *gas* and *blas*; the former came into use, the latter was forgotten. We may call it a Dutch word, as *gas* is the Du. spelling. ¶ Van Helmont says that it was suggested by the Gk. *chaos*: ‒ 'Halitum illum *gas* vocavi, non longe a *Chao* veterum secretum;' Ortus Medicinæ, ed. 1652, p. 59 a (N.E.D.). **Der.** *gas-e-ous*, *gas-o-meter*.

GASCONADE, boasting, bragging. (Gascony.) 'That figure of speech which is commonly distinguished by the name of *Gasconade*;' The Tatler, no. 115 (part 2). ‒ F. *gasconnade*, boasting; said to be a vice of the Gascons. ‒ F. *Gascon*, an inhabitant of Gascony, formerly Vasconia. **Der.** *gasconade*, verb, *gasconad-ing*, *gasconad-er*.

GASH, to hack, cut deeply. (F. ‒ Late L. ‒ Gk.) 'His *gashed* stabs;' Macbeth, ii. 3. 119. A corruption of an older form *garsh* or *garse*. 'A *garse* or *gashe*, incisura;' Levins, 33. 14. 'Garsshe in wode or in a knife, *hoche*;' Palsgrave. The pl. sb. *garcen* (another MS. has *garses*) occurs in the Ancren Riwle, p. 258, in the sense of 'gashes caused by a scourge.' ‒ OF. *garser*, to scarify, pierce with a lancet (Roquefort, and see *jarser*, *garser* in Godefroy); *garscher*, to chap, as the hands or lips (Cotgrave). Cf. Late L. *garsa*, scarification, or the making of numerous small incisions in the skin and flesh; an operation called by the Greeks ἐγχάραξις; Ducange. β. Origin obscure; it is possible that OF. *garser* represents Late L. *caraxāre*, short for *incaraxāre*, *incharaxāre*, to pierce, incise; from Gk. χαράσσειν, to furrow, scratch. See **Character**. ¶ Diez suggests a Late L. form **carptiāre*, founded on *carpere*, to pluck. Note ME. *carsare*, as a gloss to *scarificator*, Voc. 652. 7. **Der.** *gash*, sb.

GASP, to gape for breath. (Scand.) ME. *gaspen*, Gower, C. A. ii. 260; bk. v. 3975. Also *gaispen* (Northern), Allit. Morte Arthure, 1462. The latter is from Icel. and Norw. *geispa*, to yawn; Swed. *gäspa*; cf. Dan. *gispe*. The former suggests a cognate AS. **gāspan* (not found). Note that *sp* commonly represents an earlier *ps*; thus *clasp* is ME. *clapsen*, *hasp* was formerly *haps*, and *aspen* is from *aps*. Hence Icel. *geispa* is for **geipsa*; from a Teut. base **geip* (weak grade *gip*); cf. Du. *gijpen*, to gasp, AS. *gipung*, a gaping. **Der.** *gasp*, sb.

GASTRIC, belonging to the belly. (Late L. ‒ Gk.) Coles (1684) has *gastrick*; so also Blount, ed. 1656. ‒ Late L. *gastricus*, gastric; formed with suffix *-c-* from *gastri-* = *gastro-*. ‒ Gk. γαστρό-, for γαστήρ, the belly (stem γαστερ-). **Der.** from the same root, *gastro-nomy*; from Gk. γαστρό-, and *-νομία*, derivative of νόμος, usage.

GATE (1), a door, opening, way. (E.) [In Prov. E. and ME. we often find *gate* = a street; see below.] ME. *gate*, *ȝate*, *yate*. Spelt *gate*, O. Eng. Homilies, ed. Morris, i. 237, l. 31; *ȝate*, Will. of Palerne, 3757; *ȝet*, Ancren Riwle, p. 74. AS. *geat*, a gate, opening; Matt. vii. 13 (whence ME. *yate*); pl. *gatu* (whence ME. *gate*). ╉ Du. *gat*, a hole, opening, gap, mouth; Icel. *gat*, an opening; OFries., OSax., and Low G. *gat*. See **Gate** (2). **Der.** *gat-ed*, *gate-way*.

GATE (2), a street. (Scand.) Common in the North; it also means 'a way.' 'Whilest foot is in the *gate*;' Spenser, F. Q. i. 1. 13. ME. *gate*, Ormulum, 12749. ‒ Icel. and Norw. *gata*, Swed. *gata*, a way, path, street, lane; Dan. *gade*; cf. Goth. *gatwō*, a street, G. *gasse*. Perhaps allied to **Gate** (1). β. *Gate* (1) answers to Teut. type **gatom*, n.; but *gate* (2) to Teut. type **gatwōn-*, f. See **Gait**, **Gantlet** (2).

GATHER, to draw into a heap, collect. (E.) Just as *father* corresponds to ME. *fader*, so *gather* corresponds to ME. *gaderen* or *gaderien*, to gather; as also mod. E. *together* corresponds to ME. *togideres*. 'And *gadred* hem alle *togideres*' = and gathered them all together; P. Plowman, B. xvi. 80. AS. *gædrian*, *gaderian*; Luke, vi. 44; Grein, i. 366, 373. β. Formed, with causal suffix *-ian*, from AS. *gador*, together, preserved in the compound *gader-tang*, associated with (Grein, i. 365), and also as *gador-* or *geador*, together (Grein, i. 491); see **Together**. γ. From a base *gad-*; cf. AS. *gæd*, society, fellowship, company; whence also the AS. *ge-gada*, a companion, and AS. *gæd-el-ing*, an associate, comrade; cf. Goth. *gad-il-iggs* (= *gad-il-ings*), a sister's son, Col. iv. 10. ╉ Du. *gaderen*, to collect, from *gader*, together; Low G. *gadden*, to collect (Berghaus), the base appears in Du. *gade*, a spouse, consort; cf. G. *gatte*, a husband, *gattin*, a wife. The base **gad-* prob. meant 'fit' or 'suitable;' cf.

Low G. *gad*, pleasant (Berghaus); Russ. *godnuii*, suitable, OSlav. *godŭ*, fit season. See **Good**. Der. *gather*, sb. ; *gather-ing*, *gather-er*.

GAUD, a show, ornament. (F. – L.) Also spelt *gawd*, Shak. Mids. Nt. Dr. i. 1. 33. Chaucer uses *gaude* in the sense of 'specious trick ;' C. T. 12323 (C 389). – OF. *gaudir*, to rejoice, to jest at. – L. *gaudium*, gladness, joy ; used in Late L. of 'a large bead on a rosary ;' whence ME. *gauded*, furnished with large beads. 'A peire of bedes *gauded* al with grene ;' Chaucer, C. T. 159. – L. *gaudēre*, to rejoice, pt. t. *gāvīsus sum* ; from a base *gau*-.+Gk. γηθέειν, to rejoice ; allied to γαίειν (= γαϝ-ίειν), to rejoice ; γαῦρος, proud. Brugmann, i. § 589 : ii. § 694. Der. *gaud-y*, i. e. show-y ; *gaud-i-ly*, *gaud-i-ness*.

GAUFFER, the same as **Goffer**, q.v.

GAUGE, **GAGE**, to measure the content of a vessel. (F. – Low L.) In Shak. Merch. of Ven. ii. 2. 208 (where the old edd. have *gage*). 'Or bore and *gage* the hollow caues uncouth ;' Surrey, tr. of Virgil, Æneid, ii. 52. – O. North F. *gauger* (printed *gaugir* in Roquefort), Norm. dial. *gauger* (Moisy), Central F. *jauger*, 'to gage, or measure a piece of [or ?] cask ;' Cot. – OF. *gauge* (Norman ; see quot. in Moisy, s. v. *gauge*), old form of *jauge*, 'a gage, the instrument wherewith a cask is measured, also an iron leaver ;' Cot. Cf. Low L. *gaugia*, the standard measure of a wine-cask (A.D. 1446) ; Ducange. Also Low L. *gaugātum*, the gauging of a wine-cask ; *gaugettum*, a tribute paid for gauging, a gauge ; *gaugiātor*, a gauger. Origin unknown. Cf. *gaugeour*, a gauger ; Stat. of the Realm, i. 331 (1353). Der. *gaug-ing*, *gaug-er*.

GAULT, clay and marl. See **Galt** (1).

GAUNT, thin, lean. (Scand.) In Shak. Rich. II, ii. 1. 74. 'His own *gaunt* eagle ;' Ben Jonson, Catiline, iii. 1. '*Gawnt*, or lene ;' also '*Gawnte*, or slendyr ;' Prompt. Parv. p. 189. '*Gant*, slim, slender ;' Ray's South- and East-Country Words, ed. 1691. Also mentioned in Forby as a Norfolk, and in Moor as a Suffolk word ; also in Yks. Linc. Lanc. ; see E.D.D. It corresponds to Norweg. *gand*, a thin pointed stick, a tall and thin man, an overgrown stripling (Aasen) ; we also find Swed. dial. *gank*, a lean and nearly starved horse (Rietz). Cf. 'arm-*gaunt* steed,' i.e. slender in the fore-leg, Shak. Ant. and Cleop. i. 5. 48. Der. *gaunt-ly*, *gaunt-ness*.

GAUNTLET (1), an iron glove. (F. – Scand.) In Spenser, F. Q. i. 4. 43. ME. *gauntelet*, Sir T. Malory, Morte Darthur, bk. xix. c. 4 (end). – OF. *gantelet*, 'a gantlet, or arming-glove ;' Cot. Formed, with dimin. suffixes *-el-* and *-et*, from OF. *gant*, a glove. Of Scand. origin. – OSwed. *wante*, a glove (Ihre) ; whence Low L. *wantus* and OF. *gant* by the usual change of *w* to *g* in French ; see **Garnish** ; Dan. *vante*, a mitten ; Icel. *vöttr* (stem *vatt* = *vant*), a glove. OTeut. type **wantuz*. β. The most probable source is Teut. **windan*- (pt. t. *wand*), to wind, hence to involve, wrap, E. *wind*, verb. See **Wind** (2). Cf. G. *gewand*, a garment ; Low G. *want*, cloth (Lübben). Noreen, § 257 (5).

GAUNTLET (2). (Scand.) In the phr. 'to run the *gauntlet*,' we have a corruption of an older *gantlope*. It appears as *run the gantlope* in Bailey (1735), Kersey (1715), Philips (1706), and Blount (1674). Bailey correctly defines it as 'to run through a company of soldiers, standing on each side, *making a lane*, with each a switch in his hand to scourge the criminal.' See further under **Gantlet** (2).

GAUZE, a thin silken fabric. (F. – Palestine?) '*Gawz*, a thin sort of silk-stuff ;' Kersey's Dict. ed. 1715. – MF. *gaze*, 'cushion canvas, the thin canvas that serves women for a ground unto their cushions or pursework ; also, the sleight stuffe tiffany ;' Cot. And see Hatzfeld. Perhaps so called because first brought from Gaza, in Palestine. Cf. Low L. *gazetum*, wine brought from Gaza ; *gazzātum*, (perhaps) gauze. ¶ Several kinds of stuffs are named from places ; e.g. *damask* from Damascus, *calico* from Calicut, &c. ; but in this instance evidence is lacking.

GAVELKIND, a peculiar sort of tenure. (E.) In Minsheu, ed. 1627. '*Gavelkind*, a tenure, or custom, whereby the lands of the father are equally divided at his death among all his sons ;' Blount's Nomolexicon, ed. 1691. ME. *gauelkind* ; earliest spelling *gauelikind* in 1205 (N.E.D.). The latter answers to AS. *gafelgecynd* ; from AS. *gafel*, tribute, payment, and *gecynd*, kind, sort ; see **Kind**. β. The AS. *gaf-ol* (whence Low L. *gabulum*) is from Teut. **gab-*, 2nd grade of the verb *to give* ; see **Give**. ¶ Early misunderstood and misrepresented ; and wrongly supposed to be of Celtic origin.

GAVIAL, the crocodile of the Ganges. (F. – Hind.) First in 1825. – F. *gavial* (a corrupt form). – Hind. *ghaṛiyāl*, a crocodile (Forbes).

GAVOTTE, a kind of dance. (F. – Prov.) Spelt *gavot* in Arbuthnot and Pope's Martinus Scriblerus, as quoted in Todd's Johnson. – MF. *gavote*, 'a kind of brawle [dance], danced, commonly by one alone ;' Cot. – Prov. *gavoto*, f. a gavotte (Mistral). Fem. of *Gavot*, a mountaineer of the Upper Alps (id.). Of historical origin ; 'orig. a dance of the Gavotes, i. e. people of Gap ;' Brachet. Gap is in the department of the Upper Alps, and in the old province of Dauphiné.

GAWK, awkward. (F. – Scand.) The orig. sense is left-handed. It is short for E. dial. *gauk-handed*, left-handed (E.D.D.) ; and *gauk* is contracted from *gallack*, *gaulick*, adj., left (of the hands) ; where *-ick* is a suffix (N.E.D.). Of F. origin ; cf. Burgund. *gôle*, numb with cold, said of the fingers (Mignard). – Swed. Dan. *valen*, benumbed ; whence Swed. dial. *val-händt*, Norw. *val-hendt*, having numbed hands. ¶ Not from F. *gauche* (N.E.D.) Der. *gawk-y*, awkward, ungainly.

GAY, lively, merry, sportive. (F. – OHG.) ME. *gay*, Chaucer, C. T. 3213 ; Will. of Palerne, 816 ; King Alisaunder, ed. Weber, 3204. – OF. *gai*, merry ; spelt *gay* in Cotgrave. – OHG. *wâhi*, fine, beautiful. Der. *gai-ly*, Will. of Palerne, 1625 ; *gai-e-ty*, used by Bp. Taylor, Holy Dying, c. 5. s. 5 [*not* 15], from OF. *gayeté*, 'mirth,' Cot.

GAZE, to behold fixedly, stare at. (Scand.) ME. *gasen*. 'When that the peple *gased* up and down ;' Chaucer, C. T. 8879 (E 1003). Of Scand. origin, and preserved in Swed. dial. *gasa*, to gaze, stare, as in the phrase *gasa åkring se*, to gaze or stare about one (Rietz) ; and in Norw. *gasa*, to stare, gaze (Aasen). Der. *gaze*, sb., *gaz-ing-stock*.

GAZELLE, a kind of antelope. (F. – Span. – Arab.) Formerly *gazel*. '*Gazel*, a kind of Arabian deer, or the antilope of Barbary ;' Kersey's Dict., ed. 1715. – MF. *gazel*, *gazelle*, 'a kind of wild goat ;' Cot. – MSpan. *gacelo*, 'a wild goat ;' Minsheu. – Arab. *ghazāl*, 'a fawn just able to walk ; a wild goat ;' Richardson's Dict. p. 1050. Explained as 'a gazelle' in Palmer's Pers. Dict. col. 440.

GAZETTE, a small newspaper. (F. – Ital.) 'As we read a *gazett* ;' Bp. Taylor, vol. ii. ser. 1 (R.). [Ben Jonson has the (supposed) Ital. pl. *gazetti* ; Volpone, v. 2 (l. 7 from end).] – MF. *gazette*, 'a certain Venetian coin scarce worth our farthing ; also, a bill of news, or a short relation of the generall occurrences of the time, forged most commonly at Venice, and thence dispersed, every month, into most parts of Christendom ;' Cot. β. The word is certainly from Ital. *gazzetta*, but that word has *two* meanings, viz. (1) 'a yoong piot or magot a pie' [mag-pie] ; and (2) 'a small coine in Italie ;' Florio. Now the value of the latter (less than a farthing) was so small, that Mr. Wedgwood's objection would seem to be sound, viz. 'that it never could have been the price either of a written or a printed sheet ;' so that this (the usual) explanation is to be doubted. But in Hatzfeld, it is suggested that the coin *gazzetta* was paid, not for the gazette itself, but for the *privilege of reading* it ; and it is added that it was a periodical which appeared at Venice about the middle of the 16th century. γ. *Gazzetta*, a small coin, is prob. a dimin. from L. *gaza*, treasure, wealth, a word borrowed from Gk. γάζα, wealth, a treasury ; which, again, is said to be from Pers. *ganj*, a treasure. ¶ The word *gazet*, a small coin, occurs in Massinger, Maid of Honour, iii. 1 (speech by *Jacomo*), and in Ben Jonson, The Fox, ii. 1 (speech by *Peregrine*). Der. *gazett-eer*, orig. a writer for a gazette, now used to denote a geographical dictionary (since 1704).

GEAR, dress, harness, tackle. (Scand.) ME. *gere*, Chaucer, C. T. 354 (A 352). – Icel. *gervi*, *görvi*, gear, apparel. Cf. *görr*, *geyrr*, skilled, dressed, pp. of *göra*, to make.+AS. *gearwe*, pl. fem., preparation, dress, ornament ; Grein, i. 495 ; whence was formed the verb *gearwian*, to prepare ; allied to AS. *gearo*, yare, ready. Also to OHG. *garawi*, MHG. *garwe*, gear ; whence OF. *garbe*, and E. *garb* ; see **Garb** (1). See **Gar** (2) ; and **Yare**. Der. *gear*, verb ; *gear-ing*.

GECK, a dupe. (Du.) In Tw. Nt. v. 351. – Du. *gek*, MDu. *geck*, a fool, sot ; cf. G. *geck* (the same) ; Dan. *gjek*, a fool ; Icel. *gikkr*, a pert, rude person ; Norw. *gjekk*, a fool (Aasen). ¶ Distinct from *gawk*.

GECKO, a nocturnal lizard. (Malay.) Spelt *gekko* by Goldsmith in 1774 (N.E.D.). – Malay *gēkoq*, a gecko : so named from an imitation of its cry.

GED, the fish called a pike. (Scand.) A North. E. word. – Icel. *gedda*, a pike ; Swed. *gädda* ; Dan. *gedde* (Larsen). Allied to Icel. *gaddr*, a goad ; see **Gad** (1). Named from the sharp thin head ; whence also the name 'pike.' So also *gar-fish*, q.v.

GEHENNA, the place of torture, hell. (L. – Gk. – Heb.) '*Gehenna*, hell ;' Cockeram (1623) ; cf. Milton, P. L. i. 405. – L. *gehenna* ; Matt. v. 22 (Vulg.). – Gk. γέεννα ; Matt. v. 22. – Late Heb. *gē(i)hinnōm*, hell, the valley of Hinnom ; more fully, 'the valley of the son of Hinnom ;' Jer. vii. 31.

GELATINE, a substance which dissolves in hot water and cools as a jelly. (F. – Ital. – L.) '*Gelatina*, any sort of clear gummy juice ;' Kersey's Dict., ed. 1715. The mod. form is French. – F. *gélatine*. – Ital. and Late L. *gelatina*, as cited by Kersey ; formed from L. *gelātus*, pp. of *gelāre*, to congeal. – L. *gelu*, frost ; see **Gelid**. Der. *gelatin-ate*, *gelatin-ous*. From the same source, *jelly*.

GELD, to emasculate. (Scand.) ME. *gelden* ; Wyclif, Matt. xix. 12. '*Geldyn*, castro, testiculo, emasculo ;' Prompt. Parv. p. 190. – Icel. *gelda* ; Swed. *gälla* (for *gälda*) ; Dan. *gilde*. Cf. Icel. *geldr*, Swed. *gall*, barren ; and see **Galt** (2). Possibly related to Goth. *giltha*, a sickle ; Mark, iv. 29. Der. *geld-er* ; also *geld-ing*, Chaucer, C. T. 693 (A 691), from Icel. *gelding*, a gelding = Swed. *gälling* = Dan. *gilding*. On the suffix *-ing*, see March, A. S. Gram. sect. 228.

GELID, cool, cold. (L.) 'Dwells in their *gelid* pores;' Thomson, Autumn, 642. 'Or *gelid* hail;' Chapman, tr. of Homer, Il. xv. 162. — L. *gelidus*, cool, cold. — L. *gelu*, frost. Brugmann, i. § 481. See **Cool**. Der. *gelid-ly*, *gelid-ness*.

GEM, a precious stone. (F. — L.) ME. *gemme*; Chaucer, C. T. 8130 (E 254). — OF. *gemme*, 'a gem;' Cot. — L. *gemma*, a swelling bud; also a gem, jewel; whence also AS. *gim*. β. Of uncertain origin; prob. connected with Skt. *janman*, birth, production; so that *gemma* is for *gen-ma* (√ GEN). Brugmann, i. § 413 (4). Der. *gemmi-fer-ous*, bud-bearing (L. *ferre*, to bear); *gemmi-par-ous*, bud-producing (L. *parere*, to produce); *gemmate*, having buds (L. *gemmātus*, pp. of *gemmāre*, to bud); *gemmat-ion*.

GEMINI, twins. (L.) The name of a sign of the Zodiac. 'He was that time in *Geminis*;' Chaucer, C. T. 10096 (E 2222); where *Geminis* is the ablative case. — L. *geminī*, pl., twins; pl. of *geminus*, double. Der. *gemin-ous*, double (= L. *geminus*, double), Sir T. Browne, Vulg. Errors, b. iii. c. 15. § 4; *gemin-at-ion*, a doubling, Bacon, Colours of Good and Evil, sect. 8.

GEMSBOK, a large antelope in S. Africa. (Du. — G.) The *Oryx capensis*; a misapplied name, as it orig. meant a male chamois. — Du. *gemsbok*, chamois-buck, male chamois (Calisch). — G. *gemsbock*, chamois-buck. — G. *gems*, *gemse*, chamois; and *bock*, buck, male. See **Chamois** and **Buck**.

GENDER (1), kind, breed, sex. (F. — L.) ME. *gendre*; Chaucer, Ho. of Fame, i. 18. The *d* is excrescent, as so commonly the case after *n* in English; cf. *tender*, and see *engender*. — OF. (and mod. F.) *genre*, 'kind;' Cot. — L. *genere*, abl. case of *genus*, kind, kin, cognate with E. *kin*; see **Genus** and **Kin**. ¶ The unusual deriv. from the abl. case is due to the frequent use of the L. ablative in such phrases as *genere natus*, *hōc genere*, *omnī genere*, &c.; cf. Ital. *genere*, kind. See below. **Doublet**, *genre*.

GENDER (2), to engender, produce. (F. — L.) ME. *gendren*, Wyclif, Acts, vii. 8 (where the Vulgate has *genuit*). — OF. *gendrer* (Godefroy). — L. *generāre*, to beget. — L. *gener-*, for *genes*, stem of *genus*, kind, kin (above). Der. *en-gender*.

GENEALOGY, a pedigree of a family, descent by birth. (F. — L. — Gk.) ME. *genologie*, Wyclif, Heb. vii. 3 (where the Vulgate has *genealogia*). — OF. *genealogie*, 'a genealogy, pedegree;' Cot. — L. *genealogia*. — Gk. γενεαλογία, an account of a family; 1 Tim. i. 4. — Gk. γενεά, birth, race, descent; and -λογία, an account, from λέγειν, to speak of. Cf. Gk. γένος, birth, race, descent; see **Genus** and **Logic**. Der. *genealog-ic-al*, *genealog-ic-al-ly*, *genealog-ist*.

GENERAL, relating to a genus or class, common, prevalent. (F. — L.) 'The viker *general* of alle;' Gower, C. A. i. 253; bk. ii. 2804. Chaucer has the adv. *generally*, C. T. 17277 (H 328). — OF. *general*, 'generall, universall;' Cot. — L. *generālis*, belonging to a genus. — L. *gener-*, for *genes*, stem of *genus*, a race. See **Genus**. Der. *general*, sb., esp. in the phrase *in general*, Gower, C. A. iii. 189; bk. vii. 3088, and in the sense of 'leader,' All's Well, iii. 3. 1; *general-ly*; *general-ship*; also *general-ise*, *general-is-at-ion*; also *general-i-ty* (Hooker, Eccl. Polity, ed. Church, b. i. sect. 6. subsect. 4), from OF. *generalité*, 'generality, generallness,' Cot.; also *general-iss-i-mo*, supreme commander (see examples in Todd's Johnson), from Ital. *generalissimo*, a supreme commander, formed with the superlative suffix -*is-simo*-, which has not been fully explained (Brugmann, ii. § 73).

GENERATE, to produce. (L.) Orig. a pp., as in 'all other . . from them *generate*,' i.e. born, Hawes, Past. of Pleasure, ch. 44, st. 14. The verb is in Bacon, Nat. Hist. § 758. — L. *generātus*, pp. of *generāre*, to procreate, produce; see **Gender** (2). Der. *generat-or*, *generat-ive*; also *generation* (Wyclif, Mark, viii. 12), from OF. *generation* < L. acc. *generātiōnem*, from nom. *generātio*.

GENERIC, pertaining to a genus. (L.) The older word, in E., is *generical*. '*Generical*, pertaining to a kindred;' Blount's Gloss., ed. 1674; and found in a fifteenth century tr. of Higden; vol. i. p. 27. A coined word, with suffix -*c* (or -*c-al*) from L. *generi-*, decl. stem of *genus*; see **Genus**. Der. *generical-ly*.

GENEROUS, of a noble nature. (F. — L.) 'The *generous* [noble] and gravest citizens;' Meas. for Meas. iv. 6. 13. — MF. *genereux* [older form *genereus*], 'generous;' Cot. — L. *generōsus*, of noble birth; formed with suffix -*ōsus* from *gener-*, for *genes*, stem of *genus*; see **Genus**. Der. *generous-ly*, *generous-ness*; also *generos-i-ty* (Coriol. i. 1. 215), from OF. *generosité* < L. acc. *generōsitātem*, from nom. *generōsitās*.

GENESIS, generation, creation. (L. — Gk.) L. *genesis*, the name of the first book of the Bible in the Vulgate version. — Gk. γένεσις, origin, source. From √ GEN, to beget.

GENET, a carnivorous animal, allied to the civet. (F. — Span. — Arab.) '*Genet*, a kind of cat;' Kersey's Dict., ed. 1715. Spelt *gennet* in Skinner, ed. 1671. Caxton has *genete*, Reynard the Fox, ch. 31. — F. *genette*, 'a kind of weesell, black-spotted, and bred in

Spain;' Cot. — Span. *gineta*, a genet. — Arab. *jarneit*, cited by Dozy, who refers to the Journal Asiatique, Juin, 1849, p. 541.

GENIAL, cheering, merry. (F. — L.) In Spenser, Epithalamium, 399. — MF. *genial*, 'geniall, belonging to luck or chance, or to a man's nature, disposition, inclination;' Cot. — L. *geniālis*, pleasant, delightful. — L. *genius*, genius; also, social enjoyment. See **Genius**. Der. *genial-ly*, *genial-ness*, *genial-i-ty*.

GENICULATE, jointed. (L.) A botanical term. Bailey gives it in the L. form, viz. '*geniculatus*, jointed;' vol. ii., ed. 1731. [Cockeram has the verb *geniculate*, 'to ioynt.'] — L. *geniculum*, a little knee, a knot or joint in a plant. Formed, with suffixes -*cu*- and -*l*-, from *geni*-, for *genu*, a knee; cognate with E. *knee*. See **Knee**.

GENIE, a demon; see **Jinn**.

GENITAL, belonging to generation. (F. — L.) In Wyclif, Numb. xxv. 8. — OF. *genital*, 'genitall, fit for breed, apt to beget;' Cot. — L. *genitālis*, generative. — L. *genitum*, supine of *gignere*, to beget. *Gignere* (= *gi-gn-ere*) is a reduplicated form, from √ GEN, to beget; cf. Gk. γίγνομαι = γί-γν-ομαι; and Skt. *jan*, to beget. See **Genus**. Der. *genitals*, pl. sb., which occurs in Gower, C. A. ii. 156; bk. v. 855.

GENITIVE, the name of a case in grammar. (F. — L.) In Shak. Merry Wives, iv. 1. 59. The suffix -*ive* is a substitution for an older -*if*, answering to F. -*if*, from L. -*īuus*. — OF. *genitif*, 'the genitive case;' Cot. — L. *genetīuus*, lit. of or belonging to generation or birth, applied in grammar to a particular case of nouns. — L. *genitum*, supine of *gignere*, to beget. See above.

GENIUS, a spirit; inborn faculty. (L.) See Shak. Macb. iii. 1. 56; Jul. Cæsar, ii. 1. 66; Spenser, F. Q. ii. 12. 47; Gower, C. A. i. 48; bk. i. 196. — L. *genius*, the tutelar spirit of a person; also, inclination, wit, talent; lit. 'inborn nature.' From the weak grade of √ GEN, to produce, beget. See **Genus**. Der. *genii*, pl., *genius-es*, pl.; also *geni-al*, q. v.

GENNET, a Spanish horse; see **Jennet**.

GENRE, a style of painting, depicting ordinary life. (F. — L.) A peculiar use of F. *genre*, kind, style; see **Gender** (1).

GENTEEL, lit. belonging to a noble race, well-bred, graceful. (F. — L.) ''Tis the most *genteel* [old ed. *gentile*] and received wear now, sir;' Ben Jonson, Cynthia's Revels, i. 1 (Asotus). A doublet of *gentle*; it arose at the end of the 16th century, and was at first spelt *gentile*, with the *i* sounded as in French (N. E. D.). — MF. *gentil*, 'gentle, . . . gracious, . . . also Gentile;' Cot. — L. *gentīlis*, orig. belonging to the same clan; also, a gentile. See **Gentile**. Der. *genteel-ly*, *genteel-ness*; also *gentil-i-ty*, As You Like It, i. 2. 22. **Doublet**, *gentle*; also *gentile*.

GENTIAN, the name of a plant. (F. — L.) In Minsheu. ME. *genciane*; Med. Wks. of 14th cent., ed. Henslow, p. 131. — OF. *gentiane*, 'gentian, bitterwort;' Cot. — L. *gentiāna*, gentian. So named after the Illyrian king *Gentius* (about B.C. 180), who was the first to discover its properties; see Pliny, Nat. Hist. xxv. 7.

GENTILE, a pagan. (F. — L.) In Shak. Merch. of Ven. ii. 6. 51. Fabyan has *Gentyle*; Pt. v. ch. 82 (end). — OF. *gentil*, 'gentle, . . . Gentile;' Cot. — L. *gentīlis*, a gentile, lit. belonging to the same clan. — L. *genti-*, decl. stem of *gens*, a tribe, clan, race. From √ GEN, to beget, produce. **Doublet**, *gentle*; also, *genteel*.

GENTLE, docile, mild. (F. — L.) ME. *gentil*. 'So hardy and so *gentil*;' Rob. of Glouc. p. 167; l. 3482. 'Noble men and *gentile* and of heh burðe' [high birth]; O. Eng. Homilies, i. 273. — OF. *gentil*, 'gentle;' Cot. — L. *gentīlis*. See **Gentile** and **Genteel**. Der. *gentl-y*, *gentle-ness*; *gentle-man* (ME. *gentelman*, Gower, C. A. ii. 78; bk. iv. 2275); *gentle-woman* (ME. *gentilwomman*, Chaucer, C. T. 15893; G 425); *gentle-man-ly*, *gentle-folks*; also *gent-ry*, q. v.

GENTRY, rank by birth; gentlefolks. (F. — L.) ME. *gentrie*. 'To pryde him of his *gentrye* is ful greet folye; for ofte tyme the *gentrye* of the body binimeth [taketh away] the *gentrye* of the soule;' Chaucer, Pers. Tale, De Superbia; I 461. Shortened from the older form *gentrise*; see P. Plowman, C. xxi. 21, where we find the various spellings *gentrise*, *gentrice*, *genterise*, and *gentrye*. — OF. *genterise*, rank, formed from OF. *gentilise*, by the change of *l* into *r* (Godefroy). *Gentilise* is formed, with OF. suffix -*ice*, -*ise* (-*itia*), from the adj. *gentil*, gentle. See **Gentle**.

GENUFLECTION, GENUFLEXION, a bending of the knee. (F. — L.) Spelt *genuflexion* in Howell's Letters, b. iii. let. 2. § 2. — F. *genuflexion*, 'a bending of the knee;' Cot. — Late L. acc. *genūflexiōnem*, from nom. *genūflexio*; Ducange. — L. *genū*, the knee; and *flexus*, pp. of *flectere*, to bend. See **Knee** and **Flexible**. ¶ The correcter spelling is with *x*; cf. L. *flexio*, a bending.

GENUINE, of the true stock, natural, real. (L.) 'The last her *genuine* laws which stoutly did retain;' Drayton, Polyolbion, s. 9. l. 14. — L. *genuīnus*, innate, genuine. From the base *genu*- (for *genwo*-), an extension of the base *gen*- as seen in *genus*, &c. — √ GEN, to beget. See **Genus**. Der. *genuine-ly*, *genuine-ness*.

GENUS, breed, race, kin. (L.) In Blount's Gloss., ed. 1674.

First in 1551, as a term in logic. — L. *genus* (stem *gener-*, for *genes-*), race; cognate with E. *kin*; see **Kin**. —√GEN, to beget; cf. Skt. *jan*, to beget; Gk. γέν-ος, race; &c. Brugmann, i. § 604. **Doublet**, *kin*, q.v. Der. *gener-a*, pl.; *gener-ic*, *gener-ic-al*, *gener-ic-al-ly*. From the same root, *gener-al*, *gener-ate*, *gener-ous*; *gender*, *en-gender*, *con-gener*; *gen-i-us*, *gen-i-al*, *gen-it-al*, *con-gen-it-al*; *gen-it-ive*, *gen-u-ine*, *gen-t-ile*, *gen-t-le*, *gen-t-eel*; *con-gen-i-al*; *de-gen-er-ate*, *indi-gen-ous*, *in-gen-i-ous*, *in-gen-u-ous*, *pro-gen-i-tor*, *pro-gen-y*, *re-gener-ate*, &c. Also, from the Gk., *gen-e-a-logy*, *gen-esis*, *hetero-gen-e-ous*, *homo-gen-e-ous*; *endo-gen*, *exo-gen*, *hydro-gen*, *oxy-gen*, *nitro-gen*, &c.

GEOGRAPHY, a description of the earth. (F. — L. — Gk.) In Minsheu (1627). — MF. *geographie*, 'geography;' Cot. — L. *geographia*. — Gk. γεωγραφία, geography, lit. earth-description. — Gk. γεω- = γηο-, combining form of γῆ, earth, land; and -γραφία, description, from γραφεῖν, to write. Der. *geograph-er*, *geograph-ic-al*. From the same form *geo-* as a prefix, we have numerous derivatives, such as *geo-centr-ic* (see **Centre**), *geo-logy* (from Gk. λέγειν, to speak of), *geo-mancy* (from Gk. μαντεία, divination, through the French); and other scientific terms. See also **Geometry** and **Georgic**.

GEOMETRY, the science of measurement. (F. — L. — Gk.) ME. *geometrie*, Gower, C. A. iii. 90; bk. vii. 178. — OF. *geometrie*, 'geometry;' Cot. — L. *geōmetria*. — Gk. γεωμετρία, lit. 'the measurement of land.' — Gk. γεω- (as above), belonging to land; and -μετρια, measurement, from μετρέω, I measure, which is from μέτρον, a measure. See **Metre**. Der. *geometr-ic*, *geometr-ic-al*, *geometr-ic-al-ly*, *geometr-ic-i-an*, *geometer*.

GEORGIC, a poem on husbandry. (L. — Gk.) 'Georgicks, bookes intreating of the tillage of the ground;' Minsheu, ed. 1627. The title of four books on husbandry by Virgil. — L. *geōrgica*, neut. pl. (for *georgica carmina* = georgic poems). — L. *geōrgicus*, relating to husbandry. — Gk. γεωργικός, relating to husbandry. — Gk. γεωργία, tillage. — Gk. γεωργεῖν, to till. — Gk. γεω- (as above), relating to the earth; and *ἔργγειν* > ἔρδειν, to work. See **Geography** and **Work**. Der. *George* = Gk. γεωργός, a farmer.

GERANIUM, a kind of plant. (L. — Gk.) Sometimes called *crane's-bill* or *stork's-bill*. First in Turner (1548). ' *Geranium*, storkbill or herb robert;' Kersey's Dict., ed. 1715. — L. *geranium*, Latinised from Gk. γεράνιον, a geranium, crane's bill (from the shape of the seed-pod). — Gk. γέρανος, a crane; cognate with **Crane**.

GERFALCON, a kind of falcon; see **Gyrfalcon**.

GERM, a seed. (F. — L.) Sir T. Browne speaks of the 'germ of . . . an egg;' Vulg. Errors, b. iii. c. 28, § 3. — F. *germe*, 'a young shute, sprout;' Cot. — L. *germen* (stem *germin-*), a sprout, shoot, bud. Der. *germin-al*, *germin-ate*, *germin-at-ion*, from the s^tem *germin-*; from the same source, *german*, q.v., *germane*. **Doublet**, *germen*, Macbeth, iv. 1. 59.

GERMAN, **GERMANE**, akin. (F. — L.) Nearly obsolete, except in quotations and in the phrase *cousins-german* or *cousinsgermans*, i.e. cousins having the same grandfather. In Shak. Wint. Ta. iv. 4. 802; Timon, iv. 3. 344; Hamlet, v. 2. 165. Formerly also spelt *germain*, as in Cotgrave, and orig. derived rather from the French than Latin. The phrase ' cosins *germains*' (with the pl. adj. in *s* according to the F. idiom) is in Chaucer, Tale of Melibeus, C. T. Group B, 2558. — OF. *germain*, 'germaine, come of the same stock;' Cot. — L. *germānus*, fully akin, said of brothers and sisters having the same parents. Allied to **Germ**.

GERMANDER, a plant. (F. — Late L. — Gk.) In Bacon, Essay 46 (Of Gardens). ' *Germandre*, herbe, *germandré*;' Palsgrave. — F. *germandrée*, germander (Cotgrave). — OF. *gemandree* (Supp. to Godefroy, s.v. *germandree*); cf. G. *gamander*. — Late L. *gamandria*, a popular alteration of Late Gk. χαμανδρυά. — Gk. χαμαίδρυς, germander, lit. 'ground-tree,' or low-growing tree. — Gk. χαμαί, on the ground; δρῦς, tree. See **Chameleon** and **Tree**.

GERMEN, **GERMINAL**, **GERMINATE**; see **Germ**.

GERUND, a part of a Latin verb. (L.) The derivative *gerundive*, misprinted *gerundine*, is used as a coined word in Beaum. and Fletcher, Wit at Several Weapons, i. 2 (speech of Wittypate). — L. *gerundium*, a gerund. — L. *gerundum*, that which is to be done or carried on; an adj. formed from *gerere*, to carry on, perform; pp. *ges-tus*. (√GES.) Der. *gerund-i-al* (from *gerundi-um*). See also below.

GESTATION, the carrying of young in the womb. (F. — L.) It occurs in the Index to Holland's tr. of Pliny. — MF. *gestation*, 'a bearing, or carrying;' Cot. — L. acc. *gestātiōnem*, from nom. *gestātio*, a carrying. — L. *gestā-re*, to carry; frequentative form of *gerere*, to carry. See above. Der. *gestat-or-y*.

GESTICULATE, to make gestures. (L.) 'Or what their servile apes *gesticulate*;' Ben Jonson, Poetaster, To the Reader (an Epilogue). — L. *gesticulātus*, pp. of *gesticulāri*, to make mimic gestures. — L. *gesticulus*, a mimic gesture; formed, with suffixes *-cu-* and *-l-*, from *gesti-* = *gestu-*, for *gestus*, a gesture. — L. *gestus*, pp. of *gerere*,

to carry; reflexively, to behave. See **Gerund**. Der. *gesticulat-ion*, *gesticulat-or*, *gesticulat-or-y*.

GESTURE, a movement of the body. (L.) In Shak. Temp. iii. 3. 37. ME. *gestúre*, Sir Cleges (Weber), l. 483. — Late L. *gestūra*, a mode of action. — L. *gest-us*, pp. of *gerere*, to carry; reflexively, to behave oneself. See **Gerund** and **Gesticulate**.

GET, to seize, obtain, acquire. (Scand.) ME. *geten*, pt. t. *gat*, pp. *geten*; Chaucer, C. T. 5792, 293 (D 210, A 291). — Icel. *geta*, pt. t. *gat*, pp. *getinn*. + AS. *-getan*, *-gietan*, only in the compounds *on-gitan*, *and-gitan*, *for-gitan*, *be-gitan*, &c.; Grein, ii. 346, i. 511; Goth. *-gitan*, in the comp. *bi-gitan*, to find, obtain. + L. *-hendere* (base *hed*), in the comp. *prehendere*, to seize; Gk. χανδάνειν (base χαδ), to seize; Russ. *gad-ate*, to conjecture. (√GHwED.) Brugmann, i. § 632. Der. *gett-er*, *gett-ing*; *be-get*, *for-get*; from the same root are *ap-pre-hend*, *com-pre-hend*, *re-pre-hend*, &c.; also *apprise*, *comprise*, *enterprise*, *surprise*; *impregnable*, &c.

GEWGAW, a plaything, specious trifle. (Scand.?) 'Gewgaws and gilded puppets;' Beaum. and Fletcher, Four Plays in One, Triumph of Time, sc. 1. Spelt *gewgaudes*, id. Woman's Prize, i. 4 (Rowland). Also *gugawes*, Holinshed, Descr. of Ireland, c. 4. 'He counteth them for *gygawis*;' Skelton, Why Come Ye Nat to Court, 1060. Cotgrave explains *babiole* as 'a trifle, whimwham, *gugaw*, or small toy;' and *fariboles* as 'trifles, nifles, flim-flams, *why-whaws*, idle discourses.' The latter form *why-whaw* is a mere imitation of the older *gugaw*. [The form *gugaw* seems to answer to ME. *giuegoue* (= *givegove*?); 'worldes weole, ant wunne, ant wurschipe, ant oðer swuche *giuegouen*' = the world's wealth and joy and worship, and other such gewgaws; Ancren Riwle, p. 196; but the pronunciation of this ME. word is uncertain; and it cannot be safely identified with *gewgaw*.] β. One sense of *gewgaw* is a Jew's harp; cf. Walloon *gawe*, a Jew's harp (Grandgagnage). Cf. Swed. dial. *guva*, to blow; Norw. *guva*, *gyva* (pt. t. *gauv*), to reek; *gufs*, a puff. The ME. *gwgawe* (Prompt. Parv., p. 168) means a flute or pipe. See Notes on E. Etym., p. 116.

GEYSIR, a hot spring in Iceland. (Icelandic.) 'Geysir, the name of a famous hot spring in Iceland. . . . The word *geysir* = "a gusher," must be old, as the inflexive *-ir* is hardly used but in obsolete words;' Cleasby and Vigfusson. — Icel. *geysa*, to gush; formed (with mutation of *au* to *ey*) from *gaus*, as seen in the pt. t. of *gjósa*, to gush; see **Gush**.

GHASTLY, terrible. (E.) The *h* has been inserted, for no very good reason. ME. *gastly*; 'gastly for to see;' Chaucer, C. T. 1986 (A 1984). Formed, with suffix *-ly*, from the ME. *gasten*, AS. *gǣstan*, to terrify. Allied to Goth. *us-gais-jan*, to terrify, and *us-geis-nan*, to be astonished. See further under **Aghast**. ¶ Not to be confused with *ghostly*, q.v. Der. *ghastli-ness*; cf. also *gasted*, K. Lear, ii. 1. 57; *gastness*, Oth. v. 1. 106.

GHAUT, a landing-place, quay, way down to a river, mountainpass. (Hind.) For quotations, see Yule. — Hind. *ghāṭ*; Bengali *ghāṭ* (H. H. Wilson; Forbes, 1848, p. 450).

GHAZAL, an Oriental lyric poem. (Arab.) Spelt *gazel* in T. Moore; Twopenny Postbag, vi. 69. — Arab. *ghazal*, an ode; Rich. Dict. p. 1050.

GHEE, clarified butter. (Hind. — Skt.) See Yule. — Hind. *ghī*. — Skt. *ghṛta*, clarified butter; orig. pp. of *ghṛ*, to sprinkle. (H. H. Wilson.)

GHERKIN, a small cucumber. (Du. — Slav. — Low L. — Gk. — Pers.) The *h* is inserted to keep the *g* hard. 'Gherkins or Guerkins, a sort of pickled cucumbers;' Kersey's Dict., ed. 1715. Spelt *gherkin* in Skinner, ed. 1671. Shortened from **agherkin*. — Du. *agurkje*, a gherkin; cf. 'Gherkins, *agurkes*' in Sewel's Eng.-Du. Dict. ed. 1754. β. Note that the Du. dimin. suffix *-ken* was formerly used (as explained by Ten Kate) where the dimin. suffix *-je* now occurs; so that *agurkje* stands for an older form *agurkken*, whence the E. *gherkin* must have been borrowed, with the loss merely of initial *a*. Koolman gives *augurken* as the EFriesic form. γ. From Polish *ogurek*, Bohem. *okurka*. — Low L. *angūrius*, a water-melon (MItal. *anguria*, a cucumber, Florio). — Late Gk. ἀγγούριον, a water-melon. — Pers. *angārah*, a melon, a cucumber; Rich. Dict. p. 194.

GHOST, a spirit. (E.) The *h* has been inserted. ME. *goost*, *gost*; Chaucer, C. T. 2770 (A 2768). AS. *gāst*, a spirit; Grein, i. 371. + Du. *geest*; G. *geist*, a spirit. Teut. type **gaistoz*. Of uncertain origin; but apparently allied to Icel. *geis-a*, to rage (like fire), and to Goth. *us-gais-jan*, to terrify. Perhaps also to *ghastly*. See **Ghastly**. Cf. Skt. *hēda-s*, anger, wrath of the gods (Macdonell) Brugmann, i. § 785 (c). Der. *ghost-ly*, *ghost-li-ness*.

GHOUL, a kind of demon. (Arab.) Pron. *gool*, to rime with *cool*. — Pers. *ghōl*, an imaginary sylvan demon; supposed to devour men and animals; Arab. *ghuwal* (the same). — Arab. *ghawl*, attacking suddenly and unexpectedly; Rich. Pers. Dict. p. 1062. See Yule.

GIANT, a man of great size. (F. — L. — Gk.) ME. *giant*, more frequently *geant*, *geaunt*; Chaucer, C. T. 13738 (B 1997); King Alisaunder, 3465. – OF. *geant*, 'a giant;' Cot. – L. acc. *gigantem*, from nom. *gigas*, a giant. – Gk. γίγας, a giant (stem γιγαντ-). β. Sometimes explained from Gk. γῆ, the earth, as if the word meant 'earth-born.' Der. *gigant-ic*, q. v.; *giant-ess*.

GIAOUR, an infidel. (Ital. – Pers.) 'In Dr. Clarke's Travels, this word, which means *infidel*, is always written *djour*. Lord Byron adopted the Ital. spelling usual among the Franks of the Levant;' note 14 to Lord Byron's poem of The Giaour. – Pers. *gāwr*, an infidel; Rich. Dict. p. 1227. A variant of Pers. *gabr*, a Gueber; see **Gueber**.

GIBBERISH, nonsensical talk. (E.) Holinshed speaks of 'gibberishing Irish;' Descr. of Ireland, c. 1. 'All kinds of *gibb'rish* he had learnt to know;' Drayton, The Mooncalf, l. 913. Cotgrave has : '*Bagois*, gibridge, strange talke. The hard *g* seems to separate it from the old verb *gibber*, to gabble; Hamlet, i. 1. 116; which is allied to *jabber* and *gabble*. But the *g* in *gibber* may have been sometimes hard, as in *gibble-gabble* (N. E. D.). If so, the derivation is from *gib-*, variant of *gab-*, an imitative utterance; see **Gabble**. β. Johnson's derivation, from *Gebir*, an alchemist of the 8th cent., is unlikely, as the word is not spelt *gebirish*.

GIBBET, a gallows. (F.) ME. *gebet*, *gibet*, Chaucer, Ho. of Fame, i. 106; 'hongen on a *gibet*;' Ancren Riwle, p. 116. – OF. *gibbet*, 'a gibbet;' Cot. (mod. F. *gibet*). β. Of unknown origin; Littré suggests a comparison with OF. *gibet*, a large stick (Roquefort); apparently a dimin. of OF. *gibbe*, a sort of arm, an implement for stirring the earth and rooting up plants, apparently a hoe (Roquefort). Perhaps Scand.; cf. Swed. dial. *gippa*, to jerk up, Norw. *gippa*, *gjeppa*, to jerk up. This form *gippa* seems to be imitated from Swed. *vippa*, to see-saw, to tilt up; cf. MDu. *wippe*, 'a gibbit' (Hexham), Swed. *vipp-galge*, a gibbet.

GIBBON, a kind of ape. (F.) Cf. F. *gibbon*, in Buffon.

GIBBOSE, swelling. (L.) The L. form of the word below.

GIBBOUS, humped, swelling. (F. – L.) 'Its round and *gibbous* back;' Sir T. Browne, Vulg. Errors, b. iii. c. 26. § 5. The suffix *-ous* is for F. *-eux*, by analogy with other words in which *-ous* represents OF. *-ous* (later *-eux*). – F. *gibbeux*, 'hulch, bunched, much swelling;' Cot. – L. *gibbōsus*, hunched. Formed, with suffix *-ōsus*, from L. *gibbus*, a hump, hunch; cf. *gibbus*, bent; *gibber*, a hump. Der. *gibbous-ness*.

GIBE, to mock, taunt. (E.) 'And common courtiers love to *gybe* and fleare;' Spenser, Mother Hubberd's Tale, 714. Of imitative origin; cf. EFries. *gibeln*, to mock; Du. *gijbelen*, to sneer. Note also Swed. dial. *gipa*, to gape, also, to talk rashly and foolishly (Rietz); Icel. *geipa*, to talk nonsense; Icel. *geip*, idle talk; Norw. *geipa*, to make grimaces. ¶ Also spelt *jibe*. Der. *gibe*, sb.

GIBLETS, the various parts of a fowl that are removed before cooking. (F.) 'And set the hare's head against the goose *gyblets*;' Harrington's tr. of Orlando Furioso, b. xliii. st. 136 (R.); the date of the 1st edition is 1591. 'May feed on *giblet-pie*;' Dryden, tr. of Persius, vi. 172. 'Sliced beef, *giblets*, and pettitoes;' Beaum. and Fletcher, Woman-hater, i. 2. ME. *gibelet*; see Wright's Vocab. i. 179. – OF. *gibelet*, which, according to Littré, is the old form of F. *gibelotte*, stewed rabbit. Of unknown origin; not necessarily related to OF. *gibier*, game.

GIDDY, unsteady, dizzy. (E.) ME. *gidi*, *gydi*; Rob. of Glouc. p. 68; l. 1542. Late AS. *gidig*, frantic; in Napier's Glosses; for earlier **gydig*, as shown by the hard *g*. Teut. type **gudigoz*, i.e. possessed by a god (like Gk. ἔνθεος). – Teut. type **gudom*, a god. See **God**. Der. *giddi-ly*, *giddi-ness*.

GIER-EAGLE, a kind of eagle. (Du. and F.) In Levit. xi. 18. The first syllable is Dutch, from Du. *gier*, a vulture; cognate with G. *geier*, MHG. *gīr*, a vulture. Allied to G. *gier-ig*, greedy, and to E. **Yearn**. See **Gyrfalcon**. The word *eagle* is F. See **Eagle**.

GIFT, a thing given, present. (E.) ME. *gift*, commonly *jift*, *jeft*; Rob. of Glouc. p. 122, l. 2600; P. Plowman, B. iii. 99. [The word is perhaps rather Scand. than E.] AS. *gift*, *gyft*, rare in the sing., but common in the pl. (when it often has the sense of 'nuptials,' with reference to the marriage dowry). In Bosworth's Dict. is given a passage from the Laws of Ine, no. 31, in which the word *gyft* appears as a fem. sing., with the sense of 'dowry;' see Thorpe's Ancient Laws, i. 122, sect. 31. Or from Icel. *gift*, *gipt* (pron. *gift*), a gift. **+** Du. *gift*, a gift, present; Goth. *-gibts*, *-gifts*, only in comp. *fragibts*, *fragifts*, promise, gift, espousal; G. *-gift*, in comp. *mitgift*, a dowry. β. All from the corresponding verb, with the suffix *-t*, for *-ti-*; Teut. type **giftiz*, fem. See **Give**. Der. *gift-ed*; *heavengifted*, Milton, Samson Agon. 36.

GIG, a light carriage, a light boat. (Scand.) The orig. idea is that of anything that easily whirls or twirls about. In Shak. *gig* means a boy's top; L. L. L. iv. 3. 167; v. 1. 70, 73. Cf. *whirligig*. [In Chaucer, Ho. of Fame, iii. 852, we have : 'This hous was also ful of *gigges*;' where the sense is uncertain; it may be 'full of whirling

things;' since we find 'ful .. of other werkinges'=full of *other* movements, immediately below.] β. The hard *g* shows it to be of Scand. origin, as distinguished from *jig*, the French form. Cf. Norw. *giga*, to totter, shake about; *gigra*, *gigla*, to shake about (Ross); the latter is the prov. E. *jiggle*, E. D. D. Also Norw. *geiga*, to swing one's arms about (Ross). See **Jig**.

GIGANTIC, giant-like. (L. – Gk.) In Milton, P. L. xi. 659; Sams. Agon. 1249. A coined word, from the decl. stem *giganti-* of L. *gigas*, a giant; see **Giant**.

GIGGLE, to laugh lightly, titter. (E.) '*Giggle*, to laugh out, laugh wantonly;' Kersey's Dict., ed. 1715. 'A set of *gigglers*;' Spectator, no. 158. 'Some *gygyll* and lawgh;' Barclay, Ship of Fools, i. 63. An attenuated form of ME. *gagelen*, 'to gaggle,' or make a noise like a goose. '*Gagelin*, or cryyn as gees, *clingo*;' Prompt. Parv. p. 184. Cf. Icel. *gagl*, a goose; EFries. *gicheln*, Low G. *giggeln* (Danneil), G. *kichern*, to giggle. A frequentative form, from an imitative root. See **Cackle**. Der. *giggle*, sb., *giggl-er*.

GIGLET, **GIGLOT**, a wanton woman. (Scand.; with F. suffix.) In Shak. Meas. for Meas. v. 352; 1 Hen. VI, iv. 7. 41. Earlier, in Prompt. Parv. p. 194; and see the note. Cf. *giglotrye*, giddiness; How the Good Wife taught her Daughter, l. 159 (in Barbour's Bruce, ed. Skeat). A dimin., with suffix *-et* or *-ot*, from an older *giggle* or *gigle*. Cotgrave has : 'Gadrouillette, a minx, *gigle*, flirt, callet, *gixie*.' Here again, *gig-le* and *gixie* (=*gig-sy*) are connected with ME. *gigge*, a flighty girl, Plowman's Tale, 759 (cf. Ancren Riwle, p. 204; N. E. D.). Prob. from the base *gig*, applied to rapid motion, and thence to lightness of behaviour. See **Gig, Giggle**.

GILD, to overlay with gold. (E.) ME. *gilden*, Wyclif, Exod. xxvi. 29. AS. *gyldan*; only in the pp. *gegyld*, A. S. Psalter, ed. Spelman, xliv. 11 (xlv. 9); and in comp. *be-gyldan*, *ofer-gyldan*. Teut. type **gulthjan-*. The *y* is the usual substitution, by vowelchange, for an original *u*, which appears in the Goth. *gulth*, gold. Cf. Icel. *gylla* (for *gylda*), to gild. See **Gold**. Der. *gilt*, contracted form of *gild-ed*; *gild-er*, *gild-ing*.

GILL (1), an organ of respiration in fishes. (Scand.) '*Gylle* of a fische, *branchia*;' Prompt. Parv. Spelt *gile*, Wyclif, Tobit, vi. 4. Allied to Dan. *giælle*, a gill; Swed. *gäl*; MDan. *gælle*, MSwed. *gel*. Cf. Gk. χεῖλος, Æolic χέλλος, a lip.

GILL (2), a ravine, yawning chasm. (Scand.) Also spelt *ghyll*; common in place-names, as Dungeon *Ghyll*. – Icel. *gil*, a deep narrow glen with a stream at the bottom; Norw. *gil*; and cf. Icel. *geil*, a ravine; Swed. dial. *gilja*, a defile.

GILL (3), with *g* soft; a quarter of a pint. (F. – L. ?) ME. *gille*, *gylle*; P. Plowman, B. v. 346 (where it is written *Ille*=*jille*). – OF. *gelle*, a sort of measure for wine; Roquefort. Cf. Low L. *gillo*, a wine-vessel; *gella*, a wine-vessel, wine-measure; Ducange. Godefroy equates OF. *gille*, *gelle* with OF. *gerle*, a jar; cf. Ital. *gerla*, a basket. Possibly from Late L. *gerula*, a basket carried on the back, also, a measure of wine (Ducange). From L. *gerere*, to carry (Körting, § 4233).

GILL (4), with *g* soft; a woman's name; ground-ivy. (F. – L.) The name *Gill* is short for *Gillian*, which is in Shak. Com. Errors, iii. 1. 31. And *Gillian* is from F. *Juliane*, from L. *Iuliāna*. This personal fem. name is formed from L. *Iulius*; see **July**. β. The ground-ivy was hence called *Gill-creep-by-the-ground* (Halliwell); or briefly *Gill-go-by-the-ground* (Hall.); the herb ale-hoof (Hall.); *Gill-burnt-tail*, an ignis fatuus; *Gill-hooter*, an owl; *Gill-flirt*, a wanton girl; *flirt-gill*, the same, Romeo, ii. 4. 162. St. Juliana's day is Feb. 16.

GILLIE, a boy, page, menial. (C.) Used by Sir W. Scott; but Spenser also speaks of 'the Irish horse-boyes or *cuilles*, as they call them;' View of the State of Ireland, Globe ed., p. 641, col. 2. – Gael. *gille*, *giolla*, Irish *giolla*, a boy, lad, youth, man-servant, lacquey; OIrish *gilla*, a servant.

GILLYFLOWER, a kind of flower, a carnation, a stock. (F. – L. – Gk.) Spelt *gelliflowres* in Spenser, Shep. Kal. April, 137. Spelt *gilloflower* by Cotgrave. By the common change of *r* to *l*, *gilloflower* stands for *giroflower*, spelt *gerafloure* in The Kingis Quair, st. 190; where the ending *flower* is a mere E. corruption, like the *fish* in *crayfish*, q. v. – MF. *giroflée*, 'a gilloflower; and most properly, the clove gilloflower;' Cot. β. Here we have *clove-gilloflower* as the full form of the name, which is Chaucer's *clowe gilofre*, C. T. 13692 (B 1952); thus confirming the above derivation. γ. From F. *clou de girofle*, where *clou* is from L. *clāuus*, a nail (see **Clove**); and *girofle* is from Late L. *caryophyllum*, a Latinised form of Gk. καρυόφυλλον, strictly 'nut-leaf,' a clove-tree. (Hence the name means 'nut-leaf,' or 'nut-leaved clove.') – Gk. κάρυο-, for κάρυον, a nut; and φύλλον, a leaf (=L. *folium*, whence E. *foli-age*).

GIMBALS, a contrivance for suspending a ship's compass so as to keep it always horizontal. (F. – L.) The contrivance is one which admits of a double movement. The name *gimbals* is formed (with excrescent *b*) from the older word *gimmals*, also called a *gemmow* or *gemmow-ring*. See also *gimbol* and *gimmal* in Halliwell; and the remarks in Nares. 'Gemmow, or Gemmow-ring, a double ring, with two or more links;' Kersey's Dict., ed. 1715. In Shak. 'a gimmal bit' is a horse's bit made with linked rings; Hen. V, iv. 2. 49. 'Item,... pro haspis, *gemewis*, et clauis;' Earl of Derby's Expeditions, p. 221, l. 29 (1392). The forms *gemmow* and *gimmal* correspond to MF. *gemeau* and OF. *gemel*, a twin. ─ L. *gemellus*, a twin; a dimin. form from L. *geminus*, double. See **Gemini**.

GIMLET, GIMBLET, a tool for boring holes. (F. ─ Teut.) 'And see there the *gimblets*, how they make their entry;' Ben Jonson, The Devil is an Ass, i. 1. ME. *gymlot*, Lydgate, Assembly of Gods, l. 357. ─ MF. *guimbelet*, 'a gimlet or piercer;' Cot. = mod. F. *gibelet* (by loss of *m*). Formerly (better) spelt *guimbelet* (Godefroy); Norm. dial. *guimblet*, *vimblet* (Moisy). Spelt *guinbelet* in 1412 (Godefroy). A dimin. of *wimble*, as shown by the Norm. dial. *vimbl-et*. See **Wimble**. And cf. Icel. *vindla*, to wind up, Norw. *vindel*, a gimlet (Ross).

GIMMAL, GIMMAL-RING; see **Gimbals**.

GIMP (with hard *g*), a kind of trimming, made with twisted silk, wool, or cotton. (F. ─ Teut.) 'My *guimp* petticoat;' Dryden, Marriage-a-la-Mode, iii. 1. 'Gimp, a sort of mohair thread covered with the same, or a twist for several works formerly in use;' Bailey's Dict., vol. ii. ed. 1731. [It seems to have been influenced by confusion with F. *guimpe*, a wimple, OF. *guimple*, whence OF. *guimpler*, to adorn, attire (Godefroy), and MF. *guimpier*, a maker of wimples. See **Wimple.**] Cf. also Low G. *gimpen*, gimp (Berghaus). In sense it answers to the F. *guipure*, a thread of silk lace. The F. *guipure* is of Teutonic origin, from the base *wip-, to twist or bind round, appearing in Goth. *weipan*, to crown. See **Guipure.**

GIN (1), to begin. (E.; pron. with *g* hard.) Obsolete; or only used as a supposed contraction of *begin*, though really the orig. word whence *begin* is formed. It need not be denoted by '*gin*; the apostrophe should be omitted. Common in Shak. Macb. i. 2. 25, &c. ME. *ginnen*; Chaucer, C. T. 3020 (A 3018). AS. *-ginnan*, to begin; only used in the compounds *on-ginnan*, to begin, Matt. iv. 7; and *be-ginnan*, to begin; so that perhaps ME. *ginnen* is for *a-ginnen*. ╬ Du. *be-ginnen*; the simple *ginnen* being unused; OHG. *bi-ginnan*; G. *be-ginnen*; Goth. *-ginnan*, only in the comp. *du-ginnan*, to begin. See Brugmann, i. § 376. **Der.** *be-gin*.

GIN (2), a trap, snare. (F. ─ L.) ME. *gin*; 'uele ginnes heþ þe dyeuel uor to nime þet uolk' = many snares hath the devil for to catch the people; Ayenbite of Inwyt, ed. Morris, p. 54. (Pron. *jin*.) Also in a far wider sense, and certainly a contraction of F. *engin* < L. *ingenium*, a contrivance or piece of ingenuity. Thus, in describing the mechanism by which the horse of brass (in the Squieres Tale) was moved, we are told that 'therein lyth th'effect of al the *gin*' = therein is the pith of all the contrivance; C. T. 10636 (F 322). See **Engine.** ¶ Particularly note the use of the word in P. Plowman, B. xviii. 250; 'For *gygas* the geaunt with a *gynne engyned*' = for Gigas the giant contrived by a contrivance.

GIN (3), a kind of spirit. (F. ─ L.) Formerly called *geneva*, whence *gin* was formed by contraction. Pope has *gin-shops*; Dunciad, iii. 148. '*Geneva*, a kind of strong water;' Kersey's Dict. ed. 1715. So called by confusion with the town in Switzerland of that name; but really a corruption. ─ MF. *genevre*, 'juniper;' Cot. [It is well known that *gin* is flavoured with berries of the juniper.] ─ L. *iūniperum*, acc. of *iūniperus*, a juniper. See **Juniper.**

GINGER, the root of a certain plant. (F. ─ L. ─ Gk. ─ Skt. ─ Malay-ālam.) So called in Skt. (but by a popular etymology) because shaped like a horn; the resemblance to a deer's antler is striking. In early use. ME. *ginger*; whence *ginger-bred* (ginger-bread); Chaucer, C. T. 13783 (B 2044). An older form *gingiuere* (= *gingivere*) occurs in the Ancren Riwle, p. 370. ─ OF. *gengibre*, *gingibre* (Supp. to Godefroy), s.v. *gingembre*); Norm. dial. *gengivre* (Moisy, ed. 1895); mod. F. *gingembre*. ─ Late L. *gingiber*; L. *zingiber*, ginger. ─ Gk. ζιγγίβερις, ginger. ─ Skt. *çṝṅgavēra*, ginger. ─ Skt. *çṝṅga-*, a horn; and *vēra-*, body (i. e. shape); adapted from Malayālam *inchi-ver*, green ginger; from *inchi*, a root (Yule). **Der.** *ginger-bread*.

GINGERLY, with soft steps. (F. ─ L.) 'Go *gingerly*;' Skelton, Garl. of Laurell, l. 1203; see Dyce's note. Palsgrave has: '*Gyngerly*, a pas menu;' as, *allez a pas menu, ma fille*.' Prob. formed, with E. suffix *-ly*, from OF. *gensor*, *genzor*, properly a comparative from OF. *gent*, but also itself used as a positive, with the sense 'pretty, delicate.' ─ OF. *gent*, gentle, orig. well-born. ─ Folk-L. *gentum*, for L. *genitum*, acc. of *genitus*, born, pp. of *gignere*, to beget. See **Gentle.** (So in N. E. D.; cf. *gent* in Hatzfeld.)

GINGHAM, a kind of cotton cloth. (F. ─ Malay.) Spelt *gingham* in 1615 (Yule). ─ F. *guingan*. ─ Malay *ginggang*, a striped or checkered cotton. (C. P. G. Scott.)

GINGLE, another spelling of **Jingle,** q. v.

GIPSY, the same as **Gypsy,** q. v.

GIRAFFE, the camelopard, an African quadruped with long neck and legs. (F. ─ Span. ─ Arab.) '*Giraffa*, an Asian beast, the same with *Camelopardus*;' Kersey's Dict., ed. 1715. First in 1594, spelt *gyraffa*; spelt *giraffe* in 1605. [Here *giraffa* = Span. *girafa*. We now use the F. form.] ─ MF. *giraffe* (F. *girafe*). ─ Span. *girafa*. ─ Arab. *zarāf* or *zarāfa(t)*, a camelopard; Rich. Dict. p. 772, col. 2. See Dozy, who gives the forms as *zarāfa*, *zorāfa*, and notes that it is also called *jorāfa*.

GIRD (1), to enclose, bind round, surround, clothe. (E.) ME. *gurden*, *girden*, *gerden*; the pp. *girt* is in Chaucer, C. T. 331 (A 329). AS. *gyrdan*, to gird, surround; Grein, i. 536. ╬ Du. *gorden*; Icel. *gyrða*, to gird; Dan. *gjorde*; Swed. *gjorda*; G. *gürten*; OSax. *gurdian*. β. These are weak verbs, of which the Teut. type is *gurdjan-*; from *gurd-*, weak grade of Teut. *gerdan-* (pt. t. *gard*) to enclose; as in Goth. *bi-gairdan*, to begird. **Der.** *gird-er*; *gird-le*, q. v.; *girth*, q. v. From the same root we also have *garden*, *yard*; and even *horticulture*, *cohort*, *court*. See **Yard** (1).

GIRD (2), to jest at, jibe. (E.) A peculiar use of ME. *girden*, *gurden*, to strike, cut. 'Gurdeth of Gyles hed,' cut off Guile's head; P. Plowman, B. ii. 201. Of obscure origin. Hence, *to gird at* = to strike at, jest at; a *gird* is a cut, sarcasm; Tam. Shrew, v. 2. 58. ¶ Not from AS. *gerd*, *gyrd*, a rod, as that became E. *yard* (2); a connexion with MDu. *geerde*, a rod (Hexham) is possible; but not very probable.

GIRDLE, a band for the waist. (E.) ME. *girdel*, *gerdel*; Chaucer, C. T. 360 (A 358). AS. *gyrdel*, a girdle; Mark, i. 6. ╬ Du. *gordel*; Icel. *gyrðill*; Swed. *gördel*; G. *gürtel*. β. From the AS. *gyrdan*, to gird, with suffix *-el*; see **Gird** (1). Allied to *girth*.

GIRL, a female child, young woman. (E.) ME. *girle*, *girle*, *gyrle*, formerly used of either sex, and signifying either a boy or girl. In Chaucer, C. T. 3767 (A 3769) *gerl* is a young woman; but in C. T. 666 (A 664), the pl. *girles* means young people of both sexes. In Will. of Palerne, 816, and King Alisaunder, 2802, it means 'young women;' in P. Plowman, B. i. 33, it means 'boys;' cf. B. x. 175. Answering to an AS. form *gyr-el-*, Teut. *gur-wil-*, a dimin. form from Teut. base *gur-*. Cf. NFries. *gör*, a girl; Pomeran. *goer*, a child; O. Low G. *gör*, a child; see Bremen Wörterbuch, ii. 528. Cf. Swiss *gurre*, *gurrli*, a depreciatory term for a girl; Sanders, G. Dict. i. 609, 641; also Norw. *gorre*, a small child (Aasen); Swed. dial. *gårrä*, *gurre* (the same). Root uncertain. **Der.** *girl-ish*, *girl-ish-ly*, *girl-ish-ness*, *girl-hood*.

GIRON, GYRON, in heraldry, an eighth part of a shield. (F. ─ OHG.) It is made by drawing a diagonal line from the top (dexter) corner to the centre, and from the centre horizontally to the same side; a right-angled triangle. Spelt *gyron*, *geron* in Blount (1681). ─ MF. *gyron*, *guyron*, 'a tearme of blasonrie;' Cot. ─ MHG. *gēre*, OHG. *gēro*, G. *gehre*, a gusset, a gore. ─ OHG. *gēr*, a spear; see **Gore** (2).

GIRTH, the measure round the waist; the bellyband of a saddle. (Scand.) ME. *gerth*. 'His *gerth* and his stiropes also;' Richard Coer de Lion, 5733; and see Prompt. Parv. This is a Scand. form. ─ Icel. *gjörð*, a girdle, girth; *gerð*, girth round the waist; Swed. *gjord*; Dan. *giord*, a girdle, Mark, i. 6. Teut. type *gerdā*, f. From the Teut. base *gerd-*, to enclose; see **Gird.** **Der.** *girth*, verb; also written *girt*. Allied to *girdle*.

GIST, the main point or pith of a matter. (F. ─ L.) Not in Todd's Johnson. A legal term (see Blackstone, Comment. iv. 333) denoting the real ground of an indictment, or the point wherein the action lies. ─ OF. *gist* (F. *gît*), it lies. Cf. the old F. proverb, given by Cotgrave, s. v. *lievre*. 'Ie scay bien ou *gist* le lievre, I know well which is the very point, or knot of the matter,' lit. I know well where the hare lies. This *gist* is the mod. F. *gît*, and similarly we have, in modern French, the phrase 'tout *gît* en cela,' the whole turns upon that; and again, 'c'est là que *gît* le lièvre,' there lies the difficulty, lit. that's where the hare lies; Hamilton's F. Dict. β. From the vb. *gésir*, to lie, of which the 3 pers. pres. was *gist* (mod. F. *gît*). ─ L. *iacēre*, to lie; an intransitive verb allied to *iacere*, to throw. See **Jet** (1).

GITTERN, a kind of guitar. (F. ─ L. ─ Gk.) ME. *gitern* (with one *t*); Chaucer, C. T. 12400 (C 466); P. Plowman, B. xiii. 233. ─ OF. *guiterne*, a guitar (Godefroy). A variant of *cittern* or *cithern*; see **Cithern** and **Guitar.**

GIVE, to bestow, impart, deliver over. (E.) ME. *yeuen*, *yiuen*, *ȝeuen*, *ȝiuen* (with *u* for *v*); Chaucer, C. T. 232. In old Southern and Midland English, the *g* almost always appears as *y* (often written ȝ); the modern hard sound of the *g* seems to be due to the influence of Northern English. '*Gifand* and takand woundis wyd;' Barbour's Bruce, xiii. 160. The pt. t. is *yaf* or *ȝaf*, Northern *gaf*, changing to *yeuen* or *ȝiuen* in the pl. number; pp. *yiuen*, *ȝiuen*, *ȝouen*, *yoven*, rarely *ȝifen*, *gifen*. AS. *giefan*, *geofan*, *giefan*, *gifan*, Grein, i. 505; pt. t. ic *geaf*, pl. wē *gēafon*, pp. *gifen*. ╬ Du. *geven*; Icel. *gefa*; Dan. *give*; Swed. *gifva*; Goth. *giban*; G. *geben*. Teut. type *geban-*, pt. t. *gab*. Cf. OIrish *gab-im*, I give, I take. **Der.** *giv-er*; also *gif-t*, q. v.

GIZZARD, a second stomach in birds. (F.—L.) Spelt *gisard* in Minsheu. The *d* is excrescent. ME. *giser*. 'The fowl that highte voltor that eteth the stomak or the *giser* of Tityus' = the bird that is named the vulture, that eats the stomach or gizzard of Tityus; Chaucer, tr. of Boethius, b. iii. met. 12. l. 28.—OF. *gezier, jugier, juisier* (mod. F. *gésier*; Norm. dial. *gisier, gigier*; Picard *gigier*); see Littré, who quotes a parallel passage from Le Roman de la Rose, 19506, concerning 'li *juisier* Ticius' = the gizzard of Tityus.—L. *gigērium,* only used in the pl. *gigēria,* the cooked entrails of poultry.

GLABROUS, smooth. (L.) Rare. 'French elm, whose leaves are thicker, and more florid, *glabrous*, and smooth;' Evelyn, Sylva, i. iv. § 1 (Todd's Johnson). Coined, by adding the suffix *-ous,* from L. *glabr-,* base of *glaber,* smooth. Idg. stem **gladh-ro-*; see **Glad.** Brugmann, i. § 589.

GLACIAL, icy, frozen. (F.—L.) 'Glacial, freezing, cold;' Blount's Gloss., ed. 1674. 'White and *glacious* bodies;' Sir T. Browne, Vulg. Errors, bk. ii. c. 1. § 3.—F. *glacial,* 'icy;' Cot.—L. *glaciālis,* icy.—L. *glaciēs,* ice. Cf. L. *gelu,* cold (Bréal); see **Gelid.** Der. From same source, *glacier,* q. v.; *glacis,* q. v.

GLACIER, an ice-slope or field of ice on a mountain-side. (F.—L.) First in 1744. 'The *glacier's* cold and restless mass;' Byron, Manfred, i. 1. 68. A Savoy word.—F. *glacier,* as in 'les *glaciers* de Savoie;' Littré.—F. *glace,* ice.—Folk-L. *glacia,* for L. *glaciēs,* ice. See above.

GLACIS, a smooth slope, in fortification. (F.—L.) In Kersey's Dict., ed. 1715.—F. *glacis,* 'a place made slippery, . . . a sloping bank or causey;' Cot.—MF. *glacer,* 'to freeze, harden, cover with ice;' id.—F. *glace,* ice. See above.

GLAD, pleased, cheerful, happy. (E.) ME. *glad,* Chaucer, C. T. 310 (A 308); also *gled,* Ancren Riwle, p. 282. AS. *glæd,* shining, bright, cheerful, glad; Grein, i. 512. + Du. *glad,* bright, smooth, sleek; Icel. *glaðr,* bright, glad; Dan. *glad,* Swed. *glad,* joyous; G. *glatt,* smooth, even, polished. Cf. Russ. *gladkii,* even, smooth, polished, spruce; L. *glaber,* smooth. See **Glabrous.** Der. *glad-ly, glad-ness;* also *gladsome* = ME. *gladsum,* Wyclif, Psalm ciii. 15, Chaucer, C. T. 14784 (B 3968); *glad-some-ly, glad-some-ness;* also *gladd-en,* in which the suffix *-en* is modern and due to analogy; cf. '*gladeth* himself' = gladdens himself, Chaucer, C. T. 10923 (F 609). And see *glade.*

GLADE, an open space in a wood. (Scand.) 'Farre in the forrest, by a hollow *glade*;' Spenser, F. Q. vi. 4, 13. '*Gladden,* a glade;' A Tour to the Caves (E. Yorksh., 1781). '*Gladden,* a void place,' Yks.; Thoresby (1703); see E.D.D.; *gladen,* Wars of Alexander, ed. Skeat, 131, and Glossary. Of Scand. origin; closely connected with Icel. *glaðr,* bright, shining (see **Glad**), the orig. sense being an opening for light, a bright track, hence an open track in a wood (Nares), or a passage cut through reeds and rushes, as in Two Noble Kinsmen, ed. Skeat, iv. 1. 64. Cf. Swed. dial. *glad-yppen,* completely open, said of a lake from which the ice has all melted away (Rietz); Swed. dial. *glatt* (= *gladt*), completely, as in *glatt öppet,* completely open; id.

GLADEN, GLADDEN, a plant, *Iris pseudacorus.* (L.) Spelt *gladon* in Palsgrave; *gladone* in Prompt. Parv.; see Way's note, and Turner's Names of Herbes. AS. *glædene;* Cockayne's Leechdoms, Gloss. to vol. ii. Altered from L. *gladiolus,* 'a sword-lily;' Lewis and Short.—L. *gladius,* a sword; see **Gladiator.**

GLADIATOR, a swordsman. (L.) 'Two hundred *gladiators*;' Dryden, tr. of Persius, vi. 115.—L. *gladiātor,* a swordsman.—L. *gladius,* a sword. See **Glaive.** Der. *gladiator-i-al;* also, from the same source, *gladi-ole,* a plant like the lily, from L. *gladi-ol-us,* a small sword, dimin. of *gladius.* And see *gladen.*

GLADSOME, glad, cheerful; see **Glad.**

GLAIR, the white of an egg. (F.—L.) Little used now. ME. *gleyre* of an ey = white of an egg; Chaucer, C. T. 16274 (G 806); and Prompt. Parv.—OF. *glaire;* 'la *glaire* d'vn œuf, the white of an egge;' Cot. β. Here *glaire* is a later form of *claire,* as evidenced by related words, esp. by Ital. *chiara d'un ovo,* 'the white of an egge,' Florio (where Ital. *chi* = L. *cl,* as usual); and by Span. *clara de huevo,* glair, white of an egg.—L. *clāra,* fem. of *clārus,* clear, bright; whence Late L. *clāra ōui,* the white of an egg (Ducange). See **Clear, Clarify.**

GLAIVE, a sword. (F.—L.) ME. *gleiue* (with *u* = *v*); Havelok, 1770; *glayue,* Allit. Poems, ed. Morris, i. 653 (or 654).—OF. *glaive,* 'a gleave, or sword; also, a launce, or horseman's staffe;' Cot.—L. *gladius,* a sword; see Brachet. ¶ Contrary to the statement in N. E. D., the AF. *glaive* had the sense of 'sword' as early as in P. de Thaun, Bestiaire, 888; see my Notes on E. Etym., p. 119.

GLAMOUR, gramarye, magic. (F.—L.—Gk.) Orig. Lowl. Scotch; spelt *glamer* (ab. 1700). Introduced into the literary language by Scott. '*Glamour,* or *deceptio visus*;' Scott, Demonology, letter iii. § 18. A corruption of *grammar.* See **Gramarye.**

GLANCE, a swift dart of light, a glimpse, hasty look; as a verb, to glide off or from, to graze, to flash. (F.—L.) The sb. is from the

vb. Spenser has *glaunce* as a verb: 'The *glauncing* sparkles through her bever glared;' F. Q. v. 6. 38. It occurs often in Shak., both as vb. and sb.; Two Gent. i. 1. 4; Mids. Nt. Dr. v. 13. Apparently a nasalised form (influenced by ME. *glenten,* to glance) of obs. ME. *glace,* OF. *glacer,* to glide, slip, glance (Godefroy).—F. *glace,* ice.—Folk-L. *glacia,* for L. *glaciēs;* see **Glacier.** ¶ The ME. *glenten* answers to the causal form of the str. vb. *glinta,* still in use in Swed. dial. (Rietz.) See **Glint.**

GLAND, a cell or fleshy organ in the body which secretes animal fluid. (F.—L.) '*Gland,* a flesh-kernel;' Kersey, ed. 1715.—MF. *glande,* 'a kernell, a fleshy substance filled with pores, and growing between the flesh and skin;' Cot.; OF. *glandre* (Supp. to Godefroy, s. v. *glande*).—L. *glandula,* a gland; dimin. of *glans* (stem *gland-*), an acorn. Cognate with Gk. βάλ-αν-ος, an acorn. Brugmann, i. § 665 (2). Der. *glandi-form,* from L. *glandi-,* decl. stem of *glans;* *glandi-fer-ous* (from L. *-fer,* bearing); *gland-ule,* from L. *glandula* (above), whence *glandul-ar, glandul-ous;* *gland-ers,* a disease of the glands of horses, Taming of the Shrew, iii. 2. 51, from OF. *glandre* (above); see Palsgrave, p. 183, l. 7.

GLARE, to shine brightly, to stare with piercing sight. (E.) ME. *glaren.* 'Swiche *glaring* eyen hadde he, as an hare;' Chaucer, C. T. 686 (A 684). 'Hit is not al gold that *glareth*;' id. House of Fame, i. 272. 'Thet gold thet is bricht and *glareth*;' Kentish Sermons, in An Old Eng. Miscellany, ed. Morris, p. 27, l. 31. Probably a true E. word; cf. AS. *glær* or *glêr,* a pellucid substance, amber (Bosworth, Leo).+Low G. *glaren,* to glow; WFlem. *glarien,* to glare, stare. Cf. also E. dial. *glore,* Norw. *glora,* to glare. Probably it is closely connected with **Glass,** q. v. Der. *glar-ing-ly, glar-ing-ness.*

GLASS, a well-known hard, brittle, transparent substance. (E.) Perhaps named from its transparency. ME. *glas,* Chaucer, C. T. 198. AS. *glæs,* glass; Grein, i. 513.+Du. *glas;* Dan. *glar;* MSwed. *glar* (Ihre); Icel. *gler;* G. *glas,* OHG. *clas.* β. Perhaps from a Teut. type **glazom,* neuter; and it may even be ultimately related to AS. *glōwan,* to glow. Der. *glass-blow-er, glass-wort, glass-y, glass-i-ness;* also *glaze* = ME. *glasen,* P. Plowman, B. iii. 49, 61; whence *glaz-ing, glaz-i-er* (= *glaz-zer,* like *bow-y-er, law-y-er* = *bow-er, law-er*).

GLAUCOUS, grayish blue. (L.—Gk.) A botanical word; see Bailey's Dict., vol. ii. ed. 1731. First in 1671 (Ray). Formed with suffix *-ous* from L. *glauc-us,* blueish.—Gk. γλαυκός, gleaming, glancing, silvery, blueish; whence γλαύσσειν (= γλαύκγειν), to shine. Allied to γελ-εῖν, to shine (Hesychius).

GLAZE, to furnish a window with glass. (E.) See **Glass.**

GLEAM, a beam of light, glow. (E.) ME. *gleam, gleem, glem;* Havelok, 2122; Ancren Riwle, p. 94. AS. *glǣm,* splendour, gleam, brightness, Grein, i. 513; Leo. Cf. *gliomu, glimu,* brightness, ornament; Grein, i. 515. Also OSax. *glimo,* brightness; 'glītandi glīmo' = glittering splendour; Heliand, 3146; OHG. *glimo,* a glowworm. β. Teut. type **glaimiz,* m.; from **glaim,* 2nd grade of **gleim-,* to shine. γ. Related words further appear in the Gk. χλιαρός, warm, χλί-ω, I become warm; (Prellwitz). See **Glimmer, Glitter.** Der. *gleam,* vb., *gleam-y.*

GLEAN, to gather small quantities of corn after harvest. (F.) ME. *glenen,* P. Plowman, C. ix. 67.—OF. *glener, glaner,* to glean; mod. F. *glaner.*—Late L. *glenāre,* found in a document dated A. D. 561 (Brachet). Of unknown origin; see Körting, § 4332. β. We may notice the later by-form *gleam* or *gleme.* 'To *gleame* corne, *spicili-gere*;' Levins, 208. 20. 'To *gleme* corne, *spicilegium facere; Gleamer* of corne, *spicilegus*;' Huloet. Apparently due to some confusion with *gleam;* cf. prov. E. *gleen,* to shine (E. D. D.). Der. *glean-er.*

GLEBE, soil; esp. land attached to an ecclesiastical benefice. (F.—L.) 'Have any *glebe* more fruitful;' Ben Jonson, The Fox, A. v. sc. 1 (Mosca). ME. *glebe,* Trevisa, tr. of Higden, i. 397. The comp. *glebe-land* is in Gascoigne, Fruits of War, st. 21.—OF. *glebe,* 'glebe, land belonging to a parsonage;' Cot.—L. *glēba,* soil, a clod of earth. Der. *gleb-ous, gleb-y;* *glebe-land.*

GLEDE (1), the bird called a kite. (E.) ME. *glede,* Allit. Poems, ed. Morris, ii. 1696. AS. *glida,* a kite, lit. 'the glider,' from the sailing motion of the bird; Grein, i. 56; from *glid-,* weak grade of *glidan,* to glide. See **Glide.**

GLEDE (2), **GLEED,** a glowing coal; obsolete. (E.) ME. *glede,* Chaucer, C. T. 1999 (A 1997). AS. *glēd,* Grein, i. 513. [Here *ē* results from *ō,* by mutation.]—AS. *glōwan,* to glow; see **Glow.** So also Dan. *glöd,* a live coal; cf. Icel. *glōa,* to glow.

GLEE, joy, mirth, singing. (E.) ME. *gle, glee;* Will. of Palerne, 824; also *gleu, glew,* Havelok, 2332. AS. *glēo,* earlier form *gliu,* joy, mirth, music; Grein, i. 515.+Icel. *glȳ,* glee, gladness; Swed. dial. *gly,* mockery, ridicule (Rietz). Cf. Gk. χλεύη, a jest, joke. β. Form of the root, **ghleu;* Brugmann, i. § 633.

GLEEK (1), a scoff, a jest. (F.—Du.?) It means a 'scoff' in Shak. 1 Hen. VI, iii. 2. 123; 'a glance of the eye' in Beaum. and Fletcher,

Maid in the Mill, ii. 2. See examples in Nares. Prob. a peculiar use of the word below. *To gleek* sometimes meant to beat at the game of gleek.

GLEEK (2), a game at cards. (F.—Du.) So in Ben Jonson, Alchem. v. 2 (Subtle); it is said that Catharine of Arragon played 'at *gleeke*;' Warton, Hist. of Eng. Poetry, sect. liv; vol. iii. p. 258, note *c*, ed. 1840. See Nares. The earliest quotation in N. E. D. is dated 1533; but we find mention of the card-games 'post and *glyeke*' in Roy, Rede Me (ed. Arber), p. 117 (1528). It should rather have been spelt *glik*, but the E. *ee* represents the F. *i*. The expression 'I shall *gleek* some of you' occurs in Greene's Tu Quoque (Nares).—OF. *glic*, an old F. game at cards (mentioned in Rabelais, bk. i. c. 22), Roquefort; also spelt *ghelicque* (Godefroy). One object in the game was to get three cards *alike* (as three kings); this was called a *gleek*.—MDu. *gelijck*, alike.—MDu. *ge-*, *ghe-*, prefix (=AS. *ge-*, G. *ge-*, Goth. *ga-*); and MDu. *-lijck*, Du. *-lijk*, cognate with E. *like*; see **Like.** ¶ Hexham has MDu. *gelijk ofte ongelijk spelen*, 'to play at even or odds.'

GLEN, a narrow valley. (C.) In Spenser, Sheph. Kalendar, April, 26.—Gael. and Irish *gleann*, a valley, glen; W. *glyn*; Corn. *glyn*; OIrish *glenn*. Celtic type *glennos*. Stokes-Fick, p. 120.

GLIB (1), smooth, slippery, voluble. (E.) The orig. sense is 'slippery;' Shak. has '*glib* and oily;' K. Lear, i. 1. 227; '*glib* and slippery;' Timon, i. 1. 53. We also find *glibbery*. 'What, shall thy lubrical and *glibbery* muse,' &c.; Ben Jonson, Poetaster, Act v (Tibullus). A native word; common in dialects; see E. D. D. Cf. EFries. *glibberig*, slippery; *glippen*, to slip.+Du. *glibberig*, slippery; *glibberen*, to slide; related to *glippen*, to slip away; Low G. *glibbrig*, slippery (Berghaus), *glippig*, glib, smooth (Schambach), Low G. *glippen*, v.; Dan. *glippe*, to fall, to slip. β. We also find a somewhat similar prov. E. *gliddery*, slippery, which is related to AS. *glidan*, to glide. **Der.** *glib-ly*, *glib-ness*.

GLIB (2), a lock of hair. (C.) 'Long *glibbes*, which is a thick curled bush of heare, hanging downe over their eyes;' Spenser, View of State of Ireland; Globe ed. p. 630, col. 2.—Irish and Gael. *glib*, also Irish *clib*, a bushy lock of hair.

GLIB (3), to castrate; *obsolete*. (E.) In Shak. Wint. Tale, ii. 1. 149. The *g* is merely prefixed, and may have been suggested by Du. *ge-*, as in MDu. *ge-lubt*, 'gelt;' Hexham. The orig. form is *lib*. '*Accaponare*, to capon, to gelde, to *lib*, to splaie;' Florio, ed. 1612. Here *lib* answers to an AS. *lybban*, where *y* arose, by mutation, from an older *u*. Clearly cognate with Du. *lubben*, to castrate. See **Left,** adj.

GLIDE, to slide, flow smoothly. (E.) ME. *gliden*, pt. t. *glod* or *glood*; Chaucer, C. T. 10707 (F 393). AS. *glídan*, Grein, i. 516.+Du. *glijden*; Dan. *glide*; Swed. *glida*; G. *gleiten*. Teut. type *gleidan-*, pt. t. *glaid*, pp. *glidanoz*.

GLIMMER, to shine faintly. (E.) ME. *glimeren*, whence the pres. part. *glimerand*, Will. of Palerne, 1427. The AS. form does not occur.+Low G. *glimmern*, frequent. of *glimmen*, to shine; MSwed. *glimra* (Ihre); Dan. *glimre*, to glimmer; *glimmer*, glitter, also mica; Swed. dial. *glimmer*, to glitter, *glimmer*, a glimmer, glitter; Swed. *glimmer*, mica (from its glitter); G. *glimmer*, a glimmer, mica; *glimmern*, to glimmer. β. The simple forms appear in Dan. *glimme*, to shine, Swed. *glimma*, to glitter, Du. *glimmen*, G. *glimmen*, to shine. Cf. also prov. G. *glimm*, a spark (Flügel); Swed. dial. *glim*, a glance (Rietz). We even find the sb. *glim*, brightness, in Allit. Poems, ed. Morris, A. 1088; and AS. *gleomu* (for *glímu*), splendour. All from Teut. *glim-*, weak grade of *gleim-*; see **Gleam. Der.** *glimmer*, sb.; and see below.

GLIMPSE, a short gleam, weak light; hurried glance or view. (E.) The *p* is excrescent; the old word was *glimse*. ME. *glimsen*, to glimpse; whence the sb. *glimsing*, a glimpse. 'Ye have som *glimsing*, and no parfit sighte;' Chaucer, C. T. 10257 (E 2383). Formed by suffixing *-s-* to the base *glim-*. See above.

GLINT, to glance, to shine. (Scand.) Obsolete; but important as having influenced the form of *glance*; see **Glance.** For ME. *glenten*, to move quickly aside, to glance aside; in later E., to shine. 'Hir eyen *glente* Asyde;' Chaucer, Troil. iv. 1223; cf. Allit. Poems, ed. Morris, A. 70, 114, 671, 1026; B. 218.—Swed. dial. *glänta*, *glinta*, to slip or glance aside.+G. *glänzen*, to make bright; from G. *glanz*, brightness. β. We also find (really from a different root) MDan. *glinte*, to shine, a nasalised form of *glit-* (in *glitter*); MHG. *glinzen*, to shine.

GLISSADE, a sliding; a gliding step. (F.—Teut.) F. *glissade*, a sliding.—F. *glisser*, to slide, glide.—OF. *glier*, to glide; influenced by OF. *glacier*, F. *glacer*, to slide (Hatzfeld). β. OF. *glier* is from OHG. *glîtan* (G. *gleiten*), to glide; see **Glide.** OF. *glacier* is from *glace*, ice; see **Glacier.** ¶ It seems simpler to derive *glisser* from Low G. *glidschen* or *glisken*, both meaning 'to glide,' and secondary formations from the weak grade of Teut. *gleidan-*.

GLISTEN, GLISTER, to glitter, shine. (E.) These are mere extensions from the E. base *glis-*, to shine, which appears in ME. *glisien*, to shine; 'in *glysyinde* wede'=in glistening garment; An Old Eng. Miscellany, ed. Morris, p. 91, l. 21. AS. *glisian*, to shine; Voc. 121. 25; *glisnian*, to gleam, Grein, i. 516; cf. Swed. dial. *glis-a*, to shine. **A.** *Glisnian* is formed from the base *glis-* by the addition of the *n* so often used to extend such bases; and hence we had ME. *glisnien*, with pres. part. *glisnande*, glittering; Allit. Poems, ed. Morris, A. 165. This ME. *glisnian* gave a later E. *glissen*, but the word is now spelt *glis-t-en*, with an excrescent *t*, which is usually, however, not sounded. **B.** Similarly, from the base *glis-*, with suffixed *-t* and the frequentative *-er*, was formed ME. *glisteren* or *glistren*. 'The water *glistred* over al;' Gower, C. A. ii. 252; bk. v. 3734. Cf. MDu. *glisteren* (Oudemans); now nasalised into mod. Du. *glinsteren*, to glitter.

GLITTER, to gleam, sparkle. (Scand.) ME. *gliteren* (with one *t*), Chaucer, C. T. 979 (A 977); '*glytered* and glent;' Gawain and the Grene Knight, 604.—Icel. *glitra*, to glitter; frequentative of *glita*, to shine, sparkle; Swed. *glittra*, to glitter; *glitter*, sb. glitter, spangle. Cf. AS. *glitinian*, to glitter, Mark, ix. 3; Goth. *glitmunjan*, to shine, Mark, ix. 3. β. Shorter forms appear in AS. *glitian*, to shine, Mone, Quellen, p. 355; Icel. *glit*, sb. glitter. γ. All from Teut. base *glit-*, weak grade of *gleit-*, as in OSax. *glîtan*, G. *gleissen*, to shine. Cf. Gk. χλιδ-ή, luxury. From Idg. base GHLEI, whence also *gleam*. See **Gleam. Der.** *glitter*, sb.; and see *glisten*, *glister*.

GLOAMING, twilight. (E.) 'Darker *gloaming* brought the night;' Burns, Twa Dogs, 232. But Hogg has: 'Tween the *gloaming* and the mirk;' Song. Here the *gloaming* means the evening glow of sunset. 'Fra the *glomyng* of the nycht;' Wyntoun, Chron. iv. 7. 827. The *oa* is from AS. short *o*; as in ǽfen-glommung, twilight, in A. S. Hymnary (Surtees Soc.), 16. 16. But the *ō* is usually long; as in ǽfen-glōm, evening glow, twilight; Grein, i. 64. Here *glō-m* is from Teut. root *glō-*, as in AS. *glówan*, to glow. See **Glow.** ¶ Distinct from **Gloom.**

GLOAT, to stare, gaze with admiration. (Scand.) Also spelt *glote*. 'So he *glotes* [stares], and grins, and bites;' Beaum. and Fletcher, Mad Lover, ii. 2. '*Gloting* [peeping] round her rock;' Chapman, tr. of Homer, Odyssey, xii. 150.—Icel. *glotta*, to grin, smile scornfully; Swed. dial. *glotta*, *glutta*, to peep (Rietz); G. *glotzen*, to stare (Flügel).

GLOBE, a ball, round body. (F.—L.) In Shak. Temp. iv. 153.—OF. *globe*, 'a globe, ball;' Cot.—L. *globum*, acc. of *globus*, a ball; allied to *glomus*, a ball, clue. See below. **Der.** *glob-ate* (L. *globātus*, globe-shaped); *glob-ose* (L. *globōsus*). Milton, P. L. v. 753, also written *glob-ous*, id. v. 649; *glob-y*; *glob-ule* (L. *glob-ul-us*, dimin. of *globus*); *glob-ul-ar*, *glob-ul-ous*, *glob-ul-ar-i-ty*.

GLOMERATE, to gather into a mass or ball. (L.) 'A river, which after many *glomerating* dances, increases Indus;' Sir T. Herbert, Travels, ed. 1665, p. 70 (p. 69 in R.).—L. *glomerātus*, pp. of *glomerāre*, to collect into a ball.—L. *glomer-*, for *glomes*, stem of *glomus*, a ball or clew of yarn; allied to L. *globus*, a globe. See **Globe. Der.** *glomerat-ion*, Bacon, Nat. Hist. § 832; also *ag-glomerate*, *con-glomerate*.

GLOOM, cloudiness, darkness, twilight. (E.) In Milton, P. L. i. 244, 544. Seldom found earlier except as a verb. 'A *glooming* peace;' Romeo, v. 3. 305. 'Now *glooming* [frowning] sadly;' Spenser, F. Q. vi. 6. 42. Cf. ME. *gloumen*, to lower, as in 'The wedire *gloumes*,' Wars of Alexander, 4142; also *gloumben* (with excrescent *b*), to frown; Rom. of the Rose, 4356. The ME. *gloumen* answers to AS. *glúmian* (not found); cf. E. *room* < ME. *roum* < AS. *rúm*. Allied to **Glum. Der.** *gloom-y*, Shak. Lucrece, 803; *gloom-i-ly*, *gloom-i-ness*; but not *gloam-ing*.

GLORY, renown, fame. (F.—L.) ME. *glorie*, Ancren Riwle, p. 358.—OF. *glorie*, later *gloire*.—L. *glōria*, glory; prob. for *clōria*; cf. L. *inclytus* (*in-clu-tus*), renowned; Gk. κλέος, glory; κλυτός, renowned; Irish *clú*, glory (Bréal). **Der.** *glori-ous*, in early use, Rob. of Glouc. p. 483; *glori-ous-ly*, P. Plowman, C. xx. 15; *glori-ous-ness*; also *glori-fy*, ME. *glorifien*, Wyclif, John, vii. 39 (F. *glorifier*, L. *glōrificāre*, to make glorious, from *glōri-*=*glōria*, and *fic-* (=*fac-ere*), to do, make); also *glori-fic-at-ion* (from L. acc. *glōrificātiōnem*).

GLOSS (1), brightness, lustre. (Scand.) In Shak. Much Ado, iii. 2. 6. Milton has *glossy*, P. L. i. 672.—Icel. *glossi*, a blaze; *glys*, finery. Cf. Swed. dial. *glossa*, to glow, shine; Norw. *glosa*, to glow; MHG. *glosen*, to glow; *glose*, a glow, gleam. Perhaps allied to **Glare** and **Glass. Der.** *gloss*, verb. ¶ Quite distinct from *gloss* (2). Der. *gloss-y*, *gloss-i-ly*, *gloss-i-ness*.

GLOSS (2), a commentary, explanation. (L.—Gk.) ME. *glose* (with one *s*), in early use; P. Plowman, C. xx. 15. [But the verb *glosen*, to gloss or gloze, was much more common than the sb.; see Chaucer, C. T. 7374, 7375 (D 1792); P. Plowman, B. vii. 303.] This ME. *glose* is from the OF. *glose*, 'a glosse;' Cot. But the L. form *glosse* (with double *s*) was substituted for the F. form in the 16th century; as, e.g. in Udal on S. Matt. xxiii. 18.—L. *glōssa*, a difficult word requiring explanation.—Gk. γλῶσσα, the tongue; also, a tongue, language, a word needing explanation. **Der.** *gloss*, verb; *gloze*, q. v.; *gloss-ar-y*, q. v.; *glosso-graphy*, *glosso-logy*, q. v.

GLOSSARY, a collection of glosses or words explained. (L.—Gk.) In Kersey's Dict. ed. 1715. Spelt *glosarye*, Caxton, Golden Legend, St. Clement, § 1.—L. *glōssārium*, a glossary; formed with suffix *-āri-um* from L. *glōss-a*, a hard word needing explanation (above). **Der.** *glossari-al*, *glossar-ist*. See below.

GLOSSOGRAPHER, a writer of glossaries or glosses. (Gk.) In Blount's *Glossographia*, ed. 1674. Coined from *glosso-*, for Gk. γλῶσσα, a hard word; and Gk. γράφ-ειν, to write. See **Gloss** (2).

GLOTTIS, the entrance to the windpipe. (Gk.) ' *Glottis*, one of the five gristles of the larynx;' Kersey, ed. 1715. First in 1578.—Gk. γλῶττις, the mouth of the windpipe (Galen).—Gk. γλῶττα, Attic form of γλῶσσα, the tongue (above). **Der.** *glott-al*, adj.; *epi-glottis*.

GLOVE, a cover for the hand. (E.) ME. *gloue* (with *u* for *v*), *glove*, Chaucer, C. T. 2876 (A 2874); King Alisaunder, 2033. AS. *glóf*, glove; Grein, i. 516. † Icel. *glófi*; prob. borrowed from AS. *glóf*. **β.** Possibly the initial *g* stands for *ge-* (Goth. *ga-*), a common prefix; and the word may be related to Goth. *lōfa*, Icel. *lófi*, the flat or palm of the hand; Scottish *loof*. **Der.** *glov-er*, *fox-glove*.

GLOW, to shine brightly, be ardent, be flushed with heat. (E.) ME. *glowen*, Chaucer, C. T. 2134 (A 2132). AS. *glówan*, to glow; very rare, but found in Ælfric, Hom. i. 424; the pt. t. *gléow* occurs in his Saints' Lives, vii. 240. † Icel. *glóa*; Dan. *glo*, to glow; Swed. dial. *glo*, *gloa*, to glow; Du. *gloeijen*, to glow, to heat; G. *glühen*. Allied to Gk. χλωρός, light green; Brugmann, i. § 156. Also to W. *glo*, a coal. **Der.** *glow*, sb.; *glow-worm*, Hamlet, i. 5. 89. Also *glede* (2).

GLOWER, to look angrily, to scowl. (E.) Spelt *glowir* in Dunbar's Poems, ed. Small, xlix. 24. ' *Glowres*, is dull or lowering;' Pegge, Derbicisms, p. 102 (1791). EFries. *glüren*. Cf. Low G. *gluren*, to be overcast (said of the weather); MDu. *gloeren*, 'to look awry, to leare;' Hexham; Du. *gluren*, to peep, to leer. Cf. **Lower** (2).

GLOZE, to interpret, deceive, flatter. (F.—L.—Gk.) In Rich. II, ii. 1. 10. ME. *glosen*, to make glosses; from the sb. *glose*, a gloss. See further under **Gloss** (2).

GLUE, a sticky substance. (F.—L.) ME. *glue*, Gower, C. A. ii. 248; bk. v. 3603.—OF. *glu*, ' glew, birdlime;' Cot.—Late L. *glūtem*, acc. of *glūs* (gen. *glūtis*), glue; a form used by Ausonius. Allied to L. *glūten*, glue; *glūtus*, tenacious; and to Gk. γλοιός, mud, gum. Allied to **Clay**. Brugmann, i. § 639. **Der.** *glue-y*; and see *glutin-ous*, *agglutin-ate*.

GLUM, sullen, gloomy, sad. (E.) ' With visage sad and *glum*;' Drant, tr. of Horace; to translate L. *saeuus*, Epist. ii. 2. 21. But the word was formerly a verb. ME. *glommen*, to look gloomy, frown; Towneley Myst. xxx. 596; Halliwell's Dict. p. 404. Allied to ME. *gloumen*, to be gloomy. EFries. *glumen*, *glümen*, to look sullen. † Low G. *glum*, turbid; *glumen*, to make turbid; *gluum*, a sullen look; Norw. *glyme*, a sullen look, *glyma*, *gloma*, to look sullen; see **Gloom**.

GLUME, a bracteal covering, in grasses. (L.) A botanical term. Borrowed, like F. *glume*, from L. *glūma*, a husk, hull.—L. *glūbere*, to peel, take off the husk; whence *glubma = *glūma*. Cf. Gk. γλύφειν, to hollow out. Allied to E. *cleave*, to split asunder. See **Cleave** (1). Brugmann, i. § 672 (1). **Der.** *glum-ac-e-ous* (L. *glūmāceus*).

GLUT, to swallow greedily, gorge. (F.—L.) In Shak. Temp. i. 1. 63. ' Til leade (for golde) do *glut* his greedie gal;' Gascoigne, Fruits of War, st. 68. ME. *glotien*, P. Plowman, C. x. 76 (Ilchester MS.).—OF. *glotir*, *gloutir*, to gulp down (Godefroy).—L. *glūtīre*, *glūttīre*, to swallow, gulp down. Cf. L. *gula*, the throat. **Der.** *glutt-on*, q. v.; from the same root, *de-glut-it-ion*, *gullet*, *gules*.

GLUTINOUS, gluey, viscous, sticky. (L.) 'No soft and *glutinous* bodies;' Ben Jonson, Sejanus, i. 1. 8. Englished from L. *glūtinōsus*, sticky.—L. *glūtin-um*, glue; also *glūten* (stem *glūtin-*), glue. See **Glue**. **Der.** *glutinous-ness*; also Cot. has ' glutinosité, glutinositie, glewiness;' *glutin-at-ive*; *ag-glutin-ate*.

GLUTTON, a voracious eater. (F.—L.) ME. *gloton*, Chaucer, C. T. 12454 (C 520); also *glutun*, Ancren Riwle, p. 214; whence *glotonie*, gluttony, Chaucer, C. T. 12446 (C 512).—OF. *gloton*, later *glouton*, 'a glutton;' Cot.—L. acc. *glūtōnem*, from *glūto*, a glutton.—L. *glūtīre*, to devour. See **Glut**. **Der.** *glutton-y*, *glutton-ous*.

GLYCERINE, a certain viscid fluid, of a sweet taste. (F.—Gk.) Modern. Named from its sweet taste. F. *glycérine*; coined from Gk. γλυκερός, sweet, an extension of γλυκύς, sweet. **Der.** from the same source, *liquorice*, q. v.

GLYPTIC, relating to carving in stone. (Gk.) Mere Greek.—Gk. γλυπτικός, carving; γλυπτός, carved, fit for carving.—Gk. γλύφειν, to hollow out, engrave. Allied to **Glume** and **Cleave** (1).

GNARL, to snarl, to growl. (E.) Perhaps obsolete. Shak. has ' *gnarling* sorrow hath less power to bite;' Rich. II, i. 3. 292; ' Wolves are *gnarling*;' 2 Hen. VI, iii. 1. 192. *Gnar-l* (with the usual added *-l*) is the frequentative of *gnar*, to snarl. ' For and this curre do *gnar*' = for if this cur doth snarl; Skelton, Why Come Ye Nat to Court, 297. This word is imitative; cf. AS. *gnyrran*, to snarl; Wulfstan, p. 139. We find, however, EFries. *gnarren*, to creak, snarl.+Du. *knorren*, to grumble, snarl; Dan. *knurre*, to growl, snarl; cf. *knarre*, *knarke*, to creak, grate; *knur*, a growl, the purring of a cat; Swed. *knorra*, to murmur, growl; *knorr*, a murmur; G. *knurren*, to growl, snarl; *knarren*, *knirren*, to creak.

GNARLED, twisted, knotty. (E.) ' *Gnarled* oak;' Meas. for Meas. ii. 2. 116. *Gnarled* means 'full of gnarls,' where *gnar-l* is a dimin. form of *gnar* or *knar*, a knot in wood. ME. *knarre*, a knot in wood; Wyclif, Wisdom, xiii. 13; whence the adj. *knarry*, full of knots. ' With knotty *knarry* barein treës olde;' Chaucer, C. T. 1979 (A 1977). **β.** The spelling *knur* or *knurr* (for *knar*) also occurs; 'A bounche [bunch] or *knur* in a tree;' Elyot's Dict., ed. 1559, s.v. *Bruscum*. This word has also a dimin. form *knurl*, with the same sense of ' hard knot.' These words may be considered E., though not found in AS. Cf. EFries. *knarre*, *knar*, a knotty piece of wood; Icel. *gnerr*, a knot, knob. See **Knurr**.

GNASH, to grind the teeth, to bite fiercely. (Scand.) A modification of ME. *gnasten*, to gnash the teeth; Wyclif, Isaiah, v. 29; viii. 19.—MDan. *knaske*, to crush between the teeth, to gnash; Swed. *knastra*, to crash (between the teeth); Icel. *gnastan*, sb. a gnashing; *gnesta*, to crack; G. *knastern*, to gnash, crackle; Low G. *gnastern*, the same (Berghaus). **β.** Of imitative origin; so also Dan. *knase*, to crackle; cf. Icel. *gnista*, EFries. *gnisen*, to gnash.

GNAT, a small stinging insect. (E.) ME. *gnat*, Chaucer, C. T. 5929 (D 347). AS. *gnæt*, Matt. xxiii. 24. **β.** It has been suggested that the insect was so named from the whirring of its wings; cf. Icel. *gnata*, to clash; *gnat*, the clash of weapons.

GNAW, to bite furiously or roughly. (E.) ME. *gnawen*; the pt. t. *gnow* occurs in Chaucer, C. T. 14758 (B 3638); and *gnew* in Rich. Coer de Lion, ed. Weber, 3089. AS. *gnagan*; the compound *for-gnagan*, to devour entirely, occurs in Ælfric's Homilies, ii. 194, l. 1.+Du. *knagen*; OIcel. *gnaga*, mod. Icel. *naga*; Dan. *gnave*; Swed. *gnaga*. **β.** Without the *g*, we have Icel. *naga*, Dan. *nage*, G. *nagen*, to gnaw; Swed. *nagga*, to nibble; whence the prov. E. *nag*, to tease, worry, irritate, scold. See **Nag** (2).

GNEISS, a species of stratified rock. (G.) Modern. A term in geology. Borrowed from G. *gneiss*, a name given to a certain kind of rock; from its sparkling.—OHG. *gneistan*, to sparkle; *gneista*, a spark.+AS. *gnāst*, Icel. *gneisti*, a spark. **Der.** *gneiss-o-id*, with a Gk. suffix, as in **Asteroid**.

GNOME, a kind of sprite. (F.—Gk.) In Pope, Rape of the Lock, i. 63.—F. *gnome*, a gnome. Littré traces the word back to Paracelsus; it seems to be an adaptation of Gk. γνώμη, intelligence, from the notion that the intelligence of these spirits could reveal the secret treasures of the earth; but this is conjecture. The gnomes were spirits of *earth*, the *sylphs* of air, the *salamanders* of *fire*, and the *nymphs* of *water*. **β.** The Gk. γνώμη is from γνῶναι, to know (below).

GNOMON, the index of a dial, &c. (L.—Gk.) ' The style in the dial called the *gnomon*;' Holland's Pliny, b. ii. c. 72.—L. *gnōmōn*, which is merely the Gk. word.—Gk. γνώμων, an interpreter, lit. ' one who knows;' an index of a dial.—Gk. γνῶναι, to know.—√GEN; whence also E. **Know**, q.v. **Der.** *gnomon-ic*, *gnomon-ics*, *gnomon-ic-al*.

GNOSTIC, one of a certain sect in the second Christian century. (Gk.) ' The vain science of the *Gnosticks*;' Gibbon, Rom. Empire, c. 15. § 11. And see Blount's Gloss., ed. 1674.—Gk. γνωστικός, good at knowing.—Gk. γνωστός, longer form of γνωτός, known.—Gk. γνῶναι, to know. See **Gnomon**. **Der.** *Gnostic-ism*.

GNU, a kind of antelope. (Kaffir.) Found in S. Africa. Orig. a Kaffir word; see the Kaffir Dict. by Davis, who gives it in the form *ngu*, where the *q* represents a click. It was sometimes written *quu*, whence *gnu* by an erroneous substitution of *g* for *q*. (N. and Q., 9 S. v. 45.)

GO, to move about, proceed, advance. (E.) ME. *gon*, *goon*, *go*; Chaucer, C. T. 379 (A 377); common. AS. *gān*, to go, Grein, i. 368, 369.+Du. *gaan*; (Icel. lost); Dan. *gaae*; Swed. *gå*; G. *gehen*, to go. Distinct from Goth. *gangan*, OHG. *kankan*, Icel. *ganga*, E. *gang*. The OHG. *gā-m*, I go, shows that the OTeut. **gai-* belonged to the class of ' verbs in *-mi*.' **Der.** *go-by*, *go-cart*, *go-er*, *go-ing*; also *gait*, q. v. ☞ The pt. t. *went* is from *wend*; see **Wend**.

GOAD, a sharp pointed stick for driving oxen. (E.) ME. *gode*. ' Wiþ a longe *gode*;' P. Plowman's Crede, ed. Skeat, l. 433. AS. *gād*, not common; but we find ' ongēan þa *gāde*' = against the goad (cf. Acts, ix. 5); Ælfric's Hom. i. 386. l. 9. We find also the early form *gaad*; O. E. Texts, p. 99, l. 1937. Teut. type *gaidā, fem.; verified by the Lombardic form *gaida* (Ducange). From the Teut. base **gai-*, whence also AS. *gā-r*, Icel. *gei-rr*; cf. OIrish *gai*, a spear. See **Gore** (2). ¶ Not allied to *gad* or *yard* (2).

GOAL, the winning-post in a race. (E.) A term in running races. 'As, in rennynge, passynge the *gole* is accounted but rasshenesse;' Sir T. Elyot, The Governour, b. iii. c. 21. 'No person . . . should haue wone the ryng or gott the *gole* before me;' Hall's Chron. Rich. III, an. 2. § 2. ME. *gōl*, a limit; Shoreham's Poems, p. 145, l. 4. It answers to an AS. form *gāl (not found), which may have meant 'barrier' or 'impediment;' whence *gǣlan*, to impede, *ā-gǣlan*, to delay. ¶ Not of F. origin, as often said.

GOAT, the name of a well-known quadruped. (E.) ME. *goot, gote*; Chaucer, C. T. 690 (A 688). AS. *gāt*; Grein, i. 373.+Du. *geit*; Dan. *ged*; Swed. *get*; Icel. *geit*; G. *geiss, geisse*; Goth. *gaits*.+L. *haedus*, a kid. Idg. base **ghaid-*. Der. *goats-beard, goat-moth, goat-sucker*.

GOBBET, a mouthful, a little lump, small piece. (F.–C.) The short form *gob* is rare. '*Gob* or *Gobbet*, a great piece of meat;' Kersey's Dict., ed. 1715. ME. *gobet*, a small piece; P. Plowman, C. vi. 100; Chaucer, C. T. 698 (A 696). 'Thei tooken the relifs of brokun *gobetis*, twelue cofyns ful;' Wyclif, Matt. xiv. 20.–OF. *gobet*, a morsel of food (Godefroy); not given in Burguy or Cotgrave, but preserved in the modern F. *gobet*, in use in the Norman dialect (Du Bois). A dimin. form, with suffix *-et*, allied to MF. *gob*, a gulp, as used in the phrase 'l'avalla tout de *gob* = at one gulpe, or, as one gobbet, he swallowed it;' Cot.–OF. *gober*, 'to ravine, devour, feed greedily;' Cot. β. Of Celtic origin; cf. Gael. *gob*, the beak or bill of a bird, or (ludicrously) the mouth; Irish *gob*, mouth, beak, snout; see Macbain. ¶ The prov. E. *gob*, the mouth, is borrowed from Celtic directly. And see **Gobble**.

GOBBLE, to swallow greedily. (F.–C.; *with* E. *suffix*.) '*Gobble up*, to eat gobs, or swallow down greedily;' Kersey's Dict., ed. 1715. First in 1601. A frequentative, formed by adding *-le*, of OF. *gober*, 'to ravine, devour, feed greedily, swallow great morsels, let downe whole gobbets;' Cot. See **Gobbet**. ¶ At a late period the word *gobble* was adopted as being a suitable imitative word (cf. *gabble*), to represent the sound made by turkeys. In this sense, it occurs in Prior, The Ladle, l. 74: 'Fat turkeys *gobbling* at the door.'

GOBELIN, a rich French tapestry. (F.) 'So named from a house at Paris, formerly possessed by wool-dyers, whereof the chief (Giles *Gobelin*) in the reign of Francis I. [1515–1547] is said to have found the secret of dyeing scarlet;' Haydn, Dict. of Dates.

GOBLET, a large drinking-cup. (F.–L.) 'A *goblet* of syluer;' Berners, tr. of Froissart, v. ii. c. 87. 'In grete *goblettez*;' Morte Arthure, l. 207.–F. *gobelet*, 'a goblet, bole, or wide-mouthed cup;' Cot. Dimin. (with suffix *-et*) of OF. *gobel*, (later form *gobeau*) which Cot. explains by 'a mazer or great goblet.'–Late L. *cūpellum*, acc. of *cūpellus*, a cup; a dimin. of L. *cūpa*, a tub, cask, vat. See **Coop**. Cf. Picard *gobe*, a great cup. (Körting, § 2693; but doubtful.)

GOBLIN, a kind of mischievous sprite, fairy. (F.–Low L.–G.) Formerly *gobeline*, in 3 syllables. 'The wicked *gobbelines*;' Spenser, F. Q. ii. 10. 73. ME. *gobelyn*; Wyclif, Ps. xc (xci). 6.–OF. *gobelin*, 'a goblin, or hob-goblin;' Cot.–Low L. *gobelinus*, a goblin; prob. from the same source as G. *kobold*, a goblin (see Kluge). If so, it is from MHG. *kobel*, a hut, with L. suffix *-inus*. The sense is to be explained from the cognate AS. *cof-godas*, 'penates,' or household gods. β. MHG. *kobel* is the dimin. of MHG. *kobe*, a stall, cognate with Icel. *cofi*, a hut, AS. *cofa*, a chamber; see **Cove**. ¶ So in Kluge, and Körting, § 2279. Diez derives it from Gk. κόβᾰλος, a rogue, a knave, also, a goblin invoked by knaves. But *kobold* (at any rate) is prob. Germanic.

GOBY, a kind of sea-fish. (L.–Gk.) '*Gobio* or *Gobius*, the gudgeon or pink, a fish;' Kersey's Dict., ed. 1715. The *goby* is a mere corruption of L. *gōbius* (cf. F. *gobie*), orig. applied to the gudgeon; also spelt *cōbius*.–Gk. κωβιός, a kind of fish, gudgeon, tench. See **Gudgeon**.

GOD, the Supreme Being. (E.) ME. *god* (written in MSS. with small initial letter); Chaucer, C. T. 535 (A 533). AS. *god*; Grein, i. 517.+Du. *god*; Icel. *guð*; Dan. *gud*; Swed. *gud*; Goth. *guth*; G. *gott*. β. Teut. type *guthom; Idg. type *ghutom, perhaps 'the being who is worshipped;' a pp. form from Idg. *ghu, to worship, as in Skt. *hu*, to sacrifice (to), whence Skt. *huta-*, one to whom sacrifice is offered. ¶ In no way allied to *good*, adj. **Der.** *godd-ess*, q. v.; *god-child*; *god-father*, q. v.; *god-head*, q. v.; *god-less, god-like, god-ly, god-send, god-son*; also *good-bye*, q. v.; *gospell*, q. v.; *gossip*, q. v.

GODDESS, a female divinity. (E.; *with* F. *suffix*.) ME. *goddesse* (better *godesse*), a hybrid compound, used by Chaucer, C. T. 1103 (A 1101). Made by adding to *God* the OF. suffix *-esse* (= L. *-issa* = Gk. *-ισσα*). ¶ The AS. word was *gyden* (Grein, i. 536); correctly formed by vowel-change and with the addition of the fem. suffix *-en* (Teut. *-īna*), as in **Vixen**, q.v. Cf. G. *göttin*, fem. of *gott*.

GODFATHER, a male sponsor in baptism. (E.) ME. *god-fader*, Rob. of Glouc. p. 69; l. 1571. Earlier, in William of Shoreham's Poems, ed. Wright, p. 69 (temp. Edw. II). From *god*, God;

and *fader*, father. β. Other similar words are *godchild*, Ancren Riwle, p. 210; ME. *goddoȝter* = god-daughter, Ayenbite of Inwyt, p. 48; ME. *godmoder* = god-mother, id. same page; ME. *godsune* = god-son, Wright's Vocab. i. 214, col. 2. And see **Gossip**.

GODHEAD, divinity, divine nature. (E.) ME. *godhed*, Chaucer, C. T. 2383 (A 2381); spelt *godhod*, Ancren Riwle, p. 112. The suffix is wholly different from E. *head*, being a variant of the suffix which is commonly written *-hood*. This *-hood* is from the AS. *hād*, office, state, dignity; as in 'þrī on *hādum*' = three in (their) Persons; Ælfric's Hom. ii. 42. β. This AS. *hād* properly passed into *-hood*, as in E. *man-hood*; but in ME. we also find the suffix *-hede* or *-hed*, as in *manhede*, Will. of Palerne, 431; as if from an AS. mutated form *-hǣd-*; cf. OFries. *-hēd*, Du. *-heid*, OSax. *-hēd*, equivalents of AS. *-hǣdu*; Teut. type *haidjā, f. AS. *hād* < Teut. *haidoz, m. This accounts for the double form *maiden-hood* and *maiden-head*.

GODWIT, the name of a bird. (E.) 'Th' Ionian *godwit*;' Ben Jonson, tr. of Horace's Odes, lib. v. od. 2, l. 53. Of unknown origin; but the former syllable may well be a shortened form of *gōd*, good, as it was famous as a delicacy. The latter syllable *-wit* probably stands for ME. *wight*, AS. *wiht*, a wight, a creature, which could be used (in AS.) of a bird; see Cynewulf, Crist, l. 981. Variously corrupted to *god-wike* in 1612 (N. E. D.); *god-wipe* (1579).

GOFFER, to flute or crimp a frill, &c. (F.–O. Low G.) Not in Johnson, and not much used before 1800. (The *o* is long.)–MF. *gauffrer*, 'to print (a garment); also, to deck or set out with puffes;' Cot. Orig. to mark like the edging of pie-crust, or like wafers.– MF. *gauffre, goffre*, 'a wafer; also, a honny-combe;' Cot. See further under **Wafer**.

GOGGLE-EYED, having rolling and staring eyes. (E.) 'They *gogle* with their eyes hither and thither;' Holinshed, Descr. of Ireland, c. 1. '*Glyare*, or *gogul-eye*, limus, strabo;' Prompt. Parv. p. 199. '*Gogyl-eyid, gogelere*, limus, strabo;' id. p. 201. Wyclif translates L. *luscum* by 'gogil-iȝed' = goggle-eyed; Mark, ix. 46. '*Goggle-eyed* man, *louche*;' Palsgrave. The suffix *-le* is, as usual, frequentative; the base appears to be imitative; cf. prov. E. *goggle*, to shake, *gog*, a quagmire (because it shakes). We find also Irish and Gael. *gogshuileach*, goggle-eyed, having wandering eyes; from *gog*, to move slightly, and *suil*, the eye, look, glance; but this *gog* seems to be of E. (and imitative) origin. Cf. prov. E. *coggle*, Bavar. *gageln*, to be unsteady; and E. *jog*, **joggle**. **Der.** *goggle*, verb, to roll the eyes (Butler, Hudibras, ii. 1. 120); *goggles*, i. e. a facetious name for spectacles.

GOITRE, a swelling in the throat. (F.–Prov.–L.) Spelt *goytre* in Howell, Letters, i. 1. 43. Used in speaking of the Swiss peasants who are afflicted with it.–F. *goitre*, a swelled neck; a back-formation from the adj. *goitreux*, afflicted with goitre (Hatzfeld).–Prov. *goitros*, adj.; from *goit*, sb., the throat (in Mistral).–L. *guttur*, the throat; see Juvenal, Sat. xiii. 162.

GOLD, a precious metal. (E.) ME. *gold*, Chaucer, C. T. 12704 (C 770). AS. *gold*; Grein, i. 519.+Du. *goud* [for *gold*]; Icel. *gull*; Swed. and Dan. *guld*; G. *gold*; Goth. *gulth*; 1 Tim. ii. 9. Teut. type *gul-thom, neuter; Idg. type *ghəl-tom; cf. Russ. *zoloto*, Skt. *hātaka-*, gold. Allied to Pers. *zar*, gold, Zend *zaranya-*, Skt. *hiranya-*, gold. Named from its yellow colour; and allied to **Yellow**. (√GHEL.) Brugmann, i. § 506; ii. § 79. **Der.** *gold-en* (AS. *gyld-en*, by the usual letter change, but altered in ME. to *gold-en*); *gold-beater, gold-dust, gold-finch* (Chaucer, C. T. 4365), *gold-fish, gold-leaf, gold-smith* (Prompt. Parv. p. 202); *mary-gold* or *mari-gold*. Also *gild*.

GOLF, the name of a game. (Du.) Mentioned in Acts of James II., of Scotland; 1457, c. 71, ed. 1566: 'the futball and the *golf*.' The name is usually supposed to have been taken from that of a Du. game played with a mall and ball.–Du. *kolf*, 'a club to strike little bouls or balls with, a mall-stick;' Sewel's Du. Dict.+Icel. *kölfr*, the (rounded) clapper of a bell, a bulb, a bolt for a crossbow; *kylfa*, a club; Dan. *kolbe*, the butt-end of a weapon; *kolv*, a bolt, shaft, arrow; Swed. *kolf*, a butt-end, bolt; Low G. *kulf*, a club with which boys play a kind of hockey (Brem. Wört.); G. *kolbe*, a club, mace, knob, butt-end of a gun. ¶ Or it may be allied to prov. E. *gouff*, to strike, to hit (E. D. D.); which is possibly of imitative origin. Cf. *cuff*.

GOLOSH. The same as **Galoche**, q. v.

GONDOLA, a Venetian pleasure-boat. (Ital.–Gk. ?) Shak. has *gondola*, Merch. of Ven. ii. 8. 8; and *gondolier*, Oth. i. 1. 126.–Ital. *gondola*, a boat used (says Florio) only at Venice; a dimin. of *gonda* (Torriano), with the same meaning.–Gk. κόνδυ, a drinking-vessel; which the *gondola* was supposed to resemble (Diez). But this is doubtful. Or from L. *cūnula*, a little cradle; see Körting, § 2402.

GONFANON, GONFALON, a kind of standard or banner. (F.–MHG.) ME. *gonfanon*, Rom. of the Rose, 1201, 2018. [The form *gonfalon* is from Ital. *gonfalone*.] The sb. *gunfaneur* = bannerbearer, occurs in the Ancren Riwle, p. 300.–OF. *gonfanon, gunfanon*.–MHG. *gundfano*, a banner, lit. battle-standard.–MHG. *gunt, gund*, battle (chiefly preserved in female names, as *Rhadegund*); and *fano*, *vano* (mod. G. *fahne*), a standard, banner. β. The MHG. *gund* is cognate with AS. *gúð* (for **gunð*), war, battle; Icel. *gunnr*, *guðr*, battle; from √GHwEN, to strike; cf. Skt. *han*, to strike,kill. Brugmann, i. § 678. γ. G. *fahne* is cognate with E. *vane*; see Vane.

GONG, a metallic disc, used as a bell. (Malay.) Spelt *gongo* in 1590; *gong* in 1686; see Yule.—Malay *agōng* or *gōng*, 'the gong, a sonorous instrument;' Marsden's Malay Dict., p. 12, col. 1.

GOOD, virtuous, excellent, kind. (E.) ME. *good*, *gode*, Chaucer, C. T. 479 (A 477). AS. *gód*; Grein, i. 520.+Du. *goed*; Icel. *gōðr*; Dan. and Swed. *god*; Goth. *gōds*; G. *gut*. Teut. type **gōdoz*; from **gōd-*, strong grade of **gad-*, to suit, fit; for which see Gather. Cf. Russ. *godno*, suitably; *godnuii*, suitable. Der. *good*, sb., pl. *goods* (ME. *goodes*, P. Plowman, C. ix. 251); *good-day*; *good-Friday* (ME. *gode fridaye*, P. Plowman, B. x. 414); *good-ly* =AS. *gōdlic*, Grein, i. 523; *good-li-ness* (ME. *goodlines*, also in A.V. of Bible, Isaiah, xl. 6, and Fairfax, tr. of Tasso, b. xx. st. 107); *good-natured*; *good-ness* =AS. *gōdnes*, Grein, i. 523; *good-will*. Also *good-man*, q.v.

GOOD-BYE, farewell. (E.) A familiar (but meaningless) contraction of *God be with you*, the old form of farewell. Very common in Shak., where old edd. often have *God buy you*. 'God buy you, good Sir Topas;' Tw. Nt. iv. 2. 108 (first folio). 'God be with you; I haue done;' Oth. i. 3. 189 (first folio). Strictly, *God buy* (also *God b'w'y*) = God be with you; and the added *you* was needless, and is not preserved.

GOODMAN, the master of the house. (E.) In the Bible, A.V. Luke, xii. 39, &c. See Eastwood and Wright's Bible Wordbook. ME. *godeman*, in the Seven Sages, Thornton Romances, Introd. xliv, l. 5. Observe especially the occurrence of *godeman*, as a tr. of L. *pater-familias*, in An O. Eng. Miscellany, ed. Morris, p. 33. 'Two bondmen, whyche be all vnder the rule and order of the *good man* and the *good wyfe* of the house;' Sir T. More's Utopia (E. version), ed. Arber, p. 75. Compounded of *good* and *man*. Cf. Lowland Scotch *gude man*, the master of a family; Jamieson.

GOOSANDER, the largest species of *Mergus*. (Scand. ?) The *Mergus merganser*; formerly *gossander*, as in Drayton, Polyolb. song xxv. 65. Of obscure formation; apparently 'goose-duck;' from Norw. *gaas*, Icel. *gās*, goose (modified by E. *goose*), and Norw. *and*, a duck, Icel. *önd* (pl. *andir*), a duck, cognate with AS. *ened*. See Newton, Dict. of Birds.

GOOSE, the name of a bird. (E.) ME. *gos*, *goos*, pl. *gees*; Chaucer, C. T. 4135 (A 4137). AS. *gōs*, pl. *gēs*; Grein, i. 523 (where *gōs* stands for an older **gons*<**gans*, the lengthening of *o* causing loss of *n*).+Du. *gans*; Dan. *gaas* (for **gans*), pl. *gæs*; Swed. *gås* (for **gans*); Icel. *gās* (for **gans*); G. *gans*.+L. *ans-er*; Gk. χήν; Skt. *haṃsas*, a swan; OIrish *geis*, a swan; Lithuan. *żasis*. Teut. type **gans*, Idg. base **ghans-*. ¶ From the Idg. base **ghan-* we have also *gann-et* and *gan-d-er*. See Gannet, Gander. The occurrence of these words favours the theory that Gk. χήν is allied to χαίνειν (for **χάν-γειν*), to gape. Der. *goose-grass* (so called because geese are fond of it), *goose-quill*, *gos-hawk*, q.v., *gos-ling*, q.v. And see below.

GOOSEBERRY, the berry of a well-known shrub. (E.) 'Not worth a *gooseberry*;' 2 Hen. IV, i. 2. 196. 'A goo̅seberrie, *vua* [*uva*] *crispa*;' Levins, 104. 28. 'Gose berrys, *groiselles*;' Du Wes (in Palsgrave), p. 912. From *goose* and *berry*; cf. *goose-grass*, &c. ¶ Plant-names are often whimsical and inappropriate; it is possible that the name was suggested by North E. *grosers*, gooseberries (Halliwell, Brockett). Burns has *grozet*, a gooseberry; To a Louse, st. 5. These forms are, apparently, from an OF. **grose*, which occurs not only in OF. *grosele*, *groisele*, a gooseberry, but also in Irish *grois-aid*, Gael. *grois-eid*, W. *grwys-en*, a gooseberry, all borrowed from E. (Turner has *groser-bushe* in 1548.) The OF. *groisele* is of Teutonic origin; viz. from MHG. *krūs*, curling, crisped; whence mod. G. *krausbeere*, a cranberry, rough gooseberry. Cf. Swed. *krusbär*, a gooseberry. [Du. *kruisbezie* (lit. a cross-berry), is a singular corruption of *kroesbezie*, by confusion between *kruis*, a cross, and *kroes*, crisp, frizzled.] The G. *kraus*, Swed. *krus*, Du. *kroes*, crisp, frizzled, refer to the short crisp curling hairs upon the rougher kinds of the fruit; cf. the L. name *uva crispa* in Levins, given above.

GOPHER, a kind of wood. (Heb.) In A.V. Gen. vi. 14.—Heb. *gōpher*, a kind of wood; supposed to be pine or fir.

GORBELLIED, having a fat belly. (E.) In Shak. 1 Hen. IV, ii. 2. 93. Compounded of E. *gore*, lit. filth, dirt (here used of the contents of the stomach and intestines); and *belly*. β. All doubt as to the origin is removed by comparing Swed. dial. *går-bälg*, a fat paunch, compounded of Swed. dial. *går* (Swed. *gorr*), dirt, the contents of the intestines, and *bälg*, the belly. See Rietz, p. 225. See Gore (1). And see below.

GORCROW, the carrion-crow. (E.) 'Raven and *gorcrow*, all my birds of prey;' Ben Jonson, The Fox, Act i. Compounded of E. *gore*, filth, dirt, carrion (a former sense of the word); and *crow*. See Gore (1). And see above.

GORDIAN, intricate. (Gk.) Chiefly in the phr. 'Gordian knot;' Cymb. ii. 2. 34. Named from the Phrygian king *Gordius* (Gk. Γόρδιος), father of Midas, who, on being declared king, 'dedicated his chariot to Zeus, in the Acropolis of Gordium. The pole was fastened to the yoke by a knot of bark; and an oracle declared that whosoever should untie the knot should reign over all Asia. Alexander, on his arrival at Gordium, cut the knot with his sword, and applied the oracle to himself;' Smith's Classical Dict.

GORE (1), clotted blood, blood. (E.) It formerly meant also dirt or filth. It occurs in the sense of 'filthiness' in Allit. Poems, ed. Morris, B. 306. AS. *gor*, dirt, filth; Grein, i. 520.+Icel. *gor*, gore, the cud in animals, the chyme in men; Swed. *gorr*, dirt, matter; MDu. *goor*, OHG. *gor*. Origin uncertain. Der. *gor-belly*, q.v., *gor-crow*, q.v. Also *gor-y*, Macbeth, iii. 4. 51.

GORE (2), to pierce, bore through. (E.) In Shak. As You Like It, ii. 1. 25. Formed, as a verb, from ME. *gare*, *gore*, *gar*, a spear. 'Brennes . . . lette glide his *gar*' = Brennus let fall his spear; Layamon, 5079. AS. *gār*, a spear; Grein, i. 370. (The vowel-change is perfectly regular; cf. *bone*, *stone*, *loaf*, from AS. *bān*, *stān*, *hláf*.)+Icel. *geirr*, a spear; OHG. *gēr*, a spear. Teut. type **gaizoz*, m.; allied to Gaulish L. *gaesum*, a javelin; OIrish *gai*, a spear. Brugmann, i. § 210 (3). Perhaps allied to *goad*. Allied to *gore* (3); see below.

GORE (3), a triangular piece let into a garment; a triangular slip of land. (E.) ME. *gore*, Chaucer, C. T. 3237. AS. *gāra*, a projecting point of land; Ælfred, tr. of Orosius, i. 1, ed. Sweet, p. 24, l. 3. From AS. *gār*, a spear; see Gore (2). β. Similarly we have Icel. *geiri*, a triangular piece of land; from *geirr*, a spear. Also G. *gehre*, a wedge, gusset; Du. *geer*, a gusset, gore. Der. *giron*, q.v.

GORGE, the throat; a narrow pass. (F.—L.) ME. *gorge*, the throat; Allit. Morte Arthure, ed. Brock, 3760.—OF. *gorge*, the throat, gullet. [Ital. *gorga*.]—Folk-L. **gorga*, gullet (Hatzfeld); prob. a popular form of L. *gurgulio*, the gullet. Perhaps allied to L. *gurgēs*, a whirlpool; with which cf. Skt. *gargara-*, whirlpool. Der. *gorge*, verb, Romeo, v. 3. 46; *gorg-et*, a piece of armour to protect the throat, Troilus, i. 3. 174; Spenser, F. Q. iv. 3. 12. And see *gorgeous*.

GORGEOUS, showy, splendid. (F.—L.) 'Of *gorgeous* aray;' Sir T. More, Works, p. 808 c; 'they go *gorgeously* arayed;' id. 808 a. A corruption of *gorgias*; 'That were ioly and *gorgyas* in theyr gere;' Justes of May and June, in Hazlitt's Early Pop. Poet. ii. 117.—OF. *gorgias*, 'gorgeous, gaudy, flaunting, brave, gallant, gay, fine, trimme, quaintly clothed;' Cot. Cf. *se gorgiaser*, 'to flaunt, brave, or gallantise it;' id. β. Perhaps formed from OF. *gorgias*, 'a gorget;' id.; as though to wear a gorget were a fine thing; or from the swelling of the throat considered as a symbol of pride. γ. Either way, the word depends upon F. *gorge*, the throat; and much light is thrown upon the word by another entry in Cotgrave, viz. '*se rengorger*, to hold down [let sink down] the head, or thrust the chin into the neck, as some do *in pride*, or to make their faces look the fuller; we say, to bridle it.' δ. Note also Span. *gorja*, the throat; *gorjal*, a gorget, the collar of a doublet; *gorguera*, a gorget; *gorguero*, a kind of neckcloth, of ladies of fashion; *gorguerin*, a ruff round the neck. See Gorge. The editor of the F. poems of G. Coquillart has: '*Gorgias*, élégant. qui se rengorge, fat qui se pavane, dont la poitrine est couverte d'étoffes précieuses et de riches bijoux.' Der. *gorgeous-ly*, *gorgeous-ness*.

GORGON, a terrible monster. (L.—Gk.) In Shak. Macb. ii. 3. 77.—L. *Gorgon*, *Gorgō*.—Gk. Γοργώ, the Gorgon, a monster of fearful aspect. ☛ Gk. γοργός, fearful, terrible. Cf. OIrish *garg*, fierce; perhaps Skt. *garj*, to roar. Der. *Gorgon-ian*, Milton, P. L. ii. 611.

GORILLA, a kind of large ape. (OAfrican.) The word is an old one, lately revived. It occurs just at the end of a treatise called the *Periplūs* (περίπλους), i.e. 'circumnavigation,' written by a Carthaginian navigator named Hanno. This was originally written in the Punic language, and afterwards translated into Greek. He there describes some creatures 'which the interpreters called γορίλλας.'

GORMANDIZE, to eat like a glutton. (F.—Scand.) In Shak. Merch. of Ven. ii. 5. 3. Cotgrave has: '*Gourmander*, to ravine, devour, glut, gormandize or gluttonize it.' The E. form was suggested by the previous existence in E. of the sb. *gourmandyse*, as in 'they eate withoute *gourmandyse*;' Sir T. Elyot, Castle of Helth, b. ii. c. 1. This is from OF. *gourmandise*, gluttony; Cot. Both the sb. *gourmandise* and the vb. *gourmander* are from the OF. *gourmand*, 'a glutton, gormand, belly-god;' Cot. See Gourmand. Der. *gormandiz-er*, *gormandiz-ing*.

GORSE, a prickly shrub, furze. (E.) For *gorst*. ME. *gorst*, furze; Wyclif, Isaiah, lv. 13. AS. *gorst*. 'On gorste;' Luke, vi. 44; A.V. 'of a bramble-bush;' Vulgate, 'de rubo.' β. So named from its prickles. Cf. Skt. *hṛsh*, to bristle; L. *hirsūtus*, *horridus*, bristly; L. *hordeum*, Du. *gerst*, barley. Brugmann, i. § 882. See **Hirsute.**

GOSHAWK, a kind of hawk. (E.) Lit. a 'goose-hawk.' ME. *goshauk*, Wyclif, Job, xxxix. 13. The connexion with *goose* is proved by two successive entries in Voc. 131. 21, 22; viz. '*Auca*, gos;' and '*Aucarius*, gos-hafuc.' Here *gos* = AS. *gōs*, a goose; and *hafuc* = a hawk. The Vocabulary is ascribed to the tenth century. ✛ Icel. *gās-haukr*, similarly formed. And see below.

GOSLING, a young goose. (E.) In Shak. Cor. v. 3. 35. ME. *goselynge*; Prompt. Parv. Here *gose* = ME. *gos* = AS. *gōs*, a goose. The suffix *-ling* is a double diminutive, = *l-ing*. Cf. *duckling*, from *duck*. See **Goose.**

GOSPEL, the life of Christ. (E.) ME. *gospel*, Chaucer, C. T. 483 (A 481). Also *godspel*, P. Plowman, C. xiii. 100. AS. *godspell*, Grein, i. 519. The orig. sense was 'good story,' to translate L. *euangelium*. We find: '*Euuangelium* (sic), *id est, bonum nuntium, godspell*;' Voc. 314. 8. But the *o* (of AS. *gōd, good*) was soon shortened before *dsp*, and a more obvious popular etymology arose, as if *god-spell* meant 'story of God,' i.e. Christ. Hence, when the AS. word was introduced into Iceland, it took the form *guðspjall* = God-story, and not *gōð-spjall* = good story. And the OHG. word was likewise *gotspel* (= God-story), and not *guot spel*. ¶ It is interesting to find the orig. interpretation in the Ormulum, l. 157 of the Introduction.

GOSSAMER, fine spider-threads seen in fine weather. (E.) ME. *gossomer*, Chaucer, C. T. 10573 (F 259). Spelt *gosesomer* by W. de Bibbesworth (13th cent.); Wright's Vocab. i. 147, last line; and in Nominale, ed. Skeat, l. 625, we have 'a web of *gossomer*.' ME. *gossomer* is lit. *goose-summer*, and the prov. E. (Craven) name for gossamer is *summer-goose*; see Craven Gloss. It is named from the time of year when it is most seen, viz. during St. Martin's summer (early November); geese were eaten on Nov. 11 formerly. Cf. Lowl. Sc. (popular variant) *go-summer*, Martinmas. β. We may note, further, that Jamieson's Scottish Dict. gives *summer-cout*, i.e. summer-colt, as the name of exhalations seen rising from the ground in hot weather; and the Yorkshire expression for the same is very similar. 'When the air is seen on a warm day to undulate, and seems to rise as from hot embers, it is said, "see how the *summer-colt* rides!"' Whitby Glossary, by F. K. Robinson; quoted from Marshall. γ. In the same Whitby Glossary, the word for 'gossamer' is entered as *summer-gauze*. This may be confidently pronounced to be an ingenious corruption, as the word *gauze* is quite unknown to Middle-English and to the peasants of Craven, who say *summer-goose*; see Carr's Craven Glossary, where the *summer-colt* and *summer-goose* are synonymous. δ. The G. *sommer* means not only 'summer,' but also 'gossamer,' in certain compounds. The G. name for 'gossamer' is not only *sommerfäden* (summerthreads), but also *mädchen-sommer* (Maiden-summer), *der-alte-Weiber-sommer* (the old women's summer), or *Mechtildesommer*; see E. Müller. It was also simply known as *der fliegende sommer*, the flying summer (Weigand). This makes G. *sommer* = summer-film; and gives to *gossamer* the probable sense of 'goose-summer-film.' The connexion of the word with *summer* is further illustrated by the Du. *zomerdraden*, gossamer, lit. 'summer-threads,' and the Swed. *sommerträd*, gossamer, lit. 'summer-thread.' It may be observed that the spelling *gossamer* (with *a*) is certainly corrupt. It should rather be *gossomer* or *gossummer*.

GOSSIP, a sponsor in baptism, a crony. (E.) The old sense was 'sponsor in baptism,' lit. 'god-relative.' The final *p* stands for *b*, and *ss* for *ds*. ME. *gossib*, Chaucer, C. T. 5825 (D 243); earlier spelt *godsib*. See Poems of Will. of Shoreham, ed. Wright, pp. 68–70, where occur the words *gossibbe, sibbe,* and *gossibrede* (also spelt *godsibrede*), a derivative from *godsib* by suffixing ME. *-rede* (= AS. *rǣden*, E. *-red* in *kind-red*). β. Thus *gossip* stands for *god-sib*, i.e. related in God; AS. *godsibb*, Wulfstan, ed. Napier, p. 160; m. pl. *god-sibbas*. The f. sb. *sib* in AS. means 'peace,' but there was a derived word meaning 'relative.' Thus, in Luke, xiv. 12, the Northumb. glosses to Latin *cognatos* are (in one MS.) *sibbo* and (in the other) *gisibbe*; and again, in the Ormulum, l. 307, it is said of Elizabeth that she was 'Sante Marȝe sibb,' i.e. Saint Mary's relative. Cf. Icel. *sif*, affinity; *sifi*, a relative; G. *sippe*, affinity; pl. *sippen*, kinsmen; Goth. *sibja*, relationship, adoption as sons, Gal. iv. 5; *unsibis*, lit. unpeaceful, hence, lawless, wicked, Mark, xv. 28; *unsibja*, iniquity, Matt. vii. 23. These are further related to Skt. *sabhya-*, relating to an assembly, fit for an assembly, trusty, faithful; from *sabhā*, an assembly. Brugmann, i. §§ 124 (4), 567.

GOTH, one of a certain early Germanic tribe. (Late L. – Gothic.) 'Theodoric, the king of *Gothes*;' Chaucer, tr. of Boethius, bk. i. pr. 4. 53. – Late L. *Gōthi*, pl. Goths. – Goth. *Gutōs, or *Gutans, pl.; cf. Goth. *Gut-þiuda*, the Gothic people, where *þiuda* (AS. *þēod*) means 'people.' Der. *Goth-ic*.

GOUGE, a chisel with a hollowed blade. (F. – Late L. – C.?)

Formerly *googe*. 'By *googing* of them out;' Ben Jonson, The Devil is an Ass, A. ii. sc. 1 (Meercraft). 'An yron *goodg*;' Naval Accounts, p. 240 (1497). – F. *gouge*, 'a joyners googe;' Cot. Cf. Span. *gubia*, a gouge; Ital. *sgubia, sgubbia* (Torriano); Port. *goiva*. – Late L. *guvia*, a kind of chisel, in Isidore of Seville, lib. xix. De Instrumentis Lignariis (Brachet); also *gulbium* (Ducange). β. Of obscure origin; but perhaps Celtic. – OIrish *gulban*, a beak; W. *gylf* (N. E. D.).

GOURD, a large fleshy fruit. (F. – L.) ME. *gourd*, Chaucer, C. T. 17031 (H82). – F. *gourde*, formerly spelt *gouhourde* or *cougourde*, both of which spellings are in Cotgrave. *Gourde* is short for *gouhourde*, which is a corruption of *cougourde*. – L. *cucurbita*, a gourd; evidently a reduplicated form.

GOURMAND, a glutton. (F. – Scand.) Also *gormand, gormond*. 'To that great *gormond*, fat Apicius;' Ben Jonson, Sejanus, A. i. sc. 1. 'To *gurmander*, abligurire;' Levins, 83. 22. – F. *gourmand*, 'a glutton, gormand, belly-god;' Cot. β. Of Scand. origin. – Norw. *gurmen*, inclined to gorge oneself (Ross); from *gurma*, (1) to stir up mud; (2) to eat steadily and continually; (3) to gorge oneself (Aasen, Ross). Cf. Icel. *gormr*; Norw. *gurm*, ooze, mud, grounds of coffee, &c., allied to *gor*, gore; see **Gore** (1). The Span. *gormar* means 'to vomit.' Der. *gormand-ize* or *gormand-ise*, q.v.

GOUT (1), a drop, a disease. (F. – L.) '*Gouts* of blood;' Macb. ii. 1. 46. 'And he was al-so sik mid *goute*,' i.e. with the disease; Rob. of Glouc. p. 564; l. 11865. The disease was supposed to be caused by a defluxion of humours; so that it is the same word as *gout*, a drop. – OF. *goute, goutte*, a drop; also, 'the gowt;' Cot. – L. *gutta*, a drop. Der. *gout-y, gout-i-ness*.

GOUT (2), taste. (F. – L.) Merely borrowed from F. *goût*, taste. – L. *gustus*, taste; cf. *gustāre*, to taste; from the same root as E. *choose*. See **Choose.**

GOVERN, to steer, direct, rule. (F. – L. – Gk.) ME. *gouernen*, (with *u* for *v*), Rob. of Glouc. p. 44; l. 1036. – OF. *governer*, later *gouverner*. – L. *gubernāre*, to steer a ship, guide, direct. (Borrowed from Gk.) – Gk. κυβερνᾷν, to steer. Cf. Lithuan. *kumbriti*, to steer. Der. *govern-able*; *govern-ess*, Mids. Nt. Dream, ii. 1. 103; *government*, Tempest, i. 2. 75 (the older term being *govern-ance*, as in Chaucer, C. T. 12007, C 73); *govern-ment-al*; *govern-or*, ME. *gouernour* (*u* for *v*), Wyclif, James, iii. 4, from OF. *governeur* < L. acc. *gubernātōrem*, a steersman; *governor-ship*.

GOWAN, a daisy. (Scand.) 'And pu'd the *gowans* fine;' Burns, Auld Lang Syne, st. 2. Also formerly, a buttercup; North E. *gowlan*, Sc. *yellow gowan*, corn marigold. Named from the colour. – Icel. *gulr*, Swed. *gul*, Dan. *guul*, yellow. See **Yellow.**

GOWK, a cuckoo; a foolish person. (Scand.) 'Thare galede the *gowke*,' there sang the cuckoo; Allit. Morte Arthure, l. 927. And see E. D. D. – Icel. *gaukr*, a cuckoo; Swed. *gök*. ✛ AS. *gēac* (prov. E. *yeke*), a cuckoo; G. *gauch*. Teut. type *gaukoz, m.

GOWN, a loose robe. (F. – Late L.) ME. *goune*, Chaucer, C. T. 393; P. Plowman, B. xiii. 227. – OF. *gone, gonne, goune*, a long coat (Godefroy). – Late L. *gunna*, a skin, fur (scholiast on Geo. iii. 383); also a garment of fur (8th cent.) Ducange. Hence also Ital. *gonna*, OSpan. and Prov. *gona*, a woman's gown. Cf. also Byzantine Gk. γοῦνα, a coarse garment. ¶ Sometimes said to be Celtic, which is doubtful; see Stokes-Fick, p. 281. Cf. W. *gwn*, a gown, loose robe; Irish *gunn*, Gael. and Corn. *gun*, a gown; Manx *goon*; but these may be borrowed from E. Der. *gown-s-man*.

GRAB, to seize, clutch. (E.) A somewhat vulgar word, but given in Rider, Eng.-Lat. Dict. (1589). Prob. of native origin; cf. EFries. *grabbig*, greedy, *grabbelen*, to grab at. ✛ Du. *grabbel*, a scramble, *grabbelen*, to scramble for; Low G. *grabbeln*, to grab at; Swed. *grabba*, to grasp. Very near to OSkt. *grabh*, to seize, a Vedic form, of which the later form is *grah*; cf. OSlav. *grabiti*, to plunder. The standard E. word is *gripe*. See **Grapple, Gripe, Grasp.**

GRACE, favour, mercy, pardon. (F. – L.) ME. *grace*, in early use; Layamon, 6616 (later text). – OF. *grace*, L. *grātia*, favour. – L. *grātus*, dear, pleasing. Brugmann, i. §§ 524, 632. Der. *grace-ful, grace-ful-ly, grace-ful-ness*; *grac-i-ous*, Chaucer, C. T. 8489 (E 613); *grac-i-ous-ly, grac-i-ous-ness*; *grace-less, grace-less-ly, grace-less-ness*. And see *grateful*.

GRADATION, an advance by short steps, a blending of tints. (F. – L.) In Shak. Oth. i. 1. 37. – OF. *gradation*, 'a gradation, step, degree;' Cot. – L. *gradātiōnem*, acc. of *gradātio*, an ascent by steps. Cf. L. *gradātim*, step by step. – L. *gradus*, a step. See **Grade.** Der. *gradation-al, gradation-ed*.

GRADE, a degree, step in rank. (F. – L.) Of late introduction into E.; see Todd's Johnson; though used as a mathem. term (= degree) as early as 1511. [But the derived words *graduate*, &c., have been long in use; see below.] – F. *grade*, 'a degree;' Cot. – L. *gradum*, acc., a step, degree. – L. *gradi* (pp. *gressus*), to step, go. Brugmann, i. § 635; ii. § 707; Stokes-Fick, p. 118. Der. *grad-at-ion*, q.v., *grad-ient*, q.v., *grad-u-al*, q.v., *grad-u-ate*, q.v. Doublet, *gradus*. From the same source are *de-gree, de-grade, retro-grade*; *in-gred-i-ent*; also *ag-gress-ion, con-gress, di-gress, e-gress, in-gress, pro-gress, trans-gress.*

GRADIENT, gradually rising; a slope. (L.) A coined word, used in modern mechanics.—L. *gradient-*, stem of *gradiens*, pres. part. of *gradī*, to walk, advance. See **Grade**.

GRADUAL, advancing by steps. (L.) ' By *gradual* scale ; ' Milton, P. L. v. 483. [Also as sb., a *gradual* (see Blount), a service-book called in Latin *graduāle*, and more commonly known in ME. by the F. form *grayl*.]—Late L. **graduālis*, but only used in the neut. *graduāle* (often *gradāle*), to signify a service-book ' containing the portions to be sung by the choir, so called from certain short phrases after the Epistle sung *in gradibus* ' [upon the steps] ; Proctor, On the Common Prayer, p. 8. Formed, with suffix *-ālis*, from *gradu-*, decl. stem of *gradus*, a step. See **Grade**. Der. *gradual-ly*. And see *grail* (1).

GRADUATE, one who has received a university degree ; *as verb*, to take a degree, to mark off degrees. (L.) Cotgrave has : ' *Gradué*, *graduated*, having taken a degree ; ' and also : ' *Gradé*, *graduate*, or having taken a degree.' ' I would be a *graduate*, sir, no freshman ; ' Beaum. and Fletcher, Fair Maid, A. iv. sc. 2 (Dancer). And as sb., in Barclay, Ship of Fools, i. 2.—Late L. *graduātus*, one who has taken a degree ; still in use at the universities.—L. *gradu-*, decl. stem of *gradus*, a degree ; with pp. suffix *-ātus*. Der. *graduation, graduat-or*.

GRAFT, GRAFF, to insert buds on a stem. (F.—L.—Gk.) The form *graft* is due to a confusion with *graffed*, which was orig. the pp. of *graff*. Shak. has *grafted*, Macb. iv. 3. 51 ; but he also rightly has *graft* as a pp. ' Her royal stock *graft* with ignoble plants ; ' Rich. III, iii. 7. 127. Also the verb to *graff*, As You Like It, iii. 2. 124. Cf. Rom. xi. 17. ME. *graffen*, to graft ; P. Plowman, B. v. 137. β. The verb is formed from the sb. *graff*, a scion ; found in 1398 (N. E. D.). ' This bastard *graff* shall never come to growth ; ' Shak. Lucr. 1062. —OF. *graffe, grafe*, a style for writing with, a sort of pencil ; also *greffe*, ' a graff, a slip or young shoot ; ' Cot. [So named from the resemblance of the cut slip to the shape of a pointed pencil. Similarly we have L. *graphiolum*, (1) a small style, (2) a small shoot, scion, graff.]—L. *graphium*, a style for writing with.—Gk. γραφίον, another form of γραφεῖον, a style, pencil.—Gk. γράφειν, to write, grave. See **Graphic**. Der. *graft-er*.

GRAIL (1), a gradual, or service-book. (F.—L.) ME. *graile, grayle*. ' *Grayle*, boke, gradale, vel gradalis ; ' Prompt. Parv. p. 207 ; and see Way's note.—OF. *graël* ; Godefroy.—Late L. *gradāle* ; see explanation s. v. **Gradual**.

GRAIL (2), the Holy Dish at the Last Supper. (F.—L.) In Spenser, F. Q. ii. 10. 53. ' Fulfille the meruails of the *greal* ; ' Arthur and Merlin, ed. Kölbing, 2222. See my Pref. to Joseph of Arimathie, published for the Early Eng. Text Society. It is there shown that the true etymology has, at an early period, deliberately falsified by a change of *San Greal* (Holy Dish) into *Sang Real* (Royal Blood, but perversely made to mean Real Blood).—OF. *graal, greal, grasal*, a flat dish, Prov. *grasal*, Late L. *gradāle, grasāle*, a flat dish, a shallow vessel. [The various forms in OF. and Low L. are very numerous ; see the articles in Godefroy, Ducange, and Charpentier's Supplement to Ducange.] β. The word would appear to represent a Folk-L. type **crātālis*, formed from Late L. *crātus*, a cup, substituted for *crāter*, a bowl. See **Crater**. It was, fabulously, the dish in which Joseph of Arimathea is said to have collected our Lord's blood.

GRAIL (3), fine sand. (F.) Spenser uses the word in a way peculiarly his own ; he seems to have meant ' fine particles ; ' he speaks of ' sandie *graile*,' and of ' golden *grayle* ; ' F. Q. ii. 7. 6 ; Visions of Bellay, st. 12. Perhaps suggested by MF. *graisle*, 'thinne, small, little ; ' Cot. (mod. F. *grêle*).—L. *gracilis*, slender. ¶ It is, of course, possible that Spenser was merely coining a new form of *gravel*.

GRAIN, a single small hard seed. (F.—L.) ME. *grein, greyn, grain* ; Chaucer, C. T. 598 (A 596) ; P. Plowman, B. x. 139.—OF. *grain*.—L. *grānum*, a grain, corn.+Irish *grān*, W. *gronyn*. Cognate with E. *corn*. See **Corn**. Der. *grain-ed* ; also *granule*, q.v., *grange*, q. v., *granary*, q. v., *granite*, q.v. ☞ *Grain* in the sense of fibre of wood is the same word ; cf. F. *grain des pierres*, the grain of stones (Hamilton). The phrase ' to dye in grain ' meant to dye of a fast colour, by means of kermes, &c. ; whence *grained*, deeply dyed, Hamlet, iii. 4. 90. The phrase is an old one ; see P. Plowman, B. ii. 15, and the note.

GRALLATORY, long-legged, said of birds. (L.) A term applied to wading birds. Coined from L. *grallātor*, a walker on stilts.—L. *grallæ*, stilts, contracted from **gradlæ*, formed from the base *grad-* in L. *gradī*, to walk. See **Grade**. Brugmann, i. § 587 (4). Der. *grallatori-al*.

GRAMARYE, magic. (F.—L.—Gk.) Used by Scott, Lay of the Last Minstrel, iii. 11, vi. 17 ; who took it from ' King Estmere ' in Percy's Reliques, where it occurs in a passage the genuineness of

which is doubtful ; see Percy Folio MS., ii. 604, l. 144, ii. 607, l. 274. The same word as ME. *gramery, gramory*, skill in grammar, or (jestingly) skill in magic. ' Cowthe ye by youre *gramery* reche us a drynk, I shuld be more mery ; ' Towneley Myst. p. 90. ' I se thou can of *gramory* and som what of arte ; ' id. p. 311.—OF. *gramaire*, grammar ; see **Grammar**. ☞ I desire here to record my opinion, that the word *glamour*, magic, also used by Scott in the same poem (iii. 9), and taken by him from the expression ' They coost the *glamer* o'er her ' in Johnny Faa (printed in Ritson's Sc. Poems, ii. 176), is nothing but another form of *gramere*, i.e. grammar. The note in Vigfusson's Dict. asserting the identity of *glamour* with Icel. *glâmr*, the moon, cannot be seriously entertained. I see that Littré (s. v. *grimoire*) agrees with me as to *glamour* ; cf. *grimoire* in Hatzfeld. [This note, now confirmed (see N. E. D.), first appeared in 1884.]

GRAMERCY, thanks ! (F.—L.) In Shak. Merch. of Ven. ii. 2. 128. Formerly *grand mercy*, Chaucer, C. T. 8964 (E 1088).—F. *grand merci*, great thanks. See **Grand** and **Mercy**.

GRAMINEOUS, relating to grass. (L.) In Blount's Gloss., ed. 1674. Coined from L. *grāmin-*, stem of *grāmen*, grass. Der. *graminivorous*, grass-eating, from *grāmini-*, decl. stem of *grāmen*, and *uorāre*, to devour ; see **Voracious**. And see **Grass**.

GRAMMAR, the science of the use of language. (F.—L.—Gk.) ME. *grammere*, Chaucer, C. T. 13466 (B 1726).—OF. *gramaire* (12th cent.)—Late L. *grammatica*, grammar (Hatzfeld). —Gk. γραμματική, grammar.—Gk. γραμματικός, knowing one's letters (see below). Der. *grammar-i-an, grammar-school* ; from the same source, *grammatical* ; see below.

GRAMMATICAL, belonging to grammar. (F.—L.—Gk.) ' Those *grammatic* flats and shallows ; ' Milton, Of Education (R.). *Grammaticall* is in Palsgrave, page v.—F. *grammatical*, ' grammaticall ; ' Cot. Formed, with suffix *-al*, from L. *grammaticus*, grammatical.—Gk. γραμματικός, versed in one's letters, knowing the rudiments.—Gk. γραμματ-, stem of γράμμα, a letter.—Gk. γράφειν, to write. Der. *grammatical-ly*.

GRAMPUS, a kind of fish. (F.—L.) ' *Grampus*, a fish somewhat like a whale, but less ; ' Kersey, ed. 1715. Sir T. Herbert mentions ' porpice, *grampasse* (the *sus marinus*), mullet,' &c. ; Travels, p. 404, ed. 1655 (or p. 384, Todd's Johnson). Spelt *graundepose* in Skelton, Speke Parrot, l. 309.—AF. *grampais*, Black Book of Admiralty, i. 152 ; a changed form of OF. *craspois, crapois, graspois, grapois* (Godefroy) ; by substituting OF. *grand*, great, for OF. *cras, gras*, fat. Cf. Late L. *craspiscis* in Thorpe, Anc. Laws, i. 300.—L. *crassum piscem*, acc., fat fish. See **Grease** and **Fish**. ¶ The word *porpoise* is similarly formed. See **Porpoise**.

GRANARY, a storehouse for grain. (L.) ' *Granary* or *Garner* ; ' Kersey, ed. 1715. Also *granarie* in Levins, 104. 24.—L. *grānārium* (pl. *grānāria*), a granary.—L. *grānum*, corn. See **Grain** and **Garner**. Doublet, *garner* ; also, *grange*.

GRAND, great, large. (F.—L.) In Shak. Temp. i. 2. 274. ME. *grant, graunt* ; not much used formerly, except in compounds. The comp. *grandame* occurs in St. Marharete, ed. Cockayne, p. 22, l. 32. *Graund-father* is in Berners, tr. of Froissart, vol. i. c. 3. Fabyan has *graund-mother*, vol. i. c. 124 ; ed. Ellis, p. 102.—OF. *grand*, great. —L. *grandem*, acc. of *grandis*, great. Der. *grand-child, grandame, grand-sire, grand-father, grand-son, grand-mother, grand-daughter ; grand-ly, grand-ness*. And see below.

GRANDEE, a Spanish nobleman. (Span.—L.) Spelt *grandy* ; ' in a great person, right worshipful sir, a right honourable *grandy* ; ' Burton, Anat. of Melancholy, To the Reader, ed. 1651, p. 35. Spelt *grande*, B. Jonson, Alchemist, A. iii.—Span. *grande*, great ; also, a nobleman.—L. *grandem*, acc. of *grandis*, great. See **Grand**.

GRANDEUR, greatness. (F.—L.) In Milton, P. R. iv. 110. —F. *grandeur*, ' greatnesse ; ' Cot. Formed, with suffix *-eur*, from F. *grand*, great. See **Grand**.

GRANDILOQUENT, pompous in speech. (L.) Not in early use. The adj. and the sb. *grandiloquence* are in Blount's Glossary (1681). Formed (in rivalry of L. *grandiloquus*, grandiloquent) from *grandi-*, decl. stem of *grandis*, great, and *loquent-*, stem of pres. part. of *loquī*, to speak. See **Grand** and **Loquacious**. Der. *grandiloquence*.

GRANGE, a farmhouse. (F.—L.) ME. *grange, graunge* ; Chaucer, C. T. 12996 (B 1256) ; P. Plowman, B. xvii. 71.—OF. *grange*, ' a barn for corn ; also, a grange ; ' Cot. [Cf. Span. *granja*, a farmhouse, villa, grange.]—Late L. *grānica, grānea*, a barn, grange.—L. *grānum*, corn. See **Grain**.

GRANITE, a hard stone. (Ital.—L.) ' *Granite* or *Granita*, a kind of speckled marble ; ' Kersey, ed. 1715.—Ital. *granito*, ' a kind of speckled stone ; ' Florio.—Ital. *granito*, pp. of *granire*, ' to reduce into graines ; ' Florio ; hence, to speckle.—Ital. *grano*, corn.—L. *grānum*, corn. See **Grain**.

GRANT, to allow, bestow, permit. (F.—L.) ME. *graunten*, *granten*, in very early use; Layamon, 4789, later text; Ancren Riwle, p. 34.—OF. *graanter*, *graunter*, later spellings of OF. *craanter*, *creanter*, to caution, to assure, guarantee; whence the later senses of promise, yield. Cf. Late L. *crēantāre* (for *crēdentāre*), to assure, guarantee; *creantium*, a caution, guarantee; Ducange.—Late L. *crēdentāre*, to guarantee, not found; closely related to Late L. crēdentia, a promise, whence F. *créance*.—L. *crēdent-*, stem of pres. part. of *crēdere*, to trust. See **Creed**. Der. *grant*, sb., *grant-or*, *grant-ee*.

GRANULE, a little grain. (L.) 'Granule, a little grain, or barley-corn;' Blount's Gloss., ed. 1674. (Prob. directly from L.; but cf. F. *granule*.)—L. *grānulum*, a little grain; dimin. of *grānum*, a grain. See **Grain**. Der. *granul-ar*, *granul-ate*, *granul-at-ion*, *granul-ous*.

GRAPE, the fruit of the vine. (F.—O. Low G.) In Chaucer, C. T. 17032 (H 83); P. Plowman, B. xiv. 30.—OF. *grape*; MF. *grappe*, 'a bunch, or cluster of grapes;' Cot. [The orig. sense was 'a hook,' whence OF. *graper*, to gather clusters with a hook. The Rouchi dial. has *crape*, a bunch (Hécart). In E., the sense has altered from 'cluster' to 'single berry.' But cf. Norman dial. *grape*, a grape (Moisy; ed. 1895). Cf. Span. *grapa*, a hold-fast, cramp-iron; Ital. *grappare*, to seize; *grappo*, a clutching; *grappolo*, a cluster of grapes.]—Teut. type *krappo-*, whence O. Low G. *crappo*, a hook (Gallée), Low G. *krappe*, a hook (Berghaus), OHG. *chrapho*, a hook. Allied to E. *cramp*. See **Cramp**. Der. *grape-ry*, *grape-shot*. ☞ The senses of 'hook' and 'cluster' or 'handful' result from that of 'clutching.' See *grapnel*.

GRAPHIC, pertaining to writing; descriptive. (L.—Gk.) 'The letters will grow more large and *graphicall*;' Bacon, Nat. Hist. § 503. 'Each line, as it were *graphic*, in the face;' Ben Jonson, An Elegy on My Muse, Underwoods, xxi. ix. 154.—L. *graphicus*, belonging to painting or drawing.—Gk. γραφικός, the same.—Gk. γράφειν, to write. See **Carve**. Der. *graphic-al*, *graphic-al-ly*.

GRAPNEL, a grappling-iron. (F.—O. Low G.) ME. *grapenel* (trisyllabic); Chaucer, Legend of Good Women, 640 (Cleopatra).—OF. *grapin* (Supp. to Godefroy), F. *grappin*, a grapnel; with dim. suffix *-el*, thus giving *grapinel*, in three syllables. Formed, with suffix *-in*, from OF. *grape*, F. *grappe*, a hook. See **Grape**, **Grapple**.

GRAPPLE, to lay fast hold of, clutch. (F.—O. Low G.) In Shak. L. L. L. ii. 218; Spenser, F. Q. iv. 4. 29. Properly to seize with a *graple*, i. e. a grapnel (Palsgrave, p. 227), and formed from the sb.—MF. *grappil*, 'the *grapple* of a ship;' Cot. The same in sense as F. *grappin*. Both *grapp-il* and *grapp-in* are formed from F. *grappe*, formerly used in the sense of 'hook;' cf. the phrase *mordre à la grappe*, to bite at the hook, to swallow the bait (Hamilton). See further under **Grape**.

GRASP, to seize, hold fast. (E.) ME. *graspen*, used in the sense of 'grope,' to feel one's way; as in 'And *graspeth* by the walles to and fro;' Chaucer, C. T. 4291 (A 4293); also in Wyclif, Job, v. 14, xii. 25 (earlier version), where the later version has *grope*. Just as *clasp* was formerly *claps*, so *grasp* stands for *graps*. The ME. *graspen* stands for *grap-sen*, 'That *grapsest* here and there as doth the blynde;' Hoccleve, De Reg. Princ., ed. Wright, p. 8, st. 31 (l. 212). Prob. from AS. type *grǣpsan* (Teut. type *graipisōn*), from *grāpan*, to grope. Cp. EFries. *grapsen*, to seize. See **Grope**. ¶ Similar transpositions of *sp* are seen in the prov. E. *wops* for *wasp*, in AS. *hæps*, a hasp, AS. *æps*, an aspen-tree; &c. The extension of the stem by the addition of *s* occurs in AS., and remains in E. *clean-se* from *clean*.

GRASS, common herbage. (E.) ME. *gras*, *gres*; also *gers*. Spelt *gras*, Chaucer, C. T. 7577 (D 1995); *gres* and *gresse*, Prompt. Parv. p. 210; *gers*, Ayenbite of Inwyt, ed. Morris, p. 111. AS. *gærs*, *græs*, Grein, i. 373, 525.+Du. and Icel. *gras*; Swed. and Dan. *græs*; Goth. *gras*; G. *gras*. Teut. type *gra-som*, neut. From *gra-*, a weak grade of Teut. *grō-*, to grow; cf. MHG. *gruose*, young plants; and E. *green*. See **Grow**. Der. *grass-plot*, *grass-y*; *grass-hopper* = AS. *gærshoppa*, Ps. lxxvii. 51, ed. Spelman; *graze*<ME. *grasien*, Prompt. Parv. p. 210, from AS. *grasian* (Icel. *gresja*); *graz-i-er*=*graz-er* (cf. *bow-yer*, *law-yer*).

GRATE (1), a frame-work of iron-bars. (Late L.—L.) ME. *grate*. 'Grate, or trelys wyndowe, cancellus;' Prompt. Parv. p. 207.—Late L. *grāta*, a grating; cf. Ital. *grata*, a grate, gridiron. A variant of Late L. *crāta*, a grating, crate.—L. *crātes*, a hurdle. See **Crate**. Thus *grate* is a mere variant of *crate*, due to a weakened pronunciation. Der. *grat-ing*, *grat-ed*.

GRATE (2), to rub, scrape, scratch, creak. (F.—Teut.) ME. *graten*. 'Grate brede [to grate bread], *mico*;' Prompt. Parv. p. 207. 'Gratynge of gyngure, *frictura*;' id.—OF. *grater*, to scratch, to scrape;' Cot.; Norm. dial. *grater* (Moisy); F. *gratter*. Cf. Ital. *grattare*, to scratch, rub; Late L. *cratare*, found in the Germanic codes; 'si quis alium unguibus *cratauerit*;' Lex Frisonum, app. 5.—Teut. type *krattōjan*, as seen in Swed. *kratta*, to scrape; Dan. *kratte*, to scrape; OHG. *chrazzōn*, G. *kratzen*, to scratch. Der. *grat-er*, *grat-ing*, *grat-ing-ly*. Cf. *scratch*.

GRATEFUL, pleasant, thankful. (Hybrid; F. *and* E.) In Shak. All's Well, ii. 1. 132. The suffix *-ful* is E., from AS. *-ful*, full. The first syllable appears again in *in-grate*, and is derived from OF. *grat*, likewise preserved in OF. *in-grat*, 'ungrateful;' Cot.—L. *grātus*, pleasing. See **Grace**. Der. *grate-ful-ly*, *grate-ful-ness*; also *gratify*, q. v.; and see *gratis*, *gratitude*, *gratuitous*, *gratulate*; also *agree*.

GRATIFY, to please, soothe. (F.—L.) In Shak. Merch. of Ven. iv. 1. 406.—MF. *gratifier*, 'to gratifie;' Cot.—L. *grātificāre*, *grātificārī*, to please.—L. *grāti-* < *grāto-*, decl. stem of *grātus*, pleasing; and *-ficāre* (=*facere*), to make. See **Grateful**, **Grace**. Der. *gratific-at-ion*, from L. acc. *grātificātiōnem*, which is from *grātificārī*.

GRATIS, freely. (L.) In Shak. Merch. of Ven. i. 3. 45.—L. *grātīs*, adv. freely; for *grātiis*, abl. pl. of *grātia*, favour. See **Grace**.

GRATITUDE, thankfulness. (F.—L.) In Shak. Cor. iii. 1. 291.—F. *gratitude*; Cot.—Late L. *grātitūdinem*, acc. of *grātitūdo*, thankfulness. Formed (like *beātitūdo* from *beātus*) from *grātus*, pleasing; see **Grateful**.

GRATUITOUS, freely given. (L.) 'By way of gift, merely *gratuitous*;' Bp. Taylor, Rule of Conscience, b. ii. c. 3. rule 81.—L. *grātuīt-us*, freely given; with suffix *-ous*. Extended from *grātu-*, for *grātus*, pleasing. See **Grateful**. Der. *gratuitous-ly*; and see below.

GRATUITY, a present. (F.—L.) So called because given freely or *gratis*. 'To be given me in *gratuity*;' Ben Jonson, The Humble Petition of Poor Ben to K. Charles, l. 10. And in Cotgrave.—OF. *gratuité*, 'a gratuity, or free gift;' Cot.—Late L. *grātuītātem*, acc. of *grātuītas*, a free gift. Allied to *grātuītus*, freely given. See above.

GRATULATE, to congratulate. (L.) In Shak. Rich. III, iv. 1. 10.—L. *grātulātus*, pp. of *grātulārī*, to wish a person joy. Formed as if from an adj. *grātulus*, joyful; an extension of *grātus*, pleasing. See **Grateful**. Der. *gratulat-ion*, *gratulat-or-y*; also *con-gratulate*, which has now taken the place of the simple verb.

GRAVE (1), to cut, engrave. (E.) ME. *grauen* (with *u* for *v*), to grave, also to bury; Chaucer, C. T. 8557 (E 681); Layamon, 9960. AS. *grafan*, to dig, grave, engrave; Grein, i. 523.+Du. *graven*, to dig; Dan. *grave*; Icel. *grafa*; Swed. *grafva*, to dig; Goth. *graban*, Luke, vi. 48; G. *graben*. Teut. type *graban-*, pt. t. *grōb*; Idg. type *ghrabh-*; whence also Russ. *grob'*, a tomb, a grave. Der. *grave*, sb., Chaucer, C. T. 12599 (C 665); lit. 'that which is dug out;' also *grav-er*, *grav-ing*, *groove*.

GRAVE (2), solemn, sad. (F.—L.) Lit. 'heavy.' In Spenser, F. Q. v. 7. 18.—F. *grave*, 'grave, stately;' Cot.—L. *grauem*, acc. of *grauis*, heavy, grave.+Goth. *kaurus*, heavy, burdensome, 2 Cor. x. 10; Gk. βαρύς, heavy; Skt. *guru-*, heavy. Brugmann, i. § 665. Der. *grave-ly*, *grave-ness*; also *grav-i-ty* (Shak.), from F. *gravité* (Cot.), from L. acc. *grauitātem*; *gravi-t-ate*, *gravi-t-at-ion*; *gravi-d*, from L. *grauidus*, burdened. From the same root, *grief*, q. v.; also *ag-grav-ate*, *ag-grieve*, *baro-meter*.

GRAVEL, fine small stones. (F.—C.) ME. *grauel* (with *u* for *v*), in early use; in King Horn, ed. Lumby, l. 1465.—OF. *gravele*, later *gravelle* (Godefroy, Cot.); dimin. of OF. *grave*, rough sand mixed with stones (Brachet).—Celt. base *gravo-*, as in Bret. *grouan*, gravel, Corn. *grow*, gravel, sand; W. *gro*, pebbles; Stokes-Fick, p. 117. Der. *gravell-y*.

GRAVY, juice from cooked meat. (F.—L.) In Shak. 2 Hen. IV, i. 2. 184. Also spelt *greavy*, or *greauy* (with *u* for *v*). 'In fat and *greauy*;' Chapman, tr. of Homer, Odyss. xviii. 166. 'With all their fat and *greauie*;' id. xviii. 63. ME. *graué*, *grauey*, the name of a dressing for meats made of broth, milk of almonds, spices, and wine or ale. 'Conyngus in *graué*, rabbits in gravy;' Liber Cure Cocorum, ed. Morris, p. 8; cf. pp. 24, 25. And see *grauey* in Two Cookery-books, ed. Austin (glossary).—OF. *grané*, a similar sauce, which seems to have been misread as *graué*; cf. 'conyns en grané' (misprinted *gravé*), Wright, Vol. of Vocab., i. 174. See Godefroy.—L. *grānātus*, full of grains (with apparent allusion to the thickened broth).—L. *grānum*, a grain; see **Grain** and **Grenade**. ☞ Thus *gravy* appears to be an error for *grainy*. Torriano explains Ital. *granato*, *granito*, as 'kernelly or corny as honey, figs, soap, or oyl is sometimes in winter.' See N. E. D.

GRAY, ash-coloured; white mixed with black. (E.) ME. *gray*, *grey*. 'Hire eyen *grey* as glas;' Chaucer, C. T. 152. OMerc. *grei* (O. E. Texts); AS. *grǣg*; Grein, i. 525.+Du. *graauw*; Icel. *grár*; Dan. *graa*; Swed. *grå*; G. *grau*. Teut. type *grǣgwoz*; whence *grǣg-*, *grǣw-*. Cf. Low G. *grag*, gray (Berghaus). Der. *gray-ish*, *gray-beard*; *gray-l-ing* (with double dimin. suffix). Cf. *graile* as a fish-name in Harrison's Descr. of England, iii. 3.

GRAZE (1), to feed cattle. (E.) Merely formed from *grass*. ME. *grasen*. 'And lich an oxe, under the fot, He *graseth* as he nedes mot;' said of Nebuchadnezzar; Gower, C. A. i. 142; bk. i. 2973. AS. *grasian*, to graze.+Icel. *gresja*; Dan. *græsse*; Du. *grazen*; G. *grasen*. See **Grass**. Der. *graz-i-er*.

GRAZE (2), to touch lightly in passing and glance off. (E.) It appears to be merely a peculiar use of *graze* (1); and was used of cannon-balls that rebounded from the grass. 'That being dead, like to the bullet's *grazing*, Break out into a second course of mischief;' Hen. V, iv. 3. 105. 'Those bullets which *graze* on the ground do most mischief;' Fuller, Holy and Profane State, v. 1. 2. So also G. *grasen*, to graze (pasture), also to roll and bound, as cannon-balls (Flügel); so also Dan. *græsse* (Larsen).

GREASE, animal fat, oily matter. (F.—L.) ME. *grece, grese*; Chaucer, C. T. 135, 6069 (A 135, D 487).—OF. *graisse, gresse*, earlier *creisse* (Supp. to Godefroy); F. *graisse*.—Folk-L. **crassia* (Hatzfeld).—L. *crassus*, thick, fat. See **Crass**. Der. *greas-y, greas-i-ness*; also *cresset*, q. v.

GREAT, large, ample, big. (E.) ME. *gret, grete*; Chaucer, C. T. 1279. AS. *gréat*, Grein, i. 527. **+** Du. *groot*; G. *gross*. Teut. type **grautoz*. Der. *great-ly, great-ness*; *great-coat, great-hearted*; also *great-grandfather, great-grandson*. And see *groat*.

GREAVES (1), **GRAVES**, the sediment of melted tallow. (E.) 'Chandlers *graiues* [pr. *graines*] . . . the offall of rendred Tallow;' G. Markham, Husbandry (1614), p. 97 (N. E. D.). 'To *Grave* a ship, to preserve the calking, by laying over a mixture of tallow or train-oil, rosin, &c. boiled together;' Kersey's Dict. ed. 1715. This verb merely means to smear with *grave* or *graves*, i. e. a tallowy mess. Perhaps a native word; the AS. *gréofa*, glossed *olla* (pot) may have meant 'melting-pot.' Cf. EFries. *gräfen*, pl., greaves. Also MSwed. *grefwar*, dirt, *ljus-grefwar*, candle-dirt, refuse of tallow (Ihre); Swed. dial. *grevar*, sb. pl. leavings of tallow, greaves (Rietz); Westphal. *graiwe*; Low G. *greven*, greaves; Bremen Wörterbuch, ii. 541. **+** G. *griebe*, the fibrous remains of lard, after it has been fried (Flügel); OHG. *griupo, griebo*.

GREAVES (2), armour for the legs. (F.) In Milton, Samson, 1121. ME. *greues*, pl.; Gawain and Grene Knt. 575.—OF. *greves*, 'boots, also greaves, or armour for the legs;' Cot. Cf. Span. *grebas* (pl. of *greba*), greaves.—OF. *greve*, 'the shank, shin, or forepart of the leg;' Cot.; Picard *greve*.

GREBE, an aquatic bird. (F.) Not in Johnson. First found in Pennant (1766).—F. *grèbe*, a grebe (Hamilton); also *grépe*, in the dial. of Lyons (Puitspelu). Of unknown origin; Cot. gives *griaibe*, 'a sea-mew,' as a Savoyard word.

GRECE, a flight of steps. (F.—L.) 'A *grece* ther was of steppis fijftene;' Cursor Mundi, l. 10584. Really a pl.; = *gree-s*, pl. of *gree*, a step.—OF. *gré*, a step (Roquefort).—L. *gradum*, acc. of *gradus*, a step. See **Grade** and **Degree**. β. Hence *grece* was often improperly used to mean 'a (single) step;' Shak. spells it *grise*; Oth. i. 3. 200.

GREEDY, hungry, voracious. (E.) ME. *gredi, gredy*; Ancren Riwle, p. 416; whence *gredinesse*, id. p. 416. AS. *grǽdig, grédig*; Grein, i. 525. **+** Icel. *gráðugr*; MSwed. *grådig, grådig* (Ihre); Dan. *graadig*; Goth. *grēdags*. Teut. type **grēdugoz*; an adj. formed from Teut. *grǽduz*, hunger, greed; as seen in Goth. *grēdus*, hunger, Icel. *gráðr*, hunger, and in AS. *grǽd-um*, greedily, a dat. pl. form. Further allied to Skt. *grdhra-*, greedy, *grdh*, to be greedy; *gardha-s*, greed; Macdonell. (✓GERDH.) Der. *greed-i-ly, greed-i-ness*. The sb. *greed*, though not found before 1609, is a perfectly correct form.

GREEN, of the colour of growing plants. (E.) ME. *green, grene*, Chaucer, C. T. 6443 (D 861); used as sb., 6580 (D 998). AS. *gréne*, Grein, i. 526. [Here *ē* represents the *i-* mutation of *ō*, so that the base is *grō-*.] **+** Du. *groen*; Icel. *grænn* (for *grœnn*); Dan. and Swed. *grön*; G. *grün*, MHG. *gruene*, OHG. *kruoni*. Teut. type **grōn-joz*, earlier type **grō-niz* (Sievers). Allied to AS. *grōwan*, to grow. Teut. base **gra-, *grō-*; see **Grass**. Thus *green* is the colour of growing herbs. Der. *green-s*; the phrase 'wortes of *grenes*' is used to translate *holera herbarum* in The Anglo-Saxon and Early English Psalters, ed. Stevenson (Surtees Soc.), vol. i. p. 111; Ps. xxxvi. 2. Also *green-cloth, green-crop, greengage, green-grocer* (see *grocer*), *green-house, green-ish, green-ish-ness, green-room, green-sand, green-stone*; also *green-sward* (s.v. *sward*).

GREENGAGE, a kind of plum. (E.) This stands for *green Gage*, where *Gage* is a personal name. It is the French plum called *la grosse Reine Claude*, and is written as *Green Gage* in P. Miller, Gardener's Dictionary, 7th ed. 1759, s. v. *Prunus*. There is also a *blue Gage* and a *purple Gage*. 'Plum; of the many sorts, the following are good: *Green* and *blue gage*, Fotheringham,' &c.; C. Marshall, Introd. to Gardening, 1796, p. 350. In R. Hogg's Fruit Manual, 4th ed. 1875, it is said to have been introduced 'at the beginning of the last century, by Sir T. Gage, of Hengrave Hall, near Bury, who procured it from his brother, the Rev. John Gage, a Roman Catholic priest then resident in Paris.' The following account is more explicit, and gives the name as Sir *William* Gage. In Hortus Collinsonianus, p. 60, are some Memoranda by Mr. Collinson, written 1759-1765, where is the following entry. 'On Plums. *Mem.* I was on a visit to

Sir William Gage, at Hengrave, near Bury: he was then near 70. He told me that he first brought over, from France, the *Grosse Reine Claude*, and introduced it into England; and in compliment to him the Plum was called the *Green Gage*; this was about the year 1725.' (J. A. H. Murray.) β. It must be added, that Mr. Hogg shows that there is reason for supposing that this plum was known in England at least a century earlier than the above date, but was then called the *Verdoch*, from the Ital. *verdochia*, obviously derived from *verde* (L. *uiridis*), green. But this does not affect the etymology of the present name. 'The green gages' occurs, with reference to plums, in Foote's Lame Lover, A. iii. (1770).

GREET (1), to salute. (E.) ME. *greten*, Chaucer, C. T. 8890 (E 1014); Ancren Riwle, p. 430. AS. *grétan*, to approach, visit, address; Grein, i. 526. **+** Du. *groeten*, to greet, salute; OSax. *grótian*; MHG. *gruezen*, G. *grüssen*, to greet. Teut. type **grótjan-*; from the sb. **grōt-oz*, m., seen in Du. *groet*, G. *gruss*, a greeting. Der. *greet-ing*.

GREET (2), to weep, cry, lament. (E.) In Northern E. only. ME. *greten*, Havelok, 164, 241, 285. AS. *grǽtan, grétan*, to weep; Grein, i. 525. **+** Icel. *gráta*; Dan. *grǽde*; Swed. *gråta*; Goth. *grētan*, to weep, pt. t. *gai-grót*. Teut. type **grǽtan-*, with reduplic. pt. t. Perhaps allied to Skt. *hrad*, to resound, roar, *hrād-as*, noise.

GREGARIOUS, associating in flocks. (L.) 'No birds of prey are *gregarious*;' Ray, On the Creation, pt. i. (R.).—L. *gregārius*, belonging to a flock (with suffix *-ous*).—L. *greg-*, base of *grex*, a flock; with suffix *-ārius*. Cf. OIrish *graig*, a herd of horses; W. *gre*, a flock; Stokes-Fick, p. 117. Also Gk. ἀγείρειν, to assemble (Prellwitz). Der. *gregarious-ly, gregarious-ness*; from the same source, *ag-greg-ate, con-greg-ate, se-greg-ate, e-greg-ious*.

GRENADE, a kind of war-missile. (F.—Span.—L.) Formerly also *granado*, which is the Span. form. 'Granado, an apple filled with delicious grains; there is also a warlike engine, that being filled with gunpowder and other materials, is wont to be shot out of a wide-mouthed piece of ordnance, and is called a *granado* for the likeness it hath with the other *granado* in fashion, and being fully stuffed as the other *granado* is, though the materials are very different;' Blount's Gloss. ed. 1674. Spelt *granados*, Evelyn, Diary, June 1, 1667.—OF. *grenade*, 'a pomegranet; also a ball of wildfire, made like a pomegranet;' Cot.—Span. *granada*, a pomegranate, a hand-grenade.—Span. *granado*, full of seeds.—L. *grānātus*, full of seeds.—L. *grānum*, a grain. See **Grain, Garnet**. Der. *grenad-ier* (spelt *granadier*, Evelyn, Diary, June 29, 1678).

GREY, the same as **Gray**, q. v.

GREYHOUND, a swift slender hound. (E.) 'Grehoundes he hadde as swift as fowel in flight;' Chaucer, C. T. 190. Also spelt *greahund*, Ancren Riwle, p. 332, last line. AS. *grighund*, Voc. 276. 3; where *grig-* = *grieg-* (Icel. *grey-*), for Teut. **graujo-*. Cf. Icel. *greyhundr*, a greyhound; composed of *grey*, a dog, and *hundr*, a hound. The Icel. *grey* is also used alone in the sense of greyhound or dog; and the Icel. *greybaka* means a bitch. ¶ Whatever be the source of Icel. *grey*, there is no pretence for connecting it with E. *gray*, adj., for which the Icel. word is *grár*.

GRIDDLE, a pan for baking cakes. (F.—L.) ME. *gredil*, a gridiron (in the story of St. Lawrence), Ancren Riwle, p. 122. Called a *girdle* (= *gridle*) in North. E.—AF. *gridil* (OF. *greil*), used to gloss L. *craticulam* in Neckam; see Wright, Vol. Vocab. i. 102, l. 9. So also AF. *gridile*, glossed by 'rosting-hiron;' Nominale, ed. Skeat, l. 488. [Cf. Norm. dial. *grédil*, Moisy.]—Late L. **crāticulum*, for L. *crāticula*, a griddle, dimin. of *crātis*, a hurdle. [W. *greidyll* is from E.] See **Crate**, and see **Grill**. Der. From the same ME. *gredil*, by a slight change, was made the ME. *gredire*, a griddle, P. Plowman, C. iii. 130. Very likely, this was at first a mere change of *l* to *r*, but the latter part of the word thus became significant, the ME. *ire* meaning 'iron;' hence our *grid-iron*, spelt *gyrdiron* in Levins, 163. 39.

GRIDE, to pierce, cut through. (E.) A favourite word with Spenser; see F. Q. ii. 8. 36; Sheph. Kal. February, l. 4; Virgil's Gnat, 254. And cf. 'griding sword;' Milton, P. L. vi. 329. A mere metathesis of *gird*, ME. *girden*, to strike, pierce, cut through, used by Chaucer, and borrowed from him by later poets. 'Thurgh *girt* [pierced through] with many a grevous blody wound;' Chaucer, C. T. 1012. See **Gird** (2). ¶ The same word is used metaphorically in the phrase 'to *gird* at,' i. e. to strike at, try to injure; see Shak. 2 Hen. IV, i. 2. 7; so also a *gird* is a cut, a sarcasm, Tam. Shrew, v. 2. 58.

GRIDIRON; see under **Griddle**.

GRIEF, great sorrow. (F.—L.) In early use. ME. *grief, gref*; spelt *gref*, Floriz and Blauncheflur, ed. Lumby, 187.—OF. *grief, gref*, adj. burdensome, heavy, sad; as sb., grief (Godefroy).—L. *grauem*, acc. of *grauis*, heavy, sad, grave. See **Grave** (2). Der. *grieve*, &c. See below.

GRIEVE, to afflict; to mourn. (F.—L.) ME. *greuen* (with *u* = *v*), Rob. of Glouc. p. 41, l. 969; P. Plowman, C. v. 95.—OF.

grever, to grieve, burden, afflict. — L. *grauāre*, to burden. — L. *grauis*, heavy (above). **Der.** *griev-ous* (ME. *greuous*, P. Plowman, C. xvii. 77); *griev-ous-ly*, *griev-ous-ness*; *griev-ance*, ME. *greuance*, Gower, C. A. i. 289, bk. iii. l. 296; and see above.

GRIFFIN, GRIFFON, an imaginary animal. (F.—L.—Gk.) *Griffin* is a weakened spelling; a better spelling is *griffon*. ME. *griffon*, Chaucer, C. T. 2135 (A 2133); King Alisaunder, 496. — F. *griffon*, 'a gripe, or griffon;' Cot. Formed, with suffix *-on*, from Late L. *griffus*, a griffin. — L. *grȳphus*, an extended form of *gryps*, a griffin. — Gk. γρύψ (stem γρυπ-), a griffin, a fabulous creature named from its hooked beak. — Gk. γρυπός, curved; also, hook-nosed, hook-beaked. Allied to G. *krauen*, to claw (Prellwitz).

GRIG (1), a small lively eel. (Scand.) 'A *grigge*, a young eele. A merie *grigge*;' Minsheu, ed. 1627. '*Anguillette*, a *grig*, or little eele;' Cot. Cf. Lowland Sc. *crike*, *crick*, a tick, a louse (Jamieson). Probably Scandinavian. — Scand. dial. *kräk*, also *krik*, a little creature, esp. a crawling creature; allied to *kräka*, to creep (Rietz); Norw. *krek*, a creeping thing; *kreka* (pt. t. *krak*), to creep. [Distinct from G. *kriechen*.] ☞ The phrase *as merry as a grig* is probably due to this word, though it was early changed to (or confused with) the equivalent phrase *as merry as a Greek*; see quotations in Nares, amongst which we may note 'she's *a merry Greek* indeed;' Troilus, i. 2. 118; 'the *merry Greeks*,' id. iv. 4. 58. *Merygreek* is a character in Udall's Roister Doister; A.D. 1553. Cf. L. *græcāri*, to live like Greeks, i.e. effeminately, luxuriously; Horat. Sat. ii. 2. 11.

GRIG (2), a cricket. (E.) Prov. E. *grig*; see E. D. D. Prob. due to prov. E. *crick*, to make a sharp noise; and to E. *cricket*, q. v. Cf. Du. *kriek*, a cricket. Apparently of imitative origin; and distinct from **Grig** (1).

GRILL, to broil on a gridiron. (F.—L.) Extended to *grilly* by Butler. 'Than have them *grillied* on the embers;' Hudibras, pt. iii. c. 2. l. 15 from end. — F. *griller*, 'to broile on a gridiron, to scorch;' Cot. — F. *gril*, 'a gridiron;' id. Formerly spelt *greil*, Godefroy. — Late L. acc. **crāticulam*, a masc. form of *crāticula*, a small gridiron, Martial, xiv. 221 (whence F. *grille*, a grating). These are dimin. forms from L. *crātis*, a hurdle. See **Grate** (1), **Crate**, **Griddle**.

GRILSE, the young salmon on its first return to the river from the sea. (F.—OHG.?) The forms in the N. E. D. suggest that the older form *grilles* was a plural, so that *grilse* = *grills*. An Act of 22 Edw. IV, c. 2, mentions 'grillez ou salmons' (N. E. D.). And perhaps *grill* represents OF. *grisle*, *grille*, grayish, applied (like the variant OF. *grisel*) to a horse. If so, it is from OF. *gris*, gray. — OHG. *gris*, gray. ¶ Some refer *grilse* to Irish *grealsach*, 'a kind of fish;' but (if connected) the derivation may run the other way.

GRIM, fierce, angry-looking. (E.) ME. *grim*, Chaucer, C. T. 11458 (F 1146). AS. *grim*, fierce, cruel, severe, dire, Grein, i. 527; for **grem-*, and allied to AS. *gram*, angry, furious, hostile; id. i. 523. Cf. also AS. *grimetan*, to rage, roar, grunt. + Du. *grimmig*, angry; cf. *grimmen*, to foam with rage; Icel. *grimmr*, grim, stern; *gramr*, wrathful; Dan. *grim*, ugly, grim; *gram*, wrathful; + G. *grimmig*, furious; *grimmen*, to rage; *grimm*, fury; *gram*, hostile. From Teut. root **grem-* (2nd grade, **gram-*). β. Further allied to Gk. χρόμη, χρόμος, noise; χρεμίζειν, χρεμετίζειν, to neigh; see Brugmann, i. § 572.

GRIMACE, an ugly look, smirk. (F.—Teut.?) 'Annotations of *grimaces*;' Butler, Hudib. iii. 2. 1004. '*Grimace* and affectation;' Dryden, Poet. Epist. to H. Higden, l. 10. — F. *grimace*, 'a crabd looke;' Cot. Of uncertain origin; but probably from G. *grimm*, fury, or from Icel. *grimr*, Norw. *grimm*, angry, furious; cf. EFries. and Low G. *grimlachen*, to laugh maliciously. (Körting, § 4355.) **Der.** *grimace*, verb.

GRIMALKIN, a cat. (E.; partly OHG.) See Nares, who suggests that it stands for *gray malkin*, 'a name for a fiend, supposed to resemble a grey cat.' He is probably right. See Macb. i. 1. 8. [Cf. the proverb 'All cats are grey in the dark.'] In this view, *Malkin* is for *Mald-kin*, dimin. of Maud (Matilda), with suffix *-kin*. The name *Maud*, AF. *Mald*, is from OHG. *Maht-hilt*; from *maht*, might, and *hilt*, battle. The ME. *Malkin*, as a dimin. of Maud, was in very common use; see Chaucer, C. T. 4450 (B 30). It was a name for a slut or loose woman. The Prompt. Parv. (1440) has : '*Malkyne*, or *Mawt*, propyr name, *Molt*, *Mawde*, Matildis, Matilda.'

GRIME, dirt that soils deeply, smut. (Low G.) In Shak. Com. of Errors, iii. 2. 106. As a verb, K. Lear, ii. 3. 9. — WFlem. *grijm*, grime (De Bo); cf. MDu. *grijmsel*, *grimsel*, soot, smut (Kilian); *grimmelen*, to soil, begrime (Oudemans). Also Dan. *grim*, *griim*, lampblack, soot, grime; whence *grimet*, streaked, begrimed (Ferrall); MDan. *grim*, soot on a kettle (Kalkar); Swed. dial. *grima*, a spot or smut on the face; Rietz. Probably allied further to AS. *begriwan*, to smear (?), Ælf. Hom. i. 384, ii. 368; and to Gk. χρί-ειν, to anoint, to smear. See **Chrism**. **Der.** *grim-y*.

GRIN, to snarl, grimace. (E.) ME. *grennen*, Ancren Riwle, p. 212; Layamon, 29550. AS. *grennian*, to grin; Grein, i. 525. + OHG.

grennan, to mutter, MHG. *grennen*, to grin. From a Teut. base **gran-*; whence also Icel. *grenja*, to howl. β. Perhaps influenced by derivatives from a Teut. base **grein-*; whence Du. *grijnen*, to weep, cry, fret, grumble; *grijnsen*, to grumble, to grin; Dan. *grine*, to grin, simper; Swed. *grina*, to distort the face, grimace, grin; G. *greinen*, to grin, grimace, weep, cry, growl; all of the latter set being related to E. *groan*; see **Groan**. **Der.** *grin*, sb.

GRIND, to reduce to powder by rubbing. (E.) ME. *grinden*, Chaucer, C. T. 14080 (B 3264); Ancren Riwle, p. 70. AS. *grindan*, Grein, i. 528. Teut. type **grendan-*, pt. t. **grand*, pp. **grundanoz*; whence also Du. *grint*, gravel, grit. **Der.** *grind-er*, *grind-stone*; also *grist*, q. v.

GRIP, sb., a firm grasp; vb., to grasp firmly. (E.) 1. ME. *gripe*; pl. *gripen*, Layamon, l. 15273; vol. ii. p. 215. The pl. *grippis* is in the Kingis Quair, st. 171. AS. *gripe*, a grip (Bosworth). 2. ME. *grippen*; 'he *gript* his mantel;' Will. of Palerne, 744. ONorthumb. *grippa*; whence *gegrippde*, pt. t., Luke, ix. 39. β. Both from *grip-*, weak grade of Teut. **greipan-*, to gripe (below).

GRIPE, to grasp, hold fast, seize forcibly. (E.) In Shak. Macb. iii. 1. 62; K. John, iv. 2. 190. ME. *gripen*, P. Plowman, B. iii. 248. AS. *gripan*, to seize; Grein, i. 529. + Du. *grijpen*; Icel. *gripa*; Dan. *gribe*; Swed. *gripa*; Goth. *greipan*; G. *greifen*. Teut. type **greipan-*, pt. t. **graip*, pp. **gripanoz*. Cf. Lithuan. *graibyti*, to grasp at. And see **Grope**. **Der.** *gripe*, sb., *gripes*.

GRISE, GRIZE, a step. (Shak.) See **Grece**.

GRISETTE, a gay young Frenchwoman of the lower class. (F.—MHG.) Borrowed (1723) from F. *grisette*, orig. a cheap dress of gray colour, whence they were named. — F. *gris*, gray. — MHG. *gris*, gray; cf. G. *greis*, a grayhaired man. See **Grizzly**. ¶ Hence also F. *gris*, the fur of the gray squirrel; Chaucer, C. T. 194.

GRISKIN, the loin of a pig; prov. E. (Scand.) The lit. sense is 'a little pig' (still found in Angus); it is formed by the dimin. suffix *-kin* from the once common word *gris* or *grice*, a pig. 'Bothe my gees and my *grys*' = both my geese and pigs; P. Plowman, B. iv. 51. '*Gryce*, swyne, or *pygge*, *porcellus*,' Prompt. Parv. p. 211; and see Way's note. — Icel. *griss*, a young pig; Dan. *griis*, a pig; Swed. *gris*, a pig. Cf. OSax. *grīs*, gray.

GRISLED, the same as **Grizzled**, q. v.

GRISLY, hideous, horrible. (E.) ME. *grisly*, Chaucer, C. T. 1973 (A 1971). AS. *grislic*, horrible (see Clark Hall); perhaps shortened from *angrislic*, terrible, Ps. lxxxviii. 8 (ed. Spelman). Formed with suffix *-lic* (like) from *grīs-an*, *ā-grīs-an* (pt. t. *ā-grās*), to shudder. 'And for helle *āgrīse*' = and shudder at the thought of hell; Laws of Cnut, i. 25; see Ancient Laws, ed. Thorpe, vol. i. p. 374. + Du. *af-grijselijk*, horrible; *af-grijzen*, horror; Low G. *grisen*, *griseln*, to shudder (Berghaus).

GRIST, a supply of corn to be ground. (E.) ME. *grist*. 'And moreouer . . . *grynd* att the Citeis myllis . . . as long as they mey have sufficiaunt *grist*;' Eng. Gilds, ed. Toulmin Smith, pp. 335, 336. AS. *grist*, as a gloss to L. *molitūra*; Wright's Vocab. i. 34, col. 2. It represents a type **grin(d)-st-*, from the verb *grindan*, to grind. See **Grind**. ¶ Cf. *bla-st* from *blow* (as wind), *blossom* (= (blō-st-ma) from *blow* (to flourish). The *i* was shortened before *st*; cf. *fist*. **Der.** *grist-le*.

GRISTLE, cartilage. (E.) 'Seales have *gristle*, and no bone;' Holland, tr. of Pliny, b. xi. c. 37; vol. i. p. 345 a. The word *gristly* occurs in the preceding clause. It was especially used with reference to the nose. '*Grystylle of the nose*, cartilago;' Prompt. Parv. '*Nease-gristles*,' i. e. gristles of the nose (speaking of many people together); O. Eng. Homilies, ed. Morris, i. 251. AS. *gristle*, as a gloss to *cartilago*; Ælfric's Gloss. in Voc. 158. 22. OMerc. *naes-gristle*, gloss to *cartilago*; Voc. 10. 20. Cf. OFries. *gristel*, *gristl*, *grestel*, *gerstel*; Richtofen. β. The word may be the dimin. of *grist*, and derivable from *grind*; with reference to the necessity of crunching it if eaten. So also Du. *knarsbeen*, gristle, from *knarsen*, to crunch (Wedgwood). See **Grist**. ¶ The AS. *grost* (O. E. Texts, p. 112, l. 56) also means 'gristle,' but has a different vowel; cf. NFries. *grössel*, *grüssel* (Outzen), OHG. *crustula*, gristle (Schade). These may be connected with Du. *gruizen*, to crush, EFries. *grüsen*, to crunch; from a Teut. root **greus-*, noted by Franck, s. v. *griesmeel*. Cf. **Grit** (2). **Der.** *gristl-y*.

GRIT (1), gravel, coarse sand. (E.) Formerly *greet*. '*Greete*, sabulum;' Levins, 89, 11. '*Sablonniere*, a sand-bed, . . a place full of sand, *greet*, or small gravel;' Cotgrave. ME. *greot*, Ancren Riwle, p. 70. AS. *grēot*, grit, dust; Grein, i. 527. OFries. *grēt*. + Icel. *grjōt*; G. *gries*; Swed. dial. *grut*, gravel. Closely allied to **Grout**, q. v. See **Grit** (2). ¶ The short vowel is due to confusion with *grit* (2). **Der.** *gritt-y*, *gritt-i-ness*; see also *groats*, *grout*.

GRIT (2), coarse oat-meal. (E.) Usually in pl. *grits*. The oldest sense is bran or chaff. From AS. *gryttan*, pl.; as in *hwǣte gryttan*, wheat-grits, Voc. 141. 20. Cf. MDu. *grutte*, 'barlie,' Hexham; G. *grüüze*, f., grit, groats. Teut. type **grut-jōn-*, fem.; from **grut-*, weak grade of *greut-* (2nd grade *graut*), Idg. root *ghreud*, to crush, pound (whence Lith. *gruzti*, to crush, pound, O. Church Slav. *grud-a*, a clod). ¶ Grit (1). AS. *grēot*, is from the prime grade *greut-*.

GRIZZLY, GRIZZLED, of a grey colour. (F. – MHG.; with E. *suffix*.) Shak. has *grizzled*, Hamlet, i. 2. 240 (in some copies *grisly*); also *grizzle* as sb., a tinge of gray, Tw. Nt. v. 168. Formed with suffix -*y* (or -*ed*) from ME. *grisel*, a gray-haired man. ' That olde *grisel* is no fole' [fool]; Gower, C. A. iii. 356; bk. viii. 2407. *Grisel* is formed, with suffix -*el*, from F. *gris*, gray. – MHG. *gris*, gray; cf. G. *greis*, a gray-haired man. **Der.** From the same source, *gris-ette*, q. v.

GROAN, to moan. (E.) ME. *gronen*, Chaucer, C. T. 14892 (B 4076); Ancren Riwle, p. 326. AS. *grānian*, to groan, lament; Grein, i. 524. Teut. type *grain-ōjan*; from a root *grei-*, as in OHG. *grinan*, G. *greinen*, to grin, weep, growl. **Der.** *groan-ing*.

GROAT, a coin worth 4*d*. (O. Low G.) ME. *grote*, Chaucer, C. T. 7546 (D 1964); P. Plowman, B. iii. 137 (and see the note). – O. Low G. *grote*, a coin of Bremen, described in the Bremen Wörterb. ii. 550. The word (like Du. *groot*) means ' great;' the coins being greater than the small copper coins (Schwaren) formerly in use in Bremen. Cognate with E. *great*. See **Great**.

GROATS, the grain of oats without the husks. (E.) ME. *grotes*, Liber Cure Cocorum, ed. Morris, p. 47. In the A. S. Leechdoms, iii. 292, appears the weak pl. *grotan* [miswritten *gratan* in the late MS.]. This represents a weak sb. closely allied to AS. *grot*, an atom, particle, whence ME. *grotes*, bits, in Havelok, 472. The AS. *grot* is from *grut-*, weak grade of *greut-*; see **Grit** (2). Cf. AS. *grūt*, coarse meal, whence E. *grout*, coarse meal, *grouts*, dregs. See **Grout**.

GROCER, a dealer in tea and sugar. (F. – L.) Formerly also spelt *grosser*, as in Holinshed's Chron. Rich. II, an. 1382 (R.); Hakluyt's Voyages, vol. i. p. 193. Spelt *grocer*, Libell of Eng. Policye, l. 346; AF. *grossour*, Liber Custumarum, i. 304. **A.** In old times, those whom we *now* call *grocers* were called *spicers*. Dealers were of two kinds, as now; there were wholesale dealers, called *grossers* or *engrossers*, and retail dealers, called *regrators*; see Liber Albus, ed. Riley, p. 547, note 1. Thus the word *grosser*, properly ' a whole-sale dealer,' is now spelt *grocer*, and means ' a spicer.' **B.** Borrowed from OF. *grossier*, ' a grocer; *marchant grossier*, that sels only by great, or utters his commodities by wholesale;' Cot. – OF. *gros*, fem. *grosse*, great. See **Gross**. Cf. Norm. dial. *grossier*, a spicer, a grocer (Moisy). **Der.** *grocer-y*, formerly *grossery*, from OF. *grosserie*, ' great worke; also *grossery*, wares uttered, or the uttering of wares, by whole-sale;' Cot.

GROG, spirits and water, not sweetened. (F. – L.) ' O'er *grog* or ale;' Byron, The Island, iii. 19. 4. An abbreviation of *grogram*. ' It derived its name from Admiral Edward Vernon, who wore *grogram* breeches, and was hence called "Old Grog." About 1745 [rightly, Aug. 1740], he ordered his sailors to dilute their rum with water. . . He died 30 Oct., 1757;' Haydn, Dict. of Dates. See **Grogram**.

GROGRAM, a stuff made of silk and mohair. (F. – L.) Formerly *grogran*, a more correct form (Skinner). ' He shall have the *grograns* at the rate I told him;' Ben Jonson, Every Man in his Humour, ii. 1. 9. Spelt *grograyn* in Cavendish, Life of Wolsey (ab. 1557), ed. 1893, p. 147. So called because of a coarse grain or texture. – OF. *grosgrain*, ' the stuffe *grogeran*;' Cot. – F. *gros*, gross, great, coarse; and *grain*, grain. See **Gross** and **Grain**. **Der.** *grog*, q. v.

GROIN, the fold or depression between the abdomen and each of the upper thighs. (E.) In Shak. 2 Hen. IV, ii. 4. 227. But *groin* is an incorrect variant of *grine* or *gryne*, a common form in the 16th century, from the still older form *grind* or *grynd*. Thus Cotgrave has: ' *Aines*, f., the *grine* or *groyne* of man or woman.' Palsgrave has: ' *Grynde* bytwene the thyghe and the belly, *ayne*.' Spelt *grynde* in Lanfranc's Cirurgie, p. 41 (ab. 1400). Prob. from AS. *grynde*, an abyss; the lit. sense being ' depression.' Teut. type *grundjom*, from *grunduz*, ground; see **Ground**. Cf. prov. E. *grindle*, a small gutter (E. D. D.); Bavar. *grund*, a valley. See Notes on E. Etym., p. 124. **Der.** *groin-ed*, i.e. having angular curves which intersect or *fork off*.

GROMWELL, a plant. (F. – L.?) The letter *w* is a modern insertion; Cotgrave, s. v. *gremil*, gives *gromill*, *grummell*; Palsgrave has *gromell*; the Prompt. Parv. has *gromaly* or *gromely sede*; *grummel* occurs in the 14th century, in Reliquiæ Antiquæ, i. 52, l. 1; and the Cath. Angl. has both *grumelle* and *gromelle*. [The *gromwell* or *Lithospermum* is remarkable for its hard, stony seeds; whence *Lithospermum* (stony seed) as the name of the genus.] – OF. *gromil*, 13th cent.; Hatzfeld (s. v. *gremil*). Also found as OF. *gremil*, *gremil*, *grenil* (Godefroy). Origin uncertain. **1.** The form *grenil* seems to rest upon L. *grānum*, a grain; cf. ' *granum solis*, gromylle;' Voc. 587. 9. **2.** Gromil perhaps is from OF. *grume*, stone of a grape (Godefroy), Prov. *grum*, the same (Mistral). – L. *grūmus*, a little heap. (Körting,

§ 4372.) ¶ Roquefort gives OF. *grumel*, ' pelote, peloton;' dimin. of *grume*, used to mean all kinds of grain. Cotgrave also gives *grum* as a Languedoc word synonymous with F. *grain*, grain. It would seem that the L. *grūmus* came to mean a mere clot of earth. Cf. Span. *grumillo*, a small clot, a curd; from *grumo*, a clot. We may note that *gromwell* is also called in E. *gray millet* or (in Cotgrave) *graymill*, which is merely the F. *grémil* ingeniously made partly significant, and was clearly suggested by the fact that *gromwell* was sometimes called *milium solis* as well as *granum solis*; see Cath. Anglicum.

GROOM, a servant, lad. (F.) Now esp. used of men employed about horses; but orig. of wider use. It meant a lad, servant in waiting, or sometimes, a labourer, shepherd. ME. *grom*, *grome*; Chaucer, Ho. of Fame, iii. 135; P. Plowman, C. ix. 227; Havelok, 790; Ancren Riwle, p. 422; Polit. Songs (C. S.), p. 237, l. 3. **β.** Of uncertain origin; Stratmann cites the MDu. *grom* and OIcel. *gromr*, a boy, as parallel forms; but neither of these forms are authorised or have any obvious etymology, and may be borrowed from ME. *grome*, which occurs in the Ancren Riwle (ab. 1225). **γ.** It seems to be from an OF. *grome*, only found in the dimin. form *gromet*; or else it was shortened from the form *gromet* itself. Godefroy has OF. *gromet*, *grummet*, *groumet*, *gourmet* (F. *gourmet*), a servant, valet, groom. Cf. Span. *grumete*, a ship-boy. Referred by Diez to L. *grūmus*, a small heap, a clot. See Notes on E. Etym., p. 125. See **Grume, Grummet**.

GROOVE, a trench, furrow, channel. (Du.) In Skinner; rare in early books. ' *Groove*, a channel cut out in wood, iron, or stone;' Kersey, ed. 1715. Also: ' *Groove* or *Grove*, a deep hole or pit sunk in the ground, to search for minerals;' id.; see Manlove's poem on Leadmines (E. D. S. Glos. B. 8, ll. 18, 22, and the Glossary), printed A.D. 1653. Cf. ME. *grofe*, a mine; Wars of Alex., 5394. – Du. *groef* (Du. *oe* = E. *oo*) or *groeve*, a trench, channel, groove; also, a mine, quarry. – Du. *graven* (pt. t. *groef*), to dig; cognate with AS. *grafan*. See **Grave** (1). ¶ The ME. *grofe* may be from Icel. *grōf*, a pit (cognate with Du. *groef*); but mod. E. *groove*, a channel, first found in 1659, is borrowed from the 2nd grade of the Dutch verb.

GROPE, to feel one's way. (E.) ME. *gropen*, C. T. 646 (A 644); used in the sense of ' grasp,' King Alisaunder, ed. Weber, 1957. AS. *grāpian*, to seize, handle, Grein, i. 524; a weak verb, and un-original. Teut. type *graipōjan*, from *graipā*, f. sb., as seen in AS. *grāp*, the grip of the fingers, grasp of the hand; id. From *graip*, 2nd grade of Teut. *greipan-*, AS. *grīpan*, to gripe. See **Gripe**. **β.** Similarly the Icel. *greip*, grip, grasp, is allied to *grīpa*, to gripe; and the OHG. *greifa*, a two-pronged fork (cited by Fick, iii. 111) to OHG. *grīfan*, to gripe. And see **Grasp**. **Der.** *grop-ing-ly*.

GROSS, fat, large. (F. – L.) Very common in Shak.; Merry Wives, iii. 3. 43, &c. ' This *grosse* imagination;' Frith's Works, p. 140, col. 2. Spelt *grosse* in Palsgrave. – OF. *gros* (fem. *grosse*), ' grosse, great, big, thick;' Cot. – L. *grossus*, thick (a late form). **Der.** *gross-ly*, *gross-ness*, *gros-beak* or *gross-beak* (F. *gros bec*, great beak, the name of a bird), *grocer*, q.v., *grocer-y*; also *gross*, sb., *engross*, *in-gross*, *gro-gram*, *grog*.

GROT, a cavern. (F. – Ital. – L. – Gk.) ' Umbrageous *grots* and caves;' Milton, P. L. iv. 257. – F. *grotte*, ' a grot, caue;' Cot. – Ital. *grotta*, ' a caue, a grot;' Florio. (Cf. Prov. *croto* (Mistral), formerly *cropta*, cited by Littré.) – Late L. *crupta*, L. *crypta*, a crypt, cave, grotto. From Greek; see **Crypt**. And see **Grotto**. Doublet, *crypt*; also *grotto*. **Der.** *grot-esque*, q.v.

GROTTO, a cavern. (Ital. – L. – Gk.) A corruption of the older form *grotta*. ' And in our *grottoes*;' Pope, tr. of Homer's Odyss. b. x. 480. (Pope had his own *grotto* at Twickenham.) ' A *grotta*, or place of shade;' Bacon, Essay 45 (Of Building). – Ital. *grotta*, a grotto, whence F. *grotte*. See **Grot**.

GROTESQUE, ludicrous, strange. (F. – Ital. – L. – Gk.) ' *Grotesque* and wild;' Milton, P. L. iv. 136. ' And this *grotesque* design;' Dryden, Hind and Panther, iii. 1044. – OF. *grotesque*; pl. *grotesques*, ' pictures wherein all kinds of odde things are represented;' Cot. – Ital. *grottesca*, ' antick worke;' Florio. [So called because such paintings were found in old crypts and grottoes.] – Ital. *grotta*, a grotto. See **Grot, Grotto**. ¶ Sir T. Herbert uses the Ital. form. ' The walls and pavements, . . . by rare artificers carved into story and *grotesco* work;' Travels, ed. 1665, p. 147.

GROUND, the surface of the earth. (E.) ME. *grund*, *ground*, Chaucer, C. T. 455; Havelok, 1979; Layamon, 2296. AS. *grund*; Grein, i. 530.+Du. *grond*; Goth. *grundus*, only in the comp. *grunduwaddjus*, a ground-wall, foundation; Luke, vi. 48, 49; OHG. *grunt*, G. *grund*. Teut. type *grunduz*; also *grunthoz*, as in Icel. *grunnr*, bottom (Dan. Swed. *grund*). We also find Gael. *grunnd*, Irish *grunnt*, ground, bottom (from Norse or E.). **Der.** *ground*, verb (Chaucer, C. T. 416, A 414); *ground-less*, *ground-less-ly*, *ground-less-ness*, *groundling*, q.v., *ground-sill*, q.v.; also *ground-floor*, -*ivy*, -*plan*, -*rent*, -*swell*, -*work*. Also *grounds*, q.v.

GROUNDLING, a spectator in the pit of a theatre. (E.) In Shak. Hamlet, iii. 2. 12; Beaum. and Fletcher, Prophetess, i. 3. 32. A term of contempt; made by suffixing -*ling*, a double dimin. ending (-*l-ing*), to the sb. *ground*. 2. There is also a fish called the *groundling*, so called because it keeps near the bottom of the water; the Low G. name is *gründlink* (Berghaus).

GROUNDS, dregs. (E.) In Minsheu, ed. 1627. 'Grounds, the settling or dregs of drink;' Kersey, ed. 1715. This peculiar use of the word occurs also in Gael. *grunndas*, lees, dregs; Irish *gruntas*, dregs, *grunndas*, lees, dross; both borrowed from E. See **Ground**.

GROUNDSEL, a small plant. (E.) Corruptly written *greneswel* in Levins. Better *groundswell*, as in Holland's Pliny, b. xxv. c. 13. AS. *grundeswylige*, *grundeswelge*, *grundeswilie*, with numerous references; Cockayne's Leechdoms, iii. 329. 'Senecio, *grundswylige*;' Wright's Vocab. i. 68, col. 2, l. 1. β. The lit. sense would thus seem to be 'ground-swallower,' i.e. occupier of the ground, abundant weed; as if from AS. *grund*, ground, and *swelgan*, to swallow; but this seems to be, after all, only a popular etymology, as a much older form appears in *gundae-suelgiae*, Epinal gloss. 976 (also spelt *gundae-suelgae*, *gundesuilge*, O. E. Texts, pp. 97, 98). Thus the orig. sense was 'swallower or absorber of pus;' from AS. *gund*, pus; and in fact the leaves are still used for reducing abscesses.

GROUNDSILL, the timber of a building next the ground; a threshold. (E.) Spelt *grunsel*, Milton, P. L. i. 460. 'And so fyll downe deed on the *groundsyll*;' Berners, tr. of Froissart, vol. i. c. 176 (R). Compounded of *ground* and *sill*; see **Sill**.

GROUP, a cluster, assemblage. (F.—Ital.—G.) 'Group, in painting, a piece that consists of several figures;' Kersey, ed. 1715. 'The figures of the *groups*;' Dryden, Parallel of Painting and Poetry, ed. Yonge, 1882, p. 164.—F. *groupe*, a group; not in Cot.—Ital. *groppo*, a knot, heap, group, bag of money.—Teut. type **kroppoz*, as seen in G. *kropf*, a crop, craw, maw, wen on the throat; orig. a bunch. Cf. Icel. *kroppr*, a hunch or bunch on any part of the body. See **Crop**, of which *group* is a doublet. **Der.** *group-ing*, *group*, verb.

GROUSE, the name of a bird. (F. ?) 'Growse, a fowl, common in the North of England;' Kersey, ed. 1715. Prof. Newton has kindly sent me an earlier instance of the word. 'Attagen, perdix Asclepica, the Heath-cock or *Grouss*. . . . Hujus in Anglia duas habemus species, quarum major vulgo dicitur, *the black game*, . . minor vero, *the grey game*;' Charleton, Onomasticon Zoïcon, London, 1668, p. 73. Earlier examples are given in N.E.D. In Household Ordinances (1531), as given in Archæologia, iii. 157, we have the pl. forms '*grows* and *peions*' [pigeons]. In Household Ordinances (1547), ed. 1790, p. 220, the pl. is *grewes*. In 1674, the pl. is *grooses*. It is possible that *grows* was at first a plural form, from a sing. *grow* or *grou*. Of unknown origin; though the form seems to be French. Giraldus Cambrensis, Topog. Hib. (Opera, Rolls Series, v. 47), has: 'gallinæ campestres, quas vulgariter *grutas* vocant.' ¶ Cotgrave, s. v. *griesche*, has 'the hen of the *grice* or moorgame.' This seems to be a mistake, as the form *grice* is otherwise unknown.

GROUT, coarse meal; in pl. grounds, dregs. (E.) Holland, tr. of Pliny, bk. xx. c. 7 (v. ii. p. 46) has: 'drie *grout*, or barley meale.' AS. *grút*, groats, coarse meal; Codex Diplomaticus, ed. Kemble, Charter 235 (vol. i. p. 311). + Du. *gruit*, dregs. Cf. Icel. *grautr*, porridge; Dan. *gröd*, boiled groats; Swed. *gröt*, thick pap; G. *grütze*, groats. Allied to Lithuan. *grudas*, corn. Also to *groats*, q. v.; *grit*, q. v. **Der.** *gru-el*, q. v.

GROVE, a collection of trees. (E.) In Shak. M. N. Dr. iii. 1. 390. ME. *groue* (with *u* for *v*), Chaucer, C. T. 1480 (A 1478); Layamon, 469. AS. *gráf*, a grove (Lye); but the word is very scarce. Leo refers to Codex Diplomaticus, ed. Kemble, Charter 305 (vol. ii. p. 100; see also vol. iii. p. 436). It is both masc. and neut. Teut. types **graibos*, **graibom*; from a root **greib*, which is wholly unknown. No cognate forms appear; unless we may compare Norw. *greiv-la*, a tree whose branches spread out wide like horns, *greiv-la*, v., to branch out, &c. (Ross).

GROVEL, to fall flat on the ground. (Scand.) In Shak. K. John, ii. 305. (Not found earlier.) The formation of the verb *to grovel* was due to a singular grammatical mistake. *Groveling* was in use as an adverb with the suffix -*ling*, but this was readily mistaken for the pres. part. of a verb, and, the -*ing* being dropped, the new verb *to grovel* emerged. β. Spenser uses the form *groveling* only. 'Streight downe againe herselfe, in great despight She *groveling* threw to ground;' F. Q. ii. 1. 45. 'And by his side the Goddesse *groveling* Makes for him endlesse mone;' F. Q. iii. 1. 38. 'Downe on the ground his carkas *groveling* fell;' F. Q. iii. 5. 23. In the last instance, the sense is 'flatly' or 'flat.' γ. The ME. *groveling* or *grovelings* is a mere adverb. '*Grouelyng* to his fete thay felle;' Allit. Poems, ed. Morris, A. 1120. '*Grovelynge*, or *grovelyngys*, adv. Suppine, resupine;' Prompt. Parv. p. 215. After which is added: '*Grovelynge*, nom. Suppinus, resupinus;' showing that, in A. D. 1440, the

word was beginning to be considered as being sometimes a nom. pres. part. Note also: 'Therfor *groflynges* thou shall be layde;' Towneley Myst. p. 40. Way notes that in Norf. and Suff. the phrase 'to lie *grubblins*,' or with the face downwards, is still in use. δ. The correct ME. form is *grofling* or *groflinges*, where the -*ling* or -*lings* is the adv. suffix that appears in other words, such as *dark-ling*, *flat-ling*; see **Darkling, Headlong**. The former part of the word could be used *alone*, with exactly the same adverbial sense; as 'they fillen *gruf*;' Chaucer, C. T. 951 (A 949). The phrase is of Scand. origin. —Icel. *grúfa*, in the phr. *liggja á grúfu*, to lie grovelling, to lie on one's face, *symja á grúfu*, to swim on one's belly. Cf. also *grúfa*, verb, to grovel, couch, or cower down. Also *grufla*, to grovel, which justifies the E. verb, though proof of *direct* connexion between the words is wanting; Swed. dial. *gruva*, flat on one's face; *ligga á gruve*, to lie on one's face; Rietz. Root uncertain; perhaps related to **Grub**. **Der.** *grovell-er*.

GROW, to increase, become enlarged by degrees. (E.) ME. *growen*, P. Plowman, B. xx. 56; C. xiii. 177. AS. *grówan*, pt. t. *gréow*, pp. *grówen*; Grein, i. 529. + Du. *groeijen* (weak); Icel. *gróa*; Dan. *groe*; Swed. *gro*. β. Esp. used of the growth of vegetables, &c., and hence closely connected with the word *green*, from the same root. Teut. root **grō-*, **gra-*. See **Green** and **Grass**. ¶ The AS. word for the growth of *animals* is properly *weaxan*, mod. E. *wax*, q. v. **Der.** *grow-er*; *growth*, Othello, v. 2. 14, not an AS. word, but of Scand. origin, from Icel. *gróðr*, *gróði*, growth.

GROWL, to grumble. (F.—Teut.) In Skinner, ed. 1671; and in Pope, Moral Essays, iii. 195. Lowl. Sc. has the form *gurle*. Wyclif, Select Works, ed. Arnold, ii. 249, has: 'A mete, not defied [digested] makith mannis bodi to *groule*' [rumble].—AF. *grouler*, to make a noise like a crane; Nominale, ed. Skeat, l. 837; Picard *grouler*, to murmur, grumble (Corblet).—EFries. *grullen*; WFlem. *grollen*, to rumble (De Bo); Du. *grollen*, to grumble. + G. *grollen*, to bear ill-will against, to be angry; also, to rumble (as thunder). β. Of imitative origin; see **Grumble**. And see *grol* in Franck. **Der.** *growl*, sb., *growl-er*.

GROWTH, sb.; see under **Grow**.

GRUB, to grope in the dirt. (E.) ME. *grubben*, *grobben*. 'To *grobbe* vp metal;' Chaucer, Ætas Prima, l. 29. 'So depe thei *grubbed* and so fast;' Legends of the Holy Rood, ed. Morris, p. 94, l. 268. Cf. EFries. *grubbeln*, to grope about. From Teut. type **grubjan*-; from **grub*, weak grade of **graban*-, to dig; see **Grave** (1). From the same grade are Low G. *grubbeln*, to grope about; G. *grübeln*, OHG. *grubilón*, to rake, dig, grub up; and ON. *gryfja*, a pit. Cf. **Grovel**. **Der.** *grub*, sb., an insect; *grubb-er*, *grubb-y*.

GRUDGE, to grumble, murmur. (F.) ME. *grochen*, *gruchen*, *grucchen*, to murmur. 'Why *grucchen* we?' Chaucer, C. T. 3060 (A 3058). The weakened form *grugge* occurs in The Dictes and Sayinges by Lord Rivers, pr. by Caxton, 1477, fol. 17, back, l. 8. 'ʒif þe gomes *grucche*'= if the men murmur, P. Plowman, B. vi. 219. Spelt *grochi*, Ayenbite of Inwyt, p. 67; *grucchen*, Ancren Riwle, p. 186. The earliest spelling was *grucchen*, then *gruggen*, and finally *grudge*, Tempest, i. 2. 249.—OF. *groucier*, *grousser*, *groucher*, to murmur, Godefroy; later *gruger*, 'to grudge, repine;' Cot. Cf. Low L. *groussáre*, to murmur, found in a passage written A. D. 1358 (Ducange). Godefroy also gives the spelling *croucier*, evidently an older form. β. Of uncertain origin, but prob. Scandinavian; cf. Icel. *krytja* (pt. t. *krutti*), to murmur, *krutr*, a murmur; Swed. dial. *kruttla*, to murmur (Rietz); Norw. *grutta*, to grunt, to growl (Ross); MDan. *krutte*, to grumble (Kalkar). ¶ Different from mod. F. *gruger*, to crunch. **Der.** *grudge*, sb., *grudg-ing-ly*.

GRUEL, liquid food, made from meal. (F.—O. Low G.) 'Or casten al the *gruwel* in the fyr;' Chaucer, Troilus, iii. 711.—OF. *gruel* (Burguy) > mod. F. *gruau*.—Late L. *grútellum*, a dimin. of *grútum*, meal, in a Carolingian text (Brachet).—O. Low G. *grút*, cognate with AS. *grút*, groats, grout, coarse meal. See **Grout**.

GRUESOME, horrible, fearful. (Scand.) Also *grewsome*, *grusome*, *grousum*. 'Death, that *grusome* carl;' Burns, Verses to J. Rankine. And see Jamieson's Sc. Dict., s. v. *grousum*. '*Growsome*, horridus;' Levins, 162. 10.—Dan. *grusom*, cruel; (Kalkar has M Dan. *grusommelig*, cruel, violent); Norw. *gruvsam*, frightful, also timid (Aasen).—Dan. *gru*, horror, terror; with Dan. suffix -*som*, as in *virk-som*, active. Cf. Dan. *grue*, to dread, *gruelig*, horrid; Norw. *gruva*, to dread; Swed. *gruflig*, dreadful, dismal, horrid, dire. + Du. *gruwzaam*, terrible, hideous; MHG. *grüwesam*, *grúsam*, G. *grausam*, cruel, horrible. Further allied to E. dial. *growze*, EFries. *grüsen*, G. *grausen*, to shiver, shudder.

GRUFF, rough, surly. (Dutch.) A late word. 'Such an one the tall, . . . such an one the *gruff*;' Spectator, no. 433. First in Lowl. Sc., in 1533; and in 1563 we find '*grof* stanis,' coarse, rough stones, in Winyet's Works, i. 114 (S. T. S.).—Du. *grof*, coarse, plump, loud, blunt, great, heavy. + EFries. and Westphal. *grof*; EFries.

gruffig, coarse; Swed. *grof*, coarse, big, rude, gross; Dan. *grov*, the same; G. *grob*, coarse; OHG. *gerob*, *grop*. β. The OHG. form shows that the initial *g* stands for *ge* (= AS. *ge-* = Goth. *ga-*), a mere prefix. The syllable *-rob* may perhaps be allied to the weak grade corresponding to AS. *hrēof*, rough. Der. *gruff-ly*, *gruff-ness*.

GRUMBLE, to growl, murmur. (F. – G.) In Shak. Temp. i. 2. 249; &c. – Picard *grumeler*, *groumeler* (Corblet); F. *grommeler*, 'to grumble, repine;' Cot. – Low and prov. G. *grummelen*, to grumble; frequentative of the verb *grummen*, *grumen*, or *grommen*; cf. Bavarian *sich grumen*, to be vexed, fret oneself, Schmeller, 997; MDu. *grommelen*, frequent. of Du. *grommen*, to grumble, growl. From **grumm-*, weak grade of Teut. **gremman-*, to rage, as in MHG. and AS. *grimman*, to rage, str. vb. β. The orig. sense is 'to be angry,' and the word is closely connected with G. *gram*, vexation; see further under **Grim**. Der. *grumbl-er*, *grumbl-ing-ly*.

GRUME, a clot, as of blood. (F. – L.) Very rare; first used in 1619 (N. E. D.). Eden has *groume*, a lump; Decades, p. 145 (1555); ed. Arber, p. 182. Commoner in the adj. *grum-ous*. 'Grumous, full of clots or lumps;' Kersey, ed. 1715. – OF. *grume*, 'a knot, bunch, cluster;' Cot. Cf. F. *grumeau*, a clot of blood; id. – L. *grūmus*, a little heap or hillock of earth. Der. *grum-ous*.

GRUMMET (1), **GROMET**, a ship's boy, cabin-boy. (F.) Rare in books. 'In everie ship .. a boye, which is called a *gromet*;' Lambarde, Peramb. of Kent, ed. 1826, p. 110. – OF. *gromet*, a servant, groom; see further under **Groom**.

GRUMMET (2), **GROMMET**, a ring of rope. (F. – C.) 'Grommets, little rings on the upper side of the yard, to which the caskets are fastned;' Coles (1684). Spelt *grummets*; Capt. J. Smith, Works, ed. Arber, p. 793 (1626). – OF. *gromette* (Hatzfeld), s. v. F. *gourmette*, the curb of a bridle (affected by F. *gourmer*, to curb). According to Thurneysen, p. 102, the OF. *gromette* is from Bret. *chadenn gromm*, lit. 'bent chain,' the chain of a curb; where *gromm* is the fem. of Bret. *kroumm*, bent, W. *crwm*. Celt. type **krumbos*, bent; Stokes-Fick, p. 100.

GRUNSEL, used for **Groundsill**, q. v.

GRUNT, to make a sound like a pig. (E.) ME. *grunten*, Ancren Riwle, p. 326. AS. *grunnettan* (O. E. Texts, p. 559), an extension of *grunian*, to grunt, found in Ælfric's Grammar (Bosworth). + Dan. *grynte*, to grunt; Swed. *grymta*, to grunt; G. *grunzen*. + L. *grunnire*, OL. *grundire*; Gk. γρυ̂ζειν. β. All of imitative origin; cf. Gk. γρῦ, the noise made by a pig. Der. *grunt-er*.

GUAIACUM, a genus of trees in the W. Indies; also, the resin of the lignum vitæ. (Span. – Hayti.) In Minsheu, ed. 1627, and in Kersey, ed. 1715. Latinised from Span. *guayaco* or *guayacan*, lignum vitæ. From the language of Hayti; see Frampton, tr. of Monardes, Joyfull Newes, p. 10, back. *Gua-*, in Haytian, is a prefix or article (R. Eden, p. 168). See Notes on E. Etym., p. 347.

GUANACO, a kind of Peruvian sheep. (Span. – Peruv.) Spelt *guancos*, pl., in E. G., tr. of Acosta (1604); bk. i. c. 21, p. 70. – Span. *guanaco*, 'a beast in the West Indies, like a great sheep;' Pineda. – Peruv. *huanacu*, a wild sheep; see Skeat, Notes on E. Etym., p. 343.

GUANO, the dung of a certain sea-fowl of S. America, used for manure. (Span. – Peruvian.) See E. G., tr. of Acosta, 1604, p. 311 (bk. iv. c. 37); Prescott, Conq. of Peru, c. 5. – Span. *guano* or *huano* (Pineda). – Peruvian *huanu*, dung; see Skeat, Notes on E. Etym., p. 343.

GUARANTEE, **GUARANTY**, a warrant, surety. (F. – OHG.) *Guarantee* appears to have been misused in place of *guaranty*, *garanty*, or *garranty*, probably owing to the use of words such as *lessee*, *feoffee*, and the like; but the final *-ee* is (in the present case) incorrect. Blount's Nomo-lexicon gives the spellings *garanty* and *waranty*. Cotgrave has *garrantie* and *warrantie*. – AF. *guarantie*; OF. *garrantie* (better *garantie*), 'garrantie, warrantie, or warrantise,' Cot.; fem. form of *garanti*, warranted, pp. of *garantir*, to warrant. – OF. *garant*, also spelt *guarant*, *warant* (Burguy), and explained by Cotgrave as 'a vouchee, warrant, warranter, supporter, maintainer.' See further under **Warrant**. ¶ The OHG. *w* became in OF. first *w*, then *gu*, and finally *g*. Thus OF. *garant* and E. *warrant* are the same word. Der. *guarantee*, vb.

GUARD, to ward, watch, keep, protect. (F. – Teut.) Common in Shak. both as verb and sb. [He also has *guardage*, Oth. i. 2. 70; *guardant*, Cor. v. 2. 67; *guardian*, Macb. ii. 4. 35. But the verb does not seem to be much older, though the sb. is in Lydgate, De Deguil. Pilgrimage, 8793. Rich. cites *guardens* (= guardians) from Surrey, tr. of Virgil's Æn. b. ii. l. 1013 (E. version).] – OF. *garder*, 'to keep, ward, guard,' Cot.; also spelt *guarder*, as in the Chanson de Roland, l. 9; and, in the 11th century, *warder*. – OSax. *wardōn*, to watch; cognate with E. *ward*, vb. See further under **Ward**. ¶ The sb. *guard* is older than the verb; from OF. *garde*, *guarde*; from OTeut. **wardā*, a guard. Der. *guard-age*, *guard-ant*, *guard-ian* (= OF. *gardien*, which Cot. explains by 'a warden, keeper, gardien');

guard-ed, *guard-ed-ly*, *guard-ed-ness*; *guard-room*, *guard-ship*. Doublet, *ward*; the doublet of *guardian* is *warden*, q. v.

GUAVA, a genus of trees and shrubs of tropical America. (Span. – W. Indian.) The Span. name *guayaba* is no doubt borrowed from the W. Indian name; see Skeat, Notes on E. Etym., p. 347. Spelt *guayva* in 1593; Eng. Garner, ed. Arber, v. 532; in an account of Drake's expedition to Panama, &c. The pl. is spelt *guayavos* in E. G., tr. of Acosta, bk. iv. c. 24 (1604). The *guava* is found within the tropics in Mexico, the W. Indies, and S. America.

GUDGEON, a small fresh-water fish. (F. – L. – Gk.) In Shak. Merch. of Ven. i. 1. 102. ME. *gojone*. 'Goione, fysche;' Prompt. Parv. – F. *goujon*, 'a gudgeon-fish, also the pin which the truckle of a pully runneth on; also, the gudgeon of the spindle of a wheele; any gudgeon;' Cot. – L. *gōbiōnem*, acc. of *gōbio*, a by-form of *gōbius*, a gudgeon. – Gk. κωβιός, a kind of fish, gudgeon, tench. The Sicilian name was κω̂θος (Liddell and Scott).

GUELDER-ROSE, a species of *Viburnum*, bearing large white ball-shaped flowers. (Du. *and* F.) So named from some resemblance of the flower to a white rose. See **Rose**. The word *guelder* stands for *Gueldre*, the F. spelling of the province of *Gelderland* in Holland.

GUERDON, a reward, recompense. (F. – OHG.) In Chaucer, C. T. 7460 (D 1878). He also has the verb *guerdonen* = to reward; Pers. Tale, Group I, l. 283, Six-text ed.; but this is derived from the sb. *Guerdonles* occurs in Lydgate, Complaint of Black Knight, l. 399. – OF. *guerdon*, 'guerdon, recompence, meed;' Cot. Equivalent to Ital. *guiderdone*, a guerdon. – Low L. *widerdōnum*, which, according to Littré, is found in the time of Charles the Bald. β. This is a singular hybrid compound from OHG. *wider* (G. *wieder*), against, back again, and the L. *dōnum*, a gift; but the whole word is a mere adaptation of OHG. *widarlōn*, a recompence. γ. The OHG. word has its exact cognate in the AS. *wiðer-lēan*, a recompence, Grein, ii. 697; which is compounded of the prefix *wiðer*, against, back again (connected with E. *with-* in the word *with-stand*) and the sb. *lēan*, payment, which is from AS. *lēon*, to lend; and *lēon* is also allied to E. *loan*. See **With, Donation,** and **Loan.** ¶ The same notion of 'back' occurs in the synonymous words *re-ward*, *re-compence*, *re-muneration*.

GUERILLA, **GUERRILLA**, an irregular warfare carried on by small bands of men. (Span. – OHG.) We speak of 'guerilla warfare,' making the word an adj., but it is properly a sb. – Span. *guerrilla*, a skirmish, lit. a petty war; dimin. of *guerra*, war (= F. *guerre*.) – OHG. *werra*, discord, the same word as E. *war*. See **War**.

GUESS, to form an opinion at hazard, to conjecture. (Scand.) The insertion of *u* was merely for the purpose of preserving the *g* as hard. ME. *gessen*; Chaucer, C. T. 82. – Dan. *gisse*; Swed. *gissa*, to guess; MDan. *gidze*, *gitse*, *getse* (Kalkar); NFriesic *gezze*, *gedse* (Outzen); the oldest form being *getze* = **getsa*, from the base **get-*. β. Closely related to Dan. *gjette*, to guess; the mod. Icel. *gizka* = **git-ska*, a denominative vb. from a base **git-isko-*, for **get-isko-*, i.e. acquisitive, is from Icel. *geta* (1), to get, (2) to guess. The latter word is cognate with AS. *gitan*, and mod. E. *get*; and it is highly probable that *guess* meant originally 'to be ready to get,' being a secondary (desiderative) verb formed from *get*. See **Get.** Der. *guess*, sb.; *guess-work*.

GUEST, a stranger who is entertained. (E.) The *u* is inserted to preserve the *g* as hard. The word is prob. Anglian or Scand., as the AS. *gi* > *y*. ME. *gest*, Hampole, Pricke of Conscience, 1374; also *gist*, Ancren Riwle, p. 68. AS. *gæst*; also *gist*, *giest*; Grein, i. 373. Cf. Icel. *gestr*; Dan. *gæst*; Swed. *gäst*. + Du. *gast*; Goth. *gasts*; G. *gast*. Teut. type **gastiz*. Idg. type **ghostis*, whence L. *hostis*, a stranger, guest, enemy; Russ. *gost(e)*, a guest, alien. β. The orig. sense appears to be that of 'alien,' whence the senses of 'enemy' and 'guest' arose. See **Hostile.** Der. *guest-chamber*, Mark, xiv. 14. From the same root, *host* (2), *hostile*.

GUIACUM, a genus of trees. See **Guaiacum**.

GUIDE, to lead, direct, regulate. (F. – Teut.) ME. *gyden*, Chaucer, C. T. 13410 (B 1670). [The ME. form *gyen* is also common (C. T. 1952); see **Guy**.] The sb. is *gyde*, C. T. 806 (A 804). – OF. *guider* (14th cent.), from older *guier*, to guide; the *d* being inserted by the influence of OProv. *guidar* (Bartsch). Cf. also Ital. *guidare*; and Span. *guiar*. Romanic type **guidāre*. – OSax. *witan* (AS. *witan*), to pay heed to; OHG. *wizan*. – Teut. root **weit-*, **wit-*; Idg. root WEID, to know; whence also AS. *wīs*, wise, knowing, *wīsa*, a leader, director, *wīsian*, to guide, lead, show the way. See **Wit, Wise.** Der. *guide*, sb., *guide-post*, *guid-on*, *guise*, *guy-rope*.

GUIDON, a pennon; or a bearer of a pennon. (F. – Teut.) 'With *guidons* trail'd on earth;' Sandys, Travels (1632), p. 84. – F. *guidon*, 'a standard, or banner, under which a troop of men of arms do serve; also, he that bears it;' Cot. – F. *guid-er*, to guide; as pointing also the way. See above.

GUILD, GILD, an association of men of one class for mutual aid. (E.) The insertion of *u*, though common, is quite unnecessary, and is unoriginal. See English Gilds, ed. Toulmin Smith, Early Eng. Text Soc., 1870. ME. *gilde*, *ȝilde*; the pl. *ȝilden* = guilds, occurs in Layamon, 32001. Cf. AS. *gegyldscipe*, a guild, *gegilda*, a member of a guild, in Thorpe's Ancient Laws, Æthelst. v. 8. 6; vol. i. p. 236. These words are formed from AS. *gild*, a payment, a guild (from the fee paid); also spelt *gield*, *gyld*. *geld*; from the AS. *gildan*, to pay, whence also mod. E. *yield*; see Yield; cf. also Icel. *gildi*, a payment, a guild, from *gjalda* (pres. t. *geld*), to pay; Dan. *gilde*, a feast, a guild. + Du. *gild*, a guild, company, society; Goth. *gild*, tribute-money, Lu. xx. 22. ¶ The hard *g* is remarkable, as the AS. form would rather have given *yild*. It is usually referred to the influence of Icel. *gildi*, but we must not forget the possible influence of Latin and AF., which adopted the word very early. The N. E. D. cites L. *gildis* ab. 1009, L. *gildam* ab. 1189; and AF. forms with *gui-* appear early likewise. It is unlikely that L. *g* was sounded as *y*, and it is certain that AF. *gu* was hard. Der. *guild-hall*, ME. *gild-halle*, *yeldhalle*, Chaucer, C. T. 372 (A 370).

GUILDER, a Dutch coin. (Du.) In Shak. Com. Errors, i. 1. 8; iv. 1. 4. A corrupt form of Du. *gulden*, a guilder, 'a piece of 20 stivers' (Sewel). Hexham has *Carolus gulden*, 'a Charles gilder;' *Philippus gulden*, 'a Philip's gilder;' the former evidently refers to Charles V. Cf. G. *gulden*, *gülden*, a florin; as the name implies, the coin was at first of gold, though afterwards made of silver. The MHG. name was *guldin*, or *guldîn pfenninc*, the golden penny (L. *aureus denârius*). + Goth. *gultheins*, golden. From Teut. adj. type *gulthinoz*, golden; formed (with suffix -*inoz* = L. -*înus*), from Teut. *gulth-om*, gold. See **Gold**.

GUILE, a wile, cunning, deceit. (F. – Teut.) In early use. ME. *gile*, *gyle*; Layamon, 3198, 16382 (later text); and common later. – OF. *guile*, *guille* (Godefroy). From a Teut. source; see **Wile**. Der. *guile-ful* (ME. *gileful*, Wyclif, Job, xiii. 7, Ps. v. 7), *guile-ful-ly*, *guile-ful-ness* (ME. *gilefulnesse*, Wyclif, Ecclus. xxxvii. 3); *guile-less*, *guile-less-ness*. **Doublet**, *wile*.

GUILLEMOT, a sea-bird. (F. – Teut.) 'A *guillemot* or sea-hen;' Ray, Willughby's Ornithol., p. 324 (1678); N. E. D. '*Wilmots*, Nodies, Gulles;' Hakluyt's Voy. iii. 76. – F. *guillemot* (1555, Hatzfeld). Dimin. of F. *Guillaume*, as *wilmot* and prov. E. *willock* (guillemot) are of *William*. – OHG. *Wilhelm*. In the Norm. dialect *roi Guillemot* means our William I. (Robin).

GUILLOTINE, an instrument for beheading men. (F. personal name.) 'Named after the supposed inventor, a physician named Joseph Ignatius Guillotin, who died in 1814. The first person executed by it was a highway robber named Pelletier, April 25, 1792;' Haydn, Dict. of Dates. Der. *guillotine*, verb.

GUILT, crime, punishable offence. (E.) The *u* is inserted to preserve the *g* as hard. ME. *gilt*, Gower, C. A. ii. 122 (bk. iv. 3610); Chaucer, C. T. 5057 (B 637); commonly also *gult*, as in Ancren Riwle, p. 258. AS. *gylt*, a crime; Grein, i. 536. Teut. type *gultiz*, m. Some have connected it with AS. *geldan*, to pay; but this seems to be inadmissible. No cognate word is known. Der. *guilt-less* = ME. *giltlees*, Chaucer, C. T. 5063 (B 643); *guilt-less-ly*, *guilt-less-ness*; also *guilt-y* = AS. *gyltig*, Matt. xxiii. 18; *guilt-i-ly*, *guilt-i-ness*.

GUINEA, the name of a (former) gold coin. (African.) 'So named from having been first coined of gold brought by the African company from the coast of Guinea in 1663, valued then at 20s.; but worth 30s. in 1695. Not coined since 1813. Reduced at various times; in 1717 to 21s.;' Haydn, Dict. of Dates. Der. *guinea-fowl*, *guinea-hen*, named from the same country. ¶ The *guinea-pig* is from S. America, chiefly Brazil; so that the name is an erroneous one, as in the case of *turkey*.

GUIPURE, a kind of lace; a kind of gimp. (F. – Teut.) First in 1843; see N. E. D. – F. *guipure*, which Cotgrave defines as 'a grosse black thread, covered or whipt about with silk.' – F. *guiper*, to cover (thus) with silk; Godefroy gives the pp. *guipé*. – Teut. *wîpan*, to wind; as in Goth. *weipan*, to crown (whence *waips*, a wreath); G. *weifen*, to reel, to wind. Cf. MDan. *gimpe*, fringe; mod. Dan. *gimpe*, to whip about with silk (Larsen).

GUISE, way, manner, wise. (F. – OHG.) ME. *gise*, *gyse*, Chaucer, C. T. 995 (A 993). Also *guise*, *guyse*; first used in Layamon, 19641, later text, where the earlier text has *wise*. – OF. *guise*, way, wise; cf. Prov., Port., Span., and Ital. *guisa*. [The *gu* stands for an older *w*.] – OHG. *wîsa*, MHG. *wise* (G. *weise*), a way, wise, guise; cognate with AS. *wîse*, whence E. *wise*, sb. See **Wise** (2). Doublet, *wise* (2).

GUITAR, a musical stringed instrument. (F. – L. – Gk.) In Skinner, ed. 1671. ['Give me my *guittara*;' Ben Jonson, Gipsies Metam. § 1 (end); from Span. *guitarra*.] – F. *guitare* (Littré). – L. *cithâra* (accented as in Gk.). – Gk. κιθάρα, a kind of lyre. ¶ The ME. form of the word is *giterne*, Chaucer, C. T. 3333. This also is of F. origin; Cotgrave gives '*Guiterne*, or *Guiterre*, a gitterne.'

GULES, the heraldic name for red. (F. – L.) ME. *goules*; Gawain and Grene Knt., 619. Richardson cites: 'And to bere armes than

are ye able Of gold and *goules* sete with sable;' Squier of Low Degre, l. 203, in Ritson's Metrical Romances, vol. iii. At p. 484 of Rob. of Glouc., ed. Hearne, is a footnote in which we find: 'that bere the armes of *goules* with a white croys.' – F. *gueules*, 'gules, red, or sanguine, in blazon,' Cot.; OF. *goles*, *goules*, *geules*; AF. *goules*, gules, P. Langtoft, ii. 430, answering to Late L. *gulæ*, gules. ¶ Ducange shows that L. *gulæ* also meant 'skins of ermine dyed *red*.' Cf. also OF. *goler*, to border with fur; *engoulé*, *engolé*, *angolé*, trimmed with fur. Cf. 'murium rubricatas pelliculas, quas *gulas* vocant;' S. Bernard, Epist. 42. c. 2. The origin of Late L. *gulæ* (in this sense) is doubtful.

GULF, a hollow in the sea-coast, a bay, a deep place, whirlpool. (F. – Ital. – Gk.) Formerly spelt *goulfe*, *gulph*. 'Hast thou not read in bookes Of fell Charybdis *goulfe*?' Turberville, Pyndara's Answer to Tymetes. ME. *goulf*; 'the *goulf* of Venyse;' Mandeville, Trav. ch. v. p. 54. Milton has the adj. *gulphie*, Vacation Exercise, l. 92; Spenser has *gulphing*, Virgil's Gnat, 542. – F. *golfe* (formerly also *goulfe*), 'a gulph, whirlpool;' Cot. – Ital. *golfo*, a gulf, bay. – Late Gk. κόλφος, variant of Gk. κόλπος, the bosom, lap, a deep hollow, bay, creek. [Cf. the various senses of L. *sinus*.] Der. *gulf-y*, *en-gulf*.

GULL (1), a web-footed sea-bird. (C.) 'Timon will be left a naked *gull*, Which flashes now a Phœnix;' Timon, ii. 1. 31. – Corn. *gullan*, *gwilan*, a gull (Williams); W. *gwylan*; Bret. *gwelan*; Gael. and Irish *faoileann*, Gael. *faoileag*, Irish *faoileag*, OIrish *foilenn*. Celtic type *woilenno-*. The prob. sense was 'wailer,' from its cry; cf. Bret. *gwel-a*, to weep. Stokes-Fick, p. 285.

GULL (2), a dupe. (Low G.) 'Yond *gull* Malvolio;' Tw. Nt. iii. 2. 73. There seems to have been a false notion that the *gull* was a stupid bird. Thus a person who entraps dupes is called a *gull-catcher*, Tw. Nt. ii. 5. 204; and it is possible that popular etymology wrongly associated this word with **Gull** (1); cf. *owl*, *goose*, *dotterel*. But it is probably quite a distinct word, and borrowed from Du. or Low G. – Low G. *gull*, adj., soft, mild, good-natured, open-hearted (Berghaus); MDu. *gulle*, 'a great wench without wit,' Hexham; EFries. *gul*, soft, mild, liberal (Koolman). Der. *gull*, verb, Tw. Nt. ii. 3. 145; *gull-ible*.

GULLET, the throat. (F. – L.) ME. *golet*, *gullet*; Chaucer, C. T. 12477 (C 543). '*Golet*, or throte, *guttur*, *gluma*, *gula*;' Prompt. Parv. – F. *goulet*, 'the gullet;' Cot. Dimin. of OF. *gole*, *goule* (mod. F. *gueule*), the throat. – L. *gula*, the throat. Brugm. i. § 499. From the same source we have *gules*, q. v. Doublet, *gully*, q. v.

GULLY, a channel worn by water. (F. – L.) In Capt. Cook's Third Voyage, b. iv. c. 4 (R.). Formerly written *gullet*. 'It meeteth afterward with another *gullet*,' i.e. small stream; Holinshed, Desc. of Britain, c. 11 (R.). – F. *goulet*, 'a gullet, . . . a narrow brook or deep gutter of water;' Cot. Thus the word is the same as **Gullet**, q. v.

GULP, to swallow greedily and quickly. (E.) 'He has *gulped* me down, Lance;' Beaum. and Fletcher, Wit without Money, A. i. sc. 2. ME. *gulpen*, *gloppen*, *glubben*; 'Til Gloton hedde *i-gloupet* (v. r. *ygloppid*, *ygultid*) a galoun;' P. Plowman, A. v. 191. Of imitative origin. Cf. EFries. and Du. *gulpen*, to swallow eagerly; MDu. *golpen*, *gulpen*, to quaff (Hexham); Du. *gulp*, a great billow, wave, draught, gulp. β. Further allied to Swed. *glupande*, Dan. *glubende*, voracious; Swed. *glup-sk*, Dan. *glub-sk*, ravenous. From Teut. root *gleup-*; as in Swed. dial. *gliopa* (pt. t. *glop*, pl. *glupum*), to swallow, Norw. *glupa* (pt. t. *glaup*), to swallow. Der. *gulp*, sb.

GUM (1), the flesh of the jaws. (E.) ME. *gome*. In Legends of the Holy Rood, ed. Morris, p. 218, l. 250, where it means 'palate.' '*Gome* in mannys mowthe, pl. *goomys*, *Gingiva*, *vel gingive*, *plur*.;' Prompt. Parv. AS. *gôma*, the palate, jaws; Grein, i. 523. + Icel. *gômr*, the palate; Swed. *gom*, the palate; OHG. *guomo*, G. *gaumen*, the palate. β. Allied to Gk. χαῦνος, gaping; Lith. *gomurys*, the palate. See Brugm. i. § 196; where the AS. *ô* is explained as from *ôu*. Der. *gum-boil*.

GUM (2), the hardened adhesive juice of certain trees. (F. – L. – Gk. – Egypt.) ME. *gomme*, Chaucer, Good Women, 121; P. Plowman, B. ii. 226. – F. *gomme*, gum. – L. *gummi*. – Gk. κόμμι, gum; but not orig. a Gk. word. Prob. of Egyptian origin; cf. Coptic *komē*, gum; Peyron, Dict., p. 67. Der. *gum*, verb; *gummi-ferous*, from L. suffix -*fer*, bearing, which from *ferre*, to bear; *gumm-y*, *gumm-i-ness*.

GUN, an engine for throwing projectiles. (Scand.) ME. *gonne*, Chaucer, Ho. of Fame, 1643; P. Plowman, C. xxi. 293; King Alisaunder, ed. Weber, 3268. See note by Way in Prompt. Parv. p. 218. [W. *gwn*, Irish *gunna*, gun, are from E.] Shortened from Icel. *Gunnhildr*, a fem. proper name (whence *Gunnild* in Havelok), a name once given to war-engines, and appropriately enough, because the element *gunn-* (Icel. *gunnr*) signifies 'war,' and *hildr* signifies 'battle.' This is confirmed by an account of munitions at Windsor Castle in 1330–1 (Exchequer Accts. Q. R. Bundle 18, no. 34), which mentions 'una magna balista de cornu quæ vocatur *Domina Gunilda*.' In ME. *Gunne* would be the regular pet-name for *Gunnhildr*. A *Gunnild* is mentioned in the A. S. Chron. an. 1045 (MS. D) ; and *Gunn* is now a surname. Cf. also *gonnylde gnoste*, a spark of a gun ; Polit. Songs, ed. Wright, p. 237. ¶ In Icel. poetry, *gunn-eldr* (war-fire) meant ' a sword,' and *gunn-māni* (war-moon) meant ' a shield.' Der. *gunn-er, gunn-er-y, gun-barrel, -boat, -carriage, -cotton, -powder, -shot, -smith, -stock*; also *gun-wale*, q. v.

GUNNY, a coarse kind of sacking for bags. (Hind.—Skt.) See Yule.—Hind. and Mahratti *gōṇ, gōṇi*, a sack, sacking.—Skt. *gōṇi*, a sack. Perhaps orig. made of hide ; cf. Skt. *gāus* (stem *gō-*), an ox (Uhlenbeck).

GUNWALE, the upper edge of a ship's side. (Scand. *and* E.) Corruptly pronounced *gunnel* [gun·l]. In Skinner, ed. 1671. ' *Gun-wale*, or *Gunnel of a Ship*, a piece of timber that reaches from the halfdeck to the forecastle on either side ;' Kersey, ed. 1715. ' *Wales or Wails*, those timbers on the ship's sides, which lie outmost, and are usually trod upon, when people climb up the sides to get into the ship ;' id. β. Compounded of *gun* and *wale*; see **Wale**. So called because the guns used once to rest upon it ; cf. ' some guns, that went with a swivel upon their *gunnal* ;' Dampier, Voy., ed. 1729, i. 400. The sense of *wale* is ' stick ' or ' beam,' and secondly, ' the mark of a blow with a stick.'

GURGLE, to flow irregularly, with a slight noise. (Ital.—L.) ' To *gurgling* sound Of Liffy's tumbling streams ;' Spenser, Mourning Muse of Thestylis, l. 3. Imitated from Ital. *gorgolare*, ' to gurgle as water doth running;' Florio ; also *gorgogliare*, to gargle, purl, bubble, boil ; cf. *gorgoglio*, a warbling, the gurgling of a stream. The latter answers to a L. type *gurguliāre*, formed as if from L. *gurgulio*, the gullet. See **Gorge**. Brugmann, i. § 499. ¶ To be distinguished from *gargle*, though they were confused.

GURNARD, GURNET, a kind of fish. (F.—Prov.—L.; *with* Teut. *suffix*.) ' *Gurnard*, fysche ;' Prompt. Parv. ' *Gurnarde*, a fysshe, *gournault* ;' Palsgrave. See Levins. Shak. has *gurnet*, 1 Hen. IV, iv. 2. 13. Cotgrave has : ' *Gournauld*, a gurnard fish ;' but the E. word answers rather to OF. *gornard* (Godefroy), F. **gournard* (the suffixes *-ard, -ald, -auld* being convertible) ; and this again stands, by the not uncommon shifting of *r*, for **grounard*. The latter form is represented in Cotgrave by ' *Grougnaut*, a gurnard,' marked as being a Languedoc word ; cf. Prov. *gournau, grougnau*, a gurnard (Mistral), from Prov. *gourgna, grougna*, to grunt (which shows that the word is really of Prov. origin). β. Again, we find another form of the word in MF. *grongnard* (mod. F. *grognard*), explained by Cotgrave as ' grunting ;' and, in fact, the word *gurnard* means ' grunter.' Godefroy has OF. *groignart, gruinard*, ' grondant.' ' The *gurnards* . . . derive their popular appellation from a grunting noise which they make when taken out of the water ;' Eng. Cyclop. s. v. *Trigla*. γ. The F. *grognard* is formed by the suffix *-ard* (=OHG. *hard, hart*) from F. *grogner*, for OF. *grognir, gronir*, to grunt.—L. *grunnire*, to grunt. See **Grunt**. The Prov. word is similar.

GUSH, to flow out swiftly. (E.) ME. *guschen*, Morte Arthure, ed. Brock, 1130. Cf. EFries. *güsen*, to gush out ; Low G. *gusen* (Berghaus). Allied to MDu. *guysen*, to gush out (Kilian) ; Icel. *gusa*, to gush, spirt out, a derivative of the strong verb *gjōsa* (pt. t. *gauss*, pp. *gosinn*), to gush, break out as a volcano. Also Du. *gudsen*, to gush ; ' het bloed *gudsde* uyt zyne wonde, the blood did gush out of his wound ;' Sewel. From Idg. √GHEU, to pour (Gk. χέ-ειν) ; whence √GHEUD, to pour (L. *fundere* (E. *fuse*), Goth. *giutan*, G. *giessen*, Icel. *gjuta*, Swed. *gjuta*, Dan. *gyde*, AS. *gēotan*, to pour). See **Gut, Geysir**, and **Fuse**. ¶ The final *sh* suggests a Teut. base **gut-sk*, extended from **gut-*, weak grade of Teut. **geut-*, Idg. **gheud-*. Der. *gush-ing, gush-ing-ly*; cf. *gust* (1), q. v.

GUSSET, a small insertion of cloth in a garment, for the purpose of enlarging it. (F.) Particularly used of a piece of chain-mail protecting a joint in armour (see gloss. to Fairholt's Costume), or an insertion in the armhole of a shirt. ME. *guschet*, Wallace, bk. ii. 63. The word occurs in Du Wes ; see Palsgrave's Dict., p. 906, col. 3. —F. *gousset*, ' a gusset ; the piece of armour, or of a shirt, whereby the arme-hoole is covered ;' Cot. β. Named from some fancied resemblance to the husk of a bean or pea ; the word being a dimin. of F. *gousse*, ' the huske, swad, cod, hull of beanes, pease, &c.;' Cot. ✝ Ital. *guscio*, a shell, husk ; a word of unknown origin.

GUST (1), a sudden blast or gush of wind. (Scand.) In Shak. Mer. of Ven. iv. 1. 77.—Icel. *gustr*, a gust, blast ; cf. also *gjōsta*, a gust. Cf. Swed. dial. *gust*, a stream of air from an oven (Rietz) ; Norw. *gust*, a gust.—Icel. *gus-*, weak grade of *gjōsa*, to gush. See **Gush**. Der. *gust-y, gust-i-ness*.

GUST (2), relish, taste. (L.) In Shak. Tw. Nt. i. 3. 33 ; and in Spenser, F. Q. vii. 7. 39.—L. *gustus*, a tasting, taste (whence F. *goût*) ; cf. *gustāre*, to taste.—√GEUS, to choose ; whence also Skt. *jush*, to enjoy, like, Gk. γεύειν, to taste, and E. *choose*. See **Choose**. Doublet, *gusto*, the Ital. form of the word. Der. *dis-gust*, q. v.

GUT, the intestinal canal. (E.) [The same word as prov. E. *gut*,

a water-course, wide ditch ; ME. *gote*, Prompt. Parv. p. 205 ; see Way's note.] ME. *gutte, gotte* ; P. Plowman, B. i. 36 ; Rob. of Glouc. p. 289, l. 5865. AS. *gutt* ; pl. *guttas*, ' receptacula viscerum ;' A. S. Gloss. in Mone's Quellen und Forschungen, i. 1830, p. 333, l. 198. β. The orig. sense is ' channel ;' cf. Swed. *gjuta*, a mill-leat (Rietz) ; Dan. *gyde*, a lane ; MDu. *gote*, a channel (Hexham) ; G. *gosse*, a drain ; ME. *gote*, prov. E. *gut*, a drain, water-course. γ. All from the Idg. weak grade **ghud-* (Teut. **gut-*) of √GHEUD, to pour ; see **Gush, Fuse**. ☞ Not connected with *gutter*, which is of Latin origin. Der. *gut*, verb.

GUTTA-PERCHA, a solidified juice of certain trees. (Malay.) ' Made known in England in 1843 ;' Haydn, Dict. of Dates. The trees yielding it abound in the Malayan peninsula and in Borneo.— Malay *gatah, guttah*, gum, balsam (Marsden's Malay Dict., p. 283) ; and *percha*, the name of the tree producing it (though now obtained from other trees). Hence the sense is ' gum of the Percha-tree.' β. The spelling *gutta* is obviously due to confusion with the L. *gutta*, a drop, with which it has nothing whatever to do. ' *Gutta* in Malay means *gum*, *percha* is the name of the tree (Isonandra gutta), or of an island from which the tree was first imported (Pulo-percha) ;' Max Müller, Lect. on Language, 8th ed., i. 231. The former seems to be right ; see C. P. G. Scott, Malayan Words in E.

GUTTER, a channel for water. (F.—L.) ME. *gotere* ; Prompt. Parv. The pl. *goteres* is in Trevisa, i. 181.—OF. *gutiere, goutiere* ; see quotations in Littré, s. v. *gouttière*, a gutter ; cf. Span. *gotera*, a gutter. β. Esp. used of the duct for catching the drippings of the eaves of a roof ; from OF. *gote, goute* (mod. F. *goutte*), a drop.—L. *gutta*, a drop. See **Gout** (1). Der. *gutter*, verb.

GUTTURAL, pertaining to the throat. (F.—L.) In Cotgrave.— F. *guttural*, ' gutturall, belonging to the throat ;' Cot.—L. *gutturālis* ; formed with suffix *-ālis* from *guttur*, the throat. Der. *guttural-ly* (2).

GUY (1), a hideous creature, a fright. (F.—Ital.—Teut.) Orig. an effigy of Guy Fawkes ; carried about and burnt on Nov. 5 ; see Hone, Every-day Book, i. 1430.—F. *Guy*.—Ital. *Guido* ; a name of Teut. origin.

GUY (2), **GUY-ROPE,** a rope used to steady a weight. (F.— Teut.) A nautical term. Spelt *guie* in Capt. J. Smith, Works, ed. Arber, p. 795. Dunbar has *guye*=a guide ; p. 278, l. 1 (S. T. S.). In Skinner, ed. 1671. ' *Guy*, a rope made use of to keep anything from falling or bearing against a ship's side, when it is to be hoised in ;' Kersey's Dict., ed. 1715.—OF. *guie, guye*, a guide ; cf. Span. *guia*, a guide, leader, guy.—F. *guier*, to guide ; earlier form of F. *guider*, to guide. See **Guide**.

GUZZLE, to swallow greedily. (F.) ' *Guzzle*, to drink greedily, to tipple ;' Kersey, ed. 1715. Cotgrave explains OF. *martiner* by ' to quaffe, swill, *guzzle*.' Prob. suggested by OF. *goziller, gosillier*, to vomit, also to prattle, talk (Godefroy) ; whence (in Cotgrave) the comp. *desgoziller*, ' to gulp, to swallow down.' But OF. *desgosiller* had *both* senses. Cf. also F. *s'égosiller*, to make one's throat sore with shouting ; clearly connected with OF. *gosillier*, the throat (Godefroy), and F. *gosier*, the throat. β. Littré connects *gosier* with Lorraine *gosse*, the throat, the stomach of fatted animals. Remoter source unknown ; see Körting, § 4237. Der. *guzzl-er*.

GYMNASIUM, a place for athletic exercises. (L.—Gk.) In Blount's Gloss., ed. 1674.—L. *gymnasium*.—Gk. γυμνάσιον, an athletic school ; so called because the athletes were naked when practising their exercises.—Gk. γυμνάζειν, to train naked, to exercise.—Gk. γυμνάς, more commonly γυμνός, naked. See Prellwitz. Der. From the same source are *gymnast*=Gk. γυμναστής, a trainer of athletes ; *gymnast-ic, gymnast-ics* ; also *gymnick*, from L. *gymnicus*, Gk. γυμνικός, Milton, Samson Agon. 1324 ; also *gymno-sophist*, Ben Jonson, Fortunate Isles (Merefool), from L. pl. *gymno-sophistæ*, Gk. pl. γυμνο-σοφισταί, lit. ' naked sophists.' Also *gymnotus*, an electric eel ; lit. ' naked back,' from the absence of dorsal fins upon it ; short for *gymno-nōtus*, from Gk. γυμνό-s, naked, and νῶτον, back.

GYNARCHY, government by a woman. (Gk.) Spelt *gunarchy* by Lord Chesterfield (Todd). Coined from Gk. γυν-ή, a woman, and *-αρχία, ἀρχή*, rule, from ἄρχειν, to rule ; cf. *olig-archy, tetr-archy*, &c. See **Queen**.

GYPSUM, a mineral containing sulphate of lime and water. (L.— Gk.—Arab.) ' *Gypsum*, parget, white-lime, plaister ; also, the pargetstone ;' Kersey, ed. 1715.—L. *gypsum*, chalk.—Gk. **γύψον*, for γύψος, chalk ; Herod. vii. 69. β. Prob. of Eastern origin ; cf. Pers. *jabsīn*, lime ; Arab. *jibs*, plaster, mortar ; Rich. Dict. p. 494.

GYPSY, GIPSY, one of a certain nomad race. (F.—L.—Gk.— Egypt.) Spelt *gipsen* by Spenser, Mother Hubbard's Tale, l. 86 ; see *Giptian* in Nares. This is a mere corruption of ME. *Egypcien*, an Egyptian. Chaucer calls St. Mary of Egypt ' the *Egipcien* Marie ;' C. T., B 500 (l. 4920) ; and Skelton, swearing by the same saint, says ' By Mary *Gipcy* !' Garland of Laurell, 1455.—OF. *Egyptien, Egiptien*. — Late L. *Ægyptiānus*, formed with suffix *-ānus* from L. *Ægyptius*, an

Egyptian.—Gk. Αἰγύπτιος, an Egyptian.—Gk. Αἴγυπτος, Egypt. From the name of the country. ☞ The supposition that they were Egyptians was false; their orig. home was India. Der. Hence perhaps *gyp*, a college scout (at Cambridge); cf. *Gip* (dog's name) in David Copperfield. The common fable that *gyp* is from Gk. γύψ, a vulture, is unsupported.

GYRE, a circle, circular course. (L.—Gk.) 'Or hurtle rownd in warlike *gyre*;' Spenser, F. Q. ii. 5. 8; cf. iii. 1. 23.—L. *gȳrus*, a circle, circuit.—Gk. γῦρος, a ring, circle; cf. γῦρος, adj. round. Der. *gyrate*, from L. *gȳrātus*, pp. of *gȳrāre*, to turn round, formed from *gȳrus*; *gyrat-ion*, *gyrat-or-y*.

GYRFALCON, GERFALCON, a bird of prey. (F.—Teut. *and* L.) '*Gyrfalcon*, a bird of prey;' Kersey, ed. 1715; spelt *gerfaulcon* in Cotgrave; *girefaucoun* in Trevisa, i. 323, to translate L. *gȳrofalco*. α. The prefix is French, the word being from OF. *gerfaucon*, *girfaucon* (Godefroy), MF. *gerfault*, 'a gerfaulcon, the greatest of hawks, called also *falcon gerfault*;' Cot. Cf. Ital. *gerfalco*, *girfalco*, *girifalco*, a gerfalcon.—Low L. *gērofalco*, a gerfalcon; *gīrefalco*, in 55 Hen. III, Excerpta Historica, p. 20; and (corruptly) *gȳrofalco* (as if named from his circling flight; see **Gyre** above). The right form is *gīrefalco.*—MHG. *gīrvalke*; where *gir* is from OHG. *gīr-*, for *giri*, greedy (whence also G. *geier*, a vulture); and *valke* represents L. *falco*, a falcon. See **Gier-eagle.**

GYRON, a term in heraldry. See **Giron.**

GYVES, fetters. (AF.—E.?) In early use; only in the plural. ME. *giues*, *gyues* (with *u* for *v*); Layamon, 15338; P. Plowman, C. xvi. 254. The *g* was orig. hard; we find '*guyvies de ferro*' in Records of Nottingham, iii. 100 (1505); *ghywes* (for *guyves*), Allit. Morte Arthure, 3621. From AF. *guives*, pl., spelt *gives*, Fr. Chron. of London, p. 89. Of unknown origin; presumably Teutonic, and perhaps E.; probably from AS. *wiððe*, a thong, cord; see Layamon, 15338, 22833 (N. E. D.).

H

HA, an exclamation. (E.) '*A ha!* the fox!' Chaucer, C. T. 15387 (B 4571). When reduplicated, it signifies laughter. '*Ha! ha! ha!*' Temp. ii. 1. 36. Common in Shak. as an exclamation of surprise. Of onomatopoetic origin; see also **Ah.**+OFries. *haha*, to denote laughter; MHG. *hā*, G. *he*; MHG. *hahā*; OF. *ha*.

HABERDASHER, a seller of small wares. (AF.) 'An *haberdasher*;' Chaucer, C. T. 363 (A 361). 'The *haberdasher* heapeth wealth by hattes;' Gascoigne, Fruits of War, st. 64. '*Haberdasher*, a hatter, or seller of hats; also, a dealer in small wares;' Kersey. 'A *haberdasher*, mercier; a poore, petty *haberdasher* of small wares, mercerot;' Sherwood, index to Cotgrave. α. So named from selling a stuff called *hapertas* in Anglo-French, of which (possibly) hats were sometimes made. In the Liber Albus, ed. Riley, p. 225, is mentioned 'la charge de *hapertas*;' in the E. version by Riley, 'the load of hapertas.' And again, at p. 230, we find 'les feez de leyne d'Espagne, wadmal, mercerie, canevas, . . feutre, lormerie, peil, *haberdassherie*, esquireux, . . . et des autres choses qe l'em acustument par fee, vi. d;' thus Englished by Riley: 'the fixed charge upon wool of Spain, wadmal, mercery, canvas, . . . felt, lymere, pile, *haberdassherie*, squirrel-skins, . . and upon other articles that pay custom at a fixed rate, is six pence.' β. The word is probably of Teutonic origin; but its history is not known. Der. *haberdasher-y.*

HABERGEON, a piece of armour to defend the neck and breast. (F.—OHG.) ME. *habergeon*, Chaucer, C. T. 76; *hawberioun*, Wyclif, 1 Kings, xvii. 5.—OF. *haubergeon*, *hauberjon*, a small hauberk (Supp. to Godefroy); dimin. of OF. *hauberc*; see **Hauberk.**

HABILIMENT, dress, attire. (F.—L.) 'The whiche furnysshynge his people with all *habylymentys* of warre;' Fabyan's Chron., Charles VII. (of France); ed. Ellis, p. 553.—F. *habillement*, 'apparell, clothing;' Cot. Formed with suffix -*ment* from *habiller*, 'to cloth, dresse, apparell;' Cot. β. The verb *habiller* signified orig. 'to get ready,' from the F. *habile*, able, ready; which is from the L. *habilis*, manageable, fit. See **Able.** Der. from the same source, *dis-habille*, q. v.

HABIT, practice, custom, dress. (F.—L.) ME. *habit*, *abit*; the latter spelling being common. Spelt *habit*, P. Plowman, B. prol. 3; *abit*, id. C. prol. 3; Ancren Riwle, p. 12, l. 8.—OF. *habit*, 'a garment, raiment, . . . also, an habit, a fashion settled, a use or custom gotten;' Cot.—L. *habitum*, acc. of *habitus*, condition, habit, dress, attire.—L. *habitus*, held in a certain condition, pp. of *habēre*, to have, hold, keep. See Brugmann, i. § 638. Der. *habit*, verb; pp. *habited*, i.e. dressed, Wint. Tale, iv. 4. 557; *habit-u-al*, from MF. *habituel* (mod. F. *habitu-el*), explained 'habituall' by Cotgrave, and from Late L. *habitu-ālis*,

formed with suffix -*ālis* from *habitu-*, for *habitus*, habit; *habit-u-al-ly*; *habitu-ate*, from L. *habituātus*, pp. of *habituāre*, to bring into a certain habit or condition. Also, from the same source, *habit-ude*, q. v., *habit-able*, q. v., *habit-at*, q. v., *habit-at-ion*, q. v., *hab-ili-ment*, q. v. From the L. *habēre* are also numerous derivatives, as *ex-hibit*, *in-hibit*, *in-habit*, *pro-hibit*; *ab-le*, *ab-ili-ty*, *dis-hab-ille*; *debt*; *prebend*; *binnacle*, *malady.*

HABITABLE, that can be dwelt in. (F.—L.) In Milton, P. L. viii. 157; earlier, in Gower, C. A. iii. 104; bk. vii. 586.—F. *habitable*, 'inhabitable;' Cot.—L. *habitābilis*, habitable; formed with suffix -*bilis* from *habitā-re*, to dwell, frequentative form of L. *habēre*, to have (supine *habit-um*). See **Habit.** Der. *habitabl-y*, *habitable-ness*, *inhabitable.*

HABITANT, an inhabitant. (F.—L.) In Milton, P. L. viii. 99; x. 588. Spelt *habitaunt* in Palsgrave.—F. *habitant*, 'an inhabitant;' Cot.; pres. part. of F. *habiter*, to dwell.—L. *habitāre*, to dwell (above). Der. *in-habitant.*

HABITAT, the natural abode of an animal or plant. (L.) A word coined for use in works on natural history. It means 'it dwells (there).'—L. *habitat*, 3 pers. s. pres. of *habitāre*, to dwell.

HABITATION, a dwelling. (F.—L.) In Shak. Mids. Nt. Dr. v. 17. ME. *habitacioun*, Chaucer, C. T. 2928 (A 2926).—F. *habitation*, 'a habitation;' Cot.—L. *habitātiōnem*, acc. of *habitātio*, a dwelling.—L. *habitāre*, to dwell. See **Habitable.**

HABITUDE, usual manner, quality. (F.—L.) In Shak. Complaint, 114.—F. *habitude*, 'custom, use;' Cot.—L. *habitūdo*, condition; formed with suffix -(*t*)*ū-do* from *habit-*, pp. stem of *habēre*, to have.

HACIENDA, a farm, estate, farmhouse. (Span.—L.) Since 1760; chiefly with relation to former Spanish colonies.—Span. *hacienda*, an estate, orig. employment; OSpan. *facienda*.—L. *facienda*, neut. pl., things to be done; from the gerundive of *facere*, to do. See **Fact.**

HACK (1), to cut, chop, mangle. (E.) ME. *hakken*. 'To *hakke* and hewe;' Chaucer, C. T. 2867 (A 2865). '*Hackeð* of his heued' = hacks off his head; Ancren Riwle, p. 298. AS. -*haccian*, to cut; in comp. *tō-haccian*, of which the pt. t. *tō-haccode* occurs in St. Veronica, ed. Goodwin, p. 36, l. 22.+Du. *kakken*, to hew, chop; Dan. *hakke*, to hack, hoe; Swed. *hacka*, to chop; G. *hacken*, to chop, cleave. Teut. type, *hakkōn-*, or *hakkōjan-*. ☞ Mr. Oliphant calls attention to ONorthumb. *hackande*, troublesome, in Early Eng. Psalter, Surtees Soc., Ps. xxxiv. 13. 'Hence, perhaps, our "*hacking* cough."'

HACK (2), a hackney. See **Hackney.**

HACKBUT, an arquebus, an old kind of musket. (F.—O. Low G.) In Holinshed, Hist. Scotland, an. 1583; *hackbutter*, a man armed with a hackbut, id. an. 1544. Rich. says that 'the 33 Hen. VIII. c. 6, regulates the length in stock and gun of the *hagbut* or *demihaque*, and sets forth who may keep and use them.' Also spelt *hagbut*, less correctly.—MF. *haquebute*, 'an haquebut, or arquebuze, a caliver;' Cot. β. A less correct form of *hackbush*, formerly *hakebusse*, as in Naval Accounts of Hen. VII (1485), p. 50; see **Arquebus.** A mere corruption of Low G. *hakebüsse*, Du. *haakbus* (*haeckbusse* in Hexham), an arquebus; due, apparently, to some confusion with OF. *buter*, to thrust.

HACKERY, a bullock-cart. (Hindī—Skt.?) Anglo-Indian. See Supp. to Yule, who suggests Hindī *chakra*, a wheel, a cart; from Skt. *chakra-*, a wheel. Forbes gives Hind. *chhakṛā*, a kind of carriage, car.

HACKLE (1), **HATCHEL**, an instrument for dressing flax or hemp. (E.) Also spelt **Heckle**, q.v.

HACKLE (2), long shining feathers on a cock's neck; or a fly for angling, dressed with such feathers. (E.) It appears to be the same word as the above; see N. E. D.

HACKNEY, HACK, a horse let out for hire. (E.) ME. *hakeney*, Chaucer, C. T. 16027 (G 559); P. Plowman, B. v. 318. Late L. *hackeneius*, as early as 1292; 'pro *hackeneio* ferente tunicam nocturnam et res alias;' Expenses of John of Brabant; in The Camden Miscellany, vol. ii. p. 2. Cf. AF. *un hakenay*, Stat. Realm, i. 288 (1340); *sur hakenai*, P. Langtoft's Chron. ii. 250 (1307). *Hackeneius* means 'belonging to Hackney,' spelt *Hakeneia* in 1199, Rotuli Curiæ Regis, ed. Palgrave, i. 216; ME. *Hakeney* (Middlesex); Inquis. p. Mortem (1285). See Supplement. Der. *hackney-ed.*

HADDOCK, a sea-fish. (E.) ME. *haddoke*. '*Hic morus*, a haddoke;' Wright's Vocab. i. 222, col. 2. Spelt *haddok*, Prompt. Parv.; and in Liber Albus, p. 376. Of unknown origin; the Gael. *adag*, a haddock, is a borrowed word from English; similarly, the OF. *hadot*, 'a salt haddock' (Cotgrave), is plainly a less original form. The suffix -*ock* is perhaps diminutive, as in *hill-ock*. The Irish name is *codog*.

HADES, the abode of the dead. (Gk.) Spelt *Ades*, Milton, P. L. ii. 964.—Gk. ᾁδης, ᾁδης (Attic), ἀΐδης (Homeric), the nether world. 'Usually derived from α, privative, and ἰδεῖν, to see [as though it meant 'the unseen']; but the aspirate in Attic makes this very doubtful;' Liddell and Scott. See Homer, Il. i. 3. And see the account in Prellwitz.

HADJI, HAJJI, one who has performed the pilgrimage to Mecca. (Arab.) First in 1612.—Arab. *ḥāji*, 'a Christian who has performed the pilgrimage to Jerusalem, or a Muhammedan [who has performed] that to Mecca;' Rich. Dict., p. 549. Orig. the latter.

HÆMATITE, HÆMORRHAGE; see **Hematite, Hemorrhage.**

HAFT, a handle. (E.) ME. *haft, heft.* 'Los in the *haft*' = loose in the handle; Polit. Songs, ed. Wright, p. 339. Spelt *haft,* Wyclif, Deut. xix. 5; *heft,* Prompt. Parv. AS. *hæft,* a handle; Grein, ii. 20. +Du. *heft, hecht*; Icel. *hepti* (pron. *hefti*); G. *heft,* a handle, hilt, portion of a book. β. The orig. sense is 'that which is seized, or caught up;' cf. the pp. seen in Icel. *haftr,* one who is taken, a prisoner, and Goth. *hafts,* joined together; with which compare L. *captus,* taken. γ. All from the verb seen in AS. *hebban,* L. *capere.* See **Heave.**

HAG, an ugly old woman. (E.) ME. *hagge*; P. Plowman, B. v. 191. The pl. *heggen* is in the Ancren Riwle, p. 216. The AS. form is fuller, viz. *hægtis, hægtesse,* used to translate L. *pythonissa,* a prophetess or witch; Wright's Vocab. i. 60, col. 1. In the same column, we also find: 'Tisiphona, *wælcyrre*; Parcæ, *hægtesse*;' on which Mr. Wright remarks: 'The Anglo-Saxon of these words would appear to be transposed. *Hægtesse* means properly a fury, or in its modern representative, a *hag,* and would apply singly to Tysiphone, while *wælcyrian* was the name of the three fates of the A.S. mythology.' +G. *hexe,* a witch; OHG. *hāzissa,* apparently short for *hagazissa,* also *hagazussa.* β. The suffix *-tesse,* OHG. *-zissa,* contains a feminine ending; the base is possibly (as has been suggested) the AS. *haga* (G. *hag*), a hedge, bush; it being supposed that witches were seen in bushes by night. See **Hedge,** and **Haggard.** Schade refers the AS. *-tesse* to *teswian,* to harm, from *tesu, teosu,* harm; thus *-tesse* = 'harmer.' **Der.** *hag-gard* (2), q.v.; and even *haggard* (1) is from the same base.

HAGGARD (1), wild, said of a hawk. (F.–G.) Orig. the name of a wild, untrained hawk. 'As *hagard* hauke;' Spenser, F. Q. i. 11. 19. 'For *hagard* hawkes mislike an emptie hand;' Gascoigne's Flowers, Memories, John Vaughan's Theme, l. 26.—OF. *hagard,* 'hagard, wild, strange, froward . . . Faulcon *hagard,* a hagard, a faulcon that preyed for herself long before she was taken;' Cot. β. The orig. sense is 'living in a hedge,' hence, wild. Formed with suffix *-ard* (of G. origin, G. *-hart*), from MHG. *hag* (OHG. *hac*), a hedge; see **Hedge, Haw.** See Hatzfeld.

HAGGARD (2), lean, hollow-eyed, meagre. (F.–G.) 'With *haggard* eyes they stare;' Dryden, tr. of Virgil, Georg. iv. 370. Altered sometimes to *hagged,* as if 'hag-like.' 'The ghostly prudes with *hagged* face;' Gray, A Long Story, 4th stanza from end. Wedgwood cites from Lestrange's Fables: 'A *hagged* carrion of a wolf and a jolly sort of dog with good flesh upon 's back fell into company.' A peculiar use of the word above; 'wild,' hence 'gaunt.' See Hatzfeld.

HAGGIS, a dish commonly made in a sheep's maw, of the minced lungs, heart, and liver of the same animal. (Scand.; *with* AF. *suffix.*) ME. *hagas, hageys, hakkys,* Prompt. Parv. Also spelt *haggas, hagges, hakeys*; see notes to Prompt. Parv., and to the Catholicon Anglicum, p. 169; also the account in Jamieson. The AF. form is *hagiz*; see Wright's Vocab. i. 172, l. 6: 'Estrere le *hagiz* du pocenet,' to take the haggis out of the pot. Formed, with AF. suffix *-iz, -eis,* from the verb *hag,* to cut, found also in the E. frequentative *haggle*; see **Haggle** (1); cf. Norm. dial. *haguer,* to cut up (Moisy). Cf. also Du. *haksel,* minced meat, and Low G. *haks un plüks,* a kind of hash or mince. ¶ The Gael. *taigeis,* a haggis, is merely borrowed from English.

HAGGLE (1), to cut awkwardly, mangle. (Scand.) 'York, all *haggled* over;' Hen. V, iv. 6. 11. A frequentative of Lowland Sc. *hag,* to cut, to hew.—Icel. *höggva,* to hew, from a base **haggw-* (Noreen, § 72, note 8); Swed. dial. *hagga,* to hew (Rietz); allied to E. *hew*; see **Hew.**

HAGGLE (2), to be slow in making a bargain. (Scand.) Cotgrave explains OF. *harceler* by 'to vex, harry, . . . also, to haggle, hucke, hedge, or paulter long in the buying of a commodity.' He similarly explains *barguigner* by 'to chaffer, . . . dodge, haggle, brabble, in the making of a bargain.' It is plain that *higgle* is a weakened form of the same word. β. It seems probable that *haggle* is ultimately the same as the word above. Similarly we have Du. *hakkelen,* to mangle, to stammer; explained by Sewel as 'to hackle, mangle, faulter;' also Du. *hakketeren,* to wrangle, cavil; both derivatives of Du. *hakken,* to hack. **Der.** *haggl-er*; and see **higgle.**

HAGIOGRAPHA, holy writings. (Gk.) A name given to the last of the three Jewish divisions of the Old Testament, contain-

---

ing Ps., Prov., Job, Dan., Ez., Nehem., Ruth, Esther, Chron., Cant., Lam., and Eccles.—Gk. ἁγιόγραφα (βιβλία), books written by inspiration.—Gk. ἁγιο-, for ἅγιος, devoted to the gods, sacred, holy; and γράφ-ειν, to write. β. ἅγιος is allied to Skt. *yaj,* to worship. For γράφειν, see **Graphic. Der.** *hagiograph-y* (in Minsheu), *hagiograph-er*; cf. *hagio-logy,* sacred literature.

HA-HA, HAW-HAW, a sunk fence. (F.) 'Leap each *ha-ha* of truth and common sense;' Mason, Ep. to Sir W. Chambers, l. 14.—F. *haha,* an obstacle that interrupts one suddenly; called *ha! ha!* because it laughs at the man's surprise who meets it.—F. *ha!* interjection of laughter. ¶ With the pron. *haw-haw* compare E. *ς*aw for *ς*pa. 'Just by the *haw-haw*;' Murphy, Three Weeks after Marriage, A. i. sc. 1 (1776).

HAIL (1), frozen rain. (E.) ME. *haȝel,* Layamon, 11975; spelt *hawel* in the later text. Later *hayl* (by loss of *ȝ* or *w*), Chaucer, Good Women, Cleop. 76. AS. *hagl, hagol*; Grein.+Icel. *hagl*; Du., Dan., Swed. *hagel*; G. *hagel.* Teut. types **hag(a)loz,* m., **hag(a)lom,* n. Allied to Gk. κάχληξ, a round pebble; so that *hail-stone* is tautological. **Der.** *hail,* verb, ME. *hailen,* Prompt. Parv.; also *hail-stone,* ME. *hailstone,* Wyclif, Wisdom, v. 23 (later text).

HAIL (2), to greet, call to, address. (Scand.) ME. *heilen.* 'Heylyn, or gretyn, *saluto*;' Prompt. Parv. Spelt *heȝȝlenn* (for *heȝlen*), Ormulum, 2814. A verb formed from Icel. *heill,* sb., prosperity, good luck; a sb. formed from Icel. *heill,* adj., hale, sound. This sb. was particularly used in greeting, as in *far heill,* farewell! β. The usual Icel. verb is *heilsa,* to say hail to one, to greet one, whence ME. *hailsen,* to greet. In P. Plowman, B. v. 101, we have: 'I *hailse* hym hendeliche, as I his frende were' = I greet him readily, as if he were his friend; and, in this very passage, the Bodley MS. reads: 'I *haile* him.' Cf. Swed. *hel, hale,* Dan. *heel, hale,* whole. See **Hale** (1), and **Whole.**

HAIL! (3), an exclamation of greeting. (Scand.) 'All *hail,* great master! grave sir, *hail,* I come!' Temp. i. 2. 189. '*Hayl* be þow, mary' = Lat. *aue Maria*; Myrc's Instructions for Parish Priests, ed. Peacock, l. 422.—Icel. *heill,* hale, whole, adj., *heill,* good luck, sb. See **Hail** (2). ☞ Similar is the use of AS. *wes hāl,* lit. be whole, may you be in good health; but the AS. *hāl* produced the E. *whole,* and the Northern E. *hale.* See **Wassail.**

HAIR, a filament growing from the skin of an animal. (E.; *but influenced by* F.) ME. *heer, her,* Chaucer, C. T. 591 (A 589); Ancren Riwle, p. 424. AS. *hær, hêr,* Grein, ii. 24.+Du. *haar*; Icel. *hār*; Dan. *haar*; Swed. *hår*; G. *haar,* OHG. *hār.* Teut. type **hærom,* n. β. But this would have given a mod. E. form *hear* or *here*; cf. *heares* in Spenser, F. Q. iv. 8. 4. The form now in use is due to the influence of ME. *heire, heyre,* a hair shirt; P. Plowman, B. v. 66; from OF. *haire,* a hair shirt; and this OF. form is from OHG. *hārra* (<*hār-jā), hair-cloth, a fem. derivative from OHG. *hār,* hair. γ. The AS. *hær* is further related to Icel. *haddr,* hair (Teut. type **hazdoz*); and to Lith. *kassa,* plaited hair; L. *cārere,* to card wool. **Der.** *hair-y,* ME. *heeri,* Wyclif, Gen. xxvii. 11; *hair-i-ness*; also *hair-breadth, -cloth, -powder, -splitting, -spring, -stroke, -trigger, -worm.*

HAIRIF, HAYRIF, goose-grass; *Galium Aparine.* (E.) AS. *hege-rife,* goose-grass.—AS. *hege,* a hedge (see **Hay** (2)); and *-rife,* prob. allied to **Rife,** and meaning 'abundant.'

HAKE, a sea-fish of the cod family. (Scand.) 'Hake, fysche, *squilla*;' Prompt. Parv.—Norw. *hakefisk* (lit. hook-fish), a fish with hooked under-jaw, esp. of salmon and trout (Aasen); from Norw. *hake,* a hook; see **Hook.** β. Compare AS. *hacod,* glossed by L. *lucius*; Wright's Vocab. i. 55, col. 2; whence Prov. E. *haked,* a large pike (Cambridgeshire); Blount's Gloss.; allied to G. *hecht* MHG. *hechet,* OHG. *hachit,* a pike. We may explain AS. *hac-od* as furnished with sharp teeth; from Teut. **hak-,* to pierce, as in OHG. *hecchen,* MHG. *hecken* (from **hak-jan-*), to pierce, sting; see **Hack.**

HAKIM, a physician, doctor. (Arab.) 'The Doctors are named *hackeems*;' Sir T. Herbert, Trav. (ed. 1638), p. 234.—Arab. *ḥakim,* wise; also a doctor, physician.—Arab. root *ḥakama,* he exercised authority; Rich. Dict., p. 577.

HALBERD, HALBERT, a kind of pole-axe; a combination of spear and battle-axe, with a long handle. (F.–MHG.) In Shak. Com. Errors, v. 185; and in Naval Accounts (1497); ed. 1896, p. 99. An AF. *halebarde* occurs in 1372; Antiq. Repertory, ii. 27, col. 2. Ben Jonson has *halberdiers,* Every Man, ed. Wheatley, iii. 5. 14.—OF. *halebarde,* 'an halberd;' Cot.—MHG. *helmbarte,* later *halenbarte,* mod. G. *hellebarte,* an axe with which to split a helmet, furnished with a conveniently long handle, derived from MHG. (and G.) *helm,* a helmet; and MHG. (and G.) *barte,* OHG. *barta,* a broad axe. The latter element is derived from G. *bart,* a beard; just as Icel. *skeggja,* an axe, is from *skegg,* a beard; and see **Barb** (1). Cf. Icel. *barða,* a halberd. β. The former element has also been explained as 'long handle;' from MHG. *halm,* a helve, handle; see **Helm** (1); but this explanation is no longer favoured; see Kluge and Darmesteter. The *halberd* may have been named from the jagged and irregular shape of the iron head. **Der.** *halberd-ier*, OF. *halebardier*, 'an halberdier;' Cot.

HALCYON, a king-fisher; as adj., serene. (L.–Gk.) '*Halcyon* days'=calm days, 1 Hen. VI, i. 2. 131. It was supposed that the weather was always calm when the kingfishers were breeding. 'They lay and sit about midwinter, when daies be shortest; and the time whiles they are broody, is called the *halcyon* daies; for during that season, the sea is calme and nauigable, especially in the coast of Sicilie;' Holland's Pliny, b. x. c. 32.–L. *halcyon*, commonly as *alcyon*, a kingfisher.–Gk. ἀλκυών, ἁλκυών, a kingfisher. β. The aspirate seems to be wrong, and due to association with Gk. ἅλς, sea, combined with κύων, 'conceiving,' by popular etymology; but the Gk. name is clearly cognate with L. *alcēdo*, the true L. name for the bird.

HALE (1), whole, healthy, sound. (E.) 'For they bene *hale* enough, I trowe;' Spenser, Sheph. Kal., July, 107. A Northern E. form; spelt *hale* in Cursor Mundi, 24888. It is the Northern form corresponding to AS. *hāl*, whence ME. *hool*, E. *whole*. See **Whole.**

HALE (2), **HAUL**, to drag, draw violently. (F.–OHG.) ME. *halien*, *halen*; whence mod. E. *hale* and a later form *haul*; it appears as *hall* in 1581. Spelt *halie*, P. Plowman, B. viii. 95; *hale*, Chaucer, Parl. of Foules, 151.–F. *haler*, to pull; which first appears in the 12th cent. (Hatzfeld).–OHG. *halōn*, *holōn* (G. *holen*), to summon, to fetch. **+** OFries. *halia*, to fetch; OSax. *halon*, to bring, fetch; Du. *halen*, to fetch, draw, pull; Low G. *halen* (whence Dan. *hale*, Swed. *hala*), to pull, haul. Allied to AS. *ge-holian*, to acquire, get; L. *calāre*, to summon; Gk. καλεῖν, to summon. See **Calends.** **Der.** *haul*, sb., *haul-er*, *haul-age*; also *halyard*, q. v. ☞ *Hale* is the older form; we find '*halede* hine to grunde'=haled him to the ground, Layamon, 25888 (later text); *haul* first occurs in the pp. *ihauled*, Life of Beket, ed. W. H. Black, l. 1497.

HALF, one of two equal parts of a thing. (E.) ME. *half*; '*half* a bushel;' Chaucer, C. T. 4242 (A 4244). OMerc. *half*; AS. *healf*, Northumb. *half*, Luke, xix. 8; where the later AS. text has *half*. **+** Du. *half*; Icel. *hálfr*; Swed. *half*; Dan. *halv*; Goth. *halbs*; G. *halb*, OHG. *halp*. β. In close connexion with this adj. we find ME. *half*, AS. *healf* (Gen. xiii. 9), Icel. *hálfa*, Goth. *halba*, OHG. *halpa*, used with the sense of 'side,' or 'part;' and this may have been the orig. sense. It occurs, e. g. in the Goth. version of 2 Cor. iii. 10, where the Gk. ἐν τούτῳ τῷ μέρει is translated by *in thizai halbai*. γ. A late example of the sb. is in the phrase *left half*=left side, or left hand; P. Plowman, B. ii. 5. It survives in mod. E. *behalf*; see **Behalf.** Cf. Skt. *kalp-aya* (causal of *klp*), to arrange, to distribute (Uhlenbeck). **Der.** *halve*, verb, ME. *haluen* (=*halven*), Wyclif, Ps. liv. 24; *halv-ed*; *half-blood*, *half-breed*, *half-bred*, *half-brother*, *half-sister*, *half-moon*, *half-pay*, *half-way*, *half-witted*, *half-yearly*. Also *half-penny*, in which the *f* (as well as the *l*) has long been lost in pronunciation; spelt *halpeny*, P. Plowman, B. vi. 307. Also *be-half*.

HALIBUT, a large flat-fish. (E.) '*Hallibut*, a fish like a plaice;' Kersey's Dict., ed. 1715. Cotgrave translates OF. *flatelet* by 'a hallibut (fish).' Spelt *halybut* in Fabyan's Chron., ed. Ellis, p. 587. Compounded of ME. *hali*, holy (see **Holy**), and *butte*, a flounder, plaice, which occurs in Havelok, 759. See **Butt** (4). So called because excellent eating for holidays; the sense being 'holy (i.e. holiday) plaice.' The fish often attains to a large size, and weighs as much as 400 lbs. The cognate languages have similar names for it. **+** Du. *heilbot*; from *heilig*, holy, and *bot*, a plaice. Cf. Swed. *helgflundra*, from *helg*, holidays, and *flundra*, a flounder; Dan. *helle-flynder*, from *hellig*, holy, and *flynder*, a flounder.

HALIDOM, a holy relic. (E.) ME. *halidom*, *halidam*. 'That dar y swere on the *halydom*;' Rob. of Brunne, Handlyng Synne, l. 5629. AS. *hāligdōm*; 'on þām *hāligdōme* swerian,' swear on the halidom, Laws of Ethelred, sect. 3, c. 2; in Thorpe, Anc. Laws, i. 293.–AS. *hālig*, holy; and *-dōm*, suffix, orig. the same as *dōm*, doom. See **Holy** and **Doom.** **+** Du. *heiligdom*; Icel. *helgidómr*, Dan. *helligdom*; G. *heiligthum*. ¶ *By my halidam* (with *-dam* for *-dom*) was imagined to refer to our Lady (Dame).

HALIMOTE, a court of a lord of a manor, held in a hall. (E.) ME. *halimote*, *halimot*. 'Vel *halimoto*;' Laws of Hen. I., in Thorpe, Anc. Laws, i. 517. Lit. 'hall-moot;' from ME. *hal*, hall; and AS. *gemōt*, ME. *imot*, a moot, a meeting. See **Hall** and **Moot.** For the form of the word, cf. **Handiwork.**

HALL, a large room. (E.) ME. *halle*, Chaucer, C. T. 2523 (A 2521). OMerc. *hall*; AS. *heall*, *heal*, Grein, ii. 50; the acc. *healle* occurs in Mark, xiv. 15, where the latest text has *halle*. **+** Du. *hal*; Icel. *hall*, *höll*; OSwed. *hall*. (The G. *halle* is a borrowed word.) Teut. type *hallā*, f., for *halnā*; from *hal*, 2nd grade of *helan*-, to cover, shelter; cf. AS. *helan*, to hide, conceal, cover; just as the L. *cella* is allied to L. *cēlāre*, to conceal, cover; the orig. sense being

'cover,' or place of shelter. See **Cell. Der.** *hall-mark*, *guild-hall*, *halimote*. ☞ Quite unconnected with L. *aula*.

HALLELUJAH, the same as **Alleluiah**, q. v.

HALLIARD, the same as **Halyard**, q. v.

HALLOO, HALLOW, to shout. (F.) ME. *halowen*, to chase with shouts; Chaucer, Book Duch. 379; Rich. Redeles, iii. 228; cf. '*Halow*, schypmannys crye, *Celeuma*;' Prompt. Parv.–OF. *halloer*, to pursue with shouts (Godefroy). Of imitative origin. Cotgrave has F. *halle*, 'an interj. of cheering or setting on a dog,' whence *haller*, 'to hallow, or incourage dogs with hallowing.'

HALLOW, to sanctify, make holy. (E.) ME. *halзien*, Layamon, 17496; later *halwe*, P. Plowman, B. xv. 557; *halewe*, *halowe*, Wyclif, John, xi. 55. AS. *hālgian*, to make holy; from *hālig*, holy. See **Holy.** And see below.

HALLOWMASS, the feast of *All Hallows* or All Saints. (Hybrid; E. *and* L.) In Shak. Rich. II, v. i. 80. A familiar abbreviation for *All Hallows' Mass*=the mass (or feast) of All Saints. In Eng. Gilds, ed. Toulmin Smith, p. 351, we have the expression *alle halowene tyd*=all hallows' tide; and again, *the tyme of al halowene* =the time of all hallows. β. Here *hallows* is the gen. pl. of *hallow*, ME. *halwe*, a saint; just as *halowene* is the ME. gen. pl. of the same word. The pl. *halwes* (=saints) occurs in Chaucer, C. T. 14. γ. The ME. *halwe*=AS. *hālga*, definite form of the adj. *hālig*, holy; so also the ME. *halowene* = AS. *hālgena*, definite form of the gen. pl. of the same adj. See **Holy**, and see **Mass** (2). 2. Similarly, *hallowe'en* = all hallows' even.

HALLUCINATION, wandering of mind. (L.) 'For if vision be abolished, it is called *cæcitas*, or blindness; if depraved, and receive its objects erroneously, *hallucination*;' Sir T. Browne, Vulg. Errors, b. iii. c. 18. § 4. Also in Minsheu, ed. 1627. Formed, by analogy with F. sbs. in *-tion*, from L. *hallūcinātio*, *allūcinātio*, or *ālūcinātio*, a wandering of the mind.–L. *hallūcinārī*, *allūcinārī*, or *ālūcinārī*, to wander in mind, dream, rave. Cf. Gk. ἀλύειν, ἁλύειν, to wander in mind; ἠλεός, distraught. **Der.** *hallucinate*, verb, *hallucinat-or-y*.

HALM, the same as **Haulm**, q. v.

HALO, a luminous ring round the sun or moon. (F.–L.–Gk.) 'This *halo* is made after this manner;' Holland's Plutarch, p. 681 (R.).–F. *halo* (16th c.); Hatzfeld.–L. acc. *halō*, from nom. *halos*, a halo.–Gk. ἅλως, a round threshing-floor, in which the oxen trod out a circular path; a halo.

HALSER (in Minsheu), the same as **Hawser**, q. v.

HALT (1), lame. (E.) ME. *halt*, Havelok, 543. OMerc. *halt*, AS. *healt*, Northumb. *halt*, Luke, xiv. 21. **+** Icel. *haltr*; Dan. *halt*; Swed. *halt*; Goth. *halts*; OHG. *halz*. Teut. type *haltoz*. Cf. L. *claudus*, lame. **Der.** *halt*, verb=ME. *halten*, AS. *healtian* (Ps. xvii. 47); *halt-ing*, *halt-ing-ly*.

HALT (2), as sb., a sudden stop; as a verb, to stop quickly at the word of command. (F.–G.) 'And in their march soon made a *halt*;' Sir W. Davenant, The Dream, st. 19. A military term. Dr. Murray says it first came in as an Ital. term, without initial *h*; and Richardson quotes the form *alt* from Milton, P. L. vi. 532, where mod. editions have *halt*. The *h* is due to F.–F. *halte* (Hatzfeld); cf. Ital. *alto*; as in *fare alto*, to make a halt, to stop.–G. *halt*, halt! lit. hold! from *halten*, to hold, check, cognate with E. **Hold** (1), q. v. The word has passed, from G., into several languages.

HALTER, a rope for leading a horse, a noose. (E.) ME. *halter*, Gower, C. A. ii. 47; bk. iv. 1357. Also *helfter*=halter, in O. Eng. Hom., ed. Morris, i. 53, l. 18. AS. *healfter* (rare); the dat. on *healftre*=with a halter, occurs as a translation of L. *in camo* in Ps. xxxi. 12 (Camb. MS.), ed. Spelman; also spelt *hælftre*; we find '*capistrum*, hælftre,' Wright's Vocab. i. 84, col. 1; cf. Thorpe's Analecta, p. 28, l. 1. **+** MDu. *halfter* (Hexham); G. *halfter*, a halter; OHG. *halftra*; O. Low G. *haliftra* (Schade). Teut. types *halftr-*, *halftr-* (Franck). From the base *halb-*, apparently signifying 'to hold;' see **Helve.** Lit. 'something to hold by;' cf. L. *cap-istrum*, a halter, from L. *capere*, to take hold. **Der.** *halter*, verb.

HALVE, to divide in half. (E.) See **Half.**

HALYARD, HALLIARD, a rope for hoisting or lowering sails. (E.) Both spellings are in Kersey's Dict., ed. 1715. A form due to popular etymology, as if the ropes were so called because fastened to the *yards* of the ship from which the sails are suspended, and so *hale* or draw the yards into their places. But the *d* is excrescent; from ME. *halier*, lit. 'a haler,' or 'hauler.' 'Oon uptye with 2 *haliers*;' Riley, Mem. of London, p. 370 (A.D. 1373); *halliers*, Hakluyt, Voy. iii. 847. See **Hale** (2).

HAM, the inner or hind part of the knee; the thigh of an animal. (E.) ME. *hamme*, *homme*; the pl. is spelt both *hommen* and *hammes*, Ancren Riwle, p. 122. AS. *hamm*; '*poples*, hamm;' Wright's Vocab. i. 44, col. 2; '*suffragines*, hamma' (pl.); id. **+** Du. *ham*; Icel. *höm* (gen. *hamar*); OHG. *hamma*, prov. G. *hamme*. β. Connected by

Brugmann (i. § 421) with Gk. κνήμη, the lower part of the leg. (But see **Gambol**.) Der. *ham-string*, sb., Shak. Troil. i. 3. 154; *ham-string*, verb.

HAMADRYAD, a dryad or wood-nymph. (L. – Gk.) Properly used rather in the pl. *Hamadryades*, whence the sing. *hamadryad* was (incorrectly) formed, by cutting off the suffix *-es*. Chaucer, C. T. 2930 (A 2938), has the corrupt form *Amadrydes*. – L. pl. *hamadryades* (sing. *hamadryas*), wood-nymphs. – Gk. pl. Ἁμαδρυάδες, wood-nymphs ; the life of each nymph depended on that of the tree to which she was attached. – Gk. ἅμα, together with (i. e. coexistent with) ; and δρῦς, a tree. Ἅμα is co-radicate with *same* ; and δρῦς with *tree*. See **Same** and **Tree**.

HAME, one of the two bent sticks round a horse collar. (E.) Usually in the pl. *hames*. ME. *hame* ; Catholicon Anglic. (1483). In Wright's Vocab. i. 168, the AF. *esteles* is glossed by *hames* ; and *boceles* by *beru-hames* ; cf. prov. E. *bargham* (E. D. D.). + Du. *haam*. Cf. MDu. *hamme*, 'a cratch of wood to tie beasts to, or a yoke ;' Hexham. Further allied to Skt. *çamyā*, the pin of a yoke ; Pers. *sīm*, *saym*, 'the neck-yoke of oxen,' Rich. Dict., p. 866. (Horn, § 764 ; Uhlenbeck.) Cf. **Hem** (1).

HAMLET, a small village. (F. – O. Low G.) ME. *hamelet*, of three syllables ; Rob. of Brunne, tr. of Langtoft, p. 269 ; spelt *hamelat*, Barbour, Bruce, ix. 195 ; *hamillet*, id. ix. 403 (Edinb. MS.) ; *hamlet*, id. ix. 403 (Camb. MS.). – AF. *hamelet*, Year-books of Edw. I, 1292–3, p. 25 ; dimin. of OF. *hamel* (whence mod. F. *hameau*). *Hamel* is used by Froissart, ii. 2. 232 (Littré). The suffix *-el* is also dimin. ; the base being *ham-*. – OFriesic *hām*, a home, dwelling ; cognate with AS. *hām*, whence E. *home*. See **Home**. ¶ The fact that the word is *French* explains the difference of vowel.

HAMMER, a tool for driving nails. (E.) ME. *hamer*, *hammer* ; Chaucer, C. T. 2510 (A 2508) ; Havelok, 1877. AS. *hamor*, Grein, ii. 11. + Du. *hamer* ; Icel. *hamarr* ; Dan. *hammer* ; Swed. *hammare* ; G. *hammer* ; OHG. *hamar*. β. Of doubtful origin ; Curtius (i. 161) connects it with Church Slavonic *kameni* (Russ. *kamene*), a stone. Perhaps orig. 'a stone implement ;' Icel. *hamarr* also means 'a rock.' Der. *hammer*, verb, K. John, iv. 1. 67 ; *hammer-head* (a kind of shark).

HAMMERCLOTH, the cloth which covers a coach-box. (Hybrid ; Du. *and* E. ?) The N. E. D. quotes, from Mann. and Househ. Exp. (1465), p. 315, 'My mastyr bout [bought] . . xlj elles of *hamer-clothe*.' Also, from Archæol. xvi. 91 (Document of the time of Queen Mary), '*Hamer-clothes*, with our arms and badges of our colours . . apperteininge unto the same wagon.' Of unknown origin. β. But perhaps the form *hammer* is an E. adaptation of the Du. word *hemel* (which was not understood) ; with the addition of E. *cloth*. Du. *hemel* (1) heaven, (2) a tester of a bed, roof of a coach, canopy, daïs, baldachin (Calisch). 'Den *hemel* van een koetse, the seeling of a coach,' Hexham ; explained by Sewel as 'the testern of a coach.' Cf. also MDu. *hemelen*, 'to hide, cover, adorne ;' Hexham. Also WFlem. *hemelwagen*, a triumphal car (De Bo). γ. Cognate with Swed., Dan., and G. *himmel*, heaven, a canopy, tester. See *hemel* in Franck.

HAMMOCK, a piece of strong netting slung to form a hanging bed. (West Indian.) 'Those beds which they call *hamacas*, or Brasill beds ;' Hakluyt's Voyages, iii. 641. 'Cotton for the making of *hamaccas*, which are Indian beds ;' Ralegh, Discovery of Guiana, ed. 1596, p. 32 (Todd). 'Beds or *hamacks* ;' Sir T. Herbert, Travels, p. 6 (id.). Columbus, in the Narrative of his First Voyage, says : 'a great many Indians came to-day for the purpose of bartering their cotton, and *hamacas*, or nets, in which they sleep' (Webster). Cf. Span. *hamaca*, a hammock. Of West Indian origin ; prob. Caribbean. Eden has *amacca*, ed. Arber, p. 192 ; *hamaca*, p. 230. ¶ Ingeniously corrupted in Dutch to *hangmat*, i. e. a hanging mat ; but the older Du. form was *hammak* (Sewel).

HAMPER (1), to impede, hinder, harass. (E.) ME. *hamperen*, *hampren* ; the pp. is *hampered* and *hampred*, Will. of Palerne, 441, 4694. 'For, I trow, he can *hampre* thee ;' Rom. of the Rose, 6426. A difficult word ; but it seems to be a nasalised form allied to Low G. *hapern*, EFries. *haperen*, to stop short. Cf. Alsace *haperen*, *hamperen*, to hesitate, proceed with difficulty ; '*s hampert*, it goes hard (E. Martin) ; Low G. *hampern*, occasional form of *happern*, *happeln*, to be stuck fast (Berghaus) ; Du. *haperen*, to stop, stagnate, flag, fail ; *de machine hapert*, the machine flags, is hampered ; *er hapert iets aan*, there is a hitch ; Pomeran. *happern*, *hapern*, to meet with difficulties ; Swed. dial. *happla*, to stammer ; *happe*, to back a horse ; Dan. *happe*, to stutter. Cf. **Hopple**. Der. *hamper*, a fetter (rare).

HAMPER (2), a kind of basket. (F. – G.) 'An *hamper* of golde ;' Fabyan's Chron., an. 1431–2 ; ed. Ellis, p. 607. 'An *hampyr* of gold ;' Lydgate, Minor Poems, p. 20. 'Cophinus, *hampere* ;' Voc. 659. 10. A shortened form of **Hanaper**, q.v. '*Clerk of the Hamper* or *hanaper* (*Clericus hanaperii*) is an officer in Chancery (Anno 2 Edw. iv. c. 1) otherwise called *Warden of the Hamper* in the same statute ;'

Blount's Law Lexicon. – OF. *hanapier* ; Low L. *hanaperium*, a large vessel for keeping cups in. – OF. *hanap* (Low L. *hanapus*), a drinking-cup. – OFrankish **hnapp-* (Du. *nap*) ; OHG. *hnapf* (MHG. *napf*), a drinking-cup. + AS. *hnæp*, as a gloss to L. *ciatus* (*cyathus*) ; Wright's Vocab. i. 24, col. 2. Doublet, *hanaper*.

HAMSTER, a species of rodent, allied to the rat. (G.) 'The skins of *hamsters* ;' Topsell, Four-footed Beasts, ed. 1658, p. 413. – G. *hamster*, 'German marmot ;' Flügel.

HANAPER, the old form of **Hamper** (2). Cf. '*hanypere*, or *hamper*, canistrum ;' Prompt. Parv., p. 226. 'The Hanaper office in the Court of Chancery derives its name from the *hanaperium*, a large basket in which writs were deposited,' &c. ; Way's note.

HAND, the part of the body used for seizing and holding. (E.) ME. *hand*, *hond*, Chaucer, C. T. 843 (A 841). AS. *hand*, *hond* ; Grein, ii. 11. + Du. *hand* ; Icel. *hönd*, *hand* ; Dan. *haand* ; Swed. *hand* ; Goth. *handus* ; G. *hand* ; OHG. *hant*. Teut. type **handuz*, fem. Root uncertain. Some connect it with Goth. *hinthan*, to seize, a strong verb (pt. t. *hanth*, pp. *hunthans*), only found in the compounds *frahinthan*, to take captive, *ushinthan*, to take captive. Der. *hand*, verb, Temp. i. 1. 25 ; *hand-er* ; *hand-barrow*, *hand-bill*, *hand-book* (imitated from G. *handbuch*, see Trench, Eng. Past and Present) ; *hand-breadth*, Exod. xxv. 25 ; *hand-cart* ; *hand-ful* (Wyclif has *hondfullis*, pl., Gen. xxxvii. 7) ; *hand-gallop* ; *hand-glass*, *hand-grenade*, *hand-kerchief* (see **Kerchief**), *hand-less*, *hand-maid* (Gen. xvi. 1), *hand-maiden* (Luke, i. 48), *hand-spike*, *hand-staves* (Ezek. xxxix. 9), *hand-weapon* (Numb. xxxv. 18), *hand-writing*. And see *hand-cuff*, *hand-i-cap*, *hand-i-craft*, *hand-i-work*, *hand-le*, *hand-sel*, *hand-some*, *hand-y*.

HANDCUFF, a manacle, shackle for the hand. (E.) In Todd's Johnson, without a reference ; rare in books. The more usual word (in former times) was *hand-fetter*, used by Cotgrave to translate OF. *manette*, *manicle*, and *manotte*. From *hand* and *cuff*. ¶ Too late to be an adaptation of ME. and AS. *handcops*, a handcuff. We find '*manica*, *hond-cops*' in a vocabulary of the 12th century ; Wright's Vocab. i. 95, col. 2.

HANDICAP, a race for horses of all ages. (E.) In a *handicap*, horses carry different weights according to their ages, &c., with a view to equalising their chances. The word was formerly the name of a game. 'To the Miter Taverne in Woodstreete . . . Here some of us fell to *handycapp*, a sport that I never knew before ;' Pepys' Diary, Sept. 18, 1660. Orig. the same as the *Newe Feire*, described in P. Plowman, B. v. 327 ; which shows that it was a custom to barter articles, and to settle by arbitration which of the articles was more valuable, and how much (by way of 'amends') was to be given to the holder of the inferior one. From this settlement of 'amends' arose the system known as *handicapping*. The etymology is from *hand i' cap* (= hand in cap) ; from the mode of drawing lots. See the N. E. D. and my Notes on P. Plowman ; also N. and Q., June 23, 1855.

HANDICRAFT, manual occupation, by way of trade. (E.) Cotgrave translates OF. *mestier* by 'a trade, occupation, mystery, *handicraft*.' A corruption of *handcraft* ; the insertion of *i* being due to an imitation of the form of *handiwork*, in which *i* is a real part of the word. AS. *handcræft*, a trade ; Canons under K. Edgar, sect. xi ; in Thorpe's Ancient Laws, ii. 246. See **Hand** and **Craft**. Der. *handicrafts-man*.

HANDIWORK, HANDYWORK, work done by the hands. (E.) ME. *handiwerk*, *hondiwerc* ; spelt *hondiwerc*, O. Eng. Homilies, ed. Morris, i. 129, l. 20. AS. *handgeweorc*, Deut. iv. 28. – AS. *hand*, hand ; and *geweorc*, a collective form of *weorc*, work. See **Hand** and **Work**. ¶ The prefix *ge-* in AS. is extremely common, and makes no appreciable difference in the sense of a word. In later E., it is constantly rendered by *i-* or *y-*, as in *y-clept*, from AS. *gecleoped*.

HANDLE, to treat of, manage. (E.) ME. *handlen*, Chaucer, C. T. 8252 (E 376). AS. *handlian*, Gen. xxvii. 12. Formed with suffix *-l* and causal *-ian* from AS. *hand*, hand. + Du. *handelen*, to handle, trade ; Icel. *höndla* ; Dan. *handle*, to treat, use, trade ; Swed. *handla*, G. *handeln*, to trade. All similarly formed. See **Hand**. Allied to *handle*, sb., lit. a thing by which to manage a tool ; the dat. pl. *hondlen* occurs early, in St. Juliana, ed. Cockayne and Brock, p. 59 ; from AS. *handle*, a handle, Corpus Gloss. 1904. Cf. Dan. *handel*, a handle.

HANDSEL, HANSEL, a first instalment or earnest of a bargain. (Scand.) 1. In making bargains, it was formerly usual to pay a small part of the price at once, to conclude the bargain and as an earnest of the rest. The lit. sense of the word is 'delivery into the hand' or 'hand-gift.' The word often means a gift or bribe, a new-year's gift, an earnest-penny, the first money received in a morning, &c. See *Hansel* in Halliwell. ME. *hansele*, P. Plowman, C. vii. 375 ; B. v. 326 ; *hansell*, Rich. Redeles, iv. 91. 2. Another sense of the word was 'a giving of hands,' a shaking of hands by way of concluding a bargain; see *handsal* in Icel. Dict. Cf. AS. *handselen*, a delivery into the hand; cited by Lye from a Glossary (Cot. 136); see Voc. 449. 29. [The AS. word is rare, and the word is rather to be considered as Scand.]—Icel. *handsal*, a law term, the transaction of a bargain by joining hands; 'hand-shaking was with the men of old the sign of a *transaction*, and is still used among farmers and the like, so that *to shake hands* is the same as to conclude a bargain' (Vigfusson); derived from Icel. *hand*, hand, and *sal*, a sale, bargain. Cf. Dan. *handsel*, a handsel, earnest; Swed. *handsöl*. Der. *handsel* or *hansel*, verb, used in Warner's Albion's England, b. xii. c. 75, l. 7; spelt *hanselle*, Cath. Angl. (1483).

HANDSOME, comely, orig. dexterous. (E.) Formerly it signified able, adroit, dexterous; see Trench, Select Glossary; Shak. has it in the mod. sense. ME. *handsum*. '*Handsum*, or esy to hond werke, esy to han hand werke, *manualis*;' Prompt. Parv.—AS. *hand*, hand; and suffix *-sum*, as in *wyn-sum*, winsome, joyous; but the whole word *handsum* does not appear.+Du. *handzaam*, tractable, serviceable. β. The suffix *-sum* is a weaker grade of Du. *-zaam*, G. *-sam* (in *lang-sam*); see **-some**, suffix. Der. *handsome-ly*; *handsomeness*, Troil. ii. 1. 16; spelt *hansom-nesse* in Palsgrave.

HANDY (1), dexterous, expert. (E.) 'With *handy* care;' Dryden, Baucis and Philemon, l. 61. From *hand* and *-y*. ¶ Somewhat different from ME. *hendi*, which occurs in King Horn, ed. Lumby, 1336. 'Theonne beo ȝe his *hendi* children' = then ye are his dutiful children; Ancren Riwle, p. 186; from AS. *hendig*, appearing in the comp. *list-hendig*, having skilful hands (Grein); which is composed of AS. *list*, skill, and *hendig*, an adj. regularly formed from the sb. *hand* by the addition of the suffix *-ig* and the consequent vowel change from *a* to *e*. See **Hand**.+Du. *handig*, handy, expert; cf. Dan. *hændig*, usually *behændig*, expert, dexterous; Swed. *händig*, dexterous; Goth. *handugs*, clever, wise. Cf. G. *behend*, agile, dexterous; and see **Handy** (2).

HANDY (2), convenient, near. (E.) Also from *hand* and *-y*. 'Very *handy* and convenient;' T. Fuller, Pisgah Sight, i. 400 (N.E.D.). 'Ah! though he lives so *handy*, He never now drops in to sup;' Hood's Own, i. 44. ¶ Different in form from ME. *hende*. 'Nade his help *hende* ben' = had not help been near him; William of Palerne, 2513. AS. *gehende*, near; 'sumor is *gehende*' = summer is nigh at hand, Luke, xxi. 30; 'he wæs *gehende* þam scipe' = he was nigh unto the ship, John, vi. 19. [The prefix *ge-* could always be dropped, and is nearly lost in mod. English.] The AS. *gehende* is an adv. and prep., formed from *hand* by suffixed *-e* (for *-jo-*) and vowel-change. See **Handy** (1).

HANDYWORK, the same as **Handiwork**, q. v.

HANG, to suspend; to be suspended. (E.) Here two E. verbs and the ON. *hengja* have been mixed together. See the full account in the N. E. D. A. Trans. and weak verb, pt. t. and pp. *hanged*. 'Born to be *hanged*;' Temp. i. 1. 35. But the pt. t. is generally turned into *hung*, as in '*hung* their eyelids down;' 1 Hen. IV, iii. 2. 81. ME. *hangien*, *hongien*; also *hangen*, *hongen*. 'Honged hym after' = he hanged himself afterwards; P. Plowman, B. i. 68; pp. *hanged*, id. B. prol. 176. AS. *hangian*, *hongian*, but with intransitive sense, Grein, ii. 14; the pt. t. *hangode* occurs in Beowulf, ed. Grein, 2085. Cf. Icel. *hengja*, to hang up (weak verb), G. *hängen* (weak verb). Teut. type **hangjan-*. B. ME. *hangen*, pt. t. *heng* (sometimes *hing*), pp. *hongen*. 'And theron *heng* a broche of gold ful schene;' Chaucer, C. T. 160. 'By ounces *henge* his lokkes that he hadde;' id. 679. The ME. infin. *hangen* is conformed to the causal and Icel. forms, the AS. infin. being always contracted. AS. *hōn*, to hang, but transitive in sense (contr. from *hāhan* or *hanghan*); pt. t. *hēng*, pp. *hangen*; Grein, ii. 95. Cf. Icel. *hanga*, to hang, intr.; pt. t. *hekk*, pp. *hanginn*; Goth. *hāhan*, pt. t. *haihāh* (formed by reduplication), pp. *hāhans*; G. *hangen*, pt. t. *hieng*, *hing*, pp. *gehangen*. Allied to L. *cunctari*, to hesitate, delay, and Skt. *çank*, to hesitate, be in uncertainty, doubt, fear. Brugmann, i. § 420. ¶ The Du. *hangen*, Dan. *hænge*, Swed. *hänga*, are forms used with both trans. and intrans. senses. Der. *hang-er*, (1) one who hangs, (2) a suspended sword, orig. part of a sword-belt whence the sword was suspended, Hamlet, v. 2. 157; *hanger-on*, *hang-ing*; *hang-ings*, Tam. Shrew, ii. 351; *hang-man*, Meas. iv. 2. 18; *hang-dog*, Pope, Donne Versified, Sat. iv. 267.

HANGNAIL; for *angnail*, a form of **Agnail**, q. v.

HANK, a skein or coil of thread or yarn. (Scand.) Cotgrave translates OF. *bobine* by 'a skane or *hanke* of gold or silver thread.' 'An *hank*;' Catholicon Angl. (1483). Cf. prov. E. *hank*, a skein, a loop to fasten a gate, a handle (Halliwell). The rare ME. verb *hanken*, to fetter, occurs in Cursor Mundi, 16044.—Icel. *hanki*, the hasp or clasp of a chest; *hönk*, a hank, coil; Dan. *hank*, a handle, ear of a vessel; Swed. *hank*, a string, tie-band. Also Low G. *hank*, a handle (Lübben); G. *henkel*, a handle, ring, ear, hook. β. The orig. sense seems to be 'a loop,' or 'hasp,' or 'hook;' and the sb.

is a nasalised form allied to Icel. *haki*, a hook, G. *haken*, a hook, AS. *haca*, a fastening of a door. See **Hatch** (1), **Hook**.

HANKER, to long importunately. (E.) Not in early use. 'And felt such bowel-*hankerings* To see an empire, all of kings;' Butler, Hudibras, pt. iii. c. 2. l. 239. Cf. prov. E. *hank*, to hanker after (North); Halliwell. This verb is a frequentative allied to prov. E. *hake*, to wander about, loiter, hanker after; also to tease; further allied to prov. E. *hake*, a hook, and to *hank* (above). And see *hanker* in the E. D. D.+MDu. *anckeren* (surely for *hanckeren*), 'to long or desire much after anything;' Hexham. Cf. WFlem. *hankeren*, with the same sense as mod. Du. *hunkeren*, to hanker after, formerly *honkeren* (= *hankeren*); see Sewel. ¶ Perhaps it has often been associated with the verb *to hang*.

HANSEATIC, pertaining to the Hanse Towns in Germany. (F.—OHG.) 'The chiefe cities of the *Hans*;' Hakluyt, Voy. i. 155. The *Hanse* towns were so called because associated in a league. —OF. *hanse*, 'the hanse; a company, society, or corporation of merchants;' Cot.—OHG. *hansa*, mod. G. *hanse*, an association, league (Flügel).+Goth. *hansa*, a band of men, Mk. xv. 16; Luke, vi. 17.+AS. *hōs* [for **hans*], a band of men; Beowulf, 924. The Finnish *kansa*, people, was borrowed from Teutonic. ¶ The league began about A.D. 1140 (Haydn).

HANSEL, the same as **Handsel**, q. v.

HANSOM, a kind of cab. (E.) Modern. An abbreviation for 'Hansom's patent safety cab.' From the name of the inventor (1834). *Hansom* is prob. a variant of *Hanson* (son of Hans); see Bardley's E. Surnames.

HAP, fortune, chance, accident. (Scand.) ME. *hap*, *happ*; P. Plowman, B. xii. 108; Layamon, 816, 3857.—Icel. *happ*, hap, chance, good luck. Cf. AS. *gehæp*, fit; Ælfric's Colloquy, in Voc. 92. 8; also AS. *mægenhæp*, full of strength, *mōdhæp*, full of courage, Grein, ii. 219, 259. ¶ The W. *hap*, luck, hap, chance, must be borrowed from E.; but the OIrish *cob*, Irish *cobh*, victory, triumph, is cognate. Der. *happ-y*, orig. lucky, Pricke of Conscience, 1334; *happ-i-ly*, *happi-ness*; *hap-less*, Gascoigne, Fruits of War, st. 108; *hap-less-ly*; *hap-ly*, Shak. Two Gent. i. 1. 32 (*happily* in the same sense, Meas. iv. 2. 98); *hap-hazard*, Holland, tr. of Livy, p. 578 (R.); *happ-en*, verb, q.v.; *mis-hap*, *per-haps*.

HAPPEN, to befal. (Scand.) ME. *happenen*; Gower has *hapneth* = it happens; C. A. iii. 62; bk. vi. 1815. 'ȝif me þe lyffe *happene*' = if life be granted me; Morte Arthure, ed. Brock, 1269. β. The form *happenen* is an extension of the commoner form *happen* (mod. E. *hap*). 'In any cas that mighte falle or *happe*;' Chaucer, C. T. 587 (A 585). The latter verb is formed directly from the sb. *hap* above. ¶ With the ending *-enen* compare Goth. verbs in *-nan*.

HARAKIRI, a form of suicide. (Japan.) Also known as 'happy dispatch;' but lit. suicide by disembowelment.—Jap. *hara*, belly; *kiri*, to cut (N.E.D.).

HARANGUE, a popular address. (F.—OHG.) In Milton, P. L. xi. 663. ME. *arang*, Ratis Raving, i. 244.—MF. *harangue*, 'an oration, . . . set speech, long tale;' Cot. Cf. Span. *arenga*, Ital. *aringa*, *arringa*, an harangue. β. The Ital. *aringa* signifies a speech made from an *aringo*, which Florio explains by 'a pulpit;' *aringo* also meant an arena, lists, place of declamation. The more lit. sense is a speech made in the midst of a *ring* of people.—OHG. *hring* (mod. G. *ring*), a ring, a ring of people, an arena, circus, lists; cognate with E. *ring*. See **Ring**. ¶ The vowel *a* (for *i*) reappears in the sb. *rank*; see **Rank**, **Range**. The prefix *ha-* in F., and *a-* in Span. and Ital., are due to the OHG. *h-*, now dropped. Der. *harangue*, verb, Butler, Hudibras, pt. iii. c. 2. l. 438.

HARASS, to torment, vex, plague. (F.—OHG.) Also spelt *harras*. 'To *harass* and weary the English;' Bacon, Life of Hen. VII, ed. Lumby, p. 61 (spelt *harrasse* in R.).—MF. *harasser*, 'to tire, or toile out, . . . vex, disquiet;' Cot. β. Of disputed origin; but it seems best to suppose it to be an extension of OF. *harer*; '*harer vn chien*, to hound a dog at, or set a dog on a beast;' Cot.—OHG. *haren*, to cry out; allied to Goth. *hazjan*, to praise. Der. *harass*, sb., Milton, Samson, 257; *harass-er*.

HARBINGER, a forerunner. (F.—OHG.) In Shak. Macb. i. 4. 45. See Trench, Select Glossary. The *n* stands for *r*, and the older form is ME. *herbergeour*, one who provided lodgings for a host or army of people. This sense is retained in Bacon, who says: 'There was a *harbinger* who had lodged a gentleman in a very ill room;' Apophthegms, no. 54 (or 63). 'The fame anon thurgh Rome toun is born . . . By *herbergeours* that wenten him biforn;' Chaucer, C. T. 5417 (B 995). In the title of the legend of St. Julian, in Bodley MS. 1596, fol. 4, he is called 'St. Julian the gode *herberour*,' i.e. the good harbourer. *Herbergeour* is formed (by help of the suffix *-our*, L. *-ātō-rem*, denoting the agent) from the OF. *herberger*, 'to harbour, lodge, or dwell in a house;' Cot. (and see Godefroy).—OF. *herberge*, 'a house, harbour, lodging;' Cot.; mod. F. *auberge.* ─MHG. *herberge,* OHG. *heriberga,* a lodging, harbour; see further under **Harbour.**

HARBOUR, a lodging, shelter, place of refuge. (Scand.) ME. *herberwe,* Chaucer, C. T. 767 (A 765); whence mod. E. *harbour* by change of *-erwe* to *-our,* and the use of *ar* to represent the later sound of *er.* The *w* stands for an older *ȝ,* and this again for *g*; the spelling *herberȝe* is in Layamon, 28878. ─Icel. *herbergi,* a harbour, inn, lodging, lit. a 'host-shelter;' derived from Icel. *herr,* an army, and *barg,* 2nd grade of *bjarga,* to save, help, defend. Cf. MSwed. *hærberge,* an inn; derived from *hær,* an army, and *berga,* to defend (Ihre). ✛ OHG. *heriberga,* a camp, lodging; from OHG. *heri* (G. *heer*) an army, and *bergan,* to shelter; whence come mod. F. *auberge,* Ital. *albergo,* an inn and mod. E. *harbinger,* q. v. β. For the former element, see **Harry.** For the latter element, cf. Goth. *bairgan,* AS. *beorgan,* to preserve; and see **Bury.** ¶ It is usual to cite AS. *hereberga* as the original of *harbour*; but it is hardly native; though the word may have been borrowed very early. **Der.** *harbour,* verb, ME. *herberwen,* P. Plowman, B. xvii. 73, from Icel. *herbergja,* to shelter, harbour, a verb formed from the sb. *herbergi*; also *harbour-er*; *harbour-age,* K. John, ii. 234; *harbour-less*; *harbour-master*; also *harbinger,* q. v.

HARD, firm, solid, severe. (E.) ME. *hard,* Chaucer, C. T. 229 (and common). AS. *heard,* John, vi. 60; OFries. *herd.* ✛ Du. *hard*; Dan.; Swed. *hård*; Icel. *harðr*; Goth. *hardus*; G. *hart.* Teut. type **harduz,* allied to Gk. κρατύς, strong; cf. κρατερός, καρτερός, valiant, stout. See Brugmann, i. § 792. **Der.** *hard-ly, hard-ness* = AS. *heardnes,* Mark, x. 5; *hard-en* = ME. *hardnen,* Ormulum, 1574, 18219, which is an extension of the commoner ME. *harden,* of which the pp. *yharded* occurs in Chaucer, C. T. 10559 (F 245); *hard-en-ed*; *hard-ship,* ME. *heardschipe,* Ancren Riwle, p. 6, l. 9; *hard-ware, hard-featured, hard-fisted, hard-handed, hard-headed, hard-hearted, hard-mouthed, hard-visaged*; also *hard-y,* q. v.

HARDOCK, HORDOCK, prob. the corn-bluebottle; *Centaurea cyanus.* (E.) *Hardokes,* pl., King Lear, iv. 4. 4 (1623); the quartos have *hordocks.* The same as *haudods,* used in Fitzherbert's Husbandry; see Glossary, and Pref. p. xxx. Mr. Wright (note to K. Lear) shows that *hardhake* meant the *Centaurea nigra.* Both plants were called, indifferently, *knobweed, knotweed,* and *loggerhead.* Named from the *hardness* of the head of the *Centaurea nigra*; also called *knapweed, iron-weed, iron-head,* &c. See Plant-names, ed. Britten and Holland. ¶ No kind of dock is suitable for a wreath, or grows among corn.

HARDS, fibres of flax. (E.) ME. *herdes.* 'Hempen *herdes*;' Chaucer, Rom. Rose, 1233. AS. *heordan,* pl. 'Stuppa, *heordan*;' Corp. Gloss. 1908. ✛ MDu. *heerde, herde* (Kilian); later *hēde* (Hexham); EFries. *hēde.* Teut. type **hizdōn-*; cf. **Meed.** ¶ Not allied to *hard.* **Der.** *hard-en,* adj.

HARDY, stout, strong, brave. (F.─OHG.) ME. *hardi, hardy,* P. Plowman, B. xix. 285; the comp. *hardiere* is in Layamon, 4348, later text. ─OF. *hardi,* 'hardy, daring, stout, bold;' Cot. *Hardi* was orig. the pp. of OF. *hardir,* of which the compound *enhardir* is explained by Cotgrave to mean 'to hearten, imbolden.'─OHG. *hartjan* (MHG. *herten*), to harden, make strong.─OHG. *harti* (G. *hart*), hard; cognate with AS. *heard,* hard. See **Hard.** Der. *hardi-ly, hardi-ness,* P. Plowman, B. xix. 31; *hardi-head,* Spenser, F. Q. i. 4. 38; *hardi-hood,* Milton, Comus, 650. ☞ *Hardi-ly, hardi-ness, hardi-head, hardi-hood* are all hybrid compounds, with E. suffixes; showing how completely the word was naturalised.

HARE, the name of an animal. (E.) ME. *hare,* Chaucer, C. T. 13626 (B 1886). AS. *hara,* as a gloss to L. *lepus,* Ælfric's Gloss., in Voc. 119. 11. ✛ Du. *haas*; Dan. and Swed. *hare*; Icel. *hēri* (formerly *here*); G. *hase*; OHG. *haso.* Teut. types **hazon-, *hason-,* m. Idg. type **kas-on-*; cf. OPruss. *sasnis* (for **kasnis*), W. *cein-ach,* f. (Rhys); and Skt. *çaça,* orig. *çasa,* a hare. See Stokes-Fick, p. 74; Brugmann, i. § 826. Uhlenbeck connects Skt. *çaças* with AS. *hasu,* gray. **Der.** *hare-brained,* 1 Hen. IV, v. 2. 19; *hare-lip,* K. Lear, iii. 4. 123; *hare-lipped*; *harr-i-er,* q. v.; *hare-bell,* q. v.

HAREBELL, the name of a flower. (E.) In Cymb. iv. 2. 222. The word does not appear among AS. names of plants; but we find ME. *hare-belle,* Voc. 713. 9. Certainly compounded of *hare* and *bell*; but, owing to the absence of reason for the appellation, it has been supposed to be a corruption of *hair-bell,* with reference to the slenderness of the stalk of the true 'hair-bell,' the *Campanula rotundifolia.* The apparent absence of reason for the name is, however, rather *in favour* of the etymology from *hare* than otherwise, as will be seen by consulting the fanciful AS. names of plants given in Cockayne's Leechdoms, vol. iii. To name plants from animals was the old custom; hence *hare's beard, hare's ear, hare's foot, hare's lettuce, hare's palace, hare's tail, hare-thistle,* all given in Dr. Prior's Popular Names of British Plants; to which add AS. *haran-hyge* (hare's foot trefoil), *haran-specel* (now called viper's bugloss), *haran-wyrt* (hare's wort), from Cockayne's Leechdoms. The spelling *hair-bell* savours of

modern science, but certainly not of the principles of English etymology. ¶ A similar modern error (invented in 1851, by Fox Talbot) is to derive *fox-glove* from *folks'-glove* (with the silly interpretation of *folks* as being 'the good folks' or fairies), in face of the evidence that the AS. name was *foxes glōfa* = the glove of the fox.

HAREM, the set of apartments reserved for females in large Eastern houses. (Arab.) Not in Todd's Johnson. Spelt *haram* in Sir T. Herbert's Travels, ed. 1634, p. 62 (N. E. D.); and in Moore's Lalla Rookh; 'And the light of his *haram* was young Nourmahal.' Also in Byron, Bride of Abydos, c. i. st. 14.─Arab. *ḥaram,* women's apartments; lit. 'sacred;' Palmer's Pers. Dict. col. 197.─Arab. root *ḥarama,* he prohibited; the *haram* is the place which men are prohibited from entering; Rich. Dict., p. 563.

HARICOT, (1) a stew of mutton, (2) a kidney bean. (F.) 'Haricot, in cookery, a particular way of dressing mutton-cutlets; also, a kind of French beans;' Kersey's Dict., ed. 1715.─F. *haricot,* 'mutton sod with little turneps, some wine, and tosts of bread crumbled among,' &c.; Cotgrave (who gives two other methods of preparing it, showing that it was sometimes served with 'chopped herbs'). β. See Littré, who discusses it; it is found that the sense of 'bean' is later, whilst the sense of 'minced mutton with herbs' is old. Perhaps the bean was so named from its use in the dish called *haricot,* or from their being cut up; cf. Du. *snijboon,* French bean, from *snijden,* to cut. γ. Of unknown origin, but presumably Teutonic. Hatzfeld quotes *febves de haricot,* haricot beans (1642), *hericoq de mouton,* haricot of mutton, 14th c. Perhaps connected with OF. *haligoter, harigoter,* to cut in pieces; *haligote, harigote,* a piece, a rag (Godefroy).

HARK! listen! (E.) ME. *herke,* Coventry Mysteries, 55 (Stratmann). The imp. mood of ME. *herkien*; 'And *herke* why,' Chaucer, C. T. 9187 (E 1323). Cf. *herkien,* inf., O. E. Hom. i. 31, l. 6. OFries. *herkia, harkia.* Closely allied to ME. *herknen,* to hearken. See **Hearken.**

HARLEQUIN, the leading character in a pantomime. (F.─Ital.) 'The joy of a king for a victory must not be like that of a *harlequin* upon a letter from his mistress;' Dryden (in Todd's Johnson; no reference). He also has: 'Those nauseous *harlequins*;' Epil. to Man of Mode, l. 3.─F. *arlequin,* a harlequin; spelt *harlequin* in the 16th cent.─Ital. *arlecchino,* a harlequin, buffoon, jester. β. It seems best to connect it with the OF. *hierlekin* or *hellequin* (13th century) for which Littré gives quotations. This word was used in the phrase *la maisnie hierlekin* (Low L. *harlequini familias*) which meant a troop of demons that haunted lonely places, called in Middle-English *Hurlewaynes kynne* or *Hurlewaynes meynè* = Hurlewain's kin or troop, mentioned in Richard the Redeles, i. 90, and in the Prologue to the Tale of Beryn, l. 8. The orig. signification of OF. *hellequin* (see Godefroy) seems to have been 'a troop of demons,' sometimes also a demon, a devil. Cf. also Ital. *Alichino,* the name of a demon in Dante, Inf. xxi. 118. The origin of the name is wholly unknown. See note to Rich. Redeles, ed. Skeat, i. 90. ¶ I shall here venture my guess. Perhaps *hellekin* may have been of Teut. origin; thus OHG. *hella cunni,* OFriesic *helle kin* (AS. *helle cyn,* Icel. *heljar kyn*) would mean 'the kindred of hell' or 'the host of hell,' hence a troop of demons. The sense being lost, the OF. *maisnie* would be added to keep up the idea of 'host,' turning *hierlekin* into (apparently) a personal name of a single demon. The change from *hellekin* to *herlequin,* &c., arose from a popular etymology which connected the word with *Charles Quint* (Charles V.); see the story in Max Müller, Lectures, ii. 581. It may also have been confused with OF. *herle, hierle,* tumult.

HARLOT, a wanton woman. (F.─Teut.) Orig. used of either sex indifferently; in fact, more commonly of men in Mid. Eng. It has no very bad sense, and means little more than 'fellow.' 'He was a gentil *harlot* and a kind;' Chaucer, C. T. 649 (A 647). 'A sturdy *harlot* [a stout fellow] wente ay hem behinde;' id. 7336 (D 1753). 'Dauwe the dykere with a dosen *harlotes* of portours and pykeporses and pylede toth-drawers' = Davy the ditcher with a dozen fellows who were porters and pick-purses and hairless (?) tooth-drawers; P. Plowman, C. vii. 369. 'Beggen ase on *harlot*' = beg like a vagabond, Ancren Riwle, p. 356. Undoubtedly of Romance origin.─OF. *herlot, arlot,* explained by Godefroy as 'fripon, coquin, ribaud,' a vagabond; for which Diez gives a reference to the Romance of Tristran, i. 173 (where it is misprinted *berlot* by Michel). β. The Prov. *arlot,* a vagabond, occurs in a poem of the 13th century; Bartsch, Chrestomathie Provençale, 207. 20; and Mistral explains Prov. *arlot* by 'pillard, ribaud, goujat qui suivait les armées.' Florio explains Ital. *arlotto* by 'a lack-Latin, a hedge-priest,' and *arlotta* as a harlot in the modern E. sense. Ducange explains Late L. *arlotus, erlotus,* to mean a glutton. γ. Of disputed origin, but presumably Teutonic, viz. from OHG. *heri, hari* (G. *heer*), an army, and a suffix *-lot.* This suffix occurs in Du. *labber-lot,* a blackguard, which Franck mentions in connexion with Du. *leuteren,* to loiter, linger, the sense of *lot* being 'loiterer.' The fem. of *lot* occurs in WFlem. *lutte*; De Bo explains *dronke-lutte* as a drunken woman, a slut; and *jenever-lutte* as a gin-drinking woman. Allied to OHG. *lotar*, MHG. *lotar*, *lotter*, useless, vagabond-like, OHG. *lotar*, a frivolous fellow; cf. prov. G. *lotter-bube*, a vagabond (Flügel); Bavar. *lotter* (Schmeller). Thus *her-lot* meant 'army-loafer,' a camp-follower. ¶ We find also W. *herlod*, a stripling, lad; but this is merely the E. word borrowed; the Cornish not only borrowed the E. *harlot* unchanged (with the sense of 'rogue'), but also the word *harlutry*, corruption, which is plainly the ME. *harlotrie*, with a suffix (-*rie*) which is extremely common in French. See Williams, Cornish Lexicon, p. 211. **Der.** *harlot-ry* = ME. *harlotrie*, of which one meaning was 'ribald talk;' see Chaucer, C. T. 563, 3147 (A 561, 3145). The suffix -*ry* is of F. origin, as in *caval-ry*, *bribe-ry*, &c.

HARM, injury, wrong. (E.) ME. *harm*, P. Plowman, C. xvi. 113; spelt *herm*, Ancren Riwle, p. 116. AS. *hearm*, *herm*, grief of mind, also harm, injury; Grein, ii. 60.+Icel. *harmr*, grief; Dan. *harme*, wrath; Swed. *harm*, anger, grief, pity; G. *harm*, grief. Teut. type *harmoz*, m. Cf. Russ. *srame*, shame. Brugmann, ii. § 72. **Der.** *harm*, verb, ME. *harmen*, spelt *hearmin* in O. Eng. Homilies, ed. Morris, p. 263, l. 7; *harm-ful*, Wyclif, Prov. i. 22; *harm-ful-ly*, *harm-ful-ness*; *harm-less* = ME. *harmles*, Will. of Palerne, 1671; *harm-less-ly*, *harm-less-ness*.

HARMONY, concord, esp. of sounds. (F.—L.—Gk.) ME. *armonie*, Gower, C. A. iii. 90; bk. vii. 165. 'There is a melodye in heven, whiche clerkes clepen *armony*;' Testament of Love, ii. 9. 9.— F. *harmonie*.—L. *harmonia*.—Gk. ἁρμονία, a joint, joining, proportion, harmony.—Gk. ἁρμός, a fitting, joining.—Gk. *ἄρειν*, ἀραρίσκειν (fut. ἀρῶ), to fit, join together.—√AR, to fit; whence also E. *arm*, *article*, &c. **Der.** *harmon-ic*, Milton, P. L. iv. 687; *harmoni-cs*, *harmoni-c-al*, *harmoni-c-al-ly*; *harmoni-ous*, Temp. iv. 119; *harmoni-ous-ly*, *harmoni-ous-ness*; *harmon-ise* (Cudworth), *harmon-is-er*, *harmon-ist*, *harmoni-um* (about A.D. 1840).

HARNESS, equipment for a horse. (F.—C.) In old books, it often means body-armour for soldiers; 1 Kings, xx. 11; &c. ME. *harneis*, *harneys*, Chaucer, C. T., A 1613; spelt *herneys*, P. Plowman, B. xv. 215. 'He dude quyk *harnesche* hors' = he commanded horses to be quickly harnessed, King Alisaunder, 4708.—OF. *harneis*, *hernois*, armour. Of unknown origin. ¶ The G. *harnisch*, Du. *harnas*, &c., are borrowed from French; so also the Bret. *harnez*, old iron, armour (Thurneysen). **Der.** *harness*, verb, = OF. *harnaschier*.

HARP, a stringed musical instrument. (E.) ME. *harpe*, Gower, C. A. iii. 301; bk. viii. 764; Layamon, 4898. AS. *hearpe*, Grein, ii. 62; and see Ælfred, tr. of Boethius, c. xxxv. § 6 (b. iii. met. 12).+ Du. *harp*; Icel. *harpa*; Swed. *harpa*; Dan. *harpe*; G. *harfe*; OHG. *harpha*. Teut. type *harpōn-*, f. Root unknown. **Der.** *harp-er* = AS. *hearpere*, in Ælfred, as above; *harp*, verb, AS. *hearpian*, id.; also *harpsichord*, q. v.

HARPOON, a dart for striking whales. (F.—L.—Gk.) 'Some fish with *harpons*' (late edd. *harpoons*), Dryden, Art of Love, 875. Also spelt *harpon* in J. Davis, Voyages, 1599, p. 137 (Hakluyt Soc.). The dart is also called 'a harping-iron' in Kersey's Dict.—F. *harpon*, orig. 'a crampiron wherewith masons fasten stones together' (Cotgrave); hence, a grappling-iron (whence also Du. *harpoen*).—OF. *harpe*, 'a dog's claw or paw;' Cot.; cf. '*se harper l'vn à l'autre*, to grapple, grasp, hasp, clasp, imbrace, cope, close together, to scuffle or fall together by the ears;' id. [Cf. Span. *arpon*, a harpoon, *arpeo*, a grappling-iron, *arpar*, to tear to pieces, rend, claw. Also Ital. *arpagone*, a harpoon, *arpe e*, a cramp-iron, clamp, *arpicare*, to clamber up, *arpino*, a hook, *arpione*, a hinge, pivot, hook, tenter.] β. The OF. *harpe*, claw, is from Late L. *harpē*, a sickle-shaped sword.—Gk. ἅρπη, a sickle (Körting, § 4501). Allied to OLat. *sarpere*, to prune; Russ. *serp'*, 'a sickle.' **Der.** *harpoon-er*.

HARPSICHORD, an old harp-shaped instrument of music. (F.—Teut. *and* Gk.) Also spelt *harpsicon* or *harpsecol*. 'On the *harpsicon* or virginals;' Partheneia Sacra, ed. 1633, p. 144 (Todd). '*Harpsechord* or *Harpsecol*, a musical instrument;' Kersey. Spelt *harpsechord* in Minsheu, ed. 1627. The corrupt forms of the word are not easy to explain; in particular, the letter *s* seems to have been intrusive.—OF. *harpechorde*, 'an arpsichord or harpsichord;' Cot. Compounded of OF. *harpe*, a harp (from a Teutonic source); and *chorde*, more commonly *corde*, a string. See **Harp**, **Chord**, and **Cord**. Cf. Ital. *arpicordo* (Florio).

HARPY, a mythological monster, half bird and half woman. (F.—L.—Gk.) In Shak. Temp. iii. 3. 83. Trevisa speaks of 'þe *arpies*;' tr. of Higden, ii. 363.—OF. *harpie*, or *harpye*, 'a harpy;' Cot. —L. *harpȳia*, chiefly used in pl. *harpȳiæ*, Verg. Æn. iii. 226.—Gk. pl. ἅρπυιαι, harpies; lit. 'the spoilers.'—Gk. ἁρπ-, the base of ἁρπάζειν, to seize; allied to L. *rapere*, to seize. See **Rapacious**.

HARQUEBUS, the same as **Arquebus**, q. v.

HARRIDAN, a worn-out wanton woman. (F.) In Pope,

Macer, a Character, l. 24. It seems to be a variant of MF. *haridelle*, which Cot. explains by 'a poor tit, or leane ill-favored jade;' i. e. a worn-out horse. Some connect this with MF. *hardelle*, a herd; 'also, a girl, a young maid, lasse,' Cot. Of unknown origin; cf. Körting, § 4548. ¶ It is remarkable that Godefroy has OF. *harre-banne*, a debauched woman.

HARRIER (1), a hare-hound. (E.) Formerly *harier*, more correctly. So spelt in Minsheu, ed. 1627. The word occurs also in Blount, Ancient Tenures, p. 39 (Todd). Formed from *hare*, with suffix -*ier*; cf. *bow-yer* from *bow*, *law-yer* from *law*.

HARRIER (2), a kind of falcon. (E.) 'A sort of puttock called a *hen-harrier*;' Ray, Collection of Words, pref. p. 3 (E. D. S.). Named from its *harrying* or destroying small birds. See **Harry**.

HARROW, a frame of wood, fitted with spikes, used for breaking the soil. (E.) ME. *harwe*, P. Plowman, B. xix. 268; spelt *haru*, *harou*, *harwe*, Cursor Mundi, 12388. NFries. *harwe*. Not found in AS.+ Icel. *herfi*, a harrow; Dan. *harv*, a harrow; *harve*, to harrow; Swed. *harf*, a harrow; *harfva*, to harrow. Apparently allied to MDan. *harge*, Du. *hark*, Swed. *harka*, G. *harke*, a rake. ¶ The F. *herce* a harrow, is a different word; see **Hearse**. **Der.** *harrow*, verb, ME. *harwen*, P. Plowman, C. vi. 19.

HARRY, to ravage, plunder, lay waste. (E.) Also written *harrow*, but this is chiefly confined to the phrase 'the *Harrowing* of Hell,' i. e. the despoiling of hell by Christ. ME. *herȝien*, later *herien*, *herwen*, *harwen*. 'By him that *harwed* helle;' Chaucer, C. T. 3512. 'He that *heried* helle;' Will. of Palerne, 3725. AS. *hergian*, to lay waste, Grein, ii. 38. Lit. to 'over-run with an army;' cognate with Icel. *herja*, Dan. *hærge*, OHG. *harjon*, to ravage. Teut. type *harjōjan-*, to harry; from *harjoz*, an army, which appears in AS. *here*, an army, a word particularly used in the sense of 'destroying host;' Grein, ii. 35. β. The AS. *here* is cognate with Icel. *herr*, Dan. *hær*, Swed. *här*, G. *heer*, and Goth. *harjis*, a host, army. Allied to OPruss. *karjis*, an army (Uhlenbeck); OSlav. *kara*, strife; Lithuan. *karas*, war, army. **Der.** *harrier* (2).

HARSH, rough, bitter, severe. (Scand.) ME. *harsk*, rough to the touch, Morte Arthure, ed. Brock, 1084. '*Harske*, or *haske*, as sundry frutys;' Prompt. Parv.—Dan. *harsk*, rancid; Swed. *härsk*, rank, rancid, rusty; MSwed. *harsk* (Ihre).+G. *harsch*, harsh, rough. β. Cf. Lithuan. *kartùs*, harsh, bitter (of taste); see **Hard**. **Der.** *harsh-ly*, *harsh-ness*.

HART, a stag, male deer. (E.) ME. *hert*, Chaucer, C. T. 11503 (F 1191); spelt *heort*, Layamon, 26762. AS. *heort*, *heorot*, Grein, ii. 69; also *herut*.+Du. *hert*; Icel. *hjörtr*; Dan. *hjort*; Swed. *hjort*; G. *hirsch*, OHG. *hiruz*. Teut. stem *herut-*, i. e. 'horned.' Allied to L. *ceruus*, a hart, W. *carw*, a hart, stag, horned animal; OSlav. *krava*, Russ. *korova*, a cow; cf. Gk. κεραός (for *κεραϝος), horned; from the base which appears in the Gk. κέρας, a horn, and is related to E. *horn*. The orig. sense is 'horned animal.' See further under **Horn**. See Stokes-Fick, p. 79. **Der.** *harts-horn*, so called because the horns of the hart abound with ammonia; *harts-tongue*.

HARVEST, the ingathering of crops, the produce of labour. (E.) Sometimes used in the sense of 'autumn;' see Wyclif, Jude, 12; Shak. Temp. iv. 116. ME. *heruest* (with *u* for *v*), P. Plowman, B. vi. 292, 301. AS. *hærfest*, autumn, Grein, ii. 24; the orig. sense being 'crop.'+Du. *herfst*, autumn; Icel. *haust*, autumn (contracted form); Dan. *höst*, harvest, crop (contr. form); Swed. *höst*, autumn (contr. form); G. *herbst*, autumn, harvest; MHG. *herbest*, OHG. *herpist*. β. All with a suffix -*is-toz* (-*us-toz*) from Teut. base *harb-*, allied to the base καρπ- of the cognate Gk. καρπός, fruit.—√SQLRP, to shear; as in L. *carp-ere*, to pluck, gather, Lith. *kerp-u*, I shear. Brugmann, i. § 631. Cf. Gk. κείρειν, to shear; and see **Shear**. **Der.** *harvest*, verb; *harvest-home*, 1 Hen. IV, i. 3. 35; *harvest-man*, Cor. i. 3. 39; *harvest-moon*, *harvest-time*.

HASEL, the name of a tree; see **Hazel**.

HASH, a dish of meat cut into small slices. (F.—G.) '*Hash*, cold meat cut into slices and heated again with spice, &c.;' Kersey, ed. 1715. An abbreviation of an older form *hachey* or *hachee*, in Cotgrave.—OF. *hachis*, 'a hachey, or hachee; a sliced gallimaufrey or minced meat;' Cot.—OF. *hacher*, 'to hack, shread, slice;' id.— OF. and F. *hache*, an ax.—OHG. *happja*, whence OHG. *heppa*, MHG. *hepe*, a bill, a sickle. See **Hatchet**. **Der.** *hash*, vb., perhaps directly from F. *hacher*; and see *hatch* (3).

HASHISH, HASHEESH, an intoxicating drink. (Arab.) See **Assassin**.

HASLETS, HARSLETS, HASTELETS, the inwards of a pig, &c., for roasting. (F.—L.) ME. *hastelets*, *hastlettes*; Gawaine and the Grene Knt., l. 1612.—OF. *hastelet*, meat roasted on a spit.— OF. *haste*, a spit.—L. *hasta*, a spear, a spit; see **Hastate**.

HASP, a clasp. (E.) ME. *haspe*, Chaucer, C. T. 3470. '*Hespe* of a dore, *pessulum*;' Prompt. Parv. [*Haspe* stands for *hapse*, by the same change as in *clasp* from ME. *clapsen*, *aspen* from AS. *æps*.] AS.

hæpse, as a gloss to *sera* (a bolt, bar), in Voc. 326. 36. + Icel. *hespa*; Dan. *haspe*, a hasp, reel; Swed. *haspe*, a hasp; G. *haspe*, a hasp; *haspel*, a staple, reel, windlass; cf. Du. *haspel*, a windlass, reel. β. All from a Teut. type *hap-sōn-*, f. Cf. Low G. *happen, hapsen*, to snatch, clutch; F. *happer*, to lay hold of; NFries. *happe*, to snatch at. The sense of *hasp* is 'a catch.'

HASSOCK, a stuffed mat for kneeling on in church. (E.) 'Hassock, a straw-cushion us'd to kneel upon;' Kersey, ed. 1715. Also in Phillips, New World of Words, 1706, in the same sense; see Trench, Select Glossary. So called from the coarse grass of which it was made; ME. *hassok*. 'Hassok, ulphus;' Prompt. Parv.; see Way's Note, showing the word to be in use A.D. 1147; whilst in 1465 there is mention of 'segges, soddes, et *hassokes*' = sedges, sods, and hassocks. Forby explains Norfolk *hassock* as 'coarse grass, which grows in rank tufts on boggy ground.' AS. *hassuc*, a tump or clump of coarse grass or sedge; in Kemble, Cod. Dipl. iii. 223. ¶ Distinct from W. *hesg*, pl. sedges.

HASTATE, shaped like the head of a spear. (L.) Modern, and botanical. — L. *hastātus*, spear-like; formed from *hasta*, a spear, which is co-radicate with E. *gad*. See **Gad** (1).

HASTE, HASTEN, to go speedily; **Haste,** speed. (F.—Teut.) The form *hasten* appears to be nothing more than an extended form of the verb *to haste*; the pt. t. and pp. *hastened* (or *hastned*) do not occur in early authors; one of the earliest examples is that of the pp. *hastened* in Spenser, Shep. Kal., May, 152. Strictly speaking, the form *haste* (pt. t. *hasted*) is much to be preferred, and is commoner than *hasten* both in Shak. and in the A.V. of the Bible. ME. *hasten* (pt. t. *hastede*), where the *n* is merely the sign of the infin. mood, and was readily dropped. Thus Gower has: 'Cupide . . Syh [saw] Phebus *hasten* him so sore, And, for he sholde him *haste* more, . . A dart throughout his herte he caste;' C.A. i. 336; bk. iii. 1697. 'To *hasten* hem;' Chaucer, C.T. 8854: (E 978). 'But *hasteth* yow' = make haste, id. 17383 (I 72). 'He *hasteth* wel that wysly can abyde; and in wikked *haste* is no profit;' id., Six-text, B 2244. β. It is hard to say whether the vb. or sb. first came into use in English; both occur in the Cursor Mundi, 5198, 26737; where we also find the phr. *in hast* = in haste, 13402. Neither is found in AS. —OF. *haste* (F. *hâte*), sb. —WGerm. *hai(f)sti-*, violence; as seen in OFries. *haest* (Richtofen, s.v. *hast*), AS. *hǣst*, violence, fury. Cf. AS. *hǣste*, violent, vehement, OHG. *heisti*, violent; also Goth. *haifsts*, f., strife; Icel. *heipt* (= *heift*), war. ¶ Du. *haast*, G., Dan., Swed. *hast*, haste, are all borrowed from French. **Der.** *hast-y*, Will. of Palerne, 475; *hast-i-ly, hast-i-ness.* ☞ We also find ME. *hastif*, hasty, Allit. Poems, ed. Morris, iii. 520; this is from OF. *hastif*, adj. formed from the OF. *haste* (mod. F. *hâte*), haste, which was borrowed from the Teutonic (as above).

HAT, a covering for the head. (E.) ME. *hat*, Chaucer, C.T. 472, 1390 (A 470, 1388). AS. *hæt*; 'Galerus, vel pileus, *fellen hæt*;' Voc. 118. 14; 'Calamanca, *hæt*;' id. 153. 22. + Icel. *hǫtt*, a hood, later *hattr*; Swed. *hatt*; Dan. *hat*. Teut. type *hattuz*, m. If it is related to *hood*, this form stands for an earlier type *hadnuz*. **Der.** *hatt-er, hat-band* (Minsheu).

HATCH (1), a half-door, wicket. (E.) A word presenting some difficulty. 'Leap the *hatch*;' King Lear, iii. 6. 76. It is the same as North of E. *heck*, an enclosure of open-work, of slender bars of wood, a hay-rack; a *heck-door* is a door only partly panelled, the rest being latticed (Halliwell); cf. Lowland Sc. *hack* or *heck*, a rack for cattle, a frame for cheeses (Jamieson). It seems to have been specially used of anything made with parallel bars of wood. Palsgrave has: 'Hatche of a door, *hecq*.' In a 15th-cent. vocabulary we find: 'Hoc osticulum, *a hatche*;' Voc. 778. 14. Also: 'Hoc ostiolum, *hek*;' id. 668. 4. AS. *hæc*, f. (gen. *hæcce*); 'tō þǣre ealdan wude hæcce,' to the old wood hatch; Thorpe, Diplom. Ævi Saxon. p. 395. + Du. *hek*, a fence, rail, gate, Swed. *häck*, a coop, a rack. Teut. type *hakjā*, f. Prob. named from being lightly fastened with a hook. Cf. AS. *haca*, a fastening of a door; Epinal Gloss. 803. All, probably, from the same source as *hook*; cf. prov. E. *hatch*, to fasten (Halliwell); and see Shak. Per. iv. 2. 37. See **Hake** and **Hook.** **Der.** *hatch-es*, q.v.; also *hatch-way.*

HATCH (2), to produce a brood by incubation. (E.) ME. *hacchen*. 'This brid [bird] . . hopith for to *hacche*;' Richard the Redeles, Pass. iii. l. 44. The pt. t. *haȝte* occurs in The Owl and Nightingale, l. 105. Not found earlier; but prob. E. + Swed. *häcka*, to hatch, to breed; Dan. *hække*, to breed, whence *hækkebuur*, a breeding-cage (lit. a hatch-bower), and *hækkefugl*, a breeder (lit. a hatch-fowl). In German, we have *hecken*, to hatch, MHG. *hecken*. Origin unknown.

HATCH (3), to shade by minute lines, crossing each other, in drawing and engraving. (F.—G.) 'Hatch, to draw small strokes with a pen;' Kersey, ed. 1715. A certain kind of ornamentation on a sword-hilt was called *hatching*, and is spelt *hachyng* in 1389; see

Riley, Memorials of London, p. 513; hence '*hatched* in silver,' Shak. Troil. i. 3. 65; 'my sword well *hatcht*;' Beaum. and Fletcher, Bonduca, ii. 2. — F. *hacher*, 'to hack, . . also to hatch a hilt;' Cot. — F. *hache*, an ax. — OHG. *happja*, whence OHG. *heppa*, a bill, a sickle. See **Hash.** **Der.** *hatch-ing* (perhaps sometimes confused with *etching*); and see *hatch-et.*

HATCHES, a frame of cross-bars laid over an opening in a ship's deck. (E.) ME. *hacches*, Chaucer, Good Women, 648; Will. of Palerne, 2770. Merely the pl. of **Hatch** (1), q.v. **Der.** *hatch-way*, from the sing. *hatch.*

HATCHET, a small axe. (F.—G.) ME. *hachet.* 'Axe other [or] *hatchet*;' P. Plowman, B. iii. 304. Spelt *hachet*, John de Garlande; in Wright's Vocab. i. 137.—F. *hachette*, 'a hatchet, or small axe;' Cot. Dimin. of F. *hache*, 'an axe;' id.; see **Hatch** (3), and **Hash.**

HATCHMENT, the escutcheon of a deceased person, publicly displayed. (F.—L.) In Shak. Hamlet, iv. 5. 214. Well known to be a corruption of *atch'ment*, the shortened form of *atchievement* (mod. E. *achievement*), the heraldic name for the same thing. Dryden uses *achievement* in the true heraldic sense; Palamon and Arcite, l. 1620; *átcheament* is in Ferne (1586); and *hachement* in Hall (1548). See N.E.D. See **Achieve.**

HATE, extreme dislike, detestation; to detest. (E.) **A.** The sb. is ME. *hate*, Chaucer, C.T. 14506 (B 3778). AS. *hete*, Grein, ii. 39; the mod. E. sb. takes its vowel from the vb. (AS. *hatian*).+Du. *haat*; Icel. *hatr*; Swed. *hat*; Dan. *had*; Goth. *hatis*; G. *hass*, hate. These forms suggest a Teut. type *hatoz*, neut., gen. *hatizos*; Idg. type *kodos*, gen. *kodesos*; whence a form *hatiz* in W. Germanic. Cf. Gk. κῆδειν, to vex; W. *cawdd*, displeasure. Stokes-Fick, p. 68. **B.** The verb is AS. *hatian*, OFries. *hatia*, OSax. *hatōn*, OHG. *hazzōn*; allied to Goth. *hatan*, to hate; from the same base *hat-*. **Der.** *hate-ful*, Chaucer, C.T. 8608 (E 732); *hate-ful-ly, hate-ful-ness*; also *hat-red*, q.v.; from the same source, *heinous*, q.v.

HATRED, extreme dislike. (E.) ME. *hatred*, P. Plowman, B. iii. 140; fuller form *hatreden*, Pricke of Conscience, 3363. Not found in AS.; but the suffix is the AS. suffix -*rēden*, signifying 'law,' 'mode,' or 'condition,' which appears in *frēondrēden*, friendship (Gen. xxxvii. 4), &c.; see **Kindred.** And see **Hate.**

HAUBERK, a coat of ringed mail. (F.—OHG.) Orig. armour for the neck, as the name implies. ME. *hauberk*, Chaucer, C.T. 2433 (A 2431); *hawberk*, King Alisaunder, 2372. — OF. *hauberc, halberc* (Burguy). — OHG. *halsberc, halsberge*, a hauberk. — OHG. *hals* (G. *hals*), the neck, cognate with AS. *heals*, L. *collum*, the neck; and OHG. *bergan*, to protect, cognate with AS. *beorgan*, to protect, hide. See **Collar** and **Bury.** **Der.** *habergeon*, q.v.

HAUGH, a piece of alluvial land beside a river. (E.) Northern; also *halgh*, as in Greenhalgh. AS. *healh*, a nook, a corner; see N.E.D. ¶ From the dat. case *heale, hale*, we have ME. *hale*, a nook; common in place-names as a suffix, and often written -*hall.*

HAUGHTY, proud, arrogant. (F.—L.) **a.** The spelling with *gh* is a mistake, as the word is not E.; it is a corruption of ME. *hautein*, loud, arrogant. 'I peine me to have an *hautein* speech' = I endeavour to speak loudly; Chaucer, C.T. 12264 (C 330); cf. Rob. of Glouc., l. 1504. 'Myn *hauteyn* herte' = my proud heart; Will. of Palerne, 472. β. The corruption arose from the use of the adj. with the E. suffix -*ness*, producing a form *hautein-ness*, but generally written *hautenesse*, and easily misdivided into *hauti-ness* (like *naughti-ness*). 'For heo [she, i.e. Cordelia] was best and fairest, and to *hautenesse* drow lest' [drew least]; Rob. of Glouc. p. 29 (where the best MS. has *hautesce*); l. 687. Later forms *hautyn*, Book of St. Alban's, fol. a 5, *hauty* in Palsgrave. — OF. *hautain*, also spelt *hauttain* by Cotgrave, who explains it by 'hauty, proud, arrogant.' — OF. *haut*, formerly *halt*, high, lofty; with suffix -*ain* = L. -*ānus*. — L. *altus*, high; see **Altitude.** **Der.** *haughti-ly; haughti-ness* (for *hautin-ness* = *hautein-ness*, as explained above).

HAUL, to hale, draw; see **Hale** (2). This spelling occurs early. 'I-hauled hi were . . out of the lond;' Beket, l. 1497.

HAULM, HALM, HAUM, the stem or stalk of grain. (E.) Little used, but an excellent E. word. 'The *hawme* is the strawe of the wheat or the rie;' Tusser's Husbandry, sect. 57, st. 15 (E.D.S.). 'Halm, or stobyl [stubble], *Stipula*;' Prompt. Parv. OMerc. *halm*; Vesp. Psalter, Ps. lxxxii. 14 (lxxxiii. 13); AS. *healm*, in the compound *healm-streaw*, lit. haulm-straw, used to translate L. *stipulam* in Ps. lxxxii. 12, ed. Spelman.+Du. *halm*, stalk, straw; Icel. *hálmr*; Dan. and Swed. *halm*.+Russ. *soloma*, straw; L. *culmus*, a stalk; *calamus*, a reed (borrowed from Gk.); Gk. κάλαμος, a reed; καλάμη, a stalk or straw of corn; W. *calaf*, a stalk. See Brugmann, ii. § 72; Stokes-Fick, p. 73. β. From the same root as **Culminate**, q.v.

HAUNCH, the hip, bend of the thigh. (F.—OHG.) ME. *hanche*, Morte Arthure, ed. Brock, 1100; spelt *haunche*, Ancren Riwle, 280. — F. *hanche*, 'the haunch or hip;' Cot. Cf. Span. and Ital. *anca*, the haunch; the F. word was also sometimes spelt *anche* (Cotgrave). Of Teut. origin; from Frankish *hankā, fem., represented by MDu. *hancke*, 'the haunch or the hip,' Hexham: whence also O. North F. *hanke*, Norm. dial. *hanque*, haunch (Moisy). Körting, §§ 663, 4479.

HAUNT, to frequent. (F.) ME. *haunten*, *hanten*, to frequent, use, employ. 'That *haunteden* folie' = who were ever after folly; Chaucer, C. T. 12398 (C 464). 'We *haunten* none tauernes' = we frequent no taverns; Pierce Plowman's Crede, ed. Skeat, 106. '*Haunted* Maumetrie' = practised Mohammedanism, Rob. of Brunne, tr. of Langtoft, p. 320. The earliest use of the word is in Hali Meidenhad, ed. Cockayne, p. 25, l. 15. – OF. *hanter*, 'to haunt, frequent, resort unto;' Cot. β. Origin unknown, and much disputed. Suggestions are: (1) Icel. *heimta*, lit. to fetch home, to draw, claim, recover; but neither form nor sense suit: (2) Bret. *hent*, a path: (3) a nasalised form of L. *habitāre*, to dwell (Littré): (4) a Late L. form *ambitāre (not found), to go about, from L. *ambitus*, a going about (Scheler). The last seems to me the most likely; there are many such formations in F. **Der.** *haunt*, sb.

HAUTBOY, a kind of musical instrument. (F. – L.) [Also called *oboe*, the Ital. name.] In Shak. 2 Hen. IV, iii. 2. 351; where the old edd. have *hoeboy*. Spelt *hau'boy* (sic) in Ben Jonson, tr. of Horace's Art of Poetry, where the L. has *tibia*; Ars Poet. 202. Spelt *hoboies*, *hoboy* in Cotgrave. – MF. *haultbois* (or *hautbois*), 'a hobois, or hoboy;' Cot. – OF. *hault*, later *haut*, high, from L. *altus*, high; and F. *bois*< Late L. *boscus*, wood. See **Altitude** and **Bush**. Thus the lit. sense is 'high wood;' the *hautboy* being a wooden instrument of a high tone. **Doublet**, *oboe*.

HAUT-GOÛT, a high flavour. (F. – L.) Spelt *haugou* in Howell's Letters, vol. i. § 5. let. 38. – F. *haut*, high; *goût*, taste. – L. *altus*, high; *gustus*, taste; see **Gust** (2).

HAVE, to possess, hold. (E.) ME. *hauen*, pt. t. *hadde*, pp. *had* (common). AS. *habban*, pt. t. *hæfde*, pp. *gehæfd*.+Du. *hebben*; Icel. *hafa*; Swed. *hafva*; Dan. *have*; Goth. *haban*; G. *haben*. Teut. stem **habē-*. If cognate, as some hold, with L. *habēre*, to have, the Idg. stem is **khabhē-*. Streitberg, § 206, p. 307.

HAVEN, an inlet of the sea, harbour, port. (E.) ME. *hauen* (with *u* for *v*), Chaucer, C. T. 409 (A 407); spelt *hauene*, Layamon, 8566. Late AS. *hæfene* (acc. *hæfenan*), A. S. Chron. an. 1031. – Icel. *höfn*; Dan. *havn*, Swed. *hamn*.+Du. *haven*; G. *hafen*. β. Allied to AS. *hæf* (Grein, ii. 19), Icel. and Swed. *haf*, Dan. *hav*, MHG. *hab*, the open sea, main.

HAVERSACK, a soldier's bag for provisions. (F. – G.) Lit. 'oat-bag' or 'oat-sack.' A late importation. It occurs in Smollett's tr. of Gil Blas, b. ii. c. 8 (R.). – F. *havresac*, a haversack, knapsack (Hamilton). – G. *habersack*, *hafersack*, a sack for oats. – G. *haber*, *hafer*, oats (cognate with Icel. *hafr*, Du. *haver*, Swed. *hafre*, Dan. *havre*, oats), from MHG. *habere*, OHG. *habaro*, oats; and G. *sack*, cognate with E. *sack*.

HAVILDAR, a sepoy non-commissioned officer, corresponding to a sergeant. (Pers. – Arab.) So in Yule. From Pers. *ḥawāl-dār*, a military officer of inferior rank; Rich. Dict., p. 585. – Arab. *ḥawāla(h)*, commission, charge; and Pers. *dār*, holding (as in *sir-dar*).

HAVOC, general waste, destruction. (F. – Teut.) 'Cry *havoc*,' Shak. Cor. iii. 1. 275; Jul. Cæs. iii. 1. 273; 'cries on *havoc*,' Haml. v. 2. 375. 'Pell-mell, *havoc*, and confusion;' 1 Hen. IV, v. 1. 82. 'They entrid in-to Ylion and pillyd hit, and after did do *crye hauok* upon all the tresours;' Caxton, Troy-book, fol. 175. 'To *crye havok*' occurs in 1419; Excerpta Historica, p. 32. From the AF. phrase *crier havok*; Black Book of Admiralty, i. 455. An Eng. adaptation of OF. *havot*, pillage, plunder (Godefroy), used in precisely the same way; esp. in the phrase *crier havot*, to cry out 'plunder,' of which Godefroy gives two examples. It is clearly connected with OF. *havee*, a handful (Godefroy), which Cotgrave explains by 'a gripe, or handfull, also a booty, or prey;' from the OF. verb *haver*, 'to hooke, or to grapple with a hook,' Cot. Cf. *havet*, 'a little hooke,' Cot.; *havecq*, the same (Godefroy). W. de Bibbesworth explains *havet* by 'a flesh-hook;' Wright, Vocab. i. 172. Apparently from the Teut. base **haf-* seen in Goth. *hafjan*, to heave, lift up; see **Heave** and **Haft**. 'To cry havoc' was to give the signal for seizing upon the spoil. Notes on E. Etym., p. 128. **Der.** *havoc*, verb (rare), Hen. V, i. 2. 173, where a cat is said 'to tear and *havoc* more than she can eat.'

HAW, a hedge; a berry of the haw-thorn. (E.) The sense of 'inclosure' or 'hedge' is the older one. In the sense of 'berry,' the word is really a short form for *haw-berry* or *hawthorn-berry*; still it is of early use in this transferred sense. ME. *hawe*. Chaucer uses *hawe*, lit. a haw-berry, to signify anything of no value, C. T. 6241 (D 659); but he also has it in the orig. sense. 'And eke ther was a polkat in his *hawe*' = there was a polecat in his yard; C. T. 12789 (C 855). AS. *haga*, an enclosure, yard, house, Grein, ii. 5; whence the usual change to later *hage*, *haʒe*, *hawe*, by rule.+Icel. *hagi*,

a hedged field, a pasture; Swed. *hage*, an enclosed pasture-ground; Dan. *have* [for *hage*], a garden; Du. *haag*, a hedge; whence 's Gravenhage, i. e. the count's garden, the place called by us *the Hague*. Teut. type **hagon-*, m. Allied to G. *hag*, a fence, hedge; and further, to W. *cae*, an enclosure. See **Quay**. Stokes-Fick, p. 66. **Der.** *haw-finch*; *haw-thorn* = AS. *hægþorn*, which occurs as a gloss to *alba spina*, Voc. 139. 23; ONorthumb. *hagoþorn*, Matt. vii. 16. Also *hedge*, q. v.

HAWK (1), a bird of prey. (E.) ME. *hauk*, Chaucer, C. T. 4132, 5997 (A 4134, D 415). Earlier *hauek* (= *havek*), Layamon, 3258. AS. *hafoc*, more commonly *heafoc*, Grein, ii. 42.+Du. *havic*; Icel. *haukr*; Swed. *hök*; Dan. *hög*; G. *habicht*, OHG. *hapuh*. β. All probably from the Teut. base *hab, to seize, hold; see **Heave**, and cf. L. *capere*. Cf. Low L. *capus*, a falcon, from L. *cap-ere*; and L. *accipiter*, a hawk. **Der.** *hawk*, verb, ME. *hauken*, Chaucer, C. T. 7957 (E 81); *hawk-er*.

HAWK (2), to carry about for sale. (O. Low G.) Not in early use. Rich. quotes from Swift, A Friendly Apology, the line: 'To hear his praises *hawk'd* about.' The verb is a mere development from the sb. *hawker*, which is an older word. See **Hawker**.

HAWK (3), to force up phlegm from the throat, to clear the throat. (E.) 'Without *hawking* or spitting;' As You Like It, v. 3. 12. Apparently an imitative word; cf. W. *hochi*, to throw up phlegm; *hoch*, the throwing up of phlegm; Dan. *harke*, Swed. *harska*, to hawk. And (perhaps) Norw. *hauka*, to shout, call out (Aasen); F. *hoquet*, hiccough.

HAWKER, one who carries about goods for sale, a pedlar. (O. Low G.) Minsheu tells us that the word was in use in the reign of Hen. VIII; it is much older, in E., than the verb to *hawk*. '*Hawkers*, be certain deceitfull fellowes, that goe from place to place buying and selling brasse, pewter, and other merchandise, that ought to be vttered in open market.. You finde the word An. 25 Hen. VIII, cap. 6, and An. 33 eiusdem, cap. 4;' Minsheu. 'Those people which go up and down the streets crying newsbooks and selling them by retail, are also called *Hawkers*;' Blount's Gloss., ed. 1674. [The earliest trace of a similar word is in P. Plowman, B. v. 227, where the trade of the pedlar is denoted by *hokkerye*, spelt also *hukkerye* and *hukrie*; where the base of the word is the same as that of the word *huckster*.] β. A word introduced from abroad; cf. Low G. *höker*, a retail-dealer, Du. *heuker*; MDu. *heukeren*, to sell by retail, to huckster; *heukelaar*, a huckster, retailer (Sewel). We find also Dan. *höker*, a chandler, huckster, *hökeri*, a hawker's trade, *hökre*, to hawk; Swed. *hökeri*, higgling, *hökare*, a chandler, cheesemonger. Also G. *höcker*, a retailer of goods. See further under **Huckster**.

HAWSE, HAWSE-HOLE. (Scand.) '*Hawses*, two large round holes in a ship, under the head or beak, through which the cables pass, when the ship lies at anchor;' Phillips, ed. 1706. Cf. 'I was forced to cut cable in the *hawse*;' Eng. Garner, vii. 83 (ab. 1606). So called because made in the 'neck' or bow of the ship. – Icel. *háls*, *hals*, the neck; also (as a sea-term) part of the bow of a ship or boat. Cf. Du. *hals*, neck; *halsblok*, a hawse-block; Dan. and Swed. *hals*, neck, also a tack (as a sea-term). Also AS. *heals*, G. *hals*, Goth. *hals*, neck; cognate with L. *collum*, neck. ¶ Distinct from *hawser*; see below.

HAWSER, HALSER, a small cable. (F. – L.) '*Hawser*, a three-stroud [-strand] rope, or small cable;' Kersey. In Sherwood's index to Cotgrave, *halser* means a tow-rope by which boats are drawn along. In Grafton's Chron., Rich. III, an. 3, we read: 'He wayed up his ancors and *halsed* up his sayles.' 'Two *hancers* pour boy-ropes;' (1373) Riley's Mem. of London, p. 369. 'With well-wreathed *halsers* raise Their white sails;' Chapman, tr. of Od. ii. 609. From the old verb *hause*, to lift, raise, as in Rom. of Partenay, 3083. – OF. *halcier*, F. *hausser* (Hatzfeld). to raise. – Late L. *altiāre*, to elevate. – L. *altus*, high. See **Altitude**. Similarly the MItal. *alzaniere*, 'a halsier [hawser] in a ship' (Florio) is from Ital. *alzare*, to raise. ¶ Often associated with *hawse* (above), though of different origin.

HAWTHORN, from *haw* and *thorn*; see **Haw**.

HAY (1), grass cut and dried. (E.) Formerly used also of uncut growing grass. ME. *hey*, hay; Chaucer, C. T. 16963 (H 14). 'Vpon grene *hey*' = on green grass; Wyclif, Mark, vi. 39. From OMerc. *hēg* (faenum), Vesp. Psalter, xxxvi[i]. 2. AS. *hig*, grass, hay; 'ofer þæt grēne *hig*' = on the green grass; Mark, vi. 39.+Du. *hooi*; Icel. *hey*; Dan. and Swed. *hö*; Goth. *hawi*, grass; G. *heu*, MHG. *houwe*. β. The true sense is 'cut grass;' the sense of 'growing grass' being occasional. The Teut. type is *hau-jom, n. From the base **hau(w)-* of the verb to *hew*, i.e. to cut. See **Hew**. **Der.** *hay-cock*, *hay-maker*. But not ME. *hay-ward*, where *hay* = hedge (below).

HAY (2), a hedge. (E.) ME. *heie*, *heye*; 'bi the *heie*,' by the hedge; Owl and Night., 817. AS. *hege*; see Corpus Gloss., 606. Teut. type *hagiz; allied to **Haw**. Cf. OF. *haie*, a hedge, of Low

G. origin. **Der.** *hay-ward*, an officer who had charge of fences and enclosures ; P. Plowman, C. vi. 16, and note.

HAZARD, chance, risk. (F.—Span.—Arab.) ME. *hasard*, the name of a game of chance, generally played with dice ; Chaucer, C. T. 12525 (C 591). Earlier, in Havelok, 2326.—F. *hasard*, 'hazard, adventure ;' Cot. The orig. sense was certainly 'a game at dice' (Littré). β. We find also Span. *azar*, an unforeseen accident, hazard, MSpan. *azar*, 'an ill token, a pricke or note in a die, a hucklebone ;' also *azar en el dado*, 'a game at dice called hazard ;' Minsheu. Cf. MItal. *zara*, 'a game at dice called hazard, also a hazard or a nicke at dice ;' Florio. It is probab'e that F. *ha-*, Span. *a-*, answers to the Arab. article *al*, turned into *az* by assimilation. Thus the F. word is from Span., and the Span. from Arab. *al zahr*, the die, a word only found in the vulgar speech ; see Devic's Supplement to Littré. But Arab. *zahr* is a word of doubtful authority ; and the etym. is uncertain. **Der.** *hazard*, verb, *hazard-ous*.

HAZE, vapour, mist. (Low G.) Not in early use. The earliest trace of the form *haze* is in Ray's Collection of Northern-English Words, 1691 (1st ed. 1674). He gives : 'it *hazes*, it misles, or rains small rain.' As a sb., it occurs in Phillips, ed. 1706 : '*Haze*, a Rime or thick Fog.' '*Hazy* weather' is in Dampier's Voyages, ed. 1684 (R.) ; and 'thicke and *hawsey*' occurs in 1625 (N. E. D.). Apparently due to the Low G. phrase *de Hase Brouet*, i. e. a mist or haze is rising ; see Bremen Wörterbuch. *Brouet* = brews, is brewing. Berghaus enters the phrase under *Hase*, a hare ; but does not explain the connexion. Rietz gives *hås*, a slight shower of rain, as a Swed. dial. word. Note also prov. E. *haar*, a cold sea-fog or mist (E. D. D.) ; Du. dial. *harig*, foggy, misty (Boekenoogen). **Der.** *haz-y*, *haz-i-ness*.

HAZEL, the name of a tree or shrub. (E.) ME. *hasel*. 'The *hasel* and the ha‑horne' [haw-thorn] ; Gawayne and the Grene Knight, ed. Morris, 744. AS. *hæsel*. '*Corilus*, hæsel. *Saginus*, hwit hæsel ;' Wright's Vocab. i. 32, col. 1. '*Abellana*, hæsl, vel hæsel-hnutu' [hazel-nut] ; id. 33, col. 2 (Voc. 137. 16, 139. 17).+ Du. *hazelaar* ; Icel. *hasl*, *hesli* ; Dan. and Swed. *hassel* ; G. *hasel* ; OHG. *hasala.*+L. *corulus* (for *cosulus*) ; W. *coll* ; OIrish *coll* (for *cosl*). Stokes-Fick, p. 92. Teut. type *hasaloz*, Idg. type *kosolos*. **Der.** *hazel-nut* = AS. *hæselhnutu*, as above ; *hazel-twig*, Tam. Shrew. ii. 255.

HE, pronoun of the third person. (E.) ME. *he* ; common. AS. *hē* ; declined as follows. *Masc. sing.* nom. *hē* ; gen. *his* ; dat. *him* ; acc. *hine*. *Fem. sing.* nom. *hēo* ; gen. and dat. *hire* ; acc. *hi*. *Neut. sing.* nom. and acc. *hit* ; gen. *his* ; dat. *him*. *Plural* (for all genders) ; nom. and acc. *hi*, *hig* ; gen. *hira*, *heora* ; dat. *him*, *heom.*+Du. *hij* ; OSax. *he*, *hi* ; allied to Goth. neut. *hi-ta*. Allied to Lith. *szis*, this, L. *ci-trā*, on this side, Gk. *ἐ-κεῖ*, there, *κεῖνος*, that one. Brugmann, i. §§ 83, 604. **Der.** *hence*, *here*, *hither*.

HEAD, the uppermost part of the body. (E.) ME. *hed*, *heed* ; earlier *heued* (= *heved*), from which it is contracted. 'His *heed* was balled' [bald] ; Chaucer, C. T. 198. In P. Plowman, B. xvii. 70, it is spelt *hed* ; but in the corresponding passage in C. xx. 70, the various readings are *hede*, *heed*, and *heuede*. AS. *hēafod*, Mark, vi. 24, where the latest MS. has *hēafed.*+Du. *hoofd* ; Goth. *haubith* ; G. *haupt* ; OHG. *houbit*. Also OIcel. *haufoð*, later *höfuð* ; Dan. *hoved* ; Swed. *hufvud*. Teut. types *hauƀuð-*, *hauƀið-*, n. ; which have no equivalents. The L. *caput* (with short *a*) is allied to AS. *hafela*, *heafola*, head. **Der.** *head*, vb. ; *head-ache*, *-band* (Isa. iii. 20), *-dress*, *-gear*, *-land*, *-less*, *-piece* (K. Lear, iii. 2. 26), *-quarters*, *-stall* (Tam. Shrew. iii. 2. 58), *-stone* (Zech. iv. 7), *-strong* (*heed-strong* in Palsgrave), *-tire* (1 Esdras, iii. 6), *-way*, *-wind*. Also *head-ing*, a late word ; *head-s-man* (All's Well, iv. 3. 342) ; *head-y* (2 Tim. iii. 4), *headi-ly*, *head-i-ness*. Also *head-long*, q. v.

HEADLONG, rashly ; rash. (E.) Now often used as an adj., but orig. an adv. ME. *hedling*, *heedling*, *hedlynges*, *heuedlynge* ; Wyclif, Deut. xxii. 8 ; Judg. v. 22 ; Matt. viii. 32 ; Luke, viii. 33. 'Heore hors *hedlyng* mette' = their horses met head to head ; King Alisaunder, 2261. The suffix is adverbial, answering to the AS. suffix *-ling*, which occurs in *bæc-ling*, backwards. In this suffix, the *-l-* is separable ; the common form being *-inga* ; as in *fær-inga*, suddenly.

HEAL, to make whole. (E.) ME. *helen*. 'For he with it coude bothe *hele* and dere ;' i.e. heal and harm, Chaucer, C. T. 10554 (F 240). AS. *hælan*, to make whole ; very common in the pres. part. *hælend* = the healing one, saviour, as a translation of *Jesus*. Regularly formed (with *i-* mutation of *ā* to *æ*) from AS. *hāl*, whole ; see **Whole.**+Du. *heelen*, from *heel*, whole ; Icel. *heila*, from *heill* ; Dan. *hele*, from *heel* ; Swed. *hela*, from *hel* ; Goth. *hailjan*, from *hails* ; G. *heilen*, from *heil*. **Der.** *heal-er*, *heal-ing* ; and see *health*.

HEALTH, soundness of body, or of mind. (E.) ME. *helth*, P. Plowman, C. xvii. 137. AS. *hǣlð* (acc. *hǣlðe*), Ælfric's Hom. i. 466, l. 8 ; ii. 396, l. 21. Formed from AS. *hāl*, whole. Teut. type *hailithā*, f. The suffix *-thā* denotes condition, like L. *-tās*. ¶ Not a very common word in old writers ; the more usual form is ME. *hele*

(P. Plowman, C. vi. 7, 10), from AS. *hǣlu*, Grein, ii. 22. **Der.** *health-y*, *health-i-ly*, *health-i-ness* ; *health-ful*, *health-ful-ly*, *health-ful-ness* ; *health-some*, Romeo, iv. 3. 34.

HEAP, a pile of things thrown together. (E.) ME. *heep* (dat. *heepe*, *hepe*), Chaucer, C. T. 577 (A 575) ; P. Plowman, B. vi. 190. AS. *hēap*, a heap, crowd, multitude ; Grein, ii. 56.+Du. *hoop* ; (whence Icel. *hópr* ; Dan. *hob* ; Swed. *hop*) ; G. *haufe*, OHG. *hūfo.*+Russ. *kupa*, a heap, crowd, group ; Lithuanian *kaupas*, a heap (Fick, iii. 77). Brugmann, i. § 421 (7). **Der.** *heap*, vb., AS. *hēapian*, Luke, vi. 38. **Doublet,** *hope* (2).

HEAR, to perceive by the ear. (E.) ME. *heren* (sometimes *huyre*), pt. t. *herde*, pp. *herd* ; Chaucer, C. T. 851 (A 849) ; 13448 (B 1708). OMerc. *hēran* ; AS. *hȳran*, pt. t. *hȳrde*, pp. *gehȳred* ; Grein, ii. 132.+ Du. *hooren* ; Icel. *heyra* ; Dan. *höre* ; Swed. *höra* ; Goth. *hausjan* ; G. *hören*, OHG. *hōrjan*. Teut. type *hauzjan-*. Cf. Gk. *ἀ-κού-ειν*, to hear. ¶ It does not seem possible so to ignore the initial *h* as to connect it with the word *ear*, though there is a remarkable similarity in form between Goth. *hausjan*, to hear, and Goth. *auso*, the ear. See **Ear.** **Der.** *hear-er*, *hear-ing*, *hear-say*, q. v., *hearken*, q. v.

HEARKEN ; see under **Hark.**

HEARSAY, a saying heard, a rumour. (E.) From *hear* and *say*. 'I speake unto you since I came into this country by *hearesay*. For I *heard say* that there were some homely theeves,' &c. : Bp. Latimer, Ser. on the Gospel for St. Andrew's Day (R.). The verb *say*, being the latter of two verbs, is in the infin. mood, as in AS. 'Ful ofte time I haue *herd sein* ;' Gower, C. A. i. 367 ; bk. iii. 2622. 'He . . . *secgan hȳrde*' = he heard say ; Beowulf, ed. Grein, 875.

HEARSE, a carriage in which the dead are carried to the grave. (F.—L.) Much changed in meaning. ME. *herse*, *herce*. First (perhaps) used by Chaucer, 'Adoun I fel when that I saugh the *herse* ;' Complaint to Pity, st. 3. '*Heerce* on a dede corce' (*herce* vpon dede corcys), *Pirama*, *piramis* ;' Prompt. Parv. p. 236. Mr. Way's note says : 'This term is derived from a sort of pyramidal candlestick, or frame for supporting lights, called *hercia* or *herpica*, from its resemblance in form to a harrow, of which mention occurs as early as the xiith century. It was not, at first, exclusively a part of funeral display, but was used in the solemn services of the holy week . . . Chaucer appears to use the term *herse* to denote the decorated bier, or funeral pageant, and not exclusively the illumination, which was a part thereof ; and towards the 16th century, it had such a general signification alone. Hardyng describes the honours falsely bestowed upon the remains of Richard II. when cloths of gold were offered "upon his *hers*" by the king and lords ;' &c. See the whole note ; also Rock, Church of our Fathers, ii. 495. The changes of sense are (1) a harrow, (2) a triangular frame for lights in a church service, (3) a frame for lights over a tomb, (4) a frame to support a pall, (5) a carriage for a dead body ; the older senses being quite forgotten.—OF. *herce*, 'a harrow, also, a kind of portcullis, that's stuck, as a harrow, full of sharp, strong, and outstanding iron pins' [which leads up to the sense of a frame for holding candles] ; Cot. Mod.F. *herse*, Ital. *erpice*, a harrow. —L. *hirpicem*, acc. of *hirpex*, a harrow, also spelt *irpex*. ¶ A remarkable use of the word is in Berners' tr. of Froissart, cap. cxxx, where it is said that, at the battle of Crecy, 'the archers ther stode in maner of a *herse*,' i.e. drawn up in a triangular form, the old F. harrow being so shaped. See Specimens of English, ed. Skeat, p. 160. **Der.** *re-hearse*.

HEART, the organ of the body that circulates the blood. (E.) ME. *herte*, properly dissyllabic. 'That dwelland in his *herte* sike and sore, Gan faillen, when the *herte* felt deth ;' Chaucer, C. T. 2806, 2807 (A 2804). AS. *heorte*, fem. (gen. *heortan*), Grein, ii. 69.+Du. *hart* ; Icel. *hjarta* ; Swed. *hjerta* ; Dan. *hjerte* ; Goth. *hairto* ; G. *herz*, OHG. *herza*. Teut. type *herton-* n. ; which afterwards became fem. +Irish *cridhe* ; Russ. *serdtse* ; L. *cor* (gen. *cord-is*) ; Gk. *κῆρ*, *καρδια* ; W. *craidd* ; Lith. *szirdis*, Streitberg, § 86 ; Stokes-Fick, p. 95. **Der.** *heart-ache*, Hamlet, iii. 1. 62 ; *heart-blood* = ME. *herte-blod*, Havelok, 1819 ; *heart-breaking*, Ant. i. 2. 74 ; *heart broken*, *heart-burn*, *heart-burning*, L. L. L. i. 280 ; *heart-ease*, *heart-en*, 3 Hen. VI, ii. 2. 79 ; *heart-felt*, *heart-less* = ME. *herteles*, Wyclif, Prov. xii. 8 ; *heart-less-ly*, *heart-less-ness*, *heart-rending*, *heart-sick*, *heart-sickness*, *heart-whole*. Also *heart's-ease*, q. v., *heart-y*, q. v.

HEARTH, the floor in a chimney on which the fire is made. (E.) ME. *herth*, *herthe* ; a rare word. '*Herthe*, where fyre ys made ;' Prompt. Parv. AS. *heorð*, as a gloss to *foculare* ; Wright's Vocab. i. 27, col. 1 (Voc. 127. 4).+Du. *haard* ; MDan. *hærd* (Kalkar) ; Swed. *hard*, the hearth of a forge, a forge ; G. *herd*, a hearth ; OHG. *hert*, ground, hearth. Teut. type *herthoz*, m. Idg. base *ker-* ; cf. L. *cremāre*, to burn. **Der.** *hearth-stone* (in late use).

HEART'S-EASE, a pansy. (E.) '*Hearts-ease*, or *Pansey*, an herb ;' Kersey, ed. 1715. '*Hartysease*, a floure ;' Palsgrave. Lit. *ease of heart*, i.e. pleasure-giving.

HEARTY, cordial, encouraging. (E.) ME. *herty*. '*Herty*, cordialis;' Prompt. Parv. An accommodation of the older ME. *hertly.* 'ʒe han *hertely* hate to oure hole peple' = ye have hearty hate against our whole people; Alexander and Dindimus, ed. Skeat, 961. Der. *hearti-ly, hearti-ness.*

HEAT, great warmth. (E.) ME. *hete,* Chaucer, C. T. 16876 (G 1408). AS. *hǣtu, hǣto;* Grein, ii. 24; from **haitin-,* heat, fem. Formed from the adj. *hāt,* hot. β. The Icel. *hiti,* heat, Du. *hitte,* G. *hitze,* are not precisely parallel forms; but are formed from the weak grade *hit-.* See further under **Hot. Der.** *heat,* verb = AS. *hǣtan,* in The Shrine, ed. Cockayne, p. 16, l. 15; formed rather from the adj. *hāt,* hot, than from the sb.; *heat-er.*

HEATH, wild open country. (E.) ME. *hethe* (but the final *e* marks the dat.); Chaucer, C. T. 6; spelt *heth,* P. Plowman, B. xv. 451. AS. *hǣð,* Grein, ii. 18. + Du. *heide;* Icel. *heiðr;* Swed. *hed;* Dan. *hede;* Goth. *haithi,* a waste; G. *heide.* Teut. type **haithjā,* f. Further allied to W. *coed,* a wood; L. *-cētum* in comp. *bū-cētum,* a pasture for cows; where *bū-* is allied to *bōs,* a cow. Stokes-Fick, p. 76. Der. *heath-y;* also *heath-en,* q. v.

HEATHEN, a pagan, unbeliever. (E.) Simply orig. 'a dweller on a heath;' see Trench, Study of Words; and cf. L. *pāgānus,* a pagan, lit. a villager, from *pāgus,* a village. The idea is that dwellers in remote districts are among the last to be converted. ME. *hethen.* 'Hethene is to mene after heth and vntiled erthe' = heathen takes its sense from heath and untilled land; P. Plowman, B. xv. 451. AS. *hǣðen,* a heathen; Grein, ii. 18. — AS. *hǣð,* a heath. See **Heath.** β. So also Du. *heiden,* a heathen, from *heide,* a heath; Icel. *heiðinn,* from *heiðr;* Swed. *heden,* from *hed;* Dan. *heden,* from *hede;* Goth. *haithnō,* a heathen woman, *haithiwisks,* wild, from *haithi;* G. *heiden,* from *heide.* And note AS. *hǣðen,* a wild creature, monster; Bēowulf, 986. **Der.** *heathen-dom* = AS. *hǣðendōm,* Grein, ii. 19; *heathen-ish, heathen-ish-ly, heathen-ish-ness, heathen-ise, heathen-ism.*

HEATHER, a small evergreen shrub. (E.) Usually associated with *heath.* But *heather* is quite a late form; and the old name is *hadder.* 'Hadder, heath or ling;' Ray, N. Country Words (1691). ME. *haddyr;* Wallace, v. 300. So that the words seem to be distinct. ¶ MDan. *hede* meant (1) a heath; (2) ling (Kalkar).

HEAVE, to raise, lift or force up. (E.) ME. *heuen* (with *u* for *v*); Chaucer, C. T. 552 (A 550); earlier form *hebben,* Rob. of Glouc., p. 17, l. 8; or l. 389. From AS. *hef-,* a pres. stem of AS. *hebban,* Grein, ii. 28; pt. t. *hōf,* pp. *hafen;* orig. a strong verb, whence the later pt. t. *hove,* occasionally found. Cf. OFries. *heva,* to heave. + Du. *heffen;* Icel. *hefja;* Swed. *häfva;* Dan. *hæve;* Goth. *hafjan;* G. *heben,* OHG. *heffan.* Teut. type **hafjan-,* pt. t. **hōf;* corresponding to L. *capio,* I seize; cf. Gk. κώπη, a handle. ¶ Distinct from *have.* **Der.** *heav-er, heave-offering;* also *heav-y,* q. v.

HEAVEN, the dwelling-place of the Deity. (E.) ME. *heuen* (with *u* for *v*), Chaucer, C. T. 2563 (A 2561). AS. *heofon, hiofon, hefon,* Grein, ii. 63. + OSax. *heban.* Cf. AS. *hūs-heofon,* a ceiling; so that the sense may have been 'canopy' or 'cover.' β. Another word for 'heaven' is the Icel. *himinn;* Goth. *himins,* heaven; and G. *himmel,* heaven (with altered suffix). The two forms can hardly be connected. **Der.** *heaven-ly* = AS. *heofonlic; heaven-ward, heaven-wards,* as to which see **Towards.**

HEAVY, hard to heave, weighty. (E.) ME. *heui, heuy* (with *u* = *v*). Chaucer has *heuy* and *heuinesse;* C. T. 11134, 11140 (F 822, 828). AS. *hefig,* heavy; Grein, ii. 29; lit. 'hard to heave,' from AS. *haf-,* stem of *hebban* (pt. t. *hōf*), to heave. + Icel. *hōfigr,* heavy; from *hefja,* to heave; OHG. *hepig, hebig* (obsolete), heavy; Low G. *hevig.* **Der.** *heavi-ly; heavi-ness* = AS. *hefignes* (Grein).

HEBDOMADAL, weekly. (L. — Gk.) 'As for *hebdomadal* periods or weeks;' Sir T. Browne, Vulg. Errors, b. iv. c. 12, § 11. — L. *hebdomadālis,* belonging to a week. — L. *hebdomad-,* stem of *hebdomas,* a number of seven, a week; with suffix *-ālis.* — Gk. ἑβδομάς, a number of seven, a week; cf. ἕβδομος, seventh. — Gk. ἑπτά (for **σεπτά*), seven; cognate with E. *seven.* See **Seven.**

HEBETUDE, dulness, obtuseness. (L.) '*Hebetude,* bluntness, dulness;' Bailey (1735). — L. *hebetūdo,* bluntness. — L. *hebes* (*hebet-*), blunt, dull.

HEBREW, a descendant of Abraham. (F. — L. — Gk. — Heb.) In Merch. of Ven. i. 3. 58, 179. — F. *hébreu,* spelt *hebrieu* in Cotgrave. — L. *Hebræus.* — Gk. ἑβραῖος. — Heb. *'ivrī,* a Hebrew (Gen. xiv. 13); of uncertain origin, but supposed to mean one of a people dwelling in *Heber,* i.e. in the land 'beyond' the Euphrates; from Heb. *'āvar,* he crossed over.

HECATOMB, a sacrifice of a large number of victims. (F. — L. — Gk.) Lit. a sacrifice of a hundred oxen. In Chapman's tr. of Homer's Iliad, b. i. l. 60. — MF. *hecatombe;* Cot. — L. *hecatombē.* — Gk. ἑκατόμβη, a sacrifice of a hundred oxen; or any large sacrifice. — Gk. ἑκατόν, hundred (cognate with Skt. *çata,* L. *centum,* AS. *hund*); and βοῦς, an ox (cognate with E. *cow*). See **Hundred** and **Cow.**

HECKLE, HACKLE, HATCHEL, an instrument for dress-

ing flax or hemp. (E.) ME. *hekele, hechele.* 'Hekele, mataxa;' Prompt. Parv. 'I *heckell* (or *hetchyll*) flaxe;' Palsgrave. 'Hec mataxa, a *hekylle*;' Wright's Vocab. i. 269, col. 2 (Voc. 668. 32). EFries. *hekel, häkel.* + Du. *hekel,* a heckle; Dan. *hegle,* a heckle; Swed. *häckla;* G. *hechel.* Teut. type **hakilā,* fem.; from a Teut. base **hak-,* to pierce, bite, as in OHG. *hecchen,* MHG. *hecken* (for **hakjan*), to pierce, bite as a snake; cf. AS. *hacod,* a pike (fish), from its sharp teeth. Cf. **Hack** (1). **Der.** *hackle* (1), *hackle* (2), q. v.

HECTIC, continual; applied to a fever. (F. — L. — Gk.) 'My fits are like the fever *ectick* fits;' Gascoigne, Flowers, The Passion of a Lover, st. 8. Shak. has it as a sb., to mean 'a constitutional fever;' Hamlet, iv. 3. 68. — F. *hectique,* 'sick of an hectick, or continuall feaver;' Cot. — Late L. **hecticus,* for which I find no authority, but it was doubtless in use as a medical word. — Gk. ἑκτικός, hectic, consumptive (Galen). — Gk. ἕξις, a habit of body; lit. a possession. Gk. ἕξ-ω, fut. of ἔχειν, to have, possess. — √ SEGH, to hold in, stop; whence also Skt. *sah,* to hold in, stop, bear, undergo, endure, &c. **Der.** *hectic,* sb.

HECTOR, a bully; as a verb, to bully, to brag. (Gk.) 'The *hectoring* kill-cow Hercules;' Butler, Hudibras, pt. ii. c. 1. l. 352. From the Gk. *Hector* (Ἕκτωρ), the celebrated Trojan hero. The lit. sense of Gk. ἕκτωρ is 'holding fast;' from the Gk. ἔχειν, to hold. See **Hectic.**

HEDGE, a fence round a field, thicket of bushes. (E.) ME. *hegge,* Chaucer, C. T. 15224 (B 4408). AS. *hecg* (dat. *hecge*); A. S. Chron. an. 547; Cart. Saxon., ed. Birch, i. 339; iii. 532. Teut. type **hagjā,* f.; formed from *hag-* with suffix *-jā,* causing vowel-change of *hag-* to *heg-;* i. e. it is a secondary form from AS. *haga,* a hedge, preserved in mod. E. in the form *haw;* see **Haw.** + Du. *hegge, heg,* a hedge; cf. *haag,* a haw; Icel. *heggr,* a kind of tree used in hedges; cf. *hagi,* a haw (see Icel. Dict. p. 774); G. *hecke.* **Der.** *hedge,* verb (Prompt. Parv. p. 232), *hedge-bill, hedge-born,* 1 Hen. VI, iv. 1. 43; *hedge-hog,* Temp. ii. 2. 10; *hedge-pig,* Macb. iv. 1. 2; *hedge-priest.* L. L. L. v. 2. 545; *hedge-row,* Milton, L'Allegro, 58; *hedge-school; hedge-sparrow,* K. Lear, i. 4. 235; also *hedg-er,* Milton, Comus, 293.

HEED, to take care, attend to. (E.) ME. *heden,* pt. t. *hedde;* Layamon, 17801; Allit. Poems, ed. Morris, A. 1050 (or 1051). AS. *hēdan,* to take care; pt. t. *hēdde;* Grein, ii. 29. A weak verb, formed by vowel change from a sb. **hōd,* care, not found in AS. but occurring in OFries. *hōde, hūde,* care, protection, and allied to G. *hut,* OHG. *huota,* heed, watchfulness. + OSax. *hōdian,* to heed; Du. *hoeden,* to heed, guard, from *hoede,* guard, care, protection; G. *hüten,* to protect (OHG. *huaten*), from G. *hut* (OHG. *huota*), protection. β. For the vowel-change, cf. *bleed* (AS. *blēdan*) from *blood* (AS. *blōd*). Brugmann, i. § 754. Prob. allied to **Hood.** The notion of 'guarding' is common to both words. **Der.** *heed,* sb. = ME. *hede,* Chaucer, C. T. 305 (A 303); *heed-ful, heed-ful-ly, heed-ful-ness, heed-less, heed-less-ly, heed-less-ness.*

HEEL (1), the part of the foot projecting behind. (E.) ME. *heel, heele;* Wyclif, John, xiii. 18. AS. *hēla,* the heel; Grein, ii. 30. We find also the gloss: 'Calx, héla, hóh niþeweard' = the heel, the lower part of the heel;' Wright's Vocab. i. 283, col. 2 (Voc. 266. 8). + Du. *hiel* (from OFriesic *hēla*); Icel. *hæll;* Swed. *häl;* Dan. *hæl.* β. It is probable that AS. *hēla* is a contraction of **hōh-ila,* with the usual vowel-change from *ō* (followed by *i*) to *ē;* this would make the word a diminutive of AS. *hōh,* which also means 'the heel,' and is a commoner word. See **Hough. Der.** *heel-piece.*

HEEL (2), to lean over, incline. (E.) A corrupted form; the word has lost a final *d,* wh.lst the vowel has been lengthened. It is modified from ME. *helden, hilden.* Cf. the EFries., Du. and Swed. forms. Palsgrave has: 'I *hylde,* I leane on the one syde, as a bote or shyp, or any other vessell, *ie encline de cousté.* Sytte fast, I rede [advise] you, for the bote begynneth to *hylde.*' 'Heldyn, or bowyn, *inclino, flecto, deflecto*;' Prompt. Parv. p. 234; see Way's note. β. The ME. *helden* or *hilden* was frequently transitive, meaning (1) to pour, esp. by tilting a vessel on one side; and (2) intransitively, to heel over, to incline. Wyclif has: 'and whanne the boxe of alabastre was brokun, she *helde* it [poured it out] on his heed;' Mark, xiv. 3. AS. *hyldan, heldan,* trans. to tilt, incline, intrans. to bow down; Grein, ii. 131. 'Þū gestaðoladest ... eorðan swā fǣste, þæt hīo on ǣnige healfe ne *heldeð*' = Thou hast founded the earth so fast, that it will not *heel* over on any side; Ælfred's Metres, xx. 164. It is a weak verb, related to the (participial) adjective *heald,* inclined, bent down, which occurs in *niðer-heald,* bent downwards; Grein, ii. 295. + Icel. *halla* (for **haiða*), to lean sideways, heel over, esp. used of a ship; from *hallr* (< **halth-*), leaning, sloping; Dan. *helde,* to slant, lean, tilt (both trans. and intrans.); cf. *held,* an inclination, slope; Swed. *halla,* to tilt, pour; cf. EFries. *hella,* to heel over. The adj. is AS. *-heald,* OFries. *hald,* Icel. *hallr,* OHG. *hald,* inclined, bent forward; Teut. type **halthoz.* Allied to AS. *hold,* G. *hold,* faithful, true (to a master), Goth. *hulths,* gracious; Teut. type **hulthoz.* Cf.

Goth. *wilja-halthei*, inclination of will, partiality (which see in Uhlenbeck).

HEFT, a heaving. (E.) In Shak. Wint. Ta. ii. 1. 45. Formed from the verb *to heave*, and closely allied to *haft*. ¶ *Heft* also occurs as another spelling of *haft*.

HEGEMONY, leadership. (Gk.) Chiefly modern. — Gk. ἡγεμονία, leadership. — Gk. ἡγεμον-, from ἡγεμών, a leader. — Gk. ἡγέομαι, I lead. — Gk. ἡγ-, as in ἡγ-αγον, 2 aor. of ἄγ-ειν, to lead, cognate with L. *ag-ere*. See **Agent**.

HEGIRA, the flight of Mohammed. (Arab.) In Blount's Gloss., ed. 1674. 'The era of the *Hegira* dates from the flight of Mohammed from Mecca to Medina, on the night of Thursday, July 15, 622. The era begins on the 16th;' Haydn, Dict. of Dates. — Arab. *hijrah*, separation (here flight); the Mohammedan era; Palmer's Pers. Dict. col. 695. From the Arab. root *hajara*, he separated, he went away. Cf. Arab. *hajr*, separation, absence; id. ¶ Hence, pronounce the E. word as *hejra*, with soft *g* and no *i*.

HEIFER, a young cow. (E.) ME. *hayfare, hekfere*. 'Juvenca, *hayfare*;' Wright's Vocab. i. 177, l. 4; 'Hec juvenca, a *hekfere*;' id. 250, col. 2. (Voc. 624. 14; 758. 3, with *kf* < *hf*.) AS. *hēahfore*. 'Annicula, vel vaccula, *hēahfore*' also, 'Altilium, *fæt hēahfore*' [a fat heifer]; id. p. 23, col. 2 (Voc. 120. 29, 35). Also spelt *hēahfru*; Voc. 274. 20. β. The first syllable (*hēah* or *heah*) is prob. the same as AS. *hēah*, high; but the rest is obscure. The forms *-fore*, *-fru*, may be referred to AS. *faran*, to go; hardly to AS. *fearr*, bull.

HEIGH-HO, an exclamation of weariness. (E.) Also, in Shak., an exclamation of joy; As You Like It, iv. 3. 169; ii. 7, 180, 182, 190; iii. 4. 54. 'But sung *hey-howe*;' The Frere and the Boy (Hazlitt; E. E. Pop. Poetry, iii. 62), l. 50. Compounded of *heigh*, a cry to call attention, Temp. i. 1. 6; and *ho*! interjection. Both words are of natural origin, to express a cry to call attention.

HEIGHT, the condition of being high; a hill. (E.) A variant of *highth*, a form common in Milton, P. L. i. 24, 92, 282, 552, 723; &c. *Height* is common in Shak. Merch. Ven. iv. 1. 72; &c. ME. *highte, hyghte*, as in Chaucer, C. T. 1786 (where it rimes with *lyghte*); also *heȝþe* (= *heghthe*), Allit. Poems, ed. Morris, B. 317; *heighthe*, Mandeville's Travels, p. 40. AS. *hēahðu, hēhðu*, also *hīehðu* (Bosworth); from *hēah*, high. + Du. *hoogte*, height; Icel. *hæð*; Swed. *höjd*; Dan. *höide*; Goth. *hauhitha*. See **High**. Der. *height-en*, Shak. Cor. v. 6. 22; formed by analogy with *length-en, strength-en*, &c.; not an orig. form.

HEINOUS, hateful, atrocious. (F. — O. Low G.) Properly trisyllabic. ME. *heinous, hainous*; Chaucer, Troilus, ii. 1617. — OF. *haïnos*, odious; formed with suffix *-os* (= L. *ōsus*, mod. F. *-eux*) from the sb. *haïne*, hate. — OF. *haïr*, to hate. From an O. Low G. form, well exemplified in Goth. *hatjan* (= *hatian*), to hate; OFries. *hatia*. See **Hate**. Der. *heinous-ly, heinous-ness*.

HEIR, one who inherits property. (F. — L.) The word being F. the *h* is silent. ME. *heire, heyre*; better *heir, heyr*; Chaucer, C. T. 5186 (B 766); also *eyr*, Will. of Palerne, 128; *eir*, Havelok, 410. — OF. *heir, eir* (later *hoir*), an heir. — Late L. *hērem*, for L. *hērēdem*, acc. of *hērēs*, an heir. See Brugmann, i. § 477. Der. *heir-dom, heir-ship*, hybrid words, with E. suffixes; *heir-apparent*, 1 Hen. IV, i. 2. 65; *heir-ess*, with F. suffix, Blackstone's Comment., b. iv. c. 15 (R.); *heir-less*, Wint. Ta. v. 1. 10; *heir-presumptive, heir-male*; also *heir-loom*, q. v.

HEIR-LOOM, a piece of property which descends to an heir along with his inheritance. (Hybrid; F. *and* E.) 'Which he an *heir-loom* left unto the English throne;' Drayton, Polyolbion, s. 11 (near the end). Also (in 1424) in E. E. Wills, p. 56. Compounded of *heir* (see above); and *loom*, a piece of property, furniture, the same word as *loom* in the sense of a weaver's frame. See **Loom** (1).

HELIACAL, relating to the sun. (L. — Gk.) A term in astronomy, used and defined in Sir T. Browne, Vulg. Errors, b. iv. c. 13. § 7; 'We term that .. the *heliacal* [ascension of a star], when a star which before, for the vicinity of the sun, was not visible, being further removed, beginneth to appear.' — Late L. *hēliacus*, Latinised from the Gk. ἡλιακός, belonging to the sun. — Gk. ἥλιος, the sun; allied to L. *sōl*. See **Solar**. Der. *heliacal-ly*.

HELIOCENTRIC, considered with reference to the sun as a centre. (Gk.) An astronomical term; in Kersey, ed. 1715. Coined from *helio-* = Gk. ἥλιο-, for ἥλιος, the sun; and *centric*, adj. coined from Gk. κέντρον, centre. See **Heliacal** and **Centre**. β. Similar formations are *helio-graphy*, equivalent to photography, from γράφειν, to write; *helio-latry*, sun-worship, from λατρεία, service, worship; *helio-trope*, q. v.

HELIOTROPE, the name of a flower. (F. — L. — Gk.) In Blount's Gloss., ed. 1674; Ben Jonson, Sejanus, iv. 5. — F. *heliotrope*, 'the herbe turnsole;' Cot. — L. *heliotropium*. — Gk. ἡλιοτρόπιον, a heliotrope. — Gk. ἡλιο-, for ἥλιος, the sun; and τροπ-, 2nd grade of τρέπειν, to turn; lit. 'sun-turner,' or the flower which turns to the sun. See **Heliacal** and **Trope**.

HELIX, a spiral figure. (L. — Gk.) '*Helix*, barren or creeping ivy; in anatomy, the outward brim of the ear; in geometry, a spiral figure;' Kersey, ed. 1715. — L. *helix*, a volute, spiral; kind of ivy. — Gk. ἕλιξ, anything twisted, a tendril, spiral, volute, curl. — Gk. ἑλίσσειν, to turn round. — Gk. root Ϝελ; allied to L. *uoluere*, to roll. See **Volute**. Der. *helices*, the pl. form; *helic-al, helic-al-ly*.

HELL, the place of the dead; the abode of evil spirits. (E.) ME. *helle*; Chaucer, C. T. 1202 (A 1200). AS. *hel*, a fem. sb., gen. *helle*; Grein, ii. 29. + Du. *hel*; Icel. *hel*; G. *hölle*, OHG. *hella*; Goth. *halja*, hell. Teut. type *haljā*, f.; from *hal-*, 2nd grade of the Teutonic base *hel-*, to hide, whence AS. *helan*, G. *hehlen*, to hide; so that the orig. sense is 'that which hides or covers up.' The AS. *helan* is allied to L. *cēlāre*, to hide, from the root *kel*, to hide, whence also L. *cella*, E. *cell*. Der. *hell-ish, hell-ish-ly, hell-ish-ness*; *hell-fire* = AS. *helle-fýr*, Grein, ii. 31; *hell-hound*, ME. *helle-hund*, Seinte Marherete, ed. Cockayne, p. 6, l. 4 from bottom.

HELLEBORE, the name of a plant. (F. — L. — Gk.) Also spelt *ellebore*, as frequently in Holland, tr. of Pliny, b. xxv. c. 5. — OF. *ellebore*, 'hellebore;' Cot. Properly *hellebore*. — L. *helleborus*. — Gk. ἑλλέβορος, the name of the plant. Of uncertain origin.

HELM (1), the instrument by which a ship is steered. (E.) Properly used of the tiller or handle of the rudder. ME. *helme*; Allit. Poems, ed. Morris, iii. 149. AS. *helma*, masc., Ælfred's tr. of Boethius, cap. xxxv. § 4; lib. iii. pr. 12. + Icel. *hjálm*, a rudder; G. *helm*, a helve, handle. β. Closely allied to ME. *halm*, a handle, Gawaine and Grene Knt., l. 330. Another kindred word is *helve*. See **Helve**. Der. *helms-man*; where *helms* = *helm's* (the possessive case).

HELM (2), **HELMET**, armour for the head. (E.) ME. *helm*, Chaucer, C. T. 2611 (A 2609). AS. *helm*, masc., (1) a protector, (2) a protection, helm; Grein, ii. 31. + Du. *helm* (also *helmet*), a helm, casque; Icel. *hjálmr*, a helmet; Dan. *hielm*; Swed. *hjelm*; G. *helm*; Goth. *hilms*. Teut. type *hel-moz*, m., lit. 'a covering.' β. All formed with suffix *-mo-* from the base *kel-* (Teut. *hel-*), a grade of the root *kel*, to cover, protect. See **Hell**. Der. *helm-ed*, Chaucer, C. T. 14376 (B 3560); *helm-et*, a dimin. form, with suffix *-et* of F. origin, from OF. *helmet*.

HELMINTHOLOGY, the natural history of worms. (Gk.) A scientific word. Coined from Gk. ἑλμινθο-, decl. stem of ἕλμινς, a worm; and *-λογια*, a discourse, from λέγειν, to speak. The Gk. ἕλμινς is also found as ἕλμις, i.e. 'that which curls about;' from the same source as ἑλ-ιξ, a helix. See **Helix**. Der. *helminthologi-c-al*.

HELOT, a slave, among the Spartans. (L. — Gk.) 'The *Helots*;' Sir P. Sidney, Arcadia; (1638) p. 16. The pl. *helots* answers to L. pl. *Hēlōtes*, borrowed from Gk. Εἵλωτες, pl. of Εἵλως, a helot, bondsman; fabled to have meant originally a man of *Helos* (Ἕλος), a town of Laconia, whose inhabitants were enslaved under the Spartans. Der. *helot-ism*.

HELP, to aid, assist. (E.) ME. *helpen*, pt. t. *halp*, pp. *holpen*; Chaucer, C. T. 10244 (E 2370). AS. *helpan*, pt. t. *healp*, pp. *holpen*; Grein, ii. 33. + Du. *helpen*; Icel. *hjálpa*; Dan. *hielpe*; Swed. *hjelpa*; Goth. *hilpan*; G. *helfen*, OHG. *helfan*. Teut. type *helpan-* (pt. t. *halp*, pp. *hulpanoz*). Allied to Lithuan. *szelpti*, to help. Der. *help*, sb. = AS. *helpe* (Grein); *help-er, help-ful, help-ful-ness, help-less, help-less-ly, help-less-ness*; also *help-meet*, a coinage due to a mistaken notion of the phrase *an help meet* (Gen. ii. 18, 20); later form *help-mate*; thus Rich. quotes from Sharp's Sermons, vol. iv. ser. 12: 'that she might be a *help-mate* for the man.'

HELVE, a handle of an axe. (E.) ME. *helue* (= *helve*), Wyclif, Deut. xix. 5; spelt *hellfe* (for *helfe*), Ormulum, 9948. AS. *hielf*, of which the dat. *hielfe* occurs in Gregory's Pastoral, ed. Sweet, p. 166, l. 8; also *helfe*, as in 'Manubrium, hæft and helfe;' Wright's Vocab. i. 35, col. 1 (Voc. 142. 21). + MDu. *helve*, a handle; Oudemans; Low G. *helft*, a handle; Pomeran. *helfter*. Allied to **Helm** (1) and **Halter**.

HEM (1), the border of a garment. (E.) ME. *hem*; pl. *hemmes*, Wyclif, Matt. xxiii. 5. AS. *hemm, hem*; 'Limbus, stemning vel hem;' Wright's Vocab. i. 26, col. 1 (Voc. 125. 13). Orig. 'an enclosure;' cf. OFries. *ham, hem*; NFries. *ham*, an enclosure; EFries. *ham*, an enclosure surrounded by ditches. Der. *hem*, verb, chiefly in the phr. *to hem in* (cf. G. *hemmen*, to stop, check, hem, from Fries. *ham*; Swed. *hämma*, to withhold, keep in), Shak. Troilus, iv. 5. 193.

HEM (2), a slight cough to call attention. (E.) 'Cry hem! when he should groan,' Much Ado, v. 1. 16; cf. As You Like It, i. 3. 19. An imitative word, formed from the sound. Allied to **Hum**. In Dutch, we also find the same word *hem*, used in the same way. Der. *hem*, verb, As You Like It, i. 3. 18.

HEMATITE, an ore of iron. (F. — L. — Gk.) The sesqui-oxide of iron ; so called because of the red colour of the powder (Webster). 'The sanguine load-stone, called *hæmatites* ;' Holland's Pliny, b. xxxvi. c. 16. – OF. *hematite* (Supp. to Godefroy). – L. *hæmatitēs* ; Pliny. – Gk. αἱματίτης, blood-like. – Gk. αἱματ-, stem of αἷμα, blood.

HEMI-, half. (Gk.) From a L. spelling (*hēmi-*) of the Gk. prefix ἡμι-, signifying half ; cognate with L. *sēmi-*, half. See **Semi-**.

HEMICRANIA, megrim ; see **Megrim**.

HEMISPHERE, a half sphere, a half globe. (F. – L. – Gk.) In Cotgrave. – MF. *hemisphere*, 'a hemisphere ;' Cot. – L. *hēmisphærium*. – Gk. ἡμισφαίριον, a hemisphere. – Gk. ἡμι-, prefix, signifying half ; and σφαῖρα, a ball, sphere. See **Hemi-** and **Sphere**. Der. *hemispheri-c-al* ; Sir T. Browne, Vulg. Errors, b. ii. c. 1, § 13.

HEMISTICH, half a line, in poetry. (L. – Gk.) Not from F. *hemistique* (Cotgrave), but directly from L. *hēmistichium*, by dropping the two latter syllables. Kersey has : '*Hemistichium*, a half verse.' – Gk. ἡμιστίχιον, a half verse. – Gk. ἡμι-, half ; and στίχος, a row, order, line, verse. See **Hemi-** and **Distich**.

HEMLOCK, a poisonous plant. (E.) ME. *hemlok* ; spelt *humloke*, *humlok*, Wright's Vocab. i. 226, col. 1, 265, col. 1 ; *hemelok*, id. i. 191, col. 2 (Voc. 711.34 ; 786.16 ; 645.21). AS. *hemlic*, *hymlice* ; Gloss. to Cockayne's Saxon Leechdoms ; early form *hymblicæ*, Epinal Gloss. 185. Of unknown origin.

HEMORRHAGE, a great flow of blood. (F. – L. – Gk.) Spelt *hemorragy* by Ray, On the Creation, pt. 1 (R.). – MF. *hemorrhagie*, 'an abundant flux of blood ;' Cot. – Late L. *hæmorrhagia*, Latinised from Gk. αἱμορραγία, a violent bleeding. – Gk. αἱμο-, for αἷμα, blood ; and ϝραγ-, a grade of ῥήγνυμι, I break, burst ; the lit. sense being 'a bursting out of blood.' Gk. ϝραγ is allied to E. *wreak*.

HEMORRHOIDS, EMERODS, painful bleeding tubercles round the margin of the anus. (F. – L. – Gk.) '*Hemorroides* be vaynes in the foundement ;' Sir T. Elyot, Castel of Helth, b. iii. c. 9. – MF. *hemorrhoïde*, 'an issue of blood by the veins of the fundament ;' Cot. – L. *hæmorrhoidæ*, hemorrhoids, pl. of *hæmorrhoida*. – Gk. αἱμορροΐδες, pl. of αἱμορροΐς, adj., liable to flow of blood. – Gk. αἱμο-, for αἷμα, blood ; and ῥέειν, to flow, cognate with Skt. *sru*, to flow, and allied to E. *stream*. Der. *hemorrhoid-al*. Doublet, *emerods*.

HEMP, a kind of plant. (L. – Gk.) ME. *hemp*, Havelok, 782. Contracted from a form *henep* ; the *n* becoming *m* by the influence of the following *p*. AS. *henep*, *hænep* ; Cockayne's A. S. Leechdoms, i. 124. ll. 1, 3, and note. [Cf. Du. *hennep* ; Icel. *hampr* ; Dan. *hamp* ; Swed. *hampa* ; G. *hanf* ; OHG. *hanaf*.] All from L. *cannabis* ; Gk. κάνναβις ; hemp. Cf. Skt. *çana-s*, hemp ; prob. not an Idg. word. β. The L. word is merely borrowed from Gk. 'Grimm and Kuhn both consider the Gk. word borrowed from the East, and the Teutonic one from the L. *cannabis* which certainly made its way to them ;' Curtius, i. 173. The word was borrowed so early that it suffered consonantal change. Der. *hemp-en*, with adj. suffix, as in *gold-en* ; Hen. V, iii. chor. 8. Also *canvas*, q. v.

HEN, the female of a bird, especially of the domestic fowl. (E.) ME. *hen*, Chaucer, C. T. 15445 ; pl. *hennes*, id. 14872 (B 4629, 4056). AS. *henn*, *hen*, *hæn* ; Grein, ii. 23. Teut. type **hanjā*, f. ; from AS. *hana*, a cock ; Grein, ii. 11.+Du. *hen*, fem. of *haan*, a cock ; Icel. *hæna*, fem. of *hani* ; Dan. *höne*, fem. of *hane*, a cock ; Swed. *höna*, fem. of *hane* ; G. *henne*, fem. of *hahn*, a cock. Cf. Goth. *hana*, a cock. β. Thus *hen* is the fem. of a word for cock (obsolete in English), of which the old Teutonic type was **han-on-*. γ. The AS. *hana* means, literally, 'singer,' the suffix *-a* denoting the agent, as in AS. *hunt-a*, a hunter. – √KAN, to sing ; whence L. *canere*, to sing. Der. *hen-coop*, Prompt. Parv. p. 235 ; lit. 'fowl-poison ;' see **Bane**. Also *hen-coop*, *hen-harrier*, a kind of hawk (see **Harrier**) ; *hen-pecked*, i.e. pecked by the hen or wife, as in the Spectator, no. 176 : 'a very good sort of people, which are commonly called in scorn the *henpeckt*.' ' My *henpecked* sire ;' Dryden, tr. of Virgil, Past. iii. 49.

HENCE, from this place or time. (E.) ME. *hennes*, P. Plowman, B. iii. 108 ; whence the shorter form *hens*, occurring in Lydgate's Minor Poems, p. 220. In the modern *hence*, the *-ce* merely records that the ME. *hens* was pronounced with voiceless *s*, not with a final *z*-sound. β. In the form *hennes*, the suffixed *s* was due to a habit of forming adverbs in *-s* or *-es*, as in *twy-es*, twice, *need-es*, needs ; an older form was *henne*, Havelok, 843, which is found as late as in Chaucer, C. T. 2358 (A 2356). γ. Again, *henne* represents a still older *henen* or *heonen*, spelt *heonene* in Ancren Riwle, p. 230, l. 8. AS. *heonan*, *hionan*, hence ; Grein, ii. 67. Here *heonan* stands as usual for an older **hinan*. A shorter form appears in the AS. *heona* (for *hina*), hence, Grein, ii. 67 ; closely allied to *hi-ne*, acc. masc. of the pron. *hē*, *he*. See **He**. ¶ Similarly, L. *hinc*, hence, is connected with L. *hic*, this. Der. *hence-forth*, compounded of *hence* and *forth*, and answering to AS. *forð heonan*, used of time ; see examples in Grein, ii. 68, ll. 1–4 ; *hence-forward*, comp. of *hence* and *forward*.

HENCHMAN, a page, servant. (E.) In Shak. Mids. Nt. Dr. ii. 1. 121. 'Compare me the fewe .. disciples of Jesus with the

solemne pomp . . . of such as go before the bishop, of his *hensemen*, of trumpets, of sundry tunes,' &c. ; Udal, on St. Mark, c. 11. vv. 1–10. ' And every knight had after him riding Three *henshmen* on him awaiting ;' The Flower and the Leaf, l. 252 (a poem wrongly ascribed to Chaucer, and belonging to the fifteenth century). ME. *henksman* ; the pl. *henksmen* occurs in 1392, in the Earl of Derby's Expedition (Camden Soc.), p. 163 ; cf. p. 280. Spelt *henxtman* in 1402. The full (Latinised) form *hengestmannus* occurs in the Issue Roll for 1380 (Easter) ; see N. E. D. β. We also find *Hinxman* as a proper name in Wilts. (in the Clergy List, 1873) ; showing that the right etymology is from ME. *hengest* (cognate with Du. and G. *hengst*, Swed. and Dan. *hingst*), a horse, and E. *man*. We find similar formations in Icel. *hestvörðr* (lit. horse-ward), a mounted guard (Cleasby) ; and in Swed. *kingstridare* (lit. horse-rider), 'a groom of the king's stable, who rides before his coach ;' Widegren's Swed. Dict. In this view, the sense is simply 'groom,' which is the sense required in The Flower and the Leaf. γ. The ME. *hengest* occurs in Layamon, l. 3546, and is from AS. *hengest*, a horse (Grein, ii. 34), once a common word. It is cognate with Icel. *hestr*, Swed. and Dan. *hingst* and *häst*, G. *hengst* ; from an orig. Teutonic **hangistoz*. The orig. sense of *henchman* was 'horseman ;' then 'a page,' usually a young man of high rank. See A Student's Pastime (index). ¶ I find in Blount's Nomolexicon, ed. 1691, the following : '*Henchman*, qui equo innititur bellicoso, from the G. *hengst*, a war-horse : with us it signifies one that runs on foot, attending upon a person of honor or worship. [Mentioned] Anno 3 Edw. 4. cap. 5, and 24 Hen. 8. cap. 13. It is written *henxman*, anno 6 Hen. 8. cap. 1.'

HENDECAGON, a plane figure of eleven sides and angles. (Gk.) So called from its eleven angles. – Gk. ἕνδεκα, eleven ; and γωνία, an angle. Ἕνδεκα = ἕν, one, and δέκα, ten. See **Heptagon**.

HENDECASYLLABIC, a term applied to a verse of eleven syllables. (Gk.) From Gk. ἕνδεκα, eleven (= ἕν, one, and δέκα, ten) ; and συλλαβή, a syllable. See **Decasyllabic**.

HENNA, the Egyptian privet ; also a dye made from the leaves to stain the nails, &c. (Arab.) 'Their women .. with a certaine colour in their hand called *Hanna* which will staine ;' Purchas, Pilgrimage, 1614, p. 637 (N. E. D.). – Arab. *ḥinnā'*, the dyeing or colouring shrub ; *Lawsonia inermis* ; Rich. Dict., p. 582.

HENT, a seizure, an intention. (E.) In the latter sense, Shak. Haml. iii. 3. 88. A doublet of *hint* ; see **Hint**.

HEP, HIP, the fruit of the dog-rose. See **Hip** (2).

HEPATIC, pertaining to the liver. (F. – L. – Gk.) Spelt *epatike*, Book of St. Alban's, fol. C 5, back, l. 7. '*Hepatiques*, obstructions of the liver ;' Blount's Gloss., ed. 1674. – MF. *hepatique*, 'hepatical, of or belonging to the liver ;' Cot. – L. *hēpaticus*. – Gk. ἡπατικός, belonging to the liver. – Gk. ἡπατ-, stem of ἧπαρ, the liver.+L. *iecur*, the liver ; Skt. *yakṛt*, the liver. Der. *hepatic-al* ; *hepatic-a*, a flower, the liver-wort ; see *hepathique*, *hepatique* in Cotgrave.

HEPTAGON, a plane figure with seven sides and angles. (Gk.) In Blount's Gloss., ed. 1674. So called from its seven angles. – Gk. ἑπτά, seven, cognate with E. *seven* ; and γωνία, an angle, allied to γόνυ, a knee. See **Seven** and **Knee**. Der. *heptagon-al*.

HEPTAHEDRON, a solid figure with seven bases or sides. (Gk.) Spelt *heptaedron* in Kersey, ed. 1715. – Gk. ἑπτά, seven, cognate with E. *seven* ; and ἕδρα, a seat, base, from the same base as E. *seat* and *sit*. See **Seven** and **Sit**.

HEPTARCHY, a government by seven persons. (Gk.) In T. Fuller, Worthies of England, ch. 3. Applied to seven Old-English kingdoms, viz. those of Kent, Sussex, Wessex, Essex, Northumberland, Mercia, and East Anglia. The term is not a good one ; see Freeman, Old Eng. Hist. for Children, p. 40. – Gk. ἑπτ-, for ἑπτά, seven ; and -αρχία, government. See **Seven** and **Anarchy**.

HER, possessive and objective case of the fem. of the third pers. pronoun. (E.) ME. *hire*, the usual form ; also *here*, Chaucer, C. T. 4880 (B 460) ; *hure*, P. Plowman, C. iv. 45–48. AS. *hire*, gen. and dat. case of *hēo*, she ; the possessive pronoun being made from the gen. case, and indeclinable ; see Sweet's A. S. Reader, Grammat. Introduction. The word is to be divided as *hi-re*, where *hi-* is to be referred to a Teut. pronominal base, signifying 'this ;' and *-re* is the usual AS. fem. inflection in the gen. and dat. of adjectives declined according to the strong declension. See **He**. Der. *her-s*, ME. *hires*, Chaucer, C. T. 4647 (B 227) ; not found much earlier ; *her-self*.

HERALD, an officer who makes proclamations. (F. – OHG.) ME. *herald*, *heraud* ; Chaucer, C. T. 2601 (A 2599) ; P. Plowman, B. xviii. 16. – OF. *heralt*, *heraut*, a herald ; Low L. *heraldus* ; cf. Ital. *araldo*, a herald ; OHG. *herolt* (G. *herold*), a herald (from OF.). β. Nevertheless, the OF. word is of Teut. origin ; and prob. from OHG. *harēn*, to proclaim, cry aloud ; with the usual F. suffix *-alt* for *-ald* < G. *-wald* (Toynbee, Gr. § 692. xx) ; the sense being 'crier' or 'proclaimer.' Cf. OHG. *fora-haro*, a herald ; from *for-harēn*, to proclaim. γ. The OHG. *harēn* is cognate with Goth. *hazjan*, AS.

herian, to praise. Körting, § 4491. Der. *herald-ic*; also *herald-ry*, Mids. Nt. Dr. iii. 2. 213, spelt *heraldie*, Gower, C. A. i. 173; bk. ii. 399.

HERB, a plant with a succulent stem. (F. – L.) The word being of F. origin, the *h* was probably once silent, and is still sometimes so considered; there is a tendency at present to sound the *h*, the word being a short monosyllable. ME. *erbe*, *herbe*, Chaucer, C. T. 14972, 14955 (B 4156, 4139); King Alisaunder, 331. – F. *herbe*, 'an herb;' Cot. – L. *herba*, grass, a herb; properly herbage, food for cattle. β. Supposed to be allied to OL. *forbea*, food, and to Gk. φορβή, pasture, fodder, forage, φέρβειν, to feed. Der. *herb-less*, *herb-ac-eous*, in Sir T. Browne, Vulg. Errors, b. ii. c. 6, § 15, from L. *herbāceus*, grassy, herb-like; *herb-age*, from F. *herbage*, 'herbage, pasture' (Cot.), answering to a L. form *herbāticum*; *herb-al*; *herb-al-ist*, Sir T. Browne, Vulg. Errors, b. ii. c. 6, § 4; *herb-ar-ium*, from L. *herbārium*, a book describing herbs, a herbal, but now applied to a collection of plants; *herbivorous*, herb-devouring, from L. *uorāre*, to devour (see **Voracious**). And note ME. *herbere*, a herb-garden, from L. *herbārium* through the French; a word discussed under **Arbour**.

HERD (1), a flock of beasts, group of animals. (E.) ME. *heerde*, *heorde*. 'Heerde, or flok of beestys;' Prompt. Parv. p. 236. 'Ane *heorde* of hoerten' = a herd of harts, Layamon, 305. AS. *heord*, *herd*, *hyrd*, (1) care, custody, (2) herd, flock, (3) family; Grein, ii. 68.╋ Icel. *hjorð*; Dan. *hiord*; Swed. *hjord*; G. *heerde*; Goth. *hairda*. Teut. type *herdā*, f. Cf. Skt. *çardha(s)*, a herd, troop. Brugmann, i. § 797. Der. *herd*, vb., ME. *herdien*, to draw together into a herd, P. Plowman, C. xiv. 148; *herd-man*, ME. *herdeman*, *hirdeman*, Ormulum, 6852; later form *herd-s-man*, Shak. Wint. Ta. iv. 4. 344. Der. *herd* (2).

HERD (2), one who tends a herd. (E.) Generally used in the comp. *shep-herd*, *cow-herd*, &c. ME. *herde*, Chaucer, C. T. 605 (A 603); Will. of Palerne, 6; spelt *hurde*, P. Plowman, C. x. 267. AS. *hierde*, *hirde*; Grein, ii. 77.╋Icel. *hirðir*; Dan. *hyrde*; Swed. *herde*; G. *hirt*, *hirte*; Goth. *hairdeis*. Teut. type *herdjoz*, i. e. keeper of the herd (*herdā*). See above. Cf. Lithuan. *kerdzus*, a cow-herd. Der. *cow-herd*, *goat-herd*, *shep-herd*.

HERE, in this place. (E.) ME. *her*, *heer*; Chaucer, C. T. 1610, 1612. AS. *hēr*; Grein, ii. 34.╋Du. *hier*; Icel. *hér*; Dan. *her*; Swed. *här*; G. *hier*; OHG. *hiar*; Goth. *hēr*. β. All from the pronominal base HI (Fick, iii. 74); so that *here* is related to *he* just as *where* is related to *who*. See **He**. Der. *here-about*, Temp. ii. 2. 41; *here-abouts*; *hereafter*, ME. *her-after*, Genesis and Exodus, ed. Morris, 243; *here-by*, ME. *her-bi*, Owl and Nightingale, 127; *here-in*, ME. *her-inne*, Havelok, 458; *here-of*, ME. *her-of*, Havelok, 2585; *here-tofore*, 1 Sam. iv. 7; *here-unto*, 1 Pet. ii. 21; *here-upon*, answering to ME. *her-on*, P. Plowman, B. xiii. 130; *here-with*, Malachi, iii. 10.

HEREDITARY, descending by inheritance. (L.) In Shak. Temp. ii. 1. 223; and in Cotgrave, to translate MF. *hereditaire*. Englished from L. *hērēditārius*, hereditary. – L. *hērēditās*, heredity. – L. *hērēdi-*, decl. stem of *hērēs*, an heir. See **Heir**. Der. *hereditari-ly*. From the same base we have *heredita-ble*, a late and rare word, for which *heritable* (MF. *heritable*) was formerly used, as in Blackstone's Comment. b. ii. c. 5 (R.); also *heredita-ment*, in Fabyan's Chron., ed. Ellis, p. 650; *heredit-y* (F. *hérédité*, L. acc. *hērēdītātem*).

HERESY, the choice of an opinion contrary to that usually received. (F. – L. – Gk.) The word means, literally, no more than 'choice.' ME. *heresye*, Ayenbite of Inwyt, p. 267 (see Spec. of English, ed. Morris and Skeat, p. 103, l. 149); *eresie*, Wyclif, Acts, xxiv. 14; Ancren Riwle, p. 82. – OF. *heresie*, 'heresie, obstinate or wicked error;' Cot. – L. type *hæresia*, for L. *hæresis*. – Gk. αἵρεσις, a taking, choice, sect, heresy. – Gk. αἱρεῖν, to take, αἱρεῖσθαι, to choose. Der. *heretic*, q.v.

HERETIC, the holder of a heresy. (F. – L. – Gk.) ME. *eretik*, *heretik*, Wyclif, Tit. iii. 10. – OF. *heretique*, 'an heretick;' Cot. – L. *hæreticus*. – Gk. αἱρετικός, able to choose, heretical. – Gk. αἱρεῖν, to take, αἱρεῖσθαι, to choose. See **Heresy**. Der. *heretic-al*.

HERIOT, a tribute paid to the lord of a manor on the decease of a tenant. (E.) See Blackstone, Comment. b. ii. capp. 6, 28; and see *Hariot* in Blount's Law Lexicon; and *Heriot* in Jamieson's Scot. Dict. [Sir D. Lyndesay speaks of a *herield hors*, a horse paid as a heriot, The Monarche, b. iii. l. 4734; but this represents AS. *heregield*, war-tax.] ME. *heriet*; 'And [h]is beste beest [beast] to *heriet*;' S. E. Legendary, ed. Horstmann, p. 445, l. 480. From AF. *heriet*, Year-books of Edw. I (1392-3), p. 213. From AS. *heregeatu*, lit. military apparel; Grein, ii. 36. The *heregeatu* (-*geatwa*, -*geatwe*) consisted of 'military habiliments or equipments, which, after the death of the vassal, escheated to the sovereign or lord, to whom they were delivered by the heir;' Thorpe, Ancient Laws, b. ii. glossary, s.v. In later times, horses and cows, and many other things were paid as *heriots* to the lord of the manor. 'And þām cinge minne *hæregeatwa*, fēower sweord, and fēower spæra, and fēower scyldas, and fēower beagas, .. fēower hors, and twā sylfrene fata;' i. e. And [I bequeath]

to the king my *heriots*, viz. four swords, and four spears, and four shields, and four torques, .. four horses, and two silver vessels; Will dated about 946-955; in Thorpe's Diplomatarium Ævi Saxonici, p. 499. – AS. *here*, an army (hence, belonging to war); and *geatu*, pl. *geatwe*, apparel, adornment; Grein, i. 495.

HERITAGE, an inheritance. (F. – L.) In early use. ME. *heritage*, Hali Meidenhad, ed. Cockayne, p. 25, last line but one; King Horn, ed. Lumby, 1281; also *eritage*, Alexander and Dindimus, ed. Skeat, 981. – OF. *heritage*, 'an inheritance, heritage;' Cot. Formed, with suffix -*age* (answering to L. -*āticum*) from OF. *heriter*, to inherit. – L. *hērēditāre*, to inherit; the loss of a syllable is exemplified by Low L. *hēritātor*, used for *hērēditātor*; it would seem as if the base *hēri-* was substituted for *hērēdi-*. – L. *hērēdi-*, decl. stem of *hērēs*, an heir; see **Heir**. Der. from same source, *herit-able*, *herit-or*.

HERMAPHRODITE, an animal or plant of both sexes. (L. – Gk.) In Gascoigne, The Steele Glas, l. 53. See Sir T. Browne, Vulg. Errors, b. iii. c. 17. – L. *hermaphroditus*. – Gk. ἑρμαφρόδιτος; a coined word, made up from Gk. Ἑρμῆς, Hermes (Mercury), as representing the male principle; and Ἀφροδίτη, Aphroditē (Venus), the female. Hence the legend that Hermaphroditus, son of Hermes, and Aphrodite, when bathing, grew together with Salmacis, the nymph of a fountain, into one person; see Ovid, Met. iv. 383. Der. *hermaphrodit-ic*, -*ic-al*, -*ism*; also *hermaphrodism*.

HERMENEUTIC, explanatory. (Gk.) A modern word. From Gk. ἑρμηνευτικός, skilled in interpreting. – Gk. ἑρμηνευτής, an interpreter; of which a shorter form is ἑρμηνεύς. Connected (perhaps) with L. *sermo*, speech (Prellwitz). Der. *hermeneutic-al*, *hermeneutic-al-ly*, *hermeneutics* (the science of interpretation).

HERMETIC, chemical, &c. (Gk.) 'Their seals, their characters, *hermetic* rings;' Ben Jonson, Underwoods, lxi. An Execration upon Vulcan, l. 73. – Low L. *hermēticus*, relating to alchemy; a coined word, made from the name *Hermēs* (= Gk. Ἑρμῆς); from the notion that the great secrets of alchemy were discovered by *Hermēs Trismegistus* (Hermes the thrice-greatest). Der. *hermetic-al*, *hermetic-al-ly*. ¶ *Hermetically* was a term in alchemy; a glass bottle was said to be *hermetically* (i. e. perfectly) sealed when the opening of it was fused and closed against the admission of air.

HERMIT, one who lives in solitude. (F. – L. – Gk.) ME. *eremite*, *heremite*; in early use. [It first appears in Layamon, 18763, where the earlier text has *æremite*, the later *heremite*. This form was taken *directly* from L. *herēmita*, the later form *hermite* being from the French. *Heremite* occurs in P. Plowman, B. vi. 190, and even as late as in Holinshed's Description of Britain, b. i. c. 9 (R.).] The shorter form *armyte* also occurs in Layamon, 18800; and *hermyte* is in Berners' tr. of Froissart, vol. ii. c. 204 (R.). – F. *hermite*, 'an hermit;' Cot. – Late L. *heremita*, for *herēmita*, in P. Plowman, B. xv. 281; but usually *erēmita*. – Gk. ἐρεμίτης, a dweller in a desert. – Gk. ἐρημία, a solitude, desert. – Gk. ἔρημος, deserted, desolate. Root uncertain; perhaps allied to Goth. *arms*, poor (Prellwitz). Der. *hermit-age*, Spenser, F. Q. i. i. 34, spelt *heremytage*, Mandeville's Travels, p. 93, from F. *hermitage*, 'an hermitage;' Cot. Also *hermit-ic-al*, spelt *heremiticall* in Holinshed, Desc. of Britain, b. i. c. 9 (R.), from L. *herēmiticus* (better *erēmiticus*), solitary.

HERN, the same as **Heron**, q.v.

HERNIA, a kind of rupture; a surgical term. (L.) In Kersey, ed. 1715; *hirnia* in Chaucer, C. T. Pers. Tale (I 423). – L. *hernia*, a rupture, hernia.

HERO, a warrior, illustrious man. (F. – L. – Gk.) In Hamlet, ii. 2. 270. – MF. *heroe*, 'a worthy, a demygod;' Cot. – L. *hērōem*, acc. of *hērōs*, a hero. – Gk. ἥρως, a hero, demi-god. ¶ The mod. F. *héros* is now accommodated to the spelling of the L. nom. The L. acc. is, however, still preserved in the Span. *heroe*, Ital. *eroe*. Der. *hero-ic*, spelt *heroicke* in Spenser, F. Q. v. i. 1, from MF. *heroïque* (Cot.), which from L. *hērōicus*; *hero-ic-al-ly*, *hero-ism*; also *hero-ine*, q. v.

HEROINE, a famous woman. (F. – L. – Gk.) In Minsheu. 'A *heroine* is a kinde of prodigy;' Evelyn, Memoirs; Mrs. Evelyn to Mr. Bohun, Jan. 4, 1672 (R.). – MF. *heroïne*, 'a most worthy lady;' Cot. – L. *hērōïnē*. – Gk. ἡρωίνη, f. of ἥρως, hero (above).

HERON, a long-legged water-fowl. (F. – OHG.) ME. *heroune*, Chaucer, Parliament of Foules, 346. Also *hayron*, Wright's Vocab. i. 177; (Voc. 625. 4). 'Heern, byrde, heryn, herne, ardea;' Prompt. Parv. p. 237. – OF. *hairon*, 'a heron, herne, hernshaw;' Cot. (Mod. F. *heron*; OProv. *aigros*; Ital. *aghirone*, *airone*; Span. *airon*.) – OHG. *heigir*, *heiger*, a heron; with suffixed -*on* (Ital. -*one*). Allied to Swed. *häger*, a heron; Dan. *heire*, a heron; Icel. *hegri*, a heron; OHG. *hehara*, G. *häher*, *heher*, a jackdaw; AS. *higora*, a magpie; Gk. κίσσα (for *κικ-ya*), Skt. *kiki-*, a jay (Prellwitz); of imitative origin. Brugmann, i. §§ 86, 639. ¶ The AS. name was *hrāgra*, Wright's Vocab. i. 29, col. 1 (Voc. 6. 37); with which cf. G. *reiher*, a heron; Du. *reiger*; allied to Gk. κριγή, a creaking, κρίζειν, to screech. Der. *heron-er*, ME. *heronere*, Chaucer, Troilus, iv. 413;

from OF. *haironnier*; Cotgrave explains *faulcon haironnier* as 'a herner, a faulcon made only to the heron.' Also *heron-ry*. And see **Heronshaw, Egret.**

HERONSHAW, HERNSHAW, (1) a young heron, (2) a heronry. (F. – OHG.) Spenser has *herneshaw*, a young heron; F. Q. vi. 7. 9. Two distinct words have been confused here. **1.** *Hernshaw*, a heron, is a corruption of *heronsewe*; the name *heronsew* for the heron is still common in Lincolnshire and Yorkshire. Mr. Peacock's Glossary of Manley and Corringham (Lincoln) words has: '*Heronsew*, the common heron. "There were vewed at this present survey certayne *heronsewes* whiche have allwayes used to brede there to the number of iiij."—Survey of Glastonbury, temp. Hen. VIII, *Mon. Ang.* i. 11. See Chaucer, Squyeres Tale, F. 68.' The etymology of this *heronsewe* is given by Tyrwhitt, who cites the F. *heronçeau* from 'the glossary,' meaning probably that in Urry's ed. of Chaucer; but it is verified by the fact that the OF. *herouncel* (older form of *heronçeau*) occurs in the Liber Custumarum, p. 304, and means 'a young heron.' And again, Palsgrave has '*heronceau*, an hernshawe;' p. 187. The suffix *-c-el* is a double dimin., as in *lion-c-el*, later *lionçeau*. For *ew* < F. *eau*, cf. ME. *bew-tee* = F. *beau-té*. **2.** *Hernshaw* in its other sense is due to a (false) popular etymology, as if it were from *heron*, and *shaw*, a wood. This sense is given by Cotgrave, who explains OF. *haironniere* by 'a heron's neast, or ayrie; a *herneshaw*, or *shaw* of wood wherein *herons* breed.' Hence *heronshaw* (1) is (F. – OHG.); *heronshaw* (2) is hybrid.

HERRING, a small fish. (E.) ME. *hering* (with one *r*), Havelok, 758. AS. *hǣrincg*; the pl. *hǣrincgas* is in Ælfric's Colloquy, in Thorpe's Analecta, p. 24; also *hǣring*, Wright's Vocab. i. 56, l. 4 (Voc. 94. 13; 181. 4). **+** Du. *haring*; G. *häring*; OHG. *hāring* (Kluge). **β.** The explanation that the fish is named 'from its appearance in large shoals,' from the Teut. type **harjoz*, an army (as seen in Goth. *harjis*, AS. *here*, G. *heer*), seems to be phonetically impossible. The word remains unexplained.

HESITATE, to doubt, stammer. (L.) Spelt *hesitate, hæsitate* in Minsheu, ed. 1627. [Perhaps suggested by the sb. *hesitation*, which occurs in Cotgrave to translate F. *hesitation*, whereas he explains *hesiter* only by 'to doubt, feare, stick, stammer, stagger in opinion.']— L. *hæsitātus*, pp. of *hæsitāre*, to stick fast; a frequentative formed from *hæsum*, supine of *hærēre*, to stick, cleave. **+** Lithuanian *gaiszti, gaiszoti*, to tarry, delay (Nesselmann); Fick, i. 576.—√GHAIS, to stick, cleave; where the *gh* is not palatal. Brugmann, i. § 627. **Der.** *hesitat-ion, hesit-anc-y*; from the same root, *ad-here, co-here, in-her-ent*.

HESPERIAN, western. (L. – Gk.) 'Your feigned Hesperian orchards;' Massinger, Virgin Martyr, A. iv. sc. 3 (where it refers to the Hesperides).—L. *Hesperi-us*, western; with suffix *-an*.—L. *Hesperi-a*. —Gk. Ἑσπερία, the western land; fem. of ἑσπέριος, evening, western. —Gk. ἕσπερος, evening. **+** L. *uesper*, evening; see **Vesper. Der.** Closely allied to the adj. ἑσπέριος is the fem. ἑσπερίς, whence the pl. Ἑσπερίδες, the daughters of Night, who dwelt in a western isle, and guarded a garden with golden apples; Hesiod, Th. 215.

HEST, a command. (E.) ME. *hest, heste*, a command; also, a promise; Chaucer, C. T. 11376 (F 1064). The final *t* is properly excrescent, as in *whils-t, agains-t, amongs-t, amids-t*, from ME. *whiles, againes, amonges, amiddes*. AS. *hǣs*, a command, Grein, i. 24; Teut. type **haittiz*, f. (> **haissiz*, with *ss* for *tt*).—AS. *hātan*, to command; Teut. type **haitan*-. **+** Icel. *heit*, a vow, from *heita*, to call, promise; OHG. *heiz* (G. *geheiss*), a command, from OHG. *heizan* (G. *heissen*), to call, bid, command. Cf. Goth. *haitan*, to name, call, command.

HETEROCLITE, irregularly inflected. (L. – Gk.) A grammatical term; hence used in the general sense of irregular, disorderly. 'Ther are strange *heteroclites* in religion now adaies;' Howell, Familiar Letters, vol. iv. let. 35.—L. *heteroclitus*, varying in declension.—Gk. ἑτερόκλιτος, otherwise or irregularly inflected. — Gk. ἑτερο-, decl. stem of ἕτερος, other; and *-κλιτος*, formed from κλίνειν, to lean, hence, to vary as a case does, cognate with E. *lean* (1).

HETERODOX, of strange opinion; heretical. (Gk.) In Blount's Gloss., ed. 1674. Compounded from Gk. ἑτερο-, decl. stem of ἕτερος, another, other; and δόξα, opinion, from δοκεῖν, to think. **Der.** *heterodox-y*, Gk. ἑτεροδοξία.

HETEROGENEOUS, dissimilar in kind. (Gk.) Blount's Gloss., ed. 1674, gives the adjectives *heterogene, heterogeneal*, and the sb. *heterogeneity*. Compounded from Gk. ἑτερο-, decl. stem of ἕτερος, another, other; and γένος, kind, kin, cognate with E. *kin*. **Der.** *heterogeneous-ly, -ness*; *heterogene-it-y*.

HETMAN, a captain; (of Cossacks, or in Poland. (Pol. – G.) First in 1710, in Whitworth, Acc. of Russia (ed. 1758, p. 19).— Polish *hetman* (Russ. *ataman'*), a captain.—G. *hauptman*, a captain. —G. *haupt*, head; and *mann*, man.

HEW, to hack, cut. (E.) ME. *hewen*, Chaucer, C. T. 1424 (A 1422). AS. *hēawan*, to hew; Grein, ii. 62. **+** Du. *houwen*; Icel. *hǫggva*; Swed. *hugga*; Dan. *hugge*; G. *hauen*; OHG. *houwan*. Teut.

type **hauwan*-. **+** Russ. *kovate*, to hammer, forge; Lith. *kauti*, to fight; cf. Lith. *kowà*, battle. Allied to L. *cūdere*, to strike, pound, beat. Brugmann, i. § 639. The root appears to be KEU, to strike, beat. **Der.** *hew-er*; also *hay* (1), q. v.; *hoe*, q. v.

HEXAGON, a plane figure, with six sides and angles. (L. – Gk.) *Hexagonal* is in Blount's Gloss., ed. 1674. *Hexagone* in Minsheu, ed. 1627. Named from its six angles.—L. *hexagōnum*, a hexagon. — Gk. ἑξάγωνος, six-cornered.—Gk. ἕξ, six, cognate with E. *six*; and γωνία, an angle, corner, allied to γόνυ, knee, cognate with E. *knee*. See **Six** and **Knee. Der.** *hexagon-al, hexagon-al-ly*.

HEXAMETER, a certain kind of verse having six feet. (L. – Gk.) 'This provoking song in *hexameter* verse;' Sidney's Arcadia, b. i. (R.) 'I like your late Englishe *hexameters*;' Spenser, letter to Harvey, qu. in Globe ed. of Spenser, p. xxviii.—L. *hexameter*; also *hexametrus*.—Gk. ἑξάμετρος, a hexameter; properly an adj. meaning 'of six metres' or feet.—Gk. ἕξ, six, cognate with E. *six*; and μέτρον, a measure, metre. See **Six** and **Metre.**

HEY, interjection. (E.) ME. *hei*, Legend of St. Katharine, l. 579; *hay*, Gawayn and Grene Knight, 1445. A natural exclamation. **+** G. *hei*, interjection; Du. *hei*, hey! ho!

HEYDAY (1), interjection (G. or Du.) In Shak. Temp. ii. 2. 190. '*Heyda*, what Hans Flutterkin is this? what Dutchman does build or frame castles in the air?' Ben Jonson, Masque of Augurs. 'Ioly rutterkin, *heyda*!' Skelton, Magnif. 757. Borrowed either from G. *heida*, ho! hallo! or from Du. *hei daar*, ho! there. It comes to much the same thing. The G. *da*, Du. *daar*, are cognate with E. *there*. **β.** But note that Cotgrave has MF. *hadea*, 'interj. of perceiving or surprising, ha! are you there?'; cf. OF. *hé dea, hé dia*, interj. (Godefroy, s. v. *dea*). **¶** The interj. *hey* is older; see above.

HEYDAY (2), frolicsome wildness. (E.) 'At your age the *heyday* in the blood is tame;' Hamlet, iii. 4. 69. I take this to be quite a different word from the foregoing, though the commentators confuse the two. In this case, and in the expression '*heyday* of youth,' the word may well stand for *high day* (ME. *hey day*); and it is not surprising that the old editions of Shakespeare have *highday* in place of *heyday*; only, unluckily, in the wrong place, viz. Temp. ii. 2. 190. So also 'in the *highday* of blood;' Macklin, Love-a-la-Mode, A. i (Sir Archy); 'in the *highday* of youth;' Smollett, Hum. Clinker, 1771, ii. 50. Cf. 'that sabbath day was an *high day*;' John, xix. 31. For the old spellings of *high*, see **High.**

HIATUS, a gap, defect, &c. (L.) In Bailey's Dict., vol. ii. ed. 1731.—L. *hiātus*, a gap, chasm; cf. *hiātus*, pp. of *hiāre*, to yawn, gape; cognate with E. *yawn*. See **Yawn. Doublet,** *chasm*, q. v.

HIBERNAL, wintry. (F. – L.) In Sir T. Browne, Vulg. Errors, b. iv. c. 13, § 10, where it is spelt *hybernal*.—F. *hibernal*, 'wintery;' Cot.—L. *hibernālis*, wintry (Wisdom, xvi. 29, Vulg.); lengthened from L. *hibernus*, wintry. **β.** *Hi-bernus* is allied to Gk. χειμερινός, wintry, χεῖμα, winter; and to L. *hi-ems*, winter, Gk. χι-ών, snow, Skt. *hi-ma-s*, cold, winter; the form of the root is GHEI. **Der.** from same source, *hibern-ate*.

HICCOUGH, HICCUP, HICKET, a spasmodic inspiration, with closing of the glottis, causing a slight sound. (E.) Now generally spelt *hiccough*. Spelt *hiccup* (riming with *prick up*), Butler's Hudibras, pt. ii. c. 1. 346. Also *hicket*, as in the old edition of Sir T. Browne, Vulg. Errors, b. iv. c. 9, § 5; and in Minsheu. Also *hichcock*; Florio explains Ital. *singhiozzi* by 'yeaxings, *hichecocks*.' Also *hickock*; Cotgrave has: '*Hoquet*, the *hickock*, or yexing;' also '*Hocqueter*, to yex, or clock [cluck], to have the *hickup* or *hickcock*.' **β.** It seems to be generally considered that the second syllable is *cough*, but it is ascertained (see N. E. D.) that *hiccough* is an accommodated spelling, due to popular etymology. The evidence takes us back to the forms *hick-ock, hick-et*, both formed from *hick* by the help of the usual dimin. suffixes *-ock, -et*. Cf. F. *hoqu-et*, the hiccough, in which the final *-et* is certainly a dimin. suffix; Walloon *hikett*, a hiccough, *hiket*, a shaking (Remacle). **γ.** The former syllable *hic, hik*, or *hick* is of imitative origin, to denote the spasmodic sound or jerk; and is preserved in English. **+** MDu. *huck-up*, 'the hick or hock;' also *hick*, 'the hick-hock,' Hexham; Du. *hik*, the hiccough, *hikken*, to hiccough; Dan. *hikke*, the hiccough; also, to hiccough; Swed. *hicka*, the hiccough; also, to hiccough. And cf. W. *ig*, a hiccough, sob; *igio*, to sob; Breton, *hik*, a hiccough, called *hâk* in the dialect of Vannes, whence (perhaps) F. *hoquet*. **δ.** All from an imitative base HIK, variant form of KIK, used to denote convulsive movements in the throat; see **Chincough.**

HICKORY, an American tree of the genus *Carya*. (N. Amer. Indian.) Short for *pohickery*, recorded in 1653 as the Amer. Indian name; Virginian *powcohicora* (Trumbull).

HIDALGO, a Spanish nobleman of the lowest class. (Span. – L.) The word occurs in Terry, Voyage to East India, ed. 1655, p. 169 (Todd); *fidalgo*, Sir T. Herbert's Travels, ed. 1665, p. 116.—Span.

hidalgo, a nobleman; OSpan. *fidalgo*, Port. *fidalgo*, a nobleman; also MSpan. *hijodalgo* (Minsheu). Lit. ' son of something,' i.e. a son to whom a father has left an estate. (So Körting; the explanation from *filius Italicus* is baseless.) β. *Hijo*, OSpan. *fijo*, is from L. *filium*, acc. of *filius*, son; see **Filial**; -*d'algo* is from L. *dē aliquō*, of something.

HIDE (1), to cover, conceal. (E.) ME. *hiden*, *huden*; Chaucer, C. T. 1479 (A 1477); Ancren Riwle, p. 130. AS. *hȳdan*, Grein, ii. 125. + Gk. *κεύθειν*, to hide. And cf. L. *cus-tōs*, a custodian (see **Custody**); W. *cuddio*, to hide (base *coud*-). ─ √KEUDH, to hide. Der. *hid-ing*. Brugmann, i. § 699.

HIDE (2), a skin. (E.) ME. *hyde*, Pricke of Conscience, l. 5299; *hude*, Ancren Riwle, p. 120. AS. *hȳd*, the skin; Grein, ii. 125. + Du. *huid*; Icel. *hūd*; Dan. and Swed. *hud*; OHG. *hūt*; G. *haut*. + L. *cutis*, skin; Gk. *κύτος*, *σκῦτος*, skin, hide; OPruss. *keuto*, hide. ─ √SKEU, to cover; Fick, i. 816. See **Sky**. Der. *hide-bound*, said of a tree the bark of which impedes its growth, Milton's Areopagitica, ed. Hales, p. 32, l. 2; also *hide* (3).

HIDE (3), to flog, castigate. (E.) Colloquial; ' to skin' by flogging. Cf. Icel. *hȳða*, to flog; from *hūð*, the hide. Der. *hid-ing*.

HIDE (4), a measure of land. (E.) ' *Hide of land*;' Blount's Law Dict., ed. 1691. Of variable size; estimated at 120 or 100 acres; or even much less; see Blount. Low L. *hida*; Ducange. AS. *hīd*; Ælfred's tr. of Bede, b. iii. c. 24; b. iv. c. 13, 19. (See Kemble's Saxons in England, b. i. c. 4; and the Appendix, showing that the estimate at 120 or 100 acres is too large.) β. This word is of a contracted form; the full form is *higid*; Thorpe, Diplomatarium Ævi Saxonici, p. 657; Kemble, Codex Diplomaticus, no. 243. This form *higid* is equivalent to *hiwisc*, another term for the same thing; and both words orig. meant (as Beda says) an estate sufficient to support *one family* or *household*. They are, accordingly, closely connected with AS. *hīwan*, domestics, those of one household, and with the Goth. *heiwa-frauja*, the master of a household; see further under **Hind** (2). ¶ Popular etymology has probably long ago confused the *hide* of land with *hide*, a skin; but the two words must be kept entirely apart. The former is AS. *hīgid*, the latter AS. *hȳd*.

HIDEOUS, ugly, horrible. (F. ─ L.?) The central *e* has crept into the word, and it has become trisyllabic; the true form is *hidous*. It is trisyllabic in Shak. Merry Wives, iv. 3. 34. ME. *hidous* (the invariable form); Chaucer, C. T., A 3520; he also has *hidously*, C. T., A 1701. ─ OF. *hidos*, *hidus*, *hideus*, later *hideux*, hideous; the earliest form is *hisdos*. β. Of uncertain origin; if the former *s* in *hisdos* is not an inserted letter, the probable original is L. *hispidōsus*, roughish, an extended form of L. *hispidus*, rough, shaggy, bristly. (Körting, § 4581.) Der. *hideous-ly*, *hideous-ness*.

HIE, to hasten. (E.) ME. *hien*, *hyen*, *hiȝen*; P. Plowman, B. xx. 322; cf. Chaucer, C. T. 10605 (F 291). The ME. sb. *hie* or *hye*, haste, is also found; id. 4629 (B 209). AS. *hīgian* (*higian?*), to hasten; Grein, ii. 72. β. Allied to Du. *hijgen*, to pant; which seems to be of imitative origin.

HIERARCHY, a sacred government. (F. ─ Gk.) Gascoigne has the pl. *hierarchies*; Steel Glas, 993; ed. Arber, p. 77; spelt *hierarches*, Sir T. Elyot, The Governour, i. 1. § 4. ─ F. *hierarchie*, ' an hierarchy;' Cot. ─ Gk. *ἱεραρχία*, the power or post of an *ἱεράρχης*. ─ Gk. *ἱεράρχης*, a steward or president of sacred rites. ─ Gk. *ἱερ*-, for *ἱερός*, sacred; and *ἄρχειν*, to rule, govern. β. The orig. sense of *ἱερὸς* was ' vigorous;' cognate with Skt. *ishiras*, vigorous, fresh, blooming (in the Peterb. Dict.); see Brugmann, i. § 851. For *ἄρχειν*, see **Arch-**, prefix. Der. *hierarchi-c-al*; we also find *hierarch* (Milton, P. L. v. 468), from Gk. *ἱεράρχης*.

HIEROGLYPHIC, symbolical; applied to picture writing. (L. ─ Gk.) ' The characters which are called *hieroglyphicks*;' Holland, tr. of Plutarch, p. 1051 (R.). ' An *hieroglyphical* answer;' Ralegh, Hist. of the World, b. iii. c. 5. s. 4 (R.). ─ L. *hieroglyphicus*, symbolical. ─ Gk. *ἱερογλυφικός*, hieroglyphic. ─ Gk. *ἱερο*-, decl. stem of *ἱερός*, sacred; and *γλύφειν*, to hollow out, engrave, carve, write in incised characters. See **Hierarchy** and **Glyptic**. Der. *hieroglyphic-al*, -*al-ly*; also the sb. *hieroglyph*, coined by omitting -*ic*.

HIEROPHANT, a revealer of sacred things, a priest. (Gk.) In Warburton's Divine Legation, b. ii. s. 4 (R.). ─ Gk. *ἱεροφάντης*, teaching the rites of worship. ─ Gk. *ἱερο*-, for *ἱερός*, sacred; and *φαίνειν*, to show, explain. See **Hierarchy** and **Phantom**.

HIGGLE, to chaffer, bargain. (E.) ' To *higgle* thus;' Butler, Hudibras, pt. ii. c. 2. l. 491. And used by Fuller, Worthies, Northumberland (R.). A weakened form of *haggle*; see **Haggle** (2). Der. *higgl-er*.

HIGH, tall, lofty, chief, illustrious. (E.) ME. *heigh*, *high*, *hey*, *hy*; Chaucer, C. T., A 316; P. Plowman, B. x. 155. AS. *hēah*, *hēh*; Grein, ii. 44. + Du. *hoog*; Icel. *hār*; Swed. *hög*; Dan. *höi*; Goth. *hauhs*; G. *hoch*; OHG. *hôh*. Teut. type **hauhoz*. β. The orig. sense is ' knoblike,' humped or bunched up; cf. G. *hügel*, a bunch, knob, hillock; Icel. *haugr*, a mound. The still older sense is simply

' rounded;' cf. Lith. *kaukaras*, a hill, *kaukas*, a boil, a swelling; Skt. *kucha-s*, the female breast. √KEUK, to bend, make round; cf. Skt. *kuch*, to contract, bend. Der. *height*, q. v.; *high-ly*; also *high-born*, K. John, v. 2. 79; *high-bred*; *high-coloured*, Ant. and Cleop. ii. 7. 4; *high-fed*; *high-flown*; *high-handed*; *high-minded*, 1 Hen. VI, i. 5. 12; *high-minded-ness*; *high-ness*, Temp. ii. 1. 172; *high-priest*; *high-road*; *high-spirited*; *high-way* = ME. *heigh weye*, P. Plowman, B. x. 155; *high-way-man*; *high-wrought*, Othello, ii. 1. 2; with numerous similar compounds. Also *high-land* (below); and see *how* (2).

HIGHLAND, belonging to a mountainous region. (E.) ' A generation of *highland* thieves and redshanks;' Milton, Observ. on the Art. of Peace (quoted in Todd). AS. *hēahlond*, a high land; from *hēah*, high, and *lond*, land; Cædmon, Exod. 385. Der. *highland-er*; *highlands*.

HIGHT, was or is called. (E.) Obsolete. A most singular word, presenting the sole instance in English of a *passive* verb; the correct phrase was *he hight* = he was (or is) called, or he was named. ' This grisly beast, which lion *hight* by name' = which is called by the name of lion; Mids. Nt. Dr. v. 140. ME. *highte*. ' But ther as I was wont to *highte* [be called] Arcite, Now *highte* I Philostrat;' Chaucer, C. T., A 1557. Older forms *hatte*, *hette*. ' Clarice *hatte* that maide' = the maid was named Clarice; Floriz and Blauncheflur, ed. Lumby, l. 479. ' Thet *hetten* Calef and Iosue' = that were named Caleb and Joshua; Ayenbite of Inwyt, p. 67. And see Stratmann's Dict., s. v. *hāten*. From AS. *hātte*, I am called, I was called; pres. and pt. t. passive or middle, of AS. *hātan*, active verb, to bid, command, call; Grein, ii. 16, 17. + Icel. *heiti*, I am named, from *heita*, to call; G. *ich heisse*, I am named, from *heissen*, to call. β. Best illustrated by Gothic, which has *haitan*, to call, name, pt. t. *haihait*; whence was formed the passive pres. tense *haitada*, I am called, he is called; as in ' Thomas, saei *haitada* Didymus' = Thomas, who is called Didymus; John, xi. 16. See **Hest**.

HILARITY, cheerfulness, mirth. (F. ─ L. ─ Gk.) ' Restraining his ebriety into *hilarity*;' Sir T. Browne, Vulg. Errors, b. v. c. 23, § 16. ─ F. *hilarité*, mirth; omitted by Cotgrave, but see Littré. ─ L. *hilaritātem*, acc. of *hilaritās*, mirth. ─ L. *hilaris*, *hilarus*, cheerful, gay. Not an orig. L. word; but borrowed. ─ Gk. *ἱλαρός*, cheerful, gay. Cf. Gk. *ἵλαος*, propitious, kind; *ἵλημι*, I am gracious. √SEL; whence E. *silly*. Brugmann, iv. § 594. Der. Hence the late word *hilari-ous*, formed as if from a L. **hilariōsus*; *hilarious* does not occur in Todd's Johnson. From same source, *ex-hilarate*. ¶ *Hilary* Term is so called from the festival of St. Hilary (L. *Hilarius*); Jan. 13.

HILDING, a base, menial wretch. (E.) In Shak. used of both sexes; Tam. Shrew, ii. 26; &c. [Not derived, as Dr. Schmidt says, from AS. *healdan*, to hold; which is impossible.] We also find *helding*, *hilding*, *heilding*, applied to a worthless horse, a jade (N. E. D.). Prob. from ME. *helden*, to incline, to bend down. Cf. ME. *heldinge*, a bending aside; AS. *hylding*, a bending (Voc. 382. 2). See **Heel** (2).

HILL, a small mountain. (E.) ME. *hil* (with one *l*); Havelok, 1287; also *hul*, Ancren Riwle, p. 178. AS. *hyll*; Grein, ii. 132. ' Collis, *hyll*;' Wright's Vocab. i. 54, col. 1 (Voc. 177. 24). And see Northumbrian version of St. Luke, xxiii. 30. + MDu. *hil*, *hille*; Oudemans. β. Further allied to Lithuan. *kalnas*, L. *collis*, a hill; *culmen*, a top; Gk. *κολωνός*, a hill. Brugmann, i. § 633. See **Culminate**, and **Holm**. From √QEL, to be elevated, rise up. Der. *hill-y*, *hill-i-ness*; dimin. *hill-ock*, in Shak. Venus and Adonis, 237. ¶ Not connected with G. *hügel*, a hill; for that is related to E. *how*, a hill; see **How** (2).

HILT, the handle of a sword. (E.) In Shak. Hamlet, v. 2. 159; it was common to use the pl. *hilts* with reference to a single weapon; Jul. Cæsar, v. 3. 43. ME. *hilt*; Layamon, 6506. AS. *hilt*, Grein, ii. 75; *helt*, O. E. Texts. + Icel. *hjalt*; Dan. *hjalte*; North Fries. *heelt*; OHG. *helza*, a sword-hilt. Cf. OF. *helt* (from Teutonic). Perhaps allied to Low G. *helft*, an ax-handle, and to **Helve**. Der. *hilt-ed*.

HIM, the objective case of *he*; see **He**.

HIN, a Hebrew liquid measure. (Heb.) In Exod. xxix. 40, &c. Supposed to contain about 6 quarts. ─ Heb. *hin*, a hin; said to be a word of Egyptian origin.

HIND (1), the female of the stag. (E.) ME. *hind*, *hynde*; P. Plowman, B. xv. 274. AS. *hind*, fem.; Grein, ii. 76. + Du. *hinde*, a hind, doe. + Icel., Dan., and Swed. *hind*; OHG. *hinta*, MHG. *hinde*; whence G. *hindin*, a doe, with suffixed (fem.) -*in*. Perhaps allied to Gk. *κεμ-άς*, a young deer. Der. *hind-berry*, a wild raspberry.

HIND (2), a peasant. (E.) In Spenser, F. Q. vi. 8. 12. The *d* is excrescent. ME. *hine*, Chaucer, C. T. 605 (A 603); *hyne*, P. Plowman, B. vi. 133. AS. **hīna*, a domestic; but the word is unauthenticated as a nom. sing., and was orig. a gen. pl.; so that *hīna* really stands for *hīna man* = a man of the domestics. We find *hīna ealdor* = elder of the domestics, i. e. master of a household; Ælfred's tr. of Beda, iii. 9. **β.** Further, *hina* stands for *higna*, gen. pl. of *hiwan* (pl. nom.), domestics; Grein, ii. 78. Cf. *hiwen*, a family; *hiwrǣden*, a household; also G. *hei-rath*, marriage; Goth. *heiwa-frauja*, master of a household. Allied to L. *ciuis*, a citizen. Brugmann, i. § 609.

HIND (3), adj. in the rear. (E.) We say 'hind feet,' i. e. the two feet of a quadruped in the rear. But the older expression is 'hinder feet,' as in St. Brandan, ed. Wright, p. 30, the positive degree not being used; we also find *hynderere*, *hyndrere*, Wyclif, Gen. xvi. 13; *hyndrest*, Chaucer, C. T. 624 (A 622). AS. *hindan*, only as adv., at the back of; *hindeweard*, hindwards, backwards; *hinder*, adv. backwards; Grein, ii. 76. **+** Goth. *hindar*, prep. behind; *hindana*, prep. beyond; G. *hinter*, prep. behind; *hinten*, adv. behind; OHG. *hintar*, comp. adj., hinder. We also find Goth. *hindumists*, hindmost. All from the base which appears in AS. *hin-an* (*heon-an*), hence; while the comp. suffix *-der* answers to Gk. *-τερο-*. See **Hence, He, Behind.** **Der.** *hind-ward*, Wyclif, Ps. xlix. 17, lxix. 4; also *hind-most*, q. v.; *hinder*, verb, q. v.; *be-hind*.

HINDER, to put behind, keep back, check. (E.) ME. *hindren*, *hyndren*; Gower, C. A. i. 311; bk. iii. 937. He also has the sb. *hinderer*; i. 330; iii. 111; bk. iii. 1526; bk. vii. 803. AS. *hindrian*; A. S. Chron. an. 1003. — AS. *hinder*, adv. behind; cf. *hindan*, behind. **+** Icel. *hindra*, to hinder; G. *hindern*. See **Hind** (3). **Der.** *hinder-er*; also *hindr-ance* (for *hinder-ance*), with F. suffix *-ance*; 'damages, hurt, or *hinderaunce*;' Frith's Works, p. 15; and see La Belle Dame sans Merci, 602.

HINDMOST, last. (E.) In Shak. Sonnet, 85. 12; 2 Hen. VI, iii. 1. 2; cf. *henmast*, Barbour, Bruce, viii. 245. The suffix is the word *most*, and the compound is of late formation. **β.** Distinct from AS. *hindema*, hindmost; Grein, ii. 76; where the suffix *-ma* is the same as that seen in L. *opti-mus*, *optu-mus*, best; see **Aftermost**; cf. Goth. *hindumists*, hindmost, Matt. viii. 12; to be divided as *hind-u-m-ists*; cf. Goth. *fru-ma*, first. See **Hind** (3). ¶ Also spelt *hindermost*, as in Holinshed, Hist. Scotland, an. 1290 (R.). And again, we have ME. *hind-r-est*, as in Chaucer, C. T. 624 (A 622).

HINGE, the joint on which a door turns. (E.) The *i* was formerly *e*. ME. *henge* (with hard *g*), a hinge; with dimin. form *hengel*, a hinge. 'As a dore is turned in his *hengis*' [earlier version, *in his heeng*]; Wyclif, Prov. xxvi. 14. 'Hengyl of a dore;' Prompt. Parv. p. 235. 'Hic gumser, a hengylle;' Wright's Vocab. i. 261, col. 1 (Voc. 779. 3). **β.** So called because the door *hangs* upon it; from ME. *hengen*, to hang. 'Henged on a tre;' Havelok, 1429. *Hengen* is a later variant (cf. Icel. *hengja*) of ME. *hangien*, AS. *hangian*, to hang; see **Hang**. Cf. AS. *henge-clif*, a steep cliff, and *stone-henge*; Dan. dial. *hinge*, *hænge*, a hinge (Dan. *hængsel*); Low G. *henge*; MDu. *henge*, *hengene*, a hinge (Du. *hengsel*). For the sound, cf. *singe*, *swinge*. **Der.** *hinge*, verb.

HINT, a slight allusion. (E.) **α.** The verb is later than the sb. 'As I have *hinted* in some former papers;' Tatler, no. 267. First found in 1648. Only the sb. occurs in Shak., where it is a common word; Oth. i. 3. 142, 166. Esp. used in the phrases 'to take the *hint*,' or 'upon this *hint*.' **β.** *Hint* properly signifies 'a thing taken,' i. e. a thing caught or apprehended; being a derivative of the ME. *henten* (pp. *hent*), to seize upon. Palsgrave has: 'I *hente*, I take by vyolence;' also spelt *hinten*. Cf. *hint*, sb., a sudden seizure, Dunbar, Fenyeit Friar, l. 88. 'Hyntyd, raptus; Hyntyn, or revyn, or *hentyn*, rapio, arripio;' Prompt. Parv. p. 240. The earlier spelling of the verb was *henten*, pt. t. *hente*, Chaucer, C. T. 700 (A 698); the pp. *hent* occurs even in Shak. Meas. iv. 6. 14. AS. *hentan*, to seize, to hunt after; Grein, ii. 34. Cf. Goth. *-hinthan*, to seize. See **Hunt. Der.** *hint*, verb.

HIP (1), the haunch, upper part of the thigh. (E.) ME. *hupe*, *hipe*, *hippe*. 'About hire *hipes* large;' Chaucer, C. T. 474 (A 472). 'Hupes had hue faire' = she had fair hips; Alisaunder, l. 190; printed with Will. of Palerne, ed. Skeat. AS. *hype*; Gregory's Pastoral, ed. Sweet, p. 383, l. 2. **+** Du. *heup*; (Dan. *hofte*; Swed. *höft*; from G. *hüfte*); Goth. *hups*; OHG. *huf*. **β.** The suffixed *-t* or *-te* in some of these words stands for the Idg. suffix *-to-*; the older Teut. type is **hupiz*. Perhaps allied to Gk. *κύβος*, the hollow near the hips of cattle. **Der.** *hip-bone*, AS. *hype-bān*; Wright's Vocab. i. 44, col. 1, last line (Voc. 159. 24). ☞ The word *hipped*, depressed, is connected with *hypochondria*; see **Hippish**.

HIP (2), also **HEP**, the fruit of the dog-rose. (E.) ME. *hepe*. 'And swete as is the bremble flour That bereth the rede *hepe*;' Chaucer, C. T. 13677 (B 937). AS. *hēope* (Voc. 133. 36); whence the comp. *hēop-brȳmel*, a hip-bramble; Wright's Vocab. i. 33, col. 1; to translate L. *rubus* (Voc. 138. 37). **+** Dan. *hyben*, pl.; MDan. *hjuben-torn*, hip-thorn; MHG. *hiefe*, OHG. *hiufo*, a bramble-bush.

HIPPISH, hypochondriacal. (Gk.) In Byron, Beppo, st. 64. The word is merely a colloquial substitute for *hypochondriacal*, of which only the first syllable is preserved. Hence *hippish* is for *hyp-ish*. See Somerville's poem entitled 'The Hip.'

HIPPOCAMPUS, a kind of fish. (Gk.) *Hyppocamps* ends a line in W. Browne's Britannia's Pastorals, bk. ii. song 1. It has a head like a horse, and a long flexible tail; whence the name. — Gk. *ἱπποκάμπος*, *ἱπποκάμπη*, a monster, with a horse's head and fish's tail. — Gk. *ἱππο-*, for *ἵππος*, a horse; and *κάμπος*, masc. of *κάμπη*, a caterpillar, also a sea-monster, allied to *κάμπ-τειν*, to bend.

HIPPOPOTAMUS, the river-horse. (L. — Gk.) ME. *ypotamus*, Alexander and Dindimus, ed. Skeat, 157. Also *ypotanos*, King Alisaunder, 6554. Both corrupted from L. *hippopotamus*. — Gk. *ἱπποπόταμος*, the river-horse of Egypt; also called *ἵππος ποτάμιος* = river-dwelling horse. — Gk. *ἱππο-*, for *ἵππος*, a horse; and *ποταμός*, a river. **β.** The Gk. *ἵππος* has a dial. by-form *ἵκκος*, cognate with L. *equus*, a horse; see **Equine.** *Ποταμός* is 'running' water; cf. Gk. *ποτ-ή*, flight, *πέτ-ομαι*, I fly (Prellwitz). ☞ From the same Gk. *ἵππος* we have *hippo-drome*, a race-course for horses; *hippo-phagy*, a feeding on horse-flesh; *hippo-griff*, a monster, half horse, half griffin; &c.

HIRE, wages for service. (E.) ME. *hyre*, Chaucer, C. T. 509 (A 507); also *hure*, *huyre*, *hyre*, P. Plowman, A. ii. 91; B. ii. 122. AS. *hȳr*, fem. (gen. *hȳre*), Luke xix. 23. **+** Du. *huur*, wages, service; Swed. *hyra*, rent, wages; Dan. *hyre*, hire; prov. G. *heuer*, hire (Flügel's Dict.). Teut. type **hūr-ja*, f. **Der.** *hire*, verb, AS. *hȳrian*, Matt. xx. 7; *hire-ling*, AS. *hȳrling*, Mark, i. 20.

HIRSUTE, rough, shaggy, bristly. (L.) In Blount's Gloss., ed. 1674; and in Bacon, Nat. Hist., § 616. — L. *hirsūtus*, rough, bristly. Allied to Gk. *χέρσος*, dry, hard; L. *horrēre*, to bristle. See **Horror. Der.** *hirsute-ness* (Todd).

HIS, of him, of it. (E.) Formerly neut. as well as masc. AS. *his*, gen. m. and n. of *hē*, he. See **He, Its.**

HISS, to make a sound like a serpent or a goose. (E.) Wyclif has *hisshing*, a hissing, 2 Chron. xxix. 8; and *hisse*, v., Isa. v. 26. The L. *sibilat* is glossed by *hyssyt*, i. e. hisses; Wright's Vocab. i. 180, l. 1 (Voc. 627. 15). **+** MFlem. *hisschen*, to hiss; Kilian, Oudemans; Norw. *hyssa*; MSwed. *hyss*, a noise to drive away pigs (Ihre); Gascon *hissa*, to hiss (Moncaut). **β.** Formed from the sound; the Du. *sissen*, G. *zischen*, to hiss, are even more expressive; cf. *fizz*, *whizz*, *whistle*. **Der.** *hiss*, sb.; *hiss-ing*, Jer. xviii. 16, &c.; and see *hist*, *hush*.

HIST, an interjection enjoining silence. (E.) In Shak. Romeo, ii. 2. 159. In Milton, Il Penseroso, 55, the word *hist* appears to mean 'to summon by saying *hist*;' so that 'And the mute silence *hist* along' = summon (and bring) along the mute Silence by saying *hist*. Also *ist*, *'st*. Cf. Dan. *hys*, interj. silence! *hysse*, to hush.

HISTOLOGY, the science which treats of the minute structure of the tissues of plants and animals. (Gk.) A modern scientific term. Coined from Gk. *ἱστο-*, for *ἱστός*, a web; and *-λογία*, from *λόγος*, a discourse, from *λέγειν*, to speak. **β.** The orig. sense of *ἱστός* is a ship's mast, also the bar or beam of a loom, which in Greek looms stood upright; hence, a warp or web. **γ.** So called because standing upright; from Gk. *ἵστημι*, to make to stand, set, place; from √STA, to stand; see **Stand.**

HISTORY, also **STORY,** a narrative, account. (L. — Gk.) *Story* (q. v.) is an abbreviated form. Gower has *histoire*, C. A. iii. 48; bk. vi. 1383. Fabyan gave to his Chronicle (printed in 1516) the name of The Concordance of *Histories*. In older authors, we commonly find the term *storie*, which is of F. origin. *Historie* is Englished directly from L. *historia*, a history. — Gk. *ἱστορία*, a learning by enquiry, information, history. — Gk. *ἱστορ-*, stem of *ἵστωρ* or *ἴστωρ*, knowing, learned; for **ἴδ-τωρ*, from the weak grade *ἰδ-* of *εἰδέναι*, to know. — √WEID, to know; see **Wit. Der.** *histori-an*, formerly *historien*, Sir T. Elyot, The Governour, b. i. c. 24; *histori-c-al*, Tyndal's Works, p. 266, col. 2; *histori-c-al-ly*: *histori-c*; *histori-o-grapher*, a writer of history from Gk. *γράφειν*, to write), Gascoigne's Steel Glas, 981; *histori-o-graphy*.

HISTRIONICAL, relating to the stage. (L.) In Minsheu. 'And is a *histrionical* contempt;' Ben Jonson, Magnetic Lady, A. iii. sc. 4. Coined with suffix *-al*, from L. *histriōnic-us*, of or belonging to a player. — L. *histriōni-*, decl. stem of *histrio*, a player, actor. From Etruscan *hister*, a player; Livy, vii. 2.

HIT, to light upon, to strike, to attain to. (Scand.) ME. *hitten*, P. Plowman, B. xii. 108; xvi. 87; Layamon, l. 1550. — Icel. *hitta*, to hit upon, meet with; Swed. *hitta*, to find, discover, light upon; Dan. *hitte*, to hit upon. **Der.** *hit*, sb.

HITCH, to move by jerks, catch slightly, suddenly. (E.) ME. *hicchen*. '*Hytchyn*, *hychyn*, *hytchen*, or remevyn, *Amoveo*, *moveo*, *removeo*;' Prompt. Parv. p. 239; where the word should have been printed as *hycchyn* or *hycchen*. We also find: '*Hatchyd* [read *hacchyd*], or *remevyd*, *hichid*, *hychyd*, *Amotus*, *remotus*;' ibid. Cf. Lowland Scotch *hatch*, *hotch*, to move by jerks; Jamieson. Also prov. E. *hotch*, *hutch*, to jerk, to hitch; *huck*, to draw near, to hitch (E.D.D.). Of obscure origin. Perhaps related to prov. E. *huck*, to hunch up; Du. *hokken*, to squat, to crouch, also to stick; as *het hokt*, there is an obstacle (or hitch); Calisch. If so, it is allied to *huckster*. See Phil. Soc. Trans. 1903, p. 150. **Der.** *hitch*, sb.

HITHE, HYTHE, a small haven. (E.) ME. *hithe*; as in *Garleke-hithe*, P. Plowman, B. v. 324; and see Prompt. Parv., p. 242, note 1. AS. *hȳð*, a haven; Grein, ii. 126. Teut. type **hūthjā*, f.

HITHER, to this place. (E.) ME. *hider*, *hither*, Chaucer, C. T. 674 (A 672); the right form in Chaucer being probably *hider*, since he rimes *thider* with *slider*; C. T. 1265 (A 1263). [So also ME. *fader, moder* are now *father, mother*.] AS. *hider* (common); Grein, ii. 71.+ Icel. *heðra* (for *hiðra*); Goth. *hidrē.*+L. *citrā*, on this side. β. From the Teutonic pronominal base *hi-* (see **He**); with a suffix allied to the Idg. comparative suffix *-ter*. **Der.** *hither-to*; *hither-ward*, ME. *hiderward*, P. Plowman, B. vi. 323.

HIVE, a basket for bees. (E.) The old sense is 'hood.' ME. *hyue* (with *u* for *v*), Chaucer, C. T. 15398 (B 4582). Spelt *hyfe*, Wright's Vocab. i. 223, col. 2 (Voc. 706. 41). AS. *hȳf*, f.; Voc. 123. 16; '*Aluearia*, hyfi;' Corpus Gloss. 543. Teut. type **hūfiz.*+Du. *huif*, a hood, a hive (see Franck); Dan. dial. *hyve*. Allied to L. *cūpa*, a tub, a cup. See **Cupola**.

HO, HOA, a call to excite attention. (E.) 'And cryed *ho*!' Chaucer, C. T., A 1706. Merely a natural exclamation; cf. Icel. *hō*, interj. ho!, also Icel. *hōa*, to shout out ho!

HOAR, white, grayish white. (E.) ME. *hor, hoor*; Chaucer, C. T. 3876, 7764 (A 3878, D 2182); P. Plowman, B. vi. 85. AS. *hār*, Grein, ii. 14.+Icel. *hārr*, hoar, hoary; G. *hehr*, exalted, OHG. *hēr*, proud, lofty, orig. 'reverend.' Teut. type **hairoz* (= *hai-roz*), lit. 'shining;' hence, white. The base *hai-* appears in Goth. *hais*, a torch, G. *hei-ter*, orig. 'bright,' Icel. *hei-ð*, brightness; cf. Skt. *kētu-s*, a sign, a meteor (Kluge). ¶ To be kept distinct from Icel. *hār*, which is the E. *high* (the *r* being merely the sign of the nom. case); and also from E. *hair*. **Der.** *hoar-y*, occurring in the comp. *horilocket*, having hoary locks, Layamon, 25845; *hoar-i-ness*; also *hoar-frost*, ME. *hoorfrost*, Wyclif, Exod. xvi. 14; also *hoar-hound*, q.v.

HOARD, a store, a treasure. (E.) ME. *hord*, Chaucer, C. T. 3262; Gower, C. A. iii. 155; bk. vii. 2094. AS. *hord*, Grein, ii. 96. +Icel. *hodd*; G. *hort*; Goth. *huzd*, a treasure. β. The Teutonic type is **huzdo-*, due to Idg. **kudh-dho-*, 'a thing hidden;' from **kudh*, weak grade of √KEUDH, whence Gk. κεύθ-ειν, AS. *hȳd-an*, to hide. See **Hide** (1). Brugmann, i. § 699. **Der.** *hoard*, verb, AS. *hordian* in Sweet's A. S. Reader; cf. Goth. *huzdjan*, to hoard; *hoard-er*, AS. *hordere* (Bosworth).

HOARDING, HOARD, a fence enclosing a house while builders are at work. (F.−Du.; *or* Du.) Rare in books; it is difficult to say how long it may have existed in E. as a builder's term. *Hoard* occurs in 1757 (N. E. D.). Either taken directly from Du. *horde*, a hurdle; or from OF. *hourd*, 'a scaffold,' in Froissart (Godefroy, s. v. *hourt*), which is borrowed from it. The suffix *-ing* is, of course, English. Cf. Picard *hourdage*, a scaffold (Corblet); AF. *hurdys*, a scaffold, in Liber Albus; p. 477. The true E. word is **Hurdle**, q.v.

HOARHOUND, HOREHOUND, the name of a plant. (E.) The true *hoarhound* is the white, *Marrubium vulgare*; the first part of the word is *hoar*, and the plant is so called because its bushy stems 'are covered with white woolly down;' Johns, Flowers of the Field. The final *d* is excrescent; the ME. form being *horehune*. '*Marubium, horehune*;' Wright's Vocab. i. 139 (Voc. 554. 2). AS. *hārhūne*; or simply *hūne*; for numerous examples of which see Cockayne's A.S. Leechdoms, iii. 334; where we also find: 'the syllable *hār*, hoary, describes the aspect, so that "black horehound" shows how we have forgotten our own language.' The words are also found separate; *þa hāran hūnan*. We also find *hwite hāre hūnan*, white horehound, an early indication of the black horehound, *Ballota nigra*, a very strong-smelling plant. β. The first syllable is obvious; see **Hoar**. The second syllable is unexplained. ¶ It thus appears that the right names should have been *hoar houn* and *black houn*; *white hoarhound* involves a reduplication; and *black hoarhound*, a contradiction.

HOARSE, having a rough, harsh voice. (E.) The *r* in this word is probably intrusive, and is (generally) not sounded; still, it was inserted at an early period. ME. *hoos, hos, hors*; all three spellings occur in P. Plowman, B. xvii. 324 (and various readings); *hors*, Chaucer, Book of the Duchesse, 347. AS. *hās*, Grein, ii. 14.+Dan. *hæs*; Swed. *hes*; Du. *heesch*; G. *heiser*. β. All from a Teutonic type **haisoz*; or (if the *r* be original) **hairsoz*; perhaps the latter is indicated by the Icel. form *hāss*. See N. E. D. **Der.** *hoarse-ly, hoarseness*.

HOARY, white; see **Hoar**.

HOAX, to trick, to play a practical joke. (Low L.) In Todd's Johnson; not found in early writers. The late appearance of the word suggests that it is a corruption of *hocus*, used in just the same sense. '*Legerdemain*, with which these jugglers *hocus* the vulgar;' Nalson, in Todd. 'This gift of *hocus-pocussing*;' L'Estrange (Todd). See **Hocus-Pocus**. **Der.** *hoax*, sb.

HOB (1), **HUB,** the nave of a wheel, part of a grate. (E.) The true sense is 'projection.' Hence *hub*, 'the nave of a wheel (Oxfordshire); a small stack of hay, the mark to be thrown at in quoits, the hilt of a weapon; *up to the hub*, as far as possible;' Halliwell. The mark for quoits is the same word as *hob*, 'a small piece of wood of a cylindrical form, used by boys to set on end, to put half-pence on to chuck or pitch at;' Halliwell. *Hob* also means the shoe (projecting edge) of a sledge. The *hob* of a fire-place is explained in the N. E. D. as having been orig. 'a boss or mass of clay behind the fire-place.' EFries. *hobbe*, a rough tump of grassy land rising out of water; *hubbel*, a projection.+Du. *hobbel*, a knob; G. *hübel*, OHG. *hubel*, a hillock. [Cf. Du. *heuvel*, a hill; AS. *hofer*, a hump.] Lith. *kup-stas*, a tump of grass. **Der.** *hob-nail*, a nail with a projecting head, 1 Hen. IV, ii. 4. 398; 2 Hen. VI, iv. 10. 63; *hob-nail-ed*.

HOB (2), a clown, a rustic, a fairy. (F.−OHG.) 'The *hobbes* as wise as grauest men;' Drant's tr. of Horace's Art of Poetry (R.). 'From elves, *hobs*, and fairies That trouble our dairies;' Beaumont and Fletcher, Monsieur Thomas, iv. 6. See Nares; also *Hob* in Atkinson's Cleveland Glossary, where, however, the suggestion of identifying *hob* with *elf* is to be rejected. It is quite certain that *Hob* was a common personal name, and in early use. 'To beg of Hob and Dick;' Cor. ii. 3. 123. That it was in early use is clear from its numerous derivatives, as *Hobbs, Hobbins, Hobson, Hopkins, Hopkinson*. β. That *Hob*, strange as it may seem, was a popular corruption of *Robin* is clearly borne out by the equally strange corruption of *Hodge* from *Roger*, as well as by the name of *Robin Goodfellow* for the hob-goblin Puck; (Mids. Nt. Dr. ii. 1. 40). Robert Bruce was nicknamed 'kyng Hobbe;' Polit. Songs, p. 216. γ. The name *Robin* is French, and, like *Robert*, is of OHG. origin; Littré considers it as a mere pet corruption from *Robert*, a name early known in England, as being that of the eldest son of Will. I. **Der.** *hob-goblin* (see goblin); spelt *hob-goblyng* in Palsgrave, who translates it by F. *goblin*.

HOBBLE, to limp, walk with a limp. (E.) ME. *hobelen* (with one *b*), P. Plowman, A. i. 113; P. Plowman's Crede, 106; and see Barbour's Bruce, iv. 447. Practically, the frequentative of *hop*; so that the lit. sense is 'to hop often.'+Du. *hobbelen*, to toss, ride on a hobby-horse, stammer, stutter (all with the notion of repetition of uneven motion); frequent. of *hobben*, to toss up and down; allied to *huppen, huppelen*, to hop, skip. Cf. EFries. and Westphal. *hubbelen*, to hobble; OF. *hober*, to move, bestir oneself; prov. G. *hoppeln*, to hop, hobble (Flügel). See **Hop** (1). **Der.** *hobble*, sb.

HOBBLEDEHOY, a youth approaching manhood. (E.) A jocose word, very variously spelt (see N. E. D.). Palsgrave, in 1540, has *hobledehoye*; Cotgrave explains F. *marmaille* as 'young rascals . . a troop of . . unprofitable *hoberdihoies*.' The true origin is unknown. Perhaps suggested by E. *hobble*, expressive of clumsy movement, and *hoy*! as an interjection. Cf. F. *hober*, 'to remove from place to place, a rustic word;' Cot. Low G. *hop-hei*, an assembly of common people who dance about; Alsace *hoppetihopp*, a giddy, flighty, eccentric man (Martin); Low G. *hupperling*, a boy who jumps about, and cannot be still. *Hobby* was also a pet name for *Robert*; see **Hobby** (1).

HOBBY (1), **HOBBY-HORSE,** an ambling nag, a toy like a horse, a favourite pursuit. (F.−OHG.) See *Hobby* in Trench, Select Glossary. A *hobby* is now a favourite pursuit, but formerly a toy in imitation of a prancing nag, the orig. sense being a kind of prancing horse. In Hamlet, iii. 2. 142. 'They have likewise excellent good horses, we term the *hobbies*;' Holland, Camden's Ireland, p. 63. A corruption of ME. *hobin*, a nag; Barbour's Bruce, ed. Skeat, xiv. 68, 500; [whence OF. *hobin*, 'a hobby, a little ambling and short-maned horse;' Cot.] β. But this ME. *Hobin* was a horse's name (see N. E. D.); of which *Dobbin* is a familiar variant. And *Hobin* is but an E. variant of F. *Robin*; see further under **Hob** (2).

HOBBY (2), a small species of falcon. (F.−Du.) Obsolete. Cotgrave translates MF. *hobreau* by 'the hawke tearmed a hobby.' ME. *hobi, hoby* (with one *b*). '*Hoby*, hawke;' Prompt. Parv.; pl. *hobies*, Sir T. Elyot, The Governour, cap. xviii; see Spec. of English, ed. Skeat, p. 204. Like other terms of falconry, it is of F. origin; being from OF. *hobet*, a hobby, allied to the MF. *hobreau* mentioned above. So named from its movement.−OF. *hober*, 'to stirre, move, remove from place to place;' Cot.−MDu. *hobben*, to toss, move up and down. See **Hobble**. ¶ This etymology is confirmed by noting that the OF. verb *hober* was sometimes spelt *auber* (Cot.); corresponding to which latter form, the hobby was also called *aubereau* (Cot.).

HOBGOBLIN, a kind of fairy. (F.−OHG.) In Minsheu, ed. 1627; and in Mids. Nt. Dr. ii. 1. 40; *hobgoblyng* in Palsgrave. Compounded of *hob* and *goblin*. See **Hob** (2) and **Goblin**.

HOBNAIL, a kind of nail. (E.) See **Hob** (1).

HOBNOB, HABNAB, take or leave, in any case, at random. (E.) Compounded of *hab* and *nab*, derived respectively from AS. *habban*, to have, and *nabban*, not to have. **1.** In one aspect it means 'take it or leave it ;' implying free choice, and hence a familiar invitation to drink, originating the phrase ' to hob-nob together.' ' Hob-nob is his word ; give't or take't ;' Twelfth Night, iii. 4. 262. 2. In another aspect, it means hit or miss, at random ; also, in any case. ' Philautus determined, hab, nab, to sende his letters ;' i.e. whatever might happen ; Lyly's Euphues, ed. Arber, p. 354. ' Although set down hab-nab, at random ;' Butler's Hudibras, pt. ii. c. 3. l. 990. **β.** Hab is from AS. habban ; see **Have.** Nab is from AS. nabban, a contracted form of ne habban, not to have.

HOCK (1), the hough ; see **Hough.**

HOCK (2), the name of a wine. (G.) ' What wine is it ? Hock ;' Beaum. and Fletcher, The Chances, A. v. sc. 3. Shortened from Hockamore (Stanford Dict.), which was an Anglicised form of Hochheimer, i.e. wine of Hochheim, the name of a place in Germany, on the river Main, whence the wine came. It means ' high home ;' see **High** and **Home.**

HOCKEY, the name of a game. (E.) Also called hawkey ; so named because played with a hooked stick ; see **Hook.** ¶ In some places called bandy, the ball being bandied backwards and forwards.

HOCUS-POCUS, a juggler's trick, a juggler. (Low L.) Hokos-Pokos is the name of the juggler in Ben Jonson, Magnetic Lady, Chorus at end of Act i. In Butler's Hudibras, it means a trick ; ' As easily as hocus-pocus ;' pt. iii. c. 3. l. 716. If the word may be said to belong to any language at all, it is bad Latin, as shown by the termination -us. The reduplicated word was a mere invention, used by jugglers in playing tricks. ' At the playing of every trick, he [a juggler in the times of James I] used to say "hocus pocus, tontus, talontus, vade celeriter, jubeo," ' Ady's Candle in the Dark, Treat. of Witches, &c. p. 29 ; cited in Todd. See the whole article in Todd. ¶ The ' derivations' sometimes assigned are ridiculous ; the word no more needs to be traced than its companions tontus and talontus. **Der.** hocus, to cheat ; see Todd. Hence also hoax, q. v.

HOD, a kind of trough for carrying bricks on the shoulder. (MDu.) ' A lath-hammer, trowel, a hod, or a traie ;' Tusser. Five Hundred Points of Husbandry, sect. 16, st. 16 (E. D. S. edition, p. 37, last line). Cotgrave has : ' Oiseau, a bird . . also, a Hodd, the Tray wherein Masons carry their Mortar.'—MDu. hodde, ' a basket or a maund ;' given by Hexham, s. v. Botte. Cf. Swed. dial. hodda, hudda, f., a hut ; MDan. hodde, a hut, hudde, a small room ; cognate with Alsace hutte, G. hotte, a wooden vessell, a tub, a vintager's dosser (Flügel) ; [whence F. hotte, ' a scuttle, dosser, basket to carry on the back ; the right hotte is wide at the top and narrow at the bottom ;' Cot.] **β.** All (perhaps) from Teut. *hud-, weak grade of *heud- = Gk. κευθ-, to hide ; the orig. sense being ' cover ' or ' case.' See Phil. Soc. Trans., 1902, p. 671. ¶ Note that E. has the Low G. form, but F. the HG. form ; whence ME. hotte, in Chaucer, Hous of Fame, 1940 ; see my note.

HODGE-PODGE, a mixture ; see **Hotchpot.**

HOE, an instrument for cutting up weeds, &c. (F.—G.) ' How, pronounced as [i.e. to rime with] mow and throw ; a narrow iron rake without teeth, to cleanse gardens from weeds ; rastrum Gallicum ' [a French rake] ; Ray's Collection of South-Country Words, ed. 1691. Written haugh by Evelyn (R.).—F. houe, ' an instrument of husbandry, which hath a crooked handle, or helve of wood, some two foot long, and a broad and in-bending head of iron ;' Cot. ; Norm. dial. hoe.—OHG. houwa, G. haue, a hoe.—OHG. houwan, to hew ; cognate with E. hew. See **Hew.** **Der.** hoe, vb.

HOG, the name of an animal, a pig. (E.) ME. hog ; Wyclif, Luke, xv. 16 ; King Alisaunder, 1885. Also hogge, ' maialis, est enim porcus carens testiculis ;' Cathol. Anglicum, p. 187. Cf. hog-sheep, one clipped the first year. It occurs as AS. hocg in Hocges tūn, Kemble, Cod. Dipl. Moisy, ed. 1895, gives Norm. dial. hogge, a six-months' lamb, a pig ; and hogastre, a two-year-old sheep (both prob. from E.). AS. hogg, Cambridge Phil. Soc. Proceedings, lxi-lxiii (1902), p. 13, l. 2. **β.** Cf. also the prov. E. hog, vb., to cut short a horse's mane, to cut a hedge, to pollard a tree, to hack off (E. D. D.). —Norw. hogga, to cut (Aasen) ; allied to Icel. höggva (base hagg-), to hew. See Phil. Soc. Trans., 1903, p. 151. **Der.** hogg-ish, hogg-ish-ly, hogg-ish-ness ; hog-ring-er ; hog's-lard.

HOGSHEAD, a measure containing about 52½ gallons ; a half-pipe. (E.) In Shak. Temp. iv. 252 ; L. L. L. iv. 2. 88 ; &c. Also in Cotgrave, to translate F. tonneau ; it seems to have meant a large cask. Minsheu, ed. 1627, refers us to ' An. 1 Rich. III, cap. 13.' Cf. ' ij pipes, v hogges-hedes,' in The Earl of Derby's Expeditions (Camden Soc.), p. 156 (A. D. 1392). Certainly derived from ME. hogges hed, ' hog's head ;' a fanciful name, of which the origin is not known ; but it seems as sensible as pipe in ' pipe of wine.' Hence were borrowed MDan. hogshoved, a hog's head, modified into Dan. oxehoved, as if it meant ' ox-head ;' Low G. hukeshovet, a hogshead (Lübben) ; also Swed. oxhufvud, a hogshead, lit. ' ox-head ;' G. oxhoft, a hogshead ; Du. oxhooft. Cf. also prov. E. hogget, a hogshead, a large cask.

HOIDEN, HOYDEN, a romping girl. (MDu.) See hoyden in Trench, Select Glossary ; in old authors, it is usually applied to the male sex, and means a clown, a lout, a rustic. ' Badault, a fool, dolt, sot, . . . gaping hoydon ;' Cot. ' Falourdin, a luske, lowt, . . . lumpish hoydon ;' id. ' Hilts. You mean to make a hoiden or a hare Of me, to hunt counter thus, and make these doubles ;' Ben Jonson, Tale of a Tub, A. ii. sc. 1.—MDu. heyden (mod. Du. heiden), a heathen, gentile ; also a gipsy, vagabond ; Sewel.—MDu. heyde, a heath. See **Heathen, Heath.** ¶ This derivation, proposed by Skinner, is probable enough. The W. hoeden, having only the modern E. meaning of ' coquette,' must have been borrowed from English, and is not the original, as some have supposed.

HOIST, to heave, raise with tackle. (MDu.) The t is excrescent, and due to confusion with the pp. The verb is properly hoise, with pp. hoist = hoised. ' Hoised up the main-sail ;' Acts, xxvii. 40. Shak. has both hoise and hoist, and (in the pp.) both hoist and hoisted ; Rich. III, iv. 4. 529 ; Temp. i. 2. 148 ; Hamlet, iii. 4. 207 ; Antony, iii. 10. 15, iv. 12. 34, v. 2. 55. ' We hoyse up mast and sayle ;' Sackville's Induction, st. 71 (A.D. 1563). ' I hyse up the sayle ;' Palsgrave. ' Made the saylles to be hyssed uppe ;' Caxton, Eneydos, ch. 31, p. 116. ' With anker hoist ;' Lydgate, Troy-book, bk. iii. c. 13 ; fol. I. i (1555).—MDu. hyssen, to hoise (Sewel) ; mod. Du. hijschen. [The MDu. y (mod. ij) being sounded like English long i, the vowel-change is slight.]—Low G. hisen, hiessen, to hoist ; whence Dan. heise, hisse, to hoist ; Swed. hissa, to hoist ; hissa upp, to hoist up. Cf. F. hisser, to hoist a sail, borrowed from the Du. or Low G. ; quite distinct from F. hausser, to exalt, which is from L. altus, high (F. haut).

HOLD (1), to keep, retain, defend, restrain. (E.) ME. holden, Chaucer, C. T. 12116 (C 182). AS. healdan, haldan, Grein, ii. 50. + Du. houden ; Icel. halda ; Swed. hålla ; Dan. holde ; Goth. haldan ; G. halten. Teut. type *haldan- ; pt. t. *he-hald. **Der.** hold, sb., Chaucer, C. T. 10481 (F 167) ; hold-fast, hold-ing ; be-hold, up-hold.

HOLD (2), the ' hold ' of a ship. (Du.) ' A hulk better stuffed in the hold ;' 2 Hen. IV, ii. 4. 70. Not named, as might be supposed, from what it holds ; but a nautical term, borrowed (like most other such) from the Dutch. The d is really excrescent, and due to a natural confusion with the E. verb. The right sense is ' hole.'—Du. hol, a hole, cave, den, cavity ; Sewel gives also ' het hol van een schip, the ship's hold or hull.' Cognate with E. **Hole,** q. v.

HOLE, a cavity, hollow place. (E.) ME. hole, hol ; Chaucer, C. T. 3440, 3442 ; Havelok, 1813. AS. hol, a cave ; Grein, ii. 92. + Du. hol ; Icel. hol ; Dan. hul ; Swed. hål. Cf. also Goth. hulundi, a hollow, cave ; us-hulōn, to hollow out, Matt. xxvii. 60. **β.** Teut. type *hulom, n. ; orig. neut. of *huloz, adj. hollow, as in AS. hol, Du. hol, Icel. holr, Dan. hul, G. hohl. Prob from *hul-, weak grade of Teut. *helan-, to cover ; see **Hell.** ¶ Not allied to Gk. κοῖλος, hollow.

HOLIBUT, a fish. (E.) See **Halibut.**

HOLIDAY, a holy day, festival, day of amusement. (E.) For holy day. Spelt holy day ; Chaucer, C. T. 3309 ; haliday, P. Plowman, B. v. 409. See **Holy** and **Day.**

HOLINESS, a being holy. (E.) See **Holy.**

HOLLA, HALLO, stop, wait ! (F.) Not the same word as halloo, q. v., but somewhat differently used in old authors. The true sense is stop ! wait ! and it was at first used as an interjection simply, though easily confused with halloo, and thus acquiring the sense of to shout. ' Holla, stand there !' Othello, i. 2. 56. ' Cry holla [stop !] to thy tongue ;' As You Like It, iii. 2. 257.—F. holà, ' an interjection, hoe there, enough ; . . also, hear you me, or come hither ;' Cot.—F. ho, interjection ; and là, there. **β.** The F. là is an abbreviation from L. illāc, that way, there, allied to illic, pron. he yonder. **Der.** holla, hollo, verb ; K. Lear, iii. 1. 55 ; Twelfth Night, i. 5. 291. ¶ The form hallo is due to confusion with halloo.

HOLLAND, Dutch linen. (Du.) In Shak. 1 Hen. IV, iii. 3. 82. ' A sheet of feyn Holond ;' Cov. Myst. p. 241. From the name of the country ; Du. Holland. Orig. form Holt-land, i.e. wood-land ; see **Holt.** (N. E. D.) **Der.** from the same source, hollands, i. e. gin made in Holland.

HOLLOW, vacant, concave ; as sb., a hole, cavity. (E.) ME. holwe, Chaucer, C. T. 291, 1365 (A 291, 1363). Regularly formed from AS. holʒe, dat. form of holh, only as a sb., signifying a hollow place, vacant space ; also spelt holg ; see Cockayne's A. S. Leechdoms, iii. 365 ; Gregory's Pastoral, ed. Sweet, p. 218, ll. 1, 3, 4, 9 ; p. 241, l. 7. Cf. OHG. huliwa, a pool, puddle. An extended form from AS. hol, a hole ; see **Hole.** **Der.** hollow, verb ; ' hollow your body more, sir, thus ;' Ben Jonson, Every Man in his Humour, ed. Wheatley, i. 5. 136 ; hollow-ly, Temp. iii. 1. 70 ; hollow-ness, ME. holownesse, Chaucer, Troil. v. 1809 ; hollow-eyed, Com. Errors, v. 240 ; hollow-hearted, Rich. III, iv. 4. 435.

HOLLY, the name of a prickly shrub. (E.) The word has lost a final n. ME. holin, holyn. The F. hous [holly] is glossed by holyn in Wright's Vocab. i. 163, l. 17; the spellings *holin, holie* both occur in the Ancren Riwle, p. 418, note *l*. AS. *holen, holegn*; Cockayne's A. S. Leechdoms, iii. 332. + W. *celyn*; Corn. *celin*; Bret. *kelen, helly*; Gael. *cuilionn*; Irish *cuileann*, holly. Idg. type **kolenno-*; Stokes-Fick, p. 91. **β**. The base of the AS. word is also preserved in Du. *hulst*, Low G. *hulse*, holly; and from the older form (*hulis, huls*) of the G. word the F. *houx* is derived. Der. *holm-oak*, q. v.

HOLLYHOCK, a kind of mallow. (E.) It should be spelt with one *l*, like *holiday*. ME. *holihoc*, to translate L. *althea* and OF. *ymalue*, in a list of plants; Wright's Vocab. i. 140, col. 1, l. 6 (Voc. 556. 24). [Here the OF. *ymalue* = mod. F. *guimauve*, the marsh mallow (Cot.).] Also spelt *holihocce, holihoke*; see Cockayne's Leechdoms, iii. 332, col. 1, bottom. Compounded from ME. *holi*, holy; and *hocce, hoke, hoc*, a mallow, from AS. *hoc*, a mallow; id. Minsheu, ed. 1627, gives '*Holie hocke*, i.e. *malua sacra*.' **β**. The mallow was also called in AS. *hocléaf*. Cf. W. *hocys*, mallows; *hocys bendigaid*, hollyhock, lit. 'blessed mallow' (where *bendigaid* is equivalent to L. *benedictus*); but this W. form is merely borrowed from the AS. nom. pl. *hoccas*. **γ**. 'Of hagiological origin; another name was *caulis Sancti Cuthberti*;' N. E. D.

HOLM, an islet in a river; flat land near a river. (Scand.) '*Holm*, a river-island;' Coles, ed. 1684. '*Holm*, in old records, an hill, island, or fenny ground, encompassed with little brooks;' Phillips, ed. 1706. The true sense is 'a mound,' or any slightly rising ground; and, as such ground often has water round it, it came to mean an island. Again, as a rising slope is often situate beside a river, it came to mean a bank, wharf, or dockyard, as in German. The most curious use is in AS., where the main sea itself is often called *holm*, from its convex shape; the later senses are Scandinavian. ME. *holm*. '*Holm*, place besydone a water, *Hulmus*;' Prompt. Parv. p. 243; see Way's note, which is full of information about the word. [The Low L. *hulmus* is nothing but the Teutonic word Latinised.]—Icel. *hólmr, hólmi, holmr*, an islet; 'even meadows on the shore with ditches behind them are in Icelandic called *holms*;' Dan. *holm*, a holm, quay, dockyard; Swed. *holme*, a small island; whence G. *holm*, a hill, island, dockyard, wharf (Flügel). + L. *culmen*, a mountain-top; cf. L. *collis*, a hill. See **Culminate** and **Hill.**

HOLM-OAK, the evergreen oak. (E.) Cotgrave translates MF. *yeuse* by 'the *holme oake*, barren scarlet oak, French oak.' The tree is the *Quercus Ilex*, or common evergreen oak, 'a most variable plant, .. with leaves varying from being as prickly as a holly to being as even at the edge as an olive;' Eng. Cyclop. s. v. *Quercus*. Whether because it is an evergreen, or because its leaves are sometimes prickly, we at any rate know that it is so called from its resemblance to the *holly*. **β**. The ME. name for *holly* was *holin*, sometimes phonetically varied to *holm* or *holy*. '*Holme*, or holy;' Prompt. Parv. p. 244; and see Way's note. '*Hollie*, or *Holmtree*;' Minsheu. The form *holm* is in Chaucer, C. T. 2923 (A 2921). Thus *holm-oak* = *holly-oak*. See **Holly.**

HOLOCAUST, an entire burnt sacrifice. (L. — Gk.) So called because the victim offered was burnt entire. It occurs early, in the Story of Genesis and Exodus, ed. Morris, 1319, 1326, where it is plainly taken from the Vulgate version of Gen. xxii. 8. — L. *holocaustum*; Gen. xxii. 8. — Gk. ὁλόκαυστον, neut. of ὁλόκαυστος, ὁλόκαυτος, burnt whole. — Gk. ὁλο-, for ὅλος, whole, entire; and καίειν (fut. καύσ-ω), to burn. **β**. The Gk. ὅλος is cognate with Skt. *sarva(s)*, all. Brugmann, i. § 319. For καίειν see **Caustic.**

HOLOTHURIAN, belonging to the genus of sea-slugs; as sb., a sea-slug, sea-cucumber, trepang. (L. — Gk.) Modern. — Modern L. *holothūria*, neut. pl. of Gk. ὁλοθούριον, a kind of zoophyte (Aristotle).

HOLSTER, a leathern case for a pistol. (Du. — G.) Merely 'a case;' though now restricted to a peculiar use. In Butler, Hudibras, pt. i. c. 1. l. 391. — Du. *holster*, a pistol-case, holster; also, a soldier's knapsack (Sewel). **β**. The word is not orig. E., though we find *hulstred* = covered, Rom. of the Rose, 6146; and AS. *heolstor*, a hiding-place, cave, covering, Grein, ii. 67; as well as Icel. *hulstr*, a case, sheath; Goth. *hulistr*, a veil, 2 Cor. iii. 13. **γ**. But any real connexion with these words is very doubtful; as the Du. word appears to have been borrowed (with change of *ft* to *st*) from G. *holfter, hulfter*, a holster; MHG. *hulfter*, a quiver; from OHG. *hulft*, a cover, case (Franck, Kluge). Hexham has MDu. *huelfte*, 'a galloch to weare with shoes or bootes.'

HOLT, a wood, woody hill. (E.) '*Holt*, a small wood, or grove;' Kersey, ed. 1715. ME. *holt*, Chaucer, C. T. 6. 'Hoc virgultum, a *holt*;' Wright's Vocab. i. 270, col. 1 (Voc. 796. 29). AS. *holt*, a wood, grove; Grein, ii. 95. + Du. *hout* (MDu. *holt*), wood, timber; Icel. *holt*, a copse; G. *holz*, a wood, grove; also wood, timber. Teut. stem **hulto-*, Idg. stem **kəldo-*. Allied to OIrish *caill, coill* (for **cald-*), a wood; W. *celli*, a grove; Russ. *koloda*, a log; Gk. κλάδος, a twig. Stokes-Fick, p. 82.

HOLY, sacred, pure, sainted. (E.) The word is nothing but ME.

hool (now spelt *whole*) with suffix *-y*. ME. *holi, holy*; Chaucer, C. T. 178; AS. *hālig*; Grein, ii. 7. + Du. *heilig*; Icel. *heilagr*, often contracted to *helgr*; Dan. *hellig*; Swed. *helig*; G. *heilig*; Goth. *hailag*, neut., in an inscription. Teut. type **hailagoz*, a derivative of Teut. **hailoz*, whole (AS. *hāl*) or of **hailoz* or **hailiz*, sb., a good omen. Cf. Irish *cél*, W. *coel*, an omen; Stokes-Fick, p. 88. See **Whole. Der.** *holi-ly*; *holi-ness*, AS. *hālignes*; *holi-day*, q. v.; *holly-hock* (for *holy hock*), q. v.; *hali-but* (= *holy but*), q. v.

HOMAGE, the submission of a vassal to a lord. (F. — L.) In early use. In Rob. of Glouc. p. 46, l. 5; l. 1061; P. Plowman, B. xii. 155. — OF. *homage*, later *hommage*, the service of a vassal. Late L. *homāticum* (also *homināticum*), the service of a vassal or 'man.' — L. *homo* (stem *homin-*), a man; hence, a servant, vassal. See **Human.** ¶ The AS. *guma*, a man, is cognate with L. *homo*; see **Bridegroom.**

HOME, native place, place of residence. (E.) ME. *hoom, home*; Chaucer, C. T. 2367 (A 2365); P. Plowman, B. v. 365; vi. 203; common in the phrase 'to go *home*.' AS. *hām*, home, a dwelling; Grein, ii. 9. The acc. case is used adverbially, as in *hām cuman*, to come home; cf. L. *īre domum*. + Du. *heem*, a farm; *heim*, in the comp. *heimelijk*, private, secret; Icel. *heimr*, an abode, village, *heima*, home; Dan. *hjem*, home; also used adverbially, as in E.; Swed. *hem*, home; and used as adv.; G. *heim*; Goth. *haims*, a village. + Lithuanian *kēmas*, OPruss. *caymis*, a village (Fick, iii. 75). Teut. types **haimoz, *haimiz*. Some compare Skt. *kshēma(s)*, safety, safe abode, from *kshi*, to dwell; but this is to be rejected. Cf. Brugmann, i. § 920. Der. *home-bred*, Rich. II, i. 3. 187; *home-farm*; *home-felt*; *home-keeping*, Two Gent. of Verona, ii. 1. 2; *home-less*, AS. *hāmlēas* (Grein); *home-less-ness*; *home-ly*, Chaucer, C. T. 330 (A 328); *home-li-ness*, ME. *homlinesse*, Chaucer, C. T. 8305 (E 429); *home-made*; *home-sick*; *home-sick-ness*; *home-spun*, Mids. Nt. Dr. iii. 1. 79; *home-stall*; *home-stead* (see **Stead**); *home-ward*, AS. *hāmweard*, Gen. xxiv. 61; *home-wards*.

HOMER, a large Hebrew measure. (Heb.) As a liquid measure, it has been computed at 80 gallons (more or less). Also used as a dry measure. — Heb. *khōmer*, a homer, also a heap or mound (with initial *cheth*); from the root *khāmar*, to undulate, surge up, swell up.

HOMESTEAD, a dwelling-place, mansion-house, with its enclosures. (E.) In Bp. Hall, Contemplations, New Test. b. ii. cont. 3. § 6 (Todd). 'Both house and *homestead* into seas are borne;' Dryden (quoted in Todd; no reference). Compounded of *home* and *stead*.

HOMICIDE, man-slaughter; a man-slayer. (F. — L.) 1. Chaucer has *homicide* in the sense of manslaughter; C. T. 12591 (C 657). — F. *homicide*, 'manslaughter;' Cot. — L. *homicīdium*, manslaughter. — L. *homi-*, short for *homin-*, stem of *homo*, a man (see **Homage**); and *-cīdere*, for *cædere*, to cut, to kill. 2. Chaucer also has: 'He that hateth his brother is *homicide*;' Pers. Tale, De Ira, § 4 (I 565). — F. *homicide*, 'an homicide, man-killer;' Cot. — L. *homicīda*, a man-slayer; similarly formed from *homi-* and *-cīdere*. Der. *homicid-al*.

HOMILY, a plain sermon, discourse. (F. — L. — Gk.) In As You Like It, iii. 2. 164. And see Pref. to the Book of Homilies. ME. *omelye*, Trevisa, tr. of Higden, ii. 183. — OF. *omelie* (F. *homélie*, Hatzfeld). — L. *homīlia*, a homily. — Gk. ὁμιλία, a living together, intercourse, converse, instruction, homily. — Gk. ὅμιλος, an assembly, throng, concourse. — Gk. ὁμ-, short for ὁμο-, for ὁμός, like, same, cognate with E. **Same**; and (possibly) ἴλη, εἴλη, a crowd, band, from εἴλειν, to press or crowd together, compress, shut in. **Der.** *homiletic*, from the Gk. ὁμιλητικός, sociable, an adj. allied to ὁμιλία, used in E. as the adj. belonging to *homily*; hence *homiletic-al, homiletic-s*. Also *homil-ist* (= *homily-ist*).

HOMINY, maize prepared for food. (West Indian.) 'Milke *Homini*;' Capt. J. Smith, Works, p. 886. 'From Indian *auhúminea*, parched corn;' Webster. Trumbull gives *appumínneoash*, with the same sense.

HOMMOCK, a hillock; see **Hummock.**

HOMŒOPATHY, a particular treatment of disease. (Gk.) The system is an attempt to cure a disease by the use of small doses of drugs such as would produce the symptoms of the disease in a sound person. Hence the name, signifying 'similar feeling.' Proposed (ab. 1796) by Dr. Hahnemann, of Leipsic (died 1843). Englished from Gk. ὁμοιοπάθεια, likeness in feeling or condition, sympathy. — Gk. ὁμοιο-, for ὅμοιος, like, similar; and παθεῖν, aorist infin. of πάσχειν, to suffer. The Gk. ὅμοιος is from ὁμός, same, like. See **Same** and **Pathos.** Der. *homœopath-ic, -ist*.

HOMOGENEOUS, of the same kind or nature throughout. (Gk.) '*Homogeneal*, of one or the same kind, congenerous;' Blount's Gloss., ed. 1674. 'Of *homogeneous* things;' State Trials, Earl of Strafford, an. 1640 (R.). Englished from Gk. ὁμογενής, of the same race. — Gk. ὁμο-, for ὁμός, cognate with E. *same*; and γένος, race, cognate with E. *kin*. See **Same** and **Kin.** Der. *homogeneous-ness*.

HOMOLOGOUS, agreeing, corresponding. (Gk.) 'Homologous, having the same reason or proportion;' Phillips, ed. 1706. Englished from Gk. ὁμόλογος, agreeing, lit. saying the same. – Gk. ὁμο-, for ὁμός, cognate with E. same; and λόγος, a saying, from λέγειν, to say. See Same and **Logic**. Der. so also *homology*, agreement, from Gk. ὁμολογία.

HOMONYMOUS, like in sound, but differing in sense. (L. – Gk.) Applied to words. In Blount's Gloss., ed. 1674. – L. *homōnym-us*, of the same name; with suffix *-ous*. – Gk. ὁμώνυμος, having the same name. – Gk. ὁμο-, for ὁμός, cognate with E. *same*; and ὄνυμα, Æolic form of ὄνομα, a name, cognate with E. *name*. See Same and **Name**. The Gk. ω is due to the double o. Der. *homonymous-ly*; also *homonym*, sb., from F. *homonyme*, ' a word of divers significations;' Cot. Hence *homonym-y*. ¶ Similarly we have *homo-phonous*, like-sounding; from Gk. φωνή, a voice, sound.

HONE, a stone for sharpening various implements. (E.) 'Hoone, barbarys instrument, cos;' Prompt. Parv. p. 245. AS. *hān*, a hone, but only found in the sense of 'stone;' as in 'to þǣre *hāne*;' Birch, Cart. Saxon. ii. 458; whence the derived verb *hǣnan*, to stone, John, x. 32. +Icel. *hein*, a hone; Swed. *hen*, a hone (Widegren); MDan. *hen*. Teut. type *hainā*, f. Cf. Skt. *çi*, to sharpen. Brugmann, i. § 200.

HONEST, honourable, frank, just. (F. – L.) ME. *honest*, frequently in the sense of ' honourable;' Chaucer, C. T. 246; *honeste*, King Alisaunder, ed. Weber, 158. – OF. *honeste* (Littré); later *honneste*, ' honest, good, virtuous,' Cot.; mod. F. *honnête*. – L. *honestus*, honourable; for *hones-tus*, related to L. *honos*, honour. See **Honour**. Der. *honest-ly*; *honest-y*, ME. *honestee*, Chaucer, C. T. 6849 (D 1267), from OF. *honestet* (Ste. Eulalie, l. 18), from L. acc. *honestātem*, from nom. *honestās*, honourableness.

HONEY, a fluid collected by bees from plants. (E.) ME. *hony*, Rob. of Glouc., p. 43, l. 1013; P. Plowman, B. xv. 56; *huni*, Ancren Riwle, p. 404. AS. *hunig*, Mark, i. 6. +Du. *honig*; Icel. *hunang*; Dan. *honning*; Swed. *honing*; G. *honig*, MHG. *honec*, OHG. *honang*. Teut. type *huna(n)gom*, neut. Allied to Gk. κνηκός, pale yellow, Skt. *kanaka-m*, gold. Der. *honey-bag*, Mid. Nt. Dr. iii. 1. 171; *honey-bee*, Hen. V, i. 2. 187; *honey-comb*, q.v.; *honey-dew*, Titus, iii. 1. 112; *honey-fag*, Hen. V, i. 1. 50; *honey-moon*, 'the first sweet month of matrimony,' Kersey, ed. 1715; *honey-mouthed*, Wint. Ta. ii. 2. 33; *honey-suckle*, q.v.; *honey-tongued*, L. L. L. v. 2. 334.

HONEYCOMB, a mass of cells in which bees store honey. (E.) ME. *honycomb*, Chaucer, C. T. 3698. AS. *hunig-camb*; Bosworth, Lye. – AS. *hunig*, honey; and *camb*, a comb. See **Honey** and **Comb**. ¶ The likeness to a comb is fanciful, but there is no doubt about the word. It seems peculiar to E.; cf. G. *honig-scheibe* = a 'shive' or slice of honey, a honey-comb; Swed. *honingskaka*, Dan. *honningkage* (honey-cake); Icel. *hunangsseimr* (honey-string); Du. *honigraat* (honey-mass). Der. *honeycomb-ed*.

HONEY-MOON, the first month after marriage. (E.) Wedded love was compared to the full moon, that soon wanes; Huloet, 1552. See N. E. D. There was at first no reference to the period of a month.

HONEYSUCKLE, the name of a plant. (E.) So named because *honey* can be easily *suckled* or *sucked* from it. ME. *honysocle*, Prompt. Parv. p. 245; also *hunisuccles*, Voc. 558. 15. Extended from AS. *huni(g)sūce*, Voc. 298. 23. See **Honey, Suckle**.

HONOUR, respect, excellence, mark of esteem, worth. (F. – L.) In early use. ME. *honour*, Chaucer, C. T. 46; earlier *honure*, Layamon, 6084 (later text). The verb *honouren* is in Rob. of Glouc., p. 14, l. 16; l. 325. – AF. *honur*; OF. *honur*, *honeur*. – L. *honōrem*, acc. of *honos*, *honor*, honour. Der. *honour*, v., *honour-able*, Chaucer, C. T. 12574 (C 640); *honour-abl-y*, *honour-able-ness*, *honour-ed*, *honour-less*; *honor-ar-y*, used by Addison (Todd), from L. *honorārius*; also *honest*, q.v. ¶ The spelling *honor* assumes that the word is from the L. nominative, which is not the case. But it is now more phonetic.

HOOD, a covering, esp. for the head. (E.) ME. *hood*, Chaucer, C. T. 195; P. Plowman, B. v. 329; *hod*, Ancren Riwle, p. 56. AS. *hōd*, a hood; Voc. 199. 18; spelt *hood*, Epinal Gloss. 239.+Du. *hoed*, a hat; Pomeran. *hōd*, *hood*, a hat; G. *hut*, OHG. *huot*, *hōt*, a hat. β. Allied to E. *heed*; cf. G. *hüten*, to protect. Also to **Hat**. Der. *hood-ed*; *hood-man-blind*, Hamlet, iii. 4. 77; *hood-wink*, Romeo, i. 4. 4, lit. to make one *wink* or close his eyes, by covering him with a *hood*.

-HOOD, -HEAD, suffix. (E.) AS. *hād*, state, quality; cognate with Goth. *haidus*, manner, way; and Skt. *kētu(s)*, a sign by which a thing is known, from *kit*, to perceive, know (Vedic). Brugmann, ii. § 104. The form *-head* (as in *God-head*) may be compared with the OFries. *hēd*, *hēde*, OSax. *hēd*, cognate with AS. *hād*.

HOOF, the horny growth which sheathes the feet of horses, &c. (E.) ME. *hoof*, *hof*; dat. sing. *hufe*, Prick of Conscience, 4179; pl. *hoves*, Gawayn and the Grene Knight, 459. AS. *hōf*, to translate L. *ungula*; Wright's Vocab. i. 43. col. 2, 71. col. 2 (Voc. 158. 20). +Du. *hoef*; Icel. *hōfr*; Dan. *hov*; Swed. *hof*; G. *huf*. Teut. type

hōfoz, m. Allied to Skt. *çapha-s*, a hoof, esp. a horse's hoof. Der. *hoof-ed*, *hoof-less*.

HOOK, a bent piece of metal, &c. (E.) ME. *hok*, Havelok, 1102; pl. *hokes*, P. Plowman, B. v. 603. AS. *hōc*, Ælfric's Homilies, i. 362; also *hooc*; 'Arpago, vel palum, *hooc*;' Wright's Vocab., i. 16, col. 2. +Du. *hoek*; also (with *a*-grade), Du. *haak*; Icel. *haki*, Dan. *hage*, Swed. *hake*, a hook, clasp, hinge, G. *haken*, a hook, clasp, AS. *haca*, a hook, clasp, hinge. See **Hake**. Der. *hook*, v.; *hook-ed*, ME. *hoked*, P. Plowman, B. prol. 53; *hook-er*; *hook-nosed*, 2 Hen. IV, iv. 3. 45; also *arquebus*, q.v. ¶ Hence ' by *hook* or by crook;' Spenser, F. Q. v. 2. 27.

HOOKAH, HOOKA, a kind of pipe for smoking. (Arab.) 'Divine in *hookas*, glorious in a pipe;' Byron, The Island, c. ii. st. 19. – Arab. *ḥuqqa(h)*, a casket, bowl, a pipe for smoking; properly, the bottle through which the fumes pass. Cf. Arab. *ḥuqq*, a hollow place. Palmer's Pers. Dict. col. 201; Rich. Dict. p. 575.

HOOP (1), a pliant strip of wood or metal bent into a band. (E.) ME. *hoop*, *hope*, *hoope*. ' Hoope, hope, cuneus, circulus;' Prompt. Parv. p. 245. ' Hic circulus, a *hope*;' Wright's Vocab. i. 276, col. 1. AS. *hōp*, a hoop; rare, but found in Holy Rood, ed. Napier, p. 22, l. 9, and l. 14; p. 24, l. 6.+Du. *hoep*, a hoop. Teut. type *hōpoz*, m. Der. *hoop*, verb; *hoop-er*.

HOOP (2), **WHOOP**, to call out, shout. (F. – Teut.) *Whoop* is a late spelling; as in Spenser, F. Q. vi. 8. 11; and Palsgrave has: 'I *whoope*, I call, *je huppe*.' ME. *houpen*, to call out; Chaucer, C. T. 15406 (B 4590); P. Plowman, B. vi. 174. – OF. *houper*, ' to hoop unto, or call afar off;' Cot. Of imitative origin; from F. *houp*! interj. used in calling to dogs (Hatzfeld); cf. Goth. *hwōpan*, to boast; Romans, xi. 18. **Doublet**, *whoop*; see **Whoop**; and cf. **Hoot**. Der. *hoop-ing-cough*, a cough, accompanied with a *hoop* or convulsive noisy inspiration; formerly called the *chincough*. See **Chincough**. ¶ Also spelt *whooping-cough*, but this makes no real difference.

HOOPOE, the name of a bird. (L.) α. The old name for the bird was *houpe* or *hoope*, as in Minsheu's Dict., ed. 1627; spelt *houpe* in 1580 (N. E. D.). This is the F. form; from F. *huppe*, OF. *hupe*, *huppe*; spelt *huppe* in Philip de Thaun, The Bestiary, l. 1263, pr. in Wright's Popular Treatises on Science, p. 119. β. Also called *hoopoop* in 1668 (N. E. D.), in imitation of the L. name. Cf. also OF. *pupu*, a hoopoe; Low G. *huppupp* (Danneil). All from L. *upupa*, a hoopoe; the initial *h* in the mod. E. form being borrowed from the *h* in the F. form. γ. Called ἔποψ in Greek; both L. *up-up-a* and Gk. ἔπ-οψ are words of onomatopoetic origin, due to an imitation of the bird's cry. ¶ The bird has a remarkable tuft on its head; hence F. *huppe*, a tuft of feathers. But the tuft is named from the bird; not vice versâ.

HOOT, to shout in derision. (Scand.) ME. *houten*, whence the pp. *yhouted*, *yhowted* – hooted at; P. Plowman, B. ii. 218; also *huten*, Ormulum, 2034. Of Scand. origin; the original being preserved in MSwed. *huta*, in the phrase *huta ut en*, lit. to hoot one out, to cast out with contempt, as one would a dog (Ihre); Swed. *huta ut*, to take one up sharply; Norw. *huta*, to shout, *hut* (with *ū*), a cry to a dog (Aasen). Hence also Norm. dial. *houter*, as a variant of *houper*, to whoop. β. Formed from the Swed. interj. *hut*, begone! a word of imitative origin; cf. Norw. *hūt* (above), W. *hwt*, off! away! Irish *ut*, out! psha! Gael. *ut! ut*! interjection of dislike. So also MHG. *hiuzen*, *hūzen*, to call to the pursuit, from the interjection *hiu* (mod. G. *hui*), hallo! So also Dan. *huje*, to shout, hoot, halloo, from *hui*, hallo! OF. *huer*, to shout. The regular modern form would be *hout*, but the expressive *ū* has been preserved. Der. *hoot*, sb.; cf. *hue*, in the phrase *hue and cry*; see **Hue** (2).

HOP (1), to leap on one leg. (E.) Formerly used of dancing on both legs. ME. *hoppen*, *huppen*. ' At every bridal wolde he singe and *hoppe*,' i. e. dance; Chaucer, C. T. 4373 (A 4375). ' To *huppe* abowte ' = to dance about, P. Plowman, C. xviii. 279. AS. *hoppian*, to leap, dance; Ælfric's Homilies, i. 202, l. 18. +Du. *hoppen*, to hop; Icel. *hoppa*, to hop, skip; Swed. *hoppa*, to leap, jump, hop; Dan. *hoppe* (the same); cf. G. *hüpfen* (the same). Teut. type *huppōjan-*, from Idg. base *qup-n-*; allied to Russ. *kipiete*, to boil. Brugmann, i. § 421 (7). Der. *hop*, sb. (we still sometimes use *hop* in the old sense of 'a dance'); *hopp-er* (of a mill), ME. *hoper* or *hopper*, Chaucer, C. T. 4034 (A 4036); *hop-scotch*, a game in which children *hop* over lines *scotched* or traced on the ground (see **Scotch**); *hopp-le*, a fetter for horses, causing them to *hop* or progress slowly, a frequentative form. Also *hobb-le* (= *hopp-le*); see **Hobble**. Also *grass-hopper*, q.v.

HOP (2), the name of a plant. (Du.) In Cotgrave, to translate MF. *houbelon* (= F. *houblon*). Also in Minsheu's Dict., ed. 1627. ' Hoppes, humulus, lupulus;' Levins, ed. 1570. ' Hoppes in biere' [beer]; Sir T. Elyot, Castel of Helth, b. ii. c. 21. The pl. *hoppis* occurs as early as 1502, in Arnold's Chron.; ed. 1811, pp. 236, 246; and hops are frequently mentioned in the Northumberland Household-book, 1512. '*Hoppe*, sede for beyre (*v. r.* bere), *Hummulus, secundum extraneos*;' (i.e. it is a foreign word); Prompt. Parv. (1440). – MDu. *hoppe* (Franck), Du. *hop*, the hop-plant.+G. *hopfen*, the hop. β. We also find AS. *hymele*, Icel. *humall*, Swed., Dan. *humle*, MDu. *hommel*, the hop (Kilian); whence the Late L. *humulus*, now used as the botanical name. [The F. *houblon* is of Walloon origin, and ultimately from the Dutch.] But these can hardly be related words. ¶ An old note of the word occurs in an Old Westphalian gloss. : '*volubilis major, hoppe* ;' Mone, Quellen, p. 292. Cf. O. Low G. *hoppo, hupo*, the hop (Gallée). Dr. E. Scott writes :—' One of the Westminster Abbey documents, temp. Henry I or late 11th century, begins— " Hec est firma . . . ad panem vj. cumbas . . . xx *hopis* de brasio." ' **Der.** *hop-vine, hop-bind* (corruptly *hop-bine*).

HOPE (1), expectation ; as a verb, to expect. (E.) The verb is weak, and seems to be derived from the sb. ME. *hope*, sb., Chaucer, C. T. 88. ME. *hopen*, verb, sometimes in the sense ' to expect ;' as, ' Our manciple, I *hope* he wil be deed' = I fear he will be dead ; Chaucer, C. T. 4027 (A 4029). See P. Plowman, C. xviii. 313, and the note. AS. *hopa*, sb., in Ælfric's Hom. i. 350, l. 24 ; i. 568, l. 8 ; also used in the comp. *tōhopa*, Grein, ii. 545 ; *hopian*, v. to hope, Grein, ii. 96.+Du. *hoop*, sb., *hopen*, v.; Dan. *haab*, sb., *haabe*, v.; Swed. *hopp*, sb., whence the reflexive verb *hoppas*, to hope ; MHG. *hoffe*, sb., represented by mod. G. *hoffnung* ; G. *hoffen*, to hope. **Der.** *hope-ful, hope-ful-ly* ; *hope-less, -ly, -ness*.

HOPE (2), a troop. (Du.) Only in the phr. *forlorn hope*, North's Plutarch, ed. 1631, p. 372. The phr. also occurs in An Eng. Garner, vii. 128, where Sir F. Vere describes the battle of Nieuwport (S.W. of Ostend) in the year 1600 ; here it is at once connected with Du. *verloren hoop*; see **Forlorn**. Here *hoop* = band, troop, as in ' een *hoop krijghs-volck*, a troupe or a band of souldiers ;' Hexham. Cf. *verloren hoop* (Kilian). It is now obsolete in Dutch. The usual sense of Du. *hoop* is *heap* ; see **Heap**.

HOPLITE, a heavy-armed foot-soldier. (Gk.) Modern. From Gk. ὁπλίτης, a hoplite. – Gk. ὅπλ-ον, a weapon, piece of armour ; with suffix -ιτης (E. *-ite*) ; allied to ὅπλομαι, I prepare for myself, and to ἔπω, I am busy with (Prellwitz).

HOPPLE, to fetter a horse, &c. (E.) ' To *hopple* an horse, to tye his feet with a rope ;' Kersey (1721) ; and in Coles (1684). Lit. to make to hopple, or hobble ; see E. D. D. Cf. MDu. *hoppelen*, to hobble ; see **Hobble**, and **Hop**.

HORDE, a wandering troop or tribe. (F. – Turk. – Tatar.) Spelt *hoord* in Sir T. Herbert's Travels, ed. 1665, p. 61 ; and in Hakluyt, Voy. i. 491. – F. *horde*, first in use in the 16th century (Littré). – Turk. *urdū*, a camp (Zenker, p. 117) ; cf. Pers. *ōrdū*, ' a court, camp, horde of Tartars ;' also *urdū*, a camp, an army ; Rich. Pers. Dict., pp. 56, 201. – Tatar *ūrdū*, a royal camp, horde of Tatars (Tartars) ; see Pavet de la Courteille, p. 54. First applied to the Tatar tribes.

HORDOCK ; see **Hardock**.

HOREHOUND, a plant ; see **Hoarhound**.

HORIZON, the circle bounding the view where earth and sky seem to meet. (F. – L. – Gk.) In Shak. 3 Hen. VI, iv. 7. 81. [But we also find ME. *orizonte*, Chaucer, Treatise on the Astrolabe, prol. l. 7. This is (through the OF.) from the L. acc. *horizontem*.] – F. *horizon*, ' a horizon ;' Cot. – L. *horizōn* (stem *horizont-*). – Gk. ὁρίζων, the bounding or limiting circle ; orig. the pres. pt. of the vb. ὁρίζειν, to bound, limit. – Gk. ὅρος, a boundary, limit ; perhaps allied to Gk. ἕρκος, an enclosure (Prellwitz). **Der.** *horizont-al, horizont-al-ly.*

HORN, the hard substance projecting from the heads of some animals. (E.) ME. *horn*, Chaucer, C. T. 116. AS. *horn*, Grein, ii. 98. + Icel., Dan., and Swed. *horn* ; Du. *horen* [for *horn*, the *e* being due to the trilling of the *r*] ; G. *horn* ; Goth. *haurn*. Teut. type *hornom*, n. + Gael., and Irish *corn* ; L. *cornu*. β. The Celtic forms are from the Idg. base *kor-no-*; Stokes-Fick, p. 79. Further allied to Gk. κέρ-ας, a horn ; and to **Hart**. **Der.** *horn-beam*, a tree ; *horn-bill*, a bird ; *horn-blende*, a mineral term, wholly borrowed from G. *horn-blende*, where *-blende*, i.e. a ' deceitful ' mineral, yielding little ore, is from *blenden*, to dazzle, lit. to make blind ; *horn-book*, L. L. L. v. 1. 49 ; *horn-ed*, Mids. Nt. Dr. v. 243, spelt *hornyd* in Prompt. Parv. p. 247 ; *horn-owl* or *horn-ed owl* ; *horn-pipe*, Wint. Tale, iv. 3. 47, a dance so called because danced to an instrument with that name, mentioned in the Rom. of the Rose, 4250 ; *horn-stone* ; *horn-work*, a term in fortification, named from its projections ; *horn-less* ; *horn-y*, Milton, P. R. ii. 267 ; also *horn-et*, q. v. From the same source are *corn* (2), *corn-er, corn-et*, &c.

HORNET, a kind of large wasp. (E.) So called from its resounding hum. In Holland's Pliny, b. xi. c. 21. AS. *hyrnet*, *hyrnīs* ; the pl. *hyrnytta* occurs in Exod. xxiii. 28. ' Crabro, *hyrnet* ;' Ælfric's Gloss., De Nominibus Insectorum. Formed, with suffix *-et*, from *korn*, a horn, by regular vowel-change ; cf. *hyrned* = horned, Grein, ii. 133. The vowel has, however, reverted in mod. E. to the

original *o*, for clearness. See **Horn**.+EFries. *hörnetje* ; Westphal. *horntje* ; LowG. *horneke* (Schambach). Cf. OSax. *horno-bero*, a hornet, lit. a ' horn-bearer ;' AS. *horn-bera*, a trumpeter. Hexham has MDu. *horener, hornte*, a hornet, *horentoren*, a wasp ; from *horen*, a horn. ¶ It is curious that G. *hornisse*, OHG. *hornaz* (without vowel-change) is referred to a Teut. type *hurznatoz* (cf. Du. *horz-elen*, to buzz), allied to L. *crābro* (for *cras-ro*), a hornet, Lith. *szirszū* (gen. *szirsz-ens*), a hornet ; lit. ' a buzzer ;' see Brugmann, i. § 626.

HOROLOGE, an instrument for telling the hours, a clock. (F. – L. – Gk.) In Shak. Oth. ii. 3. 135. Nearly obsolete. ME. *orloge*, Chaucer, C. T. 14860 (B 4044). – OF. *horologe, horloge* ; ' *Horloge*, a clock or dyall ;' Cot. – L. *hōrologium*, a sun-dial, a water-clock. – Gk. ὡρολόγιον, the same. – Gk. ὡρο-, for ὥρα, a season, period, hour ; and -λογιον, formed from λέγειν, to tell. See **Hour** and **Logic**. **Der.** *horolog-y, horolog-i-c-al*.

HOROSCOPE, an observation of the sky at a person's nativity. (F. – L. – Gk.) A term in astrology. In Cotgrave. [Chaucer uses the L. term *horoscopum* ; Treatise on the Astrolabe, ed. Skeat, pt. ii. § 4.] – F. *horoscope*, ' the horoscope, or ascendant at a nativity ;' Cot. – L. *hōroscopus*, a horoscope ; from *hōroscopus*, adj., that shows the hour. – Gk. ὡροσκόπος, a horoscope ; from the adj. ὡροσκόπος, observing the hour. – Gk. ὡρο-, for ὥρα, season, hour ; and σκοπεῖν, to consider, related to σκέπτομαι, I consider. See **Hour** and **Sceptic**. **Der.** *horoscop-y, horoscop-i-c, horoscop-ist*.

HORRIBLE, dreadful, fearful. (F. – L.) ME. *horrible*, also written *orrible*, Chaucer, C. T. 4893 (B 473). – OF. *horrible*, ' horrible, terrible ;' Cot. – L. *horribilis*, terrible, lit. to be trembled at ; formed with suffix *-bilis* from *horrēre*, to tremble, shake. See **Horror**. **Der.** *horribl-y*, Chaucer, C. T. 14535 (B 3807) ; *horrible-ness*.

HORRID, dreadful. (L.) Directly from Latin. Spenser uses it in the L. sense of ' rough.' ' His haughty helmet, *horrid* all with gold ;' F. Q. i. 7. 31. – L. *horridus*, rough, bristly, &c. – L. *horrēre*, to be rough. See **Horror**. **Der.** *horrid-ly, horrid-ness*.

HORRIFY, to make afraid, scare. (L.) A late word ; not in Johnson. Coined, by analogy with words in *-fy* (mostly of F. origin), from L. *horrificāre*, to cause terror. – L. *horrificus*, causing terror. – L. *horri-*, from *horrēre*, to dread ; and *-fic-*, for *facere*, to make. **Der.** From L. *horrificus* has also been coined the adj. *horrific*, Thomson's Seasons, Autumn, 782. See **Horror**.

HORROR, dread, terror. (F. – L.) Formerly also spelt *horrour* (Minsheu), because at first taken from the French. Sir T. Elyot has *horrour* ; Castel of Helth, bk. iii. ch. 1 ; and so in Chaucer, C. T. Pers. Tale (I 224). We find ' sad *horror*' in Spenser, F. Q. ii. 7. 23 ; and *horrors* in Hamlet, ii. 1. 84, in the first folio edition. – OF. *horrour* ; later *horreur*, ' horror ;' Cot. – L. *horrōrem*, acc. of *horror*, terror, dread. – L. *horrēre*, to bristle, be rough ; also, to dread, with reference to the bristling of the hair through terror. Cf. Skt. *hrsh*, to bristle, said of the hair, esp. as a token of fear or of pleasure. Thus *horrēre* is for *horsēre* (cf. L. *hirsutus*, rough, shaggy) ; from √ GHERS, to be rough. **Der.** From L. *horrēre* we have *horrent* (from the stem of the pres. part.) ; also *horri-ble*, q. v., *horri-d*, q. v. ; *horri-fy*, q. v. ; and *horri-fic*. Cf. *hirsute, urchin*.

HORSE, the name of a well-known quadruped. (E.) The final *e* merely marks that the *s* is hard, and is not to be pronounced as z. ME. *hors* ; pl. *hors* (unchanged), also *hors-es*, as now. Chaucer, C. T. 74, 10504 (A 74, F 190). ' Thei sellen bothe here *hors* and here harneys' = they sell both their horses and their harness ; Mandeville's Travels, p. 38. AS. *hors*, neut. ; pl. *hors*, Grein, ii. 98. + Icel. *hross* ; also *hors* ; Du. *ros* ; G. *ross*, MHG. *ros, ors*, OHG. *hros*. β. Teut. type *horsom*, n. ; Idg. stem *curs-o-*; prob. allied to *curs-us*, pp. of L. *currere*, to run, whence also E. *courser* with the sense of ' horse.' See **Courser**. γ. This supposition is made more probable by the fact that the same base will account for AS. *horsc*, swift, Grein, ii. 98 ; cf. MHG. *rosch*, swift. Brugmann, i. § 516 ; ii. § 662. **Der.** *horse*, verb, Wint. Ta. i. 2. 288 ; *horse-back*, ME. *hors-bak*, Gower, C. A. iii. 256 ; bk. vii. l. 4908 ; *horse-block, horse-breaker, horse-fly, horse-guards* ; *horse-hair*, Cymb. ii. 3. 33 ; *horse-leech*, Hen. V, ii. 3. 57 ; *horse-man*, Wint. Ta. iv. 3. 67 ; *horse-man-ship*, Hen. V, iii. 7. 58 ; *horse-power, horse-race, horse-racing* ; *horse-shoe*, Merry Wives, iii. 5. 123 ; *horse-tail, horse-trainer, horse-whip*, sb. and vb. Also numerous other compounds, as *horse-bread, horse-flesh, horse-pond*, all readily understood. Also *horse-chestnut*, said to be so called because the nuts were ground and given to horses ; the word also occurs in several plant-names, as *horse-foot, horse-knop, horse-radish, horse-tail, horse-thistle, horse-tongue, horse-vetch*. Also *wal-rus*.

HORSE-COURSER, HORSE-SCORSER, a jobbing dealer in horses. (Hybrid ; E. *and* F. – L.) The latter form is corrupt ; see examples in Nares, s. v. *Horse-courser, Scorse*. And *courser* is for *cosser, coser* ; ' Hic *mango*, a cosyr ;' Voc. 684. 40. And cf. Gloss. to Elyot's Governour, ed. Croft, s. v. *Skocer*. From

AF. *cossour* (1310), a broker, in Riley, Mem. of London, p. xxii. — Late L. *cōciātōrem*, acc. of *cōciātor*, a broker (Duc.). Cf. L. *cōcio*, a broker. See my Notes on E. Etym., p. 136.

HORTATORY, full of encouragement. (L.) 'He animated his soldiers with many *hortatorie* orations;' Holland, Ammianus, p. 202 (R.). Formed as if from L. **hortātōrius*, a coined word from *hortātor*, an encourager. — L. *hortā-*, as in *hortārī*, to encourage; prob. connected with *horiri* (pres. tense *horior*), to urge, incite. Perhaps allied to E. *yearn* (Prellwitz, s. v. χαίρω). **Der.** So also *hortative* (Minsheu), a better form, from L. *hortātiuus*, encouraging; also *ex-hort*, q. v.

HORTICULTURE, the art of cultivating gardens, gardening. (L.) First in Phillips, ed. 1678. From L. *hortī*, gen. of *hortus*, a garden; and *culture*, Englished form of L. *cultūra*, cultivation. See **Culture.** L. *hortus* is allied to E. *yard*; see **Yard** (1). **Der.** *horticultur-al*, *horticultur-ist*.

HOSANNA, an expression of praise. (Gk. — Heb.) In Matt. xxi. 9, 15; &c. It is rather a form of prayer, as it signifies 'save, we pray.' — Gk. ὡσαννά, Matt. xxi. 9. — Heb. *hōshī'āh nnā*, save, we pray; Ps. cxviii. 25. — Heb. *hōshīa'*, save, from *yāsha'*, to save; and *nā*, a particle signifying entreaty.

HOSE, a covering for the legs and feet; stockings. (E.) ME. *hose*, pl. *hosen*; Chaucer, C. T. 458 (A 456); Ancren Riwle, p. 420. AS. *hosa*, pl. *hosan*; 'Caliga vel ocrea, *hosa*;' Wright's Vocab. i. 81, col. 2 (Voc. 327. 29). + Du. *hoos*, hose, stocking, spout, water-spout; Icel. *hosa*, the hose covering the leg between the knee and ankle, a kind of gaiter; Dan. *hose*, pl. *hoser*, hose, stockings; G. *hose*, breeches (whence OF. *hose*). Perhaps cf. Skt. *kōsha-s*, a sheath. **Der.** *hos-i-er*, where the inserted *i* answers to the *y* in *law-y-er*, *bow-y-er*; *hos-i-er-y*.

HOSPICE, a house for the reception of travellers as guests. (F. — L.) Modern; chiefly used of such houses in the Alps. — F. *hospice*, a hospice. — L. *hospitium*, a hospice. — L. *hospiti-*, decl. stem of *hospes*, a guest; also, a host. See **Host** (1), **Hospital.**

HOSPITABLE, showing kindness to strangers. (F. — L.) In K. John, ii. 244; Cor. i. 10. 26. — F. *hospitable*, 'hospitable;' Cot. Coined, with suffix *-able*, from Late L. *hospitāre*, to receive as a guest; Ducange. — L. *hospit-*, stem of *hospes*, a guest, host. See **Host** (1). **Der.** *hospitabl-y*, *hospitable-ness*.

HOSPITAL, a building for receiving guests; hence, one for receiving sick people. (F. — L.) ME. *hospital*, *hospitalle* in Mandeville's Travels, ed. Halliwell, p. 81; *hospytal*, Eng. Gilds, ed. T. Smith, p. 350, l. 25. — OF. *hospital*, 'an hospitall, a spittle;' Cot. — Late L. *hospitāle*, a large house, palace, which occurs A.D. 1243 (Brachet); a sing. formed from L. pl. *hospitālia*, apartments for strangers. — L. *hospit-*, stem of *hospes*; see **Host** (1). **Der.** *hospitall-er*, ME. *hospitalier*, Chaucer, C. T. Persones Tale, De Luxuria (I 891); *hospital-i-ty*, ME. *hospitalité*, Lydgate, Minor Poems, p. 96. **Doublets,** *hostel*, *hotel*, *spital*.

HOST (1), one who entertains guests. (F. — L.) ME. *host*, *hoste*, Chaucer, C. T. 749 (A 747). — OF. *hoste*, 'an hoste, inn-keeper;' Cot. Cf. Port. *hospede*, a host, a guest. — L. *hospitem*, acc. of *hospes*, (1) a host, entertainer of guests, (2) a guest. β. The base *hospit-* is commonly taken to be short for **hosti-pot-*, where *hosti-* is the decl. stem of *hostis*, a stranger, a guest, an enemy; see **Host** (2). Again, the stem *-pot-* is supposed to have meant 'lord,' being allied to L. *pot-ens*, powerful; cf. Skt. *pati-*, a master, governor, lord; see **Possible.** γ. Thus *hospes* = **hostipotis*, guest-master, a master of a house who receives guests. Cf. Russ. *gospode*, the Lord, *gospodare*, governor, prince; from *goste*, a guest, and *-pode* = Skt. *pati-*, a lord. Brugmann, i. § 240. **Der.** *host-ess*, from OF. *hostesse*, 'an hostesse,' Cot.; also *host-el*, q. v., *host-ler*, q. v., *hotel*, q. v.; and from the same source, *hospital*, q. v., *hospice*, q. v., *hospitable*, q. v.

HOST (2), an army. (F. — L.) The orig. sense is 'enemy' or 'foreigner.' ME. *host*, Chaucer, C. T. 1028 (A 1026); frequently spelt *ost*, Will. of Palerne, 1127, 1197, 3767; Cursor Mundi, 6160. — OF. *host*, 'an host, or army, a troop;' Cot. — L. *hostem*, acc. of *hostis*, a stranger, an enemy; hence, a hostile army, host. + Russ. *go te*, a guest, visitor, stranger, alien; AS. *gæst*; see **Guest.** **Der.** *host-ile*, Cor. iii. 3. 97, from F. *hostile*, which from L. *hostīlis*; *host-ile-ly*; *host-il-i-ty*, K. John, iv. 2. 247, from F. *hostilite*, which from L. acc. *hostilitātem*. **Doublet,** *guest*.

HOST (3), the consecrated bread of the eucharist. (L.) 'In as many *hoostes* as be consecrate;' Bp. Gardner, Of the Presence in the Sacrament, fol. 35 (R.). And in Holland's Plutarch, p. 1097 (R.). ME. *oste*, Rob. of Brunne, Handlyng Synne, l. 8849. Coined by dropping the final syllables of L. *hostia*, a victim in a sacrifice; afterwards applied to the host in the eucharist. β. The old form of *hostia* was *fostia* (Festus), and it signified 'that which is struck or slain.' — L. *hostire* (old form *fostīre*), to strike.

HOSTAGE, a person delivered to the enemy as a pledge for the performance of the conditions of a treaty. (F. — L.) In early use. —

ME. *hostage*, Layamon, 4793, 8905 (later text only). — OF. *hostage*, 'an hostage, pawne, surety,' Cot.; mod. F. *otage*. Cf. Ital. *ostaggio*; OProv. *ostatge*, Bartsch, Chrestomathie Prov. col. 173, l. 18. Perhaps from a Late L. **obsidāticum*, acc. of **obsidāticus*, not found, yet preserved also in Ital. *statico*, a hostage, and regularly formed from Late L. *obsidātus*, the condition of a hostage, hostage-ship. *Obsidātus* is formed (by analogy with *principātus* from *princip-*, stem of *princeps*) from L. *obsid-*, stem of *obses*, a hostage, one who remains behind with the enemy. — L. *obsidēre*, to sit, stay, abide, remain. — L. *ob*, at, on, about; and *sedēre*, to sit, cognate with E. *sit*. See **Sit.** ¶ Another explanation is from a Late L. form **hospitāticum*, a receiving as a guest; from L. *hospit-*, for *hospes*, a host; see **Host** (1). So Körting. The words may have been confused.

HOSTEL, an inn. (F. — L.) Now commonly *hotel*, q. v. ME. *hostel*, Genesis and Exodus, ed. Morris, 1397; Sir Gawayn and the Grene Knight, 805. — OF. *hostel*, an inn. Regularly contracted from Late L. *hospitāle*; see **Hospital.** Doublets, *hotel*, *hospital*, *spital*. **Der.** *hostel-ry*, ME. *hostelrie*, Chaucer, C. T. 23; *hostler*, q. v.

HOSTLER, OSTLER, a man who takes care of horses at an inn. (F. — L.) '*Host'ler*, the horse-groom, but properly the keeper of an *hostelry*;' Coles, ed. 1684. Orig. the inn-keeper himself, and so named from his *hostel*. ME. *hostiler*, Chaucer, C. T. 241. — OF. *hostelier*, 'an inn-keeper;' Cot. — OF. *hostel*; see **Hostel.**

HOT, very warm, fiery, ardent. (E.) The vowel was formerly long. ME. *hot*, *hoot*, Chaucer, C. T. 687. 'Nether cold, nether *hoot*;' Wyclif, Rev. iii. 16. AS. *hāt*, hot; Grein, ii. 15. + Du. *heet*; Icel. *heitr*; Swed. *het*; Dan. *hed*; G. *heiss*, OHG. *heiz*. Teut. type **haitoz*. The weak grade **hit-* appears in Icel. *hiti*, heat, G. *hitze*. Cf. also Goth. *hais*, a torch, *heitō*, fever; Lithuan. *kaitra*, heat. **Der.** *hot-bed*; *hot-blooded*, Merry Wives, v. 5. 2; *hot-headed*; *hot-house*, Meas. ii. 1. 66; *hot-ly*, *hot-spur*. Also *heat*, q. v.

HOTCH-POT, HODGE-PODGE, a farrago, confused mass. (F. — Du.) *Hodge-podge* is a mere corruption; the old term is *hotch-pot*. The intermediate form *hotch-potch* is in Sir T. Herbert's Travels, ed. 1665, p. 336. 'A *hotchpot*, or mingle-mangle;' Minsheu. 'An *hotchpotte*, incisium;' Levins. 'A *hotchepotte* of many meates;' Palsgrave. ME. *hochepot*, Chaucer, Tale of Melibeus, C. T. B 2447. — F. *hochepot*, 'a hotch-pot, or gallimaufrey, a confused mingle-mangle of divers things jumbled or put together;' Cot. Cf. F. *hocher*, 'to shake, wag, jog, nob, nod;' id. — MDu. *hutsepot* (Hexham), *hutspot*, 'hodge-podge, beef or mutton cut into small pieces;' Sewel. So called from shaking or jumbling pieces of meat in a pot. — MDu. *huts-*, base of *hutsen*, to shake, jolt (Oudemans); and Du. *pot*, a pot. From *hutsen* was also formed the frequentative verb *hutselen*, 'to shake up and down, either in a tub, bowl, or basket;' Sewel. The verb *hutsen* was also spelt *hotsen* (Sewel), which comes still closer to the French; so also EFries. *hotjen*, *hutjen*, to shake up. Cf. WFlem. *hotteren*, to shake up (De Bo). See **Hustle** and **Pot.**

HOTEL, an inn, esp. of a large kind. (F. — L.) A modern word; borrowed from mod. F. *hôtel* = OF. *hostel*. See **Hostel.**

HOTTENTOT, a native of the Cape of Good Hope. (Du.) The word is traced in Wedgwood, who shows that the Dutch gave the natives this name in ridicule of their peculiar speech, which sounded to them like stuttering. He cites the word from Schouten (1653). *En* is Dutch for 'and;' hence *hot en tot* = 'hot' and 'tot;' where these words indicate stammering. Cf. *hateren*, to stammer, *tateraer*, a stammerer, in Hexham's Du. Dict., 1647; *tateren* to tattle (Sewel); Pomeran. *hütentüt*, a quack (a derisive name). See also Phil. Soc. Trans. 1866; p. 15.

HOUDAH, HOWDAH, a seat to be fixed upon an elephant's back. (Hind. — Arab.) Used in works of travel; and in The Surgeon's Daughter, c. xiv. by Sir W. Scott. — Hind. *haudah* (Forbes). — Arab. *hawdaj*, a litter carried by a camel, in which Arabian ladies travel; a seat to place on an elephant's back; Rich. Dict. p. 1694; Palmer's Pers. Dict. col. 709. (See Yule.)

HOUGH, HOCK, the joint in the hind-leg of a quadruped, between the knee and fetlock, corresponding to the ankle-joint in man; in man, the back part of the knee-joint. (E.) Now generally spelt *hock*; but formerly *hough*. 'Unto the camel's *hough*;' 2 Esdras, xv. 36 (A.V.). Cotgrave translates F. *jarret* by 'the hamme, or hough.' ME. *houch*, Wallace, ed. Jamieson, i. 322. The pl. *hoȝes* occurs in Sir Gawayn and the Grene Knight, l. 1357. AS. *hōh*, the heel; Grein, ii. 92. + Icel. *hā-*, in the comp. *hāsinn* = hock-sinew. Teut. type **hanhoz*. The E. *heel* is related; see **Heel.** β. Hock is a later form; and may have arisen in the comp. 'hough-sinew,' spelt *hōhsinu* in AS., and *hōxene*, *hōxne* in OFriesic. (AS. *hs* > *x*.) See G. *hechse* (in Kluge); and see **Hox.** Allied to L. *coxa*, the hip; Skt. *kaksha-s*, the arm-pit. **Der.** *hough*, verb, to cut the ham-string of a horse, Josh. xi. 6, 2 Sam. viii. 4; often altered to *hox*, sometimes spelt *hocks*; see Shak. Wint. Ta. i. 2. 244; *hoxe*, Wyclif, Josh. xi. 6 (later version).

HOUND, a dog. (E.) ME. *hound, hund*; P. Plowman, B. v. 261; Havelok, 1994. AS. *hund*, Matt. vii. 6; Du. *hond*; Icel. *hundr*; Dan. and Swed. *hund*; G. *hund*; Goth. *hunds*. Teut. type *hundoz*, m. Further allied to L. *can-is*, a dog, Gk. κύων (genitive κυν-ός), Skt. *çvan*, a dog; also Irish *cu*, Gael. *cu*, W. *ci*, a dog; Russ. *suka*, a bitch; Lith. *szù* (stem *szun-*), a dog. Brugmann, i. § 609. The final *d* may have been suggested by confusion with Teut. *henthan-*, to catch. See **Hunt.** Der. *hound*, verb, in Otway, Caius Marius, Act iv. sc. 2 (R.); *hound-fish*, Chaucer, C. T. 9699 (E 1825); *hound's-tongue*.

HOUR, a certain definite space of time. (F.—L.—Gk.) ME. *houre*, Chaucer, C. T. 14733 (B 3613).—AF. *houre*, Statutes of the Realm, p. 30 (1275); OF. *hore* (mod. F. *heure*).—L. *hōra*.—Gk. ὥρα, a season, hour; cf. ὥρος, a season, a year. Allied to *year*. See **Year.** Der. *hour-ly*, adj. Temp. iv. 108, adv. Temp. i. 2. 402; *hour-glass*, Merch. of Ven. i. 1. 25; *hour-plate*. Also (from L. *hōra*) *hor-ar-y*, Blount's Gloss., ed. 1674; *hor-al*, Prior, Alma, c. 3. Also *horo-loge, horo-scope*, which see.

HOURI, a nymph of Paradise. (F.—Pers.—Arab.) 'With Paradise within my view And all his *houris* beckoning through;' Byron, The Giaour; see note 39 to that poem. Also in Dr. Johnson's Irene, iv. 5. 10.—F. *houri*.—Pers. *hūrī*, a virgin of Paradise; *hūrā, hūr*, a virgin of Paradise, a black-eyed nymph; so called from their fine black eyes.—Arab. *hūr*, pl. of Arab. *hawrā*, fem. of *ahwar*, having fine black eyes; Rich. Arab. Dict. pp. 585, 33; Palmer's Pers. Dict. col. 206.—Arab. root *hawira*, to be black-eyed like a doe. (Devic.)

HOUSE, a dwelling-place; a family. (E.) ME. *hous*, Chaucer, C. T. 252. AS. *hūs*, Matt. xii. 25.+Du. *huis*; Icel. *hūs*; Dan. *huus*; Swed. *hus*; Goth. *-hus*, in the comp. *gud-hus*, a house of God; G. *haus*, OHG. *hūs*. Teut. type *hūsom*, n. β. Probably allied to **Hoard,** and **Hide** (1). From √ KEUDH, to hide. Brugm. i. § 796. Der. *house*, verb, now 'to provide a house for,' as in Gower, C. A. iii. 18 (bk. vi. 498), but the ME. *housen* also meant 'to build a house,' as in Rob. of Glouc. p. 21, l. 13 (cf. 'howsyn, or puttyn yn a howse, *domifero*;' 'howsyn, or makyn howsys, *domifico*;' Prompt. Parv. p. 251); *house-breaker, house-breaking; house-hold*, ME. *houshold*, Chaucer, C. T. 5681 (D 99), so called because held together in one house; *house-hold-er*, ME. *householder*, Chaucer, C. T. 341; *house-keeper*, Cor. i. 3. 55, Macb. iii. 1. 97; *house-keeping*, L. L. L. ii. 104; *house-leek*, ME. *hows-leke*, Prompt. Parv. p. 251; *house-less*, K. Lear, iii. 4. 26; *house-maid, house-steward, house-warming, house-wife*, spelt *huswif*, Ancren Riwle, p. 416, also *hosewijf* or *huswijf*, Wyclif, 3 Kings, xvii. 17, and frequently *huswife*, as in Shak. Cor. i. 3. 76, Romeo, iv. 2. 43; *house-wife-ry*, or *hus-wife-ry*, Oth. ii. 1. 113, with which cf. 'huswyfery, yconomia;' Prompt. Parv. See also **Husband, Hussy, Hustings, Hoard.**

HOUSEL, the eucharist or sacrament of the Lord's Supper. (E.) The orig. sense is 'sacrifice.' ME. *housel*, Rom. of the Rose, 6386; P. Plowman, C. xxii. 394. AS. *hūsel* (for *hunsel*), the eucharist; Grein, ii. 112.+Goth. *hunsl*, a sacrifice, Matt. ix. 13. The orig. sense was prob. 'holy rite.' Allied to Lith. *szwentas*, holy, consecrated; Zend *spənta-*, holy. Brugmann, i. § 377. Der. *housel*, verb, ME. *hoselen, houselen*, P. Plowman, C. xxii. 3; *unhousel'd*, Hamlet, i. 5. 77.

HOUSINGS, trappings of a horse. (F.—Arab.) Unconnected with *house*, but probably often supposed to be related to it; the old form was *houss*, the addition -*ings* being English. 'The cattle used for draught . . . are covered with *housings* of linnen;' Evelyn, Diary, end of May, 1645. 'A velvet bed of state drawn by six horses, *houss'd* with the same;' Evelyn, Diary, Oct. 22, 1658. 'Spread on his back, the *houss* and trappings of a beast;' Dryden, tr. of Ovid's Metam. b. xii. 582. 'Housse, the cloth which the king's horseguards wear behind the saddle;' Coles' Dict., ed. 1684. 'A *howse* of a horse;' Cath. Angl. (1483).—OF. *houce* (Godefroy); F. *housse*, 'a short mantle of course cloth (and all of a peece) worn in ill weather by country women about their head and shoulders; also a footcloth for a horse; also a coverlet;' Cot. Cf. Low L. *hūcia*, a long tunic; *housia*, a long tunic, coverlet for a horse, also spelt *hūsia, hussia*. Ducange dates *hūcia* in A.D. 1326, and *hūsia* in A.D. 1259, so that the word is of some antiquity. The sense is clearly 'covering.' β. Perhaps from OHG. *hulst*, a cover (Schade).+Icel. *hulstr*, AS. *heolstor*, Goth. *hulistr*, a cover. From *hul-*, weak grade of Teut. *helan-*, to cover, hide; cf. AS. *helan*, to hide, OHG. and Du. *hullen*, to cover. γ. But Devic suggests as the origin Arab. *ghushiah*, a covering, veil (Mém. de la soc. de ling. de Paris; V. 37). Körting, § 4666. Cf. Arab. *ghushwa(t)*, a veil, covering; Rich. Dict. p. 1052. ¶ The W. *hws*, a covering, is borrowed from E. *houss.*

HOVEL, a small hut. (F.—Teut.) ME. *hovel, hovil.* 'Hovylle, lytylle howse, *Teges*;' Prompt. Parv. p. 250. 'Hovyl for swyne, or oþer beestys;' ibid. Perhaps from an AF. *huvel*; cf. OF. *huvelet*, a penthouse (Godefroy), a double diminutive. Apparently

(like OF. *huvet*, a cap, helmet, from OF. *huve*, a cap, covering for the head) from AS. *hūfe*, a hood; cf. OHG. *hūba* (G. *haube*), a hood; MDu. *huyve*, a tilt of a cart, a coif (Hexham); Norw. *huva*, Icel. *hūfa*, a hood. Note prov. E. *hovel, huvel*, a finger-stall; from AS. *hūfe.* See **Hive.**

HOVER, to fluctuate, hang about, move to and fro. (E.) In Macb. i. 1. 12. 'Hover, to stay, wait for. "Will you *hover* till I come?"' E. D. S. Gloss. B. 22, p. 96. A frequentative, with suffix -*er*, of ME. *houen* (= *hoven*), sometimes used in precisely the same sense, and once a common word. 'O night! alas! why niltow [wilt thou not] over us *hove*;' Chaucer, Troil. iii. 1427; also in P. Plowman, C. xxi. 83 (see the note); 'Where that she *hoved* and abode;' Gower, C. A. iii. 63; bk. vi. 1848; 'He *hovede* and abode;' Seven Sages, ed. Wright, 2825; 'He *houede*' = he waited, Rob. of Glouc. p. 172, l. 12. In the earliest examples, it had the sense of 'hover,' or 'be poised.' In the Bestiary, l. 69, it is said of the eagle that 'he *houeð* in ðe sunne,' he soars or is poised in the sunlight. The *o* in ME. *hōven* was long (N. E. D.). The origin is unknown; but if the orig. idea was that of soaring or being lifted up, it may be related to *hōf*, the strong grade of AS. *hebban*, to heave. See **Heave.** ¶ The W. *hofio*, to hover, to fluctuate, to suspend, was borrowed from English.

HOW (1), in what way. (E.) ME. *how, hou, hu*; spelt *hu*, Ancren Riwle, p. 182, l. 20; also *hwu*, id., p. 256, l. 10; also *whow*, P. Plowman's Crede, l. 141. AS. *hū*; Grein, ii. 110.+OFries. *hū, hō*, how; Du. *hoe*; Goth. *hwaiwa.* β. The Goth. form shows that the word is closely related to the pronoun *who*, which is Goth. *hwas*, AS. *hwā.* Cf. Gk. πώς, how; 'and G. *wie.* See **Who, Why.** Der. *how-be-it*, Hen. V, i. 2. 91, Cor. i. 9. 70; *how-ever*, K. John, i. 173; *how-so-ever*, Haml. i. 5. 84.

HOW (2), a hill. (Scand.) Chiefly in place-names; as Silver *How*, near Grasmere. ME. *how*; Hampole's Psalter mentions 'howys . . and hilles;' Ps. lxxi. 3.—Icel. *haugr*, a how, mound; Swed. *hög*, a heap, pile, mound; Dan. *höi*, a hill. Allied to E. *high*, Goth. *hauhs.* Cf. Icel. *hār*, Swed. *hög*, Dan. *hoi*, high; also Lithuan. *kaukaras*, a hill. See **High.**

HOWDAH, the same as **Houdah,** q.v.

HOWITZER, a short light cannon. (G.—Bohemian.) Sometimes spelt *howitz*; a mod. word, in Todd's Johnson. Borrowed from G. *haubitze*, a howitzer; a word formerly spelt *haufnitz.*—Bohemian *haufnice*, orig. a sling for casting a stone; Jungmann, Bohem. Dict. i. 662. The F. *obus*, a bomb-shell, is from the same G. word.

HOWL, to yell, cry out. (E.) ME. *houlen*, Chaucer, C. T. 2819 (A 2817); Gower, C. A. ii. 265. An imitative word; and prob. native; cf. MDu. *huylen*, to howl; Dan. *hyle*; Icel. *ýla*; Swed. *yla*; G. *heulen.* Similar forms are L. *ululāre*, to shriek, howl (whence OF. *huller*); Gk. ὑλάω, I bark (said of a dog), I howl or cry out (said of a man); ὀλολυγή, a cry. ¶ As Scheler remarks, the *h* in OF. *huller* was due to German influence. Der. *howl*, sb.; cf. *hurly-burly*, q. v. And see **Owl.**

HOX, to hamstring. (E.) ME. *hoxe*, Wyclif, Josh. xi. 6. To cut the *hox* or hamstring; this sb. occurs in Wyclif, 2 Sam. viii. 4; and is short for *hoxen, huxen*, or *hockshin*, lit. 'hock-sinew,' AS. *hōhsinu.*—AS. *hōh*, heel, also hock, hough; and *sinu*, a sinew. See **Hough** and **Sinew.**

HOY (1), a kind of sloop. (Du.) In Spenser, F. Q. ii. 10. 64. 'Equyppt a *hoye*, and set hir under sayle;' Gascoigne, Fruits of War, st. 136. 'An *hoye* of Dorderyght;' Paston Letters, iii. 388.—MDu. *hoei* (Verwijs), variant of MDu. *heu, heude*, 'a boate or a ship' (Hexham); a kind of flat-bottomed merchantman, a hoy; whence also MF. *heù*, explained by Cotgrave to mean 'a Dutch hoy.' Of uncertain origin.

HOY (2), interj. stop! (E.) A nautical term. 'When one ship hails another, the words are, What ship, *hoy*? that is, stop, and tell the name of your ship;' Pegge, Anecdotes of the English Language, p. 16 (Todd). Also an exclamation, sometimes of joy; ME. *hoy*, P. Plowman, C. ix. 123. Cf. Du. *hui*, hoy! come! well! Dan. *hui*, hallo! See **Ho!** Der. *a-hoy*, q.v.

HOYDEN, the same as **Hoiden,** q.v.

HUB, the projecting nave of a wheel; a mark at which quoits are cast; &c. (E.) The orig. sense is 'projection.' 'Hubs, naves of wheels;' Marshall's Leicestershire and Warwickshire Words, ed. 1790 (E. D. S.). Also (in many dialects), the back of a grate, or the side-ledge of it; see N. E. D. The same word as *hob*; see **Hob** (1).

HUBBUB, a confused noise. (C.) Another spelling is *whoobub*, Wint. Ta. iv. 4. 629; Two Noble Kinsmen, ed. Skeat, ii. 5. 35. Spenser has 'shrieking *hububs*;' F. Q. iii. 10. 43; also 'a terrible yell and *hubbabowe*;' View of State of Ireland, p. 632 (Globe ed.). An imitative word; and perhaps suggested by Gael. *ub*! interj. of aversion; Irish *abu*! a warcry. *Hubbub* was confused with E. *hoop-hoop*, and *whoobub* with E. *whoop-hoop.* See **Hoop** (2).

HUCKABACK, a sort of linen cloth. (Low G.?) 'Huckaback, a sort of linen cloth that is woven so as to lie partly raised;' Bailey, vol. ii. ed. 1731. First in 1690 (N. E. D.). The word bears so remarkable a resemblance to Low G. *hukkebak*, G. *huckeback*, pick-a-back, that it seems reasonable to suppose that it at first meant 'peddler's ware;' see **Huckster**. Cf. Pomeran. *eenen hukbak drägen*, to carry one pick-a-back; Low G. *hokeboken*, to carry on the back (Lübben). Weigand (i. 828) explains G. *Huckepack* as (1) a humped back for carrying a thing; (2) a burden borne on the back.

HUCKLE-BERRY, a berry of the *Gaylussacia*, a low berry-bearing shrub, common in N. America. (E.) In Hawthorne, Twice-told Tales, ed. 1851; I. xvi. 249: 'a lot of *huckleberries*.' The same as *whortleberry*, formerly *hurtleberry*. Spelt *hurtilberyes*; Babees Book, p. 123, l. 82. See **Whortleberry**.

HUCKLE-BONE, the hip-bone. (E.) 'The hip . . . wherein the joint doth move The thigh, 'tis called the *huckle-bone*;' Chapman, tr. of Homer, Iliad, v. 297. 'Ache in the *huckle-bones*;' Sir T. Elyot, Castel of Helth, b. iv. c. 6. *Huckle* is the dimin. of prov. Eng. *huck*, which is a mere variant of *hock*; thus *huck-le* = *hock-le*. See E. D. D. And see **Hough**. Dunbar has *hukebanis*, hip-bones or hock-bones; Flyting with Kennedie, 181. ¶ In dialects, the *hock*, orig. the heel, is confused with the ham and the hip.

HUCKSTER, a peddler, hawker, retailer of small articles. (O. Low G.) Properly a *feminine* form, the corresponding masc. form being *hawker*, as now spelt, though *huckster* answers better to *hucker*. We have the expression 'she hath holden *hokkerye*,' i. e. followed a huckster's trade; P. Plowman, B. v. 227. But the AS. distinction in gender between the terminations *-er* and *-ster* was lost at an early period, so that the word was readily applied to men. '*Hwk-stare, hukstere*, auxionator, auxionatrix, auxionarius. *Hukstare of frute*, colibista;' Prompt. Parv. p. 252. *Hucster*, as a gloss to *institorem*; Wright's Vocab. i. 123. 'Forr þatt teȝȝ turrndenn Godess hus inntill *huccsterress boþe*' = for that they turned God's house into a huckster's booth; Ormulum, 15816, 7. β. An O. Low G. word, but it does not appear in AS. The related words are Du. *heuker*, a retailer, *heuken*, to retail; also '*heukeren*, to sell by retail, to huckster; *heukelaar*, a huckster, retailer;' Sewel's Du. Dict. Also Swed. *hökare*, a cheesemonger (Widegren); Dan. *höker*, a chandler, huckster, *hokeri*, the huckster's trade; *hökerske*, a 'huxteress' (this form is the Dan. equivalent of E. *huckster*); *hökre*, to huckster. γ. The word was imported, about A.D. 1200, probably from the Netherlands; the termination *-ster* being Dutch as well as English, as shown by Du. *spin-ster*, a spinster, &c. δ. The etymology is much disputed; but it is well illustrated by Hexham's MDu. Dict., which gives us *hucken*, to stoop or bow; *een hucker*, a stooper, bower, or bender; *onder eenen swaren last hucken*, to bow under a heavy burden; *een hucker*, a huckster, or a mercer. Compare also the Icel. *hokra*, to go bent, to crouch, creep, slink about, on which it is noted that 'in modern usage *hokra* means to live as a small farmer, whence *hokr*, in *bū-hokr*, small farming;' Vigfusson. Nothing could be more fitting than to describe the peddler of olden times as a croucher, creeper, or slinker about; his bent back being due to the bundle upon it. (See Sir W. Scott's description of Bryce Snailsfoot in The Pirate.) ε. Cf. also MDu. *huycken, huken*, Du. *huiken*, to stoop down, crouch (Oudemans); Icel. *hūka*, to sit on one's hams, with its deriv. *hokra*; Low G. *huken*, to crouch (Brem. Wört.); *hoker*, a huckster (Lübben). So also Icel. *hucke* is properly the *bent* back, whence G. *huckeback*, pick-a-back; G. *hocken* is to squat, also to carry on the back, and G. *hocker* means (1) a hump on the back, and (2) a huckster. See **Hawker**.

HUDDLE, to throw together confusedly, to crowd together. (E.) Used in late authors in the sense of performing a thing hastily; see examples in Todd; but it simply meant, originally, to hide in a heap, hence to crowd up, or to crowd; see Merch. of Ven. iv. 1. 28; Much Ado, ii. 1. 252. 'To *hudle* up together;' Minsheu. Not found in early writers; but the equivalent form *to hudder* (the suffixes *-er, -le* being similarly used to express a frequentative) is represented by ME. *hodren* = *hoderen* (with one *d*). 'For scatred er thi Scottis, and *hodred* in þer hottes' = for thy Scots are scattered, and huddled (dispersedly) in their huts; Rob. Manning, tr. of Langtoft, ed. Hearne, p. 273. β. But again, this ME. *hoderen* also had the sense of 'cover;' as in '*hodur* and happe' = cover and wrap up; Le Bone Florence, 112, in Ritson's Met. Romances, vol. iii; and the true notion of *huddle* or *hudder* was to crowd together for protection or in a place of shelter, a notion still preserved when we talk of cattle being huddled together in rain. So also Low G. *hudern*, to huddle oneself up (Schambach), Kurhessen *huttern*, to cover up warm. γ. From Teut. base *hud-*, weak grade allied to ME. *huden*, to hide, Ancren Riwle, p. 174, more frequently written *hiden*, whence mod. E. *hide*; see **Hide** (1). Thus to *huddle* is to hide closely, to crowd together for protection, to crowd into a place of shelter. Cf. also the ME. sb. *hudels* (= AS. *hȳdels*), a hiding-place; Ancren Riwle, p. 146; Wyclif, Deut. xxvii. 15. δ. The notion of doing things hastily may have

been due to the influence of Du. *hoetelen*, 'to doe a thing unskilly;' Hexham. This is allied to G. *hudeln*, to bungle, of which the Alsatian form is *hudlen*; cf. Swed. *hutla*, Dan. *hutle*, to bungle.

HUE (1), show, appearance, colour, tint. (E.) ME. *hewè*, often a dissyllabic word; Chaucer, C. T. 396 (A 394); but properly monosyllabic, and spelt *heu*, Havelok, 2918. AS. *hīw, hēow*, appearance, Grein, ii. 78.+Swed. *hy*, skin, complexion; Goth. *hiwi*, form, show, appearance, 2 Tim. iii. 5. Teut. type *hiwjom*, n. Cf. Skt. *chhavi*, skin, complexion, beauty. **Der.** *hue-d*, ME. *hewed*, Chaucer, C. T. 11557 (F 1245); *hue-less*.

HUE (2), clamour, outcry. (F. — Teut.) Only in the phr. *hue and cry*, Merry Wives, iv. 5. 92; 1 Hen. IV, ii. 4. 556. See *Hue and cry* in Blount's Nomolexicon; he notes that '*hue* is used alone, anno 4 Edw. I. stat. 2. In ancient records this is called *hutesium et clamor*;' for the latter phrase he cites a passage from the Close Rolls, 30 Hen. III. m. 5. ME. *hue*, a loud cry; Allit. Poems, ed. Morris, i. 872 (or 873). — OF. *hu*, a cry (Godefroy); *huer*, 'to hoot, . . . make hue and cry;' Cot. Cotgrave also gives *huée*, 'a showting, . . . outcry, or hue and cry.' Of Teut. origin. — MHG. *hū*, interj.; *hūzen*, to hoot; MSwed. *huta*, to hoot; see **Hoot**.

HUFF, to puff, bluster, bully. (E.) 'A *huff*, a huffing or swaggering fellow. *Huff*, to puff or blow, to rant or vapour;' Kersey's Dict., ed. 1715. 'And still you *huff* it;' Ben Jonson, Every Man, i. 2. 35. Hence *huffer*, a braggart; 'By such a braggadocio *huffer*;' Butler, Hudibras, pt. ii. c. 3, l. 1034. The old sense was 'to blow' or 'puff up.' 'When as the said winde within the earth, able to *huffe* up the ground, was not powerful enough to breake forth and make issue;' Holland's Pliny, b. ii. c. 85. β. Of imitative origin; we find *huf, puf*, and *haf, paf* in Reliq. Antiq. i. 240, to represent forcible blowing; cf. *puff*. Cf. Lowl. Sc. *hauch*, a forcible puff; *hech*, to breathe hard. See **Puff, Whiff**. **Der.** *huff*, at draughts, simply means 'to blow;' it seems to have been customary to blow upon the piece removed; Jamieson gives '*blaw*, to blow, also, to huff at draughts; I *blaw*, or *blow you*, I take [i. e. huff] this man.' (So also in Danish; *blæse en brikke*, to huff (lit. blow) a man at draughts.) Also *huff-er*, in Hudibras, as above; *huff-ish, huff-ish-ly, huff-ish-ness, huff-y, huff-i-ness*.

HUG, to embrace closely. (Scand.?) In Shak. Merch. of Ven. ii. 6. 16; Rich. III, i. 4. 252; &c. [Quite distinct from *hug*, to shrink, shudder; Palsgrave has: 'I *hugge*, I shrinke me in my bed. It is a good sporte to se this lytle boye *hugge* in his bedde for cold.'] β. Of uncertain origin. Perhaps (but with a change of sense) from Icel. *hugga*, to soothe, to comfort; *hugga barnið*, to soothe a child; allied to *huga*, to mind; *hugna*, to please; cf. Swed. *hugna*, to delight, gratify; Dan. *hue*, to like. Kalkar has MDan. *hugge*, to console, to encourage. This is not far from the sense of *hug*, in Comus, 164: 'and *hug* him into snares,' i. e. entice, lure.

HUGE, very great, vast. (F.) ME. *huge*, Chaucer, C. T. 2953 (A 2951); P. Plowman, B. xi. 242; Will. of Palerne, 2569. Oddly spelt *hogge*; 'an *hogge* geant;' Rob. of Brunne, tr. of Langtoft, p. 31, l. 17. The etymology is much disguised by the loss of an initial *a*, mistaken for the E. indef. article; the right word is *ahuge*. (The same loss occurs in ME. *avow*, now always *vow*, though this is not quite a parallel case, since once *vow* has a sense of its own.) — OF. *ahuge*, huge, vast; a 12th-century word. In the account of Goliath, in Les Livres des Rois, we find: 'E le fer de la lance sis cenz, e la hanste fud grosse e *ahuge* cume le suble as teissures' = and the iron of his lance weighed six hundred (shekels), and the shaft (of it) was great and *huge* as a weaver's beam; Bartsch, Chrestomathie Française, col. 45, l. 36. Also *ahoge, ahoje* (Godefroy). β. Of unknown origin; but perhaps connected with OHG. *irhōhen* (G. *erhohen*), to exalt; and the OHG. *hōh*, Icel. *hár*, AS. *hēah*, high. Cf. Norw. *hauga*, to heap up; Icel. *haugr*, a hill, whence OF. *hoge, hogue*, a hill; Norm. dial. *hogu*, arrogant (Moisy). See **How** (2). **Der.** *huge-ly*; *huge-ness*, Cymb. i. 4. 157.

HUGGER-MUGGER, secrecy. (E. and Scand.) In Hamlet, iv. 5. 84, in phr. in *hugger-mugger*. A reduplicated form; orig. *hucker-mucker*, as in More, Dialoge, ii. 52 b, iv. 121 b (N. E. D.). The E. prefix *hucker* is unmeaning, but rimes to *mucker*, from ME. *mukren, mokeren*, to heap up, hoard, conceal, from Norw. *mukka*, a heap. See **Muck**.

HUGUENOT, a French protestant. (F. — G.) '*Huguenots*, Calvinists, Reformists, French Protestants;' Blount's Gloss. ed. 1674. And in Minsheu. — F. *huguenots*, s. pl. 'Huguenots, Calvinists, Reformists;' Cot. As if from some person of the name of *Huguenot*. This name was in use as a Christian name two centuries before the time of the Reformation. 'Le 7 octobre, 1387, Pascal *Huguenot* de Saint Junien en Limousin, docteur en decret;' Hist. Litt. de la France, t. xxiv. p. 307 (Littré). *Huguenot* is a dimin. of *Hugues*, Hugh. — MHG. *Hūg*, Hugh. β. But this form was due to popular etymology; and was perverted from G. *eidgenoss*, a confederate, or from the equivalent Low G. form *eedgenoot* (MDu. *eedtgenoot* in Hexham). Wedgwood cites the Swiss Romance forms *einguenot*, *higuenot*, a protestant, also from G. Cf. Körting, § 3215.

HULK, a heavy ship. (Late L. – Gk.) Sometimes applied to the body of a ship, by confusion with *hull*; but it is quite a different word, meaning a heavy ship of clumsy make; Shak. Troil. ii. 3. 277. *The hulks* were old ships used as prisons. ME. *hulke*. 'Hulke, shyppe, Hulcus;' Prompt. Parv. p. 252. '*Hulke*, a shyppe, *hevrcque*;' Palsgrave. '*Orque*, a hulk or huge ship;' Cot. Late AS. *hulc*; '*Liburna, hulc*;' Voc. 181. 28. – Late L. *hulka*, a heavy merchant-ship, a word used by Walsingham; see quotation in Way's note to Prompt. Parv.; also spelt *hulcus*, as quoted above. Also spelt (more correctly) *holcas*; Ducange. – Gk. ὁλκάς, a ship which is towed, a ship of burden, merchantman. – Gk. ἕλκειν, to draw, drag; whence also ὁλκή, a dragging, ὁλκός, a furrow, a machine for dragging ships on land; from the base *selk-. Allied to L. *sulcus*, a furrow, AS. *sulh*, a plough. Brugmann, i. § 645. Der. *hulk-ing*, *hulk-y*, i. e. bulky or unwieldy. ☞ Not the same word as ME. *hulke*, a hovel, Wyclif, Isaiah, i. 8; which is from AS. *hulc*, a hut; Wright's Vocab. i. 58.

HULL (1), the husk or outer shell of grain or of nuts. (E.) ME. *hule, hole, hoole*. 'Hoole, hole, holl, or huske, Siliqua;' Prompt. Parv. p. 242. '*Hull* of a beane or pese, *escosse*. Hull or barcke of a tree, *escorce*;' Palsgrave; and see Way's note in Prompt. Parv. *Peese hole* (or *pese hule*) = pea-shell; P. Plowman, B. vii. 194, in two MSS.; see the footnote. AS. *hulu*, a husk; see index to Napier's glosses. Allied to G. *hülse*, a husk. From Teut. *hul-, weak grade of *helan-, to hide, to cover, as in AS. *helan*. Lit. 'covering.' See Hell. Allied words are OSaxon *bihullean*, to cover, Heliand, 1406 (Cotton MS.); Du. *hullen*, to put a cap on, mask, disguise; Goth. *huljan*, to hide, cover; G. *ver-hüllen*, to wrap up; Icel. *hylja*, to hide, cover; Swed. *hölja*, to cover, veil; Dan. *hylle*, to wrap. Der. see *housings*.

HULL (2), the body of a ship. (E.) Not in very early use. First in 1571. 'She never saw aboue one voyage, Luce, And, credit me, after another, her hull Will serue again;' Beaumont and Fletch. Wit Without Money, i. 2. 17. The *hull* is, literally, the 'shell' of the ship, being the same word with the above; see Hull (1). β. But it is probable that its use with respect to a ship was due to some confusion with ME. *holl*, Du. *hol*, the hold of a ship; see Hold (2). Cf. '*Hoole (holle)* of a schyppe, *Carina*;' Prompt. Parv. Der. *hull*, verb, to float about, as a ship does when the sails are taken down, Shak. Tw. Nt. i. 5. 217; Rich. III, iv. 4. 438; Hen. VIII, ii. 4. 199. So in Blount's Gloss., ed. 1674, we find: '*Hull*, the body of a ship, without rigging. *Hulling* is when a ship at sea takes in all her sails in a calm.'

HUM (1), to make a low buzzing or droning sound. (E.) ME. *hummen*; Chaucer, Troilus, ii. 1199; Palladius on Husbandry, ed. Lodge, vii. 124. Of imitative origin.+G. *hummen*, to hum. Cf. also Du. *hommelen*, to hum; the frequentative form; and Hem (2). Also MSwed. *hum*, a rumour (Ihre). Der. *hum* (2), q. v., *hum-bug*, q. v., *hum-drum*, q. v., *humble-bee*, q. v.; also *humm-ing-bird*, Pope's Dunciad, iv. 446, and in Evelyn's Diary, July 11, 1654; called a *hum-bird*, Sir T. Browne, Vulg. Errors, b. vi. c. 8. § 10.

HUM (2), to trick, to cajole. (E.) A particular use of the word above. In Shak. *hum* not only means to utter a low sound, as in Temp. ii. 1. 317, but also to utter a sound expressive of indignation, as in 'turns me his back And *hums*,' Macb. iii. 6. 42; 'to bite his lip and *hum* At good Cominius,' Cor. v. 1. 49. See Richardson and Todd, where it further appears that applause was formerly expressed by *humming*, and that to *hum* was to applaud; from applause to flattery, and then to cajolery, is not a long step. See the passage in Ben Jonson, The Alchemist, Act i. sc. 1, where Subtle directs his dupe to 'cry *hum* Thrice, and then *buz* as often;' showing that the word was used in a jesting sense. β. Wedgwood well points out a similar usage in Port. *zumbir*, to buzz, to hum, *zombar*, to joke, to jest; to which add Span. *zumbar*, to hum, resound, joke, jest, make one's-self merry, *zumbon*, waggish. Der. *hum*, sb. a hoax (Todd); *hum-bug*, q. v. Cf. *humh!* interj., Beaum. and Fletcher, Mons. Thomas, i. 2.

HUMAN, pertaining to mankind. (F. – L.) Formerly *humaine*, but now conformed to the L. spelling. 'All *humaine* thought;' Spenser, F. Q. vi. 3. 51. 'I meruayle not of the inhumanities that the *humain* people committeth;' Golden Book, lett. 11, § 2. – MF. *humain*, 'gentle, ... humane, manly;' Cot. – L. *hūmānus*, human; perhaps for *humnānus* (Bréal); allied to L. *hom-o*, a man. See Homage. Der. *human-ly*, *human-ise*, *human-is-at-ion*, *human-ist*, *human-kind*; also *human-i-ty*, ME. *humanitee*, Chaucer, C. T. 7968 (E 92), from OF. *humaniteit*, which is from L. acc. *hūmānitātem*, nom. *hūmānitās*; hence *humanit-ar-i-an*. And see Humane. ☞ The *accent* distinguishes *human*, of *French* origin, from *humane*, taken directly from Latin.

HUMANE, gentle, kind. (L.) In Shak., *humane* (so spelt) does duty both for *human* and *humane*, the accent being always on the *former* syllable; see Schmidt, Shak. Lexicon. Hence it has the sense of 'kind;' Temp. i. 2. 346. We have now differentiated the words, keeping the accent on the latter syllable in *humáne*, to make it more like the L. *hūmánus*. We may therefore consider this as the L. form. Both L. *hūmānus* and F. *humain* have the double sense (1) human, and (2) kind. See Human. Der. *humane-ly*, *humane-ness*.

HUMBLE, lowly, meek, modest. (F. – L.) ME. *humble*, Chaucer, C. T. 8700 (E 824). Spelt *umble* in O. Kentish Sermons, in An O. Eng. Miscellany, ed. Morris, p. 30. – OF. (and F.) *humble*, 'humble;' Cot. (With excrescent *b*.) – L. *humilem*, acc. of *humilis*, humble; lit. near the ground. – L. *humus*, the ground; *humi*, on the ground. Cf. Gk. χαμαί, on the ground; Russ. *zemlia*, earth, land. Brugmann, i. § 604. Der. *humbl-y*; *humble-ness*, formerly *humblesse*, Chaucer, C. T. 1783 (A 1781). Also, from L. *humilis*, *humili-ty*, q. v., *humili-ate*, q. v. Also, from L. *humus*, *ex-hume*, q. v. And see Chameleon.

HUMBLE-BEE, a humming bee. (E.) To *humble* is to hum; or more literally, to hum often, as it is the frequentative form, standing for *humm-le*; the *b* being excrescent. 'To *humble* like a bee;' Minsheu. ME. *humblen*, for *hummelen*. 'Or elles lyk the last *humblinge* After the clappe of a thundringe;' Chaucer, Ho. of Fame, 1039. Hence *hombel-be* or *hombul-be*; Reliquiæ Antiquæ, ed. Wright and Halliwell, i. 81. 'Hic tabanus, a *humbyl-bee*;' Wright's Vocab. i. 255 (Voc. 767. 20).+Du. *hommelen*, to hum, a frequentative form; *hommel*, a humble-bee, a drone, G. *hummel*, a humble-bee; *hummen*, to hum. Swed. *humla*, a humble-bee. See Hum (1).

HUMBLE-PIE; see under Umble.

HUMBUG, a hoax, a piece of trickery, an imposition under fair pretences. (E.) '*Humbug*, a false alarm, a bugbear;' Dean Milles MS. (written about 1760), cited in Halliwell. The word occurs in a long passage in The Student, vol. ii. p. 41, ed. 1751, cited in Todd. An alleged earlier trace of the word is on the title-page of an old jest-book, viz. 'The Universal Jester, or a pocket companion for the wits; being a choice collection of merry conceits, drolleries, ... bon-mots, and *humbugs*,' by Ferdinando Killigrew, London, said to be about 1735–40; but it is no older than 1754 (N. E. D.). See the Slang Dictionary, which contains a good article on this word. It is probably a compound of *hum*, to cajole, to hoax, and the old word *bug*, a spectre, bugbear, ghost; the orig. sense being 'sham bugbear' or 'false alarm,' as given by Dean Milles. [The N. E. D. makes *hum*, v., to cajole, a shortened form of *humbug*, but it is of the same date at least; and see Hum (1).] See Hum (2) and Bug. Der. *humbug*, verb, as in '*humbugged*, egad!' Smollett, Peregrine Pickle, ch. 85 (1751); *humbug*, sb., improperly used for *humbugger*.

HUMDRUM, dull, droning. (E.) Used as an adv., with the sense of 'idly' or 'listlessly' in Butler. 'Shall we, quoth she, stand still *hum-drum*?' Hudibras, pt. i. c. 3. l. 112. But it is properly an adj., signifying monotonous, droning, tedious, as in 'an old *humdrum* fellow;' Addison, Whig Examiner (1710), No. 3 (Todd); and is thus found as early as 1553. The sb. *humdrum*, a dull fellow, is in Ben Jonson, Every Man, i. 1. Merely formed, as a reduplicated word, from *hum*, a humming noise, and *drum*, a droning sound, made to rime with *hum*. See Hum (1).

HUMERAL, belonging to the shoulder. (L.) '*Humeral muscle*, the muscle that moves the arm at the upper end;' Kersey, ed. 1715. – Late L. *humerālis*, belonging to the shoulder; cf. L. *humerāle*, a cape for the shoulders. – L. *humerus*, better *umerus*, the shoulder. +Gk. ὦμος, the shoulder; Goth. *amsa*, the shoulder; Skt. *aṁsa-s*, the shoulder. Brugmann, i. § 163.

HUMID, moist. (F. – L.) In Milton, P. L. iv. 151; and in Cotgrave. – F. *humide*, 'humid, moist;' Cot. – L. *hūmidus*, better *ūmidus*, moist. – L. *hūmēre*, better *umēre*, to be moist; allied to *ūuens*, moist, *ūuidus*, *ūdus*, moist.+Gk. ὑγ-ρός, moist; Icel. *vokr*, moist. Brugmann, i. §§ 658, 667. Der. *humid-ness*, *humid-i-ty*, Merry Wives, iii. 3. 43; and see *humour*.

HUMILIATE, to make humble. (L.) A late word, really suggested by the sb. *humiliation*, used in Chaucer, C. T. Pers. Tale (I 480). The verb is formed from L. *humiliātus*, pp. of *humiliāre*, to humble. – L. *humili-*, decl. stem of *humilis*, humble. See Humble. Der. *humiliat-ion* (formed by analogy with other words in -*ation*) from L. acc. *humiliātiōnem*, nom. *humiliātio*.

HUMILITY, humbleness, meekness. (F. – L.) ME. *humilitee*, Chaucer, C. T. 13405 (B 1665). – OF. *humiliteit*, later *humilite*. – L. acc. *humilitātem*, from nom. *humilitās*, humility. – L. *humili-*, decl. stem of *humilis*, humble. See Humble.

HUMOUR, moisture, temperament, disposition of mind, caprice. (F. – L.) See Trench, Select Glossary, and Study of Words. 'He knew the cause of euery maladye, And wher engendred, and of what *humour*;' Chaucer, C. T. 423 (A 421). [The *four humours*, according to Galen, caused the four temperaments of mind, viz. choleric, melancholy, phlegmatic, and sanguine.]—OF. *humor* (Littré), later *humeur*, 'humour, moisture;' Cot.—L. *hūmōrem*, acc. of *hūmor*, better *ūmor*, moisture.—L. *hūmēre*, better *ūmēre*, to be moist. See **Humid**. Der. *humour*, verb; *humor-ous, humor-ous-ly, humor-ous-ness, humour-less, humor-ist*; from the same source, *hum-ect-ant*, moistening (rare).

HUMMOCK, HOMMOCK, a mound, hillock, mass. (E.) 'Common among our voyagers,' Rich.; who refers to Anson, Voyage round the World, b. ii. c. 9; Cook, Second Voyage, b. iii. c. 4. 'Round *hoommockes* or *hyllockes*;' R. Eden, ed. Arber, p. 381 (1555). It appears to be related to *hump* and *hunch*. Cf. EFries. *hümmel*, variant of *humpel, hümpel*, a hillock; Du. *homp*, a hump, hunch; '*een homp kaas*, a lunch [i. e. hunch] of cheese;' Sewel. 'Hompelig, rugged, cragged;' id. So too Low G. *hümpel*, a little heap or mound; Bremen Wörterb. ii. 669. *Hummock* is formed with dimin. -*ock*, as in *hill-ock*; whilst the EFries. *hümmel* is formed with the dimin. -*el*. See **Hump, Hunch**.

HUMP, a lump, bunch, esp. on the back. (E.) '*Hump*, a hunch, or lump, *Westmoreland*;' Halliwell. Of O. Low G. origin, and may be claimed as E., though not in early use. 'Only a natural *hump*' [on his back]; Addison, Spectator, no. 558. 'The poor *hump-backed* gentleman;' id. no. 559.+Du. *homp*, a hump, lump; cf. Low G. *hümpel*, a small heap, Bremen Wörterbuch, ii. 669; Dan. *humpel*, a hummock; Norw. *hump*, a knoll, a hillock; Swed. dial. *hump*, a clot or piece of earth, &c.; Low G. *humpe, hompe*, a hunch of bread (Berghaus). Cf. also Skt. *kubja-s*, hump-backed. Der. *hump-backed*; *humm-ock*, q. v.; *hunch*, q. v.

HUNCH, a hump, bump, a round or ill-shaped mass. (E.) A variant of *hump*. *Hunch-backed* occurs in the later quarto edd. of Shak. Rich. III, iv. 4. 81 (Schmidt). 'Thy crooked mind within *hunch'd* out thy back;' Dryden, qu. in Todd (no reference); it occurs in Œdipus, i. 6, by Dryden and Lee (N. E. D.). A palatalised form of prov. E. *hunk*, a lump; which agrees with WFlem. *hunke*, as in *hunke brood*, a hunch of bread (De Bo). And see Franck, s. v. *honk*. Der. *hunch*, vb., *hunch-backed*.

HUNDRED, ten times ten. (E.) ME. *hundred*, Chaucer, C. T. 2155 (A 2153); also *hundreth*, Pricke of Conscience, 4524. AS. *hundred*, Grein, ii. 111. A compound word.—AS. *hund*, a hundred, Grein, ii. 111; and -*red*, with the sense of 'reckoning' or rate, to denote the rate of counting; cf. Icel. *hund-rað*, which orig. meant 120; and G. *hund-ert*. This suffix is allied to Goth. *rathjo*, number (L. *ratio*); cf. Goth. *garathjan*, to reckon, number, Matt. x. 30; and see **Rate** (1). Thus the word grew up by the unnecessary addition of -*red* (denoting the rate of counting) to the old word *hund*, used by itself in earlier times. β. Dismissing the suffix, we have the cognate OHG. *hunt* (also once used alone), Goth. *hund*; cf. also W. *cant*, Gael. *ciad*, Irish *cead*, L. *centum*, Gk. ἑ-κατ-όν, Lith. *szimtas*, Russ. *sto*, Pers. *sad*, Skt. *çatam*, all meaning a hundred. γ. All from an Idg. type *kəmtóm*, prob. a docked form of *dekəm-tóm*, a decad; and allied to Goth. *taihuntē-hund*, a hundred, which Brugmann explains as δεκάδων δεκάς (a decad of decads). See Brugmann, i. § 431; ii. § 179. And see **Ten**. ¶ The ME. *hun-dreth* is a Scand. form; from the Icel. *hundrað*. Der. *hundred-th, hundred-fold, hundred-weight*, often written *cwt.*, where *c* = L. *centum*, and *wt* = Eng. *weight*.

HUNGER, desire of food. (E.) ME. *hunger*, Chaucer, C. T. 14738 (B 3618). AS. *hungor*, Grein, ii. 111.+Icel. *hungr*; Swed. and Dan. *hunger*; Du. *honger*; G. *hunger*; Goth. *hūhrus*, hunger; whence *huggrjan* (= *hungrian*), to hunger. Teut. types *hungruz, *hunhruz*, m. Allied to Lith. *kanka*, suffering. Brugm. i. § 639. Der. *hunger*, verb = AS. *hyngran* (with vowel-change of *u* to *y*); *hungry* = AS. *hungrig* (Grein); *hungri-ly*; *hunger-bitten*, Job, xviii. 12.

HUNT, to chase wild animals. (E.) ME. *hunten, honten*, Chaucer, C. T. 1640. AS. *huntian*; see Ælfric's Colloquy, in Voc., p. 92. Properly 'to capture;' a secondary verb related to *hentan*, to seize, also a weak verb; Grein, ii. 34. β. We also find Goth. *hunths*, captivity, Eph. iv. 8; formed from the weak grade (*hunth*-) of the verb *hinthan* (pt. t. *hanth*), to seize, capture, only used in the comp. *fra-hinthan*, with pp. *fra-hunthans*, a captive, Luke, iv. 19. It would hence appear that *hunt*- is a variant of *hunth*-, though the variation is not easy to explain. 'On an apparent pre-Teutonic change of *nt* to *nd* in these and some other words, see Prof. Napier in *Mod. Quart. Lang. & Lit.*, July, 1898, p. 130; cf. Brugmann, i. § 701.'—N. E. D. Der. *hunt*, sb.; *hunt-er*, Chaucer, C. T. 1638, later form of AS. *hunta*, a hunter, in Ælfric's Colloquy; *hunt-r-ess*, with F. suffix -*ess*, As You Like It, iii. 2. 4; *hunt-ing*, sb., *hunt-ing-box, hunt-ing-seat*; *hunt-s-man* (= *hunt's man*), Mid. Nt. Dr. iv. 1. 143;

hunts-man-ship; *hunts-up* (= *the hunt is up*, i. e. beginning), Rom. iii. 5. 34, replaced by *the hunt is up*, Tit. Andron. ii. 2. 1.

HURDLE, a frame of twigs interlaced or twined together, a frame of wooden bars. (E.) ME. *hurdel*; pl. *hurdles*, K. Alisaunder, 6104. AS. *hyrdel*; 'cleta, cratis, *hyrdel*;' 'crates, i. e. flecta, *hyrdel*;' Wright's Vocab. i. 26. col. 2, 34. col. 1 (Voc. 126. 16; 140. 23). Also OMerc. *hyrðil*, Voc. 16. 7. A dimin. from a Teut. base *hurd*-; see the cognate words.+Du. *horde*, a hurdle; Icel. *hurð*; G. *hürde*, MHG. *hurt*; Goth. *haurds*, a door, i. e. one made of wicker-work, Matt. vi. 6. Further allied to L. *crātis*, a hurdle, Gk. κάρταλος, a (woven) basket, from √QERT, to weave; whence also Skt. *kṛt*, to spin, *chṛt*, to connect together. Cf. also Skt. *kaṭa-s*, a mat. Brugmann, §§ 529, 633; also Stokes-Fick, p. 80, where we find Irish *certle*, glossed by L. 'glomus.' Der. *hurdle*, verb, pp. *hurdled*, Milton, P. L. iv. 186. Doublet, *crate*, q. v.

HURDY-GURDY, a kind of violin, but played by turning a wheel. (E.) 'Hum! plays, I see, upon the *hurdy-gurdy*;' O'Hara's play of Midas, Act i (1764). Suggested by Lowl. Sc. *hirdy-girdy*, a confused noise; cf. also *hirdum-dirdum*, with the same sense. Note also: 'Som vseþ straunge wlafferynge, chiterynge, harrynge and garrynge,' i. e. some people use a strange babbling, chattering, snarling and growling; Trevisa, tr. of Higden, ii. 159. Cf. Lowland Sc. *hur*, to snarl; *gurr*, to snarl, growl, purr; Jamieson. 'R is the dog's letter, and *hurreth* in the sound;' Ben Jonson, Eng. Grammar. The word seems to have been fashioned on the model of *hurly-burly*.

HURL, to throw rapidly and forcibly, to push forcibly, drive. (Scand.) 'And *hurlest* [Tyrwhitt has *hurtlest*] al from est till occi-dent' = and whirlest all from east to west; Chaucer, C. T. Group B, 297 = l. 4717. 'Into which the flood was *hurlid*;' Wyclif, Luke, vi. 49, in six MSS.; but seventeen MSS. have *hurtlid*. So again, in Luke, vi. 48, most MSS. have *hurtlid*, but eight have *hurlid*. In the Ancren Riwle, p. 166, we find 'mid a lutel *hurlunge*' = with a slight collision; where another reading is *hurtlinge*. β. It is plain that *hurl* was often confused with *hurtle*, both being used in the sense of to push violently, jostle, strike with a forcible collision. For those who wish to make the comparison, further references are (1) for *hurlen*: Polit. Songs, ed. Wright, p. 211; Poems and Lives of Saints, ed. Furnivall, xxiii. 25; Will. of Palerne, 1243; Legends of the Holy Rood, p. 140; Allit. Poems, ed. Morris, B. 44, 223, 376, 413, 874, 1204, 1211; Destruction of Troy, 1365; Rob. of Glouc. p. 487, l. 9974; Fabyan's Chron., an. 1380-1 (R.); Spenser, F. Q. i. 5. 2, &c.; (2) for *hurtlen*, Wyclif, Jerem. xlviii. 12; Prompt. Parv. p. 253; Will. of Palerne, 5013; Pricke of Conscience, 4787; Chaucer, Legend of Good Women, Cleopatra, 59; &c. β. Nevertheless, they seem to have *no* etymological connexion. *Hurl* is not found in AS., nor earlier than 1225; so that it is prob. of Scand. origin. Explained by Swed. dial. *hurra*, to whir, to whirl round; whence *hurrel*, a whirl, *hurrel-wind*, a whirlwind. So also Dan. *hurre*, to buzz; whence *hurle*, to whir (Larsen); Norw. *hurra*, to whirl, hum; *hurla*, to buzz; cf. Icel. *hurr*, a noise. And cf. EFries. *hurrel*, a gust of wind; *hurreln*, to blow in gusts; *hurrel-wind*, a whirlwind. We likewise find E. *hurleblast*, a hurricane, *hurlepool*, a whirlpool; *hurlewind*, a whirlwind. See **Hurry**. And compare **Whirl**, of which *hurl* is perhaps a 'weak-grade' form. Der. *hurl-er*.

HURLY-BURLY, a tumult. (F. and E.) In Macb. i. 1. 3; as adj., 1 Hen. IV, v. 1. 78. Spelt *hurly-burlye*, in Bale's Kynge Johan, p. 63 (before 1560). A reduplicated word, the second sylla-ble being an echo of the first, to give more fulness. The simple form *hurly* is the original; see K. John, iii. 4. 169; 2 Hen. IV, iii. 1. 25.—OF. *hurlee*, a howling, great noise, orig. fem. pp. of *hurler*, 'to howle, to yell;' Cot. Cf. Ital. *urlare*, to howl, yell. Both these forms are corrupt, and contain an inserted *r*. The OF. form was orig. *huller*, to howl, also in Cot.; cf. Bartsch, Chrestomathie Française, col. 354, l. 24; and the correct Ital. form is *ululare*, to shriek, also to howl or yell as a wolf (Florio).—L. *ululāre*, to howl; *ulula*, an owl. ¶ The MF. *hurluburlu*, a heedless, hasty person, used by Rabelais, does not seem to be immediately connected. But we may note MDan. *hulder-bulder*, noise, racket (Kalkar); Swed. *huller om buller*, pell-mell. The mod. E. *hullabaloo* seems to be a corruption.

HURRAH, an exclamation of joy. (G.) Spelt *whurra* in Addison, The Drummer (near the end). From G. *hurra*, MHG. *hurrā*. Of imitative origin; see **Hurl**. The older word is **Huzzah**, q. v.

HURRICANE, a whirlwind, violent storm of wind. (Span.—Caribbean.) Formerly *hurricano*. 'The dreadful spout, Which shipmen do the *hurricano* call;' Shak. Troilus, v. 2. 172.—Span. *huracan*, a hurricane; spelt *hurracan* in Pineda.—Caribbean *huracan*, as written by Littré, who refers to Oviedo, Hist. des Indes. 'Great tempestes which they caule *furacanas* or *haurachanas*;' Eden, ed. Arber, p. 216. See also Washington Irving's Life of Columbus, b. viii. c. 9 (Trench); Rich. quotes from Dampier's Voyages, v. ii.

pt. ii. c. 6, that hurricanes are 'violent storms, raging chiefly among the Caribbee islands.' Hence also Port. *furacão*, a hurricane.

HURRY, to hasten, urge on. (Scand.) Quite different from *harry*, with which Richardson confuses it. In Shak. Romeo, v. 1. 65; Temp. i. 2. 131. Extended by the addition of *y* from an older form *hurr*, just as *scurry* is from *skirr*. It is probably the same word with the rare ME. *horien*, to hurry. 'And by the hondes hym hent and *horyed* hym withinne' = and they [the angels] caught him [Lot] by the hand, and *hurried* him within; Allit. Poems, ed. Morris, B. 883.—MSwed. *hurra*, to swing or whirl round (Ihre); Swed. dial. *hurra*, to whirl round, to whiz; Swed. dial. *hurr*, great haste, hurry (Rietz); Dan. *hurre*, to buzz, to hum; Icel. *hurr*, a noise. **β.** Of imitative origin, and a weaker form of the more expressive and fuller form *whir*; see **Whir, Whiz**. Ben Jonson says of the letter R that it is 'the dog's letter, and *hurreth* in the sound.' **Der.** *hurry*, sb.

HURST, a wood. (E.) In Drayton's Polyolbion, s. 2, l. 187: 'that, from each rising *hurst*.' ME. *hurst* (Stratmann). Very common in place-names in Kent, e. g. *Pens-hurst*. AS. *hyrst*, i. e. Hurst in Kent; Thorpe, Diplomatarium, p. 65.+MHG. *hurst*, a shrub, thicket; Low G. *horst*; EFries. *hörst*; MDu. *horst, horscht*, 'the wood of osieres or withes;' Hexham. Perhaps allied to **Hurdle**.

HURT, to strike or dash against, to injure, harm. (F.) In early use. ME. *hurten, hirten*, used in both senses (1) to dash against, push; and (2) to injure. Ex. (1) 'And he him *hurteth* [pusheth] with his hors adoun,' Chaucer, C. T. 2618 (Six-text, A 2616), according to 4 MSS.; 'heo *hurten* heora hafden' = they dashed their heads together, Layamon, 1878. (2) 'No man *hurte* other = that none injure other; P. Plowman, B. x. 366. In the Ancren Riwle, it has both senses; see the glossary.—OF. *hurter*, later *heurter*, 'to knock, push, jur, joult, strike, dash, or hit violently against;' Cot. 'Se *heurter* à une pierre, to stumble at a stone,' id. **β.** Hardly of Celtic origin; and not from W. *hyrddu*, to ram, push, impel, butt, make an assault, *hwrdd*, a push, thrust, butt; see Thurneysen, p. 81. We find also OProv. *urtar, hurtar* (Gloss. to Bartsch, Chrest. Provençale), Ital. *urtare*, to knock, hit, dash against; perhaps from a late L. type **urtare*, as if from **urtum*, unused supine of *urgēre*, to urge, to press on. See Körting, § 9924. ¶ MDu. *horten*, and Low G. *hurten*, to push, are from F. **Der.** *hurt*, sb., Ancren Riwle, p. 112, Chaucer, C. T. 10785 (F 471); *hurt-ful, hurt-ful-ly, hurt-ful-ness; hurt-less, hurt-less-ly, hurt-less-ness.*

HURTLE, to come into collision with, to dash against, to rattle. (F.; *with* E. *suffix.*) Nearly obsolete, but used in Gray's Fatal Sisters, st. 1; imitated from Shak. Jul. Cæsar, ii. 2. 22. ME. *hurtlen*, to jostle against, dash against, push; see references under **Hurl**. To these add: 'And he him *hurtleth* with his hors adoun;' Chaucer, C. T. 2618 (Six-text, A 2616), in the Ellesmere MS., where most other MSS. have *hurteth*. **β.** In fact, *hurt-le* is merely the frequentative of *hurt* in the sense 'to dash.' And this *hurt* is the ME. *hurten*, to dash, also to dash one's foot against a thing, to stumble. 'If ony man shal wandre in the day he *hirtith* not,' i. e. stumbles not; Wyclif, John, xi. 9. Du Wes has MF. *hurteler*, 'to hurtle together;' perhaps from E.; see Palsgrave, p. 948, col. 2. See further under **Hurt**.

HURTLEBERRY, a bilberry. (E.) Hakluyt has *hurtilberies*, Voy. i. 477. Also called *huckleberries, hurts, horts, hearts, hartberries*; E. Plant-names (E. D. S.). Spelt *hurtes*, A. Boorde, Dyetary, ed. Furnivall, p. 267. AS. *heorotberge*, a berry of the buckthorn; AS. Leechdoms, iii. 331; but cf. Voc. 33. 12, 203. 22, 409. 13, 443. 28. From AS. *heorot*, a hart; and *berge, berie*, a berry. See **Hart** and **Berry**.

HUSBAND, the master of a house, the male head of a household, a married man. (Scand.) The old sense is 'master of a house.' ME. *husbonde, husebonde*. 'The *husebonde* ... warneð his hus þus' = the master of the house guardeth his house thus; OEng. Homilies, ed. Morris, i. 247. 'Till a vast *husbandis* houss' = to an empty [waste] house of a farmer; Barbour's Bruce, vii. 151. AS. *hūsbonda*; 'æt hira *hūsbondum*' = from their fellow-dwellers in the same house; Exod. iii. 22. Not a true AS. word, but borrowed from Scandinavian.—Icel. *hūsbōndi*, the master or 'goodman' of a house; a contracted form from *hūsbūandi*.—Icel. *hūs*, a house; and *būandi*, dwelling, inhabiting, pres. part. of *būa*, to abide, dwell. See **Boor, Busk**. **Der.** *husband-man*, ME. *housbonde-man*, a householder, Wyclif, Matt. xx. 1; *husband-ry*, ME. *housbonderye*, P. Plowman, B. i. 57, spelt *housbondrye*, Chaucer, E 9172 (E 1296).

HUSH, to enjoin silence. (E.) Chiefly used in the imp. mood and in the pp. ME. *hushen, hussen*; 'and *husht* was al the place,' Chaucer, C. T. 2983, ed. Tyrwhitt; spelt *hust, huyst* in Six-text, A 2981. 'Tho weren the cruel clariouns ful *whist* [Camb. MS. *hust*] and full stille;' Chaucer, tr. of Boethius, b. ii. met. 5, l. 16 (*or* 25). 'After iangling wordes cometh "*huissht*! pees, and be stille";' Test. of Love, bk. i. ch. 5, l. 90. **β.** The word is purely imitative, from

the use of the word *hush* or *husht* to signify silence (*husht* being afterwards looked upon as a pp.); and it is seen that *whist* is but another expression of the same kind. See **Whist**. Cf. Low G. *husse bussee*, an expression used in singing children to sleep; Bremen Wörterb. ii. 678; Hamburgh *hüssen*, to hush to sleep (Richey). So also G. *husch*, hush! quick! Pomeran. *hüsch*, Dan. *hys*, hush! also Swed. *hyssa*, Dan. *husse*, MDan. *hvisse*, to hush. And see **Hist**. **Der.** *hush-money*, Guardian, no. 26, April 10, 1713. ¶ In the form *husht*, the *t* was at first an integral part of the word, just as in *whist*. 'I *huste*, I styll,' Palsgrave; 'to *huste*, silere;' Levins.

HUSK, the dry covering of some fruits, &c. (E.) ME. *huske*. '*Huske* of frute or oþer lyke;' Prompt. Parv. p. 254. 'The note [nu'] of the haselle hathe an *husk* with-outen;' Mandeville, Trav. ch. xviii. p. 188. The *k* is a dimin. suffix. From AS. *hūs*, a house. Cf. Low G. *huuske*; (1) a little house; (2) core of an apple (Berghaus); Pomeran. *hūseken*, the same; EFries. *hūske*, a little house, core of an apple, small case; MDu. *huysken*, a little house, case, husk of fruit (Kilian). And note AS. *pisan hosa*, pea-shell, as a gloss to L. *siliqua*; Corpus Gloss. 1867. **Der.** *husk*, verb, to take off the shells; *husk-ed*.

HUSKY, hoarse, as applied to the voice. (E.) A peculiar use of *husky*, i. e. full of husks (N. E. D.). '*Huskye*, or ful of huskes, *siliquōsus*;' Huloet (1552). And see the other examples. But perhaps influenced by prov. E. *hask*, dry, parching, tart, hoarse (E. D. D.); *husk*, hoarse, dry, also hoarseness (id.). **Der.** *husk-i-ness*.

HUSSAR, a cavalry soldier. (G.—Hungarian.—Servian.—Gk.—L.) '*Hussars, Husares*, Hungarian horsemen;' Coles' Dict. ed. 1684. 'After the manner of the *Hussars*;' Spectator, no. 576. '*Hussars*, light cavalry in Poland and Hungary, about 1600. The British Hussars were enrolled in 1759;' Haydn, Dict. of Dates.—G. *Husar*.—Hungar. *huszar*, a free-booter, later, a light horseman.—Serv. χusar, a hussar, free-booter, robber, sea-robber; Popović.—Late Gk. κουρσάριος, a corsair, pirate (Ducange).—Late L. *cursārius*, a corsair.—L. *curs-us*, a course. See **Corsair**; of which *hussar* is a doublet. ¶ The word is older than the story about Mathias Corvinus (1458); see N. and Q. 8 S. ii. 156; Miklosich, p. 148.

HUSSIF, a case containing thread, needles, and other articles for sewing. (E.) '*Hussif*, that is, house-wife; a roll of flannel with a pin-cushion attached, used for the purpose of holding pins, needles, and thread;' Peacock, Gloss. of words used in Manley and Corringham, co. Lincoln. Spelt *husswife* in Garrick, Miss in her Teens, Act 2. sc. 1 (1747). The sense is 'housewife's companion.' [It is remarkably like Icel. *hūsi*, a case; but this is accidental.] From **House** and **Wife**. The ME. word was *nedyl-hows*, i. e. needle-house; Voc. 659. 37.

HUSSY, a pert girl. (E.) 'The young *husseys*;' Spectator, no. 242. *Hussy* is a corruption of *huswife*; cf. 'Doth Fortune play the *huswife* with me now?' Hen. V, v. 1. 85. And again, *huswife* stands for *house-wife* = woman who minds a house; from *house* and *wife* in the general sense of woman; cf. 'the good *housewife* Fortune,' As You Like It, i. 2. 33; 'Let *housewives* make a skillet of my helm;' Oth. i. 3. 273. Cf. ME. *hoswyf*, mater familias; Voc. 794. 9. See **House** and **Wife**. And see **Hussif**.

HUSTINGS, a platform used by candidates for election to parliament. (Scand.) The modern use is incorrect; it means rather a 'council,' or assembly for the choice of such a candidate; and it should rather be used in the singular *husting*. Minsheu has *hustings*, and refers to 11 Hen. VII. cap. 21. ME. *husting*, a council; 'hulden muchel *husting*' = they held a great council; Layamon, 2324. AS. *hūsting*, a council (of Danes); A. S. Chron. an. 1012. Not an AS. word, but used in speaking of Danes.—Icel. *hūsþing*, 'a council or meeting, to which a king, earl, or captain summoned his people or guardsmen.'—Icel. *hūs*, a house; and *þing*, (1) a thing, (2) as a law term, 'an assembly, meeting, a general term for any public meeting, esp. for purposes of legislation; a parliament, including courts of law.' Cf. Swed. *ting*, a thing, an assize; *hålla ting*, to hold assizes; Dan. *ting*, a thing, court, assize. **β.** The Icel. *hūs* is cognate with E. *house*; and *þing* with E. *thing*. See **House** and **Thing**.

HUSTLE, to push about, jostle in a crowd. (Du.) It should have been *hutsle*, but the change to *hustle* was inevitable, to make it easier of pronunciation. In Johnson's Dict., but scarce in literature. First in 1684.—Du. *hutselen*, to shake up and down, either in a tub, bowl, or basket; *onder malkanderen hutselen*, to huddle together [lit. to hustle one another]; Sewel. A frequentative form of MDu. *hutsen*, Du. *hotsen*, to shake, jog, jolt. '*Hutselen*, or *huisen*, to shake something in a hat;' Hexham. Cf. Lowland Sc. *hotch, hott*, to move by jerks, *hotter*, to jolt; prov. G. *hotze*, a cradle, a swing (Schade). See **Hotchpot**.

HUT, a cottage, hovel. (F.—OHG.) ME. *hotte*. 'For scatred er þi Scottis, and hodred in þer *hottes*' = for scattered are thy Scots, and huddled in their huts; Rob. Manning, tr. of Langtoft, ed. Hearne, p. 273. – F. *hutte*, 'a cote [cot] or cottage;' Cot. – OHG. *hutta*, G. *hütte*, a hut, cottage; whence also Span. *huta*, a hut; and probably Du. *hut*, Dan. *hytte* (since these words have not the Low G. *d* for HG. *t*). + Swed. *hydda*, a hut; MDan. *hodde*, a hut, *hudde*, a nook (Kalkar). From Teut. **hud-*, weak grade of **heud-*, to hide. See **Hide** (1), **Hod**.

HUTCH, a box, chest, for keeping things in. (F. – Low L.) Chiefly used now in the comp. *rabbit-hutch*. Shak. has *bolting-hutch*, a hutch for bolted (or boulted) flour; 1 Hen. IV, ii. 4. 495. Milton has *hutch'd* = stored up; Comus, 719. ME. *huche, hucche*, P. Plowman, B. iv. 116; Hampole's Psalter, Ps. 131 (132). 8. – OF. (and F.) *huche*, 'a hutch or binne;' Cot. – Low L. *hūtica*; 'quadam cista, vulgo *hutica* dicta;' Ducange. β. Of unknown origin; but prob. Teutonic; and prob. from OHG. *huotan*, MHG. *hüeten*, to take care of, from OHG. *huota*, heed, care, cognate with E. *heed*. See **Heed**.

HUZZAH, a shout of approbation. (E.) 'Loud *huzzas*;' Pope, Essay on Man, iv. 256. 'They made a greate *huzza*, or shout, at our approch, three times;' Evelyn's Diary, June 30, 1665. Of imitative origin; cf. G. *hussa*, huzza; *hussa rufen*, to shout huzza. We find also Dan. *hurra*, hurrah! Swed. *hurra*, hurrah! *hurrarop*, a cheer (*rop* = a shout); *hurra*, v., to salute with cheers; MHG. *hurrā*, hurrah! Cf. Dan. *hurre*, to hum, to buzz. See **Hurrah**, **Hurry**.

HYACINTH, a kind of flower. (F. – L. – Gk.) In Cotgrave and Minsheu; and in Milton, P. L. iv. 701. Spelt *hyacint* in Daniel, Sonnet 34. – F. *hyacinthe*, 'the blew or purple jacint, or hyacinth flower; we call it also crow-toes;' Cot. – L. *hyacinthus*. – Gk. ἱάκινθος, an iris or larkspur (not what is now called a hyacinth); said, in Grecian fable, to have sprung from the blood of the youth Hyacinthos; but, of course, the fable is later than the name. Cf. Brugmann, i. § 280. **Der.** *hyacinth-ine*, i.e. curling like the hyacinth, Milton, P. L. iv. 301; Pope, Odys. vi. 274. **Doublet**, *jacinth*.

HYADES, a group of stars in Taurus. (Gk.) In G. Douglas, tr. of Virgil, bk. iii. ch. 8, l. 21. – Gk. ὑάδες, pl., the Hyades; lit. 'little pigs;' allied to Gk. ὗς, a sow; see **Sow** (2). Called in Latin *suculæ*, with the same sense. ¶ Connected in popular etymology with ὕειν, to rain; hence Virgil has 'pluuiasque Hyadas;' Aen. iii. 516.

HYÆNA, the same as **Hyena**, q. v.

HYALINE, crystalline, glassy. (L. – Gk.) See Milton, P. L. vii. 619. – L. *hyalinus*. – Gk. ὑάλινος, glassy; see Rev. iv. 6. – Gk. ὕαλος, ὕελος, crystal.

HYBRID, mongrel, an animal or plant produced from two different species. (L. – Gk.) 'She's a wild Irish born, sir, and a *hybride*;' Ben Jonson, New Inn, A. ii. sc. 2 (Host); also spelt *hybride* in Minsheu. – L. *hibrida, hybrida*, a mongrel, hybrid; esp. with reference to a wild boar and a sow; Pliny, bk. viii. c. 53. β. Sometimes derived from Gk. ὕβριδ-, stem of ὕβρις, insult, wantonness, violation; but this is doubtful. Rather, from Gk. ὕ-, for ὗς, a sow; and ἰβρο-, only known from the comp. ἰβρί-καλοι = χοῖροι, i. e. hogs (Hesychius). So M. Warren, in Amer. Journal of Philology; vol. v. no. 4.

HYDATID, a cyst containing a watery fluid. (Gk.) The pl. *hydatides* occurs in 1683; Phil. Trans. xiii. 284. – Gk. ὑδατιδ-, stem of ὑδατίς, a watery vesicle. – Gk. ὑδατ-, stem of ὕδωρ, water. See **Hydra**.

HYDRA, a many-headed water-snake. (L. – Gk.) In Shak. Cor. iii. 1. 93. – L. *hydra*. – Gk. ὕδρα, a water-snake; also written ὕδρος; from the base ὑδ- which appears in ὕδωρ, water. + Skt. *udra-s*, a water-animal, otter; cited by Curtius, i. 308; Russ. *vuidra*, an otter; Lithuan. *udrà*, an otter; AS. *oter*, an otter. See **Otter** and **Water**. Brugmann, i. § 572. **Der.** *hydra-headed*, Hen. V, i. 1. 35; also *hydr-ant*, barbarously coined, with L. suffix *-ant-*; also *hydr-ate*.

HYDRANGEA, a kind of flower. (Gk.) A coined name, referring to the cup-form of the capsule, or seed-vessel; Johnson's Gardeners' Dict., 1877. First in 1753. Made from Gk. ὑδρ-, for ὕδωρ, water; and ἀγγεῖον or ἄγγος, a vessel.

HYDRAULIC, relating to water in motion, conveying or acting by water. (F. – L. – Gk.) 'Hydraulick, pertaining to organs, or to an instrument to draw water, or to the sound of running waters (Bacon);' Blount's Gloss., ed. 1674. Bacon has *hydraulicks*, Nat. Hist. § 102. – F. *hydraulique*, 'the sound of running waters, or music made thereby;' Cot. – L. *hydraulicus*. – Gk. ὑδραυλικός, belonging to a water-organ. – Gk. ὕδραυλις, an organ worked by water. – Gk. ὕδρ-, for ὕδωρ, water; and αὐλός, a tube, pipe; from the base αϝ, to blow; cf. ἄημι, I blow. ¶ For a description of what the *hydraulic organ* really was, see Chappell's Hist. of Music.

HYDRODYNAMICS, the science relating to the force of water in motion. (Gk.) A scientific term; coined (in 1738) from

Gk. ὕδρο-, from ὕδωρ, water; and Late L. *dynamicus*, a word of Gk. origin. See **Water** and **Dynamic**.

HYDROGEN, a very light gas. (F. – Gk.) F. *hydrogène* (1787). Spelt *hydrogene*, E. Darwin, Botanic Garden, c. iii. l. 260 (note); 1791. A scientific term; coined from *hydro-*, for Gk. ὕδρο-, from ὕδωρ, water; and *-gène*, for Gk. root γέν-, to produce, generate. The name means 'generator of water.' See **Water** and **Genesis**.

HYDROPATHY, the water-cure. (Gk.) First in 1843. Coined from *hydro-*, standing for Gk. ὕδρο-, from ὕδωρ, water; and Gk. πάθ-ος, suffering, hence, endurance of treatment. See **Water** and **Pathos**. **Der.** *hydropath-ic, hydropath-ist*.

HYDROPHOBIA, fear of water. (L. – Gk.) In Kersey's Dict., ed. 1715; spelt *hydrophobie*, a French form, in Minsheu. First in 1547. A symptom of the disease due to a mad dog's bite. Coined from Gk. ὕδρο-, from ὕδωρ, water; and Gk. φόβ-ος, fear, fright, allied to φέβομαι, I flee.

HYDROPSY, the old spelling of **Dropsy**. (F. – L. – Gk.) ME. *ydropesie*, Wyclif, Luke, xiv. 2; where the later text has *dropesie* (with loss of *y*). – MF. *hydropisie*, 'dropsie;' Cot. – L. *hydrōpisis, hydrōpisia*. – Late Gk. *ὑδρώπισις, not found; extended from Gk. ὕδρωψ, dropsy, a disease due to excess of water. – Gk. ὕδρο-, for ὕδωρ, water. See **Water**.

HYDROSTATICS, the science which treats of fluids at rest. (Gk.) In Kersey, ed. 1715; first in 1660. Coined from *hydro-* = Gk. ὕδρο-, from ὕδωρ, water; and E. *statics*. See **Water** and **Statics**.

HYENA, a sow-like quadruped. (L. – Gk.) Also spelt *hyæna*; Milton, Samson, 748. [Older authors use the French form, as *hyen*, Shak. As You Like It, iv. 1. 156. ME. *hyene*, Chaucer, La Respounse de Fortune au Pleintif, st. 2.] – L. *hyæna*. – Gk. ὕαινα, a hyena, lit. 'sow-like;' thought to resemble a sow. – Gk. ὕ-, stem of ὗς, a sow, cognate with E. *sow*; with fem. adj. suffix *-αινα*. See **Sow** (2).

HYGIENE, sanitary science. (F. – Gk.) *Hygiene* occurs in 1671 (N. E. D.). – F. *hygiène*; in Dict. Acad. 1762. – Gk. ὑγιεινή (τέχνη), fem. of ὑγιεινός, healthful. – Gk. ὑγιής, healthy.

HYMEN, the god of marriage. (L. – Gk.) In Shak. Temp. iv. 1. 23. – L. *hymen*. – Gk. Ὑμήν, the god of marriage. **Der.** *hymenean* or *hymenæan*, Milton, P. L. iv. 711, from MF. *hymenean*, 'of or belonging to a wedding,' Cot., from L. *Hymenæus*, Gk. ὑμέναιος, another name of Hymen, though the proper signification is a wedding-song; later turned into *hymen-eal*, as in 'hymeneal rite,' Pope's Homer, Il. xviii. 570. Allied to *hymn*; Brugmann, i. § 294.

HYMN, a song of praise. (F. – L. – Gk.) ME. *ympne*, Wyclif, Matt. xxvi. 30; in which the *p* is excrescent after *m*, as in ME. *solempne* = *solemn*. – OF. *ymne* (Littré), later *hymne*, 'a hymne,' Cot. – L. *hymnum*, acc. of *hymnus*. – Gk. ὕμνος, a song, festive song, hymn. β. Some explain ὕμνος as 'a stitching or joining together' (cf. **Rhapsody**), and connect it with Skt. *syūman*, a thread (Macdonell) and E. *seam* (1) and *sew*; Brugmann, i. § 294. **Der.** *hymno-logy*.

HYPALLAGE, an interchange. (L. – Gk.) In Blount's Gloss., ed. 1674; and in Puttenham, Eng. Poesie, ed. Arber, bk. iii. ch. 15, p. 183. – L. *hypallagē*, 'a rhetorical figure, by which the relations of things seem to be mutually interchanged; as, *dare classibus austros* (= to give the winds to the fleet) instead of *dare classes austris* (to give the fleet to the winds);' Virgil, Æn. iii. 61;' White. – Gk. ὑπαλλαγή, an interchange, exchange, hypallage. – Gk. ὑπ-, for ὑπό, under (see **Sub-**); and ἀλλαγή, a change, from ἀλλάσσειν, to change; from Gk. ἄλλ-ος, another, other. See **Alien, Else**.

HYPER-, prefix, denoting excess. (L. – Gk.) L. *hyper*, for Gk. ὑπέρ, above, beyond, allied to L. *super*, above. See **Super-**. Hence *hyper-baton*, a transposition of words from their natural order, lit. 'a going beyond,' from βαίνειν, to go, cognate with E. *come*; *hyper-critical*, coined from *hyper-* and *critical*; *hyper-borean*, extreme northern (Minsheu), from L. *boreas*, Gk. βορέας, the north wind; *hyper-metrical*, &c. And see below.

HYPERBOLE, a rhetorical exaggeration. (L. – Gk.) In Shak. L. L. L. v. 2. 407. – L. *hyperbolē*. – Gk. ὑπερβολή, excess, exaggeration. – Gk. ὑπέρ, beyond (see **Hyper-**); and βάλλειν, to throw, cast. **Der.** *hyperbol-ic-al*, Cor. i. 9. 51. **Doublet**, *hyperbola*, as a mathematical term.

HYPHEN, a short stroke (-) joining two parts of a compound word. (L. – Gk.) In Blount's Gloss., ed. 1674. – L. *hyphen*, which is merely a Latinised spelling of Gk. ὑφέν, together, lit. 'under one.' – Gk. ὑφ-, for ὑπό, under (see **Hypo-**); and ἕν, one thing, neuter of εἷς, one, which is prob. allied to L. *sim-* in *sim-plex*.

HYPNOTISM, the process of artificially producing a deep sleep. (Gk.) Introduced in 1842; due to *hypnotic*, adj., which occurs as early as 1625. 'Hypnoticks, medicines that cause sleep;' Kersey, ed. 1721. – Gk. ὑπνωτικός, sleepy, narcotic. – Gk. ὑπνό-ειν, to put to sleep. – Gk. ὕπνος, sleep, for *sup-nos, where sup- is the weak grade of √SWEP, to sleep; cognate with L. somnus (< *swep-nus); see **Somniferous**. Brugmann, i. §§ 97, 121.

HYPO-, prefix, lit. 'under.' (Gk.) Gk. ὑπό, under; cognate with L. sub. See **Sub-**.

HYPOCHONDRIA, a mental disorder, inducing gloominess and melancholy. (L. – Gk.) The adj. hypocondriack occurs in Blount's Gloss., ed. 1674. Named from the spleen, which was supposed to cause hypochondria, and is situate under the cartilage of the breast-bone. – L. hypochondria, sb. pl., the parts beneath the breast-bone. – Gk. ὑποχόνδρια, pl. sb., the same. – Gk. ὑπό, under, beneath; and χόνδρος, a corn, grain, gristle, and esp. the cartilage of the breast-bone (cognate with G. grand, gravel, and allied to E. grind). **Der.** hypochondria-c, hypochondria-c-al; also hip, to depress the spirits, hipp-ish. See **Hippish**.

HYPOCRISY, pretence to virtue. (F. – L. – Gk.) ME. ipo-crisye, Chaucer, C. T. 12344 (C 410); ypocrisie, P. Plowman, B. xv. 108. – OF. hypocrisie, 'hypocrisie, dissembling;' Cot. – L. hypocrisis, in 1 Tim. iv. 2 (Vulgate). – Gk. ὑπόκρισις, a reply, answer, the playing of a part on the stage, the acting of a part, hypocrisy. – Gk. ὑποκρίνο-μαι, I reply, make answer, play a part. – Gk. ὑπό, under; and κρίνομαι, I contend, dispute, middle voice of κρίνειν, to judge, discern. See **Critic**. from the same source, hypocrite, ME. ypocryte, Chaucer, C. T. 10828 (F 514), F. hypocrite, L. hypocrita, hypocritēs, from Gk. ὑποκριτής, a dissembler, Matt. vi. 2; hypocrit-ic, hypocrit-ic-al, hypocrit-ic-al-ly.

HYPOGASTRIC, belonging to the lower part of the abdomen. (F. – L. – Gk.) Spelt hypogastrick in Blount's Gloss., ed. 1674. 'The hypogaster or paunch;' Minsheu. – MF. hypogastrique, 'belonging to the lower part of the belly;' Cot. – Late L. hypogastricus. – Gk. ὑπογάστριον, the lower part of the belly. See **Hypo-** and **Gastric**.

HYPOSTASIS, a substance, personality of each Person in the Godhead. (L. – Gk.) In Kersey's Dict., ed. 1715; and in Minsheu, ed. 1627. 'The hypostatical union is the union of humane nature with Christ's Divine Person;' Blount's Gloss., ed. 1674. – L. hypo-stasis. – Gk. ὑπόστασις, a standing under, prop, groundwork, subsistence, substance, Person of the Trinity. – Gk. ὑπό, under; and στάσις, a placing, a standing, from √STA, to stand. See **Hypo-** and **Stand**. **Der.** hypostatic = Gk. ὑποστατικός, adj. formed from ὑπό-στασις; hypostatic-al.

HYPOTENUSE, HYPOTHENUSE, the side of a right-angled triangle which is opposite the right angle. (F. – L. – Gk.) Hypothenuse in Kersey, ed. 1715; but it should rather be hypotenuse. – F. hypoténuse. – L. hypotēnūsa. – Gk. ὑποτείνουσα, the subtending line (γραμμή, a line, being understood); fem. of ὑποτείνων, pres. pt. of ὑποτείνειν, to subtend, i. e. to stretch under. – Gk. ὑπό, under; and τείνειν, to stretch, from √TEN, to stretch. See **Subtend**.

HYPOTHEC, a kind of pledging or mortgage. (F. – L. – Gk.) A law term. The adj. hypothecary is in Blount's Gloss., ed. 1674. Hypothec is Englished from MF. hypotheque, 'an ingagement, mortgage, or pawning of an immovable;' Cot. – L. hypothēca, a mortgage. – Gk. ὑποθήκη, an under-prop, also a pledge, mortgage. – Gk. ὑπό, under; and base θη-, to place, from √DHĒ, to place. See **Hypothesis**. **Der.** hypothec-ate, to mortgage; hypothec-at-ion.

HYPOTHESIS, a supposition. (L. – Gk.) In Minsheu, ed. 1627. The pl. hypotheses is in Holland's Plutarch, p. 623 (R.). – Late L. hypothesis. – Gk. ὑπόθεσις, a placing under, basis, supposition. – Gk. ὑπό, under; and base θε-, to place, from √DHĒ, to place. See **Hypo-** and **Thesis**. **Der.** hypothetic, adj. = Gk. ὑποθετικός, supposed, imaginary; hypothetic-al, hypothetic-al-ly.

HYSON, a kind of tea. (Chinese.) First mentioned in 1740. In the Amoy dialect called chhun-tê, lit. 'spring tea,' from chhun, spring, and tê, tea (Douglas). Said to have been orig. from hi chhun, lit. 'blooming spring;' i. e. early crop. From Amoy hi, blooming; chhun, spring; Chinese hei-ch'un.

HYSSOP, an aromatic plant. (F. – L. – Gk. – Heb.) Spelt hysope in Minsheu. ME. ysope, Wyclif, Hebrews, ix. 19. – OF. hyssope, 'hisop;' Cot. – L. hyssōpus. – Gk. ὕσσωπος, an aromatic plant, but different from our hyssop; Heb. ix. 19. – Heb. ēzōbh, a plant, the exact nature of which is not known; see Concise Dict. of the Bible.

HYSTERIC, convulsive, said of fits. (F. – L. – Gk.) Kersey has hysteric and hysterical; only the latter is in Blount's Gloss., ed. 1674. – MF. hysterique; 'affection hysterique, the suffocation of the matrix;' Cot. – L. hystericus; whence hysterica passio, called in E. 'the mother;' see K. Lear, ii. 4. 56. – Gk. ὑστερικός, suffering in the womb, hysterical. – Gk. ὑστέρα, the womb; allied to Skt. udara-m, the belly, the womb; which see in Uhlenbeck. Brugmann, i. § 706. **Der.** hysteric-al, -al-ly; hysterics, hysteria.

I

I, nom. case of first personal pronoun. (E.) ME. (Northern) ik, i; (Southern) ich, uch, i. AS. ic.+Du. ik; Icel. ek; Dan. jeg; Swed. jag; Goth. ik; G. ich; OHG. ih.+Russ. ia; Lith. asz; L. ego; Gk. ἐγώ, ἐγών; Skt. aham. Idg. base EGH-, EG- ; see Brugmann, ii. § 434; Streitberg, § 183. See **Me**, which is, however, from a different base.

I-, prefix with negative force. (L.) Only in i-gnoble, i-gnominy, i-gnore, as an abbreviation of L. in-; see **In-** (3).

IAMBIC, a certain metre or metrical foot, denoted by ∪ –, for short followed by long. (L. – Gk.) 'Iambick, Elegiack, Pastorall;' Sir P. Sidney, Apologie for Poetrie (1595); ed. Arber, p. 28. – L. iambicus. – Gk. ἰαμβικός, iambic. – Gk. ἴαμβος, an iamb or iambic foot, also iambic verse, a lampoon. Origin doubtful. ¶ Iamb is sometimes used to represent Gk. ἴαμβος.

IBEX, a species of goat. (L.) Ibexe in Minsheu. A scientific name. – L. ibex, a kind of goat, chamois.

IBIS, a genus of wading birds. (L. – Gk. – Egyptian.) 'A fowle in the same Egypt, called ibis;' Holland, tr. of Pliny, b. viii. c. 27. 'Sikonyes, that thei clepen ibes;' Mandeville's Trav. ch. 5, p. 45. – L. ibis. – Gk. ἶβις, an Egyptian bird, to which divine honours were paid; Herod. ii. 75, 76. Of Egyptian origin; cf. Coptic hippen (Peyron), occurring as a bird-name in Levit. xi. 17, Deut. xiv. 16, where the LXX version has ἶβις, and the Vulgate has ibis.

ICE, any frozen fluid, esp. water. (E.) ME. is, iis; spelt ijs (= iis), P. Ploughman's Crede, 436; yse (dat. case), Rob. of Glouc. p. 463, l. 4; l. 9511. AS. īs, ice; Grein, ii. 147.+Du. ijs; Icel. íss; Dan. iis; Swed. is; G. eis; OHG. īs. Teut. type *īsom, neut. **Der.** ice-berg, found in 1774, but not in Todd's Johnson; in which the latter element is the Du. and Swed. berg, Dan. bjerg, G. berg, a mountain, hill; whence Du. ijsberg, Swed. isberg, Dan. iisbjerg, G. eisberg, an iceberg. We prob. borrowed it from Dutch. Also ice-blink, from Dan. iisblink, Swed. isblink, a field of ice extending into the interior of Greenland; so named from its shining appearance; from Dan. blinke, to gleam; see **Blink**. Also ice-boat, ice-bound, ice-cream (abbreviated from iced-cream), ice-field, ice-float, ice-floe, ice-house, ice-island, ice-land, ice-man, ice-pack, ice-plant. Also ice, vb., ic-ing. Also ic-y = AS. īsig; Grein, ii. 147; ic-i-ly, ic-i-ness. And see **Icicle**.

ICHNEUMON, an Egyptian carnivorous animal. (L. – Gk.) In Holland's Pliny, b. viii. c. 24; Gosson, School of Abuse, ed. Arber, p. 38 (1579). – L. ichneumon (Pliny). – Gk. ἰχνεύμων, an ichneumon; lit. 'a tracker;' so called because it tracks out the eggs of the crocodile, which it devours. See Aristotle, Hist. Animals, 9. 6. 5. – Gk. ἰχνεύειν, to track, hunt after. – Gk. ἴχνος, a track, footstep. **Der.** From the same source is ichno-graphy, a design traced out, ground-plan, a term in architecture (Vitruvius).

ICHOR, the fluid in the veins of gods. (Gk.) 'The sacred ichor;' Pope, tr. of Homer, Il. v. 516. – Gk. ἰχώρ, juice, the blood of gods. **Der.** ichor-ous.

ICHTHYOGRAPHY, a description of fishes. (Gk.) A scientific term. Coined from Gk. ἰχθυο-, decl. stem of ἰχθύς, a fish; and γράφειν, to describe. β. So also ichthyology, spelt icthyology by Sir T. Browne, Vulg. Errors, b. iii. c. 24. § 1; from Gk. ἰχθύς, a fish, and λόγος, a discourse, from λέγειν, to speak of.

ICICLE, a hanging point of ice. (E.) ME. isikel; spelt ysekel, iseyokel, isykle, isechel, P. Plowman, B. xvii. 227; C. xx. 193. Compounded of ME. ys, ice (see **Ice**); and ikyl, also used alone in the same sense of 'icicle,' as in Prompt. Parv., p. 259. Levins also has ickles = icicles. AS. īsgicel, compounded of īs, ice, and gicel, a small piece of ice; orig. written īses gicel, where īses is in the gen. case. 'Stiria, īses gicel;' Ælfric's Gloss., in Wright's Vocab. i. 21, col. 2 (Voc. 117. 14). β. Gicel appears in the older form gecilae, Epinal Gloss. 954, which is cognate with Icel. jökull, used by itself to signify 'icicle;' cf. Low G. is-hekel, is-jäkel, icicle. γ. Icel. jökull is the dim. of Icel. jaki, a piece of ice, cognate with Irish aig, W. ia, ice (from an OCeltic type yagi-); Stokes-Fick, p. 222. Cf. also Pers. yakh, ice; Rich. Dict. p. 1705; Horn, § 1126. Also prov. E. ickle, an icicle; and the comp. ice-shockle. Thus the word really = ice-ice-l, though the second ice is not the same word with the first. ¶ Observe that -ic- in ic-ic-le is totally different from -ic- in art-ic-le, part-ic-le.

ICONOCLAST, a breaker of images. (Gk.) 'Iconoclasts, or breakers of images;' Bp. Taylor, Of the Real Presence, xii. § 28. A coined word; from Gk. εἰκόνο-, for εἰκών (Latinised as īcōn), an image; and κλάστης, a breaker, one who breaks, from κλάειν, to break. **Der.** iconoclast-ic.

ICOSAHEDRON, a solid figure, having twenty equal triangular faces. (Gk.) Spelt icosaedron in Kersey's Dict., ed. 1715. Coined from Gk. εἴκοσι, twenty; and ἕδρα, a base, lit. a scat, from base ἑδ-, to sit, cognate with E. **Sit**. **Der**. *icosahedr-al*.

IDEA, a (mental) image, notion, opinion. (L.—Gk.) 'Idea is a bodiless substance,' &c.; Holland, tr. of Plutarch, p. 666. 'The fayre *Idea*;' Spenser, Sonnet 45.—L. *idea*.—Gk. ἰδέα, the look or semblance of a thing, species.—Gk. ἰδεῖν, to see.—√WEID, to see; cf. Skt. *vid*, to perceive, know. See **Wit**, verb. **Der**. *ide-al*, from MF. *ideal*, 'ideall' (Cot.), which is from L. *ideālis*; hence *ide-al-ly*, *ide-al-ise*, *ide-al-ism*, *ide-al-ist*, *ide-al-is-at-ion*, *ide-al-ist-ic*, *ide-al-i-ty* (most of these terms being rather modern).

IDENTICAL, the very same. (L.) 'Of such propositions as in the schools are called *identicall*;' Digby, Of Man's Soul, c. 2 (R.) Coined by adding -*al* to the older term *identic*, spelt *identick* in Kersey's Dict., ed. 1715. 'The beard's th' *identique* beard you knew;' Butler, Hudibras, pt. ii. c. 1. l. 149. *Identic* is formed as if from a Late L. **identicus*, suggested by the older *identitās*; see **Identity**. **Der**. *identic-al-ly*, -*ness*.

IDENTITY, sameness. (F.—Late L.—L.) 'Of *identity* and of diversity;' Holland's Plutarch, p. 54 (R.); and in Minsheu.—F. *identité*, 'identity, likeness, the being almost the very same;' Cot.—Late L. *identitātem*, acc. of *identitās*, sameness; a word which occurs in Marcianus Capella.—L. *identi-*, occurring in *identi-dem*, repeatedly; with suffix -*tās*.—L. *idem*, the same; for **is-dem* >**iz-dem*; Brugmann, ii. § 416.—L. *i-*, from base I, pronominal base of the 3rd person; and -*dem*, from base DE, likewise a pronom. base of the 3rd person. **Der**. From the same L. *identi-* we have *identi-fy* = F. *identifier* (Littré); whence *identi-fic-at-ion*; see *identical*.

IDES, the 15th day of March, May, July, and October, and the 13th of other months. (F.—L.) 'The *ides* of March;' Jul. Cæsar, i. 2. 18, 19.—F. *ides*, 'the ides of a month;' Cot.—L. *īdūs*, the ides. Rob. of Brunne has the Lat. form *Idus*; tr. of Langtoft, p. 341.

IDIOM, a mode of expression peculiar to a language. (F.—L.—Gk.) 'The Latine and Greek *idiom*;' Milton, Of Education (R.) Spelt *idiome* in Minsheu.—F. *idiome*, 'an ideom, or proper form of speech;' Cot.—L. *idiōma*.—Gk. ἰδίωμα, an idiom, peculiarity in language.—Gk. ἰδιόω, I make my own.—Gk. ἴδιο-, decl. stem of ἴδιος, one's own, peculiar to one's self. (See Prellwitz.) **Der**. *idiom-at-ic*, from ἰδιώματ-, stem of ἰδίωμα; *idiom-at-ic-al*, *idiom-at-ic-al-ly*. Also *idio-pathy*, a primary disease not occasioned by another, from ἴδιο-, for ἴδιος, and παθ-, as seen in παθεῖν, to suffer (see **Pathos**); *idio-path-ic*, *idio-path-ic-al-ly*. And see below.

IDIOSYNCRASY, peculiarity of temperament, a characteristic. (Gk.) 'Whether quails, from any *idiosyncracy* or peculiarity of constitution,' &c.; Sir T. Browne, Vulg. Errors, b. iii. c. 28, last section.—Gk. ἰδιοσυγκρασία, a peculiar temperament or habit of body.—Gk. ἴδιο-, for ἴδιος, peculiar to one's self; and σύγκρασις, a mixing together, blending. For Gk. ἴδιος, see **Idiom**. The Gk. σύγκρασις is compounded of σύν, together, and κρᾶσις, a mingling; see **Crasis**.

IDIOT, a foolish person, one weak in intellect. (F.—L.—Gk.) See Trench, Study of Words. ME. *idiot*, Chaucer, C. T. 5893 (D 311).—F. *idiot*, 'an ideot (*sic*) or naturall fool;' Cot.—L. *idiōta*, an ignorant, uneducated person.—Gk. ἰδιώτης, a private person, hence one who is inexperienced or uneducated. (See I Cor. xiv. 16, where the Vulgate has *locum idiōtæ*, and Wyclif 'the place of an *ydiote*.')—Gk. ἰδιόω, I make my own.—Gk. ἴδιο-, for ἴδιος, one's own. See **Idiom**. **Der**. *idiot-ic*, *idiot-ic-al*, *idiot-ic-al-ly*, *idiot-ism* (= *idiom*); also *idioc-y*, in Kersey's Dict., ed. 1715, formed from *idiot* as *prophec-y* is from *prophet*.

IDLE, unemployed, useless, unimportant. (E.) ME. *ydel*, Chaucer, C. T. 2507 (A 2505); hence the phr. *in idel* = in vain, id. 12576 (C 642). AS. *īdel*, vain, empty, useless; Grein, ii. 135.+Du. *ijdel*, vain, frivolous, trifling; (whence Dan. and Swed. *idel*); G. *eitel*, vain, conceited, trifling; OHG. *ītal*, empty, useless, mere. The orig. sense seems to have been 'empty' or 'clear;' cf. Low G. *īdel*, pure, unmixed (Lübben); cf. Gk. ἰθαρός, pure, αἰθήρ, a clear sky. See **Ether**. **Der**. *idl-y*; *idle*, verb; *idl-er*, *idle-ness*, Ormulum, 4736, from AS. *īdelnes*, Grein, ii. 135.

IDOL, a figure or image of a god. (F.—L.—Gk.) ME. *idole*, Chaucer, C. T. 15753 (G 285).—OF. *idole*; see Sherwood's index to Cot.—L. *idōlum*, 1 Cor. viii. 4 (Vulg.); also *idōlon*.—Gk. εἴδωλον, an image, likeness.—Gk. εἴδομαι, I appear, seem; cf. Gk. εἶδον, I saw, ἰδεῖν, to see.—√WEID, to see; cf. Skt. *vid*, to perceive, and see **Wit**, verb. **Der**. *ido-latry* (contraction of *idolo-latry*), ME. *ydolatrie*, Chaucer, C. T. Pers. Tale, De Avaritia, § 2 (I 748), from F. *idolatrie* = Late L. *idōlatrīa*, shortened form of *idōlolatrīa*, from Gk. εἰδωλολατρεία, service of idols, Coloss. iii. 5; composed of εἰδωλο-, for εἴδωλον, and λατρεία, service, from λάτρον, hire. Also *idolater*, from OF. *idolatre*, 'an idolater' (Cot.); also *idolastre* in OF., whence MF. *idolastre*, an idolater, Chaucer, C. T. Pers. Tale, De Avaritia, § 3 (I 749); the OF. *idolatre* is developed from OF.

idolatr-ie, explained above. Hence also *idolatr-ess*, *idolatr-ise*, *idolatr-ize*, *idolatr-ous-ly*. Also *idol-ise* (Kersey), *idol-is-er*; see *idyl*.

IDYL, IDYLL, a pastoral poem. (L.—Gk.) 'Amatorious *eidyls*;' Holland's Pliny, bk. xxviii. ch. 2 (ii. 296). '*Idyl*, a poem consisting of a few verses;' Blount's Gloss., ed. 1674.—L. *idyllium*.—Gk. εἰδύλλιον, a short descriptive pastoral poem; so called from its descriptive representations.—Gk. εἶδος, shape, figure, appearance, look.—Gk. εἴδομαι, I appear, seem (above). **Der**. *idyll-ic*.

IF, a conjunction, expressive of doubt. (E.) ME. *if*, Chaucer, C. T. 145; *ȝif*, P. Plowman, B. prol. 37; *giff*, Barbour, Bruce, i. 12. AS. *gif*, if; Grein, i. 505. Cf. Icel. *ef*, *if*, if; OFries. *ief*, *gef*, *ef*, if; OSax. *ef*, if; Goth. *iba*, *ibai*, interrog. particle, *jabai*, if. Cf. also Du. *of*, OFries. *of*, OSax. *of*, G. *ob*; OHG. *iba*, condition, stipulation, whence the instrum. case *ibu*, *ipu*, used in the sense of 'if,' lit. 'on the condition;' also OHG. *upi*, *upa*, *ube*, mod. G. *ob*, whether. β. The OHG. *ibu* is the instrumental case of *iba*, as said above; so also the Icel. *ef*, *if*, is closely related to (and once a case of) Icel. *ef* (*if*), doubt, hesitation, whence also the verb *efa* (*ifa*), to doubt. See Kluge, s. v. *ob*. ¶ The guess of Horne Tooke, that AS. *gif* is the imperative mood of AS. *gifan*, to give, has been copied only too often. It is plainly wrong, (1) because the AS. use of the words exhibits no such connexion, and (2) because it fails to explain the cognate forms.

IGNITION, a setting on fire. (F.—L.) 'Not a total *ignition*;' Sir T. Browne, Works, b. ii. c. 2. § 6.—F. *ignition*, 'a burning, firing;' Cot. Coined (as if from L. **ignītio*, a burning) from L. *ignītus*, pp. of *ignīre*, to set on fire.—L. *ignis*, fire.+Skt. *agni*, fire; base **egni-*. Cf. Russ. *ogone*, Lith. *ugnìs*, fire; base **ogni-*, Brugmann, i. § 148. See also **Ingle** (2). **Der**. Hence *ignite*, a later word, though perhaps formed directly from L. pp. *ignītus*; *ignit-ible*. Also *igneous*, Englished from L. *igneus*, fiery, by the common change from L. -*us* to E. -*ous*. Also, directly from the Latin, *ignis fatuus*, lit. 'foolish fire,' hence a misleading meteor; see **Fatuous**. 'Fuller (Comment. on Ruth, p. 38) would have scarcely spoken of "a meteor of foolish fire," if *ignis fatuus*, which has now quite put out "firedrake," the older name for these meteors, had not been, when he wrote, still strange to the language, or quite recent to it;' Trench, Eng. Past and Present, lect. iv. (ed. 1875).

IGNOBLE, not noble, mean, base. (F.—L.) In Shak. Rich. III, ii. 7. 127.—F. *ignoble*, 'ignoble;' Sherwood's index to Cotgrave.—L. *ignōbilis*.—L. *i-*, short for *in-*, not; and *gnōbilis*, later *nōbilis*, noble. See **I-** and **Noble**. **Der**. *ignobl-y*, *ignoble-ness*. And see **Ignominy**.

IGNOMINY, disgrace, dishonour. (F.—L.) In Shak. I Hen. IV, v. 4. 100.—F. *ignominie*, 'ignominy;' Cot.—L. *ignōminia*, disgrace.—L. *i-*, short for *in-*, not; and *gnōmini-*, decl. stem of -*gnōmen* (as in *a-gnōmen*, *co-gnōmen*), something by which one is known; from *gnō-scere*, to know; see **Know**. ¶ Distinct from L. *nōmen*, a name; see **Name**. **Der**. *ignomini-ous*, *ignomini-ous-ly*, -*ness*. See **Ignore**.

IGNORE, not to know, to disregard. (F.—L.) In Cotgrave.—F. *ignorer*, 'to ignore, or be ignorant of;' Cot.—L. *ignōrāre*, not to know.—L. *i-*, short for *in-*, not; and the base *gnō-*, seen in *gnōscere*, later *noscere*, to know. See **Know**. **Der**. *ignorant*, in the Remedie of Love, st. 34, pr. in Chaucer's Works, ed. 1561, fol. 323 b, from F. *ignorant* (Cot.), which from L. *ignōrant-*, stem of pres. pt. of *ignōrāre*; *ignorant-ly*; also *ignorance*, in early use, Ancren Riwle, p. 278, l. 7, from F. *ignorance* (Cot.), which is from L. *ignōrantia*, ignorance. Also *ignoramus*, formerly a law term; '*Ignorāmus* (i. e. we are ignorant) is properly written on the bill of indictments by the grand enquest, empanelled on the inquisition of causes criminal and publick, when they mislike their evidence, as defective or too weak to make good the presentment;' Blount's Law Dict. 1691 (from Cowel, 1607).

IGUANA, a kind of American lizard. (Span.—Caribbean.) 'The *yguana*' is described in a translation by E. G. of Acosta's Hist. of the Indies, p. 313. Spelt *iuanna* in Eden, ed. Arber, pp. 167. Also called *guana*.—Span. *iguana*. β. Eden (ed. Arber, pp. 85, 167) gives *iuanna* as the (Caribbean) name in Hayti; he spells *yuana* at p. 220. Littré gives *yuana* as a Caribbean word, cited by Oviedo in 1525.

IGUANODON, a fossil dinosaur, with teeth like an iguana. From *iguana*, and Gk. ὀδον-τ-, stem of ὀδούς, a tooth.

IL- (1), the form assumed by the prefix *in-* (=L. *in*, prep.) when followed by *l*. Exx.: *il-lapse*, *il-lation*, *il-lision*, *il-lude*, *il-luminate*, *il-lusion*, *il-lustrate*, *il-lustrious*. See **In-** (2).

IL- (2), the form assumed by the L. prefix *in-*, used in a negative sense, when followed by *l*. Exx.: *il-legal*, *il-legible*, *il-legitimate*, *il-liberal*, *il-licit*, *il-limitable*, *il-literate*, *il-logical*. See **In-** (3).

ILIAC, pertaining to the smaller intestines. (F.—L.) 'The *iliacke* passion is most sharpe and grieuous;' Holland, tr. of Pliny,

b. xxx. c. 7.—F. *iliaque*, 'of or belonging to the flanks;' Cot. Formed from Late L. *iliacus*, adj. (Lewis); from L. *ilia*, sb. pl. the flanks, groin. β. But interpreted as if from Late L. *ileos*, for Gk. εἰλεός, a severe pain in the intestines; from Gk. εἰλεῖν, εἴλειν, to press hard. See also **Jade** (2).

ILIAD, an epic poem by Homer. (L.—Gk.) Called 'Homer's *Iliads*' by the translator Chapman.—L. *Iliad*-, stem of *Ilias*, the Iliad.—Gk. Ἰλιάδ-, stem of Ἰλιάς, the Iliad.—Gk. Ἴλιος, Ἴλιον, Ilios, Ilion, the city of Ilus; commonly known as Troy.—Ἶλος, Ilus, the (mythical) grandfather of Priam, and son of *Tros* (whence *Troy*).

ILK, same. (E.) Hence, *of that ilk*, of the same (territorial) name; e.g. Guthrie *of that ilk*, i. e. Guthrie of Guthrie. ME. (Northern) *ilk*; AS. *ilca*, the same. From the pronominal stem *i-* (as in Goth. *i-s*, L. *i-s*, he), and AS. *lic*, like. Cf. *such, which* (North. *swilk, quhilk*).

ILL, evil, bad, wicked. (Scand.) The comp. and superl. forms are **Worse, Worst**, q. v. ME. *ill, ille*, Ormulum, 6647; common as adv., Havelok, 1165; chiefly used in poems which contain several Scand. words.—Icel. *illr*, adj. ill; also written *illr*; Dan. *ilde* (for *ille*), adv. ill, badly; Swed. *illa*, adv. ill, badly. [It is not allied to the AS. *yfel*, whence the mod. E. *evil*.] Der. *ill*, adv., *ill*, sb.; *ill-ness*, Macb. i. 5. 21 (not in early use); *ill-blood, ill-bred, ill-breeding, ill-favoured, ill-natured, ill-starred, ill-will*.

ILLAPSE, a gliding in, sudden entrance. (L.) Rare. 'The *illapse* of some such active substance or powerful being, *illapsing* into matter,' &c.; Hale, Origin of Mankind, p. 321 (R.) Coined (in imitation of *lapse*) from L. *illapsus*, a gliding in.—L. *il-* (for *in*), in; *lapsus*, a gliding, from the same stem as the pp. of *lābī*, to glide. See **Il-** (1) and **Lapse**. Der. *illapse*, vb.

ILLATION, an inference, conclusion. (F.—L.) '*Illation*, an inference, conclusion;' Blount's Gloss., ed. 1674; and in Cotgrave. —F. *illation*, 'an illation, inference;' Cot.—L. acc. *illātiōnem*, from nom. *illātio*, a bringing in, inference.—L. *il-*=*in-*, prefix, in; and *lāt-*, as in *lātus*=*tlātus*, borne, brought (= Gk. τλητός, borne), from √TEL, to lift. See **Il-** (1) and **Tolerate**. ¶ Since *lātus* is used as the pp. of *ferre*, to bear, whence *in-fer-ence*, the senses of *illation* and *inference* are much the same. Der. *il-lative, il-lative-ly*.

ILLEGAL, contrary to law. (L.) 'Not an *illegal* violence;' Milton, Reason of Church Government, b. ii (R.) And in Selden, Table Talk, ed. Arber, p. 75. From **Il-** (2) and **Legal**. Der. *illegal-ity*, from F. *illegalité*, 'illegality;' Cot.; *illegal-ly, illegal-ise*.

ILLEGIBLE, not to be read. (F.—L.) 'The secretary poured the ink-box all over the writings, and so defaced them that they were made altogether *illegible*;' Howell, Dodona's Grove, ed. 1645, p. 55 (N. E. D.). Coined from **Il-** (2) and **Legible**. Der. *illegibl-y, illegible-ness*; also *illegibil-i-ty*.

ILLEGITIMATE, not born in wedlock. (L.) In Shak. Troil. v. 7. 18. From **Il-** (2) and **Legitimate**. Der. *illegitimate-ly, illegitimac-y*.

ILLIBERAL, niggardly, mean. (F.—L.) In Marlowe, Faustus, i. 1. Bacon has *illiberalitie* ; Essay vii (Of Parents). From **Il-** (2) and **Liberal**. Der. *illiberal-ly, illiberal-i-ty*.

ILLICIT, unlawful. (F.—L.) '*Illicitous, Illicite*, unlawful;' Blount's Gloss., ed. 1684.—F. *illicite*, 'illicitous;' Cot.—L. *illicitus*, not allowed.—L. *il-*=*in-*, not; and *licitus*, pp. of *licēre*, to be allowed, to be lawful. See **License**. Der. *illicit-ly, illicit-ness*.

ILLIMITABLE, boundless. (L.) In Spenser, Hymn of Heavenly Love, l. 57; Milton, P. L. ii. 892. From **Il-** (2) and **Limitable**; see **Limit**. Der. *illimitabl-y, illimitable-ness*.

ILLISION, a striking against. (L.) In Holland's Plutarch, p. 867 (R.); and Sir T. Browne, Vulg. Errors, b. iii. c. 27, part 10. Formed (by analogy with F. sbs. from L. accusatives) from L. *illisio*, a striking or dashing against; cf. *illīs-us*, pp. of *illīdere*, to strike against.—L. *il-* (for *in*), upon); and *lædere*, to strike, hurt. See **Il-** (1) and **Lesion**.

ILLITERATE, unlearned, ignorant. (L.) In Shak. Two Gent. iii. i. 296.—L. *illitterātus*, less correctly *illiterātus*, unlettered.—L. *il-*=*in-*, not; and *litterātus, literātus*, literate. See **Il-** (2) and **Literal**. Der. *illiterate-ly, -ness*.

ILLOGICAL, not logical. (L. *and* Gk.) In Blount's Gloss., ed. 1674. From **Il-** (2) and **Logical**; see **Logic**. Der. *illogical-ly, -ness*.

ILLUDE, to deceive. (L.; *or* F.—L.) 'I cannot be *illuded*;' Sir T. More, Works, p. 166 g. Cf. F. *illuder*, 'to illude, delude, mock;' Cot.—L. *illūdere*, pp. *illūsus*, to make sport of, mock, deceive.—L. *il-* =*in-*, on, upon; and *lūdere*, to play. See **Il-** (1) and **Ludicrous**. Der. *illus-ion*, q. v.; also *illus-ive*, Thomson, to Seraphina, l. 2 ; *illus-ive-ly, illus-ive-ness*.

ILLUMINATE, to enlighten, light up. (L.) In the Bible, A. V., Heb. x. 32; Shak. Jul. Cæsar, i. 3. 110. But properly a pp., as in Bacon, Adv. of Learning, b. i. 7. § 3; G. Douglas, tr. of Virgil,

prol. to bk. xii., l. 54. [Older writers use *illumine*; see Dunbar, Thrissill and Rois, st. 3. We also find the shortened form *illume*, Hamlet, i. 1. 37. Both from F. *illuminer*; Cot.]—L. *illūminātus*, Heb. x. 32 (Vulgate); pp. of *illūmināre*, to give light to.—L. *il-*, for *in*, on, upon; and *lūmināre*, to light up, from *lūmin-*, for *lūmen*, light. See **Il-** (1) and **Luminary**. Der. *illuminat-ion, illuminat-ive, illuminat-or*; also *illumine* (see above), for which Gower uses *enlumine*, C. A. iii. 86 (bk. vii. 64), whence the short form *illume* (see above), with which cf. *relume*, Oth. v. 2. 13.

ILLUSION, deception, false show. (F.—L.) In Chaucer, C. T. 11446 (F 1134).—F. *illusion*, 'illusion;' Cot.—L. acc. *illūsiōnem*, from nom. *illūsio*, a deception; cf. *illūsus*, pp. of *illūdere*, to mock. See **Illude**; which also see for *illusive*.

ILLUSTRATE, to throw light upon. (L.) In Shak. Hen. VIII, iii. 2. 181; and in Palsgrave. Properly a pp.; see L. L. L. iv. 1. 65; v. 1. 128.—L. *illustrātus*, pp. of *illustrāre*, to light up, throw light on.—L. *il-*, for *in*, upon; and *lustrāre*, to enlighten. See **Illustrious**. Der. *illustrat-or, illustrat-ion, illustrat-ive, illustrat-ive-ly*; and see below.

ILLUSTRIOUS, bright, renowned. (F.—L.; *or* L.) In Shak. L. L. L. i. 1. 178. A badly coined word; either from F. *illustre*, by adding *-ous*, or from the corresponding L. *illustris*, bright, renowned. [Its form imitates that of *industrious*, which is correct.] β. The L. *illustris* is derived from *il-*, for *in*, on, upon; and *-lūstris*, for **louc-s-tris*, from *louc*, base *leuc-* > *lūc-*, as in *lūc-idus*, bright. See **Lucid**. Brugmann, i. § 760. Der. *illustrious-ly, -ness*.

IM- (1), prefix. (F.—L.) In some words, *im-* stands for *em-*, the OF. form of L. *im-*, prefix. Exx.: *im-brue, im-mure, im-part*.

IM- (2), prefix. (E.) For E. *in-*; as in *im-bed*, for *in-bed*. But due to the influence of **Im-** (1).

IM- (3), prefix. (L.) L. *im-* (for *in*), in; when *b, m*, or *p* follows. Exx.: *im-bue, im-merge, im-migrate, im-mit, im-pel*, &c.

IM- (4), prefix. (F.—L.; *or* L.) Negative prefix; for L. *in-*, not. Exx.: *im-material, im-mature, im-measurable, im-memorial, im-modest, im-moderate, im-moral, im-mortal, im-movable, im-mutable; im-palpable, im-parity, im-partial, im-passable, im-passive, im-patient, im-peccable, im-penetrable, im-penitent, im-perceptible, im-perfect, im-perishable, im-personal, im-pertinent, im-perturbable, im-piety, im-pious, im-placable, im-polite, im-politic, im-ponderable, im-possible, im-potent, im-practicable, im-probable, im-proper, im-provident, im-prudent, im-pure*; for which see *material*, &c.

IMAGE, a likeness, statue, idol, figure. (F.—L.) In Chaucer, C. T. 420 (A 418). And in St. Katherine, l. 1476.—F. *image*, 'an image;' Cot.—L. *imāginem*, acc. of *imāgo*, a likeness. Formed, with suffix *-āgo*, from the base *im-* seen in *im-itārī*, to imitate. See **Imitate**. Der. *image-ry*, Chaucer, Ho. of Fame, iii. 100; *ymagerie*, Gower, C. A. ii. 320; bk. v. 5771; also *imag-ine*, q. v.

IMAGINE, to conceive of, think, devise. (F.—L.) ME. *ima-ginen*; Chaucer, C. T. 5309 (B 889).—F. *imaginer*, 'to imagine, think;' Cot.—L. *imāgināri*, pp. *imāginātus*, to picture to one's self, imagine.—L. *imāgin-*, stem of *imāgo*, a likeness; see **Image**. Der. *imagin-er*; *imagin-able*, Sir T. More, Works, p. 1193 d ; *imagin-abl-y, imagin-able-ness*; *imagin-ar-y*, Com. of Errors, iv. 3. 10; *imagin-at-ion*, ME. *imaginacioun*, Chaucer, C. T. 15223 (B 4407); *imagin-at-ive* =ME. *imaginatif*, Chaucer, C. T. 11406 (F 1094); *imagin-at-ive-ness*.

IMAM, IMAUM, a Muhammedan priest. (Arab.) Arab. *imām*, a leader, chief, prelate, priest.—Arab. root *amma*, 'he tended towards;' Rich. Dict., p. 163.

IMBALM, the same as **Embalm**, q. v. (F.) Milton has *im-balm'd*, Areopagitica, ed. Hales, p. 6, l. 7.

IMBANK, the same as **Embank**, q. v. (F. *and* E.)

IMBARGO, the same as **Embargo**, q. v. (Span.) In Coles' Dict. 1684.

IMBARK, the same as **Embark**, q. v. (F.) In Minsheu, ed. 1627.

IMBECILE, feeble. (F.—L.) 'We in a manner were got out of God's possession; were, in respect to Him, become *imbecile* and lost;' Barrow, Sermons, vol. ii. ser. 22 (R.) [Formerly a rare word as an adj.; but the verb to *imbécill* (accented on the penultimate) was rather common; see note below.] *Imbecility* is in Shak. Troil. i. 3. 114.—MF. *imbecille*, 'weak, feeble;' Cot.—L. *imbēcillum*, acc. of *imbēcillus*, feeble. Root unknown. Der. *imbecil-i-ty*. ☞ The examples in R. show that the verb to *imbécill* or *imbécel*, to weaken, enfeeble, was once tolerably well known. It also meant 'to diminish' or 'subtract from,' and was repeatedly confused with the verb *to embezzle*, to purloin. An example from Udal, on the Revelation of St. John, c. 16, shows this sense. It runs as follows: 'The second plage of the second angell is the second iudgement of God against the regiment of Rome, and this is *imbeselynge* and diminishyng of theyr power and domynion, many landes and people fallynge from them.' The quotations (in R.) from Drant's tr. of Horace, b. i. sat. 6 and sat. 5, introduce the lines : 'So tyrannous a monarchie *imbecelyng* freedome, than' [then]; and: 'And so *imbecill* all theyr strengthe that they are naught to me.' These lines completely establish the accentuation of this verb, and further illustrate its sense. See **Embezzle**. The old word *bezzle*, to squander, is, however, the real original of *im-bezzle*; from OF. *besiler*, to destroy, waste.

IMBED, to lay, as in a bed. (E.; *with* F. *prefix*.) In Todd's Johnson. From **Im-** (2) and **Bed**. For *in-bed* or *em-bed*.

IMBIBE, to drink in. (F.—L.; *or* L.) In Blount's Gloss., ed. 1674. Cf. *enbibing* in Chaucer, C. T., G 814.—MF. *imbiber*, in use in the 16th cent.—L. *imbibere*, to drink in.—L. *im-* = *in*, in; and *bibere*, to drink. See **Bib**. ¶ Or taken immediately from Latin. Der. *imbibit-ion*, once a common term in alchemy; see Ben Jonson, Alchemist, ii. 1 (Subtle). Der. *imbue*, q. v.; *imbrue*, q. v.

IMBITTER, to render bitter. (E.; *with* F. *prefix*.) 'Why loads he this *imbitter'd* life with shame?' Dryden, tr. of Homer's Iliad, b. i. l. 494. From **Im-** (1) and **Bitter**.

IMBODY, the same as **Embody**. (E.; *with* F. *prefix*.) In Milton, P. L. i. 574; Comus, 468. See **Im-** (1).

IMBORDER, to border. (F.) From **Im-** (1) and **Border**. In Milton, P. L. ix. 438.

IMBOSOM, the same as **Embosom**. (E.; *with* F. *prefix*.) In Milton, P. L. iii. 75, v. 597. See **Im-** (1).

IMBOWER, to shelter with a bower. (E.; *with* F. *prefix*.) From **Im-** (1) and **Bower**. In Milton, P. L. i. 304.

IMBRICATED, bent and hollowed like a gutter-tile; covered with scales that overlap. (L.) A term in botany. Both *imbricated* and *imbrication* are in Kersey, ed. 1715. Blount (1656) has *imbricate*, i. e. formed like a gutter-tile.—L. *imbricātus*, pp. of *imbrīcāre*, to cover with a gutter-tile.—L. *imbric-*, stem of *imbrex*, a gutter-tile.—L. *imbri-*, decl. stem of *imber*, a shower of rain.+Gk. ἀφρός, foam; Skt. *abhra-*, a rain-cloud. Brugmann, i. § 466. Der. *imbricat-ion*.

IMBROGLIO. (Ital.) In Gray, A Long Story, l. 66.—Ital. *imbroglio*, perplexity, trouble, intrigue; hence, a confused heap.— Ital. *imbrogliare*, to entangle, perplex, confuse.—Ital. *im-* (for *in*), in; *broglio*, a broil, confusion; see **Broil** (2).

IMBROWN, to make brown. (E.; *with* F. *prefix*.) From **Im-** (1) and **Brown**. In Milton, P. L. iv. 246.

IMBRUE, IMBREW, EMBRUE, to moisten, drench. (F.— L.) '[Mine eyes] With teares no more *imbrue* your mistresse face;' Turberville, The Lover Hoping Assuredly. '*Imbrew'd* in guilty blood;' Spenser, F. Q. i. 7. 47. 'With mouth *enbrowide*;' Lydgate, Stans Puer, l. 38.—OF. *embruer*; Cot. gives '*s'embruer*, to imbrue or bedable himself with.' Variant of OF. *embevrer*, *embreuver*, to moisten; allied to MItal. *imbevere*, which Torriano gives as equivalent to *imbuire*, 'to sinke into, to moist or wet, to embrue;' Florio. Cf. mod. Ital. *imbevere*, to imbibe. β. The OF. *embreuver* is formed, like mod. F. *abreuver*, from a causal verb *-bevrer*, to give to drink, turned into *-brever* in the 16th century, and thence into *-bruer*. See *abreuver* in Brachet. γ. This causal verb (as if L. **biberāre*) is founded on OF. *bevre* (F. *boire*), to drink; from L. *bibere*, to drink. δ. Hence *imbrue* is the causal of to imbibe, and signifies 'to make to imbibe,' to soak, drench. See **Imbibe**. ☞ Probably it has often been confounded with *imbue* (below). Unconnected with E. *brew*, with which it is sometimes supposed to be allied.

IMBUE, to cause to drink, tinge deeply. (L.) 'With noysome rage *imbew'd*;' Spenser, Ruines of Rome, st. 24, l. 6. Cf. Milton, P. L. viii. 216.—L. *imbuere*, to cause to drink in.—L. *im-*, for *in*, in; and *-buere*, a causal form, apparently allied to L. *bibere*, to drink. Cf. Norm. dial. *embu*, saturated with wet (Moisy). ¶ Early exx. have only the pp. *imbued*, suggested by the L. pp. *imbūtus*.

IMITATE, to copy, make a likeness of. (L.) '*Imitate* and follow his passion;' Sir T. More, 1346 b.—L. *imitātus*, pp. of *imitāri*, to imitate. *Imitāri* is a frequentative form of **im-āre*, not found; cf. **Image**. Root uncertain. Der. *imitat-ion*, *imitat-or*, *imitat-ive*, *imitat-ive-ly*, *imit-a-ble*, *imit-a-bil-i-ty*.

IMMACULATE, spotless. (L.) 'The moste pure and *immaculate* lambe,' Udal, on St. Matt. c. 26. v. 26; Shak. Rich. II, v. 3. 61. And in Lydgate, Minor Poems, p. 79. — L. *immaculātus*, unspotted.—L. *im-* = *in-*, not; and *maculātus*, pp. of *maculāre*, to spot, from *macula*, a spot. See **Mail** (1). Der. *immaculate-ly*, *immaculate-ness*.

IMMANENT, indwelling. (L.) In Sir D. Lyndesay, Satyre, l. 3460.—L. *immanent-*, stem of pres. pt. of *immanēre*, to dwell within.—L. *im-*, for *in*, within; and *manēre*, to remain, dwell. See **Mansion**.

IMMATERIAL, not material. (F.—L.) In Shak. Troil. v. 1. 35.—MF. *immateriel*, 'immateriall;' Cot. See **Im-** (4) and **Material**. ¶ The final syllable has been changed to *-al*, to make it nearer the Latin. Der. *immaterial-ly*, *-ise*, *-ism*, *-ist*, *-i-ty*.

IMMATURE, not mature. (L.) In Milton, P. L. vii. 277. See **Im-** (4) and **Mature**. Der. *immature-ly*, *-ness*, *immatur-ed*.

IMMEASURABLE, not to be measured. (F.—L.) 'Theire *immesurable* outrage;' Sir T. More, Works, p. 590 b. See **Im-** (4) and **Measurable**. Der. *immeasurable-ness*, *immeasurabl-y*. Doublet, *immense*.

IMMEDIATE, without intervention, direct, present. (F.—L.) 'Their authoritye is so hygh and so *immediate* of [not to] God;' Sir T. More, Works, p. 893 d.—MF. *immediat*, 'immediate;' Cot. See **Im-** (4) and **Mediate**. Der. *immediate-ly*, *-ness*.

IMMEMORIAL, beyond the reach of memory. (F.—L.) 'Their *immemorial* antiquity;' Howell, Familiar Letters, b. ii. let. 59 (R.); let. 60, ed. 1678; dated 1630.—F. *immemorial*, 'without the compasse, scope, or reach of memory;' Cot. See **Im-** (4) and **Memorial**. Der. *immemorial-ly*.

IMMENSE, immeasurable, very large. (F.—L.) In Milton, P. L. i. 790; and in Daniel, Musophilus, st. 27 from end.—F. *immense*, 'immense;' Cot.—L. *immensus*, immeasurable.—L. *im-* = *in-*, not; and *mensus*, pp. of *metiri*, to measure. See **Im-** (4) and **Mete**. Der. *immense-ly*, *immense-ness*, *immens-i-ty*, *immeas-ur-able*, from *mensūrus*, fut. pp. of *metiri*; *immens-ur-abil-i-ty*.

IMMERGE, to plunge into. (L.) '*Immerged*, or *Immersed*, dipt in or plunged;' also '*Immerse*, to plunge or dip over head and ears;' Kersey, ed. 1715. *Immerse* occurs as a pp. in Bacon, Nat. Hist. s. 114.—L. *immergere*, pp. *immersus*, to plunge into.—L. *im-* = *in*, into; and *mergere*, to plunge, sink. See **Im-** (3) and **Merge**. Der. *immerse*, from pp. *immersus*; *immers-ion*.

IMMIGRATE, to migrate into a country. (L.) 'Hitherto I have considered the Saracens, either at their *immigration* into Spain about the ninth century,' &c.; Warton, Hist. Eng. Poetry, Diss. i.; ed. 1840, vol. i. p. xviii. The verb is in Cockeram (1623).—L. *immigrātus*, pp. of *immigrāre*, to migrate into. See **Im-** (3) and **Migrate**. Der. *immigrat-ion*, *immigrant*.

IMMINENT, projecting over, near at hand. (L.) 'Against the sinne *imminent* or to come;' Sir T. More, Works, p. 370 b. ME. *imminent*, Libell of E. Policye, l. 739.—L. *imminent-*, stem of pres. part. of *imminēre*, to project over.—L. *im-* = *in*, upon, over; and *minēre*, to jut out. See **Eminent**. Der. *imminent-ly*; *imminence*, Shak. Troil. v. 10. 13.

IMMIT, to send into, inject. (L.) '*Immit*, to send in, to put in;' Cockeram (1642). *Immission* is in Bp. Taylor, Great Exemplar, pt. ii. dis. 12 (R.)—L. *immittere*, pp. *immissus*, to send into. See **Im-** (3) and **Missile**. Der. *immiss-ion*, from pp. *immissus*.

IMMOBILITY, steadfastness. (F.—L.) 'The earth's settledness and *immobility*;' Wilkins, That the Earth may be a Planet, b. ii. prop. 5 (R.)—F. *immobilité*, 'steadfastnesse;' Cot.—L. acc. *immōbilitātem*, from L. *immōbilitās*, immobility.—L. *immōbilis*, immovable. See **Im-** (4) and **Mobile**.

IMMODERATE, not moderate. (L.) '*Immoderate* slepe;' Sir T. Elyot, Castell of Helthe, bk. ii. ch. 30. Sir T. More has *immoderately*; Works, p. 87 a, l. 1.—L. *immoderātus*, not moderate. See **Im-** (4) and **Moderate**. Der. *immoderate-ly*.

IMMODEST, not modest. (F.—L.) In Spenser, F. Q. b. ii. c. 6. st. 37.—F. *immodeste*, 'immodest;' Cot.—L. *immodestus*. See **Im-** (4) and **Modest**. Der. *immodest-ly*, *immodest-y*.

IMMOLATE, to offer in sacrifice. (L.) Cotgrave has *immolated*, to explain F. *immolé*.—L. *immolātus*, pp. of *immolāre*, to sacrifice; lit. to throw meal upon a victim, as was the custom.—L. *im-* = *in*, upon; and *mola*, meal, cognate with E. *meal*. See **Im-** (3), **Meal** (1). Der. *immolat-ion*, from F. *immolation*, 'an immolation, sacrifice;' Cot.

IMMORAL, not moral, wicked. (F.—L.) In Kersey, ed. 1715. From **Im-** (4) and **Moral**. Der. *immoral-ly*, *-ity*.

IMMORTAL, not mortal. (F.—L.) ME. *immortal*, Chaucer C. T. 5059 (B 639).—MF. *immortel*, 'immortall;' Cot.—L. *immortālis*. See **Im-** (4) and **Mortal**. Der. *immortal-ly*, *immortal-ise*, 1 Hen. VI, i. 2. 148; *immortal-i-ty*, Shak. Lucrece, 725.

IMMOVABLE, not movable. (F.—L.) ME. *immouable*; Test. of Love, bk. iii. ch. 4. l. 207. From **Im-** (4) and **Movable**; see **Move**. Der. *immovable-ness*, *immovabl-y*.

IMMUNITY, freedom from obligation. (F.—L.) In Hall's Chron. Edw. IV, an. 10. § 19. Wyclif has *ynmunité*, 1 Macc. x. 34. —F. *immunité*, 'immunity;' Cot.—L. *immūnitātem*, acc. of *immūnitās*, exemption.—L. *immūnis*, exempt from public services.—L. *im-* = *in-*, not; and *mūnis*, serving, obliging (whence also *commūnis*, common). Cf. L. *mūnus*, duty; see **Common**.

IMMURE, to shut up in prison. (F.—L.) In Shak. L. L. L. iii. 126; Merch. Ven. ii. 7. 52. Shak. also has *immures*, sb. pl. fortifications, walls, Troilus, prol. l. 8; spelt *emures* in the first folio. Similarly *immure* stands for *emmure*.—MF. *emmurer*, 'to immure, or wall about;' Cot.—F. *em-*, from L. *im-* = *in*, in, within; and F. *murer*, 'to wall;' Cot., from L. *murāre*, to wall, from *mūrus*, a wall. See **Im-** (1) and **Mural**.

IMMUTABLE, not mutable. (F.—L.) 'Of an *immutable* necessitie,' Sir T. More, Works, p. 838 h [not p. 839]; and in Lydgate, Minor Poems, p. 25.—F. *immutable*, with same sense as *immuable*, which is the better form; both are in Cotgrave.—L. *immūtābilis*. See Im- (4) and **Mutable.** Der. *immutabl-y, immutable-ness, immuta-bili-ty.*

IMP, a graft, offspring, demon. (Late L.—Gk.) Formerly used in a good sense, meaning 'scion' or 'offspring.' 'Well worthy *impe*;' Spenser, F. Q. i. 9. 6. 'And thou, most dreaded *impe* of highest Jove;' id. Introd. to b. i. st. 3. ME. *imp, ymp,* a graft on a tree; *impen, ympen,* to graft. 'I was sumtyme a frere [friar], And the couentes [convent's] gardyner, for to graffe *ympes*; On limitoures and listres lesynges I *ymped*;' P. Plowman, B. v. 136-8. 'Of feble trees ther comen wrecched *impes*;' Chaucer, C. T. 13962 (B 3146). The pl. sb. *impen* occurs in the Ancren Riwle, p. 378, l. 24; and the pp. *i-imped,* i. e. grafted, in the same, p. 360, l. 6. (The verb is due to the sb.) AS. *impian,* to graft; Gerefa, § 12; in Anglia, ix. 262. AS. *impan,* s. pl., grafts; Gregory's Past. Care, ed. Sweet, p. 381, l. 17.—Late L. *impotus,* a graft, occurring in the Lex Salica; see the text called Lex Emendata, c. xxvii. § 8.—Gk. ἔμφυτος, engrafted; James, i. 21.—Gk. ἐμφύειν, to implant.—Gk. ἐμ- for ἐν, in; and φύειν, to produce, from √BHEU, to be. See In and Be. ¶ From the same source are W. *impio,* to graft, *imp,* a graft, scion; Dan. *ympe,* Swed. *ympa,* G. *impfen,* OHG. *impitôn, imphôn,* to graft; also F. *enter,* to graft; showing that the word was widely spread at an early period. Der. *imp,* vb. Rich. II, ii. 1. 292, ME. *impen,* AS. *impian,* as above.

IMPACT, a striking against, collision. (L.) Modern. 'The quarrel [crossbow-bolt] by that *impact* driven, True to its aim, fled fatal;' Southey, Joan of Arc, b. viii. l. 228.—L. *impactus,* pp. of *impingere,* to impinge. See **Impinge.** ¶ The right form of the sb. should rather have been *impaction.* The word *impacted* occurs in Holland's Pliny, b. xx. c. 21. '*Impacted,* dashed or beaten against, cast or put into;' Blount's Gloss., ed. 1674.

IMPAIR, to make worse, injure, weaken. (F.—L.) 'Whose praise hereby no whit *impaired* is;' Spenser, Colin Clout, l. 755. ME. *empeiren,* also written *enpeiren*; Chaucer, tr. of Boethius, b. iv. pr. 3, l. 35; b. iv. pr. 6, l. 170.—OF. *empeirer* (Burguy); later *empirer,* 'to impaire;' Cot.—Late L. *impēiōrāre,* to make worse.—L. *im-=in,* with an intensive force; and L. *pēior,* worse; a comparative form from a lost positive, and of uncertain origin. Cf. **Pessimist.**

IMPALE, the same as **Empale,** q. v. (F.—L.) In Blount's Gloss., ed. 1674; and in Minsheu, ed. 1627. In Shak. it means 'to surround;' Troilus, v. 7. 5; but it is the same word. Der. *impalement.*

IMPALPABLE, not palpable. (F.—L.) In Holland's Plutarch, p. 913 (R.); and in Cotgrave.—F. *impalpable,* 'impalpable;' Cot. See Im- (4) and **Palpable.** Der. *impalpabl-y.*

IMPANEL, IMPANNEL, the same as **Empanel,** q. v.

IMPARITY, want of parity. (F.—L.) In Blount's Gloss., ed. 1674. From Im- (4) and **Parity**; cf. L. *imparitās.* See **Par.** [No MF. *imparité* in Cotgrave; but OF. *imparité* is in Godefroy.]

IMPARK, EMPARK, to enclose for a park. (F.) '*Impark,* to enclose . . . a piece of ground for a park;' Kersey, ed. 1715. 'Not . . . held nor *emparked* within any laws or limits;' Bp. King, Vine Palatine, 1614, p. 32 (Todd).—AF. *enparker,* Stat. Realm, i. 197.—F. *en,* for L. *in,* in; and F. *parc,* from Late L. *parcus.* See **Park.**

IMPART, to give a part of, communicate. (F.—L.) 'The secrete thoughts *imparted* with such trust;' Surrey, Prisoned in Windsor, l. 37; see Specimens of English, ed. Skeat, p. 220.—MF. *impartir,* 'to impart;' Cot.—L. *impartīre, impertīre,* to bestow a share on.—L. *im-,* for *in,* on, upon; and *partīre, partīrī,* to share, from *parti-,* decl. stem of *pars,* a part. See **Part.** Der. *impart-ible.*

IMPARTIAL, not partial. (F.—L.) In Shak. Rich. II, i. 1. 115. From Im- (4) and **Partial.** Der. *impartial-ly, impartial-i-ty.*

IMPASSABLE, not to be passed through. (F.—L.) In Milton, P. L. x. 254. From Im- (4) and **Passable;** see **Pass.** Der. *impassabl-y, impassable-ness.*

IMPASSIBLE, incapable of feeling. (F.—L.) 'This most pure parte of the soule, . . . diuyne, *impassible,* and incorruptible;' Sir T. Elyot, The Governour, b. iii. c. 24. § 2. *Impassibilitie* is in Sir T. More's Works, p. 1329 b.—F. *impassible,* 'impassible, sencelesse;' Cot.—L. *impassibilis,* incapable of passion or suffering.—L. *im-=in-,* not; and *passibilis,* capable of suffering, allied to *passus,* pp. of *pati,* to suffer. See Im- (4) and **Passion, Patient.** Der. *impassible-ness, impassibili-ty.*

IMPASSIONED, roused to strong feeling. (F.—L.) In Milton, P. L. ix. 678. From the prefix *im-=*L. *in,* with an intensive force; and **Passion.** Der. A similar formation is *impassionate,* rarely used.

IMPASSIVE, not susceptible of feeling, not showing feeling. (F.—L.) In Milton, P. L. vi. 455. From Im- (4) and **Passive.** Der. *impassive-ly, -ness;* Burton has *impassionate* in a like sense; Anat. of Melancholy, i. 3. 1. 3.

IMPATIENT, not patient. (F.—L.) ME. *impacient.* '*Impacient* is he that wol nat been y-taught;' Chaucer, C. T. Pers. Tale, De Superbia, I 401.—F. *impatient,* 'impatient;' Cot. See Im- (4) and **Patient.** Der. *impatient-ly, impacience, impacienc-y.*

IMPAWN, to pledge. (F.) In Shak. Hen. V, i. 2. 21; Hamlet, v. 2. 155, 171. From *im-,* prefix, a substitute for F. *em-=*L. *im-,* in; and *pawn*; see Im- (1) and **Pawn.**

IMPEACH, to charge with a crime. (F.—L.) The orig. sense is 'to hinder;' and it was once so used. 'The victorie was much hindered and *impeached*;' Holland, tr. of Livy, p. 308 (R.) 'To *impeach* and stop their breath;' Holland, tr. of Pliny, b. xi. c. 3. ME. *empechen*; 'no man [schal], *empeche* hem;' Wyclif, Works, ed. Arnold, iii. 294.—OF. *empescher,* 'to hinder, let, stop, bar, impeach;' Cot. β. Littré and Scheler connect it with Prov. *empedegar,* which they cite; from Late L. *impedicāre,* to fetter. *Impedicāre* is from the prefix *im-=in,* in, on; and *pedica,* a fetter, from *pedi-,* decl. stem of *pēs,* a foot; see Im- (1) and **Foot.** γ. At the same time some (at least) of the senses of OF. *enpescher* are due to OF. *empacher,* Span. *empachar,* Ital. *impacciare,* to delay; these represent a Late L. frequent. form **impacticāre,* a derivative from *impingere,* pp. *impactus,* to fasten upon. *Impingere* is compounded of *im-=in,* in, on; and *pangere,* to fasten. See **Pact,** and see **Despatch.** Der. *impeach-er, impeach-able, impeach-ment,* spelt *impechement,* Sir T. Elyot, The Governour, b. i. c. 15 (end); *empeschement,* Dictes of the Philosophers, pr. by Caxton, fol. 13, back, l. 5.

IMPEARL, to adorn with pearls. (F.) In Milton, P. L. v. 747. From Im- (1) and **Pearl.**

IMPECCABLE, not liable to sin. (L.) '*Impeccable,* that cannot offend or do amiss;' Blount's Gloss., ed. 1674.—L. *impeccābilis,* faultless.—L. *im-* for *in-,* negative prefix; and *peccābilis,* peccable. See Im- (4) and **Peccable.** Der. *impeccabili-ty.*

IMPECUNIOUS, in want of money. (L.) 'Put him out, an *impecunious* creature;' Ben Jonson, Cynthia's Revels, A. v. sc. 2 (Anaides).—L. *im-,* for *in-,* not; and *pecūniōsus,* rich, from *pecūnia,* money; see **Pecuniary.**

IMPEDE, to obstruct. (L.) In Macbeth, i. 5. 29. The sb. *impediment* is commoner, and earlier; Hoccleve, De Regimine Principum, l. 1807.—L. *impedīre,* to intangle the feet, obstruct.—L. *im-=in,* in; and *ped-,* stem of *pēs,* a foot; see Im- (3) and **Foot.** Der. *impedi-ment, impedi-t-ive.*

IMPEL, to drive forward, urge. (L.) 'The flames *impell'd*;' Dryden, Annus Mirabilis, st. 230. And in Caxton, Eneydos, ch. xxii. p. 78, l. 17.—L. *impellere,* pp. *impulsus,* to urge on.—L. *im-=in,* on, forward: and *pellere,* to drive. See Im- (3) and **Pulsate.** Der. *impell-ent, impell-er*; and (from pp. *impulsus*) *im-pulse,* Milton, P. L. iii. 120; *impuls-ion,* id. Sams. Agon. 422; *impuls-ive, impuls-ive-ly, impuls-ive-ness.*

IMPEND, to hang over, be near. (L.) Milton has *impendent,* P. L. ii. 177, v. 891. 'Vengeance *impending* on you;' Massinger, The Old Law, A. v. sc. 1.—L. *impendēre,* to hang over.—L. *im-=in,* on, over; and *pendēre,* to hang. See Im- (3) and **Pendant.** Der. *impend-ing*; also *impend-ent,* from the stem of the pres. part.

IMPENETRABLE, not penetrable. (F.—L.) In Sir T. Elyot, The Governour, b. i. c. 23. § 5; Shak. Merch. Ven. iii. 3. 18.—MF. *impenetrable,* 'impenetrable;' Cot. See Im- (4) and **Penetrate.** Der. *impenetrabl-y,* Milton, P. L. vi. 400; *impenetrabili-ty.*

IMPENITENT, not penitent. (F.—L.) Sir T. More has both *impenitent* and *impenitence*; Works, p. 573 a. From Im- (4) and **Penitent.** Der. *impenitent-ly, impenitence*; *impenitenc-y,* Bible A. V. heading to Isa. ix.

IMPERATIVE, authoritative. (F.—L.) In Palsgrave (Of Verbs).—MF. *imperatif,* 'imperative, imperious; the imperative mood in grammer;' Cot.—L. *imperātīuus,* due to a command.—L. *imperātum,* a command; neut. of *imperātus,* pp. of *imperāre,* to command.—L. *im-=in*; and *parāre,* to make ready, order. See Im- (3) and **Parade.** Der. *impera-tive-ly*; and see *imperial.*

IMPERCEPTIBLE, not perceptible. (F.—L.) 'Hang on such small *imperceptible* strings' [*not* things]; Cowley, Davideis, b. iv; l. 323.—F. *imperceptible,* 'imperceptible;' Cot. See Im- (4) and **Perceive.** Der. *imperceptibl-y, imperceptible-ness, imperceptibili-ty.*

IMPERFECT, not perfect. (F.—L.) Really of *French* origin, but conformed to the Latin spelling. ME. *imparfit, inparfit, inperfit*; P. Plowman, B. xv. 50; Chaucer, tr. of Boethius, b. iii. pr. 9, l. 16.—OF. *imparfait* (Hatzfeld); *imperfaict* (Cotgrave).—L. *imperfectus.* See Im- (4) and **Perfect.** Der. *imperfect-ly, imperfect-ness, imperfect-ion.*

IMPERIAL, relating to an empire. (F.—L.) ME. *imperial,*

Gower, C. A. iii. 61; bk. vi. 1785.—OF. *emperial* (Burguy); later *imperial* (Cot.).—L. *imperiālis*, belonging to an empire.—L. *imperium*, an empire. See **Empire**. **Der.** *imperial-ly, imperial-ism, imperial-ist*; also (from L. *imperium*) *imperi-ous*, Hamlet, v. 1. 236, Oth. ii. 3. 276; *imperi-ous-ly, imperi-ous-ness*.

IMPERIL, to put in peril. (F.—L.) In Ben Jonson, Magnetic Lady, at the end of Act ii; Probee's second speech; Spenser, F. Q. iv. 4. 10. From **Im-** (1) and **Peril**.

IMPERISHABLE, not perishable. (F.—L.) In Milton, P. L. vi. 435.—MF. *imperissable*, 'unperishable;' Cot. See **Im-** (4) and **Perish**. **Der.** *imperishabl-y, imperishable-ness, imperishabil-i-ty*.

IMPERSONAL, not personal. (F.—L.) In Levins. Ben Jonson treats of *impersonal* verbs; Eng. Grammar, b. i. c. 16.—F. *impersonnel*, 'impersonall;' Cot.—L. *impersonālis*. See **Im-** (4) and **Person**. **Der.** *impersonal-ly, impersonal-i-ty*.

IMPERSONATE, to personify, to personate or represent a person's qualities. (L.) 'The masques . . . were not only furnished by the heathen divinities, but often by the virtues and vices *impersonated*;' Warton, Hist. Eng. Poetry, sect. lxi; ed. 1840, iii. 400. From L. *im-=in*, used as a prefix; and *personate*. See **Im-** (3) and **Person**. **Der.** *impersonat-ion*.

IMPERTINENT, not pertinent, trifling, rude. (F.—L.) ME. *impertinent*; Chaucer, C. T. 7930 (E 54).—F. *impertinent*, 'impertinent, unfit;' Cot.—L. *impertinent-*, stem of *impertinens*, not belonging to. See **Im-** (4) and **Pertinent, Pertain**. **Der.** *impertinence*, Milton, P. L. viii. 195; *impertinenc-y*, K. Lear, iv. 6. 178; *impertinent-ly*.

IMPERTURBABLE, not easily disturbed. (L.) In Ash's Dict., ed. 1775.—L. *imperturbābilis*, that cannot be disturbed. See **Im-** (4) and **Perturb**. **Der.** *imperturbabili-ty*.

IMPERVIOUS, impassable. (L.) In Cowley, Ode upon Dr. Harvey, st. ii. l. 6; and in Milton, P. L. x. 254.—L. *imperuius*, impassable; the L. *-us* being turned into E. *-ous*, as in *arduous, conspicuous*, &c.—L. *im-=in* (= E. *un-*), not; *per*, through; and *uia*, a way. See **Viaduct**. **Der.** *impervious-ly, -ness*.

IMPETRATE, to procure by entreaty. (L.) '*Impetrate*, to obtaine;' Cockeram (1642); and in Minsheu.—L. *impetrāt-us*, pp. of *impetrāre*, to procure.—L. *im-*, for *in*, prep., to; *patrāre*, to bring to pass, to achieve, perhaps orig. 'to act as father,' and allied to *pater*, father.

IMPETUS, sudden impulse, violent push. (L.) In Boyle's Works, vol. i. p. 138 (R.).—L. *impetus*, an attack, impulse; lit. 'a falling on.'—L. *im-=in*, on, upon; and *petere*, to seek, tend to, lit. to fly or fall.—√PET, to fall, fly; cf. Skt. *pat*, to fly; see **Im-** (3). **Der.** *impetu-ous*, Caxton, Troy-book, leaf 174 back, l. 19, from F. *impetueux*, which is from L. *impetuōsus*; *impetu-ous-ly, impetu-ous-ness, impetu-os-i-ty*.

IMPIETY, want of piety. (F.—L.) In Shak. Much Ado, iv. 1. 105.—F. *impieté*, 'impiety;' Cot.—L. *impietātem*, acc. of *impietās*. See **Im-** (4) and **Piety**. And see **Impious**.

IMPINGE, to strike or fall against. (L.) '*Impinge*, to hurl or throw against a thing;' Blount's Gloss., ed. 1678.—L. *impingere*, pp. *impactus*, to strike upon or against.—L. *im-=in*, on; and *pangere*, to fasten, also to strike. See **Pact**. **Der.** *impact*, q.v.

IMPIOUS, not pious, wicked. (F.—L.) In Shak. Haml. i. 2. 94. Coined from **Im-** (4) and **Pious**. [The OF. word is *impie*.] **Der.** *impious-ly, -ness*; and see *impiety*.

IMPLACABLE, not to be appeased. (F.—L.) 'Bering *implacable* anger;' Sir T. More, Works, p. 83 a.—F. *implacable*, 'unplacable;' Cot.—L. *implācābilis*. See **Im-** (4) and **Placable**. **Der.** *implacabili-ty*.

IMPLANT, to plant in. (F.—L.) In Milton, P. L. xi. 23; and Barnes, Works, p. 323, col. 1.—F. *implanter*, 'to implant, to fix, or set into;' Cot.—L. *im-=in*, in; and *plantāre*, to plant. See **Im-** (1) and **Plant**. **Der.** *implant-at-ion*.

IMPLEAD, to urge a plea or suit at law. (F.—L.) In Acts, xix. 38 (A. V.); and Fuller, Hist. of Waltham Abbey, § 16 (p. 10, ed. 1655). ME. *enpleden, empleden*, Trevisa, tr. of Higden, vii. 481. —AF. *enpleder*, Stat. Realm, i. 49 (1278); MF. *emplaider*, 'to sue, to implead;' Cot. See **Im-** (1) and **Plead**. **Der.** *implead-er*.

IMPLEMENT, a utensil, tool. (Late L.—L.) In Hamlet, i. 1. 74.—Late L. *implēmentum*, an accomplishing, filling up; furniture, necessaries, an instrument.—L. *implēre*, to fill, discharge, execute.—L. *im-=in*, in; and *plēre*, to fill; see **Im-** (3) and **Full**.

IMPLICATE, to involve. (L.) Cot. has *implication*, to translate F. *implication*; the verb is noted by Cockeram (1642); and the pp. form *implicat* occurs as early as 1536.—L. *implicātus*, pp. of *implicāre*, to infold, involve.—L. *im-=in*, in; and *plica*, a fold. See **Im-** (3) and **Ply**. **Der.** *implicat-ion*, from F. *implication*; also *implicit*, Milton, P. L. vii. 323, from L. *implicitus*, also a pp. of *implicāre*; *implicit-ly, -ness*; and see *imply*.

IMPLORE, to entreat, beg earnestly. (F.—L.) In Spenser, F. Q. iii. 11. 18; used as a sb., id. ii. 5. 37.—F. *implorer*, 'to implore;' Cot.—L. *implōrāre*, to implore.—L. *im-=in*, on, upon; and *plōrāre*, to wail. See **Im-** (3) and **Deplore**. **Der.** *implor-ing-ly*.

IMPLY, to mean, signify. (F.—L.) 'It *implyeth* fyrst repugnaunce;' Sir T. More, Works, p. 1127 b. A coined word; from **Im-** (1) and **Ply**, as if from an OF. *emplier*; but the OF. form was *empleier*, later *emploier*. [According to stress, an infin. *emplier* would answer to L. *implicāre*, inf., whilst *empleie* would answer to L. *implicō*; but Godefroy gives no example of the stem *empli-*.] Doublets, *implicate*, q. v.; *employ*, q. v.

IMPOLITE, not polite. (L.) 'I never saw such *impolite* confusion at any country wedding in Britain;' Drummond, Trav. (let. 3. 1744), p. 76 (Todd). First in 1612.—L. *impolitus*, unpolished, rude. See **Im-** (4) and **Polite**. **Der.** *impolite-ly, -ness*.

IMPOLITIC, not politic. (L. *and* L.—Gk.) 'They [the merchants] do it so *impoliticly*;' Bacon, Report on the Petition of the Merchants (R.). Spelt *impolitick* in Phillips and Kersey. From **Im-** (4) and **Politic**. **Der.** *im-politic-ly*.

IMPONDERABLE, without sensible weight. (L.) Modern. The older word is *imponderous*; Sir T. Browne, Vulg. Errors, b. ii. c. 5. § 10. From **Im-** (4) and **Ponderable** or **Ponderous**.

IMPORT, to bring in from abroad, to convey, signify, interest. (F.—L.; *or* L.) In the sense 'to bring in from abroad,' the word is Latin. 'It *importeth* also plaine and open blasphemy;' Sir T. More, Works, pp. 325, 326 a.—F. *importer*; 'cela *importe* much, that is of great consequence;' Cot.—L. *importāre*, to import, bring, introduce, cause.—L. *im-=in*, in; and *portāre*, to carry; see **Port** (1). **Der.** *import*, sb.; *import-ant*, L. L. L. v. 1. 104, from F. *important*, pres. pt.; *important-ly*; *importance*, Wint. Ta. v. 2. 20, from F. *importance*; also *import-er, import-at-ion*.

IMPORTABLE, intolerable. (F.—L.) Obsolete. In the Prayer of Manasses (A. V.); Spenser, F. Q. ii. 8. 35; and earlier, in Chaucer, C. T. 9020 (E 1144).—F. *importable*, 'intollerable;' Cot.—L. *importābilis*, that cannot be borne. See **Im-** (4), **Port** (1).

IMPORTUNE, to molest, urge with eager solicitation. (F.—L.) In Ant. and Cleop. iv. 15. 19; Meas. i. 1. 57. Formed from ME. *importune*, adj., molesting, troublesome; cf. 'And for he nill be *importune* Unto no wight, ne onerous;' Rom. of the Rose, 5632.—OF. *importun*, 'importunate, urgent, earnest with, troublesome;' Cot. —L. *importūnus*, unfit, unsuitable, troublesome, grievous, rude. **β.** The L. *importūnus* (with prefix *im-=in-*, not) and *opportūnus* (with prefix *ob*) are both related to L. *portus*, a harbour, with reference to approach or access to it; so that *importūnus*=hard of access, unsuitable, &c. Cf. L. *Portūnus*, the protecting god of harbours. See **Port** (2). **Der.** *importun-i-ty* (Levins), from F. *importunité* = L. acc. *importūnitātem*; also *importun-ate* (Levins), a coined word; *importun-ate-ly, importun-ate-ness*.

IMPOSE, to lay upon, enjoin, obtrude, palm off. (F.—L. *and* Gk.) In Spenser, F. Q. v. 8. 49.—F. *imposer*, 'to impose;' Cot. —F. *im-*=L. *im-=in*, on, upon; and *poser*, to place; see **Im-** (1) and **Pose**. ¶ The F. *imposer* was confused with L. *impōnere* (below). **Der.** *impos-ing, impos-ing-ly*.

IMPOSITION, a laying on, tax, deception. (F.—L.) 'Thy fader sette on us . . . grete *imposicions*;' Caxton, Golden Legend, Hist. of Roboas.—F. *imposition*.—L. acc. *impositiōnem*, from nom. *impositio*, a laying on; cf. *impositus*, pp. of *impōnere*, to lay on.—L. *im-=in*, on; and *pōnere*, to put, lay; see **Im-** (3) and **Position**. **Der.** from same source: *impost*, from F. *impost*, 'an impost, custom' (Cot.), which from L. pp. *impositus*; *impostor*, Temp. i. 2. 477, from L. *impostor*, a deceiver; *impost-ure*, Hall's Chron. Hen. VI, an. 26. § 2, from F. *imposture*, 'imposture, guile' (Cot.).

IMPOSSIBLE, not possible. (F.—L.) ME. *impossible*, Chaucer, C. T. 6270 (D 688).—F. *impossible*, 'impossible;' Cot.—L. *impossibilis*. See **Im-** (4) and **Possible**. **Der.** *impossibili-ty*.

IMPOSTHUME, an abscess. (F.—L.—Gk.) 'A boyle or *imposthume*;' Sir T. Elyot, Castel of Helth, b. ii. c. 25. Also (better) spelt *apostume*, as in Prompt. Parv.—OF. *apostume*, 'an apostume, an inward swelling full of corrupt matter;' Cot. Also (better) spelt *aposteme*; Cot.—L. *apostēma*, an abscess.—Gk. ἀπόστημα, a standing away from; hence, a separation of corrupt matter.—Gk. ἀπό, from; cognate with E. *of, off*; and στη-, base of ἵστημι, I set, place, stand, from √STĀ, to stand. See **Apo-** and **Stand**. **Der.** *imposthum-ate, imposthum-at-ion*. ☞ Here the prefix *im-* is due to mere corruption; the right form was *aposteme* or *apostem* (N. E. D.).

IMPOSTOR, IMPOST; see under **Imposition**.

IMPOTENT, not potent, feeble. (F.—L.) ME. *impotent*; Gower, C. A. iii. 383; bk. viii. 3127.—F. *impotent*, 'impotent;' Cot. —L. *impotentem*, acc. of *impotens*, unable. See **Im-** (4) and **Potent**. **Der.** *impotent-ly, impotence, impotenc-y*.

IMPOUND, to put into a pound, as cattle. (E.) In Shak. Hen. V, i. 2. 160. From **Im-** (2) and **Pound** (2). Der. *impound-age*.

IMPOVERISH, to make poor. (F.—L.) 'Him and his subjects still *impoverishing*;' Drayton, Barons' Wars, b. v. st. 8; and in Baret. From OF. *empoviriss*-, stem of pres. part. of *empovrir*, to impoverish (Godefroy).—F. *em*-, for L. *in*, extremely; and OF. *povre*, poor. See **Poor**. Der. *impoverish-ment* (Cotgrave).

IMPRACTICABLE, not practicable. (Late L.—Gk.) In Phillips, ed. 1706, and Kersey, ed. 1715; see Tatler, no. 187, § 3. From **Im-** (4) and **Practicable**. Der. *impracticabl-y*, *impracticableness*, *impracticabili-ty*.

IMPRECATE, to invoke a curse on. (L.) [The sb. *imprecation* (from F. *imprecation*) is in earlier use than the verb, and occurs in Puttenham, Eng. Poetrie, ed. Arber, bk. iii. ch. 19; p. 221. 'The *imprecation* of the vestall nun Tuccia;' Holland, tr. of Pliny, b. xxviii. c. 2.]—L. *imprecātus*, pp. of *imprecārī*, to call down by prayer.—L. *im*-=*in*, upon, on; and *precārī*, to pray. See **Im-** (3) and **Pray**. Der. *imprecat-ion* (above); *imprecat-or-y*.

IMPREGNABLE, not to be taken or seized upon. (F.—L.) '*Impreignable* cities and stronge holdes;' Sir T. Elyot, The Governour, b. i. c. 27. § 10. [The *g* is inserted much as in *sovereign*, and was sometimes silent; or *gn* was pronounced as *ny*.] Caxton has *imprenable*, Golden Legend, Moses, § 5 from end.—OF. *imprenable*, 'impregnable;' Cot.—F. *im*-=L. *im*-=*in*-, negative prefix; and F. *prendre*, to take, from L. *prehendere*, to seize. See **Comprehend**. Der. *impregnabl-y*, *impregnabili-ty*.

IMPREGNATE, to render pregnant. (L.) Milton uses *impregn*, P. L. iv. 500, ix. 737; this is a mere abbreviation. Sir T. Brown has *impregnate*, Vulgar Errors, bk. iii. ch. 12. § 9.—L. *impraegnātus*, pp. of an (unused) *impraegnāre*, to make pregnant.—L. *im*-=*in*, in; and *praegnā*-, seen in *praegnans*, *praegnas*, pregnant. See **Im-** (3) and **Pregnant**. Der. *impregnat-ion*.

IMPRESE, an heraldic device, with a motto. (F.—Ital.—L.) In Shak. Rich. II, iii. 1. 25. Also spelt *impresa* (Nares).—MF. *imprese*.—Ital. *impresa*, 'an imprese, an embleme; also an enterprise;' Florio. Fem. of *impreso*, undertaken (hence, adopted), pp. of *imprendere*, to undertake.—L. *in*, in; and *prehendere*, to lay hold of; see **Prehensile**. Doublet, *emprise*, an enterprise; Spenser, F. Q. ii. 4. 12, from F. *emprise*, fem. pp. of *emprendre*, to undertake, Cot. Der. *impresario*, an undertaker, stage manager, from Ital. *impresa*, an undertaking.

IMPRESS, to imprint, make an impression, press. (L.) ME. *impressen*, Chaucer, Troil. iii. 1543; Gower, C. A. i. 257; bk. ii. 2900. The sb. *impressioun* is in Chaucer, C. T. 3613.—L. *impressāre*, frequentative of *imprimere*, to impress.—L. *im*-=*in*, upon; and *premere*, to press. See **Im-** (3) and **Press**. Der. *impress*, sb., Two Gent. iii. 2. 6; *impress-ion*, Gower, C. A. ii. 14; bk. iv. 389; *impress-ible*, *impress-ibl-y*, *impress-ible-ness*, *impress-ive*, *impress-ive-ly*, *impress-ive-ness*. ¶ But *impress-ment*, a seizing of provisions or sailors for public service, is a coined word allied to the *press* in **Press-gang**; see **Press** (2).

IMPRINT, to print upon, impress deeply. (F.—L.) '*Imprinted* that feare so sore in theyr ymaginacyon;' Sir T. More, Works, 1196 d [*not* 1197]. ME. *empreinten*, Chaucer, tr. of Boethius, bk. v. met. 4. l. 12.—OF. *empreinte*, 'a stamp, print;' Cot. Orig. fem. of pp. of *empreindre*, 'to print, stamp;' id.—L. *imprimere*, to impress (above). ☞ The OF. verb is *empreindre*. Der. *imprint*, sb. (first in 1480).

IMPRISON, to put in prison. (F.—L.) ME. *enprisonen*, Rob. of Glouc., ed. W. A. Wright, l. 9521. For *emprison*.—OF. *emprisonner*, 'to imprison;' Cot.—F. *em*-=L. *im*-=*in*, in; and F. *prison*, a prison. See **Im-** (1) and **Prison**. Der. *imprison-ment*.

IMPROBABLE, not probable. (F.—L.) In Shak. Tw. Nt. iii. 4. 141.—F. *improbable*, 'improbable;' Cot. See **Im-** (4) and **Probable**. Der. *improbabl-y*, *improbabili-ty*.

IMPROMPTU, off hand; a thing composed extempore. (F.—L.) 'They were made *ex tempore*, and were, as the French call them, *impromptus*;' Dryden, A Discourse on Satire; in Dryden's Poems, ed. 1856, p. 366.—F. *impromptu*; 'L'Impromptu de Versailles' is the title of a comedy by Molière.—L. *in promptū*, in readiness; where *promptū* is the abl. of *promptus*, a sb. formed from *prōmere*, to bring forward. See **In** and **Prompt**.

IMPROPER, not proper. (F.—L.) ME. *improper*. '*Improprelich* he demeth fame;' Gower, C. A. i. 21; prol. 537.—F. *impropre*, 'unproper;' Cot. From **Im-** (4) and **Proper**. Der. *improper-ly*; so also *impropriety*, in Selden's Illustrations to Drayton's Polyolbion, s. 2, note to l. 110, from *im-* and *propriety*.

IMPROPRIATE, to appropriate to private use. (L.) 'Canst thou *impropriate* to thee Augustus' worthy praise?' Drant, tr. of Horace, Ep. to Quinctius (Ep. i. 16, l. 29). Coined from L. *im*-=*in*, in, hence to (a person); and *propriāre*, to appropriate, from *proprius*, one's own; see **Im-** (3) and **Proper**. Der. *impropriat-ion*.

IMPROVE, to make better. (F.—L.) In Shak. Jul. Cæsar, ii. 1. 159. '*Approve* and *improve*, *approvement* and *improvement*, are used in our old law as respectively equivalent;' Richardson. See Blount's Nomolexicon. *Improve* is altered from the late ME. *enprowen* (see Skelton, Philip Sparowe, 793), which was a parallel form to ME. *approwen*, to 'approve,' to benefit.—AF. *emprouwer*, to benefit, parallel to OF. *aproer*, *approuer*, to benefit. These are formed (with prefix *em-* for L. *in*, or prefix *a-* for L. *ad*) from OF. *prou*, sb. profit, benefit; which is allied to Ital. *prode*, sb. benefit; and Ital. *prode*, adj. good, valiant. See **Prowess**. The AF. forms *enprouver*, *emprover*, both occur in Britton. ¶ Not allied to *prove*, with which it was confused in form. Der. *improv-able*, *improv-abl-y*, *improv-able-ness*, *improv-ing-ly*, *improve-ment*, Bacon, Essay 34, Of Riches.

IMPROVIDENT, not provident. (L.) In Shak. 1 Hen. VI, ii. 1. 58. From **Im-** (4) and **Provident**; see **Provide**. Der. *improvident-ly*, *improvidence*. Doublet, *imprudent*.

IMPROVISE, to recite extemporaneously, bring about on a sudden. (F.—Ital.—L.) Quite modern. Not in Todd's Johnson. —F. *improviser*.—Ital. *improvvisare*, to sing extempore verses.—Ital. *improvviso*, sudden, unprovided for.—L. *improuīsus*, unforeseen.—L. *im*-=*in*-, negative prefix; and *prōuīsus*, pp. of *prōuidēre*, to foresee. See **Im-** (4) and **Provide**. Der. *improvis-er*, *improvis-ate*, *improvis-at-ore* (Ital.), *improvis-at-ion*; we even find *improvis-at-ise*, Chambers, Cyclop. of Eng. Literature, 1860, ii. 499, col. 2.

IMPRUDENT, not prudent. (F.—L.) In Chaucer, C. T., B 309. Milton has *imprudence*, P. L. xi. 686.—F. *imprudent*, 'imprudent;' Cot. ◄L. *imprūdent*-, stem of *imprūdens*, not prudent. See **Im-** (4) and **Prudent**. Der. *imprudent-ly*, *imprudence*.

IMPUDENT, shameless. (F.—L.) In Spenser, F. Q. iii. 12. 5; Chaucer, C. T., I 397.—F. *impudent*, 'impudent;' Cot.—L. *impudent*-, stem of *impudens*, shameless.—L. *im*-=*in*-, not; and *pudens*, modest, properly pres. part. of *pudēre*, to feel shame (a word of doubtful origin). Der. *impudent-ly*; *impudence*, from F. *impudence*, 'impudence' (Cot.).

IMPUGN, to attack, call in question. (F.—L.) In rather early use. ME. *impugnen*; P. Plowman, B. vii. 147.—F. *impugner*, 'to impugne, fight or stirre against;' Cot.—L. *impugnāre*, to fight against.—L. *im*-=*in*, against; and *pugnāre*, to fight. See **Im-** (1) and **Pugnacious**. Der. *impugn-er*, *impugn-able*.

IMPULSE, IMPULSION, IMPULSIVE; see **Impel**.

IMPUNITY, safety from punishment. (F.—L. *and* Gk.) 'As touching both the *impunitie* and also the recompense of other the informers;' Holland, tr. of Livy, p. 1035 (R.); and in Cotgrave. —F. *impunité*, 'impunity;' Cot.—L. *impūnitātem*, acc. of *impūnitās*, impunity.—L. *impūni*-, decl. stem of *impūnis*, without punishment. —L. *im*-=*in*-, not; and *poena*, penalty, from Gk. ποινή. See **Im-** (4) and **Pain**.

IMPURE, not pure. (F.—L.) '*Impure* and uncleane;' Tyndall, Works, p. 193, col. 2.—F. *impur*, 'impure;' Cot.—L. *impūrus*. See **Im-** (4) and **Pure**. Der. *impure-ly*, *impure-ness*, *impur-i-ty*, Shak. Lucrece, 854.

IMPUTE, to place to the account of, reckon against as a fault, ascribe, charge. (F.—L.) In Levins. 'Th' *imputed* blame;' Spenser, F. Q. ii. 1. 20. And in Caxton, Eneydos, ch. 20; p. 73.—F. *imputer*, 'to impute, ascribe, or attribute unto;' Cot.—L. *imputāre*, to bring into a reckoning.—L. *im*-=*in*, in; and *putāre*, to reckon, suppose, orig. to cleanse. See **Im-** (1) and **Putative**. Der. *imput-er*, *imput-able*, *imput-abl-y*, *imput-able-ness*, *imputabil-i-ty*; *imput-at-ion*, Merch. Ven. i. 3. 13; *imput-at-ive*, *imput-at-ive-ly*.

IN, prep. denoting presence or situation in place, time, or circumstances. (E.) ME. *in*; passim. AS. *in*; passim.+Du. *in*; Icel. *í*; Swed. and Dan. *i*; Goth. *in*; G. *in*.+W. *yn*; OIrish *in* (Fick, i. 486); OPruss. *en*; L. *in*; Gk. ἐνί, ἐν. β. L. *in* is a weakened form of *en*, as in OL. *en-do*; cf. Gk. ἐν, ἔν-δον. Der. *inn-er*, from AS. *innera*, a comparative adj., Grein, ii. 143; *in-most*, ME. *inemaste* (written for *innemest*), Castel of Love, ed. Weymouth, l. 809 (Stratmann), from AS. *innemest*, an authorised form (Bosworth). ☞ The form *innermost* is doubly corrupt, having an inserted *r*, and *o* substituted for older *e*; the correct form is *innemest* = AS. *innemest* above. Even this is a double superlative, with the suffix *-est* added to the formative *-m-* which in itself denotes the superlative (as in Latin *prī-m-us*); see this explained under **Aftermost, Foremost**. Similarly *inmost* should rather have been *inmest*. Der. (continued): *in-ward*, q. v.; also *there-in*, *where-in*, *with-in*, *in-as-much*, *in-so-much*; and cf. *in-ter-*, *in-tro-*; also *inn*, q. v.

IN- (1), *prefix*, in. (E.) In some words, the prefix *in-* is purely E., and is merely the prep. *in* in composition. Exx.: *in-born*, *in-breathe*, *in-bred*, *in-land*, *in-lay*, *in-let*, *in-ly*, *in-mate*, *in-side*, *in-sight*, *in-snare*, *in-stall*, *in-step*, *in-twine*, *in-twist*, *in-weave*, *in-wrap*, *in-wrought*. See **In**.

IN- (2), *prefix*, in. (L.; *or* F.−L.) In some words, the prefix is not the E. prep. *in*, but the cognate L. form. Exx.: *in-augurate*, *in-carcerate*, *in-carnate*, *in-cidence*, &c. These words are rather numerous. β. Sometimes the L. word has passed through F. before reaching E. Exx.: *in-cise*, *in-cite*, *in-cline*, *in-dication*, &c. ¶ In- (2) becomes *il-* before *l*, as in *il-lusion*; *im-* before *m* and *p*, as in *im-bue*, *im-peril*; *ir-* before *r*, as in *ir-rigate*.

IN- (3), *prefix*, with negative force. (L.; *or* F.−L.) In numerous words, the prefix *in-* has a negative force; from L. neg. prefix *in-*, which is cognate with E. *un-* (with the same force), OIrish *an-*, Skt. *an-* (frequently shortened to *a-*), Gk. *ăv-* (often shortened to *ă-*), Zend *an-*, *a-*. See **Un-** (1), **An-**, **A-** (9). β. In many words, the L. word has reached us through the medium of French. Exx.: *in-capable*, *in-certainty*, *in-clement*, *in-compatible*, &c. ¶ In- (3) becomes *i-* before *gn*, as in *i-gnoble*; *il-* before *l*, as in *il-legal*; *im-* before *m* and *p*, as in *im-mense*, *im-pure*; *ir-* before *r*, as in *ir-rational*.

INABILITY, lack of ability. (F.−L.) ME. *inabylité*; in A Goodly Balade, a poem wrongly ascribed to Chaucer, l. 68; see Chaucerian Poems, p. 407. See **In-** (3) and **Able**.

INACCESSIBLE, not accessible. (F.−L.) In Shak. Temp. ii. 1. 37.−F. *inaccessible*; Cot. From **In-** (3) and **Accessible**; see **Accede**. Der. *inaccessible-ness*, *inaccessibili-ty*.

INACCURATE, not accurate. (L.) 'Very *inaccurate* judgments;' Warburton, Divine Legation, b. ii. s. 6 (R.) *Inaccuracy* is in Bailey's Dict., vol. ii. ed. 1731. From **In-** (3) and **Accurate**. Der. *inaccurate-ly*, *inaccuracy*.

INACTION, want of action. (F.−L.) In Bailey, vol. ii. ed. 1731. From **In-** (3) and **Action**; see **Act**. Der. *inact-ive*, *inactive-ly*; *in-activity*, Swift, Horace, b. iv, ode 9, l. 2.

INADEQUATE, not adequate. (L.) In Phillips, ed. 1706. From **In-** (3) and **Adequate**. Der. *inadequate-ly*, *inadequate-ness*, *inadequac-y*.

INADMISSIBLE, not admissible. (F.−L.) In late use. Used by Burke, On a Regicide Peace, let. 1, note (R.)−F. *inadmissible*, 'unadmittable;' Cot. From **In-** (3) and **Admissible**; see **Admit**.

INADVERTENT, unattentive, heedless. (L.) Spelt *inadvertant* in Bailey, vol. ii. ed. 1731; first found in 1653. *Inadvertence* is in earlier use; Coles' Dict., ed. 1684; first found in 1568; *inadvertency* in Bp. Taylor, vol. i. ser. 5 (R.) *Inadvertent* is of L. origin; *inadvertence* is from the F. *inadvertence*, 'inconsideration;' Cot. See **In-** (3) and **Advert**. Der. *inadvertent-ly*; also *in-advertence*, *in-advertenc-y*, as above.

INALIENABLE, not alienable. (F.−L.) In Howell, Letters, vol. ii. let. x. § 4.−F. *inalienable*, 'unalienable;' Cot. From **In-** (3) and **Alienable**; see **Alien**.

INAMORATO, a lover. (Ital.−L.) In Greene, Upstart Courtier, fol. D 4 (1592).−MItal. *inamorato*, a lover, spelt *innamorato* in Florio; pp. of *innamorare*, to enamour.−L. *in*, in; and *amōr-*, stem of *amor*, love, allied to *amāre*, to love; see **Enamour**. Der. *inamorata*, fem. of the same.

INANE, empty, void, silly, useless. (L.) 'We speak of place, distance, or bulk, in the great *inane*' [i. e. void, used as a sb.]; Locke, On Human Underst. b. ii. c. 15. s. 7. [Not from F., but suggested by F. *inanité*, 'emptiness, inanity' (Cot.), which is from L. *inānitātem*, acc. of *inānitās*, emptiness.]−L. *inānis*, void, empty. Of uncertain etymology. Der. *inan-i-ty*; *inan-it-ion*, q. v.

INANIMATE, lifeless. (L.) '*Inanimate*, without life;' Blount's Gloss., ed. 1674. And in Cockeram (1642).−L. *inanimātus*, lifeless. See **In-** (3) and **Animate**. Der. *inanimat-ion*.

INANITION, emptiness, exhaustion from lack of food. (F.−L.) Spelt *inanisioun*, Lanfranc's Surgery, p. 100 (1380). 'Repletion and *inanition* may both doe harme;' Burton, Anat. of Melancholy, p. 235 (R.)−F. *inanition*, 'an emptying;' Cot. Allied to the pp. *inānitus* of L. *inānīre*, to empty; from *ināni-*, decl. stem of *inānis*, empty. See **Inane**.

INAPPLICABLE, not applicable. (L.) Bailey has *inapplicable-ness*, vol. ii. ed. 1731. From **In-** (3) and **Applicable**; see **Apply**. Der. *inapplicable-ness*, *inapplicabili-ty*.

INAPPRECIABLE, not appreciable. (L.) A rather late word; not in Todd's Johnson. First in 1787. From **In-** (3) and **Appreciable**; see **Appreciate**.

INAPPROACHABLE, not approachable. (F.−L.) A late word; not in Todd's Johnson, but in Webster (1828). From **In-** (3) and **Approachable**; see **Approach**.

INAPPROPRIATE, not fit. (L.) Late; not in Todd. From **In-** (3) and **Appropriate**. Der. *inappropriate-ly*, *inappropriate-ness*.

INAPT, not apt. (F.−L.) First in 1744; but *ineptitude* is in Howell, Familiar Letters, b. i. s. 1. let. 9; dated 1619. From **In-** (3) and **Apt**. ¶ Note that *ineptitude* is a correct spelling, from

L. *ineptitūdo*; so too the L. adj. is *ineptus*, not *inaptus*. Der. *inapt-ly*, *inapt-i-tude*. Doublet, *inept*, q. v. (a better form).

INARTICULATE, not distinct. (L.) 'The *inarticulate* sounds of music;' Giles Fletcher, Poems; Pref. to the Reader.−L. *inarti-culātus*, indistinct. From **In-** (3) and **Articulate**. Der. *inarticu-late-ly*, *-ness*; *inarticulat-ion*.

INARTIFICIAL, without artifice. (L.) 'An *inartificial* argument;' Sir T. Browne, Vulg. Errors, b. i. c. 7. § 2.−L. *inartificiālis*, not according to the rules of art. From **In-** (3) and **Artificial**; see **Artifice**. Der. *inartificial-ly*.

INASMUCH, seeing that. (E.) Merely the three words *in as much* run together. We find North. E. *in als mekil als*, Cursor Mundi, 19596; also *inasmyche as*, Wyclif's Works, ed. Arnold, ii. 206. Cf. '*be als moche as* that ryvere may serve' = by as much as that river, &c.; Mandeville's Travels, ed. Halliwell, p. 45.

INATTENTION, lack of attention. (F.−L.) 'This universal indolence and *inattention* among us;' Tatler, no. 187. From **In-** (3) and **Attention**; see **Attend**. Der. *inattent-ive*, *inattent-ive-ly*.

INAUDIBLE, not audible. (L.) In Shak. All's Well, v. 3. 41. See **In-** (3) and **Audience**. Der. *inaudibl-y*, *inaudibili-ty*.

INAUGURATE, to consecrate, install, enter upon or invest with an office formally, begin formally. (L.) 'The seat on which her kings *inaugurated* were;' Drayton, Polyolbion, s. 17. l. 188. Properly a pp., as in 'being *inaugurate* and invested in the kingdome;' Holland, tr. of Livy, p. 14 (R.) 'When is the *inauguration*?' Beaum. and Fletcher, Valentinian, v. 5. 1.−L. *inaugurātus*, pp. of *inaugurāre*, to consult the divining birds, practise augury, inaugurate.−L. *in-* = prep. *in*, for, towards; and *augurāre*, to act as augur. See **In-** (2) and **Augur**. Der. *inaugurat-ion* (above); *inaugurat-or*; *inaugural*.

INAUSPICIOUS, not auspicious. (L.) In Shak. Romeo, v. 3. 111. See **In-** (3) and **Auspice**. Der. *inauspicious-ly*, *-ness*.

INBORN, born within one, native. (E.) 'And straight, with *inborn* vigour, on the wing;' Dryden, Mrs. Anne Killigrew, l. 191. Late AS. *inboren*, in-born. From *in*, prep.; and *born*, pp. of *bear*. See **In-** (1) and **Bear** (1). So also Icel. *innborinn*, inborn.

INBREATHED, breathed in. (E.) 'Dead things with *in-breathed* sense;' Milton, At a Solemn Musick, l. 4. See **In-** (1) and **Breathe**.

INBRED, bred within, innate. (E.) 'My *inbred* enemy;' Milton, P. L. ii. 785. From *in*, prep.; and *bred*, pp. of **Breed**.

INCA, a royal title. (Peruvian.) 'The Indian Inca;' Howell, Fam. Letters, 2nd Introd. Poem, l. 19. Dryden has the pl. *Incas*; Fables, Dedication, § 7.−Peruv. *inca*, a title. Cf. Peruv. *çapay kapac Inca*, king of Peru (*çapay* = only; *kapac* = lord); Peruv. Dict. *Inca* was orig. the chief of a tribe (Oviedo). Garcilasso de la Vega explains *capa Inca* as 'sole lord;' and complains that the Span. form *inga* is corrupt.

INCAGE, to put in a cage. (F.−L.) Better *encage*. In Shak. Rich. II, ii. 1. 102.−F. *encager*, 'to incage, to shut within a cage;' Cot.−F. *en* = L. *in*, in; and *cage*, a cage. See **In-** (2) and **Cage**.

INCALCULABLE, not to be counted. (L.) 'Do mischiefs *incalculable*;' Burke, On Scarcity (R.) From **In-** (3) and **Calculable**; see **Calculate**. Der. *incalculabl-y*.

INCANDESCENT, glowing hot. (L.) *Incandescence* is in Blount's Gloss., ed. 1674.−L. *incandescent-*, stem of pres. part. of *incandescere*, to glow.−L. *in*, towards; and *candescere*, inceptive form of *candēre*, to glow. See **In-** (2) and **Candle**. Der. *incan-descence*.

INCANTATION, a magical charm. (L.) ME. *incantacion*, Gower, C. A. iii. 45; bk. vi. 1309.−OF. *incantation*; see N. E. D.−L. *incantātiōnem*, acc. of *incantātio*, an enchanting; cf. *incantātus*, pp. of *incantāre*, to sing charms. See **Enchant**.

INCAPABLE, not capable. (F.−L.) In Drayton, Moses his Birth, b. i. l. 250; Milton, P. L. ii. 140, v. 505; Shak. Sonnet 113.− F. *incapable*, 'uncapable;' Cot. From **In-** (3) and **Capable**. Der. *incapabili-ty*; and see below.

INCAPACITY, want of capacity. (F.−L.) In Minsheu.− F. *incapacité*, 'incapacity;' Cot. Cf. L. *incapax*, incapable. From **In-** (3) and **Capacity**; see **Capacious**. Der. *incapacit-ate*; *incapacit-at-ion*, Burke, Thoughts on the Present Discontents, ed. E. J. Payne (Clar. Press), p. 63, l. 3.

INCARCERATE, to put in prison. (L.) In Blount's Gloss. ed. 1674. As a pp. in Roy, Rede Me, ed. Arber, p. 48, l. 6.−L. *in*, in; and *carcerātus*, pp. of *carcerāre*, to imprison, from *carcer*, a prison; a word of uncertain origin. Der. *incarcerat-ion*.

INCARNADINE, to dye of a red colour. (F.−Ital.−L.) In Shak. Macb. ii. 2. 62; see Nares.−F. *incarnadin*, 'carnation, of a deep, rich, or bright carnation;' Cot.−Ital. *incarnadino*, 'carnation or flesh colour;' Florio. Also spelt *incarnatino* (Florio), as in mod. Italian.−Ital. *incarnato*, incarnate, of flesh colour.−L. *incarnātus*, incarnate. See **Incarnation**.

INCARNATION, embodiment in flesh. (F.—L.) ME. *incarnacion,* Rob. of Glouc. p. 9; l. 197.—F. *incarnation.*—Late L. *incarnātiōnem,* acc. of *incarnātio;* cf. *incarnātus,* pp. of *incarnāre,* to clothe with flesh.—L. *in,* in; and *carn-,* stem of *caro,* flesh. See **Carnal. Der.** *incarnate,* Merch. Ven. ii. 2. 29, from pp. *incarnātus;* *incarnat-ive,* i. e. causing flesh to grow, Holland, tr. of Pliny, b. xxvii. c. 11 (near end).

INCASE, the same as **Encase.** (F.—L.) In Pope, tr. of Homer, Od. i. 333.

INCAUTIOUS, not cautious. (L.) 'You treat adventurous, and *incautious* tread;' Francis, tr. of Horace, b. ii. ode 1 (R.). From **In-** (3) and **Cautious;** see **Caution. Der.** *incautious-ly, ness.*

INCENDIARY, one who sets fire to houses, &c. (L.) 'Others called him . . . *incendiarie;*' Holland, tr. of Suetonius, p. 238.—L. *incendiārius,* setting on fire.—L. *incendium,* a burning.—L. *incendere,* to kindle. See **Incense** (1). **Der.** *incendiar-ism.*

INCENSE (1), to inflame. (L.) 'Much was the knight *incenst;*' Spenser, F. Q. v. 3. 36.—L. *incensus,* pp. of *incendere,* to kindle, inflame.—L. *in,* in, upon; and **candere,* to burn (found also in comp. *accendere*), allied to *candēre,* to glow. See **In-** (2) and **Candle. Der.** *incend-iary,* q. v.; *incense-ment,* Twelfth Nt. iii. 4. 260.

INCENSE (2), spices, odour of spices burned. (F.—L.) ME. *encens,* Chaucer, C. T. 2279 (A 2277).—F. *encens,* 'incense, frankincense;' Cot.—L. *incensum,* incense, lit. what is burnt; orig. neuter of *incensus,* pp. of *incendere;* see **Incense** (1). **Der.** *frank-incense, censer.*

INCENTIVE, provoking, inciting. (L.) 'Part *incentive* reed Provide, pernicious with one touch to fire;' Milton, P. L. vi. 519. [Yet not connected with L. *incendere,* to kindle.]—L. *incentiuus,* that which strikes up or sets a tune; hence, that provokes or incites; cf. L. **incentus,* unused pp. of *incinere,* to blow or sound an instrument.—L. *in,* into; and *canere,* to sing. See **Enchant, Chant.**

INCEPTIVE, beginning. (L.) In Phillips' Dict. ed. 1706. Formed, with suffix *-ive* (=L. *-īuus*), from *incept-um,* supine of *incipere,* to begin, lit. to seize on.—L. *in,* on; and *capere,* to seize; see **In-** (2) and **Capable. Der.** *inceptive-ly;* and see *incipient.*

INCERTITUDE, uncertainty. (F.—L.) In Holland, tr. of Pliny, bk. xviii. c. 25, p. 586 h.—F. *incertitude,* 'incertainty;' Cot.—L. *in-,* not; and Late L. *certitūdo,* certainty (Duc.), from *certus,* sure. See **Certain.**

INCESSANT, ceaseless. (L.) In Levins. And in Shak. Hen. V, ii. 2. 38.—L. *incessant-,* stem of *incessans,* unceasing.—L. *in-,* negative prefix; and *cessans,* pres. pt. of *cessāre,* to cease. See **In-** (3) and **Cease. Der.** *incessant-ly.*

INCEST, impurity. (F.—L.) In early use. ME. *incest,* Ancren Riwle, p. 204, l. 20.—F. *inceste,* 'incest;' Cot.—L. *incestus* (gen. *-ūs*), sb. incest.—L. *incestus,* adj., unchaste.—L. *in-,* not; and *castus,* chaste. See **In-** (3) and **Chaste. Der.** *incest-u-ous,* Hamlet, i. 2. 157; *incest-u-ous-ly.*

INCH (1), the twelfth part of a foot. (L.) ME. *inche,* Prompt. Parv. p. 261. Older spelling also *unche;* 'feouwer *unche* long;' Layamon, 23970. AS. *ynce;* Laws of Æthelberht, 67; in Thorpe's Ancient Laws, i. 18.—L. *uncia,* an inch; also, an ounce. See **Ounce** (1), which is the doublet. **Der.** *inch-meal,* Temp. ii. 2. 3 (see **Piecemeal**); *inch-thick,* Wint. Tale, i. 2. 186. ☞ The AS. *y* = *ü,* derived from *u* by vowel-change; the changes from L. *u* to AS. *y,* and thence to ME. *i,* are quite regular.

INCH (2), an island. (Gael.) In Shak. Macb. i. 2. 61; Henry, Wallace, bk. ix. 1147.—Gael. *innis,* an island.+Irish *inis,* an island; W. *ynys;* Bret. *enez;* Corn. *enys.* Cf. L. *insula.*

INCHOATE, just begun. (L.) First in 1534 (N.E.D.).—L. *inchoātus,* more correctly *incohātus,* pp. of *incohāre,* to begin.

INCIDENT, falling upon, liable to occur. (F.—L.) In Levins; and in Shak. Timon, iv. 1. 21. Also used as sb. Lydgate *incydentes,* sb. pl., Troye Book, bk. v. last ch.; fol. Ddij, back.—F. *incident,* 'an incident, circumstance;' Cot.—L. *incident-,* stem of pres. pt. of *incidere,* to befall.—L. *in,* on; and *cadere,* to fall. See **Cadence. Der.** *incident-al, -ly, -ness; incidence; incidenc-y,* Wint. Tale, i. 2. 403.

INCIPIENT, beginning. (L.) Found in 1669. '*Incipient* apoplexies;' Boyle, Works, vol. iv. p. 641 (R.).—L. *incipient-,* stem of *incipiens,* pres. pt. of *incipere,* to begin; see **Inceptive. Der.** *incipient-ly, incipience.*

INCIRCLE, the same as **Encircle.** (F.—L.) In Kersey, ed. 1715.

INCISE, to cut into, gash. (F.—L.) 'But I must be *incised* first, cut, and opened;' Beaum. and Fletcher, Mad Lover, ii. 1. 17. —F. *inciser,* 'to cut into, make an incision;' Cot.—L. *incisus,* pp. of *incidere,* to cut into.—L. *in,* into; and *cædere,* to cut. See **In-** (2) and **Cæsura. Der.** *incis-ion,* L. L. L. iv. 3. 97, from F. *incision* (Cot.); *incis-ive,* from F. *incisif,* 'cutting;' Cot.; *incis-ive-ly, incis-ive-ness; incis-or,* from L. *incisor; incis-or-y.*

INCITE, to rouse, instigate. (F.—L.) In K. Lear, iv. 4. 27.—

F. *inciter,* 'to incite;' Cot.—L. *incitāre,* to urge forward.—L. *in,* towards, forwards; and *citāre,* to urge. See **In-** (2) and **Cite. Der.** *incite-ment,* from F. *incitement,* 'an inciting,' Cot.; *incit-at-ion,* spelt *incitacion,* Sir T. More, Works, p. 551 c.

INCIVIL, uncivil, rude. (F.—L.) In Shak. Cymb. v. 5. 292.—F. *incivil,* 'uncivill;' Cot.—L. *inciuilis,* rude. From **In-** (3) and **Civil. Der.** *incivil-it-y,* Com. Errors, iv. 4. 49, from F. *incivilité,* 'incivility;' Cot.

INCLEMENT, not clement. (F.—L.) In Milton, P. L. iii. 426.—F. *inclement,* 'unclement;' Cot. From **In-** (3) and **Clement. Der.** *inclement-ly; inclemenc-y,* used by Cot. to translate F. *inclemence.*

INCLINE, to lean towards, bow towards. (F.—L.) ME. *enclinen,* Gower, C. A. i. 168; bk. ii. 271; also in Chaucer, C. T. 13908 (B 3092).—F. *incliner,* 'to incline;' Cot.—L. *inclināre,* to incline.—L. *in,* towards; and **clināre,* to lean, cognate with E. *lean.* See **Lean. Der.** *inclin-at-ion,* Hamlet, iii. 3. 39, ME. *inclynacioun,* Lydgate, Minor Poems, p. 91, from F. *inclination,* 'an inclination,' Cot.; also *inclin-able,* Cor. ii. 2. 60.

INCLOSE, the same as **Enclose.** (F.—L.) In Spenser, F. Q. iii. 2. 31; Dunbar, Thistle and Rose, st. 23. **Der.** *enclos-ure,* Milton, P. L. iv. 133. See **Include.**

INCLUDE, to shut in, contain. (L.) In Barnes, Works, p. 228, col. 2.—L. *inclūdere,* pp. *inclūsus,* to shut in.—L. *in,* in; and *claudere,* to shut. See **In-** (2) and **Close** (1). **Der.** *inclus-ion; inclus-ive,* Rich. III, iv. 1. 59; *inclus-ive-ly.*

INCOGNITO, in concealment. (Ital.—L.) In Dryden, Kind Keeper, Act i. sc. 1; and in Blount's Gloss., ed. 1674.—Ital. *incognito,* unknown.—L. *incognitus,* unknown.—L. *in-,* not; and *cognitus,* known. See **In-** (3) and **Cognition.** ¶ Shortened to *incog,* Tatler, no. 230.

INCOHERENT, not coherent. (L.) 'Two *incoherent* and uncombining dispositions;' Milton, On Divorce, b. i. c. 1. 'Besides the *incoherence* of such a doctrine;' id. b. ii. c. 2. See **In-** (3) and **Cohere. Der.** *incoherent-ly, incoherence.*

INCOMBUSTIBLE, that cannot be burnt. (L.) 'Stories of *incombustible* napkins;' Sir T. Browne, Vulg. Errors, b. iii. c. 14, § 3. From **In-** (3) and **Combustible;** see **Combustion. Der.** *incombustible-ness, incombustibili-ty.*

INCOME, gain, profit, revenue. (E.) Properly, the 'coming in,' and hence, accomplishment, fulfilment. ME. *income,* coming in; Cursor Mundi, 11127. 'Pain pays the *income* of each precious thing;' Shak. Lucrece, 334. From **In-** (1) and **Come.**

INCOMMENSURABLE, not commensurable. (F.—L.) In Blount's Gloss., ed. 1674.—F. *incommensurable,* 'unmeasurable;' Cot.—L. *incommensūrābilis.* See **In-** (3) and **Commensurate. Der.** *incommensurabl-y, incommensurable-ness, incommensurabili-ty.*

INCOMMENSURATE, not commensurate. (F.—L.) In Boyle, Works, vol. iv. p. 780 (R.). From **In-** (3) and **Commensurate.**

INCOMMODE, to cause inconvenience to. (F.—L.) In Florio (1594), s.v. *Incomodare.*—F. *incommoder,* 'to incommodate, hinder;' Cot.—L. *incommodāre,* to cause inconvenience to.—L. *incommodus,* inconvenient.—L. *in-,* not; and *commodus,* convenient. See **In-** (3) and **Commodious. Der.** *incommod-i-ous,* North's Plutarch, p. 77 (R.); *incommod-i-ous-ly, -ness;* also *incommod-i-ty,* Sir T. Elyot, Castel of Helth, b. ii. c. 31.

INCOMMUNICABLE, not communicable. (F.—L.) In Blount's Gloss., ed. 1674.—F. *incommunicable,* 'uncommunicable;' Cot. See **In-** (3) and **Commune. Der.** *incommunicabl-y, incommunicable-ness, incommunicabili-ty;* so also *in-communic-at-ive.*

INCOMMUTABLE, not commutable. (F.—L.) 'The *incomutable* deyté;' Caxton, Golden Legend; Pentecost, § 1.—F. *incommutable;* Cot. See **In-** (3) and **Commute. Der.** *incommutabl-y, incommutable-ness, incommutabili-ty.*

INCOMPARABLE, matchless. (F.—L.) In Shak. Timon, i. 1. 10; and Lydgate, Troye Book, bk. i. ch. 6, fol. D 4 (end).—F. *incomparable,* 'incomparable;' Cot. See **In-** (3) and **Compare. Der.** *incomparabl-y, incomparable-ness.*

INCOMPATIBLE, not compatible. (F.—L.) In Beaum. and Fletcher, Four Plays in One, Triumph of Love, sc. 1, l. 7.—F. *incompatible;* Cot. See **In-** (3) and **Compatible. Der.** *incompatibl-y; incompatibil-i-ty,* from F. *incompatibilité* (Cot.).

INCOMPETENT, not competent. (F.—L.) In Minsheu.—F. *incompetent,* 'incompetent, unfit;' Cot. See **In-** (3) and **Competent. Der.** *incompetent-ly, incompetence;* also *incompetenc-y,* used by Cot. to translate F. *incompetence.*

INCOMPLETE, not complete. (L.) 'A most imperfect and *incompleat* divine;' Milton, Animad. upon Remonstrants Defence against Smectymnuus (R.). ME. *incompleet,* Wyclif, Works, ed. Arnold, iii. 342, l. 9.—L. *incomplētus.* See **In-** (3) and **Complete. Der.** *incomplete-ly, -ness.*

INCOMPREHENSIBLE, not to be comprehended. (F.—L.)

'How *incomprehensible* are his waies;' Frith, Works, p. 84, col. 2, last line. And in Wyclif, Jerem. xxxii. 19.—F. *incomprehensible*; Cot. From **In-** (3) and **Comprehensible**; see **Comprehend**. Der. *incomprehensibl-y, incomprehensibili-ty*; so also *incomprehens-ive, incomprehens-ive-ness*.

INCOMPRESSIBLE, not compressible. (L.) In Bailey, vol. ii. ed. 1731. From **In-** (3) and **Compressible**; see **Compress**. Der. *incompressibili-ty*.

INCONCEIVABLE, not to be conceived. (F.—L.) First in 1631. Bailey has *inconceivable-ness*, vol. ii. ed. 1731. A coined word; see **In-** (3) and **Conceive**. Der. *inconceivabl-y, inconceivableness*.

INCONCLUSIVE, not conclusive. (L.) First in 1707. See Todd's Johnson. From **In-** (3) and **Conclusive**; see **Conclude**. Der. *inconclusive-ly, -ness*.

INCONDITE, ill-constructed, crude, rude. (L.) 'Carol *incondite* rhythms;' Philips, Cyder, bk. ii. —L. *inconditus*, ill put together. —L. *in-*, not; *conditus*, pp. of *condere*, to put together, from *con-*, for *cum*, together, and *-dere*, to put, place, allied to Gk. τί-θη-μι, I place. See **Thesis**. Brugmann, i. § 573.

INCONGRUOUS, inconsistent, unsuitable. (L.) In Cotgrave, to translate F. *incongrue*.—L. *incongruus*; with *-ous* for *-us*. From **In-** (3) and **Congruous**; see **Congrue**. Der. *incongru-i-ty*, in Minsheu, and used by Cot. to translate F. *incongruité*.

INCONSEQUENT, not following from the premises. (L.) Kersey has *inconsequency*, ed. 1715; Bailey has *inconsequentness*, vol. ii. ed. 1731.—L. *inconsequent-*, stem of *inconsequens*, inconsequent. See **In-** (3) and **Consequent**. Der. *inconsequent-ly, -ness; inconsequence, inconsequenc-y*; also *inconsequent-ial, inconsequent-ial-ly*.

INCONSIDERABLE, unimportant. (F.—L.) In Milton, P. R. iv. 457. From **In-** (3) and **Considerable**; see **Consider**. Der. So also *inconsider-ate*, Shak. K. John, ii. 67; *inconsider-ate-ly, inconsider-ate-ness; inconsider-at-ion*, in Cotgrave, to translate F. *inconsideration*.

INCONSISTENT, not consistent. (L.) 'Though it be *inconsistent* with thy calling;' Howell, Foreign Travel, ed. 1642, s. 18; ed. Arber, p. 76. From **In-** (3) and **Consistent**; see **Consist**. Der. *inconsistent-ly, inconsistence, inconsistenc-y*.

INCONSOLABLE, not to be consoled. (F.—L.) In Minsheu.—F. *inconsolable*, 'inconsolable;' Cot.—L. *inconsolabilis*. See **In-** (3) and **Console**. Der. *inconsolabl-y*.

INCONSTANT, not constant. (F.—L.) '*Inconstant* man;' Spenser, F. Q. i. 4. 26. ME. *inconstaunt*, Hoccleve, Letter of Cupid, l. 101.—F. *inconstant*, 'inconstant;' Cot. See **In-** (3) and **Constant**. Der. *inconstant-ly; inconstanc-y*, used by Cot. to translate F. *inconstance*.

INCONSUMABLE, that cannot be consumed. (L.) 'Coats, *inconsumable* by fire;' Sir T. Browne, Vulg. Errors, b. iii. c. 14, § 4. A coined word. See **In-** (3) and **Consume**.

INCONTESTABLE, not contestable. (F.—L.) 'By necessary consequences, as *incontestable* as those in mathematicks;' Locke, Of Human Underst. b. iv. c. 3. s. 18 (R.).—F. *incontestable*, 'not to be contested or stood on;' Cot. See **In-** (3) and **Contest**. Der. *incontestabl-y*.

INCONTINENT (1), unchaste. (F.—L.) In Shak. As You Like It, v. 2. 42.—F. *incontinent*, 'incontinent, immoderate;' Cot.—L. *incontinent-*, stem of *incontinens*.—L. *in-*, not; and *continens*, containing, pres. pt. of *continēre*, to contain. See **In-** (3) and **Contain**. Der. *incontinent-ly; incontinence*, used by Cot. to translate F. *incontinence*; also *incontinenc-y*, spelt *incontinencie* in Sir T. More, Works, p. 297 f.

INCONTINENT (2), immediately. (F.—L.) In Spenser, F. Q. i. 9. 19. ME. *incontinent*, Generydes, l. 1571.—F. *incontinent*, 'adverb, incontinently, instantly;' Cot. Lit. 'immoderately;' and due to the word above. Der. *incontinent-ly*, Oth. i. 3. 306.

INCONTROLLABLE, not to be controlled. (F.—L.) 'An *incontroullable* conformity;' Sir T. Browne, Vulg. Errors, b. iv. c. 12, § 15. A coined word. See **In-** (3) and **Control**. Der. *incontrollabl-y*.

INCONTROVERTIBLE, not to be gainsaid. (L.) In Sir T. Browne, Vulg. Errors, b. vii. c. 13, § 4 [*not* c. 23]. A coined word. See **In-** (3) and **Controversy**. Der. *incontrovertibl-y, incontrovertibili-ty*.

INCONVENIENT, not suitable, incommodious. (F.—L.) 'I wene that non *inconuenient* shalt thou fynde betwene Goddes forweting and liberté of arbitrement;' Test. of Love, b. iii. c. 3. 77. 'Withouten any *inconuenience* thereof to folow;' id. c. 4. 139.—F. *inconvenient*; Cot.—L. *inconuenient-*, stem of *inconueniens*, unsuitable. See **In-** (3) and **Convenient**. Der. *inconvenient-ly, inconvenience, inconvenienc-y*.

INCONVERTIBLE, not convertible. (L.) 'And accompanieth the *inconvertible* portion;' Sir T. Browne, Vulg. Errors, b. ii. c. 5,

§ 8 [reference in R. wrong].—L. *inconuertibilis*, unchangeable. See **In-** (3) and **Convert**. Der. *inconvertibili-ty*.

INCONVINCIBLE, not convincible. (L.) 'Yet it is not much less injurious unto knowledge, obstinately and *inconvincibly* [*inconvincedly*, R.] to side with any one;' Sir T. Browne, Vulg. Errors, b. i. c. 7, § 6. A coined word; from **In-** (3) and **Convince**. Der. *inconvincibl-y*.

INCONY, adj., rare, fine, delicate, pretty, very dear. (E.) In Shak. L. L. L. iii. 1. 136; iv. 1. 144; Marlowe, Jew of Malta, iv. 5 (*or* 6). Perhaps for *in-conny*; where *in-* is intensive, as in ME. *in-ly*, very; and *conny* (also *canny*) is North E., meaning skilful, gentle, pleasant, dainty, &c. (E.D.D.) From E. *can*, I know (how); cf. Icel. *kunnigr*, knowing, wise; Swed. *kunnig*, skilful.

INCORPORATE, to form into a body. (L.) In Shak. Romeo, ii. 6. 37. Orig. a pp. as in Mids. Nt. Dr. iii. 2. 208; and much earlier (spelt *incorporat*) in Trevisa, tr. of Higden, i. 329.—L. *incorporātus*, pp. of *incorporāre*, to furnish with a body.—L. *in*, in; and *corpor-*, decl. stem of *corpus*, a body. See **In-** (2) and **Corporal** (2). Der. *incorporat-ion*, Sir T. More, Works, p. 1045 h; so also *incorpor-eal*, Milton, P. L. i. 789; *incorpor-eal-ly*.

INCORRECT, not correct. (F.—L.) In Hamlet, i. 2. 95.—F. *incorrect*, 'incorrect;' Cot.—L. *incorrectus*, uncorrected. See **In-** (3) and **Correct**. Der. *incorrect-ly, -ness*; so also *incorrigible*, in Minsheu, and used by Cot. to translate F. *incorrigible; incorrigibleness, incorrigibili-ty*.

INCORRUPT, not corrupt. (L.) 'The most iuste and *incorrupt* iuge' [judge]; Joye, Exposicion of Daniel, c. 7. And in Trevisa, tr. of Higden, vii. 149.—L. *incorruptus*, uncorrupted. See **In-** (3) and **Corrupt**. Der. *incorrupt-ly; incorrupt-ion*, Sir T. More, Works, p. 1345 d; *incorrupt-ness*; also *incorrupt-ibl-*, Bible, 1551, 1 Cor. xv. 52, from F. *incorruptible*, Cot.; *incorruptibl-y, incorruptible-ness*.

INCRASSATE, to make thick. (L.) 'Liquors which time hath *incrassated* into jellies;' Sir T. Browne, Urn-burial, c. iii. § 3.—L. *incrassātus*, pp. of *incrassāre*, to make thick.—L. *in*, in, into; and *crassāre*, to thicken, from *crassus*, thick. See **Crass**. Der. *incrassation, incrassat-ive*.

INCREASE, to grow in size, to augment. (F.—L.) ME. *incresen*, Prompt. Parv. p. 261. Earlier, *encresen*, Chaucer, C. T. 13394 (B 1654).—AF. *encress-*, a stem of *encrestre*, to increase; Stat. Realm, p. 284.—F. *en*, in; and AF. *cres-*, stem of *creistre*, to grow (OF. *croistre*, F. *croître*). 'Un arbresu ki eu munt fu *cresant*'=a small tree which was *growing* on the mount; Vie de St. Auban, ed. Atkinson, 1172. Cf. L. *increscere*, to increase.—L. *in*, in; and *crescere*, to grow. See **In-** (2) and **Crescent**. Der. *increase*, sb., Bible, 1551, Ezek. xxxiv. 27. And see *increment*.

INCREDIBLE, not credible. (F.—L.) 'Reioysyng *incredibly*;' Sir T. Elyot, The Governour, b. ii. c. 2; Shak. Tam. Shrew, ii. 308.—F. *incredible*, 'incredible;' Cot.—L. *incrēdibilis*. From **In-** (3) and **Credible**; see **Creed**. Der. *incredibl-y, incredibili-ty*; so also *incred-ul-ous*, 2 Hen. IV, iv. 5. 154, from L. *incrēdulus*, by change of *-us* to *-ous*, as in numerous other instances; *incredulous-ly; incredul-i-ty*, from F. *incredulité*, 'incredulity,' Cot.

INCREMENT, increase. (L.) Used by Bp. Taylor, Liberty of Prophesying, § 16. '*Increment*, incrementum;' Levins, ed. 1570.—L. *incrēmentum*, increase. Formed with suffix *-mentum* from *incrē-*, base of *increscere*, to increase. See **Increase**.

INCROACH, the same as **Encroach**. (F.) In Minsheu; and in Cotgrave, to translate MF. *enjamber*.

INCRUST, to cover with a crust. (F.—L.) 'The chapell is *incrusted* with such precious materials;' Evelyn, Diary, Nov. 10, 1644. '*Incrustate*, incrustare;' Levins, ed. 1570.—F. *incruster*, 'to set a scab or crust on;' Cot.—L. *incrustāre*, to cover with a crust.—L. *in*, on; and *crusta*, a crust. See **In-** (2) and **Crust**. Der. *incrustat-ion*, Blount's Gloss., ed. 1674. ☞ Better than *encrust*.

INCUBATE, to sit on eggs to hatch them. (L.) The verb is late, and suggested by the sb. *incubation*. 'The daily *incubation* of ducks;' Sir T. Browne, Vulg. Errors, b. iii. c. 7, § 9.—L. *incubātus*, pp. of *incubāre*, to lie upon, sit upon eggs. See **Incubus**. Der. *incubat-ion, incubat-or*.

INCUBUS, a nightmare, oppressive weight. (L.) 'Ther is noon other *incubus* but he;' Chaucer, C. T. 6462 (D 880).—L. *incubus*, a nightmare.—L. *incubāre*, to lie upon.—L. *in*, upon; and *cubāre*, to lie down, lit. to be bent down. Cf. Gk. κύπτειν, to stoop down.

INCULCATE, to enforce by admonitions. (L.) 'To *inculcate*, inculcare;' Levins.—L. *inculcātus*, pp. of *inculcāre*, lit. to tread in. —L. *in*, in; and *calcāre*, to tread. See **Calk**. Der. *inculcat-ion*.

INCULPABLE, not culpable. (L.) 'As one that was *inculpable*;' Chapman, Homer's Iliad, b. iv. l. 103; and in Minsheu. —L. *inculpābilis*. See **In-** (3) and **Culpable**. Der. *inculpabl-y*.

INCULPATE, to bring into blame. (L.) First in 1799. Not in Todd's Johnson. — Late L. *inculpāre*, to bring blame upon, accuse; Ducange. — L. *in*, upon; and *culpa*, blame; see **In-** (2) and **Culpable.** Der. *inculpat-ion, inculpat-or-y.*

INCUMBENT, lying upon, resting upon as a duty. (L.) 'Aloft, *incumbent* on the dusky air;' Milton, P. L. i. 226. — L. *incumbent-*, stem of pres. pt. of *incumbere*, to lie upon; a nasalised form allied to *incubāre*, to lie upon. See **Incubus.** Der. *incumbent*, sb., one who holds an ecclesiastical office, see Minsheu, and Blount's Gloss., ed. 1674; *incumbent-ly, incumbenc-y.*

INCUMBER, the same as **Encumber.** (F.—L.) In Minsheu; and in Milton, P. L. vi. 874, ix. 1051.

INCUR, to become liable to, bring on. (L.) In Shak. Merch. Ven. iv. 1. 361. — L. *incurrere*, to run into, fall into, run upon, attack, befal, occur. — L. *in*, upon; and *currere*, to run. See **In-** (2) and **Current.** Der. *incursion, q. v.*

INCURABLE, not curable. (F.—L.) ME. *incurable*, P. Plowman, B. x. 327; Gower, C. A. ii. 119; bk. iv. 3509. — F. *incurable*; Cot. — L. *incūrābilis*. — L. *in-*, not; and *cūrābilis*, curable, from *cūrāre*, to cure. See **In-** (3) and **Cure.** Der. *incurabl-y, incurable-ness, incurabili-ty.*

INCURSION, an inroad, encounter. (F.—L.) In Shak. 1 Hen. IV, iii. 2. 108. — F. *incursion*, 'an incursion, inrode;' Cot. — L. *incursiōnem*, acc. of *incursio*, an attack; allied to L. *incursus*, pp. of *incurrere*, to attack. See **Incur.**

INCURVATE, to bend, crook. (L.) In Cockeram, pt. ii. s. v. *bow*. '*Incurvation*, a crook'ning or bowing;' Kersey, ed. 1715. — L. *incurvātus*, pp. of *incurvāre*, to bend into a curve. — L. *in*, in, into; and *curvāre*, to curve, from *curvus*, crooked; see **In-** (2) and **Curve.** Der. *incurvat-ion.*

INDEBTED, being in debt. (F.—L.) In Luke, xi. 4 (A. V.). ME. *endetted*; Chaucer, C. T. 16202 (G 734). — OF. *endetter*, MF. *endebter*, 'to bring into debt;' Cot. — F. *en*, in, into; and OF. *dette*, MF. *debte*, a debt. See **In-** (2) and **Debt.** Der. *indebted-ness.*

INDECENT, not decent. (F.—L.) In Spenser, b. ii. c. 9. st. 1. — F. *indecent*, 'undecent;' Cot. — L. *indecent-*, stem of *indecens*, unbecoming. See **In-** (3) and **Decent.** Der. *indecent-ly, indecenc-y.*

INDECISION, want of decision. (F.—L.) Used by Burke (R.). — F. *indecision*, 'an undecision;' Cot. See **In-** (3) and **Decide.** Der. *indecis-ive, indecis-ive-ly, -ness.*

INDECLINABLE, that cannot be declined. (L.) A grammatical term. In Palsgrave, Introd. p. xxxvii. — L. *indēclīnābilis*, indeclinable. — L. *in-*, neg. prefix; and *dēclīnāre*, to decline, inflect a substantive. See **In-** (4) and **Decline.** Der. *indeclinabl-y.*

INDECORUM, want of propriety. (L.) 'To entermingle merie iests in a serious matter is an indecorum;' Gascoigne, On Verse, ed. Arber, p. 32. And in Minsheu's Dict., ed. 1627. — L. *indecōrum*, what is unbecoming; neut. of *indecōrus*, unbecoming. See **In-** (3) and **Decorum.** Der. *indecor-ous*, used by Burke (R.); directly from L. *indecōrus*, with *-ous* for *-us*; hence *indecor-ous-ly.*

INDEED, in fact, in truth. (E.) ME. *in dede*, in reality, according to the facts. 'And how that al this proces fil *in dede*' = and how all this series of events happened in reality; Chaucer, C. T. 14327 (B 3511). We find nearly the modern usage in the following. 'Made her owne weapon do her finger blede, To fele if pricking wer so good *in dede*;' Sir T. Wiat, Of his Love that pricked her finger with a nedle. From *in*, prep.; and *dede*, dat. case of *deed*. See **In** and **Deed.**

INDEFATIGABLE, that cannot be wearied out. (F.—L.) In Milton, P. L. ii. 408; and in Minsheu. — F. *indefatigable*, 'indefatigable;' Cot. — L. *indēfatigābilis*, not to be wearied out. — L. *in-*, negative prefix; and *dēfatigāre*, to weary out, from *dē*, down, extremely, and *fatigāre*, to weary. See **In-** (3) and **Fatigue.** Der. *indefatigabl-y, indefatigable-ness.*

INDEFEASIBLE, not to be defeated or made void. (AF.—L.) An AF. law-term. Spelt *indefeosable* in Cockeram (1642). 'An *indefeasible* title;' Burnet, Hist. Reformation, an. 1553 (R.). Also spelt *indefeasable*; Tatler, no. 187. From **In-** (3) and **Defeasible**; see **Defeasance, Defeat.** Der. *indefeasibl-y, indefeasibili-ty.*

INDEFENSIBLE, not defensible. (L.) Used by Sir T. More, Works, p. 151. From **In-** (3) and **Defensible.** See **Defend.** Der. *indefensibl-y.*

INDEFINABLE, that cannot be defined. (L.) Modern. Added by Todd to Johnson's Dict. From **In-** (3) and **Definable.** See **Indefinite.**

INDEFINITE, not definite, vague. (F.—L.) 'It was left somewhat *indefinitely*;' Bacon, Life of Hen. VII, ed. Lumby, p. 102, l. 25. From **In-** (3) and **Definite.** See **Define.** Der. *indefinite-ly, -ness.*

INDELIBLE, not to be blotted out. (F.—L.) In Cotgrave. Misspelt for *indeleble*. Owing to the lack of E. words ending in *-eble*, it has been made to end in *-ible*, by analogy with *terr-ible, horr-ible,*

and the like. The correct spelling *indeleble* often occurs (see Rich. and Todd) and is given in Blount's Gloss., ed. 1674. 'Might fix any character *indeleble* of disgrace upon you;' Bacon, Letters, ed. 1657, p. 13 (Todd). — MF. *indelebile*, 'indelible;' Cot. — L. *indēlēbilis*, indelible. — L. *in-*, not; and *dēlēbilis*, destructible, from *dēlēre*, to destroy. See **In-** (3) and **Delete.** Der. *indelibl-y, indelibili-ty.*

INDELICATE, not delicate, coarse. (F.—L.) 'If to your nice and chaster ears That term *indelicate* appears;' Churchill, The Ghost, b. iii. l. 283. *Indelicacy* is in the Spectator, no. 286. From **In-** (3) and **Delicate.** Der. *indelicate-ly, indelicac-y.*

INDEMNIFY, to make good for damage done. (F.—L.) 'I believe the states must at last engage to the merchants here that they will *indemnify* them from all that shall fall out on this occasion;' Sir W. Temple, to Lord Arlington (R.). Cf. MF. *indemniser*, 'to indemnize, or *indamnifie*;' Cot. [A clumsy and ignorantly formed compound, made as if from an OF. *indemnifier* or Late L. *indemnificāre*, neither of which is used; the true words being OF. *indemniser* and Late L. *indemnisāre*.] — L. *indemni-*, decl. stem of *indemnis*, unharmed; and F. suffix *-fier* = L. *-ficāre*, forms due to L. *facere*, to make; see **Fact.** β. L. *indemnis* is from *in-*, neg. prefix; and *damnum*, harm, loss; see **In-** (3) and **Damage.** Der. *indemnific-at-ion.* And see **Indemnity.**

INDEMNITY, security from loss, compensation for loss. (F.—L.) 'Sufficiently prouide for *thindemnity* [i. e. the indemnity] of the wytnes;' Sir T. More, Works, p. 970 b. — F. *indemnité*, 'indemnity;' Cot. — L. *indemnitātem*, acc. of *indemnitās*, security from damage. — L. *indemni-*, decl. stem of *indemnis*; see **Indemnify.**

INDEMONSTRABLE, not demonstrable. (L.) 'Undiscernable, and most commonly *indemonstrable*;' Bp. Taylor, Liberty of Prophesying, s. 2. — L. *indēmonstrābilis*, not to be shown. — L. *in-*, not; and *dēmonstrābilis*, demonstrable, from *dēmonstrāre*, to show. See **In-** (3) and **Demonstrate.**

INDENT (1), to notch, cut into points like teeth. (Law L.) A law term. In making duplicates of deeds, it was usual to cut or *indent* the edges exactly alike so that they would tally with each other upon comparison. The deeds with edges so cut were called *indentures*, and the verb to *indent* came also to mean to execute a deed or make a compact. See *indentura* in Ducange. 'Shall we buy treason, and *indent* with fears, When they have lost and forfeited themselves?' 1 Hen. IV, i. 3. 87. It was also used as a term in heraldry, as in the following. 'His baner, . . . the which was goules, . . . bordred syluer *indented*;' Berners, tr. of Froissart, vol. i. c. 60 (R.). Hence used in a general sense. 'With *indented* glides;' As You Like It, iv. 3. 113. — Law L. *indentāre*, to notch or cut into teeth; whence also MF. *endenter* (Cotgrave). — L. *in*, in, into; and *dent-*, stem of *dens*, a tooth, cognate with E. **Tooth,** q. v. Der. *indenture*, Hamlet, v. 1. 119 (= Law L. *indentūra*, Ducange), formed with F. suffix *-ure* (*-ūra*) by analogy with F. sbs. such as *blessure* from *bless-er*, &c. Also *indentat-ion* (in one sense).

INDENT (2), to make a dint in. (E.) 'Deep scars were seen *indented* on his breast;' Dryden, Juvenal, vi. 151. From E. *in*, prep.; and *dent*, a dint. See **Dent.** Suggested and much affected by *indent* (1), though really a different word. Der. *indent-ation.*

INDEPENDENT, not dependent. (L.) The *Independents* formed a sect famous in history. 'Robert Brown preached these views [i. e. such views as they held] in 1585 . . . A church was formed in London in 1593, when there were 20,000 *independents* . . . Cromwell, himself an Independent, obtained them toleration;' Haydn, Dict. of Dates. From **In-** (3) and **Dependent**; see **Depend.** Der. *independent-ly, independence, independenc-y.*

INDESCRIBABLE, not to be described. (L.) A late word; added by Todd to Johnson's Dict. From **In-** (3) and **Describable**; see **Describe.**

INDESTRUCTIBLE, not to be destroyed. (L.) 'Primitive and *indestructible* bodies;' Boyle, Works, vol. i. p. 538 (R.). From **In-** (3) and **Destructible**; see **Destroy.** Der. *indestructibl-y, indestructible-ness, indestructibili-ty.*

INDETERMINATE, not fixed. (L.) 'Any sterre . . . *indeterminat*;' Chaucer, Astrolabe, pt. ii. § 17 (rubric). — L. *indēterminātus*, undefined. — L. *in-*, not; and *dēterminātus*, pp. of *dētermināre*, to define, limit, fix; see **In-** (3) and **Determine.** Der. *indeterminate-ly, indeterminat-ion*; so also *indetermin-able, indetermin-abl-y*; and *indetermin-ed.*

INDEX, a hand that points out, a table of contents to a book. (L.) See Nares. In Shak. Rich. III, ii. 2. 149; Troil. i. 3. 343; Hamlet, iii. 4. 52. [The L. pl. is *indices*; the E. pl. is *indexes*.] — L. *index* (stem *indic-*), a discloser, informer, index, indicator; allied to *indicāre*, to point out. See **Indicate.** Der. *index*, verb (modern), *index-learning*, Pope, Dunciad, ii. 279.

INDIAMAN, a large ship employed in trade with India; from *India* and *man*. See **Indigo** and **Man.**

INDIAN RUBBER, INDIA-RUBBER, caoutchouc, so named from its rubbing out pencil marks, and because often brought from the W. Indies; from *India* and **Rubber.** ¶ The use of *Indian* with reference to the *West* Indies was once common; see Temp. ii. 2. 34; Pope, Horace, Ep. I. i. 69. See **Indigo.**

INDICATE, to point out, show. (L.) In Kersey's Dict., ed. 1715; first in 1651. *Indication* is earlier, in Bacon, Nat. Hist. § 479. − L. *indicātus*, pp. of *indicāre*, to point to, point out. − L. *in*, towards; and *dicāre*, to proclaim, make known. From *dic-*, weak grade of √DEIK, to show; whence also E. **Token,** q. v. Der. *indicat-or*, *indicat-or-y*, *indicat-ion*; also *indicat-ive*, a grammatical term, used in the F. grammar prefixed to Palsgrave's F. Dict., p. xxxi; *indicative-ly*; also *index*, q. v.

INDICT, to accuse. (L.; *rather* F. − L.) The spelling is Latin; but the pronunciation is invariably *indite* [i. e. rhyming with *bite*], showing that it is really French. See further under **Indite.** Shak. has *indict* (old editions *indite*) in Haml. ii. 2. 464; Oth. iii. 4. 154. Der. *indict-able*; *indict-ment*, Wint. Ta. iii. 2. 11; and see **Indiction.**

INDICTION, a cycle of 15 years. (F. − L.) Lit. an imposition of a tax, an impost, tax. Specially applied to the period called the *Indiction*, 'a cycle of tributes orderly disposed for 15 years, not known before the time of Constantine . . . In memory of the great victory obtained by Constantine over Mezentius, 8 Cal. Oct. 312, the council of Nice ordained that the accounts of years should be no longer kept by the Olympiads, but by the Indiction, which has its epocha 1 Jan. 313. It was first used by the Latin church in 342 [Sept. 1];' Haydn, Dict. of Dates. Given and explained in Minsheu and Blount. − F. *indiction*, 'a tearme of 5, 10, or 15 years used by the ancient Romans in their numbring of years; also an imposition, taxe, or tallage;' Cot. − L. *indictiōnem*, acc. of *indictio*, an imposition of a tax; cf. L. *indictus*, pp. of *indīcere*, to appoint, impose. − L. *in*, in, to; and *dīcere*, to say, speak, tell, appoint. See **In-** (2) and **Diction.**

INDIFFERENT, impartial, neutral, unimportant. (F. − L.) In Palsgrave; and Ecclus. xlii. 5 (A. V.). See Bible Wordbook and Nares. And see Shak. Rich. II, ii. 3. 116; Jul. Cæsar i. 3. 115; Tam. Shrew, iv. 1. 94. − F. *indifferent*, 'indifferent, equall, tollerable, in a mean between both;' Cot. − L. *indifferent-*, stem of *indifferens*, indifferent, careless. From **In-** (3) and **Different;** see **Differ.** Der. *indifferent-ly*, Jul. Cæsar, i. 2. 87; Titus Andron. i. 430; Haml. iii. 2. 41; *indifference*.

INDIGENOUS, native, born in, naturally produced in. (L.) 'Negroes . . . not *indigenous* or proper natives of America;' Sir T. Browne, Vulg. Errors, b. vi. c. 10. § 7. − L. *indigenus*, native; by change of *-us* to *-ous*, as in very numerous instances. − L. *indi-*, for *indu*, Old L. extension from the prep. *in* (cf. Gk. ἔνδον, within); and *gen-*, as in *gen-i-tus*, born, pp. of *gignere*, to beget, formed from √GEN, to beget. See **Genus.**

INDIGENT, destitute, needy, poor. (F. − L.) ME. *indigent*; the sb. *indigence* is in Chaucer, C. T. 4524 (B 104); Gower, C. A. iii. 153; bk. vii. 2028. − F. *indigent*, 'indigent;' Cot. − L. *indigent-*, stem of *indigens*, a needy person, lit. needing; orig. pres. pt. of *indigēre*, to need, to be in want. − L. *ind-*, shortened from *indu*, an Old L. extension from the prep. *in* (cf. Gk. ἔνδον, within); and *egēre*, to be in want. β. *Egēre* is allied to **egus*, adj., only found in comp. *ind-igus*, needy. Cf. Gk. ἀχήν, poor, needy (rare); Theocritus, 16. 33. Both L. and Gk. words appear to be from √EGH, to be in want; Fick, i. 482. Der. *indigent-ly*, *indigence*.

INDIGESTED, not digested, unarranged. (L.) *Indigested* in the sense of 'unarranged' is now commonly so written, as if to distinguish it from *undigested*, applied to food; but the words had once the same sense. 'Hence, heap of wrath, foul *indigested* lump;' 2 Hen. VI, v. 1. 157. The shorter form *indigest* also occurs; 'monsters and things *indigest*;' Shak. Sonnet 114, l. 5. − L. *indigestus*, (1) unarranged, (2) undigested. − L. *in-*, not; and *digestus*, pp. of *digerere*, to arrange, digest. See **In-** (3) and **Digest.** Der. *indigest-ible* (cf. *digestible* in Chaucer, C. T., A 437), from F. *indigestible*, 'indigestible,' Cot., from pp. *indigestus*; *indigest-ibl-y*; also *indigest-ion*, from F. *indigestion*, 'indigestion,' Cot.

INDIGNATION, anger at what is unworthy. (F. − L.) ME. *indignacion*. 'The hates and *indignaciouns* of the accusour Ciprian;' Chaucer, tr. of Boethius, b. i. pr. 4, l. 74. − F. *indignation*, 'indignation;' Cot. − L. *indignātiōnem*, acc. of *indignātio*, displeasure; cf. *indignātus*, pp. of *indignāri*, to consider as unworthy, be displeased at. − L. *indignus*, unworthy. − L. *in-*, not; and *dignus*, worthy. See **In-** (3) and **Dignity.** Der. So also *indignant*, Spenser, F. Q. iii. 5. 23, from L. *indignant-*, stem of pres. part. of *indignāri*; *indignant-ly*; also *indignity*, Spenser, F. Q. iv. 7. 36, from MF. *indigneté*, 'indignity' (Cot.), from L. *indignitātem*, acc. of *indignitās*, unworthiness, indignity, indignation.

INDIGO, a blue dye obtained from a certain plant. (F. − Span. − L. − Gk. − Pers. − Skt.) Most of it comes from India, whence the name. The mod. name *indigo* is French, a word borrowed from Spanish. Holland uses the Span. form. 'There commeth from India . . . store enough not only of *indico*;' tr. of Pliny, b. xxxv. c. 7. − F. *indigo*. − Span. *indico*, indigo; lit. 'Indian.' − L. *Indicum*, indigo; neut. of *Indicus*, Indian. − Gk. ἰνδικόν, indigo; neut. of Ἰνδικός, Indian. − Pers. *Hind*, India; Rich. Dict. p. 1691. The name is due to the *Indus*, a large river. − Skt. *sindhu-*, the river Indus, a river. ¶ The Persian changes initial *s* into *h*; see Max Müller, Lectures, i. 265.

INDIRECT, not direct, crooked. (F. − L.) In Shak. Merch. Ven. iv. 1. 350; Caxton, Chesse, bk. iv. c. 2. − F. *indirect*, 'indirect, not right;' Cot. − L. *indīrectus*. See **In-** (3) and **Direct.** Der. *indirect-ly*, *-ness*, *indirect-ion*, Hamlet, ii. 1. 66.

INDISCERNIBLE, not discernible. (L.) Spelt *indiscernable* in Kersey, ed. 1715. From **In-** (3) and **Discernible;** see **Discern.** Der. *indiscernibl-y*.

INDISCREET, not discreet. (F. − L.) ME. *indiscret*; spelt *indyscrete* in Myrc's Instructions for Parish Priests, ed. Peacock, l. 825. − F. *indiscret*, 'indiscreet;' Cot. − L. *indiscrētus*, unseparated, indiscriminate; also, that does not discern or distinguish. See **In-** (3) and **Discreet.** Der. *indiscreet-ly*, *-ness*; also *indiscretion*, from F. *indiscretion*, 'indiscretion;' Cot. See below.

INDISCRIMINATE, confused. (L.) 'The use of all things *indiscriminate*;' Bp. Hall, b. v. sat. 3, l. 25. Here it is used as an adverb. − L. *indiscriminātim*, adv., without distinction. − L. *in-*, not; and *discriminātim*, with a distinction. − L. *discrimin-*, decl. stem of *discrimen*, a separation, distinction. See **In-** (3) and **Discriminate.** Der. *indiscriminate-ly*.

INDISPENSABLE, that cannot be dispensed with. (L.) In Bale's Apology, fol. 133 (R.). From **In-** (3) and **Dispensable;** see **Dispense.** Der. *indispensabl-y*, *indispensable-ness*.

INDISPOSED, disinclined, unwell in health. (F. − L. *and* Gk.) 'The *indisposed* and sickly;' K. Lear, ii. 4. 112. − MF. *indisposé*, 'sickly, crazie, unhealthful, ill-disposed;' Cot. − F. *in-* = L. *in-*, not; and MF. *disposé*, 'nimble, well disposed in body,' Cot.; from the verb *disposer*. See **In-** (3) and **Dispose.** Der. Hence the verb *in-dispose*, which is quite modern; *indisposed-ness*. ¶ But *indisposit-ion*, Timon, ii. 2. 139, from F. *indisposition*, Cot., is wholly Latin; see **Disposition.**

INDISPUTABLE, not disputable, certain. (F. − L.) 'Indisputably certain;' Sir T. Browne, Vulg. Errors, b. v. c. 12. § 1. From **In-** (3) and F. *disputable*, 'disputable,' Cot.; see **Dispute.** Der. *indisputabl-y*, *indisputable-ness*.

INDISSOLUBLE, not dissoluble. (F. − L.) 'The *indissoluble* knot;' Udal, on St. Matthew, c. 19; vv. 1–9. − F. *indissoluble*, 'indissoluble;' Cot. − L. *indissolūbilis*. − L. *in-*, not; and *dissolūbilis*, that may be dissolved, from *dissoluere*, to dissolve. See **In-** (3) and **Dissolute.** Der. *indissolubl-y*, *indissoluble-ness*, *indissolubili-ty*.

INDISTINCT, not distinct. (F. − L.; *or* L.) In Ant. and Cleop. iv. 14. 10. − F. *indistinct*, 'indistinct;' Cot. − L. *indistinctus*. From **In-** (3) and **Distinct.** Der. *indistinct-ly*, *-ness*; so also *indistinguish-able*, Shak. Troil. v. 1. 33; *indistinguishabl-y*.

INDITE, to dictate for writing, compose, write. (F. − L.) It should rather be *endite*. ME. *enditen*, Chaucer, C. T. 1874 (A 1872). '*Indyted* or *endyted* of clerkly speche, Dictatus;' Prompt. Parv. p. 261. '*Indytyd* be [by] lawe, for trespace, Indictatus;' id. − OF. *enditer*, MF. *endicter*, 'to indict, accuse, impeach;' Cot. Spelt *enditer*, with the sense 'to point out;' Bartsch, Chrest. Française. − Late L. *in-dictāre*, to accuse; frequentative of L. *indīcere*, to proclaim, enjoin, impose. − L. *in*, upon; and *dīcere*, to say; see **Diction.** It would seem that the senses of the related words *indicāre*, to point out, and *dictāre*, to dictate, have influenced the sense of *indite*. ¶ The spelling *indict* is reserved for the sense 'to accuse.' Der. *indit-er*, *indite-ment*. Doublet, *indict*, q. v.

INDIVIDUAL, separate, pertaining to one only. (L.) 'If it were not for two things that are constant . . . no *individuall* would last one moment;' Bacon, Essay 58, Of Vicissitude. Formed, with suffix *-al*, from L. *indiuidu-us*, indivisible, inseparable; hence, distinct, apart. − L. *in-*, not; and *diuiduus*, divisible, from *diuidere*, to divide; see **In-** (3) and **Divide.** Der. *individual-ly*, *individual-ise*, *individual-is-at-ion*; *-ism*, *-i-ty*; also *individu-ate* (rare), *individu-at-ion*; and see below.

INDIVISIBLE, not divisible. (F. − L.) 'That *indivisible* point or centre;' Hooker, Eccl. Polity, ed. Church, b. i. sect. viii. subsect. 8. Also in Cotgrave. − F. *indivisible*, 'indivisible;' Cot. − L. *indiuisibilis*. From **In-** (3) and **Divisible;** see **Divide.** Der. *indivisibl-y*, *indivisible-ness*, *indivisibili-ty*.

INDOCILE, not docile. (F. − L.) 'Hogs and more *indocile* beasts;' Sir W. Petty, Adv. to Hartlib (1648), p. 23; Todd. − F. *in-*

docile, 'indocible;' Cot. — L. *indocilis*, not teachable. See **In-** (3) and **Docile**. Der. *indocil-i-ty*.

INDOCTRINATE, to instruct in doctrine. (L.) 'His *indoctrinating* power;' Milton, Apology for Smectymnuus (R.). Coined as if from Late L. **indoctrināre*, not found. — L. *in*, in; and *doctrina*, learning. See **In-** (2) and **Doctrine**. Der. *indoctrinat-ion*.

INDOLENCE, idleness. (F.—L.; *or* L.) Also *indolency*. '*Indolence or Indolency*;' Kersey, ed. 1715. Only *indolency* is given in Coles and Blount, and occurs in Holland's Plutarch, p. 480 (R.). *Indolence* and *indolent* both occur in the Spectator, no. 100; the former is from F. *indolence*. *Indolency* is Englished from L. *indolentia*, freedom from pain; hence, ease. — L. *in-*, neg. prefix; and *dolent-*, stem of *dolens*, pres. part. of *dolēre*, to grieve. See **In-** (3) and **Dolour**. Der. *indolent* (later than *indolence*); *indolent-ly*.

INDOMITABLE, untameable. (L.) 'It is so fierce and *indomitable*;' Sir T. Herbert, Travels, p. 383 (R.). A coined word; from L. *in-*, not; and *domitāre*, frequentative of *domāre*, to tame, cognate with E. *tame*; see **In-** (3) and **Tame**. Der. *indomitabl-y*.

INDORSE, the same as **Endorse**. (L.) ¶ The OF. is *endosser*; the Late L. is *indorsāre*. Der. *indors-er*, *indors-ee*, *indorse-ment*.

INDUBITABLE, not to be doubted. (F.—L.) 'He did not *indubitably* believe;' Sir T. Browne, Vulg. Errors, b. i. c. 1. § 6. — F. *indubitable*, 'undoubtable;' Cot. — L. *indubitābilis*, indubitable. — L. *in-*, not; and *dubitābilis*, doubtful, from *dubitāre* to doubt. See **Doubt**. Der. *indubitabl-y*, *indubitable-ness*; so also *in-dubious*.

INDUCE, to lead to, prevail on. (L.) '*Induceth* in many of them a loue to worldly thinges;' Sir T. More, Works, p. 880 h; Caxton, Eneydos, ch. 24; p. 90. — L. *indūcere*, to lead in, conduct to. — L. *in*, towards; and *dūcere*, to lead. See **In-** (2) and **Duct**. Der. *induc-er*, *induc-ible*; *induce-ment*, Spenser, F. Q. vii. 6. 32; also *induct*, q.v.

INDUCT, to introduce, put in possession. (L.) '*Inducted* and brought in thither;' Holland, tr. of Livy, p. 1029 (R.); and in Palsgrave. — L. *inductus*, pp. of *indūcere*, to bring in; see above. Der. *induct-ion*, from F. *induction*, 'an induction, entry, or leading into' (Cot.), from L. *inductiōnem*, acc. of *inductio*, an introducing; *induct-ive*, *induct-ive-ly*. ¶ *Induction* was formerly used for 'introduction;' as in Sackville's *Induction* to the Mirror for Magistrates.

INDUE (1), to invest or clothe with, supply with. (L.) 'Infinite shapes of creatures there are bred . . . Some fitt for reasonable sowles t'*indew*;' Spenser, F. Q. iii. 6. 35. '*Indu'd* with robes of various hue;' Dryden, tr. of Ovid's Metam. b. xi. l. 264; where the Lat. has '*induitur* uelamina mille colorum,' Metam. xi. 589. — L. *induere*, to put into, put on, clothe with. And see Higden's Polychronicon, iii. 453, where *induenge* occurs in the 15th cent. translation, and Higden has *induit*. β. Connected with *induuiæ*, clothes, *ex-uuiæ*, spoils; the prefix is *ind-* rather than *in-*, there being no connexion with Gk. ἐνδύειν, ἐνδύειν, to put on. See **Exuviæ**. Der. *indue-ment* (rare). And see below.

INDUE (2), a corruption of **Endue**, to endow, q.v. (F.—L.) This word is distinct from the above, but some of our best writers seem to have confused them. For instances, see Shak. Tw. Nt. i. 5. 105, Oth. iii. 4. 146, &c.; Spenser, F. Q. ii. 2. 6. See Todd's Johnson. The mistake chiefly arises in the phrase 'indued with,' miswritten for 'endued with,' in the sense of 'endowed with;' see Shak. Two Gent. v. 4. 153, Com. Errors, ii. 1. 22. Dryden uses 'indued with' correctly, in the instance cited under **Indue** (1).

INDULGENCE, permission, licence, gratification. (F.—L.) ME. *indulgence*, P. Plowman, B. vii. 193; Chaucer, C. T. 5666 (D 84). — F. *indulgence*, 'indulgence;' Cot. — L. *indulgentia*, indulgence, gentleness. — L. *indulgent-*, stem of pres. part. of *indulgēre*, to be courteous, to indulge. β. Origin doubtful; it is not even certain whether the prefix is *in-* or *ind-*. Bréal explains *indulgentia* as from **indu-licentia*; but Prellwitz connects it with Gk. ἐν-δελεχής, continuous, Goth. *tulgus*, steadfast, and E. *long*; see **Long** (2). Der. *indulg-ent*, Ant. and Cleop. i. 4. 16, from F. *indulgent*, 'indulgent,' Cot. Hence the (later) verb *indulge*, Dryden, tr. of Persius, Sat. v. 74, answering to L. *indulgēre*.

INDURATE, to harden. (L.) *Indurated* occurs four times, and *induration* twice, in Barnes, Works, p. 282. Properly a pp., as in Tyndal, Works, p. 28, col. 1; 'for their harts were *indurate*;' cf. Caxton, Golden Legend, Moyses, § 10. — L. *indūrātus*, pp. of *indūrāre*, to harden. See **Endure**. Der. *indurat-ion*, ME. *induracioun*, Chaucer, C. T., G 855.

INDUSTRY, diligence. (F.—L.) In Shak. Two Gent. i. 3. 22; spelt *industree*, Spenser, F. Q. i. 10. 45. — F. *industrie*, 'industry;' Cot. — L. *industria*, diligence. — L. *industrius*, diligent. β. Of uncertain origin; perhaps for **industruus = *indu-stru-us*, from *indu*, OLat. extension from *in*, in; and the base *stru-*, occurring in *struere*, to arrange, build (hence, to toil); see **Instruct**. Der. *industri-al*, *industri-al-ly*; also *industri-ous*, Temp. iv. 33, from F. *industrieux*,

'industrious' (Cot.), which from L. *industri-ōsus*, abounding in industry; *industri-ous-ly*.

INDWELLING, a dwelling within. (E.) 'The personal *indwelling* of the Spirit;' South's Sermons, vol. v. ser. 7 (R.). From **In-** (1), and **Dwelling**, sb. formed from **Dwell**. Der. So also *indwell-er*, Spenser, F. Q. vii. 6. 55.

INEBRIATE, to intoxicate. (L.) In Levins. — L. *inēbriātus*, pp. of *inēbriāre*, to make drunk. — L. *in*, in, used as an intensive prefix; and *ēbriāre*, to make drunk, from *ēbri-us*, drunk. See **Ebriety**. Der. *inebriat-ion*, Sir T. Browne, Vulg. Errors, b. v. c. 23, part 16; also *in-ebriety*.

INEDITED, unpublished. (L.) First in 1760; see Todd. From **In-** (3) and **Edit**.

INEFFABLE, unspeakable. (F.—L.) In Tindale; 2 Cor. ix. 15; and in Caxton, Golden Legend; Holy Sacrament, § 1. — F. *ineffable*, 'ineffable;' Cot. — L. *ineffābilis*, unutterable. — L. *in-*, not; and *effabilis*, utterable, from *effārī*, to speak out, utter. — L. *ef- < ex*, out; and *fārī*, to speak; see **Fame**. Der. *ineffabl-y*, Milton, P. L. vi. 721.

INEFFACEABLE, not to be effaced. (F.—L.) Modern; not in Todd's Johnson. — MF. *ineffaçable*, 'uneffaceable;' Cot. See **In-** (3) and **Efface**. Der. *ineffaceabl-y*.

INEFFECTIVE, not effective. (L.) 'An *ineffective* pity;' Bp. Taylor, vol. i. ser. 12 (R.). From **In-** (3) and **Effective**; see **Effect**. Der. *ineffective-ly*; so also *ineffect-u-al*, Milton, P. L. ix. 301; *ineffectual-ly*, *-ness*. And see below.

INEFFICACIOUS, that has no efficacy. (F.—L.) In Phillips, ed. 1706. From **In-** (3) and **Efficacious**; see **Efficacy**. Der. *inefficacious-ly*; so also *inefficient*, a late word, added by Todd to Johnson's Dict.; whence *inefficient-ly*, *inefficienc-y*.

INELEGANT, not elegant. (L.) In Levins; and Milton, P. L. v. 335. — L. *inēlegant-*, stem of *inēlegans*. See **In-** (3) and **Elegant**. Der. *inelegance*, *ineleganc-y*.

INELIGIBLE, not eligible. (F.—L.) Modern; not in Todd's Johnson. From **In-** (3) and **Eligible**. Der. *ineligibl-y*, *ineligibili-ty*.

INELOQUENT, not eloquent. (F.—L.) In Milton, P. L. viii. 219. — MF. *ineloquent*, 'uneloquent;' Cot. See **In-** (3) and **Eloquent**.

INEPT, not apt, inexpert, foolish. (F.—L.) In Cotgrave and Blount's Gloss., ed. 1674. — MF. *inepte*, 'inept, unapt;' Cot. — L. *ineptus*, improper, foolish. — L. *in-*, not; and *aptus*, fit, proper. See **Apt**. Der. *inept-ly*, *inept-i-tude*. Doublet, *inapt*, q.v.

INEQUALITY, want of equality. (F.—L.) 'But onely considerynge the *inequalitie*;' Sir T. Elyot, The Governour, b. iii. c. 1. end. — MF. *inequalité*, 'inequality;' Cot. — Late L. *inæquālitās*. — L. *in-*, not; and *æquālitās*, equality, from *æquālis*, equal. See **In-** (3) and **Equal**. ¶ The adj. *inequal* (for *unequal*) is in Chaucer, C. T. 2273 (A 2271).

INERT, dull, inactive. (L.) 'Inertly strong;' Pope, Dunciad, iv. 7. — L. *inert-*, stem of *iners*, unskilful, inactive. — L. *in-*, not; and *ars* (gen. *art-is*), art, skill. See **Art**. Der. *inert-ly*, *inert-ness*; also *inert-ia = L. inertia*, inactivity.

INESTIMABLE, that cannot be valued, priceless. (F.—L.) In Shak. Rich. III, i. 4. 27; Chaucer, tr. of Boethius, bk. ii. pr. 5. 137. From **In-** (3) and **Estimable**; see **Estimate**. Der. *inestimabl-y*.

INEVITABLE, that cannot be avoided. (F.—L.) '*Inevitable* destiny;' Sir T. More, Works, p. 645 d. — MF. *inevitable*, 'inevitable;' Cot. — L. *inēuitābilis*, unavoidable. — L. *in-*, not; and *ēuitābilis*, avoidable, from *ēuitāre*, to avoid; from L. *ē-*, out, away; and *uītāre*, to shun (of doubtful origin). Der. *inevitabl-y*, *inevitable-ness*.

INEXACT, not precise. (L.) Modern; not in Todd; coined from **In-** (3) and **Exact**. Der. *inexact-ly*, *-ness*.

INEXCUSABLE, not excusable. (F.—L.) In Bible, 1551, and in Tindale; Rom. ii. 1. — F. *inexcusable*, 'unexcusable;' Cot. — L. *inexcūsābilis*, Rom. ii. 1 (Vulgate). — L. *in-*, not; and *excūsāre*, to excuse. See **In-** (3) and **Excuse**. Der. *inexcusabl-y*, *inexcusableness*.

INEXHAUSTED, not spent. (L.) In Dryden, On Mrs. Anne Killigrew, l. 28. From **In-** (3) and **Exhausted**; see **Exhaust**. Cf. L. *inexhaustus*, inexhausted. Der. *inexhaust-ible*, in Cowley's Pref. to Poems, on his Davideis; *inexhaustibl-y*, *inexhaustibili-ty*.

INEXORABLE, unrelenting. (F.—L.) In Shak. Merch. Ven. iv. 1. 128; Romeo, v. 3. 38. — F. *inexorable*, 'inexorable;' Cot. — L. *inexōrābilis*, that cannot be moved by entreaty. — L. *in-*, not; and *exōrābilis*, easily entreated, from *exōrāre*, to gain by entreaty; which is from *ex*, from, and *ōrāre*, to pray. See **Adore, Oral**. Der. *inexorabl-y*, *inexorable-ness*, *inexorabili-ty*.

INEXPEDIENT, unfit. (F.—L.) In Phillips, ed. 1706. From **In-** (3) and **Expedient**; see **Expedite**. Der. *inexpedient-ly*, *inexpedience*, *inexpedienc-y*.

INEXPERIENCE, want of experience. (F. – L.) In Milton, P. L. iv. 931. – MF. *inexperience* (Godefroy, Supp.). – L. *inexperientia,* want of experience. See **In-** (3) and **Experience.** Der. *inexperienc-ed.*

INEXPERT, not expert. (F. – L.) In Tindale, Heb. v. 13. – OF. *inexpert* (Godefroy). – L. *inexpertus,* untried. – L. *in-,* not ; and *expertus,* experienced. See **Expert.** Der. *inexpert-ly, -ness.*

INEXPIABLE, that cannot be expiated. (F. – L.) In Levins ; and in Milton, Samson, 839. – MF. *inexpiable* (Supp. to Godefroy). – L. *inexpiābilis.* – L. *in-,* not ; and *expiābilis.* See **Expiate.** Der. *inexpiabl-y, inexpiable-ness.*

INEXPLICABLE, that cannot be explained. (F. – L.) In Sir T. Elyot, The Governour, b. ii. c. 12, § 2 ; and Hamlet, iii. 2. 13. – F. *inexplicable,* 'inexplicable ;' Cot. – L. *inexplicābilis.* – L. *in-,* not ; and *explicāre,* to unfold, explain. See **Explicate.** Der. *inexplicabl-y, inexplicabili-ty.*

INEXPRESSIBLE, that cannot be expressed. (L.) In Milton, P. L. v. 595 ; viii. 113. From **In-** (3) and **Expressible ;** see **Express.** Der. *inexpressibl-y ;* so also *inexpress-ive, inexpress-ive-ly, -ness.*

INEXTINGUISHABLE, that cannot be quenched. (F. – L.) In Hawes, Pastime of Pleasure, ch. xlv. st. 3. From **In-** (3) and **Extinguish.** ¶ The old form is *inextinguible,* Sir T. More, Works, p. 825 g, from F. *inextinguible* (Cot.), L. *inextinguibilis,* Matt. iii. 12 (Vulgate). Der. *inextinguishabl-y.*

INEXTRICABLE, that cannot be extricated. (F. – L.) In Cotgrave ; and Milton, P. L. v. 528. – F. *inextricable,* 'inextricable ;' Cot. – L. *inextrīcābilis.* – L. *in-,* not ; and *extrīcāre,* to extricate. See **In-** (3) and **Extricate.** Der. *inextricabl-y.*

INFALLIBLE, quite certain. (F. – L.) In Shak. Meas. iii. 2. 119 ; see Palsgrave, p. 896, l. 7. – F. *infallible,* 'infallible ;' Cot. From **In-** (3) and **Fallible.** Der. *infallibl-y, infallibili-ty.*

INFAMY, ill fame, vileness. (F. – L.) In Spenser, F. Q. vi. 6. 1 ; Caxton, Eneydos, ch. xxvi. p. 93. – F. *infamie,* 'infamy.' – L. *infāmia,* ill fame. – L. *infāmi-s,* of ill report, disreputable. – L. *in-,* not ; and *fām-a,* fame ; see **Fame.** Der. So also *in-fam-ous,* accented *infámous,* Spenser, F. Q. i. 12. 27, from *in-* and *famous.*

INFANT, a babe, person not of age. (L.) [The ME. *enfaunt* (shortened to *faunt,* P. Plowman, B. vii. 94), from F. *enfant,* has been supplanted by the Law Lat. form.] In Spenser, F. Q. vi. 9. 14. – L. *infant-,* stem of *infans,* a babe, lit. one who cannot speak. – L. *in-,* not ; and *fans,* speaking, pres. part. of *fāri,* to speak. See **Fame.** Der. *infanc-y,* Temp. i. 2. 484, suggested by F. *enfance ;* infancy ; *infant-ile,* from MF. *infantile* (Cot.), which is from L. *infan-tilis ; infant-ine,* from MF. *infantin,* 'infantine,' Cot. ; *infanti-cide* = F. *infanticide,* 'child-murthering' (Cot.), from L. *infanticīdium,* child-murder : and this from L. *infanti-,* decl. stem of *infans,* and *-cīd-* (= *cæd-*) in *cæd-ere,* to kill (see **Cæsura**) ; *infanticid-al ;* and see **Infantry.** Also *infante,* a prince of Portugal or Spain who is not the heir to the throne (Port. *infante*) ; *infanta,* a princess (Port. *infanta*).

INFANTRY, a band of foot-soldiers. (F. – Ital. – L.) 'The principal strength of an army consisteth in the *infantry* or foot ;' Bacon, Hist. Hen. VII, ed. Lumby, p. 72. – F. *infanterie,* 'the infantry or footmen of an army ;' Cot. – Ital. *infanteria,* 'infantery, souldiers on foot ;' Florio. β. The lit. sense is 'a band of infants,' i. e. of young men or servants attendant on knights. – Ital. *infante,* an infant. – L. *infantem,* acc. of *infans,* an infant ; see **Infant.**

INFATUATE, to make foolish, besot. (L.) In Skelton, Speke Parrot, l. 377. Properly a pp., as : ' There was never wicked man that was not *infatuate* ;' Bp. Hall, Contemplations on O. T., b. xviii. c. 4. par. 7. – L. *infatuātus,* pp. of *infatuāre,* to make a fool of. – L. *in-,* as intensive prefix ; and *fatu-us,* foolish ; see **Fatuous.** Der. *infatuat-ion.*

INFECT, to taint. (F. – L.) Properly a pp., as : ' the prynce, whose mynd in tender youth *infect,* shal redily fal to mischief ;' Sir T. More, Works, p. 39 b. So also *infect* in Chaucer, C. T. 322 (A 320), where Tyrwhitt has ' in suspect.' Hence ME. *infecten,* to infect, Prompt. Parv. p. 261. – OF. *infect,* ' infect, infected ;' Cot. – L. *infectus,* pp. of *inficere,* to put in, dip, mix, stain, tinge, infect. – L. *in,* in ; and *facere,* to make, put ; see **Fact.** Der. *infect-ion, infect-i-ous, infect-i-ous-ly, infect-i-ous-ness ; infect-ive* (Levins), from L. *infectīuus.*

INFELICITY, misfortune. (F. – L.) ME. *infelicitee,* Complaint of Creseide, st. 6. – OF. *infelicité* (omitted by Cot.). – L. *infēlicitātem,* acc. of *infēlicitās,* ill luck. See **In-** (3) and **Felicity.** Der. *infelicit-ous.*

INFER, to bring into, deduce, imply. (F. – L.) In Sir T. More, Works, p. 840 h. – MF. *inferer,* 'to inferre, imply ;' Cot. – L. *inferre,* to bring into, introduce, infer. – L. *in,* into ; and *ferre,* to bring, cognate with E. *bear ;* see **Bear.** Der. *infer-able,* or *inferr-ible, infer-ence, infer-ent-i-al, infer-ent-i-al-ly.*

INFERIOR, lower, secondary. (F. – L.) Now conformed to the L. spelling. Spelt *inferiour* in some edd. of Spenser, F. Q. iii. 3. 54 (R.) ; and in Sir T. Elyot, The Governour, bk. i. c. 1. § 7. Spelt *inferioure* in Levins. – MF. *inferieur,* 'inferiour, lower ;' Cot. – L. *inferiōrem,* acc. of *inferior,* lower, compar. of *inferus,* low, nether. β. Strictly, *infer-ior* is a double comparative ; *inferus* itself is a comp. form, answering to Skt. *adhara(s),* lower, from *adhas,* adv. underneath, low, down. Der. *inferior-i-ty ;* and see **Infernal.**

INFERNAL, hellish. (F. – L.) ME. *infernal,* Chaucer, C. T. 2686 (A 2684). – F. *infernal* (Burguy). – L. *infernālis,* belonging to the lower regions, infernal. – L. *infernus,* lower ; extended from *inferus,* low. See **Inferior.** Der. *infernal-ly.*

INFEST, to disturb, harass, molest. (F. – L.) In Spenser, F. Q. ii. 1. 48. – F. *infester,* 'to infest ;' Cot. – L. *infestāre,* to attack, trouble. – L. *infestus,* attacking, hostile. For *in-fest-us ;* probably allied to *of-fend-ere,* to offend ; see **Offend.**

INFIDEL, faithless, unbelieving ; a heathen. (F. – L.) 'Oute of the handes of the *infydelles* ;' Berners, tr. of Froissart, vol. ii. c. 40 (R.). – OF. *infidele,* 'infidell ;' Cot. – L. *infidēlis,* faithless. – L. *in-,* not ; and *fidēlis,* faithful. See **In-** (3) and **Fidelity.** Der. *infidel-i-ty,* from F. *infidelité,* 'infidelity ;' Cot.

INFINITE, endless, boundless. (L.) ME. *infinit,* Chaucer, C. T. 2829 (A 2827). – L. *infinitus,* infinite. See **In-** (3) and **Finite.** ¶ The MF. form is *infini ;* but there was (see Hatzfeld) an older form *infinit,* from which the ME. word was really taken. Der. *infinite-ly ; infinit-y* (ME. *infinitee*), from F. *infinité,* which from L. acc. *infinitātem ; infinit-ude,* from F. *infinitude* (Cot.) ; *infinit-ive,* from F. *infinitif* (Sherwood's index to Cot.), from L. *infinitīuus,* the unlimited, indefinite mood (in grammar) ; also *infinit-esimal,* a late and coined word, in which the suffix is imitated from that of *cent-esimal,* q. v. ; *infinit-esimal-ly.*

INFIRM, feeble, weak. (L.) '*Infirm* of purpose ;' Macb. ii. 2. 52. ME. *infirme,* Chaucer, tr. of Boethius, bk. v. met. 2. l. 3. – L. *infirmus,* not firm, weak. See **In-** (3) and **Firm.** Der. *infirm-ly ;* also *infirm-ar-y,* q. v., *infirm-i-ty,* q. v.

INFIRMARY, a hospital for the infirm. (F. – L.) Modified from ME. *fermerye* so as to bring it nearer to the Lat. spelling. The ME. *fermerye,* shortened from **enfermerie,* occurs in the Prompt. Parv. p. 157. – OF. *enfermerie,* 'an hospitall ;' Cot. – Late L. *infirmāria,* a hospital. – L. *infirmus ;* see **Infirm.**

INFIRMITY, feebleness. (F. – L.) ME. *infirmitee,* spelt *infirmyte,* Wyclif, 2 Cor. xi. 30. – F. *infirmité,* 'infirmity ;' Cot. – L. *infirmitātem,* acc. of *infirmitās,* weakness. – L. *infirmus ;* see **Infirm.**

INFIX, to fix into. (L.) '*Infixed* into his flesh ;' Sir T. More, Works, p. 1114 a. – L. *infixus,* pp. of *infigere,* to fix in. – L. *in,* in ; and *figere,* to fix ; see **Fix.**

INFLAME, to cause to burn, excite. (F. – L.) In Shak. K. John, v. 1. 7 ; and in Palsgrave. Modified from OF. *enflamber,* 'to inflame' (Cot.), so as to bring it nearer to L. *inflammāre,* to set in a flame. – L. *in,* in ; and *flamma,* a flame. See **Flame.** Der. *inflamm-able,* from F. *inflammable,* 'inflammable' (Cot.), formed from L. *inflammāre ; inflamm-a-bili-ty ; inflamm-at-ion,* 2 Hen. IV, iv. 3. 103 ; *inflamm-at-or-y.*

INFLATE, to blow into, puff up. (L.) In Palsgrave ; and in Sir T. Elyot, Castel of Helth, b. ii. c. 7 (Of Fylberdes). Orig. a pp., as in The Complaint of Creseide, st. 7 (l. 463). – L. *inflātus,* pp. of *inflāre,* to blow into. – L. *in,* into ; and *flāre,* cognate with E. **Blow** (1), q. v. Der. *inflat-ion,* Lanfranc, Cirurgie, p. 204, l. 16 ; from F. *inflation,* 'an inflation ;' Cot.

INFLECT, to bend, bend in, modulate the voice ; (in grammar) to vary the terminations. (L.) 'Somewhat *inflected,*' i. e. bent ; Sir T. Browne, Vulg. Errors, b. iii. c. 1. § 4. And in Cockeram (1642). – L. *inflectere,* to bow, curve, lit. bend in. – L. *in,* in ; and *flectere,* to bend ; see **Flexible.** Der. *inflect-ion* (better spelt *inflex-ion,* as in Sir T. Browne, Vulg. Errors, b. iii. c. 1. § 2), from L. *inflexio ;* cf. *inflex-us,* pp. of *inflectere ; inflex-ion-al ; inflect-ive.*

INFLEXIBLE, that cannot be bent. (F. – L.) In Lanfranc, Cirurgie, i. 2. 1, p. 24 ; and Milton, Samson, 816. – F. *inflexible,* 'inflexible ;' Cot. – L. *inflexibilis,* not flexible. See **In-** (3) and **Flexible.** Der. *inflexibl-y, inflexibili-ty.*

INFLICT, to lay on, impose. (L.) In Spenser, F. Q. vi. 8. 22. – L. *inflictus,* pp. of *infligere,* to inflict. – L. *in,* upon ; and *fligere,* to strike. See **Afflict.** Der. *inflict-ion,* Meas. i. 3. 28 ; *inflict-ive,* from MF. *inflictif,* 'inflictive ;' Cot.

INFLORESCENCE, mode of flowering, said of plants. (F. – L.) A modern botan. term. – F. *inflorescence* (Littré). Coined from L. *inflōrescent-,* stem of pres. part. of *inflōrescere,* to burst into blossom. – L. *in,* in ; and *flōrescere,* to flourish ; see **Flourish.**

INFLUENCE, an inspiration, authority, power. (F. – L.) Properly a term in astrology ; see quotation from Cotgrave below. 'O *influences* of thise hevenes hye ;' Chaucer, Troil. iii. 618. – OF.

influence, 'a flowing in, and particularly an influence, or influent course, of the planets; their vertue infused into, or their course working on, inferiour creatures;' Cot. – Late L. *influentia*, an inundation, lit. a flowing into. – L. *influent-*, stem of pres. part. of *influere*, to flow into. – L. *in*, in; and *fluere*, to flow; see **Fluid.** Der. *influence*, verb; *influenti-al*, from L. *influenti-*; *influenti-al-ly*; *influx*, q. v. Doublet, *influenza.*

INFLUENZA, a severe catarrh. (Ital. – L.) 'The new *influenza*;' Foote, Lame Lover, A. i. (ab. 1770). – Ital. *influenza*, lit. influence, also (according to Littré) an epidemic catarrh. A doublet of **Influence,** q. v.

INFLUX, a flowing in, abundant accession. (L.) Formerly used as we now use 'influence.' 'That dominion, which the starres have . . . by their *influxes*;' Howell, Forraine Travell, sect. vi; ed. Arber, p. 36. – L. *influxus*, a flowing in. – L. *influxus*, pp. of *influere*, to flow in; see **Influence.**

INFOLD, to inwrap. (E.) Sometimes written *enfold*, but badly. In Shak. Macb. i. 4. 31. From **In-** (1) and **Fold.**

INFORM, to impart knowledge to. (F. – L.) ME. *enformen*, Gower, C. A. i. 87; bk. i. 1340. – OF. *enformer* (Godefroy); MF. *informer*, 'to informe;' Cot. – L. *informāre*, to put into form, mould, tell, inform. – L. *in*, into; and *forma*, form; see **Form.** Der. *inform-er*; *inform-ant*; *inform-at-ion*, ME. *enformacion*, Gower, C. A. iii. 145; bk. vii. 1780.

INFORMAL, not formal. (L.) In Shak. Meas. v. 236. From **In-** (3) and **Formal;** see **Form.** Der. *informal-ly*, *informal-i-ty.*

INFRACTION, a violation, esp. of law. (F. – L.) Used by Waller (Todd's Johnson; without a reference); and in Cockeram (1642). – F. *infraction*, the same as *infracture*, 'an infracture, infringement;' Cot. – L. *infractiōnem*, acc. of *infractio*, a weakening; cf. *infractus*, pp. of *infringere*; see **Infringe.**

INFRANGIBLE, that cannot be broken. (F. – L.) In Minsheu; and in Holland's tr. of Plutarch, p. 661 (R.). – F. *infrangible*, 'infrangible, unbreakable;' Cot. See **In-** (3) and **Frangible.** Der. *infrangibili-ty.*

INFREQUENT, not frequent. (L.) In Sir T. Elyot, The Governour, b. iii. c. 22. – L. *infrequent-*, stem of *infrequens*, rare. See **In-** (3) and **Frequent.** Der. *infrequent-ly*, *infrequenc-y.*

INFRINGE, to break into, violate, esp. law. (L.) In Shak. L. L. L. iv. 3. 144, 146. – L. *infringere*, to break into. – L. *in*, into; and *frangere*, to break. See **Fraction.** Der. *infringe-ment.*

INFURIATE, to enrage. (L.) Properly a pp., as in Milton, P. L. vi. 486. – Late L. *infuriātus*, pp. of *infuriāre*, to rouse to fury (Ducange). [Perhaps suggested by Ital. *infuriato*, pp. of *infuriare*, 'to grow into fury or rage;' Florio. – Ital. *in furia*, 'in a fury, ragingly;' Florio.] – L. *in*, in; and *furia*, properly a Fury, hence, fury. See **Fury.**

INFUSE, to pour into (F. – L.) In Shak. Merch. Ven. iv. 1. 132, 137. The pp. *enfused* is in Palladius on Husbandry, iii. 755. – F. *infuser*, 'to infuse;' Cot. – L. *infūsus*, pp. of *infundere*, to pour into. – L. *in*, in; and *fundere*, to pour; see **Fuse** (1). Der. *infus-ion*, Wint. Ta. iv. 4. 816; *infus-or-i-a*, *infus-or-i-al.*

INFUSIBLE, not fusible. (F. – L.) In Sir T. Browne, Vulg. Errors, b. ii. c. 1, § 11. From **In-** (3) and **Fusible;** see **Fuse** (1).

INGATHERING, a gathering in. (E.) In Bible, ed. 1551, and A. V.; Exod. xxiii. 16. From **In-** (1) and **Gather.**

INGENDER, the same as **Engender.** (F. – L.) In Minsheu; and Milton, P. L. ii. 794, iv. 809, x. 530.

INGENIOUS, witty, skilful in invention. (F. – L.) In Caxton, Golden Legend, St. Machaire, § 1; and in Shak. Tam. Shrew, i. 1. 9. Shak. often uses it indiscriminately with *ingenuous* (Schmidt). Cf. *ingeniously*, Timon, ii. 2. 230. – F. *ingenieux*, 'ingenious, witty, inventive;' Cot. – L. *ingeniōsus*, clever. – L. *ingenium*, temper, natural capacity, genius. See **Engine, Genius.** Der. *ingenious-ly*, *-ness.* And see below.

INGENUOUS, frank, honourable. (L.) In Shak., who confuses it with *ingenious* (Schmidt); see L. L. L. i. 2. 29; iii. 59; iv. 2. 80. – L. *ingenuus*, inborn, free-born, frank, candid; with change of *-us* to *-ous.* – L. *in*, in; and *gen-*, base of *gignere*, to beget (pt. t. *gen-ui*), from √GEN, to beget. Der. *ingenuous-ly*, *-ness*; also *ingenu-i-ty*, Ben Jonson, Every Man out of his Humour, Act iii. sc. 3 (some edd., sc. 9, Macilente's speech), from F. *ingenuité*, 'ingenuity' (Cot.), which is from L. acc. *ingenuitātem.* And see above.

INGLE (1), fire. (C.) Burns has *ingle-lowe*, blaze of the fire, The Vision, st. 7. Spelt *ingill*, G. Douglas, tr. of Virgil, bk. v. ch. 11. 117. – Gael. and Irish *aingeal*, fire; allied to L. *ignis*, Skt. *agni-*, fire. See **Ignition.**

INGLE (2), a darling, paramour. (Du. *or* Fries. – L. – Gk.) See Nares. Spelt *enghle*, Ben Jonson, Poetaster, A. i. (Ovid sen.). – MDu. *ingel*, *engel*, an angel; Koolman notes EFries. *engel*, an angel, as being commonly used as a term of endearment and as a female

name; cf. Low G. *miin engel*, the usual term of endearment between a married couple (Berghaus); whence E. *my ningle* (Nares). – L. *angelus.* – Gk. ἄγγελος; see **Angel.**

INGLORIOUS, not glorious. (F. – L.) In Shak. K. John, v. 1. 65. – F. *inglorieux*, 'inglorious;' Cot. – Late L. *inglōriōsus*, formed from L. *inglōrius*, inglorious. See **In-** (3) and **Glory.** Der. *inglorious-ly*, *-ness.* ¶ Perhaps borrowed directly from L. *inglōrius*, like *arduous* from L. *arduus*, &c.

INGOT, a mass of metal poured into a mould, a mass of unwrought metal. (E) See my note to Two Noble Kinsmen, i. 2. 17. ME. *ingot*, Chaucer, C. T. 16677, 16691, 16696, 16701 (G 1209-33); where it means 'a mould in which metal is cast;' see the passages. But the true sense is that which is still preserved, viz. 'that which is poured in,' a mass of metal. From AS. *in*, in; and *goten*, poured, pp. of *gēotan*, to pour, shed water, fuse metals; Grein, i. 504. Cf. Du. *ingieten*, Swed. *ingjuta*, to pour in. β. The AS. *gēotan* is cognate with Du. *gieten*, G. *giessen*, Icel. *gjóta* (pp. *gotinn*), Dan. *gyde*, Swed. *gjuta* (pp. *guten*), Goth. *gjutan*, to pour, shed, fuse; all from √GHEUD, to pour, seen also in L. *fundere* (pt. t. *fūdi*, pp. *fūsus*); which is an extension of √GHEU, to pour. See **Fuse, Chyle.** ☞ A. From the E. *ingot* is derived the F. *lingot*, an ingot, which stands for *l'ingot*, by that incorporation of the article which is not uncommon in French; cf. *lendemain* (= *le en demain*), *loriot* (from L. *aureolus*), *luette* (from L. *uua*), *lierre* (from L. *hedera*). And again, from F. *lingot* (found in 1405) was formed the Low Lat. *lingotus*, which is not an early word, but assigned by Ducange to A. D. 1440. This Low Lat. word has been by some fancifully derived from L. *lingua*, the tongue; owing to a supposed resemblance of a mass of molten metal to the shape of the tongue; much as the countryman described the size of a stone as being 'as big as a lump of chalk.' B. Scheler hesitates to accept the derivation here given, from the notion that the AS. verb *gēotan* soon became obsolete. This is quite a mistake, as it is still extant; see '*Yote*, to pour,' in Halliwell, and cf. Cleveland *yetling*, a small iron pan; and more E. dialect words from the same source might be adduced. The ME. verb ȝeten was long in use also; see examples in Stratmann, s. v. ȝeoten, 3rd ed., p. 262. 'Hys mase [mace] he toke in hys honde tho, That was made of *yoten* bras,' i. e. brass formed in a mould; Rich. Coer de Lion, ed. Weber, 370. 'The lazar tok forth his coupe [cup] of gold; Bothe were *yoten* in o mold,' i. e. both the lazar's cup and another were *cast* in one mould; Amis and Amiloun, ed. Weber, 2023. 'Mawmez *igoten* of golde' = idols cast out of gold; Juliana, ed. Cockayne, p. 38, l. 13. C. Moreover, there was a derivative sb. *gote*, a channel; see Prompt. Parv., p. 205, and note; it occurs in the statutes 33 Hen. VIII, c. 33, 2 and 3 Edw. VI, c. 30; *still in use* in the forms *gote, gowt, gut, got*, in various parts of England; cf. Du. *goot*, a gutter; Low G. *güte, gete*, a can for pouring out, the beak of such a can; *göte*, a pouring out; see Bremen Wörterb. ii. 502. D. And note particularly that the whole word *ingot* has its parallel in the cognate (yet independent) G. *einguss*, 'infusion, instillation, pouring in, potion, drink (given to horses); as a technical term, jet, ingot;' Flügel's G. Dict. Cf. also Swed. *ingöte*, the neck of a mould for casting metals (Öman); Low G. *ingote* = G. *einguss* (Berghaus). The objection that the ME. pp. was usually *yoten* rather than *goten*, is not fatal; cf. E. *give* with ME. *yeven, yiven.*

INGRAFT, ENGRAFT, to graft upon. (F. – L. – Gk.) See *Engraffed* and *Engraft* in Schmidt, Shak. Lexicon. Spelt *ingraft*, Milton, P. L. xi. 35. Coined from **In-** (1) or **In-** (2) and **Graft,** q. v.

INGRAILED, a term in heraldry; see **Engrailed.**

INGRAIN, to dye of a fast colour. (F. – L.) ME. *engreynen*, P. Plowman, B. ii. 15, xiv. 20; cf. P. Plowman's Crede, l. 230. See the excellent note by Mr. Marsh, in his Lect. on the E. Language, ed. Smith, p. 55, on the signification of to *dye in grain*, or of a fast colour. And see Shak. Tw. Nt. i. 5. 255, Haml. iii. 4. 90; Milton, Il Pens. 33, Comus, 750. – F. *en graine*, in grain; Cot. gives 'graine, the seed of herbs, also grain wherewith cloth is died in grain, scarlet die, scarlet in graine.' β. The F. *en* = L. *in*, in; the F. *graine* is from Late L. *grāna*, the dye produced from cochineal, which appears also in Span. and Ital. *grana*, grain, seed, cochineal. So named from the resemblance of the dried cochineal to fine *grain* or seed; from L. *grānum*, a grain; see **Grain.**

INGRATIATE, to commend to the favour of. (L.) In Bacon, Life of Hen. VII, ed. Lumby, p. 93, l. 2. Coined from L. *in*, into; and *grātia*, favour; see **Grace.** Cf. Ital. *ingratiare*, 'to engrace;' *ingratiarsi*, 'to ingratiate, or to insinuate ones self into favour' (Torriano).

INGRATITUDE, want of gratitude. (F. – L.) ME. *ingratitude*, Ayenbite of Inwyt, ed. Morris, p. 18, l. 4. – F. *ingratitude*, 'ingratitude;' Cot. – L. *ingrātitūdo*, unthankfulness. – L. *ingrati-*, from the decl. stem of *ingrātus*, unpleasant, unthankful. See **In-** (3) and

Grateful. Der. *ingrate*, Tam. Shrew, i. 2. 270, from F. *ingrat* = L. *ingrātus*; whence *ingrate-ful*, Tw. Nt. v. 80.

INGREDIENT, that which enters into a compound. (F.—L.) In Shak. Wint. Ta. ii. 1. 43.—F. *ingredient*, 'an ingredient, a beginning or entrance; also, in physick, a simple put into a compound medicine;' Cot.—L. *ingredient-*, stem of pres. pt. of *ingredi* (pp. *ingressus*), to enter upon, begin.—L. *in*, in; and *gradi*, to walk; see **Grade.** And see **Ingress.**

INGRESS, entrance. (L.) In Holland, Pliny, b. xxi. c. 14; and in Palladius on Husbandry, bk. i. 964.—L. *ingressus*, an entering.—L. *ingredi*, to enter upon (above).

INGUINAL, relating to the groin. (L.) A medical term; used in 1681.—L. *inguinālis*, belonging to the groin.—L. *inguin-*, stem of *inguen*, the groin.

INGULF, the same as **Engulf.** (F.) Spelt *ingulfe* in Minsheu.

INHABIT, to dwell in, occupy. (F.—L.) In Shak. Tw. Nt. iii. 4. 391. ME. *enhabiten*, Wyclif, Acts, xvii. 26.—F. *inhabiter*, 'to inhabit;' Cot.—L. *inhabitāre*, to dwell in.—L. *in*, in; and *habitāre*, to dwell; see **Habit.** Der. *inhabit-able*; *inhabit-ant*, Macb. i. 3. 41; *inhabit-er*, Rev. viii. 13 (A. V.).

INHALE, to draw in the breath. (L.) A late word. In Thomson, Spring, 834.—L. *inhālāre*, to breathe upon.—L. *in*, upon; and *hālāre*, to breathe. ¶ The E. sense assumes the L. verb to mean 'to draw in breath,' which is not the case. *Inhale* is used in contrast with **Exhale,** q. v. Der. *inhal-at-ion.*

INHARMONIOUS, not harmonious. (F.—L.—Gk.) A mod. word; in Cowper, The Task, i. 207. Coined from **In-** (3) and **Harmonious;** see **Harmony.** Der. *inharmonious-ly*, *-ness.*

INHERENT, existing inseparably, innate. (L.) 'A most *inherent* baseness;' Shak. Cor. iii. 2. 123.—L. *inhaerent-*, stem of pres. part. of *inhaerēre*, to stick fast in.—L. *in*, in; and *haerēre*, to stick. See **Hesitate.** Der. *inherent-ly*; *inherence*, from F. *inherence*, an inherence; *inherenc-y.* Somewhat rarely, *inhere* is used as a verb.

INHERIT, to possess as an heir, come to property. (F.—L.) '*Inheryte*, or receyue in heritage, Heredito;' Prompt. Parv. p. 261.—OF. *enheriter*, to inherit (Godefroy).—Late L. *inhērēditāre*.—L. *in*, in; and *hērēditāre*, to inherit.—L. *hērēdi-* or *hærēdi-*, decl. stem of *hēres* or *hæres*, an heir. See **Heritage, Heir.** Der. *inherit-able*, *inherit-or*, *inherit-ress*; *inherit-ance*, K. John, i. 72.

INHIBIT, to check, restrain. (L.) In Palsgrave; and in Shak. All's Well, i. 1. 157; Oth. i. 2. 79.—L. *inhibitus*, pp. of *inhibēre*, to have in hand, check.—L. *in*, in; and *habēre*, to have. See **Habit.** Der. *inhibit-ion*, Dunbar, Thrissill and Rois, st. 10, from F. *inhibition*, 'an inhibition,' Cot.; *inhibit-or-y.*

INHOSPITABLE, not hospitable. (F.—L.) In Levins; and in Shak. Per. v. 1. 254.—F. *inhospitable*, 'unhospitable;' Cot. See **In-** (3) and **Hospitable.** Der. *inhospitabl-y*, *inhospitable-ness*; so also *in-hospi-tality.*

INHUMAN, not human, barbarous, cruel. (F.—L.) Also written *inhumane* in old authors; Shak. Merch. Ven. iv. 1. 4. Cf. *inhumayne* in Caxton, Golden Legend, St. Vincent, § 2.—F. *inhumain*, 'inhumane, ungentle;' Cot.—L. *inhūmānus.* See **In-** (3) and **Human.** Der. *inhuman-ly*, *inhuman-i-ty.*

INHUME, to inter, deposit in the earth. (F.—L.) In Minsheu, ed. 1627.—F. *inhumer*, 'to bury, inter;' Cot.—L. *inhumāre*, to bury in the ground.—L. *in*, in; and *humus*, the ground. See **Humble.** Der. *inhum-at-ion*, Sir T. Browne, Urn Burial, c. 1, § 4.

INIMICAL, like an enemy, hostile. (L.) 'Inimical to the constitution;' Brand, Essay on Political Associations, 1796; Todd's Johnson.—L. *inimīcālis*, extended from *inimicus*, unfriendly.—L. *in-*, not; and *amicus*, a friend; see **In-** (3) and **Amity.** Der. *inimical-ly.*

INIMITABLE, that cannot be imitated. (F.—L.) 'For the natiue and *inimitable* eloquence;' Sir T. Elyot, The Governour, b. i. c. 23, § 6.—F. *inimitable*, 'unimitable;' Cot.—L. *inimitābilis.*—L. *in-*, not; and *imitābilis*, that can be imitated; see **In-** (3) and **Imitate.** Der. *inimitabl-y.*

INIQUITY, wickedness, vice, crime. (F.—L.) ME. *iniquitee*, Chaucer, C. T. 4778 (B 358).—F. *iniquité*, 'iniquity;' Cot.—L. *inīquitātem*, acc. of *inīquitās*, injustice, lit. unequalness.—L. *in-*, not; and *æquitās*, equality, uniformity, justice; see **In-** (3) and **Equity.** Der. *iniquit-ous*, *iniquit-ous-ly.*

INITIAL, commencing, pertaining to the beginning. (L.) In Phillips, ed. 1706.—L. *initiālis*, incipient.—L. *initium*, a beginning.—L. *initum*, supine of *inīre*, to enter into.—L. *in*, into; and *īre*, to go, from √EI, to go. Der. from same source, *commence*, q. v. And see **Initiate.**

INITIATE, to instruct in principles. (L.) The participial form occurs in Shak. Macb. iii. 4. 143; 'the *initiate* fear that wants hard use.'—L. *initiātus*, pp. of *initiāre*, to begin.—L. *initium*, a beginning (above). Der. *initiat-ion*, *initiat-ive*, *initiat-or-y.*

INJECT, to throw into, cast on. (L.) 'Applied outwardly or

iniected inwardly;' Holland, tr. of Pliny, b. xxvi. c. 15. 'The said *iniection*;' id. b. xx. c. 22 (Of Horehound).—L. *iniectus*, pp. of *inicere* (*injicere*), to throw into.—L. *in*, into; and *iacere*, to throw; see **Jet.** Der. *inject-ion.*

INJUDICIOUS, not judicious. (F.—L.) In Phillips, ed. 1706; and Bp. Hall, Cases of Conscience, dec. 3, cas. 9 (R.). From **In-** (3) and **Judicious.** Der. *injudicious-ly*, *-ness*; so also *in-judicial.*

INJUNCTION, an enjoining, order. (L.) 'After the special *injunccion* of my lorde and master;' Bale, Image, pt. i; and in Shak. Merch. of Venice, ii. 9. 17. Formed, by analogy with F. sbs. in *-ion*, from L. *iniunctiōnem*, acc. of *iniunctio*, an injunction, order; cf. *iniunctus*, pp. of *iniungere*, to join into, enjoin. See **Enjoin.**

INJURE, to hurt, harm. (F.—L.) (Really made from the sb. *injury*, which was in much earlier use.) In Shak. As You Like It, iii. 5. 9. Cf. F. *injurier*, 'to wrong, injure, misuse;' Cot.—Late L. *iniūriāre*; for L. *iniūriārī*, to do harm to.—L. *iniūria*, an injury.—L. *iniūrius*, wrongful, unjust.—L. *in-*, neg. prefix; and *iūr-*, stem of *iūs*, law, right; see **Just.** Der. *injur-y*, ME. *iniurie*, Wyclif, Col. iii. 25, from AF. *injurie*, Phil. de Thaun, Bestiary, l. 395, rather than from OF. *injure*, an injury (the usual form), both forms answering to L. *iniūria*, an injury; *injuri-ous*, *injuri-ous-ly*, *-ness.* And see below.

INJUSTICE, want of justice. (F.—L.) 'If he be sene to exercise *injustyce* or wrong;' Sir T. Elyot, The Governour, b. iii. c. 4.—F. *injustice*, 'injustice;' Cot.—L. *iniustitia.* See **In-** (3) and **Justice.**

INK, a fluid for writing with, usually black. (F.—L.—Gk.) '*Inke*, encaustum;' Prompt. Parv. p. 261. Older form *enke*, Wyclif, Jer. xxxvi. 18.—AF. *enke*, A. Neckam, in Wright's Vocab. i. 116, last line; OF. *enque*, ink (Littré); the mod. F. form being *encre*, with inserted *r.*—L. *encaustum*, the purple red ink used by the later Roman emperors; neut. of *encaustus*, burnt in, encaustic.—Gk. ἔγκαυστος, burnt in. See **Encaustic.** ¶ Littré remarks that the accent on the L. *encaustum* varied; from *éncaustum* was derived the OF. *enque*, whilst from *encaústum* was derived the Ital. *inchiostro* (ink). Der. *ink-y*; *ink-bottle*, *ink-stand*; *ink-horn*, Ezek. ix. 2 (A.V.), but otherwise almost obsolete.

INKLE, a kind of tape. (Du.?) In Shak. L. L. L. iii. 140; Wint. Ta. iv. 4. 208. 'White *ynkell*;' Harman, Caveat (E.E.T.S.), p. 65. Spelt *inkyll* in Arnold's Chron.; ed. 1811, p. 237; '*brod enkell*,' broad tape; Wills and Inventories from Durham, p. 103 (1582). Prob. from MDu. *inckel* (Oudemans), Du. *enkel*, single (as opposed to double), which may have been applied to a commoner sort of tape. No certain connexion is known; but WFlem. *inkelooge* or *enkelooge*, lit. 'single-eye,' is a term in lace-making, referring to the edging of the lace (De Bo). Koolman has *enkel däken*, a single coverlet; cf. Dan. *enkelt-garn*, single yarn (Larsen).

INKLING, a hint, intimation. (Scand.?) In Shak. Hen. VIII, ii. 1. 140; Cor. i. 1. 59. 'What cause hee hadde soo to thynke, harde it is to say, whyther hee, being toward him, any thynge knewe that hee suche thynge purposed, or otherwyse had any *inkelynge* thereof; for hee was not likelye to speake it of noughte;' Sir T. More, Works, p. 38 a. *Inkling* is a verbal sb. formed from the ME. verb *incle.* 'To *incle* the truthe;' Alisaunder, ed. Skeat, 616 (in Appendix to Will. of Palerne). '[Alexander] herd a *nyngk-iling* [whispered mention] of his name;' Wars of Alexander, l. 2968; where *a nyngkiling* = *an yngkiling.* Origin unknown; perhaps allied to Swed. *enkel*, single, Dan. *enkelt.* Cf. Swed. *et enkelt ord*, a single word; Dan. *enkelte bemærkninger*, a few stray remarks; MDu. *enckelinge*, 'a falling or a diminishing of notes;' Hexham. Kilian has MDu. '*eenckelen den sanck* [song], ornare cantum symphonia; . . . voce remittente canere.' See **Inkle.**

INLAND, an inner part of the country. (E.) Orig. a sb., signifying a place near some great town or centre, where superior civilisation is supposed to be found. The counties lying round London are still, in a similar spirit, called 'home' counties. Used in contrast to *upland*, which signified a remote country district where manners were rough. See Shak. Tw. Nt. iv. 1. 52; Hen. V, i. 2. 142; &c. Cf. AS. *inland* (a legal term), a domain; see Laws of King Edgar, i. 1, in Thorpe, Ancient Laws, i. 263; also p. 432, last line but one.—AS. *in*, within; and *land*, land, country. Cf. Icel. *inlendr*, native. See **In** and **Land.** Der. *inland*, adj. As You Like It, ii. 7. 96; *inland-er*, Holland, tr. of Pliny, b. iii. c. 11, l. 7 (end).

INLAY, to lay within, ornament with inserted pieces. (E.) In Shak. Merch. Ven. v. 59; Cymb. v. 5. 352. From **In** and **Lay.** Der. *inlay-er*; *inlaid* (pp. of the verb).

INLET, a place of ingress; a small bay. (E.) The orig. sense is 'admission' or 'ingress;' hence, a place of ingress, esp. from the sea to the land. Spelt *inlate*: 'The king o blis will haf *inlate*' = the king of glory will have admission, must be admitted; Cursor Mundi,

1807%. From AS. *in*, in ; and *lǽtan*, to let. Cf. the phr. ' to *let in*.'
+G. *einlass*, place of ingress ; Low Gk. *inlāt* (Schambach). See **In**
and Let (1).

INLY, adj., inward ; adv., inwardly. (E.) As adj. in Two Gent.
ii. 7. 18 ; commonly an adv., Temp. v. 200. ME. *inly* (chiefly as
adv.), Chaucer, Troil. i. 640. AS. *inlic*, adj. inward, Ælfred, tr. of
Beda, b. iii. c. 15 ; whence *inlice*, adv. inwardly. — AS. *in*, in ; and
lic, like ; see **In and Like**.

INMATE, one who lodges in the same place with another,
a lodger, co-inhabitant. (E.) In Minsheu ; and Milton, P. L. ix.
495, xii. 166. First in 1589. From **In**, prep. within ; and **Mate**,
a companion, q. v.

INMOST, INNERMOST ; see under **In**.

INN, a large lodging-house, hotel, house of entertainment. (E.)
ME. *in*, inn ; Ancren Riwle, p. 260, l. 6 ; dat. *inne*, P. Plowman,
B. viii. 4. AS. *in*, inn, sb. ; Grein, ii. 140. Allied to AS. *in*, inn,
adv. within ; AS. *in*, prep. in ; see **In.**+Icel. *inni*, an inn ; cf. *inni*,
adv. indoors ; *inn*, adv. indoors ; from *in*, the older form of *ī*, prep.
in. Der. *inn*, verb (see **Inning**) ; *inn-holder* ; *inn-keeper*, 1 Hen. IV,
iv. 2. 51.

INNATE, in-born, native. (L.) ' Your *innat* sapience ;' Hoccleve, De Regimine Principum, 2130. Also formerly spelt *innated* ;
see examples in Nares. — L. *innātus*, in-born ; pp. of *innascī*, to be
born in. — L. *in*, in ; and *nascī*, to be born ; see **Native**. Der.
innate-ly, -ness.

INNAVIGABLE, impassable by ships. (F. — L.) In Cockeram
(1642). ' Th' *innavigable* flood ;' Dryden, tr. of Virgil, vi. 161. —
F. *innavigable*. — L. *innāuigābilis*. From **In-** (3) and **Navigable**.

INNER, INNERMOST ; see under **In**.

INNING, the securing of grain ; a turn at cricket. (E.) As
a cricket term, invariably used in the pl. *innings*, though only one
side has an *inning* at a time (first in 1746). Merely a peculiar use
of the verbal sb. formed from the verb to *inn*, i. e. to house or secure
corn when reaped, also to lodge. Cf. ' All was *inned* at last into the
king's barn ;' Bacon, Hist. Hen. VII, ed. Lumby, p. 65, l. 6. The
verb *to inn* is from the sb. **Inn**, q. v. Cf. AS. *innung*, a dwelling ;
Liber Scintillarum, 11. 18.

INNOCENT, harmless, not guilty. (F. — L.) ME. *innocent*,
Chaucer, C. T. 5038 (B 618). *Innocence* also occurs, id. 11905
(F 1601). — F. *innocent*, ' innocent ;' Cot. — L. *innocent-*, stem of
innocens, harmless. — L. *in-*, not ; and *nocens*, harmful, pres. part. of
nocēre, to hurt ; see **In-** (3) and **Noxious**. Der. *innocent-ly, innocence* ; *innocenc-y*, Gen. xx. 5 (A. V.). And see **Innocuous**.

INNOCUOUS, harmless. (L.) Sir T. Browne has *innocuously*,
Vulg. Errors, b. iii. c. 28, § last. Englished from L. *innocuus*, harmless ; by change from *-us* to *-ous*, as in numerous instances. — L. *in-*,
not ; and *nocuus*, harmful, from *nocēre*, to harm ; see **Innocent**.
Der. *innocuous-ly, -ness*. Doublet, *innoxious*.

INNOVATE, to introduce something new. (L.) In Levins.
Shak. has *innovation*, Haml. ii. 2. 347 ; *innovator*, Cor. iii. 1. 175. —
L. *innouātus*, pp. of *innouāre*, to renew. — L. *in*, in ; and *nouāre*, to
make new, from *nouus*, new ; see **In-** (2) and **Novel**. Der.
innovat-ion, innovat-or.

INNOXIOUS, harmless. (L.) ' Benign and of *innoxious* qualities ;' Sir T. Browne, Vulg. Errors, b. iv. c. 13, § 25. — L. *innoxius*,
harmless. From **In-** (3) and **Noxious**. Der. *innoxious-ly*.

INNUENDO, INUENDO, an indirect hint. (L.) The
spelling *inuendo*, though not uncommon, is incorrect. ' *Innuendo* is
a law term, most used in declarations and other pleadings ; and the
office of this word is onely to declare and ascertain the person or
thing which was named uncertain before ; as to say, he (*innuendo*, the
plaintiff) is a thief ; when as there was mention before of another
person ;' Blount's Gloss., ed. 1674. — L. *innuendō*, i. e. by intimation ;
gerund of *innuere*, to nod towards, intimate. — L. *in*, in, towards ;
and *nuere*, to nod. See **In-** (2) and **Nutation**.

INNUMERABLE, that cannot be counted. (F. — L.) ME.
innumerable, Ayenbite of Inwyt, p. 267, l. 17. — F. *innumerable*, ' innumerable ;' Cot. — L. *innumerābilis*. — L. *in-*, not ; and *numerābilis*,
that can be counted, from *numerāre*, to number ; see **Number**.
Der. *innumerabl-y*.

INNUTRITIOUS, not nutritious. (L.) *Innutrition*, sb., first
found in 1796 ; the adj. appears to be of the same date. From **In-**
(3) and **Nutritious**. Der. So also *in-nutrition*.

INOBSERVANT, not observant, heedless. (L.) *Inobservance*
is used by Bacon (R.). — L. *inobseruant-*, stem of *inobseruans* ; from
In- (3) and **Observant** ; see **Observe**. Der. *inobservance*.

INOCULATE, to engraft, introduce into the human system. (L.)
' The Turkish *inoculation* for the small pox was introduced to this
country under the name of *ingrafting*' (R.) ; he refers to Lady Mary
W. Montague's Letters, let. 31. But *inoculate* in old authors signifies to engraft ; see Holland, tr. of Pliny, b. xix. c. 8, sect. on

' graffing herbs ;' and Hamlet, iii. 1. 119. — L. *inoculātus*, pp. of
inoculāre, to engraft, insert a graft. — L. *in*, in ; and *oculus*, an eye,
also a bud or burgeon of a plant ; see **Eye**. Der. *inoculat-ion*.

INODOROUS, not odorous. (L.) In Kersey, ed. 1715. — L.
inodōrus, inodorous. From **In-** (3) and **Odorous** ; see **Odour**.

INOFFENSIVE, giving no offence. (F. — L.) In Milton,
P. L. v. 345, viii. 164. From **In-** (3) and **Offensive** ; see **Offend**.
Der. *inoffensive-ly, -ness*.

INOFFICIAL, not official. (F. — L.) Modern ; but once in
1632. From **In-** (3) and **Official** ; see **Office**. Der. *inofficial-ly*.

INOPERATIVE, not operative. (F. — L.) In South's Sermons,
vol. vi. ser. 4 (R.). From **In-** (3) and **Operative**.

INOPPORTUNE, not opportune, unfitting. (F. — L.) ' An
inopportune education ;' Bp. Taylor, Great Exemplar, pt. iii. *ad* s. 15.
From **In-** (3) and **Opportune**. Der. *inopportune-ly*.

INORDINATE, unregulated, immoderate. (L.) Skelton has
inordinat, Why Come Ye Nat to Court, 1228 ; and *inordinatly*, 701.
And see Chaucer, C. T. (I 414). — L. *inordinātus*, irregular. — L. *in-*,
not ; and *ordinātus*, pp. of *ordināre*, to set in order, from *ordin-*,
stem of *ordo*, order ; see **Order**. Der. *inordinate-ly, -ness* ; *in-
ordinat-ion*.

INORGANIC, not organic. (F. — L. and Gk.) Formerly *inorganical* ; Blount's Gloss., ed. 1674. ' Organical or *inorganical* ;'
Burton, Anat. of Melancholy, p. 26 (R.). From **In-** (3) and **Organic**: see **Organ**. Der. *inorganic-al-ly* ; *inorgan-is-ed*.

INQUEST, a judicial inquiry. (F. — L.) ' And seththe thoru
enqueste [MS. anqueste] he let thorugh the contreies anquere ;' Beket,
l. 387 ; in S. Eng. Legendary, p. 117. — OF. *enqueste*, ' an inquest ;'
Cot. — Late L. *inquesta*, sb. ; from *inquesta*, fem. of *inquestus*, late substitution for *inquisītus*, pp. of *inquīrere*, to search into. See **Inquire**.
Doublet, *inquiry*.

INQUIETUDE, want of rest, disquiet. (F. — L.) In Phillips,
ed. 1658. — MF. *inquietude*, ' disquiet ;' Cot. — L. *inquiētūdo*, restless-
ness. — L. *in-*, not ; and *quiētūdo*, rest, from *quiētus*, quiet. See
Quiet.

INQUIRE, ENQUIRE, to search into or after. (L.) The
spelling *inquire* is Latin, but the word is really a modification of
the ME. *enquire*, (also) *enqueren* (see quot. under **Inquest**) ; from
OF. *enquerre* (Godefroy). Spelt *inquyre*, Spenser, F. Q. b. ii. introd.
st. 4. — L. *inquīrere*, pp. *inquisītus*, to search into. See **Enquire**.
Der. *inquir-er, inquir-ing, inquir-ing-ly* ; *inquir-y*, Spenser, F. Q.
vi. 4. 24 ; also *inquisit-ion*, Temp. i. 2. 35, from F. *inquisition*<L.
inquisītiōnem, acc. of *inquisītio*, a searching for, from pp. *inquisīt-us* ;
inquisit-ion-al ; *inquisit-or* (Levins), from L. *inquīsītor*, a searcher ;
inquisit-or-i-al, *inquisit-or-i-al-ly* ; *inquisit-ive*, ME. *inquisitif*, Gower,
C. A. i. 226 ; bk. ii. 1987, an OF. spelling of L. *inquisītiuus*, searching
into ; *inquisit-ive-ly, -ness*. And see *inquest*.

INROAD, a raid into an enemy's country. (E.) ' Many hot
inroads They make in Italy ;' Ant. and Cleop. i. 4. 50. ' An *inrode*,
an invasion ;' Baret (1580). Compounded of *in*, prep., and *road*, the
Southern E. equivalent of North E. *raid*, a riding, from AS. *rād*,
a riding. See **Road, Raid, Ride**. ¶ The change from AS. *ā* to
later *oa* is the usual one.

INSANE, not sane, mad. (L.) In Macb. i. 3. 84. — L. *insānus*,
not sane. See **In-** (3) and **Sane**. Der. *insane-ly, insan-i-ty*.

INSATIABLE, not satiable. (F. — L.) ' Gredynes *insaciable* ;'
Hoccleve, De Regimine Principum, l. 1172. — F. *insatiable*, ' insatiate,
unsatiable ;' Cot. — L. *insatiābilis*. — L. *in-*, not ; and *satiāre*, to satiate.
See **In-** (3) and **Satiate**. Der. *insatiabl-y, insatiable-ness, insatia-
bili-ty*. Also *insatiate*, Skelton, Colyn Cloute, 1181 ; from L. *in-
satiātus*, not sated.

INSCRIBE, to engrave as on a monument, engrave, imprint
deeply. (L.) In Shak. Hen. VIII, iii. 2. 315. — L. *inscrībere*, pp.
inscriptus, to write upon. — L. *in*, upon ; and *scribere*, to write. See
Scribe. Der. *inscrib-er* ; also *inscription*, Merch. Ven. ii. 7. 4, from
F. *inscription*<L. *inscriptiōnem*, acc. of *inscriptio*, an inscription, from
pp. *inscriptus* ; *inscript-ive*.

INSCRUTABLE, that cannot be scrutinised. (F. — L.) ' God's
inscrutable will ;' Barnes, Works, p. 278, col. 1. — F. *inscrutable*,
' inscrutable ;' Cot. — L. *inscrūtābilis*. — L. *in-*, not ; and **scrūtābilis*
(not found), formed from *scrūtārī*, to scrutinise. See **Scrutiny**.
Der. *inscrutabl-y, inscrutable-ness, inscrutabili-ty*.

INSECT, a small invertebrate animal, as described below.
(F. — L.) ' Wel may they all be called *insecta*, by reason of those
cuts and *diuisions*, which some haue about the necke, others in the
breast and belly, the which do go round and part the members of
the body, hanging together only by a little pipe and fistulous con-
ueiance ;' Holland, tr. of Pliny, b. xi. c. 1. — F. *insecte*, ' an insect ;'
Cot. — L. *insectum*. ' Iure omnia *insecta* appellata ab *incisuris*, quæ
nunc ceruicum loco, nunc pectorum atque alui, præcincta separant
membra, tenui modo fistula cohærentia ;' Pliny, b. xi. c. 1, § 1. —

L. *insectus*, pp. of *insecāre*, to cut into. — L. *in*, into; and *secāre*, to cut. See **Section**. ¶ The L. *insectum* is a rendering of Gk. ἔντομον, an insect. Der. *insect-ile*; *insecti-vorous* (from L. *uorāre*, to devour).

INSECURE, not secure. (L.) Bp. Taylor has '*insecure* apprehensions;' The Great Exemplar, pt. i. *ad* s. 2; also '*insecurities* and inconveniencies;' id. ib. pt. i. *ad* s. 6 (R.). — L. *insēcūrus*, not secure. See **In-** (3) and **Secure**. Der. *insecure-ly*, *insecur-i-ty*.

INSENSATE, void of sense. (L.) In Milton, P. L. vi. 787; and Skelton, Works, i. 209. — L. *insensātus*, irrational. — L. *in-*, not; and *sensātus*, gifted with sense, from *sensus*, sense; see **In-** (3) and **Sense**.

INSENSIBLE, devoid of feeling. (F. — L.) In Levins; and Shak. Cor. iv. 5. 239. — F. *insensible*, 'insensible.' — L. *insensibilis*. From **In-** (3) and **Sensible**; see **Sense**. Der. *insensibl-y*, *insensibili-ty*. So also *in-sentient*.

INSEPARABLE, not separable. (F. — L.) In Sir P. Sidney, Apol. for Poetry, ed. Arber, p. 49, l. 36. — F. *inseparable*, 'inseparable;' Cot. — L. *insēparābilis*. From **In-** (3) and **Separable**; see **Separate**. Der. *inseparabl-y*, *inseparable-ness*, *inseparabili-ty*.

INSERT, to join into, introduce into. (L.) 'I haue . . . *inserted*;' Sir T. More, Works, p. 1053 f. — L. *insertus*, pp. of *inserere*, to insert, introduce into. — L. *in*, into; and *serere*, to join, bind, connect; see **In-** (2) and **Series**. Der. *insert-ion*.

INSESSORIAL, having feet (as birds) formed for perching on trees. (L.) Scientific and modern. Formed, in imitation of L. *sessor*, a sitter, from *insess-us*, pp. of *insidēre*. to sit upon. — L. *in*, upon; and *sedēre*, to sit; see **Sit**.

INSHRINE, the same as **Enshrine**. (E. *and* L.)

INSIDE, the inward side or part. (E.) Sir T. More, Works, p. 1256 f, has 'on the *outsyde*' opposed to ' on the *insyde*.' Formed from **In** and **Side**.

INSIDIOUS, ensnaring, treacherous. (F. — L.) In Blount's Gloss., ed. 1674. — F. *insidieux*, 'deceitfull;' Cot. — L. *insidiōsus*, cunning, deceitful. — L. *insidiæ*, sb. pl. (1) troops of men who lie in wait, (2) a plot, snare, cunning wiles. — L. *insidēre*, to sit in, take up a position, lie in wait. — L. *in-*, in; and *sedēre*, to sit, cognate with E. *sit*; see **In-** (2) and **Sit**. Der. *insidious-ly*, *-ness*.

INSIGHT, the power of seeing into. (E.) ME. *insight*, *insiht*. 'Salomon, Which hadde of euery thing *insihte*' = Solomon, who had insight into everything; Gower, C. A. ii. 80; bk. iv. 2340. Spelt *insiht*, Layamon, 30497. From **In** and **Sight**. + Du. *inzicht*, insight, design; G. *einsicht*, insight, intelligence.

INSIGNIA, signs or badges of office. (L.) Borrowed from L. *insignia*, pl. of *insigne*, a distinctive mark, which was orig. the neut. of the adj. *insignis*, remarkable. See **Ensign**.

INSIGNIFICANT, poor, mean, vile. (L.) ' Little *insignificant* monk;' Milton, A Defence of the People of England (R.). From **In-** (3) and **Significant**; see **Sign**. Der. *insignificant-ly*, *insignificance*, *insignificanc-y*. So also *in-significative*.

INSINCERE, not sincere. (F. — L.) ' But ah! how *insincere* are all our joys;' Dryden, Annus Mirabilis, st. 209. From **In-** (3) and **Sincere**. Der. *insincere-ly*, *insincer-i-ty*.

INSINUATE, to introduce artfully, hint. (L.) In Levins; and in Shak. Rich. II, iv. 165. — L. *insinuātus*, pp. of *insinuāre*, to introduce by winding or bending. — L. *in*, in; and *sinuāre*, to wind about, from *sinus*, a bend. See **Sinuous**. Der. *insinuat-ing*, *insinuat-ing-ly*; *insinuat-ion*, K. John, v. 1. 68, from F. *insinuation*, ' an insinuation,' Cot.; *insinuat-or*, *insinuat-ive*.

INSIPID, tasteless. (F. — L.) ' His salt, if I may dare to say so, [is] almost *insipid*,' spoken of Horace; Dryden, Discourse on Satire; Poems, ed. 1856, p. 377, l. 7. — F. *insipide*, 'unsavory, smacklesse;' Cot. — L. *insipidus*, tasteless. — L. *in-*, not; and *sapidus*, welltasting, savoury. See **Savour**. Der. *insipid-ly*, *insipid-i-ty*.

INSIST, to dwell upon in discourse. (F. — L.) In Shak. Jul. Cæs. ii. 1. 245. — F. *insister*, ' to insist on;' Cot. — L. *insistere*, to set foot on, persist. — L. *in*, upon; and *sistere*, to set, causal verb formed from *stāre*, cognate with E. **Stand**.

INSNARE, the same as **Ensnare**. (E.)

INSOBRIETY, intemperance. (F. — L.) In Howell, Familiar Letters, vol. iii. let. 26 (end). From **In-** (3) and **Sobriety**; see **Sober**.

INSOLENT, contemptuous, rude. (F. — L.) ME. *insolent*, Chaucer, C. T. Pers. Tale, De Superbia (I 399). — F. *insolent*, 'insolent, malapert, saucy;' Cot. — L. *insolent-*, stem of *insolens*, not customary, unusual, haughty, insolent. — L. *in-*, not; and *solens*, pres. part. of *solēre*, to be accustomed, to be wont (root unknown); or from L. *in-*, against, and *sol-*, weak grade of the vb. *to swell* (AS. *swellan*). Der. *insolent-ly*; *insolence*, Court of Love, l. 936; Chaucer, C. T., I 391; *insolenc-y*, in the Bible Wordbook.

INSOLIDITY, want of solidity. (F. — L.) Used in 1578. From **In-** (3) and **Solidity**; see **Solid**.

INSOLUBLE, not soluble, that cannot be solved. (F. — L.) *Insolubles*, in the sense of ' insoluble problems,' occurs in Sir T. More, Works, p. 355 b; cf. p. 165, col. 2. See Wyclif, Heb. vii. 16 (earlier version). — F. *insoluble*, 'insoluble;' Cot. — L. *insolūbilis*. See **In-** (3) and **Soluble**. Der. *insolubl-y*, *insoluble-ness*, *insolubili-ty*. And see below.

INSOLVENT, unable to pay debts. (L.) In Kersey's Dict., ed. 1715. 'If his father was *insolvent* by his crime;' Bp. Taylor, Rule of Conscience, b. iii. c. 2. Formed from L. *in-*, not; and *soluent-*, stem of *soluens*, pres. part. of *soluere*, to solve, to pay; see **Solve**. Der. *insolvenc-y* (Kersey).

INSOMNIA, sleeplessness. (L.) First as *insomnie*; in Cockeram (1623). — L. *insomnia*. — L. *insomnis*, adj., sleepless. — L. *in-*, not; and *somnus*, sleep. See **Somnolence**.

INSOMUCH, to such a degree. (E.) '*Insomuch* I say I know you are;' As You Like It, v. 2. 60. From **In**, **So**, and **Much**. See **Inasmuch**.

INSPECT, to look into, examine. (L.) In Kersey, ed. 1715; Cockeram (1623) has *inspected*. [But the sb. *inspeccioun* is in much earlier use, and occurs in Gower, C. A. iii. 46; bk. vi. 1349.] — L. *inspectāre*, to observe; frequent. of *inspicere*, to look into. — L. *in*, in; and *specere*, to spy; see **Spy**. Der. *inspect-or*, *inspect-or-ship*; also *inspect-ion* = F. *inspection*, ' an inspection ' (Cot.), from L. *inspectiōnem*, acc. of *inspectio*, a looking into.

INSPIRE, to breathe into, infuse, influence. (F. — L.) ME. *enspiren*, Chaucer, C. T. 6; Gower, C. A. iii. 226; bk. vii. 4003. — OF. *enspirer*, later *inspirer*, the latter being the form in Cotgrave. — L. *inspirāre*, to breathe into, inspire. — L. *in*, into; and *spirāre*, to breathe; see **Spirit**. Der. *inspir-able*, *inspir-at-ion*, Robert of Brunne, Handlyng Synne, l. 7746, *inspir-at-or-y*, *inspir-er*; also *in-spirit* (Pope, To Mrs. M. B., l. 13), from *in* and *spirit*.

INSPISSATE, to make thick, as fluids. (L.) ' The sugar doth *inspissate* the spirits of the wine;' Bacon, Nat. Hist. § 726. — L. *inspissātus*, pp. of *inspissāre*, to thicken. — L. *in*, into, here used as intensive prefix; and *spissāre*, to thicken, from *spissus*, dense.

INSTABILITY, want of stability. (F. — L.) ' For some, lamentyng the *instabilitee* of the Englishe people;' Hall's Chron. Hen. IV, an. 1. § 15. — F. *instabilité*, 'instability;' Cot. — L. *instābilitātem*, acc. of *instābilitās*. — L. *instābilis*, unstable. See **In-** (3) and **Stable**, adj.

INSTALL, INSTAL, to place in a stall, seat, or office. (F. — Low L. — OHG.) Though the word might easily have been coined from Eng. elements, yet, as a fact, it was borrowed. ' To be *installed* or inthronised at Yorke;' Hall's Cron. Hen. VIII, an. 22. § 9. — F. *installer*, ' to install, settle, establish, place surely in ;' Cot. — Low L. *installāre*, to install. — L. *in*, in; and Low L. *stallum*, a stall, seat, place to sit in; Ducange. β. The Low L. *stallum* is from OHG. *stal*, G. *stall*, a stall, place, cognate with E. *stall*. See **Stall**. Der. *install-at-ion*, from MF. *installation* (Cot.) ; *instal-ment*, formerly used in the sense of installation, Shak. Rich. III, iii. 1. 163; a coined word.

INSTANCE, solicitation, occasion, example. (F. — L.) ' At his *instance*;' Chaucer, C. T. 9485 (E 1611). — F. *instance*, 'instance, earnestness, urgency, importunitie;' Cot. — L. *instantia*, a being near, urgency. — L. *instant-*, stem of *instans*, present, urgent; pres. part. of *instāre*, to be at hand, press, urge. — L. *in*, upon, near; and *stāre*, to stand, cognate with E. **Stand**, q. v. Der. *instant*, adj. urgent, Luke, xxiii. 23, from L. *instant-*, stem of *instans*; *instant-ly* = urgently, Luke, vii. 4; also *instant*, sb. = moment, Spenser, F. Q. ii. 5. 11, from F. *instant*, 'an instant, moment' (Cot.), from the same L. *instant-*. Also *instant-an-e-ous*, Thomson, To the Memory of Lord Talbot, l. 27, coined as if from a L. **instant-āneus*, made by analogy with L. *mōment-āneus* ; *instant-an-e-ous-ly*.

INSTATE, to put in possession. (F. — L.) In Shak. Meas. v. 249. Coined from *in-*, equivalent to F. *en-*, prefix; and *state*. See **In-** (2) and **State**. Der. *re-instate*.

INSTEAD, in the place. (E.) ME. *in stede*, Mandeville's Travels, ch. 21, ed. Halliwell, p. 227. We also find *on stede* nearly in the same sense. ' And he toc him *on sunes stede*' = and he took him *in place of a son*, received him as a son; Genesis and Exodus, ed. Morris, 2637. From AS. *on stede*, lit. in the place. ' On þæra nægla *stede*' = in the place of the nails; John, xx. 25. See **In** and **Stead**.

INSTEP, the upper part of the foot, rising from the toes to the ankle. (E.) In The Spectator, no. 48. A somewhat rare word; formerly also spelt *instup* or *instop*. ' Coudepied, the *instup*;' Cot. Minsheu, ed. 1627, refers, under *Instep*, to *Instop*; and also gives: ' the *instop* of the foot,' as well as '*Instuppe*, vide *Instoppe*.' But Palsgrave, in 1530, has the form *insteppe*; and A. Borde, ab. 1542, has *instep*, Introd. of Knowledge, ed. Furnivall, p. 189, l. 26. β. It would seem that *instep* and *instop* (or *instup*) were both in use; the former must be from *in*, prep. in, and ME. *steppen*, to step. The latter may contain the strong grade *stŏp-* of AS. *steppan*, to step; cf. AS. *stŏp-el*, a footprint, OSax. *stŏp-o*, a step. The reference seems to be to the movement of the instep in walking. See **Step**.

INSTIGATE, to urge on, incite. (L.) In Shak. Merry Wives, iii. 5. 77; and in Levins. — L. *instīgātus*, pp. of *instīgāre*, to goad on, incite. — L. *in*, in, on; and **stig-*, to stick, prick, sting, allied to L. *stinguere*, to prick or scratch out, to quench. See **Sting, Distinguish**. See Brugmann, i. § 633. **Der.** *instigat-ion*, Wint. Ta. ii. 1. 163, from F. *instigation*, 'an instigation;' Cot.; *instigat-or*; and see *instinct*.

INSTIL, to infuse drop by drop. (F.—L.) 'A fayhfull preacher . . . doth *instill* it into us;' Fryth, Works, p. 166, col. 2. — F. *instiller*, 'to drop, trill, drizle;' Cot. — L. *instillāre*, to pour in by drops. — L. *in*, in; and *stilla*, a drop. See **Still** (2). **Der.** *instill-at-ion*, from F. *instillation*, 'an instillation;' Cot.

INSTINCT, a natural impulse or instigation, esp. that by which animals are guided aright. (F.—L.; *or* L.) 'A secrete inward *instincte* of nature;' Sir T. More, Works, p. 521 c. — F. *instinct*, 'an instinct or inclination;' Cot. [Or perhaps directly from Latin.] — L. *instinctum*, acc. of *instinctus*, an instigation, impulse; cf. *instinctus*, pp. of *instinguere*, to goad on, instigate. — L. *in*, on; and *stinguere*, to stick, prick; see **Instigate**. **Der.** *instinct-ive*, *instinct-ive-ly*, Temp. i. 2. 148; also *instinct*, adj. = instigated, moved, Pope, tr. of Iliad, b. xviii. l. 442, from L. pp. *instinctus*.

INSTITUTE, to establish, set up, erect, appoint. (L.) In Shak. 1 Hen. VI, iv. 1. 162; Tam. Shrew, i. 1. 8; and in Palsgrave. — L. *institūtus*, pp. of *instituere*, to set, plant, establish. — L. *in*, in (with little force); and *statuere*, to place, from *status*, a position. See **Statute, State**. **Der.** *institute*, sb.; *institut-ion*, Meas. for Meas. i. 1. 11, from F. *institution*, 'an institution;' Cot.; *institut-ion-al*, *institut-ion-ar-y*, *institut-ive*.

INSTRUCT, to inform, teach, order. (L.) 'But *instructe* hem,' i. e. them; Lord Rivers, Dictes and Sayings, pr. by Caxton, fol. 4, l. 7. Properly a pp. as in 'informed and *instructe* in all thynges;' Caxton, Golden Legend, Conv. of St. Paul, § 6. — L. *instructus*, pp. of *instruere*, to build into, instruct. — L. *in*, into; and *struere*, to build; see **Structure**. **Der.** *instruct-ible*; *instruct-ion*; L. L. L. iv. 2. 81, from F. *instruction*, 'an instruction,' Cot.; *instruct-ive*, *instruct-ive-ly*, *-ness*; *instruct-or*, *-ress*; and see *instrument*.

INSTRUMENT, a tool, machine producing music, contract in writing, a means. (F.—L.) ME. *instrument* = a musical instrument, Chaucer, Parl. of Foules, 197. — F. *instrument*, 'an instrument, implement, engine,' &c.; Cot. — L. *instrūmentum*, formed with suffix *-mentum*, and prefix *in-*, from *struere*, to build; see **Instruct**. **Der.** *instrument-al*, *instrument-al-ly*, *instrument-al-i-ty*, *instrument-al-ist*, *instrument-at-ion*.

INSUBJECTION, want of subjection. (F.—L.) A late word; added to Johnson by Todd. From **In-** (3) and **Subjection**.

INSUBORDINATE, not subordinate. (L.) Quite modern. From **In-** (3) and **Subordinate**. **Der.** *insubordinat-ion*.

INSUFFERABLE, intolerable. (F.—L.) 'Perceiving still her wrongs *insufferable* were;' Drayton, Polyolbion, s. 6. l. 141. Coined with prefix *in-* (= not) and suffix *-able* from **Suffer**, q. v. **Der.** *insufferab-ly*, Milton, P. L. ix. 1084.

INSUFFICIENT, not sufficient. (L.) Chaucer has *insufficient*, C. T., D 1960. Shak. has *insufficience*, Wint. Ta. i. 1. 16; also *insufficiency*, Mid. Nt. Dr. ii. 2. 128. — L. *insufficient-*, stem of *insufficiens*. From **In-** (3) and **Sufficient**; see **Suffice**. **Der.** *insufficient-ly*, *insufficience*, *insufficienc-y*.

INSULAR, belonging to an island. (L.) In Cotgrave, to translate F. *insulaire*. — L. *insulāris*, insular. — L. *insula*, an island. Perhaps allied to Gael. *innis*, an island; see **Inch** (2). **Der.** *insular-ly*, *insular-i-ty*; also *insul-ate*, from L. *insulātus*, made like an island; *insul-at-or*, *insul-at-ion*. And see **Isle, Isolate**.

INSULT, to treat with indignity, affront. (F.—L.) In Shak. Rich. II, iv. 254. — F. *insulter*, 'to insult;' Cot. — L. *insultāre*, to leap upon or against, scoff at, insult; frequent. form of *insilīre*, to leap into, spring upon. — L. *in*, upon; and *salīre*, to leap. See **Salient**. **Der.** *insult*, sb. = MF. *insult*, 'an affront,' Cot.; *insult-er*, *insult-ment*, Cymb. iii. 5. 145.

INSUPERABLE, insurmountable. (F. — L.) In Caxton, Eneydos, ch. xii. p. 44; and Milton, P. L. iv. 138. — F. *insuperable*, 'insuperable;' Cot. — L. *insuperābilis*, insurmountable. — L. *in-*, not; and *superāre*, to surmount, from *super*, above. See **Super-**. **Der.** *insuperabl-y*, *insuperabili-ty*.

INSUPPORTABLE, intolerable. (F.—L.) Accented as *insúpportable*, Spenser, F. Q. i. 7. 11. — F. *insupportable*, 'unsupportable;' Cot. — F. *in-* < L. *in-*, not; and F. *supportable*, from *supporter*, to support; see **Support**. **Der.** *insupportab-ly*, *insupportable-ness*.

INSUPPRESSIBLE, that cannot be suppressed. (L.) A coined word; first in 1610. Also used by Young, On Orig. Composition (R.). Shak. has *insuppressive*, Jul. Cæs. ii. 1. 134. From **In-** (3) and **Suppress**.

INSURE, to make sure, secure. (F.—L.) ME. *ensure*, Chaucer, C. T. 12971 (B 1231; Petworth MS.; most MSS. have *assure*). — AF. *enseurer* (Godefroy); used instead of OF. *asseurer* (Cot.), *aseurer* (Burguy), by the substitution of the prefix *en* (< L. *in*) for the prefix *a* (< L. *ad*). The form *-seurer* is from OF. *seur*, sure. See **In-** (2) and **Sure**; also **Assure**. **Der.** *insur-able*, *insur-er*, *insur-ance*; *insur-anc-er*, Dryden, Threnodia Augustalis, 186.

INSURGENT, rebellious. (L.) A late word, added by Todd to Johnson's Dict. — L. *insurgent-*, stem of pres. part. of *insurgere*, to rise up. — L. *in*, upon; and *surgere*, to rise; see **Surge**. **Der.** *insurgenc-y*; and see *insurrection*.

INSURMOUNTABLE, not surmountable. (F.—L.) In Phillips, ed. 1696. — F. *insurmontable*, 'unsurmountable;' Cot. — F. *in-* < L. *in-*, not; and *surmontable*, from *surmonter*, to surmount; see **Surmount**. **Der.** *insurmountabl-y*.

INSURRECTION, rebellion. (F.—L.) In Shak. 1 Hen. IV, v. 1. 79. — OF. *insurrection* (Hatzfeld). — L. *insurrectiōnem*, acc. of *insurrectio*, an insurrection; cf. *insurrectus*, pp. of *insurgere*, to rise up, rebel; see **Insurgent**. **Der.** *insurrection-al*, *insurrection-ar-y*, *insurrection-ist*.

INTACT, untouched. (L.) In Bailey, ed. 1721. — L. *intactus*, untouched. — L. *in-*, not; and *tactus*, pp. of *tangere*, to touch; see **Tangent, Tact, Intangible**.

INTAKE, an enclosure from a moor. (Scand.) Northern; see E. D. D. — Norw. *inntak*, a taking in; from *inn*, in, and *taka*, to take. See **Take**. Cf. Swed. *intaga*, an enclosed space that was formerly part of a common; *intaga*, to take in (Widegren).

INTANGIBLE, that cannot be touched. (L.) 'Intactible or Intangible;' Kersey, ed. 1715. From **In-** (3) and **Tangible**.

INTAGLIO, an engraving, esp. a gem in which the design is hollowed out. (Ital.—L.) Evelyn has *intaglias*, Diary, 1 Mar., 1644; and *intaglios*, 23 Oct., 1654. — Ital. *intaglio*, an engraving, sculpture, carving. — Ital. *intagliare*, to cut into, engrave. — Ital. *in* < L. *in*, in; and *tagliare*, to cut, from Late L. *taleāre*, to cut, esp. to cut twigs, from *talea*, a rod, stick, bar, twig. See **Entail** and **Tally**. **Der.** *intagli-at-ed*.

INTEGER, that which is whole or entire; a whole number. (L.) In Kersey, ed. 1715, as an arithmetical term; first in 1509. — L. *integer*, adj. whole, entire; lit. untouched, unharmed. — L. *in-*, not; and *tag-*, base of *tangere*, to touch; see **Tangent**. **Der.** *integr-al*, Blount's Gloss., ed. 1674, formed from *integr-um*, neut. of *integer* used as sb.; *integr-al-ly*, *integr-ate*, *integr-at-ion*, *integr-ant*; also *integr-i-ty*, Sir T. More, Works, p. 1337 h, from F. *integrité* (Cot.) < L. *integritātem*, acc. of *integritās*, soundness, blamelessness. Doublet, *entire*, q. v.

INTEGUMENT, a covering, skin. (L.) In Chapman, tr. of Homer, Il. xxii. l. 7 from end. — L. *integumentum*, a covering. — L. *in*, upon; and *tegere*, to cover. See **Teguement**. **Der.** *integument-ar-y*.

INTELLECT, the thinking principle, understanding. (F.—L.) ME. *intellect*, Chaucer, C. T. 2805 (A 2803). — OF. *intellect*, 'the intellect;' Cot. — L. *intellectum*, acc. of *intellectus*, perception, discernment; cf. *intellectus*, pp. of *intelligere*, to discern; see **Intelligence**. **Der.** *intellect-u-al*, Sir T. Elyot, The Governour, b. iii. c. 24. § 2; *intellect-u-al-ly*; *intellect-ion*, *intellect-ive*.

INTELLIGENCE, intellectual skill, news. (F.—L.) ME. *intelligence*, Gower, C. A. iii. 85; bk. vii. 28. — F. *intelligence*; Cot. — L. *intelligentia*, perception. — L. *intelligent-*, stem of *intelligens*, pres. part. of *intelligere*, to understand, lit. 'to choose between.' — L. *intel-*, for *inter*, between, before *l* following; and *legere*, to choose; see **Legend**. **Der.** *intelligenc-er*, Rich. III, iv. 4. 71; *intelligenc-ing*, Wint. Ta. ii. 3. 68; also *intelligent*, Wint. Ta. i. 2. 378, from L. *intelligent-*, stem of *intelligens*; *intelligent-ly*, *intelligent-i-al*; also *intelligible*, Wyclif, Wisdom, vii. 23, from F. *intelligible*, 'intelligible' (Cot.), from L. *intelligibilis*, perceptible to the senses, Wisdom, vii. 23 (Vulgate); *intelligibl-y*, *intelligibil-i-ty*.

INTEMPERANCE, want of temperance, excess. (F.—L.) Spelt *intemperaunce*, Spenser, F. Q. ii. 4. 36. — F. *intemperance*, 'intemperance;' Cot. — L. *intemperantia*, want of mildness or clemency, intemperance, excess. See **In-** (3) and **Temperance**. **Der.** (from L. *intemperātus*, untempered) *intemperate*, Meas. v. 98, and in Levins; *intemperate-ly*, *intemperate-ness*.

INTEND, to fix the mind upon, purpose. (F.—L.) ME. *entenden*, Gower, C. A. i. 12; prol. 253; later spelt *intend*, to bring it nearer Latin. — F. *entendre*, 'to understand, conceive, apprehend,' Cot.; whence *entendre à*, 'to study, mind, heed,' id. — L. *intendere*, to stretch out, extend, stretch to, bend, direct, apply the mind. — L. *in*, towards; and *tendere*, to stretch; see **Tend**. **Der.** *intend-ant*,

Kersey, ed. 1715, from MF. *intendant*, one of 'the foure overseers or controllers of the exchequer, at first brought in by king Francis the First' (Cot.), formed as a pres. part. from L. pres. part. *intendens*; *intend-anc-y*; *intend-ed*; *intend-ment*, As You Like It, i. 1. 140; also *intense*, q. v.: *intent*, q. v.

INTENSE, highly increased, esp. in tension, severe. (L.) In Milton, P. L. viii. 387.—L. *intensus*, stretched out, pp. of *intendere*, to stretch out; see **Intend.** Der. *intense-ly*, *intense-ness*, *intens-i-ty*; *intens-i-fy* (from F. suffix *-fier*<L. *-ficare*, for *facere*, to make); *intens-ive*, *intens-ive-ly*, *intens-ive-ness*.

INTENT, design, intention. (F.—L.) ME. *entente*, Chaucer, C. T. 960 (A 958); Ancren Riwle, p. 252, note *a*. Later, *intent*, Gower, C. A. ii. 262; bk. v. 4038.—F. *entente*, 'intention, purpose, meaning;' Cot. *Entente* is a participial sb. formed from the vb. *entendre*; see **Intend.** The adj. *intent* (Milton, P. L. ix. 786) is directly from L. *intentus*, pp. of *intendere*; *intent-ly*, *intent-ness*. Also *intent-ion*, Wint. Ta. i. 2. 138 (spelt *intencyone* in Prompt. Parv.), from F. *intention*, 'an intention, intent,' from L. *intentiōnem*, acc. of *intentio*, endeavour, effort, design; *intent-ion-al*, *intent-ion-al-ly*, *intention-ed*.

INTER, to bury. (F.—L.) ME. *enterren*. 'And with gret dule *entyrit* wes he;' Barbour's Bruce, xix. 224. Later, *inter*, K. John, v. 7. 99.—F. *enterrer*, 'to interre, bury;' Cot.—Late L. *interrāre*, to put into the ground, bury.—L. *in*, in; and *terra*, the earth; see **Terrace.** Der. *inter-ment* = ME. *enterement*, Gower, C. A. ii. 319, bk. v. 5727, from F. *enterrement*, 'an interring;' Cot.

INTER-, *prefix*, among, amongst, between. (L.) L. *inter-*, prefix; from *inter*, prep. between, among. A comparative form, answering to Skt. *antar*, within; and closely connected with L. *interus*, interior. See **Interior.** In a few cases, the final *r* becomes *l* before *l* following, as in *intel-lect*, *intel-ligence*. Most words with this prefix are purely Latin, but a few, as *inter-weave*, are hybrid. In some cases. *inter-* stands for the F. *entre-*.

INTERACTION, mutual action. (L.; *and* F.—L.) Modern; not in Todd's Johnson. Coined from **Inter-** and **Action.**

INTERCALATE, to insert between, said of a day in a calendar. (L.) In Raleigh, Hist. of World, b. ii. c. 3. s. 6. *Intercalation* is explained in Blount's Gloss., ed. 1674.—L. *intercalātus*, pp. of *intercalāre*, to proclaim that something has been inserted.—L. *inter*, between, among; and *calāre*, to proclaim; see **Calends.** Der. *intercalat-ion*; also *intercalar* = L. *intercalāris*; *intercalar-y* = L. *intercalārius*.

INTERCEDE, to go between, mediate, plead for one. (F.—L.) Milton has *intercede*, P. L. xi. 21; *intercession*, P. L. x. 228; *intercessour*, P. L. iii. 219.—MF. *interceder*; 'interceder *pour*, to intercede for;' Cot.—L. *intercēdere*, lit. to go between.—L. *inter*, between; and *cēdere*, to go; see **Inter-** and **Cede.** Der. *interced-ent*, *interced-ent-ly*; also (like pp. *intercessus*) *intercess-ion* = F. *intercession*, 'intercession,' Cot.; *intercession-al*; *intercess-or*, formerly *intercessour*, from F. *intercesseur*, 'an intercessor' (Cot.), which is from L. acc. *intercessōrem*; hence *intercessor-i-al*, *intercessor-y*.

INTERCEPT, to catch by the way, cut off communication. (F.—L.) Orig. a pp.; thus Chaucer has *intercept* = intercepted; On the Astrolabe, pt. ii. § 39, l. 24. 'To *intercept*, intercipere;' Levins (1570).—F. *intercepter*, 'to intercept, forestall;' Cot.—L. *interceptus*, pp. of *intercipere*, lit. to catch between.—L. *inter*, between; and *capere*, to catch, seize. See **Inter-** and **Capable.** Der. *intercept-er*: *intercept-ion*, Hen. V, ii. 2. 7.

INTERCESSION, INTERCESSOR; see **Intercede.**

INTERCHANGE, to change between, exchange. (F.—L.) Formerly *enterchange*. 'Full many strokes . . . were *enterchaungèd* twixt them two;' Spenser, F. Q. iv. 3. 17.—F. *entrechanger*; *s'entrechanger*, to interchange;' Cot.—F. *entre* < L. *inter*, between; and *changer*, to change. See **Inter-** and **Change.** Der. *interchange-able*; *interchange-abl-y*, Rich. II, i. 1. 146; *interchange-ment*, Tw. Nt. v. 162.

INTERCOMMUNICATE, to communicate mutually. (L.) In Phillips (1706). Coined from **Inter-** and **Communicate**; see **Commune.** Der. *intercommunicat-ion*; so also *intercommun-ion*.

INTERCOSTAL, lying between the ribs. (F.—L.) In Blount's Gloss., ed. 1674.—F. *intercostal*, 'between the ribs;' Cot. From L. *inter*, between; and *costa*, a rib. See **Inter-** and **Costal.**

INTERCOURSE, commerce, connexion by dealings, communication. (F.—L.) In Milton, P. L. ii. 1031, vii. 571. Spelt *entercourse* in Fabyan's Chron., an. 1271–2; ed. Ellis, p. 368. Modified from F. *entrecours*, intercourse; omitted by Cotgrave, but in use in the 16th century in the sense of 'commerce;' see Littré.—Late L. *intercursus*, commerce; L. *intercursus*, interposition. See **Inter-** and **Course.** Der. So also *inter-current*, *inter-currence*.

INTERDICT, a prohibitory decree. (L.) A law term, from Law Latin. [The F. form *entredit* is in early use; Rob. of Glouc.,

p. 495, l. 6 (and note), l. 10173; *enterdite*, Gower, C. A. i. 259; bk. ii. 2979. Hence the ME. verb *entrediten*, Rob. of Glouc., p. 495, l. 10184.] 'An *interdicte*, that no man shal rede, ne syngen, ne crystene chyldren, ne burye the deede, ne receyue sacramente;' Caxton, tr. of Reynard the Fox, ch. 28; ed. Arber, p. 70, last line.—Law L. *interdictum*, a kind of excommunication, Ducange; L. *interdictum*, a decree of a judge.—L. *interdictus*, pp. of *interdicere*, to pronounce judgment between two parties, to decree.—L. *inter*, between; and *dīcere*, to speak, utter. See **Inter-** and **Diction.** Der. *interdict*, vb.; *interdict-ion*, Macb. iv. 3. 106; *interdict-ive*, *interdict-or-y*.

INTEREST (1), profit, advantage, premium for use of money. (F.—L.) Differently formed from the word below. 'My well-won thrift, Which he calls *interest*;' Merch. Ven. i. 3. 52.—OF. *interest* (mod. F. *interêt*), 'an interest in, a right or title unto a thing; also interest, or use for money;' Cot.—L. *interest*, it is profitable, it concerns; 3 p. s. pres. indic. of *interesse*, to concern, lit. to be between.—L. *inter*, between; and *esse*, to be. See **Inter-** and **Essence.** ¶ Littré remarks that the F. has considerably modified the use of the L. original; see his Dict. for the full history of the word. He also bids us observe that the Span. *interes*, Port. *interesse*, Ital. *interesse*, interest, are all taken from the *infinitive mood* of the L. verb, not from the 3 p. s. pres., as in French; cf. Late L. *interesse*, interest. Besides this, the use of this sb. helped to modify the verb below; q. v. ☞ Spenser has the Ital. form *interesse*, F. Q. vii. 6. 33; cf. *intresse*, Chaucer, Fortune, 71; *interesse*, Lydgate, Minor Poems, p. 170.

INTEREST (2), to engage the attention, awaken concern in, excite in behalf of another. (F.—L.) A very curious word; formed (by partial confusion with the word above) from the pp. *interess'd* of the obsolete verb *to interess*. The very same confusion occurs in the formation of **Disinterested,** q. v. 'The wars so long continued between The emperor Charles and Francis the French king, Have *interess'd*, in either's cause, the most Of the Italian princes;' Massinger, Duke of Milan, i. 1. '*Tib.* By the Capitol, And all our gods, but that the dear republic, Our sacred laws, and just authority Are *interess'd* therein, I should be silent;' Ben Jonson, Sejanus, iii. 1. 'To *interess* themselves for Rome, against Carthage;' Dryden, On Poetry and Painting, § 13 (R.). 'To *interess* or *interest*, to concern, to engage;' Kersey, ed. 1715.—MF. *interessé*, 'interessed, or touched in;' Cot. Cf. Ital. *interessare* (pp. *interessato*), Span. *interesar* (pp. *interesado*), to interest.—L. *interesse*, to concern; see **Interest** (1). Der. *interest-ed* (really a reduplicated pp.), first used in 1665; *interest-ing* (first in 1711), *interest-ing-ly*; also *dis-interest-ed*, q. v.

INTERFERE, to interpose, intermeddle. (F.—L.) A word known in the 15th cent., but not much used. Chiefly restricted to the peculiar sense of hitting one leg against another; said of a horse; see Palsgrave, s. v. *Entrefyer*. '*Entyrferyn*, interrnisceo;' Prompt. Parv. 'To *interfeere*, to hacke one foot or legge against the other, as a horse doth;' Minsheu, ed. 1627. 'To *enterfeir*, to rub or dash one heel **against** the other, to exchange some blows;' Blount's Gloss., ed. 1674.—MF. *entreferir*, 'to interchange some blows; to strike or hit, at once, one another; **to interfeere, as a horse**;' Cot.—F. *entre*, between; and *ferir*, to strike.—L. *inter*, between; and *ferīre*, to strike. See **Inter-** and **Ferule.** Der. *interfer-er*, *interfer-ence*.

INTERFUSE, to pour between. (L.) Milton has *interfus'd*, P. L. vii. 89.—L. *interfūsus*, pp. of *interfundere*, to pour between. See **Inter-** and **Fuse** (1). Der. *interfus-ion*.

INTERIM, an interval. (L.) At least 14 times in Shak.; see Jul. Cæsar, ii. 1. 64; &c.—L. *interim*, adv. in the mean while.—L. *inter*, between; and *im*, allied to *is*, demonst. pronoun.

INTERIOR, internal. (L.) In Shak. Rich. III, i. 3. 65.—L. *interior*, compar. of *interus*, which is itself a comparative form. Thus *interior* (like *inferior*) is a double comparative. The L. *interus* and *intimus* correspond to Skt. *antara-* (interior) and *antima-₃*Vedic *antama-* (last), which are, respectively, compar. and superl. forms. The positive form appears in L. and E. *in.* Brugmann, i. § 466. Der. *interior*, sb., Merch. Venice, iii. 9. 28; *interior-ly*; and see *internal.*

INTERJACENT, lying between. (L.) In Kersey, ed. 1715. *Interjacency* is in Blount's Gloss., ed. 1674.—L. *interiacent-*, stem of pres. part. of *interiacēre*, to lie between.—L. *inter-*, between; and *iacēre*, to lie. See **Inter-** and **Gist.** Der. *interjacenc-y*.

INTERJECTION, a word thrown in to express emotion. (F.—L.) In Shak. Much Ado, iv. 1. 22; and in Palsgrave.—F. *interjection*, 'an interjection;' Cot.—L. *interiectionem*, acc. of *interiectio*, a throwing between, insertion, interjection; cf. *interiectus*, pp. of *intericere*, to cast between.—L. *inter*; and *iacere*, to cast; see **Inter-** and **Jet** (1). Der. *interjection-al*; also *interject*, verb (rare).

INTERLACE, to lace together. (F.—L.) In Spenser, F. Q. v. 3. 23; and in Sir T. More, Works, p. 739 b. Spelt *enterlace* in Baret (1580); and Chaucer, tr. of Boethius, iii. pr. 12. 118. Modified from MF. *entrelasser*, 'to interlace;' Cot.—F. *entre*, between; **and**

lasser, lacer, to lace ; Cot. See **Inter-** and **Lace.** Der. *interlace-ment.*

INTERLARD, to place lard amongst. (F. – L.) 'Whose grain doth rise in flakes, with fatness *interlarded* ;' Drayton, Polyolbion, s. 26, l. 255. Caxton has *entrelarded,* Troy-bk, fol. 62, l. 7. – F. *entrelarder,* 'to interlard, mingle different things together ;' Cot. See **Inter-** and **Lard.**

INTERLEAVE, to insert blank leaves in a book between the others. (Hybrid; L. and E.) In The Spectator, no. 547, § 2. Coined from **Inter-** and **Leave,** the latter being a coined verb from the sb. **Leaf** (pl. *leaves*).

INTERLINE, to write between the lines. (L.) 'I *interline,* I blot, correct, I note ;' Drayton, Matilda to K. John, l. 36 ; and in Cotgrave, to translate F. *entreligner.* – Late L. *interlineāre,* to write between lines for the purpose of making corrections ; used A.D. 1278 ; Ducange. – L. *inter,* between ; and *linea,* a line. See **Inter-** and **Line.** Der. *interline-ar,* from Late L. *interlineāris ;* whence *inter-line-ar-y,* Milton, Areopagitica, ed. Hales, p. 41, l. 3 ; *interline-at-ion.*

INTERLINK, to connect by uniting links. (Hybrid ; L. *and* Scand.) 'With such infinite combinations *interlinked* ;' Daniel, Defence of Rhyme, § 19. Coined from L. *inter* and *link.* See **Inter-** and **Link.**

INTERLOCUTION, a conference, speaking between. (F. – L.) 'A good speech of *interlocution* ;' Bacon, Essay 32, Of Discourse. – F. *interlocution,* 'an interlocution, interposition ;' Cot. – L. *inter-locūtiōnem,* acc. of *interlocūtio.* – L. *inter,* between ; and *locūtus,* pp. of *loquī,* to speak ; see **Inter-** and **Loquacious.** Der. So also *interlocut-or,* Bp. Taylor, Great Exemplar, pt. iii. s. 11 (R.), from L. *inter* and *locūtor,* a speaker ; *interlocut-or-y.*

INTERLOPER, an intruder. (Hybrid ; L. *and* E.) '*Interlopers* in trade ;' Minsheu's Dict., ed. 1627. '*Interlopers,* leapers or runners between ; it is usually applied to those merchants that intercept the trade or traffick of a company, and are not legally authorised ;' Blount's Gloss., ed. 1674. – L. *inter,* between ; and E. dial. *loper,* a runner (as in *land-loper*), from E. dial. *lope,* dial. form of E. *leap.* See **Inter-** and **Leap ;** and see **Elope.** ¶ Low G. and Du. *enterloper* are said to be from E. Der. *interlope,* vb., coined from the sb.

INTERLUDE, a short piece played between the acts of a play. (L.) In Shak. Mids. Nt. Dr. i. 2. 6 ; and in G. Douglas, ed. Small, v. i. p. 45, l. 18. ME. *enterlude,* Gawaine and G. Knight, 472 ; *entyrlude,* Rob. of Brunne, Handlyng Synne, 8993. – Anglo-Lat. *inter-lūdium* (Ducange). Coined from L. *inter,* between ; and *lūdus,* a play, or *lūdere,* to play ; see **Inter-** and **Ludicrous.** Der. *interlud-er.*

INTERLUNAR, between the moons. (L.) 'Hid in her vacant *interlunar* cave ;' Milton, Samson Agon., 89. Applied to the time when the moon, about to change, is invisible. Coined from L. *inter,* between ; and *lūna,* moon. See **Inter-** and **Lunar.**

INTERMARRY, to marry amongst. (Hybrid ; L. *and* F.) See examples in R. from Bp. Hall and Swift. Coined from L. *inter,* amongst ; and *marry,* of F. origin ; see **Inter-** and **Marry.** Der. *intermarri-age.*

INTERMEDDLE, to mingle, meddle, mix with. (F. – L.) ME. *entermedlen ;* 'Was *entermedled* ther among ;' Rom. of the Rose, 906. – OF. *entremedler,* a variant of *entremesler,* 'to inter-mingle, interlace, intermix ;' Cot. [For this variation, see *mesler, medler,* in Godefroy.] – OF. *entre,* from L. *inter,* among ; and OF. *medler,* to meddle. See **Inter-** and **Meddle.** Der. *intermeddl-er.*

INTERMEDIATE, intervening. (F. – L.) In Kersey, ed. 1715. – F. *intermediat,* 'that is between two ;' Cot. – L. *inter,* be-tween ; and *mediātus,* pp. of *mediāre,* to halve. See **Inter-** and **Mediate.** Der. *intermediate-ly.*

INTERMINABLE, endless. (L.) In Chaucer, tr. of Boethius, b. v. pr. 6, l. 29. – L. *interminābilis,* endless. – L. *in-,* not ; and *termināre,* to terminate, from *terminus,* an end. See **In-** (3) and **Term.** Der. *interminabl-y, interminable-ness.*

INTERMINGLE, to mingle together. (Hybrid ; L. *and* E.) In Shak. Oth. iii. 3. 25 ; earlier, in Surrey, tr. of Virgil, Æn. b. iv. l. 691. From L. *inter,* amongst ; and *mingle.* See **Inter-** and **Mingle.**

INTERMIT, to interrupt, cease for a time. (L.) In Shak. Jul. Cæs. i. 1. 59. – L. *intermittere,* to send apart, interrupt. – L. *inter,* between ; and *mittere,* to send ; see **Inter-** and **Missile.** Der. *intermitt-ent,* as in ' an *intermittent* ague,' Holland, tr. of Ammianus, p. 420, from the pres. part. ; *intermitt-ing-ly ;* also *intermiss-ion,* Macb. iv. 3. 232, from F. *intermission* (Cot.) < L. *intermissiōnem,* acc. of *intermissio,* allied to *intermissus,* pp. of *intermittere ; inter-miss-ive,* 1 Hen. VI, i. 1. 88.

INTERMIX, to mix together. (L.) Shak. has *intermixed ;* Rich. II, v. 5. 12. Coined from L. *inter,* among, and *mix,* of L. origin ; see **Inter-** and **Mix.** Der. *inter-mixture,* from *inter-* and *mixture,* q. v.

INTERNAL, being in the interior, domestic, intrinsic. (L.) In Spenser, F. Q. iii. 10. 59. Coined, with suffix *-al,* from L. *internus,* inward ; extended from *inter-,* inward ; see **Interior.** Der. *internal-ly.* Allied to *denizen,* q. v., *entrails,* q. v.

INTERN, to confine within certain limits. (F. – L.) Modern. – F. *interner,* to relegate into the interior (Hamilton). – F. *interne,* internal. – L. *internus* (above).

INTERNECINE, thoroughly destructive. (L.) '*Internecine* war ;' Butler, Hudibras, pt. i. c. 1. l. 774. – L. *internecīnus,* thoroughly destructive. – L. *interneci-o,* utter slaughter. – L. *inter,* thoroughly (see Lewis) ; and *necāre,* to kill. See **Inter-** and **Necromancy.**

INTERPELLATION, an interruption, summons, hindrance. (F. – L.) In Minsheu, ed. 1627. – F. *interpellation,* 'an interruption, disturbance ;' Cot. – L. *interpellātiōnem,* acc. of *interpellātio,* an in-terruption, hindrance ; cf. *interpellātus,* pp. of *interpellāre,* to drive between, hinder. – L. *inter,* between ; and *pellere,* to drive ; see **Inter-** and **Pulsate.**

INTERPOLATE, to insert a spurious passage. (L.) 'Although you admit Cæsar's copy to be therein not *interpolated* ;' Drayton, Polyolbion, s. 10 ; Illustrations (end). – L. *interpolātus,* pp. of *inter-polāre,* to furbish up, patch, interpolate. – L. *interpolus, interpolis,* polished up. – L. *inter,* between, here and there ; and *polīre,* to polish. See **Inter-** and **Polish.** Der. *interpolat-ion,* from F. *interpolation,* 'a polishing ;' Cot.

INTERPOSE, to put between, thrust in, mediate. (F. – L. *and* Gk.) In Shak. Jul. Cæs. ii. 1. 98. – F. *interposer,* 'to interpose, to put or set between ;' Cot. See **Inter-** and **Pose.** Der. *interpos-er,* Merch. Ven. iii. 2. 329.

INTERPOSITION, intervention, mediation. (F. – L.) 'By reason of the often *interposicion* ;' Sir T. More, Works, p. 1291 d. – F. *interposition,* 'an interposition, or putting between ;' Cot. See **Inter-** and **Position** (which is *not* from *pose*).

INTERPRET, to explain, translate. (F. – L.) ME. *interpreten,* Wyclif, 1 Cor. xiv. 27 ; *interpretour* is in verse 28. – F. *interpreter,* 'to interpret ;' Cot. – L. *interpretārī,* to expound. – L. *interpret-,* stem of *interprēs,* an interpreter ; properly an agent, broker, factor, go-between. β. Of uncertain origin ; the former part of the word is L. *inter,* between ; the base *-pret-* is perhaps allied to L. *pretium,* price. Der. *interpret-able, interpret-er* (in Wyclif, as above) ; also (cf. L. pp. *interpretātus*) *interpretat-ion* = F. *interpretation,* 'an inter-pretation' (Cot.) ; *interpretat-ive, interpretat-ive-ly.*

INTERREGNUM, an interval between two reigns. (L.) '*In-terreign* or *Interregnum* ;' Kersey, ed. 1715. – L. *interregnum.* – L. *inter,* between ; and *regnum,* a reign, rule. See **Inter-** and **Reign.**

INTERROGATE, to examine by questions, question. (L.) In Minsheu, ed. 1627. Shak. has *interrogatory,* K. John, iii. 1. 147 ; shortened to *intergatories,* Merch. Ven. v. 298. – L. *interrogātus,* pp. of *interrogāre,* to question. – L. *inter,* thoroughly (see Lewis) ; and *rogāre,* to ask ; see **Rogation.** Der. *interrogat-or, interrogat-or-y ; interrogat-ion* = F. *interrogation,* 'an interrogation' (Cot.), from L. acc. *interrogātiōnem ; interrogat-ive,* from L. *interrogātiuus ; inter-rogat-ive-ly.*

INTERRUPT, to break in amongst, hinder, divide continuity. (L.) 'Your tale for to *interrupte* or breke ;' Hoccleve, De Regimine Principum, l. 1231. – L. *interruptus,* pp. of *interrumpere,* to burst asunder, break up, hinder. – L. *inter,* between ; and *rumpere,* to break. See **Inter-** and **Rupture.** Der. *interrupt-ed-ly, inter-rupt-ive, interrupt-ive-ly ;* also *interruption,* ME. *interrupcioun,* Gower, C. A. i. 37 (prol. 985) = F. *interruption* (Cot.), from L. acc. *inter-ruptiōnem.*

INTERSECT, to cut between, cross as lines do. (L.) '*Inter-secteth* not the horizon ;' Sir T. Browne, Vulg. Errors, b. vi. c. 7. § 4. – L. *intersectus,* pp. of *intersecāre,* to cut apart. – L. *inter,* between, apart ; and *secāre,* to cut. See **Inter-** and **Section.** Der. *inter-sect-ion.*

INTERSPERSE, to disperse amongst, set here and there. (L.) '*Interspersed,* bestrewed, scattered or sprinkled between ;' Blount's Gloss., ed. 1674. – L. *interspersus,* pp. of *interspergere,* to sprinkle amongst. – L. *inter,* amongst ; and *spargere,* to scatter ; see **Sparse.** Der. *interspers-ion.*

INTERSTELLAR, lit. between the stars. (L.) 'The *inter-stellar* sky ;' Bacon, Nat. Hist. § 354. Coined from L. *inter,* amongst ; and E. *stellar,* adj. dependent on L. *stella,* a star ; see **Stellar.**

INTERSTICE, a slight space between things set closely together. (F. – L.) 'For when the airy *interstices* are filled ;' Sir T. Browne, Vulg. Errors, b. ii. c. 5. § 14. – MF. *interstice,* in use in the 16th century ; Littré. – L. *interstitium,* an interval of space. – L. *inter,* between ; and *status,* pp. of *sistere,* to place, a causal verb formed from *stāre,* to stand ; see **State.** Der. *interstiti-al,* from L. *interstiti-um.*

INTERTWINE, to twine amongst. (Hybrid; L. *and* E.) In Milton, P. R. iv. 405. From L. *inter*, amongst; and E. **Twine**, q.v. ¶ So also *inter-twist*.

INTERVAL, a space or period between. (F. — L.) ME. *inter-ualle*, Chaucer, C. T. (B 2723). — OF. *intervalle*, 'an interval;' Cot. — L. *interuallum*, lit. the space between two palisades; or the space within the breastwork of a camp. — L. *inter*, between; and *uallum*, a rampart, whence E. *wall*. See **Inter-** and **Wall**.

INTERVENE, to come between, interpose. (F. — L.) In Bacon, Adv. of Learning, bk. i. 4. 1. — F. *intervenir*, 'to interpose himselfe;' Cot. — L. *interuenire*, to come between. — L. *inter*, between; and *uenire*, to come, cognate with E. **Come**, q.v. Der. *inter-vent-ion* = F. *intervention*, 'an intervention' (Cot.), from L. acc. *interuentiōnem*, allied to L. pp. *interuentus*.

INTERVIEW, a mutual view or sight, a meeting. (F. — L.) In Shak. L. L. L. ii. 167; spelt *enterveue* in 1520; Royal Letters, ed. Ellis, i. 166. — OF. *entrevue* (Supp. to Godefroy), a verbal sb. allied to *entreveu*, pp. of *entrevoir*; cf. 's'*entrevoir*, to behold or visit one another;' Cot. — F. *entre*, from L. *inter*, between; and OF. *veu*, pp. of *voir*, from L. *uidēre*, to see; see **View**.

INTERWEAVE, to weave together. (Hybrid; L. *and* E.) The pp. *interwoven* is in Milton, P. R. ii. 263. Coined from L. *inter*, between; and **Weave**, q.v.

INTESTATE, without a will. (L.) 'Or dieth *intestate*;' P. Plowman, B. xv. 134. — L. *intestātus*, that has made no testament or will. — L. *in-*, not; and *testātus*, pp. of *testāri*, to be a witness, to make a will; see **Testament**. Der. *intestac-y*.

INTESTINE, inward, internal. (F. — L.) In Shak. Com. Errors, i. 1. 11. — F. *intestin*, 'intestine, inward;' Cot. — L. *intestīnus*, adj. inward. β. Formed from L. *intus*, adv. within; cognate with Gk. ἐντός, within. These are extensions from L. *in*, Gk. ἐν, in; see **In**. Der. *intestines*, pl. sb., in Kersey, ed. 1715, from F. *intestin*, 'an intestine' (Cot.), which is from L. *intestīnum*, neut. of *intestīnus*. Also *inte-tin-al*, from F. *intestinal* (Cot.). Cf. **Entrails**.

INTHRAL, the same as **Enthral**, q.v., but with E. prefix. (E.) Spelt *inthrall* in Kersey, ed. 1715; and in Phineas Fletcher, Purple Island, c. 5. st. 7. Der. *inthral-ment*.

INTIMATE (1), to announce, hint. (L.) In Shak. L. L. L. ii. 129. Properly a pp., as: 'their enterpryse was *intimate* and published to the kyng;' Hall's Chron. Hen. IV, an. 1. § 11. — L. *intimātus*, pp. of *intimāre*, to bring within, to announce. — L. *intimus*, innermost; superl. corresponding to comp. *interior*; see **Interior**. Der. *intimat-ion*, from F. *intimation*, 'an intimation;' Cot. And see **Intimate** (2).

INTIMATE (2), familiar, close. (L.) The form of this word is due to confusion with the word above. A better form is *intime*, as in : 'requires an *intime* application of the agents;' Digby, On Bodies, b. 5. s. 6. This is MF. *intime*, 'inward, secret, hearty, especiall, deer, intirely affected' (Cot.), from L. *intimus*, innermost, closely attached, intimate; see above. Der. *intimate-ly*, *intimac-y*.

INTIMIDATE, to frighten. (Late L. — L.) In Blount's Gloss., ed. 1674. [Probably suggested by MF. *intimider*, 'to fear, to skare;' Cot.] — Late L. *intimidātus*, pp. of *intimidāre*, to frighten; in the Acta Sanctorum (Ducange). — L. *in-*, intensive prefix, from the prep. *in*; and *timidus*, timid, fearful; see **Timid**. Der. *intimidat-ion*, from F. *intimidation*, 'a fearing, a skaring;' Cot.

INTITULED, entitled. (F. — L.) In Shak. L. L. L. v. 1. 8; and in Caxton, Godefroy of Bologne, rubric to ch. 1. — F. *intitule*, 'intitled or intituled,' Cot.; *intituler*, 'to intitle,' id. See **Entitle**.

INTO, prep. denoting passage inwards. (E.) ME. *into*, Chaucer, C. T. 2431 (A 2429); Layamon, 5150. — AS. *in tō* (two words), where *in* is used adverbially, and *tō* is the preposition. Cf. *up to*, *down to*. 'Ne gā þū mid þīnum esne *in tō* dóme' = go not thou *into* judgment [lit. *inwards to* judgment] with thy servant; Psalm cxlii. 2 (metrical version); Grein, ii. 142. See **In** and **To**.

INTOLERABLE, not tolerable. (F. — L.) 'For lenger to endure it is *intollerable*;' Lament of Mary Magdalen, st. 54; and see st. 10. — F. *intolerable*, 'intollerable;' Cot. — L. *intolerābilis*; see **In-** (3) and **Tolerable**. Der. *intolerabl-y*, *intolerable-ness*. So also *in-tolerant*, a late word, in Todd's Johnson; *intolerance* = F. *in-tolérance*, 'impatiency,' Cot.

INTOMB, the same as **Entomb**. (F. — L. — Gk.; *with* E. *prefix*.) In Shak. Macb. ii. 4. 9 (first folio).

INTONE, to chant. (Late L. — L. *and* Gk.) Formerly *entone* (from OF. *entoner*); G. Douglas, tr. of Virgil, bk. vii. ch. 12. 5. 'Ass *intones* to ass;' Pope, Dunciad, ii. 253. — Late L. *intonāre*, to sing according to tone. — L. *in tonum*, according to tone; where *tonum* is acc. of *tonus*, not a true L. word, but borrowed from Gk. τόνος; see **Tone**. Der. *inton-at-ion*. ¶ Note that *intonation* was also formerly used in the sense of 'loud noise.' Thus Minsheu (ed. 1627) has: '*Intonation*, loud noise or sound, a thundering.'

This is from the *classical* L. *intonāre*, to thunder forth, compounded of *in* (used as intensive prefix) and *tonāre*, to thunder, which is from OL. *tonus*, thunder. See **Thunder**.

INTOXICATE, to make drunk. (Late L. — L. *and* Gk.) In Shak. Hen. V, iv. 7. 39. *Intoxycat* in Palsgrave. Lydgate has *intoxycate* = invenomed, Troy-Book, bk. ii. c. 24; fol. Q 2, back, col. 1. Used as a pp. in Fryth's Works, p. 77 : 'their mynde is so *intoxicate*.' — Late L. *intoxicātus*, pp. of *intoxicāre*, to poison. — L. *in*, into; and *toxicum*, poison, a word borrowed from Gk. τοξικόν, poison in which arrows were dipped, from τόξον, a bow; of which the pl. τόξα = (1) bow and arrows, (2) arrows only. Der. *intoxicat-ion*.

INTRA-, *prefix*, within. (L.) L. *intrā*, on the inside, within; for **interā*, abl. fem. of **interus*, whence the compar. *interi-or*; see **Interior**.

INTRACTABLE, not tractable. (F. — L.) In Minsheu, ed. 1627. — F. *intractable*, 'intractable;' Cot. — L. *intractābilis*. See **In-** (3) and **Tractable**, **Trace**. Der. *intractabl-y*, *intractable-ness*.

INTRAMURAL, within the walls. (L.) Modern; not in Todd's Johnson. — L. *intrā*, within; and *mūrus*, a wall; see **Mural**.

INTRANSITIVE, not transitive. (L.) In Kersey, ed. 1715. — L. *intransitīuus*, that does not pass over to another person; used of verbs in grammar. See **In-** (3) and **Transitive**. Der. *intransitive-ly*.

INTREAT, the same as **Entreat**. (F. — L.; *with* E. *prefix*.) Minsheu, ed. 1627, gives both spellings; and see the Bible Word-book and Nares. Spelt *intreate* in Palsgrave.

INTRENCH, the same as **Entrench**. (F. — L.; *with* E. *prefix*.) In Shak. 1 Hen. VI, i. 4. 9. Der. *intrench-ment*.

INTREPID, dauntless, brave. (L.) 'That quality [valour] which signifies no more than an *intrepid* courage;' Dryden; Dedic. to Virgil's Æneid. — L. *intrepidus*, fearless. — L. *in-*, not; and *trepidus*, restless, alarmed; see **In-** (3) and **Trepidation**. Der. *intrepid-ly*; *intrepid-i-ty*, Spectator, no. 122.

INTRICATE, perplexed, obscure. (L.) In Shak. Com. Errors, v. 269. 'With mundane affections *intricate*;' Roy, Rede me, ed. Arber, p. 91, l. 15. — L. *intricātus*, pp. of *intricāre*, to perplex, embarrass, entangle. — L. *in*, in; and *tricæ*, pl. sb., hindrances, vexations, wiles (whence also **Extricate**). Der. *intricate-ly*, *intricate-ness*; *intricac-y*, Milton, P. L. viii. 182. And see **Intrigue**.

INTRIGUE, to form secret plots. (F. — Ital. — L.) 'In*triguing* fops;' Dryden, Absalom and Achitophel, pt. ii. l. 521. — F. *intriguer*, formerly also spelt *intriquer*, 'to intricate, perplex, pester, insnare;' Cot. — Ital. *intrigare*, 'to intricate, entrap;' Florio. — L. *intricāre*, to perplex; see above. Der. *intrigue*, sb.; *intrigu-er*.

INTRINSIC, inward, genuine, inherent. (F. — L.) A mistake for *intrinsecal*. *Intrinsecal* was formerly in use, as in Minsheu, ed. 1627. Shak. has *intrinse*, K. Lear, ii. 2. 81; and *intrinsicate*, Antony, v. 2. 307. '*Intrinsecal* or *Intrinsick*, inward or secret;' Kersey, ed. 1715. — MF. *intrinseque*, 'intrinsecal, inward;' Cot. — L. *intrinsecus*, inwards; lit. following towards the inside. — L. **intrim*, allied to *intr-ā*, within; and *secus*, lit. following, connected with L. *secundus*, second, and *sequi*, to follow. Brugmann, i. § 413 (2). See **Intra-** and **Second**. ¶ Similarly **Extrinsic**, q.v. Der. *intrinsic-al* (for *intrinsec-al*), *intrinsic-al-ly*.

INTRO-, *prefix*, within. (L.) L. *intrō*, an adv. closely allied to L. *intrā*, within; from *interus*, inner. See **Interior**.

INTRODUCE, to lead or conduct into, bring into notice or use. (L.) 'With whiche he *introduceth* and bringeth his reders into a false vnderstanding;' Sir T. More, Works, p. 341 e. 'Who hath *intro-duced* the[e] to do this;' Caxton, Troy-book, fol. 248, l. 5. — L. *introdūcere*, pp. *introductus*, to bring in. — L. *intrō*, short for *interō*, orig. abl. of *interus*, inward (see **Interior**); and *dūcere*, to lead; see **Duke**. Der. *introduct-ion*, Chaucer, C. T. 16854 (G 1386), from F. *introduction* < L. acc. *introductiōnem* (nom. *introductio*); *introduct-ive*; *introduct-or-y*, Chaucer, On the Astrolabe, prol. 73; *introduct-or-i-ly*.

INTROIT, an antiphon sung as the priest approaches the altar. (F. — L.) 'The *introyte* of the masse;' Caxton, Golden Legend; The Purification, § last. — OF. *introit*, F. *introït* (Hatzfeld). — L. *introïtum*, acc. of *introïtus*, lit. 'entrance.' — L. *introïtus*, pp. of *introïre*, to enter. — L. *intrō*, within; *īre*, to go.

INTROMISSION, a letting in, admission. (L.) '*Intromission*, a letting in;' Blount's Gloss., ed. 1674. A rare word. Formed, by analogy with F. sbs. in *-ion*, from *intrōmissum*, supine of the verb *intrōmittere*, to introduce. — L. *intrō*, within (see **Introduce**); and *mittere*, to send; see **Mission**. Der. Sometimes the verb *intromit* is used, but it is not now common.

INTROSPECTION, a looking into. (L.) In Kersey, ed. 1715. Formed, by analogy with F. sbs. in *-ion*, from L. acc. *introspectiōnem*, from nom. *introspectio*, a looking into. — L. *intrō*, within (see **Introduce**); and the base *spec-*; cf. *spectus*, pp. of *specere*, to look; see **Spy**.

INTRUDE, to thrust oneself into. (L.) In Hamlet, iii. 4. 31. —L. *intrūdere*, to thrust into, obtrude (oneself). —L. *in*, into; and *trūdere*, to thrust. See **Thrust**. Der. *intrud-er*; also *intrus-ion*, Sir T. More, Works, p. 640 b = F. *intrusion*, 'an intrusion' (Cot.), allied to L. pp. *intrūsus*; *intrus-ive*, Thomson, Liberty, pt. i. l. 299; *intrus-ive-ly*, *intrus-ive-ness*.

INTRUST, to give in trust, commit to one's care. (Scand.; *with* E. *prefix*.) Sometimes *entrust*, but *intrust* is much better, as being purer English; the latter part of the word being of Scand. (not F.) origin. In Dryden, Character of a Good Parson, l. 57. Compounded of **In** and **Trust**.

INTUITION, a looking into, ready power of perception. (F.—L.) Used by Bp. Taylor in the sense of 'looking upon;' Great Exemplar, pt. i. s. 36; and Rule of Conscience, b. iv. c. 2 (R.). [*Intuitive* is in Cotgrave, and in Milton, P. L. v. 488.]—MF. (*and* F.) *intuition* (Hatzfeld). Formed by analogy with *tuition*; allied to L. *intuitus*, pp. of *intuēri*, to look upon. —L. *in*, upon; and *tuēri*, to look; see **Tuition, Tutor**. Der. *intuit-ive* = F. *intuitif*, 'intuitive' (Cot.); *intuit-ive-ly*.

INTUMESCENCE, a swelling. (F.—L.) In Blount's Gloss., ed. 1674.—F. *intumescence*, 'a swelling, puffing;' Cot. Formed (as if from a Late L. *intumescentia*), from L. *intumescent-*, stem of pres. pt. of *intumescere*, to begin to swell.—L. *in*, used intensively; and *tumescere*, inceptive form of *tumēre*, to swell. See **Tumid**.

INTWINE, another form of **Entwine**, q. v. (E.) Really a better form, as being purer English. ¶ So also *in-twist*; see **Entwist**.

INUNDATION, an overflowing of water, a flood. (L.) In Palsgrave; and in Shak. K. John, v. 1. 12; v. 2. 48. [Imitated from F. *inondation*.]—L. *inundātiōnem*, acc. of *inundātio*, an overflowing; cf. *inundātus*, pp. of *inundāre*, to overflow, spread over in waves.—L. *in*, upon, over; and *unda*, a wave. See **Undulate**. Der. *inundate*, vb., really suggested by the sb., and of later date.

INURE, to habituate, accustom. (F.—L.) In Shak. Tw. Nt. ii. 5. 160. Also *enure*, as in Spenser, F. Q. iv. 2. 29; v. 9. 39; vi. 8. 14; and Sonnet 14, l. 7. 'A fayre company, and well *enewred* to the warre;' Caxton, Four Sons of Aymon, ch. viii. p. 187.—OF. *enovrer*, to work; whence pp. *enovré* à, employed in.—L. *inoperāre*, to effect; from *in*, in, and *operāre*, to work, from *opera*, work. See **Operate**. β. The word may have also been influenced by the phrase *in* (F. *en*) *ure*, i.e. in operation, in work, in employment; which was formerly common. Thus, in Ferrex and Porrex, Act iv. sc. 2, we have: 'And wisdome willed me without protract [delay] In speedie wise to put the same *in ure*,' i.e. *in operation*, not *in use*; see the passage in Morley's Library of Eng. Literature, Plays, p. 59, col. 1. And again, 'I wish that it should streight be put *in ure*;' id. Act v. sc. 1. γ. Hence was also formed the verb to *ure*, used in the same sense as *inure*. 'Ned, thou must begin Now to forget thy study and thy books, And *ure* thy shoulders to an armour's weight;' Edw. III, Act i. sc. 1, l. 159 (in the Leopold Shakspere, p. 1038). δ. The etymology of *ure* is from the OF. *ovre, oevre, nevre, eure*, work, action, operation. [Mr. Wedgwood well remarks upon the similar sound-changes by which the F. *man-œuvre* has become the E. *man-ure*.] Der. *inure-ment* (rare). ☞ The word *ure* here treated of is quite distinct from ME. *ure*, fate, destiny, luck, as used in Barbour's Bruce, i. 312, ii. 434, &c.; see glossary to my edition. In this case, *ure* is the OF. *eur, aur* (mod. F. *heur* in *bon-heur*), from L. *augurium*; see **Augur**.

INURN, to put into a sepulchral urn. (F.—L.; *or* L.) In Shak. Hamlet, i. 4. 49. See **In-** (1) and **Urn**.

INUTILITY, uselessness. (F.—L.) In Cotgrave.—F. *inutilité*, 'inutility;' Cot.—L. *inūtilitātem*, from nom. *inūtilitās*. See **In-** (3) and **Utility**.

INVADE, to enter an enemy's country, encroach upon. (F.—L.) 'And streight *inuade* the town;' Lord Surrey, tr. of Æneid, b. ii. l. 336.—F. *invader*, 'to invade;' Cot.—L. *inuādere*, to go into, enter, invade.—L. *in*, in, into; and *uādere*, to go. See **Wade**. Der. *invad-er*: *invas-ion*, K. John, iv. 2. 173 = F. *invasion*, 'an invasion' (Cot.), from L. *inuāsiōnem*, acc. of *inuāsio*; cf. pp. *inuāsus*; also *invas-ive*, K. John, v. 1. 69.

INVALID, not valid. (L.; *or* F.—L.) **A.** Accented *inválid*, Milton, P. L. viii. 116.—L. *inualidus* (below). **B.** Accented *invalíd*, and pronounced as a sb. 'As well stow'd with gallants as with *invalids*;' Tatler, no. 16.—F. *invalide*, 'impotent, infirme;' Cot.—L. *inualidus*, not strong, feeble.—L. *in-*, not; and *ualidus*, strong; see **Valid**. Der. *invalid-ate*, Burnet, Own Time, an. 1680 (R.); *invalid-at-ion*; *invalid-i-ty*.

INVALUABLE, that cannot be valued. (F.—L.) 'For rareness of *invaluable* price;' Drayton, Moses, his Birth and Miracles, bk. i. l. 550. From **In-** (3) and **Valuable**. Der. *invaluabl-y*.

INVARIABLE, not variable. (F.—L.) In Sir T. Browne, Vulg. Errors, b. i. c. 6, § last.—F. *invariable*, 'unvariable;' Cot. From **In-** (3) and **Variable**. Der. *invariabl-y*, *invariable-ness*.

INVASION, an entry into an enemy's country. (F.—L.) See **Invade**.

INVECKED, INVECTED, in heraldry, the reverse of *engrailed*, said of an edge indented with successive cusps. (L.) Formerly used with a slightly different meaning; see the diagram in the Boke of St. Albans, pt. ii. fol. d 4 (1486). Lit. 'carried in.' —L. *inuectus*, carried inwards, pp. of *inuehere* (below).

INVEIGH, to attack with words, rail. (L.) In Shak. Lucrece, 1254. The close connexion of *inveigh* with the sb. *invective* at once points out the etymology. In this word, the L. *h* is expressed by the guttural *gh*, just as the AS. *h* was replaced by the same combination; see Mätzner, Eng. Gram. i. 149. Cf. Span. *invehir*, to inveigh.—L. *inuehere* (pp. *inuectus*), to carry into or to, to introduce, attack, inveigh against.—L. *in*, into; and *uehere*, to carry; see **Vehicle**. Der. *invect-ive*, sb. from F. *invective*, 'an invective' (Cot.); also, as adj., as in 'inuectyue monycyons,' Caxton, Eneydos, ch. 16, p. 65, l. 1, from L. adj. *inuectiuus*, scolding, from the pp. *inuectus*; hence *invect-ive*, adj.; *invect-ive-ly*, As You Like It, ii. 1. 58. Also *invecked* (above). Also (obs.) *invect*, to inveigh, from the pp. *inuectus*; as in 'Fool that I am, thus to *invect* against her;' Beaumont and Fletcher, Faithful Friends, iii. 3.

INVEIGLE, to seduce, entice. (AF.—L.) 'Achilles hath *inveigled* his fool from him;' Shak. Troil. ii. 3. 99. 'Yet have they many baits and guileful spells To *inveigle* and invite the unwary sense;' Milton, Comus, 537, 538. And see Spenser, F. Q. i. 12. 32. 'The sayd duke of Glouceter *inuegelyd* so the arbysshop of Caunterbury;' Fabyan, ed. Ellis, p. 668. [Indirectly from F. *aveugler*, to blind; cf. E. *aveugle*, to cajole, seduce, in Froude's Hist. v. 132 (A. D. 1547); and State Papers, ix. 287 (A. D. 1543).]—AF. *enveoglir*, to blind, in Will. of Wadington's Manuel des Peches, l. 10639; and in N. Bozon. Altered, ignorantly, from F. *aveugler*, to blind.—F. *aveugle* (AF. *enveogle* in Bozon), adj., blind.—Late L. *aboculum*, acc. of *aboculus*, blind. [Ducange has *avoculus*, also *aboculis*, adj.]—L. *ab*, without; *oculus*, eye. ¶ Baret (1580) has: 'inveigle ones minde, *occæcare animum*.' Der. *inveigle-ment* (rare).

INVENT, to find out, devise, feign. (F.—L.) In Spenser, F. Q. iii. 5. 10; with the sense 'to find.'—F. *inventer*, 'to invent;' Cot. —L. *inuent-us*, pp. of *inuenīre*, to come upon, discover, invent.—L. *in*, upon; and *uenīre*, to come, cognate with E. **Come**, q. v. Der. *invention*, ME. *inuencion*, Testament of Creseide, st. 10 = F. *invention*, 'an invention' (Cot.), from L. *inuentiōnem*, acc. of *inuentio*; *inventive* < F. *inventif*, 'inventive' (Cot.); *invent-ive-ly*, *invent-ive-ness*; *invent-or*, ME. *inuentor*, Sir T. Elyot, The Governour, b. i. c. 20, § 11 < F. *inventeur*, from L. acc. *inuentōrem*; *invent-or-y*, Cor. i. 1. 21.

INVERSE, inverted, opposite. (F.—L.) ME. *invers*, Gower, C. A. iii. 3; bk. vi. 70.—OF. *invers*, 'inverse' (Cot.).—L. *inuersus*, pp. of *inuertere*; see **Invert**. Der. *inverse-ly*, *invers-ion*, Sir T. Browne, Vulg. Errors, b. iii. c. 15, § 6, formed by analogy with F. sbs. in *-ion*, from L. acc. *inuersiōnem*.

INVERT, to turn upside down, reverse. (L.) In Shak. Temp. iii. 1. 70.—L. *inuertere*, to invert.—L. *in*, signifying motion towards, or up; and *uertere*, to turn. See **Verse**. Der. *invert-ed-ly*; also *inverse*, q. v.

INVERTEBRATE: see **In-** (3) and **Vertebrate**. (L.)

INVEST, to dress with, put in office, surround, lay out money. (F.—L.) 'This girdle to *invest*;' Spenser, F. Q. iv. 5. 18.—F. *investir*, 'to invest, inrobe, install;' Cot.—L. *inuestīre*, to clothe, clothe in or with.—L. *in*, in; and *uestīre*, to clothe, from *uestis*, clothing; see **Vest**. Der. *invest-ment*, Hamlet, i. 3. 128; *invest-i-ture*, in Tyndal's Works, p. 362 [misnumbered 374] < F. *investiture* (Cot.), resembling L. *inuestītūra*, fem. of fut. part. of *inuestīre*.

INVESTIGATE, to track out, search into. (L.) 'She [Prudence] doth *inuestigate* and prepare places apt and conuenient;' Sir T. Elyot, The Governour, b. i. c. 22, § 2.—L. *inuestīgātus*, pp. of *inuestīgāre*, to track out, search into a track.—L. *in*, in; and *uestīgāre*, to trace. See **Vestige**. Der. *investigat-ion*, ME. *inuestigacioun*, Libell of E. Policy, l. 904; *investigat-ive*, *investigat-or*, *investigat-or-y*; also *investiga-ble*. ¶ Note that *investigable* also sometimes means 'unsearchable,' from L. *inuestīgābilis*, unsearchable (distinct from *inuestīgābilis*, that may be investigated); where the prefix *in-* has a negative force.

INVETERATE, grown old, firmly established or rooted. (L.) In Shak. Temp. i. 2. 122; Rich. II, i. 1. 14.—L. *inueterātus*, pp. of *inueterāre*, to retain for a long while.—L. *in*, with intensive force; and *ueter-*, decl. stem of *uetus*, old. See **Veteran**. Der. *inveterate-ly*, *inveterate-ness*, *inveterac-y*.

INVIDIOUS, envious, productive of odium. (L.) '*Invidious* crimes;' Dryden, tr. of Virgil, Æn. xi. 518. Formed by analogy with adjectives in *-ous* (of F. origin) from L. *inuidiōsus*, envious, productive of odium. ‒ L. *inuidia*, envy. See **Envy**. Der. *invidious-ly, invidious-ness.*

INVIGORATE, to give vigour to. (L.) 'This polarity . . . might serve to *invigorate* and touch a needle;' Sir T. Browne, Vulg. Errors, b. ii. c. 2, § 6. A coined word, formed as if from a L. **invigorāre* (not found); from *in*, prefix, and *uigor*, vigour. See **Vigour**.

INVINCIBLE, unconquerable. (F. ‒ L.) In Shak. Cor. iv. 1. 10; and Caxton, Golden Legend, St. Vincent, § last. ‒ F. *invincible*, 'invincible;' Cot. ‒ L. *inuincibilis.* ‒ L. *in-*, not; and *uincibilis*, vincible. See **In-** (3) and **Vincible**. Der. *invincibl-y, invincible-ness, invincibili-ty.*

INVIOLABLE, that cannot be violated or profaned. (F. ‒ L.) In Sir T. More, Works, p. 527 g: and in Spenser, F. Q. iv. 10. 35. ‒ F. *inviolable*, 'inviolable;' Cot. ‒ L. *inuiolābilis.* ‒ L. *in-*, not; and *uiolābilis*, that may be violated, from *uiolāre.* See **In-** (3) and **Violate**; and see below. Der. *inviolabl-y, inviolabili-ty.*

INVIOLATE, not profaned. (L.) In Spenser, tr. of Virgil's Gnat, l. 425; ME. *inuiolat*, Hoccleve, De Regim. Principum, l. 3696. ‒ L. *inuiolātus*, unhurt, inviolate. ‒ L. *in-*, not; and *uiolātus*, pp. of *uiolāre*, to violate; see **In-** (3) and **Violate**.

INVISIBLE, that cannot be seen. (F. ‒ L.) ME. *inuisible*, Chaucer, Legend of Good Women, 1021; Gower, C. A. ii. 247; bk. v. 3574. ‒ F. *invisible*; in Sherwood's index to Cotgrave. ‒ L. *inuīsibilis*. See **In-** (3) and **Visible**. Der. *invisibl-y, invisibili-ty.*

INVITE, to ask, summon, allure. (F. ‒ L.) 'God *inuited* men vnto the folowing of himselfe;' Sir T. More, Works, p. 1205 e. ‒ F. *inviter*, 'to invite;' Cot. ‒ L. *inuītāre*, to ask, bid, request, invite. Allied to **uit-us*, willing; as seen in *in-uītus*, unwilling; Brugmann, i. § 343. Der. *invitat-ion*, Merry Wives, i. 3. 50 < F. *invitation*, 'an invitation,' Cot.; *invit-er, invit-ing-ly.*

INVOCATE, to invoke. (L.) In Shak. Rich. III, i. 2. 8. ‒ L. *inuocātus*, pp. of *inuocāre*; see **Invoke**. Der. *invocat-ion*, ME. *inuocacioun*, Gower, C. A. iii. 46 (bk. vi. 1329), from F. *invocation*, 'an invocation' (Cot.), from L. acc. *inuocātiōnem*.

INVOICE, a particular account of goods sent. (F. ‒ L.) '*Invoice*, is a particular of the value, custom, and charges of any goods sent by a merchant in another man's ship, and consigned to a factor or correspondent in another countrey;' Blount's Gloss., ed. 1674. The word is certainly a corruption of *invoyes*, an English plural of F. *envoi*, OF. *envoy*, a sending. See *Invoy* also in N.E.D. Compare the phrases in Littré: 'par le dernier *envoi*, j'ai reçu' = by the last conveyance, I have received, &c.; 'j'ai reçu votre *envoi*' = I have received your last consignment; 'lettre d'*envoi*,' an invoice. See **Envoy**. ¶ A somewhat similar example occurs in the pronunciation of ' bourgeois ' type, called by printers *burjoice*.

INVOKE, to call upon. (F. ‒ L.) ' Whilst I *invoke* the Lord, whose power shall me defend;' Lord Surrey, Psalm 55, l. 27; and in Shak. Hen. V, i. 2. 104. ‒ F. *invoquer*, 'to invoke;' Cot. ‒ L. *inuocāre*, to call on. ‒ L. *in*, on; and *uocāre*, to call, allied to *uōc-*, stem of *uōx*, voice; see **Voice**. Doublet, *invocate*, q. v.

INVOLUNTARY, not voluntary. (L.) In Pope, Imit. of Horace, Odes, iv. 1, l. 38; and Sir T. Elyot, The Governour, bk. iii. c. 1, § 3. ‒ L. *inuoluntārius*. See **In-** (3) and **Voluntary**. Der. *involuntari-ly, involuntari-ness.*

INVOLUTE, involved, rolled inward. (L.) '*Involute* and *Evolute* Figures, certain geometrical figures;' Kersey, ed. 1715. ‒ L. *inuolūtus*, pp. of *inuoluere*; see **Involve**. Der. *involution*, from F. *involution*, ' an involution, enwrapping, enfolding,' Cot., from L. *inuolūtiōnem*, acc. of *inuolūtio*, a rolling up.

INVOLVE, to infold, wrap up. (F. ‒ L.) 'That reuerende studie is *inuolued* in so barbarouse a langage;' Sir T. Elyot, The Governour, b. i. c. 14, § 1. In Hoccleve, De Regimine Principum, l. 2657. ‒ F. *involver*, 'to involve;' Cot. ‒ L. *inuoluere*, to roll in or up. ‒ L. *in*, in; and *uoluere*, to roll; see **Voluble**. Der. *involve-ment*; *involucre*, an envelope, from F. *involucre*, L. *inuolūcrum*; and see **Involute**.

INVULNERABLE, not vulnerable. (F. ‒ L.) In Spenser, F. Q. vi. 4. 4. ‒ F. *invulnerable*, 'invulnerable;' Cot. ‒ L. *inuulnerābilis.* See **In-** (3) and **Vulnerable**. Der. *invulnerabl-y, invulnerable-ness, invulnerabili-ty.*

INWARD, internal. (E.) ME. *inward*, adj., St. Juliana, p. 44, l. 12; commonly adv., as in Ancren Riwle, p. 272. [The adv. is also *inwardes*, id. p. 92.] AS. *inneweard, innanweard*, adj.; Grein, i. 143. ‒ AS. *innan, inne*, adv. within, formed from prep. *in*, in; and suffix *-weard*, with the notion of 'towards;' see **Toward**, **Towards**. Der. *inward-s*, adv., where *-s* answers to ME. adverbial suffix *-es*, orig. the inflection of the gen. case; *inward-ly*, AS. *inweardlice*; Grein, i. 144. Also *inwards*, sb. pl., Milton, P. L. xi. 439.

INWEAVE, to weave in, intertwine. (E.) Milton has *inwove*, P. L. iii. 352; *inwoven*, P. L. iv. 693. Compounded of **In-** (1) and **Weave**.

INWRAP, the same as **Enwrap**, q. v. (E.)

INWREATHE, to wreathe amongst. (E.) Milton has *inwreath'd*, P. L. iii. 361. From **In-** (1) and **Wreathe**.

INWROUGHT, wrought in or amongst. (E.) '*Inwrought* with figures dim;' Milton, Lycidas, 105. From **In-** (1) and **Wrought**, i. e. worked.

IODINE, an elementary body, in chemistry. (Gk.) First in 1814. So named from the violet colour of its vapour. Formed, with suffix *-ine* (as in *chlor-ine, brom-ine*), from Gk. ἰώδης. contr. form of ἰοειδής, violet-coloured. ‒ Gk. ἴο-ν, a violet; and εἶδ-ος, appearance. See **Violet** and **Idyl**. Der. *iod-ide.*

IOTA, a jot. (Gk.) The name of the Gk. letter ι. See **Jot**.

IPECACUANHA, a medicinal West-Indian root. (Port. ‒ Brazilian.) So defined in Bailey's Dict., vol. ii. ed. 1731. ‒ Port. *ipecacuanha*, given in the Eng.-Port. part of Vieyra's Dict. Cf. Span. *ipecacuana*. Both Port. and Span. words are from the Guarani (Brazilian) name of the plant, *ipé-kaa-guaña*; where *ipé* = peb, small; *kaa*, plant; *guaña*, causing sickness (Cavalcanti). See Notes on E. Etym., p. 337. ¶ Spelt *ipecacoanha* in Historia Naturalis Braziliæ, 1648; p. 17.

IR- (1), *prefix.* (L.; or F. ‒ L.) The form assumed by the prefix *in-* (= prep. *in*), when the letter *r* follows. See **In-** (2). Exx.: *ir-radiate, ir-rigate, ir-rision, ir-ritate, ir-ruption.*

IR- (2), *prefix.* (L.; or F. ‒ L.) For *in-*, negative prefix, when the letter *r* follows. See **In-** (3). Exx.: all words beginning with *ir-*, except those given under **Ir-** (1).

IRE, anger. (F. ‒ L.) In Chaucer, C. T. 7587 (D 2005). ‒ F. *ire*, 'ire;' Cot. ‒ L. *īra*, anger (of doubtful origin). Der. *ire-ful*, Com. Errors, v. 151; *ir-asc-i-ble*, in Palsgrave, from F. *irascible*, 'cholerick' (Cot.), which from L. *īrascibilis*, adj. formed from *īrasci*, to become angry; *irascibl-y, irascibili-ty.*

IRIS, a rainbow. (L. ‒ Gk.) In Shak. All's Well, i. 3. 158. ‒ L. *iris*, a rainbow. ‒ Gk. ἶρις, Iris, the messenger of the gods; ἶρις, a rainbow (Homer). Root uncertain. Der. *irid-esc-ent*, a coined word, as if from pres. part. of a L. verb *īrid-esc-ere*, to become like a rainbow, formed with inceptive suffix *-esc-* from *īrid-*, stem of *iris* (gen. *irid-is*); hence *iridescence*; also *iridi-um* (from the decl. stem *iridi-*). *Iris*, a flower, is the same word; and see **orrice**.

IRK, to weary, distress. (E.) Now used impersonally, as in Shak. As You Like It, ii. 1. 22. **A.** Formerly used personally. ME. *irken*, (1) to make tired, (2) to become tired. Of these, the transitive (orig.) sense does not often appear, though preserved in the mod. phrase 'it *irks* me,' and in the word *irksome* = tiring. '*Irkesoum*, fastidiosus; *Irkesumnesse*, fastidium; *Irkyn*, fastidio, accidior;' Prompt. Parv. The intrans. sense is common. 'To preche also þow myȝt not *yrke*' = you must not grow weary of preaching; Myrc, Instructions for Parish Priests, 526. *Irked* = shrank back, drew back; Gawain and Grene Knight, 1573. 'Swa þat na man moght *irk* withalle' = so that none may grow tired withal; Pricke of Conscience, 8918. 'Men schuld *yrke* to telle them alle;' Rob. of Brunne, Chron. (Rolls Series), l. 11122. **B.** We also find ME. *irk* = tired, oppressed. 'Owre frendis of us wille sone be *irke*' = our friends will soon be tired of us; Sir Isumbras, 118. 'Syr Arther wos *irke*,' i. e. tired; Anturs of Arthur, st. vi. 'Thof he was *irk* [tired];' Cursor Mundi, 6425. Hence *for-hirked*, for *for-irked*, very weary; Gen. and Exodus, 3658. Palsgrave has: 'I waxe *yrke*, *Il me ennuye*.' **C.** The verb *irken*, to be tired, is from the adj. *irk*, tired, weary, sluggish; apparently a back-formation from the AS. *irgþ* (which came to be pronounced as *irk-þ*; cf. *length, strength*), with the meaning 'sluggishness;' see *irgþ* in Toller. And *irgþ, iergþ* was formed (with suffix *-þi*) from AS. *earg*, inert, sluggish, weak, timid; cognate with Lowl. Scotch *ergh*, timid, Icel. *arg*, Du. *erg*, G. *arg*, cowardly. Cf. G. *es ärgert mich*, it irks me. See Phil. Soc. Trans. 1903, p. 151. Der. *irk-some, irk-some-ness*, in the Prompt. Parv., as above.

IRON, a common metal. (E.; or C.) ME. *iren*, Chaucer, C. T. 502 (A 500); *yzen* (for *isen*), Ayenbite of Inwyt, p. 139, l. 31. AS. *iren*, both adj. and sb., Grein, ii. 145; older form *isen*, both adj. and sb., id. 147; also *īsern*, adj., Ælfred, tr. of Gregory, p. 165; shortened form of **īsern-en*, as the Goth. form shows. ✛ Du. *ijzer*, formerly *yzer*; Icel. *jārn*, contracted from the old form *īsarn*; Dan. and Swed. *jern*; OHG. *īsarn*; MHG. *īsern, īsen*; G. *eisen*; Goth. *eisarn*, sb.; *eisarneins*, adj. And cf. W. *haiarn*, Irish *iarann*, Bret. *houarn*, iron. β. The Teut. forms are all from the base **īsarno-*; and the Celtic forms are likewise from an OCeltic **isarno-, *eisarno-*; see Stokes-Fick, p. 25. And it is suggested that the Teut. forms were borrowed from Celtic. Cf. also Goth. *aiz*, L. *aes*, brass; Skt. *ayas*, iron. Der. *iron-bound, -clad, -founder, -foundry, -grey, -handed, -hearted,*

-*master*, -*mould* [see *mould* (3)], -*ware*, -*work*, -*witted*, Rich. III, iv. 2. 28. Also *iron-monger*, q. v.

IRONMONGER, a dealer in iron goods. (E.) In Minsheu's Dict., 1627; Pepys' Diary, Feb. 6, 1668-9; Beaum. and Fletcher, Cupid's Revenge, iv. 3; also *irenmanger*, York Mysteries, p. xxii. See **Iron** and **Monger.** Der. *iron-monger-y*.

IRONY, dissimulation, satire. (F.–L.–Gk.) '*Ironic*, a speaking by contraries, a mocke, a scoffe;' Minsheu's Dict., ed. 1627.–F. *ironie* (not in Cotgrave, but cited by Minsheu).–L. *īrōnīa*.–Gk. εἰρωνεία, dissimulation, irony.–Gk. εἴρων, a dissembler, one who says less than he thinks or means. β. This Gk. word is a pres. part. from ἐρέω (εἴρομαι, ἔρομαι), I ask, I question; and is an Ionic form. Cf. εἰρωτέω, Ionic for ἐρωτάω, I ask; ἔρευνα, enquiry (base *reu*); see Prellwitz. Der. *ironi-c-al*, *ironi-c-al-ly*.

IRRADIATE, to throw rays of light upon, light up. (L.) In Cockeram (1623); Milton, P. L. iii. 53.–L. *irradiātus*, pp. of *irradiāre*, to cast rays on.–L. *ir-=in-*; and *radius*, a ray. See **Ir-** (1) and **Ray.** Der. *irradiat-ion*; also *irradiant*, from stem of pres. pt. of *irradiāre*; *irradiance*, Milton, P. L. viii. 617.

IRRATIONAL, not rational. (L.) In Milton, P. L. ix. 766, x. 708; and in Henrysoun, The Cock and Fox.–L. *irratiōnālis*. See **Ir-** (2) and **Rational.** Der. *irrational-ly*, *irrational-i-ty*.

IRRECLAIMABLE, that cannot be reclaimed. (F.–L.) First in 1662 (in its present sense). Coined from **Ir-** (2) and **Reclaim.** Der. *irreclaimabl-y*.

IRRECONCILABLE, that cannot be reconciled. (F.–L.) In Minsheu, ed. 1627; in Cotgrave; and in Milton, P. L. i. 122.–F. *irreconciliable*, 'irreconcilable;' Cot.–F. *ir-*<L. *ir-=in-*, not; and F. *reconcilier*, 'to reconcile;' Cot. See **Ir-** (2) and **Reconcile.** Der. *irreconcilabl-y*, *irreconcilable-ness*.

IRRECOVERABLE, that cannot be recovered. (F.–L.) In Shak. 2 Hen. IV, ii. 4. 360. Milton has *irrecoverably*, Samson Agon. 81. Coined from *ir-*, for *in-*, not; and F. *recouvrable*, 'recoverable;' Cot. See **Ir-** (2) and **Recover.** Der. *irrecoverabl-y*. Doublet, *irrecuperable*.

IRRECUPERABLE, irrecoverable. (F.–L.) 'Ye [yea], what *irrecuperable* damage;' Sir T. Elyot, The Governour, b. i. c. 27. § 11.–OF. *irrecuperable*, 'unrecoverable;' Cot.–L. *irrecuperābilis*.–L. *ir-=in-*, not; and *recuperāre*, to recover. See **Ir-** (2) and **Recover.** Doublet, *irrecoverable*.

IRREDEEMABLE, not redeemable. (F.–L.) A coined word; first in 1609. From **Ir-** (2) and **Redeem.** Der. *irredeemabl-y*.

IRREDUCIBLE, not reducible. (L.) In Boyle's Works, vol. i. p. 50 (R.); first in 1633. From **Ir-** (2) and **Reduce.** Der. *irreducibl-y*, *irreducible-ness*.

IRREFRAGABLE, that cannot be refuted. (F.–L.) In More's Works, p. 1031, col. 1; and Minsheu, ed. 1627.–MF. *irrefragable*, 'irrefragable, unbreakable;' Cot.–L. *irrefrāgābilis*, not to be withstood.–L. *ir-=in-*, not; and *refrāgāri*, to oppose, thwart, withstand. β. *Refrāgāri* is of doubtful origin. Perhaps from *re-*, back, and *frag-*, base of *frangere*, to break; the orig. sense perhaps being 'to break back;' but see Bréal. See **Fragment.** ¶ The long *a* appears also in L. *suffrāgium*, prob. from the same root. Der. *irrefragabl-y*, *irrefragable-ness*, *irrefragabili-ty*.

IRREFUTABLE, that cannot be refuted. (F.–L.) In Kersey, ed. 1715; first in 1620. From **Ir-** (2) and **Refute.** Der. *irrefutabl-y*.

IRREGULAR, not regular. (F.–L.) In Shak. K. John, v. 4. 54; and in Cath. Anglicum (1483).–OF. *irreguler*.–L. *irrēgulāris*. See **Ir-** (2) and **Regular.** Der. *irregular-ly*; *irregular-i-ty*, from MF. *irregularité*, 'irregularity,' Cot.

IRRELEVANT, not relevant. (F.–L.) Used by Burke (R.). From **Ir-** (2) and **Relevant.** Der. *irrelevant-ly*, *irrelevance*.

IRRELIGIOUS, not religious. (F.–L.) In Shak. Merry Wives, v. 5. 242.–MF. *irreligieux*, 'irreligious;' Cot.–L. *irreligiōsus*. See **Ir-** (2) and **Religious.** Der. *irreligious-ly*; *irreligious-ness* (Bible Wordbook). So also *ir-religion*, Holland's Pliny, b. ii. c. 7, ed. 1634, p. 4 i.

IRREMEDIABLE, that cannot be remedied. (F.–L.) In Minsheu, ed. 1627; first in 1547.–MF. *irremediable*, 'remediless;' Cot.–L. *irremediābilis*.–L. *ir-*, for *in-*, not; and *remediābilis*, remediable, from *remedium*, a remedy. See **Ir-** (2) and **Remedy.** Der. *irremediabl-y*, *irremediable-ness*.

IRREMISSIBLE, that cannot be remitted or forgiven. (F.–L.) 'Your sinne is *irremissible*;' Fryth, Works, p. 3, col. 1.–MF. *irremissible*, 'unremittable;' Cot.–L. *irremissibilis*, unpardonable. See **Ir-** (2) and **Remit.** Der. *irremissible-ness*.

IRREMOVABLE, not removable, firm. (F.–L.) In Shak. Wint. Tale, iv. 4. 518. Coined from *ir-=in-*, not; and *removable*; see **Ir-** (2) and **Remove.** Der. *irremovabl-y*.

IRREPARABLE, that cannot be repaired. (F.–L.) In Shak. Temp. iv. 140; and Hoccleve, De Regim. Principum, l. 2082.–MF. *irreparable*, 'irreparable, unrepairable;' Cot.–L. *irreparābilis*. See **Ir-** (2) and **Repair.** Der. *irreparabl-y*, *irreparable-ness*.

IRREPREHENSIBLE, free from blame. (F.–L.) In Minsheu, ed. 1627; ME. *irreprehensyble*, Wyclif, 1 Tim. iii. 2 (earlier text).–MF. *irreprehensible*, 'irreprehensible, blamelesse;' Cot.–L. *irreprehensibilis*, unblamable. See **Ir-** (2) and **Reprehend.** Der. *irreprehensibl-y*, *irreprehensible-ness*.

IRREPRESSIBLE, not repressible. (F.–L.) Modern; added by Todd to Johnson. Coined from *ir-=in-*, not; and *repressible*. See **Ir-** (2) and **Repress.** Der. *irrepressibl-y*.

IRREPROACHABLE, not reproachable. (F.–L.) In Kersey, ed. 1715; first in 1634.–MF. *irreprochable*, 'unreprochable;' Cot.–F. *ir-=in-*, not; and MF. *reprochable*, 'reprochable;' Cot. See **Ir-** (2) and **Reproach.** Der. *irreproachabl-y*.

IRREPROVABLE, not reprovable, blameless. (F.–L.) In Minsheu, ed. 1627.–MF. *irreprovable*, 'unreprovable;' Cot. See **Ir-** (2) and **Reprove.** Der. *irreprovabl-y*, *irreprovable-ness*.

IRRESISTIBLE, that cannot be resisted. (F.–L.) In Milton, P. L. vi. 63. Coined from **Ir-** (2) and *resistible*; see **Resist.** Der. *irresistibl-y*, *irresistible-ness*, *irresistibili-ty*.

IRRESOLUTE, not resolute. (L.) In Shak. Hen. VIII, i. 2. 209; first in 1573. Coined from **Ir-** (2) and **Resolute.** Der. *irresolute-ly*, *irresolute-ness*; also *irresolut-ion*.

IRRESPECTIVE, not respective. (F.–L.) 'God's absolute *irrespective* decrees of election;' Hammond, Works, v. i. p. 462 (R.). From F. *ir-=in-*, not; and F. *respectif*, 'respective;' Cot. See **Respect.** Der. *irrespective-ly*.

IRRESPONSIBLE, not responsible. (L.) 'Such high and *irresponsible* licence over mankind;' Milton, Tenure of Kings (R.). From **Ir-** (2) and *responsible*; see **Response.** Der. *irresponsibl-y*, *irresponsibili-ty*.

IRRETRIEVABLE, not retrievable. (F.–L.) 'The condition of Gloriana, I am afraid, is *irretrievable*;' Spectator, no. 423. From F. *ir-=in-*, not; and *retrievable*; see **Retrieve.** Der. *irretrievabl-y*, *irretrievable-ness*.

IRREVERENT, not reverent. (F.–L.) In Milton, P. L. xii. 101.–MF. *irreverent*, 'unreverent;' Cot.–L. *irreuerent-*, stem of *irreuerens*, disrespectful.–L. *ir-=in-*, not; and *reuerens*, respectful, properly pres. part. of *reuerērī*, to revere. See **Revere.** Der. *irreverent-ly*; *irreverence*, Chaucer, C. T. Pers. Tale, De Superbia, sect 1 (I 391).

IRREVOCABLE, that cannot be recalled. (F.–L.) In Spenser, F. Q. vi. 2. 15; and in Palsgrave.–F. *irrevocable*, 'irrevocable;' Cot.–L. *irreuocābilis*.–L. *ir-=in-*, not; and *reuocābilis*, revocable, from *reuocāre*, to recall. See **Revoke.** Der. *irrevocabl-y*, *irrevocable-ness*.

IRRIGATE, to water. (L.) '*Irrigate*, to water ground;' Blount's Gloss., ed. 1674. And earlier, in Minsheu, ed. 1627.–L. *irrigātus*, pp. of *irrigāre*, to moisten, irrigate, flood.–L. *in*, upon, or as an intensive prefix; and *rigāre*, to wet, moisten. Der. *irrigat-ion*; also *irrig-u-ous*, Milton, P. L. iv. 255, from L. *irriguus*, adj. irrigating, allied to *irrigāre*.

IRRISION, mocking, scorn. (F.–L.) Rare; in Minsheu, ed. 1627.–MF. *irrision*, 'irrision, mocking;' Cot.–L. *irrisiōnem*, acc. from *irrīsio*, a deriding; cf. *irrīsus*, pp. of *irrīdēre*, to laugh at.–L. *ir-=in*, at; and *rīdēre*, to laugh. See **Risible.**

IRRITATE, to provoke. (L.) '*Irritate* [provoke] the myndes of the dauncers;' Sir T. Elyot, The Governour, b. i. c. 19.–L. *irrītātus*, pp. of *irrītāre*, perhaps, to cause to snarl, also to provoke, tease, irritate. β. Prob. a frequentative from *irrīre*, also spelt *hirrīre*, to snarl as a dog, which seems to be an imitative word. Der. *irritat-ion*=F. *irritation*, 'an irritation' (Cot.), from L. acc. *irrītātiōnem*; *irritat-ive*, *irritat-or-y*; *irrit-ant*, from the stem of pres. pt. of *irrītāre*; also *irrit-able*, in Minsheu, ed. 1627, from L. *irrītābilis*; *irrit-abl-y*, *irrit-able-ness*, *irrit-abili-ty*.

IRRUPTION, a bursting in upon, sudden invasion. (F.–L.) 'An *irruption*, or violent bursting in;' Minsheu, ed. 1627.–F. *irruption*, 'an irruption, a forcible entry;' Cot.–L. *irruptiōnem*, acc. of *irruptio*, a bursting into.–L. *ir-=in*, in, upon; and *ruptio*, a bursting; cf. *ruptus*, pp. of *rumpere*, to burst. See **Rupture.** Der. *irrupt-ive*, *irrupt-ive-ly*, from pp. *irruptus* of *irrumpere*, to burst in.

IS, the 3 pers. pres. of the verb substantive. (E.) AS. *is*; see further under **Are, Essence.**

ISINGLASS, a glutinous substance made from a fish. (Du.) '*Ising-glass*, a kind of fish-glue brought from Island [Iceland], us'd in medicines;' Kersey's Dict., ed. 1715. Spelt *ison-glass* in 1662 (N. E. D.). A singular perversion of MDu. *huyzenblas*, mod. Du. *huisblad*. '*Isinglass*, *huyzenblas*;' Sewel's Eng.-Du. Dict.; 1754. The lit. sense is 'sturgeon-bladder;' isinglass being obtained from the bladder of the sturgeon (*Accipenser sturio*).–MDu. *huys*, a sturgeon; *blaese*, a bladder (Kilian).+G. *hausenblase*, isinglass; from *hausen*, a kind of sturgeon (answering to MDu. *huyzen*); and *blase* (= Du. *blas*), a bladder, from *blasen*, to blow, allied to E. **Blast**.

ISLAM, the religious system of Mohammed. (Arab.) 'The revolt of Islam;' Shelley.–Arab. *islâm*, lit. 'submission,' or 'resignation.'–Arab. root *salama*, he was resigned; whence also *salaam*, *Moslem*, *Mussulman*.

ISLAND, an isle, land surrounded by water. (E.) The *s* is ignorantly inserted, owing to confusion with *isle*, a word of F. origin; see below. In Spenser, F. Q. ii. 6. 11, the word is spelt *island* in the Globe edition, but *iland* in the passage as quoted in Richardson. ME. *iland*, *ilond*, *yland*, *ylond*; spelt *ilond* in Octovian Imperator, l. 539 (Weber's Met. Romances, iii. 179); *ilond*, Layamon, l. 1133 (later text). AS. *îgland*, Grein, ii. 136. β. The AS. *îg-land* is compounded of *îg*, an island, and *land*, land; prob. by association with *êa-land*, an island, from *êa*, water. Grein (ii. 136) gives *ig*, *ieg* as equivalent forms, with references; the word is also written *êg* in Mercian (id. i. 233); and in Eng. local names appears as *-ea* or *-ey*, as in *Batters-ea*, *Aldern-ey*, *Angles-ey*. γ. Cognate words are: Du. *eiland*, an island, formerly written *eyland* (Sewel); Icel. *eyland*; Swed. *iland*, used as a proper name for an island in the Baltic Sea; G. *eiland*. δ. Dropping the syllable *-land*, we also find AS. *îg*, *îeg*, Mercian *êg* (as above); Icel. *ey*, an island; Dan. and Swed. *ö*, an island; also G. *aue*, a meadow near water. All from Teut. **agwiâ*, fem. of **agwioz*, adj., belonging to water; an adj. formed from Teut. **ahwa*, water, represented by AS. *êa*, OHG. *aha*, Goth. *ahwa*, a stream, cognate with L. *aqua*, water. See **Aquatic**. Thus the AS. *êa* signifies 'water;' whence *îeg*, *îg*, 'a place near water,' lit. 'aqueous;' and *îg-land*, an island. Der. *island-er*, Temp. ii. 2. 37.

ISLE, an island. (F.–L.) Quite distinct from the E. *island*, in which the *s* was ignorantly inserted. It is singular that, in the word *isle*, the *s* was formerly dropped, thus tending still further to confound the two words. ME. *ile*, *yle*; Rob. of Glouc., p. 1, l. 3; Wyclif, Deeds [Acts], xxviii. 1.–OF. *ille*, *ile*; MF. *isle*, 'an isle;' Cot.; mod. F. *île*.–L. *insula*, an island. See **Insular**. Der. *isl-et*, in Drayton's Polyolbion, s. 24, note, from MF. *islette*, 'a little island' (Cot.), a dimin. form. And see *isolate*.

ISOCHRONOUS, performed in equal times. (Gk.) In Phillips' Dict., ed. 1706 (s. v. *Isochrone*). Imitated from Gk. *ἰσόχρονος*, consisting of an equal number of times (a grammatical term).–Gk. *ἰσο-*, for *ἶσος*, equal; and *χρόνος*, time, whence also E. **Chronicle**. β. The Gk. *ἴσος* or *ἶσος* is perhaps allied to Gk. *εἶδος*, form; Brugmann, i. § 345 (c). Cf. Skt. *vishu-*, adv., equally. Der. *isochron-ism*.

ISOLATE, to insulate, place in a detached situation. (Ital.–L.) The word occurs in the Preface to Warburton's Divine Grace, but was censured in 1800 as being a novel and unnecessary word (Todd). And see note in Trench, Eng. Past and Present. Todd remarks, further, that *isolated* was properly a term in architecture, signifying detached. It was thus at first a translation of Ital. *isolato*, detached, separate, formed as an adj. (with pp. form) from *isola*, an island.–L. *insula*, an island; also, a detached house or pile of buildings, whence *insulâtus*, insulated, answering to Ital. *isolato*. See **Insular**. ¶ The F. *isolé* is likewise borrowed from the Ital. *isolato*; the E. word was not taken from F., but directly from the Italian. Der. *i-olat-ion*. Doublet, *insulate*.

ISOSCELES, having two sides equal, as a triangle. (L.–Gk.) In Phillips' Dict., ed. 1706.–L. *isosceles*.–Gk. *ἰσοσκελής*, with equal legs or sides.–Gk. *ἰσο-*, for *ἶσος*, equal (see **Isochronous**); and *σκέλος*, a leg, which see in Prellwitz.

ISOTHERMAL, having an equal degree of heat. (Gk.) Modern.–Gk. *ἰσο-*, for *ἶσος*, equal; and *θέρμ-η*, heat; with adj. suffix *-al*. See **Isochronous**, **Thermometer**.

ISSUE, that which proceeds from something, progeny, produce, result. (F.–L.) ME. *issue*. 'To me and to myn *issue*;' P. Plowman, C. xix. 259. 'An *issue* large;' Chaucer, Troil. v. 205.–OF. *issuë*, 'the issue, end, success, event;' Cot. A fem. form of *issu*, 'issued, flowen, sprung, proceeded from;' pp. of *issir*, 'to issue, to go, or depart out;' id.–L. *exire*, to go out of; from *ex*, out, and *ire*, to go; see **Exit**. The F. pp. *issu* answers to Folk-L. **exûtus*, for L. *exitus*. Der. *issue*, verb, borrowed from the sb.; 'we issued out' is in Surrey's tr. of Virgil, where the L. text has 'iuuat ire,' Æneid, ii. 27; ME. *isuen*, Rich. Coer de Lion, 4432. [The ME. Northern verb was *isch*, common in Barbour's Bruce, and borrowed from the F. vb. *issir*.] Also *issu-er*; *issue-less*, Wint. Ta. v. 1. 174.

ISTHMUS, a neck of land connecting a peninsula with the mainland. (L.–Gk.) In Minsheu, ed. 1627; spelt *istmus* in Cotgrave, to translate MF. *isthme*.–L. *isthmus*.–Gk. *ἰσθμός*, a narrow passage, neck of land; allied to *ἴθμα*, a step; from √EI, to go.

IT, the neuter of the third personal pronoun. (E.) Formerly also *hit*, P. Plowman, A. i. 85, C. ii. 83; but *it* in the same, B. i. 86.

AS. *hit*, neuter of *hê*; see **He**.+Icel. *hit*, neut. of *hinn*; Du. *het*, neut. of *hij*; Goth. *hita*. ☞ The gen. case *its* was just coming into use in Shakespeare's time, and occurs in Temp. i. 2. 95, &c., but the usual form in Shak. is *his*, as in AS. We also find *it* in Shak. (with the sense of *its*) in the first folio, in 13 passages, Temp. ii. 1. 163, &c. See the articles in The Bible Wordbook and in Schmidt's Shak. Lexicon. *Its* does not once occur in the Bible, ed. 1611, which has *it* where mod. editions have *its* in Levit. xxv. 5; but first appears in Florio's Ital. Dict. (1598), s. v. *Spontaneamente*. The use of *hit* for *his* (=*its*) occurs early, viz. in the Anturs of Arthur, st. viii. l. 11, and in Allit. Poems, B. 264. The AS. neuter form is *hit*, nom.; *his*, gen.; *him*, dat.; *hit*, acc. Der. *it-self*; see **Self**.

ITALICS, the name given to letters printed thus—*in sloping type*. (L.) So called because invented by Aldo Manuzio (Aldus Manutius), of Venice, about A. D. 1500. Aldo was born in 1449, and died in 1515. Letters printed in this type were called by the Italians *corsivi* (cursive, or running hand), but were known to other nations as *Italics*; see Engl. Cyclop. s. v. Manuzio.–L. *Italicus*, Italian.–L. *Italia*, Italy (Gk. *Ἰταλία*). The initial *I* is long. Der. *italic-ise*.

ITCH, to have an irritating sensation in the skin. (E.) Like *if* (=ME. *yif*, *ʒif*=AS. *g'f*) this word has lost an initial ME. *y* or *ʒ*=AS. *g*. ME. *iken*, *icchen*, *ʒichen*, *ʒiken*; see Prompt. Parv. pp. 259, 538. The pp. occurs in Chaucer, C. T. 3684, where the Six-text (A 3682) has the various spellings *icched*, *yched*, and *ʒechid*. AS. *giccan*, for **gyccan*, to itch; in AS. Leechdoms, ed. Cockayne, vol. iii. p. 50, l. 13; whence AS. *gyhða*, an itching, in Ælfric's Hom. i. 86.+Du. *jeuken*, to itch; whence *jeuking*, *jeukte* (= AS. *gyhþa*), an itching; G. *jucken*, to itch; OHG. *jucchan*. Teut. type **jukjan-* or **jukkjan-*. Der. *itch*, sb., *itch-y*.

ITEM, a separate article or particular. (L.) The mod. use of *item* as a sb. is due to the old use of it in enumerating particulars. Properly, it is an adv. meaning 'also' or 'likewise,' as in Shak. Tw. Nt. i. 5. 265: 'as, *item*, two lips, indifferent red; *item*, two grey eyes;' &c.–L. *item*, in like manner, likewise, also; closely related to *ita*, so; cf. *is*, he. Cf. Skt. *ittham*, thus; *itthâ*, thus; *iti*, thus.

ITERATE, to repeat often. (L.) Bacon has *iterations* and *iterate* in Essay 25 (Of Dispatch). Shak. has *iterance*, Oth. v. 2. 150 (folio edd.); *iteration*, 1 Hen. IV, i. 2. 101.–L. *iterâtus*, pp. of *iterâre*, to repeat.–L. *iterum*, again; a comparative adverbial form (with suffix *-ter-*) from the pronom. base I of the third person; see **Item**. Cf. Skt. *i-tara(s)*, other. Der. *iterat-ion*, *iterat-ive*.

ITINERANT, travelling. (L.) 'And glad to turn *itinerant*;' Butler, Hudibras, pt. iii. c. 2. l. 92.–L. *itinerant-*, stem of pres. pt. of the verb *itinerârî*, to travel.–L. *itiner-*, stem of *iter*, a journey.–L. *it-um*, supine of *îre*, to go.–√EI, to go; cf. Skt. *i*, to go. Der. *itinerant-ly*, *itineranc-y*, *itinerac-y*. Also *itinerary* (Levins), from L. *itinerârium*, an account of a journey, neut. of *itiner-ârius*, belonging to a journey, from the base *itiner-* with suffix *-ârius*.

IVORY, a hard white substance chiefly obtained from the tusks of elephants. (F.–L.) ME. *ynory*, *iuorie* (with *u* for *v*), Chaucer, C. T. 7323 (D 1741); also spelt *euery*, Trevisa, i. 79.–AF. *ivorie*, Charlemagne, ed. Michel, l. 353; OF. *ivurie*, ivory, a 12th-century form, cited by Littré; later *ivoire*, 'ivory;' Cot. [Cf. Prov. *evori*, Bartsch, Chrestomathie Provençale, 29. 20, whence perhaps the ME. form *euery*. Also Ital. *avorio*, *avolio*.]–L. *eboreus*, adj. made of ivory.–L. *ebor-*, stem of *ebur*, sb. ivory. β. Supposed by some to be connected with Skt. *ibha-s*, an elephant. Der. *ivory*, adj., *ivory-black*, *ivory-nut*.

IVY, the name of a creeping evergreen. (E.) 'He moot go pypen in an *ivy-leef*;' Chaucer, C. T. 1840 (A 1838). AS. *îfig*, ivy; see Gloss. to AS. Leechdoms, ed. Cockayne; also *ifegn*, an old form in the Corpus glossary, l. 718. [The AS. *f* between two vowels was sounded as *v*, and the change of AS. *-ig* to E. *-y* is regular, as in AS. *stân-ig* = E. *ston-y*].+OHG. *ebahewi*, ivy (cited by Kluge); G. *epheu*. β. The AS. *îf-ig* seems to be a compound word. The syllable *îf-* is equivalent to Du. *ei-* in *ei-loof*, ivy (lit. ivy-leaf); and to OHG. *eba(h)-* in *ebahewi*; but the orig. sense is unknown. Der. *ivy-mantled*, *ivi-ed*.

IWIS, certainly. (E.) ME. *ywis*, *iwis*; Chaucer, C. T. 3277, 3705. Common in Shak., as in Merch. Ven. ii. 9. 68, Tam. Shrew, i. 1. 62, Rich. III, i. 3. 102. AS. *gewis*, adj. certain; *gewislîce*, adv. certainly; Grein, i. 43.+Du. *gewis*, adj. and adv., certain, certainly; G. *gewiss*, certainly. Cf. Icel. *viss*, certain, sure. β. All from Teut. type **wissoz*, for **wittoz* (Idg. **wid-tos*), pp. from the base *wit-* in Teut. **wit-an-*, to know. See **Wit** (1). From √WEID, to know. ☞ It is to be particularly noted that the ME. prefix *i-* (= AS. *ge-*) was often written apart from the rest of the word, and with a capital letter. Hence, by the mistake of editors, it is sometimes printed *I wis*, and explained to mean 'I know.' Hence, further, the imaginary verb *wis*, to know, has found its way into many dictionaries.

IZARD, a kind of antelope. (F.) Modern.—F. *isard*; perhaps of Iberian origin (Hatzfeld).

IZZARD, the letter Z. (F.—Gk.) Written *ezod* in 1597 (N. E. D.); *izzard* in Goldsmith, She Stoops to Conquer, A. iv.—F. *ézed*, a F. name for the letter (see my Notes on E. Etym., p. 146); Prov. *izèdo*, *izèto* (Mistral).—Gk. ζῆτα, the name of the 6th letter of the Gk. alphabet.

J

JABBER, to chatter, talk indistinctly. (F. ?) Formerly *jaber* or *jable*. 'Whatsoeuer the Jewes would *jaber* or iangle agayn;' Sir T. More, Works, p. 665 c. 'To *iabil*, multum loqui;' Levins, ed. 1570. ME. *iaberen*, to chatter; see under *Tateryn* in Prompt. Parv. And cf. *gibber*, Hamlet, i. 1. 116. *Jabber*, *Jabble* are imitative words, similar to *gabber*, *gabble*, which are from the base *gab*, seen in Icel. *gabba*, to mock, scoff. More immediately, they may be referred to OF. *jaber*, given by Godefroy as a variant of *gaber*, to mock. Cf. also MF. *javioler*, 'to gabble, prate, or prattle;' Cot. Of imitative origin. See **Gabble**; and cf. Du. *gabberen*, 'to jabber' (Sewel). Der. *jabber-er*.

JABIRU, a large wading bird of tropical America. (Brazil.) From the Tupi-Guarani (Brazilian) *jabiru*; see Hist. Nat. Brasiliæ, 1648; ii. 200.

JACAMAR, a bird of the family *Galbulidæ*. (F.—Brazil.) F. *jacamar* (with *c* as *s*), Brisson.—Tupi-Guarani (Brazilian) *jacamaciri*; Hist. Nat. Brasiliæ, 1648; ii. 202; Newton, Hist. Birds.

JACANA, a grallatorial aquatic bird. (Brazil.) From Tupi-Guarani (Brazilian) *jasaná*; written *jacana* (for *jaçana*); see Newton, Hist. Birds; and Hist. Nat. Brasiliæ, 1648; ii. 190.

JACINTH, a precious stone. (F.—L.—Gk.) In the Bible, Rev. ix. 17; xxi. 20. 'In Rev. ix. 17, the hyacinthine, or dark purple, colour is referred to, and not the stone; as in Sidney's Arcadia (B. i. p. 59, l. 28), where mention is made of "Queene Helen, whose *Iacinth* haire curled by nature," &c.;' Bible Wordbook, ed. 1866. [But I should explain '*iacinth* haire,' like '*hyacinthine* locks' in Milton, P. L. iv. 301, to mean 'hair curling like the hyacinth,' without reference to colour.] ME. *iacynte*, Wyclif, 2 Chron. ii. 7 (earlier version), *iacynct* (later version). Gower has *jacinctus*; C. A. iii. 112; bk. vii. 842.—OF. *jacinthe*, 'the precious stone called a jacint;' Cot.—Late L. *iacintus*, *hiacinthus*, for *hyacinthus*, a jacinth, Rev. xxi. 20 (Vulgate).—Gk. ὑάκινθος; Rev. xxi. 20. See **Hyacinth**. ¶ Thus *jacinth* is for *hyacinth*, like *Jerome* for *Hierome* or *Hieronymus*, and *Jerusalem* for *Hierusalem*.

JACK (1), a saucy fellow, sailor. (F.—L.—Gk.—Heb.) The phrase 'thou Sire John' is in Chaucer, C. T. 14816 (B 4000); on which Tyrwhitt remarks: 'I know not how it has happened, that in the principal modern languages, John, or its equivalent, is a name of contempt, or at least of slight. So the Italians use *Gianni*, from whence *Zani*; the Spaniards *Juan*, as *bobo Juan*, a foolish John; the French *Jean*, with various additions; and in English, when we call a man *a John*, we do not mean it as a title of honour. Chaucer, in l. 3708, uses *Jacke fool*, as the Spaniards do *bobo Juan*; and I suppose *jack-ass* has the same etymology.' 'Go fro the window, *Jacke fool*, she said;' Chaucer, C. T. 3708. This ME. *Jacke* has been supposed to have been borrowed from the F. *Jaques*; but it is hard to believe that this common French name should have been regarded as an equivalent to the E. common name *John*, since it really answers to *Jacob*. Indeed, a strong case has been made out by Mr. E. B. Nicholson (in his Pedigree of Jack, 1892) for regarding it as short for *Jacken* (found in 1327) which is a variant of *Jankin*, the regular dimin. of *John*, and so used by Chaucer, C. T., B 1172. See further under **Zany**. B. It is difficult to tell to what extent the various senses of the word *jack* depend upon the name above. **α.** It is, however, clearly to be traced in the phrase *Jack o' the clock*, Rich. II, v. 5. 60, where it means a figure which, in old clocks, used to strike upon the bell. **β.** In a similar way, it was used to name various implements which supplied the place of a *boy* or attendant, as in *boot-jack* and in the *jack* which turns a spit in a kitchen. **γ.** Similarly, it denoted the key of a virginal; Shak. Sonnet 128. **δ.** Hence perhaps also a familiar name for the *small* bowl aimed at in the game of bowls; Shak. Cymb. ii. 1. 2. **ε.** And for a *small* pike (fish), as distinct from a full-grown one; and in many other instances (see N. E. D.). Der. *Jack-o-lent* = Jack of Lent, a puppet thrown at in Lent, Merry Wives, iii. 3. 27; *Jack-a-lantern* = Jack o' lantern, also called *Jack-with-the-lantern*, an ignis fatuus (see Todd's Johnson); *Jack-pudding*, Milton, Defence of the People of England, c. 1 (R.), compounded of *Jack* and *pudding*, just as a buffoon is called in French *Jean-pottage* (John-

pottage) and in German *Hans-wurst* (Jack-sausage); *Jack-an-apes* (for which see below); *Jack-by-the-hedge*, 'an herb that grows by the hedge-side,' Kersey, ed. 1715, i. e. *Sisymbrium Alliaria*, see Lyte, tr. of Dodoens, bk. v. c. 72; *jack-ass*; *jack-daw*, Pliny, b. x. c. 29 (and not a corruption of *chough-daw*, as it has been desperately guessed to be): cf. MF. *jaquette*, 'a proper name for a woman, a piannat, or megatapy' [magpie], Cot. Also *jack-screw*, a screw for raising heavy weights, &c.

JACKANAPES, a tame ape, a man who displays tricks like an ape; used as a term of contempt. (F.—L.—Gk.) Tyndall has *Iack an apes* (*Iacke a napes* in ed. 1528); Works, 1572, p. 132, col. 1, l. 11. 'He grynnes and he gapis As it were *iack napis*;' Skelton, Why Come ye nat to Courte, l. 651. History shows that the orig. form was *Iack Napes*, and it is first known as a nick-name of Wm. de la Pole, duke of Suffolk (murdered in 1450), whose badge was an ape's clog and chain, such as was usually attached to a tame ape. It is possible that, at the same time, there was a covert meaning in *Napes* (which also then meant *Naples*), because he advocated the king's marriage with Margaret, daughter of René, titular king of Jerusalem, Sicily, and *Naples*; which made him unpopular.

JACK (2), a coat of mail, a military coat worn over the coat of mail. (F.—L.—Gk.—Heb.) '*Iakke* of defence, *iak* of fence, garment, Baltheus;' Prompt. Parv. p. 256, and note, showing that the word was in use as early as 1375. 'Iacke, harnesse, *iacq*, *iaeque*;' Palsgrave.—OF. *Jaque*, 'James, also a Iack, or coat of maile, and thence, a Iack for the body of an Irish grey-hound . . . put on him when he is to coap' [with a wild boar]; Cot. Cf. Ital. *giaco*, a coat-of-mail, Span. *jaco*, a soldier's jacket; also Du. *jak*, G. *jacke*, Swed. *jacka*, a jacket, jerkin. **β.** Of obscure origin. Most likely Ducange is right in assigning the origin of it to the *Jacquerie* or revolt of the peasantry nicknamed *Jacques Bonhomme*, A. D. 1358. That is, it is from the OF. name *Jacques*.—L. *Iacōbus*.—Gk. Ἰάκωβος.—Heb. *Ya'aqōb*, Jacob, lit. 'one who seizes by the heel.'—Heb. root *'āqab*, to seize by the heel, to supplant. ¶ In some instances, *jack* (1) and *jack* (2) were doubtless confused; as, e. g. in *black-jack*. Der. *jack-et*, q. v.; also *jack-boots*, boots worn as armour for the legs, in the Spectator, no. 435; *black-jack* (Nares, s. v. *jack*).

JACKAL, a kind of wild animal. (Turk.—Pers.) In Dryden, Annus Mirabilis, st. 82, l. 327; Sir T. Herbert, Travels, ed. 1665, p. 115. Spelt *Iaccal* in Sandys, Trav. p. 205.—Turk. *chakāl*.—Pers. *shaghāl*; Palmer's Pers. Dict. col. 383. Cf. Skt. *çṛgāla-s*, a jackal, a fox.

JACKET, a short coat. (F.—L.—Gk.—Heb.) 'In a blew *jacket*' Spenser, Mother Hubberd's Tale, l. 205. Palsgrave has *Iacket*.—OF. *jaquette*, 'a jacket, or short and sleevelesse country-coat;' Cot. Dimin. of OF. *jaque*, 'a jack, or coat of mail;' Cot. See **Jack** (2). Der. *jacket-ed*.

JACOBIN, a friar of the order of St. Dominick. (F.—L.—Gk.—Heb.) 'Now frere menour, now *Iacobyn*;' Rom. of the Rose, l. 6338.—F. *jacobin*, 'a jacobin;' Cot.—Low L. *Jacōbinus*, adj. formed from *Jacōbus*; see **Jack** (2). B. Hence one of a faction in the French revolution, so called from the *Jacobin* club, which first met in the hall of the Jacobin friars in Paris, Oct. 1789; see Haydn, Dict. of Dates. C. Also the name of a *hooded* (friar-like) pigeon; F. *jacobine*, fem. of *jacobin*. Der. *Jacobin-ic-al*, *Jacobin-ism*.

JACOBITE, an adherent of James II. (L.—Gk.—Heb.) Formed with suffix -*ite* (= L. -*ita*), from *Jacōb-us*, James. See **Jack** (2). Der. *Jacobit-ism*.

JACONET, a cotton fabric. (Hind.—Skt.) At first imported from India; spelt *jaconot* in 1769. 'Corrupted from Urdū [Hind.] *Jagannāthī*, from *Jagannāth* (Juggernaut) or *Jagannāthpurī* in Cuttack, where it was originally manufactured;' N. E. D. See **Juggernaut**. (Hind. *pūr* = a town.)

JADE (1), a sorry nag, an old woman. (Scand. ?) ME. *jade* (MS. *Iade*), Chaucer, C. T. 14818 (B 4002). Also found as *jaud*, *jad* (E. D. D.). Of unknown origin; unless it can be a variant of Lowl. Sc. *yaud*, *yad*, *yade*, which seems probable; see E. D. D. If so, it is from Icel. *jalda*, a mare; cf. prov. Swed. *jäldä*, a mare (Rietz). Der. *jade*, vb. to tire, spurn, Antony, iii. 1. 34.

JADE (2), a hard dark green stone. (F.—Span.—L.) In Bailey's Dict., vol. ii. ed. 1731. Cf. F. *jade*, Span. *jade*, jade. Florio's Ital. Dict. gives the form *iada*. The jade brought from America by the Spaniards was called *piedra de ijada*, because it was believed to cure pain in the side (see Pineda, s. v. *piedra*); for a similar reason it was called *nephritis* (from Gk. νεφρός, kidney). Hence F. *jade* is from Span. *ijada*, the flank; cf. Port. *ilhal*, *ilharga*, the flank, side.—L. *ilia*, pl., the flanks. Körting, § 4708.

JAG, a notch, a pointed shred. (F. ?) 'Jagge, or dagge of a garment;' Prompt. Parv. p. 255. 'I iagge or cutte a garment; *Iagge*, a cuttyng;' Palsgrave. Cf. *iaggen*, to pierce, strike through; Morte Arthure, 2087. Apparently coined as a parallel form to *dag*;

and as *dag* may have been (in some of its senses) suggested by F. *dague*, a dagger (see Morte Arthure, 2102), so *jag* may have been suggested by an OF. **jagaye*, variant of *zagaye* or *azagaye* or *archegaie*, an assagai (Cot., Godefroy). Godefroy and Cotgrave quote the dimin. form *jagayette*; and *archigaie* occurs in Froissart; see **Assagai**. Der. *jagg-ed*, spelt *iaggde* in Gascoigne, Steel Glas, 1161; whence *to-iagged*, Skelton, Elinour Rummyng, l. 124; *jagg-ed-ness*; *jagg-y*.

JAGGERY, a coarse brown sugar. (Port.—Canarese—Skt.) Spelt *gagara*, Hakluyt, Voy., ii. pt. 1. 252.—Port. *jagara*, *jagra*.—Canarese *sharkare* (H. H. Wilson).—Skt. *çarkarā*. See **Sugar**.

JAGUAR, a S. American beast of prey. (Brazilian.) In a translation of Buffon's Nat. Hist., London, 1792. The word is Brazilian; see Buffon, Quadruped. t. iii. pp. 289, 293 (Littré). '*Jagua* in the Guarani [Brazilian] language is the common name for tygers and dogs. The generic name for tygers in the Guarani language is *Jaquarete*;' Clavigero, Hist. of Mexico, tr. by Cullen, ii. 318 (ed. 1787). Cavalcanti gives Brazil. *yáuára*, a dog, *yáuira-eté*, *iáuára-eté*, a jaguar; Granada, in his Vocab. Rioplatense, gives '*jaguar*, tigre.' See my Notes on E. Etym., p. 338.

JAIL, another spelling of **Gaol**, q. v. (F.—L.)

JALAP, the root of a Mexican plant. (Mexican.) '*Jalap*, the root of a kind of Indian night-shade;' Phillips' Dict., ed. 1706. And in Coles, ed. 1684. Named from *Jalapa* or *Xalapa*, in Mexico. From Aztec *Xalapan*, lit. 'sand by the water;' from *xal(li)*, sand, *a(tl)*, water, and *pan*, on, near; where *-li*, *-tl* are suppressed in composition. See my Notes on E. Etym., p. 332.

JALOUSIE, a blind made with slats sloping upward from without. (F.—L.—Gk.) First in 1824.—F. *jalousie*, 'jealousie; also a lattice window, or grate to look through;' Cot. So called because it prevents strangers from seeing in. — F. *jaloux*, jealous; see **Jealous**.

JAM (1), to press, squeeze tight. (E.) '*Jam*, to squeeze;' Halliwell. '*Jammed* in between the rocks;' Swinburne, Travels through Spain (1779), let. 3, p. 8. '*Jam*, to render firm by treading, as cattle do land they are foddered on;' Marshall's Rural Economy of Norfolk (E. D. S. Gloss. B. 3). The same word as *cham*, or *champ*. 'I *chamme* a thyng small bytwene my tethe, or *champe*;' Palsgrave. '*Champ* [with excrescent *p*], to tread heavily, Warwickshire; to bite or chew, Suffolk;' Halliwell. Whence also: '*Champ*, hard, firm, Sussex;' id.; i. e. *chammed* or *jammed* down, as if by being trodden on; and see E. D. D. See **Champ**, which is of imitative origin. ¶ For the common and regular change from *ch* to *j*, see **Jaw, Jowl**.

JAM (2), a conserve of fruit boiled with sugar. (E.) In Johnson's Dict.; and in Ashe (1775). Apparently from **Jam** (1). The following quotation suggests that it may mean a soft substance, resembling what has been chewed. 'And if we haue anye stronger meate, it must be *chammed* afore by the nurse, and so putte into the babe's mouthe;' Sir T. More, Works, p. 241 h. See **Champ**.

JAMB, the side-post of a door. (F.—L.) '*Jaum* of the door, the side-post. This word is also used in the South, where they say the *jaum* of the chimney;' Ray, Collection of North-Country Words, 1691. Spelt *jaumbe* in Cotgrave. 'Yea, the *jambes*, posts, principals, and standards, all of the same mettall;' Holland, tr. of Pliny, b. xxxiii. c. 3, § 7. And in Baret (1580).—F. *jambe*, 'the leg or shank, . . . the jaumbe or side-post of a door;' Cot. Cf. Ital. *gamba*, Span. *gamba*, the leg; Port. *gambias*, pl. the legs.—Late L. *gamba*, a hoof; Vegetius, 1. 56, near the end; 3. 20. From an older form *camba*, which appears in the book of Cerne (see **Gambol**), and in O. Spanish (Diez, whom see). Closely allied to O. Celtic **kambos*, crooked (Stokes-Fick); so that the word was orig. used of the bent leg or the knee. Cf. W. *cam*, crooked. And see **Ham**. Der. *giamb-eux*, leggings, greaves, Spenser, F. Q. ii. 6. 29; *jambeaux*, Chaucer, C. T., B 2065; pl. from an AF. **iambel*, OF. *jambe*.

JANE, a twilled cotton cloth; see **Jean**.

JANGLE, to sound discordantly, to quarrel. (F.—Scand.) 'A *jangling* of the bells;' Shak. Per. ii. 1. 45. Hence *jangle*=to make discordant; 'like sweet bells *jangled*;' Haml. iii. 1. 166. ME. *janglen*, to quarrel, talk loudly. 'To *jangle* and to jape;' P. Plowman, B. ii. 94. Spelt *gangle*, Alisaunder, ed. Weber, 7413.—OF. *jangler*, 'to jangle, prattle, talk saucily or scurvily;' Cot. β. Of Scand. origin.—Swed. dial. and Norw. *jangla*, to quarrel; cf. Du. *jangelen*, to importune (Sewel), a frequentative form (with suffix *-el*) from Du. *janken*, to howl, yelp as a dog (Sewel). Cf. Low G. *janken*, to yelp as a dog; Bremen Wörterb. ii. 636; also Westphal. *jänglen*, to play out of tune. Of imitative origin; cf. L. *gannire*, to yelp as a dog, talk loudly. Der. *jangl-er*, *jangl-ing*; see *jingle*.

JANIZARY, JANISSARY, a soldier of the old Turkish footguard. (F.—Ital.—Turkish.) Bacon speaks of 'the Janizaries'

in Essay 19, Of Empire, near the end. There is an earlier reference to them in Sir T. More, Works, p. 279 f. '*Janissaries*, an order of infantry in the Turkish army: originally, young prisoners trained to arms; were first organised by Orcan, about 1330, and remodelled by his son Amurath I. 1360. . . . A firman was issued on 17 June, 1826, abolishing the Janizaries;' Haydn, Dict. of Dates. And see Gibbon, Roman Empire, c. 64.—MF. *Jannissaires*, 'the Janizaries;' Cot.—M. Ital. *ianizzeri*, 'the Turkes gard;' Florio. Of Turkish origin; the word means 'new soldiery;' from Turk. *yeñi*, new, and *cheri*, soldiery (Devic). The *ñ* represents *saghir noon*, a nasal letter peculiar to Turkish. And *cheri* is from Pers. *charik*, auxiliary forces (Zenker); see Rich. Dict., p. 537.

JANUARY, the first month of the year. (L.) ME. *January* (MS. *Ianuary*), Chaucer, C. T. 9267 (E 1393). Englished from L. *Iānuārius*, January, named from the god *Iānus*. *Iānus* (for **Diānus*) is allied to *Diāna* (Bréal).

JAPAN, a name given to certain kinds of varnished work. (Japan.) Properly '*Japan* work,' where *Japan* is used adjectivally. Named from the country; see Yule. Pope playfully alludes to 'shining altars of *Japan*;' Rape of the Lock, iii. 107. Der. Hence *japan*, verb, to varnish like Japan work, to polish; *japann-er*, a polisher of shoes, shoe-black, Pope, Imit. of Horace, Epist. i. 1. 156.

JAPE, to jest, mock, befool. (F.—Scand.) Obsolete. In Chaucer, C. T. 1731; P. Plowm. B. i. 67. Apparently suggested by OF. *japer* (Hatzfeld), F. *japper*, to bark as a dog, to yap, of imitative origin; but in sense answering rather to OF. *juber* (Godefroy), variant of *gaber*, 'to mock, flout, gull, cheat,' Cot.; which has just the same sense as *jape*. Roquefort has *gap*=*gab*, mockery. —Icel. *gabba*, to mock; *gabb*, mockery. Puitspelu gives Lyons dial. *japia*, foolish stories. See **Gabble, Jabber**.

JAR (1), to make a discordant noise, creak, clash, quarrel. (E.) 'All out of ioynt ye *iar*;' Skelton, Duke of Albany, l. 378. And see Shak. Tam. Shrew, iii. 1. 39, 47; v. 2. 1. *Jar* stands for an older form *char*, only found in the prov. E. *char*, to chide, and in the derivative *charken*, to creak like a cart or barrow (Prompt. Parv.), also to creak like a door (Gower, C. A. ii. 102); cf. also AS. *ceorian*, *cerian*, to murmur, MDu. *karren*, *kerren*, 'to crake [creak] like a cart,' Hexham; OHG. *kerran*, to give a loud harsh sound; cf. **Jargon** and **Garrulous**. Der. *jar*, sb., spelt *jarre*, Spenser, F. Q. iii. 3. 23.

JAR (2), an earthen pot. (F.—Span.—Arab.) 'A great *jar*;' Ben Jonson, tr. of Horace's Art of Poetry; l. 28. And in Cotgrave. The Latinized form *jarrus* occurs in The Earl of Derby's Expeditions (Camden Soc.), p. 228, l. 18.—OF. *jare*, 'a jarre,' Cot.; mod. F. *jarre*. [Cf. Span. *jarra*, a jug, pitcher; Ital. *giara*, *giarra*, 'a iarre;' Florio.]—Span. *jarra*, *jarro*, a jar (Pineda); *jarro* (Minsheu).—Arab. *jarrah*, a jar (Devic); cf. Pers. *jurrah*, a little cruise, or jar; Rich. Dict. p. 504, col. 2. Probably borrowed by the Spanish from the Arabs.

JARGON, a confused talk. (F.—L.?) ME. *jargon*, *jergon*, chattering. 'And ful of *jargon*'=very talkative; Chaucer, C. T. 9722 (E 1848). Particularly used of the chattering of birds; Gower, C. A. ii. 264; bk. v. 4103; Rom. of the Rose, 716.—F. *jargon*, 'gibridge, fustian language,' Cot.; *jargonner*, 'to speak fustian, jangle, chatter,' id. The word is old, and appears also as OF. *gergon*, *gargon* (Godefroy). Cf. Span. *gerigonza*, jargon; *gerigonzar*, to speak a jargon; Ital. *gergo*, jargon. β. All perhaps from an imitative base *garg*- (cf. *garg-le*, *gurg-le*), prob. allied to L. *garrire*; see **Jar** (1). This extended form GARG, answering to a Teut. base KARK, is exactly represented in English by ME. *charken*, to creak as a cart, and the AS. *cearcian*, to gnash the teeth (Ælfric's Homilies, i. 132). An attenuated form of *charken* is the ME. *chirken*, to chirp, to make a harsh noise. 'Al ful of *chirking* [=jargon] was that sory place;' Chaucer, C. T. 2006 (A 2004).

JARGONELLE, a variety of pear. (F.—Ital.—Arab.—Pers.) In Johnson's Dict.—F. *jargonelle*, a variety of pear, very stony or gritty (Littré). Formed (according to Littré) as a dimin. from F. *jargon*, a yellow diamond, a small stone. —Ital. *giargone*, a sort of yellow diamond; E. *zircon*.—Arab. *zarqūn*.—Pers. *zargūn*, gold-coloured, from *zar*, gold, and *gūn*, colour; see Devic, Supp. to Littré, and Yule.

JASEY, JAZY, a wig made of worsted or tow. (Jersey.) 'The old gentleman in the flaxen *jazy*;' Scott, Redgauntlet, ch. xxi [*not* xx]. For *Jersey*, because made of Jersey yarn; see Forby, Vocab. of E. Anglia. See **Jersey**.

JASMINE, JESSAMINE, a genus of plants. (F.—Pers.) Spelt *jasmin*, *jessemin*, *jelsomine*, *jesse*, in Cotgrave. Milton has *jessa-mine*, P. L. iv. 698; Lycidas, 143. The spelling *jasmin* agrees with MF. *jasmin*; Cot. *Jessemin*, *jelsomine* answer to the Ital. forms *gesmino*, *gelsomino*. The Span. form is *jazmin*. All are from Pers. *yāsmin*, jasmine; of which another form is *yāsamin*, jessamine; Rich. Pers. Dict. p. 1703; Palmer's Pers. Dict. col. 715.

JASPER, a precious stone. (F.—L.—Gk.—Arab.) ME. *Iaspre*, *Iasper*. ' What is bettre than gold: *Iaspre*;' Chaucer, C. T., Tale of Melibeus, B 2297. Also spelt *Iaspis*, Gower, C. A. iii. 112; bk. vii. 841.—OF. *jaspre* (see Littré), an occasional spelling of OF. and F. *jaspe*, ' a jasper stone;' Cot. [Thus the *r* is an addition, and no real part of the word.]—L. *iaspidem*, acc. of *iaspis*, a jasper.—Gk. ἴασπις.—Arab. *yasb*, *yasf*, also spelt *yashb*, jasper; whence Pers. *yashp*, *yashf*, jasper; Rich. Pers. Dict. p. 1707; Palmer's Pers. Dict. col. 719. Cf. Heb. *yāshpheh*, a jasper.

JAUNDICE, a disease caused by bile. (F.—L.) In Shak. Merch. Ven. i. 1. 85. The *d* is purely excrescent, as commonly in E. words after *n*; cf. *sound* from F. *son*. ME. *Iaunys*, Pricke of Conscience, l. 700; spelt *iaundys*, Trevisa, ii. 113; further corrupted to *iawndres*, in a 15th-cent. tr. of Higden, on the same page as the last reference.—OF. (and F.) *jaunisse*, so spelt in the 13th cent. (Littré); but Cot. gives it as *jaulnisse*, ' the jaundies.' Formed with suffix *-isse* (=L. *-itia*) from F. *jaune*, yellow; because the disease is characterized by yellowness of the skin and eyes. The oldest spelling of *jaune* is *jalne* (Littré).—L. *galbinus*, also *galbineus*, greenish yellow.—L. *galbus*, yellow. The likeness of L. *galbus* to G. *gelb* is so close as to suggest that it is of Teutonic origin; the true L. form being *heluus*. See **Yellow**. Der. *jaundic-ed*.

JAUNT, a tiring ramble, an excursion. (F.) It would seem from the exx. in Shak. that *jaunt* and *jaunce* are equivalent terms. *Jaunt* is a wild and fatiguing ramble, Romeo, ii. 5. 26; where another reading is *jaunce*; cf. *geances*, fatiguing journies, in Ben Jonson, A Tale of a Tub, A. ii (Hilts). It also means to ramble, rove, id. ii. 5. 53, where another reading for *jaunting* is *jaunsing*. Again, Shak. has: 'Spurred, galled, and tired by *jauncing* Bolingbroke,' i.e. hard-riding Bolingbroke. This *jaunce* is from ME. *jancer*, of which Cotgrave says: ' *Jancer un cheval*, to stirre a horse in the stable till he sweat with-all, or as our *jaunt*; an old word.' Not found in OF. Cf. E. dial. *jankit*, jaded; Swed. dial. *jank*, useless trouble, slow motion (Rietz); Norw. *janka*, to stagger. Der. *jaunt*, vb., to ramble. ¶ I suggest that *jaunt* arose from *jaunts*, a corrupt form of *jaunce*, taken as a plural form.

JAUNTY, JANTY, genteel, stylish, fantastical. (F.—L.) 'We owe most of our *janty* fashions now in vogue to some adept beau among them' [the French]; Guardian, no. 149; dated 1713. As if formed with suffix *-y* from the verb *jaunt*, to ramble idly about; but formerly *janty* or *jantee*, also *jentee*, variants of *genteel*, and used in the same sense. See therefore **Genteel**. β. Exx.: ' This *jantee* sleightness to the French we owe;' T. Shadwell, Timon, p. 71 (1688). ' A *jaunty* [genteel] part of the town;' Spectator, no. 503. ' Turn you about on your heel with a *jantee* air;' Farquhar, The Inconstant, Act I. Cf. also 'Sae jimpy lac'd her *genty* waist;' Burns, Bonie Ann. Der. *jaunt-i-ness*, Spectator, no. 530.

JAVELIN, a kind of spear or dart. (F.—C.?) Used in the sense of boar-spear, Shak., Venus, 616. ' *Iavelyn*, a speare, *iauelot*;' Palsgrave.—MF. *javelin*, m., *javeline*, f., ' a javeling, a weapon of a size between the pike and partizan;' Cot. Cf. MF. *javelot*, ' a gleave, dart, or small javelin;' Cot. Also Span. *jabalina*, Ital. *giavellotto*, a javelin. β. Perhaps of Celtic origin. The Breton *gavlin* and *gavlod* are merely borrowed from the French; but the origin is shown by the Irish *gabhla*, a spear, lance; *gabhlach*, forked, divided, peaked, pointed; *gabhlan*, a branch, a fork of a tree; *gabhlog*, any forked piece of timber; *gabhal*, OIrish *gabul*, a fork. Cf. Gael. *gobhal*, a fork; *gobhlach*, forked, pronged; *gobhlag*, a small fork, two-pronged instrument; *gobhlan*, a prong, small fork, weeding-hook. Also W. *gafl*, a fork; *gaflach*, a fork, a dart. See **Gaff**. γ. Hence may also be explained the ME. *gavelok*, a javelin, dart, in King Alisaunder, l. 1620; AS. *gafeluc*, Voc. 143. 6; also MHG. *gabilōt*, a javelin (from F.). See Thurneysen, p. 63; Macbain, s. v. *gobhal*.

JAW, part of the mouth. (F.—L.) ME. *jowe*; ' *Jowe* or chekebone, Mandibula;' Prompt. Parv. 'ʒit drow [drew] I him out of þe *Iowes*, scilicet faucibus, of hem þat gapeden;' Chaucer, tr. of Boethius, b. i. pr. 4, l. 70. 'Þe ouer *iawe*' = the upper jaw, Trevisa, iii. 109; with various readings, *jawe*, *geowe*.—AF. *jowe*, glossed ' cheke;' W. de Bibbesworth, in Wright's Voc. i. p. 145; Norm. dial. *joe*, Guernsey *jaue* (Moisy); F. *joue*, the cheek; OF. *joe* (with *o* for later *ou*), Chanson de Roland, l. 3921; corresponding to Ital. *gota*, ' a cheek, a iaw' (Florio), Prov. *gauta*; which Diez derives from Late L. *gavata*, L. *gabata*, a kind of platter, a bowl; from the rounding of the jaw. Körting, § 4103. ¶ Palsgrave has *chawebone*; this alteration to *chaw* is later, and due to association with the verb *to chew*. Somewhat similar is the MDu. *kouwe*, the cavity of the mouth, from MDu. *kouwen* (Du. *kaauwen*), to chew; Kilian. Der. *jaw-bone*, Bible, 1551, Judg. xv. 15; *jaw-teeth*; *jaw-fallen*, Fuller, Worthies, Essex (R.); *lantern-jaw-ed*.

JAY, a bird with gay plumage. (F.—OHG.) ME. *jay*, *Iay*; Chaucer, C. T. 644; King Alisaunder, l. 142.—MF. *jay* (older

spellings *gay*, *gai*), a jay; Cot. Mod. F. *geai*; Gascon *gaï*; Norm. dial. *gai*. So also Span. *gayo*, a jay, *gaya*, a magpie. β. Hardly from OHG. *gāhi* (MHG. *gæhe*, G. *jäh*), adj., quick, lively (Kluge). But rather allied to *gay*, OF. *gai*; and to be derived from OHG. *wāhi*, fine, beautiful. Körting, § 1718.

JEALOUS, suspicious of rivalry, tender of honour. (F.—L.—Gk.) ME. *jalous*, Chaucer, C. T. 1331 (A 1329). Earlier *gelus*, Ancren Riwle, p. 90, where it occurs to translate L. *zēlotes*.—OF. *jalous*, later *jaloux*, ' jealous;' Cot. Cf. Ital. *geloso*, Span. *zeloso*, jealous.—Late L. *zēlōsus*, full of zeal; related to L. *zēlōtēs*, one who is jealous.—L. *zēlus*, zeal.—Gk. ζῆλος, zeal; see **Zeal**. Der. *jealous-ly*; *jealous-y*, ME. *jalousye*, Chaucer, C. T. 12300 (C 366), from F. *jalousie*; also *jalousie*, q. v. **Doublet**, *zealous*.

JEAN, JANE, a twilled cotton cloth. (F.—Ital.) ' *Gene* fustian;' in 1589; H. Hall, Society in Eliz. Age, p. 210. Cf. ME. *Gene*, Genoa; spelt *Geane* in The Paston Letters, ii. 293.—MF. *Genes*, Genoa.—Ital. *Genova*, Genoa; whence it was brought.

JEER, to mock, scoff. (F.—L.?) In Shak. Com. Errors, ii. 2. 22. ' He saw her toy, and gibe, and *geare*;' Spenser, F. Q. ii. 6. 21. ' There you named the famous *jeerer*, That ever *jeered* in Rome or Athens;' Beaum. and Fletcher, Nice Valour, v. 1 (Song). It seems to have been regarded as a foreign word; see Ben Jonson, Staple of News, iv. 1. 5: ' Let's *jeer* a little. *Jeer*? what's that? Expect, sir,' i. e. wait a bit, and you will find out. Not found before 1553. β. The origin of the word is doubtful. If it were a slang term, it might be a corruption of Du. *scheren*, *scheeren*. From the Du. *gek*, a fool, and *scheeren*, to shear, was formed the phrase *den gek scheeren* (lit. to shear the fool), to mock, jeer, make a fool of one. Soon these words were run together, and the word *gekscheeren* was used in the sense of jeering. See Sewel's Du. Dict., which gives the above forms, as well as the sb. *gekscheeren*, ' a jeering, fooling, jesting: *Ik laat my niet gekscheeren*, I will not be trifled with.' This is still preserved in mod. Du. *gekscheeren*, to jest, banter, and in the phrase *het is geen gekscheren*, it is no laughing matter. The phrase was also used as *scheeren den gek*, to play the fool; whence simply *scheeren*, ' to gibe, or to jest' (Hexham). γ. But it accords better with phonetic laws to derive it from OF. (or AF.) *giere*, an occasional variant of OF. *chiere*, whence E. *cheer*. Godefroy has: 'S'aucuns hons te fait d'amere *giere*,' if any man makes you bitter **cheer** (jeers at you). Again, in his Supplement: ' Mas faites bale, *giere*, ioie, solas, et ris,' but dance, make cheer and joy, and pleasure, and laughter. From the phr. *faire male chere*, to make ill cheer, to frown upon. See **Cheer**. ¶ See my Note; Phil. Soc. Trans., 1902. Der. *jeer*, sb., Oth. iv. 1. 83.

JEHOVAH, the chief Hebrew name of the Deity. (Heb.) In Exod. vi. 3.—Heb. *yahōvāh*, or more correctly *yhwh* (not pronounced); see article on Jehovah in the Concise Dict. of the Bible.

JEJUNE, hungry, meagre, empty. (L.) ' We discourse *jejunely*, and falsely, and unprofitably;' Bp. Taylor, pref. to Great Exemplar.—L. *iēiūnus*, fasting, hungry, dry, barren, trifling, poor. Of uncertain origin. Der. *jejune-ly*, *jejune-ness*.

JELLY, anything gelatinous, the juice of fruit boiled with sugar. (F.—L.) In Hamlet, i. 2. 205. ME. *Iely*; Lydgate, Hors, Shepe, and Goos; l. 70. Hence *geli-cloth*; Earl of Derby's Expeditions (Camd. Soc.), p. 234. Sometimes spelt *gelly*.—F. *gelée*, ' a frost, also gelly;' Cot. Properly the fem. form of *gelé*, frozen, pp. of *geler*, ' to freeze, to thicken or congeale with cold;' Cot.—L. *gelāre*, to congeal.—L. *gelu*, frost. See **Gelatine, Gelid, Congeal**. Der. *jelly-fish*.

JEMADAR, a native officer in a sepoy regiment. (Hind.—Arab. and Pers.) See Yule.—Hind. *jama'dār*, a jemadar.—Arab. *jamā'at*, a body of men (from Arab. root *jama'a*, he collected); and Pers. *dār*, a holder, master. See N. E. D.; and Rich. Dict., pp. 518, 646.

JENNET, GENNET, a small Spanish horse. (F.—Span.—Arab.) *Jennets*; Shak. Oth. i. 1. 113. ' A breeding *jennet*;' Shak. Venus, 260. 'We have xx. thousande of other mounted on *genettes*;' Berners, tr. of Froissart, vol. i. c. 236. ' *Iennettes* of Spayne;' Squyr of Lowe Degre, l. 749.—MF. *genette*, ' a genet, or Spanish horse;' Cot.—Span. *ginete*, a nag; but the orig. sense was a horse-soldier, esp. a light-armed horse-soldier. Minsheu (1623) has: ' *ginete*, a light horseman that rideth *a la gineta*;' also ' *cavalgar a la Gineta*, to ride with the legs trussed up in short stirrups, with a target and a ginnet launce.' Of Moorish origin. The word is traced by Dozy (Glos. p. 276) to Arab. *zenāta*, a tribe of Barbary celebrated for its cavalry; see Devic, Supp. to Littré.

JENNETING, an early apple. (F.—L.—Gk.—Heb.) ' In July come ... plummes in fruit, *ginnitings*, quadlins;' Bacon, Essay 46, Of Gardens. ' Contrariwise, pomgranat-trees, fig-trees, and apple-trees, liue a very short time; and of these, the hastie kind or *ieniting*s, continue nothing so large as those that bear and ripen later;' Holland, tr. of Pliny, b. xvi. c. 44. So called because they were ripe about St. John's day (June 24) in France and Italy; but in England sometimes later. See Hogg's Fruit Annual, pp. 361, 522. Cf. *pere-*

Ionettes [Jeannot pears] in P. Plowman, C. xiii. 221, and the note. Sometimes spelt *geniton* (N. E. D.).—F. *Jeanneton, Jeannet*; from *Jean*, John. Cotgrave has: '*Pomme de S. Jean*, or *Hastivel*, a soon ripe apple called the St. John's apple.' Cf. G. *Johannisapfel*, 'John apple, geniting;' Flügel. See **Jack** (1). ¶ Commonly said to be a corruption of *June-eating* apples!

JEOPARDY, hazard, peril, danger. (F.—L.) ME. *jupartie*, later *ieopardy* or *jeopardy*. 'Hath lost his owen good thurgh *jupartye*;' Chaucer, C. T. 16211 (G 743). The various readings in this line are *Iupartie, Iopardy, Iopardye*, and *Iepardye*. Spelt *Iupartye*, Chaucer, Troilus, ii. 465. The original sense was a game in which the chances are even, a game of hazard, hence hazard or chance; as in: 'To putte that sikernes in *jupartye* = to put in hazard that which is secure; Troil. iv. 1512.—OF. *jeu parti*, lit. a divided game. 'A *jeu parti* is properly a game, in which the chances are exactly even. See Froissart, v. i. c. 234; Ils n'estoient pas à *jeu parti* contre les François (= for they were unequal in numbers to the French) (Johnes' translation]: and vol. ii. c. 9, si nous les voyons à *jeu parti*. From hence it signifies anything uncertain or hazardous. In the old French poetry, the discussion of a problem, where much might be said on both sides, was called a *jeu parti*. See Poesies du Roy de Navarre, chanson xlviii.'—Tyrwhitt's note to Chaucer, C. T. 16211.—Late L. *iocus partītus*, an alternative, a phrase used when a choice was given, of choosing one side or the other; see Ducange.—L. *iocus*, a joke, jest, sport, play, game; and *partītus*, divided, pp. of *partīri*, to part, from *part-*, stem of *pars*, a part. See **Joke** and **Part**. Der. *jeopard*, to hazard (coined by dropping *-y*), Judges, v. 18, ME. *Iuparten*, Chaucer, Troil. iv. 1566; *jeopardise*, vb.; also *jeopard-ous*, spelt *ieopardeous* in Hall's Chron. Hen. VIII, an. 25, § 10; *jeopard-ous-ly*. ¶ Observe the AF. diphthong *eo*, representing the F. *eu*.

JERBOA, a small rodent quadruped. (Arabic.) Mentioned in an E. translation of Buffon's Nat. Hist., London, 1792. The animal takes its name from the strong muscles in its hind legs.—Arab. *yarbū'*, '(1) the flesh of the back or loins, an oblique descending muscle; (2) the jerboa, an animal much resembling the dormouse, which makes prodigious bounds by means of its long hind legs; see Nat. Hist. of Aleppo, by Russell;' Rich. Pers. Dict. p. 1705, col. 2.

JEREED, JERID, a wooden javelin, used in a game. (Arab.) 'The hurl'd on high *jereed*;' Byron, Giaour, ix.—Arab. *jarīd*, a palmbranch stripped of its leaves, a lance. Rich. Dict., p. 505.

JERK, to give a sudden movement, throw with a quick action. (E.) Cotgrave has: '*Fouetter*, to scourge, lash, *yerke*, or *jerke*.' In Shak. as a sb., L. L. L. iv. 2. 129. 'A *ierk*, verber;' Levins, ed. 1570. 'With that which *jerks* [lashes] the hams of every jade;' Bp. Hall, Satires, b. iii. sat. 5, l. 26. Lowland Sc. *yerk*, to beat, strike smartly; a smart blow. 'To *jerke* or *gerke*;' Minsheu, ed. 1627. 'A *girke* or *yerke* of a rod or whip;' Minsheu's Span. Dict. (E. index). Halliwell also gives: '*Girk*, a rod; also, to beat.' β. Another form is *jert*. Cotgrave has: '*Attainte*, a reach, hit, blow, stroke, . . . a gentle nip, quip, or *jert*, a sleight *gird*, or taxation.' γ. Moreover, the words *jert* and *gird* were regarded as equivalent; thus Sherwood has, in his index to Cotgrave: 'A *jert* or *gird*, Attainte.' The words *jerk, jert*, and *gird* are probably all connected, and all had once the same meaning, viz. to strike, esp. with a whip or rod. δ. The only one of these three forms found in ME. is *gurden, girden*, to strike; see *gurden* in Stratmann. See **Gird** (2). ¶ It may be added that the usual meaning of *jerk* in old authors is to whip, to lash; as partly shown above. Der. *jerk*, sb.

JERKED BEEF, dried beef. (Peruvian.) The beef thus called is cut into thin slices and dried in the sun to preserve it. The process is explained in Capt. Basil Hall's Extracts from a Journal written on the coasts of Chili, Peru, and Mexico, vol. i. c. 4. The name is a singular corruption of *ccharqui*, the S. American name for it, which is a Peruvian word. 'The male deer and some of the coarser kind of the Peruvian sheep were slaughtered ; . . . and their flesh, cut into thin slices, was disjointed among the people, who converted it into *charqui*, the dried meat of the country;' Prescott, Conquest of Peru, c. v. β. An earlier form is *jerkin beef*. 'Their fish and flesh they boyle . . or broyle . . ; or else . . putting it on a spit, they turne first the one side, then the other, till it be as drie as their *ierkin beefe* in the West Indies;' Capt. J. Smith, Works, ed. Arber, p. 63.—Peruv. *ccharquini*, to make jerked (or hung) beef. Cf. Peruv. *ccharqui*, sb., a slice of flesh or hung beef or dried beef. Still common in the form *charqui*, sb., dried flesh, unsalted, in long strips; Granada, Vocabulario Rioplatense. See my Notes on Eng. Etym., p. 343.

JERKIN, a jacket, short coat. (Low G.) 'With *Dutchkin* dublets, with *Ierkins* iaggde;' Gascoigne, Steel Glass, l. 1161 (in Spec. of Eng. ed. Skeat). Similar forms are Westphal. *jürken*, a kind of overcoat; EFries. *jurken*, a child's frock. The origin is unknown; but perhaps it is from some name. Thus under EFries. *Djure*, Koolman notes that EFries. *Djurko, Diurko* is their form of

Du. *Dirk* (G. *Dietrich*, Theodoric), whence also the surnames *Djurken* and *Jurken*. *Jerkin* may represent *Djurken*, whilst the forms *jurken, jürken* (above) may come from *Jurken*; so also may the late Du. *jurk*, a frock (Sewel). β. I prefer the solution suggested by Berghaus; that Low G. *Juri* is a pet name for *George*, and that it also takes the dimin. form *Jürgen*, and in Hamburg *Jürken*; cf. OF. *Georget*, a sort of *casaque* (Godfrey). And cf. E. *jacket* (Athenæum, Jan. 10, 1903); Phil. Soc. Trans., 1903, p. 153.

JERSEY, fine wool, a woollen jacket. (Jersey.) '*Jersey*, the finest wooll taken from other sorts of wooll, by combing it;' Kersey, ed. 1715. Lit. 'Jersey wool,' and named from *Jersey*, one of the Channel islands. On the termination *-ey*, meaning 'island,' see **Island**. Of Scand. origin.

JERUSALEM ARTICHOKE, a kind of sunflower. (Ital.—L.) 'There is a soup called Palestine soup. It is made, I believe, of artichokes called *Jerusalem artichokes*, but the Jerusalem artichoke is so called from a mere misunderstanding. The artichoke, being a kind of sun-flower, was called in Italian *girasole*, from the Latin *gyrus*, circle, and *sol*, sun. Hence Jerusalem artichokes and Palestine soups!' Max Müller, Lect. on Language, 8th ed. ii. 404.—Ital. *girasole*, a sun-flower.—Ital. *girare*, to turn; and *sole*, sun.—L. *gyrāre*, to turn round, from *gyrus* (= Gk. γῦρος), a circle; and *sōlem*, acc. of *sōl*, sun. See **Gyre** and **Solar**.

JESSAMINE, the same as **Jasmine**, q. v.

JESSES, straps of leather or silk, with which hawks were tied by the legs. (F.—L.) In Shak. Oth. iii. 3. 261. 'That like an hauke, which feeling herselfe freed From bels and *jesses* which did let her flight;' Spenser, F. Q. vi. 4. 19. '*Jesses* for a hauke, *get*;' Palsgrave. ME. *ges*, both s. and pl. 'Me ofhalt thane uogel be the *ges*,' one restrains the bird by the jess; Ayenbite of Inwyt, p. 254. '*Gesse* made of leder' [leather]; Book of St. Albans, fol. b 5, back.—OF. *ges, gies*, nom., *get, giet*, acc.; pl. *ges, gies* (Godfroy, s. v. *giet*); MF. *jects*, pl. '*Gect*, a cast or throw, as at dice; *les jects d'un oyseau*, a hawkes Jesses;' Cot. So called from their use in letting the hawk fly.—L. *iactus*, nom., a cast, throw (acc. *iactum*).—L. *iactus*, pp. of *iacere*, to throw. Cf. also OF. *jeter*, MF. *jecter*, 'to cast, hurl;' id.—L. *iactāre*, to hurl, throw, frequentative of *iacere*, to throw. See **Jet** (1).

JEST, a joke, fun. (F.—L.) In Shak. Temp. iv. 241. Orig. a story, tale. ME. *geste*, a story, a form of composition in which tales were recited. 'Lat see wher [whether] thou canst tellen aught in *geste*;' Chaucer, C. T. 13861 (B 212). 'I cannot *geste*' = I cannot tell tales like a *gestour*, or professed tale-teller; id. 17354 (I 43). *Geste* = a tale, a saying; Allit. Poems, ed. Morris, A. 277.—OF. *geste*, an exploit, a history of exploits, romance, tale; *chansons de geste*, heroic poems; see Burguy.—L. *gesta*, used for *rēs gesta*, a deed, exploit, lit. 'a thing performed;' or from L. *gesta*, neut. pl.—L. *gestus*, pp. of *gerere*, to carry on, do, perform. See **Gesture**. Der. *jest*, vb., *jest-ing-ly*; also *jest-er* = ME. *gestour*, a reciter of tales, as in: 'And *gestours* for to tellen tales,' Chaucer, C. T. 13775 (B 2036). From L. *gerere* are also formed *gest-ure, gest-i-cu-late, con-gest-ion, di-gest, in-di-gest-ion, sug-gest, re-gist-er*; also *belli-ger-ent, con-ger-ies, ex-ag-ger-ate*.

JESUIT, one of the Society of Jesus. (F.—Span.—L.—Gk.—Heb.) In Cotgrave. The order was founded in 1534 by Ignatius Loyola; see Haydn, Dict. of Dates.—MF. *Jesuite*, 'a Jesuite;' Cot.—Span. *Jesuita* (the order being of Spanish foundation). Formed with suffix *-īta* (= L. *īta* as in L. *erēm-īta* = Gk. *-ιτης* as in ἐρημίτης, a hermit) from L. *Iēsū-*, for *Iēsūs*, q. v. Der. *jesuit-ic, jesuit-ic-al, jesuit-ic-al-ly, jesuit-ism*; all words with a sinister meaning, craft being commonly attributed to the Jesuits.

JESUS, the Saviour of mankind. (L.—Gk.—Heb.) In Wyclif's Bible.—L. *Iēsūs* (Vulgate).—Gk. Ἰησοῦς.—Heb. *Yēshū'a* (Jeshua, Nehem. viii. 17, a later form of Joshua); contracted form of *Yehōshū'a* (Jehoshua, Numb. xiii. 16), signifying 'Jehovah is salvation' or 'Saviour.'—Heb. root *yāsha'*, to be large; in the Hiphil conjugation, to save. Der. *Jesuit*, q. v. Doublets, *Joshua, Jeshua, Jehoshua*. ☞ In ME. commonly written in a contracted form (Ihs), which by editors is often printed *Jhesus*. This is really an error, the *h* standing for the Gk. H (long *ē*), so that 'Ihs' = *Iēsus*. So also 'Ihū' = *Iēsu*. In Gk. capitals, it is IHϹ, where H = long *ē* and Ϲ = *s*, being a form of the Gk. *sigma*; the mark above signifying that the form is contracted. In later times IHϹ became IHS. Lastly (the H being misunderstood) the ingenious fiction arose that IHS meant *Iesus Hominum Salvator* = Jesus Saviour of Men. The mark, being then unmeaning, was turned into a little cross, as on modern altarcloths.

JET (1), to throw out, fling about, spout. (F.—L.) In Tudor-English it commonly means to fling about the body, to strut about, to stalk about proudly. 'How he *jets* under his advanced plumes;' Tw. Nt. ii. 5. 36. 'Then must ye stately goe, *ietting* vp and downe;'

Ralph Roister Doister, A. iii. sc. 3. l. 121 (in Spec. of Eng. ed. Skeat). ME. *getten, ietten*; see Prompt. Parv. pp. 192, 258, and Way's notes; also Hoccleve, De Regimine Principum, 428. 'I *iette*, I make a countenaunce with my legges, *ie me iamboye*; I *iette* with facyon and countenaunce to sette forthe myselfe, *ie braggue*;' Palsgrave. — OF. *jetter*, also *getter*, 'to cast, hurl, throw, fling, dart or send out violently, put or push forth;' Cot. — L. *iactāre*, to fling, frequent. of *iacere*, to throw: whence *iactāre sē*, to boast. **Der.** *jet*, sb., ME. *get*, in early use in the sense of 'fashion;' cf. 'Get, or maner of custome, Modus, consuetudo,' Prompt. Parv.; 'al of the newe *Iet*' = all in the new fashion, Chaucer, C. T. 684 (A 682); this answers to OF. *iet* or *get* (mod. F. *jet*), which Cot. explains by 'a cast or throw, as at dice.' [The mod. sense of *jet* is a spout of water, as in Pope, Dunciad, ii. 177.] Hence also *jetteau*, Spectator, no. 412, for Ital. *getto*, a jet, by confusion with F. *jet d'eau* = a spout of water, a fountain (where F. *eau* = L. *aqua*, water). Also *jet-sam*, q. v., *jett-y*, q. v. ☞ From L. *iacere* (pp. *iactus*) are numerous derivatives; as, *ab-ject, ad-ject-ive, con-ject-ure, de-ject, e-ject, in-ject, inter-ject-ion, ob-ject, pro-ject, re-ject, sub-ject*; also *ad-jac-ent, circum-jac-ent, sub-jac-ent, e-jac-ulate*; also *amice* (1), *agistment, gist, joist, jesses*.

JET (2), a black mineral, used for ornaments. (F. — L. — Gk.) 'His bille was blak, and as the *Ieet* it shoon;' Chaucer, C. T. 14867 (B 4051). — OF. *iaiet* (Hatzfeld, s. v. *jais*), *iayet* (Godefroy); MF. *jet, jaet*, 'jet;' Cot. — L. *gagātem*, acc. of *gagātēs*, jet (whence the forms *gayet, jaet, jet* in successive order of development); see Trevisa, ii. 17, where the L. has *gagates*, Trevisa has *gagates*, and the later E. version has *iette*. Described in Pliny, xxxvi. 19. — Gk. γαγάτης, jet; so called from Γάγαι, a town in Lycia, in the S. of Asia Minor. **Der.** *jet-black*; *jett-y*, Chapman, tr. of Homer, Il. ii. 629; *jett-i-ness*.

JETSAM, JETSON, JETTISON, things thrown overboard from a ship. (F. — L.) '*Jetson* is a thing cast out of the ship, being in danger of wreck, and beaten to the shore by the waters, or cast on the shore by mariners;' Coke, vol. vi. fol. 106. *a*;' Blount's Gloss., ed. 1674 (s. v. *flotson*); *jetson*, in Minsheu. — AF. *getesone*, Black Book of the Admiralty, i. 96, 170; OF. *getaison* (Godefroy). — L. *iactātiōnem*, acc., a casting. — L. *iactāre*, to cast out. Cf. F. '*faire le iect*, to throw the lading of a ship overboard;' Cot. See Jet (1).

JETTY, a projection, a kind of pier. (F. — L.) Lit. 'thrown out.' ME. *gettey*; Lydgate, Troy-book, fol. N 1, back, col. 2, l. 2 (bk. ii. c. 21). The same as Jutty, q. v. — OF. *g tee*, MF. *jettée*, 'a cast, hurle, throw, fling, also a *jetty* or *jutty*; also, the bank of a ditch, or the earth cast out of it when it is made;' Cot. Properly the fem. of the pp. of OF. *geter*, F. *jeter*, to throw. See Jet (1).

JEW, a Hebrew. (F. — L. — Gk. — Heb.) ME. *Iewes*, pl. Jews; Chaucer, C. T. 12409 (C 475); earlier, *Giwes, Giws*, Ancren Riwle, p. 106. — AF. *Ieu, Geu*, a Jew; F. *Juif*; Cotgrave. — Late L. *Iūdæum*, acc. of *Iūdæus*. — Gk. Ἰουδαῖος, an inhabitant of Judæa. — Gk. Ἰουδαία, Judæa. — Heb. *Yehūdāh*, Judah, son of Jacob; lit. 'celebrated' or 'illustrious.' — Heb. root *yādāh*, to throw; in the Hithpiel conjugation, to praise, celebrate. **Der.** *Jew-ess* (with F. suffix); *Jew-ish*; *Jew-ry*, ME. *Iewerie*, Chaucer, C. T. 13419 (B 1679), earlier *Giwerie*, Ancren Riwle, p. 394, signifying 'a Jew's district,' from OF. *Juierie* (Littré) = mod. F. *Juiverie*. Also *Jews-harp*, Hakluyt, Voy. iii. 665, l. 21, sometimes called *Jews-trump*, as in Beaum. and Fletcher, Humorous Lieutenant, A. v. sc. 2. l. 10: a name given in derision, prob. with reference to the harp of David.

JEWEL, a precious stone, valuable ornament. (F. — L.) ME. *iowel*, Ayenbite of Inwyt, p. 112, l. 6; *iuel*, id. p. 77, l. 1. — AF. *iuel, iouel*; OF. *joiel, joel, jouel* (Godefroy); later *joyau*, 'a jewell;' Cot. Origin disputed; either (1) from Late L. *iocāle*, usually in pl. *iocālia*, jewels (lit. trinkets), from L. *iocārī*, to play (OF. *joer, jouer*). — L. *iocus*, play; see Joke. Or (2) a dimin. (with suffix *-el*) of OF. and F. *joie*, joy, pleasure; so that the sense is 'a little joy,' i. e. a toy, trinket. Cf. Span. *joyel*, a jewel, trinket, dimin. of *joya*, a jewel, present (answering in form to F. *joie*, though not used in same sense). Also Ital. *giojello*, a jewel, dimin. of *gioja*, (1) joy, (2) a jewel. See further under Joy. ☞ The use of Span. *joya* and Ital. *gioia* in the sense of 'jewel' supports the latter etymology; hence some think that the word was misunderstood in the middle ages, so that 'jewel' was translated into Late L. in the form *jocāle*, preserving the sense of 'toy,' but missing the etymology, which was thought to be from L. *iocus* instead of from *gaudium*, the sense of the two words being not very different. See Toynbee, §§ 76, 143; Körting, §§ 4188, 5182. **Der.** *jewell-er*, with which cf. MF. *joyallier*, a 'jeweller,' Cot.; *jewell-er-y* or *jewel-ry*, with which cf. MF. *joyaulerie*, 'jewelling, the trade or mystery of jewelling,' Cot.

JIB (1), the foremost sail of a ship. (Du.) '*Jib*, the foremost sail of a ship;' Ash's Dict., ed. 1775. First, spelt *gibb*, in 1661. Perhaps so called because readily shifted from side to side; the sb. being derived from the verb. See Jib (2). **Der.** *jib-boom* (Ash).

JIB (2), to shift a sail from side to side. (Du.) '*Jib*, to shift

the boom-sail from one side of the mast to the other;' Ash's Dict, ed. 1775. 'To *jib* round the sail;' Cook, Third Voyage, b. ii. c. 3 (R.). Also spelt *jibe*. '*Jibing*, shifting the boom-sail from one side of the mast to the other (Falconer);' id. Also spelt *gybe*. '*Gybing*, the act of shifting the boom-sail,' &c.; id.; cf. Dan. *gibbe*, 'to gybe, a naut. term;' Ferrall (from E. or Du.). — Du. *gijpen* (of sails), to turn suddenly: Calisch. Sewel gives: '*Gypen*, 't overslaan der zeylen [the overturning of a sail] a sail's being turned over by an eddy wind.' Cf. Jutland *gippe*, to shift the sails; Swed. dial. *gippa*, verb, used of a sudden movement or jerk; thus, if a man stands on the lower end of a slanting plank, and a sudden weight falls on the upper end and tips it up, he is *gippad*, i.e. jerked up; Reitz. Cf. Swed. *guppa*, to move up and down, to rock. And see Gibbet.

JIB (3), to move restively, as a horse. (F. — Scand.) '*Jib*, said of a draught-horse that goes backwards instead of forwards;' Halliwell. A very early use of a compound from this verb occurs in ME. *regibben*, to kick. 'Hit *regibbeth* anon; ase uet kelf and idel' = it kicks back again, like a fat and idle calf; Ancren Riwle, p. 138. Cf. 'Wynsyng of an horse, *regibement*;' Palsgrave. — OF. *giber*, 'se débattre des pieds et des mains, s'agiter, lutter,' i. e. to struggle with the hands and feet, Roquefort; *giber*, to shake (Godefroy). Whence OF. *regiber* (Roquefort), mod. F. *regimber*, to kick; accounting for the ME. *regibben*. Cf. also OF. *giper*, to kick (as a horse); Godefroy; Burgundy *gipai*, to gambol (Mignard). β. Of Scand. origin; cf. Swed. dial. *gippa*, to jerk. See Jib (2).

JIBBAH, the same as Jubbah. (Arab.) See Jupon.

JIBE, the same as Gibe, q.v. (Scand.)

JIG, a lively tune or dance. (F. — MHG.) As sb. in Shak. Much Ado, ii. 1. 77; Hamlet, ii. 2. 522. As vb., Hamlet, iii. 1. 150. — OF. *gige, gigue*, a sort of wind instrument, a kind of dance (Roquefort); but it was rather a stringed instrument, as noted by Littré and Burguy; which may be verified by consulting the Ital. use of the word *giga* in Paradiso, xiv. 118. Cf. Norm. dial. *giguer*, to dance (Moisy); Span. *giga*, a jig, lively tune or dance; Port. *giga*, a jig; Ital. *giga*, 'a fiddle, a croud, a kit, a violin' (Florio). — MHG. *gige*, mod. G. *geige*, a fiddle. **Der.** *jig*, verb, *jig-maker*, Hamlet, iii. 2. 131. Doublet, *gig*, q. v.

JILT, a flirt, inconstant woman. (L.) 'Where dilatory fortune plays the *jilt*;' Otway, The Orphan, i. 1. 65. 'And who is *jilted* for another's sake;' Dryden, tr. of Juvenal, Sat. vi. 530. A contraction of *jillet*. 'A *jillet* brak his heart at last;' Burns, On a Scotch Bard, Gone to the W. Indies, st. 6. A diminutive (with suffix *-et*) of *Jill*, a personal name, but used in the same sense as *jilt* or *flirt*. Hence the compounds *flirt-gill*, Romeo, ii. 4. 162; and *flirt-Gillian*, Beaum. and Fletcher, The Chances, i.i. 1 (Landlady). Cf. '*Bagasse*, a baggage, queane, *jyll*, punke, flirt;' Cot. Gill is short for *Gillian*, i. e. *Juliana*; see Gill (4). See Gillott, Gillett, in Bardsley, Dict. of Surnames. **Der.** *jilt*, verb.

JINGLE, to make a clinking sound. (E.) ME. *gingelen, ginglen*; Chaucer, C. T. 170. A frequentative verb from the base *jing*, by-form of prov. E. *jink*, to chink, to jingle, allied to and probably the same word as *chink*, a word of imitative origin; see Chink (2). A fuller form appears in *jangle*; hence Palsgrave has *gyngle-geangle*; see Jangle. **Der.** *jingle*, sb.

JINN, a demon. (Arab.) Formed from the Arab. pl. *jinna(t)*, demons; so that the form is properly a plural. The Arab. sing. is *jinnī, jinnīy*, which is Englished as *jinnee* or (more frequently) as *genie* (as if connected with L. *genius*).

JINRIKSHA, a light two-wheeled vehicle drawn by one or more men. (Japan.) See *Jennyrickshaw* in Yule. — Japan. *jinrikisha*; from *jin*, a man; *riki*, strength; and *sha*, a car. 'A car drawn by strength of man.'

JOB (1), to peck with the beak, as a bird. (E.?) '*Becquade*, a pecke, *job*, or bob with a beake;' Cot. '*Iobbyn* wythe the bylle' = to job with the beak; Prompt. Parv. Prob. of imitative origin; cf. *chop, dab, bob*. Cf. Irish and Gael. *gob*, the beak or bill of a bird.

JOB (2), a small piece of work. (F. — C.?) In Pope, Epilogue to Satires, i. 104; ii. 40; Donne versified, Sat. iv. 142. He also has the verb: 'And judges *job*,' Moral Essays, to Bathurst, 141. Spelt *jobb* in Kersey, ed. 1715. First in 1627. It seems to be equivalent to *gob*. '*Gob*, a portion, a lump; hence the phrase, to work by the *gob*;' Halliwell. Dimin. forms are seen in: '*Gobbet*, a morsel, a bit; a large block of stone is still called a *gobbet* by workmen;' Halliwell. '*Jobbel, Jobbet*, a small load, generally of hay or straw, Oxfordshire;' id. And see E. D. D. β. In earlier authors, only *gobbet* is found; ME. *gobet*, Chaucer, C. T. 698. — OF. *gob*, lit. a mouthful. 'L'avalla tout de *gob*, at one gulpe, or as one gobbet, he swallowed it;' Cot. Cf. *gober*, 'to ravine, devoure, swallow great morsels, let downe whole gobbets;' Cot. Of Celtic origin; cf. Gael. and Irish *gob*, the bill or beak of a bird, also, ludicrously, the mouth. See Gobbet, and Job (1). **Der.** *job*, verb; *jobb-er, jobb-er-y*.

JOCKEY, a man who rides a race-horse. (F.−L.−Gk.−Heb.) 'As *jockies* use;' Butler, Hudibras, pt. iii. c. 1. l. 6 from end. 'Whose *jockey-rider* is all spurs;' id. pt. iii. c. ii. last line. A Northern E. pronunciation of *Jackey*, dimin. of *Jack* as a personal name; see **Jack** (1). A name given to the lads who act as grooms and riders. *Jocky*, for *Jack*, occurs in Skelton, Works, ed. Dyce, i. 185, l. 91. **Der.** *jockey*, verb; *jockey-ism*, *jockey-ship*.

JOCOSE, merry. (L.) *Jocose* is in Kersey, ed. 1715. *Jocosity*, in Blount's Gloss., ed. 1674.−L. *iocōsus*, sportive.−L. *iocus*, a joke, sport. See **Joke**. **Der.** *jocose-ly*, *jocos-i-ty*.

JOCULAR, droll. (L.) 'My name is *Johphiel*, ... An airy *jocular* spirit;' Ben Jonson, Masques, The Fortunate Isles.−L. *iocu-lāris*, jocular.−L. *ioculus*, a little jest; dimin. of *iocus*, a jest; see **Joke**. And see **Juggle**. **Der.** *jocular-ly*, *jocular-i-ty*.

JOCUND, merry, pleasant. (F.−L.) ME. *ioconde*, *Iocunde*; Chaucer, C. T. 16064 (G 5,6).−OF. *jocond*, pleasant, agreeable (Godefroy); Roquefort gives the derived adj. *jocondeux*, and the derived sb. *jocondite*.−L. *iūcundus*, pleasant, agreeable; from L. *iuuāre* (pt. t. *iū-ui*), to help, aid; so that the orig. sense was 'helpful.' See **Adjutant**. **Der.** *jocund-ly*, *jocund-i-ty*.

JOG, to push slightly, jolt. (E. ?) Prob. imitative. Cf. Kentish *jock*, to jolt, shake; E. D. D. Cooper's Thesaurus (1565) has: '*Succutio*, To shake a thyng, to *iogge* vp.' Not found earlier. De Bo gives the WFlem. *djokken*, to jolt, to jog, as equivalent to F. *choquer*, to knock; cf. also Low G. *jukkeln*, *jukkern*, to jog on, to ride badly (Berghaus); Norw. and Swed. dial. *jukka*, to jog up and down in riding. Cf. also E. *shog*, as used in Hen. V, ii. 1. 47. And see **Shock**. **Der.** Hence *jog* as a neuter verb, to move by jolts, ride roughly, trot, Wint. Ta. iv. 3. 132, Tam. Shrew, iii. 2. 213; *jog-trot*; *jogg-le*, frequentative form.

JOHN DORY, the name of a fish. (F.−L.) *John Dory* is the vulgar name of the fish also called the *dory*. It occurs in Todd's Johnson, spelt *John Dory*, *dory*, and *doree*. 1. *Dory* or *doree* is merely borrowed from the F. *dorée*, the vulgar F. name of the fish, signifying 'golden' or 'gilded,' from its yellow colour. *Dorée* is the fem. of the pp. of the verb *dorer*, to gild.−L. *deaurāre*, to gild, lit. 'cover with gold.'−L. *dē*, prep. of, with; and *aurum*, gold. See **Aureate**. 2. The prefix *John* is nothing but the ordinary name; cf. *jack-ass*. It is usually explained as a corruption of F. *jaune*, yellow; but there is no reason why Englishmen should have prefixed this F. epithet, nor why Frenchmen should use such a tautological expression as *jaune dorée*. This suggested corruption is not a 'well-known fact,' but given as a mere guess in Todd's Johnson. 3. In fact, the prefixing of the name *John* was due to the popularity of an extremely well-known ballad, entitled *John Dory*, pr. in 1609; see Ritson's Anc. Songs. It is alluded to in Beaum. and Fletcher, The Chances, A. iii. sc. 2. See Nares.

JOIN, to connect, unite, annex. (F.−L.) ME. *ioynen*, *ioignen*; P. Plowman, B. ii. 136; A. ii. 106.−OF. *joign-*, pr. pl. stem of *joindre*, to join.−L. *iungere*, pp. *iunctus*, to join (base *iug-*).−√YEUG, to join; cf. Skt. *yuj*, to join, connect; also Gk. ζεύγνυμι, to join, yoke. From the same root is E. *yoke*; see **Yoke**. **Der.** *join-er*, Sir T. More, Works, p. 345 d; *join-e-ry*; *joind-er* (from F. *joindre*), Tw. Nt. v. 160; and see *joint*, *junct-ure*, *junct-ion*, *junta*. From F. *joindre* we also have *ad-join*, *con-join*, *dis-join*, *en-join*, *re-join*, *sub-join*. From L. *iungere* (pp. *iunct-us*) we have *ad-junct*, *con-junct-ure*, *con-junct-ion*, *dis-junct-ion*, *in-junct-ion*, *sub-junct-ive*; whilst the L. base *iug-* appears in *con-jug-al*, *con-jug-ate*, *sub-jug-ate*, *jug-ul-ar*.

JOINT, a place where things are joined, a hinge, seam. (F.−L.) ME. *ioynt*, P. Plowman, B. xvii. 175, C. xx. 142; 'out of *ioynte*,' id. C. x. 215.−F. *joint*, 'a joint, joining;' Cot.−OF. *joint*, pp. of *joindre*, to join; see **Join**. **Der.** *joint*, adj. (from the pp.); *joint-ly*, *joint-stock*; *joint*, verb, Ant. and Cleop. i. 2. 96; *joint-ure*, Merry Wives, iii. 4. 50, from MF. *joincture*, 'a joining, coupling, yoaking together' (Cot.), from L. *iunctūra*, from the pp. stem of *iungere*, to join; *joint-ress* (short for *joint-ur-ess*), Hamlet, i. 2. 9.

JOIST, one of a set of timbers which support the boards of a floor. (F.−L.) Sometimes called *jist* (with *i* as in *Christ*); and vulgarly *jice*, riming with *mice*. 'They were fayne to lay pavesses [large shields] and targes on the *joystes* of the bridg to passe ouer;' Berners, tr. of Froissart, vol. i. c. 415 (R.). ME. *giste*, *gyste*. 'Gyyste, balke, Trabes;' Prompt. Parv. p. 196. 'The *gistes*;' Wright's Vocab. i. 170 (Walter de Bibbesworth). 'Gyst that gothe ouer the florthe, *soliue*, *giste*;' Palsgrave.−OF. *giste*, 'a bed, couch, lodging, place to lie on' (Cot.); also a joist, as in Palsgrave; mod. F. *gite*. So called because these timbers form a support for the floor to lie on.−OF. *gesir*, to lie, lie on. See **Gist**, which is related. **Der.** *joist*, verb.

JOKE, a jest, something mirthful. (L.) '*Joking* decides great things;' Milton, tr. of Horace (in Minor Poems).−L. *iocus*, 'a joke, jest.' Cf. OF. *joquer*; in Ducange, s. v. *Iocare*. Brugmann, i. § 302.

Der. *joke*, vb.; and see *joc-ose*, *joc-ul-ar*. ☞ The Du. *jok*, a joke, is merely borrowed (like the E. word) from Latin.

JOLE, another form of *Jowl*, q. v. (E.)

JOLLY, merry, plump. (F.−Scand. *or* L.) ME. *Ioly*, *ioly*, *ioli*, Chaucer, C. T. 3263. He also has *iolily*, id. 4368 (A 4370); *iolinesse*, id. 10603 (F 289); *iolitee*, id. 10592 (F 278). The older form is *Iolif* or *iolif*; King Alisaunder, l. 155.−OF. *jolif*, later *joli*, 'jolly, gay, trim, fine, gallant, neat;' Cot. β. Perhaps the orig. sense was 'festive\'−Icel. *jōl*, Yule, a great feast in the heathen time; see *jōl* in Icel. Dict. See **Yule**. γ. But this solution is by no means certain. Perhaps from Late L. **gaudīvus*, joyful; from *gaudium*, joy, *gaudēre*, to rejoice (P. Meyer). **Der.** *jolli-ly*, *jolli-ty*, *jolli-ness*.

JOLLY-BOAT, a small boat belonging to a ship. (Scand.) In Todd's Johnson. Apparently, the element *jolly* is the adj. above, but this may have been substituted for Dan. *jolle*, a yawl, jolly-boat; Swed. *julle*, a yawl; cf. Du. *jol*, a yawl, skiff. See **Yawl**. *Boat* is then a needless addition, due to the corruption into the E. adj. *jolly*. β. Perhaps suggested by *jolywat*, which seems to have been a sort of boat. 'Grete boat and *jolywat*;' Naval Accts. of Hen. VII (1896), p. 181. And this is (doubtfully) derived from Port. *galeota*, a galliot; see *Gallevat* in Yule; and see **Galliot**.

JOLT, to shake violently, to jerk. (E.) Formerly also *joult*. Cotgrave explains F. *heurtade* as 'a shock, knock, jur [jar], jolt, push;' and *heurter* as 'to knock, push, jur, *joult*, strike.' Also found in the comp. *jolt-head*, a thick-headed fellow, Two Gent. iii. 1. 290; Tam. Shrew, iv. 1. 169. '*Teste de bœuf*, a *joult-head*, jobernoll, *loger-head*, one whose wit is as little as his head is great;' Cot. In North's Plutarch, p. 133 (R.), or p. 158, ed. 1631, we find some verses containing the word *jolt-head*, as well as the expression 'this heavy *jolting* pate,' said of Jupiter, when regarded as a stupid tyrant. β. The frequent association of *jolt* with *head* or *pate* suggests a connexion with *joll* or *jowl* in the sense of 'head.' '*Iol*, or heed, *iolle*, Caput;' Prompt. Parv. '*Iolle* of a fysshe, *teste*;' Palsgrave. 'Ther they *jollede* [beat on the head] Jewes thorowe;' MS. Calig. A. ii. f. 117; cited in Halliwell. 'They may *joll* horns [knock heads] together;' As You Like It, i. 3. 59. 'How the knave *jowls* it [viz. a *skull*] to the ground;' Hamlet, v. 1. 84. 'I *jolle* one aboute the eares, Ie *soufflette*;' Palsgrave. Cf. prov. E. *jow*, *jowl*, to knock (the head); *jollock*, to jolt. We may also compare prov. E. *jot*, to jerk, spelt *jotte* in Palsgrave. γ. It may be added that *jolt* seems to have acquired a frequentative sense, 'to knock often,' and was soon used generally of various kinds of jerky knocks. 'He whipped his horses, the coach *jolted* again;' Rambler, no. 34 (R.). See further under **Jowl**. **Der.** *jolt*, sb.

JONQUIL, a kind of narcissus. (F.−Span.−L.) In Kersey's Dict. ed. 1715. Accented *jonquíl*, Thomson's Seasons, Spring, 548.−Mod. F. *jonquille*, a jonquil. So named from its rush-like leaves; whence it is sometimes called *Narcissus juncifolius*.−Span. *junquillo*, jonquil.−Span. *junco*, a rush.−L. *iuncus*, a rush. See **Junket**. ¶ So also Ital. *giunchiglia*, a jonquil; from *giunco*, a rush.

JORDAN, a pot, chamber-pot. (L. ?−Gk. ?−Heb. ?) ME. *Iordan*, Chaucer, C. T. 12239 (C 305); see Tyrwhitt's note. Also *Iurdon*, *Iordeyne*; see Prompt. Parv., and Way's note; p. 267. Halliwell explains it as 'a kind of pot or vessel formerly used by physicians and alchemists. It was very much in the form of a soda-water bottle, only the neck was larger, not much smaller than the body of the vessel; &c.'−Late L. *iurdānus*; as in Prompt. Parv. β. Origin uncertain; but it may very well have been named from the river Jordan (L. *Iordānes*, Gk. Ἰορδάνης, Heb. *Yardēn*, i. e. flowing down). 'We must remember this was the time of the Crusades. It was the custom of all pilgrims who visited the Holy Land to bring back a bottle of water from the Jordan for baptismal purposes. ... It was thus that *Jordan* as a surname has arisen. I need not remind students of early records how common is *Jordan* as a Christian name, such cognomens as 'Jordan de Abingdon' or 'Jordan le Clerc' being of the most familiar occurrence;' Bardsley, Our English Surnames, p. 53. Thus *Jordan* may be short for 'Jordan-bottle.' Halliwell further explains how the later sense (as in Shakespeare) came about; the bottle being, in course of time, occasionally used for baser purposes. ¶ Not from Dan. or Swed. *jord*, earth; the adj. from which is *jordisk*, and means 'terrestrial.'

JOSS, a Chinese figure of a deity. (Port.−L.) 'Critic in jars and *josses*;' Epilogue to A Jealous Wife, by Colman (1761). Not Chinese; but a corruption of Port. *deos*, God. Cognate with Span. *dios*, OF. *deus*.−L. *Deus*, God; nom. case. See **Deity**.

JOSTLE, JUSTLE, to strike or push against. (F.−L.; with E. suffix.) [Not in P. Plowman, as said in R.] 'Thou *justlest* nowe too nigh;' Roister Doister, iii. 3. 129 (in Spec. of Eng., ed. Skeat). Formed, with E. frequentative suffix *-le*, from *just* or *joust*; see **Joust**.

JOT, a tittle. (L.−Gk.−Heb.) In Spenser, Sonnet 57. Spelt *iote* in Udall, Prol. to Ephesians, and Phaer's Virgill, Æn. b. xi; see Richardson. Englished from L. *iōta*, Matt. v. 18 (Vulgate). — Gk. ἰῶτα, the name of the Gk. letter ι. — Heb. *yōd* (*y*), the smallest letter of the Heb. alphabet. β. Hence also Du. *jot*, Span. and Ital. *jota*, a jot, tittle. See the Bible Word-book. Der. *jot*, verb, in the phr. 'to jot down' = to make a brief note of. ¶ Not the same word as prov. E. *jot*, to jolt, jog, nudge; which appears as *jotte* in Palsgrave.

JOURNAL, a day-book, daily newspaper, magazine. (F. — L.) 'Iurnall, a boke, *journal*;' Palsgrave. Properly an adj., signifying 'daily.' 'His *journal* greeting;' Meas. iv. 3. 92. 'Their *journall* labours;' Spenser, F. Q. i. 11. 31. — F. *journal*, adj. 'journall, dayly;' Cot. — L. *diurnālis*, daily; from *diēs*, a day. See **Diurnal, Diary.** Der. *journal-ism, journal-ist, journal-ist-ic.* And see *journey, ad-journ.* Doublet, *diurnal.*

JOURNEY, a day's travel, travel, tour. (F. — L.) ME. *Iornee, Iournee.* It means 'a day's travel' in Chaucer, C. T. 2740 (A 2738). Spelt *jurneie*, Ancren Riwle, p. 352, l. 29. — F. *journée*, 'a day, or whole day; also . . . a daies worke or labour; a daies journy, or travell;' Cot. β. F. *journée* answers to Span. *jornada*, Ital. *giornata*, Late L. *jornāta*, a day's work; all formed with the fem. ending of a pp. as if from a verb **jornāre*, from the stem *jorn-* (< *diurn-*), which appears in Late L. *jorn-āle* (= E. *journal*). — L. *diurn-us*, daily. See **Journal.** Der. *journey*, verb, Rich. III, ii. 2. 146; *journey-man*, Rich. II, i. 3. 274.

JOUST, JUST, to tilt, encounter on horseback. (F. — L.) ME. *Iusten, Iousten*; Chaucer, C. T. 96; P. Plowman, B. xviii. 82. — OF. *jouster*, 'to just, tilt, or tourney;' Cot. (mod. F. *jouter*). [Cf. Ital. *giostrare*, Span. *justar*, to tilt.] β. The orig. sense is merely 'to meet' or 'to approach,' a sense better preserved in OF. *adjouster*, to set near, to annex; (not E. *adjust*). [The hostile sense is easily added as in other cases; cf. E. to *meet* (often in a hostile sense), to *encounter*, and ME. *assemblen*, to fight, contend, so common in Barbour's Bruce. So also F. *rencontre*.] — Late L. *iuxtāre*, to approach, cause to approach, join; see Ducange. — L. *iuxtā*, near, close, hard by; whence OF. *jouste*, 'neer to, hard by;' Cot. γ. The form *iuxtā* = *iūg-is-tā*, fem. abl. of the superl. form of adj. *iūg-is*, continual; from base *iūg-* of *iungere*, to join. — √YEUG, to join; see **Join.** Brugmann, i. § 760 (1), note 1. Der. *joust*, sb., ME. *Iuste, Iouste*, P. Plowman, B. xvii. 74. Also *jost-le*, q.v.

JOVIAL, mirthful. (F. — L.) In the old astrology, Jupiter was 'the joyfullest star, and of the happiest augury of all;' Trench, Study of Words. 'The heavens, always *joviall*,' i. e. propitious, kindly; Spenser, F. Q. ii. 12. 51. — OF. *Jovial*, 'joviall, sanguine, born under the planet Jupiter;' Cot. — L. *Iouiālis*, pertaining to Jupiter. — L. *Ioui-*, for OLat. *Iouis*, Jove, only used in later Lat. in the form *Iū-piter* (= Jove-father), Jupiter. β. Again *Iouis* stands for an older *Diouis* (cf. Oscan dat. *Diuv-ei*), allied to *diēs*, day, and to *deus*, God; cf. Gk. Διός, gen. case of Ζεύς. See **Deity, Tuesday.** Brugmann, i. §§ 120, 223. Cf. Skt. *div*, to shine, whence *deva-*, a deity, *daiva-*, divine; also Skt. *dyu-*, inflectional base of *Dyaus*. See Max Müller, Lect. on Lang. vol. ii. Der. *jovial-ly, jovial-ness, jovial-i-ty.*

JOWL, JOLE, the jaw or cheek. (E.) 'Cheek by *jowl*;' Mids. Nt. Dream, iii. 2. 338. β. A corruption of *chowl*; cf. *cheek* and *chowl*, and *cheek for chowl* in E. D. D. [We also find *chowl* in a somewhat different sense. 'The *chowle* or crop adhering unto the lower side of the bill [of the pelican], and so descending by the throat; a bag or sachel very observable;' Sir T. Browne, Vulg. Errors, b. v. c. 1. § 5. 'His *chyn* with a *chol* lollede' = his chin wagged with the hanging flesh beneath it; Piers Ploughman's Crede, l. 224 (in Spec. of Eng. ed. Skeat).] γ. There is also a form *chaul*, meaning (apparently) 'jaw.' 'Bothe his *chaul* [jowl] and his chynne;' Alisaunder, fragment A, ed. Skeat, 1119 (in App. to Wm. of Palerne). This *chaul* is a corruption of an older form *chauel* = *chavel*. Thus in the Cursor Mundi, l. 7510, when David describes how he slew the lion and the bear, he says: 'I scok þam be þe berdes swa þat I þair *chafftes* raue in twa' = I shook them by the beards so that I reft their chaps in twain; where other MSS. read *chauelis, chaulis,* and *chaules.* So also: '*Chavylbone,* or *chawl-bone* or *chaule-bone,* Mandibula;' Prompt. Parv. p. 70; and see Way's note, who cites: 'A *chafte,* a chawylle, a chekebone, *maxilla*;' and: '*Brancus,* a gole, or a chawle.' And again: 'And þat deor to-dede his *chæfles*' (later text, *choules*) = and the beast opened (?) his jaws; Layamon, 6507. — AS. *ceafl,* the jaw; pl. *ceaflas,* jaws, chaps; Grein, i. 157. 'Dauid . . . his *ceaflas* tō-tær' = David tare asunder the chaps (of the bear); Ælfric on the Old Test.; Liber Regum. + OSax. *kaflōs,* pl. the jaws. Allied to Icel. *kjaptr,* the mouth, jaw, esp. of a beast; for **kjaf-tr*; cf. Swed. *käft,* jaw, Dan. *kjæft.* The *l* in AS. *ceafl* is a mere suffix, and the word must have originated from a Teutonic base **kaf-.* See **Chafer.** δ. But the connexion of *chowl* with *chaul* is doubtful, and the word cannot be said to be satisfactorily solved; see N. E. D.

¶ The change from *ch* to *j* is well illustrated by the Norfolk *jig-by-jole* = cheek by jowl = Ayrshire *cheek for chow,* cheek by chowl; see E. D. D.

JOY, gladness, happiness. (F. — L.) ME. *Ioyè, ioyè* (dissyllable), Chaucer, C. T. 1873 (A 1871); earlier, in Ancren Riwle, p. 218. — OF. *joye, joie,* 'joy, mirth;' Cot. Cf. Ital. *gioia,* joy; Gascon *goy.* — L. neut. pl. *gaudia,* which was turned into a fem. sing. as in other cases (see **Antiphon**); from sing. *gaudium,* joy. — L. *gaudēre,* to rejoice. See **Gaud.** Der. *joy,* verb, 2 Cor. vii. 13 (A. V.); *joy-ful,* ME. *joiefull,* Gower, C. A. i. 191, bk. ii. 931; *joy-ful-ly, joy-ful-ness; joy-less,* ME. *joy-less-ly, joy-less-ness; joy-ous,* ME. *joy-ous,* Shoreham's Poems, ed. Wright, p. 120, l. 14; *joy-ous-ly, joy-ous-ness.*

JUBBAH, a kind of tunic. (Arab.) See **Jupon.**

JUBILATION, a shouting for joy. (L.) In Cotgrave; ME. *Iubilacioun,* Wyclif, Ps. cl. 5. — F. *jubilation,* 'a jubilation, exultation;' Cot. — L. *iūbilātiōnem,* acc. of *iūbilātio,* a shouting for joy; cf. L. *iūbilātus,* pp. of *iūbilāre,* to shout for joy. — L. *iūbilum,* a shout of joy. β. There is nothing to connect this with the following word; the resemblance is accidental. Nevertheless, the words were confused at an early date. Der. *jubil-ant,* from pres. pt. of *iūbilāre.*

JUBILEE, a season of great joy. (F. — L. — Heb.) ME. *Iubilee,* Chaucer, C. T. 7444 (D 1862). — OF. *jubilé,* 'a jubilee, a year of releasing, liberty, rejoicing;' Cot. — L. *iūbilæus,* the jubilee, Levit. xxv. 11; masc. of adj. *iūbilæus,* belonging to the jubilee; Levit. xxv. 28. An alteration of L. **iōbēlæus* (due to the influence of L. *iūbilum,* a shout of triumph), which is the true rendering of Late Gk. ἰωβηλαῖος, adj. formed from ἰωβήλος, jubilee (Josephus, Antiq. iii. 12. 3). — Heb. *yōbēl,* a blast of a trumpet, a shout of joy; orig. a blast on a ram's horn. Distinct from the word above.

JUDGE, an arbitrator, one who decides a cause. (F. — L.) ME. *Iuge, iuge,* Chaucer, C. T. 15931 (G 463). — F. *juge,* 'a judge;' Cot. — L. *iūdicem,* acc. of *iūdex,* a judge. β. The stem is *iū-dic-,* and signifies 'one who points out what is law;' from *iū-s,* law, and *dic-āre,* to point out, make known. For *ius,* see **Just.** For *dicāre,* see **Indicate.** Der. *judge,* verb, ME. *Iugen, iuggen,* Rob. of Glouc., p. 345, l. 7082; *judge-ship; judg-ment,* ME. *iugement* (three syllables), Chaucer, C. T. 807 (A 805); *judgment-day, judgment-seat;* and see *judicature, judicial, judicious.* Also *ad-judge, pre-judge.*

JUDICATURE, judgment. (F. — L.) In Cotgrave and Palsgrave. — F. *judicature,* 'judicature;' Cot. — L. *iūdicātūra,* office of a judge; cf. *iūdicāt-us,* pp. of *iūdicāre,* to judge. — L. *iūdic-,* stem of *iūdex,* a judge. See **Judge.** Der. (from L. *iūdicāre*) *judic-able* (like pp. *iūdicātus*), *judicat-ive* (L. *iūdicātīuus*), *judicat-or-y* (L. *iūdicātōrius*).

JUDICIAL, pertaining to courts of law. (F. — L.) In Cotgrave; and in Wyclif, Nehem. iii. 30. — OF. *judiciel,* 'judiciall;' Cot. — L. *iūdiciālis,* pertaining to courts of law. — L. *iūdici-um,* a trial, suit, judgment. — L. *iūdici-,* decl. stem of *iūdex,* a judge. See **Judge.** Der. *judicial-ly; judiciar-y* (L. *iūdiciārius*); and see below.

JUDICIOUS, full of judgment, discreet. (F. — L.) In Shak. Macb. iv. 2. 16. — F. *judicieux,* 'judicious;' Cot. — L. **iūdiciōsus,* not found, but regularly formed with suffix -*ōsus* from L. *iūdici-,* decl. stem of *iūdex,* a judge. Der. *judicious-ly, judicious-ness.*

JUG, a kind of pitcher. (Heb.?) 'A *iugge,* poculum;' Levins, ed. 1570. 'A *iugge* to drink in;' Minsheu, ed. 1637. Of uncertain origin. Mr. Wedgwood's suggestion is probably right; he connects it with '*Jug* or *Judge,* formerly a familiar equivalent of Joan or Jenny.' In this case, the word is of jocular origin; which is rendered probable by the fact that a drinking-vessel was also called a *jack,* and that another vessel was called a *jill.* 'A *jacke* of leather to drink in;' Minsheu. *Jack* seems to have been the earlier word, and *Jill* was used in a similar way to go with it. 'Be the *Jacks* fair within, the *Jills* fair without;' Tam. of Shrew, iv. 1. 51; on which Steevens remarks that it is 'a play upon the words, which signify two drinking-measures as well as men and maid-servants.' β. The use of *Jug* or *Joan* appears in Cotgrave, who gives: '*Jehannette,* Jug, or Jinny;' and again: '*Jannette,* Judge, Jenny, a woman's name.' [How *Jug* came to be used for *Joanna* is not very obvious; but pet names are liable to strange confusion. The forms *Jug* and *Judge* are more like the Heb. *Judith* (Gen. xxvi. 34).] Similarly, Wedgwood cites '*Susan,* a brown earthenware pitcher,' used in the district of Gower (Philol. Proceedings, iv. 223). Cf. also 'a *jack* of beer,' Dodsley's O. Plays, ed. Hazlitt, vii. 218, ix. 441. As *Jug* was a female name, we also find *jug,* a mistress, as a term of endearment; id. iv. 183, vi. 511, viii. 400, xii. 115. ¶ The curious word *jubbe,* in the sense of bottle, occurs in Chaucer, C. T. 13000 (B 1260); but *jug* can hardly be a corruption of it.

JUGGERNAUT, the name of an Indian idol. (Hindi — Skt.) See Southey, Curse of Kehama, c. xiv; and see Yule. — Hindi *Jagannātha,* vernacularly *jagannāth,* a name esp. applied to Kṛṣṇa, as worshipped at Puri in Orissa (H. H. Wilson). = Skt. *jagannātha-*, lord of the world. = Skt. *jagat*, world; *nātha-*, protector, lord.

JUGGLER, one who exercises sleight of hand. (F. – L.) ME. *Iogelour, iogelour*, Chaucer, C. T. 7049, 10533 (D 1467, F 219). ' Ther saugh I pleyen *iogelours*, Magiciens, and tregetoures;' Chaucer, Ho. Fame, iii. 169. Spelt *juglur*, with the sense of ' buffoon;' Ancren Riwle, p. 210, l. 30. – OF. *jogleor, jugleor, jougleor* (Burguy); later *jongleur*, with inserted *n*; hence *jongleur*, a jugler;' Cot. – L. *ioculātōrem*, acc. of *ioculātor* a jester. – L. *ioculāri*, to jest. – L. *ioculus*, a little jest, dimin. of *iocus*, a joke; see **Joke.** **Der.** *juggler-y*, ME. *Iogelrie*, Chaucer, C. T. 11577 (F 1265). Hence also was developed the verb *juggle*, formerly *iuglen*, used by Tyndall, Works, p. 101, col. 2, l. 7 from bottom (see Spec. of Eng. ed. Skeat, p. 169, l. 70, p. 170, l. 101); *juggl-ing, juggle*, sb.

JUGULAR, pertaining to the side of the neck. (L.) Also *jugulary*. '*Jugularie*, of or belonging to the throat;' Minsheu, ed. 1627. Formed with suffix *-ar* or *-ary* (= L. *-ārius*) from *iugul-um* or *iugul-us*, the collar-bone (so called from its joining together the shoulders and neck); also, the hollow part of the neck above the collar-bone; also the throat. Dimin. of *iugum*, that which joins, a yoke. – √YEUG, to join. See **Yoke.**

JUICE, sap, fluid part of animal bodies. (F. – L.) ME. *Iuse, iuce*; Gower, C. A. ii. 265; bk. v. 4120; spelt *Iuys*, S. E. Legendary, St. Cuthbert, l. 52. – OF. *jus*, ' juice, liquor, sap, pottage, broath;' Cot. – L. *iūs*, broth, soup, sauce, pickle; lit. ' mixture.' ✚ Skt. *yūsha-*, soup. – √YEU, to bind, mix; cf. Skt. *yu*, to bind, join, mix; Gk. ζύμη, leaven. **Der.** *juic-y, juice-less, juic-i-ness*.

JUJUBE, the fruit of a certain tree. (F. – L. – Gk. – Pers.) The tree is the *Rhamnus zizyphus* or *Rhamnus jujuba*. ' *Iuiubes*, or iuebefruit;' Minsheu, ed. 1627. See Lanfranc, Cirurgie, p. 74, l. 14. – OF. *jujubes*, ' the fruit or plum called jujubes;' Cot. A pl. form. – Late L. *jujuba* (Ital. *giugiuba*, Florio); altered from the pl. of L. *zizyphum*, the jujube; fruit of the tree *zizyphus*. – Gk. ζίζυφον, fruit of the tree ζίζυφος. – Pers. *zayzafūn, zizfūn, zizafūn*, the jujube-tree; Rich. Dict. p. 793.

JULEP, a sweet drink, demulcent mixture. (F. – Span. – Arab. – Pers.) ' This cordial *julep* here;' Milton, Comus, 672. ' Good wine . . . made in a *iulep* with suger;' Sir T. Elyot, Castel of Helth, b. iii. c. 18. See Lanfranc, Cirurgie, p. 76, l. 9. – F. *julep*, ' a julep, or juleb, a drink made either of distilled waters and syrops mixed together; or of a decoction sweetned with hony and sugar, or else mingled with syrops;' Cot. – Span. *julepe*, julep. – Arab. *julāb*, julep; from Pers. *gulāb*, rose-water, also, julep; Rich. Dict. pp. 512, 1239. – Pers. *gul*, a rose; and *āb*, water; id. pp. 1238, 1.

JULY, the name of the seventh month. (F. – L.) Chaucer, Treat. on the Astrolabe, calls the month *Iulius, Iuyl, Iuylle*; pt. i. § 10. *July* is from AF. *Julie*, L. *Iūlius*, a name given to this month (formerly called *Quinctīlis*) in honour of Caius Julius Cæsar, who was born in this month. Hence the E. form was accented as *July* (rhyming with *newly*) as late as in Dr. Johnson's time; cf. ' Then came hot *July*, boyling like to fire;' Spenser, F. Q. vii. 7. 36. Now *Ju-lý*, prob. to distinguish it more clearly from *June* (N. and Q., 9 S. x. 426). ¶ *Quinctīlis* is from *quintus*, fifth, because this was formerly the fifth month, when the year began in March. *Quintus* is from *quinque*, five; see **Five.**

JUMBLE, to mix together confusedly. (E.) ' I jum'byll, I make a noyse by removyng of heavy thynges. I *jumble*, as one dothe that can [not] play upon an instrument, *je brouille*;' Palsgrave. Here it means to make a confused noise. Cf. prov. E. *jum*, a jolt; whence *jummle, jumble*, to jolt (frequentative). Of imitative origin. ¶ Chaucer uses the equivalent form *jompren*. ' Ne *jompre* eek no discordaunt thing yfere' = do not jumble discordant things together; Troilus, ii. 1037. But Sir T. More uses the word in the sense of ' to mingle harmoniously;' as in : ' Let vs . . . see how diffinicion of the churche and hys heresies will *jumper* and agree together among themselfe;' Works, p. 612 a. Compare this with the phr. ' to *jump* together ' (= to agree with). **Der.** *jumble*, sb.; *jumbl-ing-ly*.

JUMP (1), to leap, spring, skip. (Scand. ?) In Shak. As You Like It, ii. 1. 53, and in Palsgrave; but not found earlier. The frequentative form *jumper* occurs in Sir T. More, and *jompren* in Chaucer; see quotations s. v. *Jumble*. Hence the word *jump* may have been known to our dialects at an earlier date. Cf. Sc. *jump* (pt. t. *jamp*) in E. D. D. Perhaps it is of Scand. origin. Cf. Jutland *jumpe*, to be in oscillating motion, also, to jump, spring (Feilberg); allied to Swed. dial. *jómpa*, to jog up and down, as in riding (Rietz). Note also Swed. dial. *gumpa*, to spring, jump, or wag about heavily and clumsily (Rietz); Swed. *guppa*, to move up and down; Dan. *gumpe*, to jolt; *gimpa*, to wriggle (Rietz); Norw. *gimpa*, to swing oneself about (Ross); Norw. *gimpe*, to see-saw, *gamp*, a nag (Larsen). As Rietz remarks, there must have been a strong verb **gimpa*, pt. t.

*gamp, pp. *gumpinn*. ✚ MHG. *gumpen*, to jump; *gumpeln*, to play the buffoon; *gempeln*, to jump, dimin. form of prov. G. *gampen*, to jump, spring, hop, sport; see Schmeller's Bavarian Dict.; cf. MHG. *gampelmann*, a buffoon, jester, one who plays antics; mod. G. *gimpel*, a simpleton. But the history of the verb is very obscure. **Der.** *jump*, sb., used in the sense of ' lot ' or ' hazard,' Anthony, iii. 8. 6. Also *jump* (2).

JUMP (2), exactly, just, pat. (Scand. ?) ' *Jump* at this dead hour;' Hamlet, i. 1. 65; cf. v. 2. 386; Oth. ii. 3. 392. From the verb above, in the sense to agree or tally, commonly followed by *with*, but also used without it. ' Both our inventions meet and *jump* in one;' Tam. Shrew, i. 1. 195. ' They *jump* not on a just account;' Oth. i. 3. 5. See **Jump** (1).

JUNCTION, a joining. (L.) Used by Addison, Spectator, no. 165, § 5 : ' Upon the *junction* of the French and Bavarian armies.' Formed, by analogy with F. sbs. in *-ion*, from L. *iunctiōnem*, acc. of *iunctio*, a joining; cf. L. *iunctus*, pp. of *iungere*, to join. See **Join.**

JUNCTURE, a union, critical moment. (L.) ' Signes workings, planets *iunctures*, and the eleuated poule ' [pole]; Warner, Albion's England, b. v. c. 27. ' *Juncture*, a joyning or coupling together;' Blount's Gloss., ed. 1674. – L. *iunctūra*, a joining; cf. *iunct-*, stem of pp. of *iungere*, to join. See **Join.** ¶ The sense of ' critical moment ' is probably of astrological origin; cf. the quotation from Warner.

JUNE, the sixth month. (L.) Chaucer, On the Astrolabe, pt. i. § 10, has *Iunius* and *Iuyn*; the latter answering to F. *Juin*. Englished from L. *Iūnius*, the name of the sixth month and of a Roman *gens* or clan.

JUNGLE, country covered with trees and brushwood. (Hind. – Skt.) Not in Johnson; first in 1776 (N. E. D.). – Hind. *jangal*, wood, jungle (Forbes). – Skt. *jañgala-*, adj. dry, desert. Hence *jungle* = waste land. ¶ The Skt. short *a* is sounded like *u* in *mud*; hence the E. spelling. **Der.** *jungl-y*.

JUNIOR, younger. (L.) In Levins, ed. 1570. – L. *iūnior*, comparative of *iuuenis*, young; so that *iunior* stands for *iuuenior*. Cf. Skt. *yuvan*, young. See **Juvenile.** **Der.** *junior-ship, junior-i-ty*.

JUNIPER, an evergreen shrub. (L.) In Levins, ed. 1570. Spelt *junipere*; Spenser, Sonnet 26; *ieniper*, Palladius on Husbandry, bk. i. l. 397. – L. *iūniperus*, a juniper-tree. Of doubtful origin. **Der.** *gin* (3), q. v.

JUNK (1), a Chinese three-masted vessel. (Port. – Malay.) ' China also, and the great Atlantis, . . . which have now but *junks* and canoas' [canoes]; Bacon, New Atlantis, ed. 1639, p. 12. Also in Sir T. Herbert's Travels, ed. 1665, pp. 42, 384. – Port. (and Span.) *junco*, a junk. – Malay *jōng*, also *ajōng*, a junk; Javanese *jong*. ¶ Not allied, as often said, to Chinese *chw'an*, ' a ship, boat, bark, junk, or whatever carries people on the water;' Williams, Chinese Dict., 1874, p. 120; unless the Chinese word is borrowed from Malay.

JUNK (2), pieces of old cordage, used for mats and oakum. (Port. – L.) ' *Junk*, pieces of old rope;' Ash's Dict., ed. 1775. ' *Junk*, a sea-word for any piece of old cable;' Kersey's Dict., ed. 1715. – Port. *junco*, a rush; (in a ship) the junk; Vieyra's Dict. [As if so called from rush-made ropes; but there is no obvious connexion.] – L. *iuncus*, a rush. **B.** Salt meat is also facetiously termed *junk* by the sailors, because it is as tough as old rope. ¶ *Junk*, a lump (Halliwell), is a different word, being for *chunk*, a log of wood; see **Chump.**

JUNKET, a kind of sweetmeat. (F. – Ital. – L.) Also spelt *juncate*; Spenser, F. Q. v. 4. 49. In Shak. Tam. Shrew, iii. 2. 250; Milton, L'Allegro, 102. The orig. sense was a kind of cream-cheese, served up on rushes, whence its name. Also used as a name for various delicacies made of cream. Cf. *Iuncade*; Voc. 590. 44. ' Milke, crayme, and cruddes, and eke the *Ioncate*;' I. Russell, Boke of Nurture, l. 93; in Babees Book, p. 124. – MF. *joncade*, ' a certain spoon-meat, made of cream, rose-water, and sugar;' Cot. – Ital. *giuncata*, ' a kind of fresh cheese and creame, so called because it is brought to market upon rushes; also a iunket;' Florio. [Cf. MF. *jonchée*, ' a bundle of rushes; also, a green cheese or fresh cheese made of milk thats curdled without any runnet, and served in a fraile [basket] of green rushes;' Cot.; Norm. dial. *jonquette*, a junket (Moisy).] Formed as a pp. from Ital. *giuncare*, ' to strewe with rushes;' Florio. – Ital. *giunco*, a rush. – L. *iuncum*, acc. of *iuncus*, a rush. **Der.** *junket*, vb., *junket-ing*, Spectator, no. 466. From the same source, *jonquil*, q. v., *junk* (2).

JUNTA, a congress, council. (Span. – L.) In Howell's Letters, vol. i. sect. 3, let. 21. – Span. *junta*, a junta, congress. – L. *iuncta*, f. of *iunctus*, pp. of *iungere*, to join; see **Join.** And see **Junto.**

JUNTO, a knot of men, combination, confederacy, faction. (Span. – L.) ' And these to be set on by plot and consultation with a *junto* of clergymen and licensers;' Milton, Colasterion (R.).

Erroneously used for *junta* (above); as if from Span. *junto*, united, conjoined. — L. *iunctus*, pp. of *iungere*, to join.

JUPON, a tight-fitting tunic, a skirt. (F. — Arab.) ME. *gipoun*, Chaucer, C. T. 75; *Iupon*, Allit. Morte Arthure, 905. — OF. *Iupon*, *gippon*, ' a short cassock;' Cot.; also *Iuppon*. Extended form of F. *jupe*, MF. *juppe*, ' a gaberdine, cassock,' Cot.; OF. *Iupe*, *Iuppe*. — Arab. *jubba*(*t*), ' a waistcoat with cotton quilted between the outside and lining;' Rich. Dict. p. 494; whence also E. *jubbah*, *jibbah*, a kind of tunic. See Notes on E. Etym., p. 149.

JURIDICAL, pertaining to a judge or to courts of law. (L.) Blount, in his Glossographia, ed. 1674, has *juridical* and *juridick*. First in 1502. Formed with suffix -*al*, from L. *iūridic-us*, relating to the administration of justice. — L. *iūri*-, decl. stem of *iūs*, law; and *dicāre*, to proclaim. See **Just** and **Diction**. Der. *juridical*-*ly*.

JURISDICTION, authority to execute laws. (F. — L.) ME. *Iurisdiction*, Chaucer, C. T. 6901 (D 1319). — F. *jurisdiction*, ' jurisdiction;' Cot. — L. *iūrisdictiōnem*, acc. of *iūrisdictio*, administration of justice. — L. *iūris*, gen. of *iūs*, justice; and *dictio*, a saying, proclaiming. See **Just** and **Diction**.

JURISPRUDENCE, the knowledge of law. (F. — L.) In Blount's Gloss., ed. 1674. — F. *jurisprudence*; Cot. — L. *iūrisprūdentia*, the science of law. — L. *iūris*, gen. of *iūs*, law; and *prūdentia*, skill, prudence. See **Just** and **Prudence**.

JURIST, a lawyer. (F. — L.) ' *Jurist*, a lawyer;' Blount's Gloss., ed. 1674. First in 1481. — F. *juriste*, ' a lawyer;' Cot. — Late L. *iūrista*, a lawyer. Formed, with suffix -*ista* (Gk. -*ιστης*), from *iūr*-, stem of *iūs*, law. See **Just**.

JUROR, one of a jury. (F. — L.) In Shak. Hen. VIII, v. 3. 60. ME. *iuroure*, P. Plowman, B. vii. 44. — AF. *iurour*, Yearbooks of Edw. I, 1292–3, p. 43. [Cf. F. *jureur*, ' a swearer or deposer, a juror;' Cot.] — L. *iūrātōrem*, acc. of *iūrātor*, a swearer. — L. *iūrā*-, stem of *iūrāre*, to swear; with agential suffix -*tor*. See **Jury**.

JURY, a body of sworn men. (F. — L.) ' I durst as wel trust the truth of one iudge as of two *iuries*;' Sir T. More, Works, p. 988 d. ME. *iuree*, Allit. Morte Arthure, 662. — F. *jurée*, ' a jury,' Cot.; lit. a company of sworn men. Properly the fem. pp. of F. *jurer*, to swear. — L. *iūrāre*, to swear; lit. to bind oneself by an oath. Cf. Skt. *yu*, to bind; *yōs*, health (Macdonell). Der. *jury*-*man*, Tw. Nt. iii. 2. 17. From same source, *con*-*jure*. And see *juror*.

JURY-MAST, a temporary mast. (F. — L. ?) ' *Jury-mast*, a yard set up instead of a mast that is broken down by a storm or shot, and fitted with sails, so as to make a poor shift to steer a ship;' Kersey, ed. 1715. And in Capt. J. Smith, Works, p. 221 (1616). Perhaps short for *ajúry mast*, where *ajury* = OF. *ajuirie*, aid, succour (Godfrey). From L. *adjūtāre*, to aid; see **Aid**. Cf. ' *iuwere*, remedium;' Prompt. Parv. Also mod. Prov. *ajudaire*, *ajuaire*, auxiliary (Mistral); OF. *ajuer*, one who aids (Roquefort).

JUST (1), righteous, upright, true. (F. — L.) ME. *Iust*, *iust*; Wyclif, Luke, i. 17. — F. *juste*, ' just;' Cot. — L. *iustus*, just. Extended from *iūs*, right, law, lit. what is fitting; with suffix -*tus*. See **Jury**. Der. *just* = exactly, Temp. ii. 1. 6; *just*-*ly*, -*ness*; and see *justice*, *justify*.

JUST (2), the same as **Joust**, q. v. (F. — L.)

JUSTICE, integrity, uprightness; a judge. (F. — L.) ME. *Iustice*, *iustice*, generally in the sense of judge; Chaucer, C. T. 316. — OF. *justice*, (1) justice, (2) a judge (Burguy); the latter sense is not in Cotgrave. — L. *iustitia*, justice; Late L. *iustitia*, a tribunal, a judge (Ducange). — L. *iusti*- = *iusto*-, for *iustus*, just; with suffix -*ti-a*. See **Just** (1). Der. *justice*-*ship*, *justic*-*er*, K. Lear, iii. 6. 59; *justic*-*i-a-ry*, from Late L. *iustitiārius*.

JUSTIFY, to show to be just or right. (F. — L.) ME. *Iustifien*, *iustifien*; Wyclif, Matt. xii. 37; Gower, C. A. i. 84; bk. i. 1250. — F. *justifier*, ' to justifie;' Cot. — L. *iustificāre*, to justify, show to be just. — L. *iusti*- = *iusto*-, for *iustus*, just; and -*ficāre*, used (in composition) for *facere*, to make. See **Just** and **Fact**. Der. *justifi*-*able*, *justifi*-*abl*-*y*, *justifi*-*able*-*ness*, *justifi*-*er*; also *justificat*-*ion*, Gower, C. A. i. 169; bk. ii. 296; Wyclif, Rom. v. 16, from F. *justification*, from L. acc. *iustificātiōnem*, allied to the pp. *iustificātus*; also *justificat*-*ive*, *justificat*-*or-y*.

JUSTLE, the same as **Jostle**, q. v. In Temp. v. 158.

JUT, to project. (F. — L.) ' *Jutting*, proiectus;' Levins. ' *For-jetter*, to jut, leane out, hang over;' Cot. A phonetic variant of **Jet** (1), q. v. Der. *jutt*-*y*, sb. a projection, Macb. i. 6. 6, from MF. *jettée*, ' a cast . . a jetty, or jutty,' Cot.; hence *jutt*-*y*, vb. to project over, Hen. V, iii. i. 13. See **Jetty**.

JUTE, a substance resembling hemp. (Bengāli. — Skt.) ' The jute of commerce is the product of two plants of the order of *Tiliaceæ*, viz. *Corchorus capsularis* and *Corchorus olitorius* . . the leaves . . are employed in medicine . . dried leaves prepared for this purpose being found in almost every Hindu house in some districts of Bengal . . Its recognition as a distinct plant [from hemp] dates from the year 1795,

when Dr. Roxburgh, Superintendent of the East India Company's Botanical Garden at Seebpoor, forwarded a bale prepared by himself, under its present name of *jute*;' Overland Mail, July 30, 1875, p. 17 (which contains a long article on Jute). — Bengāli *jūt*, *joot*, ' the fibres of the bark of the *Corchorus olitorius*, much used for making a coarse kind of canvas, and the common *ganni* bags; it is also sometimes loosely applied to the plant;' H. H. Wilson, Gloss of Indian Terms, p. 243. From *jhōto*, vulgarly *jhuto*, the native name in Orissa (Yule). Perhaps from Skt. *jūṭa*-, more commonly *jaṭā*, the matted hair of Çiva, a braid of hair.

JUVENILE, young. (F. — L.) *Juvenile* is in Bacon's Essays, Of Vicissitudes, § last; *juvenilitie* in Minsheu, ed. 1627. — F. *juvenile*, ' youthful;' Cot. — L. *iuuenīlis*, youthful. — L. *iuuenis*, young; cognate with E. **Young**, q. v. Der. *juvenile*-*ness*, *juvenil*-*i-ty*. Cf. *juvenal* (from L. *iuuenālis*, by-form of *iuuenīlis*), jocularly used, L. L. L. i. 2. 8. And see *junior*.

JUXTAPOSITION, contiguity, nearness. (F. — L.) In Kersey, ed. 1715. — F. *juxtaposition* (1690); Hatzfeld. A coined word, from L. *iuxtā*, near; and F. *position*, position. See **Joust** and **Position**.

K

KAFTAN, a Turkish robe. See **Caftan**.

KAIL, **KALE**, a cabbage. (North. E. — L.) *Kail* or *kale* is the North E. form of *cole* or *cole-wort*. Spelt *keal* in Milton, Apology for Smectymnuus (R.). ' *Cale*, *olus*;' Cath. Anglicum (1483). ME. *caul*; AS. *cāul*, *cawel*. — L. *caulis*, a stalk, a cabbage; whence were also borrowed Icel. *kāl*, Dan. *kaal*, Swed. *kål*; see **Cole**.

KAILS, nine-pins. (O. Low G.) Perhaps obsolete. Formerly also *keyles*. ' A game call'd nine-pins, or *keils*;' Ben Jonson, Chloridia. ' *Quille*, the keel of a ship, also a *keyle*, a big peg, or pin of wood, used at nine-pins or *keyles*;' Cotgrave. Spelt *kayles*; Reliquiæ Antiquæ, i. 292; *caylys*, id. ii. 224. Of O. Low Ger. origin; Du. *kegel*, ' a pin, kail; *mid kegels spelen*, to play at nine-pins;' Sewel. (It may be observed that *kails* were shaped like a cone.) Cf. Dan. *kegle*, a cone; *kegler*, nine-pins; Swed. *kegla*, a pin, cone; both borrowed from Low G. + OHG. *chegil*, G. *kegel*, a cone, nine-pin, bobbin (whence F. *quille*). β. Evidently a dimin. form; from a Teut. base **kagil*-. Related to Du. *keg*, *kegge*, a wedge; Swed. dial. *kage*, stubs, stumps.

KALEIDOSCOPE, an optical toy. (Gk.) Modern. Invented by Sir D. Brewster, and named by him in 1817. Coined from Gk. *καλ-ός*, beautiful, *εἰδο*-, for *εἶδος*, appearance, and *σκοπ-εῖν*, to behold, survey. Thus the sense is an instrument for ' beholding beautiful forms.'

KALENDAR, **KALENDS**; see **Calendar**, **Calends**.

KALI, soda-ash; see **Alkali**.

KANGAROO, the name of a quadruped. (Australian.) ' The *kangaroo* is one of the latest discoveries in the history of quadrupeds;' tr. of Buffon's Nat. Hist., London, 1792. ' The animals called by the natives *kangooroo* or *kanguru*;' Cook, Journal, Aug. 4, 1770. But the name is no longer in use in the Australian dialects, which change rapidly. See Austral English, by E. E. Morris. Der. *kangaroo*-*rat*.

KAVASS, an armed constable. (Turk. — Arab.) Modern. From Turk.-Arabic *qawwās*, lit. a bowmaker; from Arab. *qaws*, a bow; Rich. Dict. pp. 1152, 1153.

KAYAK, a light Greenland canoe. (Eskimo.) An Eskimo word; common in all the dialects (N. E. D.).

KAYLES, ninepins; see **Kails**.

KEDGE (1), to warp a ship. (F. — L.) ' *Kedge*, to set up the foresail, and to let a ship drive with the tide, lifting up and letting fall the kedge-anchor, as often as occasion serves;' Kersey's Dict. ed. 1714. And see the longer description in Todd's Johnson. ' A *caggeewy* cable;' Naval Accounts, Henry VII, 1485, ed. 1896, p. 12. Allied to *cadge*, to fasten, to tie, which seems to be a variant of *catch*. Cf. *catch-anchor*, under *catch*, sb. (3), in N. E. D. See **Catch**. Cf. also: ' let fall a *cadge* anker;' Hakluyt, Voy. iii. 107 (last line). Der. *kedg-er*, *kedge-anchor*. ' *Kedge-anchors*, or *Kedgers*, small anchors used in calm weather, and in a slow stream;' Kersey. So called because used to assist in *kedging*; see Todd's Johnson.

KEDGE (2), **KIDGE**, cheerful, lively. (E.) ' *Kedge*, brisk, lively;' Ray's Gloss., ed. 1691; see reprint, ed. Skeat (Eng. Dial. Soc.), pref. p. xviii. Also called *kidge* (Forby). An East Anglian word. ' *Kygge*, or ioly, *kydge*, *kyde*, jocundus, hillaris, vernosus;' Prompt. Parv. Cf. prov. E. *cadgy*, cheerful; and perhaps Swed. dial. *kägg*, wanton, *kägas*, to be eager.

KEEL (1), the bottom of a ship. (Scand.) ME. *kele* (rare). 'The schippe [Noah's ark] was . . . thritty cubite high from the *cule* to the hacches vnder the cabans;' i.e. from the *bottom* to the hatches; where [instead of *cule* = bottom, from F. *cul*] another reading is *kele* = keel; Trevisa, tr. of Higden, ii. 233. Of Scand. origin; answering to Icel. *kjölr*, Dan. *kjöl*, Swed. *köl*, the keel of a ship; Teut. type *keluz. ¶ Distinct from AS. *cēol*, a ship, OHG. *kiol*, MHG. *kiel*, a ship. But Du. and G. *kiel*, a keel, are borrowed from Scand. Der. *keel-ed*; also *keel-son*, q.v. Also *keel-haul*, q.v.

KEEL (2), to cool. (E.) 'While greasy Joan doth *keel* the pot;' L. L. L. v. 2. 930. The proper sense is not to *scum* the pot (though it may sometimes be so used) but to *keep it from boiling over* by stirring it round and round; orig. merely to cool it or keep it cool. 'Keel, to keep the pot from boiling over;' A Tour to the Caves, 1781; see Eng. Dial. Soc. Gloss. B. 1. 'Faith, Doricus, thy brain boils; *keel* it, *keel* it, or all the fat's in the fire;' Marston, [Induction to] What You Will, 1607; in Anc. Drama, ii. 199 (Nares). ME. *kelen*, to cool, once a common word; see Ormulum, 19584; OEng. Homilies, i. 141; Prompt. Parv., p. 270; Court of Love, 775; Gower, C. A. ii. 360; bk. v. 6908. AS. *cēlan*, to cool.—AS. *cōl*, cool; see **Cool**. ¶ Note the *regular* change from *ō* to *ē*, as in *fōt*, foot, pl. *fēt*, feet; so also *feed* from *food*, &c.

KEELHAUL. (Du.) Also *keelhale*, 'to punish in the seaman's way, by dragging the criminal under water on one side of the ship and up again on the other;' Johnson. 'Hawling vnder the *keele*;' Capt. Smith, Works, p. 790. Formerly called *keel-raking* (Phillips). A less severe punishment was *ducking at the main-yard* (Phillips). From *keel* (1) and *hale* (2); like Du. *kielhalen*, G. *kielholen*. The E. word was imitated from Dutch. See N. E. D.

KEELSON, KELSON, a piece of timber in a ship next to the keel. (Scand.) 'Keelson, the second piece of timber, which lies right over the keel;' Kersey, ed. 1715. Spelt *kelsine*, Chapman, tr. of Homer, Iliad, i. 426.—Swed. *kölsvin*, the keelson; Dan. *kjölsviin*; Norweg. *kjölsvill* (Aasen); whence G. *kielschwein*, a keelson. β. For the former syllable, see **Keel**. The latter syllable wholly agrees, in appearance, with Swed. *svin*, Dan. *sviin*, G. *schwein*, which = E. swine (see **Swine**). And such may have been the original sense; for animal names are strangely applied. Perhaps a better sense is given by Norweg. *kjölsvill*, where *svill* answers to G. *schwelle*, E. *sill*; see **Sill**. It is not known in which direction the alteration was made.

KEEN, sharp, eager, acute. (E.) ME. *kene*, Chaucer, C. T. 1968 (A 1966); Havelok, 1832. AS. *cēne*; Grein, i. 157. Here *ē* comes from an older *ō*; the orig. sense is 'knowing' or 'skilful.'+Du. *koen*, bold, stout, daring; Icel. *kænn* (for *kœnn*), wise; OHG. *chuoni*, *kuani*, MHG. *kuene*, G. *kühn*, bold. Teut. type *kōnjoz, able, wise; from *kōn-*, *ō*-grade of the Teut. root *ken (√GEN), to know; see **Ken**, **Can** (1). Der. *keen-ly*, *keen-ness*, Merch. of Ven. iv. 1. 125.

KEEP, to regard, have the care of, guard, maintain, hold, preserve. (E.) ME. *kepen*, pt. t. *kepte*, pp. *kept*; Chaucer, C. T. 514 (or 512). AS. *cēpan* (weak verb), to keep, guard, observe, heed; also to seize, lay hold of, &c. Teut. *kōpjan; root unknown; prob. allied to AS. *gecōp*, fit, suitable. [Distinct from AS. *cēpan*, variant of *cȳpan*, to buy (see **Cheap**).] In Ælfric's Homilies, i. 412, we find 'gif he dysigra manna herunga *cēpð* on arfæstum weorcum' = if he *seek after* the praises of men in pious works. 'Georne ðaes āndagan *cēpton*' = they earnestly *awaited* the appointed day; Ælf. Hom. ii. 172. '*Cēpað* heora tīman ' = they observe (or keep) their times; id. ii. 324. Der. *keep*, sb., *keep-er*, *keep-er-ship*; *keep-ing*, As You Like It, i. 1. 9; also *keep-sake*, i. e. something which we *keep* for another's *sake*, first known in 1790, and added by Todd to Johnson's Dict.

KEG, a small cask or barrel. (Scand.) Formerly also spelt *cag*. 'Cacque, Caque, a cag;' Cot. And in Sherwood's Index to Cotgrave, we find: '*A kegge*, caque; voyez *a Cag*.'—Icel. *kaggi*, a keg, cask; Swed. *kagge*, 'a cag, rundlet, runlet,' Tauchnitz, Swed. Dict.; Norwegian *kagge*, a keg, a round mass or heap, a big-bellied animal or man (whence prov. E. *kedge-bellied*, pot-bellied). And see **Kails**, which is probably related.

KELP, a kind of large sea-weed; hence, the calcined ashes of sea-weed. (E.) Formerly *kilp* or *kilpe*. 'As for the reits [sea-weeds] *kilpe*, tangle, and such like sea-weeds, Nicander saith they are as good as treacle. Sundry sorts there be of these reits, going under the name of *Alga*;' Holland, tr. of Pliny, b. xxxii. c. 6. ME. *culp*; 'as *culpes* of the see waggeth with the water;' Trevisa, tr. of Higden, ii. 181. Not found in AS.

KELPIE, in Scotland, a fabulous demon assuming various shapes, usually that of a horse. (C.) 'Be thou a *kelpie*;' Burns, Let. to Mr. Cunningham, Sept. 10, 1792. And see Brand, Antiq., ed. Ellis, ii. 513; the kelpie is a kind of horse, that makes a bellowing or neighing sound, and browses beside a lake. Prob. from Gael. *calpach*, *cólpach*, a heifer, bullock, colt; *colpa*, a cow, a horse; Irish *colpach*,

colpa, a cow, a colt. And perhaps the Gael. word is from Icel. *kálfr*, a calf (Macbain). See my Notes on E. Etym. p. 150.

KELSON, the same as **Keelson**, q.v. (Scand.)

KELT, the same as **Celt**, q.v.

KEMB, to comb. (E.) See **Unkempt**.

KEN, to know. (Scand.) Not E., but Scand. ME. *kennen*, to know, discern. 'That *kenne* myght alle,' that all might know; Allit. Poems, ed. Morris, C. 357.—Icel. *kenna*, to know; Swed. *känna*; Dan. *kjende*.+Du. *kennen*; G. *kennen*. β. The sense 'to know' is Scand.; but it is not the *original* sense. The verb is, etymologically, a *causal* one, signifying *to make* to know, to teach, show; a sense frequently found in ME. '*Kenne* me on Crist to bileue ' = teach me to believe in Christ; P. Plowman, B. i. 81. Such is also the sense of AS. *cennan*, Grein, i. 156; and of Goth. *kannjan*, to make known, John, xvii. 26. Teut. type **kannjan-*, to make known, causal of the verb which appears as *cunnan* in AS. and *kunnan* in Gothic, with the sense 'to know.' For further remarks, see **Can** (1). Der. *ken*, sb., Cymb. iii. 6. 6; a coined word, not in early use; *kenn-ing*, the range of sight, as far as one can see.

KENNEL (1), a house for dogs, pack of hounds. (F.—L.) Properly 'a place for dogs;' hence, the set of dogs themselves. ME. *kenel* (with one *n*), Prompt. Parv.; Sir Gawayn and Grene Knight, 1140.—Norm. French *kenil, answering to OF. *chenil*, a kennel. β. The Norman form is proved by the *k* being still preserved in English, and by the Norman F. *kenet*, a little dog, occurring in a Norman poem cited in Way's note in Prompt. Parv., p. 271, where the ME. *kenet* also occurs. This *kenet* is dimin. of a Norman F. *ken*, answering to Picard *kien*, OF. *chen* (Littré), mod. F. *chien*, a dog. So also in OF. *chen-il*, the former syllable = the same OF. *chen*. γ. From Late L. *canile*, 'domus canis;' Voc. 198. 29.—L. *can-*, base of *canis*, a dog; with the termination *-ile*, occurring in *ou-ile*, a house or place for sheep, a sheepfold, from *ou-is*, a sheep; cf. Ital. *canile*, a kennel. See **Canine**. Der. *kennel*, vb.; *kennell'd*, Shak. Venus, 913.

KENNEL (2), a gutter. (F.—L.) In Shak. Tam. Shrew, iv. 3. 98. A later form of the ME. *canel* or *canell*, of which ME. *chanell* (= mod. E. *channel*) is a variant with palatalisation.—AF. *canel*, a channel; in Charlemagne, ed. Michel, l. 556.—L. *canālem*, acc. of *canālis*, a canal; hence, a channel or kennel. See **Channel**, of which *kennel* is a doublet; also **Canal**.

KERAMIC, the same as **Ceramic**, q.v.

KERBSTONE, CURBSTONE, a stone laid so as to form part of the edging of stone or brick-work. (Hybrid; F.—L.; *and* E.) 'Kerbstone, a stone laid round the brim of a well;' Kersey's Dict., ed. 1715. A phonetic spelling of *curbstone*; so called from its *curbing* the stone-work, which it retains in its place. See **Curb** and **Stone**.

KERCHIEF, a square piece of cloth used to cover the head; and later, for other purposes. (F.—L.) Better spelt *curchief*. Spelt *kerchiefe* in Shak. Merry Wives, iii. 3. 62, iv. 2. 74. ME. *couerchief* (= *coverchef*), Chaucer, C. T. 6172 (D 590); also spelt *couerhcief* (= *coverchief*), id. 455 (A 453). Also *kerchef*, Chaucer, Parl. of Foules, 272.—OF. *covre-chef*, later *couvre-chef*; cf. 'Couvre-chef, a kerchief;' Cot.—OF. *covrir*, later *couvrir*, to cover; and *chef*, *chief*, the head, which is from L. *caput*, the head. See **Cover** and **Chief**. ¶ A word of similar formation is *curfew*, q.v. Der. *hand-kerchief*, *pocket-hand-kerchief*.

KERMES, the dried bodies of insects used in dyeing crimson. (Arab.—Skt.) See **Crimson**.

KERN (1), **KERNE**, an Irish soldier. (Irish.) In Shak. Macb. i. 2. 13, 30; v. 7. 17. 'The *kearne* . . . whom only I tooke to be the proper Irish souldiour;' Spenser, View of the State of Ireland; in Globe ed. of Spenser, p. 640, col. 1.—Irish *ceatharn*, a troop, but used in the sense of *ceatharnach*, a (single) soldier; from OIrish *ceithern*, a troop (Macbain). Cp. L. *caterua*, a troop. See **Cateran**. (Stokes-Fick, p. 76).

KERN (2), another spelling of **Quern**, q.v.

KERNEL, a grain, the substance in the shell of a nut. (E.) ME. *kirnel* (badly *kirnelle*), P. Plowman, B. xi. 253; *curnel*, id. C. xiii. 146. AS. *cyrnel*, to translate L. *grānum*; Voc. 138. 22. Formed (with dimin. suffix and vowel-change from Teut. *u* to *y*) from AS. *corn*, grain. Teut. stem. **kurnilo-*. See **Corn**.

KEROSENE, a lamp-oil made from petroleum. (Gk.) Ill coined from Gk. κηρός, wax; with suffix *-ene*.

KERSEY, coarse woollen cloth. (E.) In Shak. L. L. L. v. 2. 413. 'Carsey cloth, *cresy*;' Palsgrave. 'Pro tribus ulnis de *kersey*;' Earl of Derby's Expedition, 1390 (Camd. Soc.), p. 89, l. 3. The word is certainly English, and the same word as the personal name *Kersey*; named from Kersey, 3 miles from Hadleigh, in the S. of Suffolk, where a woollen trade was once carried on. A little weaving still goes on at Hadleigh. The place of the manufacture of *kersey* is now the North of England, but it was once made in the South (Phillips' Dict.). AS. *Cæres-īg*, 'Cær's island;' Birch, Cart. Saxon. iii. 603. ¶ The F. *carizé*, 'kersie' (Cot.), Du. *karsaai*, Swed. *kersing*, are all from the E. word.

KERSEYMERE, a twilled cloth of fine wool. (Cashmere.) A modern corrupt spelling of *cassimere*, an old name for the cloth also called *Cashmere*. See **Cassimere, Cashmere**. The corruption is clearly due to confusion with *kersey*, a coarse cloth of a very different texture.

KESTREL, a base kind of hawk. (F.—L.) In Spenser, F. Q. ii. 3. 4; spelt *castrel*, Beaum. and Fletcher, Pilgrim, i. 1; *kastril*, Ben Jonson, Epicœne, iv. 4; see Nares. The *t* is excrescent (as after *s* in *whils-t, amongs-t*); it stands for *kas'rel, kes'rel*, short for *casserel, ksererel*.—OF. *quercerelle*, 'a kastrell;' Cot. Also *cresserelle*, *crecerelle*, 'a kestrel,' id. Probably for **quercelelle*, the regular dimin. of *quercelle*, 'a kastrell,' Cot.—L. *querquēdula*, a kind of teal; see Diez and Scheler. Prob. of imitative origin. β. See also, in Cotgrave, the forms *cercelle*, a teal; *cercerelle*, a kestrel, teal; *crecerelle*, a kestrel; mod. F. *crécerelle*. The form *cercelle* is mod. F. *sarcelle*; see Littré, under *crécelle*, *crécerelle*, *sarcelle*; Diez, under *cerceta*, the Spanish form. The Ital. *tristarello*, a kestrel (Florio), represents a form **cristarello*; cf. Burgundian *cristel*, a kestrel, a form cited by Wedgwood. (See my letter to The Academy, Oct. 7, 1882, p. 262.)

KETCH, a small yacht or hoy. (F.—L.) '*Ketch*, a vessel like a hoy, but of a lesser size;' Kersey, ed. 1715. 'We stood in for the channel: about noon we saw a sail having but one mast; judged it to be a *ketch*; but, drawing nearer, found it was a ship in distress, having lost her main and mizen masts;' Randolph's Islands in the Archipelago, 1687, p. 103 (Todd). Formerly also *catch*; Capt. J. Smith, Works, ed. Arber, p. 51. Supposed to be a particular use of *catch*, from the verb *to catch*. See **Catch**; and see *Catch, sb.* (2) in N. E. D.

KETCHUP, a sauce. (Malay.) 'Shall I use *ketch-up*?' W. King, Art of Cookery, let. 8; in Eng. Poets (1810); ix. 252. Spelt *ketchup* in 1711 (N. E. D.).—Malay *kēchup, kichup*, à sauce; soy. (In Du. spelling *ketjap*.) See C. P. G. Scott; Malayan Words in English. Perhaps ult. of Chinese origin; see N. E. D.

KETTLE, a metal vessel for boiling liquids. (Scand.—L.) ME. *ketel* (with one *t*), Prompt. Parv.; Wyclif, Levit. xi. 35. As the *k* is hard, it is prob. from Icel. *ketill*, a kettle; we find also AS. *cetel*, AS. Leechdoms, ii. 86; spelt *cetil* in the Epinal Glossary, 168. Cf. also Du. *ketel*, G. *kessel*. The Mœso-Goth. form is *katils*, occurring in the gen. pl. *katilē* in Mark, vii. 4 (Gk. χαλκίων, Lat. *æramentorum*, A. V. 'brazen vessels'). β. Borrowed from L. *catillus*, a small bowl, also found in the form *catinulus*; dimin. form of L. *catīnus*, a bowl, a deep vessel for cooking food. The L. *catīnus* is a kindred word to Gk. κότυλος, a cup, κοτύλη, a small cup; see **Cotyledon**. ¶ From the L. *catillus* were also borrowed Icel. *ketill*, Swed. *kittel*, Dan. *kedel*, Du. *ketel*, G. *kessel*, and even Russ. *kotel'*. Der. *kettle-drum*, Hamlet, i. 4. 11.

KEX, hemlock; orig. a hollow stem. (C.?) 'Bundles of these empty *kexes*;' Beaum. and Fletcher, Elder Brother, iii. 5. 13. ME. *kex, kix*; P. Plowman, B. xvii. 219; Prompt. Parv. In Walter de Bibbesworth, *the kex* seems to mean 'dry stalks,' and translates OF. *le frenole*; Wright, Vocab., vol. i. p. 157. Cf. prov. E. *keggas*, tall umbelliferous plants; answering to Corn. *cegas*, hemlock. Prob. of Celtic or Latin origin; cf. Welsh *cegid*, hemlock; L. *cicūta*, hemlock. ¶ Hence also prov. E. *kecksies* = *kexes*, in Shak. Hen. V, v. 2. 52; a pl. sb. of which the proper singular form is not *kecksy*, but *kex*. See Way's note in Prompt. Parv., s.v. *kyx*. Note also that *kex* really = *kecks*, and is itself a plural; *kexes* being a *double* plural. W. *cecys*, pl., is merely the E. word borrowed.

KEY, that which opens or shuts a lock. (E.) Formerly called *kay*, riming with *may*, Merch. of Ven. ii. 7. 59; and with *survey*, Shak. Sonnet 52. ME. *keye* (riming with *pleye*, to play), Chaucer, C. T. 9918 (E 2044). AS. *cǣg, cǣge*, Grein, i. 156; whence ME. *keye* by the usual change of *g* into *y*, as in *day* from AS. *dæg*; OFries. *kai*, *kei*, a key. Der. *key-board, key-hole, key-note, key-stone*.

KHALIF, KHALIFA, the same as **Calif**, q. v.

KHAN, a prince, chief, emperor. (Pers.—Tatar.) Common in Mandeville's Travels, spelt *Cham, Cane, Chane, Can, Chan*; pp. 42, 215, 216, 224, 225.—Pers. *khān*, lord, prince (a title); Palmer's Pers. Dict., col. 212. But the word is of Tatar origin; the well-known title *Chingīs Khan* signifies 'great khan' or 'great lord,' a title assumed by the celebrated conqueror Temugin, who was proclaimed Great Khan of the Moguls and Tatars, A.D. 1205. He is always known by the sole *title*, often also spelt Gengis Khan, corrupted (in Chaucer) to Cambuscan. See Introd. to Chaucer's Prioresses Tale, &c., ed. Skeat, p. xlii. Der. *khan-ate*, where the suffix is of L. origin.

KHEDIVE, a prince. (F.—Pers.) A Turkish title given to the governor of Egypt; the word itself is, however, not Turkish, but borrowed from Persian.—F. *Khédive*.—Pers. *khadīw, khidīw, khudīw*, a king, a great prince, a sovereign, Rich. Dict. p. 601; spelt *khidiv*, a king, Palmer's Dict. col. 216, where the name for the viceroy of Egypt is given as *khidēwī*. Cf. Pers. *khodā*, God (Vullers, p. 663).

KHIDMUTGAR, KITMUTGAR, a male servant who waits at table; in India. (Hind.—Pers.—Arab.) First in 1765.—Hind. *khidmatgār*, a male domestic who waits at table (Forbes).—Pers. *khidmat-gār*, the same; lit. 'rendering service;' Rich. Dict., p. 601. Formed with Pers. *-gār*, agential suffix, from Arab. *khidmat*, service, employment, from Arab. root *khadama*, he served; ib. (See Yule.)

KIBE, a chilblain. (C.) In Hamlet, v. 1. 153. 'She halted of [owing to] a *kybe*;' Skelton, Elynour Rummyng, l. 493. 'He haltith often that hath a *kyby* hele;' id. Garland of Laurell, l. 502. 'Gibbus, *kybe*,' Voc. 586. 25. '*Kybis* on the fete;' Lanfranc, Cirurgie, p. 5 (ab. 1400).—W. *cibi*, a kibe (D. Silvan Evans); also *cibwst*, 'chilblains, kibes;' Spurrell. β. Explained in Pughe's Welsh Dict. as standing for *cib-gwst*, from *cib*, a cup, seed-vessel, husk, and *gwst*, a humour, malady, disease. Thus the sense would appear to be 'a malady in the shape of a cup,' from the swelling or rounded form.

KICK, to strike or thrust with the foot. (Scand.) ME. *kiken*, Chaucer, C. T. 6523 (D 941); P. Plowman, C. v. 22. [W. *cicio*, to kick, given in the Eng.-Welsh portion of Spurrell's Dict., and Gael. *ceig*, to kick, are both from E.] We find also prov. E. *kink*, to kick, also to jerk, twist the body, to sprain.—Norw. *kikka*, for *kinka*, to over-drive a horse, so as to sprain him; *kikla*, to jerk, to go jerkily, like a capricious horse; *kikk*, a spraining or straining of a sinew (Ross). Evidently related to **Kink**. Cf. Swed. *kik-hosta*, Low G. *kinkhoost*, the chincough, hooping-cough. A *kink* is a twist in a rope; hence, a hitch, jerk, kick, sprain. See *kick, kink*, in E. D. D.

KICKSHAWS, a delicacy, fantastical dish. (F.—L.) 'Any pretty little tiny *kickshaws*;' 2 Hen. IV, v. 1. 29. The pl. is *kickshawses*. 'Art thou good at these *kickshawses*?' Twelfth Nt. i. 3. 122. At a later time, *kickshaws* was incorrectly regarded as being a pl. form. *Kickshaws* is a curious corruption of F. *quelque chose*, lit. something, hence, a trifle, small delicacy. This can be abundantly proved by quotations. '*Fricandeaux*, short, skinlesse, and dainty puddings, or *quelkchoses*, made of good flesh and herbs chopped together, then rolled up into the form of liverings, &c., and so boiled;' Cotgrave's F. Dict. 'I made bold to set on the board *kickeshoses*, and variety of strange fruits;' Featley, Dippers Dipt, ed. 1645, p. 199 (Todd). 'Fresh salmon, and French *kickshose*;' Milton, Animadversions upon Remonstrant's Defence (R.). 'Nor shall we then need the monsieurs of Paris . . . to send [our youth] over back again transformed into mimicks, apes, and *kicshoes*;' Milton, Treatise on Education (Todd). 'As for French *kickshaws*, Cellery, and Champaign, Ragous, and Fricasees, in truth we've none;' Rochester, Works, 1777, p. 143. 'Some foolish French *quelquechose*, I warrant you. *Quelquechose*! oh! ignorance in supreme perfection! He means a *kek shose*!' Dryden, Kind Keeper, A. iii. sc. 1.—F. *quelque chose*, something.—L. *quāl-is*, of what kind, with suffix *-quam*; and *caussa*, a cause, thing. *Quālis* answers to E. *which*; *quam* is fem. acc. of *quī*, answering to E. *who*. See **Which, Who**, and **Cause**.

KID, a young goat. (Scand.) ME. *kid*, Chaucer, C. T. 3260, 9238 (E 1364); Ormulum, 7804.—Norw. and Dan. *kid*, a kid; Swed. *kid*, in Widegren's Swed. Dict., also *kidling*; Icel. *kið, kiðlingr*, a kid.+ OHG. *kizzi*, MHG. and G. *kitze*, a kid. Der. *kid*, verb; *kid-ling*, with double suffix *-l-ing*; *kid-fox*, a young fox, Much Ado, ii. 3. 44; also *kid-nap*, q.v.

KIDDLE, a kind of weir formed of basket-work, placed in a river to catch fish. (AF.) AF. *kidel*, pl. *kideux*, Statutes of the Realm, i. 316 (1351); MF. *quideau*, 'a wicker engine whereby fish is caught;' Cot. F. *guideau*; which cannot be derived from F. *guider* (Hatzfeld), though it may have been modified by it. Cf. E. *kit*, a tub, basket for fish; prov. E. *kid*, a tub, basket. See **Kit** (1).

KIDNAP, to steal children. (Scand.) 'People that lye in wait for our children, and may be considered as a kind of *kidnappers* within the law;' Spectator, no. 311 (Richardson, Johnson). 'Thou practisest the craft of a *kidnapper*;' said by Giant Maul in Bunyan, Pilg. Prog. pt. 2. Compounded of *kid*, a child, in thieves' slang; and *nap*, more commonly *nab*, to steal. *Kid* is of Scand. origin; see **Kid**. *Nap* is also of Scand. origin; from Dan. *nappe*, to snatch, Swed. *nappa*, to catch, to snatch, lay hold on; see **Nab**. Der. *kid-napp-er*.

KIDNEY, a gland which secretes the urine. (E.) 'And the two *kydneers*;' Wyclif, Exod. xxix. 13 (earlier version); 'and twey *kidneris*;' (later version). But the ending *-eris, -eers* seems to be a substitution for *-eren, -eiren* (see N. E. D.); and, in the same passage, three MSS. have *kideneiren*. In W. de Bibbesworth, we find the sing. form *kidenei*; Wright's Voc. vol. i. p. 149. Comparing *kiden-ei*, pl. *kiden-eiren*, with ME. *ei, ey*, an egg, pl. *eiren*, eggs, we see the probability that ME. *ei* (pl. *eiren*) constitutes the second element in kid(e)n-ey. **β.** This ME. _ei_ is from AS. _æg_ (pl. _ǣgru_, whence ME. _eire_, later _eire-n_, a double pl. form), meaning 'egg;' from the shape. Cf. Du. _ei_, an egg, pl. _eijeren_. The former element is unknown; perhaps it represents an AS. adj. form *_cydden_, or an AS. *_cyddan_, formed from AS. _codd_, a bag, husk, which in ME. also meant 'belly.' Cf. prov. E. _kid_, a pod, husk; _kiddon_, a kidney; Swed. dial. _kudde_, a pod. ¶ The ME. _nere_, a kidney, seems to be a different word; from Icel. _nȳra_, Dan. _nyre_, cognate with G. _niere_, a kidney. **Der.** _kidney-bean_. The phrase 'of his _kidney_' means 'of his size or kind;' see Merry Wives, iii. 5. 116.

KILDERKIN, a liquid measure of 18 gallons. (Du.—F.—Span.—Arab.—L.) In Levins, ed. 1570; spelt _kylderkin_. 'Take a _kilder-kin_ ... of 4 gallons of beer;' Bacon, Nat. Hist., § 46. The size of the measure appears to have varied. A corruption (by change of the liquid _n_ to _l_) of MDu. _kindeken_. Spelt _kylderken_ in Palsgrave; _kil-derkyn_ in 1390; see Riley, Memorials of London, p. 517; but _kin-derkin_ in 1598 and 1691, _kynterkyn_ in 1530 (N. E. D.). Kilian gives: '_Kindeken, kinneken_, the eighth part of a vat.' In mod. Du., _kinnetje_ means 'a firkin,' which in English measure is only half a kilderkin. **β.** The form resembles that of Du. _kindekin_, 'a little child,' Sewel; formed, with dimin. suffix _-ken_ (= E. _-kin_ = G. _-chen_), from Du. _kind_, a child; but the real origin is very different. It is ascertained to be a derivative, with the same suffix _-ken_, from a Du. spelling of OF. _quintal_, 'a quintal, or hundredweight;' Cot. See further under **Quintal**. 'See Grimm, Wört., s. v. _Kindlein_ (2); Verwijs and Verdam, s. v. _Kindekijn_ (2);' N. E. D.

KILL, to slay, deaden. (E.) ME. _killen_, more commonly _cullen_; a weak verb. Spelt _cullen_, P. Plowman, A. i. 64; _kullen_ (various reading, _killen_), id. B. i. 66. The old sense appears to be simply 'to hit' or 'strike.' 'We _kylle_ of thin heued'=we strike off thy head; Allit. Poems, ed. Morris, B. 876. '.Þauh a word _culle_ þe ful herde up o þine herte'=though a word _strike_ thee full hard upon the heart; Ancren Riwle, p. 126, l. 13; with which compare: 'þe _cul_ of þer _eax_'=the _stroke_ of the axe; id. p. 128, l. 1. 'Ofte me hine _culde_,' often people struck him; Layamon, l. 20319. If a native word, it answers to an AS. type *_cyllan_, from the weak grade, _c(w)ul_, of _cwel-an_, to die; of which E. _quell_ is the causal form. The sense 'to strike' is somewhat against this; but there is a parallel form in EFries. _küllen_, to vex, strike, beat; which suits very well; cf. also OHG. _chollen_, to vex, kill, martyr, allied to _quellan_, with the same sense. For the loss of _w_, cf. _dull_, which is related to _dwell_. See **Quell**. ¶ It bears some resemblance to Icel. _kolla_, to hit on the head, to harm; from _kollr_, top, summit, head, crown, shaven crown, pate; cf. Norweg. _kylla_, to poll, to cut the shoots off trees; from Norweg. _koll_, the top, head, crown; Aasen. But this hardly seems the right solution. **Der.** _kill-er_.

KILN, a large oven for drying corn, bricks, &c.; bricks piled for burning. (L.) '_Kylne, Kyll_, for malt dryynge, Ustrina;' Prompt. Parv., p. 274; _kulne_, Reliquiæ Antiquæ, ii. 81. AS. _cyln_, a drying-house; 'Siccatorium, _cyln_, vel _ast_;' Wright's Vocab. i. 58 (where _ast_ = _āst_ = E. _oast_ in _oast-house_, a drying-house). Also spelt _cyline_ in the Corpus glossary, l. 906. **β.** Merely borrowed from L. _culīna_, a kitchen; whence the sense was easily transferred to that of 'drying-house.' The Icel. _kylna_, Swed. _kölna_, a kiln, are from the same source; so also W. _cylyn, cyl_, a kiln. See **Culinary**.

KILOGRAMME, KILOGRAM, a weight containing 1000 grammes; about 2·205 lb. avoirdupois. (F.—Gk.) F. _kilogramme_ (1795).—F. _kilo-_, for Gk. χίλιοι, a thousand; and F. _gramme_, for Gk. γράμμα, a letter, also taken to mean a small weight.

KILOMETRE, a length of 1000 metres; nearly five furlongs. (F.—Gk.) F. _kilomètre_ (1795).—F. _kilo-_, for Gk. χίλιοι, a thousand; and F. _mètre_, a metre. See **Metre**.

KILT, a very short petticoat worn by the Highlanders of Scotland. (Scand.) The sb. is merely derived from the verb _kilt_, to tuck up, added by Todd to Johnson's Dict.; he makes no mention of the sb. 'Her tartan petticoat she'll _kilt_,' i. e. tuck up; Burns, Author's Earnest Cry, st. 17. '_Kilt_, to tuck up the clothes;' Brockett's North-Country Words. G. Douglas translates Virgil's _Nuda genu_ (Æn. i. 320) by _kiltit_. 'To _kylte_, succingere;' Cath. Anglicum (1483).—Dan. _kilte_, to truss, tuck up; Swed. dial. _kilta_, to swathe or swaddle a child (Rietz); MSwed. _upkilta_, to tuck up (Ihre). Cf. Icel. _kilting_, a skirt. **β.** There is an allied sb., signifying 'lap;' occurring in Swed. dial. _kilta_, the lap; cf. Icel. _kjalta_, the lap, _kjöltu-barn_, a baby in the lap, _kjöltu-rakki_, a lap-dog.

KIMBO; see this discussed under **Akimbo**.

KIN, relationship, affinity, genus, race. (E.) ME. _kun, kyn, kin_. 'I haue no _kun_ þere'=I have no kindred there; P. Plowman, A. vi. 118, where some MSS. have _kyn_; spelt _kynne_, id. B. v. 639. AS. _cynn_; Grein, i. 177. + OSax. _kunni_; Icel. _kyn_, kin, kindred, tribe; cf. _kynni_, acquaintance; Du. _kunne_, sex; Goth. _kuni_, kin, race, tribe. **β.** Teut. type *_kunjom_, neut. From Teut. *_kun_, weak grade of the

root KEN, equivalent to Idg. √GEN, to generate; whence L. _genus_. See **Genus, Generate**. **Der.** from the same source are _kind_, q. v., _kindred_, q. v., _king_, q. v. Also _kins-man_ = _kin's man_ = man of the same kin or tribe, Much Ado, v. 4. 112; _kins-woman_, id. iv. 1. 305; _kins-folk_, Luke, ii. 44.

KIND (1), sb., nature, sort, character. (E.) ME. _kund, kunde, kind, kinde_; Chaucer, C. T. 2453 (A 2451); spelt _kunde_, Ancren Riwle, p. 14, l. 10. AS. _cynd_, generally _gecynd_, Grein, i. 387, 388; the prefix _ge-_ making no difference to the meaning; the most usual sense is 'nature.' Teut. type *_kundiz_, fem.; from *_kun-_, base of *_kun-jom_, kin, with suffix _-di-_ = Idg. _-ti-_. See **Kin**. **Der.** _kind-ly_, adj., ME. _kyndli_ = natural, Wyclif, Wisdom, xii. 10, and so used in the Litany in the phr. '_kindly_ fruits;' whence also _kindli-ness_. Also _kind_ (2) below.

KIND (2), adj., natural, loving. (E.) ME. _kunde, kinde_; Chaucer, C. T. 8478 (E 602). 'For þe _kunde_ folk of þe lond'=for the native people of the land; Rob. of Glouc. p. 40, l. 937. A common meaning is 'natural' or 'native.' AS. _cynde_, natural, in-born; more usually _gecynde_, where the common prefix _ge-_ does not alter the sense; Grein, i. 178, 388. Teut. type *_kund-oz_, from the sb. *_kundiz_; see the sb. above. **Der.** _kind-ness_, ME. _kindenesse_ (four syllables), Chaucer, C. T. 5533 (B 1113); _kind-l-y_, adv.; _kind-hearted_, Shak. Sonnet 10.

KINDLE (1), to set fire to, inflame. (Scand.) ME. _kindlen_; Chaucer, C. T. 12415 (C 481); Havelok, 915; Ormulum, 13442. Formed from Icel. _kynda_, to light a fire, kindle; Swed. dial. _kinda, kynda, kvända_, to kindle. **β.** But Icel. _kyndill_, Swed. dial. _kyndel_, a torch, has evidently been affected by AS. _candel_, a candle (from L. _candēla_); as shown by Icel. _kyndill-messa_, Candlemas; adapted from AS. _candel-mæsse_, Candlemas, at the time of the introduction of Christianity into Iceland. **Der.** _kindl-er_.

KINDLE (2), to bring forth young. (E.) 'The cony that you see dwell where she is _kindled_;' As You Like It, iii. 2. 358. ME. _kindlen, kundlen_. 'Thet is the uttre uondunge thet _kundleð_ wreððe'=it is the outward temptation that _produces_ wrath, Ancren Riwle, p. 194, l. 20: where we also find, immediately below, the sentence: 'thus beoð theo inre uondunges the seouen heaued-sunnen and hore fule _kundles_'=thus the inward temptations are the seven chief sins and their foul _progeny_. Cf. also: '_Kyndlyn_, or brynge forthe yonge kyndelyngis, Feto, effeto;' Prompt. Parv. p. 275. And in Wyclif, Luke, iii. 7, we find '_kyndlis_ of eddris' in the earlier, and '_kyndlyngis_ of eddris' in the later version, where the A. V. has 'generation of vipers.' **β.** The verb _kindlen_, to produce, and the sb. _kindel_, a generation, are due to the sb. _kind_; see **Kind** (1). We may probably regard the sb. _kindel_ as a derivative of _kind_, and the verb as formed from it. Both words refer, in general, to a _numerous_ progeny, a litter, esp. with regard to rabbits, &c.

KINDRED, relatives, relationship. (E.) The former _d_ is excrescent, the true form being _kinred_, which occurs occasionally in Shakespeare; as, e. g. in Much Ado, ii. i. 68 (first folio). 'All the _kinred_ of Marius;' Shakespeare's Plutarch, ed. Skeat, p. 47, l. 27. ME. _kinrede_, Chaucer, C. T. 2792 (A 2790); spelt _cunreden_, St. Juliana, ed. Cockayne, p. 60, l. 13. Composed of AS. _cyn_ (see **Kin**), and the suffix _-rǣden_, signifying 'condition,' or more literally 'rule.' The AS. _cynrǣden_ does not appear, but we find the parallel word _hīwrǣden_, a household, Matt. x. 6; and the same suffix is preserved in E. _hat-red_. _Rǣden_ is connected with the Goth. _garaideins_, rule, and the adj. **Ready**, q. v. **Der.** _kindred_, adj., K. John, iii. 4. 14.

KINE, cows. (E.) Not merely the plural, but the _double_ plural form; it is impossible to regard it as a contraction of _cowen_, as some have absurdly supposed. **a.** The AS. _cū_, a cow, made the pl. _cȳ_, with the usual vowel-change of _ū_ to _ȳ_; cf. _mūs_ (E. _mouse_), pl. _mȳs_ (E. _mice_). Hence the ME. _ky_ (= cows), Barbour, Bruce, vi. 405, and still common in Lowland Scotch. 'The _kye_ stood rowtin i' the loan'; Burns, The Twa Dogs, l. 5 from end. **β.** By the addition of _-en_, a weakened form of the AS. plural-ending _-an_, was formed the double plural _ky-en_, so spelt in the Trinity-College MS. of P. Plowman, B. vi. 142, where other MSS. have _kyene, kyne, kijn, ken_. Hence kine in Gen. xxxii. 15; &c. See **Cow**. Cf. _ey-ne_ for _ey-en_ (AS. _ēag-an_), old pl. of _eye_ (AS. _ēage_). Also MDu. _koeyen_, pl. of _koe_, a cow. **γ.** Or _kine_ may represent the AS. gen. pl. _cȳna_, used with numerals; but the evidence is insufficient.

KINEMATIC, relating to motion. (Gk.) From Gk. κινημᾰτ-, stem of κίνημα, movement; from κινεῖν, to move; with adj. suffix _-ic_.

KINETIC, causing motion. (Gk.) From Gk. κινητικός, moving; from κινεῖν, to move.

KING, a chief ruler, monarch. (E.) ME. _king_, a contraction of an older form _kining_ or _kyning_. Spelt _king_, Ancren Riwle, p. 138, last line; _kining_, Mark, xv. 2 (Hatton MS.). AS. _cyning_, also _cyningc, cyninc, cynyng_, Mark, xv. 2; Grein, i. 179.—AS. _cyn_, a tribe, race, kin; with suffix _-ing_. The suffix _-ing_ means 'belonging to,' and is frequently used with the sense 'son of,' as in 'Ælfred Æþel-wulfing' = Ælfred son of Æthelwulf; A. S. Chronicle, an. 871. Thus *cyn-ing* = son of the tribe, i. e. chosen of the tribe, or man of rank.✛ OSax. *kuning,* a king, from *kuni, kunni,* a tribe; OFriesic *kining, kening,* from *ken,* a tribe; Icel. *konungr,* a king, with which cf. OIcel. *konr,* a noble, Icel. *kyn,* a kind, kin, tribe; Swed. *konung;* Dan. *konge;* Du. *koning;* G. *könig,* MHG. *künic,* OHG. *chuning, kunninc;* from MHG. *künne,* OHG. *chunni,* a race, kind. See **Kin.** β. Or else *cyn-ing* is 'son of a noble,' from AS. *cyn-e,* royal; the ultimate result is the same. See below. Der. *king-crab, king-craft, king-cup,* Spenser, Shepherd's Kalendar, April, l. 141; *king-fisher* (so called from the splendour of its plumage), Sir T. Browne, Vulg. Errors, b. iii. c. 10; *king-less,* Rob. of Glouc. p. 105 (l. 2289); *king-let,* a double diminutive, with suffixes *-l-* and *-et;* *king-like, king-ly,* ME. *kingly,* Lydgate's Minor Poems, p. 20; *king-li-ness.* Also *king's bench,* so called because the king used to sit in court; *king's evil,* Holland, tr. of Pliny, b. xx. c. 4 (end), and in Palsgrave, so called because it was supposed that a king's touch could cure it. And see *kingdom.*

KINGDOM, the realm of a king. (E.) ME. *kingdom, kyngdom;* P. Plowman, B. vii. 155. Evidently regarded as a compound of *king* with suffix *-dom;* and AS. *cyningdōm* occurs thrice in the poem of Daniel. But, as a fact, the commoner form was *kinedom;* 'þene *kinedom* of heouene' = the kingdom of heaven, Ancren Riwle, p. 148, l. 3. AS. *cynedōm,* a kingdom; Grein, i. 179. β. The former is cognate with OSax. *kuningdōm,* ONorse *konungdōmr.* The latter was formed (with suffix *-dōm*) from the adj. *cyne,* royal, very common in composition, but hardly used otherwise. This adj. answers nearly to Icel. *konr,* a man of royal or noble birth; and is related to **Kin** and **King.** Thus the alteration from ME. *kine-* to E. *king-* makes little practical difference. ¶ So also, for *king-ly,* there is an AS. *cynelic,* royal; Grein, i. 179.

KINK, a twist in a rope. (Du.) '*Kink,* a twist or short convolution in a rope;' Brockett, Gloss. of North Country Words, ed. 1846.—Du. *kink,* a twist in a rope; but prob. of Scand. origin. Cf. Norw. and Swed. *kink,* a twist in a rope; also Low G. *kinke,* a twist in a thread. β. From a Teut. base KEIK, to bend; appearing in Icel. *kikna,* to sink at the knees through a heavy burden, *keikr,* bent backwards, *keikja,* to bend backwards. The base is well preserved in Norw. *kika,* to twist, *keika,* to bend back or aside, *kinka,* to writhe, twist, *kink,* a twist (Aasen). ¶ There is an ultimate relation to **Chincough,** q.v. And see **Kick.**

KIOSK, a Turkish open summer-house, small pavilion. (F.—Turk.—Pers.) In Byron, Corsair, iii. 1. Spelt *kiosque* in French.—Turk. *kushk, köshk* (with *k* pronounced as *ki*), a kiosk; Zenker's Dict. p. 774.—Pers. *kūshk,* a palace, a villa; a portico, or similar projection in a palace, Rich. Dict. p. 1217; a palace, kiosk, Palmer's Dict. col. 496. Devic remarks that the *i* is due to the Turkish practice of inserting a slight *i* after *k.*

KIPPER, to cure or preserve salmon. (E.) This meaning is quite an accidental one, arising from a practice of curing *kipper-salmon,* i. e. salmon during the spawning season. Such fish, being inferior in kind, were cured instead of being eaten fresh. '*Kipper-time,* a space of time between May 3 and Twelfth-day, during which salmon-fishing in the river Thames was forbidden;' Kersey, ed. 1715. But some explain *kipper* to mean a salmon *before* spawning. It answers exactly, in form, to AS. *cypera,* a kind of salmon; though the precise sense is not known. 'Eow fōn lysteð leax oððe *cyperan,*' You wish to catch a salmon or a kipper; Metres of Boethius, xix. 12.

KIRK, a church. (North. E.—Gk.) The North. E. form; see Burns, The Twa Dogs, l. 19. ME. *kirke,* P. Plowman, B. v. 1; Ormulum, 3531. Cf. Icel. *kirkja;* Dan. *kirke;* Swed. *kyrka;* borrowed from AS. *cirice, circe,* a church. Of Gk. origin. See **Church.**

KIRTLE, a sort of gown or petticoat. (L.; *with* E. *suffix.*) Used rather vaguely. ME. *kirtel,* Chaucer, C. T. 3321; *kurtel,* Ancren Riwle, p. 10. AS. *cyrtel,* to translate L. *palla;* Ælfric's Gloss., in Voc. 107. 26. Also ONorthumbrian *cyrtel,* to translate L. *tunica;* Matt. v. 40 (Lindisfarne MS.)✛Icel. *kyrtill,* a kirtle, tunic, gown; Dan. *kjortel,* a tunic; Swed. *kjortel,* a petticoat. β. Evidently a diminutive, with suffixed *-el,* for *-il.* From L. *curtus,* short; which also appears in Du. *kort,* G. *kurz,* short. See **Curt.**

KISMET, fate, destiny. (Turk.—Pers.—Arab.) First in 1849.—Turk. *qismet,* fate.—Pers. *qismat,* fate.—Arab. *qisma(t),* a portion; fate, destiny.—Arab. root *qasama,* he divided.

KISS, a salute with the lips, osculation. (E.) ME. *cos, kos, cus, kus;* later *kisse, kiss.* The vowel *i* is really proper only to the verb, which is formed from the *sb.* by vowel-change. 'And he cam to Jhesu, to *kisse* him; And Jhesus seide to him, Judas, with a *coss* thou bytrayest mannys sone;' Wyclif, Luke, xxii. 47, 48. The form *kusse* is as late as Skelton, Phylyp Sparowe, 361. In the Ancren Riwle, p. 102, we find *cos,* nom. sing., *cosses,* pl., *cosse,* dat. sing.;

as well as *cus,* verb in the imperative mood. AS. *coss,* sb., a kiss, Luke, xxii. 48; whence *cyssan,* to kiss, id. xxii. 47.✛Du. *kus,* sb., whence *kussen,* vb.; Icel. *koss,* sb., whence *kyssa,* vb.; Dan. *kys,* sb., *kysse,* vb.; Swed. *kyss,* sb., *kyssa,* vb.; G. *kuss,* MHG. *kus,* whence *küssen,* vb. β. All from a Teut. type *kussuz,* sb. Cf. Goth. *kukjan,* to kiss; EFries. *kük,* a kiss. Der. *kiss,* verb; as shown above.

KISTVAEN, the same as **Cistvaen,** q.v.

KIT (1), a vessel of various kinds, a milk-pail, tub; hence, an outfit. (Du.) 'A *kit,* a little vessel, *Cantharus,*' Levins. 'Hoc mul[c]trum, a *kytt;*' Voc. 696. 14. In Barbour's Bruce, b. xviii. l. 168, we are told that Gib Harper's head was cut off, salted, put into 'a *kyt,*' and sent to London.—MDu. *kitte,* 'a great wodden bowle, or tancker,' Hexham; Du. *kit,* 'a wooden can;' Sewel. Cf. Norweg. *kitte,* a large corn-bin in the wall of a house (Aasen). *Kit,* an outfit, a collection, set, lot, is the same word (N. E. D.).

KIT (2), a small violin. (F.—L.—Gk.) 'I'll have his little gut to string a *kit* with;' Beaum. and Fletcher, Philaster, Act v. sc. 4 (4th Citizen). Abbreviated from MF. *quiterne,* a cittern, or cithern, Cot.; OF. *quitterne* (Roquefort); which is borrowed from L. *cithara.* See **Cithern, Gittern.** Godefroy, s. v. *guiterneur,* a player on a cittern, quotes the by-form *quiterneur.* The form is North. F.; Norm. dial. *quiterne,* Moisy, ed. 1895.

KIT-CAT, KIT-KAT, the name given to portraits of a particular size. (Personal name.) a. A portrait of about 28 by 36 in. in size is thus called, because it was the size adopted by Sir Godfrey Kneller (died 1723) for painting portraits of the members of the *Kit-kat* club. β. This club, founded in 1703, was so named because the members used to dine at the house of *Christopher Kat,* a pastry-cook in King's Street, Westminster [or in Shire Lane, near Temple Bar; see Spectator, no. 9, and note in Morley's edition;] Haydn, Dict. of Dates. 'Immortal made, as *Kit Kat* by his pies;' W. King, Art of Poetry, letter viii; pr. in 1708. γ. *Kit* is a familiar abbreviation of *Christopher,* a name of Gk. origin, from Gk. Χριστο-φόρος, lit. 'Christ-bearing.'

KITCHEN, a room where food is cooked. (L.) The *t* is inserted. ME. *kichen, kychene, kechene,* Will. of Palerne, 1681, 1707, 2171; *kychyne,* P. Plowman, B. v. 261. Spelt *kuchene,* Ancren Riwle, p. 214. AS. '*cycene,* coquina;' Voc. 283. 12.—Late L. *cucīna,* for L. *coquīna,* a kitchen.—L. *coquere,* to cook; see **Cook.** Der. *kitchen-maid, kitchen-stuff, kitchen-garden.*

KITE, a voracious bird; a toy for flying in the air. (E.) ME. *kitë, kytë* (dissyllabic), Chaucer, C. T. 1181 (A 1179). AS. *cýta;* we find the entry 'Butio (*sic*), *cyta*' in Ælfric's Gloss. (Nomina Auium); and in the Corpus Glossary, 333. The L. *butio* is properly a bittern; but doubtless *buteo* is meant, signifying a kind of falcon or hawk. The *y* was long, as shown by the modern sound; cf. E. *mice* with AS. *mýs.* β. Teut. type *kūt-jon,* an agential form. Prob. from its swift flight; cf. Norw. *kuta* (pt. t. *kaut*), to run, go swiftly (Aasen). γ. The toy called a *kite* is mentioned in Butler, Hudibras, pt. ii. c. 3. l. 414; and is named from its hovering in the air.

KITH, kindred, acquaintance, sort. (E.) Usual in the phrase '*kith* and kin.' ME. *cuððe, kiþþe, kith;* see Gower, C. A. ii. 267, bk. v. 4180; P. Plowman, B. xv. 497. AS. *cýððu,* native land, *cýð,* relationship; Grein, i. 181, 182.—AS. *cúð,* known; pp. of *cunnan,* to know; see **Can** (1) and **Kythe.**

KITLING, a kitten. (Scand.) Palsgrave has *kytlyng* (1530).—Icel. *ketlingr,* a kitten; dimin. of *köttr* (stem *kattu-*), a cat. Cognate with E. *cat;* see **Cat.** ¶ The ME. *kitling, ketling,* also meant a whelp, or young of any animal; perhaps it was influenced by L. *catulus,* a whelp. It first appears in 'the *kitelinges* of liouns;' E. Eng. Psalter, lvi. 5; where the Vulgate has *catulorum leonum.*

KITTEN, a young cat. (F.—L.) ME. *kyton,* P. Plowman, C. i. 204, 207; *kitoun,* id., B. prol. 190, 202. From an AF. *kitoun,* variant of OF. *chitoun,* a kitten, used by Gower, Mirour de l'Omme, l. 8221. Again, AF. *kitoun* is a variant of Norm. F. *caton,* Northern form of *chaton,* a kitten, formed from F. *chat,* a cat, with suffix *-on* (< L. *-ōnem*).—Folk-L. *cattum,* acc. of *cattus,* for L. *cātus,* a cat. See **Cat.** Cf. MF. *chatton.* '*Chatton,* a kitling or young cat;' Cot. For the *i-* sound, cf. Low G. *kette, kitte, kettin, kittin,* f., a female cat; *kitten,* a kitten (Schambach). The true E. form is *kit-ling;* see above. Note also the old verb *to kittle,* to produce young as a cat does. Cf. Norw. *kjetling,* a kitling or kitten, *kjetla,* to kittle or kitten; Aasen. 'I *kyttell,* as a catte dothe, *je chatonne.* Gossyppe, whan your catte *kytelleth,* I praye you let me haue a *kytlynge* (*chatton*),' Palsgrave; cf. Way's note in Prompt. Parv. p. 277.

KIWI, the apteryx, a wingless bird. (Maori.) First in 1835. The native name in New Zealand; so called from the note of the bird. See Austral English; by E. E. Morris.

KLEPTOMANIA, an irresistible propensity to theft. (Gk.)

Spelt *cleptomania* in 1830.—Gk. κλεπτο-, for κλεπτής, a thief; and μανία, frenzy; see **Mania**.

KNACK, a snap, quick motion, dexterity, trick. (E.) 'The more queinte *knakkes* that they make'=the more clever tricks they practise; Chaucer, C. T., A 4051 (Harl. MS.). On which Tyrwhitt remarks: 'The word seems to have been formed from the *knacking* or snapping of the fingers made by jugglers.' For this explanation, he refers us to Cotgrave. '*Matassiner des mains*, to move, knack, or waggle the fingers, like a jugler, plaier, jeaster, &c.;' Cot. '*Niquet*, a *knick*, tlick, snap with the teeth or fingers, a trifle, nifle, bable [bauble], matter of small value;' id. '*Faire la nique*, to threaten or defie, by putting the thumbe naile into the mouth, and with a jerke (from the upper teeth) make it to *knack*;' id. The word is clearly (like *crack, click*) of imitative origin; cf. EFries. *knakken* (base *knakan*), pt. t. *knuok, knōk*, to snap, make a snapping noise.+Du. *knakken*; Norw. *knaka*, Swed. *knaka*, Dan. *knage*, to crack. [Gael. *cnac*, a crack, is from E. *crack*.] The senses are (1) a snap, crack, (2) a snap with the finger or nail, (3) a jester's trick, piece of dexterity, (4) a joke, trifle, toy. See Shak. Mids. Nt. Dr. i. 1. 34; Tam. Shrew, iv. 3. 67; Wint. Tale, iv. 4. 360, 439. ¶ A similar succession of ideas is seen in Du. *knap*, a crack; *knappen*, to crack, snap; *knap*, clever, nimble; *knaphandig*, nimble-handed, dexterous. See **Knap**. Der. *knick-knack*, q. v. ☞ The F. *nique* (above) is from Du. *knikken*, to crack slightly, an attenuated form of *knakken*. And see **Knock**.

KNACKER, a dealer in old horses. (E.) Now applied to a dealer in old horses and dogs' meat. Prob. it meant at first a dealer in *knacks*, i. e. trifles or worthless articles. See **Knack**, above. 2. We also find: '*Knacker*, one that makes collars and other furniture for cart-horses;' Ray, South and East Country Words, 1691 (E. D. S. Gloss. B. 16). Perhaps from Icel. *hnakkr*, a man's saddle; cf. *hnakkmarr*, a saddle-horse.

KNAG, a knot in wood, a peg, branch of a deer's horn. (E.) 'I schall hyt hynge on a *knagg*'=I shall hang it on a peg; Le Bone Florence, l. 1795; in Ritson, Metrical Romances, v. iii. 'A *knagge* in wood, *Bosse*;' Sherwood's Index to Cotgrave. We read also of the 'sharp and branching *knags*' of a stag's horn; Holland, tr. of Plutarch, p. 1039. Not found in AS. EFries. *knagge*, a knot in wood, a stump. Cf. also Low G. *knagge*, knot, peg (Lübben); Norw. *knagg*, a knag, short branch; Swed. *knagg*, a knag, knot; Dan. *knag*, a peg, cog. We also find Irish *cnag*, a knob, peg, *cnaig*, a knot in wood; Gael. *cnag*, a pin, peg, knob; borrowed from E. Der. *knagg-y*.

KNAP, to snap, break with a noise. (E.) 'He hath *knapped* the speare in sonder;' Ps. xlvi. 9, in the Bible of 1535, also of 1551; still preserved in the Prayer-book version. 'As lying a gossip as ever *knapped* ginger;' Merch. Ven. iii. 1. 10. 'Thow can *knap* doun [knock down] caponis;' Henryson, Wolf and Fox. Not in AS. *knappen*. Of imitative origin; cf. EFries. *knap*, a cracking, a snap.+Du. *knappen*, to crack, snap, catch, crush, eat; whence *knapper*, (1) hard gingerbread, (2) a lie, untruth [this brings out the force of Shakespeare's phrase]; Dan. *kneppe*, to snap, crack with the fingers; *knep*, a snap, crack, fillip. Cf. Swed. *knep*, a trick, artifice; *bruka knep*, to play tricks; which illustrates the use of the parallel word *knack*, q.v. Der. *knap-sack*.

KNAPSACK, a provision-bag, case for necessaries used by travellers. (Du.) 'And each one fills his *knapsack* or his scrip;' Drayton, The Battle of Agincourt, 6th st. from end.—Du. *knapzak*, a knapsack; orig. a provision-bag.—Du. *knap*, eating, *knappen*, to crack, crush, eat; and *zak*, a bag, sack, pocket. Cf. Westphalian *knapp*, a piece of bread (Franck). See **Knap** and **Sack**.

KNAP, a hill-top; **KNAPWEED**, knopweed; see **Knop**.

KNAR, a knot in wood. (E.) See **Gnarled** and **Knurr**.

KNAVE, a boy, servant, sly fellow, villain. (E.) The older senses are 'boy' and 'servant.' ME. *knaue* (with *u* for *v*). 'A *knaue* child'=a male child, boy; Chaucer, C. T. 8320, 8323 (E 444, 447). 'The kokes *knaue*, thet wassheð the disshes;'=the cook's boy, that washes the dishes; Ancren Riwle, p. 380, l. 8. AS. *cnafa*, a boy, another form of *cnapa*, a boy; *cnapa* occurs in Matt. xii. 18, and in Ps. lxxxv. 15, ed. Spelman, where another reading (in the latter passage) is *cnafa*.+Du. *knaap*, a lad, servant, fellow; Icel. *knapi*, a servant-boy; Swed. *knäfvel*, a rogue (a dimin. form); G. *knabe*, a boy; OHG. *knappo*, also *knabo*, as to which see Streitberg, § 131 (5). β. The origin of the word is doubtful; but it is generally supposed that the initial *kn-* corresponds to the weak grade of the √GEN, to beget. Cp. **Genus**. And see **Knight**. Der. *knav-ish*, Chaucer, C. T. 17154 (H 205); *knav-ish-ly; knav-er-y*, Spenser, F. Q. ii. 3. 9.

KNEAD, to work flour into dough, mould by pressure. (E.) ME. *kneden*, Chaucer, C. T. 4092 (A 4094); Ormulum, 1486. AS. *cnedan*, to knead, very rare; in the ONorthumbrian versions of Luke, xiii. 21, the L. *fermentaretur* is glossed by *sie gedærsted* vel *gecnoeden* in the Lindisfarne MS., and by *sie gedærstad* vel *cneden* in the Rushworth MS.; hence we infer the strong verb *cnedan*, with pt. t. *cnæd*, and pp. *cneden*. We also find the form *gecnedan*, Gen. xviii. 6; where the prefix *ge-* does not affect the force of the verb. The verb has become a weak one, the pp. passing from *knoden* to *kneded* in the 15th century, as shown by the entry: '*Knodon, kneded*, Pistus;' Prompt. Parv. p. 280.+Du. *kneden*; Icel. *knoða*, Swed. *knåda* (both from the weak grade); G. *kneten*, OHG. *chnetan*. Teut. type *knedan-*, pt. t. *knad*, pp. *knedanoz*. Further allied to Russ. *gnetate, gnesti*, to press, squeeze, from an Idg. base *gnet-*, to press. Der. *knead-ing-trough*, ME. *kneding-trough*, Chaucer, C. T. 3548.

KNEE, the joint of the lower leg with the thigh. (E.) ME. *kne, knee*; pl. *knees*, Chaucer, C. T. 5573 (B 1153); also *cneo*, pl. *cnecn* (=*kneen*), Ancreh Riwle, p. 16, last line but one. AS. *cneō, cneow*, a knee; Grein, i. 164.+Du. *knie*; Icel. *knē*; Dan. *knæ*; Swed. *knä*; G. *knie*, OHG. *chniu*; Goth. *kniu*. Teut. type *knewom*, neut. Allied to L. *genu*; Gk. γόνυ; Skt. *jānu*, knee. β. The Idg. related bases are *genu-* (as in L.), *gonu-* (as in Gk.), and *gneu-* (answering to Teut. *kneu-*). The loss of vowel in the weak grade is well illustrated by the Gk. γνύ-πετος, fallen upon the knees. Der. *knee-d; knee-pan*; also *kneel*, q.v. And see *geni-culate, genu-flection, penta-gon, hexa-gon*, &c.

KNEEL, to fall on the knees. (E.) ME. *knelen*, Havelok, 1320; Ormulum, 6138. AS. *cneowlian*, to kneel, various reading for *gecneowigan* in Canons under k. Edgar; see N. E. D., and Thorpe, Anc. Laws, ii. 282, § xvi.+Du. *knielen*; Low G. *knelen* (Lübben); whence Dan. *knæle*, to kneel. Formed from *knee* (AS. *cneow*) by adding *-l-*, to denote the action.

KNELL, KNOLL, to sound as a bell, toll. (E.) 'Where bells have *knolled* to church;' As You Like It, ii. 7. 114; 'I *knolle* a belle, *Ie frappe du batant*;' Palsgrave. ME. *knillen*; 'And lete also the belles *knille*;' Myrc's Instructions for Parish Priests, ed. Peacock, l. 779. '*Knyllynge* of a belle, *Tintillacio*;' Prompt. Parv., p. 279. The orig. sense is to beat so as to produce a sound. AS. *cnyllan*, to beat noisily; in the ONorthumb. version of Luke, xi. 9, we find: '*cnyllað* and ontyned bið iow'=knock and it shall be opened to you (Rushworth MS.). We find also AS. *cnyl*, a knell, the sound of a bell (Bosworth). The AS. verb=Teut. *knul-jan*, whence ME. *knillen*, of which knell and knoll are later variants (prob. of imitative origin). From a Teut. base *knel-* (whence *knal, *knul-* by gradation); as in the OHG. strong verb *er-knellan*, to resound. Cp. Du. *knallen*, to give a loud report; *knal*, a clap, a report; Dan. *knalde* (=*knalle*), to explode; *knalde med en pidsk*, to crack a whip; *knald* (=*knall*), a crack; Swed. *knalla*, to make a noise, to thunder; *knall*, a report, loud noise; G. *knallen*, to make a loud noise; *knall*, a report, explosion; Icel. *gnella*, to scream. β. All words of imitative origin, like *knack, knap, knock*. ¶ We find also W. *cnill*, a passing-bell, *cnul*, a knell; borrowed from E. Der. *knell*, sb., Temp. i. 2. 402.

KNICKERBOCKERS, loose knee-breeches. (Du.) First in 1859. 'The name is said to have been given to them because of their resemblance to the knee-breeches of the Dutchmen in Cruikshank's illustrations to W. Irving's Hist. of New York;' N. E. D. This book came out under the pseudonym of Diedrich *Knickerbocker*.

KNICK-KNACK, a trick, trifle, toy. (E.) A reduplication of *knack* in the sense of 'trick,' as formerly used; or in the sense of 'toy,' as generally used now. 'But if you use these *knick-knacks*,' i. e. these tricks; Beaum. and Fletcher, Loyal Subject, ii. 1 (Theodore). The reduplication is effected in the usual manner, by the attenuation of the radical vowel *a* to *i*; cf. *click-clack, ding-dong, pit-a-pat*. Cf. Du. *knikken*, to crack, snap, weakened form of *knakken*, to crack. See further under **Knack**.

KNIFE, an instrument for cutting. (E.) ME. *knif, cnif*; pl. *kniues* (with *u*=*v*), Chaucer, C. T. 233. The sing. *knif* is in the Ancren Riwle, p. 282, last line but one. AS. *cnīf*, a knife (late), Voc. 329. 17. EFries. *knīf*, also *knīp*.+Du. *knīf*; Icel. *knīfr, hnīfr*; Dan. *kniv*; Swed. *knif*; G. (provincial) *kneif*, a hedging-bill, clasp-knife (Flügel); Low G. *knīf, knīp* (Lübben). β. The root is uncertain; if we may take *knīp-* as the Teut. base, we may perhaps connect it with the verb which appears in Du. *knijpen*, to pinch, nip; G. *kneipen*, to pinch, *kneifen*, to nip, squeeze. See **Nip**. ¶ The F. *canif* is of Teut. origin. Der. *knife-edge*.

KNIGHT, a youth, servant, man at arms. (E.) ME. *knight*; see Chaucer's *Knightes* Tale. AS. *cniht*, a boy, servant; Grein, i. 165; OMerc. *cneht* (O. E. Texts).+Du. *knecht*, a servant, waiter, whence Dan. *knegt*, a servant, knave (at cards); Swed. *knekt*, a soldier, knave (at cards); G. *knecht*, a man-servant. β. Origin uncertain; the AS. suffix *-eht, -iht* is adjectival, as in *stān-iht*=stony. Probably *cn-eht* is from *cn-*, weak grade of *cen-*, Idg. *gen-*, as in Gk. γέν-ος, kin; cf. Gk. γν-ήσιος, legitimate, allied to γένος. Thus *cn-eht* may = *cyn-eht*, i. e. belonging to the 'kin' or tribe; it would thus signify one of age to be admitted among the men of the tribe. Der. *knight*, verb, *knight-ly*, Wyclif, 2 Macc. viii. 9, with which cf. AS. *cnihtlic*, boyish (Bosworth); *knight-hood*, ME. *kny3thod*, P. Plowman, B. prol. 112, from AS. *cnihthād*, lit. boyhood, youth (Bosworth); *knight-errant*. 2 Hen. IV, v. 4. 24; *knight-errant-r-y*.

KNIT, to form into a knot. (E.) ME. *knitten*, Chaucer, C. T. 1130 (A 1128); P. Plowman, B. prol. 169. AS. *cny'tan*, *cnittan*; '*Necto*, *ic cnytte*,' Ælfric, Gram., ed. Zupitza, p. 214; the comp. *becnittan* is used in Ælfric's Homilies, i. 476, l. 5. Formed by vowel-change from Teut. **knut-*, base of AS. *cnotta*, a knot. ✛ Icel. *knyta*, *knytja*, to knit; cf. *knū'tr*, a knot; Dan. *knytte*, to tie in a knot, knit; Swed. *knyta*, to knit, tie; *knut*, knot. See **Knot**. Der. *knitt-er*, *knitt-ing*.

KNOB, allied to **Knop**, q.v. (E.) In Levins; and Chaucer, C. T. 635 (A 633). Cf. Low G. *knobbe*, a knob; Du. *knobbel*. Der. *knobb-ed*, *knobb-y*, *knobb-i-ness*.

KNOCK, to strike, rap, thump. (E.) ME. *knokken*; Chaucer, C. T. 3432. AS. *cnucian*, later *cnokien*, Matt. vii. 7; Luke, xi. 10. Also *ge-cnocian*, *ge-cnucian*, AS. Leechdoms, i. 168, note 8. ✛ Icel. *knoka*, to knock. An imitative word; from Teut. **knuk-*, weak grade allied to **knak-*. See **Knack**. Cf. Low G. *knuk*, a knock. Der. *knock*, sb., *knock-kneed*, *knock-er*.

KNOLL (1), the top of a hill, a hillock, mound. (E.) ME. *knol*, a hill, mount; Genesis and Exodus, ed. Morris, l. 4129. AS. *cnoll*; ' *þæra munta cnollas*' = the tops of the hills; Gen. viii. 5. ✛ Du. *knol*, a turnip; from its roundness; Dan. *knold* (for **knoll*), a knoll; Swed. *knöl*, a bump, knob, bunch, knot; G. *knollen*, a knoll, clod, lump, knot, knob, bulb (provincially, a potato); MHG. *knolle*. And cf. Swed. dial. *knall*, a knoll. We also find W. *cnol*, a knoll, hillock; from E.

KNOLL (2), the same as **Knell**, q.v. (E.)

KNOP, KNOB, a protuberance, bump, round projection. (E.) *Knob* is a derivative, yet occurs in Chaucer, C. T. 635 (A 633), where we find the pl. *knobbes*, from a singular *knobbë* (dissyllabic). *Knop* is in Exod. xxv. 31, 33, 36 (A. V.). The pl. *knoppis* is in Wyclif, Exod. xxvi. 11; spelt *knoppes*, Rom. of the Rose, 1683, 1685, where it means ' rose-buds.' It also occurs in the sense of a hill-top (N. E. D.; E. D. D.). [It is perhaps allied to *knap*, in the sense of ' hill-top;' as in : ' some high *knap* or tuft of a mountaine;' Holland, tr. of Pliny, b. xi. c. 11.] ✛ Du. *knop*, a knob, pummel, button, bud; allied to *knoop*, a knob, button, knot, tie; Dan. *knop*, a knob, bud; Swed. *knopp*, a knob; allied to *knop*, a knot; G. *knopf*, a knob, button, pummel, bud. Teut. stem **knuppo-*; and Du. *knoop* is from Teut. stem **knaupo-*; both from a Teut. base **knup-* (Franck). β. With a different vowel, we find E. *knap* (as above), from AS. *cnæpp*, a hill-top, Luke, iv. 29; Numb. xiv. 44; allied to Icel. *knappr*, a knot, stud, button; MSwed. *knapp*, a button; Dan. *knap*, a knob, button; Low G. *knap*, a hill (Schambach). And this may be allied to *knap*, to strike; cf. *bump*. See **Knap**. *Knap*, in the sense of ' to beat,' occurs in King Lear, ii. 4. 125. Der. *knop-weed* or *knap-weed*.

KNOT, a tight fastening, bond, cluster. (E.) ME. *knottë* (dissyllabic), Chaucer, C. T. 10715 (F 401). AS. *cnotta*, a knot; Ælfric's Hom. ii. 386, l. 22. ✛ Du. *knot*, Low G. *knutte*. Teut. type **knutton-* (whence E. *knit*); from a base **knuþ-*. β. We also find OHG. *knodo*, a knob, from a Teut. type **knuþon-*, Idg. type **gnuton-*; as well as OHG. *knoto*, G. *knoten*, a knob, a knot, from a Teut. type **knuðōn-*, Idg. type **gnutōn-*. γ. Also (with a long vowel), Icel. *knū'tr*, a knot, Swed. *knut*, Dan. *knude*. δ. Also (with original *a*) Icel. *knöttr*, a ball; Teut. type **knattuz*. For this change, cf. *knop*, *knap*; see **Knop**. ¶ Not connected with L. *nōdus*, a knot. Der. *knot*, verb; *knit*, q.v.; *knott-y*, *knot-less*, *knot-grass*.

KNOUT, a whip used as an instrument of punishment in Russia. (Russian—Scand.) Not in Todd's Johnson. ◆ Russ. *knute*, a whip, scourge; but spelt as in French. Not a Slavonic word. ◆ Swed. *knut* (Icel. *knū'tr*), a knot. See **Knot** (γ). Der. *knout*, verb.

KNOW, to be assured of, recognise. (E.) ME. *knowen*; pt. t. *knew*, Chaucer, C. T. 5474 (B 1054); pp. *knowen*, id. 5310 (B 890). AS. *cnāwan*, pt. t. *cnēow*, pp. *cnāwen*; gen. used with prefix *ge-*, which does not affect the sense; Grein, i. 386. ✛ Icel. *knā*, I know how to, defective verb; OHG. *chnāan*, to know, only in the compounds *bi-chnāan*, *ir-chnāan*, *int-chnāan*; cited by Fick, iii. 41. ✛ Russ. *znate*, to know, OSlavon. *zna-ti*; L. *nōscere* (for *gnōscere*), to know; Gk. γι-γνώσκειν (fut. γνώσομαι), a reduplicated form; Skt. *jnā*, to know. Cf. also Pers. *far-zān*, knowledge; OIrish *gnāth*, known, accustomed; W. *gnawd*, a custom. β. All from **gnē*, **gnō-*, to know. secondary forms from √GEN, to know; whence **Can** (1), **Ken**, **Keen**, &c. Brugmann, i. § 304. Der. *know-ing*, *know-ing-ly*; also *know-ledge*, q.v.

KNOWLEDGE, assured belief, information, skill. (E.) ME. *knowlege*, Chaucer, C. T. 12960; spelt *knoweliche*, *knoweleche* in Sixtext ed., B 1220. In the Cursor Mundi, 12162, the spellings are *knaulage*, *knawlage*, *knauleche*, *knoweleche*. The *d* is a late insertion;

and *-lege* is for older *-leche*. For *know-*, see above. As to the suffix, it is of verbal origin; the *ch* is a palatalised form of *c* as usual; and the ME. suffix *-lechen* represents the AS. suffix *-lācan*, as in *nēah-lācan*, to draw nigh. β. The origin of this *-lācan* is not quite certain; I regard it as representing **-lācian*, from the substantival suffix *-lāc*, preserved in E. **Wedlock**, q.v. γ. The AS. *-lāc* corresponds to Icel. *-leikr*; and we find a related word in Icel. *kunnleikr*, knowledge. Der. *acknowledge*, a bad spelling of *a-knowledge*; see **Acknowledge**.

KNUCKLE, the projecting joint of the fingers. (E.) ME. *knokil*. '*Knokyl* of an honde, *knokil-bone*, Condilus;' Prompt. Parv. '*Knokylle-bone* of a legge, Coxa;' id. 'The *knokelys* of the fete;' Rel. Antiq. i. 190 (ab. 1375). Not found in AS.; the alleged form *cnucl*, due to Somner, appears to be a fiction. Yet some such form probably existed, though not recorded; it occurs in OFriesic as *knokele*, *knokle*. ✛ Du. *knokkel*, a knuckle (Sewel); dimin. of *knoke*, *knake*, a bone, or a knuckle (Hexham); Low G. *knukkel*; Dan. *knokkel*; Swed. *knoge*, a knuckle (in which the dimin. suffix is not added); G. *knöchel*, a knuckle, joint; connected with *knochen*, a bone. Note MDu. *knoke*; Hexham has: '*De knoest*, *knoke*, *ofte Weere van een boom*, the knobb or knot of a tree.' All from a Teut. base **knuk-*; perhaps allied to **Knock**. And cf. **Knop**.

KNURR, KNUR, a knot in wood, wooden ball. (E.) 'A *knurre*, bruscum, gibbus;' Levins, 190. 16. '*Bosse*, a knob, knot, or *knur* in a tree;' Cot. ME. *knor*. 'Without knot or *knor*, or eny signe of goute;' Tale of Beryn, ed. Furnivall, l. 2514. Not found in AS., but prob. a native word. EFries. *knure*. Cf. also MDu. *knorre*, a hard swelling, knot in wood (Kilian, Oudemans); Dan. *knort*, a knot, gnarl, knag; Swed. dial. *knurr*, *knurra*, a round knob on a tree; G. *knorren*, a hunch, lump, protuberance, knot in reed or straw; prov. G. *knorz*, a knob, knot (Flügel). β. It is evidently allied to ME. *knarre*, a knot in wood; see Wyclif, Wisd. xiii. 13; see **Gnarled**.

KOPJE, a small hill. (Du.) Common in S. Africa. ◆ Du. *kopje*, lit. ' little head;' dimin. of *kop*, head. Cf. E. *cop*, AS. *cop*, top, esp. of a hill; G. *kopf*, head.

KORAN, the sacred book of the Mohammedans. (Arab.) Also *Alcoran*, where *al* is the Arabic def. article. Bacon has *Alcoran*, Essay 16 (Of Atheism). ◆ Arab. *qurān*, Palmer's Pers. Dict., col. 469; explained by ' reading, a legible book, the *kurān*,' Rich. Pers. and Arab. Dict. p. 1122. ◆ Arab. root *qara'a*, he read; Rich. Dict. p. 1121. ¶ The *a* is long, and bears the stress; but Byron has *kórans*, Corsair, ii. 2.

KOUMISS, a fermented liquor prepared from mare's milk. (F.—Russ.—Tatar.) Spelt *chumis* in 1607; Topsell, Fourfooted Beasts, p. 32. ◆ F. *koumis*. ◆ Russ. *kymuis*; Reiff. ◆ Tatar *kumiz* (N. E. D.).

KRAAL, a Kaffir village. (Du.—Port.—L.) 'This shews the *koral*, or *kraal*, to be a village;' Voyages (1745); vol. ii. p. 120 (note); under the date 1714. ◆ Du. *kraal*. ◆ Port. *curral*, an enclosure for cattle, a fold for sheep; Span. *corral*. ◆ Port. *corr-o*, a ring in which to bait bulls; with suffix *-al*. ◆ L. *currere*, to run; see **Current**. From the Span. phrase *correr toros*, to run bulls, to hold a bull-fight (Diez). Körting, § 2705.

KYTHE, KITHE, to make known. (E.) In Burns, Hallowe'en, st. 3. ME. *kythen*, *kithen*; Chaucer, C. T. 5056 (B 636). AS. *cȳðan*, to make known; formed by regular vowel-change from *cūð*, known, pp. of *cunnan*, to know. See **Uncouth**, **Can** (1).

L

LAAGER, a camp, a temporary lodgement surrounded by waggons. (Du.) SAfrican Du. *lager*; Du. *leger*; cf. G. *lager*, a camp, MHG. *leger*. See **Leaguer**, **Lair**.

LABEL, a small slip of paper, &c. (F.) Variously used. In heraldry, it denotes a small horizontal strip with (usually) three pendants or tassels. Also, a strip or slip of silk, parchment, or paper. ME. *label*; Chaucer, On the Astrolabe, pt. i. § 22; where it denotes a movable slip or thin rule of metal, used on the front of the astrolabe, revolving on a central pin, and used as a sort of pointer. ◆ OF. *label*, also *lambel* (F. *lambeau*), in the heraldic sense; see Hatzfeld. Cotgrave has: '*Lambel*, a label of three points; *Lambeau*, a shread, rag, or small piece of stuffe or of a garment.' Of uncertain origin; perhaps allied to OLat. *lamberāre*, to tear in pieces (Ascoli). Körting, § 5399. β. But the OF. *label* may be of Teut. origin; from OHG. *lappa* (G. *lappen*), a flap, rag, shred; see **Lap** (1). Der. *label*, verb; Twelfth Night, i. 5. 265.

LABELLUM, a pendulous petal. (L.) A botanical term. ◆ L. *labellum*, a little lip. For **labrellum*, dimin. of *labrum*, a lip, akin to *labium*, a lip; see **Labial**.

LABIAL, pertaining to the lips. (L.) 'Which letters are *labiall*;' Bacon, Nat. Hist. § 198. [The *labial* letters are *p*, *b*, *f*, *v*, *w*; closely allied to which is the nasal *m*.]—Late L. *labiālis*, belonging to the lips; coined from L. *labium*, the lip. See **Lip.**

LABIATE, having lips or lobes. (L.) A botanical term. Coined, as if from a L. pp. **labiātus*, from L. *labium*, the lip. See **Labial.**

LABORATORY, a chemist's workroom. (L.) '*Laboratory*, a chymists workhouse;' Kersey, ed. 1715. And in Ben Jonson, Mercury Vindicated. Shortened from *elaboratory*, by loss of *e*. '*Elaboratory*, a work-house;' Blount's Gloss., ed. 1674. Cf. MF. *elaboratoire*, 'an elaboratory, or workhouse;' Cot. Formed, as if from a L. **ēlabōrātōrium*, from *ēlabōrāre*, to take pains, compounded of L. *ē*, out, extremely, and *labōrāre*, to work. See **Elaborate, Labour.**

LABORIOUS, toilsome. (F.—L.) ME. *laborious*; Gower, Conf. Amant. ii. 90; bk. iv. 2636.—F. *laborieux*, 'laborious;' Cot.—L. *labōriōsus*, toilsome; formed with suffix *-ōsus* from *labōri-*, decl. stem of *labor*. See **Labour.** Der. *laborious-ly, -ness.*

LABOUR, toil, work. (F.—L.) ME. *labour* (accented on *-our*); Chaucer, C. T. 2195 (A 2193).—OF. *labour*, later *labeur*.—L. *labōrem*, acc. of *labor* (oldest form *labōs*), labour, toil. β. Perhaps allied to *labāre*, to totter, to sink, from the idea of struggling with a heavy weight (Bréal). Der. *labour*, verb, ME. *labouren*, Chaucer, C. T. 186; *labour-ed*; *labour-er*, ME. *laborer*, Chaucer, C. T. 1411 (A 1409); and see *labor-i-ous, labor-at-or-y*. ☞ The spelling with final *-our*, answering to OF. *-our*, shows that the derivation is not from L. nom. *labor*, but from the acc. *labōrem*.

LABURNUM, the name of a tree. (L.) In Holland, tr. of Pliny, b. xvi. c. 18.—L. *laburnum*; Pliny, xvi. 18. 31.

LABYRINTH, a place full of winding passages, a maze. (F.—L.—Gk.) In Shak. Troil. ii. 3. 2.—F. *labyrinthe*; Cot.—L. *labyrinthus*.—Gk. λαβύρινθος, a maze, place full of lanes or alleys. Prob. of Egypt. origin. ¶ Cotgrave spells the E. word 'laborinth;' so also Late L. *laborintus*, Trevisa, i. 9; by confusion with L. *labor*. Der. *labyrinth-ine, labyrinth-i-an*.

LAC (1), a resinous substance. (Hind.—Skt.) A resinous substance produced mainly upon the banyan-tree by an insect called the *Coccus lacca*. '*Lacca*, a kind of red gum;' Kersey's Dict., ed. 1715.—Hind. *lākh*, the same as Pers. *lak, luk*, 'the substance commonly called gum-lac, being the nidus of an insect found deposited on certain trees in India, and from which a beautiful red lake is extracted, used in dyeing;' Richardson's Pers. Dict. p. 1272.—Skt. *lākshā*, lac, the animal dye; also *laktaka-*, lac; *raktā*, lac, from *rakta-*, pp. of the verb *rañj*, to dye, to colour, to redden; cf. Skt. *ranga-*, colour, paint (Benfey). Doublet, *lake* (2). Der. *lacqu-er, gum-lac, shel-lac*.

LAC (2), a hundred thousand. (Hind.—Skt.) Imported from India in modern times; we speak of 'a lac of rupees' = 100,000 rupees. — Hind. *lākh*, a hundred thousand. — Skt. *lakshā*, a lac, a hundred thousand; orig. 'a mark;' cf. Skt. *laksh*, to mark. According to H. H. Wilson, the reference is to the great number of *lacca* insects in a nest. See *Lack* in Yule. See **Lac** (1).

LACE, a cord, tie, plaited string. (F.—L.) ME. *las, laas*, King Alisaunder, 7698; Chaucer, C. T. 394 (A 392).—OF. *las*, a snare; MF. *laqs* (F. *lacs*); cf. *laqs courant*, a noose, running knot; Cot.—L. *laqueum*, acc. of *laqueus*, a noose, snare, knot. β. Perhaps allied to L. *lacĕre*, to allure, used in the comp. *allicere*, to allude, *ēlicere*, to draw out, *dēlicere*, to entice, delight. See **Delight.** Der. *lace*, verb, Spenser, F. Q. v. 5. 3. Doublet, *lasso*. ☞ The use of *lace* in the orig. sense of 'snare' occurs in Spenser, Muiopotmos, 427.

LACERATE, to tear. (L.) In Cotgrave, to translate F. *lacerer*; and in Minsheu, ed. 1627.—L. *lacerātus*, pp. of *lacerāre*, to tear, rend.—L. *lacer*, mangled, torn.+Gk. λακερός, torn; cf. λακίς, a rent. Der. *lacerat-ion, lacerat-ive*.

LACHRYMAL, LACRIMAL, pertaining to tears. (L.) The usual spelling *lachrymal* is false; it should be *lacrimal*. In anatomy, we speak of 'the lachrymal gland.' Spelt *lachrymall* in Holland, tr. of Pliny, bk. xxix. c. 6; p. 367 e; we find '*lachrymable, lamentable*,' '*lachrymate*, to weep,' and '*lachrymatory*, a tear-bottle' in Blount's Gloss., ed. 1674. All formed from L. *lacryma*, a tear, better spelt *lacruma* or *lacrima*. β. The oldest form is *dacrima* (Festus); cognate with Gk. δάκρυ, a tear, and with E. *tear*. See **Tear,** sb. Der. from the same L. *lacrima* are *lachrym-ose, lachry-mat-or-y*.

LACK (1), want. (E.) The old sense is often 'failing,' 'failure,' or 'fault.' ME. *lak*, spelt *lac*, Havelok, l. 191; the pl. *lakkes* is in P. Plowman, B. x. 262. Not found in AS., but cf. EFries. *lak*, defect, blame; OFries. *lek*, damage, harm, *lakia*, to attack.+Du. *lak*, blemish, stain; whence *laken*, to blame; Low G. *lak*, defect, blame; MSwed. *lack*, defect, blame. We also find Icel. *lakr*, defective, lacking. Der. *lack*, verb; see below.

LACK (2), to want, be destitute of. (E.) ME. *lakken*, Chaucer, C. T. 758, 11498 (A 756, F 1186); P. Plowman, B. v. 132. The verb is formed from the sb.; hence the verb is a *weak* one; and the pt. t. is *lakkede*, as in Chaucer. See therefore **Lack** (1) above.

LACKER, another form of **Lacquer,** q. v.

LACKEY, LACQUEY, a footman, menial attendant. (F.—Span.?—Arab.?) In Shak. As You Like It, iii. 2. 314; Tam. Shrew, iii. 2. 66. Also spelt *alakay* in Lowl. Sc.; see Rolland, Court of Venus, ii. 1035 (S. T. S.).—MF. *laquay*, 'a lackey, footboy, footman;' Cot. ModF. *laquais*. There was also an OF. form *alacay*; see Littré, who shows that, in the 15th cent., a certain class of soldiers (esp. crossbow-men) were called *alagues, alacays*, or *lacays*. (The prefix *a-* suggests *al*, the Arab. def. article.)—Span. *lacayo*, a lackey; cf. Port. *lacaio*, a lackey, *lacaia*, a woman-servant in dramatic performances. β. The use of *a-* (for *al*) in OF. *alacays* suggests an Arab. origin.—Arab. *luka'*, worthless, slavish, and, as a sb., a slave. The fem. form *lak'ā*, mean, servile (applied to a woman) may account for the Port. *lacaia*. Allied words are *laki'*, abject, servile, *lakā'i*, slovenly; *alka'*, sordid, servile. See Richardson, Pers. Dict. pp. 1272, 1273, 159. γ. However, this is but a guess; the etymology is quite uncertain; Diez connects it with Ital. *leccare*, G. *lecken*, to lick; see **Lick.** Der. *lackey*, verb, Ant. and Cleop. i. 4. 46; Spenser, F. Q. vi. 2. 15.

LACONIC, brief, pithy. (L.—Gk.) '*Laconical*, that speaks briefly or pithily;' Blount's Gloss., ed. 1674. 'With *laconic* brevity;' Beaum. and Fletcher, Little Fr. Lawyer, v. 1 (Cleremont).—L. *Lacōnicus*, Laconian.—Gk. Λακωνικός, Laconian.—Gk. Λάκων, a Laconian, an inhabitant of Lacedæmon or Sparta. These men were proverbial for their brief and pithy style of speaking. Der. *laconic-al, laconic-al-ly, laconic-is m*; also *lacon-ism*, from Gk. Λάκων.

LACQUER, LACKER, a sort of varnish. (F.—Port.—Hind.—Skt.) '*Lacker*, a sort of varnish;' Kersey, ed. 1715. '*Lacquer'd* chair;' Pope, Horace, Ep. ii. 1. 337. 'The *lack* of Tonquin is a sort of gummy juice, which drains out of the bodies or limbs of trees. . . . The cabinets, desks, or any sort of frames to be *lackered*, are made of fir or pone-tree (*sic*). . . . The work-houses where the *lacker* is laid on are accounted very unwholesom;' Dampier, Voyages, an. 1688; ed. 1699; vol. ii. pt. 1, p. 61.—MF. *lacre*, 'a confection or stuffe made of rosin, brimstone, and white wax mingled, and melted together,' &c.; Cot. — Port. *lacre*, sealing-wax; allied to Port. *laca*, gum-lac.—Hind. *lākh*, lac.—Skt. *lākshā*, lac. See **Lac** (1). Der. *lacquer*, verb.

LACROSSE, a Canadian game; played with a *crosse*, or large stringed bat. (F.—L.) F. *la crosse*; from *la*, f., the, and *crosse*, a bent stick.—L. *illa*, f. of *ille*, that; Late L. type **croccia, *croccea*, fem. of adj. formed from Late L. *croccus*, a hook.

LACTEAL, relating to milk, conveying chyle. (L.) '*Lacteal, Lacteous*, milky;' Blount's Gloss., ed. 1674. '*Lactory* [read *lactary*] or milky plants, which have a white and *lacteous* juice;' Sir T. Browne, Vulg. Errors, b. vi. c. 10, § 2. Formed with suffix *-al* from L. *lacte-us*, milky.—L. *lact-*, stem of *lac*, milk.+Gk. γαλακτ-, stem of γάλα, milk. Der. *lacte-ous* (= L. *lacteus*); *lactesc-ent*, from pres. part. of *lactescere*, to become milky; whence *lactescence*. Also *lacti-c*, from *lacti-*, decl. stem of *lac*; whence also *lacti-ferous*, where the suffix is from L. *-fer*, bearing, from *ferre*, to bear, cognate with E. *bear*. Also *lettuce*, q. v.

LACUNA, a hiatus, gap in a MS. (L.) First in 1663.—L. *lacūna*, a hole, pit.—L. *lacu-s*, a lake; see **Lake** (1), **Lagoon.**

LACUSTRINE, pertaining to a lake. (L.) First in 1830. Formed from L. *lacus*, a lake; like L. *palustri-*, from *palus*, a marsh,

LAD, a boy, youth. (E.) ME. *ladde*, pl. *laddes*; Havelok, l. 1786; P. Plowman, B. xix. 32; Allit. Poems, ed. Morris, B. 36. Of obscure origin; perhaps (as suggested in N. E. D.) the orig. sense was 'one led,' i. e. a follower, dependant. From ME. *lad*, led, pp. of *lēden*, to lead. See **Lead** (1). (H. Bradley, in Athenæum, June 1, 1894.) ¶ Larsen has Dan. *aske-ladd* (Norw. *oske-ladd*) the youngest son in Norw. nursery tales, a (male) Cinderella; where *aske* = ash.

LADANUM, the same as **Laudanum,** q. v.

LADDER, a frame with steps, for climbing up by. (E.) ME. *laddre*, P. Plowman, B. xvi. 44; Rob. of Glouc. p. 333, l. 6830. The word has lost an initial *h*. AS. *hlǣdder, hlǣder*, a ladder; Grein, ii. 80.+Du. *ladder*, a ladder, rack or rails of a cart; OHG. *hleitra*, G. *leiter*, a ladder, scale. β. Allied to Gk. κλίμαξ, a ladder; see **Climax.** Named from sloping; see **Lean** (1). (√KLEI.)

LADE (1), to load. (E.) 'And they *laded* their asses with the corn;' Gen. xlii. 26. Formerly a strong verb; we still use the pp. *laden* = loaded; Ant. and Cleop. iii. 11. 5; v. 2. 123. ME. *laden*, pp. *laden*, Genesis and Exodus, ed. Morris, l. 1800. AS. *hladan*, to heap together, to lade, to burden; also, to lade out (water); pt. t. *hlōd*, pp. *hladen*.+Du. *laden*; Icel. *hlaða*, Dan. *lade*, Swed. *ladda*; Goth. *-hlathan* (in comp. *af-hlathan*); G. *laden*, OHG. *hladan*. β. All from a Teut. base *hlad (not *hlath), to lade (Kluge). Allied to Russ. klade, a load. **Der.** lad-ing, a load, cargo, Merch. Ven. iii. 1. 3. And see **Lade** (2).

LADE (2), to draw out water, drain. (E.) 'He'll lade it [the sea] dry;' 3 Hen. VI, iii. 2. 139. ME. hladen, laden; 'lhade out thet weter'=lade out the water, Ayenbite of Inwyt, p. 178, l. 19 [where lh is written for hl]. AS. hladan, to heap together, to load, to lade out; Grein, ii. 79. 'Hlōd wæter'=drew water; Exod. ii. 19. The same word as **Lade** (1). **Der.** lad-le, q. v.

LADLE, a large spoon. (E.) So called because used for lading or dipping out water from a vessel. ME. ladel, Chaucer, C. T. 2022; P. Plowman, B. xix. 274. AS. hlædel; in Glosses, ed. Napier. Formed with suffix -el from AS. hladan, to lade; see **Lade** (2). β. The suffix -el in this case denotes the means or instrument, as in E. sett-le (=AS. set-l), a seat, a thing to sit upon.

LADY, the mistress of a house, a wife, woman of rank. (E.) ME. lady, Chaucer, C. T. 88. Older spellings læfdi, Layamon, 1256; lefdi, leafdi, Ancren Riwle, pp. 4, 38; lheuedi (=hlevedi), Ayenbite of Inwyt, p. 24; lafdiȝ, Ormulum, 1807. AS. hlǣfdige, a lady; Grein, ii. 81; ONorthumb. hlāfdīa, in the margin of John, xx. 16, in the Lindisfarne MS. β. Of uncertain origin; the syllable hlāf is certainly from the word hlāf, a loaf; see **Loaf, Lord**. But the suffix -dige remains uncertain; the most reasonable guess is that which identifies it with a supposed *dige, a kneader, from a verb cognate with Goth. deigan, to knead. This gives the sense 'bread-kneader,' or maker of bread, which is a very likely one; see **Lord**. Cf. Icel. deigja, a dairy-maid; and see further under **Dairy, Dough.** ¶ The Icel. lafði, a lady, is merely borrowed from English. **B.** The term Lady was often used in a special sense, to signify the blessed Virgin Mary; hence several derivatives, such as lady-bird, lady-fern, lady's-finger, lady's-mantle, lady's-slipper, lady's-smock, lady's-tresses. Cf. G. Marien-käfer (Mary's chafer), a lady-bird; Marien-blume (Mary's flower), a daisy; Marien-mantel (Mary's mantle), lady's-mantle; Marien-schuh (Mary's shoe), lady's-slipper. **Der. A.** (in the general sense), lady-love, lady-ship, ME. ladiship, Gower, C. A. ii. 301, bk. v. 5208; written lefdischip (=deference), Ancren Riwle, p. 108; lady-like. **B.** (in the special sense) lady-bird, &c., as above. Also lady-chapel, lady-day, which strictly speaking are not compound words at all, since lady is here in the gen. case, so that lady chapel = chapel of our Lady, and lady day = day of our Lady. The ME. gen. case of this word was lady or ladie, rather than ladies, which was a later form; this is remarkably shown by the phrase 'in his lady grace' = in his lady's favour, Chaucer, C. T. 88; where Tyrwhitt wrongly prints ladies, though the MSS. have lady. The contrast of Lady day with Lord's day is striking, like that of Fri-day with Thur-s-day, the absence of s marking the fem. gender; the AS. gen. case is hlǣfdig-an.

LAG, sluggish, coming behind. (E.) 'Came too lag [late] to see him buried;' Rich. III, ii. 1. 90. Cf. prov. E. lag, late, last, slow; lag-last, a loiterer; lag-teeth, the grinders, so called because the last in growth; Halliwell. A difficult word, prob. due to confusion of lag, in other senses (see N. E. D.) with ME. lak, E. lack, failure, deficiency. Cf. prov. E. lack, to be absent, to loiter, lackish, slow, backward, lacky, laggy, a turn last, last of all; ME. Dan. lakke, to go slowly (Kalkar); Norw. lagga, to go slowly (Ross); Icel. lakra, to loiter, to lag behind. ¶ The obs. lagg, remnant of liquor in a cask, seems to answer to Norw. lagg(a)hall, with the same sense (Ross), which is prob. derived from Icel. lögg, the end of a cask, and Norw. hald, inclined. This may have influenced the form. **Der.** lag, verb, Spenser, F. Q. i. 1. 6; spelt lagge in Palsgrave; also lagg-ing-ly, lagg-er; lag-end, 1 Hen. IV, v. 1. 24; lagg-ard (a late word), where the suffix -ard is French (of Teut. origin) and is affixed even to English bases, as in drunk-ard.

LAGAN, wreckage lying on the bed of the sea. (F.—Scand.) 'Lagan, such a parcel of goods as the mariners in danger of shipwrack cast out of the ship; and because they sink, they fasten to them a buoy;' Cowel, Interpreter (1701). He adds that they are called ligan, from Lat. ligandō, i. e. fastening. But they are called lagan.—AF. lagan, used by Edw. II in 1315 (Godefroy); whence Late L. laganum. Allied to Icel. lögn, pl. lagnir, a net laid in the sea.—Icel. lag, 2nd stem of liggja, to lie; see **Lie** (1). So called because sunk.

LAGER-BIER, a light German bier. (G.) From G. lager-bier, beer brewed for keeping.—G. lager, a store (see **Leaguer**); and bier, beer (see **Beer**).

LAGOON, LAGUNE, a shallow lake. (Ital. or Span.—L.) Ray speaks of 'the lagune, . . . about Venice' in 1673 (N. E. D.). And Dampier of a lagune in Mexico; New Voy. (1699), i. 241. We speak of 'the lagoons of Venice;'—Ital. and Span. laguna, a pool.—L. lacūna, a pool.—L. lacus, a lake; see **Lake** (1).

LAIC, LAICAL, pertaining to the people. (L.—Gk.) 'A Laicke, or Lay-man;' Minsheu, ed. 1627.—L. lāicus; of Gk. origin. See **Lay** (3), the more usual form of the word.

LAIR, the den or retreat of a wild beast. (E.) ME. leir; the dat. case leire occurs in OEng. Homilies, ed. Morris, 2nd Series, p. 103, l. 11, where it means 'bed.' Spelt layere, meaning 'camp,' Morte Arthure, ed. Brock, l. 2293. AS. leger, a lair, couch, bed; Grein, ii. 167; from AS. *leg-, base of licgan, to lie down. See **Lie** (1).+ Du. leger, a bed, couch, lair; liggen, to lie.+MHG. leger, OHG. legar, now spelt lager, a couch; OHG. liggan, to lie; Goth. ligrs, a couch; ligan, to lie. **Doublet**, leaguer.

LAITY, the lay people. (F.—L.—Gk.; F. suffix.) In Kersey, ed. 1715; laitie, Cockeram (1642). A coined word; AF. laieté, lay property, Yearbooks of Edw. I, 1304–5, p. 411; from the adj. lay, with the F. suffix -té, due to L. acc. suffix -tātem. Formed by analogy with du-ty from due; &c. See **Lay** (3).

LAKE (1), a pool. (F.—L.) ME. lac; Layamon, 1280; also AF. lac, as in 'þās meres and laces' = these meres and lakes; in MS. E. of the AS. Chron. an. 656; see Plummer's ed. p. 31.—L. lacum, acc. of lacus, a lake. The lit. sense is 'a hollow' or depression.+Gk. λάκκος, a hollow, hole, pit, pond. **Doublet**, loch. **Der.** lag-oon, q. v.

LAKE (2), a colour, a kind of crimson. (F.—Pers.—Skt.) A certain colour is called 'crimson lake.' 'Vermillian, lake, or crimson;' Ben Jonson, Expostulation with Inigo Jones, l. 11 from end.—F. laque, 'sanguine, rose or rubie colour;' Cot.—Pers. lāk, lake produced from lac; Rich. Dict. p. 1253; Pers. lak, lac; see **Lac** (1).

LAMA (1), a high priest. (Thibetan.) We speak of the Grand Lama of Thibet. 'Offered to a living Lama;' Murphy, Orphan of China (1759), A. ii. sc. 2. First in 1654.—Thibetan blama, a priest, the b being silent; Jäschke, Dict., p. 650.

LAMA (2), the same as **Llama**, q. v.

LAMB, the young of the sheep. (E.) ME. lamb, lomb; Chaucer, C. T. 5037 (B 617). AS. lamb, Grein, ii. 154; pl. lambru.+Du. lam; Icel. lamb; Dan. lam; Swed. lamm; G. lamm; Goth. lamb. β. All from Teut. type *lamboz; root unknown. **Der.** lamb, verb, lamb-like, lamb-skin; also lamb-k-in (with double dimin. suffix), Hen. V, ii. 1. 133.

LAMBENT, flickering. (L.) 'Was but a lambent flame;' Cowley, Pindaric Odes, Destiny, st. 4.—L. lambent-, stem of pres. part. of lambere, to lick, sometimes applied to flames; see Virgil, Æn. ii. 684. From √LAB, to lick; whence also E. labial, lip, and lap, verb. See **Lap** (1).

LAME, disabled in the limbs, esp. in the legs. (E.) ME. lame, Wyclif, Acts, iii. 2; Havelok, 1938. AS. lama (weak form only), Matt. viii. 6.+Du. lam; Icel. lami; Dan. lam, palsied; Swed. lam; MHG. lam; G. lahm. β. The orig. sense is maimed, bruised, broken; from the base LEM, to break (second grade LOM), preserved in Russ. lomate, to break; Fick, iii. 267. Cf. Icel. lama, to bruise, prov. E. lam, to beat; whence lamming, a beating, Beaum. and Fletcher, King and No King, A. v. sc. 3. **Der.** lame, verb; lame-ly, lame-ness.

LAMENT, to utter a mournful cry. (F.—L.) Though the sb. is the orig. word in Latin, the verb is the older word in English, occurring in John, xvi. 20, in Tyndal's version, A. D. 1526.—F. lamenter, 'to lament;' Cot.—L. lāmentārī, to wail.—L. lāmentum, a mournful cry; formed with suffix -mentum from the base lā-, to utter a cry, which appears again in lā-trāre, to bark. β. Cf. Russ. laiate, to bark, snarl, scold. Of imitative origin. **Der.** lament, sb.; lament-able, Lydgate, Minor Poems, p. 145; lament-at-ion, ME. lamentacioun, Chaucer, C. T. 937 (A 935), from F. lamentation.

LAMINA, a thin plate or layer. (L.) In Blount's Gloss., ed. 1674.—L. lāmina, a thin plate of metal. Cf. **Omelette. Der.** lamin-ar, lamin-at-ed, lamin-at-ion.

LAMMAS, a name for the first of August. (E.) ME. lammasse; P. Plowman, B. vi. 291; see note on the line (Notes, p. 173). AS. hlāfmæsse, Grein, i. 80; AS. Chron. an. 921; at a later period spelt hlammæsse, AS. Chron. an. 1009. K. Ælfred has: 'on þǣre tide calendas Agustus, on þæm dæge þe wē hātað hlāfmæsse;' Orosius, v. xiii. § 2. β. The lit. sense is 'loaf-mass,' because a loaf was offered on this day as an offering of first-fruits; see Chambers, Book of Days, ii. 154.—AS. hlāf, a loaf; and mæsse, mass. See **Loaf** and **Mass** (2). Another AS. name for lammas was hlāf-sēnung, i. e. loaf-blessing; The Shrine, p. 112. ¶ Not from lamb and mass, as the fiction sometimes runs.

LAMMERGEYER, the bearded vulture. (G.) First in 1817. —G. lämmergeier, lit. 'lambs-vulture.'—G. lämmer, pl. of lamm, a lamb; geier, a vulture. See **Lamb** and **Gyrfalcon**.

LAMP, a vessel for giving light. (F.—L.—Gk.) In early use. ME. lampe; St. Margaret, ed. Cockayne, p. 20, l. 21.—OF. lampe, 'a lampe;' Cot.—L. lampas.—Gk. λαμπάς, a torch, light.—Gk. λάμπειν, to shine. **Der.** lamp-black; lantern, q. v.

LAMPOON, a personal satire. (F.—O. Low G.) In Dryden,

Essay on Satire, l. 47.—F. *lampon*, orig. a drinking song; so called from the exclamation *lampons !*=let us drink, frequently introduced into such songs. (See Littré, who gives an example.)—F. *lamper*, to drink; a popular or provincial word; given in Littré. Perhaps a nasalised form of OF. *lapper*, 'to lap or lick up;' Cot. Cf. Picard *lamper*, to drink. Of O. Low G. origin; see **Lap** (1). Der. *lampoon-er*.

LAMPREY, a kind of fish. (F.—L.) ME. *laumprei*, *laumpree*; Havelok, ll. 771, 897.—AF. *lamprey*, Liber Albus, p. 382; OF. *lamproie*, spelt *lamproye* in Cot. Cf. Ital. *lampreda*, a lamprey.—Late L. *lamprēda*, a lamprey, of which an older form was *lampetra* (Ducange). β. So called from its cleaving to rocks; lit. 'licker of rocks;' coined from L. *lamb-ere*, to lick, and *petra*, a rock. See **Lambent** and **Petrify**. ¶ Scientifically named *Petromyzon*, i.e. stone-sucking.

LANCE, a shaft of wood, with a spear-head. (F.—L.) ME. *launce*; P. Plowman, B. iii. 303; King Alisaunder, l. 936.—F. *lance*, 'a lance;' Cot.—L. *lancea*, a lance. Root uncertain. Der. *lance*, verb, Rich. III, iv. 4. 224 (sometimes spelt *lanch*)=ME. *launcen*, spelt *lawncyn* in Prompt. Parv., p. 290; *lanc-er*, formerly written *lanceer*, from F. *lancier*, 'a lanceer' (Cot.); also *lancegay*, q. v., *lanc-et*, q.v., *lance-ol-ate*, q. v. (But not *lansquenet*.)

LANCEGAY, a kind of spear. (Hybrid; F.—L.; *and* F.—Span.—Moorish.) Obsolete. In Chaucer, C. T. 13682, 13751 (Six-text, B 1942, 2011). A corruption of F. *lance-zagaye*, compounded of *lance*, a lance (see **Lance**) and *zagaye*, 'a fashion of slender . . . pike, used by the Moorish horsemen;' Cot. Cf. Span. *azagaya*=*al zagaya*, where *al* is the Arab. def. art., and *zagaya* is an OSpan. word for *assegay* or 'dart,' a word of Berber or Algerian origin. See my note to Chaucer, loc. cit., and Way's note, Prompt. Parv., p. 290. ¶ *Assegai* is from Port. *azagaia*.

LANCEOLATE, lance-shaped. (L.) A botan. term, applied to leaves which in shape resemble the head of a lance.—L. *lanceolātus*, furnished with a spike.—L. *lanceola*, a spike; dimin. of *lancea*, a lance; see **Lance**. ¶ Esp. applied to the leaf of the plantain; cf. F. *lancelée*, 'ribwort plantaine' (Cot.).

LANCET, a surgical instrument. (F.—L.) ME. *launcet*, also spelt *lawnset*, *lawncent*, Prompt. Parv., p. 290.—OF. *lancette*, 'a surgeon's launcet;' also, a little lance;' Cot. Dimin. of F. *lance*; see **Lance**.

LANCH, another spelling of **Lance**, verb, and of **Launch**.

LAND, earth, soil, country, district. (E.) ME. *land*, *lond*; Chaucer, C. T. 4912 (B 492). AS. *land*; Grein, ii. 154.+Du. *land*; Icel., Dan., and Swed. *land*; Goth. *land*; G. *land*; MHG. *lant*. Teut. type *landom, neut.; closely allied to Celtic type *landā, whence Irish *lann*, land, open space, W. *llan*, a yard, churchyard; whence F. *lande*, a moor. See **Lawn** (1). Der. *land*, verb, AS. *lendan* (=*landian*), Grein, ii. 168; *land-breeze*, *land-crab*, *land-flood*, *land-grave*, q. v., *land-holder*, *land-ing*, *land-lady*; *land-lord*, Tyndal's Works, p. 210, col. 1, AS. *land-hlāford*; *lands-man* (=*land-man*, Ant. and Cleop. iv. 3. 11); *land-mark*, Bible, 1551, Job, xxiv. 2; *land-rail*, q.v.; *land-scape*, q.v.; *land-slip*, *land-steward*, *land-tax*, *land-waiter*, *land-ward*.

LANDAU, a kind of coach. (G.) Added by Todd to Johnson's Dict. In E. Darwin, Botanic Garden, pt. ii. c. i. 344. Named from *Landau*, a town in Bavaria. Here, *Land*=E. *land*; for -*au*, see **Island**.

LAND-GRAVE, a count of a province. (Du.) 'Landgrave, or Landsgrave, the earl or count of a province, whereof in Germany there are four;' Blount's Gloss., ed. 1674. Spelt *langraue*, Fabyan, Chron., ed. 1811, p. 328.—Du. *landgraaf*, a landgrave.—Du. *land*, land, province; and *graaf*, a count, earl. So also G. *landgraf*, from *land* and *graf*. B. The word was borrowed from the Du. rather than the G., at any rate in the fem. form *landgravine*, which answers to Du. *landgravin* rather than to G. *landgräfinn*. See **Land** and **Margrave**. Der. *landgrav-in*, as above; *landgrav-i-ate*, 'that region or country which belongs to a landgrave;' Blount.

LANDRAIL, a kind of bird; see **Rail** (3).

LANDSCAPE, the prospect of a country. (Du.) In Milton, L'Allegro, l. 70. Formerly spelt *landskip*, Trench, Select Glossary. 'The *landskipp* . . which is in the Dutch cabinett;' (1648); Bury Wills, ed. Tymms, p. 216. And see Blount's Gloss., ed. 1674, which gives it as a painter's term, to express 'all that part of a picture which is not of the body or argument;' answering somewhat to the mod. term *back-ground*. It was borrowed from the Dutch painters.—Du. *landschap*, a landscape, province; cf. *landschap-schilder*, a landscape painter.—Du. *land*, cognate with E. *land*; and -*schap*, a suffix=AS. -*scipe*=E. -*ship* (in *friend-ship*, *wor-ship*), allied to the verb which in Eng. is spelt *shape*. See **Land** and **Shape**. ¶ The Du. *sch* is sounded more like E. *sk* than E. *sh*; hence the mod. sound.

LANE, an open space between hedges, a narrow passage or street.

(E.) ME. *lane*, *lone*; Chaucer, C. T. 16126 (G 658); P. Plowman, A. ii. 192, B. ii. 216. AS. *lane*, *lone*, a lane; Codex Diplomaticus, ed. Kemble, vol. i. p. 1. l. 13; vol. iii. p. 33 (no. 549). [Cf. Prov. E. *lone* (Cleveland), *lonnin* (Cumberland).] OFriesic *lona*, *lana*, a lane, way; North Fries. *lona*, *lana*, a narrow way between houses and gardens (Outzen).+Du. *laan*, an alley, lane, walk. Teut. type **lanōn-*, fem.

LANGUAGE, speech, diction. (F.—L.) ME. *langage*, King Alisaunder, l. 6857; Chaucer, C. T. 4936 (B 516).—F. *langage*, language; formed with suffix -*age* (< L. -*āticum*) from *langue*, the tongue.—L. *lingua*, the tongue. See **Lingual, Tongue**.

LANGUID, feeble, exhausted, sluggish. (L.) In Blount's Gloss., ed. 1674.—L. *languidus*, languid.—L. *languēre*, to be weak. See **Languish**. Der. *languid-ly*, *languid-ness*.

LANGUISH, to become enfeebled, pine, become dull or torpid. (F.—L.) ME. *languishen*, Chaucer, C. T. 11262 (F 950); Cursor Mundi, 14138.—F. *languiss-*, stem of pres. part. of *languir*, 'to languish, pine;' Cot.—L. *languēre*, to be weak; whence *languescere*, to become weak, which furnishes the F. stem *languiss-*. β. From √SLEG, to be slack or lax, whence also E. *lax*, q.v. See **Slack**. Brugmann, i. § 193; ii. § 632. Der. *languish-ing-ly*, *languish-ment*; and see *languid*, *languor*.

LANGUOR, dulness, listlessness. (F.—L.) ME. *langour*, Will. of Palerne, 918, 986; *langur*, Cursor Mundi, 3596. [Now accommodated to the L. spelling.]—F. *langueur*, 'langor;' Cot.—L. *languōrem*, acc. of *languor*, languor.—L. *languēre*, to be weak. See **Languish**.

LANIARD, the same as **Lanyard**, q.v.

LANIFEROUS, wool-bearing. (L.) A scientific term in zoology. In Coles (1676). Coined from L. *lānifer*, producing wool.—L. *lāni-*, for *lāna*, wool; and *ferre*, to bear. β. The L. *lāna* is allied to **Wool**, q.v.; L. *ferre* is cognate with E. *bear*. Der. So also *lani-gerous*, wool-bearing, from L. *gerere*, to carry.

LANK, slender, lean, thin. (E.) ME. *lank*, *lonk*; spelt *lonc*, OE. Homilies; ed. Morris, i. 249, l. 9: '*lonc* he is ant leane'=he is lank and lean. AS. *hlanc*, slender; Grein, ii. 80. β. The orig. sense was 'bending,' weak; cf. G. *lenken*, to turn, bend; see further under **Link** (1). Der. *lank-ly*, *lank-ness*.

LANNER, a species of falcon. (F.) ME. *laner*, Voc. 761. 10; *lanner*, Newton, Dict. of Birds.—OF. *lanier*, 'a lanner;' Cot. Perhaps the same word as OF. *lanier*, cowardly. (N. E. D.)

LANSQUENET, a German foot-soldier; a game at cards. (F.—G.) Corruptly spelt *lanceknight* in old authors, by a popular blunder. See Ben Jonson, Every Man, ed. Wheatley, A. ii. sc. 4. l. 21. 'Lansknyght, *lancequenet*;' Palsgrave.—F. *lansquenet*, 'a lanceknight, or German footman; also, the name of a game at cards;' Cot.—G. (and Du.) *landsknecht*, a foot-soldier.—G. *lands*, for *landes*, gen. case of *land*, land, country; and *knecht*, a soldier. *Land*=E. *land*; and *knecht*=E. *knight*. Thus the word is *land's-knight*, not *lance-knight*. ¶ The term means a soldier of the flat or Low Countries, as distinguished from the men who came from the highlands of Switzerland; see Revue Britannique, no. for Sept. 1866, p. 29 (Littré).

LANTERN, a case for carrying a light. (F.—L.—Gk.) ME. *lanterne*, Floriz and Blauncheflur, ed. Lumby, l. 238.—F. *lanterne*.—L. *lanterna*, *lāterna*, a lantern; the spelling *lanterna* occurs in the Lindisfarne MS., in the L. text of John, xviii. 3. *Lanterna*=*lamterna=*lampterna; not a true L. word, but borrowed from Gk. λαμπτήρ, a light, torch.—Gk. λάμπειν, to shine. See **Lamp**. ¶ Sometimes spelt *lanthorn* (Kersey), by a singular popular etymology which took account of the *horn* sometimes used for the sides of lanterns.

LANUGINOUS, covered with down or soft hair. (L.) In Blount's Gloss. (1681). From L. *lanūginōsus*, downy.—L. *lanūgin-*, stem of *lanūgo*, down: from *lāna*, wool. See **Wool**.

LANYARD, LANIARD, a certain small rope in a ship. (F.) The spelling *laniard* is the better one, since the word has nothing to do with *yard*. The *d* is excrescent; the old spelling was *lannier*. 'Lanniers, Lanniards, small ship-ropes that serve to slacken or make stiff the shrowds, chains,' &c.; Kersey, ed. 1715. 'Laniers, vox nautica;' Skinner, ed. 1671. '*Lanyer* of lether, *lasniere*;' Palsgrave.—MF. *laniere*, 'a long and narrow band or thong of leather;' Cot. β. Origin uncertain; but Cotgr. has *lanieres*, 'hawks lunes,' i.e. jesses; perhaps from F. *lanier*, a species of falcon. See **Lanner**.

LAP (1), to lick up with the tongue. (E.) ME. *lappen*, *lapen*, Wyclif, Judges, vii. 7; Gower, C. A. iii. 215; bk. vii. 3671. AS. *lapian*, to lap: rare, but found in Ælfric's Grammar, De Tertia Conj. § 6; and in Glosses to Prudentius (Leo). The derivative *læpelder*, a dish, is in Ælfric's Homilies, ii. 244, l. 4.+Icel. *lepja*, to lap like a dog; Dan. *labe*, to lap; MHG. *laffen*, OHG. *laffan*, to lap up; MDu. *lappen*, *lapen*, 'to lap or licke like a dogge;' Hexham.+L. *lambere* (with inserted *m*), to lick. All from √LAB, to lap, lick up; Brugmann, ii. § 632. **Der.** from the same base are *lab-i-al*, *lamb-ent*, *lip*.

LAP (2), the loose part of a coat, an apron, part of the body covered by an apron, a fold, flap. (E.) ME. *lappe* (dissyllabic), Chaucer, C. T. 688 (A 686); P. Plowman, B. ii. 35, xvi. 255; often in the sense of 'skirt of a garment;' see Prompt. Parv., and Way's note. AS. *læppa*, a loosely hanging portion; 'lifre-*læppan*' = portions of the liver; Ælfric's Gloss., in Voc. 160. 39. OFries. *lappa*, a piece of a garment.**+**Du. *lap*, a remnant, shred, rag, patch; Dan. *lap*, a patch; Swed. *lapp*, a piece, shred, patch; G. *lappen*, a patch, shred. β. The Teut. type is **lappon-*, m.; allied to Icel. *lapa*, to hang down (not given in Cleasby, but cited by Fick and others). Cf. Gk. λοβός, a lobe of the ear, or of the liver (Prellwitz). See **Lobe**. **Der.** *lap-ful*; *lap-el*, i.e. part of a coat which laps over the facing (a mod. word, added by Todd to Johnson), formed with dimin. suffix -*el*; *lapp-et*, dimin. form with suffix -*et*, used by Swift (Johnson); *lap-dog*, Dryden, tr. of Juvenal, Sat. vi. 853; also *dew-lap*. Perhaps connected with *lap* (3). Cf. *lop-eared* = *lap-eared*, with hanging ears, applied to rabbits.

LAP (3), to wrap, involve, fold. (E.) Prob. derived from the word above; whence also ME. *bi-lappen*, to enfold; Ormulum, 14267. ME. *lappen*, to wrap, fold, Will. of Palerne, 1712; 'lapped in cloutes' = wrapped up in rags, P. Plowman's Crede, ed. Skeat, l. 438. β. The puzzling form *wlappen* is misleading; thus in Wyclif, Matt. xxvii. 59, the L. *inuoluit* is translated in the later version by '*lappide* it,' but in the earlier one by '*wlappide* it.' But this ME. *wlappen* is a later form of *wrappen*, to wrap, by the frequent change of *r* to *l*; so that *wlap* is a mere corruption or later form of *wrap*, prob. influenced by *lap*, to enfold. See **Wrap**.

LAPIDARY, one who cuts and sets precious stones. (L.) Cotgrave translates F. *lapidaire* by 'a *lapidary* or jeweller.' 'Werk of the *lapidarie*;' Wyclif, Ecclus. xlv. 13 (A. V. 11). Englished from L. *lapidārius*, a stone-mason, a jeweller.—L. *lapid-*, stem of *lapis*, a stone. Allied to Gk. λέπας, a bare rock, λέπις, a scale, flake. From the base LEP, to scale off, peel; seen in Gk. λέπειν, to peel. **Der.** from the same source, *lapidi-fy*, *lapid-esc-ent*, *lapid-esc-ence*, *lapid-esc-enc-y*, Sir T. Browne, Vulg. Errors, b. iii. c. 23. § 5. Also *di-lapid-ate*, q. v.

LAPIS LAZULI, a silicate containing sulphur, of a bright blue colour. (L. and Arab.) From L. *lapis*, a stone; and *lāzulī*, gen. of Med. L. *lāzulum*, azure; see **Azure**.

LAPSE, to slip or fall into error, to fail in duty. (L.) In Shak. Cor. v. 2. 19; the sb. *lapse* is in All's Well, ii. 3. 170.—L. *lapsāre*, to slip, frequentative of *lābī* (pp. *lapsus*), to glide, slip, trip. Cf. F. *laps*, a slip. Allied to **Sleep**. Cf. Skt. *lamb*, to hang down; Brugmann, i. § 553. **Der.** *lapse*, sb., from L. *lapsus*, a slip; hence also some senses of the vb.; cf. AF. *laps de temps*, lapse of time, Stat. Realm, i. 318 (1351). Also *col-lapse*, *e-lap:e*, *il-lapse*, *re-lapse*.

LAPWING, the name of a bird. (E.) ME. *lappewinke* (four syllables), Gower, C. A. ii. 329, bk. v. 6041; later *lapwinke*, Prompt. Parv. p. 288; spelt *lhapwynche*, Ayenbite of Inwyt, p. 61, l. 31. AS. *hléapewince*; Voc. 260. 2. β. The first part is *hléape-*, connected with *hléapan*, to run, spring, leap; see **Leap**. γ. The second part of the word is, literally, 'winker;' but we must assign to the verb *wink* its original sense. This orig. sense appears in the OHG. *winchan*, MHG. *winken*, to move from side to side, a sense preserved in mod. G. *wanken*, to totter, stagger, vacillate, reel, waver, &c. Thus the sense is 'one who turns about in running or flight,' which is fairly descriptive of the habit of the male bird. δ. We find, however, an AS. form *laepae-uincæ* (OE. Texts, p. 504), which has not been explained. ¶ Popular etymology explains the word as 'wing-flapper;' but *lap* does not really take the sense of *flap*; it means, rather, to droop, hang down loosely; see **Lap** (2). This interpretation is wrong as to *both* parts of the AS. form of the word, and is too general.

LARBOARD, the left side of a ship, looking from the stern. (E.) Cotgrave has: '*Babort*, the *larboord* side of a ship.' It is also spelt *larboord* in Minsheu, ed. 1627. The spelling is, however, probably corrupt; the ME. spelling appears to be *laddebord*. In Allit. Poems, ed. Morris, C. l. 106, some sailors are preparing to set sail, and after spreading the mainsail, 'þay layden in on *ladde-borde* and the lofe wynnes' = they laid in [hauled in?] on the *larboard* and set right the loof (see **Luff**). Again, in the Naval Accounts of Henry VII, ed. Oppenheim, p. 192, we find *sterborde* and *latheborde*; and, at p. 203, *latebord*; so that the former syllable was once *lathe*, *late*, or *ladde*. It was obviously altered to *leerebord* (Hakluyt, Voy. i. 4) and to *larboard* (Milton, P. L. ii. 1019) by the influence of *steerboard*, later *starboard*; see **Starboard**. β. The only word which answers in form to ME. *ladde* is Swed. *ladda*, to lade, load, charge, answering to Icel. *hlaða*, AS. *hladan*, E. *lade*. We find Icel. *hlaða seglum* = to take in sail. γ. Beyond this, all is uncertainty; we may conjecture that the sails, when taken down, were put on the left side

of the ship, to be out of the way of the steersman, who originally stood on the *starboard* (= steer-board) or right side of the ship. δ. But it is worth notice that Icel. *hlaðask ā mara bōgu*, lit. 'to lade oneself on the shoulders of a horse,' meant 'to mount a horse;' and one mounts a horse on the *left* side. ¶ The F. *babord* = G. *backbord*, where *back* means 'behind' the steersman, who used his paddle on the right side of the ship.

LARCENY, theft, robbery. (F.—L.) In Cotgrave, who explains OF. *larrecin* by '*larceny*, theft, robbery.' An old law term; see Blount's Nomolexicon.—OF. *larrecin*, *larcin* (both forms are in Cotgrave); mod. F. *larcin*. The spelling *larrecin* occurs in the Laws of William the Conqueror, § xiv; in Thorpe's Ancient Laws of England, i. 472; and *larcin* in Britton, bk. i. c. 25. [The suffix -*y* appears to be an E. addition, to conform the word to *forger-y*, *burglar-y*, *felon-y*, and the like; but it is unnecessary.]—L. *latrōcinium*, freebooting, marauding, robbery; formed with suffix -*cinium* (occurring also in *tīrō-cinium*) from *latro*, a robber. β. Curtius (i. 453) considers *latro* as borrowed from Gk. It is, rather, allied to Gk. λάτρις, a hireling, used in a bad sense. The suffix -*tro* or -τρις denotes the agent, and the base is *lē-* or *la*, discussed by Prellwitz, s. v. λάτρον. **Der.** *larcen-ist*.

LARCH, a kind of tree like a pine. (G.—L.) Spelt *larche* in Minsheu, ed. 1627. Also spelt *larche* by Turner, Names of Herbes (1548), who seems to have introduced the spelling directly from G. *lärche*, a larch, though the *ch* naturally took the E. sound.—G. *lärche*.—L. *laricem*, acc. of *larix*, the larch-tree (whence Late Gk. λάριξ). The L. *larix* is for *darix (cf. *lingua* for *dingua*); cognate with Irish *dair*, W. *dar*, an oak (Stokes-Fick, p. 147); cf. Skt. *dāru*, wood, a kind of pine. Allied to **Tree**.

LARD, the melted fat of swine. (F.—L.) 'Larde of flesche, *larda*, *vel lardum*;' Prompt. Parv. p. 288.—OF. (and F.) *lard*, 'lard;' Cot.—L. *lardum*; also *larda*, shortened form of *lāridum* (also *lārida*), lard, fat of bacon. Akin to Gk. λαρός, pleasant to the taste, nice, dainty, sweet, λαρινός, fat. **Der.** *lard*, verb, ME. *lard:n* (Prompt. Parv.), from F. *larder*, to lard (see note to Ben Jonson, Every Man, ed. Wheatley, A. iii. sc. 5, l. 174); *lard-er*, Gower, C. A. iii. 124, with which cf. AF. *larder*, OF. *lardier*, 'a tub to keep bacon in' (Cotgrave), hence applied to a room in which bacon and meat are kept, called by Palsgrave a *larder-house*; *lard-y*, *lard-ac-e-ous*; *inter-lard*.

LARGE, great, bulky, vast. (F.—L.) In early use. ME. *large* (which usually has the sense of liberal), O. Eng. Homilies, ed. Morris, i. 143, l. 32.—F. *large*.—L. *larga*, fem. of *largus*, large, long. Cf. OF. *larc*, *larg*, m. (superseded by *large*, f.) **Der.** *large-ly*; *large-ness*, King Alisaunder, l. 6879; *large-heart-ed*; *large-hand-ed*, Timon of Ath. iv. 1. 11; and see *largess*, *en-large*.

LARGESS, a liberal gift, donation. (F.—L.) ME. *largesse*, P. Plowman, A. vi. 112; Ancren Riwle, p. 166.—F. *largesse*, bounty; Cot.—Late L. *largitia (not found), for L. *largitio*, a bestowing, giving; cf. L. *largītus*, pp. of *largīrī*, to bestow.—L. *largus*, large, liberal; see **Large**.

LARIAT, a rope with a noose, a lasso. (Span.—L.) '*Lariats*, or noosed cords;' W. Irving, Tour on the Prairies, 1835, p. 26.—Span. *la rea·a*, lit. 'the rope that ties together.'—L. *illa*, fem. of *ille*, he; and Span. *reatar*, lit. 'to retie,' attach together, from L. *re-*, again, and *aptāre*, to adjust, from *aptus*, fit. See **Apt**.

LARK (1), the name of a bird. (E.) *Lark* also appears as *lavrock*; see Burns, Holy Fair, st. 1. ME. *larke*, Chaucer, C. T. 1493 (A 1491); spelt *laverock*, Gower, C. A. ii. 264; bk. v. 4100. AS. *lāwerce*, later *lāuerce*, *lāverce*, *lāferce*. The spelling *lawerce* is in Voc. 286. 17; *lauerce* in Voc. 131. 28. *Laferc:* is in the comp. *lafercan-beorh*, a place-name cited in Kemble. But the oldest spelling is *laurice*, Corpus Gloss. 1173.**+**Icel. *lævirki*, a lark; Low G. *lewerke* (Bremen Wörterbuch); OHG. *lērehha*; G. *lerche*; Du. *leeuwrik*, *leeuwerik*; Swed. *lärka*; Dan. *lærke*. β. The Icel. *læ-virki* = skilful worker or worker of craft, from *læ*, craft, and *virki*, a worker; cf. Icel. *læ-visi*, craft, skill, *læ-vīss*, crafty, skilful; and (as to *virki*), *ill-virki*, a worker of ill, *spell-virki*, a doer of mischief. But the general Teut. form poin·s rather to an original **laiwirakjōn-* (N. E. D.), which may perhaps mean 'revealer of treachery;' from **rakjan-* (AS. *reccan*, to relate, expound). Cf. *læwa*, a traitor, betrayer, Mark, xiv. 44; also Goth. *lēw*, an occasion, opportunity (Rom. vii. 8, 11), whence *lēwjan*, *leiwjan*, to betray. Such a name would point to some superstition which may have connected the bird with the rising sun; but no such legend is known. Thus the true origin remains wholly unknown: and the oldest spelling (*laurice*) is obscure.

LARK (2), a game, sport, fun. (E.) Spelt *lark* in modern E., and now a slang term. Also used as *sky-lark*, and probably due to a peculiar use of **Lark** (1); from its cheerful note. ¶ Often (but perhaps wrongly) connected with ME. *lak*, *lok*; also *laik*, which is a Scand. form. See Will. of Palerne, 678; P. Plowman, B. xiv.

243; Ormulum, 1157, 2166; Ancren Riwle, p. 152, note *b*; &c. (Stratmann). Cf. AS. *lác*, play, contest, prey, gift, offering; Grein, ii. 148; Icel. *leikr*, a game, play, sport.

LARUM, short for **Alarum,** q. v. In Shak. Cor. i. 4. 9.

LARVA, an insect in the caterpillar state. (L.) A scientific term. – L. *larua*, a ghost, spectre, mask; the insect's first stage being the mask (disguise) of its last one; a fanciful term. Root unknown. Der. *larv-al*, Blount's Gloss., ed. 1674.

LARYNX, the upper part of the windpipe. (L. – Gk.) In Kersey, ed. 1715; and in P. Fletcher, Purple Island, c. 4, note 29. – L. *larynx*, Gk. λάρυγξ, the larynx, throat, gullet; gen. case, λάρυγγος. Der. *laryng-e-al*, *laryng-e-an*, *laryng-itis*.

LASCAR, a native E. Indian sailor. (Pers.) 'Lascars, or Indian seamen;' W. Dampier, A New Voyage, vol. ii. pt. i. p. 112 (1669). First in 1625. – Pers. *lashkar*, an army; whence *lashkarī*, military; hence, a soldier, camp-follower; Rich. Pers. Dict. p. 1265. See Yule.

LASCIVIOUS, lustful. (L.) In Shak. Rich. II, ii. 1. 19; Lydgate, Assembly of Gods, l. 686. – Late L. *lasciviōsus*, lustful. – L. *lasciuia*, sb.; from L. *lasciuus*, lascivious. Lengthened from an older form **lascus* (not found), as *fest-īuus* is from *fest-us*. Cf. Skt. *lash*, to desire, covet, akin to Gk. λι-λαίομαι, I desire, and to E. *lust*. See **Lust.** Der. *lascivious-ly*, *lascivious-ness*.

LASH (1), to fasten firmly together. (F. – L.) 'Lash (in sea affairs), to fasten or bind up anything to the ship's sides;' Kersey, ed. 1715. 'Her ordnance being *lashed* so fast;' Capt. Smith, Works, ed. Arber, p. 674. – OF. *lachier*, variant of *lacier* (Godefroy), to fasten with a lace or string. – OF. *lache* (Godefroy), a lace, also a hinge. – Folk-L. **lacium*, for L. *laqueum*, acc. of *laqueus*, a snare. See **Lace.** Cf. Norm. dial. *lacher*, to fasten with thongs (Moisy). ¶ We also find Du. *lasschen*, to join, scarf together; *lasch*, sb., a piece, joint, seam, notch; Swed. *laska*, to stitch, *lask*, a scarf, joint; Dan. *laske*, to scarf, *lask*, a scarf; but it is not clear that they have influenced the E. word. See *lasch* in Franck, sb.

LASH (2), a thong, flexible part of a whip, a stroke, stripe. (F. – L.) ME. *lasche*. 'Lasche, stroke, *ligula*, *flagrum*;' Prompt. Parv. p. 288. 'Whippes *lasshe*;' Chaucer, Parl. of Foules, 178. Perhaps formed from **Lash** (1). Cf. Norm. dial. *laschier*, to lash, whip with a cord (Le Héricher). β. Or, from OF. *lache*, a lace (Godefroy); see above. Der. *lash*, verb, to flog, scourge; cf. 'Laschyn, betyn, *ligulo*, *verbero*;' Prompt. Parv.

LASS, a girl. (Scand.) ME. *lasse*, spelt *lasce* in Cursor Mundi, l. 2608. ME. *lasce* may be regarded as allied to Icel. *löskr* (base *lask-*), weak; MSwed. *lösk*, a person having no fixed abode; OSwed. *loska kona*, a spinster (cited by Vigfusson). – H. Bradley; in Athenæum, June 16, 1894. Cf. Bavarian *lasch*, a woman (a term of contempt); Schmeller. β. OIcel. *löskr* is for **lat-kwaz*, allied to Goth. *lat-s*, idle, E. *late*, q. v.; Brugmann, ii. § 85.

LASSITUDE, weariness. (F. – L.) 'The one is callyd cruditie, the other *lassitude*;' Sir T. Elyot, Castel of Helth, b. iv. c. 1. – F. *lassitude*; Cot. – L. *lassitūdo*, faintness, weariness. – L. *lassi-*, for *lassu-* tired, wearied; with suffix *-tū-den-*. β. *Lassus* is for **lad-tus*, where *lad-* corresponds to *lat-* in Goth. *lats*, slothful, cognate with E. *late*. See **Late.** Brugmann, i. § 197.

LASSO, a rope with a noose. (Span. – L.) Modern; not in Todd's Johnson. The pron. is that used in Texas, which is archaic. – OSpan. *laso* (Minsheu, 1623); Span. *lazo*, a snare, slip-knot; and cf. F. *lacs*. – Folk-L. **lacium*, for L. *laqueum*, acc. of *laqueus*, a snare. See **Lace.** ¶ Not from mod. Spanish, for the Span. *z* is sounded like our voiceless *th*. Der. *lasso*, verb.

LAST (1), latest, hindmost. (E.) *Last* is a contraction of *latest*, through the intermediate form *latst* (= *lat'st*), for which see Ormulum, l. 4168. See **Late.** Cf. Du. *laatst*, last, which is the superl. of *laat*, late.

LAST (2), a wooden model of the foot on which shoes are made. (E.) ME. *last*, *leste*. 'Hec formula, *last*;' Voc. 654. 35; in a glossary of the 15th cent. 'Leste, sowtarys [shoemaker's] forme, *formula*;' Prompt. Parv. p. 298. AS. *lást*, a foot-track, path, trace of feet; Grein, ii. 160; also AS. *lǽste*, a model of the foot; 'Calopodium, uel mustricula, *lǽste*;' Voc. 125. 32.+Du. *leest*, a last, shape, form; Icel. *leistr*, the foot below the ankle; Swed. *läst*, a shoemaker's last; Dan. *læst*, the same; G. *leisten*, the same; Goth. *laists*, a track, way, footstep; 2 Cor. xii. 18. β. The Teut. types are all from a base *laist-*, and the original sense is foot-track, trace of a man's path; cf. G. *gleise* (*ge-leise*), a track. Formed from Teut. **lais*, as in Goth. *lais*, I know (Phil. iv. 12); the trace being that whereby a man's path is *known*. This word *lais* was orig. used in the sense 'I have experienced,' and it is the pt. t. of Goth. *leisan*, to track, to find out. From Teut. base **leis*, to find out, whence E. *learn*; allied to L. *lira*, a furrow, a track, whence E. *de-lir-ious*. See **Learn.** Der. *last* (3).

LAST (3), to endure, continue. (E.) ME. *lasten*, Havelok, 538; also *lesten*, Prompt. Parv. p. 299. AS. *lǽstan*, to observe, perform, last, remain; the orig. sense being 'to follow in the track of,' from *lást*, a foot-track; see **Last** (2).+Goth. *laistjan*, to follow, follow after; from *laists*, a foot-track; G. *leisten*, verb, to perform, follow out, fulfil, allied to *leisten*, sb., a form, model, shoemaker's last. Der. *last-ing-ly*, *ever-last-ing*. ¶ The train of ideas in *learn*, *last* (2), and *last* (3) is: trace (whence learn, know), follow out, fulfil, continue.

LAST (4), a load, a large weight, ship's cargo. (E.) ME. *last*. 'A thousand *last* quad yere' = a thousand cargoes of bad years; Chaucer, C. T. 13368 (B 1628); and see Deposition of Rich. II, ed. Skeat, iv. 74. AS. *hlǽst*, a burden; Grein, ii. 81. – AS. *hladan*, to load; see **Lade, Load.**+Icel. *lest*, a load, from *hlaða*, to load; Dan. *last*, a weight, burden, cargo, from *lade*, to load; Swed. *last*, a burden, allied to *ladda*, to load; Du. and G. *last*, from *laden*, to load. Idg. type **klat-sto-* (-sti-), from **klat-*, to lade; whence also Idg. **klat-to-*, as in Icel. *hlass*, a cart-load, Swed. *lass*, the same.

LATCH, a catch, fastening. (E.) ME. *lacche*, used by Walter de Bibbesworth to translate OF. *cliket*; Wright's Vocab. i. 170. [See *cliket* in Chaucer, C. T. 9920 (E 2046)] 'Latche, *lahche*, *lach*, or *snekke*, Clitorium, vel *pessula*;' Prompt. Parv. p. 283. From ME. verb *lacchen*, to seize, catch hold of, Will. of Palerne, 666, 671; P. Plowman, B. xviii. 324. AS. *lǽccan*, to seize, lay hold of, Grein, ii. 161; also *ge-lǽccan*, Ælfric's Homilies, i. 182, ii. 50. β. AS. *lǽccan* is a weak verb (pt. t. *lǽhte*), from a base **lakk-*. It is perhaps ultimately connected with L. *laqueus*, a snare. ¶ The assertion in Trench's Select Glossary that *lace* and *latch* are 'the same word,' may be true for *some* senses of the latter; thus ME. *lacche* occurs in the sense of 'snare' in Ch., Rom. Rose, 1624. The E. and F. words were prob. confused. For the F. word see **Latchet.** Der. *latch*, verb, to fasten with a latch, merely formed from the sb., and not the same as ME. *lacchen*; also *latch-key*.

LATCH, to moisten. (E.) In Shak. Mid. Nt. Dream, iii. 2. 36: 'But hast thou yet *lacht* the Athenians eyes With the loue-iuyce, as I did bid thee doe?' ed. 1623. Oberon had bidden Puck to 'annoint his eyes;' ii. 1. 261. A variant of North E. *leck*, to moisten, which exactly represents AS. *leccan*, to moisten, water; *latch* has the vowel of prov. E. *lache*, a gutter, AS. *lacu*, a stream, closely allied to *leccan*. Cf. MDu. *laken*, to flow (Oudemans), Swed. *laka på*, to pour on to. See Notes on E. Etym., p. 158.

LATCHET, a little lace, a thong. (F. – L.) In the Bible, Mark, i. 7, Isa. v. 27. The former *t* is intrusive. ME. *lachet*, as in 'lachet of a schoo;' Prompt. Parv. p. 284. 'Lachet outher loupe' = latchet or loop; Sir Gawayne and the Grene Knight, l. 591. – OF. *lachet*, Norman and Picard form of OF. *lacet*, 'the lace of a petticote, a woman's lace or lacing, also a snare or ginne;' Cot. Dimin. (with suffix *-et*) of OF. *lache* (Godefroy), variant of *las*, a snare. See **Lace.** ☞ Observe that *latchet* is the dimin. of *lace*, and distinct from *latch* in most of its senses.

LATE, tardy, coming behind, slow, delayed. (E.) 1. ME. *lat*, rare as an adj. in the positive degree. 'A *lat* mon' = a man slow of belief; Joseph of Arimathie, ed. Skeat, l. 695. The adv. is *late*, as in 'late ne rathe' = late nor early, P. Plowman, B. iii. 73. 2. The compar. form is *later* or *latter*, spelt *lættere* in Layamon, l. 5911. 3. The superl. is *latest*, *latst*, or *last*, the intermediate form appearing in the Ormulum, l. 4168. AS. *lǽt*, slow, late; Grein, ii. 165.+Du. *laat*, late; Icel. *latr*, slow, lazy; Dan. *lad*, lazy, slothful; Swed. *lat*, lazy, idle; Goth. *lats*, slothful, Luke, xix. 22; G. *lass*, weary, indolent. Allied to L. *lassus* (= **lad-tus*), weary. β. All from the weak grade of Teut. base **lēt*, to let, let go, let alone; so that *late* means let alone, neglected, hence slothful, slow, coming behindhand. See **Let** (1). Brugmann, i. § 197. Der. *late-ly*, *late-ness*, *lat-ish*, *latt-er*, *latt-er-ly*, *last* (1), q. v., *last-ly*. Also *let* (2). From the same source, *lassitude*, q. v.

LATEEN, triangular, applied to sails. (F. – L.) In Ash's Dict., ed. 1775. Vessels in the Mediterranean frequently have *lateen* sails, of a triangular shape. The E. spelling preserves the pronunciation of the F. word *latine*, the fem. of *Latin*, Latin; the lit. sense being 'Latin sails,' i. e. Roman sails. See **Latin.** 'Voile *Latine*, a mizen or smack saile;' Cot. 'Latina, the mizen saile of a ship; also, the Latine toong;' Florio, Ital. Dict. ed. 1598. So also Span. *latina vela*, a lateen sail; *a la Latina*, of a triangular form.

LATENT, lying hid, concealed. (L.) In Blount's Gloss., ed. 1674; and in Cockeram (1642). – L. *latent-*, stem of pres. pt. of *latēre*, to lie hid. Der. *latent-ly*, *latenc-y*.

LATERAL, belonging to the side. (L.) In Milton, P. L. x. 705. 'A *lateral* view;' Ben Jonson, Underwoods, xxiii. l. 9. – L. *laterālis*, belonging to the side. – L. *later-*, for **lates-*, stem of *latus*, the side.+Irish *leth*, W. *led*, side. Der. *lateral-ly*.

LATH, a thin slip of wood. (E.) In Shak. Tw. Nt. iv. 2. 136.

In the North of England, the form used is *lat*; see Ray, Halliwell, and the Holderness Glossary (E. D. S.). This corresponds with ME. *latte*, a lath. 'Hic asser, a *latt*;' Voc. 729. 4. AS. *lætt*, pl. *lætta*; 'Asseres, *lætta*;' Ælfric's Gloss., in Voc. 126. 14; also *latta*, pl., Voc. 185. 20.+Du. *lat*, a lath; G. *latte*, a lath, whence F. *latte* is borrowed. β. The exact correspondence of the dental sound in AS. *lætt* and G. *latte* presents a difficulty. Perhaps the modern E. form was influenced by the W. *llath*, a rod, staff, yard, which is cognate with Irish *slat*, a rod, from a Celtic type *slattā. The pl. *lathes* occurs in 1350; Riley, Memorials of London, p. 261. **Der.** *latt-ice*, q. v., *latt-en*, q. v.

LATHE (1), a machine for 'turning' wood and metal. (Scand.) 'Could turn his word, and oath, and faith, As many ways as in a *lathe*;' Butler, Hudibras, pt. iii. c. 2. ll. 375, 376. Cotgrave explains F. *tournoir* by 'a turner's wheel, a *lathe* or *lare*.' Prob. of Scand. origin; from a form represented by Dan. *lad*, as in *dreie-lad*, a turning-lathe; which also means 'frame,' as in *væver-lad*, a loom (weaving-frame). This Dan. *lad* is prob. the same as Icel. *hlað*, a pile, a stack; from *hlaða*, to lade; see **Lade** (2). β. We may also compare AS. *hlæd-hwēogl* (lit. lade-wheel), an engine or wheel of a well, to draw water (Bosworth); also AS. *hlæd-trendel*, a wheel for drawing water (id.); which are clearly derived from AS. *hladan*, to lade out water. A transference of name from the water-wheel to the lathe would be easy. ¶ The entry *löð*, a lathe, in Vigfusson's Icel. Dict., is incorrect (N.E.D.).

LATHE (2), a division of a county. (E.) Kent is divided into five *lathes* or portions; see Pegge's Alphabet of Kenticisms; E.D.S. Gloss. C. 3. AS. *lǽð*, a portion of land; 'ne gyrne ic þines, ne *lǽðes* ne landes' = I covet not thine, neither lathe nor land; Thorpe's Ancient Laws, i. 184. 'In quibusdam vero provinciis Anglice vocabatur *leð*, quod isti dicunt *tithinge*;' id. i. 455, note 3; and see Glossary in vol. ii.+Icel. *láð*, land, landed possession. Teut. type *læðom, neuter. Cf. Goth. *un-lēds*, poor, lit. 'landless.'

LATHER, foam or froth, esp. when made with soap and water. (E.) ME. *lather*, for which Stratmann gives no reference; but we find the derived verb *letherien*, as in 'he *leþerede* a swote' = he was in a lather with sweat; Layamon, l. 7489 (later text). AS. *lēaðor*, lather, Voc. 456. 14; also in the comp. *lēaðor-wyrt*, lit. lather-wort, i. e. soap-wort; Gloss. to AS. Leechdoms, ed. Cockayne; whence the verb *lēðrian*, to anoint, John, xi. 2 (Lindisfarne MS.).+Icel. *lauðr*, later *löðr*, froth, foam, scum of the sea, soap; whence *lauðra*, *löðra*, to foam, also to drip with blood; *leyðra*, to wash. Teut. type *lauðrom, neut.; Idg. type *loutrom, as in Gk. λουτρόν, for λοϝετρόν, a bath, from λούω, Homeric λόω (for *λοϝω), I wash (Prellwitz). Cf. L. *lauāre*, to wash; for which see **Lave**. **Der.** *lather*, vb.

LATIN, pertaining to the Romans. (F.—L.) ME. *Latin*; Chaucer, C. T. 4939 (B 519); and earlier, in St. Juliana, p. 3.—F. *Latin*.—L. *Latīnus*, Latin, belonging to Latium.—L. *Latium*, the name of a country of Italy, in which Rome was situate. **Der.** *Latin-ism*, *Latin-ist*, *Latin-i-ty*, *Latin-ise*. Also *latim-er* = *Latin-er*, an interpreter, Layamon, 14319; well known as a proper name. Also *lateen*, q. v.

LATITUDE, breadth, scope, distance of a place N. or S. of the equator. (F.—L.) ME. *latitude*; Chaucer, C. T. 4433.—F. *latitude*.—L. *lātitūdo*, breadth.—L. *lātus*, broad; from an OL. *stlātus*, appearing in *stlāta*, a broad ship. See Brugmann, i. § 529 (2). **Der.** *latitudin-al*, from stem *lātitūdin-* of the sb. *lātitūdo*; *latitudin-ar-i-an*, *latitudin-ar-i-an-ism*, *latitudin-ous*.

LATTEN, a mixed metal, a kind of brass. (F.—G.?) 'This *latten* bilbo;' Merry Wives, i. 1. 165. ME. *latoun*, *laton*; Chaucer, C. T. 701 (A 699).—OF. *laton* (13th cent., see Littré); mod. F. *laiton*. Cotgrave has: 'Laiton, lattin (metall).' Cf. Span. *laton*, latten, brass; Port. *latão*, brass; Ital. *ottone* (corrupted from *lottone* or *lattone*), latten, brass, yellow copper. β. According to Diez, the OF. *laton* is from *latte*, a lath (also spelt *latz*, as in Cotgrave); because this metal was hammered into thin plates. This is rendered probable by the Ital. *latta*, tin, a thin sheet of iron tinned, answering in form to Low L. *latta*, a lath (occurring in Voc. 729. 5); so also Span. *latas*, laths, *hoja de lata*, tin-plate, tinned iron plate [where *hoja* = foil, leaf]; also Port. *lata*, tin plate, *latas*, laths. γ. If this be right, these words are of G. origin viz. from G. *latte*, a lath; see **Lath**.

LATTER, another form of *later*; see **Late**. (E.)

LATTICE, a network of crossed laths. (F.—G.) Here, as in other words, the final *-ce* stands for *s*; a better form is *lattis*, as in Spenser, F. Q. iii. 12. 15. ME. *latis*, *latys*; Wyclif, Prov. vii. 6.— AF. *latys*, Liber Albus, p. 333, l. 4; F. *lattis*, lath-work (Hamilton). —F. *la'te*, a lath. — G. *latte*, a lath; see **Lath**. **Der.** *lattice-work*.

LAUD, to praise. (L.) ME. *lauden*. 'If thou *laudest* and ioyest any wight;' Test. of Love, b. i. ch. 10. 76; '*laude* it nought;' P. Plowman, B. xi. 102.—L. *laudāre*, to praise.—L. *laud-*, stem of

laus, praise. Root uncertain. **Der.** *laud-er*, *laud-able*, *laud-able-ness*, *laud-abl-y*; also *laud-at-or-y* (from pp. *laud-ātus*); *laud*, sb., Troil. iii. 3. 179; Hamlet, iv. 7. 178. And see *allow* (2).

LAUDANUM, a preparation of opium. (L.—Gk.—Pers.) '*Laudanum* or *Opiate Laudanum*, a medicine so called from its excellent qualities;' Kersey, ed. 1715; and in Sir T. Browne, Religio Medici, pt. ii. § 12. Kersey's remark refers to a supposed connexion with L. *laudāre*, to praise; on which Mahn (in Webster) remarks: 'this word cannot be derived from L. *laudandum*, to be praised, nor was it invented by Paracelsus, as it previously existed in Provençal.' The *name*, in fact, was an old one; but was transferred from one drug to another. '*Laudanum*, *Ladanum*, or *Labdanum*, a sweet-smelling transparent gum gathered from the leaves of *Cistus Ledon*, a shrub, of which they make pomander; it smells like wine mingled with spices;' Blount's Gloss., ed. 1674. Cf. MSpan. *laudano*, 'the gum labdanum vsed in pomanders;' Minsheu (1623). Spelt *labdanum* in Cotgrave, s. v. *labdane*; but *laudanum* in Bullein's Dialogue (1578), p. 43, l. 13. Spelt *ludanum*, Ben Jonson, Cynthia's Revels, v. 2 (Perfumer).—L. *lādanum*, *lēdanum*, the resinous substance exuding from the shrub *lada*; Pliny, xxvi. 8. 30, § 47; xii. 17. 37, § 45.—Gk. λήδανον, λάδανον, the same.—Gk. λῆδον, an oriental shrub, *Cistus Creticus*.—Pers. *lādan*, the gum-herb lada; Rich. Pers. Dict., p. 1251, col. 2, last line.

LAUGH, to make the noise denoting mirth. (E.) ME. *laughen*, Chaucer, C. T. 3847 (A 3849). Various spellings are *lauhwen*, *lauhen*, *laghen*, *lehȝen*, *lihȝen*, &c.; see Stratmann. OMerc. *hlæhhan*, AS. *hlehhan*, *hlihhan*, *hlihan*, pt. t. *hlōh*; Grein, ii. 81.+Du. *lagchen*, Icel. *hlæja*, pt. t. *hlō*; Dan. *lee*; Swed. *le*; G. *lachen*; Goth. *hlahjan*, pt. t. *hlōh*. β. All imitative words from a Teut. base HLAH, corresponding to an Aryan base KLAK, to make a noise. Cf. Lith. *kleg-éti*, to laugh, Gk. κλώσσειν, to cluck. Somewhat similar words are κλώζειν, to cry as a jackdaw, κρώζειν, to caw, κλάζειν, to clash, κράζειν, to croak, &c.; L. *crocitāre*, *glocīre*; and cf. E. *crake*, *creak*, *crack*, *click*, *clack*, *cluck*, &c. **Der.** *laugh*, sb., *laugh-er*, *laugh-able*, *laugh-abl-y*, *laugh-able-ness*, *laugh-ing-ly*, *laugh-ing-gas*, *laugh-ing-stock*. Also *laugh-ter*, Chaucer, Troil. ii. 1169, from AS. *hleahtor*, Grein, ii. 82, cognate with Icel. *hlātr*, Dan. *latter*, G. *lachter*.

LAUNCH (1), **LANCH**, to throw forward like a spear, hurl, send forth, speed (a ship) into the water. (F.—L.) ME. *launchen* to pierce, Destr. of Troy, 6811; variant of *launcen*, to hurl, Will. of Palerne, l. 2755; cf. P. Plowman's Crede, 551. 'Lawncyn, lawnchyn, or stynge with a spere or blode-yryne, lanceo;' Prompt. Parv.—OF. *lanchier*, variant of *lancier*, Picard *lancher*, F. *lancer*, 'to throw, fling, hurle, dart; also, to prick, pierce;' Cot.—F. *lance*, a lance; see **Lance**. Doublet, *lance*, verb.

LAUNCH (2), the largest boat of a man of war, a kind of long-boat. (Span.—Port.—Malay.) Formerly *lanch*. 'The craft was.. a *lanch*, or long-boat;' Dampier, Voy. (ed. 1729), i. 2.—Span. *lancha*, 'the pinnace of a ship;' Pineda.—Port. *lancha*, pinnace of a ship; also *lanchara*.—Malay *lanchar*, swift, nimble; *lanchar*, to proceed quickly. See Notes on E. Etym., p. 158.

LAUNDRESS, a washerwoman. (F.—L.) Formerly *launderess* (see below), formed by adding the F. suffix -*ess* to the old word *launder* or *lavender*, which had the same sense. ME. *lavender*, Chaucer, Legend of Good Women, l. 358; spelt *lauender*, *laynder*, *landar*, Barbour's Bruce, ed. Skeat, xvi. 273, 292.—OF. *lavandier*, masc. one who washes; (whence the fem. *lavandiere*, 'a launderesse or washing-woman;' Cot).—Late L. *lavandārius*, one who washes; Ducange.—L. *lavand-a*, things to be washed; from *lauāre*, to wash; see **Lave**. **Der.** *laundr-y* (= *launder-y*), spelt *lauendrye* in P. Plowman, B. xv. 182.

LAUREATE, crowned with laurel. (L.) ME. *laureat*, Chaucer, C. T. 14614 (B 3886).—L. *laureātus*, crowned with laurel.—L. *laurea*, a laurel crown; fem. form of adj. *laureus*, made of laurel, from *laurus*; see **Laurel**. **Der.** *laureate-ship*.

LAUREL, the bay-tree. (F.—L.) In Shak. Troil. i. 3. 107. Formed, by the common substitution of *l* for *r*, from ME. *laurer*, a laurel, Chaucer, C. T. 9340 (E 1466); spelt *lorer*, Gower, C. A. i. 337; bk. iii. 1716; *lorel*, Will. of Palerne, l. 2983.—F. *laurier*, 'a laurell, or bay-tree;' Cot.—Late L. *laurārius* (not found), an adjectival formation with suffix -*ārius*.—L. *laurus*, a laurel-tree. **Der.** *laurell-ed*; also *laur-e-ate*; see above.

LAURUSTINUS, an evergreen shrub. (L.) Used by Evelyn in 1664. Really compounded of two separate words.—L. *laurus*, a laurel; *tinus*, a laurustinus.

LAVA, the matter which flows down a burning mountain. (Ital. —L.) In Keats, Lamia, i. 157. A late word; added by Todd to Johnson's Dict.—Ital. *lava*, 'a running gullet, streame, or gutter sodainly caused by raine;' Florio's Ital. Dict., ed. 1598.—Ital. *lavare*, to wash.—L. *lauāre*, to wash; see **Lave**.

LAVATORY, a place for washing. (L.) In Levins; and in

Wyclif, Exod. xxx. 18. Cotgrave explains F. *lavatoire* as 'a lavatory, a place or vessell to wash in.'—L. *lauātōrium*, a lavatory; neut. of *lauātōrius*, belonging to a washer.—L. *lauātor*, a washer.—L. *lauāre*, to wash; see **Lave.**

LAVE, to wash, bathe. (F.—L.) ME. *lauen*; 'And *laueth* hem in the *lauandrie*' [laundry]; P. Plowman, C. xvii. 330; cf. Layamon, 7489.—F. *laver*, to wash.—L. *lauāre*, to wash.+Gk. λούειν, to wash. From the Idg. base LOU, to wash. See **Lather.** Der. *lav-er* (Exod. xxxviii. 8), ME. *lavour*, *lauour*, Chaucer, C. T. 5869 (D 287), from OF. *laveoir*, *lavoer* (Godefroy), *lavoir*, 'a washing poole' (Cot.), from L. *lauātōrium* (above). And see *laundress*, *lotion*. From the same base are *de-luge*, *al-luvial*.

LAVEER, to beat to windward, to tack. (Du.—F.—Du.) 'But those that 'gainst stiff gales *laveering* go;' Dryden, Astræa Redux, l. 65.—Du. *laveeren*, MDu. *laveren*, *loeveren*, 'to saile up and downe,' Hexham.—MF. *lovêer* (Littré); F. *louvoyer*.—F. *lof*, luff, weatherside.—Du. *loef*. See **Luff.** See Notes on E. Etym., p. 159.

LAVENDER, an odoriferous plant. (F.—Late L.) Spelt *lavendre* in Palsgrave; cf. Shak. Wint. Ta. iv. 104. 'Lavendere, herbe, *Lavendula*;' Prompt. Parv. — AF. *lavendre*, Voc. 557. 9.—Late L. *lavendula*, as in Prompt. Parv. and Voc. 557. 9. Other forms are *lavandula*, *livendula* (N. E. D.). Also F. *lavande*, 'lavender,' Cot.; Ital. *lavanda*, lavender; Ital. *lavendola*, Span. *lavándula*. β. The plant was often laid with fresh-washed linen, and thus came to be associated (in popular etymology) with L. *lauāre*, to wash. But the early form *livendula* tends rather to associate it with *liuēre*, to be livid, from its blueish colour. The exact source is unknown.

LAVISH, adj., profuse, prodigal. (F.—L.) α. The adj. is due to an obs. sb., also spelt *lavish*; also *lavas*, *lavess*, which is explained below. β. Examples of the adj. are as follows. 'In al other thing so light and *laues* [are they] of theyr tong;' Sir T. More, Works, p. 250 b. 'Punishing with losse of life the *lavesnes* of the toung;' Brende, Quintus Curtius, fol. 67 (R.). 'Although some *lauishe* lippes, which like some other best;' Gascoigne, In Praise of Lady Sandes, l. 7 (Poems, ed. Hazlitt, vol. i. p. 53). 'Lavish Nature;' Spenser, Muiopotmos, l. 163. Spelt *lavas* in 'Romeus and Juliet,' p. 20 (Halliwell); so also '*lavas* of theyr tungys;' Paston Letters, iii. 323. γ. The adj. arose from the use of *lavas*, sb., in the sense of lavishness or prodigality. 'There was no *lauas* [profusion, excess] in their speche;' Caxton, Golden Legend, fol. 364, back (N. E. D.). Whence also the vb., as in; 'Those, who did prodigally *lauesse* out and waste their substaunce;' Udall, tr. of Erasmus' Apophthegms, Diogenes, § 161. The sb. is of F. origin.—OF. *lavasse*, an inundation, abundant rain (Godefroy); cf. Rouchi *lavache*, as in *flouvoir à lavache*, to rain abundantly (Hécart).—F. *laver*, to wash; Norm. dial. *laver*, to lavish, to squander (Moisy).—L. *lauāre*, to wash. See **Lave.** Compare: 'He *lauez* hys gyftez as water of dyche' = God *lavishes* his gifts as (freely as one would take) water out of a ditch; Allit. Poems, ed. Morris, A. 607; see the whole passage, which treats of God's profuseness of reward to the souls in heaven. Der. *lavish-ly*, *lavish-ness*, *lavish-ment*; also *lavish*, verb (Levins).

LAW, a rule of action, edict, statute. (Scand.) ME. *lawe* (two syllables), Chaucer, C. T. 1167 (A 1165). AS. *lagu*, a late word, used in place of the early AS. *ǣ*, law. Borrowed from prehistoric ON. *lagu, answering to Icel. *lög* (below). Cf. OSax. *lag* (pl. *lagu*), a statute, decree; Icel. *lög* (s. pl., but used in the sing. sense), for older *logu, a law; it is the pl. of *lag*, a stratum, order, due place, lit. 'that which lies' or is placed; Swed. *lag*; Dan. *lov*. Teut. type *logom, n. β. The sense is 'that which lies' or is in due order; from Teut. base *lag, 2nd grade of **liggan-*, to lie; see **Lie** (1). Der. *law-ful*, ME. *laweful*, Trevisa, iii. 193; *law-ful-ly*, ME. *lawefulliche*, P. Plowman, C. x. 59; *law-ful-ness*, see Owl and Nightingale, ed. Stratmann, l. 1741; *law-giver*; *law-less*, ME. *laweles*, Trevisa, iii. 73; *law-less-ly*, *law-less-ness*; *law-book*, see Ormulum, l. 1953; *law-suit*; also *law-yer*, q. v.

LAWN (1), a space of ground covered with grass in a garden. (F.—C.) Properly an open space, esp. in a wood; a glade (see **Glade**). The spelling *lawn* is not old; the older spelling is invariably *laund*, which was still in use in the 18th century. 'Laund or *Lawn*, in a park, plain untilled ground;' Kersey's Dict., ed. 1715. Spelt *laund* in Shak. Venus, 813; 3 Hen. VI, iii. 1. 2. ME. *laund*, Chaucer, C. T. 1691; (observe that Dryden substitutes *lawn* in his Palamon and Arcite, l. 845); P. Plowman, C. i. 8.—OF. *launde* (Godefroy), also *lande*, 'a land or *laund*, a wild, untilled, shrubby, or bushy plain;' Cot. Cf. Ital. and Span. *landa*, a heath, tract of open country.—OCeltic *landā, fem.; whence Bret. *lann*, a bushy shrub, of which the pl. *lannou* is only used to signify waste land, like the F. *landes*. The Bret. *lann* is also used in a variety of senses, corresponding to those of Gael. and Irish *lann*; and W. *llan*; one of these senses is *land* or territory, though most often used of an inclosure. Spurrell gives W. *llan*, 'an area, yard, church;' but the Gael. *lann*

means 'an inclosure, a house, a church, a repository, land;' and the Irish *lann* is 'land, a house, church, repository.' In fact, the Irish *lann* and E. *land* are cognate words; see **Land.**

LAWN (2), a sort of fine linen. (F.?—L.?) In Shak. Wint. Ta. iv. 4. 209, 220. 'In the third yeare of the raigne of Queene Elizabeth, 1562, beganne the knowledge and wearing of *lawne* and cambrick, which was then brought into England by very small quantities;' Stow, King James, an. 1604 (R.). But this misleading statement is entirely wrong, as the word is known to English as early as 1415 (N. E. D.). It also occurs in Lydgate's London Lickpenny, l. 66 (Minor Poems, p. 105); and in Henrysoun, Test. Cressid, 423. In 1502, *lawn* is enumerted among the wares of Flanders; Arnold's Chron., ed. 1811, p. 205. And Palsgrave (1530) has: '*Laune lynen*, crespe.' I understand *Laune lynen* to mean 'linen of *Laon*,' formerly also *Lan*, not far N.W. of Rheims; cf. '*Lawne*, or fine linnen cloth called cloth of Remes;' Baret. Linen manufacture was carried on at Laon for many centuries (*Romania*, xxix. 182). For the spelling *Lan*, see Calendar of State Papers, vi. 203, 224; and for OF. *Lan* (Laon) see Ménage.—L. *Laudūnum*, *Lugdūnum*, a name of Celtic origin. Cf. *fawn* (2), from OF. *fan*, *faon*; *pawn* (2), from OF. *paon*.

LAWYER, one versed in the law, one who practises law. (E.) ME. *lawyer*, *lawier*; P. Plowman, B. vii. 59. From *law*, with suffix -*yer*. This suffix originated in the use of the suffix -*ien* in place of -*en* in causal verbs, and verbs derived from sbs. Thus, from the AS. *lufu*, love, was formed the vb. *lufigan* or *lufian*, to love, which became *lov-ien* in ME. Hence the sb. *lov-ier* or *lov-yer*, a lover, another form of *lov-er* or *lov-ere*, a lover; see the readings in the Petworth and Lansdowne MSS. in Chaucer, C.T., A 1347. By analogy, from *lawe*, law, was formed *law-ier* or *law-yer*. So also *bow-yer*, one who uses a bow; *saw-yer*, one who uses a saw.

LAX, slack, loose, soft, not strict. (L.) In Milton, P. L. vii. 162. —L. *laxus*, lax, loose.—L. base LAG, to be weak; whence also *langu-ēre*, to be languid, with inserted *n*. Allied to *slack*; see **Slack.** Brugmann, i. § 193. Der. *lax-ly*, *lax-ness*; *lax-i-ty*, from F. *laxité* (Cot.), which from L. acc. *laxitātem*; and see *lax-at-ive*.

LAXATIVE, loosening. (F.—L.) ME. *laxatif*, Chaucer, C. T. 14949 (B 4133).—F. *laxatif*, 'laxative;' Cot.—L. *laxātiuus*, loosening; cf. *laxātus*, pp. of *laxāre*, to render lax.—L. *laxus*; see **Lax.** Der. *laxative-ness*.

LAY (1), to cause to lie down, place, set. (E.) The causal of *lie*, from which it is derived. ME. *leggen*; weak verb, pt. t. *leide*, pp. *leid*; Chaucer, C. T. 81, 3935 (A 3937). AS. *lecgan* (where *cg*=*gg*), to lay; pt. t. *legde*, pp. *gelegd*; Grein, ii. 166. Formed (by vowel-change of *a* to *e*) from *lag*, orig. form of AS. *læg*, pt. t. of *licgan*, to lie; see **Lie** (1).+Du. *leggen*, pt. t. *legde*, *leide*, pp. *gelegt*; Icel. *leggja*, pt. t. *lagði*, pp. *lagiðr*, *lagðr*; Dan. *lægge*, pt. t. *lagde*, pp. *lagt*; Swed. *lägge*, pt. t. *lade*, pp. *lagd*; Goth. *lagjan*, pt. t. *lagida*, pp. *lagiths*; G. *legen*, pt. t. *legte*, pp. *gelegt*. Teut. type **lagjan-*; from *lag*, 2nd grade of **legjan-*, to lie. β. The form *lay* is due to the base *leg-*, occurring in AS. *leg-est*, *leg-ð*, 2nd and 3rd pers. sing. of the present tense. Der. *lay-er*, q. v.

LAY (2), a song, lyric poem. (F.—OHG.) ME. *lai*, O. Eng. Homilies, ed. Morris, i. 199, l. 167; *lay*, P. Plowman, B. viii. 66.—OF. *lai*, spelt *lais* in Cotgrave; cf. Prov. *lais*, a lay. [The *lay* was regarded as specially belonging to the Bretons; Mr. Wedgwood cites from Marie de France: 'Les cuntes ke jo sai verais Dunt li Breton unt fait lor *lais* Vus cunterai assez briefment' = the tales which I know to be true, of which the Bretons have made their *lays*, I will briefly relate to you. See further in note 24 to Tyrwhitt's Introductory Discourse to the Cant. Tales; and see Chaucer, C. T. 11021 (F 709).] Of doubtful origin; but most probably from OHG. *leih*, *leich*, a game, sport; also melody, song (see Schade).+Icel. *leikr*; AS. *lāc*, sport; Goth. *laiks*, dancing (Lu. xv. 25). Teut. type *laikoz, m.; whence also OSlav. *likŭ*, Russ. *lik'*, a chorus, choir. ¶ Not from Celtic; and not from G. *lied*; see under **Lark** (2).

LAY (3), **LAIC,** pertaining to the laity. (F.—L.—Gk.) ME. *lay*; 'Lered men and *lay*' = learned men and laymen; Rob. of Brunne, tr. of Langtoft, p. 171, last line.—OF. *lai*, 'lay, secular, of the laity;' Cot.—L. *lāicus*, belonging to the people (whence the E. *laic*).—Gk. λαϊκός, belonging to the people.—Gk. λαός (Ionic ληός, Attic λεώς), the people. Root uncertain. Der. *laic-al*, *lay-man*, Trevisa, v. 289; also *lai-ty*, used by Cotgrave (as cited above), formed with suffix -*ty* by analogy with words such as *chasti-ty*, *quanti-ty*, &c.

LAY FIGURE, a jointed wooden model of the human body, used by artists. (Du. and F.) *Figure* is from F. *figure*, L. *figūra*. *Lay* is properly a part of the older word *layman* (used in the same sense as *lay figure*).—Du. *leeman*, lit. 'joint man,' i.e. jointed figure; where *lee* is for *lede-*, in compounds (Sewel); from MDu. *ledi*, *lidt* (Hexham), Du. *lid*, a joint, limb, which is cognate with AS. *lið*, a limb, G. *g-lied*, Goth. *lithus*, a limb. See Franck. See Notes on E. Etym., p. 159.

LAYER, a stratum, row, tier, bed. (E.) '*Layer*, a bed or channel in a creek, where small oisters are thrown in to breed; among gardeners, it is taken for a young sprout covered with mould, in order to raise its kind;' Kersey, ed. 1715. *Lay-er* = that which lays, hence a mode of laying or propagating. It was extended to mean anything carefully laid in due order. See **Lay** (1). ¶ Distinct from *lair*, which is from the *intrans.* verb to *lie*. Der. *layer-ing*.

LAZAR, a leper. (F. — L. — Gk. — Heb.) ME. *lazar*, Chaucer, C. T. 242. — F. *Lazare*; see Littré. — L. *Lazarus.* — Gk. Λάζαρος, the name of the beggar in the parable; Luke, xvi. 20; contracted from the Heb. name *Eleazar.* — Heb. *El'āzār*, 'he whom God helps.' Der. *lazar-like*, Hamlet, i. 5. 72; *lazar-house*, Milton, P. L. xi. 479; also *lazar-etto*, from Ital. *lazzeretto*, a plague-hospital.

LAZY, slow, sluggish, slothful. (Low G.?) In Shak. Temp. iii. 1. 28; spelt *laesie* in Spenser, Shep. Kal. Feb., 9; July, 33; *lazie* in Minsheu, ed. 1627. We also find the verb to *laze*. '*S'endormir en sentinelle*, to sleep when he hath most cause to watch; *to laze it* when he hath most need to looke about him;' Cot.; this is a back formation from the adj. Spelt *laysy* in 1549 (N. E. D.). Of obscure origin; but prob. from Low G. *lasich*, variant of *losich*, languid, idle (Lübben); *läösig*, lazy (Danneil); Pomeran. *läsig*; Hamburgh *lösig*, slow, tired, lazy (Richey); cf. *laassam*, lazy (Bremen); Du. *leuzig*, idle (Calisch). Allied to **Loose.** The phonology offers difficulties; it does not appear to be connected with G. *lässig*, weary, lazy (though the sense corresponds); which is from G. *lass*, cognate with E. *late*. Of course we did not borrow words from High German in the 16th century, except in very rare and peculiar instances, such as *carouse*. Der. *lazi-ly*, *lazi-ness*.

LEA (1), **LEY, LAY,** a tract of open ground. (E.) 'On the watry *lea*,' i.e. plain; Spenser, F. Q. iv. 2. 16. Often spelt *ley, leigh*, in E. place-names, as in *Brom-ley, Haw-ley, Had-leigh*. 'Thy rich leas;' Tempest, v. 1. 60. AS. *lēah, lēa*, gen. case *lēages*, also *lēage*; see Thorpe, Diplomatarium Ævi Saxonici, p. 109, l. 8, p. 292, l. 4; also p. 526, where the place-name *Hǽd-lēah* (Hadleigh) occurs; also p. 658. β. Just as AS. *flēah* (= E. *flea*) is cognate with G. *floh*, so *lea* is cognate with prov. G. *loh*, a morass, bog, wood, forest (Flügel), which also appears in place-names, such as *Hohen-lohe*, i.e. high leas. So also we find the Low G. *loge*, which in place-names near Bremen signifies a low-lying tract, a grassy plain; Bremen Wörterb. iii. 80. So also *Water-loo* = water-lea. Teut. types *lauhoz*, m., *lauhā*, f. Further cognates occur in Lithuanian *laukas*, an open field (Nesselmann); L. *lūcus*, a grove, glade, open space in a wood (?); Skt. *lōka-s*, a region; Idg. type *louqos*. Orig. sense 'a clearing, cleared land.' Allied to **Lucid.** Brugmann, i. § 221. ¶ No connexion whatever with *lay* (1); but see below.

LEA (2), **LEY, LAY,** fallow land, arable land under grass, pasture-land. (E.) Often very difficult to distinguish from **Lea** (1). '*Leys*, to falowe or to sowe upon;' Fitzherbert, Husbandry, § 8. '*Lay*, londe not telyd;' Prompt. Parv. Short for *ley-land*, from *ley*, adj. 'Thi lond that lith *leie*;' Gamelyn, l. 161. AS. *lǣge*; as in *lǣh-hrycg*, 'lea rig;' Birch, Cart. Saxon. iii. 96. From *lǣg-*, 3rd stem of *licgan*, to lie; see **Lie** (1). Cf. Icel. *-lǽgr*, as in *gras-lǽgr*, lying in the grass. See N. E. D.

LEAD (1), to bring, conduct, guide, precede, direct, allure. (E.) ME. *leden*, pt. t. *ladde, ledde*, pp. *lad, led*; Chaucer, C. T. 4777, 4862, 5066 (B 357, 442, 646). AS. *lǣdan*, pt. t. *lǣdde*, pp. *lǣded*; Grein, ii. 161; lit. 'to show the way.' — AS. *lād*, a way, path; Grein, ii. 150. — AS. *līðan*, strong verb, to travel, go; Grein, ii. 183; of which *lǣdan* may be regarded as the causal form. + Icel. *leiða*, to lead, from *leið*, a way; which from *līða*, to go, pass, move along; Swed. *leda*, to lead, from *led*, a way, course; which from *lida*, to pass, go on; Dan. *lede*, to lead, from *led*, a gate; which from *lide*, to glide on; G. *leiten*, to lead; causal of OHG. *lîdan*, to go, go away, undergo, endure, suffer = mod. G. *leiden*, to suffer; cf. G. *begleiten* (= *be-geleiten*), to accompany, go on the way with. Cf. Du. *leiden*, to lead. β. Teut. type *laidjan-*; from *laith*, 2nd grade of *leithan-*, to travel, as in AS. *līðan*, Goth. *ga-leithan*, to go (pt. t. *ga-laith*, pp. *ga-lithans*). Der. *lead*, sb., *lead-er*, *lead-er-ship*, *lead-ing-strings*. And see *lode, load*.

LEAD (2), a well-known metal. (E.) ME. *leed, led*; dat. *lede*, Chaucer, Ho. of Fame, iii. 341; P. Plowman, B. v. 600; cf. Havelok, 924. — AS. *lēad*; Grein, ii. 168. + Du. *lood*, lead, a plummet; M. Low G. *lōd* (whence Swed. *lod*, a weight, plummet; Dan. *lod*, a weight, plummet); G. *loth*, a plummet, bullet; MHG. *lôt*, lead. Teut. type *laudom*, neut. Cognate with OIrish *luaidhe*, Gael. *luaidh*, lead (Macbain). Der. *lead-en*, ME. *leden*, Chaucer, C. T. 16196 (G 728), with suffix as in *gold-en*; *lead-pencil*; also *lead*, vb., *lead-ed*.

LEAF, part of a plant, two pages of a book. (E.) ME. *leef, lef*, pl. *leues* (= *leves*); Chaucer, C. T. 1840 (A 1838). AS. *lēaf*, pl. *lēaf*; Grein, ii. 168. OFries. *lāf.* + OSax. *lōf*; Du. *loof*, foliage; Swed. *löf*; Dan. *löv*, foliage; Goth. *laufs*, pl. *laubōs*; OHG. *laup*, MHG. *loup*, a leaf; OHG. *laup*, MHG. *loup*, leaves, G. *laub*, leaves,

foliage. β. All from Teut. types *lauðom*, n., or *lauðoz*, m. Further allied to Russ. *lupite*, to peel, OSlav. *lupiti*, Lithuanian *lùpti*, to strip. Der. *leaf-age* (made in imitation of *foli-age*), *leaf-less, leaf-let, leav-ed, leaf-y* (also *leavy*, i.e. *leav-y*, in ed. 1623 of Shak. Macb. v. 6. 1), *leaf-i-ness, inter-leave.*

LEAGUE (1), a bond, alliance, confederacy. (F. — Ital. — L.) In Shak. Mer. Wives, iii. 2. 25. Spelt *lyge* in G. Douglas, tr. of Virgil, bk. iii. ch. 7, l. 63. — F. *ligue*, 'a league or confederacy;' Cot. — Ital. *liga*, variant of *lega*, 'a league, confederacie;' Florio; Late L. *liga* (sometimes *lega*), a league, confederacy. — L. *ligāre*, to clasp, bind, fasten, tie, ratify an agreement. See **Ligament.** Der. *league*, verb, Oth. ii. 3. 218; cf. '*se liguer l'un à l'autre*, to make a league;' Cot. And see *ligature.*

LEAGUE (2), a distance of about three miles. (Prov. — L. — C.) The distance varied. 'A *league* or myle;' Levins, ed. 1570. Cotgrave, s. v. *lieue*, notes that German or long leagues are about 4 miles long, those of Languedoc, about 3 miles, and Italian or short leagues are about 1 mile. 'A hundred *leages* fro the place;' Berners, tr. of Froissart, Chron. vol. i. c. 81. 'The space of iii *leges*;' Gesta Romanorum, c. 78; p. 397. — Prov. *legua*; OF. *legue*, a league (Godefroy, Supp., s. v. *lieue*); Bordeaux *lègue* (Mistral); but the usual OF. form was *liue*; mod. F. *lieue.* Cf. Gascon *lega*; mod. Prov. *lego*; Ital. *lega* (Florio); Span. *legua.* — Low L. *lēga*, which occurs A. D. 1217, Ducange; another form being *leuca*, which is the more original; L. *leuca* (more correctly *leuga*), a Gallic mile of 1500 Roman paces; a word of Celtic origin. β. The Celtic word remains in Bret. *leō* or *lev*, a league; in the district of Vannes, *leu*. From Celtic type *leugā*; Stokes-Fick, p. 244. Observe that the F. form from which the E. word is derived is a *Southern* F. or Provençal form; and the E. league of 3 miles coincides, as to length, with that of Languedoc. See Phil. Soc. Trans. 1903, p. 154. Der. *seven-leagu-ed.*

LEAGUER, a camp. (Du.) In All's Well, iii. 6. 27. — Du. *leger*, a lair; also, a camp, army. See **Beleaguer.** Doublet, *lair.*

LEAK, to ooze through a chink. (Scand.) ME. *leken.* 'That humoure oute may *leke*' = that the moisture may leak out; Palladius on Husbandry, ed. Lodge, b. vi. l. 33. — Icel. *leka* (pt. t. *lak*), to drip, dribble, leak as a ship. Cf. Swed. *läcka*; Dan. *lække*; Du. *lekken*, to leak, drop; G. *lecken*, to leak, run, trickle; AS. *leccan*, to wet, to moisten; Ps. vi. 6 (ed. Spelman); all weak verbs from the same root. Teut. type *lekan-*, pt. t. *lak*, pp. *lekanoz.* See **Lack.** Cf. also AS. *hlec*, leaky; Westphal. *lek*, leaky. + Irish and Gael. *leagh*, to melt; W. *llaith*, moist; base *leg.* Der. *leak*, sb., from Icel. *leki*, a leak; *leak-y*, Temp. i. 1. 51; *leak-i-ness*; also *leak-age*, a late word, with F. suffix -*age* (= L. -*āticum*). Also *lack* (1), *lack* (2).

LEAL, loyal, true. (F. — L.) Spelt *leale* in Levins, ed. 1570. A Northern word; in Burns, Halloween, st. 3. ME. *lel*; 'And be *lel* to the lord;' Will. of Palerne, l. 5119. — AF. *leal*; see Vie de St. Auban, ed. Atkinson; OF. *leel*, mod. F. *loyal.* See further under **Loyal,** of which it is a doublet.

LEAN (1), to incline, bend, stoop. (E.) ME. *lenen*, P. Plowman, B. prol. 9, xviii. 5. The trans. and intrans. forms are now alike; properly, the intrans. form is the more primitive, and the mod. E. verb may have arisen from this form only, as the causal form was rare. AS. *hleonian, hlinian*, intrans. weak verb, to lean, Grein, i. 85; whence *hleonian*, to make to lean, id. i. 81. + OSax. *hlinōn*, intrans. form; OHG. *hlinēn*, MHG. *lenen*, G. *lehnen*, intrans. form. All from Teut. root *hlei-*, Idg. √KLEI; whence L. *clīnāre*, obsolete, occurring in *inclināre*; see **Incline.** Gk. κλίνειν (with long ι), to make to bend, cause to lean. See **Clinical.** From the same root, *in-cline, de-cline, re-cline, en-cline, ac-cliv-i-ty, de-cliv-i-ty.*

LEAN (2), slender, not fat, frail, thin. (E.) ME. *lene* (two syllables). 'As *lenè* was his hors as is a rake;' Chaucer, C. T. 289. AS. *hlǣne*, lean; used of Pharaoh's lean kine; Gen. xli. 3. + Low G. *leen*, lean. β. Perhaps the orig. sense was leaning, bending, stooping; hence weak, thin, poor. Cf. L. *dēclīuis*, bending down, declining; *ætāte dēclīuis*, in the decline of life; OFries. *lānig*, yielding, weak; OIrish *clóen*, sloping, bad. See **Lean** (1). ☞ The occurrence of the initial *h* in AS. *hlǣne* at once separates it from AS. *lǣne*, adj. transitory, which is connected with *lend* and *loan.* Der. *lean-ly, lean-ness.*

LEAP, to bound, spring, jump. (E.) ME. *lepen*, pt. t. *leep, lep*, pp. *lopen*; Chaucer, C. T. 4376, 2689 (A 4378, 2687); P. Plowman, B. v. 198. AS. *hlēapan*, to run, leap, spring; a strong verb; pt. t. *hlēop*, pp. *gehlēapen*; Grein, ii. 82, and i. 24 (s. v. *āhlēapan*). OFries. *hlāpa* (cf. prov. E. *lope*). + OSax. *hlōpan*, to run; in comp. *āhlōpan*; Du. *loopen*, to run, flow; pt. t. *liep*; pp. *geloopen*; Icel. *hlaupa*, to leap, jump, run; pt. t. *hljóp*, pp. *hlaupinn*; Dan. *löbe*, to run; Swed. *löpa*, to run; Goth. *-hlaupan*, to leap, only in comp. *us-hlaupan*; pt. t. *hlaihlaup* (reduplicated); OHG. *hlaufan*, MHG. *loufen*, G. *laufen* (pt. t. *lief*, pp. *gelaufen*), to run. β. All from Teut. type *hlaupan-*, pt. t. *hle-hlaup*, to leap, run. Der. *leap*, sb., AS. *hlyp*, Grein, ii. 89.

cognate with Icel. *hlaup*, a leap, G. *lauf*, a course. Also *leap-frog*; *leap-year*, ME. *lepeƷeer*, Mandeville's Travels, p. 77.

LEARN, to acquire knowledge of. (E.) ME. *lernen*, Chaucer, C. T. 310 (A 308). AS. *leornian*, to learn; Grein, ii. 179.+OSax. *linōn*, to learn, contracted form of **liznōn*; OHG. *lirnēn*, G. *lernen*. Teut. type **liznōjan-*; in which LIS is the base, and *-n-* is a formative element used in certain verbs; see Streitberg, § 208. Cf. Goth. *full-nan*, to become full, *and-bund-nan*, to become unbound, *af-lif-nan*, to be left remaining, *ga-hail-nan*, to become whole, *ga-wak-nan*, to become awake. β. From Teut. type **liz(a)noz*, pp. of **leisan-*, to trace out, of which the pt. t. *lais* occurs in Gothic with the sense 'I know,' i. e. I have found out. Hence also Teut. **laizjan-*, to teach, as in AS. *lǽran*, ME. *lēren*, G. *lehren*, to teach; and Teut. **laizā*, sb., as in AS. *lār*, E. *lore*. See **Last** (2), **Lore**. Brugmann, i. § 903 (c). **Der.** *learn-ed*, orig. merely the pp. of the verb; *learn-ed-ly*, *learn-ed-ness*, *learn-er*, *learn-ing*.

LEASE (1), to let tenements for a term of years. (F.–L.) 'To *lease* or *let leas*, locare, dimittere; the *lease*, *letting*, locatio, dimissio;' Levins, ed. 1570. An AF. law term; see Blount's Nomolexicon, ed. 1691.–AF. *lesser*, Year-book of Edw. I (1292–3), p. 43; F. *laisser*, 'to leave, relinquish;' Cot. [Cf. Ital. *lasciare*, to quit.] *Laisser* is still used in the sense 'to part with' or 'let go' at a fixed price; see Littré. [The AF. form *lesser* at once accounts for E. *less-or*, *less-ee*.]–L. *laxāre*, to slacken, let go.–L. *laxus*, lax, slack; see **Lax**. ¶ Not related to G. *lassen*, which=E. *let*; see **Let** (1). **Der.** *lease-hold*; also *less-or* (spelt *leassor* in Blount's Nomolexicon), signifying 'one who leases,' with suffix *-or* of the agent; *less-ee* (spelt *leassee* in Blount), signifying 'one to whom a lease is granted,' with suffix *-ee* in place of OF. *-é* (<L. *-ātus*), the pp. ending, with a passive sense.

LEASE (2), to glean. (E.) In Dryden, tr. of Theocritus, Idyl 3, l. 72. ME. *lesen*, P. Plowman, B. vi. 68. AS. *lesan*, to glean (Grein).+Du. *lezen*, to gather, read; Icel. *lesa*, to glean, to read; G. *lesen*; Goth. *lisan*, to gather; pt. t. *las*. Teut. type **lesan-*, pt. t. **las*; allied to Lith. *lèsti*, to pick up with the bill.

LEASE (3), a pasture, meadow-land. (E.) ME. *lese*, pasture, Will. of Palerne, 175. AS. *lǽs*, a pasture; gen., dat., acc. *lǽswe*. Teut. type *lǽswā*, fem. Prob. connected with *lǽt-an*, to let alone; so that the sense was 'land not tilled.' See N. E. D. **Doublet**, prov. E. *leasow*; see E. D. D. ¶ Often confused with **Lea** (1).

LEASH, a thong by which a hawk or hound is held; a brace and a half. (F.–L.) 1. ME. *lees*, *leese*, *leece*. 'Alle they renne in o *lees*'=they all run in one leash; Chaucer, C. T. Pers. Tale, De Septem Peccatis (Six-text, Group I, 387). And see Prompt. Parv. p. 291.–OF. *lesse* (mod. F. *laisse*), 'a leash, to hold a dog in;' Cot. Cot. also gives: '*Laisse*, the same as *Lesse*, also, a leash of hounds, &c.' Cf. Ital. *lascio*, a leash, band; also a legacy, will.–Late L. *laxa*, a lease, thong; lit. a loose rope; cf. '*Laxa*, a lees;' Voc. 592. 5.–L. *laxa*, fem. of *laxus*, loose, lax; see **Lax**. 2. The sense of 'three' arose from the application of the word to the number usually leashed together (Richardson); see Shak. 1 Henry IV, ii. 4. 7. 'A Brace of grehoundis, of *ij*; a *Lece* of Grehoundis, of *iij*;' Book of St. Alban's, fol. f 6, col. 2. **Der.** *leash*, verb, Hen. V, prol. 7.

LEASING, falsehood, lying. (E.) In Ps. iv. 2, v. 6; A. V. ME. *lesynge*, *lesinge*; Chaucer, C. T. 1929 (A 1927). AS. *lēasing*, *lēasung*, a falsehood; Grein, ii. 179; from AS. *lēasian*, to lie.–AS. *lēas*, false, orig. empty; the same word with AS. *lēas*, loose. Cf. Icel. *lausung*, falsehood; Du. *loos*, false; Goth. *laus*, empty, vain; *lausa-waurds*, loose-worded, speaking loose and random words, Tit. i. 10. See **Loose**.

LEAST; see under **Less**.

LEAT, a duct, open water-course. (E.) See *Leat* in E. D. D. From AS. *ge-lǽt*, outlet, course; 'oþ þera strǽta gelǽto,' to the cross-roads; Earle, Land Charters, p. 292, l. 4; also *wæter-gelǽt*, a conduit; Voc. 211. 13.–AS. *lǽtan*, to let, allow, let out; see **Let** (1). Cf. WFlem. *laat*, a leat; De Bo.

LEATHER, the prepared skin of an animal. (E.) ME. *lether*, Chaucer, C. T. 3250. AS. *leðer*, in comp. *geweald-leðer*, lit. 'wield-leather,' i. e. a bridle; Grein, i. 478. '*Bulgæ*, leþer-coddas,' i. e. leathern bags; Ælfric's Gloss., in Voc. 117. 3.+Du. *leder*; Icel. *leðr*; Dan. *læder*; Swed. *läder*; G. *leder*. Teut. type **lethrom*, neut; Idg. type **letrom*, as in OIrish *lethar*, W. *lledr*. Stokes-Fick, p. 248. **Der.** *leather-n*, ME. *letheren*, P. Plowman, B. v. 192, formed with suffix *-en*, as in *gold-en*; also *leather-y*.

LEAVE (1), to quit, abandon, forsake. (E.) ME. *leuen* (*u* = *v*), pt. t. *lafte*, *lefte*, pp. *laft*, *left*; Chaucer, C. T. 8126, 14204, 10500 (E 250, B 3388, F 186). AS. *lǽfan*, Grein, ii. 162. The lit. sense is 'to leave a heritage,' to leave behind one. – AS. *lāf*, a heritage, residue, remnant. OFries. *lēva*, to leave.+Icel. *leifa*, to leave, leave a heritage; from *leif*, a leaving, patrimony. β. The Goth. form is *laibjan*, only in comp. *bi-laibjan*, to leave behind; from the sb. *laiba*, a remnant. Teut. type **laibjan-*, to leave; from **laib-*, as in AS. *lāf*, Icel. *leif*, Goth. *laiba*, above. And **laib-* is the 2nd stem of Teut. *leiðan-*, to remain, as in AS. *be-līfan*, G. *b-leiben* from OHG. *bi-līban*. From the Idg. √LEIP, whence Gk. λίπ-αρής, persistent; the weaker grade **lip* is in Skt. *lip*, to smear, Gk. λίπ-ος, grease, Russ. *lip-kii*, sticky, Lith. *lip-ti*, to adhere to. See **Live**. Brugmann, i. § 87. ¶ The Gk. λείπειν answers to L. *linquere*, and to Goth. *leihwan*, G. *leihen*, to lend (orig. to let go). See **Loan**. **Der.** *leav-ings*.

LEAVE (2), permission, farewell. (E.) In the phr. 'to take *leave*,' the word is the same as *leave*, permission. The orig. sense was, probably, 'to take permission to go,' hence, 'to take a formal farewell.' Cf. 'to give leave.' We may, then, remember that the sb. is entirely independent of the verb above. ME. *leue*, *leaue* (with *u*=*v*). 'By your *leue*'=with your permission; Chaucer, C. T. 13377. 'But taketh his *leue*'=but takes his leave; id. 1219. AS. *lēaf*, permission; Grein, ii. 168; whence was formed the verb *lȳfan* (OAnglian *lēfan*), to permit=ME. *lēuen*, to permit, grant (now obsolete), one of the most troublesome words in old authors, as it is frequently confounded with ME. *lenen*, to lend, and misprinted accordingly; see note to Chaucer's Prioress's Tale, ed. Skeat, l. 1873. The orig. sense of *leave* is 'that which is acceptable or pleasing,' or simply 'pleasure;' and the Teut. type is **laubā*, fem.; from **lauð-*, 2nd grade of Teut. root **leuð*, whence AS. *lēof*, pleasing, lief, dear; see **Lief**.+Du. *-lof*, only in the comp. *oor-lof*, permission, *ver-lof*, leave; cf. also Icel. *leyfi*, leave; *leyfa*, to permit; *lofan*, permission; G. *ur-laub*, leave, furlough; *ver-laub*, leave, permission; *er-lauben*, to permit. See **Furlough** and **Love**.

LEAVEN, the ferment which makes dough rise. (F.–L.) ME. *leuain*, *leuein* (with *u* for *v*). 'He is the *leuein* of the bred' [bread]; Gower, C. A. i. 294; bk. iii. 446; cf. Prompt. Parv. p. 300.–F. *levain*, 'leaven;' Cot.–L. *leuāmen*, an alleviation, mitigation; but used (here) in the orig. sense of 'that which raises.' [Ducange records the sense of 'leaven' for Late L. *leuāmentum*, a parallel form to *leuāmen*.]–L. *leuāre*, to raise. See **Lever**. Similarly, Ital. *lievito*, leaven, is from Ital. *lievare*, to raise (<L. *leuāre*). **Der.** *leaven*, verb.

LECHER, a man addicted to lewdness. (F.–G.) In early use. ME. *lechur*, *lechour*; O. Eng. Homilies, ed. Morris, i. 53, l. 27; Ancren Riwle, p. 216; Rob. of Glouc. p. 119; l. 2529.–OF. *lecheor* (Godefroy), *lecheur* (Cotgrave), lit. one who licks up.–OF. *lechier*, to lick, to live in gluttony (Godefroy), mod. F. *lécher*, to lick.–OHG. *lecchōn*, G. *lecken*, to lick; cognate with E. **Lick**, q.v. **Der.** *lecher-ous*, P. Plowman, C. ii. 25; *lecher-ous-ly*, *lecher-ous-ness*; *lecher-y*, ME. *lecherie*, *leccherie*, Hali Meidenhad, ed. Cockayne, p. 11, l. 3. Cf. *lickerish*.

LECTERN, LECTURN, a reading-desk. (F.–L.) '*Leterone*, *lectorne*, *lectrone*, *lectrun*, deske, *Lectrinum*;' Prompt. Parv. p. 299. Spelt *lecterne* in Minsheu, ed. 1627. Adapted from OF. *letrun*, a lectern (Godefroy), with *c* added from the Late L. form.–Late L. *lectrum*, a reading-desk or pulpit (attributed to Isidore of Seville). For **leg-trum*; from *leg-ere*, to read (below). [Cf. L. *mulc-trum*, a milking-pail; from *mulg-ēre*, to milk.] See **Legend**. Some forms, as OF. *leitrin*, F. *lutrin*, were influenced by Late L. *lectrīnum*, by-form of *lectrum*. Hence *lectryne*, a lectern; Trevisa, tr. of Higden, vi. 447.

LECTION, a reading, portion to be read. (F.–L.) 'Other copies and various *lections*;' Milton, A Defence of the People of England. (R.)–OF. *lection*, a reading, a lesson (Godefroy).–L. *lectiōnem*, acc. of *lectio*, a reading; cf. L. *lectus*, pp. of *legere*, to gather, read; see **Legend**. **Der.** *lection-ary*; and see below. **Doublet**, *lesson*.

LECTURE, a discourse, formal reproof. (F.–L.) 'Wherof oure present *lecture* speaketh;' Sir T. More, p. 1301 c.–F. *lecture*, 'a lecture, a reading;' Cot.–Late L. *lectūra*, a commentary; cf. *lectus*, pp. of *legere*, to read; see **Legend**. **Der.** *lecture*, verb, *lectur-er*, *lecture-ship*.

LEDGE, a slight shelf, ridge, small moulding. (E.) Palsgrave has: '*Ledge* of a shelfe, *apuy*,' i. e. support; also: '*Ledge* of a dore, *barre*.' See *Legge* in Prompt. Parv. In Norfolk, a bar of a gate, or stile, of a chair, table, &c., is termed a *ledge*, according to Forby. A door made of three or four upright boards, fastened by cross-pieces, is called a *ledger-door*; a *ledger* is a horizontal slab of stone, a horizontal bar, and is also called a *ligger* (Halliwell). A *ligger* is 'a lier,' that which lies, from AS. *licgan*, to lie; and *ledge* is from a like source, as it was evidently formed from ME. *leggen* [*gg*=*dj*], to lay, the causal of *liggen*, AS. *licgan* (above). So also MHG. *lekke*, *legge*, a layer, stratum, from OHG. *lekkan*, to lay. We may also note Norw. *lega*, a lying, couch, lair, bed, a support upon which anything rests. See **Lay** (1), **Lie** (1).

LEDGER, a book in which a summary of accounts is preserved. (E.) Formerly called a *ledger-book*; Kersey, ed. 1715. Spelt *lidger* in 1538, with reference to a bible that was always to lie in the same place (N. E. D.). The word had other meanings, most of them involving the sense of 'lying still.' Thus a *ledger* was a horizontal slab of stone (Halliwell); *leger* ambassadors were such as *remained* for some time at a foreign court; see *leiger* in Shak. Meas. iii. 1. 59. A *ledger-bait* was a bait that was 'fixed or made to rest in one certain place;' I. Walton, Angler, pt. i. c. 8. 'A rusty musket, which had lien long *leger* in his shop;' Fuller's Worthies, London (R.). Formed, like *ledge* above, from ME. *leggen* [*gg* = *dj*], to lay, or from ME. *liggen* [*gg* = *dj*], to lie; which were much confused. Cf. prov. E. *lidge*, to lie (E. D.D.). A similar formation occurs in Du. *legger*, 'one that lyes down' (Sewel); hence mod. Du. *legger*, the nether mill-stone [answering to E. *ledger*, a horizontal slab of stone]; MDu. *ligger*, 'a dayly Booke kept for ones use,' i. e. a ledger (Hexham); MDu. *leggen*, to lie, once in common use, though the true form is *liggen*, and the proper sense of *leggen* is to lay. We know how these words are constantly confused in English. 'Te bed *leggen*, to ly a-bed. Neêr *leggen*, to lie down. Waar *legt* hy t'huys, where does he ly, or lodge?' Sewel. See **Lie** (1). ¶ Thus a *ledger-book* is one that lies always ready in one place. The etymology of the word was ill-understood, and it was confused with OF. *legier*, light; see **Ledger-line**. Hence it was sometimes spelt *ligier* (see Richardson); and Howell goes so far as to use a *leger-book* in the sense of a portable memorandum-book, apparently from thus mistaking the true sense. 'Some do use to have a small *leger-booke* fairely bound up table-book-wise,' i.e. like a memorandum-book; Howell, Forraine Travell, sect. iv, ed. Arber, p. 27. N.B. The earliest quotation in the N. E. D. is dated 1481, with reference to 'a large copy of the breviary;' but Wylie, Hist. Henry IV, iv. 198, cites '19 portos, 3 *liggers*' in 1401.

LEDGER-LINE, in music; one of the short lines added above or below the stave to accommodate notes lying beyond the usual five lines. (Hybrid; E. *and* L.) Not in Todd's Johnson. Spelt *leger-line* in Ash's Dict., 1775. 'You add a line or two to the five lines, . . . those lines . . . being called *Ledger-lines*;' Playford, Skill of Music, i. 6; ed. 1700 (N. E. D.). So called from lying flat; cf. *ledger*, a horizontal timber (N. E. D.). ¶ Not from F. *léger*, OF. *legier*, light; the F. name is *ligne additionnelle*.

LEE, a sheltered place, shelter; part of a ship away from the wind. (Scand.) ME. *lee*, shelter. 'We lurked vndyr *lee*,' we lay hid under shelter; Mort Arthure, ed. Brock, l. 1446. A-*lee* = on the lee; Deposition of Rich. II., ed. Skeat, iv. 74. The word and its use are perhaps both Scand.; the E. word is *lew*, a shelter, still in use provincially (E. D.D.), though *lee* also occurs. Prob. from Icel. *hlé*, lee, used only by seamen; *sigla ā hlé*, to stand to leeward; *hlé-borð*, the lee-side; Dan. *læ*; Swed. *lä*.+Du. *lij*. Cognate with AS. *hléo*, *hleow*, a covering, protection, shelter; Grein, ii. 82; whence prov. E. *lew*, a shelter, also, as adj., warm; see **Lew.** β. From AS. *hléo* was formed the sb. *hléoð*, *hleowð*, a shelter (Grein, ii. 83); the same word as prov. E. *lewth*, shelter, warmth. With these forms we may compare Icel. *hlý*, warmth, *hlær*, *hlýr*, warm, *hlýja*, to shelter. All from a Teut. type *hlewoz*, adj. warm. ¶ Note the pronunciation *lew-ard*, for *lee-ward*, due to E. *lew*. Der. *lee-shore*, *lee-side*, *lee-ward*. Also *lee-way*. Also allied to MDu. *lywaard*, lee-ward (Sewel); the mod. Du. form being *lijwaarts*.

LEECH (1), a physician. (E.) In Shak. Timon, v. 4. 84. ME. *leche*, Chaucer, C. T. 15524 (G 56). AS. *læce*, a physician; Matt. ix. 12; Lu. iv. 23. Connected with AS. *lācnian*, to heal; Grein, ii. 150. Cf. Icel. *læknir*, a physician; *lækna*, to cure, heal; Dan. *læge*, a physician; *læge*, to heal; Swed. *läkare*, a physician; from *läka*, to heal; Goth. *leikeis*, *lēkeis*, a physician, Lu. iv. 23; connected with *leikinon*, *lēkinon*, to heal; OHG. *lāhhi*, *lāchi*, a physician; connected with OHG. *lāhhinon*, to heal, MHG. *lāchenen*, to employ remedies, MHG. *lāchen*, a remedy. β. The AS. *læce*, Dan. *læge*, Goth. *lēkeis*, are all from a Teut. type *lækjoz*, a healer; from Idg. base *lēg-*. γ. We may further compare Irish and Gael. *leigh*, OIrish *liaig*, a physician.

LEECH (2), a blood-sucking worm. (E.) ME. *leche*, Prompt. Parv. p. 291. AS. *læce*; we find 'Sanguisuga, vel hirudo, *læce*' in Ælfric's Gloss., Nomina Insectorum; Voc. 121. 36. Lit. 'the healer;' and the same word as the above.

LEECH (3), **LEACH**, the border or edge of a sail at the sides. (Scand.) '*Leech*, the edge of a sail, the goring;' Ash's Dict., ed. 1775. 'The *leetch* of a sail, vox nautica;' Skinner, ed. 1671. '*Penne d'une voile*, the *leech* of a saile;' Cot. Ultimately allied to Icel. *lik*, a leech-line; Swed. *lik*, a bolt-rope, *stående liken*, the leeches; Dan. *lig*, a bolt-rope, *staaende lig*, a leech.+MDu. *lyken*, a bolt-rope (Sewel); Du. *lijk* (see Franck).

LEEK, a kind of onion. (E.) ME. *leek*, Chaucer, C. T. 3877 (A 3879); P. Plowman, B. v. 82. AS. *léac*; Voc. 295. 22.+Du. *look*; Icel. *laukr*; Dan. *lög*; Swed. *lök*; G. *lauch*. Teut. types *laukoz*, m.; *laukom*, n. Root unknown; perhaps from Teut. type *lauk*, as in AS. *léac*, pt. t. of *lúcan*, to weed, to pull up. Der. *gar-lic*, *char-lock*, *hem-lock*.

LEER, to cast side-glances. (E.) 'I *leare* or *lere*, as a dogge dothe underneth a dore;' Palsgrave. Cf. Shak. L. L. L. v. 2. 480, 2 Hen. IV. v. 5. 7; Troil. v. 1. 97. The verb is a later development from the ME. *lere*, meaning the cheek, also the face, complexion, mien. 'A loveli lady of *lere*' = a lady of lovely mien; P. Plowman, B. i. 3. It was orig. almost always used in a good sense, but in Skelton we find it otherwise in two passages. 'Her lothely *lere* Is nothynge clere, But vgly of chere' = her loathsome look is not at all clear, but ugly of aspect; Elynoure Rummynge, l. 12. 'Your lothesum *lere* to loke on;' 2nd Poem against Garnesche, l. 5. Shakespeare has it in two senses; (1) the complexion, aspect, As You Like It, iv. 1. 67, Titus Andron. iv. 2. 119; (2) a winning look, Merry Wives, i. 3. 50. At a later period it is generally used in a sinister sense.—AS. *hléor*, the cheek; hence the face, look, Grein, ii. 85.+OSax. *hlior*, the cheek; MDu. *lier* (Oudemans); Icel. *hlýr*, pl. the cheeks. Der. *leer*, sb., a side-glance.

LEES, dregs of wine. (F.) In A. V.-Isa. xxv. 6, Jer. xlviii. 11. 'Verily the *lies* of wine are so strong;' Holland, tr. of Pliny, b. xxiii. c. 2. ME. *lyes*, pl.; Chaucer, House of Fame, iii. 1040. Gower has *lie*, sing., sediment; Conf. Amant. i. 309; bk. iii. 895. A pl. sb., from a sing. not much used.—F. *lie*, 'the lees, dregs, grounds, thick substance that settles in the bottome of liquor;' Cot. Of unknown origin; the Late L. form is *lia*; the phr. 'fecla sive *lias* uini' occurs in a MS. of the 10th century (Littré). Moncaut has Gascon *lio*, 'lie de vin.' Perhaps Celtic; cf. Bret. *lec'hid*, sediment, W. *llaid*, mire. Körting, § 5574; Thurneysen, p. 66.

LEET, a special court of record held by certain lords of manors. (E.?) 'Amercyn in a corte or *lete*;' Prompt. Parv. Spelt *lēta* in Law Latin (Cowell); and *lete* in AF., as in Stat. Realm, i. 342 (1353); Year-books of Edw. I., 1392, p. 297. *Lete* is perhaps the AF. spelling and adaptation of AS. *læð*; for which see **Lathe** (2). β. Or perhaps it was adapted from Icel. *leið*, which, according to Vigfusson, means precisely 'a leet.' γ. Or perhaps a particular use of *leat*, q.v. Cf. Low G. *gelaat*, G. *gelass*, room, space.

LEFT, a term applied to the (usually) weaker hand. (E.) ME. *left*, *lift*, *luft*. Spelt *left*, Chaucer, C. T. 2955 (A 2593); *lift*, Will. of Palerne, 2961; *luft*, P. Plowman, A. ii. 5; Layamon, 24461. Rare in AS., which has the term *winster* instead; see Grein, ii. 716. We do, however, find 'inanis, *left*,' in a Gloss (Mone, Quellen, i. 443), and the same MS. has *senne* for *synne* (sin); so that *left* is the Kentish form of *lyft*, with the sense of 'worthless' or 'weak;' cf. AS. *lyft-ādl*, palsy. NFriesic *leeft*, *leefter hond* (left hand); Outzen.+MDu. *luft*, left (Oudemans); Kilian also gives the form *lucht*. β. The *t* is a suffix; cf. EFries. *luf*, weak. All from Teut. base *luð-*; cf. Du. *lubben*, to geld. See **Lib.** (So H. Sweet; in Anglia, iii. 155; 1880.) Der. *left-handed*, -*ness*.

LEG, one of the limbs by which animals walk, a slender support. (Scand.) ME. *leg* (pl. *legges*), Chaucer, C. T. 593 (A 591); Layamon, l. 1876 (later text, the earlier text has *sconken* = shanks).—Icel. *leggr*, a leg, hollow bone, stem of a tree, shaft of a spear; Dan. *læg*, the calf of the leg; Swed. *lägg*, the calf or bone of the leg. Teut. type *lag-joz*. Cf. Icel. *hand-leggr* (lit. hand-stem), the fore-arm, *arm-leggr*, the upper arm; L. *lac-ertus*, the upper arm; Skt. *lak-uṭa-*, a cudgel (Macdonell). Der. *leg-less*, *legg-ings*.

LEGACY, a bequest of personal property. (F.—L.) ME. *legacie*, 'Hir *legacy* and lamentatioun;' Henrysoun, Complaint of Creseide, l. 597; Wyclif, 2 Cor. v. 20 (earlier version). Cf. MF. *legat*, 'a legacy;' Cot. The ME. *legacie* also meant 'office of a legate;' Trevisa, tr. of Higden, viii. 260.—OF. *legacie*, office of a legate (Godefroy).—Late L. *lēgātia* (Ducange).—L. *lēgātus*, a legate; see **Legate.** Cf. also L. *lēgātum*, a legacy, bequest; orig. neut. of pp. of L. *lēgāre*, to appoint, bequeath.—L. *lēg-*, stem of *lex*, law. See **Legal.** Der. *legacy-hunter*; also *legat-ee*, a barbarously formed word, coined by adding the F. suffix -*é* (= L. -*ātus*), denoting the pp., to the stem of L. *lēgāt-us*, pp. of *lēgāre*.

LEGAL, pertaining to the law. (F.—L.) In Minsheu's Dict., ed. 1627.—MF. *legal*, 'legall, lawful;' Cot.—L. *lēgālis*, legal.—L. *lēg-*, stem of *lex*, law. Allied to L. *legere*, Gk. λέγειν, to collect. Brugmann, i. § 134. (√LEG.) Doublets, *leal*, *loyal*. Der. *legal-ly*, *legal-ise*; *legal-i-ty*, from F. *legalité*, 'lawfulness' (Cot.), which from Late L. acc. *lēgālitātem*. And see *legacy*, *legate*, *legislator*, *legitimate*; *allege*, *delegate*, *relegate*, *college*, *colleague*, *privilege*, &c.

LEGATE, a commissioner, ambassador. (F.—L.) ME. *legate*, *legat*; Rob. of Glouc. p. 499; l. 10276; Layamon, l. 24501; AS. Chron. an. 1123 (Laud MS.).—OF. *legat*, 'a legat, the pope's ambassador;' Cot.—L. *lēgātus*, a legate, deputy; pp. of *lēgāre*, to appoint, send. ─ L. *lĕg-*, stem of *lex*, law. See **Legal**. Der. *legate-ship*; *legat-ion*, from MF. *legation*, 'a legateship' (Cot.), which from L. acc. *lĕgātiōnem*; also *legat-ine*, adj., Hen. VIII, iii. 2. 339.

LEGATEE; see under **Legacy**.

LEGEND, a marvellous or romantic story. (F. ─ L.) ME. *legende*, Chaucer, C. T. 3143 (A 3141); P. Plowman, C. xii. 206. ─ OF. *legende*, 'a legend, a writing, also the words that be about the edge of a piece of coyne;' Cot. ─ Late L. *lĕgenda*, as in *Aurea legenda* = the Golden Legend; fem. sing. from L. *lĕgenda*, neut. pl. of fut. pass. part. of *legere* (pp. *lectus*), to read, orig. to gather, collect.+ Gk. λέγειν, to collect, gather, speak, tell. β. From √LEG, to gather. Brugmann, i. § 134. Der. *legend-a-ry*; also (from L. *leg-ere*) *leg-ible*, *leg-ibl-y*, *leg-ible-ness*, *leg-i-bili-ty*; together with numerous other words such as *lection*, *lecture*, *legion*, *lesson*; *col-lect*, *coil* (1), *cull*, *di-lig-ent*, *e-leg-ant*, *e-lect*, *e-lig-ible*, *intel-lect*, *intel-lig-ent*, *neg-lect*, *neg-l-g-ent*, *re-col-lect*, *se-lect*, *pre-di-lect-ion*, *sacri-lege*, &c. Also (from Gk. λέγειν) *lexicon*, *dialect*, *ec-lect-ic*; *log-ic*, *log-arithm*, and the suffixes *-logue*, *-logy*; *syllogism*.

LEGERDEMAIN, sleight of hand. (F. ─ L.) 'And of *legier-demayne* the mysteries did know;' Spenser, F. Q. v. 9. 13. 'Perceiue theyr *leygier demaine*;' Sir T. More, Works, p. 813 g. Also in Lydgate, Dance of Macabre (The Tregetour). ─ OF. *legier de main*, lit. light of hand. The OF. *legier*, F. *léger*, light, slight, is from a Late L. type *leviārius*; from L. *leuis*, light; whence also Span. *ligero*, Ital. *leggiero*. The F. *de* is from L. *dē*, prep. The F. *main* is from L. *manum*, acc. of *manus*, the hand; see **Manual**.

LEGER-LINE, in music; see **Ledger-line**.

LEGIBLE, that can be read. (F. ─ L.) In Minsheu, ed. 1627. '*Legibylle*, legibilis;' Cath. Anglicum (1483). ─ OF. *legible*, 'legible, readable;' Cot. ─ L. *legibilis*, legible. ─ L. *legere*, to read; see **Legend**. Der. *legibl-y*, *legible-ness*, *legibil-i-ty*.

LEGION, a large body of soldiers. (F. ─ L.) In early use. ME. *legiun*, Layamon, 6024; later, *legioun*, *legion*. ─ OF. *legion*, 'a Roman legion;' Cot. ─ L. *legiōnem*, acc. of *legio*, a Roman legion, a body of troops of from 4200 to 6000 men. ─ L. *legere*, to gather, select, levy a body of men. See **Legend**. Der. *legion-ar-y*.

LEGISLATOR, a law-giver. (L.) In Bacon, Life of Henry VII, ed. Lumby, p. 69, l. 30. ─ L. *lēgis-lātor*, lit. proposer of a law. ─ L. *lēgis*, gen. case of *lex*, a law; and *lātor*, a proposer of a law, lit. a carrier, bearer, allied to *lātum*, to bear, used as supine of *ferre*, to bear, but from a different root. β. For L. *lex*, see **Legal**. L. *lātum* stands for *tlātum*, from √TEL, to lift; see **Tolerate**. Der. *legislat-ion*, *legislat-ive*, *legislat-ure*; hence was at last developed the verb to *legislate*. And see **Legist**.

LEGIST, one skilled in the laws. (F. ─ L.) 'A great iuryst and *legyst*;' Berners, tr. of Froissart, vol. ii. c. 210 (R.). ─ OF. *legiste*, in use in the 13th century; mod. F. *légiste*; Littré. ─ Late L. *lēgista*, a legist. ─ L. *lēg-*, stem of *lex*, law; with (Gk.) suffix *-ista*. See **Legal**.

LEGITIMATE, lawful, lawfully begotten, genuine, authorised. (L.) In Shak. K. John, i. 116. 'Without issu *legyttymat*;' Fabyan's Chron., ed. Ellis, p. 253. ─ Late L. *lēgitimātus*, pp. of *lēgitimāre*, to declare to be lawful. ─ L. *lēgitimus*, pertaining to law, legitimate; formed with suffix *-timus* from *lēgi-*, decl. stem of *lex*, a law; see **Legal**. Der. *legitimate-ly*, *legitimac-y*, *legitim-ist* (from *legitim-us*).

LEGUME, a pod. (F. ─ L.) A botanical term. In Todd's Johnson. Formerly, the L. *legumen* was used, as in Kersey's Dict., ed. 1715. ─ F. *légume*, pulse; in botany, a pod. ─ L. *legūmen*, pulse, bean-plant; applied to that which can be gathered or picked, as opposed to crops that must be cut. ─ L. *legere*, to gather; see **Legend**. Der. *legumin-ous*, from stem *legūmin-* (of *legūmen*).

LEISURE, freedom from employment, free time. (F. ─ L.) ME. *leyser*, *leysere*; Chaucer, Book of the Duchess, l. 172; Rob. of Brunne, tr. of Langtoft, p. 229, l. 1. ─ OF. *leisir* (Godefroy), later *loisir* (Cot.), leisure. The OF. *leisir* was orig. an infin. mood, signifying 'to be permitted;' Littré. ─ L. *licēre*, to be permitted. See **Licence**. Der. *leisure-ly*. ☞ We may note the bad spelling; it should be *leis-er*, *leis-ir*, or *lezir*; but is now mispronounced.

LEMAN, LEMMAN, a sweetheart, of either sex. (E.) In Shak. Merry Wives, iv. 2. 172; Tw. Nt. ii. 3. 26. ME. *lemman*, Havelok, 1283; older form *leofmon*, Ancren Riwle, p. 90, l. 14. From AS. *lēof*, dear; and *mann*, a man or woman. See **Lief** and **Man**.

LEMMA, in mathematics, an assumption. (L. ─ Gk.) In Kersey's Dict., ed. 1715. First in 1570. ─ L. *lĕmma*. ─ Gk. λῆμμα, a thing taken; in logic, a premiss taken for granted. ─ Gk. εἴ-λη-μμαι, perf. pass. of λαμβάνειν, to take; base λαβ-, for *σλαβ-; Brugmann, i. § 852.

LEMMING, LEMING, a kind of Norwegian rat. (Norwegian.) Described as 'the *leming* or Lapland marmot' in a translation of Buffon's Nat. Hist., London, 1792; cf. Goldsmith, Nat.

Hist., 1774, ii. 283. Not in Todd's Johnson. ─ Norweg. *lemende*; also used in many various forms, as *læmende*, *limende*, *lemende*, *lömende*, *lemming*, *lemelde*, &c.; see Aasen; Swed. *lemel*; Icel. *lōmundr*; Swed. dial. *lemming*. There is also, according to Ihre (Lexicon Lapponicum), a Lapp form, *luomek*. β. Origin obscure; Aasen thinks that the word means 'laming,' i.e. spoiling, very destructive, and connects it with Norweg. *lemja*, to palsy, strike, beat; but this is 'popular etymology.' Perhaps it is of Lapp origin, after all.

LEMNISCATE, one of certain closed curves, resembling the figure 8. (L. ─ Gk.) First in 1781. From L. *lēmniscātus*, adorned with a ribbon; from the ribbon-like form. ─ L. *lēmniscus*, a pendent ribbon. ─ Gk. λημνίσκος, a fillet. Said to be from Gk. λῆνος, wool; see **Wool**.

LEMON, an ovate fruit, with acid pulp. (F. ─ Late L. ─ Pers. ─ Malay.) Formerly *limon*; as in Levins, ed. 1570; *lymon*, Lydgate, Minor Poems, p. 15. ─ F. *limon*, 'a lemmon;' Cot. ─ Late L. *limōnem*, acc. of *limo*, a lemon. [The pl. *limōnes* occurs about A. D. 1200; Yule.] ─ Pers. *līmū*, lemon, citron. ─ Malay *līmau*; Javanese *limo*, lime, citron, lemon; Uhlenbeck (on Skt. *nimbū*). The final *-n* may be Latin; whence, perhaps, Pers. *līmūn*, *līmūnā*, a lemon, citron; Richardson's Pers. Dict., p. 1282, col. 1. Cf. Turk. *līmūn*; Arab. *laimūn*, a lemon; Palmer's Pers. Dict. col. 517. Der. *lemon-ade*, from F. *limonade*.

LEMUR, a nocturnal mammal. (L.) First in 1795. From its habit of going about at night, it has been nicknamed 'ghost' by naturalists. ─ L. *lemur*, a ghost.

LEND, to let for hire, allow the use of for a time. (E.) The final *d* is excrescent, as in *sound* from F. *son*. ME. *lenen*, pt. t. *lenede*, *lende*, *lente*, pp. *lened*, *lend*, *lent*. Thus the mod. final *d* was easily suggested by the forms of the pt. t. and pp. 'Leen me your hond' = lend me your hand; Chaucer, C. T. 3084 (A 3082). 'This lond he hire *lende*' = he lent [granted] her this land; Layamon, l. 228. AS. *lǣnan*, to lend, also, to give, grant; Grein, ii. 163. ─ AS. *lǣn*, a loan, Grein, ii. 163.+Du. *leenen*, to lend; from *leen*, a fee, fief; Icel. *lāna*, to lend; from *lān*, a loan; Dan. *laane*, to lend; from *laan*, a loan; OHG. *lēhanōn*, G. *lehnen*, to lend (a provincial word); from OHG. *lēhan*, *lehen*, *lehn*, a fief. See further under **Loan**. Der. *lend-er*; *lend-ings*, K. Lear, iii. 4. 113.

LENGTH, extent, the quality of being long. (E.) ME. *lengthè* (two syllables), Chaucer, C. T. 83, 4428 (B 8). AS. *lengðu*; the dat. *lengðe* occurs in the AS. Chron. an. 1122. For *langiða*. Formed with suffix *-ðu* and vowel-change of *a* to *e* from AS. *lang*, long.+Du. *lengte*, from *lang*; Dan. *længde*, from *lang*; Swed. *längd*, from *lång*; Icel. *lengd*, from *langr*. See **Long**. Der. *length-en*, in which the final *-en* has a causal force, though this peculiar formation is conventional and unoriginal; in the ME. *lengthen*, the final *-en* merely denoted the infinitive mood, and properly produced the verb to *length*, as in Palsgrave, and in Shak. Passionate Pilgrim, l. 210. Also *length-y*, *length-i-ly*, *length-i-ness*; *length-wise*, *length-ways*.

LENIENT, mild, merciful. (L.) In Milton, Samson, 659. ─ L. *lēnient-*, stem of pres. part. of *lēnire*, to soften, soothe. ─ L. *lēnis*, soft, mild. See **Lenity**, **Lithe**. Der. *lenient-ly*, *lenienc-y*.

LENITY, mildness, clemency. (F. ─ L.) In Shak. Hen. V, iii. 2. 26, 6. 118. ─ OF. *lenité*, mildness (obsolete). ─ L. *lēnitātem*, acc. of *lēnitās*, softness, mildness. ─ L. *lēni-*, decl. stem of *lēnis*, soft, gentle, mild; with suffix *-tās*. Root uncertain; but *re-lent* and *lithe* are related words. Der. *lenit-ive* = OF. *lenitif*, a 'lenitive' (Cot.), from Late L. *lēnitīvus*. And see **Lenient**.

LENS, a piece of glass used for optical purposes. (L.) In Kersey, ed. 1715. So called, from the resemblance in shape to the seed of a lentil, which is like a *double-convex lens*. ─ L. *lens*; see **Lentil**. Der. *lenticul-ar*, from L. *lenticula*, a little lentil.

LENT, a fast of forty days, beginning with Ash Wednesday. (E.) The fast is in the spring of the year, and the old sense is simply 'spring.' ME. *lenten*, *lente*, *lent*; spelt *lenten*, P. Plowman, B. xx. 359. AS. *lencten*, the spring; Grein, ii. 167.+Du. *lente*, the spring; G. *lenz*, spring; OHG. *lenzo*, *lenzin*, *lengizen*, spring. β. Supposed to be derived from AS., Du., and G. *lang*, long, because in spring the days *lengthen*; Kluge suggests that the orig. Teut. type was *langi-tino-*, i.e. 'long day;' where *-tino-* is allied to Skt. *dina-*, Lith. *dēna*, a day. Der. *lenten*, adj., Hamlet, ii. 2. 329; here the suffix *-en* is *not* adjectival (as in *gold-en*), but the whole word is the ME. *lenten* fully preserved; so also *Lenten-tide* = AS. *lencten-tīd*, spring-time, Gen. xlviii. 7.

LENTIL, an annual plant, bearing pulse for food. (F. ─ L.) ME. *lentil*; Genesis and Exodus, ed. Morris, l. 1488. ─ OF. *lentille*, 'the lintle or lentill;' Cot. ─ L. *lenticula*, a little lentil; double dimin. (with suffix *-cu-l-*) from *lenti-*, decl. stem of *lens*, a lentil. See **Lens**. Der. *lenticul-ar*, resembling a lens or lentil.

LENTISK, the mastic-tree. (F. ─ L.) In Turner's Herbal (1562); and in Cotgrave. ─ F. *lentisque*, 'the lentiske or mastick-tree;' Cot. ─ L. *lentiscum*, *lentiscus*, a mastic-tree; named from the clamminess of the resin yielded by it.—L. *lenti-*, decl. stem of *lentus*, tenacious, sticky, pliant. See **Relent** and **Lithe**.

LEO, a lion. (L.—Gk.—Egypt.) As the name of a zodiacal sign; Chaucer, On the Astrolabe, ed. Skeat, i. 8. 2. We even find AS. *leo*, Grein, ii. 171.—L. *leo*, a lion; see **Lion**. Der. *leon-ine* = F. *leonin* (Cot.), from L. *leōn-in-us*, from *leōn-*, stem of *leo*.

LEOPARD, the lion-pard, an animal of the cat kind. (F.—L.—Gk.) ME. *leopard*, *leopart*, P. Plowman, B. xv. 293.—OF. *leopard*, 'a leopard, or libbard, a beast ingendred between a lion and a panther;' Cot.—L. *leopardus*, a leopard.—Gk. λεόπαρδος, λεοντόπαρδος, a leopard; supposed to be a mongrel between a pard or panther and a lioness; Pliny, Nat. Hist. b. viii. c. 16.—Gk. λεό-, λεοντο-, secondary form or decl. stem of λέων, a lion; and πάρδος, a pard. See **Lion** and **Pard**.

LEPER, one afflicted with leprosy. (F.—L.—Gk.) The form of the word is founded on a mistake; the word properly means the *disease itself* (2 Kings, v. 11), now called *leprosy*; the old term for 'leper' was *leprous man*. 'And loo! a *leprouse man* cam ... And anon the *lepre* of him was clensid;' Wyclif, Matt. viii. 2, 3. And see Henryson, Test. of Cresseid, ll. 43⁸, 451, 474, 480, &c.—F. *lepre*, 'a leprosie;' Cot.—L. *lepra*.—Gk. λέπρα, leprosy. So called because it makes the skin scaly.—Gk. λεπρός, scaly, scabby, rough.—Gk. λέπος, a scale, husk, rind.—Gk. λέπειν, to strip, peel, take off the husk or rind, scale. Cf. Russ. *lupite*, to peel, bark; Lithuanian *lùpti*, to scale, peel. Der. *lepr-ous* = OF. *leprous*, from L. *leprōsus*, adj.; whence was coined the sb. *lepros-y*, Matt. viii. 3.

LEPIDOPTERA, s. pl., a certain order of insects. (Gk.) Modern, and scientific; due to Linnæus. Used of the butterfly, and other insects whose four *wings* are covered with very fine *scales*. Coined from Gk. λεπίδο-, decl. stem of λεπίς, a scale; and πτερά, pl. of πτερόν, a wing. Λεπίς is from λέπειν, to scale (see **Leprosy**); and πτερόν is allied to E *feather*, from πτ-, weak grade of √PET, to fly; see **Feather, Pen**. Der. *lepidopter-ous*.

LEPORINE, pertaining to the hare. (L.) In Blount's Gloss., ed. 1656. Either from F. *leporin*, 'of or belonging to a hare' (Cot.), or rather directly from L. *leporinus*, with the same sense.—L. *lepor-*, for *lepos-*, stem of *lepus*, a hare. See **Leveret**.

LEPROSY; see under **Leper**. (F.—L.—Gk.)

LESION, an injury, wound. (F.—L.) In Blount's Gloss., ed. 1674.—MF. *lesion*, 'hurt, wounding, harme;' Cot.—L. *læsiōnem*, acc. of *læsio*, an injury; cf. *læsus*, pp. of *lædere*, to hurt. Der. (from L. *lædere*), *col-lide*, *col-lis-ion*, *e-lide*, *il-lis-ion*.

LESS, smaller. (E.) Used as compar. of *little*, but from a different root; the coincidence in the first letter is accidental. ME. *lessè*, *lassè*, adj., *les*, adv. 'The *lesse* luue' = the less love; Ancren Riwle, p. 92, l. 7. *Les* as adv., id. p. 30, l. 7. AS. *lǽssa*, adj., *lǽs*, adv.; Grein, ii. 164.+OFries. *lêssa*, less. β. *Lǽssa* stands for *lǽs-ra*, by assimilation; and *lǽs* represents the Teut. type *lais-iz*, both formed (with comp. suffix -*iz*-) from a base *lais-*, for *lais-o-*, small; allied to Lith. *lēsas*, thin, small. From Idg. base *leis-*.

LEAST, the superl. form, is the ME. *lestè*, adj., P. Plowman, B. iii. 24; *lest*, adv., Gower, C. A. i. 153; bk. i. 3285. AS. *lǽsest* (whence *lǽst* by contraction), Grein, ii. 164; from the same base *lais-*, with the usual suffix -*est* (for -*ist*, Gk. -ιστος). Der. *less*, sb.; *less-er*, a double comparative, Gen. i. 16; *less-en*, vb., from ME. *lassen*, Sir Gawain and the Grene Knight, l. 1800, *lessin* (for *lessen*), Prompt. Parv., p. 298; with a new suffix -*en* (as in *length-en*) added, after the loss of the ME. infin. suffix -*en*, -*e*. And see *lest*.

-LESS, suffix. (E.) AS. *léas*, cognate with **Loose**, q.v.

LESSEE, LESSOR; see under **Lease**.

LESSON, a reading of scripture, portion of scripture read, a task, lecture, piece of instruction. (F.—L.) ME. *lesson*, Chaucer, C. T. 9069 (E 1193); spelt *lescun*, Ancren Riwle, p. 282, l. 3.—OF. *lecon*, F. *leçon*.—L. *lectiōnem*, acc. of *lectio*, a reading; from *legere*, to read; see **Legend**. Doublet, *lection*.

LEST, for fear that, that not. (E.) Not for *least*, as sometimes erroneously said, but due to *less*. It arose from the AS. equivalent expression ðӯ lǽs ðe, as in the following sentence. 'Nelle we ðas race nā leng téon, ðӯ lǽs ðe hit eōw ǽþryt þynce' = we will not prolong this story farther, lest it seem to you tedious; Sweet's A. S. Reader, p. 94, l. 211. Here ðӯ lǽs ðe literally = *for the reason less that* (L. *quō minus*); where ðӯ (= for the reason) is the instrumental case of the def. article; lǽs = less, adv.; and ðe (= that) is the indeclinable relative. β. At a later period ðӯ lǽs was dropped, lǽs became *les*, and lǽs ðe, coalescing, became one word *lesthe*, altered (regularly) to *leste*, and lastly to *lest*, for ease of pronunciation. The form *leste* occurs in the Ancren Riwle, p. 58, l. 12, whilst the older expression þi les þe occurs in O. Eng. Homilies, ed. Morris, i. 117, l. 2 from bottom; so that the word took the form *leste* about the beginning of the 13th century. See **Nevertheless**.

LET (1), to allow, permit, suffer, grant. (E.) ME. *leten* (with one *t*), a strong verb; pt. t. *lat*, *let*, *leet*; pp. *laten*, *leten*, *lete*. See Chaucer, C. T. 128, 510 (A 508). AS. *lǽ.an*, *lǽtan*, to let, allow; pt. t. *lēt*, *leort*, pp. *lǽten*; Grein, ii. 165.+Du. *laten*, pt. t. *liet*, pp. *gelaten*; Icel. *lāta*, pt. t. *lēt*, pp. *lātinn*; Dan. *lade*, pt. t. *lod*, pp. *ladet*; Swed. *lâta*, pt. t. *lät*, pp. *lâten*; Goth. *lētan*, pt. t. *lailōt*, pp. *lētans*; G. *lassen*, pt. t. *liess*, pp. *gelassen*. β. The Teut. type is *lēt-an-*, pt. t. *lelōt*, pp. *lētanoz*. Idg. √LĒ(I)D; from the weak grade *lad* comes E. *late*. See **Late**. Brugmann, i. § 478. Cf. Lith. *léidmi*, I let (base *lēid*). And see **Let** (2).

LET (2), to hinder, prevent, obstruct. (E.) ME. *letten* (with double *t*), a weak verb. 'He *letted* nat his felawe for to see' = he hindered not his fellow from seeing; Chaucer, C. T. 1894 (A 1892). AS. *lettan*, to hinder; also *gelettan*; Grein, ii. 168. A causal verb, with the sense 'to make late,' just as *hinder* is derived from the -*hind* in *behind*.—AS. *lǽt*, slow; see **Late**.+Du. *letten*, to impede; from *laat*; Icel. *letja*, from *latr*; Goth. *latjan*, intrans., to be late, to tarry; from *lats*, slothful. Teut. type *lat-jan-*; from *lat-*, slow. See above.

LETHAL, deadly, mortal. (F.—L.; *or* L.) Spelt *lethall* in Minsheu, ed. 1627.—F. *lethal*, 'deadly, mortal;' Cot. [Or directly from Latin.]—L. *lēthālis*, better *lētālis*, mortal.—L. *lētum*, death. Der. *lethi-ferous*, deadly; from *lēthi-*, for *lēthum*, and -*fer-ous* = -*fer-us*, bearing, from *ferre*, to bear.

LETHARGY, heavy slumber, great dulness. (F.—L.—Gk.) In Shak. Wint. Ta. iv. 4. 627. Spelt *letharge*, Sir T. Elyot, Castel of Helth, b. ii. c. 34.—MF. *lethargie*, 'a lethargy;' Cot.—L. *lēthargia*, drowsiness.—Gk. ληθαργία, drowsiness.—Gk. λήθαργος, forgetting, forgetful.—Gk. λήθη, oblivion. See **Lethe**. Der. *lethargi-c*, from Gk. ληθαργικός, drowsy; *lethargi-c-al*; *lethargi-ed*, K. Lear, i. 4. 249.

LETCH, to moisten. (E.) AS. *leccan*, to moisten; see **Latch** (2). The usual spelling is *leach*, to remove by percolation; see N. E. D.

LETHE, forgetfulness, oblivion. (L.—Gk.) In Shak. Hamlet, i. 5. 33.—L. *lēthē*.—Gk. λήθη, a forgetting; also Lethe, the river of oblivion in the lower world. Allied to Gk. λαθ-, base of λανθάνειν, to lie hid. Der. *leth-argy*, q. v.; *lethe-an*; *lethe'd*, Antony, ii. 1. 27.

LETTER, a character, written message. (F.—L.) ME. *lettre*, Genesis and Exod, ed. Morris, l. 993.—F. *lettre*.—L. *littera* (older forms *lītera*, *leitera*), a letter. Brugmann, i. § 930. Der. *letter-ed*, Will. of Palerne, l. 4088; *letter-founder*, *letter-ing*, *letter-press*; *letters-patent*, Rich. II, ii. 1. 202, where *patents* is the F. *plural* adjective.

LETTUCE, a succulent plant. (F.—L.) ME. *letuce*, Palladius on Husbandry, b. ii. st. 29, l. 202; *letus*, Cursor Mundi, 6079. Of obscure formation; it seems to be a plural form, from a singular *letu*.—AF. *letue*; Voc. 558. 27.—L. *lactūca*, lettuce; named from its juiciness; Varro, De Lingua Latina, v. 104.—L. *lact-*, stem of *lac*, milk. See **Lacteal**. Cf. F. *laitue*.

LEUCOMA, a white opacity in the cornea of the eye. (Gk.) In Phillips (1706).—Gk. λεύκωμα, whiteness.—Gk. λευκοῦν, to make white.—Gk. λευκός, white. Allied to **Lucid**.

LEVANT, the East of the Mediterranean Sea. (F.—Ital.—L.) *Levant* and *Ponent*, lit. rising and setting (with ref. to the sun) are old terms for East and West. 'Forth rush the *Levant* and the *Ponent* winds;' Milton, P. L. x. 704.—F. *levant*, 'the Levant, the East;' Cot.—Ital. *levante*, 'the east winde, the cuntrey lying toward or in the east;' Florio.—L. *leuant-*, stem of pres. part. of *leuāre*, to raise, whence *sē leuāre* to rise; see **Lever**. Der. *levant-ine*. Cf. slang E. *levant*, from Span. *levantar*, lit. to raise; *levantar la casa*, to break up house, move away.

LEVEE, a morning assembly. (F.—L.) 'The good man early to the *levee* goes;' Dryden, tr. of Juvenal, Sat. vi. l. 428. As if from F. *levée* (see **Levy**), but really an alteration of F. *lever*, infin. used as a sb. in the sense of *levee* (see Littré).—F. *lever*, to raise; see **Levy**.

LEVEL, an instrument by which a thing is determined to be horizontal. (F.—L.) ME. *liuel*, *leuel* (with *u* for *v*); P. Plowman, A. xi. 135; B. x. 179.—OF. *livel*, preserved in the expression '*d'un livel*, levell;' Cot. Later spelt *liveau*, afterwards corrupted to *niveau*; both spellings are in Cotgrave, who explains it by 'a mason's or carpenter's levell or triangle.' He also gives the verb *niveler* (corruption of *liveler*), 'to levell.'—L. *libella*, a level; dimin. of *libra*, a level, balance; see **Librate**. ¶ Not an AS. word, as sometimes said. Der. *level*, verb, spelt *levell* in Palsgrave, of which the pp. *leaueld* (= *levell'd*) occurs in Sir P. Sidney, Apology for Poetry, ed. Arber, p. 55; *level-er*, *level-ness*.

LEVER, a bar for raising bodies. (F.—L.) ME. *leuour* (with *u* = *v*), Rob. of Glouc. p. 126, l. 2680; *leuer*, Romance of Partenay, ed. Skeat, l. 4177.—OF. *leveor* (Godefroy), MF. *leveur*, 'a raiser, lifter;' Cot. [Not quite the same word as F. *levier*, a lever, which differs in the suffix.]—L. *leuātōrem*, acc. of *leuātor*, a lifter.—L. *leuāre*, to lift, lit. to make light.—L. *leuis*, light. See **Levity.** Der. *lever-age*.

LEVERET, a young hare. (F.—L.) Spelt *lyueret* in Levins, ed. 1570. ME. *leveret*, Voc. 592. 22.—AF. *leveret*, pl. *leveres*, Gaimar, Chron. 6239; pl. *leverez*, Rel. Antiq. i. 155; allied to OF. *levrault*, a 'leveret, or young hare;' Cot. β. The suffix *-ault* = Late L. *-aldus*, from OHG. *wald*, power; see Introd. to Brachet, Etym. Dict., § 195; but the AF. suffix *-et* is diminutive; cf. Ital. *lepretta*, a leveret. The base *levr-* is from L. *lepor-*, for **lepos*, stem of *lepus*, a hare. See **Leporine.**

LEVIATHAN, a huge aquatic animal. (L.—Heb.) In Minsheu, ed. 1627; and in Shak. Mids. Nt. Dr. ii. 1. 174.—Late L. *leviathan*, Job, xl. 20 (Vulgate), where Wyclif has *leuyathan*.—Heb. *livyāthān*, an aquatic animal, dragon, serpent; so called from its twisting itself in curves.—Heb. root *lāvāh*, Arab. root *lawa'*, to bend, whence *lawā*, the twisting or coiling of a serpent; Rich. Dict. pp. 1278, 1275.

LEVIGATE, to make smooth. (L.) Now little used. [Richardson cites an example from Sir T. Elyot, where *levigate* = lightened, from L. *leuigāre*, to lighten, which from *leuis*, light; see **Levity.** But this is quite another word.] 'When use hath *levigated* the organs, and made the way so smooth and easie;' Barrow, vol. iii. ser. 9 (R.).—L. *lēuigātus*, pp. of *lēuigāre*, to make smooth.—L. *lēu-*, stem of *lēuis*, smooth; with suffix *-ig-* weakened from *ag-ere*, to drive. The L. *lēuis* is cognate with Gk. λεῖος, smooth; which see in Prellwitz. Der. *levigat-ion.*

LEVIN, lightning. (Scand.) 'The flashing *levin*;' Spenser, F. Q. v. 6. 40; 'Thunder and *leuene*;' Genesis and Exodus, 3265. Cf. MDan. *löffn*, lightning; Kalkar, s. v. *ljune*; Swed. dial. *lyvna, lygna*; Rietz, s. v. *ljuna*. Teut. **leugnó-*. (√LEUQ).

LEVITE, one of the tribe of Levi. (L.—Gk.—Heb.) In A. V. Lu. x. 32; P. Plowman, B. xii. 115.—L. *Leuīta*, Lu. x. 32.—Gk. Λευΐτης, Lu. x. 32. Formed with suffix *-της* from Λευΐ, Rev. vii. 7.—Heb. *Lēvī*, one of the sons of Jacob. Der. *Levit-i-c-us, Levit-i-c-al.*

LEVITY, lightness of weight or of conduct. (F.—L.) In Shak. All's Well, i. 2. 35.—OF. *levité*, lightness (Godefroy); obsolete.—L. *leuitātem*, acc. of *leuitās*, lightness.—L. *leuis*, light; usually considered as allied to Gk. ἐλαχύς, small, Skt. *laghu-s*, light; see Prellwitz and Uhlenbeck.

LEVY, the act of raising men for war; a force raised. (F.—L.) In Shak. Macb. iii. 2. 25. 'Make *leuy* of my dettys;' Bury Wills (Camd. Soc.), p. 43 (1463). 'Whanne kynge Iohn had *leuyed* many great summes of money;' Fabyan, Chron., Edw. III, an. 30. [The verb is from the sb.]—F. *levée*, 'a bank, or causey; also, a levy, or levying of money, souldiers, &c. ;' Cot. Properly the fem. of the pp. of the vb. *lever*, to raise.—L. *leuāre*, to raise; lit. 'to make light.'—L. *leuis*, light; see **Levee.** Der. *lev-ee, lev-er, lev-ant, al-lev-iate, e-lev-ate, leav-en, legerdemain, re-lev-ant, re-lieve.* Doublet, *levee.*

LEW, warm. (E.) 'The sunne, briht and *lewe*;' Havelok, 2921. AS. *hlēow*, warm; as in comp. *ge-hlēow* (Bosworth).+Icel. *hlȳr*, warm, mild. Der. *lew-warm*, tepid; also *lew*, sb., warmth, shelter; prov. E. *lew-th*, shelter. See **Lee.**

LEWD, ignorant, base, licentious. (E.) Contracted for *lewed*. ME. *lewed*, Chaucer, C. T. 576. AS. *læwede*, adj. lay, i. e. belonging to the laity; '*þæt læwede* folc' = the lay-people, Ælfric's Homilies, ed. Thorpe, ii. 74, l. 17. 'Laicus, *læwede* mann,' Voc. 308. 15. The word thus originally merely meant 'the laity,' hence the untaught, ignorant, as opposed to the clergy. The phrase *lered and lewede* = clergy and laity, taught and untaught, is not uncommon; see P. Plowman, B. iv. 11. β. The form *læwede* is not participial in form, and the assumed connexion or confusion with the verb *læwan*, to betray, does not suit the sense or help the development. γ. It has been derived from L. **lāicātus*, belonging to the laity, parallel to Late L. *clēricātus*, whence *clergy*; and if so, is from L. *lāicus*, a word of Gk. origin; see **Laic.** So Sievers, § 173; Pogatscher, § 340. But the phonetic difficulties seem too great for this. Der. *lewd-ly*, *lewd-ness* = ignorance, Acts, xviii. 14.

LEXICON, a dictionary. (Gk.) In Blount's Gloss., ed. 1674.—Gk. λεξικόν (with βιβλίον, a book, understood), a lexicon; properly neut. of λεξικός, adj., of or for words.—Gk. λέξι-s, a saying, speech. —Gk. λέγειν, to speak; see **Legend.** Der. *lexico-graph-y, lexico-graph-i-c-al, lexico-graph-i-c-al-ly, lexico-graph-er*; all from γράφειν, to write; see **Graphic.**

LEY, a meadow; see **Lea.** (E.)

LIABLE, responsible, subject. (F.—L.) In Shak. John, ii. 490; v. 2. 101. In the latter passage it means 'allied, associated, compatible;' Schmidt. Formed, with the common suffix *-able*, from F. *lier*, 'to tie, bind, fasten, knit, ... unite, oblige, or make beholden to;' Cot.—L. *ligāre*, to tie, bind; see **Ligament.** Der. *liabil-i-ty*.

LIAISON, an illicit intimacy between a man and woman. (F.—L.) 'Some chaste *liaison*;' Byron, Don Juan, iii. 25.—F. *liaison*. —L. *ligātiōnem*, acc. of *ligātio*, a binding; from *ligāre*, to bind. See **Ligament.**

LIANE, LIANA, a climbing tropical plant. (F.—L.) 'The *nebees*, called by the French *liannes*;' Stedman, Surinam, vol. i. p. 231.—F. *liane*, the same; from Norm. and Picard *lian*, a band.—L. *ligāmen*, a tie.—L. *ligāre*, to bind (above). See **Lien.**

LIAS, a formation of limestone, underlying the oölite. (F.) Modern in E. as a geological term; but found in Northern E., and spelt *lyas*, as early as 1404 (N. E. D.).—F. *liais*, formerly *liois*. '*Liais*, a very hard free-stone whereof stone-steps and tombe-stones be commonly made;' Cot. Spelt *liois* in the 13th cent. (Littré, Hatzfeld.) Of unknown origin. Der. *liass-ic*.

LIB, to castrate; now dialectal. (E.) Florio, ed. 1598, has: '*Accaponare*, to geld, splaie, or *lib*.' Cf. EFries. *lübben*, Du. *lubben*, to lib. See **Glib** (3).

LIBATION, the pouring forth of wine in honour of a deity. (F.—L.) In Minsheu, ed. 1627; and in Wyclif, Ezek. xx. 28.—F. *libation* (Cot.).—L. *libātiōnem*, acc. of *libātio*, a libation.—L. *lībāre*, to sip, taste, drink, pour out. + Gk. λείβειν, to pour out, offer a libation, let flow, shed. Brugmann, i. § 553.

LIBEL, a written accusation, defamatory publication. (F.—L.) The orig. sense is merely 'a little book' or 'a brief piece of writing.' Hence Wyclif has: 'зyue he to hir a *libel* of forsakyng;' Matt. v. 31.—OF. *libel* (Godefroy).—L. *libellum*, acc. of *libellus*, a little book, writing, written notice; hence '*libellum* repudii' in Matt. v. 31 (Vulgate). Dimin. of *liber*, a book; see **Library.** ¶ Perhaps taken directly from the Latin. Der. *libel*, verb, *libell-er, libell-ous, libell-ous-ly.*

LIBERAL, generous, candid, free, noble-minded. (F.—L.) ME. *liberal*, Gower, C. A. iii. 114; bk. vii. 876.—OF. *liberal*, 'liberall;' Cot.—L. *liberālis*, befitting a free man, generous.—L. *liber*, free. Der. *liberal-ly*; *liberal-i-ty* = F. *liberalité* (Cot.), from L. acc. *liberālitātem*; *liberal-ism, liberal-ise*. And see *liberate, liberty, libertine.*

LIBERATE, to set free. (L.) In Minsheu, ed. 1627.—L. *liberātus*, pp. of *liberāre*, to set free.—L. *liber*, free; see **Liberal.** Der. *liberat-ion, liberat-or.*

LIBERTINE, a licentious man. (L.) In Shak. Much Ado, ii. 1. 144. 'Applied at first to certain heretical sects, and intended to mark the licentious *liberty* of their creed;' Trench, Select Glossary; q. v. Wyclif has *libertyns* in Acts, vi. 9.—L. *libertīnus*, adj., of or belonging to a freed man; also, as sb., a freed man; used in the Vulgate in Acts, vi. 9. An extended form of L. *libertus*, a freed man.—L. *liber*, free; with participal suffix *-tus*. See **Liberal.** Der. *libertin-ism.*

LIBERTY, freedom. (F.—L.) ME. *liberté, libertee*, Chaucer, C. T. 8047 (E 171).—OF. *liberte*, later *liberté*, 'liberty, freedom;' Cot.—L. *libertātem*, acc. of *libertās*, liberty.—L. *liber*, free; see **Liberal.**

LIBIDINOUS, lustful. (F.—L.) In Minsheu, ed. 1627; 'His *lybidynous* desire;' Caxton, Eneydos, ch. ix. p. 36.—F. *libidineux*, 'libidinous, lascivious;' Cot.—L. *libidinōsus*, eager, lustful.—L. *libidin-*, stem of *libido*, lust, pleasure.—L. *libet*, it pleases; also (better) spelt *lubet*. Cf. Skt. *lubh*, to desire. Allied to **Lief, Love.** Der. *libidinous-ly, libidinous-ness.*

LIBRARY, a collection of books, a room for books. (F.—L.) ME. *librarie*, Chaucer, tr. of Boethius, b. i. pr. 4, l. 10.—F. *librairie*; which in OF. meant a library (Godefroy).—Late L. type *librāria*; allied to L. *librārius*, of or belonging to books.—L. *libr-*, stem of *liber*, a book, orig. the bark of a tree, which was the earliest writing material; with suffix *-ārius*. β. Prob. connected with Gk. λέπις, a scale, rind; from √LEP, to peel; Brugmann, i. § 499. Der. *librari-an, librari-an-ship.*

LIBRATE, to balance, be poised, move slightly as things that balance; **LIBRATION,** a balancing, slight swinging motion. (L.) The verb is rare, and prob. suggested by the sb. '*Libration*, a ballancing or poising; also, the motion of swinging in a pendulum;' Kersey, ed. 1715. First in 1603. Formed, by analogy with F. sbs. in *-ion*, from L. *librātiōnem*, acc. of *librātio*, a poising.—L. *lībrāre*, to poise.—L. *lībra*, a balance, a level, machine for levelling, a pound of 12 ounces.+Gk. λίτρα, a pound of 12 ounces, a coin. β. L. *lī-bra* = Gk. λῖ-τρα, the words being cognate. Brugmann, i. § 589. Der. *librat-or-y*; from the same source as *de-liber-ate, equi-libri-um, level*. Also F. *litre*, from Gk. λίτρα; *lira*, q. v.

LICENCE, LICENSE, leave, permission, abuse of freedom, excess. (F.—L.) 'Leue and *lycence*' = leave and licence; P. Plowman, A. prol. 82. 'A *lycence* and a leue;' id. B. prol. 85. [The right spelling is with *c*; the spelling with *s* is reserved for the verb, by analogy with *practice, practise, &c.*]—F. *licence*, 'licence, leave;'

Cot.—L. *licentia*, freedom to act.—L. *licent-*, stem of pres. pt. of *licēre*, to be allowable, to be permissible; see Brugmann, ii. § 587. Der. *licence*, or more commonly *license*, verb, 1 Hen. IV, i. 3. 123; *licens-er*, spelt *licenc-er*, Milton's Areopagitica, ed. Hales, p. 24, l. 8; also *licentiate*, q. v., *licentious*, q. v. See also *leisure*, *il-licit*.

LICENTIATE, one who has a grant to exercise a function. (L.) ME. *licentiat*, Chaucer, C. T. 220. Englished from Late L. *licentiātus*, pp. of *licentiāre*, to license.—L. *licentia* (above).

LICENTIOUS, indulging in excess of freedom, dissolute. (F.—L.) 'A *licentious* libertie;' Spenser, F. Q. v. 5. 25.—OF. *licentieus* (Godefroy); F. *licencieux*.—L. *licentiōsus*, full of licence.—L. *licentia*, licence. See **Licence**. Der. *licentious-ly*, *-ness*.

LICHEN, one of an order of cellular flowerless plants; also, an eruption on the skin. (L.—Gk.) See Holland, tr. of Pliny, b. xxvi. c. 4; p. 245. Also Kersey's Dict., ed. 1715.—L. *lichēn*, in Pliny, Nat. Hist. xxvi. 4. 10, § 21; xxiii. 7. 63, § 117.—Gk. λείχην, lichen, tree-moss; also, a lichen-like eruption on the skin, a tetter. Generally connected with Gk. λείχειν, to lick, to lick up; from its encroachment; see **Lick**. Cf. Russ. *lishai*, a tetter, a lichen.

LICH-GATE, a church-yard gate with a porch under which a bier may be rested. (E.) In Johnson's Dict. The word is scarce, though its component parts are common. Chaucer has *lich-wake* [or rather *liche-wake* in 4 syllables] to signify the 'waking' or watching of a dead body; C. T. 2960 (A 2958). The lit. sense is ' corpse-gate.' ME. *lich*, the body, most often a dead body or corpse (sometimes lengthened to *liche* in two syllables, as above); see Layamon, 6682, 10434; Ormulum, 8183, 16300; St. Marharete, ed. Cockayne, p. 5; Genesis and Exodus, ed. Morris, 2441, 2447, 2488, 4140; P. Plowman, B. x. 2; &c. AS. *lic*, the body, almost always used of the *living* body; Grein, ii. 179. The orig. sense is 'form,' shape, or likeness, and it is from the same root as *like*, adj., with which it is closely connected; see **Like** (1).+Du. *lijk*, a corpse; Icel. *lík*, a living body (in old poems); also a corpse; Dan. *lig*, a corpse; Swed. *lik*, a corpse; Goth. *leik*, the body, Matt. v. 29; a corpse, Matt. xxvii. 52; G. *leiche*, OHG. *lih*, the body, a corpse; whence G. *leichnam*, a corpse. Teut. type *līkom*, n. And see **Gate**.

LICK, to pass the tongue over, to lap. (E.) ME. *licken*, *likken*; Wyclif, Luke, xvi. 21. AS. *liccian*, Luke, xvi. 21; Grein, ii. 180. +Du. *likken*; G. *lecken*. Teut. type *likkōn-* (whence F. *lécher*). Allied to Goth. *laigōn*, only in the comp. *bi-laigōn*, Luke, xvi. 21. +Russ. *lizate*; L. *lingere*; Gk. λείχειν; Lith. *lèsz-ti*; OIrish *lig-im*, I lick; Pers. *lish-tan*; Skt. *lih*, Vedic form *rih*, to lick. β. All from √LEIGH, to lick. Brugmann, i. § 604. Der. *lecher*, q. v.

LICKERISH, LIQUORISH, fond of dainties; greedy; lecherous. (F.—G.) 'The *liquorish* hag rejects the pelf with scorn;' Dryden, Wife of Bath, 319. Adaptations of ME. *likerous*; 'she had a *likerous* yë' [eye]; Chaucer, C. T., A 3244.—AF. *likerous*, *lekerous*, Northern variant of OF. *licherous*, *lecherous*, lecherous; cf. Norman dial. *liquer*, *lequer*, for F. *lécher*, to lick (Moisy).—North F. *lequer*, for F. *lécher*, to lick.—OHG. *lecchōn* (G. *lecken*), to lick. See **Lecher**.

LICORICE, LIQUORICE, a plant with a sweet root, used in medicine. (F.—L.—Gk.) ME. *licoris*. In early use; Layamon, 17745; Chaucer, C. T. 3207.—AF. *lycorys*, Liber Albus, p. 224; OF. *licorice*, spelt *licorece*, Vie de St. Gilles, 854; MF. *liquerice*, 'lickorice,' in Cotgrave. [Littré gives also the corrupt (but old) spellings *reculisse*, *regulisse*, whence mod. F. *réglisse*. So also in Ital., we have the double form *legorizia*, *regolizia*.]—L. *liquiritia*, liquorice, a corrupted form; the correct spelling being *glycyrrhiza*, which is found in Pliny, Nat. Hist. xxii. 9. 11.—Gk. γλυκύρριζα, the liquorice-plant; so called from its sweet root.—Gk. γλυκύ-, for γλυκύς, sweet; and ρίζα, a root, cognate with E. *wort*. The Gk. γλυκύς is often regarded as cognate with L. *dulcis*, sweet; but this is very doubtful.

LICTOR, an officer in Rome, who bore an axe and fasces. (L.) In Shak., Antony, v. 2. 214.—L. *lictor*; so called (perhaps) from the fasces or bundles of bound rods which he bore, or from binding culprits. Connected with *ligāre*, to bind (Bréal). See **Ligament**.

LID, a cover. (E.) ME. *lid* (rare, see exx. in Stratmann); spelt *led*, Sir Cleges, l. 272, in Weber's Met. Romances, vol. i. AS. *hlid*, Matt. xxvii. 60.+Du. *lid*, a lid; (not the same word as *lid*, a joint). +Icel. *hlið*, a gate, gateway, gap, space, breach; OHG. *hlit*, MHG. *lit*, a cover (whence G. *augen-lied*, eye-lid). Teut. type *hlīdom*, n. β. From *hlið-*, weak grade of Teut. *hleidan-*, *hlīdan-*, to cover; as in AS. *hlīdan*, to shut, cover, Grein, ii. 86; cf. OSax. *hlīdan*, to cover. Der. *lid-gate*, a swing-gate; also occurring as a poet's name, from a place-name in Suffolk.

LIE (1), to rest, lean, lay oneself down, repose, abide, be situate. (E.) A strong verb. ME. *liggen*, *lien*, pt. t. *lei*, *lai*, *lay*, pp. *leien*, *lein*, *lain*; Chaucer, C. T. 3651, 20; P. Plowman, B. iii. 175, i. 30,

iii. 38. AS. *licgan*, pt. t. *læg*, pp. *legen*; Grein, ii. 181.+Du. *liggen*, pt. t. *lag*, pp. *gelegen*.+Icel. *liggja*, pt. t. *lā*, pp. *leginn*; Dan. *ligge*; Swed. *ligga*; G. *liegen*, pt. t. *lag*, pp. *gelegen*. Goth. *ligan*, pt. t. *lag*, pp. *ligans*. Teut. type *lig-jan-* (except in Gothic); pt. t. *lag*, pp. *leganoz*. Teut. root *leg*; Idg. √LEGH. Further related to Russ. *lejate*, to lie; L. base *leg-*, to lie; only in *lectus*, a bed; Gk. base λεχ-, appearing in aorist ἐλεξα, Homer, Iliad, xiv. 252; λέχος, a bed. ¶ As to the modern E. form, which depends on the AS. stem *lig-*, occurring in the 2nd and 3rd person sing. indic. and in the imp. sing., see Sweet, E. Gram. § 1293. The pp. *lien* occurs in Gen. xxvi. 10, Ps. lxviii. 13. Der. *lay*, q. v., *law*, q. v.

LIE (2), to tell a lie, speak falsely. (E.) ME. *liȝen*, *lien*, *lyen*, a strong verb; Layamon, 3034, Chaucer, C. T. 765 (A 763); pt. t. *leh*, Layamon, 12942, 17684; pp. *lowen*, P. Plowman, B. v. 95. AS. *lēogan*, pt. t. *lēag*, pp. *logen*; Grein, ii. 176.+Du. *liegen*, pt. t. *loog*, pp. *gelogen*; Icel. *ljūga*, pt. t. *laug*, pp. *loginn*; Dan. *lyve*, pt. t. *löj*, pp. *löjet*; Swed. *ljuga*, pt. t. *lög*, pp. *ljugen*; Goth. *liugan*, pt. t. *lauh*, pp. *lugans*; G. *lügen*, pt. t. *log*, pp. *gelogen*. β. Teut. type *leugan-*, pt. t. *laug*, pp. *luganoz*. Teut. root *leug*; Idg. √LEUGH. Cf. Russ. *lgate*, *luigate*, to lie; *loje*, a lie. Der. *lie*, sb. = AS. *lyge*, *lige*, Grein, ii. 199; *li-ar*, cf. AS. *lēogere*; *ly-ing*, *ly-ing-ly*.

LIEF, dear, beloved, loved, pleasing. (E.) Now chiefly used in the phr. 'I had as *lief*,' which is common in Shak.; see Hamlet, iii. 2. 4. ME. *lief*, *leef*, *lef*, Chaucer, C. T. 3790 (A 3792); vocative and pl. *leue* (=*leve*), id. 1138; compar. *leuer* (=*lever*), id. 295; superl. *leuest* (=*levest*), P. Plowman's Crede, ed. Skeat, l. 16. AS. *lēof*, *liof*, vocative *lēofa*, pl. *lēofe*; compar. *lēofra*, superl. *lēofesta*, Grein, ii. 174, 175 (a common word).+Du. *lief*, dear; Icel. *ljúfr*; Swed. *ljuf*; Goth. *liubs*; G. *lieb*, MHG. *liep*, OHG. *liup*. Teut. type *leuboz*; Idg. type *leubhos*. Cf. also Russ. *lioboi*, agreeable; *liobite*, to love. β. All from Teut. base LEUB, to be pleasing to; cf. L. *lubet*, *libet*, it pleases; Skt. *lubh*, to covet, desire.—√LEUBH, to desire. Der. (from the same root) *love*, *leave* (2), *believe*, *furlough*, *lib-idinous*.

LIEGE, faithful, subject, true, bound by feudal tenure. (F.—OHG.) α. The etymology is disguised by a change both of sense and usage. We now say 'a liege vassal,' i. e. one bound to his lord; it is easy to see that this sense is due to a false etymology which connected the word with L. *ligātus*, bound, pp. of *ligāre*, to bind; see **Ligament**. β. But the fact is, that the older phrase was ' a liege lord,' and the older sense ' a lord entitled to feudal allegiance.' The phrase ' my lege man' occurs twice, and ' my lege men' once, in Will. of Palerne, 1174, 2663, 3004. The expression ' vr [our] lige louerd' occurs in Rob. of Glouc. p. 457, l. 9376; and in Chaucer, C. T. 12271 (Six-text, C 337, where the MSS. have lige, lege, liege). In Barbour's Bruce, ed. Skeat, v. 165, we find: ' Bot and I lif in *lege* pouste ' = but if I survive in sovereignty entitled to homage; or, in free sovereignty.—OF. *lige*, 'liege, leall, or loyall; *Prince lige*, a liege lord; *Seigneur lige*, the same;' Cot. Also (better) spelt *liege* in the 12th cent. (Littré).—OHG. *ledec*, *ledic*, also *lidic*, *lidig* (mod. G. *ledig*), free, unfettered, free from all obligations; which seems to have been the orig. sense. The expression ' *ligius* homo, quod Teutonicè dicitur *ledighman*' occurs A.D. 1253; Ducange. ' A *liege* lord' seems to have been a lord of a free band; and his *lieges*, though serving under him, were privileged men, free from other obligations. B. Further; the OHG. *lidic* is cognate with Icel. *liðugr*, free, also ready, willing; and is prob. allied to OHG. *lidan*, to go, depart, experience, take one's way; cognate with AS. *līðan*, to go, to go, travel. Also, the Icel. *liðugr*, ready, free, is from Icel. *liða*, to travel; see **Lead** (1). ¶ For further information on this difficult word, see Diez, Scheler, and Littré; and the MDu. *ledig*, free, in Kilian. And see Körting, § 5506. ' *Leecheyt* [= *ledigheid*] is moeder van alle quaethede ' = idleness is mother of all vices; O. Du. Proverb, cited in Oudemans. Ducange's attempt to connect the word with Late L. *litus*, a kind of vassal, is a failure.

LIEGER, LEIGER, an ambassador; see **Ledger**.

LIEN, a legal claim, a charge on property. (F.—L.) A legal word; not in Todd's Johnson; preserved as a law term from the 16th century.—F. *lien*, a band, or tye, ... anything that fasteneth or fettereth;' Cot.—L. *ligāmen*, a band, tie.—L. *ligāre*, to tie; see **Ligament**. And see **Liane**.

LIEU, place, stead. (F.—L.) In the phr. ' in lieu of' = in place of; Temp. i. 2. 123.—F. *lieu*, 'a place, roome;' Cot. Spelt *liu* in the 10th century.—L. *locum*, acc. of *locus*, a place; see **Locus**. Der. *lieu-tenant*, q. v.

LIEUTENANT, a deputy, vicegerent, &c. (F.—L.) ME. *lieutenant*, Gower, C. A. i. 73; bk. i. 947; P. Plowman, B. xvi. 47.—F. *lieutenant*, 'a lieutenant, deputy;' Cot.—L. *locum-tenentem*, acc. of *locum-tenens*, one who holds another's place, a deputy.—L. *locum*, acc. of *locus*, a place; and *tenens*, pres. part. of *tenēre*, to hold. See **Locus** and **Tenant**. Der. *lieutenanc-y*. ¶ The pron.

as *leftenant* is old; cf. *luftenand* in Barbour, Bruce, xiv. 139. Cf. OF. *luef*, for *lieu* (Godefroy).

LIFE, animate existence. (E.) ME. *lif*, *lyf*, gen. case *lyues*, dat. *lyue*, pl. *lyues* (with *u*=*v*); Chaucer, C. T. 2757, 2778, 14100 (A 2755, 2776, B 3284). AS. *lif*, gen. *lifes*, dat. *life*, pl. *lifas*; Grein, ii. 183. +Icel. *lif*, *lift*; Dan. *liv*; Swed. *lif*; OHG. *lib*, *leip*, life; mod. G. *leib*, the body. Cf. Du. *lijf*, the body. β. Teut. type *libom*, n. This sb. is a derivative from Teut. root *lib* (weak grade *lib*), to remain, occurring in Icel. *lifa*, to be left, to remain, to live, AS. *lifian*, to be remaining, to live; OHG. *liban*, *lipan*, only used in the comp. *beliban*, MHG. *beliben*, G. *bleiben*, to remain, be left. γ. The sense 'remain' arose from that of 'to cleave;' and thus *life* is connected with Lithuanian *lipti*, to cleave, stick, Skt. *lip*, to anoint, smear, Gk. ἀλείφειν, to anoint, λῑπ-αρής, persistent; the form of the root being LEIP; Fick, i. 754. Der. *life-blood*, *life-boat*, *life-estate*, *life-guard*, q. v., *life-hold*, *life-insurance*, &c.; also *life-less*, *life-less-ly*, *life-less-ness*, *life-long*. Also *live*, *live-ly*, *live-lihood*, *live-long*. From the same source, *leave* (1). And see **Alive**.

LIFEGUARD, a body-guard. (Hybrid; E. *and* F.) 'The Cherethites were a kind of *lifeguard* to king David;' Fuller, Pisgah Sight of Palestine, ed. 1650, p. 217. From **Life** and **Guard**. ¶ See Trench, Eng. Past and Present. The word is *not* borrowed from the G. *leibgarde*, a body-guard; and it is much to the purpose to observe that, if it were so, it would make no difference; for the G. *leib* is the G. spelling of the word which we spell *life*, despite the difference in sense. The MHG. *lip* meant 'life' as well as 'body.'

LIFELONG, lasting for a life-time. (E.) Modern; suggested by *livelong*; see **Livelong**.

LIFT (1), to elevate, raise. (Scand.) ME. *liften*, to raise; Prompt. Parv. p. 303; P. Plowman, B. v. 359; Havelok, 1028; spelt *leften* (*leff-enn*) Ormulum, 2658, 2744, 2755, 6141, 7528, &c. The orig. sense is to raise *aloft*, to exalt *into the air*.—Icel. *lypta* (pronounced *lyfta*), to lift; allied to *loft*, the air; Dan. *löfte*, to lift; *loft*, a loft, a cock-loft, orig. 'the air;' Swed. *lyfta*, to lift; *loft*, a loft, garret, orig. 'the air.' Teut. type *luftjan*-; from *luftuz*, the air; see **Loft**. The *i*=*y*, mutation of *u* (*o*).

LIFT (2), to steal. (E.) 'But if night-robbers *lift* [steal from] the well-stored hive;' Dryden, Annus Mirabilis, st. 228, l. 916. The sb. *lifter*, a thief, occurs in Shak., Troil. i. 2. 129. This sense arose from that of lifting up and carrying away; and the word is ult. the same as **Lift** (1). See N. E. D. Skelton has: 'Conuey it be [by] crafte, *lyft* and lay asyde;' Magnificence, l. 1373.

LIGAMENT, a band, the membrane connecting the moveable bones. (F.—L.) In Minsheu, ed. 1627. ME. *ligament*, Lanfranc, Cirurgie, p. 24, l. 1.—F. *ligament*, 'a ligament, or ligature;' Cot.— L. *ligamentum*, a tie, band.—L. *liga-re*, to tie; with suffix -*mentum*. Der. *ligament-al*, *ligament-ous*. From L. *ligāre* we have also *liga-ture*, *liable*, *liane*, *lictor*, *lien*, *lime-hound*, *ally*, *alligation*, *alloy*, *ally*, *league* (1), *oblige*, *rally* (1).

LIGAN, as if from L. *ligāre*; corrupt form of **Lagan**, q. v.

LIGATURE, a bandage. (F.—L.) In Minsheu, ed. 1627; and in Lanfranc, Cirurgie, p. 177, l. 17.—F. *ligature*, 'a ligature, tie, band;' Cot.—L. *ligātūra*, a binding, bandage; from *ligāre*, to bind; see **Ligament**.

LIGHT (1), illumination. (E.) ME. *light*, Chaucer, C. T. 1989, 1991 (A 1987, 1989). AS. *leoht*, Grein, ii. 177 (cf. *lyhtan*, *lihtan*, to shine, id. ii. 200); OMerc. *leht*, whence ME. *liht*, *light*.+Du. *licht*; G. *licht*, OHG. *lioht*; Goth. *liuhath*, light. β. Observe that the *t* is a mere suffix; Teut. type *leuh-tom*, n., related to *leuh-toz*, adj., 'bright,' as in E. *light*, adj. The Goth. *liuh-ath* answers to Teut. type *leuh-a-thom*, Idg. type *leuk-o-tom*. γ. Neglecting the final *t*, we have cognate words in Icel. *ljōs* (Teut. type *leuh-som*), light, Icel. *logi*, a flame (whence Lowland Scotch *lowe*, a flame). Idg. root LEUQ; whence L. *lūx*, light, L. *lūmen* (=*luc-men*), light, *lūna* (=*louc-sna*), moon; with numerous connected terms; also Gk. λευκ-ός, white, bright, λύχνος (=λύκ-νος), a light, lamp, &c. Cf. Skt. *ruch*, to shine. See **Lucid**. Der. *light-house*. Also *light*, verb, ME. *lighten*, Chaucer, C. T. 2428, AS. *lyhtan*, *lihtan*, Grein, ii. 200; whence *light-er*, sb. Also *light-en* (1), q. v., *light-ning*, q. v. Connected words are *luc-id*, *luc-i-fer*, *e-luc-idate*, *il-lu-minate*, *lu-nar*, *lu-natic*, *luc-ubration*, *lea* (1), q. v., *lustre*, *il-lu-strate*, *il-lu-strious*, *lu-minous*, *lynx*, &c.

LIGHT (2), active, not heavy, unimportant. (E.) ME. *light*, Chaucer, C. T. 9087 (E 1211); *lightly*, adv., id. 1463 (A 1461). AS. *leoht*, adj., Grein, ii. 176; OMerc. *liht*, Matt. xi. 30 (Rushworth MS.).+Du. *ligt*; Icel. *lēttr*; Dan. *let*; Swed. *lätt*; Goth. *leihts*, 2 Cor. i. 17; G. *leicht*, MHG. *lihte*, OHG. *lihti*, *liht*. Teut. type *lihtoz*, for *linχtoz*, *lenχtoz*. Allied to Lith. *lengwas*, light; from Idg. base *lengh(w)*. From the weak grade of the same we have Gk. ἐ-λαχ-ύς, Skt. *lagh-u(s)*, light. Allied further to Skt. *langh*, to jump over. See Brugmann, i. § 684; Sievers, § 84. Thus the orig. sense is

'springy,' active, nimble; from which the other senses are easily deduced. Der. *light-ly*, *light-ness*, *lights*, q. v., *light-fingered*, *light-headed*, *light-hearted*, *light-minded*, &c.; *light-some*, Rom. of the Rose, l. 936; *light-some-ness*; *light-en* (2), q. v.; *light-er*, q. v. From the same root we have (from L. *leu-is*) *lev-ant*, *lev-er*, *lev-ity*, *lev-y*, *al-leviate*, &c. And see **Lung**.

LIGHT (3), to settle, alight, descend. (E.) ME. *lighten*, *lihten*; 'adun heo gunnen *lihten*'=they alighted down; Layamon, 26337; 'he *lighte* a-doun of lyard'=he lighted down from his horse, P. Plowman, B. xvii. 64. β. The sense is to relieve a horse of his burden, and the word is identical with ME. *lighten* in the sense of to relieve of a burden. The derivation is from the adj. *light*, not heavy; see **Light** (2). γ. When a man *alights* from a horse, he not only relieves the horse of his burden, but completes the action by descending or *alighting* on the earth; hence *light* came to be used in the sense of to descend, settle, often with the prep. *on*. 'New *lighted* on a heaven-kissing hill;' Hamlet, iii. 4. 59; 'this murderous shaft Hath yet not *lighted*;' Macb. ii. 3. 148. Hence this verb is (in sense) a doublet of **Lighten** (2), q. v., as well as of **Lighten** (3). Der. *light-er*, q. v. And see **Alight**, verb.

LIGHTEN (1), to illuminate, flash. (E.) The force of the final -*en* is somewhat dubious, but appears to have arisen in the transitive form. 1. Intrans. to shine as lightning; 'it *lightens*,' Romeo, ii. 2. 120. ME. *lightenen*, Prompt. Parv. p. 304; also *lightn-en*, to shine; Wyclif, Gen. i. 15. 2. Trans. The trans. use is in Shak. Hen. VIII, ii. 3. 79, Titus And. ii. 3. 227, with the sense 'to illuminate.' ME. *lightenen*; as in 'that *lightend* has ur ded sa dim;' Cursor Mundi, 18600. From *light*, sb. with causal suffix -*en*, as in *length-en*, *strength-en*. We also find the simple form *l'ight*, as in: 'the eye of heaven that *lights* the lower world;' Rich. II, iii. 2. 38. This is the ME. *lighten*, *lightè* (where the final -*en* is merely the mark of the infin. mood, often dropped); Chaucer, C. T. 2428 (A 2426). AS. *leohtan*, to illuminate; Grein, ii. 178.—AS. *leoht*, light; see **Light** (1). Der. *lightn-ing*.

LIGHTEN (2), to make lighter, alleviate. (E.) The final -*en* is merely formative, as in *strength-en*, *length-en*, *short-en*, *weak-en*. It is intended to have a causal force. We also find the simple form to *light*, answering to ME. *lighten*, *lightè* (in which the final -*en* is merely the mark of the infin. mood, and is often dropped). 'Lyghteyn, or make wyghtys [weights] more esy, *lightyn* burdens, heuy weightis, *Allevio*;' Prompt. Parv. p. 304. 'To *lihten* ower heaued'=to take the weight [of hair] off your head: Ancren Riwle, p. 422. From the adj. *light*; see **Light** (2), and **Light** (3). So also Dan. *lette*, to lighten, from *let*, light.

LIGHTEN (3), to descend, settle, alight. (E.) 'O Lord, let thy mercy *lighten* upon us;' Te Deum, in the Prayer-book (L. 'fiat'). Here *lighten* is a mere extension of **Light** (3), q. v.

LIGHTER, a boat for unlading ships. (Du.) In Skinner, ed. 1671; and in Pope, Dunciad, ii. 287. '*Lyghter*, a great bote;' Palsgrave. Probably borrowed from Du. *ligter*, a lighter (Sewel); spelt *lichter* in Skinner. Hence also *lighter-man*, from Du. *ligterman*, a lighter-man (Sewel).—Du. *ligt*, light (not heavy); see **Light** (2). ¶ Thus the sense is the same as if the word had been purely English; it means 'unloader;' from the use made of these vessels. Der. *lichter-man* (as above); *lighter-age*.

LIGHTNING, an illuminating flash. (E.) 'Thi *lightnyngis* schyneden;' Wyclif, Ps. lxxvii (lxxviii). 19. Verbal sb. from **Lighten** (1).

LIGHTS, lungs. (E.) ME. *lightes*, Destruction of Troy, 10705; þa *lihte*=the lights, Layamon, 6499, answering to AS. ðā *lihtan*, i. e. the light things. So called from their lightness. So also Russ. *legkiia*, lights; from *legkii*, light. See **Light** (2).

LIGN-ALOES, the bitter drug aloes. (Hybrid; L. *and* Gk.) In Numbers, xxiv. 6 (A. V.) 'A kind of odoriferous Indian tree, usually identified with the *Aquilaria Agallochum* which supplies the aloes-wood of commerce. Our word is a partial translation of the L. *lignum aloēs*, Gk. ξυλαλόη. The bitterness of the aloe is proverbial;' Bible Wordbook, ed. Eastwood and Wright. Chaucer has: 'As bittre . . . as is *ligne aloes*, or galle;' Troilus, iv. 1137.—L. *lignum*, wood; and *aloēs*, of the aloe, gen. case of *aloē*, the aloe, a word borrowed from Gk. ἀλόη, the aloe. ¶ On the true distinction between *aloe* and *aloes-wood*, see note to **Aloe**. And see **Ligneous**.

LIGNEOUS, woody, wooden, wood-like. (L.) 'Of a more *ligneous* nature;' Bacon, Nat. Hist. § 504. Formed by mere change of L. -*us* into E. -*ous* (as in *ingenuous*, *arduous*, and many others), from L. *ligneus*, wooden.—L. *lignum*, wood; a word of disputed origin. Der. from *ligni*- (for *ligno*-) we have *ligni-fer-ous*=wood-producing (from *ferre*, to bear); *ligni-fy*=to turn to wood; and from the stem *lign*- has been formed *lign-ite*, coal retaining the texture of wood, where the suffix -*ite* is Gk.

LIGULE, a strap-shaped petal. (L.) A mod. botanical term;

also applied to the flat part of the leaf of a grass. — L. *ligula*, a little tongue, a tongue-shaped extremity; by-form of *lingula*. Dimin. of *lingua*, a tongue; see **Lingual**. But Brugmann (i. § 604) derives *lig-ula* immediately from *lig-*, base of *ling-ere*, to lick. See **Lick**.

LIGURE, a precious stone. (L. — Gk.) In the Bible, A. V., Ex. xxviii. 19, xxxix. 12. 'Our translators have followed the Septuagint λιγύριον and Vulgate *ligurius* in translating the Heb. *leshem* by *ligure*, which is a precious stone unknown in modern mineralogy;' Bible Wordbook, by Eastwood and Wright. — L. *ligūrius*. — Gk. λι-γύριον, also spelt λιγγούριον, λιγκούριον, λυγκούριον, a sort of gem; acc. to some, a reddish amber, acc. to others, the hyacinth (Liddell).

LIKE (1), similar, resembling. (E.) ME. *lyk*, *lik*; Chaucer, C. T. 414, 1973 (A 412, 1971). AS. *lic*, in comp. *ge-lic*, like, in which form it is common; Grein, i. 422. The prefix *ge-* was long retained in the weakened form *i-* or *y-*; Chaucer has *yliche* as an adv., C. T. 2528 (A 2526).+Du. *ge-lijk*, like; where *ge-* is a prefix; Icel. *likr*, *glikr*, like; where *g-* = *ge-*, prefix; Dan. *lig*; Swed. *lik*; Goth. *ga-leiks*, Mark, vii. 8; G. *gleich*, MHG. *ge-lich*, OHG. *ka-lih*. β. All signifying 'resembling in form,' and derived from the Teut. sb. **likom*, a form, shape, appearing in AS. *lic*, a form, body (whence **Lich-gate**, p. 347), OSax. *lik*, Icel. *lik*, Goth. *leik*, the body, &c. Cf. Lith. *lygus*, like; Skt. *linga(m)*, a mark, sign; W. *cyffe-lyb*, like, similar; Stokes-Fick, p. 251. **Der.** *like-ly*, Chaucer, C. T. 1174 (A 1172); *like-li-hood*, ME. *liklihed*, id. 13526 (B 1786); *like-li-ness*, ME. *likliness*, id. 8272 (E 396); *like-ness*, ME. *liknes*, P. Plowman, B. i. 113, formerly *i-licnes*, Ancren Riwle, p. 230, from AS. *ge-licnes*; *like-wise*, short for *in like wise* (see **Wise**, sb.); *like* (2), q. v.; *like*, sb.; *lik-en*, q. v. ☞ All adjectives ending in *-ly* have adopted this ending from AS. *-lic*, lit. 'like;' all adverbs in *-ly* take this suffix from AS. *-lice*, the same word with the adverbial final *-e* added. The word *like-ly* = *like-like*, a reduplication.

LIKE (2), to approve, be pleased with. (E.) The mod. sense is evolved by an alteration in the construction. The ME. verb *lyken* (or *liken*) signified 'to please,' and was used impersonally. We have, in fact, changed the phrase *it likes me* into *I like*, and so on throughout. Both senses are in Shak.; see Temp. iii. 1. 43, Hamlet, v. 2. 276. Chaucer has only the intrans. verb. 'And if *you lyketh*' = and if it please you; C. T. 779 (A 777); still preserved in the mod. phrase 'if you like.' 'That oghte *lyken* yow' = that ought to please you; id. 13866 (B 2128). AS. *lician*, to please, rarely *lican*; Grein, ii. 182. The lit. sense is to be like or suitable for. — AS. *lic*, *ge-lic*, like; see **Like** (1).+Du. *lijken*, to be like, resemble, seem, suit; from *ge-lijk*, like; Icel. *lika*, to like; from *likr*, like; Goth. *leikan*, *ga-leikan*, to please; from *ga-leiks*, like; MHG. *lichen*, *ge-lichen*, to be like; from *ge-lich*, like (G. *gleich*). **Der.** *lik-ing*, ME. *lykynge*, P. Plowman, B. xi. 20, O. Eng. Homilies, ed. Morris, i. 271. Also *well-liking* = well-pleasing, Ps. xcii. 13, Prayer-book.

LIKEN, to consider as similar, to compare. (E.; *or* Scand.) ME. *liknen*. 'The water is *likned* to the worlde;' P. Plowman, B. viii. 39, A. ix. 34. 'And *lyknez* hit to heuen ly3te' = and likens it to the light of heaven; Allit. Poems, ed. Morris, A. 500. But the orig. sense was perhaps *intransitive*, as in the case of Goth. verbs in *-nan*, and several Swed. verbs in *-na*; and the peculiar use and form of the word seem to be Scand. It is intrans. in Allit. Poems, B. 1064. — Swed. *likna*, (1) to resemble, (2) to liken; from *lik*, like; Dan. *ligne*, (1) to resemble, (2) to liken; from *lig*, like. See **Like** (1).

LILAC, a flowering shrub. (F. — Span. — Arab. — Pers.) 'The *lelacke* tree;' Bacon, Essay 46. Spelt *lilach* in Kersey, ed. 1715. — MF. *lilac*, Cot.; now spelt *lilas*. — Span. *lilac*, *lila*, a lilac. Of Oriental origin. — Arab. *lilak*, *lilāk* (Devic). Derived from the Pers. *lilaj*, *lilanj*, or *lilang*, of which the proper sense is the indigo-plant; Rich. Pers. Dict. p. 1282. Here the initial *l* stands for *n*, and the above forms are connected with Pers. *nil*, the indigo-plant; whence *nilak* (dimin. form, whence Arab. *lilak*), blueish; Rich. Dict. pp. 1619, 1620. Cf. Skt. *nila-s*, dark-blue, *nili*, the indigo-plant. Named from the blueish tinge on the flowers in some varieties (Devic).

LILLIPUTIAN, diminutive, very small. (E.) 'The stairs are of *lilliputian* measurement;' Dickens, American Notes (1850), p. 33. Formed with suffix *-ian*, from *Lilliput*, the name of an imaginary country in Gulliver's Travels, inhabited by pygmies six inches high. Coined by Swift (1726).

LILT, to sing cheerfully. (Scand.) Cf. ME. *lilting-horn*, Chaucer, Ho. of Fame, 1223. The pp. *lulted* occurs in Early E. Allit. Poems, A. 1207. Connected with Norw. *lilla*, to sing in a high tone; OSwed. *lylla*, to lull to sleep (Rietz, s. v. *lulla*). — Swed. *lulla*, Dan. *lulle*, to hum, to lull. See **Lull**. See Notes on E. Etym., p. 163.

LILY, a bulbous plant. (L. — Gk.) ME. *lilie*; Chaucer, C. T. 15555 (G 87). AS. *lilie*, *lilian*; Matt. vi. 28; Ælfric's Gloss., Nomina Herbarum. — L. *lilium*; Matt. vi. 28. — Gk. λείριον, a lily; the change of Gk. ρ to L. *l* being in accordance with usual laws.

¶ The more usual Gk. name is κρίνον, as in Matt. vi. 28. **Der.** *lili-ac-e-ous* = L. *liliāceus*.

LIMB (1), a member of the body, branch of a tree. (E.) ME. *lim*, pl. *limes*; Chaucer, C. T. 4881 (B 461). AS. *lim*, pl. *leomu*; Grein, ii. 188; Icel. *limr*; Dan. and Swed. *lem*. Teut. types **li-mom*, n.; **li-moz*, m.; allied to AS. *li-þ*, Goth. *li-þus*, a limb. See **Lay figure**. Cf. Lith. *lēmŭ*, trunk, stature.

LIMB (2), the edge or border of a sextant, &c. (L.) 'Limb, in mathematics, the outermost border of an astrolabe; .. in astronomy, the utmost border of the disk or body of the sun or moon, when either is in eclipse;' Kersey, ed. 1715. Kersey also gives the form *limbus*. — L. *limbus*, a border, edging, edge. Cotgrave gives MF. *l'mbe de bouteille*, 'the mouth or brink of a bottle.' **Doublet**, *limbo*.

LIMBECK, the same as **Alembic**, q. v. Palsgrave has: 'Lembyke for a styllatorie, *lembic*;' where *lembic* is a F. form.

LIMBER (1), flexible, pliant. (E.) Not found very early. 'With *limber* vows;' Wint. Tale, i. 2. 47. Richardson quotes an earlier and better example. 'Ne yet the bargeman, that doth rowe With long and *limber* oare;' Turbervile, A Myrrour of the Fall of Pride. Cooper's Thesaurus has: '*Lentus*, softe, pliant, *limber*' (1565). Perhaps allied to *limp*, flexible, pliant; or to prov. E. *limmock*, flexible, pliant. The suffix *-er* is adjectival, as in *bitt-er*, *fair-er* (= AS. *fæg-er*), &c.; see Mätzner, Engl. Gramm. i. 435. See **Limp** (1).

LIMBER (2), part of a gun-carriage consisting of two wheels and a shaft to which horses are attached. (F.) Taken up from prov. E. '*Limbers*, thills or shafts (Berkshire); *Limmers*, a pair of shafts (North);' Grose's Prov. Eng. Glossary, ed. 1790; and see E.D.D. It appears that *b* is excrescent, and the form *limmers* is the older one. β. Further, *limmer* was formerly spelt *limour* (in 1480), and *lymowr*, as in: 'The cartis stand with *lymowris*;' Douglas, tr. of Virgil, bk. ix. ch. 6, l. 23. In Douglas, Palice of Honour, st. 33, the form used is *lymnaris*, pl. of *lymnar*, for *limner*. The spelling *limours* seems to be an E. variant of F. *limons*, pl. of *limon*, 'the thill of a waine,' which was mostly used in the pl.; Cot. Similarly, *limner* may well represent F. *limonier*, as in 'Cheval *limonier*, a thill-horse;' Cot.

LIMBO, LIMBUS, the borders of hell. (L.) In Shak. All's Well, v. 3. 261. The orig. phrase was *in limbo*, Com. Errors, iv. 2. 32; or more fully, *in limbo patrum*, Hen. VIII, v. 4. 67. — L. *limbō* (governed by the prep. *in*), abl. case of *limbus*, a border; see **Limb** (2). 'The *limbus patrum*, in the language of churchmen, was the place bordering on hell, where the saints of the Old Testament remained till Christ's descent into hell;' Schmidt. The Ital. word is also *limbo*, derived (not from the ablative, but) from the acc. *limbum* of the same L. word. Cf. P. Plowman, B. xvi. 84. **Doublet**, *limb* (2).

LIME (1), viscous substance, bird-lime, mortar, oxide of calcium. (E.) The orig. sense is 'viscous substance.' ME. *lym*, *liim*, *lyme*. 'Lyme, to take with byrdys [to catch birds with], *viscus*; Lyme, or mortare, *Calx*;' Prompt. Parv. p. 305. And see Chaucer, C. T. 16274 (G 806). AS. *lim*, bitumen, cement; Grein, ii. 188.+Du. *lijm*, glue, lime; Icel. *lim*, glue, lime, chalk; Dan. *lim*, glue; Swed. *lim*, glue; G. *leim*, glue; MHG. *lim*, bird-lime.+L. *limus*, mud, slime. β. Teut. type **limoz*, Idg. type **leimos*, from √LEI; of which the weak grade (*li*) appears in L. *li-nere*, to smear, daub; cf. Russ. *lite*, to pour, flow; cf. Skt. *li*, to melt, to adhere; allied to Skt. *ri*, to distil. See **Loam** (which is allied). **Der.** *lime*, verb, Ancren Riwle, p. 226, Hamlet, iii. 3. 68; *lim-y*; *lime-kiln*, Merry Wives, iii. 3. 86; *lime-stone*; *lime-twig*, Lydgate, Minor Poems, p. 189; *lime-rod*, spelt *lymrod*, Chaucer, C. T. 14694 (B 3574).

LIME (2), the linden-tree. (E.) In Pope, Autumn, 25. A corruption of the earlier spelling *line*. 'Linden-tree, or Line-tree;' Kersey, ed. 1715. 'In the line-grove' (modern edd. *lime-grove*); Shak. Temp. v. 10. The change from *line* to *lime* does not seem to be older than about A. D. 1625. The form *lime* is in Bailey's Dict., vol. ii. ed. 1731; Bacon has 'the *lime-tree*;' Essay 46. β. Again, *line* is a corruption of *lind*, the older name, by loss of final *d*. See **Linden**. **Der.** *lime-tree*.

LIME (3), a kind of citron. (F. — Span. — Arab. *or* Pers. — Malay.) First in 1638. '*Lime*, a sort of small lemmon;' Phillips, ed. 1706. — F. *lime*, a lime; Hamilton. — Span. *lima*. — Arab. *limah* (below); Pers. *limū*, a lemon, citron; Rich. Dict. p. 1282. — Malay *limau*, Javanese *limo*, a generic name for a lime or citron. And see **Lemon**. Dozy gives Arab. *limah*, a lime; see Devic.

LIME-HOUND, a dog led by a cord; a dog used for hunting the wild boar. (F. — L.; *and* E.) Lime-hound is short for *liam-hound*, a hound held by a *liam* or leash. 'The string wherewith wee leade a Grey hounde is called a *leqse*, and for a hounde a *lyame*;' Turberville, Booke of Hunting, ed. 1575, p. 240. See Croft's Gloss. to Sir T. Elyot's The Governour. Spenser has *lime-hound*; F. Q. v. 2. 25. — OF. *liem*; F. *lien*; see Littré, s. v. *lien*; and cf. Norm.

dial. *lian*, a tie, a cord. = L. *ligāmen*, a fastening; see **Lien**. And see **Hound**. See Notes on E. Etym., p. 164.

LIMIT, to assign a boundary; a boundary. (F.—L.) The verb is in older (general) use in E. than the sb. *limit*, though really the derived word. ME. *limiten*, to limit. 'To *limite* us or assigne us;' Chaucer, Tale of Melibeus, Six-text, B 2956. [Hence the sb. *limit-or*, Chaucer, C. T. 209.] = F. *limiter*, 'to limit;' Cot. = F. *limite*, a limit; id. = L. *limitem*, acc. of *līmes*, a boundary; akin to L. *limen*, a threshold. Prob. allied to L. *limus*, transverse (Bréal). **Der.** *limit-ed*, *limit-ed-ly*, *limit-ed-ness*, *limit-less*, *limit-able*; also *limit-at-ion* = F. *limitation*, 'a limitation' (Cot.), from L. acc. *limitātiōnem*.

LIMN, to illuminate, paint. (F.—L.) ME. *limnen*, a contracted form of *luminen*. '*Lymnyd*, or *lumynid*, as bookys;' Prompt. Parv. p. 317. '*Lymnore, luminour*, Alluminator, illuminator;' id. β. Again, *luminen* is short for *enluminen*, by loss of the prefix. Chaucer has *enlumined* = enlightened; C. T. 7909 (E 33). = MF. *enluminer*, 'to illuminate, inlighten; . . also to sleek, burnish; also to *limn*;' Cot. = Late L. *inlūmināre*; for L. *illūmināre*, to enlighten; see **Illuminate**. **Der.** *limn-er* = ME. *luminour*, as above, short for *enluminour*; '*Enlumineur de livres*, a burnisher of bookes, an alluminer;' Cot.

LIMP (1), flaccid, flexible, pliant, weak. (E.) '*Limp*, limber, supple;' Kersey, ed. 1715. Scarce in books, but known to our E. dialects, and doubtless an old E. word. β. Allied words are perhaps 'Swiss *lampig*, *lampelig*, faded, loose, flabby, hanging,' and similar words, cited in Wedgwood. Also Bavarian *lampecht*, flaccid, *lampende Ohren*, hanging ears (answering to E. *lop-ears*, as in 'a *lop-eared* rabbit'); *lāmp*, *lemp*, a rag, a hanging shred; from the verb *lampen*, to hang loosely down; Schmeller, Bav. Dict. 1474. Cf. Skt. *lamba-*, depending, *lambana-*, falling; from the verb *lamb*, to fall, hang downwards. **Der.** *limp-ness*; cf. *limber* (1).

LIMP (2), to walk lamely. (E.) In Shak. Merch. Ven. iii. 2. 130; and in Levins (1570). Palsgrave has: '*lympe-hault, boiteux*.' Not easily traced earlier, and the orig. form is uncertain. Allied to AS. *lemp-healt*, limp-halting, halting, lame, of which the earliest form is *læmpi-halt*, Epinal Gloss., 589; cf. *lemp-halt*, Corpus Gloss., 1250. Allied also to MDan. *limpe*, to limp (Kalkar); MHG. *limphin*, to limp. Possibly connected with **Limp** (1), rather than (as some think) with **Lame**. ¶ We also find Low G. *lumpen*, to limp (Bremen Wörterbuch); which seems to be connected with *limp* by gradation. So also Dan. dial. *lumpe*, to limp; *lumpen*, lame.

LIMPET, a small shell-fish, which cleaves to rocks. (L.) Cotgrave explains OF. *berdin* by 'the shellfish called a *lympyne* or a *lempet*.' Holland, tr. of Pliny, b. xxxii. c. 9, translates L. *mituli* by '*limpins*.' ME. *lempet*, Durham Acc. Rolls (Surtees Soc.), p. 10 (:313). AS. *lempedu*, (properly) a lamprey. = Late L. *lemprida*, for *lamprēda*, late form of *lampetra*, a lamprey; see **Lamprey**, of which *limpet* is a doublet. We find in Wülker's Gloss., 438, 17: '*lemprida*, *lempedu*;' where *lempedu* is the AS. form. See Notes on E. Etym., p. 164.

LIMPID, pure, clear, shining. (F.—L.) In Blount's Gloss. ed. 1674. 'Most pure and *limpid* juice;' Sir T. Browne, Vulg. Errors, bk. ii. c. 1. § 16. = F. *limpide*, 'clear, bright;' Cot. = L. *limpidus*, limpid, clear. Allied to L. *lympha*, pure water; see **Lymph**. Brugmann, i. § 102. **Der.** *limpid-i-ty*, *limpid-ness*.

LINCH-PIN, a pin to fasten the wheel on to the axle. (E.) Formerly also spelt *lins-pin*, as Kersey, ed. 1715; Coles, ed. 1684; Skinner, ed. 1671. [*Linch* appears to be a corrupted form, obviously by confusion with *link*.] The pl. *linses* in Will. of Shoreham's Poems, p. 109, means 'linch-pins.' AS. *lynis*, an axle-tree; Epinal Gloss., 8. +Du. *luns*, a linch-pin; whence *lunzen*, to put the linch-pin to a wheel; Low G. *lunse*, a linch-pin; Bremen Wörterbuch; G. *lünse*, a linch-pin. β. Cf. also OHG. *lun*, a linch-pin.

LIND, LINDEN, the lime-tree. (E.) Here (as in the case of *asp-en*) the true sb. is *lind*, whence *lind-en* was formed as an adjective, with the suffix *-en* as in *gold-en*, *birch-en*, *beech-en*. The true name is *lind*, or, in longer phrase, *linden tree*. *Lind* was in time corrupted to *line*, and later to *lime*; see **Lime** (2). ME. *lind*, *lynd*; Chaucer, C. T. 2924 and 2922. AS. *lind*, Grein, ii. 128. 'Seno vel tilia, *lind*;' Ælfric's Gloss., Nomina Arborum. Hence the adj. *linden* (Grein, ii. 189), as in *linden bord* = the linden shield, shield made of lind.+Du. *linde*, *linde-boom*; Icel. *lind*; Dan. *lind*, *lind-træ*; Swed. *lind*; G. *linde*, OHG. *linta*. Teut. type *lendā* (?). Idg. base *lent-*; the weak grade appears in Gk. ἐλάτη, silver fir. Cf. Lith. *lenta*, a board.

LINE, a thread, thin cord, stroke, row, rank, verse. (L.; or F.—L.) In all senses the word is of L. origin; the only difference is that, in some senses, the word was borrowed from L. *directly*, in other senses *through the French*. We may take them separately, as follows. 1. *Line* = a thin cord or rope, a thread, rope of a ship. ME. *lyne*; P. Plowman, B. v. 355. AS. *line*, a cord; Grein, ii. 189. = L. *linea*, a string of hemp or flax, hempen cord; properly

the fem. of adj. *lineus*, made of hemp or flax. = L. *linum*, flax. Prob. rather cognate with than borrowed from Gk. λίνον, flax. [The G. *lein*, &c. are probably borrowed from Latin.] 2. *Line* = a verse, rank, row; Chaucer, C. T. 1553 (A 1551); P. Plowman, B. vii. 110. = F. *ligne*, a line. = L. *linea*, a line, stroke, mark, line of descent; the same word as above. **Der.** *line*, verb, in various senses; to *line* garments is properly to put *linen* inside them (see **Linen**); also *lin-ing*, *lineal*, q. v., *linear*, q. v., *lineage*, q. v., *lineament*, q. v. And see *linnet*, *linseed*, *linsey-woolsey*, *lint*, *de-lineate*, *a-lign*.

LINEAGE, race, family, descent. (F.—L.) ME. *linage* (without the medial *e*), Chaucer, C. T. 1552 (A 1550); Romance of Partenay, 5033; *lignage*, Gower, C. A. i. 344; bk. iii. 1944. = F. *lignage*, 'a lineage;' Cot. [Here E. *ne* = F. *gn*.] Made with suffix *-age* (= L. *-āticum*) from F. *ligne*, a line. = L. *linea*, a line; see **Line**.

LINEAL, belonging to a line. (L.) In Spenser, F. Q. iv. 11. 12. '*Lineally* and in the genelogye;' Lydgate, Minor Poems, p. 17. = L. *lineālis*, belonging to a line. = L. *linea*, a line; see **Line**. **Der.** *lineal-ly*. Doublet, *linear*.

LINEAMENT, a feature. (F.—L.) 'In the *liniamentes* and fauor of his visage;' Sir T. More, Works, p. 61 b. = MF. *lineament*, 'a lineament or feature;' Cot. = L. *lineāmentum*, a drawing, delineation, feature. = L. *lineāre*, to draw a line; with suffix *-mentum*. = L. *linea*, a line; see **Line**.

LINEAR, consisting of lines. (L.) In Blount's Gloss., ed. 1674. = L. *lineāris*, belonging to a line. = L. *linea*; see **Line**. Doublet, *lineal*, which is an older word. **Der.** *linear-ly*.

LINEN, cloth made of flax. (L.) Used as a sb., but really an adj., with adj. suffix *-en* as in *wooll-en*, *gold-en*; the orig. sb. was *lin*, preserved in *lin-seed*. ME. *lin*, sb. *linen*, adj. The sb. is rare. 'The bondes . . . That weren of ful strong *line*' = the bonds that were of very strong flax; Havelok, 539. The adj. is common. 'Clothid with *lynnun* cloth . . . he lefte the *lynnyn* clothing;' Wyclif, Mark, xiv. 51, 52. It was also used as a sb., as now. 'In *lynnen* yclothed' = clothed in linen; P. Plowman, B. i. 3. = AS. *līn*, flax, linen; in comp. *līn-wǣd*, a linen garment; John, xiii. 5. Thence was formed the adj. *līnen*, as in *līnen hrægl* = a linen cloth, John, xiii. 4. = L. *linum*, flax; cognate with Gk. λίνον, flax. See **Line**. And see *linseed*, *linnet*.

LING (1), a kind of fish. (E.) '*Lynge*, fysshe;' Palsgrave. Spelt *leenge* in Prompt. Parv. p. 296; and see Way's note. Spelt *lenge*, Havelok, l. 832. Not found in AS., but answering to Teut. *lang-jōn-*, f., from *lang*, long; i.e. 'the long one.' EFries. *leng*, *leng-fisk*. So called from its slender shape.+Du. *leng*, a ling; from *lang*, long; Icel. *langa*, a ling; from *langr*, long; Norw. *langa*, *longa* (Aasen); Swed. *långa*; G. *länge*, a ling; also called *längfisch*, i.e. long fish.

LING (2), heath. (Scand.) '*Lynge*, or heth;' Prompt. Parv. p. 305; and see Way's note. 'Dede in the *lyng*' = lying dead on the heath; Sir Degrevant, l. 336, in Thornton Romances, ed. Halliwell. (Not AS.) = Icel. *lyng*, ling, heather; Dan. *lyng*; Swed. *ljung*, ling, heather; Swed. dial. *ling* (Rietz). Teut. type *lengwo-*; cf. Swed. *lingon*, the whortleberry.

LINGER, to loiter, tarry, hesitate. (E.) 'Of *lingring* doutes such hope is sprong, pardie;' Surrey, Bonum est mihi, l. 10; in Tottell's Miscellany, ed. Arber, p. 31. Formed by adding the frequentative suffix *-er* or *-r* to the ME. *lengen*, to tarry; with further thinning of *e* to *i* before *ng*. This ME. verb is by no means rare. 'I may no *lenger lenge*' = I may no longer linger; P. Plowman, B. i. 207. Cf. Will. of Palerne, 5421; Havelok, 1734. = AS. *lengan*, to prolong, put off; Grein, i. 168; formed by the usual vowel-change (of *a* to *e*) from AS. *lang*, long; see **Long**. Cf. Icel. *lengja*, to lengthen, from *langr*, long; G. *verlängern*, to prolong, from *lang*, long; Du. *lengen*, to lengthen, *verlengen*, to prolong.

LINGO, speech, language. (Prov.—L.) A contemptuous term. 'Well, well, I shall understand your *lingo* one of these days;' Congreve, Way of the World, A. iv. sc. 1 (Sir Wilfull). = Prov. *lengo*, *lingo*, speech (Mistral); *lingo* is the precise form used at Marseilles, and *lengo* is Gascon (Moncaut). = L. *lingua*, tongue, speech (below). Cf. Port. *lingoa*.

LINGUAL, pertaining to the tongue. (L.) A late word (with few exceptions); not in Todd's Johnson. Coined, as if from an adj. *lingŭālis*, from L. *lingua*, the tongue, of which the OL. form was *dingua* (see Lewis' Dict.); cognate with E. **Tongue**, q. v. **Der.** (from L. *lingua*) *lingu-ist*, q. v., *language*, q. v.

LINGUIST, one skilled in languages. (L.) In Shak. Two Gent. iv. 1. 57; and in Minsheu, ed. 1627. Coined, with suffix *-ist* (= L. *-ista*, from Gk. *-ιστης*), from L. *lingu-a*, the tongue; see **Lingual**. **Der.** *linguist-ic*, *linguist-ic-s*.

LINIMENT, a salve, soft ointment. (F.—L.) The word occurs 3 or 4 times in Holland, tr. of Pliny, b. xxii. c. 21. = F. *liniment*.

'a liniment, a thin ointment;' Cot. – L. *linimentum*, smearing-stuff, ointment. Formed, with suffix -*mentum*, from *linīre*, to smear; allied to *linere*, to smear. Cf. Skt. *ri*, to distil, ooze, drop; *li*, to melt, adhere. Brugmann, i. § 476 (5); ii. § 608.

LINING, a covering on the inner surface of a garment. (L.) In Shak. L. L. L. v. 2. 791. Formed, with E. suffix -*ing*, from the verb to *line*, meaning to cover the inside of a garment with *line*, i.e. *linen*; see **Line, Linen**.

LINK (1), a ring of a chain, joint. (Scand.) In Shak. Cor. i. 1. 73. Cf. 'Trouth [truth] and mercy *linked* in a chain;' Lydgate, Storie of Thebes, pt. ii (How trouth is preferred). – OIcel. **hlenkr*, Icel. *hlekkr* (by assimilation); Dan. *lænke*; Swed. *länk*.+AS. *hlence* (which would have given *linch*); as in the comp. sb. *wælhlence*, a slaughter-link, i.e. linked coat of mail, Grein, ii. 646. Teut. type **hlankjoz*, m.; cf. also G. *gelenk*, a joint, link, ring; G. *lenken*, to turn, bend. **Der.** *link*, verb.

LINK (2), a torch. (Scand.) 'A *link* or torch;' Minsheu's Dict., ed. 1627. '*Links* and torches;' Shak. 1 Hen. IV, iii. 3. 48. 'Lynke, *torche*;' Palsgrave. Of obscure origin; but it is prob. the same as the word above, in the sense of 'length of rope;' cf. 'a *link* of sausages.' Such seems to be the sense in Shak. 2 Hen. IV, v. i. 23: 'Now, sir, a new *link* to the bucket must needs be had.' Links for torches were made of handy lengths of rope.

LINN, a pool; also a cascade, torrent. (C.) Two words have been confounded: (1) AS. *hlynn*, a torrent; Rushworth Gospels, John, xviii. 1; and (2) Gael. *linne*, Irish *linn*, W. *llyn*, a pool. See Notes on E. Etym., p. 165.

LINNET, a small singing-bird. (F. – L.) ME. *lynet*, Court of Love, l. 1412. – OF. *linette* (Godefroy); F. *linotte*, 'a linnet;' Cot. [So called from feeding on the seed of flax and hemp, as is clearly shown by similar names in other languages, e.g. G. *hänfling*, a linnet, from *hanf*, hemp, G. *lein-finke*, a linnet (cited by Wedgwood), lit. a lin-finch, flax-finch.] – F. *lin*, flax. – L. *linum*, flax; see **Linen, Line**. ¶ The E. name is *lintwhite*, Scotch *lintquhit*; see Complaint of Scotland, ed. Murray, p. 39, l. 24. From AS. *linetwige*, a linnet; Ælfric's Gloss., Nomina Avium. This name is also (probably) from L. *linum*, flax. So also W. *llinos*, a linnet; from *llin*, flax.

LINSEED, flax-seed. (Hybrid; L. *and* E.) ME. *lin-seed*; spelt *lynne-seed* in P. Plowman, C. xiii. 190; *linseed* (to translate OF. *lynoys*) in Walter de Bibbesworth; Wright's Vocab. i. 156. From ME. *lin* = AS. *lin*, flax, borrowed from L. *linum*, flax; and E. *seed*. See **Line, Linen**, and **Seed**. **Der.** *linseed-oil*, *linseed-cake*.

LINSEY-WOOLSEY, made of linen and wool mixed. (Hybrid; L. *and* E.) '*Lynsy-wolsye*, linistema, vel linostema;' Cathol. Anglicum (1483). Used facetiously in Shak. All's Well, iv. 1. 13; Minsheu (ed. 1627) has: '*linsie-woolsie*, i.e. of linnen and woollen.' As if from ME. *lin*, linen; and E. *wool*; with -*sy* or -*sey* as a suffix twice over; cf. *tip-sy*; see **Linen** and **Wool**. β. But *linsey* may represent *Lindsey*, near *Kersey* (Suffolk); see **Kersey**. In fact, *Lindsey* was formerly *Lynsey, Lylsey, Lelesey*; Skelton has the form *Lylse wulse*; see further in the Supplement.

LINSTOCK, LINTSTOCK, a stick to hold a lighted match. (Du.) In Dryden, Annus Mirabilis, st. 188; spelt *linstock* in Marlowe, Jew of Malta, v. 4. 4. '*Lint-stock*, a carved stick (about half a yard) with a cock at one end to hold the gunner's match, and a sharp pike at the other, to stick it anywhere;' Coles' Dict., ed. 1684. – Du. *lontstok*, 'a lint-stock;' Sewel. – Du. *lont*, a match; and *stok*, a stick, for which see **Stock**.+Dan. *lunte-stok*, a lint-stock; from *lunte*, a match, and *stok*, a stick; Swed. *lunt-stake*; from *lunta*, a match, an old bad book (fit to be burnt), and *stake*, a stick, candle-stick. β. The derivation of Du. *lont*, Swed. *lunta*, is uncertain; but it would appear from Kilian that Du. *lomp*, a rag, tatter, MDu. *lompe*, was also used in the same sense as *lont*, MDu. *lonte*. Perhaps *lonte* arose from **lomp-te*; cf. MDu. *lonte*, a match, rag, with MDu. *lompe*, a rag, tatter; and Swed. *lunta*, a match, with Swed. *lumpor*, rags (only used in the plural). See Ihre, s. v. *lunta*; and see **Lump**.

LINT, scraped linen. (F. – L.; *or* L.) '*Lynt*, schauynge of lynen clothe, *Carpea*;' Prompt. Parv. p. 306. Spelt *lynnet* in Lanfranc, Cirurgie, p. 83; but *lynt* (flax) in Barbour, Bruce, bk. xvii. 612. Either from F. *lin*, flax, with F. suffix -*et* or -*ette* (cf. OF. *linette*, linseed, in Godefroy); or perhaps borrowed directly from L. *linteum*, a linen cloth. – L. *linteus*, made of linen. – L. *linum*, flax. See **Line, Linen**. ¶ And see Du. *lint* in Franck.

LINTEL, the head-piece of a door or casement. (F. – L.) ME. *lintel, lyntel*; Wyclif, Exod. xii. 22. – OF. *lintel* (see Littré), later F. *linteau*, 'the lintell, or head-piece, over a door;' Cot. – Late L. *lintellus*, a lintel; which (as Diez suggests) stands for **limitellus*, dimin. of L. *limes* (stem *limit-*), a boundary, hence a border; see **Limit**. Prob. confused with *limen*, a threshold. ¶ A similar contraction is found in Span. *linde*, from L. acc. *limitem*, a boundary.

LION, a large and fierce beast of prey. (F. – L. – Gk. – Egypt.)

In early use. In Layamon, 1463, we find *leon* in the earlier text, *lion* in the later. A still earlier form was *leo*, but this was borrowed from the Latin *directly*; see **Leo**. – OF. *leon, lion*. – L. *leōnem*, acc. of *leo*, a lion. – Gk. λέων, a lion. Also Gk. λέαινα, for **λέϝαινα, a lioness; from Egypt. *labai, lawai*; which was also the name of the hieroglyphic for L. Cf. Heb. *lābī*, a lion; also of Egypt. origin. See Notes on E. Etym., p. 165. We also find G. *löwe*, OHG. *leo, lewo*; Russ. *lev'*; Lithuanian *lēvas, lavas*; Du. *leeuw*; &c. **Der.** *lion-ess*, As You Like It, iv. 3. 115, from F. *lionnesse*; *lion-hearted*; also *lion-ise*, orig. to show strangers the lions which used to be kept in the Tower of London. See Capt. Smith, Works, ed. Arber; p. 872.

LIP, the muscular part forming each of the upper and lower edges of the mouth. (E.) ME. *lippe*, Chaucer, C. T. 128, 133. AS. *lippa*. '*Labium*, ufeweard lippa' = upper lip; Ælfric's Gloss., in Voc. 157. 22. '*Labrum*, niðera lippe' = nether lip; id.+Du. *lip*; Dan. *læbe*; Swed. *läpp*; G. *lippe, lefze*; OHG. *lefs, leffur*. Further allied to L. *lab-rum, lab-ium*, the lip; Pers. *lab*, the lip, Palmer's Pers. Dict. col. 511. See Brugmann, i. § 563. Perhaps allied to *lambere*, to lick (Bréal). The AS. *lippa* represents a Teut. type **lep-jon-*, m. **Der.** *lipp-ed*; from the same root are *lab-ial, lab-iate, lamb-ent*.

LIQUEFY, to make liquid. (F. – L.) Also 'to become liquid,' but this is a later sense. 'The disposition not to *liquefie*' = to become liquid; Bacon, Nat. Hist. § 840. – MF. *liquefier*; but only found in Cot. as a pp.; he gives '*liquefié*,' dissolved, melted, made liquid.' β. The E. *liquefy* is formed by analogy with other words in -*fy*, which answers to F. -*fier* = L. -*ficāre*, used in place of *facere*, to make. But in the intrans. sense the word corresponds to L. *liquefierī*, to become liquid, used as pass. of *liquefacere*, to make liquid. – L. *lique-*, from *liquēre*, to be fluid; and *facere*, to make. See **Liquid** and **Fact**. **Der.** *lique-fact-ion*, Minsheu, ed. 1627; allied to *liquefactus*, pp. of *liquefacere*.

LIQUESCENT, melting. (L.) Modern; in Todd's Johnson; and in Bailey, vol. ii. – L. *liquescent-*, stem of pres. pt. of *liquescere*, to become liquid; inceptive form of *liquēre*, to be liquid. See **Liquid**. **Der.** *liquescenc-y, de-liquescent*.

LIQUEUR, a cordial. (F. – L.) In Pope; Dunciad, iv. 317. A modern F. form of the older term **Liquor**, q. v.

LIQUID, fluid, moist, soft, clear. (F. – L.) 'The playne [flat] and *liquide* water;' Tyndal, Works, p. 265, col. 2. – F. *liquide*, 'liquid, moist, wet;' Cot. – L. *liquidus*, liquid, moist. – L. *liquēre*, to be liquid or moist or clear. See Bréal. **Der.** *liquid*, sb., *liquid-i-ty, liquid-ness*; also *liquid-ate*, q. v.; *liquor*, q. v., *lique-fy*, q. v.

LIQUIDATE, to make clear, clear or pay off an account. (L.) Bailey has *liquidated*, vol. ii. ed. 1727. '*Liquidate*, to make moist or clear;' Blount, Gloss., 1681. – Late L. *liquidātus*, pp. of *liquidāre*, to clarify, make clear. – L. *liquidus*, liquid, clear; see **Liquid**. **Der.** *liquid-at-ion* = F. *liquidation*; *liquidat-or*.

LIQUOR, anything liquid, moisture, strong drink. (F. – L.) The word is really F., but has been accommodated to the orig. L. spelling; yet we retain somewhat of the F. pronunciation, the *qu* being sounded as *c* (*k*). ME. *licour*, Chaucer, C. T. 1. 3; spelt *licur*; Ancren Riwle, p. 164, l. 13. – AF. *licur*, Tristan, i. 136; F. *liqueur*, 'liquor, humor;' Cot. – L. *liquōrem*, acc. of *liquor*, moisture. – L. *liquēre*, to be liquid; see **Liquid**. **Doublet**, *liqueur*.

LIQUORICE, the same as **Licorice**, q. v.

LIRA, an Italian silver coin. (Ital. – L.) First in 1617. – Ital. *lira*. – L. *libra*, a pound. **Doublet**, *litre*.

LISP, to pronounce imperfectly, utter feebly, in speaking. (E.) ME. *lispen, lipsen*; Chaucer, C. T. 266 (Six-text, A 264, where 5 MSS. have *lipsed* for *lisped*). AS. **wlispian*, to lisp; in *ā-wlispian*, in Napier's Additions. – AS. *wlisp*, imperfect in utterance, lisping, Voc. 8. 29; also spelt *wlips*, Voc. 192. 11.+Du. *lispen*, to lisp; Dan. *læspe*, to lisp; Swed. *läspa*; G. *lispeln*, to lisp, whisper. β. An imitative word, similar to **Whisper**, q. v. **Der.** *lisp*, sb.; *lisp-ing-ly*.

LISSOM, pliant, agile. (E.) A contr. form of *lithesome*; from E. *lithe*, with suffix -*some*. See **Lithe**.

LIST (1), a stripe or border of cloth, selvage. (E.) ME. *list, liste*. 'With a brode *liste*' = with a broad strip of cloth; P. Plowman, B. v. 524. AS. *liste*; 'Lembus, liste;' Corp. Gloss., 1228. Teut. type **list-jon-*, f.+Du. *lijst*, list, a border; G. *leiste*, list, border; OHG. *lista*, whence Ital. *lista*. **Der.** *list* (3).

LIST (2), a catalogue. (F. – G.) In Shak. Hamlet, i. 1. 98, i. 2. 32. – F. *liste*, 'a list, roll, catalogue; also, a list, or selvage;' Cot. The older sense is the latter, viz. border; hence it came to mean a strip, roll, list of names. – OHG. *lista*, G. *leiste*, a border; cognate with AS. *liste*, whence *list*, a border. See **List** (1). ¶ Thus *list* (1) and *list* (2) are the same word, but the latter is used in the F. sense. **Der.** *list*, verb, *en-list*.

LIST (3), gen. used in the pl. **Lists**, q. v.

LIST (4), to choose, to desire, have pleasure in. (E.) In Shak.

1 Hen. VI, i. 5. 22. Often used as an impers. verb in older authors. ME. *listen, lusten*; 'if thee *lust*' or 'if thee *list*'=if it pleases thee; Chaucer, C. T. 1185; cf. l. 1054 (A 1183, 1052). AS. *lystan*, to desire, used impersonally; Grein, ii. 200. Formed (by regular vowel-change from *u* to *y*) from AS. *lust*, pleasure; see **Lust.**+Du. *lusten*, to like; Icel. *lysta*, to desire; Dan. *lyste*; Swed. *lysta*; Goth. *lustōn*; G. *gelüsten*. Teut. type *lustjan-; from *lustuz, sb. **Der.** *list*, sb., Oth. ii. 1. 105. And see *list-less*.

LIST (5), an inclination (of a ship) to one side. (E.) A variant of *lust*, desire, inclination, which was formerly used in the same sense. 'The ship at low water had a great *lust* to the offing;' T. James, Voy. (1633), p. 82 (N. E. D.). '*Lust* of a ship;' Phillips (1658); prov. E. *lust* (E. D. D.). Cf. Dan. *lyst*, inclination. See **List** (4).

LIST (6), to listen. (E.) In Hamlet, i. 5. 22. ME. *listen, lusten*. '*Listeth*, lordes;' Chaucer, Sir Thopas, l. 1. 'And *lust* hu ich con be bitelle;' Owl and Night., 263. AS. *hlystan*, Grein, ii. 90.—AS. *hlyst*, hearing, the sense of hearing, id. Teut. type *hlustiz, Idg. type *clustis; cf. Icel. *hlust*, the ear, W. *clust*, the ear; Skt. *çrustis*, hearing, obedience (Uhlenbeck). All from √KLEUS, extended form of √KLEU, to hear, whence L. *clu-ere*, Gk. κλύ-ειν, Skt. *çru*, to hear. See **Loud.**

LISTEN, to hearken, give ear. (E.) In Shak. Macb. iv. 1. 89; ii. 2. 29. We also find *list*, as above. So we also find both ME. *lustnen* or *listnen*, and *lusten* or *listen*. 1. 'Or *lysteneth* to his reson,' P. Plowman, B. xiv. 307; where the Trinity MS. has *listneth*, ed. Wright, l. 9534. Here *list(e)neth* stands for the older *listneth*, the *e* being inserted for greater ease of pronunciation, and still retained in mod. E. spelling, though seldom sounded. We further find the pt. t. *lustnede*, Layamon, 26357; and the pp. *lustned*, id. 25128. This form *lus(t)nen* is derived from an AS. form *hlysnan* (see below) by an insertion of *t*, due to confusion with the closely allied **List** (5), AS. *hlystan*, used in the same sense. The AS. *hlysnan* is inferred from O. North. *lysna* (for *hlysna*) in Matt. xiii. 18; cf. AS. *hlosnian*, to listen (Bosworth). Here *lysna* represents a Teut. type *hlusinōjan-, and *hlosnian* represents a Teut. type *hlusnōjan; both from Teut. *hlus-, weak grade of *hleus, to hear; √KLEUS (above). Cf. Swed. *lyssna*, to listen; EFries. *lüstern*, Westphal. *lustern*.

LISTLESS, careless, uninterested. (E.) The lit. sense is 'devoid of desire.' Not immediately derived from the verb to *list* (see **List** (4)), but put in place of the older form *lustless*. We find *lystles* in Prompt. Parv. p. 307; but *lustles* in Gower, C. A. ii. 104; bk. iv. 3262. Formed from *lust* with the suffix *-less*. See **Lust** and **-less.** Cf. Icel. *lystarlauss*, having no appetite, from *lyst*=*losti*, lust. **Der.** *list-less-ly*, *list-less-ness*.

LISTS, the ground enclosed for a tournament. (E.) Scarcely used in the singular. Used to translate OF. *lices* in the Rom. of the Rose, 4199; and much affected by the influence of that word. ME. *listes*, pl. sb., the lists, Chaucer, C. T. 63, 1864. Really the pl. of E. *list*, a stripe, border, which took up the further sense of limit or boundary; as in Eng. Gilds (E. E. T. S.), p. 44: 'Any brother or sister that duellen wyt[h]outen the *lystys* of thre myle fro the cyte.' See therefore **List** (1). **β.** Note also OF. *lisse, lice* (mod. F. *lice*), 'a list or tiltyard;' Cot. Cf. Ital. *liccia*, a barrier, palisade, list; Span. *liza*, a list for tilting; Port. *liça, liçada*, list, enclosed ground in which combats are fought: whence Low Lat. *liciæ*, s. pl., barriers, palisades; *liciæ duelli*, the lists. Hatzfeld thinks this OF. *lice* may be derived from a Romanic type *listea, formed from OHG. *lista* (G. *leiste*), a border. If so, it is closely related to E. *list* (1); and this explains the way in which the two were so readily confused.

LITANY, a form of prayer. (F.—L.—Gk.) ME. *letanie*, Ancren Riwle, p. 20, l. 4; altered to *litanie, litany*, to bring it nearer to the L. spelling.—OF. *letanie*, a litany; so spelt in the 13th century (Littré); mod. F. *litanie*.—L. *litanīa*.—Gk. λιτανεία, a prayer.—Gk. λιταίνειν, to pray.—Gk. λιτανός, a suppliant; from λιτή, supplication, prayer, allied to λίτομαι, λίσσομαι, I pray, beg, beseech.

LITERAL, according to the letter. (F.—L.) 'It hath but one simple *litterall* sense;' Tyndal, Works, p. 1, col. 2.—OF. *literal*, MF. *litéral*, 'literall;' Cot.—L. *litterālis*, literal.—L. *littera*, a letter; see **Letter.** **Der.** *literal-ly*, *-ness*; also *liter-ar-y*, Englished from L. *litterārius*, belonging to learning; and see **Literature.**

LITERATURE, the science of letters, literary productions. (F.—L.) In Wyntoun, Chron. v. 3633.—MF. *literature*, 'literature, learning;' Cot.—L. *litterātūra*, scholarship; allied to the pp. form *litterātus*, learned.—L. *littera*, a letter; see **Letter.** **Der.** *literate*, from L. *litterātus*; *literatur-ed*, Hen. V, iv. 7. 157.

LITHARGE, protoxide of lead. (F.—L.—Gk.) Lit. 'stone-silver.' ME. *litarge*, Chaucer, C. T. 631, 16243 (A 629, G 775).—OF. *litarge*, F. *litharge*, 'litargie, white lead;' Cot.—L. *lithargyrus*.—Gk. λιθάργυρος, litharge.—Gk. λιθ-, base of λίθος, a stone (root unknown); and ἄργυρος, silver (see **Argent**).

LITHE, pliant, flexible, active. (E.) ME. *lithe*, Chaucer, Ho. of

Fame, i. 118. AS. *līðe* (for *linðe*), gentle, soft; Grein, ii. 183; *līð*, gentle, id. 182.+G. *ge-lind, ge-linde*, OHG. *lindi*, soft, tender. Teut. type *linthjoz. **β.** Shorter forms appear in Icel. *linr*, soft, L. *lēnis*, gentle, *len-tus*, pliant; see **Lenient.** **Der.** *lithe-ness*; *lissom*=*lithe-some*. And see *lenity, lentisk, re-lent*.

LITHER, foul, pestilential, of the air. (E.) 'Two Talbots winged through the *lither* skie;' 1 Hen. VI, iv. 7. 21. Also explained as 'yielding,' owing to the influence of *lithe*, which is unconnected; but see '*luther eir*' in P. Plowman, C. xvi. 220. ME. *lither, luther*; AS. *lȳðer*, evil, poor, bad (hence, dull). See Stratmann and E. D. D. Cf. G. *liederlich*, vicious.

LITHOGRAPHY, writing on stone. (Gk.) Modern. Coined from Gk. λίθο-, decl. stem of λίθος, a stone; and γράφειν, to write. **Der.** *lithograph-er*, *lithograph-ic*; *lithograph*. Also *lith-ia*, *lith-ium*.

LITHOTOMY, the operation of cutting for stone. (L.—Gk.) Englished from Late L. *lithotomia*, the form given in Kersey's Dict., ed. 1715.—Gk. λιθοτομία.—Gk. λίθο-, decl. stem of λίθος, a stone; and τομ-, 2nd grade of τεμ-, base of τέμνειν, to cut; see **Tome.** **Der.** *lithotom-ist*.

LITIGATION, a contest in law. (L.) In Blount's Gloss., ed. 1674. Formed, by analogy with F. words in *-ion*, from Late L. *lītigātio*, a disputing.—L. *lītigāre*, to dispute.—L. *lit-*, stem of *līs*, strife, law-suit; and *-ig-*, weakened form of *ag-ere*, to drive, conduct (see **Agent**). **β.** The L. *līs* was in OL. *stlīs* (Festus). **Der.** *litigate*, a late verb, really due to the sb.; *litigant*=L. *lītigant-*, stem of pres. pt. of *lītigāre*; also *litigious*, q. v.

LITIGIOUS, contentious. (F.—L.) In old authors it also means 'debatable' or doubtful; see Trench, Select Glossary. *Litigious*=precarious; Shak. Pericles, iii. 3. 3.—F. *litigieux*, 'litigious, debatefull;' Cot.—L. *lītigiōsus*, (1) contentious, (2) doubtful.—L. *lītigium*, strife; cf. *lītigāre*, to dispute; see **Litigation.** **Der.** *litigious-ly*, *litigious-ness*.

LITMUS, a kind of dye. (Du.) Spelt *litmose-blew* in Phillips, ed. 1706. It appears in AF. as *lytemoise*, Liber Albus, p. 238. Put for *lakmose*; prob. by association with the old E. word *lit*, to dye.—Du. *lakmoes*, a blue dye-stuff (Sewel).—Du. *lak*, lac; and *moes*, pulp. Hence also G. *lackmuss*, litmus. See **Lac.**

LITRE, a unit of capacity in the metric system. (F.—Late L.—Gk.) It contains about 1¾ pints.—F. *litre* (1793).—Late L. *li'tra*.—Gk. λίτρα, a pound. See **Librate, Lira.**

LITTER (1), a portable bed. (F.—L.) ME. *litere*, Cursor Mundi, 13817; Wyclif, Isa. lxvi. 20. Spelt *lytier* in Caxton, Reynard the Fox, ed. Arber, p. 61, l. 1.—AF. *littere*, Livere de Reis, 86; OF. *litiere* (F. *litière*), 'a horse-litter;' Cot.—Late L. *lectāria*, a litter.—L. *lectus*, a bed. Cf. Gk. λέκτρον, a bed, λέχος, a couch.—L. and Gk. base LEGH, to lie; see **Lie** (1). Allied to **Lectern.**

LITTER (2), materials for a bed, a heap of straw for animals to lie on, a confused mass of objects scattered about; &c. (F.—L.) Really the same word as the above; with allusion to beds of straw for animals, and hence a confused heap. Thus Cotgrave has: '*Litiere*, a horse-litter, also *litter* for cattell, also old dung or manure.' See **Litter** (1). **β.** Hence also *litter* in the sense of 'a brood;' see the various senses of *lytere* in Prompt. Parv.; and cf. F. *accoucher*, and E. 'to be in the straw.' And see Wright, Vocab. p. 156. **Der.** *litter*, verb, Temp. i. 2. 282.

LITTLE, small. (E.) ME. *litel, lutel* (with one *t*); Chaucer, C. T. 492 (A 490); Havelok, 481; Layamon, 9124. AS. *lytel, lȳtel*, Grein, ii. 201.+OSax. *luttil*; Du. *luttel*, little, few; MHG. *lützel*; OHG. *luzzil*; Teut. type *luttiloz. **β.** All from a base LEUT, to deceive, in connexion with which we also find AS. *lytig*, deceitful, Ælfric's Colloquy, in Voc. 101. 2; also AS. *lot*, deceit, Grein, i. 194; and the Goth. *liuts*, deceitful, *liuta*, dissembler, *lutōn*, to betray. **γ.** Further, the Teut. base LEUT meant orig. to stoop, to bow down (hence to creep, or sneak), as in AS. *lūtan*, to stoop, 'lout,' incline to; see **Lout.** **Der.** *little-ness.* ☞ It is remarkable that the Icel. *litill*, Swed. *liten*, Goth. *leitils*, little, are unrelated; being from a base *leit. The forms *less, least*, are from a different source. But see **Loiter.**

LITTORAL, belonging to the sea-shore. (L.) Spelt *littoral* in Kersey; *litoral* in Blount, ed. 1674. Mere Latin.—L. *li'torālis*, better *litorālis*, belonging to the sea-shore.—L. *litor-*, for *litos*, stem of *lītus*, the sea-shore.

LITURGY, public worship, established form of prayer. (F.—Late L.—Gk.) Spelt *litturgie* in Minsheu, ed. 1627.—MF. *lyturgie*, 'a liturgy, or form of service;' Cot.—L. *liturgia*.—Gk. λειτουργία, public service.—Gk. λειτουργός, performing public service or duties.—Gk. λεῖτο-, for λεῖτος, public; and ἔργον, work, cognate with E. **Work.** **β.** λεῖτος, λήϊτος, λάϊτος, public, is derived from λαός, λεώς, the people; whence E. **Laic, Laity. Der.** *liturgi-c*, *liturgi-c-al*, *liturg-ist*.

LIVE (1), to continue in life, exist, dwell. (E.) ME. *liuien, liuen*

(with *u* for *v*); Chaucer, C. T. 508 (A 506); Havelok, 355. AS. *lífian*; Grein, ii. 185; also *libban*, id. 179; where *bb* stands for *fi*.+ Du. *leven*; also used as sb., with sense of 'life;' Icel. *lifa*, to be left, to remain behind, also to live; Dan. *leve*; Swed. *lefva*; Goth. *liban*; G. *leben*, to live (whence *leben*, sb. life), MHG. *leben*, *lepen*, to live (also spelt *libjan*, *lipjan*); allied to *b-leiben*, MHG. *beliben*, OHG. *belíban*, to remain, be left. From Teut. stem **lib-*, weak grade cf **leib-*, to remain. β. The sense of 'live' is unoriginal; the older sense is to remain, to be left behind. See further under **Life**. Der. *liv-er*, *liv-ing*; and see **live** (2).

LIVE (2), adj. alive, having life, active, burning. (E.) 'Upon the next *live* creature that it sees;' Mids. Nt. Dr. ii. 1. 172. The use of this adj. is really due to an attributive use of *live*, aphetic form of *alive*, which is not a true adj., but a phrase consisting of a prep. and a dat. case; see **Alive**. β. The use as an adj. arose the more easily owing to the currency of the words *live-ly* and *liv-ish*. The former is still in use, but the latter is obsolete; it occurs as *lifissh* in Gower, C. A. iii. 93; bk. vii. 257. Der. *live-stock*.

LIVELIHOOD, means of subsistence. (E.) α. Cotgrave translates F. *patrimoine* by 'patrimony, birthright, inheritance, *livelihood*.' And Drayton speaks of a man 'Of so fair *livelihood*, and so large rent;' The Owl. The metre shows that the word was then, as now, trisyllabic. β. But it is a singular corruption of the ME. *livelode*, *liuelode*, i.e. life-leading; due to confusion with *livelihood* in the sense of 'liveliness,' as used (quite correctly) in Shak. Venus, 26; All's Well, i. 1. 58. γ. Again *livelode* is better spelt *liflode*, as in P. Plowman, B. prol. 30. Cf. 'Lyflode, liyflode, lyuelode, or warysome, *Donativum*;' Prompt. Parv. p. 308; indeed, we find *livelode* as late as in Levins, ed. 1570. An older spelling is in St. Marharete, ed. Cockayne, p. 20, l. 16, where we find *liflade*, meaning 'way of life,' lit. leading of life. δ. Late AS. *liflád*, course of life; Rule of St. Bennet, ed. Schröer, c. 1; p. 13, l. 24. Compounded of AS. *lif*, life; and AS. *lád*, a leading, way, also provisions to live by, Grein, ii. 150. Another sense of AS. *lád* is a course, as preserved in mod. E. *lode*. See **Life** and **Lode**.

LIVELONG, long-lasting, long as it is. (E.) 'The *livelong* night;' Macb. ii. 3. 65. Orig. *lief-long*, i.e. 'dear long;' but altered to *live-long* at the end of the 16th cent., where *live* represents the verb to *live*, the *i* being short. Sometimes understood as *live-long* (with long *i*) as if connected with *life*. Really from **Lief** and **Long**. β. Cf. 'Alle the *lefe longe* daye;' Sowdan of Babylon, l. 832; 'Al that *leve* longe nyht;' H. Lovelich, The Holy Grail, c. xxxix. l. 319.

LIVELY, vigorous, active. (E.) A corruption of *lifely*. 'Lyvely, liyfly, or qwyk, or fulle of lyyf, *Vivax*;' Prompt. Parv. p. 308. Chaucer uses *lyfly* in the sense of 'in a life-like manner,' C. T., A 2087. AS. *líflic*. Compounded of **Life** and **Like**. Der. *liveli-ness*, in Holinshed, Conquest of Ireland, c. 9 (R.). Cf. *lively*, adv., in a life-like manner, Two Gent. iv. 4. 174; Chaucer (as above).

LIVER, an organ of the body, secreting bile. (E.) ME. *liuer* (with *u*=*v*); Chaucer, C. T. 7421 (D 1839). AS. *lifer*, Grein, ii. 184.+Du. *lever*; Icel. *lifr*; Dan. *lever*; Swed. *lefver*; G. *leber*, MHG. *lebere*, OHG. *lepara*, *lipara*. Cf. Russ. *liver'*, the pluck (of animals); (from Teut.) Teut. type **librā*, f.; cognate with Armenian *leard*, liver; but not with L. *iecur*. Brugmann, i. §§ 280, 557 (2). Der. *liver-coloured*; also *liver-wort*, Prompt. Parv. p. 309.

LIVERY, a thing delivered, as e. g. a uniform worn by servants; a delivery. (F.−L.) ME. *liuerè* (with *u* for *v*, and trisyllabic), Chaucer, C. T., A 363.−AF. *liveré* (Britton); F. *livrée*, 'a delivery of a thing that's given, the thing so given, hence, a livery;' Cot. Properly the fem. of the pp. of *livrer*, to deliver, give. Cf. Ital. *liberare*, to deliver.−Late L. *liberāre*, to give, give freely; a particular use of L. *liberāre*, to set free; see **Liberate**. Der. *livery-man*; *livery-stable*, a stable where horses are kept *at livery*, i.e. at a certain rate or on a certain allowance; *liveri-ed*. ☞ The word is fully explained in Spenser, View of the State of Ireland, Globe ed., p. 623, col. 2; and Prompt. Parv. p. 308.

LIVID, black and blue, discoloured. (F.−L.) 'Purple or *livid* spots;' Bacon, Life of Hen. VII, ed. Lumby, p. 12, l. 31.−F. *livide* (Cot.).−L. *liuidus*, leaden-coloured, bluish.−L. *liuēre*, to be bluish. Cf. W. *lliw*, OIrish *lí*, colour, hue. Brugmann, i. § 94. Der. *lividness*.

LIZARD, a kind of four-footed reptile. (F.−L.) ME. *lesarde*, Prompt. Parv. p. 298; *lusarde*, P. Plowman, B. xviii. 335.−OF. *lesard*, m., *lesarde*, f., 'a lizard;' Cot.−L. *lacerta*, a lizard; also *lacertus*. Root unknown. Cf. **Alligator**.

LLAMA, a Peruvian quadruped. (Peruvian.) See Prescott, Conquest of Peru, c.v. 'Llama, according to Garcilasso de la Vega, is a Peruvian word signifying *flock*; see Garcilasso, Com. Real. parte i. lib. viii. c. xvi;' note in Prescott. But the Peruv. Dict. gives 'llama, carnero de la tierra,' i.e. sheep of the country. Cf. 'Llamas, or sheepe of Peru;' Hakluyt, Voy. iii. 735.

LLANO, a treeless plain in S. America. (Span.−L.) Usually in the pl. *llanos*; spelt *lanos* in E. G., tr. of Acosta, b. iii. c. 20.−Span. *llano* (pl. *llanos*), a plain.−Span. *llano*, plain, flat.−L. *plānus*, flat. See **Plain**.

LO, interj. see, behold. (E.) ME. *lo*, Chaucer, C. T. 3019 (A 3017). AS. *lá*, lo! Grein, ii. 148. β. Lo is gen. considered as equivalent to *look*; and we actually find a ME. *lo* (with close *o*), prob. from *lō-*, short for AS. *lōca*, look thou! But this would have become *loo* in modern E., and is obsolete; though it may have affected the sense of the surviving form. The AS. *lá* is a natural interjection, to call attention. Cf. Gk. ἀλαλή, a loud cry, ἀλαλάζειν, to utter a war-cry, L. *lā-trāre*, to bark; &c.

LOACH, LOCHE, a small river-fish. (F.) ME. *loche*; Prompt. Parv. p. 310. Also *lochefissh*, Stat. of the Realm, i. 355 (1357).−F. *loche*, 'the loach;' Cot. Cf. Norm. dial. *loque*, a loach, a slug (Moisy); Ital. *locca*, *locchia*, 'a cob, or gudgeon-fish;' Florio. Of unknown origin.

LOAD, a quantity carried, a burden. (E.) Most probably this word has been extended in meaning by confusion with the unrelated verb to *lade*. *Load* is common in Shakespeare both as a sb. and verb, but in ME. it is a sb. only, and is identical with **Lode**, q. v., notwithstanding the difference in sense. The AS. *lád* means only way, course, journey; but ME. *lode* has also the sense of 'burden.' An early example of this is 'hors and *lode*,' Ancren Riwle, p. 268; cf. also *carte-lóde*, a cart-load, in Havelok, l. 895. It should be particularly noticed, however, that the derived verb to *lead* is constantly used in prov. E. in the sense 'to carry corn;' and, in the Prompt. Parv. p. 62, we find: 'Cartyn, or *lede* wythe a carte, *Carruco*.' Chaucer has *y-lad*=carried, Prologue, 530. 'Se geneat sceal . . . lade lædan,' the tenant shall carry loads;' Birch, Cart. Saxon. iii. 102. Hence *load*=ME. *lode*=AS. *lád*, a derivative from the 2nd grade of the verb *líðan*, to go, travel. See **Lode, Lead** (1). Der. *load*, vb.

LOAD-STAR, LOAD-STONE, the same as **Lode-star, Lode-stone**.

LOAF, a mass of bread; also of sugar. (E.) ME. *lof*, *loof*. 'A pese-*lof*'=a loaf made of peas; P. Plowman, B. vi. 181; pl. *looues* (=*loaves*), Wyclif, Matt. iv. 3. AS. *hláf*, a loaf; Grein, ii. 79.+Icel. *hleifr*; Goth. *hlaifs*; G. *laib*, MHG. *leip*. Cf. also Lithuanian *klëpas*, Lettish *klaipas*, bread; Russ. *khlieb*, bread; prob. borrowed from Teutonic. β. Perhaps named from its 'rising,' when leavened; cf. AS. *hlífian*, to rise high; NFries. *lif*, a loaf; MSwed. *lef* (Ihre). Der. *loaf-sugar*; *lady, lord, lammas*.

LOAM, a mixed soil of clay, sand, &c. (E.) ME. *lam*, dat. *lame*; Cursor Mundi, 11985; where one MS. has *cley* (clay). AS. *lám*; Grein, ii. 153; Du. *leem*; G. *lehm*, OHG. *leim*. β. Teut. types **laimo-*, **laimon-*; from the base **lai*, 2nd grade of **lei-* (> **li-*), as in *lím*, lime, to which *loam* is closely allied. See **Lime** (1). Also akin to Icel. *leir*, loam (Teut. type **lai-zom*). Der. *loam-y*, ME. *lami*, Hali Meidenhad, ed. Cockayne, p. 47, l. 28.

LOAN, a lending, money lent. (Scand.) ME. *lone*, Chaucer, C. T. 7443 (D 1861); P. Plowman, B. xx. 284. This corresponds to an AS. *lán*, but we only find *lǽn*, Grein, ii. 163; Ælfric's Homilies, ii. 176, last line. We once find *lán-land* for *lǽn-land*, Kemble, Cod. Dipl. iii. 165; from Norse.−Icel. *lán*, a loan; Dan. *laan*, a loan; Swed. *lån*. Cognate with AS. *lǽn*, a loan (whence E. *lend*, q.v.); Du. *leen*; G. *lehn*. β. These words answer to Teut. types **laihwniz*, **laihwnoz*, n.; from **laihw-*, 2nd grade of the verb appearing in Goth. *leihwan*, to lend (Luke, vi. 34), AS. *léon*, for *lihan*, to lend, give (Grein, ii. 187), Icel. *ljá*, to lend, G. *leihen*, OHG. *lihan*. γ. The Teut. base **leihw* answers to Idg. √LEIQ, whence the L. *linquere* (pt. t. *liqu-i*), to leave; which is closely related to Gk. λείπειν, Skt. *rich*, to leave; OIrish *lec-im*, I leave. ¶ Quite distinct from AS. *lǽan*, Icel. *laun*, G. *lohn*, a reward; see **Lucre**. Der. *len-d*, q. v.

LOATH, disliking, reluctant, unwilling. (E.) ME. *loth* (opposed to *leef*, dear, willing), Chaucer, C. T. 1839 (A 1837); Havelok, 261. AS. *láð*, hateful (very common), Grein, ii. 150.+Icel. *leiðr*, loathed, disliked; Dan. *led*, loathsome; Swed. *led*, odious; OHG. *leit*, odious; orig. mournful. β. All from a Teut. type **laithoz*, mournful, in which *-thoz* is prob. a suffix. Allied to G. *leiden*, to suffer; but prob. *not* to AS. *líðan*, to travel (pt. t. *láð*), as usually said (Kluge). Der. *loath-ly*=AS. *láðlic*, Grein, ii. 151; *loathe*, verb =AS. *láðian*, Ælfric's Hom. ii. 506, l. 24; *loath-ing*, sb., ME. *lothynge*, Prompt. Parv. p. 316; *loath-some*, ME. *lothsum*, Prompt. Parv. p. 314, spelt *laithsum*, Cursor Mundi, 23229 (Gött. MS.), where the suffix *-some*=AS. *-sum* as in *win-some*; also *loath-some-ness*.

LOBBY, a small hall, waiting-room, passage. (Low L.−G.) In Hamlet, ii. 2. 161, iv. 3. 39. Becon (1553) has: 'Our recluses neuer come out of their *lobbeis*;' Reliques of Rome, 53. [Hence we may suppose that it was a monastic term, and was taken up into E. directly from the Low L.]−Low L. *lobia*, a portico, gallery, covered way, Ducange ; also spelt *lobium*. Also *laubia*; as if from a Teut. type *laubjā. MHG. *loube*, an arbour, a bower, also an open way up to the upper story of a house. The latter sense will be at once intelligible to any one who has seen a Swiss *châlet* ; and we can thus see also how it easily passed into the sense of a gallery to lounge or wait in. The same word as mod. G. *laube*, a bower. So called from being formed orig. with branches and foliage. MHG. *loub*, *loup*, OHG. *laup*, mod. G. *laub*, a leaf ; cognate with E. **Leaf**, q. v. Doublet, *lodge*.

LOBE, the flap or lower part of the ear, a division of the lungs or brain. (F. Late L. Gk.) In Cotgrave. F. *lobe*, 'the lap or lowest part of the ear, also a *lobe* or lappet of the liver ;' Cot. Late L. *lobum*, acc. of *lobus*, not given in Ducange, but it may (I suppose) be found in old works on medicine as a transliteration of the Gk. word ; Cooper's Thesaurus (1565) has *lobos*. Gk. λοβός, a lobe of the ear or liver ; allied to L. *legula*, the lobe of the ear. Brugmann, i. § 667. Der. *lob-ate*, mod. and scientific ; *lob-ed*.

LOBELIA, a genus of herbaceous plants. (Personal name.) First in 1739 ; but named after Matthias de *Lobel* (15381616), botanist and physician to James I. (N. E. D.)

LOBSTER, a kind of crustacean. (L.) ME. *lopstere*, *loppester*, *loppister*. 'A *loppyster* or a crabbe ;' Voc. 624. 12 ; 'Hic polupus, *lopstere* ;' id. 642. 22. AS. *loppestre* ; Voc. 181. 2 ; a corruption of an earlier form *lopust* ; Voc. 30. 36. β. The word had no sense in AS., *lopust* being a mere corruption of L. *locusta*, meaning (1) lobster, (2) locust ; see **Locust**. Hence the entry : '*Locusta*, lopust ;' in Voc. 30. 36.

LOCAL, belonging to a place. (F. L.) Spelt *locall* in Frith, Works, p. 139, last line. F. *local*, 'locall ;' Cot. L. *locālis*, local. L. *locus*, a place ; see **Locus**. Der. *local-ly*, *local-ise*, *local-is-at-ion*, *local-i-ty*, Blount's Gloss., ed. 1674 ; also *loc-ate*, q. v.

LOCATE, to place. (L.) A late word, added by Todd to Johnson's Dict. L. *locātus*, pp. of *locāre*, to place. L. *locus*, a place ; see **Local**. Der. *locat-ion*, in Cockeram, 1623 ; *locat-ive*.

LOCH, a lake. (Gaelic.) In place-names, as *Loch* Lomond, *Loch* Ness. Gael. and Irish *loch*, a lake, arm of the sea ; cf. Corn. *lagen* ; Bret. *laguenn*, *lagen*.+L. *lacus* ; see **Lake**. Doublets, *lake*, *lough*.

LOCK (1), a contrivance for fastening doors, an enclosure in a canal ; &c. (E.) ME. *loke*, Prompt. Parv. p. 311 ; pl. *loken*, also *locun*, *lokes*, Layamon, 5926. AS. *loca*, pl. *locan* ; Grein, ii. 191 ; allied to *loc*, a hole.+Icel. *loka*, a lock, latch ; *lok*, a cover, lid of a chest ; Swed. *lock*, a lid ; cf. G. *loch*, a dungeon, hole ; orig. a locked-up place. β. All from Teut. *luk-, weaker grade of the strong verb *lūkan-, to lock, enclose, appearing in the AS. strong verb *lūcan*, to enclose, Grein, ii. 194 ; also in Icel. *lūka*, to shut, finish (strong verb) ; MHG. *lūchen*, to shut ; Goth. *galūkan*, to shut, shut up. Der. *lock*, verb, ME. *lokken*, *locken*, Chaucer, C. T. 5899, D 317 ; (observe that this verb is a secondary formation from the sb., and not to be confused with the old strong verb *luken*, *louken* = AS. *lūcan*, now obsolete, of which the pp. *loken* occurs in Chaucer, C. T. 14881, B 4065) ; also *lock-er*, a closed place that locks = ME. *lokere*, Prompt. Parv. p. 311, answering to OFlemish *loker*, a chest (Kilian) ; also *lock-jaw*, for *locked-jaw* ; *lock-keeper* ; *lock-smith* ; *lock-up*. And see *lock-et*.

LOCK (2), a tuft of hair, flock of wool. (E.) ME. *lok* ; pl. *lokkes*, *lockes*, Chaucer, C. T. 81. AS. *locc*, *loc*, Grein, ii. 191 ; pl. *loccas*.+Du. *lok*, a lock, tress, curl ; Icel. *lokkr* ; Dan. *lok* ; Swed. *lock* ; OHG. *loch*, G. *locke*. β. The form of the Teut. type is *lukkoz, m. ; Idg. type *lugnos; from a Teut. base *luk, weak grade of Teut. *leuk, Idg. LEUG ; whence also Icel. *lykkr*, a loop, bend, crook. From the same root are Gk. λύγος, a pliant twig, withy ; λυγίζειν, to bend ; Lith. *lugnas*, pliable.

LOCKET, a little gold case worn as an ornament. (F. Scand.) ME. *loket*, Polit. Songs, ed. Wright, p. 154. The old sense is a small lock, something that fastens. 'With wooden *lockets* 'bout their wrists,' with reference to the pillory ; Butler, Hudibras, pt. ii. c. 1. l. 808. F. *loquet*, 'the latch of a door ;' Cot. Cf. Guernsey dial. *loquet*, 'cadenas.' Dimin. of OF. *loc*, a lock ; Godefroy. Borrowed from Icel. *loka*, a lock, latch ; see **Lock** (1).

LOCKRAM, a cheap kind of linen. (F. Breton.) In Shak. Cor. ii. 1. 225 ; see Nares and Halliwell. 'A *lockerom* kercher ;' Bury Wills, ed. Tymms (Camd. Soc.), p, 147 (1556). F. *locrenan*, the name given to a sort of unbleached linen ; named from the place in Brittany where it is manufactured ; Dict. de Trévoux. F. *Locrenan*, also called *S. Renan*, the name of a place in Basse Bretagne, a few miles N. by W. from Quimper. Bret. *Lok-ronan*, the Bret. name for the same place. The sense of the name is 'St. Ronan's cell ;' from Bret. *lók*, a cell, and *Ronan*, St. Ronan ; see Legonidec's Bret. Dict., where this very name is cited as an instance of the use of *Lok*- as a prefix in place-names. ¶ Cf. *dowlas*, similarly named ;

'dowlas and lockeram' are mentioned in 1529, Act 21 Hen. 8. c. 14.

LOCOMOTION, motion from place to place. (L.) 'Progression or animal *locomotion* ;' Sir T. Browne, Vulg. Errors, b. iii. c. 1, § 2. Coined from L. *locō*, abl. of *locus*, a place ; and *motion*. See **Locus** and **Motion**. Der. *locomot-ive*, adj., Kersey's Dict., ed. 1715 ; hence *locomotive*, sb. = locomotive engine, the first of which was used A. D. 1814, Haydn, Dict. of Dates.

LOCUS, a place. (L.) '*Locus*, a place, room, or stead ;' Phillips, ed. 1706. He also gives instances of its technical use in astronomy and philosophy. L. *locus*, a place ; a later form of OL. *stlocus*, a place. Prob. allied to Skt. *sthala-m*, firm ground, also, a place. Brugmann, i. § 585. Cf. G. *stelle*, a place. See **Stall**. Der. *loc-al*, q. v., *loc-ate*, *al-locate*, *allow* (1), *col-locate*, *dis-locate*, *lieu*, *lieu-tenant*, *loco-motive* ; also *couch*.

LOCUST, a winged insect. (L.) In Kersey, ed. 1715, it also means 'a fish like a lobster, called a long-oister ;' see **Lobster**. ME. *locust*, Cursor Mundi, 6041 ; Wyclif, Rev. ix. 3. L. *locusta*, a shell-fish ; also a locust. Doublet, *lobster*, q. v.

LODE, a vein of ore. (E.) In Halliwell. Also spelt *load*, as in Carew's Survey of Cornwall, p. 10 (R.). An old mining term. The lit. sense is 'course.' AS. *lād*, a way, course, journey ; *on lāde* = in the way, Beowulf, ed. Grein, l. 1987. Teut. type *laidā, f. ; closely allied to *laidjan-, to lead ; see **Lead** (1).+Icel. *leið*, a lode, way, course ; Dan. *led*, a gate ; Swed. *led*, a way, course. Der. *lode-star*, *lode-stone* ; also *lead* (1).

LODESTAR, **LOADSTAR**, the pole-star. (E.) Lit. 'way-star ;' i. e. the star that shows the way, or that leads. ME. *lode-sterre*, Chaucer, C. T. 2061 (A 2059). Compounded of *lode*, a way, course ; and *star*. See **Lode** and **Star**.+Icel. *leiðar-stjarna* ; from *leiðar*, for *leið*, a way, and *stjarna*, a star ; Swed. *led-stjerna* ; G. *leit-stern*.

LODESTONE, **LOADSTONE**, an ore that attracts pieces of iron. (E.) 'For lyke as the *lodestone* draweth unto it yron ;' Udall, on S. Mark, c. 5, v. 21. And see Robinson's tr. of More's Utopia (1556), ed. Arber, p. 32. Spelt *lodestone*, *loadstone*, in Minsheu, ed. 1627. Compounded of *lode* and *stone*, similarly to *lodestar* ; see above.+Icel. *leiðarsteinn* ; from *leiðar*, for *leið*, a lode ; and *steinn*, stone.

LODGE, a small house, cottage, cell, place to rest in. (F. Low L. G.) ME. *loge*, *logge* ; Chaucer, C. T. 14859 (D 4043) ; Seven Sages, ed. Weber, 2603. OF. *loge*, 'a lodge, cote, shed, small house ;' Cot. [Cf. Ital. *loggia*, a gallery, a lodge.] Low L. *laubia*, a porch ; cf. *lobia*, a gallery. 'We find in an act of A. D. 904, "In palatio quod est fundatum juxta basilica beatissimi principis apostolorum, in *laubia* . . . ipsius palatii ;"' Brachet (see Ducange). Teut. type *laubjā; cf. OHG. *louba* (MHG. *loube*, G. *laube*), an arbour, a hut of leaves and branches. OHG. *laup* (MHG. *loub*, G. *laub*), a leaf ; cognate with E. **Leaf**, q. v. Der. *lodge*, verb, ME. *loggen*, Chaucer, C. T. 14997 (B 4181), Ancren Riwle, p. 264 ; from OF. *loger*, 'to lodge, lie, sojourne' (Cot.) ; *lodg-ing* = ME. *logging*, Chaucer, C. T. 15001 (B 4185) ; *lodg-er* ; *lodg-ment*, in Kersey, ed. 1715. Doublet, *lobby*, q. v.

LOFT, a room in a roof, attic, upper room. (Scand.) See Bible Word-book. ME. *loft*, Gawain and the Grene Knight, ed. Morris, l. 1096. The proper sense of *loft*, is 'air,' as in **Aloft**, q. v. The peculiar sense is Scand. Icel. *lopt* (pron. *loft*), meaning (1) air, sky, (2) an upper room, balcony ; cf. the prov. E. *sky-parlour* as applied to an attic ; Dan. *loft*, a loft, cock-loft ; Swed. *loft*, a garret.+AS. *lyft*, air, sky, Grein, ii. 198 ; whence ME. *lift*, sky, P. Plowman, B. xv. 351 ; Goth. *luftus*, the air ; Du. *lucht* [for *luft*], air, sky ; G. *luft*, the air. Root unknown. Der. *loft-y*, Shak. Lucrece, 1167, Rich. II, iii. 4. 35 ; *loft-i-ly* ; *loft-i-ness*, Isa. ii. 17 ; also *lift*, q. v. ; *a-loft*, q. v.

LOG (1), a block, piece of wood. (E.) 'A long *log* of timbre ;' Sir T. More, Works, p. 54 g. '*Logges*, buches ;' Du Wes, Sup. to Palsgrave, p. 914, col. 1. ME. *logge* (1398). An obscure word ; perhaps allied to prov. E. *lug*, ME. *lugge*, a long stick, a pole. The prov. E. *lug* also means a tree-trunk. Cf. E. *clog*. Der. *log-cabin*, *log-hut* ; *log-man*, Temp. iii. 1. 67 ; *logg-et*, a small log (with dimin. suffix -*et*, of F. origin), Ben Jonson, Tale of a Tub, A. iv. sc. 5, Puppy's 5th speech ; *logg-ats*, another spelling of *logg-ets*, the name of a game, Hamlet, v. 1. 100 ; *log-wood*, so called because imported in logs, for which reason it was also called *block-wood*, as appears from Kersey's Dict. and the Stat. 23 Eliz. c. 9, cited in Wedgwood ; also *log* (2), q. v. ; *logger-head*, q. v.

LOG (2), a piece of wood with a line, for measuring the rate of a ship. (E.) In Kersey, ed. 1715. The same as **Log** (1). But Swed. *logg*, a log (as a sea-term), whence *log-lina*, log-line, *log-bok*, log-book, *logga*, to heave the log (Widegren), Dan. *log-line*, *log-bog*, *logge*, Du. *log*, *log-lijn*, *log-boek*, *loggen*, do not seem to be old words and were prob. taken from E. Der. *log-board*, *-book*, *-line*, *-reel*.

LOG (3), a Hebrew liquid measure. (Heb.) The twelfth part of a *hin*. In Levit. xiv. 10. – Heb. *lōg*, a word which orig. signified ' a basin ; ' Smith, Dict. of the Bible.

LOGARITHM, the exponent of the power to which a given number or base must be raised in order to produce another given number. (Gk.) In Blount's Gloss., ed. 1674; and in Ben Jonson, Magnetic Lady, A. i. sc. 1 (Compass). Logarithms were invented by Napier, who published his work in 1614; Haydn. Coined from Gk. λογ-, stem of λόγος, a word, a proportion; and ἀριθμός, a number; the sense being ' ratio-number.' See **Logic** and **Arithmetic.** Der. *l garithm-ic, -ic-al, -ic-al-ly.*

LOGGER-HEAD, a dunce; a piece of round timber (in a whale-boat) round which a line is passed to make it run more slowly. (E.) In Shak. it means a blockhead; L. L. L. iv. 3. 204. The word evidently means much the same as *log-head* and is a similar formation to *block-head*; the difficulty is to account for the syllable *-er*. However, the prov. E. *logger* means a clog fastened to a horse's leg, to hamper its movements. See **Log** (1) and **Head.**

LOGIC, the science of reasoning correctly. (F. – L. – Gk.) ME. *logike,* Chaucer, C. T. 288 (A 286). – OF. *logique,* ' logick; ' Cot. – L. *logica* (= *ars logica*), logic; properly fem. of *logicus,* logical. – Gk. λογική (= λογική τέχνη), logic; properly fem. of λογικός, belonging to speaking, reasonable. – Gk. λόγος, a speech. – Gk. λέγειν, to collect, gather, select, tell, speak. + L. *legere,* to collect, select, read; see **Legend.** Der. *logic-al, logic-al-ly, logic-i-an* (Levins). Also (from Gk. λογιστής, a calculator, λογιστικός, skilled in calculating), *logistic, logistic-al.* Also *logo-machy,* a strife about words = Gk. λογομαχία, 1 Tim. vi. 4, from Gk. λόγο-, for λόγός, and μάχομαι, I fight or contend. From the same Gk. source we have numerous words, as *ana-logue, apo-logue, cata-logue, deca-logue, dia-logue, ec-logue, epi-logue, mono-logue, pro-logue;* also *syl-log-ism;* also *log-arithm;* also *ana-logy, apo-logy, etymo-logy, eu-logy;* also all scientific terms in *-logy,* such as *bio-logy, concho-logy,* &c. And (from λέγειν), *dia-lect, ec-lectic, lex-icon.*

LOIN, part of an animal just above the hip-bone. (F. – L.) ME. *loine, loyne;* Prompt. Parv. p. 3 2; Polit. Songs, ed. Wright, p. 191, in a song written temp. Edw. II. – OF. *loigne, loгne* (Godefroy), also *longe,* ' the loyne or flank; ' Cot. – Late L. **lumbea* (not found), fem. of an adj. **lumbeus,* formed from L. *lumbus,* the loin. ¶ We may note that the AS. *lendenu,* pl. sb., the loins, is cognate with the L. word; hence came ME. *lendis, leendis,* the loins, in Wyclif, Matt. iii. 4, &c. See **Lumbar.**

LOITER, to delay, linger. (Du.) ' *Loyter* and goe a-begging; ' Tyndall's Works, p. 217, col. 1; see Trench, Select Glossary, where the orig. bad sense of the word is noted; and see Palsgrave. ME. *loitren.* ' *Loytron,* or byn ydyl, *Ocior;* ' Prompt. Parv. p. 311. – Du. (and MDu.) *leuteren,* to linger, loiter, trifle, waver; also MDu. *loteren,* to delay, linger, act negligently, deceive, waver, vacillate (Kilian, Oudemans); cf. MFlemish *lutsen,* with the same senses (Kilian); WFlem. *lutteren,* to totter (De Bo); Norw. *lutra,* to loiter. Perhaps allied to **Lout.** Der. *loiter-er.*

LOLL, to lounge about lazily. (E.) ME. *lollen;* ' And wel loseliche *lolleth* there ' = and very idly he lounges there; P. Plowman, B. xii. 213. ' He that *lolleth* is lame, other his leg out of ioynte, Other meymed in som membre ' = he who lounges is lame, or his leg is out of joint, or he is maimed in some member; id. C. x. 215. See also id. B. v. 192; P. Plowman's Crede, ed. Skeat, l. 224. Cf. Icel. *lolla,* ' segniter agere,' Haldórsson; MDu. *lollen,* to sit over the fire. ' Wie sit en *lolt* of sit en vrijt Verlet sijn werck, vergeet sijn tijt ' = he who sits and warms himself, or sits and wooes, neglects his work and loses his time; Cats, ed. 1828, i. 428, a; cited by Oudemans. Kilian also gives *lollebancke,* a sleeping-bench, as a Zealand word. The older sense was prob. to ' doze,' to sleep, hence to brood over the fire, to lounge about. It appears to be allied to *lull,* i. e. to sing to sleep; see **Lull.** Der. *loll-er;* and see **Lollard.**

LOLLARD, a name given to the followers of Wyclif. (MDu.) The history of the word is a little difficult, because it is certain that several words have been purposely mixed up with it. 1. In the first place, the ME. word most commonly in use was not *lollard,* but *loller* = one who lolls, a lounger, an idle vagabond. ' I smelle a *loller* in the wind, quod he; ' Chaucer, C. T. 12913 (B. 1173). That ' lounger ' is the true sense of *this* form of the word, is clear from a passage in P. Plowman, C. x. 188–218, the whole of which may be consulted. The most material lines are: ' Now kyndeliche, by Crist, beth suche callyd *lolleres,* As by englisch of oure eldres of olde menne techynge; He that *lolleth* is lame other his leg out of ioynte Other meymed in som membre,' i.e. such fellows are naturally called *lollers* in the English of our forefathers; he that *lolls about* is lame, or broken-jointed, or maimed; see **Loll.** 2. At the same time, the name *lollard* was *also* in use as a term of reproach; and this was a MDu. term, Latinised as *Lollardus.* It had been in use *before*

Wyclif. Ducange quotes from Johannes Hocsemius, who says, under the date 1309: ' Eodem anno quidam hypocritae gyrovagi, qui *Lollardi* sive Deum laudantes vocabantur, per Hannoniam et Brabantiam quasdam mulieres nobiles deceperunt ; ' i. e. In this year certain vagabond hypocrites, called *Lollards* or God-praisers, deceived certain noblewomen in Hainault and Brabant. He adds that Trithemius says in his Chronicle, under the date 1315: ' ita appellatos a Gualtero *Lolhard,* Germano quodam.' This latter statement makes no difference to the etymology, since *Lolhard* as a surname (like our surnames Fisher, Baker, or Butcher) is precisely the same word as when used in the sense of ' God-praiser.' The lit. sense is ' a singer,' one who chants. – MDu. *lollaerd* (1) a mumbler of prayers or hymns (L. *mussitator*), one who hums; (2) a Lollard; Kilian, Oudemans. This is a mere dialectical variation of a form *lull-ard,* formed regularly from the MDu. *lullen* (also *lollen*), to sing, hum, with the suffix *-ard* as in E. *drunk-ard, slugg-ard,* &c., denoting the agent. This MDu. *lullen* is our E. word **Lull,** q. v. Hexham has: ' *lol,* or *lule,* a harmonious sound.' 3. Besides the confusion thus introduced, it was common to compare the *Lollards* to tares, by help of a bad pun on the L. *lolia,* tares; this has, however, nothing to do with the etymology. See my note on Chaucer, C. T., B 1173, in the Prioresses Tale, &c. (Clarendon Press). ¶ Since *loll* and *lull* are allied words, it makes no very great difference to which verb we refer *loller* and *Lollard;* still *loller* = *loll-er,* and *Lollard* = *lull-er.*

LONE, solitary, retired, away from company. (E.) Not in early use; the word does not appear in Minsheu or Levins, and I find no example much earlier than Shakespeare, who has: ' a poor *lone* woman; ' 2 Hen. IV, ii. 1. 35. It probably was at first a colloquial or vulgar word, recommended by its brevity for more extended use. It is known to be a short form of *alone,* as has generally been explained by lexicographers; even Shakespeare brings it in as a pun: ' a long *loan* for a poor *lone* woman to bear.' Observe: ' I go *alone,* Like to a *lonely* dragon; ' Cor. iv. 1. 30. Todd cites a slightly earlier instance: ' Moreover this Glycerie is a *lone* woman; ' Kyffin, transl. of Terence, ed. 1588; but Palsgrave has ' lone, onely, *seul;* ' and see P. Plowman, B. xvi. 20. See **Alone.** β. Other examples of loss of initial *a* occur in the words *mend, purtenance, limbeck, vanguard.* Der. *lone-ly,* Cor. iv. 1. 30; *lone-li-ness,* Hamlet, iii. 1. 46; also *lone-some,* spelt *lonesom* in Skinner, ed. 1671; *lone-some-ness;* also *lone-ness:* ' One that doth wear himself away in *lone-ness,*' Fletcher, Faithful Shepherdess, A. i. sc. 2 (Amarillis).

LONG (1), extended, not short, tedious. (E.) ME. *long,* Northern *lang;* Chaucer, C. T. 3021 (A 3019); Pricke of Conscience, l. 632. AS. *lang, long;* Grein, ii. 156. + Du. *lang;* Icel. *langr;* Dan. *lang;* Swed. *lång;* Goth. *laggrs* (= *langrs*); G. *lang;* L. *longus.* Brugmann, i. § 642. Der. *long,* adv.; *long-boat, long-measure, long-run, long-sight-ed, long-stop, long-suffering.* Also *a-long* (1), *a-long* (2), and *be-long,* verb (see N. E. D.). Also (from L. *longus*) *long-evity,* q. v., *long-itude,* q. v. Also *length,* q. v.; *ling* (1), q. v.; *ling-er,* q. v., *lunge,* q. v. Cf. *lumber* (1).

LONG (2), to desire, yearn; to belong. (E.) Often used with *for* or *after.* Very common in Shak. ME. *longen, longien.* ' Than *longen* folk to goon on pilgrimages ' = then people desire, &c.; Chaucer, C. T. 12. AS. *langian,* impers. vb. with acc. of person. ' Langað þe āwuht,' dost thou desire ought ? ' Hæleð *langode* ' = the heroes longed; Grein, ii. 157. [Distinct from *langian,* to grow long.] + OSax. *langōn,* impers.; Icel. *langa,* impers. and pers.; OHG. *langōn,* impers. Cf. G. *verlangen,* to long for. Not allied to *long* (1), but rather to G. *gelingen,* to succeed, prosper; to AS. *lungre,* quickly; and Gk. ἐλαφρός, light, nimble. See Kluge; and Brugmann, i. § 684. But the N. E. D. connects it with *long* (1). Der. *long-ing,* sb.; *long-ing,* adj., *long-ing-ly.*

LONGEVITY, length of life. (L.) ' In *longevity* by many conceived to attain unto hundreds ' [of years]; Sir T. Browne, Vulg. Errors, b. iii. c. 9. § 1. Spelt *longæuitie* in Minsheu, ed. 1627. Coined, by analogy with F. words in *-ité* (= E. *-ity*), from L. *longæuitas,* long life. – L. *long-,* stem of *longus,* long; and *æuitas,* full form of the word commonly written *ætas,* age. See **Long** and **Age.**

LONGITUDE, lit. length; distance in degrees from a given meridian. (F. – L.) ' *Longitudes* and latitudes; ' Chaucer, On the Astrolabie, Prol. l. 57. – F. *longitude.* – L. *longitūdo* (gen. *longitūdin-is*), length, long duration; in Late L., longitude. – L. *longi-,* for *longo-,* decl. stem of *longus,* long; with suffix *-tūdo.* See **Long.** Der. *longitudin-al* (from stem *longitūdin-*); *longitudinal-ly.*

LOO, a game at cards. (F.) Spelt *lu* in Pope, Rape of the Lock, c. iii. l. 62 (l. 350). Formerly called *Lanterloo* (Engl. Cycl. Supp.). ' Pam in *lanterloo;* ' Farquhar, Sir Harry Wildair, ii. 2 (1701). – F. *lanturelu* or *lanturlu,* interj. nonsense ! fiddlestick ! fudge! (Hamilton); also a game at cards, *jeu de la bê e* (i.e. loo); see Littré and Hamilton. [The more usual F. name for loo is *mouche.*] β. The expression was orig. the refrain of a famous vaudeville in the time of Cardinal

Richelieu (died 1642); hence used in order to give an evasive answer. As the expression is merely nonsensical, it admits of no further analysis.

LOOBY, a simpleton, a lubber. (E.) ME. *loby*, Rich. the Redeles, ii. 170. Allied to **Lubber**, q.v.

LOOF, another spelling of **Luff**, q.v.

LOOK, to behold, see. (E.) ME. *loken, lokien*; Chaucer, C. T. 1697. AS. *lōcian*, to look, see; Grein, ii. 192.+OSax. *lōkōn*, to look; cf. prov. G. *lugen*, to look out, OHG. *luogēn*, MHG. *luogen*, to mark, behold. Brugmann, i. § 421 (7). Der. *look*, sb., ME. *loke*, Chaucer, C. T. 3342; *look!* interj.; *look-er, look-out, look-ing, look-ing-glass.*

LOOM (1), a machine for weaving cloth. (E.) In Spenser, Muiopotmos, l. 272. ME. *lome*, a tool, instrument; P. Plowman, C. vi. 45; and see Prompt. Parv., p. 312. The pl. *lomen*=implements for tilling the soil, occurs in the Ancren Riwle, p. 384. AS. *gelōma*, a tool, implement, Ælfred, tr. of Beda, iv. 28, ed. E. E. T. S., p. 366, l. 23; cf. AS. *and-lōma*, a tool, implement, utensil; Voc. 549. 9. The mod. E. *loom* has the sense of ME. *weblome*, a weaving loom; see Test. Eboracensis, i. 191; Records of Nottingham, ii. 22 (1404).

LOOM (2), to appear faintly or at a distance. (Scand.) The orig. sense is to glimmer or shine faintly. Rare; and usually used of a ship. '*Looming of a ship*, is her prospective [appearance] or shew. Hence it is said, *such a ship looms a great sail*, i. e. she appears or seems to be a great ship;' Kersey's Dict. ed. 1715. So also Skinner, ed. 1671, who adds: 'she *looms* but small,' i. e. looks small. The orig. sense may have been 'to come slowly towards;' answering to EFries. *lōmen*, Swed. dial. *loma*, to move slowly; cf. MHG. *luomen*, to be weary, from the adj. *luomi*, slack. Kilian has MDu. *lome*, slow, inactive. From Teut. base **lōm-*, 2nd grade of **lam-*, as in E. *lame*. See **Lame, Loon** (2). Der. *loom-ing*, sb.

LOON (1), **LOWN**, a base fellow. (E.) Spelt *loon* in Macbeth, v. 3. 11; *lown* in Oth. ii. 3. 95. The latter passage is 'he called the tailor *lown*,' cited from an old ballad. In the Percy Folio MS., ed. Hales and Furnivall, ii. 324, l. 52, the line appears as: 'therfore he called the taylor *clowne*.' Lowl. Sc. *loun*, used frequently by Dunbar (see Small's Glossary); see *loon* in E. D. D. Cf. MDu. *loen*, 'homo stupidus;' Kilian.

LOON (2), a water-bird, diver. (Scand.) A corruption of the Shetland name *loom*; see Gloss. of Shetland Words by T. Edmondston; Phil. Soc. 1866.—Icel. *lōmr*, a loon; Swed. and Dan. *lom*; Norw. *lom*. Prob. from the *lame* or awkward motion of such birds on land; cf. Swed. dial. *loma*, EFries. *lōmen*, to move slowly; see **Loom** (2). For derogatory use of the names of birds, cf. *booby, gull, goose, owl*, &c.

LOOP, a bend, a bend in a cord leaving an opening. (C.) Spelt *loupe* in the Bible of 1551, Exod. xxvi. 4, 5. The ME. *loupe* is also used in the sense of 'loop-hole,' but it is prob. the same word, denoting a small hole in a wall shaped like a loop in a piece of string. In this sense it occurs in P. Plowman, C. xxi. 288; and Romance of Partenay, l. 1175. The pl. *loupis*, loops, occurs in the allit. Troy-book (see Glossary). Palsgrave has: '*Loupe* in a towne-wall, *creneau*; *Loupe* to holde a button, *fermeau*.' G. Douglas has *lowpis*, Æn. bk. v. ch. 5. 66; and *lowpit*, looped, id. 13. Jamieson has Lowl. Scotch *loops*, the windings of a river. The word appears to be Northern, and borrowed from Gaelic.—Gael. *lub*, a bend, loop, noose, winding, meander; *luib*, a fold, corner, or angle, a turn of a stream, a bending of the shore; Macleod. Cf. Irish *lub*, a loop, bow, staple, plait, fold, thong, meander; and note the sense of 'thong' in Cath. Anglicum, which has: 'a *lowpe*, *Amentum*.'—Gael. and Irish *lub*, to bend; cf. OIrish *lubtha*, bent (Windisch). And see Macbain. Der. *loop*, verb; *loop-ed*, full of holes, K. Lear, iii. 4. 31; *loop-hole*, Shak. Lucr. 1383, the older term being ME. *loupe*, as above; *loop-hol-ed*. ☞ But the N. E. D. connects *loop-hole* with Du. *luipen*, MDu. *lūpen*, to lurk (hence, to spy).

LOOSE, free, slack, unfastened, unconfined. (Scand.) ME. *laus, loose*, Chaucer, C. T. 4062 (A 4064); where the Camb. MS. has *los*, and the Petworth MS. has *louse*. Spelt *lowse, lousse*, in the Ancren Riwle, p. 228, note *d*. α. The form *laus* is Scand.; from Icel. *lauss* (Swed. Dan. *lös*); it is the Norse equivalent of ME. *lees*, false; see Prompt. Parv. p. 298. The latter is from AS. *lēas*, (1) loose, (2) false; cognate with Icel. *lauss*, loose, vacant, Dan. and Swed. *lös*, loose. +OSax. *lōs*, MDu. *loos*, (1) loose, (2) false (Oudemans); the mod. Du. separates the two senses, having *los*, loose, and *loos*, false. Further cognate words appear in Goth. *laus*, empty, vain; G. *los*, loose. Teut. type **lausoz*; from **laus*, 2nd grade of Teut. **leusan-*, to lose. See **Lose**; and see **Loosen**. See Notes on E. Etym., p. 173. Der. *loose-ly, loose-ness*. Note that *-l ss* (AS. *lēas*) is the commonest suffix in E.; see **-less**. And see **Leasing**.

LOOSE, LOOSEN, to make loose, set free. (E.) The suffix *-en* is due to analogy with words like *lengthen, strengthen*, and has been added. ME. *losen, lousen, lowsen*; where the final *n* merely

marks the infinitive mood, without having the causal force which is implied by the final *n* at present. 'The boondis of alle weren *lousid*' =the bonds of all were loosed; Wyclif, Acts, xvi. 26. From the adj. above.+OSax. *lōsian*, 'to make free.' So also Du. *lossen*, to loosen, release; Icel. *leysa*, to loosen; Swed. *lösa*; Dan. *löse*; G. *lösen*; Goth. *lausjan*; all from the adjective.

LOOT, plunder, booty. (Hindi.—Skt.) A modern term, imported from India.—Hindi *lūṭ* (with cerebral *ṭ*), loot, plunder. The cerebral *ṭ* shows that an *r* is elided.—Skt. *lōtram*, short form of *lōptram*, booty, spoil.—Skt. *luṭ*, to break, spoil; the neut. pp. *luptam* is also used in the sense of 'booty,' like the deriv. *loptram*; see Benfey, p. 798.—✓REUP, to break; whence L. *rumpere*, G. *rauben*, and E. *rob*. See **Rob, Rupture.** Cf. Horn, Pers. Dict., § 608. ¶ Thus *loot*=that which is robbed. Der. *loot*, verb.

LOOVER, the same as **Louver**, q. v.

LOP, to maim, to cut branches off trees. (E.) In Levins, ed. 1570; and in Shak. Cymb. v. 4. 141. Spelt *loppe* in Palsgrave. Ducange quotes *loppāre* as an Anglo-Latin word; Birch (Cart. Saxon. iii. 240) has '*æt loppede* thorne;' as if from an AS. verb *loppian*, to lop. Der. *lop*, sb., small branches cut off, Henry VIII, i. 2. 96. And see *glib* (3), *left*.

LOQUACIOUS, talkative. (L.) In Milton, P. L. x. 161. A coined word, formed by adding *-ious* to L. *loquāc-*, stem of *loquax*, talkative. [Prob. suggested by the sb. *loquacity*, which had previously been introduced into the language from F. *loquacité*, 'loquacity;' Cot. *Loquacity* occurs in Minsheu, ed. 1627.]—L. *loqui*, to speak. Der. *loquacious-ly, -ness*. Also *loquac-i-ty*, from F. *loquacité*, which from L. acc. *loquācitātem*. From the same root are *col-loqu-ial, e-loqu-ence, ob-loqu-y, soli-loqu-y, ventri-loqu-ist*; also (like L. pp. *locūt-us*) *al-locut-ion, circum-locut-ion, e-locut-ion, inter-locut-ion, pro-locutor*.

LORD, a master, ruler, peer. (E.) ME. *louerd* (=*lŭverd*), Havelok, l. 96; gen. contracted to *lord*, Chaucer, C. T. 47. AS. *hlāford*, a lord; Grein, ii. 80. Fuller form *hlāfweard* (misprinted *hālfweard*), Ps. civ. 17 (ed. Thorpe). β. Thus the word is a compound, and the former syllable is AS. *hlāf*, a loaf. It also appears that *-ord* stands for a warden, keeper, master; whence *hlāf-weard*=loaf-keeper, i. e. the master of the house, father of the family. See **Loaf** and **Ward.** The simple word *weard* is used nearly synonymously with the comp. *hlāf-weard*; and cf. *hord-weard*, a treasure-keeper, lord (Grein). Der. *lord*, verb (gen. used with *it*), 2 Hen. VI, iv. 8. 47; *lord-ed*, Temp. i. 2. 97; *lord-ing* (with dimin. suffix *-ing*), Wint. Ta. i. 2. 62=ME. *lauerd-ing*, Layamon, 27394; *lord-l-ing* (with double dimin.), Bp. Hall's Satires, b. ii. sat. 2, l. 12 =ME. *louerd-ling*, Layamon, 12664, later text; *lord-ly*=ME. *lorde-liche*, P. Plowman, B. xiii. 302; *lord-li-ness*, Shak. Ant. v. 2. 161; *lord-ship*=ME. *lordeship*, P. Plowman, B. iii. 206.

LORE, learning, doctrine. (E.) ME. *lore*, Chaucer, C. T. 529, 4424 (A 527, B 4). [The final *e* is unessential, and due to the frequent use of the oblique cases.] AS. *lār*, lore; gen., dat., acc. *lāre*; Grein, ii. 158.+Du. *leer*, doctrine; G. *lehre*, MHG. *lēre*, OHG. *lēra* (whence Dan. *lære*). Teut. type **laizā*, f.; cf. Goth. *laisjan*, to teach; *laiseins*, doctrine. From **lais*, 2nd grade of **leisan-*, to trace out. See further under **Learn.**

LOREL, a variant of **Losel**, q. v.

LORGNETTE, an opera-glass. (F.) F. *lorgnette.*—F. *lorgner*, to spy.

LORIKEET, a small lory. (Malay; *with* Span. *suffix.*) From *lory*, q.v.; with dimin. suffix *-keet*, borrowed from *parrakeet*.

LORIMER, a maker of bits and spurs. (F.—L.) Also *loriner*; both forms are in Blount's Gloss. (1681). '*Loremar* that maketh byttes;' Palsgrave.—OF. *loremier, lorenier* (Godefroy); F. *lormier.*—OF. *lorain*, rein, bridle, bit.—Late L. *lōrānum*, a rein, bit.—L. *lōrum*, a thong.

LORIOT, the golden oriole. (F.—L.) '*Loriot*, a bird otherwise called a witwall;' Kersey, ed. 1715.—F. *loriot*, 'the bird called a witwall, yellowpeake, hickway;' Cot. Corruptly written for *l'oriot, l'oriol*, the prefixed *l* being the def. article (=L. *ille*). Cotgrave has: '*Oriot*, a heighaw, or witwall;' also spelt *Oriol*, id. The latter form is the same as E. **Oriole**, q. v.

LORN, old pp. of the verb to *lose*. (E.) See **Lose, Forlorn.**

LORY, a small bird of the parrot kind. (Malay.) In Webster. Also called *lury*, and (better) *nory, nury.*—Malay *lūri*, a bird of the parrot kind, also called *nūri*; Marsden's Malay Dict., p. 311. *Nūri*, the lury, a beautiful bird of the parrot kind, brought from the Moluccas; id. p. 350.

LOSE, to part with, be separated from. (E.) The mod. E. *lose* appears to be due to confusion between three ME. forms, viz. (1) *losien*, (2) *lōsen*, (3) *lēosen*. 1. *Losien* is recorded in Stratmann, p. 405; it occurs in the sense 'to be lost,' or 'to perish,' as in O. Eng. Homilies, ed. Morris, i. 117, ll. 28, 35; and in Layamon, 20538, it is used exactly in the sense of 'lose.'—AS. *losian*, to become loose, to escape, Grein, ii. 194. From *los-*, weak grade of *lēosan*, to lose. 2. ME. *lōsen*, to loose, set free, is from the adj. *lōs*, *lous*, loose; see **Loose.** 3. The ME. *lēosen*, more commonly *lēsen*, is in Stratmann, at p. 394. This is the verb which invariably has the force of 'lose,' but it should rather have produced a mod. E. *leese*. It is a strong verb, with pt. t. *lees*, and pp. *loren*, *lorn*; see Chaucer, C. T. 1217, 3536; P. Plowman, B. v. 499. AS. *-lēosan*, to lose; pt. t. *lēas*, pp. *loren*; only used in comp. *for-lēosan*, to lose entirely, Luke, xv. 4, 9, Grein, i. 328.+Du. *-liezen*, only in comp. *ver-liezen*, to lose; pt. t. *verloor*, pp. *verloren*; G. *-lieren*, only in comp. *ver-lieren*, pt. t. *verlor*, pp. *verloren*; Goth. *-liusan*, only in comp. *fra-liusan*, to lose, Luke, xv. 8, with which cf. *fra-lusnan*, to perish, 1 Cor. i. 18. β. All three forms are from different grades of the Teut. verb **leusan-*, to lose; pt. t. **laus*, pp. **luzanoz*. From the Teut. base LEUS, to lose, become loose (Fick, iii. 273). This base is an extension of √LEU, to set free, whence Gk. λύειν, to set free, release; L. *luere*, to set free. A still older sense, 'to set free by cutting a bond,' is suggested by Skt. *lū*, to cut, clip; Benfey, p. 799. ¶ Note the double form of the pp., viz., *lost*, *lorn*; of which *lost* (= *los-ed*) is formed from ME. *losien*: but *lorn* (= *lor-en*) is the regular strong pp. of *lēosen* = AS. *lēosan*. Der. *los-er*, *los-ing*; from the same Teut. base are *loose*, vb., also spelt *loosen*, q.v., *loose*, adj.; *leasing*, q.v.; *lorn*, *for-lorn*; *loss*, q.v. From the root LEU we also have *solve*, *solution*, *ana-ly-sis*, *para-ly-sis*, *palsy*.

LOSEL, LOREL, a worthless fellow, a scamp. (E.) In Shak., Wint. Tale, ii. 3. 109. ME. *losel*, P. Plowm. B. vi. 124; also *lorel*, id., vii. 136. Cf. AS. *los-ian*, to lose. From Teut. **lus-*, weak grade of **leusan*, AS. *lēosan*, to lose, of which the pp. was *lor-en* (for older **los-en*); whence *lor-el*. See **Lose** (above). The sense is 'devoted to perdition;' for the suffix, cf. AS. *wac-ol*, watchful.

LOSS, a losing, damage, waste. (E.) ME. *los*, Chaucer, C. T. 4447 (B 27). AS. *los*, destruction; *tō lose wurdon*, i. e. perished, Ælfred, tr. of Beda, lib. v. c. 9 (or c. 10). ONorthumb. *los*, Matt. vii. 13 (Lindisfarne MS.). From Teut. **lus-*, weak grade of **leusan-*, AS. *lēosan*, to lose; see **Lose.**

LOT, a portion, share, fate. (E.) ME. *lot*, a share; Rich. Cuer de Lion, 4262, in Weber's Met. Romances. AS. *hlot*; Matt. xxvii. 35, Luke, xxiii. 34; also *hlȳt*, Grein, ii. 90. The AS. *hlot*, n. (Teut. type **hlutom*) is from *hlut-*, the weak grade of Teut. **hleutan-*, AS. *hlēotan*, to cast lots, a strong verb.+Du. *lot*, a lot; *loten*, to cast lots; Icel. *hluti*, a part, share; from the strong verb *hljóta*, to obtain by lot; Dan. *lod*, a lot; Swed. *lott*, a lot; *lotta*, to cast lots. Cf. also G. *loos*, a lot; *loosen*, to cast lots; Goth. *hlauts*, a lot, Mark, xv. 24; from Teut. **hlaut*, 2nd grade of **hleutan-* (above). Der. *lot*, vb.; *lott-er-y*, q.v.; *al-lot*, q.v.

LOTH, reluctant; the same as **Loath,** q.v.

LOTION, a washing, external medicinal application. (L.) 'Lotion, a washing or rinsing;' Blount's Gloss., ed. 1674. Formed, by analogy with F. words in *-ion*, from L. *lōtio*, a washing; cf. *lōtus*, pp. of *lauāre*, to wash; see **Lave.** Brugmann, i. § 352 (3).

LOTO, LOTTO, the name of a game. (Ital.—Teut.) Modern; the spelling *lotto* is the correct Ital. spelling; *loto* is a F. form of the Ital. word.—Ital. *lotto*, a lot, lottery. Of Teut. origin; cf. OHG. *hlōz* (G. *loos*), a lot; see **Lot.**

LOTTERY, a distribution by lot or chance. (Ital.—Teut.) In Levins, ed. 1570; and in Shak. Merch. Ven. i. 2. 32, ii. 1. 15. —Ital. *lotteria*, *lottaria*, 'a lottery;' Torriano (1688).—Ital. *lotto* (above). ¶ The F. *loterie* is borrowed from Italian, but is in much later use; thus it is omitted by Cotgrave, and Sherwood's index to Cotgrave only gives *balotage*, *sort*, as equivalent words to E. *lottery*.

LOTUS, the Egyptian water-lily. (L.—Gk.) 'Lotos, or Lotus, the lote-tree;' Kersey, ed. 1715. Minsheu, ed. 1627, speaks of the *lothe-tree* or *lote-tree*. It is spelt *lote* by Chapman, tr. of Odyssey, ix. 163.—L. *lōtus*, *lōtos*.—Gk. λωτός, a name given to several shrubs; (1) the Greek lotus; (2) the Cyrenean lotus, an African shrub, the eaters of which were called *Loto-phagi* = Lotus-eaters, from Gk. φαγεῖν, to eat; (3) the lily of the Nile; see Liddell and Scott. Der. *Lo'o-phagi*; *lotus-eater*.

LOUD, making a great sound, noisy. (E.) ME. *loud*; more common in the adv. form *loude* = loudly; Chaucer, C. T. 674, 15339 (A 672, B 4523). AS. *hlūd*, loud, Grein, ii. 88.+Du. *luid*; G. *laut*, OHG. *hlūt*. β. Teut. type **hlūdoz*, for **hlūthós* (with accent on o); allied to the Idg. type **klutós* (with weak grade *klu* as seen in L. *-clutus*, in comp. *in-clutus*, renowned; Gk. κλυτός, renowned; Skt. *çruta-*, heard, from *çru*, to hear, Gk. κλύειν. √KLEU, to hear. Brugmann, i. §§ 100, 113. Der. *loud-ly*, *loud-ness*; from the same root is *cli-ent*.

LOUGH, a lake. (Irish.) The written Irish form of *loch.*—Irish *loch*, a lake, lough, arm of the sea; see **Loch.**

LOUNGE, to loll about, move about listlessly. (F.—L.) In Skinner's Dict., ed. 1671; not before 1508. 'A very flourishing society of people called *loungers*, gentlemen whose observations are mostly itinerant;' The Guardian, no. 124, dated Aug. 3, 1713. The verb seems to have been suggested by the term *lungis*, defined in Minsheu, ed. 1627, as meaning 'a slimme, a tall and dull slangam, that hath no making to his height;' and even as late as in Kersey, ed. 1715, we find *lungis* explained as 'a drowsy or dreaming fellow.' It was once a well-known term, and occurs in Decker's Satiromastix; Beaum. and Fletcher, Knight of the Burning Pestle, Act ii. sc. 3, speech 1; Lyly's Euphues and his England, ed. Arber, p. 325; and the Play of Misogonus, written about 1560; see Nares and Halliwell. —F. *longis*, 'a lungis; a slimme, slow-back, dreaming luske [idle fellow], drowsie gangrill; a tall and dull slangam, that hath no making to his height, nor wit to his making; also, one that being sent on an errand is long in returning;' Cot. Cf. Norm. dial. *longis*, or *seint-longis*, a dolt, a slow fellow (Moisy). β. Littré supposes that the sense of F. *longis* was due to a pun, having reference to L. *longus*, long; see **Long.** For, strictly, *Longis* was a proper name, being the OF. form of L. *Longis*, or *Longinus*, the name of the centurion who pierced the body of Christ. This name *Longinus* first appears in the Apocryphal Gospel of Nicodemus, and was probably suggested by the Gk. λόγχη, a lance, the word used in John, xix. 34; hence the Picard form *longin*, with the sense of F. *longis*. See my note to P. Plowman, C. xxi. 82. See the word **Lunge,** which is certainly due to L. *longus*. Der. *loung-er*.

LOUSE, the name of an insect. (E.) ME. *lous*, pl. *lys* or *lis*; P. Plowman, B. v. 197, 198. AS. *lūs*, as a gloss to L. *pediculus*; Ælfric's Gloss., Nomina Insectorum; the pl. form was *lȳs*.+Du. *luis*; Dan. *lus*, pl. *lus*; Swed. *lus*, pl. *löss*; Icel. *lūs*, pl. *lȳss*; G. *laus*, pl. *läuse*. All from Teut. **lūs*, fem. Cf. W. *lleuen*, a louse; Stokes-Fick, p. 256. Der. *lous-y*, *lous-i-ness*; *louse*, v.

LOUT, a clown, awkward fellow. (E.) The lit. sense is 'stooping' or 'slouching.' In Levins; and in K. John, ii. 509, iii. 1. 220. Sidney has: 'this *lowtish* clown;' Arcadia, b. i. (R.) From the old verb *lout*, to stoop, bow: 'he humbly *louted*;' Spenser, F. Q. i. 10. 44. ME. *louten*, to stoop, bow down; Chaucer, C. T. 14168 (B 3352); P. Plowman, B. iii. 115. AS. *lūtan*, to stoop, str. vb.; pt. t. *lēat*; Grein, ii. 197.+Icel. *lūta*, to bow down; whence *lūtr*, adj. bent down, stooping, which may have suggested our modern *lout*; Swed. *luta*, to lean; Dan. *lude*, to stoop. Teut. type **lūtan-*, pt. t. **laut*, pp. *lutanoz*. Der. *lout-ish*, *lout-ish-ness*, *loit-er*.

LOUVER, LOOVER, an opening in the roofs of ancient houses. (F.—Teut.) ME. *lover*, Prompt. Parv. p. 315; see Way's note. He cites: 'A *loouer*, or tunnell in the roofe, or top of a great hall, to auoid smoke, *fumarium*, *spiramentum*;' Baret. Also in P. Plowman, C. xxi. 288; Romance of Partenay, 1175. In the latter passage we find: 'At *louers*, lowpes, archers had plente, To cast, draw, and shete, the diffence to be' = it (the town) had plenty of archers at openings and loop-holes, to cast, draw (bow), and shoot.—OF. *lovier*, a louver; see Godefroy, who has *lovier*, *luvier*, *lover*, with three instances in which it is used to translate Late L. *lōdium*.—Romanic type **lōdārium*, adj. form due to Late L. *lōdium*, a louver. (For the intercalated *v*, cf. F. *pouvoir*, from OF. *pooir* = Span. *poder*.) β. The orig. sense was prob. an opening over a fireplace; from Icel. *hlóð*, n. pl. a hearth, a fire-place; ult. allied to Icel. *hlaða*, to lade, to pile, build up. See **Lade.** (See Academy, Dec. 1894.)

LOVAGE, an umbelliferous plant. (F.—L.) In Levins, ed. 1570, and in Cotgrave. Spelt *loueache* in Palsgrave; and ab. 1400, in Henslow's Medical Works of 14th cent., p. 8, l. 18. From OF. *levesche* (mod. F. *livèche*), 'common lovage, Lombardy lovage,' Cot.; spelt *livesche*, *liuvesche*, *luvesche*, *lovache* in Godefroy; cf. *luvesche*, as in Voc. 555. 11, whence the E. form. Cf. Ital. *levistico*, lovage.—L. *ligusticum*, lovage, a plant indigenous to Liguria; whence its name. —L. *Ligusticus*, belonging to Liguria.—L. *Liguria* (prob. formerly **Ligusia*), a country of Cisalpine Gaul, of which the principal town was *Genua*, the modern Genoa. Similarly, we have *Etruscan* from *Etruria* [*Etrusia*?].

LOVE, affection, fondness, attachment. (E.) ME. *loue* (with *u* for *v*), Chaucer, C. T. 1137, 1161 (A 1135, 1159). AS. *lufu*, love; Grein, ii. 196. From the weak grade (**lub*) of Teut. base **leub-*.+ Goth. *lubō*; OHG. *luba*; cf. G. *liebe*, OHG. *liupa*, love; Russ. *liobov'*, love; Skt. *lobha-*, covetousness, *lubh*, to desire. Closely allied to **Lief.** (√LEUBH.) Der. *love*, verb, ME. *louen* (= *loven*), older forms *louien*, *luuien*, AS. *lufigan*, *lufian*, Grein, ii. 195; also *lov-able*, *lov-er* (Chaucer, C. T., A 1347), *lov-ing*, *lov-ing-ly*, *lov-ing-ness*, *lov-ing-kind-ness*; also *love-ly*, ME. *luuelich*, Ancren Riwle, p. 428, l. 25; *love-li-ness*; also *love-less*, *love-bird*, *love-knot*, *love-lorn*. Also *be-love*, ME. *bi-luʒien*, to love greatly.

LOW (1), inferior, deep, mean, humble. (Scand.) ME. *low*, pl.

lowe; Chaucer, C. T. 17310 (H 361); older spellings *louh*, Ancren Riwle, p. 140, l. 2; *lah*, Ormulum, 15246, *loogh* (in the comp. *biloogh* = below), Allit. Poems, B. 116. Late AS. *lāh*, in l. 8 of The Grave; in Thorpe's Analecta, p. 153.—Icel. *lāgr*, low; Swed. *låg*; Dan. *lav*.+Du. *laag*. β. The orig. sense is 'that which lies down,' or lies low (as we say). From Icel. *lāg*-, 3rd (pt. pl.) stem of *liggja*, to lie. See **Lie** (1). Der. *low-ness*, P. Plowman's Crede, ed. Skeat, l. 513; *low-ly*, Chaucer, C. T. 99, *low-li-ness*; *low-er*, verb = to make or become more low, formed from the comparative of the adj. (cf. *better*), Shak. Ant. i. 2. 129; *low-church*, *low-land*, *low-lander*, *low-spirited*. Also *be-low* (= by low).

LOW (2), to bellow as a cow or ox. (E.) ME. *loowen*, *lowen*, Wyclif, Job, vi. 5; Jer. li. 52. AS. *hlōwan*, to bellow, resound; Grein, ii. 88.+Du. *loeijen*, to low; MHG. *luejen*, OHG. *hlōjan*, to low. Cf. L. *clā-māre*, to exclaim, cry out; Gk. κέ-κλη-μαι, perf. pass. of καλ-εῖν, to call. Der. *low-ing*, 1 Sam. xv. 14.

LOW (3), a hill. (E.) In place-names; as *Lud-low*, *Bart-low*, *Trip-low*. AS. *hlāw*, a hill, a slope; also spelt *hlǣw*, Grein, ii. 81. It also means a mound, a grave.+Goth. *hlaiw*, a grave, tomb; allied to Goth. *hlains*, a hill. From Teut. base *hlai-, 2nd grade of *hlei- (Idg. KLEI), to incline, slope. Hence it is related to L. *cliuus*, a hill; *clīnāre*, to lean; and E. *lean*, verb. See **Lean** (1).

LOW (4), flame. (Scand.) In Burns, The Weary Pund o' Tow, l. 10. ME. *loȝhe*, Ormulum, 16185.—Icel. *logi*, a flame; NFries. *lowe* (Outzen); MDan. *loge*, Dan. *lue*. From Teut. *luh, weak grade of *leuh- (Idg. LEUK), to shine; allied to L. *lux*; see **Lucid**.

LOWER (1), to let down, abase, sink. (E.) See **Low** (1).

LOWER (2), to frown, look sour. (E.) ME. *louren*, Chaucer, C. T. 6848 (D 1266); P. Plowman, B. v. 132; spelt *luren*, K. Horn, ed. Lumby, l. 270. Not found in AS.+EFries. and Low G. *lūren*, to lower, frown, peer; MDu. *loeren* (with *oe* for *ū*, Franck), 'to leere, to frowne;' Hexham. Also G. *lauern*, to lurk, lie on the watch; a sense which appears in the E. derivative *lur-k*; see **Lurk**.

LOYAL, faithful, true. (F.—L.) Common in Shak.; as in Rich. II, i. 1. 148, 181.—F. *loyal*, 'loyall, faithfull, also lawfull;' Cot.—L. *lēgālis*, legal.—L. *lēg*-, stem of *lex*, law. See **Legal**. Doublets, *leal*, *legal*. Der. *loyal-ly*, *loyal-ty*, *loyal-ist*.

LOZENGE, a rhombus; a small cake of flavoured sugar, &c., orig. of a diamond shape. (F.—Prov.—L.) Formerly spelt *losenge*; and esp. used as an heraldic term, to denote a shield of a diamond shape; see Romaunt of the Rose, l. 893, where the OF. word is also *losenges*. The word *losenges* in Chaucer, Ho. of Fame, 1317, is prob. the same word.—OF. *losenge*, *lozenge*, 'a losenge, a lozenge, a little square cake of preserved herbs, flowers, &c.;' Cot. Mod. F. *losange*; Prov. *lausange* (Mistral).—OProv. *lauza*, Prov. *lauso* (Gascon *lu͞o*), a square stone, a tomb-stone (Mistral); Low L. *lausa*, *lauza*, the same. Allied to Span. *laude*, a tomb-stone (Pineda).—L. acc. *lapidem*, from nom. *lapis*, a stone, also a tomb-stone, grave-stone. See **Lapidary**. ¶ See N. and Q. 9 S. x. 84. The phonology is quite regular; the L. *d*, between two vowels, becomes OProv. *z*, mod. Prov. *s*, as in L. *laudāre*, to praise, OProv. *lauzar*, mod. Prov. *lausa*. With Span. *laude*<L. *lapidem*, compare Span. *raudo*, rapid<L. *rapidum*. But *lauza* may represent an adj. form *lapidea*. Cf. also Span. *losa*, a flag-stone, marble-slab, a square stone used for paving; whence *losar*, to pave; OF. *lauze*, Port. *lousa*, a flat-stone, a slate for covering roofs; all from Prov. Thus the word meant grave-stone, square slab; and finally a flat square cake.

LUBBER, a clumsy fellow, dolt. (E.) ME. *lobre*, *lobur*, P. Plowman, A. prol. 52; B. prol. 55; where some MSS. have *loby*. Palsgrave has: 'I *lubber*, I playe the *lubber*.' We find similar forms in Du. *lobbes*, a booby; Swed. dial. *lubber*, a thick, clumsy, lazy man (Rietz); *lubba*, the same, from *lubba*, v., to be slow or dull; MDu. *lobben*, 'a lubbard, a clown;' Norw. *lubb*, *lubba*, one of round thick figure, *lubben*, short and thick. Cf. W. *llob*, a dolt, lubber; *llabi*, a stripling, looby; Pomeranian *lobbe*, a lubber; EFries. *lobbe*, *lob*, a flabby lump. Shak. has *lob*, Mids. Nt. Dr. ii. 1. 16, which is exactly the W. word; also to *lob down* = to droop, Hen. V, iv. 2. 47. Der. *lubber-ly*, Merry Wives, v. 5. 195. And see *lump*.

LUBRICATE, to make smooth or slippery. (L.) Used by Ray, On the Creation, pt. ii. (R.) Kersey, ed. 1715, has *lubricitate*, to make slippery. The adj. *lubrick* occurs in Cotgrave to translate F. *lubrique*; and the sb. *lubricity*, for F. *lubricité*.—L. *lūbricātus*, pp. of *lūbricāre*, to make slippery.—L. *lūbricus*, slippery (whence F. *lubrique*). Allied to **Slip**, q. v. Der. *lubricat-ion*, *lubricat-or*; also *lubricity* = F. *lubricité*, as above.

LUCE, a fish, prob. the pike. (F.—L.) 'Luce, fysche, Lucius;' Prompt. Parv.; and see Chaucer, C. T. 352 (A 350).—OF. *lus*, 'a pike;' Cot.—L. *lūcius*, a fish, perhaps the pike. ☞ It is probable that *luce* in Shak. Merry Wives, i. 1. 16, means a louse, by a pun upon the word; see note in Schmidt.

LUCID, bright, shining, clear. (L.) 'Lucid firmament;' Spenser, Mother Hubbard's Tale, l. 1259. [There is no MF. *lucide* in Cot.; the E. word was taken directly from Latin.]—L. *lūcidus*, bright, shining.—L. *lūcēre*, to shine; L. *lūc-*, stem of *lux*, light. From √LEUK or √REUK, to shine; whence also Skt. *ruch*, to shine, *ruch*, light, Gk. λευκός, white, &c. Der. *lucid-ly*, *lucid-ness*, *lucid-i-ty*. Also *Luci-fer*, Chaucer, C. T. 14005 (B 3189), from L. *lūci-fer* (bringer of light, morning-star), from L. *lūci-*, decl. stem of *lux*, and *fer-re*, to bring. Also *lucent*, Ben Jonson, Epigram 76, l. 8, from L. *lūcent-*, stem of pres. pt. of *lūcēre*, to shine. Also *lucubration*, q.v. From the same root we have *lu-nar*, *lu-min-ous*, *lu-min-ary*, *e-lu-cid-ate*, *il-lu-min-ate*, *limn*, *pel-lu-cid*, *lu-s-trat-ion*, *il-lu-s-trate*, *trans-luc-ent*, *lu-natic*, *lustre* (1), *lynx*. And see **Light** (1).

LUCK, fortune, chance, good hap. (MDu.) 'Lukke and good happe;' Caxton, Hist. of Troye, leaf 216, back, l. 7. Not found in AS.—Du. *luk*, *geluk*, good fortune, happiness.+MHG. *gelücke*, good fortune; whence G. *glück* (for *gelück*). Prob. allied to G. *locken*, MHG. *locken*, OHG. *lokôn*, to entice, allure, decoy; cf. the Shetland word *luck*, to entice, to entreat (Edmondston). The EFries. *luk*, Swed. *lycka*, Dan. *lykke*, are all from G. Der. *luck-y*, Much Ado, v. 3. 32; *luck-i-ly*, *luck-i-ness*, *luck-less*, *luck-less-ly*, *-ness*.

LUCRE, gain, profit. (F.—L.) ME. *lucre*, Chaucer, C. T. 16870 (G 1402).—F. *lucre*.—L. *lucrum*, gain. Allied to Irish *luach*, value, price, wages, hire; G. *lohn*, a reward; Gk. λεία, booty; Russ. *lov'*, catching or prey, *lovite*, to capture. All from √LEU, to win, capture as booty; Fick, i. 755. Der. *lucr-at-ive*, from F. *lucratif*, 'lucrative,' Cot.<L. *lucrātīuus*, from *lucrātus*, pp. of *lucrāri*, to gain, which is from *lucrum*. sb.; also *lucrative-ly*, *-ness*.

LUCUBRATION, a production composed in retirement. (L.) 'Lucubration, a studying or working by candle light;' Phillips' Dict. ed. 1706. Coined, in imitation of F. words in *-tion*, from L. *lūcubrātio*, a working by lamp-light, night-work, lucubration.—L. *lūcubrāre*, to bring in lamps, to work by lamp-light.—L. *lūcubrum*, a faint light (Isidore); formed from *lūc-*, stem of *lux*, light. See **Lucid**, **Light** (1).

LUDICROUS, laughable, ridiculous. (L.) 'Some *ludicrous* schoolmen;' Spectator, no. 191, l. 1. Formed (like *arduous*, &c.) immediately from L. *lūdicrus*, done in sport; by change of *-us* to *-ous*.—L. *lūdi-*, for *ludo-*, decl. stem of *lūdus*, sport.—L. *lūdere*, to play. Root unknown. Der. *ludicrous-ly*, *-ness*; also (from *lūdere*), *al-lude*, *col-lude*, *e-lude*, *de-lude*, *inter-lude*, *pre-lude*; and (like pp. *lūsus*), *al-lus-ion*, *col-lus-ion*, *de-lus-ion*, *il-lus-ion*.

LUFF, LOOF, to turn a ship towards the wind. (E.?) The pp. *loofed* is in Shak. Ant. iii. 10. 18. 'To *loof*, usually pron. to *luff*;' Phillips' Dict. ed. 1706. Shak. prob. took the word from North's Plutarch, since we find 'he was driven also to *loof* off to have more room' in the description of the battle of Actium; see Shakespeare's Plutarch, ed. Skeat, p. 212, note 1. The verb answers to Du. *loeven*, to luff, to keep close to the wind. B. But the verb is due to an older sb., found in ME. more than once. This is the ME. *lof*, a 'loof,' the name of a certain contrivance on board ship, of which the use is not quite certain. We find it in Layamon, ll. 7859, 9744; the pl. being *loues* (= *loves*), 20949, 30922; see Sir F. Madden's remarks in vol. iii. p. 476 of his edition; and cf. OF. *lof*, *loef*, *louf* in Godefroy, used in the same sense. See also Richard Cuer de Lion, l. 71; Allit. Poems, ed. Morris, C. 106; Ancren Riwle, p. 104, l. 1 (though this passage is of doubtful meaning). The word seems to have had different senses at different times; thus the mod. Du. *loef* is 'weather-gage,' like mod. E. *luff*; but Kilian explains the MDu. *loef* by *scalmus*, i. e. a thole-pin. In Falconer's Marine Dict. we find *loof* explained as 'the after-part of a ship's bow;' whilst in Layamon and other passages in ME. we find (as Sir F. Madden says) that it is 'applied to some part of a ship, the agency of which was used to alter its course.' Sir F. Madden quotes from the Supplement to Ducange, s.v. *dracena*, which L. word is used as equivalent to E. *loof*, and explained by *gubernaculum*. The reader should consult Sir F. Madden's note. The *loof* was certainly, as Mr. Wedgwood remarks, 'a timber of considerable size, by which the course of the ship was directed.' It was not, however, what we now call a rudder. C. In my opinion, the passages in which the word occurs go to prove that it was orig. a kind of paddle, which in large ships became a large piece of timber, perhaps thrust over *the after-part of a ship's bow* (to use Falconer's expression) to assist the rudder in keeping the ship's head right. D. In any case, we may perhaps infer that the orig. sense was 'paddle;' and the word may be an English one, though we may have also re-borrowed the word, in the 16th century, from the cognate Du. *loef*. Cf. also Dan. *luv*, luff, weather-gage; *luve*, to luff; Swed. *lof*, weather-gage; but these may have been borrowed from Dutch. We find, however, the cognate Bavarian *laffen*, the blade of an oar, flat part of a rudder (Schmeller). These words are further to be connected with Icel. *lófi*, the flat hand,

Goth. *lôfa*, the flat hand, palm of the hand, the Lowland Scotch form being *loof*.   E. Recapitulating, we may conclude that the flat or palm of the hand was the original *loof* which, thrust over the side of the primitive canoe, helped to direct its course when a rude sail had been set up; this became a paddle, and, at a later time, a more elaborate piece of mechanism for keeping the ship's head straight; which, being constantly associated with the idea of the wind's direction, came at last to mean 'weather-gage,' esp. as in the Du. *loef houden*, to keep the luff, *de loef afwinnen*, to gain the luff, *te loef*, windward; &c. A similar idea is seen in L. *palma*, (1) the palm of the hand, (2) the blade of an oar. The *verb* is from the older sb. ¶ Napier's Collection of Glosses contains the entry: 'Redimicula, *lôfas*;' 5241; otherwise, *lôf* is unrecorded. We must not connect Du. *loef*, luff, with Du. *lucht*, air; nor with our own word *loft*. Der. *a-loof*, q. v.

LUG, to pull, haul, drag. (Scand.) 'To *lugge*, trahere, vellere;' Levins. The old sense was 'to pull by the hair.' In Gower, iii. 148 (bk. vii. 1892), we have: 'And be the chin and be the cheke She *luggeth* him riht as hir liste,' i. e. she pulls him by his beard and whiskers as she pleases. So also: '*to-lugged* of manye' = pulled by the hair by many people; P. Plowman, B. ii. 216. − Swed. *lugga*, to pull by the hair; cf. Swed. *lugg*, the fore-lock; Norw. *lugga*, to pull by the hair; *lugg*, the hair of the head. β. Perhaps a variant (with *k* for *g*) appears in Low G. *luken*, to pull, esp. to pull by the hair; Brem. Wörterbuch, iii. 97; cf. prov. E. *louk*, to weed, pull up weeds (see *loukers* = weeders, in Halliwell), from AS. *lûcan*, str. vb., to pull up weeds; cf. Dan. *luge*, the same. 'Ceorl of his æcere *lȳcð* yfel wēod monig' = a peasant lugs many an evil weed out of his field; Ælfred's tr. of Boethius, met. xii. 28. Der. *lugg-age* (with F. suffix *-age*), Temp. iv. 231. And see **Lugsail**. ☞ The alleged AS. *geluggian*, due to Somner, is unauthorised.

LUGSAIL, a sort of square sail. (Hybrid; Scand. *and* E.) '*Lugsail*, a square sail hoisted occasionally on a yard which hangs nearly at right angles with the mast;' Ash's Dict., ed. 1775. [He does not mention *lugger*, which appears to be a later word; the Dan. *lugger*, Du. *logger*, a lugger, may be borrowed from E.] Apparently from the verb to *lug*, it being so easily hoisted by a mere pull at the rope which supports the yard. Der. *lugg-er*, a ship rigged with *lug-sails*; unless the derivation runs the other way; in which case the *lugsail* is named from the *lugger*, which may be from Du. *logger*, 'slow ship,' from Du. *log*, EFries. *lug*, slow. (Uncertain.)

LUGUBRIOUS, mournful. (L.) Spelt *lugubrous* and *lugubrious* in Kersey, ed. 1715; but *lugubrous* only in Blount's Gloss., ed. 1674. Suggested by L. *lūgubris*, mournful. − L. *lūgēre*, to mourn. Cf. Gk. λυγρός, sad; prob. also Skt. *ruj*, to break, bend. Der. *lugubrious-ly*, *-ness*.

LUKEWARM, partially warm, not hot. (E.) '*Leuke warme* or blodde warme;' Palsgrave. *Luke* means 'tepid,' and can correctly be used alone, as by Sam Weller in Dickens, Pickwick Papers, ch. 33: 'let me have nine penn'orth o' brandy and water *luke*.' It is sufficient to trace this word alone. ME. *leuk*, *leuke*, *luke*, warm, tepid. 'Als a *leuke* bath, nouther hate ne calde;' = as a tepid bath, neither hot nor cold; Pricke of Conscience, l. 7481 (Harl. MS.). 'Tha blod com forð *luke*' = the blood came forth warm; Layamon, 27557. Not in AS. Cf. Du. *leuk*, lukewarm; EFries. *lük*, *luke*, tepid, weak, slack. Root uncertain; see Du. *leuk* in Franck. ¶ Distinct from the older word *lew*, with the same sense, but perhaps affected by it. 'Thou art *lew*, nether cold nether hoot;' Wyclif, Rev. iii. 16, where one MS. has *lewk*. This *lew* is closely allied to AS. *hlēo*, *hleow*, a shelter, a place that is protected from cold wind, &c., allied to the mod. E. *lee*; see **Lee**. Der. *luke-warm-ly*, *luke-warm-ness*.

LULL, to sing to rest, quiet. (E.?) ME. *lullen*, Chaucer, C. T. 8429, 9697 (E 553, 1823). Earlier, in Walter de Bibbesworth, l. 9; in Wright, Vocab. i. 143. Not in AS. + Swed. *lulla*, to hum, to lull; Dan. *lulle*, to lull; MDu. *lullen*, to sing in a humming voice, sing to sleep; Oudemans; WFlem. *lullen*, the same; De Bo. β. Purely an imitative word, from the repetition of *lu*, *lu*, which is a drowsier form of the more cheerful *la! la!* used in singing. Cf. G. *lallen*, to lisp as children do, to babble (lit. to say *la la*); so also Gk. λαλεῖν, to speak. Der. *lull*, sb.; *lull-a-by*; and see *loll*, *loll-ard*, *lilt*.

LUMBAGO, pain in the loins. (L.) In Phillips' Dict., ed. 1706. − L. *lumbāgo* (a rare word), pain in the loins. − L. *lumb-us*, the loin. See **Lumbar**.

LUMBAR, belonging to the loins. (L.) '*Lumbar* or *Lumbary*, belonging to the loins;' Phillips, ed. 1706. − L. *lumbāris*, adj., only found in the neut. *lumbāre*, used as sb. to signify 'apron;' Jerem. xiii. 1 (Vulgate). − L. *lumbus*, the loin. Cf. AS. *lendenu*, pl. the loins, Matt. iii. 4; Du. *lendenen*, s. pl.; Swed. *länd*, Dan. *lænd*, the loin; G. *lende*, the haunch. Root unknown. Brugmann, i. § 360. Der. (from L. *lumbus*) *lumb-ago*; also *loin*, q. v.

LUMBER (1), cumbersome or useless furniture. (F. − G.) See Trench, Select Glossary, where we find: 'The *lumber*-room was orig. the Lombard-room, or room where the Lombard banker and broker stowed away his pledges. . . . As these would naturally often accumulate here till they became out of date and unserviceable, the steps are easy to be traced by which the word came to possess its present meaning.' So in Webster, Northward Ho, A. v. sc. 1: 'for though his apparel lie i' the *Lombard*.' 'To put one's clothes to *lumber*, pignori dare;' Skinner's Dict., ed. 1671. '*Lombardeer*, an usurer or broaker, so called from the Lombards . . . hence our word *lumbar*, which signifies refuse household stuff. *Lombard* is also used for a bank for usury or pawns;' Blount's Gloss., ed. 1674; so also in Fuller, Church Hist., III. v. 10. Minsheu, ed. 1627, gives *Lumbar*, *Lombar*, or *Lombard*, 'a bancke for vsury or pawnes.' He also gives: '*Lumber*, old baggage of household stuffe, so called of the noise it maketh when it is remoued, *lumber*, *lumber*, &c.;' and if any reader prefer this fancy, he may do so; see **Lumber** (2). But, on the other hand, Butler uses *lumber* to mean 'money for pledges;' as: 'The *lumber* for their proper goods recover;' Upon Critics, l. 94. And the word had reference to quite small articles; as 'a brasse ladle, and other *lomber*;' Unton Inventories, p. 27. 'A panne of brasse, with other *lombor*;' Will of R. Morton (1488); pr. by E. M. Thompson. β. The *Lombards* were early known as lenders of money on pawn; see P. Plowman, C. vii. 241, B. v. 242, and the note. − F. *Lombard*, 'a Lombard;' Cot.; OF. *Lombart*, a usurer (Godefroy). (It also formerly meant a pawn-broker's shop; Littré.) − Late L. *Longobardus*, *Langobardus*; for G. *Langbart*, Long-beard; a name given to the men of this tribe (Littré). See **Long** and **Beard**. ¶ Or the sb. may have been originally due to the verb *to lumber*, to rumble, to move heavy furniture, make a noise thus; cf. *lumber*, v., in Palsgrave, and Swed. dial. *lomra*, to roar. See N. E. D. The word may have been influenced by *both* sources. See **Lumber** (2). Der. *lumber-room*.

LUMBER (2), to make a great noise, as a heavy rolling object. (Scand.) 'The *lumbering* of the wheels;' Cowper, John Gilpin, st. 6 from end. 'I *lumber*, I make a noise above ones head, *Ie fais bruit*. You *lumbred* so above my head I could not sleep for you;' Palsgrave. 'They *lumber* forth the lawe;' Skelton, Colin Clout, l. 95. A frequentative verb of Scand. origin; preserved in Swed. dial. *lomra*, to resound, frequent. of *ljumma*, or *ljomma*, to resound, thunder; from *ljumm*, a great noise; Rietz. [Similarly *lumber* (with excrescent *b*) stands for *lumm-er*, where *-er* is the frequentative suffix.] β. The Swed. *ljumm* is cognate with Icel. *hljómr*, a sound, tune, voice; but differs from AS. *hlyn*, a loud noise (Grein), in the suffix and quantity. The Goth. *hliuma* means 'hearing;' Mk. vii. 35. γ. Swed. *ljumm*, Icel. *hljómr*, Goth. *hliuma*, are from the Teut. base *hleu-*, to hear; √KLEU. See **Loud**.

LUMINARY, a bright light. (F. − L.) 'O radiant *Luminary*;' Skelton, Prayer to the Father of Heaven, l. 1. − OF. *luminarie* (Littré); later *luminaire*, 'a light, candle, lampe;' Cot. − L. *lūmināre*, a luminary, neut. of *lūmināris*, light-giving. − L. *lūmin-*, stem of *lūmen* (=*lūc-men*), light. Cf. L. *lūcēre*, to shine; see **Lucid**. And see **Luminous**.

LUMINOUS, bright, shining. (F. − L.) 'Their sunny tents, and houses luminous;' Giles Fletcher, Christ's Triumph after Death; ii. st. 31. − F. *lumineux*, 'shining;' Cot. − L. *lūminōsus*, luminous. − L. *lūmin-*, stem of *lūmen*, light; see **Luminary**. Der. *luminous-ly*, *-ness*. Also (from L. *lūmen*) *lumin-ar-y*, *il-lumin-ate*. See **Lucid**. ¶ Perhaps taken *directly* from Latin.

LUMP, a small shapeless mass, clot. (Scand.) ME. *lompe*, *lumpe*; 'a *lompe* of chese' = a lump of cheese; P. Plowman, C. x. 150. Of Scand. origin; cf. Swed. dial. *lump*, a piece hewn off a log (Rietz); Norweg. *lump*, a block, knop, stump (Aasen). β. Allied words are Du. *lomp* (MDu. *lompe*), a rag, tatter, lump; Du. *lomp*, clumsy, dull, awkward; EFries. *lump*, clumsy, thick, vile, lumpy; Swed. and Dan. *lumpen*, shabby, mean. Perhaps allied to **Limp** (2) by gradation; cf. Dan. dial. *lumpe*, Low G. *lumpen*, to limp. Der. *lump-ing*; *lump-ish*, Two Gent. iii. 2. 62; *lump-y*, *lump-fish*. Also *lunch*, q. v.

LUNAR, belonging to the moon. (L.) In Minsheu, ed. 1627. [The older word was *lunary*, used by Cot. to tr. F. *lunaire*.] − L. *lūnāris*, lunar. − L. *lūna* (<*loucsnā*), the moon, lit. light-giver. Cf. L. *lūcēre*, to shine; see **Lucid**. Brugmann, i. § 218. Der. (from L. *lūna*) *lun-ate*, i. e. moon-shaped, crescent-like; *lun-at-ion*, in Kersey, ed. 1715; *lun-at-ic*, q. v.; *lun-ette*, 'in fortification, a small work gen. raised before the courtin in ditches full of water,' Phillips = F. *lunette*, dimin. of F. *lune*, the moon. Also *inter-lunar*.

LUNATIC, affected with madness. (F. − L.) ME. *lunatik*, P. Plowman, C. x. 107; used as sb. id. B. prol. 123. − F. *lunatique*, 'lunatick;' Cot. − L. *lūnāticus*, insane; lit. affected by the moon, which was supposed to cause insanity. − L. *lūnātus*, moon-like;

—L. *lūna*, the moon; see **Lunar**. Der. *lunac-y*, Hamlet, ii. 2. 49, iii. 1. 14.

LUNCH, a lump, large piece of bread, &c. (Scand.) 'Lunches, slices, cuts of meat or bread;' Whitby Glossary. Minsheu (ed. 1627) mentions *lunch*, as being equivalent to 'gobbet, or peece.' 'Cheese an' bread . . in *lunches*;' Burns, Holy Fair, st. 23. Rietz has Swed. dial. *lunk*, a ball of flour in broth. The word is a variant of *lump*; just as *bunch*, *hunch*, are variants of *bump* and *hump*; see those words. Similarly, Swed. *linka*, to limp. And see **Lump**. Der. *lunch-eon*, q. v.

LUNCHEON, LUNCH, a slight meal between breakfast and dinner. (Scand.) *Lunch*, in the modern sense, seems at first to be an abbreviation of *luncheon*, though we shall trace the latter back to *lunch* in the sense mentioned in the article above. Cotgrave translates OF. *caribot* by 'a *lunchion*, or big piece of bread, &c.;' also OF. *horion* by 'a dust, cuff, rap, knock, thump, also, a *luncheon*, or big piece.' 'A *lunch*, or a *luncheon* of bread;' Gazophylacium Anglicanum (1689). We may suspect the spellings *lunch-ion*, *lunch-eon*, to be merely literary English for *lunch-in*. 'A huge *lunshin* of bread, i. e. a large piece;' Thoresby's (Yorkshire) Letter to Ray, 1703 (E. D. S. Gloss. B. 17, p. 103). And this *lunchin* is probably nothing but *lunching*, with *n* for *ng*. At any rate, *luncheon*, *lunchion*, or *lunchin*, is nothing but an old provincial word, and a mere extension of *lunch*, a lump, without, at first, any change of meaning. It was easily extended to mean a slight meal, just as we now say 'to take a snack,' i. e. a snatch of food. Quite distinct from **Nuncheon**, q. v. Der. *lunch*, verb.

LUNE, a leash; as, the *lune* of a hawk. (F.—L.) 'Lunes, or small thongs of leather;' Strutt, Sports, bk. i. c. 2. § 9. Prob. a variant of ME. *loigne*, the same; Rom. Rose, 3882.—OF. *loigne*, *longne*, a lune.—Late L. *longia*, a thong; formed from L. *longus*, long; see **Long**. Cf. MF. *longe*, 'a hawk's *lune* or leash;' Cot.

LUNG, one of the organs of breathing. (E.) Gen. in the pl. *lungs*. ME. *lunge* (sing.), Gower, C. A. iii. 100; bk. vii. 465; *lunges* (pl.), id. iii. 99; bk. vii. 452. Also *longes*, pl., Chaucer, C. T. 2754 (A 2752). AS. *lungen*, fem. sing.; pl. *lungena*. 'Pulmo, *lungen*;' Voc. 160. 34; *lungena*, 306. 18.+Du. *long*, s. pl., lungs, lights; Icel. *lunga*, neut. sing.; usually in pl. *lungu*; Dan. *lunge*; pl. *lunger*; Swed. *lunga*; G. *lungen*, pl.   β. Allied to AS. *lungre*, quickly (orig. *lightly*), Grein, ii. 196; also to E. *light* (2), which is allied to Gk. ἐλαχύς, Skt. *laghu-*, light; see **Light** (2). Thus the *lungs* are named from their lightness; indeed, they are also called *lights*. Finally, *lungs*, *light*, *levity* are all from the same root. Cf. also Russ. *legkoe*, lung, as compared with Russ. *legkii*, light; Port. *leves*, lights, from *leve*, light. Brugmann, i. § 691. Der. *lung-wort*, AS. *lungenwyrt*, Gloss. to Cockayne's A. S. Leechdoms.

LUNGE, a thrust, in fencing. (F.—L.) In Todd's Johnson; formerly *longe*, used by Smollett (Johnson). 'I have my passees, . . . My *longes*;' Dekker, Wonder of a Kingdom, A. i. sc. 1; spelt *longees*, Butler, Hud. pt. iii. c. 1. 159. The E. *a longe* is a mistaken substitute for F. *allonge* (formerly also *alonge*), 'a lengthening,' Cot. So named from the extension of the body in delivering the thrust.— F. *allonger* (formerly *alonger*), to lengthen; cf. Ital. *allongare*, *allungare*, to lengthen (Florio). Compounded of F. *à* (L. *ad*) and **longāre*, only in comp. *ē-longāre*, to lengthen; see **Elongate**.

LUPINE, a kind of pulse. (F.—L.) The pl. is both *lupines* and *lupins* in Holland, tr. of Pliny, b. xxii. c. 25. ME. *lupines*, pl., Lanfranc's Cirurgie, p. 88, l. 20.—F. *lupin*, 'the pulse lupines;' Cot.—L. *lupīnum*, a lupine, kind of pulse; neut. of *lupīnus*, wolfish, though the reason of the name is not apparent; perhaps 'because it exhausts the soil' (Webster).—L. *lupus*, a wolf; see **Wolf**.

LURCH (1), to lurk, dodge. (Scand.) Merely a variant of *lurk*, due to a palatalised pronunciation; see **Lurk**. It means to lie in wait, lurk; Merry Wives, ii. 2. 26. Der. *lurch-er*, 'one that lies upon the lurch, or upon the catch, also a kind of hunting-dog,' Phillips, ed. 1706; 'false *lorchers*,' Roy, Rede Me, ed. Arber, p. 98, l. 7.

LURCH (2), the name of a game. (F.—G.) The phr. 'to leave in the *lurch*' was derived from its use in an old game; to *lurch* is still used in playing cribbage. 'But rather leave him in the lurch;' Butler, Hudibras, pt. ii. c. 3. l. 1151. The game is mentioned in Cotgrave.—F. *lourche*, 'the game called Lurche, or, a Lurch in game; *il demoura lourche*, he was left in the lurch;' Cot. He also gives: '*Ourche*, the game at tables called lurch.'   β. This suggests that *lourche* stands for *l'ourche*, the initial *l* being merely the def. article; but this is doubtful, as we find also Ital. *lurcio*, 'the game lurch;' Torriano.   γ. Apparently from OF. *lourche*, deceived, duped (Godefroy).—Bavar. *lurzen*, to deceive; *lurz*, left (of the hands), perverse, beaten at draughts; Schmeller, i. 1503. Der. *lurch*, v., to cheat, rob; see Coriolanus, ii. 2. 105.

LURCH (3), to devour; *obsolete*. (F.?—G.?) Bacon says that proximity to great cities '*lurcheth* all provisions, and maketh every

thing deare;' Essay xlv, Of Building. That is, it absorbs them, lit. gulps them down. 'To *lurch*, deuour, or eate greedily, *Ingurgito*;' Baret, Alvearie. '*Lurcher*, an exceding eater;' Palsgrave. Perhaps a peculiar use of *lurch* (2), as if to devour before others. Cf. 'I *lurtche*, as one dothe his felowes at meate with etynge to hastyly;' Palsgrave. But influenced by Ital. *lurcare*, to lurch or devour greedily;' Torriano; Late L. *lurcāre*, to devour greedily; L. *lurcāri*, the same; L. *lurco*, a glutton.

LURCH (4), a sudden roll sideways. (Scand.?) Not in Todd's Johnson. 'A lee lurch, a sudden jerky roll of a ship to the leeward, as when a heavy sea strikes her on the weather side;' Cent. Dict. A sea term. Of obscure origin; but probably due to *lurch* (1) in the sense of to stoop or duck like one who skulks or tries to avoid notice. See **Lurch** (1).

LURE, a bait, enticement, decoy. (F.—G.) ME. *lure*, Chaucer, C. T. 17021 (H 72). The pp. *lured*, enticed, occurs in P. Plowman, B. v. 439; cf. Chaucer, C. T. 5997 (D 415). A term of the chase; and therefore of F. origin.—OF. *loerre*, *loirre* (see Littré), later *leurre*, 'a faulconer's lure;' Cot.—Teut. type **lōthrom*, n.; as in MHG. *luoder* (G. *luder*), a bait, decoy, lure. Der. *lure*, vb.

LURID, wan, gloomy. (L.) 'Lurid, pale, wan, black and blew;' Blount's Gloss., ed. 1674.—L. *lūridus*, pale, yellow, wan, ghastly. Prob. allied to Gk. χλωρός, green (Prellwitz); see **Chlorine**.

LURK, to lie in wait, skulk, lie hid. (Scand.) ME. *lurken*, *lorken*, Chaucer, C. T. 16126 (G 658); P. Plowman, B. ii. 216. Of Scand. origin.—Norw. *lurka*, to sneak away, to go slowly; Swed. dial. *lurka*, to do anything slowly; EFries. *lurken*, to shuffle along.   β. The *-k* appears to be a suffix; cf. Norw. and Swed. *lura*, Dan. *lure*, to lurk, outwit, G. *lauern*, to lurk. See **Lower** (2).   **Doublet**, *lurch* (1); perhaps *lurch* (4).

LURY, the same as **Lory**, q. v.

LUSCIOUS, delicious, very sweet, fulsome, nice. (F.—L.?) Also spelt *lushious*, Spenser, F. Q. ii. 12. 54; and in Skinner. Wedgwood cites from Palsgrave: 'Fresshe or *lussyouse*, as meate that is nat well seasoned or that hath an unplesante swetnesse in it, *fade*.' 'The strong may eate good *looshiouse* meate;' Drant, tr. of Horace, bk. ii. sat. 4 (1566). It seems to be formed from prov. E. *lush*, sweet, juicy, abundant, said of vegetation (E. D. D.).   β. Possibly influenced by ME. *lucius*, variant of *licius*, short for *delicious*; as in 'with *lucius* drinkes;' Robson, Three Met. Romances, p. 17; cf. 'with *licius* drinke;' id. p. 38. So also: '*licious* quails;' Bp. Hacket, Cent. of Sermons, fol. p. 515. And it may also have been influenced by ME. *lusty*, pleasant. 'How *lush* and *lusty* the grass looks;' Temp. ii. 1. 52. See **Lush**. Der. *luscious-ness*.

LUSH, fresh, luxuriant, juicy, said of vegetation. (F.—L.) 'Then green and voyd of strength and *lush* and foggy is the blade;' Golding, tr. of Ovid, Metam. xv. leaf 182 (1603). Cf. Tempest, ii. 1. 52. A parallel form to *lash*, relaxed, tender, soft and watery (E. D. D.). And see N. E. D.—MF. *lasche*, 'slack, flagging, weak;' Cot.—MF. *lascher* (F. *lâcher*), to slacken.—Late L. **lascāre*, for L. *laxāre*, to slacken.—L. *laxus*, lax; see **Lax**.

LUST, longing desire. (E.) The old sense is 'pleasure.' ME. *lust*, Chaucer, C. T. 192. AS. *lust*, pleasure; Grein, ii. 196.+Du. *lust*, delight; Icel. *lyst*, *losti*; Dan. *lyst*; Swed. *lust*; Goth. *lustus*; G. *lust*. Allied to Skt. *lash*, to desire; Gk. λιλαίομαι, Brugmann, i. § 518 (2). Der. *lust*, verb, K. Lear, iv. 6. 166, the older form being *list* = AS. *lystan*; *lust-y*, ME. *lust-y*, Chaucer, C. T. 80; *lust-i-ly*, *lust-i-ness*; *lust-ful*, Ayenbite of Inwyt, p. 80; *lust-ful-ness*, O. Eng. Homilies, ed. Morris, i. 21; *list-less* (=*lust-less*), Gower, C. A. ii. 111, bk. iv. 3262; Prompt. Parv. p. 307; *list-less-ness*.

LUSTRATION, a purification by sacrifice, a sacrifice. (L.) 'The doctrine of *lustrations*, amulets, and charms;' Sir T. Browne, Vulg. Errors, b. i. c. 11. sect. 12. Formed, by analogy with F. words in *-tion*, from L. *lustrātio*, an expiation, sacrifice.—L. *lustrāre*, to purify.—L. *lustrum*, an expiatory sacrifice. See **Lustre** (2).

LUSTRE (1), splendour, brightness. (F.—Ital.—L.) 'Lustre of the dyamonte;' Sir T. More, Works, p. 73 e. Spelt *luster* in Minsheu, ed. 1627.—F. *lustre*, 'a luster, or gloss;' Cot.—Ital. *lustro*, 'a lustre, a glasse, a shining;' Florio; cf. Late L. *lustrum*, a window; lit. a place for admitting light; connected with L. *lustrāre*, to enlighten, illumine.   β. This verb *lustrāre* appears to be quite distinct from *lustrāre*, to purify; for which see **Lustre** (2). It is prob. formed from a lost adjective **lustrus*, shining, an abbreviation of **lūc-strus*; in any case, it is to be connected with *lūcēre*, to shine; see **Lucid**. Der. *lustr-ous*, All's Well, ii. 1. 41; *lustrous-ly*; *lustre-less*; also *lutestring*. q. v.

LUSTRE (2), **LUSTRUM**, a period of five years. (F.—L.) Spelt *lustrum* in Minsheu, ed. 1627; which is the L. form. In Du Wes, Sup. to Palsgrave, p. 1078, we find the pl. *lustres*, both E. and F.—OF. and F. *lustre*, 'a tearm of . . fifty months;' Cot.—L. *lustrum*, an expiatory offering, a lustration; also a period of five years, because every five years a *lustrum* was performed. β. The orig. sense is 'a washing' or purification; connected with L. *luere*, to cleanse, purify, and *lauāre*, to wash; see **Lave**. Der. *lustr-al*, adj.; *lustr-at-ion*, q. v.

LUTE (1), a stringed instrument of music. (F.—Prov.—Span.—Arab.) ME. *lute*, Chaucer, C. T. 12400 (C 466). It is not easy to say *how* the word came to us; but prob. it was through the French, viz. OF. *leut*.—Prov. *laut*.—Span. *laud*.—Arab. *al 'ūd* (below). The forms are: OF. *leut*, pl. *leus* (Hatzfeld); MF. *lut* (Cot.), mod. F. *luth*; Prov. *laut*, Span. *laud*, Port. *alaude*, Ital. *liuto, leuto*; also MDu. *luyte* (Kilian), Du. *luit*, Dan. *lut*, G. *laute*. β. The Port. form *alaude* clearly shows the Arab. origin of the word, the prefix *al-* being the Arab. def. article, which in other languages appears merely as an initial *l*. The sb. is Arab. *'ūd* (with initial *ain*), wood, timber, the trunk or branch of a tree, a staff, stick, wood of aloes, lute, or harp; Rich. Dict. p. 1035, col. 1. Der. *lute-string*, Much Ado, iii. 2. 61; and in Palsgrave.

LUTE (2), a composition like clay, loam. (F.—L.) Chaucer has *enluting*, Six-text, Group G, l. 766, on which see my note. We also find the pp. *luted*, i.e. protected with lute; see Bacon, Nat. Hist. § 99; Massinger, A Very Woman, iii. 1. 38.—OF. *lut*, 'clay, mould, loam, durt;' Cot.—L. *lutum*, mud, mire; lit. that which is washed over or washed down.—L. *luere*, to wash, lave; see **Lave**. Der. *lut-ing*.

LUTESTRING, a lustrous silk. (F.—Ital.—L.) In Skinner, ed. 1671. 'The price of *lutestring*;' Spectator, no. 21. A curious corruption of *lustring* or *lustrine*. '*Lustring* or *Lutestring*, a sort of silk;' Kersey.—F. *lustrine*, lustring; Hamilton.—Ital. *lustrino*, lutestring (a shining silk), tinsel; Meadows. β. So called from its glossiness.—Ital. *lustrare*, to shine.—L. *lustrāre*, to shine; see Lustre (1). ☞ Distinct from *lute-string* under *lute* (1).

LUXATION, dislocation. (F.—L.) In surgery.—F. *luxation*, 'a luxation; a being out of joint;' Cot.—L. *luxā[t]iōnem*, acc. of *luxātio*, a dislocation.—L. *luxāre*, to dislocate.—L. *luxus*, adj., out of joint. Cf. Gk. λοξός, bent sideways, oblique. Brugmann, ii. § 635. Der. *luxate* (Davies); from pp. *luxāt-us*.

LUXURY, free indulgence in pleasure, a dainty. (F.—L.) ME. *luxurie*, Chaucer, C. T. 12484 (C 484).—AF. *luxurie*, Phil. de Thaun, Bestiary, 566; F. *luxure*, 'luxury;' Cot.—L. *luxuria*, luxury. An extended form from L. *luxus*, pomp, excess, luxury. Der. *luxuri-ous*, Chaucer, tr. of Boethius, b. i. pr. 4, l. 224; *luxuri-ous-ly, -ness*; *luxuri-ate*, from L. *luxuriātus*, pp. of *luxuriāre*, to indulge in luxury; *luxuri-ant*, Milton, P. L. iv. 260, from L. *luxuri-ant-*, stem of pres. pt. of *luxuriāre*; *luxuri-ant-ly, luxuri-ance, luxuri-anc-y*.

-LY, a common adj. and adv. ending. (E.) As an adj. ending, in *man-ly*, &c.; the AS. form is *-lic*. As an adv. ending, the AS. form is *-lice*. The suffix *-lic* is the same word as AS. *lic*, like; see **Like**.

LYCANTHROPY, a belief in werwolves. (Gk.) From Gk. λυκανθρωπία, a madness in which one imagines himself a wolf.—Gk. λυκάνθρωπος, a man-wolf, werwolf.—Gk. λύκ-ος, a wolf; ἄνθρωπος, a man. See **Wolf**. Der. From Gk. λύκος we also have *lyco-podium*, a genus of cryptogamous plants; where *-podium* is from Gk. ποδ-, from πούς, the foot; from the claw-like shape of the root; N. E. D.

LYDDITE, an explosive. (E.) Named from *Lydd*, a place in Kent; see N. and Q., 9 S. v. 185 (1900).

LYE, a mixture of ashes and water, water impregnated with alkaline salt imbibed from wood-ashes. (E.) 'Ley for waschynge, lye, *leye*, Lixivium;' Prompt. Parv. p. 294; dat., Ayenbite of Inwyt, p. 145, l. 22. AS. *lēah*, f., gen. *lēage*, 'lie, lee' [lye], AS. Leechdoms, ii. 338, 397.+Du. *loog*; G. *lauge*, OHG. *louga*. Teut. type *laugā*, f. β. Further allied to Icel. *laug*, a bath; from a Teut. base LAU, to wash, akin to L. *lauāre*, to wash; see **Lave** and **Lather**.

LYM, a lime-hound. (F.—L.) In Shak., K. Lear, iii. 6. 72. Short for *lime-hound*, q. v.

LYMPH, a colourless fluid in animals. (L.) A shortened form of *lympha*, the older term. '*Lympha*, a clear humour;' Kersey, ed. 1715.—L. *lympha*, water, lymph; also, a water-nymph. β. The spelling with *y* is due to a supposed derivation from the Gk. νύμφη, a nymph, which is false. The word is rather to be spelt *limpa*, *lumpa*, and to be connected with L. *limpidus*, clear; see **Limpid**. Brugmann, i. §§ 102, 763 (b). Der. *lymph-at-ic*, Evelyn's Diary, Jan. 10, 1657; from F. *lymphatique* (Cot.), L. *lymphāticus*.

LYNCH, to punish summarily, by mob-law. (E.) Not from John Lynch (Haydn), but from *Charles Lynch*, his brother, a Virginia planter (1736–96), who 'undertook to protect society . . in the region where he lived, on the Staunton river, by punishing with stripes or banishment such lawless or disaffected persons as were accused.'—Cent. Dict. The name *Lynch* is from AS. *hlinc*, a ridge of land; see **Link** (1). Der. *lynch-law*.

LYNX, a keen-sighted quadruped. (L.—Gk.) ME. *lynx*; Ayen-

bite of Inwyt, ed. Morris, p. 81, l. 6.—L. *lynx*.—Gk. λύγξ, a lynx; allied to λεύσσειν (for *λευκ-γειν), to see, λεύκος, bright, and named from its bright eyes.—√REUK, to shine; cf. Skt. *ruch*, to shine, *loch*, to see. The corresponding Teut. base is LEUH, to shine, whence G. *luchs*, Swed. *lo*, OSax. *lohs*, Du. *losch*, AS. *lox*, a lynx. Cf. also Lith. *luszis*, a lynx, Russ. *ruise*, Polish *rys*, and prob. Zend *raozha*. See A Student's Pastime, p. 393. See **Lucid**. Der. *lynx-eyed*.

LYRE, a stringed musical instrument. (F.—L.—Gk.) In Milton, P. L. iii. 17; he also has *lyrick*, P. R. iv. 257.—F. *lyre*, 'a lyra [sic], or harp;' Cot.—L. *lyra*.—Gk. λύρα, a lyre, lute. Der. *lyre-bird*; *lyr-ic*, spelt *liricke* in Sir P. Sidney, Apol. for Poetry, ed. Arber, p. 45, last line; *lyr-ic-al, lyr-ic-al-ly, lyr-ate*.

M

MACADAMISE, to pave a road with small, broken stones. (Hybrid; Gael. *and* Heb.; *with* F. *suffix*.) '*Macadamising*, a system of road-making devised by Mr. John Macadam, and published by him in an essay, in 1819,' &c.; Haydn, Dict. of Dates. *Macadam* = son of Adam; from Gael. *mac*, son; and Heb. *ādām*, a man, from the root *ādām*, to be red.

MACARONI, MACCARONI, a paste made of wheat flour. (Ital.—L.) 'He doth learn to make strange sauces, to eat anchovies, *maccaroni*, bovoli, fagioli, and caviare;' Ben Jonson, Cynthia's Revels, A. ii (Mercury). '*Macaroni*, gobbets or lumps of boyled paste,' &c.; Minsheu, ed. 1627.—MItal. *maccaroni*, 'a kinde of paste meate boiled in broth, and drest with butter, cheese, and spice;' Florio. The mod. Ital. spelling is *maccheroni*, properly the plural of *maccherone*, used in the sense of a 'macarone' biscuit. β. Of somewhat doubtful origin; but prob. to be connected with MItal. *maccare*, 'to bruise, to batter,' i.e. to pound; cf. Ital. *macco*, 'a kind of dish made of beans boiled to a mash;' Torriano.—L. *māc-*, base of *mācerāre*, to macerate. See **Macerate**. γ. Thus the orig. sense seems to have been 'pulp;' hence anything of a pulpy or pasty nature. Der. *Macaron-ic*, from F. *macaronique*, 'a macaronick, a confused heap or huddle of many severall things' (Cot.), so named from *macaroni*, which was orig. a mixed mess, as described by Florio above. Cf. Ital. *maccheronea*, 'Macaronics;' Baretti. The name *macaroni*, according to Haydn, Dict. of Dates, was given to a poem by Theophilo Folengo (otherwise Merlinus Coccaius) in 1509; *macaronic* poetry is a kind of jumble, often written in a mixture of languages. And see *macaroon*. *Maccaroni*, a fop, a dandy, belongs here. Garrick has 'rake and *maccaroni*;' Bon Ton, A. i. sc. 1 (Sir J. Trotley). Florio has: '*maccarone*, a gul, a dolt, a loggerhead;' so that the E. word for 'fop' should have ended in *-e*. See the long extract under *macaroni* in Davies, Suppl. Glossary.

MACAROON, a kind of cake or biscuit. (F.—Ital.—L.) In Albumazar, A. ii. sc. 3 (Davies). Formerly *macaron*, as in Cotgrave.—F. *macaron*; pl. *macarons*, 'macarons, little fritter-like buns, or thick losenges, compounded of sugar, almonds, rose-water, and musk, pounded together and baked with a gentle fire; also [the same as] the Ital. *macaroni*;' Cot.—Ital. *macarone*, a macaroon. See further under **Macaroni**. ☞ The sense of the word has been somewhat altered.

MACAW, a kind of parrot. (Brazil.) Gay has *mockaw*, The Toilette, l. 9. Spelt *maccaw* by Willughby, Ornithologia (1676), p. 73; but *machao* by Charleton, Onomasticon (1668), p. 66.—Brazil. *macao*; see *Macaw* in Newton, Dict. of Birds.

MACE (1), a kind of club. (F.—L.) In early use. ME. *mace*, King Alisaunder, 1901.—AF. *mace*, Stat. Realm, i. 231; OF. *mace, mache* (Burguy), mod. F. *masse*, a mace.—L. *matea, a mace; only preserved in the dimin. *mateola*, a beetle, mallet; Pliny, 17. 18. 29. Körting, § 6000. Der. *mace-bearer*.

MACE (2), a kind of spice. (F.—L.—Gk.) A pl. form *maces* occurs in Sir T. Elyot, Castel of Helth, b. ii. c. 10; cf. 'item, in *maces*;' Earl of Derby's Expedition, 1392–3; p. 221, l. 25.—AF. *maces*, Liber Albus, p. 230.—F. *macis*, 'the spice called mace;' Cot.; OF. *macis, maceis, maceys* (Godefroy); so that the E. form should be *maces*, sing., not plural. β. The etym. is very obscure; the L. *macis* or *maceis* (gen. *maccidis*) is a doubtful word, the name of a fictitious spice in Plautus (Lewis). It is possible that the F. *macis* was confused with OF. *macer*, of which Cot. says that it 'is not mace, as many imagine, but a reddish, aromaticall, and astringent rind of a certain Indian root.' This OF. *macer* is the word concerning which we read in Holland, tr. of Pliny, b. xii. c. 8, that 'the *macir* is likewise brought out of India; a reddish bark or rind it is of a great root, and beareth the name of the tree itselfe.' Cf. L. *macir*,

i. e. 'macir;' Pliny. — Gk. μακερ; doubtless a borrowed word from the East.

MACERATE, to soften by steeping, to soak. (L.) In Spenser, Virgil's Gnat, l. 94. — L. *mācerātus*, pp. of *mācerāre*, to steep; a frequentative from a base *māc-*; from an Idg. base **mak*. **Der.** *macerat-ion.*

MACHICOLATION, an opening in the floor of a projecting gallery of a tower, for pouring down molten lead and the like. (Low L.) Coined from Late L. *machicolāre*, to provide with machicolations; cf. MF. *machecoulis, maschecoulis,* 'the stones at the foot of a parapet (especially over a gate) resembling a grate, through which offensive things are thrown upon assailants;' Cot. Of uncertain origin; perhaps from MF. *mache-*, as in MF. *mache-rave,* 'a turnip-eater,' Cot., and other words, but here meaning 'bruising' or 'killing;' and OF. *coleïs,* MF. *coulis,* adj., gliding, or as sb., a groove; L. type **cōlāticius,* from *cōlāre,* to strain; see **Cullis** and **Portcullis.** Here *mache-* (F. *mâche-*) is from the OF. *mascher, macher,* to chew, also used in the sense of to crush, to murder (see OF. *mascher* in Godefroy). Hence it may mean 'a groove for crushing foes.' The OF. *mascher* is from L. *masticāre;* see **Masticate.**

MACHINE, a contrivance, instrument. (F. — L. — Gk.) In Shak. Hamlet, ii. 2. 124; first in 1549. — F. *machine.* — L. *māchina.* — Gk. μηχανή, a device, machine; cf. μῆχος, means, contrivance. β. From the base μηχ, 2nd grade of the Idg. √MAGH, Teut. MAG, to have power; whence also the E. verb *may;* Curtius, i. 416. See **May** (1). **Der.** *machin-er-y, machin-ist; machin-ate,* from L. *māchinātus,* pp. of *māchinārī,* to contrive, which is from the sb. *māchina;* *machin-at-ion,* K. Lear, i. 2. 122, v. 1. 46; AF. *machinacion,* Stat. Realm, i. 342 (1353); *machin-at-or.*

MACKEREL, the name of a fish. (F. — L.?) ME. *makerel,* Havelok, 758. — OF. *makerel,* in Neckam's Treatise de Utensilibus; Wright's Vocab. i. 98, l. 1; *makerelle,* Liber Albus, p. 235. (Mod. F. *maquereau.*) From Late L. *maquerellus;* of unknown origin. ¶ The suggestion in Mahn's Webster, that the F. *maquereau,* a mackerel, is the same word as OF. *maquereau,* a pandar (Cotgrave), from 'a popular tradition in France that the mackerel, in spring, follows the female shads, which are called *vierges* or maids, and leads them to their mates,' is one which is open to doubt. It may be that the story arose out of the coincidence of the name, and that the name was not derived from the story. The etymology of OF. *maquereau,* a pandar, is from the Teut. source preserved in Du. *makelaar,* a broker, pandar, from Du. *makelen,* to procure, bring about, frequentative form of *maken,* to make.

MACKINTOSH, a waterproof overcoat. (Gael.) From the name of the inventor.

MACROCOSM, the whole universe. (Gk.) In Phillips, ed. 1706; and in Howell's Letters, vol. i. let. 34 (1621). ME. *macrocosme,* Lydgate, Assembly of Gods, 995. Spelt *macrocosmus* in Blount's Gloss., ed. 1674. Coined from Gk. μακρό-, for μακρός, long, great; and κόσμος, the world. See **Microcosm.**

MACULATE, to defile. (L.) Used as a pp. in The Two Noble Kinsmen, ed. Skeat, v. 1. 134. — L. *maculātus,* pp. of *maculāre,* to spot. — L. *macula,* a spot; a dimin. form. **Der.** *maculat-ion.* Shak. Troil. iv. 4. 66; *im-maculate,* q.v. And see *mail* (1).

MAD, insane, foolish. (E.) The vowel was at first long. ME. *mad,* spelt *maad* in Li Beau Disconus, l. 2001, in Ritson's Met. Romances, vol. ii.; *made* in The Seven Sages, ed. Wright, 2091. Cf. *mēdschipe* = madness; Ancren Riwle, p. 148, l. 1. The ME. *mad* is from AS. (*ge-*)*mǣded,* maddened, shortened to (*ge-*)*mǣdd* (cf. *fat*), pp. of *ge-mǣdan,* to madden, to drive mad. Cf. AS. *ge-maad,* mad, Corpus Gloss. 2105. + OSax. *ge-mēd,* foolish; OHG. *ka-meit, gi-meit,* vain; Icel. *meiddr,* pp. of *meiða,* to maim, hurt; Goth. *ga-maids,* bruised, maimed; Luke, iv. 19, xiv. 13, 21. β. Thus the Teut. sense appears to be 'maimed.' Teut. type **maiđoz,* Idg. type **moitós,* pp. from the root MEI, to change; cf. L. *mūtāre,* to change; see **Mutable.** ¶ Not connected with Ital. *matto,* mad (see **Mate** (2)); nor with Skt. *matta-s,* mad (pp. of *mad,* to be drunk). **Der.** *mad-ly, mad-ness;* also ME. *madden,* to be mad, Wyclif, John, x. 20 (*obsolete*); also *madd-en,* to make mad, for which Shak. uses the simple form *mad,* Rich. II, v. 5, 61, &c.; *mad-cap* (from *mad* and *cap*), K. John, i. 84; *mad-house; mad-man,* L. L. L. v. 2. 338; *mad-wort.*

MADAM, my lady, a lady. (F. — L.) In early use. ME. *madame,* King Alisaunder, 269. — F. *madame* = *ma dame,* my lady. — L. *mea domina,* my lady. See **Dame.** Doublet, *madonna.*

MADDER, the name of a plant. (E.) ME. *madir, mader* (with one *d*); Prompt. Parv. AS. *mædere,* in Cockayne's Leechdoms, iii. 337; cf. *feld-mædere,* field-madder, Voc. 300. 10. + Icel. *maðra;* Du. *mede, mee.* Cf. Skt. *madhura-,* sweet, tender; whence fem. *madhurā,* the name of several plants (Benfey). See **Mead** (1).

MADEIRA, a sort of wine. (Port. — L.) In Shak. 1 Hen. IV, i. 2. 128. So named from the island of *Madeira,* off the N. W. coast of Africa. The name is Port., and signifies that the island was well-wooded. — Port. *madeira,* wood, timber. Cf. Span. *madera* (the same). — L. *matēria,* stuff, wood, timber; see **Matter** (1). See Diez, p. 465; also Hakluyt, Voy. vol. ii. pt. 2. p. 7.

MADEMOISELLE, miss: lit. my damsel. (F. — L.) Milton, Apology for Smectymnuus, speaks slightingly of 'grooms and *madamoisellaes*' (R.). Spelt *madamoiselle,* Caxton, Blanchardyn, ch. 16. — F. *mademoiselle,* spelt *madamoiselle* in Cotgrave. — F. *ma,* my; and *demoiselle,* formerly *damoiselle,* a damsel. See **Madame** and **Damsel.**

MADONNA, my lady, Our Lady. (Ital. — L.) In Shak. Tw. Nt. i. 5. 47. — Ital. *madonna.* — Ital. *ma,* my; and *donna,* lady. — L. *mea,* my; and *domina* lady, dame. See **Dame.** Doublet, *madame.*

MADREPORE, the common coral. (F. — Ital. — L. *and* Gk.) Modern; not in Todd's Johnson. — F. *madrépore,* madrepore. — Ital. *madrepora,* explained in Meadows as 'a petrified plant.' β. Of somewhat uncertain origin; but prob. the first part of the word is Ital. *madre,* mother, used in various compounds, as *madre-selva* (lit. mother-wood), honeysuckle, *madre-bosco* (lit. mother-bush), woodbine (Florio), *madre perla,* mother of pearl (Florio); from L. *mātrem,* acc. of *māter,* mother; see **Mother.** γ. The part *-pora* appears to be from the Gk. πῶρος, a light, friable stone, also a stalactite. Hence *madre-pore* = mother-stone, a similar formation to *madre perla* (lit. mother-pearl). ¶ If this be right, it has nothing to do with F. *madré,* spotted, nor with *pore.* But it has certainly been *understood* as connected with the word *pore,* as shown by the numerous similar scientific terms, such as *catenipora, tubipora, dentipora, gemmipora,* &c.; see the articles in Engl. Cycl. on *Madrephyllicea* and *Madreporæa.* It does not follow that the supposed connexion with *pore* was originally right; it only shews that this sense was substituted for that of the Gk. πῶρος. In fact, the Ital. *poro* (πῶρος) was misunderstood as representing L. *porus* in 1599; N. E. D.

MADRIGAL, a pastoral song. (Ital. — L. — Gk.) 'Melodious birds sing *madrigals;*' Marlowe, Passionate Shepherd; cited in Shak. Merry Wives, iii. 1. 18, 23. — Ital. *madrigale,* pl. *madrigali, madriali,* 'madrigals, a kind of short songs or ditties in Italie;' Florio. It stands for **mandrigale,* and means 'a shepherd's song;' cf. *mandriale, mandriano,* 'a heardesman, a grasier, a drover; [also] as *madrigale;*' Florio. — Ital. *mandra,* 'a herde, drove, flocke, folde;' Florio. — L. *mandra,* a stall, stable, stye. — Gk. μάνδρα, an inclosure, fold, stable. + Skt. *mandurā,* a stable for horses; prob. from *mand,* to sleep. ¶ The suffix *-gale* = L. *-cālis.* Perhaps through F. *madrigal.*

MÆNAD, a priestess of Bacchus. (Gk.) From Gk. μαινάδ-, stem of μαινάς, mad, raving; as sb., a female Bacchanal. — Gk. μαίνομαι, I am mad, I rave; allied to μανία, madness; see **Mania.**

MAGAZINE, a storehouse, store, store of news, pamphlet. (F. — Ital. — Arab.) In Milton, P. L. iv. 816. Spelt *magason,* Hakluyt, Voy. ii. pt. 1. p. 234. — MF. *magazin,* 'a magazin,' Cot.; mod. F. *magasin.* — Ital. *magazzino,* a storehouse. [Cf. Span. *magacen,* also *almagacen,* where *al* is the Arab. article.] — Arab. *makhzan* (pl. *makhāzin*), a storehouse, granary, cellar; Rich. Dict. p. 1366. Cf. also *khizānat,* a magazine, treasure-house; from *khazn,* a laying up in store; id. pp. 609, 610. **Der.** *magazine,* vb., to store; North, Examen, 1740, p. 222.

MAGGOT, a grub, worm. (E.) ME. *magot, magat* (with one *g*), given as a variant of 'make, mathe, wyrm yn the fleshe;' Prompt. Parv. p. 321. Cf. *maked* in Wright's Vocab. i. 255, col. 1, to translate L. *tarinus* [misprint for *tarmus*] or *simax* [= L. *cimex*]. *Maggot* is an AF. perversion of ME. *maddok,* a maggot; see Voc. 594. 3; Lanfranc's Cirurgie, p. 44, l. 18; Henslow, Medical Works of the 14th Cent., p. 141; also *maðek,* O. Eng. Homilies, ed. Morris, i. 326. A dimin. from AS. *maþa, maþu,* a worm; Voc. 122. 3; 205. 8. + Du. *made;* G. *made,* OHG. *mado;* Goth. *matha,* a worm. Cf. Icel. *maðkr,* a maggot; Dan. *maddik, madike,* a maggot. See **Mawkish. Der.** *maggot-y.*

MAGI, priests of the Persians. (L. — Gk. — Pers.) In P. Plowman, C. xxii. 85. Borrowed from L. *magi,* Matt. ii. 1 (Vulgate). — Gk. μάγοι, Matt. ii. 1; pl. of μάγος, a Magian, one of a Median tribe (Herod. i. 101), hence, an enchanter, wizard, juggler. Properly, one of the priests or wise men in Persia who interpreted dreams, &c. (Liddell.) β. From OPers. *magu-* (nom. *magus*), Pers. *mugh, mūgh,* one of the Magi, a fire-worshipper; Horn, § 984; Rich. Dict. p. 1527. **Der.** *mag-ic,* q.v. ☞ It is interesting to note that the word *magus,* which Sir H. Rawlinson translates by 'the Magian,' occurs in cuneiform characters in an inscription at Behistan; see Schleicher, Indogerm. Chrestomathie, p. 151; Nineveh and Persepolis, by W. S. W. Vaux, ed. 1851, p. 405.

MAGIC, enchantment. (F. — L. — Gk. — Pers.) ME. *magike,* sb., Chaucer, C. T. 4634 (B 214). — F. *magique,* adj. 'magicall;' Cot.

—L. *magicus*, magical. —Gk. μαγικός, magical. —Gk. μάγος, one of the Magi, an enchanter. See **Magi**. β. The sb. *magic* is an abbreviation for 'magic art,' L. *ars magica*. **Der.** *magic-al*, *magic-al-ly*; *magic-ian*, ME. *magicien*, Chaucer, C. T. 14213 (B 3397), from F. *magicien*, 'a magician;' Cot.

MAGISTERIAL, master-like, authoritative. (L.) In Phillips, ed. 1706. Coined, with suffix *-al*, from L. *magisteri-us*, magisterial, belonging to a master. —L. *magister*, a master. See **Magistrate**. **Der.** *magisterial-ly*, *magisterial-ness*.

MAGISTRATE, a justice of the peace. (F.—L.) ME. *maiestrat* (= *majestrat*), Wyclif, Luke, xxiii. 13. — F. *magistrat*, 'a magistrate, ruler;' Cot. —L. *magistrātus*, (1) a magistracy, (2) a magistrate. —L. *magister*, a master. See **Master**. **Der.** *magistrac-y*.

MAGNANIMITY, greatness of mind. (F.—L.) ME. *magnanimitee*, Chaucer, C. T. 15578 (G 110). —F. *magnanimité*, 'magnanimity;' Cot. —L. *magnanimitātem*, acc. of *magnanimitās*, greatness of mind. —L. *magn-*, stem of *magnus*, great; and *animi-*, for *animus*, the mind; with suffix *-tās*. See **Magnate** and **Animus**.

MAGNANIMOUS, high-minded, noble. (L.) In Shak. All's Well, iii. 6. 70. Formed (by changing *-us* to *-ous*, as in *ardu-ous*, &c.) from L. *magnanimus*, great-souled. —L. *magn-*, stem of *magnus*, great; and *animus*, the mind. **Der.** *magnanimous-ly*.

MAGNATE, a great man, noble. (L.) A late word; not in Todd's Johnson. From Late L. *magnātem*, acc. of *magnās*, a prince (Judith, v. 26). —L. *magn-*, stem of *magnus*, great. β. L. *magnus* is cognate with Gk. μέγας, great, Skt. *mahant-*, great, and E. *much*; see **Much**. ¶ *Magnate* is a Hungarian and Polish use of the L. word; the F. *magnat* (in Littré, but little used) is, more strictly, due to the pl. *magnats* = L. *magnātes*. For derivatives from L. *magnus*, see **Magnitude**.

MAGNESIA, the oxide of magnesium. (Late L.—Gk.) The name *magnesia*, apparently formerly applied to *manganese*, occurs in Chaucer, C. T. 16923 (G 1455); and in Ben Jonson's Alchemist, Act ii (Surly). Added by Todd to Johnson's Dict. Coined from some supposed resemblance to the mineral called by a similar name in Gk., from L. *Magnesia*, fem. of *Magnesius*, of or belonging to the country called Magnesia. —Gk. Μαγνήσιος, belonging to Magnesia, in Thessaly; whence λίθος Μαγνήτης or λίθος Μαγνῆσιος, lit. Magnesian stone, applied to (1) the magnet, (2) a metal that looked like silver. See Schade, p. 1395. **Der.** *magnesi-um*. See **Magnet**.

MAGNET, the loadstone, a bar having magnetic properties. (F.—L.—Gk.) ME. *magnete*, Prompt. Parv. p. 325. — AF. *magnete*, Bozon, p. 51; OF. *magnete* (Godefroy), also found as *manete*, in a F. MS. of the 13th cent.; see Littré, s.v. *magnétique*. —L. *magnēta*, acc. of *magnēs*, for *magnēs lapis* = Magnesian stone, the loadstone. —Gk. Μάγνης (stem Μάγνητ-), Magnesian; also Μαγνῆτις, whence λίθος Μαγνῆτις, the Magnesian stone, magnet. See **Magnesia**. ¶ Spenser has the L. form *magnes*, F. Q. ii. 12. 4. **Der.** *magnet-ic*, *magnet-ic-al*, *magnetic-al-ly*, *magnet-ism*, *magnet-ise*.

MAGNIFICENT, doing great things, pompous, grand. (L.) In Shak. L. L. L. i. 1. 193. —L. *magnificent-*, stem of *magnificens*, doing great things. —L. *magni-*, for *magnus*, great; and *-fic-*, for *fac-*, base of *facere*, to do; with suffix *-ent* of a pres. part. See **Magnify**. **Der.** *magnificent-ly*; *magnificence* (Chaucer) = F. *magnificence*, 'magnificence,' Cot. So also *magnific-al*, A. V. 1 Chron. xxii. 5, from L. *magnificus*, grand.

MAGNIFY, to enlarge, praise highly. (F.—L.) ME. *magnifien*, Wyclif, Matt. xxiii. 5. — F. *magnifier*, 'to magnifie;' Cot. —L. *magnificāre*, to make large. —L. *magni-*, for *magnus*, great; and *-fic-*, for *fac-*, base of *facere*, to make, do. See **Magnate** and **Fact**.

MAGNILOQUENCE, elevated or pompous language. (L.) Modern; added by Todd to Johnson's Dict. Coined, by analogy with F. words in *-ence* (= L. *-entia*), from L. *magniloquentia*, elevated language. —L. *magni-*, for *magnus*, great; and *loquentia*, discourse, from *loquent-*, stem of pres. part. of *loqui*, to speak. See **Magnate** and **Loquacious**. **Der.** *magniloquent*, a coined word.

MAGNITUDE, greatness, size. (L.) In Minsheu, ed. 1627. [There is no F. *magnitude*.] —L. *magnitūdo*, greatness. —L. *magni-*, for *magnus*, great; with suffix *-tūdo*, expressive of quality. See **Magnate**. ☞ The derivatives from L. *magnus* are numerous, viz. *magn-animity*, *magn-animous*, *magn-ate*, *magni-ficent*, *magni-fy*, *magni-loquence*, *magni-tude*. From the base *mag-* of the same word we have also *mag-istrate*, *mag-isterial*, *master*, *majesty*, *major*, *mayor*. And see **Much** and **May** (1).

MAGNOLIA, the name of a genus of plants. (F.) 'A genus of plants named in honour of Pierre *Magnol*, who was professor of medicine and prefect of the botanic garden of Montpellier [in France]. He was born in 1638, and died in 1715;' Engl. Cycl. See his Botanicum Monspeliense, 1686.

MAGPIE, the name of a bird. (Hybrid; F.—L.—Gk.; *and* F. —L.) 1. Called *magot-pie* in Macbeth, iii. 4. 125. We also find

prov. E. *maggoty-pie*; and *madge*, meaning (1) an owl, (2) a magpie. The prefixes *Mag*, *Magot*, *Maggoty* (like *Madge*) are various forms of the name *Margaret*; cf. *Robin* as applied to the red-breast, *Jenny* to the wren, *Philip* to the sparrow. *Mag* may be taken to be short for *Magot* = F. *Margot*, which is (1) a familiar form of F. *Marguerite*, and (2) a name for the magpie. —F. *Margot*, for *Marguerite*. —L. *margarīta*, a pearl. —Gk. μαργαρίτης, a pearl, a word of Eastern origin; cf. Pers. *murwārīd*, a pearl; Rich. Dict. p. 1396; Skt. *mañjarī*, a pearl. 2. The syllable *pie* = F. *pie*, from L. *pica*, a magpie; see **Pie** (1).

MAGUEY, the American aloe. (Cuba.) According to Oviedo, it is of Cuban origin. ¶ Not Mexican, which has no *g*. The Mex. name is *metl*.

MAHARAJAH, a title of some Indian princes. (Skt.) From Skt. *mahā-rājā*, m., lit. 'great king.' —Skt. *mahā-*, for *mahant-*, great, allied to L. *magnus*, great; and *rājā*, king, allied to L. *rex*, king.

MAHDI, an Arabian Messiah. (Arab.) From Arab. *mahdī*, one who is (divinely) guided; from *ma*, prefix, and *hady*, to guide. Cf. *hādī*, a guide (Rich. Dict., pp. 1661, 1670).

MAHLSTICK, the same as **Maulstick**, q. v.

MAHOGANY, the name of a tree and a wood. (W. Indian.) See *mahogany* in index to Boswell's Life of Johnson. Added by Todd to Johnson's Dict.; 'said to have been brought to England by Raleigh, in 1595;' Haydn, Dict. of Dates. Spelt *mohogeney* in 1671, with a reference to Jamaica. Of W. Indian origin; but from what dialect is unknown.

MAHOMETAN; see **Mohammedan**.

MAHOUT, an elephant-driver. (Hind.) 'The *mahout* of his elephant had been pulled off his seat;' Thackeray, Vanity Fair, ch. iv. —Hind. *mahāwat*, an elephant-driver (Forbes). And see Yule.

MAID, MAIDEN, a girl, virgin. (E.) 1. *Mayde* occurs in Rob. of Glouc. p. 13, l. 297. It is not common in *early* ME., and is, practically, merely a corruption of *maiden*, by the loss of final *n*, rather than a form derived from AS. *mægð* or *mægeð*, a maiden (Grein, ii. 216). 2. The usual *early* ME. word is *maiden* or *meiden*, Ancren Riwle, pp. 64, 166. AS. *mægden*, a maiden (Grein, ii. 216); also *mǣden*, Mark, v. 41; later text, *maide*. β. AS. *mægden*, cognate with OHG. *magatīn*, is formed from *mægd-* (for *mægeð*) by adding the suffix *-īn* (cf. L. *-īn-us*); see March, A. S. Gram. art. 228. γ. *Mægeð* is cognate with Goth. *magaths*, a virgin, maid (= G. *magd*), where the suffix *-ths* answers to the Idg. suffix *-to-s*. The base *mæg-* is allied to Goth. *mag-us*, a boy, a child, Luke, ii. 43; also to Icel. *mögr*, a boy, youth, son. δ. The orig. sense of *magus* is 'a growing lad,' one increasing in strength; from the Teut. base MAG, to have power, whence also *might*, *main*. See **May** (1). See Stokes-Fick, p. 198. **Der.** *maiden-hood* = AS. *mægdenhād*, Grein, ii. 216; also spelt *maiden-head* = ME. *meidenhed* or *maydenhede*, Gower, C. A. ii. 230, bk. v. 3068, which is a mere variant of *maiden-hood*; *maiden-ly*, Mids. Nt. Dr. iii. 2. 217, Skelton, Garden of Laurel, l. 865; *maiden-li-ness*; *maiden-hair*; also *maid-child*, Levit. xii. 5.

MAIL (1), steel network forming body-armour. (F.—L.) 'For though thyn housbonde armed be in *maille*;' Chaucer, C. T. 9078 (E 1202); the pl. *mayles* is in the Anturs of Arthur, st. xxx. Cf. '*macula*, mayl;' Voc. 594. 18.—OF. *maille*, 'maile, or a link of maile, whereof coats of maile be made; . . any little ring of metall; . . also, a mash [mesh] of a net;' Cot.—L. *macula*, a spot, speck, hole, mesh of a net, net. See **Maculate**.

MAIL (2), a bag for carrying letters. (F.—OHG.) ME. *male*, a bag, wallet; Chaucer, C. T. 3117, 12854 (A 3115, C 920); Havelok, 48.—OF. *male* (mod. F. *malle*), 'a male, or great budget;' Cot.— OHG. *malaha*, MHG. *malhe*, a leathern wallet. Cf. Gael. and Irish *mala*, a bag, sack (from E.).+Gk. μολγός, a hide, skin. **Der.** *mail-bag*, *mail-coach*, *mail-cart*.

MAIL (BLACK), a forced tribute. (Scand.) *Mail* is a Scottish term for rent. Jamieson cites the phr. *burrow-mailles*, duties payable within boroughs, from the Acts of Jas. I. c. 8 (A.D. 1424). *Black-maill* is mentioned in the Acts of Jas. VI. c. 21 (1567), and in the Acts of Elizabeth, an. 43, cap. 13, as a forced tribute paid to moss-troopers; see Jamieson and Blount. Spelman is right in supposing that it meant black rent or black money, a jocose allusion to tribute paid in cattle, &c., as distinct from rent paid in silver or white money; Blount shows that the term *black money* occurs in 9 Edw. III. cap. 4, and *white money* is not uncommon. Blount also cites the term *black-rents*. A Northern form.—Icel. *māl*, speech, law-suit, agreement; *māli*, agreement, payment. Cognate with AS. *mæþel*, *mæl*, a meeting, speech; Goth. *mathl*, a meeting-place.

MAIM, a bruise, injury, crippling hurt. (F.—OHG.) Also spelt *mahim* in Law-books; Blount's Nomolexicon, ed. 1691. ME. *maim*, pl. *maimes*, Ayenbite of Inwyt, p. 135, l. 27; the pp. *y-maymed* is in the preceding line. The verb occurs also in Chaucer, C. T. 6714

(D1132).—AF. *mahaym*, Liber Albus, p. 281; OF. *meshain* (Godefroy); MF. *mehaing*, 'a maime, or … abatement of strength … by hurts received;' Cot. Whence the verb *mehaigner*, 'to maime;' id. Cf. Ital. *magagna*, a defect, blemish; whence *magagnare*, to spoil, vitiate. β. Of uncertain origin; Bret. *machañ*, mutilation (whence *machaña*, to maim, mutilate), is borrowed from F. (Thurneysen). Some derive the Ital. word from OHG. *mann*, a man, and **hamjan*, to mutilate, from the OHG. adj. *ham*, maimed (Körting). In the OF. form, the prefix is *mes-*; see **Mis-** (2). **Der.** *maim*, verb.

MAIN (1), sb., strength, might. (E.) To be distinguished from *main* (2), though both are from the same Idg. root. ME. *main*, dat. *maine*, Gower, C. A. iii. 4; bk. vi. 90; also *mein*, as in 'with al his *mein*,' Floriz and Blauncheflor, ed. Lumby, l. 17. AS. *mægen*, strength; Grein, ii. 217. + Icel. *megin*, strength; OSax. *megin*, strength; OHG. *megin*. Also OHG. *magan*, Icel. *magn*, mighty; allied to *megin*, strength (above). Cf. Icel. *meginland*, main-land; *megin-sjōr*, main sea, the main. **Der.** *main-ly*; also *main-deck*, *-mast*, *-sail* (Palsgrave), *-spring*, *-stay*, *-top*, *-yard*; *main-land* (Palsgrave).

MAINOUR. (F.—L.) In the phr. 'taken with the *mainour*,' or later, 'taken in the manner;' see 1 Hen. IV, ii. 4. 347. See note to **Manner.** We find *pris ov meinoure* (where *ov* = F. *avec*), Stat. of the Realm, i. 30, an. 1275. Blount, in his Nomolexicon, explains *mainour* as meaning 'the thing that a thief steals;' and 'to be taken with the mainour,' as 'with the thing stoln about him, *flagrante delicto*.' It is lit. 'with the manœuvre,' and therefore refers rather to the *act* than the *thing*; see Cotgrave, s.v. *flagrant*; E. Webbe, Travels, 1590, ed. Arber, p. 28. The Anglo-F. *meinoure*, also *mainoure* (Stat. Realm, i. 161) answers to OF. *manouvre* (Littré). See **Manœuvre.**

MAINTAIN, to keep in a fixed state, keep up, support. (F.—L.) ME. *maintenen*, *mayntenen*, K. Alisaunder, l. 1592.—F. *maintenir*, 'to maintain;' Cot.—L. *manū tenēre*, to hold in the hand; or more likely, in Late Latin, to hold by the hand, to support or aid another, as shown by the use of ME. *mainteinen*, to aid and abet, P. Plowman, B. iii. 90, and note.—L. *manū*, abl. case of *manus*, the hand; and *tenēre*, to hold. See **Manual** and **Tenable.** **Der.** *maintain-able*, *maintain-er*; *mainten-ance*, ME. *meintenaunce*, spelt *mentenaunce* in Shoreham's Poems, p. 100, l. 19, from OF. *maintenance*, 'maintenance;'. Cot.

MAIZE, Indian corn or wheat. (Span.—W. Indian.) 'Indian *maiz*;' Bacon, Nat. Hist. § 49; and in Essay 33. Also in Dampier's Voyages, an. 1681 (R.).—Span. *maiz*, maize.—W. Indian *mahiz*, *mahis*, in the old Carib dialect of the island of Hayti (S. Domingo); see R. Eden (ed. Arber), pp. 67, 116, 118; Acosta, Hist. Indies, bk. iv. c. 16.

MAJESTY, grandeur, dignity. (F.—L.) ME. *magestee*, Chaucer, C. T. 4320 (A 4322); E. E. Psalter, Ps. 71. 20.—OF. *majestet*, *majeste*, later *majesté*, 'majesty;' Cot.—L. *maiestātem*, acc. of *maiestās*, dignity, honour.—L. *māies-*, related by gradation to *mā-ior*, comp. of *mag-nus*, great, with the addition of a comparative suffix; see Brugmann, ii. § 135. The sense of *maiestas* is the 'condition of being greater,' hence, dignity. See **Major, Magnitude.** **Der.** *majest-ic*, a coined word, Temp. iv. 118; *majest-ic-al*, L. L. L. v. 2. 102; *majest-ic-al-ly*, 1 Hen. IV, ii. 4. 479.

MAJOLICA, usually with *ware*; decorative enamelled pottery. (Ital.—Span.—L.) From Ital. *maiolica*, also *maiorica*, 'the earth we call porcelane, whereof China dishes are made;' Florio.—Span. *Mallorca*, Majorca, formerly *Majolica* (Ducange), whence the first specimens came. From L. *māior*, greater.

MAJOR, greater; the title of an officer in the army. (L.) Early used (as an adj.) as a term in logic, as in 'this *maior* or first proposition;' Fryth, Works, p. 147, col. 1. 'The *major* part;' Cor. ii. 1. 64.—L. *māior*, greater; comparative of *magnus*, great; see **Magnitude. Der.** *major-ship*, *major-general*; *major-domo*, spelt *maiordomo* in Puttenham, Art of Poesie, b. iii. c. 4. (ed. Arber, p. 158), imitated from Span. *mayor-domo*, a house-steward (see **Domestic**); also *major-i-ty*, 1 Hen. IV, iii. 2. 109, from F. *majorité*, 'majority;' Cot. **Doublet,** *mayor*.

MAJUSCULE, a capital or uncial letter; not a minuscule. (L.) From L. *māiusculus*, somewhat larger; allied to *māior*, greater; see **Major.**

MAKE, to fashion, frame, cause, produce. (E.) ME. *maken*, *makien*; pt. t. *makede*, *made*, pp. *maked*, *maad*, *mad*; Chaucer, C. T. 9, 33, 396. AS. *macian*, pt. t. *macode*, pp. *macod*; see Sweet, A. S. Reader; also *ge-macian* (Grein). + Du. *maken*; G. *machen*, OHG. *machōn*, to make. Allied to **Match** (1). **Der.** *make*, sb., Gower,

C. A. ii. 204; bk. v. 2096; *mak-er*, P. Plowman, B. x. 240; *make-peace*, Rich. II, i. 1. 160; *make-shift*, *make-weight*; and see *match* (1).

MALACHITE, a hard green stone. (Gk.) '*Malachites*, *Molochites*, a kind of precious stone of a dark green colour, like the herb mallows;' Phillips, ed. 1706. Formed, with suffix *-ites* (= Gk. *-ιτης*) from Gk. *μαλάχ-η*, a mallow. See **Mallow.**

MALADMINISTRATION, bad administration. (F.—L.) Spelt *maleadministration* in Swift, Sentiments of a Church of Eng. Man, s. 2 (R.).—F. *male*, fem. of *mal* (= L. *malus*), bad; and F. *administration.* See **Malice** and **Administer.** ¶ So also *mal-adjus!m·nt*, *mal-adroit*, *mal-apert*, *mal-conformation*, *mal-content*, &c.; these have the same F. adj. (or *mal*, adv.) as a prefix.

MALADROIT, clumsy. (F.—L.) F. *maladroit*; for *mal* (L. *male*), ill, badly; and *adroit.* See **Adroit.**

MALADY, disease, illness. (F.—L.) ME. *maladie*, *maladye*, Chaucer, C. T. 421, 1375 (A 419, 1373). Also earlier, in O. Eng. Miscellany, ed. Morris, p. 31, l. 13.—AF. *maladie*, Edw. Conf. 1511; F. *maladie*, 'malady;' Cot.—F. *malade*, sick, ill; oldest spelling *malabde* (Littré). Cf. Prov. *malaptes*, *malautes*, *malaudes*, sick, ill; Bartsch, Chrestomathie.—L. *male habitus*, out of condition; cf. *male habens*, sick, Matt. iv. 24 (Vulgate).—L. *male*, adv., badly, ill, from *malus*, bad; and *habitus*, held, kept, kept in a certain condition, pp. of *habēre*, to have. See **Malice** and **Habit.** ¶ The usual derivation is that given by Diez, who imagined F. *malade* to answer to *male aptus*; there appears to be no authority for the phrase, which (like *ineptus*) would mean 'foolish' rather than 'ill.' See Körting, § 5833.

MALAPERT, saucy, impudent, ill-behaved. (F.—L.) The true sense is 'ill-skilled,' 'ill-bred.' In The Court of Love, 737 (after A.D. 1500); also in Chaucer, Troil. iii. 87.—OF. *mal appert*, insolent (see Godefroy).—OF. *mal*<L. *male*, adv., badly, ill; and *appert*, 'expert, ready, dexter, prompt, active, nimble; feat, handsome in that he does;' Cot. Also spelt *aspert*, *espert*; from L. *expertus*, expert; see **Expert.** [The OF. *apert*, 'open, evident,' is a different word, and der. from L. *apertus*, open; but the OF. *apert* and *appert* were much confused, as, e.g. in Godefroy, though kept apart by Cotgrave.] ¶ By a complete confusion of L. *apertus* and *expertus*, we find OF. *espert* used in the sense of 'open.' **Der.** *malapert-ly*, *malapert-ness.*

MALARIA, miasma, noxious exhalation. (Ital.—L. and Gk.) Modern. Not in Todd's Johnson.—Ital. *mal' aria*, for *mala aria*, bad air. *Mala* is fem. of *malo*, bad, from L. *malus*, bad; see **Malice.** *Aria* represents Late L. **āria*, for *āeria*, f. of *āerius*, adj. formed from L. *āēr*, air, Gk. *ἀήρ.* See **Air.**

MALCONTENT, MALECONTENT, discontented. (F.—L.) In Shak. 3 Hen. VI, iv. 1. 10, 60.—OF. *malcontent*, 'male-content;' Cot.—F. *mal*, adv., from L. *male*, badly; and F. *content.* See **Malice** and **Content.**

MALE, masculine. (F.—L.) ME. *male*. 'Male and *female*;' Wyclif, Matt. xix. 4. Cf. Chaucer, C. T. 5704 (D 122).—OF. *masle* (later *male*), 'a male,' Cot. (who gives *both* spellings); mod. F. *mâle*; earliest spelling *mascle* (Hatzfeld).—L. *masculum*, acc. of *masculus*, male; formed with suffixes *-cu-* and *-l-* from *mas-*, stem of *mās*, a male creature, man (gen. *mār-is* = **mās-is*). See **Masculine.** **Der.** *mascul-ine*, *mallard*. ¶ Nowise connected with *female.*

MALEDICTION, a curse, execration. (F.—L.) In Shak. K. Lear, i. 2. 160. Spelt *malediccion* in the Bible of 1551, Gal. iii. 10.—F. *malediction*, 'a malediction;' Cot.—L. *maledictiōnem*, acc. of *maledictio*, a curse; cf. *maledictus*, pp. of *maledicere*, to speak evil against.—L. *male*, adv., badly; and *dīcere*, to speak. See **Malice** and **Diction.** **Doublet,** *malison.*

MALEFACTOR, an evil-doer. (L.) 'Heretik or any *malefactour*;' Sir T. More, Works, p. 941 h; and in Dictes of the Philosophers, pr. by Caxton, fol. 11 b, l. 18.—L. *malefactōrem*, acc. of *malefactor*, an evil-doer.—L. *male*, adv., badly; and *factor*, a doer, from *facere*, to do. See **Malice** and **Fact.** **Der.** So also *malefaction*, Hamlet, ii. 2. 621, from *factiōnem*, acc. of *factio*, a doing.

MALEVOLENT, ill-disposed to others, envious. (L.) Lit. 'wishing ill.' In Shak. 1 Hen. IV, i. 1. 97.—L. *maleuolent-*, stem of *maleuolens*, wishing evil.—L. *male*, adv., badly, ill; and *uolens*, pres. pt. of *uelle*, to wish. See **Malice** and **Voluntary.** **Der.** *malevolent-ly*; *malevolence*, from OF. *malivolence* (Godefroy).

MALFORMATION, an ill formation. (F.—L.) Coined from *mal-* and *formation*; see **Maladministration.**

MALIC, made from apples. (L.) Formed with suffix *-ic* (L. *-ic-us*) from L. *māl-um*, an apple. + Gk. *μῆλον*, a fruit, an apple.

MALICE, ill will, spite. (F.—L.) ME. *malice*, Rob. of Glouc. p. 570; l. 12027.—F. *malice.*—L. *malitia*, badness, ill will.—L. *mali-*, for *malus*, bad; with suffix *-ti-a.* Root unknown. **Der.** *malici-ous*, ME. *malicious*, K. Alisaunder, 3323, 5045, from F. *malicieux*; *malicious-ly*, *-ness.*

MALIGN, unfavourable, malicious. (F.—L.) 'The spirit

malign;' Milton, P. L. iii. 553; cf. iv. 503, &c. ME. *maligne*; in Shoreham's Poems, p. 72, l. 25. [The derived verb *malign*, to curse, is found in Sir T. More, Works, p. 37 b.]—OF. *maling*, fem. *maligne*, 'malignant;' Cot. (Mod. F. *malin*.)—L. *malignus*, ill-disposed, wicked; for *mali-gen-us, ill-born; like *benignus* for *beni-gen-us.—L. *mali*-, for *malus*, bad; and *gen*-, base of *gignere*, to produce. See **Malice** and **Generate**. Der. *malign*, verb (as above), due to L. *malignāre*, to act spitefully; *malign-ly*, *malign-er*; also *malign-ant*, Temp. i. 2. 257, from L. *malignant*-, stem of pres. pt. of *malignāre*, to act spitefully; *malign-ant-ly*; *malign-anc-y*, Tw. Nt. ii. 1. 4; *malign-i-ty*, ME. *malignitee*, Chaucer, Persones Tale, De Invidia (Six-text, I 513), from F. *malignité* < L. *malignitātem*, acc. of *malignitās*, malignity.

MALINGER, to feign sickness. (F.—L. and G.) Modern. Not in Todd's Johnson. Coined from F. *malingre*, adj. diseased, sickly, or 'sore, scabby, ugly, loathsome;' Cot.—F. *mal*, badly; and OF. *haingre*, *heingre*, Norm. dial. *haingre*, thin, emaciated (Godefroy, Moisy).—L. *male*, adv. badly, from *malus*, bad; and G. *hager*, thin, lean. Cf. Körting, § 306; where another solution is offered, viz. from L. *mal*- (for *male*), and the suffix *-ing-* (of G. origin); § 5825; which fails to explain the *h*.

MALISON, a curse. (F.—L.) In early use. ME. *malison*, spelt *malisun* in Havelok, 426.—AF. *malicoun*, Polit. Songs, ed. Wright, p. 234; OF. *maleison*, in Godefroy. A doublet of *malediction*, just as *benison* is of *benediction*; see **Malediction** and **Benison**.

MALKIN, a kitchen wench. (F.—OHG.) In Chaucer, C. T. B 30 (see note); P. Plowm. B. i. 182 (see note). Orig. a reduced form (not of Mary, but) of Matilda. 'Malkyne, or Mawt, Molt, Mawde, propyr name, *Matildis*;' Prompt. Parv. Dimin. of AF. *Mald*, *Maud*, Matilda.—OHG. *Maht-hilt*; where *maht* means 'might,' and *hilt*, 'battle.' Cf. Macbeth, i. 1. 8. Der. *Gri-malkin*.

MALL (1), a large wooden hammer or beetle. (F.—L.) Also *maul*. It occurs in the Spectator, no. 195, near the beginning; and in Spenser, F. Q. i. 7. 51. ME. *malle*, St. Brandan, ed. Wright, p. 48; spelt *mealle* in O. Eng. Homilies, ed. Morris, i. 253, l. 12; *melle*, Hampole, Pricke of Conscience, 6572.—OF. *mail*, *mal*, *maul* (Godefroy); F. *mail*, 'a mall, mallet, or beetle;' Cot.—L. *malleum*, acc. of *malleus*, a hammer. [The vowel *a* in the E. word was perhaps suggested by the L. form.] Der. *mall* (2), q. v.; *mall-e-able*, q. v., *mall-et*, q. v.

MALL (2), the name of a public walk. (F.—L.) Preserved in the name of the street called *Pall Mall*, and in *The Mall* in St. James's Park. In Pope, Rape of the Lock, v. 133. 'To walk in *the Mall*;' Parsons, Wapping Old Stairs, l. 9. Named from MF. *pale-maille*, 'a game wherein a round box bowle is with a mallet struck through a high arch of iron,' &c. [i. e. the game imitated in mod. croquet]; Cot. A representation of the game is given in Knight's Old England, vol. ii. fig. 2152.—MItal. *palamaglio*, 'a stick with a mallet at one end to play at a wooden ball with; also, the name of such a game;' Florio. Better spelt *pallamaglio*, as in Baretti's Dict. Lit. 'a ball-mallet' or 'ball-mall.'—Ital. *palla*, a ball; and *maglio* (= F. *mail*), a mace, mall, hammer. β. A hybrid word; from OHG. *palla*, *pallo* (MHG. *balle*, G. *ball*), a ball, cognate with E. **Ball**, q. v.; and L. *malleum*, acc. of *malleus*, a hammer; see **Mall** (1). ¶ It is contended that Ital. *pallamaglio* really meant 'mallet-ball,' not 'ball-mallet;' if so, it was misunderstood. See my Notes on E. Etym., p. 204; s. v. *Pall-mall*.

MALLARD, a wild drake. (F.—L.) ME. *malard*. 'Malarde, anas;' Prompt. Parv.—OF. *malard*, also *maslard*, 'a mallard, or wild drake;' Cot. Formed with suffix *-ard* (of G. origin); and certainly from OF. *masle* (mod. F. *mâle*), male; see **Male**. β. The suffix *-ard* (= Goth. *hardus*, G. *hart*, hard) was much used in forming masculine proper names, to give the idea of force or strength; hence it was readily added to OF. *masle*, producing a form *masl-ard*, in which the notion of 'male' is practically reduplicated. See Introd. to Hatzfeld, Etym. Dict. § 147. γ. As this etymology, given by Diez, offers some difficulty, Hatzfeld suggests that *Malart* (*Malard* in Godefroy) was a proper name, playfully given to the bird; and that this name is from OHG. *Madal-hard*, a proper name cognate with AS. *Mathelheard* (Birch, Cart. Saxon. i. 280). And in fact the ME. form *mawdelarde*, 'mallard' occurs in the Liber Cure Cocorum, p. 27. But it represents the OF. *madlarde*, f., wild duck (Godefroy), f. of *madlard*; from AF. *madle*, male, variant of OF. *masle* (above). For AF. *dl* = OF. *sl*, cf. *medlar*, *medley*.

MALLEABLE, that can be beaten out by the hammer. (F.—L.) In Shak. Per. iv. 6. 152; and even in Chaucer, C. T. 16598 (G 1130). —OF. *malleable*, 'mallable, hammerable, pliant to the hammer;' Cot. Formed with suffix *-able* from obs. L. *malleāre, to hammer, of which the pp. *malleātus* occurs.—L. *malleus*, a hammer; see **Mall** (1). Der. *malleabili-ty*, **malleable**-*ness* (see Locke, On Hum. Underst.;

b. iii. c. 6. s. 6, c. 10. s. 17); *malleat-ed*, Blount's Gloss., ed. 1674, from L. pp. *malleāt-us*; *malleat-ion*.

MALLECHO, mischief; lit. 'malefaction.' (Span.—L.) In Hamlet, iii. 2. 147.—Span. *malhecho*, 'misdone; an evil deed;' Minsheu.—Span. *mal*, evil; *hecho*, done, pp. of *hacer*, to do.—L. *male*, ill; *factus*, pp. of *facere*, to do. See **Fact**.

MALLET, a small mall, a wooden hammer. (F.—L.) 'Bear-ynge great *malettes* of iron and stele;' Berners, tr. of Froissart, vol. i. c. 422 (R.). ME. *maillet*, Romance of Partenay, 4698; *malyet*, Wyntoun, Chron. iii. 104.—F. *maillet*, 'a mallet or hammer;' Cot. Dimin. of F. *mail*; see **Mall** (1).

MALLOW, the name of a plant. (L.) ME. *malwe*; Prompt. Parv. AS. *malwe*, *mealewe*; Voc. 135. 27; 297. 27. Not a Teut. word, but borrowed from L. *malua*, a mallow.+Gk. μαλάχη (for *μαλϜάκη), a mallow. β. Named from its supposed emollient properties; cf. Gk. μαλάσσειν (= *μαλακ-yειν), to make soft, from μαλακός, soft, mild. Der. *marsh-mallow*, AS. *mersc-mealewe*, Voc. 296. 21. Also *malv-ac-e-ous* (= L. *maluāceus*, adj.). ☞ Mr. Wedgwood shows that the Arabs still use mallows for poultices to allay irritation. And see **Malachite**.

MALM, a kind of earth. (E.) Common in prov. E. AS. *mealm*, as seen in *mealm-iht*, sandy, chalky; *mealm-stān*, malm-stone, maum-stone.+Icel. *málmr*, sand; Goth. *malma*, sand. Teut. base *mal-m-, from *mal-an*, to grind, allied to L. *mol-ere*, to grind. See **Meal** (1).

MALMSEY, a strong sweet wine. (F.—Gk.) In Shak. L. L. L. v. 2. 233. Spelt *malmesay* in Tyndall, Works, p. 229, col. 2. Also called *malvesye*, Chaucer, C. T. 13000 (B 1260). — AF. *malvesy* (Ducange); OF. *malvoisie*, 'malmesie;' Cot. From *Malvasia*, now called *Napoli di Malvasia* (see Black's Atlas), the name of a town on the E. coast of Lacedaemonia in the Morea; for *Monemvasia* (Gk. μον-εμβασία, lit. 'single entrance.' — Gk. μόν-η, fem. of μόνος, single; ἐμ-βασία, entrance, from ἐν, in, βαίνειν, to go. Cf. Span. *malvasia*, Ital. *malvagia*, malmsey. ¶ The second *m* in *Malmsey* is due to the form *Monemvasia*.

MALT, grain steeped in water, and dried in a kiln, for brewing. (E.) ME. *malt*, Chaucer, C. T. 3989 (A 3991). AS. *mealt*, Voc. 196. 22; whence *mealt-hūs*, a malt-house, Voc. 185. 24. From Teut. *malt (AS. *mealt*), 2nd grade of *meltan-, strong verb, to melt; hence, to steep, soften.+Du. *mout*; Icel. *malt*, whence the weak verb *melta*, to malt (not the same as E. *melt*); Dan. and Swed. *malt*; G. *malz*, malt; cf. MHG. *malz*, soft, weak. Cf. Skt. *mṛdu-s*, L. *mollis*, soft. See **Melt**. Der. *malt*, vb., ME. *malten*, Prompt. Parv.; *malt-house*, Com. Errors, iii. 1. 32; *malt-worm*, 1 Hen. IV, ii. 1. 83; also *malt-ster*, ME. *malte-stere*, Prompt. Parv. ¶ The suffix *-ster* was once looked upon as a fem. termination, as in *brew-ster*, *baxter* for *bake-ster*, *web-ster*, *spin-ster*; and the baking, brewing, weaving, and spinning were once all alike in the hands of females. See **Spinster**.

MALTREAT, to treat ill. (F.—L.) 'Yorick indeed was never better served in his life; but it was a little hard to *maltreat* him after;' Sterne, Tristram Shandy, vol. ii. c. 17, not far from the end. —F. *maltraiter*, to treat ill. Cf. Ital. *maltrattare*, to treat ill.—L. *male*, adv., ill, badly; and *tractāre*, to treat, handle. See **Malice** and **Treat**. Der. *maltreat-ment*, MF. *maltraictement*, 'hard deal-ing;' Cot.

MALVERSATION, fraudulent behaviour. (F.—L.) 'Malversation, ill conversation, misdemeanure, misuse;' Blount's Gloss., ed. 1674.—F. *malversation*, 'misdemeanor;' Cot. Regularly formed (with suffix *-a-tion*) from F. *malverser*; Cot. gives 'malverser en son office, to behave himself ill in his office.'—L. *male*, adv., badly; and *uersāri* (pp. *uersātus*), to dwell, be engaged in, from *uersāre*, frequentative form of *uertere*, to turn. See **Malice** and **Verse**.

MAMALUKE, MAMELUKE, an Egyptian light horse-soldier. (F.—Arab.) In Sir T. More, Works, p. 279 f. Also in Skelton, Why Come Ye Nat to Courte, l. 476; see Spec. of Eng. ed. Skeat, p. 143, and the note.—MF. *Mamaluc*, 'a Mameluke, or light-horseman;' Cot. [Cf. Span. *Mameluco*, Ital. *Mammalucco*.] They were a corps of slaves.—Arab. *mamlūk*, a purchased slave or captive; lit. 'possessed.'—Arab. root *malaka*, he possessed; Rich. Dict. pp. 1494, 1488.

MAMMA, an infantine term for mother. (E.) Seldom found in books, except of late years; it occurs in Prior's poems, entitled 'Venus Mistaken,' and 'The Dove.' 'The babe shall now begin to tattle and call her *Mamma*;' Lily, Euphues, ed. Arber, p. 129. In Skinner and Cotgrave it is spelt *mam*; Cot. gives: *Mammam*, the voice of infants, *mam*.' Skelton has *mammy*, Garl. of Laurel, l. 974. The spelling *mamma* is doubtless pedantic, and due to the L. *mamma*; it should rather be *mama*, as it is merely a repetition of *ma*, an infantine syllable. It may also be considered as an E. word; most other languages have something like it. Cf. MF. *mammam*, cited above, mod. F. *maman*; Span. *mama*, Ital. *mamma*, Du. *mama*,

G. *mama*, *mümme*, *memme*, all infantine words for mother; also W. *mam*, mother, L. *mamma*, mother, Gk. μάμμη, Russ. *mama*, &c. ¶ We have no evidence *against* the borrowing of the word from French; still it was. most likely, not so borrowed. Brugmann, ii. § 179, 947.

MAMMALIA, the class of animals that suckle their young. (L.) Modern and scientific; not in Johnson. Formed from L. *mammālis*, belonging to the breasts. — L. *mamma*, the breast. β. There is a doubt whether the word is the same as L. *mamma*, mother; if it be, we may consider it as of infantine origin; see above. γ. Brugmann separates them (i. § 587), and explains this *mamma* as *mad-ma, from *mad-ēre*, to be wet; cf. Gk. μαζός (< *μαδ-yos), μαστός (< *μαδ-τύs), breast; μαδ-άειν, to flow away. **Der.** *mammalian*; we also use *mammal* as a convenient short term for 'one of the mammalia.'

MAMMILLARY, pertaining to the breasts. (L.) 'The *mammillary* teats;' Dr. Robinson, Endoxa (ed. 1658), p. 51; Todd's Johnson. Coined from L. *mammillāris*, adj. formed from *mammilla*, a teat, dimin. of *mamma*, a breast. See **Mammalia.**

MAMMON, riches, the god of riches. (L. — Gk. — Syriac.) In A. V. Matt. vi. 24; Luke, xvi. 9. — L. *mammōna*, Matt. vi. 24 (Vulgate). — Gk. μαμωνᾶς; ibid. — Syr. *mamōnā*; a word which often occurs in the Chaldee Targums of Onkelos, and later writers, and in the Syriac version, and means 'riches;' Dict. of the Bible. Cf. Heb. *matmōn*, a hidden treasure; from *tāman*, to hide (*t* = *teth*).

MAMMOTH, an extinct species of elephant. (Russ. — Tatar?) 'An entire *mammoth*, flesh and bones, was discovered in Siberia, in 1799;' Haydn, Dict. of Dates. — Russ. *mamant'*, a mammoth. — Siberian *mammont*. 'From Tartar *mamma*, the earth, because the Tungooses and Yakoots believed that this animal worked its way in the earth like a mole;' Webster. But it does not appear that there is any such Tatar word. See N. and Q. 9 S. xi. 286.

MAN, a human being. (E.) ME. *man*, Chaucer, C. T. I. 43. AS. *mann*, also *mon*; Grein, ii. 105.╋Du. *man*; Icel. *maðr* (for *mannr); also *mann*; Swed. *man*; Dan. *mand* (with excrescent *d*); Goth. *manna*; G. *mann*; [the G. *mensch* = *männisch*, i.e. mannish, human]. Allied to Skt. *manu-*, Vedic *manus-*, a man. β. Connected by some with Skt. *man*, to think; see **Mind.** But it is unlikely that the orig. sense could have been 'thinker.' **Der.** *man-child*, Gen. xvii. 10; *man-ful*, Lydgate, Complaint of the Black Knight, st. 60; *man-ful-ly*, Two Gent. iv. 1. 28; *man-ful-ness*; *man-hood*, Chaucer, C. T. 758 (A 756); *man-of-war*, Luke, xxiii. 11; *man-kind*, q. v.; *man-ly*, ME. *manlich*, P. Plowman, B. v. 260, from AS. *manlic*, man-like, see Grein, ii. 211; *man-li-ness*; *man-slaughter*, ME. *man-slaghter*, Cursor Mundi, 25772; *man-slay-er*, ME. *mansleer*, Trevisa, iii. 41, l. 8, Wyclif, John, viii. 44. Also *man*, vb., Rich. II, ii. 3. 54. Also *man-like*, Antony, i. 4. 5; *man-ly*, adv., Macb. iv. 3. 235; *mann-ish*, As You Like It, i. 3. 123, Chaucer, C. T. 5202 (B 782); *man-queller*, 2 Hen. IV, ii. 1. 58, Wyclif, Mark, vi. 27; *man-ik-in*, q. v.

MANACLE, a fetter, handcuff. (F. — L.) Better spelt *manicle*, as in Cotgrave. ME. *manycle*, Wyclif, Ps. cxlix. 8, earlier text; where the later text has *manacle*. — AF. *manicle*, Vie de St. Auban; OF. *manicle*, pl. *manicles*, 'manicles, hand-fetters, or gyves;' Cot. — L. *manicula*, dimin. of *manica*, a long sleeve, glove, gauntlet, manacle, handcuff. — L. *manus*, the hand; see **Manual.** **Der.** *manacle*, vb., Temp. i. 2. 461.

MANAGE, government of a horse, control, administration. (F. — Ital. — L.) Orig. a sb., but now superseded by *management*. 'Wanting the *manage* of unruly jades;' Rich. II, iii. 3. 179. — MF. *manege*, 'the manage, or managing of a horse;' Cot. Mod. F. *manège*. — Ital. *maneggio*, 'a busines, a managing, a handling, . . . an exercise;' Florio. Particularly used of managing horses; the mod. Ital. *maneggio* means 'a riding-school.' The lit. sense is 'a handling,' the word being formed from *maneggiare*, 'to manage, handle.' — Ital. *mano*, the hand. — L. *manum*, acc. of *manus*, the hand; see **Manual.** **Der.** *manage*, vb., to handle, Rich. II, iii. 2. 118; *manag-er*, L. L. L. i. 2. 188; *manage-able*, *manage-able-ness*; *manage-ment* (a coined word), used by Bp. Hall in a Fast Sermon, April 5, 1628 (R.). **Doublet,** *menage*, from mod. F. *manège*. ☞ Not to be confused with ME. *menage*, a household, K. Alisaunder, 2087, from OF. *maisnage*, MF. *mesnage* (Cot.), mod. F. *ménage*; this OF. *maisnage* stands for *maison-age*, extended from F. *maison*, a mansion; see **Mansion.** (Scheler.)

MANATEE, a sea-cow, a dugong. (Span. — Carib.) The word occurs in Sir T. Herbert's Travels, ed. 1665, p. 404; spelt *manate* in R. Eden, ed. Arber, p. 231, l. 2 (1555). — Span. *manati*, a sea-cow; also written *manato*. A West Indian word; spelt *manattoüi* in Raymond Breton's Dictionaire Caraibe-François; Auxerre, 1665; p. 349. ☞ The Malay name is *dugong*, s. v.

MANCHET, a loaf of fine wheaten bread. (F. — L.?) 'Of breade

. . the most excellent is the *mainchet*,' v. r. 'manchet;' Harrison, Desc. of England, bk. ii. ch. 6. ME. *manchete*, Liber Cure Cucorum, p. 53. β. The word seems to refer to quality; and, if so, is prob. different from Norm. dial. *manchette*, bread made in the shape of a crown, and also called *couronne*; i.e. of an annular shape; Moisy, Robin; prob. from *manchette*, 'a cuff or hand-ruff;' Cot.; which is also annular. Dimin. of *manche*, a sleeve. — L. *manica*, a sleeve; from L. *manus*, the hand; see **Manacle.**

MANCHINEEL, a W. Indian tree. (F. — Span. — L.) '*Man-chinelo-tree*, a tree that grows wild in the woods of Jamaica, the fruit of which is as round as a ball;' Phillips, ed. 1706. Spelt *manchineel*, W. Dampier, New Voy. (1699), iii. 67; *mancinell*, Capt. Smith, Works, p. 905. — F. *mancinelle* (Hatzfeld). [Mahn gives Ital. *mancinello*, but it must be modern, and borrowed from Spanish; the name, like many W. Indian words, is certainly Span., not Italian.] — Span. *manzanillo*, a little apple-tree; hence, the manchineel tree, from the apple-like fruit; dimin. of Span. *manzana*, an apple, also a pommel. Cf. Span. *manzanal*, an orchard of apple-trees. — L. *Matiāna*, neut. pl. of *Matiāna*, adj.; we find *Matiāna māla*, and *Matiāna pōma*, applied to certain kinds of apples. The adj. *Matiānus*, Matian, is from L. *Matius*, the name of a Roman gens (Lewis).

MANCIPLE, a purveyor, esp. for a college. (F. — L.) Not obsolete; still in use in Oxford and Cambridge. ME. *manciple*, Chaucer, C. T. 569 (A 567). The *l* is an insertion, as in *principle*, *syllable*, *participle*. — OF. *mancipe*, a slave; also *manciple* (Godefroy). Cf. MItal. *mancipio*, 'a slave, vassal, subject, captive, manciple, farmer, baily,' &c.; Florio. — L. *mancipium*, a slave, orig. possession, property, lit. a taking in the hand; see Maine, Ancient Law, p. 317. Cf. L. *mancipi-*, decl. stem of *manceps*, a taker in hand. — L. *man-*, base of *man-us*, the hand; *cip-*, weakened form of *cap-*, base of *cap-ere*, to take. See **Manual** and **Captive.**

MANDARIN, a Chinese governor of a province. (Port. — Malay — Skt.) Not a Chinese, but a Malay word; brought to us by the Portuguese. In Sir T. Herbert's Travels, ed. 1665, p. 395; and in E. G[rimston], tr. of Acosta, 1604, p. 370. — Port. *mandarim*, a mandarin. — Malay (and Hindu) *mantri*, 'a counsellor, minister of state; *ferdana mantri*, the first minister, vizir;' Marsden, Malay Dict., p. 334. — Skt. *mantrin-*, a counsellor; *mahā-mantrin-*, the prime minister. — Skt. *mantra-*, a holy text, charm, prayer, advice, counsel. Formed, with suffix *-tra*, from Skt. *man*, to think, mind, know; cf. Skt. *man-tu-*, *man-tṛ*, an adviser. — √MEN, to think; see **Mind.** (See Yule.)

MANDATE, a command, order, charge. (F. — L.) In Hamlet, iii. 4. 204. — MF. *mandat*, 'a mandate, or mandamus, for the preferment of one to a benefice;' Cot. — L. *mandātum*, a charge, order, commission. — L. *mandātus*, pp. of *mandāre*, to commit to one's charge, enjoin, command. β. Lit. 'to put into one's hand,' from *man-*, base of *manus*, the hand, and *dare*, to give. [So also *manceps* = a taker by the hand; from *man-* and *capere*, to take.] See **Manual** and **Date** (1). Brugmann, i. § 589 (2, b). **Der.** *man-dat-or-y*. **Doublet,** *maundy*, in the term *Maundy Thursday*, q. v. From L. *mandāre* are also *counter-mand*, *com-mand*, *de-mand*, *re-mand*, *com-mend*, *re-com-mend*, *commodore*. Also *mandamus*, a writ that enjoins a duty; from L. *mandāmus*, we command, the first word in it.

MANDIBLE, a jaw. (L.) '*Mandibula*, the mandible, or jaw;' Phillips, ed. 1706. — L. *mandibula*, a jaw. — L. *mandere*, to chew, eat. **Der.** *mandibul-ar*, adj., from L. *mandibula*.

MANDILION, a soldier's cloak. (Ital. — Span. — Arab. — L.) See examples in Nares. — Ital. *mandiglione*, 'a mandillion, souldier's iacket;' Florio. — Span. *mandil*, a coarse apron. — Arab. *mandīl*, a table-cloth, towel, mantle. — L. *mantile*, a napkin.

MANDOLIN, a kind of guitar. (F. — Ital. — Gk.) Added by Todd to Johnson's Dict. 'Lutes and mandolins;' T. Moore, Oh! come to me when daylight sets; l. 7. — F. *mandoline*, a mandolin. — Ital. *mandolino*, dimin. of *mandola*, a kind of guitar (there were several kinds). *Mandola* is a corruption of *mandora* (cf. F. *mandore*), and, again, this is for *bandora* = Ital. *pandora*. See further under **Banjo.**

MANDRAKE, a narcotic plant. (AF. — L. — Gk.) In Gen. xxx. 14, where the Bible of 1551 has pl. *mandragoras*. Also *mandrake* in Palsgrave. ME. *mandragores*, Old Eng. Miscellany, ed. Morris, p. 19, l. 613. AS. *mandragora*, Cockayne's Leechdoms, i. 244. *Mandrake* (also spelt *mandrage* in Minsheu) is the AF. *mandrake*, also *mandrage* (Bozon); a shortened form of *mandragora*, the form used by Shak. in Oth. iii. 3. 330. Cf. OF. *mandragore*, Ital. *mandragora*, Span. *mandragora*. — L. *mandragoras*, gen. *-æ*; Gen. xxx. 14. — Gk. μανδραγόρας, the name of the plant; of uncertain origin.

MANDREL, the revolving shank in which turners fix their work in a lathe. (F. — L.) '*Mandril*, a kind of wooden pulley, that is part of a turner's leath;' Bailey's Dict. vol. ii. ed. 1731. Corrupted from F. *mandrin*, a punch, a mandrel (Hamilton). β. Marked by Littré as of unknown origin; but. prob. derived from a L. type **mandar-*

inum, allied to Oscan *mamphur*, (apparently) a mandrel or part of a lathe (Lewis). Cf. also Icel. *möndull*, handle of a handmill; Lith. *menturė*, something that twirls; Skt. *mantha-s*, a churning-stick, *manthana-s* (the same), from *math*, *manth*, to churn. See Brugmann, i. §§ 571, 589 (2, b), 757.

MANDRILL, a kind of baboon. (E.) Nares, s.v. *Drill*, shows that *mandrill* occurs in Smith's Voyage to Guinea (1744), who thought the animal was so called from its likeness to a *man*. Compounded of E. *man*, and *dril*, 'a large overgrown ape or baboon;' Blount's Gloss. The origin of *dril* or *drill* is unknown; perhaps allied to MDu. *drillen*, 'to goe, trot, or run up and downe,' Hexham; whence also E. *drill*, v. See *Drill* in Nares, and in the N. E. D.

MANE, long hair on the neck of a horse, &c. (E.) ME. *mane*, King Alisaunder, 1957. AS. *manu*, mane; Erfurt gloss., 1182.+ Icel. *mön* (gen. *manar*, pl. *manar*), a mane; Swed. and Dan. *man*; Du. *maan* (Sewel); MDu. *mane* (Hexham); G. *mähne*, OHG. *mana*. Cf. W. *myngen*, a horse's mane, *mwng*, a mane; from *mwn*, the neck. So also Irish *mong*, a mane, *muince*, a collar (W. *mynci*, the hame of a horse-collar) from Irish *muin*, the neck. Hence E. *mane* is plainly connected with Skt. *manyā*, the tendon forming the nape of the neck; and with L. *monile*, a necklace (Stokes-Fick, p. 216).

MANEGE, the control of horses; see **Manage**.

MANGANESE, the name of a metal. (F. – Ital. – L. – Gk.) The metal was discovered in 1774 (Littré). But the term is much older, otherwise used. 'Manganese, so called from its likeness in colour and weight to the *magnes* or loadstone, is the most universal material used in making glass;' Blount's Gloss., ed. 1674. – MF. *manganese*, 'a certain minerall which, being melted with glasse, amends the colour thereof;' Cot. – Ital. *manganese*, 'a stuffe or stone to make glasses with; also a kind of mineral stone;' Florio. β. A perverted form of *magnesia*, also written *mangnesia*. See Cent. Dict., and Schade, p. 1395; and see **Magnesia**. Palsgrave has *mangnet* for *magnet*.

MANGE, the scab or itch in dogs, &c. (F. – L.) Minsheu, ed. 1627, gives 'the *mange*' as sb., and *mangie* as adj. Cf. 'a *mangy* dog,' Timon, iv. 3. 371; 'In wretched beggary And *maungy* misery,' Skelton, How the Douty Duke of Albany, &c., ll. 137, 138. But earlier, the sb. is *mangie*, as in 'the *mangie*, or the scurvie,' in E. G., tr. of Acosta, p. 465. ME. *maniewe* (= *manjewe*); see N. E. D. – OF. *manjue*, mange; cf. mod. Norman *manjure*, Guernsey *manjue* (Moisy). – OF. *manjuer*, *mangier*, F. *manger*, to eat. [The MF. sb. for 'mange' is *mangeson*.] See further under **Manger**. Der. *mangi-ness*.

MANGEL-WURZEL, a variety of beet. (G.) For *mangold-wurzel*, also sometimes used. – G. *mangold-wurzel*, beet-root. – G. *mangold*, MHG. *mangolt*, beet, derived by Schade from the personal name *Manegolt*; and *wurzel*, root, allied to **Wort** (1).

MANGER, an eating-trough for cattle. (F. – L.) In Sir T. More, Works, p. 1139 h. ME. *maungeur*, Cath. Anglicum (1483). – OF. *mangeure* (Godefroy); F. *mangeoire*, 'a manger;' Cot. – F. *manger*, to eat. – L. *mandūcāre*, to eat. – L. *mandūcus*, a glutton. – L. *mandere*, to chew. See **Mandible**.

MANGLE (1), to render maimed, tear, mutilate. (F. – G.) In Sir T. More, Works, p. 538 f. – AF. *mangler*, to maim (Godefroy); for *mahangler*, to maim, Langtoft, i. 254. Frequent. form of OF. *mahaigner*, to maim. – OF. *mahaing*, a maim, a hurt; see **Maim**. Der. *mangl-er*.

MANGLE (2), a roller for smoothing linen; vb., to smooth linen. (Du. – Late L. – Gk.) A late word; added by Todd to Johnson's Dict. 'A movement capable of being applied to *mangles* and calenders;' Ann. Reg. (1799), p. 399. Borrowed from Dutch; cf. Du. *mangelen*, to roll with a rolling-pin; *linnen mangelen*, to roll linen on a rolling-pin; *mangelstok*, a rolling-pin (Sewel); *een mangelstok*, 'a smoothing role, or a battle-dore' (Hexham). The corresponding MItal. word is *mangano*, 'a kind of presse to presse buckrom;' Florio. Both Du. and Ital. words are modifications of Late L. *manganum*, *mangona*, a very common word as the name of a military engine for throwing stones; see **Mangonel**. The mangle, being worked with an axis and winch, was named from its resemblance to the old war-engine; sometimes it was reduced to an axis or cylinder worked by hand. The Ital. *mangano* also means 'a mangonel.' – Gk. μάγγανον, a machine for defending fortifications; also, the axis of a pulley. See Prellwitz.

MANGO, the fruit of an E. Indian tree. (Span. – Port. – Malay. – Tamil.) In Sir T. Herbert's Travels, ed. 1665, p. 350. – Span. *mango*. – Port. *manga*. – Malay *manggā*, 'the mango-fruit, of which the varieties are numerous;' Marsden's Dict., p. 327. Formerly *mangkā* (see Yule). – Tamil *mān-kāy*, i.e. *mān*-fruit, or fruit of the tree called *māmaram*, i.e. *mān*-tree (from *mān* and *maram*, wood, tree); cf. **Catamaran** (Yule).

MANGONEL, a war-engine for throwing stones. (F. – Late L. – Gk.) ME. *mangonel*, in a MS. of the time of Edw. II; Polit.

Songs, ed. Wright, p. 69. – AF. *mangonel*, Langtoft, i. 494; OF. *mangonel*, later *mangonneau*, 'an old-fashioned sling or engine,' &c.; Cot. – Late L. *mangonellus*, dimin. of *mangona*, *manganum*, a war-engine. – Gk. μάγγανον; see **Mangle** (2).

MANGOSTEEN, a fruit. (Malay.) Formerly *mangostan*. – Malay *manggustan* (C. P. G. Scott); *manggista* (Marsden).

MANGROVE. (Hybrid; Malay *and* E.) 'A sort of trees called *mangroves*;' Eng. Garner, vii. 371 (ab. 1689). My belief is that the second syllable is nothing but the E. word *grove*, and has reference to the peculiar growth of the trees, which form a close thicket of some extent. Again, the tree is sometimes called the *mangle* (F. *mangle*, from Span. *mangle*); so that *mangrove* may well stand for *mang-grove* or 'grove of *mangs* or *mangles*.' The syllable *mang* may be due to the Malay name for the tree, viz. *manggi-manggi*; see Pijnappel's Malay-Dutch Dict. p. 133. β. On the other hand, the Span. *mangle*, a mangrove, appears to be of S. American origin (Yule). Cf. Brazil. *mangue*, Hist. Nat. Brasil. i. 113.

MANIA, madness, frenzy. (L. – Gk.) In Phillips, ed. 1706. [ME. *manie*, Chaucer, C. T. 1376, is from F. *manie*, 'madnesse;' Cot.] – L. *mania*. – Gk. μανία, madness, frenzy. β. The orig. sense is 'mental excitement:' cf. μένος, mind, spirit, force; Skt. *manyu-*, anger, fury. See **Mind**. Der. *mania-c*, spelt *maniack* in Blount's Gloss., ed. 1674, from F. *maniaque*, 'mad,' Cot.; as if from a Lat. *maniacus*. Hence *maniac-al*.

MANIFEST, evident, apparent. (F. – L.) ME. *manifest*, Chaucer, tr. of Boethius, b. iii. pr. 10, l. 104. – F. *manifeste*, 'manifest;' Cot. – L. *manifestus*, evident. β. The lit. sense is (probably) 'struck by the hand,' hence, palpable. – L. *mani-*, for *manu-*, from *manus*, the hand; and *-festus* = *-fed-tus*, pp. of obs. verb **fendere*, to strike, occurring in the compp. *dē-fendere*, *of-fendere*; cf. *in-festus*, *in-fensus*, hostile. – √GwHEN, to strike; see **Defend** (Bréal). And see **Manual**. Der. *manifest-ly*, *manifest-ness*; *manifest*, vb., ME. *manifesten*, Chaucer, Boeth. bk. ii. pr. 7, l. 31; *manifest-at-ion*; also *manifesto*, q.v.

MANIFESTO, a written declaration. (Ital. – L.) 'Manifesto or evidence;' Sir T. Browne, Vulg. Errors, b. iii. c. 17. § 5. – Ital. *manifesto*, sb., a manifesto. – Ital. *manifesto*, adj., manifest. – L. *manifestus*; see **Manifest**.

MANIFOLD, various. (E.) ME. *manifold*, *manyfold*, Gower, C. A. i. 344; bk. iii. 1952. AS. *manigfeald*, manifold; Grein, ii. 210. – AS. *manig*, many; and *-feald*, suffix (E. *-fold*), connected with *fealdan*, to fold. See **Many** and **Fold**.

MANIKIN, **MANAKIN**, a little man, dwarf. (F. – Du.) In Tw. Nt. iii. 2. 57. [Not an E. word.] – MF. *manequin*, 'a puppet;' Cot. – MDu. *manneken*, a little man (Hexham); mod. Du. *mannetje*, by alteration of the suffix. Formed, with double dimin. suffix *-k-en*, from Du. *manne-*, for *man*, a man. See **Man**. Cf. G. *männchen*, from *mann*.

MANIOC, the cassava-plant. (Port. – Brazil.) Better spelt *mandioc*. – Port. *mandioca* (Span. *mandiocha* in Pineda). – Brazil. *mandioca*, the root of the cassava-plant. Cp. 'mandiiba, maniiba, cujus radix *mandioca* vocatur;' Hist. Brasil. ii. 65. It is spelt *mandihoca* in the same, i. 52. Granada gives the Guarani name as *mandióg*.

MANIPLE, a handful; small band of soldiers, a kind of priest's scarf. (F. – L.) 'Our small divided *maniples*,' i.e. bands of men; Milton, Areopagitica, ed. Hales, p. 48, l. 6. Also *manypule*, a scarf; Supp. to Palsgrave, p. 1068, l. 31. – MF. *manipule*, 'a fistfull;' Cot. – L. *manipulus*, a handful; hence, a wisp of straw, &c. used as an ensign; and hence, a company of soldiers under the same standard, a band of men. – L. *mani-*, for *manu-*, for *manus*, the hand; and *-pulus*, lit. filling, from the weak grade (*pəl*) of the root **plē-*, to fill; cf. L. *plēnus*, full, and AS. *full*. See **Manual** and **Full**. Der. *manipul-ate*, q.v.

MANIPULATE, to handle. (L.) A modern word; not in Johnson; the sb. *manipulation* (but not the verb) was added by Todd to Johnson's Dict. The verb was prob. suggested by the sb. *manipulation*, which appears in F. in 1716. Even the sb. is quite a coined word, there being nothing nearer to it than the L. *manipulātim*, by troops, an adv. formed from *manipulus*, a troop. The word *manipulate* should mean 'to *fill* the hands' rather than merely to *use* them. Altogether, the word has little to recommend it on etymological grounds; but it is now well established. Perhaps the suffix has been confused with that of *inter-polate*. Der. *manipulat-ion*, *-ive*, *-or*.

MANITO, a spirit, a fetish. (Algonkin.) 'Gitche *Mánito*, the mighty;' Longfellow, Hiawatha, xiv. From the Algonkin *manitu*, *manito*, a spirit, a demon (Cuoq).

MANKIND, the race of men. (E.) ME. *mankinde*, Gower, C. A. ii. 83; bk. iv. 2443. The final *d* is excrescent, the older form being *mankin*, Ormulum, 799. AS. *mancynn*, mankind; Grein, ii. 207. – AS. *man*, a man; and *cynn*, kind, race; see **Man** and **Kin**.

MANNA, the food supplied to the Israelites in the wilderness of

Arabia. (L. — Gk. — Heb.) In A. V. Exod. xvi. 15; Numb. xi. 7; Deut. viii. 3; &c. — L. *manna*, Deut. viii. 3 (Vulgate); but in Exod. xvi. 15 the Vulgate has *manhu*, and in Numb. xi. 7 it has *man*. — Gk. μάννα. — Heb. *mān*, manna. **β.** Two explanations are given: (1) from Heb. *mān hu*, what is this? from the enquiry which the Hebrews made when they first saw it on the ground, where *mān* is the neuter interrogative pronoun; see Exod. xvi. 15. But this is a popular etymology; since *mān* is not Hebrew, but Aramaic (Gesenius). And (2) that the sense of *mān* is 'it is a gift' (cf. Arab. *mann*, beneficence, grace, favour, also manna, Rich. Dict. p. 1495). See Gesenius, Heb. Dict. (1883), p. 468.

MANNER, way, fashion, habit, sort, kind, style. (F. — L.) In early use. ME. *manere*, O. Eng. Homilies, ed. Morris, i. 51, l. 30. — AF. *manere*, Stat. Realm, i. 27 (1275); OF. *maniere*, 'manner;' Cot. Mod. F. *manière*; properly 'habit.' Orig. fem. of OF. *manier*, adj. manual, easily managed (Godefroy); allied to OF. *manier*, 'to handle, hand, manage, wield;' Cot. — Late L. type *manārius*, for L. *manuārius*, handy. — L. *manu-*, for *manus*, the hand; see **Manual.** Der. *manner-ly*, in Skelton, who wrote a poem called *Manerly Margery Mylk and Ale*; *manner-li-ness*; *un-manner-ly*, Hamlet, iii. 2. 364; *manner-ism*. ☞ The phrase *to be taken in the manner* (a law phrase) is a corruption of *to be taken with the mainour*; the L. phrase is *cum manuopere captus*. Here *mainour* is the same word as *manœuvre*, q.v. See *maynure* in Croft's gloss. to Sir T. Elyot's Governour. And see **Mainour.**

MANŒUVRE, dexterous management, stratagem. (F. — L.) Introduced into E. in the 18th cent. Added to Johnson's Dict. by Todd, who cites it from Burke, but without a satisfactory reference. — F. *manœuvre*, a manœuvre, properly a work of the hand. — Late L. *manuopera* (more commonly *manopera*), a working with the hand. [Cf. Span. *maniobra*, handiwork; *maniobrar*, to work with the hands, manœuvre; Ital. *manovra*, the working of a ship; *manovrare*, to steer a ship.] — L. *manū operāri*, to work with the hand. — L. *manū*, abl. of *manus*, the hand; and *operāri*, to work, from *opera*, work. See **Manual** and **Operate.** Der. *manœuvre*, vb., *manœuvr-er*. **Doublet, *manure*.**

MANOR, a place of residence for a nobleman in former times; estate belonging to a lord. (F. — L.) In Shak. Merry Wives, ii. 2. 19. ME. *manere*, P. Plowman, B. v. 595. — OF. *manoir* (a mansion, mannor, or mannor-house,' Cot.; formerly also spelt *menoir* (Godefroy). Properly 'a place to dwell in;' from OF. *manoir, menoir*, to dwell (Godefroy). — L. *manēre*, to dwell, remain; see **Mansion.** Der. *manor-house*, L. L. L. i. 1. 208; *manor-seat*; *manor-i-al*.

MANSE, a clergyman's house, in Scotland. (L.) 'Manse, a habitation, a farm;' Blount's Law Lexicon, ed. 1691. An old law term. — Late L. *mansa*, a farm. — L. *mansa*, fem. of *mansus*, pp. of *manēre*, to dwell; see **Mansion.**

MANSION, a large house, dwelling-place. (F. — L.) ME. *mansion*, Chaucer, C. T. 1976 (A 1974). — OF. *mansion*, a dwelling-place; Burguy. — L. *mansiōnem*, acc. of *mansio*, a stopping, a place of abode; cf. *mansus*, pp. of *manēre*, to dwell. + Gk. μένειν, to stay, remain; allied to μόνιμος, staying, steadfast. — √MEN, to remain. Der. *mansion-house*; *mansion-ry*, Macb. i. 6. 5; from L. *manēre* are also *manse, manor, permanent, remain, remnant*. And see *menial, menagerie, messuage*.

MANTEL, a shelf over a fire-place. (F. — L.) Hardly used except in the comp. *mantel-piece* and *mantel-shelf*; formerly used in the comp. *mantle-tree*, which occurs in Cotgrave, s.v. *manteau*. In old fire-places, the mantel slopes forward like a hood, to catch the smoke; the word is a mere doublet of **Mantle**, q.v. 'Mantyltre of a chymney, *manteau dune cheminee*;' Palsgrave. ¶ The difference in spelling between *mantel* and *mantle* is an absurdity. Der. *mantel-piece, -shelf*.

MANTLE, a cloak, covering. (F. — L.) Better spelt *mantel*, as it is the same word as that above. In early use. ME. *mantel*, Layamon, 14755, 15274. [Cf. AS. *mentel*, a mantle, Ps. cviii. 28.] — OF. *mantel* (Godefroy), later *manteau*, 'a cloke, also the mantle-tree of a chimney;' Cot. — L. *mantellum*, a napkin; also, a means of covering, a cloak (in a figurative sense); cf. L. *mantēle, mantile*, a napkin, towel. A shortened form appears in the Late L. *mantum*, a short cloak, used by Isidore of Seville, whence Ital. and Span. *manto*, F. *mante*, a mantle. For the origin, see Brugmann, i. §§ 134, 483 (7). Der. *mantle*, vb., to cloak, cover, Temp. v. 67; also *mantle*, vb., to gather a scum on the surface, Merch. Ven. i. 1. 89; *mantle-et* (with dimin. suffix), 'a short purple mantle, ... in fortification, a moveable pent-house,' Phillips, ed. 1706, from F. *mantelet*, 'a little mantle, a movable pent-house,' &c., Cotgrave. Also *mantilla*, a long head-dress, from Span. *mantilla*, dimin. of *manto*, a cloak, a veil.

MANTUA, a lady's gown. (Ital.) Seldom used except in the comp. *mantua-maker*, a lady's dressmaker. 'Mantoe or Mantua gown,'

a loose upper garment, now generally worn by women, instead of a straight body'd gown;' Phillips, ed. 1706. 'By th' yellow *mantos* of the bride;' Butler, Hudibras, pt. iii. c. 1. l. 700. *Manto* is from Ital. (or Span.) *manto*, a mantle, or even from F. *manteau*; but *Mantua gown* must refer to *Mantua* in Italy, though this connexion seems to have arisen from mere confusion. As to Ital. *manto*, see **Mantle.**

MANUAL, done by the hand, suitable for the hand. (F. — L.) We recognize it as a F. word from its use *after* its sb., in such phrases as 'sign *manual*,' or 'seal *manual*;' the spelling has been conformed to the L. vowel in the final syllable. Shak. has *seal manual*, Venus, l. 516. Formerly spelt *manuel*, as in Cotgrave. Cf. '*syne manuell*,' sign manual; Fifty Eng. Wills, ed. Furnivall, p. 83, l. 18 (1428). — F. *manuel*, 'manuel, handy, of the hand;' Cot. — L. *manuālis*, manual. — L. *manu-*, for *manus*, the hand. **β.** The sense of *manus* is 'the measurer;' formed (with suffix -*nu*-) from **mə*, weak grade of √ME, to measure, whence also Skt. *mā*, to measure, a verb which when used with the prep. *nis*, out, also means to build, cause, create, compose; cf. also Skt. *māna-*, sb., measuring, measure; Brugmann, ii. § 106. Der. *manual*, sb., a hand-book; *manual-ly*. From L. *manus* we also have *man-acle, man-age, man-ciple, man-ege, mani-fest, mani-ple, mani-pul-ate, mann-er, man-œuvre, man-ure; manu-facture, manu-mit, manu-script, a-manu-ensis*; also *main-tain, e-man-cip-ate, quadru-man-ous*, &c.

MANUFACTURE, a making by hand. (F. — L.) In Bacon, Life of Henry VII, ed. Lumby, p. 58, l. 19; p. 196, l. 4. Also spelt *manifacture*, as in Cotgrave. — F. *manufacture* (also *manifacture* in Cot.), 'manifacture, workemanship;' Cot. Coined from Latin. — L. *manū*, by the hand, abl. of *manus*; and *factūra*, a making, from *facere*, to make. See **Manual** and **Fact.** Der. *manufacture*, vb., *manufactur-al, manufactur-er, manufactur-or-y*.

MANUMIT, to release a slave. (L.) 'Manumitted and set at liberty;' Stow, Edw. III, an. 1350. The pp. *manumissed* occurs in North's Plutarch, p. 85 (R.); or p. 103, ed. 1631. — L. *manūmittere* (pp. *manūmissus*), to set at liberty a slave, lit. 'to release from one's power,' or 'send away from one's hand.' — L. *manū*, abl. of *manus*, the hand; and *mittere*, to send. See **Manual** and **Missile.** Der. *manumission*, from F. *manumission*, 'a manumission or dismissing' (Cot.), from L. *manūmissionem*, acc. of *manūmissio*, a dismissal, formed like the pp. *manūmissus*.

MANURE, to enrich with a fertilising substance. (F. — L.) The old sense was simply 'to work at with the hand.' 'Arable land, which could not be *manured* [tilled] without people and families, was turned into pasture;' Bacon, Henry VII, ed. Lumby, p. 70, l. 26. 'Manured with industry;' Oth. i. 3. 328. Cf. *manure* in G. Douglas, tr. of Virgil, bk. iv. ch. 5. l. 72. See Trench, Select Glossary. *Manure* is a contracted form of *manœuvre*; see **Manœuvre** and **Inure.** Der. *manure*, sb., *manur-er, manur-ing*.

MANUSCRIPT, written by the hand. (L.) Properly an adj., but also used as a sb. 'A *manuscript*;' Minsheu, ed. 1627. — Late L. *manuscriptum*, a manuscript; L. *manū scriptum*, written by the hand. — L. *manū*, abl. of *manus*, the hand; and *scriptum*, neut. of *scriptus*, pp. of *scribere*, to write. See **Manual** and **Scribe.**

MANY, not few, numerous. (E.) ME. *mani, many, moni*, frequently followed by *a*, as 'many a man;' Chaucer, C. T. 229, 3905 (A 3907). The oldest instances of this use are in Layamon, 7993, 16189, 29131. AS. *manig, monig*, Grein, ii. 209. + Du. *menig*; Dan. *mange*; Swed. *månge*; Icel. *margr* (with a singular change from *n* to *r*); see Noreen, § 369; Goth. *manags*; G. *manch*, MHG. *manec*, OHG. *manac*. **β.** All from a Teut. type **managoz*. Further allied to Irish *minic*, Gael. *minig*, W. *mynych*, frequent, Russ. *mnogie*, pl. many.

MAP, a representation of the earth, or of a part of it. (F. — L.) The oldest maps were maps of the world, and were called *mappe-mounde*, as in Gower, C. A. iii. 102; bk. vii. 530. This is a F. form of the L. name *mappa mundī*, which occurs in Trevisa, i. 27, and in the corresponding passage of Higden's Polychronicon. **β.** The original sense of L. *mappa* was a napkin; hence, a painted cloth. According to Quinctilian, it is a Punic word. See **Napkin.**

MAPLE, the name of a tree. (E.) ME. *maple, mapul*; Chaucer, C. T. 2925 (A 2923). AS. *mapul-der*, the maple-tree; 'Acer, *mapulder*,' Voc. 138. 15; we also find *mapolder*, a maple, *Mapulder-stede*, now Maplestead (in Essex), in Thorpe's Diplomatarium Ævi Saxonici, pp. 146, 403; and Kemble has *Mapeles baruue* in his index. Hence the AS. name is *mapul, mapel*; cf. *mapel-trēow*, Birch, Cart. Saxon. i. 290. The Icel. *möpurr* is borrowed from E.

MAR, to injure, spoil, damage. (E.) ME. *merren*, less commonly *marren*, P. Ploughman's Crede, l. 66; Will. of Palerne, 664. OMerc. **merran*, in comp. *ā-merran*, to hinder; Vesp. Ps. 77. 31. Also AS. *ā-myrran*, used in various senses, such as to dissipate, waste, lose, hinder, obstruct; see Matt. x. 42, Luke, xv. 14; Ælfric's

Hom. i. 372, l. 3; Grein, i. 28, 29. Cf. also AS. *mirran*, to impede; Exod. v. 4; *gemearr*, an impediment, Ælfred, tr. of Gregory's Past Care, ed. Sweet, p. 401, ll. 17, 20.+MDu. *merren*, to stay, retard (Hexham); Du. *marren*, to tarry; OHG. *marrjan*, to hinder, disturb, vex; whence mod. F. *marri*, vexed, sad; Goth. *marzjan*, to offend, cause to stumble. Teut. type *marzjan-; base *marz-. Brugmann, i. 903 b.

MARABOU, MARABOUT, a kind of African stork; also, its downy feathers. (F.—Port.—Span.—Arab.) F. *marabout*.—Port. *marabuto* (Hatzfeld).—Span. *morabito*, a Moorish anchorite, a religious man (Pineda). The bird obtained its name from its sage-like appearance; the Indian variety is called the adjutant-bird, for a similar reason.—Arab. *murābiṭ*, quiet, still; a hermit, sage; a religious sage among the Berbers; see Devic. And see **Maravedi**.

MARANATHA, our Lord cometh. (Syriac.) In 1 Cor. xvi. 22. 'It is a Græcised form of the Aramaic words *māran athā*, our Lord cometh;' Dict. of the Bible. Cf. Arab. *mār*, lord (from Syriac).

MARASCHINO, a cordial. (Ital.—L.) It is said to have come originally from Dalmatia, where the cherries grow.—Ital. *maraschino*, an adj. form from *marasca*, *amarasca*, a kind of sour cherry (Baretti).—L. *amārus*, bitter, sour.

MARAUD, to wander in quest of plunder. (F.) 'Marauding, ranging about as soldiers in quest of plunder, forage, &c.;' Bailey's Dict. v. ii. ed. 1731.—MF. *marauder*, 'to beg, to play the rogue;' Cot.—F. *maraud*, 'a rogue, begger, vagabond, varlet, rascall;' Cot. β. The etymology is much disputed; see Scheler and Körting. Bugge suggests a Late L. form *malaldus, from L. *malus*, evil; whence *maraud* by dissimilation.

MARAVEDI, a small coin, less than a farthing. (Span.—Arab.) In Minsheu, ed. 1627.—Span. *maravedi*, the smallest Span. coin. Called in Port. both *marabitino* and *maravedim*. The name is an old one, the coin being so called because first struck during the dynasty of the Almoravides at Cordova, A.D. 1094–1144 (Haydn, Dict. of Dates, s.v. *Spain*). *Maravedi* is derived from the Arab. name of this dynasty.—Arab. *Murābiṭin*, the name of an Arab. dynasty: pl. of *murābiṭ*, a hermit, a sage; see **Marabou**. Rich. Pers. Dict. p. 1382.

MARBLE, a sort of stone. (F.—L.) Gen. called *marbreston* (=marble-stone) in ME.; afterwards shortened to *marbre*, and thence changed to *marbel* or *marble*. Spelt *marbre-ston*, Layamon, 1317 (later text); *marbelston*, P. Plowman, A. x. 101; *marbel*, Chaucer, C. T. 1895 (A 1893).—OF. *marbre*, 'marble;' Cot.—L. *marmorem*, acc. of *marmor*, marble, considered as a masc. sb.; but it is commonly neuter.+Gk. μάρμαρος, explained as a glistening white stone, whence μαρμαίρειν, to sparkle, glitter; cf. μαρμάρεος, sparkling, μαῖρα, the dog-star, lit. 'sparkler.' But named rather from its hardness; cf. μάρμαρ, explained as στερεόν, i.e. a hard body; see Prellwitz. Der. *marbl-y*; also *marble-hearted*, K. Lear, i. 4. 281, &c.

MARCASITE, a kind of iron pyrites. (F.—Span.—Arab.) 'Other metals and *marcasites*;' Evelyn's Diary, June 21, 1650.—F. *marcasite*, *marcassite*, 'the marcassite, or fire-stone;' Cot.—Span. *marquesita*, 'a stone found in the copper-mines;' Pineda.—Arab. *marqashīthā*, marcasite; Devic. And see Vüllers.

MARCESCENT, withering. (L.) Botanical. In Bailey's Dict. vol. ii. ed. 1731.—L. *marcescent-*, stem of pres. pt. of *marcescere*, inceptive form of *marcēre*, to wither, lit. to grow soft. Brugmann, i. § 413 (8).

MARCH (1), a border, frontier. (F.—OHG.) Usually in the pl. *marches*, as in Hen. V, i. 2. 140. ME. *marche*, sing., P. Plowman, B. xv. 438. AF. *marche*, Liber Albus, p. 229; Stat. Realm, i. 211.—F. *marche*, 'a march, frontire;' Cot.—OHG. *marka*, a boundary. See **Mark** (2), of which *march* is a doublet.

MARCH (2), to walk with regular steps, as a soldier. (F.—L.? or G.?) In Spenser, F. Q. v. 10. 33.—F. *marcher*, 'to march, goe, pace;' Cot. β. Of disputed origin; a good suggestion is Scheler's, who sees in it the notion of regular beating (cf. E. 'to be on the *beat*,' 'to *beat* time'), and connects it with L. *marcus*, a hammer, whence a verb *marcāre, to beat, could easily have arisen in Late L., and would well express the regular tramp of a marching host. γ. Otherwise, from F. *marche*, a frontier, from OHG. *marka*, cognate with AS. *mearc*; see **March** (1). Cotgrave has: '*Marche*, . . a march, frontire, . . . a march, marching of soldiers.' Diez cites an OF. phr. *aller de marche en marche*, to go from land to land, to make expeditions. Der. *march*, sb., K. John, ii. 60.

MARCH (3), the name of the third month. (F.—L.) ME. *March*, Chaucer, C. T. 10361 (F 47). Not from OF. and F. *mars*, but from *Marche*, the ONF. (Picard) form, also found in the dial. of Rouchi (Hécart).—L. *Martium*, acc. of *Martius*, the month of Mars, lit. belonging to Mars.—L. *Marti-*, decl. stem of *Mars*, the god of war.

MARCHIONESS, the fem. of **Marquis**, q.v.

MARCHPANE, a sweet cake, made with almonds and sugar.

(F.—Ital.—L.?) In Romeo and Jul. i. 5. 9. ME. *march payne*, in a list temp. Hen. V; Fabyan, repr. 1811, p. 587. From a dial. form (prob. Picard) of MF. *marcepain*, which occurs in 1544 (Hatzfeld); corrupted to *massepain* in F.—Ital. *marciapane*, *marzapane* (Florio). The origin of *marcia* is unknown, but it prob. represents a name, such as L. *Martia*; *pane* is from L. *pānem*, acc. of *pānis*, bread.

MARE, the female of the horse. (E.) ME. *mere*, Chaucer, C. T. 543 (A 541). AS. *mere*; we find 'equa, *mere*' in Voc. 119. 36. This is the fem. form of AS. *mearh*, a horse, Grein, ii. 238; also spelt *mearg*, *mear*.+Icel. *merr*, a mare, *mer-hross*, *mer-hryssi*, a mare-horse, used as fem. of *marr*, a steed; Dan. *mær*, a mare; Swed. *märr*, a mare; Du. *merrie*, a mare; G. *mähre*, OHG. *meriha*, a mare; fem. of OHG. *marah*, a battle-horse. β. The AS. *mearh*, Icel. *marr*, OHG. *marah*, a battle-horse, steed, are cognate with Irish and Gael. *marc*, W. and Corn. *march*, a horse, a stallion. Root uncertain. Teut. type *markoz, Idg. type *mark-os, m., a horse; whence Teut. type *marh-jōn-, f., a mare. Der. *mar-shal*, q.v. ☞ The mare in *night-mare* (q.v.) is a different word.

MARGARINE, a pearl-like substance extracted from hog's lard; and (by misapplication), a substitute for butter. (F.—L.—Gk.—Pers.) A barbarous formation from *margar-ic* (acid), a substance supposed to be present in certain fats; from *margar-*, as in *margar-et*, F. *marguerite*, lit. 'pearl.'—L. *margarīta*, pearl.—Gk. μαργαρίτης, pearl.—Pers. *murwārīd*, a pearl; Rich. Dict. p. 1396.

MARGIN, an edge, border. (L.) ME. *margin*; spelt *margyne*, P. Plowman, B. vii. 18. Trevisa (i. 41) translates L. *margines* by *margyns*.—L. *margin-*, stem of *margo*, a brink, margin, border; cognate with E. **Mark** (2), q.v. Der. *margin-al*, *margin-al-ly*, *margin-at-ed*. Doublets, *margent*, with excrescent *t*, Tyndal, Works, p. 32, col. 2; *marge*, Spenser, F. Q. iv. 8. 61, from F. *marge*; also *mark* (2).

MARGRAVE, a marquis, a lord of the marches. (Du.) 'The *maregraue*, as thei call him, of Bruges;' tr. of Sir T. More's Utopia, 1551, ed. Arber, p. 28. Cf. *meregrave* in Liber Custumarum, p. 634.—Du. *markgraaf*, a margrave.—Du. *mark*, a mark, also a march, border, border-land; and *graaf*, a count, earl.+G. *markgraf*, similarly compounded. β. For the first element, see **Mark** (2). The second element is Du. *graaf*, G. *graf*, MHG. *grāve*, OHG. *krāvjo*, *grāveo*, *grāvo*, a lord chief justice, administrator of justice, count. Of unknown origin. Franck and Kluge reject the explanations from Late L. or Celtic. Kluge dissociates it from AS. *gerēfa*, a reeve, but connects it with Goth. *ga-grēfts*, a decree (Luke, ii. 1). Franck admits association with AS. *gerēfa*; for which see **Reeve** (2). Der. *margrav-ine*, from Du. *markgravin*, where *-in* is a fem. suffix. See *marquis*.

MARIGOLD, the name of a plant. (Hybrid; Heb. *and* E.) The pl. *mary-goulden* occurs in Medical Works of the 14th cent., ed. G. Henslow, p. 81 (from MS. Harl. 2378, fol. 29). Spelt *marygould* in Levins; *marygild* in G. Douglas, Palace of Honour, Prol. st. 5. In Shak. Wint. Ta. iv. 4. 105. It bears a yellow flower, whence also the Du. name *goud-bloem* (gold-bloom), a marigold. Compounded of **Mary** and **Gold**. Chaucer has *gold* for marigold; C. T. 1931 (A 1929). The Gaelic name is *lus-mairi*, Mary's leek or plant. Flowers named from the Virgin Mary are numerous; hence our *lady's-slipper*, *lady's tresses*, &c. The name *Mary* (from F. *Marie*, L. *Maria*, Gk. Μαρία) is Hebrew, and is the same as Heb. *Miryām* or Miriam.

MARINE, belonging to the sea. (F.—L.) In Cotgrave. [The sb. *mariner* is in much earlier use, spelt *marineer*, Chaucer, C. T. 13367 (B 1627).]—F. *marin*, 'marine, of the sea;' Cot.—L. *marinus*, adj., of the sea.—L. *mare*, the sea; cognate with E. **Mere** (1). Der. *mariner*, which occurs in Floriz and Blancheflur, ed. Lumby, l. 71; from AF. *mariner*, Liber Albus, p. 381 (footnote); F. *marinier*, 'a mariner;' Cot.

MARIONETTE, a puppet. (F.—L.—Gk.—Heb.) Cotgrave has *marionnette*, 'little Marian; .. also, a puppet.' Dimin. of F. *Marion*, Marian; from *Marie*, Mary; see **Marigold**.

MARISH, a marsh. (F.—L.—Gk.—Heb.) In Ezek. xlvii. 11. Variant of ME. *mareis*, Chaucer, C. T. 6552 (D 970).—OF. *mareshe* (Godefroy); also *mareis* (Hatzfeld); Late L. type *mariscus*.—L. *mar-e*, the sea; cognate with **Mere** (1); with suffix *-iscus*. ¶ The F. *marais* is preserved in the name *Beaumaris*, in Anglesey. Doublet, *morass*.

MARITAL, belonging to a husband. (F.—L.) In Blount's Gloss., ed. 1674.—F. *marital*, 'belonging to a mariage, esp. on the husband's side;' Cot.—L. *maritālis*, adj., formed from *maritus*, a husband; see **Marry**.

MARITIME, pertaining to the sea. (F.—L.) In Shak. Ant. i. 4. 51.—F. *maritime*, 'maritime;' Cot.—L. *maritimus*, adj., formed with suffix *-timus* from *mari-*, for *mare*, the sea, cognate with E. **Mere** (1), q.v.

MARJORAM, an aromatic plant. (F.—Late L.) The former *r* is often omitted in various languages. ME. *majoran*, Gower, C. A. iii. 133; bk. vii. 1433.—OF. *majorane* (Godefroy); Late L. *majorāna* (Ducange). Cf. Ital. *majorana*, Span. *mayorana*, Port. *maiorana*, marjoram. β. Doubtfully connected with Late L. *majoraca*, marjoram, Ducange; thought to be a disfigured form of L. *a-māracus*, marjoram, with loss of initial *a*. – Gk. ἀμάρακος, marjoram.

MARK (1), a stroke, outline, trace, line, sign. (E.) ME. *merke*, Chaucer, C. T. 6201 (D 619). AS. *mearc*, fem. a mark, sign. + Du. *merk*; Icel. *mark*; Swed. *märke*; Dan. *mærke*; G. *marke*, MHG. *marc*, a mark, token. Cf. Lithuan. *margas*, marked, variegated. Prob. the same as Mark (2), which seems to be older. Der. *mark*, vb., AS. *mearcian* (Grein); *mark-er*, *mark-ing ink*; marksman, Dryden's Meleager (from Ovid, bk. viii), l. 188; also *mark-man*, Romeo, i. 1. 212.

MARK (2), a march, limit, boundary. (E.) Not common in ME., the usual form being *merche* or *marche*. ME. *merke*; as in ' *merke* of felde,' Gen. and Exodus, ed. Morris, 440. AS. *mearc*, fem. a boundary. + OSax. *marka*; Du. *mark*; G. *mark*, fem., OHG. *marcha*; Goth. *marka*, a confine, coast. So also Icel. *mörk*, f., a forest; orig. a boundary. Teut. type *markā*, f. Allied to L. *margo*, a margin; Zend *merezu*, Pers. *marz*, a border; OIrish *mruig*, a mark, province. See Mark (1). The sense of ' boundary ' suggested that of ' mark to indicate a boundary.' Doublet, *march* (1). Cf. *margin*.

MARK (3), the name of a coin. (Scand.) The Old E. *mark* was valued at 13*s*. 4*d*. ME. *mark*, Chaucer, C. T. 12324 (C 390). AS. *marc*; ' i. *marc* goldes ' = 1 marc of gold, Diplomatarium Ævi Saxon., ed. Thorpe, p. 379. – Icel. *mörk*; Dan. and Swed. *mark*, a mark + G. *mark*, a certain weight of silver, viz. 8 oz.; also a coin. β. Perhaps a particular use of Mark (1), as denoting (1) a fixed weight, and (2) a fixed value. Cf. the use of *token* to denote a coin.

MARKET, a place of merchandise. (F. – L.) In early use. ME. *market*, Old Eng. Miscellany, ed. Morris, p. 16, l. 491. Late AS. *market*, Birch, Cart. Saxon. iii. 582; l. 23. – OF. *market*, NF. variant of *marchet* (Roland, 1150), mod. F. *marché*. Cf. Walloon *markié*, Prov. *mercatz* (Bartsch), Ital. *mercato*, Span. *mercado*, a market. – L. *mercātum*, acc. of *mercātus*, traffic, trade, also a market (whence also G. *markt*, Du. *markt*, Icel. *markaðr*, &c.). – L. *mercātus*, pp. of *mercāri*, to trade. Closely connected with L. *merx*, merchandise. See Mercantile. Doublet, *mart*. Der. *market-able*, Temp. v. 266; *market-cross*, *-town*. And see *merchant*.

MARL, a rich earth. (F. – L.) ME. *marle*, *marl*, Trevisa, ii. 15; see Spec. of Eng. ed. Morris and Skeat, p. 236, ll. 25, 27. Dissyllabic in *marle-pit*, Chaucer, C. T. 3460. – OF. *marle*, *merle*, *malle*, now spelt *marne*; cf. Picard and Walloon *marle*, Gascon *merle*; and see Littré, s.v. *marne*. Cot. has the derivative *marliere*, ' a marle-pit.' – Late L. *margila*, marl; dimin. of Late L. *marga*, marl (a common word); Ducange. It occurs in Pliny, xvii. 6. 4, § 42, who considers it to be a word of Gaulish origin. ¶ The Irish and Gael. *marla*, W. *marl*, must be borrowed from E.; the G., Du., Dan., and Swed. *mergel* are from the L. *margila*. Der. *marl-y*, *marl-pit*.

MARLINE, a small cord used for binding large ropes, to protect them. (Du.) ' Some the galled ropes with dauby *marling* bind;' Dryden, Annus Mirabilis, st. 148. – Du. *marling*, *marlijn*, a marline; also called *marlreep* (corruption of *marreep*). So called from its use in binding ropes. – Du. *marren*, to tie (MDu. *marren*, *maren*, ' to bynde, or to tye knots,' Hexham); and *lijn* (corruptly *ling*), a line, borrowed from F. *ligne*, L. *linea*, a line. Similarly *mar-reep*, from *reep*, a rope. The MDu. *maren* = E. *moor*, in the expression ' to moor a ship.' See Moor (2) and Line. Der. *marline-spike*.

MARMALADE, a jam or conserve, gen. made of oranges, but formerly of quinces. (F. – Port. – L. – Gk.) ' *Marmalet*, Marmelade, a kind of confection made of quinces, or other fruit;' Phillips. Spelt *marmalat*, *marmalet* in Levins; *marmelet* in Baret; *marmelad* in Tyndall, Works, p. 229, col. 2. – MF. *mermelade*, ' marmelade;' Cot. Mod. F. *marmelade*. – Port. *marmelada*, marmelade; orig. made of quinces. Formed with suffix *-ada* (like that of a fem. pp.) from *marmel-o*, a quince; thus the sense is ' made of quince.' – L. *melimēlum*, lit. a honey-apple, sometimes applied to the quince, as shown by the allied word *melomeli*, the syrup of preserved quinces. – Gk. μελίμηλον, a sweet apple, an apple grafted on a quince; cf. μηλόμελι, honey flavoured with quince. – Gk. μέλι-, honey, cognate with L. *mel*, honey; and μῆλον, an apple. See Mellifluous and Melon.

MARMOSET, a small variety of American monkey. (F. – L.) Formerly applied to a different animal, as the word is older than Columbus. ME. *marmosette*, *marmozette*. ' Apes, *marmozettes*, babewynes [baboons], and many other dyverse bestes;' Mandeville's Travels, ed. Halliwell (1866), p. 210; see Wright's note to Temp. ii. 2. – F. *marmouset* (OF. *marmoset*), ' the cock of a cestern or fountaine, made like a woman's dug; any antick image, from whose teats water trilleth; any puppet, or antick; any such foolish or odd representation; also, the minion, favorite, or flatterer of a prince;' Cot. It would seem that the word was applied to some kind of ape because of its grotesque antics. β. The origin of OF. *marmoset* (Cotgrave) looks uncertain; and Scheler's statement that the Late L. *vicus mar-*

morētōrum occurs as a translation of F. *rue des Marmousets* turns out to be a mistake; as the L. form is *marmosētōrum*. γ. At the same time, it is perfectly clear that one reason for the use of this particular word as meaning a kind of ape was due to a connexion with the F. word *marmot* (not to be confused with E. *marmot*, which may be a different word). Cotgrave has: ' *Marmot*, a marmoset, or little monky;' also: ' *Marmotte*, a she marmoset, or she monky.' The etym. of this F. *marmot* is uncertain; the most likely explanation is Scheler's; he takes it to be a dimin. with suffix *-ot* from OF. *merme*, little, tiny, lit. very small. This OF. *merme* is a curious derivative of L. *minimus* (like OF. *arme* from L. *animus*); see Minim. This gives to F. *marmot* the sense of ' dear little creature,' and accounts for the mod. use in the senses of ' puppet' and ' little child' (Hamilton); cf. Ital. *marmotta*, ' a marmoset, a babie for a childe to play withall, a pugge;' Florio. Körting, § 1678.

MARMOT, a mountain-rat, a rodent animal. (F. – Rom. – L.) Sometimes introduced into Eng. from Ital. Ray speaks of ' the *Marmotto* or *mus Alpinus*, a creature as big [as] or bigger than a rabbet;' On the Creation, pt. ii (R.). ' *Marmotto*, a mountain-rat;' Kersey, ed. 1715. Also Englished from F. *marmotte*; cf. Ital. *marmotta*, ' a marmotte;' Baretti; substituted for *marmotana*, ' the mountain-rat, a marmotan;' Torriano. [Cf. OF. *marmotaine*, *marmotan*, ' the Alpine mouse, or mountain-rat;' Cot.] – Romansch (Grisons) *murmont*; cf. OHG. *murmunti*, *muremunto*, a marmot. – L. *mūr-*, for *mūs*, a mouse, and *montis*, gen. of *mons*, a mountain. Thus the sense is ' mountain-mouse.' See Mountain and Mouse. ¶ So in Diez. But Körting (§ 6387) rejects this etymology, and proposes to refer *marmotte* to OF. *merme*, very small, from L. *minimus*; cf. Romania, xxiii. 237, and see Marmoset.

MAROON (1), brownish-crimson. (F. – Ital.) Not in Todd's Johnson. ' *Marones* or great chesnuts;' Passenger of Benvenuto (1612). Lit. ' chesnut-coloured.' – F. *marron*, ' the great chestnut;' Cot. – Ital. *marrone*; Florio gives the pl. as *marroni*, *maroni*, ' a kind of greater chestnuts then any we haue.' Of unknown origin; Diez suggests a connexion with the L. name *Maro*. Cf. late Gk. μάραον, the fruit of the cornel-tree, in Eustathius (12th cent.).

MAROON (2), to put ashore on a desolate island. (F. – Span. – L. – Gk.) It occurs in Scott, The Pirate, c. xli. Dampier has: ' I was . . . *marooned* or lost;' Voy. (1699); v. ii. pt. 2. p. 84; cf. p. 95. And see *Maroons* in Haydn, Dict. of Dates. – F. *marron*, adj., an epithet applied to a fugitive slave; *nègre marron*, a fugitive slave who takes to the woods and mountains (Littré); hence the E. verb *to maroon* = to cause to live in a wild country, like a fugitive slave. See Scheler, who points out that the F. word is a clipt form of Span. *cimarron*, wild, unruly; hence, savage. Of unknown origin. β. Some have connected it with Span. *cima*, a mountain-summit. Cf. Ital. and Port. *cima*, F. *cime*, a mountain-top; according to Diez, the OSpan. *cima* also meant a twig, sprout; from L. *cȳma*, a young sprout of a cabbage. – Gk. κῦμα, anything swollen, a wave, young sprout. ¶ Mr. Wedgwood says that ' the fugitive negroes are mentioned under the name of *symarons* in Hawkins' Voyage, § 68, where they are said to be settled near Panama.' He also cites the following: ' I was in the Spanish service, some twenty years ago in the interior of Cuba, and *negro cimarrón* or briefly *cimarrón*, was then an every-day phrase for fugitive or outlawed negroes hidden in the woods and mountains;' Notes and Queries, Jan. 27, 1866. Verified by Granada's Vocab. Rioplatense, which has *cimarron*, adj., belonging to the hills, said of animals and plants; applied in Span. to slaves.

MARQUE, LETTERS OF, letters authorising reprisals. (F. – Prov. – G.) The old sense of *letter of marque* was a letter signed by a king or prince authorising his subjects to make reprisals on another country, when they could not otherwise get redress. It is now only used in naval affairs, to show that a ship is not a pirate or a corsair. Palsgrave has: ' I sende forthe a *letter of marke*,' &c. ' *Law of Marque*, or [corruptly] *Mart*; this word is used 27 Edw. III, stat. 2. c. 17, and grows from the German word *march* [which, however, is the *English* form of the word], i. e. *limes*, a bound or limit. And the reason of this appellation is because they that are driven to this law of reprizal, take the goods of that people (of whom they have received wrong and can get no ordinary justice) when they catch them within their own territories or precincts;' Blount's Gloss., ed. 1674. ' *Marque* . . . signifies in the ancient statutes of our land as much as reprisals; as An. 4 Hen. V, c. 7, *Marques* and *Reprisals* are used as synonima; and *letters of marque* are found in the same signification in the same chapter;' id. See also Ducange, s.v. *Marcha*. In one instance, cited by Wedgwood and Littré, the OF. *marquer* seems to mean ' to pillage,' the lit. sense being ' to catch within one's borders.' Littré also shows that the spelling *marche* was used in the same sense as *marque*, in this connexion; it would hence appear that *marque* is lit. a border, and hence a catching within one's borders, as explained by Blount above. – OF. *marque*, properly a boundary;

explained by Cot. as 'a distresse, arrest, or seisure of body or goods.' He also gives: '*Droict de Marque*, power to arrest the body, and seize the goods of another; granted by the king, and in old time given by the parliament, against a stranger or forreiner.' — Prov. *marca* (mod. *marco*), verbal sb. from *marcar*, to seize by way of reprisal (Hatzfeld); cf. also Prov. *marca*, a mark. — MHG. *marke*, OHG. *marcha*, a march, boundary, border. See **March** (1) and **Mark** (2). ☞ The corrupt form *letters of mart* occurs in Beaum. and Fletcher, Wife for a Month, ii. 1 (Tony).

MARQUEE, a large field-tent. (F. — G.) Modern; not in Todd's Johnson. This is one of the words in which a final *s* has been cut off, from a false idea that *marquees* is a plural form; so also we have *sherry* for *sherris*, *pea* for *pease*, and '*Chinee*' for Chinese, &c. *Marquees* is nothing but an E. spelling of F. *marquise*, an officer's tent, large tent, marquee. β. Littré says that *marquise*, a tent, a little elegant construction, was no doubt so named from *marquise*, a marchioness, or lady of rank who was to be protected from the inclemency of the weather. That is, it is short for ' tent of the marchioness.' The F. *marquise* is the fem. of *marquis*, a marquis; see **Marquis**.

MARQUETRY, inlaid work. (F. — MHG.) In Sir T. Herbert's Travels, ed. 1665, p. 146. — F. *marqueterie*, 'inlaied work of sundry colours;' Cot. — F. *marqueter*, 'to inlay, to diversifie, flourish, or work all over with small pieces of sundry colours, also, to spot ;' id. Lit. 'to mark slightly, or with spots;' iterative form of *marquer*, to mark. — F. *marque*, a mark. — MHG. *mark*, G. *marke*, a mark, token ; cognate with E. *mark*; see **Mark** (1).

MARQUIS, a title of nobility. (F. — Low L. — G.) ME. *markis*, *marquis*; Chaucer, C. T. 7940, 8473 (E 64, 597). — OF. *marchis* (Hatzfeld), later *marquis*, 'a marquesse, in old time the governour of a frontire, or frontire town ;' Cot. Cf. Prov. and Span. *marques*, Port. *marquez*, Ital. *marchese*. — Low L. *marchensis*, a prefect of the marches. — Low L. *marcha*, a march, boundary. — OHG. *marcha*, a march, boundary; see **March** (1) and **Mark** (2). ¶ The true OF. form was *marchis*; altered to *markis* by the influence of Ital. *marchese* (with *ch* as *k*); Hatzfeld. Der. *marquis-ate*, in Minsheu; also *marchioness* = Low L. *marchiōnissa*, formed with fem. suffix -*issa* (= Gk. -ισσα) from Low L. *marchiōn-em*, acc. of *marchio*, a prefect of the marches, which is a variant of *marchensis*. Also *marquee*, q. v. **Doublet**, *marquess*, Merch. Ven. i. 2. 125, from Span. *marques*; cf. *margrave*, q. v.

MARROW (1), pith, soft matter within bones. (E.) ME. *marow*, *marwhe*, *marughe* (with one *r*), Prompt. Parv. p. 326. More commonly *mary*, Chaucer, C. T. 12476 (C 542). AS. *mearh*, marrow, dat. *mearge*, Voc. 159. 32. OMerc. *merg*, dat. *merge*, Corpus gloss. 1308.+Du. *merg*, marrow, pith; Icel. *mergr*, marrow; Swed. *merg*; Dan. *marv*; G. *mark*, OHG. *marag*, marrow. Teut. types *mazgom, n., *mazgoz*, m. Further allied to Russ.-*mozg'*, marrow; Zend *mazga*-, Pers. *maghz*; and Skt. *majjan* (for *masjan), marrow of bones, pith or sap of trees. Root unknown. ¶ The Gael. *smior*, marrow, strength, Irish *smear*, grease, W. *mer*, marrow, do not belong here, but are related to E. *smear*. **Der.** *marrow-bone*, ME. *mary-bone*, Chaucer, C. T. 382.

MARROW (2), a companion, partner. (Scand.) ME. *marwe*, 'socius;' Prompt. Parv. — Icel. *margr*, (1) many; (2) friendly; see Vigfusson. Cognate with E. *many*; see **Many**.

MARRY, to take for a husband or wife. (F. — L.) Properly 'to provide with a husband.' ME. *marien* (with one *r*), Rob. of Glouc. p. 30, l. 700. — F. *marier*, to marry. — L. *marītāre*, (1) to give a woman in marriage, (2) to take a woman in marriage. — L. *marītus*, a husband; the fem. *marīta* means lit. provided with a husband, or joined to a male. — L. *mari*-, for *mās*, a male. See **Male**. D:r. *marri-age*, ME. *mariage* (with one *r*), Rob. of Glouc. p. 31, l. 726, from F. *mariage*, which from Late L. *marītāticum*, a woman's dowry, in use A. D. 1062, later *marītāgium* (Ducange); *marriage-able*, *marriage-able-ness*. And see *marital*.

MARSALA, a wine. (Ital.) From *Marsala*, a town on the W. coast of Sicily.

MARSH, a morass, swamp, fen. (E.) ME. *mersche*, Wyclif, Gen. xli. 18 (earlier text). AS. *mersc*, a marsh; Grein, ii. 234. [The change from *sc* to *sh* is usual and regular.] *Mersc* is a contraction of *mer-isc*, orig. an adj. signifying full of meres or pools (= mere-ish); Teut. type **mar-isk-*; formed with suffix -*isc* (-*ish*) from Teut. *mari-, AS. *mere*, a mere, pool, lake; see **Mere**.+Low G. *marsch*, Bremen Wörterbuch, iii. 133. **Der.** *marsh-y*, *marsh-i-ness*.

MARSHAL, a master of the horse; variously applied as a title of honour. (F. — OHG.) The orig. sense is ' horse-servant,' a farrier or groom; it rose to be a title of honour, like *constable*, q. v. ME. *mareschal*, Rob. of Glouc. p. 491, l. 10081; *marschal*, P. Plowman, B. iii. 200. — OF. *mareschal* (mod. F. *maréchal*), 'a marshall of a kingdom or of a camp (an honourable place), also, a blacksmith, farrier ;' Cot. — OHG. *maraschalh* (MHG. *marshalc*, G. *marschall*),

an attendant upon a horse, groom, farrier. — OHG. *marah*, a battle-horse, whence the fem. *meriha*, a mare, cognate with E. **Mare**, q.v.; and *schalh*, MHG. *shalc*, a servant, whence G. *schalk*, a knave, a rogue (by a change of sense parallel to that of E. *knave*). β. The latter element is cognate with AS. *scealc*, a servant, man (Grein), Du. *schalk*, a knave, Icel. *skǫlkr*, a servant, knave, rogue, Swed. *skalk*, a rogue; the oldest form and sense being preserved in Goth. *skalks*, a servant, Mat. viii. 9. **Der.** *marshal*, vb., Macb. ii. 1. 42, the sense being 'to act as marshal,' it being orig. a part of his duty to arrange for tournaments and to direct ceremonies; *marshall-er*, *marshal-ship*. ☞ The syllable -*shal* occurs also in *sene-schal*, q. v.

MARSUPIAL, belonging to a certain family of animals. (L. — Gk.) Modern. Applied to such animals as have a pouch in which to carry their young. — L. *marsūpium*, a pouch. — Gk. μαρσύπιον, μαρσίπιον, a little pouch; dimin. of μάρσυπος, μάρσιπος, a bag, pouch (Xenophon, Anab. 4. 3. 11).

MART, a contracted form of **Market**, q. v. In Hamlet, i. 1. 74.

MARTELLO TOWER, a circular fort on the S. coast of England. (Ital. — L. — Pers.) ' The English borrowed the name of the tower from Corsica in 1794;' Webster. More correctly *Mortella*, because the fort taken in 1794 by the English was situate in *Mortella* bay, Corsica (Davies). The Ital. *mortella* means a myrtle. ¶ Some have thought that these towers were called *torri di martello* because the watchmen gave the alarm by striking the bell with a hammer; Sir G. C. Lewis, Letters, 1862, p. 419 (see quot. in Davies, Suppl. Glossary). Torriano has *sonare le campane a martello*, to sound the bells with a hammer, to give an alarm ; and see Ariosto's Orlando, x. 51 ; xiv. 100. Hence the mistaken spelling. Cf. N. and Q. 10 S. iii. 193. See **Myrtle**.

MARTEN, a kind of weasel. (F. — Low L. — Teut.) α. *Marten* is a contraction of the older form *martern*, in Harrison's Description of England, b. ii, c. 19, ed. Furnivall, p. 310, and in Palsgrave; ME. *martryn*, properly 'marten's fur,' used by Lydgate (Halliwell's Dict.). β. Again, *martrin* an adj. form; from OF. *martrin*, adj., belonging to the marten (Godefroy); cf. OF. *martrine*, f., marten's fur. The E. sb. is *marter* or *martre*; it is spelt *martre* in Caxton, tr. of Reynard the Fox, ed. Arber, p. 112, l. 18.— F. *martre* (also *marte*), 'a martin,' Cot.; spelt *martre* in the 11th cent. (Littré). Cf. Ital. *martora*, Span. *marta*, Low L. *marturis, of which Ducange gives the pl. *martures*, as being a common word; also *martalus* (with the common change of *l* for *r*).— Teut. type *marþ-uz, a marten; cf. MHG. and G. *marder* ; Du. *marter*; AS. *meard*, a marten, Orosius, i. 1; see Sweet's A. S. Reader; Icel. *mǫrðr* (gen. *marðar*); Swed. *mård*; Dan. *maar* (for *maard). Root unknown. ¶ 1. The supposed L. *martes*, a marten, is due to a doubtful reading in Martial, 10. 37. 18, and cannot be relied on. It is curious that the AS. name was lost, and replaced by the F. one; but many terms of the chase are Norman.

MARTIAL, warlike, brave. (F. — L.) In Shak. Hen. V, iv. 8. 46 ; Lydgate, Minor Poems, p. 5.— F. *martial*, 'martiall;' Cot.— L. *Martiālis*, dedicated to Mars.— L. *Marti*-, decl. stem of *Mars*, the god of war; see **March** (3). **Der.** *martial-ly*; also *martial-ist* (obsolete), Two Noble Kinsmen, i. 2. 16.

MARTIN, a bird of the swallow kind. (F.) In Minsheu, ed. 1627, the name of the bird is given as *martin*, *marten*, *martinet*, and *martelet*. Palsgrave has *martynet*. Of these forms, *marten* is corrupt; and *martinet*, *martelet* are dimin. forms, for which see **Martlet**.— F. *martin*, (1) a proper name, Martin, (2) the same name applied to various birds and animals (Scheler); thus *martin-pêcheur* is a king-fisher (Hamilton), and *oiseau de S. Martin* is ' the ring-taile or hen-harm,' Cot.; whilst the MF. name for the martin was *martinet*; Cot. A note to Dunbar's Poems (S. T. S.), ii. 223, says that the hen harrier was called in F. *oiseau de Saint-Martin* because it traverses France about Nov. 11 (St. Martin's day). **Der.** *mart-let*, q. v. Also (from the name *Martin*) *Martin-mas* or (corruptly) *Martle-mas*, 2 Hen. IV, ii. 2. 110 ; *martin-et*, q. v.

MARTINET, a strict disciplinarian. (F.) ' You *martinet* rogue ;' Wycherley, Plain Dealer (1677), A. iii. sc. 1. ' So called from an officer of that name, whom Voltaire describes as the regulator of the French infantry under Louis XIV' (A. D. 1643-1715) ; Todd's Johnson. See Sir S. D. Scott, The British Army, iii. 302. The name is a dimin. of the name *Martin*; see **Martin**.

MARTINGALE, **MARTINGAL**, a strap fastened to a horse's girth to hold his head down; in ships, a short spar under the bowsprit. (F. — Prov.) The ship's *martingale* is named from its resemblance, in situation, to the horse's. The word, spelt *martingal*, is given in Johnson only with respect to the horse. Minsheu, ed. 1627, speaks of 'a *martingale* for a horse's taile ;' the word also occurs in Cotgrave. — F. *martingale*, 'a martingale for a horse;' Cot. He also gives: ' *a la martingale*, absurdly, foolishly, untowardly, . . . in the homeliest manner.' β. See the account in Littré, who shows that the term arose from an oddly made kind of breeches, called *chausses à la martingale*, a phrase used by Rabelais. Cf. Span. *martingal*, an old kind of breeches; Ital. *martingala*, an old kind of hose. γ. The explanation of Ménage is accepted by Littré and Scheler. He says the breeches were named after the *Martigaux* (pl. of *Martigal*), who were the inhabitants of a place called *Martigues* in Provence (S. of France). See Mistral, who gives Prov. *martingalo*, *martegalo*, a martingale (both for horse and ship). ‒ Prov. *Martingau*, *Martezau*, an inhabitant of Martegue. ‒ Prov. *Martegue*, *Martigue*, near the mouths of the Rhone; said to be named from St. Martha, who was supposed to be buried at Tarascon.

MARTINMAS, MARTLEMAS, the feast of St. Martin; Nov. 11. (Hybrid; F. *and* L.) Palsgrave has *Martylmas*. The corruption to *Martlemas* (2 Hen. IV, ii. 2. 110) is due to the easy change of *n* to *l*; see **Lilac.** ME. *Martynmesse*, Rob. of Brunne, tr. of Langtoft, p. 230, l. 1. Compounded of the F. proper name *Martin*; and ME. *messe* = AS. *mæsse*, from L. *missa*, a mass. See **Martin** and **Mass** (2).

MARTLET (1), a kind of bird, a martin. (F.) In Levins; and in Shak. Merch. Ven. ii. 9. 28. *Martinet* in Baret (1580). A corruption of the older name *martnet* or *martinet* by the same change of *n* to *l* as is seen in *Martlemas* for *Martinmas*. ‘*Martnet*, *martenet*, byrd;’ Prompt. Parv. p. 327. ‒ F. *martinet*, ‘a martlet or martin;’ Cot. Picard *martinet*, a martin; also *martelot*, in the department of la Meuse (Corblet). Dimin. of F. *martin*, a martin; with suffix *-et*. See **Martin.**

MARTLET (2), a swift; in heraldry. (F.‒L.) The name was orig. *merlette*, altered to *martlet* by confusion with *martlet* (1), which meant ‘a martin,’ a bird closely allied to the swift. The alteration was earlier than Cotgrave’s time, as he gives F. *merlette*, f., ‘a martlet, in blason.’ But the true sense of *merlette* was ‘a little blackbird.’ ‒ F. *merle*, blackbird. ‒ L. *merula*; see **Merle.** ¶ We find OF. *merlos*, pl. of *merlot*, in the sense of ‘martlets’ or swifts, in the Roll of Caerlaverock (1300), p. 7. See Notes on E. Etym., p. 179.

MARTYR, one who suffers for his belief. (L.‒Gk.) Lit. ‘a witness’ to the truth. ME. *martir*, O. Eng. Homilies, ed. Morris, ii. 185, l. 10. AS. *martyr*, Ælfred, tr. of Beda, lib. i. c. 7. ‒ L. *martyr*. ‒ Gk. μάρτυρ, μάρτυς, a witness; lit. one who remembers, records, or declares. Cf. Skt. *smṛ*, to remember, desire, record, declare. ‒ √SMER, to remember; whence also E. *memory*, Gk. μέριμνα, care, &c. **Der.** *martyr-dom*, AS. *martyr-dōm*; also *martyro-logy*, from Gk. μάρτυρο-, decl. stem of μάρτυς, with the common suffix *-logy* of Gk. origin, from λέγειν, to speak; *martyro-log-ist*.

MARVEL, a wonder. (F.‒L.) ME. *mervaile*; King Alisaunder, l. 218. ‒ F. *merveille*, ‘a marvell;’ Cot. [Cf. Span. *maravilla*, Ital. *maraviglia*, Port. *maravilha*.] ‒ L. *mīrābilia*, neut. pl., wonderful things; according to the common confusion in Late L. between the fem. and neut. pl.; from the adj. *mīrābilis*, wonderful. ‒ L. *mīrārī*, to wonder at. ‒ L. *mīrus*, wonderful; formed with suffix *-rus* from the base *mī-*, later form of *smi-*. See **Miracle. Der.** *marvell-ous*, ME. *meruailous*, Rob. of Brunne, tr. of Langtoft, p. 174, l. 20; *marvell-ous-ly*, *marvell-ous-ness*; also *marvel*, vb., ME. *meruailen*, *merueillen*, P. Plowman, B. xi. 342.

MASCLE, in heraldry; a perforated lozenge. (F.‒L.) An erroneous spelling of OF. *macle*. ‒ OF. *macle*, a mascle, or lozenge-shaped plate of steel, used in making scale-armour (Godefroy); MF. (and F.) *macle*, ‘the mash [mesh] of a net; also, in blazon, a *mascle*, or short lozenge, having a square hole in the middest;’ Cot. ‒ L. *macula*, a mesh; whence also **Mail** (1), q. v. Perhaps confused with OHG. *masca*, a mesh. Doublet, *mail* (1). See Notes on E. Etym., p. 181.

MASCULINE, male. (F.‒L.) ME. *masculin*, Chaucer, tr. of Boethius, b. ii. pr. 3. l. 28. ‒ F. *masculin*, ‘masculine;’ Cot. ‒ L. *masculīnus*, lengthened from *masculus*, male; see **Male. Der.** *masculine-ly*, *masculine-ness*.

MASH, to beat into a mixed mass. (E.) The old sense was ‘to mix.’ ‘To *masche*, miscere;’ Levins, 35. 10. ‘*Maschyn*, yn brewynge, misceo; *Maschynge*, mixtura, mixtio;’ Prompt. Parv. Also ME. *mēshen*, to mash; Owl and Nightingale, 84; as if from AS. *mǣscan, from *māsc, sb. To *mash* is, in particular, to steep malt; the tub into which the refuse grains are put is called the *mash-tub*, whence pigs are fed. A *mash* for horses is a mixture of malt and bran. Cf. Lowland Scotch *mask-fat*, a vat for brewing; *masking-fat*, a mashing-vat; *masking-pat*, a tea-pot, lit. a pot for steeping or infusing tea (see Burns, When Guildford good our pilot steed, st. 1). See Halliwell and Jamieson. Apparently E.; cf. AS. *māx-wyrt* (for *māsc-wyrt), wort, new beer, Cockayne’s Leechdoms, ii. 87, 97, 107. Here *māx* stands for *māsc*, as usual, whence Sc. *mask*, E. *mash*; the sense of *māsc* was probably a mixture, esp. brewers’ grains. + Swed. dial. *mask*, brewers’ grains (Rietz), Swed. *mäsk*, grains; Swed. *mäska*, to mash; Dan. *mask*, a mash; whence *mask-kar*, a mashing-tub; *mæske*, to mash, to fatten pigs (with grains); North Friesic *mǎsk*,

grains, draff (Outzen); Norw. *meisk*, sb., *meiska*, vb.; G. *meisch*, a mash (of distillers and brewers); whence *meischfass*, a mash-vat, *meischen*, to mash, mix. β. Thus the verb to *mash* is due to the sb. *mash* (from AS. *māsc-*, with vowel-shortening), meaning ‘a mixture;’ and it is probable that the base **māsc-* (Teut. **maisk-*) is allied by gradation to *misc-*, as in AS. *miscian*, to mix; see **Mix.** The Irish *masgaim*, I infuse, mash malt, Gael. *masg*, to mix, infuse, steep, are borrowed from E. But Irish *measgaim*, I mix, Gael. *measg*, to mix, W. *mysgu*, to mix, as well as Lithuan. *maiszyti*, to stir things in a pot, from *miszti*, to mix (Nesselmann), are cognate. ¶ Unconnected with OF. *mascher*, F. *mâcher*, which is merely L. *masticāre*, to chew.

MASK, MASQUE, a disguise for the face; a masked entertainment. (F.‒Span.‒Arab.) It is usual to write *mask* in the sense of visor, and *masque* in the sense of masquerade; there is no reason for this distinction. Perhaps we may call *mask* the E., and *masque* the F. spelling. No doubt it is, and long has been, gen. supposed that the entertainment takes its name from the visor, according to the F. usage; but it is remarkable that the sense of entertainment is an old one, the use of the visor being accidental. The sense of entertainment is a common one in old authors. ‘A jolly company In maner of a *maske*;’ Spenser, F. Q. iii. 12. 5. ‘The whiles the *maskers* marched forth in trim array;’ id. iii. 12. 6. ‘Some haue I sene ere this, full boldlye come daunce in a *maske*, whose dauncing became theym so well, that yf theyr vysours had beene of [off] theyr faces, shame woulde not haue suffred theym to set forth a foote;’ Sir T. More, Works, p. 1039 e. ‘Cause them to be deprehended and taken and their *maskers* taken of [off] and theyr hipocrisie to be dyscouered;’ id. p. 758 b. Note here the use of *maskers* in the sense of *masks*; it is not a mistake, but correct according to the Span. spelling, as will appear. ‒ F. *masque*, ‘a mask, a visor;’ Cot. β. This F. *masque* is probably due to the Late L. *masca*, a mask, or a spectre, in the Corpus Glossary, l. 1275. But we must further consider the fuller forms evidenced by MF. *masquarizé*, ‘masked,’ Cot.; as well as by *masquerie*, *masquerade*, *mascarade*, ‘a mask or mummery.’ γ. The last form, *mascarade*, is plainly borrowed from Span. *mascarada*, a masquerade, assembly of maskers, from *mascara*, a masker, masquerader, also a mask. Cf. Ital. *mascherata*, a masquerade; *mascherare*, to mask, *maschera*, a mask; so that Sir T. More’s use of *masker* = mask, is fully accounted for. ‒ Arab. *maskharat*, ‘a buffoon, a fool, jester, a droll, a wag, a man in masquerade; a pleasantry, anything ridiculous or mirthful, sport; Pers. *maskharah kardan*, to ridicule or deride, to play the buffoon;’ Rich. Pers. Dict. p. 1416. ‒ Arab. root *sakhira*, he ridiculed; id. p. 815. ¶ Both sources seem real; as M. Devic remarks, in the Supplement to Littré, it is needless to give all the details in full by which the latter etymology can be proved. It is sufficient to refer to Dozy, Glossaire des Mots Espagnols tirés de l’Arabe. **Der.** *mask-er*; also *masquer-ade*, explained above; whence *masquerad-er*.

MASON, a worker in stone. (F.‒Late L.‒G.?) In early use. ME. *mason*, King Alisaunder, l. 2370; spelt *mascun*, Floriz and Blauncheflor, l. 326. ‒ OF. *maçon*, *masson* (F. *maçon*), ‘a mason;’ Cot. ‒ Late L. *maciōnem*, acc. of *macio*, a mason; we find also the forms *machio*, *macho*, *maco*, and even *marcio*, *mactio*, *matio*, *mattio*. β. The difficulty is to tell the true Low Lat. form; *marcio* is probably wrong, and *mactio* may be a misreading of *mattio*. If we take *matio* or *mattio* as the standard form, we may perhaps suppose *machio*, *macho*, *macio*, *maco* to come from it; the difficulty of distinguishing between *c* and *t* in MSS. is often very great. γ. *Mattio* may be referred to a Teut. stem **matjon-*, m., i.e. a cutter, from a base **mat-*, to hack, or cut; whence possibly E. *mat-tock*. Cf. OHG. *mezzo*, a mason, G. *steinmetz*, a stonemason. **Der.** *mason-ic*; also *mason-ry*, Rom. of the Rose, l. 302, from F. *maçonnerie*, from the verb *maçonner*, to do mason’s work.

MASQUE, MASQUERADE; see **Mask.**

MASS (1), a lump of matter, quantity, size. (F.‒L.‒Gk.) ME. *masse*, Prompt. Parv. ‒ F. *masse*, ‘a masse, lump;’ Cot. ‒ L. *massa*, a mass. (Prob. not a true L. word, but taken from Gk.) ‒ Gk. μᾶζα, a barley-cake, closely allied to μάγμα, any kneaded mass. ‒ Gk. μάσσειν (for *μάκ-γειν), to knead. Cf. Lith. *minkyti*, to knead. **Der.** *mass*, vb.; *mass-ive*, from F. *massif*, ‘massive,’ Cot.; *mass-ive-ly*, *mass-ive-ness*; also *mass-y* (an older adj., with E. suffix *-y* = AS. *-ig*), Spenser, F. Q. iii. 11. 47; *mass-i-ness*.

MASS (2), the celebration of the Eucharist. (L.) ME. *messe*, *masse*, P. Plowman, B. v. 418, C. viii. 27; Chaucer has *masse-peny*, C. T. 7331 (D 1749). Spelt *messe* in Havelok, 188. [Not from F. *messe*, but directly from L.] OMerc. *messe*, Matt. viii. 4; AS. *mæsse*, (1) the mass, (2) a church-festival, Grein, ii. 226; Ælfred, tr. of Beda, b. iv. c. 22, ed. Whelock, p. 319. ‒ Late L. *missa*, (1) dismissal, (2) the mass; see Ducange. β. The name is usually accounted for by supposing that the allusion is to the words *ite*, *missa est* (go, the congregation is dismissed), which were used at the conclusion of the service. 'Come I to *ite, missa est*, I holde me yserued' = If I come in time to hear the last words of the service, it suffices for me; P. Plowman, B. v. 419. Wedgwood suggests that it meant rather the dismissal of the catechumens who were not allowed to remain during the celebration of the eucharist; for which he cites the following passage from Papias: '*Missa tempore sacrificii est quando catecumeni foras mittuntur, clamante leuita* [the deacon], *Si quis catecumenus remansit, exeat foras; et inde missa, quia sacramentis altaris interesse non possunt, quia nondum regenerati sunt.*' **γ.** It matters little; for we may be sure that *missa* is, in any case, derived from L. *missa*, fem. of *missus*, pp. of *mittere*, to send, send away; see **Missile**. ¶ The change of vowel from L. *i* to AS. *æ* is remarkable, but we find a similar change in Icel. *messa*, Swed. *messa*, Dan. *messe*; and still more clearly in G. *messe* from OHG. *messa* and *missa*; also in OF. *messe*, Ital. *messa*. (All these words are, of course, borrowed from Romanic, which substitutes *e* for L. short *i*; cf. F. *vert* from L. *uiridem*.) **Der.** *Candle-mas, Christ-mas, Hallow-mas, Lam-mas, Martin-mas, Michael-mas*; q.v.

MASSACRE, indiscriminate slaughter, carnage. (F.—O. Low G.?) Pronounced *massácre* in Spenser, F. Q. iii. 11. 29; he also has *massácred*, id. iii. 3. 35.—F. *massacre*, 'a massacre;' Cot. Also *massacrer*, 'to massacre;' id. The OF. sb. is *maçacre, machacre* (Godefroy). **β.** Of disputed origin; perhaps extended from Low G. *matsken*, to cut, to hew (Bremen Wörterb. iii. 137), Du. *matsen*, to maul, to kill. Cf. G. *metzeln*, an extension of *metzen*, to cut, to kill (Flügel); G. *metzelei*, a massacre, butchery, slaughter; see **Mason**. ¶ The F. word is one of much difficulty; the above solution is very doubtful. See Norm. dial. *machacre*, a massacre (Moisy), allied to ONF. *macheclier*, a butcher (Wace); cf. Late L. *macellārius*, a butcher (Ducange), from L. *macellum*, shambles, meat-market. Cf. also OF. *maceclier, macheclier, macacrier, macecrier*, &c., a butcher (Godefroy). This seems to lead to a right solution, though the forms are abnormal.

MAST (1), a pole to sustain the sails of a ship. (E.) ME. *mast*, Chaucer, C. T. 3264. AS. *mæst*, the stem of a tree, bough, mast of a ship; Grein, ii. 226 (whence Icel. *mastr* was prob. borrowed).+Du. *mast*; Swed. and Dan. *mast*; G. *mast*. Prob. cognate with L. *mālus* (<*mazdos*), a mast; Brugmann, i. § 587. **Der.** *mast-less, dis-mast*.

MAST (2), the fruit of beech and forest trees. (E.) The orig. sense is 'edible fruit,' with reference to the feeding of swine. ME. *mast*. 'They eten *mast*;' Chaucer, Ætas Prima, l. 7. AS. *mæst*; '*þrim hund swīna mæst*' = mast for three hundred swine; Thorpe, Diplomatarium Ævi Saxonici, p. 70.+G. *mast*, (1) mast, (2) stall-feeding, fattening; whence *mästen*, to fatten. **β.** Doubtless allied to Skt. *mēdas*, sb., fat; see Brugmann, i. § 698.

MASTER, a superior, lord, teacher. (F.—L.) In early use. ME. *maister, meister*, spelt *meister*, O. Eng. Homilies, ed. Morris, i. 41, l. 29.—OF. *maistre, meistre*; mod. F. *maître*, a master.—L. *magistrum*, acc. of *magister*, a master. **β.** L. *mag-is-ter* is a double comparative form; the base *mag-* is the same as in *mag-nus*, great, Gk. *μέγ-as*, great; so that the sense is 'great-er-er' = much more great. **Der.** *master*, verb; *master-ly, master-ship, master-y*, q.v.; also *master-builder, -hand, -key, -less, -piece, -work*, &c.

MASTERY, lordship, dominion. (F.—L.) In early use. ME. *maistrie, meistrie*; spelt *meistrie* in Ancren Riwle, p. 140.—AF. *maisterie*, Philip du Thaun, Livre des Creatures, l. 1564; OF. *maistrie, meistrie*, mastery (Burguy).—OF. *maistre*, a master; see **Master**.

MASTIC, MASTICH, a kind of gum resin. (F.—L.—Gk.) The tree yielding it is also called *mastic*, but should rather be called the *mastic-tree*, spelt *mastick-tree* in the Bible, Story of Susanna, v. 54. Another name for the tree is *lentisk*. 'The lentiskes also haue their rosin, which they call *mastick*;' Holland, tr. of Pliny, b. xiv. c. 20. ME. *mastyk*, Prompt. Parv.; *mastic*, Palladius, xi. 410.—F. *mastic*, 'mastick, a sweet gum;' Cot.—L. *mastichē.*—Gk. *μαστίχη*, the gum of the tree *σχῖνος*, called in L. *lentiscus*. **β.** So called because it was used for chewing in the East; from the base *μαστ-*, seen in *μάσταξ*, the mouth, *μαστάζειν*, to chew.—Gk. *μασάομαι*, I chew. **Der.** *mastic-ate*, q.v.

MASTICATE, to chew. (L.—Gk.) The E. verb was suggested by the previous use of the sb. *mastication*, which alone appears in Minsheu, ed. 1627, and in Cotgrave, who uses it to translate the F. *mastication*.—L. *masticātus*, pp. of *masticāre*, to chew; a late word, marked by Lewis as 'post-classical.' **β.** Formed, like most verbs in *-āre*, from a sb. The orig. sense was probably 'to chew mastic,' from L. *masticē, mastichē*, mastic, Gk. *μαστίχη*; see **Mastic**. ¶ The true L. word for 'chew' is *mandere*. The explanation under **Mastic**, that *mastic* is so named from being chewed, only applies to Greek; in Latin, the verb is derived from the sb. **Der.** *mastication*, from F. *mastication*, as above; *masticat-or-y*.

MASTIFF, a large dog. (F.—Late L.—L.) ME. *mestif*,

mastif. 'Als grehound or *mastif*' (riming with *hastif*), Rob. of Brunne, tr. of Langtoft, p. 189, l. 8. '*Mastyf*, or *mestyf*, hownde;' Prompt. Parv. But the AF. form was *mastin*; see Polit. Songs, ed. Wright, p. 283; Langtoft, ii. 100.—OF. *mastin*, a mastiff, lit. 'house-dog' (Supp. to Godefroy); also 'a domestic;' see Godefroy.—Late L. type *mansuētinum*, acc. of *mansuētinus*, tame, domestic; extended from *mansuētus*, tame.—L. *mansuētus*, pp. of *mansuescere*, to tame; lit. 'to accustom to the hand.'—L. *man-*, for *manus*, the hand; and *suescere*, to accustom, make one's own, which is allied to *suus*, one's own. See Körting, § 5906. Cf. L. *mansuētārius*, a tamer (Lewis). **β.** The Late L. *mastinus* seems to have been mistakenly changed to *mastīuus* (*mastivus*); see Ducange. Confusion also set in with ME. *masty*, fat (adj. formed from *mast* (2)), and OF. *mestif*, mongrel, Late L. *mixtivus*, from L. *mixtus*, pp. of *miscēre*, to mix.

MASTODON, the name of an extinct elephant. (Gk.) Modern; so called from the conical or nipple-like projections on its molar teeth. Coined from Gk. *μαστ-*, base of *μαστός*, the female breast (connected with *μαδάειν*, L. *madēre*, to be moist); and *ὀδον-*, short for *ὀδοντ-*, stem of *ὀδούς*, a tooth; see **Tooth**.

MAT, a texture of sedge, rushes, or other material, to be laid on a floor, &c. (L.) ME. *matte*. '*Matte*, or *natte*, *Matta, storium*;' Prompt. Parv. AS. *meatta*; '*Storea, vel psiata, meatta*;' Voc. 154. 2. [L. *storea* means 'a mat.' Observe the variant ME. *natte* given in the Prompt. Parv.]—L. *matta*, a mat; cf. Low L. *natta*, a mat (Ducange). **β.** From the form *matta* were borrowed E. *mat*, Du. *mat*, G. *matte*, Swed. *matta*, Dan. *maatte*, Ital. *matta*, Span. *mata*; whilst the form *natta* is preserved in F. *natte*. Precisely a similar interchange of *m* and *n* occurs in F. *nappe* from L. *mappa*; see **Map**. **γ.** Root uncertain; the curious shifting of *m* and *n* suggests that (as in the case of *map*) the word may have been a Punic word; indeed, it would not be surprising if the words *mappa* and *matta* were related. **Der.** *mat*, verb; *matt-ed, matt-ing*.

MATADOR, the slayer of the bull in bull-fights. (Span.—L.) In Dryden, Span. Friar, A. i. sc. 2. Spelt *matadore*, Pope, Rape of the Lock, iii. 33, 47.—Span. *matador*, lit. 'the slayer;' formed with suffix *-dor* (= L. acc. *-tōrem*) from *matar*, to kill.—L. *mactāre*, (1) to honour, (2) to honour by sacrifice, to sacrifice, (3) to kill.—L. *mactus*, honoured; allied to *mag-nus*, great (Bréal).

MATCH (1), one of the same make, an equal, a contest, game, marriage. (E.) ME. *macche, mache*. Spelt *macche* = mate, companion; P. Plowman, B. xiii. 47. 'This was a *mache* vnmete' = this was an unfit contest; Morte Arthure, ed. Brock, 4070; whence the pp. *machede* = matched, id. 1533, 2904. The orig. sense was 'companion' or 'mate,' hence an equal, giving the verb *to match* = to consider equal; the senses of 'contest, game, marriage,' &c., are really due to the verb. AS. *-mæcca*, generally *ge-mæcca*, a companion, comrade, spouse; Grein, i. 426. [The prefix *ge-*, often and easily dropped, makes no difference.] The change of sound from final *-cca* to *-cche*, and later to *-tch*, is perfectly regular. **β.** The form *gemæcca* or *mæcca* is one of secondary formation; from the more original form *maca*, a companion, as in *gi-maca*, gloss to *compar* in Durham Ritual, p. 165, l. 6; whence ME. *make*, a companion (Chaucer).+Icel. *maki*, Swed. *make*, Dan. *mage*, OSax. *gi-mako*, a mate, a comrade. **β.** Allied to AS. *gemæc*, adj., like, Icel. *makr*, adj., suitable, MHG. *gemach*, suitable; and to AS. *macian*, to make, to 'fit together.' See **Make**. ¶ Distinct from **Mate** (1). **Der.** *match*, verb, see exx. above, and see P. Plowman, B. ix. 173; also *match-less, match-less-ly, match-less-ness*.

MATCH (2), a prepared cord for firing a cannon, a 'lucifer.' (F.—L.—Gk.) ME. *macche*; 'the *macche* brenneth' = the match burns (used of a smouldering wick); P. Plowman, B. xvii. 213.— OF. *mesche, meiche*, 'the wicke or snuffe of a candle; the match of a lamp; also, match for a harquebuse, &c.;' Cot. Mod. F. *mèche*. The corresponding Late L. type is *micca* or *mycca*, which may be connected with Gk. *μύκης*, the snuff of a lamp-wick; and with Late L. *myxus*, the wick of a candle (Ducange); and Martial (14. 41. 2) uses the acc. pl. *myxas*, as if from nom. *myxa*, i.e. the nozzle of a lamp, the part through which the wick protrudes.—Gk. *μύξα*, the nozzle of a lamp; the more orig. senses being (1) mucus, discharge from the nose, (2) a nostril. See further under **Mucus**. **Der.** *match-lock*, i.e. a lock of a gun holding a match, and hence the gun itself; added by Todd to Johnson's Dict. Körting, § 6429.

MATE (1), a companion, comrade, equal. (Low G.) Spelt *mate* in Prompt. Parv., p. 329; Sir Ferumbras, l. 1372. [Distinct from AS. *gemaca*, and borrowed from Low German.]—Mid. Low G. *mate* (Franck); Low G. *maat*, a companion; MDu. *maet*, 'a mate or fellow-companion;' Hexham; Du. *maat*.+OHG. *gimazzo*, a companion at table; cf. Goth. *matjan*, to eat, from *mat-*, base of *mats*, meat. See **Meat**. The sense is 'one who eats with you;' the prefix *gi-* (Goth. *ga-*), meaning 'together,' is lost in the MDu. form. **Der.** *mate*, vb., All's Well, i. 1. 102; *mate-less*.

MATE (2), to check-mate, confound. (F.—Pers.—Arab.) Used by Shak. in the sense 'to confound;' as in 'My mind she has *mated*, and amazed my sight;' Macb. v. 1. 86. It is the same word as is used in chess, the true form being *check-mate*, which is often used as a verb. β. Properly, *check mate* is an exclamation, meaning 'the king is dead;' this occurs in Chaucer, Book of the Duchess, 659.—OF. *eschec et mat*, 'check-mate;' Cot.; so also in Rom. Rose, ed. Méon, 6676. Cf. AF. *maté*, mated; Gaimar, 3320. Here the introduction of the conj. *et* is unnecessary and unmeaning, and due to ignorance of the sense.—Pers. *shāh māt*, the king is dead.—Pers. *shāh*, king; and *māt*, he is dead, Palmer's Pers. Dict. col. 518. γ. *Shāh* is a Pers. word (see **Shah**); but *māt* is not, being of Arab. origin.—Arab. root *māta*, he died; Rich. Dict. p. 1283; whence is derived the Turk. and Pers. *māt*, 'astonished, amazed, confounded, perplexed, conquered, subjected, ... receiving check-mate,' id.; also Pers. *māt kardan*, 'to give check-mate, to confound;' id. Cf. Heb. *mūth*, to die. ¶ We have here the obvious original of OF. *mat*, 'deaded, mated, amated, quelled, subdued,' Cot. Also of ME. *mate*, confounded, Ancren Riwle, p. 382, Will. of Palerne, 2441, &c.; a word merely borrowed from OF. See also **Check, Chess.**

MATERIAL, substantial, essential. (F.—L.) 'Hys *materiall* body;' Tyndall, Works, p. 460, col. 2. And in Chaucer, C. T., I 182.—OF. *materiel*, 'materiall;' Cot.—L. *mātēriālis*, material. —L. *mātēria* (also *mātēriēs*), matter; see **Matter. Der.** *material-ly, material-ness, material-i-ty, material-ise, material-ism, material-ist, material-ist-ic, material-ist-ic-al.*

MATERNAL, belonging to a mother. (F.—L.) Spelt *maternall* in Minsheu and Cotgrave. Caxton has: 'our *maternal* tongue;' Godfrey of Boloyne, prol.; p. 4, l. 24.—F. *maternel*, 'maternall;' Cot.—Late L. *māternālis*, extended from L. *māternus*, motherly. This adj. is formed with suffix -*nus* (Idg. -*nos*) from L. *māter*, cognate with E. *mother* : see **Mother. Der.** *maternal-ly*; also *matern-i-ty*, from F. *maternité*, 'maternity' (Cot.), which from L. acc. *māternitātem.*

MATHEMATIC, pertaining to the science of number. (F.—L.—Gk.) Gower speaks of 'the science ... *mathematique*;' C. A. iii. 87; bk. vii. 72.—OF. *mathematique*, 'mathematical;' Cot.—L. *mathēmaticus.*—Gk. μαθηματικός, disposed to learn, belonging to the sciences, esp. to mathematics.—Gk. μαθηματ-, stem of μάθημα, that which is learnt, a lesson, learning, science.—Gk. μαθη-, appearing in μαθήσομαι, I shall learn, fut. of μαν-θά-νειν, to learn; one of the derivatives from √MEN, to think; cf. μάντις, a seer, μένος, mind, Skt. *man*, to think. The syllable -θα- prob. represents Idg. *dhə*, weak grade of √DHĒ, to put, place (Gk. τί-θη-μι). See **Mind. Der.** *mathematic-al, -al-ly, mathematic-i-an*; also *mathematic-s*, sb. pl.

MATINS, MATTINS, morning prayers. (F.—L.) 'Masse and *matines*;' Rob. of Glouc. p. 369, l. 7605. '*Matynes* and masse;' P. Plowman, B. v. 418.—F. *matins*, 'matins, morning praier;' Cot. A pl. sb. from F. *matin*, properly an adj., but used as a sb. to mean 'the morning.'—L. *mātūtīnum*, acc. of *mātūtīnus*, belonging to the morning; which passed into F. with the loss of *u*, thus producing *mat'tin*, contracted to *matin*; cf. Ital. *mattino*, morning.—L. *Mātūta*, the goddess of morning or dawn; cf. Lucretius, v. 655; as if from a masc. **mātūtus*, with the sense of 'timely,' or 'early;' closely related to L. *mātūrus* (Bréal); see **Mature. Der.** *matin*, sb. morning (in later use), Hamlet, i. 5. 89, from F. *matin*, the morning; hence *matin*, adj., as in 'the *matin* trumpet,' Milton, P. L. vi. 526. And see *matutinal.* ¶ The spelling with double *t* may be due to Ital. *mattino*, or simply to the doubling of *t* to keep the vowel *a* short, as in *matter*, *mattress.*

MATRASS, a long-necked glass bottle; in chemistry. (F.— Span.—Arab.?) From F. *matras*, the same. Cotgrave has *matraz*, *matrac*, also *matelas*, 'a streight, long, narrow-necked, and great, wide, round-bellied bottle or violl, of strong and thick glasse.' Perhaps from Span. *matraz*, a matrass. Devic thinks it is of Arab. origin.

MATRICIDE, the murderer of one's mother. (F.—L.) 1. The above is the correct sense, but rare; see Blount's Gloss., ed. 1674.— F. *matricide*, adj., 'mother-killing;' Cot.—L. *mātricīda*, a murderer of a mother.—L. *mātri-*, decl. stem of *māter*, a mother (see **Mother**); and -*cīda*, killing, formed from *cædere* (pt. t. *ce-cīdi*), to kill (see **Cæsura**). 2. Sir T. Browne has the word in the sense 'murder of one's mother;' Vulg. Errors, b. iii. c. 16, § 5. In this case, it is coined directly from L. *mātricīdium*, a killing of a mother. —L. *mātri-*, as before; and -*cīdium*, a killing, from *cædere*, as before. ¶ *Fratricide*, *parricide*, are equally ambiguous. **Der.** *matricid-al.*

MATRICULATE, to admit to membership, esp. in a college, to register. (L.) Used as a pp., with the sense of 'enrolled,' in Skelton, Garland of Laurel, l. 1281.—Late L. *mātriculātus*, pp. of *mātriculāre*, to enrol, a coined word.—L. *mātricula*, a register; a dimin. of *mātrix*, (1) a breeding animal, (2) a womb, matrix,

(3) a public register, roll, list, lit. a parent-stock. See **Matrix. Der.** *matriculat-ion.*

MATRIMONY, marriage. (F.—L.) ME. *matrimoine*, Chaucer, C. T. 3097 (A 3095).—AF. *ma'rimonie*, Year-book of Edw. I, 1304–5, p. 251; OF. *matrimonie*; MF. *matrimoine*, 'matrimony,' Cot.; of which another form was *matrimoine.*—L. *mātrimōnium*, marriage.—L. *mātri-*, decl. stem of *māter*, a mother (see **Mother**); with suffix -*mōn-io-*. **Der.** *matrimoni-al, matrimoni-al-ly.*

MATRIX, the womb, a cavity in which anything is formed, a mould. (L.) Exod. xiii. 12, 15. [Written *matrice* in Numb. iii. 12 in A. V., ed. 1611. Minsheu has both *matrice* and *matrix*; the former is the F. form. Cf. '*matrice*, the matrix,' Cot.; from the L. *mātricem*, the acc. case.]—L. *mātrix*, the womb.—L. *mātri-*, decl. stem of *māter*, mother, cognate with E. **Mother**, q. v.

MATRON, a married woman, elderly lady. (F.—L.) ME. *matrone*, Gower, C. A. i. 98; bk. i. 1657.—F. *matrone*, 'a matron;' Cot.—L. *mātrōna*, a matron; extended from *mātr-*, for *māter*, a mother; see **Mother. Der.** *matron-ly*, *matron-al*, *matron-hood*; also (from L. *mātri-*), *matrix*, q. v., *matri-c-ul-ate*, q. v., *matri-cide*, *matri-mony*; and see *mater-nal.*

MATTER (1), the material part of a thing, substance. (F.—L.) ME. *matere* (with one *t*), Chaucer, C. T. 6492 (D 910). Earlier form *materie*, Ancren Riwle, p. 270, l. 7.—OF. *matiere*, *matere*; mod. F. *matière*.—L. *mātēria*, matter, materials, stuff; so called because useful for construction, building, &c. See Brugmann, i. § 407. **Der.** *matter*, vb., not in early use; *matter-less*; *materi-al*, q. v. Also *matter* (2), q. v.

MATTER (2), pus, a fluid in abscesses. (F.—L.) '*Matter*, that which runs out of a sore;' Kersey, ed. 1715. Really the same word as the above; see Littré, s. v. *matière*, sect. 8, who gives: 'Matière purulente, ou simplement matière, le pus qui sort d'une plaie, d'un abscès.' So also in the Dict. de Trevoux. Littré gives the example: 'Il est sorti beaucoup de *matière* de cette plaie'=much matter has come out of this sore. See **Matter** (1).

MATTINS, the same as **Matins**, q. v.

MATTOCK, a kind of pickaxe. (E.) ME. *mattok*. 'Hoc bidens, a *mattok*;' Voc. 726. 29; and see Prompt. Parv. AS. *mattuc*, Orosius, b. iv. c. 8. § 2. β. Hence probably W. *matog*, a mattock, hoe; cf. Gael. *madag*, a mattock, pickaxe (from E.); Russ. *motuika*, Lithuan. *matikkas*, a mattock (from Teut.). See **Mason.**

MATTRESS, a quilt to lie upon. (F.—Arab.) 'A *mattress*, culcitra;' Levins. ME. *materas*, Voc. 583. 21.—OF. *materas*, 'a matteresse, or quilt to lie on;' Cot. Picard and Walloon *matras* (AF. *materas*; Royal Wills, p. 181). Mod. F. *matelas* (by change of *r* to *l*); cf. Span. and Port. *al-madraque*, a quilted cushion, mattress (where *al* is the Arab. def. article).—Arab. *maṭraḥ*, 'a place, station, post, situation, foundation, a place where anything is thrown; *muṭraḥ*, thrown away, rejected;' Rich. Dict. p. 1440. This Arab. word came to mean anything hastily thrown down, hence, something to lie upon, a bed (Devic); just as the L. *strātum*, lit. 'anything spread,' came to mean a bed. The Arab. *maṭraḥ* is derived from the Arab. root *ṭaraḥa*, he threw prostrate; Rich. Dict. p. 967.

MATURE, ripe, completed. (L.) '*Maturity* is a mean between two extremities, ... they be *maturely* done;' Sir T. Elyot, The Governour, b. i. c. 22. 'Peres right *mature*;' Palladius, iii. 827.— L. *mātūrus*, mature, ripe, arrived at full growth. See **Matins. Der.** *mature-ly*, *matur-i-ty*, from F. *maturité*, 'maturity' (Cot.), which from L. acc. *mātūritātem*; *mature-ness*; *matur-at-ion*, from MF. *maturation*, 'a maturation, ripening' (Cot.), which from L. acc. *mātūrātiōnem*, allied to *mātūrātus*, pp. of *mātūrāre*, to ripen; *matur-at-ive*, from MF. *maturatif*, 'maturative, ripening' (Cot.), a coined word; *matur-esc-ent*, from the stem of the pres. pt. of *mātūrescere*, inceptive form of *mātūrāre*. Closely related words are *matin*, *matutinal.*

MATUTINAL, pertaining to the morning, early. (L.) *Matutinal* is in Blount's Gloss., ed. 1674; *matutine* in Kersey, ed. 1715.— L. *mātūtinālis*, belonging to the morning; formed with suffix -*ālis* from *mātūtin-us*, belonging to the morning; see further under **Matins.**

MAUDLIN, sickly sentimental. (F.—L.—Gk.—Heb.) The orig. sense was 'shedding tears of penitence,' like Mary Magdalene, who was taken as the type of sorrowing penitence. Hence the expression 'their *maudlin* eyes' in Dryden's Prol. to Southerne's play of The Loyal Brother, l. 21 (A.D. 1682). Corrupted from ME. *Maudeleyne*, or *Magdalene*, Chaucer, C. T. 412 (A 410); P. Plowman, B. xv. 289.—OF. *Maudeleine*, *Magdaleine*.—L. *Magdalēnē*.— Gk. Μαγδαληνή, i. e. belonging to Magdala; Luke, viii. 2. Here 'Magdala' answers to Heb. *migdol*, a tower; Smith's Dict. of the Bible. ¶ Observe the spelling *Maudlin* (for *Magdalen*) in All's Well, v. 3. 68.

MAUGRE, in spite of. (F.—L.) Obsolete, except in imitating archaic writing. In Shak. Tw. Nt. iii. 1. 163; Tit. And. iv. 2. 110; K. Lear, v. 3. 131. In P. Plowman, B. ii. 204, it means 'in spite of;' but in B. vi. 242, it is (rightly) a sb., signifying 'ill will.' — OF. *malgre, maugre, maudgre*; Cot. has 'maulgré eux, mauger their teeth, in spite of their hearts, against their wils.' The lit. sense of *malgre* is 'ill will' or 'displeasure.' Compounded of *mal*, from L. *malum*, acc. of *malus*, bad, ill; and OF. *gre, gret*, from L. *grātum*, a pleasant thing. See **Malice** and **Agree**.

MAUL, to beat grievously, to bruise greatly, disfigure. (F.—L.) Formerly *mall*. 'Then they malled the horsses legges, that their mightie coursers lefte praunsynge;' Bible, 1551, Judges, v. 22. ME. *mallen*, to strike with a mall or mace, Joseph of Arimathie, ed. Skeat, l. 508. Merely formed from ME. *malle*, a mall, mace; see **Mall** (1). ¶ Even the sb. is spelt *maul* in A. V. Prov. xxv. 18.

MAULSTICK, a stick used by painters to steady the hand. (Du.) In Phillips, ed. 1706. — Du. *maalstok*, a maulstick. — Du. *malen*, to paint; *stok*, stick. Cf. G. *malerstock*, a maulstick, lit. 'painter's stick;' from G. *malen*, to represent, paint, and *stock*, a stick, staff. β. G. *malen*, OHG. *mālōn*, to mark (hence to delineate, draw, paint), is der. from G. *mahl*, MHG. and OHG. *māl*, a mark; see **Meal** (2). γ. G. *stock* is cognate with E. *stock, stake*; see **Stock**.

MAUND (1), a basket. (F.—Low G.) ME. *mawnd*, 'sportula;' Prompt. Parv. [This word, now nearly obsolete, occurs as early as the 8th century, in the gloss: 'Qualus, mand;' Voc. 42. 26; but it became obsolete, and was replaced by AF. *mande*.] — OF. *mande*, a basket (Godefroy); Picard *mande* (Corblet). — Du. *mand*, a basket, hamper; prov. G. *mand, mande, manne*, a basket (Flügel), whence F. *manne*; EFries. *mande*.

MAUND (2), a (very variable) weight. (Arab.) From Arab. *mann*; Pers. *man*. Cf. Heb. *māneh*, Gk. μνᾶ (Yule).

MAUNDY THURSDAY, the day preceding Good Friday. (F.—L.; *and* E.) *Thursday* is the E. name of the fifth day of the week; see **Thursday**. *Maundy* is ME. *maundee, maunde*, a command, used with especial reference to the text 'Mandatum novum,' &c.; John, xiii. 34. 'He made his *maundee*,' He [Christ] performed his own command, i.e. washed his disciples' feet; P. Plowman, B. xvi. 140. 'Lord, where wolte thou kepe thi *maunde*?' Coventry Mysteries, ed. Halliwell, p. 259. The 'new commandment' really is 'that ye love one another;' but in olden times it was, singularly enough, appropriated to the particular form of devotion to others exemplified by Christ when washing his disciples' feet, as told in earlier verses of the same chapter. 'The Thursday before Easter is called *Maundy Thursday*, *dies mandati*, a name derived from the ancient custom of washing the feet of the poor on this day, and singing at the same time the anthem—*Mandatum novum*, &c.; John, xiii. 34 . . . The notion was, that the washing of the feet was a fulfilling of this command, and it is so called in the rubric, *conveniunt clerici ad faciendum mandatum*. This rite, called *mandatum* or *lavipedium*, is of great antiquity, both in the Eastern and Western church;' &c.; Humphrey on the Common Prayer, p. 179. See my long note to P. Plowman, B. xvi. 140, and *Maundy Thursday* in the Index to the Parker Society's publications. *Maundy*, for *mandatum*, occurs in Grindal's Works, p. 51; Hutchinson, pp. 221, 259, 346; Tyndale, i. 259, iii. 236 (Parker Soc.). β. From OF. *mandé*, that which is commanded. Cot. has 'mandé, commanded, . . . directed, appointed.' —L. *mandātum*, a command, lit. that which is commanded, neut. of *mandātus*, pp. of *mandāre*, to command. See **Mandate**, of which *maundy* is, in fact, the doublet. ¶ Not connected with *maund*, a basket, for which see **Maund** (1). Cf. OHG. *mandāt*, the washing of feet (Otfrid); obviously from L. *mandātum*.

MAUSOLEUM, a magnificent tomb. (L.—Gk.) 'This mausoleum was the renowned tombe or sepulchre of Mausolus, a petty king of Caria;' Holland, tr. of Pliny, b. xxxvi. c. 5. — L. *mausōlēum*, a splendid tomb, orig. the tomb of Mausolus. — Gk. Μαυσωλεῖον, the tomb of Mausolus. — Gk. Μαύσωλος, king of Caria, to whom a splendid monument was erected by his queen Artemisia.

MAUVE, the name of a colour. (F.—L.) Modern. So named from its likeness to the tint of the flowers of a mallow. — F. *mauve*, a mallow. — L. *malua*, a mallow; see **Mallow**.

MAVIS, the song-thrush. (F.—C.) ME. *mavis*, Rom. of the Rose, 619. — F. *mauvis*, 'a mavis, a throstle;' Cot.; and see Roman de la Rose, 614. Cf. Span. *malvis*, a thrush. Supposed to be derived from or related to Bret. *milvid*, also *milfid*, a mavis; called *milchouid* (with guttural *ch*) in the neighbourhood of Vannes. Cf. Corn. *melhues*, OCorn. *melhuet*, a lark (Williams). See Thurneysen, p. 107.

MAVOURNEEN, my darling. (Irish.) 'Erin *mavournin*;' Campbell, Exile of Erin; last line. — Irish *mo*, my; *mhuirnin* (with *mh=v*), mutated form of *muirnin*, darling, from *muirn*, affection. See Gael. *muirn* in Macbain.

MAW, the stomach, esp. in the lower animals. (E.) ME. *mawe* (disyllabic), Chaucer, C. T. 4906 (B 486). AS. *maga*, the stomach; Voc. 48. 39.+Du. *maag*; Icel. *magi*; Swed. *mage*; Dan. *mave*; G. *magen*, OHG. *mago*. Root unknown. ¶ The change from *maga* to *mawe, maw*, is quite regular; cf. AS. *haga*, ME. *hawe*, E. *haw*. Der. *maw-worm*, i.e. stomach-worm, parasite, Beaum. and Fletcher, Bonduca, i. 2 (3rd Soldier).

MAWKISH, squeamish. (Scand.; *with* E. *suffix*.) 'Mawkish, sick at stomach, squeamish;' Phillips, ed. 1706. Dryden has 'mawkish joys;' tr. of Lucretius, bk. iii. l. 307. The older sense is 'loathsome,' or, more literally, 'maggoty.' Formed with suffix *-ish* from ME. *mauk, mawk*, a maggot; cf. *mawky*, adj., 'cimicosus;' Cath. Anglicum. 'Hic cimex, Anglicè *mawke*;' Voc. 643. 2. *Mauk* is a contraction of the older form *maðek*, a maggot, which occurs (in another MS.) as a variant of *meaðe*, a maggot; O. Eng. Homilies, i. 251, l. 19; cf. note on p. 326. — Icel. *maðkr*, a maggot; Dan. *maddik*, a maggot; whence the Norweg. *makk* (Aasen) = E. *mawk*. β. This is a dimin. form with suffix -*k*, from the older form appearing in AS. *maða*, Goth. *matha*, Du. and G. *made*, a maggot; prob. allied to **Moth**. Der. *mawkish-ly, mawkish-ness*.

MAXILLAR, MAXILLARY, belonging to the jaw-bone. (L.) Blount, ed. 1674, gives both forms. Bacon has 'maxillary bones;' Nat. Hist. § 747. — L. *maxillāris*, belonging to the jaw-bone. — L. *maxilla*, the jaw-bone; allied to *māla*, the cheek-bone (Bréal).

MAXIM, a proverb, general principle. (F.—L.) Lit. 'a saying of the greatest importance.' In Shak. Troil. i. 2. 318. — F. *maxime*, 'a maxime, principle;' Cot. — L. *maxima*, greatest (for *maxima sententiārum*, the chief of opinions); fem. of *maximus*, greatest, superl. of *magnus*, great. See **Magnify**.

MAXIMUM, the greatest value or quantity. (L.) A mathematical term. — L. *maximum*, neut. of *maximus*, greatest; see **Maxim**.

MAY (1), I am able, I am free to act, I am allowed to. (E.) There is no infinitive in use; if there were, it would rather take the form *mow* than *may*. *May* is the present tense (once, the past tense of a strong verb); *might* is the past tense (really a secondary past tense or pluperfect). ME. infin. *mown* (for *mowen*), Prompt. Parv. p. 346; pres. t. sing. *I may*, Chaucer, C. T. 4651 (B 231); pt. t. *I mighte*, id. 322, 634 (A 320, 632). AS. *mugan*, infin., to be able; pres. t. *ic mæg*, I may or can; pt. t. *ic mihte*, I might.+OSax. *mugan*; pres. t. *ik mag*; pt. t. *mahta*; Icel. *mega*; pres. t. *ek mā*; pt. t. *ek mātti*; Du. *mogen*; pres. t. *ik mag*; pt. t. *ik mogt*; Dan. pres. t. *maa*; pt. t. *maatte*; Swed. pres. t. *må*; pt. t. *måtte*; G. *mögen*; pres. t. *mag*; pt. t. *mochte*; Goth. *magan*; pres. t. *ik mag*; pt. t. *ik mahta*. β. All from a Teut. base MAG, to have power. Further allied to Russ. *moche*, to be able; cf. *moche*, sb., power, might; Gk. μηχανή, means. All from √MAGH, to have power. Der. *might*; also *dis-may*. And cf. *machine, mechanic*.

MAY (2), the fifth month. (F.—L.) ME. *Mai, May*; Chaucer, C. T. 1502 (A 1500). — OF. *May, Mai*, 'the month of May;' Cot. — L. *Māius*, May; so named as being the month of 'growth.' It was dedicated to *Māia*, i.e. 'the increaser.' Allied to *māior*, greater, *magnus*, great (Bréal). See **Magnitude**. Der. *May-day, -flower, -fly, -pole, -queen*.

MAYOR, the chief magistrate of a town. (F.—L.) ME. *maire*, P. Plowman, B. iii. 87. There were mayors of London much earlier; cf. AF. *meire*, Stat. Realm, i. 52 (1281). — F. *maire*, a mayor. — L. *māior*, greater; hence, a superior. See **Major**. ☞ It is most remarkable that the sixteenth century spelling, viz. *mayor*, resembles the Span. spelling *mayor*. Spelt *maior* in Shak. Rich. III, iii. 1. 17 (first folio); it answers to OF. *maior*, from L. *māiōrem*, the acc. case. The word *maire* was first used temp. Hen. III; Liber Albus, p. 13. Der. *mayor-ess*, a coined word, formed by adding the F. fem. suffix *-esse* (= L. *-issa*, Gk. *-ισσα*); Ben Jonson speaks of 'the lady may'ress' in An Elegy, Underwoods, lx. l. 70. Cf. Norm. dial. *mairesse*, wife of a mayor (Moisy). Also *mayor-al-ty*, Lord Bacon, Life of Hen. VII, ed. Lumby, p. 209, l. 24; a coined word, as if from a Lat. acc. *māiōrālitātem*. Also *mayor-ship, mayor-dom*, in Cotgrave, s.v. *mairie*.

MAY-WEED, stinking camomile; *Anthemis Cotula*. (E.) Short for *maythe-weed*; where *maythe* represents AS. *mægþa, mageþe*, camomile. See Notes on E. Etym., p. 183.

MAZE, a labyrinth, confusion, perplexity. (E.) ME. *mase*, P. Plowman, B. i. 6. Prob. from the verb; we find ME. *masen*, to confuse, puzzle; Chaucer, C. T. 4946 (B 526). The AS. **masian*, vb., appears in the comp. pp. *ā-masod*; Wulfstan, Homil. (ed. Napier), p. 137, l. 23; cf. Norweg. *masa-st* (where the final -*st* = -*sk* = *sik*, oneself), a verb of reflexive form, to fall into a slumber, to lose one's senses and begin to dream; *masa*, to be continually busy at a thing, to have a troublesome piece of work to do, also, to prate, chatter (Aasen). Icel. *masa*, to chatter, prattle; Swed. dial. *masa*,

(1) to warm, (2) to bask before the fire or in the sun, ... (4) to be slow, lazy, work slowly and lazily ; *mas*, adj., slow, lazy (Rietz). β. These senses of lounging, poring stupidly over work, dreaming, and the like, agree with the E. phrase to be *in a maze*, i.e. in a dreamy perplexity. Compare the following : 'Auh þe *bimasede* Isboset, lo ! hwu he dude *maseliche*' = but the stupid Ishbosheth, lo ! how stupidly he acted ; Ancren Riwle, p. 272. Prob. the orig. sense was ' to be lost in thought ;' hence to be in perplexity. **Der.** *maz-ed*, Mids. Nt. Dr. ii. 1. 113 (cf. ME. *mased*, *bimased*) ; *maz-y*, *maz-i-ness*. Also *a-maze*, q.v.

MAZER, a large drinking-bowl. (F.—OHG.) Obsolete. '*Mazer*, a broad standing-cup, or drinking-bowl ;' Phillips, ed. 1706. ME. *maser*, Prompt. Parv. ; pl. *masers*, Testamenta Ebor. i. 160 (1391).— AF. *maser*, Royal Wills, p. 25 (1360) ; *mazer* (Bozon, p. 50) ; OF. *masere*, a bowl of maple-wood [explained by Godefroy as made of a kind of streaked precious stone, but see *madre* in Diez].—OHG. *masar*, a knot in wood, also maple-wood. *Mazers* were so called because often made of maple, which is a spotted wood ; the orig. sense of the word being ' a spot,' a knot in wood, &c. Cf. Icel. *mösurr*, 'a maple-tree, spot-wood ;' *mösur-bolli*, a mazer-bowl ; *mösurtrē*, a maple-tree. β. The word is allied to the form which appears in MHG. *mase*, a spot, mark of a blow ; whence also E. **Measles**, q.v. **Der.** *masel-yn* (= *maser-in*), a dimin. form, used in the same sense, Chaucer, C. T. 13781 (B 2042).

MAZURKA, a lively Polish dance. (Pol.) From Pol. *Mazurka*, lit. a woman of Massovia or Mazovia, a province of Poland containing Warsaw. Similarly, *Polonaise* means both a Polish woman and a dance ; and cf. **Polka**.

MAZZARD, MAZARD, the head, the skull. (F.—OHG.) In Hamlet, v. 1. 97. Formed from *mazer*, a bowl ; with excrescent *d*. See **Mazer**. See Notes on E. Etym., p. 183.

ME, pers. pron. the dat. and obj. case of *I*. (E.) ME. *me*. AS. *mē* ; fuller form *mec*, in the acc. only. + Du. *mij* ; Icel. *mēr*, dat. ; *mik*, acc. ; Swed. and Dan. *mig* ; Goth. *mis*, dat. ; *mik*, acc. ; G. *mir*, dat. ; *mich*, acc. + Corn. *me*, *mi* ; Bret. *me* ; Irish, Gael., and W. *mi*. + L. *mihi*, dat. ; *mē*, acc. ; Gk. μοί, ἐμοί, dat. ; μέ, ἐμέ, acc. ; Skt. *mahyam*, *mē*, dat. ; *mām*, *mā*, acc. **Der.** *mine* (1), *my*.

MEAD (1), a drink made from honey. (E.) ME. *mede*, Legends of the Holy Rood, p. 138, l. 202. Also spelt *meth*, *meeth*, Chaucer, C. T. 3261, 3378. AS. *medu*, *meodu*, *medo*, *meodo*, Grein, ii. 239. + Du. *mede* ; Icel. *mjöðr* ; Dan. *miöd* ; Swed. *mjöd* ; G. *meth* ; OHG. *meto* ; W. *medd* ; Lithuan. *middus*, mead ; *medùs*, honey ; Russ. *med'* ; Gk. μέθυ, intoxicating drink ; Skt. *madhu*, sweet ; also, as sb., honey, sugar. Idg. type *medhu* ; Brugmann, ii. § 104.

MEAD (2), **MEADOW**, a grass-field, pasture-ground. (E.) So called because ' mown.' **1.** ME. *mede*, Chaucer, C. T. 89. AS. *mǣd* ; 'Pratum, *mǣd* ;' Voc. 147. 16. Allied to the prov. E. *math*, a mowing, used only in the comp. *after-math*, an after-mowing, a second crop ; and to AS. *māwan*, to mow ; see **Mow** (1). Cf. G. *mahd*, a mowing ; MHG. *māt*, a mowing, a crop, a mead ; MHG. *mate*, *matte*, a meadow ; Swiss *matt*, a meadow, in the well-known names *Zermatt*, *Andermatt* ; also OHG. *māen*, to mow, cognate with E. *mow* ; also Gk. ά-μητος, a harvest, ἀμάειν, to mow. **2.** The fuller form *meadow* is due to the inflected form, dat. *mǣd-we*, of the same word ; the change from final *-we* to later *-ow* is the usual one, as in *sparrow*, *arrow*, &c. 'Mid *lǣswe* and mid *mǣdwe*' = with leasow and with meadow ; A. S. Chron., an. 777, MS. E. (see Thorpe's edit. p. 92, note 1). Teut. type *mǣ-d-wā*, nom. f. ; from Teut. root *mǣ* = Idg. *mē*, to mow, as in Gk. ά-μη-τος (above). **Der.** *meadow-y*.

MEAGRE, lean, thin, poor, scanty. (F.—L.) ME. *megre*, P. Plowman, B. v. 128 ; Allit. Poems, ed. Morris, B. 1198. (Not in earlier use ; and not from AS. *mæger*, in A. S. Leechdoms, ii. 242.) — AF. *megre*, Sir Bevis, 1101 ; F. *maigre*, thin.— L. *macrum*, acc. of *macer*, thin, lean ; whence also AS. *mæger*, Icel. *magr*, Dan., Swed., and G. *mager*, thin, lean, were borrowed at an early period ; unless they be cognate, which is possible. Cf. Gk. μακρός, long. **Der.** *meagre-ly*, *-ness*. From the same source, *e-mac-i-ate*.

MEAL (1), ground grain. (E.) ME. *mele*, Chaucer, C. T. 3993 (A 3995). AS. *melu*, *melo*, gen. *melewes*, Matt. xiii. 33. + Du. *meel* ; Icel. *mjöl*, later form *mēl* ; Dan. *meel* ; Swed. *mjöl* ; G. *mehl*. Teut. type *melwom*, n. β. All from the Idg. √MEL, to grind ; as in OIrish *mel-im*, OSlav. *mel-jǫ*, I grind. The 2nd grade occurs in L. *mol-ere*, Lith. *mal-ti*, to grind, and in Teut. *mal-*, as in Icel. *mala*, Goth. *malan*, OHG. *malan*, to grind. See **Mill, Molar**. **Der.** *meal-y*, *meal-i-ness*, *meal-y-mouth-ed*.

MEAL (2), a repast, share or time of food. (E.) ME. *meel*, Chaucer, C. T. 4886 (B 466). AS. *mǣl* (1), a portion of time, stated time, Grein, ii. 221. Hence the orig. sense was ' time for food ;' cf. mod. E. ' regular *meals*.' It has reference to the common meal at a stated time, not to a hastily snatched repast. + Du. *maal*, (1) time, (2) a meal ; Icel. *māl*, (1) a measure, (2) time, nick of time, (3) a

meal ; Dan. *maal*, measure, dimension ; *maaltid*, a meal (lit. mealtime) ; Swed. *mål*, measure, due size, meal ; Goth. *mēl*, time, season ; G. *mahl*, a meal ; *mal*, a time. β. Teut. type *mǣlom*, n. ; base *mǣl-*, from Idg. √MĒ, to measure ; cf. Skt. *mā*, to measure ; see **Mete**. **Der.** *meal-time*, *meal-tide*.

MEAN (1), to have in the mind, intend, signify. (E.) ME. *menen*, Chaucer, C. T. 2065 (A 2063). AS. *mǣnan*, to intend ; Grein, ii. 222. + Du. *meenen*, to think, believe, fancy, mean ; Dan. *mene*, to mean, think ; Swed. *mena*, to mean, think ; G. *meinen*, OHG. *meinjan*, to think upon, mean, signify. β. These are all secondary verbs, as shown by the OHG. form, and derived from the sb. which appears as MHG. *meine*, OHG. *meina*, thought, intent, signification. Further allied to Icel. *minni*, remembrance, memory, mind ; see **Mind**. **Der.** *mean-ing*, ME. *mening*, Chaucer, C. T. 10465 (F 151), cognate with G. *meinung* ; *mean-ing-less*. See *moan*.

MEAN (2), common, vile, base, sordid. (E.) ME. *mene* ; 'þe *mene* and þe *riche* ;' P. Plowman, B. prol. 18. AS. *mǣne*, usually *ge-mǣne*, common ; OFries. *mēne*, common ; and cf. Goth. *gamains*, common, Titus, i. 4 ; see **Common**. ¶ The peculiar sense of ' base, vile' is prob. due to confusion with **Mean** (3), which sometimes meant ' middling.' The AS. *gemǣne* is further allied to the AS. *mǣne*, wicked, false, evil, from *mān*, sb., wickedness. Cf. Icel. *meinn*, mean, base, hurtful ; *mein*, a hurt, harm ; Dan. *meen*, Swed. *men*, hurt, injury ; MHG. *mein*, false ; *mein*, a falsehood ; cf. G. *meineid*, perjury. **Der.** *mean-ly*, L. L. L. v. 2. 328 ; *mean-ness* (not in early use).

MEAN (3), coming between, intermediate, moderate. (F.—L.) ME. *mene*. 'And a *mene* [i.e. an intermediate one, a mediator] bitwene þe kyng and þe comune' [commons] ; P. Plowman, B. i. 158. 'In þe *mene* while ;' Will. of Palerne, 1148.— AF. *meen*, Stat. Realm, i. 140 (1300) ; OF. *meien*, *moien* (Godefroy) ; mod. F. *moyen*, mean, intermediate.— L. *mediānus*, extended form from *medius*, middle ; see **Mediate**. **Der.** *mean*, sb., ME. *mene*, Rom. of the Rose, 6527 ; *mean-s*, ME. *menes*, Chaucer, C. T. 11195 (F 883).

MEAN (4), to moan. (E.) In Mid. Nt. Dream, v. 1. 330 (first folio). ME. *mēnen*, AS. *mǣnan*, to moan ; see **Moan**. So also in Merch. Ven. iii. 5. 82, I explain *mean it* by ' lament, sorrow.'

MEANDER, a winding course. (L.—Gk.) 'Through forthrights and *meanders* ;' Temp. iii. 3. 3.— L. *Mæander*.— Gk. Μαίανδρος, the name of a river, remarkable for its circuitous course ; Pliny, b. v. c. 29. **Der.** *meander*, vb., *meander-ing*.

MEASLES, a contagious fever accompanied by small red spots on the skin. (E.) [The remarks in Trench, Select Glossary, are founded on a misconception. The word is *quite distinct* from ME. *mesel*, a leper, which will be explained below.] 'The *maysilles*, variolæ ;' Levins, 125. 15. '*Rougeolle*, the *meazles* ;' Cot. In Shak. Cor. iii. 1. 78, the sense is ' measles,' not ' leprosy,' as explained in Schmidt. The use of the term was quite definite. 'The *maisils*, a disease with many reddish spottes or speckles in the face and bodie, much like freckles in colour ;' Baret. ME. *maseles*, to translate OF. *rugeroles* (14th cent.), in Wright's Voc. i. 161, l. 23. AS. *mǣsle-*, a spot ; in composition. Cf. ' eruca, *mǣl-sceafa*,' Voc. 121. 34 ; ' eruca, *mǣsle-sceafa*,' Voc. 544. 13 ; so that *mǣsle* has the same sense as *mǣl*, i.e. a spot, mark. + Du. *maselen*. 'De *maselen*, ofte [or] *masel-sieckte*, the measels, or sick of the measels. De *masel-sucht*, the measell-sicknesse ;' Hexham. The same word as MDu. *masselen*. ' *Masselen ofte masseren*, black spots or blemishes of burning upon one's body or leggs ;' Hexham. β. It is obvious that the word simply means ' spots,' or rather ' little spots ;' the Du. form *masel* being a dimin. of an older form *mase*, allied to the MHG. *mâse*, OHG. *mâsa*, a spot, the mark of a wound ; cf. also G. *maser* [= *masel*], a spot, speckle, and *masern*, pl. measles. γ. Precisely the same form *maser*, 'a spot,' is the source whence is derived the E. **Mazer**, q.v. ¶ It thus appears that *measle* means ' a little spot.' It is therefore wholly unconnected with ME. *mesel*, which invariably means ' a leper' (see Stratmann) ; whence *meselrie*, i.e. leprosy. Both *mesel* and *meselrie* occur in Chaucer, Pers. Tale, I. 624-5. This word is borrowed from OF. *mesel*, which is from L. *misellus*, wretched, unfortunate, dimin. of *miser*, wretched ; see **Miser**. The confusion between the words is probably quite modern ; when, e. g., Cotgrave explains MF. *mesel*, *meseau* by ' a meselled, scurvy, leaporous, lazarous person,' he clearly uses *meselled* as equivalent to *leprous* ; whilst he reserves the spelling *meazles* to translate *rougeolle*. Cf. Skt. *masurikā*, a kind of eruption or small pox (Macdonell). **Der.** *measl-ed*, *measl-y*.

MEASURE, extent, proportion, degree, moderation, metre. (F.—L.) ME. *mesure*, P. Plowman, B. i. 35 ; Ancren Riwle, p. 372, l. 1 ; O. Eng. Homilies, 2nd Ser. p. 55, l. 8. — OF. *mesure*.— L. *mensūra*, measure ; cf. *mensus*, pp. of *mētīri*, to measure. From Idg. √MĒ, to measure, whence Skt. *mā*, to measure, Gk. μῆ-τις, counsel. See Brugmann, ii. § 771. **Der.** *measure*, vb., ME. *mesuren*, Chaucer, tr. of Boethius, b. iii. pr. 2, l. 28 ; *measur-able*, ME. *mesurable*,

P. Plowman, B. i. 19; *measur-abl-y, measur-ed, measure-less, measure-ment.*

MEAT, food, flesh of animals used as food. (E.) ME. *mete,* Chaucer, C. T. 1615. AS. *mete,* John, iv. 32, 34. Teut. type **matiz,* m.+Icel. *matr,* food; Dan. *mad,* victuals, food; Swed. *mat,* victuals; Goth. *mats,* food (whence *matjan,* to use as food, eat); OHG. *maz,* food. β. Prob. allied to Skt. *mad,* to be glad, *madaya,* to exhilarate, to be satisfied (Uhlenbeck). Der. *meat-offering.*

MECHANIC, pertaining to machines. (F.—L.—Gk.) First used as a sb., with the sense 'mechanic art.' ME. *mechanike, mechanique.* 'Whos arte is cleped *mechanique*' = whose art is called *mechanic*; Gower, C. A. iii. 142; bk. vii. 1693.—OF. *mechanique, mecanique,* 'mechanicall;' Cot.—L. *mēchanica,* mechanic; also used as sb., the science of mechanics.—Gk. μηχανική, sb., the science of mechanics; fem. of adj. μηχανικός, relating to machines.—Gk. μηχανή, a machine; see **Machine.** Der. *mechanic-al* (see Trench, Select Glossary); *mechanic-al-ly*; *mechanic-s, mechanic-i-an*; also *mechan-ist, mechan-ism.*

MEDAL, a piece of metal in the form of a coin. (F.—Ital.—Gk.) Shak. has *medal* to signify 'a piece of metal stamped with a figure;' Wint. Ta. i. 2. 307.—MF. *medaille,* 'a medall, an ancient and flat jewel,' &c.; Cot. (Mod. F. *médaille.*)—Ital. *medaglia,* a medal, coin; equiv. to OF. *meaille,* whence mod. F. *maille,* a small coin.—Folk-L. type **metallea,* adj. fem.—L. *metallum,* metal; a word of Gk. origin; see **Metal.** Cf. Late L. *medālia,* a small coin. Der. *medal-ist* or *medall-ist*; *medall-i-on,* in Blount's Gloss., ed. 1674, from MF. *medaillon* (F. *médaillon*), 'a little medall,' Cot., which is from the Ital. *medaglione,* formed from *medaglia.*

MEDDLE, to mix or interfere with. (F.—L.) To *meddle* with is to *mix* with. The ME. verb *medlen* simply means 'to mix.' '*Medled togideres*' = mixed together, P. Plowman, B. ix. 3. Also frequently spelt *mellen*; thus, for '*imedled* togidres,' another reading is *ymelled,* in Trevisa, iii. 469, l. 4.—AF. *medler,* Langtoft, i. 248; OF. *mesler, meller,* to mix, interfere or meddle with (Godefroy). Cotgrave has: '*mesler,* to mingle, mix, . . jumble; *se mesler de,* to meddle, inter-meddle, deal with, have a hand in.' Mod. F. *mêler.* Cf. Span. *mezclar,* Port. *mesclar,* Ital. *meschiare* [for *mesclare,* by usual change of *cl* to *chi*], to mix.—Late L. *misculāre,* to mix; cf. L. *miscellus,* mixed.—L. *miscēre,* to mix; see **Miscellaneous.** β. The orig. OF. form was *mesler,* whence AF. **mezdler, medler.* An intrusive *d* occurs, similarly, in *medlar,* q.v. Der. *meddl-er, meddle-some* (with E. suffix), *meddl-ing.* Also *medley,* q.v.

MEDIATE, middle, acting by or as a means. (L.) Rare as an adj., and not very common in the adv. form *mediate-ly.* 'Either *immediatly* or *mediatly*;' Fryth's Works, p. 18.—L. *mediātus,* pp. of *mediāre,* to be in the middle.—L. *medius,* middle; cognate with AS. *midd,* middle; see **Medium.** Der. *mediate,* verb (rare in old books); Rich. quotes: 'employed to *mediate* A present marriage, to be had between Him and the sister of the young French queen;' Daniel, Civil War, b. viii. st. 49. Also *mediat-ion,* q.v., *mediat-or,* q.v. Also *im-mediate.* Also *medial,* from L. *medi-ālis.*

MEDIATION, intercession, entreaty for another. (F.—L.) ME. *mediation, mediacioun,* Chaucer, C. T. 4654 (B 234).—OF. *mediation,* 'mediation;' Cot. Formed as if from a L. acc. **mediā-tiōnem,* from a nom. **mediātio.*—L. *mediāre,* to be in the middle, be between; see **Mediate.**

MEDIATOR, an intercessor. (F.—L.) Now conformed to the L. spelling. ME. *mediatour,* Wyclif, 1 Tim. ii. 5.—OF. *media-teur.*—L. *mediātōrem,* acc. of *mediātor,* one who comes between, a mediator.—L. *mediāre*; see **Mediate.** Der. *mediator-i-al, mediator-i-al-ly.*

MEDIC, a kind of clover. (L.—Gk.) Botanical. Lit. 'Median.' Phillips, ed. 1706, has both *medick* and the L. form *mēdica.*—Gk. Μηδική, for Μηδική πόα, Median grass; fem. of Μηδικός, Median. From *Media,* the name of a country in Asia; Pliny, b. xviii. c. 16.

MEDICAL, relating to the art of healing diseases. (L.) In Blount's Gloss., ed. 1674.—Late L. *medicālis,* medical.—L. *medicus,* a physician.—L. *medēri,* to heal. See **Medicine.** Der. *medical-ly.*

MEDICATE, to impregnate with anything medicinal. (L.) Rich. quotes 'his *medicated* posie at his nose' from Bp. Hall, A Sermon of Thanksgiving.—L. *medicātus,* pp. of *medicāri,* to heal.—L. *medicus,* a physician. See **Medicine.** Der. *medicat-ed, medicat-ion, medicat-ive.* Also *medica-ble,* Blount's Gloss., ed. 1674, from L. *medicābilis*; *medicament,* from OF. *medicament,* 'a medicament, salve' (Cot.), which is from L. *medicāmentum.*

MEDICINE, something given as a remedy for disease. (F.—L.) In early use. ME. *medicine,* in O. Eng. Homilies, ed. Morris, i. 187, l. 4 from bottom.—OF. *medecine* (for *medicine*).—L. *medicīna,* medi-cine.—L. *medicus,* a physician.—L. *medēri,* to heal. β. Fick (i. 714) compares also Zend *madh,* to treat medically, *madha,* medical science. Der. *medicine,* vb., Oth. iii. 3. 332; *medicin-al,* Wint. Ta. ii. 3. 37;

medicin-al-ly; *medicin-able,* Much Ado, ii. 2. 5. And see *medical, medicate.*

MEDIEVAL, relating to the middle ages. (L.) Also written *mediæval.* Modern; not in Todd's Johnson. Coined from L. *medi-,* for *medius,* middle; and L. *æu-um,* an age; with suffix *-al.* See **Mediate** and **Age.**

MEDIOCRE, middling, moderate. (F.—L.) 'A very *mediocre* poet, one Drayton;' Pope, To Dr. Warburton, Nov. 27, 1742 (R.). —F. *médiocre,* middling.—L. *mediocrem,* acc. of *mediocris,* middling; extended from *medius,* middle. (Cf. *ferox* from *ferus.*) See **Mid.** Der. *mediocri-ty,* F. *médiocrité,* from L. acc. *mediocritātem.*

MEDITATE, to think, ponder, purpose. (L.) In Shak. Rich. III, iii. 7. 75. [The sb. *meditation* is in much earlier use, spelt *meditaciun* in the Ancren Riwle, p. 44, l. 4.]—L. *meditātus,* pp. of *meditāri,* to ponder. Cf. Gk. μέδομαι, I attend to; Brugmann, i. § 591. See **Mete.** Der. *meditat-ion,* from OF. *meditation*<L. acc. *meditātiōnem*; *meditat-ed, meditat-ive, meditat-ive-ly, meditat-ive-ness.*

MEDITERRANEAN, inland. (L.) In Shak. Temp. i. 2. 234; and in Cotgrave, who translates MF. *Mediterranée* by 'the mediterranean or mid-earth sea.'—L. *mediterrāne-us,* situate in the middle of the land; with suffix *-an* (=F. *-an,* L. *-ānus*).—L. *medi-,* for *medius,* middle; and *terra,* land; with suffix *-ne-o-.* See **Mid** and **Terrace.** ¶ Chiefly applied to the *Mediterranean Sea,* which appeared to the ancients as nearly in the middle of the old world; but the word was sometimes used more generally; see Trench, Select Glossary.

MEDIUM, the middle place, means, or instrument. (L.) In Dryden, Art of Poetry, c. iv. l. 888; Bacon, Nat. Hist. § 293.— L. *medium,* the midst, a means; neut. of *medius,* middle; see **Mid.**

MEDLAR, a small tree with a fruit somewhat like an apple or pear. (F.—L.—Gk.) Palsgrave has *medlar* for both the fruit and the tree. Properly, *medlar* is the name of the *tree*; the *fruit* should be called a *medle,* but the word is obsolete; the *medlar* is so called because it bears *medles.* ME. *medler,* a medlar-tree; Rom. of the Rose, 1375. Also called *medle-tre,* Sir Beves of Hamptoun, ed. Turnbull, 52 (Stratmann).—AF. *medler,* OF. *meslier,* a medlar-tree; both in Godefroy, Supp., s. v. *nesplier* (sic); MF. *meslier,* 'a medlar-tree;' Cot.—AF. *medle,* OF. *mesle* (both in Godefroy, Supp., s.v. *nesple*); MF. *mesle,* 'a medlar (a Picard word);' Cot.—L. *mespilum,* a medlar; cf. *mespilus,* a medlar-tree; Pliny, b. xvii. c. 10.—Gk. μέσπιλον, a medlar. ¶ The introduction of *d* before *l* in this word is curious; but the same phenomenon occurs also in *meddle* and *medley*; it arose from the OF. *sl,* which became *zdl,* and finally *dl.*

MEDLEY, a confused mass, confusion, mixture. (F.—L.) ME. *medlè, medlee.* 'Medle, mixtura;' Prompt. Parv. p. 331. Also spelt *mellè* (dissyllabic), which occurs in Barbour's Bruce in the sense of 'mixture,' b. v. l. 404, and over and over again in the sense of 'fray,' 'contest,' exactly corresponding to the mod. F. *mêlée,* which is in fact the same word. See Trench, Select Glossary. Chaucer has *medlee* in the sense of 'mixed in colour,' as in: 'He rood but hoomly in a *medlee* cote,' Prol. to C. T. 330 (A 328).—AF. *medlee,* a combat, Life of Edw. Conf., p. 15; cf. OF. *mesle, melle* (fem. forms *meslee, mellee*), pp. of *mesler,* or *meller* (mod. F. *mêler*), to mix. See further under **Meddle.** ¶ The verb to *meddle* also appears as *mell,* All's Well, iv. 3. 257; Barbour's Bruce, v. 409; and see Nares.

MÉDOC, a red wine. (F.) From *Médoc,* a region of France, in the department of Gironde.

MEDULLAR, MEDULLARY, belonging to the marrow. (L.) *Medullar* is in Blount's Gloss., ed. 1674. Kersey, ed. 1715, has both forms.—L. *medullāris,* belonging to the marrow.—L. *medulla,* the marrow. Cf. L. *medius,* middle.

MEED, reward, wages, hire, reward of merit. (E.) ME. *mede,* P. Plowman, B. ii. 20, 27, 34, 36, 39, &c. AS. *mēd,* Matt. vi. 1; allied form *meord* (with *r* for older *s*), John, iv. 36, Rushworth MS. +G. *miethe,* hire; MHG. *miete,* OHG. *mieta.* Cf. Goth. *mizdō,* reward; Russ. *mzda,* remuneration; Gk. μισθός, pay; Pers. *muzd,* wages; Skt. *midha,* reward. Idg. types **meizdhā, *mizdhā,* f.; **mizdhos,* m.; **mizdhom,* n. Brugmann, i. § 226.

MEEK, mild, gentle. (Scand.) ME. *meke,* Chaucer, C. T. 69; Havelok, 945; spelt *meoc,* Ormulum, 667.—Icel. *mjúkr,* soft, agile, meek, mild; Swed. *mjuk,* soft, pliable, supple; Dan. *myg,* pliant, soft; NFries. *mjöck.* Cf. also Du. *muik,* soft; Goth. **mūks,* only in comp. *mūka-mōdei,* gentleness. Teut. types **meukoz, *mūkoz.* (AS. *mēoc,* from Scand., only occurs in *Mēoces dūn,* a place-name; Birch, Cart. Sax. ii. 557. Der. *meek-ly, meek-ness.*

MEERSCHAUM, a substance used for making tobacco-pipes. (G.) Modern.—G. *meerschaum,* lit. sea-foam.—G. *meer,* sea, cognate with E. **Mere** (1); and *schaum,* foam, cognate with E. **Scum.**

MEET (1), fitting, according to measure, suitable. (E.) ME. *mete,* Chaucer, C. T. 2293 (A 2291). [We also find ME. *mete* with the sense of moderate, small, scanty; P. Plowman's Crede, l. 428.

This is the same word, from the notion of fitting tightly.] OMerc. *mēte*, measurable, as in *or-mēte*, excessive, Epinal Gloss. 640; AS. *mǣte*, small, scanty, lit. tight-fitting; whence *unmǣte*, immense, immeasurable; Grein, ii. 227, 624.—AS. *mǣt-*, 3rd grade of *metan*, pt. t. pl. *mǣt-on*, to mete; see **Mete**. Cf. G. *mässig*, moderate, frugal; from *messen*, to measure. Der. *meet-ly*, *meet-ness*.

MEET (2), to encounter, find, assemble. (E.) ME. *meten*, Chaucer, C. T. 1526 (A 1524). AS. *mētan*, to find, meet; Grein, ii. 234; OMerc. *mœtan* (Sweet, OE. Texts). (Formed with the usual vowel-change from *ō* to *ē*, as in *fōt*, pl. *fēt*.)—AS. *mōt*, *gemōt*, a meeting; see **Moot**.+OSax. *mōtian* (the exact equivalent of AS. *mētan*), from *mōt*; Du. *moeten*, only in comp. *ontmoeten*, to meet, from *gemoet*, a meeting; Icel. *mæta*, *mœta*, to meet, from *mōt*, a meeting; Swed. *möta*, to meet, from *mot*, preserved only in the prep. *mot*, against, towards; Dan. *møde*, to meet; cf. *mod*, against; Goth. *gamōtjan*, to meet. All from Teut. base *mōt-, of uncertain meaning. Perhaps cf. Gk. μήδ-ομαι, I devise, plan. Der. *meet-ing*, AS. *gemēting*, Grein, i. 429; *meet-ing-house*.

MEGALOSAURUS, a fossil animal. (Gk.) Lit. 'great lizard.' —Gk. μεγάλο-, decl. stem extended from μέγας, for μέγας, great, cognate with E. **Much**, q. v.; and σαῦρος, a lizard.

MEGATHERIUM, a fossil quadruped. (Gk.) Lit. 'great wild beast.'—Gk. μέγα, n. of μέγας, great, cognate with E. **Much**, q. v.; and *therium*, for Gk. θηρίον, dimin. of θήρ, a wild beast.

MEGRIM, a pain affecting one side of the head. (F.—L.—Gk.) ME. *migrim*, *migreim*, *migrene*. 'Mygreyme, migrym, mygrene, sekenesse, *Emigranea*;' Prompt. Parv. Here *migrim* is a corruption, by change of *n* to *m*, of the older form *migrene*.—F. *migraine*, 'the megrim, head-ach;' Cot.—Late L. *hēmigrānea*, megrim, Ducange; cf. *ēmigrānea* in Prompt. Parv., just cited.—L. *hēmicrānia*, a pain on one side of the face.—Gk. ἡμικρανία, megrim.—Gk. ἡμι-, half (see **Hemi-**); and κρανίον, the cranium, skull (see **Cranium**).

MELANCHOLY, depression or dejection of spirits, sadness. (F.—L.—Gk.) Supposed to be caused by an excess of *black bile*; whence the name. ME. *melancolie*, *malencolie*, Gower, C. A. i. 39; prol. 1069; cf. 'engendred of humour *malencolyk*,' Chaucer, C. T. 1377 (A 1375). — OF. *melancolie*, MF. *melancholie*, 'melancholy, black choler;' Cot.—L. *melancholia*.—Gk. μελαγχολία, melancholy. —Gk. μελάγχολος, jaundiced, filled with black bile.—Gk. μέλαν-, stem of μέλας, black, dark, gloomy (allied to Skt. *mala*-, dirty, *malina*-, black); and χολή, bile, cognate with E. **Gall**, q. v. Der. *melanchol-ic*, MF. *melancholique*, 'melancholick' (Cot.), from L. *melancholicus*.

MELANITE, a black variety of garnet. (Gk.) From Gk. μέλαν-, stem of μέλας, black; with suffix *-ite* (Gk. -ιτης).

MELÉE, a confused conflict. (F. — L.) Explained under **Medley**.

MELILOT, the name of a plant. (F.—L.—Gk.) In Levins and Cotgrave.—MF. *melilot*, 'melilot;' Cot.—L. *melilōtos*.—Gk. μελίλωτος, μελίλωτον, a kind of clover; so called from the honey it contained.—Gk. μέλι, honey; and λωτός, lotus, clover. See **Mellifluous** and **Lotus**.

MELIORATE, to make better, improve. (L.) Bacon has *meliorate* and *melioration*, Nat. Hist. §§ 232, 434.—L. *meliōrātus*, pp. of *meliōrāre*, to make better (Lewis).—L. *melior*, better. β. Cognate with Gk. μᾶλλον, rather, compar. of μάλα, adv., very much, exceedingly. Der. *meliorat-ion*, *a-meliorate*.

MELLIFLUOUS, flowing sweetly, sweet. (L.) In Milton, P. L. v. 429; P. R. iv. 277. And in Shak. Tw. Nt. ii. 3. 54.—L. *mellifluus*, flowing like honey (by change of *-us* to *-ous*, as in numerous other instances).—L. *melli-*, decl. stem of *mel*, honey; and suffix *-fluus*, flowing, formed from *fluere*, to flow. β. L. *mel* is cognate with Gk. μέλι, Goth. *milith*, honey; Irish *mil*, W. *mêl*. For L. *fluere*, see **Fluent**. Der. So also *melli-fluent*, from *melli-* (as above) and *fluent-*, stem of pres. pt. of *fluere*. So also *melli-ferous*, i. e. honey-bearing, from L. *ferre*, to bear. And see *melilot*, marmalade.

MELLOW, fully ripe. (E.) '*Melwe*, *melowe*, or rype, *Maturus*;' Prompt. Parv. Hence *mellow-y*, as in 'not mellowy,' for L. 'necdum *mitia*;' Palladius, iv. 523. Pegge notes that, in Derbyshire, a mellow apple or pear is called a *mealy* one; and perhaps *mellow* is an adjectival use of *meal*. The ME. *melwe* may be due to AS. *melw-*, as in *melw-e*, dat. of *melu*, meal. See **Meal** (1). Cf. Du. *malsch*, Low G. *mals*, soft, mellow; Du. *mul*, soft, *mollig*, soft (see Franck). ¶ Perhaps confused with OMerc. *merwe*, tender (Matt. xxiv. 32); AS. *mearu*, G. *mürbe*, mellow. Der. *mellow-ness*.

MELOCOTON, a peach grafted on a quince. (Span.—Ital.—L. —Gk.) Spelt *malakatoon*; Webster, Devil's Law-case; A. i. sc. 2; and see Nares.—Span. *melocoton*, a quince, a peach grafted on a quince.—Ital. *melocotogno*, a quince.—Late L. *mēlum cotōneum*, a quince (Ducange).—Gk. μῆλον κυδώνιον, a quince; lit. a Cydonian apple. See **Quince**.

MELODRAMA, MELODRAME, a theatrical performance, with songs. (F.—Gk.) Given in Todd's Johnson only in the form *melodrame*, noted by Todd as a modern word lately borrowed from French. It is now written *melodrama*.—F. *mélodrame*, properly, acting with songs. A coined word.—Gk. μέλο-, for μέλος, a song (see **Melody**); and δρᾶμα, an action, drama (see **Drama**). Der. *melodramat-ic*, *melodramat-ist*, from the stem δράμα τ-.

MELODY, an air or tune, music. (F.—L.—Gk.) ME. *melodie*, *melodye*, Chaucer, C. T. 9; Legend of St. Christopher, l. 18.—OF. *melodie*.—L. *melōdia*.—Gk. μελῳδία, a singing.—Gk. μελῳδός, adj., singing, musical.—Gk. μελ-, for μέλος, a song, music; and ᾠδή, a song, ode (see **Ode**). Der. *melodi-ous*, *-ly*, *-ness*.

MELON, a kind of fruit. (F.—L.—Gk.) 'Of *melones*;' see Sir T. Elyot, Castel of Helth, b. ii. c. 7; ME. *meloun*, Wyclif, Numb. xi. 5.—OF. *melon*, 'a melon;' Cot.—L. *mēlōnem*, acc. of *mēlō*, an apple-shaped melon.—Gk. μῆλον, (1) an apple, (2) fruit of various kinds. Cf. L. *mālum*, an apple (possibly borrowed from Gk.). Der. *mar-mal-ade*, q. v.

MELT, to become liquid, dissolve. (E.) ME. *melten*; pt. t. *malt*, Genesis and Exodus, ed. Morris, 1017; pp. *molten*, P. Plowman, B. xiii. 82. AS. *meltan*, pt. t. *mealt*, Grein, ii. 230.+Gk. μέλδειν, to melt. Allied to Skt. *mṛdu*-, soft, and the OSlavonic *mladu*, soft (cited by Max Müller, Lect. on Language, 8th edit., ii. 363). Brugmann, i. § 580, ii. § 690. (√MEL). Der. *melt*, trans. vb., AS. *mieltan*, *miltan*; *melt-ing*, *melt-ing-ly*. Also *malt*, q. v., *milt* (1), q. v.

MEMBER, a limb, a clause, one of a community. (F.—L.) ME. *membre*, Rob. of Glouc. p. 511, l. 10525.—F. *membre*, a member.—L. *membrum*, a member. Brugmann, i. § 875. Der. *member-ship*, with E. suffix. Also *membr-ane*, q. v.

MEMBRANE, a thin skin or film. (F.—L.) 'The skin is a *membrane* of all the rest the most large and thick;' P. Fletcher, Purple Island, c. 2, note 13.—F. *membrane*, 'a membrane;' Cot.— L. *membrāna*, a skin covering a member of the body, a membrane. —L. *membr-um*, a member; see **Member**. Der. *membran-ous*, *membran-ac-e-ous*.

MEMENTO, a memorial or token whereby to remember another. (L.) A Lat. word, adopted into E.; as early as 1401; see Polit. Poems, ii. 103. From the first word in one of two prayers in the Canon of the Mass. The phrase *memento mori* (remember you must die) is in Shak. 1 Hen. IV, iii. 3. 35; but this is used in a different connexion. 'That *memento* would do well for you too, sirrah;' Dryden, Kind Keeper, A. iv. sc. 1. We find 'for *memento* sake' as early as in P. Plowman, B. v. 474, where there is a special allusion to the text 'Remember him,' Luke, xxiii. 42.—L. *memento* (see Luke, xxiii. 42, Vulgate); imperative of *memini*, I remember; see **Mention, Mind**. Brugmann, ii. § 846. (√MEN).

MEMOIR, a record, short biographical sketch, collection of recollections. (F.—L.) Commonly in the pl. *memoirs*, spelt *memoires* in Phillips' Dict., ed. 1706.—MF. *memoires*, 'notes of, writings for, remembrance, ... records;' Cot. Pl. of MF. *memoire*, memory.— L. *memoria*, memory; also, a historical account, record, memoir. See **Memory**.

MEMORY, remembrance, recollection. (F.—L.) ME. *memorie*, Chaucer, C. T. 10118 (E 2244); King Alisaunder, 4790. — OF. *memoire*, memory (of which the AF. form *memorie* is in Gaimar).— L. *memoria*, memory.—L. *memor*, mindful. β. The L. *me-mor* appears to be a reduplicated form (like *me-min-i*, I remember); cf. Gk. μέρ-μερος, anxious, μερ-μηρίζειν, to be anxious, to ponder earnestly (with which the notion of *memory* is closely associated); the simpler form in Gk. appears in μέρ-ιμνα, care, thought. γ. Thus the base is MER, a later form of √SMER, to remember, as in Skt. *smṛ*, to remember; cf. E. **Martyr**, q. v. Brugmann, ii. § 846. Der. *memori-al*, Gower, C. A. ii. 19; bk. iv. 532; from OF. *memorial*, 'a memoriall' (Cot.), from L. *memoriālis*; *memori-al-ist*, *memori-al-ise*. Also *memor-able*, Hen. V, ii. 4. 53, from MF. *memorable*, 'memorable' (Cot.)<L. *memorā-bilis*, from *memorāre*, which from *memor*. Hence *memor-abl-y*. Also *memorandum*, pl. *memorandums*, 1 Hen. IV, iii. 3. 179, from L. *memorandum*, neut. of fut. pass. part. of *memorāre*, to record. Also *com-memor-ate*, *im-memor-ial*, *re-mem-ber*. **Doublet**, *memoir*. Not allied to *memento*.

MENACE, a threat. (F.—L.) ME. *menace*, *manace*; spelt *manas*, King Alisaunder, l. 843. 'Now cometh *manace*, that is an open folye; for he that ofte *manaceth*,' &c.; Chaucer, Pers. Tale, De Ira (I 646). —OF. *menace*, *menache*, *manace* (Supp. to Godefroy); MF. *menace* (Cot.), a threat.—L. *mināciă*, a threat, of which the pl. *mināciæ* is used by Plautus.—L. *mināci-*, decl. stem of *minax*, full of threats; also, projecting.—L. *minæ*, pl., things projecting, hence (from the idea of threatening to fall) threats, menaces; cf. *minārī*, to threaten. Perhaps allied to L. -*minēre*, as in *ē-minēre*, to jut out, project. Der. *menace*, verb, as above; *menac-ing*, *menac-ing-ly*. From the same source, *com-min-at-ion*, *de-mean* (1); perhaps allied to *e-min-ent*, *pro-min-ent*.

MENAGERIE, a place for keeping wild animals. (F.—Late L. —L.) 'The *menagerie* in the tower;' Burke, On a Regicide Peace, let. 1 (R.).—F. *ménagerie*, 'properly a place where the animals of a household are kept, then by extension a place in which are kept rare and foreign animals;' Brachet. (So also Scheler.)—F. *ménager*, to keep house.—F. *ménage*, a household, housekeeping; OF. *mesnage*, 'houshold stuffe, businesse, or people, a houshold, family, or meyney;' Cot. See further under **Menial, Mansion.**

MEND, to remove a fault, repair. (F.—L.) ME. *menden*, Will. of Palerne, 647. The sb. *mendyng* is in King Alisaunder, 5206. *Mend* is an aphetic form of *amend*, by the loss of the initial vowel. See **Amend.** Der. *mend-er*, *mend-ing*.

MENDACITY, falsehood, lying. (L.) 'The *mendacity* of Greece;' Sir T. Browne, Vulg. Errors, b. i. c. 6. § 9. Formed, by analogy with F. words in *-ty*, from L. acc. *mendācitātem*, from nom. *mendācitās*, falsehood.—L. *mendāci-*, decl. stem of *mendax*, false, lying. Allied to *mentīrī*, to lie. β. The orig. meaning of L. *mentīrī* was 'to think out, invent, devise;' cf. *commentum*, a device, a falsehood, *comminisci*, to devise. γ. Hence the base *men-t-* is plainly an extension from the common √MEN, to think. See **Mention, Mentor.** Der. *mendaci-ous*, formed with suffix *-ous* from *mendāci-* above; *mendaci-ous-ly*, *-ness*.

MENDICANT, a beggar. (L.) Properly an adj., as 'the *mendicant* (or begging) friars.' The word came in with these friars, and must have been well known, as a *Latin* word at least, in the 14th century. Chaucer has the F. form *mendinant*, C. T. 7488 (D 1906). Palsgrave has: '*mendycante*, an order of freres, *mendicant*.'—L. *mendicant-*, stem of pres. part. of *mendicāre*, to beg.—L. *mendīcus*, beggarly, poor; cf. L. *menda*, a fault. Der. *mendicanc-y*. Also *mendic-it-y*, ME. *mendicite*, Rom. of the Rose, 6525, from OF. *mendicité*, 'mendicity,' Cot.

MENHIR, a tall monumental stone. (Bret.) A modern name; from Bret. *men*, also *mean*, a stone; and Bret. *hir*, long. The former is from the Celtic type *maini-*, as in W. *maen*, Bret. *mean*, a stone; allied to L. *mœnia*, walls. The latter is from the Celtic type *sēros*, long, as in Irish *sir*, W. *hir*, Corn. and Bret. *hir*; cf. L. *sērus*, late.

MENIAL, one of a household, servile. (F.—Late L.—L.) Properly an adj., but also used as sb. 'His seruauntes *menyall*;' Skelton, Why Come Ye Nat to Courte, 592. ME. *meineal*, *meyneal*. ' Grete ʒe wel her *meyneal* chirche,' i.e. the church of their household, Wyclif, Rom. xvi. 5. This adj. is formed, by help of the common suffix *-al* (=F. *-al*, L. *-ālis*) from the ME. sb. *meine*, *meinee*, *maine*, *mainee*, a household, now obsolete, but once in common use; see Rob. of Glouc., pp. 167, l. 3484; Rob. of Brunne, tr. of Langtoft, p. 15; Will. of Palerne, 184, 416; Havelok, 827; Wyclif, Matt. x. 25, Luke, ii. 4; Chaucer, C. T. 7627 (D 2045). β. [Note that this word is entirely unconnected with E. *many*, with which Richardson confuses it. In Spenser, prob. owing to such confusion, the word is badly spelt *many* or *manie*, F. Q. v. 11. 3.]—OF. *mesniee*, *maisnee*, *meisnee*, *mainsniee* (Godefroy); cf. '*Mesnie*, a meyny, family;' Cot. The same word as Ital. *masnada*, a family, troop, company of men. —Late L. *mansiōnāta*, for which Ducange gives the forms *mansnada*, *maisnada*, a family, household; whence the derivative *mansiōnāticum*, expenses of a household, as explained in Brachet, s.v. *ménage*. γ. Formed, with fem. pp. suffix *-āta*, from *mansiōn-*, stem of L. *mansio*, a dwelling. See **Mansion, Menagerie.**

MENINGITIS, inflammation of the membranes of the brain or spinal cord. (Gk.) From Gk. μηνιγγ-, stem of μῆνιγξ, a membrane, esp. of the brain; with suffix *-itis* (Gk. *-ιτις*).

MENISCUS, a crescent-shaped lens. (Gk.) From Gk. μηνίσκος, a crescent; dimin. of μήνη, the moon. See **Moon.**

MENIVER, MINEVER, MINIVER, a kind of fur. (F.—L.) ME. *meniver* (with *u* for *v*); spelt *menyuere*, P. Plowman, B. xx. 137.—AF. *meniver*, Liber Albus, p. 283; OF. *menu ver*; '*menu ver*, *ou verk*, the furre minever, also, the beast that bears it;' Cot. Also spelt *menu vair*, 'minever, the furre of ermins mixed or spotted with the furre of the weesell called *gris*;' Cot.—OF. *menu*, 'little, small,' Cot.; and *vair*, 'a rich fur of ermines powdered thick with blue hairs;' Cot. β. The F. *menu* is from L. *minūtus*, small; see **Minute.** The F. *vair* is from L. *uarius*, variegated, spotted; see **Vair, Various.** Thus the sense is 'little spotted' fur or animal.

MENSES, the monthly discharge from the womb. (L.) A L. medical phrase. In Phillips, ed. 1706.—L. *mensēs*, with the same sense; pl. of *mensis*, a month; from the same root as E. **Month**, q.v. Der. *menstruous*, q.v.

MENSTRUOUS, having or belonging to menses. (L.) In Isaiah, xxx. 22 (A. V.); Palladius, i. 859.—L. *menstruus*, monthly. —L. *mensis*, a month. See **Month.** Der. *menstru-ate*, from *menstruāre*. Also *menstruum*, a solvent, Sir T. Browne, Vulg. Errors,

b. ii. c. i. § 11; considered as a solvent liquid, and likened, by the alchemists, to menstrual blood; see N. E. D.

MENSURATION, measuring, measurement. (L.) In Phillips, ed. 1706. Formed, by analogy with F. words in *-tion*, from L. *mensūrātiōnem*, acc. of *mensūrātio*, a measuring.—L. *mensūrāre*, to measure.—L. *mensūra*, measure; see **Measure.**

-MENT, a common suffix. (F.—L.) F. *-ment*, from L. *-mentum*, answering to Gk. *-μα-το-*, Idg. *-mn̥-to-*.

MENTAL, pertaining to the mind. (F.—L.) In Shak. Timon, i. 1. 31.—F. *mental*, 'mentall;' Cot.—Late L. *mentālis*, mental.—L. *ment-*, stem of *mens*, mind; see **Mind.** Brugmann, i. § 431 (2). Der. *mental-ly*.

MENTION, a notice, remark, hint. (F.—L.) ME. *mencioun*, Chaucer, C. T. 895 (A 893).—F. *mention*, 'mention.'—L. *mentiōnem*, acc. of *mentio*, a mention. Closely related to *mens* (decl. stem *menti-*), the mind, and to *me-min-i*, I remember. See **Mind.** Der. *mention*, vb., Wint. Tale, iv. 1. 22; *mention-able*.

MENTOR, an adviser, monitor. (Gk.) Not in Todd's Johnson. Simply adopted from the story in Homer, where Athene takes the form of *Mentor* with a view to give advice to Telemachus. See Pope's Homer, Od. b. ii.—Gk. Μέντωρ, proper name; it means 'adviser,' and is equivalent to L. *monitor*. Doublet, *monitor*, q.v.

MENU, a bill of fare. (F.—L.) From F. *menu*, a brief account or minute; substantival use of *menu*, small.—L. *minūtus*, small; see **Minute.**

MEPHITIS, a pestilential exhalation. (L.) In Phillips, World of Words, ed. 1706. The adj. *mephitick* is in Blount's Gloss., ed. 1674; spelt *mephiticke* in Cockeram (1623).—L. *mephītis*, a pestilential exhalation; Æn. vii. 84. Der. *mephit-ic*.

MERCANTILE, commercial. (F.—Ital.—L.) 'That I may use the *mercantile* term;' Howell, Familiar Letters, vol. i. let. 29; A. D. 1621.—MF. *mercantil*, 'merchantly;' Cot.—Ital. *mercantile*, mercantile.—L. *mercant-*, stem of pres. part. of *mercārī*, to trade; with suffix *-ilis*. See **Merchant.**

MERCENARY, hired for money, greedy of gain. (F.—L.) ME. *mercenarie*, Chaucer, C. T. 516 (A 514).—F. *mercenaire*, 'mercenary;' Cot.—L. *mercēnārius*, older form *mercennārius*, a hireling; for *merced-nārius*.—L. *merced-*, stem of *mercēs*, a reward, pay.—L. *merc-*, stem of *merx*, merchandise. Brugmann, i. § 762 (2). See **Mercy.**

MERCER, a dealer in silks and woollen cloths. (F.—L.) The sense is simply 'a trader.' In early use. ME. *mercer*; Ancren Riwle, p. 66, l. 18.—F. *mercier*.—L. type *merciārius*; cf. Late L. *mercērius*, a mercer, trader.—L. *merc-*, decl. stem of *merx*, merchandise; with suffix *-ārius*, denoting the agent. See **Merchant.** Der. *mercer-y*, from AF. *mercerie*, Liber Albus, p. 225.

MERCHANDISE, a merchant's goods, wares. (F.—L.) ME. *marchandise*, P. Plowman, B. prol. 63.—F. *marchandise*, 'merchandise;' Cot.—F. *marchand*; see **Merchant.**

MERCHANT, a trader. (F.—L.) ME. *marchant*, Chaucer, C. T. 272 (A 270); Floriz and Blauncheflur, ed. Lumby, 42.—OF. *marchant* (Burguy), F. *marchand*, a merchant.—L. *mercant-*, stem of pres. pt. of *mercārī*, to barter.—L. *merc-*, stem of *merx*, merchandise. Perhaps allied to *merēre*, to gain, buy, purchase; see **Merit.** So Bréal. Der. *merchantman*, Matt. xiii. 45; *merchand-ise*, q.v. And see *com-merce*.

MERCURY, the messenger of the gods; quicksilver. (F.—L.) ME. *mercurie*, with the sense of quicksilver, Chaucer, C. T. 16240, 16242 (G 772, 774); as the name of the god, id. 1387.—AF. *mercurie*, Livre des Creatures, by Philippe de Thaun, l. 264 (in Wright, Popular Treatises on Science); F. *mercure*.—L. *Mercurium*, acc. of *Mercurius*, Mercury, the god of traffic.—L. *merc-*, stem of *merx*, merchandise; see **Merchant.** Der. *mercuri-al*, Cymb. iv. 2. 310; *mercurial-ise*.

MERCY, favour, clemency. (F.—L.) In early use. ME. *merci*, Old Eng. Homilies, ed. Morris, i. 43; Ancren Riwle, p. 30.— F. *merci*; OF. *mercit*.—L. *mercēdem*, acc. of *mercēs*, reward, pay; which in Late L. had the sense of mercy or pity.—L. *merc-*, stem of *merx*, merchandise, traffic. Der. *merci-ful*, spelt *merciuol*, Ayenbite of Inwyt, p. 188; *merci-ful-ly*, *merci-ful-ness*; *merci-less*, *merci-less-ly*, *merci-less-ness*; *mercy-seat*, Exod. xxv. 17; *gra-mercy*.

MERE (1), a lake, pool. (E.) ME. *mere*, Allit. Poems, ed. Morris, A. 158. AS. *mere*, a mere; Grein, ii. 232.+Du. *meer*; Icel. *marr*, the sea; G. *meer*, OHG. *mari*, sea; Goth. *marei*, sea.+Russ. *moré*, sea; Lithuan. *mārės*, pl.; W. *môr*; Gael. and Irish *muir*; L. *mare*. β. Some explain it as 'that which is dead,' hence a desert, waste, a pool of stagnant water or the waste of ocean; cf. Skt. *maru-*, a desert, allied to *mṛ*, to die. But this is too far-fetched. Der. *mar-sh*, q.v.; *mar-ish*, q.v. ¶ Probably allied to *moor* (1).

MERE (2), pure, simple, absolute. (L.) Very common in Shak.;

see Meas. for Meas. iii. 1. 30, &c. See Trench, Select Glossary. —
L. *merus*, pure, unmixed; esp. used of wine. Der. *mere-ly*.

MERE (3), a boundary. (E.) Spelt *meare*; Spenser, F. Q. iii. 9.
46. ME. *mere*, Trevisa, tr. of Higden, i. 137. AS. *gemǣre*, a
boundary (the prefix *ge-* makes no difference). Cf. Icel. *landa-mæri*,
a land-mark. Teut. type *(ga)mairjom*, n.; allied to L. *mūrus* (for
moiros), a wall. See **Mural.** Der. *mere-stone*; spelt *meere-stone*,
Bacon, Essay 56, § 1.

MERETRICIOUS, alluring by false show. (L.) In Minsheu,
ed. 1627. Formed, by the common change of *-us* to *-ous*, from L.
meretrīcius, pertaining to a courtesan. — L. *meretrīci-*, decl. stem of
meretrix, a courtesan. Formed with fem. suffix *-tr-ix* (signifying an
agent) from *merē-re*, to gain, receive hire. See **Merit.** Der.
meretricious-ly, *-ness*.

MERGANSER, a bird resembling a duck. (L.) Compounded
of L. *merg-us*, a diver, diving-bird, from *merg-ere*, to dive; and
anser, a goose, cognate with E. *goose*. See **Merge** and **Goose.**

MERGE, to sink, plunge under water. (L.) It occurs in
Prynne's Breviate of the Prelates, ed. 1637, p. 64; Todd's Johnson.
The sb. *mersion* is in Blount's Gloss., ed. 1674. — L. *mergere*, to dip.
+Skt. *majj*, to dive, bathe, sink. Brugmann, i. § 816. Der. *merg-er*;
mers-ion, from *mersiōnem*, acc. of *mersio*, a dipping, cf. *mersus*, pp. of
mergere; also *merg-anser* (above). Also *e-merge*, *im-merge*.

MERIDIAN, pertaining to mid-day. (F. — L.) ME. *meridian*;
'the altitude *meridian*;' Chaucer, On the Astrolabe, prol. 1. 56 (or
60). Also used as sb. — OF. *meridien*, 'meridian, south; also as sb.,
the meridian;' Cot. — L. *merīdiānus*, belonging to mid-day. — L. *meri-
diēs*, mid-day; as if *merī-diē* signified 'in the clear day,' from *merus*,
pure, and *diēs*, a day; but really for *medī-diē*, at mid-day, from
medius, middle, and *diēs*. Brugmann, i. § 587 (7). See **Medium**
and **Diurnal.** Der. *meridion-al*, Chaucer, C. T. 10577 (F 263),
from OF. *meridional*, L. *merīdiōnālis*; *meridion-al-ly*.

MERINO, a variety of woollen. (Span. — L.) Not in Todd's
Johnson. — Span. *merino*, roving from pasture to pasture; a name
given to a certain kind of sheep. — Span. *merino*, an inspector of
pastures and sheep-walks. — Late L. *mājōrīnus*, a major-domo, steward
of a household; cf. Late L. *mājōrālis*, a head-shepherd. See Ducange
and Diez. Formed from L. *māior*, greater; see **Major.**

MERIT, excellence, worth, desert. (F. — L.) ME. *merite*, Gower,
C. A. iii. 187; bk. vii. 3029. — OF. *merite*, 'merit;' Cot. — L. *meritum*,
lit. a thing deserved; orig. neut. of *meritus*, pp. of *merēre*, to deserve.
β. The orig. sense of *merēre* was perhaps 'to receive as a share;' i.e.
if it is allied to Gk. μείρομαι, I obtain a portion, μέρος, a portion,
share. Der. *merit-or-i-ous*, Tyndall's Works, p. 171, col. 1, Englished
from L. *meritōrius*, deserving; *meritor-i-ous-ly*, *-ness*. And see *meretricious*.

MERLE, a blackbird. (F. — L.) In Henrysoun's Testament of
Creseide, l. 430. — OF. *merle*, 'a mearle, owsell, blackbird;' Cot. —
L. *merula*, a blackbird. See **Titmouse.** And see *merl-in*.

MERLIN, a kind of hawk. (F. — Teut.) ME. *merlion*, Chaucer,
Parl. of Foules, 339; cf. AF. *merilun*, in MS. Digby 86, desc. by
Stengel (p. 10). — OF. *emerillon*, *esmerillon*, 'the hawk termed a
marlin;' Cot. Cf. Ital. *smerlo*, a kind of hawk, whence *smeriglione*,
a merlin; Span. *esmerejon*, a merlin. Of Teut. origin; cf. OHG.
smirl, Icel. *smyrill*, mod. G. *schmerl*, a merlin. β. Diez supposes the
Romance words to have been formed from L. *merula*, a blackbird;
the initial *s* being unoriginal. See **Merle.** But L. *merula* may be
cognate; with *m* for *sm*. Cf. Körting, § 6124.

MERMAID, a fabled marine animal. (E.) ME. *mermaid*,
Chaucer, C. T. 15276 (B 4460); also *mermaidens*, Rom. of the Rose,
682. — AS. *mere*, a lake, mere; and *mægd*, a maid; cf. AS. *mere-wif*,
a mere-woman, Grein, ii. 233. See **Mere** and **Maid.** ¶ The
sense of *mere* was easily exchanged for that of *sea* under the influence
of F. *mer*, the cognate word. Der. *mer-man*, similarly formed.

MERRY, sportive, cheerful. (E.) ME. *merie*, *mirie*, *murie* (with
one *r*), Chaucer, C. T. 235, 1388 (A 1386). Best form *murie*, as in
Layamon, 10147. AS. *merg[e]*, merry, Grein, ii. 233. Better spelt
myrge (see *mirige* in Bosworth); cf. *murge*, adv. (Grein). β. The
orig. sense of AS. *myrg-e* was 'making the time short' (cf. OHG.
murg-fāri, transitory). Cognate with Gk. βραχ-ús, short; from the
common base *mrgh-* (Brugmann, ii. § 104). Hence the AS. *myrge*
(from Teut. type *murgjoz*) means 'lasting a short time,' and so
'making the time short;' cf. Goth. *ga-maurgjan*, to shorten. See
Brief (1). ¶ First explained in Engl. Studien, viii. 465. The form
merie is Kentish. Der. *merri-ly*, *merri-ness*, L. L. L. i. 1. 202; also
merriment (a hybrid word, with F. suffix, which has almost displaced
merriness), Spenser, F. Q. ii. 6. 3. Also *merry-andrew*, where *Andrew*
is a personal name, asserted by Hearne (Benedict. Abbas, ed. 1735,
tom. i. pref. p. 50) to have been given to jesters in remembrance of
the once famous *Andrew Boorde*, Doctor of Physic in the reign of
Henry VIII; several jest-books were ascribed to him, perhaps

wrongly; see Mr. Furnivall's preface to his edition of Andrew
Boorde's Introduction of Knowledge, and see the passage from Hearne
cited at length in Todd's Johnson. Also *merry-thought*; Cot. translates F. *lunette* by 'the *merry-thought*, the forked craw-bone of
a bird, which we use in sport to put on our noses.' See further in
N. E. D. And see *mirth*.

MESENTERY, a membrane in the middle of the intestines.
(L. — Gk.) In Minsheu, ed. 1627. Englished from L. *mesenterium*.
— Gk. μεσεντέριον, also μεσέντερον, the membrane by which all the
intestines are connected. — Gk. μεσ-, for μέσος, middle, cognate with
L. *medius* (see **Mid**); and ἔντερον, a piece of the entrails (see
Entrails). Der. *mesenter-ic*.

MESH, the opening between the threads of a net. (E.) Sometimes *mash*. Surrey has *meash* as a verb. 'How smal a net may take
and *meash* a hart of gentle kinde;' Description of the Fickle Affections, l. 44; in Tottel's Misc., ed. Arber, p. 7. [ME. *maske*; 'maske
of nette, *macula*;' Prompt. Parv.; but this is a Scand. form; cf.
Icel. *möskvi*, Dan. *maske*, a mesh.] AS. *max*, a net (equivalent to
masc, by the frequent interchange of *x* and *sc*, as in *ask* = AS. *āxian*,
ācsian). We find '*max* mīne,' glossed by *retia mea*; Ælfric's Colloquy, in Thorpe's Analecta, p. 23, l. 5 (or in Voc. 92. 8). The very
rare dimin. *mæscre*, a mesh, is glossed by L. *macula* in a gloss; Voc.
450. 10.+Du. *maas*, a mesh, net; Icel. *möskvi*, a mesh; Dan. *maske*;
OHG. *masca*; G. *masche*. β. The orig. sense seems to have been
'a knot,' from the use of knots in netting; this sense appears in
Lithuanian *mazgas*, a knot, *magztas*, a knitting-needle, allied to the
verb *megsti* (pres. t. *mezgù*), to knot, to weave nets; forms cited by
Fick, iii. 236; Nesselmann, p. 387. Der. *mesh*, vb., as above.

MESMERISE, to induce an extraordinary state of the nervous
system, in which the operator controls the action of the patient.
(G. proper name.) Formed with verbal suffix *-ise* (= F. *-iser*), from
Mesmer, the name of a German physician, of Mersburg, who first
published his doctrines in 1766. See Haydn, Dict. of Dates. Der.
mesmer-ist, *mesmer-ism*, *mesmer-ic*.

MESNE, intermediate. (F. — L.) Given in Cowell's Interpreter,
with a wrong derivation from OF. *maisne*, younger by birth. But it
is a variant of AF. *meen*, mean, intermediate; see **Mean** (3).

MESO-, middle. (Gk.) From Gk. μέσο-, for μέσος, middle,
cognate with L. *medius*, middle; see **Medium, Mid.** Hence *meso-
cephalic*, having a head of medium size; and many scientific terms.

MESS (1), a dish of meat, portion of food. (F. — L.) 'A *mease*
of meat, *ferculum*;' Levins, 204. 36. 'A *messe*, or dish of meate
borne to the table, *ferculum*;' Baret, Alvearie. And see Gen. xliii.
34. ME. *messe* 'Messe of mete, *ferculum*;' Prompt. Parv. 'His
furste *mes*,' his first dish; King of Tars, 86; in Ritson, Met. Rom.
ii. 160. [Cf. ME. *entremesse*, a side dish, on which see my note to
Barbour's Bruce, b. xvi. l. 457.] — OF. *mes*, a dish, course at table
(Godefroy; Burguy). Cotgrave has : '*més*, a messe, or service of
meat, a course of dishes at table.' Mod. F. *mets* (which also appears
in Cotgrave), is a misspelt form due to a wish to point out more distinctly its connexion with the verb *mettre*, of which the old pp. was
mes. Cf. Ital. *messo*, a course of dishes at table; also, a messenger
(the former = L. *missum* : the latter = L. *missus*). — OF. *mes* (< Late L.
missum), that which is set or placed, viz. on the table; pp. of *mettre*,
to place. — Late L. *mittere*, to place; L. *mittere*, to send. See
Mass (2) and **Message.** ¶ Not to be derived from AS. *myse*,
a table, nor from L. *mensa*, nor from OHG. *maz*, meat; all of which
have been (absurdly) suggested. Der. *mess*, sb., a number of persons
who eat together, the orig. number being *four*; see Levins, and
Trench, Select Glossary; also L. L. L. iv. 3. 207. 'A *fourth*, to
make us a full *messe* of guests;' Heywood, Witches of Lancs., A. i.
sc. 1. 'Euery *messe* being *fiue* persons;' Hakluyt, Voy., iii. 100;
l. 1. Also *mess*, vb., to eat of a mess, to associate at table; also
mess-mate.

MESS (2), a mixture, disorder. (F. — L.) 'As pure a *mess*
almost as it came in;' Pope, Epilogue to Satires, Dial. ii. 176. The
same as *mess* (1); see N. E. D.

MESSAGE, a communication sent to another, an errand. (F.
— L.) In early use. In Rob. of Glouc. p. 359, l. 7405. — F. *message*,
'a message;' Cot. — Late L. *missāticum*, message. Extended from
L. *miss-us*, pp. of *mittere*, to send; see **Mission.** Der. *messenger*, q. v.
And see *mess* (1), *mass* (2).

MESSENGER, the bearer of a message. (F. — L.) The *n* is
excrescent, as in *scavenger* for *scavager*, *passenger* for *passager*; so
also *messenger* is for *messager*. ME. *messager*, Chaucer, C. T. 5163,
5191, 5205 (B 743, 771); Ancren Riwle, p. 190, l. 20. AF. *messager*,
Polit. Songs, p. 243 (1307); *messanger*, Langtoft's Chron., ii. 210.
Formed from *message* with suffix *-er* of the agent; see **Message.**
¶ We also find ME. *message* in the sense of 'messenger,' as in
Allit. Poems, ed. Morris, B. 454. This form answers to Late L.
missāticus, m.

MESSIAH, the anointed one. (Heb.) In Dan. ix. 25.—Heb. *māshiakh,* anointed; from *mashakh,* to anoint.

MESSUAGE, a dwelling-house with offices, &c. (F.—L.) 'Messuage (*messuāgium*), a dwelling-house; but by that name may also pass a curtilage, a garden, an orchard, a dove-house, a shop, a mill, a cottage, a toft, as parcel of a *messuage*,' &c.; Blount, Nomolexicon, ed. 1691. ME. *messuage,* Chaucer, C. T. 3977.—AF. *mesuage,* Year-books of Edw. I, 1292-3, p. 219; OF. *mesuage,* a manor-house (Roquefort); cf. Late L. *mesuāgium, messuāgium,* a manor-house (Ducange), also *mansuāgium,* a farm-house.—Late L. type **mansuāticum* (cf. *mansuārius,* a dweller in a house); allied to *mansiōnāticum,* a mansion, *mansāticus,* a mansion. All from Late L. *mansa,* a small farm with a house, a manse.—L. *mansa,* fem. of *mansus,* pp. of *manēre,* to remain, dwell. See **Manse, Mansion.** Thus *messuage = mansu-age;* cf. OF. *mes,* a manse, MF. *metz,* 'a mesuage;' Cot.

META-, prefix. (Gk.) From Gk. μετά, prep., among, with, after; frequently used as a prefix, when it commonly implies 'change.' Cognate with Goth. *mith,* AS. *mid,* G. *mit,* with. Der. *met-al, meta-morphosis, meta-phor, meta-phrase, meta-physics, meta-thesis, met-empsychosis, met-eor, meth-od, met-onymy;* &c.

METAL, a name given to certain solid opaque substances, as gold. (F.—L.—Gk.) ME. *metal,* Rob. of Glouc. p. 28, l. 665; also *metel,* id. p. 6, l. 144.—OF. *metal,* 'mettal, mettle;' Cot.—L. *metallum,* a mine, metal.—Gk. μέταλλον, a pit, cave, mine, mineral, metal. Cf. μεταλλάω, I search after, search carefully, explore. Of unexplained origin. It prob. contains the prep. μετά. Der. *metall-ic,* Milton, P. L. i. 673, immediately from L. *metallicus; metalli-fer-ous,* from *metalli- = metallo-,* for *metallum,* and *-fer,* producing, from *ferre,* to bear; also *metalloid,* i.e. metal-like, from Gk. μέταλλο-, for μέταλλον, and εἶδος, form; also *metallurgy,* q.v. **Doublet,** *mettle.*

METALLURGY, a working in metals. (F.—L.—Gk.) In Phillips, World of Words, ed. 1706.—MF. *metallurgie,* 'a search for metall in the bowels of the earth,' Cot. [But this would appear to be but a partial explanation.]—Low L. **metallurgia,* not recorded, but such a form must have existed as a transcription from the Gk.—Gk. μεταλλουργός, adj., working in metals, mining; μεταλλουργεῖν, to smelt ore or work metals.—Gk. μέταλλο-, decl. stem of μέταλλον, a metal; and ἔργον, work, cognate with E. *work.* See **Metal** and **Work.** ¶ The vowel *u* = Gk. ov, resulting from o and ε. Der. *metallurgic-al, metallurg-ist.*

METAMORPHOSIS, change of form, transformation. (L.—Gk.) Chaucer has *Metamorphoseos,* short for *Metamorphoseos liber,* book of metamorphosis, C. T. 4513 (B 93). He alludes to the celebrated *Metamorphoseon Libri,* books of metamorphoses, by Ovid; and there is no doubt that the word became widely familiar because Ovid used it.—L. *metamorphōsis* (gen. sing. *metamorphōsis* or *metamorphōseos,* the latter being the Gk. form; gen. pl. *metamorphōseōn*), a transformation.—Gk. μεταμόρφωσις, a transformation.—Gk. μεταμορφόομαι, I am transformed.—Gk. μετά, which in comp. has the sense of 'change;' and μορφόω, I form, from μορφή, form. β. The etymology of μορφή is uncertain; some connect it with L. *forma,* form. Brugmann, i. § 413 (8). Der. *metamorphose,* Two Gent. i. 1. 66, ii. 1. 32, a verb coined from the sb. above; also used by Gascoigne, Complaint of Philomene, l. 18 from end. Also *metamorph-ic,* a geological term, likewise a coined word.

METAPHOR, a transference in the meaning of words. (F.—L.—Gk.) 'And make therof a *metaphore*;' Gascoigne, Complaint of Philomene (near the end); ed. Arber, p. 116.—MF. *metaphore,* 'a metaphor;' Cot.—L. *metaphora.*—Gk. μεταφορά, a transferring of a word from its proper signification to another.—Gk. μεταφέρειν, to transfer.—Gk. μετά, which in comp. often gives the sense of 'change;' and φέρειν, to bear, carry, cognate with E. *bear.* See **Meta-** and **Bear** (1). Der. *metaphor-ic, -ical, ic-al-ly.*

METAPHRASE, METAPHRASIS, a literal translation. (Gk.) '*Metaphrasis,* a bare translation out of one language into another;' Phillips, World of Words, ed. 1706.—Gk. μετάφρασις, a paraphrasing.—Gk. μεταφράζειν, to paraphrase, translate, lit. to change the style of phrase.—Gk. μετά, signifying 'change;' and φράζειν, to speak. See **Meta-** and **Phrase.** Der. *metaphrast* = Gk. μεταφράστης, a translator; *metaphrast-ic.*

METAPHYSICS, the science of mind. (L.—Gk.) Formerly called *metaphysic*; thus Tyndall speaks of 'textes of logike, . . . of *metaphysike*;' Works, p. 104, l. 1. ME. *methaphesik,* tr. of Higden, iii. 365.—L. *metaphysicus,* metaphysical; whence *metaphysica,* sb. pl., metaphysics.—Gk. μετὰ τὰ φυσικά, after physics; because the study was supposed fitly to follow the study of physics or natural science. The name is due to editors of Aristotle. See **Physics.** Der. *metaphysic-al,* Levins; *-al-ly, -i-an.*

METASTASIS, a change of condition. (Gk.) From Gk. μετάστασις, a removal, change; allied to μεθιστάναι, to remove.—Gk. μετά, implying change, and ἱστάναι, to place.

METATHESIS, transposition of some letters of a word. (L.—Gk.) In Blount's Gloss., ed. 1674.—L. *metathesis,* transposition.—Gk. μετά, signifying 'change;' and θέσις, a setting, place. See **Meta-** and **Thesis.**

METE, to measure. (E.) ME. *meten,* P. Plowman, B. i. 175. AS. *metan, gemetan,* to measure; Grein, ii. 234.+Du. *meten*; Icel. *meta,* to tax, value; Swed. *mäta,* to measure; Goth. *mitan*; G. *messen.* Cf. Gk. μέδ-ομαι, I provide for; L. *modus,* measure, moderation. See **Mode.** (√MED.) Brugmann, i. § 412 (1). Der. *mete-yard,* Levit. xix. 35, from AS. *met-geard,* a measuring-rod, Voc. 147. 20 (see **Yard**); *meet* (1).

METEMPSYCHOSIS, the transmigration of souls. (Gk.) '*Metempsychosis,* a passing of the soul from one body to another;' Blount's Gloss., ed. 1674. Spelt *metempsichosis* in Herbert's Travels, ed. 1665, p. 53.—Gk. μετεμψύχωσις, a transferring of the soul.—Gk. μετεμψυχόω, I make the soul pass from one body to another.—Gk. μετ-, for μετά, denoting 'change;' εμ-, for ἐν, in, into, before the ψ following; ψυχ-, for ψυχή, the soul. See **Psychology.**

METEOR, an apparition in the sky. (F.—Gk.) Frequent in Shak.; see Rich. II, ii. 4. 9, &c.—MF. *meteore,* 'a meteor;' Cot.—Gk. μετέωρος, adj., raised up above the earth, soaring in air; hence μετέωρον, a meteor.—Gk. μετ-, for μετά, among; and ἐώρα, allied to αἰώρα, anything suspended, from ἀείρειν, to lift, raise up. See Prellwitz. Der. *meteor-ic*; *meteoro-logy,* from λόγος, a discourse, λέγειν, to speak; *meteoro-logi-c-al, meteoro-log-ist.*

METHEGLIN, mead. (W.) In Sir T. Elyot, Castel of Helth, b. ii. c. 22; L. L. L. v. 2. 233.—W. *meddyglyn,* mead; lit. medical liquor.—W. *meddyg,* from L. *medicus,* healing, curative; and *llyn,* liquor (Spurrell, pt. i. p. 189). See J. Davies, Welsh-Lat. Dict. 1632.—A. L. Mayhew.

METHINKS, it seems to me. (E.) ME. *me thinkes,* Will. of Palerne, 430; also *me thinketh,* id. 839. AS. *mē þynceð,* it seems to me; Grein, ii. 613. Here *mē* is the dat. case of the 1st pers. pronoun; and þynceð is from the impersonal verb þyncan, to seem, distinct from þencan, to think (Grein, ii. 579). β. Cognate with AS. þyncan are OSax. *thuncian,* Icel. þykkja (= þynkja), Goth. *thugkjan* (= *thunk-an*), G. *dünken,* OHG. *dunchan,* to seem. These answer to a Teut. type **thunkjan-*; from **thunk-,* weak grade of **thenk-*; see **Think.**

METHOD, arrangement, system, orderly procedure, way. (F.—L.—Gk.) In Shak. Meas. for Meas. iii. 2. 52.—MF. *methode,* 'a method, a short, ready, and orderly course for the teaching, learning, or doing of a thing;' Cot.—L. *methodus.*—Gk. μέθοδος, an enquiry into, method, system.—Gk. μεθ-, for μετά, after; and ὁδός, a way; the lit. sense being 'a way after,' or 'a following after.' β. The Gk. ὁδός is from √SED, to go; cf. Skt. *sādaya* (with *ā*), to approach (Benfey, p. 999); Russ. *chodite,* to go, walk, march, *chod',* a going, course. See Prellwitz; Brugmann, i. § 907, n. 1. Der. *method-ic-al, method-ic, method-ist* (Blount's Gloss., ed. 1674, and see Trench, Select Glossary), *method-ise, Method-ism.*

METHYLATED, mixed with methyl. (Gk.) *Methyl* is the radical of wood-spirit or methylic alcohol. From Gk. μέθυ, wine; and ὕλη, wood. As if 'spirit of wood;' see N. E. D.

METONYMY, a rhetorical figure. (L.—Gk.) 'I understand your *metonýmy*;' Butler, Hudibras, pt. ii. c. 3. l. 588. '*Metonymie,* a putting one name for another; a figure, when the cause is put for the effect, or contrarily;' Blount's Gloss., ed. 1674.—L. *metōnymia.*—Gk. μετωνυμία, a change of names, the use of one word for another.—Gk. μετά, implying 'change;' and ὄνομα, a name, cognate with E. *name*; see **Name.** Der. *metonym-ic-al, -ic-al-ly.*

METRE, METER, poetical arrangement of syllables, rhythm, verse. (F.—L.—Gk.) ME. *metre,* Chaucer, C. T. 13987 (B 3170). —OF. *metre,* 'meeter;' Cot.—L. *metrum.*—Gk. μέτρον, that by which anything is measured, a rule, metre. β. From base με-, with suffix -τρον, signifying the agent; see Brugmann, ii. § 62. From the weak grade (με-) of √ME, to measure; cf. Skt. *mā,* to measure. ¶ The word *meter* occurs in A. S. (see Bosworth), from L. *metrum*; but Chaucer took it from the French. Der. *metr-ic-al* (Skelton, A Replycacion, 338), *metr-ic-al-ly; dia-meter.* Also *metro-nome,* a musical time-measurer, from μέτρο-, for μέτρον, and νόμος, distribution, from νέμειν, to distribute. Also *baro-meter, chrono-meter, hexa-meter, hydro-meter, hygro-meter, penta-meter, thermo-meter, tri-meter; geo-metry, trigono-metry,* &c.

METROPOLIS, a mother city. (L.—Gk.) Ecclesiastically, it is applied to the chief *cathedral* city; thus Canterbury is the *metropolis* of England, but London is not so, except in a secular sense. In K. John, v. 2. 72; and Blount's Gloss., ed. 1674. The adj. *metropolitan* (= L. *mētropolitānus*) was in much earlier use, having a purely ecclesiastical sense. 'Bysshoppes *metropolitanes*' = metropolitan bishops; Sir T. More, Works, p. 1091 h. (Here Sir T. More uses the word as a F. adj., with added *s*, and following its sb.)—L. *mē·ro-polis*.—Gk. μητρόπολις, a mother-state; ecclesiastically, the city of a primate.—Gk. μήτρο-, for μήτηρ, a mother, cognate with E. **Mother**; and πόλις, a city, for which see **Police**. ¶ In St. Erkenwald, ed. Horstmann, l. 26, London is called 'þe *metropol* and þe *mayster-tone*.' 'And thereof is *metropolis* called the chiefe citee, where the Archbishop of any prouince hath his see, .. as Caunterbury and Yorke;' Udall, tr. of Erasmus' Apophthegms; Diogenes, § 110. **Der.** *metropol:!-an*, from L. *metropolitānus* (cf. Gk. πολίτ-ης, a citizen).

METTLE, spirit, ardour. (F.—L.—Gk.) Absolutely the same word as *me:al*, though the difference in sense is now indicated by a difference in the spelling. Common in Shak.; see K. John, ii. 401, Jul. Cæsar, i. 1. 66, i. 2. 313, ii. 1. 134, iv. 2. 24, &c. 'No distinction is made in old editions between the two words, either in spelling or in use;' Schmidt. The allusion is to the temper of the *metal* of a sword-blade. See **Metal**. **Der.** *mettl-ed*; *mettle-some* (with E. suffix).

MEW (1), to cry as a cat. (E.) In Shak. Macb. iv. 1. 1; Hamlet, v. 1. 315; 'cry *mew*!' 1 Hen. IV, iii. i. 129. ME. *mawen*. 'Tybert [the cat] coude not goo awaye, but he *mawede* and galped so lowde,' i. e. mewed and yelped so loudly; Caxton, tr. of Reynard the Fox, ed. Arber, p. 22. Of imitative origin.+Low G. *mauen, miauen*. So also Pers. *maw*, the mewing of a cat; Arab. *mua*, a mewing; Rich. Dict. p. 1517. **Der.** *mew-l*, As You Like It, ii. 7. 144; this is a F. form, from MF. *miauler*, 'to mewl or mew like a cat,' Cot.

MEW (2), a sea-fowl, gull. (E.) ME. *mawe*. 'Hec fuliga, *semawe*' [sea-mew]; Voc. 641. 1. AS. *mǣw*. 'Alcedo, vel alcion, *mǣw*;' id. 131. 30; also *mēau*, id. 5. 16; *mēu*, 432. 9.+NFries. *mēwe*; Du. *meeuw*; Icel. *mār*; Dan. *maage*; Norw. *maake*; G. *möwe*. β. Teut. types *mai(g)wiz, *maihwoz*; Idg. types *moiqis, *moigos (N. E. D.). Perhaps allied to Skt. *mēchaka-s*, dark-blue.

MEW (3), a cage for hawks, &c. (F.—L.) The sense of 'cage' gave rise to the verb *mew*, to enclose. [The verb *mew* also meant 'to moult,' which is the orig. sense in French; cf. ME. *mewen*, to change; Chaucer, Troil. ii. 1258.] ME. *mewe, mewwe, mue*. 'And by hire beddes heed she made a *mewe*;' Chaucer, C. T. 10957 (F 643). 'In *mexwe*;' Will. of Palerne, 3336. 'In *mue*;' Knight de la Tour Landry, ch. 64; ed. Wright, p. 85, l. 3 from bottom.—OF. *mue*, 'a change, or changing; any casting of the coat or skin, as the *mewing* of a hawke; ... also, a hawks *mue*; and a *mue*, or coope wherein fowle is fattened;' Cot. So also Guernsey *mue*, a mew.—F. *muer*, 'to change, to *mue*, to cast the head, coat, or skin;' Cot.—L. *mūtāre*, to change. β. For **moutāre*, frequentative form of *movēre*, to move; see **Move**. Cf. *prūdens* for *prouidens*, *būbus* for *bouibus* (Bréal). **Der.** *mew-s*, s. pl., a range of stabling, orig. a place for falcons; the reason for the change of name is given in Stow's Survey of London, ed. 1842, p. 167. 'Then is the *Mewse*, so called of the king's falcons there kept by the king's falconer, which of old time was an office of great account, as appeareth by a record of Rich. II, in the 1st year of his reign ... After which time [A. D. 1534] the fore-named house called the *Mewse*, by Charing-cross, was new built, *and prepared for stabling of the king's horses*, in the reign of Edw. VI and Queen Mary, and *so remaineth to that use.*' Also *mew*, vb., to cage up, confine, of which the pp. *mued* occurs in The Knight de la Tour Landry, ch. 64, p. 85, l. 29. Also *mew*, vb., to moult, cast the coat; 'But I have *mew'd* that coat,' Beaum. and Fletcher, Little French Lawyer, iii. 2. See **Moult**.

MEWL; see under **Mew** (1).

MEWS, a range of stabling; see **Mew** (3).

MEZZOTINTO, a mode of engraving. (Ital.—L.) See Evelyn's Diary, Mar. 13, 1661.—Ital. *mezzo tinto*, half tinted.—Ital. *mezzo* (L. *medius*); and *tinto*, pp. of *tingere*, to tinge. See **Mediate** and **Tinge**.

MIASMA, pollution, infectious matter. (Gk.) In Phillips, ed. 1706.—Gk. μίασμα, pollution, stain.—Gk. μιαίνειν, to stain.

MICA, a glittering mineral. (L.) '*Mica*, a crum, or little quantity of anything that breaks off; also glimmer, or cat-silver, a metallick body like silver, which shines in marble and other stones, but cannot be separated from them;' Phillips, ed. 1706. Cf. mod. F. and Span. *mica*, mica. Apparently from L. *mica*, a crumb (see **Microcosm**); but it seems to have been applied to the mineral from a notion that this word is related to L. *micāre*, to shine, glimmer; which is not the case. **Der.** *mic-ac-e-ous*, a coined adj.

MICH, to skulk, hide, play truant. (E.) ME. *michen*, Prompt. Parv. The sb. *micher*, a skulking thief, occurs in the Rom. of the Rose, 6541; and, much earlier, spelt *muchare*, in Ancren Riwle, p. 150, last line. The ME. *muchen, michen*, result from an AS. form **myccan*, not found. But it is allied by gradation to OHG. *mūhhon*, to lie in wait secretly; whence G. *meucheln*, to assassinate, *meuch-lings*, insidiously, maliciously. See *meuchel-* in Kluge. **Der.** *mich-er*,

1 Hen. IV, ii. 4. 450, and in Ancren Riwle (as above); *mich-ing*, Hamlet, iii. 2. 146.

MICHAELMAS, the feast of St. Michael. (Hybrid; F.—Heb. and L.) ME. *michelmesse, mychelmesse*, P. Plowman, B. xiii. 240. **1.** *Michel* is from F. *Michel*, the F. form of Heb. *Mīkhāēl*, a proper name, signifying 'who is like unto God?' from Heb. *mī*, who? *ke*, like, *El*, God. **2.** The suffix *-mas*, ME. *messe*, AS. *mæsse*, is from L. *missa*, a mass; see **Mass** (2).

MICKLE, great. (E.) ME. *mikel, mukel, michel, muchel, mochel*; used as adv. in Chaucer, C. T. 260 (A 258). And see Havelok, 1025; Ormulum, 788; &c. AS. *micel*; Grein, ii. 242.+Icel. *mikill* (*mykill*); Goth. *mikils*; MHG. *michel*, OHG. *mihil*.+Gk. μεγάλ-η, fem., great. Allied to Gk. μέγας, great, L. *magnus*. See **Much**.

MICROBE, a very minute living being. (F.—Gk.) F. *microbe*, due to Sédillot (1878); and prob. meant to express 'small living being;' but it should mean 'short-lived.'—Gk. μικρόβιος, short-lived. —Gk. μικρός, also σμικρός, little; and βίος, life.

MICROCOSM, a little world. (F.—L.—Gk.) This term, meaning 'a little universe,' was applied in old times to man, who was regarded as a model or epitome of the universe. In Minsheu, ed. 1627. 'This word is sometimes applied to man, as being a compendium of all other creatures, his body being compared to the baser part of the world, and his soul to the blessed angels;' Blount, ed. 1674. Also in Shak. Cor. ii. 1. 68.—F. *microcosme*, 'a little world;' Cot.—L. *microcosmus*.—Gk. μικρόκοσμος, a little world.—Gk. μικρο-, decl. stem of μικρός, also σμικρός, small, little; and κόσμος, a world (see **Cosmetic**).

MICROSCOPE, an instrument for viewing small objects. (Gk.) In Milton, P. R. iv. 57. Coined from Gk. μικρό-, decl. stem of μικρός, small; and σκοπ-εῖν, to behold, see. Cf. Gk. ἐπί-σκοπος, an overseer, bishop. See **Microcosm** and **Scope**. **Der.** *microscop-ic, microscop-ic-al*. So also *micro-meter*, an instrument for measuring small distances; see **Metre**. Many compounds begin with *micro-*.

MID, middle. (E.) ME. *mid, midde*; only used in compounds and phrases; see Stratmann. AS. *mid, midd*, adj., middle; Grein, ii. 248.+Du. *mid-*, used in composition, as *mid-dag*, mid-day; Icel. *miðr*, adj.; Swed. and Dan. *mid-*, in composition; Goth. *midjis*; OHG. *mitti*, adj.+L. *medius*, adj.; Gk. μέσος, Æolic μέσσος (=*μίθ-yos); Skt. *madhya-*, adj., middle. Teut. type *medjoz; Idg. type *medhjos, adj. **Der.** *amid*, q. v., whence the use of *mid* (for 'mid) as a preposition, like Russ. *mejdu, mej*', amid; *a-mid-s-t*, q. v. Also *mid-day*, AS. *mid-dæg*, John, iv. 6; *mid-land*, 2 Macc. viii. 35 (A.V.); *mid-night*, AS. *mid-niht*, Voc. 175. 38; *mid-rib*, a modern botanical term, not in Todd's Johnson; *mid-riff*, q. v.; *mid-ship*, short for *amid-ship*, whence also the term *midship-beam*, Phillips, World of Words, ed. 1706; *mid-ship-man*; *mid-summer*, AS. *midsumor*, A. S. Chron., an. 1052; *mid-way*, ME. *midwei*, Ancren Riwle, p. 412. Also *mid-dle*, q. v.; *mid-st*, q. v. Also (from L. *medi-us*), *mediate*, &c.

MIDDEN, a dunghill. (Scand.) Common in dialects. ME. *midding*; spelt *myddyng*, Palladius, i. 750.—Dan. *möddyng*, a dunghill (for **mögdynge*).—Dan. *mög* (Icel. *myki*), muck; Dan. *dynge*, a heap. Lit. 'muck-heap.' Dan. *dynge*=Swed. *dynga*, dung; allied to E. *dung*. See **Muck** and **Dung**.

MIDDLE, adj., intervening, intermediate. (E.) ME. *middel*, adj. 'In the *myddel* place;' Mandeville's Travels, p. 2 (in Spec. of English, p. 165, l. 34). Also *middel*, sb. 'Aboute hir *middel*;' Gower, C. A. ii. 47, l. 12; bk. iv. 1356. AS. *middel*, sb., Grein, ii. 249. β. Formed with suffix *-el* from AS. *midd*, adj.; see **Mid**.+Du. *middel*, adj., adv., and sb.; G. *mittel*, sb., means; OHG. *mittil*, adj., middle. Cf. Icel. *meðal*, prep. among. **Der.** *middle-man*, given in Phillips, ed. 1706, as a military term, signifying 'he that stands middlemost in a file;' *middl-ing*, used by L'Estrange and Dryden (Johnson), not an early word; *middle-most*, Ezek. xlii. 5 (in the Bible of 1551 and in the A. V.), an ill-coined superlative on the model of *fore-most* and *after-most*.

MIDGE, a small fly or gnat. (E.) ME. *migge, mygge*. 'Hec sicoma, a *myge*' [better *mygge*]; Voc. 707. 4. AS. *micge*, Ælfric's Gloss., Nom. Insectorum; in Voc. 122. 7; 'Culix, *mygc*' [for *mycg*]; id. Voc. 261. 6; *mygg*, 16. 23. Here *micge* is for *mycge*, where *y* is due to an earlier *u*, with the usual vowel-change.+Du. *mug*, a gnat; Low G. *mugge*, Bremen Wörterbuch; Swed. *mygg*; Dan. *myg*; G. *mücke*, OHG. *mucca, mugga*. β. Teut. types *mugjōn-, f.; *mugjoz, m.; perhaps the orig. sense was 'buzzer,' from the noise made by the insect's wings. Cf. Gk. μύζειν, to mutter, μυῖα, a fly (Prellwitz); also Icel. *mȳ*, a midge. **Der.** *mug-wort*, q.v.

MIDRIFF, the diaphragm, separating the heart from the stomach, &c. (E.) ME. *midrif, myc.ryf*, Prompt. Parv. AS. *midrif*. '*Disseptum*, midrif; *Exta*, midrif;' Voc. 159. 40, 42. Older form *midhrif*; A. S. Leechdoms, ii. 260.—AS. *mid*, middle; and *hrif*, the belly, the womb, Grein, ii. 104. Cf. Du. *rif*, in the sense of 'carcase;' OHG. *href*, the body, OFries. *rif*, *ref*, the belly, *midref*, the midriff. ¶ With AS. *hrif* compare L. *corp-us*, body.

MIDST, the middle. (E.) 'In the *midst*,' Com. Errors, i. 1. 104; and 11 other times in Shakespeare. 'In *middest* of his race;' Spenser, F. Q. vi. 3. 25. *In the midst* is from this older phrase *in middest*. Moreover, the *t* is excrescent, as in *whils-t*, *amongs-t*; and *in middest* answers to ME. *in middes*, as in '*in myddes* the se' = in the midst of the sea, Pricke of Conscience, l. 2938. A parallel phrase is *amyddes*, P. Plowman, B. xiii. 82. **β**. Here the *s* gives the phrase an adverbial force, and is due to the habit of forming adverbs from the AS. gen. case in *-es*. The older form is without the *s*, as in *a midde*, Layamon, 4836, also spelt *a midden*, id. 8154. Still earlier, we have *on midden*, Luke, xxiv. 36, in the latest version of the A. S. Gospels, where the earlier version has *on mydlene*. **γ**. The ME. form *midde* answers to AS. *middan*, dat. case of the sb. *midde*, formed from the adj. *mid*, middle. See **Mid**; and see **Amidst**.

MIDWIFE, a woman who assists another in childbirth. (E.) ME. *mydwyf*, P. Plowman's Crede, l. 78; *mydwyf*, Myrc's Duties of Parish Priest, ed. Peacock, l. 98; *mydewyf*, id. l. 87; *mydwijf*, Wyclif, Gen. xxxviii. 27 (later version); *medewife*, id. (earlier version). The false spelling *medewife* (not common) is due to confusion with *mede*, i. e. meed, reward; this has misled Verstegan and others as to the etymology. In Cursor Mundi, 5543, the Fairfax MS. has the pl. *midwyues*; but the Cotton MS. has *midwimmen* (mid-women). **β**. The prefix *mid-* is certainly nothing but the once common AS. and ME. *mid*, prep., together with; it occurs again as a part of the ME. *midþolinge*, compassion (lit. suffering with), Ayenbite of Inwyt, p. 157. There are several such compounds in AS.; as *mid-wyrcan*, to work with, Mk. xvi. 20, *mid-wyrhta*, a worker together with, co-adjutor, A. S. Chron. an. 945; see Bosworth. This AS. *mid* is cognate with Du. *mede*, with (whence *medebroeder*, a companion, lit. mid-brother, *medegenoot*, a partner, *medehelpen*, to assist); also with G. *mit* (whence G. *mit-bruder*, a comrade, *mithelfer*, a helper, *mitmachen*, to take a part in, &c.); also with Gk. μετά, with (whence μεταλαμβάνειν, to participate). The sense of *mid* in this compound is clearly 'helping with,' or 'assisting.' **γ**. The ME. *wif* means no more than 'woman;' see **Wife**, **Woman**. And see **Meta-**. Der. *midwif-er-y*, spelt *midwifry* in Bp. Hall, Sat. i. 1. 25, a clumsy compound, with F. suffix *-ery* (= F. *-erie*).

MIEN, look, bearing, demeanour. (F. – C.) Spelt *meen* in Blount's Gloss., ed. 1674. He has: '*Meen* (F. *mine*), the countenance, figure, gesture, or posture of the face.' [*Meane* in Spenser, F. Q. vi. 7. 39, is a different word.] – F. *mine*, 'the countenance, look, cheer;' Cot. **β**. The F. word is not found earlier than the 15th century; still, Ital. *mina* is borrowed from it (Hatzfeld). Prob. of Celtic origin. – Bret. *min*, muzzle, beak (also used of men); cf. W. *min*, lip; Irish *mēn*, mouth; Corn. *mein*, *min*, lip, mouth (Thurneysen). Celtic types **maknā*, **mekno-*, open mouth; Stokes-Fick, 197. (So Hatzfeld; Körting, § 6172).

MIGHT (1), power, strength. (E.) ME. *might*, *miȝt*; Chaucer, C. T. 5580 (B 1160). AS. *miht*, *meht*, *mæht*; Grein, ii. 235. + Du. *magt*; Goth. *mahts*; G. *macht*, OHG. *maht*. **β**. Teut. type **mahtiz*, for **mag-tiz*, might (Fick, iii. 227); from MAG, to be able; see **May** (1). Cf. Russ. *moche*, might, from *moche*, to be able. Der. *might-y*, AS. *mihtig*, *meahtig*, Grein, ii. 237; *might-i-ly*, *might-i-ness*.

MIGHT (2), was able. (E.) AS. *meahte*, *mihte*, pt. t. of *mugan*, to be able; Grein, ii. 267. See **May** (1).

MIGNONETTE, an annual plant. (F. – G.) Modern. Added by Todd to Johnson. – F. *mignonette*, fem. dimin. of *mignon*, a darling. See **Minion**.

MIGRATE, to remove from one country to another. (L.) The sb. *migration* is in Cotgrave, and in Blount's Gloss., ed. 1674. – L. *migrātus*, pp. of *migrāre*, to wander; connected with Gk. ἀμείβειν, to change (Prellwitz). Der. *migration*, from F. *migration*, 'a migration' (Cot.), from L. acc. *migrātiōnem*. Also *migrat-or-y*, *e-migrate*, *im-migrate*.

MIKADO, the emperor of Japan. (Japan.) From Jap. *mikado*, said to mean 'high gate;' like the Turkish *Sublime Porte*. – Jap. *mi*, august, exalted; *kado*, gate, door.

MILCH, milk-giving. (E.) In Gen. xxxii. 15. 'A hundred *r ch* kine;' Tam. Shrew, ii. 1. 359. '*Mylch cowe*, vacca mulsaria;' Prompt. Parv., p. 337. Also *melche*, as in Lay le Freine, 196; in Weber, Met. Rom., vol. i. From AS. *melc*, adj., milch (see Bosworth; The Shrine, p. 130, l. 3. Allied to **Milk**, q. v. Cf. Icel. *mjólk*, milk; *milkr*, *mjólkr*, adj., milk-giving; *milk ær*, a milch ewe. So G. *melk*, adj., milch; Low G. *melsch* (Schambach).

MILD, gentle, kind, soft. (E.) ME. *mild*, *milde*; Rob. of Glouc. p. 72, l. 1625. AS. *milde*, Grein, ii. 250. + Du. *mild*; OSax. *mildi*; Icel. *mildr*; Dan. and Swed. *mild*; G. *mild*, OHG. *milti*; Goth. *mildeis*, only in comp. *un-mildeis*, without natural affection, 2 Tim. iii. 3. Allied to Gk. μαλθακός, soft, mild; OIrish *meld*, pleasant;

Skt. *mṛdh*, to grow weary of, disregard (Macdonell); root **meldh*. Brugmann, i. § 591, ii. § 690. Der. *mild-ly*, *mild-ness*.

MILDEW, a kind of blight. (E.) ME. *meldew*, Wyclif, Gen. xli. 6. AS. *meledēaw*, honey-dew, Grein, ii. 230; *mildēaw*, Voc. 455. 19. Cf. OHG. *militou*, mildew, cited by Grein. **β**. The sense is prob. 'honey-dew,' from the sticky honey-like appearance of some kinds of blight, as, e. g. on lime-trees. Cf. Goth. *milith*, honey; allied to L. *mel*, Gk. μέλι, honey; Irish *mil*, honey, *milcheo*, mildew. See **Mellifluous** and **Dew**. ¶ The mod. G. word is *mehlthau*, i. e. meal-dew; but this is an altered form, as it does not agree with the OHG. *militou*; the OHG. for 'meal' being *melo*.

MILE, a measure of distance, 1760 yards. (L.) ME. *mile*, pl. *mile*, Chaucer, C. T. 16023 (G 555). AS. *mil*, a mile; fem. sb., with pl. *mīla*, *mīle*; Grein, ii. 250. Formed from L. pl. *mīlia*, more commonly *millia*, used in the sense of a Roman mile; the proper sense is 'thousands.' The older name for the Roman mile was *mille passus*, or *mille passuum*, a thousand paces. **β**. Hence also G. *meile*, OHG. *mila*, a mile; Du. *mijl*, a mile, &c. ¶ The ME. unchanged pl. *mile* explains such a phrase as 'a ten-mile stage.' Der. *mile-age* (with F. suffix); *mile-stone*. And see *millenary*, *milfoil*, *million*.

MILFOIL, the name of a plant. (F. – L.) In a Vocabulary of Plant-names, said to be of the thirteenth century, we find '*Mille-folium*, milfoil;' Wright's Vocab. i. 139. The sense is 'thousand-leaf,' from the minute and numerous sections into which the leaf is divided. – OF. *milfoil*; from F. *mille*, a thousand, and OF. *fuil*, *foil*, m., a leaf. – L. *mīlifolium*, *millefolium*, milfoil; from *mille*, a thousand, and *folium*, a leaf. See **Foil**. ¶ The true E. name is *yarrow*, q. v.

MILITATE, to contend, fight, be opposed to. (L.) Modern. Added by Todd to Johnson's Dict. [But *militant*, chiefly used of 'the church *militant*,' occurs in Barnes, Works, p. 253, col. 2.] – L. *mīlitātus*, pp. of *mīlitāre*, to serve as a soldier, fight. – L. *mīlit-*, stem of *mīles*, a soldier. Root uncertain. Der. *militant*, from L. *mīlitant-*, stem of pres. pt. of *mīlitāre*. From L. *mīlit-* we have also *milit-ar-y*, All's Well, i. 1. 132; *milit-ar-ist*, a coined word, All's Well, iv. 3. 161. Also *milit-ia*, q. v.

MILITIA, a body of soldiers for home service. (L.) 'Except his *militia* of natives be of good and valiant soldiers;' Bacon, Essay 29, Of Greatness of Kingdoms. – L. *mīlitia*, (1) warfare, (2) troops, army. – L. *mīlit-*, stem of *mīles*, a soldier. See **Militate**. Der. *militia-man*.

MILK, a white fluid secreted by female mammals for feeding their young. (E.) ME. *milk*, Chaucer, C. T. 360 (A 358). OMerc. *milc* (in Sweet, O. E. Texts). AS. *meolc*, sometimes *meoluc*; Grein, ii. 240. + Du. *melk*; OSax. *miluk*; Icel. *mjólk*; Dan. *melk*; Swed. *mjölk*; Goth. *miluks*; G. *milch*. Teut. stem **meluk-*, f. Allied to AS. *melcan*, str. vb., pt. t. *mealc*; G. *melken* (pt. t. *molk*, pp. *gemolken*), OHG. *melchan*, to milk; orig. 'to stroke,' from the action employed in milking a cow. **β**. Teut. type **melkan-*, pt. t. **malk*, str. vb.; allied to Gk. ἀμέλγειν, to milk, L. *mulgēre*, to milk; Lith. *milsz-ti*, to milk, OIrish *blig-im*, I milk. From √MELG; Brugmann, i. § 628. The older sense appears in Skt. *mṛj*, to wipe, rub, stroke, sweep; from √MERG, to rub, wipe. Der. *milk-er*, *milk-y*; *milk-maid*, *milk-pail*, *milk-tree*; *milk-sop*, q. v.; *milch*, q. v.

MILKSOP, an effeminate man. (E.) 'Allas, she seith, that euer I was shape To wedde a *milksop*, or a coward ape;' Chaucer, C. T. 13916 (B 3100). The lit. sense is 'bread soaked in milk;' hence, a soft, effeminate man. From ME. *milk*, milk; and *soppe*, a sop, bread soaked in milk. See **Milk** and **Sop**.

MILL, a machine for grinding corn, &c. (L.) ME. *melle* (riming with *telle*); Chaucer, C. T. 3921 (A 3923). Also *mulle*, in comp. *windmulle*, a windmill, Rob. of Glouc. p. 547, l. 11383. *Mill* is a corruption, for ease of pronunciation, of *miln*, still in use provincially; cf. the name *Milner*, equivalent to the commoner *Miller*. Similarly, ME. *mulle* is for ME. *mulne*, which occurs in Sir Gawain, ed. Morris, 2203. In P. Plowman, A. ii. 80, we have as various readings the forms *mulnere*, *mylnere*, *myllere*, *mellere*, a miller, corresponding respectively to *mulne*, *mylne*, *mylle*, *melle*, a mill. AS. *myln*, a mill; '*Molendinum*, *myln*;' Voc. 330. 19. Also spelt *mylen*, Grein, ii. 270. Not an E. word, but borrowed from Late L. *mulina*, for L. *molina*, a mill; whence also Icel. *mylna*, a mill. Extended from L. *mola*, a mill, lit. 'that which grinds;' cf. *molere*, to grind. – √MEL, to grind, rub; whence also Lithuan. *malti*, Goth. *malan*, G. *mahlen*, to grind. Brugmann, i. § 121 (2). Der. *mill-cog*, *mill-dam*, *mill-race*, *mill-stone*, *mill-wright*, *mill-wheel*. Also *mill-er*, *mill-er's-thumb* (a fish). See **Meal** (1).

MILLENNIUM, a thousand years. (L.) In Johnson's Dict. – Mod. L. **millennium*, a period of a thousand years. – L. *mille*, a thousand; and *annus*, a year; see **Annual**. The same change of vowel occurs in *bi-ennial*, *tri-ennial*, &c. Der. *millenni-al*. ☞ We also find *millenary*, Bp. Taylor, Sermons, vol. ii. ser. 12 (R.). This is from L. *millēnārius*, belonging to a thousand, a derivative of pl. adj. *millēni*, extended from *mille*, a thousand.

MILLET, the name of a plant. (F.—L.) In Holland, tr. of Pliny, bk. xviii. c. 7.—F. *millet*, 'millet, mill;' Cot. Dimin. of F. *mil*, 'mill, millet;' Cot.—L. *milium*, millet; whence also AS. *mil*, millet (Bosworth).+Gk. μελίνη, millet. Root uncertain. **Der.** *mili-ar-y*, directly from L. *milium*.

MILLINER, one who makes bonnets, &c. (Ital.) In Shak. Wint. Ta. iv. 4. 192. 'A *millaner's* wife;' Ben Jonson, Every Man (ed. Wheatley), i. 3. 120; see the note. A *milliner* or *millaner* was formerly of the male sex. Spelt *millener* in Phillips; *millenier* in Minsheu. Origin somewhat disputed; but probably for *Milaner*, a dealer in wares from *Milan*, in Italy. Milan steel was in good repute at an early period; we find 'And a *Millaine* knife fast by my knee' in the Percy Folio MS., ed. Hales and Furnivall, i. 68; where a note says: 'The dealers in miscellaneous articles were also called *milliners*, from their importing *Milan* goods for sale, such as brooches, aiglets, spurs, glasses, &c.; Saunders's Chaucer, p. 241.' Chapman has: 'Milan, a rich state of haberdashers;' The Ball, Act v. See examples in Palmer, Folk-Etymology. The Ital. *Milano*, L. *Mediolānum*, is a name of Celtic origin; see Bacmeister, Kelt. Briefe, pp. 71, 102. We must also remember that the old sense of *milliner* was a haberdasher, or seller of small wares; see Minsheu, ed. 1627, whose suggestion that *milliner* is derived from L. *mille* (a thousand) is to be rejected, though it shows that their wares were of a very miscellaneous character, and that they had 'a thousand small wares to sell.' ¶ We also have the term *mantua-maker*, as if from the Italian town of *Mantua*, but this is a corruption of Ital. *manto*. **Der.** *milliner-y*.

MILLION, a thousand thousand. (F.—L.) ME. *millioun*; Chaucer, C. T. 7267 (D 1685).—F. *million*, 'a million;' Cot.—Late L. *milliōnem*, acc. of *millio*; Ducange. Evidently a coined word, extended from L. *mille*, a thousand. See **Mile**. **Der.** *million-th*; *million-aire*, from F. *millionnaire*.

MILREIS, a Portuguese coin. (Port.—L.) Formerly *milree*. '*Mill-Ree* or a Thousand Rees, a Portuguese coin, worth 6s. 8½d. sterling;' Phillips (1706). Now worth ab. 4s. 6d.—Port. *milreis*; from *mil*, a thousand, and *reis*, pl. of *real*, 'a Port. coin called ree, equal to 27/400d.;' Vieyra. He also gives: '*mil réis*, a milree, equal to 5s. 7½d.;' (1857).—L. *mille*, a thousand; *rēgālem*, acc. of *rēgālis*, royal. See **Real** (2).

MILT (1), the spleen. (E.) ME. *milte*, O. Eng. Miscellany, ed. Morris, p. 178, l. 171. AS. *milte*; 'Splen, *milte*;' Voc. 160. 35. +Du. *milt*, the spleen; Icel. *milti*, the spleen; Dan. *milt*; Swed. *mjälte*; G. *milz*, milt; OHG. *meltjōn-*. Teut. stem **meltjo-*, **meltjōn-*. β. All from the verb to *melt*, in the sense 'to digest;' cf. Icel. *melta*, (1) to malt for brewing, (2) to digest; see **Melt**.

MILT (2), soft roe of fishes. (MDu.) In Walton's Angler, with the spelling *melt*; see Todd. Palsgrave has: '*Mylte* [in] a fysshe, *laicte de poisson*.' In this sense, it was prob. borrowed from MDu. *milte*, 'the milt of a fish,' Hexham; cf. Norw. *mjelte*, the same. Doubtless confused with *milk*, sometimes used in the same sense; cf. '*Lactes*, mylke of fyshe;' Voc. 591. 16. This use of the word is known elsewhere. Cf. Swed. *mjölk*, milk; *mjölke*, milt of fishes; *mjölkfisk*, a milter, lit. milk-fish; Dan. *fiske-mælk*, soft roe, lit. fish-milk. So also G. *milch*, (1) milk, (2) milt of fishes; MDu. *melcker van een visch*, 'the milt of a fish,' Hexham; Low G. *melk*, milk, also milt (Lübben). **Der.** *milt*, vb., *milt-er*.

MIMIC, imitative, apt in imitating. (L.—Gk.) 'Mimic Fancy;' Milton, P. L. v. 110. The sb. *mimick* occurs in Milton, Samson, 1325; and once in Shak. Mids. Nt. Dr. iii. 2. 19, spelt *mimmick* in the folios.—L. *mīmicus*, farcical.—Gk. μιμικός, imitative, belonging to or like a mime.—Gk. μῖμος, an imitator, actor, mime. **Der.** *mimic*, sb., *mimic*, vb., *mimic-ry*. We sometimes find *mime*, directly from Gk. μῖμος; also *mim-et-ic*, from Gk. μιμητικός, imitative, from μιμη-τής, an imitator.

MINARET, a turret on a mosque. (Span.—Arab.) Added by Todd to Johnson; it occurs in Swinburne's Travels through Spain; letter 44.—Span. *minarete*, a high slender turret.—Arab. *manārat*, a candle-stick, lamp, light-house, a turret on a mosque; Rich. Dict. p. 1496.—Arab. *manār*, the same, id.; connected with *nār*, fire, p. 1548.+Heb. *manōrāh*, a candle-stick; from *nūr*, to shine.

MINCE, to chop small. (F.—L.) ME. *mincen*; the pp. *mincid*, spelt *myncyd*, occurs in the Liber Cure Cocorum, ed. Morris, p. 18. —OF. *mincier*, MF. *mincer*, 'to mince, to shred;' Cot.—Late L. type **minūtiāre*, to mince, make small (see Schwan, § 199); from Late L. *minūtia*, a small piece.—L. *minūtus*, small; see **Minute**. Cf. F. dial. *mincer* (Berry); Norm. dial. *mincher*, to break up (Moisy). ¶ From the same root we have AS. *minsian*, to become small, to fail. It only occurs twice: '*wērigra wlite minsode*' = the comeliness of the accursed ones failed; Daniel, 268, ed. Grein; and again,

'*swiðe ne minsade*' = it did not greatly fail; Reimlied, 29. From the adj. *min*, small, Grein, ii. 252. Cf. Du. *min*, less; L. *min-or*, less; see **Minish**. See Körting, § 6202. **Der.** *minc-ing* = taking small steps, Isa. iii. 16; *mince-pie*, formerly *minced-pie*, Spectator, no. 629; *mince-meat*, formerly *minced-meat* (Baret).

MIND, the understanding, intellect, memory. (E.) ME. *mind*, *mynd*, often in the sense of memory; Chaucer, C. T. 1908, 4972 (A 1906, B 552). AS. *gemynd*, memory, mind, thought (where the prefixed *ge-* makes no difference); Grein, ii. 432. Formed (with the usual vowel-change of *u* to *y*) from AS. *munan*, to think, *gemunan*, to remember; id. i. 431; ii. 268.+Goth. *gamunds*, remembrance, f.; from *gamunan*, to remember. Teut. type **mundi-z*, f.; for **munthiz*, by Verner's law. Idg. type **mṇn-ti-s*; cf. L. *mens* (decl. stem *menti-*), mind; Skt. *ma-ti-*, f., mind. β. All from the weak grade of √MEN, to think; cf. Skt. *man*, to think, L. *me-min-i*, I remember. **Der.** *mind*, verb, from the sb.; cf. AS. *gemyndgian*, to remember, Grein, ii. 433; *mind-ed*; *like-mind-ed*; *mind-ful*, Shak. Lucrece, l. 1583; *mind-ful-ly*, *mind-ful-ness*; *mind-less*, Pricke of Conscience, 2088. From the same root, *mental*, *mentor*, *mania*, *mandarin*, *money*, *mint* (1), *mendacious*, *com-ment*, &c.

MINE (1), belonging to me. (E.) ME. *min*, pl. *mine*, Chaucer, C. T. 1146 (A 1144); frequently shortened to *my*, as in id. 1145. AS. *mīn*, poss. pron. (declinable), Grein, ii. 252; from AS. *mīn* (unchangeable), gen. case of the 1st pers. pronoun; see **Me**.+Goth. *meins*, poss. pron. (declinable), mine; from *meina*, gen. case of 1st personal pronoun. So in other Teut. tongues. **Doublet**, *my*.

MINE (2), to excavate, dig for metals. (F.—C.) In King Alisaunder, l. 1216; cf. l. 1218. 'And therupon anon he bad His mynours for to go and *myne*;' Gower, C. A. ii. 198; bk. v. 2120.— F. *miner*, 'to mine, or undermine;' Cot. Cf. Ital. *minare*, Span. and Port. *minar*, to mine. All of Celtic origin, according to Thurneysen (p. 67). Cf. Irish and Gael. *mein*, ore, vein of metal; OIrish *mianach*, ore (Windisch); W. *mwn*, ore, a mine; W. *mwn-glawdd*, a mine (from *clawdd*, a pit); Bret. *men-gleuz*, a mine (cf. *cleuz*, hollow), pron. *men-glé* in the dialect of Vannes. Celtic type **meini* (Stokes). **Der.** *mine*, sb.; *min-er*, ME. *minour*, as above; *min-ing*; *min-er-al*, q.v. Also *counter-mine*, *under-mine*.

MINERAL, what is dug out of mines. (F.—C.) ME. *mineral*. 'The thridde stone in special By name is cleped *mineral* Whiche the metalls of every *mine* Attempreth, til that thei ben fyne;' Gower, C. A. ii. 87; bk. iv. 2554.—F. *mineral*, 'a minerall;' Cot. Formed as adj. to accompany the sb. *miniere*, 'a mine of metals or minerals,' Cot.—F. *miner*, to mine; see **Mine** (2). Cf. Span. *minera*, a mine. **Der.** *mineral-ise*, *mineral-ist*, *minera(l)-logy* (where the final *l* is dropped, owing to the *l* following), a coined word from Gk. λόγος, discourse, from λέγειν, to speak; *minera-logi-c-al*, *mineralog-ist*.

MINEVER, MINIVER, the same as **Meniver**, q.v.

MINGLE, to mix, confuse. (E.) Common in Shak.; both trans. and intrans. K. Lear, i. 1. 242; Macb. iii. 4. 3. Spelt *myngell* in Palsgrave; but cf. *mengling*, sb., a mingling, More, Life of Rich. III, ed. Lumby, p. 70. A frequentative form, lit. 'to mix often,' from the older verb *ming*, ME. *mengen*, *mingen*. 'The busy bee, her honye now she *minges*;' Surrey, Desc. of Spring; see Spec. of Eng. ed. Skeat, p. 217 (C), l. 11. The ME. verb occurs as *ming*, imp., in Henrysoun, Test. of Cresseid, l. 613; it is more often *mengen*, and mostly used in the pp. *meint* (contracted form of *menged*), or *meind*, or *meynd*, Gower, C. A. ii. 262; bk. v. 4049. AS. *mengan*, to mix, also to become mixed; also spelt *mencgan*, *mængan*, Grein, ii. 231. β. The vowel-change (of *a* to *æ* or *e*) shows that *mengan* is a causal verb, derived from the older form *mang*, a mixture, preserved in the forms *ge-mang*, *ge-mong*, a mixture, crowd, assembly (where the prefixed *ge-* makes no difference), Grein, i. 425.+Du. *mengelen*, to mingle; from *mengen*, to mix; OFries. *mengia*, to mix; cf. *mong*, prep. *among*; Icel. *menga*, to mingle; G. *mengen*, to mingle. γ. These forms are all due to the sb. *mang*, a mixture, crowd, as above. ¶ Not allied to *mix*, nor to Gk. μίγνυμι. **Der.** *mingl-ing*; *com-mingle*, q.v. And see **Among**, **Monger**, and **Mongrel**.

MINIATURE, a painting on a small scale. (Ital.—L.) '*Miniature* (from *minium*, i. e. red lead), the art of drawing pictures in little, being done with red lead. *Miniated*, painted or inlaid, as we read of porcellane dishes *miniated* with gold;' Blount's Gloss. ed. 1674.— Ital. *miniatura*, a miniature; cf. Ital. *miniato*, pp. of *miniare*, 'to die, to paint, to colour or limne with vermilion or sinople or red lead;' Florio.—L. *minium*, cinnabar, red lead. β. Said to be an Iberian word, the Romans getting their *minium* from Spain; see Pliny, b. xxxiii. c. 7.

MINIKIN, a little darling. (Du.) In Baret (1580). Florio translates Ital. *mignone* by 'a minion, a fauorit, a minikin, a darling.' —Du. *minnekyn*, a cupid; Sewel's Du. Dict.; 'Minne, Minneken, my love;' Hexham's Du. Dict. ed. 1658. Dimin. of Du. *minne*, love, cognate with OHG. *minna*, love, allied to E. *mind*. See **Mind, Minion**. Der. *minikin*, adj., i.e. dear little, K. Lear, iii. 6. 45.

MINIM, a note in music; $\frac{1}{60}$th of a drachm. (F.–L.) *Mynym* in Palsgrave. The *minim* was once the shortest note, a quarter of the *breve*, or short note. The modern *semibreve* is so long a note that the breve is out of use. Formerly also spelt *minum*; Romeo, ii. 4. 22, second quarto (Schmidt).–OF. *minime*; '*minime blanche*, a minume in musick [so called from its open head]; *minime noire*, a crochet' [because wholly black]; Cot.–L. *minimum, minumum*, acc. of *minimus, minumus*, very small; a superlative form with Idg. suffix -*mo*- (Brugmann, ii. § 72) from a base *min*-, small. See **Minor**. Doublet, *minimum*, directly from L. neut. *minimum*, the smallest thing.

MINION, a favourite, flatterer. (F.–OHG.) Palsgrave has *mignyon*. In Shak. Temp. iv. 98; see Trench, Select Glossary.–F. *mignon*, 'a minion, favorite;' Cot.–F. *mignon*, adj., 'minion, dainty, neat, spruce; also pleasing, gentle, kind;' Cot. [The use as a sb., with a sinister sense, appears more clearly in Ital. *mignone*, 'a minion, a favorite, a dilling, a minikin, a darling;' Florio.] β. The F. -*on*, Ital. -*one*, is a mere suffix; the base *mign*- is due to MHG. *minne*, OHG. *minna, minni*, memory, remembrance, love; well-known by its derivative *minnesinger*=singer of love. γ. This OHG. *minna*, memory, is allied to L. *me-min-ī*, and to E. *mind*; see **Mind, Minikin**.

MINISH, to make little, diminish. (F.–L.) In Exod. v. 19; see Bible Word-book. ME. *menusen*. '*Menusid*, or maad lesse;' Wyclif, John, iii. 30, earlier version. Chaucer has the comp. *amenuse*, Pers. Tale, I 377 (Six-text).–F. *menuiser*, 'to minish, extenuate;' Cot. Cf. Ital. *minuzzare*, to mince, cut small.–Late L. *minūtiāre, not found; cf. Late L. *minūtāre*, to reduce to fragments.–L. *minūtia*, smallness.–L. *minūtus*, small (whence F. *menu*); see **Minute, Minor**. Der. *di-minish*; see *mince*.

MINISTER, a servant. (F.–L.) ME. *ministre*, Chaucer, C. T. 1665 (A 1663); Rob. of Brunne, tr. of Langtoft, p. 312, l. 13. [Afterwards altered to the L. form.]–F. *ministre*.–L. *ministrum*, acc. of *minister*, a servant. β. Formed with compar. suffix -*ter* from *min-es, related by gradation to *min-us*, adv. less, and to *min-or*, adj.; see **Minor, Minim**. Der. *minister*, vb., ME. *ministren*, Rob. of Brunne, p. 80, from F. *ministrer*, L. *ministrāre*; *minister-i-al*, *minister-i-al-ly*; *ministr-ant*, from the stem of pres. pt. of L. *ministrāre*; *ministr-at-ion*, from L. acc. *ministrātiōnem*, from *ministrāre*; *ministr-at-ive*; *ministr-y*. Also *minstrel*, q.v.

MINIVER, the same as **Meniver**, q.v.

MINK, a small stoat-like animal. (Low G.) 'Powlecats, weessels, and *minkes*;' Capt. J. Smith, Works, p. 60. 'Mynkes, a furre, *minques*;' Palsgrave.–Low G. *mink, menke*, a sort of otter (Lübben). Cf. MDan. *minke*, Swed. *menk*, a mink (Kalkar).

MINNESINGER, a German lyric poet of early times. (G.) 'Songs of the *Minnesingers*;' Longfellow, Hyperion; bk. i. ch. 8 (conclusion). They composed love-songs in the 12th and 13th centuries.–G. *minne*, love; *singer*, a singer. See **Minikin, Minion**.

MINNOW, the name of a very small fish. (E.) There are *two* similar names for the fish in early books; one corresponds to *minn-ow*, and is prob. **a** pure E. word; the other corresponds to OF. *menuise*. 1. ME. *menow*, spelt *menawe* in a Nominale of the 15th cent., in Voc. 704. 44; spelt *menoun*, pl. *menounys*, Barbour's Bruce, ii. 577. The suffix -*ow* cannot be traced to the earliest period; we find only AS. *myne*. 'Capito, *myne*, vel ǣlepūte' [eel-pout];' Voc. 180. 38. We also find, in Ælfric's Colloquy (Voc. 94. 13), with the acc. pl. *mynas* and *ǣlepūtan* as a gloss to Late L. *menas et capitones*. This AS. *myne* is cognate with OHG. *muniwa*, a minnow (Kluge). It is not a mere borrowing from L. *mena*. Similarly, the AS. *pyle*, a pillow, answers to E. *pillow*. 2. The ME. *menuse* occurs (spelt *menuce*) in the Prompt. Parv. p. 333; and (spelt *menuse*) in the Babees Book, ed. Furnivall, p. 168, l. 747. Cf. 'Hec menusa, a *menys*;' Voc. 763. 33.–OF. *menuise*, 'small fish of divers sorts, the small frie of fish;' Cot. Clearly connected with L. *minūtia*, smallness, also, a small particle; from L. *minūtus*, minute; see **Minute**. ¶ The Late L. *mēna*, L. *maena*, is not the same word, being borrowed from Gk. μαίνη, a small sea-fish, often salted.

MINOR, less, inferior. (L.) Like *major*, it was a term familiar in logic. It occurs in Sir T. More, Works, p. 504 d.–L. *minor*, less; compar. from a base *min*, small, not found in Latin, but occurring in the very form *min* in NFriesic and Low G.+Icel. *minnr*, less (no positive); Goth. *minniza*, less (no positive). β. All from *mi, weak grade of √MEI, to diminish; Brugmann, i. § 84. Der. *minor-i-ty*, Rich. III, i. 3. 11, coined in imitation of *major-ity*.

MINOTAUR, a fabulous monster. (L.–Gk.) ME. *Minotaure*, Chaucer, C. T. 982 (A 980).–L. *Minōtaurus*.–Gk. Μινώταυρος, a monster, half man, half bull; born, according to the story, of

Pasiphaë, wife of Minos.–Gk. Μίνω-, for Μίνως, Minos, king of Crete; and ταῦρος, a bull.

MINSTER, a monastery. (L.–Gk.) ME. *minster*; in the name *West-minster*, of frequent occurrence; P. Plowman, B. iii. 12; &c. AS. *mynster*, Grein, ii. 271. Borrowed early from L. *monastērium*, a monastery. See **Monastery**, which is a doublet.

MINSTREL, a musical performer. (F.–L.) ME. *minstrel*, *minstral*; spelt *mynstral*, P. Plowman, B. prol. 33; *ministral*, Chaucer, C. T. 10392 (F 78); *menestral*, Ayenbite of Inwyt, p. 192. The pl. *menestraus* occurs in Ancren Riwle, p. 84, l. 11.–OF. *menestrel*, 'a minstrell;' Cot. Also *menestral* (whence pl. *menestraus*).–Late L. *ministrālis, ministeriālis*, a retainer; hence applied to the lazy train of retainers who played instruments, acted as buffoons and jesters, and the like.–L. *minister*, a servant; see **Minister**. Der. *minstrel-sy*, Lydgate, London Lyckpeny, st. 12; see Spec. of English, ed. Skeat, p. 26; spelt *minstralcye*, Chaucer, C. T. 2673 (A 2671).

MINT (1), a place where money is coined. (L.) ME. *mint*; spelt *mynt*, Myrc's Instructions for Parish Priests, l. 1775; *menet*, Ayenbite of Inwyt, p. 241. AS. *mynet, mynyt*, a coin; Matt. xxii. 19. Not an AS. word, but borrowed from L. *monēta*, (1) a mint, (2) money. β. *Monēta* was a surname of Juno, in whose temple at Rome money was coined. The lit. sense is 'the warning one,' from *monēre*, to warn, admonish, lit. 'to cause to remember;' cf. L. *me-min-ī*, I remember. See Bréal; and Brugmann, ii. § 79. Cf. G. *münze*, mint; MDu. *munte*. Der. *mint*, vb., *mint-er*, *mint-age*. Doublet, *money*.

MINT (2), the name of an aromatic plant. (L.–Gk.) ME. *minte, mynte*, Wyclif, Matt. xxiii. 23. AS. *minte*, Matt. xxiii. 23; Voc. 2. 7. Not an E. word, but merely borrowed from L. *menta, mentha*, Matt. xxiii. 23 (Vulgate).–Gk. μίνθα, μίνθος, mint.

MINUET, the name of a dance. (F.–L.) '*Menuet* or *Minuet*, a sort of French dance, or the tune belonging to it;' Phillips, ed. 1706. So called from the short steps in it.–F. *menuët*, 'smallish, little, pretty;' Cot. Dimin. of F. *menu*, small.–L. *minūtus*; see **Minute**.

MINUS, the sign of subtraction. (L.) Mathematical.–L. *minus*, less; neuter of *minor*, less; see **Minor**.

MINUSCULE, small, as applied to a letter in early MSS. (L.) '*Minuscule* letters are cursive forms of the earlier uncials;' Is. Taylor, The Alphabet, i. 71.–L. *minuscula* (sc. *littera*), fem. of *minusculus*, rather small; dimin. of *minus* (*minor*), less.

MINUTE, very small, slight. (L.) An accentuation on the first syllable occurs in: 'With *minute* drops;' Milton, Il Penseroso, l. 130. But the word first came into use as a sb., in which use it is much older. ME. *minute*, meaning (1) a minute of an hour, (2) a minute of a degree in a circle. 'Foure *minutes*, that is to seyn, *minutes* of an houre;' Chaucer, On the Astrolabe, pt. i. § 7. l. 8. 'A degree of a signe contieneth 60 *minutes*;' id. pt. i. § 8. l. 11.–L. *minūtus*, small (whence F. *menu*); Late L. *minūta*, fem., a small portion, a mite (of money). Pp. of *minuere*, to make small.–L. *min*-, small, only found in *min-or*, less, *min-imus*, least; but cognate with NFries. *min*, small.+Gk. μινύ-θειν, to make small.–√MEI, to diminish; cf. Skt. *mī*, to hurt. See **Minor, Minish**. Der. *minute-ly*, *minute-ness*; and from the sb., *minute-book*, *minute-glass*, *minute-gun*, *minute-hand*.

MINX, a pert, wanton woman. (Low G.) In Shak. Tw. Nt. iii. 4. 133; Oth. iii. 3. 475. An adaptation of Low G. *minsk*, (1) m., a man, (2) n., a pert female. Cf. G. *mensch*, neut., a wench; Du. *mensch*, n. (vulgar), a woman; *het oude mensch*, the old woman (Calisch). The G. *mensch* was orig. an adj.=*mann-ish*, from *mann*, a man. Cf. AS. *mennisc*, human, from *mann*, a man; EFries. *minske*, *minsk*, a man; West Flem. *minsch* (De Bo).

MIOCENE, less recent, in geology. (Gk.) A coined word, signifying 'less recent.'–Gk. μείο-, for μείων, less; and καιν-ός, new, recent.

MIRABOLAN, in Hakluyt; see **Myrobolan**.

MIRACLE, a wonder, prodigy. (F.–L.) In very early use. ME. *miracle*, Chaucer, C. T. 4897 (B 477). The pl. *miracles* is in the A. S. Chron. an. 1137 (last line).–F. *miracle*.–L. *mirā-culum*, anything wonderful. Formed with suffixes -*cu*- and -*lu*- (=Idg. suffixes *ko*-, *lo*-) from *mirā-rī*, to wonder at.–L. *mīrus*, wonderful (base *smī-ro*).–√SMEI, to smile, laugh, wonder at; see **Smile**. Cf. Skt. *smi*, to smile, whence *smaya*-, wonder. Der. *miracul-ous*, Macb. iv. 3. 147, from F. *miraculeux*, 'miraculous' (Cot.), answering to a L. type *mīrācul-ōsus, not used; *miracul-ous-ly*, -*ness*. From L. *mirārī* we have also *mir-age*, *mirr-or*.

MIRAGE, an optical illusion. (F.–L.) Modern.–F. *mirage*, an optical illusion by which very distant objects appear close at hand; in use in 1753 (Hatzfeld).–F. *mirer*, to look at.–Late L. *mirāre*, to behold.–L. *mirāri*, to wonder at. See **Miracle, Mirror**.

MIRE, deep mud. (Scand.) ME. *mire*, *myre*; Chaucer, C. T. 510 (A 508); *myre*, Rob. of Brunne, tr. of Langtoft, p. 70, l. 18; *mire*, Will. of Palerne, 3507.—Icel. *myrr*, mod. *myri*, a bog, swamp; Swed. *myra*, a bog, marsh; Dan. *myr*, *myre*, a marsh.+OHG. *mios*, MHG. *mies*, moss, swamp; NFries. *myrre*; AS. *meos*, moss. Teut. base *meus-*>*meuz-*>*meur-*. Allied to **Moss**, q. v. The sense is 'mossy ground,' bog, deep mud. I cannot find authority for an alleged AS. *myre*, mire. **Der.** *mire*, vb., Much Ado, iv. 1. 135; *mir-y*, Tam. Shrew, iv. 1. 77.

MIRKY; see **Murky.**

MIRROR, a looking-glass. (F.—L.) ME. *mirour*, *myroure* (with one *r*); P. Plowman, B. xi. 8.—OF. *mireor*, later *miroir*, 'a myrror;' Cot. This form answers to a L. type *miratorium*, not found. Evidently from the Late L. *mirare*, to behold.—L. *mirari*, to wonder at. See **Miracle.**

MIRTH, merriment, pleasure, jollity. (E.) ME. *mirthe*, Chaucer, C. T. 775 (A 773). AS. *myrgð*, *myrð*, *mirhð*, *mirigð*, mirth, Grein, ii. 271. Formed from AS. *myrge*, merry. Cf. Gael. and Irish *mear*, merry (Macbain). See **Merry. Der.** *mirth-ful*, *mirth-ful-ly*, *-ness*.

MIS- (1), prefix. (E. *and* Scand.) The AS. prefix *mis-* occurs in *mis-dæd*, a misdeed, and in other compounds. It answers to Du., Dan., and Icel. *mis-*, Swed. *miss-*, G. *miss-*; Goth. *missa-* (with the sense of 'wrong'), as in *missa-deds*, a misdeed. Teut. type *misso-*; Idg. type *mit-to-*; allied to OHG. *midan* (G. *meiden*), to avoid; L. *mittere*, to send away, pp. *missus*. Brugmann, i. § 794. Hence the verb to *miss*; see **Miss** (1). It is sometimes Scand., as in *mis-take*. **Der.** *mis-become*, *-behave*, *-deed*, *-deem*, *-do*, *-give*, *-lay*, *-lead*, *-like*, *-name*, *-shape*, *-time*, *-understand*. Also prefixed to words of F. and L. origin, as in *mis-apply*, *-apprehend*, *-appropriate*, &c. Also to Scand. words, as in *mis-call*, *-hap*, *-take*. And see **Mis-** (2).

MIS- (2), prefix. (F.—L.) Not to be confused with *mis-* (1). The proper old spelling is *mes-*, as in OF. *mes-chief*, mischief. The comparison of this with Span. *menos-cabo*, diminution, Port. *menos-cabo*, contempt, &c. shows that this prefix undoubtedly arose from L. *minus*, less, used as a depreciatory prefix. At the same time, Scheler's observation is just, that the number of F. words beginning with *mé-* (OF. *mes-*) was considerably increased by the influence of the G. prefix *miss-* (see above) with which it was easily confused. Clear examples of this F. prefix occur in *mis-adventure*, *mis-alliance*, *mis-chance*, *mis-chief*, *mis-count*, *mis-creant*, *mis-nomer*, *mis-prise*.

MISADVENTURE, ill luck. (F.—L.) ME. *misauenture*; spelt *messauenture*, King Horn, ed. Lumby, l. 710.—OF. *mesaventure* (Burguy).—OF. *mes-*, prefix (< L. *minus*); and F. *aventure*, adventure. See **Mis-** (2) and **Adventure.**

MISALLIANCE, an improper alliance. (F.—L.) A late word; added by Todd to Johnson's Dict.—F. *mésalliance*. See **Mis-** (2) and **Ally.**

MISANTHROPE, a hater of mankind. (Gk.) 'I am *misanthropos*;' Timon, iv. 3. 53.—Gk. μισάνθρωπος, adj., hating mankind.—Gk. μισ-εῖν, to hate, from μῖσ-ος, hatred; and ἄνθρωπος, a man. See **Anthropology. Der.** *misanthrop-ic*, *misanthrop-ic-al*, *misanthrop-ist*, *misanthrop-y* (Gk. μισανθρωπία).

MISAPPLY, to apply amiss. (Hybrid; F.—L.; *with* E. *prefix.*) In Shak. Romeo, ii. 3. 21. From **Mis-** (1) and **Apply. Der.** *mis-appli-ca-tion.*

MISAPPREHEND, to apprehend amiss. (Hybrid; E. *and* L.) In Phillips, ed. 1706. From **Mis-** (1) and **Apprehend. Der.** *misapprehens-ion.*

MISAPPROPRIATE, to appropriate amiss. (Hybrid; E. *and* L.) Late; not in Johnson. From **Mis-** (1) and **Appropriate. Der.** *misappropriat-ion.*

MISARRANGE, to arrange amiss. (Hybrid; E. *and* F.) From **Mis-** (1) and **Arrange.**

MISBECOME, not to suit. (E.) In Shak. L. L. L. v. 2. 778; and in Palsgrave. From **Mis-** (1) and **Become.**

MISBEHAVE, to behave amiss. (E.) In Shak. Romeo, iii. 3. 143; and in Palsgrave. From **Mis-** (1) and **Behave. Der.** *misbehav-iour*, spelt *mysbehavour* in Palsgrave; see **Behaviour.**

MISBELIEVE, to believe amiss. (E.) ME. *misbeleuen*, Gower, C. A. ii. 152, l. 5; bk. v. 739. From **Mis-** (1) and **Believe. Der.** *misbelief*, spelt *mysbylyefe*, Pricke of Conscience, 5521; *misbileaue*, St. Katharine, 348.

MISCALCULATE, to calculate amiss. (Hybrid; E. *and* L.) Late. In Johnson. From **Mis-** (1) and **Calculate. Der.** *miscalculat-ion.*

MISCALL, to abuse, revile. (Hybrid; E. *and* Scand.) In Spenser, F. Q. iv. 8. 24. From **Mis-** (1) and **Call.**

MISCARRY, to be unsuccessful, to fail, to bring forth prematurely. (Hybrid; E. *and* F.) In Shak. Meas. for Meas. iii. 1. 217. **ME.** *miscarien*. 'Yet had I leuer dye than I sawe them *myscarye* to-fore myn eyen;' Caxton, tr. of Reynard Fox, ed. Arber,

p. 79, l. 10; and see Chaucer, C. T., A 513. From **Mis-** (1) and **Carry. Der.** *miscarri-age.*

MISCELLANEOUS, various, belonging to or treating of various subjects. (L.) 'An elegant and *miscellaneous* author;' Sir T. Browne, Works, b. i. c. 8, part 6.—L. *miscellaneus*, miscellaneous, varied (by change of *-us* to *-ous*, as in *arduous*, &c.).—L. *miscellus*, mixed.—L. *miscere*, to mix. See **Mix. Der.** *miscellaneous-ly*, *-ness*. Also *miscellany*, which appears to be due to L. neut. pl. *miscellanea*, various things. 'As a *miscellany*-madam, [I would] invent new tires;' Ben Jonson, Cynthia's Revels, iv. 1 (Phantaste's long speech).

MISCHANCE, mishap, ill luck. (F.—L.) ME. *meschance*, Rob. of Glouc. p. 137, l. 14; l. 2902.—OF. *meschance*, 'a mischiefe, or mischance;' Cot. See **Mis-** (2) and **Chance.**

MISCHIEF, an ill result, misfortune, damage, injury, evil. (F.—L.) ME. *myschief*; P. Plowman, B. prol. 67. Opposed in ME. to *bonchief*, i. e. a good result. 'Good happes and *boonchief*, as wel as yuel happes and *meschief*;' Trevisa, i. 87, l. 19.—OF. *meschief*, a bad result, misadventure, damage. Cf. Span. *menoscabo*, diminution, loss; Port. *menoscabo*, contempt; which are varied forms of the same word. From **Mis-** (2) and **Chief.** (The L. words in the compound are *minus* and *caput*.) **Der.** *mischiev-ous*, a coined word, As You Like It, ii. 7. 64; *mischiev-ous-ly*, *-ness*.

MISCONCEIVE, to conceive amiss. (Hybrid; E. *and* F.—L.) 'He that *misconceyueth*, he misdemeth;' Chaucer, C. T. 10284 (E 2410). A coined word. From **Mis-** (1) and **Conceive. Der.** *misconcept-ion.*

MISCONDUCT, ill conduct. (Hybrid; E. *and* L.) It occurs in the Spectator; no. 256, § 4. From **Mis-** (1) and **Conduct. Der.** *misconduct*, verb.

MISCONSTRUE, to interpret amiss. (Hybrid; E. *and* L.) In Shak. Merch. Ven. ii. 2. 197; Chaucer, Troilus, i. 346. From **Mis-** (1) and **Construe. Der.** *misconstruct-ion.*

MISCOUNT, to count wrongly. (F.—L.) ME. *miscounten*, Gower, C. A. i. 147, l. 12; bk. i. 3112.—OF. *mesconter*, to miscount (Godefroy). From **Mis-** (2) and **Count.**

MISCREANT, a vile fellow, wretch. (F.—L.) Orig. an unbeliever, infidel; see Trench, Select Glossary. Formerly also used as an adjective. 'Al *miscreant* [unbelieving] painyms;' Sir T. More, Works, p. 774 a. 'This *miscreant* [unbeliever] now thus baptised;' Frith's Works, p. 91, col. 1. Gower has the pl. *mescreantz*, in his Praise of Peace, 268.—OF. *mescreant*, 'miscreant, misbelieving;' Cot. β. The prefix *mes-* answers to L. *minus*, less, used in a bad sense; see **Mis-** (2). By comparing OF. *mescreant* with Ital. *miscredente*, incredulous, heathen, we at once see that OF. *creant* is from L. *credent-*, stem of pres. part. of *credere*, to believe; see **Creed.** And see **Recreant.**

MISDATE, to date amiss. (Hybrid; E. *and* F.—L.) 'Oh! how *misdated* on their flattering tombs!' Young's Night Thoughts, Night, v. l. 778. From **Mis-** (1) and **Date.**

MISDEED, a bad deed. (E.) ME. *misdede*, Ancren Riwle, p. 124, l. 22. AS. *misdæd*, Grein, ii. 255.+Du. *misdaad*; Goth. *missadeths*; G. *missethat*, OHG. *missitaat*. From **Mis-** (1) and **Deed.**

MISDEEM, to judge amiss. (E.) ME. *misdemen*, Chaucer, C. T. 10284 (E 2410). From **Mis-** (1) and **Deem.** (Icel. *misdæma*.)

MISDEMEANOUR, ill conduct. (Hybrid; E. *and* F.—L.) In Shak. Tw. Nt. ii. 3. 106. From **Mis-** (1) and **Demeanour.** ¶ It is possible that the prefix is French; see **Mis-** (2). But I find no proof of it.

MISDIRECT, to direct amiss. (Hybrid; E. *and* L.) Added by Todd to Johnson. From **Mis-** (1) and **Direct. Der.** *mis-direction.*

MISDO, to do amiss. (E.) ME. *misdon*, *misdo*; P. Plowman, B. iii. 122. We find 'yfle vel mis *doeð*' as a gloss to 'male agit' in the ONorthumb. glosses of John, iii. 20. + Du. *misdoen*; G. *missthun*. From **Mis-** (1) and **Do. Der.** *misdo-er*, ME. *misdoer*, *mysdoer*, Wyclif, 1 Pet. ii. 12. And see *misdeed*.

MISEMPLOY, to employ amiss. (Hybrid; E. *and* F.—L.) In Dryden, Absalom, l. 613. From **Mis-** (1) and **Employ. Der.** *misemploy-ment.*

MISER, an avaricious man, niggard. (L.) It sometimes means merely 'a wretched creature;' Spenser, F. Q. ii. 1. 8. See Trench, Select Glossary.—L. *miser*, wretched. Cf. Ital. and Span. *misero*, (1) wretched, (2) avaricious. Prob. connected with Gk. μῖσος, hatred; Curtius, ii. 225. **Der.** *miser-ly*; *miser-y*, ME. *misérie*, Chaucer, C. T. 14012 (B 3196), from OF. *miserie* (Littré, mod. F. *misère*), which from L. *miseria*, wretchedness; also *miser-able*, q. v.

MISERABLE, wretched. (F.—L.) Skelton has *miserably* and *miserableness*; Why Come Ye Nat to Court, 865, 1029.—F. *miserable*, 'miserable;' Cot.—L. *miserabilis*, pitiable.—L. *miserari*, to pity.—L. *miser*, wretched; see **Miser. Der.** *miserabl-y*, *miser-able-ness.*

MISFORTUNE, ill fortune. (Hybrid; E. *and* F.—L.) In the Bible of 1551, Nehem. i. 3. Palsgrave has: '*Mysfortune*, desfortune;' so that the prefix is not French. From **Mis-** (1) and **Fortune.**

MISGIVE, to fail, be filled with doubt. (E.) In Shak. Julius, iii. 1. 145. From **Mis-** (1) and **Give.** Der. *misgiv-ing.*

MISGOVERN, to govern amiss. (F.—L.) In Shak. Rich. II, v. 2. 5; and in Palsgrave. — MF. *mesgouverner*, recorded by Palsgrave. — OF. *mes-*, mis-; and F. *gouverner*, to govern; see **Mis-** (2) and **Govern.** Der. *misgovern-ment*, Much Ado, iv. 1. 100.

MISGUIDE, to guide wrongly. (Hybrid; E. *and* F.—Teut.) ME. *misguide*, Gower, C. A. iii. 373, l. 14; bk. viii. 2920; where it is contrasted with *guide*. Also *misgyen*, Chaucer, C. T. 14451 (B 3723). From **Mis-** (1) and **Guide.** ¶ The prefix does not seem to be French. Der. *misguid-ance.*

MISHAP, ill hap. (Hybrid; E. *and* Scand.) In Prompt. Parv. The verb *mishappen*, to mishap, fall out ill, occurs in Chaucer, C. T., A 1646. From **Mis-** (1) and **Hap.**

MISHNAH, MISHNA, a digest of Jewish traditions; the 'second Law.' (Heb.) 'Their *Mishna* or Talmud text;' Purchas, Pilgrimage, bk. ii. ch. 12. § 1. par. 7. — Heb. *mishnah*, a repetition; a second part; instruction (in oral tradition). — Heb. *shānāh*, to repeat.

MISINFORM, to inform amiss. (Hybrid; E. *and* F.—L.) ME. *misenformen*, Gower, C. A. i. 178; bk. ii. 559. From **Mis-** (1) and **Inform.** Der. *mis-inform-at-ion.*

MISINTERPRET, to interpret amiss. (Hybrid; E. *and* F.— L.) In Shak. Rich. II, iii. 1. 18. From **Mis-** (1) and **Interpret.** Der. *misinterpret-at-ion.*

MISJUDGE, to judge amiss. (F.—L.) 'And therefore no more *mysse-iudge* any manne;' Sir T. More, Works, p. 952 h. — OF. *mes-juger*, to misjudge (Godefroy). See **Mis-** (2) and **Judge.** Der. *mis-judg-ment.*

MISLAY, to lay in a wrong place, lose. (E.) 'The *mislaier* of a meere-stone [boundary-stone] is to blame;' Bacon, Essay lvi, Of Judicature. From **Mis-** (1) and **Lay.** (Icel. *misleggja*.)

MISLEAD, to lead astray. (E.) '*Misleder* [misleader] of the papacie;' Gower, C. A. i. 261; bk. ii. 3021. AS. *mislǣdan*, to mislead, seduce (Bosworth). From **Mis-** (1) and **Lead,** verb.

MISLIKE, to dislike. (E.) In Shak. Merch. Ven. ii. 1. 1. ME. *misliken*, to displease (usually impersonal); Will. of Palerne, 2039. AS. *mislician*, to displease; Exod. xxi. 8. Der. *mislike*, sb., 3 Hen. VI, iv. 1. 24.

MISNAME, to name amiss. (E.) In Skelton, A Replycacion, l. 59. From **Mis-** (1) and **Name.**

MISNOMER, a wrong name. (F.—L.) '*Misnomer*, French Law-Term, the using of one name or term for another;' Phillips, ed. 1706. It properly means 'a misnaming.' Also in Blount's Nomolexicon, ed. 1691, where the prefix is said to be the F. *mes-*, which is correct. The E. word answers to an OF. *mesnommer* (Godefroy). — OF. *mes-* (< L. *minus*), badly; and *nommer*, to name, from L. *nōmināre*, to name. See **Mis-** (2) and **Nominate.**

MISOGAMY, a hatred of marriage. (Gk.) In Blount's Glossary (1656). From μῖσο-, hating, from μῖσεῖν, to hate; and -γαμία, from γάμος, marriage. So also *misogynist*, from μῖσο-, hating, and γυνή, a woman.

MISPLACE, to place amiss. (Hybrid; E. *and* F.—L.) In As You Like It, i. 2. 37. From **Mis-** (1) and **Place.** Der. *misplace-ment.*

MISPRINT, to print wrongly. (Hybrid; E. *and* F.—L.) 'By misse-writing or by *mysse-pryntynge*;' Sir T. More, Works, p. 772 b. From **Mis-** (1) and **Print.** Der. *misprint*, sb.

MISPRISE, MISPRIZE, to slight, undervalue. (F.—L.) In As You Like It, i. 1. 177. Spenser has the sb. *misprise* = contempt; F. Q. iii. 9. 9. — MF. *mespriser*, 'to disesteem, contemn,' Cot.; OF. *mesprisier* (Godefroy). — OF. *mes-* (< L. *minus*), badly; and Late L. *pretiāre*, to prize, esteem, from L. *pretium*, a price. See **Mis-** (2) and **Prize, Price.** But see below.

MISPRISION, a mistake, neglect. (F.—L.) See Blount's Nomolexicon, ed. 1691. He says: '*misprision* of clerks (Anno 8 Hen. VI. c. 15) is a neglect of clerks in writing or keeping records ... *Misprision* also signifies a mistaking (Anno 14 Edw. III. stat. 1. cap. 6).'— OF. *mesprison* (Godefroy); MF. *mesprison*, 'misprision, error, offence, a thing done, or taken, amisse;' Cot. β. This OF. *mesprison* or *mesprision* has the same sense and source as mod. F. *méprise*, a mistake (Littré). It is written *misprisio* in Low L. (Ducange); but this is only the OF. word turned into Latin. γ. From OF. *mes-* < L. *minus*, badly; and Late L. *prensiōnem*, acc. of *prensio*, a taking, contracted form of L. *prehensio*, a seizing. The latter is from L. *prehensus*, pp. of *prehendere*, to take. See **Mis-** (2) and **Prison.** Cf. *mispris'd*, mistaken; Mid. Nt. Dr. iii. 2. 74.

¶ *Misprision* was ignorantly confused with *misprise*, in the sense of contempt. Thus Blount, in the article already cited, says: '*misprision* of treason is a neglect or light account made of treason;' and he derives the word from MF. *mespris*, contempt. Milton wrongly has *misprision* in the sense of 'scorn;' Cent. Dict.

MISPRONOUNCE, to pronounce amiss. (Hybrid; E. *and* F.—L.) 'They *mis-pronounced*, and I mislik'd;' Milton, Apology for Smectymnuus; Works (1852), iii. 268. From **Mis-** (1) and **Pronounce.** Der. *mispronunci-at-ion.*

MISQUOTE, to quote amiss, misinterpret. (Hybrid; E. *and* F.—L.) In Shak. 1 Hen. IV, v. 2. 13. From **Mis-** (1) and **Quote.** Der. *misquot-at-ion.*

MISREPRESENT, to represent amiss. (Hybrid; E. *and* F. —L.) In Milton, Samson, 124. From **Mis-** (1) and **Represent.** Der. *misrepresent-at-ion.*

MISRULE, want of rule, disorder. (Hybrid; E. *and* F.—L.) Gower has it as a verb. 'That eny king himself *misreule*;' C. A. iii. 170; bk. vii. 2509. Stow mentions 'the lord of *misrule*' under the date 1552 (R.); and it occurs in 1503, in the Privy Expenses of Elizabeth of York, p. 91; and first in 1491. From **Mis-** (1) and **Rule.**

MISS (1), to fail to hit, omit, feel the want of. (E.) ME. *missen*, Will. of Palerne, 1016. Rather a Scand. than an E. word, but the prefix *mis-*, which is closely connected with it, is sufficiently common in AS. AS. *missan* (rare). 'þy læs þe him *misse*,' lest aught escape his notice, *or*, go wrong with him; Canons under King Edgar, 32; in Thorpe, Ancient Laws, ii. 250. And in Beowulf, 2439. A weak verb, formed from a base **mith-*, weak grade of **meith-*, as in AS. and OS. *miðan*, to conceal, avoid, escape notice (also in G. *meiden*, OHG. *mīdan*, to avoid). Cf. the prefix *mis-*, signifying amiss or wrongly.+Du. *missen*, to miss; *mis*, sb., an error, mistake; *mis*, adv., amiss; *mis-*, as prefix, amiss; Icel. *missa*, to miss, lose; *mis*, or *ā mis*, adv., amiss; *mis-*, prefix; Dan. *miste* (for *missa*), to lose; *mis-*, prefix; Swed. *mista* (for *missa*), to lose; *miste*, adv., wrongly, amiss; *miss-*, prefix; Goth. *missō*, adv., reciprocally, interchangeably; *missa-*, prefix, wrongly; MHG. *missen*, OHG. *missan*, to miss; OHG. *mis* or *missi*, variously; OHG. *missa-*, prefix; MHG. *misse*, an error. Allied to L. *mittere*, to send; see **Missile,** and see **Mis-** (1). Brugmann, i. § 794. Der. *miss*, sb., ME. *misse*, a fault; 'to mende my *misse*' = to repair my fault, Will. of Palerne, l. 532. Also *miss-ing.*

MISS (2), a young woman, a girl. (F.—L.) Merely a contraction from **Mistress,** q. v. One of the earliest instances in dramatic writing occurs in the introduction of *Miss* Prue as a character in Congreve's Love for Love. An early example occurs in the following: 'she being taken to be the Earle of Oxford's *misse*, as at this time they began to call lewd women;' Evelyn's Diary, Jan. 9, 1662. Thus Shak. has: 'this is *Mistress* Anne Page,' where we should now say '*Miss* Anne Page;' Merry Wives, i. 1. 197. Cf. 'The virtuous matron and the *miss*;' Butler, Hudibras, pt. iii. c. 1. 864.

MISSAL, a mass-book. (L.) ME. *myssalle*, Voc. 719. 33; cf. *mass-book*, ME. *messebok*, Havelok, 186. In Minsheu, ed. 1627. In Sherwood's Index to Cotgrave we find L. *missal*, given as equivalent to OF. *messel, missel*; but Cotgrave himself explains the OF. words as 'masse-book.' The E. word is rather taken directly from the familiar Latin term than borrowed from OF. — Late L. *missāle*, a missal. — Late L. *missa*, the mass. See further under **Mass** (2).

MISSEL-THRUSH, MISTLE-THRUSH, the name of a kind of thrush. (E.) So called because it feeds on the berries of the *mistle-toe*. The name is not recorded early. 'We meet in Aristotle with one kind of thrush [ἰξοβόρος] called the *miselthrush*, or feeder upon *miseltoe*;' Sir T. Browne, Vulg. Errors, b. ii. c. 6. § 21 (part 3). +G. *mistel-drossel*, a mistle-thrush; from *mistel*, mistletoe, and *drossel*, a thrush. See **Mistletoe** and **Thrush.**

MISSHAPE, to shape amiss. (E.) Chiefly in the pp. *misshaped*, 3 Hen. VI, iii. 2. 170; or *misshapen*, Temp. v. 268. ME. *misshapen*, pp., spelt *mysshape* (with loss of final *n*), P. Plowman, B. vii. 95. From **Mis-** (1) and **Shape.**+MDu. *misscheppen*, to misshape, used by Vondel (Oudemans); G. *missschaffen*, to misshape (rare).

MISSILE, that may be thrown; a missile weapon. (L.) Properly an adj., now chiefly used as a sb. Taken directly from L. rather than through the F. Cotgrave gives '*feu missile*, a squib or other firework thrown,' but the word is not in Littré, and probably not common. 'His *missile* weapon was a lying tongue;' P. Fletcher, The Purple Island, c. vii. st. 68. — L. *missilis*, adj., that can be thrown; the neut. *missile* is used to mean a missile weapon (*tēlum* being understood). — L. *missus*, pp. of *mittere*, to throw. β. Perhaps for **mitere*; cf. pt. t. *mi-sī*.+OHG. *mīdan*, to avoid; see **Miss** (1). Brugmann, i. § 930. Der. From L. *mittere* are also derived *ad-mit*, *com-mit*, *e-mit*, *im-mit*, *inter-mit*, *manu-mit*, *o-mit*, *per-mit*, *preter-mit*, *re-mit*, *sub-mit*, *trans-mit*, with their derivatives; from the pp. *miss-us* are also *mass* (2), *mess* (1), *miss-al*, *miss-ion*, q.v., *miss-ive*, q.v., *dis-miss*, *di-missory*, *e-miss-ar-y*, *pro-miss-or-y*; *com-pro-mise*, *de-mise*, *pre-mise*, *pre-mises*, *pro-mise*, *sur-mise*, *message*, &c.

MISSION, a sending, an embassy. (L.) In Shak. Troil. iii. 3. 189. [The MF. *mission* merely means 'expence, disbursement;' Cot.] Formed by analogy with F. words in -*ion*, from L. *missiōnem*, acc. of *missio*, a sending; cf. *missus*, pp. of *mittere*, to send. See **Missile**. Der. *mission-er*, a missionary, Dryden, Hind and Panther, ii. 565; *mission-ar-y*, Tatler, no. 270, Dec. 30, 1710.

MISSIVE, a thing sent. (F.—L.) Used by Shak. to mean 'a messenger;' Macb. i. 5. 7. And in G. Douglas, Palice of Honour, pt. ii. st. 5. K. Edw. IV employs the phr. 'our lettres *missiues*,' in 1477; Orig. Letters, ed. Ellis, i. 17.—MF. *missive*, 'a letter missive, a letter sent;' Cot. Coined, with suffix -*ive* (=L. -*iuus*), from L. *miss-us*, pp. of *mittere*, to send; see **Missile**.

MISSPEND, to spend ill, to squander. (Hybrid; E. *and* L.) 'That folke in folyes *myspenden* her fyue wittes;' P. Plowman, B. xv. 74. From AS. *mis-*, prefix, wrongly, amiss; and AS. *spendan*, in the compounds *āspendan*, *forspendan*; see Sweet's A. S. Reader. But *spendan* is not a true E. word; it is borrowed from L. *dispendere*. See **Mis-** (1) and **Spend**.

MIST, watery vapour, fine rain. (E.) ME. *mist*, P. Plowman, A. prol. 88; B. prol. 214. AS. *mist*, gloom, darkness; Grein, ii. 256.+Icel. *mistr*, mist; Swed. *mist*, foggy weather at sea; Du. *mist*, fog. β. Teut. type *mih-stoz, m. Apparently from the base *mig* (Idg. *migh*, Skt. *mih*) which appears in Lithuan. *mig-la*, mist (Nesselmann), Russ. *mgla* (for *mig-la*), mist, vapour, Gk. ὀ-μίχ-λη, mist, fog, Skt. *mih-ira-*, a cloud; cf. also Skt. *mēgh-a-*, a cloud. γ. All from √MEIGwH, to darken; different from √MEIGH, which appears in L. *mingere*. Brugmann, i. §§ 604, 633. Der. *mist-y*, AS. *mist-ig* (Grein); *mist-i-ness*.

MISTAKE, to take amiss, err. (Scand.) ME. *mistaken*, Rom. of the Rose, l. 1540.—Icel. *mistaka*, to take by mistake, to make a slip.—Icel. *mis-*, cognate with AS. *mis-*, prefix; and *taka*, to take. See **Mis-** (1) and **Take**. Der. *mistake*, sb., *mistak-en*, *mis-tak-en-ly*.

MISTER, MR., a title of address to a man. (F.—L.) The contraction *Mr.* occurs on the title-page of the first folio edition of Shakespeare (1623); but it is probably to be read as *Master*. Cotgrave explains *monsieur* by 'sir, or master.' It is difficult to trace the first use of *mister*, but it does not appear to be earlier than 1550, and is certainly nothing but a corruption of *master* or *maister*, due to the influence of the corresponding title of *mistress*. See **Master**, **Mistress**. β. Richardson's supposition that it is connected with ME. *mister*, a trade, is as absurd as it is needless; notwithstanding the oft-quoted 'what *mister* wight,' Spenser, F. Q. i. 9. 23. ¶ It may be remarked that ME. *mister* is from OF. *mestier* (F. *métier*), L. *ministerium*, and is therefore a doublet of *ministry*.

MISTERM, to term or name amiss. (Hybrid; E. *and* F.—L.) In Shak. Romeo, iii. 3. 21. From **Mis-** (2) and **Term**.

MISTIME, to time amiss. (E.) ME. *mistimen*, to happen amiss, Ancren Riwle, p. 200, note *e*. AS. *mistimian*, to happen amiss, turn out ill (Bosworth). From **Mis-** (1) and **Time**.

MISTLE-THRUSH; see **Missel-thrush**.

MISTLETOE, a parasitic plant. (E.) In Shak. Titus, ii. 3. 95. Scarcely to be found in ME., but it must have existed. The variant form *mystyldene* is in MS. Sloane 2584, p. 90; see Henslow, Medical Werkes, p. 130. AS. *misteltān*. 'Viscarago, *mistiltan*' (sic); Ælfric's Gloss., Nomina Herbarum; in Voc. 136. 11. [The *a* is of course long; cf. E. *stone* with AS. *stān*, &c.] This should have produced *mistletone*, but the final *n* (*ne*) was dropped, probably because the ME. *tone* (better *toon*) meant 'toes,' which gave a false impression that the final *n* was a plural-ending, and unnecessary.+ Icel. *mistilteinn*, the mistletoe. β. The final element is the easier to explain; it simply means 'twig.' Cf. AS. *tān*, a twig (Grein), Icel. *teinn*, Du. *teen*, MHG. *zein*, Goth. *tains*, a twig, Dan. *ten*, Swed. *ten*, a spindle; all from a Teut. type *tain-oz, m., a twig, rod. γ. The former element is AS. *mistel*, which could be used alone to mean 'mistletoe,' though it was also called *āc-mistel* (oak-mistle), to distinguish it from *eorð-mistel* (earth-mistle), a name sometimes given to wild basil or calamint; see Cockayne's A. S. Leechdoms. In Danish, the mistletoe is called either *mistel* or *mistelten*. In Swed. and G. the mistletoe is simply *mistel*. δ. The word *mist-el* is clearly a mere dimin. of *mist*, which in G. has the sense of 'dung;' cf. MDu. *mest*, *mist*, dung (Hexham). As to the reason for the name, cf. 'it [the mistletoe] comes onely by the mewting of birds .. which feed thereupon, and let it passe through their body;' Holland, tr. of Pliny's Nat. Hist., bk. xvi. ch. 44. ε. The G. *mist* is cognate with Goth. *maihstus*, dung; which see in Uhlenbeck. Der. *missel-thrush*, q.v.

MISTRESS, a lady at the head of a household. (F.—L.) Also written *Mrs.*, and called *Missis*. In Shak. Macb. iii. 5. 6. ME.

maistresse, Chaucer, C. T. 10691 (F 377).—OF. *maistresse*, 'a mistress, dame;' Cot. (Mod. F. *maîtresse*.) Formed with F. suffix -*esse* (< L. -*issa*, Gk. -*ισσα*) from OF. *maistre*, a master; see **Master**. Der. *mistress-ship*, Titus Andron. iv. 4. 40.

MISTRUST, to regard with suspicion. (Scand.) ME. *missetrost*, Coventry Plays, ed. Halliwell, 126 (Stratmann); *mistraist*, Bruce, x. 327 (in Hart's edition, see the footnote); *mistriste*, Chaucer, C. T. 12303 (C 369). Rather Scand. than E. See **Mis-** (1) and **Trust**. Der. *mistrust*, sb.; *mistrust-ful*, 3 Hen. VI, iv. 2. 8; *mistrust-ful-ly*, -*ness*.

MISTY (1), nebulous, foggy. (E.) 'A ful *misty* morow;' Chaucer, Troil. iii. 1060. AS. *mistig*, adj.; from *mist*, mist; see **Mist**.

MISTY (2). (F.—L.—Gk.) Used for *mystic*; in the Prompt. Parv., we find a distinction made between '*mysty*, nebulosus' and '*mysty*, or prevey to mannes wytte, misticus.' So also *mysty*, mystic, in Wyclif, Eng. Works, ed. Matthew, p. 344; and *mystily*, mystically, in the same, p. 343. Cf. *mistier*, with the double meaning, in P. Plowman, B. x. 181. See Palmer, Folk-Etymology. For the loss of the final letter, cf. E. *jolly* from OF. *jolif*. See **Mystic**.

MISUNDERSTAND, to understand amiss. (E.) ME. *misunderstanden*, Rob. of Glouc. p. 42, l. 990. From **Mis-** (1) and **Understand**. Der. *misunderstand-ing*.

MISUSE, to use amiss. (F.—L.) 'That *misuseth* the might and the power that is yeven him;' Chaucer, C. T. (Melibeus), Group B, 3040 (Six-text); Gower, C. A. ii. 279, l. 12.—OF. *mesuser*, to misuse; Godefroy.—OF. *mes-*, *mis-*; and *user*, to use. See **Mis-** (2) and **Use**. Der. *misuse*, sb., 1 Hen. IV, i. 1. 43, OF. *mesus*, sb. (Godefroy); *misusage*, OF. *mesusage*.

MITE (1), a very small insect. (E.) ME. *mite*, Chaucer, C. T. 6142 (D 560). AS. *mīte*. 'Tomus, maða, mīte;' Ælfric's Gloss., Nom. Insectorum; Voc. 122. 6.+Low G. *mite*, a mite; Du. *mijt*; OHG. *mīza*, a mite, midge, fly. β. The word means 'cutter' or 'biter,' from the Teut. root MEIT, to cut small; whence Goth. *maitan*, to cut, Icel. *meita*, to cut, also Icel. *meitill*, G. *meissel*, a chisel. Der. *mit-y*. And see *emmet*.

MITE (2), a very small portion. (F.—Du.) ME. *mite*; 'not worth a *myte*;' Chaucer, C. T., A 1558. 'A *myte* [small coin] that he offreþ;' P. Plowman, C. xiv. 97.—OF. *mite* (Godefroy).—MDu. *mijt*, a small coin, the sixth part of a doit; *mite*, *myte*, a small coin, worth a third of a *penning*, according to some, or a *penning* and a half, according to others; anything small; *niet eener myte*, not worth a mite (Oudemans). From the Teut. base MEIT, to cut small; see **Mite** (1).

MITIGATE, to alleviate. (L.) *Mytigate* in Palsgrave. 'Breake the ordinaunce or *mitigat* it;' Tyndall's Works, p. 316, col. 1.—L. *mītigātus*, pp. of *mītigāre*, to make gentle.—L. *mīt-*, stem of *mītis*, soft, gentle; with suffix -*ig-*, for *agere*, to make. Root uncertain. Der. *mitigation*, ME. *mitigacioun*, P. Plowman, B. v. 477, from F. *mitigation*, 'mitigation,' Cot.; *mitigat-or*; *mitigat-ive*, from MF. *mitigatif*, 'mitigative,' Cot.; also *mitiga-ble*, L. *mitigābilis*, from *mitigā-re*.

MITRAILLEUSE, a machine-gun. (F.—Du.) F. *mitrailleuse*, fem. agential sb. from *mitrailler*, to fire small missiles.—F. *mitraille*, small bits of grape-shot; 'lumps consisting of divers metals' in Cot. Variant of MF. *mitaille*, 'great file-dust,' Cot. Extended from OF. *mite*, a mite, small piece; see **Mite** (2).

MITRE, a head-dress, esp. for a bishop. (F.—L.—Gk.) 'Thy *mytrede* bisshopes' = thy mitred bishops; P. Plowman, C. v. 193. 'On his *mitere*,' referring to a bishop; Rob. of Brunne, tr. of Langtoft, p. 302, l. 2.—OF. *mitre*, 'a bishop's miter;' Cot.—L. *mītra*, a cap.—Gk. μίτρα, a belt, girdle, head-band, fillet, turban. β. Perhaps allied to Gk. μίτος, a thread of the woof (Prellwitz).

MITTEN, a covering for the hand. (F.) ME. *mitaine*; spelt *miteyn*, Chaucer, C. T. 12307 (C 373); *myteyne*, P. Plowman's Crede, ed. Skeat, l. 428.—OF. *mitaine*; Cot. gives: '*mitaines*, mittains, winter-gloves.' Cf. Gascon *mitano*, a mitten. β. Of disputed origin; see Hatzfeld, Scheler, and Körting, § 6043. Mistral has Prov. *mito*, a mitten, as well as *mitano*.

MITTIMUS, a warrant of commitment to prison. (L.) 'Take a *mittimus*;' Massinger, A New Way, l. 47 from end. From L. *mittimus*, we send; from the first word in the warrant.—L. *mittere*, to send; see **Missile**.

MIX, to mingle, confuse. (L.) In Shak. 2 Hen. IV, v. 2. 46. Rich. cites '*mixed* with faith' from the Bible of 1561, Heb. iv. 2. But in earlier books it is extremely rare; Stratmann cites the pp. *mixid* from Songs and Carols, ed. Wright, no. VI. *Mix* (see N. E. D.) is a back-formation from the pp. *mixt*, in use as a law-term, as in Shillingford's Letters (Camden Soc.), App. 39: 'Any action real, personal, and *myxte*;' A.D. 1448. Cf. AF. *mixte*, Britton, ii. 64. Hence Palsgrave has: 'I *myxte* or *myngell*.'—L. *mixtus*, pp. of *miscēre*, to mix.+W. *mysgu*, to mix; *cymmysgu*, to mix together; Gael. *measg*, to mingle, mix, stir; Irish *measgaim*, I mix, mingle, stir, move; Russ. *mieshate*, to mix; Lithuan. *maiszyti*, to mix. Cf. Skt. *miçra-*, mixed. **β.** All from a √MEIK, to mingle; see Brugmann, i. § 707, 760. Der. *mix-er*, *com-mix*; also *mix-ture*, Romeo, iv. 3. 21, Sir T. More, Works, p. 83 a, from L. *mixtūra*, a mixing, mixture, allied to *mixt-us*, pp. of *miscēre*.

MIXEN, a dung-hill. (E.) In Chaucer, C. T., I 911. AS. *mixen*, *meoxen*, a dung-hill; from *meox*, dung. Allied to G. *mist*, Goth. *maihstus*, dung; from the verbal root seen in AS. *migan*, L. *mingere*, Gk. ὀ-μιχ-εῖν, to make water. Brugmann, i. § 796 (b).

MIZEN, MIZZEN, the hindmost of the fore and aft sails, in a three-masted vessel. (F.—Ital.—L.) Spelt *misen* in Minsheu, ed. 1627, and in Florio, ed. 1598; *meson* in Naval Accts. of Hen. VII, p. 36. '*Meson* sayle of a shyppe, *mysayne*;' Palsgrave.—MF. *misaine*, which Cotgrave defines as 'the foresaile of a ship.'—Ital. *mezzana*, 'a saile in a ship called the poope or misen-saile;' Florio, ed. 1598. Cf. *mezzano*, 'a meane or countertenour in singing, a meane man, betweene great and little;' id. **β.** The sense had reference to its *original* position, which was that of 'a fore-sail' (see Cotgrave), and in mod. F. it still signifies a sail between the bowsprit and the main-mast, occupying the middle position between the jib and main-sail of a cutter.—Late L. *mediānus*, middle; whence also F. *moyen*, and E. *mean* (3). Extended from L. *medius*, middle; see **Mid.** Doublet, *mean* (3). Der. *mizen-mast* or *mizzen-mast*.

MIZZLE, to rain in fine drops. (E.) 'As the *miseling* vpon the herbes, and as the droppes vpon the grasse;' Deut. xxxii. 2, in the Bible of 1551. 'Immoysturid with *mislyng*;' Skelton, Garland of Laurell, 698. 'To *miselle*, to *mysylle*, pluitare;' Cathol. Anglicum; p. 241. Cf. MDu. *mieselen*, to drizzle (Hexham); Low G. *miseln* (Berghaus). From the base *mis-*, as in EFries. *mis-ig*, damp, gloomy; allied to EFries. *mis*, *mis-ig*, damp, moist. Cf. **Mist.**

MNEMONICS, the science of assisting the memory. (Gk.) '*Mnemonica*, precepts or rules, and common places to help the memory;' Phillips, ed. 1706.—Gk. μνημονικά, mnemonics; neut. pl. of μνημονικός, belonging to memory.—Gk. μνήμον-, from μνήμων, mindful.—Gk. μνάομαι, I remember; Skt. *mnā*, to remember. From the base *mnā*, lengthened grade of √MEN, to think; see **Mind.**

MOAN, a complaint, a low sound of pain. (E.) ME. *mone*, Chaucer, C. T. 11232 (F 920). This corresponds to an AS. form *mān*, which does not appear with the modern sense; but the derived verb *mǣnan* to moan, to lament, is common; see exx. in Grein, ii. 222. **β.** This AS. verb passed into the ME. *menen*, to moan; whence *mened hire* = bemoaned herself, made her complaint, P. Plowman, B. iii. 169. After a time this verb fell into disuse, and its place was supplied by the sb. form, used verbally. 'Than they of the towne began to *mone*;' Berners, tr. of Froissart, vol. i. c. 348. **γ.** Some identify AS. *mǣnan*, to moan, with AS. *mǣnan*, to mean; see **Mean** (1); but there is no connexion in sense. Ettmüller compares AS. *mān*, adj., evil, wicked, sb. evil, wickedness. Note that the Icel. *mein* (cognate with AS. *mān*, wickedness) means a hurt, harm, disease, sore, whence there is but a step to a *moan* as the expression of pain; but this is unsatisfactory. ¶ Cf. *means* (some edd. *moans*) in Shak., M. Nt. Dr. v. 330. Der. *moan*, verb, as explained above; also *be-moan*, q.v.

MOAT, a trench round a fort, filled with water. (F.—Teut.) ME. *mote*, P. Plowman, B. v. 595.—OF. *mote*, 'chaussée, levée, digue,' i.e. a causeway, embankment, dike, Roquefort; and see Godefroy. Norm. dial. *motte*, a moat, foss. [Just as in the case of *dike* and *ditch*, the word *moat* originally meant either the trench dug out, or the embankment thrown up; and in OF. the usual sense was certainly an embankment, hill. It is therefore the same word as mod. F. *motte*, a mound, also a clod, or piece of turf. '*Motte*, a clod, lumpe, round sodd, or turfe of earth; also, a little hill or high place; a fit seat for a fort or strong house; hence, also, such a fort, or house of earth; . . a butt to shoot at;' Cotgrave. The orig. sense is clearly a sod or turf, such as is dug out, and thrown up into a mound; and the word is associated with earthen fortifications, whence it was transferred to such a trench as was used in fortification. Thus Shak. speaks of a *moat* defensive to a house;' Rich. II, ii. 1. 48; and in P. Plowman, the 'mote' is described as being 'the manere aboute,' i.e. all round the manor-house. Cf. also: '*Mothe*, a little earthen fortresse, or strong house, built on a hill;' Cotgrave.] Cf. also Low L. *mota*, *motta*, (1) a mound, (2) a mound and moat together; Ital. *motta*, a heap of earth, also a hollow, trench (as in E.); Span. *mota*, a mound; Romansch *muota*, *muotta*, a rounded hill. **β.** Of Teut. origin, but rarely found; it occurs, however, in the Bavarian *mott*, peat, esp. peat such as was dug up, burnt, and used for manure; whence *motten*, to burn peat; Schmeller, Bavarian Dict., col. 1693. This Bavarian word is prob. related to E. *mud*.

see **Mud.** Cf. also MHG. *mot*, peaty earth. Der. *moat-ed*, Meas. for Meas. iii. 1. 277.

MOB (1), a disorderly crowd. (L.) Used by Dryden, in pref. to Cleomenes, 1692; as cited in Nares. A contraction from *mobile uulgus*. 'I may note that the rabble first changed their title, and were called "the mob" in the assemblies of this [The King's Head] Club. It was their beast of burden, and called first *mobile vulgus*, but fell naturally into the contraction of one syllable, and ever since is become proper English;' North's Examen (1740), p. 574; cited in Trench, Study of Words. In the Hatton Correspondence, ed. E. M. Thompson (Camden Soc.), the editor remarks that *mob* is always used in its full form *mobile* throughout the volumes (see ii. 40, 99, 124, 156); but, as Mr. Thompson kindly pointed out to me, he has since noted that it occurs once in the short form *mob*, viz. at p. 216 of vol. ii. Thus, under the date 1690, we read that 'Lord Torrington is most miserably reproached by the *mobile*' (ii. 156); and under the date 1695, that 'a great *mob* have been up in Holborn and Drury Lane' (ii. 216). In Shadwell's Squire of Alsatia (1688), we find *mobile* in A. i. sc. 1, but *mob* in A. iv. sc. 2. And see Spectator, no. 135.—L. *mōbile*, neut. of *mōbilis*, movable, fickle; *mōbile uulgus*, the fickle multitude. See **Mobile** and **Vulgar.** Der. *mob*, verb. See Notes on E. Etym., p. 190.

MOB (2), a kind of cap. (Dutch.) '*Mob*, a woman's night-cap;' Bailey's Dict., vol. ii. ed. 1731. We also say *mob-cap*.—Du. *mop-muts*, a woman's night-cap; where *muts* means 'cap;' MDu. *mop*, a woman's coif (Sewel); Low G. *mopp*, a woman's cap (Danneil). Cf. prov. E. *mop*, to muffle up (Halliwell).

MOBILE, easily moved, movable. (F.—L.) 'Fyxt or els *mobyll*;' Skelton, Why Come Ye Nat to Courte, l. 522. [The expression '*mobil* people' occurs, according to Richardson, in The Testament of Love, b. i; but the reading is really *mokil*, i.e. much; ch. 6, l. 73.]—F. *mobile*, 'movable;' Cot.—L. *mōbilis*, movable (for *mǒuibilis*).—L. *mouēre*, to move; see **Move.** Der. *mobili-ty*, from F. *mobilité*, which from L. acc. *mōbilitātem*; also *mobil-ise*, from mod. F. *mobiliser*; hence *mobil-is-at-ion*. And see *mob* (1).

MOCCASIN, MOCCASSIN, MOCASSIN, a shoe of deer-skin, &c. (N. American Indian.) Spelt *mocassin* in Fenimore Cooper, The Pioneers, ch. i. A North-American Indian word. From Powhatan *mǒckasin*; Algonquin *makisin* (Cuoq); Micmac *mkūsun* (S. T. Rand). Capt. Smith (Works, ed. Arber, p. 44) cites Indian '*mockasins*, shoaes.'

MOCK, to deride. (F.—L.) ME. *mokken*, Prompt. Parv.—OF. *mocquier*, late *moquer*. '*Se mocquer*, to mock, flowt, frumpe, scoffe;' Cot. According to Körting, § 6330, it is the Picard form of *moucher*, to wipe the nose; Corblet gives the Picard form as *mouker*, and Moisy has Norm. dial. *mouquer*, to wipe the nose (so that the vowel does not quite correspond); but Mistral has mod. Prov. *mouca*, *moucha*, to wipe the nose, and *se mouca*, to mock. Cotgrave has MF. *moucher*, 'to snyte or make cleane the nose; also to frumpe, mocke, scoff, deride.' Cf. Ital. *moccare*, 'to blow the nose, also to mocke;' Florio.—Late L. *muccāre*, to blow the nose.—L. *muccus*, *mūcus*, mucus. See **Mucus.** Der. *mock*, sb.; *mock-er*; *mock-er-y*, spelt *mocquerye* in Caxton, Hist. of Troye, fol. 95, l. 8, from F. *moquerie*; *mock-ing*, *mock-ing-bird*.

MODE, a manner, measure, rule, fashion. (F.—L.) 'In the first figure and the third *mode*;' Sir T. More, Works, p. 504 d; where it is used in a logical sense.—F. *mode*, 'manner, sort, fashion;' Cot.—L. *modum*, acc. of *modus*, a measure, manner, kind, way. **β.** Akin to Gk. μέδομαι, I think upon, plan, L. *meditor*, I meditate, Gk. μῆδος, a plan, μήδομαι, I intend, plan; from √MED (Teut. MET), to measure, to plan, best exemplified in E. *mete*; cf. Icel. *māti*, a mode, manner, way; see **Mete.** Brugmann, i. § 412. Der. *mod-al*, a coined word from L. *mod-us*; *mod-ish*, coined from F. *mode*; *mod-el*, q.v., *mod-er-ate*, q.v., *mod-ern*, q.v., *mod-est*, q.v.; *mod-ic-um*, q.v., *mod-i-fy*, q.v.; *mod-ul-ate*, q.v. From the L. *modus* we also have *accom-mod-ate*, *com-mod-ious*. Doublet, *mood* (2).

MODEL, a pattern, mould, shape. (F.—Ital.—L.) See Shak. Rich. II, iii. 2. 153; Hen. V, ii. chor. 16; &c.—MF. *modelle* (F. *modèle*), 'a modell, pattern, mould;' Cot.—Ital. *modello*, 'a model, a frame, a plot, a mould;' Florio. Formed as if from a L. type *modellus*, dimin. of *modulus*, a measure, standard, which again is a dimin. of *modus*. See **Modulate, Mode.** Der. *model*, vb., *modell-er*, *modell-ing*; *re-model*.

MODERATE, temperate, within bounds, not extreme. (L.) '*Moderat* speche;' Hoccleve, Reg. of Princes, 2436. '*Moderately* and with reuerence;' Sir T. More, Works, p. 361 h.—L. *moderātus*, pp. of *moderāri*, to fix a measure, regulate, control. From a stem *moder-*, answering to an older *modes-*, extended from *mod-*, as in *modus*, a measure; see **Modest, Mode.** Der. *moderate*, verb, Shak. Troil. iv. 4. 5; *moderate-ly*, *moderate-ness*, *moderat-or*, Sir P. Sidney, Apology for Poetrie, ed. Arber, p. 32, from L. *moderātor*;

moderat-ion, Troil. iv. 4. 2, from OF. *moderation*, 'moderation' (Cot.), which from L. acc. *moderātiōnem*.

MODERN, belonging to the present age. (F.—L.) Used by Shak. to mean 'common-place;' Macb. iv. 3. 170, &c.—F. *moderne*, 'modern, new, of this age;' Cot.—L. *modernus*, modern; lit. of the present mode or fashion; formed from a stem *moder-, for *modes-; from *mod-*, as in *modus*, a measure; cf. *modo*, adv., just now. See **Moderate.** Der. *modern-ly, modern-ness, modern-ise.*

MODEST, moderate, decent, chaste, pure. (F.—L.) *Modestly* is in Gascoigne, Fruites of Warre, st. 208 (and last). *Modestie* is in Sir T. Elyot, The Governour, b. i. c. 25, § 6.—F. *modeste*, 'modest;' Cot.—L. *modestus*, modest, lit. keeping within bounds or measure. From a stem *modes- (extended from *mod-us*, with Aryan suffix *-to*; the same stem, weakened to *moder-*, gives *moder-ate, moder-n.*—L. *modus*, a measure; see **Mode.** Der. *modest-ly, modest-y.*

MODICUM, a small quantity. (L.) In Shak. Troil. ii. 1. 74. Merely L. *modicum*, neut. of *modi-c-us*, moderate. From *modi-*, for *modus*, a measure; see **Modify, Mode.**

MODIFY, to moderate, change the form of. (F.—L.) ME. *modifien*, Gower, C. A. iii. 157; bk. vii. 2153; Chaucer, C. T., A 2542.—F. *modifier*, 'to modifie, moderate;' Cot.—L. *modificāre.* —L. *modi-*, for *modus*, a measure; and *-fic-*, for *fac-ere*, to make. See **Mode** and **Fact.** Der. *modifi-er, modifi-able; modific-at-ion* = F. *modification*, 'modification' (Cot.), from L. acc. *modificā-tiōnem.*

MODULATE, to regulate, vary. (L.) 'To *modulate* the sounds;' Grew, Cosmographia Sacra (1701), b. i. c. 5. sect. 16 (R.). [But the verb was prob. suggested by the sb. *modulation*, given as both a F. and E. word by Cotgrave; from the L. acc. *modulātiōnem.*] —L. *modulātus*, pp. of *modulāri*, to measure according to a standard. —L. *modulus*, a standard; dimin. of *modus*, a measure. See **Mode.** Der. *modulat-ion*, as above; *modulat-or*, from L. *modulātor.* So also *module*, from F. *module*, 'a modell or module' (Cot.), from L. *modulus.* Also *modulus* = L. *modulus.*

MOGUL, a Mongolian. (Mongolia.) In Sir T. Herbert, Travels, ed. 1665, p. 75; Milton, P. L. xi. 391. 'Mr. Limberham is the *mogul* [lord] of the next mansion;' Dryden, Kind Keeper, iv. 1. The word *Mogul* is only another form of *Mongol*; the Great Mogul was the emperor of the Moguls in India. 'The Mogul dynasty in India began with Baber in 1525;' Haydn, Dict. of Dates. Cf. Pers. *Moghōl*, a Mogul; Rich. Pers. Dict. p. 1460.

MOHAIR, cloth made of fine hair. (Arab.) The E. spelling is a sophisticated one, from a ridiculous attempt to connect it with E. *hair*; just as in the case of *cray-fish.* Spelt *mohaire* in Skinner, ed. 1691; older spelling *mockaire*, Hakluyt, Voy. ii. 273; whence was borrowed the MF. *mouäire*, cited by Skinner; the mod. F. is *moire.* Other MF. forms are *mohère, mouhaire*, cited by Scheler. The name was given to a stuff made from the hair of the Angora goat (Asia Minor).—Arab. *mukhayyar*, 'a kind of coarse camelot or hair-cloth;' Rich. Dict. p. 1369, col. 2. See Devic, in Supp. to Littré. Doublet, *moire*, from F. *moire.*

MOHAMMEDAN, a follower of Mohammed. (Arab.) From the well-known name.—Arab. *muḥammad*, praiseworthy; Rich. Dict. p. 1358.—Arab. root *ḥamada*, he praised; id. p. 581.

MOHUR, a gold coin current in India. (Pers.) From Pers. *muhr, muhur*, 'a seal, a gold coin current in India for about £1 16s.;' Rich. Dict. p. 1534, col. 1; Pers. *muhr, muhar*, a seal, a gold coin worth 16 rupees (H. H. Wilson).—Skt. *mudrā*, a seal.

MOIDORE, a Portuguese gold coin. (Port.—L.) '*Moidore*, a Portugal gold coin, in value 27 shillings sterling;' Bailey's Dict., vol. ii. ed. 1731.—Port. *moeda d'ouro* or *moeda de ouro*, a moidore, £1 7s. Lit. 'money of gold.'—L. *monēta*, money; *dē*, of; *aurum*, gold. See **Money** and **Aureate.**

MOIETY, half, a portion. (F.—L.)· See K. Lear, i. 1. 7, where it means 'a part' merely. It means 'a half' in All's Well, iii. 2. 69. —AF. *moyté*, Year-books of Edw. I, ii. 441; F. *moitié*, 'an half, or half part;' Cot.—L. *medietātem*, acc. of *medietās*, a middle course, a half.—L. *medius*, middle; see **Mediate.**

MOIL, to toil or drudge. (F.—L.) Skinner, ed. 1691, explains *moil* by 'impigrè laborare,' i.e. to toil, drudge. But it is prob. nothing but a peculiar use of the word *moile*, given in Minsheu, ed. 1627, with the sense 'to defile, to pollute;' cf. *moil*, 'to drudge, to dawb with dirt;' Phillips, ed. 1706. As Mr. Wedgwood suggests, *moil*, to drudge, is probably 'only a secondary application from the laborious efforts of one struggling through wet and mud;' or simply, from the dirty state in which hard labour often leaves one. γ. We find earlier quotations for both senses; Halliwell cites 'we *moyle* and toyle' from the Marriage of Wit and Humour, A. D. 1579. Rich. quotes from Gascoigne: 'A simple soule much like myself did once a serpent find, Which, almost dead for cold, lay *moyling* in the myre;' i.e. wallowing in the dirt; see Gascoigne, ed. Hazlitt, i. 94. So also Spenser uses *moyle* for 'to wallow;' see his Hymn of Heavenly

Love, st. 32. Still earlier, the sense is simply to wet or moisten. ME. *moillen*, to wet. 'A monk ... *moillid* al hir patis,' i.e. moistened all their heads by sprinkling them with holy water; Introd. to Tale of Beryn, ed. Furnivall, p. 6, l. 139.—OF. *moiller, moiler* (Littré), later *mouiller*, 'to wet, moisten, soake;' Cot. The orig. sense was 'to soften,' which is effected, in the case of clay, &c., by wetting it. The OF. *moiller* answers to a L. type *molliāre, to soften (not found), formed directly from L. *molli-*, stem of *mollis* (OF. *mol*), soft. See **Mollify.**

MOIRE, watered silk. (F.—E.—Arab.) A later F. form of E. **Mohair,** q. v.; in a slightly altered sense. Körting suggests that, in the sense of 'watered silk,' it may represent L. *marmoreus*, shining like marble, from *marmor*, marble; because *moire* cannot well represent the Arabic form. But Hatzfeld derives F. *moire* from E. *mohair*; which explains the matter. We then reborrowed this F. form *moire.*

MOIST, damp, humid. (F.—L.) ME. *moiste*; 'a *moiste* fruit with-alle;' P. Plowman, B. xvi. 68. The peculiar use of ME. *moiste* is suggestive as to the derivation of the F. word. It means 'fresh' or 'new;' thus the Wife of Bath's shoes were 'ful *moiste* and newe;' Chaucer, C. T. 459 (A 457). The Host liked to drink '*moiste* and corny ale;' id. 12249 (C 315). And again '*moisty* ale' is opposed to old ale; id. 17009 (H 60).—OF. *moiste* (Littré), later *moite*, 'moist, liquid, humid, wet;' Cot. But the old sense of F. *moiste* must have agreed with the sense with which the word was imported into English. Etym. disputed. Either (1) from L. *musteus*, of or belonging to new wine or must, also new, fresh; as *musteus cāseus*, new cheese (Pliny).—L. *mustum*, new wine; a neut. form from *mustus*, adj., young, fresh, new. See Körting, § 6414; and cf. Prov. *mousti*, moist, allied to *moust*, new wine (Mistral). β. Or (2) from L. *muccidus, mūcidus*, mouldy; from L. *mūcus*, mucus (Körting); see **Mucus.** γ. Or from L. *muscidus, for L. *mūcidus*, the same (Hatzfeld). Perhaps the two L. words coalesced in French (N. E. D.). Der. *moist-ly, moist-ness; moist-en*, Spenser, F. Q. iii. 6. 34, where the final *-en* is really of comparatively late addition (by analogy with other verbs in *-en*), since Wyclif has 'bigan to *moiste* hise feet with teeris,' Luke, vii. 38; *moist-ure*, Gower, C. A. iii. 109; bk. vii. 730; from OF. *moisteur*, mod. F. *moiteur* (Littré).

MOLAR, used for grinding. (L.) '*Molar* teeth or grinders;' Bacon, Nat. Hist. § 752.—L. *molāris*, belonging to a mill, molar.— L. *mola*, a mill.—√MEL, to grind; see **Mill.** Brugmann, ii. § 690.

MOLASSES, syrup made from sugar. (Port.—L.) Also *molosses*; in Phillips, ed. 1706. It ought rather to be *melasses*; as in Stedman's Surinam, i. 317 (1796). Spelt *malasses*, Hakluyt, Voy. ii. pt. 2, p. 4. As it came to us from the West Indies, where the sugar is made, it is either a Port. or a Span. word. The Span. spelling is *melaza*, where the *z* (though now sounded like *th* in *bath*) may well have had (ab. 1600) the sound of E. *ss*; see **Lasso.** Cf. also Port. *melaço*, molasses; where the *ç* is sounded like E. *ss*; and this Port. form better represents the L. neuter sb. [We also find Ital. *melassa*, F. *mélasse.*]—L. *mellāceum*, a kind of must (Lewis); neuter of *mellāceus*, made with honey, hence honey-like; cf. Port. *melado*, mixed with honey. Formed with ending *-āc-e-us* from *mell-, mel*, honey. See **Mellifluous** (with which cf. also *marmalade*, another decoction).

MOLE (1), a spot or mark on the body. (E.) ME. *mole*. 'Many *moles* and spottes;' P. Plowman, B. xiii. 315. [As usual, the ME. *o* answers to AS. *ā*.] AS. *māl*, also written *maal* (where *aa* = *ā*). '*Stigmentum*, fūl *maal* on rægel' = a foul spot on a garment; Ælfric's Gloss., in Voc. 125. 19.+OHG. *meil*, a spot; Goth. *mail*, a spot, blemish. Teut. type *mailom, n. Root unknown.

MOLE (2), a small animal that burrows. (E.) *Mole* seems to be quite distinct from another name of the animal, viz. *moldwarp.* Shak. has both forms, viz. *mole*, Temp. iv. 194; and *moldwarp*, 1 Hen. IV, iii. 1. 149. Palsgrave has *mole.* In the 15th cent., we find 'Talpa, *molle*;' Voc. 639. 14.+MDu. and Du. *mol*; Low G. *mull* (Berghaus). Teut. type *mulloz or *mulluz, m. (Franck). Prob. related to MDu. *mul*, 'the dust or crumblings of turf,' Hexham; ME. *mul*, AS. *myl*, dust; which are further related to **Mould** (1). The sense may have been 'earth-grubber' or 'crumbler,' from the weak grade of √MEL, to pound; see **Molar.** Cf. EFries. *mullen*, to grub; *mulle*, a child that grubs in the ground; *mulle, mul*, a mole; Low G. *mull-worm*, a mole (Danneil). 2. The other form appears as ME. *mold-werp*; Wyclif, Levit. xi. 30. From ME. *molde*, mould; and *werpen*, to throw up, end. E. to *warp.* See **Mould** and **Warp.** So also MDu. *molworp* (Kilian); Icel. *moldvarpa*, a mole, similarly formed. Cf. Swed. *mull-sork, mull-vad*, a mole; from *mull*, mould. And note Icel. *mylja*, to crush. Der. *mole-hill*, Cor. v. 3. 30.

MOLE (3), a breakwater. (F.—Ital.—L.) '*Mole* or peer' [pier]; Blount's Gloss., ed. 1674. 'The Mole, that .. defendeth the hauen;' Sandys, Trav. (1632); p. 255.—MF. *mole*, 'a peer, a bank, or causey on the sea-side;' Cot. F. *môle.*—Ital. *molo, mole,* 'a great pile;' Florio.—L. *mōlem,* acc. of *mōles,* a great heap, vast pile. A word of doubtful origin. **Der.** From L. *mōles* we also have *molecule,* q. v.

MOLECULE, an atom, small particle. (L.) Formerly written *molecula.* 'Molecula, a little mass or part of anything;' Bailey's Dict. vol. ii. ed. 1751. A coined word; formed with double dimin. suffix *-c-ul-* (in imitation of *particula,* a particle) from L. *mōles,* a heap. See **Mole** (3). **Der.** *molecul-ar.*

MOLEST, to disturb, annoy. (F.—L.) ME. *molesten,* Chaucer, Troilus, b. iv. l. 880.—F. *molester,* 'to molest;' Cot.—L. *molestāre,* to annoy.—L. *molestus,* adj., troublesome, burdensome. β. Formed (with suffix *-tus* = Idg. *-to-s*) from a stem *moles-,* which is usually associated with *mōles;* see **Mole** (3). **Der.** *molest-er; molest-at-ion,* Oth. ii. 1. 16.

MOLLA, the same as **Mullah,** q. v.

MOLLIFY, to soften. (F.—L.) In Isa. i. 6 (A. V.). 'It [borage] *mollyfyeth* the bealy;' Sir T. Elyot, Castel of Helth, b. ii. c. 9. Hoccleve has *mollifie,* Reg. of Princes, 2638. [The sb. *mollificacioun* is in Chaucer, C. T. 16322; G 854.]—OF. *mollifier,* 'to mollifie;' Cot.—L. *mollificāre,* to soften. β. L. *molli-,* for *mollis,* soft; and *-fic-,* for *facere,* to make. β. L. *mollis* is akin to Skt. *mṛdu-,* soft; O. Ch. Slav. *mladŭ,* young, tender (Russ. *molodoi*); and to Gk. μέλδειν, E. *melt;* see **Melt.** Brugmann, ii. § 690. **Der.** *mollifi-able, mollifi-er;* also *mollific-at-ion,* allied to *mollificātus,* pp. of *mollificāre.* And see *moil, mollusc.*

MOLLUSC, an invertebrate animal, with a soft fleshy body, as a snail. (L.) Modern. Not in Todd's Johnson. Cf. F. *mollusque,* a mollusc (Littré).—L. *mollusca,* a kind of nut with a soft shell, which some molluscs were supposed to resemble; from *molluscus,* softish; allied to *mollescere,* to become soft.—L. *mollis,* soft; see **Mollify.**

MOLTEN, melted. (E.) In Exod. xxxii. 4; &c. The old pp. of *melt;* see **Melt.**

MOLY, the name of a certain plant. (L.—Gk.) In Spenser, Sonnet 26.—L. *mōly.*—Gk. μῶλυ; Homer, Od. x. 305; cf. Skt. *mūla-m,* an edible root.

MOMENT, importance, value, instant of time. (F.—L.) 'In a *moment;*' Wyclif, 1 Cor. xv. 52.—F. *moment,* 'a moment, a minute, a jot of time; also moment, importance, weight;' Cot.—L. *mōmentum,* a movement, hence an instant of time; also moving force, weight. β. For *mouimentum;* formed with the common suffix *-ment-* from *mouēre,* to move; see **Move.** **Der.** *moment-ar-y,* Temp. i. 2. 202, from L. *mōmentārius; moment-ar-i-ly, -ness; moment-an-y* (obsolete), Mids. Nt. Dr. i. 1. 143, from L. *mōmentāneus; moment-ly; moment-ous,* from L. *mōmentōsus; momentous-ly, -ness.* **Doublets,** *momentum* (= L. *mōmentum*); also *movement.*

MONAD, a unit, &c. (L.—Gk.) The pl. *monades* was formerly used as synonymous with digits. 'Monades, a term in arithmetick, the same as digits;' Phillips, ed. 1706.—L. *monad-,* stem of *monas,* a unit.—Gk. μονάς, a unit.—Gk. μόνος, alone, sole. See **Mono-.**

MONARCHY, sole government, a kingdom. (F.—L.—Gk.) The word *monarchy* is (perhaps) older than *monarch* in English. Sir David Lyndsay's book entitled 'The Monarchè,' written in 1552, treats of monarchies, not of monarchs; see l. 1979 of the poem. ME. *monarchie,* Gower, C. A. i. 27; prol. 695.—F. *monarchie,* 'a monarchie, a kingdom;' Cot.—L. *monarchia,* a kingdom.—Gk. μοναρχία, a kingdom.—Gk. μόναρχος, adj., ruling alone.—Gk. μον-, for μόνος, alone; and ἄρχειν, to be first. See **Mono-** and **Arch-.** **Der.** *monarch,* Hamlet, ii. 2. 270, from F. *monarque* < L. *monarcha,* from Gk. μονάρχης, a sovereign; *monarch-al,* Milton, P. L. ii. 428; *monarch-ic,* from F. *monarchique* (Cot.), Gk. μοναρχικός; *monarch-ic-al; monarch-ise,* Rich. II, iii. 2. 165; *monarch-ist.*

MONASTERY, a house for monks, convent. (L.—Gk.) The older word was *minster,* q. v. Sir T. More has *monastery,* Works, p. 135 e. Also in Caxton, Golden Legend; Mary Magd. § 12. Englished from L. *monastērium,* a minster.—Gk. μοναστήριον, a minster.—Gk. μοναστής, dwelling alone; hence, a monk.—Gk. μονάζειν, to be alone.—Gk. μόνος, alone. See **Mono-.** **Der.** From Gk. μοναστής we also have *monast-ic,* As You Like It, iii. 2. 441 = Gk. μοναστικός, living in solitude; hence *monast-ic-al, monastic-ism.* **Doublet,** *minster.*

MONDAY, the second day of the week. (E.) ME. *monenday,* Rob. of Glouc. p. 495, l. 10180; later *Moneday, Monday.* AS. *Mōnan dæg,* Monday; rubric to John, vii. 32. The lit. sense is 'day of the Moon.'—AS. *mōnan,* gen. of *mōna,* the moon (a masc. sb. with gen. in *-an*); and *dæg,* a day. See **Moon** and **Day.**

MONETARY, relating to money. (L.) Modern; not in Todd's Johnson. Imitated from L. *monētārius,* which properly means 'belonging to a mint,' or a mint-master.—L. *monēta,* (1) a mint, (2) money; see **Mint** (1).

MONEY, current coin, wealth. (F.—L.) ME. *moneie;* Chaucer,

C. T. 705 (A 703).—OF. *moneie;* mod. F. *monnaie.*—L. *monēta,* (1) a mint, (2) money. See further under **Mint** (1). **Der.** *money-bag,* Merch. Ven. ii. 5. 18; *money-ed,* Merry Wives, iv. 4. 88; *money-changer; money-less.* Also *monetary,* q. v.

MONGER, a dealer, trader. (L.) Generally used in composition. ME. *wol-monger,* a wool-monger; Rob. of Glouc. p. 539, l. 11173. AS. *mangere,* a dealer, merchant; the dat. case *mangere* occurs in Matt. xiii. 45. Formed with suffix *-ere* (= mod. E. *-er*) from *mangian,* to traffic, barter, gain by trading, Luke, xix. 15. Cf. *mangung,* merchandise, Matt. xxii. 5. β. The form *mangian* is from L. *mango,* a dealer, of which *mangere* is a translation or equivalent. ¶ Prob. sometimes confused with AS. *mengan,* to mingle, already treated of under **Mingle,** q. v.; AS. *mang,* a mixture, preserved in the forms *ge-mang, ge-mong,* a mixture, crowd, assembly, Grein, i. 425. **Der.** *cheese-monger, fell-monger, fish-monger, iron-monger,* &c.

MONGOOSE; see **Mungoose.**

MONGREL, an animal of a mixed breed. (E.) In Macbeth, iii. 1. 93. Spelt *mungrel, mungril* in Levins, ed. 1570. The exact history of the word fails, for want of early quotations; but we may consider it as short for *mong-er-el,* with double dimin. suffixes as in *cock-er-el, pick-er-el* (a small pike), so that it was doubtless orig. applied to puppies and young animals. β. As to the stem *mong-,* we may refer it to AS. *mang,* a mixture. The sense is 'a small animal of mingled breed.' See **Mingle.** ¶ We also find late ME. *mengrell,* Book of St. Albans, fol. f 4, back. If not an error for *mongrell,* it is from AS. *mengan,* to mix; from *mang,* as above.

MONITION, a warning, notice. (F.—L.) 'With a good *monicion;*' Sir T. More, Works, p. 245 g. Caxton has *monycion,* Golden Legend, St. Juliana, § 2.—F. *monition,* 'a monition, admonition;' Cot.—L. *monitiōnem,* acc. of *monitio,* a reminding; cf. *monitus,* pp. of *monēre,* to remind; lit. to bring to mind or make to think.—√MEN, to think. Brugmann, ii. § 794. **Der.** *monit-or,* from L. *monitor,* an adviser, from *monēre;* hence *monit-or-y,* Bacon, Henry VII, ed. Lumby, p. 73, l. 6; *monit-or-ship; monit-r-ess* (with fem. suffix *-ess* = F. *-esse,* L. *-issa,* Gk. *-ισσα*); *monit-or-i-al.* And see **Admonish.** The doublet of *monitor* is *mentor.*

MONK, a religious recluse. (L.—Gk.) ME. *monk,* Chaucer, C. T. 165. AS. *munec,* Grein, ii. 269; also *munuc,* Sweet's A. S. Reader.—L. *monachus.*—Gk. μοναχός, adj. solitary; sb. a monk. Extended from Gk. μόν-ος, alone; see **Mono-.** **Der.** *monk-ish; monk's-hood.* Also (from L. *monachus*) *monach-ism.* And see *monastery, minster.*

MONKEY, an ape. (Low G.—F.—Ital.—L.) Spelt *munkie* in Levins and Baret, *monkey, munkey,* in Palsgrave; perhaps not found much earlier. Borrowed from Low G. *Moneke,* the name of the ape's son in Reinke de Vos (1479); where *-ke* is for *-ken,* dimin. suffix; so that the F. version has *Monnekin* (Godefroy). Formed (with Low G. suffix *-ke* = *-ken* = G. *-chen*) from MF. *monne,* an ape.—MItal. *monna, mona,* 'an ape, a munkie, a pug, a kitlin [kitten], a munkie-face; also a nickname for women, as we say gammer, goodie, good-wife such a one;' Florio. He notes that *mona* is also spelt *monna;* cf. mod. Ital. *monna,* mistress, dame, ape, monkey (Meadows). [Cf. also Span. *mona,* Port. *mona,* a she-monkey; Span. and Port. *mono,* a monkey.] The order of ideas is: mistress, dame, old woman, monkey, by that degradation of meaning so common in all languages. β. The orig. sense of Ital. *monna* was 'mistress,' and it was used as a title; Scott introduces *Monna Paula* as a character in the Fortunes of Nigel. As Diez remarks, it is a familiar corruption of *madonna,* i. e. my lady, hence, mistress or madam; see **Madonna, Madam.** ¶ The Span. and Port. *mona* were, apparently, borrowed from Italian; being feminine sbs., the masc. sb. *mono* was coined to accompany them. The MItal. has also *monicchio,* 'a pugge, a munkie,' Florio; which is the Ital. equivalent of the Low G. form.

MONO-, *prefix,* single, sole. (Gk.) From Gk. μόνο-, for μόνος, single. Shortened to *mon-* in *mon-arch, mon-ocular, mon-ody;* see also *mon-ad, mon-astery, mon-k.* Words with this prefix are numerous; e. g. *mono-ceros,* a unicorn, from Gk. κέρας, a horn; *mono-chrome,* painting in one colour, from χρῶμα, colour; *mon-œcious,* having stamens and pistils in different flowers on the same plant, from οἶκος, a house, dwelling.

MONOCHORD, a musical instrument with one chord. (F.—L.—Gk.) Spelt *monacorde;* in Hall's Chron. Hen. VII, an. i. § 9.—F. *monocorde.*—L. *monochordon.*—Gk. μονόχορδον.—Gk. μόνο-; and χορδή, the string of a musical instrument. See **Mono-** and **Chord.**

MONOCOTYLEDON, a plant with one cotyledon. (Gk.) Modern and botanical. See **Mono-** and **Cotyledon.**

MONOCULAR, with one eye. (Hybrid; Gk. *and* L.) A coined word; used by Howell (R.). From Gk. μον-, for μόνο-, from μόνος, sole; and L. *oculus,* an eye. See **Mono-** and **Ocular.**

MONODY, a kind of mournful poem. (Gk.) 'In this *monody,*' &c.; Milton, Introd. to Lycidas. So called because sung by a single person. — Gk. μονῳδία, a solo, a lament. — Gk. μον-, for μόνος, alone; and ᾠδή, a song, ode, lay. See **Mono-** and **Ode**. **Der.** *monod-ist.*

MONOGAMY, marriage to one wife only. (L. — Gk.) Spelt *monogamie* in Minsheu, ed. 1627. Used by Bp. Hall, Honour of the Maried Clergie, sect. 19, in speaking of a book by Tertullian. — L. *monogamia*, monogamy, on which Tertullian wrote a treatise. — Gk. μονογαμία, monogamy; μονόγαμος, adj., marrying but once. — Gk. μόνο-, for μόνος, alone, sole; and γαμεῖν, to marry, γάμος, marriage. See **Mono-** and **Bigamy**. **Der.** *monogam-ist*, Goldsmith, Vicar of Wakefield, ch. xiv.

MONOGRAM, a single character, a cipher of characters joined together. (L. — Gk.) Used by Ben Jonson, but in a different sense; Underwoods, Poet to Painter, lxx. 11. — L. *monogramma*, a monogram. — Gk. μονογράμματον, a mark formed of one letter; neut. of μονογράμματος, consisting of one letter. — Gk. μόνο-, sole; and γραμματ-, stem of γράμμα, a letter, from γράφειν, to grave, write. See **Mono-** and **Graphic**. **Der.** So also *mono-graph*, a modern word, from Gk. γραφή, writing.

MONOLOGUE, a soliloquy. (F. — Gk.) 'Besides the chorus or *monologues*;' Dryden, Essay of Dramatic Poesie. But Minsheu, ed. 1627, distinguishes between *monologue*, a sole talker, and *monologie*, 'a long tale of little matter.' — F. *monologue*, given by Cotgrave only in the sense 'one that loves to hear himselfe talke;' but, as in *dia-logue*, the last syllable was also used in the sense of 'speech.' — Gk. μονόλογος, adj., speaking alone. — Gk. μόνο-, alone; and λέγειν, to speak. See **Mono-** and **Logic**.

MONOMANIA, mania on a single subject. (Gk.) A coined word; from **Mono-** and **Mania**. First in 1823.

MONOPOLY, exclusive dealing in the sale of an article. (L. — Gk.) 'Monopolies were formerly so numerous in England that parliament petitioned against them, and many were abolished, about 1601-2. They were further suppressed by 21 Jas. I, 1624;' Haydn, Dict. of Dates. 'Thou hast a *monopoly* thereof;' Sir T. More, Works, p. 1303 h. — L. *monopōlium*. — Gk. μονοπώλιον, the right of monopoly; μονοπωλία, monopoly. — Gk. μόνο-, sole (see **Mono-**); and πωλεῖν, to barter, sell; connected with Icel. *fal-r*, adj., venal, for sale (Prellwitz); Skt. *paṇya-*, saleable, *paṇ* (for *paln*), to buy. **Der.** *monopol-ise*, spelt *monopol-ize* in Bacon, Hist. Hen. VII, ed. Lumby, p. 147, l. 33; a coined word, formed by analogy, since the MF. word was simply *monopoler* (Cotgrave).

MONOSYLLABLE, a word of one syllable. (F. — L. — Gk.) In Minsheu, ed. 1627; he makes it an adjective. Altered from F. *monosyllabe*, adj., 'of one syllable;' Cot. — L. *monosyllabus*, adj. — Gk. μονοσύλλαβος, adj., of one syllable. See **Mono-** and **Syllable**. **Der.** *monosyllab-ic*.

MONOTONY, sameness of tone. (Gk.) Bailey, vol. ii. ed. 1731, gives it in the form *monotonia*. — Gk. μονοτονία, sameness of tone. — Gk. μονότονος, adj., of the same tone, monotonous. See **Mono-** and **Tone**. **Der.** *monoton-ous*, formed from Gk. μονότονος, by change of -ος into -ous; like the change of L. -us into E. -ous (as in *ardu-ous*, &c.). Also *monotone*, a late term. Also *monoton-ous-ly, -ness.*

MONSOON, a periodical wind. (Du. — Port. — Arab.) Spelt *monson* in Hakluyt's Voyages, ii. 278. Sir T. Herbert speaks of the *monzoones*; Travels, ed. 1665, pp. 409, 413. Ray speaks of 'the *monsoons* and trade-winds;' On the Creation, pt. 1 (R.). — MDu. *monssoen*, in 1596 (Yule). — Port. *monção*, monsoon. — Arab. *mausim*, a time, a season; Rich. Dict. p. 1525; whence also Malay *mūsim*, 'a season, monsoon, year;' cf. also *awal mūsim*, 'beginning of the season, setting in of the monsoon;' Marsden, Malay Dict. pp. 340, 24. (See *Monsoon* in Yule.)

MONSTER, a prodigy, unusual production of nature. (F. — L.) ME. *monstre*, Chaucer, C. T. 11656 (F 1344). — F. *monstre*, 'a monster;' Cot. — L. *monstrum*, a divine omen, portent, monster. To be resolved into *mon-es-tru-m* (with Idg. suffixes -*es*- and -*tro*-, for which see Brugmann) from *mon-ēre*, to warn, lit. to make to think. — √MEN, to think; see **Mind**. **Der.** *monstr-ous*, formerly *monstruous*, as in Chaucer, tr. of Boethius, B. iv. met. 3, l. 22, from OF. *monstrueus* (Godefroy), MF. *monstrüeux*, 'monstrous' (Cot.), which from L. *monstruōsus* (also *monstrōsus*), monstrous; *monstrous-ly, monstrous-ness; monstros-i-ty*, spelt *monstruosity*, Troilus, iii. 2. 87. Also *de-monstrate, re-monstrate*. **Doublet**, *muster*.

MONTH, the period of the moon's revolution. (E.) Properly 28 days; afterwards so altered as to divide the year into 12 parts. ME. *moneth* (of two syllables), Rob. of Glouc., p. 59, l. 1369; sometimes shortened to *month*. AS. *mōnaþ*, sometimes *mōnð*, a month; Grein, ii. 262; properly 'a lunation.' Cf. AS. *mōna*, moon; see **Moon**. + Du. *maand*; Icel. *mānuðr, mānaðr, mōnoðr*; Dan. *maaned*; Swed. *månad*; Goth. *mēnōþs*; G. *monat*. Teut. type *mēnōth-. Cf. also Lithuan. *mėnesis*, a month, *mėnū*, moon; Russ. *miesiats'*, a month, also the moon; L. *mensis*, a month; Irish and W. *mis*, Gael. *mios*,

a month; Gk. μήν, month, μήνη, moon; Pers. *māh*, a moon, a month; Skt. *mās*, a month. **Der.** *month-ly*, adj., K. Lear, i. 1. 134; *month-ly*, adv., Romeo, ii. 2. 110.

MONUMENT, a record, memorial. (F. — L.) Tyndall speaks of 'reliques and *monumentes*;' Works, p. 283, col. 1. — F. *monument*, 'a monument;' Cot. — L. *monumentum*, a monument. β. Formed, with suffix -*ment-um*, from *mon-u-* = *mon-i-*, seen in *moni-tus*, pp. of *monēre*, to remind, cause to think. — √MEN, to think; see **Moni-tion**. **Der.** *monument-al*, All's Well, iv. 3. 20.

MOOD (1), disposition of mind, temper. (E.) It is probable that the sense of the word has been influenced by confusion with *mood* (2), and with *mode*. The old sense is simply 'mind,' or sometimes 'wrath.' ME. *mood*; 'aslaked was his *mood*' = his wrath was appeased; Chaucer, C. T. 1762 (A 1760). AS. *mōd*, mind, feeling, heart (very common); Grein, ii. 257. + Du. *moed*, courage, heart, spirit, mind; Icel. *mōðr*, wrath, moodiness; Dan. and Swed. *mod*, courage, mettle; Goth. *mōds*, wrath; G. *muth*, courage. β. All from a Teut. type *mō-do-*; where -*do*- is a suffix. Cf. Gk. μέ-μα-α, I strive after. Brugmann, i. § 196. **Der.** *mood-y*, AS. *mōdig*, Grein, ii. 260; Sweet, New E. Gr. § 1608; *mood-i-ly, mood-i-ness.*

MOOD (2), manner, grammatical form. (F. — L.) A variant of *mode*, in the particular sense of 'grammatical form of a verb.' Spelt *mode* in Palsgrave. 'Mood, or Mode, manner, measure, or rule. In Grammar there are 6 moods, well known;' Blount's Gloss., ed. 1674. See **Mode**. ¶ Perhaps it has often been confused with **Mood** (1); see *Mood* in Trench, Select Glossary.

MOON, the planet which revolves round the earth. (E.) ME. *monè*, of two syllables; Chaucer, C. T. 9759 (E 1885). AS. *mōna*, a masc. sb.; Grein, ii. 262. + Du. *maan*, masc. sb.; Dan. *maane*; Swed. *måne*, masc.; Goth. *mēna*, masc.; G. *mond*, masc.; OHG. *māno*. Teut. type *mē-non-*, m. + Lithuan. *mėnū*, masc.; Gk. μήνη. Cf. Skt. *mās*, a month; which Benfey refers to *mā*, to measure. — √MĒ, to measure, as it is a chief measurer of time. See also **Month**. **Der.** *moon-beam, moon-light, moon-shine; moon-calf*, Temp. ii. 2. 111; *moon-ish*, As You Like It, iii. 2. 430.

MOONSHEE, a secretary. (Hind. — Arab.) Hind. *munshī*, 'a writer, a secretary; applied by Europeans usually to teachers or interpreters of Persian and Hindustani;' H. H. Wilson, Gloss. of Indian Terms, p. 356. — Arab. *munshi'*, a writer, secretary, tutor, language-master; Rich. Dict. p. 1508. (See *Moonshee* in Yule.)

MOOR (1), a heath, extensive waste ground. (E.) ME. *more*, King Alisaunder, 6074. AS. *mōr*, a moor, morass, bog; Grein, ii. 262. + MDu. *moer*, 'mire, dirt, mud;' *moerlandt*, 'moorish land, or turfie land of which turfe is made,' Hexham; OHG. *muor*. Teut. types *mōroz*, m., *mōrom*, n.; prob. related, by gradation, to Goth. *marei*, sea, lake; see **Mere** (1). **Der.** *moor-ish, moor-land, moor-cock; moor-hen*, ME. *mor-hen*, Polit. Songs, ed. Wright, p. 158, l. 6. Also *mor-ass*, q. v.

MOOR (2), to fasten a ship by cable and anchor. (E.) In Minsheu, ed. 1627; Milton, P. L. i. 207. Not found in ME. or AS., but prob. E., and representing AS. form *mārian*, to moor a ship; for we find, as derivatives, AS. *mǣrels*, a mooring-rope or painter, Voc. 288. 28, and *mǣrels-rāp*, the same, Voc. 182. 30. Cognate with Du. *maaren, meeren* (Sewel), to tie, to moor a ship; MDu. *marren, maren*, to bind, or tie knots (Hexham); Du. *meren* (Franck); whence perhaps ME. *marlen*, to moor; Prompt. Parv. **Der.** *moor-ing, moor-age*; and see *marline*.

MOOR (3), a native of North Africa. (F. — L.) 'A *Moore*, or one of Mauritania, a blacke moore, or neger;' Minsheu, ed. 1627. ME. *Mowres*, pl. Moors; Mandeville's Travels, ch. xiv. p. 156. — F. *More*, 'a Moor, Maurian, blackamore;' Cot. — L. *Maurus*, a Moor; see Smith's Class. Dict. **Der.** *Moor-ish*; and see *morris, morocco, Morian*. Also *black-a-moor*, spelt *blackamore*, in Cotgrave, as above; a corruption of *black moor* in Minsheu, as above; also spelt *blackmoor* in Beaum. and Fletcher, Mons. Thomas, v. 2.

MOOSE, the American elk. (N. Amer. Indian.) 'Moos, a beast bigger than a stagge;' Capt. Smith, Works, p. 207. The native Virginian name; Abenaki *mos*, Penobscot *muns*; see N. and Q. 9 S. xii. 504. Cuoq cites Algonquin *mons* (with *n*).

MOOT, to discuss or argue a case. (E.) Little used, except in the phr. 'a moot point.' 'To *moote*, a tearme vsed in the innes of the Court, it is the handling of a case, as in the Vniuersitie, their disputations, problemes, sophismes, and such other like acts;' Minsheu, ed. 1627. The true sense is 'to discuss in or at a meeting,' and the verb is unoriginal, being due to AS. *mōt*, ME. *mote*, later *moot*, an assembly or meeting, whence also *moot-hall*, i. e. a hall of assembly, occurring in P. Plowman, B. iv. 135; cf. also *ward-mote*, i. e. meeting of a ward, id. prol. 94. Cf. ME. *motien, moten*, to moot, discuss, also to cite, plead, P. Plowman, B. i. 174; AS. *mōtian*, to cite, summon (to an assembly or court); 'gif man ... þane mannan *mōte*' = if one summon (or cite) the man; Laws of Hlothhære, sect. 8; see

Thorpe, Ancient Laws, i. 31.—AS. *mōt*, a meeting, an assembly; usually spelt *gemōt*, a word familiar in the phrase *witena gemōt*, an assembly of wise men, a parliament.+Icel. *mōt*, a meeting, court of law; MHG. *muoz*, *mōz*, a meeting. β. From a Teutonic type *mōtom, n. Der. *moot-able*, *moot-case*, i.e. case for discussion; *moot-point*, i.e. point for discussion; *moot-hall*, a hall of assembly, law court. Also *meet*, q.v. ¶ Observe that *meet* is a mere derivative of *moot*, as shown by the vowel-change.

MOP (1), an implement for washing floors, &c. (F.—L.) In Torriano's Ital. Dict., the word *pannatore* is explained by 'a maulkin, a *map* of rags or clouts to rub withal;' ed. 1688. Halliwell gives prov. E. *mop*, a napkin, as a Glouc. word. 'Not such *maps* as you wash houses with, but *maps* of countries;' Middleton, Span. Gipsy (acted in 1623); A. ii. sc. 2. Most likely borrowed from OF. *mappe*, a napkin, though this word was later corrupted to *nappe*. See *Nappe* in Littré, who cites the spelling *mappe* as known in the 15th century, though the corrupt form with initial *n* was already known in the 11th century. Both *mappe* and *nappe* are from L. *mappa*, a napkin; whence also **Map** and **Napkin**, the former being taken from the form *mappe*, whilst the latter was due to *nappe*. L. *mappa* is a word of Punic origin. See **Map**. We find Walloon *map*, a table-cloth, *mappe*, a napkin (Remacle); W. Flem. *moppe*, a (ship's) mop (De Bo). ¶ Cf. *strop*, *knop*, with *strap*, *knap*. The Celtic forms are from E. Der. *mop*, verb.

MOP (2), a grimace; to grimace. (E.) Obsolete. 'With *mop* and mow;' Temp. iv. 47. Also as a verbal sb.; '*mopping* and mowing;' K. Lear, iv. 164. The verb to *mop* is allied to **Mope**, q.v. Hence also ME. *moppe*, a foolish person; in Weber, Met. Rom. iii. 56.

MOPE, to be dull or dispirited. (E.) In Shak. Temp. v. 240. Allied to ME. *mopisch*, foolish; Beket, l. 78. We also find *mop*, to grimace; see **Mop** (2). Cf. 'in the *mops*, sulky;' Halliwell. +Du. *moppen*, to pout; whence to grimace, or to sulk; MSwed. *mopa*, to mock (Ihre); Westphal. *möpen*, to grimace; Dan. *maabe*, to mope; cf. prov. G. *muffen*, to sulk (Flügel). Also ME. *mappen*, to bewilder, stupefy; Legends of the Holy Rood, p. 216. And see **Mow** (3). Der. *mop-ish*, *mop-ish-ness*.

MORAINE, a line of stones at the edges of a glacier. (F.—Teut.) Modern; well known from books of Swiss travel.—F. *moraine*, a moraine; Littré. [Cf. Port. *morraria*, a ridge of shelves of sand; *morro*, a great rock, a shelf of sand; Ital. *mora*, a pile of stones. (But not Span. *moron*, a hillock.)] β. Of Teut. origin; cf. Bavarian *mur*, sand and broken stones, fallen from rocks into a valley; Schmeller, Bayerisches Wörterbuch, col. 1642. Schmeller notes the name *moraine* as used by the peasants of Chamouni, according to Saussure. γ. The radical sense is 'mould' or 'crumbled material;' hence fallen rocks, sand, &c.; cf. G. *mürbe*, soft, OHG. *muruwi*, soft, brittle; Icel. *merja*, to crush (Körting).

MORAL, virtuous, excellent in conduct. (F.—L.) 'O moral Gower;' Chaucer, Troilus, b. v, last stanza but one.—F. *moral*, 'morall;' Cot.—L. *mōrālis*, relating to conduct.—L. *mōr-*, from *mōs*, a manner, custom. Root uncertain. Der. *moral*, sb., *morals*, sb. pl.; *moral-er*, i.e. one who moralises, Oth. ii. 3. 301; *moral-ly*; *morale* (a mod. word, borrowed from F. *morale*, morality, good conduct); *moral-ise*, As You Like It, ii. 1. 44; *moral-ist*; *moral-i-ty*, Meas. for Meas. i. 2. 138, from F. *moralité*, 'morality,' Cot.

MORASS, a swamp, bog. (Du.—F.—Teut.) 'Morass, a moorish ground, a marsh, fen, or bog;' Phillips, ed. 1706. Todd says that P. Heylin, in 1656, noted the word as being 'new and uncouth;' but he omits the reference. It occurs in a list of 'uncouth words' at the end of Heylin, Obs. on the Hist. of K. Charles I, published by H[amon] L[estrange]; but Heylin should rather have attributed it to Fuller.—Du. *moeras*, marsh, fen (Sewel). The older Du. form is *moerasch*, adj., 'moorish' (Hexham); as if from the sb. *moer*, 'mire, dirt, or mud' (id.). But this *moerasch* is an altered form of MDu. *marasch*, *maerasch*, a marsh, pool (Kilian).—OF. *maresque*, *maresche*, adj., marshy; also, as sb.; a marsh, a pool; Low L. *mariscus*.—Teut. *mari, the sea; see **Marish**. Cf. G. *morast*, from Du. or Low G. (see *Morast* in Kluge); whence also Swed. *moras*; Dan. *morads* (a corrupt form). Doublet, *marish*.

MORBID, sickly, unhealthy. (F.—L.) 'Morbid (in painting), a term used of very fat flesh very strongly expressed;' Bailey's Dict., vol. ii. ed. 1731.—F. *morbide*, sometimes similarly used as a term in painting (Littré).—L. *morbidus*, sickly (which has determined the present sense of the E. word).—L. *morbus*, disease. Allied to *mor-i*, to die, *mors*, death; see **Mortal**. Brugmann, ii. § 701. Der. *morbid-ly*, *morbid-ness*; also *morbi-fic*, causing disease, a coined word, from *morbi-*, for *morbus*, and L. suffix -*fic-us*, due to *facere*, to make.

MORDACITY, sarcasm. (F.—L.) Little used. It occurs in Cotgrave.—F. *mordacité*, 'mordacity, easie detraction, bitter tearms;' Cot.—L. acc. *mordācitātem*, from nom. *mordācitas*, power to bite.—

L. *mordāci-*, decl. stem of *mordax*, biting; with suffix -*tās*.—L. *mordēre*, to bite. Cf. Skt. *mardaya*, to rub, break in pieces; from *myd*, to rub. Brugmann, ii. § 794. (√MERD, SMERD.) β. Prob. from the same root as E. **Smart**, q.v. Der. *mordaci-ous*, little used, from the stem *mordaci-*; *mordaci-ous-ly*. Also *mordant*, biting, F. *mordant*, from L. *mordent-*, stem of pres. pt. of *mordēre*, to bite.

MORE, additional, greater. (E.) The mod. E. *more* does duty for *two* ME. words which were, generally, well distinguished, viz. *mo* and *more*, the former relating to number, the latter to size. 1. ME. *mo*, more in number, additional. '*Mo* than thries ten' = more than thirty in number; Chaucer, C. T. 578 (A 576). AS. *mā*, both as adj. and adv.; Grein, ii. 201. Thus 'þær byð wundra mā' = there are wonders more in number, lit. more of wonders (Grein). This AS. *mā* was originally an adverbial form; it is cognate with Goth. *mais*, more, adv. 2. ME. *more*, larger in size, bigger; '*more* and *lesse*' = greater and smaller, Chaucer, C. T. 6516 (D 934). [The distinction between *mo* and *more* is not *always* observed in old authors, but very often it appears clearly enough.] AS. *māra*, greater, larger; Grein, ii. 212. Cognate with Icel. *meiri*, greater; Goth. *maiza* (stem *maizon-*), greater. See **Most**. Allied to OIrish *mār*, *mōr*, W. *mawr*, great; AS. *mǣre*, illustrious. ¶ *Mo* is an adverbial, but *not* a positive form; the positive forms are *much*, *mickle*, many. The -*r*- in *more* represents Teut. -*z*-, which in the adv. *mais (being final) was (regularly) lost in AS. Brugmann, i. § 200. Der. *more-over*.

MOST, the superl. form, answers to ME. *moste*, Chaucer, C. T. 2200 (A 2198), also spelt *meste*, *maste*, *measte*, in earlier authors (see Stratmann). AS. *mǣst*, most; Grein, ii. 226. Cognate with Du. *meest*, Icel. *mestr*, G. *meist*, Goth. *maists*; Teut. type *mais-toz, the superl. form allied to the comp. **maiz-on-* (above). Altered from ME. *mēste* to later *mōst* by the influence of *more* and *mo*.

MOREL, an edible fungus. (F.—OHG.) 'Spungy moréls;' Gay, Trivia, iii. 203. [Properly *morille*, but confused with another *morel*, the name of a herb, but lit. 'mulberry-colored;' MF. *morelle*, 'the herb morell, garden nightshade,' Cot. (cf. MF. *morelles*, 'morell cherries,' Cot.), ultimately from L. *mōrum*, a mulberry.]—F. *morille*, 'the smallest and daintiest kind of red mushrome;' Cot.—OHG. *morhila* (G. *morchel*), a morel; from OHG. *morha*, a root, a carrot, allied to AS. *more*, an edible root. See *morchel* in Kluge.

MORGANATIC, used with reference to a marriage of a man with a woman of inferior rank. (Low L.—G.) 'When the left hand is given instead of the right, between a man of superior and a woman of inferior rank, in which it is stipulated that the latter and her children shall not inherit the rank or inherit the possessions of the former. The children are legitimate. Such marriages are frequently contracted in Germany by royalty and the higher nobility. Our George I was thus married;' Haydn, Dict. of Dates.—Low L. *morganātica*. Ducange explains that a man of rank contracting a morganatic marriage was said 'accipere uxorem ad *morganāticam*.' This L. word was coined, with suffix -*ātica*, from the G. *morgen*, morning, which was in this case understood as an abbreviation for MHG. *morgengabe*, morning-gift, a term used to denote the present which, according to the old usage, a husband used to make to his wife on the morning after the marriage-night; esp. if the wife were of inferior rank. This G. *morgen* is cognate with E. *morn*; see **Morn**.

MORIAN, a blackamoor, a Moor. (F.—L.) 'The Morians' land;' Ps. lxviii. 31 (P. B.).—OF. *Morien*, a Moor (Godefroy); also *Moriaine* (15th cent.). From a Late L. type *Mauritānus or *Mauritānius, a man of *Mauritānia*, the country of the *Mauri* or Moors. (A Student's Pastime, p. 254.)

MORION, an open helmet, without visor. (F.—Span.) In Spenser, Muiopotmos, l. 322.—F. *morion*, 'a murrian, or head-peece;' Cot.—Span. *morrion*. Cf. Port. *morrião*, Ital. *morione*, a morion. The word is Spanish, if we may accept the very probable derivation of Span. *morrion* from *morra*, the crown of the head. The latter word has no cognate form in Ital. or Port. Cf. Span. *morro*, anything round; *moron*, a hillock. Perhaps from Basque *murua*, a hill, heap (Diez).

MORMONITE, one of a sect of the Latter-day Saints. (E.; *but a pure invention*.) The *Mormonites* are the followers of Joseph Smith, 'called the prophet, who announced in 1823, at Palmyra, New York, that he had had a vision of the angel Moroni. In 1827 he said that he found the book of *Mormon*, written on gold plates in Egyptian characters;' Haydn, Dict. of Dates, q.v. We may call the word E., as used by English-speaking people; but it is really a pure invention. β. Joseph Smith's own explanation was that it meant 'more good;' from E. *more*, and Egypt. *mon*, good. (This was probably an afterthought.) See The Mormons; London, 1851. Der. *Mormon-ism*.

MORN, the first part of the day. (E.) ME. *morn*, a North E. form. 'On the *morn*' = on the morrow; Barbour's Bruce, i. 601;

to-morn = to-morrow; id. i. 621. *Morn* and *morrow* are merely doublets; the former being contracted from ME. *morwen*, and the latter standing for ME. *morwe*, the same word with loss of final *n*. The form *morwe* is in Chaucer, C. T., A 1492; the older form *morwen* is in the Ancren Riwle, p. 22, l. 16. AS. *morgen*, morn, morrow, Grein, ii. 264; whence *morwen* by the common change of *g* to *w*. Cf. OFries. *morn*, morning.+Du. *morgen*; Icel. *morginn*; Dan. *morgen*; Swed. *morgon*; G. *morgen*; Goth. *maurgins*. Cf. Lith. *merk-ti*, to blink. Orig. sense prob. 'dawn.' Doublet, *morrow*.

MORNING, dawn, morn. (E.) ME. *morning*, P. Plowman, B. prol. 5; contracted from the fuller form *morwening*, Chaucer, C. T. 1064 (A 1062). *Morwening* signifies 'a dawning,' or 'a becoming morn;' formed with the substantival (not participial) suffix *-ing* (AS. *-ung*) from ME. *morwen* = AS. *morgen*, morn; see **Morn**. Cf. *even-ing*; from *even*. **Der.** *morning-star*.

MOROCCO, a fine kind of leather. (Morocco.) Added by Todd to Johnson's Dict. Named from Morocco, in N. Africa; whence also F. *maroquin*, morocco leather. So called from the *Moors*.

MOROSE, ill-tempered, gloomy, severe. (L.) In Blount's Gloss., ed. 1674. See Trench, Select Gloss., who shows that the word was once used as if it owed its derivation to L. *mora*, delay; but this use is obsolete. – L. *mōrōsus*, self-willed; (1) in a good sense, scrupulous, fastidious, (2) in a bad sense, peevish, morose. – L. *mōr-*, decl. stem of *mōs*, (1) self-will, (2) usage, custom, character. See **Moral**. **Der.** *morose-ly*, *morose-ness*. Also *moros-i-ty*, in Minsheu, ed. 1627, from OF. *morosité*, 'morosity, frowardnesse,' Cot.; but now obsolete.

MORPHIA, MORPHINE, the narcotic principle of opium. (Gk.) Modern; coined words from Gk. *Morpheus* (Μορφεύς), the god of sleep and dreams, lit. 'the shaper,' i.e. creator of shapes seen in dreams. – Gk. μορφή, a shape, form. **Der.** *meta-morph-osis*, *a-morph-ous*; from μορφ-ή.

MORRIS, MORRIS-DANCE, an old dance on festive occasions. (Span. – L.) In Shak. Hen. V, ii. 4. 25. See Nares' Glossary. G. Douglas has the pl. *morisis*, Aen. bk. xiii. ch. ix. l. 112. The dance was also called a *morisco*, as in Beaum. and Fletcher, Wild Goose Chase, v. 2. 7. A morris-dancer was also called a *morisco*, 2 Hen. VI, iii. 1. 365; and it is clear that the word meant 'Moorish dance,' though the reason for it is not quite certain, unless it was from the use of the tabor as an accompaniment to it. – Span. *Morisco*, Moorish. Formed with suffix *-isco* (= L. *-iscus*, E. *-ish*) from Span. *Moro*, a Moor. – L. acc. *Maurum*, a Moor; see **Moor** (3). See Brand, Popular Antiquities. ¶ We also find *morris-pike*, i.e. Moorish pike, Com. Errors, iv. 3. 28. Spelt *morys-pike*, Sir T. Elyot, Castel of Helth, b. ii. c. 33. 'The Mourish daunce' is mentioned in 1494; Excerpta Historica, p. 95.

MORROW, morning, morn. (E.) A doublet of *morn*. From ME. *morwe* by the change of final *-we* to *-ow*, as in *arr-ow*, *sparr-ow*, *sorr-ow*, &c. 'A *morwe*' = on the morrow, Chaucer, C. T. 824 (A 822). Again, *morwe* is from the older *morwen*, by loss of final *n*; and *morwen* = mod. E. morn. See **Morn**. **Der.** *to-morrow* = AS. *tō morgene*, where *tō* = mod. E. *to*; the sense is 'for the morrow;' see Grein, ii. 264.

MORSE, a walrus. (F. – Finnish.) Spelt *morsse*, Hakluyt's Voyages, i. 5 (margin). 'The tooth of a *morse* or sea-horse;' Sir T. Browne, Vulg. Errors, b. iii. c. 23. § 5. – F. *morse*. – Finnish *mursu*, a morse (Renvall); whence also Russ. *morj'*, a morse (with *j* sounded as *zh*, i.e. as F. *j*). Cf. Lapp. *morsha*, a morse (Früs). The Russ. name is *morskaia korova*, i.e. sea-cow.

MORSEL, a mouthful, small piece. (F. – L.) ME. *morsel*, Chaucer, C. T. 128. Also *mossel*, Rob. of Glouc. p. 342, l. 7025; 'thys *mossel* bred' = this morsel of bread. The corrupt form *mossel* is still in common use in prov. E. – OF. *morsel*, *morcel*, mod. F. *morceau*, 'a morsell, bit,' Cot. (And see Burguy.) Cf. Ital. *morsello*. Dimin. from L. *morsum*, a bit. – L. *morsus*, pp. of *mordēre*, to bite; see **Mordacity**.

MORTAL, deadly. (F. – L.) See Trench, Select Glossary. ME. *mortal*, Chaucer, C. T., A 61, 1592. – OF. *mortal* (Burguy); *mortel* (Cot.) – L. *mortālis*, mortal. – L. *mort-*, stem of *mors*, death. The decl. stem *mor-ti-* contains the Idg. suffix *-ti-*. √MER, to die; cf. Skt. *mṛ*, to die, pp. *mṛta-*, dead; L. *morī*, to die. **Der.** *mortal-ly*; *mortal-i-ty*, from F. *mortalité*, 'mortality' (Cot.), from L. acc. *mortālitātem*; *morti-fer-ous*, Blount's Gloss., ed. 1674, from L. *fer-re*, to bring, cause. And see *mort-gage*, *morti-fy*, *mort-main*, *mort-u-ary*.

MORTAR (1), **MORTER**, a vessel in which substances are pounded with a pestle. (L.) [A certain kind of ordnance was also called a *mortar*, from its orig. resemblance in shape to the *mortar* for pounding substances in. This is a French word.] ME. *morter*, P. Plowman, B. xiii. 44; King Alisaunder, l. 332. AS. *mortere*, a mortar; A. S. Leechdoms, ed. Cockayne, i. 142. [Cf. OF. *mortier*, 'a morter to bray (pound) things in, also, the short and wide-

mouthed piece of ordnance called a *morter*,' &c.; Cot.] – L. *mortārium*, a mortar. Cf. L. *marculus*, a hammer. See *mortar* (2).

MORTAR (2), cement of lime, sand, and water. (F. – L.) ME. *mortier*, Rob. of Glouc., p. 128, l. 2715. – OF. *mortier*, 'morter used by dawbers;' Cot. – L. *mortārium*, mortar; lit. stuff pounded together; a different sense of the word above; see **Mortar** (1).

MORTGAGE, a kind of security for debt. (F. – L.) ME. *mortgage*, spelt *morgage* in Gower, C. A. iii. 234; bk. vii. 4228. – OF. *mortgage*, *mortgaige*, 'morgage, or mortgage;' Cot. 'It was called a *mortgage*, or *dead pledge*, because, whatever profit it might yield, it did not thereby redeem itself, but became lost or dead to the mortgager on breach of the condition;' Webster. – F. *mort*, dead, from L. *mortuus*, pp. of *morī*, to die; and F. *gage*, a pledge. See **Mortal** and **Gage** (1). **Der.** *mortgag-er*; *mortgag-ee*, where the final *-ee* answers to the F. *-é* of the pp.

MORTIFY, to destroy the vital functions, vex, humble. (F. – L.) ME. *mortifien*, used as a term of alchemy, Chaucer, C. T. 16594 (G 1126). – OF. *mortifier*, 'to mortifie,' Cot. – L. *mortificāre*, to cause death. – L. *morti-*, decl. stem of *mors*, death; and *-fic-*, for *fac-ere*, to make, cause; see **Mortal** and **Fact**. **Der.** *mortify-ing*; *mortific-at-ion*, Sir T. More, Works, p. 700 f, from OF. *mortification* (Cot.), from L. acc. *mortificātiōnem*.

MORTISE, a hole in a piece of timber to receive the tenon, or a piece made to fit it. (F.) Spelt *mortesse* in Palsgrave; *mortaise* in Cot. Shak. has *mortise* as a sb., Oth. ii. 1. 9; and the pp. *mortised*, joined together, Hamlet, iii. 3. 20. ME. *morteys*, Prompt. Parv.; Mandeville, Trav. ch. 7, p. 76. – F. *mortaise*, 'a mortaise in a piece of timber;' Cot. Cf. Span. *mortaja*, a mortise. β. Of unknown origin; it cannot be from L. *mordēre*, to bite, which could not have given the *t*. Devic (in a supplement to Littré) thinks the Span. word may be of Arabic origin. **Der.** *mortise*, verb.

MORTMAIN, the transfer of property to a corporation. (F. – L.) 'Agaynst all *mortmayn*;' Sir T. More, Works, p. 333 h. ME. *mayn mort*, Trevisa, tr. of Higden, viii. 265. The Statute of Mortmain was passed A.D. 1279 (7 Edw. I). Property transferred to the church was said to pass into *main mort* or *mort main*, i.e. into a dead hand, because it could not be alienated. – F. *mort*, dead; and *main*, a hand (L. *manus*). See **Mortgage** and **Manual**.

MORTUARY, belonging to the burial of the dead. (F. – L.) The old use of *mortuary* was in the sense of a fee paid to the parson of a parish on the death of a parishioner. 'And [pore over] Linwode, a booke of constitutions to gather tithes, *mortuaries*, offeringes, customes,' &c.; Tyndall's Works, p. 2, col. 1. Lyndwode, to whom Tyndall here refers, died A.D. 1446. – AF. *mortuarie*, Year-books of Edw. I, 1302-3, p. 443. – Late L. *mortuārium*, a mortuary; neut. of L. *mortuārius*, belonging to the dead. – L. *mortu-us*, dead, pp. of *morī*, to die; see **Mortal**.

MOSAIC, MOSAIC-WORK, ornamental work made with small pieces of marble, &c. (F. – L. – Gk.) Spelt *mosaick*, Milton, P. L. iv. 700. 'Mosaicall-worke, a worke of small inlayed peeces;' Minsheu's Dict., ed. 1627. – MF. *mosaïque*, 'mosaicall work;' Cot. – Ital. *mosaico*, mosaic; [Span. *mosaica obra*, mosaic work.] Formed from a Late L. *mūsāicus*, adj., an extended form from L. *mūsæum opus* (also called *mūsīuum opus*), mosaic work. The Late L. form *mūsāicus* answers to a Late Gk. *μουσαϊκός*, an extended form in some way related to the Late Gk. *μουσεῖον*, mosaic work; neut. of *μουσεῖος*, of or belonging to the Muses (hence artistic, ornamental). – Gk. μοῦσα, a Muse; see **Muse** (2).

MOSLEM, a Mussulman or Mohammedan; *as adj.*, Mahommedan. (Arab.) 'This low salam Replies of *Moslem* faith I am;' Byron, The Giaour (see note 29). – Arab. *muslim*, 'a musulman, a true believer in the Muhammedan faith;' Rich. Dict. p. 1418. A mussulman is one who professes *islām*, i.e. 'obedience to the will of God, submission, the true or orthodox faith;' id. p. 91. A participial form, from the 4th conj. of *salama*, to be safe, be at rest. The words *moslem*, *mussulman*, *islam*, and *salaam* are all from the same root *salama*. Doublet, *mussulman*.

MOSQUE, a Mahommedan temple or church. (F. – Span. – Arab.) 'Mosche or Mosque, a temple or church among the Turks and Saracens;' Blount's Gloss., ed. 1674. Spelt *musque*, Sandys, Trav. (1632), p. 27. – F. *mosquée*, 'a temple or church among the Turks;' Cot. – Span. *mezquita*, a mosque. – Arab. *masjid*, a mosque, temple; Rich. Dict. p. 1415. Cf. Arab. *sajjādah*, 'a carpet, &c., place of adoration, mosque;' id. p. 812. – Arab. root *sajada*, to adore, prostrate oneself.

MOSQUITO, a kind of gnat. (Span. – L.) Spelt *muskitto* in Sir T. Herbert, Travels, ed. 1665, p. 128; *muskyto*, Hakluyt, Voy. iii. 107. – Span. *mosquito*, a little gnat; dimin. of *mosca*, a fly. – L. *musca*, a fly. Cf. Gk. μυῖα, a fly; Lithuan. *musé*, a fly.

MOSS, a cryptogamic plant. (E.) ME. *mos*, P. Plowman, C. xviii. 14; *mosse* (dat.), id. B. xv. 282. AS. *mos* (Bosworth).+Du. *mos*;

Icel. *mosi*, moss; also, a moss, moorland; Dan. *mos*; Swed. *mossa*; G. *moos*, MHG. *mos*, moss; also a moss, swamp. Teut. base **mus-*, weak grade allied to MHG. *mies*, OHG. *mios*, moss; AS. *mēos*, moss (Teut. base **meus-*); and to **Mire**. β. Further allied to Russ. *mokh'*, moss; L. *muscus*, moss. Brugmann, i. § 105. ¶ We may note the E. use of *moss* in the sense of bog or soft moorland, as in Solway *Moss*, Chat *Moss*; this sense comes out again in E. *mire*, which is certainly related to *moss*. Der. *moss-land*, *moss-rose*; *moss-trooper*, i.e. a trooper or bandit who rode over the mosses on the Scottish border; *moss-ed*, As You Like It, iv. 3. 105; *moss-grown*, 1 Hen. IV, iii. 1. 33; *moss-y*, *moss-i-ness*. See *mire*.

MOST, greatest. (E.) ME. *most*, *mēst*. AS. *mǣst*.+Du. *meest*; Icel. *mestr*; G. *meist*; Goth. *maists*. Teut. type *ma-ist-oz, superl. form allied to **More**, q.v. ¶ The *o* (for early ME. *ē*) is due to association with the *o* in *more*.

MOTE, a particle of dust, speck, spot. (E.) ME. *mot*, *mote*; Chaucer has the pl. *motes*, C. T. 6450 (D 868). AS. *mot*, Matt. vii. 3. +Du. *mot*, saw-dust; EFries. *mut*, rubbish.

MOTET, a short piece of sacred music. (F.—L.) In Blount's Gloss., ed. 1674. ME. *motetis*, pl.; Wyclif, Works; ed. Matthew, p. 91.—F. *motet*, 'a verse in musick, or of a song, a poesie, a short lay;' Cot. [Cf. MItal. *mottetto*, 'a dittie, a verse, a iigge, a short song; a wittie saying;' Florio.] Dimin. of F. *mot*, 'a word; the note winded by a huntsman on his horne;' Cot.—L. *muttum*, a murmur; see **Motto**.

MOTH, a lepidopterous insect. (E.) ME. *moththe*, Chaucer, C. T. 6142 (D 560); also spelt *moþþe*, *mouþe*, *mouȝte*, P. Plowman, C. xiii. 217. AS. *moððe*, Grein, ii. 261; also *mohðe*, Matt. vi. 20, latest text; O. Northumbrian *mohðe*, *mohða*, Matt. vi. 20.+Du. *mot*; Icel. *motti*; Swed. *mätt*, a mite; G. *motte*, a moth. Origin doubtful. β. We also find AS. *maðu*, a maggot, bug; 'Cimex, *maðu*,' Ælfric's Gloss., Nomina Insectorum, in Wright's Vocab. i. 24; cognate forms being Du. and G. *made*, a maggot, Goth. *matha*, a worm; but connexion with *moth* is doubtful. A late example of ME. *mathe*, a maggot, occurs in Caxton's tr. of Reynard the Fox, ed. Arber, p. 69; 'a dede hare, full of *mathes* and wormes.' γ. Perhaps the latter word meant 'a biter' or 'eater;' Fick refers AS. *maðu* to the root of E. *mow*, to cut grass. Der. *moth-eaten*, ME. *moth-eten*, P. Plowman, B. x. 362.

MOTHER (1), a female parent. (E.) ME. *moder*, Chaucer, C. T. 5261 (B 841), where Tyrwhitt prints *mother*; but all the six MSS. of the Six-text ed. have *moder* or *mooder*. [The ME. spelling is almost invariably *moder*, and it is difficult to see how *mother* came to be the present standard form; it was probably due to dialectal influence.] AS. *mōder*, *mōdor*, *mōdur*; Grein, ii. 261.+Du. *moeder*; Icel. *mōðir*; Dan. and Swed. *moder*; G. *mutter*, OHG. *muotar*.+Irish and Gael. *mathair*; Russ. *mat(e)*; Lithuan. *motė* (Schleicher); L. *māter*; Gk. μήτηρ; Pers. *mādar*; Skt. *mātā*, *mātṛ*. β. All formed from a root *mā, of uncertain meaning. Der. *mother-ly*, *mother-li-ness*, *mother-hood*, *mother-less*. Cf. *matrix*, *matron*.

MOTHER (2), the hysterical passion. (E.) In K. Lear, ii. 4. 56. Spelt *moder* in Palsgrave; the same word as the above. So also Du. *moeder* means 'mother, womb, hysterical passion;' cf. G. *mutterbeschwerung*, mother-fit, hysterical passion.

MOTHER (3), lees, sediment. (E.) 'As touching the *mother* or lees of oile oliue;' Holland, tr. of Pliny, b. xxiii. c. 3. It is prob. the same word as **Mother** (1), as the dregs seem to be bred in the liquid. So also in mod. Du. we have *moer* signifying both sediment or dregs, also a matrix or female screw; G. *mutter*, mother, sediment in wine or other liquids. Cf. Gk. γραῦς, an old woman; also, scum, mother. Perhaps affected by E. *mud*, MDu. *modder*, mud, lees, dregs; G. *moder*, mould. Der. *mother-v*.

MOTION, movement. (F.—L.) 'Of that *mocyon* his cardynalles were sore abashed;' Berners, tr. of Froissart, vol. i. c. 326.—F. *motion*, omitted in Cotgrave, but used by Froissart in this very passage, as quoted by Littré.—L. *mōtiōnem*, acc. of *mōtio*, a movement; cf. *mōtus*, pp. of *mouēre*, to move; see **Move**. Der. *motion-less*, Hen. V, iv. 2. 50.

MOTIVE, an inducement. (F.—L.) Properly an adj., but also used as a sb. ME. *motif*, a motive, Chaucer, C. T. 5048, 9365 (B 628, E 1491).—OF. *motif*, 'a motive, a moving reason;' Cot.—Late L. *mōtiuum*, a motive; found A.D. 1452; but certainly earlier.—Late L. *mōtiuus*, moving, animating; found A.D. 1369. Formed with L. suffix *-iuus* from *mōt-*, stem of *mōtus*, pp. of *mouēre*; see **Move**. Der. *motiv-i-ty* (modern). Also *motor*, i.e. a mover, Sir T. Browne, Vulg. Errors. b. ii. c. 2. § 2, borrowed from L. *mōtor*, a mover.

MOTLEY, of different colours. (F.—G.) ME. *mottelee*, Chaucer, C. T. 273 (A 271). So called because spotted or clotted. Apparently formed, with pp. suffix *-é*, from OF. *motel*, *mottel, MF. *motteau*, 'a clot of congealed moisture,' Cot.; also used in the sense of MF. *mottelet*, 'a little clod, lump of earth,' id. A dimin. of OF. *mote*,

motte, MF. *motte*, 'a clod, lump, round sodd, or **turfe of earth**; also a little hill;' Cot. See **Moat**. Cf. Languedoc *moutel*, a clot of anything adhesive, dimin. of *mouto*, a clod (D'Hombres). Mistral gives Prov. *mouteloun*, 'petite pelote;' *à mouteloun*, 'en grumeaux.' β. Perhaps affected by OF. *mattelé*, 'clotted, knotted, curdled, or curd-like;' Cot. Cf. OF. *mattonné*, in the expression *ciel mattonné*, 'a curdled [i.e. mottled] skie, or a skie full of small curdled clowds;' id. The OF. *mattelé* answers to a pp. of a verb *matteler, representing an OHG. *matteln, a frequentative verb regularly formed from Bavarian *matte*, curds; Schmeller's Bayerisches Wörterbuch, col. 1685; MDu. *matte*, curds (Hexham). Der. *mottled*, Drayton, Muses' Elysium, Nymph. 6. l. 57.

MOTTO, a sentence added to a device. (Ital.—L.) In Shak. Per. ii. 2. 38.—Ital. *motto*, 'a word, a mot, a saying, a posie or briefe in any shield, ring, or emprese' [device]; Florio.—L. *muttum*, a mutter, a grunt, a muttered sound; cf. *mūtire*, *muttire*, to mutter, mumble. Formed from √MEU, to make a low sound; cf. Gk. μῦ, a muttered sound. See **Mutter**. And cf. **Motet**.

MOULD (1), earth, soil, crumbling ground. (E.) ME. *molde*, P. Plowman, B. prol. 67, iii. 80. AS. *molde*, dust, soil, earth, country; Grein, ii. 261.+Du. *moude*, *molde*, mould; cf. *molm*, mould; Icel. *mold*, mould, earth; Dan. *muld*; Swed. *mull* (for *muld*); Goth. *mulda*, dust; Mk. vii. 11; prov. G. *molt*, *molten*, garden mould (Flügel); OHG. *molta*. β. All from a Teut. type *mul-dōn, f.; from *mal, weak grade of √MEL, to grind; see **Meal** (1). Der. *mould-warp*, the old name for a mole (see *mole*); also *mould-er*, a frequentative verb, 'to crumble often,' hence, to decay, cf. 'in the *mouldring* of earth in frosts and sunne,' Bacon, Nat. Hist. § 337. ¶ The adj. *mouldy*, in its commonest sense, is unconnected.

MOULD (2), a model, pattern, form, fashion. (F.—L.) ME. *molde*, P. Plowman, B. xi. 341. ONorth F. *molde*, Les Rois, p. 244 (Moisy); OF. *molle*, *mole*, mod. F. *moule*, a mould. Littré gives *molle* as the spelling of the 14th century; a still earlier form was *modle*, in the 13th cent.—L. *modulum*, acc. of *modulus*, a measure, standard, size. See **Model**. Cf. Span. *molde*, from *modulus*, by transposition. Der. *mod-el*, a dimin. form. Also *mould*, vb., Mids. Nt. Dr. iii. 2. 211; *mould-er*, *mould-ing*.

MOULD (3), rust, spot. (E.) Spenser has: 'Upon the litle brest . . a litle purple *mold*;' F. Q. vi. 12. 7. But chiefly in the compound *iron-mould*. Here *mould* is a mere extension of *mole*, a spot; the added *d* was prob. due to confusion with *moled*, i.e. spotted. 'One droppe of poyson infecteth the whole tunne of Wine; . . one *yron Mole* defaceth the whole peece of Lawne;' Lyly, Euphues, ed. Arber. p. 39. See further under **Mole** (1).

MOULDY, musty, fusty. (Scand.) In Shak. 1 Hen. IV, ii. 4. 134; iii. 2. 119. This is an extremely difficult word. It has probably been confused with *mould* (1), supposed to mean dirt, though it properly means only friable earth. It has also probably been confused with *mould* (3), rust, spot of rust. But with neither of these words has it anything to do. It is formed from the sb. *mould*, fustiness, which is quite an unoriginal word, as will appear. For an example of this sb., compare: 'we see that cloth and apparell, not aired, doe breed moathes and *mould*;' Bacon, Nat. Hist. § 343. This sb. is due to the ME. verb *moulen*, to become mouldy, to putrefy or rot, as in: 'Let us not *moulen* thus in idlenesse;' Chaucer, C. T., Group B, 32. The pp. *mouled* was used in the precise sense of the mod. E. *mouldy*, and it is easy to see that the sb. was really due to this pp., and in its turn produced the adj. *mouldy*. Stratmann cites 'þi *mowlid* mete,' i.e. thy mouldy meat, Political Poems, &c., ed. Furnivall, p. 181; *moullyde brede*, i.e. mouldy bread, Reliquiæ Antiquæ, i. 85; 'Pannes *mouled* in a wyche,' clothes lying mouldy in a chest; Test. of Love, b. ii. ch. ii. l. 29. So also *mowled*, *mowlde*, mucidus; from *mowle*, mucidare, Catholicon Anglicum, q.v. Todd cites: 'Sour wine, and *mowled* bread;' Abp. Cranmer, Ans. to Bp. Gardiner, p. 299. With which compare: 'Very coarse, hoary, moulded bread,' Knollys, Hist. of the Turks (Todd). β. The oldest spelling of the ME. verb is *muwlen*. 'Oðer leten þinges *muwlen* oðer rusten' = or let things grow mouldy or rusty; Ancren Riwle, p. 344, l. 4. We also find '*mulede* þinges' = mouldy things, id. p. 104, note *h*. Hence *mowly*, adj.; 'All the brede [bread] . . waxed anon *mowly*;' Caxton, Golden Legend, St. Thomas, § 10. Cf. prov. E. *mouly*, mouldy; E.D.D. Of Scand. origin. Cf. ME. *moul*, sb., mouldiness, answering to MDan. *mul*, Swed. dial. *mul*, *muel*, *mujel*, Swed. *mögel*, mould. Cf. also Dan. *mullen*, mouldy, *mulne*, to become mouldy; Swed. dial. *nulas*, Swed. *möglas*, to grow mouldy; Icel. *mygla*, to grow musty, formed, by vowel-change of *u* to *y*, from Icel. *mug-*, as in *mugga*, mugginess. See **Muggy**. Thus *mould* is *mugginess*; the notions of muggy and mouldy are still not far apart. Der. *mouldi-ness*; also *mould*, verb, for *moul*, Spenser. F. Q. ii. 3. 41. See note on **Mould** (1) above.

MOULT, to cast feathers, as birds do. (L.) The *l* is intrusive, just as in *fault* from ME. *faute*; see **Fault**. ME. *mouten*; 'his haire *moutes*,' i.e. falls off, Pricke of Conscience, l. 781. '*Mowtyn*, as fowlys, *Plumeo*, *deplumeo*;' Prompt. Parv. '*Mowter*, *moulter*, quando auium pennæ decidunt;' Gouldman, cited by Way to illustrate '*Mowtare*, or *mowtard* [i.e. moulter, moulting bird], byrde, *Plutor*;' Prompt. Parv. AS. *bi-mūtian*, to exchange (Bosworth). —L. *mūtāre*, to change; whence F. *muer*, to moult; see **Mew** (3). So also OHG. *mūzōn*, to moult, is merely borrowed from L. *mūtāre*; now spelt *mausen* in mod. G. **Der.** *moulting*; also *mews*; and see *mutable*.

MOUND, an earthen defence, a hillock. (F.—L.) 'Compast with a *mound*;' Spenser, F. Q. ii. 7. 56. The sense of 'hillock' or 'heap' is found also in F. *mont*, Ital. *monte*, and Walloon *mont*, a heap, a mass (Sigart); as well as in L. *mons*. *Mound* is merely a variant of *mount* (1).—AF. *mund*, variant of *munt*, a hill; Vie de St. Auban, 848, 875; OF. *mont*.—L. *montem*, acc. of *mons*, a mountain, a heap. See below. ¶ Perhaps confused with AS. *mund*, protection; thus Baret (1580) has: 'A hedge, a mound, *sepes*.' Cf. prov. E. *mound*, a hedge.

MOUNT (1), a hill, rising ground. (L.) ME. *munt*, OEng. Homilies, ed. Morris, i. 11, l. 14. AS. *munt*, Grein, ii. 269. [*Immediately* from Latin, but affected by AF. *munt*.]—L. *montem*, acc. of *mons*, a mountain; stem *mon-ti-*. Formed (with suffix *-ti-*) from the second grade (*mon-*) of √MEN, to project, seen in L. *ē-min-ēre*, to jut out; cf. E. *pro-mon-tor-y*. See **Eminent**. **Der.** *mount-ain*, q.v.; *mount* (2), q.v.

MOUNT (2), to ascend. (F.—L.) ME. *mounten*, P. Plowman, B. prol. 67; older form *monten*, King Alisaunder, 784.—F. *monter*, 'to mount;' Cot.—F. *mont*, a mountain, hill. [The verb is due to the use of the OF. adverb *a mont*, up-hill; so also the adv. *a val*, down-hill, produced F. *avaler*, to swallow, and *avalanche*.]—L. *montem*, acc. of *mons*, a hill. See **Mount** (1). **Der.** *mount-er*, *mount-ing*; also *mount-e-bank*, q.v. Also *a-mount*, q.v.; *para-mount*, *re-mount*, *sur-mount*, *tanta-mount*, *tra-montane*.

MOUNTAIN, a hill. (F.—L.) In early use. ME. *montaine*, Layamon, l. 1282.—OF. *montaigne*, *montaine*; mod. F. *montagne*, a mountain.—Late L. *montānea*, by-form of *montāna*, a mountain; Ducange.—L. *montāna*, neut. pl., mountainous regions; from *montānus*, adj., hilly.—L. *mont-*, stem of *mons*, a mountain. See **Mount** (1). **Der.** *mountain-ous*, Cor. ii. 3. 127, from MF. *montaigneux*, 'mountainous,' Cot.; *mountain-eer*, Temp. iii. 3. 44, with suffix *-eer* = F. *-ier*.

MOUNTEBANK, a charlatan, quack doctor. (Ital.—L. and G.) Lit. 'one who mounts on a bench,' to proclaim his nostrums. See Trench, Select Glossary. In Shak. Hamlet, iv. 7. 142. 'Fellows, to *mount a bank*! Did your instructor In the dear tongues, never discourse to you Of the *Italian mountebanks*?' Ben Jonson, Volpone, ii. 1 (Sir Politick).—Ital. *montambanco*, a mountebank; MItal. *monta in banco*, 'a mountibanke,' *montar' in banco*, 'to plaie the mountibanke;' Florio. β. Hence the *e* stands for older *i*, which is short for *in*; the mod. Ital. must be divided *monta-m-banco*, where *-m-* (for *in*) has become *m* before the following *b*.—Ital. *montare*, to mount, cognate with F. *monter*, to mount; *in* = L. *in*, in, on; and Ital. *banco*, from OHG. *banc*, a bench, money-table. See **Mount** (2), **In**, and **Bank** (2). Cf. Ital. *saltimbanco* (for *saltar' in banco*), a quack.

MOURN, to grieve, be sad. (E.) ME. *moornen*, *mournen*, *mornen*; Chaucer, C. T., A 3704. AS. *murnan*, to grieve; Grein, ii. 269.+Icel. *morna*; Goth. *maurnan*; OHG. *mornēn*. β. The Goth. *-n-* before *-an* is a mere suffix, giving the verb an intransitive character; and the Teut. type is *mur-n-an-*. Allied to AS. *meornan*, to care; Gk. *μέρ-ιμνα*, sorrow. From √SMER; cf. Skt. *smr̥*, to remember, to long for. **Der.** *mourn-ful*, Spenser, F. Q. i. 1. 54; *mourn-ful-ly*, *mourn-ful-ness*; *mourn-ing*, sb., AS. *murnung*.

MOUSE, a small rodent quadruped. (E.) ME. *mous* (without final *e*), Chaucer, C. T. 144. AS. *mūs*, in Ælfric's Gloss., Nomina Ferarum; Voc. 120. 16. The pl. is *mȳs*, by vowel-change; whence E. *mice*.+Du. *muis*; Icel. *mūs*, pl. *mȳss*; Dan. *muus*; Swed. *mus*; G. *maus*; Russ. *muish(e)*; L. *mūs*; Gk. *μῦς*; Pers. *mūsh*; Rich. Dict. p. 1325; Skt. *mūsha-*, a rat, a mouse. β. The sense is 'the stealing animal.'—√MEUS, to steal; whence Skt. *mush*, to steal, *mūsha-*, a stealer. **Der.** *mouse*, vb., Macb. ii. 4. 13, *mous-er*; *mouse-ear*, a plant, *mouse-tail*, a plant. Also *muscle*. (But not *tit-mouse*.)

MOUSTACHE, MUSTACHE, the hair on the upper lip. (F.—Ital.—Gk.) Formerly *mustachio*, Shak. L. L. L. v. 1. 110; this is taken from the Ital. form given below. Both *mustachio* and *mustache* are given in Blount's Gloss., ed. 1674.—F. *moustache*, 'a mustachoe;' Cot.—Ital. *mostaccio*, 'a face, a snout, a mostacho;' Florio. [Cf. Span. *mostacho*, a whisker, moustache; answering to the E. form *mostacho* in Florio.]—Gk. *μύσταξ*, stem of *μύσταξ*, the upper lip, a moustache; Doric and Laconic form of *μάσταξ*, that

wherewith one chews, the mouth, the upper lip; cf. *μαστάζειν*, to chew, eat. See **Mastic**.

MOUTH, the aperture between the lips, an aperture, orifice, outlet. (E.) ME. *mouth*, Chaucer, C. T. 153. AS. *mūð*, Grein, ii. 266.+Du. *mond*; Icel. *munnr* (for *munðr*); Dan. *mund*; Swed. *mun*; G. *mund*; Goth. *munths*. β. Teut. type *munthoz*, m.; Idg. type *mantos*; cf. L. *mentum*, the chin. **Der.** *mouth*, vb., Hamlet, iv. 2. 29; *mouth-ful*, Pericles, ii. 1. 35; *mouth-piece*.

MOVE, to set in motion, stir, impel. (F.—L.) ME. *mouen*, *moeuen*, *meuen*; P. Plowman, B. xvii. 194 (where all three spellings occur in the MSS. The *u* is written for *v*; the form *meuen* is common). Also in Chaucer, Parl. of Foules, l. 150.—OF. *movoir*, mod. F. *mouvoir*.—L. *mouēre*, to move; pp. *mōtus*. Allied to Skt. *mīv*, to push (with pp. *mūta-*, moved, corresponding to L. *mōtus*; also Gk. *ἀμεύομαι*, I surpass. **Der.** *mov-er*, Chaucer, C. T. 2989 (A 2987); *mov-able*, of which the ME. form was *meble* or *moeble*, P. Plowman, B. iii. 267, borrowed from F. *meuble*, L. *mōbilis*, movable; *mov-abl-y*, *mov-able-ness*; *move-ment*, Gower, C. A. iii. 107, bk. vii. 674, from OF. *movement* (Burguy); *mov-ing*, *mov-ing-ly*. Also *mobile*, from L. *mōbilis*, movable, often contracted to *mob*; see **Mob**. Also *mot-ion*, q.v., *mot-ive*, q.v., *mot-or*; cf. L. pp. *mōtus*. Also *mo-ment*, *com-mot-ion*, *e-mot-ion*, *pro-mote*, *re-mote*, *remove*, *mutiny*.

MOW (1), to cut down with a scythe. (E.) ME. *mowen*; 'Mowe other *mowen*' (other MSS. *mouwen*), i. e. mow (hay) or stack (in a mow); P. Plowman, C. vi. 14. The old pt. t. was *mew*, still common in Cambridgeshire; see Layamon, 1942. AS. *māwan*, Grein, ii. 213. (The vowel-change from AS. *ā* to E. *o* is regular; cf. *stān*, stone.)+Du. *maaijen*; G. *mähen*, OHG. *māan*, to mow. β. Teut. type *mǣwan-*; allied to Gk. *ἀ-μά-ω*, I reap, L. *me-t-ere*, to reap. Brugmann, ii. § 680. **Der.** *mow-er*. *mow-ing*; also *mea-d*, *mea-d-ow*, *after-math*.

MOW (2), a heap, pile of hay or corn. (E.) ME. *mowe*; 'mowe of scheues' = heap of sheaves, given as a various reading in Wyclif, Ruth, iii. 7 (later text). AS. *mūga*, a mow, Exod. xxii. 6, where the Vulgate has *aceruus frugum*. Oldest form *mūha*, Corpus Glos., 46.+Icel. *mūga*, *mūgi*, a swathe in mowing, also a crowd of people, a mob; Norw. *muga*, *mua*, a heap (of hay). β. The change from AS. *g* to ME. *w* is common; so also in ME. *morwe* (morrow) from AS. *morgen*; ME. *hawe*, a haw, AS. *haga*.

MOW (3), a grimace; *obsolete*. (F.—MDu.) 'With mop and *mow*;' Temp. iv. 47. 'Mopping and *mowing*;' K. Lear, iv. 1. 64. 'I *mowe*, I mocke one; he useth to mocke and *mowe*;' Palsgrave. Chaucer has ME. *mowes*, pl.; C. T., I 258.—OF. *moe*, mouth, lip, grimace; F. *moue*, 'a moe, or mouth, an ill-favoured extension or thrusting out of the lips;' Cot.—MDu. *mouwe*, the protruded underlip; see Oudemans, who cites the phrase *maken die mouwe* = to make a grimace, deride, in two passages. ¶ The word *mop*, its companion, is also foreign; see **Mop** (2).

MUCH, great in quantity. (E.) ME. *moche*, *muche*, *miche*. Formerly also used with respect of size. 'A *moche* man' = a tall man; P. Plowman, B. viii. 70; where one MS. reads *mykil*. '*Muche* and lyte' = great and small; Chaucer, C. T. 496 (A 494), where other MSS. have *moche*, *miche*, *meche*. β. When we compare ME. *miche*, *moche*, *muche*, with the older forms *michel*, *mochel*, *muchel*, we see at once that the former result from the latter by the loss of final *l*. *Muche* occurs in Layamon, 10350; but not in AS. *Muchel*, *mochel*, are variants of *michel* (the orig. form) due to form-association with ME. *lutel*, from AS. *lȳtel*. γ. The orig. form was AS. *micel* (cf. Lowl. Sc. *mickle*), great.+Icel. *mikill*, great; OHG. *mihhil*; Goth. *mikils*. Allied to Gk. *μεγάλ-η*, great, *μέγας*, great; and to L. *magnus*. See **Magnitude**.

MUCILAGE, a slimy substance, gum. (F.—L.) Richardson cites the word from Bacon's Philosophical Remains. The adj. *mucilaginous* is in Blount's Gloss., ed. 1674.—F. *mucilage*, 'slime, clammy sap, glewy juice;' Cot.—L. *mūcilāgo* (stem *mūcilāgin-*), mouldy moisture; used by Theodorus Priscianus (iv. 1), a physician of the 4th century (Lewis). Extended from *mūcilus*, for *mūcidus*, an adj. formed from *mūcus*; see **Mucus**. **Der.** *mucilagin-ous* (from the stem).

MUCK, filth, dung, dirt. (Scand.) ME. *muck*; spelt *muk*, Gower, C. A. ii. 290; bk. v. 4853; *muc*, Genesis and Exodus, ed. Morris, 2557.—Icel. *myki*, dung; whence *myki-reka*, a muck-rake, dung-shovel; cf. *moka*, to shovel dung out of a stable; Dan. *møg*, dung; Norw. *mok-dunge*, a muck-heap; prob. allied to Norw. *mukka*, a heap. Cf. Swed. *mocka*, to throw dung out of a stable, like prov. E. 'to *muck out*.' ¶ Not allied to AS. *meox*, dung, whence prov. E. *mixen*, a dung-heap. **Der.** *muck-y*, *muck-i-ness*; *muck-heap*, *muck-rake* (Bunyan's Pilg. Progress).

MUCK, AMUCK, a term applied to malicious rage. (Malay.) Only in the phrase 'to run *amuck*;' the word has been absurdly turned into *a muck*. Dryden goes further, and inserts an adjective between *muck* and the supposed article ! ' And *runs an Indian muck* at all he meets ;' Hind and Panther, iii. 1188. To *run amuck* is to run about in a mad rage.—Malay *āmuk*, ' engaging furiously in battle, attacking with desperate resolution, rushing in a state of frenzy to the commission of indiscriminate murder, running amuck. It is applied to any animal in a state of vicious rage ;' Marsden, Malay Dict. p. 16.

MUCKINDER, a handkerchief. (Prov.—L.) ' Take my *muck-inder*, And dry thine eyes ;' Ben Jonson, Tale of a Tub, iii. i (Turfe). ME. *mokadour*, Lydgate, Minor Poems, p. 30.—Prov. *mocadovr*, mod. Prov. *moucadou* (Mistral) ; the same as F. *mouchoir*.—L. type **muccā-tōrium*, the same as *mūcātōrium*, a wiper ; given by Ducange in the sense of ' pair of snuffers.'—Late L. *muccāre*, to free from mucus.—L. *muccus*, *mūcus* ; see **Mucus**.

MUCUS, slimy fluid. (L.) The adj. *mucous* is in older use, the sb. being modern. Sir T. Browne says the chameleon's tongue has ' a *mucous* and slimy extremity ;' Vulg. Errors, b. iii. c. 21. § 7.—L. *mūcus*, *muccus*, slime from the nose ; whence the adj. *mūcōsus*, Englished by *mucous*. Allied to Gk. μύξα, the discharge from the nose, μύκης, snuff of a wick ; cf. Gk. ἀπομύσσειν (= ἀπο-μύκ-γειν), to wipe the nose ; L. *ē-mungere*, to wipe the nose. Der. *muc-ous* ; and see *mucilage*, *match* (2).

MUD, wet, soft earth, mire. (E.) ME. *mud* ; the dat. *mudde* occurs in Allit. Poems, ed. Morris, B. 407 ; see Spec. of Eng., ed. Morris and Skeat, p. 156, l. 407. Not found in AS. Of Old Low G. origin, and prob. a native word. EFries. *mudde*. Cf. OLow G. *mudde*, mud ; whence the adj. *muddig*, muddy, Bremen Wörterbuch ; MSwed. *modd*, mud (Ihre) ; Pomeran. *modde*. Also in an extended form ; cf. Du. *modder*, mud. β. The cognate High German form is found in the Bavarian *mott*, peat, already mentioned as the origin of E. *moat* ; see **Moat**. This establishes it as a Teut. word. Cf. Skt. *mūtra-m*, urine. Der. *mudd-y*, *mudd-i-ly*, *mudd-i-ness*, *mudd-le*.

MUDDLE, to confuse. (E.) ' *Muddle*, to rout with the bill, as geese and ducks do ; also, to make tipsy and unfit for business ;' Kersey, ed. 1715. A frequentative verb, formed with the usual suffix *-le*, from the sb. *mud*. Thus to *mudd-le* is to go often in mud, to dabble in mud ; hence, to render water turbid, and, generally, to confuse. Similarly, Dan. *muddre*, to stir up mud in water, said of a ship, from Dan. *mudder*, mud (from Du.). Cf. EFries. *muddelen*, to dirty ; MDu. *moddelen*, ' to mudd water,' Hexham ; Pomeran. *muddeln*, to disorder. See **Mud**.

MUEZZIN, a Mohammedan crier of the hour of prayer. (Arab.) Spelt *muezin* in Sir T. Herbert, Travels, ed. 1665, p. 339.—Arab. *mu'zin*, *mu'azzin*, ' the public crier, who assembles people to prayers by proclamation from a minaret ;' Rich. Dict. p. 1523 ; *mu'azzin*, ' the crier of a mosque ;' Palmer's Pers. Dict. col. 617. Connected with Arab. *azan*, the call to prayers, Palmer, col. 17 ; *uzn*, the ear, Rich. p. 48, Palmer, col. 17 ; *azina*, he listened, Rich. p. 48. (Here z = ʒ, with the sound of E. *th* in *that*.)

MUFF (1), a warm, soft cover for the hands. (Walloon—F.— Late L.) Spelt *muffe* in Minsheu, ed. 1627. Prob. from Walloon *mouffe* (Sigart), *mof* (Remacle), a muff. [Cf. Du. *mof*, Low G. *muff* (Berghaus) ; EFries. *muf* ; from the same.] A shortened form of F. *moufle*, a kind of *muff* ; see further under **Muffle**.

MUFF (2), a silly fellow, simpleton. (E.) A prov. E. word, of imitative origin. It simply means ' a mumbler' or indistinct speaker. Cf. prov. E. *muff*, *muffle*, to mumble (Halliwell) ; *moffle*, to do any-thing ineffectually ; *id*. So also prov. E. *maffle*, to speak indistinctly, an old word, occurring in Richard the Redeles, ed. Skeat, iv. 63 : ' And somme *mafflid* with the mouth, and nyst [knew not] what they mente.' Cf. Du. *muffen*, to dote ; prov. G. *muffen*, to be sulky (Flügel) ; EFries. *muf*, a muff, simpleton ; Du. *mof*, a (Westphalian) boor, a clown, used as a nickname. ¶ Cf. ' Almains, Rutters, *Muffes*, and Danes ;' Marlowe, Tamb. pt. ii. A. i. sc. 1. 22. This is the same word ; *Muffe* (Du. *mof*) was a nickname given by one Germanic people to another. ' The Low Dutch call the High *muffes* .. up-braiding them with their heavinesse ;' Sir J. Reresby, Travels (1657). And see Addit. to Nares.

MUFFIN, a kind of tea-cake. (F. ?) Lanc. dial. *mowfin*, *moufin*, a wheat-cake baked upon a bake-stone over the fire ; tea-cake in general (E. D. D.). Cp. Norm. dial. *mouflu*, adj., said of bread swollen up in the baking, Moisy, Corblet ; OF. *mouflet*, soft bread (Roquefort) ; OF. *mofflet*, bread of a finer sort (Ducange) ; Prov. *pan moʋflet*, soft bread (Mistral) ; OF. *pain moflet*, soft bread (Godefroy). Probably related to EFries. *muffeln*, to mumble food, as a toothless person does. See **Muff** (2).

MUFFLE, to cover up warmly. (F.—Late L.) Levins, ed. 1570, gives : ' A *muffle*, focale [i. e. a neck-cloth] ; to *muffle* the face, velare ; to *muffle* the mouth, obturare ;' col. 184. ' I *muffyll*, je em-mouffle ;' Palsgrave. The pp. *muffeld* is in Malory, ed. Caxton,

bk. viii. ch. 25 ; l. 34. Only the verb is now used, but it is derived from the sb. here given.—OF. *mofle*, *moufle* (13th cent., Littré) ; the same as *mouffle*, which Cot. explains by ' a winter mittaine.' [Cf. MDu. *moffel*, ' a muff, or muffe lined with furre ;' Hexham ; Norweg. *muffel*, a half-glove, mitten ; Aasen ; from OF.]—Late L. *muffula* (occurring A. D. 817), a winter glove (Ducange) ; also spelt *mulfola*. Of unknown origin. β. From the sb. *muffle* came the verb to *muffle*, in common use owing to analogy with the numerous frequentative verbs ending in *-le*. See **Muff** (1). To *muffle* a bell is to wrap a cloth round the clapper ; a *muffled peal* is a peal rung with such bells, rung on the 31st of December. At midnight, the muffles are taken off, and the New Year is rung in. Hence the phrase ' a *muffled sound* :' the sense of which approaches that of prov. E. *muffle*, to mumble, from a different source, as explained under **Muff** (2). Der. *muffl-er*, Merry Wives, iv. 2. 73.

MUFTI, an expounder of the law, magistrate. (Arab.) In Sir T. Herbert's Travels, ed. 1665, pp. 175, 285 ; spelt *mufiti*, Howell, Directions for Travel, ed. Arber, p. 85 ; *mufti* in Sandys, Trav. 1632, p. 36 (end).—Arab. *muftī*, ' a magistrate' (Palmer, col. 590) ; ' wise, one whose sentence has the authority of the law, an expounder of the Muhammedan law, the mufti or head law-officer amongst the Turks ;' Rich. Dict. p. 1462. Connected with *fatwā*, ' a judicious or religious decree pronounced by a mufti, a judgment, sentence ;' id. p. 1070. ¶ The phrase ' in mufti' means in civilian costume, as opposed to military dress. See Yule.

MUG, a cylindrical cup for liquor. (Low G.) ' A *mugge*, potte, *Ollula*;' Levins, 184. 24. ' Clay *mugis*,' pl. ; G. Douglas, tr. of Virgil, prol. to bk. viii. st. 8. Perhaps from EFries. *mukke*, a cylindrical earthen vessel ; Groningen *mokke* (Molema, p. 543) ; whence also Norm. dial. *moque*, Guernsey *mogue* (Moisy) ; Norw. *mugge*, *mugga*, an open can or pitcher ; see Aasen, Larsen. The Irish *mugan*, a mug, is prob. from E. Cf. prov. E. *muggen*, made of earthenware.

MUGGY, damp and close, said of weather. (Scand.) Both *muggy* and *muggish* are in Ash's Dict., ed. 1775.—Icel. *mugga*, soft drizzling mist ; whence *mugguveðr*, muggy, misty weather. Cf. Norw. *mugg*, fine rain ; *muggen*, moist, muggy. Perhaps allied to Dan. *muggen*, musty, mouldy ; *mugne*, to grow musty ; Swed. dial. *muggen*, mouldy, from *mugg*, mould. Cf. also Swed. *mögel*, mould, Icel. *mygla*, to grow musty. Der. *muggi-ness* ; cf. *mouldy*.

MUGWORT, the name of a wild flower. (E.) Spelt *mogworte* in Palsgrave. AS. *mucgwyrt*, the Artemisia ; see numerous examples of the word in Cockayne's A. S. Leechdoms, iii. 339. It prob. means ' midge-wort ;' see **Midge**. Perhaps regarded as being good against midges ; cf. *flea-bane*. For the form, cf. OSax. *muggia*, Du. *mug*, Low G. *mügge*, a midge, *muggert*, mugwort. Note also Dan. *myg-blomst*, ' midge-bloom,' bog orchis.

MULATTO, a child of a white person and a negro. (Span.—L.) Used by E. Young, The Centaur (1754), letter 2 ; Todd's Johnson. —Span. *mulato*, ' a mulatto, a son of a black and of a white ;' Pineda (1740) ; ' the sonne of a black Moore and one of another nation ;' Minsheu (1623). From Span. *mul-o*, a mule, with dimin. suffix *-at-* ; see Diez.—L. *mūlum*, acc. of *mūlus* ; see **Mule**.

MULBERRY, the fruit of a certain tree. (Hybrid ; L. and E.) ME. *moolbery*. Trevisa translates *sycomoros* by *moolberyes*, i. 11, l. 4. Here the *l* stands for *r* ; cf. ME. *murberie*, Voc. 557. 31. The AS. name for the tree was *mōr-bēam* ; see Cockayne's A. S. Leech-doms, iii. 339. ' *Morus, vel rubus*, mōr-bēam ;' Ælfric's Gloss., Nomina Arborum, in Wright's Vocab. i. 32, col. 2. [The AS. *bēam*, a tree, is mod. E. beam.] β. *Berry* is an E. word ; *mul* = ME. *mool* = AS. *mōr-*. The AS. *mōr-* is from L. *mōrus*, a mulberry-tree. Cf. Gk. μῶρον, μόρον, a mulberry, μορέα, a mulberry-tree ; perhaps μῶρον is the origin of L. *mōrum*, a mulberry. ¶ The G. *maulbee·e* (OHG. *mūrberi*) is similarly compounded, from L. *mōrus* and G. *beere*. See **Sycamore**. Der. *murrey*.

MULCT, a fine, penalty. (L.) Given as a sb. in Minsheu, ed. 1627.—L. *mulcta*, a fine, penalty ; whence also OF. *multe* (Cot-grave). The older and better L. form is *multa*. Said to be of Sabine or Oscan origin. Der. *mulct*, vb.

MULE, the offspring of the horse and ass. (F.—L.) ME. *mule*, Rob. of Glouc. p. 189, l. 3913.—F. *mule*.—L. *mūlum*, acc. of *mūlus*, a mule. β. The long *ū* points to a loss ; the word is cognate with Gk. μύκλος, an ass, μυχλός, a stallion ass. (See Prellwitz.) ¶ The L. *mūlus* is also the origin of AS. *mūl*, which is obsolete ; it would have given the mod. E. form as *moul* or *wowl*. Der. *mul-ish* ; *mul-et-eer*, spelt *muleter* in old edd. of Shakespeare, 1 Hen. VI, iii. 2. 68, from F. *muletier*, ' a muletor' (Cot.), which from F. *mulet*, ' a moyle, mulet, or great mule' (id.), formed with suffix *-et* from F. *mule* < L. *mūlum*, acc. of *mūlus*.

MULLAH, MOLLA, a Mohammedan title of respect given to some religious dignitaries. (Arab.) Arab. *maulā*, a judge, the magistrate of a large city, a lord, a master; Rich. Dict. p. 1528; commonly pronounced *mollā* in Turkey (Devic).

MULLED, a term applied to sweetened ale or wine. (F–L.?) Apparently from ME. *mullen*, to break to powder, crumble (Prompt. Parv. p. 348), from the sb. *mull*, powder, the sense of which was perhaps transferred (as Way suggests) to the 'powdered condiments' which the ale contained, esp. grated spices, and the like. Cf. ME. *mul*, AS. *myl*, dust, powder. But Blount's Gloss. has: '*Mulled sack* (*vinum mollitum*), because softened and made mild by burning and a mixture of sugar.'–F. *mollir*, to soften.–L. *mollīre*, to soften.–L. *mollis*, soft; see **Mollify**. Cf. *mull'd*, weak; Cor. iv. 5. 239.

MULLEIN, a kind of wild flower. (F.) The *great mullein* is *Verbascum thapsus*. Spelt *mullein* in Minsheu, ed. 1627. ME. *moleyn*, Prompt. Parv.–AF. *moleine*, Voc. 556. 31; F. *molène*. The ME. name was *softe*, i.e. the soft. This suggests a der. from OF. *mol*, soft; from L. *mollis*, soft.

MULLET (1), a kind of fish. (F.–L.) ME. *molet*; '*Molet*, *fysche*, *Mullus*;' Prompt. Parv. Older form *mulet*, occurring as a gloss to L. *mūlus* in a list of fishes of the 12th cent.; see Wright's Vocab. i. 98, l. 1.–OF. *mulet*, 'the mullet-fish;' Cot. Formed, with dimin. suffix -*et*, from L. *mullus*, Late L. *mūlus*, the red mullet. Cf. Gk. μύλλος, a sea-fish.

MULLET (2), a five-pointed star. (F.–L.) In Blount's Gloss., ed. 1674. A term in heraldry. ME. *molet*, a mullet (in heraldry); Book of St. Alban's, pt. ii. fol. f 7, back; pl. *molettys*, id. fol. b 3, back.–OF. and F. *molette*, a rowel; '*molette d'esperon*, the rowell of a spur,' Cot.; *mollette*, 'a mullet, the ramhead of a windlesse, the rowell of a spur;' id. Hatzfeld explains F. *molette* as the dimin. of F. *meule*, a mill-stone.–L. *mola*, a mill. See **Molar, Mill**. ¶ The transference of sense was from 'wheel of a water-mill' to any wheel, including the spur-rowel, which the mullet resembled.

MULLIGATAWNY, a hot soup. (Tamil.) It occurs in 1784; see Yule. From Tamil *milagu-tannīr*, lit. pepper-water (Yule). Cf. Malayālam *muḷaka*, pepper; Tamil *tannīr*, water (H. H. Wilson).

MULLION, an upright division between the lights of windows. (F.) A variant of *munnion*, with the same sense, which is still in use in Dorsetshire; Halliwell. It occurs in some edd. of Florio; see below.–F. *moignon*, 'a stump, or the blunt end of a thing; *moignon des ailes*, the stumps, or pinions of the wings; *moignon du bras*, the brawn, or brawny part of the arm;' Cot. β. Hence *munnion*, just as OF. *troignon* gives E. *trunnion*. Cf. MItal. *mugnone*, 'a carpenter's munion or trunion;' Torriano. As Wedgwood well observes, 'the munnion or mullion of a window is the stump of the division before it breaks off into the tracery of the window.' It clearly took its name from the likeness to the stump of a lopped tree, which is one of the senses of F. *moignon*; see Littré. The word also occurs as Span. *muñon*, the brawn or muscle of the arm, the stump of an arm or leg cut off; Port. *munhões*, pl. of *munhão*, the trunnions of a gun. Further allied to Span. *muñeca*, the wrist, Port. *munheca*. γ. From OF. *moing*, maimed (Diez, 4th ed. p. 725). Of uncertain origin; see Körting, § 6369. ¶ The E. form may be Walloon. Sigart has: '*Mouyon, mouillon (d'cabiau)*, tranche de cabillaut; peut-être de *moignon*.'

MULTANGULAR, having many angles. (L.) In Kersey, ed. 1715.–L. *mult-*, stem of *multus*, many; and *angulāris*, angular. See **Multitude** and **Angular**. ¶ Similarly, *multi-lateral*, from *multi* = *multo-*, from *multus*, and E. *lateral*, q. v. So also *multi-form*.

MULTIFARIOUS, manifold, diversified. (L.) In Blount's Gloss., ed. 1674; he says it occurs in Bacon. Englished (by change of -*us* to -*ous*, as in *ardu-ous*, &c.) from L. *multifārius*, manifold, various. The orig. sense appears to be 'many-speaking,' i. e. speaking on many subjects.–L. *multi* = *multo-*, from *multus*, much; and -*fārius*, prob. connected with *fāri*, to speak. Cf. the rare word *fāriāri*, to speak. See **Multitude** and **Fate**.

MULTIPLE, repeated many times. (L.) In Kersey, ed. 1715. A coined word, analogous to *tri-ple, quadru-ple*, &c., the suffix being due to the L. suffix -*plex*; see **Multiply**.

MULTIPLY, to increase many times, make more numerous. (F.–L.) ME. *multiplien*, Chaucer, C. T. 16303 (G 835). He also has *multiplying*, sb., C. T. 12308 (C 374); and *multiplication*, C. T. 16317 (G 849).–F. *multiplier*, 'to multiply;' Cot.–L. *multiplicāre*, to render manifold.–L. *multiplic-*, stem of *multiplex*, manifold.–L. *multi-* = *multo-*, from *multus*, much; and the suffix -*plex*, with the sense of 'fold.' See **Multitude** and **Complex, Plait**. Der. *multiplic-and*, from the fut. pass. part. *multiplicandus*; *multiplic-at-ion*, from F. *multiplication* < L. acc. *multiplicātiōnem*; *multiplic-at-ive*; *multipli-er*; *multiplic-i-ty*, Drayton, The Mooncalf, l. 401 (R.).

MULTITUDE, a great number, a crowd. (F.–L.) ME. *multitude*, Gower, C. A. i. 220; bk. ii. 1810.–F. *multitude*, 'a multitude;' Cot.–L. *multitūdinem*, acc. of *multitūdo*, a multitude.

Formed (with suffix -*tūdo*) from *multi-* = *multo-*, from *multus*, many, much. Root unknown. Der. *multitudin-ous*, Macb. ii. 2. 62, from the stem *multitūdin-*.

MULTURE, a toll or fee taken for grinding corn at a mill. (F.–L.) MF. *moulture*, 'a multure; a grist, or grinding; the corne ground; also, the toll or fee that's due for grinding;' Cot. (F. *mouture*.)–L. *molitūra*, a grinding; from *molere* (pp. *molitus*), to grind. See **Molar**.

MUM (1), an interjection, impressing silence. (E.) In Shak. Temp. iii. 2. 59. ME. *mom, mum*, expressive of the least possible sound with the lips; P. Plowman, B. prol. 215; Lydgate, London Lyckpeny, st. 4, in Spec. of Eng. ed. Skeat, p. 24. So also L. *mu*, Gk. μῦ, the least sound made with the lips. Evidently of imitative origin. Der. *mum-ble*; and see *mummer*. Compare *mew, murmur, mutter, myth*.

MUM (2), a kind of beer. (Low G.) 'Cold roast beef and *mum*;' Guardian, no. 34 (1713). 'Mugs of *mum*;' Pope, Dunciad, ii. 385. Named after Christian *Mumme*, a brewer of Brunswick (ab. 1492). Cf. Du. *mom*, G. *mumme* (in Weigand).

MUMBLE, to speak indistinctly, to chew inefficiently. (E.) The *b* is excrescent, and due to emphasis; the final -*le* is the usual frequentative ending. ME. *momelen, mamelen*, to speak indistinctly or weakly; P. Plowman, A. v. 21, B. v. 21. Formed with the frequent. suffix -*el-* from ME. *mum*, a slight sound. See **Mum** (1). Cf. Du. *mommelen*, EFries. and G. *mummeln*, to mutter, mumble; similarly formed; Low G. *mummeln*, to mumble food (Schambach.) Der. *mumbl-er, mumbl-ing*.

MUMMER, a masker, buffoon. (F.–Du.) 'That goeth a *mummynge*;' Tyndall, Works, p. 13, col. 2, l. 1. 'As though he came in in a *mummary*;' Sir T. More, Works, p. 975 b. 'Made prouysyon for a dysguysynge or a *mummynge*;' Fabyan's Chron. an. 1399–1400. 'Mommery, *mommerie*;' Palsgrave. ME. *mummerye, mommynge*, a rude dramatic entertainment; Trevisa, tr. of Higden, viii. 539, 540. This early use of the F. form *mummery* shows that we took the word through the French, though it was orig. a Dutch or Platt-deutsch word. Cotgrave gives, however, no *verb*; but this was easily developed.–MF. *mommeur*, 'a mummer, one that goes a mumming;' also *mommerie*, 'a mummery, a mumming;' Cot.–MDu. *mommen*, 'to goe a moming, or in a maske;' also *mom, mommer*, or *mommekans*, 'a mommer, or a masker;' also *mommerye*, 'momming, or masking' (with F. suffix); Hexham. He also gives *mom-aensicht*, 'a vizard, or a mommers vizard.' Cf. Low G. *mummeln, bemummeln*, to mask, *mumme*, a mask; Bremen Wörterbuch. (Hence G. *vermummen*, to mask.) β. The origin is imitative, from the sound *mum* or *mom*, used by nurses to frighten children, like the E. *bo!* See Wedgwood, who refers to the habit of nurses who wish to frighten or amuse children, and for this purpose cover their faces and say *mum!* or *bo!* whence the notion of masking to give amusement. Cf. G. *mummel*, a bugbear. Thus the origin is much the same as in the case of *mum, mumble*; see **Mum** (1). Der. *mummer-y*.

MUMMY, an embalmed human body. (F.–Ital.–Pers.) Formerly used of stuff derived from mummies. '*Mumy, Mummy*, a thing like pitch sold by the apothecaries; .. one [kind] is digged out of the graves, in Arabia and Syria, of those bodies that were embalmed, and is called *Arabian Mummy*;' Blount's Gloss., ed. 1674. '*Mummy* hath great force in staunching of bloud;' Bacon, Nat. Hist. § 980.–MF. *mumie*, 'mummy; man's flesh imbalmed; or rather the stuffe wherewith it hath been long imbalmed;' Cot.–Ital. *mummia, mumia* (cf. Span. *momia*).–Pers. *mūmiyā*, a mummy.–Pers. *mūm, mōm*, wax (much used in embalming); Rich. Dict. p. 1520.

MUMP, to mumble, sulk, whine, beg. (Du.) A *mumper* was an old cant term for a beggar; and to *mump* was to beg, also to be sulky; see Nares, ed. Halliwell and Wright. The original notion was to mumble, hence to mutter, to be sulky, to beg; used derisively with various senses. 'How he *mumps* and bridles!' where the sense appears to be 'grimaces;' Beaum. and Fletcher, Maid in the Mill, iii. 2 (Pedro).–Du. *mompen*, to mump, to cheat (Sewel). Cf. MDu. *mompelen*, to mumble (Sewel); *mommelen, mompelen*, to mumble (Hexham). β. The form *mompelen* is nothing but an emphasised form of *mommelen*, and *mompen* of *mommen*, to say mum, to mask. That is, *mump* is merely a strengthened form of the imitative word *mum*; see **Mum** (1), **Mumble, Mummer**. Cp. Norw. *mumpa*, to munch; WFlem. *mompe*, a mouthful, also, one who pouts (De Bo). The curious Goth. verb *bi-mamp-jan*, to deride, mock at, Luke, xvi. 14, has a similar origin. Der. *mump-er, mump-ish* (sullen); *mumps*, q. v.

MUMPS, a swelling of the glands of the neck. (Du.) This troublesome disease renders speaking and eating difficult, and gives the patient the appearance of being sullen or sulky. 'To have the mumps' or 'to be in the *mumps*' was, originally, to be sullen; the sense was easily transferred to the disease which gave such an appearance. It is derived from the verb **Mump**, q.v. We find *mumps* used as a term of derision. 'Not such another as I was, *mumps!*' Beaum. and Fletcher, Scornful Lady, v. 1 (Elder Loveless). 'Sick o' the *mumps*,' i.e. sulky; B. and F., Bonduca, i. 2 (Petillius), near the end.

MUNCH, to chew, masticate. (E.) In Macb. i. 3. 5 (where ed. 1623 has *mouncht*). Udall has *maunch*, Apoph. of Erasmus, § 23. ME. *monchen*, Chaucer, Troil. i. 914. *Monch*- answers to an older form *monk*-, apparently an imitative word parallel to the base *mom*- in ME. *momelen*, to mumble; see **Mumble**. Kilian has MDu. *moncken*, *mompelen*, 'mussitare.' Cf. EFries. and Low G. *munkeln*, to mumble; and see **Mump**. ¶ We cannot deduce it from F. *manger*, for phonetic reasons; yet it is quite possible that this common F. word may have helped to suggest the special sense. The F. *manger* is from L. *mandūcāre*, to chew, extended from *mandūcus*, a glutton, which is from *mandere*, to chew; see **Mandible**. Der. *munch-er*.

MUNDANE, worldly. (F.—L.) Taken from F., but now spelt as if from Latin. 'For folowinge of his pleasaunce *mondayne*;' Skelton, Book of Three Fooles, ed. Dyce, i. 205.—F. *mondain*, 'mundane;' Cot.—L. *mundānus*, worldly.—L. *mundus*, the world (lit. order, like Gk. κόσμος).—L. *mundus*, clean, adorned.

MUNGOOSE, MONGOOSE, an Indian ichneumon. (Telugu.) Spelt *mongoose* in 1673; *mangus* in 1685; see Yule, who says: 'The word is Telugu, *mangīsu*. Jerdon gives *mangūs* however as a Deccani and Mahratti word.' Forbes, in his Hind. Dict., has: '*mangūs*, a weasel, a mongoose.'

MUNICIPAL, pertaining to a township or corporation. (F.—L.) In Cotgrave.—F. *municipal*, 'municipall;' Cot.—L. *mūnicipālis*, belonging to a *mūnicipium*, i.e. a township which received the rights of Roman citizenship, whilst retaining its own laws.—L. *mūnicipi*-, from *mūniceps*, a free citizen, lit. one who takes office or undertakes duties.—L. *mūni*-, for *mūnus*, obligation, duty, and *capere*, to take; see **Capture**; and see below. Der. *municipal-i-ty*.

MUNIFICENCE, bounty, liberality. (F.—L.) Both *munificence* and *munificent* are in Minsheu, ed. 1627. The sb. is the more orig. word.—F. *munificence*, 'munificence;' Cot.—L. *mūnificentia*, bounty, bountifulness. Formed as if from an adj. *munificent*-, with secondary suffix -*ent*; the only related word found is the adj. *mūnificus*, bountiful, liberal, formed upon *mūni*-, for *mūnus*, a duty, a present, and *facere*, to make; so that *mūni-ficus* = present-making. [The verb *mūnificāre* is a mere derivative of *mūnificus*.] β. For the verb *facere*, see **Fact**. The L. *mūnus* signifies orig. 'obligation;' from an Idg. base *moi*-, whence also E. *munition*, *muniment*, *common*, *com-mune*, *com-muni-c-ate*, *im-muni-ty*, *re-muner-ate*. See Bréal and Brugmann, i. § 208. From √MEI, to exchange; see **Common**. Der. *munificent*, coined to suit the sb.; *muni-ficent-ly*.

MUNIMENT, a defence, a record of a claim, title-deed. (F.—L.) In Shak. *muniments* means expedients or instruments; Cor. i. 1. 122.—F. *muniment*, 'a fortifying; also used in the sense of *munition*;' Cot.—L. *mūnimentum*, a defence, safeguard. Formed with suffix -*mentum* from *mūni-re*, to fortify, for an older form *moenire*, to furnish with a wall.—L. *moenia*, neut. pl., ramparts, walls, defences. Allied to *munition*. Brugmann, i. § 208.

MUNITION, materials used in war; also, a fortress. (F.—L.) In Isaiah, xxix. 7, xxxiii. 16; and in Shak. K. John, v. 2. 98.—F. *munition*, 'munition, store, provision, provant or victuals for an army;' Cot.—L. *mūnītiōnem*, acc. of *mūnitio*, a blockading, defending, securing; cf. *mūnītus*, pp. of *mūnire*, to fortify. See **Muniment**. Der. *am-munition*.

MUNNION, the older and correct form of **Mullion**, q.v.

MURAL, belonging to a wall. (F.—L.) 'He [Manlius Capitolinus] . . . was honoured with a *murall* crown of gold;' Holland, tr. of Pliny, b. vii. c. 28.—F. *mural*, 'murall, of or belonging to a wall;' Cot.—L. *mūrālis*, mural.—L. *mūrus*, a wall; OL. *moerus*, *moirus*. β. Probably akin to *moenia*, walls. See **Muniment**. Der. *im-mure*.

MURDER, MURTHER, wilful killing of another man. (E.) ME. *mordre*, *morder*; Chaucer, C. T. 15057 (B 4241). Also *morthre*, Rob. of Glouc. p. 560, l. 11736. AF. *murdre*, Laws of Will. I, § 22. AS. *morðor*, *morður*; Grein, ii. 263.+Goth. *maurthr*. β. The word appears without the suffix -*or* in AS. and OSax. *morð*, OFriesic *morth*, *mord*, Du. *moord*, G. *mord*, Icel. *morð*, death, murder, cognate with L. *mors* (base *mort*-), death; see **Mortal**. The change from *th* (as in AS. *morðor*) to *d* was due to Norman influence; note the AF. forms *murdre*, *murdrir*. Der. *murder*, vb., AF. *murdrir*, ME. *mortheren*, P. Plowman, B. xvii. 278; *murder-er*; *murder-ess*, spelt *moerdrice* in Gower, C. A. i. 351; bk. iii. 2162; *murder-ous* or *murther-ous*, Macb. ii. 3. 147; *murder-ous-ly*.

MURIATIC, briny, pertaining to brine. (L.) In Johnson. L. *muriāticus*, pickled or lying in brine.—L. *muria*, salt liquor, brine, pickle.

MURICATED, prickly. (L.) '*Muricated*, in botany, prickly, full of sharp points;' Ash's Dict., ed. 1775.—L. *mūricātus*, adj. of the form of a pp. formed from *mūric*-, stem of *mūrex*, a fish having sharp prickles; also, a sharp pointed stone, a spike.

MURKY, MIRKY, dark, obscure, gloomy. (Scand.) The -*y* is a modern addition. 'Hell is *murky*;' Macb. v. 1. 41. ME. *mirke*, *merke*. 'The *merke* dale;' P. Plowman, B. i. 1. 'The *mirke* nith' [night]; Havelok, 404.—Icel. *myrkr* (for *mirkwoz*, Noreen); Dan. and Swed. *mörk*, dark, murky. +AS. *mirce*; OSax. *mirki*. ¶ The AS. *mirce* would have become *mirch*; the final *k* shows that the origin is Scand. Cf. Skt. *marka*-, an eclipse (Macdonell); see Uhlenbeck, Skt. Dict. Der. *murki-ly*, *murki-ness*.

MURMUR, a low muttering sound; to mutter, complain in a low voice. (F.—L.) ME. *murmur*, sb., Chaucer, C. T. Pers. Tale, De Invidia (I 503); *murmuren*, vb., id. 10518 (F 204).—F. *murmure*, 'a murmure;' also *murmurer*, 'to murmure;' Cot.—L. *murmur*, a murmur; whence the verb *murmurāre*.+Gk. μορμύρειν, to rush and roar as water; Skt. *marmara*-, the rustling sound of the wind. β. Evidently a reduplicated form from the imitative √MUR, expressive of a rustling noise; as in Icel. *murra*, G. *murren*, to murmur. Brugmann, i. § 499. Der. *murmur-ous*, Pope, tr. of Odyssey, b. xx. l. 19.

MURRAIN, an infectious disease among cattle. (F.—L.) ME. *moreyne*, *moreine*, P. Plowman, C. iv. 97.—OF. *moreine*, not found; closely allied to OF. *morine*, a carcase of a beast, a malady or murrain among cattle. See Roquefort, who cites an OF. translation of Levit. xi. 8; 'tu eschiveras mortes *morines*' = thou shalt eschew dead carcases. [Cf. Norm. dial. *morine*, Span. *morriña*, Port. *morrinha*, murrain.]—OF. *morir* (mod. F. *mourir*), to die (Burguy).—Folk-L. *morire*, for L. *mori*, to die; see **Mortal**.

MURREY, dark red; *obsolete*. (F.—L.—Gk.) 'The leaves of some trees turn a little *murry* or reddish;' Bacon, Nat. Hist. § 512. Spelt *murrey*, Palsgrave; *murreye*, Hoccleve, De Regim. Principum, 695.—OF. *morée*, 'a kind of murrey, or dark red colour;' Cot. This OF. *morée* answers to a Late L. *mōrāta*, fem. of *mōrātus*. We actually find Late L. *mōrātum* in the sense of a kind of drink, made of thin wine coloured with mulberries; see Ducange. Cf. Ital. *morato*, mulberry-coloured, from Ital. *mora*, a mulberry; Span. *morado*, mulberry-coloured, from Span. *mora*. Hence the derivation is from L. *mōrum*, a mulberry; and the sense is properly 'mulberry-coloured.' See **Mulberry**.

MURRION, another spelling of **Morion**, q.v.

MUSCADEL, MUSCATEL, MUSCADINE, a rich fragrant wine, a fragrant pear. (F.—Ital.—Gk.—Pers.) Shak. has *muscadel*, a wine, Tam. Shrew, iii. 2. 174. '*Muscadell*, mulsum apianum;' Levins. Spelt *muscadine*, Beaum. and Fletcher, Loyal Subject, iii. 4, last line. And see Nares.—MF. *muscadel*, 'the wine muscadell or muscadine;' Cot.—MItal. *moscadello*, *moscatello*, 'the wine muscadine;' cf. *moscardino*, 'a kinde of muske comfets, the name of a kind of grapes and peares;' *moscatini*, 'certaine grapes, peares, and apricocks, so called;' Florio. Dimin. forms from MItal. *moscato*, 'sweetened or perfumed with muske; also the wine muskadine;' id. —MItal. *musco*, 'muske; also, a muske or civet cat;' id.—L. *muscum*, acc. of *muscus*, musk; see **Musk**.

MUSCLE (1), the fleshy parts of the body by which an animal moves. (F.—L.) Sir T. Elyot has the pl. *muscules*; Castel of Helth, b. ii. c. 33. But this is a Latinised form. Spenser has *muscles*, Astrophel, 120.—F. *muscle*.—L. *musculum*, acc. of *musculus*, (1) a little mouse, (2) a muscle, from its creeping appearance. (Cf. F. *souris*, (1) a mouse, (2) a muscle.) Dimin. of *mūs*, a mouse, cognate with E. *mouse*; see **Mouse**. Der. *muscul-ar*, in Kersey, ed. 1715, substituted for the older term *musculous* (Blount's Gloss., ed. 1674), from L. *musculōsus*, muscular.

MUSCLE (2), **MUSSEL**, a shell-fish. (L.) Really the same word as the above, but borrowed at a much earlier period, and directly from Latin. ME. *muscle*, Chaucer, C. T. 7682 (D. 2100); P. Plowman, C. x. 94; which follows the F. spelling. AS. *muxle*; 'Muscula, *muxle*;' Voc. 319. 22; and again, 'Geniscula, *muxle*;' Voc. 261. 34. [Here the *x* stands for *cs*, by metathesis for *sc*, just as in AS. *axian* for *āscian*; see **Ask**.]—L. *musculus*, a small fish, sea-muscle; the same word as *musculus*, a little mouse; see **Muscle** (1). ¶ The double spelling of this word can be accounted for; the L. *musculus* became AS. *muscle* (Mone, Quellen, p. 340), early turned into *muxle*, whence E. *mussel*, the final -*el* being regarded as the AS. dimin. suffix. The spelling *muscle* is French. ☞ The remarkable change of sense in L. *musculus* from 'little mouse' to 'muscle' has its counterpart in Dan. *mus-ling*, a muscle (the fish), lit. 'mouse-ling.' Cf. Swed. *mus*, a mouse; *mussla*, a muscle (fish); Gk. μῦς, (1) mouse, (2) muscle, in both E. senses. We even find, as Mr. Wedgwood points out, F. *souris*, 'a mouse, also, the sinewy brawn of the arm;' Cot.

MUSCOID, moss-like. (Hybrid; L., *with* Gk. *suffix*.) Botanical. Coined from L. *musco-*, for *muscus*, moss; and the Gk. suffix -ειδης, like, from ειδος, form. See **Moss**.

MUSE (1), to meditate, be pensive. (F.—L.) ME. *musen*, Chaucer, C. T. 5453 (B 1033); P. Plowman, B. x. 181. [We also find ME. *musard*, a dreamer, Rob. of Brunne, tr. of Langtoft, pp. 229, 266; from F. *musard*, sb. 'a muser, dreamer,' also as adj. 'musing, dreaming,' &c.; Cot.]—F. *muser*, 'to muse, dreame, study, pause, linger about a matter;' Cot.—OF. *muse*, the mouth, snout of an animal, Godefroy; whence the dimin. *musel*, later *museau*, whence E. *muzzle*; see **Muzzle**. β. Strange as it may seem, this etymology, given by Diez, is probably the right one; it is well borne out by Florio's Ital. Dict., where we find: ' *Musare*, to muse, to thinke, to surmise, also to muzle, to muffle, to mocke, to iest, to gape idlie about, *to hould ones musle or snout in the aire*.' This is plainly from Ital. *muso*, 'a musle, a snout, a face.' The image is that of a dog snuffing idly about, and *musing* which direction to take; and arose as a hunting term. Thus in the Book of St. Alban's, fol. e 6, we find: 'And any hound fynd or *musyng* of hir mace,' i.e. If any hound find her [a hare], or makes a scenting of her. See the OF. *musart, muse, musel, muser*. ¶ Disputed; see Diez, Körting, Scheler. Der. *mus-er, a-muse*.

MUSE (2), one of the nine fabled goddesses who presided over the arts. (F.—L.—Gk.) In Shak. Hen. V, prol. 1.—F. *muse*.—L. *mūsa*, a muse.—Gk. μοῦσα, a muse. Der. *mus-eum*, q.v., *mus-ic*, q.v., *mos-aic*, q. v.

MUSEUM, a repository for works of art, &c. (L.—Gk.) '*Museum*, a study, or library; ... The *Museum* or *Ashmole's Museum*, a neat building in the city of Oxford . . . founded by Elias Ashmole, Esq.;' Phillips, World of Words, ed. 1706. This building was finished in 1683. 'That famous *Musæum*;' Sandys, Trav. 1632; p. 111.—L. *mūsēum*.—Gk. μουσεῖον, the temple of the muses, a study, school.—Gk. μοῦσα, a muse; see **Muse** (2).

MUSHROOM, a kind of fungus. (F.—OHG.) In Shak. Temp. v. 39. The final *m* is put for *n*. ME. *muscheron*, explained as 'toodys hatte, *boletus, fungus*;' Prompt. Parv.—MF. *mouscheron, mousseron*, 'a mushrome;' Cot. Extended from OF. *mousse*, moss (Hatzfeld); where mushrooms grow.—OHG. *mos* (G. *moos*), moss; cognate with E. *moss*; see **Moss**.

MUSIC, the science of harmony. (F.—L.—Gk.) ME. *musik, musyk*, P. Plowman, B. x. 172.—F. *musique*, 'musick;' Cot.—L. *mūsica*.—Gk. μουσική, any art over which the muses presided, esp. music; fem. of μουσικός, belonging to the muses.—Gk. μοῦσα, a muse; see **Muse** (2). Der. *music-al*, L. L. L. iv. 3. 342; *music-al-ly*; *music-i-an*, Merch. Ven. v. 106, from F. *musicien*.

MUSIT, a small gap in a hedge; *obsolete*. (F.—C.) In Shak. Venus, 683; and see Two Noble Kinsmen, iii. 1. 97, and my note thereon; also Nares.—MF. *mussette*, 'a little hole, corner, or hoord to hide things in;' Cot. Hence applied to the hole in a hedge through which a hare passes. Dimin. of OF. *musse*, 'a secret corner;' Cot.—F. *musser*, 'to hide, conceale;' id. Of Celtic origin; cf. OIrish *mūch-aim*, I hide (Thurneysen, p. 108).

MUSK, a strong perfume obtained from the musk-deer. (F.—L. —Gk.—Pers.) In Shak. Merry Wives, ii. 2. 68. Spelt *muske* in Palsgrave.—MF. *musque* (Palsgrave); F. *musc*, 'musk;' Cot.—L. *muscum*, acc. of *muscus*, musk.—Late Gk. μόσχος.—Pers. *musk, misk*, musk; Rich. Dict. p. 1417. Cf. Skt. *mushka-s*, a testicle; because the musk was obtained from a bag behind the musk-deer's navel. Another sense of *mushka-s* was (probably) 'little mouse;' from *mush*, to steal. See **Mouse**. Der. *musc-adel*, q. v., *nut-meg*, q. v.; *musk-apple, musk-rose* (from the scent); *musk-y*.

MUSKET, a small hawk; a hand-gun. (F.—Ital.—L.) α. The old guns had often rather fanciful names. One was called the *falconet*, a dimin. of *falcon*; another a *saker*, also the name of a hawk; another a *basilisk*; another a *culverin*, i.e. snake-like; see **Culverin**. So also the *musket* was called after a small hawk of the same name. β. Shak. has *musket*, a hand-gun; All's Well, iii. 2. 111. ME. *musket*, spelt *muskytte* in Prompt. Parv., and explained as a 'byrde.' '*Musket*, a lytell hauke, *mouchet*;' Palsgrave. See Way's note, who remarks that 'the most ancient names of fire-arms were derived from monsters, dragons, or serpents, or from birds of prey, in allusion to velocity of movement.'—MF. *mousquet*, 'a musket (hawke, or piece);' Cot. [Here *piece* = gun.] [Cotgrave also gives MF. *mouchet, mouschet*, 'a musket, the tassel of a spar-hauke; also the little singing-bird that resembles the *friquet*, [which is] a kind of sparrow that keeps altogether about walnut-trees.']—Ital. *mosquetto*, 'a musket; also, a musket-hawke;' Florio. γ. Just as MF. *mouchet, mouschet*, is related to MF. *mouche, mousche*, a fly, so Ital. *mosquetto* is related to Ital. *mosca*, a fly. [The connexion is

not very obvious, but see the remarks in Scheler, who shows that small birds were sometimes called flies; a clear example is in G. *gras-mücke*, a hedge-sparrow, lit. a 'grass-midge.' The particular hawk here spoken of was so named from his small size.]—L. *musca*, a fly. Observe also, in Florio, the forms *moscardo*, 'a kind of birde, also a musket hauke;' *moscherino*, 'a kind of flie, the name of a birde;' *moschetti*, 'a kinde of sparowes in India, so little, as with feathers and all one is no bigger then [than] a little walnut;' all of which words are derived from *mosca*. We may also compare the Span. and E. *mosquito*; see **Mosquito**. Der. *musket-eer*, spelt *musqueteer* in Hudibras, pt. i. c. 2, l. 567, from MF. *mousquetaire*, 'a musketeer, a souldier that serves with a musket;' Cot.; *musket-oon*, 'a short gun, with a very large bore,' Kersey, ed. 1715, from Ital. *moschettone*, a blunderbuss (Baretti); cf. *moschettone*, a great horse-fly (Florio); *musket-r-y*.

MUSLIN, a fine thin kind of cotton cloth. (F.—Ital.—Syriac.) Spelt *musselin* and *muslin* in Phillips, ed. 1706.—F. *mousseline*, muslin.—Ital. *mussolino*, muslin; a dimin. form of *mussolo*, also used in the same sense.—Syriac *Mosul* (Webster), the name of a city in Kurdistan, in the E. of Turkey in Asia, where it was first manufactured, according to Marco Polo. The Arab. name of the city is *Mawsil*; Rich. Dict. p. 1526.

MUSQUASH, a rodent quadruped. (N. Amer. Indian.) Capt. Smith has the pl. *musquassus*, Works, p. 207; in his description of New England. From the old N. Amer. Indian name.

MUSQUITO, MUSSEL; see **Mosquito, Muscle** (2).

MUSSULMAN, a true believer in the Mohammedan faith. (Pers.—Arab.) 'The full-fed *Mussulman*;' Dryden, Hind and Panther, i. 377. 'A *Musselman*, which is a true beleeuer;' Sandys, Trav. 1632, p. 56. In Richardson's Arab. and Pers. Dict., p. 1418, the form *musulmān*, an orthodox believer, is marked as Persian. The Arab. form is *muslim*, answering to E. *moslem*; see **Moslem**.

MUST (1), part of a verb implying 'obligation.' (E.) This verb is extremely defective; nothing remains of it but the *past tense*, which does duty both for past and present. The infinitive (*mote*) is obsolete; even in AS. the infin. (*mōtan*) is not found. But the present tense is common in the Middle-English period. ME. *mot, moot*, pres. t., I am able, I can, I may, I am free to, very seldom with the sense of obligation; pt. t. *moste* (properly dissyllabic), I could, I might, I ought. 'As euer *mote* I drinke wyn or ale ' = as sure as I can (or hope to be free to) drink wine or ale; Chaucer, C. T. 834 (A 832). In Ch. C. T. 734, 737, 740, 744, Tyrwhitt wrongly changed *moot* into *moste*, against both the MSS. and the metre. The right readings are: 'He *moot* reherse' = he is bound to relate; 'he *moot* telle' = he will be sure to tell; 'He *moot* as wel' = he is bound as well; 'The wordes *mote* be' = the words should be. The pt. t. *moste, muste*, occurs in l. 714; 'He *muste* preche' = he will have to preach; where many MSS. have the spelling *moste*. AS. *mōtan*, not used in the infinitive; preterito-pres. t. *ic mōt*, I am able, I may, can, am free to, seldom with the sense of obligation; new pt. t. *ic mōste*; see Grein, ii. 265. +OSax. *mōtan* (not found); pres. t. *ik mōt, ik muot*; pt. t. *ik mōsta*; OFries. pres. t. *ik mōt*; pt. t. *ik mōste*; Du. *moeten*, to be obliged; pres. t. *ik moet*, pt. t. *ik moest*; Swed. *måste*, I must, both as pres. and pt. tense; so that the similar use in E. may be partly due to Scand. influence; G. *müssen*, MHG. *muezen*, OHG. *mōzan*, of which the old sense was 'to be free to do ' a thing, to be allowed; pres. t. *ich muss*; pt. t. *ich musste*; Goth. *mōtan*, not found; pres. t. *ik ga-mōt*; pt. t. *ik ga-mōsta*. In Mark ii. 2, Goth. *ni gamōsēdun* = 'they could not find room;' so that the orig. sense of *mōtan* was 'to find room.' β. Root uncertain; it may be connected with *meet, moot*; but this is not at all made out. Some connect it with the E. vb. *mete*, to measure.

MUST (2), new wine. (L.) In early use. ME. *must, most*; P. Plowman, B. xviii. 368; Layamon, 8723. AS. *must*, in a gloss (Bosworth).—L. *mustum*, new wine; neut. of *mustus*, young, fresh, new. Der. *must-ard*.

MUSTACHE, MUSTACHIO; see **Moustache**.

MUSTANG, a wild horse of the prairies. (Span.—L.) MSpan. *mestengo*, used in the same sense as *mostrenco*, adj., stray, having no owner; the spelling *mest-* shows confusion with *mesteño*, meaning (1) belonging to the *mesta* or graziers, and (2) the same as *mostrenco*, i.e., stray; see Minsheu, Pineda, Neumann. It is difficult to estimate the extent to which these words respectively influenced the form *mestengo*. 1. *Mostrenco* answers to a L. type *monstrānicum*, a stray animal, which the finder was bound to have publicly cried; from L. *monstrāre*, to show, inform (hence, to cry); see Diez, and cf. **Muster**. 2. *Mesteño* is from Span. *mesta*, a company of graziers; from L. *mixta*, fem. of pp. of *miscēre*, to mingle, to mix; cf. Span. *mestura*, a mixture. β. Minsheu shows how much the two words were confused in 1623; he gives: '*Mesta*, a monethly faire among herdmen; also, the ordinance that all owners and keepers of cattell are to observe.' Also: '*Mestengo*, or *Mostrenco*, a strayer.' Also: '*Mostrenco*, a straier, a bill signed: belonging to shepherds faires.'

MUSTARD, a condiment made from a plant with a pungent taste. (F.—L.; with Teut. *suffix*.) ME. *mustard*, Prompt. Parv.; *mostard*, Ayenbite of Inwyt, ed. Morris, p. 143, l. 30.—OF. *mostarde* (Hatzfeld), later *moustarde* (Cotgrave), mod. F. *moutarde*. Cf. Ital. and Port. *mostarda* [Span. *mostaza* (with a different suffix)]. β. The suffix -*ard* (fem. -*arde*) is of Teut. origin; from G. *hart*, lit. 'hard;' see Toynbee, Hist. F. Gr. The condiment took its name from the fact that it was made by mixing the pounded seeds of the mustard-plant with *must* or vinegar (Littré). The name was afterwards given to the plant itself (L. *sinapi*). γ. From OF. *most, only found in the form *moust* (Supp. to Godefroy), mod. F. *moût*, must. Cf. Ital., Span., and Port. *mosto*.—L. *mustum*, must, new wine; see **Must** (2).

MUSTER, an assembling in force, display, a fair show. (F.—L.) The E. sb. is older than the verb, and is nearly a doublet of *monster*. ME. *moustre*. 'And the *moustre* was thretti thousandis of men;' Wyclif, 3 Kings, v. 13, earlier version; the later version has *summe* [sum]. 'And made a gode *moustre*'=and made a fair show; P. Plowman, B. xiii. 362.—OF. *mostre* (13th cent.), another form of MF. *monstre*, fem. 'a pattern, also a muster, view, shew, or sight;' Cot. Mod. F. *montre*, which see in Littré. Cf. Port. *mostra*, a pattern, sample, muster, review of soldiers, *mostrar*, to show; Ital. *mostra*, a show, review, display, *mostrare*, to show.—Late L. *monstra*, a review of troops, show, sample.—L. *monstrāre*, to show.—L. *monstrum*, a divine omen, portent. See **Monster**, which differs in gender, being orig. neuter. Der. *muster*, vb., ME. *mustren*, Romance of Partenay, ed. Skeat, 3003; *muster-master*. Cf. OF. *moustrer*, variant of *monstrer*, ONorman *mustrer*, Gascon *mustra*, to show.

MUSTY, mouldy, sour, spoiled by damp. (Prov.—L.) 'Men shall find little fine flowre in them, but all very *mustie* branne, not worthy so muche as to fede either horse or hogges;' Sir T. More, Works, p. 649 h (not p. 694, as in Richardson). See Hamlet, iii. 2. 359. Minsheu (1623) has Span. *mosto*, new wine; *mostoso*, 'mustie, of sweet wine.' Godefroy (Supp.) gives OF. *muste, moste, moete, muiste, moite*, all as variants of *muiste*, moist; also *moiste* and *muste* with the sense '*moisi*.' The simplest solution is to take it as having come straight from Provence, with which we were connected by the wine trade from Bourdeaux.—Prov. *mousti, musti* (Gascon), adj., moist, humid (Mistral).—Prov. *moust*, must, new wine; see **Must**, and cf. '*moisty* ale' in Chaucer, C. T., H 60. We may suspect some confusion with OF. *moisi*, explained by Cotgrave as 'mouldy, musty, fusty.' But to *derive* the word from OF. *moisi* is, phonetically, impossible. Der. *must-i-ly*, -*ness*.

MUTABLE, subject to change. (L.) ME. *mutable*, Chaucer, tr. of Boethius, b. iv. pr. 6, l. 110.—L. *mūtābilis*, subject to change.—L. *mūtāre*, to change; see **Moult**. For older *moitāre; allied to L. *mūt-uus*, mutual, and to Gk. *μοῖτος*, thanks, favour (Prellwitz). Goth. *maidjan*, to change, corrupt; Skt. *mēth*, to associate with. Der. *mutabili-ty*, Chaucer, Troilus, i. 851. Also *mut-at-ion*, ME. *mutacioun*, Chaucer, Boeth. b. i. pr. 6, l. 61, from F. *mutation* (Cot.), from L. acc. *mūtātiōnem*. Also (from *mūtāre*) *com-mute, per-mute, trans-mute, mew* (3), *moult*. Cf. *mut-ual*.

MUTCHKIN, an E. pint. (Du.) 'Ix. pyntis and three *mutchkinnis*;' Acts of Jas. I (1426), c. 80; ed. 1566 (Jam.). The Scotch pint was 4 E. pints.—MDu. *mudseken*, 'our halfe common pinte;' Hexham. For *mutseken: lit. 'small cap;' a dimin., with suffix -*ken*, of MDu. *mutse*, Du. *muts*, a cap. Cf. G. *mütze*, a cap. See **Amice** (2).

MUTE (1), dumb. (L.) In Shak. Temp. iv. 1. 126.—L. *mūtus*, dumb. β. The form is that of a pp. from √MEU, to mutter with closed lips; cf. Gk. *μύ*, alas! *μυεῖν*, to close; and esp. Skt. *mūka-*, dumb, Gk. *μύδος*, dumb; from the notion of attempting to mutter low sounds; from the imitative L. *mu*, Gk. *μῦ*, a muttered sound. See **Mumble, Mutter, Mum**. ¶ The ME. *muet* (Chaucer, Troil. v. 194) is from OF. *muet*; from a L. type *mūt-ett-us, a dimin. form. Der. *mute-ly, mute-ness*; also *mutter*.

MUTE (2), to dung; used of birds. (F.—MDu.) In Tobit, ii. 10 (A. V.); and in Palsgrave.—MF. *mutir*, 'to mute, as a hawke;' Cot. A clipped form of OF. *esmeutir*, 'to mute, as birds doe;' id. Spelt *esmeltir* in the 13th cent. (Littré, s. v. *émeutir*), to give the etymology, which is to be found in Scheler).—MDu. *smelten*, also *smilten*, to smelt, to liquefy; also used of liquid animal discharge, as in Hexham. See **Smelt**.

MUTILATE, to maim. (L.) Formerly a pp. 'Imperfect or *mutilate*,' i.e. mutilated; Frith, Works, p. 90, col. 1.—L. *mutilātus*, pp. of *mutilāre*, to maim.—L. *mutilus*, maimed.+Gk. *μίτυλος*, also *μύτιλος*, curtailed, docked. Der. *mutilat-ion*, from F. *mutilation*, 'a mutilation,' Cot., from L. acc. *mutilātiōnem*.

MUTINY, a rebellion, insurrection, tumult. (F.—L.) *Mutin-y* is allied to the old verb to *mutine*. 'If thou canst *mutine* in a

matron's bones;' Hamlet, iii. 4. 83. [Hence were also formed *mutin-er*, Cor. i. 1. 254; *mutin-eer*, Temp. iii. 2. 40; *mutin-ous*, Temp. v. 42.]—MF. *mutiner*, 'to mutine;' Cot.—MF. *mutin*, 'mutinous, tumultuous;' id. β. MF. *mutin* stands for *meutin*, extended from OF. *muete, mute, meute*, an armed expedition (Godefroy); better known by the mod. F. derivative *émeute*. The mod. F. *meute*, though the same word, is only used in the sense of 'a pack of hounds;' answering to Late L. *mōta canum* (Ducange).—Late L. *movita*, a movement, contention, strife; used in place of L. *mōta*, fem. of *mōtus*, pp. of *mouēre*, to move; see **Move**. γ. Thus the orig. sense is 'movement,' well expressed by our 'commotion.' Parallel forms are MItal. *mutino*, 'a mutinie' (Florio), *mutinare*, 'to mutinie' (id.), whence mod. Ital. *ammutinarsi*, to mutiny; also Span. *motin*, a mutiny, sedition, Port. *motim*, a mutiny, uproar. Der. *mutiny*, verb, As You Like It, i. 1. 24; *mutin-er* (as above), *mutin-eer* (as above), *mutin-ous* (as above), *mutin-ous-ly, mutin-ous-ness*.

MUTTER, to murmur, speak in a low voice. (E.) ME. *motren*, Chaucer, Troil. ii. 541. Also *moteren*, whence the pres. part. *moteringe*, used to tr. L. *mussitantes*, Wyclif, 2 Kings, xii. 19. The word is rather E. than borrowed from L. *mūtīre*, to mutter. To be divided as *mot-er-en*, where -*er* is the usual frequentative verbal suffix, and *mot-* or *mut-* is an imitative sound, to express inarticulate mumbling; see **Mum**. Cf. EFries. *motjen*, to mutter; Swed. dial. *mutla, muttra*, Norw. *mutra*; also prov. G. *mustern*, to whisper, similarly formed from a base *must-*; L. *mut-īre, mutt-īre, muss-āre*, to mutter, *muttum*, a muttered sound; &c.

MUTTON, the flesh of sheep. (F.—C.) ME. *motoun* (with one *t*), spelt *motone* in Prompt. Parv. In P. Plowman, B. iii. 24, the word *motoun* means a coin of gold, so called because stamped with the image of a sheep. The older spelling *moltoun* is in Gower, C. A. i. 39; prol. 1060.—OF. *moton* (mod. F. *mouton*), a sheep; a still older spelling is *multon* (Godefroy).—Low L. *multōnem*, acc. of *multo*, a sheep, also a gold coin (as in P. Plowman). Cf. Ital. *montone*, 'a ram, a mutton,' Florio; where *n* is substituted for *l*, preserved in the Venetian form *moltone*, cited by Diez. β. Of Celtic origin; from a Celtic type *moltos, a sheep; as in Irish and Manx *molt*, Gael. *mult*, W. *mollt*, Bret. *maout, meut* (for *molt), a wether, sheep. See Stokes-Fick, p. 212. Miklosich cites Russ. *molit(e)*, to castrate, s. v. *moli-*. Der. *mutton-chop*.

MUTUAL, reciprocal, given and received. (F.—L.) 'Conspyracy and *mutuall* promise;' Sir T. More, Works, p. 1019 c; *mutuall* in Palsgrave.—OF. *mutuël*, 'mutuall, reciprocall;' Cot. Extended from L. *mūtu-us*, mutual, by help of the suffix -*el* (<L. -*ālis*). β. The orig. sense is 'exchanged;' from L. *mūtāre*, to change; see **Mutable**. Cf. *mort-u-us*, from *mort-*. Der. *mutual-ly, mutual-i-ty*.

MUZZLE, the snout of an animal. (F.—L.) ME. *mosel*, Chaucer, C. T. 2153 (A 2151).—OF. *musel* (Burguy), *muzel* (A. D. 1521, Godefroy); later *museau*, 'the muzzle, snout, or nose of a beast;' Cot.; Norm. dial. *musel* (Du Bois). As Diez shows, an older form *morsel* is indicated by the Bret. *morzeel*, which (like Bret. *muzel*) means 'muzzle,' and is merely a borrowed word from OFrench. β. Again, the Provençal (according to Diez) not only has the form *mus*, but also *mursel*, in which the *r* is again preserved; but it is lost in Ital. *muso*, the muzzle, and in the E. **Muse** (1). γ. The OF. *morsel thus indicated is a dimin. (with suffix -*el*) from a form *mors; cf. Ital. *muso*, standing for an older *morso, which may have meant 'muzzle' as well as 'bit, bridle, or snaffle for a horse' (Florio). Cf. F. *mors*, 'a bitt, or biting;' Cot.—Late L. *morsus*, (1) a morsel, (2) a buckle, (3) remorse, (4) a beak, snout, in which sense it is found A.D. 1309; L. *morsus*, a bite, a tooth, clasp of a buckle, grasp, fluke of an anchor.—L. *morsus*, pp. of *mordēre*, to bite. See **Morsel**. ¶ Disputed; see Körting, §§ 244, 6307, 6411; and add. note on § 244. Der. *muzzle*, verb, spelt *mosell* in the Bible of 1551, Deut. xxv. 4.

MY, possessive pronoun. (E.) ME. *mi*, formed from ME. *min*, mine, by dropping the final *n*. 'Ne thenkest nowt of *mine* oþes That ich haue *mi* louerd sworen?' Havelok, 578; where grammar requires '*min* louerd' to answer to the plural '*minè* oþes.' See **Mine**. ¶ The final *n* is often retained before vowels, as in the case of *an*. Der. *my-self*, ME. *mi self*, a substitution for *me self*; see Stratmann, s. v. *self*.

MYOPIA, shortsightedness. (Gk.) Bailey has: '*Myopia*, purblindness;' vol. ii. ed. 1731.—Gk. *μυωπία*, shortsightedness.—Gk. *μυωπ-*, from *μύωψ*, closing the eyes, blinking, shortsighted.—Gk. *μύ-ω*, I am shut, said of the eyes, I wink or wince; and *ὤψ*, the eye, face. See **Optic**.

MYRIAD, ten thousand, a vast number. (Gk.) In Milton, P. L. i. 87, &c.; Ben Jonson, Fortunate Isles (Johphiel). Englished from Gk. *μυριάδ-*, stem of *μυριάς*, the number of 10,000.—Gk. *μυρίος*, numberless.

MYRMIDON, one of a band of men. (L.—Gk.) Gen. in pl.

myrmidons; the *Myrmidons* were the followers of Achilles; in Chapman, tr. of Homer, Iliad ii. 604; Surrey, tr. of Æneid, ii. l. 10; and Lydgate, Hist. of Troye, fol. M 5. col. 1.—L. *Myrmidones*, Verg. Æn. ii. 7.—Gk. Μυρμιδόνες, a warlike people of Thessaly, formerly in Ægina (Homer). There was a fable (to account for the name) that the Myrmidons were ants changed into men; Ovid, Met. vii. 635-654. Cf. Gk. μυρμηδών, an ant's nest; μύρμηξ, an ant, cognate with Pers. *mūr*, L. *formīca*.

MYROBALAN, the dried drupaceous fruit of some *Terminalia*, having an astringent pulp. (F.—L.—Gk.) Spelt *mirabolan*, Hakluyt, Voy. ii. 1. 276.—F. *myrobalan*, 'an East-Indian plumb;' Cot.—L. *myrobalanum*.—Gk. μυροβάλανος, lit. 'acorn producing an unguent.'—Gk. μύρο-, for μύρον, a sweet juice, unguent; and βάλανος, acorn, allied to L. *glans*, whence E. *gland*.

MYRRH, a bitter aromatic gum. (F.—L.—Gk.—Arab.) ME. *mirre*, Ancren Riwle, p. 372, l. 7; now adapted to the L. spelling.—OF. *mirre* (11th cent.); mod. F. *myrrhe* (Littré).—L. *myrrha*.—Gk. μύρρα, the balsamic juice of the Arabian myrtle.—Arab. *murr*, (1) bitter, (2) myrrh, from its bitterness; Rich. Dict., p. 1381.✛ Heb. *mōr*, myrrh; allied to *mar*, bitter.

MYRTLE, the name of a tree. (F.—L.—Gk.—Pers.) In Shak. Meas. for Meas. ii. 2. 117.—MF. *myrtil*, 'a mirtle-berrie; also, the lesse kind of mirtle, called noble mirtle;' Cot. Dimin. of *myrte*, *meurte*, 'the mirtle-tree;' id.—L. *murtus*, *myrtus*, myrtle.—Gk. μύρτος.—Pers. *mūrd*, the myrtle; Palmer, col. 617; Rich. Dict. p. 1524.

MYSTERY (1), anything kept concealed or very obscure, a secret rite. (L.—Gk.) ME. *mysterie*, Wyclif, Rom. xvi. 25. Englished from L. *mytērium*, Rom. xvi. 25 (Vulgate).—Gk. μυστήριον, Rom. xvi. 25.—Gk. μύστης, one who is initiated.—Gk. μυεῖν, to initiate into mysteries.—Gk. μύειν, to close the eyes; suggested by Gk. μῦ, a slight sound with closed lips; of imitative origin. See **Mute, Mum**. Der. *mysteri-ous*, from F. *mysterieux*, 'mysterious,' Cot.; *mysteri-ous-ly*, *-ness*. And see *mystic*, *mystify*.

MISTERY (2), **MYSTERY**, a trade, handicraft. (F.—L.) Cotgrave translates OF. *mestier* by 'a trade, occupation, *mystery*, handicraft.' Spenser, Mother Hubbard's Tale, 221, speaks of the soldier's occupation as being 'the noblest *mysterie*.' This is a different word from the above, but often confused with it. It should rather be spelt *mistery*. Indeed, it owes to the word above not only the former *y*, but the addition of the latter one; being an extension of ME. *mistere*, a trade, craft, Chaucer, C. T. 615 (A 613).—AF. *mister*, Stat. Realm, i. 311 (1351); OF. *mestier* (as above); mod. F. *métier*. [Cognate with Span. *menester*, want, need, employment, trade; Ital. *mestiere*, with same sense.]—L. *ministerium*, service, employment.—L. *minister*, a servant; see **Minister**.

MYSTIC, secret, allegorical. (F.—L.—Gk.) Milton has *mystick*, P. L. v. 178, ix. 442; also *mystical*, P. L. v. 620.—F. *mystique*, 'mysticall;' Cot.—L. *mysticus*.—Gk. μυστικός, mystic.—Gk. μύστης, fem. μύστις, one who is initiated into mysteries; see **Mystery** (1). Der. *mystic-al*, in Skelton, ed. Dyce, i. 222; *mystic-ism*; and see *mystify*.

MYSTIFY, to involve in mystery, puzzle. (F.—Gk. *and* L.) Quite modern; not in Todd's Johnson.—F. *mystifier*, to mystify. An ill-formed jumble, from Gk. μυστι-κός, mystic (not well divided), and L. *-ficāre*, for *facere*, to make. See Littré, who remarks that it was not admitted into the F. Dict. till 1835 (rather in 1798); Hatzfeld.) See **Mystic**. Der. *mystific-at-ion*, from mod. F. *mystification*.

MYTH, a fable. (Gk.) Now common, but quite a mod. word and formed directly from Gk. μῦθος, a fable; see **Mythology**, which is a much older word in our language. Der. *myth-ic*, *myth-ic-al*, *myth-ic-al-ly*.

MYTHOLOGY, a system of legends, the science of legends. (F.—L.—Gk.) In Sir T. Browne, Vulg. Errors, b. i. c. 8, Of Ctesias. Lydgate has *methologies*, Hist. Troye, fol. H 2, back, col. 2.—F. *mythologie*, 'an exposition, or moralising of fables;' Cot.—L. *mythologia*.—Gk. μυθολογία, legendary lore, a telling of fables.—Gk. μῦθο-, for μῦθος, a fable; and λέγειν, to tell. β. The Gk. μῦ-θος is from μῦ, a slight sound, hence a word, saying, tale; see **Mute, Mum**. Der. *mytholog-ic*, *mytholog-ic-al*, *mytholog-ist*.

N

N. A few remarks upon this letter are necessary. An initial *n*, in English, is very liable to be prefixed to a word which properly begins with a vowel; and again, on the other hand, an original initial *n* is sometimes dropped. **A**. In the former case, the *n* is probably due to the final letter of *an* or *mine*; thus *an ewt* becomes

a newt, *mine uncle* becomes *my nuncle*, and hence *newt* and *nuncle*, used independently. Another example occurs in *nickname* for *eke-name*. In Middle-English, numerous similar examples occur, such as *a noke* for *an oke*, an oak (cf. John Nokes = John an-oaks, i. e. John of the oaks); *a naye* = *an aye*, an egg; *thi nye* = *thin ye*, thine eye; *thi nynon* = *thin ynon*, thine eyes; examples of all these are given in Halliwell, under *noke*, *naye*, *nye*, and *nynon* respectively. In the case of *for the nonce*, the *n* belongs to the old dat. case of the article, the older phrase being *for then ones*; see **Nonce**. **B**. On the other hand, an original *n* is lost in *auger* for *nauger*, in the sense of a carpenter's tool; in *umpire* for *numpire*, *adder* for *nadder*, *apron* for *anpron*, *ouch* for *nouch*. See my note to P. Plowman, C. xx. 306.

NAB, to seize. (Scand.) A dialect word; also found as *nap*. Added by Todd to Johnson's Dict.—Swed. *nappa*, Dan. *nappe*, to catch, snatch at. ¶ Rich. cites the word *nab-cheats* from Beaum. and Fletcher, Beggar's Bush, ii. 1, with the sense of *caps*. This is a totally different word; here *nab* = knob, the head; *cheat* = a thing, in the cant language; and *nab-cheat* = head-thing, cap; see Harman's Caveat, ed. Furnivall, p. 82.

NABOB, an Indian prince, very rich man. (Hind.—Arab.) See Burke, Speech on the *Nabob* of Arcot's debts. The word signifies 'deputy' or vice-roy, esp. applied to a governor of a province of the Mogul empire (Webster). Also *nobobb*, a nobleman; so spelt by Sir T. Herbert, Travels, ed. 1665, p. 104, who assigns it that meaning 'in the language of the Mogul's kingdom, which hath mixt with it much of the Persian.'—Hind. *nuwwāb* (pl. of *nā'ib*), 'vice-gerents, deputies; *nawwāb*, vulg. nabob;' Forbes. But the word is merely borrowed from Arabic; Devic notes that Hind. often employs Arab. plurals as sing.—Arab. *nawwāb*; which is properly a plural form (used honorifically), signifying vice-gerents, deputies; pl. of *nā'ib*, a vice-gerent, lieutenant, deputy. Cf. Arab. *nawb*, supplying the place of another. See Rich. Dict. pp. 1606, 1557, 1608. Palmer's Pers. Dict. col. 665, has: Arab. *nawwāb*, 'a viceroy, governor; in Persia, this title is given to princes of the blood;' cf. col. 639. Cf. Port. *nababo*, a nabob; see Yule.

NACRE, mother-of-pearl. (F.—Span.—Arab.) In Cotgrave.—F. *nacre*, 'a naker, a great and long shell-fish, the outside of whose shell is rugged .. the inside smooth and of a shining hue;' *nacre de perles*, 'mother of pearle, the beautiful shell of another fish, wherein the best, and most pearles be found;' Cot.—Span. *nacar*.—Arab. *naqrah*, a cavity (from the hollow inside of the shell); from Arab. root *naqara*, he hollowed out; Rich. Dict., p. 1596.

NADIR, the point of the sky opposite the zenith. (Arab.) Chaucer uses *nadir* to signify the point of the zodiac opposite to that in which the sun is situate; Treatise on the Astrolabe, pt. ii. sect. 6, l. 1.—Arab. *nazīru 'samt* (or simply *nazīr*), the point of the sky opposite the zenith.—Arab. *nazīr*, over against, corresponding to; and *as' samt*, the azimuth, or rather an abbreviation of *as' samtu'r'ras*, the zenith. Rich. Dict. pp. 1586, 848. See **Azimuth, Zenith**. The Arab. *z* (or *ḍ*) here used is the 17th letter of the Arab. alphabet, an unusual letter with a difficult sound, which came to be rendered by *d* in Low L. and E.

NAG (1), a small horse. (MDu.) In Minsheu, ed. 1627. ME. *nagge*. 'Nagge, or lytylle beest, *bestula*, *equillus*;' Prompt. Parv. 'He neyt [neighed] as a *nagge*;' Destruction of Troy, ed. Panton and Donaldson, l. 7727.—MDu. *negghe*, a small horse (Kilian); *negge*, 'a nagg, a small horse,' Hexham; Du. *neg*; Du. dial. *knagge* (Molema). And compare Low G. *nikkel*, a nag; and perhaps Norw. *kneggja*, Icel. *gneggja*, *hneggja*, to neigh.

NAG (2), to worry, tease. (Scand.) Provincial; but a good word.—Norw. and Swed. *nagga*, to nibble, peck; Dan. *nage*, Icel. *gnaga*, to gnaw; Low G. *nagen*, *naggen*, to gnaw, vex, nag, *gnaggen*, to nag (Berghaus). Allied to **Gnaw**, q. v.

NAIAD, a water-nymph. (L.—Gk.) In Shak. Temp. iv. 128.—L. *naiad-*, stem of *naias*, a water-nymph.—Gk. ναϊάς (gen. ναϊάδ-ος), a water-nymph.—Gk. νάειν, to flow; Æolic form ναύειν (= νάϝειν). From √SNĀ; cf. Skt. *snā*, to bathe; OIrish *snáim*, I swim. And see **Natation**.

NAIL, the horny scale at the end of the human fingers and toes; a spike of metal. (E.) ME. *nail*, *nayl*; the pl. *nayles*, used of the human nails, is in Havelok, 2163; the pl. *nailes*, i. e. iron spikes, is in Chaucer, C. T. 6351 (D 769). AS. *nægel*, in both senses, Grein, ii. 274. [The loss of *g* is regular, and occurs in *hail*, *sail*, &c.]✛Du. *nagel*, in both senses; Icel. *nagl*, the human nail; *nagli*, a spike, peg; Dan. *nagle*, in both senses; Swed. *nagel*, in both senses; Goth. **nagls*, only in the derived verb *ganagljan*, to nail; G. *nagel*, in both senses. β. Teut. type **nagloz*, m. Allied to Lithuan. *nagas*, a claw, nail, Russ. *nogot(e)*, a nail, Skt. *nakhá-m*, n., *nakhá-s*, m., a nail of the finger or toe; Pers. *nākhun*, the same. γ. The Gk. ὄνυξ, a nail, claw, L. *unguis*, Gael. and Irish *ionga*, OIrish *inga*, W. *ewin*, go back to forms with a different gradation. Brugmann, §§ 539, 658, 702. **Der.** nail, vb., AS. *næglian*, whence the pp. *nægled*, in Grein; *nail-er*. Cf. *onyx*.

NAILBOURN, an intermittent stream. (E.) Given in N. E. D. s. v. *eylebourn*, as it was spelt in 1719. But spelt *nailbourne* in 1667, and *naylborne* in 1480. We find in Birch, Cart. Saxon. ii. 172:— 'thonne . . . of dune on stream on *næglesburnan*.' I cannot explain the form; cf. Phil. Soc. Trans. 1903–6, p. 364.

NAIVE, artless, simple, ingenuous. (F.—L.) A late word; the adv. *naively* is used by Pope in a letter; see the quotation in Richardson. Dryden has: 'it was so *naive*,' and ''twas such a *naiveté*;' Marriage à la Mode, iii. 1.—F. *naive*, fem. of *naïf*, which Cot. explains by 'lively, quick, naturall, kindly, . . no way counterfeit.'—L. *natiuus*, native, natural; see **Native.** ¶ The fem. form *naïve* was chosen, because it appears in the adv. *naïvement*, and in the sb. *naïveté*; and, in fact, it is nearer the Latin original than the masc. *naïf*. **Der.** *naive-ly*, for F. *naïve-ment*; and *naive-té*, sb., directly from the French. **Doublet,** *native*.

NAKED, bare, uncovered, exposed. (E.) Always dissyllabic. ME. *naked*, Chaucer, C. T. 2068 (A 2066). AS. *nacod* (= *nac-od*), which is plainly an old pp., with the pp. suffix *-od*; Grein, ii. 272. +OFries. *nakad*, *naken*; Du. *naakt*; Icel. *nakinn*, *nökviðr*; Dan. *nögen*; Swed. *naken*; G. *nackt*, MHG. *nacket*, OHG. *nachot*, *nakot*; Goth. *nakwaths* (where *-aths* is the usual pp. suffix). β. Most of these point to an old pp. form; the Du. *-t*, Icel. *-iðr*, G. *-t*, Goth. *-aths*, are all pp. suffixes of a weak verb, and lead us back to the orig. Teut. type *nákwathóz* (> *nákwadóz*); Idg. type *nog(w)otós*. γ. But Icel. *nak-inn*, Dan. *nög-en*, Swed. *nak-en*, OFries. *nak-en*, adopt the pp. suffixes of a strong verb from a base NAQ, answering to an Idg. √ NOGw, to strip, lay bare; cf. Skt. *nagna-*, naked, Russ. *nagoi*, naked, Lith. *nugas*, naked, L. *nūdus* (= *noudos* for *nogwedos*). Further allied words are the Irish and Gael. *nochd*, naked, bare, exposed, desolate, W. *noeth*, Bret. *noaz*. δ. Lastly, it is remarkable that English has evolved a verb from this pp. by back-formation, viz. ONorthumb. *ge-nacian*, Mark, ii. 4; ME. *naken*. The following are examples. 'He *nakide* the hous of the pore man,' Wyclif, Job, xx. 19, early version; the later version has 'he *made nakid* the hows.' 'O *nyce* men, why *nake* ye youre bakkes' = O foolish men, why do ye expose your backs (to the enemy, by turning to flee); Chaucer, tr. of Boethius, b. iv. met. 7, l. 45. It is also found much later. 'Lus. Come, be ready, *nake* your swords, Think of your wrongs;' Tourneur, The Revenger's Tragedy, Act v. sc. 1. We even find a derived verb *naknen*; 'A! nu *nacnes* mon mi lef' = Ah! now men strip my beloved; O. Eng. Homilies, ed. Morris, i. 283, l. 10. Cf. Brugmann, i. § 165; Rhys, W. Phil. p. 95. **Der.** *naked-ly*, ME. *nakedliche*, Ancren Riwle, p. 316; *naked-ness*, ME. *nakidnesse*, Wyclif, Rev. iii. 18. Also *stark-naked*, q. v. **Doublet,** *nude*.

NAKER, a kettle-drum. (F.—Arab.) Chaucer has *nakers*, pl., C. T., A 2511.—OF. *nacaire* (Godefroy).—Arab. *naqqārah*, a kettledrum; Palmer's Pers. Dict.

NAMBY-PAMBY, weakly sentimental. (E.) Coined from *Ambrose*, i. e. Ambrose Philips (d. 1749), a poet whose style was ridiculed by Carey and Pope. Johnson, in his Life of Philips says: 'The pieces that please best are those which, from Pope and Pope's adherents, procured him the name of *Namby Pamby*;' see Chalmers, Eng. Poets, xiii. 103.

NAME, that by which a thing or person is called, a designation. (E.) ME. *name* (orig. dissyllabic); Chaucer, C. T. 3939 (A 3941). AS. *nama*, Grein, ii. 273.+Du. *naam*; Icel. *nafn*, *namn*; Dan. *navn*; Swed. *namn*; Goth. *namo*; G. *name*, OHG. *namo*. Teut. type *namon-*. β. Further allied to L. *nōmen*; Gk. ὄνομα, Pers. *nām*, Skt. *nāman*; and to Irish *ainm*, W. *enw*, name; Russ. *imia*. Brugmann, i. §§ 399, 425. ¶ Not allied to **Know**; see Prellwitz. **Der.** *name*, vb., AS. *nemnan*, Grein, ii. 280; *nam-er*; *name-ly*, ME. *name-liche*, *nomeliche*, Ancren Riwle, p. 18, l. 16; *name-less*, ME. *nameles*, Chaucer, tr. of Boethius, b. iv. pr. 5, l. 5; *name-less-ly*, *name-less-ness*; also *name-sake* (= *name's sake*, the *s* being dropped before *s* following), i. e. one whose name is given him for the sake of another's fame, Dryden, Absalom, pt. ii. l. 323 (see **Sake**). Allied words are *nominal*, *de-nominate*. **Doublet,** *noun*.

NANKEEN, NANKIN, a kind of cotton cloth. (China.) Added by Todd to Johnson. So called from Nankin in China.—Chinese *nan-king*, 'south court;' cf. *Pekin*, from *pe-king*, 'north court' (Yule).

NAP (1), a short sleep. (E.) We now say 'to take a *nap*,' and treat *nap* as a sb. We also say 'to be caught *napping*.' It was formerly a verb; ME. *nappen*, to doze. 'See! how he *nappeth*;' Chaucer, C. T. 16958 (H 9). AS. *hnæppian*, to nap; *hnæppað* is a gloss upon *dormit*, Ps. xl. 9, ed. Spelman. Cf. Bavarian *knappen*, to nod with the head (Schmeller); OHG. *hnaffezen*, to nap. **Der.** *napp-ing*, sb., AS. *hnappung*, Grein, ii. 90.

NAP (2), the roughish surface of cloth. (MDu.) In Spenser, Muiopotmos, l. 333. Shak. has *napless* = threadbare; Cor. ii. 1. 250. The older form is *noppe* (Palsgrave). ME. *noppe*; 'noppe of a cloth, *villus*;' Prompt. Parv. See Way's note, where he cites passages to show that *noppe* 'denotes those little knots, which, after cloth has passed through the fulling-mill, are removed by women with little nippers; a process termed *burling* cloth.' He cites: 'noppy, as cloth is that hath a gross woffe [woof];' Palsgrave. Also: 'Clarisse, the *nopster* (*esbourysse*) can well her craft, syth whan she lerned it, cloth for to *noppe*;' Caxton, Book for Travellers. We now apply the term, not to the rough surface, but to the *sheared* surface, by a natural change in the sense, due to our not seeing the cloth till the process is completed. Prob. introduced by Du. clothworkers. [AS. *hnoppa* is unauthorised.]—MDu. *noppe*, 'the nap of wooll or cloath,' Hexham; cf. MDu. *noppen*, 'to sheare of [off] the nap,' id. Cf. Du. *nop*, nap; Dan. *noppe*, frizzed nap of cloth; MSwed. *nopp*, nap; Low G. *nobben*, nap; Bremen Wörterbuch. Also Norw. *napp*, nap, and Norw. *nuppa*, to pluck off with the fingers; AS. *hnoppian*, to pluck, Voc. 480. 23; AS. *ā-hnēapan*, to pluck off; Goth. *dis-hnupnan*, to be torn in pieces; *dis-hniupan*, to tear to pieces. All from Teut. base *hneup*, to pluck, pull. **Der.** *napless*, as above.

NAPE, the joint of the neck behind. (E.) In Shak. Cor. ii. 1. 43. ME. *nape*, Prompt. Parv. 'Dedly woundid through the *nape*;' King Alisaunder, l. 1347. The orig. sense is projection or 'knob;' and the term must have been first applied to the slight knob at the back of the head, felt on passing the finger upwards from the neck; cf. OFries. *halsknap*, nape of the neck. It is, in fact, a mere variant of ME. *knappe*, a knob, button, P. Plowman, B. vi. 272. Cf. Icel. *knappr*, a knob, stud, button; AS. *cnæp*, the top of a hill. See **Knop, Neck.**

NAPERY, linen for the table. (F.—L.) 'Manie farmers . . . have learned also to garnish their cupbords with plate, . . and their tables with fine *naperie*;' Harrison, Descr. of England, ed. Furnivall, b. ii. c. 12, p. 239. Palsgrave has: 'Naprie, store of lynen.'—OF. *naperie*, table-linen (Godefroy); orig. the office in a household for providing table-linen (Roquefort).—Late L. *nāpāria*, the same; Ducange; also spelt *mapparia*.—Late L. *nāpa*, a cloth; corrupted from L. *mappa*, a cloth. See **Napkin.**

NAPHTHA, an inflammable liquid. (L.—Gk.—Pers.) In Milton, P. L. i. 729. Spelt *nephta* by Sir T. Herbert, Travels, p. 182 (Todd).—L. *naphtha*.—Gk. νάφθα.—Pers. *naft*, *nift*, naphtha; Rich. Dict. p. 1591. Allied to Zend *napta-*, moist; Horn, § 1035. Cf. Arab. *naft*, *nift*, 'naphtha, bitumen;' Rich. Dict. p. 1593. The final letter of the Arab. word is the 16th letter of the alphabet, sometimes rendered by *th*; and the Arab. form is unoriginal; prob. from Gk.

NAPKIN, a cloth used at the table, a small cloth. (F.—L.; with E. suffix.) ME. *napekin*. 'Napet or *napekyn*, Napella, manupiarium, mapella;' Prompt. Parv. Both these forms, *nap-et* and *nape-kyn*, are formed with dimin. suffixes from F. *nappe*, 'a tablecloth;' Cot.; OF. *nape*, *mape* (Supp. to Godefroy).—Late L. *nāpa*; corruption of L. *mappa*, a cloth. See **Map.** **Der.** *ap-ron* (for *nap-ron*); *nap-er-y*, q. v.

NARCISSUS, a kind of flower. (L.—Gk.) In Cotgrave, to translate F. *narcisse*.—L. *narcissus*.—Gk. νάρκισσος, the narcissus; named from its narcotic properties; see **Narcotic.**

NARCOTIC, producing torpor; an opiate. (F.—Gk.) Chaucer has the pl. *nercotikes* as a pl. sb., C. T. 1474 (A 1472). It is properly an adj.—F. *narcotique*, 'stupefactive, benumming;' Cot. [The L. form does not appear.]—Gk. ναρκωτικός, benumbing.—Gk. ναρκόω, I benumb; ναρκάω, I grow numb.—Gk. νάρκη, numbness, torpor. For *σνάρκη*, i. e. contraction; see **Snare.** **Der.** *narcissus*, from νάρκη.

NARD, an unguent from an aromatic plant. (F.—L.—Gk.—Pers.) In the margin of A. V., Mark, xiv. 3, where the text has *spikenard*; and in Holland, tr. of Pliny, b. xii. c. 12. ME. *nard*, Wyclif, John, xii. 3.—F. *nard*, 'spikenard;' Cot.—L. *nardus*, Mk. xiv. 3 (Vulgate). —Gk. νάρδος, Mk. xiv. 3.—OPers. type *narda-* (Horn, § 1060), whence also Heb. *nērd*, and Skt. *nalada-*, the Indian spikenard, Nardostachys jatamansi; Benfey. β. The name is Persian; the Arab. *nardīn* is borrowed, like the Skt. and Heb. forms. The interchange of *l* and *r* is common in many languages. **Der.** *spike-nard*.

NARGILEH, NARGILE, NARGILI, a pipe or smokingapparatus in which the smoke is passed through water. (Pers.) 'Making believe to puff at a *narghile*;' Thackeray, Van. Fair, bk. ii. c. 16. From Pers. *nārgīl*, a coco-nut; because these pipes were orig. made with a coco-nut, which held the water; Rich. Dict., p. 1548. Cf. Skt. *nārikera-s*, *nārikela-s*, a coco-nut. See Yule and Devic.

NARRATION, a tale, recitation. (F.—L.) [The verb *narrate* is late.] *Narration* is in Minsheu, ed. 1627. It occurs earlier, in The Monk of Evesham, p. 65 (1482).—F. *narration*, 'a narration;'

Cot. — L. *narrātiōnem*, acc. of *narrātio*, a tale. — L. *narrāre*, to relate, tell; lit. to make known. — L. *nārus*, another form of *gnārus*, knowing, acquainted with. From **gnā*, allied to √GEN, to know; cf. Skt. *jnā*, to know, Russ. *znate*, E. *know*; see **Know**. Der. From L. *narrāre* we also have *narrate*, vb., in Johnson's Dict.; *narrat-ive*, adj., from F. *narratif*, 'narrative' (Cot.); *narrat-ive*, sb., Bacon, Life of Hen. VII, ed. Lumby, p. 54, l. 14; *narrat-or*.

NARROW, of little breadth or extent. (E.) ME. *narowe*, *narewe*, *narwe* (with one *r*); Chaucer has *narwe* (= narrowly) as an adv., C. T. 3224; also as an adj., C. T. 627 (A 625). AS. *nearu*, *nearo*, adj.; *nearwe*, adv., Grein, ii. 287, 288. + OSax. *naru*, adj., *narawo*, adv.; Du. *naar*, dismal, sad (see Franck). Teut. type **narwoz*. Connected by Curtius (i. 392) with *nerve*. Der. *narrow-ly*, *narrow-ness*, *narrow-mind-ed*.

NARWHAL, the sea-unicorn. (Scand.) In Ash's Dict., ed. 1775. 'Teeth of *narwhals*;' Sir T. Browne, Vulgar Errors, bk. iii. c. 23. § 6. — Dan. and Swed. *narhval*; Icel. *nāhvalr*, a narwhal. β. The latter part of the word is the same as E. *whale*. As to the sense of the prefix, the lit. sense of Icel. *nā-hvalr* is 'corpse-whale,' from Icel. *nār* (in compounds *nā-*), a corpse, and the fish is often of a pallid colour. Such is the usual explanation; perhaps it is only a 'popular' etymology.

NASAL, belonging to the nose. (F. — L.) In Kersey, ed. 1715. Burton uses *nasals* for medicines operating through the nose; Anat. of Melancholy, p. 384 (R.); or p. 393 (Todd). — F. *nasal*, belonging to the nose; Cot. — Late L. *nāsālis*, nasal; a coined word, not used in good Latin. — L. *nās-us*, the nose, cognate with E. *nose*; see **Nose**. Der. *nas-turt-ium*, q.v.

NASCENT, springing up, arising. (L.) A late word, added by Todd to Johnson. — L. *nascent-*, stem of pres. part. of *nasci*, to be born, to arise, an inceptive form with pp. *nātus*. See **Natal**.

NASTURTIUM, the name of a flower. (L.) In Ash's Dict., ed. 1775. 'Cresses tooke the name in Latine *nasturtium, a narium tormento*, as a man would say, nose-wring, because it will make one writh and shrink vp his nosthrils;' Holland, tr. of Pliny, b. xix. c. 8. — L. *nasturtium*, cress; better spelt *nasturcium*. — L. *nās-*, stem of *nāsus*, the nose; and *turc-* = *torc-*, from *torquēre*, to twist, torment. see **Nose** and **Torture**.

NASTY, dirty, filthy, unpleasant. (Scand.) In Hamlet, iii. 4. 94. Formerly also (as Wedgwood points out) written *nasky*. '*Maulavé*, ill-washed, slubbered, *naskie, nasty*, foul;' Cot. In such cases, the form with *k* is the older; cf. ME. *naxty*; as in '*naxty*, and needy, and nakut;' Three Met. Romances, ed. Robson, A. st. xv. Of Scand. origin; preserved in Swed. dial. *naskug*, nasty, dirty, foul (used of weather); we also find the form *nasket*, dirty, sullied (Rietz); cf. Dan. dial. *nasken, nasket*, old, worn out (said of clothes), Molbech. β. Perhaps allied to Swed. dial. *snaskig*, nasty, swinelike; Swed. *snuskig*, slovenly, nasty; Swed. dial. *snaska*, to eat like a pig, to eat greedily and noisily, to be slovenly (Rietz); Dan. *snaske*, to champ one's food with a smacking noise. These words are of imitative origin, like various other suggestive words of a like character. The word appears also in Low G. *nask*, nasty, Bremen Wörterbuch; and may be allied to Norweg. *nask*, greedy, *naska*, to eat noisily. Cf. Dan. *knaske, gnaske*, to crunch; and E. *gnash*. Der. *nasti-ly*, *nasti-ness*.

NATAL, belonging to one's birth. (F. — L.) 'By *natall* Joves feest' = by the feast of Jove, who presides over nativity; Chaucer, Troilus, iii. 150. — F. *natal*, in use at least as early as the 15th cent. (Littré); though the true OF. form is *noel*. — L. *nātālis*, natal; also presiding over a birth. — L. *nātus* (for *gnātus*), born. Cf. Gk. -γνητος, in κασί-γνητος, a blood relation. From the base *gnā-*, allied to √GEN, to beget, produce; see **Kin, Genus**. Der. From L. *nātus* are *in-nate*, *cognate*; and see *nat-ion*, *nat-ive*, *nat-ure*.

NATATION, swimming. (L.) Used by Sir T. Browne, Vulgar Errors, bk. iv. c. 6. § 2. From the acc. of L. *natātio*, a swimming. — L. *natāre*, to swim; frequent. of L. *nāre*, to swim. Cf. Gk. νή-χειν, to swim; OIrish *snā-im*, I swim. See **Naiad**.

NATION, a race of people. (F. — L.) ME. *nation*, Chaucer, C. T. 4688 (B 268). — F. *nation*. — L. *nātiōnem*, acc. of *nātio*, a race; cf. *nātus*, born; see **Natal**. Der. *nation-al*, *nation-ally*, *nation-al-i-ty*, *nation-al-ise*.

NATIVE, original, produced by nature, due to birth. (F. — L.) 'O *natiue* land!' Surrey, tr. of Æneid, b. ii. l. 305; where the L. text has *patria*; see Spec. of English, ed. Skeat, p. 207. 'His *natiue* countrey;' Sir T. More, Works, p. 306 a. — F. *natif*, masc. *native*, fem. 'native;' Cot. — L. *nātiuus*, natural, native. — L. *nātus*, born; see **Natal**. Der. *native-ly*, *native-ness*; also *nativ-i-ty*, ME. *natiuitee*, Chaucer, C. T. 14022 (B 3206), from F. *nativité*, from L. acc. *nātiuitātem*. **Doublet**, *naive*.

NATRON, native carbonate of sodium. (F. — Span. — Arab. — Gk. — Heb.) F. *natron*. — Span. *natron*. — Arab. *naṭrūn, niṭrūn*, natron,

nitre; Rich. Dict., p. 1585. — Gk. νίτρον. — Heb. *nether*, nitre, Prov. xxv. 20. **Doublet**, *nitre*.

NATTER-JACK, a kind of toad. (E. *and* F. — L. — Gk. — Heb.) In Pennant (1769). 'It has a deep, hollow voice, which may be heard at a considerable distance;' Cent. Dict. Perhaps from prov. E. *natter*, *gnatter*, to make a rattling noise; see E. D. D. And see **Jack**.

NATTY, neat. (F. — L.) Formerly *nettie*; Tusser, Husbandry, § 68, l. 6. From *net*, adj.; see **Net** (2), **Neat** (2).

NATURE, kind, disposition. (F. — L.) ME. *nature*, in OEng. Miscellany, Ser. i., ed. Morris, p. 35, l. 29. — F. *nature*. — L. *nātūra*, nature. — L. *nātus*, born, pp. of *nasci*, to be born; see **Natal**. Der. *natur-al*, ME. *naturel*, OEng. Miscellany, Ser. i. p. 30, l. 17, from F. *naturel* < L. *nātūrālis*; *natur-al-ly*, *natural-ness*, *natur-al-ism*, *natur-al-ise*, *natur-al-ist* (see Trench, Select Gloss.), *natur-al-is-at-ion* (Minsheu); also *un-natural*, *preter-natural*, *super-natural*.

NAUGHT, NOUGHT, nothing. (E.) ME. *naught*, Chaucer, C. T. 758. Older spelling *nawiht*, Layamon, 473. AS. *nāwiht*, often contracted to *nāht*, Grein, ii. 274. — AS. *nā*, no, not; and *wiht*, a whit, thing; Grein, ii. 272, 703. See **No** and **Whit**. Der. *naught*, adj., i. e. worthless, As You Like It, i. 2. 68, 69, iii. 2. 15; whence *naught-y*, i. e. worthless (Prov. vi. 12), Sir T. More, Works, p. 155 e; *naught-i-ly*, *naught-i-ness*. **Doublet**, *not*.

NAUSEOUS, disgusting. (L. — Gk.) *Nauseous* and *nauseate* are in Blount's Gloss., ed. 1674. Englished from L. *nauseōsus*, that produces nausea. — L. *nausea*, *nausia*, sea-sickness, sickness. — Gk. ναυσία, sea-sickness. — Gk. ναῦς, a ship, cognate with L. *nāuis*; see **Nave** (2). Der. *nauseous-ly*, *-ness*; *nause-ate*, from L. *nauseātus*, pp. of *nauseāre*, to feel sick, from *nausea*, sickness. We have also adopted the sb. *nausea*, which occurs in Phillips, ed. 1706.

NAUTCH, a kind of ballet-dance by women. (Hind. — Prakrit — Skt.) Spelt *nāch* by Bp. Heber in 1825, who speaks of 'the *nāch*-women.' — Hind. (and Mahratti) *nāch*, a dance; Prakrit *nachcha*. — Skt. *nṛtya-*, dancing, acting; orig. fut. pass. part. of *nṛt*, to dance, act. (See Yule.) Der. *nautch-girl*, a dancing girl.

NAUTICAL, naval, belonging to ships. (L. — Gk.) Blount's Gloss., ed. 1674, has *nautical* and *nautick*, the latter being the more orig. form. — L. *nauticus*, nautical. — Gk. ναυτικός, pertaining to ships. Gk. ναύτης, a sea-man. — Gk. ναῦς, a ship, cognate with L. *nāuis*; see **Nave** (2). Der. *nautical-ly*.

NAUTILUS, a kind of shell-fish. (L. — Gk.) 'The *Nautilus* or Sailer, a shell-fish, that swims like a boat with a sail;' Phillips, ed. 1706. — L. *nautilus*. — Gk. ναυτίλος, a sea-man, also, the nautilus. — Gk. ναύτης, a sea-man; see **Nautical**.

NAVAL, belonging to ships, marine. (F. — L.) In Cotgrave. F. *naval*, 'navall;' Cot. — L. *nāuālis*, naval. — L. *nāuis*, a ship; see **Nave** (2).

NAVE (1), the central portion or hub of a wheel, through which the axle passes. (E.) ME. *naue* (with *u* = *v*), Chaucer, C. T. 7848 (D 2266). AS. *nafu*, *nafa*; Ælfred, tr. of Boethius, b. iv. pr. 6, cap. xxxix, § 7. + Du. *naaf*; Icel. *nöf*; Dan. *nav*; Swed. *naf*; G. *nabe*, OHG. *naba*. Teut. type *nabā*, fem. Allied to Skt. *nābhi-*, the navel, the nave of a wheel, the centre. See **Navel**. Der. *auger*, for *nau-ger*.

NAVE (2), the middle or body of a church. (F. — L.) In Phillips, World of Words, ed. 1706. Spelt *nef* in Addison, Travels in Italy, description of the church of St. Justina in Padua. — F. *nef*, 'a ship; also, the body of a church;' Cot. — Late L. *nāuem*, acc. of *nāuis*, the body of a church. The similitude by which the church of Christ is likened to a ship tossed by waves was formerly common. See my note to P. Plowman, C. xi. 32, where I cite the passage from Augustine about 'nauis, i.e. ecclesia;' S. Aug. Sermo lxxv. cap. iii. ed. Migne, v. 475. — L. *nāuis*, a ship. + Gk. ναῦς, a ship; Skt. *nāu-*, a ship, boat; OIrish *nau*. Brugmann, i. § 184; Prellwitz. Der. *nav-al*, q. v., *nau-ti-c-al*, q. v., *nau-ti-lus*, q. v., *argo-naut*, q. v., *nav-ig-ate* (see *navigation*), *nav-y*. From the same root are *nai-ad*, *nau-sea*.

NAVEL, the central point of the belly. (E.) A dimin. of *nave* (1). We find *nave* used for *navel*, Macb. i. 2. 22; and conversely *nauels* (= navels) for the *naves* of a wheel, Bible, ed. 1551, 3 Kings, vii. 33. ME. *nauel* (= navel), Chaucer, C. T. 1959 (A 1957). AS. *nafela*; Ælfred, tr. of Orosius, b. iv. c. 1. § 5. + Du. *navel*; Icel. *nafli*; Dan. *navle*; Swed. *nafle*; G. *nabel*. Teut. type **nabalon-*, from **nabā*, a nave. Cf. also Pers. *nāf*, navel (Horn, § 1020); Skt. *nābhi-*, navel, nave, centre. See **Nave** (1). β. Further related, with a difference of gradation, to Gk. ὀμφαλός, navel, L. *umbilicus*, OIrish *imbliu*. So also *nave* (1) is related to L. *umbō*, the boss of a shield. Brugmann, ii. § 76.

NAVEW, the wild turnip. (F. — L.) 'Rape-rotes and *Nauews*;' Sir T. Elyot, Castel of Helth, bk. ii. c. 9. — MF. *naveau*, 'the navew gentle;' Cot. — Late L. *nāpellum*, acc. of *nāpellus*; dimin. of L. *nāpus*, a kind of turnip, a navew. Cf. *tur-nip*.

NAVIGABLE, that may be travelled over by ships. (F.—L.) In Palsgrave.—F. *navigable*, 'navigable;' Cot.—L. *nāuigābilis*, navigable.—L. *nāuigāre*, to navigate; see **Navigation**. Der. *navigabl-y, navigable-ness.*

NAVIGATION, management of a ship. (F.—L.) In Shak. Macb. iv. 1. 54.—F. *navigation*, 'navigation, sailing;' Cot.—L. *nāuigātiōnem*, acc. of *nāuigātio*, a sailing.—L. *nāuigāre*, to sail, manage a ship.—L. *nāu-*, stem of *nāuis*, a ship; and *-ig-*, for *ag-*, base of *agere*, to drive. See **Nave** (2) and **Agent**. Der. *navigate*, from L. *nāuigātus*, pp. of *nāuigāre*, but suggested by the sb.; *navigator*, familiarly contracted to *navvy*, formerly applied to the labourers on canals for internal navigation, and now applied to labourers on railways! Also *circum-navigate*.

NAVY, a fleet of ships. (F.—L.) ME. *nauie*, Chaucer, Ho. of Fame, i. 216.—OF. *navie*, a fleet (Burguy); the orig. sense was a single ship.—L. *nāuia*, a ship, vessel.—L. *nāui-*, decl. stem of *nāuis*, a ship; see **Nave** (2).

NAWAB, the same as **Nabob**.

NAY, no, a form of denial. (Scand.) There was a difference in usage between *nay* and *no* formerly; the former answered simple questions, the latter was used when the form of the question involved a negative expression. Besides this, *nay* was the simple, *no* the emphatic form, often accompanied by an oath. The distinction went out of use in the time of Henry VIII; see Skeat, Eng. Lang. p. 192, l. 22, and the note; Student's Manual of the Eng. Language, ed. Smith, pp. 414, 422. Moreover, *nay* is of Scand. origin, whilst *no* is E. ME. *nay*, Chaucer, C. T., A 1667, 8693 (E 817); spelt *næi*, *nai*, Layamon, 13132.—Icel. *nei*, no, Dan. *nei*, Swed. *nej*; cognate with E. *no*; see **No**. Opposed to **Aye**.

NAZARITE, a Jew who made vows of abstinence, &c. (Heb.; with Gk. *suffix*.) 'To vowe a vowe of a *Nazarite* to separate [himself] vnto the Lorde;' Geneva Bible, 1561, Numb. vi. 5 (R.); [rather, vi. 2]. Formed with suffix *-ite* (=L. *-ita*, from Gk. *-ιτης*) from Heb. *nāzar*, to separate oneself, consecrate oneself, vow, abstain. Der. *Nazarit-ism*.

NEAP, scanty, very low; said of a tide. (E.) ME. *neep*; very rare. 'In the *neep-sesons*,' i.e. in the neap-tide seasons, when boats cannot come to the quay; Eng. Gilds, ed. Toulmin Smith, p. 425.—AS. *nēp*, in the term *nēp-flōd*, as opposed to *hēah-flōd*=high flood; Voc. 182. 38; also Voc. i. 14. The spelling *neap* indicates an open *ē*; prob. *nēp* is an OMercian form, for **nǣp*; from Teut. root **nīpan* (**neipan*), to pinch; whence Du. *nijpen*, to pinch, *neep*, a pinch, nip. Thus the sense is 'pinched,' or 'scanty.' Cf. EFries. *nēp-tange*, a pair of pincers. See Phil. Soc. Trans. 1903–6; p. 254. ¶ Quite a distinct word from *ebb*. Der. *neap-tide*.

NEAR, nigh, close at hand. (E.) By a singular grammatical confusion, this word, orig. used as the comparative of *nigh*, came to be used as a *positive*, from which the new comparative *nearer* was evolved. In Schmidt's Shakespeare Lexicon, the explanation is given wrongly; he says that *near* is put by contraction for *nearer*, whereas it is the old form of the word. Shak. uses both *near* and *nearer* as comparatives; both forms occur together, Macb. ii. 3. 146: cf. 'nor *near* nor farther off;' Rich. II, iii. 2. 64; 'being ne'er the *near*,' id. v. 1. 88. The form *near-er* is late, not found in the 14th cent., perhaps in the 15th. Dr. Morris (Outlines of E. Accidence) observes that '*near*, for *nigh*, first came into use in the phrase *far and near*, in which *near* is an adverb.' But it first appears in 'comen *ner*;' Genesis and Exod. 2611 (ab. 1250). [He goes on to cite an AS. *neorran*, not given in the dictionaries.] It is clear that the precise form was first of all adverbial; the ME. form of *nigher* was *nerre*, whilst the adv. was *ner*, or *neer*. 'Cometh *neer*'=come near; Chaucer, C. T. 841 (A 839). AS. *nēar*, comp. adverb from *nēah*, nigh; Grein, ii. 283.+Icel. *nær*, adv.; both pos. and comp.; orig. the latter. See **Nigh**. Der. *near-ly*, Macb. iv. 2. 67; *near-ness*, Rich. II, i. 1. 119; *near-sight-ed*.

NEAT (1), black cattle, an ox, cow. (E.) ME. *neet*, both sing. and pl.; used as pl. in Chaucer, C. T. 599 (A 597). AS. *nēat*, neut. sb., unchanged in the plural (like *sheep*, *deer*, also neuters); Grein, ii. 288.+Icel. *naut*, neut. sb., unchanged in the plural, and gen. used to mean cattle, oxen; Swed. *nöt*; Dan. *nöd*; MHG. *nōz*, neut. sb., cattle. Teut. type **nautom*, n. β. So named from their usefulness and employment. From **naut*, 2nd grade of Teut. **neut-an-*, to employ, as seen in AS. *nēotan*, *nīotan*, to use, employ; Grein, ii. 292; Icel. *njóta*, to use, enjoy; MHG. *niezen*, OHG. *niozan*, G. *geniessen*, to enjoy, have the use of; Goth. *niutan*, to receive joy (or benefit) from. From Idg. √NEUD; whence Lithuan. *naudà*, usefulness, *naudingas*, useful (Nesselman). Brugmann, i. § 221. Der. *neatherd*.

NEAT (2), tidy, unadulterated. (F.—L.) '*Neat* and fine;' Two Gent. of Verona, i. 2. 10. Also spelt *nett*; Spenser, F. Q. iii. 12. 20. 'To kepe it cleen and *nette*;' Caxton, Godfrey of Boloyne, ch. 6.

—F. *net*, masc., *nette*, fem., 'neat, clean, pure;' Cot. [Cf. *beast* from OF. *beste*.]—L. *nitidum*, acc. of *nitidus*, shining, clear, handsome, neat, elegant.—L. *nitēre*, to shine. Der. *neat-ly*, *neat-ness*. **Doublet**, *net* (2).

NEB, the beak of a bird, the nose. (E.) In Winter's Tale, i. 2. 183. ME. *neb*. '*Ostende mihi faciam*, scheau thi *neb* to me'=shew me thy face; Ancren Riwle, p. 90. AS. *nebb*, the face, John, xi. 44.+Du. *neb*, bill, beak, nib, mouth; Icel. *nef*, the nose; Dan. *næb*, beak, bill; Swed. *näbb*, beak, bill. β. The word has lost an initial *s*; we also find Du. *sneb*, a bill, beak, *snavel*, a bill; G. *schnabel*, a bill, beak, nib. The MHG. *snabel*, a bill, is derived from MHG. *snaben*, to snap. And cf. Lith. *snapas*, a bill. **Doublet**, *nib*.

NEBULA, a misty patch of light; a cluster of very faintly shining stars. (L.) Modern and scientific.—L. *nebula*, a mist.+Gk. νεφέλη, a cloud; dimin. of νέφος, cloud, mist.+G. *nebel*, mist, fog; Du. *nevel*, Icel. *nifl*. β. The Gk. νέφος is cognate with W. *nef*, OIrish *nem*, heaven, Russ. *nebo*, heaven; Skt. *nabhas*, sky, atmosphere, æther. Brugmann, i. § 554. Der. *nebul-ar*, *nebul-ose*, *nebul-ous*, *nebul-os-i-ty*.

NECESSARY, needful, requisite. (F.—L.) ME. *necessarie*, Chaucer, C. T. 12615 (C 681).—OF. *necessaire*, 'necessary;' Cot. —L. *necessārius*, needful.—L. *necesse*, neut. adj., unavoidable, necessary. β. The usual derivation from *ne*, not, and *cēdere*, to give way, is not satisfactory. Der. *necessari-ly*, also *necessity*, ME. *necessitee*, Chaucer, C. T. 3044 (A 3042), from OF. *necessite* < L. acc. *necessitātem*; hence *necessit-oys*, *-ly*, *-ness*, *necessit-ate*, *necessit-ar-ian*.

NECK, the part of the body joining the head to the trunk. (E.) ME. *nekke* (dissyllabic), Chaucer, C. T. 5859 (D 277). AS. *hnecca*, Deut. xxviii. 35.+Du. *nek*, the nape of the neck; G. *genick*, MHG. *genicke*. Teut. type **hnakjon-*. Cf. Icel. *hnakki*, the nape of the neck, back of the head; Dan. *nakke*, the same; Swed. *nacke*, the same; G. *nacken*, nape, neck, crag; from Teut. type **hnakkon-*. Cf. Norw. *nakk*, a knoll, *nakke*, nape, neck; the orig. sense being 'projection,' as in the parallel form *nape*. Further allied to Irish *cnoc*, a hill, *cnoc*, a hill. Der. *neck-cloth*, *neck-kerchief* (for *neck-kerchief*, see **Kerchief**), *neck-band*, *neck-tie*; *neck-lace*, Winter's Tale, iv. 4. 244, compounded of *neck* and *lace*; *neck-verse*, Tyndall's Works, p. 112, col. 1, on which see my note to P. Plowman, C. xv. 129.

NECROLOGY, a register of deaths. (Gk.) Added by Todd to Johnson. From Gk. νεκρό-, stem of νεκρός, a corpse; and *-λογία*, due to λόγος, discourse, from λέγειν, to speak. See **Necromancy**.

NECROMANCY, divination by communion with the dead. (F.—L.—Gk.) The history of the word is somewhat concealed by our modern knowledge of Gk., which enables us to spell the word correctly. But the ME. forms are *nigromaunce*, *nigromancie*, and the like. Precisely the same 'correction' of the spelling has been made in modern French. Spelt *nygremauncye* in King Alisaunder, l. 138'; *nigromancye* in P. Plowman, A. xi. 158, on which see my Notes to P. Pl., p. 246. Trench rightly remarks, in his Eng. Past and Present, that 'the Latin mediæval writers, whose Greek was either little or none, spelt the word *nigromantia*, as if its first syllables had been Latin.'—OF. *nigromance*, 'nigromancy, conjuring, the black art;' Cot. Spelt *nigromancie* in the Vie de S. Aubar, l. 997.—Late L. *nigromantia*, corrupt form of *necromantīa*.—Gk. νεκρομαντεία, necromancy.—Gk. νεκρό-, for νεκρός, a corpse; and μαντεία, prophetic power, power of divination. β. The Gk. νεκρός is allied to νέκυς, a corpse, dead body.—√NEK, to perish, to kill; whence Skt. *naç*, to perish, *nāçaya*, to destroy, L. *necāre*, to kill, and E. *inter-nec-ine*, q. v. γ. The Gk. μαντεία is from μάντις, a prophet, seer, inspired one; cf. Gk. μαίνομαι, I rage; see **Mania**. Der. *necromanc-er*, Deut. xviii. 11 (A. V.); *necromantic*, from Gk. νεκρο-, and μαντικός, prophetic; *necromantic-al*. ☞ From the singular confusion with L. *niger*, black, above mentioned, the art of *necromancy* came to be called *the black art!*

NECTAR, a delicious beverage. (L.—Gk.) In Spenser, Sonnet 39, l. 13.—L. *nectar*.—Gk. νέκταρ, the drink of the gods; Homer, Il. xix. 38, Od. v. 93. Perhaps 'overcoming death;' cf. Gk. νέκ-υς, a corpse, and Skt. *tar-a-*, overcoming. Der. *nectar-e-an*, *nectar-e-ous*, *nectar-ous*, *nectar-y*; also *nectar-ine*, the name given to a variety of the peach, orig. an adj., as in 'Nectarine fruits,' Milton, P. L. iv. 332.

NEED, necessity, distress. (E.) ME. *need*, *nede*, Chaucer, C. T. 4523 (B 103). OMerc. *nēd*; AS. *nȳd*, *nīed* (*nēad*); Grein, ii. 301.+Du. *nood*; Icel. *nauð*; Dan. and Swed. *nöd*; Goth. *nauths*; G. *noth*, OHG. *nōt*. β. The Teut. stem is **naudi-* (>**naudi-*); answering to Idg. stem **nau-ti-*: as in OPruss. *nautin*, need. (But *nēad* represents Teut. **naudā*.) Brugmann, i. § 427 b. ¶ Confused in late AS. texts with *nēod*, *nīed*, *nyd*, desire; which is related to OSax. *niud*, OHG. *niot*, earnestness; from the Teut. base **neud-*. Der. *need-ful*, ME. *neodful*, Ancren Riwle, p. 260, l. 10; *need-less*, *need-less-ly*, *need-less-ness*; *need-y*, ME. *nedy*, P. Plowman, B. xx. 40, 41; 47, 48; *need-i-ly*, *need-i-ness*. Also *need-s*, adv., ME. *needes*, *nedes*,

Chaucer, C. T. 1171 (A 1169), where the final *-es* is an adverbial ending, orig. due to AS. gen. cases in *-es*; but in this case *nedes* supplanted an older form *nede*, Layamon, l. 1051, which originated in AS. *nȳde*, gen. case of *nȳd*, which was a fem. sb. with gen. in *-e*.

NEEDLE, a sharp pointed steel implement, for sewing with. (E.) ME. *nedle, nedel*, also spelt *nelde, neelde*; P. Plowman, C. xx. 56, and various readings. AS. *nǣdl*, Grein, ii. 274; earlier forms *nǣðl, nēþl* (OE. Texts).+Du. *naald* (for *naadl*); Icel. *nāl* (for contraction); Dan. *naal*; Swed. *nål*; G. *nadel*, OHG. *nādela*; Goth. *nēthla*. β. The Teut. type is **nǣ-thlā*, from a base *nǣ* = Idg. √NĒ, to sew, fasten with thread, preserved in OHG. *nāhen*, G. *nähen*, to sew, and also in L. *nēre*, Gk. *νήθειν, νέειν*, to spin. The suffix denotes the agent. γ. This is clearly one of the rather numerous cases in which an initial *s* has dropped off; the orig. root is √SNĒ; as in Irish *snathad*, a needle, *snathaim*, I thread, or string together, *snaidhe*, thread, Gael. *snathad*, a needle, *snath*, thread, yarn; OIrish *snim*, a spinning. Stokes-Fick, p. 315; Brugmann, i. § 136. Der. *needle-book, -ful, -gun, -woman, -work*.

NEESE, NEEZE, to breathe hard, sneeze. (Scand.) 'To *neeze*' = to sneeze, Mids. Nt. Dr. ii. 1. 56. The sb. *neesing* is in Job, xli. 18 (A.V.). ME. *nesen*, vb., *nesing*, sb.; see Prompt. Parv., and Way's note. Not found in AS. – OIcel. *hnjōsa*; Dan. *nyse*; Swed. *nysa*.+Du. *niezen*, G. *niesen*, OHG. *niusan*. Teut. type **hneusan-*. Like the parallel form *sneeze*, it is of imitative origin; cf. Skt. *kshu*, to sneeze. ¶ In the later version of Wyclif, Job, xli. 9, the reading is *fnesynge*; this is not quite the same word, though of similar formation. The sense of *fnesynge* is 'violent blowing,' but it also means sneezing; cf. AS. *fnēosung*, sneezing, *fnæst*, a puff, Du. *fniezen*, to sneeze. Cf. 'And *fneseth* faste' = and puffs hard, Chaucer, C. T., H 62. Teut. type **fneusan-*. It reminds us of Gk. *πνέειν*, to blow. Der. *nees-ing*, *neez-ing*, as above.

NEFARIOUS, unlawful, very wicked. (L.) In Butler, To the Memory of Du-Val, l. 20. Englished from L. *nefārius*, impious, very wicked; by change of *-us* to *-ous*, as in *arduous*, &c. – L. *nefās*, that which is contrary to divine law, impiety, great wickedness. – L. *ne-*, for *nē*, not; and *fās*, divine law, orig. that which is divinely uttered; cf. *fārī*, to speak; see **Fate**. Der. *nefarious-ly, -ness*.

NEGATION, denial. (F. – L.) In Shak. Troilus, v. 2. 127. – F. *negation*, 'a negation;' Cot. – L. acc. *negātiōnem*, from nom. *negātio*; cf. *negātus*, pp. of *negāre*, to deny. β. *Negāre* is opposed to *āiere*, to affirm; but is unconnected with it. Brugmann, ii. § 774, explains *neg-āre* by comparing Lith. *ne-gi*, not at all; cf. L. *neg-ōtium*. Der. *negat-ive*, adj., Wint. Tale, i. 2. 274, ME. *negatif*, *negative*, Usk, Test. of Love, bk. iii. ch. 2. 92, from F. *negatif* < L. *negātīuus*; *negative-ly, negative-ness*; also *negative*, sb., Twelfth Nt. v. 24. From the same L. *negāre* we have *de-ny, ab-negate, re-negate, re-negade*.

NEGLECT, to disregard. (L.) Orig. a pp. 'Because it should not be *neglect* or left undone;' Tyndall, Works, p. 276, col. 2. 'To *neglecte* and set at nought;' Sir T. More, Works, p. 257 g. – L. *neglectus*, pp. of *negligere*, to neglect. *Negligere* = *neg-legere*. – L. *neg-*, a particle of negation, and *legere*, to gather, collect, select. See **Negation** and **Legend**. Der. *neglect-ful, neglect-ful-ly, neglect-ful-ness*; *neglect-ion*, a coined word, 1 Hen. VI, iv. 3. 49; and see *negligence*.

NEGLIGENCE, disregard. (F. – L.) ME. *negligence*, Chaucer, C. T. 1883 (A 1881). – F. *negligence*, 'negligence;' Cot. – L. *negligentia*, carelessness. – L. *negligent-*, stem of pres. part. of *negligere*, to neglect; see **Neglect**. Der. *negligent*, ME. *negligent*, Chaucer, C. T. 7398 (D 1816), from F. *negligent* (Cot.) < L. *negligentem*, acc. of pres. part. of *negligere*; *negligent-ly*; also *negligee*, from F. *negligé*, pp. of *negliger*, to neglect < L. *negligere*.

NEGOTIATE, to do business, transact. (L.) In Minsheu, ed. 1627. 'She was a busy *negociating* woman;' Bacon, Life of Hen. VII, ed. Lumby, p. 24, l. 14. – L. *negōtiātus*, pp. of *negōtiārī*, to transact business. – L. *negōtium*, business. Compounded of L. *neg-*, negative particle (see **Negation**); and *ōtium*, leisure. Der. *negotiat-or*, from L. *negōtiātor*; *negotiat-ion*, from F. *negociation*, 'negociation,' Cot., from L. acc. *negōtiātiōnem*; *negotia-ble*; *negotiat-or-y*. ☞ The right (historical) spelling is *negotiate* for the verb, *negociation* for the sb.; but this is not regarded.

NEGRO, one of the black race of mankind. (Span. – L.) In Shak. Merch. Ven. iii. 5. 42. 'Black as *negros*;' Hakluyt, Voy. iii. 649. – Span. *negro*, a black man. – L. *nigrum*, acc. of *niger*, black; see **Nigrescent**. ¶ Minsheu gives the form *neger*; this is from the OF. *negre* (mod. F. *nègre*), 'a negro' (Cot.), and answers to mod. E. *nigger*, q.v.

NEGUS (1), a beverage of wine, water, sugar, &c. (E.) 'The mixture now called *negus* was invented in Queen Anne's time by Colonel *Negus*;' Malone, Life of Dryden, p. 484 (Todd's Johnson). Col. Francis Negus died in 1732; N.E.D. The Neguses are a

Norfolk family; see Notes and Queries, 1 Ser. x. 10, 2 Ser. v. 224; Gent. Maga. Feb. 1799, p. 119.

NEGUS (2), a title of the kings of Abyssinia (Abyssinian). 'Th' empire of *Negus*;' Milton, P. L. xi. 397. '*Neguz* [which signifieth] a king;' John Pory, tr. Lee's Hist. Africa, Introd. p. 21 (Stanford Dict.).

NEIF, NEAF, the fist. (Scand.) In Shak. Mids. Nt. Dr. iv. 1. 20; 2 Hen. IV, ii. 4. 200. ME. *neue* (= *neve*, dat. case), Havelok, 2405. – Icel. *hnefi*, the fist; Swed. *näfve*; Dan. *næve*.

NEIGH, to make a noise as a horse. (E.) ME. *neȝen*, Wyclif, Isa. xxiv. 14, earlier version. AS. *hnǣgan*, to neigh; Ælfric's Grammar, p. 192, l. 8; whence the sb. *hnǣgung*, a neighing, id. p. 4, l. 15 (Zupitza).+Low G. *neigen* (Lübben); MDu. *neyen*, to neigh. Cf. Icel. *gneggja, hneggja*; Swed. *gnägga*; Dan. *gnegge*. An imitative word.

NEIGHBOUR, one who dwells near. (E.) ME. *neighebour*, Chaucer, C. T. 9423 (E 1549). AS. *nēahgebūr*, a neighbour, John, ix. 8; so that the trisyllabic form *neigh-e-bour* in Chaucer is easily explained. The AS. form *nēahbūr* also occurs, but more rarely. – AS. *nēah*, nigh; and *gebūr*, a husbandman, for which see the Laws of Ine, sect. vi, in Thorpe's Ancient Laws, i. 106. The AS. *gebūr* or *būr* is cognate with Du. *boer*, a boor (the prefix *ge-* making no difference).+MHG. *nāchgebūr, nāchbūr*; mod. G. *nachbar*. See **Nigh** and **Boor**. Der. *neighbour*, adj., Jerem. xlix. 18, l. 40 (A.V.); *neighbour-hood*, ME. *neyghbourhede*, Prompt. Parv.; *neighbour-ing*, All's Well, iv. 1. 18; *neighbour-ly*, Merch. Ven. i. 2. 85; *neighbour-li-ness*.

NEITHER, not either. (E.) ME. *neither*, Havelok, 458. [Distinct from *noither, nouther, nother* (whence the contracted form *nor*); earlier *nowther* (Ormulum, 3124), *nawther, nauther*; see examples in Stratmann.] Formed by prefixing *ne*, not, to ME. *either* = AS. *ǣgðer* = *ǣghwæðer*, for *ā + ge + hwæðer*; where *ā* means 'ever.' Thus *neither* = *no-whether*; see **No** and **Whether**. With AS. *ne*, not, compare OSax. *ne, ni*; Goth. and OHG. *ni*, not.

NEMESIS, retributive justice. (L. – Gk.) In Shak. 1 Hen. VI, iv. 7. 78. – L. *Nemesis*. – Gk. *νέμεσις*, distribution of what is due, retribution. – Gk. *νέμειν*, to distribute; see **Nomad**.

NEMORAL, belonging to a grove. (L.) Phillips (1658) has '*nemoral* or *nemorous*.' – L. *nemorālis* or *nemorōsus*, woody. – L. *nemor-*, for **nemos*, in *nemus*, a grove.+Gk. *νέμος*, a pasture; from *νέμειν*, to distribute, to pasture; from √NEM. See **Nomad**.

NENUPHAR, a kind of water-lily. (F. – Pers. – Skt.) '*Nenuphar*, water-lillie;' Baret (1580); and see the Stanford Dict. – MF. *nenuphar*, 'nenuphar, the water-lilly, or water-rose;' Cot. – Pers. *nīnūfar*, for *nīlūfar, nīlūpar, nīlūpal*, a water-lily (Devic). – Skt. *nīlōtpala*, a blue lotus. – Skt. *nīla-*, blue; *utpala-*, a lotus, lit. 'bursting out,' from *ud*, out, and *paṭ*, to burst.

NEOLOGY, the introduction of new phrases. (Gk.) Modern. Compounded from Gk. *νέο-*, for *νέος*, new; and *-λογία*, from *λόγος*, discourse, which is from *λέγειν*, to speak. See **New** and **Logic**. Der. *neologi-c, neologi-c-al, neolog-ise, neolog-ism, neolog-ist*.

NEOPHYTE, a new convert, a novice. (L. – Gk.) 'There stands a *neophite* glazing of his face;' Ben Jonson, Cynthia's Revels, iii. 2 (Crites). – L. *neophytus*. – Gk. *νεόφυτος*, lit. newly planted, hence, a novice; 1 Tim. iii. 6. – Gk. *νέο-*, for *νέος*, new; and *φυτόν*, a plant, *φυτός*, grown, from the vb. *φύειν*, (1) to cause to grow, (2) to grow, allied to E. *be*. See **New** and **Be**.

NEOTERIC, recent, novel. (L. – Gk.) Spelt *neoterique* in Minsheu, ed. 1627; but not given in Cotgrave or Littré. – L. *neōtericus*. – Gk. *νεωτερικός*, novel; expanded from *νεώτερος*, comp. of *νέος*, new, which is cognate with E. *new*. See **New**. Der. *neoteric-al*.

NEPENTHE, NEPENTHES, a drug which lulled sorrow. (Gk.) Spelt *nepenthe* in Spenser, F. Q. iv. 3. 43; better *nepenthes*, as in Holland, tr. of Pliny, b. xxi. c. 21. – Gk. *νηπενθές*, an epithet of a soothing drug in Homer, Od. iv. 221; neut. of *νηπενθής*, free from sorrow. – Gk. *νη-*, negative prefix allied to E. *no*; and *πένθος*, grief, allied to *πάθος*, suffering. See **No** and **Pathos**.

NEPHEW, a brother's or sister's son. (F. – L.) An older meaning is 'grandson,' as in 1 Tim. v. 4, &c. The *ph* is a substitute for the older *v*, often written *u*. ME. *neuew* (= *nevew*), Chaucer, Legend of Good Women, l. 2659; *neueu* (= *neveu*), Rob. of Glouc. p. 169; l. 3529. – OF. *neveu*, 'a nephew;' Cot. – L. *nepōtem*, acc. of *nepōs*, a grandson, a nephew.+Pers. *nawāda*, a grandson; Skt. *napāt*, a grandson.+AS. *nefa*, a nephew; Ælfred, tr. of Beda, b. iii. c. 6 (near the end). [This AS. word was supplanted by the F. form;] OHG. *nefo, nevo*, G. *neffe*; Du. *neef*. Idg. type **nepōt-*; whence orig. Teut. type **nefōd-*, later **nefon-*. The fem. type is Idg. **neptī-*, whence Skt. *naptī*, L. *neptis*; Teut. type **neftī* > **niftī*, as in AS. *nift*, Du. *nicht*. Brugmann, i. § 149. Der. *nepot-ism*, i.e. favouritism to relations, from L. stem *nepōt-*, with suffix *-ism*. See *niece*.

NEREID, a sea-nymph. (L. – Gk.) Minsheu has the pl. form

Nereides. — L. *Nēreid-*, stem of *Nēreis* (pl. *Nēreides*), a sea-nymph, a daughter of Nereus. — Gk. Νηρείς, a sea-nymph, a daughter of Nereus. — Gk. Νηρεύς, an ancient sea-god. — Gk. νηρός, wet; an allied word to ναίς, ναιάς, a naiad; see **Naiad.**

NERVE, physical strength, firmness, a fibre in the body conveying sensation. (F. — L.) ME. *nerfe,* Chaucer, Troilus, b. ii. l. 642. — F. *nerf,* 'a sinew, might;' Cot. — L. *neruum,* acc. of *neruus,* a sinew. Prob. allied to Gk. νεῦρον, a sinew, string; cf. Gk. νευρά, a string; Skt. *snāva-,* a tendon. Der. *nerve,* verb, not in early use; *nerv-ous,* formerly used in the sense of 'sinewy' (Phillips), from F. *nerveux,* 'sinewy' (Cot.), which from L. *neruōsus,* full of nerve; *nervous-ly, nervous-ness*; also *nerv-y,* i. e. sinewy (obsolete), in Shak. Cor. ii. 1. 177; *nerve-less*; cf. *neur-algia.*

NESCIENT, ignorant. (L.) Coles (1684) has *nescient* and *nescience.* — L. *nescient-,* stem of *nesciens,* pres. part. of *nescire,* not to know. — L. *ne-,* not; *scire,* to know. See **Nice** and **Science.**

NESH, tender, soft. (E.) Still in use in prov. E. ME. *nesh;* 'tendre *nesh*;' Court of Love, l. 1092 (16th cent.); 'That tendre was, and swithe [very] *nesh*;' Havelok, 2743. AS. *hnæsce, hnesce,* soft; Grein, ii. 91. — Goth. *hnaskwus,* soft, tender, delicate, Matt. xi. 8.

NESS, a promontory. (E.) Preserved in place-names, as *Tot-ness, Sheer-ness.* AS. *næss, ness,* (1) the ground, (2) a promontory, headland, as in Beowulf, ed. Grein, l. 1360; the form *næssa* also occurs, Grein, ii. 277. + Icel. *nes*; Dan. *næs*; Swed. *näs.* β. The sense of 'promontory' suggests association with AS. *nasu,* nose, and E. *nose.*

NEST, the bed formed by a bird for her young. (E.) ME. *nest,* P. Plowman, B. xi. 336. AS. *nest,* a nest; Grein, ii. 282. + Du. *nest*; G. *nest.* + Gael. and Irish *nead*; OIrish *net*; W. *nyth*; L. *nīdus* (for *niz-dus*); Lithuan. *lizdas* (for *nizdas*), Nesselmann; Skt. *niḍa-,* a nest, a den. β. Now usually explained as representing a form *nizdos = ni-sd-os,* 'a place to sit down in;' from *ni,* down, and the weak grade of the root SED, to sit. Cf. Skt. *ni-sad,* to sit down. See **Sit.** Brugmann, i. § 81. Der. *nest,* vb.; *nest-le,* AS. *nestlian,* to make a nest, a frequentative form, orig. 'to frequent a nest;' *nest-ling,* with double dimin. suffix (= -*l-ing*), as in *gos-ling, duck-ling.*

NET (1), an implement made of knitted or knotted twine for catching fish, &c. (E.) ME. *net, nett,* Wyclif, John, xxi. 6. AS. *net, nett,* Grein, ii. 282. + Du. *net*; Icel. and Dan. *net*; Swed. *nät*; Goth. *nati*; G. *netz.* Teut. type *natjom,* n. Cf. L. *nassa,* a wicker creel; Icel. *nōt,* a net. ¶ Not connected with *knit,* which has initial *k.* Der. *net,* verb, (1) to use a net, (2) to make a net; *nett-ing, net-work.*

NET (2), clear of all charges. (F. — L.) Merely a doublet of *neat*; see **Neat** (2). Caxton has: 'the ayer [air] was pure and *net*;' Troy-book, leaf 95, back, l. 23.

NETHER, lower. (E.) ME. *nethere*; 'the overe lippe and the *nethere*' = the upper lip and the lower one, Wright's Vocab. i. 146, l. 14. AS. *neoðera, neoðra,* Ps. lxxxvii. 6, ed. Spelman. A comparative adj. due to the compar. adv. *niðer, nioðor,* downward; Grein, ii. 294. Related forms are *niðe,* adv. below, *neoðan,* adv. below, Grein, ii. 294, 290; but these are really forms suggested by *niðer,* and not original ones. β. The word is to be divided as *ne-ther,* the suffix *-ther* being comparative, as in *o-ther,* and answering to the *-ter* in *af-ter,* and the Skt. *-tara-* (Gk. *-τερος*). + Icel. *neðri,* nether, lower; *neðarr,* adv. lower; cf. *neðan,* from below; Dan. *neder-,* in comp. *nederdel,* the lower part of a thing; cf. *neden,* adv. below, *nede, ned,* down; Swed. *nedre,* nether, as in *nedre läppen,* the nether lip; cf. *nedre,* below, *nedre, ned,* down; Du. *neder*; G. *nieder,* nether, lower. γ. As said above, the base is *ni-*; cf. Skt. *ni-tarām,* adv., excessively; a comp. form from *ni,* downward, into. Cf. also Russ. *nije,* lower. Der. *nethermost,* 1 Kings, vi. 6; a false form, due to a popular etymology which connected the ending with *most*; but really a corruption of AS. *niðemesta,* in Ælfred, tr. of Boethius, b. ii. pr. 2 (cap. vii. § 3); and AS. *ni-ðe-m-est-* is from *ni,* down, with the Idg. suffixes *-te-mo-* (as in L. *op-ti-mus,* best) and the usual AS. superl. suffix *-est.* Cf. *be-neath.*

NETTLE, a well-known stinging plant. (E.) ME. *netle, nettle* (better with one *t*); '*Netle* in, dokke out;' Chaucer, Troil. iv. 461. AS. *netele, netle*; Cockayne, A. S. Leechdoms, iii. 340. + Du. *netel*; Dan. *nelde* (MDan. *nædle*); Swed. *nässla* (MSwed. *nätla*); G. *nessel*; OHG. *nezzila, nezila.* β. A dimin. form; Teut. type *nat-il-ōn-,* f.; the simple form appears in Swed. dial. *näta,* OHG. *nazza* a nettle. Cf. OIrish *nenaid,* nettles. Der. *nettle-rash*; *nettle,* vb., Phillips, ed. 1706.

NEURALGIA, pain in the nerves. (Gk.) Modern; not in Todd's Johnson. Coined from Gk. νευρ-, stem of νεῦρον, a nerve; and Gk. ἀλγ-, stem of ἄλγος, pain; with Gk. suffix *-ia* (-ια). Perhaps the Gk. νεῦρον is allied to L. *neruus*; see **Nerve.** Der. *neuralg-ic-i.*

NEUTER, neither, sexless, taking neither part. (L.) 'The duke . . . abode as *neuter* and helde with none of both parties;'

Berners, tr. of Froissart, vol. i. c. 252 (R). — L. *neuter,* neither. Compounded of *ne,* not; and *uter,* whether of the two; which some connect with **Whether.** Der. *neutr-al,* Macb. ii. 3. 115, from L. *neutrālis*; *neutr-al-ly, neutral-ise, neutral-is-at-ion*; *neutral-i-ty* = F. *neutralité* (Cotgrave), from L. acc. *neutrālitātem.*

NEVER, not ever, at no time. (E.) ME. *neuer* (with *u* for *v*), Chaucer, C. T. 1135 (A 1133). AS. *næfre*; compounded of *ne,* not, and *æfre,* ever; Grein, ii. 275. See **Ever.** Der. *never-the-less,* ME. *neuerþeles,* Rob. of Brunne, tr. of Langtoft, p. 16, l. 9, substituted for the earlier form *napeles* = AS. *nā þi læs* (= no-the-less, not the less). In this phrase, the AS. *þi,* also written *þȳ,* is the instrumental case of the def. article *se,* and is cognate with Goth. *thē,* on that account, instrum. case of *sa*; for examples, see *læs* in Grein, ii. 164. See **The** (2).

NEW, recent, fresh. (E.) ME. *newe* (dissyllabic), Chaucer, C. T. 459, 8733 (A 457, E 857). AS. *nīwe, nēowe, nīowe,* Grein, ii. 298. + Du. *nieuw*; Icel. *nȳr*; Dan. and Swed. *ny*; Goth. *niujis*; G. *neu,* OHG. *niuwi*; L. *nouus*; W. *newydd*; Irish *nua, nuadh,* Gael. *nuadh*; Lithuan. *naujas*; of which an older form was perhaps *nawas* (Nesselmann); Russ. *novuii*; Gk. νέος; Skt. *nava-,* new. Idg. types *newos, newios*; Brugmann, i. §§ 120, 318; ii. § 63. Allied to Skt. *nu, nū,* now; see **Now.** Thus *new* means 'that which is now,' recent. Der. *new-ly*; = AS. *nīwlīce,* Grein, ii. 299; *new-ness,* spelt *newenesse* in Sir T. More, Works, p. 1328 g; *new-ish, new-fashioned*; and see *new-fangled, news, re-new*; also *nov-el, nov-ice.*

NEWEL, the upright column about which a circular staircase winds. (F. — L.) 'The staires, . . . let them bee upon a faire open *newell,* and finely raild in;' Bacon, Essay 45, Of Building. Cotgrave, s. v. *noyau,* spells it *nuell,* which is an older and better spelling. The right sense is much the same as that of *nucleus,* with which word it is connected. The form seems to show that the word was borrowed early. — OF. *nuel, noiel* (Godefroy); later F. *noyau,* 'the stone of a plumme, also, the *nuell* or spindle of a winding staire;' Cot. So called because it is the centre or nucleus of the staircase, round which the steps are ranged. — L. *nucāle,* neut. of *nucālis,* lit. belonging to a nut; hence applied to the kernel of a nut or the stone of a plum. — L. *nuc-,* stem of *nux,* a nut; with suffix *-ālis.* See **Nucleus.** Cf. F. *nueil,* a nut (dial. of La Meuse).

NEWFANGLED, fond of what is new, novel. (E.) The old sense is 'fond of what is new;' see Shak. L. L. L. i. 1. 106, As You Like It, iv. 1. 152; and in Palsgrave. The final *-d* is a late addition to the word, due to a loss of a sense of the old force of *-le* (see below); the ME. form is *newefangel* (4 syllables), fond of novelty, Chaucer, C. T. 10932 (F 618). So also Gower, C. A. ii. 273; l. 4366: 'Bot euery newe loue quemeth To him, that *newefongel* is' = but every new love pleases him who is fond of what is new. β. Compounded of *newe,* new; and *fangel,* ready to seize, snatching at, formed from the base *fang-,* to take (occurring in AS. *fang-en,* pp. of *fōn,* to take), with the suffix *-el* (= AS. *-ol*) used to form adjectives descriptive of an agent. γ. This suffix is preserved in mod. E. *witt-ol* = one who knows, sarcastically used to mean an idiot; cf. AS. *sprec-ol,* fond of talking, talkative; *wac-ol,* vigilant; and see **Nimble.** So also *fangel* = fond of taking, readily adopting, and *new-fangle* = fond of taking up what is new; whence *new-fangle-d,* by later addition of *d.* See **Fang.** Der. *newfangled-ness,* for ME. *newefangelnesse,* Chaucer, C. T. 10924 (F 610); formed by adding *-nes* (-ness) to ME. *newe-fangel.*

NEWS, what is new, tidings. (E.) Formerly *newes,* which does not seem to be older than about A. D. 1400. 'Desyrous to here *newes*;' Berners, tr. of Froissart, vol. i. c. 66. 'What *newes* he brought;' Surrey, tr. of Virgil, Æn. ii. l. 95. 'I bring the *newis* glad;' James I, The Kingis Quair, st. 179. It is nothing but a plural, formed from *new* treated as a sb.; so also *tidings.* It is a translation of F. *nouvelles,* news, pl. of *nouvelle,* new (Cotgrave); so also L. *noua* = new things, i.e. news. In Wyclif, Ecclus. xxiv. 35, *in diebus novorum* is translated by 'in the dayes of *newes*;' later version, 'of *newe thingis.*' See **New.** Notes on E. Etym., p. 196. Der. *news-boy, -monger,* 1 Hen. IV, iii. 2. 25, *-paper, -room, -vendor.*

NEWT, a kind of lizard. (E.) This is one of the words which has taken to itself an initial *n,* borrowed from the indef. art. *an*; see remarks on the letter **N.** A *newt* = an *ewt.* ME. *newte, ewte.* '*Newte,* or ewte, wyrme, *lacertus*;' Prompt. Parv. p. 355. *Ewte* is a contraction of the older form *euete* (= *evete*). The OF. *lesard,* a lizard, is glossed by *evete* (the MS. prob. has *euete*), in Walter de Biblesworth; see Wright's Vocab. i. 159. AS. *efeta*; 'Lacerta, *efeta,*' in a gloss; Wright's Voc. i. 78, col. 2. ¶ The mod. prov. E. *eft* is a contraction of AS. *efeta.* For further references, see King Alisaunder, l. 6126, Mandeville's Travels, p. 61, &c.; see Stratmann.

NEXT, nighest, nearest. (E.) *Next* is a doublet of *nighest,* of which it is an older spelling. 'When þe bale is *hest,* þenne is þe bote *nest'* = when the sorrow is highest, then is the remedy nighest; Proverbs of Hendyng, st. 23. This is often cited in the form: 'When bale is *hext*, then bote is *next*;' and just as *hext* or *hest* is a contraction of ME. *hehest* (highest), so is *next* or *nest* a contraction of ME. *nehest* (nighest). See Stratmann, s.v. *neh*. The AS. forms are *nēahst*, *nēhst*, *nȳhst*, *nīhst*, *nīehst*; Grein, ii. 283. See **Nigh.**

NIAS, a young hawk; also, a ninny. (F.—L.) See Nares' Glossary. The correct form of **Eyas,** q. v.

NIB, the point of a pen. (E.) Another form of *neb*, which is the older spelling. The spelling *nib* is in Johnson's Dict., but is not older than 1585. See **Neb.** Cf. EFries. *nibbe*, *nib*, Low G. *nibbe*, a neb; Norw. *nibba*, a sharp point. Der. *nipp-le*, q. v.

NIBBLE, to eat in small portions. (E.) In Shak. Temp. iv. 1. 62. Not connected with *nib*, or *neb*, but with *nip*, of which it is the frequentative form, and means 'to nip often.' In fact, it has lost an initial *k*, and stands for *knibble*, just as *nip* does for *knip*. G. Douglas has *knyp*, with the sense of 'nibbled;' tr. of Virgil, prol. to bk. xii. l. 94. + Low G. *nibbeln*, *knibbeln*, to nibble, gnaw slightly; Bremen Wört.; Westphalian *nibbeln*, *nippeln*, to nibble. Cf. also Du. *knibbelen*, to cavil, haggle; the same word, differently employed. See **Nip.** Cf. Du. *knabbelen*, to nibble, allied to E. *knap*. Cotgrave has: '*Brouter*, to knap or nible off.' Der. *nibbl-er*.

NICE, hard to please, fastidious, dainty, delicious. (F.—L.) ME. *nice*, foolish, simple; later, it took the sense of fastidious; and lastly, that of delicious. In Chaucer, C. T. 5508, 6520 (B 1088, D 938); in the latter passage 'wise and nothing *nice*' = wise and not simple at all. So also in P. Plowman, B. xvi. 33. 'For he was *nyce*, and ne couthe no wisdom' = for he was foolish, and knew no wisdom; Rob. of Glouc. p. 106; l. 2326.—OF. *nice*, 'lazy, slothful, idle, faint, slack, dull, simple;' Cot. The orig. sense was 'ignorant.'—Romanic type **necium* (cf. Span. *necio*); for L. *nescium*, acc. of *nescius*, ignorant.—L. *ne*, not; and *sci-*, related to *scire*, to know. See **No** and **Science.** ¶ The remarkable changes in the sense may have been due to some confusion with E. *nesh*, which sometimes meant 'delicate' as well as 'soft.' Der. *nice-ty*, ME. *nicetee*, Chaucer, C. T. 4044 (A 4046), from OF. *nicete*, 'sloth, simplicity' (Cot.); *nice-ness*.

NICHE, a recess in a wall, for a statue. (F.—Ital.—L.) In Minsheu, ed. 1627.—F. *niche*, 'a niche;' Cot.—Ital. *nicchia*, a niche; closely allied to *nicchio*, a shell, hence a shell-like recess in a wall, so called (probably) from the early shape of it. Florio explains *nicchio* as 'the shell of any shell-fish, a nooke or corner, also such little cubboords in churches as they put images in or as images stand in.'—L. *mitulum*, *mȳtilum*, acc. of *mītulus*, *mȳtilus*, a sea-muscle. 'Derived in the same way as Ital. *secchia* from *situla*, a bucket, and Ital. *vecchio*, from L. *uetulus*, old; as to the change of initial, cf. Ital. *nespola* with L. *mespilum*, a medlar;' Diez. A similar change of initial occurs in E. *napkin*, due to L. *mappa*, and in F. *natte*, a mat. β. Referred by some to Gk. μυτίλος, a muscle; but the Gk. word may be of Lat. origin. The L. *mȳtilus* is also found in the form *mūtulus*, and is by some connected with *musculus*, a little mouse, also a sea-muscle. ¶ The similarity to E. *nick* is accidental.

NICK (1), a small notch, a cut. (E.) 'Though but a stick with a *nick*;' Fotherby, Atheom., p. 62, ed. 1622 (Todd's Johnson). 'To *nick*, to hit the time right; I *nick'd* it, I came in the *nick* of time, just in time. *Nick* and *notch*, i.e. *crena*, are synonymous words, and to *nick* a thing seems to me to be originally no more than to hit just the notch or mark;' J. Ray, pref. to Collection of English (dialectal) Words, ed. 1691. Palsgrave has: 'I *nycke*, I make *nyckes* on a tayle, or on a *stycke*;' where *tayle* = tally. *Nick* is an attenuated form of *nock*, and means a little notch; so also *tip* from *top*. See **Nock.** β. Hence *nick*, a score on a tally, a reckoning; 'out of all *nick*' = past all counting, Two Gent. iv. 2. 76. Der. *nick*, to notch slightly, Com. Errors, v. 175.

NICK (2), the devil. (F.—L.—Gk.) In the phrase 'Old *Nick*,' i. e. 'Old *Nicholas*' or 'Old *Nicolas*.' [Not really connected with AS. *nicor*, a water-sprite; Beowulf, ed. Grein, ll. 422, 575, 845, 1427; Icel. *nykr*, a fabulous water-goblin; Dan. *nök*; OHG. *nichus*, a water-sprite, fem. *nicchessa*; G. *nix*, fem. *nixe*. See *Nix* in Kluge.] —F. *Nicolas*.—L. *Nicolāus*.—Gk. Νικόλαος; cf. Acts, vi. 5.

NICKEL, a grayish white metal. (Swed.—G.) One of the few G. words in E. Added by Todd to Johnson's Dict. From Swed. *nickel*; so named by Cronstedt, a Swede, in 1754; he abbreviated the G. word *kupfernickel* to *nickel*, to denote the metal which he had discovered in 1751 (Weigand). The origin of the G. name is doubtful.

NICKNACK, the same as **Knickknack,** q. v.

NICKNAME, a surname, soubriquet. (E.) In Shak. Romeo, ii. 1. 12. One of the words which has acquired an unoriginal initial *n*; see remarks on the letter **N.** ME. *nekename*, corruption of *ekename*, an additional name; in later times changed to *nickname*,

from a popular etymology which connected the word with the verb *nick*, which properly means 'to notch,' not 'to clip.' It may further be remarked that a *nickname* is not so much a docking of the name, as an addition to it, a *sur-name*. '*Neke-name*, or *eke-name*, agnomen;' Prompt. Parv. p. 352. Way cites in his note similar glosses, such as: '*Agnomen*, an *ekename*, or a surename (*sic*),' Medulla; 'An *ekname*, agnomen;' Catholicon. Spelt *ekename*, Testament of Love; bk. ii. ch. 1. 96. There can be no doubt as to the purely E. origin of the word, which has just the sense of L. *agnōmen*, and is parallel to ME. *toname*, a to-name, additional name, surname (cognate with G. *zuname*, a nickname), for which see P. Plowman, C. xiii. 211, Layamon, 9383. Thus the word is simply compounded of *eke* and *name*; see **Eke, Name.** + Icel. *auknafn*, a nickname; from *auka*, to eke, and *nafn*, a name; Swed. *öknamn*, from *öka*, to eke, and *namn*, a name; Dan. *ögenavn*, from *öge*, to eke. Der. *nickname*, verb, Hamlet, iii. 1. 151.

NICOTIAN, belonging to tobacco. (F.) 'Your *Nicotian* [tobacco] is good too;' Ben Jonson, Every Man, ed. Wheatley, A. iii. sc. 5, l. 89.—MF. *Nicotiane*, 'Nicotian, tobacco, first sent into France by *Nicot* in 1560;' Cot. Coined, with fem. suffix *-iane* (= L. *-iāna*), from the F. name *Nicot*. Der. Hence also *nicot-ine*.

NIECE, the daughter of a brother or sister. (F.—L.) The fem. form of *nephew*. ME. *nece*, Rob. of Glouc. p. 353, l. 7252; spelt *neyce*, King Alisaunder, l. 1712.—OF. *niece*, mod. F. *nièce*. Cf. Prov. *nepta*, a niece, in Bartsch, Chrestomathie Provençale.—Late L. *neptia*, which occurs A.D. 809 (Brachet).—L. *neptis*, a granddaughter, a niece; used as fem. of *nepōs* (stem *nepōt-*); see **Nephew.**

NIGGARD, a miser. (Scand.) ME. *nigard* (with one *g*), Chaucer, C. T. 5915 (D 333); cf. *nigardye*, sb., id. 13102 (B 1362). The suffix *-ard* is of F. origin, as usual; and the F. *-ard* is of OHG. origin; see Brachet, Introd. to F. Etym. Dict. § 196. But this suffix was freely added to E. words, as in *drunk-ard*; and we find a parallel form in ME. *nygun*. '[He was] a *nygun* and auarous' = he was a niggard and an avaricious man; Rob. of Brunne, Handlyng Synne, l. 5578. We also find an adj. *niggish* (Richardson), from the sb. *nig*, a niggardly person; see Plowman's Tale, l. 757. Of Scand. origin.—Icel. *hnöggr*, niggardly, stingy; Swed. *njugg*, niggardly, scanty; cf. MDan. *nygger*, Swed. dial. *nugger*, stingy; MDu. *nugger*, 'nimble, carefull, or diligent;' Hexham; Swed. dial. *gnugger*, a miser, from *gnugga*, to be stingy. + AS. *hnēaw*, sparing. The orig. sense was prob. 'scraping;' from Teut. base **hneu-*, allied to Gk. κνύειν, to scratch, scrape; see Prellwitz. Der. *niggard*, adj., Hamlet, iii. 1. 13; *niggard-ly*, Hen. V, ii. 4. 46; *niggard-ly*, adv., Merry Wives, ii. 2. 205; *niggard-li-ness*.

NIGGER, a negro. (F.—Span.—L.) 'He takes us all for a parcel of *negers*;' Garrick, A Peep behind the Curtain, A. i. sc. 2. —MF. *negre*, 'a negro;' F. *nègre*.—Span. *negro*, a negro; see **Negro.**

NIGGLE, to trifle, fret, mock. (Scand.) 'Take heed . . You *niggle* not with your conscience;' Massinger, Emp. of the East, A. v. sc. 3. Cf. Norw. *nigla*, *gnigga*, to pinch, spare, save; Low G. *gnegeln*, to spare, save; Norw. *gnika*, to rub, scrape, save.

NIGH, near, not far off, close. (E.) ME. *neh*, *neih*, *ney*, *neigh*, *ny*; Chaucer, C. T. 1528 (A 1526); Havelok, 464; &c. AS. *nēah*, *nēh*, Grein, ii. 282, used as adj., adv., and prep. + Du. *na*, adv., nigh; Icel. *nā-*, adv., nigh; only used in composition, as *nā-būi*, a neighbour; Goth. *nēhw*, *nēhwa*, adv., nigh; whence *nēhwjan*, to draw nigh; G. *nahe*, adj., *nach*, prep., nigh, next, &c. β. These forms belong to a Teut. type **næhwoz*, adj., nigh; root unknown. Der. *near*, q. v., *neighbour*, q. v., *next*, q. v.

NIGHT, the time of the sun's absence. (E.) ME. *niht*, *night*; Chaucer, C. T. 23. AS. *niht*, *neht*, *neaht*, Grein, ii. 284. + Du. *nacht*; Icel. *nātt*, *nōtt*; Dan. *nat*; Swed. *natt*; Goth. *nahts*; G. *nacht*. + W. *nos*; Irish *nochd*; Lithuan. *naktis*; Russ. *noch(e)*; L. *nox* (stem *noct-*); Gk. νύξ (stem *νυκτ-*); Skt. *nakta-*. β. All from the Idg. type **nokt-*; whence Teut. **naht-*. Brugmann, i. §§ 420, 658 b. Der. *night-cap*, *-dress*, *-fall*, *-jar* (from its jarring noise), *-piece*, *-watch*; also *night-ly*, ME. *nihtliche*, Reliquiæ Antiquæ, i. 131, *night-less*, *night-ward*; also numerous compounds in Shak., as *-bird*, *-crow*, *-dog*, *-fly*, *-foe*, *-gown*, &c. And see *night-mare*, *night-shade*, *night-in-gale*, *nocturn*. Also *fort-night*, *sen-night*.

NIGHTINGALE, the bird that sings by night. (E.) The *n* before *g* is excrescent, as in *messenger* for *messager*, *passenger* for *passager*, &c. ME. *nightingale*, Chaucer, C. T. 98; earlier form *niȝtegale*, Reliquiæ Antiquæ, i. 241. AS. *nihtegale*, Voc. 247. 11. Lit. 'singer of [or in] the night.'—AS. *nihte*, gen. and dat. case of *niht*, *neaht*, night; and *gale* = singer, from *galan*, to sing (Grein). + Du. *nachtegaal*; Dan. *nattergal*; Swed. *näktergal*; G. *nachtigall*, OHG. *nahtagala*, *nahtegala*, *nahtigala*. β. The verb *galan* became *galen* in ME., and occurs in Chaucer, C. T. 6414 (D 832); it is cognate with Dan. *gale*, Swed. *gala*, to crow as a cock, OHG. *kalan*, to sing; and is derived from *gal, 2nd stem of the Teut. verb which appears as E. yell. See **Yell.**

NIGHTMARE, an incubus, a dream at night accompanied by pressure on the breast. (E.) ME. *nightemare.* 'Nyghte *mare,* or *mare,* or *wytche,* Epialtes, vel effialtes' [ephialtes]; Prompt. Parv. — AS. *neaht, niht,* night; and *mare,* a night-mare, a rare word, occurring in Cockayne's A. S. Leechdoms, ii 306, l. 12; older forms *mera,* m., Epinal gloss., 558; *maere,* f., Corpus gloss., 1111. ✠ Du. *nacht-merrie,* a night-mare; an accommodated spelling, due to confusion with Du. *merrie,* a mare, with which the word has no connexion. A like confusion is probably common in modern English, though the AS. forms are distinct; Icel. *mara,* the nightmare, an ogress; Swed. *mara*; Dan. *mare*; Low G. *moor, nagt-moor*; Bremen Wörterbuch, iii. 184, where the editor, against the evidence, confuses *moor* with 'mare;' OHG. *mara,* a nightmare, incubus. ✠ Polish *mora,* nightmare. β. The sense perhaps is 'crusher;' from a root *mer; cf. Icel. *merja,* to crush (pt. t. *mar-ði*). The AS., Icel., and OHG. suffix *-a* (fem. *-e*) may denote the agent, as in numerous other cases; e. g. AS. *hunt-a,* a hunter, huntsman.

NIGHTSHADE, a narcotic plant. (E.) AS. *nihtscadu, niht-scada,* nightshade; Cockayne's A. S. Leechdoms, iii. 340. Compounded of *niht,* night, and *scadu,* shade; perhaps because thought to be evil, and loving the shade of night. See **Night, Shade.** β. But this may be 'popular' etymology. Cf. Du. *nachtschade,* MDu. *nachtschaede,* G. *nachtschatten,* nightshade. But the MHG. for 'night-shade' is *nahtschate,* and the Swed. dial. form is *nattskate-gräs,* lit. ' bat-grass,' from *naht-skata,* a bat. Notes on E. Etym., p. 197.

NIGRESCENT, growing black. (L.) In Todd's Johnson. — L. *nigrescent-,* stem of pres. pt. of *nigrescere,* to become black, inceptive form of *nigrēre,* to be black. — L. *nigr-,* stem of *niger,* black. **Der.** *nigritude,* from L. *nigritūdo,* blackness; see Hood's Poems, A Black Job, last line but one. Also *negro,* q. v.

NIHILIST, one who rejects all positive beliefs. (L.) Formed with suffix *-ist* from L. *nihil,* nothing.

NILGAU, the same as **Nylghau,** q. v.

NIMBLE, active. (E.) The *b* is excrescent. ME. *nimel, nimil*; see '*Nymyl,* capax' in Prompt. Parv., and Way's note. Formed from AS. *nim-an,* to take, catch, seize, with the AS. suffix *-ol,* still preserved in E. *witt-ol,* lit. a wise man, used sarcastically to mean a simpleton. We find the parallel AS. forms *numol, numul, numel,* occurring in the compounds *scearp-numul,* lit. 'sharp-taking,' i. e. efficacious, and *teart-numul,* also lit. 'tart-taking,' i. e. efficacious; Cockayne's A. S. Leechdoms, i. 134, l. 10, 152, l. 3, and footnotes; these are formed from *num-,* the weak grade of the same verb *niman.* The sense is 'quick at seizing,' hence active, nimble. So also Icel. *næma,* keen, quick at learning, from *nema,* to take; Dan. *nem,* quick, apprehensive, adroit, from *nemme,* to apprehend, learn. β. The AS. *niman,* to seize, is cognate with Icel. *nema,* Dan. *nemme,* G. *nehmen,* Goth. *niman,* to take; a strong verb, with AS. and Goth. pt. t. *nam.* The orig. sense is 'to take as one's share.' —√NEM, to apportion, distribute, allot; whence also Gk. *νέμειν,* to distribute, L. *num-erus,* a number. &c.; see Prellwitz. **Der.** *nimbl-y, nimble-ness.* From the same root, *nem-esis, nom-ad, num-b-er, num-ism-at-ic.* And see **Numb.**

NIMBUS, a cloud, halo. (L.) L. *nimbus,* a cloud; allied to **Nebula.**

NINCOMPOOP, a simpleton. (L.) 'An old ninnyhammer, a dotard, a nincompoop;' The Guardian, no. 109 (1713). A corruption (by association with *ninny*) of L. *non compos,* short form of *non compos mentis,* not in possession of one's mind. 'Bo! the man's *non compos*;' Murphy, The Upholsterer, A. i. sc. 3. — L. *nōn,* not; *compos,* in control of, from *com-* (for *cum,* prep., with) and *-pos,* allied to *potis,* capable; see **Potent.**

NINE, a numeral, one less than ten. (E.) ME. *nyne, nine,* Chaucer, C. T. 24. Here the final *-e* is the usual pl. ending, and *nyne* stands for an older form *niȝene,* extended form of *niȝen,* Layamon, 2804. AS. *nigon, nigen,* Grein, ii. 296. ✠ Du. *negen*; Icel. *níu*; Dan. *ni*; Swed. *nio*; G. *neun*; Goth. *niun.* ✠ W. *naw*; Irish and Gael. *naoi,* L. *nouem*; Gk. *ἐννέα* (= ἐ-νέϝα); Zend *nava,* Pers. *nuh,* Skt. *nava.* Idg. type *newṇ; Brugmann, ii. § 173. **Der.** *nine-fold, nine-pins*; *nine-teen,* AS. *nigontȳne* (Grein); *nine-ty,* AS. *nigontig* (Grein); *nin-th,* AS. *nigoða, nigeða* (id.); *nine-teen-th, nine-ti-eth*; *nin-th-ly.* And see *Novem-ber.*

NINNY, a simpleton. (E.) 'What a pied *ninny*'s this!' Temp. iii. 2. 71. Prov. E. *ninny, nonny,* or *nunny,* a simpleton; *ninny-hammer* (the same); E. D. D. Of imitative origin (see below). Cf. Westphal. *ninne,* an infant (Woeste); Picard *ninette* (Corblet); Ital. *ninno,* a child, a dialectal form cited by Diez, not given in Florio nor in Meadows' Dict., but the same word with Span. *niño,* a child, infant, one of little experience. Cf. also Span. *nene* (colloq.), an infant; Gascon *nenet, ninet,* an infant (Mistral). Cf. Ital. *ninna,* a lullaby, nurse's song to rock a child to sleep, *ninnare,* to lull to

sleep, *nanna,* 'a word that women use to still their children with' (Florio). From the repetition of the syllables *ni, ni,* or *na, na,* in humming or singing children to sleep. Körting, § 6545. See **Nun.**

NIP, to pinch, break off the edge or end. (E.) ME. *nippen*; '*nyppyng* hus *lyppes*'=biting his lips, pressing them with his teeth, P. Plowman, C. vii. 104. For *knip*; see G. Douglas, Prol. to XII Book of the Æneid, l. 94. Not found in AS., though the (possibly) cognate *cnif,* a knife, occurs; see **Knife.** From the weak grade (*knip-*) of a Teut. verb **kneipan-,* to pinch, as seen in Du. *knijpen,* to pinch; Dan. *knibe,* to pinch, nip; Swed. *knipa,* to pinch, squeeze, catch; G. *kneifen,* to pinch, nip; *kneipen,* to pinch, twitch. Perhaps allied to Lith. *knèbti,* to pinch; or to Lith. *gnybti,* to pinch. **Der.** *nip,* sb., a cut, Tam. Shrew, iv. 3. 90; *nipp-er, nipp-ers, nibb-le.* And see *knife.*

NIPPLE, a teat, a small projection with an orifice. (E.) In Shak. Macb. i. 7. 57; and in Minsheu, ed. 1627. A dimin. of *nib,* just as *neble* is the dimin. of *neb.* '*Neble* of a womans pappe, *bout de la mamelle*;' Palsgrave. *Nib* and *neb* are the same word; see **Nib, Neb.** Cf. Low G. *nibbe,* a beak; whence OF. *nifle, niffle,* a nose, Ital. *niffa, niffolo,* a snout. Körting, § 6526. **Der.** *nipple-wort.*

NIT, the egg of a louse or small insect. (E.) ME. *nite, nyte,* also used to mean a louse. '*Nyte,* wyrme, Lens;' Prompt. Parv. AS. *hnitu,* to translate L. *lens*; Voc. 30. 2; 122. 2. ✠ Du. *neet*; Icel. *nitr,* pl., OIcel. *gnit*; Dan. *gnid*; Swed. *gnet*; G. *niss,* MHG. *niz.* Cf. Russ. *gnida,* a nit, Gk. *κόνις* (stem *κόνιδ-*); W. *nedd,* pl. nits. β. Teut. base **hnit,* which may be the weak grade of the verb seen in AS. *hnītan,* only used of an ox, meaning 'to gore,' Exod. xxi. 28, Icel. *hníta,* to attack, strike. The corresponding Idg. root is KNEID, appearing in Gk. *κνίζειν* (= κνίδ-yειν), to scrape, tease, make to itch. See Prellwitz.

NITRE, saltpetre. (F. — L. — Gk. — Heb.) Spelt *niter* in Minsheu, ed. 1627. — F. *nitre,* 'niter;' Cot. — L. *nitrum.* — Gk. *νίτρον,* 'natron, a mineral alkali, our potassa or soda, or both (not our nitre, i. e. saltpetre);' Liddell and Scott. This means that the *sense* of the word has changed; but the *form* is the same. — Heb. *nether,* nitre; Prov. xxv. 20; cf. Arab. *nitrūn, natrūn,* natron, native alkaline salt; Rich. Dict. p. 1585. **Der.** *nitr-ate, nitr-ic, nitr-ous, nitr-i-fy, nitr-ite.* Also *nitro-gen,* i. e. that which produces nitre, from *νίτρο-,* for *νίτρον,* and *γεν-,* base of *γίγνειν,* to produce; see **Generate.**

NIZAM, the title of a ruler in the Deccan, in Hindustan. (Hind. — Pers. — Arab.) Found in 1793; see Stanford Dict. Short for Hind. *nizām-ul-mulk,* administrator of the empire (Forbes). — Arab. *niḍhām,* government; which the Persians pronounce as *nizām.* Though the proper sense is 'government,' in the phrase *nizam-'l-mulk* it is used as a title, meaning 'governor of the empire.' First used by Asaf Jāh in 1713 (Yule). From Arab. root *naḍhama,* he arranged or ordered. See Devic and Richardson.

NO (1), a word of refusal or denial. (E.) ME. *no,* Will. of Palerne, 2701, 3115. There is a clear distinction in ME. between *no* and *nay,* the former being the stronger form; see **Nay,** which is of Scand. origin. AS. *nā,* adv., never, no. Compounded of *ne,* not, and *ā,* aye. The form *ā* became *oo* in ME., occurring in Genesis and Exodus, ed. Morris, l. 111; but this form was entirely superseded by the cognate word *ai, ay,* mod. E. *ay, aye,* which is of Scand. origin. See **Aye,** adv., ever. B. The neg. particle *ne,* signifying 'not,' is cognate with OHG. *ni,* MHG. *ne,* not; Goth. *ni,* not; Russ. *ne,* not; Irish, Gael., and W. *ni,* not; L. *ne,* in *non-ne*; Skt. *na,* not. C. In mod. E. this neg. particle is represented by the initial *n-* of *n-ever, n-aught, n-one, n-either, n-ay, n-or,* and the like. ¶ It is quite a mistake to suppose that ME. *ne,* not, so common in Chaucer, is of F. origin. It is rather the AS. *ne,* which happens to coincide in form with F. *ne,* of L. origin; and that is all.

NO (2), none. (E.) Merely a shortened form of *none,* as *a* is of *an*; see **None.** **Der.** *no-body,* q. v.

NOBLE, illustrious, excellent, magnificent. (F. — L.) In early use. ME. *noble,* O. Eng. Homilies, ed. Morris, i. 273, l. 16. — F. *noble.* — L. *nōbilem,* acc. of *nōbilis* (= *gnō-bilis*), well-known, notable, illustrious, noble. — L. *gnō-,* base of *noscere* (= *gnoscere*), to know, cognate with E. *know*; with suffix *-bilis.* See **Know.** **Der.** *nobl-y,* adv.; *noble-man,* in O. Eng. Homilies, as above; *noble-ness* (a hybrid word, with E. suffix), Wint. Tale, ii. 3. 12. Also *nobil-i-ty,* K. John, v. 2. 42, from OF. *nobilite,* nobilitet < L. acc. *nōbilitātem.*

NOBODY, no one. (E.) In Shak. Merry Wives, i. 4. 14. Compounded of *no,* short for *none,* and *body*; not in early use. It took the place of ME. *no man,* which is now less used. See **None** and **Body.**

NOCK, an indentation. (MDu.) 'The *nocke* of the shafte;' Ascham, Toxophilus, bk. ii. ed. Arber, p. 127. ME. *nokke,* Prompt. Parv., p. 357. '*Nokked* and fethered aright,' said of arrows; Chaucer,

Rom. Rose, 942. — MDu. *nocke* (Kilian); also *nock*, ' *een nock .. in een pijl*, a notch in the head of an arrow;' Hexham. **+**MSwed. *nocka*, an incision (Ihre); Swed. dial. *nokke, nokk*, an incision or a cut in timber (Rietz). **β.** The MSwed. *nocka* also denotes the same as Icel. *hnokki*, i. e. one of the small metal hooks holding the thread in a distaff. **¶** Constantly confused with *notch*, which is a different word. The Norman dial. *noque* (Du Bois), Ital. *nocca*, a nock (see Florio), are of Germanic origin.

NOCTURN, the name of a service of the church. (F. — L.) See Palmer, Origines Liturgicæ, i. 202, ed. 1832. 'A *nocturne* of the Psalter;' Lord Berners, tr. of Froissart, vol. ii. c. 26 (R.). ME. *nocturne*, Ancren Riwle, p. 270, l. 1. — F. *nocturne*, nocturnal; also, a nocturn. — Late L. *nocturna*, a nocturn; orig. fem. of L. *nocturnus*, belonging to night. **β.** To be divided as *noct-urnus*, from *noct-*, stem of *nox*, night, with a suffix imitating *di-urnus*. See **Night**. Der. *nocturn-al*, spelt *nocturnall*, Hardyng's Chron., ch. 95, st. 10; and in Milton, P. L. iii. 40, viii. 134, from Late L. *nocturnālis*, extended from *nocturnus*; *nocturn-al-ly*.

NOD, to incline the head forward. (E.) ME. *nodden*, Chaucer, C. T. 16996 (H 47). Not found in AS., and difficult to trace. But it answers to a G. form **notten*, found in the frequentative form *notteln*, a prov. G. word, meaning to shake, wag, jog (Flügel). To *nod* is to shake the head by a sudden inclination forwards, as is done by a sleepy person; to make a butting movement with the head. Schmeller gives *notteln* as Bavarian. The orig. notion seems to be that of butting or pushing; and there is a connexion with Icel. *hnjōða*, to hammer, clinch, rivet, *hnyðja*, a rammer for beating turf; G. *nieten*, to rivet. Teut. base **hnud-*, weak grade of **hneud-*. **¶** Not connected with L. *nuere*, to nod (base *nu*). Der. *nod*, sb.

NODDLE, a name for the head. (E.) In Shak. Tam. Shrew, i. 1. 64. Wedgwood well says: 'the *noddle, noddock*, or *niddock* is properly the projecting part at the back of the head, the nape of the neck, then ludicrously used for the head itself.' ME. *nodle, nodil*. ' *Nodyl*, or *nodle* of the heed, or nolle, *Occiput*;' Prompt. Parv. **β.** It really stands for *knoddel*, and is the dimin. of *knod*, a word lost in Early E., but preserved in E. dial. *nod*, nape, and in other languages; cf. MDu. *knodde*, a knob (Hexham); Icel. *hnúðr*, a knob, ball; G. *knoten*, a knot, a knob; Du. *knod*, a club. Cf. Low G. *knuddel*, a ball of yarn, a hard swelling under the skin (Berghaus). **γ.** This *knod* is a variant of **Knot**, q. v.

NODE, a knot. (L.) ' *Nodes*, in astronomy, are the points of the intersection of the orbit of the sun or any other (!) planet with the eclipse;' Phillips, ed. 1706. ' *Nodus* or *Node*, a knot, or noose, &c.;' id. — L. *nōdus*, a knot. Allied to Skt. *naddha-*, tied, bound, pp. of *nah* (for *nadh*), to tie. From Idg. root NEDH, to fasten. Brugmann, i. § 700 (a), note 2. Der. *nod-al*, adj.; *nod-ous*, Sir T. Browne, Vulg. Errors, b. iv. c. 4, § 1, Englished from L. *nōdōsus*; *nod-os-i-ty*, id. b. v. c. 5, § 2, from F. *nodosité*, 'knottiness' (Cot.) <L. acc. *nōdōsitātem*; *nod-ule*, Englished from L. *nōdulus*, a little knot, dimin. of *nōdus*.

NOGGIN, a wooden cup, small mug. (Scand.) ' Of drinking-cups .. we have .. mazers, broad-mouthed dishes, *noggins*, whiskins, piggins, &c.;' Heywood, Drunkard Opened, &c., ed. 1635, p. 45 (Todd). Also in Minsheu, ed. 1627. [Cf. Irish *noigin*, 'a noggin, a naggin, quarter of a pint,' O'Reilly; Gael. *noigean*, a wooden cup; Gael. *cnagan*, a little knob, peg, pin, an earthen pipkin; Gael. *cnagaire*, a knocker, a noggin; all from E. (Macbain).] We also find Lowl. Sc. *noggin, noggie*, spelt *knoggin* by Swift, in Lines to Dr. Sheridan (1719). For **knoggen*, with *-en* as in *wood-en*, from *knog*, a small cask, a firkin (E.D.D.), variant of *knag*, a keg (E.D.D.), which is prob. the same word as **Knag**, a knot in wood, a peg; q. v.; whence also *knaggie*, a keg.

NOISE, a din, troublesome sound. (F. — L. — Gk.) In early use. ME. *noise*, Ancren Riwle, p. 66, l. 18. — F. *noise*, 'a brabble, brawle, debate, .. also a noise;' Cot. **β.** The OF. form is also *nose*; and the Provençal form is *nausa, nauza, noisa, nueiza* (Bartsch). The origin is uncertain; it is discussed by Diez, who decides that the Prov. form *nausa* could only have been derived from L. *nausea*, so that a *noise* is so called because *nauseous*; see **Nausea**. If this be right, the word is really of Greek origin. So Körting § 6471. Der. *nois-y*, for which formerly *noise-ful* was used, as in Dryden, Annus Mirabilis, st. 40; *nois-i-ly, nois-i-ness*; *noise-less, -ly, -ness*; also *noise*, verb, ME. *noisen*, Chaucer, tr. of Boethius, b. iii. met. 6, l. 7.

NOISOME, annoying, troublesome. (F. — L.; *with* E. *suffix*.) Formed from ME. *noy*, annoyance, injury; with E. suffix *-some* = AS. *-sum*, as in **Winsome**, q. v. We find three forms in use formerly, viz. *noy-ous*, Wyclif, 2 Thess. iii. 2; *noy-ful*, Sir T. More, Works, p. 481 e; and *noy-some*, id. p. 1389 h. **β.** *Noy* is a mere contraction of ME. *anoy, anoi*; see Romaunt of the Rose, 4404, &c. The derivation is from the L. phrase *in odiō habēre*, as explained s. v. **Annoy**, q. v. **¶** Not connected with L. *nocēre*, to hurt.

NOLE, NOLL, the head; see **Noule**.

NOMAD, wandering; one of a wandering tribe. (Gk.) 'The Numidian *nomades*, so named of changing their pasture;' Holland, tr. of Pliny, b. v. c. 3. — Gk. νομάδ-, stem of νομάς, roaming, wandering, esp. in search of pasture. — Gk. νομός, a pasture, allotted abode. — Gk. νέμειν, to assign, allot. — √NEM, to assign; cf. Skt. *nam*, to bow to, bow, bend, *upa-nam*, to fall to one's share. Hence also *nem-esis, nim-ble, num-ber*; and the suffix *-nomy* in *astro-nomy, auto-nomy, gastro-nomy, anti-nomi-an*. Der. *nomad-ic*.

NOMENCLATOR, one who gives names to things. (L.) 'What? will Cupid turn *nomenclator*?' Ben Jonson, Cynthia's Revels, A. v. sc. 3 (2nd Masque). In Minsheu, ed. 1627. — L. *nōmenclātor*, one who gives names, lit. 'name-caller;' fuller form *nōmenculātor*. — L. *nōmen*, a name; and *calāre*, to call. See **Name** and **Calendar**. Der. *nomenclat-ure*, from L. *nōmenclātūra*, a calling by name, naming.

NOMINAL, pertaining to a name, existing only in name. (L.) 'One is a *reall*, another a *nominall*;' Tyndal's Works, p. 104, col. 1; see Spec. of English, ed. Skeat, p. 176, l. 316. This refers to the famous dispute between the *Nominalists* and *Realists*; the founder of the former sect was condemned by a council at Soissons, A.D. 1092; Haydn, Dict. of Dates. — L. *nōminālis*, nominal. — L. *nōmin-*, for *nōmen*, a name, cognate with E. **Name**, q. v. See **Nominate**.

NOMINATE, to name. (L.) In Shak. L. L. L. i. 2. 16. — L. *nōminātus*, pp. of *nōmināre*, to name. — L. *nōmin-*, for *nomen*, a name, cognate with E. **Name**, q. v. Der. *nominat-ion*, Fryth's Works, p. 58, col. 2, from F. *nomination*, 'a nomination' (Cot.); *nomina-tor*; *nominat-ive*, ME. *nominatif*, Trevisa, i. 327, from OF. *nominatif*, in use in the 13th century (Littré), from L. *nōminātiuus*. Also *nomin-ee*, a term of law, formed as if from a F. verb **nominer*, with a pp. *nominé*; but the real F. verb is *nommer*.

NON-, prefix, not. (L.) In compounds, such as *non-appearance, non-compliance*. — L. *nōn*, not; orig. none, not one; compounded of L. *ne*, not, and *oinum*, old form of *ūnum*, neut. of *ūnus*, one (Bréal). Thus L. *nōn* is of parallel formation with E. **None**, q. v.

NONAGE, minority. (F. — L.) In Shak. Rich. III, ii. 3. 13. Orig. a law-term. AF. *nonage*, Stat. Realm, i. 38 (1275). Compounded of F. *non*, from L. *nōn*, not, and *age*; see **Non-**, **Age**.

NONCE, in phr. *for the nonce*. (E.) ME. *for the nones*, Chaucer, C. T. 381 (A 379). The sense is 'for the once,' for the occasion or purpose. The older spelling is *for then ones*, still earlier *for then anes*, as in St. Juliana, ed. Cockayne, p. 71. Thus the *n* really belongs to the dat. case of the article, viz. AS. *ðām*, later *ðan*, *then*. *Ones* = mod. E. *once*; see **Once**. We may note that *ones* was first a gen. case, then an adv., and was lastly used as a sb., as here.

NONCHALANT, careless. (F. — L.) In R. North's Examen, p. 463 (Davies). — F. *nonchalant*, 'careless,' Cot.; pres. pt. of OF. *nonchaloir*, 'to neglect, or be carelesse of;' Cot. — F. *non*, not; *chaloir*, 'to care, take thought for;' id. Cf. OF. *chaloir, caloir*, in Bartsch, orig. 'to glow,' hence, to be hot over, be fervent; also Anglo-F. *nunchaler*, to be careless, Life of Edw. Conf. 4519. **+**L. *nōn*, not; *calēre*, to glow, to be animated. See **Caldron**. Der. *nonchalance*, sb., Whitehead's Poems, Variety, l. 284, from F. *nonchalance*, carelessness, indifference.

NONCONFORMING, refusing to conform. (L.; *and* F. — L.; *with* E. *suffix*.) The Act of Uniformity came into operation on 24 Aug. 1662; Haydn, Dict. of Dates. Hence arose the name *nonconformist*, and the adj. *nonconforming*. Compounded of L. *nōn*, not; and **Conform**, q. v. Der. *nonconform-ist, non-conform-i-ty*.

NONDESCRIPT, not yet described, novel, odd. (L.) 'Such as are *non-descripts*;' Letters of Eminent Men, ed. Ellis (Cam. Soc.) p. 203; A.D. 1696. Added by Todd to Johnson's Dict. — L. *nōn*, not; and *descriptus*, pp. of *describere*, to describe; see **Describe**.

NONE, not one. (E.) ME. *noon, non*; as in 'non other' = no other, Rob. of Brunne, tr. of Langtoft, p. 5. Before a consonant it commonly becomes *no*, as in mod. E.; but in very early authors we find *non* even before a consonant, as in 'none tonge;' Rob. of Glouc. p. 285, l. 5806. AS. *nán*, none; compounded of *ne*, not, and *ān*, one; see **No** (1) § B, and **One**.

NONENTITY, a thing that does not exist. (L.) In The Tatler, no. 118, § 6 (1710). From **Non-** and **Entity**.

NONES, the ninth day before the ides. (L.) Also used of the old church service at the ninth hour, which is the older use in E. See P. Plowman, B. v. 378. This ninth hour or *nones* was orig. 3 P.M., but was changed to midday; whence our *noon*. See further under **Noon**.

NONJUROR, one who refuses to take the oath of allegiance. (L.; *and* F. — L.) First used of those who refused allegiance to Will. III. in 1689. From **Non-** and **Juror**.

NONPAREIL, one without equal, matchless. (F. — L.) In Shak. Temp. iii. 2. 108. — F. *non*, not, from L. *nōn*; and *pareil*, equal, from Late L. *pariculus*, double dimin. from L. *par*, equal. See **Apparel**, and **Par**.

NONPLUS, a state of perplexity; to perplex. (L.) Most commonly a verb. ' He has *non-plus'd* me ; ' Dryden, Kind Keeper, iii. I. The orig. phrase was ' to be at a *non-plus*,' which occurs in Cotgrave, s. v. *Latin*. A half-ludicrous coined term for a state of perplexity, in which one can do no more, nor go any further.—L. *nōn plūs*, no more. See **Non-** and **Plural**.

NONSENSE, language without meaning. (L.; *and* F.—L.) It occurs in Cowley, The Mistress; The Incurable, l. 2. From **Non-** and **Sense**. Der. *nonsens-ic-al*.

NONSUIT, a withdrawal of a suit at law. (L.; *and* F.—L.) In Blount's Gloss., ed. 1674, which see; and in Baret (1580); AF. *nonsute*. From **Non-** and **Suit**. Der. *nonsuit*, verb.

NOOK, a corner, recess. (E.) ME. *nōk*, Havelok, 820; pl. *nōkes*, Cursor Mundi, 17675. The comp. *feower-nōked* = four-cornered, occurs in Layamon, ii. 500, l. 21999. The Lowland Sc. form is *neuk* (Jamieson); whence, probably, Irish and Gael. *niuc*, a nook, corner. The AS. *nōc* is not found.+Norw. *nōk*, a nook, corner (Supp. to Aasen, p. 970); cf. Norw. *nakke*, a corner cut off (Ross); and perhaps even Dan. dial. *nogg*, a bend in a river.

NOON, midday. (L.) Orig. the ninth hour of the day, or 3 P.M., but afterwards the time of the church-service called *nones* was shifted back, and the term came to be applied to midday as early as the twelfth century; see Hampson, Medii Ævi Calendarium, i. 87. ME. *none*, Layamon, 17063; *nones*, pl., P. Plowman, B. v. 378, vi. 147 (see notes). AS. *nōn-tid* (= noon-tide), the ninth hour, Mark, xv. 33, 34.—L. *nōna*, for *nōna hōra*, ninth hour; where *nōna* is the fem. of *nōnus*, ninth. *Nōnus* = *nouimus*, from *nouem*, nine; cf. *decimus* from *decem*, ten. The L. *nouem* is cognate with E. **Nine**, q. v. Der. *noon-tide*, AS. *nōn-tīd*, as above; *noon-day*, Jul. Cæsar, i. 3. 27. Also *nones*, *nun-chion*.

NOOSE, a slip-knot. (Prov.—L.) ' Caught in my own *noose* ; ' Beaum. and Fletcher, Rule a Wife, iii. 4 (Perez). Cotgrave explains F. *laqs courant* as ' a noose, a running knot.' Imported from Gascony by sailors.—Gascon *nus*, Prov. *nous*, a noose, a loop of cord.—L. *nōdus*, a knot. Cf. Prov. *nous courrént*, a running noose; pl. *nouses* ; also *nous de l'araire*, a noose for mooring ships (whence the nautical word); see Mistral. Also Gascon *nouset*, a knot; *nousera*, to tie a knot. ¶ The F. *nœud* is from L. acc. *nōdum* ; whereas Prov. *nous* is from the nom. *nōdus*. See **Node**. Der. *noose*, verb.

NOR, neither. (E.) ME. *nor*, short for ME. *nother*, *nauther* ; from AS. *nāhwæðer* (no-whether); but partly confused with other forms of *or*. ' Vor hor hors were al astoned, and nolde after wylle Sywe *noþer* spore no brydel ' = for their horses were all astonied, and would not, according to their will, obey *nor* spur nor bridle ; Rob. of Glouc. p. 396; l. 8169. For a full account of the word, see N. E. D. See **Or**.

NORMAL, according to rule. (L.) A late word; added by Todd to Johnson.—L. *normālis*, made according to a carpenter's square.—L. *norma*, a carpenter's square, rule, pattern. Contracted from a form *gnōrima*, and perhaps merely a borrowed word from Gk. The corresponding Gk. word is γνωρίμη, fem. of γνώριμος, well-known, whence the sense of ' exact ' in Latin; allied to Gk. γνώμων, that which knows or indicates, an index, a carpenter's square. See **Gnomon**. Der. *normal-ly* ; also *e-norm-ous*, q. v., *ab-norm-al* (modern). We also find *norm*, a rule, model; from L. *norma*.

NORMAN, a Northman. (F.—Scand.) ME. *Norman*, Rob. of Glouc. p. 360; l. 7418.—OF. *Normand*, ' a Norman ; ' Cot.—Dan. *Normand* ; Icel. *Norðmaðr* (= *Norðmannr*), pl. *Norðmenn*, a Northman, Norwegian. See **North**. Der. *Norman-d-y*, ME. *Normandy*, Rob. of Glouc. p. 345, l. 7074, F. *Normandie*, Dan. *Normandi*, Icel. *Norðmanndi*, Normandy, Norman's land, where the suffix is French (F. *-ie*, L. *-ia*).

NORSE, Norwegian. (Scand.) Short for *Norsk*, the Norwegian and Dan. spelling of Norse = Icel. *Norskr*, Norse, adj., which appears in the 14th cent. instead of the older Icel. *Norrœnn*. *Norsk* is short for *North-isk*, i. e. *North-ish* ; see **North**.

NORTH, the cardinal point opposite to the sun's place at noon. (E.) ME. *north*, Wyclif, Luke, xiii. 29. AS. *norð*, Grein, ii. 300.+Du. *noord* ; Icel. *norðr* ; Dan. and Swed. *nord* ; G. *nord*. Root unknown. Some compare the Umbrian *nertru*, on the left hand (to one looking eastwards) ; Gk. νέρτερος, lower. Der. *north-ern*, ME. *northren*, Chaucer, C. T. 1989 (A 1987), AS. *norðern* (Grein), cognate with Icel. *norr-œnn*, OHG. *nord-r-ōni*, northern ; where the latter suffix is like the L. *-āneus*. Also *north-east*, *-west*, &c. Also *north-ward* ; *north-er-ly* (short for *northern-ly*), &c. Also *Nor-man*, *Nor-se*.

NOSE, the organ of smell. (E.) ME. *nose* (orig. dissyllabic), Chaucer, C. T. 123, 152. AS. *nosu*, Grein, ii. 300.+Du. *neus*. Teut. type *nas-ā*, f., related by gradation to Teut. type *nas-ā*, f.; cf. AS. *nas-u*, nose; Icel. *nös* ; Dan. *næse* ; Swed. *näsa* ; G. *nase* ; Russ. *nos'* ;

Lithuan. *nosis*.+L. *nāsus* ; also *nar-es*, pl.; Skt. *nāsā*, dual. Der. *nose-bag*, *nose-less* ; *nose*, v., Hamlet, iv. 3. 38; *nose-gay*, Mids. Nt. Dr. i. 1. 34, and Palsgrave, with which cf. *gay*, sb., a gay flower, as in ' *gayes* To make a Posie,' in Golding's Ovid, fol. 47, back, l. 4; and prov. E. (Essex) *gay*, a painted picture in a child's book, derived from *gay*, adj. And see *nos-tril*, *nozz-le*, *nuzz-le*.

NOSOLOGY, the science of diseases. (Gk.) In Bailey's Dict. —Gk. νόσο-, for νόσος, disease ; and -λογία, from λόγος, a discourse, which is from λέγειν, to speak.

NOSTRIL, one of the orifices of the nose. (E.) *Nostril* = *nose-thrill* or *nose-thirl*, Chaucer, C. T. 559 (A 557). AS. *nosðyrl* ; the pl. *nosðyrla* (= *nosðyrlu*, the sb. being neuter) is used to translate L. *nāres* in Voc. 157. 15.—AS. *nos-*, for *nosu*, the nose ; and *ðyrel*, *þyrel*, a perforation, orifice, Grein, ii. 613. See further under **Thrill**.

NOSTRUM, a quack medicine. (L.) In Pope, Prol. to Satires, l. 29.—L. *nostrum*, lit. ' our own,' i. e. a special drug peculiar to the seller of it. Neut. of *noster*, ours, possess. pron. formed from *nōs*, we. Cf. Skt. *nas*, us.

NOT (1), a word expressing denial. (E.) ME. *not*, often spelt *nought* or *noght*, Chaucer, C. T. 304. The less stressed form of **Naught**, q. v.

NOT (2), I know not, or he knows not. (E.) Obsolete. ME. *not*, *noot*, Chaucer, C. T. 286 (A 284). AS. *nāt*, I know not, or he knows not ; Grein, ii. 274. Equivalent to *ne wāt* ; from *ne*, not, and *wāt*, I know or he knows. See **Wot**, **Wit**.

NOT (3), to crop, shear closely; see **Not-pated**.

NOTABLE, remarkable. (F.—L.) ME. *notable*, Chaucer, C. T. 13615 (B 1875).—F. *notable*, ' notable ; ' Cot.—L. *notābilis*, remarkable.—L. *notāre*, to mark.—L. *nota*, a mark, note ; see **Note**. Der. *notabl-y*, *notable-ness* ; *notabil-i-ty*, ME. *notabilitee*, Chaucer, C. T. 15215 (B 4399), answering to F. *notabilité*, as if from L. acc. *notābilitātem*, from nom. *notābilitās*, a word not recorded.

NOTARY, a scrivener, one who takes notes. (F.—L.) The pl. *notaryes* occurs in the Ayenbite of Inwyt, p. 40, l. 8. Englished from AF. *notarie*, Langtoft, ii. 392; OF. *notaire*, ' a notary, a scrivener ; ' Cot.—L. *notārium*, acc. of *notārius*, a short-hand writer, one who makes notes ; formed with the adj. suffix *-rius* from *notā-*, stem of *nota*, a mark ; see **Note**.

NOTATION, a system of symbols. (L.) In Ben Jonson's Eng. Grammar, cap. viii is on ' the *notation* of a word,' by which he means the etymology. The word was really taken directly from Latin, but was put into a French form, by analogy. Formed as if from a F. *notation* (not in Cotgrave) ; from L. *notātiōnem*, acc. of *notātio*, a designating, also, etymology ; cf. *notātus*, pp. of *notāre*, to mark ; from *nota*. a mark ; see **Note**.

NOTCH, to make an indentation, or a small cut in an arrow-head, &c. (F.—L.) Much confused with *nock*, with the same sense ; but it appears to be of different origin. The vb. to *notch* seems to be older than the sb.; Cotgrave has both (see below). ' He .. *notched* him like a carbonado ; ' Cor. iv. 5. 199. It seems to have acquired an initial *n*; from ME. *ochen*, to cut, as in Morte Arthure, 2565, 4246, where it occurs as ' he *oches* in sondire,' and ' he *ochede* it in sondyre.'—MF. *ocher*, OF. *oschier* (*hoschier* in Godefroy), *ochier*, ' to nick, nock, notch, to cut as a tally ; ' Cot. Cognate with Prov. dial. *auscar* (Körting), spelt *ousca* in Mistral, Catalan *oscar*, to cut into ; cf. Prov. *osco*, a notch (Mistral), Catalan *osca*.—L. *absecāre*, to cut off, whence L. *absegmen*, a piece cut off (Lewis).—L. *ab*, off ; and *secāre*, to cut ; see **Section**. Der. *notch*, sb. ; cf. MF. *oche*, ' a nock, nick, or *notch*,' Cot. ; Norm. dial. *oche*, *noche*, a notch (Le Héricher) ; F. *hoche*. ¶ So Körting, § 49 ; but the MF. *ocher* also answers to Late L. *occāre*, to cut (Duc.), L. *occāre*, to harrow ; from *occa*, a harrow.

NOTE, a mark, sign. (F.—L.) In early use. ME. *note*, Chaucer, C. T. 13477 (B 1737) ; Layamon, 7000.—F. *note*.—L. *nota*, a mark, sign, note. β. The *o* is short, and perhaps *nota* stands for *gnōta*, allied to *nōtus* (for *gnō'us*), known. The shortening of the syllable appears still more decisively in *cognĭtus* = *cognōtus*, known (Bréal). See **Notice**. Thus a *note* is ' a mark whereby a thing is known.' Der. *note*, verb, ME. *noten*, Gower, C. A. iii. 164 ; bk. vii. l. 2340 ; *not-ed*, ibid. ; *not-ed-ly*, *note-less*, *not-er* ; *note-book*, Jul. Cæs. iv. 3. 98 ; *note-worthy* (= *worthy of note*), Two Gent. of Verona, i. 1. 13. And see *not-able*, *not-ary*, *not-at-ion*, *not-ice*, *not-ify*, *not-ion*, *not-or-i-ous*.

NOTHING, absence of being, insignificance. (E.) Merely an abbreviation, in pronunciation, of *no thing*. The words were formerly written apart. Thus, in Chaucer, C. T. 1756 (Six-text, A 1754), the Ellesmere and Hengwrt MSS. have *no thyng*, where the Camb. MS. has *nopyng*. See **No** (2) and **Thing**. Der. *nothing-ness*, in Bp. Hall, Select Thoughts, § 22 (R.).

NOTICE, an observation, warning, information. (F.—L.) In Shak. Hen. V, iv. 7. 122.—F. *notice*, ' notice ; ' Cot.—L. *nōtitia*, a being known, knowledge, acquaintance. Extended from *nōtus*, known, pp. of *nōscere*, to know. See **Note, Know.** Der. *notice*, verb, *notice-able, notice-abl-y.*

NOTIFY, to signify, declare. (F.—L.) In Minsheu, ed. 1627; cf. Oth. iii. 1. 31. ME. *notifyen*, Chaucer, Troil. ii. 1591. —F. *notifier*, 'to notifie;' Cot. —L. *nōtificāre*, to make known. —L. *nōti-*, for *nōtus*, known; and *-fic-*, for *fac-ere*, to make. See **Notice** and **Fact.** Der. *notific-at-ion.*

NOTION, an idea. (F.—L.) Formerly, intellectual power, sense, mind; see Shak. Cor. v. 6. 107. —F. *notion*, omitted by Cotgrave, but given in Sherwood's Index to the same. —L. *nōtiōnem*, acc. of *nōtio*, an investigation, notion, idea; cf. *nōtus*, known; see **Notice.** Der. *notion-al.*

NOTORIOUS, manifest to all. (L.) In Shak. All's Well, i. 1. 111. *Notoriously* is in Sir T. More, Works, p. 960 f. Englished from L. *nōtōrius*, by changing *-us* into *-ous*, as in *arduous*, &c. This L. word is only represented in Lewis's Dict. by the fem. and neut. forms *nōtōria, nōtōrium*, both used substantively; cf. OF. *notoire*, 'notorious' (Cot.), which points back to the same L. adj. Formed from L. *nōtor*, a voucher, witness; which again is formed with agential suffix *-tor* from *nō-*, base of *noscere*, to know, cognate with E. *know*; see **Know.** Der. *notorious-ly, -ness.*

NOTORIETY, notoriousness. (F.—L.) Used by Addison, On the Christian Religion (Todd). —MF. *notorieté*, 'notoriousness;' Cot.; mod. F. *notoriété.* —Late L. *nōtōrietātem*, acc. of *nōtōrietās* (Ducange). —L. *nōtōrius*; see **Notorious.**

NOT-PATED, closely shorn or cropped. (E. *and* Late L.) See Shak. 1 Hen. IV, ii. 4. 78. Chaucer has *not-heed*, a closely cropped head; C. T. prol. 109. Cf. 'To *Notte* his haire, *comas recidere*;' Baret (1580). From AS. *hnot*, close shorn, smooth; and **Pate.**

NOTWITHSTANDING, nevertheless. (E.) ME. *noght with-stondende*, Gower, C. A. ii. 181; bk. v. 1611. From *noght*=*naught*; and *withstanding*, pres. part. of *withstand*. Perhaps suggested by L. *nōn obstante.* See **Naught** and **Withstand.**

NOUCH, the same as **Ouch,** q. v.

NOUGHT, the same as **Naught,** q. v.

NOULE, NOWL, NOLE, NOLL, a head. (E.) 'An Asses *nole*;' Mids. Nt. Dream, iii. 2. 17 (1623). And see Nares. ME. *nol*. AS. *hnoll*, the crown of the head.+OHG. *hnol*, top.

NOUN, the name of a thing. (F.—L.) Used so as to include adjectives, as being descriptive. Rich. quotes 'that *nowne* knowledging, and that verbe knowledge' from Sir T. More, Works, p. 437 a. Also *nowne* in Cathol. Anglicum (1483); but the word is older, and belongs to the 14th cent.; first appearing in 1398 (N.E.D.). —OF. *non, nun, nom, num* (Godefroy); mod. F. *nom*, a name, a noun. In Philip de Thaun, Livre des Creatures, we have the AF. forms *nun*, l. 241, *num*, l. 233; see Wright's Popular Treatises on Science. —L. *nōmen*, a name, noun; cognate with E. **Name,** q. v. **Doublet,** *name.*

NOURISH, to feed or bring up. (F.—L.) In early use. ME. *norisen, norysen*, Rob. of Glouc. p. 238, l. 4901; whence the sb. *norysynge* in the preceding line. —OF. *noris-* (mod. F. *nourriss-*), stem of parts of the verb *norir* (mod. F. *nourrir*), to nourish. —L. *nutrire*, to suckle, feed, nourish. Der. *nourish-er*, Macb. ii. 2. 40, *nourish-able*; *nourish-ment*, Spenser, F. Q. vi. 9. 20. And see *nurse, nurture, nutri-ment, nutri-ti-ous, nutri-tive.*

NOVEL, new, strange. (F.—L.) In Shak. Sonnet 123. It seems to be less old in the language than the sb. *novelty*, which is ME. *noveltee*, Chaucer, C. T., E 1004. And it follows the OF. spelling of the sb. —OF. *novel* (Godefroy), later *nouvel*, mod. F. *nouveau.* —L. *nouellus*, new; dimin. form from *nouus*, which is cognate with E. **New,** q. v. Der. *novel-ty*, ME. *noveltee* (as above), OF. *noveliteit*, from L. *nouellitātem*, acc. of *nouellitās*, newness; *novel*, sb., a late word in the mod. sense, but the pl. *novels* (=news) occurs in the Towneley Mysteries (see Trench, Select Glossary); *novel-ist*, formerly an innovator (Trench); and see *nov-ice, in-nov-ate.*

NOVEMBER, the eleventh month. (L.) In Chaucer, On the Astrolabe, pt. i. § 10, l. 11. —L. *Nouember*, the ninth month of the Roman year. —L. *nouem*, nine. See **Nine.**

NOVICE, a beginner. (F.—L.) In Shak. Meas. i. 4. 18. ME. *novys, novice*, Chaucer, C. T. 13945 (B 3129). —F. *novice*, 'a novice, a young monke or nunne;' Cot. —L. *nouicius, nouitius*, new, fresh, a novice; Juvenal, Sat. iii. 265. Extended from *nouus*, new; see **Novel, New.** Der. *noviti-ate*, Blount's Gloss., ed. 1674, from F. *novitiat*, 'the estate of a novice,' from Late L. *nouitiātus*, sb.; see *nouītiāri* in Ducange.

NOW, at this present time. (E.) ME. *now*, Chaucer, C. T. 763 (A 761); also spelt *nou*, for older *nu*. AS. *nū*, Grein, ii. 301.+Du. *nu*; Icel. *nū*; Dan. and Swed. *nu*; OHG. *nu*; Goth. *nu.*+Skt. *nu, nū*, now (Vedic). β. The G. *nu-n*, Gk. *vṽ-v*, L. *nu-n-c*, are extended forms from the same source. Brugmann, i. § 1042. **Der.** *now-a-*

days (=now on days), Mids. Nt. Dr. iii. 1. 148, Chaucer, C. T. 16864 (G 1396); see **A-** (2), prefix. Hence also *new, novel.*

NOWAY, NOWAYS, in no way. (E.) The older form is *noways*, for ME. *nanes weies*, in no way, by no way, Layamon, 11216. This answers to AS. *nānes weges*, the gen. case used adverbially, as usual. —AS. *nānes*, gen. of *nān*, none; and *weges*, gen. of *weg*, a way. See **No** (2) and **Way.**

NOWHERE, in no place. (E.) AS. *nāhwær*, nowhere; Grein, ii. 273.—AS. *nā*, no; and *hwær*, where. See **No** (1) and **Where.**

NOWISE, in no way. (E.) Short for *in no wise*, ME. *on none wise*, Castell of Love, ed. Weymouth, 573 (Stratmann). Here *on* = *in*, is a prep.; *none* is dat. case of ME. *noon*, AS. *nān*, none; *wise*=*wisan*, dat. of AS. *wise*, a wise, a way. See **No** (2) and **Wise,** sb.

NOXIOUS, hurtful. (L.) In Milton, Par. Reg. iv. 460. Englished from L. *noxius*, hurtful, by change of *-us* to *-ous*, as in *ardu-ous*, &c.—L. *noxa*, harm, hurt; cf. *nocēre*, to hurt; *nex* (stem *nec-*), destruction. —√NEK, to perish, or cause to perish; whence also Skt. *naç*, to be lost, disappear, Gk. *νέκυς*, a corpse. Brugmann, i. § 143; ii. § 794. Der. *noxious-ly, -ness.* From the same root are *nec-ro-mancy, inter-nec-ine, per-nic-i-ous, ob-nox-i-ous, nuis-ance*, &c.

NOYAU, a cordial flavoured with orange-peel and kernels of stone-fruits. (F.—L.) Found in 1818; see Stanford Dict. —F. *noyau*, lit. 'kernel' of a fruit. —L. *nucāle*, neut. of *nucālis*, like a nut. —L. *nuc-*, stem of *nux*, a nut. See **Newel.**

NOZZLE, a snout. (E.) Rare in books. Spelt *nozle* in Arbuthnot and Pope, Martinus Scriblerus (Todd); *nozzle* (E. D. D.). Cp. 'a candylstyk *nosled*;' Archæol. Cantiana, xvi. 315 (A. D. 1500). The dimin. of *nose*, with suffix *-le* (or *-el*); so also Westphal. *nüəsel*, a nozzle (Woeste). See **Nose, Nuzzle.**

NUANCE, a shade of a colour, gradation of colour. (F.—L.) It occurs in 1781; see Stanford Dict. —F. *nuance*, a shade. —F. *nuer*, to shade. —F. *nue*, a cloud. —Folk-L. **nūba*, for L. *nūbēs*, a cloud. Allied to L. *nimbus*, a cloud; see **Nimbus, Nebula.**

NUCLEUS, the kernel of a nut, core. (L.) In Phillips, ed. 1706. —L. *nucleus*, a small nut, a kernel; cf. *nucula*, a small nut. Dimin. from L. *nux*, a nut (stem *nuc-*). Root uncertain. ¶ *Not* allied to E. *nut*. Allied to *newel*, q. v.

NUDE, naked, bare. (L.) In Minsheu, ed. 1627. Taken from the L. directly; cf. *nude contract*, Englished from L. law-term *nūdum pactum*, Blount's Nomolexicon. —L. *nūdus*, naked. L. *nūdus* =**nugdus*, for **nogwedos*, allied to Skt. *nagna-*, naked, and to E. **Naked,** q. v. Brugmann, i. § 165. Der. *nude-ly*; *nud-i-ty*, spelt *nuditie* in Minsheu, from F. *nudité*, 'nudity' (Cot.), from L. acc. *nūditātem.*

NUDGE, a slight push. (Scand.) '*Knudge*, v. to kick with the elbow;' E. D. S. Glos. B. 1; A. D. 1781. Lowland Sc. *nodge*, 'a push or strike, properly with the knuckles, *nodge*, to strike with the knuckles;' Jamieson; North E. *nog*, to jog; Lowland Sc. *gnidge*, to press, squeeze; Jam. Cf. Norw. *gnugga, nugga*, to rub, push; allied to *gnyggja, nyggja* (pt. t. *nogg*), to push; Swed. dial. *nogga*, to move slightly. Also NFries. *nocke*, to jog. Allied to **Knock.** Cf. also Icel. *knūi*, a knuckle, *knȳja*, to press down with the fists and knees; Swed. *knoge*, a knuckle; Dan. *knuge*, to press.

NUGATORY, trifling, vain. (L.) In Bacon, Adv. of Learning, bk. ii. 7. 5. —L. *nūgātōrius*, trifling. —L. *nūgātor*, a trifler. —L. *nūgāri*, to trifle. —L. pl. *nūgæ*, trifles. Root unknown. Cf. L. *naucum*, a trifle; and perhaps L. *nux*, a nut (Bréal).

NUGGET, a lump or mass of metal. (E.) Formerly also *niggot*. 'After the fire was quenched, they found in *niggots* of gold and silver mingled together, about a thousand talents;' North, tr. of Plutarch's Lives, p. 499; cited in Trench, Eng. Past and Present, without a statement of the edition used; it is not that of 1631. I find 'siluer *niggots*' in the same, ed. 1631, p. 425 (Marius). Cf. prov. E. *nug*, a block of wood; *nigg*, a small piece (Essex); *nog*, *knog*, a block of wood, knob, peg; allied to **Knag.** See **Noggin.** Ross gives Norw. *knugg*, a rounded projection, a 'knot' on the body.

NUISANCE, a troublesome or annoying thing. (F.—L.) Spelt *nuissance* in Minsheu, ed. 1627; but *nuisance* is better, as in Cotgrave. ME. *nusance*, Hoccleve, De Regim. Princ., 810. —F. *nuisance*, 'nuisance, hurt, offence;' Cot. —F. *nuisant*, 'hurtfull,' id.; pres. part. of *nuire*, to hurt. —L. *nocēre*, to hurt; see **Noxious.**

NULL, of no force, invalid. (F.—L.) In Dryden, tr. of Juvenal, Sat. i. 87. Cf. *nullity*, which occurs in Minsheu, ed. 1627. —AF. *nul* (in law); Stat. of Realm, i. 334. —L. *nullum*, acc. of *nullus*, none, not any. —L. *ne*, not, related to E. *no*; and *ullus*, any, short for **ūnulus*, dimin. from *ūnus*, one. See **No** (1) and **One.** Der. *null-i-ty*, from F. *nullité*, 'a nullity' (Cot.), from Late L. acc. *nullitātem*; *nulli-fy*, formed (as if from F. *nullifier*) from L. *nullificāre*, to make void, from *nulli-*, for *nullus*, and *-fic-*, for *facere*, to make; also *null*, verb, Milton, Samson, 935. Also *an-nul*, *dis-an-nul*.

NULLAH, a water-course, bed of a torrent. (Hind.) In 1776 (Yule). — Hind. *nāla*, a water-course (Yule); *nālā*, a ravine, rivulet (Forbes).

NUMB, deprived of sensation. (E.) The *b* is excrescent; spelt *numme* in Shak. 1 Hen. VI, ii. 5. 13 (first folio). ME. *nome*, a shortened form of *nomen*, which was orig. the pp. of ME. *nimen*, to take. Thus *nome* = taken, seized, hence overpowered, and lastly, deprived of sensation. 'Whan this was seid, into wepinge Sche fel, as sche that was thurgh-*nome* With love, and so fer overcome' = when this was said, she fell a-weeping, as being thoroughly *overcome* by love, &c.; Gower, C. A. ii. 249; bk. v. 3634. Gower uses the same word *nome* elsewhere in the ordinary sense of 'taken;' C. A. ii. 227 (bk. v. 2993); ii. 386 (bk. v. 7524). — AS. *numen*, pp. of *niman*, to take; see **Nimble**. So also Icel. *numinn*, the pp. of *nema*, to take, is similarly used; as in *numinn māli*, bereft of speech; *fjörvi numna*, life-bereft. Der. *be-numb*, q. v.; also *numb*, verb, Spenser, F. Q. vi. 11. 45; *numb-ness*, Wint. Tale, v. 3. 102 (spelt *numnesse* in the first folio). Also *num-scull*.

NUMBER, a unit in counting, a quantity. (F. — L.) The *b* is excrescent in the F. form. ME. *nombre*, *noumbre*, Rob. of Glouc. p. 60, l. 1397; Chaucer, C. T. 718 (A 716). — F. *nombre*; Norman F. *numbre* (see Philip de Thaun, Livre des Creatures, l. 127, in Wright, Popular Treatises on Science, p. 24). — L. *numerum*, acc. of *numerus*, a number. — √NEM, to distribute; cf. Gk. νόμ-ος, law, νέμ-ειν, to distribute. Brugmann, i. § 442. Der. *number*, verb, ME. *nombren*, *noumbren*, Rob. of Glouc. p. 61, l. 1398; *number-er*; *number-less*; and see *numer-al*, *numer-ation*, *numer-ous*.

NUMBLES, the entrails of a deer. (F. — L.) '*Noumbles* of a dere or beest, *entrailles*;' Palsgrave. ME. *noumbles*, Gawaine and Grene Knight, 1347. — OF. *nombles* (*d'un cerf*), 'the numbles of a stag,' Cot.; and see *nomble* in Godefroy. *Nomble* is for OF. *lomble*, by confusion with F. *nombril*, navel (from L. *umbilīcus*). See *lomble* in Godefroy, who quotes the AF. *li mien lumble*, Ps. xxvii. 8, where the Vulgate version has *lumbi mei*, i. e. my reins or loins. — L. *lumbulum*, acc. of *lumbulus*, dimin. of *lumbus*, loin; see **Loin**.

NUMERAL, a figure expressing a number. (L.) Orig. an adj. '*Numeral*, of or belonging to number;' Blount's Gloss., ed. 1674; and in Palsgrave, p. 372. — L. *numerālis*, belonging to number. L. *numerus*, a number; see **Number**. Der. *numeral-ly*.

NUMERATION, numbering. (F. — L.) In Sir T. Browne, Pseudodoxia, iii. 5. § 2. — F. *numération*; in use in the 15th cent. — L. *numerātiōnem*, acc. of *numerātio*, a counting out; cf. *numerātus*, pp. of *numerāre* to number. — L. *numerus*, number; see **Number**. Der. *numerate* (really due to the sb.), formed from L. *numerātus*; *numera-tor* = L. *numerātor*, a counter, numberer. Also *e-numerate*, *in-numer-able*.

NUMEROUS, many. (F. — L.) In Milton, P. L. i. 675, &c. — MF. *numereux*, a less usual form than *nombreux*; both are in Cotgrave. — L. *numerōsus*, numerous. — L. *numerus*, a number; see **Number**. Der. *numerous-ly*, *numerous-ness*; also (obsolete) *numer-osity* = F. *numerosité*, 'numerosity, a great number' (Cot.). So also *numer-ic*, Butler, Hudibras, pt. i. c. 3, l. 461, as if from L. **numericus* (not used); *numeric-al*, *-al-ly*.

NUMISMATIC, relating to coins. (L. — Gk.) The pl. sb. *numismaticks* was added by Todd to Johnson's Dict. Coined from L. *numismat-*, stem of *numisma*, current coin. — Gk. νόμισμα, a custom, also, current coin. — Gk. νομίζειν, to practise, adopt, to use as current coin. — Gk. νόμος, usage. — Gk. νέμειν, to distribute; see **Nomad**. Der. *numismatic-s*; *numismato-logy*, from -λογία, which from λόγος, a discourse, from λέγειν, to speak.

NUN, a female celibate, living in seclusion. (L.) ME. *nonne*, Chaucer, C. T. 118; but this is an alteration to the F. spelling; cf. F. *nonne*, a nun. The mod. E. agrees with the AS. spelling, and with ME. *nunne*, as found in the Ancren Riwle, p. 316, last line. AS. *nunne*, a nun; Laws of Ælfred (political), sect. 8; in Thorpe's Ancient Laws, i. 66. — Late L. *nunna*, more commonly *nonna*, a nun, orig. a title of respect, esp. used in addressing an old maiden lady, or a widow who had devoted herself to sacred duties. The old sense is 'mother,' answering to L. *nonnus*, father, later, a monk; a word of great antiquity. + Gk. νάννη, νέννα, an aunt; νάννας, νέννος, an uncle; Skt. *nanā*, a familiar word for mother, used by children; see the St. Petersburg Dict. iv. 25; answering to Skt. *tata*, father. β. Formed by repetition of the syllable *na*, used by children to a father, mother, aunt, or nurse; just as we have *ma-ma*, *da-da* or *daddy*, and the like. Compare **Mamma**, and **Dad**. Der. *nunn-er-y*, ME. *nonnerie*, Rob. of Glouc. p. 291, l. 5918, from OF. *nonnerie*, spelt *nonerie* in Roquefort, which was formed from QF. *nonne*, a nun, from L. *nonna*.

NUNCHION, a luncheon. (Hybrid; L. *and* E.) In Butler,

Hudibras, i. 1. 346. Cotgrave explains MF. *ressie* by 'an afternoons *nunchion*, or drinking;' and rightly, for the old sense had relation to drinking, not to eating, as will appear. Florio has: '*merenda*, a repast betweene dinner and supper, a *nunchin*.' The ME. spelling, in one instance at least, is *nonechenche*. We find that certain donations for drink to workmen are called in the [London] Letter-book G, fol. iv (27 Edw. III), *nonechenche*; see Riley, Memorials of London, p. 265, note 7; see my note to P. Plowman, C. ix. 146. It should rather be spelt *noneschenche*. β. The etymology is obvious, viz. from ME. *none*, noon; and *schenche*, a pouring out or distribution of drink. The *none-schenche* or 'noon-drink' was the accompaniment to the *none-mete* or 'noon-meat,' for which see *nunmete* in the Prompt. Parv. p. 360, and Way's note upon it. γ. The ME. *none*, noon, is from L. *nōna*, the ninth hour, as explained s. v. **Noon**. δ. ME. *schenche*, a pouring out of drink, is a sb. made from ME. *schenchen*, to pour out drink. 'Bachus the wyn hem *schenchith* al aboute' = Bacchus pours out the wine for them all round; Chaucer, C. T. (Harleian MS.), ed. Wright, l. 9596. Tyrwhitt's ed. has *skinketh*, l. 9596; the Six-text edition (E 1722) has *skynketh*, *shynketh*, *shenketh*, *schenketh*, as various readings. All these are various forms from the verb *skenken*, AS. *scencan*, to pour out drink, occurring in Beowulf, ed. Grein, l. 496. This AS. verb is cognate with Du. *schenken*, to pour out, fill, give, present, Icel. *skenkja*, to serve drink, fill one's cup, Dan. *skjenke*, G. *schenken*, *ein-schenken*. ε. The derivation of AS. *scencan* is very curious; it is a causal verb, derived with the usual vowel-change of *a* to *e*, from AS. *scanc*, usually written *sceanc*, a shank; see **Shank**. The explanation is, that a *shank* also meant a hollow bone, a bone of the leg, shin-bone, and hence 'a pipe;' in particular, it denoted the pipe thrust into a cask to tap it and draw off the liquor. Thus prov. E. *shank* means 'a tunnel for a chimney' (Halliwell), i. e. a chimney-pipe; the MDu. *schenkkan* means 'a pot with a pipe or a gullet to pour out,' Sewel. A precisely parallel interchange of sense occurs in G. *rohr*, a reed, tube, pipe; whence *röhrbein*, the hollow bone of a leg, shin-bone; *röhrbrunnen*, a jet of a fountain; *röhre*, a pipe, also a funnel, shaft, or tunnel (like the use of prov. E. *shank*). ¶ We can now understand the full force of the quotation in Way's note from Kennett's MS., viz. '*Nooning*, beavre, drinking, or repast *ad nonam*, three in the afternoon, called . . . in the North parts a *noonchion*, an afternoon's *nunchion*.' In many parts, the use of *nuncheon* was driven out by the use of *bever* (lit. a drinking) in the same sense, and in East Anglia by the more intelligible word *nooning*. Lastly, by a curious confusion with the prov. E. *lunch*, a lump of bread, *nuncheon* was turned into the modern *luncheon*; see **Luncheon**. The same change of initial *n* to *l* occurs in *lilac*, from Pers. *nil*, blue; see **Lilac**. The verb *schenchen* was afterwards supplanted by *skink*, and occurs in Shakespeare in the deriv. *under-skinker*, 1 Hen. IV, ii. 4. 26.

NUNCIO, a messenger, esp. a papal ambassador. (Ital. — L.) In Minsheu, ed. 1627; and in Shak. Tw. Nt. i. 4. 28. — Ital. *nuncio*, *nuntio*, 'an ambassador;' Florio. — L. *nuntium*, acc. of *nuntius*, a bringer of tidings; of doubtful origin. Cf. *announce*, *de-nounce*, *pro-nounce*, *e-nounce*, *re-nounce*.

NUNCUPATIVE, declared by word of mouth. (F. — L.) '*Nuncupative*, called, named, pronounced, expresly declared by word of mouth;' Blount's Glos. ed. 1674. It occurs in *Cotgrave*; also in the sense of 'nominal,' in Hall's Chron. Hen. VII, an. 11, § 10. — F. *nuncupatif*, 'nuncupative;' Cot. — Late L. *nuncupātiuus*, nominal. — L. *nuncupātus*, pp. of *nuncupāre*, to call by name. Prob. from *nōmen*, a name, and *capere*, to take (Bréal). We find *cup-* for *cap-* in *occup-āre*, to occupy. Der. *nuncupat-or-y*, formed from L. *nuncupātor*, a namer, caller by name.

NUPHAR, a yellow water-lily. (Pers. — Skt.) A corrupt form, due to **Nenuphar**, q. v. Attributed in the Cent. Dict. to Sir J. E. Smith, 1806. The form is absurd, as the word can only be (etymologically) divided as *nen-uphar*; nevertheless, the form *nūfar* (for *nīnūfar*) occurs in Persian; see Rich. Dict., p. 1611.

NUPTIAL, pertaining to marriage. (F. — L.) 'Our *nuptial* hour;' Mids. Nt. Dr. i. 1. 1. — F. *nuptial*, 'nuptiall;' Cot. — L. *nuptiālis*, belonging to a marriage. — L. sb. pl. *nuptiæ*, a wedding. — L. *nupta*, a bride, fem. of *nuptus*, pp. of *nūbere*, to marry. Brugmann, i. § 877 (a), connects L. *nūbere* with OSlavonic *snubiti*, to love, to woo. Der. *nuptial*, sb., Meas. for Meas. iii. 1. 122, usually in pl. *nuptials*, Pericles, v. 3. 80. And see *con-nub-i-al*.

NURSE, one who nourishes an infant. (F. — L.) Contracted from ME. *nurice*, a nurse; Ancren Riwle, p. 82, l. 20. — OF. *norrice*, *nurrice* (Littré), later *nour-rice* (Cot.), a nurse. — L. *nutrīcia*, a nurse. — L. *nutric-*, stem of *nutrix*, a nurse, formed with fem. suffix from the same base as *nutrire*, to feed, nourish; see **Nourish**. Der. *nurse*, verb, Wyatt, To his Ladie, cruel ouer her yelden Louer, l. 5, in Tottell's Miscellany, ed.

Arber, p. 62 ; *nurs-er*, 1 Hen. VI, iv. 7. 46 ; *nurs-er-y*, K. Lear, i. 1. 126, Cymb. i. 1. 59, and see Trench, Select Glossary ; *nurs-ling*, spelt *noursling* in Spenser, Virgil's Gnat, 282, formed with double dimin. suffix *-l-ing*, as in *duck-ling* ; *nurs-ing-father*, Numb. xi. 12. And see *nurture*.

NURTURE, nourishment, education. (F.–L.) ME. *norture*, Rob. of Brunne, tr. of Langtoft, p. 188, l. 3.–AF. *nurture*, Stat. Realm, i. 104 ; OF. *norriture* (Godefroy), mod. F. *nourriture*, 'nourishment, nutriment, . . . also nurture ;' Cot. [Cf. Ital. *nutritura*, nutriment.]–L. *nutritūra* ; from *nutrire*, to nourish ; see **Nourish.** Der. *nurture*, verb, spelt *nourter* in the Bible of 1551, Deut. viii. 5 ; *nurtur-er*. And see *nutriment*.

NUT, the fruit of certain trees, a hard shell with a kernel. (E.) ME. *note*, Havelok, 419 ; King Alisaunder, 3293 ; *nute*, O. Eng. Homilies, ed. Morris, i. 79, l. 14. AS. *hnutu*, to translate L. *nux* ; Voc. 137. 18.+Du. *noot* ; Icel. *hnot* ; Swed. *nöt* ; Dan. *nöd* ; G. *nuss*. Teut. base *hnut-* ; allied to Irish *cnu*, Gael. *cno*, W. *cneuen*, a nut ; Stokes-Fick, p. 96. ¶ It cannot be brought under the same form with L. *nux*. Der. *nut*, verb, to gather nuts ; *nut-shell*, ME. *note-schale*, Trevisa, iv. 141 ; *nut-brown*, ME. *nute-brun*, Cursor Mundi, 18846 ; *nut-cracker* (Baret) ; *nut-hatch*, a bird also called the *nut-jobber* or *nutpecker*, ME. *nuthake*, Squire of Low Degree, 55, the sense being *nut-hacker*, the bird that hacks or pecks nuts, see **Hack** (1). And see *nut-meg*.

NUTMEG, the musk-nut. (Hybrid ; E. *and* F.–L.–Pers.) ME. *notemuge*, Chaucer, C. T. 13693 (B 1953) ; *nutmegge*, Rom. of the Rose. 1361. A hybrid word ; the former half being E. *nut* ; see **Nut.** β. The latter half is from OF. *mugue*, musk, standing for *musgue*, which is ultimately from L. *muscum*, acc. of *muscus*, musk ; see **Musk.** The OF. *mugue* and *muge* occur in quotations given by Godefroy. The form *musque* is a Southern F. (Dauphinois) form, the usual Prov. form being *musc* ; see Mistral. The *s* also appears in OF. *musguette*, by-form of *muguette* in the phr. *noix muguette*, a nutmeg (Godefroy) ; whence MF. *muguette*, 'a nutmeg,' Cot. Cf. F. *noix muscade*, 'a nutmeg,' id. ; Span. *nuez moscada*, a nutmeg, Ital. *noce moscada*, the same ; Late L. *muscāta*, a nutmeg, lit. 'musk-like,' formed with suffix *-āta* from *musc-*, stem of *muscus*. The L. *muscus* is from the Pers., as shown s. v. *musk*.

NUTATION, a nodding, vibratory movement of the earth's axis. (L.) In Pope, Dunciad, ii. 409. Astronomical. Englished from L. *nūtātio*, a nodding, swaying.–L. *nūtāre*, to nod, frequentative form of *nuere*, to nod.+Gk. νεύειν, to nod. From a base NEU, signifying 'to move slightly.' Der. Hence also *in-nu-endo*.

NUTRIMENT, nourishment, food. (L.) In Milton, P. L. v. 496.–L. *nūtrimentum*, food ; formed with suffix *-mentum* from *nūtri-re*, to nourish ; see **Nourish.** Der. *nutriment-al* ; and see *nutritious*.

NUTRITIOUS, furnishing nutriment. (L.) In Blount's Gloss., ed. 1674. Englished from L. *nūtrītius*, by change of *-us* to *-ous*, as in *ardu-ous*, &c. The L. word is also (better) spelt *nūtricius*.–L. *nūtric-*, stem of *nūtrix*, a nurse ; see **Nurse.** Der. *nutritious-ly*, *-ness*. So also *nutrition*, Pope, Essay on Man, ii. 64 ; a coined word.

NUTRITIVE, nourishing. (F.–L.) In Minsheu and Cotgrave. ME. *nutritiff*, Lydgate, Minor Poems, p. 195.–F. *nutritif*, 'nutritive ;' Cot. Formed with suffix *-if* (<L. *-iuus*) from *nūtrit-*, stem of pp. of *nūtrire*, to nourish ; see **Nourish.** Der. *nutritive-ly*, *-ness*.

NUZZLE, to thrust the nose in. (E.) Also spelt *nousle* ; Shak. Venus, 1115 ; Pericles, i. 4. 42 ; *nosyll* in Palsgrave. A frequentative verb, with suffix *-le*, from the sb. *nose*. It means 'to nose often,' i. e. to keep pushing the nose towards. Cf. Low G. *nusseln* ; EFries. *nüsseln*, Swed. dial. *nösla*, with the same sense ; Swed. *nosa på allt ting*, to thrust one's nose into every corner (Widegren) ; Du. *neuzelen*, *neusen*. See **Nose,** and cf. **Nozzle.**

NYLGHAU, a large species of antelope. (Pers.) Lit. 'blue cow ;' the males being of a bluish colour.–Pers. *nīlgāw*, 'the white-footed antelope of *Pennant*, and antelope picta of *Pallas* ;' Rich. Pers. Dict. p. 1620.–Pers. *nil*, blue ; and *gāw*, a bullock, cow, cognate with E. *cow* ; id. pp. 1619, 1226. See **Lilac** and **Cow.**

NYMPH, a bride, maiden. (F.–L.–Gk.) ME. *nimphe*, Chaucer, C. T. 2930 (A 2928).–F. *nymphe*, 'a nimph ;' Cot.–L. *nympha*.–Gk. νύμφη, a bride. Der. *nymph-like*, Milton, P. L. ix. 452.

O

O (1), **OH,** an interjection. (E.) ME. *o*, Ancren Riwle, p. 54 ; Layamon, 17126. Not in AS.+Du. *o* ; Dan. and Swed. *o* ; G. *o* ; Goth. *o*, Mk. ix. 19.+L. *o* ; Gk. ὦ, ὤ. β. A natural exclamatory sound, akin to **Ah !** ¶ There is no particular reason for the

spelling *oh*, which is not older than 1548. Some make a distinction in use between *o* and *oh* ; this is merely arbitrary.

O (2), a circle. (E.) In Shak. Hen. V, prol. 13 ; Mids. Nt. Dr. iii. 2. 188. So called because the letter *o* is of a circular shape.

OAF, a simpleton. (Scand.) 'You *oaf*, you !' Dryden, Kind Keeper, i. 1 ; where the old ed. has *auph* ; see ed. 1763, vol. iv. p. 302. In Drayton's Nymphidia, l. 79, the old ed. of 1627 has *aulf* ; Prof. Morley prints *oaf*. It is the same word as prov. E. *awf*, an elf (Halliwell). Again, *auf* or *awf* stands for *aulf*, a dialectal variety of E. *elf*.–Icel. *ālfr*, an elf, cognate with E. **Elf**, q. v. β. Thus *oaf* is the Northern or Scand. variant of *elf* ; perhaps in some counties it resulted from AS. *ælf*.

OAK, the name of a tree. (E.) ME. *oke*, better *ook*, Chaucer, C. T. 3019 (A 3017). AS. *āc*, Grein, i. 14 ; the long *a* changes into ME. *oo*, by rule.+Du. *eik* ; Icel. *eik* ; Dan. *eeg*, *eg* ; Swed. *ek* ; G. *eiche*. β. All from the Teut. type *aiks*, f. Root unknown. Cf. Gk. αἰγ-ίλωψ, a kind of oak. Der. *oak-en*, adj., AS. *ācen* (Bosworth), with adj. suffix *-en* as *gold-en*, *beech-en*, &c. Also *oak-apple*, ME. *oke-appul*, Henslow, Medical Werkes, p. 80, l. 20 ; *oak-leaf*, *oak-gall*. [But not *acorn*, as often wrongly supposed.]

OAKUM, tow, old ropes teased into loose hemp. (E.) Spelt *ockam* in Skinner, ed. 1671. Spelt *oakam* in Dampier's Voyages, v. i. p. 295, an. 1686 (R.) ; *okum*, Naval Accounts (1486) ; p. 18. AS. *ācumba*, tow, in a gloss, ed. Napier, 3293 ; cf. 'Stuppa, *æcumbe*,' Voc. 152. 15. [The L. *stuppa* means 'tow.'] β. The sense is 'that which is combed off ;' the prefix is the AS. *ā-*, 'away, off,' as in the OHG. *ā-chambi*. The rest of the word is related to AS. *cemban*, to comb, and *camb*, a comb ; see **Comb.** Mr. Wedgwood says : 'OHG. *ācambi* [*āchambi*], tow ; MHG. *hanef-ācamb*, the combings or hards of hemp, tow, what is combed out in dressing it ; as *āswinc*, the refuse *swingled* out in dressing flax. " Stuppa pectitur ferreis hamis, donec omnis membrana decorticatur ;" Pliny, xix. 1. 3, cited by Aufrecht in Philological Transactions.' Holland's translation of the passage is as follows : 'Now that part thereof which is vtmost and next to the pill [peel] or rind, is called *tow* or *hurds*, and it is the worst of the line or flaxe, good for little or nothing but to make lampe-match or candle-wiek ; and yet the same must be better *kembed* with hetchell teeth of yron, vntill it be clensed from all the grosse barke and rind among ;' vol. ii. p. 4. Hence *ācumba* is used to gloss L. *putāmen* ; Mone, Quellen, p. 407, col. 1.

OAR, a light pole with a flat blade, for rowing a boat. (E.) ME. *ore*, Havelok, 1871 ; Northern form *ar*, Barbour's Bruce, iii. 576, 691. AS. *ār*, Grein, i. 34 ; the change from *ā* to long *o* being quite regular.+Icel. *ār* ; Dan. *aare* ; Swed. *åra*. Teut. type *airā*, f. ; whence Finnish *airo* (Noreen, § 57). ¶ A connexion with Gk. ἐρέτης, an oarsman, cannot be established. Cf. rather Gk. οἴαξ (for *οἴσαξ*), a tiller. Der. *oar*, verb, Temp. ii. 1. 118 ; *oar-ed* ; *eight-oar*, i. e. eight-oared boat, &c. ; *oar-s-man*, formed like *hunt-s-man*.

OASIS, a fertile spot in a desert. (L.–Gk.–Egyptian.) First in 1613 ; and now common.–L. *oasis*.–Gk. ὄασις, αὔασις, a name of the fertile islets in the Libyan desert ; Herod. iii. 26. Of Egyptian origin ; cf. Coptic *ouahe*, a dwelling-place, oasis ; *ouih*, to dwell ; Peyron, Copt. Lexicon, 1835, pp. 159, 160.

OAST, OAST-HOUSE, a kiln for drying hops. (E.) Spelt *oast* or *east* in Ray's Collection of South-Country Words, ed. 1691. [The form *east* is from Du. *eest*.] ME. *ost* ; Palladius on Husbandry, i. 457. AS. *āst*, a kiln ; 'Siccatorium [i. e. a drying-house], cyln, vel *āst* ;' Voc. 185. 30. Thus the word is E., the change from *ā* to *oa* being quite regular ; cf. AS. *āc*, an oak, *ār*, an oar.+Du. *eest* ; MDu. *ast* ; '*een ast*, a place where barley is dryed to make malt with ;' Hexham. Teut. type *aistoz*, for *aid-toz*. β. Allied to AS. *ād*, a funeral pile (Leo), MHG. *eit*, a fire, oven ; just as L. *æstus*, glow, is related to L. *ædes*, a hearth, house. Cf. Gk. αἶθος, a burning heat ; Skt. *idh*, to burn.–√EIDH, to kindle ; see **Ether.**

OATH, a solemn vow. (E.) ME. *ooth*, *oth* ; Chaucer, C. T. 120. AS. *āð*, Grein, i. 17 ; the change from *ā* to *oa* being regular, as in *āc*, oak, *ār*, oar.+Du. *eed* ; Icel. *eiðr* ; Dan. and Swed. *ed* ; Goth. *aiths* ; G. *eid* ; OHG. *eit*. β. The Teut. type is *aithoz*, m. ; Idg. type *oitos* ; allied to O:rish *oeth*, oath (Rhys).

OATS, the name of a kind of grain. (E.) ME. *otes*, s. pl., Chaucer, C. T. 7545 (D 1963). The sing. form appears in mod. E. *oat-cake*, *oat-meal*, and the adj. *oat-en*. AS. *āte* ; we find *āta* as a gloss to *zizania* in the Northumb. gloss to Matt. xiii. 38 ; also *æcer-sæd āten*, an acre-seed of oats, AS. Chron. an. 1124, where *āten* is for *ātan*, pl. Perhaps allied to Icel. *eitill*, a nodule in stone, Norweg. *eitel*, a gland, knot, nodule in stone, Russ. *iadro*, a kernel in fruit, bullet, ball, shot, Gk. οἶδος, a swelling. If this be right, the orig. meaning of *oat* has reference to its swollen form ; from √EID, to swell. Der. *oat-en*, adj., with suffix *-en* as in *gold-en*, *oak-en* ; *oat-meal*, *oat-cake*.

OB-, prefix. (L.) A common prefix, changing to *oc-* before *c*, *of-* before *f*, and *op-* before *p*, as in *oc-cur*, *of-fer*, *op-pose*. L. *ob*, with very variable senses; as, towards, at, before, upon, over, about, near. Cf. Oscan *op*, near, Gk. ἐπι, upon; Brugmann, i. § 557.

OBDURATE, hardened, stubborn. (L.) 'Obdurate in malice;' Sir T. More, Works, p. 503 b.—L. *obdūrātus*, pp. of *obdūrāre*, to render hard.—L. *ob*, prefix (which hardly affects the sense); and *dūrāre*, to harden, from *dūrus*, hard. See **Ob-** and **Dure.** Der. *obdurate-ly, -ness; obduracy,* 2 Hen. IV, ii. 2. 50.

OBEDIENT, submissive, dutiful. (F.—L.) In early use. ME. *obedient,* Ancren Riwle, p. 424, l. 11.—OF. *obedient,* 'obedient;' Cot. —L. *obēdient-,* stem of pres. pt. of *obēdire,* to obey. β. The old L. form was *oboedire.*—L. *ob-,* prefix (of little force); and *audire,* to hear, listen to. See **Ob-** and **Audience.** Brugmann, i. § 250. Der. *obedient-ly, obedience,* O. Eng. Homilies, ed. Morris, i. 213, l. 5 from bottom, = OF. *obedience,* L. *obedientia.* And see *obeisance, obey.*

OBEISANCE, a bow or act of reverence. (F.—L.) ME. *obeisance,* formerly also used in the orig. sense of obedience or act of obedience, Chaucer, C. T. 8106, 8378 (E 230, 502); cf. Gower, C. A. i. 370, ii. 219.—OF. *obeissance,* later *obeissance,* 'obedience, obeissance, a dutiful observing of;' Cot.—OF. *obeissant,* pres. pt. of *obeir,* to obey. See **Obey.**

OBELISK, a tall tapering pillar. (F.—L.—Gk.) In Holland, tr. of Pliny, b. xxxvi. c. 8 and c. 9; and in Minsheu, ed. 1627. And see Trench, Select Glossary.—MF. *obelisque,* 'an obeliske;' Cot.— L. *obeliscum,* acc. of *obeliscus.*—Gk. ὀβελίσκος, lit. a small spit, hence a thin pointed pillar; dimin. of ὀβελός, a spit; Æolic and Doric ὀδελός. Root uncertain. See **Obolus.**

OBESE, fat, fleshy. (L.) The sb. *obeseness* is in Bailey, vol. ii. ed. 1731. [The sb. *obesity* is older, and occurs in Cotgrave to translate MF. *obesité,* der. from L. acc. *obēsitātem.*]—L. *obēsus,* (1) wasted, eaten away, (2) fat, lit. 'that which has eaten away' from something; pp. of *obedere,* to eat away.—L. *ob,* near; *edere,* to eat. See **Ob-** and **Eat.** Der. *obese-ness, obes-i-ty.*

OBEY, to submit, yield to, do as bid. (F.—L.) ME. *obeyen,* Gower, C. A. ii. 219; bk. v. 2571.—OF. *obeïr,* 'to obey;' Cot.—L. *obēdire,* to obey; see **Obedience.**

OBFUSCATE, to darken, bewilder. (L.) 'Obfuscate, or made darke;' Sir T. Elyot, The Governour, b. iii. c. 23.—L. *obfuscātus,* pp. of *obfuscāre,* to darken over, obscure; also spelt *offuscāre.*—L. *ob,* over; and *fuscāre,* to darken, from *fuscus,* dark, swarthy. See **Ob-** and **Fuscous.**

OBIT, a funeral rite. (F.—L.) Almost obsolete. 'Men shall care little for *obites* within a whyle;' Sir T. More, Works, p. 880 d. ME. *obit,* Destr. of Troy, 5357.—OF. *obit,* 'an obit, obsequy, buriall;' Cot.—L. *obitus,* a going to, a going down, downfall, death. —L. *obitum,* supine of *obire,* to go near.—L. *ob,* near; and *īre,* to go, from √EI, to go. See **Ob-** and **Itinerant.** Der. *obit-u-al,* formed with suffix *-al* (= L. *-ālis*) from *obitu-,* for *obitus;* also *obitu-ar-y,* adj. relating to a decease, whence *obitu-ar-y,* sb. notice of a decease.

OBJECT, to offer in opposition, oppose. (L.) 'The kinges mother *obiected* openly against his mariage;' Sir T. More, Works, p. 60, l. 1. 'To *obiecte* [venture] their owne bodyes and lyues for their defence;' Sir T. Elyot, Castel of Helth, b. iii. c. 12.—L. *obiectāre,* to throw against, oppose; frequentative of *obicere (objicere),* to throw towards.—L. *ob,* towards, against; and *iacere,* to throw. See **Ob-** and **Jet** (1). Der. *object,* sb., a thing thrown before or presented to the senses or mind, Merch. Ven. i. 1. 20 (from the pp. *obiectus*); *object-glass; object-ion,* 1 Hen. VI, iv. 1. 129, and in Palsgrave, from F. *objection (obiection* in Cotgrave), from L. acc. *obiectiōnem; object-ion-able; object-ive,* in Bailey, vol. ii. ed. 1731, a coined word, *object-ive-ly, object-ive-ness, object-iv-i-ty.*

OBJURGATION, a blaming, reproving. (F.—L.) In Minsheu, ed. 1627; and in Cotgrave.—F. *objurgation,* 'an objurgation, chiding;' Cot.—L. *obiurgātiōnem,* acc. of *obiurgātio,* a chiding.—L. *obiurgāre,* to chide.—L. *ob,* against; and *iurgāre,* to sue, proceed against, quarrel, chide. β. L. *iurgāre* stands for *iūr-ig-āre,* from *iūr-,* stem of *iūs,* law; and *-ig-,* for *ag-ere,* to drive (Bréal). See **Jurist** and **Agent.**

OBLATE, widened at the sides. (L.) Mathematical.—L. *oblātus,* pushed forwards, viz. at the sides, said of a sphere that is flattened at the poles, and (by comparison) protrudes at the equator.—L. *ob,* towards; and *lātus,* pushed, lit. borne, for **tlātus* (= Gk. τλητός), pp. related to *tollere,* to bear, sustain. See **Ob-** and **Tolerate.** ¶ *Oblātus* is used as the pp. of *offerre,* with which it has no etymological connexion. Der. *oblate-ness;* also *oblat-ion.* (And see *prolate.*)

OBLATION, an offering. (F.—L.) 'Blessed *oblacion* of the holy masse;' Sir T. More, Works, p. 338 f. ME. *oblacion,* Lydgate, Siege of Troy, ii. 13. 159.—F. *oblation,* 'an oblation, an offering;' Cot.—L. *oblātiōnem,* acc. of *oblātio,* an offering; cf. *oblātus,* used as pp. of *offerre,* to offer. See **Oblate.**

OBLIGE, to constrain, to bind by doing a favour, to, to do a favour to. (F.—L.) ME. *obligen,* Rob. of Glouc. p. 12, l. 280.—

F. *obliger,* 'to oblige, tie, bind;' Cot.—L. *obligāre,* to bind together, oblige.—L. *ob,* to; and *ligāre,* to bind. See **Ob-** and **Ligament.** Der. *oblig-ing,* used as adj., Pope, Prol. to Satires, 208; *oblig-at-ion,* ME. *obligacion,* Rob. of Glouc. p. 391, l. 8042, from F. *obligation* <L. acc. *obligātiōnem;* *oblig-at-or-y,* from L. *obligātōrius; oblig-at-or-i-ly, oblig-at-or-i-ness.*

OBLIQUE, slanting, perverse. (F.—L.) In Shak. Timon, iv. 3. 18.—F. *oblique,* 'crooked, oblique;' Cot.—L. *obliquus, oblīcus,* slanting, sideways, awry.—L. *ob,* towards; and a base **liqu-* or **līc-.* β. The orig. sense of this **liquus* is 'bent;' cf. L. *licinus,* bent, *limus,* for **licmus,* askew; and perhaps Lithuan. *lenkti,* to bend. Der. *obliqu-i-ty,* from F. *obliquité,* 'obliquity' (Cot.), from L. acc. *oblīquitātem; oblique-ness.*

OBLITERATE, to efface. (L.) In Minsheu, ed. 1627.—L. *oblīteratus,* pp. of *oblīterare* or *oblitterāre,* to efface, smear out.—L. *ob,* over; and *littera,* a letter; see **Letter.** β. It seems to have been associated with L. *oblitus,* pp. of *oblinere,* to smear over; but there is no etym. connexion. Der. *obliterat-ion.*

OBLIVION, forgetfulness. (F.—L.) ME. *obliuion* (for oblivion), Gower, C. A. ii. 23; bk. iv. 651.—F. *oblivion.*—L. *obliuiōnem,* acc. of *obliuio,* forgetfulness.—L. *obliu-,* base of the inceptive verb *obliuiscī,* to forget. Root uncertain; the prefix is the prep. *ob.* Perhaps connected with *liuescere,* to become livid, turn black and blue (hence, perhaps, to become dark); see **Livid.** But Bréal connects it with *oblitus,* i.e. effaced, pp. of *oblinere,* to smear over. Der. *oblivi-ous,* Minsheu, *oblyvyouse* in Palsgrave, from F. *oblivieux* (Cot.)<L. *ob-liuiōsus; oblivi-ous-ly, oblivi-ous-ness.*

OBLONG, long from side to side. (F.—L.) In Cotgrave.—F. *oblong,* 'oblong, somewhat long;' Cot.—L. *oblongus,* long, esp. long across.—L. *ob,* across, over; and *longus,* long. See **Ob-** and **Long.**

OBLOQUY, calumny. (L.) 'From the great *obloquy* in which hee was;' Sir T. More, Works, p. 44 f. Englished from L. *obloquium,* contradiction.—L. *obloquī,* to speak against.—L. *ob,* against; and *loquī,* to speak. See **Ob-** and **Loquacious.**

OBNOXIOUS, offensive, answerable. (L.) Formerly used in the L. sense of 'liable to;' as in Milton, Samson, 106; P. L. ix. 170, 1094. 'The perils that you are *obnoxious* to;' Ben Jonson, Silent Woman, ii. 1. See Trench, Select Glossary.—L. *obnoxius,* liable to hurt; confused with L. *noxius,* hurtful; whence the E. word was formed by change of *-us* to *-ous.*—L. *ob,* prefix; and *noxa,* harm. See **Ob-** and **Noxious.** Der. *obnoxious-ly, -ness.*

OBOE, a hautboy. (Ital.—F.—L.) The Ital. spelling of *hautboy.* —Ital. *oboè,* a hautboy (Meadows, Eng.-Ital. section).—F. *hautbois.* See **Hautboy.**

OBOLUS, a very small Gk. coin. (L.—Gk.) Sometimes used in mod. E.—L. *obolus.*—Gk. ὀβολός, a small coin, perhaps orig. in the shape of a small rod or nail; a collateral form of ὀβελός, a spit. See **Obelisk.**

OBSCENE, unchaste, foul. (L.) In Shak. Rich. II, iv. 1. 131. Spelt *obscœne* in Minsheu, ed. 1627.—L. *obscēnus, obscænus, obscœnus,* repulsive, foul. Etym. very doubtful; as one sense of *obscēnus* is ill-boding, inauspicious, it may be connected with L. *scœuus,* left, left-handed, unlucky, inauspicious. Der. *obscene-ness, obscen-i-ty.*

OBSCURE, dark, little known. (F.—L.) 'Now is faire, and now *obscure;*' Rom. of the Rose, 5348.—F. *obscur,* 'obscure,' Cot.— L. *obscūrus,* dark, lit. 'covered over.'—L. *ob,* over; and *-scūrus,* covered, from √SKEU, to cover. Cf. Skt. *sku,* to cover; and see **Sky.** Der. *obscure-ly, -ness; obscure,* verb, used by Surrey to translate L. *caligare* in Virgil, Æn. ii. 606; *obscur-i-ty,* ME. *obscurete,* Caxton, G. Legend, St. Hilary, § 1, from F. *obscurité,* 'obscurity' (Cot.), from L. acc. *obscūritātem;* also *obscur-at-ion,* directly from L. *obscūrātio.*

OBSECRATE, to entreat. (L.) 'Obsecrate, heartily to request;' Cockeram (1642).—L. *obsecrāt-us,* pp. of *obsecrāre,* to entreat, conjure.—L. *ob,* on account of; and *sacrāre,* to treat as sacred, from *sacr-,* for *sacer,* sacred. See **Ob-** and **Sacred.**

OBSEQUIES, funeral rites. (F.—L.) ME. *obsequies,* Chaucer, C. T. 995 (A 993).—AF. and OF. *obsequies,* MF. *obseques,* 'obsequies;' Cot.—L. *obsequiās,* acc. of *obsequiæ,* s. pl., funeral rites; lit. 'followings;' a late form, for *exsequiās* (Lewis).—L. *ob,* prep., near; and *sequī,* to follow. See **Ob-** and **Sequence;** also **Obsequious.**

OBSEQUIOUS, compliant. (L.) See Trench, Select Glossary. In Shak. Oth. i. 1. 46. [F. *obsequieux,* 'obsequious;' Cot.]—L. *obsequiōsus,* full of compliance.—L. *obsequium,* compliance.—L. *obsequī,* to comply with; lit. 'to follow near.'—L. *ob,* near; and *sequī,* to follow. See **Ob-** and **Sequence.** Der. *obsequious-ly, -ness.*

OBSERVE, to heed, regard, keep. (F.—L.) ME. *obseruen* (with *u=v*), Chaucer, C. T. 13561 (B 1821).—OF. *observer,* 'to observe;' Cot.—L. *obseruāre,* to mark, take notice of.—L. *ob* (scarcely affecting the sense); and *seruāre*, to keep, heed. See **Ob-** and **Serve**. Der. *observ-er*, *observ-able*, *observ-abl-y*; *observ-ance*, ME. *obseruaunce*, Chaucer, C. T. 1502, 10830 (A 1500, F 516), from F. *observance*, which from L. *obseruantia*; *observ-ant*, Hamlet, i. 1. 71, from F. *observant*, pres. part. of the verb *observer*; *observant-ly*; *observ-at-ion*, L. L. L. iii. 28, and in Palsgrave, directly from L. *obseruātio*; *observ-at-or*, *observ-at-or-y*.

OBSIDIAN, a vitreous stone. (L.) Bailey (1735) has: '*Obsidianum marmor*, the touchstone;' and see Holland, tr. of Pliny, bk. xxxvi. c. 26. — L. *Obsidiānus lapis*, a false reading for *Obsidius lapis*; a stone found by one *Obsidius* (false reading for *Obsius*) in Aethiopia; in Pliny, lib. xxxvi. c. 26, and lib. xxxvii. c. 10.

OBSOLESCENT, going out of use. (L.) In Johnson's Dict., s. v. *Hereout*. — L. *obsolescent-*, stem of pres. part. of *obsolescere*, to grow old, inceptive form of *obsolēre*, to decay. See **Obsolete**. Der. *obsolescence*.

OBSOLETE, gone out of use. (L.) In Minsheu, ed. 1627. — L. *obsolētus*, pp. of *obsolēre*, to grow old, decay. β. The etym. of this word is very doubtful; it is not even known how it should be divided. Perhaps from *ob*, against, and *solēre*, to be wont, as if *obsolēre* = to go against custom; cf. *ex-solescere*, to become disused (to Tertullian). Der. *obsolete-ness*; and see *obsolescent*.

OBSTACLE, a hindrance. (F. — L.) ME. *obstacle*, Chaucer, C. T. 9533 (E 1659). — F. *obstacle*. — L. *obstāculum*, a hindrance, a double dimin. form with suffixes *-cu-lu-*. — L. *obstāre*, to stand in the way. — L. *ob*, over against; and *stāre*, to stand, from √STA, to stand. See **Ob-** and **Stand**; also **Obstetric**.

OBSTETRIC, pertaining to midwifery. (L.) In Pope, Dunciad, iv. 394. Shortened from *obstetricious*, occurring in Cudworth, Intellectual System, b. i. c. 4 (R.). — L. *obstetrīcius*, obstetric. — L. *obstetrīc-*, stem of *obstetrix*, a midwife. β. In *obste-trix*, the suffix *-trix* is the fem. suffix answering to masc. suffix *-tor*; the lit. sense is 'a female who stands near or beside.' — L. *obstāre*, to stand near. — L. *ob*, near; and *stāre*, to stand. See **Obstacle**. Der. *obstetric-s*, *obstetric-al*.

OBSTINATE, stubborn. (L.) ME. *obstinat*, Gower, C. A. ii. 117; bk. iv. 3434. We find the sb. *obstinacy* 5 lines above, with the L. *obstinacio* in the margin. — L. *obstinātus*, resolute, stubborn; pp. of *obstināre*, to set about, be resolved on. — L. *ob*, over against; and a verb *stanāre*, to cause to stand, set, allied to Cretic στανύω, I set; whence also the comp. *dē-stina*, a support, stay, prop. See **Ob-** and **Destine**. The root is √STA, to stand, stand firm. Brugmann, ii. § 603 (2). Der. *obstinate-ly*; *obstinac-y*, formed by analogy with *legacy* from *legate*, &c.

OBSTREPEROUS, noisy, clamorous. (L.) In Beaum. and Fletcher, Maid in a Mill, iii. 1. 5. — L. *obstreperus*, clamorous; with change of *-us* to *-ous*. — L. *ob*, against, near; and *strepere*, to make a noise, rattle, roar, perhaps of imitative origin. Der. *obstreperous-ly*, *-ness*.

OBSTRICTION, obligation. (L.) Very rare. In Milton, Samson, 312. A coined word; made from L. *obstrictus*, bound, obliged, pp. of *obstringere*, to bind, fasten. — L. *ob*, over against; and *stringere*, to bind. See **Ob-** and **Strict**.

OBSTRUCT, to block up a way, &c. (L.) In Milton, P. L. v. 257, x. 636; and in Cotgrave, s.v. *Oppiler*. [Probably really due to the earlier sb. *obstruction*, occurring in Sir T. Elyot, Castel of Helth, b. ii. c. 32, a word taken *directly* from L. *obstructio*.] — L. *obstructus*, pp. of *obstruere*, to build in the way of anything. — L. *ob*, over against; and *struere*, to build. See **Ob-** and **Structure**. Der. *obstruct-ion*, as above; *obstruct-ive*, *obstruct-ive-ly*.

OBTAIN, to get, gain, hold. (F. — L.) 'Possible for vs in this life to *obtaine*;' Sir T. More, Works, p. 7 d. Spelt *opteyne*, Dictes and Sayings, pr. by Caxton, fol. 19, l. 24. — F. *obtenir*. — L. *obtinēre*, to hold, obtain. — L. *ob*, near, close to; and *tenēre*, to hold. See **Ob-** and **Tenable**. Der. *obtain-able*.

OBTEST, to conjure, call to witness, supplicate. (F. — L.) '[They] *Obtest* his clemency;' Dryden, tr. of Virgil, Æn. xi. 151. 'He earnestly *obtested*' [besought]; Hall's Chron., Hen. VII, an. 4, § 8. — MF. *obtester*, 'to obtest, conjure, invoke;' Cot. — L. *obtestārī*, to call as witness. — L. *ob*, near; and *testārī*, to witness, from *testis*, a witness. See **Testament**.

OBTRUDE, to thrust upon, thrust in upon. (L.) In Minsheu, ed. 1627. — L. *obtrūdere*, pp. *obtrūsus*, to thrust against, obtrude on one. — L. *ob*, against; and *trūdere*, to thrust, allied to E. *threaten*. See **Ob-** and **Threat**. Der. *obtrus-ion*, *obtrus-ive*, *obtrus-ive-ly*; from the pp. *obtrūsus*.

OBTUSE, blunt, dull. (F. — L.) In Minsheu, ed. 1627. — MF. *obtus*, 'dull, blunt;' Cot. — L. *obtūsus*, blunt; pp. of *obtundere*, to beat against or upon, to dull, deaden. — L. *ob*, upon; and *tundere*, to beat, strike, from √TEUD, to strike; cf. Skt. *tud*, to strike. Der. *obtuse-ly*, *-ness*.

OBVERSE, lit. turned towards one, used of the face of a coin, as opposed to the reverse. (L.) 'Silver pieces, ... with a rude head upon the *obverse*;' Sir T. Browne, Hydriotaphia, ch. ii. § 7. — L. *obuersus*, pp. of *obuertere*, to turn towards. — L. *ob*, towards; and *uertere*, to turn. See **Ob-** and **Verse**. Der. *obverse-ly*.

OBVIATE, to meet in the way, prevent. (L.) 'Obviate, to meet with one, withstand, resist;' Minsheu, ed. 1627. — L. *obuiātus*, pp. of *obuiāre*, to meet in the way, go towards. — L. *ob*, over against; and *uia*, a way. See **Ob-** and **Voyage**. And see **Obvious**.

OBVIOUS, evident. (L.) Orig. 'meeting in the way,' as defined by Minsheu, ed. 1627. — L. *obuius*, meeting, lying in the way, obvious. — L. *ob*, near; and *uia*, a way; see **Obviate**. Der. *obvious-ly*, *-ness*.

OCA, a name of *Oxalis crenata* and *Oxalis tuberosa*, cultivated for their tubers. (Span. — Peruvian.) 'The Papas and Ocas be the chiefe for nourishment;' E. G.; tr. of Acosta, bk. iv. c. 18; p. 261. — Span. *oca*. — Peruv. *occa*, an edible root; Peruv. Dict. p. 262.

OCCASION, opportunity, occurrence. (F. — L.) ME. *occasion*, *occasioun*, Chaucer, C. T. 12000 (C 66). — F. *occasion*. — L. *occāsiōnem*, acc. of *occāsio*, opportunity. — L. *oc-*, for *ob* before *c*; and *-cāsio*, allied to *cāsus*, pp. of *cadere*, to fall, befall; see **Ob-** and **Chance**. Der. *occasion-al*, *occasion-al-ly*. And see *occident*.

OCCIDENT, the west. (F. — L.) Not now common. ME. *occident*, Chaucer, C. T. 4717 (B 297). — OF. *occident*, 'the occident, the west;' Cot. — L. *occidentem*, acc. of pres. pt. of *occidere*, to set (as the sun), go down. — L. *oc-* (for *ob* before *c*); and *cadere*, to fall; see **Ob-** and **Chance**. Der. *occident-al*, All's Well, ii. 1. 166.

OCCIPUT, the back part of the skull. (L.) In Phillips, ed. 1706; and first in 1602. [The adj. *occipital* is found earlier, in Minsheu, ed. 1627; and first in 1541.] — L. *occiput*, the back of the head. — L. *oc-* (for *ob* before *c*), over against; and *caput*, the head. See **Ob-** and **Chief**. Der. *occipit-al*, formed from *occipit-*, decl. stem of *occiput*.

OCCULT, hidden, secret. (L.) In Blount's Gloss., ed. 1674; first in 1567. [Cf. F. *occulte*, 'hidden;' Cot.] — L. *occultus*, hidden, pp. of *occulere*, to cover over. — L. *oc-* (for *ob* before *c*); and *celere*, to hide (not found), from √KEL, to cover, hide, whence also OIrish *cel-im*, I hide, and E. *hell*. See **Ob-** and **Hell**. Der. *occult-ly*, *-ness*; *occult*, verb, Hamlet, iii. 2. 85, from F. *occulter*, 'to hide' (Cot.), which from L. *occultāre*, frequentative of *occulere*. Also *occult-at-ion*, in Palsgrave, an astronomical term, borrowed from L. *occultātio*, a hiding.

OCCUPY, to keep, hold, fill, employ. (F. — L.) ME. *occupien*, Chaucer, C. T. 4844 (B 424); P. Plowman, B. v. 409. — F. *occuper*. — L. *occupāre*, to lay hold of, occupy. — L. *oc-* (for *ob* before *c*); and *capere*, to seize. See **Ob-** and **Captive**. The final *-y* is due to the *i* in the ME. infin. ending *-ien*, which was substituted for the ordinary ending *-en*, probably to strengthen the word; cf. the suffix *-ian* for *-an* in AS. causal verbs. Der. *occupi-er*; also *occup-at-ion*, ME. *occupacion*, Gower, C. A. ii. 50, bk. iv. 1452, from F. *occupation*, which from L. acc. *occupātiōnem*; also *occup-ant*, from F. *occupant*, pres. pt. of *occuper*; *occup-anc-y*.

OCCUR, to happen. (F. — L.) The word occurs in a letter from Cromwell to Sir T. Wyat dated Feb. 22, 1538 (R.). — MF. *occurrer*, 'to occurr;' Cot. — L. *occurrere*, to run to meet, meet, appear, occur. — L. *oc-* (for *ob* before *c*); and *currere*, to run. See **Ob-** and **Course**. Der. *occurr-ent*, Bible, 1 Kings, v. 4, from MF. *occurrent*, 'occurrent, accidentall' (Cot.), which from L. *occurrent-*, stem of the pres. part. of *occurrere*. Also *occurr-ence*, 1 Hen. V, v. chor. 40, from MF. *occurrence*, 'an occurrence or accident,' Cot.

OCEAN, the main sea. (F. — L. — Gk.) ME. *ocean*, *occean*, Chaucer, C. T. 4925 (B 505). — OF. *ocean*, fem. *oceane*; Cot. gives '*la mer oceane*, the ocean, or maine sea.' — L. *ōceanum*, acc. of *ōceanus*, the main sea. — Gk. ὠκεανός, the great stream supposed to encompass the earth, Homer, Il. xiv. 245, xx. 7; a word of unknown origin. Der. *ocean-ic*.

OCELOT, a small carnivorous animal. (Mexican.) Described in a tr. of Buffon, London, 1793, i. 303. 'Ocelotl, or leopard-cat of Mexico;' Clavigero, Hist. of Mexico, tr. by Cullen, ii. 319. '*Ocelotl* in Mexican is the name of the tyger, but Buffon applies it to the leopard-cat;' id., footnote. — Mex. *ocelotl*, a tiger, jaguar.

OCHRE, a fine clay, commonly yellow. (F. — L. — Gk.) In Holland, tr. of Pliny, b. xxxiii. c. 13. The *ch* is due to Gk. χ; it is spelt *occar* in Palsgrave, *oker* in Cotgrave. — OF. *ocre*, 'painters' oker;' Cot. — L. *ōchra*. — Gk. ὤχρα, yellow ochre, so called from its pale colour. — Gk. ὠχρός, pale, wan, esp. pale-yellow. Root uncertain. Der. *ochre-ous*, *ochr-y*.

OCTAGON, a plane figure with eight sides and angles. (Gk.) In Phillips, ed. 1706. Spelt *octogon* in Blount (1656). Coined from Gk. ὀκτά, for ὀκτώ, eight, cognate with E. *eight*; and γωνία, an angle, corner, allied to γόνυ, the knee. See **Eight** and **Knee**. Der. *octagon-al*.

OCTAHEDRON, a solid figure with eight equal triangular sides. (Gk.) Spelt *octaedron* in Phillips, ed. 1706; ed. 1658 has the adj. *octohedrical.* The *h* represents the Gk. hard breathing. Coined from ὀκτά, for ὀκτώ, eight, cognate with E. *eight*; and ἕδρα, a base, a seat, from the base ἑεδ-, cognate with E. *sit.* See **Eight** and **Sit.** And see **Decahedron.**

OCTANGULAR, having eight angles. (L.) In Blount's Gloss., ed. 1674. Formed with adj. suffix *-ar* (= L. *-āris*) from L. *oct-angul-us*, eight-angled.—L. *oct-*, for *octo*, eight; and *angulus*, an angle. See **Eight** and **Angle.**

OCTANT, the aspect of two planets when distant by the eighth part of a circle. (L.) In Phillips, ed. 1706.—L. *octant-*, stem of *octans*, an instrument for measuring the eighth of a circle.—L. *octo*, eight. See **Eight.**

OCTAVE, lit. eighth; hence eight days after a festival, eighth note in music. (F.—L.) [The true old F. form of *eight* was *oit*, *uit*, whence ME. *utas*, an octave (Halliwell); occurring as late as in Palsgrave.] 'The *octauis* [octaves] of the Epyphany;' Fabyan's Chron. an. 1324-5, ed. Ellis, p. 428.—F. *octaves*, pl. of *octave*; Cot. gives 'octave, an octave, an eighth; *l'octave d'une feste*, the octave, eight days, [or] on the eighth day, after a holyday.'—L. *octāua*, fem. of *octāuus*, eighth.—L. *octo*, eight; see **Eight.** Der. *octav-o*, from L. *octāuo*, abl. case of *octāuus*; a book was said to be *in folio, in quarto, in octavo*, &c.

OCTOBER, the eighth month of the Roman year. (L.) In Chaucer, On the Astrolabe, pt. i. § 10, l. 4.—L. *Octōber*; from *octo*, eight. The origin of the suffix *-ber* is doubtful.

OCTOGENARIAN, one who is eighty years old. (L.) Added by Todd to Johnson. Coined from L. *octogēnārius*, belonging to eighty.—L. *octogēni*, eighty each; distributive form belonging to *octoginta*, eighty.—L. *octo*, eight; and *-ginta* = *-cinta*, prob. short for **decinta*, a derivative from *decem*, ten, cognate with E. *ten.* See **Eight** and **Ten.** Brugmann, ii. § 164.

OCTOPUS, a cephalopod mollusc with eight arms or feelers. (L.—Gk.) Pl. *octopodes* or *octopuses.* First in 1758.—L. *octōpūs.*—Gk. ὀκτώπους (gen. ὀκτώποδ-ος), i.e. eight-footed.—Gk. ὀκτώ, eight; and πούς (gen. ποδ-ός), foot. See **Eight** and **Foot.**

OCTOROON, the offspring of a white person and a quadroon. (L.) First in 1861. One who is, in an eighth part, black. Coined from L. *octō*, eight; in imitation of *quadroon.* See **Quadroon.**

OCTOSYLLABIC, having eight syllables. (L.—Gk.) Tyrwhitt, in his Introd. to Chaucer, § vii, speaks of 'the *octosyllable* metre,' without the suffix *-ic.*—L. *octosyllabus*, adj., having 8 syllables.—Gk. ὀκτώ, eight; and συλλαβή, a syllable. See **Eight** and **Syllable.**

OCTROI, a duty or toll on articles admitted into a town. (F.—L.) First in 1614; in the sense of 'grant.'—F. *octroi*; MF. *octroy*, 'a grant, a privilege conferred;' Cot.—MF. *octroyer*, 'to grant, allow,' Cot.; OF. *otreiier, otroier.*—Late L. type **autoridiāre*, for Late L. *auctorizāre*, to authorise.—L. *auctor*, author; see **Author.**

OCULAR, pertaining to the eye. (L.) 'Ocular proof;' Oth. iii. 3. 360.—L. *oculāris*, adj., formed from *oculus*, the eye, a dimin. of **ocus*, the eye, a form not used, but cognate with Gk. ὄμμα, the eye. Der. *ocular-ly, bin-ocular, in-oculate*; also *ocul-ist*, from L. *oculus.*

ODALISQUE, a female slave in a Turkish harem. (F.—Turk.) Blount, ed. 1681, has '*Odalisque*, a slave.' 'Sleek *odalisques*;' Tennyson, Princess, ii. 63.—F. *odalisque*, the same (Littré); better spelt *odalique* (Devic).—Turk. *ōdaliq*, a chambermaid.—Turk. *ōda*(*h*), a chamber, a room; Zenker's Dict. p. 115.

ODD, not even, strange, queer. (Scand.) ME. *odde.* 'Odde or euen;' Gower, C. A. iii. 138; bk. vii. 1580. 'None *odde* ʒerez' = no odd years, Allit. Poems, ed. Morris, B. 426. 'None *odde* wedding' = no irregular marriage; Myrc's Instructions for Parish Priests, ed. Peacock, l. 198.—Icel. *oddi*, a triangle, a point of land; metaph. from the triangle, an odd number, opp. to even; also used in the metaphorical phrase *standask ī odda*, to stand at odds, be at odds, quarrel. In composition, we find Icel. *oddamaðr*, the odd man, the third man, one who gives a casting vote; *oddatala*, an odd number. Hence it is clear that the notion of 'oddness' arose from the figure of a triangle, which has *two* angles at the base and an odd one at the vertex. Also *oddi* is closely related to *oddr*, a point of a weapon, which stands for **ozdr*, by assimilation.+AS. *ord*, point of a sword, point, beginning, chief; Dan. *od*, a point; *odde*, a tongue of land; Swed. *udda*, odd, not even; *udde*, a point, cape, promontory; *udd*, a point, prick; G. *ort*, a place, region, MHG. *ort*, an extreme point. β. The common Teut. type is **uzdoz*; and the orig. sense seems to have been sharp point or edge, esp. of a weapon. ¶ The sense of 'strange,' or 'queer,' seems to be a mere development from that of uneven. The W. *od*, notable, excellent, odd, is merely borrowed from E. The phrase *odds and ends* means 'points and ends,' hence, scraps; different from the ME. *ord and ende* =

beginning and end; see Tyrwhitt's note to Chaucer, C. T. 14639, and my note to the same line in the Monkes Tale, B 3911. ☞ Quite distinct from **Orts**, q.v. Der. *odd-ly, odd-ness, odd-i-ty, odd-fellow*; *odds*, Oth. ii. 3. 185.

ODE, a song. (F.—L.—Gk.) In Shak. L. L. L. iv. 3. 99.—F. *ode*, 'an ode;' Cot.—L. *ōda, ōdē.*—Gk. ᾠδή, a song; contracted form of ἀοιδή, a song.—Gk. ἀείδειν, to sing; related to ἀηδών, a nightingale, singing bird. β. The base of ἀείδειν is ἀϝειδ, where ἀ is prosthetic, and ϝειδ represents a √WEID, to cry out; whence also OIrish *faed*, W. *gwaedd*, a cry, shout. Stokes-Fick, p. 259. Der. *ep-ode, com-ed-y, trag-ed-y, mel-od-y, mon-od-y, palin-ode, par-od-y, psalm-od-y, pros-od-y, rhaps-od-y.*

ODIUM, hatred. (L.) In Phillips, ed. 1706. [The adj. *odious* is much older; in Chaucer, C. T., D 2190.]—L. *odium*, hatred.—L. *ōdī*, I hate; an old pt. t. used as a present. Cf. Armenian *at-eam*, I hate. Brugmann, i. § 160. Der. *odi-ous*, Test. of Creseide, st. 33, l. 229, and as above, from F. *odieux*, 'odious' (Cot.), from L. *odiōsus*, adj., formed from *odium*; *odi-ous-ly, -ness.* And see **annoy.**

ODOUR, scent, perfume. (F.—L.) ME. *odour*, Wyclif, Eph. v. 2; Cursor Mundi, 3701.—AF. *odour*, OF. *odor*, F. *odeur*, 'an odor, sent;' Cot.—L. *odōrem*, acc. of *odor*, a scent.—√OD, to smell; whence also Gk. ὄζειν (= ὀδ-γειν), to smell; and Lithuan. *ůdžiu*, I smell. Der. *odor-ous*, Mids. Nt. Dr. ii. 1. 110, from L. *odōrus*, by change of *-us* to *-ous*, and throwing back the accent; *odor-ous-ly.* Also *odori-fer-ous*, L. L. L. iv. 2. 128, Lydgate, Assembly of Gods, 336, coined from L. *odōri-fer*, odour-bearing; which from *odōri-*, decl. stem of *odor*, and *-fer*, bearing, from *ferre*, to bear; see **Bear** (1). And see **Olfactory, Osmium, Ozone, Redolent.**

ŒSOPHAGUS, the gullet. (L.—Gk.) 'The *oesophagus*, or meatpipe;' P. Fletcher, The Purple Island, c. iv. note 30.—Late L. *oesophagus.*—Gk. οἰσοφάγος, the gullet; of uncertain origin.

OF, from, belonging to, among. (E.) ME. *of*; passim. AS. *of*, of; Grein, ii. 308.+Du., Icel., Swed., Dan., and Goth. *af*; G. *ab*; OHG. *aba.*+L. *ab*; Gk. ἀπό; Skt. *apa*, away. Brugmann, i. § 560. The E. *off* is merely another spelling of *of*; see **Off.** A comparative form occurs in E. *after*; see **After.** And see **A-** (6), **Ab-, Apo-.**

OFF, away, away from. (E.) Merely another form of *of*, due to an emphatic or stressed use of it; and in old authors there is no distinction between the words, the spelling *of* doing duty for both. 'Smiteth *of* my hed' = smite off my head; Chaucer, C. T. 784 (A 782, Harl. MS.). The spelling *off* for *of* occurs in Barbour's Bruce, i. 27, &c. An early instance occurs in the line: 'For thou art mon *off* strange lond;' Rob. of Glouc. p. 115, l. 15; ed. Hearne. In the 13th century the spelling *off* is (I believe) never found. See **Of.** Der. see below, *of-fal, off-ing, off-scouring, off-set, off-shoot, off-spring.*

OFFAL, waste meat, refuse. (E.) See Trench, Select Glossary. ME. *offal*; 'Offal, that ys bleuit of a thynge, as chyppys, or other lyke, *Caducum*;' Prompt. Parv. Cf. '*Offall* of trees;' Palsgrave. Thus it was formerly used of chips of wood falling from a cut log; and is merely compounded of *off* and *fall*; see **Off** and **Fall.**+Du. *afval*, fall, windfall, refuse, offal; from *af*, off, and *vallen*, to fall; Dan. *affald*, a fall off, decline, refuse, offal; G. *abfall*, offal; from *ab*, off, and *fallen.*

OFFEND, to annoy, displease. (F.—L.) ME. *offenden*, Chaucer, C. T. 2396 (A 2394).—F. *offendre*, 'to offend, hurt;' Cot.—L. *offendere* (pp. *offensus*), to strike or dash against, hurt, injure.—L. *of-* (for *ob* before *f*), against; and **fendere*, to strike, only occurring in compounds. See **Defend.** Der. *offence* or *offense*, ME. *offence*, Chaucer, C. T. 5558 (B 1138), from OF. *offense* (Cot.), from L. *offensa*, an offence, orig. fem. of pp. *offensus*; *offens-ive*, K. Lear, iv. 2. 11, from F. *offensif* (Cot.), as if from L. **offensiuus* (not used); *offens-ive-ly, offens-ive-ness*; also *offend-er.*

OFFER, to propose, present, lay before. (L.) Directly from Latin. In very early use; found even in AS. ME. *offren*, Chaucer, C. T. 12841 (C 907); Rob. of Glouc. p. 14, l. 325. AS. *offrian*, to offer; see exx. in Sweet's A. S. Reader.—L. *offerre*, to offer.—L. *of-* (for *ob* before *f*), near; and *ferre*, to bring, to bear, cognate with E. *bear.* See **Ob-** and **Bear** (1). Der. *offer*, sb., *offer-er*; *offer-ing* = AS. *offrung*, Mark, ix. 49. Also *offer-tor-y*, ME. *offertorie*, Chaucer, C. T. 712 (A 710), F. *offertoire* (Cot.), from L. *offertōrium*, a place to which offerings were brought, an offertory, extended from *offertor*, an offerer, formed from the verb *offer-re* with agential suffix *-tor.*

OFFICE, duty, employment, act of worship, &c. (F.—L.) In early use. ME. *offiz, office.* 'On thin *offiz*' = in thy official position; Genesis and Exodus, ed. Morris, l. 2071.—F. *office.*—L. *officium*, duty, service. Perhaps from *of-* (for *ob* before *f*), and *-fic-*, for *facere*, to do (Bréal). See **Ob-** and **Fact.** Der. *office-bearer*; *offic-er*, ME. *officere*, Chaucer, C. T. 8066 (E 190), from F. *officier* < Late L. *officiārius*, one who performs an office; *offic-i-al*, P. Plowman, B. xx.

136, from OF. *official*, 'an officiall' (Cot.), which from L. *officiālis*; *offic-i-al-ly*; *offici-ate*, in Milton, P. L. viii. 22, from Late L. *officiātus*, pp. of *officiāre*, to perform an office, occurring A.D. 1314 (Ducange). Also *offici-ous* (see Trench, Select Glossary), used sometimes in a good sense, Titus Andron. v. 2. 202, from F. *officieux*, 'officious, dutifull, serviceable' (Cot.), which from L. *officiōsus*, obliging; *offici-ous-ly*, *offici-ous-ness*.

OFFICINAL, pertaining to or used in a shop or laboratory. (L.) '*Officinal*, such drugs, plants, &c. as are sold in shops;' Bailey (1735). Formed with suffix *-al* (L. *-ālis*) from L. *officin-a*, a workshop, office; contracted form of *opificīna* (Plautus). ‒ L. *opific-*, decl. stem of *opifex*, a workman. ‒ L. *opi-*, for *opus*, work; and *-fic-*, for *facere*, to do. See **Operate**.

OFFING, the part of the visible sea remote from the shore. (E.) '*Offin* or *Offing*, the open sea, that part of it which is at a good distance from the shore;' Phillips, ed. 1706. Merely formed from *off* with the suffix *-ing*. See **Off**.

OFFSCOURING, refuse. (E.) Lit. anything scoured off; hence, refuse. In 1 Cor. iv. 13 (A.V.). From **Off** and **Scour**.

OFFSET, a young shoot, &c. (E.) Used in several senses. The sense 'shoot of a plant' occurs in Ray, as cited in Todd's Johnson (without a reference). From **Off** and **Set**.

OFFSHOOT, that which shoots off. (E.) Not in Todd's Johnson. Used figuratively in The Tatler, no. 157, § 10. From **Off** and **Shoot**.

OFFSPRING, progeny, issue. (E.) ME. *ofspring*, Rob. of Glouc. p. 164, l. 3433. The odd spelling *oxspring* occurs in Cursor Mundi, l. 11415. AS. *ofspring*, Gen. iii. 15. ‒ AS. *of*, off, from; and *springan*, to spring. See **Off**, **Of**, and **Spring**.

OFFUSCATE, the same as **Obfuscate**, q.v.

OFT, OFTEN, frequently. (E.) *Oft* is the orig. form; this was lengthened into *ofte* (dissyllabic), because *-e* was a common adverbial ending in the ME. period. Lastly, *ofte* was used as *often* before a vowel or *h* in *hadde*, &c. Thus: 'Ful *ofte* tyme,' Chaucer, C. T. 358 (A 356), where Tyrwhitt prints *often* unnecessarily, the best MSS. having *ofte*. Again: 'That *often* hadde ben,' id. 312 (A 310); but Cursor Mundi has *oftin* before a consonant, 3520, &c. AS. *oft*, Grein, ii. 320.+Icel. *oft*, *opt* (pronounced *oft*); Dan. *ofte*; Swed. *ofta*; G. *oft*; OHG. *ofto*; Goth. *ufta*, adv. oft, Mk. v. 4; used as adj. in the phrase *thizō ufta sauhtē*, frequent infirmities, 1 Tim. v. 23. Origin unexplained. Hence *often*, adj., esp. in the phr. *ofte tyme* or *often-tyme*, Chaucer, C. T. 52, 358 (A 52, 356); *often-ness*. ☞ We now say *often-er*, *often-est*; the old forms were *oft-er*, *oft-est*.

OGEE, OGIVE, a double curve. (F. ‒ Span. ‒ Arab.) Sometimes absurdly written OG, as if compounded of two letters of the alphabet. *Ogee* is another form of *ogive* (with *i* as in *machine*). 'An *Ogiue* or *Ogee*, a wreath, circlet, or round band in architecture;' Minsheu, ed. 1627. It is now generally used to mean a double curve ⌒, formed by the union of a convex and concave line. An *ogee* arch is a pointed arch, with double-curved sides. ‒ OF. *augive*, 'an ogive, a wreath, circlet, round band, in architecture;' *branches d'augives*, 'branches ogived, or limmes with ogives:' Cot. He also has: '*Ogive*, an ogive, or ogee in architecture.' β. The suggestion in E. Müller is perhaps right; he compares the Span. *auge*, highest point. Excellent examples of the ogee curve are to be found in Moorish domes and arches, and we may derive the term from the pointed top of such domes, &c. Cf. Span. *cimacio ogee*, an ogee moulding, where *cimacio* is derived from *cima*, a summit, top; Late L. *cȳmatium*, an ogee curve (Vitruvius). Similarly, the F. *augive* is derived from Span. *auge*, highest point, also apogee (Pineda), which curious word is also found in Port. and Italian. γ. The Span. *auge* is from Arab. *āwj*, top, summit, vertex, altitude or ascendent of a planet; Rich. Dict. p. 200. Cf. Körting, § 1049; Devic, s. v. *auge*. ¶ Prob. not an Arab. word, but from Gk. ἀπόγαιον, apogee. **Der.** *ogiv-al*, adj., sometimes oddly corrupted to *ogee-fall*.

OGHAM, OGAM, used with reference to the alphabet of twenty characters employed by the ancient Irish and British. (Irish.) From Irish *ogham*, 'the occult manner of writing used by the ancient Irish;' O'Reilly. OIrish *ogum* (Windisch). Said to have been devised by a mythical inventor named *Ogma*.

OGLE, to look at sideways, glance at. (Du.) Not an old word in E. In Pope, Rape of the Lock, v. 23. 'I see him *ogle* still;' Dryden, Prol. to the Prophetess, 46. 'They say their wiues learn *ogling* in the pit;' T. Shadwell, Tegue o Divelly, Epilogue, p. 80 (1692); where a side-note says: 'A foolish word among the canters for glancing.' Certainly of Du. origin; answering to a Du. verb **oogelen* (not in the Dictt.), a regular frequentative of *oogen*, 'to cast sheeps eyes upon one;' Hexham. Such frequentative verbs are extremely common in Dutch, and may be numbered by hundreds;

and we actually find the Low G. *oegeln*, to ogle, in the Bremen Wörterbuch, used as a frequentative of *oegen*, to look at; Low G. *ogelen*, to ogle (Lübben); as well as MDu. *oogheler*, a flatterer, eye-servant, i.e. ogler (Oudemans). ‒ Du. *ooge*, the eye; cognate with E. **Eye**, q.v.

OGRE, a monster, in fairy tales. (F.) Late. Added by Todd to Johnson's Dict. The quotation in Todd is from the E. version of the Arabian Nights (first in 1713), which was taken from the F. version. ‒ F. *ogre*, an ogre; first used by Perrault in his *Contes*, 1697; see N.E.D. Diez proposed to connect it with Ital. *orco*, 'a sea-monster;' Florio; OSpan. *huergo*, *uerco*. ‒ L. *orcum*, acc. of *orcus*, (1) the abode of the dead, (2) the god of the infernal regions, Orcus, Pluto. ¶ But it is difficult to guess what Perrault had in mind. **Der.** *ogr-ess*, from F. *ogresse*.

OH, a later spelling of **O**, q.v.

OIL, juice from the olive-tree, a greasy liquid. (F. ‒ L. ‒ Gk.) [We find in AS. the form *ele*, in Goth. *alew*, forms borrowed ultimately from the Gk., but at a very early period.] The ME. *oile* was borrowed from French; it occurs in Chaucer, C. T. 2963 (A 2961); and in Early E. Prose Psalter, Ps. xliv. 9. ‒ AF. *oile*, St. Nicolas, by Wace, 636; OF. *oile*, later *huile* (Cotgrave). ‒ L. *oleum*, oil; *olea*, an olive-tree. ‒ Gk. ἔλαιον, oil; ἐλαία, an olive-tree, also an olive. See **Olive**. **Der.** *oil*, verb; the pp. *oyled* occurs in Hall's Satires, b. iv. sat. 4, l. 48. Also *oil-y*, K. Lear, i. 1. 227; *oil-i-ness*. Also *oil-bag*, *-cake*, *-cloth*, *-colour*, *-nut*, *-painting*. And see **Oleaginous, Oleaster**.

OINTMENT, a greasy substance for anointing wounds, &c. (F. ‒ L.) The *t* is due to confusion with ME. *ointen*, vb., to anoint; the ME. form being *oinement* or *oynement*. '[They] bouȝten [bought] swete-smelling *oynementis*, to come and to *anoynte* Jesu;' Wyclif, Mark, xvi. 1. Spelt *oinement* in Chaucer, C. T. 633 (A 631). ‒ OF. *oignement*, an anointing, also an unguent, liniment; Burguy. Formed with suffix *-ment* (= L. *-mentum*) from OF. *oigner* (Godefroy), another form of OF. (and mod. F.) *oindre*, to anoint. ‒ L. *ungere*, to anoint; see **Unguent, Anoint**.

OLD, aged, full of years, ancient. (E.) ME. *old*, def. form and pl. *olde*; Chaucer, C. T. 5240, 10023 (B 820, E 2149). OMerc. *ald*, later *āld* (written *ǎld*), Matt. ix. 16 (Rushworth MS.); AS. *eald*, ONorthumb. *ald*, Luke, i. 18.+Du. *oud* (for *old*); G. *alt*; Goth. *altheis*. Teut. type **alðoz*; Idg. type **altos*; cf. L. *ad-ultus*, an adult, one of full age. β. Like the *-ultus* in L. *adultus*, it is a pp. form from the √AL, to nourish, as seen in Goth. *alan*, to nourish, L. *alere*, to nourish; cf. Goth. *us-althan*, to grow old. It means 'nourished, grown up.' See further under **Adult, Altitude**. **Der.** *old-en*, Macbeth, iii. 4. 75; Cursor Mundi, 18100 (Trin. MS.); apparently a Scand. word from Icel. *aldinn*, old, or (more probably) the adj. suffix *-en* was merely tacked on; cf. *gold-en*. Also *old-ness*, K. Lear, i. 2. 50; cf. *eldness*, Wyclif, Rom. vii. 6. Also *eld*, sb., *eld-er* (1), *eld-est*, *ald-er-man*.

OLEAGINOUS, oily. (L. ‒ Gk.) In Blount's Gloss., ed. 1674. ‒ L. *oleāginus*, belonging to olive-oil; by change of *-us* to *-ous*, as in *arduous*, &c. An adj. form from *olea*, the olive-tree. Not a true L. word, but borrowed from Gk. ἐλαία; see **Oil**.

OLEANDER, the rose-bay-tree. (F. ‒ Late L.) '*Oleander*, rose-bay;' Minsheu. ‒ MF. *oleandre*, 'the rose-tree, rose-bay, rose-lawrell, rose-bay-tree;' Cot. The same as Ital. *oleandro*, Span. *eloendro*, 'the rose-bay-tree,' Minsheu (1623), Port. *eloendro*, *loendro*. All those forms are variously corrupted (it is supposed) from Late L. *lōrandrum*, a word cited by Isidore of Seville; Origines, xvii. 7. β. Again, Isidore has suggested that *lōrandrum* was corrupted from *rhododendron*: 'Rhododendron [v. r. *rodandarum*] quod corrupte *lorandrum* uocatur, quod sit foliis *lauri* similibus, flore ut rosa, arbor uenenata.' Perhaps we may rather guess *lorandrum* to represent *lauridendrum* (Ducange); from *lauri-* for L. *laurus*, laurel, and Gk. δένδρον, a tree. γ. The change from *lōrandrum* to *oleandrum* is clearly due to confusion with *olea*, an olive-tree.

OLEASTER, the wild olive. (L. ‒ Gk.) In Phillips, ed. 1706. Spelt *oliaster*, Palladius on Husbandry, bk. iv. 115. ‒ L. *oleaster*, Rom. xi. 17 (Vulgate). Formed with suffix *-s-ter* (as in *poeta-s-ter*) from *olea*, an olive-tree. ‒ Gk. ἐλαία, an olive-tree. See **Oil**. See Bréal.

OLFACTORY, pertaining to smell. (L.) In Phillips, ed. 1658. ‒ L. *olfactōrius*, belonging to one that smells; only appearing in the fem. and neut. forms, *olfactōria*, *olfactōrium*, a smelling-bottle. ‒ L. *olfactor*, one who smells; (but only the fem. form *olfactrix* occurs); cf. *olfactus*, a smelling, also pp. of *olfacere*, to smell, to scent; of which a fuller form *olefacere* also occurs. ‒ L. *olē-re*, to smell; and *facere*, to make; hence, to emit a scent. β. It is clear that *olēre* stands for **odēre*, whence *odor*, smell; cf. Gk. ὀδ-μή, scent. The change of *d* to *l* is a peculiarity of Latin, as in *Ulysses* for *Odysseus*, *lacruma* for *dacruma*; see **Tear** (2). See **Odour**.

OLIGARCHY, government by a few. (F. – L. – Gk.) Spelt *oligarchie* in Minsheu, ed. 1627. – F. *oligarchie*, 'an oligarchie;' Cot. – Late L. *oligarchia* (Ducange). – Gk. ὀλιγαρχία, government in the hands of a few. – Gk. ὀλίγ-, for ὀλίγος, few, little; and -αρχία, from ἄρχειν, to rule. **Der.** *oligarchi-c-al*; also *oligarch*, Gk. ὀλιγάρχης; *oligarch-al*.

OLIO, a mixture, medley. (Span. – L.) A mistaken form of *olia*, which is an E. spelling of Span. *olla*, sounded very nearly as *olia*, the Span. *ll* answering to E. *ly* or to E. *lli* in *million*. The mistake occurs in Eikon Basilike, cap. xv, and is noticed by Milton. 'Not to tax him for want of elegance as a courtier in writing *oglio* for *olla*, the Spanish word;' Milton, Answer to Eikon Basilike, cap. 15. – Span. *olla*, 'a round earthen pot, an oglio' (*sic*); Meadows. Properly, the latter sense is due to the Span. dish called *olla podrida*, a dish of various meats and vegetables, hence a mixture, medley, olio. – L. *olla*, a pot; from OL. *aula*, a pot. Root uncertain.

OLIVE, the name of an oil-yielding tree. (F. – L. – Gk.) ME. *oliue* (with *u* for *v*), O. Eng. Homilies, ed. Morris, ii. 89, l. 5 from bottom. – F. *olive*. – L. *olīua*. – Gk. ἐλαία, an olive-tree. Brugmann, i. § 121. See further under **Oil.**

OLYMPIAN, belonging to Olympus, celestial. (L. – Gk.) 'Above th' *Olympian* hill;' Milton, P. L. vii. 3. – Late L. *Olympiānus*, adj., for L. *Olympius*, Olympian. – Gk. Ὀλυμπία, a sacred region in Elis, where the Olympian games were held; Ὄλυμπος, a mountain in Thessaly, the fabled abode of the greater gods of Greece. **Der.** *Olympia-d* (from the same source), a period of four years, from one celebration of these games to another.

OMADAUN, OMADHAWN, a simpleton. (Irish.) First in 1818. Anglo-Irish. – Irish *amadán*, a simpleton. – Irish *amad* (the same). – Irish *am-*, for *an-*, negative prefix (cf. Gk. ἀν-); and -*mad*, OIrish -*met*, mind, cognate with L. *mens* and E. *mind*. Cf. L. *āmens*, mad.

OMBRE, a game at cards. (F. – Span. – L.) In Pope, Rape of the Lock, i. 56. The game came to England with Charles II, in 1660. A pamphlet called 'The Royal Game of *Ombre*' was published in that year (Chatto, p. 145). – F. *hombre*, ombre (Hamilton). – Span. *juego del hombre*, the game of ombre; lit. 'game of the man;' see Eng.-Span. part of Meadows' Dict. The Span. *juego* is from L. *iocus*; see **Joke.** The Span. *hombre* is from L. *hominem*, acc. of *homo*, a man; see **Human.** See Notes on E. Etym., p. 201.

OMEGA, the end. (Gk.) In Rev. i. 8. The sense 'end' is due to the fact that *omega* is the last letter of the Gk. alphabet. Its force is that of long *o*. – Gk. ὦ, called ὦ μέγα, i. e. great *o* or long *o*; where μέγα is the neut. of μέγας, great, allied to E. *mickle*; see **Mickle.** ¶ Opposed to *alpha*, the *first* letter; see **Alphabet.**

OMELET, a pancake made chiefly of eggs. (F. – L.) In Cotgrave. – F. *omelette*, 'an omelet or pancake of eggs;' Cot. An older form was *aumelette*; Cot. also gives: '*Aumelette d'œufs*, an omelet, or pancake made of egges.' β. The forms of the word are various; a very common old form, according to Scheler, was *amelette*, but this was preceded by the forms *alemette, alemelle,* and *alumelle*. It is clear that *amelette* is a corruption from the older *alemette*; and it seems that *alemette*, in its turn, took the place of *alemelle*. γ. Now the OF. *alemelle* signified 'a thin plate;' esp. the blade of a knife, and is still preserved in the mod. F. *alumelle* (a corrupted spelling), with the sense of 'sheathing of a ship,' as a nautical term (Hamilton). That is, the *omelet* was named from its thin, flat, shape, and has nothing to do with F. *œufs*, eggs, as some have supposed; so that the old expression in Cotgrave, viz. *aumelette d'œufs*, is quite correct, not tautological. See *alemele*, the blade of a knife, in Godefroy, who has also *alemelle*; as well as (in the Supp.) the forms *alumette, amelette, omelette, œufmolette* (!), *aumelete,* an omelet; s. v. *omelette*. δ. Lastly, *alemelle* (or *alemele*) is a mistaken form, due to confusion of *la lemelle* (the correct form) with *l'alemelle*, as if the article had been elided before a vowel. – L. *lāmella*, a thin plate, properly of metal; dimin. of *lāmina*, a thin, flat plate; see **Lamina.** ¶ There seems to be no reason for doubting the correctness of this curious etymology, due to Littré; see the articles in Littré and Scheler, under the words *omelette* and *alumelle.* Cf. Norm. dial. *amelette*, omelette (Moisy).

OMEN, a sign of a future event, prognostication. (L.) In Shak. Hamlet, i. 1. 123. – L. *ōmen*, an omen; OL. *osmen*. β. Root uncertain; Brugmann takes it to stand for **ouis-men*, which he connects with Gk. οἶο-μαι, I think, suppose; §§ 877, 352 (3). **Der.** *omen-ed*, chiefly in *ill-omened; omin-ous* (Minsheu), imitated from L. *ōmin-ōsus*, adj., formed from *ōmin-*, decl. stem of *ōmen; omin-ous-ly, omin-ous-ness.* Also *ab-omin-ate.*

OMENTUM, 'a fold or duplication of the peritoneum connecting the stomach with certain of the other viscera, as the liver, spleen, and colon; the caul;' N. E. D. (L.) Called *oment* in 1547. – L. *ōmentum.*

OMIT, to leave out, neglect. (L.) 'Nor *omitted* no charitable meane;' Sir T. More, Works, p. 887 e. – L. *ōmittere*, to omit; lit. 'to let go.' For **ommittere*, which stands (by assimilation) for **obmittere*. – L. *ob* (which often scarcely affects the sense); and *mittere*, to send, let go. See **Ob-** and **Mission.** **Der.** *omiss-ion*, Troil. iii. 3. 230, from F. *omission*, 'an omission' (Cot.), which from L. *ōmiss-iōnem*, acc. of *ōmissio*, allied to the pp. *ōmissus.* Also *omitt-ance*, a coined word, As You Like It, iii. 5. 133.

OMNIBUS, a public vehicle. (L.) The name seems to have been first used in France. They were used in Paris about 1828; and were so called because intended for the use of all classes. – L. *omnibus*, for all, dat. pl. of *omnis*, all. Root uncertain; see Supp. note to Brugmann, § 762.

OMNIPOTENT, almighty. (F. – L.) ME. *omnipotent*, Chaucer, C. T. 6005 (D 423). – F. *omnipotent*; Cot. – L. *omnipotent-*, stem of *omnipotens*, all-powerful. – L. *omni-*, for *omnis*, all; and *potens*, powerful; see **Potent.** **Der.** *omnipotent-ly, omnipotence*, from F. *omnipotence* (Cot.).

OMNIPRESENT, everywhere present. (F. – L.) Milton has *omnipresence*, P. L. vii. 590, xi. 336. Coined from *omni-*, for *omnis*, all; and **Present,** q. v. **Der.** *omnipresence.*

OMNISCIENT, all-knowing. (L.) In Milton, P. L. vi. 430. Coined from *omni-*, for *omnis*, all; and *scient-*, stem of *sciens*, pres. part. of *scīre*, to know; see **Science.** **Der.** *omniscience.*

OMNIVOROUS, all-devouring, feeding on all kinds of food. (L.) In Blount's Gloss., ed. 1674. – L. *omniuorus*, all-devouring; by change of -*us* to -*ous*. – L. *omni-*, for *omnis*, all; and -*uorus*, devouring, from *uorāre*, to devour; see **Voracious.**

OMRAH, a prince, lord. (Hind. – Arab.) 'Aigrettes by *Omrahs* worn;' Scott, Vision of Don Roderick, ii. 31. – Hind. *umarā*, a noble; lit. 'nobles,' pl., used as a title (Forbes). – Arab. *umarā*, pl. of *amīr*, a prince, emir; see **Emir.** Cf. the Arab. title *amīru'l-umarā*, prince of princes (Yule).

ON, upon, at, near. (E.) ME. *on*; passim. AS. *on*; passim. +Du. *aan*; Icel. *ā* (for *an*); Dan. *an*, prep. and adv.; Swed. *å*, prep.; G. *an*; Goth. *ana*, to, upon, on.+Gk. ἀνά; Russ. *na*. Idg. type **ana.* **Der.** *on*, adv.; *on-set, on-slaught, on-ward, on-wards*; and see *anon.*

ONCE, a single time, at a former time. (E.) ME. *ones, oones, onis*, Chaucer, C. T. 5592, 5595 (D 10, 13); cf. *at ones*, id. 767 (A 765). The final *s* was voiceless, not pronounced as *z*; and this is why the word is now spelt with *ce*, which is an attempt to show this. AS. *ānes*, once; orig. gen. case masc. and neut. of *ān*, one; the gen. case was sometimes used adverbially, as in *need-s, twi-ce, thri-ce.* See **One** (1). **Der.** *nonce*, in the phr. *for the nonce*; see **Nonce.**

ONCE, OUNCE, an animal; see **Ounce** (2).

ONE (1), single, undivided, sole. (E.) [The mod. pronunciation [wun] seems to have arisen in the W. of England; it is noticed by Jones, in 1701, as in use 'in Shropshire and some parts of Wales;' Ellis, On Early Eng. Pronunciation, p. 1012. It does not appear to be older in literature than about A.D. 1420; see N. E. D. Tindale has *wons* in Mark, vi. 31. At any rate, the ME. pronunciation was at first with long open *o*, later with long close *o*, whence the sound of -*one, on-*, in *al-one, at-one, on-ly*; we never say *wunly.* We do, however, say *wuns* (with voiceless *s*) for *once.*] ME. *oon, on*; also *oo, o*; dative *oone, one*; Chaucer, C. T. 343, 365, 681, 749 (A 341, &c.). AS. *ān*, one; Grein, i. 29.+Du. *een*; Icel. *einn*; Dan. *een*; Swed. *en*; G. *ein*; Goth. *ains*.+W. *un*; Irish and Gael. *aon*; L. *ūnus*; OL. *oinos*; Gk. **οἰνός*, one (fem. οἴνη, an ace on a die). Teut. type **ainoz*; Idg. type **oinos.* Cf. Lith. *vēnas*, one; Brugmann, ii. § 165. **Der.** *one-sided, one-sided-ness; one-ness*; and see *on-ce, on-ly, al-one, l-one, at-one; un-ique, un-ite, un-ion, un-animous, uni-son, uni-versal, on-ion*; also *n-one, n-on-ce, an-on* (=in one), *an-other.* **Doublet,** *an* or *a* (from the unstressed form). ☞ The Gk. εἷς, one (base **sem*) cannot be referred to the same source; Brugmann, i. § 408.

ONE (2), a person, spoken of indefinitely. (E.) In the phrase '*one* says,' the *one* means a single person. Cf. '*One* that moche wo wrou3te, Sleuthe was his name' = one who wrought much wo, whose name was Sloth; P. Plowman, B. xx. 157. See Mätzner, Engl. Grammatik. 'The indefinite *one*, as in *one says*, is sometimes, but wrongly, derived from the F. *on*, L. *homo*. It is merely the use of the numeral *one* for the older *man, men*, or *me*;' Morris, Hist. Outlines of Eng. Accidence, p. 143; which see for examples. And see N. E. D.; One, § 20.

ONEROUS, burdensome. (F. – L.) In the Rom. of the Rose, l. 5633. – F. *onereux*, 'onerous;' Cot. – L. *onerōsus*, burdensome. – L. *oner-*, for **ones*, stem of *onus*, a burden. β. Benfey (Skt. Dict. p. 19) compares *onus* with Skt. *anas*, a cart; and so Brugmann. i. § 159. **Der.** *onerous-ly, -ness*; also *ex-oner-ate.*

ONION, the name of a plant. (F. – L.) ME. *oynon*, Chaucer,

C. T. 636. — F. *oignon*, 'an onion;' Cot. — L. *ŭniōnem*, acc. of *ŭnio*, (1) unity, oneness, (2) a single large pearl, (3) a kind of onion. — L. *ūnus*, one; cognate with E. **One**, q. v. **Doublet**, *union*, esp. in the sense 'a large pearl,' Hamlet, v. 2. 283.

ONLY, single, singly. (E.) Both adj. and adv. ME. *oonli*, earlier *oonliche, onliche.* '*Onliche* liue' = solitary life; Ancren Riwle, p. 152, last line but one. *Onliche*, adv., Will. of Palerne, 3155. — AS. *ānlīc*, adj., unique, lit. one-like; Grein, i. 33. — AS. *ān*, one; and *līc*, like. See **One** and **Like**.

ONOMATOPŒIA, name-making, the formation of a word with resemblance in sound to that of the thing signified. (Gk.) Esp. used of words such as *click, hiss*, and the like, directly imitative of sounds. Spelt *onomatopeia* in Puttenham, Arte of E. Poesie, bk. iii. ch. 17 (ed. Arber, p. 192, sidenote). — Gk. ὀνοματοποιΐα, the making of a name; we also find ὀνοματοποίησις. — Gk. ὀνοματο-, decl. stem of ὄνομα, a name; and ποιεῖν, to make. See **Name** and **Poem**. Der. *onomato-poetic*. Also (from Gk. ὄνομα) *an-onym-ous, hom-onym, met-onym-y, par-onym-ous, syn-onym*.

ONSET, an assault, attack. (E.) In King John, ii. 326. A good word; but not in early use. Due to the phrase *to set on*, i. e. to attack. 'Percy! and *set on*!' 1 Hen. IV, v. 2. 97. See **On** and **Set**.

ONSLAUGHT, an attack. (E.) In Butler, Hudibras, pt. i. c. 3. ll. 422, 424. The ME. form would be *onslaht*; but it does not occur. Compounded of ME. *on*, on; and *slaht, slaght, slaught*, a stroke, blow, also slaughter, as in Gower, i. 348; bk. iii. 2058. — AS. *on*, on; and *sleaht*, a stroke, blow, found in the compounds *morðor-sleaht, wæl-sleaht*, Grein, ii. 264, 647, and derived from *slēan*, to strike. See **On** and **Slaughter**.

ONTOLOGY, the science of being. (Gk.) '*Ontology*, an Account of Beings (*sic*) in the Abstract;' Bailey (1735). Compounded of Gk. ὀντο-, for ὀντ-, stem of the pres. part. of εἶναι, to be; and -λογία, from λόγος, discourse, from λέγ-ειν, to speak.

ONWARD, ONWARDS, forward. (E.) Not a very old word. 'I haue driuen hym *onwarde* one steppe down;' Sir T. More, Works, p. 409 d. Peculiarly used in Chaucer, C. T., A 970. Compounded of *on* and *-ward*, in imitation of **Toward**, q. v. So also *onwards*, Shak. Sonnet 126, in imitation of *towards*.

ONYX, a kind of agate. (L. — Gk.) In Holland, tr. of Pliny, b. xxxvii. c. 6. ME. *onix*; Wyclif, Ezek. xxviii. 13. — L. *onyx*. — Gk. ὄνυξ, a claw, a nail, a finger-nail, a veined gem, onyx, from the resemblance to the colour of the finger-nail. The stem is ὀνυχ-, allied by gradation to Skt. *nakha-*, a nail, Russ. *nogote*, a nail, and E. *nail*; see **Nail**.

OOLITE, a kind of limestone. (F. — Gk.) Modern and geological. A coined word, but coined in France; an Englishman would have said *oolith*. — F. *oolithe*, with *th* pronounced as E. *t*; in Dict. Acad. 1762. — Gk. ᾠό-, for ᾠόν, an egg, cognate with L. *ōuum*; and λίθ-ος, a stone. See **Oval** and **Lithography**.

OOZE (1), moisture, gentle flow; confused with **Ooze** (2), soft mud. (E.) These words have lost an initial *w*; they should rather be *wooze*, or *woze*; see E. D. D. The vb. *to woose* is in Golding, tr. of Ovid, fol. 127. For the loss of *w*, cf. prov. E. '*ooman* for *woman*, Shropshire '*ood* for *wood*. 1. ME. *wose*, moisture; 'alle the othre *woses*,' all the other fluids, Ayenb. of Inwyt, p. 186. AS. *wōs*, juice; as in *ofetes wōs*, juice of fruit; Voc. 128. 11.+Icel. *vás*, wetness. Noreen looks upon Icel. *vás* as from a form **vans*; and if so, AS. *wōs* is from a form **wons*. But *wōs* may be allied to OHG. *waso*, turf, sod; see G. *wasen* in Kluge. 2. ME. *wose*, soft mud; 'in *wose* and in *donge*;' P. Plowm. C. xiii. 229; and see Prompt. Parv., p. 532. AS. *wāse*, sepia; as in *wāse-scīte*, a cuttle-fish, Voc. 181. 7; *wāse*, mud, Voc. 203. 45.+Icel. *veisa*, a stagnant pool; Norw. *veisa*, mud. Teut. type **wais-ōn-*, f. Der. from *ooze* (1), ooze, verb, to exude, Timon, i. 1. 21; *ooz-y*.

OPACITY, opaqueness; see **Opaque**.

OPAL, a precious stone. (F. — L. — Skt.?) In Holland, tr. of Pliny, b. xxxvii. c 6; Tw. Nt. ii. 4. 77. — F. *opale*, 'the opall stone;' Cot. — L. *opalus*, an opal; Pliny, as above. Cf. Gk. ὀπάλλιος, an opal. Apparently from Skt. *upala-s*, a stone; cf. *tapana-upalas*, a fabulous gem, *rasa-upalas*, a pearl (Benfey).

OPAQUE, not transparent, dark. (F. — L.) In Milton, P. L. iii. 619; ME. *opake*, Palladius on Husbandry, ii. 261. — F. *opaque*, 'duskie, gloomie, obscure;' Cot. — L. *opācum*, acc. of *opācus*, shady. Root unknown. Der. *opaque-ness*; also *opac-i-ty*, Minsheu, from F. *opacité*, 'opacity' (Cot.), from L. acc. *opācitātem*.

OPE, to open. (E.) A short form for *open*, verb; K. John, ii. 536. So also *ope* is used as a short form for *open*, adj., as in 'the gates are *ope*,' Cor. i. 4. 43. Seldom used except in poetry. See **Open**.

OPEN, unclosed, free of access, clear. (E.) The verb is formed from the adj., as is shown by the old forms. ME. *open*, Chaucer,

C. T. 8666 (E 790). At a later period contracted to *ope*; see **Ope**. AS. *open*, open, Grein, ii. 355. Lit. 'that which is lifted up;' the metaphor being probably taken from the lifting of the curtain of a tent, or the lifting of a door-latch; cf. *dup* (= do up), to open, Hamlet, iv. 5. 53. Allied to AS. *up*, up; see **Up**.+Du. *open*; *op*, up; Icel. *opinn*, open, also face upwards; *upp*, up; Dan. *aaben*; *op*, up; cf. the phr. *luk Dören op*, open the door, lit. 'lock the door up;' Swed. *öppen*; *upp*, up; G. *offen*; allied to *auf*, OHG. *ûf*. Teut. types **upanoz, *upenoz*; allied to **Up**, q. v. Der. *open*, verb, AS. *openian*, causal verb from adj. *open*; so also Du. *openen*, from *open*; Icel. *opna*, Dan. *aabne*, Swed. *öppna*, G. *öffnen*. Also *open-ly, open-ness, open-ing, open-handed, open-hearted*.

OPERA, a musical drama. (Ital. — L.) 'An *opera* is a poetical tale or fiction,' &c.; Dryden, pref. to Albion and Albanius; first in Evelyn, Diary, Nov. 19, 1644. — Ital. *opera*, work; hence a performance. — L. *opera*; see **Operate**. Der. *operat-ic*; *opera-glass*.

OPERATE, to produce an effect. (L.) In Shak. Cymb. v. 5. 197. [Really due to the sb. *operation*, in much earlier use; ME. *operacion*, Chaucer, C. T. 6730 (D 1148); Gower, C. A. iii. 128; bk. vii. 1282; from F. *operation*, which from L. acc. *operātiōnem*.] — L. *operātus*, pp. of *operārī*, to work. — L. *opera*, work; closely allied to L. *opus* (decl. stem *oper-*), work, labour, toil.+Skt. *apas*, work (Vedic). Der. *operat-ion*, as above; *operat-ive*, King Lear, iv. 4. 14, from F. *operatif*, 'operative' (Cot.); *operat-ive-ly*; *operat-or*, from L. *operātor*; *oper-ant*, Hamlet, iii. 2. 184, from *operant-*, stem of pres. part. of *operārī*; *oper-ance*, Two Noble Kinsmen, i. 3. 63. Also *oper-ose*, i. e. laborious, Blount's Gloss., from L. *operōsus*; *oper-ose-ly*, *oper-ose-ness*; *oper-os-i-ty*, Minsheu. From the same root we have *co-operate, en-ure, in-ure, man-ure, man-œuvre*.

OPHICLEIDE, a musical instrument. (F. — Gk.) Modern. — F. *ophicléide*, 'an ophicleid, key-serpent;' Hamilton. An odd name; due to the old twining musical instrument called 'a serpent,' to which keys were added, thus turning it into a 'key-serpent.' — Gk. ὄφι-, for ὄφις, a serpent; and κλειδ-, decl. stem of κλείς, a key. See **Ophidian** and **Clavicle**.

OPHIDIAN, relating to serpents. (Gk.) Modern; formed with E. suffix *-an* (= L. *-ānus*) from Gk. **ὀφιδι-*, an imaginary form wrongly supposed to be the stem of ὄφις, a serpent; perhaps suggested by the Gk. dimin. form ὀφίδιον. The true stem is ὀφι-, as seen in *ophi-cleide* and *Ophi-uchus* (Gk. ὀφιοῦχος, serpent-holder, from ἔχειν, to hold), Milton, P. L. ii. 709.

OPHTHALMIA, inflammation of the eye. (Gk.) Spelt *ophthalmie* in Blount's Gloss., which is borrowed from F. *ophthalmie* (Cotgrave). — Gk. ὀφθαλμία, a disease of the eye. — Gk. ὀφθαλμός, the eye; Bœotian ὄκταλλος; cf. Doric ὀπτίλος, the eye, ὀπτεύειν, to see, ὀπτήρ, one who looks, a spy, eye-witness. See **Optic**. Der. *ophthalmi-c*.

OPINION, a notion, judgement, estimation. (F. — L.) ME. *opinion*, Chaucer, C. T. 183; Gower, C. A. ii. 267; bk. ii. 3214. — F. *opinion*, 'opinion;' Cot. — L. *opīniōnem*, acc. of *opīnio*, a supposition. — L. *opīnārī*, to suppose; rarely *opīnāre*. — L. *opīnus*, thinking, expecting; only in the comp. *nec-opīnus, in-opīnus*, unexpected; perhaps connected with *ob*, near, as *sup-īnus* is with *sub* (Bréal). Der. *opinion-at-ive* (Johnson), which has taken the place of the older *opinative* (Blount's Gloss., ed. 1674), coined from L. *opīnātus*, pp. of *opīnārī*, to suppose; *opinion-at-ive-ly, opinion-at-ive-ness*. We also use the coined word *opinion-at-ed*, a clumsy formation. The verb *opine* is a perfectly correct word, from F. *opiner*, 'to opine' (Cot.), which from L. *opīnāre*, more commonly *opīnārī*, as above; it occurs in Pope, Moral Essays, iii. 9. The derivatives *opin-able, opin-at-ive, opin-at-or* (all in Blount) are obsolete.

OPIUM, a narcotic drug. (L. — Gk.) In Holland, tr. of Pliny, b. xx. c. 18; and in Milton, Samson, 630. [The ME. *opie*, Chaucer, C. T. 1474 (A 1472), answers to an OF. *opie*.] — L. *opium*; Pliny. — Gk. ὄπιον, poppy-juice, opium; dimin. from ὀπός, juice, sap. ¶ Not connected with E. *sap*; but rather with Skt. *āpas*, pl., waters. Der. *opi-ate*, Milton, P. L. xi. 133, spelt *opiat* in Cotgrave, from F. *opiate*, which from Late L. *opiātus* (Ducange), lit. 'provided with opium.'

OPODELDOC, a medical plaster, soap liniment. (*Partly* Gk.) A name believed to have been invented by Paracelsus, about 1541. He spelt it *oppodeltoch*. The first part seems to be Gk. ὀπο-, for ὀπός, juice (above).

OPOPANAX, a gum-resin orig. obtained from an umbelliferous plant, the *Opopanax Chironium*. (L. — Gk.) Spelt *opopanac* in Lanfranc's Cirurgerie, p. 60 (ab. 1400). — L. *opopanax*, Pliny, xx. 24. — Gk. ὀποπάναξ, the juice of panax. — Gk. ὀπο-, for ὀπός, juice, sap (above); and πάναξ, lit. all-heal; see **Panacea**.

OPOSSUM, an American quadruped. (W. Indian.) In a tr. of Buffon's Nat. Hist., London, 1792, i. 214. Orig. *opassom*, in the language of the Indians of Virginia; Captain Smith, Works, ed. Arber, p. 59.

OPPIDAN, at Eton, a student who boards in the town, not in the college. (L.) Formerly in more general use. ' Oppidan, a citizen or townsman ;' Blount's Gloss., ed. 1674. – L. oppidānus, belonging to a town. – L. oppidum, a town ; OL. oppedum. Cf. L. Pedum, the name of a town in Latium, Livy, ii. 39. 4. β. ' The word oppidum I derive from pedum (cf. Pedum) = Gk. πέδον, ground, country, Skt. pada-m, tread, step, place, spot, foot-print, track, and ob, on, near, over, and interpret it accordingly as orig. " What lies on or over the open ground ;" . . . hence may well also be derived the old use of oppida for the barriers of a race-course, which lie on [or] over the arena ;' Curtius, ii. 103, 303. Bréal compares Gk. ἔμπεδος, steadfast, firm (with prefix ἐμ-, for ἐν).

OPPILATION, a stopping up. (F. – L.) Sir T. Elyot has the pl. oppilations; Castel of Helthe, bk. ii. c. 7 (Of Fygges). – MF. oppilation, ' an obstruction ;' Cot. – L. acc. oppilātiōnem, allied to oppīlātus, pp. of oppīlāre, to stop up. – L. op (for ob), against ; and pīlāre, to ram, from pīlum, a pestle. L. pīlum is for *pinslom, from pinsere, to pound.

OPPONENT, one who opposes. (L.) In Minsheu, ed. 1627. – L. oppōnent-, stem of pres. pt. of oppōnere, to oppose, lit. set against. – L. op- (for ob before p) ; and pōnere, to place. See **Ob-** and **Position.**

OPPORTUNE, seasonable. (F. – L.) Spelt oportune in Lydgate, Siege of Thebes, prol. 139. – F. opportun, ' timely ;' Cot. – L. opportūnus, convenient, seasonable ; lit. near the harbour. – L. op- (for ob before p), near ; and portus, a harbour, port. Cf. im-portune ; and L. Portūnus, the protecting deity of harbours. See **Ob-** and **Port** (2). Der. opportune-ly, opportune-ness ; also opportun-i-ty, ME. opportunité, Wyclif, Matt. xxvi. 16, from F. opportunité (Cot.), which from L. acc. opportūnitātem.

OPPOSE, to resist, withstand. (F. – L. and Gk.) ME. opposen, used commonly in the special sense of to contradict in argument, as an examiner used to do in the schools ; see Chaucer, C. T. 7179 (D 1597), where Tyrwhitt prints apposen; Gower, C. A. i. 49 ; bk. i. 225. ' Aposen, or oposyn, Oppono ;' Prompt. Parv. p. 13. – F. opposer ; reflexively s'opposer, ' to oppose himself, to resist, withstand, gainsay, to object, except, or protest against ;' Cot. – F. op- = L. op- (for ob before p), against ; and F. poser, to place. See **Ob-** and **Pose.** Der. oppos-er, oppos-able.

OPPOSITE, over against, contrary, adverse. (F. – L.) ME. opposite, Chaucer, C. T., A 1894. – F. opposite, ' opposite ;' Cot. – L. oppositus, pp. of oppōnere, to set against. – L. op- (for ob before p), against ; and pōnere, to put, set ; see **Ob-** and **Position.** Der. opposite-ly, opposite-ness ; also opposit-ion, ME. opposition, Chaucer, C. T. 11369 (F 1057), from F. opposition, which from L. acc. oppositiōnem.

OPPRESS, to press against, constrain, overburden. (F. – L.) ME. oppressen, Chaucer, C. T. 11723 (F 1411). – F. oppresser, ' to oppresse ;' Cot. – Late L. oppressāre, to oppress ; Ducange. – L. op- press-us, pp. of opprimere, to oppress, press upon. See **Ob-** and **Press.** Der. oppress-ion, Chaucer, C. T. 6471 (D 889), from F. oppression, which from L. acc. oppressiōnem ; oppress-ive, oppress-ive-ly, oppress-ive-ness ; oppress-or, Hamlet, iii. 1. 71.

OPPROBRIOUS, reproachful, disgraceful. (L.) Spelt opprobrious in Trevisa, tr. of Higden, iv. 167 ; opprobrous, by a misprint, in The Remedie of Loue, st. 41, pr. in Chaucer's Works, ed. 1561, fol. 323, back. – L. opprobriōsus, full of reproach. – L. op- (for ob before p), on, upon ; and probrum, disgrace, infamy. Root uncertain. Der. opprobrious-ly, -ness. The sb. opprobrium is also sometimes used, having taken the place of the older word opprobry.

OPPUGN, to oppose, resist. (F. – L.) ' The true catholike faythe is, and euer hath been, oppugned and assaulted ;' Sir T. More, Works, p. 571 h. – F. oppugner, ' to oppugne ;' Cot. – L. oppugnāre, to buffet, beat with the fists. – L. op- (for ob before p), against ; and pugnāre, to fight, esp. with the fists, from pugnus, the fist. β. Pugnus is from a base pug-, appearing in pug-il, a boxer, pugilist. See **Ob-** and **Pugilist.** Der. oppugn-er ; oppugn-anc-y, Shak. Troil. i. 3. 111.

OPTATIVE, wishful, wishing. (F. – L.) The name of a mood in grammar, sometimes expressive of wishing. In Palsgrave, p. 84 ; and in Sherwood's Index to Cotgrave, where the F. optatif is also given. – F. optatif. – L. optātīuus, expressive of a wish ; the name of a mood. – L. optātus, pp. of optāre, to wish ; a frequentative verb from a base opt-, perhaps connected with ap-iscī, to obtain ; cf. Skt. āp, ap, to obtain, attain. Der. optative-ly ; from the same source, opt-ion, ad-opt.

OPTIC, relating to the sight. (F. – Gk.) Formerly optick. ' Through optick glass ;' Milton, P. L. i. 288. = F. optique, ' of, or belonging to, the eie-sight ;' Cot. – Gk. ὀπτικός, belonging to the sight ; cf. ὀπτήρ, a spy, eye-witness. From the base ΟΠ (for ΟϘ) occurring in Ionic ὄπ-ωπ-α, I have seen, ὄψομαι, I shall see ; Bœotian

ὄκ-ταλλος, for *ὄκταγ-λος (cf. Skt. akshan-, the eye) ; also Lith. ak-ìs, eye, L. oc-ulus, Russ. ok-o, the eye. Der. optic, sb., an eye, as in ' the cleere casements of his own optiques,' Howell, Instructions for Foreign Travel, last sentence ; optic-s, sb.; optic-al, optic-al-ly, optic-i-an. Also aut-op-s-y, cat-op-tric, di-op-tric, syn-op-sis ; and see oph-thalmia.

OPTIMISM, the doctrine that all is for the best. (L.; with Gk. suffix.) Added by Todd to Johnson's Dict. Coined by adding the suffix -ism (= Gk. -ισμος) to optim-, stem of L. optimus, best, OL. opitumus ; see Brugmann, ii. § 73. Perhaps related to L. op-ēs, riches (Bréal). Der. optim-ist, with Gk. suffix -ιστης.

OPTION, choice, wish. (F. – L.) In Minsheu. – F. option, ' option ;' Cot. – L. optiōnem, acc. of optio, choice. Allied to optāre, to wish ; see **Optative.** Der. option-al, option-al-ly.

OPULENT, wealthy. (F. – L.) In K. Lear, i. 1. 88. – F. opulent, ' opulent ;' Cot. – L. opulentus, wealthy. Extended from op-, stem of opēs, sb. pl., wealth, riches. Cf. Skt. apnas, wealth. Der. opu-lence ; opulenc-y, Timon, v. 1. 38. From the same source are c-op-y, c-op-i-ous, c-op-ul-ate, &c.

OR (1), conjunction, offering an alternative. (E.) Short for other, owther, outher, auther, the older forms. ' Amys other elles ' = amiss or else ; P. Plowman, B. i. 175 ; where the Trin. MS. (printed by Wright) has ' amys outher ellis.' ' Other catell other cloth ' = either property or cloth ; P. Plowman's Crede, ed. Skeat, l. 116. ' Auther to lenge lye, or to longe sitte ' = either to lie long, or to sit long ; Gawain and the Grene Knight, l. 88. β. This other or auther is not the mod. E. other, nor allied to either ; but seems to have been substituted for AS. oððe. Cf. AS. oððe . . . oððe, either . . . or. See N. E. D. Der. n-or.

OR (2), ere. (E.) The use of or for ere is not uncommon ; see ' or ever I had seen that day ;' Hamlet, i. 2. 183. Particularly in the phrase or ere, Temp. i. 2. 11 ; Macb. iv. 3. 173, &c. The forms or, er, ar occur as exact equivalents in the same passage in the three texts of P. Plowman, C. viii. 66, B. v. 459, A. v. 232. All are from AS. ǣr, ere, or from its equivalents in various E. dialects. See **Ere.** ¶ It is probable that or ere arose as a reduplicated expression, in which ere repeats and explains or ; and this was confused with or e'er ; whence or ever.

OR (3), gold. (F. – L.) A common heraldic term. – F. or, gold. – L. aurum, gold ; see **Aureate.**

ORACH, ORACHE, a plant of the genus Atriplex, esp. mountain-spinach. (F. – L. – Gk.) Spelt orech in Turner, Names of Herbes, s. v. Atriplex ; orach in Lyte, tr. of Dodoens, bk. v. ch. 1 ; better spelt arache (see N. E. D.). – AF. arasche ; in Voc. 559. 1 ; MF. and F. arroche, Cot. A Picard form (Hatzfeld) for OF. *arreuce (not found). – L. atriplicem, acc. of atriplex, orach ; Pliny, xix. 6. – Gk. ἀτράφαξις, ἀτράφαξυς, orach ; of unknown origin.

ORACLE, the utterance or response of a deity. (F. – L.) ME. oracle, Chaucer, Ho. of Fame, b. i. l. 11. – F. oracle, ' an oracle ;' Cot. – L. ōrāculum, a divine announcement ; formed with double dimin. suffix -cu-lu- from ōrāre, to speak, announce, pray ; from ōr- (for ōs), the mouth ; see **Oral.** Der. oracul-ar, due to L. ōrāculārius, oracular ; oracul-ar-ly, -ness.

ORAL, spoken, uttered by the mouth. (L.) In Blount's Gloss., ed. 1674. A coined word ; formed with suffix -al (= F. -al, -el, L. -ālis) from ōr-, stem of ōs, the mouth. β. Allied to Skt. āsya-m, the mouth ; Icel. ōss, the mouth of a river. Der. oral-ly ; also or-ac-le, q. v., or-at-ion, q. v., or-at-or, q. v., ori-fice, q. v. ; ori-son, q. v. ; also ad-ore, in-ex-or-able.

ORANG-OUTANG, a large ape. (Malay.) ' Orang-outang is the name this animal bears in the E. Indies ; Pongo, its denomination at Lowando, a province of Congo ;' E. tr. of Buffon, London, 1792. ' An oran-outang o'er his shoulders hung ;' Garth, Dispensary, c. v. l. 150 (1699). – Malay ōrang ūtan, ' the wild man, a species of ape ;' Marsden, Malay Dict., p. 22. – Malay ōrang, a man, id. ; and hūtan, ūtan, ' woods, a forest, wild or uncultivated parts of the country, wild, whether in respect to domestication or cultivation ;' id. p. 364. Thus it means ' wild man.'

ORANGE, the name of a fruit. (F. – Ital. – Pers.) The pl. orenges is in Sir T. Elyot, Castel of Helth, b. ii. c. 7. The colour of orenge occurs in l. 11 of a 15th-century ballad beginning ' O mossie Quince,' pr. in Chaucer's Works, ed. 1561, fol. 344, back ; and see Oronge in Prompt. Parv. Lydgate has the pl. orengis, Minor Poems, p. 15 ; the sing. orenge occurs in Allit. Poems, ed. Morris, B. 1044. – OF. orenge (14th century), Littré ; later changed into orange, ' an orange ;' Cot. [The form should rather have been narenge, but the initial n was lost, and arenge became orenge under the influence of F. or (L. aurum), gold ; because the notion arose that the name denoted the golden colour of the fruit.] – MItal. narancia, an orange (Florio) ; also arancia, id., as now. Cf. Span. naranja, Port. laranja (for naranja), an orange. – Pers. nāranj, nārinj, also nārang, an orange; Rich. Pers. Dict. p. 1548; perhaps from Skt. *náranga-s,* an orange-tree. Cf. Pers. *nār,* a pomegranate.

ORATION, a speech. (F. – L.) In Sir T. More, Works, p. 399 a. – F. *oration,* 'an oration, or harang;' Cot. – L. *ōrātiōnem,* acc. of *ōrātio,* a speech. – L. *ōrāre,* to speak, pray; from *ōr-,* stem of *ōs,* mouth. See **Oral.**

ORATOR, a speaker. (F. – L.) Formerly *oratour,* but now conformed to the L. spelling. ME. *oratour,* Chaucer, tr. of Boethius, b. 4. pr. 4, l. 183. – AF. *oratour,* F. *orateur,* 'an orator;' Cot. – L. *ōrātōrem,* acc. of *ōrātor,* a speaker. – L. *ōrāre,* to speak; see **Oration.** Der. *oratori-c-al, oratori-c-al-ly; orator-y,* ME. *oratorie,* Chaucer, C. T. 1907 (A 1905), from F. *oratorie* (Cot.), from L. *ōrātōrium,* a place of prayer, neut. of *ōrātōrius,* belonging to prayer; *orator-i-o,* from Ital. *oratorio,* an oratory, also an oratorio, from the same L. *ōrātōrius.*

ORB, a sphere, celestial body, eye. (F. – L.) In Shak. Merch. Ven. v. 60; and earlier. – F. *orbe,* an orb; omitted in Cotgrave, but given in Sherwood's Index, and in use in F. in the 13th century (Littré). – L. *orbem,* acc. of *orbis,* a circle, circuit, orb. Root unknown. Der. *orb-ed,* Haml. iii. 2. 166; *orbi-c-ul-ar,* Milton, P. L. iii. 718, from L. *orbiculāris,* circular; *orbi-c-ul-ar-ly;* also *orb-it,* Dryden, tr. of Virgil, xii. 1076, directly from L. *orbita,* a track, course, orbit, formed with suffix *-ta* from *orbi-,* decl. stem of *orbis.* Hence *orbit-al.*

ORC, ORK, a sea-monster. (L.) 'Seals and *orks;*' Milton, P. L. xi. 835. '*Epaular,* an Orke, a great sea-fish, mortal enemy to the whale;' Cot. – L. *orca,* a sea-fish; perhaps the narwhal; Pliny, ix. 6. Holland's translation has: 'The *Orcæ,* other monstrous fishes . . . deadly enemies they be vnto the foresaid whales.'

ORCHARD, a garden of fruit-trees. (L. *and* E.) ME. *orchard,* Ancren Riwle, p. 378, l. 2 from bottom; *orchærd,* Layamon, 12955. AS. *orceard,* also spelt *orcerd,* Gen. ii. 8, 16; Wright, Popular Treatises on Science, p. 10, l. 3. The older form is *ortgeard,* Ælfred, tr. of Gregory's Pastoral, c. 40; ed. Sweet, p. 292, l. 4. [We also find *wyrtgeard,* to translate L. *promptuarium,* Ps. cxliii. 16, ed. Spelman.] Cognate with Goth. *aurtigards,* a garden, John, xviii. 1; cf. *aurtja,* a gardener, husbandman, Luke, xx. 10. β. The latter element is merely the mod. E. *yard;* see **Yard** (1). The former element is merely borrowed from L. *hortus,* a garden, both in E. and Gothic; and, as L. *hortus* is cognate with E. *yard,* the form *ort-geard* merely repeats the idea of 'yard.' ¶ So in Brugmann, i. § 767; but some have considered AS. *ort-geard* as wholly Teutonic, and have connected it with AS. *wyrt-geard* above (Dan. *urt-gaard,* Swed. *örtegård*), a kitchen-garden, from AS. *wyrt,* Dan. *urt,* Swed. *ört,* a wort. But the change from *wyrt* to *ort* (before A.D. 900) is incredible, and is now generally abandoned.

ORCHESTRA, the part of a theatre for the musicians. (L. – Gk.) In Holland, tr. of Suetonius, p. 242 (R.). – L. *orchēstra.* – Gk. ὀρχήστρα, an orchestra; which, in the Attic theatre, was a space on which the chorus danced. – Gk. ὀρχέομαι, I dance. Cf. Skt. *rghāya,* to rage. Root uncertain. Der. *orchestr-al.*

ORCHIS, a name for certain plants. (L. – Gk.) In Holland, tr. of Pliny, b. xxvi. c. 10; and in Swinburne, Trav. through Spain, (1779), p. 233, l. 1. – L. *orchis* (Pliny). – Gk. ὄρχις, a testicle; hence applied to a plant with tubers of testicular shape. Der. *orchid-ac-e-ous,* a coined word, as if from *orchid-,* stem of *orchis* (but the L. *orchis* makes gen. *orchis,* and Gk. ὄρχις makes gen. ὀρχέως); also *orchid,* similarly coined. ¶ A similar mis-coinage is seen in *ophidian,* for which see under **Ophicleide.**

ORDAIN, to set in order, arrange, regulate. (F. – L.) ME. *ordeynen;* P. Plowman, B. prol. 119; Rob. of Glouc. p. 236, l. 4864. – AF. *ordeiner,* Stat. Realm; i. 157; OF. *ordener,* later *ordonner,* as in Cotgrave. – L. *ordināre,* to set in order. – L. *ordin-,* stem of *ordo,* order; see **Order.** Der. *ordin-ance,* q.v.; *ordin-ate,* adj., ME. *ordinat,* Chaucer, C. T. 9160 (E 1284), from L. pp. *ordinātus; ordin-ate,* sb. (in mathematics); *ordin-ate-ly; ordin-at-ion,* in Phillips, ed. 1706, formed, by analogy with F. words in *-tion,* from L. *ordinātio,* an ordinance, also ordination. And see *ordin-al, ordin-ar-y, ord-nance.*

ORDEAL, a severe trial, a judgement by test of fire, &c. (E.) The spelling is artificial; from about A.D. 1605; see N.E.D. It is also remarkable that this word (from complete ignorance of its etymology) is commonly pronounced *ordë-al* in three syllables, though the *-deal* is related to the *deal* spoken of in *dealing* cards. ME. *ordal,* Chaucer, Troilus, iii. 1046. AS. *ordēl, ordāl;* the spelling *ordēl* is rare, but occurs in the Laws of Edward and Guthrum, sect. ix, in Thorpe's Ancient Laws, i. 172; this form would answer to mod. E. *ordeel,* or (by shortening due to want of stress) to a form *ordel.* The usual spelling is *ordāl,* as in the Laws of Ethelred, sect. i (in Thorpe, i. 281), and sect. iv (id. i. 294), and see numerous references in Thorpe's Index; this form answers to

Chaucer's *ordal* (the *a* having been shortened by lack of stress); though the latter part of the word (*dāl*) answers to mod. E. *dole.* The orig. sense is 'a dealing out,' separation, or discrimination; hence, a judgement, decision. + OFries. *ordēl;* OSax. *urdēli,* a judgement, decision; Du. *oordeel,* judgement; G. *urtheil,* OHG. *urteili,* judgement. B. The latter part of the word is (etymologically) the same as **Dole;** as shown by Du. *deel,* G. *theil.* The prefix is the Du. *oor-,* OSax. and G. *ur-,* answering to the OHG. prep. *ur,* Goth. *us,* out, out of, hence, thorough. It was common in AS., in such words as *or-mǣte,* immense, *or-mōd,* despondent, *or-sorg,* free from care, *or-trȳwe,* wanting in trust, *or-wēna,* wanting in hope, &c.; see Grein, ii. 356–360.

ORDER, arrangement, system. (F. – L.) ME. *ordre;* occurring four times on p. 8 of the Ancren Riwle. – F. *ordre,* substituted for OF. *ordine* (Godefroy), by the not uncommon change of *n* to *r;* see **Coffer.** – L. *ordinem,* acc. of *ordo,* order, arrangement. β. Supposed to be connected with L. *ord-īrī,* to begin, esp. to begin to weave, to lay a warp; see Bréal, and Brugmann, ii. § 128. Der. *order,* verb, in Sir T. Wiat, Sat. ii. l. 87; *order-less,* K. John, iii. 1. 253; *order-ly,* adj., Cymb. ii. 3. 52; *order-ly,* adv., Two Gent. i. 1. 130; *order-li-ness, order-ing.* Also *dis-order, ordain, ordin-ance, ordn-ance, ordin-ate, ordin-at-ion, ordin-al, ordin-ar-y, in-ordin-ate, co-ordin-ate, sub-ordin-ate.*

ORDINAL, showing order or succession. (L.) In Phillips, ed. 1706; chiefly in the phr. 'an *ordinal* number.' '*Ordinall* Numerals;' Minsheu's Span. Grammar (1623); p. 12. – L. *ordinālis,* in order, used of an ordinal number. – L. *ordin-,* decl. stem of *ordo,* order; see **Order.** Der. *ordinal,* sb., 'a book of directions for bishops to give holy orders,' Blount's Gloss., ed. 1674, from Late L. *ordināle,* neut. of *ordinālis.*

ORDINANCE, an order, regulation. (F. – L.) ME. *ordennace,* Rob. of Brunne, tr. of Langtoft, p. 83, last line. – OF. *ordenance,* later *ordonnance* (Cotgrave). – Late L. *ordinantia,* a command. – L. *ordinant-,* stem of pres. part. of *ordināre,* to set in order; see **Ordain.** Doublet, *ordnance.*

ORDINARY, usual, customary. (F. – L.) 'The *ordinary* maner;' Sir T. More, Works, p. 583 d. *Ordinarily* occurs on p. 582 h. – F. *ordinaire,* 'ordinary;' Cot. – L. *ordinārius,* regular, usual. – L. *ordin-,* decl. stem of *ordo,* order; see **Order.** Der. *ordinary,* sb., from F. *ordinaire,* 'an ordinary' (Cot.), L. *ordinārius,* an overseer; *ordinari-ly.* Also *extra-ordinary.*

ORDINATE, ORDINATION; see **Ordain.**

ORDNANCE, artillery. (F. – L.) The same word as *ordinance,* which is the old spelling; see K. John, ii. 218; Hen. V, ii. 4. 126; cf. Gower, C. A. ii. 195; bk. v. 2040. It sometimes referred to the *bore* or *size* of the cannon; cf. **Caliver.** '*Engin de telle ordonnance,* of such a bulk, size, or bore;' Cotgrave.

ORDURE, excrement. (F. – L.) In Shak. Hen. V, ii. 4. 39. ME. *ordure,* Chaucer, Pers. Tale, De Superbia (Six-text, Group I, 428). – F. *ordure,* 'ordure;' Cot. – OF. *ord* (fem. *orde*) 'filthy, nasty, foule, . . . ugly, or loathsom to behold;' Cot. Cf. OF. *ordir,* 'to foule, defile, soile;' id. [So also Ital. *ordura* is from the adj. *ordo,* dirty, slovenly, soiled, deformed.] – L. *horridus,* rough, shaggy, wild, frightful; see **Horrid.** So also Ital. *ordo* answers to MItal. *horrido,* mod. Ital. *orrido,* which Florio explains by 'horride, hideous, . . . euill fauoured, . . . lothesome to behold.'

ORE, crude or unrefined metal. (E.) ME. *ore,* in Chaucer, C. T. 6646 (D 1064). From AS. *ōra;* 'hit is ēac berende on wecga *ōrum* āres and īsernes,' it is fertile in ores of lumps of brass and iron; Ælfred, tr. of Beda, lib. i. c. 1. The word *ōra* was, sooner or later, entirely confused with the (unrelated) AS. *ār,* brass, also occurring in the above quotation; and the dat. case *āre,* meaning 'bronze,' occurs in Gregory's Pastoral, c. 37, ed. Sweet, p. 266. The change from AS. *ā* to long open o is seen again in E. *oar* from AS. *ār;* whilst the change from AS. *ō* to the same is illustrated by AS. *flōr,* E. *floor.* β. The AS. *ōra* is cognate with Du. *oer.* But *ār* is cognate with Icel. *eir,* brass; OHG. *ēr,* brass; Goth. *aiz, ais,* brass, coin, money, Mark, vi. 8; cf. *aizasmitha,* a copper-smith, 2 Tim. iv. 14; L. *æs,* bronze. Cf. Skt. *ayas,* iron; Max Müller, Lect. ii. 256.

OREAD, a mountain-nymph. (L. – Gk.) 'The Nymphs and *Oreades*;' Spenser, A Pastorall Aeglogue, l. 64. – L. *Oread-,* stem of *Oreas,* a mountain-nymph. – Gk. Ὀρειάς (the same). – Gk. ὄρος, a mountain. See **Origan.**

ORGAN, an instrument, esp. of music. (F. – L. – Gk.) In old books, the instrument of music is frequently called *the organs* or *a pair of organs; orgone* or *orgoon* (answering to L. pl. *organa*) occurs in P. Plowman, C. xxi. 7; Chaucer, C. T. 14857 (B 4041); the pl. *organs* is in Chaucer, C. T. 15602 (G 134); see my note to P. Plowman, C. xxi. 7. – F. *organe,* 'an organ, or instrument wherewith anything may be made or done;' Cot. – L. *organa;* orig. pl. of *organum,* an implement. – Gk. ὄργανον, an implement; allied to ἔργον, a work; see **Work**. And see **Orgies**. Der. *organ-ic*, *organ-ic-al*, *organ-ic-al-ly*, *organ-ism*, *organ-ist*, *organ-ise*, *organ-is-at-ion*. ☞ The AS. *organan*, sb. pl., used to translate L. *organa* in Ps. cxxxvi. 2 (ed. Spelman), can hardly be called an AS. word.

ORGIES, sacred rites accompanied with revelry; revelry, drunkenness. (F.–L.–Gk.) In Milton, P. L. i. 415; Drayton, Polyolbion, s. 6, l. 111.–F. *orgies*, 'the sacrifices of Bacchus;' Cot.–L. *orgia*, sb. pl., a nocturnal festival in honour of Bacchus, orgies.–Gk. ὄργια, sb. pl., orgies, rites; from sing. *ὄργιον, a sacred act; closely connected with ἔργον, work, action. See above. ¶ The sing. *orgy* is comparatively rare.

ORGULOUS, proud. (F.–OHG.) The reading in modern editions for *orgillous*, Shak. Troil. prol. 2. Palsgrave has: 'Orguyllous, prowde, *orgueilleux*.' ME. *orgeilous*, O. E. Misc. p. 30, l. 23; cf. Sir T. Malory, Morte Arthure, bk. xxi. c. 1. Anglo-F. *orguyllus*, Langtoft's Chron. i. 54.–OF. *orguillus* (11th cent.), later *orgueilleux*, 'proud,' Cot.–OF. *orguil*, *orguel*, *orgoil*, mod. F. *orgueil*, 'pride,' id. [Cf. Span. *orgullo*, orig. *urgullo*, as shown by l. 1947 of the Poem of the Cid, Ital. *orgoglio*, pride.] From a supposed OHG. sb. *urguolî, pride; formed from OHG. *urguol*, remarkable, notable (Graff, iv. 153). See Diez, Scheler, Littré. Cf. AS. *orgellice*, arrogantly, in Ælfred, tr. of Boëthius, c. 18, § 4; though connexion with this is uncertain. β. The OHG. word is compound; the prefix *ur-* answers to AS. *or-*, Goth. *us*, out, and has an intensive force, as explained under **Ordeal**. γ. The latter part of the word is not clear; the vowel suggests a connexion with AS. *gōl*, 2nd grade of *galan*, to sing loudly.

ORIEL, a recess (with a window) in a room. (F.–L.) 'It may generally be described as a recess within a building;' Blount has *oriol*, the little waste room near the hall in some houses and monasteries, where particular persons dined, and this is clearly an authorised and correct explanation;' Halliwell's Dict., which see. Spelt *oryall* in the Squire of Low Degree, l. 93; in Ritson's Metrical Romances, vol. iii.–OF. *oriol*, *eurieul*, a porch, alley, gallery, corridor; Godefroy. We find *le oriol* glossed by 'de la chambre,' i.e. the oriel of a chamber, in Wright's Vocab. i. 166, l. 9. The Late L. form is *ōriolum*, explained as a portico in Matt. Paris, in Ducange; see the citations in N. E. D. and Halliwell. β. Also specially applied to the small apartment in which it was the privilege of sick monks to dine; 'ut non in infirmaria sed seorsim in *ōriolo* monachi infirmi carnem comederent;' Matt. Paris, v. 259; in Ducange. Also to an oriel-window, as in the Squire of Low Degree, l. 93, and in the Erl of Tolouse, l. 307; Ritson, Met. Rom. vol. iii. Of unknown origin; but the OF. *eu* points to orig. L. *ō*; see N. E. D. Perhaps the L. *ori-* is the same as in E. *ori-fice*; from L. *ōs*, a mouth, an entrance, an opening; cf. E. *usher*, q. v. ¶ There is an article on the senses of the word *Oriel* in the Archæologia, vol. xxiii.

ORIENT, eastern. (F.–L.) ME. *orient*, in Chaucer, C. T. 14320 (B 3504).–F. *orient*.–L. *orient-*, stem of *oriens*, the rising sun, the east; properly pres. part. of *orīrī*, to rise. See **Origin**. Der. *orient-al*, Chaucer, On the Astrolabe, pt. i. sect. 5, l. 4, from F. *oriental*, L. *orientālis*; *orient-al-ist*.

ORIFICE, a small opening. (F.–L.) Spelt *orifis* in Spenser, F. Q. iv. 12. 22.–F. *orifice*, 'orifice;' Cot.–L. *orificium*, an opening, lit. 'the making of a mouth.'–L. *ōri-*, decl. stem of *ōs*, a mouth; and *-fic-*, for *facere*, to make. See **Oral** and **Fact**.

ORIFLAMME, the old standard of France. (F.–L.) 'The *oryflambe*, a speciall relyke that the Frenshe kynges vse to bere before them in all battayles;' Fabyan's Chron. an. 1355, ed. Ellis, p. 467. –OF. *oriflambe*, 'the great and holy standard of France;' Cot.–Late L. *auriflamma*, the standard of the monastery of St. Denis in France. The lit. sense is 'golden flame,' hence 'a golden banner;' so called because the banner was a red pennon with streamers, and was carried on a gilt pole. Cf. L. *flammula*, a little flame, also a small banner used by cavalry.–L. *auri-*, for *aurum*, gold; and *flamma*, a flame. See **Aureate** and **Flame**. ☞ But the Chanson de Roland, 3093, has *orie flambe* (L. *auream flammam*), as if the flag itself were golden; and a drawing, showing the shape of the oriflamme, is given in Gautier's edition, p. 278.

ORIGAN, ORIGANUM, wild marjoram. (F.–L.–Gk.) [An older name is *organy*, mentioned in Cotgrave. We also find AS. *organe*, for which see Cockayne's Leechdoms, iii. 340, borrowed directly from L. *origanum*.] In Holland, tr. of Pliny, b. xx. c. 17; Spenser, F. Q. i. 2. 40.–F. *origan*, 'garden organy, wild marjerome;' Cot.–L. *origanum* (Pliny).–Gk. ὀρίγανον, ὀρίγανος, marjoram; lit. 'mountain-pride.'–Gk. ὀρι-, for ὀρει-, from ὄρος, a mountain; and γάνος, brightness, beauty, ornament, delight. β. Gk. ὄρος is perhaps allied to Skt. *varshma*, height; γάνος is perhaps from the same root as L. *gaudēre*, to rejoice. Cf. **Oread**.

ORIGIN, source, beginning. (F.–L.) In Hamlet, i. 4. 26; the adj. *original* is much older, in Chaucer, C. T. 12434 (C 500).–F.

origine, 'an originall, beginning;' Cot.–L. *originem*, acc. of *origo*, a beginning.–L. *orīrī*, to arise, begin. Allied to Gk. ὄρνυμι, I stir up. Der. *origin-al* (as above), *origin-al-ly*, *origin-al-i-ty*, *origin-ate*, *origin-at-ion*, *origin-at-or*. And see *ori-ent*, *prim-ordial*.

ORIOLE, the golden thrush. (F.–L.) Called 'the golden oriole' in a translation of Buffon, London, 1792. The old names are golden thrush, witwall, wodewale, and heighaw.–OF. *oriol*, 'a heighaw, or witwall;' Cot.–L. *aureolus*, golden; extended from *aureus*, golden.–L. *aurum*, gold; see **Aureate**.

ORISON, a prayer. (F.–L.) ME. *oryson*, *orisoun*, Rob. of Glouc. p. 235, l. 4846; Chaucer, C. T. 5016 (B 596).–AF. *orison*; OF. *orison*, *oreson*, *oreison* (Burguy), later *oraison*, 'orison, prayer;' Cot.–L. *ōrātiōnem*, acc. of *ōrātio*, a speech, prayer.–L. *ōrāre*, to pray.–L. *ōr-*, from *ōs*, the mouth; see **Oral**. Doublet, *oration*.

ORLE, in heraldry, an ordinary like a fillet round the shield within it, at some distance from the edge; in architecture, a fillet. (F.–L.) F. *orle*, fem. 'a hem, selvidge, or narrow border; in blazon, an *urle*, or open border about, and within, a coat of arms;' Cot.; Late L. *orla*, a border, edge; in use A. D. 1244 (Ducange). This answers to a L. form *ōrula*, not found, dimin. of *ōra*, border, edge, margin.

ORLOP, a deck of a ship. (Du.) 'Orlope, the uppermost deck of a great ship, lying between the main and missen mast, and otherwise called the spare-deck; the second and lowest decks of a ship that has three decks, are likewise sometimes termed *orlopes*;' Phillips, ed. 1706. Also 'the second and lower deck of a ship;' id., ed. 1658. But properly applied only to the deck over the hold, which became the lower (or lowest) deck in ships having more decks than one. Contracted from *overlop*; spelt *overloppe* in Naval Accounts of Hen. VII, p. 176; l. 21.–Du. *overloop*, 'a running over; *de overloop van een schip*, the deck of a ship, the orlope;' Sewel. So called because it runs over or traverses the ship; cf. Du. *overloopen*, 'to run over, to run from one side to the other;' Sewel.–Du. *over*, cognate with E. *over*; and *loopen*, to run, cognate with E. *leap*. See **Over** and **Leap**.

ORMOLU, a kind of brass. (F.–L.) 'Ormolu, an alloy in which there is less zinc and more copper than in brass, that it may present a nearer resemblance to gold. . . . Furniture ornamented with *ormolu* came into fashion in France in the reign of Louis XV' [1715–1774]; Beeton's Dict. of Univ. Information.–F. *or moulu*, lit. pounded gold.–F. *or*, gold, from L. *aurum*; and *moulu*, pp. of *moudre*, to grind, pound, OF. *moldre*, *molre*, from L. *molere*, to grind; see **Aureate** and **Mill**.

ORNAMENT, that which beautifies, adornment. (F.–L.) ME. *ornament*; the pl. *ornamentes* occurs in Chaucer, C. T. 8134 (Sixtext, E 258); where it is remarkable that the Ellesmere and Camb. MSS. have *aornementes*, and the Hengwrt MS. has *aournementes*. [These forms answer to OF. *aornement*, an ornament, from the verb *aorner* (< L. *adornāre*), to adorn.] Also *ornementes*, pl., Allit. Poems, ed. Morris, B. 1799.–F. *ornement*, 'an ornament;' Cot.– L. *ornāmentum*, an ornament; formed with suffix *-mentum* from *ornāre*, to adorn. β. According to Bréal, a contracted form of *ordināre*, to set in order; see **Ordain**. Der. *ornament*, verb, added by Todd to Johnson; *ornament-al* (in 1646); *ornament-al-ly*, *ornament-at-ion*; also (from L. pp. *ornātus*) *ornate*, *ornate-ly*, *ornate-ness*. Also *ad-orn*.

ORNITHOLOGY, the science of birds. (Gk.) [In Blount's Gloss., ed. 1674, where it is noted as being 'the title of a late book;' viz. Fuller's *Ornithologie*, or the Speech of Birds; which is a different usage.] First truly used by Ray (1678) in his tr. of Willughby's *Ornithologiæ Libri Tres* (1676).–Gk. ὀρνιθο-, decl. stem of ὄρνις, a bird; and -λογία, allied to λόγος, a discourse; see **Logic**. β. The Gk. ὄρνις is interesting as being cognate with AS. *earn*, an eagle, Matt. xxiv. 28. A shorter form appears in Goth. *ara*, G. *aar*, an eagle; cf. also Russ. *orél*, an eagle. Named from its soaring; cf. Gk. ὄρνυμι, I stir up. Der. *ornithologi-c-al*, *ornitholog-ist*.

ORNITHORHYNCUS, an Australian mammal. (Gk.) Lit. 'bird-snout;' so called from the resemblance of its snout to a duck's bill.–Gk. ὀρνιθο-, for ὄρνις, a bird (above); and ῥύγχος, a snout, muzzle.

ORPHAN, a child bereft of father or mother, or of both parents. (L.–Gk.) 'He will not leūe them *orphanes*, as fatherlesse children;' Sir T. More, Works, p. 173 e; with a reference to John, xiv. [This form supplanted the older F. form *orphelin*, used by Chaucer, tr. of Boethius, b. ii. pr. 3, l. 21.]–L. *orphanus*, John, xiv. 18 (Vulgate).–Gk. ὀρφανός, destitute, John, xiv. 18; A. V. 'comfortless.' Cf. Gk. ὀρφός, with the same sense; whence ὀρφοβότης, one who brings up orphans. The shorter form ὀρφός answers to L. *orbus*, deprived, bereft, destitute. Der. *orphan-age*, a coined word.

ORPIMENT, yellow trisulphide of arsenic. (F.–L.) ME. *orpiment*, Chaucer, C. T. 16291 (G 823). Lit. 'gold paint.'–F.

orpiment, 'orpiment;' Cot.—L. *auripigmentum*, orpiment.—L. *auri-*, for *aurum*, gold; and *pigmentum*, a pigment, paint. See **Aureate** and **Pigment**. Der. *orpine*.

ORPINE, ORPIN, a kind of stone-crop. (F.—L.) Also called *live-long*; whence Spenser speaks of the '*orpine* growing still,' i.e. growing continually; Muiopotmos, l. 193. ME. *orpyn*; Prompt. Parv.—F. *orpin*, 'orpin, or live-long; also orpine, orpiment, or arsenick;' Cot. Merely a docked form of F. *orpiment*, orpiment; so called from its yellow flowers. See **Orpiment**.

ORRERY, an apparatus for illustrating the motions of the planets, &c. (Ireland.) 'Constructed at the expense of Charles Boyle, [second] earl of *Orrery*, about 1715 [rather 1713];' Haydn, Dict. of Dates. Orrery is the name of a barony in the county of Cork, in Ireland; the chief town in it is Bannevant. It derives its name from the *Orbraighe*, or 'descendants of *Orb*;' see Cormac's Glossary, ed. Stokes, ed. 1868, p. 128. (A. L. Mayhew.)

ORRIS, the name of a plant. (Ital.—L.—Gk.) 'The nature of the *orris*-root is almost singular;' Bacon, Nat. Hist. § 863. Spelt *orice* in Cotgrave, who explains F. *iris* by 'the rainbow, also, a flowerdeluce; *iris de Florence*, the flowerdeluce of Florence, whose root yields our *orice*-powder.' The Spanish term for *orris*-root is *raiz de iris florentina* = root of the Florentine iris. In Holland, tr. of Pliny, b. xxi. c. 7, we read: 'but as for the flour-de-lis [commonly called *ireos*, Holland's note], it is the root only therof that is comfortable for the odor.' It appears that *orris*, *orice*, and *orrice*, are English corruptions of the Ital. *irios* or *ireos*. MItal. *irios*, 'a kinde of sweete white roote called oris-roote:' Florio, ed. 1598; cf. mod. Ital. *ireos*, corn-flag, sword-grass (Meadows). β. The form of the Ital. *irios*, *ireos* is not easy to explain; it occurs as Late L. *yreos* in Synonima Bartholomæi, p. 25; but it is certainly connected with L. *iris*, which is the very word in Pliny, b. xxi. c. 7; and this is borrowed from Gk. ἶρις, 'the plant iris, a kind of lily with an aromatic root;' Liddell and Scott. γ. *Ireos* was specially used of the dried roots of the iris; see Lyte, tr. of Dodoens, b. ii. c. 35. It is prob. short for ἴρεως ῥίζα, where ἴρεως is a variant of the gen. ἴριδις (see Prellwitz). See **Iris**.

ORT, a leaving, remnant, morsel left at a meal. (E.) Usually in the pl. *orts*, Troil. v. 2. 158; Timon iv. 3. 400. ME. *ortes*, sb. pl., spelt *ortus* in the Prompt. Parv. p. 371, which has: '*Ortus*, releef of beestys mete,' i.e. orts, remnants of the food of animals. Not found in AS., but it is in general dialectal use, and is found in MDu., Low G., and Friesic. The Friesic is *ort* (Outzen); the Low G. is *ort*, esp. used of what is left by cattle in eating; cf. Low G. *ortstro*, refuse-straw; Bremen Wörterbuch, iii. 272. The word is solved by the fuller form found in MDu., viz. *oorete*, *ooraete*, a piece left uneaten at a meal, also nausea due to over-eating; Oudemans, v. 403. β. This is a compound word, made up of MDu. *oor-*, cognate with AS. *or-*, OHG. *ur-* (mod. G. *er-*), Goth. *us*, prep. signifying 'out' or 'without;' and MDu. *aet*, victuals (Hexham). Thus the sense is 'what is left in eating,' an 'over-morsel,' if we may so express it. For the prefix, see further under **Ordeal**; and see **Eat**. Cf. AS. *æt*, food; from the 3rd grade of *etan*, to eat; whence *or-æt*. γ. We may particularly note Swed. dial. *or-äte*, *ur-äte*, refuse fodder, orts, from *ur-*, *or-*, the prefix corresponding to Du. *oor-* above, and Swed. *äta*, victuals, food (Rietz). Dan. dial. *ored*, *orret*, an ort; cf. also NFries. *örte*, to leave remnants after eating. Also Bavarian *urässen*, *urezen*, to eat wastefully, *uräss*, *urez*, refuse; where *ur-* is the OHG. form of the same prefix, and *ässen* = G. *essen*, to eat; see Schmeller, Bav. Wört. i. 134. Also Norw. *orræta* (for *oræta*), orts; MDan. *orte*.

ORTHODOX, of the right faith. (F.—L.—Gk.; *or* L.—Gk.) Blount's Gloss., ed. 1674, has *orthodox* and *orthodoxal*; so also in Cotgrave.—F. *orthodoxe*, 'orthodoxe, orthodoxall;' Cot.—Late L. *orthodoxus* (Lewis).—Gk. ὀρθόδοξος, of the right opinion.—Gk. ὀρθο-, for ὀρθός, upright, right, true; and δόξα, opinion. β. Gk. ὀρθός is cognate with L. *arduus*, high, Irish *ard*, high. γ. Gk. δόξα is from δοκεῖν, to seem, allied to L. *decet*, it is fitting; see **Decorum**. Brugmann, ii. § 143. Der. *orthodox-y*, Gk. ὀρθοδοξία.

ORTHOEPY, correct pronunciation. (Gk.) The word occurs in Bp. Wilkins, Essay towards a Real Character, pt. iii. c. 1 (R.). This work appeared in 1668. Imitated from Gk. ὀρθοέπεια, correct pronunciation.—Gk. ὀρθό-, for ὀρθός, right, true; and ἔπ-ος, a word. See **Orthodox** and **Epic**.

ORTHOGRAPHY, correct writing. (F.—L.—Gk.) In rather early use. 'Of this word the true *ortographie*;' Remedy of Love (15th cent.), st. 41, l. 6; pr. in Chaucer's Works, ed. 1561, fol. 323, back. The word was at first spelt *orto-*, as in French, but afterwards corrected.—OF. *ortographie*; Cot. only gives the verb *ortographier*, 'to ortographise, to write or use true ortography.'—L. *orthographia* (Lewis).—Gk. ὀρθογραφία, a writing correctly.—Gk. ὀρθό-, for ὀρθός, right; and γράφειν, to write; see **Orthodox** and **Graphic**. Der. *orthographi-c*, *-c-al*, *-al-ly*; *orthograph-er*, *-ist*.

ORTHOPTEROUS, lit. straight-winged; an order of insects. (Gk.) Modern and scientific: coined from ὀρθό-, for ὀρθός, right, straight; and πτερ-όν, a wing. See **Orthodox** and **Diptera**. So also *orthoptera*.

ORTOLAN, the name of a bird. (F.—Ital.—L.) See Trench, Select Glossary; the word means 'haunting gardens,' and Trench cites *ortolan* in the early sense of 'gardener' from the State Papers, an. 1536, vol. vi. p. 534.—OF. *hortolan*, 'a delicate bird,' &c.; Cot.—MItal. *hortolano*, 'a gardiner; also a daintie bird so called;' Florio.—L. *hortulānus*, a gardener, belonging to a garden.—L. *hortulus*, a little garden, dimin. of *hortus*, a garden, cognate with E. *yard* and *garth*; see **Court**, **Garth**, **Yard** (1). ¶ The change from *u* to *o* is common in Italian.

ORTS, the pl. of **Ort**, q. v.

OSCILLATE, to swing. (L.) In Blount's Gloss., ed. 1674.—L. *oscillātus*, pp. of *oscillāre*, to swing, sway.—L. *oscillum*, a swing. β. Vanicek (with a reference to Corssen in Kuhn's Zeitschrift, xv. 156) identifies *oscillum*, a swing, with *oscillum*, a little mouth, a little cavity, a little image of the face, mask or head of Bacchus which was suspended on a tree (Lewis); with the remark that it meant a puppet made to swing or dance. If so, *oscillum* is a dimin. of *osculum*, the mouth, itself a dimin. from ōs, the mouth; see **Oral**. Cf. Verg. Georg. ii. 389. Der. *oscillat-ion*, *oscillat-or-y*. And see *osculate*.

OSCULATE, to kiss. (L.) In Blount's Gloss., ed. 1674.—L. *osculātus*, pp. of *osculārī*, to kiss.—L. *osculum*, a little mouth, pretty mouth; double dimin. (with suffix *-cu-lu-*) from ōs, the mouth; see **Oral**. Der. *osculat-or-y*, *osculat-ion*.

OSIER, the water-willow. (F.—Late L.) In Shak. L. L. L. iv. 2. 112. ME. *osyere*; Prompt. Parv. p. 371; *oyser*, K. Alisaunder, ed. Weber, 6186.—F. *osier*, 'the ozier, red withy, water-willow tree;' Cot. Cf. AF. *osere*, an osier; A. Neckam; in Wright's Vocab. 1st Ser. p. 110. β. Origin uncertain; but obviously related to Late L. *ōsāria*, *ausāria*, a bundle of osiers or twigs of the willow, in Irminon's Polyptychum (9th cent.); Phil. Soc. Trans., 1902; p. 543. Godefroy has OF. *ausay*, an osier.

OSMIUM, a metal. (Gk.) Discovered in 1803 (Haydn). The oxide has a disagreeable smell; hence the name, coined from Gk. ὀσμή, a smell; earlier form, ὀδμή. Connected with ὄζειν (= ὄδ-γειν), to smell, and with L. *odor*; see **Odour**.

OSPREY, the fish-hawk. (F.—L.) In Shak. Cor. iv. 7. 34; cf. Two Noble Kinsmen, i. 1. 138. In the old texts, it is spelt *aspray* in both passages. Spelt *osprey*, *ospreie*, *orfraie* (F. *orfraie*), in Holland, tr. of Pliny, b. x. c. 3; all these forms are related to *ossifrage*, also occurring in the same chapter. Spelt *ospray* in Lydgate, Assembly of Gods, 813. The name signifies 'bone-breaker;' from the bird's strength. β. The form *orfraie* is from MF. *orfraye*, 'the osprey;' Cot. The form *osprey* appears to be an altered form of an OF. *osfraie* (not found, but the form intermediate between F. *orfraie* and the L. word); perhaps by confusion with E. *prey*. All from L. *ossifragus*, *ossifraga*, the sea-eagle, osprey.—L. *ossifragus*, bone-breaking.—L. *ossi-*, decl. stem of *os*, a bone; and *frag-*, a stem of *frangere*, to break, cognate with E. *break*. See **Osseous** and **Break**. Doublet, *ossifrage*.

OSSEOUS, bony. (L.) A late word; added by Todd to Johnson.—L. *osseus*, bony; by change of *-us* to *-ous* (common).—L. *oss-*, from *os*, a bone. β. Allied to Gk. ὀστέον, Skt. *asthi*, a bone. Brugmann, i. § 703. Der. *ossi-fy*, to turn to bone, from *ossi-*, decl. stem of *os*, and F. *-fier* < L. *-ficāre* (for *facere*), to make; *ossific-at-ion*; *ossu-ar-y*, Sir T. Browne, Urn-burial, c. v. § 4, from L. *ossuārium*, a receptacle for the bones of the dead. Also *ossi-frage*, *os-prey*.

OSSIFRAGE, an osprey; also, the bearded vulture. (L.) In Levit. xi. 13; Deut. xiv. 12.—L. *ossifragus*, also *ossifraga*, a bone-breaker; see **Osprey**.

OSTENSIBLE, that may be shown, apparent. (L.) Late; see Todd's Johnson. Coined by adding the suffix *-ble* (F. *-ble*, L. *-bilis*) to *ostensi-*, for *ostensus*, pp. of *ostendere*, to show. β. *Ostendere* is for *ops-tendere*, where *ops* is related to *ob*, near, before, and *tendere* is to stretch; hence the sense is 'to spread before' one, to show. See **Ob-** and **Tend**. Der. *ostensi-bl-y*, *ostensi-bili-ty*; we also find *ostensive* = 'that serves to shew,' a term in logic; see Bacon, Adv. of Learning, bk. ii. § xiii. 3. And see *ostent-at-ion*.

OSTENTATION, show, pomp. (F.—L.) '*Ostentacion* and shew;' Sir T. More, Works, p. 1191 c.—F. *ostentation*, 'ostentation;' Cot.—L. *ostentātiōnem*, acc. of *ostentātio*, display.—L. *ostentāre*, intensive form of *ostendere*, to show; see **Ostensible**. Der. *ostentati-ous*, in 1673; *ostentati-ous-ly*, *-ness*. We also find *ostent*, Merch. Ven. ii. 2. 205, from L. *ostentus*, display.

OSTEOLOGY, the science of the bones. (Gk.) Scientific.—Gk. ὀστέο-, decl. stem of ὀστέον, a bone; and *-λογία*, equivalent to λόγος, discourse, from λέγειν, to speak. See **Osseous** and **Logic**.

OSTLER, the same as **Hostler,** q. v. (F. –L.) Wyclif has *ostiler,* an innkeeper, Luke, x. 35.

OSTRACISE, to banish by a vote written on a potsherd. (Gk.) 'And all that worth from hence did *ostracise*;' Marvell, Lachrymæ Musarum; 1650 (R.). [The sb. *ostracisme* is in Minsheu, ed. 1627, and the MF. *ostracisme* is in Cotgrave.] ‒ Gk. ὀστρακίζειν, to banish by potsherds, to ostracise. ‒ Gk. ὄστρακον, burnt clay, a tile, potsherd, tablet for voting; also, a shell, which appears to be the orig. meaning. β. Closely allied to Gk. ὄστρεον, an oyster, and to Gk. ὀστέον, a bone. See **Oyster** and **Osseous.** Der. *ostracis-m* (= F. *ostracisme*), from Gk. ὀστρακισμός.

OSTRICH, a very large bird. (F. –L. *and* Gk.) ME. *oystryche,* Squire of Low Degree, l. 226; in Ritson, Met. Romances, vol. iii. Earlier *ostrice,* Ancren Riwle, p. 132, note *e.* *Ostrice* is a weakened form of *ostruce.* ‒ OF. *ostruce* (12th cent.), *ostruche,* Palsgrave, *ostruce,* Cotgrave, mod. F. *autruche*; see Littré. Cf. Span. *avestruz,* Port. *abestruz,* an ostrich. β. All from L. *auis strūthio,* i.e. ostrich-bird. ‒ L. *auis,* a bird; and *strūthio,* an ostrich, borrowed from Gk. στρου-θίων, an ostrich. γ. For the L. *auis,* see **Aviary.** The Gk. στρουθίων is an extension from στρουθός, a bird; which is prob. allied to Lith. *strazdas,* a thrush; see **Throstle.** ¶ The L. *auis* also occurs as a prefix in the singular word *bustard* (= *auis tarda*); see **Bustard.** N. B. We find also the spelling *estridge,* 1 Hen. IV, iv. 1. 98.

OTHER, second, different, not the same. (E.) A. The word *second* is the only ordinal number of F. origin, till we come to *millionth*; it has taken the place of *other,* which formerly frequently had the sense of 'second.' B. We constantly meet with *thet on, thet other* = the one, the other (lit. that one, that other); these phrases are often spelt *the ton, the tother,* the *t* being attached to the wrong word; and this explains the common prov. E. *the tother,* often used as *tother,* without *the.* It must be remembered that *thet* or *that* was orig. merely the neut. of the def. article. 'And euer whyl *that* on hire sorwe tolde *That other* wepte ' = and ever, whilst the one told her sorrow, the other wept; Chaucer, C. T. 10809 (F 495). AS. ōðer, other, second, Grein, ii. 305. The long ō- is due to older *on-,* for *an-,* as in *gōs* (goose) for *gans*; *tōð* (tooth) for *tanth*; hence ōðer stands for **anðer.* ✛ Du. *ander*; Icel. *annarr* (for **antharr,* by assimilation); Dan. *anden* (neut. *andet,* pl. *andre*); Swed. *andra,* next, second, other; G. *ander*; Goth. *anthar.* ✛ Lithuan. *antras,* other, second (Nesselmann). β. We also find Skt. *anya-s,* other; which at once shows the division of the word. [We must be careful, by the way, to separate Skt. *antara-s,* other, from Skt. *antara-s,* interior, connected with *antar* (L. *inter*), within.] In Skt. *an-tara-s,* Goth. *an-thar,* E. *o-ther,* the suffix is the usual comparative suffix appearing in Gk. σοφώ-τερ-ος, wiser, &c.; seen also in E. *whe-ther, ei-ther, hi-ther,* &c.; the Idg. form being -TER-. γ. The base *an-* is perhaps the Idg. pronominal base found in Lithuan. *an-as,* that one (Nesselmann, p. 5), and in Russ. *on',* he. Thus the orig. sense is 'more than that,' or 'beyond that,' used in pointing out something more remote than that which was first contemplated; hence its use in the sense of 'second.' Der. *other-wise,* ME. *other wise* = in another way, Will. of Palerne, l. 396; *an-other.*

OTIOSE, unemployed, idle, futile. (L.) First in 1794. ‒ L. *ōtiōsus,* unemployed. ‒ L. *ōtium,* leisure.

OTTER, the water-weasel. (E.) ME. *oter* (with one *t*); Old Eng. Miscellany, ed. Morris, p. 70, l. 358. AS. *otor,* as a gloss to L. *lutria* in Ælfric's Gloss., Nomina Ferarum; Voc. 118. 42; spelt *oter,* id. 320. 21. Hence the adj. *yteren,* by vowel-change; Sweet's AS. Reader. ✛ Du. *otter*; Icel. *otr*; Dan. *odder*; Swed. *utter*; G. *otter*; Russ. *vuidra*; Lithuan. *udra*; Gk. ὕδρα, a water-snake, hydra. β. The common Teutonic type is **otroz,* m.; Idg. types **udros,* m., **udrā,* f.; closely related to *water*; cf. Gk. ὕδρα, water-snake, with ὕδωρ, water. The sense is 'water-animal.' See **Water, Wet.** Doublet, *hydra.*

OTTO, a bad spelling of **ATTAR,** q.v. (Arab.)

OTTOMAN, a low stuffed seat. (F. –Arab.) F. *ottomane,* 'an ottoman, sofa;' Hamilton. ‒ F. *Ottoman,* Turkish, Turk. So named from *Othman* or *Osman,* the founder of the Ottoman or Turkish empire in A.D. 1299. From Arab. *'othmān* (Devic).

OUBIT, a hairy caterpillar. (E.) Also *oobit, woubit, woubet*; see The Oubit in Kingsley's Poems. Spelt *woubet,* Montgomery's Poems, S. T. S., p. 68, l. 268. ME. *wolbode, wollebode,* 'multipes;' Catholicon Anglicum. ‒ AS. *wull,* wool, and *budda,* a beetle; Voc. 543. 10. See Notes on E. Etym., p. 203.

OUCH, NOUCH, the socket of a precious stone, an ornament. (F. –OHG.) The orig. sense is 'socket of a gem,' but it is commonly used for gem or ornament. The true form is *nouch,* but the initial *n* is often dropped; see remarks upon the letter **N.** Spelt *ouches* in Exod. xxviii, xxxix; and in Shak. 2 Hen. IV, ii. 4. 53; *owches* in Sir T. More, Works, p. 337 d. 'As a precious stone in

a riche *ouche*;' Sir T. Elyot, The Governour, b. iii. c. 30. ME. *nouche,* Chaucer, C. T. 8258 (E 382), after a word ending with a consonant; but *an ouch* (for *a nouch*) in C. T. 6325 (D 742). 'Nowche, monile;' Prompt. Parv. p. 359, and see Way's note; he cites: '*Fermaglio,* the hangeyng *owche,* or flowre that women use to tye at the chaine or lace that they weare about their neckes,' W. Thomas, Ital. Grammar, 1548. So that one sense of the word is exactly mod. E. 'locket.' 'A golden lase or *nowche*;' Wyclif, 1 Macc. x. 89; where the A. V. has 'a buckle of gold.' ‒ AF. *nouche,* Stat. Realm, i. 380; OF. *nouche, nosche, nusche,* a buckle, clasp, given by Godefroy, s. v. *noche.* [It is, indeed, obvious that the Low L. *nouchia,* which occurs in the Inventory of jewels of Blanche of Spain (cited in Way's note) is nothing but the F. *nouche* Latinised.] The more correct Late L. form is *nusca* (Ducange). ‒ MHG. *nusche, nuske,* OHG. *nusca, nuscha,* a buckle, clasp, or brooch for a cloak. Prob. ult. of Celtic origin; cf. Irish *nasc,* a tie, chain, ring; *nasgaim,* I bind (Schade, Stokes).

OUGHT (1), past tense of **Owe,** q.v. (E.)

OUGHT (2), another spelling of **Aught,** q.v. (E.) Spelt *ouȝt* in Wyclif, Luke, ix. 36.

OUNCE (1), the twelfth part of a pound Troy. (F. –L.) ME. *unce,* Chaucer, C. T. 16224, 16589 (G 756, 1121). ‒ OF. *unce* (12th cent.), mod. F. *once* (Littré). ‒ L. *uncia,* (1) an ounce, (2) an inch. β. The orig. sense is 'a small weight;' allied to Gk. ὄγκος, bulk, mass, weight. Doublet, *inch.*

OUNCE (2), **ONCE,** a kind of lynx. (F. –L. –Gk.) In Shak. Mids. Nt. Dream, ii. 2. 30; Milton, P. L. iv. 344; and in Holland, tr. of Pliny, b. xxviii. c. 8, last section. ME. *unce,* King Alisaunder, 5228. ‒ F. *once,* an ounce; OF. *lonce,* Supp. to Godefroy, s.v. *once*; MF. *lonce,* 'the ounce;' Cot. Cf. Port. *onça,* Span. *onza,* Ital. *lonza,* an ounce. β. The OF. and MF. *lonce* show that the mod. F. *once* resulted from taking *lonce* to represent *l'once,* where *l* seemed to be the def. article. So also Florio (1598) gives an Ital. form *onza*; but *lonza* is in Dante, Inf. i. 32. All from a Late L. popular type **luncia,* for L. *lyncea,* f., lynx-like. ‒ L. *lync-,* stem of *lynx,* a lynx. ‒ Gk. λύγξ, a lynx; see **Lynx.** For F. *o* < Gk. *v,* cf. *grotto, tomb, torso.*

OUPH, OUPHE, an elf. (E.) In Merry Wᵢves, iv. 4. 49. A variant of **Oaf,** q.v. And see **Oaf** in E.D.D.

OUR, possessive pronoun of the 1st pers. plural. (E.) ME. *oure,* older form *ure*; Havelok, l. 13. AS. *ūre,* gen. pl. of 1st personal pronoun; orig. meaning 'of us.' This gen. pl. was used as a possessive pronoun, and regularly declined, with gen. *ūres,* dat. *ūrum,* &c.; see Grein, ii. 633. It then completely supplanted the older AS. possess. pron. *ūser, usser* (Grein, ii. 633), cognate with G. *unser* and Goth. *unsar.* β. Yet *ūre* is itself a contracted form for **ūsere,* cognate with Goth. *unsara,* the Gothic form of the gen. pl. of the 1st pers. pronoun. Here *-ara* is the gen. pl. suffix, and a shorter form appears in Goth. *uns,* equivalent to E. *us.* γ. Briefly, *our* is the gen. pl. corresponding to the acc. pl. *us*; see **Us.** Der. *our-s,* ME. *oures,* Chaucer, C. T. 13203 (B 1463), due to AS. *ūres,* gen. sing. of *ūre,* when declined as above; also *our-selves,* or (in regal style) *our-self*; see **Self.** ☞ As to the dispute as to whether we should write *ours* or *our's,* it cannot matter; we write *day's* for AS. *dæges* (gen. sing.), but *days* for AS. *dagas* (nom. pl.); thus marking the omission, strangely enough, only where the *weaker* vowel is omitted. The apostrophe is merely conventional, and better omitted.

OURANG-OUTANG; see **Orang-Outang.** (Malay.)

OUSEL, OUZEL, a kind of thrush. (E.) ME. *osel,* Wright's Vocab. i. 164, l. 3; *osul,* Trevisa, tr. of Higden, i. 237. AS. *ōsle,* gloss upon L. *merula,* Voc. 260. 26; older form *ōslæ,* id. 32. 27. Here, as in AS. ōðer, other = Goth. *anthar,* the long ō stands for *an* or *am*; thus *ōsle* < **ansele* or **amsele*; in this case, for the latter. ✛ G. *amsel,* OHG. *amsala,* a blackbird, ousel. The L. *merula* (whence E. *merle*) can stand for **mesula,* and may be connected with OHG. *amsala* by gradation. See **Merle.**

OUST, to eject, expel. (F. –L.) The word has come to us through Law French. '*Ousted,* from the Fr. *oster,* to remove, or put out, as *ousted* of the possession (*Pecks Case, Mich.* 9 *Car.* 1. 3 *Part Crokes Rep. fol.* 349), that is, removed, or put out of possession ;' Blount's Nomolexicon, ed. 1691. ‒ AF. *ouster* (Bozon); OF. *oster,* 'to remove, withdraw,' Cot.; mod. F. *ôter.* Cf. Prov. *ostar, hostar* (Bartsch). β. Of disputed origin; it has been proposed to derive it from L. *obstāre,* to withstand, hinder, but this does not wholly suit the sense. Yet this is prob. right. Ducange has *obstāre vel ostāre viam,* to get in one's way, from which the change to the sense of 'to turn one out of the way ' is not difficult. See Körting, § 6643; and cf. Romaunsch *dustar* (**de-obstāre*), to drive away flies, &c.; also Prov. *dousta,* to remove (Mistral). Der. *oust-er.*

OUT, without, abroad, completely. (E.) ME. *out,* prep.; ME. *oute,* older form *ūte,* adv., out. 'Out of alle charitee ;' Chaucer, C. T., A 452. 'That hii ne ssolde *out* wende' = that they should not go out; Rob. of Glouc. p. 170. AS. *ūte, ūtan,* adv., out, without; Grein, i. 634. Formed with adv. suffix *-e* (or *-an*) from AS. *ūt,* adv. 'Flēogan of hūse *ūt*' = to fly out of the house; '*ūt* of earce' = out of the ark; Grein, ii. 633. (This shows the origin of the phrase *out of* = out from.) **+** Du. *uit;* Icel. *ūt;* Dan. *ud;* Swed. *ut;* G. *aus;* OHG. *ūz;* Goth. *ūt;* whence *ūta,* adv. (= AS. *ūte);* *utana,* adv. and prep. (= AS. *ūtan*).**+**Skt. *ud,* up, out. It appears also in Gk. ὕστερος = ὕδ-τερος, corresponding to E. *utter, outer.* All from Idg. types UD, UD, up, out. Der. *with-out, there-out, out-er, ut-ter, out-m-ost, ut-m-ost* (double superlatives); see **Utter, Utmost, Uttermost.** Also as a prefix in numerous compounds, for which see below. (But not in *outrage.*)

OUTBALANCE, to exceed in weight. (Hybrid; E. *and* F.−L.) In Dryden, tr. of Ovid, Met. xiii. 397. From **Out** and **Balance.**

OUTBID, to bid above or beyond. (E.) In Shak. 2 Hen. IV, ii. 4. 363. See **Bid** (2).

OUTBREAK, an outburst. (E.) In Hamlet, ii. i. 33. See **Break.**

OUTBURST, a bursting forth. (E.) First in 1657, in imitation of *out-break;* but a good word. Neither in Rich. or Todd's Johnson. See **Burst.**

OUTCAST, one who is cast out, a wretch. (Hybrid; E. *and* Scand.) 'For yif it so be that a wikked wight be . . . the more *out cast* (L. *abiectior*);' Chaucer, tr. of Boethius, b. iii. pr. 4. l. 31. See **Cast.**

OUTCOME, result, event. (E.) An old word; ME. *utcume,* a coming out, deliverance; Ancren Riwle, p. 80. See **Come.**

OUTCRY, a crying out, clamour. (Hybrid; E. *and* F.−L.) In Shak. Romeo, v. 3. 193; and in Palsgrave. See **Cry.**

OUTDO, to surpass. (E.) In Shak. Cor. ii. 1. 150. See **Do.**

OUTDOOR, in the open air. (E.) First in 1765; a modern contraction for *out of door.* See **Door.**

OUTER, OUTERMOST; see **Utter, Uttermost.**

OUTFIT, equipment. (Hybrid; E. *and* Scand.) First in 1769; added by Todd to Johnson. See **Fit.** Der. *outfitt-er, outfitt-ing.*

OUTGO, to surpass. (E.) In Shak. Timon, i. 1. 285; and Palsgrave. See **Go.** Der. *outgo-ing,* sb., expenditure. And see *outwent.*

OUTGROW, to grow beyond. (E.) In Shak. Rich. III, iii. 1. 104. See **Grow.**

OUTHOUSE, a small house built away from the house. (E.) In Beaum. and Fletcher, The Coxcomb, iii. 1. 53. See **House.**

OUTLANDISH, foreign. (E.) Cf. AS. *ūtlendisc,* exiled, Levit. xxiv. 22.−AS. *ūt,* out; and *land,* land. See **Land.**

OUTLAST, to last beyond. (E.) In Beaum. and Fletcher, Nice Valour, iv. 1 (Shamont). See **Last** (3).

OUTLAW, one not under the protection of the law. (Scand.) ME. *outlawe,* Chaucer, C. T. 17173 (H 224). AS. *ūtlaga, ūtlah,* an outlaw; see numerous references in Thorpe, Ancient Laws, index to vol. i. Borrowed from Icel. *ūtlagi,* an outlaw. See **Out** and **Law.** ¶ The word *law* is rather Scand. than E. Der. *outlaw,* verb, K. Lear, iii. 4. 172, from AS. *ūtlagian,* A. S. Chron. an. 1014; *outlaw-ry* (with F. suffix *-rie* = *-erie*), Jul. Cæs. iv. 3. 173.

OUTLAY, expenditure. (E.) Not in Todd's Johnson; but a good word; orig. Northern; first in 1798. See **Lay.**

OUTLET, a place or means by which a thing is let out. (E.) An old word. ME. *utlete,* Owl and Nightingale, l. 1752; lit. 'a letting out.'−AS. *ūtlǣtan,* verb, to let out, let down; Luke, v. 5. See **Let** (1).

OUTLINE, a sketch. (Hybrid; E. *and* F.−L.) Used by Dryden; Parallel bet. Painting and Poetry; repr. 1882, p. 139; and in The Tatler, no. 182, § 6. Lit. a *line* lying on the *outer* edge, a sketch of the lines enclosing a figure. See **Line.**

OUTLIVE, to live beyond. (E.) In Shak. Merch. Ven. iv. 1. 269. See **Live.**

OUTLOOK, a prospect. (E.) 'Which owe's to man's short *out-look* all its charms;' Young's Night Thoughts, Night 8, l. 264 from end. See **Look.** Der. *out-look,* verb, to look bigger than, K. John, v. 2. 115.

OUTLYING, remote. (E.) Used by Sir W. Temple and Walpole; see Richardson. See **Lie** (1).

OUTPOST, a troop in advance of an army. (Hybrid; E. *and* F.−L.) Late; see quotation in Richardson. See **Post.**

OUTPOUR, to pour out. (Hybrid; E. *and* F.) In Milton, P. R. iii. 311; Samson, 544. See **Pour.** Der. *outpour-ing.*

OUTRAGE, excessive violence. (F.−L.) ME. *outrage,* to be divided as *outr-age,* there being no connexion with *out* or *rage;* Chaucer, C. T. 2014 (A 2012); Rob. of Glouc. p. 46, l. 1062.−OF. *outrage,* earlier *oultrage* (Godefroy); MF. *outrage,* 'outrage, excesse;' Cot. Cf. Ital. *oltraggio,* outrage. β. Formed with suffix *-age* (<L. *-āticum*) from OF. *oltre, outre,* beyond; spelt *oultre* in Cotgrave; cf.

Ital. *oltra,* beyond; from L. *ultrā,* beyond. See **Ulterior.** Der. *outrage,* verb, Spenser, F. Q. i. 6. 5; *outrag-e-ous,* ME. *outrageous,* Chaucer, C. T. 3996 (A 3998), from OF. *outrageux,* spelt *oultrageus* in Cotgrave; *outrageous-ly, -ness.* Also *outré,* exaggerated, pp. of *outrer,* to pass beyond, from F. *outre,* beyond.

OUTREACH, to reach beyond. (E.) In Beaum. and Fletcher, Love's Pilgrimage, v. 4 (Philippo). See **Reach.**

OUTRIDE, to ride faster than. (E.) In 2 Hen. IV, i. 1. 36. See **Ride.** Der. *outrid-er,* one who rides forth, Chaucer, C. T. 166.

OUTRIGGER, a naval term. (E. *and* Scand.) A projecting spar for extending sails, a projecting rowlock for an oar, a boat with projecting rowlocks (ab. 1840). See **Rig.**

OUTRIGHT, thoroughly, wholly. (E.) Properly an adverb. 'The frere made the foole madde *outright;*' Sir T. More, Works, p. 483 a. See **Right.**

OUTROAD, an excursion. (E.) Lit. 'a riding out.' In 1 Macc. xv. 41 (A.V.). For the sense of *road* = a riding, see **Inroad.**

OUTRUN, to surpass in running. (E.) In John, xx. 4 (A. V.); and in Tyndale's translation (1526). See **Run.**

OUTSET, a setting out, beginning. (E.) Used by Burke (R.). See **Set.**

OUTSHINE, to surpass in splendour. (E.) In Spenser, F. Q. v. 9. 21. See **Shine.**

OUTSIDE, the exterior surface. (E.) In King John, v. 2. 109. See **Side.**

OUTSKIRT, the outer border. (E. *and* Scand.) 'All that *outskirte* of Meathe;' Spenser, View of the State of Ireland; Globe ed. p. 668, col. 1, l. 27. See **Skirt.**

OUTSTRETCH, to stretch out. (E.) ME. *outstrecchen,* pt. t. *outstraughte,* Rom. of the Rose, 1515. See **Stretch.**

OUTSTRIP, to outrun. (E.) In Hen. V, iv. 1. 177. From *out,* and *strip,* to run fast. 'The swiftest Hound, when he is hallowed [i. e. urged on] *strippes* forth;' Gosson, School of Abuse, ed. Arber, p. 58. See **Strip.**

OUTVIE, to exceed, surpass. (E. *and* F.−L.) In Tam. of the Shrew, ii. 387. See **Vie.**

OUTVOTE, to defeat by excess of votes. (E. *and* F.−L.) 'Sense and appetite *outvote* reason;' South's Sermons, vol. iii. ser. 6 (R.). See **Vote.**

OUTWARD, towards the outside, exterior. (E.) ME. *outward,* earlier *utward,* adv., Ancren Riwle, p. 102, l. 3. AS. *ūteweard, ūtewerd,* Exod. xxix. 20.−AS. *ūte,* adv., out; and *-weard,* suffix indicating direction. See **Out** and **Toward.** Der. *outward,* adj., Temp. i. 2. 104; *outward,* sb., Cymb. i. 1. 23; *outward-ly,* Macb. i. 3. 54; *outward-s,* where the *-s* answers to the ME. adv. suffix *-es,* Hamlet, ii. 2. 392; *outward-bound,* as to which see **Bound** (3).

OUTWEIGH, to exceed in weight. (E.) In Shak. Cor. i. 6. 71. See **Weigh.**

OUTWENT, went faster than. (E.) In Mark, vi. 33 (A. V.). From **Out,** and *went,* pt. t. of Wend.

OUTWIT, to surpass in wit. (E.) 'To *outwit* and deceive themselves;' South's Sermons, vol. ii. ser. 7 (R.). See **Wit.**

OUTWORKS, external or advanced fortifications. (E.) 'And stormed the *outworks* of his fortress;' Butler, Hudibras, pt. iii. c. 1, l. 1136. See **Work.**

OUZEL, another form of **Ousel,** q. v.

OVAL, of the shape of an egg. (F.−L.) Spelt *ovall* in Minsheu, ed. 1627.−MF. *oval,* 'ovall, shaped like an egg;' Cot. Formed with suffix *-al* (<L. *-ālis*) from L. *ōu-um,* an egg; there was prob. a Late Latin *ōuālis,* adj., but it is not recorded. β. L. *ōuum* is cognate with Gk. ᾠόν, an egg; and they answer to the Idg. types *ōwom, ōwiom,* related by gradation to L. *auis,* a bird; see **Aviary.** Perhaps connected with E. *egg;* see **Egg.** Der. (from L. *ōuum*) *ov-ar-y,* Sir T. Browne, Vulg. Errors, b. iii. c. 28, § 5, from Late L. *ōuāria,* the part of the body where eggs are formed in birds (Ducange); *ov-ate,* i. e. egg-shaped, L. *ōuātus,* with suffix *-ātus* like the pp. suffix of the 1st conjugation; and see *ovi-form.*

OVATION, a lesser Roman triumph. (F.−L.) In Minsheu, ed. 1627.−F. *ovation,* 'a small triumph granted to a commander;' Cot. −L. *ōuātiōnem,* acc. of *ōuātio,* lit. shouting, exultation.−L. *ōuāre,* to shout.**+**Gk. εὐάζειν, to shout, call aloud; from εὐαί, εὐοῖ, interjections of rejoicing, esp. in honour of Bacchus.

OVEN, a furnace, cavity for baking bread, &c. (E.) ME. *ouen* (with *u* for *v*), Wyclif, Luke, xii. 28. AS. *ofen, ofn,* Grein, ii. 310. **+**Du. *oven;* Icel. *ofn,* later *omn;* of which an earlier form *ogn* is found; Swed. *ugn;* G. *ofen;* Goth. *auhns.* β. It would appear that the Teut. types are *uhno-, ufno-;* Idg. type *uqnos.* Allied to Skt. *ukhā,* a pot; and to Gk. ἰπνός, an oven; the older sense is remarkably preserved in AS. *ofnet,* a pot, a closed vessel.

OVER, above, across, along the surface of. (E.) ME. *ouer* (with *u* for *v*), Chaucer, C. T. 3920 (A 3922). AS. *ofer* (Grein).**+**Du.

over; Icel. *yfir*; also *ofr*, adv., exceedingly; Dan. *over*; Swed. *öfver*; G. *über*, OHG. *ubar*; Goth. *ufar*; Gk. ὑπέρ; L. *super*; Skt. *upari*, above. β. The prefixed *s* in L. *s-uper* has not been satisfactorily explained; some think it is equivalent to Gk. ἐξ. The common Idg. base is **uper-*, closely related to *uperos, upper (Skt. *upara-*, L. *s-uperus*, AS. *ufera*, Grein, ii. 614). γ. It is obvious that *up-eros is a comparative form; the superlative takes a double shape, (1) with suffix -MO, as in L. *summus* (from *s-upmos*), highest, AS. *ufema, highest (only found with an additional suffix -*est* in *ufemyst*, written for *ufemest, in Gen. xl. 17); and (2) with suffix -TO, as in Gk. ὕπατος, highest. δ. The positive form is **upo-*; this appears in Skt. *upa*, near, on, under, Gk. ὑπό, under, L. *sub*, under, Goth. *uf*, under. A closely related adverbial form occurs in AS. *ufan*, above, G. *oben*, and E. -*ove* in *ab-ove*. The Goth. form *uf* appears to be further related to E. *up*, and G. *auf*, upon; so that there are two parallel Teutonic types, viz. UF (Goth. *uf*, G. *oben*, E. *ab-ove*) and UP (E. *up*, G. *auf*); with the parallel comparative forms seen in *over* and *upper*. ε. The senses of 'under' and 'over' are curiously mixed, as in L. *sub*, under, and *super*, above; Bréal suggests that L. *sub* refers to an upward movement; cf. L. *surgere* (for *sub-regere) to rise. ζ. We may further note ME. *over*, adj., with the sense of 'upper,' Chaucer, C. T. 133; and ME. *overest*, with the sense of 'uppermost,' id. 292 (A 290). And see **Up, Sub-, Hypo-, Super-, Hyper-, Above, Sum, Summit, Supreme, Sovereign**. Der. verbs, as *over-act*, *over-awe*, &c.; adverbs, as *over-board*, &c.; sbs., as *over-coat*, &c.; adjectives, as *over-due*, &c.; see below.

OVERACT, to act more than is necessary. (E. *and* L.) Used by Ben Jonson; Catiline, ii. 3 (Curius). See **Act**.

OVERALLS, loose trowsers worn above others. (E.) Modern; from **Over** and **All**.

OVERARCH, to arch over. (E. *and* F. — L.) In Milton, P. L. i. 304. See **Arch**.

OVERAWE, to keep in complete subjection. (E. *and* Scand.) In Shak. 1 Hen. VI, i. 1. 36. See **Awe**.

OVERBALANCE, to exceed in weight. (E. *and* F. — L.) 'For deeds always *overbalance* words;' South's Sermons, vol. vii. ser. 13 (R.). See **Balance**. Cf. *out-balance*. Der. *overbalance*, sb.

OVERBEAR, to overrule. (E.) Much Ado, ii. 3. 157; pp. *overborne*, 1 Hen. VI, iii. 1. 53. See **Bear**. Der. *overbearing*, adj.

OVERBOARD, out of the ship. (E.) Rich. III, i. 4. 19. ME. *ouer bord*; Chaucer, C. T., B 922. See **Board**.

OVERBURDEN, to burden overmuch. (E.) Spelt *ouerburdein*, Sir T. More, Works, p. 824 b. See **Burden**.

OVERCAST, to throw over, to overcloud. (E. *and* Scand.) The orig. sense is 'to throw over,' ME. *ouerkasten*, Rob. of Brunne, tr. of Langtoft, p. 70. l. 14. The sense 'overcloud' is old; Chaucer, C. T. 1538 (A 1536). See **Cast**.

OVERCHARGE, to overburden, charge too much. (E. *and* F. — C.) The old sense is 'to overburden;' Gascoigne, Steel Glass, 1062; and Palsgrave. See **Charge**. Der. *overcharge*, sb.

OVERCLOUD, to obscure with clouds. (E.) In Dryden, tr. of Virgil, Æn. xi. 1193. See **Cloud**.

OVERCOAT, a coat worn above the rest of the dress. (E. *and* F. — G.) Modern; see **Coat**.

OVERCOME, to subdue. (E.) ME. *ouercomen*, Wyclif, John, xvi. 33. AS. *ofercuman*, Grein, ii. 314. — AS. *ofer*, over; and *cuman*, to come. Cf. Icel. *yfirkominn*, pp. overcome. See **Come**.

OVERDO, to do too much, to fatigue, to cook too much. (E.) ME. *ouerdon*; 'That that is *ouerdon*'= a thing that is overdone; Chaucer, C. T. 16113 (G 645). AS. *oferdōn*. — AS. *ofer*, over; and *dōn*, to do. See **Do**.

OVERDOSE, to dose too much. (E. *and* F. — Gk.) Modern; not in Todd's Johnson. See **Dose**.

OVERDRAW, to exaggerate in depicting. (E.) First in 1844, in this sense; not in Johnson. See **Draw**.

OVERDRESS, to dress too much. (E. *and* F. — L.) In Pope, Moral Essays, iv. 52. See **Dress**.

OVERDRIVE, to drive too fast. (E.) In Gen. xxxiii. 13 (A. V.); and in the Bible of 1551. AS. *oferdrifan*, Ælfred, tr. of Orosius, b. 1. c. 7; ed. Sweet, p. 40, l. 1. See **Drive**.

OVERFLOW, to flood, flow over. (E.) We find the pp. *overflown*, inundated, Spenser, F. Q. iii. 5. 17. ME. *ouerflowen*, Wyclif, Luke, vi. 38. AS. *oferflōwan*. — AS. *ofer*, over; and *flōwan*, to flow; pt. t. *flēow*, pp. *flōwen*; so that the form *overflown* for the pp. is correct. See **Flow**. Der. *overflow*, sb.; *overflow-ing*.

OVERGROW, to grow over. (E.) Pp. *ouergrowen*, Sir T. More, Works, p. 74 d; Gawayn and Grene Knight, 2190. See **Grow**.

OVERHANG, to project over, impend. (E.) Contracted to *o'erhang*, Hen. V, iii. 1. 13. See **Hang**.

OVERHAUL, to draw over, to scrutinise. (E. *and* F. — G.)

Spenser has *overhaile*, to hale or draw over; Shep. Kal. Jan. 75. See **Hale, Haul**.

OVERHEAD, above one's head. (E.) In Shak. L. L. L. iv. 3. 281. See **Head**.

OVERHEAR, to hear without being spoken to. (E.) In Shak. Meas. iii. 1. 161. See **Hear**.

OVERJOYED, transported with gladness. (E. *and* F. — L.) In Shak. Much Ado, ii. 1. 230. See **Joy**. Der. *overjoy*, sb., 2 Hen. VI, i. 1. 31.

OVERLADE, to lade with too heavy a burden. (E.) 'For men may *ouerlade* a ship or barge;' Chaucer, Legend of Good Women, Cleop. 42. The pp. *ouerladen* is in Ancren Riwle, p. 368. l. 21. See **Lade**.

OVERLAND, passing over the land. (E.) First in 1800; not in Todd's Johnson. See **Land**.

OVERLAP, to lap over. (E.) Spelt *overlop* in 1726; not in Todd's Johnson. See **Lap**.

OVERLAY, to spread over, to oppress. (E.) Often confused with *overlie*; in particular, the pp. *overlaid* is often confused with *overlain*, the pp. of *overlie*. Richardson confounds the two. Wyclif has '*ouerleiyng* of folkis' for L. pressura gentium; Luke, xxi. 25. See **Lay**.

OVERLEAP, to leap over. (E.) ME. *ouerlepen*, pt. t. *ouerleep*; P. Plowman, B. prol. 150, where the true sense is 'outran,' in conformity with the fact that ME. *lepen* (like G. *laufen*) commonly means 'to run.' AS. *oferhlēapan*; the pt. t. *oferhlēop* occurs in Ælfred's tr. of Beda, b. v. c. 6. — AS. *ofer*, over; and *hlēapan*, to run, to leap. See **Leap**.

OVERLIE, to lie upon. (E.) Often confused with *overlay*; the pp. *ouerlein*, in the sense of 'oppressed,' occurs in Gower, C. A. iii. 224; bk. vii. 3930. The verb *ouerliggen* occurs in O. Eng. Homilies, ed. Morris, i. 53. l. 16. See **Lie** (1).

OVERLIVE, to outlive, survive. (E.) ME. *ouerliuen*, Wyclif, Exod. xxi. 22 (later text). AS. *oferlibban*, in Bosworth-Toller's Dict. See **Live**.

OVERLOAD, to load overmuch. (E.) Gascoigne has *overloding*, Steel Glass, l. 1009. See **Load**. Doublet, *overlade*, q.v.

OVERLOOK, to inspect, also to neglect, slight. (E.) ME. *ouerloken*, in the sense 'to look over,' or 'peruse;' Chaucer, Book of the Duchess, l. 232. See **Look**.

OVERMATCH, to surpass, conquer. (E.) ME. *ouermacchen*, Chaucer, C. T. 9096 (E 1220). See **Match**.

OVERMUCH, too much. (E.) Spelt *ouermuchel* in Chaucer, tr. of Boethius, b. iii. pr. 7; l. 13. See **Much**.

OVERPASS, to pass over. (E. *and* F. — L.) ME. *ouerpassen*, Chaucer, tr. of Boethius, b. v. pr. 6; l. 74. See **Pass**.

OVERPAY, to pay in addition. (E. *and* F. — L.) In All's Well, iii. 7. 16. See **Pay**.

OVERPLUS, that which is more than enough. (E. *and* L.) In Antony, iii. 7. 51, iv. 6. 22; ME. *ouerpluse*, Trevisa, tr. of Higden, i. 407. From E. *over*; and L. *plūs*, more; see **Nonplus**. Doublet, *surplus*.

OVERPOWER, to subdue. (E. *and* F. — L.) Contracted to *o'erpower*, Rich. II, v. 1. 31. See **Power**. Der. *overpower*, sb., i.e. excess of power, Bacon, Ess. 58.

OVERRATE, to rate too highly. (E. *and* F. — L.) Contr. to *o'errate*, Cymb. i. 4. 41. See **Rate**.

OVERREACH, to reach beyond, to cheat. (E.) ME. *ouerrechen*, P. Plowman, B. xiii. 374. See **Reach**.

OVERRIDE, to ride over. (E.) ME. *ouerriden*, pp. *ouerriden*, Chaucer, C. T. 2024 (A 2022). AS. *oferrīdan*, to ride across (a ford); Ælfred, tr. of Beda, iii. 14. See **Ride**.

OVERRULE, to influence by greater authority. (E. *and* F. — L.) In K. Lear, i. 3. 16. See **Rule**.

OVERRUN, to spread or grow over, to outrun. (E.) ME. *ouerrennen*, Rob. of Brunne, tr. of Langtoft, p. 124, l. 10. See **Run**.

OVERSEE, to superintend. (E.) ME. *ouersen*, P. Plowman, B. vi. 115. AS. *ofersēon*, used in the sense to look down on, to despise; Ælfred, tr. of Boethius, c. 36, sect. 2. See **See**. Der. *overse-er*, Tyndall, Works, p. 252, l. 6; *over-sight*, (1) superintendence, Bible, 1551, 1 Chron. ix. 31; (2) omission, 2 Hen. IV, ii. 3. 47.

OVERSET, to upset, overturn. (E.) ME. *ouersetten*, to oppress; O. Eng. Homilies, ed. Morris, ii. 51; and see Prompt. Parv. p. 373. AS. *ofersettan*, to spread over, cover, Ælfred, tr. of Boethius, b. ii. pr. 7; c. xviii. sect. 1. See **Set**.

OVERSHADOW, to throw a shadow over. (E.) ME. *ouerschadewen*, Luke, ix. 34. AS. *ofersceadian*, Luke, ix. 34. See **Shadow**.

OVERSHOOT, to shoot beyond. (E.) The pp. *ouershotte*

(better *ouershot*) is in Sir T. More, Works, p. 1134 h. Palsgrave has I *overshote my-selfe*. See **Shoot**.

OVERSIGHT; see **Oversee**.

OVERSPREAD, to spread over. (E.) ME. *ouerspreden*, pt. t. *ouerspradde*, Chaucer, C. T. 2873 (A 2871); Layamon, 14188. AS. *ofersprǣdan*, to overspread (Bosworth). **—**AS. *ofer*, over; and *sprǣdan*; see **Spread**.

OVERSTEP, to step beyond, exceed. (E.) Contr. to *o'erstep*, Hamlet, iii. 2. 21. AS. *ofersteppan*. See **Step**.

OVERSTOCK, to stock too full. (E.) *O'erstock'd* is in Dryden, The Medal, 102. See **Stock**.

OVERSTRAIN, to strain too much. (E. and F.**—**L.) In Dryden, Art of Painting, § 54 (R.). See **Strain**.

OVERT, open, apparent, public. (F.**—**L.) 'The wey ther-to is so *ouerte*;' Chaucer, Ho. of Fame, b. ii. l. 210.**—**OF. *overt* (later *ouvert*), pp. of *ovrir* (later *ouvrir*), to open. β. The exact formation of the word is uncertain; but Littré's explanation is now accepted, that OF. *ovrir* was a perverted form of OF. *avrir*, to open; from L. *aperire*, to open; the change being due to frequent association with OF. *covrir* (F. *couvrir*), to cover. (So Körting, Hatzfeld.) For L. *aperire*, see **Aperient**. ¶ Diez cites Prov. *obrir*, *ubrir*, MItal. *oprire* (Florio), to open, which he distinguishes from Span. *abrir*, mod. Ital. *aprire*, derived directly from L. *aperire*, to open. As to *ovrir*, he supposes this to be a shorter form of OF. *a-ovrir*, *a-uvrir*, to open, words of three syllables, occurring in the Livre des Rois. These forms arose from Prov. *adubrir* (Raynouard, Lexique Roman, ii. 104), in which the prefixed *a-* (<L. *ad*) does not alter the sense, but is added as in *ablasmar*, *afranher*; whilst *dubrir* is from the L. *dē-operire*, to open wide, lit. 'uncover,' used by Celsus (White). He supports this by instancing mod. Prov. *durbir*, Piedmontese *durvi*, Walloon *drovi*, Lorraine *deurvi*, all corresponding to the same L. *dēoperire*. L. *operire* is for *op-uer-ire*, parallel to Lith. *už-wer-ti*, to shut; just as L. *aperire* (for *ap-uer-ire*) is parallel to Lith. *at-wer-ti*, to open; Brugmann, i. § 282. Cf. Skt. *vṛ*, to cover. Der. *overt-ly*; *overt-ure*, meaning 'an open, unprotected place,' Spenser, Shep. Kal. July, 28, from OF. *overture*, later *ouverture*, 'an overture, or opening, an entrance, hole, beginning made, a motion made [i. e. proposal], also an opening, manifestation, discovery, uncovering,' Cot.

OVERTAKE, to come up with, in travelling. (E. and Scand.) ME. *ouertaken*, Havelok, 1816; Ancren Riwle, p. 244, note *g*.**—**AS. *ofer*, over; and Icel. *taka*, to take. Cf. Icel. *yfirtak*, an overtaking, surpassing, transgression; which prob. suggested the E. word. See **Take**.

OVERTASK, to task too much. (E. and F.**—**L.) In Milton, Comus, 309. See **Task**. ¶ So also *over-tax*.

OVERTHROW, to throw over, upset, demolish. (E.) ME. *ouerthrowen*, King Alisaunder, 1113. See **Throw**. Der. *overthrow*, sb., Much Ado, i. 3. 69.

OVERTOP, to rise above the top of. (E.) Temp. i. 2. 81. See **Top**.

OVERTURE, a proposal, beginning. (F.**—**L.) All's Well, iv. 3. 46. Also 'a disclosure,' K. Lear, iii. 7. 89. See **Overt**.

OVERTURN, to overthrow, upset. (E. and F.**—**L.) ME. *ouerturnen*, Ancren Riwle, p. 356, l. 16. See **Turn**.

OVERVALUE, to value too much. (E. and F.**—**L.) Contracted to *o'ervalue*, Cymb. i. 4. 120. See **Value**.

OVERWEENING, thinking too highly, conceited. (E.) The pres. part. *ouerweninde* occurs in the Ayenbite of Inwyt, ed. Morris, p. 169, l. 26; where *-inde* is the Kentish form for *-inge* (*-ing*). Shak. even uses the verb *overween*, 2 Hen. IV, iv. 1. 149. AS. *oferwenian*, to be insolent. 'Insolesceret, *oberwenide*;' Corpus Gloss. 1099; spelt *oberuuaenidae*, Epinal Gloss. 538. Lit. 'going beyond what is customary.'**—**AS. *ofer*, beyond; *wenian*, to be accustomed; see **Wean**. Thus it is only remotely connected with *ween*, q.v.

OVERWEIGH, to outweigh. (E.) ME. *ouerweȝen*; 'luue *ouerweið* hit' = love overweighs it, Ancren Riwle, p. 386, l. 25. See **Weigh**. Der. *overweight*.

OVERWHELM, to turn over, bear down, demolish. (E.) ME. *ouerwhelmen*, Rom. of the Rose, 3775; Rob. of Brunne, tr. of Langtoft, p. 190, l. 10. 'The erthe sall thaim *ouer-whelme*;' St. Cuthbert, 4964. See **Whelm**.

OVERWISE, wise overmuch. (E.) In Beaum. and Fletcher, Philaster, last line of Act iv. See **Wise**. Der. *overwise-ly*, *-ness*.

OVERWORK, excess of work. (E.) The verb to *overwork* is in Palsgrave. The sb. is, etymologically, the more orig. word. See **Work**. Der. *overwork*, verb; whence the pp. *overwrought*.

OVERWORN, worn too much. (E.) In Twelfth Nt. iii. 1. 66. From *over*; and *worn*, pp. of *wear*. See **Wear**.

OVERWROUGHT, wrought to excess. (E.) In Dryden, Art of Poetry, c. i. l. 50. See **Overwork**.

OVIFORM, egg-shaped. (L.) Used by T. Burnet, Theory of the Earth, 1759 (R.).**—**L. *ōui-*, for *ōuum*, an egg; and *form-a*, form. See **Oval** and **Form**. ¶ So also *oviduct*, Phillips, ed. 1706, from L. *ductus*, a conducting, a duct; see **Duct**. Also *ovi-parous*, Phillips, ed. 1706, from L. *ōuiparus*, egg-producing, from *parere*, to produce; see **Parent**. Also *ovoid*, egg-shaped, a clumsy hybrid compound, from L. *ōuo-*, for *ōuum*, an egg, and Gk. εἶδος, form.

OWE, to possess; hence, to possess another's property, to be in debt, be obliged. (E.) ME. *aȝen*, *awen*, *oȝen*, *owen*, orig. 'to possess;' hence, to be obliged to do, to be in debt. 'The dette thet tu *owest* me' = the debt that thou owest me, Ancren Riwle, p. 126, l. 13. 'Hou myche *owist* thou?' Wyclif, Luke, xvi. 5. For this important verb, see Mätzner's O. Eng. Dict. p. 49, s.v. *aȝen*; or Stratmann, p. 23; or N. E. D. The sense 'to possess' is very common in Shakespeare; see Schmidt. AS. *āgan*, to have, possess, Grein, i. 19. The change from *ā* to *o* is perfectly regular, as in *bān*, bone, *stān*, stone; the *g* passes into *w* after *ā*, as usual.+Icel. *eiga*, to possess, have, be bound, own; Dan. *eie*, to own, possess; Swed. *äga*, to own, possess, have a right to, be able to; OHG. *eigan*, to possess; Goth. *aigan*, to possess. Teut. type *aig-an-*. β. Further related to Skt. *īç*, to possess, to be able; whence *īça-*, a proprietor, owner; the form of the root being EIK. Brugmann, i. § 701. ¶ It may be noted that the Goth. *aigan* has the old past tense *aih*, used as a present tense; so also AS. *āh*.

OUGHT. The pres. tense of AS. *āgan* is *āh*, really an old past tense; the past tense is *āhte* (Goth. *aihta*), really a secondary past tense or pluperfect; this became ME. *ahte*, *agte*, *aughte*, *oughte*, properly dissyllabic, as in '*oghté* be,' Chaucer, C. T. 16808 (G 1340); where Tyrwhitt has the inferior reading '*ought* to be.' The pp. of AS. *āgan* was *āgen*, for which see **Own** (1). Der. *ow-ing*, esp. in phr. *owing to*, i.e. due to, because of. Also *own* (1), *own* (2).

OWL, a nocturnal bird. (E.) ME. *oule*, Chaucer, Parl. of Foules, 343; pl. *oules*, id. 599. AS. *ūle*, Levit. xi. 16.+Du. *uil*; Icel. *ugla*; Dan. *ugle*; Swed. *ugla*; G. *eule*, OHG. *ūwela*. Teut. types *ūwalōn*, *uwwalōn-*, f. β. Allied to L. *ulula*, an owl, Skt. *ulūka-*, an owl. All from an imitative root, signifying to hoot, howl, screech; cf. Gk. ὑλάω, I howl, ὀλολύζειν, to howl, ἐλελεῦ, interjection; L. *ululāre*, to howl, *ulucus*, a screech-owl. γ. With a prefixed *h*, added for emphasis, we get G. *heulen*, whence OF. *huller*; see **Howl**. Somewhat similar is G. *uhu*, an owl, MHG. *hūwe*, OHG. *hūwo*; cf. E. *hoot*. Der. *owl-et*, dimin. form, also spelt *howlet*, Macb. iv. 1. 17; *owl-ish*.

OWN (1), possessed by any one, proper, peculiar, belonging to oneself. (E.) ME. *aȝen*, *awen* (North. E. *awin*), *owen*; later, contracted to *own* by omission of *e*. 'Right at min *owné* cost, and be your gyde;' Chaucer, C. T. 806 (A 804). 'Thar *awyn* fre' = their own free property; Barbour, Bruce, iii. 752. AS. *āgen*, own, Grein, i. 20; orig. the pp. of the anomalous strong verb *āgan*, to owe, i.e. to possess; see **Owe**.+Icel. *eigin*, one's own; orig. the old pp. of *eiga*, to possess; Dan. and Swed. *egen*, one's own; Goth. *aigin*, property, possessions; a neut. sb. formed from the adj. which was orig. the old pp. of *aigan*, to possess. Thus the orig. sense is 'possessed' or 'held.' Der. *own*, verb, to possess; see *own* (2), *own* (3).

OWN (2), to possess. (E.) ME. *aȝnien*, *ahnien*, *ohnien*, *ahnen*, *ohnen*; see Layamon, 11864, 25359; Ormulum, 5649. AS. *āgnian*, to appropriate, claim as one's own; Grein, i. 22. Formed with causal suffix *-ian* from *āgn*, contracted form of *āgen*, one's own; see **Own** (1).+Icel. *eigna*, to claim as one's own; from *eigin*, own; Goth. *ga-aiginōn*, to make a gain of, lit. make one's own, 2 Cor. ii. 11; from *aigin*, one's own property. ¶ It is thus evident that the verb is a derivative from the adjective. Der. *own-er*, ME. *oȝenere*, Ayenbite of Inwyt, ed. Morris, p. 37, last line but one; *owner-ship*.

OWN (3), to grant, admit. (E.) 'You will not *own* it,' i.e. admit it, Winter's Tale, iii. 2. 60. A peculiar development of *own* (2); as if 'to make one's own,' or 'to take to oneself.' ¶ The ME. *unnen* (AS. *unnan*), to grant, comes near to the sense of *own* (3); but it does not seem to have influenced it, and soon became obsolete.

OX, a ruminant quadruped. (E.) ME. *ox*, pl. *oxen*, Chaucer, C. T. 889 (A 887); *oxis*, Wyclif, Luke, xvii. 7. AS. *oxa*, pl. *oxan*, Grein, ii. 360.+Du. *os*; Icel. *uxi*, also *oxi*; pl. *yxn*, *öxn*; Dan. *oxe*, pl. *oxer*; Swed. *oxe*; G. *ochse*, *ochs*, pl. *ochsen*; OHG. *ohso*; Goth. *auhsa*, *anhsus*.+W. *ych*, pl. *ychen*; Skt. *ukshan-*, an ox, bull; also, 'a Vedic epithet of the Maruts who, by bringing rain, i.e. by sprinkling, impregnate the earth like bulls;' Benfey. The Maruts are storms; see Max Müller, Lectures, ii. 416. Teut. base *ohsan-*. Idg. base *ukson-*. β. The Skt. *ukshan* is usually derived from *uksh*, to sprinkle. Further, *uksh* is allied to Gk. ὑγρός, moist, as well as to Icel. *vökr*, moist, prov. E. *wokey*, moist (Halliwell); see Brugmann, ii. § 114; Benfey, p. 108. See **Wake** (2). Der. *ox-eye*, a plant, *ox-eyed*, *ox-fly*, *ox-goad*; *ox-stall*; also *ox-lip*, q. v.

OXALIS, wood-sorrel. (L.**—**Gk.) In Holland, tr. of Pliny, b. xx.

c. 21.—L. *oxalis* (Pliny).—Gk. ὀξαλίς, (1) a sour wine, (2) sorrel. So named from its sourness.—Gk. ὀξύς, sharp, keen, cutting, acid. Allied to L. *ācer*, sharp, pungent; Brugmann, i. §§ 161, 536. **Der.** *oxali-c*; cf. *ox-ide*, *oxy-gen*, *oxy-mel*, *oxy-tone*.

OXIDE, a compound of oxygen with a non-acid base. (Gk.) A coined word; from *ox-*, short for *oxy-*, part of the word *oxy-gen*; and *-ide*, due to Gk. -ειδής, like, which more commonly appears as *-id*, as in *ellipso-id*, *sphero-id*, *ovo-id*, and the like. See **Oxygen**. **Der.** *oxid-ise*, *oxid-is-er*, *oxid-is-able*, *oxid-at-ion*; all coined words.

OXLIP, the greater cowslip. (E.) In Mids. Nt. Dr. ii. 1. 250; Wint. Ta. iv. 4. 125. AS. *oxanslyppe*; see Cockayne's Leechdoms, iii. 340.—AS. *oxan*, gen. case of *oxa*, an ox; and *slyppe*, a slop, i.e. a piece of dung. [This confirms the etymology of *cowslip* already given; see **Cowslip**.] ¶ It should therefore be spelt *ox-slip*.

OXYGEN, a gas often found in acid compounds. (F.—Gk.) The sense is 'generator of acids;' and it is a coined word. The discovery of oxygen dates from 1774 (Haydn); but the name is French.—F. *oxygène*; in 1787 (Hatzfeld).—Gk. ὀξύ- (written *oxy-* in Roman characters), for ὀξύς, sharp, keen, acid; and γεν-, to produce, base of γί-γν-ομαι, I am produced or born. See **Oxalis** and **Generate**. **Der.** *oxygen-ate*, *oxygen-ise*, *oxygen-ous*; and see *ox-ide*.

OXYMEL, a mixture of honey and vinegar. (L.—Gk.) In early use; it occurs as AS. *oxumelle*; see Cockayne's A.S. Leechdoms, iii. 368.—L. *oxymeli* (Pliny).—Gk. ὀξύμελι.—Gk. ὀξύ-, for ὀξύς, acid; and μέλι, honey. See **Oxalis** and **Mellifluous**.

OXYTONE, having an acute accent on the last syllable. (Gk.) A grammatical term.—Gk. ὀξύτονος, shrill-toned; also, as a grammatical term.—Gk. ὀξύ-, for ὀξύς, sharp; and τόνος, a tone. See **Oxalis** and **Tone**.

OYER, a term in law. (F.—L.) An OF. law term. ' *Oyer* and *terminer* [lit. to hear and determine], is a commission specially granted to certain persons, for the hearing and determining one or more causes,' &c.; Blount's Law Dict., ed. 1691. Cf. AF. *oier et terminer*; Stat. Realm, i. 44 (1276); AF. *oyer*, as sb., a hearing, Year-books of Edw. I. i. 73.—AF. *oyer*, mod. F. *ouir*, to hear.—L. *audire*, to hear. See **Audience**. **Der.** *oyez*.

OYEZ, OYES, hear ye! (F.—L.) Henryson has: *oyas! oyas!* Parl. of Beistis, l. 53. The first word of every proclamation by a public crier; now corrupted into the unmeaning *O! yes!* ' *O yes*, a corruption from the F. *oyez*, i.e. hear ye, is well known to be used by the cryers in our courts,' &c.; Blount, Law Dict., ed. 1691.—AF. *oyez*, 2 p. pl. imp. of *oyer*, to hear; Stat. Realm, i. 211 (ab. 1286); see **Oyer**.

OYSTER, a well-known bivalve shell-fish. (F.—L.—Gk.) [The AS. form *ostre* was borrowed from Latin; cf. 'ostrea, ostre' in Voc. 261. 33. The diphthong shows the mod. E. form to be from the French.] ME. *oistre*, Chaucer, C. T. 182.—AF. *oyster*, Liber Albus, p. 244; OF. *oistre*, in the 13th cent. (Littré); whence mod. F. *huître*.—L. *ostrea*, more rarely *ostreum*.—Gk. ὄστρεον, an oyster; so called from its shell.—Gk. ὀστρέον, a bone, shell; akin to L. *os* (gen. *ossis*), a bone. See **Osseous**, **Ostracise**.

OZONE, a substance perceived by its smell in air after electric discharges. (Gk.) ' *Ozone*, a name given in 1840 by M. Schönbein of Basel to the odour in the atmosphere developed during the electric discharge;' Haydn.—Gk. ὄζων, smelling; pres. pt. of ὄζειν, to smell. Gk. ὄζειν stands for ὄδ-γειν, from the base ὀδ-, to smell, appearing also in L. *od-or*, smell; see **Odour**.

P

PABULUM, food. (L.) '*Pabulum* or food;' Bp. Berkeley, Siris (1747), § 197 (Todd).—L. *pābulum*, food. Formed with suffix *-bulu-* from *pā-*, base of *pascere*, to feed (pt. t. *pā-ui*); see **Pastor**. **Der.** *pabul-ous*, Sir T. Browne, Vulg. Errors, b. iii. c. 21. § 15; *pabul-ar*.

PACE, a step, gait. (F.—L.) ME. *pas*, *paas*, Rob. of Glouc. p. 149, l. 3129; Chaucer, C. T., A 825, 1033.—F. *pas*.—L. *passum*, acc. of *passus*, a step, pace, lit. a stretch, i.e. the distance between the feet in walking.—L. *passus*, pp. of *pandere*, to stretch. See **Expand**. **Der.** *pace*, verb, a doublet of **Pass**, q.v.; *pac-er*, Spectator, no. 104.

PACHA, the French spelling of **Pasha**, q.v.

PACHYDERMATOUS, thick-skinned. (Gk.) Modern and scientific.—Gk. παχύ-, for παχύς, thick; and δερματ-, stem of δέρμα, a skin; with suffix *-ous* (=L. *-ōsus*). β. The Gk. παχύς is cognate with Skt. *bahu-*, strong. γ. Gk. δέρμα is a hide, 'that which is flayed off;' from Gk. δέρειν, to flay, tear, cognate with E. **Tear**, verb, q.v. **Der.** *pachyderm*, an abbreviation for *pachydermatous animal*.

PACIFY, to appease, make peaceful. (F.—L.) Spelt *pacifie*, Sir T. More, Works, p. 871 b.—F. *pacifier*, 'to pacifie;' Cot.—L. *pācificāre*, *pācificāri*, to make peace.—L. *pāci-*, decl. stem of *pax*, peace; and *-ficāre*, for *facere*, to make; see **Peace** and **Fact**. **Der.** *pacifi-er*, spelt *pacyfyer*, Sir T. More, Works, p. 872 d; *pacific-at-ion*, from F. *pacification*, 'a pacification' (Cot.), which from L. acc. *pācificātiōnem*, due to *pācificāre*; *pacificat-or*, Bacon, Life of Hen. VII. ed. Lumby, p. 52, l. 10, from L. *pācificātor*; *pacific*, formerly *pacifick*, Milton, P. L. xi. 860, from F. *pacifique*, 'pacificous' (Cot.), which from L. adj. *pācificus*, peace-making; *pacific-al*, *pacific-al-ly*.

PACK, a bundle, burden, set of cards or hounds, &c. (Low G.) ME. *pakke*, P. Plowman, B. xiii. 201; pl. *packes*, Ancren Riwle, p. 166, last line.—Low G. *pakk*, *pak*; Du. *pak*, a pack; cf. Icel. *pakki*, a pack, bundle; Dan. *pakke*; Swed. *packa*; G. *pack*. β. It appears to be a true Teutonic word, though few Teutonic words begin with *p*. There is no proof that it was suggested by the L. base *pac-*, as in pp. *pac-tus*, from *pangere*, to fasten. [We also find Irish *pac*, Gall. *pac*, from E.; Bret. *pac*, borrowed from Romanic; Ital. *pacco*, F. *paqu-et*, Late L. *paccus*, from Teutonic.] **Der.** *pack*, verb, ME. *pakken*, P. Plowman, B. xv. 184; *pack-er*, *pack-horse*, 2 Hen. IV, ii. 4. 177; *pack-ing*; *pack-man*; *pack-needle* or *pack-ing-needle*, ME. *pakkenedle* or *paknedle*, P. Plowman, B. v. 212; *pack-saddle*, Cor. ii. 1. 99; *pack-thread* Romeo, v. 1. 47. Also *pack-age*, q.v., *pack-et*, q.v. ☞ Quite distinct from *bag*.

PACKAGE, a packet, small bundle. (Low G.; with F. suffix.) A late word; added by Todd to Johnson; formed by adding F. suffix *-age* (< L. *-āticum*) to *pack*; see **Pack**. Cf. *packet*.

PACKET, a small pack, package. (AF.—Low G.) In Hamlet, v. 2. 15. AF. *pacquet*, Black Book of the Admiralty, i. 277 (1463); whence MF. *pacquet*, *paquet*, 'a packet, bundle;' Cot. Formed with dimin. suffix *-et* from ME. *pakke*, a pack; cf. Low G. *pakk*, a pack (Bremen Wörterbuch); MDu. *pack*, 'a pack' (Hexham); Icel. *pakki*. See **Pack**. **Der.** *packet-boat*, a boat for carrying mail-bags, Evelyn's Diary, Oct. 10, 1641; now often shortened to *packet*. Doublet, *package*.

PACT, a contract. (L.) In Bacon, Life of Hen. VII, ed. Lumby, p. 7, l. 19; and p. 27, l. 30.—L. *pactum*, an agreement.—L. *pactus*, pp. of *paciscere*, to stipulate, agree; inceptive form of OLat. *pacere*, to agree, come to an agreement about anything.—√PAK, to bind; whence also Skt. *paç*, to bind; cf. Gk. πήγνυμι, I fasten, L. *pangere* (pp. *pac-tus*), to fasten, fix. Brugmann, i. § 200; ii. § 79. **Der.** *pact-ion*, Fox's Martyrs, p. 272 (R.), from F. *paction* (Cot.) < L. *pactiōnem*, acc. of *pactio*, an agreement. Also *appease*, *com-pact*, *im-pact*, *im-pinge*. From the same root we have *peace*, *paci-fy*, *page* (2), *pale* (1), *pay*, *pro-pag-ate*, *peel* (3), *pole* (1), *re-pay*.

PAD (1), a soft cushion, &c. (E.?) 'He was kept in the bands, hauing under him but onely a *pad* of straw;' Fox, Martyrs, p. 854 (R.). Spelt *padde*, Gascoigne, Fruits of War, st. 177. A stuffed saddle was called a *pad*; hence: '*Padde*, saddle,' in Levins, ed. 1570. It also occurs in the sense of 'bundle;' see Halliwell. Of obscure origin. β. In the prov. E. sense of paw, or animal's foot, it agrees with MDu., Low G., and Pomeranian *pad*, sole of the foot; perhaps borrowed from Slavonic. Cf. Russ. *podoshva*, sole of the foot; *podushka*, a cushion; also Lith. *padas*, sole of the foot. And cf. **Pod**. **Der.** *pad*, verb; *padd-ing*.

PAD (2), a thief on the high road. (Du.) We now speak of a *foot-pad*. The old word is a *padder*, Massinger, A New Way, ii. 1, l. 15 from end; Butler, Hudibras, pt. iii. c. 1, l. 5 from end. This means 'one who goes upon the *pad* or foot-path.' A *pad* is also a 'roadster,' a horse for riding on roads; Gay's Fables, no. 46; also (more correctly) called a *pad-nag*, i.e. 'road-horse' (R.).—Du. *pad*, a path; MDu. *padt* (Hexham); cf. Low G. *pad*. Cognate with E. *path*; see **Path**. ☞ Many cant words are of Du. origin; see Beaum. and Fletcher, Beggar's Bush. **Der.** *pad*, v., to tramp along.

PADDLE (1), to finger; to dabble in water. (E.) **1.** It means 'to finger, handle;' Hamlet, iii. 4. 185; Oth. ii. 1. 259. It is a parallel formation to *pattle*, which is the frequentative of *pat*; and cf. *patter*. **2.** The sense 'to dabble in water' is in Palsgrave, who has: 'I *paddyl* in the myre;' cf. Low G. *paddeln*, to tramp about (Danneil); frequent. of *pedden*, to tread, or *padjen*, to take short steps (Brem. Wört.); from *pad*, the sole of the foot; see **Pad** (1). **Der.** *paddle*, sb., in the sense of broad-bladed oar, but there is probably some confusion with the word below; *paddl-er*, Beaum. and Fletcher, Wit at Several Weapons, i. 1. 20; *paddle-wheel*.

PADDLE (2), a little spade, esp. one to clean a plough with. (E.) In Deut. xxiii. 13 (A. V.). It seems to be a parallel form to *spaddle*, the dimin. of *spade*. 'Others destroy moles with a *spaddle*,' Mortimer's Husbandry (R.); and see *spud* and *spittle-staff* in Halliwell. Cf. also Irish and Gael. *spadal*, a plough-staff, paddle; words borrowed from English. See **Spade**. ¶ In the sense of 'broad-bladed oar,' see **Paddle** (1).

PADDOCK (1), a toad. (Scand.) In Hamlet, iii. 4. 190; Macb. i. 1. 9. ME. *paddok*, King Alisaunder, 6126. Dimin. with suffix -*ok* or -*ock* (as in *hill-ock*, *bull-ock*), from ME. *padde*, a toad, frog; in Wyclif, Exod. viii. 9 (later version), one MS. has the pl. *paddis* for *paddokis*, which is the common reading.—Icel. *padda*, a toad; Swed. *padda*, a toad, frog; Dan. *padde*.+Du. *padde*, *pad*; EFries. *padde*. Cf. G. *schild-pati*, tortoise-shell. Origin obscure. Der. *paddock-stool*, a toad-stool.

PADDOCK (2), a small enclosure. (E.) 'Delectable country-seats and villas environed with parks, *paddocks*, plantations,' &c.; Evelyn (Todd; no reference). Here *park* and *paddock* are conjoined; and it is certain that *paddock* is a corruption of *parrock*, another form of *park*. Parrocks (Kent) is now called Paddock Wood; Hasted, Hist. Kent, 8vo, v. 286. 'Parrocke, a lytell parke,' Palsgrave. See Way's note to Prompt. Parv., p. 384. He adds that 'a fenced enclosure of nine acres at Hawsted (Suffolk), in which deer were kept in pens for the course, was termed the *Parrock*;' Cullum's Hawsted, p. 210. See also *parrock* in Jamieson, and *parrick* in Halliwell. [The unusual change from *r* to *d* may have been due to some confusion with *paddock*, a toad, once a familiar word; cf. *poddish* for *porridge*.] AS. *pearruc*, *pearroc*, a small enclosure. 'On ðisum lytlum *pearroce*' = in this little enclosure; Ælfred, tr. of Boethius, c. xviii. § 2, b. ii. prosa 7. Perhaps formed, with dimin. suffix -*oc* (=mod. E. -*ock*, as in *padd-ock* (1), *hill-ock*, *bull-ock*), from a verb *parran, to shut, enclose; only found in ME. *parren*; see **Park**.

PADDY, rice in the husk. (Malay.) Malay *pādī*, rice in the straw. (See Yule.) It seems to have been sometimes confused with Hind. *bhāt*, boiled rice (Forbes), derived from the Skt. *bhakta-*, (properly) boiled rice; orig. pp. of *bhaj*, to divide, take, possess (Benfey).

PADISHAH, great king, emperor. (Turk.—Pers.) A title given by the Turks to the Sultan and other kings.—Turk. *pādishāh*.—Pers. *pādshāh*, an emperor, sovereign; Rich. Dict., p. 315. The Pers. *pād* answers to OPers. *pati-* (=Skt. *pati-*), master, lord; and *shāh* is 'king.' See **Despot** and **Shah**; also **Pasha**.

PADLOCK, a loose hanging lock. (E.) A *padlock* is a loose hanging lock with a staple, suitable for hampers, baskets, &c., when the case to which it is affixed is not made of a solid substance. It occurs in Pope's Dunciad, iv. 162. Todd quotes from Milton's Colasterion (1645): 'Let not such an unmerciful and more than legal yoke be *padlocked* upon the neck of any Christian.' Ben Jonson has *padlock* in The Staple of News, Act v. sc. 1 (Picklock). Minsheu's Span. Dict. has: '*Candado*, a hanging locke, a padlocke' (1623); cf. *locchetto*, 'a padlocke' in Florio (1598). Of uncertain origin; perhaps formed by adding *lock* to prov. E. *pad*, a pannier (Halliwell), given as a Norfolk word. This word is more commonly written *ped*, ME. *pedde*. '*Pedde*, idem quod *panere*;' Prompt. Parv. Of unknown origin; see further under **Pedlar**.

PADUASOY, a rich silk. (F.) 'Her crimson *paduasoy*;' Goldsmith, Vicar of Wakefield, ch. iv. § 5. As if 'Padua silk;' from *Padua* (in Italy); and F. *soie*, silk, from L. *sēta*, a pig's bristle, hence strong hair, silk (like Span. *seda*). But really a popular perversion of F. *pou-de-soie*, a silken stuff (Hatzfeld). Godefroy has *pout de soye* (1389); *poul de soie* (1394). The origin of *pou-* is unknown.

PÆAN, a hymn in honour of Apollo. (L.—Gk.) 'I have ever hung Elaborate *pæans* on thy golden shrine;' Ben Jonson, Cynthia's Revels, A. v. sc. 2; near the end.—L. *pæan*, (1) a name of Apollo, (2) a religious hymn, esp. to Apollo.—Gk. Παιάν, Παιών, (1) Pæan, Pæon, the physician of the gods, who cured Hades and Ares, Homer, Il. v. 401, 899; cf. Od. iv. 232; also Apollo; also his son Æsculapius; a deliverer, saviour; (2) a choral song, hymn, chant, song of triumph. Der. *peon-y*, q. v.

PÆDOBAPTISM; the same as **Pedobaptism**, q.v.

PAGAN, a countryman, hence, a heathen. (L.) In Shak. Rich. II, iv. 95. [The ME. form is *paien* or *payen*, Chaucer, C. T. 4954 (B 534), from OF. *paien* (Burguy); which from L. *pāgānus*.]—L. *pāgānus*, (1) a villager, countryman, (2) a pagan, because the rustic people were supposed to be unconverted at a time when townsmen were converts. See Trench, On the Study of Words.—L. *pāgānus*, adj., rustic, belonging to a village.—L. *pāgus*, a district, canton. β. Some connect it with L. *pangere* (pt. t. *pēgi*), to fasten, fix, set, as being marked out by fixed limits; see **Pact**. Der. *pagan-ish*, *pagan-ism*, *pagan-ise*; and see *paynim*, *peasant*.

PAGE (1), a boy attending a person of distinction. (F.—Low Lat.—Gk?) ME. *page*, King Alisaunder, 835; Havelok, 1730.—F. *page*, 'a page;' Cot. [Cf. Span. *page*, Port. *pagem*, Ital. *paggio*.]—Late L. *pagium*, acc. of *pagius*, a servant (Ducange). ¶ See Littré, who does not admit the etymology suggested by Diez, viz. that Ital. *paggio* might have been formed from Gk. παιδίον, a little

boy, dimin. of παῖς, a boy, child; for which see **Pedagogue**. But Körting accepts this solution.

PAGE (2), one side of the leaf of a book. (F.—L.) 'If one leafe of this large paper were plucked off, the more *pages* took harme thereby;' Holland, tr. of Pliny, b. xiii. c. 12. [ME. *pagine*, Ancren Riwle, p. 286; an older form.]—F. *page*, 'a page, a side of a leafe;' Cot.—L. *pāgina*, a page, or leaf. β. Orig. 'a leaf;' and so called because the leaves were once made of strips of papyrus fastened together.—L. *pangere* (base *pāg-*), to fasten; see **Pact**. ¶ We also find ME. *pagent* (with added *t*), Romance of Partenay, prol. 79. The three forms *page*, *pagine*, *pagent*, from L. *pāgina*, are parallel to the three forms *marge*, *margin*, *margent*, from L. *marginem*. Der. *pagin-at-ion*, a modern coined word.

PAGEANT, an exhibition, spectacle, show. (Late L.—L.) A. It orig. meant 'a moveable scaffold,' such as was used in the representation of the old mysteries. A picture of such a pageant will be found in Chambers, Book of Days, i. 634. The Chester plays 'were always acted in the open air, and consisted of 24 parts, each part or *pageant* being taken by one of the guilds of the city... Twenty-four large scaffolds or stages were made,' &c.; Chambers, as above; see the whole passage. Phillips, ed. 1706, defines *pageant* as 'a triumphal chariot or arch, or other pompous device usually carried about in publick shows.' B. ME. *pagent*; also *pagyn*, as in Wyclif's Works, ed. Arnold, i. 129. The entry 'pagent, *pagina*,' occurs in Prompt. Parv. p. 377; where there is nothing to show whether a pageant is meant or a page of a book, the words being ultimately the same; see **Page** (2). But Way's excellent note on this entry is full of information, and should be consulted. He says: 'the primary signification of *pageant* appears to have been a stage or scaffold, which was called *pāgina*, it may be supposed, from its construction, being a machine *compāgināta*, framed and compacted together. The curious extracts from the Coventry records given by Mr. Sharp, in his Dissertation on the Pageants or Mysteries performed there, afford definite information on this subject. The term is variously written, and occasionally appears as *pagyn*, *pagen*, approaching closely to the L. *pāgina*. The various plays or pageants composing the Chester mysteries .. are entitled *Pagina prima*, .. *Pagina secunda*, .. and so forth; see Chester Plays, ed. Wright. A curious contemporary account has been preserved of the construction of the *pageants* [scaffolds] at Chester during the xvith century, "which *pagiants* weare a high scafold with 2 rowmes, a higher and a lower, upon 4 wheeles;" Sharp, Cov. Myst. p. 17. The term denoting the stage whereon the play was exhibited subsequently denoted also the play itself; but the primary sense .. is observed by several writers, as by Higins, in his version of Junius's Nomenclator, 1585: "*Pegma*, lignea machina in altum educta, tabulatis etiam in sublime crescentibus *compaginata*, de loco in locum portatilis, aut quæ vehi potest, ut in pompis fieri solet: *Eschaffaut*, a pageant, or scaffold."' Palsgrave has: 'Pagiant in a playe, mystère;' and Cotgrave explains MF. *pegmate* as 'a stage or frame whereon *pageants* be set or carried.' See further illustrations in Wedgwood. C. We may conclude that, just as ME. *pagent* is used as a variant of *pagine*, in the sense of page of a book, so the ME. *pagent* (or *pagiant*, &c.) was formed, by the addition of an excrescent *t* after *n*, from an older *pagen* or *pagin*, which is nothing but an Anglicised form of Late L. *pagina* in the sense of scaffold or stage. For examples of excrescent *t*, cf. *ancient*, *margent*, *tyrant*, *pheasant*. D. Though this sense of *pagina* is not given by Ducange, it was certainly in use, as shown above, and a very clear instance is cited by Wedgwood from Munimenta Gildhalliæ Londoniensis, ed. Riley, iii. 459, where we find: 'parabatur *machina* satis pulcra . . . in eadem *pagina* erigebantur duo animalia vocata antelops;' showing that (in 1432) *machina* and *pagina* were synonymous. E. The true sense of *pagina* I take to have been simply 'stage' or 'platform;' we find one sense of L. *pāgina* to be a slab of marble or plank of wood (White). Cf. L. *pāginātus*, planked, built, constructed (White). Hence the derivation is from L. *pangere* (base *pāg-*), to fasten, fix; see **Page** (2). ¶ Note that another word for the old stage was *pēgma* (stem *pēgmat-*, whence MF. *pegmate* in Cotgrave); this is the corresponding and cognate *Greek* name, from Gk. πῆγμα (stem πηγματ-), a platform, stage, derived from the base of Gk. πήγνυμι, I fix, cognate with L. *pangere*. Der. *pageant*, verb, to play, Shak. Troil. i. 3. 151; *pageant-r-y*, Pericles, v. 2. 6.

PAGODA, an Indian idol's temple. (Port.—Pers.) Spelt *pagotha* in Sir T. Herbert, Travels, ed. 1665, pp. 69, 393; *pagod* in Skinner, ed. 1671; *pagodes*, pl., in Hakluyt, Voy. ii. part 1. 221, 253.—Port. *pagoda*, now generally *pagode*; but both forms are given in the Eng.-Port. part of Vieyra's Dict. Adapted from Pers. *but-kadah*, an idol-temple; Rich. Dict. p. 241, col. 2; spelt *but-kedah* in Palmer, Pers. Dict. col. 70.—Pers. *but*, an idol, image, God, id. p. 241, col. 1; and *kadah*, a habitation, id. p. 1175. β. The initial Pers.

sound is sometimes rendered by *p*, as in Devic. Yule suggests some confusion with Skt. *bhagavatī*, f., lit. 'venerable,' as the name of a goddess.

PAH, PA, a fort. (New Zealand.) A Maori word, signifying a fort surrounded by a stockade. 'In Maori, the verb *pà* means to touch, to block up. *Pa*=a collection of houses to which access is blocked by means of stockades and ditches;' Morris, Austral English.

PAIGLE, the cowslip. (O. Low G. ?) '*Paggles*, greene and yelow;' Tusser's Husbandry, § 43. 25 (E. D. S.) '*Pagyll*, a cow-sloppe;' Palsgrave. As *cowslip*, formerly *cowslop*, orig. meant 'cow-dung,' it is possible that *paigle* may have meant 'horsedung.' Woeste's Westphal. glossary gives *pāen-wiæmel*, a dung-beetle; and he notes that the Hannover form is *pagel-worm*, where *pagel* means 'dung;' evidently from Low G. *page*, MDu. *paghe* (Oudemans), a horse.

PAIL, an open vessel of wood, &c. for holding liquids. (F.—L.) ME. *paile*, *payle*. '*Payle*, or mylke-stoppe [milk-pail];' Prompt. Parv. AF. *paile*; glossed by ME. *stoppe*; Nominale, ed. Skeat, l. 496.—OF. *paele*, a pan; 'a footless posnet,' i.e. iron cooking-pot; saucepan; Cot.—L. *patella*, dimin. of *patina*, a pan; see **Paten.** β. Or from AS. *pægel*, occurring as a gloss upon L. *gillo* in Wright's Vocab., where it is misprinted *wægel*; see Voc. 124. 2, and Toller's A. S. Dict. It is cognate with Du. and G. *pegel*, G. *peil*, a gauge for liquids; cf. Dan. *pægel*, half a pint. But it seems to have been French; note the final -*e*. Der. *pail-ful*.

PAIN, bodily suffering, anguish. (F.—L.—Gk.) ME. *peine*, *peyne*, King Alisaunder, 4522.—F. *peine*, 'a paine, penalty;' Cot.—L. *pœna*, punishment, penalty, pain.—Gk. ποινή, penalty. β. The L. word was borrowed from the Gk. very early. Idg. type *qoinā*; cf. OIrish *cin* (Ir. *cion*), a fault; Zend *kaēnā-*, punishment, Pers. *kīn*, revenge; Russ. *tsiena*, a price; Gk. τίνειν, to pay a price; Brugmann, i. § 202. Cf. **Pine** (1). Der. *pain*, verb, ME. *peinen*, Chaucer, C. T. 139; *pain-ed*; *pain-ful* (with E. suffix -*ful*=*full*), formerly used with the sense of 'industrious,' see exx. in Trench, Select Glossary; *pain-ful-ly*, *pain-ful-ness*, *pain-less*, *pain-less-ness*; also *pains-taking*, adj., i.e. taking pains or trouble, Beaum. and Fletcher, Span. Curate, iv. 5 (Diego); *pains-taking*, sb. And see *pen-al*, *pen-ance*, *pen-itent*, *pun-ish*, *pine* (2).

PAINIM; see **Paynim.**

PAINT, to colour, describe, depict. (F.—L.) ME. *peinten*, Chaucer, C. T. 11946, 11949 (C 12, 15); but the word must have been in use in very early times, as we find the derived words *peintunge*, painting, and *peinture*, a picture, in the Ancren Riwle, p. 392, l. 17, p. 242, l. 14.—OF. *peint*, *paint* (mod. F. *peint*), pp. of *peindre*, *paindre* (mod. F. *peindre*), to paint.—L. *pingere*, to paint. Allied to Skt. *piñj*, to dye, colour; *piñjara*-, yellow, tawny. β. The form of the root is PEIG, to colour; perhaps allied to √PEIK, to adorn, form, whence Skt. *piç*, to adorn, form, *pēças*, an ornament, and Gk. ποικίλος, variegated. Der. *paint*, sb. (a late word), Dryden, to Sir Robert Howard, l. 8; *paint-er*, Romeo, i. 2. 41; *paint-ing*, in early use, ME. *peintunge*, as above. And see *pict-ure*, *de-pict*, *pig-ment*, *pi-mento*, *or-pi-ment*, *or-pine*, *pint*.

PAINTER, a rope for mooring a boat. (F.—L.) '*Painter*, a rope employed to fasten a boat;' Hawkesworth's Voyages, 1773, vol. i. p. xxix; spelt *paynter*, Naval Accounts (1485), p. 37. β. Some have supposed it to have been corrupted (by assimilation to the ordinary sb. *painter*) from ME. *panter*, a snare, esp. for catching birds; see Chaucer, Legend of Good Women, 131; Prompt. Parv. p. 381; spelt *paunter*, Polit. Songs, ed. Wright, p. 344.—AF. *panter* (Godefroy); MF. *pantiere*, a kind of snare for birds (Roquefort); *panthiere*, 'a great swoop-net;' Cot. Cf. Ital. *pantiera*, 'a kinde of tramell or fowling-net,' Florio; *panthera*, 'a net or haie to catch conies with, also a kind of fowling-net;' id.—L. *panthēr*, a hunting-net for catching wild beasts; cf. *panthēra*, an entire capture.—Gk. πάνθηρος, catching all sorts of animals.—Gk. πᾶν, neut. of πᾶς, every; and θήρ, a wild beast; see **Pan-** and **Panther.** ¶ The Irish *painteir*, Gael. *painntear*, a gin, snare, are borrowed from E.; the ME. word occurs as early as the reign of Edw. II. It is remarkable that, in America, a *panther* is also called a *painter*; see Cooper, The Pioneers, cap. xxviii. γ. But ME. *panter* means 'net' rather than 'noose.' Perhaps *painter* represents MF. *penteur*, 'the name of one of the ropes which passe over the top of a mast,' Cot.; or OF. *pentoir*, *pendoir*, in Godefroy, a perch for hanging clothes to dry, part of a belt to which a sword is hung; also strong cordage; from L. *pendēre*, to hang. But the history is obscure.

PAIR, two equal or like things, a couple. (F.—L.) ME. *peire*, *peyre*, applied to any number of like or equal things, and not limited, as now, to two only. Thus 'a *peire* of bedes'=a set of beads, Chaucer, C. T. 159. 'A *pair* of cards'=a pack of cards; Ben Jonson, Masque of Christmas (Carol). 'A *pair* of organs'=a set of organ-pipes, i.e. an organ; see my note to P. Plowman, C. xxi. 7.

'A *pair* of stairs'=a flight of stairs. Yet we also find 'a *peyre* hose'=a pair of hose; Rob. of Glouc. p. 390, l. 8013.—F. *paire*, 'a paire, or couple of;' Cot.; F. *pair*, 'like, alike, equall, matching, even, meet;' Cot.—L. *paria*, neut. pl., and *parem*, acc. of *pār*, alike. See **Par, Peer.** Der. *pair*, verb, Wint. Ta. iv. 4. 154. Also *umpire*, q. v.

PAJAMAS, PYJAMAS, loose drawers. (Hind.—Pers.) Modern. Lit. 'leg-clothing.'—Hind. *pā'ejāma*, *pājāma*, drawers.—Hind. *pā'e*, leg, *pā*, foot; *jāma*, garment (Forbes, Yule).—Pers. *pāi*, cognate with E. *foot*; *jāmah*, a garment. (Horn, § 412.) See *pyjammas* in Yule.

PAL, a brother, comrade. (Gipsy.) '*Pal* is a common cant word for brother or friend, and it is purely Gipsy. On the Continent it is *prala* or *pral*;' C. G. Leland, Eng. Gipsies, vi.

PALACE, a royal house. (F.—L.) ME. *palais*, King Horn, ed. Lumby, 1256; *paleis*, Floriz and Blancheflur, 87.—F. *palais*, 'a palace;' Cot.—L. *palātium*, formerly a building on the Palatine hill at Rome. 'On this hill, the *Collis Palatinus*, stood . . . the houses of Cicero and Catiline. Augustus built his mansion on the same hill, and his example was followed by Tiberius and Nero. Under Nero, all private houses had to be pulled down on the Collis Palatinus, in order to make room for the emperor's residence . . . called the *Palatium*; and it became the type of all the palaces of the kings and emperors of Europe;' Max Müller, Lectures on Language, ii. 276. β. The Collis Palatinus is supposed to have been so called from *Pales*, a pastoral deity; see Max Müller, as above. *Pales* was a goddess who protected flocks; and the name may have meant 'protector;' cf. Skt. *pāla-*, one who guards or protects; *pā*, to protect, cherish. Der. *palati-al* (Todd), formed with suffix -*al* from I. *palāti-um*; also *palat-ine*, q. v.; *palad-in*, q. v.

PALADIN, a warrior, a knight of Charlemagne's household. (F.—Ital.—L.) In Blount's Gloss., ed. 1674.—F. *paladin*, 'a knight of the round table;' Cot.—Ital. *paladino*, 'a warrier, a valiant man at armes;' Florio.—L. *palātinus*; see **Palatine.** Properly applied to a knight of a palace or royal household. **Doublet,** *palatine*.

PALÆO-; see **Paleo-.**

PALANQUIN, PALANKEEN, a light litter in which travellers are carried on men's shoulders. (Port.—Hind.—Skt.) 'A *pallamkeen* or litter;' Sir T. Herbert, Travels, 1665, p. 72. Spelt *palankee* in Terry's Voyage to East India, 1655, p. 155 (Todd); *palanquin* in Skinner, ed. 1671; *pallanchine* in Hakluyt, Voy. ii. part i. 222.—Portuguese *palanquim*.—Hind. *palang*, a bed, bedstead; otherwise *pālkī*; Forbes, Hindustani Dict.; and (in the Carnatic) *pallakki* (H. H. Wilson); Pali *pallanko* (Yule). Cf. Pers. *palank*, *palang*, a bedstead; Rich. Dict. p. 335. All from Skt. *paryaṅka-* (Prakrit *pallaṅka-*), a couch-bed, a bed; the change from *r* to *l* being very common.—Skt. *pari*, about, round (Gk. περί); and *aṅka-*, a hook, the flank, &c. Apparently from the support given to the body. The Skt. *aṅka-* is allied to L. *uncus*, a hook, AS. *angel*, a hook. See **Peri-** and **Angle** (2).

PALATE, the roof of the mouth, taste, relish. (F.—L.) In Cor. ii. 1. 61. ME. *palet*, Wyclif, Lament. iv. 4; Prompt. Parv. p. 378.—AF. *palet*, palate, in Nominale, ed. Skeat, 29; OF. *palat*, in the 14th century; see Littré.—L. *palātum*, the palate. Root uncertain. ¶ The mod. F. *palais* answers to a Late L. *palātium*, which seems to have been used by mistake for *palātum*. See remarks in Max Müller, Lect. on Lang. ii. 276. Der. *palat-al*, *palat-able*, *palat-abl-y*. Also *palate*, verb, Cor. iii. 1. 104.

PALATINE, orig. pertaining to a palace. (F.—L.) Chiefly in the phr. 'count *palatine*,' where the adj. follows the sb., as in French; see Merch. Ven. i. 2. 49.—F. *palatin*, 'a generall and common appellation, or title, for such as have any speciall office or function in a soveraign princes palace;' Cot. He adds: '*Compte palatin*, a count palatine, is not the title of a particular office, but an hereditary addition of dignity and honour, gotten by service done in a domesticall charge.'—L. *palātinus*, (1) the name of a hill in Rome, (2) belonging to the imperial abode, to the palace or court. See **Palace.** Der. *palatin-ate*, from F. *palatinat*, 'a palatinaty, the title or dignity of a count palatine, also a county palatine;' Cot. **Doublet,** *paladin*.

PALAVER, a talk, parley. (Port.—L.—Gk.) Frequently used in works of travel, of a parley with African chiefs; a word introduced on the African coast by the Portuguese.—Port. *palavra*, a word, parole.—L. *parabola*; from Gk. See **Parole, Parable.**

PALE (1), a stake, narrow piece of wood for enclosing ground, an enclosure, limit, district. (F.—L.) ME. *paal*, Wyclif, Ezek. xv. 3 (earlier version); the later version has *stake*; Vulgate, *paxillus*. Dat. *pale*, Wyclif, Luke, xix. 43.—F. *pal*, 'a pale, stake, or pole;' Cot.—L. *pālus*, a stake. For *pacslus*, from *pac-*, to fasten; as in *pac-iscī*, to stipulate. Brugmann, ii. § 76. See **Pact.** Der. *pal-ing*, Blackstone's Comment. b. ii. c. 3 (R.); *pale*, verb, 3 Hen. VI, i. 4.

103; *im-pale*; also *pal-is-ade*, q. v. **Doublet,** *pole* (1). ☞ The heraldic term *pale* is the same word.

PALE (2), wan, dim. (F.—L.) ME. *palē*, Chaucer, C. T. 5065 (B 645).—OF. *pale, palle* (Burguy), later *pasle* (Cot.), whence mod. F. *pâle.—*L. *pallidum,* acc. of *pallidus,* pale. On the loss of the last two atonic syllables, see Brachet, Introd. § 50, 51. Allied to Gk. πολιός, gray, and to E. *fallow;* see **Fallow** (2). Der. *pale-ly, pale-ness, pal-ish.* **Doublet,** *pallid.*

PALEOGRAPHY, the study of ancient modes of writing. (Gk.) Modern; coined from Gk. παλαιό-, for παλαιός, old; and γράφ-ειν, to write. Παλαιός is from πάλαι, adv., long ago.

PALEOLOGY, archæology. (Gk.) Modern. From Gk. παλαιό-, for παλαιός, old; and -λογία, from λόγος, a discourse, which from λέγειν, to speak. See **Paleography** and **Logic.** Der. *palæolog-ist.*

PALEONTOLOGY, the science of fossils, &c. (Gk.) Modern. Lit. 'a discourse on ancient creatures.' Coined from Gk. πάλαι, long ago; ὄντο-, decl. stem of ὤν, existing; and -λογία, from λόγος, a discourse, which from λέγειν, to speak. See **Paleography, Sooth,** and **Logic.** Der. *palæontolog-ist.*

PALESTRA, a wrestling-school. (L.—Gk.) In Lyly, Euphues, ed. Arber, p. 447; *palestr-al,* adj., Chaucer, Troilus, v. 304.—L. *palæstra.—*Gk. παλαίστρα, a wrestling-school.—Gk. παλαίειν, to wrestle; cf. πάλη, wrestling. Connected with Gk. παλάμη, the palm of the hand (Prellwitz). See **Palm** (1). Der. *palestr-al,* as above.

PALETOT, a loose garment. (F.) Modern. Borrowed from mod. F. *paletot,* formerly *palletoc,* for which see below. However, the word is by no means new to English; the ME. *paltok* is not an uncommon word; see numerous references in my note to P. Plowman, B. xviii. 25, where the word occurs; and see Prompt. Parv., and Way's note; cf. AF. *paltoke* (below). This form was borrowed from OF. *palletoc,* 'a long and thick pelt, or cassock, a garment like a short cloak with sleeves, or such a one as the most of our modern pages are attired in;' Cot. Explained by Diez as *palle-toque,* a cloak with a hood; from L. *palla,* a mantle, and Bret. *tôk,* W. *toc,* a cap. β. Littré derives OF. *palletoc* from MDu. *paltrok,* a mantle; but Franck says that this MDu. form was taken (with alteration) from the OF. word. Cf. Bret. *paltok,* a peasant's robe; from L. *palla* and Bret. *tôk,* a cap. See **Pall** (1). ¶ Way says that 'Sir Roger de Norwico bequeaths, in 1370, *unum paltoke de ueluete, cum armis meis;*' &c.

PALETTE, a small slab on which a painter mixes colours. (F.—L.) '*Pallet,* a thin oval piece of wood, used by painters to hold their colours;' Kersey, ed. 1715. The word is used by Dryden; see Todd (who gives no reference).—F. *palette,* 'a lingell, tenon, slice, or flat tool wherewith chirurgians lay salve on plaisters; also, the saucer or porringer, whereinto they receive blood out of an opened vein; also, a battledoor;' Cot. Thus it orig. meant a flat blade for spreading things, and afterwards a flat slab for colours. Cf. Ital. *paletta,* 'a lingell, slice [such] as apothecaries vse;' Florio; dimin. of *pala,* 'a spade;' id.—L. *pāla,* a spade, shovel, flat-bladed 'peel' for putting bread into an oven; see **Peel** (3). **Doublet,** *pallet* (2).

PALFREY, a saddle-horse, esp. a lady's horse. (F.—Low L.—Gk. *and* C.) In early use. ME. *palefrai,* O. Eng. Homilies, ed. Morris, i. 5, l. 20; *palfrei,* Chaucer, C. T. 2497 (A 2495).—OF. *palefrei* (13th century, Littré), MF. *palefroy,* 'a palfrey,' Cot.; mod. F. *palefroi.* Spelt *palefreid* in the 11th century; Littré.—Low L. *paraverēdus,* a post-horse, lit. 'an extra post-horse' (Lewis). Brachet gives quotations for the later forms *paravrēdus, parafrēdus,* and *palafrēdus* (10th century); and OF. *palefreid* = Low L. acc. *palafrēdum;* every step being traced with certainty. β. The Low L. *paraverēdus* is a hybrid formation from Gk. παρά, beside (hence extra); and Late L. *uerēdus,* a post-horse, courier's horse (Lewis). γ. Here *veredus* stands for **voredus,* from a Celtic type **vo-reidos,* a carriage-horse.—Celtic **vo* (Irish *fo,* W. *go*), prep. under, in; and **reidā,* Gaulish L. *rhēda, rēda,* a carriage. The Celtic **vo-reidos* occurs in W. *gorwydd,* a horse. The Celtic **reidā* is from the verb seen in OIrish *riad-aim,* I travel, ride, cognate with E. *ride* (Stokes). ¶ The Low L. *parauerēdus* is also the original of G. *pferd,* Du. *paard,* a palfrey, horse.

PALIMPSEST, a manuscript which has been twice written on, the first writing being partly erased. (Gk.) *Palimpseston* in Phillips (1706).—Gk. παλίμψηστον, a palimpsest (manuscript); neut. of παλίμψηστος, lit. scraped again.—Gk. πάλιμ-, for πάλιν, again, before the following ψ; and ψηστός, rubbed, scraped, verbal adj. from ψάειν, to rub, Ionic ψέειν. Cf. Skt. *psā,* to eat.

PALINDROME, a word or sentence that reads the same backwards as forwards. (Gk.) Examples are *Hannah, madam, Eve;* Todd quotes *subi dura a rudibus* from Peacham, Experience in these Times (1638). 'Curious *palindromes;*' Ben Jonson, An Execration

upon Vulcan, Underwoods, lxi. l. 34.—Gk. παλίνδρομος, running back again.—Gk. πάλιν, back, again; and δρόμος, a running, from δραμεῖν, to run; see **Dromedary.**

PALINODE, a recantation, in song. (F.—L.—Gk.) 'You, two and two, singing a *palinode;*' Ben Jonson, Cynthia's Revels, last speech of Crites.—F. *palinodie,* 'a palinody, recantation, contrary song, unsaying of what hath been said;' Cot.—L. *palinōdia.—* Gk. παλινῳδία, a recantation, esp. of an ode.—Gk. πάλιν, back, again; and ῳδή, a song; see **Ode.**

PALISADE, a fence made of pales or stakes. (F.—L.) Shak. has the pl. *palisadoes,* 1 Hen. IV, ii. 3. 55; this is a pseudo-Spanish form; the mod. Span. word is *palizada.* Dryden has *palisades,* tr. of Virgil, b. vii. l. 214.—F. *palissade,* 'a palisadoe;' Cot.—F. *paliss-er,* 'to inclose with pales,' id.; with suffix *-ade* < L. *-āta.—*F. *palis,* a 'pale, stake, pole,' id.; extended from *pal,* a pale. See further under **Pale** (1). Der. *palisade,* verb.

PALL (1), a cloak, mantle, archbishop's scarf, shroud. (L.) ME. *pal,* Layamon, 897, 1296; pl. *pælles,* id. 2368. AS. *pæll,* purple cloth; we find *pællas and sīdan* = purple cloths and silks, as a gloss to L. *purpuram et sēricum* in Ælfric's Colloquy (the Merchant); see Thorpe, Analecta, p. 27.—L. *pallium,* a coverlet, pall, curtain, toga; allied to *palla,* a mantle, loose dress. Sievers, Gr. § 80. Der. *pall-i-ate,* q.v.

PALL (2), to become vapid, lose taste or spirit. (F.—L.) ME. *pallen.* '*Pallyn,* as ale and drynke, *Emorior;*' Prompt. Parv. Way, in the note on the passage, quotes from Lydgate's Order of Fools: 'Who forsakith wyne, and drynkithe ale *pallid,* Such foltisshe foolis, God lete hem never the' [prosper]; Minor Poems, p. 168. He also cites from Palsgrave: 'I *palle,* as drinke or bloode dothe, by longe standyng in a thynge, *ie appallys.* This drink wyll *pall* (*s'appallyra*) if it stande vncouered all nyght. I *palle,* I fade of freshenesse in colour or beautye, *ie flaitris.*' β. He also has: 'I *appalle,* as drinke dothe or wyne, whan it leseth his colour, *je appalys;*' and again: 'I *appale* ones colour, *je appalis.*' Thus *pall* is merely an aphetic form of *appal,* which meant both to wax pale and to make pale or to terrify. See **Appal.**

PALLADIUM, a safeguard of liberty. (L.—Gk.) 'A kind of *palladium* to save the city;' Milton, Of Reformation in England, B. 1 (Todd).—L. *Palladium;* Virgil, Æn. ii. 166, 183.—Gk. Παλλάδιον, the statue of Pallas on which the safety of Troy was supposed to depend.—Gk. Παλλαδ-, stem of Παλλάς, an epithet of Athene (Minerva).

PALLET (1), a kind of mattress or couch, properly one of straw. (F.—L.) ME. *paillet,* Chaucer, Troil. iii. 229.—AF. *paillete,* straw, Bestiary, 475; F. *paillet,* a heap of straw, given by Littré as a provincial word. Cotgrave only gives *pailler,* 'a reek or stack of straw, also, bed-straw.' Dimin. of F. *paille,* 'straw;' Cot.—L. *palea,* straw, chaff. Allied to Skt. *palāla-,* straw; Russ. *polova,* chaff; Lith. *pelai,* pl. chaff. See **Palliasse.**

PALLET (2), an instrument used by potters, also by gilders; also, a palette. (F.—Ital.—L.) See definitions in N. E. D.; it is, properly, a flat-bladed instrument for spreading plasters, gilding, &c., and for moulding; and is only another spelling of **Palette,** q. v.

PALLIASSE, a straw mattress. (F.—L.) Not in Todd's Johnson. The introduction of *i* is due to an attempt to represent the '*ll* mouillés' of the F. *paillasse,* which see in Littré. The MF. form in Cotgrave is *paillace,* 'a straw-bed.' The suffix *-ace, asse* (< L. *-āceus*) is a diminutive one; Brachet, Etym. Dict. Introd. § 272; and *paill-ace* is from *paille,* straw.—L. *palea;* see **Pallet** (1).

PALLIATE, to cloak, excuse. (L.) 'Being *palliated* with a pilgrim's coat and hypocritic sanctity;' Sir T. Herbert, Travels, ed. 1665, p. 341. Properly a pp., as in 'certain lordes and citezens .. in habite *palliate* and dissimuled;' Hall's Chron., Hen. IV. introd. § 11.—L. *palliātus,* cloaked, covered with a cloak.—L. *pallium,* a cloak, mantle. See **Pall** (1). Der. *palliat-ion, palliat-ive.*

PALLID, pale. (L.) '*Pallid* death;' Spenser, F. Q. v. 11. 45.— L. *pallidus,* pale. See **Pale** (2). **Doublet,** *pale* (2).

PALL-MALL, the name of an old game. (F.—Ital.—L.) Discussed under **Mall** (2), q. v. See Notes on E. Etym., p. 204.

PALLOR, paleness. (L.) Used by Bp. Taylor, Artificial Handsomeness, p. 2 (Todd).—L. *pallor,* paleness.—L. *pallēre,* to be pale. Cf. L. *pallidus,* pale; see **Pale** (2).

PALM (1), the inner part of the hand. (F.—L.) ME. *paume,* the palm of the hand, P. Plowman, B. xvii. 141, 147, 150, 153.—F. *paume,* 'the palme of the hand;' Cot.—L. *palma,* the palm of the hand.+Gk. παλάμη; Skt. *pāṇi-* (for **palni-*).+AS. *folm;* Grein, i. 311; OIrish *lām;* W. *llaw.* Brugmann, i. § 529 (2). Allied to AS. *folm* is E. *fumble;* see **Fumble.** Der. *palmate,* from L. *palmātus,* marked with the palm of the hand, shaped like the palm; *palm-ist-ry,* in Sir T. Browne, Vulg. Errors, bk. v. ch. 24, pt. 1; ME. *pawmestry,* Lydgate, Assembly of Gods, 870.

PALM (2), the name of a tree. (L.) AS. *palm*, a palm-tree; borrowed directly from Latin. '*Palma*, palm-twig, *vel* palm;' Wright's Vocab. i. 32, col. 2. So called from some resemblance of the leaves to the out-spread hand; see **Palm** (1). ¶ We may note that the L. spelling has prevailed over the French, as in *psalm*, &c. **Der.** *palm-er*, ME. *palmere*, Chaucer, C. T. 13, King Horn, ed. Lumby, 1027, i.e. one who bears a palm-branch in token of having been to the Holy Land; *palm-er-worm*, Joel, i. 4, ii. 25, a caterpillar supposed to be so called from its wandering about like a pilgrim, and also simply called *palmer* (see Eastwood and Wright's Bible Word-book); *Palm-sunday*, ME. *palme-suneday*, O. Eng. Miscellany, ed. Morris, p. 39, l. 65, AS. *palm-sunnandæg*, Luke, xix. 29 (margin); *palm-y*, Hamlet, i. 1. 113; *palm-ary*, i.e. deserving the palm (as token of a victory). ☞ The *palmer* or *palmer-worm* might have been named from prov. E. *palm*, the catkin of a willow; but we also find *palmer* in the sense of wood-louse, and in Holliband's Dict., ed. 1593, a *palmer* is described as 'a worme having a great many feete;' see Halliwell.

PALPABLE, that can be felt, obvious. (F. – L.) In Macb. ii. 1. 40; Chaucer, Ho. Fame, 869. – F. *palpable*, omitted by Cotgrave, but in use in the 15th century (Littré), and given by Palsgrave, who has: 'Palpable, apte or mete to be felte, *palpable*.' – L. *palpābilis*, that can be touched. – L. *palpāre*, to feel, *palpāri*, to feel, handle. β. An initial *s* has been lost, if it be related to Gk. ψηλαφάω, I feel; Skt. *sphālaya*, to strike, to touch. **Der.** *palpabl-y*, *palpable-ness*, *palpabili-ty*. And see *palpitate*.

PALPITATE, to throb. (L.) In Minsheu, ed. 1627. [It is not unlikely that the E. verb to *palpitate* was really due to the sb. *palpitation*.] – L. *palpitātus*, pp. of *palpitāre*, to throb; frequentative of *palpāre*, to feel, stroke, pat. See **Palpable**. **Der.** *palpitat-ion*, from F. *palpitation*, 'a panting;' Cot.

PALSY, paralysis. (F. – L. – Gk.) ME. *palesy*, Wyclif, Matt. iv. 24; *pallesye*, Rob. of Brunne, Handlyng Synne, 11922; fuller form *parlesy*, Prick of Conscience, ed. Morris, 2996. – F. *paralysie*, 'the palsie;' Cot. – L. *paralysin*, acc. of *paralysis*; see **Paralysis**. **Der.** *palsy*, verb; *palsi-ed*, Cor. v. 2. 46.

PALTER, to dodge, shift, shuffle, equivocate. (Scand.) See Macb. v. 8. 20; Jul. Cæs. ii. 1. 126. Cotgrave, s. v. *harceler*, has: 'to haggle, hucke, hedge, or *paulter* long in the buying of a commoditie.' It also means 'to babble,' as in: 'One whyle his tonge it ran and *paltered* of a cat, Another whyle he stammered styll upon a rat;' Gammer Gurton, ii. 3. Cf. prov. E. *polter*, to work carelessly, to go about aimlessly, to trifle. Prob. of Scand. origin. Cf. Swed. dial. *pallta*, to go about, to hobble about, to toddle; *paltter*, a poor wretch, who goes about aimlessly; from *pala*, to work slowly (Rietz). Perhaps of imitative origin; cf. *falter*.

PALTRY, mean, vile, worthless. (Scand.) In Shak. Merry Wives, ii. 1. 164; Marlowe, Edw. II, ii. 6. 57. Jamieson gives *paltrie*, *peltrie*, vile trash; Halliwell has *paltring*, a worthless trifle; Forby explains Norfolk *paltry* by 'rubbish, refuse, trash;' and Brockett gives *palterly* as the North. Eng. form of the adj. *paltry*. It stands for *palter-y* (North. E. *palter-ly*), formed with the adj. suffix *-y* (or *-ly*) from an old pl. *palt-er* (formed like ME. *child-er* = children, *breth-er* = brethren), which is still preserved in Swed. and Danish. This account is verified by the G. forms; see below. The sense of *palter* is 'rags,' and that of *paltr-y* is 'ragged,' hence, vile, worthless, or, as a sb., trash or refuse. – Swed. *paltor*, rags, pl. of *palta*, a rag; Ihre gives MSwed. *paltor*, old rags, with a reference to Jerem. xxxviii. 11; Dan. *pjalter*, rags, pl. of *pjalt*, a rag, tatter; hence the adj. *pjaltet*, ragged, tattered. + Low G. *palte*, *pulte*, a rag, a piece of cloth torn or cut off; whence the adj. *paltrig*, *pultrig*, ragged, torn; Bremen Wörterb. iii. 287; Prov. G. *palter* (pl. *paltern*), a rag; whence *palterig*, paltry (Flügel). Cf. also MDu. *palt*, a piece, fragment, as, *palt brods*, a piece of bread (Oudemans, Kilian); NFries. *palt*, a rag (Outzen). β. The origin is by no means clear; Ihre connects Swed. *paltor* with MSwed. *palt*, a kind of garment. See Rietz, s. v. *pallt*. Possibly of Slavonic origin; cf. Russ. *polotno*, *platno*, linen; which may be allied to E. *fold* (as of linen); cf. Skt. *pata-*, woven stuff, piece of cloth. **Der.** *paltri-ly*, *paltri-ness*.

PALUSTRAL, PALUSTRINE, of the marshes, marshy. (L.) Coined from L. *paluster*, marshy. – L. *palus*, a marsh, morass.

PAMPAS, plains in South America. (Span. – Peruvian.) *Pampas* is the Span. pl. of *pampa*, a plain. From the Peruv. *pampa*, a plain; hence *Moyo-bamba*, *Chuqui-bamba*, places in Peru, with *bamba* for *pampa* (wrongly). Garcilaso, in his Comment. on Peru, bk. vii. c. 4, complains that the Spaniards often mispronounced *pampa* as *bamba*.

PAMPER, to feed luxuriously, glut. (Flemish.) In Much Ado, iv. 1. 61. '*Pampired* with ease;' Court of Love, l. 177 (first printed 1561). 'Oure *pamperde* paunchys;' Skelton, ed. Dyce, i. 19, l. 25. But the word was known to Chaucer; 'They ne were nat *forpampred* with owtrage;' Ætas Prima, l. 5. Wedgwood quotes from Reliquiæ

Antiquæ, i. 41: 'Thus the devil farith with men and wommen; First, he stirith him to *pappe* and *pampe* her fleisch, desyrynge delicous metis and drynkis.' Not found in AS., and prob. imported from the Netherlands. The form *pamp-er* is precisely the W. Flemish *pamperen*, to pamper (De Bo); a frequentative from *pamp* (as above), meaning to feed luxuriously; and this verb is a causal form from a sb. *pamp*, a nasalised form of *pap*. – Low G. *pampen*, more commonly *slampampen*, to live luxuriously; Brem. Wörterb. iv. 800. – Low G. *pampe*, thick pap, pap made of meal; also called *pampelbry*, i.e. pap-broth; and, in some dialects, *pappe*; id. iii. 287. So also Low G. (Altmark) *pampen*, *pappen*, to cram oneself (Danneil); vulgar G. *pampen*, *pampeln*, to cram, pamper, from *pampe*, pap, thick broth; Bavarian *pampfen*, to stuff, *sich anpampfen*, *vollpampfen*, to cram oneself with pap or broth (Schmeller, i. 392). ¶ The use of the prefix *for-* in Chaucer is almost enough in itself to stamp the word as being of Teutonic origin. **Der.** *pamper-er*.

PAMPHLET, a small book, of a few sheets stitched together. (F. – L. – Gk.) Spelt *pamflet*, Testament of Love, bk. iii. ch. 9. l. 54; ed. 1561, fol. 317 b, col. 1; *pamphlet* in Shak. 1 Hen. VI, iii. 1. 2. [The mod. F. *pamphlet* is borrowed from English (Littré).] Hoccleve has the form *pamfilet* (trisyllabic) in l. 1 of a poem addressed to Richard, duke of York. It is obviously formed, with the F. suffix *-et*, from the name *Pamphil-us*, as in other similar instances. Thus the OF. *Esop-et* meant a book by Æsop, *Avion-et* meant one by Avianus (see note to P. Plowman, B. xii. 257), and *Chaton-et* one by Cato (Godefroy). Similarly, *Pamphil-et* or *Pamfil-et* meant one by *Pamphile*, i. e. Pamphilus. The allusion is to a medieval Latin poem (in 780 lines) of the 12th century referred to by Chaucer in C. T., F 1110. The title is: 'Pamphili Mauriliani Pamphilus;' there is an edition by Goldastus. See my note on the passage. [There was also a *Pamphila*, a female historian of the first century, who wrote numerous *epitomes*; see Suidas, Aul. Gellius, xv. 17, 23; Diog. Laertius, in life of Pittacus.] The earliest record of the word in England is in the Late L. *panfletus*, a little book; in Richard of Bury, Philobiblon, c. 8 (A. D. 1344). Cf. F. *pamphile*, a name for the knave of clubs (Littré), due to the Gk. name *Pamphilus*; whence *Pam*, in Pope, Rape of the Lock, 349. **Der.** *pamphlet-eer*, Bp. Hall, Satires, b. ii. sat. 1, l. 30; *pamphlet-eer-ing*.

PAN, a broad shallow vessel for domestic use. (E.?) '*Pannes* and pottes;' Sir T. Elyot, The Governour, b. i. c. 1. ME. *panne*, Chaucer, C. T. 7196 (D 1614). AS. *panne*, a pan; 'Patella, *panne*;' 'ísen *panne*' = an iron pan; *fȳr-panne* = a fire-pan; Ælfric's Vocab. Nomina Vasorum, in Voc. 123. 6; 124. 10, 11. And see Ælfred, tr. of Gregory's Pastoral, c. xxi, ed. Sweet, p. 162, last line. [Irish *panna*, W. *pan*, are from E.] Cf. Icel. *panna*, Swed. *panna*, Dan. *pande* (for *panne*), Du. *pan*, G. *pfanne*; also Low Lat. *panna*. β. Perhaps of Teut. origin. If not, it may be a corrupted form of L. *patina*, a shallow bowl, pan, bason. **Der.** *brain-pan*, with which cf. ME. *panne* in the transferred sense of skull, Chaucer, C. T. 1167 (A 1165); *knee-pan*; *pan-cake*, As You Like It, i. 2. 67, and in Palsgrave; also *pannikin*, from MDu. *panneken*, 'a small panne,' Hexham; with MDu. dimin. suffix *-ken*. Also *pan-tile*, first in 1640 (N. E. D.).

PAN-, prefix, all. (Gk.) From Gk. πᾶν, neut. of πᾶς, all. The stem is παντ-.

PANACEA, a universal remedy. (L. – Gk.) '*Panacea*, a medycine . . . of much vertue;' Udall, pref. to Luke, fol. 8, back. Oddly spelt *panachæa*, Spenser, F. Q. iii. 5. 32. – L. *panacēa*. – Gk. πανάκεια, fem. of πανάκειος, allied to πανακής, all-healing. – Gk. πᾶν, neut. of πᾶς, all; and ακ-, base of ἀκέομαι, I heal, ἄκος, a cure, remedy.

PANCREAS, a fleshy gland under the stomach, commonly known as the sweet-bread. (L. – Gk.) '*Pancreas*, the sweet-bread;' Phillips, ed. 1706. – L. *pancreas*. – Gk. πάγκρεας, the sweet-bread; lit. 'all flesh.' – Gk. πᾶν, neut. of πᾶς, all; and κρέας, flesh, for *κρέϝ-ας, allied to Skt. *kravya-m*, raw flesh, L. *crū-dus*, raw. See **Pan-** and **Crude**. **Der.** *pancreat-ic*, from the stem παγκρεατ-.

PANDECT, a comprehensive treatise, digest. (F. – L. – Gk.) 'Thus thou, by means which th' ancients never took, A *pandect* mak'st, and universal book;' Donne, Vpon Mr. T. Coryat's Crudities, l. 50. More properly used in the pl. *pandects*, as in Sir T. Elyot, The Governor, bk. i. c. 14. § 10. – MF. *pandectes*, 'pandects, books which contain all matters, or comprehend all the parts of the subject whereof they intreat;' Cot. – L. *pandectas*, acc. of pl. *pandectæ*, the title of the collection of Roman laws made by order of Justinian, A.D. 533; see Gibbon, Rom. Empire, ch. 44. The sing. *pandecta* also appears; also *pandectēs*, the true orig. form. – Gk. πανδέκτης, all-receiving, comprehensive; whence pl. πανδέκται, pandects. – Gk. πᾶν, neut. of πᾶς, all; and δεκ-, base of δέχομαι, Ionic δέκομαι, I receive, contain. See **Pan-**.

PANDEMONIUM, the home of all the demons, hell. (Gk.)

In Milton, P. L. i. 756. Coined from Gk. πᾶν, all; and δαίμονι-, from δαίμων, a demon; see **Pan-** and **Demon**.

PANDER, PANDAR, a pimp, one who ministers to another's passions. (L. – Gk.) Commonly *pander*; yet *pandar* is better. Much Ado, v. 2. 31; used as a proper name, Troil. i. 1. 98. ME. *Pandare*, shortened form of *Pandarus*; Chaucer uses both forms, Troil. i. 610, 618. – L. *Pandarus*, the name of the man 'who procured for Troilus the love and good graces of Chryseis; which imputation, it may be added, depends upon no better authority than the fabulous histories of Dictys Cretensis and Dares Phrygius;' Richardson. In other words, the whole story is an invention of later times. – Gk. Πάνδαρος, a personal name. Two men of this name are recorded: (1) a Lycian archer, distinguished in the Trojan army; see Homer (Il. ii. 827); (2) a companion of Æneas; see Smith's Classical Dict. Der. *pander*, vb., Hamlet, iii. 4. 88; *pander-ly*, adj., Merry Wives, iv. 2. 122; *pander-er* (sometimes used, unnecessarily, for the sb. *pander*).

PANDOURS, soldiers in a certain Hungarian regiment. (F. – Low L. – Teut.) 'Hussars and *pandours* (1768),' Foote, Devil upon Two Sticks, ii. 1. – F. *pandour*; from a Serbo-Croatian form *pàndūr* (earlier *bàndūr*), a constable, catchpole, mounted policeman, watcher of vineyards (N. E. D.). – Low L. *banderius*, a follower of a banner, watcher of vineyards. – Low L. *bandum*, a banner; of Teut. origin; see **Banner**.

PANE, a patch, a plate of glass. (F. – L.) 'A *pane* of glass, or wainscote;' Minsheu, ed. 1627. ME. *pane*, applied to a part or portion of a thing; see Prompt. Parv. p. 380, and Way's note. 'Vch *pane* of þat place had þre ȝatez' = each portion of that place had three gates; Allit. Poems, ed. Morris, i. 1034 (or 1033). – F. *pan*, 'a pane, piece, or pannell of a wall, of wainscot, of a glasse-window, &c.; also, the skirt of a gown, the *pane* of a hose, of a cloak, &c.;' Cot. – L. *pannum*, acc. of *pannus*, a cloth, rag, tatter; hence, a patch, piece. Allied to *pānus*, the thread wound upon a bobbin in a shuttle; and to Gk. πῆνος, πήνη, the woof. Also to Goth. *fana*, and E. *vane*; see **Vane**. Der. *pan-ed*, in the phr. *paned hose*, ornamented breeches, which see in Nares; also *pan-el*, q. v. And see *pan-icle*.

PANEGYRIC, a eulogy, encomium. (L. – Gk.) Spelt *panegyricke* in Minsheu, ed. 1627. – L. *panēgyricus*, a eulogy; from *panēgyricus*, adj., with the same sense as in Greek. – Gk. πανηγυρικός, fit for a full assembly, festive, solemn; hence applied to a festival oration, or panegyric. – Gk. πᾶν, neut. of πᾶς, all; and -ηγυρι-s, related to ἀγορά, a gathering, a crowd, ἀγείρειν, to assemble. See **Pan-** and **Gregarious**. Der. *panegyric*, adj. (really an older use); *panegyric-al*, *panegyric-al-ly*, *panegyr-ise*, *panegyr-ist*.

PANEL, PANNEL, a compartment with a raised border, a board with a surrounding frame. (F. – L.) In Shak. As You Like It, iii. 3. 89. ME. *panel*, in two other senses: (1) a piece of cloth on a horse's back, to serve as a sort of saddle, Cursor Mundi, 14982; (2) a schedule containing the names of those summoned to serve as jurors, P. Plowman, B. iii. 315. The general sense is 'a little piece,' and esp. a square piece, whether of wood, cloth, or parchment, but orig. of cloth only. – OF. *panel*, MF. *paneau*, 'a pannel of wainscot, of a saddle, &c.;' Cot. – Late L. *pannellus*, *panellus*, used in Prompt. Parv. p. 381, as equivalent to ME. *panele*. Dimin. of L. *pannus*, cloth, a piece of cloth, a rag; see **Pane**. Der. *em-panel*, *im-panel*; see **Empanel**.

PANG, a violent pain, a throe. (E.) In the Court of Love, l. 1150, we find: 'The *prang* of love so straineth thaim to crye;' altered, in modern editions, to 'The *pange* of love.' In Prompt. Parv. p. 493, we find: '*Throwe, womannys pronge, sekeness*, Erumpna;' i. e. a throe, a woman's pang. So also: 'These *prongys* myn herte asonder thei do rende;' Coventry Myst., p. 287. But the pl. *pangus* is in The Tale of Beryn, 963. The sense is 'a sharp stab, severe prick.' It is clear that the word has lost an *r*; for the etymology, see **Prong**. β. In Skelton, Philip Sparowe, l. 44, the word occurs as a verb: 'What heuyness dyd me *pange*;' it is also a sb., id. l. 62. Cf. also: 'For there be in us certayne affectionate *pangues* of nature;' Udall, Luke, c. 4, v. 12. Both sb. and vb. are common in Shakespeare. Cf. MDu. *prange*, 'oppression, or constraint;' Hexham.

PANGOLIN, the scaly ant-eater. (Malay.) See C. P. G. Scott and Yule. – Malay *peng-gōling*. Lit. 'the creature that rolls itself up.' From Malay *gōling*, a roller, that which rolls up; with the denominative prefix *pe-*, which becomes *peng-* before *g* (Marsden, Scott).

PANIC, extreme fright. (Gk.) When we speak of *a panic*, it is an abbreviation of the phrase 'a panic fear,' given in Blount's Gloss., ed. 1674. Camden has 'a *panicall* feare;' Remaines, chap. on Poems (R.). – Gk. τὸ Πανικόν, used with or without δεῖμα (= fear), Panic fear, i. e. fear supposed to be inspired by the god Pan. – Gk. Πανικός, of or belonging to Pan. – Gk. Πάν, a rural god of Arcadia, son of Hermes. Cf. Russ. *pan'*, a lord, Lithuan. *ponas*, a lord,

also, the Lord. Cf. Skt. *pā*, to cherish. Der. *panic-struck* or *panic-stricken*.

PANICLE, a form of inflorescence in which the cluster is irregularly branched. (L.) Modern and scientific. – L. *pānicula*, a tuft, panicle. Double dimin. form from *pānus*, the thread wound round the bobbin of a shuttle, a swelling; as to which see **Pane**. Der. *panicul-at-ed, panicul-ate*.

PANNAGE, food of swine in woods; money paid for such food. (F. – L.) Obsolete; see Blount's Nomo-Lexicon, Todd's Johnson, &c. Also spelt *pawnage*, and even *pounage*; see Chaucer, The Former Age, 7. Anglo-F. *panage*, Year-Books of Edw. I, i. 63, ii. 135. – OF. *pasnage*, 'pawnage, mastage, monie . . . for feeding of swine with mast;' Cot. – Late L. *pasnāticum*, short for *pastināticum, pastionāticum*, pannage (Ducange). – Late L. *pastiōnāre*, to feed on mast, as swine. – L. *pastiōn-*, stem of *pastio*, a grazing, used in Late L. with the sense of right of pannage. – L. *past-um*, supine of *pascere*, to feed; see **Pastor**.

PANNEL, the same as **Panel**, q. v.

PANNIER, a bread-basket. (F. – L.) ME. *panier* (with one *n*), Havelok, 760. – F. *panier*, 'a pannier, or dosser;' Cot. – L. *pānārium*, a bread-basket. – L. *pānis*, bread; allied to *pascere* (pt. t. *pā-ui*), to feed. See **Pastor**. Der. see *pantry* and *company*.

PANNIKIN, dimin. of Pan, q. v.

PANOPLY, complete armour. (Gk.) In Milton, P. L. vi. 527, 760. 'Than all your fury, and the *panoply*;' Ben Jonson, Magnetic Lady, A. iii. sc. 4. – Gk. πανοπλία, the full armour of an ὁπλίτης, or heavy-armed soldier. – Gk. πᾶν, neut. of πᾶς, all; and ὅπλ-α, arms, armour, pl. of ὅπλον, a tool, implement. β. Gk. ὅπ-λον is connected with ἕπω, I am busy about (whence ἕπομαι, I follow); Brugmann, ii. § 657. Der. *panopli-ed*.

PANORAMA, a picture representing a succession of scenes. (Gk.) Late; added by Todd to Johnson. Invented by R. Barker, A.D. 1788 (Haydn). Coined to mean 'a view all round.' – Gk. πᾶν, neut. of πᾶς, all; and ὅραμα, a view, from ὁράω, I see, from √WER, to protect. See **Pan-** and **Wary**. Der. *panoram-ic*.

PANSY, heart's-ease, a species of violet. (F. – L.) In Hamlet, iv. 5. 176. ME. *pensees*, pl., Assembly of Ladies, l. 62 (and note). '*Pensy* floure, *pensee*;' Palsgrave. – F. *pensée*, 'a thought; . . also, the flower paunsie;' Cot. Thus, it is the flower of thought or remembrance; cf. *forget-me-not*. The F. *pensée* is the fem. of *pensé*, pp. of *penser*, to think. – L. *pensāre*, to weigh, ponder, consider; frequentative form of *pendere*, to weigh (pp. *pensus*). See **Pensive**.

PANT, to breathe hard. (F. – L.) In Shak. Tw. Nt. iii. 4. 323. 'To *pant* and quake;' Spenser, F. Q. i. 7. 20. ME. *panten*; Prompt. Parv. p. 381. And see Skelton, Phyllyp Sparowe, l. 132. A hawk was said 'to *pante*' when it was short-winded; Book of St. Alban's, fol. b 6, back. Obviously connected with F. *panteler*, to pant, a new formation from OF. *pantaisier* (below), MF. *pantiser*, 'to breath very fast, to blow thick and short;' Cot. From the same OF. verb was formed MF. *pantois*, 'short-winded, oft-breathing, out of breath;' *pantois*, sb., 'short wind, pursiness, a frequent breathing, or a difficult fetching of wind by the shortness of breath; in hawks, we call it the *pantais*;' Cot. [In Sherwood's index to Cotgrave we find: 'The *pantasse* or *pantois* in hawkes, *le pantais*.'] This use of the term in hawking appears to be old. β. All from AF. *pantoiser*, to pant, Vie de St. Auban, 697; OF. *panteisier, pantaisier, pantoisier* (Godefroy), to breathe with difficulty; cognate with Prov. *pantaisa(r)*, to dream, to be oppressed, to pant. – Late L. **phantasiāre*, by-form of *phantasiārī*, to dream, to see visions in sleep, imagine (Ducange). – Gk. φαντασία, a fancy; see **Fancy**. ¶ So G. Paris, in Romania, vi. 628; Körting, § 7111. Cf. Gascon *pantaia*, to dream, to pant (Mistral); ME. to *panty*, Voc. 564. 7.

PANTALOON (1), a ridiculous character in a pantomime, buffoon. (F. – Ital. – Gk.) In Shak. As You Like It, ii. 7. 158; Tam. of Shrew, iii. 1. 37. – F. *pantalon*, (1) a name given to the Venetians, (2) a pantaloon; see Littré. – Ital. *pantalone*, a pantaloon, buffoon. 'The *pantalone* is the pantaloon of Ital. comedy, a covetous and amorous old dotard who is made the butt of the piece;' Wedgwood. The name, according to Zambaldi (Vocabulario Etimologico) was applied to the pantaloon as representing the old Venetian merchant; and Mahn (in Webster) says that St. *Pantaleone* was 'the patron saint of [rather, a well-known saint in] Venice, and hence a baptismal name very frequent among the Venetians, and applied to them by the other Italians as a nickname.' Lord Byron speaks of the Venetian name *Pantaleone* as being 'her very by-word;' Childe Harold, c. iv. st. 14. β. St. *Pantaleone's* day is July 27; he was martyred A.D. 303; Chambers, Book of Days, ii. 127. The name is also written *Pantaleon* (as in Chambers), which is perhaps better. It is certainly Gk., and he is said to be known in the Greek church as *Panteleēmon*; from παντ-, for πᾶς, all, and ἐλεήμων, pitying, merciful. The pres. pt. of ἐλεεῖν, to pity, would give a by-form *Panteleōn*. ¶ The etymology advocated by Lord Byron is extraordinary, and indeed ridiculous, viz. Ital. *pianta-leone* = the planter of the lion, i. e. the planter of the standard bearing the lion of St. Mark, supposed to be applied to Venice; see note 9 to c. iv of Childe Harold. **Der.** *pantaloons.*

PANTALOONS, a kind of trousers. (F.—Ital.—Gk.) 'And as the French, we conquered once Now give us laws for *pantaloons*;' Butler, Hudibras, pt. i. c. 3, l. 923; on which Bell's note says: '*The pantaloon* belongs to the Restoration. It was loose in the upper part, and puffed, and covered the legs, the lower part terminating in stockings. In an inventory of the time of Charles II pantaloons are mentioned, and a yard and a half of lutestring allowed for them.' See also Blount's Gloss., ed. 1674.—F. *pantalon,* a garment so called because worn by the Venetians, who were themselves called *Pantaloni,* i. e. *Pantaloons* (Littré). See **Pantaloon.**

PANTHEISM, the doctrine that the universe is God. (Gk.) In Waterland, Works, vol. viii. p. 81 (R.). Todd only gives *pantheist.* Coined from **Pan-** and **Theism.** And see **Pantheon. Der.** so also *pan-theist,* from *pan-* and *theist;* hence *pantheist-ic, pantheist-ic-al.*

PANTHEON, a temple dedicated to all the gods. (L.—Gk.) 'One temple of *pantheon,* that is to say, all goddes;' Udall, on the Revelation, c. 16. fol. 311 B; and in Shak. Titus, i. 242.—L. *pan-thĕon.*—Gk. πάνθειον, for πανθείον ἱερόν, a temple consecrated to all gods.—Gk. πάνθειον, neut. of πάνθειος, common to all gods.—Gk. πᾶν, neut. of πᾶς, all; and θεῖος, divine, from θεός, god. See **Pan-** and **Theism.**

PANTHER, a fierce carnivorous quadruped. (F.—L.—Gk.— Skt.) ME. *pantere,* King Alisaunder, 6820; *panter,* O. Eng. Miscellany, ed. Morris, p. 23. [Cf. AS. *pandher* (sic); Grein, ii. 361.]—OF. *panthere,* 'a panther;' Cot.—L. *panthēra;* also *panthēr.*—Gk. πάνθηρ, a panther. Foreign to Gk., and prob. of Skt. origin.— Skt. *puṇḍarīka-s,* explained by Benfey as 'the elephant of the southeast quarter;' but also 'a tiger,' according to the St. Petersburg Skt. Dict. ¶ A popular etymology from πᾶν, all, and θήρ, a beast, gave rise to numerous fables; see Philip de Thaun, Bestiaire, l. 224, in Wright's Pop. Treatises on Science, p. 82.

PANTLER, a servant who has charge of the pantry. (F.—L.) In Shak. 2 Hen. IV, ii. 4. 258. ME. *pantlere,* Prompt. Parv.; *pantelere,* Rob. of Brunne, tr. of Langtoft, p. 33. Altered from OF. *panetier,* 'a pantler;' Cot.; prob. by the influence of *but-ler.*—Late L. *panētārius* (*pānitārius,* Prompt. Parv.).—Late L. *panēta,* one who makes bread; see **Pantry.**

PANTOMIME, one who expresses his meaning by action; a dumb show. (F.—L.—Gk.) '*Pantomime,* an actor of many parts in one play,' &c.; Blount's Gloss., ed. 1674; so also in Butler, Hudibras, pt. iii. c. 2. 1287. [Such is the proper sense of the word, though now used for the play itself.]—F. *pantomime,* 'an actor of many parts in one play,' &c.; Cot.—L. *pantomīmus.*—Gk. παντόμιμος, all imitating, a pantomimic actor.—Gk. παντο-, decl. stem of πᾶς, all; and μῖμος, an imitator, from μιμέομαι, I imitate. See **Pan-** and **Mimic. Der.** *pantomim-ic, pantomim-ist.*

PANTRY, a room for provisions. (F.—L.) ME. *pantrye, pantrie;* Prompt. Parv.—OF. *paneterie,* 'a pantry;' Cot.—Late L. *pānētāria, pānitāria,* a place where bread is made (hence, where it is kept); Ducange.—Late L. *panēta,* one who makes bread.—L. *pān-,* base of *pānis,* bread. Cf. Skt. *pā,* to nourish. **Der.** from the same base, *pann-ier, com-pan-y, ap-pan-age.*

PAP (1), food for infants. (E.) 'An Englishe infant, whiche liuethe with *pappe*;' Hall's Chron. Hen. VI, an. 3. §6. The ME. *pappe* is only found in the sense of 'breast;' we have, however, '*papmete* for chylder,' Prompt. Parv. p. 382. To be considered as an E. word, and perhaps of considerable antiquity, though seldom written down. β. Of imitative origin, due to a repetition of the syllable *pa.* 'Words formed of the simplest articulations, *ma* and *pa,* are used to designate the objects in which the infant takes the earliest interest, the mother and father, the mother's breast, the act of taking or sucking food;' Wedgwood.—Du. *pap,* 'pap sod with milke or flower;' Hexham; G. *pappe,* pap, paste.—L. *pāpa, pappa,* the word with which infants call for food. Cf. Dan. *pap,* Swed. *papp,* pasteboard; also Span. *papa,* Ital. *pappa,* pap, from L. *pappa.* This is one of those words of expressive origin which are not necessarily affected by Grimm's law. See **Pap** (2), **Papa.**

PAP (2), a teat, breast. (E.) ME. *pappe,* Havelok, 2132; Ormulum, 6441. Probably a native word; see **Pap** (1). Cf. MSwed. *papp,* the breast; which, as Ihre notes, was afterwards changed to *patt.* Still preserved in Swed. *patt,* the breast. So also Dan. *patte,* suck, *give patte,* to give suck. The Swedish dialects retain the old form *pappe, papp* (Rietz). So also NFriesic *pap, pape, papke* (Outzen); Lithuan. *pápas,* the pap. β. Doubtless ultimately the same word as the preceding; and due to the infant's cry for food.

PAPA, a child's word for father. (F.—L.) Seldom written down; found in Swift, in Todd's Johnson (without a reference, but it occurs in his Directions for Servants, 1745, p. 13): 'where there are little masters and misses in a house, bribe them, that they may not tell tales to *papa* and mamma.' Spelt *pappa* by Steele in The Spectator, no. 479, § 4 (1712). Whilst admitting that the word might easily have been coined from the repetition of the syllable *pa* by infants, and probably was so in the first instance, we have no proof that the word is truly of *native* origin; the native word from this source took rather the form of *pap;* see **Pap** (1) and **Pap** (2). In the sense of father, we may rather look upon it as merely borrowed. —F. *papa,* papa; in Molière, Malade Imaginaire, i. 5 (Littré); spelt *pappa* in 1552 (Hatzfeld).—L. *pāpa,* found as a Roman cognomen. Cf. L. *pappas,* a tutor, borrowed from Gk. πάππας, papa. Nausicaa addresses her father as πάππα φίλε = dear papa; Homer, Od. vi. 57. See **Pope.**

PAPAL, belonging to the pope. (F.—L.—Gk.) ME. *papal, papall,* Gower, C. A. i. 257; bk. ii. 2925.—F. *papal,* 'papall;' Cot.—Late L. *pāpālis,* belonging to the pope.—L. *pāpa,* a bishop, spiritual father. See **Pope. Der.** *pap-ac-y,* ME. *papacie,* Gower, C. A. i. 256; bk. ii. 2895, from Late L. *pāpatia,* papal dignity, formed from *pāpat-,* stem of *pāpas, pappas,* borrowed from Gk. πάππας, papa, father. Also *pap-ist,* All's Well, i. 3. 56, from F. *pape,* pope; the word *pap-ism* occurs in Bale's Apology, p. 83 (R.); *pap-ist-ic, pap-ist-ic-al, pap-ist-ic-al-ly.*

PAPAW, a fruit. (Span.—WIndian.) 'The fair *papà*;' Waller, Battle of the Summer Islands, i. 52.—Span. *papaya* (Pineda).— Cuban *papaya* (Oviedo, qu. by Littré); from the Carib *ababai,* explained by 'grosses papaye' (sic) in R. Breton, Dict. Caraibe-François (Auxerre, 1665).

PAPER, the substance chiefly used for writing on. (F.—L.—Gk. —Egyptian.) ME. *paper,* Gower, C.A. ii. 8; bk.iv.198. Chaucer has *paper-white* = as white as paper; Legend of Good Women, 1198.— OF. (and F.) *papier.*—L. *papȳrum,* acc. of *papȳrus,* paper. See **Papyrus. Der.** *paper-faced,* 2 Hen. IV, v. 4. 12; *paper-mill,* 3 Hen. VI, iv. 7. 41; *paper,* adj., *paper,* vb., *paper-ing; paper-hangings, paper-hang-er, paper-money, paper-reed,* Isaiah, xix. 7, *paper-stainer;* and see *papier-mâché.*

PAPIER-MÂCHÉ, paper made into pulp, then moulded, dried, and japanned. (F.—L.) First in 1753. F. *papier-mâché,* lit. chewed paper. The F. *papier* is from L. *papȳrus;* and *mâché* is the pp. of *mâcher,* OF. *mascher,* from L. *masticāre,* to masticate. See **Paper** and **Masticate.**

PAPILIONACEOUS, having a winged corolla somewhat like a butterfly. (L.) Botanical; in Glossographia Nova (1719). Used of the bean, pea, &c.—L. **papilionāceus,* a coined word from *papiliōn-,* stem of *papilio,* a butterfly. See **Pavilion.**

PAPILLARY, belonging to or resembling the nipples or teats. (L.) In 1667; see examples in Todd's Johnson; Phillips, ed. 1706, gives the sb. *papilla,* a teat or nipple.—L. *papilla,* a small pustule, nipple, teat; dimin. of *papula,* a pustule. Again, *papula* is a dimin. from a base PAP, to blow out or swell. Cf. Lithuan. *pápas,* a teat, *pampti,* to swell, Gk. πομφός, a bubble, blister on the skin. See Prellwitz. s. v. πέμφιξ. **Der.** *papul-ous,* full of pimples; from *papula.*

PAPYRUS, the reed whence paper was first made. (L.—Gk.— Egyptian.) In Holland, tr. of Pliny, b. xiii. c. 11 [not 21].—L. *papȳrus.*—Gk. πάπυρος, an Egyptian kind of rush or flag, of which writing-paper was made by cutting its inner rind (βύβλος) into strips, and pressing them together transversely. The word is not Gk., but of Egyptian origin. See **Bible.**

PAR, equal value, equality of real and nominal value or of condition. (L.) 'To be at par, to be equal;' Phillips, ed. 1706.—L. *pār,* equal. **Der.** *pari-ty,* q.v.; also *pair, peer* (1), *ap-par-el, compeer, disparage, disparity, non-pareil, prial, umpire.*

PARA-, beside; prefix. (Gk.) A common prefix.—Gk. παρά-, beside. Allied to Skt. *parā,* away, from, forth, towards, *param,* beyond, *parē,* thereupon, further, *paratas,* further, &c. Also to E. *far;* see **Far.**

PARABLE, a comparison, fable, allegory. (F.—L.—Gk.) ME. *parable,* Chaucer, C. T. 6261 (D 679); Wyclif, Mark, iv. 2.—OF. *parabole,* 'a parable;' Cot.—L. *parabola,* Mark, iv. 2.—Gk. παραβολή, a comparison; also a parable, Mark, iv. 2.—Gk. παραβάλλειν, to throw beside, set beside, compare.—Gk. παρά, beside; and βάλλειν, to throw, cast. Brugmann, ii. § 713. **Doublets,** *parle* (old form of *parley*), *parole, palaver;* also *parabola,* as a mathematical term, from L. *parabola,* Gk. παραβολή, the conic section made by a plane *parallel* to a side of the cone. Hence *parabol-ic, parabol-ic-al, parabol-ic-al-ly.* And see *parley, parole, palaver.*

PARACHUTE, an apparatus like an umbrella for breaking the fall from a balloon. (F.—L.) Modern; borrowed from F. *parachute,* coined from *para-,* as in *para-sol,* and *chute;* lit. that which parries or guards against a fall. *Para-* represents Ital. *para-* (see **Parasol, Parapet**), from Ital. *parare*, to adorn, to guard; and *chute*, a fall, is all.ed to Ital. *caduto*, fallen, from L. *cadere*, to fall.

PARACLETE, the Comforter. (L.—Gk.) 'Braggynge Winchester, the Pope's *paraclete* in England;' Bale, Image, pt. iii (R.).—L. *paraclētus.*—Gk. παράκλητος, called to one's aid, a helper, the Comforter (John, xiv. 16).—Gk. παρακαλεῖν, to call to one's aid, summon.—Gk. παρά, beside; and καλεῖν, to call. See **Para-** and **Calendar.**

PARADE, show, display. (F.—Span.—L.) In Milton, P. L. iv. 780.—F. *parade*, 'a boasting appearance, or shew, also, a stop on horseback;' Cot. The last sense was the earliest in French (Littré).—Span. *parada*, a halt, stop, pause.—Span. *parar*, to stop, halt; a particular restriction of the sense 'to get ready' or 'prepare.'—L. *parāre*, to prepare, get ready. β. The sense of 'display' in F. was easily communicated to Span. *parada*, because F. *parer* (=Span. *parar*) meant 'to deck, trimme, adorn, dress,' as well as 'to ward or defend a blow' (which comes near the Spanish use); see Cotgrave. See **Pare.**

PARADIGM, an example, model. (F.—L.—Gk.) Philips, ed. 1658, gives *paradigme*, the F. form.—F. *paradigme* (Littré).—L. *paradigma.*—Gk. παράδειγμα, a pattern, model; in grammar, an example of declension, &c.—Gk. παραδείκνυμι, I exhibit, lit. show by the side of.—Gk. παρά, beside; and δείκνυμι, I point out. See **Para-** and **Diction.**

PARADISE, the garden of Eden, heaven. (F.—L.—Gk.—Pers.) In very early use; in Layamon, l. 24122.—F. *paradis*, 'paradise;' Cot.—L. *paradīsus.*—Gk. παράδεισος, a park, pleasure-ground; an Oriental word in Xenophon, Hell. 4. 1. 15, Cyr. 1. 3. 14, &c., and used in the Septuagint version for the garden of Eden. See Gen. ii. 8 (LXX version); Luke, xxiii. 43 (Gk.). Cf. Heb. *pardēs*, a garden, paradise. β. Of Pers. origin, the Heb. word being merely borrowed, and having no Heb. root.—Zend *pairidaēza*, an enclosure, place walled in.—Zend *pairi* (=Gk. περί), around; and *diz* (Skt. *dih*), to mould, form, shape (hence to form a wall of earth); from √DHEIGH; see **Dough.** γ. It appears in other forms; cf. mod. Pers. and Arab. *firdaus*, a garden, paradise, Palmer's Pers. Dict. col. 451, Rich. Dict. p. 1080; pl. *farādīs*, paradises, Rich. Dict. p. 1075. For the Zend form, see Justi. And see Max Müller, Selected Essays, 1881; i. 130. Doublet, *parvis.*

PARADOX, that which is contrary to received opinion; strange, but true. (F.—L.—Gk.) In Ben Jonson, Cynthia's Revels, A. ii. sc. 1 (Amorphus' second speech). Spelt *paradoxe* in Minsheu, ed. 1627.—F. *paradoxe*, 'a paradox;' Cot.—L. *paradoxum*, neut. of *paradoxus*, adj.—Gk. παράδοξος, contrary to opinion, strange.—Gk. παρά, beside; and δόξα, a notion, opinion, from δοκεῖν, to seem. See **Para-** and **Dogma.** Der. *paradox-ical, paradox-ic-al-ly*, Sidney, Apologie for Poetrie, ed. Arber, p. 51, l. 6 from bottom; *paradox-ic-al-ness.*

PARAFFINE, a solid substance resembling spermaceti, produced by distillation of coal. (F.—L.) 'First obtained by Reichenbach in 1830;' Haydn, Dict. of Dates. It is remarkable for resisting chemical action, having little affinity for other bodies; whence its name.—F. *paraffine*, having small affinity. Coined from L. *par-um*, adv., little; and *affinis*, akin, having affinity. See **Affinity.**

PARAGOGE, the addition of a letter at the end of a word. (L.—Gk.) In Glossographia Nova (1719). Examples are common in English; thus in *soun-d, ancien-t, whils-t, tyran-t*, the final letter is paragogic. The word has 4 syllables, the final *e* being sounded.—L. *paragōgē.*—Gk. παραγωγή, a leading by or past, alteration, variety.—Gk. παράγειν, to lead by or past.—Gk. παρ-ά, beside, beyond; and ἄγειν, to lead, drive, cognate with L. *agere*. See **Para-** and **Agent.** Der. *paragog-ic, paragog-ic-al.*

PARAGON, a model of excellence. (F.—Ital.—Gk.) In Shak. Temp. ii. 1. 75; Hamlet, ii. 2. 320.—F. *paragon*, 'a paragon, or peerlesse one;' Cot. [MSpan. *paragon*, a model of excellence.]—Ital. *paragone*, 'a paragon, a match, an equal, a touch-stone,' Florio; *paragonare*, to compare. The latter answers to Gk. παρακονάειν, to rub against a whetstone (hence, probably, to try by a whetstone, to compare).—Gk. παρ-ά, beside; ἀκόνη, a whetstone, allied to ἀκίς, a sharp point. (√AK.) See Körting, § 6859; Tobler, in Zt. für roman. Philol. iv. 373. Der. *paragon*, vb., Oth. ii. 1. 62.

PARAGRAPH, a distinct portion of a discourse; a short passage of a work. (F.—L.—Gk.) In Minsheu, ed. 1627. But the word was in rather early use, and was corrupted in various ways, into *pargrafte, pylcrafte* (by change of *r* to *l*), and finally into *pilcrow* or *pyllcrow. 'Pylcrafte*, yn a booke, *paragraphus*;' Prompt. Parv. p. 398; see Way's note for further examples. Even the sign ¶, which was used to mark the beginning of a paragraph, was called a *pilcrow*; see Tusser's Husbandry, A Lesson, &c., st. 3.—F. *paragraphe*, 'a paragraffe, or pillcrow;' Cot.—Late L. *paragraphum*, acc. of *para-*

graphus, occurring in the Prompt. Parv., as above.—Gk. παράγραφος, a line or stroke drawn in the margin, lit. 'that which is written beside.'—Gk. παρά, beside; and γράφειν, to write. See **Para-** and **Graphic.** Der. *paragraph-ic, paragraph-ic-al.*

PARAKEET; the same as **Paraquito**, q. v.

PARALLAX, the difference between the real and apparent place of a star. &c. (Gk.) In Milton, P. R. iv. 40; and Ben Jonson has 'no *parallax* at all,' i. e. no variation; Magnetic Lady, Act i. But since Milton's time, the word has acquired special senses; he may have used it for 'refraction.'—Gk. παράλλαξις, alternation, change; also, the inclination of two lines forming an angle, esp. the angle formed by lines from a heavenly body to the earth's centre and the horizon.—Gk. παραλλάσσειν, to make things alternate.—Gk. παρά, beside; and ἀλλάσσειν, to change, alter, from ἄλλος, other, cognate with L. *alius*. See **Para-** and **Alien.** See **Parallel.**

PARALLEL, side by side, similar. (F.—L.—Gk.) In Shak. Oth. ii. 3. 355.—MF. *parallele*, 'paralell;' Cot.—L. *parallēlus.*—Gk. παράλληλος, parallel, side by side.—Gk. παρ' for παρά, beside; and *ἄλληλος, one another, only found in the gen., dat., and acc. plural. β. The decl. stem ἀλλ-ηλο- stands for ἀλλ' ἄλλο, a reduplicated form; hence the sense is 'the other the other,' or 'one another,' i.e. mutual. Ἄλλος is cognate with L. *alius*, other. See **Para-** and **Alien.** Der. *parallel*, sb., Temp. i. 2. 74; *parallel*, vb., Macb. ii. 3. 67; *parallel-ism*; also *parallelo-gram*, q. v., *parallelo-piped*, q. v.

PARALLELOGRAM, a four-sided rectilineal figure, whose opposite sides are parallel. (F.—L.—Gk.) In Cotgrave.—OF. *paralelogramme*, 'a paralelogram, or long square;' Cot. [He uses only two *l*'s.]—L. *parallēlogrammum*, a parallelogram.—Gk. παραλληλόγραμμον, a parallelogram; neut. of παραλληλόγραμμος, adj., bounded by parallel lines.—Gk. παράλληλο-, for παράλληλος, parallel; and γραμμή, a stroke, line, from γράφειν, to write. See **Parallel** and **Graphic.**

PARALLELOPIPED, a regular solid bounded by six plane parallel surfaces. (L.—Gk.) Sometimes written *parallelopipedon*, which is nearer the Gk. form. In Phillips, ed. 1706. A glaring instance of bad spelling, as it certainly should be *parallelepiped* (with ε, not ο).—L. *parallēlepipedum*, used by Boethius (Lewis).—Gk. παραλληλεπίπεδον, a body with parallel surfaces.—Gk. παράλληλ', for παράλληλος, parallel; and ἐπίπεδον, a plane surface. The form ἐπίπεδον is neut. of ἐπίπεδος, on the ground, flat, level, plane; from ἐπί, upon, and πέδον, the ground. The Gk. πέδον is from the same root as πούς (gen. ποδ-ός), the foot, and E. *foot*. See **Parallel, Epi-,** and **Foot.**

PARALOGISM, a conclusion unwarranted by the premises. (F.—L.—Gk.) In Minsheu, ed. 1627.—F. *paralogisme*, cited by Minsheu.—L. *paralogismus.*—Gk. παραλογισμός, a false reckoning, false conclusion, fallacy.—Gk. παραλογίζομαι, I misreckon, count amiss.—Gk. παρά, beside; and λογίζομαι, I reckon, from λόγος, a discourse, account, reason. See **Para-** and **Logic.**

PARALYSE, to render useless, deaden. (F.—L.—Gk.) Modern; added by Todd to Johnson's Dict. Todd cites: 'Or has taxation chill'd the aguish land And *paralysed* Britannia's bounteous hand?' London Cries, or Pict. of Tumult, 1805, p. 39.—F. *paralyser*, to paralyse; Littré. Formed from the sb. *paralysie*, palsy; see further under **Paralysis.**

PARALYSIS, palsy. (L.—Gk.) In Blount, ed. 1656.—L. *paralysis.*—Gk. παράλυσις, a loosening aside, a disabling of the nerves, paralysis.—Gk. παραλύειν, to loose from the side, loose beside, relax.—Gk. παρά, beside; and λύειν, to loosen. See **Para-** and **Lose.** Der. *paralyt-ic*, from F. *paralytique* (Cot.), which from L. *paralyticus* < Gk. παραλυτικός, afflicted with palsy (Matt. iv. 24). Doublet, *palsy.*

PARAMATTA, a fabric like merino, of worsted and cotton. (New S. Wales.) So named from *Paramatta*, a town near Sydney, New South Wales. Also *Parramatta*, on a river of the same name. Said to mean 'plenty of eels;' others explain it from *para*, fish, and *matta*, water. See Morris, Austral English.

PARAMOUNT, chief, of the highest importance. (F.—L.) In Minsheu, ed. 1627. He also gives *paravail*, the term used in contrast with it. A lord *paramount* is supreme, esp. as compared with his tenant *paravail*, i.e. his inferior. 'Let him [the pope] no longer count himselfe lord *paramount* ouer the princes of the world, no longer hold kings as his seruants *parauaile*;' Hooker, A Discourse of Justification (R.). Neither words are properly adjectives, but adverbial phrases; they correspond respectively to OF. *par amont*, at the top (lit. by that which is upwards), and *par aval* (lit. by that which is downwards). Both are AF. phrases of law; see Blount's Law Lexicon. The prep. *par* = L. *per*; see **Per-,** prefix. The F. *amont* is explained under **Amount**; and F. *aval* under **Avalanche.** Der. *paramount*, sb., Milton, P. L. ii. 508.

PARAMOUR, a lover, one beloved, now usually in a bad sense. (F. – L.) In Chaucer, C. T. 6036 (D 454). But orig. an adverbial phrase, as in : ' For *par amour* I louede hire first or thou ;' id. C. T. 1157 (A 1155). – F. *par amour*, by love, with love. – L. *per*, by, with ; and *amōrem*, acc. of *amor*, love. See **Per-** and **Amour**.

PARAPET, a rampart, esp. one breast-high. (F. – Ital. – L.) In Shak. 1 Hen. IV, ii. 3. 55. – F. *parapet*, ' a parapet, or wall breast-high ;' Cot. – Ital. *parapetto*, ' a cuirace, a breast-plate, a fence for the breast or hart ; also, a parapet or wall breast-high ;' Florio. Lit. ' breast-defence.' – Ital. *para-*, for *parare*, ' to adorne, . . . to warde or defende a blow,' Florio ; and *petto*, the breast. – L. *parāre*, to prepare, adorn ; and *pectus*, the breast. See **Parry** and **Pectoral**.

PARAPHERNALIA, ornaments, trappings. (L. – Gk.) Properly used of the property which a bride possesses beyond her dowry. ' In one particular instance the wife may acquire a property in some of her husband's goods ; which shall remain to her after his death, and not go to his executors. These are called her *paraphernalia*, which is a term borrowed from the civil law ; it is derived from the Greek language, signifying *over and above her dower* ;' Blackstone's Commentaries, b. ii. c. 29 (R.). Formed from Late L. *paraphern-a*, the property of a bride over and above her dower, by adding *-ālia*, the neut. pl. form of the common suffix *-ālis*. – Gk. παράφερνα, that which a bride brings beyond her dower. – Gk. παρά, beyond, beside ; and φερνή, a dowry, lit. that which is brought by the wife, from φέρειν, to bring, cognate with E. *bear*. See **Para-** and **Bear** (1).

PARAPHRASE, an explanation or free translation. (F. – L. – Gk.) See Udall's translation of Erasmus' *Paraphrase* vpon the Newe Testamente,' 2 vols. folio, 1548–9. – MF. *paraphrase*, ' a paraphrase ;' Cot. – L. *paraphrasin*, acc. of *paraphrasis*. – Gk. παράφρασις, a paraphrase. – Gk. παραφράζειν, to speak in addition, amplify, paraphrase. – Gk. παρά, beside ; and φράζειν, to speak. See **Para-** and **Phrase**. Der. *paraphrase*, vb., in Dryden, Cymon, l. 21 ; *paraphrast*, one who paraphrases, Gk. παραφραστής ; *paraphrast-ic*, *paraphrast-ic-al*, *paraphrast-ic-al-ly*.

PARAQUITO, a little parrot. (Span. – L. – Gk.) In Shak. 1 Hen. IV, ii. 3. 88 ; pl. *paraquitoes*, Ford, Sun's Darling, A. i. sc. 1. – Span. *periquito*, a paroquet, small parrot ; dimin. of *perico*, a parrot. β. Prob. the same as *Perico*, a pet-name for ' little Peter ;' see Pineda ; a dimin. from *Pedro*, Peter. See **Parrot**.

PARASANG, a distance of over three miles. (L. – Gk. – Pers.) ' Persian myles cauled *Parasange* ;' R. Eden, ed. Arber, p. 342. From L. *parasanga* (Lewis). – Gk. παρασάγγης ; of Pers. origin. Mod. Pers. *farsang*, *ferseng*, a league (Horn, § 818). See Notes on E. Etym., p. 206.

PARASITE, one who frequents another's table, a hanger-on. (F. – L. – Gk.) In Shak. Rich. II, ii. 2. 70. – F. *parasite*, ' a parasite, a trencher-friend, smell-feast ;' Cot. – L. *parasitus*. – Gk. παράσιτος, eating beside another at his table, a parasite, toad-eater. – Gk. παρά, beside ; and σῖτος, wheat, flour, bread, food, of unknown origin. ¶ The invidious use of the word is unoriginal ; see Liddell. Der. *parasit-ic*, from Gk. παρασιτικός ; *parasit-ic-al*.

PARASOL, a small umbrella used to keep off the heat of the sun. (F. – Ital. – L.) ' Upon another part of the wall is the like figure of another great man, over whose head one officer holds a *parasol* ;' Sir T. Herbert, Travels, ed. 1665, p. 153. – F. *parasol*, ' an umbrella ;' Cot. – Ital. *parasole*, an umbrella (Torriano). – Ital. *para-*, for *parare*, to ward off, parry ; and *sole*, the sun. See **Parry** and **Solar**. We find also Span. *parasol*, Port. *parasol*. ¶ Of similar formation is F. *para-pluie*, a guard against rain, an umbrella, from *pluie*, rain, L. *pluuia*.

PARBOIL, to boil thoroughly. (F. – L.) It now means ' to boil in part,' or insufficiently, from a notion that it is made up of *part* and *boil*. Formerly, it meant ' to boil thoroughly,' as in Ben Jonson, Every Man, iv. 1. 16 (ed. Wheatley) ; on which see Wheatley's note. ' To parboyle, *præcoquere* ;' Levins. ' My liver's *par-boil'd*,' i. e. burnt up ; Webster, White Devil, near the end. ME. *parboilen* ; ' Parboylyd, parbullitus ; Parboylyn mete, semibullio, parbullio ;' Prompt. Parv. Here the use of *semibullio* shows that the word was misunderstood at an early time. – OF. *parboillir*, to cook thoroughly, also to boil gently (Godefroy) ; Cotgrave has : ' *pour-bouillir*, to parboile throughly.' – Late L. *parbullīre* (as in the Prompt. Parv.) ; L. *perbullīre*, to boil thoroughly. See **Per-** and **Boil** (1). ☞ For a somewhat similar change in sense, see **Purblind**.

PARCEL, a small part, share, division, small package. (F. – L.) ME. *parcel*, P. Plowman, B. x. 63 ; *parcelle*, Rob. of Brunne, tr. of Langtoft, p. 135, l. 13. The old sense is ' portion.' – F. *parcelle*, ' a parcell, particle, piece, little part ;' Cot. Cf. Port. *parcela*, an article of an account. Formed from Late L. *particella*, preserved in Ital. *particella*, a small portion, a word given in Florio ; a dimin. of the true L. form *particula* ; see **Particle**. Der. *parcel*, vb.

PARCENER, a co-heir. (F. – L.) A law term ; see Blackstone, Comment. II. xi. The old spelling of **Partner**, q. v.

PARCH, to scorch. (F. – L. – Gk.?) ME. *parchen*, *paarchen*. ' *Paarche* pecyn or benys [= to parch peas or beans], frigo, ustillo ;' Prompt. Parv. [Assimilated in form to the ME. *parchen*, to pierce, an occasional form of *percen*, to pierce (F. *percer*) ; see **Pierce**. ' A knyghte . . . *perchede* the syde of Iesu ;' Religious Pieces, ed. Perry (E. E. T. S.), p. 42 ; see another example in Halliwell, s. v. *perche* ; and cf. *perche*, to pierce, Cathol. Anglicum, p. 276. *Persaunt*, lit. piercing, was used as an epithet of sunbeams ; Lydgate, Compl. of Black Knight, l. 28, has : ' Til fyry Tytan, with his *persaunt hete*.' The prov. E. *pearch* means ' to pierce with cold ;' cf. Milton, P. L. ii. 594. – F. (Norm. dial. and Picard) *percher*, to pierce (Moisy, Corblet) ; cf. Walloon *percher*, to pierce (Sigart) ; variant of F. *percer* ; see **Pierce**.] β. But the sense of *percher* seems too remote. I suggest that ME. *parchen* really meant ' to dry or harden like parchment,' and was formed from OF. *parche*, a familiar contraction for *parchment* ; of which we have sufficient evidence. ' Or est issuz Noe de l'arche, Si con gel truis escrit el *parche*,' then Noah went out of the ark, As I find it written in the parchment ; Bartsch, Chrestomathie, 1887, col. 309, l. 15 ; whence Span. *parche*, the parchment end of a drum, and (probably) Rouchi *parche*, a page of a book (Hécart). In a Vocabulaire du Haut Maine, by C. R. de M. (Paris, 1859), we are told that a pea that is elsewhere called *pois sans parchemin* is there called *pois sans parche*. Compare with this the earliest example of the E. verb in 1398 :– ' Saresines put peper into an ouen whan if is new igadered and *percheth* and rostith it so, and benemeth [take away] the vertu of burginge and of springinge,' i. e. of sprouting.

PARCHMENT, the skin of a sheep or goat prepared for writing on. (F. – L. – Gk.) The *t* is excrescent. ME. *perchemin*, *parchemyn* ; P. Plowman, B. xiv. 191, 193. – F. *parchemin*, parchment. – L. *pergamīna*, *pergamēna*, parchment ; orig. fem. of *Pergamēnus*, adj., belonging to Pergamos. [Parchment was invented by Eumenes, of Pergamus, the founder of the celebrated library at Pergamus, about 190 B.C. ; Haydn.] – Gk. περγαμηνή, parchment ; from the city of Pergamos in Asia, where it was brought into use by Crates of Mallos, when Ptolemy cut off the supply of biblus from Egypt (Liddell and Scott). Crates flourished about B. C. 160. Either way, the etymology is clear. – Gk. Πέργαμος, more commonly Πέργαμον, Pergamus, in Mysia of Asia Minor ; now called *Bergamo*.

PARD, a panther, leopard, spotted wild beast. (L. – Gk.) ME. *pard*, Wyclif, Rev. xiii. 2. – L. *pardus*, a male panther ; Rev. xiii. 2 (Vulgate). – Gk. πάρδος, a pard ; used for a leopard, panther, or ounce. An Eastern word ; cf. Pers. *pārs*, *pārsh*, a pard ; *pars*, a panther, Rich. Dict. pp. 316, 325 ; Skt. *pṛdāku-*, a leopard. Der. *leo-pard*, *camelo-pard*.

PARDON, to forgive. (F. – L.) Common in Shakespeare. Rich. quotes ' nor *pardoned* a riche man' from the Golden Boke, c. 47. But the verb first appears in 1430, being formed (in English) from the ME. sb. *pardoun*, *pardun*, *pardon*, a common word, occurring in Chaucer, C. T. 12860 (C 926). And see Chaucer's description of the *Pardonere*, l. 689. – F. *pardon*, sb., due to *pardonner*, vb., to pardon. – Late L. *perdōnāre*, to remit a debt (used A. D. 819), to grant, indulge, pardon. – L. *per*, thoroughly ; and *dō . . are*, to give, from *dōnum*, a gift. See **Per-** and **Donation**. Der. *pardon*, sb. (but see above) ; *pardon-er*, *pardon-able*, *pardon-abl-y*.

PARE, to cut or shave off. (F. – L.) ME. *paren*. ' To wey pens with a peys and *pare* the heuyest' = to weigh pence with a weight, and pare down the heaviest ; P. Plowman, B. v. 243. – F. *parer*, ' to deck, trimme, . . . also to pare the hoofe of a horse ;' Cot. – L. *parāre*, to prepare. Der. *par-ing*. From L. *parāre* we have *com-pare*, *pre-pare*, *re-pair* (1), *se-par-ate*, *sever*, *em-per-or*, *im-per-ial*, *ap-par-at-us*, *para-chute*, *para-pet*, *para-sol*, *rampart*, &c. And see **Parry**, **Parade**.

PAREGORIC, assuaging pain ; a medicine that assuages pain. (L. – Gk.) ' *Paregorica*, medicines that comfort, mollify, and asswage ;' Phillips, ed. 1706. – L. *parēgoricus*, assuaging ; whence neut. pl. *paregorica*. – Gk. παρηγορικός, addressing, encouraging, soothing. – Gk. παρήγορος, addressing, encouraging ; cf. παρηγορεῖν, to address, exhort. – Gk. παρά, beside ; and ἀγορά, an assembly. Cf. Gk. ἀγείρειν, to assemble ; and **Gregarious**.

PARENT, a father or mother. (F. – L.) In the Geneva Bible, 1561, Ephes. vi. 1 (R.). – F. *parent*, ' a cousin, kinsman, allie ;' Cot. – L. *parentem*, acc. of *parens*, a parent, lit. one who produces, formed from *parere*, to produce, of which the usual pres. part. is *pariens*. Brugmann, i. § 515. Der. *parent-al*, from L. *parentālis* ; *parent-al-ly*, *parent-less* ; also *parent-age*, in Levins, from F. *parentage*, ' parentage,' Cot.

PARENTHESIS, a phrase inserted in another which would appear complete without it. (Gk.) Spelt *parentesis*, T. Heywood, Love's Mistris, Act i (last word). And in Cotgrave, to translate

MF. *parenthese.*—Gk. παρένθεσις, a putting in beside, insertion, parenthesis.—Gk. παρ', for παρά, beside; ἐν, in; and θέσις, a placing, from √DHĒ, to place, set. See **Para-, In-,** and **Thesis. Der.** *parenthet-ic,* extended from Gk. παρένθετος, put in beside, parenthetic; *parenthet-ic-al, -ly.*

PARERGON, an incidental or subsidiary work. (L.—Gk.) L. *parergon* (Pliny).—Gk. πάρεργον, a by-work, subordinate work; neut. of πάρεργος, subordinate.—Gk. παρ-, for παρ-ά, beside; and ἐργόν, a work, cognate with E. *work.*

PARGET, to plaister a wall. (F.—L.) Nearly obsolete; once rather common. In Levins, Baret, Palsgrave, &c. ME. *pargeten.* 'Pargetyn walles, Gipso, linio (sic); *Parget,* or *playster for wallys,* Gipsum, litura;' Prompt. Parv., and see Way's note. It is frequently spelt *perget.*—OF. *pargeter,* to scatter (Chanson du Roland, 2634); variant of Norm. dial. *projeter,* to re-plaster (cf. *projet,* plaster); see Moisy; also spelt (in OF.) *porgeter,* to roughcast a wall (Godefroy). [Cf. Walloon *porgeté,* to parget (Remacle).]—L. *prōiectāre,* to cast forth.—L. *prō,* forth; and *iactāre,* to cast. See **Pro-** and **Jet** (1). ¶ The form *pargeter* gave rise to a Late L. *periactāre;* cf 'Perjacio, Anglice, to perjette;' Vocab. 602. 7. See my Notes on E. Etym., p. 206.

PARHELION, a mock sun, a bright light sometimes seen near the sun. (L.—Gk.) Spelt *parhelium* and *parelium* in Phillips, ed. 1706.—L. *parēlion* (Lewis).—Gk. παρήλιον, a parhelion; neut. of παρήλιος, adj., beside the sun.—Gk. παρ', for παρά, beside; and ἥλιος, the sun. See **Para-** and **Heliacal.** ¶ The insertion of *h* is due to the aspirate in ἥλιος; it hardly seems to be needed.

PARIAH, an outcast. (Tamil.) Spelt *paria* in the story called The Indian Cottage, where it occurs frequently. From 'Tamil *paṛaiyan,* commonly, but corruptly, *pariah,* Malayālim *parayan,* a man of a low caste, performing the lowest menial services; one of his duties is to beat the village drum (called *paṛai* in Tamil), whence, no doubt, the generic appellation of the caste;' H. H. Wilson, Glossary of Indian Terms, p. 401.

PARIAN, belonging to Paros. (Gk.) *Paros* is an island in the Ægean sea.

PARIETAL, forming the sides or walls, esp. applied to two bones in the fore part of the scull. (L.) In Phillips, ed. 1706.—L. *parietālis,* belonging to a wall.—L. *pariet-,* stem of *pariēs,* a wall. **Der.** *pellitory* (1), q.v.

PARISH, a district under one pastor, an ecclesiastical district. (F.—L.—Gk.) Orig. an ecclesiastical division. ME. *parisshe,* Chaucer, C. T. 493 (A 491).—AF. *parosse,* Laws of Will. I., i. 1; F. *paroisse,* a parish.—L. *parochia,* late form of *parœcia,* a parish, orig. an ecclesiastical district.—Gk. παροικία, an ecclesiastical district, lit. a neighbourhood.—Gk. πάροικος, neighbouring, living near together.—Gk. παρ', for παρά, beside, near; and οἶκος, a house, abode, cognate with L. *uīcus.* See **Para-** and **Vicinage. Der.** *parish-ion-er,* formed by adding -*er* to ME. *parisshen,* P. Plowman, B. xi. 67; this ME. *parisshen*<OF. *paroissien*<Late L. *parochiānus,* with the same sense as (and a mere variant of) L. *parochiālis;* see **Parochial.** Also *paroch-i-al.* ☞ It follows that *parishioner* should rather have been spelt *parishener;* also that the suffix -*er* was quite unnecessary. Indeed *Paroissien* survives as a proper name; I find it in the Clergy List, 1873.

PARITORY, the same as **Pellitory** (1).

PARITY, equality, resemblance, analogy. (F.—L.) In Cotgrave. —F. *parité,* 'parity;' Cot.—L. *paritātem,* acc. of *paritās,* equality.—L. *pari-,* decl. stem of *pār,* equal; with suffix -*tās.* See **Par.**

PARK, an enclosed ground. (E.) In early use; ME. *parc,* in Layamon, l. 1432 (later text). *Park*=OF. *parc,* is a F. spelling, and is found in F. as early as in the 12th century; but the word is of E. origin, being a contraction of ME. *parrok,* from AS. *pearruc,* *pearroc,* a word which is now also spelt *paddock.* See further under **Paddock** (2). We find also Irish and Gaelic *pairc,* W. *park* and *parwg* (the latter preserving the full suffix), all from E.; and Du. *perk,* Swed. and Dan. *park,* G. *pferch* (an enclosure, sheepfold); also F. *parc,* Ital. *parco,* Span. *parque,* all from a Late L. type *parricus,* *parcus,* an enclosure. β. The AS. *pearruc* and Late L. *parricus* are from a base **parr-,* which may be Teutonic, and possibly from an older base **sparr-.* We actually find ME. *parr-en,* to enclose, confine; Havelok, 2439; Iwain and Gawain, 3228 (ed. Ritson). Also AS. *sparrian,* to shut, fasten, as in *gesparrado dure δin,* thy door being shut, Matt. vi. 6 (Lindisfarne MS.). See **Spar. Der.** *park-ed,* 1 Hen. VI, iv. 2. 45; *park-er,* i.e. park-keeper (Levins); *park-keeper; im-park.*

PARLEY, a conference, treating with an enemy. (F.—L.—Gk.) 1. Shak. has *parley* as a sb., Macb. ii. 3. 87; also as a verb, Haml. i. 3. 123. Prob. for *parlee,* as spelt in Eng. Garner, ed. Arber, iii. 375; and in Decker, Seven Deadly Sins, ed. Arber, p. 32.—OF. *parlee,* sb. f. 'tour de parole;' Godefroy.—OF. *parlee,* pp. f. of

F. *parler,* vb., to speak. 2. Shak. also has the vb. *parle,* to speak, Lucrece, l. 100, whence the sb. *parle,* a parley, Haml. i. 1. 62. This is also from F. *parler.*—Late L. *parabolāre,* to discourse, talk.—Late L. *parabola,* a talk; L. *parabola,* a parable.—Gk. παραβολή, a parable; see **Parable. Der.** *parl-ance,* borrowed from F. *parlance,* formed from F. *parlant,* pres. part. of *parler;* *parl-ia-ment,* q.v., *parl-our,* q.v. And see *parole, palaver.*

PARLIAMENT, a meeting for consultation, deliberative assembly. (F.—L.—Gk.; with L. suffix.) ME. *parlement,* Havelok, 1006; Rob. of Glouc., p. 169, l. 3519; Chaucer, C.T. 2972 (A 2970). [The spelling *parliament* is due to Late L. *parliāmentum,* frequently used in place of *parlāmentum,* the better form.]—F. *parlement,* 'a speaking, parleying, also, a supreme court;' Cot. Formed with suffix -*ment* (=L. -*mentum*) from F. *parler,* to speak. See **Parley.** ¶ AF. *parlement,* Stat. Realm, i. 26 (1275); Late L. *parlāmentum,* Matt. Paris, p. 696 (under the date 1246); Late L. *parliāmentum,* Matt. Westminster, p. 352 (1253); see Stubbs, Select Charters, pt. vi. **Der.** *parliament-ar-y, parliament-ar-i-an.*

PARLOUR, a room for conversation, a sitting-room. (F.—L.—Gk.) ME. *parlour,* Chaucer, Troil. ii. 82; *parlur,* Ancren Riwle, p. 50, l. 17.—OF. *parleor,* later *parloir,* 'a parlour;' Cot.—F. *parl-er,* to speak, with suffix -*oir* (-*eor*)<L. -*ātōrium;* so that *parloir* answers to a Late L. **parabolātōrium,* a place to talk in; cf. ME. *dortour,* F. *dortoir*<*dormītōrium,* a place to sleep in. See further under **Parley.**

PARLOUS, old form of **Perilous.** (F.—L.) 'A parlous fear,' Mids. Nt. Dr. iii. 1. 14. See **Peril.**

PAROCHIAL, belonging to a parish. (L.—Gk.) In the Rom. of the Rose, 7687.—L. *parochiālis.*—L. *parochia,* another form of *parœcia,* a parish.—Gk. παροικία; see **Parish.**

PARODY, the alteration of a poem to another subject, a burlesque imitation. (L.—Gk.) 'Satiric poems, full of *parodies,* that is, of verses patched up from great poets, and turned into another sense than their author intended them;' Dryden, Discourse on Satire [on the Grecian *Silli*]; in Dryden's Poems, ed. 1851, p. 365.—L. *parōdia.*—Gk. παρῳδία, the same as παρῳδή, a song sung beside, a parody.—Gk. παρ', for παρά, beside; and ᾠδή, an ode. See **Para-** and **Ode. Der.** *parody,* verb; *parod-ist.*

PAROLE, a word, esp. a word of honour, solemn promise; a pass-word. (F.—L.—Gk.) In Blount's Gloss., ed. 1674.—F. *parole,* 'a word, a term, a saying;' Cot. The same word as Prov. *paraula* (Bartsch), Span. *palabra* (<*parabra*<*parabla,* by the frequent interchange of *r* and *l*), Port. *palavra;* all from Late L. *parabola,* a discourse, L. *parabola,* a parable. See further under **Parable.** Doublets, *parable, parle* (old form of *parley*), *palaver.*

PARONYMOUS, allied in origin; also, having a like sound, but a different origin. (Gk.) Rather a dubious word, as it is used in two senses, (1) allied in origin, as in the case of *man, manhood;* and (2) unallied in origin, but like-sounding, as in the case of *hair, hare.* —Gk. παρώνυμος, formed from a word by a slight change; i.e. in the former sense.—Gk. παρά, beside; and ὄνομα, a name, cognate with E. *name.* See **Para-** and **Name. Der.** *paronom-as-ia,* a slight change in the meaning of a word (in Dryden's pref. to Annus Mirabilis), from Gk. παρωνομασία, better παρονομασία. Also *paronyme,* i.e. a paronymous word, esp. in the second sense.

PAROXYSM, a fit of acute pain, a violent action. (F.—L.—Gk.) 'Paroxisme, the access or fit of an ague;' Minsheu.—F. *paroxisme,* 'the return, or fit, of an ague;' Cot.—L. *paroxysmus.*—Gk. παροξυσμός, irritation, the fit of a disease.—Gk. παροξύνειν, to urge on, provoke, irritate.—Gk. παρ', for παρά, beside; and ὀξύνειν, to sharpen, provoke, from ὀξύς, sharp. See **Para-** and **Oxygen. Der.** *paroxysm-al.*

PARQUETRY, a mosaic of wood-work for floors. (F.—Teut.) Modern.—F. *parqueterie.*—F. *parqueter,* to inlay a wooden floor.—F. *parquet,* a wooden floor; orig. a small enclosure; dimin. of F. *parc,* a park; see **Park.**

PARRAKEET; the same as **Paraquito,** q.v.

PARRICIDE, (1) the murderer of a father; (2) the murder of a father. (F.—L.) 1. The former is the older sense. Both senses occur in Shakespeare, (1) K. Lear, ii. 1. 48; (2) Macb. iii. 1. 32.— F. *parricide,* 'a parricide, a murtherer of his own father;' Cot.—L. *parricīda,* for an older form *pāricīdas* (Brugmann, ii. 190), a murderer of a relative.—L. *pāri-,* a relative (cf. Gk. πηός, a relative; Prellwitz, s.v. πάομαι); and -*cīdas,* older form of -*cīda,* i.e. a slayer, from *cīd-,* a stem of *cæd-ere* (pt. t. *ce-cīd-ī*), to cut, to slay. See **Cæsura.** 2. In the latter sense, it answers to L. *parricīdium,* the murder of a father; formed from the same sb. and vb. ¶ There is the same ambiguity about *fratricide* and *matricide.* **Der.** *parricid-al.*

PARROT, a well-known tropical bird, capable of imitating the human voice. (F.—L.—Gk.) In Shak. Merch. Ven. i. 1. 53. Spelt *parat* in Levins, ed. 1570; but *parrot* in Skelton; see his poem called

'Speke, Parrot.'—F. *perrot*, ' a man's proper name, being a diminutive or derivative of Pierre;' Cot. Cf. F. *perroquet*, ' a parrat,' Cot.; also spelt *parroquet*. β. The F. *Perrot* or *Pierrot* is still a name for a sparrow; much as *Philip* was the ME. name for the same bird. The F. *perroquet* was probably an imitation of, rather than directly borrowed from, the Span. *perichito*, which may likewise be explained as a derivative of Span. *perico*, meaning both ' a parrot' and ' little Peter,' dimin. of *Pedro*, Peter. γ. For the mod. Ital. *parrocchetto* we find in Florio the MItal. forms *parochetto*, *parochito*, ' a kind of parrats, called a *parokito*;' which seems to be nothing but the Span. word adapted to Italian. We may refer all the names to L. *Petrus*, Peter.—Gk. πέτρος, a stone, rock; as a proper name, Peter.

PARRY, a defensive movement, in fencing. (F.—L.) 'Parrying, in fencing, the action of saving a man's self, or staving off the strokes offered by another;' Bailey's Dict., vol. ii. ed. 1731. Older form *parree*, a fencing-bout; ' a *parree* of wit;' R. North, Examen, ed. 1740, p. 589 (Davies).—F. *parée*, used as equivalent to Ital. *parata*, a defence, guard; properly fem. pp. of *parer*, ' to deck, trick, trimme, . . also to ward or defend a blow;' Cot.—L. *parāre*, to prepare, deck. See **Pare**. Der. *par-a-chute*, q.v., *para-pet*, q.v., *para-sol*, q.v., *ram-part*, q.v.

PARSE, to tell the parts of speech. (L.) ' Let the childe, by and by, both construe and *parse* it ouer againe;' Ascham, Schoolmaster, b. i. ed. Arber, p. 26. An old school term; to *parse* is to declare ' quæ *pars* orationis' = what *part* of speech, a word is. It is merely the L. *pars* used familiarly. See **Part**. Der. *pars-ing*.

PARSEE, an adherent of the old Persian religion, in India. (Pers.) Spelt *Persee*, Sir T. Herbert's Travels, ed. 1665, p. 55.—Pers. *pārsī*, a Persian; from *Pārs*, Persia; Palmer's Pers. Dict. col. 106.

PARSIMONY, frugality. (F.—L.) Spelt *parsimonie* in Minsheu, ed. 1627.—MF. *parsimonie*; Cotgrave.—L. *parsimōnia*, better *parcimōnia*, parsimony.—L. *parci-*, for *parcus*, sparing; with suffix *-mōnia*, formed by joining the Idg. suffixes *-mōn-* and *-yā*. Cf. L. *parcere*, to spare. Perhaps allied to E. *spare*; see **Spare**. Der. *parsimoni-ous*, *-ly*, *-ness*.

PARSLEY, a well-known pot-herb. (F.—L.—Gk.) Formerly *persely*, Sir T. Elyot, Castel of Helth, b. iii. c. 5. ME. *percil*, P. Plowman, B. vi. 288; spelt *persely* in one of the MSS., id. A. vii. 273, footnote.—F. *persil*, ' parseley;' Cot. Spelt *peresil* in the 13th cent.; Wright's Vocab. i. 139, col. 2.—Late L. *petrosillum*, at the same reference; contr. from L. *petroselinum*, rock-parsley.—Gk. πετρο-σέλινον, rock-parsley.—Gk. πέτρο-, for πέτρος, a rock; and σέλινον, a kind of parsley, whence E. **Celery**.

PARSNEP, PARSNIP, an edible plant with a carrot-like root. (F.—L.) Formerly *parsnep*; the pl. *parsnepes* occurs in Sir T. Elyot, Castel of Helth, b. ii. c. 9. Palsgrave rightly drops the *r*, and spells it *pasneppe*; also spelt *passenep*, Pistyll of Susan, 107. Corrupted from OF. *pastenaque*, ' a parsenip;' Cot. [For the change from *qu* to *p*, compare Lat. *quinque* with Gk. πέμπε (five). The *r* is due to the sound of the F. *a*; the *te* was dropped, and the latter *a* was weakened, first to *e*, and then to *i*.] Cotgrave also gives *pastenade* and *pastenaille* with the same sense.—L. *pastināca*, a parsnip. β. *Pastināca* prob. meant ' that which is dug up,' hence a parsnip, also a carrot; the root being the edible part.—L. *pastināre*, to dig up.—L. *pastinum*, a kind of two-pronged dibble for breaking the ground. ¶ The change in the final syllable may have been influenced by the AS. *næp*, L. *nāpus*, a kind of parsnip; cf. the later word *turnep* or *turnip*.

PARSON, the incumbent of a parish. (F.—L.) ME. *persone*, Chaucer, C. T. 480 (A 478). In the Ancren Riwle, p. 316, *persone* means person. It is certain that *parson* and *person* are the same word; for the Late L. *persōna* is constantly used in the sense of ' parson.' See *persōna* in Ducange; it means dignity, rank, a choirmaster, curate, parson, body, man, person; and see Selden's Table Talk, s. v. *Parson*. The sense of *parson* may easily have been due to the mere use of the word as a title of dignity; cf. ' Laicus quidam magnæ *personæ*' = a certain lay-man of great dignity; Ducange. β. The ME. *persone* is from OF. *persone*, ' curè, recteur d'une paroisse, prieur, dignitaire, bénéficier ecclésiastique;' Godefroy.—L. *persōna* (above). ¶ The quotation from Blackstone is better known than his authority for the statement. He says: ' A *parson*, *persona ecclesiæ*, is one that hath full possession of all the rights of a parochial church. He is called *parson*, *persona*, because by his person the church, which is an invisible body, is represented;' Comment. b. i. c. 11. This is the usual sense in E. civil law, but is hardly required for the etymology. See **Person**. Der. *parson-age*, a coined word with F. suffix, Bp. Taylor, vol. iii. ser. 7 (R.).

PART, a portion, piece. (F.—L.) ME. *part*, sb., Floris and Blancheflur, ed. Lumby, l. 522; hence *parten*, vb., id. 387.—F. *part*, ' a part;' Cot.—L. *partem*, acc. of *pars*, a part. From the same root as *portion*. Brugmann, i. § 527. Der. *part*, vb., ME. *parten*, as

above; *part-ible*, from L. *partibilis*; *part-ly*, Cor. i. 1. 40; *part-ing*; and see *part-i-al*, *partake*, *parti-cip-ate*, *parti-cip-le*, *parti-cle*, *part-isan*, *part-it-ion*, *part-ner*, *part-y*; also *a-part*, *com-part-ment*, *de-part*, *im-part*, *re-part-ee*, *par-c-el*, *parse*, *port-ion*.

PARTAKE, to take part in or of, share. (Hybrid; F.—L., and Scand.) For *part-take*, and orig. used as *part take*, two separate words; indeed, we still use *take part* in much the same sense. ' The breed which we breken, wher it is not [*is it not*] the delynge, or *part takynge*, of the body of the lord?' Wyclif, 1 Cor. x. 16 (earlier version; later version omits *part*). In the Bible of 1551, we find: ' is not the breade whiche we breake, *partakynge* of the body of Christ?' in the same passage. See further in a note by Dr. Chance in N. and Q. 4th Series, viii. 481. Similarly, we find G. *theilnehmen* = *theil nehmen*, to take a part. Indeed, E. *partake* may have been suggested by the corresponding Scandinavian word (viz. Dan. *deeltage*, Swed. *deltaga*, to partake, participate) since *take* is a Scand. word. See **Part** and **Take**. Der. *partak-er*, spelt *partetaker* in Coverdale's Bible (1538), Heb. xii. 8; *partak-ing*, spelt *partetakyng*, Palsgrave.

PARTERRE, a laid-out garden, a system of plots with walks, &c. (F.—L.) ' Thus . . . was the whole *parterre* environ'd;' Evelyn's Diary, 8 Oct., 1641.—F. *parterre*, ' a floor, even piece of ground, part of a garden which consists of beds, without any tree;' Cot.—F. *par terre*, along the ground.—L. *per terram*, along the ground; see **Per-** and **Terrace**.

PARTHENOGENESIS, reproduction by a virgin. (Gk.) A term in zoology.—Gk. παρθένο-, for παρθένος, a virgin; and γένεσις, birth; see **Genesis**.

PARTIAL, relating to a part only. (F.—L.) Frequently in the sense of taking one part in preference to others, hence, inclined in behalf of. ' That in thine own behalf maist *partiall* seeme;' Spenser, F. Q. vii. 6. 35.—F. *partial*, ' solitary, . . . also partiall, unequall, factious;' Cot.—Late L. *partiālis*; formed with suffix *-ālis* from L. *parti-*, decl. stem of *pars*, a part. See **Part**. Der. *partial-ly*; *partial-i-ty*, spelt *parcialité*, Lydgate, Minor Poems, p. 120, from F. *partialité*, ' partiality,' Cot.

PARTICIPATE, to partake, have a share. (L.) In Shak. Tw. Nt. v. 245; properly a pp. or adj., as in Cor. i. 1. 106.—L. *participātus*, pp. of *participāre*, to have a share, give a share.—L. *particip-*, stem of *particeps*, sharing in.—L. *parti-*, decl. stem of *pars*, a part, and *capere*, to take. See **Part** and **Capacious**. Der. *participat-ion*, ME. *participacioun*, Chaucer, tr. of Boethius, b. iii. pr. 10, l. 110, from F. *participation*, which from L. acc. *participātiōnem*; also *particip-ant*, from the stem of the pres. part.; also *particip-le*, q.v.

PARTICIPLE, a part of speech. (F.—L.) So called because partaking of the nature both of an adjectival substantive and a verb. In Ben Jonson, Eng. Grammar, c. 6. ME. *participle*, Wyclif's Bible, Prologue, p. 57, l. 29. The insertion of the *l* is curious, and perhaps due to a misapprehension of the sound of the F. word; as in *principle* and *syllable*.—F. *participe*, ' a participle, in grammer;' Cot.—L. *participium*, a participle.—L. *particip-*, decl. stem of *particeps*, partaking; see **Participate**.

PARTICLE, a very small portion, atom. (F.—L.) In Shak. Jul. Cæs. ii. 1. 139. An abbreviation for *particule*, due to loss of stress in the last syllable.—F. *particule*, not in Cot., but in use in the 16th cent. (Littré).—L. *particula*, a small part; double dimin. (with suffixes *-cu-* and *-la*) from *parti-*, decl. stem of *pars*, a part. Der. *particul-ar*, ME. *particuler*, Chaucer, C. T. 11434 (F. 1122), from F. *particulier*, which from L. *particulāris*, concerning a part; *particular-ly*; *particular-ise*, from F. *particulariser*, ' to particularize,' Cot.; *particular-i-ty*, from F. *particularité*, ' a particularity,' Cot. Doublet, *parcel*.

PARTISAN (1), an adherent of a party. (F.—Ital.—L.) ' These *partizans* of faction often try'd;' Daniel, Civil War, bk. ii. st. 4.—F. *partisan*, ' a partner, partaker;' Cot.—Ital. *partigiano*, formerly also *partegiano*, ' a partner;' Florio. Cf. Ital. *parteggiare*, ' to share, take part with,' Florio; answering to F. *partager*, to take part in. The form *partigiano* answers to a Late L. form **partensiānus*, not found; from *part-*, base of *pars*, a part; with suffixes *-ensi-* and *-ānus*. See **Part**, **Partition**. Der. *partisan-ship*.

PARTISAN (2), **PARTIZAN**, a kind of halberd. (F.—Ital.—L. ?) In Hamlet, i. 1. 140.—F. *pertuisane*, ' a partisan, or leading-staffe;' Cot. β. But the spelling *pertuisane* is an accommodated form, to make it appear as if derived from F. *pertuiser*, to pierce (cf. *pertuis*, a hole).—Ital. *partegiana*, ' a partesan, a iauelin,' Florio; cf. Late L. *partesāna* (occurring A. D. 1488); *partisāna* (1493); *pertixāna* (1468). Supposed to be closely related to the word above, as if the weapon of a partisan (Körting, § 6882).

PARTITION, a separate part, something that separates. (F.—L.) In Shak. meaning (1) division, Mid. Nt. Dr. iii. 2. 210; (2) a party-wall, id. v. 168. Spelt *particioune* in Lydgate, Minor Poems,

p. 170. — F. *partition*, omitted by Cot., but occurring in the 14th cent. (Littré). — L. *partītiōnem*, acc. of *parītio*, a sharing, partition. — L. *partīri*, to divide. — L. *parti-*, decl. stem of *pars*, a part. See **Part**. Der. *partition*, vb. So also *partit-ive*, from F. *partitif* (Littré), as if from L. **partītīuus*, not used; hence *partit-ive-ly*.

PARTNER, a sharer, associate. (F. — L.) A curious corruption, due to the *eye*, i. e. to the misreading of MSS. and books. In many MSS. *c* and *t* are just alike, and the ME. word which appears as *partener* or *parcener* is really to be read as *parcener*, with *c*, not *t*. The spelling *parcener* occurs as late as in Cotgrave, as will appear; and even in Blackstone's Commentaries, b. ii. c. 12 (R., s. v. *parcel*). For the spelling *partener*, see Wyclif, 1 Cor. ix. 12; for the spelling *parcener*, id. Rev. xviii. 4. — OF. *parcener*, MF. *parsonnier*, 'a partener, or co-parcener;' Cot. — Late L. **partītiōnārius*, not found; but we find *partiōnārius* sometimes used in the sense of 'common' or 'mutual,' which seems to be a contracted form of it, and is the original of the F. form. — L. *partītiōn-*, stem of *partītio*; see **Partition**. Thus *partner* = *partitioner*. Der. *partner-ship*.

PARTLET, a gorget or loose collar, a garment for the neck and shoulders, esp. for women. (F.) ME. *patelet*, Henryson, Garmond of Gude Ladeis, st. 7. — OF. *patelette*, dimin. of *patte*, a band of stuff (Godefroy); cf. MF. *patellette*, 'the broad piece of leather that runnes over-crosse, or through, the top of a head-stall [for a horse];' Cot. Cf. *pate*, 'a plate or band of iron for the strengthening of a thing;' Cot. Of obscure origin; see Notes on Eng. Etym., p. 208. The *r* is unoriginal. Perhaps a dimin. of Late L. *pata*, a kind of 'limbus' or border worn by some ecclesiastics (Ducange). Or for **platelette*; cf. OF. *platel*, a flat piece (Godefroy); see **Plateau**.

PARTRIDGE, a well-known bird preserved for game. (F. — L. — Gk.) ME. *partriche, pertriche*, Richard the Redeles, ed. Skeat, iii. 38. — ONorm. F. *pertrix*, in Moisy, Gloss. Comparatif Anglo-Normand; F. *perdrix*, 'a partridge;' in which the second *r* is intrusive. — L. *perdicem*, acc. of *perdix*. — Gk. πέρδιξ, a partridge; perhaps named from its cry or its noisy flight, as some connect it with Gk. πέρδομαι, Skt. *pard* (Prellwitz).

PARTURIENT, about to produce young. (L.) In Blount's Gloss., ed. 1674. — L. *parturient-*, stem of pres. part. of *parturīre*, to be ready to bring forth young. Cf. *partūr-us*, fut. part. of *parere*, to produce; see **Parent**. Der. *partur-it-ion* = F. *parturition* (Littré), from L. acc. *parturītiōnem*, which from *parturīre*.

PARTY, a company, faction, assembly. (F. — L.) ME. *partie*, King Alisaunder, 4756; *parti, party*, Cursor Mundi, 7470. — F. *partie*, 'a part, share, party, side;' Cot. We also find F. *parti*, 'a match, bargain, party, side;' Cot. The former is the fem. of the latter. — L. *partīta*, fem. of *partītus*, pp. of *partīri*, to divide. — L. *parti-*, decl. stem of *pars*, a part. See **Part**. Cf. Ital. *partita*, a share, part; Span. *partida*, a party of soldiers, crew, &c. Der. *party-coloured*, Merch. Ven. i. 3. 89; *party-verdict*, Rich. II, i. 3. 234.

PARVENU, an upstart. (F. — L.) Modern. — F. *parvenu*, lit. one who has arrived at a place, hence, one who has thriven; pp. of *parvenir*, 'to atchieve, arrive, thrive;' Cot. — L. *peruenīre*, to arrive. — L. *per-*, through; and *uenīre*, cognate with E. *come*. See **Per-** and **Come**.

PARVIS, a porch; also, a room over a church-porch for a school. (F. — L. — Gk. — Pers.) See Halliwell, and Prompt. Parv. p. 385. ME. *paruis* (= *parvis*), Chaucer, C. T. 312 (A 310); see note. — OF. *parvis*, 'the porch of a church; also (or more properly), the utter court of a palace or great house;' Cot. A variant of OF. *parevis*, *pareïs, paraïs* (Low L. *paravīsus*), lit. paradise. — L. *paradīsus*, paradise; also a church-porch, outer court. It is thus the same word as **Paradise**, q. v. Diez cites Neapolitan *paraviso* as a variant of Ital. *paradiso*. According to Littré, when the old mystery-plays were exhibited in the church-yard, the porch represented paradise. ¶ The *v* was inserted in OF. *pare-is*, to avoid hiatus.

PASCH, the Jewish passover; Easter. (L. — Gk. — Heb.) ME. *paske*, P. Plowman, B. xvi. 139; Ormulum, 15850. AS. *pascha*; the gen. *pasches* is in the A. S. Chron. an. 1122. — L. *pascha*. — Gk. πάσχα, the passover, John, vi. 4. — Heb. *pesakh*, a passing over, the passover; from Heb. root *pāsakh*, he passed over. See Exod. xii. 11, 27. Der. *pasch-al*, from F. *paschal*, 'paschall,' Cot., from L. *paschālis*; *pasch-flower* or *pasque-flower*. (The Heb. *s* is *samech*.)

PASH, to dash, strike hard. (Scand.) 'As he was *pashing* it against a tree;' Ford, Lover's Melancholy, i. 1. And in Shak. Troil. ii. 3. 213, v. 5. 10. ME. *paschen*, P. Plowman, B. xx. 99. Cf. Swed. dial. *paska*, to dabble in water, *baska*, to beat (Rietz); Norweg. *baska*, to dabble in water, tumble, work hard, fight one's way on, *baksa*, to box (Aasen); Dan. *baske*, to slap, thwack, drub; *baxes*, to box. From Swed. dial. *bas-a*, to beat. Cf. prov. E. *bash*, of which *pash* is a variant. Also G. *patschen*, to strike, to dabble; Low G. *bat*, a stroke, a blow. And see **Baste** (1), **Box** (3).

PASHA, PACHA, PASHAW, BASHAW, a prince, lord.

(Pers.) Spelt *bashaw* in Evelyn's Diary, Dec. 17, 1684; *basha* in Sir T. Herbert, Travels, ed. 1665, p. 139. — Pers. *bāshā, bādshāh*, 'a governor of a province, counsellor of state, great lord, sometimes the grand vazīr;' the same as *pādshāh*, 'an emperor, sovereign, monarch, prince, great lord;' Rich. Dict. pp. 234, 228, 315. — Pers. *pād-*, OPers. *pati-*, equivalent to the syllable *-pot* in *des-pot*; and Pers. *shāh*, whence the E. *shah*. See **Padishah**.

PASQUE-FLOWER; see under **Pasch**.

PASQUIN, PASQUINADE, a lampoon, satire. (F. — Ital.) Formerly also *pasquil*, from MF. *pasquille*, 'a pasquill;' Cot. — F. *pasquin*, 'the name of an image or post in Rome, whereon libels and defamatory rimes are fastened, and fathered; also, a pasquill;' Cot. [Hence *pasquinade*, which see in Littré.] — Ital. *Pasquino*, 'a statue in Rome on whom all libels are fathered;' Florio; whence *pasquinata*, a libel, the original of F. *pasquinade*. 'In the 16th century, at the stall of a cobbler named *Pasquin* [Pasquino], at Rome, a number of idle persons used to assemble to listen to his pleasant sallies, and to relate little anecdotes in their turn, and indulge themselves in raillery at the expense of the passers-by. After the cobbler's death the statue of a gladiator was found near his stall, to which the people gave his name, and on which the wits of the time, secretly at night, affixed their lampoons;' Haydn, Dict. of Dates. 'The statue still stands at the corner of the Palazzo Braschi, near the Piazza Navona;' note in Gloss. to Bacon, Adv. of Learning, ed. Wright.

PASS, to walk onward, pace, move on. (F. — L.) In early use; Ancren Riwle, p. 330, l. 20; Layamon, 1341 (later text). — F. *passer*, to pass. — Late L. *passāre*, to pass. — L. *passus*, a step, a pace. Diez considers *passāre* to be a frequentative from *pandere*, to stretch; but it makes little ultimate difference, since *passus* is itself derived from the same verb, and meant, originally, 'a stretch,' hence the difference of space between the feet in walking. Either way, we are led to L. *passus*, pp. of *pandere*, to stretch. See **Pace**. Der. *pass*, sb., Hamlet, ii. 2. 77; *pass-book, pass-key, pass-word*; *pass-able*, Cor. v. 2. 13; *pass-abl-y, pass-able-ness*; *pass-age*, q. v.; *pass-er, passer-by*; *pass-ing*, Two Gent. i. 2. 17; *pass-ing*, adv., L. L. L. iv. 3. 103; *passing-bell*, Shak. Venus, 702; *pass-over*, Exod. xii. 11, 27; *pass-port*, q. v.; *past*; *pastime*, q. v.

PASSAGE, a journey, course. (F. — L.) ME. *passage*, King Horn, ed. Lumby, 1323. — F. *passage*, 'a passage;' Cot. — Late L. *passāticum*, a right of passage, occurring A.D. 1095; Ducange. [Cf. Ital. *passaggio*, Span. *pasage*.] — Late L. *passāre*, to pass; see **Pass**. Der. *passeng-er*, in which the *n* is merely excrescent before the following *g*, the old spelling being *passager*, as in North's Plutarch, ed. 1631, p. 24 (Life of Romulus), where we read that some 'hold a false opinion, that the vulturs are *passagers*, and come into these parts out of strange countries.' See F. *passager* in Cotgrave.

PASSERINE, relating to sparrows. (L.) Scientific. — L. *passerīnus*, adj., formed from *passeri-*, decl. stem of *passer*, a sparrow.

PASSION, suffering, strong agitation of mind, rage. (F. — L.) In early use. ME. *passion*; spelt *passiun*, O. Eng. Homilies, ed. Morris, i. 119, l. 6 from bottom. — F. *passion*, 'passion, perturbation;' Cot. — L. *passiōnem*, acc. of *passio*, suffering, &c.; cf. *passus*, pp. of *pati*, to suffer; see **Patient**. Der. *passion-flower, passion-less, passion-week*; *passion-ate*, Mids. Nt. Dr. iii. 2. 220, from Late L. *passiōnātus*, occurring A.D. 1409 (Ducange), with which cf. F. *passioné* (Cot.); *passion-ate-ly, passion-ate-ness*; *com-passion*. Also *passible*, F. *passible*, from L. *passibilis*, capable of suffering; from *passi-*, for *passus*, with suffix *-bilis*; hence *passibili-ty*. And see **Passive**.

PASSIVE, enduring, unresisting. (F. — L.) In Shak. Timon, iv. 3. 254. — F. *passif*, 'passive, suffering;' Cot. — L. *passīuus*, suffering. — L. *passus*, pp. of *pati*, to suffer. See **Passion**. Der. *passive-ly, -ness*; *passiv-i-ty*, a coined word, in Bp. Taylor, vol. iii. ser. 10 (R.).

PASSPORT, a permission to travel. (F. — L.) 'A travelling warrant is call'd *Passport*, whereas the original is *passe par tout*;' Howell, Familiar Letters, b. iv. let. 19. 'They gave us our *passe-port*;' Hakluyt's Voyages, ed. 1598, vol. i. p. 71. Spelt *passeporte*, Gascoigne, Fruites of War, st. 116. [Howell's remark is wrong; a *passport* and a *passe-partout* are different things; one is 'leave to quit a port,' the other is 'permission to travel everywhere;' he probably means that the former word came to signify much the same as the latter. Dryden has: 'with this *passe par tout* I will instantly conduct her to my own chamber;' Kind Keeper, Act v. sc. 1.] — F. *passe-port*, 'a passe, or passe-port, or safe conduct;' Cot. — F. *passer*, to pass; and *port*, a port, a seaport, from L. acc. *portum*, a port. See **Pass** and **Port** (2).

PASTE, dough prepared for pies, flour and water, &c. (F. — L. — Gk.) 'Paste for to make;' P. Plowman, B. xiii. 250. — OF. *paste*, 'paste, or dough;' Cot. Mod. F. *pâte*; Span. and Ital. *pasta*. — Late L. *pasta*, paste, used by Marcellus Empiricus, about A.D. 400 (Lewis). — Gk. παστή, a mess of food; strictly a fem. form from παστός, besprinkled, salted, adj., formed from πάσσειν, to strew, sprinkle, esp. to sprinkle salt. Thus the orig. sense was 'a salted mess of food.' **Der.** *paste-board*; *past-y*, ME. *pastee*, Chaucer, C. T. 4344 (A 4346), from OF. *pasté* (mod. F. *pâté*), 'a pie, or pastie,' Cot.; *past-r-y*, used in Shak. in the sense of a room in which pasties were made, Romeo, iv. 4. 2 (cf. 'Pastrye, *pistorium*,' Levins), and formed accordingly on the model of *pant-r-y* and *butt-er-y* (i. e. *bottl-er-y*), but now applied to articles made of paste; *pastry-cook*; *patt-y* (as applied to oyster-patties), from mod. F. *pâté*.

PASTEL, a roll of coloured paste used like a crayon, a coloured crayon. (F.—Ital.—L.) An artist's term.—F. *pastel*, 'a pastel, crayon;' Hamilton.—Ital. *pastello*, 'a little bit of paste;' Baretti. Also 'a pastil;' Meadows. The pastel was named from being shaped like a roll of bread.—L. *pastillum*, acc. of *pastillus*, a little loaf or roll. Dimin. of *pastus*, food.—L. *pastus*, pp. of *pascere*, to feed. See **Pastor.** ☞ Sometimes written *pastil*, very like *pastille*. However, *pastel* and *pastille* are doublets: and neither is at all related to *pasty* or *paste*, which are from Gk. Doublet, *pastille*.

PASTERN, the part of a horse's foot from the fetlock to the hoof. (F.—L.) Spelt *pasterne* in Levins, ed. 1570. Palsgrave has: 'Pastron of an horse, *pasturon*.'—MF. *pasturon*, 'the pastern of a horse;' Cot. Mod. F. *pâturon*. So called because when a horse was turned out to *pasture*, he was tethered to a peg by a cord passing round the *pastern*; the tether itself was called *pasture* in Old French. 'Le suppliant frappa icellui Godart deux ou trois coups par le costé d'unes cordes appelées *pastures*' = the petitioner beat this Godart twice or thrice on the side with cords called *pastures*; in a passage dated A.D. 1460, in Ducange, s.v. *pasturāle*, and cited by Littré.—OF. *pasture*, 'pasture, grasse, fodder;' Cot. See further under **Pasture.** Thus OF. *pasturon* was formed from *pasture*, a tether, by adding the suffix *-on*, which gave various meanings to the sb.; see Brachet, Introd. § 231. So also Ital. *pasturale*, the pastern, from *pastura*, a pasture. ☞ Hence we may explain a passage in Beaum. and Fletcher, The Chances, i. 8. 16, viz. 'She had better have worn *pasterns*.' It means tethers, or clogs tied to her feet; i. e. she had better have been tethered up. Indeed Kersey, ed. 1715, gives: 'Pastern, the hollow of a beast's heel, the foot of a horse, that part under the fetlock to the hoof; also, *a shackle for a horse*.' It is remarkable that this sense should have been retained in English, though unnoticed in Cotgrave's F. Dict.

PASTILLE, a small cone made of aromatic substances, to be burnt to purify the air of a room. (F.—L.) Modern. Borrowed from F. *pastille*. Cot. gives: 'Pastilles, little lumps or loaves of wood, &c.'—L. *pastillum*, acc. of *pastillus*, a little loaf or roll. Dimin. from *pastus*, food. Also spelt *pastil*; cf. Walloon *pastil*, a pastille (Remacle). See **Pastel**, which is a doublet.

PASTIME, amusement. (Hybrid: F.—L.; *and* E.) In Shak. Temp. v. 38. For *pass-time*. Spelt *passe-tyme* in Sir T. Elyot, The Governor, b. i. c. 22. It is a sort of half translation of F. *passe-temps*, 'pastime;' Cot. We also find, in old authors, the form *pastaunce* or *pastans*, which is the F. *passe-temps* Anglicised. Gawain Douglas has *pastans*, Prol. to Æneid, bk. xii. l. 212.

PASTOR, a shepherd. (L.) In Hamlet, i. 3. 47; spelt *pastour* in Skelton, ed. Dyce, i. 203, l. 23.—L. *pastor*, a shepherd, lit. feeder; cf. *past-us*, pp. of *pascere*, to feed, an inceptive verb, pt. t. *pā-ui.*—√PA to feed; whence also E. *food*; see **Food.** **Der.** *pastor-al*, in Sir P. Sidney, Apology for Poetrie, ed. Arber, p. 43, l. 16, from F. *pastoral*, 'pastorall, shepherdly,' Cot., from L. *pastorālis*; *pastor-ship*; *pasture*, Cursor Mundi, 18445, from OF. *pasture* (mod. F. *pâture*), 'pasture' (Cot.), which from L. *pastūra*, a feeding, like *pastūrus*, fut. part. of *pasci*, to browze, from *pascere*, to feed; *pastur-able*, from OF. *pasturable*, 'pasturable,' Cot.; *pastur-age*, from OF. *pasturage* (mod. F. *pâturage*), 'pasturage,' Cot. And see *pastern*, *pabulum*.

PASTY, a patty, a pie; see **Paste.**

PAT (1), to strike lightly, tap. (E.) 'It is childrens sport, to prove whether they can rubbe upon their brest with one hand, and *pat* upon their fore-head with another;' Lord Bacon, Nat. Hist. § 63. ME. *pat*, sb. 'And gafe his sone soche a *patte*;' Sir Eglamour, 1241 (in Thornton Romances). Of imitative origin; like *tap*. Not in AS.; but a parallel formation to AS. *plættan*, to strike. 'Hi *plætton* hyne' = they smote him with their hands, John, xix. 3. So also Swed. dial. *pjätta*, to pat, to strike lightly and often (Rietz), allied to Swed. *plätta*, to tap, *plätt*, a tap, pat; MDu. *pletten*, to beat (Kilian). Cf. MF. (Gascon) *patact*, 'a tack, clack, knock, flap;' Cot.; Prov. *pata*, to beat, to pat, to tap, allied to *pato*, an animal's paw. Also Bavarian *patzen*, to pat, *patzen*, a pat on the hand; Schmeller; see **Patrol.** And see **Patch** (1). Körting, § 6917. **Der.** *pat*, sb.; *patt-er*.

PAT (2), a small lump of butter. (E.) Cf. Irish *pait*, a hump, *paiteog*, a small lump of butter; Gael. *pait*, a hump, *paiteach*, humpy, *paiteog*, a small lump of butter; all from E. *pat*. Thus the orig.

sense is 'lump.' Prob. from the vb. *pat*, above; as being patted into shape; as *dab*, a small lump, is from *dab*, verb. Cf. prov. F. (Berry) *pater*, to stick to the shoes, said of mud.

PAT (3), quite to the purpose. (E.) Orig. an adv., as in '*Pat* he comes,' K. Lear, i. 2. 146; 'it will fall [happen] *pat*,' Mids. Nt. Dr. v. 188; 'now might I do it *pat*,' Haml. iii. 3. 73. This can hardly be other than the same word as *pat*, a tap; see **Pat** (1); cf. *dab*, an adept, from *dab*, verb, and the phrase *to hit pat*, to hit with a flat blow; see exx. in N. E. D. β. But the sense may have been affected by Du. *pas*, pat, fit, convenient, in time, which is used in exactly the same way as E. *pat*; cf. *komt het te pas*, 'if it comes convenient,' i. e. pat, *te pas dienen*, 'to serve just at the time;' Hexham. So also G. *pass*, pat, fit, suitable; *zu passe*, apropos; *passen*, to fit, suit, to be just right. These are not true Teutonic words, but borrowed from F.; cf. '*se passer*, whence *il se passe à peu de chose*, he is contented, he maketh shift, he doth well enough;' Cot.

PATCH (1), a piece sewn on a garment, a plot of ground. (E.?) ME. *pacche*, *patche*, Wyclif, Mark, ii. 21; Prompt. Parv. p. 377. The letters *tch* really appear as *cch* in old MSS.; the spelling *tch* is of later date, and sometimes due to the editors. The letters *cch* answer to an AS. *cc*, as in ME. *strecchen*, to stretch, from AS. *streccan.* β. It seems to be a by-form of *platch*. We find: '*Platch*, a large spot, a patch, or piece of cloth sewed on to a garment to repair it;' Dialect of Banffshire, by W. Gregor; cf. prov. E. *plack*, a plot of ground, E. D. D.; Low G. *plakke*, *plakk* (1), a spot; (2) a piece, both a piece torn away, and a patch put on; (3) a piece of land (cf. E. *patch* of ground); ME. *plekke*, a plot of ground. Hence the verb *plakken*, to patch, fasten. 'Frisch, from Alberi Lexicon, cites: *ich plack*, reconcinno, resarcino; *ich setze einen placken an*, assuo;' Bremen Wörterbuch. The orig. sense of *plakken* was 'to strike;' cf. MDu. *placken*, (1) to strike, (2) to plaster, besmear with lime or chalk, (3) to spot, to stain; *placke*, mod. Du. *plek*, a spot (*een mooi plek grondes*, a fine spot [patch] of ground, Sewel); see Oudemans. γ. With a change of *kk* to *tt*, we have Dan. *plette*, to strike, AS. *plættan*, to strike with the hands; and Goth. *plats*, a patch, Mark, ii. 21, where Wyclif has *pacche*. ¶ The AS. *plæce* means an open space, lit. 'a place.' The phrase 'in the corners of the streets' (Lat. *in angulis platearum*) is glossed by 'huommum ðæra *plæcena* vel worðum' in the Northumb. version of Matt. vi. 5. Here the AS. *plæce* is, apparently, merely Englished from L. *platea*; see **Place.** It is remarkable that the Norman dialect has *plache* (for *place*) in the sense of 'plot of ground.' **Der.** *patch*, verb, Tw. Nt. i. 5. 52; *patch-work*.

PATCH (2), a paltry fellow. (E.) In Shak. Temp. iii. 2. 71, Com. Err. iii. 1. 32, Merch. Ven. ii. 5. 46; &c. 'In these passages, the word is by most commentators interpreted .. "a domestic fool," supposed to be so called from his parti-coloured dress;' Schmidt. 'Wolsey we find had two fools, both occasionally called *Patch*, though they had other names; see Douce, Illustrations of Shak., i. 258;' Nares. 'To *Peche*, the fole, in rewarde, 6s. 8d.;' Excerpta Historica, p. 88 (1492). The supposition that *patch* is a nick-name from the dress is most probably right; if so, the derivation is from *patch* (1); see above. In Mids. Nt. Dr. iii. 2. 9, the word merely means clown, or an ill-dressed mechanic. ¶ It is independent of Ital. *pazzo*, a fool, madman, which is used in a much stronger sense. **Der.** *patch-ock*, a dimin. form (cf. *bull-ock*, *hill-ock*); 'as very *patchockes* [clowns] as the wild Irish,' Spenser, View of the State of Ireland, Globe ed. p. 636, col. 2; this is the word spelt *pajock* in Shak. Hamlet, iii. 2. 295.

PATCHOULI, the name of a scent. (F.—Dravidian.) F. *patchouli*; of obscure origin. Apparently from E. *patcha-leaf*, i. e. green leaf, imitating the vernacular (Bengali) *pacha-pāt*, where *pāt* is Hind. for 'leaf.' Or from Dravidian words meaning 'green leaf.' Cf. Tamil *pachchai*, green, *ilai*, leaf (Knight); Malayālim *pachchila*, green leaf (Gundert); Canarese *pachcha*, green, *yele*, leaf (Reeve). Wilson gives the Telugu name as *pachchāku*, with the same sense, from Telugu *āku*, a leaf.

PATE, the head. (F.—L.) In Spenser, Shep. Kal., June, l. 16. ME. *pate*; 'bi *pate* and by polle,' Polit. Songs, ed. Wright, p. 237, in a song of the time of Edw. II. The etymology may be disguised by the loss of *l*; *pate* may stand for *plate*, i. e. the crown of the head. —MF. *pate*, not recorded in the special sense here required, but Cotgrave gives: '*Pate*, a plate, or band of iron, &c. for the strengthening of a thing;' which suggests the loss of *l*. Cf. G. *platte*, a plate, bald pate, in vulgar language, the head (Flügel); MHG. *plate*, a plate, the shaven crown of the head. β. Cf. also Late L. *platta*, the clerical tonsure from ear to ear (Ducange); MDu. *platte kruyne*, 'flat-crowned, or ball-pated,' Hexham; *platte*, the shaven crown, Kilian. γ. Even in Irish we find *plata*, a plate; *plait*, the forehead, *plaitin* (1), a little pate, a skull, the crown of the head (with the usual change of *a* to *ai*); O'Reilly. These words were prob. borrowed from OF. or ME. We may note a similar change in sense in the word *crown*, meaning (1) the clerical tonsure, (2) the top of the head, esp. if bald. See **Plate**.

PATEN, the plate for the bread in the eucharist. (F.—L.—Gk.) Spelt *patine* in Cotgrave; Shak. has *patines* = plates of metal, Merch. Ven. v. 59. ME. *pateyn*, a paten, Havelok, 187.—OF. *patene*, 'the patine, or cover of a chalice;' Cot.—Late L. *patena*, the paten in the eucharist; L. *patena, patina*, a wide shallow bowl, basin.—Gk. πατάνη, a kind of flat dish. So named from its flatness; from √PET, to spread out, whence Gk. πετάννυμι, I spread out; cf. L. *patēre*, to lie open, spread out, extend; see **Patent**. Brugmann, i. § 120, note. Doublet, *pan* (?).

PATENT, lit. open, hence conspicuous, public; gen. as sb., an official document conferring a privilege. (F.—L.) The use as an adj. is less common, but it occurs in Cotgrave. ME. *patente*, sb., a patent, Chaucer, C. T. 12271 (C 337). [The *patent* was so called because *open* to the inspection of all men.]—OF. *patent* (fem. *patente*), 'patent, wide open, discovered;' Cot.—L. *patent-*, stem of pres. part. of *patēre*, to lie open. √PET, to spread out; whence also Gk. πετάννυμι, I spread out, unfold, unfurl, and E. *fath-om*. Der. *patent*, vb. (modern); *patent-ee*, where the suffix = F. *-é* < L. *-ātus*. And see *pace, pass, paten, pan, petal, fathom, ex-pand, compass, surpass, trespass.*

PATERA, a flat round ornament, in bas-relief. (L.) L. *patera*, a flat saucer.—L. *patēre*, to lie open. Cf. **Paten**.

PATERNAL, fatherly. (F.—L.) In Shak. King Lear, i. 1. 115.—F. *paternel*, 'paternal;' Cot.—Late L. *paternālis*, extended from L. *paternus*, paternal, fatherly. Formed with Idg. suffix -*no*- from *pater*, a father; but probably *not* from √PĀ, to guard, feed, cherish; cf. Skt. *pā*, to protect, cherish, and E. *food.* +Gk. πατήρ; E. *father*; see **Father**. Der. *paternal-ly*; also *patern-i-ty*, from F. *paternité*, 'paternity, fatherhood,' Cot., from L. acc. *paternitātem*. Also *pater-noster*, Chaucer, C. T. 3485, so called from the first two words, *pater noster*, i. e. Our Father. And see *patri-arch, patri-cian, patri-mony, patri-ot, patr-istic, patr-on.*

PATH, a way, track, road. (E.) ME. *path, paþ*, P. Plowman, B. xiv. 300; pl. *paþes*, Havelok, 268. AS. *pæð, paþ*, a path, Grein, ii. 361.+Du. *pad*; G. *pfad*. Der. *path-less, path-way.*

PATHOS, emotion, deep feeling. (Gk.) In South's Sermons, vol. iv. ser. 1 (R.); and in Phillips, ed. 1706. [But the adj. *pathetical* is in earlier use, occurring in Cotgrave and is oddly used by Shak. As You Like It, iv. 1. 196, &c.]—Gk. πάθος, suffering, deep feeling; from παθεῖν, used as 2 aor. infin. of πάσχειν, to suffer (as if for *παθ-σκειν). Allied to πένθος, grief; from the weak grade παθ- (for πνθ). Der. *path-et-ic*, from MF. *pathetique*, 'pathetical, passionate,' Cot. from L. *pathēticus* (Lewis), from Gk. παθητικός, extended from παθητός, subject to suffering; *path-et-ic-al, path-et-ic-al-ly, path-et-ic-al-ness.* Also *patho-logy*, in Blount's Gloss., ed. 1674, from MF. *pathologie*, 'that part of physick which intreats of the causes, qualities, and differences of diseases,' Cot., from Gk. παθολογεῖν, to treat of diseases; which is from πάθο-, for πάθος, and λέγειν, to speak. Hence *patholog-ic*, Gk. παθολογικός, *patholog-ic-al, patholog-ist.*

PATIENT, bearing pain, enduring, long-suffering. (F.—L.) ME. *pacient, patient*, Chaucer, C. T. 486 (A 484).—OF. *patient*, 'patient.'—L. *patient-*, stem of pres. part. of *patī*, to suffer. Der. *patient-ly*; *patience*, ME. *pacience*, Ancren Riwle, p. 180, from F. *patience*, L. *patientia*. And see *passion.*

PATINE, a round plate; see **Paten**.

PATOIS, a vulgar dialect, esp. of French. (F.—L.) In Smollett, France and Italy, let. 21 (Davies). Borrowed from F. *patois*, 'gibridge, clownish language, rusticall speech;' Cot. *Patois* perhaps stands for an older (doubtful) *patrois*; see Godefroy, Diez and Littré.—Late L. *patriensis*, one who is indigenous to a country, a native; so that *patois* is the 'speech of the natives.'—L. *patria*, one's native country. See **Patriot**.

PATRIARCH, a chief father. (F.—L.—Gk.) The lit. sense is 'chief father.' ME. *patriarche*, O. Eng. Homilies, ed. Morris, i. 131, l. 4; *patriarke*, P. Plowman, B. xviii. 138.—OF. *patriarche*, 'a patriarke,' Cot.—L. *patriarcha*, also *patriarchēs*.—Gk. πατριάρχης, the father or chief of a race.—Gk. πατρι-, short for πατριά, a lineage, race, from πατρι-, for πατήρ, a father; and ἄρχειν, to rule. See **Father** and **Archaic**. Der. *patriarch-al, patriarch-ic, patriarch-ate.* ☞ 'The ecclesiastical historian Socrates gives the title of *patriarch* to the chiefs of Christian dioceses about A. D. 440;' Haydn.

PATRICIAN, a nobleman in ancient Rome. (L.) In Shak. Cor. i. 1. 16, 68, 75. Formed with suffix -*an* (< L. -*ānus*) from L. *patrici-us*, adj. patrician, noble; sb. a patrician, a descendant of the *patrēs*, senators, or heads of families.—L. *patri-*, for *pater*, a father. See **Paternal**.

PATRIMONY, an inheritance, heritage. (F.—L.) ME. *patri-*

monye, P. Plowman, C. xxiii. 234; spelt *patrimoigne*, id. B. xx. 233.—F. *patrimoine*, 'patrimony;' Cot.—L. *patrimōnium*, an inheritance. Formed (with suffix -*mōn-io-* = Idg. -*mōn-yo-*) from *patri-* decl. stem of *pater*, a father, cognate with E. *father*. See **Paternal** and **Father**. Der. *patrimoni-al.*

PATRIOT, one who loves his fatherland. (F.—Late L.—Gk.) 'A *patriot*, or countrey-man;' Minsheu, ed. 1627.—OF. *patriote*, 'a patriot, ones countreyman;' Cot.—Late L. *patriōta*, a native.—Gk. πατριώτης, properly, a fellow-countryman.—Gk. πάτριος, belonging to one's fathers, hereditary.—Gk. πατρι-, for πατήρ, a father. Der. *patriot-ic*, Gk. πατριωτικός, *patriot-ic-al-ly, patriot-ism*; also *com-patriot, ex-patriate, re-pair* (2). ☞ The peculiar use of *patriot* in its present sense arose in *French.*

PATRISTIC, pertaining to the fathers of the Christian church. (F.—Gk.) From F. *patristique*, which see in Littré. Coined from Gk. πατρ-, for πατήρ, a father; with suffix -ιστικός. ¶ Not a well-made word.

PATROL, to go the rounds in a camp or garrison; a going of the rounds. (F.—Teut.) It occurs, spelt *patroll*, in Phillips, ed. 1706, both as a sb. and verb. 'And being then upon *patrol*;' Butler, Hudibras, pt. ii. c. 3, l. 801.—MF. *patrouille*, 'a still night-watch in warre,' Cot. Lit. a paddling about, tramping about, from MF. (Picard) *patrouiller*, 'to paddle or pudder in the water;' Cot. The same word (with inserted *r*) as *patouiller*, 'to slabber, to paddle or dable in with the feet;' Cot. β. Formed, as a sort of frequentative verb, from OF. *pate* (mod. F. *patte*), 'the paw, or foot of a beast;' Cot. [Cf. Span. *pata*, a paw, beast's foot; *patullar*, to run through mud; *patrulla*, a patrol, *patrullar*, to patrol; Ital. *pattuglia*, patrol, watch, sentry (showing that the *r* is inserted).] γ. Prob. from a Teutonic base *pat-* appearing in Bavar. *patzen*, EFries. *patjen*, to splash; G. *patsche*, an instrument for striking the hand, *patsch-fuss*, web-foot of a bird, *patschen*, to strike, dabble, walk awkwardly. See **Pat** (1). The suffix -*ouiller* represents L. -*uculāre.*

PATRON, a protector. (F.—L.) ME. *patron*, Rob. of Glouc. p. 471, l. 9673.—F. *patron*, 'a patron, protector.'—L. *patrōnum*, acc. of *patrōnus*, a protector, lit. one who takes the place of a father.—L. *patr-*, for *pater*, a father, cognate with E. *father*. See **Paternal**. Der. *patron-age*, from MF. *patronnage*, 'patronage,' Cot.; *patron-ess*, Cor. v. 5. 1; *patron-ise*. Doublet, *pattern.*

PATRONYMIC, derived from the name of a father or ancestor. (F.—L.—Gk.) 'So when the proper name is used to note one's parentage, which kind of nouns the grammarians call *patronymics*;' Ben Jonson, Eng. Grammar, b. ii. c. 3.—MF. *patronymique*, 'derived of the fathers or ancestors names;' Cot.—L. *patrōnymicus*.—Gk. πατρωνυμικός, belonging to the father's name.—Gk. πατρωνυμία, a name taken from the father.—Gk. πατρο-, for πατήρ, a father; and ὄνυμα, a name, usually spelt ὄνομα. The ω results from the doubling of the o. The Gk. πατήρ is cognate with E. *father*; and Gk. ὄνομα is cognate with E. *name*. Der. *patronymic*, sb.

PATTEN, a wooden sole supported on an iron ring; a clog. (F.—Teut.) 'Their shoes and *pattens*;' Camden's Remaines, On Apparel (R.). Spelt *paten, patin* in Minsheu, ed. 1627; *paten*, Palsgrave.—F. *patin*, 'a pattin, or clog; also, the footstall of a pillar;' Cot.—OF. *pate, patte*, mod. F. *patte*, 'the paw or foot of a beast, the footstall of a pillar;' Cot. See **Patrol**. Cf. Ital. *pattino.*

PATTER, to strike frequently, as hail. (E.) 'Or *pattering* hail comes pouring on the main;' Dryden, tr. of Virgil, Æn. ix. 910. A frequentative of *pat*, with the usual suffix -*er*; the double *t* being put in to keep the vowel short. See **Pat** (1). A dialectal (Lonsdale) variant is *pattle*, to pat gently (Peacock). Cf. Swed. dial. *padra*, to patter as hail does against a window (Rietz). ☞ It is probable that ME. *pateren*, in the sense 'to repeat prayers,' was coined from *pater*, the first word of the *pater-noster*. 'And *patred* in my *pater-noster*;' P. Plowman's Crede, ed. Skeat, l. 6; so also in the Rom. of the Rose, l. 6794. Hence *patter*, to prattle, and *patter*, sb. talk.

PATTERN, an example, model to work by. (F.—L.) In many parts, as in Lincolnshire and Cambs., the common people say *patron* for *pattern*; and rightly. 'Patron, a pattern;' Peacock, Manley Words (Lincoln); E. D. S. ME. *patron*; Chaucer, Book Duch. 910. 'Patrone, from to werk by, *patron* or example, *Exemplar*;' Prompt. Parv. 'Patrons of blacke paper;' Eng. Gilds, ed. Toulmin Smith, p. 321.—F. *patron*, 'a patron, protector, . . also a pattern, sample;' Cot. See **Patron**. Doublet, *patron.*

PATTY, a little pie. (F.—L.—Gk.) Mod. F. *pâté*; OF. *pasté*, a pasty. See **Paste**. Doublet, *pasty*. Der. *patty-pan.*

PAUCITY, fewness in number. (F.—L.) Spelt *paucitie* in Minsheu, ed. 1627.—F. *paucité*, 'paucity;' Cot.—L. *paucitātem*, acc. of *paucitās*, fewness.—L. *pauci-*, for *paucus*, few; with suffix -*tās*. β. Allied to Gk. παῦρος, small; and to E. *few*; see **Few**.

PAUNCH, the belly. (F.—L.) ME. *paunche*, P. Plowman,

B. xiii. 87.—O. North F. *panche*; OF. *pance*, 'the paunch, maw, belly;' Cot.—L. *panticem*, acc. of *pantex*, the paunch.

PAUPER, a poor person. (L.) In Phillips, ed. 1706.—L. *pauper*, poor. β. The syllable *pau-* is the same as *pau-* in *paucus*, few, Gk. παῦρος; see **Paucity**. The second element in *pau-per* is prob. allied to *parāre*. See **Pare**. Der. *pauper-ise*, *pauper-ism*; and see *poor*, *poverty*.

PAUSE, a stop, cessation. (F.—L.—Gk.) In Shak. Hamlet, ii. 2. 509. Earlier, spelt *pawse*, in Prompt. Parv.—F. *pause*, 'a pause, a stop;' Cot.—Late L. *pausa*, a pause. Adapted from Gk. παῦσις, a pause, stopping, ceasing, end.—Gk. παύω, I make to cease; παύομαι, I cease. See **Few**. Der. *pause*, vb., Much Ado, iv. I. 202. Doublet, *pose*, q.v.

PAVE, to floor, as with stones. (F.—L.) ME. *pauen* (with *u=v*), Chaucer, C. T. 16094 (G 626).—OF. *pauer*, later *paver*, 'to pave,' Cot.—Late L. *pavāre*, for L. *pavīre*, to beat, strike, also, to ram, tread down. Der. *pave-ment*, ME. *pauiment* (with *u* for *v*, and trisyllabic), Rob. of Glouc. p. 476, l. 9791, *pauement*, Chaucer, C. T. 7686 (D 2104), from F. *pavement* (Cot.), which from L. *pauīmentum*, a hard floor, from *pauīre*, to ram; also *pav-i-or* the *-i-* is an English insertion, as in *law-y-er*, *bow-y-er*, *saw-y-er*, intended to give the word a causal force), from F. *paveur*, 'a paver,' Cot.

PAVILION, a tent. (F.—L.) The spelling with *li* is intended to represent the sound of the F. *ll*. ME. *pauylon* (with *u=v*), Rob. of Glouc. p. 272, l. 5510.—F. *pavillon*, 'a pavillion, tent;' Cot. So called because spread out like the wings of a butterfly.—L. *pāpiliōnem*, acc. of *pāpilio*, (1) a butterfly, (2) a tent. 'Cubicula aut tentoria, quos etiam *papiliones* uocant;' Augustine, cited in Ducange. Der. *pavilion-ed*, Hen. V, i. 2. 129; also *papilion-ac-e-ous*, q.v.

PAVIN, PAVAN, a stately Spanish dance. (F.—Span.—L.—Pers.—Tamil.) See exx. in Nares.—F. *pavane*, 'a pavane;' Cot.—Span. *pavana*, 'a daunce called a pauin, playing;' Minsheu. Prob. from a Late L. *pavānus*, peacock-like, from the row of stately dancers (Scheler); cf. Span. *pava*, a peahen, *pavo*, a peacock, *pavonear*, to walk with affected dignity.—Late L. *pāvus*, L. *pāuo*, a peacock. See **Peacock**.

PAVISE, a large shield. (F.—Ital.) Obsolete. See examples in N. E. D., Halliwell and R. Also spelt *pavese*, *pavish*, *pauesse*, *pauice*, *pauys*. 'That impenetrable *pauice*,' Sir T. More, Works, p. 1179 c. Spelt *pauys*, Reliquiæ Antiquæ, ii. 22; *paues*, Skelton, ed. Dyce, i. 8, l. 48; *pauys*, Lydgate, Minor Poems, p. 204.—OF. *pavais*, F. *pavois*, 'a great shield,' Cot. Cf. Span. *paves*, MItal. *pavese* (Florio).—Late L. *pavensis*, a large shield, occurring A.D. 1299. Usually said to have been named from the city of *Pavia*, in the N. of Italy. Godefroy has the adj. *pavinois*, *paviois*, *pavois*, *pavais*, 'de Pavie;' *escus pavais*, shields of Pavia.

PAW, the foot of a beast of prey. (F.—Teut.) ME. *pawe*, Sir Isumbras, l. 181, in the Thornton Romances, ed. Halliwell; *powe*, Rich. Cuer de Lion, l. 1082, in Weber's Met. Romances. [Hence W. *pawen*, a paw, claw, Corn. *paw*, a foot (found in the 15th century); Bret. *paô*, *pav*, a paw, being from F.]—AF. *powe*, OF. *poe*, a paw; the same word as Prov. *pauta*, Catalan *pota*, a paw. Perhaps from a Teut. source; cf. Low G. *pote*, a paw (Bremen Wörterbuch), the same word as Du. *poot*, G. *pfote*. Perhaps from an imitative root; see **Pat** (1). Or related to *potter*; see *poot* in Franck. Der. *paw*, verb, Job, xxxix. 21.

PAWL, a short bar, which acts as a catch to a windlass. (F.—L.) A mechanical term; borrowed from OF. *paul* (Godefroy), variant of *pal*, a stake.—L. *pālum*, acc. of *pālus*, whence also L. *pale*; see **Pale** (1), **Pole**. Cf. W. *pawl*, a pole, stake, bar, from E.; Du. *pal*, Swed. *pall*, a pawl; from F. or E. Der. *paul-windlass* (Halliwell).

PAWN (1), a pledge, something given as security for the repayment of money. (F.) Spelt *paune* in Minsheu, ed. 1627; Levins (ed. 1570) has the verb *to paune*.—F. *pan*, 'a pane, piece, or pannel of a wall; also a pawn, or gage, also the skirt of a gown, the pane of a hose, of a cloak, &c.;' Cot. β. But we must distinguish the senses. In the sense of 'pane' or 'skirt,' F. *pan* is of L. origin.— L. *pannum*, acc. of *pannus*, a cloth, rag, piece; see **Pane**. γ. In the sense of 'pawn or gage,' OF. *pan* is rather from Teutonic; from Du. *pand*, a pledge; cf. G. *pfand*, OHG. *phant*, a pledge. δ. Kluge connects G. *pfand* with OF. *paner*, *panner*, to seize upon, which Godefroy connects with OF. *panir*, *pannir*, to seize upon, despoil; which looks like an adaptation of OHG. *phant-jan*; cf. MHG. *phanten*, *phenten*, to pledge, also to rob of. I see no reason why all the forms may not be ultimately referred to L. *pannus*, a piece of cloth or of clothing, as being the readiest article to seize upon as a pledge. Der. *pawn*, vb., *pawn-er*, *pawn-broker*.

PAWN (2), one of the least valuable pieces in chess. (F.—L.) ME. *paune*, Chaucer, Book of the Duchess, l. 661 (Thynne); but spelt *poune*, *poun* in the Tanner and Fairfax MSS. (Chaucer Soc.).—OF. *paon*, a pawn at chess (Roquefort); spelt *poon* in the 12th cent.

(Littré); but also *peon*, *pehon*, *pedon* (Godefroy); whence also F. *pion*, explained by Cotgrave as 'a pawn at chests.' [Cf. Span. *peon*, a foot-soldier, a pawn, Port. *piāo*, one of the lower people, a pawn, Ital. *pedone*, 'a footman' (Florio), *pedona*, 'a pawne at chesse,' id.] —Late L. *pedōnem*, acc. of *pedo*, a foot-soldier; from *ped-*, stem of *pēs*, a foot, cognate with E. **Foot**. ¶ For the form, cf. E. *fawn*, F. *faon*; from Late L. *fētōnem*. Der. *pion-eer*, q.v.

PAWNEE, drink; as in *brandy-pawnee*, Thackeray, Newcomes, ch. i. (Hind.—Skt.) Hind. *pānī*, water (also in Bengáli, and other dialects); Wilson, Gloss. of Indian Terms, p. 397.—Skt. *pānīya-*, drink (Macdonell), allied to *pāna-*, drinking, beverage (Benfey).— Skt. *pā*, to drink; cf. E. *potation*.

PAX, a thin tablet bearing a picture of Christ, kissed by the congregation. (L.) In Shak. Hen. V, iii. 6. 42. '*Paxe* to kysse;' Palsgrave.—L. *pax*, peace: with reference to the kiss of peace. See **Peace**. See Hone's Year-book, 321.

PAXWAX, the strong tendon in the neck of animals. (E.) Still common provincially; also called *paxwaxy*, *packwax*, *faxwax*, *fixfax*. ME. *paxwax*, Prompt. Parv.; see Way's note. He quotes: '*Le vendon*, the fax-wax,' MS. Harl. 219, fol. 150. Again he says: 'Gautier de Biblesworth [Bibbesworth] says, of a man's body, *Et si ad le wenne* (fex wex) *au col derere*,' i.e. and he has paxwax at the back of his neck. The orig. form is *fax-wax* or *fex-wex*, and it exactly corresponds to the equivalent G. *haarwachs*, lit. 'hair-growth;' presumably because the tendon is situate just where the hair ends. Compounded of ME. *fax*, hair, as in *Fair-fax*=fair-hair; and *wax*, growth.—AS. *feax*, *fex*, hair, Luke, vii. 38; and *weaxan*, to grow; see **Wax** (1). The AS. *feax*, OHG. *fahs*, is related to Gk. πέκειν, to comb; see **Pectinal**.

PAY (1), to discharge a debt. (F.—L.) ME. *paien*, Ancren Riwle, p. 108, l. 9; Layamon, 2340 (later text). It often has the sense of 'please' or 'content' in old authors. 'Be we *paied* with these thingis'=let us be contented with these things, Wyclif, 1 Tim. vi. 8.—OF. *paier* (also *paer*), later *payer*, 'to pay, satisfie, content;' Cot.—L. *pācāre*, to appease, pacify; Late L. *pācāre*, to pay (A.D. 1338).—L. *pāc-*, stem of *pax*, peace. See **Peace**. Der. *pay*, sb., ME. *paie*, satisfaction, P. Plowman, B. v. 556; *pay-able*, *pay-er*, *pay-ee* (= F. *payé*, pp.); *pay-master*; *pay-ment*, ME. *paiement*, Chaucer. C. T. 5713 (D 131), from OF. *paiement*, later *payement*, 'a payment,' Cot.

PAY (2), to pitch the seam of a ship. (F.—L.) A nautical term, as noticed by Skinner, ed. 1671; and in the proverb: 'the devil is to *pay*, and no pitch hot.' 'To *pay* a rope, *een kabel teeren*,' lit. to tar a cable;' Sewel's Eng.-Du. Dict. 1754.—AF. *peier*, answering to O. North F. *peier*, to cover with a plaister (a peculiar use, in Wace; see Godefroy); OF. *poier*, to pitch.—L. *picāre*, to pitch.—L. *pic-*, stem of *pix*, pitch; see **Pitch**. Cf. ME. *pich*, K. Alisaunder, 1620; from AF. *peis*, OF. *pois*, pitch; from L. acc. *picem*.

PAYNIM, PAINIM, a pagan. (F.—L.) 'The *paynim* bold;' Spenser, F. Q. i. 4. 41; cf. Fairfax, tr. of Tasso, xviii. 80. ME. *paynim*. 'The *paynymys* hii ouercome'=they overcame the pagans; Rob. of Glouc. ed. Hearne, p. 401; where the better reading is *paens*, i.e. pagans, as in ed. W. A. Wright, l. 8283. This E. use of the word is due to a singular mistake. A *paynim* was not a man, but a country; it is identical with *paganism*, which was formerly extended to mean the country of pagans, or heathen lands. It is correctly used in King Horn, ed. Lumby, l. 803, where we find 'a geaunt .. fram *paynyme*'=a giant from heathen lands.—AF. *paenime*, heathen lands, Life of Edw. Conf. 336; OF. *paienisme*, spelt *païanisme* in Cotgrave, who explains it by 'paganisme.' [The sense is borrowed from that of OF. *paënie*, *paiënie*, the country inhabited by pagans (Burguy).]—Late L. *pāgānismus*, paganism; formed with suffix *-ismus* (Gk. *-ισμος*) from L. *pāgān-us*, a pagan. See **Pagan**. ¶ When a writer, wishing to use fine language, talks of a *paynim*, he had better say a *pagan* at once.

PEA, a common vegetable. (L.) [We now say *pea*, with pl. *peas*. This is due to mistaking the *s* of the older form for a plural termination; just as when people say *shay* for *chaise*, *Chinee* for *Chinese*, &c. Other words in which the same mistake is made are *cherry* (F. *cerise*), *sherry* (formerly *sherris*).] ME. *pese*, pl. *pesen* and *peses*. 'A *pese-lof*' = a loaf made of peas, P. Plowman, B. vi. 181; pl. *peses*, id. 189; *pesen*, id. 198. A later spelling of the pl. is *peason*; see examples in Nares. Shak. has *peas-cod*=pea-pod, Mids. Nt. Dr. iii. 1. 191; and otherwise only the form *pease*. We also find *pescodes* in Lydgate, London Lyckpeny, st. 9. AS. *pise*, pl. *pisan* (Bosworth). Not an E. word, but borrowed from L. *pisa*, later by-form of L. *pisum*, a pea. [The vowel-change from *i* to *ea* occurs again in the case of *pear*, q.v.]+Gk. πίσος, a pea.—√PEIS, to grind, pound, whence L. *pinsere*, to pound, Skt. *pish*, to grind; with reference to its round shape. Cf. Russ. *pesok'*, sand. Der. *pea-pod*, *peas-cod*.

PEACE, quietness, freedom from war. (F.–L.) ME. *pais*, occurring as early as in the A. S. Chron. an. 1135.–OF. *pais*, later *paix*, 'peace;' Cot.–L. *pācem*, acc. of *pax*, peace, orig. a compact made between two contending parties.–L. *pāc-*, seen in *pāc-iscī*, to make a bargain; cf. OL. *pac-ere*, to bind, to come to an agreement; see **Pact**. Der. *peace!*, interj.; *peace-able*, Much Ado, iii. 3. 61; *peace-abl-y*, *peace-able-ness*; *peace-ful*, K. John, ii. 340, *peace-ful-ly*, *peace-ful-ness*, *peace-maker*, As You Like It, v. 4. 108; *peace-offering*, *peace-officer*. Also *ap-pease*, *pay* (1), *paci-fy*.

PEACH (1), a delicious fruit. (F.–L.–Pers.) 'Of *Peaches*;' Sir T. Elyot, Castel of Helth, b. ii. c. 7. ME. *peche*, *peshe*, Prompt. Parv. p. 395; where it is also spelt *peske*, a form due to Late L. *pesca*.–OF. *pesche*, 'a peach;' Cot. [Cf. Prov. *pêcego*, Ital. *persica*, shorter form *pesca*, a peach.]–L. *Persicum*, a peach, Pliny, xv. 11. 12; so called because growing on the *Persicus* or peach-tree; where *Persicus* stands for *Persica arbor*, the Persian tree.–Pers. *Pārs*, Persia. See **Parsee**. Der. *peach-coloured*, *peach-tree*.

PEACH (2), to inform against. (F.–L.) From ME. *apechen*, by loss of *a*; and *apechen* is a variant of *impechen*, to impeach, with *a-* (<L. *ad*) for *im-* (<L. *in*); see **Impeach**.

PEACOCK, a large gallinaceous bird with splendid plumage. (Hybrid; L.–Gk.–Pers.–Tamil; *and* E.) ME. *pecok*, but also *pacok* and *pocok*. In P. Plowman, B. xii. 241, where the text has *pekok*, two other MSS. have *pokok*, *pacok*. In Chaucer, C. T. 104, the MSS. have *pekok*, *pokok*. We also find *po* used alone, Polit. Songs, ed. Wright, p. 159. The form *pekok* is due to AS. *pēa*, variant of AS. *pāwe*, a peacock, which is not a true E. word, but borrowed from L. *pāuo*. '*Pauo*, *Pauus*, pawe;' Ælfric's Gloss., Nomina Avium, in Voc. 131. 9. Here *pāwe* is the AS. form, whilst *pāuo*, *pāuus*, are L. forms. From L. *pāuo* come also Du. *pauuw*, G. *pfau*, F. *paon*, &c. β. The L. word is not a native one, but borrowed from Gk. ταῶς, ταῶν, where the aspirate is a relic of the digamma, from a form ταϝῶς. See Liddell and Scott, and Curtius, ii. 101. The curious change from initial *t* to *p* indicates that both words are from a foreign source.–Pers. *tāwus*, *tāus*, Arab. *tāwus*, a peacock; Rich. Dict., p. 962.–OTamil *tōkei*, *tōgei*, a peacock; Max Müller, Lect. i. 233. γ. The latter element of the word is E. *cock*, a native word of imitative origin. ¶ 'The name is Tamil, *tōkei*; and the peacock is still called by it in Ceylon;' Oxford Helps to the Study of the Bible. Der. *pea-hen*, similarly formed; ME. *pehen*. *pohen*, P. Plowman, B. xii. 240.

PEA-JACKET, a coarse thick jacket often worn by seamen. (Hybrid; Du. *and* F.) Prob. of modern introduction. The latter element is the ordinary word *jacket*. The former element is spelt so as to resemble *pea*, a vegetable, with which it has nothing to do. It is borrowed from Du. *pij*, *pi,e*, a coat of a coarse woollen stuff; the word *jacket* being a needless explanatory addition. '*Een pije*, a *pie-gowne*, or a rough gowne, as souldiers and seamen weare;' Hexham, 1658. As the Du. *pij* is pronounced like E. *pie*, it should rather be called a *pie-jacket*, as the form *pie-gowne* suggests. The material of which the jacket is made is called *pij-laken*, where *laken* is cloth. β. The Du. *pije* is the same word as Low G. *pije*, a woollen jacket, called *pigge*, *pyke* in the Osnabrück dialect (Bremen Wörterbuch). Prob. from F. *pie*, a magpie; cf. E. *pied*, spotted. The variant *pyke* may be immediately from L. *pica*. See **Pie** (1). ¶ Cf. ME. *courtepy* (short coat), Chaucer, C. T. 292 (A 290).

PEAK, a sharp point, top. (Low G.?) 'Seleucia, which is a great promontory, or *peake*;' Udall, on Acts, xiii. 4. Also *peake* in Palsgrave. Apparently a variant of *pike*, q. v. Cf. dial. of Normandy *pec* a hob (or mark) in the game of quoits (Godefroy, Moisy); also Low G. *peek*, a pike, a pointed weapon. Allied to **Peck**, q. v., and **Pick**, q. v. Der. *peak-ed*, not quite the same word as ME. *piked* (Prompt. Parv.) though used in the same sense; the ME. form answers rather to mod. E. *pike*, sb., with the suffix *-ed* added. Also (probably) *peak*, verb, to become thin, dwindle, Macb. i. 3. 23. Cf. *peaked*, thin, Dorsetshire (Halliwell).

PEAL, a loud sound, summons, chime of bells, sound of a trumpet. (F.–L.) 'A *peale* of gunnes, &c.;' Levins. '*Peele* of belles;' Palsgrave. 'Of the swete *pele* and melodye of bellys;' Monk of Evesham, c. lvii, ed. Arber. A shortened form of ME. *apele*, lit. 'appeal;' see '*apele* of bellis,' in Prompt. Parv., p. 13.– AF. *apel*, an appeal; 'Le clerk soune le dreyne *apel*,' the clerk rings the last peal; Wright, Vol. of Vocab., i. 149.–OF. *apeler*, to call. We speak of a trumpet's *peal*; compare this with F. *appel*, a call with drum or trumpet (Hamilton). β. Besides the form *apel*, mod. F. *appel*, there was a later derived form *appeau*, now used in the sense of 'bird-call' (Hamilton). Cotgrave has: '*Appeau*, as *Appel*, also a bird-call; *Appeaux*, chimes, or the chiming of bells.' This at once explains our common use of the phrase 'a *peal* of bells.' Note also ME. *apel*, 'an old term in hunting music, consisting of three long moots;' Halliwell. This etymology is noticed by Minsheu,

ed. 1627; he has: 'a *peal* of bells, from the F. *appeller*, i. e. vocare.' See **Appeal**. Der. *peal*, verb.

PEAN, the same as **Pæan**, q. v. (L.–Gk.)

PEAR, a well-known fruit. (L.) ME. *pere*, Chaucer, C. T. 10205 (E 2331). AS. *pere* or *peru*; Ælfric's Grammar, 6, 9 (Bosworth); spelt *pere*, Voc. 269. 33. [The AS. *pirige*, a pear-tree, occurs in '*Pirus*, pirige;' Ælfric's Gloss., in Voc. 269. 32. Hence ME. *pery*, a pear-tree, Chaucer, C. T. 10199 (E 2325), or *pirie*, P. Plowman, B. v. 16.]–Late L. *pira*, fem. sing., for L. *pira*, pl. of L. *pirum*, a pear, Pliny, xv. 15, 16; whence also Norm. dial. *peire* (Moisy); F. *poire*. ¶ The vowel-change from *i* to *e* appears again in Ital. *pera*, a pear. Der. *pear-tree*, *perr-y*.

PEARL, a well-known shining gem. (F.–L.) ME. *perle*, Allit. Poems, ed. Morris, A. 1.–F. *perle*, 'a pearle, an union, also a berrie;' Cot. β. Of disputed etymology, but prob. Latin. It is best to collect the forms; we find Ital., Span., Prov. *perla*, Port. *perola*, sometimes *perla*; OHG. *perala*, *perla*, *berala*, *berla*. All prob. from Late L. *pirula*, point of the nose, found in Isidore of Seville, in the 7th century. γ. Diez explains *pirula* as prob. meaning a little pear, from *pirum*, a pear; the change of vowel is well seen in Ital. *pera*, a pear. See **Pear**. This is perhaps the best solution; the change of sense from 'pear' to 'pearl' may easily have been suggested by the use of the L. *bacca*, which meant (1) a berry, (2) an olive-berry, (3) any round fruit growing on a tree, (4) a pearl (Horace, Epod. viii. 14). Diez also draws attention to Span. *perilla*, (1) a little pear, (2) a pear-shaped ornament. Perhaps we may add MItal. *perolo*, 'a little button or tassell of wooll on the top and middle of a knit cap;' Florio. And observe the sense of 'berry' which Cotgrave assigns to F. *perle*. δ. But it may be that a form *perula* (for *per'la*?) was a corruption of Late L. *perna*, a pearl (see *pernæ* in Duc.); cf. Norm. dial. *perne*, a pearl (from Sicil. *perna*), MItal. *perna*, 'a shell-fish called a nakre;' Florio.–L. *perna*, a sea-mussel. See *perne* in Moisy. Der. *pearl-y*, *pearl-i-ness*; *pearl-ash*, a purer carbonate of potash, named from its pearly colour.

PEARL-BARLEY. (F.–L.; *and* E.) A translation of F. *orge perlé*, lit. 'pearled barley;' but this looks like an adaptation of MF. *orge pelé*, lit. 'peeled barley;' Cot. See **Peel** (1) and **Barley**.

PEASANT, a countryman. (F.–L.) The *t* is excrescent, as in *ancien-t*, *tyran-t*, but it occurs in OF. In Gascoigne, Steele Glas, l. 647.–OF. *paisant*, 'a peasant, boor;' Cot.; Norm. dial. *paisant* (Moisy). Mod. F. *paysan*, and the more correct OF. form *paisan*, answer to Ital. *paisano*, Span. *paesano*, one born in the same country, a compatriot. β. Formed with suffix *-an* (=Ital. *-ano*, L. *-ānus*) from OF. *païs* (mod. F. *pays*), a country; answering to Ital. *paese*, Span. *pais*, Port. *pais*, *paiz*. All these latter forms answer to Late L. *pāgensem*, acc. of *pāgensis*, for *pāgensis ager*, country.–L. *pāgus*, a village. See **Pagan**. Der. *peasant-ry*, Bacon, Life of Hen. VII, ed. Lumby, p. 72, l. 16, a coined word.

PEAT, a vegetable substance like turf, found in boggy places, and used as fuel. (C.) 'There other with their spades the *peats* are squaring out;' Drayton, Polyolbion, s. 25. l. 143. 'Turf and *peat* ... are cheape fuels;' Bacon, Nat. Hist. § 775. Spelt *peit*, Gloss. to Leslie's Hist. of Scotland (1596); S. T. S. Very common in Northumbrian. ME. *pete*, in comp. *pete-pot*, a hole out of which peats have been dug; Wyntown, viii. 24. 46 (Jamieson). Latinised as *peta* (Ducange); whence also *petaria*, a place whence peats were dug. Ducange quotes: 'Cum suis ... turbariis, tresidiis, *petariis*,' &c.; and again, 'Cum ... *petariis*, turbariis, carbonariis' (1503). As a *peat* often meant 'a piece of cut turf,' it is likely that the Late L. *peta* was a by-form of Late L. *petia*, 'a piece,' from a Celtic source. We find OGael. *pett* (Book of Deer), borrowed from British; cf. W. *peth*, a thing, a piece; cognate with Gael. *cuid*, which see in Macbain. See Thurneysen, Keltoromanisches, p. 76. See **Piece**.

PEBBLE, a small round stone. (E.) In Shak. Cor. v. 3. 58; a pebble-stone, Two Gent. ii. 3. 11. ME. *pobbel*, Allit. Poems, ed. Morris, A. 117; *pibbil-ston*, Wyclif, Prov. xx. 17. AS. *papol-stān*, a pebble-stone; Ælfric's Homilies, i. 64, l. 3. Cf. AS. *pæbbel*, Birch, Cart. Saxon. ii. 403. Der. *pebbl-y*, *pebbl-ed*.

PECCABLE, liable to sin. (L.) Rare; Rich. gives quotations for *peccable* and *peccability* from Cudworth, Intellectual System (first ed. 1678, also 1743, 1820, 1837, 1845), pp. 564, 565. Englished from L. *peccābilis*, a coined word from *peccāre*, to sin. Brugmann, i. § 585. Der. *peccabili-ty*. See **Peccant**.

PECCADILLO, a slight offence, small sin. (Span.–L.) In Blount's Gloss., ed. 1674.–Span. *pecadillo*, a slight fault, dimin. of *pecado*, a sin.–L. *peccātum*, a sin; orig. neut. of *peccātus*, pp. of *peccāre*, to sin. See **Peccant**.

PECCANT, sinning. (F.–L.) Used in the phrase '*peccant* humours;' Bacon, Advancement of Learning, ed. Wright, bk. i. 4. 12, 5. 12; p. 37, l. 32, p. 43, l. 28.–F. *peccant*, 'sinning; *l'humeur* *peccante*, the corrupt humour in the body;' Cot. – L. *peccant-*, stem of pres. part. of *peccāre*, to sin. Der. *peccant-ly*, *peccanc-y*; and see *pecc-able*, *pecc-ad-illo*.

PECCARY, a hog-like quadruped of S. America. (F. – Caribbean.) ' *Pecary*, a sort of wild hogs, called here [at Bahia] *pica*;' W. Dampier, New Voy. iii. 76; spelt *peccary*, id. i. 9 (1699). – F. *pécari*, a peccary. A S. American word. – Carib. *pakira*, the name used in Guiana; see N. and Q. 9 S. iv. 496. Cf. *pachira*, 'which is the name given to this quadruped in Oronoko;' Clavigero's Hist. of Mexico, tr. by Cullen, 1787, ii. 319. It is also called, in different parts of America, *saino*, *cojametl*, and *tatabro* (id.). And cf. Span. *pacquire* (Pineda). See my Notes on Eng. Etymology, p. 209.

PECK (1), to strike with something pointed, to snap up. (E.?) A mere variant of *pick*. In Chaucer, C. T. 14973 (Six-text, B 4157) we have: ' *Pikke* hem up right as they growe,' in MS. C., where most MSS. have *Pekke* or *Pek*. *Pick* is the older form; see **Pick**. Some Swed. dialects have *pekka* for *pikka*; cf. W. Flem. *pekken* (De Bo); for Du. *pikken*. Der. *peck-er*, *wood-peck-er*.

PECK (2), a dry measure, two gallons. (F. – Low G. ?) ME. *pekke*, Chaucer, C. T. 4008. Cf. AF. *pek*, Liber Albus, p. 335; OF. *pek* (Godefroy). The word is somewhat obscure, but it is probably related to *peck*, to snap up. As in the case of most measures, the quantity was once indefinite, and prov. E. *peck* merely means 'a quantity;' we still talk of 'a *peck* of troubles.' In particular, it was a quantity for eating; cf. prov. E. *peck*, meat, victuals, from the prov. E. verb *peck*, to eat. 'We must scrat before we *peck*,' i.e. scratch (work) before we eat; Halliwell. Hence slang E. *pecker*, appetite. β. Similarly Scheler derives *picotin*, a peck, a measure, from the verb *picoter*, to peck as a bird does; and *picoter* is itself a mere extension from the Teut. root appearing also in E. *peck* and *pick*.

PECTINAL, comb-like, applied to fish with bones like the teeth of a comb. (L.) Sir T. Browne speaks of *pectinals*, i.e. pectinal fish; Vulg. Errors, b. iv. c. 1, last section. Coined from L. *pectin-*, decl. stem of *pecten*, a comb. – L. *pectere*, to comb. + Gk. πεκτεῖν, to comb; lengthened form from πέκειν, to comb, to card wool, to shear. β. From √PEK, to pluck, pull hair, comb; preserved also in Lithuanian *pesz-ti*, to pluck, pull hair. From the same root is AS. *fæx*, a head of hair, whence *Fairfax*, i.e. fair hair. Der. Hence also *pectin-ate*, *pectin-at-ed*; and see *paxwax*.

PECTORAL, belonging to the breast or chest. (F. – L.) In Minsheu, ed. 1627. – F. *pectoral*, 'pectorall;' Cot. – L. *pectorālis*, belonging to the breast. – L. *pector-*, for *pectos*, stem of *pectus*, the breast. Der. *pectoral-ly*, *ex-pector-ate*.

PECULATE, to pilfer, steal. (L.) ' *Peculator*, that robs the prince or common treasure;' Blount's Gloss., ed. 1674. – L. *pecūlātus*, pp. of *pecūlāri*, to appropriate to one's own use. Formed as if from **pecūlum*, with the same sense as *pecūlium*, private property, and allied to *pecū-nia*, property; see **Peculiar, Pecuniary**. Der. *peculat-ion*, *peculat-or*.

PECULIAR, appropriated, one's own, particular. (F. – L.) In Levins; and in Shak. Oth. i. 1. 60. – MF. *peculier*, 'peculiar;' Cot. – L. *pecūliāris*, relating to property, one's own. – L. *pecūlium*, property; allied to *pecūnia*, property, money, from which it differs in the suffix. See **Pecuniary**. Der. *peculiar-ly*, *peculiar-i-ty*.

PECUNIARY, relating to property or money. (F. – L.) Spelt *pecuniarie* in Minsheu, ed. 1627. – MF. *pecuniaire*, 'pecuniary;' Cot. – L. *pecūniārius*, belonging to property. – L. *pecūnia*, property. β. Formed from *pecu-*, as appearing in OL. *pecu*, cattle, and in L. pl. *pecu-a*, cattle of all kinds, sheep, money; the wealth of ancient times consisting in cattle. + Skt. *paçu*, cattle; Goth. *faihu*, property; AS. *feoh*, G. *vieh*, cattle. Der. *pecuniari-ly*.

PEDAGOGUE, a teacher, pedant. (F. – L. – Gk.) In Caxton's Golden Legend, St. Eutrope, § 1. – MF. *pedagogue*, 'a schoolmaster, teacher, pedant;' Cot. – L. *pædagogus*, a preceptor. – Gk. παιδαγωγός, at Athens, a slave who led a boy to school, hence, a tutor, instructor. – Gk. παιδ-, stem of παῖς, a boy; and ἀγωγός, leading, guiding, from ἄγειν, to lead. β. The Gk. παῖς is for παϝις, i.e. pau-is, from a probable √PEU, to beget, whence L. *pu-er*, a boy, Skt. *pu-tra-*, a son. The Gk. ἄγειν, to lead, is cognate with E. **Agent**, q. v. Der. *pedagog-ic*; *pedagog-y*, MF. *pedagogie* (Cot.).

PEDAL, belonging to the foot. (L.) ' *Pedal*, of a foot, measure or space;' Blount's Gloss., ed. 1674. ' *Pedalls*, or low keyes, of organs;' Sherwood, index to Cotgrave. Now chiefly used as a sb., as the *pedal* of an organ, i.e. a key acted on by the foot. – L. *pedālis*, (1) belonging to a foot, (2) belonging to a foot-measure (whence the old use, as in Blount). – L. *ped-*, stem of *pēs*, a foot; cognate with E. **Foot**, q.v.

PEDANT, a schoolmaster, vain displayer of learning. (F. – Ital. – Gk.?) In Shak. L. L. L. iii. 179. – MF. *pedant*, 'a pedant, or ordinary schoolmaster;' Cot. Borrowed from Italian (Littré). –

Ital. *pedante*, 'a pedante, or a schoolmaster, the same as *pedagogo*;' Florio. β. *Pedante* is a pres. participial form as if from a verb **pedare*, which, as Diez suggests, is probably not the MItal. *pedare*, 'to foote it, to tracke, to trace, to tread or trample with one's feete' (Florio), but rather **pædāre*, an accommodation of the Gk. παιδεύειν, to instruct, from παιδ-, stem of παῖς, a boy. See **Pedagogue**. Diez cites from Varchi (Ercol., p. 60, ed. 1570), a passage in Italian, to the effect that ' when I was young, those who had the care of children, teaching them and taking them about, were not called as at present *pedanti* nor by the Greek name *pedagogi*, but by the more honourable name of *ripititori*' [ushers]. Der. *pedant-ic*, *pedant-ic-al*, *pedant-ry*.

PEDDLE, to deal in small wares. (E.) Bp. Hall contrasts '*pedling* barbarisms' with 'classick tongues;' Satires, bk. ii [*not* iii]. sat. 3, l. 25. Here *pedling* means 'petty,' from the verb *peddle* or *pedle*, to deal in small wares; a verb coined from the sb. *pedlar*, a dealer in small wares, which was in earlier use. See **Pedlar**.

PEDESTAL, the foot or base of a pillar. (Span. – Ital. – L. and G.) Spelt *pedestall* in Minsheu, ed. 1627. – Span. *pedestal*, 'the base or foot of a pillar,' Minsheu. Cf. MF. *pied-stal* in Cotgrave. As the Span. for 'foot' is *pié*, it is not a Span. word, but borrowed wholly from Ital. *piedestallo*, 'a footstall or a treshall [threshold] of a doore;' Florio. Lit. 'foot-support.' β. A hybrid compound; from Ital. *piede*, 'a foote, a base, a footstall or foundation of anything' (Florio), which is from L. *pedem*, acc. of *pēs*, a foot; and Ital. *stallo*, a stable, a stall, from OHG. *stal*, G. *stall*, a stable, stall, cognate with E. *stall*. See **Foot** and **Stall**. ☞ *Footstall* (G. *fussgestell*) is a better word.

PEDESTRIAN, going on foot; an expert walker. (L.) Properly an adj. Blount's Gloss., ed. 1674, gives the form *pedestrial*. Both *pedestri-an* and *pedestri-al* are coined words, from L. *pedestri-*, decl. stem of *pedester*, one who goes on foot. Formed, it is supposed, from **pedit-ter*, i.e. by adding the suffix *-ter* (Idg. *-ter*) to *pedit-*, stem of *pedes*, one who goes on foot. *Ped-it-* is from *ped-*, stem of *pēs*, a foot; and *it-um*, supine of *īre*, to go, from √EI, to go. Cf. *com-es* (stem *com-it-*), a companion, one who 'goes with' another. The L. *pēs* is cognate with E. *foot*; see **Foot**. Der. *pedestrian-ism*.

PEDICEL, PEDICLE, the foot-stalk by which a flower or fruit is joined on to a tree. (F. – L.) *Pedicel* is modern, from mod. F. *pédicelle*; not a good form, since L. *pedicellus* means 'a little louse.' *Pedicle* is the better word, as used by Bacon, Nat. Hist. § 592. – MF. *pedicule*, 'the staulk of a leafe, or of fruit;' Cot. – L. *pediculum*, acc. of *pediculus*, a little foot, foot-stalk. Double dimin. from *pedi-*, decl. stem of *pēs*, cognate with E. *foot*. See **Foot**.

PEDIGREE, a register of descent, lineage, genealogy. (F. – L.) In Shak. Hen. V, ii. 4. 90. Spelt *pedegree* in Minsheu (1627); *pedigrew* in Levins (1570); *petygrewe* in Palsgrave (1530). In the Prompt. Parv., A. D. 1440, we find the spellings *pedegru*, *pedegrw*, *pedygru*, *pedegrewe*, *petygru*, *petygrwe*, and it is explained by 'lyne of kynrede and awncetrye, *Stemma*, *in scalis*.' In the Appendix to Hearne's ed. of Rob. of Gloucester, p. 585, he cites from a MS. of Rob. of Glouc. in the Herald's Office, a piece which begins: ' A *pete-greu*, fro William Conquerour .. vn-to kyng Henry the vi.' The last circumstance mentioned belongs to A.D. 1431, so that the date is about the same as that of the Prompt. Parv. Wedgwood cites from the Rolls of Winchester College, temp. Henry IV, printed in Proceedings of the Archæological Institute, 1848, p. 64, a passage relating to the expenses 'Stephani Austinwell .. ad loquendum .. de evidenciis scrutandis de *pe de gre* progenitorum hæredum de Husey.' Lydgate has *peedegrue*; in Polit. Poems, ed. Wright, ii. 138; A.D. 1426; also *peedegrewe*, Hors, Shepe and Goos, l. 9; *pee de grewe*, Troybook, fol. E e 1, back, l. 7. Thus the word does not appear till the 15th century. β. From AF. *pee de grue*, lit. 'foot of a crane;' so named from a three-line mark (like the broad arrow, or a bird's foot), which was used in denoting succession in pedigrees; indeed, the symbol ⅄ is still in use as the 'pedigree-sign.' – L. *pedem*, acc. of *pēs*, a foot; *dē*, of; *gruem*, acc. of *grus*, a crane, related to E. **Crane**. ¶ First explained by Mr. C. Sweet, in The Athenæum, March 30, 1895. See my Notes on Eng. Etymology.

PEDIMENT, an ornament finishing the front of a building. (F. – L.) ' *Fronton*, in architecture, a member that serves to compose an ornament, raised over cross-works, doors, niches, &c., sometimes making a triangle, and sometimes part of a circle; it is otherwise called a *pediment*, and *fastigium* by Vitruvius;' Phillips, ed. 1706. Evelyn, Hist. of Architecture, 1696, speaks of the *fronton*, ' which our workmen call *pediment*.' The older form was *periment*, as shown in the N. E. D.; and this was said to be a workman's term, and 'corrupt English.' β. I think it is likely that a *periment* was simply a mistaken way of pronouncing *operiment*, given in the N. E. D. with the sense of 'a covering,' and recorded with that sense in Blount's Glossographia, ed. 1656, and in Phillips, ed. 1658. – L. *operimentum*, a covering. – L. *operire*, to cover; see **Cover**. γ. When the source of (*o*)*pediment* was lost sight of, it seems to have been associated with the L. (*im*)*pedimentum*, whence the form *pediment*.

PEDLAR, PEDLER, PEDDLER, a hawker, one who travels about selling small wares. (E.) The verb to *peddle*, to sell small wares, is later, and a mere derivative from the sb. We find *pedler* in Cotgrave, to explain F. *mercerot*, and *pedlar* in Sherwood's index. But a shorter form was *peddar* or *pedder*, appearing as late as in Levins, ed. 1570; although, on the other hand, *pedlere* occurs as early as in P. Plowman, B. v. 258; and Lydgate has: 'as *pedeler* to his pakke;' Minor Poems, p. 30. The Prompt. Parv. gives: '*Pedlare*, shapmann,' i.e. chapman, hawker. '*Peddare*, calatharius [basket-maker], *piscarius*' [one who sells fish hawked about in baskets]; Prompt. Parv.; formed from *pedde*, explained by 'panere,' i.e. a pannier; id. See Way's excellent illustrative note. β. As Way remarks, in the Eastern counties, a pannier for carrying provisions to market, esp. fish, is called a *ped*; 'the market in Norwich, where wares brought in from the country are exposed for sale, being known as the *ped-market*; and a dealer who transports his wares in such a manner is termed a *pedder*.' Perhaps *pedlar* is due to a dimin. from *peddle*, i.e. little 'ped,' which is not recorded. The word *peddar* is old, and is spelt *peoddare* in the Ancren Riwle, p. 66, l. 17, where it has the exact sense of pedlar or hawker of small wares. And see Lowland Sc. *peddir*, a pedlar (Jamieson). Cf. 'A *haske* is a wicker *pad*, wherein they vse to carry fish;' Gloss by E. Kirke to Spenser, Shep. Kal. November, l. 16. See **Padlock.** Der. *peddle*, vb., q. v.

PEDOBAPTISM, infant baptism. (Gk.) In Blount's Gloss., ed. 1674. A coined word, as if from L. *pædobaptismus, Latinised form of Gk. παιδοβαπτισμός; from παιδο-, decl. stem of παῖς, a boy; and βαπτισμός, baptism. See **Pedagogue** and **Baptism.** Der. *pedobaptist*.

PEDUNCLE, a flower-stalk. (L.) Modern; cf. F. *pédoncule*; used in 1798 (Hatzfeld). – L. *pedunculus*, variant of *pediculus*, a footstalk or pedicle. – L. *ped*-, stem of *pēs*, a foot. See **Pedal, Pedicel.**

PEEL (1), to strip off the skin or bark. (F. – L.) In Shak. Merch. Ven. i. 3. 85. [Two F. verbs are mixed up here, viz. F. *peler* and F. *piller*. It is true that *peler* and *piller* are now well distinguished in French, the former meaning 'to peel, strip,' and the latter 'to plunder,' a sense preserved in E. *pillage*. But in OF. they were sometimes confused, and the same confusion appears in ME. *pilien, pillen*, used in the sense of 'peel.' 'Rushes to *pilie*'=to peel rushes, P. Plowman, C. x. 81; *pilled*=bald, Chaucer, C. T. 3933 (A 3935). A clear case is in Palsgrave, who has: 'I *pyll* rysshes, Ie pille des ioncz.' For further remarks on *pill*, see **Pillage.**] We may consider *peel*, in the present place, as due to *peler* only. – F. *peler*, 'to pill, pare, bark, unrind, unskin;' Cot. [Cf. Span. *pelar*, Ital. *pelare*, to strip, peel, MItal. *pellare*, 'to vnskin,' Florio.] – OF. *pel*, skin. – L. *pellem*, acc. of *pellis*, skin; see **Fell** (2). ¶ But some senses of F. *peler* are due to L. *pilāre*, to deprive of hair, make bald. – L. *pilus*, hair. Der. *peel-ed*; *peel*, sb.

PEEL (2), to pillage. (F. – L.) 'Peeling their provinces,' i.e. robbing them; Milton, P. R. iv. 136. This is not the same word as the above, but another spelling of the old verb *pill* (F. *piller*), to rob. See **Pillage,** and see remarks under **Peel** (1).

PEEL (3), a fire-shovel. (F. – L.) Once a common word. '*Pele* for an ouyn, *pelle à four*;' Palsgrave. – F. *pelle*, also spelt *pale*, 'a fire-shovell,' Cot. – L. *pāla*, a spade, shovel, peel. See **Palette.** Der. *pal-ette*.

PEEL (4), a small castle. (F. – L.) Used by Burns, The Five Carlins, st. 5; see Jamieson. ME. *pel* (also *pele, pell*), Chaucer, Ho. of Fame, l. 1310 (iii. 220); *peill*, pl. *pelis*, Barbour, Bruce, x. 137, 147. – OF. *pel* (given in Godefroy under *pal*), a stake, pale, stock, stockade. (The original *peels* were stockades or wooden structures; the name was retained after stone was used; see an Essay on the word Peel by G. Neilson, of Glasgow.) – L. *pālum*, acc. of *pālus*, a stake; see **Pale** (1). ¶ Different from ME. *pile*, P. Plowman, C. xxii. 366; cf. 'I dwelle in my *pile* of ston,' Torrent of Portugal, ed. Halliwell, 573; 'Grete *pylis* and castellys;' Cov. Mysteries, p. 210. See **Pile** (2).

PEEP (1), to chirp, or cry like a chicken. (F. – L.) In Isaiah, viii. 19, x. 14; see Bible Wordbook. 'Now, suete bird, say ones to me *pepe*!' Kingis Quair, st. 57. Cf. 'A *pepe* of chekennys (chickens);' Book of St. Alban's, fol. f 7, l. 4. An imitative word, but it seems nevertheless to have been borrowed from F. – OF. *pepier*, 'to peep, cheep, or pule, as a young bird in the neast,' Cot.; also *pipier* (Godefroy). Allied to *piper*, 'to whistle, or chirp, like a bird,' id.; cf. *pipée*, 'the peeping or chirping of small birds,' id. The latter form (*piper*) represents a Folk-L. *pippāre, allied to L. *pīpāre*, *pīpīre*, to peep, chirp. Of imitative origin; due to repetition of the syllable PI. Cf. Gk. πιπίζειν, πιππίζειν, to chirp. See **Pipe** (1).

PEEP (2), to look out (or in) through a narrow aperture, to look slily. (F. – L.) 'Where dawning day doth never *peepe*;' Spenser, F. Q. i. 1. 39. 'To *peepe*, inspicere;' Levins, ed. 1570. It seems to have arisen from the sound *peep*! used as an interjection. In his Du. dial. Dict., Molema explains how the exclamation *piep*! is made (as a slight guide) by a hider in the game of *peep-bo*, *bo-peep*, or hide and seek; whence Du. dial. *piepen*, (1) to cry *piep*! (2) to peep out. Prob. Palsgrave refers to this when he says: 'I peke or prie, je pipe hors,' i.e. I peep out. The F. *piper* usually meant 'to pipe;' Cot. gives: '*piper*, to whistle, chirp like a bird, cousen, deceive, cheat.' β. The old phrase 'at peep of day' answers to MF. *a la pipe du jour*, which Palsgrave explains by 'at *daye-pype*;' p. 804, col. 1; which has reference to the chirping of birds at daybreak. All from L. *pīpāre*, to chirp; see **Peep** (1), **Pipe** (1). See my Notes on Eng. Etymology. Der. *peep-bo* or *bo-peep*, a game of hide and seek; in its simplest form, a nurse says *peep* to an infant, in a squeaky voice, with her face behind her apron, and then *bo*! suddenly in a louder one, uncovering her face at the same time. Compare: '*Bo, Boe*, cucullus lugubris oculos faciemque obstruens; *Kijke-boe*, lusus puerilis, in quo alicuius oculi, manu linteove, etc., obtecti, subitò infantis in gratiam deteguntur;' Ten Kate, Anleidning tot de Kennisse van het verhevene Deel der Nederduitsche Sprake; 1723, vol. i. p. 279. Also W. Flem. *piepbeu*, peep-bo (De Bo).

PEER (1), an equal, a nobleman. (F. – L.) The orig. sense is 'equal;' the *twelve peers* of France were so called because of equal rank. ME. *pere*, Chaucer, C. T. 10990 (F 678); *per*, Havelok, 2241. – OF. *per*, *peer*, later *pair*, 'a peer, a paragon, also a match, fellow, companion;' Cot.; or, as an adj., 'like, equall,' id. [Cf. Span. *par*, equal, also a peer; Ital. *pare, pari*, alike, *pari*, a peer.] – L. *parem*, acc. of *pār*, equal. See **Par, Pair.** Der. *peer-ess*, a late word, with fem. suffix *-ess*, of F. origin, Pope, Moral Essays, ii. 70, iii. 140; *peer-age*, used in 1671 (see N. E. D.) in place of the older word *peer-dom*, used by Cotgrave to translate F. *pairie*; also *peer-less*, Temp. iii. 1. 47; *peer-less-ly*, *peer-less-ness*.

PEER (2), to look narrowly, to pry. (E.?) 'Peering [quarto, Piring] in maps for ports;' Merch. Ven. i. 1. 19. Of obscure origin; apparently altered, by confusion with *peer* (3), from ME. *piren*. 'Riht so doth he, whan that he *pireth* And toteth on hire wommanhiede;' = so does he, when he peers and looks upon her womanhood; Gower, C. A. iii. 29; bk. vi. 819. 'And preuylich *pirith* till þe dame passe' = and privily peers, or spies, till the mother-bird leaves the nest; Rich. Redeles, ed. Skeat, iii. 48. Cf. EFries. *pīren*, Westphal. *pīren*, Low G. *pīren*, to look closely; esp. Westphal. *pīren na wot*, to peer after something. Cf. also the parallel forms *plīren*, *plüren*; see Bremen Wörterbuch. For the loss of *l*, cf. **Patch.**+Swed. *plira*, to blink; Dan. *plire*, to blink. The orig. sense of Low G. *plüren* is to draw the eyelids together, in order to look closely. And see **Peer** (3).

PEER (3), to appear. (F. – L.) Distinct from the word above, though prob. sometimes confused with it. It is merely short for *appear*. ME. *peren*, short for *aperen*. 'There was I bidde, on pain of death, to *pere*;' Court of Love (16th cent.), l. 55. Cf. 'When daffodils begin to *peer*;' Shak. Wint. Ta. iv. 3. 1. As the ME. *aperen* was usually spelt with one *p*, the prefix *a-* easily dropped off, as in the case of *peal* for *appeal*; see **Peal.** Cf. Chaucer, Troil. ii. 909, where *to appere* is also written *tapere*; see further under **Appear.** ¶ In F. the simple verb *paroir* (L. *parēre*) was used in a similar way. '*Paroir*, to appear, to peep out, as the day in a morning, or the sun over a mountain;' Cot.

PEEVISH, cross, ill-natured, fretful. (E.) ME. *peuisch*; spelt *peyuesshe* in P. Plowman, C. ix. 151, where four MSS. have *peuysche*; the sense being 'ill-natured.' It occurs also in G. Douglas, tr. of Virgil, Æn. xi. 408 (Lat. text), where we find: 'Sik ane *peuyche* and cative saule as thyne' = such a perverse and wretched soul as thine. And again, Aruns is called 'thys *pewech* man of weir' [war], where it answers to L. *improbus*; Æn. xi. 767. Ray, in his North-country Words, ed. 1691, gives: 'Peevish, witty, subtil.' Florio explains *schifezza* by 'coynes, quaintnes, *peeuishnes*, fondnes, frowardnes.' *Peevish* in Shak. is silly, childish, thoughtless, forward. *Peevishnesse* = waywardness, Spenser, F. Q. vi. 7. 37. Thus the various senses are childish, silly, wayward, froward, uncouth, ill-natured, perverse, and even witty. All of these may be reduced to the sense of 'childish,' the sense of witty being equivalent to that of 'forward,' the child being *toward* instead of *froward*. β. A difficult word; but prob. of onomatopoetic origin, from the noise made by fretful children. The origin is illustrated by Lowland Sc. *peu*, to make a plaintive noise, used in the Complaint of Scotland, ed. Murray, vi. 39, to denote the plaintive cry of young birds: 'the chekyns [chickens] began to *peu*.' *Peevish* answers to MDan. *pjæven*, tearful; adj. from *pjæve*, to whimper (Kalkar); and Wedgwood cites Dan. dial. *pjæve*, to whimper or cry like a child; cf. Low G. *pau-en*, to whimper. Cf. F. *piauler*, 'to peep or cheep as a young bird, also to pule, or howle as a young whelp;' Cot. Cf. **Pewit.** In this view, the suffix *-ish* has the not uncommon force of 'given to,' as in *thievish, mop-ish.* Similarly, from Gael. *piug,* a plaintive note, we have *piugach,* having a querulous voice, mean-looking. **Der.** *peevish-ly, -ness.*

PEEWIT, another spelling of **Pewit.** (E.)

PEG, a wooden pin for fastening boards, &c. (E. ?) ME. *pegge;* '*Pegge,* or pynne of tymbyr;' Prompt. Parv. The nearest form is Swed. dial. *pegg,* variant of Swed. *pigg* (below); cf. Dan. *pig* (pl. *pigge*), weakened form of *pik,* a pike, peak; Swed. *pigg,* a prick, spike, from *pik,* a pike. Cf. also W. *pig,* a peak, point; Corn. *peg,* a prick. β. Perhaps we may also compare Du. and Low G. *pegel,* a measure of liquid capacity, such as was marked by the pegs in a 'peg-tankard.' **Der.** *peg,* verb, Temp. i. 2. 295; *pegg-ed.*

PEISE, PEIZE, to weigh, to poize. (F.—L.) 'To *peize* the time,' i.e. to weight or retard it; Shak. Merch. Ven. iii. 2. 22. ME. *peisen,* to weigh; P. Plowm. A. v. 131.—AF. *peiser,* Stat. Realm, i. 218; OF. *poiser.* See **Poise,** of which it is a doublet.

PEITREL, the AF. form of **Poitrel,** q.v. In Baret; 1580. Gaimar has AF. *peitrels,* pl.; l. 6385.

PEJORATIVE, depreciatory. (L.) From Late L. *pēiōrāt-us,* pp. of *pēiōrāre,* to impair.—L. *pēiōr-,* from *pēior,* worse, used as the comp. of *malus,* bad. See **Pessimist.** Cf. mod. F. *péjoratif.*

PEKOE, a kind of black tea. (Chinese.) '*Pekoe* Bohea;' H. Carey, Chrononhotonthologos, A. i.—Chinese (Amoy dialect) *pek-ho;* from *pek,* white, *ho,* down; the tea being picked young, with the down still on the leaves (N. E. D.).

PELARGONIUM, a flower of the order Geraniaceæ. (Gk.) From Gk. πελαργός, a stork; from the resemblance of the beaked capsules to a stork's bill. Perhaps from πελ-ιός, dusky, and ἀργός, white.

PELERINE, a kind of lady's tippet. (F.—L.) F. *pèlerine,* a tippet.—F. *pèlerin,* a pilgrim.—L. *peregrīnum,* acc. of *peregrīnus;* see **Pilgrim.**

PELF, lucre, spoil, booty, gain. (F.) 'But all his minde is set on mucky *pelfe;*' Spenser, F. Q. iii. 9. 4. ME. *pelfyr, pelfrey,* 'Spolium;' Prompt. Parv. *Pelf,* property; St. Cuthbert, 5989. *Pelf,* to rob, occurs as a verb, Cursor Mundi, l. 6149.—OF. *pelfre,* booty, allied to *pelfrer,* to pilfer (Godefroy); cf. also OF. *pelfir,* to pillage. **Der.** *pilfer.* Of unknown origin.

PELICAN, a large water-fowl. (F.—L.—Gk.) In Hamlet, iv. 5. 146. Spelt *pellican,* Ancren Riwle, p. 118.—F. *pelican,* 'a pellican;' Cot.—L. *pelicānus, pelecānus.*—Gk. πελεκάν (gen. πελεκᾶνος), πελεκᾶς, πελέκας, strictly, the wood-pecker, the joiner-bird of Aristophanes, Av. 884, 1155; also a water-bird of the pelican kind. The wood-pecker was so called from its pecking; and the pelican from its large bill.—Gk. πελεκάω, I hew with an axe, peck.—Gk. πέλεκυς, an axe, hatchet.+Skt. *paraçu-,* an axe, hatchet.

PELISSE, a silk habit, worn by ladies. (F.—L.) Formerly a furred robe. Of late introduction; added by Todd to Johnson. [The older E. form is *pilch,* q.v.]—F. *pelisse,* formerly also *pelice,* 'a skin of fur;' Cot.—L. *pellicea, pellicia,* fem. of *pelliceus, pellicius,* made of skins.—L. *pellis,* a skin, cognate with E. *fell,* a skin; see **Pell** and **Fell** (2). **Der.** *sur-plice.* Doublet, *pilch.*

PELL, a skin, a roll of parchment. (F.—L.) ME. *pell, pel* (pl. *pellis*); King Alisaunder, 7081.—OF. *pel* (Burguy); mod. F. *peau,* a skin.—L. *pellem,* acc. of *pellis,* a skin, cognate with E. *fell,* a skin; see **Fell** (2). **Der.** *pel-isse, pell-icle, pel-t* (2), *sur-plice, peel* (1).

PELLET, a little ball, as of lint or wax, &c. (F.—L.) ME. *pelet.* Formerly used to mean a gun-stone, or piece of white stone used as a cannon-ball. 'As pale as a *pelet,*' P. Plowman, B. v. 78. 'A *pelet* out of a gonne' [gun], Chaucer, Ho. of Fame, iii. 553.—OF. *pelote,* 'a hand-ball, or tennis-ball;' Cot. Cf. Span. *pelota,* a ball, cannonball, Ital. *pillotta,* a small ball. All diminutives from L. *pila,* a ball. **Der.** *pellet-ed; plat-oon,* q.v.

PELLICLE, a thin film. (F.—L.) 'A *pellicle,* or little membrane;' Sir T. Browne, Vulg. Errors, b. iii. c. 27, part 10.—F. *pellicule,* 'a little skin;' Cot.—L. *pellicula,* a small skin or hide; double dimin. from *pellis,* a skin. See **Pell.**

PELLITORY (1), **PARITORY,** a wild flower that grows on walls. (F.—L.) Often called *pellitory of the wall,* a tautological expression; spelt *pellitorie of the wall* in Baret (1580). *Pellitory* stands for *paritory,* by the common change of *r* to *l.* ME. *paritorie,* Chaucer, C. T. 16049 (G 581).—OF. *paritoire,* 'pellitory of the wall;' Cot.—L. *parietāria,* pellitory; properly fem. of adj. *parietārius,* belonging to walls.—L. *pariet-,* stem of *pariēs,* a wall.

PELLITORY (2), **PELLETER,** the plant pyrethrum. (Span. —L.—Gk.) ME. *peletyr,* Prompt. Parv. Sometimes called *pelleter of Spain,* because it grows there (Prior). It is the *Anacyclus pyrethrum,* the name of which has been assimilated to that of the plant above, which was earlier known. On account of this it is called by

Cotgrave 'bastard pellitory, or right pellitory of Spain;' but the name is not from MF. *pirette* (Cot.), but from Span. *pelitre,* pellitory of Spain.—L. *pyrethrum.*—Gk. πύρεθρον, a hot spicy plant, feverfew (Liddell). So named from its hot taste.—Gk. πῦρ, fire, cognate with E. *fire;* with suffix *-θρο-,* denoting the agent. See **Fire.**

PELL-MELL, promiscuously, confusedly. (F.—L.) In Shak. K. John, ii. 406.—MF. *pesle-mesle* (mod. F. *pêle-mêle*), 'pell-mell, confusedly,' Cot.; also spelt *pelle-melle* in the 13th cent. (Littré.) The apparent sense is 'stirred up with a shovel;' as if from F. *pelle,* a shovel, fire-shovel (E. *peel*), from L. *pāla,* a spade, peel, shovel, and OF. *mesler,* to mix. But orig. it was only a reduplicated form of *mesle;* in fact, *mesle-mesle* and *melle-melle* also occur. See Körting, § 6214. From Late L. *misculāre,* extended from *miscēre,* to mix. See **Peel** (3) and **Medley.**

PELLUCID, transparent. (F.—L.) In Blount's Gloss., ed. 1674. 'Such a diaphanous *pellucid* dainty body;' Howell, Letters, v. i. sec. 1. let. 29 (1621).—F. *pellucide,* 'bright, shining;' Cot.—L. *pellūcidus,* transparent.—L. *pellucēre, perlucēre,* to shine through.—L. *per,* through; and *lucēre,* to shine, allied to *lux,* light. See **Per-** and **Lucid.**

PELT (1), to throw or cast, to strike by throwing. (L.) 'The chidden billow seems to *pelt* the clouds;' Oth. ii. 1. 12. ME. *pelten, pilten, pulten,* to thrust, strike, drive; pt. t. *pelte, pilte, pulte;* pp. *pelt, pilt, pult.* 'And hire oðer eare *pilteð* hire tail þer-inne' = and in her other ear she [the adder] thrusts her tail; O. Eng. Homilies, ed. Morris, ii. 197. 'Fikenhild aȝen hire *pelte* Wiþ his swerdes hilte' = Fikenhild pushed against her with his sword-hilt; King Horn, ed. Lumby, 1415. The pp. *pilt* = thrust, put, is in Gen. and Exodus, ed. Morris, 2214. The pp. *ipult* = cast, thrown, is in Layamon, 10839 (later text). See further examples in Stratmann, to which add, from Halliwell: 'With grete strokes I shalle hym *pelte,*' MS. Ashmole 61; which comes very near the mod. usage. The sense of 'drive' comes out in the common mod. E. phrase *full pelt* = full drive. β. The easiest way of interpreting the vowel-sounds is to refer the word to an AS. form *pyltan,* to thrust, drive, not recorded. This would give ME. *pulten* or *pilten;* cf. AS. *pyt,* a pit, whence ME. *put, pit.* The *e* is a dialectal variety, like Kentish *pet* for *pit.* γ. Just as *pyt* is from L. *puteus,* such a form as AS. *pyltan* would result from *pult-jan,* from L. *pultāre,* to beat, strike, knock. δ. L. *pultāre,* like *pulsāre,* is an iterative form from *pellere* (pp. *pulsus*), to drive; see **Pulsate.** The simple L. *pellere* appears, perhaps, in Havelok, 810: 'To morwen shal ich forth *pelle*' = to-morrow I shall drive forth, i. e. rush forth. **Der.** *pelt-ing, pelt,* sb.

PELT (2), a skin, esp. of a sheep. (F.—L.) Used in the North for the skin of a sheep; in hawking, a *pelt* is the dead body of a fowl killed by a hawk (Halliwell). The skin of a beast with the hair on (Webster). And see E. D. D. ME. *pelt.* 'Off shepe also comythe *pelt* and eke felle' [skin]; The Hors, Shepe, and Goos, l. 43 (by Lydgate), in Political, Religious, and Love Poems, ed. Furnivall. We also find prov. E. *peltry,* a skin (E. D. D., s. v. *pelt*); formerly *peltre-ware,* as in Berners, tr. of Froissart, vol. ii. c. 170 (R.). Hakluyt's Voyages, i. 192, l. 11 from bottom, where it occurs in a reprint of The Libell of E. Policye, l. 309. β. As *peltry* = MF. *pelleterie,* 'the trade of a skinner, or peltmonger;' Cot., from MF. *pelletier,* 'a skinner;' so *pelt* answers to OF. *pelete, pellete,* a small skin (Godefroy), the sense 'sheep's skin' being preserved in Norm. dial. *pelette* (pron. *plett*), a sheep-skin (Moisy). Dimin. of OF. *pel,* a skin; see **Pell.**

PELTATE, lit. 'shield-shaped.' (L.—Gk.) In botany; said of a leaf.—L. *peltātus,* furnished with a *pelta,* or light shield.—Gk. πέλτη, a light shield; prob. allied to πέλλα, skin, hide, and to E. *fell* (2).

PELVIS, the bony cavity in the lower part of the abdomen. (L.) In Phillips, ed. 1706.—L. *peluis,* lit. a bason; hence, the pelvis, from its shape. Allied to Gk. πέλις, πέλλα, a wooden bowl, cup.

PEMMICAN, a preparation of dried meat. (N. Amer. Indian.) A Cree word; see Cree Dict. by Lacombe.—Cree *pimikkan,* pimican, a bag filled with a mixture of fat and meat; from *pimiy,* grease. Cf. Algonkin *pimite,* grease (Cuoq). The *e* is an error for *i.*

PEN (1), to shut up, enclose. (L.) ME. *pennen,* O. Eng. Homilies, ed. Morris, ii. 43; also *pinnen,* see P. Plowman, C. vii. 219, and footnote. AS. *pennian,* only recorded in the comp. *on-pennian,* to un-pen. 'Ac gif sio pynding wierð *onpennad*' = but if the waterdam is unfastened or thrown open; Ælfred, tr. of Gregory's Pastoral, ed. Sweet, c. xxxviii, p. 276. Cf. Low G. *pennen,* to bolt a door, from *penn,* a pin, peg. *Pennian* is thus connected with *pin,* and is ultimately of Latin origin. See **Pin.** Note EFries. *penne, pinne, penn, pin,* a peg, a pin. **Der.** *pen,* sb., Merry Wives, iii. 4. 41; Allit. Poems, ed. Morris, B. 322. ☞ The verb *to pen* seems to have been connected with *pindar* at an early period; but *pindar* is related to a *pound* for cattle. See **Pinfold.**

PEN (2), an instrument used for writing. (F.–L.) ME. *penne*, Polit. Songs, ed. Wright, p. 156, l. 15; P. Plowman, B. ix. 39.—OF. *penne*, 'a quill, or hard feather; a pen-feather;' Cot.–L. *penna*, a feather; in Late L. a pen. β. The old form of *penna* was *pesna* (Festus); for **petna* or **petsna*, formed with suffix *-na* or *-sna* from √PET, to fly; whence also E. *feath-er*, *im-pet-us*, *pet-it-ion*, &c. See **Feather**. Brugmann, i. § 762 (2). Der. *pen*, vb., Skelton, Phyllyp Sparowe, l. 810; *pen-knife*, *pen-man*, *pen-man-ship*; *penn-er*, a case for pens, Chaucer, C. T. 9753 (E 1879); *penn-ate*, from L. *pennātus*, winged; *penn-on*, q. v. Also *pinn-ac-le*, *pinn-ate*, *pin-ion*. Doublet, *pin*.

PENAL, pertaining to or used for punishment. (F.–L.–Gk.) In Levins, 1570.–MF. *penal*, 'penall;' Cot.–L. *pœnālis*, penal.–L. *pœna*, punishment.–Gk. ποινή, a penalty, requital. See **Pain**. Der. *penal-ty*, L. L. L. i. 1. 123, from MF. *penalité*, not in Cotgrave, but in use in the 16th century (Littré), coined as if from a L. **pœnālitas*. Also *pen-ance*, *pen-it-ence*, *pun-ish*.

PENANCE, repentance, self-punishment expressive of penitence. (F.–L.–Gk.) ME. *penance*, Rob. of Brunne, tr. of Langtoft, p. 303, l. 14; *penaunce*, in the sense of penitence or repentance, Wyclif, Matt. iii. 2.–OF. *penance*, older form *peneance*; formed from L. *pœnitentia*, penitence, by the usual loss of medial *t* between two vowels. It is thus a doublet of *penitence*; see **Penitent**.

PENATES, household gods. (L.) L. *Penātes*; allied to *penes*, with, in the house of; see **Penetrate**.

PENCHANT, a strong inclination, bias (in favour of). (F.–L.) In Dryden, Marriage-à-la-Mode, iii. 1.–F. *penchant*, sb.; orig. pres. part. of *pencher*, to lean, lean towards.–Late L. type **pendicāre*; from L. *pendēre*, to hang.

PENCIL, a small hair-brush for laying on colours, a pointed instrument for writing without ink. (F.–L.) The old use of a *pencil* was for painting in colours; see Trench, Select Glossary. ME. *pensil*; 'With sotil *pencel* was depeynt this storie;' Chaucer, C. T. 2051 (A 2049).–OF. *pincel* (13th century, Littré), later *pinceau*, 'a pensill, a white-limer's brush;' Cot.–L. *pēnicillus*, a small tail, also, a painter's brush; dimin. of *pēniculus*, a little tail, which again is a double dimin. of *pēnis*, a tail. For **pes-nis*; cf. Skt. *pasa-*, Gk. πέος; Brugmann, i. § 877. Der. *pencil*, vb.; *pencill-ed*, Timon, i. 1. 159.

PENDANT, anything hanging, esp. by way of ornament. (F.–L.) 'His earerings had *pendants* of golde;' Hakluyt's Voyages, i. 346, l. 12. 'It was a bridge . . With curious corbes and *pendants* graven faire;' Spenser, F. Q. iv. 10. 6.–F. *pendant*, 'a pendant;' Cot.–F. *pendant*, hanging, pres. part. of *pendre*, to hang.–L. *pendēre*, to hang; allied to *pendere*, to weigh. β. The L. *pendere* is further allied to Gk. σφενδόνη, a sling, Skt. *spand*, to tremble, throb, vibrate.–√SPHED, SPHEND, to tremble, vibrate. Der. *pend-ent*, hanging, Latinized form of F. *pendant*; *pend-ing*, Anglicized form of F. *pendant*, as shown by the F. phrase *pendant cela*, 'in the mean while, in the mean time,' Cot.; *pend-ence* (rare); *pend-ul-ous*, q.v., *pend-ul-um*, q. v., *pens-ile*, q. v. Also (from L. *pendēre*) *ap-pend*, *com-pend-i-ous*, *de-pend*, *ex-pend*, *im-pend*, *per-pend*, *per-pend-ic-u-lar*, *s-pend*, *sti-pend*, *sus-pend*, &c. Also (like pp. *pensus*) *pens-ion*, *pens-ive*, *com-pens-ate*, *dis-pense*, *ex-pense*, *pre-pense*, *pro-pens-i-ty*, *recom-pense*, *sus-pens-ion*; see also *poise*, *avoir-du-pois*, *counter-poise*, *pans-y*, *pent-house*, *ponder*, *pound* (1), *pre-ponderate*, *spencer*.

PENDULOUS, hanging, impending. (L.) In Shak. K. Lear, iii. 4. 69. Englished directly from L. *pendulus*, hanging, by change of *-us* to *-ous*, as in *ardu-ous*, &c.–L. *pendēre*, to hang; see **Pendant**. Der. *pendulous-ly*, *-ness*.

PENDULUM, a hanging weight, vibrating freely. (L.) 'That the vibration of this *pendulum*;' Butler, Hudibras, pt. ii. c. 3, l. 1024.–L. *pendulum*, neut. of *pendulus*, hanging; see **Pendulous**.

PENETRATE, to pierce into. (L.) In Palsgrave, ed. 1530.–L. *penetrātus*, pp. of *penetrāre*, to pierce into. β. L. *pene-trāre* is a compound. The part *pene-* is from the base of *penes*, with, *peni-tus*, within, *pen-us*, the inner part of a sanctuary; [prob. connected with *penus*, stored food, provisions kept within doors, Lithuan. *penas*, fodder.] 'The idea " stores, store-room," furnishes the intermediate step from *penus* to *penetrāre*;' Curtius, i. 336. γ. The suffix *-trāre*, to pass beyond, is the same as in *in-trāre*, to enter, connected with L. *in-trā*, within, *ex-trā*, without, *trans*, across; allied to Skt. *tara-*, a crossing. Der. *penetra-ble*, Hamlet, iii. 4. 36, immediately from L. *penetrābilis*; *impenetrable*; *penetrabl-y*, *penetrable-ness*, *penetrability*; *penetrat-ing*; *penetrat-ive*, from MF. *penetratif*, 'penetrative' (Cot.); *penetrat-ive-ly*, *penetrat-ive-ness*; *penetrat-ion*, Milton, P. L. iii. 585, immediately from L. *penetrātio*.

PENGUIN, PINGUIN, the name of an aquatic bird. (C.?) 'As Indian Britons were from *penguins*;' Butler, Hudibras, pt. i. c. 2, l. 60. It occurs still earlier, in the 15th note (by Selden) to Drayton's Polyolbion, song 9, ed. 1613, where we find: 'About the

year 1170, Madoc, brother to Dauid ap Owen, Prince of Wales, made this sea-voyage [to Florida]; and, by probability, those names of *Capo de Breton* in Norumbeg, and *pengwin* in part of the Northerne America, for a *white rock* and a *white-headed bird*, according to the British, were reliques of this discouery.' Certainly, the form *penguin* bears a striking resemblance to W. *pen gwyn*, where *pen* = head, and *gwyn* = white; and if the name was given to the bird by W. sailors, this may be the solution. We can go still further back, and show that the word existed in Sir F. Drake's time. Yule quotes from Drake's Voyage by F. Fletcher (Hakluyt Soc.), p. 72, with reference to the year 1578: 'In these Islands we founde greate relief and plenty of good victuals, for infinite were the number of fowle which the Welsh men named *Penguin*, and Magilanus [Magellan] tearmed them geese.' In a tract printed in 1588, and reprinted in An English Garner, ed. Arber, vol. ii. p. 119, we read that: 'On the 6th day of January, 1587, we put into the straits of Magellan; and on the 8th, we came to two islands named by Sir F. Drake, the one Bartholomew Island, because he came thither on that Saint's day; and the other *Penguin Island*, upon which we powdered [*salted*] three tons (!) of *penguins* for the victualling of our ship;' cf. Hakluyt, Voy. iii. 805, 806, 849. We find in the same, iii. 161: '*Insula est ea, quam vestri Penguin vocant, ab auium eiusdem nominis multitudine*,' in a letter dated Aug. 6, 1583. The etymology is open to the objection that the penguin's head is black, but the name may have been transferred to the penguin from the great auk, which has white patches below its eyes, or the puffin, with a whitish head. 2. Another story (in Littré) is that some Dutchmen, in 1598, gave the name to some birds seen by them in the straits of Magellan, intending an allusion to L. *pinguis*, fat. But this will not account for the suffix *-in*, and is therefore wrong; besides which the 'Dutchmen' turn out to be Sir F. Drake's men, some of whom named the island at least 20 years earlier than the date thus assigned. The F. *pingouin* is derived from the E. word.

PENINSULA, a piece of land nearly surrounded by water. (L.) Cotgrave has '*peninsule*, a peninsula.'–L. *pēninsula*, a piece of land nearly an island.–L. *pēn-e*, *pœn-e*, almost; and *insula*, an island; see **Isle**. Der. *peninsul-ar*, *peninsul-ate*.

PENITENT, repentant, sorry for sin. (F.–L.) ME. *penitent*, Chaucer, C. T. Persones Tale (I 81).–OF. *penitent*, 'penitent;' stem of pres. part. of *pœnitēre*, to cause to repent, frequentative form of *pœnire*, the same as *punire*, to punish; see **Punish**. Der. *penitent-ly*; *penitence*, OEng. Homilies, ed. Morris, ii. 61, l. 5 (doublet, *penance*); *penitent-i-al*, *penitent-i-al-ly*, *penitent-i-ar-y*.

PENNON, PENNANT, a small flag, banner, streamer. (F.–L.) *Pennant* is merely formed from *pennon* by the addition of *t* after *n*, as in *ancien-t*, *tyran-t*. It occurs in Drayton, Battle of Agincourt, st. 70. *Pennon* is in Shak. Hen. V, iii. 5. 49. ME. *penon*, *penoun*, Chaucer, C. T. 980 (A 978).–MF. *pennon*, 'a pennon, flag, streamer; *les pennons d'une fleiche*, the feathers of an arrow;' Cot. [Cf. Span. *pendon*, a banner (with excrescent *d*); Ital. *pennone*, a pennon, of which the old meaning was 'a great plume or bunch of feathers' (Florio).] Formed, with suffix *-on*, from L. *penna*, a wing, feather; whence the sense of 'plume,' and lastly, of streamer or standard. See **Pen** (2). Der. *pennon-cel*, a dimin. form, from MF. *pennoncel*, 'a pennon on the top of a launce, a little flag or streamer;' Cot.

PENNY, a copper coin, one twelfth of a shilling. (L.? with E. suffix.) Formerly a silver coin; the copper coinage dates from A.D. 1665. ME. *peni*, Havelok, 705; pl. *penies*, Havelok, 776, also *pens* (pronounced like mod. E. *pence*) by contraction, P. Plowman, B. v. 243. The mod. E. *pence* is due to this contracted form. AS. *pening*, a penny, Mark, xii. 15, where the Camb. MS. has *penig*, by loss of *n* before *g*; the further loss of the final *g* produced ME. *peni*. A by-form is *pending* (A.D. 833), Thorpe, Diplomatarium, p. 471, l. 26; as if formed from the base *pand-* with dimin. suffix *-ing*. β. This *pand* = Du. *pand*, a pawn, pledge, OHG. *pfant*, G. *pfand*; a word possibly of L. origin; see **Pawn** (1). In this view, a *penny* is a little pledge, 'a token.'+Du. *penning*; Icel. *penningr*; Dan. and Swed. *penning*; G. *pfennig*, OHG. *phantinc*, *phentinc*, from *pfant*. Der. *penny-weight*, *penny-worth*, *penni-less*.

PENNY-ROYAL, a herb. (F.–L.) In Sir T. Elyot, Castel of Helth, b. ii. c. 9, it is spelt *penyryall*; but the first part of the word is a singular corruption of the old name *puliol* or *puliall*; we find Cotgrave translating MF. *pulege* by 'penny royall, puliall royall,' the name being really due to L. *pūlēium rēgium*, penny-royal (Pliny, b. xx. c. 14), a name given to the plant (like E. *flea-bane*) from its supposed efficacy against fleas; from L. *pūlex*, a flea. The form *pūleium* is short for *pulegium*, whence the dimin. **pulegi-olum* > OF. *puliol*, whence ME. *puliol*. And *rēgium* is the neuter of *rēgius*, royal; from *rēg-*, stem of *rex*, a king. See **Puce** and **Royal**. So also '*Origanum*, puliol real, wde-minte,' i. e. wood-mint; Voc. 557. 20.

PENSILE, suspended. (F.–L.) 'If a weighty body be *pensile*;'

Bacon, Nat. Hist. § 763. – MF. *pensil*, 'slightly hanging;' Cot. – L. *pensilis*, pendent; from **pens-um*, unused supine of *pendĕre*, to hang; see **Pendant**.

PENSION, a stated allowance, stipend, payment. (F. – L.) In Shak. K. Lear, ii. 4. 217; *pencyon* in Palsgrave. – F. *pension*, 'a pension;' Cot. – L. *pensiōnem*, acc. of *pensio*, a payment. – L. *pensus*, pp. of *pendere*, to weigh, weigh out, pay; orig. to cause to hang, and closely connected with *pendĕre*, to hang; see **Pendant**. Der. *pension*, vb., *pension-er*, Mid. Nt. Dr. ii. 1. 10; *pension-ar-y*. And see **Pensive**.

PENSIVE, thoughtful. (F. – L.) ME. *pensif*, Gower, C. A. ii. 65; bk. iv. 1906. – F. *pensif*, 'pensive;' Cot. Formed, as if from a L. *pensiuus, from *pensare*, to weigh, ponder, consider; intensive form of *pendere* (pp. *pensus*), to weigh; see **Pension**. Der. *pensive-ly, -ness*. And see **Pansy**.

PENT, for *penned*, pp. of **Pen** (1), q. v.

PENTACLE, a magical figure. (F. – Gk.) 'Their raven's wings, their lights, and *pentacles*;' B. Jonson, The Devil an Ass, i. 2. 8. See Nares. – OF. *pentacle*, a pentacle; also, a candlestick with five branches. Variant of ME. *pentangel*, in the same sense, Gawain and the Grene Knight, 620. – Gk. πέντε, five, cognate with E. *five*; and L. suffix *-āculum* (cf. MItal. *pentacolo* in Florio), in place of L. *angulus*, an angle, as in *rect-angle*. ¶ Ignorance of Gk. caused the substitution of a *pentacle* with *six* points for the *pentangle* of *five* points; see Notes on Eng. Etym., p. 212.

PENTAGON, a plane figure having five angles. (F. – L. – Gk.) The adj. *pentagonall* is in Minsheu, ed. 1627. – F. *pentagone*, 'five-cornered;' Cot. – L. *pentagōnus*, *pentagōnius*, pentagonal. – Gk. πεντάγωνος, pentagonal; neut. πεντάγωνον, a pentagon. – Gk. πέντα-, for πέντε, fine, cognate with E. *five*; and γωνία, a corner, angle, lit. a bend, from γόνυ, a knee, cognate with E. *knee*. See **Five** and **Knee**. Der. *pentagon-al*.

PENTAMETER, a verse of five measures. (L. – Gk.) In Skelton's Poems, ed. Dyce, i. 193, l. 6. – L. *pentameter*. – Gk. πεντάμετρος. – Gk. πέντα-, for πέντε, five, cognate with E. *five*; and μέτρον, a metre. See **Five** and **Metre**.

PENTATEUCH, the five books of Moses. (L. – Gk.) In Blount's Gloss., ed. 1674. Spelt *pentateuches* in Minsheu, ed. 1627; *penthatheukes* in Palsgrave. – L. *pentateuchus*. – Gk. πέντα-, for πέντε, five, cognate with E. *five*; and τεῦχος, a tool, implement, in late Gk., a book. Hence applied to the collection of the five books of Moses. β. Τεῦχος is allied to τεύχειν, to prepare, get ready, make; allied to τύκος, τύχος, an instrument for working stones with, a mason's pick or hammer, whence τυκίζειν, to work stones. Brugmann, i. § 780. Der. *pentateuch-al*.

PENTECOST, Whitsuntide; orig. a Jewish festival on the fiftieth day after the Passover. (L. – Gk.) ME. *pentecoste*, OEng. Homilies, ed. Morris, i. 89, l. 5. AS. *pentecosten*, rubric to John vi. 44. – L. *pentēcostēn*, acc. of *pentēcostē*. – Gk. πεντηκοστή, Pentecost, Acts, ii. 1; lit. fiftieth, fem. of πεντηκοστός, fiftieth (ἡμέρα = day, being understood). – Gk. πεντήκοντα, fifty. – Gk. πέντη-, for πέντε, five; and -κοντα, tenth. Again, -κοντα is short for *δέκοντα, tenth, from δέκα, ten, cognate with E. *ten*. See **Five** and **Ten**. Der. *pentecost-al*.

PENTHOUSE, a shed projecting from a building. (F. – L.) In Shak. Much Ado, iii. 3. 110. A corruption of *pentice* or *pentis*, due to an effort at making sense of one part of the word at the expense of the rest, as in the case of *crayfish*, &c. ME. *pentice*, *pentis*. 'Pentice of an howse ende, *Appendicium*;' Prompt. Parv. Caxton, in the Boke of the Fayt of Armes, explains how a fortress ought to be supplied with fresh water, cisterns being provided 'where men may receiue inne the rayne-watres that fallen doune along the thackes of *thappentyzes* and houses;' Part ii. c. 17 (Way's note). Here *thackes* = thatches; and *thappentyzes* = the *appentices*, showing that *pentice* stands for *apentice*, the first syllable having been dropped, as in *peal* for *appeal*. Way further quotes from Palsgrave: 'Penthouse of a house, *appentis*;' and from the Catholicon: 'A pentis, *appendix*, *appendicium*.' Also spelt *pendize*, Met. Homilies, ed. Small, p. 63. The AF. pl. *pentyz* occurs in Liber Albus, p. 271; and *appentices*, pl., at p. 288. – MF. *apentis*, *appentis*, 'a penthouse;' Cot. – L. *appendicium*, an appendage; allied to *appendix*, an appendage; see **Append**. ¶ Thus a *penthouse* is an 'appendage' or out-building. See the next word.

PENTROOF, a roof with a slope on one side only. (Hybrid; F. – L. *and* E.) Given in Cent. Dict. I notice it because the F. original of this *pent-* may have affected the sense of *penthouse*. Compounded of F. *pente*, a slope; and E. *roof*. The F. *pente* is formed from *pendre*, to hang, like *vente* from *vendre*, to sell. – L. *pendĕre*, to hang; see **Pendant**.

PENULTIMATE, the last syllable but one. (L.) A grammatical term; coined from L. *pæn-e*, almost; and *ultima*, fem., last. See **Ulterior**. Der. *penult*, the contracted form.

PENUMBRA, a partial shadow beyond the deep shadow of an eclipse. (L.) In Kersey, ed. 1721. Coined from L. *pæn-e*, almost; and *umbra*, a shadow. See **Umbrella**.

PENURY, want, poverty. (F. – L.) 'In great *penury* and miserye;' Fabyan's Chron. vol. i. c. 157. 'For lacke and *penurye*;' Caxton, Golden Legend, Moses, § 17. – MF. *penurie*, 'penury;' Cot. – L. *pēnūria*, want, need. Allied to Gk. πεῖνα, hunger. Der. *penurious* (Levins); *penuri-ous-ness*.

PEON, a foot-soldier, orderly, messenger. (Port. – L.) See quotations in Yule. [Also, in Span. America, a serf; from the cognate Span. *peon*.] – Port. *piāo*, a pawn at chess; one of the lower people. – Late L. *pedōnem*, acc. of *pedo*, a foot-soldier; see **Pawn** (2). Altered to the Span. spelling.

PEONY, PÆONY, a plant with beautiful crimson flowers. (L. – Gk.) The mod. E. *peony* answers to the AS. *peonie*, Leechdoms, i. 168; L. *pæōnia*. [The ME. forms were *pione*, *pioine*, *piane*, *pianie*; P. Plowman, A. v. 155; B. v. 312; later, *peony*, Palsgrave. – OF. *pione* (mod. F. *pivoine*); Littré.] – L. *pæōnia*, medicinal, from its supposed virtues; fem. of *Pæōnius*, belonging to *Pæon*, its supposed discoverer. – Gk. Παιών, Pæon, the god of healing. See **Pæan**.

PEOPLE, a nation, the populace, (F. – L.) ME. *peple*, P. Plowman, A. i. 5; spelt *poeple*, id. B. i. 5; spelt *peple*, *poeple*, *puple*, Chaucer, C. T. 8871 (Six-text, E. 995). [The spelling with *eo* or *oe* is due to AF. *people*, *poeple* (later *pĕple*).] – OF. *pueple*, mod. F. *peuple*, people. – L. *populum*, acc. of *populus*, people. β. *Po-pul-us* appears to be a reduplicated, form; cf. L. *plē-bēs*, people. Allied to *plē-nus*, full, E. *full*. See πίμπλημι in Prellwitz. And see **Populace**.

PEPPER, the fruit of a plant, with a hot pungent taste. (L. – Gk. – Skt.) ME. *peper* (with only two *p*'s), P. Plowman, B. v. 312. AS. *pipor*; A. S. Leechdoms, ed. Cockayne, iii. 341. – L. *piper*. – Gk. πέπερι. – Skt. *pippali* (1) long pepper; (2) the fruit of the holy fig-tree; Benfey, p. 552. Cf. Pers. *pulpul*, pepper; Palmer's Dict. col. 114. Der. *pepper-corn*, *pepper-mint*.

PEPSINE, one of the constituents of the gastric juice, helpful in the process of digestion. (F. – Gk.) From mod. F. *pepsine*, formed with suffix *-ine* from Gk. πέψ-, base of πέψις, digestion; for *πεπτις <*πēq-tis, related to πέπτειν, to cook. (√PEQ.) See **Cook**. Der. So also *pept-ic*, i. e. assisting in digestion, from Gk. πεπτικός; whence *dys-peptic*.

PER-, prefix, through. (L.) L. *per*, through; whence F. *per-*, *par-*, as a prefix. Orig. used of spaces traversed; allied to Gk. παρά, πάρ, by the side of, Skt. *parā*, away, from, forth, *param*, beyond, and to E. *from*. Also to Goth. *fair-*, G. *ver-*, prefix. The prefixes *para-* and *peri-*, both Gk., are nearly related. See Curtius, i. 334, 338.

PERADVENTURE, perhaps. (F. – L.) The *d* before *v* is an insertion, as in *adventure*. ME. *perauenture* (with *u* = *v*), Rob. of Glouc. p. 358, l. 7373; often shortened to *peraunter* or *paraunter*, spelt *paraunire* in the same passage, in MS. Cotton, Calig. A. xi. – F. *par*, by; and *aventure*, adventure. – L. *per*, through, by; and see **Adventure**.

PERAMBULATE, to walk through or over. (L.) Prob. made from the earlier sb. *perambulation*; Lambarde's 'Perambulation of Kent' was printed in 1576. Cf. L. *perambulātus*, pp. of *perambulāre*, lit. to walk through. – L. *per*, through; and *ambulāre*, to walk; see **Per-** and **Amble**. Der. *perambulat-ion*; also *perambulat-or*, an instrument for measuring distances, as in Phillips, ed. 1706, but now used to mean a light carriage for a child, and sometimes shortened to *pram*.

PERCEIVE, to comprehend. (F. – L.) ME. *perceyuen* (with *u* = *v*), also *parceyuen*, P. Plowman, B. xviii. 241. – OF. *perceiv-*, stressed stem of *percevoir* (Godefroy). Cot. gives only the MF. pp. *perceu*. [The mod. F. has the comp. *apercevoir*, with the additional prefix *a-* < L. *ad*.] – L. *percipere*, to apprehend. – L. *per*, through, thoroughly, and *capere*, to take, receive. See **Per-** and **Capacious**. Der. *perceiv-er*, *perceiv-able*. Also *percept-ion*, from F. *perception*, 'a perception' (Cot.), from L. *perceptiōnem*, acc. of *perceptio*, like the pp. *perceptus*; also *percept-ive*, *percept-ive-ly*, *percept-iv-i-ty*, *percept-ive-ness*; *percept-ible*, F. *perceptible*, 'perceptible' (Cot.), from L. *perceptibilis*, perceivable; *percept-ibl-y*, *percept-ibil-i-ty*. Also *per-cipient*, from the stem of the pres. part. of *percipere*.

PERCH (1), a rod for a bird to sit on; a long measure of five and a half yards. (F. – L.) The orig. sense is 'rod;' whether for measuring or for a bird's perch. ME. *perche*, Chaucer, C. T. 2206 (A 2204). – F. *perche*, 'a pearch;' Cot. – L. *pertica*, a pole, bar, measuring-rod. Der. *perch*, vb., Rich. III. i. 3. 71, ME. *perchen*, Chaucer, Ho. Fame, 1991; *perch-er*.

PERCH (2), a fish. (F. – L. – Gk.) ME. *perche*, Prompt. Parv. p. 393; King Alisaunder, 5446. – F. *perche*. – L. *perca*. – Gk. πέρκη, a perch; so named from its dark marks. – Gk. πέρκος, πέρκνος, spotted, blackish. + Skt. *pṛ̣çni*, spotted, pied, esp. of cows; Curtius, i. 340. β. Further allied to OHG. *forh-ana*, G. *for-elle*, AS. *for-n*, a trout.

PERCHANCE, by chance. (F.–L.) In Shak. Temp. ii. 2. 17; ME. *parchaunce*, Hampole, Prick of Conscience, 2489. [Another ME. phrase is *per cas* or *parcas*, Chaucer, C. T. 12819 (C 885); from F. *par cas*; see **Case**.]–F. *par*, by; and *chance*, chance; see **Per-** and **Chance**.

PERCIPIENT; see under **Perceive**.

PERCOLATE, to filter through. (L.) In Bacon, Nat. Hist. § 396. Prob. suggested by the sb. *percolation*, in Bacon, Nat. Hist. § 3.–L. *percōlātus*, pp. of *percōlāre*, to strain through a sieve.–L. *per*, through; and *cōlāre*, to filter, from *cōlum*, a filter. See **Per-** and **Colander**. Der. *percolat-ion*, *percolat-or*.

PERCUSSION, a shock, quick blow. (L.) Bacon has *percussion*, Nat. Hist. § 163; *percussed*, id. 164; *percutient*, id. 190. Formed, by analogy with F. sbs. in -*ion*, from L. *percussio*, a striking.–L. *percussus*, pp. of *percutere*, to strike violently.–L. *per*, thoroughly; and *quatere*, to shake, which becomes -*cutere* in compounds. See **Quash**. Der. *percuss-ive*; *percuti-ent*, from the stem of the pres. participle.

PERDITION, utter loss or destruction. (F.–L.) ME. *perdicioun*, Wyclif, 2 Pet. ii. 1.–F. *perdition*; Cot.–L. *perditiōnem*, acc. of *perditio*, destruction; cf. L. *perditus*, pp. of *perdere*, to lose utterly, to destroy.–L. *per*, thoroughly, or away; and -*dere*, to put, place, representing Idg. **dhə*, weak grade of √DHĒ, to place; see **Do**. ¶ L. *per-dere* = E. *do for*. Der. *perd-u*, hidden; from F. *perdu*, pp. of *perdre*, to lose, from L. *perdere*.

PERDURABLE, long-lasting. (F.–L.) In Shak. Othello, i. 3. 343; Chaucer, C. T., B 2699.–OF. *perdurable*, 'perdurable, perpetual;' Cot.–L. *perdūrā-re*, to endure; with suffix -*bilis*.–L. *per*, through, throughout; and *dūrāre*, to last, from *dūrus*, hard, lasting. See **Dure**. Der. *perdurabl-y*, *perdura-bili-ty*.

PEREGRINATION, travel, wandering about. (F.–L.) In Cotgrave.–F. *peregrination*, 'peregrination;' Cot.–L. *peregrīnāt-iōnem*, acc. of *peregrīnātio*, travel.–L. *peregrīnārī*, to travel.–L. *peregrinus*, foreign, abroad; see **Pilgrim**. Der. *peregrinate*, verb, rare, from L. pp. *peregrīnātus*; *peregrinat-or*. Also *peregrinate*, adj., L. L. L. v. 1. 15.

PEREMPTORY, authoritative, dogmatical. (F.–L.) In Spenser, F. Q. iii [*not* iv]. 8. 16. AF. *peremptorie*, Liber Albus, p. 217; MF. *peremptoire*, 'peremptory;' Cot.–L. *peremptōrius*, destructive; hence, decisive.–L. *peremptor*, a destroyer; cf. L. *peremptus*, pp. of *perimere*, older form *peremere*, to take entirely away, destroy.–L. *per*, away (like Skt. *parā*, from); and *emere*, to take, also to buy. See **Per-** and **Example**. Der. *peremptori-ly*, -*ness*.

PERENNIAL, everlasting. (L.) In Evelyn's Diary, Nov. 8, 1644. Coined by adding -*al* (= L. -*ālis*) to *perenni-*, for *perennis*, everlasting, lit. lasting through the year.–L. *per*, through; and *annus*, a year, which becomes *enni-* in compounds. See **Per-** and **Annual**. Der. *perennial-ly*.

PERFECT, complete, whole. (F.–L.) ME. *parfit*, *perfit*, Chaucer, C. T. 72. [The word has since been conformed to the L. spelling.]–OF. *parfit*, *parfeit*, ME. *parfaict* (Cot.); mod. F. *parfait*. –L. *perfectus*, complete; orig. pp. of *perficere*, to complete, do thoroughly.–L. *per*, thoroughly; and -*ficere*, for *facere*, to make. See **Per-** and **Fact**. Der. *perfect-ly*, -*ness*; *perfect*, vb., Temp. i. 2, 79; *perfect-ible*, *perfect-ibil-i-ty*; *perfect-er*; *perfect-ion*, ME. *perfection*, Ancren Riwle, p. 372, l. 9, from F. *perfection*; *perfection-ist*.

PERFIDIOUS, faithless, treacherous. (L.) In Shak. Temp. i. 2. 68. Not a F. word, but formed (by analogy with words of F. origin) directly from L. *perfidiōsus*, treacherous. – L. *perfidia*, treachery.–L. *perfidus*, faithless, lit. one that goes away from his faith.–L. *per*, away (like Skt. *parā*, from) and *fidēs*, faith. See **Per-** and **Faith**. Der. *perfidious-ly*, -*ness*; also *perfid-y* in Phillips, ed. 1706, F. *perfidie*, in Molière (Littré), from L. *perfidia*.

PERFOLIATE, having the stem passing through the leaf. (L.) '*Perfoliata*, the herb thorough-wax;' Phillips, ed. 1706. Botanical. –L. *per*, through; and *foli-um*, a leaf; with suffix -*ate* (= L. pp. suffix -*ātus*). See **Per-** and **Folio**. ¶ Cf. MF. *perfoliate*, 'through-wax, an herb;' Cot.

PERFORATE, to bore through. (L.) Bacon uses *perforate* as a pp., Nat. Hist. § 470. 'A cros *perforatid*,' Book of St. Albans, pt. ii, fol. c 3.–L. *perforātus*, pp. of *perforāre*, to bore through.–L. *per*, through; and *forāre*, to bore, cognate with E. *bore*. See **Per-** and **Bore** (1). Der. *perforat-ion*, -*or*.

PERFORCE, by force, of necessity. (F.–L.) In Spenser, F. Q. i. 8. 38; spelt *parforce*, Lord Berners, tr. of Froissart, vol. ii. c. 38 (R.). –F. *par*, by (< L. *per*); and *force*, force. See **Per-** and **Force**.

PERFORM, to achieve. (F.–OHG.; *with* L. *prefix*). ME. *parfournen*, P. Plowman, B. v. 607; *perfourmen*, Wyclif, John, v. 36. –OF. *parfournir*, 'to perform, consummate, accomplish;' Cot. – F. *par* (< L. *per*), thoroughly; and *fournir*, to provide, furnish, a word of OHG. origin. See **Per-** and **Furnish**. ¶ The ME.

form *parfournen* is thus accounted for; the ME. *parfourmen* is prob. due to association with *form*, with which it has no real connexion. Der. *perform-er*; *perform-ance*, Macb. ii. 3. 33, a coined word.

PERFUME, to scent. (F.–L.) The verb is the original word, and occurs in Shak. Temp. ii. 1. 48.–F. *parfumer*, 'to perfume;' Cot. Lit. 'to smoke thoroughly.'–F. *par* (< L. *per*), through; and *fumer*, to smoke, from L. *fūmāre*, vb. formed from *fūmus*, smoke. See **Per-** and **Fume**. Der. *perfume*, sb., F. *parfum*; *perfum-er*, *perfum-er-y*.

PERFUNCTORY, done in a careless way. (L.) 'In a carelesse *perfunctory* way;' Howell, Foreign Travel, § 4, ed. Arber, p. 27. Englished from L. *perfunctōrius*, done in a careless way, done because it must be done; allied to *perfunctus*, pp. of *perfungī*, to perform, discharge thoroughly.–L. *per*, thoroughly; and *fungī*, to perform. See **Per-** and **Function**. Der. *perfunctori-ly*, -*ness*.

PERHAPS, possibly. (Hybrid; L. *and* Scand.) In Hamlet, i. 3. 14. A clumsy compound, which took the place of the ME. *per cas*, and formed also on the model of *perchance*; see **Perchance**. The *per* is rather from the F. *par* than the L. *per*, but it makes no difference. *Haps* is the pl. of *hap*, a chance, a word of Scand. origin. See **Hap**. Spelt *perhapis*, Roy, Rede me, ed. Arber, p. 98.

PERI, a fairy. (Pers.) See Moore's poem of 'Paradise and the Peri,' in Lalla Rookh.–Pers. *parī*, a fairy; Palmer's Pers. Dict. col. 112. See Horn, § 310.

PERI-, *prefix*, round, around. (Gk.) Gk. περί, around, about.+ Skt. *pari*, round about. Also allied to L. *per-* in *permagnus*, &c.

PERIANTH, the floral envelope, whether calyx or corolla, or both. (Gk.) Botanical.–Gk. περί, around; and ἄνθος, flower.

PERIAPT, an amulet. (F.–Gk.) In Shak. 1 Hen. VI, v. 3. 2. –MF. *periapte*, 'a medicine hanged about any part of the body.'–Gk. περίαπτον, an amulet; neut. of περίαπτος, fitted or fastened round. –Gk. περιάπτειν, to fasten round.–Gk. περί, round; ἅπτειν, to fasten.

PERICARDIUM, the sac which surrounds the heart. (L.–Gk.) In Phillips, ed. 1706. Anatomical. – Late L. *pericardium*.–Gk. περικάρδιον, the membrane round the heart.–Gk. περί, round; and καρδία, cognate with E. *heart*. See **Peri-** and **Heart**.

PERICARP, a seed-vessel. (Gk.) Botanical.–Gk. περικάρπιον, the shell of fruit.–Gk. περί, round; and καρπός, fruit, allied to E. *harvest*. See **Peri-** and **Harvest**.

PERICRANIUM, the membrane that surrounds the skull. (Late L.–Gk.) The pl. *pericraniums* occurs in Beaum. and Fletcher, The Chances, iii. 2. 10.–Late L. *pericrānium*.–Gk. περικράνιον, neut. of περικράνιος, passing round the skull. – Gk. περί, round; and κρανίου, the skull. See **Peri-** and **Cranium**.

PERIGEE, the point of the moon's orbit nearest the earth. (F.–L.–Gk.) Scientific. In Blount's Gloss., ed. 1674. Opposed to *apogee*.–MF. *perigée*; Cot.–Late L. *perigēum*.–Late Gk. περίγειον, neut. of περίγειος, near the earth. Coined from Gk. περί, about (here near); and γῆ, the earth, which appears in *geo-graphy*, &c.

PERIHELION, the point of a planet's orbit nearest the sun. (Gk.) Scientific. In Phillips, ed. 1706. Opposed to *aphelion*.– Gk. περί, around (here near); and ἥλιος, the sun. See **Peri-** and **Aphelion**.

PERIL, danger. (F.–L.) ME. *peril*, Ancren Riwle, p. 194, l. 24.–OF. *peril*, 'perill;' Cot.–L. *periclum*, *periculum*, danger; lit. a trial, proof.–L. *perīrī*, to try, an obsolete verb of which the pp. *perītus*, experienced, is common. β. Allied to Gk. πειράω, I try, prove, περάω, I press through, pass through, as well as to Goth. *faran*, to travel, fare; see **Fare**. Thus a *peril* is a *trial* which one *passes through*. Der. *peril-ous*, Chaucer, C. T. 13925 (B 3109); *peril-ous-ly*, -*ness*.

PERIMETER, the sum of the lengths of all the sides of a plane figure. (L.–Gk.) Lit. the 'measure round.' In Blount's Gloss., ed. 1674.–L. *perimetros* (Lewis).–Gk. περίμετρος, the circumference of a circle; hence, the perimeter of a plane figure.–Gk. περί, round; and μέτρον, a measure; see **Peri-** and **Metre**.

PERIOD, the time of a circuit, date, epoch. (F.–L.–Gk.) In Shak. it often means 'conclusion, end;' Rich. III, ii. 1. 44; K. Lear, iv. 7. 97, v. 3. 204.–OF. *periode*, 'a period, perfect sentence, conclusion;' Cot.–L. *periodus*, a complete sentence.–Gk. περίοδος, a going round, way round, circuit, compass, a well-rounded sentence.–Gk. περί, round; and ὁδός, a way. See **Peri-** and **Exodus**. ¶ The sense of 'time of circuit' is taken directly from the orig. Gk. Der. *period-ic*; *period-ic-al* (Blount, 1674), *period-ic-al-ly*, *period-i-ci-ty*.

PERIPATETIC, walking about. (L.–Gk.) 'Peripatetical, that disputes or teaches walking, as Aristotle did; from whence he and his scholars were called *peripateticks*;' Blount's Gloss., ed. 1674. –L. *peripatēticus*.–Gk. περιπατητικός, given to walking about, esp. while disputing; Aristotle and his followers were called περιπατητικοί. – Gk. περιπατέω, I walk about.–Gk. περί, about; and πατέω, I walk, from πάτος, a path, which is allied to L. *pons*; see **Pontoon**.

PERIPHERY, circumference. (L. – Gk.) In Blount's Gloss., ed. 1674. ME. *periferie*; 'This air in *periferies* thre Devided is,' Gower, C. A. iii. 93 (bk. vii. 265); where the sidenote is : 'Nota qualiter aer in tribus *periferiis* diuiditur.' – L. *periferia, peripheria.* – περιφέρεια, the circumference of a circle. – Gk. περί, round; and φέρειν, to carry, cognate with E. *bear*. See **Peri-** and **Bear** (1).

PERIPHRASIS, a roundabout way of speaking. (L. – Gk.) ' *Periphrase*, circumlocution;' Blount's Gloss., ed. 1674; but this is rather a F. form. 'The figure *periphrasis*;' Puttenham, Arte of Poesie, bk. iii. c. 18. – L. *periphrasis.* – Gk. περίφρασις. – Gk. περί, round; and φράσις, a speech, phrase. See **Peri-** and **Phrase**. Der. *periphrase*, vb.; *periphrast-ic*, adj., from Gk. περιφραστικός; *periphrast-ic-al*.

PERISH, to come to naught. (F. – L.) ME. *perisshen*, Cursor Mundi, 8789; *perischen*, Wyclif, John, vi. 27. – F. *periss-*, stem of some parts of the verb *perir*, 'to perish;' Cot. (The stem *periss-* is formed as if from a L. *periscere, an imaginary inceptive form). – L. *perīre*, to perish, come to naught. – L. *per*, thoroughly, but with a destructive force like that of E. *for-*; and *īre*, to go; thus *perīre* = to go to the bad. *Ire* is from √EI, to go; cf. Skt. *i*, to go. And see **For-** (2). Der. *perish-able, perish-abl-y, perishable-ness*.

PERITONEUM, the membrane lining the abdominal cavity and investing its viscera. (Gk.) Late L. *peritonæum*, for Gk. περιτόναιον, the peritoneum; neut. of περιτόναιος, stretched around. – Gk. περί, around, and τον-, 2nd grade of τεν-, base of τείνειν (for *τέν-γειν), to stretch. See **Tone**. Der. *periton-itis*, inflammation of the peritoneum.

PERIWIG, a peruke. (F. – Ital. – L.) In Shak. Two Gent. iv. 4. 196. The *i* after *r* is corruptly inserted; Minsheu, ed. 1627, gives the spellings *perwigge* and *perwicke*. Of these forms, *perwigge* is a weakened form of *perwicke* or *perwick*; and *perwick* is a corrupted form of *peruke* or *perruque*; see **Perruque**. Du Wes has : 'the *perwyke*, la *perrucque*;' Supp. to Palsgrave, p. 902, col. i. β. The form *periwig* gave rise to a notion that *peri-* was a prefix, like Gk. περί; see **Peri-**. Hence, it was sometimes dropt, the resulting form being *wig*. See **Wig**.

PERIWINKLE, (1), a genus of evergreen plants. (L.) Formed with dimin. suffix *-le*, and insertion of *i*, from ME. *peruenke* (= *peruenke*), a periwinkle; Polit. Songs, ed. Wright, p. 218, l. 11. AS. *peruince*, as a gloss to L. *uinca*, in Voc. 322. 32. – L. *peruinca*, also called *uinca peruinca*, or (in one word) *uincaperuinca* (Lewis). β. The name was doubtless orig. given to a twining plant, as it is clearly allied to *uincire*, to bind; the prefix *per* being the usual L. prep.

PERIWINKLE (2), a small univalve mollusc. (E.; *with* Gk. *prefix*.) In Levins; and Palsgrave has : ' *Perivyncle*, a shellfysshe.' A corrupt form, due to a confusion with the word above. The best name is simply *winckle*, as in Holland, tr. of Pliny, b. ix. c. 32. *Periwincle* is in Drayton, Polyolbion, song 25, l. 190; and is a corruption of the AS. name *pinewincla*; cf. 'sǣ-snǣl, vel pinewinclan,' i. e. sea-snail, or periwinkles, in Voc. 122. 24. Cf. prov. E. *penny-winkle*, a periwinkle (E. D. D.); directly from AS. *pinewincla*. The prefix *pine-* is from L. *pīna*, Gk. πίνα, a kind of mussel. See **Winkle**.

PERJURE, to forswear (oneself), swear falsely. (F. – L.) The prefix has been conformed to the L. spelling. Shak. has *perjured*, Oth. v. 2. 63; also *perjure*, to render perjured, Antony, iii. 12. 30; also *perjure*, a perjured person, L. L. L. iv. 3. 47; *perjury*, L. L. L. iv. 3. 62. Skelton has *pariured*, perjured; How the Douty Duke of Albany, &c., l. 125. So also in Dictes and Sayings, pr. by Caxton, fol. 6, l. 10. – F. *parjurer*; whence *se parjurer*, 'to forsweare himselfe;' Cot. Cf. F. *parjure* (also MF. *perjure*), a perjured person; Cot. – L. *periūrāre*, to forswear; *periūrus*, a perjured person. – L. *per-*, prefix used in a bad sense, exactly equivalent to the cognate E. *for-* in *forswear*; and *iūrāre*, to swear. See **Per-** and **Jury**. Der. *perjury*, AF. *perjurie*, Philip de Thaun, Bestiary, 1310, from L. *periūrium*; *perjur-er*.

PERK, to make smart or trim. (F. – L.) ' To be *perked* up [dressed up] in a glistering grief;' Hen. VIII, ii. 3. 21. Prov. E. *perk*, a perch; also, to perch, sit; *perk up*, to become brisk; *perked up*, elated; see E. D. D. [Cf. W. *perc*, compact, trim; *percu*, to trim, to smarten; *percus*, smart; prob. from E.] ME. *perken*, to trim its feathers, as a bird; 'The papeiayes *perken*' (another MS. *perchyn*); The Pistill of Susan, 81 (S. T. S.). From the sb. *perke*, a perch; cf. 'an hauk's *perke*,' Cavendish, Life of Wolsey, p. 81; ed. F. S. Ellis. – North F. *perque* (Norm. dial. *perque*, Moisy), a perch. – L. *pertica*, a perch. See **Perch** (1).

PERMANENT, enduring. (F. – L.) In Spenser, F. Q. vii. 6. 2; and in Skelton's Poems, ed. Dyce, i. 199, l. 19. – F. *permanent*, 'permanent;' Cot. – L. *permanent-*, stem of pres. part. of *permanēre*, to endure. – L. *per*, thoroughly; and *manēre*, to remain. See **Per-** and **Mansion**. Der. *permanent-ly*; *permanence*.

PERMEATE, to penetrate and pass through small openings or pores, pervade. (L.) In Phillips, ed. 1706. Sir T. Browne has '*permeant* parts,' Vulg. Errors, b. ii. c. 5. § 8 (in speaking of gold). – L. *permeātus*, pp. of *permeāre*, to pass through. – L. *per*, through; and *meāre*, to pass, go. See Gk. μοῖτος in Prellwitz. Der. *permeation*; *permeant* (from the stem of the pres. part.); *permea-ble*, from L. *permeābilis*.

PERMIAN, an epithet given to a certain system of rocks. (Russian.) So named from *Perm*, in E. Russia (ab. 1841).

PERMIT, to let go, let pass, allow. (L.) In Skelton, Magnificence, l. 58. 'Yet his grace . . . wolde in no wise *permyt* and suffre me so to do;' State Papers, vol. i. Wolsey to Henry VIII, 1527 (R.). – L. *permittere* (pp. *permissus*), to let pass through, lit. to send through. – L. *per*, through; and *mittere*, to send; see **Per-** and **Mission**. Der. *permit*, sb.; also (like pp. *permissus*) *permiss-ible*, *permiss-ibl-y*, *permiss-ion*, Oth. i. 3. 340; *permiss-ive*, Meas. for Meas. i. 3. 38; *permiss-ive-ly*.

PERMUTATION, exchange, various arrangement. (F. – L.) ME. *permutacion*, P. Plowman, B. iii. 256. – F. *permutation*, 'permutation;' Cot. – L. *permutātiōnem*, acc. of *permutātio*, a changing. – L. *permūtāre*, to change, exchange. – L. *per*, thoroughly; and *mūtāre*, to change; see **Per-** and **Mutation**. Der. *permute*, vb., P. Plowman, B. xiii. 110, from L. *permūtāre*; *permut-able, permut-abl-y, permutable-ness*.

PERNICIOUS, hurtful, destructive. (F. – L.) In Shak. Meas. for Meas. ii. 4. 150; *pernyciouse*, Sir T. Elyot, Castel of Helth, bk. ii. c. 3. – F. *pernicieux*, 'pernicious;' Cot. – L. *perniciōsus*, destructive. – L. *perniciēs*, destruction. – L. *per*, thoroughly; and *nici-*, for *neci-*, decl. stem of *nex*, violent death. See **Internecine**. Der. *pernicious-ly, -ness*.

PERORATION, the conclusion of a speech. (F. – L.) In Shak. 2 Hen. VI, i. 1. 105. – F. *peroration*, 'a peroration;' Cot. – L. *perōrātiōnem*, acc. of *perōrātio*, the close of a speech. – L. *perōrāre*, to speak from beginning to end, also, to close a speech. – L. *per*, through; and *ōrāre*, to speak; see **Per-** and **Oration**.

PERPENDICULAR, exactly upright. (F. – L.) ME. *perpendiculer*, Chaucer, On the Astrolabe, pt. ii. § 23, l. 28. – F. *perpendiculaire*; Cot. – L. *perpendiculāris*, according to the plumb-line. – L. *perpendiculum*, a plummet; used for careful measurement. – L. *perpendere*, to weigh or measure carefully, consider. – L. *per*, through; and *pendere*, to weigh. See **Per-** and **Pension, Pendant**. Der. *perpendicular-ly, perpendicular-i-ty*. Also *perpend*, to consider, Hamlet, ii. 2. 105, from *perpendere*.

PERPETRATE, to execute, commit. (L.) Orig. a pp. 'Which were *perpetrate* and done;' Hall, Hen. VI, an. 31 (end). – L. *perpetrātus*, pp. of *perpetrāre*, to perform thoroughly. – L. *per*, thoroughly; and *patrāre*, to make, accomplish. Der. *perpetrat-or*, from L. *perpetrāt-or*; *perpetrat-ion*.

PERPETUAL, everlasting. (F. – L.) ME. *perpetuel*, Chaucer, C. T. Pers. Tale (I 137). – F. *perpetuel*, 'perpetuall;' Cot. – L. *perpetuālis*, universal; later used in same sense as *perpetuārius*, permanent. – L. *perpetuus*, continuous, constant, perpetual. – L. *perpet-*, stem of *perpes*, lasting throughout, continuous. – L. *per*, throughout; and *pet-*, as in *pet-ere*, to seek, to direct one's course. See **Per-** and **Petition**. Der. *perpetual-ly*, ME. *perpetuelly*, Chaucer, C. T. 1344 (A 1342); *perpetu-ate*, Palsgrave, from L. pp. *perpetuātus*; *perpetu-at-ion*; *perpetu-i-ty*, from F. *perpetuité*, 'perpetuity' (Cot.), from L. acc. *perpetuitātem*.

PERPLEX, to embarrass, bewilder. (F. – L.) 'In such *perplexed* plight;' Spenser, F. Q. iii. 1. 59. Minsheu gives only the participial adj. *perplexed*, not the verb; and, in fact, the form *perplexed* was really first in use, as a translation from the French. Spelt *perplexid* in Dictes and Sayings, pr. by Caxton, fol. 1. – F. *perplex*, 'perplexed, intricate, intangled;' Cot. – L. *perplexus*, entangled, interwoven. – L. *per*, thoroughly; and *plexus*, entangled, pp. of *plectere*, to plait, braid. See **Per-** and **Plait**. Der. *perplex-i-ty*, ME. *perplexitee*, Gower, C. A. iii. 348, bk. viii. 2190, from F. *perplexité*, which from L. acc. *perplexitātem*.

PERQUISITE, an emolument, small gain. (**L**.) Applied to a special allowance as being a thing sought for diligently and specially obtained. ' *Perquisite* (L. *perquisitum*) signifies, in Bracton, anything purchased, as *perquisitum facere*, lib. ii. c. 30, num. 3, and lib. iv. c. 22. *Perquisites* of Courts, are those profits that accrue to a lord of a manor, by vertue of his *Court Baron*, over and above the certain and yearly rents of his land; as, fines for copyhold, waifes, estrays, and such like;' Blount's Gloss., ed. 1674. – L. *perquisitum*, as above; properly neut. of *perquīsitus*, pp. of *perquīrere*, to ask after diligently. – L. *per*, thoroughly; and *quaerere*, to seek; see **Per-** and **Query**.

PERRUQUE, variant of **Peruke**, q. v.

PERRY, the fermented juice of pears. (F. – L.) In Phillips, ed. 1706. '*Perrie*, drinke of peares;' Minsheu, ed. 1627. ME. *pereye*; '*Piretum, pereye*;' Voc. 603. 11. – OF. *peré*, perry, supp. to Godefroy; mod. F. *poiré*, 'perry, drink made of pears;' Cot. Cf. Norm. dial. *péré*, perry (Robin). Formed with suffix *-é* (<L. *-ātus*, i.e. made of) from OF. *peire*, F. *poire*, a pear. ‒ L. *pirum*, a pear; see **Pear.**

PERSECUTE, to harass, pursue with annoyance. (F. ‒ L.) The sb. *persecution* is older in E. than the vb., and is spelt *persecucioun* in Wyclif, Second Prologue to Apocalypse, l. 1. Shak. has *persecute*, All's Well, i. 1. 16. ‒ MF. *persecuter*, 'to persecute, prosecute;' Cot. Formed as if from a Late L. **persecūtāre*, from L. *persecūtus*, pp. of *persequī*, to pursue, follow after. ‒ L. *per*, continually; and *sequī*, to follow. See **Per-** and **Sequence.** Der. *persecut-ion*.

PERSEVERE, to persist in anything. (F. ‒ L.) Formerly accented and spelt *perséver*, Hamlet, i. 2. 92. ME. *perseueren* (with *u*=*v*), Chaucer, C. T. 15585 (G 117). ‒ OF. *perseverer*, 'to persevere;' Cot. ‒ L. *perseuērāre*, to adhere to a thing, persist in it. ‒ L. *perseuērus*, very strict. ‒ L. *per*, thoroughly; and *seuērus*, strict; see **Per-** and **Severe.** Der. *persever-ance*, ME. *perseuerance*, Ayenbite of Inwyt, p. 168, l. 22, from OF. *perseverance*, L. *perseuerantia*.

PERSIFLAGE, light banter. (F. ‒ L.) In Greville's Memoirs, Mar. 15, 1831 (Cent. Dict.). ‒ F. *persiflage*, banter (1735). ‒ F. *persifler*, to jeer. ‒ L. *per*, through, thoroughly; *sibilāre*, to hiss, from *sibilus*, adj., hissing. See **Sibilant.**

PERSIMMON, a date-plum, the fruit of a tree of the genus Diospyros. (N. Amer. Indian.) Chiefly in use in N. America; said to be a Virginian Indian word. 'The fruit like medlers, they call *putchamins*, they cast vppon hurdles on a mat, and preserue them as pruines;' Capt. Smith, Works, ed. Arber, p. 57. (The preceding sentence treats of fruits that are dried to keep.) Spelt *pessimmins* in 1612; not stressed on the second syllable (N. E. D.). 'The second element is the suffix *-min*,' i.e. grain, small fruit, N. E. D. ‒ Algonkin *pasimine*, to cause fruits to dry; from *pas*, to be dry (Cuoq).

PERSIST, to continue steadfast, persevere. (F. ‒ L.) In Shak. All's Well, iii. 7. 42. ‒ F. *persister*, 'to persist;' Cot. ‒ L. *persistere*, to continue, persist. ‒ L. *per*, through; and *sistere*, properly to make to stand, set, a causal form from *stāre*, to stand. See **Per-** and **Stand.** Der. *persistent*, from the stem of the pres. part.; *persistence*; *persistenc-y*, 2 Hen. IV, ii. 2. 50.

PERSON, a character, individual, body. (F. ‒ L.) ME. *persone*, (1) a person, Chaucer, C. T. 10339 (F 25); (2) a parson, id. 480; earlier *persun*, Ancren Riwle, p. 126, l. 15. ‒ OF. *persone*, F. *personne*, 'a person, wight, creature;' Cot. ‒ L. *persōna*, a mask used by an actor, a personage, character, part played by an actor, a person. The large-mouthed masks worn by the actors were so called from the resonance of the voice sounding through them; at any rate, in popular etymology. Perhaps the long *ō* in *persōna* was due to the Gk. πρόσωπον, a mask, a dramatic character; but Walde (whom see) connects it with Gk. ζώνη, a zone. As if from L. *personāre*, to sound through. ‒ L. *per*, through; and *sonāre*, to sound, from *sonus*, sound. See **Per-** and **Sound.** (3) Doublet, *parson*, q. v. Der. *person-able*, Spenser, F. Q. iii. 4. 5; *person-age*, id. F. Q. iii. 2. 26, from MF. *personnage* (Cot.); *person-al*, Macb. i. 3. 91, from MF. *personnel*, L. *personālis*; *person-al-ly*; *personal-i-ty*, also in the contracted form *personal-ty*, with the sense of personal property; *person-ate*, Timon, i. 1. 69, from L. pp. *personātus*; *person-at-ion*, *person-at-or*; *person-i-fy*, a coined and late word, in Johnson's Dict.; whence *person-i-fic-at-ion*.

PERSPECTIVE, optical, relating to the science of vision. (F. ‒ L.) Properly an adj., as in 'the *perspectiue* or optike art;' Minsheu, ed. 1627; but common as a sb., accented *pérspective*, in the sense of an optical glass or optical delusion; see Rich. II, ii. 2. 18; also Skelton's Poems, ed. Dyce, i. 25, l. 22. ‒ F. *perspective*, sb. f., 'the perspective, prospective, or optike art;' Cot. ‒ L. **perspectiua* (not found), sb. f., the art of thoroughly inspecting; fem. of **perspectiuus*, relating to inspection. ‒ L. *perspectus*, clearly perceived, pp. of *perspicere*, to see through or clearly. ‒ L. *per*, through; and *specere*, to see, spy. See **Per-** and **Spy.** Der. *perspective-ly*, Hen. V, v. 2. 347. And see **Perspicacity, Perspicuous.**

PERSPICACITY, keenness of sight. (F. ‒ L.) In Minsheu, ed. 1627; and in Cotgrave. ‒ F. *perspicacité*, 'perspicacity, quick sight;' Cot. ‒ L. *perspicācitātem*, acc. of *perspicācitās*, sharpsightedness. ‒ L. *perspicāci-*, from *perspicax*, sharp-sighted; with suffix *-tās*. *Perspicax* is formed with suffix *-ax* from *perspic-ere*, to see through; see **Perspective.** Der. *perspicaci-ous*, a coined word, as an equivalent to L. *perspicax*; *perspicaciously, -ness.* And see **Perspicuous.**

PERSPICUOUS, evident. (L.) In Shak. Troil. i. 3. 324. Taken immediately (by change of *-us* to *-ous*, as in *arduous*, &c.) from L. *perspicuus*, transparent, clear. ‒ L. *perspicere*, to see through; see **Perspective.** Der. *perspicuous-ly, -ness;* also *perspicu-i-ty*, from F. *perspicuité*, 'perspicuity,' Cot.

PERSPIRATION, a sweating. (F. ‒ L.) The verb *perspire* is prob. later, and due to the sb.; it occurs in Sir T. Browne, Vulg.

Errors, b. iv. c. 7. § 4: 'A man in the morning is lighter in the scale, because in sleep some pounds have *perspired*.' The sb. is in Cotgrave; *perspirable* is in Minsheu, ed. 1627. ‒ F. *perspiration*, 'a perspiration, or breathing through.' ‒ L. *perspīrātiōnem*, acc. of **perspīrātio*, not given in Lewis's Dict., but regularly formed from *perspīrāre*, to breathe or respire all over. ‒ L. *per*, through; and *spīrāre*, to breathe; see **Per-** and **Spirit.** Der. *perspirat-or-y*; also *perspire*, verb, answering to L. *perspīrāre*.

PERSUADE, to prevail on, convince by advice. (F. ‒ L.) Common in Shak., Meas. for Meas. i. 2. 191; *perswade* in Palsgrave. ‒ F. *persuader*, 'to perswade;' Cot. ‒ L. *persuādēre* (pp. *persuāsus*), to persuade, advise thoroughly. ‒ L. *per*, thoroughly; and *suādēre*, to advise; see **Per-** and **Suasion.** Der. *persuad-er*; also (from pp. *persuāsus*) *persuas-ible*, from F. *persuasible*, 'perswasible,' Cot.; *persuasible-ness*, *persuasibili-ty*; also *persuas-ion*, Temp. ii. 1. 235, Skelton, Garland of Laurel, l. 34, from F. *persuasion*, 'perswasion,' Cot.; *persuas-ive*, from F. *persuasif*, 'perswasive,' Cot.; *persuas-ive-ly*, *persuas-ive-ness.*

PERT, forward, saucy. (F. ‒ L.) In Shak. it means 'lively, alert,' L.L.L. v. 2. 272. ' *Perte*, saucy,' Palsgrave, p. 320. ME. *pert*, which, however, has two meanings, and two sources; and the meanings somewhat run into one another. 1. In some instances, *pert* is certainly a corruption of *apert*, and *pertly* is used for 'openly' or 'evidently;' see Will. of Palerne, 4930, also 53, 96, 156, 180, &c. In this case, the source is the F. *apert*, open, evident, from L. *apertus*, pp. of *aperīre*, to open; see **Aperient.** 2. But we also find 'proud and *pert*,' Chaucer, C. T. 3948 (A 3950); 'stout he was and *pert*,' Li Beaus Disconus, l. 123 (Ritson). This is likewise short for F. *apert*, better spelt *appert*, 'expert, ready, prompt, active, nimble,' Cot.; OF. *appert*, *aspert* (Godefroy); from L. *expertus*, expert; see **Expert.** γ. It is the latter sense that now prevails. See **Malapert.** Der. *pert-ly*, Temp. iv. 58; *pert-ness*, Pope, Dunciad, i. 112.

PERTAIN, to belong. (F. ‒ L.) ME. *partenen*, Will. of Palerne, 1419; Wyclif, John, x. 13. Not a common word. ‒ OF. *partenir*, to pertain; in Godefroy and Burguy, but not in Cotgrave. (It seems to have been supplanted by the comp. *apartenir*; see **Appertain.**) ‒ L. *pertinēre*, to pertain. See **Pertinent.**

PERTINACITY, obstinacy. (F. ‒ L.) Phillips, ed. 1706, gives both *pertinacity* and *pertinacy*; Minsheu, ed. 1627, has only the latter form, which is the commoner one in old authors, though now disused. *Pertinacity* is from F. *pertinacité*, omitted by Cotgrave, but occurring in the 15th century (Godefroy). *Pertinacy* is from F. *pertinace*, cited by Minsheu, but not found in Cotgrave or Littré. β. *Pertinacity* is a coined word; *pertinacy* (F. *pertinace*) is from L. *pertinācia*, perseverance. ‒ L. *pertināci-*, for *pertinax*, very tenacious. ‒ L. *per-*, very; and *tenax*, tenacious, from *tenēre*, to hold. See **Per-** and **Tenable.** Der. *pertinaci-ous*, Milton, Apology for Smectymnuus (R.), a coined word, to represent L. *pertinax*, just as *perspicacious* represents *perspicax*; *pertinacious-ly, -ness.*

PERTINENT, related or belonging to. (F. ‒ L.) In Shak. Wint. Tale, i. 2. 221. ‒ F. *pertinent*, 'pertinent;' Cot. ‒ L. *pertinent-*, stem of pres. part. of *pertinēre*, to belong. ‒ L. *per-*, thoroughly; and *tenēre*, to hold, cling to; see **Per-** and **Tenable.** Der. *pertinent-ly, pertinence;* and see *pertinacity.*

PERTURB, to disturb greatly. (F. ‒ L.) ME. *perturben*, Chaucer, C. T. 908 (A 906). ‒ F. *perturber*, 'to perturb, disturb;' Cot. ‒ L. *perturbāre*, to disturb greatly. ‒ L. *per*, thoroughly; and *turbāre*, to disturb, from *turba*, a crowd. See **Per-** and **Turbid.** Der. *perturb-at-ion*, spelt *perturbacyon*, Bp. Fisher, On the Seven Psalms, Ps. 38, ed. Mayor (E. E. T. S.), p. 53, l. 21, from F. *perturbation* (Cot.), which is from L. acc. *perturbātiōnem.*

PERUKE, an artificial head of hair. (F. ‒ Ital. ‒ L.) The same word as *periwig*, which, however, is a corrupt form of the word; see **Periwig.** For the form *peruke*, R. refers to a poem by Cotton to John Bradshaw, l. 185; and Todd refers to Bp. Taylor, Artificial Handsomeness, p. 44; and Cooper's Lat. Dict. (1565) has : ' Capillamentum, A false *perruke*.' ‒ F. *perruque*, 'a lock of haire;' Cot. ‒ Ital. *parrucca*, MItal. *paruçca*, 'a periwigge,' Florio; who also gives the form *perucca*. β. The same word with Span. *peluca*, a wig, Port. *peruca*; Littré also cites Sardinian *pilucca*, and other forms. The key to the etymology is in remembering the frequent interchange of *r* and *l*; the true forms are those with *l*, such as Span. *peluca*, Sardinian *pilucca*. These are closely related to Ital. *piluccare*, now used in the sense 'to pick a bunch of grapes,' but formerly 'to pick or pull out haires or feathers one by one;' Florio. γ. The true old sense of *pilucca* was probably 'a mass of hair separated from the head,' thus furnishing the material for a peruke. Cf. also Ital. *pelluzo*, very soft down, MItal. *pellucare*, *pelucare*, 'to plucke off the haires or skin of anything, to pick out haires;' Florio. Also F. *peluche*, 'shag, plush,' Cot.; see **Plush.** δ. The MItal. *pelucare* and Sard. *pilucca* are formed (by help of a dimin. suffix

-*ucca*) from Ital. *pel-o*, hair. **—** L. *pilum*, acc. of *pilus*, a hair. **Doublets**, *periwig*, *wig*.

PERUSE, to examine, read over, survey. (Hybrid; L. *and* F. —L.) In Shak. in the sense 'to survey, examine,' Com. Errors, i. 2. 13; also 'to read,' Merch. Ven. ii. 4. 39. 'That I *perused* then;' G. Turbervile, The Louer to Cupid for Mercy, st. 12. 'Thus hauynge *perused* the effecte of the thirde booke, I will likewise *peruse* the fourth;' Bp. Gardiner, Explication, &c., Of the Presence, fol. 76 (R.). 'To peruse, *peruti*;' Levins, ed. 1570. And see Skelton, Phyllyp Sparowe, l. 814. **β.** The older senses of the word are nearer to the etymology. Thus, in the Naval Accounts of Henry VII (1485-8), p. 57, there are notes of a ship's fittings that were 'spent and *perused*,' i.e. used up, 'in a voiage into Lumbardye.' Fitzherbert, in his Husbandry, § 131, l. 15 (E. D. S.) has a similar usage. In giving directions for stacking faggots, he shows how to lay them in courses 'and so to *peruse* them [go through with them], tyll thou haue layd all up;' which shows a truer use of the word. So also in § 124, l. 35. In § 40, l. 23, a shepherd is bidden to *peruse* all his sheep, i.e. to examine them separately, 'tyll he haue doone.' See also § 30, l. 7. **γ.** A coined word; from **Per-** and **Use.** L.; in imitation of OF. *paruser*, 'user entièrement, achever, consommer;' Godefroy. He quotes: '*paruser sa vie* en seureté,' to lead his life in safety. The difficulty lies solely in the change of sense. The old sense seems to have been 'to go through one by one,' and so to 'use up (things) till all were done with.' Thus, in Cavendish's Life of Wolsey, p. 36, some maskers paid certain compliments to all the ladies in turn, thus '*perusyng* all the ladys and gentylwomen;' and again, at p. 65, a certain choir was directed to use a particular set of words in a litany 'and so *perused* the lettany thoroughe.' It may further be noted that compounds with *per* were once far more common than they are now. I can instance *peract*, Dr. Henry More, Poems (Chertsey Worthies' Library), p. 133, l. 31; *perdure*, *perfixt*, *perplanted*, *perquire*, *persway*, all in Halliwell; *perscrute*, *pertract*, Andrew Borde, Introduction of Knowledge, ed. Furnivall, p. 144, l. 32, p. 264, l. 25; *pervestigate*, *pervigilate*, both in Minsheu; *peraction*, *perarate*, *percruciate*, *perduction*, *perendinate*, *perflation*, *perfretation*, *perfriction*, *perfusion*, *pergraphical*, *perpession*, *perplication*, *perside*, *perstringe*, *perterebrate*, *pervagation*, all in Blount's Gloss., ed. 1674. Der. *perus-al*, Hamlet, ii. 1. 90.

PERVADE, to penetrate, spread through. (L.) 'Pervade, to go over or through;' Phillips, ed. 1706.—L. *peruādere*, to go through. —L. *per*, through; and *uādere*, to go, allied to E. *wade*. See **Per-** and **Wade.** Der. *per-vas-ive* (rare), like the pp. *peruāsus*, Shenstone, Economy, pt. iii.

PERVERT, to turn aside from the right, to corrupt. (F.—L.) ME. *peruerten* (with *u* for *v*), Chaucer, tr. of Boethius, bk. ii. pr. 1. l. 9.—F. *pervertir*, 'to pervert, seduce;' Cot.—L. *peruertere*, to overturn, ruin, corrupt (pp. *peruersus*).—L. *per*, thoroughly; and *uertere*, to turn; see **Per-** and **Verse.** Der. *pervert-er*; also *perverse*, Fabyan's Chron. vol. i. c. 112, in the description of Brunechieldis, from F. *pervers*, 'perverse, cross' (Cot.), which from L. pp. *peruersus*; hence *perverse-ly*, *perverse-ness*, *pervers-i-ty*, *pervers-ion*. Also *pervert-ible*.

PERVICACIOUS, wilful, obstinate. (L.) 'Why should you be so *pervicacious* now, Pug?' Dryden, Kind Keeper, A. ii. sc. 2 (ed. Scott). Coined by adding -*ous* to *peruicāci*-, from *peruicax*, wilful, stubborn; allied to *peruicus*, stubborn. **β.** Perhaps from *per*-, thoroughly, and the base *ui*-, weak grade of *ui*-, as seen in *ui-cī*, pt. t. of *uincere*, to conquer (Bréal). See **Per-** and **Victor.**

PERVIOUS, penetrable. (L.) In Dryden, tr. of Ovid, Meleager, l. 146. Borrowed directly from L. *peruius*, passable, by change of -*us* to -*ous*, as in *arduous*, &c.—L. *per*, through; and *uia*, a way; hence, 'affording a passage through.' See **Per-** and **Voyage.** Der. *pervious-ly*, -*ness*.

PESETA, a silver coin of modern Spain. (Span.—L.) Worth 2 silver reals, or about 9½d.—Span. *peseta*; dimin. of *pesa*, a weight, allied to *peso*, a weight, a Span. dollar. *Peso* is from L. *pensum*, a portion weighed out to spinsters.—L. *pensus*, pp. of *pendere*, to weigh; see **Poise.**

PESSIMIST, one who complains of everything as being for the worst. (L.) Modern; not in Todd's Johnson. Formed with suffix -*ist* (= L. -*ista*, from Gk. -*ιστης*) from L. *pessim-us*, worst. [So also *optim-ist* from *optim-us*, best.] **β.** *Pessimus* is connected with comp. *pēior*, worse; see **Impair.** Brugmann, ii. § 73.

PEST, a plague, anything destructive or unwholesome. (F.—L.) 'The hellish *pest*;' Milton, P. L. ii. 735.—F. *peste*, 'the plague, or pestilence;' Cot.—L. *pestem*, acc. of *pestis*, a deadly disease, plague. Der. *pest-house*; *pesti-ferous*, Sir T. Elyot, The Governor, b. i. c. 4. § 2, Englished from L. *pestiferus* (the same as *pestifer*), from *pesti-*, for *pestis*, and -*fer*, bringing, from *ferre*, to bring, cognate with E. **Bear** (1); also *pesti-lent*, q. v.

PESTER, to encumber, annoy. (F.—L.) The old sense is to 'encumber' or 'clog.' 'Neither *combred* wyth ouer greate multitude, nor *pestered* with to much baggage;' Brende, tr. of Q. Curtius, fol. 23 b (1592). '*Pestered* [crowded] with innumerable multitudes of people;' North's Plutarch (in Shakespeare's Plutarch, ed. Skeat, p. 175). Hence *pesterous*, cumbersome, in Bacon, Life of Hen. VII, ed. Lumby, p. 196, l. 29 (wrongly explained as *pestiferous*). A shortened form of *impester*, by loss of the first syllable, as in the case of *fence* for *defence*, *sport* for *disport*, *story* for *history*, &c. Cotgrave explains the F. pp. *empestré* as 'impestered, intricated, intangled, incumbered.'—MF. *empestrer*, to 'pester, intricate, intangle, trouble, incumber.' Mod. F. *empêtrer*. **β.** '*Empêtrer* signifies properly to hobble a horse while he feeds afield, and *dépêtrer* is to free his legs from the bonds. These words come from the medieval L. *pastorium*, a clog for horses at pasture. *Pastorium* (derived through *pastum* from *pascere*, to feed) is common in this sense in the Germanic laws: 'Si quis in exercitu aliquid furaverit, *pastorium*, capistrum, frenum,' &c. (Lex Bavar. tit. II. vi. 1). So also in the Lex Longobard. tit. I. xx. 5: 'Si quis *pastorium* de caballo alieno tulerit;' Brachet. **γ.** Thus *empester* represents Late L.* *impastōriāre*, regularly formed from *in*, prep., and *pastorium*, a clog. *Pastorium* is a derivative from *pastus*, pp. of *pascere*, to feed, inceptive form from a base *pa*-; see **Pastor.** ¶ Unconnected with *pest*; but connected with **Pastern,** q. v.

PESTIFEROUS; see under **Pest.**

PESTILENT, bringing a plague, hurtful to health or morals. (F.—L.) In Hamlet, ii. 2. 315. [The sb. *pestilence* is much older; ME. *pestilence*, P. Plowman, B. v. 13.]—F. *pestilent*, 'pestilent, plaguy;' Cot.—L. *pestilent-*, stem of *pestilens*, unhealthy; we also find an old rare form *pestilentus*. **β.** *Pestilens* is formed as a pres. part. from a verb **pestilēre* not in use, but founded on the adj. *pestilis*, pestilential. This adj. is formed with suffix -*li*- from *pesti*- decl. stem of *pestis*, a plague; see **Pest.** Der. *pestilence*, sb. (as above), from F. *pestilence* < L. *pestilentia*; *pestilent-ly*, *pestilent-i-al*.

PESTLE, an instrument for pounding things in a mortar. (F.—L.) ME. *pestel*, Tale of Gamelyn, l. 122. '*Pestel*, of stampynge, Pila, pistillus, pistellus;' Prompt. Parv.—OF. *pestel* (Godefroy), later *pesteil*, 'a pestle or pestell;' Cot.—L. *pistillum*, a pestle; regularly formed, as a dimin. of an unused sb. **pistrum*, from *pistum*, supine of *pinsere*, to pound, rarely spelt *pisere*. See **Pistil, Piston.**

PET (1), a tame and fondled animal, a child treated fondly. (F.?) 'The love of cronies, *petts*, and favourites;' Tatler, no. 266, Dec. 21, 1710. Cf. also *peat*, as in Shak. Tam. Shrew, i. 1. 78. 'Pretty *peat*;' Gascoigne, Flowers, Hir Question; Works, ed. Hazlitt, i. 48. Ray (A.D. 1691) calls *pet* a North-country word, and explains a *pet-lamb* as 'a cade lamb.' [Cf. Irish *peat*, sb. a pet, adj. petted; Gael. *peata*, a pet, a tame animal; borrowed from E.] Of uncertain origin. Perhaps suggested by MF. *peton*, 'a little foot, the slender stalke of a leafe; *mon peton*, my pretty springall, my gentle imp (any such flattering or dandling phrase, bestowed by nurses on their suckling boies);' Cot. Used by Rabelais; see Hatzfeld. Usually considered as a derivative of F. *pied*, a foot; from L. *ped-em*, acc. of *pēs*, a foot. Cf. also F. *petiot*, a dear little child (Godefroy); Norm. dial. *petiot* (Moisy); and see **Petty.** Der. *pet*, verb; *pett-ed*; and probably *pet* (2), q. v.

PET (2), a sudden fit of peevishness. (F.?) 'In a *pet* of temperance;' Milton, Comus, 721. Shak. has *pettish*, adj., i. e. capricious, Troil. ii. 3. 139; spelt *petish*, Levins. There was also an old phrase 'to take the *pet*,' or 'to take *pet*.' Cotgrave translates F. *se mescontenter de* by 'to take the *pet*, to be ill satisfied with.' The simplest and most probable derivation is from **Pet** (1), q. v. A *pet* is a spoilt child; hence *pettish*, capricious; *to take the pet*, to act like a spoilt child; whence, finally, the sb. *pet* in its new sense of 'capricious action' or peevishness. Der. *pett-ish*, *pett-ish-ly*, *pett-ish-ness*.

PETAL, a flower-leaf; part of a corolla. (Gk.) '*Petala*, among herbalists, those fine coloured leaves of which the flowers of all plants are made up;' Phillips, ed. 1706. Here *petala* is the *Greek* plural form, showing that the word was taken from the Greek immediately.—Gk. πέταλον (pl. πέταλα), a leaf; properly neut. of πέταλος, spread out, broad, flat. Πέταλος is formed with suffix -λος from the base πετ- (whence also πετ-άννυμι, I spread out). Cf. L. *patulus*, spreading, *pat-ēre*, to lie open, be spread out.—√PET, to spread out; see **Fathom.** Der. *petal-oid*.

PETARD, a war-engine, a case filled with explosive materials. (F.—L.) In Hamlet, iii. 4. 207; spelt *petar* in the quarto edd. of Hamlet, and by all editors down to Johnson. Cotgrave has both *petard* and *petarre*.—F. *petart*, *petard*, 'a petard or petarre; an engine . . wherewith strong gates are burst open.' Lit. 'explosive.' Formed with suffix -*art* or -*ard* (of Germanic origin, from G. *hart*, hard, Brachet, Introd. § 196) from the verb *peter*, to break wind. —F. *pet*, a breaking wind, slight explosion.—L. *pēditum*, a breaking wind. — L. *pēditus*, pp. of *pēdere* (contracted from **pezdere*), to break wind. See Brugmann, i. § 857. ¶ The E. form *petar* arose from the fact that the OF. pl. of *petard* was *petars*.

PETIOLE, the footstalk of a leaf. (F. — L.) Modern; botanical. — F. *pétiole*, a petiole. — L. *petiolum*, acc. of *petiolus*, a little stem or stalk. Usually considered as a derivative of L. *pēs*, a foot.

PETITION, a prayer, supplication. (F. — L.) ME. *peticion*, *petition*; Rob. of Brunne, tr. of Langtoft, p. 313, l. 18. — F. *petition*, 'a petition;' Cot. — L. *petītiōnem*, acc. of *petītio*, a suit; cf. *petītus*, pp. of *petere*, to attack, ask; orig. to fall on. — √PET, to fly, fall; whence also E. *feather*; see **Feather, Impetus**. **Der.** *petition*, vb., *petition-ar-y*, *petition-er*, *petition-ing*.

PETREL, PETEREL, a genus of ocean-birds. (F. — G. — L. — Gk.) For the form *peterel*, see Todd. 'The *petrel* is a Bird not much unlike a Swallow. They fly sweeping like Swallows, and very near the water;' W. Dampier, A New Voyage, iii. 97. The spelling *petrel* is also used in a translation of Buffon's Nat. Hist., London, 1792, where we are told that the stormy petrels 'sometimes hover over the water like swallows, and sometimes appear to *run on the top of it*;' vol. ii. p. 128. From the latter peculiarity they take their name. — F. *pétrel* (sometimes *pétérel*); Littré cites a letter written by Buffon, dated 1782, who gives his opinion that *pétrel* is a better spelling than *pétérel*, because the derivation is from the name *Peter*, which is pronounced, he says, as *Pétre*. (The usual F. word for *Peter* is *Pierre*.) β. Thus *pétrel* is formed as a diminutive of *Pêtre* or Peter; and the allusion is to the action of the bird, which seems to walk on the sea, like St. Peter. The G. name *Petersvogel* (lit. Peter-fowl = Peter-bird) gives clear evidence as to the etymology. — G. *Peter*. — L. *Petrus*, Peter. — Gk. Πέτρος, a rock; a name given to the apostle by Christ; see John i. 42, in the orig. Gk. text. See **Petrify**. ¶ The F. *Pétre* was prob. borrowed from G. *Peter*, not from the L. directly. Or the F. word may have been borrowed from E.; in which case E. *petrel* is from L. *Petrus*.

PETRIFY, to turn into stone. (F. — Gk. and L.) Properly transitive; also used intransitively. 'When wood and many other bodies do *petrify*;' Sir T. Browne, Vulg. Errors, bk. ii. c. 1. § 3. — F. *petrifier*, 'to make stony;' Cot. Formed as if from L. **petrificāre*, a coined word, to make stony. — L. *petri-*, for *petra*, a rock, and *-ficāre*, for *facere*, to make. β. The L. *petra* is merely borrowed from Gk. πέτρα, a rock; cf. Gk. πέτρος, a mass of rock, a stone. **Der.** *petrifact-ion*, as if from a L. pp. **petrifactus*, but the older word is *petrification*, from F. *petrification*, 'a petrification, a making stony' (Cot.); *petrifact-ive*; also *petrific*, adj., Milton, P. L. x. 294.

PETROLEUM, rock-oil. (L. — Gk.) Minsheu, ed. 1627, explains *petrol* or *petroleum* as 'a kind of marle or chaulky clay;' this is the same word, differently applied. Coined from L. *petr-*, for *petra*, a rock, a word borrowed from Gk. πέτρα; and L. *oleum*, oil, from Gk. ἔλαιον, oil. See **Petrify** and **Oil**. Cooper's Thesaurus (1565) has the form *petroleon*. ¶ There is a curious mention of rock-oil in Plutarch's Life of Alexander; see North's Plutarch, ed. 1631, p. 702.

PETRONEL, a large horse-pistol. (F. — L.) 'Their peeces then are called *petronels*;' Gascoigne, Weedes; The Continuance of the Author, upon the Fruite of Fetters, st. 7; Works, ed. Hazlitt, i. 408. Spelt *petrinel*, in Ben Jonson, Every Man, ed. Wheatley, iii. 1; some edd. have *petronel*. — MF. *petrinal*, 'a petronell, or horseman's piece;' Cot. β. Wedgwood remarks that they are said to have been invented in the Pyrenees; Godefroy gives also *poictrinal* (1585), and says that it was fired by resting the butt-end against the chest (so also Fairholt). Cf. MItal. *pietranelli*, 'souldiers serving on horseback, well armed with a pair of cuirasses and weaponed with a fire-locke-piece or a snaphance or a *petronell*;' Florio. From OF. *peitrine*, *poitrine*, the chest, allied to AF. *peitral*, a poitrel; both are from L. *pector-*, for **pectos*, stem of *pectus*, the breast; see **Poitrel**.

PETTO, the breast. (Ital. — L.) In the phr. *in petto*, within the breast, in secret. — Ital. *petto*, breast. — L. *pectus*, breast.

PETTY, small, insignificant. (F. — C.) Common in Shak.; see Merch. Ven. i. 1. 12, &c. ME. *petit*, P. Plowman, B. xiv. 242. — F. *petit*, 'little, small, . . meane, petty;' Cot. β. Perhaps of Celtic origin; Diez connects it with Sardinian *piticu*, little, Wallachian *pitic*, a dwarf, OItal. *pitetto*, *petitto*, Prov. and Catalan *petit*, Wallachian *piti*, small, little, &c. All from a Gaulish stem **pett-* = Celtic **qett-*, which occurs again in **Piece**. **Der.** *petti-ly*; *petti-ness*, Henry V, iii. 6. 136; *petti-coat*, i.e. little coat, As You Like It, ii. 3. 15 (see **Coat**); *petti-fogger*, Marston, The Malcontent, A. i. sc. 6 (R.), spelt *pettie fogger* in Minsheu, ed. 1627, whence prov. E. *fog*, to hunt in a servile manner, to flatter for gain, used by Dekker (Halliwell), equivalent to MDu. *focker*, 'a monopole, or an engrosser of wares and commodities;' Hexham; and *focker* is prob. a corruption of the surname *Fugger*, Englished as *fogger*

(N. E. D.). Also *petti-toes*, usually pig's trotters, sometimes human feet (jocularly), as in Shirley, Maid's Revenge, iv. 1; see below.

PETTITOES, pig's trotters. (F. — C. and L.) Understood as *petty-toes*, whence the present sense (see end of last article). But this is popular etymology. It formerly meant giblets or garbage (see N. E. D.) — MF. *petitose*, 'garbage of fowls,' Cot.; pl. of *petitoye*, the same, Palsgrave, p. 224; *petite oye*, the same, Cot. (s. v. *oye*). Here *oye* (F. *oie*) is from Late L. *auca*, a goose; for L. *au'ca*, **aui-ca*, from *auis*, a bird.

PETULANT, peevish. (L.) In Ben Jonson, Epigram 2 (To My Book), l. 5. — L. *petulant-*, stem of *petulans*, forward, pert, petulant; lit. 'ready to attack in a small way,' as it answers to the form of a pres. part. of **petulāre*, a dimin. of *petere*, to attack, seek. See **Petition**. **Der.** *petulant-ly*; also *petulance*, from F. *petulance*, 'petulancy,' Cot.; *petulanc-y*.

PETUNIA, a plant or flower; of the order Solanaceæ. (F. — Port. — Brazil.) F. *pétunia* (Hatzfeld). Formed with suffix -*ia* from F. *petun*, MF. *petum*, 'tobacco,' Cot. — Port. *petum* (Hatzfeld). — Guarani (Brazil.) *petĩ*, tobacco (with nasalized *i*); P. Restivo, Vocab. de la Lengua Guaraní.

PEW, an enclosed seat in a church. (F. — L. — Gk.) ME. *puwe*. 'Yparroked in *puwes*' = enclosed in pews; P. Plowman, C. vii. 144. Cf. AF. *pui*, a stage, platform; in Liber Custumarum, p. 216. — OF. *puie*, an elevated place, MF. *puye*, f., 'an open and outstanding terrace or gallery, set on the outside with rails to lean on;' Cot. Cf. Span. *poyo*, a stone-bench near a door, Ital. *poggio*, a hillock. [Prob. orig. applied to a raised desk to kneel at.] — L. *podia*, pl. of *podium*, an elevated place, a balcony next the arena, where the emperor and other distinguished persons sat. [The loss of *d* and change of *po-ia* to OF. *puie*, are regular.] — Gk. πόδιον, a little foot; whence the senses of footstool, support for the feet, gallery to sit in, &c., must have been evolved; for there can be no doubt as to the identity of the Gk. and L. words. — Gk. ποδί-, from πούς, a foot; with dimin. suffix -ον. Gk. πούς is cognate with E. *foot*; see **Foot**. **Der.** *pew-fellow*, Rich. III, iv. 4. 58. ☞ The Du. *puye*, 'a pue' (Hexham), is borrowed from MF. *puye*.

PEWET, PEEWIT, the lapwing. (E.) '*Pewet* or *Puet*, a kind of bird;' Phillips, ed. 1706. '*Een Piewit-vogel, ofte* [or] *Kiewit*, a puet, or a lap-winckle;' Hexham's Du. Dict., ed. 1658. Spelt *puwyt*, Skelton, Philip Sparowe, l. 430. Named from its cry. So also Du. *piewit* or *kiewit*, G. *kibitz*; Westphal. *pīwik*, *pīwit*. See **Peevish**.

PEWTER, an alloy of lead with tin or zinc. (F. — E.?) ME. *pewtir*, *pewtyr*. '*Pewtyr*, metalle;' Prompt. Parv. '*Pewter* pottes;' Lydgate, London Lyckpeny, st. 12. 'xij pottes de *peutre*;' Earl of Derby's Expeditions, 1390–1, p. 101. — OF. *peutre*, *peautre*, *piautre*, a kind of metal (Roquefort). *Peutre* stands, as usual, for an older form **peltre*; cf. Span. *peltre*, Ital. *peltro*, pewter. Diez remarks that the Italians believe their word *peltro* was borrowed from England; but he rejects this solution, on the ground that the form *pewter* could not well become *peltro* in Italian. The Low L. form is *peltrum*; as in 'vasorum de *peltro*,' York Wills, ii. 146 (1450). The solution is, probably, that the Ital., Span., and OF. forms have lost an initial *s*, owing to the difficulty of sounding the initial *sp*; and the original word really *does* appear in E. in the form *spelter*. '*Spelter*, a kind of metall, not known to the antients, which the Germans call zink;' Blount's Gloss., ed. 1674; whence OF. *espeautre*, *espiautre*, a kind of metal (Godefroy). Cf. MDu. *peauter* or *speauter*, pewter; Hexham. Zinc and pewter are often confounded. See **Spelter**. **Der.** *pewter-er*, Prompt. Parv.

PH

PHAETON, a kind of carriage. (F. — L. — Gk.) Properly *Phaethon*, but we took the word from French. Spelt *phaëton* (trisyllabic) in Young, Night Thoughts, bk. v. l. 825. — F. *phaéton*, a phaeton; occurring in a work written in 1792 (Littré). — F. *Phaéthon*, proper name. — L. *Phaethōn*. — Gk. Φαέθων, son of Helios, and driver of the chariot of the sun. — Gk. φαέθων, radiant, pres. part. of φαέθειν, to shine; allied to φάειν, to shine. — √BHA, to shine; see **Phantom**.

PHALANX, a battalion of troops closely arrayed. (L. — Gk.) In Minsheu, ed. 1627; and Milton, P. L. i. 550, iv. 979. 'This legion he called the *phalanx*;' Holland, tr. of Suetonius, Nero, ch. 19. — L. *phalanx*. — Gk. φάλαγξ, a line of battle, battle-array, a battalion. See **Plank**. **Der.** *phalanger*, a marsupial mammal, in a tr. of Buffon, i. 292 (1792); named *phalanger* (F.) by Buffon (see Littré) from the structure of the hind feet; from F. *phalange* =

Gk. φαλαγγ-, stem of φάλαγξ, the bone between two joints of the toes. ¶ The L. pl. is *phalanges*.

PHALLUS, an emblem of the generative power in nature, honoured in Bacchic festivals. (L. – Gk.) 'Two *Phalli*;' Purchas, Pilgrimage, bk. i. c. 15; p. 79. – L. *phallus*. – Gk. φαλλός, lit. membrum virile. +Irish *ball*, a limb, member; OIrish *ball*, glossed 'membrum.'

PHANTASM, a spectre. (F. – L. – Gk.) *Phantasme*, Minsheu, ed. 1627. ME. *fantesme*, Ancren Riwle, p. 62. – OF. *fantasme*. – L. *phantasma*; see Jul. Cæs. ii. 1. 65. – Gk. φάντασμα, a spectre; see **Phantom**. Der. *phantasm-agoria*, lit. a collection of spectres, as shown by the magic lantern, from Gk. ἀγορά, an assembly, collection, which from ἀγείρειν, to assemble. Doublet, *phantom*.

PHANTASTIC, PHANTASY; see **Fantastic, Fancy**.

PHANTOM, a vision, spectre. (F. – L. – Gk.) Partly conformed to the Gk. spelling. ME. *fantome*, Chaucer, C. T. 5457 (B 1037); *fantum*, Wyclif, Matt. xiv. 26. – OF. *fantosme*, MF. *phantosme*, 'a spirit, ghost;' Cot. – L. *phantasma*. – Gk. φάντασμα, a vision, spectre, lit. an apparition, appearance. – Gk. φαντάζειν, to display; in passive, to appear; cf. the sb. -φάντης, one who shows, only used in the compounds ἱερο-φάντης, συκο-φάντης; see **Hierophant, Sycophant**. – Gk. φαν-, as seen in φαίνειν (= φάν-γειν) to show, lit. 'to cause to shine;' where φαν- is an extended form of φα-, to shine; cf. φάειν, to shine, φάος, light. – √BHĀ, to shine; cf. Skt. *bhā*, to shine. Hence also *fan-tas-y* (shorter form *fancy*), *hiero-phant*, *syco-phant*, *dia-phan-ous*, *phen-o-men-on*, *pha-se*, *em-phas-is*, *phaeton*, *photograph*, *phosphorus*. See **Fancy, Phenomenon, Phase**. Doublet, *phantasm*.

PHARISEE, one of a religious school among the Jews. (F. – L. – Gk. – Aramaic.) Partly conformed to Gk. spelling; ME. *farisee*, Wyclif, Matt. ix. 11. – OF. *pharisee*; Godefroy. – L. *pharisēus, pharisaeus*, Matt. ix. 11 (Vulgate). – Gk. φαρισαῖος, Matt. ix. 11; lit. 'one who separates himself from men.' – Aram. *Perishīn*, for Heb. *Perūshīm*, pl., 'separated;' Smith, Dict. of the Bible. Cf. Heb. *pārash*, to separate. Der. *Pharisa-ic, Pharisa-ic-al*.

PHARMACY, the knowledge of medicines; the art of preparing medicines. (F. – L. – Gk.) Partly conformed to the Gk. spelling. ME. *fermacy*, Chaucer, C. T. 2715 (A 2713). – OF. *farmacie*, later *pharmacie*, 'a curing, or medicining with drugs;' Cot. – L. *pharmacīa*. – Gk. φαρμακεία, pharmacy. – Gk. φάρμακον, a drug. β. Perhaps so called from its bringing help; allied to φέρειν, to bear, bring, cognate with E. *bear*; see **Bear** (1); cf. Skt. *bhṛtis*, nourishment, service, from *bhṛ*, to bear. Der. *pharmac-eu-t-ic*, formed with suffix *-ic* (Gk. *-ικος*) from φαρμακευτ-ής, a druggist, which again is formed with suffix *-της* from φαρμακεύ-ειν, to administer a drug, from φαρμακ-εύς, a druggist; hence *pharmaceutic-al, pharmaceutic-s*. Also *pharmaco-pœia*, from ποιεῖν, to make, prepare.

PHARYNX, the cavity forming the upper part of the gullet. (L. – Gk.) In Phillips' Dict. ed. 1706. – Late L. *pharynx*; merely the Latinized form of the Gk. word. – Gk. φάρυγξ, the joint opening of the gullet and windpipe; also, a cleft, a bore; closely allied to φάραγξ, a chasm, gulley, cleft, ravine, and to φαράειν, to plough. All from the base φαρ-, to bore, cut, pierce, hence, to cleave; allied to L. *forāre* and E. *bore*. – √BHAR, to bore, cut; see **Bore** (1).

PHASE, PHASIS, an appearance; a particular appearance of the moon or of a planet at a given time. (L. – Gk.) The form *phase* does not appear to have been borrowed from F. *phase*, but to have resulted as an E. singular from the pl. sb. *phases*, borrowed immediately from Latin. 'Phases, appearances; in astronomy, the several positions in which the moon and other planets appear to our sight, &c.;' Phillips' Dict., ed. 1706. 'Phasis, an appearance;' Bailey, vol. ii. 1731. And see Todd's Johnson. – Late L. *phasis*, pl. *phasēs*; merely the L. form of the Gk. word. – Gk. φάσις, an appearance; from the base φα-, to shine; cf. φάος, light. – √BHĀ, to shine; see **Phantom**. ☞ The Gk. φάσις not only means 'appearance,' as above; but also 'a saying, declaration,' in which sense it is connected with φημί, I speak, declare, from √BHĀ, to speak; see **Ban**. This explains the word *em-phas-is*.

PHEASANT, a gallinaceous bird. (F. – L. – Gk.) Now conformed to the Gk. spelling as far as relates to the initial *ph*. Formed with excrescent *t* (common after *n*, as in *tyran-t, ancien-t, parchmen-t*) from ME. *fesaun*, Will. of Palerne, 183; later form *fesaunt*, Chaucer, Parl. of Foules, 357. – AF. *fesaunt*, Liber Custumarum, p. 304; OF. *faisan*, 'a phesant;' Cot. – L. *phasiāna*, a pheasant; for *Phasiāna auis* = Phasian bird, where *Phasiāna* is the fem. of *Phasiānus*, adj.; we also find *phasiānus*, masc., a pheasant. – Gk. Φασιανός, a pheasant, lit. Phasian, i. e. coming from the river *Phasis* (Φᾶσις) in Colchis. β. The river Phasis is now called the Rioni; it flows from the Caucasus into the Black Sea.

PHENIX, PHŒNIX, a fabulous bird. (L. – Gk.) The word appears very early. Spelt *fenix*, it is the subject of an AS. poem

extant in the Exeter book; printed in Grein's Bibliothek, i. 215. This poem is imitated from a L. poem with the same title. – L. *phoenix*; Pliny, Nat. Hist. x. 2. 2. – Gk. φοίνιξ, a phoenix; see Herodotus, ii. 73, and Smith's Classical Dictionary. β. The same word also means Phœnician or Punic (Gk. φοίνιξ = L. *Pūnicus*); also, a palm-tree; also purple-red. ¶ Littré supposes that the phœnix was named from its bright colour; and that the colour was so named because invented by the Phœnicians.

PHENOMENON, a remarkable appearance, an observed result. (L. – Gk.) Formerly *phænomenon*, with pl. *phænomena*, as in Phillips, ed. 1706. – L. *phænomenon*, pl. *phænomena*. – Gk. φαινόμενον, pl. φαινόμενα, properly the neut. of the pass. part. of φαίνειν, to show (pass. φαίνομαι, to be shown, to appear). See **Phantom**. Der. *phenomen-al*, a coined adj.

PHEON, the broad barbed head of an arrow. (F. – Teut.?) Heraldic; spelt *feon*, Book of St. Alban's, pt. ii. fol. B 5. Perhaps for *fleon*; from Late L. *fletōnem*, acc. of *fleto, fletho*, an arrow-head (Ducange). Cf. Du. *flits*, an arrow.

PHIAL, a small glass vessel or bottle. (F. – L. – Gk.) Formerly spelt *vial, viall, viol*; altered to *phial* (a more 'learned' form) in some mod. edd. of Shakespeare. We find *phial* as well as *vial* in Blount's Gloss., ed. 1674. – MF. *phiole*, 'a violl;' Cot. – L. *phiala*. – Gk. φιάλη, a broad, shallow cup or bowl (applied in F. to a small bottle). See **Vial**.

PHILANDER, a lover. (Gk.) 'You and your *Philander*!' Congreve, Way of the World, v. 1. From the use of the name *Philander* for a lover, as e. g. in Beaumont and Fletcher's Laws of Candy. – Gk. φίλανδρος, lit. 'loving men.' Gk. φιλ-εῖν, to love; ἀνδρ-, from ἀνήρ, a man.

PHILANTHROPY, love of mankind. (L. – Gk.) Spelt *philanthropie* in Minsheu, ed. 1627. Englished from L. *philanthrōpia*. – Gk. φιλανθρωπία, benevolence. – Gk. φιλάνθρωπος, loving mankind. – Gk. φιλ-, for φίλος, friendly, kind; and ἄνθρωπος, a man. [The words *philo-sophy, philo-logy* show that φιλ- represents φίλος, adj., not φιλεῖν, verb.] See **Philosophy** and **Anthropology**. Der. *philanthrop-ic*; *philanthrop-ist*, Young, Night Thoughts, Night 4, l. 603.

PHILHARMONIC, loving music. (Gk.) Modern; not in Todd's Johnson. Coined from Gk. φιλ-, for φίλος, friendly, fond of; and *harmoni-a*, Latinised form of Gk. ἁρμονία, harmony; with suffix *-kos*; as if from Gk. φιλ-αρμονι-κός. See **Philosophy** and **Harmony**.

PHILIBEG, a kilt (Gaelic). See **Fillibeg**.

PHILIPPIC, a discourse full of invective. (L. – Gk.) In Minsheu, ed. 1627; and in Dryden, tr. of Juvenal, sat. x. l. 196. – L. *Philippicum*, used by Juvenal (Sat. x. l. 125) in the pl. *Philippica*, used to denote the celebrated orations of Demosthenes against Philip. – Gk. φίλιππος, a lover of horses; also Philip, a personal name. – Gk. φιλ-, for φίλος, fond of; and ἵππος, a horse, cognate with L. *equus*. See **Philosophy** and **Equine**.

PHILOLOGY, the study of languages. (L. – Gk.) In Skelton, Why Come Ye Nat to Courte, 514. Spelt *philologie* in Minsheu, ed. 1627; and in Chaucer, C. T., E 1734. Englished from L. *philologia*. – Gk. φιλολογία, love of talking; hence, love of learning and literature. – Gk. φιλόλογος, fond of talking; also a student of language and history. – Gk. φίλο-, for φίλος, fond of; and λόγος, discourse, from λέγειν, to speak. See **Philosophy** and **Legend**. Der. *philologi-c-al, philologi-c-al-ly*; *philolog-ist*.

PHILOMEL, a nightingale. (L. – Gk.) In Shak. Lucrece, 1079. – L. *philomēla*, a nightingale (Virgil). – Gk. Φιλομήλη, daughter of Pandion, who was changed into a nightingale.

PHILOSOPHY, love of wisdom, knowledge of the causes of phenomena. (F. – L. – Gk.) ME. *philosophie*, Rob. of Glouc. p. 130, l. 2748; Chaucer, C. T. 297 (A 295). – F. *philosophie*, 'philosophy;' Cot. – L. *philosophia*. – Gk. φιλοσοφία, love of wisdom. – Gk. φιλόσοφος, lit. loving a handicraft or art; also, a lover of true knowledge. – Gk. φίλο-, for φίλος, friendly, also, fond of; and σοφ-, base of σόφ-ος, skilful, and σοφία, skill (see **Sophist**). Der. *philosophi-c, philosophi-c-al, philosophi-c-al-ly*; *philosoph-ise*, a coined word, spelt *philosophize* by Cotgrave, who uses it to translate the F. verb *philosopher* < L. *philosophārī*, from Gk. φιλοσοφεῖν, to be a philosopher. Also *philosoph-er*, ME. *philosophre*, Chaucer, C. T. 299; here the *r* is a needless addition, as the F. word was *philosophe*, correctly answering to L. *philosophus* and Gk. φιλόσοφος.

PHILTRE, a love potion. (F. – L. – Gk.) In Minsheu, ed. 1627. – F. *philtre*, 'an amorous potion;' Cot. – L. *philtrum* (Juv. vi. 611). – Gk. φίλτρον, a love charm, love potion, drink to make one love. – Gk. φιλ-, for φίλος, dear, loving; and suffix *-τρον* (Idg. *-ter*), denoting the agent.

PHIZ, face, visage. (F. – L. – Gk.) 'What a furious *phiz* I have! Congreve, Old Bachelor, iv. 4 (Belinda). Short for *phisnomy* (ME.

fisnomie), spelt *phisnamy* in Palsgrave ; and *phisnomy* is short for **Physiognomy**, q. v.

PHLEBOTOMY, blood-letting. (F.–L.–Gk.) Spelt *phlebotomie* in Minsheu, ed. 1627 ; *flabotomye* in Dictes and Sayings, pr. by Caxton, fol. 17, l. 10.–F. *phlebotomie*, 'phlebotomy, blood-letting ;' Cot.–L. *phlebotomia*.–Gk. φλεβοτομία, blood-letting, lit. cutting of a vein.–Gk. φλεβο-, from φλέψ, a vein ; and τομός, cutting. β. The sb. φλέψ is from φλέειν, to gush, overflow, from the base φλε-, allied to L. *flēre*, to weep. Brugmann, ii. § 590. γ. For Gk. τέμνειν, see **Tome**. And see **Fleam**.

PHLEGM, slimy matter in the throat, sluggishness, indifference. (F.–L.–Gk.) Spelt *flegme* in Cotgrave. R. quotes from Arbuthnot, On Aliments, c. 6 : '*Phlegm* among the ancients signified a cold viscous humour, contrary to the etymology of the word, which is from φλέγειν, to burn ; but amongst them there were two sorts of *phlegm*, cold and hot.' The use of the word was due to the supposed influence of the four ' humours,' which were blood, choler, phlegm, and gall; phlegm causing a dull and sluggish temperament. Chaucer, C. T. 625, has *sawceflem*, a word formed from L. *salsum phlegma*, salt phlegm.–F. *phlegme*, 'flegme ;' Cot.–L. *phlegma*.–Gk. φλέγμα, base φλεγματ-, (1) a flame, (2) inflammation, (3) phlegm.–Gk. φλέγειν, to burn. β. Gk. φλέγμα (from φλέγειν) is allied to L. *flamma* (for *flagma*, from the base *flag-* in *flagrāre*, to burn). Thus *phlegm* is almost a doublet of *flame*. See **Flame, Flagrant**. Der. *phlegmat-ic*, misused by Mrs. Quickly in Merry Wives, i. 4. 79, from the Gk. adj. φλεγματικός, from the base φλεγματ- ; *phlegmat-ic-al*, *phlegmat-ic-al-ly*.

PHLOX, the name of a flower. (Gk.) It means ' flame,' from its colour. In Phillips, ed. 1706.–Gk. φλόξ, a flame.–Gk. φλογ-, 2nd grade of φλεγ-, as in φλέγειν, to burn ; see **Phlegm**.

PHOCINE, pertaining to the seal family of mammals. (L.–Gk.) Scientific.–L. *phōca*, a seal.–Gk. φώκη, a seal ; Homer, Od. iv. 404.

PHŒNIX, the same as **Phenix**, q. v.

PHOLAS, a mollusc that makes holes in stones. (Gk.) Modern. –Gk. φωλάς, lurking in a hole ; allied to φωλεός, a lurking-hole, a den. From a stem *bhŏl-*, for *bhou-l-*, where *bhŏu-* is allied to Teut. *bau-*, whence G. *bau-en*, to live, and AS. *bū-an*, to live ; see **Booth**. (So Prellwitz.)

PHONETIC, representing sounds. (Gk.) Modern ; not in Todd's Johnson ; the science of sounds was formerly called *phonics*, spelt *phonicks* in Blount's Gloss., ed. 1706.–Gk. φωνητικός, belonging to speaking.–Gk. φωνέ-ω, I produce a sound.–Gk. φωνή, a sound ; formed with suffix -νη (Idg. -nā) from φω-, allied by gradation to φη- in φημί, I speak.–√BHA, to speak ; whence also E. *ban*. See **Ban**. Der. *phonetic-al*, *phonetic-al-ly*; also, from sb. φωνή, *phon-ics* (as above); *phono-graphy*, from γράφειν, to write ; *phono-graph*, *phono-graph-er*, *phono-graph-ic*, *phono-graph-ic-al*; also *phono-logy*, from -λογία, a discourse, from λέγειν, to speak ; *phono-type*, *phono-typ-y*. Also, from Gk. φωνή, *anthem = anti-phon*.

PHOSPHORUS, a yellowish wax-like substance, of inflammable nature. (L.–Gk.) In Phillips, ed. 1706. Discovered in 1667 (Haydn). 'The very *phosphorus* of our hemisphere'; Congreve, Double-Dealer, ii. 1 (Lady Froth).–L. *phōsphorus*.–Gk. φωσφόρος, bearing, bringing, or giving light.–Gk. φῶς, light, equivalent to φάος, light, from the base φα-, to shine ; and -φορος, bringing, from φέρειν, to bring. From √BHA, to shine ; and √BHER, to bring, bear. With Gk. φῶς, cf. Irish *bān*, white ; and see **Bale-fire**. Der. *phosphor-ic*, *phosphor-ous*, *phosphur-et*, *phosphur-et-ted*, *phosphor-esc-ence*.

PHOTOGRAPHY, the art of producing pictures by the action of light. (Gk.) Modern ; Fox Talbot's photographs took the place of the old Daguerrotypes about 1839 (Haydn).–Gk. φωτο-, decl. stem of φῶς, light ; and γράφ-ειν, to write (hence, to produce impressions). The Gk. φῶς is equivalent to φά-ος, light (above). Der. *photograph*, short for *photographed picture* ; *photograph-ic*, *photograph-er*. So also *photo-meter*, an instrument for measuring the intensity of light ; see **Metre**.

PHRASE, part of a sentence, a short sentence. (F.–L.–Gk.) Frequent in Shak. Merry Wives, i. 1. 151, i. 3. 33, &c.–F. *phrase*, not in Cotgrave, but cited in Minsheu ; Littré cites the spelling *frase* in the 16th century.–L. *phrasis*.–Gk. φράσις, a speaking, speech, phrase.–Gk. φράζειν (= φράδ-yειν), to speak. β. The Gk. base φραδ- is probably allied to Irish *bard*, a poet ; see **Bard**. Cf. Gk. φραδ-ής, shrewd. Der. *phrase*, vb., Hen. VIII, i. 1. 34 ; *phrase-less*, Shak. Lover's Complaint, 226 ; *phrase-o-logy*, Spectator, no. 616, a strange compound, in which the *o* is inserted to fill out the word, and conform it to other words in -o-logy ; *phrase-o-logi-c-al*. Also *antiphrasis*, *para-phrase*, *peri-phrasis*.

PHRENOLOGY, the science of the functions of the mind. (Gk.) '*Phrenology*, a compound term of modern formation, in very common use, but not very clearly explained by those who employ it ;' Richardson.–Gk. φρενο-, decl. stem of φρήν, the mind ; and -λογία, from λόγος, a discourse, which from λέγειν, to speak. Der. *phreno-logi-c-al*, *phrenolog-ist*.

PHTHISIS, consumption of the lungs. (L.–Gk.) In Phillips, ed. 1706. [The disease was formerly called ' the *phthisick*,' as in Blount's Gloss., ed. 1674. This is an adjectival form, from L. *phthisica* (*passio*), fem. of *phthisicus* = Gk. φθισικός, consumptive. The difficulty of sounding *phth* was easily got over by the substitution of *t* for the compound sound ; hence Phillips has '*Phthisis*, the *phthisick* or *tissick* ;' and it is still called ' the *tizic*.' The spelling *tysyk* occurs as early as in Hampole, Pricke of Conscience, 701. So also Ital. *tisica*, Span. *tisica*, *tisis*, consumption. Milton speaks of ' a broken-winded *tizzic* ;' Animadversions on the Remonstrants' Defence (R.).] –L. *phthisis*.–Gk. φθίσις, consumption, a decline, decay.–Gk. φθίειν, to decay, wane, dwindle. The Gk. φθ answers to Skt. *ksh*, and φθίειν is allied to Skt. *kshi*, to destroy, whence pp. *kshita-*, decayed, and *kshitis = φθίσις* ; Curtius, ii. 370. Brugmann, i. § 652. Der. *phthisi-c*, *phthisi-c-al*.

PHYLACTERY, a charm, amulet, esp. among the Jews, a slip of parchment inscribed with four passages from scripture. (F.–L.–Gk.) Spelt *philaterie* in Tyndall's version, A.D. 1526 ; ME. *filaterie*, Wyclif, Matt. xxiii. 5.–OF. *filatere*, *filatiere*, forms given in Littré, s. v. *phylactère* ; Cotgrave spells it *phylacterie*. [The *c*, omitted in Wyclif and Tyndall, was afterwards restored.]–L. *phylactērium*, *fylactērium*.–Gk. φυλακτήριον, a preservative, amulet ; Matt. xxiii. 5. –Gk. φυλακτήρ, a guard, watchman.–Gk. φυλάσσειν (fut. φυλάξω, from φυλακ-), to guard. Cf. φύλαξ, a watchman, guard.

PHYLLOPHOROUS, leaf-bearing. (Gk.) Modern.–Gk. φυλλοφόρος, bearing leaves.–Gk. φύλλο-, for φύλλον, a leaf ; φορ-, 2nd stem of φερ-, as in φέρειν, to bear, cognate with E. *bear* (1). β. Gk. φύλλον = L. *folium*, a leaf. The prefix *phyllo-* occurs in many scientific words, as in *phyllo-xera*, the insect that attacks grapes, lit. ' leaf-drying ' or ' leaf-withering,' from Gk. ξηρ-ός, dry.

PHYSIC, the art of healing diseases ; hence, a remedy for disease. (F.–L.–Gk.) 'Throw *physic* to the dogs ;' Macb. v. 3. 47. 'A doctor of *phisike* ;' Chaucer, C. T. 413. Spelt *fisike*, Seven Sages, ed. Weber, 186.–OF. *phisike*, *phisique*. '*Phisique* est une science par le [la] quele on connoist toutes les manieres du cors de l'homme, et par le quele on garde le [la] santé du cors et remue les maladies ;' Alebrant, fol. 2 (13th cent. ; cited in Littré). In Cotgrave's time, the word had a more 'learned' meaning ; he gives '*Physique*, naturall philosophy,' and '*Physicien*, a naturall philosopher.'–L. *physica*, *physicē*, natural science.–Gk. φυσική, fem. of φυσικός, natural, physical.–Gk. φυσι-, for φύσις, nature, essence of a thing ; with suffix -κος. β. Gk. φύσις = *φύ-τις, formed with suffix -τις (Idg. -ti-) from the base φυ- appearing in φύειν, to produce, also, to grow, wax.– √BHEU, to grow, to be ; whence also Skt. *bhū*, to be, L. *fore*, and E. *be*. See **Be**. Der. *physic*, verb, As You Like It, i. 1. 92 ; *physic-s*, *physic-al*, *physic-al-ly*, *physic-ist*. Also *physic-i-an*, ME. *fisician*, *fisicien*, spelt *ficicion* in King Alisaunder, ed. Weber, 3504, from OF. *physicien*, coined as if from L. *physiciānus*. Also *physiognomy*, q. v. ; *physiology*, q. v. ; cf. *phytoid*.

PHYSIOGNOMY, visage, expression of features. (F.–L.–Gk.) Lit. ' the art of knowing a man's disposition from his features ;' but frequently used as merely equivalent to features or face. Sometimes shortened to *phiz*, as in Congreve, The Old Bachelor, iv. 4 (Belinda). ME. *fisnomie*, *visnomie*; also *fisnamy*, *fyssnamy*. 'The fairest of *fyssnamy* that fourmede was euer ;' Allit. Morte Arthure, ed. Brock, 3331 ; cf. l. 1114.–OF. *phisonomie*, which occurs in the 13th century (Littré) ; Cotgrave has '*Physiognomie*, physiognomie, a guess at the nature, or the inward disposition, by the feature, or outward lineaments ;' and he gives *physonomie* as an old form of the word. The mod. F. is *physionomie*. [Observe that, though the *g* is now inserted in the word, it is not sounded ; we follow the F. pronunciation in this respect.] Cf. Ital. and Span. *fisonomia*, features, countenance. Formed as if from a L. *physiognōmia*, but really corrupted from a longer form *physiognōmonia*, which is merely the L. form of the Gk. word.–Gk. φυσιογνωμονία, the art of reading the features ; for which the shorter form φυσιογνωμία is occasionally found.–Gk. φυσιογνώμων, skilled in reading features, lit. judging of nature.–Gk. φυσιο-, extended from φυσι-, from φύσις, nature ; and γνώμων, an interpreter ; see **Physic** and **Gnomon**. Der. *phiz*, *physiognom-ist*.

PHYSIOLOGY, the science of nature. (F.–L.–Gk.) In Blount's Gloss., ed. 1674.–F. *physiologie*, in Cotgrave.–L. *physiologia*.–Gk. φυσιολογία, an inquiry into the nature of things.–Gk. φυσιο-, extended from φυσι-, from φύσις, nature ; and -λογία, a discourse, from λόγος, speech, which from λέγειν, to speak. See **Physics** and **Legend**. Der. *physiologi-c-al*, *physiologi-c-al-ly*.

PHYTOID, plant-like ; resembling plants. (Gk.) A term

in zoology. ‒Gk. φυτό-ν, a plant; and εἶδ-ος, form, appearance. Gk. φυ-τόν (lit. 'product') contains the same base as φύ-σις, nature; see **Physic, Be.**

PI–PY

PIACULAR, expiatory, or requiring expiation. (L.) Little used now. Blount, ed. 1694, has both *piacular* and *piaculous.* ‒L. *piăculāris,* expiatory. ‒L. *piăculum,* an expiation; formed, with suffixes *-cu-lu-,* from *piāre,* to expiate, propitiate, make holy. ‒L. *pius,* sacred, pious; see **Pious, Expiate.**

PIANOFORTE, PIANO, a musical instrument. (Ital.‒L.) Generally called *piano,* by abbreviation. Added by Todd to Johnson's Dict. Invented A.D. 1717; first made in London, 1766 (Haydn). So called from producing both *soft* and *loud* effects.‒Ital. *piano,* soft; and *forte,* strong, loud. ‒L. *plānus,* even, level (hence, smooth, soft); and *fortis,* strong. See **Plain** and **Force** (1). Der. *pian-ist,* a coined word.

PIASTRE, an Italian coin. (F.‒Ital.‒L.‒Gk.) 'Piaster, a coyn in Italy, about the value of our crown;' Blount's Gloss., ed. 1674.‒F. *piastre,* in Cot.‒Ital. *piastra,* 'any kind of plate or leafe of mettal;' *piastra d'argento,* 'a coine or plate of silver used in Spaine' (Florio). [But the form of the word is Italian.] Closely allied to Ital. *piastro,* 'a plaister;' Florio. Cf. also MItal. *plasma,* 'a kind of coine or plate of silver in Spaine,' id. In fact, the word is a mere variant of **Plaster,** q.v. The lamina of metal was likened to a plaster or 'flattened piece.'

PIAZZA, a square surrounded by buildings; a walk under a roof supported by pillars. (Ital.‒L.) Properly pronounced *piatza,* as in Italian, with the Ital. vowel-sounds. First in Foxe (1583); described in Blount's Gloss., ed. 1674, at which time it was applied to the *piazza* in Covent Garden. 'The *piazza* or market-stead;' Foxe, Martyrs, p. 1621, an. 1555 (R.).‒Ital. *piazza,* 'a market-place, the chiefest streete or broad way or place in a town;' Florio.‒Folk-L. *plattea,* for L. *platea;* see **Place.** Doublet, *place.*

PIBROCH, the music of the bag-pipe, a martial tune. (Gaelic ‒E.‒L.) '*Pibrochs* or airs;' Smollett, Humphrey Clinker, letter dated Sept. 3. 'The *pibroch* resounds, to the piper's loud number, Your deeds on the echoes of dark Loch na Garr;' Byron, Lachin y Gair (1807). '*Pibroch* is not a bag-pipe, any more than duet means a fiddle;' Edinb. Review, on the same.‒Gael. *piobaireachd,* 'the art of playing on the bag-pipe, piping; a pipe-tune, a piece of music peculiar to the bag-pipe,' &c.‒Gael. *piobair,* a piper.‒Gael. *piob,* a pipe, a bag-pipe; from E. *pipe;* see **Pipe.**

PICA, a kind of printer's type. (L.) See **Pie** (1) and (2).

PICADOR, in bull-fighting; a horseman armed with a light lance. (Span.‒Teut.) Span. *picador;* lit. 'pricker;' from *picar,* to prick; see **Piccadill.**

PICANINNY, PICCANINNY, a baby, a child, esp. among the negroes. (Span.) Spelt *peekeneenee* in Stedman's Surinam, ii. 258; dimin. of *peekeen,* small, little.‒Span. *pequeño,* small; allied to Ital. *piccolo,* small. Of uncertain origin.

PICCADILL, PICKADILL, a piece set round the edge of a garment, whether at the top or bottom; most commonly the collar; Nares. (F.‒Span.‒Teut.) See *Piccadell* in Nares. '*Pickadil,* the round hem, or the several divisions set together about the skirt of a garment, or other thing, also a kind of stiff collar, made in fashion of a band;' Blount's Gloss., ed. 1674. Also in Minsheu, ed. 1627.‒ F. *piccadille, picadille;* Cot. explains the pl. *piccadilles* by 'piccadilles, the several divisions or peeces fastened together about the brimme of the collar of a doublet.' The form of the word shows it to be of Spanish origin; it is formed, with dimin. suffix *-illo,* from Span. *picado,* pp. of *picar,* to prick, to pierce with a small puncture (Neuman). Cf. *picada,* a puncture, incision made by puncture; *picadura,* a puncture, an ornamental gusset in clothes (Neuman).‒ Span. *pica,* a pike, a long lance, a word of Teut. origin; see **Pike.** Der. *Piccadilly,* the street so named, according to Blount and Nares; first applied to 'a famous ordinary near St. James's.'

PICE, a small copper coin in the E. Indies. (Marāthī.) From Hind. and Marāthī *paisā,* a copper coin, of varying value; the Company's *paisā* is fixed at the weight of 100 grains, and is rated at 4 to the *ana,* or 64 to the rupee; H. H. Wilson, Gloss. of Indian Terms, p. 389. And see Yule.

PICK, to prick with a sharp-pointed instrument; hence, to peck, to pierce, to open a lock with a pointed instrument, to pluck, &c. (E.) The sense 'to choose' or 'gather flowers' is due to a niceness of choice, as if one were picking them out as a bird with its beak. All the senses ultimately go back to the idea of using a sharply pointed instrument. ME. *pikken, picken,* Chaucer, C. T. 14973; in the Six-

text edition (B 4157) the Camb. MS. has *pikke,* where the rest have *pekke.* 'Get wolde he teteren and *pileken* mid his bile'=yet would tear in pieces and pluck with his bill; where another MS. has *pikken* for *pileken;* Ancren Riwle, p. 84. β. Allied to ME. *piken* (with one *k*), as in 'to *pyken* and to weden it,' P. Plowman, B. xvi. 17; AS. *pīcan,* to pick. 'And lēt him *pȳcan* ūt his ēagan'=and caused his eyes to be picked out; Two Saxon Chronicles, ed. Earle, an. 796, p. 267. From AS. *pīc,* a point, pike; see **Pike.** γ. Cf. also Icel. *pikka,* to pick, to prick; Du. *pikken,* to pick; G. *picken,* to pick, peck. [Also Irish *piocaim,* I pick, pluck, nibble; Gael. *pioc,* to pick, nip, nibble; W. *pigo,* to pick, peck, prick, choose; Corn. *piga,* to prick, sting; from E.] Der. *pick-er,* Hamlet, iii. 2. 348; *pick-lock, pick-pocket, pick-purse,* Chaucer, C. T. 1900; also *pickax* q.v., *picket,* q.v., *piquet.* Also *pitch-fork* = ME. *pykkforke,* Prompt. Parv. Perhaps *pick-le, pic-nic.* Doublets, *peck* (1), *pitch,* verb.

PICKAX, a tool used in digging. (F.‒Teut.) A *pickax* is not an ax at all, but very different; the name is an ingenious popular adaptation of the ME. *pikois* or *pikeys;* see my note to P. Plowman, C. iv. 465. '*Pykeys,* mattokke;' Prompt. Parv. 'Mattok is a *pykeys,* Or a pyke, as sum men seys;' Rob. of Brunne, Handlyng Synne, 940. The pl. appears as *pikoys* in the Paston Letters, ed. Gardner, i. 106; and as *pikeyses,* Riley, Memorials of London, p. 284. ‒AF. *pikeis;* OF. *picois,* MF. *picquois,* 'a pickax;' Cot.‒OF. *piquer,* 'to prick, pierce, or thrust into;' Cot.‒F. *pic,* 'a mason's pickax,' Cot.; still called 'a pick' by English workmen.‒Late L. *pīca,* a pickax; of Teut. origin; see **Pike.**

PICKET, a peg for fastening horses; a small outpost. (F.‒ Teut.) The sense of 'outpost' is secondary, and named from the *picketing* of the horses, i.e. fastening them to pegs. Not in early use; in Phillips, ed. 1706.‒F. *piquet,* spelt *picquet* in Cotgrave, who explains it as 'a little pickax, also the peg or stick thrust down into the earth by a surveyor that measures with cord or a chain.' Dimin. of *pic,* a pickax (above). Der. *picket,* verb. Doublet, *piquet.*

PICKLE, a liquid in which some eatables are preserved. (E.?) ME. *pikil, pykyl.* '*Pykyl,* sawce, *Picula;*' Prompt. Parv. Cf. Du. *pekel,* pickle, brine; Low G. *pekel,* the same (Bremen Wörterb.). β. Origin uncertain; the old story that *pickle* took its name from its inventor, whose name is given as *William Beukeler* in Pennant's British Zoology, vol. iii, and as *William Böckel* in the Bremen Wörterbuch, is an evident fable; *b* would not thus become *p.* By way of mending matters, the name is turned into *Pökel* in Mahn's Webster, to agree with G. *pökel,* pickle; but then *Pökel* will not answer to the Du. form *pekel.* γ. Wedgwood's suggestion is preferable to this, viz. that the word is E., and is the frequentative of the verb to *pick,* in the sense 'to cleanse,' with reference to 'the gutting or cleansing of the fish with which the operation is begun.' The prov. E. *pickle,* to pick, to peck at, is still in use; and the Prompt. Parv. has: '*pykelynge,* purgulacio,' derived from '*pykyn,* or clensyn, or cullyn owte the onclene, purgo, purgulo, segrego.' Also '*pykynge,* or clensynge, purgacio.' See **Pick.** Der. *pickle,* sb., brine; whence the phr. *a rod in pickle,* i.e. a rod soaked in brine to make the punishment more severe; also *to be in a pickle,* i.e. in a mess.

PICNIC, an entertainment in the open air, at which each person contributes some article to the common table. (F.‒Teut.) Added by Todd to Johnson's Dict. The word found its way into French as early as 1692 (Ménage), and was then spelt as *piquenique.* It also found its way into Swedish before 1788, as we find in Widegren's Swed. Dict. of that date the entry '*picknick,* an assembly of young persons of both sexes at a tavern, where every one pays his club,' i.e. his share. β. A coined word; from Teut. elements; there can be little doubt that the first element is MDu. *picken,* to pick up (as a bird), to reap; cf. E. *pick.* γ. The latter element is difficult to explain; in reduplicated words, with riming elements, one of the elements is sometimes unmeaning, so that we are not bound to find a sense for it. At the same time, we may, perhaps, assign to *nique* the sense of 'trifle;' cf. MF. *niquet,* 'a knick, snap with the teeth or fingers [Du. *knikken,* to snap], a trifle, matter of small value;' Cot. Cf. E. *knick-knacks,* trifles, spelt *nick-nacks* in Hotten's Slang Dictionary. Indeed Foote calls a picnic a *nicknack;* Nabob, Act 1; see Davies, Supp. Glossary.

PICOTEE, a variety of the carnation. (F.‒Teut.). Lit. 'spotted.' ‒F. *picoté,* spotted; pp. of *picoter,* to spot.‒F. *piquer,* to prick.‒ F. *pic,* a pickax. Of Teut. origin; see **Pike.**

PICRIC; as in *picric* acid, used in dyeing. (Gk.) Formed by adding *-ic* to Gk. πικρ-ός, bitter. Allied to Gk. πείκειν, to cut, shear, and to ποικίλος, variegated, AS. *fāh,* variegated (Prellwitz).

PICTURE, a painting, drawing. (L.) 'The *picture* of that lady's head;' Spenser, F. Q. ii. 9. 2. Englished (in imitation of F. *peinture,* a picture) from L. *pictūra,* the art of painting, also a picture.‒L. *pict-us,* pp. of *pingere,* to paint; see **Paint.** Der.

pictur-esque, in Johnson's Dict., ed. 1755, s.v. *Graphically*, Englished from Ital. *pittoresco*, like what is in a picture, where the suffix in the L. *-iscus*, Gk. *-ισκος*, cognate with AS. *-isc*, E. *ish*; hence *picturesquely*, *-ness*. Also *pictor-i-al*, Sir T. Browne, Vulg. Errors, b. iii. c. 24. § 2, formed with suffix *-al* from L. *pictōri-us*, pictorial, from *pictōri-*, deel. stem of *pictor*, a painter, allied to *pictus*, pp. of *pingere*.

PICUL, the same as **Pikul**, q. v.

PIDDLE, to trifle with. (Scand.) 'Neuer ceasynge *piddelynge* about your bowe and shaftes;' Ascham, Toxophilus, ed. Arber, p. 117. Perhaps a weakened form of *pittle*, to keep picking at, to trifle with (see E. D. D.) — Swed. dial. *pittla*, to keep picking at, frequent. of Swed. *peta*, to pick, poke (Rietz). Hence *piddling*, paltry, used as an adj.; see E. D. D.

PIE (1), a magpie; mixed or unsorted printer's type. (F.–L.) The unsorted type is called *pie* or *pi*, an abbreviation of *pica*; from the common use of pica-type. It is ultimately the same word as *pie* = magpie, as will appear; see **Pie** (2). ME. *pie*, *pye*, a magpie, Chaucer, C. T. 10964 (F 650). — F. *pie*, 'a pie, pyannat, meggatapy;' Cot. (See **Magpie**.) — L. *pīca*, a magpie. β. Doubtless allied to L. *pīcus*, a woodpecker; and prob. to Skt. *pika-*, the Indian cuckoo. Note also Irish *pighead*, Gael. *pigheid*, a magpie, Gael. *pighid*, a robin, W. *pi*, *pia*, *piog*, *piogen*, a magpie; from E. or L. **Der.** *pi-ed*, variegated like a magpie, L. L. L. v. 2. 904; *pi-ed-ness*, variegation, Wint. Tale, iv. 4. 87; and see *pie-bald*.

PIE (2), a book which ordered the manner of performing the divine service. (F.–L.) 'Moreover, the number and hardness of the rules called the *pie*;' Introd. to Book of Common Prayer, 1661. Here, as in the case of **Pie** (1), the word *pie* is a F. form of the L. *pīca*, which was the old name for the Ordinale: 'quod usitato vocabulo dicitur *Pica*, sive directorium sacerdotum,' Sarum Breviary, fol. 1, cited in Procter, On the Book of Common Prayer, p. 8. The name *pica*, lit. magpie, was perhaps given to these rules from their 'pied' appearance, being printed in the old black-letter type on white paper, so that they resembled the colours of the magpie. β. The word *pica* is still retained as a printer's term, to denote certain sizes of type; and a hopeless mixture of types is *pie*. ¶ In the oath 'by cock and pie,' Merry Wives, i. 1. 316, *cock* is for the name of God, and *pie* is the Ordinal or service-book.

PIE (3), a pasty. (F.–L.?) ME. *pie*, Chaucer, C. T. 386 (A 384). Probably the same as **Pie** (2); the name may be due to a medieval pleasantry, as denoting the miscellaneous nature of the contents. In the Babees Book, ed. Furnivall, pt. ii. p. 37, l. 51, we find the L. pl. *pīcē* (= *pīcae*) apparently in the sense of pies or pasties; the next word is *pastilli*, i.e. pasties; cf. 'pyes et pastellis' in quot. dated 1303 in N. E. D. ¶ Gael. *pighe*, a pie, is from E.

PIEBALD, of various colours, in patches. (Hybrid: F.–L.; and C.) 'A *piebald* steed;' Dryden, tr. of Virgil, Æn. ix. l. 54. Richardson quotes it in the form 'A *pie-ball'd* steed;' which is a correct old spelling. Compounded of *pie* and *bald*. β. Here *pie* signifies 'like the magpie,' as in the word *pied*. *Bald*, formerly *ball'd* or *balled*, signifies 'streaked,' from W. *bal*, having a white streak on the forehead, said of a horse. See further under **Pie** (1) and **Bald**. ¶ A like compound is *skew-bald*, i.e. streaked in a skew or irregular way.

PIECE, a portion, bit, single article. (F.–C.) ME. *pece*, Rob. of Glouc. p. 555, l. 11590; the spelling *piece* is rarer, but occurs in Gower, C. A. i. 295; bk. iii. 465. — OF. *piece*, mod. F. *pièce*, a piece. [Cf. Span. *pieza*, a piece; Prov. *pessa*, *pesa* (Bartsch); Port. *peça*; Ital. *pezza*.] — Late L. **pettia*, *petia*; allied to Late L. *petium*, a piece of land, used as early as A.D. 730. From a Gaulish type **petti-*, answering to OCeltic type **qetti-*, a piece, a portion; evidenced by W. *peth*, a piece, a thing, Corn. *peth*, Bret. *pez*, a piece; cf. **qotti-*, as in Irish and Gael. *cuid*, OIrish *cuit*, a piece, share. So Thurneysen, Stokes, Körting. **Der.** *piece*, vb., Hen. V, prol. 23; *piece-less*, *piec-er*, *piece-work*; also *piece-meal*, q. v.

PIECE-MEAL, by portions at a time. (Hybrid; F. *and* E.) ME. *pece-mele*; Rob. of Glouc. has *by pece-mele*, p. 216, l. 4422. The sense is reduplicated, meaning 'by piece-pieces.' For the first element, see **Piece**. β. The second element is the ME. termination *-mele*, found also in *flokmele*, in a flock or troop, lit. 'in flock-pieces,' Chaucer, C. T. 7962 (E 86); *lim-mele*, limb from limb, lit. 'in limb-pieces,' Layamon, 25618. A fuller form of the suffix is *-melum*, as in *wukemelum*, week by week, Ormulum, 536; *hipyllmelum*, by heaps, Wyclif, Wisdom, xviii. 23. See Koch, Eng. Gram. ii. 292. ME. *-melum* = AS. *mǣlum*, dat. pl. of *mǣl*, a portion; see **Meal** (2).

PIEPOWDER COURT, a summary court of justice formerly held at fairs. (F.–L.) Explained in Blount's Nomolexicon, ed. 1691; he says, 'so called because they are most usual in summer, and suiters to this court are commonly country-clowns with dusty feet.' At any rate, the L. name was *curia pedis pulverizāti*, the court of the dusty foot; see Ducange, s.v. *curia*. And see AF. *pe-poudrous* in Liber Albus, p. 67; i.e. F. *pied poudreux*. The E. *piepowder* is an adaptation of OF. *pied poudré*, i.e. dusty foot. — F. *pied*, a foot, from L. acc. *pedem*; and OF. *poudré*, dusty, pp. of *pouldrer*, *poudrer*, to cover with dust, from *pouldre*, *poudre*, dust. See **Foot** and **Powder**. ¶ Blount refers us to the statute 17 Edw. IV. cap. 2; &c. Cf. 'Les pletz .. qe lem appele *pepoudrous*;' Black Book of the Admiralty, ii. 22.

PIER, a mass of stone-work. (F.–L.–Gk.) In Shak. Merch. Ven. i. 1. 19. ME. *pere*. 'Pere, or pyle of a brygge [bridge], or other fundament' [foundation]; Prompt. Parv. Early E. *pere*, Birch, Cart. Saxon. iii. 659. — AF. *pere*, a stone; Langtoft, i. 124. — L. *petra*, stone; see **Petrify**. (And see the Supplement.) **Der.** *pier-glass*, orig. a glass hung on the stone-work between two windows.

PIERCE, to thrust through, make a hole in, enter. (F.–L.?) ME. *percen*, Rob. of Glouc. p. 17, l. 391. — F. *percer*, 'to pierce, gore;' Cot. OF. *percier* (Roland-song). β. Origin uncertain; the suggestion in Diez, that *percer* is contracted from OF. *pertuisier*, with the same sense, is ingenious, but somewhat violent; Hatzfeld equates *percer* to a Late L. type **pertūsiāre*, which may have become **pert'-siāre*. *Pertuisier*, occurring in the 12th century, is from *pertuis*, a hole, and is parallel to Ital. *pertugiare*, to pierce, from *pertugio*, a hole; and to Prov. *pertusar*, to pierce. γ. The Ital. *pertugiare* answers to a Late L. type **pertūsiāre*, from L. *pertūsus*, pp. of *pertundere*, to thrust through, bore through, pierce, a compound of *per*, through, and *tundere*, to beat; see **Contuse**. δ. The suggestion above is supported by these considerations: (1) that the L. *per*, through, seems certainly to be involved in F. *percer*; and (2) that L. *pertundere* gives the right sense. Ennius has *latu' pertudit hasta*, which is exactly 'the spear *pierced* his side.' ¶ Bartsch suggests a type **per-itiāre*, to go through; see Körting, §§ 7057, 7082. **Der.** *pierc-er*; also *pierce-able*, spelt *perceable* in Spenser, F. Q. i. 1. 7.

PIETY, the quality of being pious. (F.–L.) In Shak. Timon, iv. 1. 15; Lyly, Euphues, p. 103. — F. *piété*, piety; omitted by Cotgrave, but given in Sherwood's index. — L. *pietātem*, acc. of *pietās*, piety. Formed, with suffix *-tās*, from *pie-*, for *pius*, pious; see **Pious**. Doublet, *pity*.

PIG, a porker, the young of swine. (E.) ME. *pigge*, Ancren Riwle, p. 204, l. 9. Cf. prov. E. *peg*, a pig (Berks.). Perhaps the AS. form was **picga* (for **peg-joz*?). Cf. also the AS. form *pecg*; as in 'of swinforda oð *pecges* ford;' Birch, Cart. Saxon. iii. 223. But the connexion is doubtful. Allied to MDu. *pigge*, 'a pigge,' Hexham; and perhaps to Du. *bigge*, *big*, a pig; Low G. *bigge*, a pig, also, a little child; 'de biggen *lopet enᵐ under de vöte*,' the children run under one's feet; Bremen Wörterbuch. **Der.** *pig*, verb; *pigg-ish*, *pigg-er-y*; *pig-head-ed*, used by Ben Jonson, News from the New World (near beginning), *pig-tail*; *pig-nut*, Temp. ii. 2. 172. Also *pig-iron*: 'A *sow* of iron is an ingot; *Pano di metallo*, a mass, a *sow* or ingot of metal (Florio). When the furnace in which iron is melted is tapped, the iron is allowed to run into one main channel, called the *sow*, out of which a number of smaller streams are made to run at right angles. These are compared to a set of pigs sucking their dam, and the iron is called *sow* and *pig* iron respectively. Probably the likeness was suggested by the word *sow* having previously signified an ingot.'—Wedgwood. But probably the original use of *sow* and *pig* referred merely to size. Add to this, that *sow* may very well have been applied jocularly to an ingot, owing to its bulk and weight. Ray mentions these *sows* and *pigs* in his 'Account of Iron-work;' see Ray's Glossary, ed. Skeat (E. D. S.), Gloss. B. 15, p. 13.

PIGEON, the name of a bird. (F.–L.) Spelt *pyione* (= *pijon*) in the Prompt. Parv. p. 396; *pygeon* in Caxton, tr. of Reynard the Fox (1481), ed. Arber, p. 58. — F. *pigeon*, 'a pigeon, or dove;' Cot. [Cf. Span. *pichon*, a young pigeon; Ital. *piccione*, *pippione*, a pigeon.] — L. *pīpiōnem*, acc. of *pīpio*, a young bird, lit. 'a chirper' or 'piper.' — L. *pīpire*, to chirp, cheep, pipe; see **Pipe**, **Peep**. Of imitative origin, from the cry *pi*, *pi* of the young bird. **Der.** *pigeon-hole*, *pigeon-hearted*; *pigeon-livered*, Hamlet, ii. 2. 605.

PIGGIN, a small wooden vessel. (E.) 'Piggin, a small wooden cylindrical vessel, made with staves and bound with hoops like a pail;' Brockett. Cotgrave translates F. *trayer* by 'a milking pale, or *piggin*.' 'Iiij *piggins*,' Lanc. and Chesh. Wills, p. 113 (1541). [Cf. Gael. *pigean*, a little earthen jar, pitcher, or pot; diminutive of *pigeadh* (also *pige*), an earthen jar, pitcher, or pot; Irish *pigin*, a small pail, *pighead*, an earthen pitcher; W. *picyn*, a piggin; all from E.] Extended from *pig*, in the sense of 'earthen vessel,' as in G. Douglas, tr. of Virgil, bk. vii. ch. 14, l. 25. The suffix is the E. *-en*, as in *wood-en*; or, possibly, Gael. *-an*, dimin.

PIGHT, old form of *pitched*; see **Pitch** (2).

PIGMENT, a paint, colouring matter. (L.) In Blount's Gloss., ed. 1674.—L. *pigmentum*, a pigment; formed with suffix *-mentum* from *pig-*, base of *pingere*, to paint; see **Paint.** Der. *or-piment, or-pine.* Doublet, *pimento.*

PIGMY, the same as **Pygmy,** q. v. (F.—L.—Gk.)

PIKE, a sharp-pointed weapon, a fish. (E.) 1. ME. *pike, pyke,* in the sense of a pointed staff, P. Plowman, B. v. 482; spelt *pic,* in the sense of spike, Layamon, 30752. AS. *pic:* 'Acisculum, *piic*;' Voc. 3. 13. And cf. Northumb. *horn-pic,* as a gloss to L. *pinnam.* Luke, iv. 9. (Hence Irish *pice,* a pike, fork; *picidh,* a pike or long spear, a pickax; Gael. *pìc,* a pike, weapon, pickax; W. *pig,* a point, pike, bill, beak, *picell,* a javelin; Bret. *pik,* a pick, pickax.) β. The orig. sense is 'sharp point' or 'spike.' Allied to **Spike, Spoke;** and see **Pick.** 2. ME. *pike,* a fish; 'Bet is, quod he, a *pyk* than a *pikerel,*' Chaucer, C. T. 9293 (E 1419). So called from its sharply-pointed jaws; see **Hake.** The young pike is called a *pikerel,* or *pickerel* (Nares), formed with dimin. suffixes *-er* and *-el,* like *cock-er-el* from *cock.* Der. *pik-ed,* old form of *peaked,* Rob. of Brunne, tr. of Langtoft, p. 328, l. 8; *pike-head,* Spenser, F. Q. i. 7. 37; *pike-man; pike-staff,* i.e. *piked-staff* or staff with a spike. ME. *pyk-staf,* P. Plowman, B. vi. 105. Also *pick,* vb.; *peck, pitch,* vb.; *pickax; piccadill, picket, piquet, picnic.* **Doublets,** *peak, pick,* sb., *pique,* sb.

PIKUL, the name of a weight. (Malay.) See *Pecul* in Yule.— Malay *pikul,* the Malay name for the Chinese weight of 100 catties or *kātis.* About 133⅓ pounds avoirdupois. See **Caddy.**

PILASTER, a square pillar or column, usually set in a wall. (F.—Ital.—L.) Spelt *pilaster, pillaster* in Phillips, ed. 1706. *Pilaster* in Chapman, tr. of Homer, Od. vii. 121. Also in Cotgrave.—F. *pilastre,* 'a pilaster or small piller;' Cot.—Ital. *pilastro,* 'any kind of piller or pilaster;' Florio. Formed with suffix *-stro* from Ital. *pila,* 'a flat-sided pillar;' Florio.—L. *pila,* a pillar; see **Pile** (2). Der. *pilaster-ed.*

PILAU, an Oriental dish; see **Pillau.**

PILCH, a furred garment. (L.) For the various senses, see N. E. D. It orig. meant a warm furred outer garment. ME. *pilche,* Ancren Riwle, p. 362, last line. AS. *pylce,* in Screadunga, ed. Bouterwek, p. 20, l. 28; *ƚylece,* Voc. 328. 11.—L. *pellicea,* fem. of *pelliceus,* made of skins; see further under **Pelisse.** Cf. **Pelt.** Doublet, *pelisse.*

PILCHARD, the name of a fish. (E.?) 'A *Pilcher* or *Pilchard*;' Minsheu, ed. 1627; *pilchard,* Baret, ed. 1580. 'Pylcher, a fysshe, sardine;' Palsgrave. Spelt *pilcher* in Shak. Tw. Nt. iii. 1. 39 (first folio). Of uncertain origin; cf. Irish *pilseir,* a pilchard (from E.). β. The prov. E. *pilch* means to filch, to pick; see E. D. D. and N. E. D.; whence *pilch-er* might be derived.

PILCROW, a curious corruption of **Paragraph,** q. v. And see Notes on E. Etym., p. 215.

PILE (1), a tumour, lit. a ball; only in the pl. *piles.* See **Piles.**

PILE (2), a pillar; a heap. (F.—L.) ME. *pile, pyle;* P. Plowman, B. xix. 360; C. xxii. 366.—F. *pile,* 'a pile, heap, or stack;' Cot.—L. *pila,* a pillar; a pier or mole of stone. Der. *pile-driver;* also *pillar,* q. v., *pil-aster,* q. v. ¶ *Pile* in the heraldic sense is an imitation of a sharp stake; see **Pile** (3). In the old phrase *cross* and *pile,* equivalent to the modern *head and tail,* the allusion is to the stamping of money. One side bore a cross; the other side was the under side in the stamping, and took its name from the *pile* or short pillar (L. *pila*) on which the coin rested. Thus Cot. translates F. *pile* (which here = *pila,* not *pila*) by 'the *pile,* or under-iron of the stamp, wherein money is stamped; and the *pile-side* of a piece of monie, the opposite whereof is a crosse; whence, *Ie n'ay croix ne pile'* = I have neither cross nor pile.

PILE (3), a stake. (L.) ME. *pile,* P. Plowman, B. xvi. 86. AS. *pil,* a pointed stick, something pointed.—L. *pilum,* a javelin; orig. a pestle. For **pins-lom.*—L. *pinsere,* to pound.+Skt. *pish, piṃsh,* to pound. ¶ The heraldic *pile* is a sharp stake; from F. *pile,* m. 'a javelin,' Cot.; from L. *pilum.* Brugmann, ii. § 76.

PILE (4), a hair, fibre of wool. (L.) In Shak. All's Well, iv. 5. 103; cf. *three-piled,* L. L. L. v. 2. 407. Directly from L. *pilus,* a hair (the F. form being *poil*). Cf. Gk. πῖλος, felt. Brugmann, ii. § 76. Der. *pil-ose, three-piled.* Also *de-pil-at-or-y, pl-ush, per-uke, per-i-wig, wig.*

PILES, hemorrhoids. (L.) In Minsheu, ed. 1627. Spelt *pyles* in Sir T. Elyot, Castel of Helth, b. iii. c. 9. Small tumours; directly from L. *pila,* a ball. Cf. MF. *pile,* 'a ball to play with;' Cot.

PILFER, to steal in a small way, filch. (F.) In Shak. Hen. V, i. 2. 142.—OF. *pelfrer,* to pilfer.—OF. *pelfre,* booty, pelf. See **Pelf.** Der. *pilfer-ings,* K. Lear, ii. 2. 151.

PILGRIM, a wanderer, stranger. (Ital.—L.) ME. *pilgrim,* Chaucer, C. T. 26; earlier forms *pilegrim, pelegrim,* Layamon, 30730, 30744. [The final *m* is put for *n,* by the frequent interchange between liquids.]—Ital. *pellegrino,* 'a wandrer, pilgrim, stranger;'

Florio. (Cf. Prov. *pellegrins,* a pilgrim (Bartsch), Port. and Span. *peregrino.*)—L. *peregrinus,* a stranger, foreigner; used in Heb. xi. 13, where the A. V. has 'pilgrims.' Orig. an adj. signifying strange, foreign, formed from adv. *peregrī,* away from home; allied to the sb. *pereger,* a traveller. This sb. was also orig. an adj. signifying 'on a journey,' abroad or away from home, lit. 'passing through a (foreign) country.'—L. *per,* through; and *ager,* a land, country, cognate with E. *acre.* The vowel-change from *a* in *ager* to *e* in *pereger* is regular. See **Per-** and **Acre.** Der. *pilgrim-age,* Chaucer, C. T. 12; formed with suffix *-age* in imitation of OF. *pelerinage,* 'a peregrination or pilgrimage;' Cot. Doublet, *peregrine,* chiefly used of the *peregrine* or 'foreign' falcon, Chaucer, C. T. 10742 (F 428). And see **Peregrination.** ¶ The form is Italian, notwithstanding its early use; due to the fact that English pilgrims frequently went (like King Alfred) to Rome. The OF. *pelerin* had no *g;* but cf. Roumansch *pelegrin.*

PILL (1), a little ball of medicine. (L.) 'Pocyons, electuaryes, or *pylles*;' Sir T. Elyot, Castel of Helth, b. iii. c. 5. Contracted, like MDu. *pille,* a pill, Late L. *pilla,* from L. *pilula* (as recipes were in Latin). The Late L. *pilla* occurs in Gemma Gemmarum, Coloniæ, 1507. The same book has the spelling *pillula.* Cf. OF. *pile,* a pill; F. *pilule,* 'a physical pill;' Cot.—L. *pilula,* a little ball, globule, pill. Dimin. of *pila,* a ball; see **Piles.**

PILL (2), to rob, plunder. (F.—L.) Also spelt *peel;* see **Peel** (2). [But the words *peel,* to strip, and *peel,* to plunder, are from different sources, though much confused; we even find *pill* used in the same sense 'to strip.' The sense of 'stripping' goes back to L. *pellis,* skin, as shown under **Peel** (1).] ME. *pillen,* most MSS. *pilen,* Chaucer, C. T. 6944 (D 1362); also *pilen,* Rob. of Brunne, tr. of Langtoft, p. 42, l. 9.—F. *piller,* 'to pill, ravage, ransack, rifle, rob;' Cot.—L. type **piliāre,* for L. *pilāre,* to plunder, pillage; a rare verb, used by Ammianus Marcellinus; a later use of *pilāre,* to deprive of hair; from *pilus,* a hair. Der. *pill-age,* plunder; we find 'such as delyte them in *pyllage* and robbery' in Fabyan, Chron. vol. i. c. 114, ed. Ellis, p. 87; from F. *pillage* (as if from a L. **pilāticum*). Hence *pill-ag-er,* for which *piller* was formerly used, spelt *pilour* in Chaucer, C. T. 1009 (A 1007).

PILLAGE, plunder; see under **Pill** (2).

PILLAR, a column, support. (F.—L.) In early use. ME. *piler,* O. Eng. Homilies, ed. Morris, i. 281, l. 29.—OF. *piler* (Littré), later *pilier,* 'a pillar;' Cot. [Cf. Span. and Port. *pilar,* a pillar.]—Late L. *pilāre,* a pillar; formed (with adj. suffix) from L. *pila,* a pier of stone; see **Pile** (2).

PILLAU, PILAU, a dish of meat or fowl with rice and spices. (Pers.) In Terry, Voy. to India, p. 195 (Pegge).—Pers. *pilāw,* the same; Rich. Dict., p. 335.

PILLION, the cushion of a saddle, a cushion behind a saddle. (C.—L.) Spenser speaks of a horseman's '*shaunck-pillion* (shank-pillion) without stirrops;' View of the State of Ireland, Globe ed. p. 639, col. 2, l. 21. [Not the same word as *pylion,* a kind of hat, in P. Plowman's Crede, 839; which is from L. *pileus.*] '*Pyllyon* for a woman to ryde on;' Palsgrave. Lowl. Sc. *pilyane* (1503); N. E. D.; prob. borrowed from Gaelic. Cf. Irish *pilliun, pillin,* a pack-saddle; Gael. *pillean, pillin,* a pack-saddle, riding-cloth; allied to Irish and Gael. *peall,* a skin; all from L. *pellis,* a skin. See **Pell, Fell** (2).

PILLORY, a wooden frame with an upright post, to which criminals were fastened for punishment. (F.) ME. *pilory,* Polit. Songs, ed. Wright, p. 345; *pillory,* P. Plowman, B. iii. 78, C. iv. 79 (see my note on the line).—F. *pilori,* 'a pillory;' Cot. β. Of unknown origin; other remarkable variants occur, viz. OF. *pilorin, pellorin,* Port. *pelourinho,* Prov. *espitlori,* Late L. *pilloricum, spiliorium,* &c., cited by Littré and Scheler. There seems to have been a loss of initial *s.*

PILLOW, a cushion for the head. (L.) ME. *pilwe,* Gower, C. A. i. 142; bk. i. 2986. The change from ME. *-we* to E. *-ow* is regular; cf. *arrow,* ME. *arwe.* But it is less easy to explain the ME. form, as the usual AS. form is *pyle,* Ælfred, tr. of Orosius, b. v. c. 11. § 1. However, there is a by-form *pylu,* which is more correct; it occurs in the gloss: 'ceruical, *pylu*;' Napier's glosses, 29. 4. This AS. *pylu* is from a type **pulwi-;* from L. *puluīnum,* acc. of *puluīnus,* a cushion, pillow, bolster; a word of uncertain origin. β. The L. *puluīnus* also gave rise to Du. *peuluw,* a pillow; OHG. *phulwi,* MHG. *phulwe,* G. *pfühl,* a pillow; Westphalian *pülf.* Der. *pillow,* vb., Milton, Ode on Christ's Nativity, l. 231; *pillow-case.*

PILOT, one who conducts ships in and out of harbour. (F.—Ital.—Gk.) Spelt *pylot* in Gascoigne, Voyage into Holland, A.D. 1572, l. 44; cf. Macb. i. 3. 28.—MF. *pilot,* 'a pilot or steersman;' Cot. Mod. F. *pilote;* whence *piloter,* to take soundings, a word used by Palsgrave, ed. 1852, p. 709. Corrupted from OF. *pedot,* a pilot (Godefroy).—MItal. *pedota,* 'a pilot or guide by sea;' Florio.—Late

Gk. *πηδώτης, a steersman; regularly formed, with suffix -της (of the agent) from πηδόν, a rudder, the blade of an oar. Körting, § 6986. Der. *pilot*, vb., *pilot-age*, *pilot-cloth*, *pilot-fish*.

PIMENTO, all-spice or Jamaica pepper; or, the tree producing it. (Port.—L.) Also called *pimenta*; both forms are in Todd's Johnson.—Port. *pimenta*, pepper (Vieyra); there is also (according to Mahn) a form *pimento*. The Spanish has both *pimienta* and *pimiento*; but the E. word clearly follows the Port. form. β. The OF. *piment* meant 'a spiced drink,' and hence the ME. *piment*, Rom. of the Rose, 6027. All these forms are from L. *pigmentum*, (1) a pigment, (2) the juice of plants. See **Pigment.**

PIMP, a pandar, one who procures gratification for the lust of others. (F.—L.?) Not an old word. ' *Fol.* Let me see; where shall I chuse two or three for *pimps* now?' Middleton, A Mad World, Act iii (end). Of unknown origin; but perhaps suggested by MF. *pimpreneau, pimperneau*, 'a grig (kind of eel); also, a knave, rascall, varlet, scoundrell;' Cot. So also OF. *pimpernel*, a small eel, a lively fellow, in an unfavourable sense (Godefroy). Cf. Norm. dial. *pinperneau, piperneau*, a kind of small eel (Moisy); Late L. *pipernella, pipella* (Ducange). β. Or perhaps allied to MF. *pimper*, 'to sprucifie, or finifie it;' Cot. Allied to the Prov. verb *pimpar*, to render elegant, from the Prov. sb. *pimpa*, equivalent to F. *pipeau*, meaning (1) a pipe, (2) a bird-call, (3) a snare; with an allusion to an old proverb *piper en une chose*, to pipe in a thing, i.e. to excel in it. Hence *pimper* came to mean (1) to pipe, (2) to excel, (3) to beautify or make smart. Cf. also F. *pimpant*, 'spruce' (Cot.), especially applied to ladies whose dress attracted the eye (Littré). γ. Thus *pimper* is from *piper*, to pipe; see **Pipe.**

PIMPERNEL, the name of a flower. (F.—L.) Spelt *pympernell* in Sir T. Elyot, Castel of Helth, b. iii. c. 6. ' *Hec pimpernella*, pimpernolle;' Voc. 645. 10; 'Piponella, *pympernele*,' Voc. 603. 7. Also: 'Pinpernele, (AF.) *pinpre*, (ME.) *briddes-tunge*;' Voc. 557. 35.—MF. *pimpernelle, pimpinelle*, 'the burnet,' Cot.; mod. F. *pimprenelle*; Norm. dial. *pimpernelle* (Moisy). Cf. Span. *pimpinela*, burnet; Ital. *pimpinella*, pimpernel; Late L. *pipinella* (Hatzfeld). β. Diez derives it from L. *bipinella* < *bipennula*, a dimin. from *bipennis*, i.e. double-winged. The pimpernel was confused with burnet (see Prior), and the latter (*Poterium sanguisorba*) has a feather-like arrangement of its leaves. Cf. *Rosa pimpinellifolia*. γ. If this be right (which is highly doubtful), we trace the word back to *bi*-, for *bis*, twice; and *penna*, a wing; see **Bi-** and **Pen.** δ. Diez also cites Catalan *pampinella*, Piedmontese *pampinela*, but regards these as corrupter forms, since we can hardly connect *pimpernel* with L. *pampinus*, a tendril of a vine.

PIMPLE, a small pustule. (Scand.?) Spelt *pimpel* in Minsheu, ed. 1627; *pimple* in Baret (1580). Prov. E. *pumple* (E. D. D.). '*Pimples* or little wheales;' Udall, tr. of Erasmus' Apophthegmes, Diogenes, § 6. 'Pymple, pustule;' Palsgrave. [The alleged AS. *pinpel* is Lye's misprint for *winpel*; Voc. 125. 8.] Apparently not an E. word, but perhaps Scand. Prob. allied to Norw. *pump-en*, swollen up, particularly in the face (Ross). There seems to have been a Scand. strong verb *pimpa (pt. t. *pamp, pp. *pump-in*), of which traces are found in Swed. dial. *pimp-ug*, swelling out, *full-pemp-ad*, pregnant, Dan. dial. *pamp-er*, a thickset man, Norw. *pump*, a small fat man (Ross); cf. Bavar. *pampfen*, to stuff, *pumpf-grob*, very coarse or thick, *pumpet*, thick-set. Hence perhaps also F. *pompette*, 'a pumple or pimple on the nose, or chin,' Cot. Cf. **Pamper.**

PIN, a peg, a small sharp-pointed instrument for fastening things together. (L.) ME. *pinne*, Chaucer, C. T. 196, 10630 (F 316). AS. *pinn*, a pin, also a pointed style for writing (Toller). The ME. *pinne* or *pin* often means 'a peg' rather than a small pin in the modern sense. β. We also find Irish *pinne*, a pin, peg, spigot, stud, *pion*, a pin, peg; Gael. *pinne*, a pin, peg, spigot; W. *pin*, a pin, style, pen; Du. *pin*, pin, peg; MDu. *penne*, a wooden pin, peg (Hexham); *pinne*, a small spit or ironshod staff, the pinnacle of a steeple (id.); Swed. *pinne*, a peg, Dan. *pind*, a (pointed) stick; Icel. *pinni*, a pin; G. *pinnen*, to pin; *penn*, a peg. γ. All borrowed words from L. *pinna*, a wing, fin, pinnacle; cognate with E. *fin*. See Brugmann, ii. § 66 (note). Der. *pin*, verb, L. L. L. v. 2. 321, ME. *pinnen*, Prompt. Parv.; *pin-afore*, so called because formerly pinned in front of a child, afterwards enlarged and made to tie behind; *pyn-case*, Skelton, Elinor Rummyng, 529; *pin-cushion*; *pin-money*, Spectator, no. 295; *pin-point*; *pin-er*, (1) a pin-maker, (2) the lappet of a head-dress, Gay, Shepherd's Week, Past. 5, l. 58; *pin-t-le* (=*pin-et-el*), a little pin, a long iron bolt (Webster). And see *pinn-ac-le*, *pinn-ate*, *pin-i-on*. ¶ The sense of peg or pointed instrument arose from that of 'pinnacle,' as in *pinnam templi*, Luke, iv. 9.

PINCH, to nip, squeeze, gripe. (F.) ME. *pinchen*, Chaucer, C. T. 328 (A 326); P. Plowman, B. xiii. 371. O. North. F. *pinchier*, Norm. dial. *pincher*, Moisy; Guernsey *pinchier*, Métivier; F. *pincer*, 'to pinch, nip, twitch;' Cot. β. This is a nasalised form of M.Ital.

picciare, pizzare, 'to pinch, to snip' (Florio), mod. Ital. *pizzicare*, to pinch; see Diez for other related forms. γ. These verbs are allied to the sb. which appears as Ital. *pinzo*, a sting, a goad, *pinzette*, pincers. δ. The orig. sense seems to have been 'a slight pricking with some small pointed instrument;' the word being formed from a base *pic* (probably Teut.) allied to E. *pick*; see **Pick.** Cf. Du. *pitsen, pinsen*, to pinch (Hexham). Der. *pinch-er*; *pinch-ers* or *pinc-ers*, ME. *pynsors*, Voc. 627. 19; with which cf. F. *pinces*, 'a pair of pincers,' Cot. And cf. **Pink** (1).

PINCHBECK, the name of a metal. (Personal name.) It is an alloy of copper and zinc, made to resemble gold. Added by Todd to Johnson's Dict.; also in Ash's Dict., ed. 1775. So named from the inventor, Mr. Christopher Pinchbeck, the elder, a London watch-maker (ab. 1670–1732). See Notes and Queries, Ser. I. vol. xii. p. 341; Ser. II. vol. xii. p. 81. Cf. Mason's Ode to Mr. Pinchbeck [the younger] on his patent snuffers (1776). β. The name was probably taken from one of the villages named East and West *Pinch-beck*, near Spalding, Lincolnshire.

PINDER, PINNER, one who impounds stray cattle. (E.) See the anonymous play, 'A pleasant conceyted Comedie of George-a-Greene, the *pinner* of Wakefield,' London, 1599. Spelt *pinder* in the reprint of 1632. ME. *pinder, pinner*; spelt *pyndare, pinnar* in Prompt. Parv. p. 400; and see Way's note. Formed, with suffix -*er* of the agent, from AS. *pyndan*, to pen up; Ælfred, tr. of Gregory's Pastoral Care, c. xxxix, ed. Sweet, p. 282, l. 13. *Pyndan* is formed (with the usual vowel-change from *u* to *y*) from the AS. sb. *pund*, a pound for cattle; see **Pound** (2), **Pinfold.** ☞ The spelling *pinner* is due to a supposed connexion with the verb *to pen up*; but there is no real relationship. See **Pen** (2).

PINE (1), a cone-bearing, resinous tree. (L.) ME. *pine*, Legends of the Holy Rood, ed. Morris, p. 70, l. 307; spelt *pigne*, Gower, C. A. ii. 161; bk. v. 1010. AS. *pin*; *pin-treow*, a pine-tree; Voc. 138. 3.—L. *pinus*. β. L. *pinus* is allied to Gk. πίτυς, a pine, Skt. *pitu-daru*-, lit. 'resin-tree;' and to L. *pitu-ita*, phlegm, also 'resin'. See **Pip** (1). Der. *pine-apple*, because the fruit resembles a pine-cone, which was called a *pine-apple* in ME.; cf. Palladius on Husbandry, bk. iii. 1049, where a pine is called *pynappultree*; *pine-cone*; *pin-e-ry*, a place for pine-apples, a coined word. Also *pinn-ace*.

PINE (2), to suffer pain, waste away, be consumed with sorrow. (L.) ME. *pinen*, almost always transitive, signifying 'to torment;' Rom. of the Rose, 3511; Chaucer, C. T. 15065 (B 4249); merely formed from the sb. *pine*, pain, torment, Chaucer, C. T. 1326 (A 1324). AS. *pinian*, to torment, A.S. Chron. an. 1137; AS. *pin*, pain, torment, A.S. Chron. an. 1137. See also *pinian*, verb, in Toller. β. Not a Teut. word, but borrowed from L. *poena*, pain; see **Pain.** Hence also G. *pein*, Du. *pijn*, &c.

PINFOLD, a pound for cattle. (E.) In Shak. K. Lear, ii. 2. 9. For *pind-fold*, i.e. pound-fold; see P. Plowman, B. xvi. 264, C. xix. 282, where we find *poundfold, pondfold, pynfold*. See **Pound** (2), **Pinder.** The AS. variant *pundfold* occurs in Birch, Cart. Saxon. iii. 309.

PINION, a wing, the joint of a wing. (F.—L.) Used in Shak. to mean 'feather,' Antony, iii. 12. 4; he also has *nimble-pinioned* = nimble-winged, Rom. ii. 5. 7. ME. *pinion*. 'Pynyon of a wynge, *pennula*;' Prompt. Parv.—F. *pignon*, only given by Cotgrave in the sense of 'a finiall, cop, or small pinacle on the ridge or top of a house,' like mod. F. *pignon*, a gable-end. The sense of the E. word was derived from OF. *pignon*, a feather (Godefroy, s. v. *pennon*); and the Span. *piñon* means 'pinion,' as in English. β. Both F. *pignon* and Span. *piñon* are derivatives from L. *pinna*, variant of *penna*, a wing; whence E. *pen* (1); confused with L. *pinna*, a fin. The Late L. *pinna* means 'a peak,' whence the sense of F. *pignon*; the same sense appears in L. *pinnaculum*. See **Pin, Pinnacle.** ¶ The E. *pinion*, in the sense of 'a small wheel working with teeth into another,' is really the same word; it is taken from F. *pignon*, with the same sense (Littré), which is from L. *pinna*, in the sense of 'float of a water-wheel.' Cotgrave gives ' *pinon*, the pinnion of a clock.' Der. *pinion*, verb, lit. to fasten the pinions of a bird, hence, to tie a man's elbows together behind him, K. Lear, iii. 7. 23.

PINK (1), to pierce, stab, prick. (E.) Esp. used of stabbing so as to produce only a small hole, as, for instance, with a thin rapier. The word, though unusual, is still extant. '*Pink*, to stab or pierce; in the days of rapier-wearing a professed duellist was said to be "a regular *pinker* and driller;"' Slang Dictionary. Todd quotes from Addison's Drummer, iv. 2: 'They grew such desperate rivals for her, that one of them *pinked* the other in a duel.' Cotgrave has: '*Eschiffeur*, a cutter or pinker.' Shak. has *pink'd porringer*, i.e. a cap reticulated or pierced with small holes, Hen. VIII, v. 4. 50. ME. *pinken*, to prick. 'Heo *pynkes* with heore penne on heore parchemyn' = they prick with their pens on their parchment; Polit. Songs, ed. Wright, p. 156. β. It is best to regard *pink* as the regular nasalised form of *pick*, in the sense 'to peck, prick;' see **Pick**. In fact, the E. *pink*, to cut silk cloth in round holes or eyes (Bailey), is parallel to MF. *piquer*, with the same sense (Cotgrave). See also **Pinch**, which is an allied word.

PINK (2), half-shut, as applied to the eyes. (Du.) Obsolete. ' Plumpy Bacchus, with *pink* eyne;' Shak. Ant. ii. 7. 121. It means ' winking, half-shut;' from MDu. *pincken*, or *pinck-oogen*, to shut the eyes,' Hexham; where *ooge* = eye. The notion is that of bringing to a point, narrowing, or making small. Cf. prov. E. *pink*, to contract the eyes. The same notion comes out in the verb to *pinch*; also in prov. E. *pink*, a minnow, i. e. a very small fish. See also **Pink** (3). Der. *pink-eyed*, q. v.

PINK (3), the name of a flower, and of a colour. (E.) Spelt *pincke*, as the name of a flower, Spenser, Shep. Kal. April, l. 136. [The name of the colour is due to that of the flower, as in the case of *violet*, *mauve*. Again, the phrase ' *pink* of perfection' is prob. due to Shakespeare's ' *pink* of courtesy,' a forced phrase, as remarked by Mercutio; Romeo, ii. 4. 61.] The flower seems to have been named from the delicately cut or *peaked* edges of the petals; see **Pink** (1) and **Pink** (2). Cf. 'The iagged *pinkes*'; Baret (1580). See also Lyte, tr. of Dodoens, bk. i. c. 7. The use of *pink* in the sense to pierce, to cut silk cloth into round holes or eyes, has already been noted; see **Pink** (1). We may note ' *pink'd* porringer,' i. e. cap ornamented with eyelet-holes, in Shak. Hen. VIII, v. 4. 50. Cf. MF. *pince*, 'a pink,' Cotgrave (see also *pinces*); from *pincer*, to pinch, nip.

PINK (4), a kind of boat. (Du.) See Nares. ' Hoy's, *pinks*, and sloops;' Crabbe, The Borough, let. 1, l. 52. ' *Pinke*, a little ship;' Baret (1580).— Du. *pink*, a fishing-boat. Short for MDu. *espincke*, as shown by Hexham, who has : ' *Espincke*, or *pincke*, a pinke, or a small fisher's boat' (whence also F. *pinque*, Span. *pingue*, a pink). This is the same word as Swed. *esping*, Icel. *espingr*, a long boat; formed with suffix -*ing* from *esp*-, signifying ' aspen,' of which wood it must have been first made. Cf. Icel. *espi*, aspen-wood; MDu. *espe*, 'an aspe-tree;' Hexham. See **Aspen**.

PINK-EYED, having small eyes. (Hybrid; Du. *and* E.) ' Them that were *pinke-eied* and had very small eies, they termed *ocellæ*;' Holland, tr. of Pliny, b. xi. c. 37 (on the Eye). See Nares. ' Plumpy Bacchus, with *pink* [half-closed] eyne;' Antony, ii. 7. 121. — Du. *pinken*, to wink. Hexham has: ' *pincke*, light, or an eye; *pincken*, *ofte* [or] *pinck-oogen*, to shut the eyes; *pimpooge*, *ofte* [or] *pimpoogen*, pinck-eyes, or pinck-eyed.' See **Pink** (2).

PINNACE, a small ship. (F.—Ital.—L.) In Shak. Merry Wives, i. 3. 89.— F. *pinasse*, 'the pitch-tree; also, a pinnace;' Cot.— MItal. *pinaccia*, *pinazza*, 'a kind of ship called a pinnace;' Florio. So called because made of pine-wood.— L. *pinus*, a pine; see **Pine** (1). ¶ There is also an OF. *espinace*, a pinnace (Ducange, s. v. *spinachium*), found in 1451; perhaps it obtained its initial *es*- by confusion with MDu. *espincke*; see **Pink** (4). Cf. the form *espyne* in Barbour, Bruce, xvii. 719.

PINNACLE, a slender turret, small spire. (F.—L.) ME. *pinacle*, Gower, C. A. ii. 124; bk. iv. 3662; spelt *pynacle*, Wyclif, Matt. iv. 5.— F. *pinacle*, 'a pinacle, a spire;' Cot.— L. *pinnāculum*, a pinnacle, peak of a building; Matt. iv. 5 (Vulgate). Double dimin. (with suffixes -*cu-lu*-), from *pinna*, a wing, fin; Late L. a pinnacle (Luke, iv. 9). See **Pin**.

PINNATE, feather-like. (L.) A botanical term. ' *Pinnata folia*, among herbalists, such leaves as are deeply indented, so that the parts resemble feathers;' Phillips, ed. 1706.— L. *pinnātus*, substituted for *pennatus*, feathered.— L. *penna*, a feather. See **Pen** (2).

PINT, a measure for liquids. (F.—Span.—L.) ME. *pinte*, *pynte*; Prompt. Parv.— F. *pinte*, 'a pint;' Cot.— Span. *pinta*, a spot, blemish, drop, mark on cards, pint. So called from the pint being marked by a mark outside (or inside) a vessel of larger capacity.— Late L. *pincta*, a pint (A.D. 1249); for L. *picta*, fem. of *pictus*, painted, marked, pp. of *pingere*, to paint. Cf. Span. *pintor*, a painter, *pintura*, a painting.

PIONEER, a soldier who clears the way before an army. (F.—L.) Formerly written *pioner*, Hamlet, i. v. 163. This may have been merely an E. modification, as the whole word appears to be F. Richardson quotes the spelling *pyoner* from Berners' tr. of Froissart, vol. i. c. 138.— F. *pionnier*, 'a pioner;' Cot. β. F. *pionnier*, OF. *peonier*, is a mere extension of F. *pion*, OF. *peon*, a foot-soldier; with the more special meaning of foot-soldier who works at digging mines. For the etymology of OF. *peon*, see **Pawn** (2).

PIONY, the same as **Peony**, q.v.

PIOUS, devout. (F.—L.) In Macb. iii. 6. 12, 27; Hamlet, iii. i. 48.— F. *pieux* (fem. *pieuse*); 'pious, godly;' Cot. The OF. form was *pius* (Littré), directly from L. *pius*, holy; not from a form *piōsus*. Brugmann, ii. § 643. Der. *pious-ly*; *piety*, Timon, iv. i. 15, a coined word, and a doublet of *pity*, q.v.; *piet-ist*, borrowed from G. *pietist*,

the name of a Protestant sect in Germany instituted about 1689 (Haydn), and taking their name from their *collegia pietatis*, the word being a mere coinage (with suffix -*ist*) from a part of the stem (*piet*-) of L. *pietās*. And see *pity*.

PIP (1), a disease of fowls, in which a horny substance grows on the tip of the tongue. (Du.—L.) ME. *pippe*, *pyppe* (once dissyllabic). ' *Pyppe*, sekenesse [sickness], *Pituita*;' Prompt. Parv. ' *Pyppe*, a sickenesse, *pepye*;' Palsgrave.—MDu. *pippe*, the pip; Hexham. Cf. also Walloon, *pîpîe* (Sigart), MF. *pepie*, 'pip;' Cot.; Norm. dial. *pipie*, pip; Span. *pepita*, the pip (Neuman); Ital. *pipita*, Port. *pevide* (in the phrase *pevide de gallinhas*, the pip). β. All from L. *pītuīta*, phlegm, rheum, the pip; which must have passed into the form **pītvīta*, whence **pīpīta*, Late L. *pīpida*, and afterwards into that of *pepida*. We find also OHG. *phiphis*, the pip, cited by Diez; Du. *pip*; Swed. *pipp*, &c. γ. L. *pītuīta* is formed (with suffix -*īta*, like -*ītus* in *crīn-ītus*) from a stem *pītu*-; for which see **Pine** (1).

PIP (2), the seed of fruit. (F.—L.—Gk.) This is nothing but a contraction of the old name *pippin* or *pepin*, for the same thing. *Pippin* is in Cotgrave; *pepin* in Holland, tr. of Pliny, b. xv. c. 14, ed. 1634, p. 438 l; b. xvii. c. 10, p. 511 a, b.— MF. *pepin*, 'a pippin or kernel, the seed of fruit;' Cot. Allied to Span. *pepita*, a pip, kernel; and prob. to Span. *pepino*, a cucumber. β. It is conjectured that the name was first applied to the pips of the melon or cucumber, and that the derivation is, accordingly, from L. *pepō*, a melon, borrowed from Gk. πέπων, a melon, orig. an adj. signifying ' ripe.' The Gk. πέπων meant ' ripened by the heat of the sun,' lit. ' cooked,' from πεπ-, base of πέπτειν, to cook, allied to Skt. *pach*, to cook, and to L. *coquere*; see **Cook**. Körting, § 7023. ¶ The odd resemblance between Span. *pepita*, a pip, and *pepita*, the pip in fowls, is due to mere confusion; see **Pip** (1). They are not connected. See **Pippin**.

PIP (3), a spot on cards. (F.—L.?) Cf. prov. E. *pip*, a spot on a dress, or on the face. But the old spelling is *peep*, or *peepe*, as in Shakespeare, Tam. Shrew, i. 2. 33. It sometimes meant a small blossom. Perhaps from the verb to *peep*; cf. prov. E. *peep*, a peephole. or an eye. See **Peep** (2).

PIPE, a musical instrument formed of a long tube; hence, any long tube, or tube in general. (L.) The musical sense is the orig. one. ME. *pipe*, Wyclif, Luke, vii. 32; Chaucer, C. T. 2752. The pl. *pipen* is in Layamon, 5110. AS. *pīpe*, a pipe, A. S. Leechdoms, ed. Cockayne, ii. 126, l. 3; and in comp. *sang-pipe*, a song-pipe, in the Glosses to Prudentius, 130. An imitative word; but borrowed from Latin.— Late L. *pīpa*, a pipe; from L. *pīpāre*, to chirp. β. It well denotes a ' peeping' or chirping sound; the pipe was frequently used to imitate and decoy birds. It is very widely spread. We find Irish and Gael. *piob*, a pipe, flute, tube; Irish *pib*, a pipe, tube; W. *pib*, a pipe, tube, *pipian*, to pipe, *pibo*, to pipe, squirt. Also Du. *pijp*, Icel. *pīpa*, Swed. *pipa*, Dan. *pibe*, G. *pfeife*. Cf. also L. *pīpīre*, to peep or chirp as a young bird, Gk. πιπίζειν, to chirp. All from the repetition *pi-pi* of the cry of a young bird. Der. *pipe*, verb, Chaucer, C. T. 3874 (A 3876); *pip-er*; *pip-ing*; *pipe-clay*; and see *pip-kin*, *pib-roch*. See also *peep* (1), *peep* (2). For *pipe*, 'a tun,' see below. Doublet, *fife*.

PIPKIN, a small earthen pot. (L.; *with* E. *suffix*.) ' A *pipkin*, or little pot;' Minsheu, ed. 1627. A dimin. (with suffix -*kin*) of E. *pipe*, in the sense of a vessel, chiefly applied to a cask of wine. ' I *pipe* vinei rubei;' York Wills, iii. 14 (1400). This particular sense may have been imported. It occurs in French, Spanish, Provençal, and Dutch. ' *Pipe*, a measure called a pipe, used for corn as well as wine;' Cot. Span. *pipa*, Prov. *pipo*. ' Een pijpe met olye ofte wijn, a pipe or caske with oyle or wine;' Hexham.

PIPPIN, a kind of tart apple. (F.—L.—Gk.?) In Shak. Merry Wives, i. 2. 13; and in Minsheu, ed. 1627. Cotgrave explains F. *renette* as 'the apple called a *pippin*, or a kind thereof.' Spelt *pepyn*, Babees Book, p. 122, l. 79. AF. *pepynes*, pl.; Wright's Vocab., 1st Ser. p. 150. Sometimes said to be named from *pip* (3), because of the spots upon it, which fails to explain the suffix -*in*. We must rather connect it with *pip* (2), of which the old spelling was actually *pippin*, as has been shown. That is, it was named with reference to the pips inside it (not *outside*); ' prob. an apple raised from the *pip* or seed,' Wedgwood; cf. Norm. dial. *pépin*, an apple raised from seed (Robin). See **Pip** (2). Hence we find; 'To plante trees of greynes and *pepins*;' Arnold's Chron., 1502; ed. 1811, p. 167. ¶ Hexham has MDu. ' *pippinck*, *puppinck*, a pipping, an apple so called;' also ' *pupping*, an apple called a pippinck.' But the Du. word seems to have been borrowed from E. Thus Sewel's Du. Dict. has yet another form *pippeling*, with the example ' *Engelsche pippe-lingen*, English pippins.'

PIQUE, wounded pride. (F.—Teut.) Oddly spelt *pike* in Cotgrave, who is an early authority for it.— MF. *picque*, *pique*, 'a pike; also, a pikeman; also a *pike*, debate, quarrel, grudge; Cot.' β. Of Teut. origin; see **Pike**. Der. *pique*, verb; *piqu-ant* (as in ' *piquant* sauce,'

Howell, Familiar Letters, vol. i, sect. 5. let. 38 [*not* 36], where, by the way, the spelling is *pickant*), from F. *piquant*, pres. part. of *piquer*, verb. Hence *piquant-ly*, *piquanc-y*.

PIQUET, a game at cards. (F.—Teut.) 'Piquet, or Picket, a certain game at cards, perhaps so called from *pique*, as it were a small contest or scuffle;' Phillips, ed. 1706. This is ingenious, and perhaps true; Littré says the game is supposed to have been named from its inventor; but Hatzfeld derives it from F. *piquer*, vb., to prick, to vex. Darmesteter derives it from the phrases *faire pic*, *faire repic*, employed in the game. Cf. F. *pic*, 'a pickax, a thrust,' Cot.; MF. *picque*, 'a spade at cards,' id.; whence prov. E. *pick*, a spade (or a diamond) at cards. In any case, *piquet* is a doublet of **Picket**, q. v.

PIRATE, a sea-robber, corsair. (F.—L.—Gk.) In Shak. Merch. Ven. i. 3. 25.—F. *pirate*, 'a pirat;' Cot.—L. *pirāta*.—Gk. πειρατής, one who attempts or attacks, an adventurer (by sea). Formed with suffix -της from πειρά-ω, I attempt.—Gk. πεῖρα, an attempt, trial, essay. For *πέρ-ια; and allied to E. *ex-per-ience* and *fare*; see **Fare, Experience.** Der. *pirat-ic-al*, *pirat-ic-al-ly*; *pirate*, verb; *pirac-y*.

PIROGUE, a sort of canoe. (F.—W. Indian.) Sometimes spelt *piragua*, which is the Span. spelling. 'Pereago, or large Canoa;' W. Dampier, A New Voyage, i. 3 (1699). Both F. *pirogue* and Span. *piragua* are from the native W. Indian name. The word is said by Oviedo to be Caribbean. 'Llamanlos los Caribes *piraguas*;' Oviedo, 1851, i. 171.

PIROUETTE, a whirling round, quick turn, esp. in dancing. (F.) Formerly used as a term in horsemanship. 'Pirouette, Piroet, a turn or circumvolution, which a horse makes without changing his ground;' Bailey's Dict., vol. ii. ed. 1751.—F. *pirouette*, 'a whirligig, also a whirling about;' Cot. β. Origin unknown, according to Littré; but in Métivier's Dict. Franco-Normand appears the Guernsey word *piroue*, a little wheel or whirligig, a child's toy, also Norm. dial. *piroue*, a top (Robin), of which *pirouette* is obviously the diminutive. [The spelling has prob. been affected by confusion with F. *roue* (L. *rota*), a wheel.] Prob. allied to MItal. *pirolo*, a peg, a child's top; origin unknown. Cf. also ME. *pirle*, *prille*, a whirligig, child's toy, Prompt. Parv. p. 413; MF. *pirevollet*, a whirligig (Cot.); MItal. *pirla*, 'a top or a gigge, also a twirle;' Florio. Der. *pirouette*, vb.

PISCES, the Fish; a zodiacal sign. (L.) ME. *Pisces*, Chaucer, C. T. 6286 (D 704).—L. *piscēs*, pl. of *piscis*, a fish; cognate with E. **Fish**, q.v. Der. *pisc-ine*, *pisc-ina*, a basin, from L. *pisc-ina*, a fish-pool, basin; *pisci-vorous*, fish-eating, from L. *uorāre*, to devour; *pisc-at-or-y*, from L. *piscātōrius*, belonging to fishing, from *piscātor*, a fisherman, formed from *piscārī*, to fish.

PISH, an interjection, expressing contempt. (E.) In Shak. Oth. ii. 1. 270; iv. 1. 42. Of imitative origin; it begins with expulsion of breath, as in *pooh* !, and ends with a hiss.

PISMIRE, an ant. (Hybrid; F. *and* E.) In Shak. 1 Hen. IV, i. 3. 240. 'The old name of the ant, an insect very generally named from the sharp urinous smell of an ant-hill;' Wedgwood. ME. *pisse-mire* (four syllables), Chaucer, C. T. 7407 (D 1825).—ME. *pisse*, urine; and *mire*, an ant, Bestiary, 234. See **Piss.** β. The AS. *mire*, given in Benson's A.S. Dict., is unauthorised, but may be correct; still, the usual E. word is *emmet* or *ant*. Cf. Du. *mier*, MDu. *miere*, EFries. *mire*, an ant; Teut. type **mīr-ōn-*. γ. We also find the somewhat similar (but unrelated?) forms: Swed. *myra*, Dan. *myre*, Icel. *maurr*, an ant. Also Irish *moirbh*, W. *mor-grugyn*, Bret. *merienen*, Russ. *mur-avei*, Gk. μύρ-μηξ, Pers. *mūr*, *mōr*, all meaning 'ant.' The Cornish *murrian* means 'ants.' ¶ Wedgwood notes a similar method of naming an ant in the Low G. *miegemke*, an ant; from *miegen* = L. *mingere*. And cf. Pomeran. *pissmiren*, pl., pismires.

PISS, to discharge urine. (F.) ME. *pissen*, Mandeville's Travels, ed. Halliwell, ch. 23, p. 249.—F. *pisser*; supposed to be a Romance word, and of imitative origin. Der. *piss*, sb., Chaucer, C. T. 6311 (D 729); *pis-mire*, q.v.

PISTACHIO, PISTACHO, the nut of a certain tree. (Span.—L.—Gk.—Pers.) In Sir T. Herbert's Travels, ed. 1665, p. 80. Spelt *pistachoe* or *pistake-nut* in Phillips, ed. 1706.—Span. *pistacho* (with *ch* as in English), a pistacho, pistich-nut.—L. *pistācium*.—Gk. πιστάκιον, a nut of the tree called πιστάκη.—Pers. *pistā*, *pistah*, the pistachio-nut; Rich. Dict. pp. 331, 332. Cf. Ital. *pistacchio*, whence the form *pistachio*.

PISTIL, the female organ in the centre of a flower. (L.) In Ash's Dict., ed. 1775. Named from the resemblance in shape to the pestle of a mortar.—L. *pistillum*, a small pestle; dimin. of an obsolete form *pistrum, a pestle.—L. *pistum*, supine of *pinsere*, to pound. Cf. Skt. *pish*, to pound. (√ PIS.) See **Pestle. Doublet,** *pestle*.

PISTOL, a small hand-gun. (F.—Ital.) In Shak. Merry Wives, v. 2. 53; and as a proper name.—F. *pistole*, 'a pistoll, a great

horseman's dag;' Cot. [Here *dag* is an old name for a pistol.] Shortened from F. *pistolet*, the same. β. We also find Ital. *pistolese*, 'a great dagger,' in Florio; and it seems to be agreed that the two words are closely connected; that the word *pistolese* is the older one; and that the name was transferred from the dagger to the pistol, both being small arms for similar use. The E. name *dag* for *pistol* confirms this; since *dag* must be the F. *dague*, a dagger. γ. The Ital. *pistolese* is known to have been named from a town in Tuscany, near Florence, now called *Pistoja*. The old name of the town must have been *Pistolia*; and this is rendered extremely probable by the fact that the old Latin name of the town was *Pistōrium*, which would easily pass into *Pistolia*, and finally into *Pistoja*. 'Pistols were first used by the cavalry of England about 1544;' Haydn. Der. *pistol*, vb., Tw. Nt. ii. 5. 42; *pistol-et*. **Doublet,** *pistole*.

PISTOLE, a gold coin of Spain. (F.—Ital.) In Dryden, The Spanish Friar, A. v. Sc. 2. The dimin. form *pistolet* is, in Beaum. and Fletcher, The Spanish Curate, Act i. sc. 1 (Jamie). Yet the word is not Spanish, but French. The forms *pistole* and *pistolet*, in the sense of 'pistole,' are the same as *pistole* and *pistolet* in the sense of *pistol*. —MF. *pistolet*, 'a pistolet, a dag, or little pistoll, also, the gold coin tearmed a pistolet;' Cot. Diez cites from Claude Fauchet (died 1599) to the effect that the crowns of Spain, being reduced to a smaller size than French crowns, were called *pistolets*, and the smallest *pistolets* were called *bidets*; cf. 'Bidet, a small pistoll;' Cot. Thus the name is one of jocular origin; and the words *pistole* and *pistol* are doublets. *Pistol*, being more Anglicized, is the older word in English.

PISTON, a short cylinder used in pumps, moving up and down within the tube of the pump. (F.—Ital.—L.) In Bailey's Dict., vol. ii. ed. 1731.—F. *piston*, 'a pestell, or pounding-stick;' Cot. In mod. F. 'a piston.'—Ital. *pistone*, a piston; the same word as *pestone*, a large heavy pestle.—Ital. *pestare*, to pound.—Late L. *pistāre*, to pound; allied to *pistus*, pp. of *pinsere*, *pīsere*, to pound. See **Pestle, Pistil, Pea.**

PIT, a hole in the earth. (L.) ME. *pit*, Wyclif, Luke xiv. 5; *put*, Ancren Riwle, p. 58, l. 4. AS. *pyt*, *pytt*; Luke xiv. 5.—L. *puteus*, a well, pit; Luke xiv. 5 (Vulgate). β. Perhaps orig. a well of pure water, a spring; and so connected with L. *putus*, pure, from the same root as *pūrus*; see **Pure.** Der. *pit*, verb, to set in competition, a phrase taken from cock-fighting. 'A *pit* is the area in which cocks fight; hence, to *pit* one against the other, to place them in the same *pit*, one against the other, for a contest;' Richardson. The *pit* of a theatre was formerly called a *cock-pit*; Hen. V, prol. 11. Also *pit-fall*, Macb. iv. 2. 35; *pit-man*, *pit-saw*; *cock-pit*.

PITAPAT, with palpitation. (E.) In Dryden, Epilogue to Tamerlane. A repetition of *pat*, weakened to *pit* in the first instance. Sir T. More says the old folks 'walked *pit-pat* upon a paire of patens;' Works, p. 94 d. See **Pat.**

PITCH (1), a black sticky substance. (L.) ME. *pich*, *pych*; Rob. of Glouc. p. 410, l. 8485; O. Eng. Homilies, ed. Morris, i. 251, l. 24; older form *pik*, id. i. 269, l. 22. AS. *pic*, Exod. ii. 3.—L. *pic-*, stem of *pix*, pitch. Hence also G. *pech*. β. Allied to Gk. πίσσα (for πίκ-ya). Cf. **Pine** (1). Der. *pitch*, verb; *pitch-y*, All's Well, iv. 4. 24. Also *pay* (2).

PITCH (2), to throw, to fall headlong, to fix a camp, &c. (E.) Spelt *pytche* in Palsgrave. A palatalized form of *pick*, to throw, Cor. i. 1. 204; esp. used of throwing a pike or dart. 'I *pycke* with an arrowe, *Ie darde*;' Palsgrave. It was particularly used of forcibly plunging a sharp peg into the ground; hence the phrase 'to *pitch* a camp,' i.e. to fasten the poles, tent-pegs, palisades, &c. 'At the eest Judas schal *picche* tentis;' Wyclif, Numb. ii. 3, where the later version has 'sette tentis.' The old pt. t. was *pihte* or *pighte*, pp. *piht*, *pight*. 'A spere that is *pight* into the erthe,' Mandeville's Travels, ed. Halliwell, p. 183. 'He *pighte* him on the pomel of his heed' = he pitched [fell] on the top of his head; Chaucer, C. T. 2691 (A 2689). 'Ther he *pihte* his stæf' = there he fixed his staff; Layamon, 29653. Allied to *tick*, verb; and probably related to *pike*. See **Pick, Pike.** Der. *pitch*, sb., Tw. Nt. i. 1. 12; *pitch-fork*, allied to ME. *pikforke* = pick-fork, Prompt. Parv.; *pitch-pipe*.

PITCHER, a vessel for holding liquids. (F.—OHG.—L.) ME. *picher*, *pycher*; English Gilds, ed. Toulmin Smith, p. 354, l. 12; *pychere*, Sir Perceval, l. 454, in Thornton Romances, ed. Halliwell.—OF. *picher*, *pecher*, a pitcher; spelt *pichier* in Cotgrave, who gives it as a Languedoc word. Cf. OProv. *pichiers*, *pechiers* (Bartsch); Prov. *pichié*, *pechié* (Mistral); Haut-Maine *piche*; Span. and Port. *pichel*, a tankard, Ital. *pecchero*, *bicchiere*, a goblet, beaker.—OHG. *pechāri* (G. *becher*).—Late L. *bicārium*, a goblet, beaker, wine-cup. The suggested connexion with Gk. βῖκος, an earthen wine-vessel, is by no means certain. See **Beaker,** which is a doublet. Der. *pitcher-plant*.

PITH, the soft substance in the centre of stems of plants, marrow. (E.) ME. *pith, pithe*, Chaucer, C. T. 6057 (D 475). AS. *piða*, Ælfred, tr. of Boethius, c. xxxiv. § 10; lib. iii. pr. 11.+Du. *pit*, pith; MDu. *pitte* (Hexham); Low G. *peddik*, pith (Bremen Wörterbuch). **Der.** *pith-y*, Tam. Shrew, iii. 1. 68; *pith-i-ly, pith-i-ness; pith-less*, 1 Hen. VI, ii. 5. 11.

PITTANCE, an allowance of food, a dole, small portion. (F.) ME. *pitance* (with one *t*), *pitaunce*, P. Plowman, C. x. 92; Ancren Riwle, p. 114, l. 5.—F. *pitance*, 'meat, food, victuall of all sorts, bread and drinke excepted;' Cot. β. Of disputed etymology; cf. Span. *pitanza*, a pittance, the price of a thing, salary; Ital. *pietanza*, a pittance, portion. In all probability the Ital. *pietanza* is a popular corruption, due to a supposed connexion with *pietà*, pity, mercy, as if to give a pittance were to give alms. The Lombard form is still *pitanza* (Diez). Diez connects *pitance* with OF. *pite*, a thing of little worth, which he further connects with *petit*, small; see **Piece.** γ. The Span. *pitar* means to distribute allowances of meat, &c., and is clearly a connected word; this seems at once to set aside any connexion with *piety* or *pity*. But Ducange gives the Late L. *pictantia* as a pittance, a portion of food (given to monks) of the value of a *picta*, which he explains to be a very small coin issued by the counts of Poitiers (*moneta comitum Pictavensium*). This answers to OF. *pite*, 'the half of a maille, a French farthing;' Cot. δ. This brings us back to the same OF. *pite*, but suggests a different origin for that word, viz. Late L. *picta*, a Poitiers coin. And this L. *picta* is supposed to be due to Late L. *Pictāva*, i.e. Poitiers (5th cent.).

PITY, sympathy, mercy. (F.—L.) ME. *pité*, Floriz and Blauncheflor, ed. Lumby, 529; Ancren Riwle, p. 368, l. 14.—OF. *pite* (*pité*), 13th cent. (Littré); *pitet*, 12th cent. (id.).—L. *pietātem*, acc. of *pietās*; see **Piety.** **Der.** *pity*, verb, As You Like It, ii. 7. 117; *piti-able, piti-abl-y, piti-able-ness; piti-ful*, All's Well, iii. 2. 130; *piti-ful-ly, piti-ful-ness; piti-less*, As You Like It, iii. 5. 40; *piti-less-ly, piti-less-ness; pity-ing-ly*. Also *pite-ous*, a corruption of ME. *pit-ous*, Chaucer, C. T. 8956 (E 1080), spelt *pitos*, Rob. of Glouc., p. 204, l. 4180, from OF. *piteus*, mod. F. *piteux*, 'pitiful, merciful,' Cot.; from Late L. *pietōsus*, merciful. And hence *piteous-ly*.

PIVOT, a pin upon which a wheel or other object turns. (F.—Ital.—L.) In Cotgrave.—F. *pivot*, 'the pivot or, as some call it, the tampin of a gate, or great doore, a piece of iron, &c., made, for the most part, like a top, round and broad at one end and sharp at the other, whereby it enters into the *crappaudine* [iron wherein the pivot plays]; and serves as well to bear up the gate as to facilitate the motion thereof;' Cot. Formed with dimin. suffix *-ot*, from Ital. *piva*, a pipe.—Late L. *pīpa*, a pipe; connected with L. *pīpāre, pīpīre*, to chirp as a bird; see **Pipe.** β. The Ital. *piva* meant (1) a pipe, (2) a tube with a fine bore; and so came to mean a solid peg, as well shown in the MItal. dimin. form *pivolo*, or *piviolo*, 'a pin or peg of wood, a setting or poaking sticke to set ruffes with, also a gardeners toole to set herbes with called a dibble;' Florio. ¶Much disputed; see Diez; and see the articles *piva* and *pivolo* or *piviolo* in Florio.

PIX, an old form of **Pyx**, q.v.

PIXY, a fairy (Scand.). 'If a *pixie*, seek thy ring;' Scott, Pirate, ch. 23 (song). Also *pisky*, which is an older form.—Swed. dial. *pysk, pyske*, a little goblin (Rietz); cf. Norw. *pjusk*, an insignificant person (Ross). See Notes on E. Etym., p. 218; and E. D. D.

PLACABLE, forgiving, easy to be appeased. (L.) In Minsheu, ed. 1627; and in Milton, P. L. xi. 151. Taken directly from L. *plācābilis*, easily appeased; formed with suffix *-bilis* from *plācāre*, to appease. Allied to *placēre*; see **Please.** **Der.** *placabl-y, placable-ness*. Also *placabili-ty*, Sir T. Elyot, The Governor, b. ii. c. 6.

PLACARD, a bill stuck up as an advertisement. (F.—Du.) In Minsheu, ed. 1627; he notes that it occurs in the 2nd and 3rd years of Philip and Mary (1555, 1556).—F. *placard, plaquard*, 'a placard, an inscription set up; also a bill, or libell stuck upon a post; also, rough-casting or pargetting of walls;' Cot. The last is the orig. sense. Formed with suffix *-ard* (of OHG. origin, from G. *hart* = E. *hard*) from the verb *plaquer*, 'to parget or to rough-cast, also, to clap, slat, stick, or paste on;' Cot.—Du. *plakken*, to paste, glue; formerly also 'to dawbe or to plaister,' Hexham. [The Du. *plakkaat*, a placard, is merely borrowed back again from the French.] The Du. *plakken* is prob. of imitative origin (Franck). **Der.** *placard*, verb. And see *plack, plaque, placket*.

PLACE, a space, room, locality, town, stead, way, passage in a book. (F.—L.—Gk.) In early use. In King Horn, ed. Lumby, 718.—F. *place*, 'a place, room, stead, .. a faire large court;' Cot.—Folk-L. **plattia*; L. *platea*, a broad way in a city, an open space, courtyard. Sometimes called *platĕa*, but properly *platēa*, not a true L. word, but borrowed.—Gk. πλατεῖα, a broad way, a street; orig. fem. of πλατύς, flat, wide.+Lithuan. *platus*, broad; Skt. *pṛthu-*, large, great; cf. Skt. *prath*, to spread out. **And prob. allied to Flat.**

Hence also *plant*, q.v. **Der.** *place*, verb, K. Lear, i. 4. 156; *plac-er; place-man*, added by Todd to Johnson. And see *plaice, plant*. Doublet, *piazza*.

PLACENTA, a substance in the womb. (L.) Called *placenta uterina* in Phillips, ed. 1706.—L. *placenta*, lit. a flat cake.+Gk. πλακοῦς, a flat cake; cf. πλάξ, a flat surface. **Der.** *placent-al*.

PLACID, gentle, peaceful. (F.—L.) In Milton, P. R. iii. 217.—F. *placide*, 'calm;' Cot.—L. *placidus*, gentle, lit. pleasing.—L. *placēre*, to please; see **Please.** **Der.** *placid-ly; placid-i-ty*, directly from L. *placiditās*, the F. *placidité* being late.

PLACK, a small copper coin, worth 4 pennies Scots. (F.—Du.) First used, spelt *plak*, of a somewhat different coin, in the reign of James III of Scotland (1460–88). Ducange has *placa* as the Latinized form (1426).—F. *plaque*, a coin; 'En ce temps (1425) couroit une monnoie a Paris nommee *plaques*;' qu. in Hatzfeld. Also a flat plate (Cot.).—Du. *plakken*, 'to lay flat upon;' Cot.—Du. *plakken*, to paste, glue, &c. Cf. MDu. *placke*, 'a French sous;' Hexham. See **Placard.**

PLACKET, an apron, petticoat, a woman; a slit in a petticoat. (Du.) See Troil. and Cress. ii. 3. 22; K. Lear, iii. 4. 100. A variant of *placard*; see N. E. D.—Du. *plakkaat*, a placard; from Du. *plakken*, to stick up; with F. suffix *-ard*; see **Placard.**

PLAGIARY, one who steals the writings of another, and passes them off as his own. (F.—L.) Spelt *plagiairie* in Minsheu, ed. 1627, with the same definition as in Cotgrave (given below). [Sir T. Browne uses the word in the sense of *plagiarism*, Vulg. Errors, b. i. c. 6. § 7; yet he has *plagiarism* in the very next section. Bp. Hall has *plagiary* as an adj., Satires, b. iv. sat. 2. l. 84.]—F. *plagiaire*, 'one that steals or takes free people out of one country, and sels them in another for slaves; .. also a book-stealer, a book-theef;' Cot.—L. *plagiārius*, a man-stealer, kidnapper.—L. *plagium*, kidnapping; whence also *plagiāre*, to steal or kidnap a free person; lit. to ensnare, net.—L. *plaga*, a net. **Der.** *plagiar-ize, plagiar-ism, plagiar-ist*.

PLAGUE, a pestilence, a severe trouble. (F.—L.) ME. *plage* (not common), Wyclif, Rev. xvi. 21, to translate L. *plāgam*; the pl. *plagis* (= *plages*, plagues) is in Wyclif, Gen. xii. 17, where the Vulgate has the L. abl. *plāgis*.—OF. *plage, plague* (Godefroy). But the E. word was prob. taken directly from Latin, and spelt with final *-ue* at a later date.—L. *plāga*, a stroke, blow, stripe, injury, disaster.+Gk. πληγή, a blow, plague, Rev. xvi. 21. From the base πληγ-, as in πληγ-ή, a blow, and in πλήσσειν (for *πληγ-γειν), to strike; cf. Lithuan. *plakti*, to strike; L. *plangere*, to strike. See Brugmann, i. § 569. ¶ The spelling *plage* occurs as late as in the Bible of 1551, Rev. xvi. 21. The *u* was introduced to keep the *g* hard. **Der.** *plague*, vb., Temp. iv. 192; spelt *plaghe* in Caxton's Reynard the Fox, p. 70, l. 9; *plague-mark, plague-spot*. And see **Plaint.**

PLAICE, a kind of flat fish. (F.—L.) ME. *plaice, playce*; Havelok, 896. Spelt *place, plaise* in Minsheu, ed. 1627.—OF. *plaïs*, noted by Littré, s. v. *plie*; he also gives *plaise* as a vulgar F. name of the fish, the literary name being *plie*, as in Cotgrave.—Late L. *platisa, platissa* (Voc. 40. 7, 94. 28); for L. *platessa*, a plaice (Lewis); whence the F. forms by the regular loss of *t* between vowels, and before a stressed vowel. β. So called from its flatness; from the base PLAT, which appears also in Gk. πλατ-ύς, flat, broad. See **Place.** Cf. **Flounder** and **Flawn.**

PLAID, a loose outer garment of woollen cloth, chiefly worn by the Highlanders of Scotland. (Gael.—L.) Spelt *plad* in Sir T. Herbert, Travels, p. 313, who speaks of a 'Scotch *plad*;' also in Phillips, ed. 1706, and in Kersey, ed. 1715. 'Heland [Highland] *plaidis*;' Ane littil Interlud (Bannatyne MS.); l. 32. *Plaid* is in Johnson.—Gael. *plaide*, a blanket; cf. Irish *plaide*, a plaid, blanket. β. Macleod and Dewar consider *plaide* to be a contraction of Gael. (and Irish) *peallaid*, a sheep-skin. Cf. Gael. *peallag*, a shaggy hide, a little covering. These words are from Gael. (and Irish) *peall*, a skin, hide, also a covering or coverlet. All from L. *pellis*, a skin; cognate with E. *fell*. See **Fell** (2). **Der.** *plaid-ed*.

PLAIN, flat, level, smooth, artless, evident. (F.—L.) ME. *plein, plain*. 'Thing that I speke it moot be bare and *pleyn*;' Chaucer, C. T. 11032 (F 720). 'The cuntre was so *playne*;' Will. of Palerne, 2217. 'Upon the *pleyn* of Salesbury;' Rob. of Glouc. p. 7. l. 155; where it is used as a sb.—F. *plain*, 'plain, flat;' Cot.—L. *plān-um*, acc. of *plānus*, plain, flat. β. Idg. type **plā-nos*; cf. Celtic type **plā-ros*, flat surface, W. *llawr*; see **Floor.** Prob. **plā-* is lengthened from **pel-*; see πέλ-ανος in Prellwitz. **Der.** *plain*, sb., *plain-ly, plain-ness; plain*, adv.; *plain-dealer*, Com. of Errors, ii. 2. 88; *plain-deal-ing*, adj., Much Ado, i. 3. 33; *plain-deal-ing*, sb., Timon, i. 1. 216; *plain-hearted; plain-song*, Mids. Nt. Dr. iii. 1. 134; *plain-spoken*, Dryden, Preface to All for Love, § 3; *plain-work*. Also *ex-plain*. And see *plan, plane* (1), *planisphere, placenta, piano*.

PLAINT, a lament, mourning, lamentation. (F.—L.) ME. *pleinte*, Havelok, 134; Ancren Riwle, p. 96, l. 18.—OF. *pleinte* (11th century, Littré), later *plainte*, 'a plaint, complaint;' Cot. – Late L. *plancta*, a plaint; closely allied to L. *planctus*, lamentation. Both are allied to *planctus* (fem. *plancta*), pp. of *plangere*, to strike, beat, esp. to beat the breast as a sign of grief, to lament aloud. A nasalized form from the base PLAG, to strike; see **Plague**. Der. *plaint-iff*, q.v., *plaint-ive*, q.v.; also *com-plain*. The verb *to plain*, i.e. to mourn, is perhaps obsolete; it is equivalent to F. *plaindre* from L. *plangere*; see K. Lear, iii. 1. 39.

PLAINTIFF, the complainant in a law-suit. (F. – L.) It should have but one *f*. ME. *plaintif*; spelt *playntyf*, Eng. Gilds, ed. Toulmin Smith, p. 360, l. 18. – F. *plaintif*, 'a plaintiff;' Cot. Formed with suffix *-if* (L. *-iuus*) from L. *planct-us*, pp. of *plangere*, to lament, hence, to complain; see **Plaint**. Doublet, *plaintive*.

PLAINTIVE, mournful. (F. – L.) Really the same word as the above, but differently used. In Daniel, Sonnet iv, To Delia. – F. *plaintif*, fem. *plaintive*, adj., 'lamenting, mournful;' Cot. See **Plaintiff**. Der. *plaintive-ly*, *-ness*.

PLAIT, a fold, braid; to fold together, interweave. (F. – L.) Minsheu, ed. 1627, has 'to *platte* or wreath.' Shak. has *plat*, Hamlet, i. 4. 89. For *plaited*, in K. Lear, i. 1. 183, the quartos have *pleated*, the folios *plighted*. Cotgrave translates F. *plier* by 'to fould, *plait*.' ME. *plaiten*, *pleten*, verb; *plait*, sb. '*Playte of a clothe*, Plica; *Playtyd*, Plicatus; *Playtyn*, Plico;' Prompt. Parv. The pt. t. *plaited* is in P. Plowman, B. v. 212; spelt *pletede*, id. A. v. 126. The verb is formed from the sb., which alone is found in French. – OF. *ploit*, *pleit*, *plet*, a fold (Burguy; Godefroy gives *ploit* only); the mod. F. word is *pli*; Littré, s.v. *pli*, gives an example of the use of the form *ploit* in the 13th century. – Late L. *plic'tum*, for *plicitum*, by-form of L. *plicātum*, acc. of *plicātus*, pp. of *plicāre*, to fold. The F. verb *plier* = L. *plicāre*, and also appears as *ployer*, 'to plie,' Cot. See **Ply**. Der. *plait-er*. Doublets, *pleat*, *plight* (2).

PLAN, a drawing of anything on a plane or flat surface; esp. the ground-plot of a building; a scheme. (F. – L.) In Phillips, ed. 1706; Pope, Essay on Man, i. 6. – F. *plan*, 'the ground-plat of a building;' Cot. – F. *plan*, adj. (fem. *plane*), flat, which first occurs in the 16th century (Littré); a 'learned' form of F. *plain*. A late formation from L. *plānus*, plain, flat; the earlier F. form being *plain*; see **Plain**. Der. *plan*, verb, Pope, Satires from Horace, Ep. II. i. 374. Hence *plann-er*.

PLANE (1), a level surface. (F. – L.) In Phillips, ed. 1706, who speaks of 'a geometrical *plane*,' 'a vertical *plane*,' &c. – F. *plane*, fem. of the adj. *plan*, flat; with the E. sense of 'a plane,' it occurs in Forcadel, Éléments d'Euclide, p. 3 (Littré), in the 16th century. See **Plan**. We also find E. *plane* as an adj., as 'a plane surface.' See **Plane** (2). Der. *plani-sphere*, q.v.

PLANE (2), a tool; also, to render a surface level. (F. – L.) 1. The carpenter's plane was so called from its use; the verb is older than the sb. in Latin. We find ME. *plane*, sb., a carpenter's tool, in the Prompt. Parv. This is the F. *plane* (Cot.), from Late L. *plāna*, a carpenter's plane (Lewis). 2. The verb is ME. *planen*, Chaucer, C. T., D 1758; spelt *planyn* in the Prompt. Parv. – F. *planer*, to plane. – L. *plānāre*, to plane (Lewis). ¶ Lewis gives Corippus as the authority for the verb *plānāre*; Prof. Mayor gives me a reference to St. Augustine, de gen. c. Manich. I. § 13. See **Plain**.

PLANE (3), **PLANE-TREE**, the name of a tree, with spreading boughs. (F. – L. – Gk.) ME. *plane*; Wyclif, Gen. xxx. 37; Squire of Low Degree, ed. Ritson, l. 40; *plane-leef*, leaf of a plane, Trevisa, tr. of Higden, i. 187, l. 9. – F. *plane*, 'the great maple;' Cot. – L. *platanum*, acc. of *platanus*, a plane. – Gk. πλάτανος, the oriental plane; named from its broad leaves and spreading form (Liddell). – Gk. πλατύς, wide, broad. See Brugmann, i. § 444. ¶ Sometimes called *platane* (an inferior form) from L. *platanus*; ME. *platan*, Trevisa, tr. of Higden, ii. 303.

PLANET, a wandering star. (F. – L. – Gk.) So called to distinguish them from the fixed stars. ME. *planete*, Rob. of Glouc., p. 112, l. 2436. – OF. *planete*, 13th cent. (Littré); mod. F. *planète*. – L. *planēta*. – Gk. πλανήτης, a wanderer; lengthened form of πλανής, a wanderer, of which the pl. πλάνητες was esp. used to signify the planets. – Gk. πλανάω, I lead astray, cause to wander; pass. πλανάομαι, I wander, roam. – Gk. πλάνη, a wandering about. Der. *planet-ar-y*, Timon, iv. 3. 108; *planet-oid* (see **Asteroid**); *planet-stricken* or *planet-struck*, see Hamlet, i. 1. 162.

PLANE-TREE; see **Plane** (3).

PLANGENT, clashing, dashing, resounding, striking. (L.) Rare. In Sir H. Taylor, Philip van Artevelde, Part I, i. 1. 97. L. *plangent-*, stem of *plangens*, pres. pt. of *plangere*, to strike; see **Plaint**.

PLANISPHERE, a sphere projected on a plane. (Hybrid; L. and Gk.) 'Planisphere, a plain sphere, or a sphere projected *in plano* as an astrolabe;' Blount's Gloss., ed. 1674. A barbarous hybrid compound. From *plani-*, for L. *plānus*, flat; and *sphere*, a word of Gk. origin. See **Plain** and **Sphere**.

PLANK, a board. (F. – L.) ME. *planke*, Will. of Palerne, 2778; Rob. of Brunne, Handlyng Synne, 5261. – North F. (Picard) *planke*; Norm. dial. *planque*. – L. *planca*, a board, plank. So called from its flatness; it is a nasalized form from the base PLAK, with the idea of flatness. Cf. Gk. πλάξ (gen. πλακ-ός), a flat stone; πλακ-ίνος, made of board. See **Placenta**. Der. *plank*, verb. ☞ The Central F. form *planche* accounts for *planched*, Meas. for Meas. iv. 1. 30.

PLANT, a vegetable production, esp. a sprout, shoot, twig, slip. (L.) ME. *plante*, Chaucer, C. T. 6345 (D 763). AS. *plante*; the pl. *plantan* occurs in the entry 'Plantaria, gesāwena plantan' in Voc. 149. 22. – L. *planta*, a plant; properly, a spreading sucker or shoot. From the base PLAT, spreading, seen in Gk. πλατύς, spreading, broad. See **Place**. ¶ The L. *planta* also means the flat sole of the foot; hence 'to plant one's foot,' i.e. to set it flat and firmly down. Der. *plant*, verb, Chaucer, C. T. 6346 (D 764); AS. *geplantian*, Mercian version of Psalm, ciii. 16; *plant-er*; *plant-at-ion*, see Bacon, Essay 33, Of Plantations, from L. *plantātio*, a planting, which from *plantāre*, to plant. Also *plant-ing*, *plant-ain*, *planti-grade*.

PLANTAIN (1), the name of a plant. (F. – L.) ME. *plantain*, Chaucer, C. T. 16049 (G 581). – F. *plantain*, 'plantain, waybred;' Cot. – L. *plantāginem*, acc. of *plantāgo*, a plantain; Pliny. β. So named from its flat spreading leaf, and connected with *planta*; see **Plant**. So also arose the ME. name *waybred*, AS. *wegbrǣde*, 'properly *way-broad*, but called *way-bread*,' Cockayne's A.S. Leechdoms, vol. ii. Glossary; however, the AS. *-brǣde* represents the sb. *brǣdu*, breadth. So also the G. name *wegebreit*.

PLANTAIN (2), a tree resembling the banana. (F. – Span. – L.) 'Oranges and *plantans*, which is a fruit that groweth upon a tree;' Hakluyt, Voy. vol. ii. pt. 2, p. 129. – OF. *plantain*, variant of *platane*, orig. a plane-tree (Godefroy). – Span. *plantano*, a plantain; variant of *platano*, (1) a plane-tree, (2) a plantain. – L. *platanum*, acc. of *platanus*, a plane. See **Plane** (3).

PLANTIGRADE, walking on the sole of the foot. (L.) Scientific. Coined from *planti-*, for *planta*, the sole of the foot, also a plant; and *grad-ī*, to walk. See **Plant** and **Grade**. For the form *planti-*, cf. L. *planti-ger*, bearing shoots.

PLAQUE, an ornamental plate, a (metal) tablet for a wall. (F. – Du.) Modern. F. *plaque*, sb.; from *plaquer*, vb., to plate; MF. *plaquer*, to fix, fasten up. – Du. *plakken*, to paste up; see **Plack**, **Placard**.

PLASH (1), a puddle, a shallow pool. (E.) ME. *plasche*, Allit. Morte Arthure, ed. Brock, 2798; Prompt. Parv. AS. *plesc*, Birch, Cart. Saxon. iii. 356; now *Plash* Park, near Cardington, Salop; cf. EFries. *plas*, *plasse*, a shallow pool. + MDu. *plasch*; 'een plas ofte [or] *plasch*, a plash of water: *een plasregen*, a sudden flash [flush] of raine; cf. *plasschen in't water*, to plash, or plunge in the water;' Hexham. Hence OF. *plasceq*, *plassis*, a pool (Godefroy). β. Cf. also G. *platschen*, to splash, dabble, Dan. *pladske* (for *platske*), to splash, dabble about, Swed. *plaska* (for *platska*), to dabble, showing that a *t* has been lost before *s*, the Du. *plasch* standing for *plat-sch*. γ. The various forms are extensions from the base PLAT, to strike, beat, appearing in AS. *plættan*, to strike with the palm, slap, John, xix. 3; also in Swed. dial. *plätta*, to strike softly, slap, whence the frequentative *plättsa*, to tap with the finger-points (Rietz).

PLASH (2), another form of **Pleach**, q.v. In Nares.

PLASTER, a composition of lime, water, and sand, for walls; an external medical application for wounds. (L. – Gk.) ME. *plastre*, Chaucer, C. T. 10950 (F 636). [This is a F. spelling, from OF. *plastre*, used in the 13th and 14th century (Littré). The spelling *plaister* in English answers to the occasional 14th cent. F. spelling *plaistre*.] AS. *plaster*, a plaster for wounds; Cockayne's Leechdoms, i. 298, l. 12. – L. *emplastrum*, a plaster; the first syllable being dropped; cf. Late L. *plastreus*, made of plaster (Ducange). – Gk. ἔμπλαστρον, a plaster; a form used by Galen instead of the usual word ἔμπλαστον, a plaster, which is properly the neut. of ἔμπλαστος, daubed on or over. – Gk. ἐμπλάσσειν, to daub on. – Gk. ἐμ- for ἐν, in, before the following π; and πλάσσειν, to mould, form in clay or wax. See **In** and **Plastic**. ¶ Cf. ME. *emplaster*, sb., Reliq. Antiq. i. 54. Der. *plaster*, verb, ME. *plasteren*, Prompt. Parv., from MF. *plastrer* (F. *plâtrer*), 'to plaister,' Cot. Also *plaster-er*, *plaster-ing*. And see *piastre*.

PLASTIC, capable of moulding; also, capable of being moulded. (L. – Gk.) Used in the active sense by Pope, Essay on Man, iii. 9; Dunciad, i. 101. – L. *plasticus*. + Gk. πλαστικός, fit for, or skilful in moulding. Formed with suffix *-ικ-ος* from πλαστ-ός, formed, moulded. – Gk. πλάσσειν, to mould. β. Gk. πλάσσειν appears to be put for *πλάτ-γειν*, and to be related to E. *fold*, vb. Der. *plastic-i-ty*, from mod. F. *plasticité* (Littré).

PLAT (1), **PLOT**, a patch of ground. (E.) Now commonly written *plot*, which is also the AS. form. Spelt *plat* in 2 Kings ix.

26, A.V. 'So three in one small *plat* of ground shall ly ;' Herrick, Hesperides ; to Anthea. ' A garden *platte* ;' Udall's Erasmus, Luke xxiii. 50, fol. 182, b. See further under **Plot, Patch.** ☞ The spelling *plat* is prob. due to ME. *plat*, F. *plat*, flat ; for which see **Plate.**

PLAT (2), to plait. (F.–L.) In Shak. Romeo, i. 4. 89. The same as **Plait**, q.v.

PLATANE, a plane-tree ; see **Plane** (3).

PLATE, a thin piece of metal, flat dish. (F.–L.) ME. *plate*, Chaucer, C. T. 2123 (A 2121).–OF. and F. *plate*, in use in the 12th century ; see Littré. Hamilton, s.v. *plat* (flat), gives ' *Vaisselle plate*, hammered plate ; particularly, plate, silver plate.' *Plate* is merely the fem. of F. *plat*, flat. Cf. Late L. *plata*, a lamina, plate of metal ; Ducange ; and esp. Span. *plata*, plate, silver (whence *La Plata*). But the Span. word was derived from the French ; Littré.–Late L. *platta*, a lamina, ' plate of metal ;' fem. of Folk-L. *plattus, flat ; whence Du. and Dan. *plat*, G. and Swed. *platt*, are borrowed. Allied to Gk. πλατ-ύς, broad ; see **Place.** Der. plate, vb., Rich. II, i. 3. 28 ; *plate-glass, plat-ing.* And see *platt-er, plat-eau, plat-form, plat-ina, plat-it-ude.*

PLATEAU, a flat space, tableland. (F.–L.) 'A rising ground or flattish hill ... called a *plateau* ;' Annual Register (1807), p. 11, col. 2.–F. *plateau* ; Cotgrave gives the pl. *plateaux*, ' flat and thin stones.' The mod. F. *plateau* also means 'tableland ;' Hamilton. OF. *platel*, a small plate, used in the 12th century ; Littré. Dimin. of *plat*, a platter, dish, which is a sb. made from the adj. *plat*, flat. See **Plate.** Doublet, *platter*, q.v.

PLATFORM, a flat surface, level scaffolding. (F.–L.) In Shak. meaning (1) a terrace, Hamlet, i. 2. 213 ; (2) a scheme, plan, 1 Hen. VI, ii. 1. 77.–F. *plateforme*, ' a platform, modell ;' Cot.– F. *plate*, fem. of *plat*, flat ; and *forme*, form ; so that the sense is ' ground-plan.' See **Plate** and **Form.**

PLATINA, a heavy metal. (Span.–F.–L.) Added by Todd to Johnson's Dict.–Span. *platina*, so called from its silvery appearance.–Span. *plata*, silver. See **Plate.** Now called *platinum*.

PLATITUDE, a trite or dull remark. (F.–L.) Modern. Not in Todd's Johnson.–F. *platitude*, flatness, insipidity (Hamilton). A modern word, coined (on the model of *latitude*) from F. *plat*, flat. See **Plate.**

PLATOON, a group of men, sub-division of a company of soldiers. (F.–L.) ' *Platoon*, a small square body of 40 or 50 men,' &c. ; Bailey's Dict., vol. ii. ed. 1731. Adapted from F. *peloton*, ' pronounced *plo-tong*, a ball, tennis-ball, group, knot, platoon ;' Hamilton. Formed, with suffix *-on*, from MF. *pelote*, a ball ; whence also E. *pellet*. See **Pellet.**

PLATTER, a flat plate or dish. (F.–L.) ME. *plater* (with one *t*), Wyclif, Matt. xxiii. 25. AF. *plater* ; N. Bozon, p. 33. A parallel formation to OF. *platel*, a plate (Burguy), which is the origin of mod. F. *plateau*, still used in the sense of ' waiter, tray, tea-board ;' Hamilton. See **Plateau.**

PLAUDIT, applause. (L.) The form *plaudit* is due to mis-reading the L. *plaudite* as if it were an E. word, in which the final *e* would naturally be considered as silent. Sometimes the pronunciation in three syllables was kept up, with the singular result that the suffix *-itè* was then occasionally mistaken for the ordinary E. suffix *-ity*. Hence we find 3 forms ; (1) the correct Latin form, considered as trisyllabic. ' After the *plaudite* stryke up Our plausible assente ;' Drant, tr. of Horace, Art of Poetry, Av. (2) The form in *-ity.* ' And give this virgin crystal *plaudities* ;' Cyril Tourneur, The Revenger's Tragedy, Act ii. sc. 1 (R.). (3) The clipped E. form. ' Not only the last *plaudit* to expect ;' Denham, Of Old Age, pt. iv. l. 44.–L. *plaudite*, clap your hands ; a cry addressed by the actors to the spectators, requesting them to express their satisfaction. It is the imperative pl. of *plaudere*, to applaud, also spelt *plōdere* ; see **Plausible.** Der. *plaudit-or-y*, an ill-coined word, neither French nor Latin.

PLAUSIBLE, deserving applause, specious. (L.) In Shak. it means ' contented, willing ;' Meas. iii. i. 253. Englished from L. *plausibilis*, praiseworthy. Formed, with suffix *-bilis*, from *plausi-*, for *plausus*, pp. of *plaudere*, to strike, beat, clap hands, applaud. Der. *plausibl-y, plausibili-ty, plausible-ness.* And see *plaudit*, *ap-plaud*, *ex-plode*.

PLAY, a game, sport, diversion. (E.) ME. *play*, Chaucer, C. T. 8906 (E 1330). AS. *plega*, a game, sport, Grein, ii. 361. β. We may note how frequently the AS. *plega* was used in the sense of fight, skirmish, battle. Thus *æsc-plega*, ash-play, is the play of spears, i. e. fighting with spears ; *sweord-plega*, sword-play, fighting with swords. Even in the Bible, 2 Sam. ii. 14, *to play* really means to fight ; but this is due to the use of *ludere* in the L. version ; Wyclif uses the same word. To play on an instrument is to strike upon it. Cf. ' *tympanan plegiendra* ' = of them that strike the timbrels ;

AS. version of Ps. lxvii. 27, ed. Spelman. And again, ' *plegaδ mid handum* ' = clap hands ; Ps. xlvi. 1. Thus the orig. sense of *plega* is a stroke, blow, and *plegian* is to strike, to clap hands. Perhaps of imitative origin. ¶ E. Müller connects AS. *plega* with G. *pflege*, care ; the form answers, and the verb may have meant ' to be busy with.' See note in N. E. D. ; and see **Plight.** Der. *play*, verb, ME. *pleyen*, Chaucer, C. T. 3333, AS. *plegian* (above). Also *play-bill, -book, -fellow, -house* (AS. *pleg-hūs*, in Mone, Quellen, p. 366), *-mate, -thing* ; *play-er, play-ing, play-ing-card* ; *play-ful*, ME. *pleiful*, Old Eng. Homilies, ed. Morris, i. 205, l. 20 ; *play-ful-ly, -ness.*

PLEA, an excuse, apology. (F.–L.) ME. *plee*, Chaucer, Parl. of Foules, 485 ; *ple*, Rob. of Glouc. p. 471, l. 9679 ; *play*, Eng. Gilds, ed. Toulmin Smith, p. 350, l. 13.–AF. *plee*, N. Bozon, p. 157 ; OF. *ple, plai*, occasional forms of OF. *plait, plaid*, a plea. Littré cites the pl. forms *plez, plais, plaiz* (12th century) from Ducange, s. v. *Placitum*. Cotgrave gives *plaid*, ' sute, controversie, . . also a plea, or a pleading, also, a court of pleading.'–Late L. *placitum*, a judgement, decision, decree, sentence ; also a public assembly, conference, or council, so called because of the decisions therein determined on ; L. *placitum*, an opinion. [The order of ideas is : that which is pleasing to all, an opinion, decision, conference for obtaining decisions, public court, law-court, proceedings or sentence in a law-court, and finally pleading, plea. The word has run a long career, with other meanings beside those here cited ; see Ducange.]–L. *placitum*, neut. of *placitus*, pp. of *placēre*, to please ; see **Please.** Der. *plead*.

PLEACH, PLASH, to intertwine boughs in a hedge, to strengthen a hedge by enweaving boughs or twigs. (F.–L.) ' The hedge to *plash* ;' Hood, The Lay of the Labourer, st. 5. ' The *pleached* bower ;' Much Ado, iii. 1. 7. ME. *plechen*, used in the sense ' to propagate a vine ;' Palladius on Husbandrye, ed. Lodge, b. iii. l. 330.–OF. *plescier, plessier*, later, *plesser*, ' to plash, to bow, fold, or plait young branches one within another, also, to thicken a hedge or cover a walk by plashing ;' Cot. Norm. dial. *plesser* (Moisy). Formed from a Late L. type *plectiāre, later *plessāre*, to pleach ; from Late L. *plectia, later *plessa*, a thicket of interwoven boughs, occurring A.D. 1215 (Ducange). We also find *plesseium*, a pleached hedge ; and numerous similar forms. β. All from L. *plectere*, to weave. *Plec-t-ere* is extended from the base PLEK, to weave, appearing in Gk. πλέκ-ειν, to weave, and in L. *plic-āre*, to fold. See **Ply, Plait.** The form *pleach* answers to an OF. dial. form *plechier*.

PLEAD, to urge an excuse or plea. (F.–L.) ME. *pleden*. ' *Pledoures* shulde peynen hem to *plede* for such ' = pleaders should take pains to plead for such ; P. Plowman, B. vii. 42. [We also find the form *pleten*, id. vii. 39.] Also *plaiden*, Owl and Nightingale, 184.–OF. *plaider*, ' to plead, argue, or open a case before a judge, also, to sue, contende, goe to law ;' Cot.–OF. *plaid*, a plea ; see **Plea.** ¶ The form *pleten* is due to OF. *plet*, an occasional form of *plaid* which preserves the *t* of L. *placitum*. Der. *plead-er* = ME. *pledour*, as above, from F. *plaideur*, ' a lawyer, arguer, pleader,' Cot. Also *plead-ing, plead-ing-ly.*

PLEASE, to delight, satisfy. (F.–L.) ME. *plesen*, P. Plowman, B. xiv. 220 ; Chaucer, C. T. 11019 (F 707).–OF. *plesir, plaisir*, mod. F. *plaire*, to please.–L. *placēre*, to please. Allied to *plācāre*, to appease. Der. *pleas-er, pleas-ing, pleas-ing-ly.* Also *pleas-ant*, ME. *plesaunt*, Wyclif, Heb. x. 8, from OF. *plesant*, pres. part. of *plesir*, to please. Hence *pleas-ant-ly, -ness* ; also *pleasant-r-y*, Walpole, Anecdotes of Painting, vol. i. c. 3 (R.), from F. *plaisanterie*, ' jeasting, merriment,' Cot. And see *pleas-ure, plac-able, plac-id, com-pla-cent, dis-please, plea, plead.*

PLEASURE, agreeable emotion, gratification. (F.–L.) Formerly *plesure*, as in The Nut-brown Maid (about A.D. 1500), l. 93 ; see Spec. of Eng. ed. Skeat, p. 102. Also *pleasure*, Skelton, Phyllyp Sparowe, 1004 ; id. p. 147. Formed, by the curious change of *-ir* into *-ure*, from ME. *plesir* (spelt *plesyr*), Flower and Leaf, l. 113 ; *playsir*, Caxton, Hist. Troye, leaf 331.–F. *plaisir*, pleasure ; the same change occurs in *leis-ure*, whilst in *treas-ure* the suffix takes the place of *-or*. The object seems to have been to give the word an apparent substantival ending. β. Again, the F. *plaisir* is merely a substantival use of the OF. infin. *plaisir*, to please ; just as F. *loisir* (leisure) is properly an infinitive also. See **Please.** Der. *pleasure*, verb, in Tottell's Miscellany, ed. Arber, p. 128, l. 16 of Poem on the Death of Master Deuerox ; also *pleasure-boat, pleasure-ground* ; *pleasur-able*, a coined word ; *pleasur-abl-y, pleasure-able-ness.*

PLEAT, the same word as **Plait,** q.v.

PLEBEIAN, pertaining to the common people, vulgar. (F.–L.) In Shak. Cor. i. 9. 7 ; ii. 1. 10 ; &c.–OF. *plebeien*, mod. F. *plébéien*, omitted by Cotgrave, but in use in the 14th century ; Littré. Formed with suffix *-en* (<L. *-ānus*) from L. *plēbēius*, plebeian.–L. *plēbē-*, old stem of *plēbēs*, more usually *plebs* (stem *plēbi-*), the people. β. *Ple-bs*

orig. meant 'a crowd, a multitude,' and is connected with *plē-rique*, very many, *plē-nus*, full; Gk. πλῆθος, a multitude, πληρής. full. See **Plenary.** Der. *plebeian*, sb.

PLECTRUM, a small instrument for plucking the strings of a lyre or harp. (L.–Gk.) L. *plectrum.*–Gk. πλῆκτρον, an instrument to strike with.–Gk. πλήσσειν (for *πλήγ-yειν), to strike; cf. pt. t. πέ-πληγ-α. Allied to πληγ-ή, a stroke, L. *plāga*; see **Plague.**

PLEDGE, a security, surety. (F.–OLowG.) ME. *plegge* a hostage, Trevisa, iii. 129, l. 6, and 321, l. 8; Eng. Gilds, ed. Toulmin Smith, p. 382, l. 26; also a security, Prompt. Parv.–OF. *plege*, 'a pledge, a surety,' Cot.; mod. F. *pleige.* Connected with OF. *plevir* (Burguy), later *pleuvir*, 'to warrant, assure,' Cot.; see **Replevy.** β. Of uncertain etymology; but Kluge proposes to derive it from OSax. *plegan*, to attend to, to promise, to pledge oneself; cf. OHG. *pflegan*, to answer for (G. *pflegen*); also AS. *plēon*, to risk; *pleoh*, risk (Franck). See **Plight** (1). Der. *pledge*, verb, 3 Hen. VI, iii. 3. 250; *pledg-er.*

PLEIAD, one of the group of stars in the constellation Taurus, called the Pleiades. (L.–Gk.) 'The sweet influences of Pleiades;' Job xxxviii. 31.–L. *Plēiades*, pl.–Gk. Πλειάδες, a group of seven stars in the constellation Taurus; Ionic Πληϊάδες. (Not, as fabled, allied to πλέειν, to sail.)

PLEIOCENE, more recent; **PLEISTOCENE**, most recent. (Gk.) Terms in geology referring to strata. Coined from Gk. πλείω-ν, more, πλεῖστο-ς, most; and καινός, recent, new. β. Gk. πλείων, πλεῖστος are comp. and superl. forms from πολύς, much, allied to πλέ-ως, full; see **Plenary.** The adj. καινός is allied to Skt. *kanyā*, a maiden; Brugmann, i. § 647.

PLENARY, full, complete. (Late L.–L.) Spelt *plenarie* in Minsheu, ed. 1627. Englished from Late L. *plēnārius*, entire, occurring in St. Augustine (N. E. D.); which is extended, with suffix *-ārius*, from L. *plēnus*, full. β. L. *plē-nus* is connected with Gk. πλέ-ως, full, πίμ-πλη-μι, I fill; from the base *plē, to fill. √PEL; cf. E. **Full**, q.v. Der. *pleni-potent-i-ar-y*, q.v., *pleni-tude*, q.v., *plent-y*, q.v. From the same root are *com-plete, com-ple-ment, de-plet-ion, ex-plet-ive, im-ple-ment, re-plete, re-plen-ish, sup-ple-ment, sup-ply, ac-com-plish, pleb-eian, plu-ral*, &c. Also (of Gk. origin) *ple-o-nasm, ple-thora, plei-o-cene, police.* Also *full*, q.v.

PLENIPOTENTIARY, having full powers. (L.) Sometimes used as a sb., but properly an adj., as in 'the *plenipotentiary* ministers' in Howell, Famil. Letters, bk. ii. let. 44. Dec. 1, 1643. Coined from L. *plēni-*, for *plēnus*, full; and *potenti-*, decl. stem of *potens*, powerful; with suffix *-ārius.* See **Plenary** and **Potent.** ¶ Milton has *plenipotent*, P. L. x. 404.

PLENITUDE, fulness, abundance. (F.–L.) In Shak. Complaint, 302.–OF. *plenitude*, 'plenitude;' Cot.–L. *plēnitūdo*, fulness. –L. *plēni-*, for *plenus*, full; with suffix *-tūdo.* See **Plenary, Plenty.**

PLENTY, abundance. (F.–L.) In early use. ME. *plentè, plentee*, Ancren Riwle, p. 194, l. 6.–OF. *plente, plentet*, later *plenté*, 'plenty;' Cot.–L. *plēnitātem*, acc. of *plēnitās*, fulness.–L. *plēni-*, for *plēnus*, full; with suffix *-tās.* See **Plenary, Plenitude.** Der. *plente-ous*, ME. *plenteus*, Rob. of Glouc. p. 23, l. 531, frequently spelt *plentiuous* (= *plentivous*), Wyclif, Matt. v. 12, 1 Thess. iii. 12, from OF. *plentivos*; this form appears to be made with suffix *-os* (= L. *-ōsus*) from OF. *plentif*, answering to a L. form *plēnitīuus.* Hence *plenteous-ly, -ness.* Also *plentiful*, Hamlet, ii. 2. 202; *plenti-ful-ly*, *-ness.*

PLEONASM, redundancy of language. (L.–Gk.) Spelt *pleonasme* in Minsheu, ed. 1627.–L. *pleonasmus* (Lewis).–Gk. πλεονασμός, abundance, pleonasm.–Gk. πλεονάζειν, to abound, lit. to be more.–Gk. πλέον, neut. of πλέων, πλείων, more. See **Pleiocene.** Der. *pleonast-ic*, from Gk. *πλεοναστικός*, redundant; *pleonast-ic-al-ly.*

PLESIOSAURUS, an extinct genus of Reptilia. (Gk.) The name signifies 'like a lizard.'–Gk. πλησίο-ς, near, allied to πέλας, near; and σαῦρος, a lizard.

PLETHORA, excessive fulness, esp. of blood. (L.–Gk.) 'Fulnesse, in greke *plethora*, in latyne *plenitudo*;' Sir T. Elyot, Castel of Helth, b. iii. c. 1. The o is long. A Latinized spelling of Gk. πληθώρη, fulness.–Gk. πληθ-ος, a throng, crowd; with the suffix *-ω-ρη.* β. Gk. πλῆ-θος (like πλή-ρης, full) is from the base πλη, seen in πίμ-πλη-μι, I fill; see **Plenary.** Der. *plethor-ic.*

PLEURISY, inflammation of the *pleura*, or membrane which covers the lungs. (F.–L.–Gk.) [Quite different from *plurisy*, q.v.] Spelt *pleurisie* in Baret, ed. 1580, and in Cotgrave.–MF. *pleuresie*, 'a pleurisie;' Cot.–L. *pleurisis*, another form of *pleurītis.*–Gk. πλευρῖτις, pleurisy.–Gk. πλευρά, a rib, the side, the 'pleura.' Der. *pleurit-ic*, from Gk. πλευριτικός, suffering from pleurisy; *pleurit-ic-al.* Also *pleuro-pneumon-ia*, inflammation of the *pleura* and lungs, from Gk. πνεύμων, a lung; see **Pneumatic.**

PLIABLE, PLIANT, PLIERS; see under **Ply.**

PLIGHT (1), an engagement, promise; usually as a verb, to pledge. (E.) ME. *pliht, pligt* (1) danger, Layamon, 3897; (2) engagement, Story of Genesis and Exodus, ed. Morris, 1269. AS. *pliht*, risk, danger, used to translate L. *periculum* in Ælfric's Colloquy, in the Merchant's second speech; whence the verb *plihtan*, to endanger (and later, to promise under peril of forfeiture); see Toller. β. The sb. *pliht* is formed with the substantival suffix *-t* (Idg. *-to-*) from the strong verb *plēon* (< *pleh-an*), to risk, imperil, in Ælfred's tr. of Gregory's Pastoral Care, ed. Sweet, p. 229, l. 20; the pt. t. *pleah* occurs in the same, p. 37, l. 7.+OFries. *plicht*, peril, risk, care; we also find the OFries. *ple, pli*, danger, answering to AS. *plioh*, danger, in Ælfred, tr. of Gregory, p. 393, l. 9; MDu. *plicht*, 'duty, debt, obligation, administration, office, custom, or use;' Hexham; cf. *plegen*, 'to be accustomed, to experiment, or trie' [i.e. to risk]; id.; G. *pflicht*, duty, obligation, faith, allegiance, oath; from the OHG. strong verb *plegan*, to promise or engage to do. ¶ The base is *pleh*, whence *pleh-t>plih-t*; perhaps the same base occurs in *pleg-an*, to play. Der. *plight*, verb, ME. *plizten, plihten*, P. Plowman, B. vi. 35, AS. *plihtan*, weak verb, to imperil, Laws of King Cnut (Secular), § 67, in Thorpe's Ancient Laws, i. 410; *plight-er*, Antony, iii. 13. 126.

PLIGHT (2), to fold; as sb., a fold; also, a state, a condition. (F.–L.) Shak. has '*plighted* cunning,' K. Lear, i. 1. 283; where the quarto editions have *pleated.* Spenser has 'with many a folded *plight*;' F. Q. ii. 3. 26; also *plight* (= *plighted*) as a pp. meaning 'folded' or 'plaited,' F. Q. ii. 6. 7, vi. 7. 43. Palsgrave has: 'I *plyght* or folde; I *plyght* a gowne, I set the *plyghtes* in ordre.' β. The word is really misspelt, by confusion with *plight* (1), and should be *plite*, without *gh.* Chaucer has the verb *pliten*, to fold, Troilus, ii. 697, 1204. It is clearly a mere variant of *plait* or *pleat*, due to the *feminine* form of the L. pp.; whereas *plait* is from the masculine. See **Plait.** γ. ME. *plyte*, state, condition, is the same word; 'To bringe our craft al in another *plyte*;' Chaucer, C. T., G 952. Palsgrave has: '*Plyte* or state.'–AF. *plyte*, state, condition; given by Godefroy as a doubtful word in Littleton, Instit. 306; but it is merely the fem. of OF. *ploit*, a fold, plait, also 'manière d'être, situation;' Godefroy. See Littleton's Tenures, ed. 1612, foll. 69 and 83 back; and see Roquefort, who explains *plyte, pliste*, as 'condition, state.'–Folk-L. type *plecta*, for *plicita*, by-form of *plicāta*, pp. of *plicāre*, to fold. Cf. F. *lit* < L. *lectum.* ¶ 'Plite of lawne, &c., seemeth to be a certaine measure, or quantitie thereof. Anno 3 Edw. IV, cap. 5;' Minsheu.

PLINTH, the lowest part of the base of a column. (L.–Gk.) 'Plinthe, the neather part of a pillars foot, of the forme of a four-square bricke or tile;' Minsheu, ed. 1627. Cotgrave gives F. *plinthe*, 'a plinth,' &c.–L. *plinthus.*–Gk. πλίνθος, a brick or tile, a brick-shaped body, a plinth. Cognate with E. **Flint**, q.v.

PLIOCENE; see Pleiocene.

PLOD, to trudge on laboriously, labour unintermittingly. (E.) In Shak. Sonnet 50, Merry Wives, i. 3. 91, All's Well, iii. 4. 6. 'The primitive sense of *plod* is to tramp through the wet and, thence, figuratively, to proceed painfully and laboriously;' Wedgwood. It particularly means to wade through pools; the E. D. D. gives *plodder*, mud; also, to walk through mud; *pload, plowd*, to walk through mire and water. The ME. sb. *plod* (dat. *plodde*) meant a filthy pool or puddle; 'In a foul *plodde* in the strete suththe me hym slong' = people then threwe him into a foul puddle in the street; Rob. of Glouc. p. 536, l. 11077. So also Northern *plud*, a puddle; E. D. D.; cf. Irish *plod, plodan*, a pool, standing water, *plodach*, a puddle; Gael. *plod*, a pool, standing water, *plodan*, a small pool; the Irish and Gael. forms being from ME. *plod* (Macbain). Cf. also EFries. *pludern*, to splash about in water; Dan. dial. *pludder*, Dan. *pladder*, mud; Low G. *pladdern*, to splash about in water (cf. *plad*, to wade, in Nares). Of imitative origin; see **Plash** (1). Der. *plodd-er, plodd-ing, plodd-ing-ly.*

PLOT (1), a conspiracy, stratagem. (F.–L.) An early instance of the word seems to be in Spenser, F. Q. vii. 6. 23 (about A.D. 1590); he also has *plot* as a verb, id. iii. 11. 20. Perhaps shortened from *complot*, used in exactly the same sense, both as a sb. and verb. The sb. *complot* is in Shak. Rich. III, iii. 1. 192; and the pp. *com-plótted* in Rich. II, i. 1. 96. We have numerous examples of the loss of an initial syllable, as in *fence* for defence, *sport* for disport, *story* for history. Shak. has both *plot* and *complot*, and both words are employed by him both as sb. and verb. Minsheu, ed. 1627, gives *complot*, but does not recognise *plot*, except as a ground-plan.–F. *complot*, 'a complot, conspiracy;' whence *comploter*, 'to complot, conspire,' Cot. The OF. *complot* means (1) crowd, in the 12th century, (2) a battle, (3) a plot; and is of disputed origin. β. Complot and *plot* are nearly of the same date, and were sometimes associated. Shak. has: 'To *plot*, contrive, or *cómplot* any ill;' Rich. II, i. 3. 189. Chapman has: 'All *plots* and *cómplots* of his villany;' Alphonsus,

v. 4. **γ.** But it is not unlikely that *plot* was sometimes an abbreviation of *plotform*, a variant of *platform*, i. e. a plan, orig. a map or sketch of a place; it occurs in Gascoigne's Art of Venerie, l. 40 (1575). It is certain that *plat* was used as an abbreviation of *platform*, a map; as in Higgins, Mirror for Mag., ed. 1815, i. 315 (1574). Cf. 'I am devising a *platform* in my head;' Lyly, Campaspe, Act v. Sc. 4. 'The *platt* and fabrick of our purpose;' Letters of Eminent Men, ed. Sir H. Ellis (Camden Soc.), p. 155. 'The Captain did *plat out* and describe the situation of all the ilands;' Hakluyt, Voy. iii. 98 (we now say *plot out*). See **Platform**; and see Notes on E. Etym., p. 219. **Der.** *plot*, verb; *plott-er*.

PLOT (2), **PLAT**, a small piece of ground. (E.) A *plot* is a patch of ground; and it also meant, in ME., a spot on a garment. 'Many foule *plottes*' = many dirty spots (on a garment); P. Plowman, B. xiii. 318. [In the Prompt. Parv. p. 405, we are told that *plot* means the same as *plek*; and we also find '*Plecke*, or *plotte*, portiuncula.' Way's note adds that '*Pleck* is given by Cole, Ray, and Grose as a North-Country word, signifying a place, and is likewise noticed by Tim Bobbin;' and he correctly refers it to AS. *plæc*, Matt. vi. 5 (Northumb. version).] The expression '*plot* of floures faire' occurs in the Flower and the Leaf, l. 499 (15th century). AS. *plot*, a patch of ground; A. S. Leechdoms, ed. Cockayne, iii. 286, l. 19 (the same passage is in Schmid, Die Gesetze der Angelsachsen, App. XI, l. 5; p. 408, ed. 1858). Cf. Goth. *plats*, a patch, Mark ii. 21; MDu. *plets*, 'a peece or a patch of cloth;' Hexham; Dan. *plet*, a spot, plot; *græs-plet*, a grass-plot. We also find AS. *splott*, a plot of land (Toller). ¶ For the spelling *plat*, see **Plat** (1).

PLOUGH, an instrument for turning up the soil. (E.) ME. *plouh*, *plou*, *plow*; Chaucer, C. T. 889 (A 887); Havelok, 1017. The traces of it in AS. are but slight; we find *plóh* = a plough-land, in A. S. Leechdoms, ed. Cockayne, iii. 286, l. 19, where is the phrase 'ne plot ne *plóh*' = neither plot of ground nor plough-land. EFries. *plóg*.+Icel. *plógr*, a plough (the usual Norse word being *arðr*); Swed. *plog*; Dan. *plov*. We find also OFries. *ploch*, G. *pflug*, OHG. *pfluoc*. The Lithuan *plugas*, Russ. *pluge*, a plough, are borrowed words from the Teutonic. **Der.** *plough*, verb, Cor. iii. 1. 71; *plough-er*, see Latimer's Sermon on the Ploughers; *plough-able*; *plough-boy*; *plough-iron*, 2 Hen. IV, v. 1. 20; *plough-man*, ME. *plow-man*, Chaucer, C. T., 531 (A 529); *plough-share*, spelt *plowh-schare* in Trevisa, ii. 353, and derived from the verb to *shear*.

PLOVER, the name of a wading bird. (F. – L.) ME. *plouer* (with *u* for *v*), P. Plowman's Crede, ed. Skeat, 764; Gower, C. A. iii. 33; bk. vi. 943; Prompt. Parv. – OF. *plovier*, in the 13th century (Littré), later *pluvier*, 'a plover;' Cot. Formed as if from a Late L. type *pluvārius*, equivalent to L. *pluuiālis*, belonging to rain, because these birds were said to be most seen and caught in a rainy season. – L. *pluuia*, rain. – L. *pluit*, it rains. See **Pluvial**. ¶ 'We derive it from the F. *pluvier*, pour ce qu'on le prend mieux en temps pluvieux qu'en nulle autre saison;' Belon, Oyseaux, 260; cited in Pennant, Zoology, vol. ii (R.). Perhaps it was only a fancy. Wedgwood remarks that the G. name is *regenpfeifer*, the rain-piper.

PLUCK, to pull away sharply, to snatch. (E.) ME. *plukken*, P. Plowman, B. v. 591; xii. 249; Wyclif, Matt. xii. 1. AS. *pluccian*, Matt. xii. 1.+Du. *plukken*; Icel. *plokka*, *plukka*, perhaps a borrowed word; Dan. *plukke*; Swed. *plocka*; G. *pflücken*. **β.** Some think the word to be not orig. Teutonic, but borrowed from Late L. **piluccāre* (whence Ital. *piluccare*, to pluck out hair), from L. *pilus*, a hair; see **Pile** (3). This is doubtful. **Der.** *pluck*, sb., a butcher's term for the heart, liver, and lights of an animal, prob. because they are plucked out after killing it; Skinner, ed. 1671, has '*pluck*, a sheep's *pluck*, i. e. cor animalis,' an animal's heart. Hence *pluck* in the sense of 'spirit, courage;' whence the adj. *plucky*. Cf. the phrase '*pluck up* thy spirits,' Tam. Shrew, iv. 3. 38; '*pluck up*, my heart,' Much Ado, v. 1. 207.

PLUG, a block or peg used to stop a hole. (Du.) Skinner, ed. 1671, has 'a *plug*, or *splug*;' but that the initial *s* is a true part of the word may be doubted. The word is also in Hexham, ed. 1658, and was probably borrowed from Dutch. – MDu. *plugge*, 'a plugge, or a woodden pegg;' also *pluggen*, 'to plugge, or pegge;' Hexham. Mod.Du. *plug*, a peg, bung. We find also Swed. *plugg*, a plug; G. *pflock*, a wooden nail, plug, peg, pin; Low G. *plugge*, *plagge*, a peg (Lübben). **Der.** *plug*, verb.

PLUM, the name of a fruit. (L. – Gk.) ME. *ploume*, *plowme*, Prompt. Parv. '*Piries* and *plomtrees*' = pear-trees and plum-trees, P. Plowman, B. v. 16. AS. *plúme*, Ælfric's Grammar, ed. Zupitza, p. 20; cf. *plúm-slá*, lit. plum-sloe, *plúm-treow*, plum-tree, in Ælfric's Gloss., Nomina Arborum. Here *plúm-slá* translates L. *prúniculus*, and *plúm-treow* translates *prúnus*. **β.** The AS. *plúme* is a mere variation of L. *prúna*, pl. of *prúnum*, a plum, with change of *r* to *l*, and of *n* to *m*. The change from *r* to *l* is very common, and hardly needs illustration; the Span. *coronel* = E. colonel; cf. Westphal. *plúme*, *prúme*, a plum; and

L. *plúmum* in the Corpus Glossary, l. 1600. The change from *n* to *m* is not infrequent, as in *lime-tree* for *line-tree*, venom for L. *uenēnum*, vellum from F. *velin*, megrim from F. *migraine*. Thus *plum* is a doublet of *prune*; see **Prune**, which is of Gk. origin. The Swed. *plommon*, Dan. *blomme*, G. *pflaume*, are all alike due to *prúnum*. **Der.** *plum-tree*, as above; *plum-cake*, *plum-pudding*. Doublet, *prune* (2).

PLUMAGE, the whole feathers of a bird. (F. – L.) 'Pruning his *plumage*, cleansing every quill;' Drayton, Noah's Flood (the dove); *plumage*, Book of St. Alban's, fol. a 7, back. – F. *plumage*, 'feathers;' Cot. – F. *plume*, a feather; see **Plume**.

PLUMB, a mass of lead hung on a string to show a perpendicular direction. (F. – L.) '*Plumbe* of leed [lead], *Plumbum*;' Prompt. Parv. The older spelling is *plomb*, shortened to *plom* in the comp. *plomrewle*, a plumb-rule, Chaucer, On the Astrolabe, ed. Skeat, pt. ii. § 38, l. 6. – F. *plomb*, 'lead, also, a carpenter's plummet or plomb-line;' Cot. – L. *plumbum*, lead. **β.** Probably cognate with Gk. μόλιβος, μόλυβδος, lead. **Der.** *plumb*, verb, to sound the depth of water with a plumb-line, from F. *plomber*, 'to sound,' Cot.; *plumb-line*, *plumb-rule*, used by Cot. to translate F. *plombet*; *plumb-er*, also spelt *plummer*, as by Cot. to translate F. *plombier*; *plumb-er-y*, i. e. plumber's shop, Bp. Hall, Satires, Bk. v. sat. 1, l. 5 from end. Also *plumb-e-an*, *plumb-e-ous*, leaden, both formed from L. *plumbeus*, leaden. Also *plumb-ago*, q. v.; *plumm-et*, q. v.; *plump* (2), plunge.

PLUMBAGO, black-lead. (L.) A mineral resembling lead, but really different from it. In Ash's Dict., ed. 1777, but only as a botanical term, 'lead-wort.' – L. *plumbāgo*, a kind of leaden ore; black-lead. – L. *plumbum*, lead. Cf. *lumb-ago*, from L. *lumbus*.

PLUME, a feather. (F. – L.) In Shak. Cor. iii. 3. 126; the ME. pl. *plumes* occurs in Richard the Redeles, iii. 49. – F. *plume*, 'a feather, plume of feathers;' Cot. – L. *plúma*, a small soft feather, piece of down. **β.** Prob. so called from its floating in the air; from √PLEUGH, to fly; see **Fly** (1). Brugmann, i. § 681 (d). **Der.** *plume*, verb, esp. in pp. *plumed*, K. Lear, iv. 2. 57, Oth. iii. 3. 349; *plum-age*, q. v.; also *plum-ose*, *plum-age*, q. v.

PLUMMET, a leaden weight, a plumb-line. (F. – L.) ME. *plommet*, Wyclif, Deeds [Acts], xxvii. 28. – OF. *plommet* (Godefroy); MF. *plombet*, 'a plummet,' Cot. Dimin. of *plomb*, lead; it thus means 'a small piece of lead.' See **Plumb**.

PLUMP (1), full, round, fleshy. (E.) '*Plump* Jack,' 1 Hen. IV, ii. 4. 527; '*plumpy* Bacchus,' Antony, ii. 7. 121. ME. *plomp*, rude, clownish (as in Dutch), Caxton, tr. of Reynard the Fox, ed. Arber, p. 100, l. 12. The word is in rather early use as a sb., meaning 'a cluster, a clump,' applied either to a compact body of men, or to a clump of trees. 'Presede into the *plumpe*' = he pressed into the throng; Morte Arthure, ed. Brock, 2199. Though it cannot be traced much further back, the word may be E., as the radical verb is preserved in the prov. E. *plim*, to swell, to swell out; used in many dialects; so also prov. E. *plum*, *plump*, to swell; see E. D. D. **β.** Hence *plump* means orig. 'swollen,' and since that which is swollen becomes tight and firm, we find *plump* further used in the sense of 'hard;' as 'the ways are *plump*' = the roads are hard (Kent); E. D. S. Gloss. B. 11; C. 5. In Oxfordshire the word *plim* is also used as an adj., in the sense of *plump*. The word appears in other Teutonic tongues. Cf. EFries. and Low G. *plump*, bulky, thick. + MDu. *plomp*, 'rude, clownish, blockish, or dull;' Hexham. This is a metaphorical use, from the notion of thickness; Swed. *plump*, clownish, coarse; Dan. *plump*, clumsy, vulgar; G. *plump*, heavy, clumsy, blunt. **Der.** *plump-ly*, *plump-ness*. Also *plump-er*, a vote given at elections, when a man who has a vote for two separate candidates gives a single vote to one, thus (in my opinion) *swelling out* that candidate's number of votes as compared with the rest; see Todd's Johnson. Also *plump-y*, as above. Also *plump*, sb., a cluster, as above; *plump* or *plump out*, verb, to swell out.

PLUMP (2), straight downward. (F. – L.) Formerly also *plum*, *plumb*. '*Plumb* down he drops,' Milton, P. L. ii. 933; cf. 'Which thou hast *perpendicularly* fell,' K. Lear, iv. 6. 54. 'They do not fall *plumb* down, but decline a little from the perpendicular;' Bentley, Serm. 2 (Todd). Of French origin; but altered to *plump* by the influence of *plump* (3) below. Really due to *plumb*, and derived from F. *plomb*, L. *plumbum*, lead. 'To fall like lead' must have been a favourite metaphor from the earliest times, and Diez shows, in his article on Ital. *piombare*, to fall like lead, that this metaphor is widely spread in the Romance languages. Cf. Ital. *cadere a piombo*, to fall *plump*, lit. like lead; F. *à plomb*, 'downright;' *à plomb sur*, 'direct, or downright;' Cot. See *plumb* in N. E. D., and **Plumb** (above).

PLUMP (3), vb., to fall heavily down. (E.) 'It will give you a notion how Dulcissa *plumps* into a chair;' Spectator, No. 492. Apparently of imitative origin; cf. prov. E. *plump*, a plunge; also, to plunge heavily, to sink. ME. *plumpen*; '*Plump* hym in water;'

Liber Cure Cocorum, p. 51.+EFries. *plumpen*, to fall heavily, *plempen*, to plunge into water; so also Du. *plompen*, G. *plumpen*, Swed. *plumpa*, to fall heavily. Under the influence of this word, the adv. *tlvmb*, 'straight downward,' became *plump*; see **Plump** (2).

PLUNDER, to rob, pillage. (G.) A note in Johnson's Dict. (ed. Todd) says that 'Fuller considers the word as introduced into the language about 1642.' R. gives a quotation for it from Prynne, Treachery and Disloyalty, pt. iv. pp. 28, 29 (not dated, but after A.D. 1642, as it refers to the civil war). He also cites a quotation dated 1642; but it first occurs in 1632, in the Swedish Intelligencer, ii. 179 (N.E.D.). Hexham, in his Du. Dict., ed. 1658, gives MDu. *plunderen*, *plonderen*, 'to plunder, or to pillage;' the mod. Du. spelling is *plunderen*. It is one of the very few G. words in English, and seems to have been introduced directly rather than through the Dutch.—G. *plündern*, to plunder, pillage, sack, ransack; provincially, to remove with one's baggage. Derived from the G. sb. *plunder*, trumpery, trash, baggage, lumber; the E. keeping the vowel of the sb. β. Connected with Low G. *plunnen*, formerly also *plunden*, rags; Bremen Wörterbuch. The orig. sense of the sb. was 'rags,' hence, worthless household stuff; the verb meant, accordingly, to strip a household even of its least valuable contents. The Dan. *plyndre*, Swed. *plundra*, Du. *plunderen*, are all alike borrowed from the G. or Low G. ¶ See Trench, Eng. Past and Present. He says that '*plunder* was brought back from Germany about the beginning of our Civil Wars, by the soldiers who had served under Gustavus Adolphus and his captains.' And again, 'on *plunder*, there are two instructive passages in Fuller's Church History, b. xi. § 4, 33; and b. ix. § 4; and one in Heylin's Animadversions thereupon, p. 196.' **Der.** *plunder*, sb., which seems to be a later word in E., though really the original word; *plunder-er*.

PLUNGE, to cast or fall suddenly into water or other liquid. (F.—L.) ME. *ploungen*; 'and wenen [imagine] that it be right blisful thing to *ploungen* hem in voluptous delyt;' Chaucer, tr. of Boethius, b. iii, pr. 2, l. 29.—F. *plonger*, 'to plunge, dive, duck;' Cot. Formed from a Late L. type *plumbicāre*, not found, but the existence of which is verified by the Picard *plonquer*, to plunge, dive, due to the same form; see Diez, s.v. *piombare*. β. Thus *plonger* is a frequentative of *plomber*, to cover with lead, to sound the depth of water; from F. *plomb*, lead; see **Plumb**. Cf. Ital. *piombare*, 'to throw, to hurle, ... to fall heauilie as a plummet of leade;' Florio; also Roumantsch *plumbar*, to fall heavily (Carigiet). Cf. AF. *se plunge*, plunges, Bestiary, 832. See also **Plump** (2). **Der.** *plunge*, sb., *plung-er*, *plung-ing*.

PLUPERFECT, the name of a tense in grammar. (L.) In the Grammar prefixed to Cotgrave's F. Dict. will be found the expression 'the præterpluperfect tense;' he gives '*J'avoies esté*, I had been,' as an example. The E. word is a curious corruption of the L. name for the tense, viz. *plusquamperfectum*. We have dropped the syllable *quam*, and given to *plus* the F. pronunciation.—L. *plūs*, more; *quam*, than; and *perfectum*, perfect. See **Plural** and **Perfect**.

PLURAL, containing or expressing more than one. (F.—L.) A term in grammar. In Shak. Merry Wives, iv. 1. 59. ME. *plural*; 'þe *plural* nombre;' Trevisa, ii. 171, l. 25; *plurel*, id. ii. 173, l. 11.—OF. *plurel* (12th century, Littré); mod. F. *pluriel*.—L. *plūrālis*, plural; because expressive of 'more' than one.—L. *plūr-*, decl. base of *plūs*, more, anciently spelt *plous*. Connected with Gk. πλέ-ως, full, πλείων, more; see **Plenary**. Brugmann, ii. § 135. **Der.** *plural-ly*, *plural-ist*, *plural-ism*. Also *plural-i-ty*, ME. *pluralite*, P. Plowman, C. iv. 33, from F. *pluralité*, 'plurality, or morenesse,' Cot., which from L. acc. *plūrālitātem*. And see *plurisy*.

PLURISY, superabundance. (L.; *misformed*.) Shak. has *plurisy* to express 'plethora,' Hamlet, iv. 7. 118. So also in Massinger, The Picture, iv. 2 (Sophia): 'A *plurisy* of ill blood you must let out.' And in The Two Noble Kinsmen, v. 1. 66; and in Ford, Fancies Chaste and Noble, A. iv. sc. 1; 'Into a *plurisy* of faithless impudence.' Formed as if from L. *plūri-*, decl. stem of *plūs*, more; by an extraordinary (prob. an ignorant) confusion with **Pleurisy**, q.v.

PLUSH, a variety of cloth-like velvet. (F.—L.) 'Waistcoats of silk *plush* laying by;' Chapman, tr. of Homer's Iliad, b. xxiv, l. 576. And in Cotgrave.—F. *peluche*, 'shag, plush;' Cot. [Thus the E. has dropped e; the word should be *pelush*. The form *pluche* occurs in Walloon (Remacle); and Godefroy gives *pluchine* as a variant of the dimin. form *peluchine*.] Cf. Span. *pelusa*, down on fruit, nap on cloth; Ital. *peluzzo*, fine hair, soft down. All from the fem. of a Late L. type *pilūcius*, hairy (not found), from L. *pilus*, hair. See **Peruke**. ¶ The Du. *pluis*, fluff, plush, G. *plüsch*, are mere borrowings from French.

PLUVIAL, rainy. (F.—L.) Little used. 'Pluuiall, rainie;' Minsheu, ed. 1627.—F. *pluvial*, 'rainy;' Cot.—L. *pluuiālis*, rainy.—L. *pluuia*, rain.—L. *plu-it*, it rains.—√PLEU, to float, swim. Cf. Gk. πλέειν, to swim, Brugmann, i. § 381. **Der.** We also find

pluuious, Sir T. Browne, Vulg. Errors, b. v, c. 24, part 4, Englished from L. *pluuius*, rainy. And see *plover*.

PLY, to bend, to work at steadily, urge. (F.—L.) ME. *plien*, to bend, Chaucer, C. T. 9045; to mould, as wax, id. 93 4 (E 1169, 1430). Since moulding wax, &c. requires constant and continued application of the fingers, we might hence obtain the metaphor of toiling at; as in to *ply* a task, to *ply* an oar; but these extensions are really due to the use of *plien* for ME. *atplien*, to apply.—F. *plier*, 'to fold, plait, ply, bend, bow, turne;' Cot.—L. *plicāre*, to fold.+Gk. πλέκειν, to weave; Russ. *pleste*, to plait, wind; G. *flechten*, strong verb, to braid, plait, twist, entwine. All from √PLEK, to weave, plait. From L. *plicāre* we also have *ap-ply*, *im-ply*, *re-ply*; *accom-plice*, *ap-plic-at-ion*, *com-plic-ate*, *com-plex*, *ex-plic-ate*, *ex-plic-it*, *im-plic-ate*, *im-pli-cit*, *in-ex-plic-able*, *per-plex*; also *de-ploy*, *dis-play*, *em-ploy*. Also *sim-ple*, *sim-plic-ity*, *sim-pli-fy*; *dou-ble*, *du-plic-ity*, *du-plic-ate*; *tri-ple*, *tri-plet*, *tre-ble*; *quadru-ple*, *multi-ple*, *multi-ply*, &c. Also *plait*, *pleach*, *pleat*, *plight* (2), *splay*, *sup-ple*, *sup-plic-ate*, *sup-pli-ant*, &c. And see *flax*. See also **Apply**.

PNEUMATIC, relating to air. (L.—Gk.) Bacon speaks of '*pneumaticall* substance in some bodies;' Nat. Hist. § 842.—L. *pneumaticus*.—Gk. πνευματικός, belonging to wind, breath, or air.—Gk. πνευματ-, stem of πνεῦμα, wind, air.—Gk. πνέειν, to blow, breathe; for πνέϝειν (base πνευ-). See **Neesing**. **Der.** *pneumatic-al*, *-al-ly*; *pneumatic-s*. And see *pneumonia*.

PNEUMONIA, inflammation of the lungs. (Gk.) Modern. Todd adds to Johnson only the word '*pneumonicks*, medicines for diseases of the lungs;' but omits *pneumonia*. The o is short.—Gk. πνευμονία, a disease of the lungs.—Gk. πνευμον-, stem of πνεύμων (also πλεύμων), a lung.—Gk. πνέειν, to breathe. See **Pneumatic** and **Pulmonary**. **Der.** *pneumon-ic*.

POACH (1), to dress eggs. (F.—OLow G.) Formerly *poche*. 'Egges well *poched* are better than roasted. They be moste holesome whan they be *poched*;' Sir T. Elyot, Castel of Helth, b. ii, c. 17. Spelt *potch* in Palsgrave; Levins; Bacon, Nat. Hist. § 53; and in Cotgrave.—F. *pocher*; Cotgrave gives '*Poché*, poched, thrust or digged out with the fingers; *oeuf poché*, a potched egge.' Here two verbs have been confused; for the former sense see **Poach** (2). β. Littré unhesitatingly derives *pocher* from F. *poche*, a pouch, pocket; and Scheler explains that 'a poached egg' means 'an egg dressed in such a manner as to keep the yolk in a rounded form,' and that the sense rests upon that of 'pouch.' In this view, it is, in fact, 'a pouched egg.' Hatzfeld explains it still more simply by supposing that the egg is likened to a pouch, because the art is to dress it in such a way as not to let the yolk escape. Cf. 'eyron en *poche*,' i.e. eggs in pouch; Two Cookery Books, ed. T. Austin, p. 24. See **Pouch**.

POACH (2), to intrude on another's preserves, for the purpose of stealing game. (F.—OLow G.) 'His greatest fault is, he hunts too much in the purlieus. Would he would leave off *poaching* !' Beaum. and Fletcher, Philaster, iv. 1 (Thrasiline).—F. *pocher*; '*pocher le labeur d'autruy*, to poch into, or incroach upon, another man's imploiment, practise, or trade;' Cot. β. There is here some difficulty in assigning the right sense to F. *pocher*. Cotgrave gives it only as meaning 'to thrust, or dig at with the fingers;' perhaps from Low G. *poken*, to thrust into; see **Poke** (2). Cf. prov. E. *poach*, to tread into holes. γ. The MF. *pocher* is also spelt *poucher*, as if from *pouce*, the thumb; see Littré. Cf. Picard *pocher*, 'tâter un fruit avec le pouce;' *peucher*, 'presser avec le pouce;' Corblet; perhaps from L. *pollicem*, acc. of *pollex*, the thumb; cf. OF. *pochier*, *poucier*, the thumb, from the L. adj. *pollicāris*. **Der.** *poach-er*.

POCK, a small pustule. (E.) We generally speak of 'the small pox;' but the spelling *pox* is absurd, since it stands for *pocks*, the pl. of *poch*, a word seldom used in the singular. [We might as well write *sox* as the pl. of *sock*; indeed, I have seen that spelling used for abbreviation.] The word *pock* is preserved in the adj. *pocky*, Hamlet, v. 1. 181. The term *small pox* in Beaum. and Fletcher, Fair Maid of the Inn, ii. 2 (Clown), is spelt *pocks* in the old edition, according to Richardson. Cotgrave explains F. *morbille* by 'the small pox,' but in Sherwood's Index it is 'the small pockes;' and in fact, the spelling *pocks* is extremely common. The pl. was once dissyllabic. Fabyan has: 'he was vysyted with the sykenesse of *pockys*;' vol. ii. an. 1463, ed. Ellis, p. 653. ME. *pokke*, pl. *pokkes*, P. Plowman, B. xx. 97. AS. *poc*, *pocc*, a pustule. 'Gif *poc* sȳ on ēagan'=if there be a pustule on the eye; A.S. Leechdoms, ed. Cockayne, iii. 4. The nom. pl. is *poccas*; Voc. 520. 25.+EFries. *pok*, *pokke*; Du. *pok*; G. *pocke*, a pock. Perhaps related to **Poke** (1), with the notion of 'bag.' ¶ Macbain derives Gael. *bucaid*, a pustule, from Brittonic L. *buccātus*, from L. *bucca*, the puffed cheek. If this be so, it is unconnected with E. *pock*. **Der.** *pox* (= *pock*s); *pock-y*.

POCKET, a small pouch. (F.—Teut.) ME. *poket*, Prompt. Parv. 'Cered *pokets* '=small waxed bags; Chaucer, C. T. 16276 (G 808). From North F. (Norm. dial.) *poquette*, variant of *pouquette*, a little bag; also in the form *pouquet*, m.; Moisy. Métivier gives the modern Guernsey form as *pouquette*, dimin. of *pouque*, a sack or pouch. He cites a Norman proverb : 'Quant il pleut le jour Saint Marc, Il ne faut ni *pouque* ni sac '= when it rains on St. Mark's day (April 25), one wants neither poke nor bag. It is therefore a dimin. of O. North F. *poque*, Parisian F. *poche*.—Icel. *poki*, a bag; MDu. *poke*, a bag, Hexham; see **Pouch**, **Poke** (1). **Der.** *pocket*, verb, Temp. ii. 1. 67 ; *pocket-book*, *pocket-money*.

POD, a husk, a covering of the seed of plants. (E.) 'Pod, the husk of any pulse;' Phillips, ed. 1706. Perhaps it merely meant ' bag ;' being related to *pad*, a cushion, i. e. a stuffed bag, and to *pudding*, of which the old meaning was ' sausage,' i. e. stuffed skin. β. The nearest word, in form, is MDu. *puden*, pl. 'huskes, pilles, or shales,' i. e. shells. Cf. also AS. *puduc*, a wen (Toller); Westphal. *puddek*, a lump, a pudding; Low G. *puddig*, thick, E. dial. *poddy*. **Der.** *pod-ware*, plants having pods; R. Scot, Disc. of Witchcraft, b. xii. c. 6. See **Pudding**.

POEM, a composition in verse. (F.—L.—Gk.) In Hamlet, ii. 2. 419.—F. *poëme*, 'a poeme ;' Cot.—L. *poēma*.—Gk. ποίημα, a work, piece of workmanship, composition, poem.—Gk. ποιεῖν, to make; see **Poet**.

POESY, poetry, a poem. (F.—L.—Gk.) ME. *poesie*, Gower, C. A. ii. 36, bk. iv. 1038.—MF. *poësie*, 'poesie ;' Cot.—L. *poēsin*, acc. of *poēsis*, poetry.—Gk. ποίησις, a making, poetic faculty, poem.—Gk. ποιεῖν, to make; see **Poet**. **Der.** Hence ' a posy on a ring,' Hamlet, iii. 2. 162, because such mottoes were commonly in verse; see examples in Chambers, Book of Days, i. 221. *Posy* stands for *poesy*, by contraction. See **Posy**.

POET, a composer in verse. (F.—L.—Gk.) ME. *poete*, Wyclif, Deeds [Acts], xvii. 28 ; Gower, C. A. iii. 374, note ; bk. viii. 2942*.—F. *poëte*, 'a poet, maker ;' Cot.—L. *poēta*.—Gk. ποιητής, a maker, composer, versifier; formed with suffix -της (Idg. -*tā*-) denoting the agent, from ποιεῖν, to make. **Der.** *poet-ic*, Gk. ποιητικός; *poetic-al*, As You Like It, iii. 3. 16 ; *poetic-al-ly* ; *poet-ize*, a coined word. Also *poet-aster*, in Ben Jonson, as the name of a drama. answering to a L. form **poētaster*, formed from *poēt-a* with the double suffix -*as-ter*, with which cf. MF. *poët-astre*, 'an ignorant poet,' Cot. Also *poet-ess*, North's Plutarch, pt. ii. p. 25 (R.), formed with F. suffix -*ess(e)* = L. -*issa* = Gk. -ισσα. Also *poet-r-y*, ME. *poetrye*, Prompt. Parv., from MF. *poëterie*, 'poetry,' Cot. From the same Gk. verb. *onomato-poeia*, *pharmaco-poeia*.

POIGNANT, stinging, sharp, pungent. (F.—L.) ME. *poinant*, Chaucer, C. T. Pers. Tale, Group I, 130 ; now conformed to the F. spelling.—F. *poignant*, 'pricking, stinging,' Cot. ; pres. part. of F. *poindre*, to prick.—L. *pungere* (pt. t. *pu-pug-i*), to prick ; base PEUG. See **Pungent**, **Point**. **Der.** *poignant-ly*, *poignanc-y*. **Doublet**, *pungent*.

POINT, (1) a dot, prick ; (2) a sharp end. (F.—L.) 1. ME. *point*, Ancren Riwle, p. 178, l. 7.—F. *point* (*poinct* in Cotgrave), 'a point, a prick, a centre ;' Cot.—L. *punctum*, a point ; orig. neut. of pp. of *pungere*, to prick, pt. t. *pupugi*. See **Pungent**. 2. ME. *point*, Chaucer, Good Women, 1795.—F. *pointe*, MF. *poincte*, 'the point of a weapon ;' Cot.—L. *puncta*, fem. of pp. of *pungere*. The two forms are confused in E. **Der.** *point*, verb, ME. *pointen*, P. Plowman, C. ix. 298 ; *point-ed*, *point-ed-ly*, *point-ed-ness* ; *point-er*, a dog that points ; *point-ers*, pl., the stars that point to the pole, Greene, Looking-glass for London, ed. Collins, iii. 1. 67; *point-ing*; *point-less*; *point-s-man*, a man who attends to the *points* on a railway. Also *point-device*, L. L. L. v. 1. 21, shortened form of the phrase *at point device* = with great nicety or exactitude, as : ' With limes [limbs] wrought *at poynt-devys* ;' Rom. of the Rose, l. 830 ; a translation of OF. *à point devis*, according to a point [of exactitude] that is devised or imagined, i. e. in the best way imaginable. (The OF. *a point devis* does not appear, but see *a point* in the Supp. to Godefroy.) Also *point-blank*, with a certain aim, so as not to miss the centre, which was a *blank* or *white* spot in the old butts at which archers aimed ; Merry Wives, iii. 2. 34.

POISE, to balance, weigh. (F.—L.) ME. *poisen*, *peisen*, to weigh, P. Plowman, B. v. 217 (and various readings).—OF. *poiser* (Supp. to Godefroy, s. v. *peser*), later *peser*, 'to peise, poise, weigh ;' Cot. [Cf. OF. *pois*, *peis*, a weight ; now spelt *poids*, by confusion with L. *pondus*, from which it is *not* derived.]—L. *pensāre*, to weigh, weigh out.—L. *pensum*, a portion weighed out as a task for spinners, a task ; Late L. *pensum*, *pensa*, a portion, a weight.—L. *pensus*, pp. of *pendere*, to weigh, weigh out ; allied to *pendēre*, to hang ; see

Pendent, **Pensive**. **Der.** *poise*, sb., used in the sense of weight, Sir T. Elyot, Castel of Helth, b. ii. end of c. 33. Also *avoir-du-pois*, q.v. The form *peise* is from AF. *peiser* = OF. *poiser*.

POISON, a deadly draught. (F.—L.) Merely 'a potion ;' the bad sense is unoriginal. In early use ; spelt *poyson*, Rob. of Glouc. p. 122, l. 2605 ; *puisun*, Hali Meidenhad, ed. Cockayne, p. 33, l. 16. —F. *poison*, 'poison ;' Cot.—L. *pōtiōnem*, acc. of *pōtio*, a drink, draught, esp. a poisonous draught.—L. *pōtāre*, to drink ; *pōtus*, drunken. β. *Pōtus* is formed with Idg. suffix -*to*- from *pō*-, a grade of √PŌ, to drink ; cf. Skt. *pā*, to drink ; Gk. πό-σις, drink, πῶ-μα, drink. Brugmann, i. § 172. **Der.** *poison*, verb, ME. *poisonen*, K. Alisaunder, 600 ; *poison-er*, *poison-ous*, *poison-ous-ly*, -*ness*. **Doublet**, *potion*.

POITREL, **PEITREL**, armour for the breast of a horse. (F.—L.) *Poytrell* (Palsgrave) ; also *pewtrel* in Levins. [ME. *peitrel*, Chaucer, C. T. 16032 (G 564).]—OF. *poitral*, MF. *poictral*, *poictrail*, 'a petrel for a horse ;' Cot.—L. *pectorāle*, belonging to the breast ; neut. of *pectorālis*. See **Pectoral**. ¶ The form *peitrel* is from AF. *peitrel*, Gaimar, 6385.

POKE (1), a bag, pouch. (Scand.) 'Two pigges in a *poke* '= two pigs in a bag, Chaucer, C. T. 4276 (A 4278). Havelok, 555. [Cf. Irish *poc*, a bag ; Gael. *poca*, a bag ; from E. or Scand.] Prob. from Icel. *poki*, a bag ; cf. MDu. *poke*, 'a poke, sack,' Hexham. The relationship to AS. *poha*, *pohha*, a bag, is not clear. **Der.** *pock-et*. **Doublet**, *pouch*.

POKE (2), to thrust or push, esp. with something pointed. (E.) ME. *poken*, Chaucer, C. T. 4167 (A 4169) ; *pukken*, P. Plowman, B. v. 620, 643. [Not in AS. ; cf. Irish *poc*, a blow, a kick ; Corn. *poc*, a push, shove ; Gael. *puc*, to'push, justle ; from E.]+Du. *poken* ; E. Fries. *pokern*, frequent., to keep on poking about ; Low G. *poken*, to thrust into ; Pomeran. *pöken* ; G. *pochen*. Cf. MDu. *poke*, a dagger, lit. 'a thruster,' Hexham. Teut. base **puk* ; perhaps imitative. **Der.** *poke*, sb., *pok-er* ; and see *puck-er*.

POLACK, a Pole, an inhabitant of Poland. (Polish.) In Shak. Hamlet, ii. 2. 63.—Pol. *Polak*, a Pole. Cf. Pol. *Polska*, Poland.—Pol. *pole*, Russ. *pole*, a field, plain, flat country ; allied to E. *field*.

POLDAVY, **POLEDAVY**, a coarse cloth or canvas. (Breton). See Nares, s. v. *Polldavy* ; and Halliwell. Named from Bret. *Pouldavid*, a small village near Douarnenez, in Finistere.—Bret. *poul*, pool ; *David*, David.

POLE (1), a stake, long thick rod. (L.) ME. *pole*, P. Plowman, B. xviii. 52. The E. long o presupposes an AS. *ā*, as in *stone* from AS. *stān*, &c. Thus *pole* = AS. *pāl*. We find ' *Palus*, pal ' in Voc. 334. 2 ; where the *a* is long in both words. Merely a borrowed word, from L. *pālus*, a stake. Cf. W. *pawl*, a pole. See **Pale** (1). ¶ Similarly the G. *ffahl*, a stake, is merely borrowed from the Latin. **Doublets**, *pale* (1), *pawl*.

POLE (2), a pivot, either end of the axis of the earth. (F.—L.— Gk.) 'The north *pole* ;' L. L. L. v. 2. 699. ME. *pol*, Chaucer, On the Astrolabe, pt. i. § 14, l. 6.—MF. *pol*, 'a pole ; *pol artique*, the north pole ;' Cot.—L. *polum*, acc. of *polus*, a pole.—Gk. πόλος, a pivot, hinge, axis, pole.—Gk. πέλειν, to be in motion ; the *poles* being the points of the axis round which motion takes place. Allied to Russ. *koleso*, a wheel, (√QEL). Brugmann, i. § 652. **Der.** *pol-ar*, Milton, P. L. v. 269, from L. *polāris* ; hence *polar-i-ty*, *polar-ize*, *polar-iz-at-ion*.

POLE-AXE, a kind of ax. (E. ; *also* L. *and* E.) Spelt *polaxe* in Palsgrave. ME. *pollax*, Chaucer, C. T. 2546 (A 2544) ; Rich. Coer de Lion, 6870. β. *Axe* (more correctly *ax*) is from AS. *æx* ; see **Ax**. γ. The prefix has changed ; orig. *poll-ax*, a weapon for striking one on the *poll* or head. But later altered to *pole-ax*, and in the cognate Westphal. *pål-exe*, it is clearly Westphal. *pål*, a pole ; denoting an ax fastened to a pole. The Low G. *follexe* (as if from *tolle*, the poll, the head) is also spelt *bollexe*, which seems to represent the obs. E. *bole-ax* (N. E. D.), Icel. *bolöxi*, from the *bole* of a tree. See **Poll**.

POLE-CAT, a kind of weasel which emits a disagreeable odour. (Hybrid; F.—L. *and* E.) ME. *polcat*, Chaucer, C. T. 12789 (C 855) ; also *pulkat*, Voc. 601. 13. For the latter syllable, see **Cat**. The former syllable, ME. *pol-*, *pul-*, represents the OF. *pole*, *poule*, a hen ; the form *pole* occurs in OF. *poletier*, variant of *pouletier*, a seller of poultry ; and the mod. E. *poul-try* is sounded with the *poul-* = *pole-* in *pole-cat*. The pole-cat is well known as a chicken-thief ; cf. the quotation from Chaucer above. See further under **Poult**.

POLEMICAL, warlike, controversial. (Gk.) In Blount's Gloss., ed. 1674. Formed with suffix -*al* (=L. *ālis*), from Gk. πολεμικός, warlike.—Gk. πόλεμος, war. β. Formed with suffix -ε-μος (like ἄν-ε-μος = L. *an-i-mus*) from πολ- ; perhaps allied to L. *pell-ere*, to drive. **Der.** *polemical-ly* ; also *polemic-s*, from Gk. πολεμικ-ός.

POLICE, the regulation of a country with respect to the preservation of order ; hence, the civil officers for preserving order. (F.— L.—Gk.) The expression *the police* signifies *the police-force*, i. e.

the force required for maintaining *police*, or public order. The sb. is in Todd's Johnson; but we already find the expression 'so well a *policed* [regulated] kingdome' in Howell, Instructions for Foreign Travel, ed. Arber, p. 78, last line but one; A.D. 1642.—F. *police*, 'policy, politick regiment, civill government;' Cot.—L. *politīa*.—Gk. πολιτεία, citizenship, polity, condition of a state.—Gk. πολίτης, a citizen.—Gk. πολι-, for πόλις, a city; with suffix -της. β. Related to Gk. πολ-ύς, much; Skt. *puri*-, a town. From the same root as **Plenary**. With Skt. *puri*-, cf. Indian -*poor* in *Bhurt-poor*, *Futteh-poor*, &c. And see **Full**. Der. *polic-y*, ME. *policie*, Chaucer, C. T. 12534 (C 600), answering to OF. *policie* (< L. *politīa*), a learned form of F. *police*. Also *polity*, in Hooker, Eccl. *Polity*, from L. *politīa*; *polit-ic*, spelt *politick* in Minsheu, from L. *politĭcus*, Gk. πολιτικός; *polit-ic-ly*; *politic-s*, spelt *politickes* in Minsheu; *polit-ic-al*, Minsheu; *polit-ic-al-ly*; *polit-ic-i-an*, used as adj. in Milton, Samson, 1195. And see *acro-polis*, *metro-polis*, *cosmo-polite*.

POLICY, a warrant for money in the public funds, a writing containing a contract of insurance. (F.—Late L.—Gk.) [Quite distinct from *policy* as connected with **Police**, q.v.] 'A *policy* of insurance is a contract between A and B;' Blackstone. And see Phillips' Dict., ed. 1706. The form is prob. due to confusion with *policy* in the other sense, or the final syllable may have been due to the Span. or Ital. form.—F. *police*, a policy; *police d'assurance*, policy of insurance; Hamilton. Cf. Span. *poliza*, a written order to receive a sum of money; *poliza de seguro*, a policy of insurance; MItal. *poliza*, a schedule (Florio); Ital. *polizza*, a bill, ticket, invoice. β. The Port. form is *apólice*, a government security (Vieyra); MSpan. *póliça* (Minsheu). These forms (and MItal. *póliza*, *pólisa*) prob. represent Late L. *apódissa*, *apódixa*, 'cautio de sumpta pecunia;' Ducange. Cf. Port. *apodixe*, a plain proof. All from Late Gk. ἀπόδειξις, a showing forth, a proof.—Gk. ἀποδείκνυμι, I point out.—Gk. ἀπό, from, forth; δείκνυμι, I show. (See Körting, § 6294.) ¶ This is to be preferred to the solution in Diez, who refers it to Late L. *polypty-chum*, a register; Gk. πολύπτυχον, a piece of writing in many folds, a long register; from πολύ-, much, and πτυχο-, for πτύξ, a fold, leaf, πτύσσειν, to fold. See Notes on E. Etym., p. 220.

POLISH, to make smooth, glossy, or elegant. (F.—L.) ME. *polischen*, Chaucer, C. T. 9456 (E 1582); sometimes contracted to *polschen*, as in P. Plowman, B. v. 482. 'A marble stone *polyshed*;' Caxton, Reynard the Fox, ed. Arber, p. 11.—F. *poliss*-, stem of *polissant*, pres. part. of *polir*, to polish.—L. *polire*, to polish, to make smooth. Der. *polish-er*; also *polite*, in Phillips, ed. 1706, from L. *polītus*, pp. of *polire*; *polite-ly*, *polite-ness*.

POLKA, a dance. (Polish.) Said to have been first danced by a Bohemian peasant-girl in 1831, and to have been named *polka* at Prague in 1835.—Pol. *Polka*, a Polish woman. Similarly, another dance is called the *Polonaise*, lit. Polish woman; another the *Crocovienne*, lit. woman of Cracow; another the *Mazurka*, q.v.

POLL, the head, esp. the back of it, a register of heads or persons, the voting at an election. (OLow G.) All the meanings are extended from *poll*, the rounded part of the head; hence, a head, person, &c. ME. *pol*, pl. *polles*. '*Pol bi pol*' = head by head, separately, P. Plowman, B. xi. 57. 'Bi pate ant by *polle*' = by pate and poll; Polit. Songs, ed. Wright, p. 237, in a MS. of the reign of Edw. II. [Not in AS.] An OLow G. word, found in MDu. *polle*, *pol*, or *bol*, 'the head or the pate,' Hexham; also in Low G. *polle*, the head, Bremen Wörterbuch; Swed. dial. *pull* (Reitz), Dan. *puld* (for *pull*), the crown of the head. Cf. EFries. *pol*, round, full, fleshy. Der. *poll*, verb, to cut off the hair, Num. i. 2, iii. 47; *poll-tax*, a tax by the head, i. e. on each person. Also *pole-axe*, formerly *pollax*, Chaucer, C. T. 2546, OLow G. *pollexe*, Bremen Wörterbuch, from OLow G. *polle*, the poll, head, and *exe*, an ax (later altered to *pole*, with reference to the handle); hardly the same as Icel. *bolöxi*, which is rather an ax for lopping branches, from *bolr*, *bulr*, the trunk of a tree. Also *poll-ard*, used as a sb. in Bacon, Nat. Hist. § 424, and in Sir T. Browne, Cyrus Garden, c. iii. § 13, in which the use of the suffix -*ard* gives the sense of 'round-headed;' it is, etymologically, the same as in *drunk-ard*, i. e. F. -*ard*, from OHG. -*hart*, hard. And see **Pole-axe**.

POLLEN, the powder on the anthers of flowers. (L.) In Johnson; it is also used for fine flour.—L. *pollen*, *pollis*, fine flour. Connected with Gk. πάλη, fine sifted meal; L. *pal-ea*, straw; *pul-uis*, dust.

POLLOCK, POLLACK, a kind of codfish, the whiting. (E.) In Carew (Survey of Cornwall); Todd's Johnson. Cf. Gael. *pollag*, a kind of fish, the gwyniad (i. e. whiting); Irish *pullog*, a pollock; borrowed from E. Prob. from *poll*, the head (above); cf. E. *poll-ard*, which is a name of the chub. (Doubtful.)

POLLUTE, to defile, taint, corrupt. (L.) In Shak. Lucrece, 854, 1063, 1726. Milton has *pollute* as a pp., Hymn on Christ's Nativity, 41; but we already find *poluted* in Skelton, Ware the Hauke, 44, 161, 174; *pollutyd* in the Coventry Mysteries, p. 154; and *polut*

in Chaucer, tr. of Boethius, bk. i. pr. 4. 180.—L. *pollūtus*, pp. of *polluere*, to defile.—L. *pol-*, a prefix, of which the older form was *por-* or *port-*, towards; and **luere*, to defile (distinct from *luere*, to wash), the origin of the sb. *lūes*, filth. Der. *pollut-ion*, Lucrece, 1157, from L. acc. *pollūtiōnem*.

POLO, a game; hockey on horseback. (Balti.) 'It comes from Balti; *polo* being properly, in the language of that region, the ball used in the game;' Yule. Balti is in the high valley of the Indus.

POLONY, a kind of sausage. (Ital.) In Thackeray, Newcomes, xviii. § 1. A corruption for *Bologna sausage*; which city is 'famous for sausages;' Evelyn's Diary, May 21, 1645. So also 'Bologna sausages;' Chapman, The Ball, Act iii. And *Bolony*, Bologna; Webbe's Trav., ed. Arber, p. 30. See Hotten's Slang Dict.

POLTROON, a dastard, coward, lazy fellow. (F.—Ital.—L.) In Shak. 3 Hen. VI, i. 1. 62. Earlier, spelt *pultrowne*, in Skelton, The Douty Duke of Albany, l. 170.—F. *poltron*, 'a knave, rascall, varlet, scowndrell, dastard, sluggard;' Cot.—Ital. *poltrone*, 'a poltroon, an idle fellow, a lazy companion, a dastard;' Torriano.—Ital. *poltro*, 'a colt, ... also a bed or a couch;' Florio. He also gives *poltrare*, *poltrire*, *poltreggiare*, *poltroneggiare*, 'to play the coward, to loll or wallowe in idlenes, to lie idle a bed.' β. The old sense is clearly a sluggard, one who lies in bed; from *poltro*, a bed, couch. *Poltro* orig. meant 'a colt;' and afterwards a bedstead; cf. MF. *poutre*, 'a filly,' Cot.; F. *poutre*, a beam, from the support it gives (like E. *clothes-horse*).—Late L. *pullitrum*, acc. of *pullitrus*, a colt (Ducange).—L. *pullus*, a colt, a foal; see **Foal**. For the change of sense, cf. *pulley*, *chevron*. Der. *poltroon-er-y*, a clumsy word; it should rather be *poltroon-y* = F. *poltronie*, 'knavery,' Cot.

POLY-, many; *prefix*. (L.—Gk.) L. *poly-*, for Gk. πολυ-, from πολύ-, for πολύς, much. Cognate with Skt. *puru*-, much; and closely allied to Gk. πλέως, full, and E. *full*; see **Full**.

POLYANTHUS, a kind of flower. (L.—Gk.) A kind of primrose bearing many flowers; lit. 'many-flowered.' In Thomson, Spring, 532. A Latinized form of Gk. πολύανθος, more commonly πολυανθής, many-flowered.—Gk. πολυ-, many; and ἄνθος, a flower. See **Poly-** and **Anther**.

POLYGAMY, marriage with more than one wife. (F.—L.—Gk.) *Polygamie* in Minsheu, ed. 1627.—F. *polygamie*, 'poligamy, the having of many wives;' Cot.—L. *polygamia*.—Gk. πολυγαμία, a marrying of many wives.—Gk. πολυ-, much, many; and -γαμία, a marrying, from γάμος, marriage. See **Poly-** and **Bigamy**. Der. *polygam-ous*, *polygam-ist*.

POLYGLOT, written in or speaking many languages. (Gk.) Howell applies it to a man; 'A *polyglot*, or linguist;' Familiar Letters, b. iii. let. 8, near the end. Coined from *poly-* = Gk. πολυ-, many; and γλῶττα = γλῶσσα, the tongue. See **Poly-** and **Glottis**.

POLYGON, a plane figure having many angles. (L.—Gk.) Spelt *polygone* in Blount's Gloss., ed. 1674.—L. *polygōnum* (White). —Gk. πολύγωνον, a polygon.—Gk. πολυ-, many; and γων-ία, a corner, angle, allied to γόνυ, the knee; see **Poly-** and **Knee**. Der. *polygon-al*, *polygon-ous*. We also find *polygon-y*, knot-grass, Spenser, F. Q. iii. 5. 32, from L. *polygonium* or *polygonon*, Gk. πολύγονον, knot-grass, so called from its many bends or knots.

POLYHEDRON, a solid body with numerous sides. (Gk.) Mathematical; coined from *poly-* = Gk. πολύ-, many; and -ἕδρον, from ἕδρα, a base, from ἕδ-, cognate with E. *sit*. See **Poly-** and **Sit**. Der. *polyhedr-al*.

POLYNOMIAL, an algebraical quantity having many terms. (Hybrid; F.—L. *and* Gk.) Mathematical; an ill-formed word, due to the use of *binomial*; from F. *polynôme*, *binôme*; from πολυ-, many; and L. *nōm-en*, a name. It should rather have been *polynōminal*, and even then would be a hybrid word. See **Poly-** and **Binomial**.

POLYPUS, an animal with many feet; &c. (L.—Gk.) The pl. *polypi* is in Holland, tr. of Pliny, b. ix. c. 30, near beginning.— L. *polypus* (gen. sing. and nom. pl. *polypī*), a polypus.—Gk. πολύπος, occasional form of πολύπους, lit. many-footed.—Gk. πολυ-, many; and πούς, cognate with E. *foot*. See **Poly-** and **Foot**. ¶ Cf. F. *polype*, Ital. and Span. *polipo*; all false forms, due to treating the Gk. ending -πους as if it were -πος. Cf. *poly-podi-um*, a fern.

POLYSYLLABLE, a word of many syllables. (Gk.) In Blount's Gloss., ed. 1674. A coined word; ultimately of Gk. origin. The spelling *syllable* is due to French. See **Poly-** and **Syllable**. Der. *polysyllab-ic*, from L. *polysyllabus* = Gk. πολυσύλλαβος, having many syllables.

POLYTECHNIC, concerning many arts. (F.—Gk.) From F. *polytechnique* (1795).—Gk. πολυ-, many; and τεχνικός, belonging to the arts, from τέχνη, art; see **Technical**.

POLYTHEISM, the doctrine of a plurality of gods. (Gk.) In Johnson's Dict. Coined from Gk. πολυ-, much, many; and θε-ός, a god; with suffix -*ism* = Gk. -ισμος. See **Poly-** and **Theism**. Der. *polythe-ist*, *polythe-ist-ic-al*.

POMADE, POMMADE, a composition for dressing the hair. (F. — Ital. — L.) Properly with two *m*'s. '*Pommade*, an oyntment used by ladies;' Blount's Gloss., ed. 1674. — F. *pommade*, 'pomatum, or pomata, an ointment;' Cot. So called because orig. made with apples; cf. F. *pomme*, an apple. — Ital. *pomada, pomata*, 'a pomado to supple ones lips, lip-salue;' Florio. Formed with participial suffix -*ata* from *pom-o*, an apple. — L. *pōmum*, an apple, the fruit of a tree. Doublet, *pomatum*, Ben Jonson, Sejanus, ii. 1, which is a Latinized form. And see *pome-granate*, *pomm-el*.

POMANDER, a globe-shaped box for holding perfumes. (F. — L. and Span. — Arab.) Spelt *pomaunder*, Skelton, Garl. of Laurel, 1027; '*Pommaundre*, to smell to;' Palsgrave. For *pomamber*; spelt *pomeamber* in Bullein, Dial. against Fever (1578); p. 49, l. 25, but also *pomeander*, p. 53, l. 29. ME. *pomum ambre*; Medical Workes of 14th Cent., ed. Henslow, p. 122. — AF. *pomme ambre*, for OF. *pomme d'ambre*, 'apple of amber;' see my Notes on E. Etym., p. 223. See **Pommel** and **Amber**.

POMEGRANATE, a kind of fruit. (F. — L.) 'Of *pomegranates*;' Sir T. Elyot, Castel of Helth, b. ii. c. 7. ME. *pome-garnade*, Lydgate, Minor Poems, p. 15; *pomgarnet*, Trevisa, i. 107, l. 7. — OF. *pome grenate*, which was turned into *pome de grenate* by some confusion or misunderstanding of the sense. In Li Contes del Graal, a poem of the 12th century, we find 'Dates, figues, et noiz mugates, Girofle et *pomes de grenates*;' see Bartsch, Chrestomathie Française, col. 172, ll. 4, 5. Cf. Ital. *pomo granato*, a pomegranate; Florio. — L. *pōmum*, an apple; and *grānātum*, used also alone to signify a pomegranate. β. *Grānātum* is neut. from *grānātus*, filled with grains or seeds; the fruit abounding in hard seeds. *Grānātus* is formed, with pp. suffix -*ātus*, from *grān-um*, a grain, seed. See **Grain**.

POMMEL, a knob, the knob on a sword-hilt, a projection on a saddle-bow. (F. — L.) ME. *pomel*, a boss; P. Plowman's Crede, l. 562. — OF. *pomel* (Burguy), later *pommeau*, 'the pommell of a sword, &c.;' Cot. Lit. 'small apple.' Formed with dim. suffix -*el* (L. -*ellus*) from *pōmum*, an apple. **Der.** *pommel*, verb, to beat with the handle of a sword or any blunt instrument or with the fists. Cf. '[He] ... all too *poumleed* the same with his handes;' Udall. tr. of Erasmus's Apophthegmes, Aug. Cæsar, § 7.

POMP, great display, ostentation. (F. — L. — Gk.) ME. *pompe*, in Chaucer, C. T., A 525. — F. *pompe*, 'pomp;' Cot. — L. *pompa*, a solemn procession, pomp. — Gk. πομπή, a sending, escorting, solemn procession. — Gk. πέμπειν, to send. **Der.** *pomp-ous*, in Palsgrave, from F. *pompeux*, L. *pompōsus*, full of pomp; *pompous-ly*, -*ness*; *pomp-os-i-ty*.

POMPELMOOSE, a shaddock. (Du.) In Stedman's Surinam, i. 22. — Du. *pampelmoes*, a shaddock (Calisch).

PONCHO, a sort of cloak, resembling a narrow blanket with a slit in the middle for the head to go through. (Span. — Araucan.) The form *poncho* is Spanish; but it is adapted from an Araucan name *pontho* or *poncho*; D. D. Granada, Vocab. of La Plata words (Montevideo, 1890). The Araucans are the Indians in the S. of Chili. (Notes on Eng. Etym., p. 224.)

POND, a pool of water. (E.) ME. *pond, ponde*, Trevisa, i. 69, l. 4; pl. *pondus*, id. i. 61, l. 5. *Pond* is a pool of standing water; strictly, one caused by damming water up. It is a variant of *pound*, an inclosure. Thus the Irish *pont* (borrowed from E.) means both 'a pound for cattle' and 'a pond.' See **Pound** (2).

PONDER, to weigh in the mind, consider. (L.) 'In balance of unegall [unequal] weight he [Love] *pondereth* by aime;' Surrey, Description of the Fickle Affections, l. 8; in Tottell's Miscellany, 1557, ed. Arber, p. 6; and see Skelton, ed. Dyce, i. 132, l. 1. Lydgate has *ponder*, imp. s., in Assembly of Gods, l. 134. — L. *ponderāre*, to weigh. — L. *ponder*-, decl. base of *pondus*, a weight; see **Pound** (1). **Der.** *ponder-er*. From the stem *ponder*- we also have *ponder-ous*, Sir T. Elyot, The Governour, b. i. c. 1, from F. *pondereux*, L. *ponderōsus*; *ponder-ous-ly*, -*ness*; *ponderos-i-ty*, from F. *ponderosité*, 'ponderosity,' Cot., from L. acc. *ponderōsitātem*. Also *ponder-able*, in Sir T. Browne, Vulg. Errors, b. iii. c. 27, part 11, from L. *ponderābilis*, that can be weighed; *ponderabil-i-ty*; *im-ponderable*.

PONENT, western. (F. — L.) In Levins; and in Milton, P. L. x. 704. — F. *ponent*, 'the west;' Cot. — L. *pōnent*-, stem of pres. part. of *pōnere*, to lay, abate; with reference to *sunset*. See **Position**.

PONIARD, a small dagger. (F. — L.; *with* G. *suffix*.) In Hamlet, v. 2. 157. — F. *poignard*, 'a poinadoe, or poniard;' Cot. Formed, with suffix -*ard* < OHG. *hart* (lit. hard), from F. *poing*, the fist. Similarly, Ital. *pugnale*, a poniard, is from *pugno*, the fist. Cf. also Span. *puño*, fist, handful, hilt, *puñal*, a poniard, *puñada*, a blow with the fist. β. The F. *poing*, Ital. *pugno*, Span. *puño*, are from L. *pugnus*, the fist; see **Pugnacious**.

PONTIFF, a Roman high-priest, the Pope. (F. — L.) The pl. *pontifes* is in Bacon, Nat. Hist. § 771. — F. *pontif*, *pontife*, 'a chief bishop;' Cot. — L. *pontificem*, acc. of *pontifex*, *pontufex*, a Roman high-priest; in eccl. Lat., a bishop. — L. *ponti*-, decl. stem of *pons*, orig. a path, way, later a bridge; and -*fex* (stem -*fic*-), a maker, from *facere*, to make. Cf. Gk. πόντος, the sea. Brugmann, i. § 140. ¶ The reason for the name is not known; the lit. sense is 'pathmaker;' hence, perhaps, one who leads to the temple, or leads the way in a procession. **Der.** *pontific-al*, in Levins, from F. *pontifical*, L. *pontificālis*, from the stem *pontific*-; *pontific-ate*, from F. *pontificat*, 'a prelateship,' Cot., from L. *pontificātus*.

PONTOON, a buoyant vessel, for the quick construction of bridges. (F. — L. — C.) Formerly *ponton*. '*Ponton*, a floating bridge;' Phillips, ed. 1706. — F. *ponton*, 'a wherry, or ferry-boat;' hence, a bridge of boats; Cot. — L. *pontōnem*, acc. of *ponto*, a boat; hence, a bridge of boats. Of Celtic origin; see **Punt**.

PONY, a small horse. (F. — L.) In Johnson. Explained as 'a little Scotch horse' in Boyer's Dict., A.D. 1727 (Wedgwood). — OF. *poulenet*, a little colt (Godefroy); dimin. of *poulain*, a colt. — Late L. *pullānus*, a colt (Ducange). — L. *pullus*, a foal. The *l* is lost before *n*, as in *Colney Hatch*. Cf. Lowl. Sc. *powney*. See **Foal**.

POODLE, a fancy dog with curly hair. (G.) One of the very few G. words in English. Modern; not in Johnson. It occurs in Miss Swanwick's tr. of Goethe's Faust, 1864, p. 37. — G. *pudel* (Goethe), a poodle; Low G. *pudel*, *pudel-hund*, so called (it may be presumed) because he looks fat and clumsy on account of his thick hair; allied to Low G. *pudeln*, to waddle, used of fat persons; cf. Low G. *pudel-dikk*, unsteady on the feet, *puddig*, thick; Bremen Wörterbuch. Danneil gives Low G. *puddel*, a little dog just beginning to walk.

POOH, an interjection of disdain. (F.) Spelt *puh!* Marston, What You Will, A. ii. sc. 1. Adapted from MF. *pouac*, 'faugh!' Cot. Cf. Icel. *pū*, pooh! Cf. *puf*. '*Puf*, said the foxe;' Caxton, tr. of Reynard the Fox, ed. Arber, p. 59. So also *buf!* Chaucer, C. T. 7516 (D 1934); *baw!* P. Plowman, B. xi. 135. Due to blowing away from one. See **Puff**.

POOL (1), a pond, small body of water. (E.) ME. *pol*, *pool*; dat. *pole*, Layamon, 21748; pl. *poles*, Havelok, 2101. AS. *pōl*, Ælfred, tr. of Gregory's Pastoral Care, ed. Sweet, p. 278, l. 15. [Irish *poll*, *pull*, a hole, pit, mire, dirt; Gael. *poll*, a hole, pit, mire, bog, pond, pool; W. *pwll*, a pool; Corn. *pol*, a pool, pond, mire, pit; Manx, *poyl*; Bret. *poull*; are all borrowed words.] + Du. *poel*, a pool; G. *pfuhl*; OHG. *pfuol*. Teut. type **pōloz*; cf. Lith. *balà*, a swamp. Brugmann, i. § 567.

POOL (2), the receptacle for the stakes at cards. (F. — L.) Formerly also spelt *poule*, as in Todd's Johnson. — F. *poule*, (1) a hen, (2) a pool, at various games; Hamilton. It seems to be so named, because the stakes are regarded as eggs, to be gained from the hen. — Late L. *pulla*, a hen (Ducange); fem. of *pullus*, a young animal, allied to Gk. πῶλος, and E. *foal*; see **Foal**, **Pony**.

POOP, the stern of a ship; a deck above the ordinary deck in the after-part of a ship. (F. — Ital. — L.) In Shak. 1 Hen. IV, iii. 3. 29. Surrey (iv. 746) has *poupe* to translate L. *puppi* in Virgil, Æn. iv. 554. — F. *poupe*, *pouppe*, 'the poop or hinder part of a ship.' — Ital. *poppa*, poop (Hatzfeld). — L. *puppim*, acc. of *puppis*, the hinder part of a ship, a ship. **Der.** *poop*, verb, to strike a ship in the stern, to sink it, Pericles, iv. 2. 25.

POOR, possessed of little, needy, weak. (F. — L.) In early use. Also *pover*, as in Roy, Rede Me, ed. Arber, p. 76 (1528). ME. *poure* (perhaps = *povre*), O. Eng. Homilies, ed. Morris, 2nd Ser. p. 47, l. 18; Ancren Riwle, p. 260, l. 3. — OF. *povre*, poor; cf. F. dial. *poure* (Berry). — L. *pauperem*, acc. of *pauper*, poor. β. L. *pau-per* means 'provided with little,' or 'preparing little for oneself;' from *pau*-, little, few, as seen in L. *pau-cus*, Gk. παῦ-ρος, E. *few*; and -*per*, providing, connected with L. *par-āre*, to provide, prepare. **Der.** *poor-ly*, *poor-ness*, *poor-house*, -*laws*, -*rate*, -*spirited*; *poverty*, q. v.

POP, to make a sharp, quick, sound; to thrust suddenly, move quickly, dart. (E.) '*Popped* in between th' election and my hopes;' Hamlet, v. 2. 65. 'A *pops* me out from 500 pound;' K. John, i. 68. 'To *poppe*, coniecture;' Levins. 'I *poppe*, or stryke in-to a thyng;' Palsgrave. Chaucer has 'A joly *popper*,' i.e. thruster, dagger; C. T. 3929 (A 3931). The word is of imitative origin; and allied to ME. *poupen*, to make a loud sound, as in blowing a horn; see Chaucer, C. T. 15405 (B 4589). Hence *powpe* in the sense of 'popgun;' Prompt. Parv. Cf. **Puff**. **Der.** *pop*, sb.

POPE, the father of a church, the bishop of Rome. (L.) ME. *pope*, Owl and Nightingale, 746. In Layamon, 14886, the older version has the dat. *papen*, where the latter version has *pope*. These forms show that the word was not taken from the F. *pape*, but from AS. *pāpa* (dat. *pāpan*), which was borrowed immediately from the Latin. The AS. homily on the Birthday of S. Gregory (ed. Elstob) begins with the words 'Gregorius se hālga *pāpa*' = Gregory, the holy pope. — L. *pāpa*. + Gk. πάπα, πάππα, voc. of πάπας, πάππας, papa, father. See **Papa**. **Der.** *pope-dom*, AS. *pāpedōm*, A. S. Chron., an. 1124; *pop-ish*, Titus Andron., v. 1. 76; *pop-er-y*.

POPINJAY, a parrot; a mark like a parrot, put on a pole to be shot at; a coxcomb. (F.–G. *and* L.; *with modified suffix*.) ME. *popingay*, Chaucer, C. T. 13299, where the Ellesmere MS. has *papeiay* (=*papejay*); Six-text ed., Group B, 1559. The pl. *papeiayes* occurs in Allit. Poems, ed. Morris, B. 1465. Thus the *n* is excrescent, as in other words before a *j*-sound; cf. *messenger* for *messager*, *passenger* for *passager*, &c.–AF. *papeiay*, Royal Wills, ed. Nichols, p. 35 (1355); OF. *papegai*, *papegay*, 'a parrot or popinjay; also a woodden parrat, . . whereat there is a generall shooting once every year;' Cot. Mod. F. *papegai*, *papegaut*; the last spelling has a needless suffixed *t*, and is due to OF. *papegau*, found in the 13th century (Littré). Cf. Span. *papagayo* (whence Arab. *babaghā*), Port. *papagaio*, Ital. *papagallo*, a parrot. β. It is clear that we have here two distinct forms; (1) F. *papegai*, Span. *papagayo*, *papagaio*, in which the base *papa-* is modified by the addition of F. *-gai*, Span. *-gayo*, due to a popular etymology which regarded the bird as chattering like the *jay*; and (2) OF. *papegau*, Ital. *papagallo*, in which the bird is regarded as a kind of *cock*, L. *gallus*; and the latter form appears to be the older; i.e. *jay* was substituted for 'cock,' because the jay seemed to come nearer than the cock to the nature of a parrot. γ. I adopt the suggestion of Wedgwood, that the syllables *pa-pa-* are imitative, and were suggested by the Bavarian *pappeln*, *pappelen*, or *pappern*, to chatter, whence the sb. *pappel*, a parrot, lit. a babbler; Schmeller, i. 398, 399. δ. Bavar. *pappeln* is cognate with E. **Babble**, q.v. Cf. *bubblyjock* (i.e. babblejack), the Lowland Scotch name for a turkey-cock; so named from the gobbling sound which it makes.

POPLAR, a kind of tall tree. (F.–L.) ME. *poplere*, Chaucer, C. T. 2923 (A 2921); *popler*, Palladius on Husbandry, b. iii. l. 194. –OF. *poplier* (13th cent.), mod. F. *peuplier*, a poplar; Littré. Formed with suffix *-ier* (L. *-ārius*) from OF. **pople* (not recorded), later form *peuple*, 'the poplar;' Cot. Cf. prov. E. *popple*, a poplar; Nares, ed. Halliwell.–L. *pōpulum*, acc. of *pōpulus*, a poplar. Cf. OF. *popelin*, *poupelin*, a poplar; Godefroy.

POPLIN, a fabric made of silk and worsted. (F.) Added by Todd to Johnson's Dict.–F. *popeline*, of which an older form was *papeline*, first mentioned in A.D. 1667 (Littré). β. Origin unknown; it has been supposed to be connected with F. *papal*, papal, because it may have been first made at Avignon, where there was once a papal court, A.D. 1309-1408. The chronology does not bear out this suggestion. Cf. Span. *popelens*, *populina*, poplin. γ. The spelling *papeline* separates it from *Poppeling* or *Popperingen*, near Ypres, in W. Flanders; with which some would connect it.

POPPY, the name of a flower with narcotic properties. (L.) ME. *popi* (with one *p*), Gower, C. A. ii. 102; bk. iv. 3007. AS. *popig*; 'Papauer, *popig*,' Voc. 134. 33; also *popæg*, Voc. 16. 17. Merely borrowed from L. *papāuer*, a poppy, by change of *u* (*w*) to *g*, and loss of *-er*.

POPULACE, the common people. (F.–Ital.–L.) 'And calm the peers, and please the *populace*;' Daniel, Civil Wars, b. vii. st. 78.–F. *populace*, 'the rascall people;' Cot.–Ital. *popolazzo*, *popolaccio*, 'the grosse, base, vile, common people;' Florio. Formed with the depreciatory suffix *-azzo*, *-accio*, from Ital. *popol-o*, the people.–L. *popŭlum*, acc. of *populus*, the people; see **People**.

POPULAR, belonging to, or liked by the people. (F.–L.) In Temp. i. 2. 92.–F. *populaire*, 'popular;' Cot.–L. *populāris*, adj., from *populus*, the people; see **People**. **Der.** *popular-ly*, *-i-ty*, *-ize*.

POPULATE, to people. (L.) In Levins, ed. 1570. 'Great shoales of people, which goe on to *populate*;' Bacon, Essay 58.–Late L. *populātus*, pp. of *populāre*, to people; (whereas the classical L. *populāri* means to ravage, destroy).–L. *populus*, people; see **People**. **Der.** *populat-ion*, in Bacon, Essay 29, § 5, from Late L. *populātiōnem*, acc. of *populātio*, a population (White). Also *populous*, Rich. II, v. 5. 3, from F. *populeux*, 'populous,' Cot., which from L. *populōsus*, full of people; *popul-ous-ly*, *-ness*.

PORCELAIN, a fine kind of earthenware. (F.–Ital.–L.) In Dryden, Annus Mirabilis, st. 29; spelt *porcellan*, Sir T. Herbert, Travels, ed. 1665, pp. 391, 396; *porcellane*, Hakluyt, Voy. ii. 1. 229, l. 4; and see extract from Florio below. *Porcelain* was so named from the resemblance of its finely polished surface to that of the univalve shell of the same name, called in English the Venus' shell; as applied to the shell, the name goes back to the 13th century, when it occurs in the F. version of Marco Polo in place of the Ital. name (Littré). Cotgrave gives *porcelaine*, *pourcelaine*, 'the purple fish, also, the sea-snail, or Venus shell.'–Ital. *porcellana*, 'a purple fish, a kinde of fine earth called *porcelane*, whereof they make fine China dishes, called *porcellan* dishes;' Florio, ed. 1598. β. Again, the shell derived its name from the curved shape of its

upper surface, which was thought to resemble the raised back of a little hog. [It is very easy to make a toy-pig with a Venus' and some putty; and such toys are often for sale.]–Ital. *porcella*, 'a sow-pig, a porkelin;' *porcello*, 'a yong hog, or pig, a porkelin;' Florio. Dimin. of Ital. *porco*, a hog.–L. *porcum*, acc. of *porcus*, a pig; see **Pork**.

PORCH, a portico, covered way or entrance. (F.–L.) ME. *porche*, Rob. of Glouc., p. 271, l. 5841.–F. *porche*, a porch.–L. *porticum*, acc. of *porticus*, a gallery, arcade, porch; for the letter-changes, see Brachet. Cf. E. *perch*, from F. *perche*, L. *pertica*. β. Sometimes derived from *porti-*, for *porta*, a gate, door; see **Port** (3); but this is doubtful; see Walde. **Doublet**, *portico*.

PORCINE, relating to swine. (L.) In Todd's Johnson, who quotes an extract dated 1660.–L. *porcīnus*, adj., formed from *porcus*, a pig; see **Pork**.

PORCUPINE, a rodent quadruped, covered with spines or quills. (F.–L.) α. In Shakespeare, old edd. have *porpentine*; a spelling which also occurs in Ascham, Toxophilus, ed. Arber, p. 31. Levins has *porpin*. Huloet has: '*Porpyn*, beaste, havinge prickes on his backe.' The Prompt. Parv. has: '*Poork-poynt*, *porpoynte*, *perpoynt*, beste, *Histrix*;' p. 409. '*Porkepyn*, a beest, *porc espin*;' Palsgrave. β. We thus see that the animal had two very similar names, (1) *porkepyn*, shortly *porpin*, easily lengthened to *porpint* by the usual excrescent *t* after *n*, and finally altered to *porpentine* as a by-form of *porkepyn*; and (2) *pork-point*, *porpoint*; the latter of which forms would also readily yield *porpentine*. γ. We conclude that *porpentine* is late; that *porkpoint* was little used, and simply meant a 'pork' or pig furnished with points or sharp quills; and that the modern *porcupine* is due (by substitution of obscure *u* for obscure *e*) to the ME. form *porkëpyn*, pronounced in three syllables, and with the *y* long. δ. The ME. *porkëpyn* is obviously derived from OF. *porc espin*, a word known to Palsgrave, A.D. 1530, but now obsolete, and supplanted by *porcépic*, in the 13th century *porc espi* (Littré), a form which is also given by Cotgrave, who has : '*Porc-espi*, a porcupine.' ε. Thus the OF. names for the animal were also double; (1) *porc-espi* = *porc-espic*, the pig with spikes (see **Spike**); and (2) *porc-espin*, the pig with spines. The English has only to do with the latter, which, though obsolete in French, is preserved in Span. *puerco espin*, Port. *porco espinho*. ζ. Finally, the F. *porc* is from L. *porcus*, and OF. *espin* is a by-form of OF. *espine* (F. *épine*), from L. *spina*, a thorn. See **Pork** and **Spine**. ¶ Holland, in his tr. of Pliny, b. viii. c. 35, has *pork-pen*, where *pen*, i.e. quill, is an ingenious substitution for *-epine*.

PORE (1), a minute hole in the skin. (F.–L.–Ck.) ME. *pore*, Prompt. Parv. p. 409; Lanfranc, Cirurgie, p. 43, l. 11. The pl. *poorus* (=*pores*) is in Trevisa, i. 53.–F. *pore*, 'a pore;' Cot.–L. *porum*, acc. of *porus*, a pore.–Gk. πόρος, a ford, passage, way, pore. –√PER, to fare; see **Fare**. Brugmann, i. § 474. **Der.** *por-ous*, from F. *poreux*, 'pory,' Cot.; *porous-ly*, *-ness*; *por-os-i-ty*, *pori-form*.

PORE (2), to look steadily, gaze long. (E. ?) ME. *poren*, Chaucer, C. T. 185, 5877, 16138 (A 185, D 295, G 670). Apparently a natural word; cf. prov. E. *pore*, to cram, to thrust, to intrude; North Fries. *porre*, to stick, stir, provoke; Du. *porren*, to poke, thrust; EFries. *puren*, *porren*, to stick, thrust, bore, stir, vex; Low G. *purren*, to poke about, clean out a hole; Norw. *pora*, to finger, poke, stir, thrust; W. Flem. *peuren*, to poke after (De Bo); Swed. dial. *pora*, *pura*, *påra*, to work slowly and gradually, to do anything slowly; Rietz. β. The idea seems to be that of poking or thrusting about in a slow and toilsome way, as in the case of clearing out a stopped-up hole; hence to *pore over* a job, to think a long while about it. γ. We also find Gael. *purr*, to push, thrust, drive, urge, Irish *purraim*, I thrust; from ME. *pouren*, *poren*; cf. Lowl. Sc. *porr*, to stab.

PORK, the flesh of swine. (F.–L.) ME. *pork*, Rich. Coer de Lion, 3049.–F. *porc*, 'a pork, hog; also pork, or swines flesh;' Cot.–L. *porcum*, acc. of *porcus*, a pig.+Lithuan. *parszas*, a pig (Nesselmann), Irish *orc*, with the usual loss of initial *p*.+AS. *fearh*, a pig; whence E. *farrow*. Brugmann, i. § 486. See **Farrow**. **Der.** *pork-er*, a young pig, Pope, tr. of Homer, Od. xvii. 201; lit. an animal that supplies pork; substituted for the older term *pork-et*, from OF. *porquet*, 'a young pork,' Cot., dimin. of *porc*. Also *porcine*, q.v. And see *porc-u-pine*, *por-poise*, *porc-el-ain*.

PORPHYRY, a hard, variegated rock, of purple and white colour. (F.–L.–Gk.) ME. *porphúrie*, Chaucer, C. T. 16243 (G 775).–OF. **porphyrie* (?), not found; Cotgrave has only *porphyre*, 'porphiry;' but the E. form appears fuller and older. Abbreviated from L. *porphyrites*, porphyry.–Gk. πορφυρίτης, porphyry; so named from its purple colour. Formed with suffix *-ιτης*, signifying 'resemblance,' from πορφυρ-, πορφύρα, the purple-fish, purple-dye; cf. πορφύρεος, purple; see **Purple**. **Der.** *porphyrit-ic*, from L. *porphyrit-es*.

PORPOISE, PORPESS, the hog-fish. (F. – L.) Spelt *porpesse* in Ray, On the Creation, pt. i. (R.); *porpaise, porpuis,* in Minsheu; *porcpisce,* Spenser, Colin Clout, l. 249. ME. *purpeys,* Prompt. Parv. – AF. *purpeys,* Liber Albus, p. 236; *porpeis* (Godefroy, s. v. *porpois*); OF. *porpois,* a porpoise; a term now obsolete in F. (except Guernsey *pourpeis*), and supplanted by the name *marsouin* (lit. mere-swine), borrowed from G. *meerschwein.* For **porc-peis.* – L. *porcum,* acc. of *porcus,* a pig; and *piscem,* acc. of *piscis,* a fish, cognate with E. *fish.* See **Pork** and **Fish.** So also MItal. *pesce-porco,* 'a sea-hogge, a hogge-fish;' Florio. The mod. Ital. name is *porco marino,* marine pig; Span. *puerco marino.* Cf. Guernsey *pourpeis,* a porpoise.

PORRIDGE, a kind of broth. (F. – Teut.) In Shak. Temp. ii. 1. 10. Apparently it took the place of the older word *pottage* (Palsgrave), ME. *potage,* occurring as early as in Ancren Riwle, p. 412; whence also prov. E. *poddish.* Cotgrave has F. *potage,* 'pottage, porridge;' formed, with suffix *-age* (L. *-āticum*) from Low L. *pottus,* a pot, of Teut. origin. – Low G. *pott,* Du. *pot;* see **Pot.** [There was an intermediate form, represented by prov. E. *poddish* and by *podech* in Tyndale's Obedience of a Christian Man, 1528, fol. 109, qu. in Brand's Antiq., ed. Ellis, iii. 384.] β. It may have been influenced by ME. *porree, poré,* also with the sense of 'pottage.' We find, ' *Porré,* or *purré,* potage,' Prompt. Parv.; and Way's note gives the spelling *porray.* Way adds : ' this term implies generally pease-pottage, still called in French *purée;* . . according to the Ortus, it seems to have denoted a pottage of leeks; *poratum* est cibus de *poris* factus, Anglicé *porray;*' he also notes the Late L. form *porrata.* – OF. *porée, porrée,* ' beets, also pot-herbs, and thence also, pottage made of beets or with other herbs;' Cot. – Late L. *porrāta* (also *porrecta*), broth made with leeks; Ducange. Cf. Ital. *porrata,* leek-soup. Formed, with L. pp. fem. suffix *-āta,* from L. *porr-um* or *porr-us,* a leek. γ. *Porrum* stands for an older form **porsum,* as shown by the cognate Gk. πράσον, a leek. Der. *porring-er,* q. v.

PORRINGER, a small dish for porridge. (F. – Teut.) In Shak. Tam. Shrew, iv. 3. 64; Bacon, Nat. Hist. § 31. ' 16 *porengers,*' temp. Hen. VIII, in Strutt, Manners and Customs, iii. 65; *poreger,* Bury Wills, p. 115 (1522); *porrynger,* id., p. 136; *poddinger,* id., p. 142. The last is the intermediate form between *pottanger* and *porringer.* Suggested by, or corrupted from, *pottanger* (Palsgrave), a dish for *pottage;* spelt *potenger* ab. 1450, Excerpta Historica, p. 418, l. 1 (ed. 1831). For **pottager,* with inserted *n,* as in *messenger* for *messager.* Cf. F. *potager,* ' of, or belonging unto, pottage;' Cot. The ME. *potagere* meant ' a maker of pottage;' Piers Plowman, B. v. 157. See **Porridge.**

PORT (1), demeanour, carriage of the body. (F. – L.) ME. *port,* Chaucer, C. T. 69, 138. – F. *port,* ' the carriage, behaviour, or demeanor of a man;' Cot. Cf. Ital. *porto,* carriage; Span. *porte,* deportment. A sb. due to the F. verb *porter,* to carry. – L. *portāre,* to carry. Allied to **Fare.** Der. *port,* verb, to carry, little used except in the phr. ' to *port* arms,' and in Milton's expression ' ported spears,' P. L. iv. 980. Also *port-able,* Macb. iv. 3. 89, from L. *portābilis,* that can be carried or borne; *port-able-ness; port-age,* Prompt. Parv., from F. *portage,* ' portage, carriage,' Cot. Also *port-er,* in the sense of ' carrier of a burden' (Phillips, ed. 1706), substituted for ME. *portour* (Prompt. Parv.), from OF. *portour,* F. *porteur,* ' a carrier,' Cot. And hence *porter,* the name of malt-liquor, so called because it was a favourite drink with London porters, supposed to be not older than A.D. 1750, see Todd's Johnson; also *porter-age,* a coined word. *Port-folio,* a case large enough to carry folio paper in, a coined word, with which cf. F. *portefeuille; Port-manteau,* Middleton, Widow, iv. 2, from F. *port-manteau* (Cot.), lit. that which carries a mantle (see **Mantle**); but we also find *port-mantua,* Dryden, Kind Keeper, Act i. sc. 1, and *portmantue,* used by Cot. to translate F. *portmanteau;* here *port-mantua* is not quite the same word, but is derived from F. *port-er* and **Mantua,** q. v. Also *port-mantle,* Howell, Letters, vol. i. sec. 3, let. 15. Also *port-ly,* Merc. of Ven. i. 1. 9; *port-li-ness.* From the L. *portāre* we also have *com-port, de-port, de-port-ment, dis-port* (and *sport*), *ex-port, im-port, im-port-ant, pur-port, re-port, sup-port, trans-port.*

PORT (2), a harbour, haven. (L.) ME. *port;* Rob. of Glouc. speaks of ' the fif *portes,*' now called the Cinque Ports, p. 51, l. 1169. The pl. *porz* (for *ports*) occurs in Layamon, 24415. AS. *port.* ' to ᷒ǎm *porte* '=to the haven, Ælfred, tr. of Beda, b. iv. c. 1, near the end. – L. *portus,* a harbour; cognate with E. **Ford.** β. Closely allied to L. *porta,* a gate; see **Port** (3). Der. (from L. *portus*), *im-port-une, op-port-une.*

PORT (3), a gate, entrance, port-hole. (F. – L.) ' So, let the *ports* be guarded;' Cor. i. 7. 1. ME. *port,* Trevisa, tr. of Higden, i. 213. – F. *porte,* ' a port or gate;' Cot. – L. *porta,* a gate. β. Formed with suffix *-ta* from the base *por-* seen in Gk. πόρος, a ford, way; from √PER, to pass through, fare, travel; see **Fare.**

¶ Though *port* is not common in ME., there is an AS. form *porte* (Grein), borrowed directly from L. *porta.* Der. *port-er,* ME. *porter,* Floriz and Blauncheflur, ed. Lumby, l. 138, from OF. *portier,* L. *portārius* (Lewis); whence (with fem. suffix *-ess* = F. *-esse* < L. *-issa,* Gk. *-ισσα*), *porter-ess,* or shortly *port-r-ess,* Milton, P. L. ii. 746. Also *port-al,* Hamlet, iii. 4. 136, from OF. *portal* (Burguy), L. *portāle,* a vestibule, porch. Also *port-hole,* Dryden, Annus Mirabilis, st. 188. Also *port-cullis,* q. v. (but perhaps not *portico, porch*). And see *port* (1), *port* (2), *port* (4), and *porte.*

PORT (4), a dark purple wine. (Port. – L.) So called from *Oporto,* in Portugal; *port* being merely an abbreviation from *Oporto wine.* – Port. o *porto,* the port; where *o* is the def. art. = Span. *lo* < L. *illum;* and *porto* is from L. *portum,* acc. of *portus,* a port. See **Port** (2).

PORTCULLIS, a sliding door of cross-timbers pointed with iron, let down to protect a gateway. (F. – L.) ME. *porte-colys,* Rom. of the Rose, 4168. – AF. *porte colice,* Excerpta Historica, p. 73 (A.D. 1250); OF. *porte coleïce* (13th cent., Littré), later *porte coulisse,* or simply *coulisse,* ' a portcullis;' Cot. – F. *porte,* from L. *porta,* a gate; and OF. *coleïce,* answering to a Late L. **cōlāticia* (not found), with the sense of flowing, gliding, or sliding, regularly formed from *cōlātus,* pp. of *cōlāre,* to flow, orig. to strain through a sieve. See **Port** (3) and **Colander** and **Cullis.** We find the Late L. forms *cōlādissus, cōlācius, porta cōlācia* (port-cullis) from the same source.

PORTE, the Turkish government. (F. – L.) The Turkish government is ' officially called the *Sublime Porte,* from the *port* (gate) of the sultan's palace, where justice was administered;' Webster. See **Port** (3). It is ' a perverted F. translation of *Babi Ali,* lit. "the high gate," the chief office of the Ottoman government;' Wedgwood. Cf. Arab. *bāb,* a gate, *'aliy,* high; Rich. Dict. pp. 224, 1027.

PORTEND, to betoken, presage, signify. (L.) In K. Lear, i. 2. 113; Spenser, F. Q. v. 7. 4. – L. *portendere,* to foretell, predict. – L. *por-,* for OL. *port,* towards; and *tendere,* to stretch forth; so that *portend* is ' to stretch out towards,' or point out. See **Position** and **Tend.** Der. *portent,* Oth. v. 2. 45, F. *portente,* ' a prodigious or monstrous thing,' Cot., which from L. *portentum,* a sign, token; formed from *portentus,* pp. of *portendere.* Hence *portent-ous,* from F. *portenteux,* ' prodigious,' Cot., which from L. *portentōsus.*

PORTER (1), a carrier. (F. – L.) See **Port** (1).

PORTER (2), a gate-keeper. (F. – L.) See **Port** (3).

PORTER (3), a dark kind of beer, orig. *porter's beer* (Wedgwood); see **Port** (1).

PORTESSE, PORTOS, PORTOUS, a breviary. (F. – L.) Spelt *portesse* in Spenser, F. Q. i. 4. 19. ' *Poortos,* booke, *portiforium,* breviarium;' Prompt. Parv. ME. *portous, portos, porthos, porthors,* P. Plowman, B. xv. 122, and footnotes; and see note to the line for further examples. All various corruptions of OF. *porte-hors,* i.e. that which one carries abroad, a word compounded as the F. equivalent of L. *portiforium,* a breviary. This OF. *portehors* is given by Godefroy; and occurs in La Clef d'Amors, l. 102. Compounded of F. *porter,* from L. *portāre,* to carry; and F. *hors,* older form *fors,* out of doors, abroad, from L. *foris,* abroad, adv., due to sb. pl. *fores,* doors. See **Port** (1) and **Door.**

PORTICO, a porch. (Ital. – L.) In Chapman, tr. of Homer, Od. iv. 405, 410. – Ital. *portico.* – L. *porticum,* acc. of *porticus,* a porch; see **Porch.** Doublet, *porch.*

PORTION, a part, share. (F. – L.) ME. *portion, portioun, porcioun,* Wyclif, Luke xv. 12. – F. *portion.* – L. *portiōnem,* acc. of *portio,* a share, lit. ' a sharing;' closely allied to *part-,* stem of *pars,* a part; see **Part.** Der. *portion,* vb.; *portion-ed, portion-er, portion-less;* and see *apportion.*

PORTLY, orig. of good demeanour; see **Port** (1).

PORTRAIT, a picture of a person. (F. – L.) In Shak. Merch. of Ven. ii. 9. 54; spelt *pourtraict,* Spenser, F. Q. ii. 1. 39. – MF. *pourtraict,* ' a pourtrait;' Cot. – MF. *pourtraict, pourtrait,* pp. of *pourtraire,* to portray; see **Portray.**

PORTRAY, to draw, depict. (F. – L.) ME. *purtreye,* Chaucer, C. T. 96; *purtreyen,* King Alisaunder, l. 1520. – OF. *portraire,* later *pourtraire,* ' to pourtray, draw,' Cot.; mod. F. *portraire.* – Late L. *prōtrahere,* to paint, depict; L. *prōtrahere,* to drag or bring forward, expose, reveal. – L. *prō-,* forward; and *trahere,* to draw; see **Pro-** and **Trace** (1). Der. *portrait,* q.v.; whence *portraiture,* ME. *pourtreture,* Gower, C. A. ii. 83, bk. iv. 2421, from OF. *portraiture,* MF. *pourtraicture,* ' a pourtraiture,' Cot., as if from L. *prōtractūra.* And see *protract.*

POSE (1), a position, attitude. (F. – L. – Gk.) We speak of ' the *pose* of an actor;' see Webster. Quite modern; not in Todd's Johnson; but the word is of importance. – F. *pose,* ' attitude, posture,' Hamilton; MF. *pose,* ' a pawse, intermission, stop, ceasing, repose, resting;' Cot. – F. *poser,* ' to place, set, put,' Hamilton; ' to put, pitch, place, to seat, settle, plant, to stay, or lean on, to set, or lay down;' Cot.—Late L. *pausāre*, to cease; also, to cause to rest, and hence used in the sense of L. *pōnere*, to place (Ducange); L. *pausāre*, to halt, cease, pause, to repose (in the grave), as in the phr. *pausat in pāce* = (here) rests in peace (Lewis).—L. *pausa*, a pause; a word of Greek origin; see **Pause**. Cf. Ital. *posare*, to put, lay down, rest, from *posa*, rest; Span. *posar*, to lodge, *posada*, an inn. ¶ One of the most remarkable facts in F. etymology is the extraordinary substitution whereby the Late L. *pausāre* came to mean 'to make to rest, to set,' and so usurped the place of the L. *pōnere*, to place, set, with which it has no etymological connexion. And this it did so effectually as to restrict the F. *pondre*, the true equivalent of L. *pōnere*, to the sense of 'to lay eggs;' whilst in all compounds it completely thrust it aside, so that *compausāre* (i. e. F. composer) took the place of the L. *compōnere*, and so on throughout. **2.** Hence the extraordinary result, that whilst the E. verbs *compose, depose, impose, propose*, &c. exactly represent in sense the L. *compōnere, depōnere, impōnere, prōpōnere*, &c., we cannot *derive* the E. verbs from the L. ones, since they have (as was said) no real etymological connexion. Indeed, these words are not even of L. origin, but Greek. **3.** The true derivatives from the L. *pōnere* appear in the verbs *compound, expound*, &c., in adjectives such as *ponent, component*, and in the substantives, such as *position, composition, deposition*; see under **Position**. **Der.** *pose*, verb, to assume an attitude, merely an E. formation from the sb. *pose*, an attitude, and quite modern. Also (from F. *poser*) the compounds *ap-pose, com-pose, de-pose, dis-pose, ex-pose, im-pose, inter-pose, op-pose, pro-pose, pur-pose, re-pose* (in which the sense of L. *pausa* appears), *sup-pose, trans-pose*.

POSE (2), to puzzle, perplex by questions. (F.—L. and Gk.) 'Say you so? then I shall *pose* you quickly;' Meas. for Meas. ii. 4. 51. Here, as in the case of *peal*, the prefixed syllable *ap-* has dropped off; the older form of the verb was commonly to *appose*, ME. *apposen, aposen*; see examples in N. E. D., or in Richardson, s. v. *Appose*. To *appose* was to question, esp. in a puzzling way, to examine. 'When Nicholas Clifforde sawe himselfe so sore *aposed* [posed, questioned], he was shamfast;' Berners, Froissart's Chron. c. 373 (R.). 'She would *appose* mee touching my learning and lesson;' Stow's Chronicle, an. 1043. And see Chaucer, C. T. 7179, 15831 (D 1597, G 363); P. Plowman, B. i. 47, iii. 5, vii. 138, xv. 376. **β.** The word appears at first sight to answer to F. *apposer*, but that verb is not used in any such sense; and it is really nothing but a corruption of *oppose*, which was used convertibly with it. Thus we find '*A posen*, or *oposyn*, Opponere,' Prompt. Parv., p. 13. 'I *oppose* one, I make a tryall of his lernyng, or I laye a thyng to his charge, *Ie appose*. I am nat to lerne nowe to *oppose* a felowe, à *apposer vng gallant*;' Palsgrave. [Here the OF. *aposer, apposer*, is, in the same way, a corruption of F. *opposer*.] 'Bot sche, which al honour supposeth, The falsë prestës than *opposeth* [questions], And axeth [asks],' &c.; Gower, C. A. i. 71, bk. i. 879. **γ.** The word arose in the schools; the method of examination was by argument, and the examiner was the umpire as to questions put by an *opponent*; hence to examine was also to *oppose*, or *pose*. '*Opponere*, in philosophicis vel theologicis disputationibus contra argumentari; *argumenter contre quelqu'un*;' Ducange, ed. Migne. For the etymology, see **Oppose**. **δ.** Lastly, the confusion can be accounted for, viz. by confusion of *opponere*, to question, argue, with the word *apposite*, applied to a neat answer; see **Apposite**, which really answers to L. *appositus*. **Der.** *pos-er*, Bacon, Essay 32; on which Mr. Aldis Wright says: 'an examiner, one who *poses* or puts questions; still in use at Eton and Winchester.' Hence also ME. *posen*, to put a case, Chaucer, C. T. 1164 (A 1162). **Der.** *puzzle*, q. v.

POSE (3), a cold in the head. (C.) Probably obsolete; noted by Ray (1691). ME. *pose*, Chaucer, C. T. 4150 (A 4152). AS. *ge-pos*, a cough; '*wið geposu*, for coughs; L. ad tussim gravem;' A.S. Leechdoms, ed. Cockayne, i. 148. Not an E. word; but borrowed from an OBritish word represented by W. *pâs* or *peswch*, a cough; allied to Irish *cas-achdach*, Russ. *kash-ele*, prov. E. *hoas-t*, a cough; Skt. *kās*, to cough. (√QAS; the *q* becomes *c* in Irish, but *p* in Welsh.)

POSITION, a situation, attitude, state, place. (F.—L.) In Shak. Tw. Nt. ii. 5. 130. ME. *posicioun*, Chaucer, tr. of Boethius, b. v. pr. 4, l. 30.—F. *position*, 'a position;' Cot.—L. *positiōnem*, acc. of *positio*, a putting, placing; cf. L. *positus*, pp. of *pōnere*, to place, put. **β.** L. *pōnere* (pp. *positus*) is generally thought to stand for **pos-sinere* (Bréal), where **pos-* is a variation of what appears to be an old prep. (*port*); and *sinere* (pp. *situs*) is to let, allow, on which see **Site**. The prefix *por-, port-*, is prob. allied to Gk. προτί, towards. **Der.** *com-position, de-position, dis-position, im-position, inter-position, op-position, pro-position, sup-position, trans-position*. Also (from L. *pōnere*) *pon-ent, com-ponent, de-ponent, ex-ponent, op-ponent; com-pound, ex-pound, post-pone*. And see *ap-posite, com-posite, de-posit*,

ex-posit-or; also *post, positive, post-ure, com-post, im-postor, pro-vost*, &c. ☞ And see remarks under **Pose** (1).

POSITIVE, actual, undoubted, decisive, certain. (F.—L.) The lit. sense is 'settled;' hence, certain. ME. *positif*, Chaucer, C. T. 1169 (A 1167).—F. *positif*, omitted by Cotgrave, but in use in the 14th century.—L. *positīuus*, settled, esp. by agreement.—L. *positus*, pp. of *pōnere*, to place; see **Position**. **Der.** *positive-ly, -ness*. Also *positiv-ism*, due to Comte, born in 1798, died 1857.

POSNET, an iron pot, saucepan. (F.—Low G.) A dialect word; see E. D. D. ME. *posnet*, Prompt. Parv.; Way's note quotes the form *possenet* from Horman; spelt *pocenet*, Rel. Antiq. i. 54. —OF. *poçonet* (Godefroy), dimin. of *poçon, posson*, a pot.—Late L. type **pottiōnem*, acc. of **pottio*; from Late L. *pott-us*, a pot.—Low G. *pott*. See **Pot**.

POSSE, power. (L.) See Butler, Hudibras, iii. 2. 1166. '*Posse comitatus*, or power of the county;' Blount's Nomo-lexicon, ed. 1691. —L. *posse*, to be able; used as sb. See **Possible**.

POSSESS, to own, seize, have, hold. (L.) The verb is probably due to the sb. *possession*, which was in earlier use, occurring in Chaucer, C. T. 2244 (A 2242), and in Robert of Brunne, tr. of Langtoft, p. 239, l. 19. *Possess* is extremely common in Shak.; see L. L. L. v. 2. 383, &c.—L. *possessus*, pp. of *possidēre*, to possess, to have in possession. **β.** Prob. derived from L. **port-*, towards; and *sedēre*, to sit, remain, continue; as if the sense were 'to remain near,' hence to have in possession. See **Position**, § **β**, and **Sit**. **Der.** *possess-ed*, Much Ado, i. 1. 193; *possess-or*, Merch. Ven. i. 3. 75, from L. *possessor*; *possess-ive*, from L. *possessīuus*; *possessive-ly*. Also *possess-ion*, ME. *possessioun, possession*, as above, from F. *possession*, 'possession,' Cot., from L. acc. *possessiōnem*. Also ME. *possession-er*, P. Plowman, B. v. 144.

POSSET, a drink composed of hot milk, curdled by some strong infusion. (F. and E.) In Shak. Merry Wives, i. 4. 8; v. 5. 180; Macb. ii. 2. 6. ME. *possyt*, Voc. 666. 9; *posset*, Voc. 793. 15; *poshet*, Voc. 567. 22; cf. MF. *possette*, 'a posset of ale and mylke;' Palsgrave (not otherwise known). **β.** But we also find what is prob. an older form; ME. *poshoote*, Voc. 625. 18; *poshote* of milke, Cookery Books, ed. Austin, p. 15; *poshote* of ale, id., p. 36. **γ.** The latter element seems to be the ME. *hote*, E. *hot*; cf. ME. *possot* in Prompt. Parv. But this leaves the former element unexplained, unless it can be equated to Norm. dial. *pous*, pap, OF. *pous, pouls, pols*, L. *puls*, pap. Cf. prov. E. *pulse*, pottage; and (for the phonology) cf. ME. *possen*, to push about, from OF. *poulser* (L. *pulsāre*). [Cf. W. *posel*, curdled milk, posset; Irish *pusoid*, a posset; from E.] **Der.** *posset*, vb., to curdle, Hamlet, i. 5. 68.

POSSIBLE, that may be done, that may happen. (F.—L.) ME. *possible*, Chaucer, C. T. 8832 (E 956).—F. *possible*, 'likely, possible,' Cot.—L. *possibilis*, that may be done, possible. **β.** Not well formed; it should rather have been **potibilis*; the form *possibilis* is due to the influence of *posse*, to be able, whence *possum*, I am able. L. *possum* (short for *potissum*) is due to *potis*, powerful, properly 'lord' or 'master,' cognate with Skt. *pati-*, a master, owner, governor, lord, husband, Lithuan. *patis*, a husband (Nesselmann), Russ. *-pode* as seen in *gos-pode*, the Lord. Brugmann, i. § 158. See **Potent**. And see **Host** (1). **Der.** *possibl-y*; *possibil-i-ty*, ME. *possibilitee*, Chaucer, C. T. 1293 (A 1291), from F. *possibilité* (Cot.), which from L. acc. *possibilitātem*.

POST (1), a stake set in the ground, a pillar. (L.) ME. *post*, a pillar; see Chaucer, C. T. 214. In very early use; see Layamon, 28032. AS. *post*; 'Basis, *post*,' Voc. 164. 32; and see Judges, xvi. 3.—L. *postis*, a post, a door-post. **β.** The orig. sense was 'something firmly fixed;' cf. L. *postus*, a form used by Lucretius for *positus*, pp. of *pōnere*, to place, set; see **Position**, and see **Post** (2).

POST (2), a military station, a public letter-carrier, a stage on a road, &c. (F.—L.) Shak. has *post*, a messenger, Temp. ii. 1. 248; a post-horse, Romeo, v. 1. 21. '*A post, runner*, Veredarius;' Levins, ed. 1570. *Post* 'originally signified a fixed place, as a military post; then, a fixed place on a line of road where horses are kept for travelling, a stage, or station; thence it was transferred to the person who travelled in this way, using relays of horses, and finally to any quick traveller;' Eastwood and Wright, Bible Wordbook. See Job, ix. 25; Jer. li. 31. Four men are mentioned in 1491 as 'lying as *posts*,' i.e. messengers; Excerpta Historica, p. 113.—F. *poste*, masc. 'a post, carrier, speedy messenger,' Cot.; fem. 'post, posting, the riding post, as also, the furniture that belongs unto posting;' id. Cf. Ital. *posta*, a post, station; Span. *posta*, post, sentinel, post-house, post-horses.—Late L. *posta*, a station, site; fem. of *postus*, a shortened form (used by Lucretius) of *positus*, placed, pp. of *pōnere*, to place. See **Position**, and **Post** (1). **Der.** *post*, vb., L. L. L. iv. 3. 188; *post*, adv., in the phr. 'to travel *post*;' *post-boy, -chaise, -haste, -horse, -man, -mark, -master, -office, -paid, -town*. Also *post-al*, a modern coined word, from F. *postal*, also modern. Also *post-age*, an E. coinage, not used in

French, but used by Dryden; see his Spanish Friar, A. ii. sc. 2 (end). And see *post-illion*.

POST-, *prefix*, after, behind. (L.) L. *post*, prep., after, behind.

POST-DATE, to date a thing after the right time. (L.) 'Those, whose *post-dated* loyalty now consists only in decrying that action;' South, vol. iii. ser. 2 (R.). From **Post-** and **Date.** Similarly are formed *post-diluvial*, *post-diluvian*, &c.

POSTERIOR, hinder, later, coming after. (L.) In Shak. L. L. L. v. 1. 94, 96, 126.—L. *posterior*, comp. of *posterus*, coming after, following.—L. *post*, after; see **Post-**, prefix. ¶ Bacon, Nat. Hist., end of § 115, has *posteriour*, answering to MF. *posterieur*, 'posterior, hinder,' Cot., from the L. acc. *posteriōrem.* **Der.** *posterior-s*, s. pl., for *posterior parts*; *posterior-ly*, *posterior-i-ty*. And see *posterity*, *postern*, *posthumous*, *postil*.

POSTERITY, succeeding generations, future race of people. (F.—L.) Spelt *posteritie*, Spenser, Ruines of Rome, 434; *posteryté*, in Caxton, Golden Legend, Adam, § 7.—MF. *posterité*, 'posterity;' Cot.—L. *posteritātem*, acc. of *posteritās*, futurity, posterity.—L. *posteri-*, for *posterus*, following after; see **Posterior.**

POSTERN, a back-door, small private gate. (F.—L.) ME. *posterne*, Rob. of Glouc. p. 19, l. 447; spelt *postorne*, K. Alisaunder, 4593.—OF. *posterle*, also *posterne* (by change of *l* to *n*), Burguy; later *poterne*, 'a posterne, or posterne-gate, a back-door to a fort,' Cot.—L. *posterula*, a small back-door, postern; formed with dimin. suffix -*la* from *posteru-s*, behind; see **Posterior.**

POSTHUMOUS (better **POSTUMOUS**), born after the father's death, published after the author's decease. (L.) The spelling with *h* is false; see below. Shak. has *Posthumus* as a name in Cymb. i. 1. 41, &c. Sir T. Browne has '*posthumous* memory;' Urn-burial, c. v. § 12.—L. *postumus*, the last; esp. of youngest children, the last-born; hence, late-born, and, as sb., a posthumous child. **β.** In accordance with a popular etymology, the word was also written *posthumus*, as if derived from *post humum*, lit. after the ground, which was forced into the meaning 'after the father is laid in the ground or buried;' and, in accordance with this notion, the sense of the word was at last chiefly confined to such a usage. Hence also the F. spelling *posthume*, Port. *posthumo*; but Span. and Ital. have *postumo*; all in the usual sense attached to E. *posthumous.* **γ.** The L. *postumus* = *post-tu-mus*, a superlative formed from *post*, behind; cf. L. *op-tu-mus*, best. See **Posterior. Der.** *post-humous-ly*.

POSTIL, an explanatory note on the Bible, marginal note or commentary. (F.—L.) ME. *postille*, Wyclif, gen. prologue to Isaiah, ed. Forshall and Madden, p. 225; the word is now obsolete, except in theological writings.—F. *postille*, 'a postill, glosse, compendious exposition;' Cot. [Hence, with prefix *ap-* (= L. *ad* before *p*) was formed MF. *appostille*, 'an answer to a petition, set down in the margent thereof; and, generally, any small addition unto a great discourse in writing;' Cot.]—Late L. *postilla*, a marginal note in a bible, in use A.D. 1228; Ducange. **β.** The usual derivation, and doubtless the correct one, is that of Ducange, viz. from L. *post illa*, i.e. *post illa verba*, after those words; because the glosses were added afterwards. Cf. Ital. and Port. *postilla*, Span. *postila*, a marginal note. **Der.** *postil*, verb, to write marginal notes, to comment on, annotate, Bacon, Life of Hen. VII, ed. Lumby, p. 193, l. 3.

POSTILLION, a post-boy, rider of post-horses in a carriage. (F.—Ital.—L.) 'Those swift *postillions*, my thoughts;' Howell, Famil. Letters, vol. i. let. 8; A.D. 1619. And in Cotgrave.—F. *postillon*, 'a postillon, guide, posts-boy;' Cot. Introduced in the 16th cent. from Ital. *postiglione*, 'a postilion,' Florio (and see Brachet). Formed with suffix -*iglione* (= L. -*il-i-ōnem*) from Ital. *post-a*, a messenger, post; see **Post** (2).

POST-MERIDIAN, POMERIDIAN, belonging to the afternoon. (L.) Howell uses the form *pomeridian*, speaking of his 'privat *pomeridian* devotions;' Famil. Letters, vol. i. sect. 6. let. 32.—L. *pōmerīdiānus*, also *postmerīdiānus*, belonging to the afternoon.—L. *post*, after; and *merīdiānus*, belonging to midday. See **Post-** and **Meridian.**

POST-MORTEM, after death. (L.) A medical term.—L. *post*, after; *mortem*, acc. of *mors*, death. See **Post-** and **Mortal.**

POST-OBIT, a bond by which a person receiving money undertakes to repay a larger sum after the death of the person who leaves him money. (L.) A law term. Shortened from L. *post obitum*, after death. See **Post** and **Obit.**

POSTPONE, to put off, delay. (L.) *Postponed* is in Blount's Nomolexicon, ed. 1691, q.v. '*Postpone*, to let behind or esteem less, to leave or neglect;' Phillips, ed. 1706. 'Thow did *postpone*;' How Dumbar was desyred to be ane Freir, l. 28. [Formerly, the form was also *postpose*, which occurs in Howell, Famil. Letters, vol. i. sect. 4. let. 15, cited by Richardson with the spelling *postpone.* This is from F. *postposer*, 'to set or leave behind;' Cot. He also has: '*Postposé*, postposed.']—L. *postpōnere*, to put after.—L. *post*, after; and *pōnere*, to put; see **Post-** and **Position. Der.** *postpone-ment*, a clumsy word, with F. suffix -*ment*.

POSTSCRIPT, a part added to a writing after it was thought to be complete. (L.) In Shak. Hamlet, iv. 7. 53. From L. *post-scriptum*, that which is written after; from *post*, after, and *scriptus*, pp. of *scrībere*, to write. See **Post-** and **Scribe.**

POSTULATE, a proposition assumed without proof, as being self-evident. (L.) '*Postulates* and entreated maxims;' Sir T. Browne, Vulg. Errors, b. vi. c. 6. § 6.—L. *postulātum*, a thing demanded; hence also, a thing granted; neut. of *postulātus*, pp. of *postulāre*, to demand. **β.** It seems probable that *postulare* stands for *por-stlāre*, allied to *poscere*, for *por-scere*, to ask. **γ.** It is further proposed to assume for *poscere* a still older form *porc-scere*, thus bringing it into alliance with √PREK, to pray, whence Skt. *pracch*, to ask, L. *precārī*, to pray; see **Pray.** Brugmann, i. §§ 483(7), 502. **Der.** *postulate*, verb, Sir T. Browne, Vulg. Errors, b. ii. c. 3 [*not* 4], last section; *postulat-or-y*, id. b. ii. c. 6. § 2.

POSTURE, position, attitude. (F.—L.) In Shak. Wint. Tale, v. 3. 23.—F. *posture*, 'posture;' Cot.—L. *positūra*, position, arrangement; allied to *posit-us*, pp. of *pōnere*, to place; see **Position. Der.** *posture-master*; *posture*, verb.

POSY, a verse of poetry, a motto, a bouquet or nosegay. (F.—L.—Gk.) The word, in all its senses, is merely a contraction of **Poesy**, q.v. **1.** It was usual to engrave short mottoes on knives and on rings; and as these were frequently in verse, they were called *posies*. Thus, in Shak. Merch. Ven. v. 148, we have: 'a ring . . . whose *posy* was . . . like cutler's *poetry* Upon a knife, *Love me, and leave me not*;' see note to the line in Wright's edition. So also in Hamlet, 'the *posy* of a ring;' iii. 2. 162. See Chambers, Book of Days, i. 221, for examples, such as 'In thee, my choice, I do rejoice;' &c. As these inscriptions were necessarily brief, any short inscription was also called a *posy*, even though neither in verse nor poetically expressed. Thus, Udall, on St. Luke, c. 23, v. 38, speaking of the handwriting above the cross, calls it 'a super-scripcion or *poisee* written with on the top of the crosse' (R.). So also in the following: 'And the tente was replenished and decked with this *poysie*, After busie laboure commeth victorious reste;' Hall's Chron. Hen. V, an. 7. § 2. And see Lydgate, Minor Poems, p. 65, l. 20. [Another old name for a motto was *a reason*; see Fabyan's Chron. Hen. V, an. 8, ed. Ellis, p. 587.] **2.** Mr. Wedgwood well accounts for *posy* in the sense of bouquet, as follows: 'A nosegay was probably called by this name from flowers being used enigmatically, as is still common in the East. Among the tracts mentioned in the Catalogue of Heber's MSS., no. 1442, is "A new yeares guifte, or *a posie made upon certen flowers* presented to the Countess of Pembroke; by the author of Chloris, &c.;" see Notes and Queries, Dec. 19, 1868 (4 S. ii. 577). So also in Beaum. and Fletcher, Philaster, Act i. sc. 1 [sc. 2 in Darley's ed.]; "Then took he up his garland, and did shew What every flower, as country people hold Did signify;" and see Hamlet, iv. 5. 175.' To this I may add, that a *posy* was even sometimes expressed by precious stones; see Chambers, as above. The line 'And a thousand fragrant *posies*' is by Marlowe; The Passionate Shepherd, st. 3. See Puttenham, Arte of E. Poesie, bk. i. c. 30. Doublet, *poesy.*

POT, a vessel for cooking, or drinking from. (E.) ME. *pot*, Ancren Riwle, p. 368, l. 21. [Cf. Irish *pota*, *potadh*, a pot, vessel; Gael. *poit*; W. *pot*; all from E.] AS. *pott*; Leechdoms, i. 378.+EFries. Du. *pot*; Low G. *pott*; Icel. *pottr*, Swed. *potta*, Dan. *pote.* Teut. type **puttoz.* Hence Low L. *pottus*, also spelt *pōtus* (as if from L. *pōtāre*, to drink); F. *pot*, Bret. *pôd*, Span. *pote.* ¶ The phrase 'to go to *pot*' meant to be put into the cooking-pot; see Squire of Low Degree, 448; my Notes on Eng. Etym., p. 226; Brand, Pop. Antiq., ii. 58. **Der.** *pot-ash*, i.e. *ash* obtained from the *pot*, so called because the alkaline salt was obtained by burning vegetable substances; Chaucer mentions fern-ashes, as used for making glass, C. T. 10569 (F 255). '*Pot-ashes* (anno 12 Car. 2. cap. 4) are made of the best wood or fern-ashes,' Blount's Nomolexicon, ed. 1691; perhaps from Du. *potasch* (from *pot* and *asch*, ashes), G. *pottasche* (from *asche*, ashes); Latinized in the form *potassa*, whence *potass-ium.* We find *pot-asshes* in Arnold's Chron. (1502); ed. 1811, p. 187. Also *pot-herb*, *pot-hook*, *pot-sherd* (see **Sherd**). Also *pot*, verb; *pott-er*, ME. *potter*, Cursor Mundi, 16536 (cf. Irish *potoir*, a potter); *potter-y*, from F. *poterie* (Cot.). And see *pot-een*, *pott-age*, *pott-le*, *pot-walloper.*

POTABLE, that may be drunk. (F.—L.) In Shak. 2 Hen. IV, iv. 5. 163.—F. *potable*, 'potable, drinkable;' Cot.—L. *pōtābilis*, drinkable; formed with suffix -*bilis* from *pōtā-re*, to drink.—L. *pōtus*, drunken; formed with suffix -*tus* from a base *pō-*, as in Gk. πῶ-μα, drink; cf. Skt. *pā*, to drink, Gk. πό-τος, a drinking, πό-σις, drink. **Der.** *potable-ness*; and see *potation*, *potion.*

POTASH, POTASSIUM; see under **Pot.**

POTATION, a draught. (L.) Not a F. word. In Shak. Oth.

ii. 3. 56. Spelt *potacion*, Coventry Myst., p. 138. – L. *pŏtātiōnem*, acc. of *pŏtātio*, a drinking. – L. *pŏtāre*, to drink. – L. *pŏtus*, drunken; see **Potable.**

POTATO, a tuber of a plant much cultivated for food; the plant itself. (Span. – Hayti.) In Shak. Merry Wives, v. 5. 21. '*Potatoes*, natives of Chili and Peru, originally brought to England from Santa Fé, in America, by Sir Francis Hawkins, 1563; others ascribe their introduction to Sir Francis Drake, in 1586; while their general culture is mentioned by many writers as occurring in 1592;' Haydn, Dict. of Dates. They are also mentioned by Ben Jonson, Cynthia's Revels, Act ii. sc. 1. – Span. *patata*, a potato; also *batata*, which is a better form. – Hayti *batata*. 'Peter Martyr, speaking of Haiti, says (in Decad. 2. c. 9), "Effodiunt etiam e tellure suapte naturâ nascentes radices, indigenæ *batatas* appellant, quas ut vidi insubres napos existimavi, aut magna terræ tubera." ... Navagerio, who was in the Indies at the same time, writes in 1526, "Io ho vedute molte cose dell' Indie ed ho avuto di quelle radice che chiamano *batatas*, e le ho mangiate; sono di sapor di castagno." Doubtless these were sweet potatoes or yams, which are still known by this name in Spanish.'—Wedgwood. Spelt *botata* (as a Hayti word) in R. Eden's books on America, ed. Arber, p. 131; also *battata*, p. 159.

POTCH, to thrust, poke. (F. – L.) In Shak. Cor. i. 10. 15. merely a variant of **Poach** (2).

POTEEN, whisky illicitly distilled in Ireland. (Irish – E.) From Irish *poitín*, a little pot; dimin. of *poite*, a pot. – E. *pot*; see **Pot.**

POTENT, powerful. (L.) In Shak. Temp. i. 2. 275. Rich. gives a quotation from Wyatt, showing that the word was used in 1539. – L. *potent-*, stem of *potens*, powerful, pres. part. of *possum*, I am able; see **Possible.** Der. *potenc-y*, Hamlet, iii. 4. 170, a coined word, due to L. *potentia*, power; *potent-ial*, ME. *potencyal*, Chaucer, House of Fame, b. iii. l. 5 [but only in Thynne's edition of 1532, and later edd.; MSS. *poetical*], from F. *potentiel*, 'strong, forcible,' Cot., which from L. *potentiālis*, forcible (only found in the derived adverb *potentiāliter*), formed with suffix *-ālis* from the sb. *potentia*; whence *potential-ly*, *potential-i-ty*. Also *potent-ate*, L.L.L. v. 2. 684, from F. *potentat*, 'a potentate, great lord,' Cot., which from Late L. *potentātus*, a supreme prince (Ducange), from *potentāre*, to exercise authority (id.). Also *omni-potent*, q.v.; and *armi-potent*, Chaucer, C. T. 1984 (A 1982). **Doublet,** *puissant*, q.v.

POTHER, bustle, confusion, constant excitement. (E.) In Pope, Horace, Sat. ii. 2. 45. 'To make a *pother*, to make a noise or bustle;' Bailey's Dict., vol. i. ed. 1735. Older form *pudder*. '*Pudder*, noise, bustle; to keep a *pudder* about trifles;' Phillips, ed. 1706. Spelt *poother* in ed. 1623 of Shak. Cor. ii. 1. 234; *pudder* in K. Lear, iii. 2. 50. ME. *puðeren*, apparently in the sense 'to poke about;' see Ancren Riwle, p. 214, note *c*. Another form is *potter*; 'To *potter*, to stir or disorder anything;' Bailey, vol. i. '*Potter*, to stir, poke, confuse, do anything inefficiently;' also '*Pother*, to shake, to poke, *West*;' Halliwell. See **Potter.** The sense 'to stir about' seems the orig. one; hence that of 'turmoil' as the result of stirring. ¶ Prob. confused with *poother*, *pudder*, dust, dialect forms of *powder*; indeed, Butler has *pother* in Hudibras, i. 1. 32, but *powder* in the same, iii. 1. 1055. See **Powder.** And see **Bother.**

POTION, a drink. (F. – L.) In Shak. Romeo, v. 3. 244. ME. *pocion*, K. Alisaunder, 3509. – F. *potion*, 'a potion;' Cot. – L. *pōtiōnem*, acc. of *pōtio*, a drink; see **Poison. Doublet,** *poison*.

POTTAGE, broth, thick soup. (F. – Teut.) ME. *potage*, Ancren Riwle, p. 412, l. 27. – F. *potage*, 'pottage, porridge;' Cot. Formed, with suffix *-age* (L. *-āticum*), from F. *pot*, which is from a Teut. source; see **Pot. Doublet,** *porridge*.

POTTER, to go about doing nothing. (E.) A provincial word, but in common use. '*Potter*, to go about doing nothing, to saunter idly; to work badly, do anything inefficiently; also, to stir, poke, *North*; also, to confuse, disturb, *Yorksh*.;' Halliwell. 'To stir or disorder anything;' Bailey's Dict., vol. i. ed. 1735. It is the frequentative form, with the usual suffix *-er*, of E. *put*, to thrust; see **Put.** Cf. also MDu. *poteren*, 'to search one thoroughly' (Hexham), from the notion of poking a stick into every corner; Du. *peuteren*, to fumble, to poke about; Norw. *pota*, MSwed. *potta*, to poke. See **Pother.** And cf. E. dial. *polter*, to potter about.

POTTLE, a small measure, basket for fruit. (F. – Teut.) ME. *potel*, to translate L. *laguncula*; Wyclif, Isaiah, x. 33. – OF. *potel*, a small pot, a small measure (Godefroy); cf. AF. *potel*, Stat. Realm, i. 321. Dimin. of F. *pot*, from Low G. *pott*; see **Pot.**

POTWALLOPER, lit. one who boils a pot. (Hybrid; E. *and* F. – Teut.) '*Potwalloper*, a voter in certain boroughs in England, where all who *boil* (wallop) *a pot* are entitled to vote;' Webster. Corrupted to *pot-wabblers* (Halliwell); also found as *pot-walliners*, given as a Somersetshire word in Upton's MS. additions to Junius (Halliwell). *Wallop*, to boil fast, is from ME. *walopen*, to gallop.

Golding has: 'seething *a-wallop*,' i.e. boiling rapidly; tr. of Ovid, fol. 82. (Prob. confused with ME. *wallen*, AS. *weallan*, to boil.) See **Pot** and **Gallop.**

POUCH, a poke, or bag. (F. – Scand.) ME. *pouche*, Chaucer, C.T. 3929 (A 3931). – OF. *pouche*, found in the 14th cent. as a variant of *poche*, 'a pocket, pouch, or poke;' Cot. See Littré; and *pouche*, variant of Norm. dial. *pouque*, a pouch; Moisy. Of Scand. origin; see **Poke** (1). **Der.** *pouch*, verb. **Doublet,** *poke* (1).

POULT, a chicken, fowl. (F. – L.) *Poult* is used by W. King (died A.D. 1712), in a poem on The Art of Cookery, l. 33. Also in Chapman, Revenge for Honour, i. 1. 21. ME. *pulte*, Prompt. Parv. – F. *poulet*, 'a chicken;' Cot. Dimin. of *poule*, a hen. – Late L. *pulla*, a hen; fem. of *pullus*, a young animal, cognate with E. **Foal**, q.v. **Der.** *poult-er*, one who deals in fowls, 1 Hen. IV, ii. 4. 480, ME. *pulter*, Prompt. Parv., AF. *pulleter*, Liber Albus, p. 465; whence the later form *poult-er-er* (Dekker, Honest Whore, pt. ii, iii. 3), by the unnecessary reduplication of the suffix *-er*, denoting the agent. Also *poult-r-y*, ME. *pultrie*, Prompt. Parv., AF. *poletrie*, *pultrie*, Liber Albus, p. 231, formed with F. suffix *-er-ie*, as in the case of *pant-r-y*, &c. And see **Pullet. Doublet,** *pullet*.

POULTICE, a soft plaister applied to sores. (F. – L.) In Shak. Romeo, ii. 5. 65. Gascoigne, Steel Glas, 997 (ed. Arber, p. 77), has the pl. form *pultesses*. Burton has the pl. *pultises*, Anat. Mel. ii. 4. i. 5. Formed, with suffix *-esse* (*-esse*, *-is*) from MF. *pulte*, 'a poultice,' Cot. – L. *pultem*, acc. of *puls*, a thick pap, or pap-like substance. +Gk. πόλτος, porridge. ¶ Godefroy also has OF. *pols*, *pous*, from L. nom. *puls*, pap; sometimes used in the sense of 'poultice;' as, 'Cil qui ... metent ... lor *pols* mollificatives sor toutes plaies.' Cf. Ital. *poltiglia*, 'a pultis;' Florio. The form may have been due to L. pl. *pultes*. **Der.** *poultice*, verb.

POUNCE (1), to seize with the claws, as a bird, to dart upon suddenly. (F. – L.) Orig. a term in hawking. A hawk's claws were called *pounces*, as in Spenser, F. Q. i. 11. 19; hence *to pounce upon*, to seize with the claws, strike or pierce with them. G. Douglas speaks of an eagle's *punsys*, Æn. xiii. ch. 5 (near end); and a hawk's *pownces* are mentioned in the Book of St. Alban's, fol. a 8. The orig. sense of the verb was 'to pierce,' to prick, to adorn with pierced work. A *pounce* is also a punch or stamp; see Nares. In Chaucer, Pers. Tale, De Ira, Group I, l. 421, we read of '*pownsoned* and dagged clothynge' in three MSS., whilst two others have '*pounsed* and dagged clothyng.' β. Here *pownsoned* has the same sense, but is a derivative word, being made from the sb. *pounson* or *punsoun*, a bodkin or dagger; for which see Barbour's Bruce, i. 545, and my note on the line. The form *pounson* answers to Late L. acc. *punctionem*, OF. *ponçon*, F. *poinçon*, a punch or puncheon for piercing holes. We must refer the verb *pounsen* and the sb. *pounce* to the OF. *ponç-on* (above). [The mod. F. *poncer* is related to **Pounce** (2).] γ. We have, however, parallel forms in other languages, viz. Span. *punchar*, to prick, punch, *puncha*, a thorn, prickle, sharp point, exactly equivalent to the *pounce* or talon of the hawk; mod. Prov. *pouncha*, to prick; Ital. *punzecchiare*, to prick slightly (which presupposes a form *punzare*, to prick); *punzone*, a puncher. δ. The OSpan. *punçar*, Span. *punchar*, answer to a Late L. *punctiare*, to prick, not found, but readily formed from *punctus*, pp. of *pungere*, to prick. See **Point, Pungent, Punch** (1).

POUNCE (2), fine powder. (F. – L.) Merely a doublet of *pumice*, and orig. used for powdered pumice-stone, but afterwards extended to other kinds of fine powder, and to various uses of it. 'Long effeminate pouldred [powdered] *pounced* haire;' Prynne, Histrio-Mastix, pt. i. Act vi. sc. 15. '*Pounce*, a sort of powder strew'd upon paper to bear ink, or to soak up a blot;' Phillips, ed. 1706. – F. *ponce*; '*pierre ponce*, a pumis stone,' Cot. '*Ponce*, pumice;' Hamilton. – L. *pūmicem*, acc. of *pūmex*, pumice; whence *ponce* (= *pom'ce*) is regularly formed. **Der.** *pounce*, to sprinkle with pounce (F. *poncer*); *pounce-box*; *pounc-et-box*, 1 Hen. IV, i. 3. 38. **Doublet,** *pumice*.

POUND (1), a weight, a sovereign. (L.) The sense of 'weight' is the orig. one. ME. *pund*, later *pound*, frequently with the pl. the same as the singular, whence the mod. phrase 'a five-*pound* note.' 'An hundred *pund*' = a hundred pounds, Havelok, 1633. AS. *pund*, pl. *pund*, a weight, a pound; see Luke xix. 16, John xii. 3. – L. *pondō*, a pound, used as an indeclinable sb., though orig. meaning 'by weight;' allied to *pondus*, a weight. Hence also were borrowed G. *pfund*, &c. Allied to *pendere*, to weigh; and to *pendēre*, to hang; see **Pendant. Der.** *pound-age*; see Blount's Nomolexicon, ed. 1691. And see *ponder*.

POUND (2), an enclosure for strayed animals. (E.) The same word as *pond*. 'Which thus in *pound* was pent;' Gascoigne, A Deuise for Viscount Mountacute; see Gascoigne's Works, ed. Hazlitt, i. 84, l. 1. Rich. has the reading *pond*. ME. *pond*; in the comp. *pond-folde* (other readings *ponfolde*, *punfolde*, *pounfolde*, *pyn-*

fold), P. Plowman, B. v. 633; with the sense 'pinfold' or 'pound.' AS. *pund*, an enclosure; the compound *pund-breche*, explained by *infractura parci* = the breaking into an enclosure, occurs in the Laws of Hen. I., c. 40; see Thorpe's Ancient Laws, vol. i. p. 540. Hence AS. *forpyndan*, to shut in, repress; Grein, i. 329. Cf. Icel. *pynda*, to shut in, torment. [Irish *pont*, a pound for cattle, a pond, is borrowed from E.] Der. *pound*, verb, Cor. i. 4. 17; *im-pound*. Also *pin-fold*, K. Lear. ii. 2. 9, for *pind-fold* = *pound-fold*, as shown by ME. *pynfold* cited above, the vowel *i* being due to the *y* in the derived AS. *pyndan*; as also in *pind-ar*, q. v. Doublet, pond.

POUND (3), to beat, bruise in a mortar. (E.) Here the *d* is excrescent; it stands for *poun*, from an older form *pūn*. Cf. *soun-d* for ME. *soun*; *gown-d*, vulgar form of *gown*. ME. *pounen*, to bruise, Wyclif, Matt. xxi. 44, earlier version. AS. *pūnian*, to pound, Liber Scintillarum, p. 95, l. 18; the pp. *gepūnod* occurs as a various reading for *gecnucud* (=knocked, pounded) in Cockayne's Leechdoms, i. 176, footnote 4. Der. *pound-er*.

POUR, to cause to flow, send forth, utter, flow. (F. – L.) 'I *poore* out the lycoure;' Palsgrave. ME. *pouren*, P. Plowman, B. v. 220; often used with *out*, Gower, C. A. i. 302; bk. iii. 679. The orig. sense in F. was to purify, clarify, esp. by wringing or squeezing out; cf. Lowl. Sc. *poor*, to drain off water, E. D. D. – OF. *purer*, to clarify, also to pour out or to drip; so also *depurer*, to drip or run out; Norm. dial. *purer*, to pour, flow, drip, as in *puis soit celle eaue puree en un autre vaissel*, let this water be then poured into another vessel; Guernsey, *j'o l'cidre qui pure dans l'auge*, I hear the cider pouring into the trough (Moisy). – Late L. *pūrāre*, to purify. – L. *pūrus*, pure. ¶ The development of the vowel is exceptional; observe that it rimes with *shower*, *flower*, in Pope, Messiah, 13, and in Gay, The Fan, i. 97; cf. E. *flower* from AF. *flur*; the sound may have been affected by *pore*, sb., and *pore*, verb. See Pure.

POURPOINT, PURPOINT, a quilted doublet. (F. – L.) ME. *purpoynt*; Paston Letters, i. 482. – F. *pourpoint*, 'a dublet;' Cot. A corruption of OF. *parpoint* (Godefroy); by the frequent confusion of *pour* and *par*. – Late L. *perpunctum*. – L. *perpunct-us*, pp. of *perpungere*, to pierce with a needle; hence, to quilt. – L. *per*, through; *pungere*, to prick. Cf. Norm. dial. *parpointer*, to quilt.

POURTRAY, the same as **Portray,** q. v.

POUT (1), to look sulky or displeased, to puff out the lips or cheeks. (E.) In Shak. Cor. v. 1. 52. ME. *pouten*, in Reliquiæ Antiquæ, ii. 211. [Cf. W. *pwdu*, to pout, to be sullen, which I suppose to be a form borrowed from English.] For the derivative *eel-pout*, see Pout (2) below. We also find Du. *puit-aal*, an eel-pout, *puit*, a frog (from its swollen shape); Swed. *puta*, a cushion, Dan. *pude*, a pillow. Cf. Swed. dial. *puta*, to be blown out, to be swollen out (Rietz). Der. *pout* (2), *pout-er*, *pout-ing*.

POUT (2), a kind of fish. (E.) 'It has the power of inflating a membrane which covers the eyes and neighboring parts of the head;' Webster. '*Powt*, or *eel-powt*;' Minsheu. We find AS. *æle-pūtan*, eel-pouts, in Ælfric's Colloquy (Fisherman), in Voc. 94. 7. *Pūta* is lit. 'pouter,' from a verb **pūtan*, to pout, found in the cognate Swed. dial. *puta*, to be blown out or inflated (Rietz); and see EFries. *pūt-āl*, an eel-pout, in Koolman. Cf. Skt. *bud-bud-a-*, a bubble, from an imitative root BEU-; cf. the root BHEU in Gk. φυσάω, I puff out. ¶ The Sc. *pout*, chicken (Jamieson) = *poult*, q. v.

POVERTY, the state of being poor. (F. – L.) In early use. ME. *pouertè* (with *u* = *v*), O. Eng. Homilies, ed. Morris, i. 143, last line. – OF. *poverte*, later *povreté*, 'poverty,' Cot. Mod. F. *pauvreté*. – L. *paupertātem*, acc. of *paupertās*, poverty. – L. *pauper*, poor; see Poor.

POWDER, dust. (F. – L.) ME. *poudre*, Rob. of Glouc. p. 345, l. 7080. – F. *poudre*, 'powder,' Cot., who also gives the spelling *pouldre*. OF. *poldre*, *puldre*, in Burguy and Supp. to Godefroy. Formed with excrescent *d* after *l*; the oldest form is *polre*. – L. *puluerem*, acc. of *puluis*, dust. Allied to *pollen*, fine meal, *palea*, chaff; Gk. πάλ-η, meal. See Pulverise. Der. *powder*, verb, ME. *pouderen*, Rich. Redeles, Pass. i. l. 46; *powder-y*.

POWER, might, ability, strength, rule. (F. – L.) ME. *poër*, Popular Treatises on Science, ed. Wright, p. 133, l. 36; also *pouër*, Allit. Poems, ed. Morris, B. 1654. Hence *power*, where the *w* is used to avoid the appearance of an hiatus; Prick of Conscience, 5884. – AF. *poër*, Stat. Realm, i. 28; OF. *poër*, also *pooir*, and (in order to avoid hiatus) *povoir*, power; mod. F. *pouvoir*. The OF. *poër* stands for *poter*, as shown by Ital. *potere*, power; cf. also Span. *poder*, power. β. The word is merely due to a substantival use of an infinitive mood, as in the case of *leisure*, *pleasure*; the Ital. *potere*, Span. *poder*, are both infinitives as well as sbs., with the sense 'to be able.' – Late L. *potēre*, to be able, which (as shown by Diez) took the place of L. *posse* in the 8th century. The L. *posse* is itself a contraction for *pot-esse*, used by Plautus and Lucretius; and *pot-esse*, again, stands for *poti-esse*, to be powerful; from *potis*, powerful, and

esse, to be. See **Possible** and **Essence.** Der. *power-ful*, Spenser, F. Q. iv. 10. 36; *power-ful-ly*, *power-ful-ness*; *power-less*, *power-less-ly*, *power-less-ness*. Doublet, posse.

POX, an eruptive disease. (E.) Written for *pocks*, pl. of *pock*, a pustule; see Pock. Cf. 'small *pockes*;' Sir T. Elyot, Castel of Helth, bk. iv. [iii. in the head-line], ch. 6.

PRACTICE, a habit of doing things, performance. (F. – L. – Gk.) Spelt *practyse* in Palsgrave. A back-formation from the verb to *practyse* (in the same). – OF. *practiser*, to practise (Godefroy). – Late L. type **practiciāre*, for Late L. *practicāre*, to practise. – L. *practicus* (below). β. But the older form of the sb. was *praktike*. ME. *praktike*, Chaucer, C. T. 5769 (D 187); *practique*, Gower, C. A. ii. 89; bk. iv. 2612. – OF. *practique*, 'practise, experience,' Cot. – L. *practica*, fem. of *practicus*. – Gk. πρακτικός, fit for business, practical; whence ἡ πρακτική (ἐπιστήμη), practical science, practice. – Gk. πρακτός, to be done; verbal adj. of πράσσειν (=*πρακγειν), to do, to accomplish. From a base πρᾱ-κ; Brugmann, ii. § 86. Der. *practise*, verb, K. John, i. 214, as above (cf. *practisour* = practis-er, in Chaucer, C. T. 424); *practis-er*. Also *practic-able*, used by Bp. Taylor, vol. iii. ser. 2 (R.), formed from MF. *practiquer*, 'to practise,' Cot.; hence *practic-abl-y*, *practic-abil-i-ty*; also *practic-al*, North's Plutarch, pt. ii. p. 18 (R.), *practic-al-ly*, *-ness*. Also *practition-er*, formed with a needless suffixed *-er* from the older term *practician*, with the same sense (both *practician* and *practitioner* are in Minsheu, from MF. *practicien*, 'a practicer or practitioner in law,' Cot. And see pragmatic.

PRÆTOR, PRETOR, a Roman magistrate. (L.) In Shak. Jul. Cæs. i. 3. 143. – L. *prætor*, lit. a goer before, a leader; contracted form of **præ-itor*. – L. *præ*, before; and **itor*, a goer, from *it-um*, supine of *īre*, to go, which is from √EI, to go. See Pre- and Itinerant. Der. *prætor-ium*, the prætor's hall, Mark xv. 16; *prætor-i-an*; *prætorship*.

PRAGMATIC, well-practised, fit for business, active. (F. – L. – Gk.) 'These *pragmatic* young men;' Ben Jonson, The Devil is an Ass, Act i. sc. 3, end of Fitzdottrel's long speech. '*Pragmaticall*, practised in many matters;' Minsheu, ed. 1627. – F. *pragmatique*; chiefly in the phrase *la pragmatique sanction*, 'a confirmation of a decree made in the councill of Basil,' &c., Cot. – L. *pragmaticus*. – Gk. πραγματικός, skilled in business. – Gk. πραγματ-, stem of πρᾶγμα (=*πρακ-μα), a deed, thing done. – Gk. πράσσειν (=*πρακ-γειν), to do; see Practice. Der. *pragmatic-al*, *-al-ly*. Note also *praxis*, an example for exercise, from Gk. πρᾶξις, a deed, action.

PRAIRIE, an extensive meadow or tract of grass. (F. – L.) A word imported from America in the 18th cent. 'The wondrous, beautiful *prairies*;' Longfellow, Evangeline, part ii. iv. 12. – F. *prairie*, 'a medow, or medow ground;' Cot. – Late L. *prātāria*, meadow-land; used. A.D. 832; Ducange. – L. *prāt-um*, a meadow; with adj. fem. suffix *-āria*.

PRAISE, commendation, tribute of gratitude. (F. – L.) ME. *preis*, *preys*, Chaucer, C. T. 14565 (B 3837). [The verb *preisen*, to praise, is found much earlier, in the Ancren Riwle, p. 64, l. 22.] – OF. *preis*, price, value, merit; from OF. *preisier*, to praise. – L. *pretiāre*, to price, prize, value; from *pretium*, price, value; see Price. Der. *prais-er*; *praise-worthy*, Much Ado, v. 2. 90; *praise-worthi-ness*. Also *ap-praise*, *dis-praise*, *ap-preci-ate*, *de-preci-ate*; *precious*. Doublets, price, prize (2).

PRAM, a flat-bottomed boat. (F. – Du. – Slav.) Spelt *prame* in Johnson's Dict. – F. *prame* (1752), Hatzfeld; but AF. *prame* occurs in The Earl of Derby's Expeditions, p. 42, l. 24. – Du. *praam*. – OChSlavon. *pramŭ*; Polish *pram*, a boat, vessel; from the Idg. √PAR, whence also Goth. *far-an*, to travel, E. *fare* (Kluge).

PRANCE, to strut about; in mod. E., to bound gaily, as a horse. (E.) Spelt *praunce* in Spenser, where it is used of a giant stalking along; F. Q. i. 7. 11. In Shak. it is used of a young man, 1 Hen. VI, ii. 1. 24. The old sense is to strut about, as if for display; and the word is a variant of *prank*. Used of a horse, Skelton, Bowge of Courte, l. 411. ME. *prauncen*; 'the horse may pryk and *praunce*,' Lydgate, Horse, Sheep, and Goose, l. 29. Also *prancen*, Gower, C. A. iii. 41; bk. vi. 1191. Allied to *prank* (below); cf. Dan. dial. *prandse*, *pranse*, to go proudly, as a prancing horse; *pransk*, proud; Swed. dial. *prånga*, Swed. *prunka*, to show off; Dan. dial. *pranje*, *pranne*, to prance. So also MDu. *pronken*, 'to make a fine show, to brag, strut; *langs straat gaan pronken*, to strut along, to walk proudly along the streets;' Sewel. See Prank. Der. *pranc-ing*.

PRANK (1), to deck, to adorn. (E.) The old senses are to display gaudily, set out ostentatiously, to deck, dress up. 'Some *prancke* their ruffes;' Spenser, F. Q. i. 4. 14. ME. *pranken*, '*Prankyd*, as clothes, *plicatus*,' Prompt. Parv. 'I *pranke* ones gowne, I set the plyghtes [pleats] in order, *ie mets les plies dune robe à poynt*. Se yonder olde man, his gowne is *pranked* as if he were but a yonge man;' Palsgrave. '*Pranked* with pletes;' Skelton, Elinour Rummyng, 69; *prank*, a fold, pleat, Prompt. Parv. β. Closely connected with *prink*, used in the same sense; see examples in Nares. 'But marke his plumes, The whiche to *princke* he dayes and nights consumes;' Gascoigne, Weeds, Farewell with a Mischief, st. 6, ed. Hazlitt. [Here Rich. reads *pranke*.] *Prink* is a nasalised form of *prick*; cf. Lowland Scot. *preek* (lit. to prick), to be spruce; 'a bit *preekin* bodie, one attached to dress, self-conceited,' Jamieson; *prick-me-dainty*, finical; *prink, primp*, to deck, to prick. See **Prick**. γ. Allied words are MDu. *pronck*, 'shewe, or ostentation,' Hexham; *proncken*, to display one's dress, *pronckepinken, pronckeprincken*, to glitter in a fine dress, Oudemans. Without the nasal, we have MDu. *pryken*, 'to make a proud shew;' Sewel. Cf. also Low G. *prunken*, to make a fine show, *prunk*, show, display, Bremen Wörterbuch; G. *prunk*, show, parade; Dan. and Swed. *prunk*, show, parade; and perhaps G. *prangen*, Dan. *prange*, to make a show. δ. The forms suggest a Teut. type *preukan*, str. vb. (pt. t. *prank*, pp. *prunkanoz*). **Der.** *prank* (2), *prance*.

PRANK (2), a trick, mischievous action. (E.) In Shak. Hamlet, iii. 4. 2; K. Lear, i. 4. 259, Oth. ii. 1. 143; Skelton, Why Come Ye Nat to Courte, 365. 'Pranke, *tour, finesse*;' Palsgrave. Mr. Wedgwood well says: 'A *prank* is usually taken in a bad sense, and signifies something done in the face of others that makes them stare with amazement.' It is, in fact, an act done 'to show off;' and is the same word as *prank*, show; see above.

PRATE, to talk idly. (Low G.) ME. *praten*, Lydgate, Minor Poems, ed. Halliwell, p. 155; Coventry Plays, ed. Halliwell, 353 (Stratmann). Cf. MSwed. *prata*, to talk (Ihre); Dan. *prate*, to prate; also Swed. *prat*, Dan. *prat*, talk, prattle. — MDu. *praten*, 'to prate,' Hexham; mod. Du. *praat*, tattle; Low G. *praten*, to prate, *praat*, tattle, Bremen Wörterbuch. Perhaps of imitative origin, from a base *prat*. **Der.** *prate*, sb., *prat-er, prat-ing*. Also *pratt-le*, Temp. iii. 1. 57, the frequentative form, with the usual suffix *-le*; cf. Low G. *prateln*, to prattle (Schambach); *prattle*, sb., Rich. II, v. 2. 26; *prattl-er*.

PRAWN, a small crustacean animal, like the shrimp. (Scand.?) ME. *prane*, Prompt. Parv. Of doubtful origin. Florio has: '*Parnocchie*, a fish called shrimps or praunes;' where *parnocchie* can hardly be other than a dimin. form of L. *perna*, a sea-mussel (lit. a ham), whence MItal. *perna*, 'a shell-fish called a nakre or a narre,' Florio; also Span. *perna*, flat shell-fish. But we cannot connect *prawn* with L. *perna*. β. We find also prov. E. *prankle*, a prawn, and *prankle*, to prance (Isle of Wight). This suggests a connexion between *prawn* and *prance*; with a possible allusion to its bright appearance or quick movements; cf. Jutland *pranni*, to strut, *prannis*, a showy person (Feilberg).

PRAY, to entreat, ask earnestly. (F. — L.) In early use. ME. *preien, preyen*; O. Eng. Homilies, ed. Morris, i. 287, l. 9; Havelok, 1440. — AF. and OF. *preier*, later *prier*, 'to pray,' Cot. — L. *precāri*, to pray. — L. *prec-*, stem of *prex*, a prayer; see **Precarious**. **Der.** *pray-er*, ME. *preiere, preyere*, Chaucer, C. T. 231, 1206 (A 1204), from OF. *preiere, proiere*, mod. F. *prière* (Ital. *preghiera*), from L. *precāria*, fem. of *precarius*; see **Precarious**. Hence *prayer-ful, prayer-less*.

PRE-, prefix, beforehand. (L.; or F. — L.) Used both as a F. and L. prefix; OF. *pre-*, L. *pre-* (in *pre-hendere*), usually *præ-*. — L. *præ*, prep., before; for *prai*, a locative form. Closely connected with *pro*; see **Pro-**. Also allied to the prefixes *per-, para-, pur-*. Hence numerous compounds, of which several, like *pre-caution*, are of obvious origin.

PREACH, to pronounce a public discourse on sacred matters. (F. — L.) ME. *prechen*, Ancren Riwle, p. 70, ll. 22, 24. — OF. *prechier* (*prescher* in Cot.), mod. F. *prêcher*. — L. *prædicāre*, to make known in public, declare publicly. — L. *præ*, before, before men, publicly; and *dicāre*, to proclaim, allied to *dicere*, to say. See **Pre-** and **Diction**. **Der.** *preach-er, preach-ing; preach-ment*, 3 Hen. VI, i. 4. 72. **Doublet**, *predicate*, vb.

PREAMBLE, an introduction, preface. (F. — L.) ME. *preamble*, Chaucer, C. T. 6413 (D 831). — OF. *preambule*, 'a preamble, preface, prologue;' Cot. — L. *præambulus*, adj.; from *præambulāre*, to walk before. — L. *præ*, before; and *ambulāre*, to walk; see **Pre-** and **Amble**. **Der.** *preambul-at-ion*, Chaucer, C. T. 6419 (D 837).

PREBEND, a portion received for maintenance by a member of a cathedral church. (F. — L.) Defined in Minsheu, ed. 1627. — OF. *prebende*, 'a prebendry,' Cot.; mod. F. *prébende*, a prebend. — L. *præbenda*, a payment to a private person from a public source; fem. of *præbendus*, fut. pass. part. of *præbēre*, to afford, supply, give. — L. *præ*, before; and *habēre*, to have; whence *præhibēre*, to hold forth, proffer, offer, contracted to *præbēre*. See **Pre-** and **Habit**. **Der.** *prebend-al; prebend-ar-y*, Spenser, Mother Hubbard's Tale, 422.

PRECARIOUS, uncertain, held by a doubtful tenure. (L.)

'Powers which he but *precariously* obeys;' Sir T. Browne, Vulg. Errors, b. i. c. 10, near end of § 10. Formed (by change of *-us* to *-ous*, as in numerous instances) from L. *precarius*, obtained by prayer, obtained as a favour, doubtful, precarious. — L. *precāri*, to pray. — L. *prec-*, stem of *prex*, a prayer. + G. *frag-en*, to ask; Goth. *fraih-nan*, AS. *frig-nan*, to ask; Lith. *praszyti*; Russ. *prosite*; Pers. *persīdan*; Skt. *pracch*, to ask; W. *erchi* (for *perchi*), to ask. (√PREK). Brugmann, i. § 607. **Der.** *precarious-ly, -ness*.

PRECAUTION, a caution taken beforehand. (F. — L.) In Minsheu, ed. 1627. — ME. *precaution*, 'a precaution,' Cot. Mod. F. *précaution*. — L. *præcautiōnem*, acc. of *præcautio*; comp. of *præ*, before, and *cautio*, a caution; see **Pre-** and **Caution**. **Der.** *precautionary*.

PRECEDE, to go before. (F. — L.) In Hamlet, i. 1. 122; and in Palsgrave. — MF. *preceder*, 'to precede,' Cot.; mod. F. *précéder*. — L. *præcēdere*, to go before; comp. of *præ*, before, and *cēdere*, to go; see **Pre-** and **Cede**. **Der.** *preced-ence*, L. L. L. iii. 83, from MF. *precedence*, 'precedence,' Cot., which from L. *præcēdentia*, a going forward, an advance; *preced-enc-y*. Also *precēd-ent*, adj., Hamlet, iii. 4. 98, from MF. *precedent*, 'precedent, foregoing,' Cot.; *preced-ent-ly*. Hence, with a change of accent, *préced-ent*, sb., Temp. ii. 1. 291 (spelt *presidente*, Skelton, ed. Dyce, i. 7, l. 23), *precedent-ed*, *un-precedent-ed*; *preced-ing*. Also *precess-ion*, q.v.

PRECENTOR, the leader of a choir. (L.) In Todd's Johnson, with a quotation dated A.D. 1622. — L. *præcentor*, a leader in music, precentor. — L. *præ*, before; and *cantor*, a singer, from *cantāre*, to sing, chant; see **Pre-** and **Chant**.

PRECEPT, a rule of action, commandment, maxim. (F. — L.) ME. *precept*, Wyclif, Acts, xvi. 24. — OF. *precept*; MF. *precepte*, 'a precept,' Cot.; mod. F. *précepte*. — L. *præceptum*, a precept, rule; orig. neut. of *præceptus*, pp. of *præcipere*, to take beforehand, also, to give rules. — L. *præ-*, before; and *capere*, to take; see **Pre-** and **Capture**. **Der.** *precept-ive; precept-ial*, Much Ado, v. 1. 24; *precept-or*, from L. *præceptor*, a teacher; *precept-or-ial, precept-or-y, precept-r-ess*.

PRECESSION, a going forward. (L.) Chiefly in the phrase *precession of the equinoxes*, defined in Phillips, ed. 1706. From L. *præcessiōnem*, acc. of *præcessio*, a late word; cf. *præcessus*, pp. of *præcēdere*; see **Precede**.

PRECINCT, a territorial district. (L.) Spelt *precynct* in Fabyan, Chron. vol. i. c. 172, ed. Ellis, p. 168, l. 27; *precinct*, Will of Hen. VI, Royal Wills, ed. Nichols, p. 299. — Late L. *præcinctum*, a boundary; Ducange. — L. *præcinctum*, neut. of *præcinctus*, pp. of *præcingere*, to enclose, surround, gird about. — L. *præ*, before, used as an augmentative, with the sense of 'fully;' and *cingere*, to gird; see **Pre-** and **Cincture**.

PRECIOUS, valuable, costly, dear. (F. — L.) ME. *precious*, P. Plowman, A. ii. 12 (footnote); Wyclif, 1 Pet. ii. 6. — OF. *precios, precieus*, mod. F. *précieux*, precious. — L. *pretiōsus*, valuable. — L. *pretium*, a price, value; see **Price**. **Der.** *precious-ly, -ness*.

PRECIPICE, a very steep place, an abrupt descent. (F. — L.) In Minsheu, and in Shak. Hen. VIII, v. 1. 140. — MF. *precipice*, mod. F. *précipice* (Littré). — L. *præcipitium*, a falling headlong down; also, a precipice. — L. *præcipiti-*, decl. stem of *præceps*, head-foremost. — L. *præ*, before; and *capiti-*, decl. stem of *caput*, the head; see **Pre-** and **Capital**. **Der.** *precipit-ous*, Sir T. Browne, Vulg. Errors, b. iii. c. 6. last §, from MF. *precipiteux*, 'headlong,' Cot.; *precipit-ous-ly, -ness*. Also *precipit-ate*, adj., properly a pp., from L. *præcipitāre*, to cast headlong; used as a verb in Minsheu, and in Shak. K. Lear, iv. 6. 50; *precipit-ate-ly; precipit-ant; precipit-ance, precipit-anc-y*; also *precipit-at-ion*, from MF. *precipitation*, 'precipitation,' Cot.

PRECISE, definite, exact. (F. — L.) We find *presysely*, adv., in Fabyan, Chron. vol. i. c. 245; ed. Ellis, p. 287, l. 44. — OF. *precis*, fem. *precise*, 'strict, precise;' Cot. Mod. F. *précis*. — L. *præcisus*, cut off, shortened, brief, concise; the sense of 'strict' arose from that of 'concise,' because an abstract is precise, to the exclusion of irrelevant matter. — L. *præcīdere*, to cut off near the end. — L. *præ*, before, in front; and *cædere*, to cut. See **Pre-** and **Cæsura**. **Der.** *precise-ly, -ness; precis-ion*, a late word. Also *precis-ian*, a precise person; a coined word; see Nares.

PRECLUDE, to hinder by anticipation, shut out beforehand. (L.) First in 1618; used by Pope and Burke; see Todd's Johnson and Richardson. — L. *præclūdere*, to close, shut up, hinder from access. — L. *præ*, in front; and *claudere*, to shut; see **Pre-** and **Clause**. **Der.** *preclus-ion, preclus-ive*.

PRECOCIOUS, premature, forward. (L.) 'Many *precocious* trees;' Sir T. Browne, Vulg. Errors, b. ii. c. 6. part 4. [Evelyn, as cited in R., uses *precoce*, answering to mod. F. *précoce*.] A coined word; from *præcoci-*, decl. stem of *præcox*, ripe before its time, premature; also spelt *præcoquus, præcoquis*. — L. *præ*, before; and *coquere*, to cook, to ripen; see **Pre-** and **Cook**. **Der.** *precocious-ly, -ness; precoci-ty*.

PRECONCEIVE, to conceive beforehand. (F. – L.) Used by Bacon, Colours of Good and Evil, sec. 5, § 2. Coined from **Pre-** and **Conceive**. Der. *preconcept-ion*; from **Pre-** and **Con-ception**.

PRECONCERT, to concert or plan beforehand. (F. – Ital. – L.) 'Some *preconcerted* stratagem;' Warton, Hist. of E. Poetry, iii. 138, ed. 1840. Coined from **Pre-** and **Concert**.

PRECURSOR, a forerunner. (L.) In Shak. Temp. i. 2. 201. – L. *præcursor*, a forerunner. – L. *præ*, before; and *cursor*, a runner, from *currere*, to run; see **Pre-** and **Course**. Der. *precur-sor-y*; note also *precurse*, a forerunning, Hamlet, i. 1. 121.

PREDATORY, given to plundering. (L.) Rich. gives a quotation from Reliquiæ Wottonianæ, p. 455. First in Puttenham, Arte of E. Poesie, bk. i. c. 18. Englished from L. *prædātōrius*, plundering; from *prædātor*, a plunderer. – L. *prædārī*, to plunder, get booty. – L. *præda*, prey, booty; see **Prey**.

PREDECESSOR, one who has preceded another in an office. (L.) In Shak. Hen. V, i. 1. 181; also an ancestor, Hen. V, i. 2. 248. Spelt *predecessour* (as if from F.) in Du Wes; printed with Palsgrave, p. 897, l. 3. – L. *prædēcessor*, a predecessor. – L. *præ*, before; and *dēcessor*, one who retires from an office; cf. *dēcessus*, pp. of *dēcēdere*, to depart, which is compounded of *dē*, from, away, and *cēdere*, to go. See **Pre-**, **De-**, and **Cede**.

PREDESTINE, to destine by fate. (F. – L.) [We find ME. *predestinacioun* in Chaucer, tr. of Boethius, b. iv. pr. 6, l. 19. *Predestinate* is well used as a pp. in: 'They were *predestynate* to suffre yet more plagues,' Hall's Chron. Hen. V, an. 4. § 2.] 'From our *predistin'd* plagues that priuileged be;' Drayton, Polyolbion, song 2. *Predistin'd* is Englished from MF. *predestiné*, 'predestined, predestinated;' Cot. – L. *prædestinātus*, pp. of *prædestināre*, to determine beforehand. – L. *præ*, before; and *destināre*, to destine; see **Pre-** and **Destine**. Der. *predestin-ate*, as above, from L. *prædestinātus*; *predestin-at-or*, *predestin-at-ion*, as above, from MF. *predestination*. Also *predestin-ar-i-an*, a coined word.

PREDETERMINE, to determine beforehand. (F. – L.) 'But he did not *predetermine* him to any evil;' Bp. Taylor, vol. i. ser. 9 (R.). Coined from **Pre-** and **Determine**. Der. *predetermin-ate*, *predetermin-at-ion*.

PREDICATE, to affirm one thing concerning another. (L.) A term in logic. 'Which may as truely be *predicated* of the English play-haunters now, as of the Romans then;' Prynne, Histrio-Mastix, pt. i. Act vi. sc. 2 (R.). – L. *prædicātus*, pp. of *prædicāre*, to publish, proclaim; see **Preach**. Der. *predicat-ion*, *predica-ble*, *predicat-ive*. Also *predica-ment*, one of the most general classes into which things can be distributed; see Tyndale, Obedience of a Christian Man (1528), in Specimens of English, ed. Skeat, p. 176, l. 317, from Late L. *prædicāmentum*. Doublet, *preach*.

PREDICT, to tell beforehand, prophesy. (L.) In Milton, P. R. iii. 356. Shak. has *predict* as a sb., with the sense of 'prediction;' Sonnet xiv. 8. – L. *prædictus*, pp. of *prædīcere*, to tell beforehand. – L. *præ*, before; and *dīcere*, to say; see **Pre-** and **Diction**. Der. *predict-ion*, Macb. i. 3. 55, from MF. *prediction*, 'a prediction,' Cot.; and this sb. probably suggested the verb to *predict*, as it is in earlier use. Also *predict-ive*, from L. *predictiuus*.

PREDILECTION, a choosing beforehand, partiality, choice. (F. – L.) A late word, added by Todd to Johnson's Dict. – F. *prédilection* (first in 1519). Coined from L. *præ*, before, beforehand; and *dilectio*, choice, love, from *diligere*, to choose out from others, to love. *Diligere* is compounded of *di-*, for *dis-*, apart; and *legere*, to choose. See **Pre-**, **Dis-**, and **Legend**.

PREDISPOSE, to dispose beforehand. (F. – L. *and* Gk.) In Phillips, ed. 1706. – F. *prédisposer* (15 cent.). Coined from L. *præ*, beforehand; and F. *disposer*. See **Pre-** and **Dispose**. Der. *predispos-it-ion* (but see **Pose** and **Position**, where the difference in origin of these two words is explained).

PREDOMINATE, to rule over, reign. (L.) In Shak. Merry Wives, ii. 2. 294; Timon, iv. 3. 142. Coined from **Pre-** and **Dominate**. Der. *predomin-ant*, in Minsheu, ed. 1627, from *domin-ant-*, stem of pres. part. of *dominārī*, to rule; *predomin-ance*; *predomin-anc-y*, Bacon, Colours of Good and Evil, vii. § 3.

PRE-EMINENCE, eminence above the rest. (F. – L.) Spelt *preemynence* in Palsgrave; *preheminence*, Bacon, Essay ix. § 12; *preemynence*, Skelton, Why Come Ye Nat to Court, 406. – MF. *pré-eminence*, 'preheminence,' Cot. [The insertion of *h* was due to a wish to avoid the hiatus.] – L. *præēminentia*, a surpassing, excelling. – L. *præ*, before; and *ēminentia*, eminence; see **Pre-** and **Eminence**. Der. *pre-eminent*, from L. *præēminent-*, stem of the pres. part. of *præēminēre*, to excel; *pre-eminent-ly*.

PRE-EMPTION, a purchasing before others. (L.) 'Right of *preemption* of first choice of wines in Bourdeaux;' Howell, Famil. Letters, b. ii. let. 55 [*not* 14]; dated 1634. Coined from L. *præ*,

before; and *emptio*, a buying, allied to *emptus* or *emtus*, pp. of *emere*, to buy; see **Pre-** and **Example**.

PRE-ENGAGE, to engage beforehand. (F. – L.) Todd gives two quotations for this word from Dryden, both without references. The former is from Cymon, l. 246. From **Pre-** and **Engage**. Der. *pre-engage-ment*.

PRE-EXIST, to exist beforehand. (L.) 'But if thy *pre-existing* soul;' Dryden, On Mrs. Killigrew, l. 29. From **Pre-** and **Exist**. Der. *pre-exist-ent*, *pre-exist-ence*.

PREFACE, the introduction to a book. (F. – L.) In Shak. 1 Hen. VI, v. 5. 11; Chaucer, C. T., G 271. – OF. and MF. *preface*, fem. 'a preface,' Cot.; mod. F. *préface*. Cf. Ital. *prefazio*, Span. *prefacio*, corresponding to an OF. *preface* of the masc. gender. β. Suggested by L. *præfātio*, a preface, which produced the Ital. *prefazione* and Span. *prefacion*, and would have given a F. form *préfaison*. – L. *præfārī*, to say beforehand. – L. *præ*, before; and *fārī*, to speak. See **Pre-** and **Fate**. Der. *preface*, verb; *prefat-or-y*, as if from a L. *præfātōrius.

PREFECT, a governor, one placed in office, president. (F. – L.) ME. *prefect*, Chaucer, C. T. 15830 (G 362), (where he is translating from Latin). – OF. and MF. *prefect*; mod. F. *préfet*. – L. *præfectus*, a prefect, one set over others. – L. *præ*, before; and *factus*, made, set, pp. of *facere*, to make; see **Pre-** and **Fact**. Der. *prefect-ship*; also *prefect-ure*, from mod. F. *préfecture*, L. *præfectūra*, a prefectship.

PREFER, to regard before others, esteem more highly, to advance or exalt. (F. – L.) Common in Shak. Cor. iii. 1. 152, &c.; spelt *preferre* in Palsgrave. – OF. *preferer*, 'to prefer, like better,' Cot. – L. *præferre* (pres. t. *præfero*), to carry in front; also to set in front, prefer. – L. *præ*, before; and *ferre*, cognate with E. *bear*; see **Pre-** and **Bear** (1). Der. *prefer-able*, from MF. *preferable*, 'preferrable,' Cot., also written *prefer-ible*; *prefer-abl-y*, *prefer-able-ness*; *prefer-ence*, from MF. *preference*, 'preferment;' Cot.; *prefer-ment*, Oth. i. 1. 36.

PREFIGURE, to suggest by types. (F. – L.) '*Prefigured* by the temple of Solomon;' Bale, Ymage of both Churches (1550), pt. i (R.). From **Pre-** and **Figure**; but suggested by Late L. *præfigurāre* (Lewis). Der. *prefigure-ment*, *prefigurat-ion*, *prefigurat-ive*.

PREFIX, to fix beforehand. (F. – L.) 'I prefixe, *Je prefixe*;' Palsgrave. Spenser has the pp. *prefixed*, Sonnet 46, l. 1; Lydgate has *prefyxyd*, Assembly of the Gods, 549. This is due to the MF. *prefix*, 'prefixed, limited;' Cot. – L. *præfixus*, pp. of *præfigere*, to fix in front. – L. *præ*, before; and *figere*, to fix; see **Pre-** and **Fix**. Der. *prefix*, sb., lit. that which is prefixed.

PREGNANT (1), pressing, urgent, cogent; as a proof or reason. (F. – L.) 'A *preignant* argument;' Chaucer, Troilus, b. iv. 1179. – OF. *preignant*, *pregnant*, 'pregnant, pithy;' Cot. Here *preignant* is the pres. pt. of OF. *preindre*, *prembre*, to press (Godefroy). – L. *premere*, to press; see **Press**.

PREGNANT (2), fruitful, with child; imaginative. (F. – L.) In Milton, P. L. ii. 779. – L. *prægnantem*, acc. of *prægnans*, pregnant. *Prægnans* has the form of a pres. part. from a verb *prægnāre, to be before a birth, to be about to bear. – L. *præ*, before; and *gnāre, to bear, of which the pp. *gnātus*, usually spelt *nātus*, born, is in common use. See **Pre-** and **Natal**. Der. *pregnant-ly*; *pregnanc-y*, 2 Hen. IV, i. 2. 192.

PREHENSILE, adapted for grasping. (L.) Modern; not in Todd's Johnson. Coined with suffix *-ilis* from *prehens-us*, usually *prensus*, pp. of *prehendere*, also *prendere*, to lay hold of. – L. *pre-*, for *præ*, before; and (obsolete) *-hendere*, to seize, get, cognate with E. *get*; see **Pre-** and **Get**. Der. *prison*, *prize* (1).

PRE-HISTORIC, before history. (F. – L.) Modern; from **Pre-** and **Historic**.

PREJUDGE, to judge beforehand. (F. – L.) In Bacon, Life of Hen. VII, ed. Lumby, p. 8, l. 17. – MF. *prejuger*, 'to prejudicate, prejudge,' Cot. – L. *præiūdicāre*; from *præ*, before, and *iūdicāre*, to judge. See **Pre-** and **Judge**. Der. *prejudicate*, All's Well, i. 2. 8, from L. *præiūdicātus*, pp. of *præiūdicāre*; *prejudicat-ion*, *prejudicat-ive*; and see *prejudice*.

PREJUDICE, a prejudgement, an ill opinion formed beforehand. (F. – L.) In Shak. Hen. VIII, i. 1. 182, ii. 4. 154. ME. *prejudice*, Shoreham's Poems (Percy Soc.), p. 36, l. 21. – OF. *prejudice*, 'a prejudice,' Cot. – L. *præiūdicium*, a judicial examination previous to a trial; also, a damage, prejudice. – L. *præ*, before; and *iūdicium*, a judgement. See **Prejudge**; also **Pre-** and **Judicial**. Der. *prejudice*, verb, 1 Hen. VI, iii. 3. 91; *prejudic-ial*, 3 Hen. VI, i. 1. 144; *prejudic-ial-ly*.

PRELATE, a bishop, church dignitary. (F. – L.) In early use; in Layamon, 24502; pl. *prelaz* (for *prelats*), Ancren Riwle, p. 10, l. 8. – OF. *prelat*, 'a prelate,' Cot. – L. *prælātus*, set above, used as pp. of the verb *præferre*, to prefer, advance, but from a different root. – L. *præ*, before; and *lātus*, for *tlātus* (= Gk. τλητός), from

√TEL, to lift; see **Pre-** and **Elate**. Der. *prelat-ic*, little used; *prelat-ic-al*, Milton, Reason of Church Government, b. ii. sect. 3. ch. 1 (R.); *prelat-ic-al-ly*; *prelat-ist*; *prelac-y*, Skelton, Why Come Ye Nat to Courte, 500.

PRELIMINARY, introductory. (F.–L.) In Blount's Gloss., ed. 1674. 'Some *preliminary* considerations;' Bp. Taylor, vol. iii. ser. 3 (R.). Coined from **Pre-**, q.v., and MF. *liminaire*, 'set before the entry, or at the beginning of, dedicatory,' Cot. From L. *liminārem*, acc. of *līmināris*, of or belonging to a threshold, coming at the beginning.–L. *limin-*, decl. stem of *limen*, a threshold, allied to *limes*, a boundary; see **Limit**. Der. *preliminari-ly*.

PRELUDE, an introduction to a piece of music, a preface. (F. –L.) The L. form *preludium* was once in use, and is the form given in Minsheu, Cotgrave, and Blount. In Dryden, Britannia Rediviva, 187, *prelude* seems to be used as a verb.–MF. *prelude*, 'a preludium, preface, preamble,' Cot.–Late L. *prēlūdium*, *†prǣlūdium*, a prelude, perhaps a coined word; it is not in Ducange.–L. *prælūdere*, to play beforehand, also, to give a prelude beforehand, which is just Dryden's use of it.–L. *præ*, before; and *lūdere*, to play; see **Pre-** and **Ludicrous**. Der. *prelude*, verb; *prelus-ive*, from pp. *prælūs-us*, with suffix *-ive*.

PREMATURE, mature before the right time, happening before the proper time. (L.) In Blount's Gloss., ed. 1674. Not F., but Englished from L. *præmātūrus*, too early, untimely, premature.–L. *præ*, before; and *mātūrus*, ripe; see **Pre-** and **Mature**. ¶ Cotgrave only gives the MF. sb. *prematurité*, 'prematurity.' Der. *premature-ly*, *prematur-i-ty*, *premature-ness*.

PREMEDITATE, to meditate beforehand. (L.) In Shak. Hen. V, iv. 1. 170.–L. *præmĕditātus*, pp. of *præmĕditārī*; see **Pre-** and **Meditate**. Der. *premeditat-ion*, in Sir T. Elyot, The Governour, b. ii. c. 1. § 13, from MF. *premeditation*, 'premeditation,' Cot., from L. acc. *præmĕditātiōnem*.

PREMIER, chief or first, a chief, a prime minister. (F.–L.) The law-phrase *premier seisin*, first possession, was in use in common law; Minsheu notes this use of it, A.D. 1627. Rich. quotes 'the Spaniard challengeth the *premier* place' from Camden's Remains.– F. *premier*, 'prime, first,' Cot.–L. *prīmārium*, acc. of *prīmārius*, chief, principal; formed with suffix *-ārius* from *prim-us*, first. See **Prime** (1). Der. *premier-ship*.

PREMISE, PREMISS, a proposition, in logic, proved or assumed for the sake of drawing conclusions; one of the two propositions in a syllogism from which the conclusion is drawn. (F.– L.) The spelling *premise* stands for *premisse*, the true F. spelling; the spelling *premiss* is perhaps due to the L. form, but may also be for *premisse*. Minsheu has 'the *premises*;' but the correct pl. *premisses* is in Chaucer, tr. of Boethius, b. iii. pr. 10, l. 83.–OF. *premisse* (mod. F. *prémisse*), omitted by Cotgrave, but in use in the 14th century (Littré).–L. *præmissa* (*sententia* being understood), a premiss, lit. that which is sent or put before.–L. *præ*, before; and *missus*, pp. of *mittere*, to send; see **Pre-** and **Missile**. Der. *premise*, verb, orig. 'to send before,' as in Shak. 2 Hen. VI, v. 2. 41, from F. *pre-* (<L. *præ*), before; and *mis* (fem. *mise*), pp. of *mettre* (<L. *mittere*), to send, to put. Also *premises*, s. pl., the adjuncts of a building, a sense due to the custom of beginning leases with the *premises* setting forth the names of the grantor and grantee of the deed, as well as a description of the thing granted; later, the sense was transferred from the description of these to that of the thing leased only, and came to be used in the present vague way; so in Blount's Nomolexicon, 1691. Wedgwood explains it more simply 'from the use of the term in legal language, where the appurtenances of a thing sold are mentioned *at full* in the first place, and subsequently referred to as the *premises*,' i.e. the things premised or mentioned above. Thus, in Lady Margaret's Will (1508) we find: 'All which maners, londs, and tenements, and other *the premisses*, we late purchased;' Royal Wills, ed. Nichols, p. 378. See examples in Caxton's print of the Statutes of Hen. VII; fol. a 6, &c.

PREMIUM, profit, bounty, reward, payment for a loan, &c. (L.) In Blount's Gloss., where he not only explains it by 'recompence,' but notes the mercantile use of it in insurances.–L. *præmium*, profit, lit. 'a taking before;' for **præ-imium* (<*præ-emium*).–L. *præ*, before; and *emere*, to take, also to buy; see **Pre-** and **Example**.

PREMONISH, to warn beforehand. (F.–L.) In Minsheu, ed. 1627. A coined word, from *pre-*, before; and *monish*, a corrupted form of ME. *monesten*, to warn, Wyclif, 2 Cor. vi. 1; just as *admonish* is corrupted from ME. *amonesten*. See **Pre-**, **Admonish**, and **Monition**. Der. *premonit-ion*, Chapman, tr. of Homer, Od. ii. 321, coined from *pre-* and *monition*. Also *premonit-ive*; *premonit-or*, from L. *præmonitor*; *premonit-or-y*, *premonit-or-i-ly*. Also *premonish-ment* (obsolete), used by Bale (R.).

PRENTICE; short for **Apprentice**, q.v.

PREOCCUPY, to occupy beforehand. (F.–L.) In Shak. Cor.

ii. 3. 240.–MF. *preoccuper*, 'to preoccupate, anticipate,' Cot.–L. *præoccupāre*; from *præ*, before, and *occupāre*, to occupy; see **Pre-** and **Occupy**. ¶ The peculiar ending of *occupy* is discussed under that word. Der. *preoccupat-ion*, from MF. *preoccupation* (Minsheu), 'a preoccupation,' Cot.; also *preoccup-anc-y*.

PREORDAIN, to ordain beforehand. (F.–L.) In Milton P. R. i. 127. From **Pre-** and **Ordain**; cf. MF. *preordonner*, 'to preordinate, or fore-ordain,' Cot. ¶ The adj. *preordinate* (L. *præordinātus*) occurs in Sir T. Elyot, The Governour, b. ii. c. 12. § 3; and see Palsgrave. Der. *preordin-at-ion*, used by Bale (R.); MF. *preordination* (Hatzfeld); from MF. *pre-* and *ordination*.

PREPARE, to make ready beforehand, arrange, provide. (F.– L.) In the Bible of 1551, Luke iii. 4; and in Palsgrave.–MF. *preparer*, 'to prepare,' Cot.–L. *præparāre*; comp. of *præ*, beforehand, and *parāre*, to get ready; see **Pre-** and **Parade**. Der. *prepar-er*, *prepar-ed*, *prepar-ed-ly*, *-ness*. Also *prepar-at-ion*, Sir T. Elyot, The Governour, b. ii. c. 1. § 1, from MF. *preparation*, 'a preparation,' Cot.; *prepar-at-ive*, ME. *preparatif*, Lydgate, Minor Poems, p. 168, from MF. *preparatif*, 'a preparative, or preparation,' Cot.; *prepar-at-ive-ly*; *prepar-at-or-y*, suggested by MF. *preparatoire*, 'a preparatory,' Cot. Also *prepare*, sb., 3 Hen. VI, iv. 1. 131.

PREPAY, to pay beforehand. (F.–L.) Modern; not in Todd's Johnson. From **Pre-** and **Pay**. Der. *prepai-d*, *pre-pay-ment*.

PREPENSE, premeditated, intentional. (F.–L.) 1. As if from F. *pre-* (L. *præ*), beforehand, and F. *penser*, to think. 2. But in the phrase 'malice *prepense*;' formerly written 'malice *prepensed*,' it is an altered form of AF. *purpensé*, pp. of *purpenser*, to meditate on, with prefix *pur-* (F. *pour-*), from L. *prō*. See my Notes on Eng. Etym., p. 230; Elyot's Governor, ed. Croft, ii. 375; and the Laws of Will. I. § 2. The expression '*prepensed* murder' occurs in the Stat. 12 Hen. VII, cap. 7; see Blount's Nomolexicon, ed. 1691. 'Malice *prepensed* is malice forethought;' Blount's Gloss., ed. 1674. See **Pansy**. Der. *prepense-ly*.

PREPONDERATE, to outweigh, exceed in weight or influence. (L.) In Blount's Gloss., ed. 1674.–L. *præponderātus*, pp. of *præponderāre*, to outweigh.–L. *præ*, before, hence, in excess; and *ponderāre*, to weigh, from *ponder-*, decl. base of *pondus*, a weight; see **Pre-** and **Ponder**. Der. *preponder-at-ion*; *preponder-ant*, *preponder-ance*.

PREPOSITION, a part of speech expressing the relation between objects, and governing a case. (F.–L.) In Minsheu, ed. 1627; and in Palsgrave, p. xxiv.–MF. *preposition*, 'a preposition, in grammar;' Cot.–L. *præpositiōnem*, acc. of *præpositio*, a putting before; in grammar, a preposition.–L. *præ*, before; and *positio*, a putting, placing; see **Pre-** and **Position**. Der. *preposition-al*.

PREPOSSESS, to possess beforehand, preoccupy. (L.) '*Prepossesses* the hearts of His servants;' Bp. Taylor, vol. iii. ser. 10 (R.). From **Pre-** and **Possess**. Der. *prepossess-ing*, *prepossess-ion*.

PREPOSTEROUS, contrary to nature or reason, absurd. (L.) '*Preposterouse*, præposterus;' Levins, ed. 1570.–L. *præposterus*, reversed, inverted; lit. the last part forwards, hind side before.–L. *præ*, before, in front; and *posterus*, latter, coming after; see **Pre-** and **Posterior**. Der. *preposterous-ly*, *-ness*.

PREROGATIVE, an exclusive privilege. (F.–L.) In Spenser, F. Q. iv. 12. 31; ME. *prerogatif*, Lydgate, Minor Poems, p. 118.– MF. *prerogative*, 'a prerogative, privilege,' Cot.–L. *prærogātiua*, a previous choice or election, preference, privilege. Orig. fem. of *prærogātiuus*, one who is asked for an opinion before others.–L. *præ*, before; and *-rogātiuus*, allied to *rogātus*, pp. of *rogāre*, to ask. See **Pre-** and **Rogation**.

PRESAGE, an omen. (F.–L.) In Shak. King John, i. 28; as a verb, Merch. Ven. iii. 2. 175.–MF. *presage*, 'a presage, divining;' Cot.–L. *præsāgium*, a presage.–L. *præsāgire*, to perceive beforehand.–L. *præ*, before; and *sāgire*, to perceive quickly. See **Pre-**, **Sagacious**. Der. *presage*, verb, answering to MF. *presagier*; *presag-er*, Shak. Sonn. 23.

PRESBYTER, a priest, elder of the church. (L.–Gk.) '*Presbyters*, or fatherly guides;' Hooker, Eccl. Polity, b. v. s. 78 (R.).–L. *presbyter*.–Gk. πρεσβύτερος, elder; comp. of πρέσβυς, old; see 1 Pet. v. 1. Cf. L. *priscus*, ancient. See **Priest**. Der. *Presbyter-ian*, a term applied to tenets embodied in a formulary A.D. 1560, Haydn, Dict. of Dates, which see; *Presbyter-ian-ism*. Also *presbyter-y*, 1 Tim. iv. 14, where the Vulgate has *presbyterium*, from Gk. πρεσβυτέριον.

PRESCIENCE, foreknowledge. (F.–L.) In Chaucer, tr. of Boethius, b. v. pr. 3, l. 17.–OF. *prescience*, 'a prescience,' Cot.– L. *præscientia*, foreknowledge.–L. *præ*, before; and *scientia*, knowledge; see **Pre-** and **Science**. Der. *prescient*, Bacon (see R.), a later word, from *præscient-*, stem of pres. part. of *præscīre*, to know beforehand.

PRESCRIBE, to give directions, appoint by way of direction. (L.) In Levins, ed. 1570. – L. *præscribere*, to write beforehand, appoint, prescribe. – L. *præ*, before; and *scribere*, to write; see **Pre-** and **Scribe**. Der. *prescrib-er*; *prescript* (= prescribed), More's Utopia (English version), b. ii. c. 5, ed. Arber, p. 89, from L. pp. *præscript-us*; hence also *prescript*, sb., *prescript-ible*. Also *prescript-ion*, Cor. ii. 1. 127, from MF. *prescription*, 'a prescription,' from L. acc. *præscriptiōnem*, from nom. *præscriptio*, a prescribing, precept, whence the medical use readily follows. Also *prescript-ive*, from L. *præscriptiuus*.

PRESENCE, a being present or within view, mien, personal appearance, readiness. (F. – L.) ME. *presence*, Chaucer, C. T. 5095 (B 675). – OF. *presence*. – L. *præsentia*, presence. – L. *præ-sent-*, stem of *præsens*, present; see **Present** (1). Der. *presence-chamber*.

PRESENT (1), near at hand, in view, at this time. (F. – L.) ME. *present*, Wyclif, 1 Cor. iii. 22. – OF. *present*. – L. *præsent-*, stem of *præsens*, present, lit. being in front, hence, being in sight. – L. *præ*, before, in front; and *-sens*, being (cognate with Skt. *sant-*, being), for *es-ens*, pres. pt. of *es-se*, to be. (✓ES); see **Pre-**, **Absent**, and **Sooth**. Der. *present-ly*, Temp. i. 2. 125; *presence*, q. v.; *present* (2), q. v.

PRESENT (2), to give, offer, exhibit to view. (F. – L.) ME. *presenten*, Rob. of Brunne, tr. of Langtoft, p. 63, l. 21; Chaucer, C. T. 12190 (C 256). – OF. *presenter*, 'to present,' Cot. – L. *præsentāre*, to place before, hold out, present; lit. 'to make present.' – L. *præsent-*, stem of *præsens*, present; see **Present** (1). Der. *present-er*, *present-able*; *present-at-ion*, As You Like It, iv. 4. 112, from MF. *presentation*, 'a presentation,' Cot., from L. acc. *præsentā-tiōnem*; *present-ee*, one who is presented to a benefice, from MF. pp. *presenté* (Cot.); *present-ment*, Hamlet, iii. 4. 54, and (as a law-term) in Blount's Nomolexicon, ed. 1691. Also *present*, sb., ME. *present*, Ancren Riwle, p. 114, l. 2, p. 152, l. 12; from OF. *present*, 'a present, gift,' Cot.

PRESENTIMENT, a perceiving beforehand, a conviction of some future event. (F. – L.) 'A *presentiment* of what is to be hereafter;' Butler, Analogy of Religion, pt. i. c. 6. § 11. – OF. *presentiment*, 'a fore-feeling,' Cot.; suggested by L. *præsentīre*, to perceive beforehand; see **Pre-** and **Sentiment**.

PRESERVE, to guard, keep, save. (F. – L.) ME. *preseruen* (with *u* = *v*), Gower, C. A. iii. 221; bk. vii. 3856. – OF. *preserver*, 'to preserve,' Cot. – L. *præ*, beforehand; and *seruāre*, to keep; see **Pre-** and **Serve**. Der. *preserve*, sb.; *preserv-er*; *preserv-at-ion*, Temp. ii. 1. 7, from OF. *preservation*, omitted by Cotgrave, but in use in the 14th century (Littré); *preserv-at-ive*, Sir T. Elyot, The Governor, b. iii. c. 4. § 1, Lydgate, Minor Poems, p. 91, from MF. *preservatif*, 'preservative,' Cot.; *preserv-at-or-y*.

PRESIDE, to superintend, have authority over others. (F. – L.) In Cotgrave. – MF. *presider*, 'to preside, govern,' Cot. – L. *præsidēre*, to sit before or above, to preside over. – L. *præ*, before; and *sedēre*, to sit, cognate with E. *sit*; see **Pre-** and **Sit**. Der. *presid-ent*, Wyclif, Deeds [Acts], xxiii. 24, 26, from OF. *president*, 'a president,' Cot., from L. *præsident-*, stem of pres. part. of *præsidēre*; *president-ship*; *presidenc-y*; *president-ial*.

PRESS (1), to crush strongly, squeeze, drive forcibly, urge, push. (F. – L.) ME. *pressen*, *presen* (with voiceless *s*), Chaucer, C. T. 2582 (A 2580). – F. *presser*, 'to press, strain,' Cot. – L. *pressāre*, to press; frequentative formed from *press-um*, supine of *premere*, to press. Der. *press*, sb., ME. *presse*, Chaucer, Fortune, l. 52, Ancren Riwle, p. 168, last line, from F. *presse*, 'a prease, throng,' Cot.; *press-er*, *press-ing*, *press-ing-ly*; *press-ure*, Prompt. Parv., from OF. *pressure*, 'pressure,' Cot., from L. *pressūra*, allied to pp. *pressus*. Also *press-fat*, a pressing-vat, Haggai, ii. 16; see **Fat** (2) and **Vat**. Also *print*, *im-print*.

PRESS (2), to hire men for service, to engage men by earnest-money for the public service, to carry men off forcibly to become sailors or soldiers. (F. – L.) It is certain, as Wedgwood has shown, that *press* is here a corruption of the old word *prest*, ready, because it was customary to give earnest-money to a soldier on entering service, just as to this day a recruit receives a shilling. This earnest-money was called *prest-money*, i.e. ready money advanced, and to give a man such money was to *imprest* him, now corruptly written *impress*. 'At a later period, the practice of taking men for the public service *by compulsion* made the word to be understood as if it signified to *force* men into the service, and the original reference to earnest-money was quite lost sight of;' Wedgwood. β. *Prest* was once a common word for ready money advanced, or ready money on loan. 'And he sent thyder iii. somers [sumpter-horses] laden with nobles of Castel [Castile] and floreyns, to gyve *in prest* [as ready money] to knyghtes and squyers, *for he knewe well otherwyse he sholde not haue them come out of theyr houses*;' Berners, tr. of Froissart, vol. ii. c. 64 (R.). 'Requiring of the city a *prest* [an advance] of 6000 marks;' Bacon, Life of Hen. VII, ed. Lumby, p. 18, l. 28. See also Skelton, Colin Clout, 350-354, and Dyce's note; North's Plutarch, ed. 1594, p. 638. Both *prest-money* and *imprest-money* are in Minsheu, ed. 1627; and Cotgrave explains MF. *imprestance* by 'prest, or imprest money, received and to be imployed for another.' – MF. *prester*, 'to lend, also, to trust out [advance] or sell unto daies' [unto an appointed time], Cot. Cf. OF. *prest*, 'prest, ready, full dight, furnished, . . . prompt, nere at hand,' id. Ital. *prestare*, 'to lend,' Florio; *imprestare*, 'to lend or give to lone,' id. (Mod. F. *prêter*.) – L. *præstāre*, to come forward or stand before, surpass, to become surety for, give, offer, furnish, provide. – L. *præ*, before; and *stāre*, cognate with E. *stand*; see **Pre-** and **Stand**. Der. *im-press*, *im-press-ment*; also *press-gang*, q. v.

PRESS-GANG, a gang of men employed to 'press' sailors into the public service. (F. – L.; *and* E.) In Johnson's Dict. This word seems to be of rather late formation, and also to be associated with the notion of *compulsion* or *pressing*; at the same time, it certainly took its origin from the verb *press*, in the sense of 'to hire men for service;' see therefore **Press** (2), as orig. quite distinct from **Press** (1). Cf. *press-money*, K. Lear, iv. 6. 87. And see **Gang**.

PRESTIGE, a delusion; also, influence due to former fame or excellence. (F. – L.) This word is in the very rare position of having achieved a good meaning in place of a bad one; the reverse is more usual, as noted in Trench, Study of Words. Cf. mod. F. *prestige*, 'fascination, magic spell, magic power, prestige,' Hamilton. In some authors it had a bad sense, in E. as well as in F., but it is not an old word with us. '*Prestiges*, illusions, impostures, juggling tricks;' Phillips, ed. 1706. – F. *prestige*; Cot. gives pl. *prestiges*, 'deceits, impostures, juggling tricks.' – L. *præstigium*, a deceiving by juggling tricks, a delusion, illusion; we also find L. pl. *præstigiæ*, tricks, deception, trickery. β. For *præstrigium*, the second *r* being lost; Brugmann, i. § 483. – L. *præstringere*, to bind fast, to dull, dim, blind. – L. *præ*, before; and *stringere*, to bind. See **Stringent**.

PRESTO, quickly. (Ital. – L.) 'Well, you'll come? *Presto!*' Ben Jonson, The Case is Altered, i. 1. – Ital. *presto*, adv., quickly. – L. *præsto*, at hand, ready, present. – L. *præ*, before; and *stāre*, to stand. See **Pre-** and **State**.

PRESUME, to take for granted, suppose, to act forwardly. (F. – L.) 'When she *presumed* tasten of a tree;' Occleve, Letter of Cupid, st. 51. l. 355 (A.D. 1402). [*Presumption*, ME. *presumcioun*, occurs earlier, spelt *presumciun*, Ancren Riwle, p. 208, l. 20.] – OF. *presumer*, 'to presume, or think too well of himselfe, . . . to presume, think, ween, imagine;' Cot. – L. *præsūmere*, to take beforehand, anticipate, presume, imagine. – L. *præ*, before; and *sūmere*, to take; where *sūmere* is from *emere*, to take, buy; the prefix was prob. *subs-*. See **Pre-** and **Example**. Der. *presum-ing*, *presum-able*, *presum-abl-y*; *presumpt-ion* (as above), from OF. *presumpcion* (13th cent., Littré), later *presomption*, 'presumption,' Cot., from L. *præsumptiōnem*, acc. of *præsumptio*, allied to *præsumptus*, pp. of *præsūmere*. Also *presumpt-ive*, Daniel, Civil War, b. iii. st. 17, from MF. *presomptif*, 'likely,' Cot.; *presumpt-ive-ly*; *presumpt-u-ous*, Skelton, ed. Dyce, i. 131, l. 160, Lydgate, Minor Poems, p. 175, spelt *presumptiouse* in Levins, from OF. *presomptüeux* (13th cent. *presumptuouse*, 14th cent. *presomptueux*, Littré), which from L. *præsumptuōsus*, *præsumptiōsus*. Hence *presumptuous-ly*, *-ness*.

PRESUPPOSE, to suppose beforehand. (F. – L. *and* Gk.) 'Wherefore it is to *presuppose*;' Fabyan, Chron. an. 1284-5, ed. Ellis, p. 389; and in Palsgrave. – OF. *presupposer*, 'to presuppose;' Cot. See **Pre-** and **Suppose**. Der. *presuppos-it-ion* (really from a different root; see **Pose, Position**).

PRETEND, to affect to feel, to feign. (F. – L.) ME. *pre-tenden*, to lay claim, Chaucer, Troilus, b. iv. l. 922. – OF. *pretendre*, 'to pretend, lay claim to;' Cot. – L. *prætendere*, to spread before, hold out as an excuse, allege, pretend. – L. *præ*, before; and *tendere*, to stretch, spread; see **Pre-** and **Tend**. Der. *pretend-er*, esp. used of the Old and Young Pretenders, so called because they *laid claim* to the crown. Also *pretence*, Macb. ii. 3. 137 (first folio), a mistaken spelling for *pretense*, from Late L. *prætensus*, pp. of *prætendere* (the usual L. supine is *prætentum*, but *tendere* gives both *tensum* and *tentum*); the right spelling *pretense* is in Spenser, F. Q. iv. 5. 23, with which cf. *pretensed*, i.e. intended, in Robinson's tr. of More's Utopia, ed. Arber, p. 20, l. 7. Cf. MF. *pretente*, 'a pretence;' Cot. Also *pretension*, Bacon, Of a War with Spain (R.), formed as if from L. type *prætensio*.

PRETER-, prefix, beyond. (L.; *or* F. – L.) OF. *preter-*, prefix, from L. *præter*, beyond, which is a compar. form of *præ*, before, with Idg. suffix *-ter-*.

PRETERIT, PRETERITE, past; the past tense. (F. – L.)

ME. *preterit*, Chaucer, tr. of Boethius, b. v. pr. 6, l. 13.—OF. *preterit*, m. *preterite*, fem. 'past, overpast,' Cot.—L. *præteritus*, pp. of *præterire*, to pass by.—L. *præter*, beyond; and *ire*, to go, from √EI, to go.

PRETERMIT, to omit. (L.) In Minsheu, ed. 1627.—L. *prætermittere*, to allow to go past, let slip.—L. *præter*, past, beyond; and *mittere*, to let go, send; see **Preter-** and **Mission**. Der. *pretermiss-ion*, from MF. *pretermission*, 'a pretermission,' Cot., from L. acc. *prætermissiōnem*.

PRETERNATURAL, supernatural, extraordinary. (L.) 'Simple aire, being *preternaturally* attenuated;' Bacon, Nat. Hist. § 30. From **Preter-** and **Natural**. ¶ So also *preter-perfect, preter-imperfect, preter-pluperfect*.

PRETEXT, a pretence, false reason. (F.—L.) In Shak. Cor. v. 6. 20.—MF. *pretexte*, m. 'a pretext,' Cot.—L. *prætextum*, a pretext; orig. neut. of *prætextus*, pp. of *prætexere*, lit. 'to weave in front.'—L. *præ*, before; and *texere*, to weave; see **Pre-** and **Text**.

PRETOR, PRETORIAL; see **Prætor**.

PRETTY, pleasing, tasteful, beautiful. (E.; *or* L.—Gk.) Spelt *pretie* in Minsheu and Levins. ME. *prati, praty*, Prompt. Parv.; Destruction of Troy, ed. Panton and Donaldson, 2622, 10815, 13634. The old senses are 'comely' and 'clever,' as used in the above passages; but the true sense was rather 'tricky,' 'cunning,' or 'full of wiles;' though the word has acquired a better sense, it has never quite lost a sort of association with pettiness. AS. *prætig, prættig*, tricky, deceitful; 'Wille ge bēon *prættige*,' tr. of L. 'Vultis esse versipelles;' Ælfric's Colloquy, in Voc. 101. 1. A rare word; formed with the usual suffix *-ig* (as in *stān-ig*, E. *ston-y*) from a sb. *præt, prætt*, deceit, trickery; see *prattas*, as a gloss to L. *artēs* (in a bad sense), Mone, Quellen, p. 347, col. 1. So also we have Lowland Scotch *pratty, pretty*, tricky, from *prat*, a trick, used by G. Douglas (Jamieson).+EFries. *prettig*, jocose, droll, pleasant, from *pret*, a trick; W. Flem. *prettig*; Icel. *prettugr*, tricky, from *prettr*, a trick, *pretta*, to cheat, deceive; Norweg. *pretten, prettevis*, tricky, roguish, from *pretta*, a trick, piece of roguery, *pretta*, to play a trick (Aasen). So also MDu. *pratte, perte*, Du. *part*, a trick, deceit. ¶ Possibly all from L. *practica*; cf. E. *practice*, in the sense of 'guile.' Der. *pretti-ly*, spelt *pretily*, Court of Love, 420; *pretti-ness*, Hamlet, iv. 5. 189; also *pretty*, adv.

PREVAIL, to overcome, effect, have influence over. (F.—L.) Spelt *prevayle* in Levins; *preuaile* in Minsheu.—OF. *prevail*, 1 p. pr. of *prevaloir*, 'to prevaile,' Cot.—L. *præualēre*, to have great power. —L. *præ*, before, hence expressive of excess; and *ualēre*, to be strong, have power; see **Pre-** and **Valiant**. Der. *prevail-ing*; *preval-ent*, Milton, P. L. vi. 411, from L. *præualent-*, stem of pres. part. of *præ-ualēre*; *preval-ence*, from OF. *prevalence* (Cot.), from Late L. *præ-valentia*, superior force; *prevalenc-y*. Also *prevail-ment*, Mids. Nt. Dr. i. 1. 35.

PREVARICATE, to shift about, to quibble. (L.) 'When any of us hath *prevaricated* our part of the covenant,' i.e. swerved from it, Bp. Taylor, vol. ii. ser. 5 (R.). [*Preuaricator* and *præuarication* are both in Minsheu's Dict.; but not the verb.]—L. *præuāricātus*, pp. of *præuāricāri*, to spread the legs apart in walking, to straddle, to walk crookedly; hence to swerve, shuffle, &c.—L. *præ*, before, here used as an intensive prefix; and *uāricus*, straddling, extended (with suffix *-ic-*) from *uārus*, bent, grown awry (esp. of the legs). Cf. L. *Vārus* as a proper name, orig. a nickname. See **Varicose**. Der. *prevaricat-or*; *prevaricat-ion*, from MF. *prevarication*, 'prevarication,' Cot.

PREVENT, to hinder, obviate. (L.) The old sense is 'to go before, anticipate;' Tw. Nt. iii. 1. 94, Hamlet, ii. 2. 305; Spenser, F. Q. vi. 1. 38, vi. 8. 15; and in Palsgrave. Cf. MF. *prevenir*, 'to prevent, outstrip, anticipate, forestall;' Cot.—L. *præuent-us*, pp. of *præuenīre*, to come or go before.—L. *præ*, before; and *uenire*, cognate with E. *come*; see **Pre-** and **Come**. Der. *prevent-ion*, from MF. *prevention*, 'a prevention, anticipation,' Cot. Also *prevent-ive*, adj., Phillips, ed. 1706, a coined word; *prevent-ive*, sb.

PREVIOUS, going before, former. (L.) 'Som *previous* meditations;' Howell, Famil. Letters, vol. i. sect. 6. let. 32, § 3; A.D. 1635. Englished (by change of *-us* to *-ous*, as in *ardu-ous*, &c.) from L. *præuius*, on the way before, going before.—L. *præ*, before; and *uia*, a way; see **Pre-** and **Voyage**. Der. *previous-ly*.

PREWARN, to warn beforehand. (Hybrid; L. *and* E.) 'Comets *prewarn*;' Two Noble Kinsmen, v. 1. 51. A coined word; see **Pre-** and **Warn**.

PREY, booty, spoil, plunder. (F.—L.) ME. *preie, preye*, Rob. of Glouc. p. 270, l. 5466; p. 303, l. 6163; *praie*, O. Eng. Homilies, ed. Morris, i. 273, l. 6.—OF. *praie, preie*; mod. F. *proie*, prey.—L. *præda*, booty. β. *Præda* is thought to stand for **prai-hid-a*, that which is got or seized beforehand; from *præ*, before, and *hed-*, base

of *-hendere*, to seize, cognate with E. *get*. Similarly *prendere* is short for *prehendere*, as is well known. See **Pre-** and **Get**. See **Predatory**. From L. *præda* we also have W. *praidd*, flock, herd, booty, prey, Gael. and Irish *spreidh*, cattle of any kind. Der. *prey*, vb., Rich. III, i. 1. 133.

PRIAL, three of a sort, at cards. (F.—L.) An unmeaning corruption of *pair-royal*. See *Pair-royal* in Nares, who fully illustrates it. Fuller has: 'that *paroyal* of armies;' Pisgah Sight of Palestine. bk. iv. ch. 2. § 22.

PRICE, value, excellence, recompence. (F.—L.) ME. *pris*, Havelok, 283; Ancren Riwle, p. 392, l. 15.—OF. *pris, preis*; mod. F. *prix*.—L. *pretium*, price. See **Precious**. Der. *price-less*; *preci-ous*, *prize* (2), verb. **Doublet**, *praise*.

PRICK, a sharp point, puncture, sting, remorse. (E.) ME. *prike, pricke, prikke*, Ancren Riwle, p. 228, last line. AS. *pricu*, a point, dot, Matt. v. 18; *prician*, v., to prick, Ælfric's Hom. ii. 88.+MDu. *prick*, a prickle, whence mod. Du. *prikkel*; see Kilian; Dan. *prik*, a dot; *prikke*, to mark with dots; Swed. *prick*, a point, dot, prick, tittle; *pricka*, to point, to mark with pricks; Low G. *prik*, a dot; *prikken*, to prick. Apparently from a Teut. base **prek-*, to prick, dot; cf. OSax. *prek*, a thorn (Gallée); MDu. *prekel*, a prick (Hexham); Cornwall *preckle*, to prick. Der. *prick*, verb, ME. *priken, prikien*, Havelok, 2639, P. Plowman, B. xviii. 11; AS. *prician* (above); hence *prick-er*. Also *prick-le*, ONorthumb. *pricle*, Matt. v. 18 (Lindisfarne MS.), a dimin. form, with the orig. sense 'a little dot' or 'speck.' Hence *prick-l-y*, which seems to be formed from *prickle* rather than from *prick* with suffix *-ly*; *prick-l-i-ness*. Also *prick-et*, Spenser, Shep. Kal., Dec. l. 27, a buck in his second year, so named from his young horns; also *prick-song*, Rom. and Juliet, ii. 4. 21, for *pricked song*, i. e. song pricked down or written, spelt *prykked songe*, Bury Wills, p. 18, l. 27.

PRIDE, the feeling of being proud. (F.—L.?) ME. *pride, pryde*, P. Plowman, B. v. 15; spelt *pruide*, id. A. v. 15; *prude*, id. C. vi. 118; Ancren Riwle, p. 140, l. 6. AS. *prȳte*, pride, Ælfric's Homilies, ii. 220, l. 32. (Thus *pride* is a weakened form of *prite*.) β. The AS. *prȳte* is regularly formed from the adj. *prūt*, proud, with mutation of *ū* to *ȳ*; see **Proud**. We find also AS. *prūtung*, pride; Mone, Quellen, p. 355, col. 1. Cf. Icel. *prȳði*, an ornament, from *prūðr*, proud; both borrowed from E., but they exhibit the length of the vowel. Der. *pride*, vb. reflexive.

PRIEST, a presbyter, one in holy orders, above a deacon and below a bishop. (L.—Gk.) ME. *preest*, Chaucer, C. T. 505; *preost*, Ancren Riwle, p. 16, l. 25. AS. *prēost*, Laws of K. Edgar, i. 2 (see Thorpe's Ancient Laws, i. 262); and, earlier, in the Laws of Ethelbert, § 1 (id. p. 2). Contracted from L. *presbyter* (<Gk. πρεσβύτερος), as clearly shown by the OF. *prestre* (13th cent.), mod. F. *prêtre*; OSax. *prēstar*, G. *priester*. Cf. *Prester John* in Mandeville's Travels, where *prester* (like AS. *prēost*) seems to have arisen from **prev'ster*, for **preb(y)ster*, a mistaken form of *presbyter*. β. Πρεσβύτερος is comp. of πρέσ-βυς, Doric πρέσ-γυς, old; cf. L. *pris-cus*, ancient. Der. *priest-ess* (with F. suffix); *priest-hood*, AS. *prēost-hād*, Ælfred, tr. of Beda, b. i. c. 7 (near beginning); *priest-craft*; *priest-ly*, Pericles, iii. 1. 70; *priest-li-ness*; *priest-ridden*. **Doublet**, *presbyter*.

PRIG (1), to steal. (E.) This is a cant term of some antiquity; *prig*, sb., a thief, occurs in Shak. Wint. Ta. iv. 3. 108. It arose in the time of Elizabeth, and is merely a cant modification of E. *prick*, which orig. meant to ride, as in Spenser, F. Q. i. 1. 1, P. Plowman, B. xviii. 11, 25. Hence it came to mean to ride off, to steal a horse, and so, generally, to steal. This we learn from Harman's Caveat, 1567, where we find: 'to *prygge*, to ryde,' p. 84, col. 3; and at p. 42: 'a *prigger of praunces* be horse-stealers; for to *prigge* signifieth in their language to steale, and a *prauncer* is a horse.' Again, at p. 43, he tells how a gentleman espied a *pryggar*, and charged 'this prity *prigging* person to walke his horse well' for him; whereupon 'this peltynge *priggar*, proude of his praye, walkethe his horse vp and downe tyll he sawe the Gentleman out of sighte, and leapes him into the saddell, and awaye he goeth a-mayne.' That is how it was done. We find a similar weakening of *k* to *g* in Lowl. Sc. *prigga-trout*, a banstickle, or stickleback (evidently for *pricker-trout*), and in Lowl. Sc. *prigmedainty*, the same as *prickmedainty*, one who dresses in a finical manner (or as we now say, a *prig*). Halliwell also gives *prygman*, a thief, which occurs in Awdelay's Fraternyte of Vacabondes, ed. Furnivall, p. 3; and *prig*, to ride, in Dekker's Lanthorne, sig. C. ii. So also *trigger* stands for *tricker*.

PRIG (2), a pert, pragmatical fellow. (E.) 'A cane is part of the dress of a *prig*;' Tatler, no. 77 (1709). From the verb to *prick*, in the sense to trim, adorn, dress up; Latimer (Works, i. 253, Parker Soc.) speaks of women having 'much *pricking*,' and inveighs against their '*pricking up* of themselves.' Cf. Lowl. Sc. *prig-me-dainty* for *prick-me-dainty*, a prig, which occurs in Udall, Roister Doister, ii. 3, ed. Arber, p. 36. See **Prig** (1).

PRIM, precise, affectedly neat or nice. (F. — L.) Bailey (vol. i. ed. 1735) has: 'to *prim*, to set the mouth conceitedly, to be full of affected ways.' Phillips, ed. 1706, has: 'to *prim*, to be full of affected ways, to be much conceited.' An older example is *prym*, sb. a neat girl, in Barclay's Fifth Eclogue, cited in Nares. [From the E. word are derived the Lowland Scotch *primp* (with excrescent *p*), to assume prudish or self-important airs, to deck oneself in a stiff and affected manner (Jamieson); and *primzie*, demure, in Burns, Hallowe'en, st. 9.] β. The sense of 'slender' or 'delicate' is the orig. one, as shown in Cotgrave. — MF. *prim*, masc., *prime*, fem., 'prime, forward;' also *prin*, 'thin, subtill, piercing, sharp;' also *prime*, both masc. and fem., 'thin, slender, exile, small; as *cheveux primes*, smooth or delicate hair;' Cot. This last example comes sufficiently near to the E. use. γ. The MF. *prim* (corrupter form *prin*) is from the L. masc. acc. *primum*; the form *prime* answers to the L. fem. *prima*. The nom. case is *primus*, first, chief; see **Prime** (1). So also mod. Prov. *prim*, m., *primo*, f., fine, delicate (Mistral). Cf. also prov. E. *prime*, to trim trees; and the phrase 'to *prime* a gun;' see **Prime** (2). ¶ The sense of 'thin' as derived from that of 'first' or 'foremost' is hard to account for; perhaps there is an allusion to the growth of newly grown shoots and buds; cf. *filer prim*, 'to run thin, or by little and little;' Cot. In E., it is possible that the sense of *prim* was affected by some confusion with the old verb *prink*, to adorn, dress well, be smart and gay, to be pert or forward (Halliwell); which is merely a nasalised form of the verb *to prick*, used in the sense of 'to trim' by Palsgrave and others; cf. Lowland Scotch *prickmaleerie*, stiff and precise, *prickmedainty*, finical (Jamieson). Der. *prim-ly, prim-ness*.

PRIME (1), first, chief, excellent. (F. — L.) ME. *prime*, properly an adj. (as in Temp. i. 2. 72), but almost always used of 'prime,' the first canonical hour, as in Ancren Riwle, p. 20, Chaucer, C. T. 12596 (C 662), &c. — F. *prime*, 'the first houre of the day,' Cot. [A fem. form, the OF. masc. being *prim*.] — L. *prima*, i. e. *prima hora*, the first hour; fem. of *primus*, first. β. *Pri-mus* is a superl. form, and stands for *pris-mus; cf. *pris-cus*, ancient; Brugmann, i. § 868, ii. § 72. The suffix is the same as in *min-i-mus* (where *-mu-* is the Idg. superl. suffix *-mo-*, appearing also in AS. *for-ma*, Goth. *fru-ma*, first. See **Prior**. Der. *prime*, sb., as already explained; *prime-number, prime-minister*; Phillips, ed. 1706, from L. *primārius*; *prim-ar-i-ly*. Also *prim-ate*, ME. *primat*, Layamon, 29736, from OF. *primat*, 'a primat or metropolitan,' Cot., which from L. *primātem*, acc. of *primās*, a principal or chief man; *primate-ship*; *prim-ac-y*, from AF. *primacie*, Polit. Songs, ed. Wright, p. 311; cf. MF. *primace*, 'primacy,' Cot. Also *prim-er*, P. Plowman, C. vi. 46, from OF. *primer*, variant of *premier* (see Supplement to Godefroy), from L. *primārius*, primary; and hence, an elementary book. Also *prima-donna*, from Ital. *prima*, first, chief, and *donna*, lady, L. *domina*; see **Dame**. Also *prim-al*, Hamlet, iii. 3. 37; *prim-y*, id. i. 3. 7; *prim-er-o*, q. v. And see *prim-eval, prim-it-ive, primo-geni-ture, prim-ordial, prim-rose, prince, prior, pristine, priest, presbyter, premier*, and *prime* (2).

PRIME (2), to put powder on the nipple of a fire-arm, to make a gun quite ready. (F. — L.) 'Neither had any [of us] one piece of ordinance *primed*;' Hakluyt's Voyages, vol. ii. pt. ii. p. 61. It is not quite clear how the word came into use; perhaps we may look upon *prime* as expressing 'to put into *prime* order,' to make quite ready; from *prime* in the sense of 'ready;' see Nares. But whatever the exact history may be, we may be sure that the etymology is from the E. adj. *prime*. Cf. prov. E. *prime*, to trim trees (Halliwell). See **Prime** (1), and **Prim**. Der. *prim-ing*.

PRIMERO, an old game at cards. (Span. — L.) Cotgrave translates MF. *prime* by 'primero at cards,' &c.; and see Shak. Merry Wives, iv. 5. 104. — MSpan. *primera*, 'the game called Primero at cards,' Minsheu (1623); the E. form being incorrect. Fem. of Span. *primero*, first. But the game is obsolete, and little is known about it; it probably derives its name from some chief or principal card. — L. *primārius*, primary; from *primus*, first; see **Prime** (1).

PRIMEVAL, original, lit. belonging to the first age. (L.) Also spelt *primæval*. In Pope, Dunciad, iv. 630. A coined word; an older form was *primevous*, in Blount's Gloss., ed. 1674. — L. *primævus*, primeval. — L. *prim-*, for *primus*, first; and *ævum*, an age. See **Prime** (1) and **Age**.

PRIMITIVE, original, antiquated. (F. — L.) In Shak. Troil. v. 1. 60. — F. *primitif*, masc., *primitive*, fem., 'primitive,' Cot. — L. *primitīuus*, earliest of its kind; extended from *primus*, first. See **Prime** (1). Der. *primitive-ly, -ness*.

PRIMOGENITURE, a being born first, the right of inheritance of the eldest-born. (F. — L.) Blount, in his Gloss., ed. 1674,

says that the word is used by Sir T. Browne; see his Vulgar Errors, bk. vii. c. 5. § 2. — MF. *primogeniture*, 'the being eldest, the title of the eldest,' Cot. Formed as if from a L. *primogenitūra. — L. *primogenitus*, first-born. — L. *primo-*, for *primus*, first; and *genitus*, pp. of *gignere* (base *gen*), to beget, produce. See **Prime** (1) and **Genus**.

PRIMORDIAL, original. (F. — L.) Used as a sb., with the sense of 'beginning,' by Skelton, Why Come Ye Nat to Courte, l. 486. — F. *primordial*, 'originall,' Cot. — L. *primordiālis*, original. — L. *primordium*, an origin. — L. *prim-*, for *primus*, first; and *ordīrī*, to begin, allied to *ordo*, order. See **Prime** (1) and **Order**.

PRIMROSE, the name of a spring flower. (F. — L.) A. 'Two noble *primeroses*;' Ascham, Scholemaster, pt. i., ed. Arber, p. 66. Cf. '*Prymerose*, primula;' Prompt. Parv. — F. *prime rose*, lit. first rose, so called because it comes early in the spring. — L. *prima rosa*; see **Prime** (1) and **Rose**. B. The above is the popular and obvious etymology of the word *as it stands*; but *primrose* is, historically, a corruption (due to popular etymology) of ME. *primerole*, a primrose, Chaucer, C. T. 3268; from OF. *primerole* (Godefroy). This answers to a Late L. type *primerula, a regular dimin. of Late L. *primula*, a primrose (see Prompt. Parv.), now the botanical name. Again, *primula* is a dimin. form from *primus*; see **Prime** (1), as before. ¶ The name *primrose* was sometimes given to the daisy.

PRINCE, a chief, sovereign, son of a king. (F. — L.) ME. *prince*, St. Marharete, ed. Cockayne, p. 2, l. 15. — F. *prince*. Cf. Ital. *principe*. — L. *principem*, acc. of *princeps*, taking the first place, hence, a principal person. — L. *prin-* (for *prim-* before *c*), from *primus*, first; and *capere*, to take. See **Prime** (1) and **Capital**. Der. *prince-dom*; *prince-ly*, Temp. i. 2. 86, *prince-ly*, adv., *prince-li-ness*. Also *princ-ess*, ME. *princesse*, Prompt. Parv., from F. *princesse*, Cot. And see **Principal, Principle**.

PRINCIPAL, chief. (F. — L. ME. *principal, princypal*, Rob. of Glouc., p. 446, l. 9154. — F. *principal*, 'principall,' Cot. — L. *principālis*, chief; formed, with suffix *-ālis*, from *princip-*, stem of *princeps*; see **Prince**. Der. *principal-ly*; *principal-i-ty*, ME. *principalitee*, Prompt. Parv., from OF. *principalité*, which from L. acc. *principālitātem*, orig. meaning 'excellence.'

PRINCIPLE, a fundamental truth or law, a tenet, a settled rule of action. (F. — L.) Used by Spenser with the sense of 'beginning;' F. Q. v. 11. 2. The *l* is an E. addition to the word, as in *particle, syllable*. — F. *principe*, 'a principle, maxime; also, a beginning,' Cot. — L. *principium*, a beginning. — L. *principi-*, decl. stem of *princeps*, chief; see **Prince**. Der. *principl-ed, un-principl-ed*.

PRINT, an impression, engraving, impression of type on paper. (F. — L.) It would appear that *print* is short for *emprint*, or rather for the F. form *empreinte*; cf. *in emprinte*, i. e. in print, in Dictes and Sayings, pr. by Caxton, fol. 73 back, l. 3. The use of the word is much older than the invention of printing. ME. *printe, prente*. In Chaucer, C. T. 6186, Six-text, D 604, the Wife of Bath says: 'I hadde the *prente* of seynt Venus seel.' In three MSS. it is spelt *printe*; in one MS. it is *preente*. It is also spelt *preente, preynte* in the Prompt. Parv. 'And to a badde peny, with a good *preynte*;' Plowman, C. xviii. 73. Formed, by loss of the first syllable, from OF. *empreinte*, 'a stamp, a print,' Cot., in use in the 13th century (Littré). — OF. *empreinte*, fem. of *empreint*, pp. of *empreindre*, 'to print, stamp,' Cot. — L. *imprimere*, to impress. — L. *im-*, for *in* before *p*, upon; and *premere*, to press. See **Im-** (1) and **Press**. ¶ The MDu. *print*, a print, was prob. borrowed from English rather than from French. Der. *print*, verb, ME. *preenten*, Prompt. Parv., later *printe*, Surrey, in Tottel's Miscellany, ed. Arber, p. 7, l. 14. Also *print-er, print-ing, im-print*.

PRIOR (1), former, coming before in time. (L.) The use of *prior* as an adj. is modern; see example in Todd's Johnson. — L. *prior*, sooner, former. β. It is a comparative form from a positive *pris-*; cf. Gk. πρό-τερ-ος, former, Skt. *pra-ta-ma-*, first; and see **Pro-**. Der. *prior-i-ty*, Cor. i. 1. 251, from F. *priorité*, 'priority,' Cot., from Late L. acc. *prioritātem*. And see **Prior** (2), **Pristine**.

PRIOR (2), the head of a priory or convent. (F. — L.) Now conformed to the L. spelling. ME. *priour*, Rob. of Brunne, tr. of Langtoft, p. 333, l. 10. — OF. *priour*, later *prieur*, 'a prior,' Cot. — L. *priōrem*, acc. of *prior*, former, hence, a superior; see **Prior** (1). Der. *prior-ess*, Chaucer, C. T. 118, from OF. *prioresse*, given by Littré, s. v. *prieure*. Also *prior-y*, ME. *priorie*, Havelok, 2581; *prior-ship*.

PRISE, PRIZE, a lever. (F. — L.) '*Prise*, a lever;' Halliwell. It occurs in the legend of St. Erkenwald, l. 70. Hence 'to *prise* open a box,' or, corruptly, 'to *pry* open.' This seems to be nothing but a derivative of F. *prise* in the sense of a grasp, or hold; cf. *prise*, 'a lock or hold in wrestling, any advantage,' Cot. — F. *prise*, fem. of *pris*, pp. of *prendre*, to seize. — L. *prendere, prehendere*, to seize : see **Prehensile**. See **Prize** (1).

PRISM, a solid figure whose ends are equal and parallel planes, and whose sides are parallelograms. (L. – Gk.) In Blount's Gloss., ed. 1674. – L. *prisma*. – Gk. πρίσμα (stem πρισματ-), a prism, lit. a thing sawn off. – Gk. πρίειν (for *πρίσ-ειν), to saw. (Gk.√πρις). Der. *prism-at-ic*, Pope, Essay on Criticism, 311 ; *prism-at-ic-all*, Blount ; *prism-at-ic-al-ly*.

PRISON, a gaol, a place of confinement. (F. – L.) ME. *prison*, *prisoun*, Rob. of Glouc., p. 37, l. 875 ; *prisun*, Ancren Riwle, p. 126, l. 1 ; A. S. Chron. an. 1137. – OF. *prisun*, *prison* ; F. *prison*, 'a prison ;' Cot. Cf. OProv. *preizos* (Bartsch) ; Span. *prision*, a seizure, prison ; Ital. *prigione*. – L. acc. *prensiōnem*, acc. of *prensio*, a seizing ; with loss of *n* before *s*. β. *Prensio* is short for *prehensio*, formed from *prehensum*, supine of *prehendere*, to seize ; see **Prehensile**. Der. *prison-er*, Will. of Palerne, 1267 ; in Gen. and Exod., ed. Morris, 2042, it means 'the keeper of a prison,' a gaoler.

PRISTINE, ancient, former. (F. – L.) In Macb. v. 3. 52. [Formerly, the word *pristinate* was also in use ; Sir T. Elyot, The Governor, b. i. c. 2. § 13.] – MF. *pristine*, 'former, old, ancient ;' Cot. – L. *pristinus*, ancient, former. β. The syllable *pris-* occurs also in *pris-cus*, ancient ; cf. Gk. πρέσ-βυς, old ; and see **Prime** (1). γ. The suffix *-tinus* is the same as in *cras-tinus*, *diū-tinus* ; perhaps from *ten-*, base of *ten-ēre*, to hold.

PRIVATE, apart, retired, secret, not publicly known. (L.) Common in Shak. ; and see Minsheu and Levins. – L. *priuātus*, apart ; pp. of *priuāre*, to bereave, make single or apart. – L. *priuus*, single. Der. *private-ly*, *private-ness* ; *privat-ive*, causing privation, in Blount's Gloss., ed. 1674, from F. *privatif*, or directly from L. *priuatīuus* ; *privat-ive-ly* ; *privac-y*, Minsheu, a coined word, the MF. word being *privauté* (Cot.). Also *privat-ion*, from F. *privation*, 'privation,' Cot. Also *privat-eer*, in Phillips, ed. 1706, an armed private vessel ; a coined word. And see *privilege*, *de-prive*. **Doublet**, *privy*, q.v.

PRIVET, a half-evergreen shrub. (F. – L.) Also called *prim-print*, *prim*, and *primet*. 'Mondthout, privet, prime-print, or white-withbinde ;' Hexham's Du. Dict. 'Priuet or primprint ;' Holland's Pliny, Index to vol. ii. 'Privet or primprint ;' Topsell's Hist. of Serpents, p. 103 (Halliwell). 'Priuet or primpriuet [misprinted *prunpriuet*] tree ;' Minsheu, ed. 1627. Cotgrave explains MF. *fresillon* and *troesne* by 'privet, primprint.' Florio, ed. 1598, explains Ital. *ligustro* by 'the priuet or primeprint tree.' In Tusser's Husbandry, ed. Herrtage (E.D.S.), § 15. st. 42, we find the forms *priuie* and *prim*. In the Grete Herball (as cited in Prior, Popular Names of British Plants), we find the form *primet* applied to the *primrose* ; the confusion being due to the fact that the Lat. *ligustrum* was applied to both plants. 'Ligustrum, a primerose ;' Voc. 592. 41 ; so also OF. *primerole*, 'ligustrum ;' Godefroy. β. It thus appears that the orig. short name was *prim*, whence the dimin. *prim-et*, corruptly *priv-et*, or (by elision of the *e*) *prim't* or *print*. The form *prim-print* (= *prim-prim-et*) is a reduplicated one. And the syllable *prim-* is clearly due to a connexion with OF. *primerole* ; perhaps from association with spring-time. See **Prime** (1). γ. Sometimes said to be so named from its being formally cut and trimmed ; cf. prov. E. *prime*, to trim trees ; see **Prim** ; but this seems to be baseless, and will not explain why the OF. name was *primerole*. The mod. Prov. *primet*, adj., means 'very small.' ¶ No connexion with the river called *Pryfetes-flōd*, A. S. Chron. an. 755, or with *Privet*, near Petersfield, Hants.

PRIVILEGE, a prerogative, peculiar advantage. (F. – L.) ME. *priuilege* (with *u* = *v*) ; earliest form *priuilegie*, A. S. Chron. an. 1137. – OF. *privilege*, 'a priviledge ;' Cot. – L. *priuilēgium*, (1) a bill against a person, (2) an ordinance in favour of a person, a privilege. β. Properly a law relating to a single person. – L. *priui-* for *priuus*, single ; and *lēgi-*, decl. stem of *lex*, a law. See **Private** and **Legal**.

PRIVY, private. (F. – L.) ME. *priue*, *priuee* (with *u* = *v*), Layamon, 6877, later text. – OF. *prive*, *preve* (mod. F. *privé*) ; a pp. form. – L. *priuātus*, private ; see **Private**. Der. *privy-council*, *privy-council-lor*, *privy-purse*, *privy-seal*. Also *privy*, sb., ME. *priue*, *priuee*, Chaucer, C. T. 9828 (E 1954) ; *privi-ly* ; *privi-ty*, ME. *priuite* (= *priuitee*), Ancren Riwle, p. 152, l. 14.

PRIZE (1), that which is captured from an enemy, that which is won in a lottery or acquired by competition. (F. – L.) 'As his owne *prize* ;' Spenser, F. Q. iv. 4. 8. – F. *prise*, 'a taking, a seizing, ... a booty, or prize ;' Cot. Orig. fem. of *pris*, pp. of *prendre*, to take. – L. *prendere*, *prehendere*, to take, seize ; see **Prehensile**. Der. *prize-court*, *-fighter*, *-money*.

PRIZE (2), to value highly. (F. – L.) In Shak. Temp. i. 2. 168. ME. *prisen*, to set a price on, Prompt. Parv. – F. *priser*, 'to prise, esteem, ... to set a price on.' – OF. *pris*, 'a price, rate,' id. ; mod. F. *prix*. – L. *pretium* ; see **Price**. Der. *prize*, sb., Cymb. iii. 6. 77.

PRIZE (3), to open a box ; see **Prise**.

PRO-, prefix, before, forward, in front. (L. ; or Gk. ; or F. – L.)

This prefix may be either F., L., or Gk. If F., it is from Latin. – L. *prō-*, prefix, before ; whence *prō* (= *prōd*), an ablative form, used as a preposition. + Gk. προ-, prefix, and πρό, prep., before ; Skt. *pra-*, prefix ; *pra*, before, away. All allied to E. *for*, prep. ; see **For** (1). Der. Cf. *pre-*, prefix ; *pro-ne*, *prow*, *provost*, &c.

PROA, PROW, PRAU, a small vessel or ship. (Malay.) Sir T. Herbert, Travels, ed. 1665, p. 385, notes *praw* as a Malay word. 'Prawes and boats ;' (1599) J. Davis, Voy., Hakluyt Soc. p. 143. It is gen. spelt *proa* in mod. books of travel. – Malay *prāu*, 'a general term for all vessels between the *sampan* or canoe, and the *kapal* or square-rigged vessel ;' Marsden's Dict., p. 222.

PROBABLE, that may be proved, likely. (F. – L.) In Shak. As You Like It, iii. 5. 11. – F. *probable*, 'probable, proveable ;' Cot. – L. *probābilem*, acc. of *probābilis*, that may be proved ; formed with suffix *-bilis* from *probā-re*, to prove ; see **Prove**. Der. *probabl-y* ; *probabili-ty*, from F. *probabilité*, 'probability ;' Cot. And see *probation*.

PROBATION, a trial, time of trial or of proof. (F. – L.) In Shak. even used with the sense of 'proof,' Macb. iii. 1. 80. ME. *probacion*, Caxton, Golden Legend, Of the Resurrection, § 1. – F. *probation*, 'a probation, proof ;' Cot. – L. *probātiōnem*, acc. of *probātio*, a trial, proof. – L. *probāre*, to prove ; see **Prove**. Der. *probation-al*, *probation-ar-y*, *probation-er*. Also *probate*, proof of a will ; 'probates of testaments,' Hall's Chron., Hen. VIII, an. 17, § 21, from L. *probātus*, pp. of *probāre*. Also *probat-ive*, *probat-or-y*. And see *probable*, *probe*, *probity*.

PROBE, an instrument for examining a wound. (L.) 'Probe, a chirurgians proofe,' &c. ; Minsheu, ed. 1627. Apparently a coined word ; cf. L. *proba*, a proof. – L. *probāre*, to prove ; see **Prove**. ¶ Similarly, Span. *tienta*, a probe, is from L. *tentāre*, to search into. Der. *probe*, verb, Dryden, Hind and Panther, iii. 80.

PROBITY, uprightness, honesty. (F. – L.) In Blount's Gloss., ed. 1674. – F. *probité*, 'honesty ;' Cot. – L. *probitātem*, acc. of *probitās*, honesty. – L. *probi-*, for *probus*, honest ; with suffix *-tās*. Root uncertain. See **Prove**.

PROBLEM, a question proposed for solution, esp. a difficult one. (F. – L. – Gk.) ME. *probleme*, Chaucer, C. T. 7801 (D 2219). – OF. *probleme*, 'a problem,' Cot. Mod. F. *problème*. – L. *problēma*. – Gk. πρόβλημα, anything thrown forward, a question put forward for discussion. – Gk. πρό, forward ; and βλῆμα, a casting, formed with suffix *-μα* from βλη-, lengthened grade of βελ-, whence also βάλλειν, to cast. See **Pro-** and **Belemnite**. Der. *problemat-ic*, from the stem προβληματ- ; *problemat-ic-al*, *-ly*.

PROBOSCIS, the trunk of an eleph̄ant. (L. – Gk.) 'Their long snoute or trunke, which the Latins call a *proboscis* ;' Holland, tr. of Pliny, b. viii. c. 7. – L. *proboscis*. – Gk. προβοσκίς, an elephant's trunk ; lit. 'a front-feeder.' – Gk. πρό, before, in front ; and βόσκειν, to feed. See **Pro-** and **Botany**.

PROCEED, to advance. (F. – L.) ME. *proceden*, Gower, C. A. i. 17 ; prol. 405. – OF. *proceder*, 'to proceed,' Cot. – L. *prōcēdere*. – L. *prō-*, before ; and *cēdere*, to go ; see **Pro-** and **Cede**. Der. *pro-ceed-ing*, Two Gent. ii. 6. 41 ; *proced-ure*, from MF. *procedure*, 'a procedure,' Cot. ; *proceed-s*, sb. pl. Also *process*, ME. *processe*, Chaucer, C. T. 2969 (A 2967), OF. *proces* (14th cent.), later *procés* (mod. F. *procès*), 'a proces or sute,' Cot., from L. *processum*, acc. of *processus*, a progress, which from *processus*, pp. of *procēdere*. Also *process-ion*, ME. *processiun*, *processiun*, Layamon, 18223, from F. *procession* < L. acc. *processiōnem*, an advance. Hence *process-ion-al*.

PROCLAIM, to publish, announce aloud. (F. – L.) ME. *pro-clamen*, Gower, C. A. i. 6 ; prol. 88. – F. *proclamer*, 'to proclame,' Cot. – L. *prōclāmāre*. – L. *prō-*, before ; and *clāmāre*, to cry aloud ; see **Pro-** and **Claim**. Der. *proclaim-er* ; *proclam-at-ion*, All's Well, i. 3. 180, from F. *proclamation* < L. acc. *prōclāmātiōnem*.

PROCLITIC, a monosyllable which is so closely connected with the following word as to have no independent accent. (Gk.) In Greek grammar ; from a form *προκλιτικός*, coined (like ἐγκλιτικός) from προκλίνειν, to lean forward. – Gk. πρό, before, forward ; and κλίνειν, to lean, cognate with E. *lean* ; see **Lean** (1).

PROCLIVITY, a tendency, propensity. (L.) Spelt *procliuitie* in Minsheu, ed. 1627 ; he also has the obsolete adj. *procliue* = *proclive*. Englished directly from L. *prōclīuitas*, a declivity, propensity. – L. *prōclīuus*, sloping forward or downward. – L. *prō-*, before ; and *cliuus*, a slope, hill, allied to *clīnāre*, to bend, incline, which is allied to E. *lean*. See **Pro-**, **Declivity**, and **Lean** (1).

PROCONSUL, orig. the deputy of a consul. (L.) In Cymb. iii. 7. 8 ; and in Caxton, Golden Legend, St. John, § 6. – L. *prōconsul*. – L. *prō-*, in place of ; and *consul* ; see **Pro-** and **Consul**. ¶ Similarly, *pro-prætor*. Der. *proconsul-ate*, *proconsul-ar*.

PROCRASTINATE, to postpone, delay. (L.) In Shak. Com. Errors, i. 1. 159. – L. *procrastināt-us*, pp. of *procrastināre*, to put off till the morrow, delay. **—**L. *prŏ-*, forward, hence, off ; and *crastin-us*, put off till the morrow, belonging to the morrow. **β.** *Crastinus* is compounded of *cras*, to-morrow, and *-tinus.* perhaps allied to *tenus*, lit. stretching or reaching onward, from √TEN, to stretch. **Der.** *procrastinat-ion*, from F. *procrastination*, ' a procrastination, delay,' Cot.<L. acc. *prōcrastinātiōnem* ; *procrastinat-or.*

PROCREATE, to generate, propagate. (L.) In Minsheu, ed. 1627. **—**L. *prōcreātus*, pp. of *prōcreāre*, to generate, produce. **—**L. *prŏ-*, forth ; and *creāre*, to create, produce ; see **Pro-** and **Create.** **Der.** *procreat-ion*, Chaucer, C. T. 9322 (E 1448), from OF. *procreation*<L. acc. *prōcreātiōnem.* Also *procreat-or*, *procreat-ive* ; *procreant*, Macb. i. 6. 8, from *prōcreant-*, stem of pres. part. of L. *prōcreāre.*

PROCTOR, a procurator, an attorney in the spiritual courts, an officer who superintends university discipline. (L.) In Minsheu, ed. 1627. ME. *proketour*, spelt *proketowre* in Prompt. Parv., where it is explained by L. *prōcūrātor.* And, whilst *proctor* is a shortened form of *prokētour* (in three syllables), the latter is in its turn an abbreviated form of *prōcūrātor.* See further under **Procure.** **Der.** *proctor-ship* ; *proctor-i-al* ; *proxy.* Doublet, *procurator.*

PROCUMBENT, prostrate, lying on the ground. (L.) Kersey, ed. 1715, gives *procumbent leaves* as a botanical term. **—**L. *prōcumbent-*, stem of pres. part. of *prōcumbere*, to incline forward. **—**L. *prŏ-*, forward ; and *-cumbere*, to lean or lie upon (only used in compounds), a nasalized form of *cubāre*, to lie down. See **Pro-** and **Incubus.**

PROCURE, to obtain, cause, get. (F.—L.) ME. *procuren*, Rob. of Brunne, p. 257, l. 20. **—**F. *procurer*, to procure, get. **—**L. *prōcūrāre*, to take care of, attend to, manage. **—**L. *prŏ-*, for, in behalf of ; and *cūrāre*, to take care of, from *cūra*, care. See **Pro-** and **Cure.** **Der.** *procur-able*, *procur-er*, *procur-ess*, *procure-ment.* Also *procur-at-or*, ME. *procuratour*, also *procutour*, *procatour*, Chaucer, C. T. 7178 (D 1596, Six-text edition), from OF. *procurator*, in use in the 13th century (Littré), mod. F. *procurateur*, from L. *prōcūrātōrem*, acc. of *prōcūrātor*, a manager, agent, deputy, viceroy, administrator ; the more usual F. form is *procureur* (see Cotgrave), and the more usual E. form is the much abbreviated *proctor*, q.v. Also *procurat-ion*, Minsheu, ed. 1627, from F. *procura'ion*, ' a procuration, a warrant or letter of attorny,' Cot. Also *proxy*, q.v.

PROD, a pointed stick for making holes, a skewer, peg. (Scand.) A variant of *brod*, a goad, short nail, awl. ' A *brod*, stimulus ; ' Catholicon Anglicum (1483). **—**Norw. and MSwed. *brodd*, Icel. *broddr*, a prick, goad ; see **Brad.** **Der.** *prod*, vb. ' to poke.'

PRODIGAL, wasteful, lavish. (F.—L.) Spelt *prodigall* in Levins and Palsgrave. ' Some *prodigallie* spend and waste all their gooddes ; ' Golden Boke, c. 45. [The sb. *prodegalite* (so spelt) occurs in Gower, C. A. iii. 153 ; bk. vii. 2026.] **—**F. *prodigal*, ' prodigall,' Cot. **—**Late L. **prōdigālis*, not found, though the sb. *prōdigālitās* occurs ; see Ducange. **—**L. *prōdigus*, wasteful. **—**L. *prōdigere*, to drive forth or away, squander, waste. **—**L. *prōd*, forth, older form of *prō*, allied to *pro-*, prefix ; and *agere*, to drive. See **Pro-** and **Agent.** **Der.** *prodigal-ly* ; *prodigal-i-ty*, from F. *prodigalité*, ' prodigality,' from L. acc. *prōdigālitātem.*

PRODIGY, a portent, wonder. (F.—L.) In Shak. Jul. Cæs. i. 3. 28, ii. 1. 198. Formed from F. *prodige*, ' a prodigy, wonder,' Cot. ; by the addition of the *-y* so often appearing in words borrowed from French ; thus we have *continency*, *excellency*, *fragrancy*, as well as *continence*, *excellence*, *fragrance* ; the E. form answering to a possible AF. form **prodigie.* **—**L. *prōdigium*, a showing beforehand, sign, token, portent. **β.** Of uncertain origin ; but prob. for *prōdagium*, where *prōd*, forth, before, is an old form of *prō*, before ; and **agium* means ' a saying,' as in the compound *ad-agium*, a saying, adage. Brugmann, i. § 759. In this case, the orig. sense is ' a saying beforehand,' hence a sign, prophecy, or token. See **Pro-** and **Adage.** **Der.** *prodigi-ous*, Spenser, F. Q. iv. 1. 13, from F. *prodigieux*, ' prodigious,' Cot., which from L. *prōdigiōsus* ; *prodigious-ly*, *-ness.*

PRODUCE, to lead or bring forward, bear, yield, cause. (L.) In Shak. All's Well, iv. 1. 6 ; and in Palsgrave. **—**L. *prōdūcere*, to bring forward. **—**L. *prŏ-*, forward ; and *dūcere*, to lead, whence E. *duke.* See **Pro-, Duke.** **Der.** *produc-er* ; *produce*, sb., formerly *prodúce*, as shown by an extract from Dryden, Ep. to John Dryden, 118, in Todd's Johnson. Also *produc-ible*, *produc-ible-ness.* Also *prodúct*, sb., Pope, Messiah, 94, accented *prodúct*, Milton, P. L. xi. 683, from *prōductus*, pp. of *prōdūcere.* Also *product-ion*, from F. *production*, ' a production, proof, evidence,' Cot., which from L. acc. *prōductiōnem*, orig. a lengthening, but in Late L., the production of a document and even the document or proof itself. Also *product-ive*, *product-ive-ly*, *product-ive-ness.*

PROEM, a prelude, preface. (F.—L.—Gk.) Chaucer has the

spelling *proheme*, C. T. 7919 (E 43), where the *h* is merely inserted to keep the vowels apart. **—**OF. *proëme*, ' a proem, preface,' Cot. ; mod. F. *proême.* **—**L. *proœmium.* **—**Gk. προοίμιον, an introduction, prelude. **—**Gk. πρό, before ; and οἶμος, a way, from *oĭ-*, 2nd grade of √EI, to go, with Idg. suffix *-mo-.* See **Pro-** and **Itinerant.**

PROFANE, unholy, impious. (F.—L.) Commonly spelt *prophane* in the 16th century ; see Rich. II, v. i. 25 (first folio) ; and Robinson's tr. of More's Utopia, ed. Arber, p. 145, l. 6. **—**F. *profane*, ' prophane ; ' Cot. **—**L. *prōfānus*, unholy, profane. **β.** The orig. sense seems to have been ' before the temple,' hence, outside of the temple, secular, not sacred. **—**L. *prŏ-*, before ; and *fānum*, a fane, temple. See **Pro-** and **Fane.** **Der.** *profane*, verb, Rich. II, iii. 3. 81 ; *profane-ly*, *profane-ness* ; *profan-at-ion*, Meas. for Meas. ii. 2. 128, from F. *profanation*, ' a prophanation or prophaning,' Cot., from L. acc. *prōfānātiōnem.* Also *profan-i-ty*, Englished from L. *prōfānitās.*

PROFESS, to own freely, declare openly, undertake to do. (F.—L.) Not orig. from F. *professer*, for this is a late form, in Palsgrave. The ME. word is *professed*, used as a pp. ; ' Which in hire ordre was *professed*,' Gower, C. A. ii. 157 ; bk. v. 890. This is Englished from OF. *profes*, masc., *professe*, fem., applied in the same way ; ' Qui devant iert nonain *professe* ' = who was before a professed nun ; Rom. de la Rose, 8844 (Littré). **—**L. *prōfessus*, manifest, confessed, avowed ; pp. of *prōfitēri*, to profess, avow. **—**L. *prŏ-*, before all, publicly ; and *fatēri*, to acknowledge. See **Pro-** and **Confess.** **Der.** *profess-ed* (see above) ; *profess-ed-ly* ; *profess-ion*, ME. *professioun*, *professiun*, Ancren Riwle, p. 6, l. 20, from F. *profession* ; *profess-ion-al*, *profess-ion-al-ly* ; *profess-or*, 1 Hen. VI, v. 1. 14, ME. *professour*, Trevisa, tr. of Higden, i. 7, from L. *prōfessor*, a public teacher ; *profess-or-ial*, *profess-or-ship.*

PROFFER, to offer, propose for acceptance. (F.—L.) ME. *profren* (with one *f*), Chaucer, C. T. 8028 (E 152) ; *proferen*, K. Alisaunder, 3539. **—**OF. *profrir*, *porofrir* (Godefroy), also AF. *profrer* (Bozon). **—**OF. *por-*, prefix, L. *prō* ; and *ofrir*, *offrir*, from L. *offerre*, to offer. See **Pro-** and **Offer.** ¶ *Not* from MF. *proferer*, ' to produce,' Cot. ; as the sense and usage show. The senses of *proffer* and *offer* are very near together. **Der.** *proffer-er.*

PROFICIENT, competent, thoroughly qualified. (L.) In Shak. 1 Hen. IV, ii. 4. 19. **—**L. *prōficient-*, stem of pres. part. of *prōficere*, to make progress, advance. **—**L. *prŏ-*, forward ; and *facere*, to make ; see **Pro-, Fact**, and **Profit.** **Der.** *proficience*, *proficienc-y.*

PROFILE, an outline, the side-face. (Ital.—L.) [Not a F., but an Ital. word. The F. word was formerly spelt *porfil* or *pourfil*, which forms see in Cotgrave ; hence ME. *purfiled*, bordered, Chaucer, C. T. 193.] ' Draw it in *profile*,' Dryden, Parallel of Poetry and Painting, § 9. ' *Profile* (Ital. *profilo*) that design which shows the side, . . . a term in painting ; ' Blount's Gloss., ed. 1674. **—**Ital. *profilo*, ' a border, a limning or drawing of any picture ; ' Florio. Hence *profilare*, ' to draw, to limne, to paint ; ' id. **—**Ital. *pro-*, before (=L. *prō-*) ; and *filo*, ' a thread, a line, a strike ' [stroke], Florio ; from L. *filum*, a thread. Thus the sense is a ' front-line ' or outline. See **Pro-** and **File** (1). ¶ The mod. F. *profil* is (like the E. word) from the Italian. **Der.** *profile*, vb. ; and see *purl* (3).

PROFIT, gain, benefit. (F.—L.) ME. *profit*, P. Plowman, B. prol. 169. **—**F. *profit*, ' profit ; ' Cot. [Cf. Ital. *profitto*.] **—**L. *prōfectum*, acc. of *prōfectus*, advance, progress. **—**L. *prōfectus*, pp. of *prōficere*, to make progress, advance, be profitable. **—**L. *prŏ-*, before ; and *facere*, to make ; see **Pro-** and **Fact.** **Der.** *profit*, vb. ME. *profiten*, Wyclif, Heb. iv. 2, from F. *profiter* ; *profit-able*, Wyclif, 2 Tim. iii. 16 ; *profit-abl-y*, *profit-able-ness* ; *profit-ing*, *profit-less.*

PROFLIGATE, dissolute. (L.) Minsheu gives ; ' to *profligate*, to ouerthrow, to vndoe, to put to flight ; ' ed. 1627. But it is properly a pp. used as an adj. Cf. ' thy father, . . . which hath *profligate* [put to flight] and discomfited so many of them ; ' Hall's Chron., Hen. VI, an. 31. **—**L. *prōflīgātus*, pp. of *prōflīgāre*, to dash to the ground, overthrow ; whence *prōflīgātus*, cast down, abandoned, dissolute. **—**L. *prŏ-*, forward ; and *flīgere*, to strike, dash. See **Pro-** and **Afflict.** **Der.** *profligate-ly*, *-ness*, *profligac-y.*

PROFOUND, deep, low, abstruse, occult. (F.—L.) In Early Eng. Poems and Lives of Saints, ed. Furnivall (Phil. Soc.), xvii. 221 ; and in Fisher's Works, ed. Mayor, p. 37, ll. 12, 16. **—**F. *profond*, ' profound,' Cot. **—**L. *prōfundus*, acc. of *prōfundus*, deep. **—**L. *prŏ*, forward, hence, downward, far, deep ; and *fundus*, the ground, bottom, cognate with E. *bottom.* See **Pro-, Found** (1), and **Bottom.** **Der.** *profound-ly*, *profound-ness* ; also *profund-i-ty*, formerly *profoundyte*, Fisher, On the Seven Psalms, Ps. cii., p. 138, l. 28, from F. *profondité*, ' profundity,' Cot.

PROFUSE, liberal to excess, lavish. (L.) ' A rhetoric so *profuse* ; ' Chapman, tr. of Homer, Od. iii. 172. **—**L. *prōfūsus*, pp. of *prōfundere*, to pour out. **—**L. *prŏ-*, forth ; and *fundere*, to pour ; see **Pro-** and **Fuse.** **Der.** *profuse-ly*, *profuse-ness* ; *profus-ion*, from L. *prōfūsio.*

PROG, to search for provisions ; as sb., provisions. (L.) The sb.

is from the verb. Orig. 'to beg, demand;' see Todd's Johnson. App. a weakened form of ME. *prokken*; '*Prokkyn*, or styfly askyn, *procor*;' Prompt. Parv. Prob. a monkish word; adapted from L. *procāre*, *procārī*, to demand.—L. *procus*, a suitor.—L. *proc-*, 2nd grade of *prec-*, in *prec-ārī*, to pray. See **Pray**. Perhaps influenced by ME. *prócren*, *próker*, to procure, obtain; see Gloss. to Dest. of Troy and to Alexander and Dindimus, short for *procuren*; and a doublet of E. **Procure**.

PROGENITOR, a forefather, ancestor. (F.—L.) Now conformed to the L. spelling; but formerly *progenytour*, Sir T. Elyot, Castel of Helth, b. ii. c. 7; Fabyan, Chron. an. 1336-7, ed. Ellis, p. 416; Caxton, Reynard, p. 91.—F. *progeniteur*, 'a progenitor,' Cot.—L. *prŏgenitōrem*, acc. of *prŏgenitor*, an ancestor.—L. *prŏ-*, before; and *genitor*, a parent, from √GEN, to beget, with suffix denoting the agent; see **Pro-** and **Genus**. See **Progeny**.

PROGENY, descendants, a race, offspring. (F.—L.) ME. *progenie*, Gower, C. A. ii. 166; bk. v. 1161; *progenye*, Wyclif, Gen. xliii. 7.—OF. *progenie*, 'a progeny;' Cot.—L. *prŏgeniem*, acc. of *prŏgeniēs*, lineage, progeny.—L. *prŏ-*, forth; and stem *gen-*, as in *gen-us*, kin, from √GEN, to beget. See **Progenitor**.

PROGNOSTIC, a foreshowing, indication, presage. (F.—L.—Gk.) 'The whiche .. they adjudged for *pronostiquykys* and tokens of the kynges deth;' Fabyan, Chron. b. i. c. 246; ed. Ellis, p. 289.—OF. *pronostique* (14th cent.), *prognostique*, Cot.; mod. F. *pronostic* (Littré).—L. *prognōsticon*.—Gk. προγνωστικόν, a sign or token of the future.—Gk. πρό, before; and γνωστικόν, neut. of γνωστικός, good at knowing, which from γνωστός, γνωτός, known, γνῶναι, to know. See **Pro-** and **Gnostic**. Der. *prognostic*, adj. from Gk. προγνωστικός; *prognostic-ate*, spelt *pronostycate* in Palsgrave; *prognostic-at-ion*, spelt *pronostication* in Sir T. Elyot, Castel of Helth, b. iii. c. 4, from OF. *pronostication* or *prognostication*, 'a prognostication;' Cot.; *prognostic-at-or*.

PROGRAMME, PROGRAM, a public notice in writing, a sketch of proceedings. (F.—L.—Gk.) The etymological spelling is *programme*, according to F. *programme*; but it is quite a modern word. We find the L. form *programma* in Phillips, ed. 1706, and in Todd's Johnson.— Gk. πρόγραμμα, a public notice in writing.—Gk. προγράφειν, to give public notice in writing.—Gk. πρό, before, publicly; and γράφειν, to write. See **Pro-** and **Graphic**.

PROGRESS, advancement. (F.—L.) In Spenser, F. Q. iii. 11. 20; Court of Love, 1067.—MF. *progrez*, 'a progression, going forward,' Cot. Mod. F. *progrès*.—L. *progressum*, acc. of *progressus*, an advance.—L. *progressus*, pp. of *progredī*, to advance.—L. *prŏ-*, forward; and *gradī*, to walk, step, go. See **Pro-** and **Grade**. Der. *progress*, vb., accented *prógress*, K. John, v. 2. 46; *progress-ion*, Chaucer, C. T. 3015 (A 3013), from F. *progression* (not in Cotgrave, but found in 1425, see Hatzfeld), from L. acc. *progressiōnem*; *progress-ion-al*, Blount, ed. 1674; *progress-ive*, Phillips, ed. 1706; *progress-ive-ly*, *-ness*.

PROHIBIT, to hinder, check, forbid. (L.) In Minsheu, ed. 1627, and in Palsgrave.—L. *prōhibitus*, pp. of *prōhibēre*, to prohibit; lit. to hold before or in one's way.—L. *prŏ-*, before; and *habēre*, to have, hold; see **Pro-** and **Habit**. Der. *prohibit-ion*, Cymb. iii. 4. 79, from F. *prohibition*, 'a prohibition,' from L. acc. *prōhibitiōnem*; *prohibit-ive*; *prohibit-or-y*, from L. *prōhibitōrius*.

PROJECT, sb., a plan, purpose, scheme. (F.—L.) In Shak. Much Ado, iii. 1. 55.—MF. *project*, 'a project, purpose,' Cot. Mod. F. *projet*.—L. *prōiectum*, acc. of *prōiectus*, pp. of *prōicere* (*prōjicere*), to fling forth, cast out, hold out, extend; whence the sense to set forth, plan, not found in classical Latin.—L. *prŏ-*, forward; and *iacere*, to throw; see **Pro-** and **Jet** (1). Der. *project*, verb, to cast forward, Spenser, F. Q. vi. 1. 45; also, to plan, accented *próject*, Antony, v. 2. 121; *project-ion*, also in the sense of 'plan' in Hen. V, ii. 4. 46, from F. *projection*, 'a projection, .. extending out,' Cot.; *project-or*; *project-ile*, in Phillips, ed. 1706, a coined word.

PROLATE, extended, elongated in the direction of the polar axis. (L.) Chiefly in the phrase '*prolate* spheroid,' Bailey's Dict., vol. i. ed. 1735. [*Prolate* is used as a verb by Howell; see Rich. and Todd's Johnson.]—L. *prōlātus*, lengthened, extended.—L. *prŏ-*, forward; and *lātus* (for *tlātus*), borne, from √TEL, to lift, bear; see **Pro-** and **Oblate**.

PROLEPSIS, anticipation. (L.—Gk.) A rhetorical term; in Phillips, ed. 1706. [Blount, ed. 1674, gives *prolepsie*, from MF. *prolepsie* in Cotgrave.]—L. *prolēpsis*.—Gk. πρόληψις, an anticipation or anticipatory allusion.—Gk. πρό, before; and λῆψις, a seizing, catching, taking, from λήψ-ομαι, fut. of λαμβάνειν, to seize. See **Pro-** and **Catalepsy**. Der. *prolep-t-ic*, as in '*proleptick disease*, a disease that always anticipates, as if an ague come today at 4 o'clock, tomorrow an hour sooner,' Phillips, ed. 1706, from Gk. προληπτικός, anticipating; *prolep-t-ic-al*, Blount's Gloss., ed. 1674; *prolep-t-ic-al-ly*.

PROLETARIAN, belonging to the lower orders, vulgar. (L.) 'Low *proletarian* tything men;' Butler, Hudibras, i. 1. 720. Formed with suffix *-an* from L. *prōlētāri-us*, a citizen of the lowest class, but regarded as useful as being a parent.—L. *prōlē-*, for *prōlēs*, offspring; with suffix *-t-ārius*; see below.

PROLIFIC, fruitful. (F.—L.) Spelt *prolifick*, in Phillips, ed. 1706, and in Bp. Taylor, vol. i. ser. 23 (R.).—F. *prolifique*, 'fruitfull,' Cot.—Late L. **prōlificus*, not recorded, though Ducange gives the derivatives *prōlificātio* and *prōlificātiuus*; it means 'producing offspring.'—L. *prōli-*, for *prōlēs*, offspring; and *-ficus*, making, from *facere*, to make; see **Fact**. β. L. *prōlēs* = **pro-olēs*; from *pro-*, before; and **olere*, to grow, whence the inceptive form *olescere*, appearing in *ad-olescere*, to grow up; see **Adolescent**, **Adult**. Cf. *sub-olēs*, *ind-olēs*. Der. *prolific-al*, Blount's Gloss., ed. 1674.

PROLIX, tedious, lengthy. (F.—L.) 'A longe and *prolixe* exhortacion;' Hall's Chron., Hen. VII, an. 6. § 3. G. Douglas has the corrupt form *prolixt*, Palace of Honour, pt. ii. st. 18, ed. Small. [The sb. *prolixity*, ME. *prolixitee*, is in Chaucer, C. T. 10719 (F 405), and Troilus, b. ii, l. 1564.]—F. *prolixe*, 'prolix,' Cot.—L. *prōlixus*, extended, prolix. β. *Prōlixus* must be compared with *ēlixus*, soaked, boiled, allied to OL. *lixa*, water, and *līquī*, *liquēre*, to flow. We then get the true sense; *prōlixus* means 'that which has flowed beyond its bounds,' and the usual sense of 'broad' or 'extended' is clearly due to the common phenomenon of the enlargement of a pond by rain.—L. *prŏ-*, forward; and *-lixus*, supplying the place of the unrecorded pp. of *liquī*, to flow. See **Pro-** and **Liquid**. Der. *prolix-i-ty* (see above), from OF. *prolixite*, in use in the 13th cent. (Littré); from L. acc. *prōlixitātem*, Brugmann, i. § 665.

PROLOCUTOR, the speaker, or chairman of a convocation. (L.) '*Prolocutour of the Conuocation house*, is an officer chosen by persons ecclesiasticall, publickly assembled by the Kings Writ at euery Parliament;' Minsheu. ed. 1627.—L. *prōlocūtor*, an advocate.—L. *prŏ-*, before, publicly; and *locūtor*, a speaker, allied to *locūtus*, pp. of *loquī*, to speak. See **Pro-** and **Loquacious**.

PROLOGUE, a preface, introductory verses to a play. (F.—L.—Gk.) ME. *prologue*, Gower, C. A. prol. And see MSS. of the Cant. Tales.—F. *prologue*, 'a prologue, or fore-speech,' Cot.—L. *prologus*.—Gk. πρόλογος, a fore-speech.—Gk. πρό, before; and λόγος, a speech; see **Pro-** and **Logic**.

PROLONG, to continue, lengthen out. (F.—L.) ME. *prolongen*. '*Purlongyn* or *prolongyn*, or put fer a-wey;' Prompt. Parv. p. 417.—F. *prolonger*, 'to prolong, protract,' Cot.—L. *prōlongāre*, to prolong.—L. *prŏ-*, forward, onward; and *longus*, long. See **Pro-** and **Long**. Der. *prolong-at-ion*, from F. *prolongation*, 'a prolongation,' Cot.; cf. L. pp. *prōlongātus*. Doublet, *purloin*.

PROMENADE, a walk, place for walking. (F.—L.) In Blount's Gloss., ed. 1674, we find both *promenade* and *pourmenade*.—F. *promenade*, formerly *pourmenade*; Cot. gives only the latter form. Formed from OF. *pourmener* or *promener*, to walk, both of which forms are given in Cotgrave, the prefix being really the same (L. *prō*) in either case. The suffix *-ade* is borrowed from the Prov. suffix *-ada*, for L. *-āta*, the fem. form of *-ātus*, the pp. suffix of the 1st conjugation.—L. *prōmināre*, to drive forwards, orig. to drive on by threats.—L. *prŏ-*, forward; and Late L. *mināre*, to drive on, allied to L. *minārī*, to threaten. See **Pro-** and **Menace**. Der. *promenade*, verb. Cf. *e-minent*, *im-minent*.

PROMINENT, projecting, conspicuous, eminent. (F.—L.) 'Some *prominent* rock:' Chapman, tr. of Homer, Iliad, xvi. 389.—F. *prominent*, 'prominent;' Cot.—L. *prōminent-*, stem of pres. part. of *prōminēre*, to project.—L. *prŏ-*, forth; and *-minēre*, to jut, project. See **Menace**. Der. *prominent-ly*; *prominence*, from F. *prominence*, 'a prominence,' Cot.

PROMISCUOUS, mixed, confused. (L.) In Minsheu, ed. 1627; and in Cotgrave, to translate F. *promiscué*.—L. *promiscuus*, mixed.—L. *prŏ-*, lit. forward, but here of slight force; and *misc-ēre*, to mix, whence E. *mix*. See **Pro-** and **Miscellaneous**. Der. *promiscuous-ly*, *-ness*.

PROMISE, an engagement to do a thing, an expectation. (F.—L.) For *promes* or *promesse*. 'And this is the *promise* that he hath *promised* vs;' Bible, 1551, 1 John, ii. 25. 'Fayre behestis and promysys;' Fabyan, Chron. an. 1336-7.—F. *promesse*, 'a promise,' Cot. [Cf. Span. *promesa*, Ital. *promessa*, a promise.]—L. *prōmissa*, fem. of *prōmissus*, pp. of *prōmittere*, to send or put forth, to promise.—L. *prŏ-*, forth; and *mittere*, to send; see **Pro-** and **Mission**. Der. *promise*, verb (as above); *promis-er*, *promis-ing*, *promis-ing-ly*; *promiss-or-y*, formed with suffix *-y* (< L. *-ius*) from the (rare) L. *prōmissor*, a promiser.

PROMONTORY, a headland, cape. (L.) In Shak. Temp. v. 46. Englished from L. *prōmontōrium*, a mountain-ridge, headland; cf. F. *promontoire* (Cot.).—L. *prŏ-*, forward; *mont-*, stem of *mons*, a mountain; and the adj. neut. suffix *-ōrium*. See **Pro-** and **Mountain**.

PROMOTE, to further, advance, elevate. (L.) 'A great furtherer or *promoter*;' Fabyan, Chron. an. 1336-7, ed. Ellis, p. 445. 'He was *promoted* to so high an office;' Grafton, Chron. Hen. VI, an. 14 (R.). – L. *prōmōtus,* pp. of *prōmouēre,* to promote, further. – L. *prō-,* forward; and *mouēre,* to move; see **Pro-** and **Move.** Der. *promot-er; promot-ion,* ME. *promocion,* Prompt. Parv., from F. *promotion,* from L. acc. *prōmōtiōnem.*

PROMPT, prepared, ready, acting with alacrity. (F. – L.) 'She that was *prompte* and redy to all euyll;' Fabyan, Chron. vol. i. c. 116; ed. Ellis, p. 91, l. 1. Cf. '*Promptyd,* Promptus;' Prompt. Parv. – F. *prompt,* 'prompt;' Cot. – L. *promptum,* acc. of *promptus, promtus,* brought to light, at hand, ready, pp. of *prōmere,* to take or bring forward. – L. *prō-,* forward; and *emere,* to take; whence *prōmere,* for *prōd-imere.* See **Pro-** and **Example.** Der. *prompt-ly, prompt-ness; prompt,* verb, ME. *prompten,* Prompt. Parv.; *prompt-er,* ME. *promptare,* Prompt. Parv.; *prompt-ing; prompt-i-tude* (Levins), from F. *promptitude,* 'promptness,' Cot., from Late L. *promptitūdo,* which occurs A.D. 1261 (Ducange).

PROMULGATE, to publish. (L.) In Shak. Oth. i. 2. 21; and both as vb. and pp. in Palsgrave. – L. *prōmulgātus,* pp. of *prōmulgāre,* to publish. β. Of unknown origin; the prefix is *prō-,* as usual. Some refer it to OLat. *promellere,* 'litem promouere,' which is not satisfactory. Der. *promulgat-or, promulgat-ion.*

PRONE, with the face downward, headlong, inclined, eagerly, ready. (F. – L.) In Shak. Wint. Tale, ii. 1. 108. – F. *prone,* 'prone, ready,' Cot. – L. *prōnum,* acc. of *prōnus,* inclined towards. β. *Prōnus* has been compared with Ionic Gk. πρηνής, Doric πρᾱνής, headlong; and is connected with the prep. *prō-, prŏd;* whence **prōd-nus.* See **Pro-.** Der. *prone-ly, prone-ness.*

PRONG, the spike of a fork. (E.) 'Iron teeth of rakes and *prongs*;' Dryden, tr. of Virgil, Georg. ii. 487. 'A *prong* or pitchforke;' Minsheu, ed. 1627. 'A *prongue,* hasta furcata;' Levins, 166. 47, ed. 1570. The ME. *pronge,* a pang, sharp pain (Prompt. Parv.) is the same word. Cf. ME. *pranglen,* to constrain, Havelok, 639; from a Teut. base **prang-,* to compress, nip, push, pierce. Hence also Du. *prangen,* to press; G. *pranger,* a pillory; Goth. *ana-praggan* (=*ana-prangan*), to press; Low G. *prange,* a stake; MDu. *prange,* 'a horse-mussle (muzzle): a shackle or a neck-yron; oppression or constraint;' Hexham; Dan. *prange,* to crowd sail. See **Pang.**

PRONOUN, a word used in place of a noun, to denote a person. (F. – L.) In Ben Jonson, Eng. Grammar, c. xv; Shak. Merry Wives, iv. 1. 41. Spelt *pronowne* in Palsgrave, p. xxiv. Compounded of **Pro-** and **Noun;** and suggested by L. *pronōmen,* a pronoun, or by F. *pronom,* a pronoun, found in 1482 (Hatzfeld). Cf. Span. *pronombre,* Ital. *pronome.* Der. *pronomin-al,* from *prōnōmin-,* stem of L. *pronōmen.*

PRONOUNCE, to utter, express, speak distinctly. (F. – L.) ME. *pronouncen,* Chaucer, C. T. 16767 (G 1299). – F. *prononcer,* 'to pronounce,' Cot. – L. *prōnuntiāre,* to pronounce. – L. *prō-,* forth; and *nuntiāre,* to tell. See **Pro-** and **Announce.** Der. *pronounc-er, pronounce-able, pronounc-ing; pronunci-at-ion,* from MF. *prononciation,* 'pronunciation,' Cot., from L. acc. *prōnuntiātiōnem.*

PROŒMIUM, a proem; see **Proem.**

PROOF, a test, demonstration, evidence. (F. – L.) The vowel has undergone some alteration; we find the spelling *profe* in the Bible of 1551, 2 Cor. ii. 9. ME. *preef,* in many MSS. of Wyclif, 2 Cor. ii. 9, later text, where the reading of the text itself is *preuyng.* Earliest spelling *preoue,* Ancren Riwle, p. 52, l. 13; where *eo* is put for F. *eu,* as in E. *people* for F. *peuple.* – F. *preuve,* 'a proofe, tryall,' Cot. – Late L. *proba,* a proof (Lewis); which seems to be merely formed from the verb *probāre,* to prove; see **Prove.** Cf. Port. and Ital. *prova,* Span. *prueba,* a proof.

PROP, a support, stay. (E.) The sb. appears earlier than the verb. ME. *proppe,* a long staff; Prompt. Parv. [Whence were borrowed Irish *propa,* a prop; *propadh,* propping; Gael. *prop,* a prop, support, *prop,* to prop, pp. *propta,* propped.] Not in AS. **+** Du. *proppe,* 'an yron branch, *proppen,* to prop, stay, or beare up,' Hexham; and with a change of meaning to fastening or stopping up, Dan. *prop,* Swed. *propp,* G. *pfropf,* a cork, stopple, G. *pfropfen,* to cram, stuff, or thrust into. All from a Teut. base **prup-,* to stop up, to support; cf. MDan. *prilpfuld,* Dan. *propfuld,* chokeful; Swed. dial. *primpa, prippa,* to cram (oneself). ¶ In the sense of 'graft,' G. *pfropf* is due to L. *propāgo;* see **Propagate.** Der. *prop,* verb.

PROPAGATE, to multiply plants by layers, extend, produce. (L.) In Shak. Per. i. 2. 73; and in Levins, ed. 1570. – L. *prōpāgātus,* pp. of *prōpāgāre,* to peg down, propagate by layers, produce, beget; allied to *prōpāges, prōpāgo,* a layer, and from the same root as *com-pāges,* a joining together, structure. – L. *prō-,* forward; and *-pāg-es,* a fastening, pegging, from *pāg-,* base of *pangere,* to fasten, set (hence, to peg down); see **Pro-** and **Pact.** Der. *propagat-or.*

propagat-ion, Minsheu; *propagand-ism, propagand-ist,* coined words from the name of the society entitled *Congregatio de Propagandâ Fide,* constituted at Rome, A.D. 1622 (Haydn). And see *prune* (1).

PROPEL, to drive forward, urge on. (L.) 'The blood . . . that is *propelled* out of a vein of the breast;' Harvey (died 1657); cited in Todd's Johnson, without a reference. ME. *propellen,* Palladius on Husbandry, bk. i. 1034. [But the word *propulse* was sometimes used instead of it; see Richardson.] – L. *prōpellere* (pp. *prōpulsus*), to propel. – L. *prō-,* forward; and *pellere,* to drive; see **Pro-** and **Pulsate.** Der. *propell-er; propuls-ion, propuls-ive,* like the pp. *prōpulsus.*

PROPENSITY, an inclination. (L.; with F. *suffix*). '*Propension* or *Propensity*;' Phillips, ed. 1706. [The old word was *propension,* as in Minsheu, and in Shak. Troil. ii. 2. 133, from F. *propension,* 'a propension or proneness,' Cot.] A coined word, with suffix *-ity* (F. *-ité*), from L. *prōpens-us,* hanging forward, inclining towards, prone to; pp. of *prōpendēre,* to hang forwards. – L. *prō-,* forwards; and *pendēre,* to hang; see **Pro-** and **Pendent.** And see **Prepense.**

PROPER, one's own, belonging to, peculiar, suitable, just, comely. (F. – L.) ME. *propre,* whence *propremen*=proper man, Ancren Riwle, p. 196, l. 15; *propreliche*=properly, id. p. 98, l. 11. – F. *propre,* 'proper,' Cot. – L. *proprium,* acc. of *proprius,* one's own. β. Etym. doubtful; Bréal connects it with the phr. *prō priuō,* for one's own; from *priuus,* single, peculiar; whence also **Private.** Der. *properly;* also *proper-ly,* ME. *propreté,* Gower, C. A. i. 239; bk. ii. 2377, from OF. *propreté,* explained as 'fitness' by Cotgrave, but found in old texts with the sense of 'property' (Littré), from L. acc. *proprietātem;* see **Propriety.**

PROPHECY, a prediction. (F. – L. – Gk.) The distinction in spelling between *prophecy,* sb., and *prophesy,* verb, is unoriginal and arbitrary; both should be *prophecy.* ME. *prophecie,* Ancren Riwle, p. 158, l. 15. – OF. *prophecie,* variant of *prophetie,* 'a prophesie,' Cot. – L. *prophētīa.* – Gk. προφητεία, a prediction. – Gk. προφήτης, a prophet; see **Prophet.** Der. *prophesy,* verb, ME. *prophecien,* Trevisa, i. 421, l. 33.

PROPHET, one who predicts, an inspired teacher. (F. – L. – Gk.) ME. *prophete,* Rob. of Glouc. p. 38, l. 893; Ormulum, 5195. – OF. *prophete.* – L. *prophēta.* – Gk. προφήτης, one who declares things, an expounder, prophet. – Gk. πρό, publicly, before all; also, before; and φη-, base of φημί, I say, speak; with suffix *-της,* denoting the agent. From √BHĀ, to speak; see **Pro-** and **Fame.** Der. *prophet-ess, prophet-ic, prophet-ic-al, prophet-ic-al-ly;* also *prophec-y,* q.v.

PROPHYLACTIC, preventive, defending from disease. (F. – Gk.) From F. *prophylactique,* employed by Rabelais; see Hatzfeld. – Gk. προφυλακτικός, guarding from. – Gk. προφυλάσσειν, to keep guard before. – Gk. πρό, before; φυλάσσειν, to guard. See **Phylactery.**

PROPINE, to drink to one's health, give, offer. (L. – Gk.) 'The lovely sorceress mix'd, and to the prince Health, joy, and peace *propin'd*;' C. Smart, The Hop-garden, i. 228. – L. *propināre,* to drink to one's health, give. – Gk. προπίνειν, the same. – Gk. πρό, before; πίνειν, to drink.

PROPINQUITY, nearness. (F. – L.) ME. *propinquitee,* Chaucer, tr. of Boethius, b. ii. pr. 3, l. 24. – OF. *propinquité* (Godefroy). – L. *propinquitātem,* acc. of *propinquitās,* nearness. – L. *propinqui-,* for *propinquus,* near, with suffix *-tās.* β. *Propinquus* = **propi-n-cus,* extended from *prope,* near. Der. from the same source, *ap-proach, re-proach, prox-imity.*

PROPITIOUS, favourable. (L.) [The old adj. was *propice,* from OF. *propice,* 'propitious;' see exx. in R.] In Minsheu, ed. 1627. Englished, by change of *-us* to *-ous,* as in *arduous,* &c., from L. *propitius,* favourable. β. Prob. a term of augury; it seems to mean 'flying forwards;' the form shows the derivation from *trō-,* forwards, and *petere,* orig. to fly, from √PET, to fly. See **Pro-** and **Feather.** Der. *propitious-ly, -ness.* Also *propiti-ate,* orig. used as a pp., as in a quotation from Bp. Gardner, Explication of the Sacrament, 1551, fol. 150, cited by R.; from L. *propitiātus,* pp. of *propitiāre,* to render favourable. Hence *propitiat-ion,* Minsheu, from F. *propitiation,* 'a propitiation,' Cot.; *propitiat-or-y,* ME. *propiciatorie,* Wyclif, Heb. ix. 5, from L. *prōpitiātōrium,* Heb. ix. 5.

PROPORTION, relation of parts, equality of ratios, analogy, symmetry. (F. – L.) ME. *proporcioun,* Chaucer, C. T. 11598 (F 1286). – F. *proportion,* 'proportion,' Cot. – L. *prōportiōnem,* acc. of *prōportio,* comparative relation. – L. *prō-,* before, here used to signify as regards or in relation to; and *portio,* a portion, part; see **Pro-** and **Portion.** Der. *proportion,* vb.; *proportion-able, proportion-abl-y, proportion-al, -al-ly, -ate, -ate-ly.*

PROPOSE, to offer for consideration. (F. – L. – Gk.) In Shak. Tam. Shrew, v. 2. 69. [We also find *propone,* whence *proponing* in

Sir T. More, Works, p. 1107 g ; this is from L. *propōnere*, and is really a different word ; see **Propound**.]—F. *proposer*, 'to purpose, also, to propose,' Cot. Compounded of *pro-*, prefix ; and F. *poser*, which is not from L. *pōnere*, but is of Gk. origin, as shown under *pose* ; see **Pro-** and **Pose**. Littré remarks that in this word, as in other derivatives of F. *poser*, there has been confusion with L. *pōnere*. Der. *propos-er* ; *propos-al*, spelt *proposall* in Minsheu, a coined word, like *bestow-al*, *refus-al*, &c. Doublet, *purpose* (1), q. v. ☞ But *profound*, *proposition*, are unrelated.

PROPOSITION, an offer of terms, statement of a subject, theorem, or problem. (F.—L.) ME. *troposicioun*, in the phrase *looues of proposicioun*, to translate L. *pānēs trōpositiōnis*, Wyclif, Luke vi. 4.—F. *proposition*, 'a proposition,' Cot.—L. *prōpositiō*, acc. of *prōpositio*, a statement ; cf. *prōpositus*, pp. of *prōpōnere*, to propound ; see **Propound**. Der. *proposition-al*.

PROPOUND, to offer for consideration, exhibit. (L.) Used as equivalent to *propose*, but really distinct, and of different origin. Formed with excrescent *d* from the old verb to *propone*, Sir T. More, Works, p. 1107 g. 'Artificially *proponed* and oppugned ;' Hall's Chron. Hen. VII, an. 6. § 4. 'The glorie of God *propouned* ;' Bale, Image, pt. iii (R.).—L. *prōpōnere*, to set forth.—L. *prō-*, forth ; and *pōnere*, to put, set, pp. *positus* ; see **Pro-** and **Position**. Der. *propound-er* ; *troposit-ion*, q. v. Also *purpose* (2), q. v.

PROPRIETY, fitness. (F.—L.) 'Proprietie*, owing, specialtie, qualitie, a just and absolute power over a free-hold ;' Minsheu. I. e. it had formerly the sense of *property*, of which it is a doublet ; see Robinson, tr. of More's Utopia, ed. Lumby, p. 62, l. 32.—F. *proprieté*, 'a property, propriety, . . . a freehold in ; also, a handsome or comely assortment, &c. ;' Cot.—L. *proprietātem*, acc. of *proprietās*, a property, ownership ; also proper signification of words, whence the mod. sense.—L. *proprius*, one's own. See **Proper**. Der. *propriet-or*, an incorrect substitute for *proprietary*, from MF. *proprietaire*, 'a proprietary, an owner,' Cot., from L. *proprietārius*, an owner. Cf. also MF. *proprietaire*, adj. 'proprietary,' Cot. Doublet, *property*.

PROPULSION, PROPULSIVE ; see **Propel**.

PROROGUE, to continue from one session to another, defer. (F.—L.) Spelt *prorogue* in Minsheu, ed. 1627 ; earlier spelling *proroge*, Levins, ed. 1570 ; and in Hardyng, Chron. ch. 36. st. 3.—F. *proroger*, 'to prorogue,' Cot.—L. *prōrogāre*, to propose a further extension of office, lit. 'to ask publicly ;' hence to prorogue, defer.—L. *prō-*, publicly ; and *rogāre*, to ask ; see **Pro-** and **Rogation**. Der. *prorog-at-ion*, from F. *prorogation*, 'a prorogation,' Cot. ; from L. acc. *prōrogātiōnem*.

PROS-, *prefix*, to, towards. (Gk.) Properly Gk., but also appearing in F. and L. words borrowed from Gk.—Gk. πρός, towards ; fuller form προτί, extended from πρό, before.+Skt. *prati*, towards ; extended from *pra*, before, forward, away. See **Pro-**. Der. *pros-elyte*, *pros-ody*, *pros-opo-pœia*.

PROSCENIUM, the front part of a stage. (L.—Gk.) Not in Todd's Johnson ; merely L. *proscēnium*.—Gk. προσκήνιον, the place before the scene where the actors appeared.—Gk. πρό, before ; and σκηνή, a scene ; see **Pro-** and **Scene**.

PROSCRIBE, to publish the name of a person to be punished, to outlaw or banish, prohibit. (L.) In Levins, ed. 1570.—L. *prōscribere*, pp. *prōscriptus*, lit. 'to write publicly.'—L. *prō-*, forth, publicly ; and *scribere*, to write ; see **Pro-** and **Scribe**. Der. *proscript-ion*, Jul. Cæs. iv. 1. 17, from F. *proscription*, 'a proscription,' Cot., from L. acc. *prōscriptiōnem* ; *proscript-ive*.

PROSE, straightforward speech, not poetically arranged. (F.—L.) ME. *prose*, Chaucer, C. T. 4516 (B 96).—F. *prose*, 'prose,' Cot.—L. *prōsa*, for *prorsa*, in the phr. *prorsa orātio*, straightforward (or unembellished) speech ; fem. of *prorsus*, forward, a contracted form of *prōuersus*, lit. turned forward.—L. *prō-*, forward ; and *uersus*, pp. of *uertere*, to turn. See **Pro-** and **Verse**. ¶ The result, that *prose* is partly derived from L. *uersus*, whence E. *verse*, is remarkable. Der. *prose*, vb., *pros-er*, *pros-y*, *pros-i-ly*, *pros-i-ness* ; *pros-a-ic*, from L. *prōsaicus*, relating to prose.

PROSECUTE, to pursue, continue, follow after, sue. (L.) In Levins, ed. 1570. Spelt *prosequute*, Robinson's tr. of More's Utopia, ed. Lumby, p. 132, l. 17, p. 133, l. 32.—L. *prosecūtus*, *prosequūtus*, pp. of *prosequī*, to pursue ; see **Pursue**. Der. *prosecut-ion*, Antony, iv. 14, 65, from L. acc. *prōsecūtiōnem* ; *prosecut-or* = L. *prōsecūtor* ; *prosecut-r-ix*, formed with suffixes *-r* (<*-or*) and *-ix*, as in L. *testat-r-ix*. Doublet, *pursue*.

PROSELYTE, a convert. (F.—L.—Gk.) ME. *proselite*, Wyclif, Deeds [Acts], ii. 10 ; afterwards conformed to the L. spelling with *y*.—OF. *proselite*, 'a proselite,' Cot.—L. *prōsēlytum*, acc. of *prosēlytus*.—Gk. προσήλυτος, one who has come to a place, hence, as sb. a stranger, esp. one who has come over to Judaism, a convert, Acts ii. 10. Allied to Gk. perf. tense προσελήλυθα, 2nd aor.

προσῆλθον (=προσ-ηλυθον) ; of which the pres. tense (προσέρχομαι) is from a different root.—Gk. πρός, to ; and ἠλυθ-, as in ἠλυθον, I came, of which the fut. tense is ἐ-λεύσομαι, from √LEUDH ; whence also Skt. *ruh*, orig. *rudh*, to grow, increase, Goth. *liudan*, to grow. Der. *proselyt-ise*, *proselyt-ism*.

PROSODY, the part of grammar that treats of the laws of verse. (F.—L.—Gk.) In Ben Jonson, Eng. Grammar, c. 1. Spelt *prosodie* in Minsheu, ed. 1627 ; *prosodye*, Coventry Mysteries, p. 189.—F. *prosodie*, in use in the 16th cent. (Littré).—L. *prosōdia*.—Gk. προσῳδία, a song sung to an instrument, a tone, accent, prosody.—Gk. πρός, to, accompanying ; and ῳδή, an ode, song ; see **Pros-** and **Ode**. Der. *prosod-i-al*, *prosodi-c-al*, *prosodi-an*, *prosod-ist*.

PROSOPOPŒIA, personification. (L.—Gk.) Spelt *prosopopeia*, Sir P. Sidney, Apology for Poetry, ed. Arber, p. 24.—L. *prosōpopæia*.—Gk. προσωποποΐα, personification.—Gk. προσωποποιεῖν, to personify.—Gk. προσωπο-, for πρόσωπον, a face, person ; and ποιεῖν, to make. β. Gk. πρόσωπον is from πρός, towards ; and ὠπ-, stem of ὤψ, face, appearance. See **Pros-**, **Optic**, and **Poet**.

PROSPECT, a view, scene, expectation. (L.) In Shak. Much Ado, iv. 1. 231 ; and in Levins.—L. *prospect-us*, a look out, distant view, prospect.—L. *prospectus*, pp. of *prospicere*, to look forward.—L. *prō-*, before ; and *spicere*, *specere*, to look ; see **Pro-** and **Spy**. Der. *prospect*, vb., in Levins ; *prospect-ive*, ME. *prospective*, Chaucer, C. T. 10548 (F 234), from F. *prospective*, 'the prospective, perspective, or optick art,' Cot., from L. adj. *prospectiuus* ; *prospect-ive-ly* ; *prospect-ion* ; also *prospectus* (modern) = L. *prospectus*.

PROSPEROUS, according to hope, successful. (L.) In Levins ; and in Surrey, tr. of Virgil, Æn. iv. 773 (L. text, 579). Englished, by change of *-us* to *-ous*, as in *arduous*, &c., from L. *prosperus*, also spelt *prosper*, according to one's hope, favourable.—L. *prō-*, for, according to ; and *spa-*, weak grade of *spē-*, as in *spē-s*, hope ; with suffix *-ro-*. β. *Spēs* is related to E. *speed* ; see Brugmann, i. § 156, ii. § 74. Der. *prosperous-ly* ; *trosper*, verb, Bible of 1551, 3 John, 2, and in Palsgrave, from MF. *trosperer*, 'to prosper,' Cot., which from L *trosperāre*, v., from *prosper*, adj. Also *prosper-i-ty*, in early use ; ME. *prosperite*, Ancren Riwle, p. 194, l. 14, from OF. *prosperité*<L. acc. *prosperitātem*.

PROSTHETIC, prefixed. (Gk.) Modern ; as if for Gk. προσθετικός, lit. disposed to add, giving additional power ; allied to Gk. πρόσθεσις, added, put to ; cf. πρόσθεσις, a putting to, attaching.—Gk. πρός-, to ; θε-τός, placed, put, verbal adj. from the base θε-, weak grade of θη-, to place ; see **Theme**. Cf. Gk. ἐπι-θετικός = L *adiectiuus*.

PROSTITUTE, to expose for sale lewdly, to sell to lewdness, devote to shameful purposes. (L.) Minsheu, ed. 1627, has *prostitute*, verb, and *prostitution*. The verb is in Shak. Per. iv. 6. 201 ; and in Palsgrave.—L. *prostitūt-us*, pp. of *prostituere*, to set forth, expose openly, prostitute.—L. *prō-*, forth ; and *statuere*, to place, set ; see **Pro-** and **Statute**. Der. *prostitute*, sb.<L. *prostitūta*, fem. ; *prostitut-ion*, from F. *prostitution*, 'a prostitution,' Cot., from L. acc. *prostitūtiōnem* ; *prostitut-or* = L. *prostitūtor*.

PROSTRATE, lying on the ground, bent forward on the ground. (L.) 'It is good to slepe *prostrate* on their bealies ;' Sir T. Elyot, Castel of Helth, b. ii. c. 30. 'Prostrat byfore thi person' ; Coventry Mysteries, p. 75.—L. *prostrātus*, pp. of *prosternere*, to throw forward on the ground.—L. *prō-*, forward ; and *sternere*, to throw on the ground. See **Pro-** and **Stratum**. Der. *prostrate*, vb., Spenser, F. Q. i. 12. 6 ; *prostrat-ion*, from F. *prostration*, 'a prostrating,' Cot., from L. acc. *prostrātiōnem*.

PROTEAN, readily assuming different shapes. (L.—Gk.) 'The *Protean* transformations of nature ;' Cudworth, Intellectual System, p. 32 (R.). Coined, with suffix *-an* (<L. *-ānus*), from L. *Prote-us*, a sea-god who often changed his form ; cf. Roy, Rede me, p. 118.—Gk. Πρωτεύς, a sea-god ; cf. πρῶτος, first, chief.

PROTECT, to cover over, defend, shelter. (L.) In Shak. Tw. Nt. ii. 4. 75. [We find ME. *protectour*, Henrysoun, Test. of Creseide, l. 556 ; *proteccioun*, Chaucer, C. T. 2365 (A 2363).]—L. *prōtect-us*, pp. of *prōtegere*, to protect.—L. *prō-*, before ; and *tegere*, to cover ; see **Pro-** and **Tegument**. Der. *protect-ion*, from F. *protection*, 'protection,' Cot., from L. acc. *prōtectiōnem* ; *protect-ive* ; *protect-or*, formerly *protecteur*, from F. *protecteur*, 'a protector,' from L. acc. *prōtectōrem* ; *protect-or-al*, *protect-or-ship*, *protect-or-ate* ; *protect-r-ess*, ME. *protectrice*, Lydgate, A Ballad in Commendacion of Our Ladie, l. 57, from F. *protectrice*, 'a protectrix,' Cot., formed from the acc. case of a L. **prōtectrix*, a fem. form similar to *testātrix*. Also *protégé*, borrowed from mod. F. *protégé*, pp. of *protéger*, to protect, from L. *protegere* ; fem. form *protégée*.

PROTEST, to bear public witness, declare solemnly. (F.—L.) In Spenser, F. Q. ii. 10. 28, and Palsgrave ; the sb. *protest* occurs in The Tale of Beryn, ed. Furnivall, l. 3905.—F. *protester*, 'to protest,' Cot.—L. *prōtestāre*, *prōtestārī*, to protest.—L. *prō-*, publicly ; and *testāri,* to bear witness, from *testis,* a witness. See **Pro-** and **Testify.** **Der.** *protest,* sb., *protest-er*; *Protest-ant,* from F. *protestant,* pres. part. of *protester*; *Protest-ant-ism*; *protest-at-ion,* Chaucer, C. T. 3139 (A 3137), from F. *protestation,* 'a protestation,' from L. acc. *protestātiōnem.*

PROTHALAMIUM, a song written on the occasion of a marriage. (L.-Gk.) See the *Prothalamion* written by Spenser.-Late L. *prothalamium,* or *prothalamion.*-Gk. προθαλάμιον, a song written before a marriage; not in Liddell and Scott, but coined (with prefix προ-) as a companion word to **Epithalamium,** q. v.

PROTOCOL, the first draught or copy of a document. (F.-L.-Gk.) In Minsheu, ed. 1627.-MF. *protocole,* also *protecole,* 'the first draught or copy of a deed,' Cot. [Cf. Ital. *protocollo,* 'a booke wherein scriveners register all their writings, anything that is first made, and needeth particular correction;' Florio.]-Late L. *prōtocollum.*-Late Gk. πρωτόκολλον, not in Liddell and Scott, but explained by Scheler. It meant, in Byzantine authors, orig. the first leaf glued on to MSS., to register under whose administration, and by whom, the MS. was written; it was afterwards particularly applied to documents drawn up by notaries, because, by a decree of Justinian, such documents were always to be accompanied by such a first leaf or fly-leaf. It means 'first glued-on,' i. e. glued on at the beginning.-Gk. πρῶτο-, for πρῶτος, first; and κολλᾶν, to glue, from Gk. κόλλα, glue. β. Gk. πρῶτος is a superl. form from πρό, before; see **Pro-.** The root of κόλλα is unknown; cf. Russ. *klei,* glue.

PROTOMARTYR, the first martyr. (F.-L.-Gk.) 'The holy *prothomartyr* seynt Alboon;' Fabyan, Chron. vol. i. c. 151; ed. Ellis, p. 138.-MF. *protomartyre,* 'the first martyr,' Cot.-Late L. *prōtomartyr.*-Gk. πρωτόμαρτυρ; coined from πρῶτο-, for πρῶτος, first, superl. of πρό, before; and μάρτυρ, a martyr, later form of μάρτυς, a witness. See **Pro-** and **Martyr.**

PROTOTYPE, the original type or model. (F.-L.-Gk.) 'There, great exemplar, *prototype* of kings;' Daniel, A Panegyric to the King's Majesty, l. 177. And in Minsheu.-F. *prototype,* 'the first form, type, or pattern of,' Cot.-L. *prōtotypum,* neut. of *prōtotypus,* adj., original.-Gk. πρωτότυπον, a prototype; neut. of πρωτότυπος, according to the first form.-Gk. πρῶτο-, for πρῶτος, first, superl. of πρό, before; and τύπος, a type. See **Pro-** and **Type.** ¶ So also, with the same prefix, we have *proto-plasm, proto-phyte,* &c.

PROTRACT, to prolong. (L.) 'Without longer *protractyng* of tyme;' Hall's Chron., Henry VI. an. 38. § 6; and in Shak.-L. *protract-us,* pp. of *protrahere,* to draw forth, prolong.-L. *prō-,* forth; and *trahere,* to draw; see **Pro-, Trace, Portray.** **Der.** *protract-ion* (not F.); *protract-ive,* Shak. Troil. i. 3. 20; *protract-or.*

PROTRUDE, to push forward, put out. (L.) In Sir T. Browne, Vulg. Errors, b. iii. c. 20, § 4.-L. *protrūdere,* to thrust forth.-L. *prō-,* forth; and *trūdere,* to thrust, allied to E. *threat*; see **Pro-** and **Threat.** **Der.** *protrus-ion,* coined from L. pp. *protrūsus*; *protrus-ive.*

PROTUBERANT, prominent, bulging out. (L.) 'Protuberant, swelling or puffing up;' Blount's Gloss., ed. 1674. Phillips, ed. 1706, has both *protuberant* and *protuberance.* The rare verb *protuberate* sometimes occurs; see Rich.-L. *prōtūberant-,* stem of pres. part. of *prōtūberāre,* to bulge out.-L. *prō-,* forward; and *tūber,* a swelling; see **Pro-** and **Tuber.** **Der.** *protuberance.*

PROUD, haughty, arrogant. (E.; *or* F.?) ME. *prud* (with long *u*), Havelok, 302; Ancren Riwle, p. 176, l. 17; later *proud,* P. Plowman, B. iii. 178. Older form *prut* (with long *u*), Ancren Riwle, p. 276, l. 19; Layamon, 8828 (earlier text; later text, *prout*). AS. *prūt,* proud; a word of which the traces are slight; the various reading *prūtne* for *rancne* in the AS. Chron. an. 1006, is only found in MS. F, of the 12th century; see Earle, Two AS. Chronicles, notes, p. 336. It occurs also in the Liber Scintillarum, § 17, p. 85, and § 46, p. 152; and we find the derived words *prūtung,* pride, Mone, Quellen, p. 355, and *prȳte* in Ælfric's Homilies, ii. 220, formed by the usual vowel-change from *ū* to *ȳ*; see **Pride.** β. Moreover, we find Icel. *prūðr,* proud, borrowed from AS.; with which cf. Dan. *prud,* stately, magnificent. γ. Borrowed (according to Kluge) from OF. *prod, prud* (fem. *prode, prude*), valiant, notable (taken in a bad sense); see further under *prowess.* But the occurrence of *prȳte* in Ælfric makes this very doubtful. **Der.** *proud-ly*; also *pride,* q. v.

PROVE, to test, demonstrate, experience. (L.) In old authors, it commonly means 'to test,' as '*prove* all things,' 1 Thess. v. 21. ME. *prouen, preuen* (with *u* for *v*), P. Plowman, B. viii. 120, A. ix. 115. Older spelling *preouen,* Ancren Riwle, p. 390, l. 22. AS. *prōfian* (below). [Cf. also OF. *prover, pruver,* later *prouver,* 'to prove, try, essay, verifie, approve, assure, &c.;' Cot.]-L. *probāre,* to test, try, examine, orig. to judge of the goodness of a thing.-L. *probus,* good, excellent. β. From the L. *probāre* are also derived, not only Port. *provar,* Span. *probar,* Ital. *provare,* but also AS. *prōfian,* Laws of Ine, § 20, in Thorpe's Ancient Laws, i. 116. Du.

proeven, Icel. *prófa,* Swed. *pröfva,* Dan. *pröve,* G. *proben, probiren.* The mod. E. *prove* seems to be due to AS., in which the *o* was arbitrarily lengthened. **Der.** *prov-able, prov-abl-y, provable-ness*; and see *proof, probable, probation, probe, probity, ap-prob-ation, ap-prove, dis-ap-prove, dis-prove, im-prove, re-prove, re-prieve, re-pro-bate.*

PROVENDER, dry food for beasts, as hay and corn. (F.-L.) In Shak. Hen. V, iv. 2. 58; Oth. i. 1. 48. The final *r* is an OF. addition.-OF. *provendre* (Godefroy); usually *provende,* 'provender, also, a prebendry,' Cot., whence ME. *prouendè, provendè,* orig. a trisyllabic word. Shak. has also the shorter form *provand,* Cor. ii. 1. 267. The ME. *prouende* also meant 'prebend,' as in : '*Prouendè,* rent, or dignité;' Rom. of the Rose, 6931. According to Stratmann, *provende* occurs in the sense of 'provender' in Robert Manning's Hist. of England, ed. Furnivall, l. 11188. [In OF. it also has the sense of 'prebend;' see Littré.]-L. *prǣbenda,* a payment; in Late L. a daily allowance of provisions, also a prebend; Ducange. Fem. of *prǣbendus,* pass. fut. part. of *prǣbēre,* to afford, give; see **Prebend.** ¶ Note also ME. *prouendre,* which meant 'a prebendary,' or person enjoying a prebend. See the passages quoted in Richardson, esp. from Rob. of Brunne, tr. of Langtoft, p. 81, l. 2, p. 210, l. 27. But it also means 'prebend;' as in Trevisa, tr. of Higden, ii. 171.

PROVERB, a short familiar sentence, an adage, a maxim. (F.-L.) ME. *prouerbe* (with *u*=*v*), Wyclif, John, xvi. 29.-F. *proverbe,* 'a proverb.'-L. *prōuerbium,* a common saying, proverb.-L. *prō-,* publicly; and *uerbum,* a word. See **Pro-** and **Verb.** **Der.** *proverb-i-al,* from L. *prōuerbiālis,* formed from *prōuerbi-um* with suffix *-ālis*; *proverb-i-al-ly.*

PROVIDE, to make ready beforehand, prepare, supply. (L.) In Shak. Com. Errors, i. 1. 81; and in Palsgrave.-L. *prouidēre,* to act with foresight, lit. to foresee.-L. *prō-,* before; and *uidēre,* to see. See **Pro-** and **Vision.** **Der.** *provid-er,* Cymb. iii. 6. 53. Also *provid-ent,* Skelton, ed. Dyce, i. 11, l. 139, from L. *prōuident-,* stem of pres. part. of *prōuidēre*; *provid-ent-ly*; also *provid-ence,* ME. *prouidence,* Chaucer, tr. of Boethius, b. v. pr. 6, l. 83, from F. *providence.*<L. *prōuidentia*; whence *providenti-al, providenti-al-ly.* Also (like L. pp. *prōuīs-us*) *provis-ion,* Sir T. Elyot, The Governor, b. ii. c. 12, § 4, from F. *provision*<L. acc. *prōuīsiōnem*; *provis-ion,* verb, *provis-ion-al, provis-ion-al-ly*; *provis-or,* ME. *prouisour,* P. Plowman, B. iv. 133, from F. *proviseur,* 'a provider,' Cot.<L. acc. *prōuīsōrem*; *provis-or-y, provis-or-i-ly.* Also *provis-o,* 1 Hen. IV, i. 3. 78, from the Late L. law-phrase *prōuiso quod*=it being provided that, in use A.D. 1350 (Ducange); pl. *provisos.* **Doublet,** *purvey*; doublet of *provident, prudent.*

PROVINCE, a business or duty, a portion of an empire or state, a region, district, department. (F.-L.) ME. *prouynce, prouince* (with *u*=*v*), Wyclif, Deeds [Acts], xxiii. 34.-F. *province,* 'a province,' Cot.-L. *prōuincia,* a territory, conquest. β. Of unknown origin; Bréal says that the primary sense was 'obligation;' possibly from *prō-,* prefix, and *uincīre,* to bind. (But see Walde.) **Der.** *provinci-al,* Meas. for Meas. v. 318; *provinci-al-ly, provinci-al-ism.*

PROVISION, PROVISO; see under **Provide.**

PROVOKE, to call forth, excite to action or anger, offend, challenge. (F.-L.) ME. *prouoken,* Prompt. Parv.-F. *provoquer,* 'to provoke,' Cot.-L. *prōuocāre,* to call forth, challenge, incite, provoke.-L. *prō-,* forth; and *uocāre,* to call; allied to *uōc-,* stem of *uox,* the voice. See **Pro-** and **Vocal.** **Der.** *provok-ing, provok-ing-ly*; *provoc-at-ion,* in Fabyan's Chron. vol. i. c. 64, from F. *provocation,* 'a provocation,' Cot., from L. acc. *prōuocātiōnem*; *provoc-at-ive,* Henrysoun, Test. of Creseide, l. 226; *provoc-at-ive-ness.*

PROVOST, a principal or chief, esp. a principal of a college or chief magistrate of a Scottish town, a prefect. (L.) ME. *prouost* (with *u*=*v*), Chaucer, tr. of Boethius, b. i. pr. 4, l. 43; *prouest,* Rob. of Brunne, tr. of Langtoft, p. 268, l. 7. AS. *prāfost,* Exod. v. 15; *prōfost,* Ælfric, Hom. ii. 172. [Cf. MF. *prevost,* 'the provost or president of a college;' Cot.]-L. *prǣpositus,* a prefect; lit. 'one who is set over,' pp. of *prǣpōnere,* to set over.-L. *prǣ,* before; and *pōnere,* to place. See **Pre-** and **Position.** ¶ In Italian we find both *prevosto* and *preposto*; showing that *v* is due to the older *p.* **Der.** *provost-marshal, provost-ship.*

PROW, the fore-part of a ship. (F.-L.-Gk.) In Minsheu, ed. 1627.-OF. *prouë* (mod. F. *proue*), 'the prow, or forepart of a ship;' Cot. [Cf. Ital. *proda, prua.*]-L. *prōra,* the prow of a ship; the second *r* disappearing in order to avoid the double trill. [Cf. Prov. Span., Port. *proa,* Genoese *prua.*]-Gk. πρῷρα (also πρῷϊρα), the prow; connected with πρό, before. See **Pro-.**

PROWESS, bravery, valour. (F.-L.) Originally 'excellence.' ME. *prowes, prowesse,* Rob. of Glouc. p. 12, l. 279; p. 112, l. 2418; *pruesse,* King Horn, ed. Lumby, l. 556.-OF. *prouesse,* 'prowesse,' Cot.; formed with suffix *-esse* (<L. *-itia*) from OF. *prou,* brave,

mod. F. *preux*, 'hardy, doughty, valiant, full of prowess;' Cot. **β**. The etym. of OF. *prou* is much disputed; it occurs also in the forms *prod, prud, pros, proz*, &c., fem. *prode, prude*; we also find Prov. *proz*, Ital. *prode*. **γ**. But, besides the adj. *prou*, we also find a sb. *prou*, formerly *prod*, in the sense of 'advantage;' thus *bon prou leur face* = much good may it do them. This is the common ME. *prow*, meaning profit, advantage, benefit, as in Chaucer, C. T. 12234, 13338 (C 300, B 1598). **δ**. It is certain that *prouesse* was used to translate L. *probitas*, and that *prou* was used to translate *probus*, but the senses of the words were, nevertheless, not quite the same, and they seem to have been drawn together by the influence of a popular etymology which supposed *prou* to represent *probus*. But the *d* is very persistent; we still find the fem. *prude* even in mod. E., and we must observe that Ital. *prode* means both 'advantage' and 'valiant,' whilst the F. *prud'homme* simply meant, at first, 'brave man.' **ε**. It seems best to accept the suggestion that the word is due to the L. prep. *prōd*-, appearing in L. *prōd-esse*, to be useful to, to do good, to benefit. This would also explain the use of OF. *prod, prou*, as an adverb. Cot. has: '*Prou*, much, greatly, enough;' cf. Körting. § 7451. See **Pro-** and **Prude**.

PROWL, to rove in search of plunder or prey. (OLow G.) 'To *proule* for fishe, *percontari*; To *proule* for riches, *omnia appetere*;' Levins. ME. *prollen*, to search about; Chaucer, C. T. 16880 (G 1412). '*Prollyn*, as ratchys [dogs that hunt by scent], Scrutor,' Prompt. Parv. '*Prollynge*, or sekynge, Perscrutacio, investigacio, scrutinium;' id. '*Purlyn*, idem quod *Prollyn*;' id. 'I *prolle*, I go here and there to seke a thyng, *ie tracasse*. *Prolyng* for a promocyon, *ambition*;' Palsgrave. '*Prolle*, to search, or prowl about; to rob, poll, or steal; to plunder;' Halliwell. Of uncertain origin. Perhaps, like *plunder*, it meant 'to filch trifles;' from Low G. *trull, prulle*, a trifle, thing of small value (Bremen). Cf. Du. *prul*, 'a bawble' (Sewel), *prullen*, 'lumber, luggage, pelf, trumpery, toys' (id.); *prullen-kooper*, a ragman (Calisch); EFries. *prülle, prüll*, a trifle.

PROXIMITY, nearness. (F.—L.) Spelt *proximitie* in Minsheu, ed. 1627.—F. *proximité*, 'proximity;' Cot.—L. *proximitātem*, acc. of *proximitās*; formed with suffix -*tās* from *proximi*-, for *proximus*, very near, which is a superl. form from *prope*, near; see **Propinquity**. Der. Also *proxim-ate*, rather a late word, see exx. in R. and Todd's Johnson, from L. *proximātus*, pp. of *proximāre*, to approach, from *proximus*, very near; *proxim-ate-ly*.

PROXY, the agency of one who acts for another; also an agent. (F.—Late L.—L.) 'Vnles the King would send a *proxie*;' Foxe, Martyrs, p. 978, an. 1536 (R.). *Proxy* is merely a contraction for ME. *prokecye*, itself a contracted form of *procuracy*, which is properly an agency, not an agent. '*Procurator* is used for him that gathereth the fruits of a benefice for another man;' An. 3 Rich. II, stat. 1. cap. 2. And *procuracie* is used for the specialtie whereby he is authorized, ibid;' Minsheu, ed. 1627. *Procuracy* is from AF. *procuracie*, Liber Albus, p. 423, l. 1.—Late L. *procūrātia*, a late form used as equivalent to L. *prōcūrātio*, a management. Similarly, *proctor* is a contraction for *prōcūrātor*, a manager; see **Proctor, Procure**. The contracted forms *proketour* and *prokecye*, later *proctor* and *proxy*, seem to have come into use at the close of the 14th century. Cf. '*Prokecye*, procuracia; *Proketowre*, Procurator;' Prompt. Parv. Also *prockesy*, Palsgrave. It thus appears that the syllable -*ra*- was dropped, whilst *u* was first weakened to *e* and afterwards disappeared.

PRUDE, a woman of affected modesty. (F.—L.) In Pope, Rape of the Lock, i. 63, iv. 74, v. 36; Tatler, no. 102, Dec. 3, 1709.—F. *prude*, orig. used in a good sense, excellent, as in '*preude femme*, a chast, honest, modest matron,' Cot. MF. *prude*; from OF. *preuz*, objective case *preu*, valiant, excellent; the etymology of which is discussed under **Prowess**, q.v. **β**. The mod. F. *prud'homme* arose from misunderstanding the OF. *preu d'homme*; and hence was made a MF. *preude femme, prude femme* (for *preu de femme*), whence the fem. form *prude* was evolved. See Hatzfeld. Der. *prud-ish*; *prud-ish-ly*, Pope, Dunciad, iv. 194; *prud-e-ry*, Pope, Answer to Mrs. Howe, l. 1, from F. *pruderie*.

PRUDENT, discreet, sagacious, frugal. (F.—L.) ME. *prudent*, Chaucer, C. T. 12044 (C 110).—F. *prudent*, 'prudent,' Cot.—L. *prūdent-em*, acc. of *prūdens*, prudent. **β**. *Prūdens* is a contracted form of *prōuidens*; see **Provident**. Der. *prudent-ly*; *prudence*, ME. *prudence*, Wyclif, 1 Cor. i. 19, from F. *prudence* < L. *prūdentia*; *prudenti-al*, Blount's Gloss., ed. 1674, coined from L. *prūdentia*.

PRUNE (1), to trim trees, divest of what is superfluous. (F.—L.) The old form is *proine, proin*; see exx. of *proin* in Nares and Jamieson. In Chaucer, C. T. 9885 (E 2011), it is said of Damian, when dressing himself up smartly: 'He kembeth him [combs himself], he *proyneth* him and pyketh,' where the Harl. MS. has *pruneth*. It here means to trim, trick out, adorn. Gascoigne speaks

of *imps*, i.e. scions of trees, which 'growe crookt, bycause they be not *proynd*,' i.e. pruned; Steel Glas, 458. It was esp. used of birds, in the sense 'to pick out damaged feathers and arrange the plumage with the bill' (Schmidt), Cymb. v. 4. 118; cf. L. L. L. iv. 3. 183. **β**. Tyrwhitt, with reference to *proinen* in Chaucer, says: 'It seems to have signified, originally, to take cuttings from vines, in order to plant them out. From hence it has been used for the cutting away of the superfluous shoots of all trees, which we now call *pruning*; and for that operation, which birds, and particularly hawks, perform upon themselves, of picking out their superfluous or damaged feathers. Gower, speaking of an *eagle*, says: "For there he *pruneth* him and piketh As doth an hauke, whan him wel liketh;" Conf. Amant. iii. 75; bk. vi. 2203.' **γ**. Hence the etymology is from OF. *proignier*, to prune (Godefroy), Norm. dial. *progner* (Moisy); the same as MF. *provigner*, 'to plant or set a stocke, staulke, slip, or sucker, for increase; hence to propagate, multiply,' &c.; Cot. Littré gives the Berry forms of *provigner* as *preugner, progner, prominer*. This verb is from the F. sb. *provin*, 'a slip or sucker planted,' Cot.; OF. *provain* (Hatzfeld); cf. Ital. *propaggine*, a vine-sucker laid in the ground.—L. *propāginem*, acc. of *propāgo*, a layer, sucker. See **Propagate**. Der. *prun-er*.

PRUNE (2), a plum. (F.—L.—Gk.) In Sir T. Elyot, Castel of Helth, b. ii. c. 7.—F. *prune*, 'a plum,' Cot.—L. *prūnum*, a plum.—Gk. προῦνον, shorter form of προῦμνον, a plum; προῦνος, shorter form of προῦμνος, a plum-tree. Der. *prun-ella*, or *prun-ello*, Pope, Essay on Man, iv. 204, the name of a strong woollen stuff of a *dark* colour, so named from *prūnella*, the Latinized form of F. *prunelle*, a sloe, dimin. of *prune*. Doublet, *plum*.

PRURIENT, itching. (L.) In Blount's Gloss., ed. 1674.—L. *prūrient*-, stem of *prūriens*, pres. part. of *prūrīre*, to itch, orig. to burn; cognate with E. *freeze*; see **Freeze**. Brugmann, i. § 562. Der. *prurience, prurienc-y*.

PRY, to search inquisitively. (F.—L.) ME. *pryen, prien*, Chaucer, C. T. 3458; P. Plowman, B. xvi. 168; Will. of Palerne, 5019; Polit. Songs, ed. Wright, p. 222, l. 11.—OF. *prier, preer, preier*, to pillage [to search for plunder].—Late L. *prēdāre*, to plunder, also to investigate; Ducange.—L. *præda*, prey; see **Prey**.

PSALM, a sacred song. (L.—Gk.) ME. *psalm*, frequently *salm*, in very early use, Layamon, 23754. AS. *sealm*; see Sweet's AS. Reader.—L. *psalmus*.—Gk. ψαλμός, a touching, a feeling, esp. the twitching of the strings of a harp; hence, the sound of the harp, a song, psalm.—Gk. ψάλλειν, to touch, twitch, twang; from base PSAL, for SPAL.—Perhaps allied to Skt. *sphālaya* (with *ā*), to strike, to touch. See Prellwitz. Der. *psalm-ist*, Levins, F. *psalmiste* (Cot.), from L. *psalmista*, Late Gk. ψαλμιστής; *psalm-ody*, spelt *psalmodie* in Minsheu, F. *psalmodie* (Cot.), from Late L. *psalmōdia*, from Gk. ψαλμῳδία, a singing to the harp, which is from ψαλμ-, stem of ψαλμός, and ᾠδή, a song, ode (see **Ode**); *psalmodi-c-al, psalmodist*. Also *psaltery*, q.v.

PSALTERY, a kind of stringed instrument. (F.—L.—Gk.) In Shak. Cor. v. 4. 52. ME. *sautrie*, Chaucer, C. T. 3213.—OF. *psalterie*, in use in the 12th cent.; see Littré, s. v. *psaltérion*, which is the mod. F. form.—L. *psaltērium*.—Gk. ψαλτήριον, a stringed instrument.—Gk. ψαλτήρ, a harper; formed from ψαλ-, base of ψάλλειν, to harp; with suffix denoting the agent. See **Psalm**. Der. *psalter*, ME. *sauter*, Hali Meidenhad, ed. Cockayne, p. 3, from OF. *psaltier*, 'a psaulter, book of psalms,' Cot. from L. *psaltērium*, (1) a psaltery, (2) a song sung to the psaltery, the Psalter.

PSEUDONYM, a fictitious name. (F.—Gk.) Modern; not in Todd's Johnson. Borrowed from F. *pseudonyme*, used by Voltaire, A.D. 1772 (Littré).—Gk. ψευδώνυμος, adj., called by a false name.—Gk. ψεῦδο-, for ψεῦδος, a falsehood (cf. ψευδής, false); and ὄνυμα, ὄνομα, a name. **β**. The Gk. ψεῦδος is allied to ψυδρός (base ψυδ-), false; and to ψύθ-ος, a lie, orig. a whisper; cf. ψυθίζειν, to whisper. **γ**. For the Gk. ὄνομα, see **Name**. Der. *pseudonym-ous*.

PSHAW, interjection of disdain. (E.) 'A peevish fellow . . . disturbs all . . . with *pishes* and *pshaws*;' Spectator, no. 438 (1712). An imitative word, like *pish*; from the sound of blowing. Cf. also *pooh*.

PSYCHICAL, pertaining to the soul. (L.—Gk.) Modern; formed with suffix -*al* from *psȳchic-us*, the Latinized form of Gk. ψυχικός, belonging to the soul or life.—Gk. ψυχ-ή, the soul, life, orig. breath.—Gk. ψύχ-ειν, to blow; extended from the base ψυ-, from a √SPEU, to blow. Der. *psycho-logy*, where the suffix -*logy* = Gk. suffix -λογία, from λόγος, discourse, which from λέγειν, to speak; hence, *psycholog-i-c-al, -al-ly*; *psycholog-ist*. Also *met-em-psychosis*, q.v.

PTARMIGAN, a species of grouse. (Gaelic.) 'The *ptarmigan grous*' is mentioned in an E. translation of Buffon's Nat. Hist., London, 1792, vol. ii. p. 48. Formerly *termagant*. 'Heath-cocks, capercailzies, and *termagants*;' Taylor the Water-Poet, The Penniless

Pilgrimage, 1618 (ed. Hindley); cited in Palmer's Folk-Etymology, p. 386. Spelt *termigant* in 1617; Newton, Dict. of Birds, p. 392. The singular spelling *ptarmigan*, with a needless initial *p*, appears in Littré's Dict. – Gael. *tarmachan*, 'the bird ptarmigan;' Irish *tarmochan*, 'the bird called the termagant.' I do not know the sense of the word; the Gael. verb *tarmaich* means 'to originate, be the source of, gather, collect, dwell, settle, produce, beget.' Cf. OIrish *tor-mag-im*, I increase; cognate with L. *mag-nus*, great.

PTERODACTYL, an extinct reptile. (Gk.) Scientific. Coined from Gk. πτερό-ν, a wing; and δάκτυλος, a finger, a digit; from the long digit which helped to spread the wing. Gk. πτερόν is from πτ-, weak grade of √PET, to fly; and see **Dactyl.**

PUBERTY, the age of full development, early manhood. (F.– L.) Spelt *pubertie* in Minsheu, ed. 1627. – F. *puberté*, 'youth,' Cot. – L. *pūbertātem*, acc. of *pūbertās*, the age of maturity. – L. *pūbes*, the signs of manhood, hair. β. Allied to *pū-pus*, a boy, *pū-pa*, a girl; from √PEU, to beget; see **Puppet, Pupil.** **Der.** *pub-esc-ent*, arriving at puberty, from *pūbescent-*, pres. part. of *pūbescere*, inceptive verb formed from sb. *pūb-es*; *pubescence*. Cf. *puerile.*

PUBLIC, belonging to the people, general, common to all. (F.–L.) '*Publike* toke his [its] begynnyng of *people*;' Sir T. Elyot, The Governour, b. i. c. 1. § 2. And in Palsgrave. – MF. *public*, masc., *publique*, fem., 'publick,' Cot. – L. *publicus*, public; OLat. *poublicos, poplicos* (in inscriptions). Formed from *populus*, people; see **People.** **Der.** *public-ly, public-house, public-ist*, one skilled in public law; *public-i-ty*, a modern word, from F. *publicité*, coined as if from a L. acc. **publicitātem*. And see *public-an, public-at-ion, publish.*

PUBLICAN, a tax-gatherer; inn-keeper. (L.) ME. *publican*, Ormulum, 10147; spelt *pupplican* in Wyclif, Luke, iii. 12, where it is used to translate L. *publicānus*, with the sense of tax-gatherer. [The sense of 'inn-keeper' is modern.] – L. *publicānus*, a farmer of the public revenue, from *publicānus*, adj., belonging to the public revenue. Extended from *publicus*, public; see **Public.**

PUBLICATION, a publishing, that which is published. (F. –L.) In Shak. Troil. i. 3. 326. – F. *publication*, 'a publication,' Cot. – L. *publicātiōnem*, acc. of *publicātio.* – L. *publicāre*, to make public. – L. *publicus*, public; see **Public.**

PUBLISH, to make public. (F.–L.) ME. *publischen, puplischen.* 'He was riʒtful, and wolde not *puplische* hir;' Wyclif, Matt. i. 19. Also *publishen*, Chaucer, C. T. 8291 (E 415). This is a new formation, conformed to other E. verbs in *-ish*, which are usually formed from F. verbs in *-ir* making the pres. part. in *-issant*. It is founded on F. *publier*, 'to publish,' Cot. – L. *publicāre*, to make public. – L. *publicus*, public. See **Public.** **Der.** *publish-er.*

PUCE, the name of a colour. (F.–L.) '*Puce*, of a dark brown colour;' Todd's Johnson. – F. *puce*, a flea; *couleur puce*, puce-coloured; Hamilton. Thus it is lit. 'flea-coloured.' The older spelling of *puce* was *pulce* (Cotgrave). – L. *pūlicem*, acc. of *pūlex*, a flea. + Gk. ψύλλα (=ψύλ-ja), a flea. ¶ Todd wrongly says that *puce* is the same as *puke*, an old word occurring in Shak. in *puke-stocking*, 1 Hen. IV, ii. 4. 78. Todd also cites 'Cloths … *puke*, brown-blue, blacks' from Stat. 5 and 6 Edw. VI, c. vi. 'Blackes, *pukes*, or other sad colours;' Hakluyt, Voy. i. 357. 'That same gowne of *puke*;' Paston Letters, iii. 153. The form *puke* is difficult to explain; the Picard and Walloon form of *puce* is *puche*. See **Puke.**

PUCK, a goblin, mischievous sprite. (E.) In Shak. Mids. Nt. Dr. ii. 1. 40. ME. *pouke*, P. Plowman, C. xvi. 164, on which passage see my note. It also appears in Richard Coer de Lion, l. 566, in Weber, Met. Romances, ii. 25. AS. *pūca*, a goblin; '*larbula, pūca*,' OE. Glosses, ed. Napier, 23. 2; whence the dimin. *pūcel* (Toller). Hence also were borrowed Irish *puca*, an elf, sprite, hobgoblin; W. *pwca, pwci*, a hobgoblin. + Icel. *pūki*, a wee devil, an imp. See **Pug.**

PUCKER, to gather into folds, to wrinkle. (Scand.) '*Pucker*, to shrink up or lie uneven, as some clothes are apt to do;' Phillips, ed. 1706. '*Saccolare*, to *pucker*, or gather, or cockle, as some stuffes do being wet;' Florio, ed. 1598. 'He fell down; and not being able to rise again, had his belly *puckered* together like a sachel, before the chamberlain could come to help him;' Junius, Sin Stigmatised (1639), p. 19; in Todd's Johnson. The allusion is here to the top of a *poke* or bag, when drawn closely together by means of the string; cf. 'to *purse* up the brows,' from *purse*, sb., and Ital. *saccolare* from *sacco*; and Norm. dial. *pocher*, to crease, to pucker, from *poche*, a bag (Moisy). A frequentative form due to prov. E. *pook, poke*, a bag; from Icel. *poki*, a bag. Cf. Norm. dial. *pouque*, a bag (F. *poche*). See **Poke** (1). **Der.** *pucker*, sb.

PUDDING, an intestine filled with meat, a sausage; a soft kind of meat, of flour, milk, eggs, &c. (E.) ME. *pudding*, P. Plowman, B. xiii. 106; *puding*, as a gloss to *tucetum*, Wright's Voc. p. 104

(ab. 1200). The older sense was doubtless 'bag,' from a Teut. base **pud-*, to swell out, similar to **put-*, to swell out (see **Pout**). Cf. AS. *pud-uc*, a wen (Toller); and see **Poodle.** Hence also prov. E. *puddle*, short and fat, *poddy*, round and stout in the belly, *pod*, a large protuberant belly (Halliwell). Cf. also E. *pad, pod*; see **Pad, Pod.** β. The Low G. *pudding* has much the same sense as E. *pudding*; and is clearly related to Low G. *pudde-wurst*, a thick black-pudding, and to *puddig*, thick, stumpy; Westphal. *puddek*, a lump, a pudding. γ. For the parallel base **put-*, cf. Gael. *pùt*, a buoy, an inflated skin; W. *pwtog*, a short round body; Corn. *pot*, a bag, a pudding; all borrowed from Teutonic. The Irish *putog*, Gael. *putag*, a pudding, are borrowed from E. *pudding.*

PUDDLE (1), a small pool of muddy water. (E.) ME. *podel*, Rob. of Brunne, tr. of Langtoft, p. 54, l. 5. Spelt *poddell* in Palsgrave. Dimin., with E. suffix *-el*, from AS. *pudd*, a ditch, a furrow (Toller). **Der.** *puddle* (2).

PUDDLE (2), to make muddy; to make thick or close with clay, so as to render impervious to water; to work iron. (E.) Shak. has *puddle*, to make muddy or thick, Com. Err. v. 173; Oth. iii. 4. 143. Hence the various technical uses. From **Puddle** (1). **Der.** *puddl-er, puddl-ing.*

PUERILE, childish. (F.–L.) In Phillips, ed. 1706. [The sb. *puerility* is in much earlier use, occurring in Minsheu, ed. 1627.] – MF. *pueril*, omitted by Cotgrave, but in use in the 16th cent. (Littré); mod. F. *puéril.* – L. *puerīlis*, boyish. – L. *puer*, a boy, lit. 'one begotten.' – √PEU, to beget; cf. Skt. *pota-*, the young of any animal, *putra-*, a son. **Der.** *pueril-i-ty*, from F. *puerilité*, 'puerility,' Cot. So also *puer-peral*, relating to child-birth, from L. *puerpera*, fem. adj., child-bearing; from *puer-*, stem of *puer*, a child, and *parere*, to bear, produce, for which see **Parent.**

PUFF, to blow. (E.) ME. *puffen*, Ancren Riwle, p. 272, l. 1. Not found in AS., but cf. AS. *pyffan*, to puff, blow away (in Napier's Glosses) suggests a sb. **puf*; of imitative origin. Cf. G. *puffen*, to puff, pop, strike, Dan. *puffe*, to pop, Swed. *puffa*, to crack, to push; also W. *puff*, a puff, a sharp blast, *pwffio*, to come in puffs (borrowed from E.). Also G. *puff*, a puff; *puff!* interjection, &c. **Der.** *puff-er, puff-er-y, puff-y, puff-i-ly, puff-i-ness.* Also *puff-in*, q. v.

PUFFIN, the name of a bird. (E.) '*Puffin*, a fowle so called;' Minsheu, ed. 1627. '*Puffin*, a sort of coot or sea-gull, a bird supposed to be so called from its round belly, as it were swelling and puffing out;' Phillips, ed. 1706. And in Skelton, Phylyp Sparowe, 454. (The F. *puffin* is borrowed from E.) *Puffin Island*, near Anglesea, abounds with these birds, or formerly did so; but the W. name for the bird is *pal*. The reason assigned by Phillips is prob. the right one; Webster thinks it is named from its peculiar swelling beak, which somewhat resembles that of the parrot. The suffix is apparently diminutival, answering to E. *-en* in *kitt-en.*

PUG, a monkey, small kind of dog. (E.) The orig. sense is 'imp' or 'little demon,' as in Butler, Hudibras, pt. ii. c. 3, l. 635, and in Ben Jonson's play The Devil is an Ass, in which '*Pug*, the lesser devil,' is one of the characters. A weakened form of **Puck,** q. v. Cf. Dan. dial. *puge*, a 'puck,' sprite; and (perhaps) Dan. dial. *pugge*, a toad. 'A *pug-dog* is a dog with a short monkey-like face;' Wedgwood.

PUGGRY, PUGGERY, a scarf round the hat. (Hind.) From Hind. *pagri*, a turban (Forbes).

PUGILISM, the art of boxing. (L.) *Pugilism* and *pugilist* are late words, added by Todd to Johnson's Dict. Coined from L. *pugil*, a boxer. Allied to L. *pūg-nus*, Gk. πύγ-μη, the fist. And see *pugnacious.*

PUGNACIOUS, combative, fond of fighting. (L.) Rather a late word. R. quotes 'a furious, *pugnacious* pope as Julius II,' from Barrow, On the Pope's Supremacy. [The sb. *pugnacity* is in Bacon, Adv. of Learning, book II. viii. 4.] A coined word (with suffix *-ous* = L. *-ōsus*) from L. *pugnāci-*, decl. stem of *pugnax*, combative. – L. *pugnā-re*, to fight, allied to *pugnus*, the fist; and Gk. πυγ-μή, the fist; πύξ, adv., with the fist. **Der.** *pugnacious-ly*; also *pugnacity*, from L. acc. *pugnācitātem.* And see *ex-pugn, im-pugn, op-pugn, re-pugn-ant, pug-il-ist, poni-ard.*

PUISNE, inferior in rank, applied to certain judges in England. (F.–L.) A law term. '*Puisne or punie*, vsed in our common law-bookes … for the *younger*; as in Oxford and Cambridge they call *Junior* and *Senior*, so at Innes of Court they say *Puisne* and *Ancient*;' Minsheu, ed. 1627. The same word as **Puny,** q. v.

PUISSANT, powerful, strong. (F.–L.) In Skelton, ed. Dyce, i. 203, l. 3 from bottom. 'This is so *puyssant* an enemy to nature;' Sir T. Elyot, Castel of Helth, b. iii. c. 12. – F. *puissant*, 'puissant, mighty,' Cot. Cf. Ital. *possente*, powerful. β. The Ital. form suggests that the F. word is formed from a barbarous L. type **possiens*, for **possens* (stem *possent-*), substituted for the true form *potens*, powerful; see **Potent.** γ. This barbarism was due to confusion between the pres. part. *potens* and the infin. *posse*, to be able, have power; see **Possible**. Der. *puissant-ly*; *puissance*, Lydgate, Minor Poems, p. 25, from F. *puissance*, power. **Doublet**, *potent*.

PUKE (1), to vomit. (E.?) In Shak. As You Like It, ii. 7. 144. Prov. E. *puke*, E. D. D. Prob. imitative; and partly suggested by the verb *to spew*, with the same meaning. Cf. G. *spucken*, to spit. See **Spew, Spit**; and cf. OF. *esput*, a spitting, L. *spūtāre*, to spit.

PUKE (2), the name of a colour; *obsolete*. (MDu.) Explained by Baret as a colour between russet and black. '*Pewke*, a colour, *pers*;' Palsgrave. See Nares and Halliwell; and cf. **Puce** (above), from which it certainly differs. It prob. referred at first to the quality of the cloth; see Privy Expenses of Eliz. of York, pp. 120, 254.—MDu. *puijck*, 'wollen cloath,' Hexham; *puyck*, pannus laneus, Kilian; Du. *puik*, choice, excellent.

PULE, to chirp as a bird, whine like an infant, whimper. (F.) In Shak. Cor. iv. 2. 52; Romeo, iii. 5. 185.—F. *piauler*, 'to peep, or cheep, as a young bird; also, to *pule* or howle, as a young whelp;' Cot. In Gascon, *pioula*. Cf. Ital. *pigolare*, to chirp, moan, complain. These are imitative words; cf. L. *pipilāre*, to chirp, *pīpāre*, to chirp.

PULL, to draw, try to draw forcibly, to pluck. (E.) ME. *pullen*, P. Plowman, B. xvi. 73; Allit. Poems, ed. Morris, B. 68. 'And let him there-in *pulle*'=and caused him *to be thrust* into it; lit. and caused (men) to *thrust* him into it; Legends of the Holy Rood, ed. Morris, p. 60. Prob. an E. word; the AS. *pullian* and the pp. *āpullod*, given in Somner's Dict., are correct forms; *āpullud* is in AS. Leechdoms, i. 362, l. 10. β. We find, also, Low G. *pulen*, to pick, pinch, pluck, pull, tear, which is the same word; Brem. Wörterb. iii. 372; Dan. dial, *pulle*, to pull. Cf. also Low G. *pullen*, to drink in gulps (E. *to take a pull*). Der. *pull*, sb., Chaucer, Parl. of Fowls, l. 164.

PULLET, a young hen. (F.—L.) ME. *polete* (with one *l*), P. Plowman, B. vi. 282.—OF. *polete* (13th cent., Littré), later *poulette*, 'a young hen,' Cot. Fem. form of F. *poulet*, a chicken, dimin. of *poule*, a hen.—Late L. *pulla*, a hen; fem. of *pullus*, a young animal, cognate with E. **Foal**, q.v. **Doublet**, *poult*, q.v.

PULLEY, a wheel turning on an axis, over which a cord is passed for raising weights. (F.—L.—Gk.?) Spelt *pulley* in Minsheu, ed. 1627; *polley* in Caxton, tr. of Reynard the Fox, ed. Arber, p. 96, l. 6 from bottom. [But, in the Prompt. Parv., we have the form *poleyne*; and in Chaucer, C. T. 10498 (F 184), we find *polyuè* (*polivè*), riming with *dryuè* (*drivè*). β. The last form is difficult to explain; but we may derive *poleyne* from F. *poulain*, 'a fole, or colt, also the rope wherewith wine is let down into a seller, a pully-rope,' Cot. 'Par le *poulain* on descend le vin en cave;' Rabelais, Garg. i. 5 (Littré).—Late L. *pullānum*, acc. of *pullānus*, a colt.—L. *pullus*, a young animal; see **Pullet** (above). Cf. Late L. *polānus*, a pulley or pulley-rope. γ. The transference of sense causes no difficulty, as the words for 'horse' or 'goat' are applied in other cases to contrivances for the exertion of force or bearing a strain; thus MF. *poutre*, a filly, also means 'a beam' (Cot.); and F. *chèvre*, a goat, also means a kind of crane. The Late L. words for 'colt' are remarkably numerous, including (besides *pullanus*) the forms *pulinus, pullenus, pulletrum, polassus, poledrus, polenus, poletus*; also *poleria, polina*, a filly.] δ. But the mod. E. *pulley* is from F. *poulie*, 'a pulley;' Cot. OF. *poulie, polie, pollye*, Supp. to Godefroy; cf. Late L. *poledia*, a crane, Ital. *puleggia*, a pulley. Perhaps from Late L. **pōlidia*, pl. of **pōlidium*, representing Late Gk. **πωλίδιον*, a little colt, dimin. of Gk. *πῶλος*, a colt. Cf. OF. *poulier*, a pulley, answering to Late Gk. *πωλάριον*, a little colt. ¶ Diez derives E. *pulley* from F. *poulie*; and then, conversely, F. *poulie* from E. *pull*; which is very unlikely. G. Paris (*Romania*, July, 1898, p. 486) suggests Gk. **πολίδιον*, dimin. of *πόλος*, a pivot, axis; see **Pole** (2).

PULMONARY, affecting the lungs. (L.) Blount, Gloss., ed. 1674, has *pulmonarious*, diseased in the lungs. Englished from L. *pulmōnārius*, belonging to the lungs, diseased in the lungs.—L. *pulmōn-*, stem of *pulmo*, a lung. β. The L. *pulmo* is cognate with Gk. *πλεύμων*, more commonly *πνεύμων*, a lung; the change to the latter form being due to association with *πνεῦ-μα*, breath, from *πνέειν* (for *πνέϝειν*), to blow. But *pulmo* (for **plu-mo*?) and Gk. *πλεύμων* are from a root PLEU; whence also Lith. *plauczei*, pl. the lungs (Prellwitz). Der. *pulmon-i-c*, from L. *pulmōni-*, decl. stem of *pulmo*.

PULP, the soft fleshy part of bodies, any soft mass. (F.—L.) 'The *pulpe* or pith of plants;' Minsheu.—F. *pulpe*, 'the pulp or pith of plants;' Cot.—L. *pulpa*, the fleshy portion of animal bodies, pulp of fruit, pith of wood. Der. *pulp-y, pulp-i-ness; pulp-ous, pulp-ous-ness*.

PULPIT, a platform for speaking from. (F.—L.) ME. *pulpit*, P. Plowman's Crede, ed. Skeat, l. 661; *pulpet*, Chaucer, C. T. 12325

(C 391).—OF. *pulpite*, 'a pulpit,' Cot.—L. *pulpitum*, a scaffold, platform, esp. a stage for actors.

PULSATE, to throb. (L.) A modern word, directly from L. *pulsātus*, pp. of *pulsāre*, to beat. It is no doubt due to the use of the sb. *pulsation*, in Blount's Gloss., ed. 1674, from F. *pulsation*; from L. *pulsātiōnem*, acc. of *pulsātio*, a beating; from the same verb. β. The orig. sense of *pulsāre* was simply 'to beat;' it is a frequentative verb, formed from *puls-us*, pp. of *pellere*, to drive. L. *pello* is for **pel-no*; cf. Gk. *πίλ-να-μαι*, 'I draw near quickly;' Brugmann, ii. § 612. Der. *pulsat-ion*, as above; *pulsat-ive, pulsat-or-y; pulse* (1), q.v. From the L. *pellere* we have also *ap-peal, peal, com-pel, dis-pel, ex-pel, im-pel, inter-pell-at-ion, pro-pel, im-pulse, re-peal, re-pel, re-pulse*; and see *pelt* (1), *pursy, pulse* (1), *push*.

PULSE (1), a throb, vibration. (F.—L.) *Puls* in Palsgrave. ME. *pous* (in which the *l* is dropped), P. Plowman, B. xvii. 66.—F. *pouls*, 'the pulse,' Cot.—L. *pulsum*, acc. of *pulsus*, a beating; also the beating of the pulse, a pulse.—L. *pulsus*, pp. of *pellere*, to drive; see **Pulsate**.

PULSE (2), grain or seed of beans, pease, &c. (L.) ME. *puls*. 'All maner *puls* is goode, the fitche outetake'=every kind of pulse is good, except the vetch; Palladius on Husbandry, b. i. l. 723.—L. *puls*, a thick pap or pottage made of meal, pulse, &c., the primitive food of the Romans before they became acquainted with bread (White). Cf. Gk. *πόλτος*, porridge. ¶ Perhaps through the intermediate OF. *pols, pous* (Norm. dial. *pouls*), porridge; cf. Somersets. *pulse*, pottage. Der. *poultice*, q.v.

PULVERISE, to pound to dust. (F.—L.) 'To *pulverate* or to *pulverize*, to beate into dust;' Minsheu, ed. 1627.—MF. *pulverizer*, 'to pulverize,' Cot.—Late L. *puluerizāre*, to pulverise; L. *puluerāre*, to scatter dust, also to pulverise.—L. *puluer-*, decl. base of *puluis*, dust. The suffix *-ise* answers to the usual F. *-iser* (occasional *-izer*), Late L. *-izāre*, imitated from Gk. *-ιζειν*. β. L. *puluis* is allied to L. *pollis, pollen*, fine meal; Gk. *πάλη*, meal, dust. See **Powder**.

PUMA, a large carnivorous animal. (Peruvian.) 'The American animal, which the natives of Peru call *puma*, and to which the Europeans have given the denomination of lion, has no mane;' tr. of Buffon's Nat. Hist., London, 1792.—Peruvian *puma*.

PUMICE, a hard, spongy, volcanic mineral. (F.—L.) ME. *pomeys, pomyce*, Prompt. Parv. [AS. *pumic-stān*, pumice-stone; Voc. 148. 3.] But the ME. *pomyce* is from OF. *pomis* (Godefroy).—L. *pūmicem*, acc. of *pūmex*, pumice. β. So named from its light, spongy nature, resembling sea-foam. From an Idg. base **spoim-*, whence also AS. *fām*, foam; see **Spume**. **Doublet**, *pounce* (2).

PUMMEL, the same as **Pommel**, q.v.

PUMP (1), a machine for raising water. (F.—Teut.) ME. *pumpe*, Prompt. Parv.—F. *pompe*, 'a pump;' Cot. Of Teut. origin. —Low G. *pumpe*, a pump; of which a fuller form is *plumpe*, which is likewise an imitative form. Cf. prov. G. *plumpen*, to pump. The Low G. *plumpen* also means to plump, to fall plump, to move suddenly but clumsily; so that the sense of 'pumping' arose from the plunging action of the piston or, as it is sometimes called, the plunger, esp. when made solid, as in the force-pump. Allied to **Plump** (3), of imitative origin. Cf. prov. E. *plump*, a pump, *plumpy*, to pump (Cornwall); also Du. *pomp*, Swed. *pump*, Dan. *pumpe*, and even Russ. *pompa*, a pump; all borrowed words from Teutonic. Also the imitative forms Span. and Port. *bomba*, a pump, a bomb; and Hamburg *pümpel*, a piston (Richey). Der. *pump*, verb; spelt *pumpe* in Palsgrave.

PUMP (2), a thin-soled shoe. (F.—L.—Gk.) In Shak. Mids. Nt. Dr. iv. 2. 37; explained by Schmidt to mean 'a light shoe, often worn with ribbons formed into the shape of flowers.' So called because worn for 'pomp' or ornament, by persons in full dress.—F. *pompe*, 'pomp, state, solemnity, magnificence, ostentation; à pied de plomb et de pompe, with a slow and stately gate' [gait]; Cot. The use of this MF. proverb connects the word particularly with the foot and its ornament. Cf. Low G. *pump*, pomp; whence *pump-boxe*, old-fashioned large stockings (Bremen). See further under **Pomp**.

PUMPION, PUMPKIN, a kind of gourd. (F.—L.—Gk.) Spelt *pumkin* in W. Dampier, A New Voyage (1699), i. 203. The form *pumpkin* is a corruption from the older word *pompon* or *pumpion*, in which the suffix, not being understood, has been replaced by the E. dimin. suffix *-kin*. *Pumpion* is in Shak. Merry Wives, iii. 3. 43. Better *pompon*, as in Holland, tr. of Pliny, b. xix. c. 5.—MF. *pompon*, 'a pumpion, or melon;' Cot. [Ital. *popone* (Florio).] Formed, with inserted *m*, from L. *pepōnem*, acc. of *pepo*, a large melon, pumpkin.—Gk. *πέπων*, a kind of melon, not eaten till quite ripe.— Gk. *πέπων*, cooked by the sun, ripe, mellow; from the base *πεπ-*, seen in *πέπτειν*, to cook; see **Cook**, and **Pip** (2).

PUN, to play upon words. (E.) 'A corporation of dull *punning* drolls;' Dryden, Art of Poetry, l. 358. The older sense of *pun* was to pound, to beat; hence to *pun* is to pound words, to beat them into new senses, to hammer at forced similes. 'He would *pun* thee into shivers with his fist;' Shak. Troil. ii. 1. 42 ; and see Nares. *Pun* is a dialect form of *pound*, to bruise; see Pound (3); cf. Swed. dial. *punna*, to slap one playfully; *punn*, a playful slap on the back (Rietz). Der. *pun*, sb., Spectator, no. 61 ; *punn-ing*; *pun-ster*, Guardian, no. 29, a coined word, like *trick-ster*.

PUNCH (1), to pierce or perforate with a sharp instrument. (F.–L.) 'Punch, or Punching-iron, a shoemaker's tool to make holes with;' Phillips, ed. 1706. In Shak. Rich. III, v. 3. 125. ME. *punchen*, to prick; see Prompt. Parv. This verb seems to have been coined from the older sb. *punchion* or *punchon*, spelt *punchon* in Prompt. Parv., denoting the kind of awl used for punching or perforating; shortened to *punche*, spelt *ponche*, Wills and Invent., i. 365 (1572). See further under **Puncheon** (1). Der. *punch*, a kind of awl, as above. ☞ Distinct from *punch* (2), q. v.

PUNCH (2), to beat, bruise. (F.–L.) In the phrase 'to *punch* one's head,' the word is not the same as *punch* (1), but is a mere abbreviation of *punish*. In fact, 'to *punish* a man about the head' has still the same meaning. This is clearly shown by the entries in the Prompt. Parv., p. 416. 'Punchyn, or chastysyn, punysshen, Punio, castigo;' and again, 'Punchynge, punysshinge, Punicio.' So also: 'Punchyth me, Lorde,' i. e. punish me; Cov. Myst., p. 75. See **Punish**. ¶ For the suppression of the *i* in *punish*, cf. ME. *pulshen*, to polish, P. Plowman, A. v. 257, foot-notes; and *vanshen*, to vanish, id. C. xv. 217. In the present instance, *punchen* was readily suggested by the like-sounding word *bunchen*, with much the same sense. Hence the entry : 'Punchyn, or bunchyn, Trudo, tundo;' Prompt. Parv.

PUNCH (3), a beverage composed of spirit, water, lemon-juice, sugar, and spice. (Hindi–Skt.) 'Punch, a strong drink made of brandy, water, lime-juice, sugar, spice, &c.;' Phillips, ed. 1706. Wedgwood cites two most interesting quotations. 'At Nerule is made the best arrack or Nepo da Goa, with which the English on this coast make that enervating liquor called *pounche* (which is Hindostan for five) from five ingredients;' Fryer, New Account of East India and Persia, 1697. 'Or to drink *palepuntz* (at Goa) which is a kind of drink consisting of aqua-vitæ, rose-water, juice of citrons, and sugar;' Olearius, Travels to the Grand Duke of Muscovy and Persia, 1669. It was introduced from India, and apparently by the way of Goa; and is named from consisting of five ingredients.— Hindi *panch*, five; Bate's Dict., 1875, p. 394; cf. Hindustani *panj*.— Skt. *pánchan*, five, cognate with E. *five*; see **Five**. ¶ Perhaps it is interesting to observe that, whereas we used to speak of *four* elements, the number of elements in Sanskrit is *five*; see Benfey, p. 658, col. 2, l. 5; cf. Skt. *pañchatva-*, the five elements; *pañchaka-*, consisting of five. It is, at any rate, necessary to add that the Hindi and Skt. short *a* is pronounced like E. *u* in *mud* or *punch*; hence the E. spelling. See **Punch** in Yule.

PUNCH (4), a short, hump-backed fellow in a puppet-show. (Ital.–L.) In this sense, *Punch* is a contraction of *Punchinello*. In the Spectator, no. 14, the puppet is first called *Punchinello*, and afterwards *Punch*. 'Punch, or Punchinello, a fellow of a short and thick size, a fool in a play, a stage-puppet;' Phillips, ed. 1706. The pl. *Punchinellos* occurs twice in Butler, Sat. on our Imitation of the French, ll. 26, 99 ; it occurs as early as A.D. 1666 (Nares). β. *Punchinello* is a corruption of Ital. *pulcinello*, by the change of *l* to *n* (cf. *Palermo* from L. *Panormus*) ; and the E. sound of *chi* corresponds to Ital. *ci*. *Pulcinello* was a character in Neapolitan comedy representing a foolish peasant who utters droll truths (Scheler) ; Baretti and Meadows only give the fem. *pulcinella*, 'punch, buffoon of a puppet-show.' These are dimin. forms of Ital. *pulcino*, 'a yoong chicken,' Florio; fem. *pulcina*. The latter form is from the same source (with a different suffix) as Ital. *pulcella*, a girl, maiden (F. *pucelle*), and all the words are from L. *pullus*, the young of any animal, whence also F. *poule* (from Late L. *pulla*), a young hen. Thus the lit. sense of Ital. *pulcinello* is 'little chicken.' See further under **Pullet**. ¶ Perhaps the E. form is due to confusion with prov. E. *punch*, short, fat, *punchy*, pot-bellied (Halliwell) ; words which are prob. closely connected with **Bunch**, q.v. 'Did you hear them call their fat child *Punch*, . . . a word of common use for all that is thick and short;' Pepys's Diary, Apr. 30, 1669. In the phrase 'Punch and Judy,' *Judy* is the usual abbreviation from *Judith*, once common as a female name.

PUNCHEON (1), a steel tool for stamping or perforating; a punch. (ONorth F.–L.) Our mod. sb. *punch* is a familiar contraction of *puncheon*, which occurs rather early. ME. *punchon*, Prompt. Parv. *Punsoune*, a dagger, occurs in Barbour's Bruce, i. 545 ; see my note on the line. ONorth-F. *ponchon* (Supp. to Godefroy, s. v. *poinçon*), also *poinchon* (as in mod. Norman dial.) ; corresponding to OF. *poinçon*, MF. *poinson*, 'a bodkin, also a puncheon, also a stamp, mark, print, or seale;' Cot. Mod. F. *poinçon*; cf. Gascon *pounchoun*

(Moncaut), Prov. *pounchoun* (Mistral), Span. *punzon*, a punch; Ital. *punzone*, 'a bodkin, or any sharp pointed thing, also a piece [wine-vessel], a barell,' Florio.–L. *punctiōnem*, acc. of *punctio*, a pricking, puncture ; Diez remarks that this sb., which in L. is feminine, changes its gender to masc. in F., &c., whilst changing its sense from 'pricking' to the concrete 'pricking-instrument.' Allied to *punctus*, pp. of *pungere*, to prick; see **Pungent**. Der. *punch* (1). And see below.

PUNCHEON (2), a cask, a liquid measure of 84 gallons. (ONorth-F.–L.) 'Butte, pipe, *puncheon*, whole barrell, halfe barrell, firken, or other caske;' Hakluyt's Voyages, vol. i. p. 273.– ONorth-F. *ponchon* (see Norm. dial. *poinchon* in Moisy), OF. *poinçon* in Supp. to Godefroy); MF. *poinson*, 'a wine-vessell;' Cot. β. It is not certain that OF. *poinçon*, MF. *poinson*, a bodkin, and *poinson*, a cask, are the same word. It is gen. supposed that they are quite distinct, owing to the wide difference in sense. But I am inclined to think that F. *poinçon* remains the same word in all its senses, the wine-vessel being so named from the 'stamp, mark, print, or seale' upon it, the stamp being produced by a *puncheon* or stamping-instrument. That is, I regard **Puncheon** (2) as identical with **Puncheon** (1). Cf. MItal. *punzone*, 'a bodkin, barell, hogshead for wine, goldsmith's pouncer, little stamp;' Florio.

PUNCHINELLO, the same as **Punch** (4), q.v.

PUNCTATE, PUNCTATED, punctured. (L.) A botanical term. Coined with suffix *-ate* (= L. *-ātus*) from L. *punct-um*, a point, dot. See **Puncture, Pungent**.

PUNCTILIO, a nice point in behaviour. (Span.–L.) 'Your courtier practic, is he that is yet in his path, his course, his way, and hath not touched the *punctilio* or point of his hopes;' Ben Jonson, Cynthia's Revels, Act ii. sc. 1 (Amorphus). Rather from Span. *puntillo*, a nice point of honour, than from the equivalent Ital. *puntiglio*. In fact, the word is spelt *punctillo* in Blount's Gloss., ed. 1674. The *c* is an E. insertion, due to confusion with *punctuate*, &c. The *li* represents the sound of the Span. *ll*. β. Span. *puntillo* is a dimin. of *punto*, a point.–L. *punctum*, a point; see **Point**. Der. *punctili-ous*, *-ly*, *-ness*.

PUNCTUAL, exact in observing appointed times. (F.–L.) Minsheu, ed. 1627, has *punctuall* and the sb. *punctualitie*. See Trench, Select Glossary.–F. *ponctuel*, 'punctuall,' Cot.–Late L. **punctuālis*, not recorded; but the adv. *punctuāliter*, exactly, occurs A.D. 1440; Ducange.–L. *punctu-*, for *punctum*, a point; with suffix *-alis*. (Perhaps *punctālis*, from the stem *punct-*, would have been more correct.) See **Point**. Der. *punctual-ly*, *punctual-i-ty*.

PUNCTUATE, to divide sentences by marks. (L.) A modern word; added by Todd to Johnson's Dict. Suggested by F. *punctuer*, 'to point, . . mark, or distinguish by points;' Cot.– Late L. *punctuāre*, to determine, define. Formed from L. *punctu-*, for *punctum*, a point; see **Point**. (Perhaps *punctate*, from the stem *punct-*, would have been a more correct form.) Der. *punctuat-ion*, from F. *punctuation*, 'a pointing;' Cot.

PUNCTURE, a prick, small hole made with a sharp point. (L.) 'Wounds and *punctures*;' Sir T. Browne, Vulg. Errors, b. ii. c. 3. § 28. ME. *puncture*, Lanfrank, Science of Cirurgie, p. 16, l. 9. –L. *punctūra*, a prick, puncture. Allied to *punctus*, pp. of *pungere*, to prick; see **Pungent, Point**. Der. *puncture*, verb.

PUNDIT, a learned man. (Skt.) Not in Todd's Johnson. – Skt. *paṇḍita-* (with cerebral *n* and *d*), adj., learned; sb. a wise man, scholar.– Skt. *puṇḍ*, to heap up or together. ¶ The E. *u* represents Skt. short *a*, as in **Punch** (3).

PUNGENT, acrid to taste or smell, keen, sarcastic. (L.) In Phillips, ed. 1706. *Pungency* occurs earlier, in Blount's Gloss., ed. 1674.–L. *pungent-*, stem of pres. part. of *pungere*, to prick, pt. t. *pu-pug-i*, pp. *punctus*; from the base PEUG, to prick. See **Point**. Der. *pungent-ly*, *pungenc-y*. From the L. *pungere* we also have *point*, with its derivatives; also *punct-ate*, q. v., *puncti-lio*, q. v., *punct-u-al*, q. v., *punct-u-ate*, q. v., *punct-ure*, q. v. Also *com-punct-ion*, *ex-punge*, *pounce* (1), *punch* (1), *puncheon* (1). Doublet, *poignant*.

PUNISH, to chasten, chastise. (F.–L.–Gk.) ME. *punischen*, P. Plowman, B. iii. 78.–F. *puniss-*, stem of pres. part. of *punir*, to punish.–L. *pūnīre*, to punish, exact a penalty; OLat. *poenīre*.–L. *poena*, a penalty.–Gk. ποινή, a penalty; whence E. **Pain**, q. v. Der. *punish-able*, from F. *punissable*, 'punishable,' Cot.; *punish-ment*, L. L. L. iv. 3. 63, a coined word, substituted for ME. *punicion* (spelt *punyssyon* in Berners, tr. of Froissart, v. ii. c. 39), which is from F. *punition*, 'a punishment,' Cot., from L. acc. *pūnītiōnem*. Also *punish-er*; and (from L. *pūnīre*) *im-punity*. And see *penance, penitence, punch* (2).

PUNK, a prostitute. (Low G.) In Shak. Merry Wives, ii. 2. 141. Cotgrave explains F. *gouge* as 'a souldier's pug, or punk.' Evidently a slang word, and probably imported by soldiers from the Low Countries. According to the Bremen Wörterbuch, it may have come (ultimately) from Bremen; for *Punken-diek* was the name of a dike, with houses near it on the river Weser, in the eastern suburb of Bremen, which was formerly notorious for evil-livers; whence probably the E. word *punk*. (According to Schmeller, the Bavarian word *punken* meant a kind of cabbage.)

PUNKAH, a large fan. (Hind.—Skt.) Hind. *pankhā*, a fan; allied to *pankh*, a wing, feather; Forbes.—Skt. *paksha-*, a wing. Cf. Pers. *pankan*, 'a sieve, a fan;' Rich. Dict. p. 338.

PUNT (1), a ferry-boat, a flat-bottomed boat. (L.—C.) 'Ulysses in a punt, or small bottom;' Holland's Pliny, bk. 35, ch. x. p. 537 a. AS. *punt*; 'Pontonium, *punt*;' Voc. 166. 2; 'Caudex, *punt*;' Voc. 181. 31. (*Caudex* means a boat hollowed out of a tree.) Abbreviated from L. *ponto*, a punt, Cæsar, Bellum Civile, iii. 29; also, a pontoon. Of Celtic origin; Celt. type *qontos; Stokes-Fick, p. 62. Given by Cæsar as a Gaulish word.

PUNT (2), to play at the game of cards called basset. (F.—Span.—L.) 'I would *punt* no more;' Pope, The Basset-table, l. 68. '*Punter*, a term used at the game of cards called basset;' Phillips, ed. 1706.—F. *ponte*, 'a punter; a punt;' also *ponter*, 'to punt;' Hamilton. Hatzfeld gives F. *ponte* as a term in the game of *ombre*, meaning an ace of hearts or diamonds.—Span. *punto*, a point, also, a pip at cards.—L. *punctum*, a point; see **Point**. ¶ Perhaps immediately from Spanish.

PUNY, small, feeble, inferior in size or strength. (F.—L.) In Shak. Rich. II, iii. 2. 86; also *puisny*, As You Like It, iii. 4. 46. And see Trench, Select Glossary.—AF. *puné*, Year-books of Edw. I, i. 83; spelt *puisne*, iii. 317; MF. *puisné*, 'puny, younger, born after,' Cot. Mod. F. *puîné*, younger. Thus the lit. sense is 'born after;' hence, younger, junior, inferior.—L. *post nātus*, born after. See **Posterior** and **Natal**. Doublet, *puisne*, q. v.

PUPA, a chrysalis. (L.) A scientific term.—L. *pūpa*, a girl, doll, puppet; hence, the sense of undeveloped insect. Fem. of *pūpus*, a boy, child. Allied to *pu-tus, pu-er*, a boy; from √PEU, to beget; see **Puerile**. Der. *pup-il, pupp-et, pupp-y*.

PUPIL (1), a scholar, a ward. (F.—L.) In Spenser, F. Q. ii. 8. 7.—MF. *pupile*, 'a pupill, ward;' Cot. Mod. F. *pupille*. Properly a *masc.* sb.—L. *pūpillum*, acc. of *pūpillus*, an orphan-boy, orphan, a ward; dimin. from *pūpus*, a boy; see **Pupa**. Der. *pupil-age*, Spenser, Verses to Lord Grey, l. 2; *pupill-ar-y*, from F. *pupilaire*, 'pupillary,' Cot., L. *pūpillāris*, belonging to a pupil. Also *pupil* (2).

PUPIL (2), the central spot of the eye. (F.—L.) Spelt *pupill* in Bacon, Nat. Hist. § 868.—F. *pupille*, the pupil (Hatzfeld). A *fem.* sb.; which distinguishes it from the word above.—L. *pūpilla*, a little girl; also, the apple of the eye, or pupil. Fem. of *pūpillus*; see **Pupil** (1). ¶ The name seems to be due to the small images seen in the pupil; cf. the OE. phrase 'to look *babies* in the eyes.'

PUPPET, a small doll, little figure. (F.—L.) ME. *popet*, King Alisaunder, l. 335; Chaucer, C. T. 13631 (B 1891).—OF. *poupette*, Godefroy; MF. *poupette*, 'a little baby, puppet;' Cot. Dimin. from L. *puppa*, a doll; variant of *pūpa*; see **Pupa**.

PUPPY, (1) a whelp; (2) a dandy. (F.—L.) 1. In Shak. Oth. i. 3. 341; a *puppy-dog*, K. John, ii. 460. Here (as in *lev-y, jur-y*) the final -*y* answers to F. *-ée*.—F. *poupée*, 'a baby, a puppet;' Cot. Here, by 'baby,' Cotgrave means a doll; but it is clear that in E. the word was made to mean a lap-dog; cf. 'smale ladies *popis*;' Book of St. Alban's, fol. f 4, back. The F. *poupée* (as if from L. *puppāta*) is due to L. *pūpa*; see **Puppet**. 2. In the sense of 'dandy,' *puppy* occurs in the Guardian (Todd's Johnson). This is the same word, used in contempt, as in Henry VIII, v. 4. 30; perhaps affected by the MF. *poupin* or *popin*, 'spruce, neat, trimme, fine,' Cot. Cf. *se popiner*, 'to trimme or trick up himself,' id.; mod. F. *faire le poupin*, to play the fop. This word answers to a Late L. *puppīnus* (not found), and is a derivative from L. *pūpus*, a boy. Der. *puppy-ism*. Also *pup*, which is an abbreviation for *puppy*; whence *pup*, verb, formerly *puppy*, as in Holland, tr. of Pliny, b. xxx. c. 14.

PUR-, prefix. (F.—L.) E. *pur-* answers to OF. *pur-*, F. *pour-*, prefix, which is the F. prep. *pour*, for, a curious variation of L. *prō*, for. Thus *pur-* and *pro-* are equivalent; and words like *purvey* and *provide* are mere doublets. ¶ In the word *pur-blind*, the prefix has a different value.

PURBLIND, nearly blind. (Hybrid; F.—L., and E.) This word has suffered a considerable change of sense, almost parallel to the strange change in the case of **Parboil**, q.v. The orig. sense was *wholly* blind, as in Rob. of Glouc., l. 376, l. 7713: 'Me ssolde pulte oute boþe is eye, and makye him *pur blind*'=they should put out both his eyes, and make him quite blind. See Spec. of Eng. ed. Morris and Skeat, p. 14, l. 390. Sir T. Elyot writes *poreblynde*, The Governour, b. iii. c. 3. § 3; so also in Levins. In Wyclif,

Exod. xxi. 26, the earlier version has *pure blynde*, where the later has *oon iȝed* (i.e. one-eyed), and the Vulgate has *luscos*. So also '*purblynde*, luscus;' Prompt. Parv. Even in Shak. we have *both* senses: (1) wholly blind, L. L. L. iii. 181, Romeo, ii. 1. 12; and (2) partly blind, Venus, 679, 1 Hen. VI, ii. 4. 21. β. It is clear that 'wholly blind' is the orig. sense, and that which alone needs an etymology; whilst 'partly blind' is a secondary sense, due perhaps to some confusion with the verb *to pore*, as shown by the spelling *poreblind*; or to a mistaken derivation from Gk. πωρός, blind. *Purblind=pure-blind*, i.e. wholly blind; see **Pure** and **Blind**. For the use of *pure* as an adv., cf. '*pure* for his love'=merely for his love, Tw. Nt. v. 86. Der. *purblind-ly, purblind-ness*.

PURCHASE, to acquire, obtain by labour, obtain by payment. (F.—L.) ME. *purchasen, purchacen*, Rob. of Glouc. p. 16, l. 360; Chaucer, C. T. 610 (A 608). The usual sense is 'to acquire.'—OF. *purchacer*, later *pourchasser*, 'eagerly to pursue, .. purchase, procure,' Cot.—OF. *pur*, F. *pour*, for; and *chasser*, to chase. Formed after the analogy of F. *poursuivre* (Scheler). See **Pur-** and **Chase**; also **Pursue**. Der. *purchase*, sb., ME. *purchas, pourchas*, Chaucer, C. T. 258 (A 256), from OF. *purchas*, later *pourchas*, 'eager pursuit,' Cot.; *purchas-er; purchas-able*.

PURE, unmixed, real, chaste, mere. (F.—L.) ME. *pur*, Rob. of Glouc., p. 8, l. 184; where it rimes with *fur*=fire. Pl. *purè* (dissyllabic), Chaucer, C. T. 1281 (A 1279).—F. *pur*, masc., *pure*, fem., 'pure,' Cot.—L. *pūrum*, acc. of *pūrus*, pure, clean.—√PEU, to purify, cleanse; cf. Skt. *pū*, to purify; see **Fire**. Der. *pure-ly, pure-ness; pur-ist, pur-ism* (coined words); and see *pour, purge, pur-i-fy, pur-i-t-an, pur-i-ty, spurge*. From the same root, *fire, bureau, com-pute, de-pute, dis-pute, im-pute, re-pute, am-put-ate, de-put-y, count* (2), &c.

PURFLE, the older form of *purl*; see **Purl** (3).

PURGE, to purify, clear, carry away impurities. (F.—L.) ME. *purgen*, Chaucer, C. T. 14953 (B 4143).—F. *purger*, 'to purge,' Cot.—L. *purgāre*, to cleanse, purge. β. L. *purgāre*= *pūrigāre* (Plautus has *expūrigātio*)<L. acc. *pūrum*, pure, and -*ig-*, weakened form of *ag-* (*ag-ere*), to do, make, cause. See **Pure** and **Agent**. Der. *purg-at-ion*, ME. *purgacioun*, Wyclif, Heb. i. 3, from F. *purgation*<L. acc. *purgātiōnem*, from *purgāre*; *purgat-ive*, orig. adj., Macb. v. 3. 55, from L. *purgātiuus*; *purgat-or-y*, ME. *purgatorie*, Ancren Riwle, p. 126, l. 8, from F. *purgatoire* (of which an old form was prob. *purgatorie*), which from L. *purgātōrius*, adj., cleansing, purifying; *purgat-or-i-al*; *purg-ing*, sb., *ex-purg-ate*. And see *spurge*.

PURIFY, to make pure. (F.—L.) ME. *purifien*, Wyclif, Deeds [Acts], xxi. 26.—F. *purifier*, 'to purifie,' Cot.—L. *pūrificāre*, to make pure.—L. *pūri-*, for *pūrus*, pure; and *fic-*, for *fac-* (*facere*), to make. Der. *purifi-er, purify-ing*; also *purific-at-ion*, ME. *purificacioun*, Wyclif, John, iii. 25, from F. *purification*, from L. acc. *pūrificātiōnem*; *purific-at-or-y*, a coined word, as if from a L. adj. *pūrificātōrius*.

PURIM, an annual Jewish festival; the feast of lots. (Heb.—Pers.) In Esther, iii. 7; ix. 26.—Heb. *pūrīm*, lots; pl. of *pūr*, a lot. Of Pers. origin (Gesenius).

PURITAN, one who pretends to great purity of life. (L.) The name was first given, about A.D. 1564, to persons who aimed at greater purity of life, &c., than others (Haydn). Frequently in Shak. All's Well, i. 3. 56, 98; Tw. Nt. ii. 3. 152, 155, 159; Wint. Tale, iv. 3. 46; Pericles, iv. 6. 9. A barbarous E. formation, with suffix -*an* (=L. -*ānus*), from the word *purit-y* or the L. *pūrit-ās*. See **Purity**. Der. *Puritan-i-c-al, Puritan-ism*. ¶ The F. *puritain* is borrowed from E.

PURITY, the condition of being pure, pureness. (F.—L.) ME. *pureté*, Ancren Riwle, p. 4, l. 21; the *e* (after *r*) was afterwards altered to *i*, to bring the word nearer to the L. spelling.—F. *pureté*, 'purity,' Cot.—L. *pūritātem*, acc. of *pūritās*, purity; formed with suffix -*tās* from *pūri-*, for *pūrus*, pure; see **Pure**.

PURL (1), to flow with a soft murmuring sound. (Scand.) 'A pipe, a little moistened, .. maketh a more solemne sound, than if the pipe were dry; but yet with a sweet degree of sibilation, or *purling*;' Bacon, Nat. Hist. § 230. The word is rather Scand. than E., being preserved in Norw. *purla*, to well up, MSwed. *porla* (Ihre), Swed. *porla*, to purl, bubble as a stream. β. But it is merely a frequentative form, with the usual suffixed -*l* from the imitative prov. E. word *pirr* or *purr*, for which see **Purr**. Cf. Irish and Gael. *bururus*, a purling noise, a gurgling; Du. *borrelen*, to bubble up, Low G. *burreln, purreln*, to bubble up, AS. *bur-na*, a well; see **Bourn** (2). ¶ *Purl*, to curl, Shak. Lucr. 1407, is from the rippling of a purling stream.

PURL (2), spiced or medicated beer or ale. (F.—L.?) '*Purl*, a sort of drink made of ale mingled with the juice of wormwood;' Phillips, ed. 1706. 'A double mug of *purle*;' Spectator, no. 88.

But I suppose the spelling to be a mistaken one, due to confusion with **Purl** (1). It should surely be *pearl*, from F. *perle*, a pearl; see **Pearl**. See *perlé*, adj., and *perler*, verb, in Littré. The word was a term in cookery; thus *sucre perlé* is sugar boiled twice; *bouillon perlé*, jelly-broth (Hamilton). So also Du. *parelen*, *paarlen*, to pearl, sparkle, rise in small bubbles, like pearls (Calisch); G. *perlen*, to rise in small bubbles like pearls, to pearl (Flügel); *perle*, a pearl, drop, bubble. Hence *purl*, a drink with bubbles on the surface.

PURL (3), to form an edging on lace, to form an embroidered border, to invert stitches in knitting. (F.—L.) 'Needlework *purled* with gold;' An Eng. Garner, ed. Arber, ii. 37 (1532). Just as the word above should be spelt *pearl*, it is found, conversely, that the present word is often misspelt *pearl*; by the same confusion. It is a contraction of the old word to *purfle*, to embroider on an edge. '*Purfled* with gold and pearl of rich assay;' Spenser, F. Q. i. 2. 13. ME. *purfilen*, Chaucer, C. T. 193.—OF. *porfiler*, later *pour-filer*. '*Pourfiler d'or*, to purfle, tinsell, or overcast with gold thread, &c.;' Cot.—OF. *por*, F. *pour*, from L. *prō*, from (which is often confused, as Scheler remarks, with F. *par*, L. *per*, throughout, and such seems to be the case here); and F. *filer*, to twist threads, from *fil*, a thread. See **Pur-** and **File** (1). ¶ Cotgrave also gives MF. *pourfil* in the sense of *profile*; *profile* and *purl* (3) are really the same word, the difference in sense being due to the peculiar use of the F. prefix *pour-* as if it were=L. *per*. To *purl* is 'to work along an edge,' or 'to overcast all along with thread.' Doublet, *profile*.

PURL (4), to upset. (E.) A slang term; a huntsman who is thrown off his horse is *purled* or *spilt*. Prov. E. *pirl*, to spin round, to tumble; E. D. D. *Purl* should rather be *pirl*; from ME. *pirle*, a whirligig, formed by the frequentative suffix *-l* from the imitative word *pirr*, to whirl. So also MItal. *pirla*, a whipping-top; *pirlare*, 'to twirle round;' Florio. Allied to **Purl** (1).

PURLIEU, the borders or environs of any place (orig. only of a forest); esp. when used, as is usual, in the plural. (F.—L.) 'In the *purlieus* of this forest;' As You Like It, iv. 3. 77. '*Purlieu*, or *Purlue*, is all that ground neere any forest, which being made forest by Henry II, Rich. I, or King John, were, by perambulations granted by Henry III, seuered again from the same;' Manwood, par. 2 of his *Forest Lawes*, cap. 20. And he calleth this ground either *pourallee*, i. e. *perambulationem*, or *purlieu* and *purluy*, which, he saith, be but abusively taken for *pourallee*;' Minsheu, ed. 1627. Manwood's definition is: '*Purlieu* is a certain territorie of ground adjoyning unto the forest, meared [marked] and bounded with immoveable marks, meeres, and boundaries;' Reed's note on As You Like It. '*Purlieu*: land which having once been part of the royal forest has been severed from it by perambulationem (*pourallée*, OF. *puralee*) granted by the crown. The preamble of 33 Edw. I. c. 5 runs: "Cume aucune gentz que sount mys hors de forest *par la puralee* . . . aient requis a cest parlement quils soient quites . . . des choses que les foresters lour demandent." In the course of the statute mention is made of "terres et tenements deaforestes *par la puralee*." These [lands] would constitute the *purlieu*. A *purlieu-man* or *purlie-man* is a man owning land within the purlieu, licensed to hunt on his own land;' Wedgwood. β. It is thus clear that *purlieu* was 'land set free' from the forest laws, and hence called *pur lieu* (L. *pūrus locus*). γ. The perambulation itself was denoted by the OF. *puralee* or *poralee*. This OF. *puralee* appears to be a mere translation of L. *perambulātiōnem*, by that confusion whereby OF. *pur* (F. *pour*), though really answering to L. *prō*, is made to do duty for the L. *per*, as in several instances noted by Scheler. See AF. *pouralee* (to translate *perambulatio*) in Liber Custumarum, p. 197; from OF. *pur*=L. *prō*; and OF. *alee*, a going, for which see **Alley**.

PURLOIN, to steal, plagiarise. (F.—L.) In Shak. Lucrece, 1651. ME. *purloynen*; the pp. is ill spelt *perloyned* in the York Plays, p. 271. Cf. ME. *purlongen*; '*Purlongyn*, or *prolongyn*, or *put fer awey*, Prolongo, alieno;' Prompt. Parv. Thus the orig. sense is simply to prolong, put away, keep back, or remove. [Cf. OF. *esloigner* (<L. *elongāre*), 'to remove, banish, drive, set, put, far away;' Cot.]—OF. *porloignier*, *purloignier*, to prolong, retard, delay; Godefroy.—L. *prolongāre*, to prolong; see **Prolong**. Der. *purloin-er*. Doublet, *prolong*.

PURPLE, a very dark-red colour. (F.—L.—Gk.) In Spenser, F. Q. i. 2. 7. For ME. *purpre*, by change of *r* to *l*, as in ME. *marbre*, now *marble*, and in *Molly*, *Dolly*, for *Mary*, *Dorothy*. The ME. *purpre* is in early use, occurring in Layamon, l. 5928.—OF. *porpre* (13th cent., Littré), later *pourpre*, 'purple,' Cot. Cf. Ital. *porpora*, Span. *purpura*.—L. *purpura*, the purple-fish, purple-dye.—Gk. πορφύρα, the purple-fish; cf. G. πορφύρεος, purple. β. The orig. sense of Gk. πορφύρεος, as an epithet of the sea, seems to have been 'troubled' or 'raging,' hence dark, and lastly purple. The sea

dark with storms was also called οἶνοψ, wine-coloured, wine-dark; apparently from the dark shade of brooding clouds. Hence the etymology is from Gk. πορφύρειν, to grow dark, used of the surging sea; a reduplicated form (=*φορ-φύρ-ειν=*φυρ-φύρ-ειν) of Gk. φύρειν, to mix up, mingle, confound, orig. to stir violently. Allied to Skt. root *bhur*, to be active, L. *furere*, to rage; see **Fury**. ¶ The AS. *purpur* is borrowed directly from Latin. So also G. *purpur*, &c. Der. *purple*, verb. And see *porphyry*.

PURPORT, to imply, mean, intend. (F.—L.) In Bacon, Life of Hen. VII, ed. Lumby, p. 146, l. 27. (And prob. a much older word.)—OF. *porporter*, *pourporter*, to intend, whence the verb *porporter*, *tenour*. Not in Cotgrave; but Godefroy gives the verb *porporter*, *pourporter*, to declare, inform, and the sb. *purport*, tenour; and notes the phrase *selon le purport*, according to the purport.—OF. *pur*, F. *pour*, from L. *prō*, according to; and F. *porter*, to bear, carry, from L. *portāre*, to carry. A similar application of F. *porter* occurs in E. *import*. See **Pur-** and **Port** (1). Der. *purport*, sb., used by Spenser with the sense of 'disguise,' F. Q. iii. 1. 52, the lit. sense being rather 'declaration' or 'pretext.'

PURPOSE (1), to intend. (F.—L.—Gk.; *with* F. *prefix*.) ME. *purposen*, Gower, C. A. i. 5, prol. 53.—OF. *porposer* (Godefroy), a variant of *proposer*, to propose. Thus *purpose* and *propose* are doublets; see **Propose**, which is strictly from L. *pausāre*, of Gk. origin, though there has been confusion with L. *pōnere*. ¶ Distinct in origin from **Purpose** (2), though much confounded with it in association. Doublet, *propose*.

PURPOSE (2), intention. (F.—L.) Though from a different origin, this sb. has become altogether associated with the verb to *purpose*, owing to the extraordinary confusion, in French, of the derivatives of *pausāre* and *pōnere*. ME. *purpos*, Chaucer, C. T. 3979 (A 3981); spelt *porpos*, Rob. of Glouc., p. 121, l. 2572.—OF. *pourpos* (of which another form was *porpost*), a resolution, design (Godefroy); a variant of F. *propos*, 'a purpose, drift, end,' Cot.—L. *prōpositum*, a thing proposed, design, resolution.—L. *prōpositus*, pp. of *prōpōnere*, to propose; see **Propound**. Der. *purpose-ly*, *purpose-less*; also *a-propos*, q.v.

PURR, PUR, to utter a murmuring sound, as a cat. (E.) 'A *pur* . . of fortune's cat;' All's Well, v. 2. 20; '*Pur*, the cat is gray;' King Lear, iii. 6. 47. An imitative word, not unlike *buzz*. Cf. Scotch *pirr*, a gentle wind, Icel. *byrr*, wind; also Irish and Gael. *burburus*, a gurgling sound. Intended to imitate the sound of a gentle murmur. Der. *pur-l* (1), a frequentative form.

PURSE, a small bag for money. (L.—Gk.) ME. *purs*, *burs*; Prompt. Parv. p. 417. Spelt *pors*, P. Plowman, A. v. 110. In early use; the pl. *porses* occurs in the later text of Layamon, l. 5927. AS. *purs*; Engl. Studien, xi. 65. [Cf. OF. *borse* (Burguy), later *bourse*, 'a purse,' Cot.]—Late L. *bursa*, a purse; Ducange.—Gk. βύρση, a hide, skin; of which purses were made. ¶ The change from initial *b* to *p* is rare, but accords with Grimm's Law, and we find similar examples in E. *apricot* as compared with F. *abricot*, and mod. E. *gossip* as compared with ME. *gossib*, Chaucer, C. T. 5825 (D 243). Der. *purs-er* (doublet, *burs-ar*, q.v.); *purs-er-ship*; *purse-proud*; *purse-bearer*, Tw. Nt. iii. 3. 47. Also *purse*, verb, to wrinkle like a bag drawn together, Oth. iii. 3. 113.

PURSLAIN, PURSLANE, an annual plant, sometimes used in salads. (F.—L.) Spelt *purselaine*, Hakluyt's Voyages, vol. ii. pt. ii. p. 109, l. 43; *pourslane*, Sir T. Elyot, Castel of Helth, b. ii. c. 8. ME. *purslane*, to translate L. *portulāca*, Prompt. Parv., p. 417.—OF. *porcelaine* (Godefroy). [Cf. Ital. *porcellana*, 'the hearbe called purcelane;' Florio.] Formed from L. *porcilāca*, purslain, Pliny, b. xx. c. 20; the usual form of the word being *portulāca*. Walde derives *portulāca* from *portula*, dimin. of *porta*, a door, with reference to some peculiarity of the seed-capsules.

PURSUE, to follow after, chase, prosecute. (F.—L.) ME. *pursuen*, Wyclif, John, xv. 20, where the AV. has *persecute*; also in P. Plowman, B. xix. 158.—OF. *porsuir*, *poursuir*; Norm. dial. *porsuir*; mod. F. *poursuivre*, 'to pursue, prosecute, persecute,' Cot. Cotgrave gives the spellings *poursuir*, *poursuyr*, and *poursuivre*.—OF. *pur*, *por*, mod. F. *pour*, answering to L. *prō*; and Late L. *sequere*, in place of L. *sequī*, to follow; so that *poursuir*=L. *prōsequī*, to prosecute. See **Prosecute**; also **Pur-** and **Sue**. β. Owing to the confusion between the F. prefixes *pour* (*prō*) and *par* (*per*), the verb *poursuivre* also had the sense of *persecute*; we even find in OF. (11th cent.) the expression *à persuir son apel*=to pursue his appeal (Littré). See **Persecute**. Der. *pursu-er*, which in Scots law means 'a plaintiff,' lit. a prosecutor. Also *pursu-ant*, 'following, according, or agreeable to,' Phillips, ed. 1706, formed with the F. pres. part. suffix *-ant* from OF. *pursu-ir*, though the usual form of the pres. part. was *pursuivant* or *poursuivant* (see below); *pursu-ance*, Phillips, ed. 1706, apparently coined from the adj. *pursuant*. Also *pursuit*, spelt *poursuitt* in Spenser, F. Q. ii. 4. 1, *pursuyt* in Trevisa, tr. of Higden, i. 195, from F. *poursuite*, fem. sb., a participial form answering to L. fem. pp. *prōsecūta*; *pursuiv-ant*, an attendant on heralds, lit. 'one who is following,' Rich. III, iii. 4. 90, ME. *purseuaunt*, Chaucer, House of Fame, 1321, from F. *poursuivant d'armes*, 'herauld extraordinary, or young herauld,' Cot., from F. *poursuivant*, pres. part. of *poursuivre*.

PURSY, short-winded. (F.—L.) In Shak. Timon, v. 4. 12. Spelt *pursy* and *pursif* in Levins. ME. *purcy* (for *pursy*), Prompt. Parv. '*Purcyfe*, shorte-wynded, or stuffed aboute the stomacke, *pourcif*;' Palsgrave.—MF. *pourcif*, in Palsgrave, as just cited; which is a variant (by change of *l* to *r*) of MF. *poulsif*, 'pursie, short-winded,' Cot. Mod. F. *poussif*. Formed, with suffix -*if* (< L. -*īuus*), from MF. *poulser* (mod. F. *pousser*), 'to push,' Cot. Cotgrave also gives the form *pousser*, which he explains not only by 'to push,' but also by 'to breathe or fetch wind.'—L. *pulsāre*, to beat, push; see **Push**. The word has reference to the pantings or quick *pulsations* of breath made by a pursy person. **Der.** *pursi-ness*.

PURTENANCE, that which belongs to; the intestines of a beast. (F.—L.) In Exod. xii. 9; the usual translation of the same Heb. word being 'inwards.' Spelt *pertenaunce* in Coverdale's translation. '*Portenaunce* of a beest, *fresseure*;' Palsgrave. In P. Plowman, B. ii. 103, where most MSS. have *purtenaunces*, MS. W. has *appurtinaunces*. Thus *purtenance* is merely an abbreviation of *appurtenance*, from AF. *apurtenance*, Langtoft's Chron., i. 438; variant of *apartenance* (Burguy), from OF. *apartenir*, to appertain. Cotgrave has: '*appartenance*, an appurtenance, an appendant.' **β.** The variation in the syllable *pur*, *par*, is due to the frequent confusion between OF. *pur* (L. *prō*), and *par* (L. *per*). In the present case, the syllable is due to L. *per*. See **Appurtenance, Appertain.**

PURULENT, PURULENCE; see **Pus.**

PURVEY, to provide. (F.—L.) A doublet of *provide*. ME. *purueien*; *porueien* (with *u=v*), Rob. of Glouc. p. 39, l. 911; Rob. of Brunne, tr. of Langtoft, p. 74.—AF. *purveier*, to provide, Liber Custumarum, p. 216; OF. *porveir* (Burguy), mod. F. *pourvoir*, to provide.—L. *prōuidēre*; see **Provide**. **β.** The F. *voir*, to see, has numerous forms in OF., such as *veoir*, *veor*, *veir*, *veer*, *veeir*, *veier*, &c.; see Burguy. The E. spelling -*vey* answers to AF. *veier*; cf. E. *sur-vey*. **Der.** *purvey-ance*, ME. *porueance*, Rob. of Glouc. p. 457, l. 9387, from AF. *purveaunce*, Polit. Songs, p. 231, answering to MF. *pourvoyance*, 'providence, forecast,' Cot.; and therefore a doublet of *providence*. Also *purvey-or*, ME. *purveour*, P. Plowman, B. xix. 255, footnote, from AF. *purveour*, Stat. Realm, i. 137 (1300); answering to MF. *pourvoyeur*, 'a provider or purveyor,' Cot. **Doublet,** *provide*.

PURVIEW, a proviso, enactment. (F.—L.) Now applied to the enacting part of a statute as opposed to the preamble, and so called because it formerly began with the words *purveu est*, it is provided. Spelt *purvieu* in Blount.—AF. *purveu*, Polit. Songs, p. 231; MF. *pourveu*, provided, Cotgrave; mod. F. *pourvu*. Pp. of AF. *purveier*, OF. *porveir*, F. *pourvoir*; see **Purvey.**

PUS, white matter issuing from a sore. (L.) In Phillips, ed. 1706. [The adj. *purulent* is in Blount's Gloss., ed. 1674.]—L. *pūs* (gen. *pūr-is*), matter. + Gk. πύ-ον, matter; Skt. *pūya-*, pus; from *pūy*, to stink.—√PEU, to be corrupt, stink; whence also *pu-trid*, &c. Allied to **Foul.** Brugmann, i. § 113. **Der.** *pur-u-lent*, from F. *purulent*, 'mattary, corrupt,' Cot., from L. *pūrulentus*, full of matter, from the stem *pūr-* and suffix -*lentus.* Hence *purulence*.

PUSH, to thrust against, urge, drive forward. (F.—L.) ME. *possen*, *pussen*; infin. *posse*, K. Horn, ed. Lumby, l. 1011; pt. t. *puste*, K. Horn, ed. Ritson, l. 1079; *possed*, P. Plowman, B. prol. 151. At a later time *puss* became *push*, by change of double *s* to *sh*, as in *anguish* from *anguisse*, *brush* from F. *brosse*, *embellish* from F. *embelliss-*, &c.—OF. *pousser*, MF. *poulser*, 'to push, thrust,' Cot.—L. *pulsāre*, to beat, strike, thrust; frequentative form of *pellere* (pp. *pulsus*), to drive. See **Pulse** (1), **Pulsate. Der.** *push*, sb., Spenser, F. Q. i. 3. 35; *push-ing*; *push-pin*, L.L.L. iv. 3. 169. ¶ The prov. E. *push*, a pustule, is spelt *poushe* in Sir T. Elyot's Castel of Helth, bk. iii. c. 6; from the same verb.

PUSILLANIMOUS, mean-spirited. (L.) 'Womanish and *pusillanimous*,' Chapman, tr. of Homer, b. i. Commentary, note 7. From L. *pusillanimus*, mean-spirited, by change of -*us* to -*ous*, as frequently; the more usual form is *pusillanimis*.—L. *pusill-*, stem of *pusillus*, very small; and *animus*, mind, soul. **β.** *Pusillus* is allied to *pūsus*, a little boy, *pu-er*, a boy; see **Puerile.** For L. *animus*, see **Animosity. Der.** *pusillanimous-ly*, -*ness*. Also *pusillanim-i-ty*, ME. *pusillanimitee* (shortened to *pusillamité*), Gower, C. A. ii. 12; bk. iv. 314; from F. *pusillanimité* < L. acc. *pusillanimitātem*.

PUSS, a cat, a hare. (E.) Spelt *pusse* in Minsheu, ed. 1627; *puscat*, in Friar Bacon's Prophecie (Hazlitt, E. Eng. Popular Poetry, iv. 274). This may be called an E. word, though it is widely

spread. Prob. imitative, from the sound made by a cat spitting (Wedgwood). So also Du. *poes*, Low G. *puus*, *puus-katte*, a puss, puss-cat; Swed. dial. *pus*, a cat (Rietz), &c.; Irish and Gael. *pus*, a cat. **β.** That the word is imitative, appears from its occurrence in Tamil. '*Pusei*, a cat, esp. in the S. Tamil idiom. In the Cashgar dialect of the Affghan, *pusha* signifies a cat;' Caldwell, Comp. Grammar of Dravidian Languages, p. 465; cited in N. and Q., 3 S. ix. 288. Lithuan. *puž*, a word to call a cat.

PUSTULE, a small pimple. (F.—L.) 'A *pustule*, wheale, or blister;' Minsheu, ed. 1627. ME. *pustulis*, pl., in Lanfrank, Science of Cirurgie, p. 197, l. 17.—F. *pustule*, 'a push, blain, wheale, small blister;' Cot.—L. *pustula*, another form of *pūsula*, a blister, pimple. Allied to Lith. *puslě*, a bladder, pimple; *pústi* (1 pers. sing. *puttu*), to blow; Gk. φυσαλίς, φύσκη, a bladder, pustule, φυσάω, I blow, Skt. *pupphusa-*, *phupphusa-*, the lungs. ¶ Note that *pustule* has nothing to do with *pus*, with which it is associated by Richardson, and even in White. **Der.** *pustul-ous*, *pustul-ate*, *pustul-ar*.

PUT, to push, thrust, cast, set, lay, place, &c. (E.) ME. *putten*, *puten*; pt. t. *putte*, pp. *put*, *i-put*; P. Plowman, A. iii. 75, B. iii. 84; Havelok, 1033, 1051; the pt. t. *putte* occurs in Layamon, 18092. AS. *potian*, to thrust; Ælfric's Homilies, i. 522, l. 25; also **putian*, whence the sb. *putung*, instigation (Napier). [Hence Gael. *put*, to push, thrust; W. *pwtio*, to push, to poke; Corn. *poot*, to kick like a horse.] The orig. sense seems to have been to push, cast; cf. 'to *put* a stone.'+Du. *poten*, to plant, set; *poot*, a twig, MDu. *pote*, a scion, plant (see Franck); NFries. *putje*, Dan. *putte*, to put, place; Swed. dial. *putta*, to push; Pomeran. *putten*, to drive on. **Der.** *pott-er*, verb, q.v.

PUTATIVE, reputed, supposed. (F.—L.) In Minsheu, ed. 1627. —F. *putatif*, 'putative,' Cot.—L. *putātīuus*, imaginary, presumptive. Formed with suffix -*īuus*; cf. L. *putātus*, pp. of *putāre*, to think. The orig. sense was to make clean or clear; hence, to come to a clear result.—L. *putus*, clean. (√PEU.) Cf. **Pure.**

PUTREFY, to make or become corrupt. (F.—L.) 'Grosse meate ... makyth *putrifyed* matter;' Sir T. Elyot, Castel of Helth, b. ii. c. 1. 'Apte to receyue *putryfaction*;' id. b. ii. c. 1. (The spelling with *i* was prob. due to confusion with *putrid*.)—F. *putrefier*, 'to putrifie,' Cot. Formed by analogy with other verbs in -*fier* as if from L. **putrefīcāre*; but the true L. forms are *putrefacere*, to make putrid; and *putrefierī*, to become putrid.—L. *putre-*, as seen in *putrēre*, to be rotten, with which cf. *puter*, *putris*, rotten; and *facere*, to make, or *fierī*, to become. See **Putrid. Der.** *putrefaction*, from F. *putrefaction*, from L. acc. *putrefactiōnem* (Lewis); regularly formed from *putrefacere*. Also *putrefact-ive.* Also *putrescent*, becoming putrid, from L. *putrescent-*, stem of pres. part. of *putrescere*, inceptive form of *putrēre*; whence *putrescence.*

PUTRID, stinking, rotten, corrupt. (F.—L.). In Blount's Gloss., ed. 1674; and in Cotgrave.—F. *putride*, 'putride,' Cot.—L. *putridus*, putrid. Extended from L. *putri-*, decl. stem of *put-er*, *put-ris*, rotten; allied to *putrēre*, to be rotten. Allied to *pūt-ēre*, to stink; from √PEU, to stink. Cf. Skt. *pūy*, to stink; see **Pus** and **Foul.**

PUTTOCK, a kite, kind of hawk. (E. ?) In Shak. Cymb. i. 1. 140; see Nares and Palsgrave. ME. *puttocke*, Book of St. Alban's, fol. b 2; *potok*, Voc. 762. 5. Of unknown origin. It seems to have been used in a contemptuous sense. AS. *Puttoc* occurs as a name or nickname; Birch, Cart. Saxon., iii. 668.

PUTTY, an oxide of tin, or lead and tin, for polishing glass; more commonly a cement of whiting and oil, for windows. (F.— Low G.) '*Putty*, a powder made of calcin d tin;' Blount's Gloss., ed. 1674. '*Putty, pottain,* and *pot-brass* . . . seem all to mean the same thing;' Rich. Dict.; this opinion is supported by extracts from Holland, tr. of Pliny, b. xxxiv. c. 9, and Boyle, Works, i. 721. Pliny explains that in brass-founding, it was often found desirable to add to the ore *collectaneum*, i. e. bits of old vessels, called by Holland '*pottain* or old metall,' or *ollaria*, called by Holland '*pot-brasse*;' showing that *pottain* simply means the metal of old *pots*. **β.** The difficulty is in the history of the word rather than in its etymology. The old sense of it was 'powder made of calcin'd tin,' as in Blount, resembling what is now called *putty powder*. '*Putty powder*, a pulverised oxide of tin sometimes mixed with oxide of lead; extensively used in glass and marble works, and the best kinds are used for polishing plate;' Weale's Dict. of Terms used in the Arts, 4th ed., 1873. The same work tells us that *putty* is 'composed of whiting and linseed oil, with or without white lead.' It thus appears that the successive senses are (1) calcin'd tin or oxide of tin, (2) the same, with oxide of lead, or (3) with white lead, (4) a preparation containing white lead, the name being continued even after the white lead was omitted. The result is that the mixture *now* called *putty* frequently contains nothing that could be called *putty* in the older sense. **γ.** Adapted from MF. *potée*, 'brasse, copper, tin, pewter, &c., burnt or calcinated; also, a pot-full of anything;' Cot. The mod. F. *potée* means 'putty,' showing a similar change of meaning. '*Potée d'étain*, tin-putty;' Hamilton. The mod. F. *potée* also means (as formerly), a potful. Cf. also MF. *pottein*, 'broken pieces of metall, or of old vessels, mingled one with another;' Cot. Also MF. *pottin*, 'solder of mettall;' id. β. *Potée* is formed with suffix *-ée* (< L. *-āta*), from F. *pot*, a pot, of Teutonic origin; see **Pot**. Der. *putty*, vb.

PUZZLE, a difficult question, embarrassment, problem, perplexity. (F.–L. *and* Gk.) As a verb in Shak. Hamlet, iii. 1. 80; and it was prob. regarded as a frequentative form of *pose*, with suffix *-le*. But this was not the way in which the word arose; and, in fact, the suffix *-le* is not usually added to words of F. origin. It was orig. a sb., and stands for *opposal*, which is used in the ordinary sense of 'opposition' in Sir T. Herbert's Travels, p. 81 (R.). It has been shown, s. v. **Pose**, that *pose* is short for *appose*, which again is a corruption of *oppose*. From the F. *opposer* was formed ME. *opposaile*, a question for solution; whence mod. E. *puzzle*. 'And to pouert she put this *opposayle* [question], Lydgate, Fall of Princes, ed. Wayland, sig. B. iii, leaf lxvi; cited in Dyce's Skelton, ii. 304. Hence corruptly, *apposaile*. 'Made vnto her this vncouth *apposayle*, Why wepe ye so?' id., sig. B. v, leaf cxxviii (Dyce). 'Madame, your *apposelle* is wele inferrid,' i.e. your question is well put; Skelton, Garland of Laurel, l. 141; where the MS. copy has *opposelle* (Dyce). The ME. *opposaile* seems to have been a coined word, like *deni-al*, *refus-al*, &c. The loss of the first syllable is due to the loss of the same in *pose*. For the etymology, see **Oppose**, **Pose** (2). See A Student's Pastime, p. 129. Der. *puzzle*, verb.

PYGARG, a white-rumped antelope. (L.–Gk.) In Deut. xiv. 5. 'A kinde of fallow Deere called *Pygargi*;' Holland, tr. of Pliny, bk. viii. c. 53.–L. *pygargus*; Deut. xiv. 5.–Gk. πύγαργος, a kind of antelope.–Gk. πυγ-ή, rump; ἀργός, shining, white.

PYGMY, a very diminutive person or thing. (F.–L.–Gk.) ME. *pigmey*, Trevisa, i. 11, l. 7.–MF. *pygmé*, adj., 'dwarfie, short, low, of a small stature;' Cot.–L. *pygmaeus*, dwarfish, pygmy-like; from pl. *Pymaei*, the race of Pygmies.–Gk. Πυγμαῖοι, the race of Pygmies, fabulous dwarfs of the length of a πυγμή, which was reckoned from the elbow to the fist or knuckles, containing about 13½ inches.–Gk. πυγμή, the fist; allied to L. *pugnus*; see **Pugnacious**.

PYLORUS, the lower orifice of the stomach. (L.–Gk.) In Phillips, ed. 1706.–L. *pylōrus*.–Gk. πυλωρός, a gate-keeper; also the pylorus, because it is gate-keeper to the intestines, or at the entrance to them. Contracted from *πυλα-ϝωρος (Prellwitz).–Gk. πύλ-α = πύλα-η, a gate; and *ϝόρος, allied to οὖρος, a keeper, watcher. β. The Gk. πύλη is perhaps allied to Gk. πόλις, a city; see Prellwitz. γ. The Gk. οὖρος is from ὄρο-μαι (= ϝόρομαι), I heed, guard, from √WER, to guard; see **Wary**. Der. *pylor-ic*.

PYRAMID, a solid figure with triangular sides meeting in an apex, upon a triangular, square, or polygonal base. (L.–Gk.) The word was rather taken directly from the Latin than from the French. Thus Shak. has the sing. *pyramis*, 1 Hen. VI, i. 6. 21; pl. *pyramides* (four syllables), Antony, v. 2. 61; as well as *pyramid*, Macb. iv. 1. 57. Cotgrave strangely translates F. *piramide* by 'a pyramides.'–L. *pyramid-*, stem of *pyramis*.–Gk. πυραμίς (gen. πυραμίδος), a pyramid. Prob. of Egyptian origin. Der. *pyramid-al*, *pyramid-ic-al*.

PYRE, a pile of wood for burning a body. (L.–Gk.) In Sir T. Browne, Urn Burial; cap. v. § 13.–L. *pyra*.–Gk. πυρά, a pyre; allied to πῦρ, fire; cognate with E. **Fire**, q. v. And see *pyrethrum*, *pyretic*, *pyr-ites*, *pyrotechnic*.

PYRETHRUM, a plant; feverfew. (L.–Gk.) L. *pyrethrum*.–Gk. πύρεθρον; so named from the hot spicy taste of the root.–Gk. πῦρ, fire. Doublet, *pellitory* (2).

PYRETIC, feverish, relating to fever. (Gk.) For *pyrectic*.–Gk. πυρεκτικός, feverish.–Gk. πυρέσσειν, to be in a fever; allied to πυρετός, burning, heat, fever.–Gk. πῦρ, fire.

PYRITES, a stone which gives out sparks when struck with steel. (L.–Gk.) '*Pyrites*, a marchasite or fire-stone;' Phillips, ed. 1706.–L. *pyrites*.–Gk. πυρίτης, a flint, pyrites; orig. an adj., belonging to fire.–Gk. πῦρ, fire; cognate with E. **Fire**, q.v. Der. *pyrit-ic*.

PYROTECHNIC, pertaining to fireworks. (Gk.) *Pyrotechnick*, adj., and *pyrotechny* are given in Phillips, ed. 1706. Coined from Gk. πυρο-, used in compounds in place of πῦρ, fire, cognate with E. *fire*; and τεχνικός, artistic, technical, from τέχνη, an art, craft. See **Fire** and **Technical**. Der. *pyrotechnic-s*, *pyro-techny* (short for *pyrotechnic art*); *pyro-technist*. So also *pyro-meter*, a fire-measurer (see **Metre**); *pyro-gen-ous*, produced by fire, from Gk. base γεν, to produce (see **Genus**).

PYTHON, a large serpent. (L.–Gk.) 'The raging *Python*;' Prior, Hymn to the Sun, st. 3.–L. *Pȳthōn*, a serpent slain by Apollo near Delphi.–Gk. Πύθων (the same).–Gk. Πυθώ, a former name of Delphi.

PYX, the sacred box in which the host is kept after consecration; at the mint, the box containing sample coins. (L.–Gk.) Spelt *pixe* in Minsheu, ed. 1627. Abbreviated from L. *pyxis*, a box.–Gk. πυξίς, a box; so-called because orig. made of box-wood.–Gk. πύξος, box-wood. Allied to **Box** (1) and **Box** (2).

QUACK (1), to make a noise like a duck. (E.) An imitative word. 'The goos, the cokkow, and the doke also So cryden "*kek! kek!*" "*cuckow!*" "*quek, quek!*" hye;' Chaucer, Parl. of Foules, 499. Here the cry *kek! kek!* is assigned to the cackling goose, and *quek! quek!* to the quacking duck. In Ch. C. T. 4150 (A 4152), the dat. case *quakke* is used to mean 'hoarseness.'+Du. *kwaken*, *kwakken*, to croak, quack, chat; G. *quaken*, to quack, croak; Icel. *kvaka*, to twitter; Dan. *kvække*, to croak, quack, cackle. Cf. L. *coaxāre*, to croak, Gk. κοάξ, a croaking; Lithuan. *kwakéti*, to croak; *kwaksèti*, to cackle. Cf. **Cackle**. Der. *quack* (2), q.v. Also *quail* (2), q.v.

QUACK (2), one who cries up pretended nostrums. (Du.) Abbreviated from the older word *quacksalver* (below). Hence also *quack*, vb., to act as a quack, to sing the praises of a nostrum, to pretend to medical skill. 'To *quack off* universal cures;' Butler, Hudibras, pt. iii. c. 1. l. 330. We find also *quack-salver*, Blount's Gloss., ed. 1674, i.e. one who puffs up his *salves* or ointments, borrowed from Du. *kwak-zalver*, a quack, charlatan, cf. Du. *kvak-zalven*, to quack, puff up salves (see **Salve**) by *quacking* or prating about them; see also *quack-salvers*, in Ben Jonson, Every Man, ii. 1. 123; *quack-doctor*, a later word which took the place of *quack-salver*, Pope, note to Dunciad, iii. 192. Hence also *quack* = quack-doctor; *quack-er-y*.

QUADRAGESIMA, the forty days of Lent. (L.) '*Quadragesima* Sunday is six weeks before Easter;' Tables in the Book of Common Prayer. [Hence *quadragesimal*, adj., = Lenten, Milton, Areopagitica, ed. Hales, p. 5, l. 8.]–L. *quadrāgesima*, lit. 'fortieth,' fem. of *quadrāgesimus*, fortieth; in late authors used to mean 'Lent.' Older form *quadrāgensumus* (= *quadrāgenti-mus*).–L. *quadrāginta*, forty.–L. *quadr-us*, square, fourfold, related to *quater*, four times, *quatuor*, four; and *-ginta*, for *de-kin-ta*, tenth, from *decem*, ten. See **Four** and **Ten**; and **Forty**. Der. *quadragesim-al*.

QUADRANGLE, a square figure, or plot of ground. (F.–L.) In Shak. 2 Hen. VI, i. 3. 156; and in Levins.–F. *quadrangle*, 'a quadrangle;' Cot.–L. *quadrangulum*, sb.; neut. of *quadrangulus*, four-cornered.–L. *quadr-us*, square, allied to *quatuor*, four; and *angulus*, an angle. See **Four** and **Angle**. Der. *quadrangul-ar*. Also *quad*, *quod*, a court (in Oxford), short for *quadrangle*.

QUADRANT, the fourth part of a circle. (L.) Chiefly used of an instrument for measuring angles (like a *sextant*), graduated with degrees along the arc. ME. *quadrant*, Prompt. Parv.–L. *quadrant-*, stem of *quadrans*, sb., a fourth part. Formed like the pres. part. of *quadrāre*, to make square; from *quadr-us*, square, allied to *quatuor*; see **Four**. Der. *quadrant-al*. From the same source are *quarrel* (2), *quarry* (1), *squad*, *squadron*, *square*.

QUADRATE, squared, well-fitted. (L.) Used as a vb. in Levins; as adj. and vb. in Minsheu; as sb. in Milton, P. L. vi. 62, to mean 'square phalanx.'–L. *quadrātus*, squared, pp. of *quadrāre*, to make or be square.–L. *quadrus*, square; see **Quadrant**. Der. *quadrat-ic*; *quadrat-ure*, Milton, P. L. x. 381; Ben Jonson, New Inn, A. ii. sc. 2.

QUADRENNIAL, once in four years. (L.) More correctly *quadriennial*, as in Blount's Gloss., ed. 1674. Formed with adj. suffix *-al* (L. *-ālis*) from *quadrienni-um*, a space of four years.–L. *quadri-*, for *quadrus*, square, fourfold; and *annus*, a year. See **Quadrant**, **Biennial**, **Annual**.

QUADRILATERAL, having four sides. (L.) In Blount's Gloss., ed. 1674.–L. *quadrilater-us*, four-sided; with suffix *-al* (= L. *-ālis*).–L. *quadri-*, for *quadrus*, square; and *later-*, decl. stem of *latus*, a side. See **Quadrant** and **Lateral**.

QUADRILLE, 1. the name of a game at cards; 2. the name of a dance. (F.–Span.–L.) The name of the dance dates from about 1773; it is added by Todd to Johnson; so called because danced by 4 persons, or by sets of four. Not improbably suggested by the game at cards, which was a game for 4 persons with 40 cards; see Pope, Moral Essays, iii. 76; Sat. i. 38. [But the Span. name was affected by confusion with F. *quadrille*, 'a squadron containing 25 (or fewer) souldiers,' Cot.; borrowed from Ital. *quadriglia*, short for MItal. *squadriglia*, 'a route, a troop, a crue, a band of men,' Florio; which is connected with **Squadron**, q. v.] On the other hand, F. *quadrille*, the game at cards, was masc.; and like *ombre*, is prob. of Span. origin. – Span. *cuadrillo*, a small square, allied to *cuadrilla*, 'a meeting of *four* or more persons,' Neuman. – Span. *cuadra*, a square. – L. *quadra*, fem. of *quadrus*, fourfold; see **Quadrant**. Cf. L. *quadrula*, a little square.

QUADRILLION, a million raised to the fourth power. (L.) An oddly coined word; made by prefixing *quadr*-(short for *quadrus*, square, fourfold) to -*illion*, which is the word *million* with the *m* left out. See **Billion** and **Quadrant**.

QUADROON, the child of a mulatto and a white person. (Span. – L.) Better *quarteroon* or *quartroon*; and spelt *quarteron* in 1707. So called because of having black blood only in a fourth part. Modern; and imported from America. – Span. *cuarteron*, the child of a creole and Spaniard (Neuman); also, a fourth part. Formed with suffixes -*er*- and -*on* from *cuarto*, a fourth part. – L. *quartum*, acc. of *quartus*, fourth. See **Quart, Quartern**.

QUADRUPED, a four-footed animal. (L.) The adj. *quadrupedal* is in Blount's Gloss., ed. 1674; *quadruped*, sb., is in Phillips, ed. 1706; the pl. *quadrupedes* is in Sir T. Browne, Vulg. Errors, bk. iii. c. 1. § 2. – L. *quadruped-*, stem of *quadrupēs, quadripēs*, four-footed. – L. *quadru-*, fourfold, four times; and *pēs*, a foot. See **Quadrant** and **Foot**. Der. *quadruped-al*.

QUADRUPLE, fourfold. (F. – L.) As a verb in Chapman, tr. of Homer, Iliad, i. 129. As adj. in Minsheu, ed. 1627. – F. *quadruple*, 'quadruple;' Cot. – L. *quadruplum*, acc. of *quadruplus*, fourfold. – L. *quadru-*, four times; and -*plus*, signifying 'fold.' See **Quadrant** and **Double**. Der. *quadruple*, verb. Also *quadruplicate*, from L. *quadruplicātus*, pp. of *quadruplicāre*, to multiply by four. Cf. **Complicate**.

QUAFF, to drink in large draughts. (E.) In Shak. Tw. Nt. i. 3. 14; &c. And in Levins. Apparently of Northern origin. [In later times, it seems to have affected the spelling of the Lowl. Sc. *quaich, quech*, a cup, which became *queff* in 1711; see *quaich* in Jamieson, and **Quaigh**.] 'I *quaught*, I drinke all oute;' Palsgrave. Spelt *quaft* by Sir T. More; N. E. D. Later forms are *quaf, quaff*. β. A Southern form of Lowl. Sc. *waucht*, to quaff, from *waucht*, sb. a deep draught (Jamieson). From ONorthumb. *waht = AS. *weaht*, moistened (Genesis, 1922), pp. of *weccan*, to moisten (Daniel, 577). Cf. Icel. *vekja*, to moisten; from *vak-*, base of *vökr*, moist; Icel. *vökva sig*, to moisten oneself, to drink, quaff. Allied to Du. *wak*, moist, *wak*, a hole in ice. See **Wake** (2). Der. *quaff-er*.

QUAGGA, a quadruped of the horse tribe. (Hottentot.) The name is said to be Hottentot; and is supposed to be imitative, from the noise made by the animal. The name is now current in the Xosa-Kaffir form *iqwara*, with clicking *q* and guttural *r*. See Athenæum, 19 May, 1901; N. and Q. 9 S. v. 3.

QUAGMIRE, boggy, yielding ground. (E.) In Shak. K. Lear, iii. 4. 54. From *quag*, variant of *quake*; and equivalent to *quake-mire*; see **Quake** and **Mire**. 'It is spelt *quake-mire* in Stanihurst's Descr. of Ireland, p. 20; *quave-myre*, in Palsgrave;' Halliwell, s. v. *quave-mire*, q. v. Cf. ME. *quauen* (=*quaven*), to quake; P. Plowman, B. xviii. 61. So also *quagg-y* (i. e. *quak-y*), adj., used of boggy ground.

QUAIGH, QUAICH, a kind of drinking-cup in Scotland, usually made of small wooden staves hooped together, with two handles. (C. – L.) See Jamieson and E. D. D. First found as *quech* in 1673. – Gael. *cuach*, a cup (cf. OIrish *cúach*, W. *cawg*). – L. *caucus*, a cup; cf. Gk. καῦκα, a cup. ¶ Also spelt *quaff*, as in Smollett, Humphrey Clinker, Sep. 3, 1771.

QUAIL (1), to cower, shrink, fail in spirit. (F. – L.) An old meaning of *quail* was 'to suffer decline, pine, fail, wither away;' hence to faint, esp. used of the spirits. 'My false spirits quail,' Cymb. v. 5. 149; 'their *quailing* breasts;' 3 Hen. VI, ii. 3. 54. 'The braunch once dead, the budde eke nedes must *quaile*,' i. e. die; Spenser, Shep. Kal. November, 91. 'This deuise *quailed*;' Sir T. More, Life of Rich. III, ed. Lumby, p. 65. The phonology shows that the word was prob. of F. origin, and not from the ME. *quelen* (AS. *cwelan*), to die; though this may have been confused with it. β. And, in spite of the change in sense, I suppose it to be ultimately the same word as the prov. E. *quail*, to curdle, used of milk; for which see Prompt. Parv. p. 418, and Way's note. [We also find confusion between *quail*, to fail, and *quell*, to kill, as in 'to *quail* and shake the orb,' Antony, v. 2. 85. Cf. Devonshire *queal*, to faint away; Halliwell.] The ME. *quailen*, to curdle, coagulate, is from OF. *coailler, quailier*, later *cailler*, to curdle (see Littré, and Supp. to Godefroy); from L. *coāgulāre*; see **Coagulate**. γ. Note Ital. *cagliare*, MItal. *quagliare*, 'to cruddle as milk, to begin to be afraid;' Torriano. Meadows explains it by 'to curdle, congeal; to want courage, to begin to fear.'

QUAIL (2), a migratory bird. (F. – Low L. – Low G.) ME. *quaille*, Chaucer, C. T. 9082 (E 1206); *quayle*, Wright's Vocab. i. 177, l. 13. – OF. *quaille* (13th cent., Littré), mod. F. *caille*. Cf. Ital. *quaglia*, a quail. – Low L. *quaquila*, a quail. – MDu. *quackel*, 'a quaile;' Hexham. Lit. 'a quacker.' – MDu. *quacken*, 'to croake,' id.; cognate with E. **Quack** (1), q.v.

QUAINT, neat, odd, whimsical. (F. – L.) ME. *queint*, Chaucer, C. T. 10553 (F 239); commonly with the sense of 'famous, excellent.' Also spelt *quoynt*, Rob. of Glouc. p. 72, l. 1635. Also *cwoint*, Ancren Riwle, p. 140, l. 21; *coint, coynt*, Will. of Palerne, 653, 1981; *koynt*, 4090. – AF. *queint*, Vie de S. Tomas, i. 194; OF. *coint*, 'quaint, compt, neat, fine, spruce, brisk, trim;' Cot. Cf. Ital. *conto*, 'known, noted, counted;' Florio. Certainly derived from L. *cognitum*, acc. of *cognitus*, known, well-known, famous; though perhaps confused (more in F. than in E.) with L. *comptus*, neat, adorned, pp. of *cōmere*, to arrange, adorn. β. *Cognitus* is used as the pp. of *cognoscere*, to know, and is compounded of *co*- (for *com* = *cum*, with) and -*gnitus* (for -*gnotus* = *gnōtus*), known, used as pp. of *gnoscere, noscere*, to know; see **Cognition**. γ. I may add that L. *cōmere* = *co-imere*, comp. of *co*- (for *com* = *cum*), and *emere*, to take. ¶ In F. the word took the sense of 'trim,' as noted; in E. it meant famous, remarkable, curious, strange, &c. Der. *quaint-ly*, *quaint-ness*, *ac-quaint*.

QUAKE, to shake, tremble. (E.) ME. *quaken*, Chaucer, C. T. 11172 (F 860); earlier *cwakien*, Ancren Riwle, p. 116, l. 20. AS. *cwacian*, to quake; Ælfred, tr. of Orosius, b. ii. c. 6. § 3. Cf. AS. *cweccan*, to wag, Mark, xv. 29. Also EFries. *quakkelen*, to be unsteady. We find variants, such as *quag, quap, quave, quab*, all meaning 'to shake about.' The author of P. Plowman has the strong pt. t. *quook*; P. Pl., C. xxi. 64. Der. *quak-er*, q.v.

QUAKER, one of the Society of Friends. (E.) 'Quakers, orig. called *Seekers*, from their seeking the truth, afterward *Friends*. Justice Bennet, of Derby, gave the Society the name of *Quakers* in 1650, because G. Fox (the founder) admonished him, and those present, to *quake* at the word of the Lord;' Haydn, Dict. of Dates. But the name seems to have been used a little earlier, in 1647. From the vb. above; see **Quake**. Der. *Quaker-ism*.

QUALIFY, to render suitable, limit, abate. (F. – L.) Frequent in Shak. Meas. i. 1. 66, &c.; and in Levins. Latimer has *qualifyeth*; Seven Sermons, ed. Arber, p. 107 (last line). – F. *qualifier*, 'to qualifie;' Cot. – Late L. *quālificāre*, to endue with a quality. – L. *quāli-*, for *qualis*, of what sort; and *fic-*, for *fac-ere*, to make. See **Quality** and **Fact**. Der. *qualific-at-ion*, due to Late L. *quālificāt-us*, pp. of *quālificāre*.

QUALITY, property, condition, sort, title. (F. – L.) ME. *qualite, qualitee*, Ayenbite of Inwyt, p. 153, l. 11. – F. *qualité*, 'a quality;' Cot. – L. *quālitātem*, acc. of *quālitās*, sort, kind. – L. *quāli-*, for *qualis*, of what sort, allied to E. **Which**, q.v. Der. *qualit-at-ive*, a coined word.

QUALM, a sudden attack of illness, prick of conscience. (E.) ME. *qualm*, often in the sense of pestilence, mortal illness; Chaucer, C. T. 2016 (A 2014). AS. *cwealm*, pestilence, Luke, xxi. 11. + OSax. *qualm*, destruction, death; Du. *kwalm*, only in the sense 'thick vapour,' from its suffocating properties; Dan. *kvalm*, suffocating air; *kvalme*, qualm, nausea; Swed. *qvalm*, sultriness; G. *qualm*, vapour. Teut. type *kwal-moz, masc.; from *kwal, 2nd grade of **kwel-an-*, AS. *cwelan*, to die. Allied to Lith. *gel-ti*, to pain; *gel-a*, pain. From Idg. root *g(w)el*; see Brugmann, i. § 656. Der. *qualm-ish*.

QUANDARY, an evil plight. (Perhaps L.) In Beaum. and Fletcher, Knight of the Burning Pestle, Act i. sc. 1 (Humphrey). 'Leaving this olde gentleman in a great *quandarie*;' Lily, Euphues, ed. Arber, p. 45. Stanihurst has *quandāre* (accent on *a*), Æn. iv. l. 1, ed. Arber, p. 94. Conjectured to be a corruption of some term of scholastic Latin. Expressly said by Mulcaster, in 1582, to be a word 'of a Latin form, .. vsed English like;' see A. J. Ellis, E. E. Pronunciation, p. 912, col. 2. Perhaps for *quantum dare*, 'how much to give.'

QUANTITY, size, bulk, large portion. (F. – L.) ME. *quantite, quantitee*; Chaucer, C. T. 4662 (B 242). – F. *quantité*, 'quantity;' Cot. – L. *quantitātem*, acc. of *quantitās*, quantity. – L. *quanti-*, for *quantus*, how much; with suffix -*tās*. Related to L. *quam*, and to *quis*, who; see **Who**. Brugmann, i. § 413. Der. *quantit-at-ive*.

QUARANTINE, a space of forty days. (F. – Ital. – L.) Spelt *quarentine* in Minsheu, who gives it the old legal sense, viz. a space of forty days during which a widow might dwell unmolested in her husband's house after his decease. Blount gives this form and sense, and derives it from OF. *quarantine*. He also gives *quarantain*, meaning (1) Lent, (2) a forty days' truce or indulgence, (3) 'the forty days which a merchant, coming from an infected port, stays on shipboard for clearing himself;' the last sense being the usual one in mod. E. – OF. *quarantine* (Roquefort), usually *quarantaine*, 'Lent, a term of forty days,' &c.; Cot. — Ital. *quarantina*, also *quarantana*, *quarantena*, the space of forty days that travellers from infected places are forced to live in outhouses (Torriano). — Ital. *quaranta*, forty, answering to F. *quarante*; this *quaranta* being nothing but a shortened form of L. *quadrāginta*, forty. See **Quadragesima**. Cf. also Ital. *fare la quarantana*, 'to keepe lent, . . . to keepe fortie daies from company, namely if one come from infected places, as they vse in Italy;' Florio. See Pepys, Diary, Nov. 26, 1663.

QUARREL (1), a dispute, brawl. (F. — L.) It should rather be *querrel*, but has been assimilated in spelling to the word below. ME. *querele* (with one *r*), Chaucer, tr. of Boethius, b. iii. pr. 3, l. 49. — OF. *querele*, later *querelle*, 'a quarrel;' Cot. (He gives both forms.) — L. *querēla*, a complaint. — L. *querī*, to complain, lament. See **Querulous**. Der. *quarrel*, verb, Romeo, i. 1. 39, 59, &c.; *quarrel-er*; *quarrel-some*, As You Like It, v. 4. 85; *quarrel-some-ness*; *quarrel-ous*, Cymb. iii. 4. 162.

QUARREL (2), a square-headed cross-bow bolt. (F. — L.) Nearly obsolete. In Spenser, F. Q. ii. 11. 24. ME. *quarel*, King Alisaunder, ed. Weber, 1594, 2781. — OF. *quarrel*, later *quarreau*, 'a diamond at cardes, a square tile, a quarrell or boult for a crosse-bow;' Cot. Mod. F. *carreau*. — Late L. *quadrellum*, acc. of *quadrellus*, a quarrel, a square tile. — L. *quadr-us*, square; with dimin. suffix. See **Quadrant**.

QUARRY (1), a place where stones are dug, esp. for building purposes. (F. — L.) In Shak. Oth. i. 3. 141. The proper sense is a place where stones are *squared* for building purposes; hence, a place where stones are procured which are afterwards squared for building; lastly, a place where stones are dug, without any reference to squaring. A better form was *quarrer*, but we also find *quarry*; which is distinct from *quarry*, sometimes used as a variant of *quarrel*, a square pane of glass (Halliwell). ME. *quarrere*, *quarrer*, Will. of Palerne, 2232, 2281, 2319, 4692; spelt *quarere*, *quarer*, *quarrye*, *quar* in Prompt. Parv. — OF. *quarriere*, 'a quarry of stone;' Cot. Mod. F. *carrière*. — Late L. *quadrāria*, a quarry for squared stones. — L. *quadrāre*, to square. — L. *quadr-us*, square; see **Quadrant**. ¶ The sense was suggested by L. *quadrātārius*, a stone-squarer, a stone-cutter; from the same source. Der. *quarry*, vb., *quarry-man*, *quarri-er*.

QUARRY (2), a heap of slaughtered game. (F. — L.) In Shak. Cor. i. 1. 202; Haml. v. 2. 375. ME. *querré*, Sir Gawain and the Grene Knight, 1324; *quirré*, Sir Tristram, 499. Altered from OF. *cuiree* (Supp. to Godefroy), *curee*, certain parts of a slain animal; the part which was given to the hounds. Cotgrave has: 'Curée, a dogs reward, the hounds fees of, or part in, the game they have killed.' So called because wrapped in the skin; see Reliq. Antiq. i. 153. — F. *cur*, a skin, hide. — L. *corium*, skin. See **Cuirass**.

QUART, the fourth part of a gallon. (F. — L.) ME. *quart*, *quarte*, Chaucer, C. T. 651 (A 649). — F. *quarte*, 'a French quarte, almost our pottle;' Cot. — L. *quarta* (i. e. *pars*), a fourth part; fem. of *quartus*, fourth. Related to L. *quatuor*, cognate with E. **Four**, q. v. Der. *quart-an*, *quart-er*, *quart-ern*, *quart-ette*, *quart-o*; and see *quatern-ary*, *quatern-ion*, *quatrain*.

QUARTAN, recurring on the fourth day. (F. — L.) Said of an ague or fever. 'Feuer *quartain*;' Cursor Mundi, 11828. 'Quarteyne, fevyr, Quartana;' Prompt. Parv. — F. *quartaine*, quartan, only used of a fever; in use in the 13th cent.; Littré. — L. *quartāna* (*febris*), a quartan fever; fem. of *quartānus*, belonging to the fourth; formed with suffix -*ānus* from *quart-us*, fourth; see **Quart**.

QUARTER, a fourth part. (F. — L.) ME. *quarter*, Rob. of Glouc. p. 528, l. 10875. — OF. *quarter* (12th cent.), Littré, also *quartier*, as in mod. F. — L. *quartārius*, a fourth part, quarter of a measure of anything; formed with suffix -*ārius* from *quart-us*, fourth; see **Quart**. Der. *quarter-day*, -*deck*, -*ly*, -*master*, -*sessions*, -*staff*. Also *quarter-n*.

QUARTERN, a fourth of a pint, a gill. (F. — L.) Short for *quarteron*. ME. *quarteroun*, *quartroun*, *quartron*, P. Plowman, B. v. 217, and footnotes. — OF. *quarteron*, 'a quarter of a pound, also a quarterne;' Cot. — Late L. *quarterōnem*, acc. of *quartero*, a fourth part of a pound; extended from Late L. *quarter-us*, which is from *quartus*; see **Quarter**. Cf. Norm. dial. *quarteron*, a fourth part.

QUARTET, QUARTETTE, a musical composition of four parts. (Ital. — L.) First in 1790; the spelling *quartette* is F., but the word is really Italian. — Ital. *quartetto*, a dimin. form from *quarto*, fourth; see **Quart, Duet**.

QUARTO, having the sheet folded into four leaves. (L.) In Johnson. First in 1589. The word is due to the L. phr. *in quarto*, i. e. in a fourth part of the orig. size; where *quarto* is the abl. case of *quartus*, fourth; see **Quart**. And see **Folio**. Der. *quarto*, sb.

QUARTZ, a mineral composed of silica. (G.) Added by Todd

to Johnson. — G. *quarz*, rock-crystal; the G. z being sounded as *ts*. MHG. *quarz*; of unknown origin.

QUASH, to crush, annihilate, annul. (F. — L.) ME. *quaschen*; see '*Quaschyn*, quasso' in Prompt. Parv. Properly transitive; but used intransitively in P. Plowman, C. xxi. 64. And see Owl and Nightingale, 1388. — AF. *quasser*, Year-books of Edw. I, 1292-3, p. 111; OF. *quasser*, later *casser*, 'to breake, . . quash asunder;' Cot. (He gives both spellings.) — L. *quassāre*, to shatter; frequentative of *quatere* (supine *quassum*), to shake. Root uncertain. ¶ The OF. *quasser* also means 'to abrogate, annul' (Cot.), as in E. 'to *quash* an indictment.' The slight likeness to AS. *cwisan*, to break, is accidental. Der. (from L. *quatere*) casque, cask, con-cuss-ion, dis-cuss, *per-cuss-ion*.

QUASSIA, a South-American tree. (Personal name.) Added by Todd to Johnson. Botanical names in -*ia* are formed by adding the L. suffix -*ia* to a personal name, as in *dahl-ia*, *fuchs-ia*. *Quassia* was named by Linnæus after a negro named *Quassi*, who first pointed out the use of the bark as a tonic about 1730; see the portrait of him in Stedman's Surinam, ii. 347. Waterton quotes a Barbadoes song in Journey 4, cap. ii: '*Quashi* scrapes the fiddle-string, And Venus plays the flute;' these lines are altered from the finale to G. Colman's Inkle and Yarico. *Quassi* is, in fact, quite a common negro name, generally given to one who is born on a Sunday. See Notes and Queries, 6 S. i. 104, 141, 166; 8 S. viii. 388; 9 S. iii. 146.

QUATERNARY, consisting of fours. (L.) Rare; see exx. in Richardson. Cf. F. *quaternaire*, 'every fourth day;' Cot. — L. *quaternārius*, consisting of four each. — L. *quaternī*, pl., four at a time; from *quatuor*, four; see **Four**.

QUATERNION, a band of four soldiers, a band of four. (L.) In Acts, xii. 4 (A.V. and Wyclif); Milton, P. L. v. 181. — L. *quaternion-*, stem of *quaternio* used in Acts, xii. 4 (Vulgate); it means 'the number four,' or 'a band of four men.' — L. *quaternī*, pl.; see **Quaternary**.

QUATRAIN, a stanza of four lines. (F. — L.) Used by Dryden, in his letter to Sir R. Howard, prefixed to Annus Mirabilis, which is written in quatrains. — F. *quatrain*, 'a staffe or stanzo of 4 verses;' Cot. Formed with suffix -*ain* (L. -*ānus*) from F. *quatre* < L. *quatuor*, four. See **Four**.

QUATREFOIL, lit. having four leaves. (F. — L.) 'With *quarter-foyles* gilt;' Fabyan, Hist., ed. Ellis (1811), p. 600. From OF. *quatre*, four; and *foil*, a leaf. — L. *quatuor*, four; *folium*, a leaf; see **Foil**.

QUAVER, to shake, to speak or sing tremulously. (E.) In Levins; and in Minsheu, ed. 1627. It is the frequentative form, with suffix -*er*, of *quave*. ME. *quauen* (with *u = v*), to tremble; Prompt. Parv. And see P. Plowman, B. xviii. 61. It first occurs as a various reading in St. Marharete, ed. Cockayne, p. 48, l. 3 from bottom. Allied to Low G. *quabbeln*, to tremble (Brem. Wört.), Norw. *kveppa*, to be shaken (Aasen). Also to ME. *quappen*, to palpitate, Chaucer, Troil. iii. 57, Legend of Good Women, 865. β. From a base KWAF, variant of KWAP, to throb, which is parallel to KWAK, to quake; see **Quake**. Der. *quaver*, sb., lit. a vibration, hence a note in music. Also *quiver* (1), q. v.

QUAY, a wharf for vessels. (F. — C.) Spelt *quay* and *kay* in Phillips, ed. 1706; *key* in Cotgrave; *keie* in Minsheu, ed. 1627. ME. *key*, spelt *keye*, Eng. Gilds, ed. Toulmin Smith, p. 374, l. 23; and see Prompt. Parv. — AF. *kaie*, Gloss. to Liber Albus; MF. *quay* (F. *quai*), 'the key of a haven;' Cot. The orig. sense is 'enclosure,' a space set apart for unloading goods. Of Celtic origin. — Bret. *kaé*, an enclosure; W. *cae*, an enclosure, hedge, field, of which the old spelling was *cai* (Rhys); cognate with OIrish *cae*, a house; whence OIr. *cerdd-chae*, 'officina.' Celtic type *kaion*, a house; from the same root as E. *home*. Stokes-Fick, p. 65.

QUEAN, a contemptible woman, a hussy. (E.) In Shak. Merry Wives, iv. 2. 180. A word very closely related to *queen*; the orig. sense being 'woman.' The difference in spelling is due to a difference in the length of the AS. vowel. The best passage to illustrate this word is in P. Plowman, C. ix. 46, where the author says that in the grave all are alike; you cannot there tell a knight from a knave, or a *queen* from a *quean*. AS. *cwene*, a woman, quean; cognate with OHG. *quena*, and Goth. *kwinō*, a woman. The former *e* in *cwene* is short; whence, by lengthening, the Tudor E. *ea*. Teut. type *kwen-ōn-*, a lengthened form of the stem *kwen-* = Idg. *g(w)en-*; whence also Idg. *g(w)enā*, as in Gk. γυνή, Russ. *jena*, a wife, Irish *ben*, Pers. *zan*, a woman. See **Queen**.

QUEASY, sickly, squeamish, causing or feeling nausea. (Scand.? or F.?) 'His *queasy* stomach;' Much Ado, ii. 1. 399. 'A *queysy* mete;' Skelton, Magnificence, 2295. '*Quaisy* as meate or drinke is, *dangereux*;' Palsgrave. *Quayss* is used as a sb., in the sense of 'nausea,' in Polit., Religious, and Love Poems, ed. Furnivall, p. 215, l. 22. Perhaps formed as adj. from a Scand. source. —

Norw. *kveis*, sickness after a debauch (Aasen); Icel. *kveisa*, a whitlow, boil; *iðra-kveisa*, bowel-pains, colic; Swed. dial. *kvesa*, a pimple, soreness, blister. Cf. Swed. *kväsa*, to bruise, wound; Low G. *quēse*, a blood-blister, *quēsig*, troubled with blisters (Schambach). β. But the form *coisy* also occurs, and the earliest sense seems to be ticklish or unsteady; as in: ‘here is a *coysy* werd’ (world); and ‘the werlde is ryght *qwesye*,’ Paston Letters, i. 497, iii. 4. This points to a F. origin; cf. OF. *coissié, coisié*, wounded, injured (Godefroy). γ. Perhaps this is allied to MF. *cuissant*, ‘smarting, itching,’ and to F. *cuire*, ‘to seeth, boyle, bake, itch, smart,’ Cot. Cf. Ital. *cocere, cuocere*, ‘to concoct, boyl, burn, grieve, molest;’ Torriano. From L. *coquere*, to cook. **Der.** *queasi-ness*, 2 Hen. IV, i. 1. 196.

QUEEN, a woman, a female sovereign. (E.) ME. *queen, queene*; P. Plowman, C. ix. 46. AS. *cwēn* (common).+Icel. *kvān*, a wife; Goth. *kwēns, kweins*, a woman, wife. Teut. type **kwǣniz*, f.; from the 3rd grade of Teut. base **kwen-*, as seen in **kwen-ōn-*, a woman; for which see **Quean**. Idg. type **g(w)ēni-*; whence also Skt. *-jāni-* (in compounds), wife. **Der.** *queen-ly, queen-mother*. Allied to *quean*.

QUEER, strange, odd. (O. Low G.) ‘A *queer* fellow;’ Spectator, no. 474, § 2. Much earlier, in Dunbar’s Flyting: ‘our awin *queir* clerk;’ l. 218. A cant word; and prob. introduced rather from Low than High German.—Low G. *queer*, across; *quere*, obliquity. In Awdeley’s Fraternity of Vagabonds, ed. Furnivall, p. 4, ‘a *quire* fellow’ is one who has just come out of prison; cf. the slang phrase ‘to be in *queer* street;’ and Low G. *in der quere liggen*, to lie across, lie queerly.+G. *quer*, transverse; *querkoff*, a queer fellow. The OHG. form is *twer*, transverse; cf. Dan. *tvær*, cross-grained, sullen, perverse (Larsen), Swed. *tvär*, cross, rude; Icel. *þverr*, whence E. *thwart*. See **Thwart**. **Der.** *queer-ly, queer-ness*.

QUELL, to crush, subdue, allay. (E.) ME. *quellen*, to kill; Chaucer, C. T. 12788 (C 854). AS. *cwellan*, to kill, Grein, i. 174.+OSax. *quellian*, to torment, causal of *quelan*, to suffer martyrdom; Du. *kwellen*, to plague, vex; Icel. *kvelja*, to torment; Swed. *qvälja*, to torment; Dan. *kvæle*, to strangle, choke; to plague, torment. β. Teut. type **kwaljan-*, causal form, ‘to make to die;’ from **kwal*, 2nd stem of **kwel-an-*, to die. Allied to Lith. *gel-ti*, to pain; *gel-a*, pain. From Idg. root **g(w)el*; Brugmann, i. § 656. See **Qualm**.

QUENCH, to extinguish, check, put out. (E.) ME. *quenchen*, Wyclif, Matt. iii. 12. (Quench is formed from an obsolete verb *quink*, to be put out, to be extinguished; just as *drench* is from *drink*.) AS. *cwencan*, in the comp. *ācwencan*, to extinguish utterly, Mark, ix. 44. Causal of AS. *cwincan*; the pt. t. *ā-cwanc* (=was extinguished) occurs in a various reading in Ælfred, tr. of Beda, b. ii. c. 7, ed. Whelock. β. Further, the verb *cwincan* is an extension of a shorter form *cwinan*, to be extinguished (which is a strong verb, with pt. t. *cwān*, pp. *cwinen*); hence ‘ðæt fŷr ācwinen wæs and ādwæsced’=the fire was put out and extinguished; Beda, ii. 7 (as above). Cf. OFries. *kwinka*, to be extinguished. **Der.** *quench-able, -less*.

QUERIMONIOUS, fretful, discontented. (L.) ‘Most *querimoniously* confessing;’ Denham, A Dialogue, l. 2. Formed with suffix *-ous* (=F. *-eux*, L. *-ōsus*) from *querimōnia*, a complaint.—L. *queri*, to complain; with Idg. suffixes *-mōn-yā*. See **Querulous**. **Der.** *querimonious-ly, -ness*.

QUERN, a handmill for grinding grain. (E.) ME. *querne*, Chaucer, C. T. 14080 (B 3264). AS. *cweorn, cwyrn*, Matt. xxiv. 41.+Du. *kweern*; Icel. *kvern*; Dan. *kværn*; Swed. *qvarn*; Goth. *kwairnus*. Teut. base **kwer-n-*, from Idg. root **g(w)er*, to grind (?); whence also Lith. *gerna*, a stone in a handmill; Russ. *jernov(e)*, a millstone, Irish *bro*; W. *breuan*, a mill-stone; Skt. *grāvan-*, a stone. Brugmann, i. § 670.

QUERULOUS, fretful. (L.) In Phillips, ed. 1658. Englished from Late L. *querulōsus* or L. *querulus*, full of complaints.—L. *queri*, to complain. The pt. t. *questus sum* points to an older form **quesi*.+Skt. *çvas*, to pant, to hiss, to sigh.—√KWES, to wheeze; whence also E. **Wheeze**, q.v. **Der.** *querulous-ly, -ness*. And see *quarrel* (1), *querimonious, cry*.

QUERY, an inquiry, question. (L.) In Phillips, ed. 1706. Formerly *quere*, as used by Warner, Albion’s England, b. vi. c. 30, l. 238; Ben Jonson, New Inn, A. ii. sc. 2. Put for *quære*, seek thou, inquire thou, 2 p. imp. of L. *quærere*, to seek. β. *Quærere* is for **quæsere* (=**quai-sere*); cf. L. *quæso*, I beg. Brugmann, ii. § 662. **Der.** *query*, verb; *quer-ist*; also *quest*, q.v., *quest-ion, quest-or*. Also (from *quærere*), *ac-quire, con-quer, dis-quis-it-ion, ex-quis-ite, in-quire, in-quis-it-ive, per-quis-ite, re-quest, re-quire, re-quis-ite*.

QUEST, a search. (F.—L.) In Levins. ME. *queste*, P. Plowman, B. xx. 161.—OF. *queste*, ‘a quest, inquirie, search;’ Cot. F. *quête*.—Folk-L. *questa*; for L. *quæsita*, a thing sought; fem. of *quæsitus*, pp. of *quærere*, to seek; see **Query**.

QUESTION, an inquiry. (F.—L.) ME. *questioun*, Wyclif, John, iii. 25.—F. *question*.—L. *quæstiōnem*, acc. of *quæstio*, a seeking, a question; formed with suffix *-tio* from *quæs-*, base of **quæs-ere*, old form of *quærere*, to seek; see **Query**. **Der.** *question*, verb, Hamlet, ii. 2. 244; *question-able*, id. i. 4. 43; *question-abl-y, question-able-ness*; *question-less*, Merch. Ven. i. 1. 176; *question-ist* (Levins). Also *questor* (Levins), from L. *quæstor*; *questor-ship* (id.).

QUEUE, a twist of hair formerly worn at the back of the head. (F.—L.) In late use. Added by Todd to Johnson.—F. *queue*, ‘a taile:’ Cot.—L. *cauda*, a tail. See **Cue**.

QUIBBLE, an evasion, shift. (L.) ‘This is some trick; come, leave your *quiblins*, Dorothy;’ Ben Jonson, Alchemist, iv. 4 (Face, to Dol). A dimin. of *quib*, with suffix *-le*. ‘*Quib*, a taunt or mock,’ Coles (Halliwell); but the word is not in ed. 1684 of Coles’ Dict. Perhaps *quib* is a weakened form of *quip* or *quippy*. See **Quip**. β. The peculiar sense of evasion is prob. due to association with *quiddity* and *quillet*; see those words. **Der.** *quibble*, verb; *quibbl-er*.

QUICK, living, moving, lively. (E.) ME. *quik*, Chaucer, C. T. 1017 (A 1015). AS. *cwic*, sometimes *cuc*, Grein, i. 175; also *cwicu, cūcu*.+Du. *kwik*; Icel. *kvikr, kykr*; Dan. *kvik*; Swed. *quick*; Prov. G. *queck, quick*, quick, lively (Flügel). β. All from a Teut. type **kwikwoz*, lively, which took the place of an older form **kwiwoz*; this older type occurs in Goth. *kwius*, living, cognate with L. *uiuus*, Lith. *gywas*, Russ. *jivoi*, alive, living; Irish *beo*, W. *byw*, alive; Idg. type **g(w)iwos*. Further allied to Skt. *jīv*, to live, L. *uiuere*, and Gk. βίος, life. See **Vivid**. Brugmann, i. §§ 85, 318, 677. **Der.** *quick*, sb., *quick-ly, quick-ness*; *quick-lime*; *quick-sand*, 3 Hen. VI, v. 4. 26; *quick-silver*, Chaucer, C. T. 16240 (G 772), AS. *cwic-seolfor*; *quick-set*, i. e. set or planted alive; *quick-sighted*. And see *quick-en*. ¶ The prov. E. *quitch-grass*=*quick-grass*; it is also spelt *couch-grass*, where *couch* is due to the occasional AS. *cūcu*.

QUICKEN, to make alive. (E.) ME. *quikenen, quiknen*, Wyclif, John, vi. 64; Chaucer, C. T. 15949 (G 481). The true form is *quik-nen*, and the suffix *-nen*=Goth. *-nan*, which was used *only* to form *intransitive* verbs; so that the true sense of *quiknen* is rather ‘to become alive,’ as in King Lear, iii. 7. 39. But this distinction was early lost, and the suffixes *-ien, -nen* were used as convertible. The Goth. keeps them distinct, having *gakwiu-jan*, to make alive, *gakwiu-nan*, to become alive. From AS. *cwic*, alive; see **Quick**. Cf. Icel. *kvikna*, Swed. *qvickna*, intr., to quicken, come to life.

QUID, a mouthful of tobacco. (E.) A dialectal variant of *cud*; ‘*Quid*, the cud’ (Halliwell); AS. *cwidu*. It occurs in Bailey’s Dict., vol. ii. ed. 1731; and see E. D. D. See **Cud**.

QUIDDITY, a trifling, nicety, cavil. (L.) A term of the schools. ‘Their predicamentes, . . *quidities*, hecseities, and relatives!’ Tyndal, Works, p. 104, col. 1, l. 8 (and in Spec. of Eng., ed. Skeat, p. 176, l. 318). Englished from Late L. *quidditās*, the essence or nature of a thing, concerning which we have to investigate ‘what it is’ (*quid est*).—L. *quid*, what, neuter of *quis*, who; see **Who**.

QUIDNUNC, an inquisitive person. (L.) Applied to one who is always saying—‘what’s the news?’ ‘The laughers call me a *quidnunc*;’ The Tatler, no. 10, § 2.—L. *quid nunc*, what now?

QUIESCENT, still, at rest. (L.) In Blount’s Gloss., ed. 1674.—L. *quiescent-*, stem of pres. part. of *quiescere*, to be at rest. See **Quiet**. **Der.** *quiescence*.

QUIET, still, at rest, tranquil. (L.) ‘A *quyet* and a pesible lijf;’ Wyclif, 1 Tim. ii. 2; where the Vulgate has *quiētam*. [Rather from L. than from F.; the F. form is **Coy**, q.v.]—L. *quiētus*, quiet; orig. pp. of **quiēre*, only used in the inceptive form *quiescere*, to rest. Cf. *quiē-s*, rest. β. Allied to OPers. *shiyāti-*, a place of delight, home; Pers. *shād*, pleased; and to E. **While**. Brugmann, i. §§ 130, 675; Horn, § 767. **Der.** *quiet*, sb., ME. *quiete*, Chaucer, C. T. 9269 (E 1395); *quiet*, verb, 1 Hen. VI, iv. 1. 115; *quiet-ly, quiet-ness*; *quiet-ude*, from Late L. *quiētūdo* (White), a contraction for **quiētitūdo*. Also *quiet-us*, a final settlement, from L. *quiētus*, adj.; *quiet-ism*, *quiet-ist*. From L. *quiescere* we also have *ac-quiesce*; and see *re-quiem, quit, quite, re-quite, ac-quit, dis-quiet*. Doublet, *coy*.

QUILL (1), a feather of a bird, a pen. (E.) ME. *quille, quylle*. ‘They take a *quil*’ (tube?); Lydgate, Troy-book, fol. E 2, col. 2. ‘*Quylle*, a stalke, Calamus;’ Prompt. Parv. Halliwell gives: ‘*Quill*, the stalk of a cane or reed, the faucet of a barrel.’ This is a difficult and doubtful word; probably the sense of ‘hollow stalk’ was the original one. The word appears to be E., and of Teut. origin.+Low G. *kiil*, a goose-quill (Berghaus); *kil* (Schambach); Westphalian *kwiele* (Woeste); G. *kiel*, Bavarian and MHG. *kil*.

QUILL (2), to pleat a ruff. (F.—L.; or E.) ‘What they called his cravat, was a little piece of white linen *quilled* with great exactness;’ Tatler, no. 257, Nov. 30, 1710. 1. Supposed to be so called from being folded as if over quills; or, to form into small folds resembling quills. See **Quill** (1). 2. Wedgwood quotes from Métivier the Guernsey word *enquiller*, to pleat, gather, wrinkle, which Métivier derives from OF. *cuillir*, to gather, collect, cull; whence also E. **Cull**, q. v. I do not know which is right. ¶ The phrase *in the quill*, in Shaks. 2 Hen. VI. i. 3. 4, certainly means 'in the collection' or 'in a body;' where *quill* (variant of *coil*) is from OF. *cuillir*, L. *colligere*, to collect, to cull.

QUILLET, a sly trick in argument. (L.) 'His quiddities, his *quillets*;' Hamlet, v. 1. 108. There is also a form *quiddit*; the N. E. D. cites from Greene (in Harl. Misc. ii. 232), 'such quibs and *quiddits*.' Prob. *quillet* is for *quiddit*, shortened from *quiddity*; see **Quiddity**. Note that, in Torriano (1688) we find Ital. *quidità*, *quiddità*, 'the quiddity, the whatness, or substance of any thing;' and, just below, *quilità*, *quillità*, 'a quillity;' which seems to prove the change from *d* to *l*.

QUILT, a bed-cover, a case filled with wool, flock, down, &c. (F.—L.) ME. *quilte*, *quylte*. 'Unum *quylt*,' York Wills, iii. 3 (1395). A. Neckam has L. *culcitra*, glossed by AF. *quilte*; Wright's Vocab. i. 100. '*Quylte* of a bedde, Culcitra;' Prompt. Parv.—OF. *cuilte* (12th cent., Littré, s. v. *couette*), also spelt *cotre* (Burguy), and *coutre*, as in *coutrepoincter*, to quilt (Cotgrave).—L. *culcita* (also *culcitra*, giving OF. *cotre*), a cushion, mattress, pillow, quilt. Root uncertain. **Der.** *quilt*, verb. And see **Counterpane** (1).

QUINARY, consisting of or arranged in fives. (L.) The L. form *quinārius*, as a sb., is in Phillips, ed. 1706; *quinary* is in Cudworth's Intellectual System, p. 625 (R.).—L. *quinārius*, arranged by fives.—L. *quīni*, pl. adj., five each. For *quinc-ni*, where *quinc* = *quinque*, five, which is cognate with E. **Five**, q. v. See **Quinquagesima**.

QUINCE, a fruit with an acid taste. (F.—L.—Gk.) In Romeo, iv. 4. 2. Spelt *quince*, *wince*, Pistill of Susan, 102; *quence* in Prompt. Parv. [Cf. MF. *coignasse*, 'a female quince, or pear-quince, the greatest kind of quince;' Cot.; *coignacier*, 'the great, or pear, quince-tree;' id.] For *quins*; orig. the pl. of *quin* or *quyne*, a quince; but the usual ME. form is *coine*, or *coin*; Rom. of the Rose, 1374. Cf. *quyns-tre*, Voc. 573. 48; *quoyn-tre*, id. 646. 35. Walter de Bibbesworth has AF. *coigner*, glossed by *coyn-tre*, *quince-tre*; Wright's Vocab. i. 163. '*Quyne-aple tre*, coingz;' Du Wes, in Palsgrave, p. 914; *quynce*, p. 260.—OF. *coin*, mod. F. *coing*, a quince. [Cf. Prov. *codoing*, Ital. *cotogna* (Littré).]—L. *cotōnium*, for *cydōnium*; (the Ital. *cotogna* representing L. *cydōnia*, a quince).—Gk. κυδωνία, a quince-tree; κυδώνιον μῆλον, a quince, lit. a Cydonian apple.—Gk. Κυδωνία, Κυδωνίς, Cydonia, one of the chief cities of Crete, named from the Κύδωνες (Cydones), a Cretan race. See Smith's Classical Dict.

QUINCUNX, an arrangement by fives. (L.) Applied to trees, &c., arranged like the five spots on the side of a die marked 5. See Sir T. Browne, Garden of Cyrus, c. 5. § 12.—L. *quincunx*, an arrangement like five spots on a die.—L. *quinc-*, for *quinque*, five, cognate with E. **Five**; and *uncia*, an ounce, hence a small mark, spot on a die; see **Ounce** (1).

QUININE, extract of Peruvian bark. (F.—Span.—Peruvian) Ab. 1820. Borrowed from F. *quinine*, an extension (with suffix *-ine* < L. *-ina*) from F. *quina*.—Span. *quina*, *quinaquina*, a Span. spelling of Peruvian *kina*, or *kina-kina*, which is said to mean 'bark,' and is applied to that which we call Peruvian bark. Granada, in his Vocab. Rioplatense, gives *quina*, a thorny shrub, good against fever; and *quinaquina*, a large tree with medicinal bark.

QUINQUAGESIMA, the next Sunday before Lent. (L.) So called because about 50 days before Easter.—L. *quinquāgēsima* (*diēs*), fiftieth day; fem. of *quinquāgēsimus*, fiftieth.—L. *quinquā-*, for *quinque*, five; and *-gēsimus*, for *-gensimus*, tenth, ultimately from *decem*, ten. See **Five** and **Ten**.

QUINQUANGULAR, having five angles. (L.) Formed from *quinque*, five, just as *quadrangular* is from *quadrus*, fourfold. See **Quadrangular**.

QUINQUENNIAL, lasting five years, recurring in five years. (L.) Formed from *quinque*, five, and *annus*, a year; see **Biennial**.

QUINSY, inflammatory sore throat. (F.—Gk.) 'The throtling *quinsey*;' Dryden, Palamon, 1682. A contraction of the older form **squinacy** or *squinancy*, spelt *squinancie* in Minsheu, ed. 1627. Sir T. Elyot has '*squynances*, or *quinces* in the throte;' Castel of Helth, bk. iii. c. 7. ME. *squynacy*, *squynancy*, Trevisa, iii. 335.—OF. *quinancie* (Supp. to Godefroy, s. v. *esquinance*); also *squinancie*; mod. F. *esquinancie*. Cot. gives *esquinance*, 'the squincy or squinancy,' and *squinancie*, 'the squinancy or squinzie.' β. Formed (sometimes with prefixed *s-* or *es-*, for OF. *es-*, L. *ex*, very) from Gk. κυνάγχη, lit. 'a dog-throttling,' applied to a bad kind of sore throat.—Gk. κυν-, stem of κύων, a dog, cognate with E. **Hound**; and ἄγχ-ειν, to choke, throttle, from ANGH, to choke; see **Anger**.

QUINTAIN, a post with arms, set up for beginners in tilting to run at. (F.—L.) In As You Like It, i. 2. 263. 'When, if neede were, they could at *quintain* run;' Sidney, Arcadia, b. i (song, l. 56). ME. *quaintan* (for *quintan*), Destr. of Troy, 1627.—F. *quintaine*, 'a quintane, or whintane, for country youths to run at;' Cot. Cf. Prov. *quintana*, Ital. *quintana* (Littré). From Late L. *quintēna*, a quintain, Matt. Paris, v. 367; also *quintāna*, a quintain, also a certain measure of land, also a part of a street where carriages could pass (Ducange). β. The form of the word is so explicit that we may connect it with L. *quintāna*, a street in the camp, which intersected the tents of the two legions in such a way as to separate the fifth maniple from the sixth, and the fifth turma from the sixth; here was the market and business-place of the camp (White). We can hardly doubt that this public place in the camp was sometimes the scene of athletic exercises and trials of skill, whence it is an easy step to the restriction of the term to one particular kind of exhibition of martial activity. And *quintāna* is the fem. of *quintānus*, formed with suffix *-ānus* from *quintus*, fifth, which is for *quinc-tus*, from *quinque*, five. See **Five**. Picard *quintaine*; described by Corblet.

QUINTAL, a hundredweight. (F.—Span.—Arab.—L.) 'Twelve pence upon euerie *quintall* of copper;' Hakluyt's Voyages, i. 137, l. 18; also *kintal*, id. ii. (part 2). 162. Spelt *quyntall*, Palsgrave.—F. *quintal*, 'a quintal or hundred-weight;' Cot.—Span. *quintal*, a quintal, hundred-weight.—Arab. *qinṭār*, a weight of 100 pounds of twelve ounces each; Rich. Dict. pp. 1150, 737.—L. *centum*, a hundred; see **Cent**. And see **Kilderkin**.

QUINTESSENCE, the pure essence of anything. (F.—L.) 'Aristoteles .. hath put down . . . for elements, foure; and for a fifth, *quintessence*, the heavenly body which is immutable;' Holland, tr. of Plutarch, p. 662 (R.). Palsgrave has *quyntessence*. Misspelt *quyntencense*, Lydgate, Minor Poems, p. 51. And see The Book of *Quinte Essence* or the Fifth Being, about A.D. 1460, ed. Furnivall, 1866 (E. E. T. S.).—F. *quintessence*, 'a quintessence, the vertue, force, or spirit of a thing extracted;' Cot.—L. *quinta essentia*, fifth essence or nature.—L. *quinta*, fem. of *quintus* (for *quinc-tus*), from *quinque*, five; see **Five**. And see **Essence**. ¶ The idea is older than Aristotle; cf. the five Skt. *bhūtam's*, or elements, which were earth, air, fire, water, and æther. Thus the fifth essence is æther, the most subtle and highest; see Benfey, Skt. Dict., p. 658, col. 1.

QUINTILLION, the fifth power of a million. (L.) Coined from L. *quint-us*, fifth; and *-illion*, part of the word *million*; see **Quadrillion**, **Billion**.

QUINTUPLE, fivefold. (F.—L.) In Sir T. Browne, Cyrus' Garden, c. 5. § 3.—F. *quintuple*, in use in the 15th cent. (Hatzfeld).—L. *quintuplus*, a coined word; formed from *quintus*, fifth, just as *duplus* is from *duo*, two. See **Quintessence** and **Double**. **Der.** *quintuple*, verb.

QUIP, a taunt, cavil. (L.) 'This was a good *quip* that he gave unto the Jewes;' Latimer, Sermon on Rom. xiii. an. 1552 (R.). Sir T. More has: 'this goodly *quyppe* agaynste me;' Works, p. 709. We also find *quippy*, as in Drant's tr. of Horace, bk. ii. sat. 1.—L. *quippe*, forsooth (used ironically). For *quid-pe*; Brugmann, i. § 585. **Der.** *quibb-le*, q. v.

QUIRE (1), a collection of so many sheets of paper, often 24. (F.—L.) Also *quair*, as in The Kingis *Quair*, i. e. small book. Spelt *quayer*, Trevisa, tr. of Higden, ii. 193. In the Ancren Riwle, p. 248, last line but 1, we find the curious form *cwaer*, in the sense of a small book or pamphlet.—AF. *quaer*, as a gloss to *quaternus*; A. Neckam, in Wright's Vocab. i. 116, l. 6; OF. *quaier* (13th cent., Littré); spelt *quayer*, *cayer*, in Cotgrave, who explains it 'a quire of written paper, a peece of a written booke;' Mod. F. *cahier*.—Late L. *quāternum*, a collection of four leaves, a small quire; from L. *quāternī*, nom. pl., four each, which from *quatuor*, four, cognate with E. **Four**. Cf. Ital. *quaderno*, a quire of paper; and the instance of F. *enfer* from L. *infernum* shows that the suffix *-num* would easily be lost.

QUIRE (2), a band of singers. (F.—L.—Gk.) Another spelling of **Choir**, q. v. **Der.** *quir-ister* (for *chorister*); Nares.

QUIRK, a cavil, subtle question. (Scand.—G.) In Minsheu, ed. 1627. The orig. sense seems to have been 'angle;' cf. prov. E. *quirk*, a twist, a clock in a stocking, a quibble. 'The quiddities and *queerks* of logique darke;' Drant, tr. of Horace, Sat. i. 5. Being found in many dialects, it may be a Scand. word. β. Prob. from Icel. *kverk*, the angle below the chin, the inner angle of an ax (Vigfusson); Molbech gives Dan. *qværk* (*kværk*) as an angle in a knee-timber of a ship (cf. E. *quirk*, an angle or groove in a moulding; see N. E. D. and E. D. D.); Jutland *kværke*, the angle between two rows of houses (Feilberg). Not of Scand. origin; but borrowed from G. *quer*, transverse; see **Queer**. Cf. MHG. *twerh*, G. *zwerch*, going across; AS. *þwearh*; see **Thwart**. Distinct from Icel. *kverkr*, pl., the throat.

QUIT, freed, released, discharged from. (F.—L.) In the phr. 'to be *quit*,' the word is really an adj., though with the force of a pp.

The verb *to quit* is derived from it, not *vice versâ*; as is easily seen by comparing the F. *quitter* (OF. *quiter*) with F. *quitte* (OF. *quite*). In the phrases 'quit rent' and 'quit claim,' the old adjectival use is retained, and the latter represents an OF. verb *quite-clamer*. Moreover, the adj. was introduced into E. before the verb, appearing as *cwite* in the Ancren Riwle, p. 6, l. 12. Cf. 'Tho was Wyllam our kyng all *quyt* of thulke fon,' i.e. all *free* of those foes; Rob. of Glouc. p. 392, l. 8062. [Hence was derived the verb *quyten*, to satisfy a claim, pay for. 'He mai *quiten* hire ale' = he will pay for her ale, Old Eng. Miscellany, ed. Morris, p. 190, l. 77; and see Chaucer, C. T. 772 (A 770).] — OF. *quite*, 'discharged, quit, freed, released;' Cot. Mod. F. *quitte*; Span. *quito*, quit. — Late L. *quitus*, *quittus*, popular forms of L. *quiētus*, at rest, hence free, satisfied. Thus *quit* is a shorter form of *quiet*. See **Quiet.** Der. *quit*, verb, from OF. *quiter*, 'to quit,' Cot. (mod. F. *quitter*). And hence *quitt-ance*, ME. *quitaunce*, spelt *cwitaunce* in Ancren Riwle, p. 126, l. 7, from OF. *quitance*, 'an acquittance,' Cot.; cf. Late L. *quiētantia*. And see *quite*.

QUITE, entirely. (F.—L.) ME. *quite*, *quyte*. 'And chaced him out of Norweie *quyte* and clene;' Rob. of Brunne, tr. of Langtoft, p. 50. This is merely an adverbial use of the ME. adj. *quyte*, now spelt *quit*. Thus the sense is 'freely,' hence 'entirely.' See **Quit.**

QUIVER (1), to tremble, shiver. (E.) Possibly allied to *quaver*, q. v. It does not appear very early, yet is probably old. 'A quiv'ring dart;' Spenser, F. Q. iii. 5. 19. 'I *quyver*, I shake;' Palsgrave. 'Dido *quyuered* and shoke;' Caxton, Eneydos, ch. 27, p. 103. Allied to the obsolete adj. *quiver*, full of motion, brisk, Shak. 2 Hen. IV, iii. 2. 301; which occurs, spelt *cwiuer* (= *cwiver*) in the Ancren Riwle, p. 140, l. 21; also as AS. *cwifer*, as in the adv. *cwiferlīce*, anxiously, eagerly; Rule of St. Benet, ed. Schröer, p. 133, l. 38. Prob. of imitative origin; cf. *quaver* and *quake*. Cf. also EFries. *kwifer*, lively, *kwifern*, to be lively (Koolman); MDu. *kuyven*, *kuyveren*, to quiver (Kilian).

QUIVER (2), a case for arrows. (F.—OHG.) 'Thair arwes in a *quiuer* sente;' E. E. Metr. Psalter, x. 3. 'Quyver, Pharetra;' Prompt. Parv. — OF. *cuivre*, *cuevre*, *coivre*, a quiver. And see Diez, s. v. *couire*. — OSax. *cokar*, a quiver; OHG. *kohhar* (cited by Diez), mod. G. *köcher*, a quiver. Cognate with AS. *cocur*, *cocer*, a quiver, Gen. xxvii. 3. Teut. type *kukuro-*, whence Med. L. *cucurum*, a quiver. Der. *quiver-ed*.

QUIXOTIC, absurdly chivalrous. (Spanish.) Formed as adj., with suffix *-ic*, from the name *Don Quixote*, or *Quijote*, the hero of the famous novel by Cervantes. (The OSpan. *x* is now commonly written as *j*; the sound of the letter is guttural, something like that of G. *ch*.)

QUIZ, an eccentric person; one who ridicules oddities; a hoax. (E.) History obscure; said to have been coined by one Daly in 1791; yet already in 1782 Madame D'Arblay, Early Diary, p. 24, has: 'He's a droll *quiz*.' The toy also called a bandalore was known as a *quiz* in 1790; which suggests a connexion with *whiz*. It seems, in any case, to have been a coined word. Perhaps suggested by *in-quis-itive*. See Davies, Supp. Glossary; Notes on E. Etym., p. 238.

QUOIF, a cap or hood. (F.—MHG.—L.) In Shak. Wint. Tale, iv. 4. 226. The same word as **Coif,** q.v.

QUOIN, a technical term, orig. a wedge. Used in architecture, gunnery, and printing. (F.—L.) The orig. sense is 'wedge;' and, as a verb, 'to wedge up.' 'A printers *quoyn*, Cuneus;' Levins, 215. 17. Merely another spelling of **Coin,** q.v. A like change of *c* to *qu* occurs in *quoit*. Der. *quoin*, verb.

QUOIT, COIT, a ring of iron for throwing at a mark in sport. (F.—L.?) The older spelling is *coit*. 'Coyte, Petreluda; Coyter, or caster of a coyte, Petreludus;' Prompt. Parv. 'Casting of *coitis*,' Pecock's Repressor (A. D. 1449); in Spec. of Eng., ed. Skeat, p. 51, l. 70. AF. *coytes*, pl. (1388); N. E. D. β. We find W. *coetan*, a quoit (where W. *oe* = E. *oi* nearly); but this is borrowed from E., having no radical, and therefore does not help us. γ. We also find, on the other hand, the Lowland Scotch *coit*, to justle or push about, occurring in Fordun's Scotichronicon, ii. 376; much like the OF. *coiter*. We there read of a woman who 'Gangis *coitand* in the curt, hornit like a gait' [goat]. δ. The spelling *coit* suggests a F. origin; and the word is prob. connected with the curious OF. *coiter*, to press, to push, to hasten, incite, instigate (Burguy); cognate with mod. Prov. *coucha*, *couita*, *coita*, to drive before one (Mistral); the Span. *coitarse* is to hurry oneself, to hasten. If the OF. *coiter* could have had the sense 'to drive,' as seems possible, we may look on a *quoit* as being a thing driven or whirled; but of this we have no evidence. *Coit*, to push along the ice, as in the game of curling (Jamieson), may have been the older sense in English, which may help. ε. The origin of OF. *coiter* is very doubtful; hardly from L. *coactāre*, to

force, from *coactus*, pp. of *cōgere*; see **Cogent.** It ought rather to represent a Late L. type *coctāre*, a frequentative of L. *coquere*, to cook, which in late authors also meant to harass or vex the mind (Lewis). See Körting, § 2297. Der. *quoit*, verb, 2 Hen. IV, ii. 4. 266.

QUORUM, a number of members of any body sufficient to transact business. (L.) In Minsheu, ed. 1627. 'Be of the *quorum*;' Stat. of Hen. VII, fol. b 5, l. 6. It was usual to enumerate the members forming a committee, *of whom* (in L., *quorum*) a certain number must be present at a meeting. L. *quōrum* is the gen. pl. of *quī*, cognate with E. *who*; see **Who.**

QUOTA, a part or share assigned to each member of a company. (L.) Used by Addison; Spectator, No. 439, § 2. — L. *quota* (*pars*), how great (a part), how much; fem. of *quotus*, how many. — L. *quot*, how many; allied to *quī*, cognate with E. **Who.** Cf. Ital. *quota*, a share (Baretti). Der. (from L. *quotus*) *quote*, q. v., *quoti-dian*; (from L. *quot*) *quot-ient*.

QUOTE, to cite, repeat the words of any one. (F.—L.) In Shak. Hamlet, ii. 1. 112. Sometimes written *cote* (Schmidt). — MF. *quoter*, 'to quote;' Cot. Mod. F. *coter*, which is also in Cotgrave. — Late L. *quotāre*, to mark off into chapters and verses; thus the real sense of *quote* is to give a reference; see *coted*, Trevisa, tr. of Higden, viii. 205 (L. *quotāvit*). The lit. sense of *quotāre* is 'to say how many,' with reference to the numbering of chapters. — L. *quota* (*pars*), fem. of *quotus*, how much, how many; see **Quota.** ¶ Sometimes from L. *quotāre*, immediately; esp. in early instances. Der. *quot-able*, *quot-er*, *quot-at-ion*.

QUOTH, he says, he said. (E.) Properly a pt. t., though sometimes used as a present. The form of the infin. is *queath*, only used in the comp. *bequeath*. ME. *quoth*, *quod*; Chaucer, C. T. 790 (A 788); and common in both forms. AS. *cwedan*, to speak, say; pt. t. *cwæð*, pl. *cwǣdon*; pp. *cweden*; Grein, i. 173.+Icel. *kveða*; pt. t. *kvað*, pp. *kveðinn*; OSax. *queðan*; OHG. *quedan*, pt. t. *quat*, *quad*; Goth. *kwithan*, to say, pt. t. *kwath*. β. All from a Teut. type *kwethan-*, to say, pt. t. *kwath*. Allied to Skt. *gad*, to speak, *gada-s*, m. speech. Der. *quotha*, for *quoth he*.

QUOTIDIAN, daily. (F.—L.) ME. *quotidian*, spelt *cotidian*, Gower, C. A. ii. 142; bk. v. 464. — OF. *cotidian* (13th cent., Littré); later *quotidien*, 'daily;' Cot. — L. *quotīdiānus*, daily. — L. *quoti-*, for *quotus*, how many; and *di-ēs*, a day; with suffix *-ānus*. Hence *quotidiānus* = on however many a day, on any day, daily. See **Quota** and **Diurnal.**

QUOTIENT, the result in arithmetical division. (F.—L.; *or* L.) In Minsheu, ed. 1627. [Perhaps directly from Latin.] — F. *quotient*, 'the part which, in the division of a thing among many, fals unto every ones share;' Cot. — L. *quotient-*, the imaginary stem of L. *quotiens*, which is really an adv., and indeclinable; it means 'how many times.' — L. *quot*, how many; see **Quota.**

R

RABBET, to cut the edges of boards so that they overlap and can be joined together. (F.—L.) ME. *rabet*, sb.; see Prompt. Parv. 'Many deep *rabbotted* incisions;' Holland, tr. of Plutarch, p. 902 (R.). 'Rabettyng of bordes, *rabetture*;' Palsgrave. The Halifax gibbet, in Harrison's Descr. of England, b. ii. c. 11, ed. Furnivall, p. 227, is described as having a block of wood 'which dooth ride vp and downe in a slot, *rabet*, or regall betweene two peeces of timber.' Bailey has: 'Rabbet, to channel boards;' and also 'Rebate, to channel, to chamfer.' Apparently from OF. *rabatre*, 'to abate, deduct, diminish,' Cot.; hence, to thin down; mod. F. *rabattre*. — F. *re-* (L. *re-*), again, back; and OF. *abatre*, to abate. See **Abate.** β. Confused, as above, with *rebate*, q. v. Also, as shown by the spelling *rabboted*, with F. *raboter*, 'to plane, levell, make or lay even,' Cot.; from F. *rabot*, 'a joyners plane,' id. See **Rebate.**

RABBI, RABBIN, sir, a Jewish title. (L.—Gk.—Heb.) 'Rabi, that is to seye maister;' Wyclif, John, i. 38. Also in the AS. version. — L. *rabbi* (Vulgate). — Gk. ῥαββί; John, i. 38. — Heb. *rabbi*, lit. my master; from *rab*, great, or as sb. master, and *ī*, my. We also find *Rabboni*, John, xx. 16; of similar import. 'Rabbi was considered a higher title than *Rab*; and *Rabban* higher than *Rabbi*;' Smith, Dict. of the Bible, q. v. — Heb. root *rābab*, to be great. Cf. Arab. *rabb*, being great; or, as sb., a master; *rabbī*, my lord; Rich. Dict. p. 719. The form *rabbin* is French. Der. *rabbin-ic-al*, *rabbin-ist*.

RABBIT, a small rodent quadruped. (Walloon—MDu.) ME. *rabet*; Prompt. Parv. The older word is *cony*. It is a dimin. form only found in Walloon *robett* (Remacle); formed with F. suffix *-et* from MDu. *robbe*, 'a rabet;' Hexham; see also Kilian and De Bo. Kilian also gives the dimin. form *robbeken*. Origin unknown; perhaps cf. Norw. *rabba*, to snatch, snap up; *rabben*, snatching, tearing, quick (Ross). See Notes on E. Etym., p. 239.

RABBLE, a noisy crowd, mob. (MDu.) Levins has *rabil*, *rable*, *rablement*. Halliwell has: '*rabble*, to speak confusedly,' with an example of ME. *rablen* used in the same sense; also: '*rabblement*, a crowd, or mob.' ME. *rabel*, a rout, Gawain and the Grene Knight, 1703, 1899. So named from the noise which they make; cf. MDu. *rabbelen*, 'to chatter, trifle, toy;' Hexham. So also prov. G. *rabbeln*, to chatter, prattle; Flügel. So also Gk. ῥαβάσσειν, to make a noise; whence ἀρράβαξ, a dancer, a brawler. The suffix *-le* gives a frequentative force; a *rabble* is 'that which keeps on making a noise.' And see **Rapparee.** Der. *rabble-ment* (with F. suffix), Jul. Cæsar, i. 2. 245.

RABID, mad, furious. (L.) 'All the *rabid* flight Of winds that ruin ships;' Chapman, tr. of Homer, Odyss. b. xii. l. 418.— L. *rabidus*, furious. — L. *rabere*, to rage; see **Rage.** Der. *rabid-ly*, *-ness.*

RACA, a term of reproach. (Chaldee.) Matt. v. 22. 'Critics are agreed in deriving it from the Chaldee *rēkā*, with the sense of worthless;' Smith, Dict. of the Bible.

RACCOON, RACOON, a carnivorous animal of N. America. (N. American Indian.) It occurs in a tr. of Buffon, London, 1792. The name of the animal in Buffon is *raton*; but this is only a F. corruption of the native name, just as *racoon* is an E. corruption. Spelt *rackoon* in Bailey, 1735. '*Arathkone*, a beast like a fox;' in a glossary of Indian words at the end of A Historie of Travaile into Virginia, by Wm. Strachey; ab. 1610-12; published by the Hakluyt Society in 1849. 'A beast they call *aroughcun*, much like a badger;' Capt. Smith, Works, ed. Arber, p. 59. Evelyn speaks of 'the Egyptian *racoon*;' Diary, May 18, 1657. From the old Virginian dialect of Algonquin. The F. *raton* is assimilated to F. *raton*, a rat.

RACE (1), a trial of speed, swift course, swift current. (E.) ME. *ras*, a Northern form. 'In a *ras*;' Met. Homilies, ed. Small; p. 141. 'In a *raiss*;' Barbour, Bruce, v. 638. [The corresponding Southern form is ME. *rees*, *res* (with long *e*), Gower, C. A. i. 335; bk. iii. 167; Tale of Gamelyn, l. 543 (Wright), or l. 547 (Six-text); from AS. *rǣs*, a rush, swift course; Luke, viii. 33.] + Icel. *rás*, a race, running. Cf. Icel. *rasa*, to rush headlong; Du. *razen* (G. *rasen*), to rage. β. The form of the Teut. base is *rǣs-*. Cf. Gk. ἐ-ρω-ή, a quick motion. Der. *race*, verb; *race-course*, *race-horse*, *rac-er*.

RACE (2), a lineage, family, breed. (F.) In Spenser, F. Q. i. 10. 60. — F. *race*, 'a race, linnage, family;' Cot. Cf. Port. *raça*, Span. *raza*, Ital. *razza*. Of unknown origin; not from OHG. *reiza*, a line, stroke, mark; as suggested by Diez. See Körting (§ 7716), who suggests rather a L. type *raptia*. Der. *rac-y*, q. v.

RACE (3), a root. (F.—L.) 'A *race* of ginger;' Wint. Tale, iv. 3. 50; spelt *raze*, 1 Hen. IV, ii. 1. 27.—OF. *raïs*, *raiz*, a root (Burguy); cf. Span. *raiz*, a root.—L. *rādīcem*, acc. of *rādix*, a root; see **Radix.**

RACEME, a cluster. (F.—L.) A botanical term; borrowed from F. *racème*, a cluster, in botany.—L. *racēmum*, acc. of *racēmus*, a cluster of grapes. Der. *racem-ed.* Doublet, *raisin.*

RACK (1), a grating above a manger for hay, an instrument of torture; a frame-work, a toothed bar. (MDu.) The word *rack* is used in a great many senses, see **Rack** (2), &c., below; and, in several of these, the origin is quite different. The word *rack* is seldom to be found in early literature, in any sense. The oldest E. word etymologically connected with *rack* (1) is AS. *reccan*, to stretch. β. The radical sense of *rack* is to extend, stretch out; hence, as a sb., that which is extended or straight, a straight bar (cf. G. *rack*, a rail, bar; hence, a frame-work, such as the bars in a grating above a manger, a frame-work used as an instrument of torture, a straight bar with teeth in which a cog-wheel can work. The ME. forms are *rakke*, *rekke*. 'A peyre *rakkes* of yryne;' E. Eng. Wills, ed. Furnivall, p. 56, l. 27; '*rakkes* and brandernes of erne' [iron]; id., p. 57, l. 27; A.D. 1424; 'pro i. pari de *rakkez*,' in a kitchen inventory, York Wills, iii. 15; A.D. 1400. 'A *rakke*, Præsepe,' i.e. a rack for hay; Prompt. Parv. '*Rekke* and manger'=rack and manger; Romance of Partenay, l. 913.—MDu. *recke*, 'a perch or a long pole,' Hexham; Low G. *rakk*, a rack, frame-work for hanging things on, a shelf (as in E.). Related words are Icel. *rekja*, to stretch, trace, *rekkja*, to strain, *rakr*, straight; MDu. *recken*, 'to stretch, reach out, also to racke,' Hexham; Swed. *rak*, straight; G. *rack*, a rack, rail, prov. G. *reck*, a scaffold, wooden horse, *reckbank*, a rack for torture, *recke*, a stretcher, *recken*, to stretch. See below.

RACK (2), to stretch a person's joints, to torture on the rack. (MDu.) Allied to **Rack** (1) above. The verb seems to have been

introduced before the sb. 'As though I had ben *racked*;' Skelton, Phillip Sparowe, l. 47. 'Worthi to been enhangid .. Or to be *rakkid*;' Lydgate, St. Edmund, ed. Horstmann, bk. ii. 277.—MDu. *racken*, 'to rack, to torture,' variant of *recken*, 'to racke,' also 'to stretch, reach out, or to extend,' Hexham; Low G. *rekken*, to stretch. + Icel. *rekja*, to stretch; Goth. *uf-rakjan*; AS. *reccan*, to stretch, extend. Teut. type *rak-jan-*, from *rak*, 2nd grade of Teut. *rek* = Idg. √REG, as in Gk. ὀρέγ-ειν, to stretch, L. *reg-ere*; see **Regent.** Brugmann, i. § 474. Der. *rack*, sb.; *rack-rent*, i.e. a rent stretched to its full value, or nearly so.

RACK (3), light vapoury clouds, the clouds generally. (Scand.) 'Still in use in the Northern counties, and sometimes there applied to a mist;' Halliwell. Used in Shak. of floating vapour; see Hamlet, ii. 2. 506, Antony, iv. 14. 10, Sonnet 33, l. 6. So also (probably) in the disputed passage in the Tempest, iv. 156; where Halliwell hesitates, though he gives instances of its use in earlier English. Thus we find: 'As Phebus doeth at mydday in the southe, Whan every *rak* and every cloudy sky Is voide clene;' Lydgate, MS. Ashmole 39, fol. 51. 'The *rac* dryuez'=the storm-cloud drives; Allit. Poems, ed. Morris, B. 433; a decisive passage. 'A *rac* [driving storm] and a royde wynde;' Destruction of Troy, 1984. 'The windes in the vpper region, which move the clouds above (which we call the *racke*) and are not perceived below;' Bacon, Nat. Hist. § 115. [Frequently confused with *reek*, but this is quite a different word.] It is the same word with *wrack*, and allied to *wreck*; but *wrack* is to be taken in the sense of 'drift,' as rightly explained in Wedgwood.—Norw. *rak*, Swed. dial. *rak* (Swed. *vrak*, Dan. *vrag*), wreckage, that which is drifted about; cf. Icel. *rek*, drift, motion; given in Vigfusson only in the sense 'a thing drifted ashore;' but Wedgwood cites *isinn er ī reki*, the ice is driving; *skȳrek*, the rack or drifting clouds; cf. '*racking* clouds' = drifting clouds, 3 Hen. VI. ii. 1. 27. From Icel. *reka*, to drive, toss, thrust, cognate with Swed. *vräka*, to reject, and E. *wreak*; see **Wreak.** Cf. Swed. *skeppet vräker*, the ship drifts. Der. *rack*, for *wrack*; as in the phr. 'to go to *rack* and ruin;' see **Wrack.**

RACK (4), to pour off liquor from the lees. (Prov.) See Halliwell. In Minsheu, ed. 1627, who speaks of '*rackt* wines, i.e. wines cleansed and purged.' 'The reboyle to *rakke* to the lies;' Russell, Boke of Nurture, 115; in Babees Book, ed. Furnivall, p. 125. Like some other words connected with the wine-trade, it is of Gascon origin. — OProv. *arracar*, Prov. *arraca* (Gascony), to decant wine (Mistral). Wedgwood quotes Languedoc *araca le bi*, to decant wine. — Prov. *raca*, mod. *raco*, *draco*, lees, husks left after pressing out wine or oil. Hence also MF. *raqué*; Cotgrave explains *vin raqué* as 'small, or corse wine, squeezed from the dregs of the grapes, already drained of all their best moisture.' Of uncertain origin; but initial *d* may have been dropped, as in **Rankle**, q. v. The mod. Prov. *draco* answers to OF. *drache*, husks of grapes; perhaps of Teut. origin. Cf. ME. *drast*, dregs (N. E. D.); and Körting, § 3109.

RACK (5), a short form of **Arrack**, q.v. Cf. Span. *raque*, *arrack*.

RACK (6), &c. We find (6) prov. E. *rack*, a neck of mutton; from AS. *hracca*, neck, according to Somner; but this is prob. an error. The AS. '*hreacca*, occiput' in OE. Texts (see p. 549) seems to be miswritten for *hnecca*; still, we find 'Occiput, *hracca*,' in Voc. 463. 21. Also (7) *rack*, for *reck*, to care; see **Reck.** Also (8) *rack*, a pace of a horse (Palsgrave); of uncertain origin. Also (9) *rack*, a track, cart-rut; cf. Icel. *reka*, to drive; see **Rack** (3).

RACKET (1), **RAQUET**, a bat with network in place of a wooden blade. (F.—Span.—Arab.) ME. *rakket.* 'Sa mony rakketis;' Dunbar, Poem xiv. l. 66 (ed. Small).—MF. *raquette*, 'a racket;' Cot. [The game of 'fives,' with the hands, preceded rackets; to this day, tennis is called in French *paume* = game of the palm of the hand.]—Span. *raqueta*, a racket, battle-dore (Minsheu). Perhaps from Arab. *rāha(t)*, the palm of the hand; Rich. Dict. p. 714. See Devic, in Supp. to Littré; who suggests that the Span. *raqueta* may have been confused with Port. *rasqueta*, the wrist, OF. *rachete*, *rasquette*; which also is prob. of Arab. origin, viz. from Arab. *rusgh*, the wrist joint; Rich. Dict. p. 733.

RACKET (2), a noise. (E.) 'After all this *Racket*;' Spectator, no. 336, § 3. Of imitative origin; cf. prov. E. *rattick*, to rattle; *rackle*, noisy talk; also *rabble*. The Gael. *racaid*, racket, is merely the E. word borrowed; but cf. Irish *racan*, noise, riot; Gael. *rac*, to make a noise like geese or ducks; Rouchi *raque*, *ric-rac*, words imitating noises.

RACOON; see **Raccoon.**

RACY, of strong flavour, spirited, rich. (F.—L. (?); *with* E. *suffix.*) *Racy* means indicative of its origin, full of the spirit of its *race*; and so is a derivative from **Race** (2); esp. in the sense of a characteristic flavour or 'raciness' of a wine, supposed to be due to the soil; see N. E. D. 'Fraught with brisk *racy* verses, in which we

The soil from whence they came taste, smell, and see;' Cowley, An Answer to a Copy of Verses sent me from Jersey, ll. 7. 8. With respect to a pipe of Canary wine, Greedy asks 'Is it of the right *race*?' Massinger, New Way to pay Old Debts, i. 3. 10. **Der.** *raci-ness.* ☞ Probably sometimes used with some notion of reference to L. *rādix*; but *race* (2) is not derived from *rādix*, which appears only in **Race** (3).

RADDLE, red ochre; for marking sheep. (E.) Fitzherbert has *radel-marke*, i. e. mark made with red ochre; Husbandry, § 52. Allied to *red*; see **Red.** And see **Ruddle.**

RADIAL, RADIANT; see **Radius.**

RADICAL, RADISH; see **Radix.**

RADIUS, a ray. (L.) In Phillips, ed. 1710. Chiefly used in mathematics. — L. *radius*, a ray; see **Ray. Der.** *radi-al*, from F. *radial*, ' of, or belonging to, the upper and bigger bone of the arme,' Cot., formed with suffix *-ālis* from L. *radius*, sometimes used to mean the exterior bone of the fore-arm. Also *radi-ant*, spelt *radyaunt* in Fisher, On the Seven Psalms, Ps. 130, ed. Mayor, p. 231, last line, from *radiant-*, stem of pres. part. of L. *radiāre*, to radiate, from *radius*; and hence *radi-ant-ly*, *radiance*. Also *radiate*, from L. *radiātus*, pp. of *radiāre*. Also *radiat-ion*, in Bacon, Nat. Hist. § 125, near the end, from F. *radiation*, 'a radiant brightness,' Cot., which is from L. *radiātiōnem*, acc. of *radiātio*, a shining, from *radiāre*.

RADIX, a root, a primitive word, base of a system of logarithms. (L.) L. *rādix* (stem *rādic-*), a root; chiefly used as a scientific term.+Gk. ῥάδιξ, a branch, rod. Cognate with E. **Root,** q. v. **Der.** *radic-al*, spelt *radycall* in Sir T. Elyot, Castle of Helth, b. iii. c. 3, from F. *radical*, ' radicall,' Cot., formed with suffix *-al* (<L. *-ālis*) from *rādic-*, stem of *rādix*; *radic-al-ly*, *radic-al-ness*; also *radic-le*, a little root, a dimin. form from the stem *rādic-*. Also *radish*, called ' *radishe rootes*' by Sir T. Elyot, Castel of Helth, b. ii. c. 9, from F. *radis*, 'a raddish root,' Cot.; not a true F. word, but borrowed from Prov. *raditz* (Littré), or from Ital. *radice* (Hatzfeld), from L. *rādicem*, acc. of *rādix*. From L. *rādix* we also have *e-radic-ate* and *rash* (3). Doublets, *radish*, *race* (3).

RAFFLE, a kind of lottery. (F. — G.) ME. *rafle* (a game at dice), Chaucer, C. T. Pers. Tale, De Avaritia; Group I, l. 793 (Six-text). — MF. *rafle* (spelt *raffle* in Cotgrave), ' a game at three dice, wherein he that throwes all three alike, winnes whatsoever is set; also, a rifling;' Cot. — F. *rafler*, ' to catch, or seise on violently;' Cot. Perhaps from G. *raffeln*, to snatch up; frequentative of *raffen*, 'to raff, sweep, carry away, carry off hastily,' Flügel. Cognate with Icel. *hrapa*, to hurry; see **Rap** (2). **Der.** *raffle*, verb.

RAFT, a collection of spars or planks, tied together to serve as a boat. (Scand.) ME. *raft*; spelt *rafte*, and used in the sense of 'spar' or 'rough beam;' Avowing of Arthur, st. 25, in Robson's Met. Rom. p. 69. The orig. sense is ' rafter.' — Icel. *raptr* (pron. *raftr*, in which *r* is merely the sign of the nom. case), a rafter; Dan. *raft*, a rafter; see **Rafter.**

RAFTER, a beam to support a roof. (E.) ME. *rafter*, Chaucer, C. T. 992 (A 990). AS. *ræfter*, Ælfred, tr. of Beda, b. iii. c. 16. An extension (with Idg. suffix *-ro-*) from the base RAFT appearing in MSwed. *raft*, Dan. *raft*, Icel. *raptr* (*raftr*), a rafter, beam. Again, Dan. *raft* is an extension (with suffix *-to-*) from the base RAF related to Icel. *ráf*, *ræfr*, a roof, which is cognate with OHG. *rāfo*, a spar, a rafter. Further allied to Gk. ἐρέφ-ειν, to cover; ὄροφος, a roof. (√REBH.) **Der.** *rafter*, verb. And see *raft*. ☞ It does not seem to be allied to *roof*, which has an initial *h*; AS. *hróf*.

RAG, a shred of cloth. (Scand.) ME. *ragge*, Gower, C. A. i. 100; bk. i. 1723. ' A *ragged* colt '= a shaggy colt, King Alisaunder, 684. We only find AS. *raggie*, adj. rough, shaggy; ' Setosa, *raggie*,' Mone, Quellen, p. 436; as if from a sb. **ragg.* — Norw. *ragg*, rough hair, whence *ragged*, shaggy (E. *ragged*); Swed. *ragg*, rough hair; *raggig*, shaggy; Swed. dial. *raggi*, having rough hair, slovenly; Icel. *rogg*, shagginess; *raggaðr*, shaggy. Thus the orig. sense is that of shagginess, hence of untidiness. Root unknown. The resemblance to Gk. ῥάκος, a shred of cloth, is accidental. **Der.** *ragg-ed*, as above, also applied by Gower to a tree, Conf. Amant. ii. 177; bk. v. 1509; *ragg-ed-ly*, *ragg-ed-ness*; *rag-stone* (a rugged stone), spelt *ragston* in Riley, Memorials of London, p. 262; *rag-wort*, spelt *rag-worte* in Levins and in a Glossary (in Cockayne's Leechdoms) apparently of the 15th century.

RAGE, fury, violent anger. (F. — L.) ME. *rage*, King Alisaunder, ed. Weber, 980. — F. *rage*. — L. *rabiem*, acc. of *rabies*, madness, rage. — L. *rabere*, to rave, to be mad. **Der.** *rage*, verb, *rag-ing*, *rag-ing-ly*. Also *en-rage*, *rave*.

RAGOUT, a dish of meat highly seasoned. (F. — L.) Spelt *ragoo* in Phillips and Kersey, to imitate the F. pronunciation. Butler has *ragusts*, pl.; Hudibras, pt. ii. c. 1. 598. — F. *ragoût*, a seasoned dish. — F. *ragoûter*, to bring back to one's appetite, with

reference to one who has been ill. — L. *re-*, back; F. *a*<L. *ad*, to; and *goût*, taste; see **Re-, A-** (5), and **Gout** (2).

RAID, a hostile invasion, inroad. (North E.) A Northern border word; and merely a doublet of the Southern E. *road*. Cf. ' That, when they heard my name in any *road*,' i. e. raid; Greene, George-a-Greene, ed. Dyce, vol. ii. p. 169; ed. Collins, A. i. sc. 3. Jamieson gives the Sc. pl. *radis* from Wyntown, viii. 34. 34. North. form of AS. *rād*; cf. Icel. *reið*, a riding, a raid; Dan. *red*, Swed. *redd*, a road. See **Road, Ride.** Doublet, *road*.

RAIL (1), a bar of timber, an iron bar for railways. (F. — L.) ME. *rail*; dat. *raile*, Gower, C. A. iii. 75; bk. vi. 2201. Not found in AS. — OF. *reille*, a rail, bar; Norm. dial. *raile* (Moisy). — L. *rēgula*, a bar; see **Rule.** Cf. Low G. *regel*, a rail, a cross-bar; Swed. *regel*, a bar, bolt; G. *riegel*, OHG. *rigil*, a bar; if these are from Latin; but Franck (s.v. *regel*) considers them to be Teutonic, and therefore distinct. **Der.** *rail*, verb, *rail-ing*, *rail-road*, *rail-way*.

RAIL (2), to brawl, to use reviling language. (F. — L.) In Skelton, Poems Against Garnesche; see Skelton, ed. Dyce, i. 130, ll. 119, 137. ' *Rayler*, a jestar, *raillevr*;' Palsgrave. — F. *railler*, ' to jest, deride, mock;' Cot. [Cf. Span. *rallar*, to grate, scrape, molest, vex; Port. *ralar*, to scrape; apparently from L. *rallum*, a scraper (Pliny); for a Lat. type **rad-lum*, from *rādere*, to scrape. The change of sense from scraping to vexing is in accordance with the usual course of metaphors.] The F. *railler* answers to a Late L. type **rādulare*, from L. *rādula*, a scraper (Lewis), formed from *rādere*, to scrape. See **Rase.** See Littré and Scheler; and Körting, §§ 7719, 7733. **Der.** *raill-er-y*=F. *raillerie*, ' jeasting, merriment, a flowt, or scoff,' Cot. Also *rally* (2).

RAIL (3), a genus of wading birds. (F.) Given by Phillips, ed. 1710, as ' a sort of bird.' Spelt *rayle* in Levins, and in the Catholicon Anglicum; but *raale* in the Book of St. Alban's, fol. f 7, back. — OF. *raale*, *raalle* (Hatzfeld); MF. *rasle*, ' the fowle called a rayle;' Cot. Mod. F. *râle*. Littré notes *raale* as the 14th cent. spelling; also that the Picard form is *reille*, showing that the mod. E. word agrees rather with the Picard than the Central F. form. β. Probably the bird was named from its cry; but we can hardly connect the form *raale* with the OF. *raller*, ' to rattle in the throat,' Cot., mod. F. *râler*.

RAIL (4), part of a woman's night-dress. (E.) For *hrail*. Obsolete; see Halliwell. ' *Rayle* for a womans necke, crevechief, *en quartre doubles*;' Palsgrave. ME. *reʒel*, Owl and Nightingale, 562; see *hræʒel* in Stratmann. AS. *hrægl*, *hreʒl*, swaddling-clothes, Luke, ii. 12.+OFries. *hreil*, *reil*, a garment; OHG. *hregil*, a garment, dress. Teut. type **hragilom*, neut. Root unknown.

RAIMENT, clothing. (F. — L. and Scand.; with F. suffix.) ' With ruffled *rayments*;' Spenser, F. Q. i. 6. 9. ME. *raiment*, Plowman's Tale, pt. iii. st. 30, l. 936 (date uncertain). Short for *arraiment*, of which the ME. form was *araiment*, and the initial *a* easily fell away. ' *Rayment*, or *arayment*, Ornatus;' Prompt. Parv. Cf. MF. *arrée-ment*, ' good array, order, equipage;' Cot. See **Array.**

RAIN, water from the clouds. (E.) ME. *rein*; spelt *reyne*, P. Plowman, B. xiv. 66. AS. *regn*, frequently contracted to *rēn*, Grein, i. 371.+Du. *regen*; Icel., Dan., and Swed. *regn*; G. *regen*; Goth. *rign*. β. All from Teut. types **reg-noz*, m., **reg-nom*, n. Prob. not allied to L. *rigāre*, to moisten; nor even to Lith. *roké*, sb., drizzling rain. **Der.** *rain*, verb, AS. *hregnian*, *regnian*, Matt. v. 45 (Northumb. version); *rain-y*, AS. *rēnig*, Grein, i. 372; *rain-bow*, AS. *rēnboga*, Gen. ix. 13; *rain-gauge*.

RAINDEER, the same as **Reindeer,** q. v.

RAISE, to lift up, exalt. (Scand.) A Scand. word; the E. form is *rear*. ME. *reisen*, Wyclif, John, xi. 11; spelt *reʒʒenn*, Ormulum, 15599. — Icel. *reisa*, to raise, make to rise; causal of *risa* (pt. t. *reis*), to rise. So also Dan. *reise*, Swed. *resa*, to raise, though these languages do not employ the verb ' to rise;' Goth. *raisjan*, causal of *reisan*. See **Rise.** Doublet, *rear*.

RAISIN, a dried grape. (F. — L.) ME. *reisin*, spelt *reisyn*, Wyclif, Judges, viii. 2 (later version); King Alisaunder, 5193. — OF. *raisin*, ' a grape, raisin, bunch, or cluster of grapes;' Cot. Cf. Span. *racimo*, a bunch of grapes. — Folk L. *racīmum*, for L. *racēmum*, acc. of *racēmus*, a bunch of grapes; see **Raceme.** Doublet, *raceme*.

RAJAH, a king, prince. (Skt.) In Sir T. Herbert's Travels, p. 53, ed. 1665. Of Skt. origin; from Skt. *rājā*, nom., a king; from the stem *rājan*, a king. The Skt. *rājan* is allied to L. *rex*; see **Regal.** See Yule and Stanford Dict.

RAJPOOT, a prince. (Hind. — Skt.) Hind. *rajpūt*, a prince, lit. the son of a rajah; Wilson, Gloss. of Indian Terms, p. 434. — Skt. *rāj-ā*, a king; *putra-*, a son; so that the lit. sense is ' son of a king.' See Yule and Stanford Dict.

RAKE (1), an instrument for scraping things together, smoothing earth, &c. (E.) ME. *rake*, Chaucer, C. T. 289 (A 287). AS. *raca*, to translate L. *rastrum* in Ælfric's Gloss., l. 9.+Du. *rakel*, a dimin.

form; Dan. *rage*, a poker; Swed. *raka*, an oven-rake (with base *rak-*); allied to Icel. *reka*, a shovel, G. *rechen*, a rake (with base *rek-*). β. From the notion of collecting or heaping up. The root appears in Goth. *rikan* (Teut. type **rekan-*, pt. t. *rak*), to collect, heap up, Rom. xii. 20. Perhaps allied to L. *rog-us*, a funeral pile. **Der.** *rake*, verb, from Icel. *raka*, to rake.

RAKE (2), a wild, gay, dissolute fellow. (E.) 'A gay, dissipated *rake*;' Sheridan, Duenna, ii. 3. First in 1653. Abbreviated from *rake-hell*; which see in Nares. The latter is usually explained to be a 'corruption' of ME. *rakel*, rash; but the examples in the N. E. D. show that this is unfounded. And in fact *rake-hell* is really compounded of *rake* and *hell*. It arose from the phrase given in Udall, Apophthegmes of Erasmus, p. 116 b :—'Suche a feloe as a manne should *rake helle* for.' Hence it meant, as it were, the off-scouring of hell, i.e. one who is very wicked. See **Rake** (1) and **Hell**. **Der.** *rak-ish*, *rak-ish-ly*.

RAKE (3), the projection of the extremities of a ship beyond the keel; the inclination of a mast from the perpendicular. (Scand.) 'In sea-language, the *rake of a ship* is so much of her hull or main body, as hangs over both the ends of her keel;' Phillips, ed. 1710. Evidently from *rake*, to reach; Halliwell. Of Scand. origin; preserved in Swed. dial. *raka*, to reach; *raka fram*, to reach over, project; see *raka* (3) in Rietz. The Dan. *rage*, to project, protrude, jut out, is borrowed from G. *ragen*, to project; perhaps the Swed. word is the same.

RAKEHELL, a rascal. (E.) See **Rake** (2).

RAKI, arrack, spirits. (Turk.—Arab.) See Stanford Dict. Turk. *rāqi*, arrack. — Arab. *'araq*, arrack. See **Arrack**.

RALLENTANDO, in music, a direction to play slower; gradually. (Ital.—L.) Ital. *rallentando*, pres. part. of *rallentare*, to slacken, retard. — Ital. *re-*, again; and *allentare*, to slacken. — L. *re-*, again; *ad-*, to; and *lentāre*, to prolong, from *lentus*, slow. Cf. *relent*, q. v.

RALLY (1), to gather together again, reassemble. (F.—L.) Properly a trans. verb; also used as intransitive. Spelt *rallie* in Cotgrave. It stands for *re-ally*; and Spenser uses *re-allie* nearly in the same sense as *rally*; F. Q. vii. 6. 23. — F. *rallier*, 'to rallie;' Cot. — L. *re-*, again; *ad*, to; and *ligāre*, to bind; see **Re-** and **Ally**. Cf. prov. F. *raller*, to rally, grow convalescent; dial. de la Meuse (Labourasse). ¶ The form *rely* in Barbour's Bruce, iii. 34, &c., is used in the same sense; and is the same word, with the omission of L. *ad*.

RALLY (2), to banter. (F.—Teut.) 'Rally, to play and droll upon, to banter or jeer;' Phillips, ed. 1710. He also gives: 'Rallery, pleasant drolling.' Here *rallery* is another form of *raillery*, and *to rally* is merely another form of *to rail*, which agrees more closely with F. *railler*. See **Rail** (2).

RAM, a male sheep. (E.) ME. *ram*, Chaucer, C. T. 550 (A 548). AS. *ram*, *rom*, Grein; also *ramm*.+Du. *ram*; OHG. *ramm*. Cf. Icel. *ramr*, strong. **Der.** *ram*, verb, to butt as a ram, hence to thrust violently forward, ME. *rammen*, Prompt. Parv., p. 422. Also *rammish*, fetid, Chaucer, C. T. 16355 (G 887). Also *ram-rod*, *ramm-er*.

RAMADAN, a great Mohammedan fast. (Arab.) Spelt *Ramazan*, in Sandys, Trav., p. 56; see Stanford Dict. So called because kept in the ninth month, named *Ramadan*. — Arab. *Ramaḍān*, pron. *Ramazān* in Turkish and Persian. As it is in the ninth month of the lunar year, it may take place in any season; but it is supposed to have been first held in a hot season. The word implies 'consuming fire;' from the Arab. root *ramaḍa*, it was hot. See Devic and Richardson.

RAMBLE, to stray, rove, roam. (E.) The frequentative of a form *rame*, of which there are no clear traces. 'Rame, to gad about, to sprawl, to spread out too much;' Holderness Glossary (E. D. S.); but this is usually *ream* or *raum*. It does not occur till after 1600, though we find ME. *romblynge*, rambling, as a variant of *romynge*, roaming, in P. Plowman, C. vi. 11; cf. Shropsh. *romble*, to ramble. Hence it may have arisen as a frequentative of *roam*. 'Nor is this lower world but a huge Inn, And men the *rambling* passengers;' Howell, Poema, prefixed to his Familiar Epistles, and dated Jan. 1, 1641. And the pl. sb. *rambles* is in Butler, Hudibras, pt. iii. c. 2. 1016 (ed. Bell, vol. ii. p. 161, l. 34). The *b* is excrescent; and *ram-b-le* is for *ramm-le*. 'Rammle, to ramble;' Whitby Glossary. ¶ Perhaps it has been somewhat influenced by the words *ramp* and *romp*; the metaphorical sense 'to wander in talk,' presents no difficulty. **Der.** *ramble*, sb., *rambl-er*, *rambl-ing*.

RAMIFY, to divide into branches. (F.—L.) 'To *ramify* and send forth branches;' Sir T. Browne, Vulg. Errors, b. ii. c. 5. part 6. — F. *ramifier*, 'to branch, put out branches;' Cot. Formed as if from L. **rāmificāre*; from *rāmi-*, for *rāmus*, a branch; and *-ficāre*, due to *facere*, to make. β. Probably *rāmus* = **wrad-mus*; allied to Gk. ῥάδαμνος, a young branch; and to L. *rādix*; Brugmann, i. § 529.

Der. *ramific-at-ion* (as if from L. **rāmificāre*, whence sb. **rāmificā-tio*). Also (from L. *rām-us*) *ram-ous*, *ram-ose*, *ram-e-ous*.

RAMP, to leap or bound, properly, to climb, scramble, rear. (F.—Teut.) 'Ramp, to rove, frisk or jump about, to play gambols or wanton tricks;' Phillips, ed. 1706; and in Palsgrave. Not much used, except in the deriv. *rampant*. ME. *rampen*, used by Chaucer in the sense 'to rage, be furious with anger;' C. T. 13910 (D 3094). Cf. mod. E. *romp*, which is the same word. Gower uses *rampend*, rearing, said of a dragon, in the same way as the F. pp. *rampant*; C. A. iii. 74; bk. vi. 2182. Cf. Prick of Conscience, 2225. — F. *ramper*, 'to creep, run, crawl, or traile itself along the ground; also, to climb;' Cot. β. From a Teut. source. Cf. Bavarian *rampfen*, explained by Schmeller, ii. 96, by the G. *raffen*, to snatch. Scheler, following Diez, says that the old sense of F. *ramper* was to clamber, preserved in mod. F. *rampe*, a flight of steps; and that it is allied to Ital. *rampa*, a claw, grip, *rampare*, to claw, and *rampo*, a grappling-iron. γ. The Ital. *rampare* (appearing in Prov. in the form *rapar*) is, according to Diez, a nasalised form of *rappare*, only used in the comp. *arrappare*, to snatch up, carry off, seize upon; and the base is Teut. RAP, to be in haste, found in Low G. *rappen*, to snatch hastily (Bremen Wörterbuch), Dan. *rappe*, to hasten, make haste, Dan. *rap*, quick, Swed. *rappa*, to snatch, *rapp*, brisk, G. *raffen*, to snatch; see **Rape** (1). δ. But Körting derives Ital. *rampa*, a grip, from Low G. *ramp* (Lübben), Bavar. *rampf*, a cramp, seizure; which is allied to OHG. *rampf*, 2nd grade of OHG. *rimpfan*, to cramp. Cf. **Ripple** (2), **Rimple**. **Der.** *ramp-ant*, chiefly used of a lion rampant, as in Skelton, Against the Scottes, 135, from F. *rampant*, pres. part. of *ramper*; hence *rampant-ly*, *rampanc-y*.

RAMPART, a mound surrounding a fortified place. (F.—L.) We frequently find also *rampire*, *rampier*, or *ramper*. Spelt *rampyre*, Tottell's Miscellany, ed. Arber, p. 172, l. 18 (Assault of Cupid, st. 5); *rampart*, Gascoigne, Fruites of Warre, st. 45. *Rampire* stands for *rampar* (without the final *t*). — MF. *rempart*, *rempar*, 'a rampier, the wall of a fortresse;' Cot. Cf. *remparer*, 'to fortifie, enclose with a rampier;' id. β. The OF. *rempar*, *rampar* (Supp. to Godefroy), is the true form; in *rempart*, the *t* is excrescent. *Rempar* corresponds (nearly) to Ital. *riparo*, a defence, and is a verbal sb. from *remparer*, to defend, answering (nearly) to Ital. *riparare*, to defend. γ. F. *remparer* is 'to put again into a state of defence;' from *re-*, again, *em-* for *en*, in, and *parer*, to defend, borrowed from Ital. *parare*, which is from L. *parāre*, to prepare, make ready. The Ital. *riparare* is the same word, with the omission of the preposition. See **Re-**, **Em-**, and **Parry**.

RAMPION, a species of bellflower, sometimes used for salads. (F.—L.?) In Tusser's Husbandrie; § 40. Apparently evolved from *rampions*, which was taken to be plural.—F. *raiponce*, 'rampions;' Cot. The *m* may have been suggested by the Ital. *ramponzoli*, pl. (Florio). Kluge, s. v. *rapunzel*, cites Late L. *rapuncium*, which he connects with L. *rāpa*, a turnip. So also in Körting, § 7759. Hatzfeld thinks the connexion with *rāpa* unlikely.

RAMSONS, broad-leaved garlic. (E.) For *hramsons*. '*Allium ursinum*, broad-leaved garlic, ramsons;' Johns, Flowers of the Field. *Ramsons* = *rams-en-s*, a double pl. form, where *-en* represents the old AS. plural, as in E. *ox-en*, and *-s* is the usual E. plural-ending. We also find ME. *ramsis*, *ramzys*, *ramseys*, Prompt. Parv. p. 422; and Way says that Gerarde calls the *Allium ursinum* by the names 'ramsies, ramsons, or buckrams.' Here again, the suffixes *-is*, *-eys*, *-ies* are pl. endings. AS. *hramsan*, ramsons; Gloss. to Cockayne, AS. Leechdoms; a pl. form, from sing. *hramsa*.+OLow G. *hramsa*, sing. (Gallée); Swed. *rams-lök* (*lök* = leek), bear-garlic; Dan. *rams*, or *rams-lög* (*lög* = leek); Bavarian *ramsen*, *ramsel* (Schmeller); Lithuan. *kermuszė*, *kermuszis*, wild garlic (Nesselmann). Further allied to Gk. κρόμυον, an onion, Irish *creamh*, garlic, W. *craf*; Stokes-Fick, p. 98; Brugmann, i. § 647. All from an Idg. base **krem-* (**krom-*).

RANCH, RANCHO, a cattle-breeding farm. (Span.—Teut.) *Ranch* is the Anglicised form of Span. *rancho*, a mess, a set of persons who eat together; applied in America to the *ranchos*, or rude huts for herdsmen to lodge and mess together. Minsheu gives Span. *rancho* with the sense of 'a ranke, an order or place where euery one is to keep or abide;' mod. *rancheria*, 'a cottage where labourers mess.' Allied to F. *rang*; see **Rank** (1). From OHG. *hring*, a ring; also (like Span. *rancho*) a clear space in the midst of a ring of people. So in Körting, § 8088. See my Notes on E. Etym., p. 241.

RANCID, sour, having a rank smell. (L.) A late word; in Bailey, vol. i. ed. 1735; first found in 1646.—L. *rancidus*, rancid.— L. **rancēre*, to stink; only used in the pres. part. *rancens*, stinking. ¶ This word has probably influenced the sense of the E. adj. *rank*; see **Rank** (2). **Der.** *rancid-ly*, *-ness*; also *ranc-our*, q. v.

RANCOUR, spite, deep-seated enmity. (F.—L.) ME. *rancour*, Chaucer, C. T. 2786 (A 2784). — OF. *rancour*, 'rankor,

hatred;' Cot.—L. *rancōrem*, acc. of *rancor*, spite, orig. rancidiness.
—L. **rancēre*, to be rancid; see **Rancid.** Cf. Norm. dial.
rancœur (Moisy). **Der.** *rancor-ous*, *rancor-ous-ly*.

RANDOM, done or said at hazard, left to chance. (F.—Teut.)
The older form is *randon*, or *randoun*; and the older sense is 'force,'
impetuosity, &c., the word being used as a sb. It was often used
with respect to the rush of a battle-charge, and the like. 'Kyng
and duyk, eorl and baroun Prikid the stedis with gret *raundoun*;'
King Alisaunder, l. 2483. It often formed part of an adverbial
phrase, such as *in a randoun*, in a furious course, Barbour's Bruce, vi.
139, xvii. 694, xviii. 130; *intill a randoun*, id. xix. 596; *in randoun
richt*, with downright force, id. v. 632. So also *at randon*, orig. with
rushing force, hence, left without guidance, left to its own force,
astray, &c. 'The gentle lady, loose *at randon* lefte, The greene-wood
long did walke, and wander wide *At wilde adventure, like a forlorne
wefte*;' Spenser, F. Q. iii. 10. 36. [The change from final *-n* to *-m* may
have been due to the influence of *whilom, seldom*; so also *ransom*.]—
OF. *randon*, 'the swiftnesse and force of a strong and violent
stream; whence *aller à grand randon*, to goe very fast, or with a
great and forced pace;' Cot. Thus the E. adv. *at random* answers
to F. *à randon*. β. A difficult word; Diez compares OF. *randir*,
to press on, Span. *de rendon, de rondon*, rashly, intrepidly, abruptly
(nearly like E. *at random*), OF. *randonner*, 'to run swiftly, violently,'
Cot., and refers them all to G. *rand*, an edge, rim, brim, margin.
Hence also Ital. *a randa*, near, with difficulty, exactly; of which the
lit. sense is 'close to the edge or brim,' Span. *randa*, lace, border of
a dress. γ. The difficulty is in the connexion of ideas; but Cotgrave really gives the solution, viz. that *randon* refers to the force of
a *brimming* river. Whoever has to cross a mountain-stream must
feel much anxiety as to whether it is *full* or not; at one time it is a
mere rill, a few hours later its force sweeps all before it. This common and natural solution is probably the right one. Cf. G. *bis am
rande voll*, full to the brim; *am rande des Todes*, on the brink of
death, at death's door; *eine sache zu rande bringen*, to bring a thing to
the brim, to fulfil or accomplish it. So also OF. *sang respandus à
gros randons*, blood shed 'by great gushes, or in great quantity,'
Cot.; lit. in brimming streams. δ. The G. *rand* is cognate with
AS. *rand*, rim, rim of a shield, verge (Grein), Icel. *rönd*, a rim, border,
Dan. *rand*, a rim, streak, Swed. *rand*, a stripe; all from a Teut.
base **rand-*, Idg. **ram-t-* (Kluge); allied to **Rim** and to **Rind.**
Cf. prov. G. *ranft*, a crust, a margin (Flügel); OHG. *ramft*, rind.

RANEE, RANI, a Hindoo queen. (Hind.—Skt.) Hind. *rānī*,
queen (Forbes).—Skt. *rājnī*, queen; fem. of *rājā*, king. See Yule.
See **Rajah.**

RANGE, to rank, or set in a row, to set in order, to rove. (F.—
OHG.) The sense of 'to rove' arose from the scouring of a
country by small troops or ranks of armed men; the orig. sense is
'to set in a rank,' to array. ME. *rengen* (corresponding to OF.
renger, the form used in the 14th cent., according to Littré), Rob.
of Brunne, p. 40, l. 26. 'The helle liun *rengeth* euer abuten' = the
lion of hell is always *ranging* (roving) about; Ancren Riwle, p. 164.
Also *rangen*: '*rangit* all on raw,' arrayed all in a row; Barbour,
Bruce, xi. 431.—F. *ranger* (OF. *ranger, renger*), 'to range, rank,
order, array;' Cot.—F. *rang*, 'a ranke,' id. See **Rank** (1).
Der. *range*, sb., Antony, iii. 13. 5. Also, *rang-er*, esp. one who
ranges a forest, Minsheu, ed. 1627 (see his explanation); *rang-er-ship*.

RANK (1), row or line of soldiers, class, order, grade, station.
(F.—OHG.) Spelt *ranck*, Spenser, F. Q. iii. 6. 35 (the verb *to
ranck* is in the same stanza). [The ME. form is *reng*, Chaucer,
C. T. 2596; also *renk*, St. Brandan, ed. Wright, p. 12 (Stratmann); see
reng in Stratmann. *Reng* became *renk*, altered afterwards to *rank* in
accordance with a similar change made in the F. original.]—OF.
reng, later *rang*, 'a ranke, row, list, range;' Cot. He gives both
forms; and Godefroy (in Supp.) has *renc, reng, rang*. Scheler
gives the Picard form as *ringue*, Prov. *renc*. — OHG. *hring* or
hrinc, a ring; cognate with E. **Ring**, q.v. And see **Harangue.**
The sense changed from 'ring' of men to a 'row' of men, or a
file irrespective of the shape in which they were ranged. The
Bret. *renk* is borrowed from OF., and the other Celtic forms from
F. or E. The G. *rang* is borrowed back again from F. *rang*.
Der. *rank*, verb (Spenser, as above); also *range*, q.v.; also *ar-range*,
de-range.

RANK (2), adj., coarse in growth, very fertile, rancid, strong-
scented. (E.) The sense 'rancid' or 'strong-scented' is late, and
perhaps due to association with L. *rancidus*, E. rancid, or with
OF. *rance*, 'musty, fusty, stale,' Cot.; but the sense may have been
developed independently of this. 'As rank as a fox;' Tw. Night,
ii. 5. 136. ME. *rank, ronk*. '*Ronk* and *ryf*;' Allit. Poems, ed.
Morris, A. 843 (*or* 844). Often with the sense of 'proud' or
'strong;' thus *ronke* is a various reading for *stronge*, Ancren Riwle,
p. 268, note *c*. AS. *ranc*, strong, proud, forward; Grein, ii. 363.+

Du. *rank*, lank, slender (like things of quick growth); MDu. *ranck*,
slender; Low G. *rank*, slender, grown high; whence (perhaps),
NFries. *rank*, Icel. *rakkr* (for **rankr*), straight, slender; Swed. *rank*,
long and thin; Dan. *rank*, erect. β. Perhaps allied to OSax.
rink, AS. *rinc*, a grown man, a warrior (N. E. D.). Apparently
from **renk*, nasalised form of **rek*, to stretch out; see **Rack** (2).

RANKLE, to fester. (F.—L.—Gk.) In Levins; spelt *rankyll*
in Palsgrave. It is rare in ME., but appears in Sir Beves of Hamptoun, ed. Kölbing, 2832; also in the Boke of St. Alban's, fol. a 3,
back: 'make the legges to *rankle*.' The corresponding AF. verb
is *rancler*; the f. pp. *ranclee*, festered, occurs in the Life of Edw.
Confessor, 4166; whence *aranclee*, putrefied, in the same, 2615.
The verb is formed from the sb. *rancle*, a festering sore, Reliq. Antiq.
i. 52; from AF. *rancle*, Edw. Conf. 2677.—OF. *rancle, raoncle*,
forms which have lost an initial *d*. Godefroy gives *draoncle, raoncle,
drancle, rancle*, an eruption on the skin; and the verb *draoncler,
rancler*, to suppurate, rankle.—Late L. *dracunculus*, a kind of ulcer
or cancer; lit. 'little dragon;' called also *dranculus morbus*
(Ducange), as dragons were thought to be venomous. Dimin. from
L. *draco*, a dragon; see **Dragon.** See my Notes on E. Etym.,
p. 243. Corblet gives the Picard *draoncler*, to fester, and its
etymology.

RANSACK, to search thoroughly. (Scand.) ME. *ransaken*,
Chaucer, C. T. 1007 (A 1005); Genesis and Exodus, ed. Morris,
2323.—Icel. *rannsaka*, to search a house, to ransack; Swed. *ransaka*,
Dan. *ransage*.—Icel. *rann*, a house, abode; and *-saka*, allied to
sækja, to seek. β. The Icel. *rann* stands for *rasn*, by the assimilation so common in Icelandic; and is cognate with Goth. *razn*,
a house, AS. *ærn*, a cot; from Teut. base **ras*, to dwell; see
Rest (1). Icel. *sækja* is cognate with AS. *sēcan*, to seek; see
Seek. Cf. Guernsey and Norm. dial. *ransaquer*, Gael. *rannsaich*;
from Scand. ¶ Not connected with AS. *rān*, Icel. *rān*, plunder,
which is quite different from Icel. *rann*.

RANSOM, redemption, price paid for redemption, release.
(F.—L.) ME. *ransoun, raunson*, Chaucer, C. T. 1178 (A 1176).
The change from final *n* to final *m* is not uncommon; cf. *random*.
Spelt *raunsun*, Ancren Riwle, p. 124, l. 24.—OF. *raenson* (12th
cent., Littré), MF. *rançon*, 'a ransome,' Cot.—L. *redemptiōnem*,
acc. of *redemptio*, redemption, by the usual loss of *d* between two
vowels and preceding an accented syllable. See **Redemption.**
Der. *ransom*, vb.; *ransom-er*. **Doublet,** *redemption*.

RANT, to use violent language. (Du.) In Hamlet, v. 1. 307.
Also in the form *rand*; as in Marston, Malcontent, iv. 4.—MDu.
ranten; '*randen*, or *ranten*, to dote, or to be enraged;' Hexham.
Cf. Low G. *randen*, to attack any one, to call out to one; West-
phal. *rantern*, to prate; prov. E. *randy*, wild, unmanageable, mad.
+G. *ranzen*, to toss about, to make a noise, to couple (as animals).
Root uncertain. **Der.** *rant-er.*

RANTIPOLE, a romping child. (MDu. *or* Low G.) See
E. D. D. First known in 1700 (N. E. D.). The word is a mere
variant of *frampold*. The former element appears in EFries. *wrante-
pot*, also *frante-pot*, a peevish man; cf. MDu. *wranten*, to chide,
MDu. *wrantigh*, quarrelsome. The second element is prob. E.
poll, head. See **Frampold.** *Rantipole* also means a see-saw
(E. D. D.); the second element is then prob. E. *pole*.

RANUNCULUS, a genus of plants, including the buttercup.
(L.) In Evelyn's Diary, Apr. 1, 1644.—L. *rānunculus*, a little frog;
also, a medicinal plant. Formed with double dimin. suffix *-cu-lu-s*
from *rān-un-*, extended from *rāna*, a frog.

RAP (1), to strike smartly, knock; as sb., a smart stroke. (E. or
Scand.) '*Rappe*, a stroke;' Palsgrave. ME. *rap*, sb., *rappen*, vb.,
Prompt. Parv. Cf. Dan. *rap*, a rap, tap; Swed. *rapp*, a stroke,
blow; *rappa*, to beat; G. *rappeln*, to rattle. From a base RAP,
allied to RAT, the base of *ratt-le*; of imitative origin. Cf. *rat-a-tat-
tat*, a knocking at a door. **Der.** *rapp-er.*

RAP (2), to snatch, seize hastily. (Scand.; *partly* L.) There is
some confusion in the forms and senses. α. The ME. *rappen*, to
hasten, is obsolete. It occurs in P. Plowm. A. iv. 23: '*rappynge
swiþe*,' hastening greatly; related to Dan. *rappe sig*, to make haste,
Swed. *rappa sig*; and to Swed. *rapp*, quick, swift. Allied to Icel.
hrapa, MSwed. *rapa*, to hasten; whence ME. *rapen*, as in 'rape þe
to shrifte,' hasten to confession; P. Plowm. B. v. 399; which is
also obsolete. β. We also find the allit. phrase *rappe and rende*,
to snatch up and carry off, as in Roy, Rede Me, ed. Arber, p. 74;
but Chaucer has *rape and renne*, C. T., G 1422. Here *rap* answers
to Swed. *rappa*, to pilfer, allied to G. *raffen*, to snatch; but *rape*
seems to correspond to AF. *raper, rapper*, to seize upon, carry off,
which may be from L. *rapere*, to seize; see Godefroy. Palsgrave
has: 'I *rappe*, I rauysshe;' also, 'I *rappe* or rende, je *rapine*.'
γ. Shak. has: 'What, dear sir, thus *raps* you?' Cymb. i. 6. 51.
Here the verb *rap* is almost certainly a back-formation from the

pp. *rapt* (from L. *raptus*, pp. of *rapere*, above); cf. 'How our partner's *rapt*!' Macb. i. 3. 142. See **Rapt**.

RAPACIOUS, ravenous, greedy of plunder. (L.) In Milton, P.L. xi. 258. 'Who more *rapacious*?' Cowley's Prose Works, ed. Lumby, p. 68, l. 10. A coined word, formed with suffix *-ous* from L. *rapāci-*, decl. stem of *rapax*, grasping. — L. *rapere*, to seize, grasp; see **Rapid**. Der. *rapacious-ly*, *-ness*; also *rapac-i-ty*, from F. *rapacité* 'rapacity,' Cot., which from L. acc. *rapācitātem*.

RAPE (1), a seizing by force, violation. (L.) Levins has: 'a *rape*, raptura, rapina;' and '*to rape*, rapere.' Caxton has: 'murdre, *rape*, and treson;' Reynard the Fox, ed. Arber, ch. 33; p. 95. The word is apparently from L. *rapere*, to seize; whence AF. *rap*, sb., rape, Stat. Realm, i. 211 (and see Britton); cf. F. *rapt*, 'a violent snatching,' Cot. β. Perhaps affected by the (obsolete) ME. *rape*, haste, occurring in the old proverb 'ofte rap reweth' = haste often repents, Proverbs of Hendyng, l. 256, in Spec. of Eng. ed. Morris and Skeat, p. 42. Chaucer accused Adam Scrivener of 'negligence and *rape*,' i.e. haste. And see King Horn, ed. Lumby, 1418; P. Plowman, B. v. 333; Gower, C. A. i. 296; bk. iii. 517. From Icel. *hrapa*, vb., to hasten; cf. *hrapaðr*, a hurry; Swed. *rapp*, Dan. *rap*, brisk, quick. See **Rap** (2). Der. *rape*, verb.

RAPE (2), a plant nearly allied to the turnip. (L.) ME. *rape*, Prompt. Parv. — L. *rāpa*, a turnip; also spelt *rāpum*; whence also MF. *rave*, 'a rape;' Cot. + Gk. ῥάπυς, a turnip; cf. ῥαφανίς, a radish; Russ. *riepa*, a turnip; G. *rübe*. Der. *rape-oil*, *rape-cake*.

RAPE (3), a division of a county, used in Sussex. (E.) Still in use. It occurs in Arnold's Chron. (1502), ed. 1811, p. 181; and also in Domesday Book in the form *rap* (N. E. D.). It is prob. a native word. It cannot be borrowed from Icel. *hreppr*, a district, as suggested by Vigfusson. The spelling *rope*, occurring in 1380, suggests an AS. form *rāp*; so that a connexion with AS. *rāp*, a rope, is possible; cf. prov. E. *rope*, a measure, a rood (of land).

RAPID, swift. (F. — L.; *or* L.) In Milton, P. L. ii. 532, iv. 227. — F. *rapide*, 'violent;' Cot. [Or directly from Latin.] — L. *rapidum*, acc. of *rapidus*, rapid, quick; lit. snatching away. — L. *rapere*, to snatch. Brugmann, i. § 477. Der. *rapid-ly*, *-ness*; *rapid-i-ty*, from F. *rapidité* < L. acc. *rapiditātem*. And see *rap-ine*, *rav-age*, *rav-en* (2), *rav-ine*, *rav-ish*, *rapt-or-i-al*, *rapt-ure*, *rapt*.

RAPIER, a light, narrow sword. (F.) In Shak. Temp. v. 84. In A.D. 1579, 'the long foining *rapier*' is described in Bullein's Dialogue between Sorenesse and Chirurge as 'a new kynd of instrument;' see note in Ben Jonson's Every Man, ed. Wheatley, introd. pp. xliv, xlv. — F. *rapiere* (mod. F. *rapière*), 'an old rusty rapier;' Cot. β. Of unknown origin, see Scheler and Littré; but Mr. Wheatley's note shows that, in 1530, la *rapiere* was 'the spanische sworde;' see Supp. to Palsgrave, p. 908, l. 1. This makes it probable that Diez's solution (rejected by Littré) is right, and that that *rapiere* is for *raspiere*, a name given in contempt, meaning a rasper or poker. Hence also 'a *proking-spit* of Spaine' means a Spanish rapier (Nares). So also mod. Prov. *raspiero*, *rapiero*, a rapier, an old sword (Mistral), allied to *raspo*, a rasp, a dough-knife (id.). Cf. Span. *raspadera*, a raker (Neuman), from *raspar*, to rasp, scrape, file, scratch; also *raspa*, a shoemaker's knife (Pineda), as well as a rasp; see **Rasp**.

RAPINE, plunder, violence. (F. — L.) In Shak. Titus, v. 2. 59. ME. *rapyne*, Hoccleve, De Regimine Principum, 4834. — F. *rapine*, 'rapine, ravine,' Cot. — L. *rapīna*, plunder, robbery. — L. *rapere*, to seize; see **Rapid**. Doublet, *ravine*.

RAPPAREE, an Irish robber. (Irish.) 'The Irish formed themselves into many bodies . . . called *rapparees*,' &c.; Burnet, Hist. of Own Time, b. v. an. 1690 (R.). '*Rapparees* and banditti;' Bolingbroke, A Letter on Archbp. Tillotson's Sermon (R.). — Irish *rapaire*, a noisy fellow, sloven, robber, thief; cf. *rapal*, noise, *rapach*, noisy. So also Gael. *rapair*, a noisy fellow. All perhaps from E. *rabble*. See **Rabble**.

RAPPEE, a kind of snuff. (F. — OHG.) Not in Todd's Johnson. ''Tis good *rapee*;' Garrick. High Life below Stairs, A. i. Sc. 2. — F. *râpé*, lit. rasped; Littré quotes: 'J'ai du bon tabac . . j'ai du fin et du *rapé*;' Lattaignant, Chanson. Pp. of *râper*, to rasp, of Teut. origin. See **Rasp**.

RAPT, carried away. (L.) 'Rapt in a chariot drawn by fiery steeds;' Milton, P. L. iii. 522. Where Higden (i. 196) has 'a Iove *raptam*,' the 15th c. E. trans. has '*rapte* by Iupiter.' — L. *raptus*, pp. of *rapere*, to seize, snatch away; see **Rapid**. And see **Rap** (2).

RAPTORIAL, in the habit of seizing. (L.) Used of birds of prey. Formed with suffix *-al* (< L. *-ālis*) from *raptōri-*, decl. stem of *raptor*, one who seizes. — L. *rapere*, to seize; see **Rapture**, **Rapid**.

RAPTURE, transport, ecstasy. (L.) In Shak. Troil. ii. 2. 122; iii. 2. 138. The word seems to be a pure coinage; there is no

F. *rapture*, nor Late L. *raptūra*. Formed with suffix *-ure* (as in *conject-ure*, &c.) from *rapt-us*, pp. of *rapere*, to seize; see **Rapid**. Der. *raptur-ous*, *raptur-ous-ly*.

RARE, thin, scarce, excellent. (F. — L.) In Levins, ed. 1570. — F. *rare*, 'rare;' Cot. — L. *rārum*, acc. of *rārus*, rare. Cf. Gk. ἀραιός, thin. Der. *rare-ly*, *rare-ness*. Also *rari-fy*, from MF. *rarefier*, 'to rarifie,' Cot., as if from L. *rārēficāre*, but the classical L. word is *rārefacere*, from *facere*, to make. Also *rarefact-ion*, from F. *rarefaction*, 'a making thin,' Cot. < L. acc. *rārefactiōnem*, from *rārefacere*. Also *rar-i-ty*, Temp. ii. 1. 58, from F. *rarité*, 'rareness, rarity,' Cot., from L. acc. *rāritātem*.

RASCAL, a knave, villain. (F.) ME. *raskaille*, used collectively, 'the common herd,' Morte Arthur, ed. Brock, 2881. See Prompt. Parv., and Way's note. 'The route of *rascaile*,' i.e. the rabble; Rob. of Brunne, tr. of Langtoft, p. 276. 'Certain animals, not accounted as beasts of chace, were so termed; . . the hart, until he was six years old, was accounted *rascayle*;' Way. He also cites: '*plebecula*, lytell folke or *raskalle*; *plebs*, folk or *raskalle*.' Cf. '*Rascall*, refuse beest;' Palsgrave. β. As the word was a term of the chase, and as it has the F. suffix *-aille*, it must needs be of F. origin. — AF. *rascaille*, Gaimar, 1826; AF. *raskayle*, rabble, Langtoft, i. 136 (F. *racaille*); OF. *rascaille*, *rescaille* (Supp. to Godefroy); 'the rascality or base and rascall sort, the scumme, dregs, offals, outcasts, of any company,' Cot. γ. Of unknown origin; but the form *rescaille* suggests a comparison with mod. Prov. *rascala*, *rescala*, *rascalha* (Mistral), to take off the inner skin of the chestnut, i.e. to 're-scale;' as if it were a sb. formed from OF. *re-*, again, and *escaille*, a scale (F. *écaille*). Hatzfeld, s.v. *écaille*, notes that this is a Normanno-Picard form. Cf. **Scale** (1). Moisy gives Norm. *écaler*, to shell oysters, to break or tear to pieces. The sense of 'fragments' or 'second scalings' would be appropriate; in fact, we find ME. '*rascaly*, or refuse, Caducum,' in Prompt. Parv., and mod. F. *racaille*, trash, rubbish. Der. *rascal-ly*, *rascal-i-ty*.

RASE, to scrape, efface, demolish, ruin. (F. — L.) Often spelt *raze*, esp. in the sense to demolish; but it makes no real difference. See **Raze**. ME. *rasen*, to scrape; Prompt. Parv. — F. *raser*, 'to shave, sheere, raze, or lay levell, to touch or grate on a thing in passing by it,' Cot. — Late L. *rāsāre*, to demolish, graze; frequentative verb formed from *rāsum*, supine of L. *rādere*, to scrape. Allied to *rōdere*, to gnaw. — √RAD, to scratch; cf. Skt. *rad*, to split, divide, *rada-s*, a tooth. Fick, i. 739. Der. *ras-ure*, from F. *rasure*, 'a razing out,' Cot.; *ab-rade*; *e-rase*, q.v., *e-ras-ure*; *ras-or-i-al*, q. v.; *raz-or*, q. v.; *rash* (2), q.v. And see *rodent*, *rat*. Doublet, *raze*.

RASH (1), hasty, headstrong. (E.) ME. *rcsh*, *rasch*, Allit. Poems, ed. Morris, A. 1166 (or 1167). The final *-sch* suggests as AS. form *rasc*, with AS. *sc* = Scand. *-sk*, as usual. + Dan. and Swed. *rask*, brisk, quick, rash; Icel. *röskr*, vigorous; Du. *rasch*, quick; G. *rasch*, quick, vigorous, rash; NFries. *radsk*, quick. Brugmann, i. § 795, connects this word with OHG. *rado*, AS. *raðe*, quickly. Der. *rash-ly*, *-ness*; perhaps *rash-er*. Cf. *rush* (2).

RASH (2), a slight eruption on the body. (F. — L.) In Johnson's Dict. 'A pimple or a *rash*;' Tatler, no. 38, § 11. — MF. *rasche*, 'a scauld, or a running scurfe, or sore; a Languedoc word,' Cot.; also spelt *rasque*. F. *rache*, an eruption on the head, scurf (Littré). Cf. Prov. *rasca*, the itch (Littré). So called because it is scratched; cf. Prov. *rascar*, Span. *rascar*, to scratch, scrape, formed from a Late L. type *rāsicāre*, to scratch, due to L. *rāsum*, supine of *rādere*, to scrape. See **Rase**.

RASH (3), to pull, or tear violently. (F. — L.) 'Rash, to snatch or seize, to tear or rend;' Halliwell. 'The second he took in his arms, and *rashed* him out of the saddle;' Arthur of Little Britain, ed. 1814, p. 83 (R.). Cf. ME. *aracen*, afterwards shortened to *racen*. 'The children from hir arm they gonne *arace*,' i.e. tore away; Chaucer, C. T. 8979 (E 1103). 'Hur heere of can she *race*' = she tore off her hair (Halliwell, s. v. *race*). — F. *arracher*, 'to root up, to pull away by violence,' Cot. — L. *exrādicāre* = *ērādicāre*, to root up; see **Eradicate**, **Radix**.

RASH (4), a kind of inferior silk. (F. — L.) See exx. in Nares. Adapted from F.; with *sh* for *s*. — MF. *ras*, 'the stuffe called serge.' [The same as Ital. *raso*, 'the stuffe called sattine; also shauen, smooth;' Florio.] Named from its smoothness. — F. *ras*, 'shaven;' Cot. — L. *rāsus*, pp. of *rādere*, to scrape. See **Rase**. ¶ Not from Ital. *rascia*, which Florio (perhaps wrongly) explains to mean 'silke rash;' see N. E. D.

RASHER, a thin slice of broiled bacon. (E.?) In Shak. Merch. Ven. iii. 5. 28. '*Rasher* on the coales, *quasi* rashly or hastily roasted;' Minsheu, ed. 1627. This etymology is prob. the right one; cf. '*rashed*, burnt in cooking, by being too hastily dressed,' Halliwell; and see his examples. 'In my former edition of Acts and Monuments, so hastily *rashed* vp at that present, in such shortnesse of time;' Foxe, Martyrs, p. 645, an. 1439 (R.). See **Rash** (1). β. If it meant 'slice,' it is from *rash*, v., to cut, variant of **Rase**, q. v.

RASORIAL, the name of a family of birds. (L.) It includes birds which, like hens, scrape the ground for food. Coined with suffix *-al* (= L. *-ālis*) from *rāsōri-*, decl. stem of *ı̄āsor*, one who scrapes; see **Razor**.

RASP, to scrape, rub with a coarse file. (F.—OHG.) ME. *raspen*, Allit. Poems, ed. Morris, B. 1545.—OF. *rasper*, mod. F. *râper*, to rasp.—OHG. *raspōn*, whence mod. G. *raspeln*, to rasp, a frequentative form. Cf. OHG. *hrespan*, MHG. *respen*, to rake together. Der. *rasp*, sb.; *rasper*; and perhaps *rapier*. Also *rasp-berry*, q. v.

RASP-BERRY, a kind of fruit. (F.—OHG.; *and* E.) The word *berry* is E.; see **Berry**. The old name was *raspis-berry* or *raspise-berry*; see Richardson. '*Raspo*, a fruit or berie called *raspise*;' Florio. 'The *raspis* is called in Latin *Rubus Idæus*;' Holland, tr. of Pliny, b. xxiv. c. 14; the chapter is headed: 'Of Cynosbatos, and the *raspice*.' 'Ampes, *raspises*;' Cot. β. *Raspice*, *raspise* may have been due to MF. *raspeux*, 'rough as a raspe,' Cot.; but this should have given a form *raspous*. But the word was evidently confused with the forms *raspise*, *raspice*, *respice*, which was the name of a thin wine; spelt *respice* in The Squire of Low Degree, 756. γ. This is also a difficult form, but answers to Late L. *raspecia*, raspis-wine, in Ducange; closely allied to Late L. *raspetum*, and to OF. *raspé*, *raspeit*, with the same sense, in Supp. to Godefroy; cf. Span. *vino raspado*, 'a small liquor made by putting water to the grapes after the wine is pressed out, and pressing them over again;' Pineda. All from Late L. *raspa*, a grape (properly, pressed grapes); cf. OF. *raspe*, pressed grapes (Supp. to Godefroy). The connexion with E. *rasp* is shown by the Prov. *raspa*, to rasp, to scrape the ground, to glean grapes (Mistral). Hence this form *raspise* also goes back to the verb to *rasp*. δ. Lastly, *raspise* became *raspis*, *raspes*, and was taken to be a pl. form, whence *raspe*, *rasp*. Indeed, the prov. E. name for *rasp-berries* is *rasps*, to this day; and *raspes* is used by Bacon, Essay 46. The Ital. *raspo* also means a rasp. See **Rasp**.

RAT, a rodent quadruped. (E.) ME. *rat*, or *ratte*, P. Plowman, B. prol. 200. AS. *ræt*, Ælfric's Gloss., Nomina Ferarum; in Wright's Voc. p. 22, col. 2.+MDu. *ratte*, 'a ratt;' Hexham; Du. *rat*; Dan. *rotte*; Swed. *rātta*; G. *ratte*, *ratz*. Cf. also Low L. *ratus*, *rato*, Ital. *ratto*, Span. *rato*, F. *rat*. Also Irish and Gael. *radan*, Bret. *raz*. β. Perhaps from √RAD, to scratch; see **Rodent**. Cf. Skt. *rada-s*, a tooth, elephant; *vajra-rada-s*, a hog. Der. *rat*, verb, to desert one's party, as rats are said to leave a falling house. Also *rat's-bane*, *ratten*.

RATAFIA, the name of a liquor. (F.—Malay.) In Congreve, Way of the World, i. 1. See Stanford Dict. '*Ratafiaz*, a delicious liquor made of apricocks, cherries, or other fruit, with their kernels bruised and steeped in brandy;' Phillips, ed. 1710.—F. *ratafia*, the same; cf. F. *tafia*, rum-arrack. The etymology is perhaps that pointed out in Mahn's Webster.—Malay *araq*, 'arrack, a distilled spirit,' Marsden's Dict., p. 5; and *tāfia*, 'a spirit distilled from molasses (the French name for rum); *araq bram tāfia*, three kinds of spirit, enumerated in an old Malayan writing,' id. p. 65. Again, at p. 39 of the same we find *araq*, *bram*, *tāfia*, arrack, bram, and rum. Omitting *bram*, we have *araq tāfia*, whence *ratafia* is an easy corruption, esp. when it is remembered that *araq* is also called *raq*, in Spanish *raque*, or in English *rack*; see **Rack** (5). β. The use of *both* words together is explicable from the consideration that *araq* is a very general term, and is not a true Malay word, being borrowed from Arabic; see **Arrack**. Thus *ratafia* may mean 'the rack (spirit) called *tafia*.'

RATCH, a rack or bar with teeth. (G.?) '*Ratch*, in clock-work, a wheel with twelve large fangs,' &c.; Phillips, ed. 1710. It is the wheel which makes the clock strike. It seems to answer to G. *ratsche* (N. E. D.). Weigand gives G. *ratsche*, a watchman's rattle, also, a clapper used during Passion Week instead of a bell in a clock-tower. From the verb *ratschen*, to rattle, MHG. *ratzen*, allied to G. *rasseln*, to rattle, and to E. *rattle*; a verb of imitative origin. The Low G. *ratsch* means 'the sound made by tearing a thing forcibly.' Cf. Bavarian *rätschen*, to rattle, &c. in Schmeller. Hence also the dimin. *ratch-et*, in watch-work, 'the small teeth at the bottom of the fusee or barrel that stop it in winding up' (Phillips); but here the *-et* is clearly due to the F. word *rochet*, as in *la roue à rochet*, the ratchet-wheel of a clock (Hatzfeld); this is a different word, and cognate with Ital. *rocchetto*, a bobbin to wind silk on, a rocket or squib, the wheel 'about which the cord or string of a clock goeth,' Torriano. From OHG. *rocco*, G. *rocken*, a distaff; see **Rock** (3) and **Rocket**.

RATE (1), a proportion, allowance, standard, price, tax. (F.—L.) In Spenser, F. Q. iv. 8. 19.—OF. *rate*, price, value (Roquefort); not

in Cotgrave.—L. *rata*, fem. of *ratus*, determined, fixed, settled, pp. of *reor*, I think, judge, deem. Both *ratum* and *rata* occur as sbs. in Late L. Cf. Brugmann, i. § 200. Der. *rate*, verb; *rat-able*, *rat-abl-y*, *rat-able-ness*, *rate-payer*. And see *ratio*, *ration*, *reason*, *rat-i-fy*.

RATE (2), to scold, chide. (F.—L.) In Shak. Merch. Ven. i. 3. 108. Sometimes supposed to be a peculiar use of the word above, as though to *rate* meant to *tax*, and so to chide. But, if this were so, we should expect to find *rate*, to value, in earlier use; whereas, on the contrary, the present word is the older of the two, being found in the 14th century. Palsgrave distinguishes between 'I *rate* one, I set one to his porcyon or stynte,' and 'I *rate* or chyde one.' ME. *raten*, to chide; 'He shal be *rated* of his studying' = he shall be scolded for his studying, Chaucer, C. T. 3463. Moreover, we find the fuller form *araten*, to reprove; see P. Plowman, B. xi. 98; 'rebuked and *arated*,' id. xiv. 163.—OF. *aratter*, variant of *areter*, to accuse (Godefroy); also *rater*, variant of *reter*, *repter*, to accuse, blame (id.).—L. **adreputāre*; from *ad*, to (prefix), and *reputāre*, to repute, which in Late L. meant to impute to, ascribe to (Lewis). See **Repute**.

RATH, early, **RATHER**, sooner. (E.) *Rather*, sooner, earlier, is the comp. form of *rath*, soon, now obsolete. We also find *rathest*, soonest. ME. *rath*, early, ready, quick, swift, *rathe*, adv., soon; comp. *rather*; superl. *rathest*, soonest. 'Why rise ye so *rathe*' = why rise ye so early, Chaucer, C. T. 3766 (A 3768). The word has lost an initial *h*, and stands for *hrath*. AS. *hraðe*, adv., quickly, comp. *hraðor*, superl. *hraðost*; from the adj. *hræð*, *hreð*, also written *hræd*, *hred*, quick, swift, Grein, ii. 99, 100.+Icel. *hraðr*, swift, fleet; MHG. *hrad*, quick; (perhaps) Du. *rad*, swift.

RATIFY, to sanction, confirm. (F.—L.) In Levins; and in Skelton, Colin Clout, 716. Spelt *ratyfye* in Palsgrave.—F. *ratifier*, 'to ratifie;' Cot.—Late L. *ratificāre*, to confirm.—L. *rati-*, for *ratus*, fixed; and *-ficāre*, for *facere*, to make. See **Rate** (1) and **Fact**. Der. *ratific-at-ion*.

RATIO, the relation of one thing to another. (L.) Mathematical; in Phillips, ed. 1706.—L. *ratio*, calculation, relation; cf. L. *ratus*, determined, pp. of *reor*, I think, deem. See **Rate** (1). Doublets, *ration*, *reason*.

RATION, rate or allowance of provisions. (F.—L.) In Phillips, ed. 1706.—F. *ration*, a ration; see Littré.—L. *ratiōnem*, acc. of *ratio*, a calculation, reckoning; so that a *ration* is a computed share for soldiers, &c., according to the reckoning of their number; cf. *ratus*, determined; see **Rate** (1). Der. *ration-al*, reasonable, Minsheu, ed. 1627, from F. *rational*, 'reasonable,' Cot.; hence, *ration-al-ly*, *ration-al-ise*, *-ism*, *-ist*, *-ist-ic*; *ration-al-i-ty*. Also *ratio-cin-at-ion*, Minsheu, from F. *ratiocination*, 'a discoursing, discussion,' from L. *ratiocinātiōnem*, acc. of *ratiocinātio*, which from *ratiocinārī*, to reckon, compute, a verb formed from the sb. *ratiocinium*, a computation = *ratio-ci-ni-um*, formed by various suffixes from the base of *ratio*. Doublets, *ratio*, *reason*.

RATLINES, RATLINS, RATTLINGS, the small transverse ropes traversing the shrouds of a ship and forming a ladder. (F.?) '*Rare-lines* or *Rattlings*, in a ship, those lines with which are made the steps ladderwise to get up the shrouds,' &c.; Phillips, ed. 1710. But the old form was *raddelyne*, or *radelynyng of the shrowdes*, Naval Accounts (1485-97), ed. Oppenheim, pp. 185, 277. Perhaps the same as prov. E. *raddlings*, or *raddles*, long rods twisted between upright stakes (which the *ratlins* resemble). *Raddle* appears to be the same word as *radyll*, the rail of a cart (Palsgrave). Perhaps from AF. *reidel*, OF. *ridelle*, *rudelle* (Supp. to Godefroy, s.v. *ridelle*), F. *ridelle*, 'raile of a cart,' Cot. β. The Du. word is *weeflijn*, i. e. weaving line or web-line, prob. because they cross the shrouds as if interwoven with them. *Rare-lines*, i. e. thin lines, is obviously a corruption.

RATTAN, a Malacca cane. (Malay.) In Sir T. Herbert, Travels, ed. 1665, p. 95. Spelt *rattoon* in Pepys, Diary, Sept. 13, 1660. See Stanford Dict. Spelt *ratan* in Todd's Johnson.—Malay *rōtan*, 'the rattan-cane, Calamus rotang;' Marsden's Dict., p. 152. Made of the peeled stem of a climbing palm.—Malay *raut*, to peel, pare.

RATTEN, to take away a workman's tools for not paying his contribution to the trades' union, or for having offended the union. (F.—Late L.—Teut.) Modern; in Halliwell. The word was frequently used in connexion with Sheffield, where *ratten* is the local word for a rat. '*Ratten*, a rat;' Hunter's Hallamshire Glossary. The usual sense is 'to do secret mischief,' which is afterwards attributed to the *rattens* or *rats*. 'I have been *rattened*; I had just put a new cat-gut band upon my lathe, and last night the *rats* have carried it off;' Notes and Queries, 3 S. xii. 192; see E. D. D. β. The prov. E. *ra'ten* is the same as ME. *raton*, *ratoun*, a rat, P. Plowman, B. prol. 158.—F. *raton*, 'a little rat;' Cot.—Late L. *ratōnem*, acc. of *rato*, the same as *ratus*, a rat; a word of Teut. origin. See **Rat**.

RATTLE, to clatter, to make a din. (E.) For *hrattle*, initial *h* being lost. ME. *ratelen*, Arthur and Merlin, 7858 (Stratmann). — AS. **hrætelan*, only preserved in AS. *hrætele, hratele,* or *hrætelwyrt,* rattle-wort, a plant which derives its name from the rattling of the seeds in the capsules; A. S. Leechdoms, ed. Cockayne, iii. 333.+Du. *ratelen,* to rattle; *ratel,* a rattle; G. *rasseln,* to rattle; *rassel,* a rattle. β. The form of the word is frequentative; and the sense is 'to keep on making a noise represented by the syllable *hrat,*' this syllable being of imitative origin; allied to Gk. κραδαίνειν, to shake. Cf. *rat-a-tat-tat* as the imitation of a knock at a door. So also Gk. κρότος, a loud knock, κροτεῖν, to knock, make to rattle, κροταλίζειν, to rattle; κρόταλον, a rattle. Der. *rattle,* sb.; *rattle-snake,* a snake with a rattle at the end of its tail; in Capt. Smith's Works, ed. Arber, p. 955; also *rattle-traps,* small knick-knacks, from *traps* =goods; see **Trap** (2).

RAUCOUS, hoarse. (L.) Added by Todd to Johnson.—L. *raucus,* hoarse; by changing -*us* to -*ous* (as often). Allied to L. *rāuus,* hoarse, Skt. *ru,* to sound; cf. **Rumour.** Der. *rauc-ity,* Bacon, Nat. Hist. § 700.

RAUGHT, pt. t. and pp. of **Reach,** q. v.

RAVAGE, plunder, devastation, ruin. (F.—L.) The sb. is the more orig. word. Both sb. and verb are in Minsheu, ed. 1627.—F. *ravage,* 'ravage, havocke, spoil;' Cot. Formed, with the usual suffix -*age* (< L. -*āticum*), from *rav-ir,* to bear away suddenly; the sb. *rav-age* was esp. used of the devastation caused by storms and torrents; see Littré.—Folk L. **rapīre,* for L. *rapere,* to seize, snatch, bear away; see **Ravish.** Der. *ravage,* vb., from F. *ravager,* 'to ravage,' Cot.; *ravag-er.*

RAVE, to be mad, talk like a madman. (F.—L.) ME. *raven,* Chaucer, C. T. 16427 (G 959).—OF. *raver,* cited by Diez (s. v. *rêver*) as a Lorraine word; the derivative *ravasser,* 'to rave, to talk idly,' is given in Cotgrave, who also explains *resver* (F. *rêver*) by 'to rave, dote, speak idly.' Godefroy has OF. *resver, raver, rever,* to stroll about, also to rave; cf. F. *râver,* dial. de la Meuse (Labourasse); mod. Prov. *rava,* to rave (Mistral). β. The word presents great difficulties; see *rêver* in Diez and Scheler; but the solution offered by Diez is plausible, viz. that OF. *râver* is allied to Span. *rabiar,* to rave, both verbs being formed from the Late L. and Span. *rabia,* rage, allied to L. *rabiēs,* rage. From L. *rabere,* to rage. See **Rage.**

RAVEL, to untwist, unweave, entangle. (MDu.) The orig. sense has reference to the untwisting of a string or woven texture, the ends of the threads of which become entangled together in a confused mass. To *unravel* is to disentangle, to separate the confused threads. 'The *ravelled* sleave [the entangled floss-silk] of care;' Macb. ii. 2. 37. To *ravel out* is hardly to disentangle (as in Schmidt), but rather to unweave. 'Must I *ravel out* My *weaved-up* folly;' Rich. II, iv. 228; cf. Haml. iii. 4. 186; and see examples in Richardson. 'To *rauell* or untwist;' Minsheu, ed. 1627.—MDu. *ravelen,* 'to ravell, or cadgell,' Hexham; he also explains *verwerren* by 'to embroile, to entangle, to bring into confusion or disorder, or to cadgill.' The same as mod. Du. *rafelen,* EFries. *rafeln,* to fray out, to unweave; Low G. *reffeln,* to fray out, ravel, pronounced *rebeln* or *rebbeln* in Hanover and Brunswick (Bremen Wörterbuch); Pomeranian *rabbeln, uprabbeln,* to ravel out; Low G. *rebbeln ut,* to ravel out (Danneil). We even find AS. *ā-rafian,* to unravel; Gregory's Pastoral Care, ed. Sweet, p. 245, l. 22. Der. *un-ravel.*

RAVELIN, a detached work in fortification, with two embankments raised before the counterscarp. (F.—Ital.) 'In bulwarks, *rav'lins,* ramparts for defence;' Ben Jonson, Underwoods, xiii, On the Poems of Sir J. Beaumont, l. 4.—F. *ravelin,* 'a ravelin;' Cot. Cf. Span. *rebellin,* Port. *rebelim,* Ital. *rivellino,* a ravelin. β. It is supposed that the Ital. word is the original, as seems indicated by the old spelling in that language.—MItal. *ravellino, revellino,* 'a rauelin, a wicket, or a posterne-gate; also the uttermost bounds of the wals of a castle, or sconces without the wals;' Florio. γ. But the origin of the Ital. word is unknown. The suggestion, from L. *re-,* back, and *uallum,* a rampart, is unlikely; see Körting, § 8046.

RAVEN (1), a well-known bird. (E.) For *hraven,* an initial *h* being lost. ME. *raven,* Chaucer, C. T. 2146 (A 2144). AS. *hræfn, hrefn,* a raven, Grein, ii. 100.+Du. *raaf,* raven; Icel. *hrafn;* Dan. *ravn;* OLow G. *hraƀan* (Gallée); G. *rabe,* OHG. *hraban.* Teut. type **hraƀnoz,* m. β. No doubt named from its cry. Cf. L. *crepāre,* to rattle.

RAVEN (2), to plunder with violence, to devour voraciously. (F.—L.) Quite unconnected with the word above, and differently pronounced. The verb is made from an obsolete sb., viz. ME. *ravine,* plunder, which accounts for the spelling *ravin* in Shak. Meas. for Meas. i. 2. 133. 'Foules of *ravyne*' = birds of prey, Chaucer, Parl. of Foules, l. 323. So also *rauyne,* plunder, Ch. tr. of Boethius, b. i. pr. 4, l. 51; *rauiner,* a plunderer, id. b. i. pr. 3, l. 57.—AF. *ravine,* plunder; Liber Custumarum, p. 18, l. 26; OF. *ravine,* rapidity, impetuosity (Burguy); mod. F. *ravine;* see **Ravine.** [This OF.

ravine must orig. have had the sense of plunder, as in AF.]—L. *rapīna,* plunder, pillage; see **Rapine.** Der. *raven-ing; raven-ous,* ME. *ravynous,* Lydgate, Minor Poems, p. 159, from F. *ravineux,* 'ravenous, violent, impetuous, like a forcible stream,' Cot.; *raven-ous-ly, -ness.* Note that ME. *ravine,* mod. E. *ravine,* and E. *rapine* are all one and the same.

RAVINE, a hollow gorge among mountains. (F.—L.) Modern; added by Todd to Johnson.—F. *ravine,* a hollow worn away by floods; explained by Cotgrave to mean 'a great floud, a ravine or inundation of waters;' showing that, even in E., a *ravine* was a flood. In still older French, it means impetuosity, violence. —L. *rapīna,* plunder, hence violence; see **Rapine.** And see **Raven** (2).

RAVISH, to seize with violence, fill with ecstasy. (F.—L.) ME. *rauischen* (with *u* for *v*), Chaucer, tr. of Boethius, b. i. pr. 3, l. 25; *rauissen,* id. b. iv. pr. 5, l. 16; b. i. met. 5, l. 3.—F. *raviss-,* stem of pres. part. of *ravir,* to ravish, snatch away hastily. Cf. Ital. *rapire.*—Folk L. **rapīre,* for L. *rapere,* to snatch; with a change of conjugation; see **Rapine, Rapid.** Der. *ravish-er, ravish-ing,* Macb. ii. 1. 55; *ravish-ment,* All's Well, iv. 3. 281, from F. *ravissement,* 'a ravishing, a ravishment,' Cot.

RAW, uncooked, unprepared, sore. (E.) For *hraw,* an initial *h* being lost. ME. *raw,* K. Alisaunder, 4932. AS. *hrēaw;* spelt *hrǣw,* Cockayne's Leechdoms, i. 254, l. 4.+Du. *raauw;* Icel. *hrár;* Dan. *raa,* raw, crude; Swed. *rå,* raw, green; OHG. *rāo* (declined as *rāwer, rouwer*), MHG. *rou,* G. *roh.* Teut. types **hrawoz, *hrēwoz.* β. Allied to L. *crūdus,* raw, and to Skt. *krūra-,* sore, cruel, hard; also to Gk. κρέας (for **κρέƑας*), raw flesh, Skt. *kravya-,* raw flesh; L. *cruor,* blood; Russ. *krove,* Lith. *kraujas,* Irish *crū,* W. *crau,* blood. Brugmann, i. § 492. (✓KREU.) See **Crude.** Der. *raw-ly, raw-ness, raw-boned.*

RAY (1), a beam of light or heat. (F.—L.) ME. *ray,* Early E. Allit. Poems, ed. Morris, A 160. The pl. 'rayes or beames' occurs in Sir T. Elyot, The Governour, b. ii. c. 12. § 2.—OF. *raye,* 'a ray, line,' Cot.; mod. F. *rai.* Cf. Span. *rayo,* Ital. *raggio.*—L. *radium,* acc. of *radius,* a ray, radius. Doublet, *radius.*

RAY (2), a class of fishes, such as the skate. (F.—L.) ME. *raye.* 'Hec ragadia, *raye;*' Wright's Vocab. i. 222, col. 2, l. 2.— AF. *raie,* Liber Albus, p. 234; OF. *raye,* 'a ray, skate,' Cot.; mod. F. *raie.*—L. *rāia,* a ray; Pliny, ix. 24.

RAY (3), a dance. (MDu.) 'Pipers of the Duche tonge, To lerne . . *reyes;*' Chaucer, Ho. Fame, 1236.—MDu. *rey, reye,* 'a round dance;' Hexham. Du. *rei;* see Franck.

RAYAH, a person, not a Mahometan, who pays the capitation-tax; a word in use in Turkey. (Arab.) In Byron, Bride of Abydos, ii. 20. It may be explained as 'subject,' though the real meaning is 'a flock,' or pastured cattle.—Arab. *ra'iyah,* a flock; from *ra'y,* pasturing, feeding, tending flocks; Rich. Dict. pp. 716, 739. Doublet, *ryot,* q. v.

RAZE, to lay level with the ground, destroy. (F.—L.) In Shak. Meas. ii. 2. 171. Also 'to graze, strike on the surface,' Rich. III, iii. 2. 11. Also 'to erase,' K. Lear, i. 4. 4. All various uses of the verb which is also spelt *rase;* see **Rase.** Der. *raz-or,* q. v., *ras-ori-al,* q. v.

RAZOR, a knife for shaving. (F.—L.) ME. *rasour,* Chaucer, C. T. 2419 (A 2417). Lit. 'a shaver;' OF. *rasor, rasour,* from F. *raser,* to shave; closely allied to mod. F. *rasoir,* from Late L. *rāsōrium.* See **Rase, Raze.** Der. *razor-strop.*

RAZZIA, a sudden raid. (F.—Arab.) F. *razzia, razia;* borrowed from an Algerine *razia,* a peculiar pronunciation of Arab. *ghāzia,* a raid, an expedition against infidels (Devic); cf. Arab. *ghāzī,* a hero, a leader of an expedition.—Arab. *ghazw,* making war; Rich. Dict., pp. 1041, 1059. ¶ Spelt *ghrazzie* in 1826 (N. E. D.).

RE-, RED-, prefix, again. (F.—L.; or L.) F. *re-, red-;* from L. *re-, red-,* again. The form *re-* is most common, and is prefixed even to E. words, as in *re-bellow, re-word* (Shak.), but this is unusual; remarkable words of this class are *re-mind, re-new.* The form *red-* occurs in *red-eem, red-integrate, red-olent, red-dition.* The true etymology of this prefix is still unsolved. ¶ As this prefix can be arbitrarily set before almost any verb, it is unnecessary to give all the words which are found with it. For the etymology of *re-address, re-adjust, re-arrange, re-bellow,* &c., &c., see the simple forms *address, adjust, arrange,* &c.

REACH (1), to attain, extend to, arrive at, gain. (E.) ME. *rechen,* pt. t. *raghte,* *raughte,* pp. *raught;* P. Plowman, B. xi. 353; Chaucer, C. T. 136. We even find *raught* in Shak. L. L. L. iv. 2. 41. &c. AS. *rǣcan, rǣcean,* to reach; pt. t. *rǣhte;* Grein, ii. 364. +Du. *reiken;* OFriesic *reka, retsia, resza;* G. *reichen.* β. Further connected with the rare sb. *ge-rǣc,* occasion, due time, occurring in Ps. ix. 9, ed. Spelman. This would give the orig. sense 'to seize the opportunity' or 'to attain to;' Teut. type **raikjan-.* Perhaps allied to *rice*, sb., power, and to the adj. *rice*, powerful; G. *reich*, kingdom. **Der. reach**, sb., Oth. iii. 3. 219; also a 'stretch' of a river.

REACH (2), to try to vomit; see **Retch**.

READ, to interpret, esp. to interpret written words. (E.) ME. *reden*, pt. t. *redde*, *radde*, pp. *red*, *rad*; P. Plowman, B. iii. 334; Chaucer, C. T. 6371, 6373 (D 789, 791). AS. *rǣdan*, to discern, advise, read; a weak verb, pt. t. *rǣdde*, pp. *gerǣd*, Grein, ii. 366. Allied to AS. *rǣd*, counsel, advice, id. 365. Also to AS. *rǣdan*, to advise, persuade; a strong verb, with the remarkable reduplicated pt. t. *reord*. β. This strong verb answers to Goth. *rēdan*, in comp. *garēdan*, to provide, a strong verb; also to Icel. *rāða*, to advise, pt. t. *rēð*, pp. *rāðinn*; also to G. *rathen*, pt. t. *rieth*, pp. *gerathen*. Observe also G. *berathen*, to assist. All ultimately from the Teut. type **rǣdan-*. Allied to Skt. *rādh*, to make favourable, propitiate, to be favourable to; Russ. *radiete*, to take care. Brugmann, i. § 136, 149. **Der. read-able**, *read-abl-y*, *read-able-ness*; *read-er*, *read-ing*, *read-ing-book*, *read-ing-room*. Also *ridd-le*.

READY, dressed, prepared, prompt, near. (E.) ME. *redi*, *redy*; spelt *rædi*, Layamon, 8651 (later text *readi*); *rædiʒ*, Ormulum, 2527. AS. *rǣde*, ready, Grein, ii. 366. [In this instance the suffix -*e* was turned into -*i* by confusion with the AS. suffix -*ig* (answering to ME. -*i*, -*y*, E. -*y*)]. The MSwed. adj. *reda*, ready, is cognate, and is connected with *reda*, to prepare. So also Dan. *rede*, ready; OHG. *reiti*, ready; mod. G. *bereit*. β. The Icel. *greiðr* (= *ga-reiðr*), ready, only differs in the prefix and suffix; so also Goth. *garaiþs*, commanded. These adjectives are closely related to Icel. *reiði*, harness, outfit, implements, gear, and to OHG. *reita*, Icel. *reið*, a raid. We may look upon *ready* as expressing either 'prepared for a raid' or 'prepared for riding, equipped.' All from a Teut. base *raid*, 2nd stem of Teut. **reidan-*, to ride; see **Ride, Raid**. Cf. G. *fertig*, ready; from *fahren*, to go. ¶ The use of *ready* in the sense of 'dressed' is found as late as the beginning of the 17th century. 'Is she *ready*?' = is she dressed; Cymb. ii. 3. 86. **Der.** *readi-ly*, *readi-ness*, *ready-made*.

REAL (1), actual, true, genuine. (L.) Spelt *reall* in Levins; and in Tyndall's Works, p. 104, col. 1, l. 5, where it is opposed to *nominall*. ME. *real*; Prompt. Parv. The famous disputes between *Realists* and the Nominalists render it probable that the word was taken immediately from the familiar Late L. *reālis* rather than the MF. *real*, 'reall,' given by Cotgrave. The mod. F. form is *réel*, also given by Cotgrave. β. The Late L. *reālis*, 'belonging to the thing itself,' is formed from *rē*-, stem of *rēs*, a thing, with suffix -*ālis*.+Skt. *rāi*-, property, wealth; cf. *rā*, to give, bestow. **Der.** *real-ly*; *real-ise*, from MF. *realiser*, 'to realize,' Cot.; *real-is-able*; *real-is-at-ion*, from MF. *realisation*, 'a realization, a making reall,' Cot.; *real-ism*, *real-ist*, *real-ist-ic*; *real-i-ty*, from F. *réalité* (Littré).

REAL (2), a small Spanish coin. (Span.—L.) In Swinburne's Travels through Spain (1779), letter 9, p. 56. And see Stanford Dict.—Span. *real*, lit. 'a royal' coin.—L. *rēgālis*, royal. See **Regal**.

REALGAR, red arsenic. (F.—Span.—Arab.) A term in chemistry and alchemy. Spelt *resalgar*, Chaucer, C. T. Group G, l. 814 (l. 16282).—F. *réalgar*; cf. the Low L. *risigallum*.—Span. *rejalgar*.—Arab. *rahj al-ghār*, powder of the mine, mineral powder. —Arab. *rahj*, dust, powder; *al*, the; and *ghār*, a cavern, hence a mine. See Rich. Dict., pp. 759, 1040. This etymology is due to Dozy; and see Devic, supp. to Littré.

REALM, a kingdom. (F.—L.) ME. *realme*, Gower, C. A. iii. 199; bk. vii. 3179; *ryalme*, Sir Gawain and the Grene Knight, l. 691; *reaume*, Will. of Palerne, 1964; *rewme*, Rom. of the Rose, 495. — OF. *realme*, *reaume*, *roialme* (Burguy); mod. F. *royaume*, a kingdom; answering to a Late L. form **rēgālimen* (not found).— L. *rēgālis*, regal; see **Regal**.

REAM, a bundle of paper, usually twenty quires. (F.—Span.— Arab.) In Skelton, Works, i. 131, l. 174; spelt *reme*. Spelt *reame*, in Minsheu, ed. 1627, and in Levins. We even find ME. *reeme* in Prompt. Parv. p. 429; and 'j *rem* papiri' in the Earl of Derby's Expeditions, 1390–3 (Camd. Soc.), p. 154. — OF. *raime*, *rayme*, (Littré), a ream; mod. F. *rame*. Palsgrave has: 'Reame of paper, *ramme de papier*.' — Span. *resma*, 'a reame of paper;' Minsheu. (Cf. Ital. *risma*.)—Arab. *rizma(t)*, (pl. *rizam*), a bundle, esp. a bundle of clothes; Rich. Dict. p. 731. See Littré, Devic's supp. to Littré, and Scheler's note on Diez; all agree that this etymology has been completely established by Dozy. Devic remarks that we even find the F. expression 'coton en *rame*,' cotton in a bundle, and that it is hopeless to connect this, as Diez proposes, with the Gk. ἀριθμός, number. Cotton paper was manufactured in Spain, where it was introduced by the Moors.

REAP, to cut, as grain, gather a crop. (E.) ME. *repen*, sometimes a strong verb; pt. t. *rep*, pl. *ropen*, P. Plowman, B. xiii. 374;

pp. *ropen*, Chaucer, Leg. of Good Women, 74. OMerc. *reopan*, Vesp. Psalter, Ps. 125. 5; AS. *repan*, pt. t. *ræp*, pt. t. pl. *rǣpon*. [But a commoner form is AS. *rīpan* (pt. t. *rāp*); allied to E. *ripe*; see **Ripe**. The occurrence of these two strong verbs with the same sense is remarkable.]+Pomeran. *reepen*, to reap.

REAR (1), to raise. (E.) ME. *reren*, Rob. of Glouc. p. 28, l. 657. AS. *rǣran*, to rear, Deut. xxviii. 30. The form *rǣran* exhibits the common substitution of *r* for *s*, and is cognate with Icel. *reisa* (mod. E. *raise*). It is the causal of *rise*; and means 'to make to rise.' Teut. type **raisjan-*, from **rais*, 2nd stem of **reisan-*, to rise. See **Rise**. **Doublet**, *raise*.

REAR (2), the back part, last part, esp. of an army. (F.—L.) 'To the abject *rear*;' Troil. iii. 3. 162. But usually in phr. 'in the *rear*,' Hamlet, i. 3. 34. ME. *rere*, but perhaps only in the compounds *rereward* (see **Rearward**) and *arere*, adv., also spelt *arrere*, P. Plowman, B. v. 354.—OF. *riere*, 'backward, behind,' Cot. The ME. *arere*, in the rear, answers to OF. *ariere* (Burguy), F. *arrière*, 'behind, backward,' adv.—L. *retro*, backward; whence *ad retro* > OF. *ariere*. See **Retro-**. **Der.** *rear-admiral*, *rear-guard*, *rear-rank*; also *rear-ward*, q. v.

REAR (3), insufficiently cooked. (E.) (For *hrear*.) Obsolete, except provincially. Dryden has: 'roasted *rare*;' Baucis and Philemon, 98. ME. *rere*; Prompt. Parv., p. 430. 'If they [eggs] be *rere*;' Sir T. Elyot, Castel of Helth, b. ii. c. 17. AS. *hrēr*, half-cooked, AS. Leechdoms, ed. Cockayne, ii. 272. Cf. Skt. *çrai*, to cook.

REARMOUSE, the same as **Reremouse**, q. v.

REARWARD, the rear-guard. (F.—L. *and* G.) Spelt *rereward*, 1 Sam. xxix. 2, Isaiah lii. 12, lviii. 8; this is merely the old spelling preserved. [Not to be read re-reward, as is sometimes done.] ME. *rerewarde*, Gower, C. A. i. 220; bk. ii. 1827; Morte Arthure, ed. Brock, 1430. Cf. AF. *rerewarde*, a rearguard, Langtoft, i. 18; *reregard*, id., ii. 282. Short for *arere-warde*, compounded of ME. *arere*, behind, and *warde*, a guard; see **Rear** (2) and **Ward**. *Warde* is an OF. form of *garde*; cf. *arriere-garde*, 'the reregard of an army,' Cot. **Doublet**, *rear-guard*.

REASON, the faculty of mind by which man draws conclusions as to right and truth, motive, cause, justice. (F.—L.) ME. *resoun*, Chaucer, C. T. 37; *reisun*, Ancren Riwle, p. 78, last line.—OF. *raisun*, *reson*; mod. F. *raison*.—L. *ratiōnem*, acc. of *ratio*, reckoning, reason; allied to L. *ratus*, pp. of *reor*, I think. See **Rate** (1). **Der.** *reason*, verb, *reason-er*, *reason-ing*; *reason-able*, ME. *resonable*, P. Plowman, C. i. 176; *reason-abl-y*, *reason-able-ness*. **Doublet**, *ration*.

REASTY, rancid, as applied to bacon. (F.—L.) 'Much bacon is *reastie*;' Tusser, Husbandry, § 20. 2. '*Restie*, attainted;' Baret. ME. *reest*, also *resty*; Prompt. Parv. In Wright's Vol. of Vocab. i. 155, the AF. *chars restez* is glossed by *resty flees*, i.e. flesh. Hence *resty* is from AF. *resté*, left over, not eaten; and therefore not fresh. —OF. *rester*, to remain; see **Rest** (2). ¶ Sometimes ingeniously altered to *rusty*; 'you *rusty* piece of Martlemas bacon;' Middleton, A Fair Quarrel, iv. 1. N.B. I now find that Wedgwood gave the same solution long ago.

REATA, a rope of raw hide, for picketing animals; a lariat. (Span.—L.) Spelt *riata* by Bret Harte; Cent. Dict.; Stanford Dict.—Span. *reata*, a rope for tying.—Span. *reatar*, to tie.—L. *re*-, back; *aptāre*, to fit together; see **Apt**.

REAVE, to rob, take away by violence. (E.) Not common in mod. E., except in the comp. *be-reave*, and in the pt. t. and pp. *reft*. '*Reaves* his son of life;' Shak. Venus, 766. And see Com. Errors, i. i. 116, Much Ado, iv. 1. 198; &c. ME. *reuen* (with *u*=*v*), Chaucer, C. T. 4009 (B 3288); pp. *raft*, *reft*, 11329 (F 1017). AS. *rēafian*, to spoil, despoil, Exod. iii. 22; lit. to take off the clothes, despoil of clothing or armour.—AS. *rēaf*, clothing, spoil, plunder, Exod. iii. 22.—AS. **rēaf*, 2nd stem of **rēof-an*, to deprive, a strong verb (pt. t. *rēaf*, pp. *rofen*), only in the comp. *birēofan*, *berēofan* (Grein). Cf. Icel. *raufa*, to rob, from sb. *rauf*, spoil; which from *rjūfa* (pt. t. *rauf*, pp. *rofinn*), to break, rip up, violate; G. *rauben*, to rob, from *raub*, plunder. Cf. Goth. *biraubon*, to despoil. β. All from the Teut. strong verb **reuðan-*, pt. t. **rauð*. Allied to L. *rumpere*, to break; see **Rupture**. Brugmann, i. § 466. **Der.** *be-reave*; and see *robe*, *rob*. **Doublet**, *rob*.

REBATE, to blunt the edge of a sword. (F.—L.) In Shak. Meas. i. 4. 60. ME. *rebate* = abate, Coventry Mysteries, p. 76.— OF. *rebattre* (Hatzfeld); MF. *rebatre*, 'to repell, repulse, beat or drive back again;' Cot.—F. *re*- (L. *re*-), back; and OF. *batre* (mod. F. *battre*), to beat, from L. *battere*, *batere*, popular forms of *batuere*, to beat. **Der.** (from OF. *batre*) *a-bate*, q. v. Also *rebate*, sb., discount; *rebate-ment*, a diminution, narrowing, 1 Kings, vi. 6, margin, where the A. V. has 'narrowed rests.' Cf. also *rebato*, *rabato*, a kind of ruff, Much Ado, iii. 4. 6, where the final -o seems to be an E.

addition, as the word is not Span. or Ital., but French; from F. *rabat*, 'a rebatee for a womans ruffe' (Cot.), which from *rabattre*, to turn back, for *re-abattre*.

REBECK, a three-stringed fiddle. (F. – Arab.) 'And the jocund *rebecks* sound;' Milton, L'Allegro, 94. *Hugh Rebeck* is a proper name in Romeo, iv. 5. 135. An old woman is called 'an old *rebekke*,' and again, 'an old *ribybe*,' in Chaucer, C. T. 7155, 6959 (D 1573, 1377). – OF. *rebec*, 'the fiddle tearmed a rebeck;' Cot. Also spelt *rebebe* (Hatzfeld, Roquefort). – Arab. *rabāb*, *rabāba*(*t*), a rebeck, an instrument played with a bow; Devic.

REBEL, adj., rebellious, opposing or renouncing authority. (F. – L.) The verb is from the sb., and the sb. was orig. an adj. ME. *rebél*, rebellious, Rob. of Glouc. p. 72, l. 1625. 'And alle that he *rébel* founde;' King Alisaunder, ed. Weber, l. 3033. 'Avaunt! *rebél!*' Lydgate, Minor Poems, Percy Soc., p. 35. – F. *rebelle*, adj., rebellious, wilful. – L. *rebellem*, acc. of *rebellis*, rebellious, lit. renewing war. – L. *re-*, again; and *bell-um*, war. See **Re-**, **Belligerent**, and **Duel**. Der. *rebel*, verb, Barbour, Bruce, x. 129 (Edinburgh MS.); *rebell-ion*, Wyclif, 3 Kings, xi. 27, from F. *rebellion*, 'rebellion,' Cot.; *rebell-i-ous*, Rich. II, v. 1. 5; *rebell-i-ous-ly*, *-ness*.

REBOUND, to bound back. (F. – L.) 'I *rebounde*, as a ball dothe, *je bondys*;' Palsgrave. And in Surrey, The Lover describes his state, l. 19; in Tottell's Misc., ed. Arber, p. 24. Trevisa has *reboundynge*, sb., tr. of Higden, i. 189. – F. *rebondir*, 'to rebound, or leap back;' Cot. – F. *re-*, back; and *bondir*, to leap, bound. See **Re-** and **Bound** (1). Der. *rebound*, sb., Antony, v. 2. 104; and in Palsgrave.

REBUFF, a sudden check or resistance, repulse. (Ital.) 'The strong *rebuff* of some tumultuous cloud;' Milton, P. L. ii. 936. – Ital. *rebuffo*, *ribuffo*, 'a check, a chiding, a taunt, a skoulding, a rating;' connected with Ital. *ribuffare*, 'to check, to chide;' Florio. Mod. Ital. *ribuffo*, a reproof; *ribuffare*, to repulse. – Ital. *ri-* (<L. *re-*), back; and *buffo*, a puff, a word of imitative origin, like E. *puff*. See **Re-** and **Puff**. Der. *rebuff*, verb.

REBUKE, to reprove, chide. (F. – L.) ME. *rebuken*, P. Plowman, B. xi. 419. – AF. *rebuker*, Langtoft, ii. 108; ONF. *rebuker*, to defeat (a plan), Chardry, Vie des Set Dormans, l. 1589; *rebukier*, OF. *rebuchier*, the same (Godefroy). – OF. *re-* (L. *re-*), again; and ONF. *bucquer*, *buskier*, OF. *buschier*, to beat, to knock, orig. to cut trees, to cut logs for the fire, to lop (Godefroy, s. v. *buschier*), mod. F. *bûcher*, 'to rough-hew, to destroy,' Hamilton. β. This OF. *buschier*, F. *bûcher*, is from OF. *busche*, F. *bûche*, a log; from Late L. *busca*, a log (Ducange). Cf. Picard *busker*, *buker*, to beat, strike, knock (Corblet); Walloon *busquer*, *buquer*, to strike, *buque*, a log (Sigart); Norm. dial. *bûquette*, a billet. Orig. 'to cut back.' Der. *rebuke*, sb., Sir Degrevant, 863; *rebuk-er*.

REBUS, an enigmatical representation of words by pictures of things. (L.) 'As round as Gyges' ring, which, say the ancients, Was a hoop-ring, and that is, round as a hoop. *Lovel.* You will have your *rebus* still, mine host;' Ben Jonson, New Inn, Act i. sc. 1. 'Excellent have beene the conceipt[s] of some citizens, who, wanting armes, have coined themselves certaine devices as neere as may be alluding to their names, which we call *rebus*;' Henry Peacham (1634), The Gentleman's Exercise, p. 155, § 2, B. 3. It refers to representing names, &c., by things; thus a *bolt* and *tun* expresses *Bolton*; and so on. – L. *rēbus*, by things, by means of things; abl. pl. of *rēs*, a thing; see **Real**. ¶ Cf. *omnibus*.

REBUT, to oppose by argument or proof. (F. – MHG.; *with* L. *prefix*.) 'Rebutit of the prey' = driven away from the prey, repulsed; Dunbar, The Golden Targe, l. 180. – AF. *reboter*, OF. *rebouter*, 'to repulse, foyle, drive back, reject,' &c.; Cot. – F. *re-* (= L. *re-*), back; and *bouter*, to thrust. See **Re-** and **Butt** (1). Der. *rebutt-er*, a plaintiff's answer to a defendant's rejoinder, a law term.

RECALL, to call back. (Scand.; *with* L. *prefix*.) In Shak. Lucrece, 1671. From **Re-** and **Call**. Der. *recall*, sb., Milton, P. L. v. 885.

RECANT, to retract an opinion. (L.) 'Which duke ... did *recant* his former life;' Contin. of Fabyan's Chron., an. 1553; ed. Ellis, p. 712. – L. *recantāre*, to sing back, re-echo, also to recant, recall (Horace, Od. i. 16. 27); the orig. sense was perhaps to reverse a charm. – L. *re-*, back; and *cantāre*, to sing; see **Re-** and **Chant**. Der. *recant-er*, *recant-at-ion*. ☞ This throws some light on the word *cant*, and renders the derivation of *cant* from L. *cantāre* more easy and probable.

RECAST, to cast or mould anew. (Scand.; *with* L. *prefix*.) Also, to throw back again; 'they would *cast* and *recast* themselves from one to another horse;' Florio, tr. of Montaigne, bk. i. c. 48. From **Re-** and **Cast**.

RECEDE, to retreat. (L.) In Phillips, ed. 1658. – L. *recēdere*, to give ground, retreat. See **Re-** and **Cede**. Der. *recess*, in Hall,

Hen. VIII, an. 34. § 7, from L. *recessus*, a retreat, which from *recessus*, pp. of *recēdere*. Also *recess-ion*, from L. *recessio*.

RECEIVE, to accept, admit, entertain. (F. – L.) ME. *receiuen*, *receyuen* (with *u* for *v*). 'He that *receyueth* other recetteth hure ys recettor of gyle;' P. Plowman, C. vii. 291. – AF. *receiv-*, a stem of *receivre*, OF. *reçoivre*; mod. F. *recevoir*. – L. *recipere* (pp. *receptus*), to receive. – L. *re-*, back; and *capere*, to take; with the usual vowel-change from *a* to *i* in composition. See **Re-** and **Capacious**. Der. *receiv-er*. Also *receipt*, ME. *receit*, Chaucer, C. T. 16821 (G 1353), from AF. *receite*, Year-books, 1304-5, p. 295, OF. *recete*, *recepte*, *recoite* (Littré), MF. *recepte*, 'a receit,' Cot., mod. F. *recette*<L. *recepta*, a thing received, fem. of *receptus*. And see *receptacle*, *recipe*.

RECENT, new, fresh, modern. (F. – L.) In Minsheu. – MF. *recent* (F. *récent*), 'recent, fresh.' – L. *recent-*, stem of *recens*, fresh, new. Der. *recent-ly*, *-ness*.

RECEPTACLE, a place in which to store things away. (F. – L.) In Shak. Romeo, iv. 3. 39. – MF. *receptacle*, 'a receptacle, store-house,' Cot. – L. *receptāculum*, a receptacle; formed with dimin. suffixes *-cu-lo-* from *receptāre*, frequentative form of *recipere*, to receive; see **Receive**. Der. (like pp. *receptus*) *recept-ion*, formerly a term in astrology, Gower, C. A. iii. 67, bk. vi. 1962, from F. *reception*, 'a reception,' Cot., from L. acc. *receptiōnem*; also *recept-ive*, from OF. *receptif* (Godefroy); hence *recept-iv-i-ty*, from mod. F. *réceptivité*, a coined word.

RECESS, RECESSION; see **Recede**.

RECHEAT, a signal of recall, in hunting. (F. – L.) In Shak. Much Ado, i. 1. 242. – AF. *rechet*, ONorth F. *rechet*, variant of *recet*, a retreat, hence, a note of retreat; see Godefroy, and cf. Norm. dial. *recheveir*, to receive (Moisy). – L. *receptum*, acc. of *receptus*, a retreating, a retreat. – L. *receptus*, pp. of *recipere*, to receive; see **Receive**. Influenced by OF. *racheter* (< L. *re-ad-captāre*), to reassemble, to rally (Godefroy).

RECIPE, a medical prescription. (L.) In Phillips, ed. 1706; he rightly explains that it is so called because it begins with the word *recipe*, i.e. take so and so. B. Jonson has the pl. *recipes*, Alchemist, ii. 1. 443. – L. *recipe*, imp. sing. of *recipere*, to take. See **Receive**. So also *recipi-ent*, one who receives, from the stem of the pres. part. of *recipere*.

RECIPROCAL, acting in return, mutual. (L.) In King Lear, iv. 6. 267. Formed by adding *-al* to L. *reciproc-us*, returning, alternating, reciprocal; whence also MF. *reciproque*, and obsolete E. *reciproque*, of which see examples in R. Lit. 'directed backwards and forwards;' from L. **re-co-*, backwards, and **pro-co-*, forwards, allied to *procul*, afar off. Brugmann, ii. § 86. Der. *reciprocal-ly*; also *reciproc-ate*, given in Phillips as a grammatical term, from *reciprocātus*, pp. of *reciprocāre*, to go backwards and forwards, to reciprocate; *reciproc-at-ion*, from F. *reciprocation*, 'a reciprocation, returning,' Cot.; *reciproc-i-ty*, from mod. F. *réciprocité*.

RECITE, to repeat aloud, narrate. (F. – L.) In Levins, ed. 1570. 'Reciteth in the gospell;' Caxton, Golden Legend, St. John Evang. § 5. – F. *reciter*, 'to recite, repeat,' Cot. – L. *recitāre*, to recite; see **Re-** and **Cite**. Der. *recit-al*, North's Plutarch, p. 14 (R.), *recit-er*; *recit-at-ion*, from F. *recitation*, in use in the 15th cent. (Littré), though omitted by Cotgrave; *recit-at-ive*, mod. F. *récitatif*, from Ital. *recitativo*, recitative in music.

RECK, to regard. (E.) ME. *rekken*, frequently also *recchen*, Chaucer, C. T. 1400, 2259; P. Plowman, B. iv. 65. The vowel has been shortened, being orig. long. AS. *reccan*, also *rēcan* (for **rōcian*); 'þu ne *rēcst*' = thou carest not, Mark, xii. 14.+OSax. *rōkian*; Icel. *rækja*; Pomeran. *röken*; MHG. *ruochen*, OHG. *rōhhjan*, *ruohhjan*, to reck, heed, have a care for. β. The *ē* results, as usual, from *ō* followed by *i* in the next syllable. The verb is a denominative, i. e. from a sb. The sb. exists in MHG. *ruoch*, OHG. *ruah*, *ruoh*, care, heed, answering to a Teut. type **rōk-oz*, m. From Teut. **rōk-*, 2nd grade of **rak-*, as seen in Icel. *rök*, a reason, AS. *racu*, account, reckoning, OSax. *raka*, an affair, OHG. *rahha*, subject, thing. See **Reckon**. Der. *reck-less*, AS. *reccelēas*, Ælfred, tr. of Gregory's Pastoral Care, ed. Sweet, p. 4, l. 23, spelt *rēcelēas*, id. p. 5, l. 23; cf. Du. *roekeloos*; *reck-less-ly*, *reck-less-ness*.

RECKON, to count, account, esteem. (E.) ME. *rekenen*, *reknen*; Chaucer, C. T. 1956 (A 1954); P. Plowman, B. ii. 61. AS. *ge-recenian*, to explain, Grein, i. 440; the prefixed *ge-*, readily added or dropped, makes no real difference. A derivative verb; allied to AS. *ge-reccan*, *reccan*, to rule, direct, order, explain, ordain, tell; Grein, i. 440, ii. 369.+Du. *rekenen*; (whence Icel. *reikna*, Dan. *regne*, Swed. *räkna*); G. *rechnen*, MHG. *rechenen*, OHG. *rehhanōn*, to compute, reckon. β. All from Teut. base **rak-*, as in AS. *rac-u*, account, Icel. *rök*, neut. pl.; a reason, ground, origin, cognate with MHG. *racha*, OHG. *rahha*, a thing, subject. Der. *reckon-er*; also *reck-on-ing*, cognate with G. *rechnung*.

RECLAIM, to tame, bring into a cultivated state, reform. (F.—L.) ME. *recleimen, reclaimen,* esp. as a term in hawking; Chaucer, C. T. 17021 (H 72).—OF. *reclaim-,* a stem of *reclamer,* 'to call often or earnestly, exclaime upon, sue, claime;' Cot. Mod. F. *réclamer.*—L. *reclāmāre,* to cry out against.—L. *re-,* back, again; and *clāmāre,* to cry out. See **Re-** and **Claim.** Der. *reclaim-able;* also *reclam-at-ion,* from MF. *reclamation,* 'a contradiction, gainsaying,' Cot., from L. acc. *reclāmātiōnem,* a cry of opposition.

RECLINE, to lean back, lie down. (L.) In Milton, P. L. iv. 333.—L. *reclīnāre,* to lean back.—L. *re-,* back; and *clīnāre,* to lean, cognate with E. **Lean** (1).

RECLUSE, secluded, retired. (F.—L.) ME. *reclus,* masc.; Fifty Early E. Wills, ed. Furnivall, p. 7, l. 31 (1395). The form *recluse* is properly feminine, and it first appears with reference to female anchorites. ME. *recluse,* Ancren Riwle (Rule of Female Anchorites), p. 10, l. 5.—OF. *reclus,* masc., *recluse,* fem., 'closely kept in, or shut up as a monk or nun;' Cot. Pp. of OF. *reclorre,* 'to shut or close up again;' Cot.—L. *reclūdere,* to unclose, but in late L. to shut up.—L. *re-,* back; and *claudere,* to shut. See **Re-** and **Clause.**

RECOGNISE, to know again, acknowledge. (F.—L.) In Levins. The MF. verb is *recognoistre* in Cot., mod. F. *reconnaître.* The E. verb is not *immediately* derived from this, but is merely made out of the sb. *recognisance,* which was in rather early use, and occurs in Chaucer as a legal term, C. T. 13260 (B 1520).—AF. *reconisaunce,* Stat. Realm, i. 53 (1283); OF. *recoignisance* (13th cent., Littré), later *recognoissance,* 'a recognizing, also an acknowledgement of tenure;' Cot.—OF. *reconoissant,* pres. part. of *reconoistre* (F. *reconnaître*).—L. *recognoscere.*—L. *re-,* again; and *cognoscere,* to know. See **Re-** and **Cognisance.** Der. *recognis-able;* also *recognit-ion,* in Blount's Gloss., ed. 1674, from L. acc. *recognitiōnem,* nom. *recognitio,* allied to *recognit-us,* pp. of *recognoscere.* And see *reconnoitre.*

RECOIL, to start back, rebound. (F.—L.) ME. *recoilen,* used transitively, to drive back, Ancren Riwle, p. 294, l. 6. Also *recule;* 'I *recule,* I go back, *ie recule;*' Palsgrave. Cf. AF. pres. pt. *recuillant,* Langtoft, ii. 176.—F. *reculer,* 'to recoyle, retire, defer, drive off,' Cot. Lit. to go backwards.—F. *re-* (= L. *re-*), back; and *cul,* the hinder part, from L. *cūlum,* acc. of *cūlus,* the hinder part, the posteriors. Der. *recoil,* sb., Milton, P. L. ii. 880.

RECOLLECT, to remember. (F.—L.) Used in Shak. in the lit. sense 'to gather,' to collect again, Per. ii. 1. 54. From **Re-** and **Collect.** Der. *recollect-ion.*

RECOMMEND, to commend to another. (F.—L.) ME. *recommenden,* ,Chaucer, C. T. 16012 (G 544). From **Re-** and **Commend;** in imitation of F. *recommander,* 'to recommend,' Cot. Der. *recommend-able, recommend-at-ion, recommend-at-or-y.*

RECOMPENSE, to reward, remunerate. (F.—L.) ME. *recompense,* Gower, C. A. ii. 278; bk. v. 4505.—OF. *recompenser* (F. *récompenser*), 'to recompence;' Cot.—L. *re-,* again; and *compensāre;* see **Re-** and **Compensate.** Der. *recompense,* sb., Timon, v. 1. 153.

RECONCILE, to restore to friendship, cause to agree. (F.—L.) ME. *reconcilen,* Gower, C. A. iii. 138; bk. vii. 1578.—OF. *reconcilier,* 'to reconcile,' Cot.—L. *reconciliāre,* to reconcile, lit. to bring into counsel again. See **Re-** and **Conciliate.** Der. *reconcil-er, reconcil-able; reconciliat-ion,* from OF. *reconciliation* (Cot.)<L. acc. *reconciliātiōnem.*

RECONDITE, secret, profound. (L.) In Phillips, ed. 1706.— L. *reconditus,* put away, hidden, secret; pp. of *recondere,* to put back again.—L. *re-,* again; and *condere,* to put together. β. The L. *condere* (in which the prefix is *con-,* for *com-* = *cum,* with), contains the weak grade of the √DHĒ, to put, place. Brugmann, i. § 573. Cf. *abs-cond.* And see **Do.**

RECONNOITRE, to survey, examine from a military point of view. (F.—L.) 'She *reconnoitres* fancy's airy band;' Young, Night Thoughts, Nt. ii. l. 265. See Spectator, no. 165, § 5.—OF. *reconoistre* (Littré), mod. F. *reconnaître,* 'to recognize; . . also, to take a precise view of;' Cot. See **Recognise.** Der. *reconnaiss-ance,* from mod. F. *reconnaissance;* of which *recognisance* is a doublet.

RECORD, to register, enrol, celebrate. (F.—L.) ME. *recorden,* to repeat, remind, Ancren Riwle, p. 256, l. 10; Chaucer, C. T. 831 (A 829).—OF. *recorder,* 'to repeat, recite, report,' Cot.—L. *recordāre,* more usually *recordāri,* to call a thing to mind.—L. *re-,* again; and *cord-,* stem of *cor,* the heart, cognate with E. *heart.* See **Re-** and **Heart.** Der. *record,* sb., Chaucer, C. T. 7631 (D 2049), from OF. *record,* 'a record, witnesse,' Cot.; *record-er, record-er-ship.*

RECOUNT, to tell again, narrate. (F.—L.) In Skelton, Philip Sparowe, l. 613. 'Who may *recounte,*' &c.; Caxton, G. Legend, St. Pawlyne, § 8.—OF. *reconter,* to tell again (Godefroy). From **Re-**

and **Count.** The F. *conter* often has the sense 'to relate;' the F. compound verb is written *raconter,* which Cotgrave explains by 'to tell, relate, report, rehearse;' where the prefix *ra-* represents L. *re-ad-.*

RECOUP, to diminish a loss by keeping back a part as a claim for damages. (F.—L. *and* Gk.) Spelt *recoupe* in Phillips, ed. 1706; whom see. It means lit. to secure a piece or shred.—F. *recoupe,* 'a shred,' Cot.—F. *recouper,* to cut again.—F. *re-* (=L. *re-*), again; and *couper,* to cut, a word of Gk. origin. See **Re-** and **Coppice.**

RECOURSE, a going to or resorting to for aid. (F.—L.) ME. *recours,* Chaucer, C. T. 10389 (F 75).—F. *recours,* 'a recourse, refuge,' Cot.—L. *recursum,* acc. of *recursus,* a running back, return, retreat.—L. *recursus,* pp. of *recurrere.* See **Recur** and **Course.**

RECOVER, to get again, regain. (F.—L.) ME. *recoeuren* (with *u* for *v*), P. Plowman, B. xix. 239; also *recoueren, rekeueren,* id. C. xxii. 245; King Alisaunder, 5835.—OF. *recovrer, recuvrer* (Burguy), F. *recouvrer,* 'to recover;' Cot.—L. *recuperāre,* to recover; also to recruit oneself. β. A difficult word; *not* connected with Sabine *cuprus,* good. Also spelt *reciperāre,* and extended from *recipere,* like *tolerāre* from *tollere.* From *re-,* back again, and *capere,* to take. Cf. Brugmann, i. § 244 (4). For the vowel *u,* cf. *oc-cup-āre.* Der. *recover-able; recover-y,* All's Well, iv. 1. 38. **Doublet,** *recuperate.*

RECREANT, cowardly, apostate. (F.—L.) ME. *recreant,* Rob. of Brunne, tr. of Langtoft, p. 9, l. 24; *recreaunt,* P. Plowman, B. xviii. 100.—OF. *recreant,* 'tired, toyled, faint-hearted,' Cot.; properly the pres. part. of *recroire,* 'to beleeve again; also, to restore, deliver, or give back;' id.; (hence, to give in). And cf. MF. *recreu,* 'tired, wearie, faint-hearted,' id. β. The pres. part. *recreant* and pp. *recreu* partook of the sense of Late L. *recrēdere,* from which MF. *recroire* is derived. This verb, lit. to believe again, or to alter one's faith, was also used in the phrase *se recrēdere,* to own oneself beaten in a duel or judicial combat. The same sense reappears in Ital. *ricreduto,* 'a miscreant, recreant, a misbeleeving wretch;' Florio.—L. *re-,* again; and *crēdere,* to believe; see **Re-** and **Creed.** Der. *recreanc-y.* And see *mis-creant.*

RECREATION, amusement. (F.—L.) ME. *recreation,* Gower, C. A. iii. 100; bk. vii. 477.—F. *recreation,* 'recreation, pastime;' Cot.—L. *recreātiōnem,* acc. of *recreātio,* recovery from illness (Pliny); cf. L. *recreātus,* pp. of *recreāre,* to refresh, revive; whence the sense of to amuse by way of invigorating the system or mind. Lit. 'to create anew.' See **Re-** and **Create.** Der. *recreate,* in Palsgrave, from L. pp. *recreātus.* Also *recreat-ive.*

RECRIMINATE, to accuse in return. (L.) In Phillips, ed. 1706.—L. *re-,* again; and *crīminātus,* pp. of *crīminārī,* to accuse of crime; from *crimin-,* stem of *crimen;* see **Crime.** Der. *recrimin-at-ion,* from MF. *recrimination,* 'a recrimination,' Cot.; *recriminat-or-y, recriminat-ive.*

RECRUDESCENCE, a reopening, renewal. (L.) In North's Examen, ed. 1740, p. 632. From L. *recrūdescent-,* stem of pres. part. of *recrūdescere,* to become raw again, to open again (as a wound).—L. *re-,* again; and *crūdus,* raw; see **Crude.**

RECRUIT, to enlist new soldiers. (F.—L.) 'To *recrute* and maintain their army when raised;' Prynne, Treachery and Disloyalty, pt. iv. p. 33 (R.). 'A *recruit* [supply] of new people;' Howell, Famil. Letters, vol. i. pt. i. let. 38, § 7.—F. *recruter,* not given in Cotgrave, but explained by Littré by 'to levy troops.' He tells us that it is an ill-formed word, first found in the 17th century. Formed from **recrute,* a mistaken or provincial form for *recrue,* fem. of *recrû,* pp. of *recroître,* to grow again. See also Hatzfeld. The sb. *recrut* occurs in Roumansch. β. The word *recrue* is used as a sb., and means 'a levy of troops.' [The *t* appears in MF. *recroist,* 'a re-increase, a new or second growth,' Cot.; cf. *recroistre,* 'to re-encrease,' id.]—F. *re-,* again; and *croître* (OF. *croistre*), to grow.—L. *re-,* again; and *crescere,* to grow; see **Re-** and **Crescent.** Der. *recruit,* sb.; *recruit-er, recruit-ing.*

RECTANGLE, a four-sided figure, of which all the angles are right angles. (F.—L.) In Phillips, ed. 1658; he says it was used to denote a right angle.—F. *rectangle,* 'a stra t or even angle;' Cot.— L. *rectangulus,* having a right angle.—L. *rect-us,* right; and *angulus,* an angle; see **Rectify** and **Angle.** Der. *rectangl-ed, rectangul-ar.*

RECTIFY, to make right, adjust. (F.—L.) 'To *rectyfye* and amend;' Skelton, Colin Clout, 1265. ME. *rectifien,* Lanfrank, Cirurgie, p. 80, l. 3.—F. *rectifier,* 'to rectifie;' Cot.—Late L. *rectificāre,* to make right.—L. *recti-,* for *rectus,* right, cognate with E. *right;* and *-fic-,* for *fac-ere,* to make. See **Right** and **Fact.** Der. *rectifi-able, rectific-at-ion, rectifi-er.*

RECTILINEAL, RECTILINEAR, bounded by right or straight lines. (L.) Spelt *rectilineal* in Phillips, ed. 1706. Formed with suffix *-al* (<L. *-ālis*) or *-ar* (<L. *-āris*) from *rectilīne-us,*

rectilineal. — L. *recti-*, for *rectus*, right; and *line-a*, a line.   See **Right** and **Line**.

RECTITUDE, uprightness. (F. — L.)   'By the *rectitude* of his justice;' Golden Book, let. 11 (R.). — F. *rectitude*, omitted by Cotgrave, but used in the 14th cent. (Littré). — L. *rectitūdo*, straightness, uprightness; formed with suffix *-tūdo* from *recti-*, for *rectus*, straight, cognate with E. **Right**, q. v.   ¶ So also *rect-or*, lit. a ruler, All's Well, iv. 3. 69, from L. *rector*, a ruler; which is for **reg-tor*; from *regere*, to rule; see **Regiment**.   Hence *rector-ship*, Cor. ii. 3. 213; *rector-ate*, *rector-al*, *rector-y*.

RECUMBENT, lying back or upon, reclining. (L.)   *Recumbency* is in Phillips, ed. 1710.   *Recumbent* seems later; it is in Cowper, The Needless Alarm, l. 47. — L. *recumbent-*, stem of pres. part. of *recumbere*, to recline. — L. *re-*, back; and see **Incumbent**.   Der. *recumbenc-y*.

RECUPERATIVE, tending to recovery. (L.)   *Recuperable*, i.e. recoverable, is in Levins, but is now disused.   *Recuperacion* (sic) is in Caxton, Godeffroy of Boloyne, p. 4, l. 16.   *Recuperator* is in Phillips, ed. 1706.   *Recuperative* appears to be modern. — L. *recuperātiuus*, (properly) recoverable. — L. *recuperātus*, pp. of *recuperāre*, to recover; see **Recover**.

RECUR, to resort, return to the mind, happen again at stated intervals. (L.)   In Phillips, ed. 1706.   *Recurrent* is in Blount's Gloss., ed. 1674. — L. *recurrere*, to run back, return, recur. — L. *re-*, back; and *currere*, to run; see **Re-** and **Current**.   Der. *recurr-ent*, from the stem of the pres. part.; whence *recurr-ence*; also *recourse*, q. v.

RECUSANT, opposing an opinion, refusing to acknowledge supremacy. (F. — L.)   In Minsheu, ed. 1627. — MF. *recusant*, 're-jecting, refusing,' Cot.; pres. part. of *recuser*. — L. *recūsāre*, to reject; properly, to oppose a cause or opinion. — L. *re-*, back, hence, with-drawing from; and *caussa*, a cause; see **Re-** and **Cause**.   β. The same change takes place in *accuse* (*accūsāre*), also from L. *caussa*.   Der. *recusanc-y*.

RED, one of the primary colours. (E.)   ME. *reed* (with long vowel), sometimes *rede*, *red*; Chaucer, C. T. 637.   AS. *rēad*, red; Grein, ii. 373. ✦Du. *rood*; Icel. *rauðr*; Dan. *röd*; Swed. *röd*; G. *roth*; Goth. *rauds*.   β. All from Teut. type **raudoz*; Idg. type **roudhos*.   Further allied to Skt. *rudhira-*, blood, Gk. ἐρεύθειν, to redden, ἐρυθρός, red, Irish and Gael. *ruadh*, W. *rhudd*, L. *ruber*, red.   Note also the strong verb appearing as AS. *rēodan*, Icel. *rjóða* (pt. t. *rauð*), to redden. (√REUDH.)   Der. *red-ly*, *red-ness*; *redd-en* (with *-en* as in *strength-en*, *length-en*); *redd-ish*, *redd-ish-ness*; *red-breast* (a bird with red breast), Skelton, Phillip Sparrow, 399, Lyd-gate, Floure of Curteisie, st. 9; *red-shank* (a bird with red shanks or legs); *red-start* (a bird with a red tail, from AS. *steort*, a tail, Exod. iv. 4), in Levins; *red-hot*, *red-heat*, *red-lead*, *red-letter*, *red-tape*.   Allied words are *ruby*, *rubescent*, *rubric*, *ruddy*, *russet*.

REDACT, to reduce, to edit. (L.)   Becon has *redact* in the sense 'reduced;' Works, i. 46 (Parker Soc.). — L. *redactus*, pp. of *redigere*, to bring back, reduce. — L. *red-*, back; and *agere*, to bring; see **Agent**.   Der. *redact-ion*.

REDDITION, a rendering, restoring. (F. — L.)   In Cotgrave; and Minsheu, ed. 1627. — F. *reddition*, 'a reddition;' Cot. — L. *red-ditiōnem*, acc. of *redditio*, a rendering; cf. *redditus*, pp. of *reddere*, to restore; see **Render**.   Der. *reddit-ive*.

REDEEM, to ransom, atone for. (F. — L.)   Lit. to buy back.   Latimer has *redemed* and *redeming*, sb., Seven Sermons, ed. Arber, p. 202.   Wyclif has *redempcion*, Luke, i. 68. — F. *redimer*, 'to redeem, ransom,' Cot.   [But the change of vowel is remarkable; perhaps partly due to L. *emere*.] — L. *redimere*, to buy back, redeem. — L. *red-*, back; and *emere*, to buy, orig. to take, from √EM, to take.   See **Re-** and **Example**.   Der. *redeem-er*, *redeem-able*; *redempt-ion*, from F. *redemption*<L. acc. *redemptiōnem*, nom. *redemptio*, allied to *redempt-us*, pp. of *redimere*; *redempt-ive*, *redempt-or-y*.   Doublet (of *redemption*), *ransom*.

REDGUM, a disease of infants. (E.)   Fully explained in my Notes to P. Plowman, C. xxiii. 83, p. 444.   ME. *reed gounde*, Prompt. Parv. — AS. *rēad*, red; *gund*, matter of a sore.

REDINTEGRATION, renovation. (L.)   Minsheu has *redin-tegration* and *redintegrate*, verb. — L. *redintegrātio*, sb.; allied to *redintegrātus*, pp. of *redintegrāre*, to restore, renovate. — L. *red-*, again; and *integrāre*, to renew, from *integr-*, for *integer*, whole.   See **Re-** and **Integer**.

REDOLENT, fragrant. (F. — L.)   In the Tale of Beryn, ed. Furnivall, l. 2765. — MF. *redolent*, 'redolent;' Cot. — L. *redolent-*, stem of pres. part. of *redolēre*, to emit odour. — L. *red-*, again; and *olēre*, to be odorous.   See **Re-** and **Olfactory**.   Der. *redolence*, Lydgate, Assembly of Gods, 1611; *redolenc-y*.

REDOUBLE, to double again. (F. — L.)   'I *redoubyll*, I doubyll agayne, *je redouble*;' Palsgrave. — F. *redoubler*; from *re-* and *doubler*, to double.   See **Re-** and **Double**.

REDOUBT, an intrenched place of retreat. (F. — Ital. — L.)   Used by Bacon, according to Todd's Johnson; Ben Jonson has *redouts*; Under-woods, lxxxix; l. 8.   Phillips, ed. 1706, gives the spellings *reduit* (which is a F. form) and *reduct* (which is Latin). — F. *redoute*. — Ital. *ridotto*, 'a withdrawing-place;' Florio.   Formed as sb. from *ridotto*, 'reduced, brought or led vnto, brought back safe and sound againe;' Florio.   This is the same word as *riduto*, pp. of *ridurre*, to bring back, bring home. — L. *redūcere*, to bring back; see **Reduce**.   ¶ The spelling *redoubt* is due to confusion with MF. *redoubter*, to dread, as if a *redoubt* were a place into which men retire out of fear!   See **Redoubtable**.

REDOUBTABLE, terrible. (F. — L.)   In Cotgrave; the verb *to redoubt*, to fear, was formerly in use, as in Minsheu.   ME. *re-doutable*, Chaucer, tr. of Boethius, b. iv. pr. 5, l. 6. — OF. *redoutable*; MF. *redoubtable*, 'redoubtable,' Cot. — OF. and F. *redouter*, to fear.   See **Re-** and **Doubt**.

REDOUND, to abound, be replete with, result. (F. — L.)   '*Re-dounding teares*;' Spenser, F. Q. i. 3. 8.   'I *redounde*, *je redonde*;' Palsgrave.   And in Caxton, Siege of Troye, lf. 205, back, l. 19. — F. *redonder*, 'to redound;' Cot. — L. *redundāre*, to overflow, abound. — L. *red-*, again, back, hence over; and *undāre*, to surge, flow, abound, from *unda*, a wave.   See **Re-** and **Undulate**.   Der. *re-dund-ant*, from the stem of the pres. part. of *redundāre*; *redund-ant-ly*, *redund-ance*, *redund-anc-y*.

REDRESS, to set right again. (F. — L.)   ME. *redressen*, Chaucer, C. T. 8307 (E. 431). — F. *redresser*, 'to redresse, straighten,' Cot. — F. *re-* (<L. *re-*) again; and *dresser*; see **Re-** and **Dress**.   Der. *redress*, sb., Skelton, Magnificence, 2438; *redress-ible*, *redress-ive*.

REDUCE, to bring down, subdue, arrange. (L.)   In Palsgrave.   Used in the sense, 'to bring back;' Rich. III, v. 5. 36. — L. *redūcere*, to bring back, restore, reduce. — L. *re-*, back; and *dūcere*, to lead, bring.   See **Re-** and **Duct**, **Duke**.   Der. *reduc-ible*, spelt *reduce-able* in Levins; also *reduct-ion*, from MF. *reduction*, 'a reduction, reducing,' Cot., from L. acc. *reductiōnem*, from nom. *reductio*, allied to *reduct-us*, pp. of *redūcere*.

REDUNDANT; see under **Redound**.

REDUPLICATE, to multiply, repeat. (L.)   In Levins. — L. *reduplicātus*, pp. of obsolete *reduplicāre*, to redouble.   See **Re-** and **Duplicate**.

RE-ECHO, to echo back. (L. *and* Gk.)   In Spenser's Fairie Queene, Mutability, c. vi. st. 52.   From **Re-** and **Echo**.

REECHY, dirty. (E.)   Lit. 'smoky;' another form of *reeky*.   In Shak. Cor. ii. 1. 225, Hamlet, iii. 4. 184; Much Ado, iii. 3. 143.   Cf. 'Auld *reekie*' as a name for Edinburgh.   See **Reek**.

REED, a common name for certain grasses. (E.)   ME. *reed*, Wyclif, Matt. xi. 7.   AS. *hrēod*, Matt. xi. 7. ✦Du. *riet*; G. *riet*, *ried*.   Teut. type **hreudom*, neut.   Der. *reed-ed*, *reed-y*.

REEF (1), a ridge of rocks. (Du.)   Formerly *riff*.   'A *riff* or ridge of rocks;' Dampier's Voyages, vol. i. an. 1681; pp. 47, 50 (R.).   Of late introduction. — Du. *rif*, a reef, riff, sand.   Sewel (ed. 1754) explains by 'a flat in sea, a *riff*.'   Hexham has *rif*, *riffe*, 'a foard, or a shallow place.' ✦Icel. *rif*, a reef in the sea; Dan. *rev*, a reef, bank; cf. *revle*, a shoal; Swed. *ref*, a sandbank; Pomeran. *reff*.   The G. *riff*, a reef, is prob. borrowed from Dutch.   β. The Du. and Icel. *rif*, Dan. *rev*, n., may represent a Teut. type **rebjom*, n.   Perhaps allied to **Rib**, q. v.   Cf. Norw. *ribbe*, a mountain-ridge, MF. *coste*, 'a rib, also a little hill, or descent of land;' Cot.   Der. *reef-y*.

REEF (2), a portion of a sail that can be drawn close together. (Du.)   Fully explained in Phillips, ed. 1706.   'Up, aloft, lads; come, *reef* both topsails;' Dryden, Enchanted Island, Act i. sc. 1 (R.).   ME. *riff*, Gower, C. A. iii. 341; bk. viii. 1983. — Du. *reef*, 'a riff in a sail;' Sewel, ed. 1754.   MDu. *rif*, also *rift* (Kilian).   'Een *rif* van een zeyl inbinden,' to binde up a peece of a saile when the wind blowes too hard;' Hexham.   Hence is formed Du. *reven*, to reeve. ✦Low G. *reff*, *riff*, a little sail, which is added to a large one when there is little wind; cf. *reffen*, to reeve; EFries. *ref*, *ref*; Pomeran. *räff*, a little extra sail, a bonnet; Swed. *ref*, a reef; *refva*, to reeve; Dan. *reb*, a reef; *rebe*, to reeve; Icel. *rif*, a reef in a sail.   Of uncertain origin; cf. Icel. *reifa*, to swaddle, AS. *rēfan*, to wrap up.   Der. *reef*, verb; also *reeve*, verb, q. v.

REEK, vapour, smoke. (E.)   ME. *reke*, Cursor Mundi, 2744; where the Trinity MS. has *reech*.   AS. *rēc*, vapour; Grein, ii. 369; OMerc. *rēc* (O. E. Texts); OFries. *rēk*. ✦Du. *rook*; Icel. *reykr*; Swed. *rök*; Dan. *rög*; G. *rauch*; OHG. *rouh*.   β. Teut. base **rauk-*; from **rauk*, 2nd grade of the str. vb. **reukan-*, to smoke, as in AS. *rēocan*, Icel. *rjūka*, OHG. *riohhan*, G. *riechen*.   Brugmann, i. § 217.   Der. *reek*, verb = AS. *rēcan*, weak verb (Grein); *reek-y*; also *reech-y*, q. v.

REEL (1), a small spindle for winding yarn. (E.)   ME. *rele*.   'Hoc alabrum, a *rele*;' Wright's Voc., p. 269, col. 1.   At p. 180 of the same vol., *alabrum* is again glossed by *reele*. AS. *hrēol*; 'alibrum (*sic*), *hreol*;' Wright's Voc. p. 59; *riul*, p. 66. Ducange explains the Late L. *alabrum* as a reel. [Not Icel. *hræll* or *ræll*, a weaver's rod or sley; EFries. *rēl*; North Fries. *reel* (Outzen). Kluge derives AS. *hrēol* from a form **hrōehil*, but this would give a form **hrēl*; see Eng. Studien, xi. 512.] **Der.** *reel*, verb, ME. *relien*, *relen*, orig. to wind on a reel (P. Plowman, C. x. 81, Prompt. Parv.), hence to turn round and round (Allit. Poems, C. 147), and so to stagger, Temp. v. 279. 'They *relyd* bacward;' Malory, Morte Arthur, bk. vii. c. 16, l. 49. Cf. NFries. *reele*, to wind on a reel. ☞ Not allied to *roll*.

REEL (2), a Highland dance. (Scand.?) Commonly called 'a Scotch reel.' Todd gives the following: 'Geilles Duncane did goe before them, playing this *reill* or daunce upon a small trump;' News from Scotland (1591), sig. B. iii; hence Gael. *righil*, a reel, a Scottish dance; also written *ruithil*. Perhaps a Scand. word. Cf. Dan. dial. *riel*, *riil*, a reel, dance; described at length by Molbech, but perhaps from E. So also Norw. *ril* (pron. *riil*); Aasen. Or possibly from *reel*, verb; see **Reel** (1).

RE-ELECT, RE-EMBARK, RE-ENACT, RE-EN- FORCE, RE-ENTER, RE-ESTABLISH, RE-EX- AMINE; see **Elect, Embark,** &c.

REEST, the mould-board or breast of a plough. (E.) Also (wrongly) *wreest*; see E. D. D. AS. *rēost*; 'sules *rēost*, dentale;' Bosworth +OLow G. *rioster*, a share-beam (Gallée).

REEVE (1), to pass the end of a rope through a hole or ring. (Du.) A nautical word; not in Todd's Johnson.—Du. *reven*, to reeve.—Du. *reef*, a reef; because a reeved rope is used for reefing. See **Reef** (2). ¶ The pt. t. is usually *rove*; but this is a mere invention, as the verb, like all other verbs derived from sbs., is properly a weak one; made by analogy, like *hove* from *heave*.

REEVE (2), an officer, steward, governor. (E.) See Chaucer's *Reve's Tale*. AS. *gerēfa*, an officer, governor; Grein, i. 441. The orig. sense was perhaps 'numberer' or registrar (of soldiers); as if for **ge-rōf-ja*, from -*rōf*, a host (as in *secg-rōf*), a host of men. Cf. OHG. **ruoba*, *ruova*, a number. See Kemble, Saxons in England, ii. 154. ¶ Not allied to G. *graf*. **Der.** *borough-reeve*, *port-reeve*; *sheriff*, q.v.

REEVE (3); a bird, the female of the ruff; see **Ruff** (2).

REFECTION, refreshment, a repast. (F.—L.) 'With a litle *refection*;' Sir T. Elyot, The Governour, b. iii. c. 22. § 4; Caxton, Siege of Troy, leaf 81, l. 6.—F. *refection*, 'a refection, repast;' Cot.—L. *refectiōnem*, a restoring, refreshment; lit. a remaking; cf. L. *refectus*, pp. of *reficere*, to remake, restore.—L. *re-*, again, and *facere*, to make. See **Re-** and **Fact. Der.** *refector-y*, Dryden, Hind and Panther, iii. 530, spelt *refectorie* in Minsheu, from Late L. *refectorium*, a hall for meals in a convent.

REFEL, to refute. (L.) In Shak. Meas. v. 94; and Palsgrave.— L. *refellere*, to show to be false, refute.—L. *re-*, back again, in reply; and *fallere*, to deceive, &c. See **Re-** and **Fail, False.**

REFER, to reduce, assign, direct to an umpire. (F.—L.) '*Re-ferre* you'=betake yourself; Henrysoun, Test. of Creseide, st. 43, l. 297.—OF. *referer* (14th cent., Littré), F. *référer*, to refer.—L. *re-ferre*, to bear back, relate, refer.—L. *re-*, back; and *ferre*, cognate with E. *bear*. See **Re-** and **Bear** (1). **Der.** *refer-able*, also spelt *referr-ible* (see exx. in N. E. D.); *refer-ee*, in which the suffix answers to F. pp. suffix -*é*, as in other cases; *refer-ence*, Oth. i. 3. 238; *refer-end-ar-y*, i. e. a referee, Bacon, Essay 49, from MF. *referendaire*, which see in Cotgrave.

REFINE, to purify, make elegant. (F.:—L.) In Spenser, Hymn 2, l. 47. Coined from *re-* and *fine*, but imitated from F. *raffiner*, 'to refine,' Cot. The F. *raffiner* is from *re-* and *affiner*, 'to refine, to fine as metalls,' Cot.; where *af-* = L. *af-*, for *ad*, to, before *f* following; also -*finer* is due to F. *fin*, fine. The E. word ignores the second element. See **Re-** and **Fine** (1). **Der.** *refin-er*, *refin-er-y*; also *refine-ment*, imitated from F. *raffinement*, 'a refining,' Cot.

REFLECT, to throw or bend back, to ponder, think. (L.) In Shak. Rich. III, i. 4. 31. 'I *reflecte*, as the sonne beames do;' Palsgrave. [The sb. *reflexion* is in Chaucer, C. T. 10544 (F. 230).] —L. *reflectere*, to bend backwards.—L. *re-*, back; and *flectere*, to bend. See **Re-** and **Flexible. Der.** *reflect-ing*; *reflect-or*; *reflective*, also *reflect-ion*, for *reflex-ion*, from F. *reflexif*, 'reflexive, reflexing,' Cot.; *reflect-ive-ly*, -*ness*; *reflex*, adj., from L. *reflexus*, pp. of *reflectere*; *reflex-ible*, *reflex-ibil-i-ty*.

REFLUENT, flowing back. (L.) Rare; in Pope, Odyss. v. 550.—L. *refluent-*, stem of pres. part. of *refluere*, to flow back. —L. *re-*, back; and *fluere*, to flow; see **Re-** and **Fluent. Der.** *reflux*, sb., in Lydgate, Minor Poems, p. 194; from F. *reflux*, 'the ebbe of the sea,' Cot.; see **Flux.**

REFORM, to shape anew, amend. (F.—L.) ME. *reformen*, Gower, C. A. i. 273; bk. ii. 3404.—F. *reformer*, 'to reforme,' Cot.— L. *re-*, again, and *formāre*, to form, from *forma*, form; see **Re-** and

Form. Der. *reform-er*; *reform-at-ion*, Skelton, Garland of Laurel, 411, from F. *reformation*, 'reformation,' Cot.<L. acc. *reformā-tiōnem*, from *reformāre*; *reform-at-ive*, *reform-at-or-y*.

REFRACT, to bend aside rays of light. (L.) 'Visual beams *refracted* through another's eye;' Selden, Introd. to Drayton's Poly-olbion (R.).—L. *refractus*, pp. of *refringere*, to break back, hence, to turn aside.—L. *re-*, back; and *frangere*, to break; see **Fragile. Der.** *refract-ion*, Chapman, Monsieur D'Olive, Act ii. sc. 1 (Van-dome's 6th speech), from F. *refraction*, 'a rebound,' Cot.; *refract-ive*, *refract-ive-ness*. Also *refract-or-y*, Troil. ii. 2. 182, a mistaken form for *refractary*, from MF. *refrectaire*, 'refractary,' Cot.<L. *refractā-rius*, stubborn, obstinate. Hence *refract-or-i-ly*, *refract-or-i-ness*. Also *refrang-ible*, a mistaken form for *refring-ible*, from L. *refringere*; *refrang-ibil-i-ty*, Phillips, ed. 1706; cf. mod. F. *réfrangible*, *réfrangi-bilité*; but the F. words were borrowed from English works on optics. And see *refrain* (2).

REFRAGABLE, that may be refuted. (L.) In Bailey; who also has *refragability*; see **Irrefragable.**

REFRAIN (1), to restrain, forbear. (F.—L.) ME. *refreinen*, *refreynen*; Wyclif, James, i. 26.—OF. *refrener*, 'to bridle, repress;' Cot. [Cf. E. *ordain*<F. *ordener*.]—L. *refrēnāre*, to bridle, hold in with a bit.—L. *re-*, back; and *frēnum*, a bit, curb, pl. *frēna*, curb and reins, a bridle. β. The L. *frē-num* may be for L. **frend-num*; from *frendere*, to champ. ¶ As Littré well remarks, Cotgrave also has MF. *refreindre*, 'to bridle, restraine, hold in:' this is from L. *re-fringere*, to break back, and it seems probable that *refrener* and *refreindre* were sometimes confused; see **Refract** and **Refrain** (2).

REFRAIN (2), the burden of a song. (F.—L.) ME. *refraine*, Chaucer, Troil. ii. 1571. The sb. *refraining*, i.e. singing of the burden of a song, occurs in the Rom. of the Rose, 749.—F. *refrain*; '*refrain d'une balade*, the refret, or burden of a ballade,' Cot. Cf. Prov. *refranhs*, a refrain, *refranher*, to repeat (Bartsch); mod. Prov. *refrin*, *refrein*, *refrain* (Mistral); Port. *refrão*, Span. *refran*, a pro-verb, short saying in common use. So called from frequent repetition; the OF. *refreindre*, to hold in, pull back (Cotgrave), is the same word as Prov. *refranher*, to repeat; both are from L. *refringere*, to break back, hence, to pull back (and so to come back to, to repeat). β. So also the MF. *refret*, OF. *refrait* (12th c.), used in the same sense (whence E. *refret*, as in Cotgrave above), is from the L. *re-fractus*, pp. of *refringere*: see **Refract.** γ. The Prov. *refranhs* has its *a* from L. *frangere*. Körting, § 7894.

REFRESH, to enliven, revive. (F.—L. *and* G.) ME. *refreshen*, *refreschen*; Chaucer, C. T. 5620 (D 38); Gower, C. A. iii. 25; bk. vi. 710.—OF. *refreschir*, 'to refresh, coole;' Cot.—F. *re-* (=L. re-), again; and OHG. *frisc* (G. *frisch*), cognate with E. *fresh*, q. v. ¶ The element *fresh* is, in fact, also native English; but the com-pound *refresh* was nevertheless borrowed from French, as shown further by the early use of the derived sb. *refreshment*. **Der.** *refresh-ment*, in the Testament of Love, pt. iii. ch. 7, l. 31, OF. *refresche-ment*; cf. MF. *refreschissement*, 'a refreshment,' Cot.

REFRIGERATE, to cool. (L.) 'Their fury was asswaged and *refrigerate*;' Hall, Chronicle, Henry VII, an. 4. § 1; where it is used as a pp. Spelt *refrigerat*, Caxton, G. Legend, St. Silvester, § 1. —L. *refrīgerātus*, pp. of *refrīgerāre*, to make cool again.—L. *re-*, again; and *frīgerāre*, to cool, from *frīgus*, sb., cold. See **Re-** and **Frigid. Der.** *refrigerat-or*, *refrigerat-ion*, *refrigerat-ive*, *refrigerat-or-y*; also *refriger-ant*, from the stem of the pres. part. of *refrīgerāre*.

REFT, pt. t. and pp. of **Reave**, q.v.

REFUGE, a shelter, retreat. (F.—L.) ME. *refuge*, Chaucer, C. T. 1722 (A 1720).—F. *refuge*, 'a refuge,' Cot.—L. *refugium*, an escape, a refuge.—L. *refugere*, to flee back, retreat.—L. *re-*, back; and *fugere*, to flee. See **Re-** and **Fugitive. Der.** *refug-ee*, Dryden, tr. of Juvenal, Sat. iii. 129, from F. *réfugié*, pp. of *se réfugier*, to take shelter.

REFULGENT, shining, brilliant. (L.) In Ben Jonson, The Barriers, Opinion's 4th speech.—L. *refulgent-*, stem of pres. part. of *refulgēre*, to shine back, glitter.—L. *re-*, back; and *fulgēre*, to shine. See **Re-** and **Fulgent. Der.** *refulgent-ly*, *refulgence*.

REFUND, to repay. (L.) '*Refund*, to melt again, reflow, cast out again, pay back;' Blount's Gloss., ed. 1674. [The sense answers to that of MF. *refonder*, 'to restore, pay back,' Cot. Perhaps it was borrowed from French, and accommodated to the L. spelling.]—L. *refundere*, to pour back, restore.—L. *re-*, back; and *fundere*, to pour. See **Re-** and **Fuse** (1). Perhaps allied to *refuse*, q.v.

REFUSE, to reject, deny a request. (F.—L.) ME. *refusen*, Rob. of Brunne, tr. of Langtoft, p. 103, l. 21.—OF. *refuser*, 'to refuse,' Cot. Cf. Port. *refusar*, Span. *rehusar* (for *refusar*), Ital. *rifusare*. β. Of disputed origin. Diez supposes it to have arisen as another form of *refute* (L. *refūtāre*), by confusion with L. *recūsāre*, to refuse. But Scheler well suggests that F. *refuser* clearly answers to a Late L. form **refūsāre*, a frequentative form of *refundere* (pp.

refūsus). The L. *refundere* meant to pour back, repay, restore, give back; and the sense of 'refusing' may have arisen from giving back a present. See above. Cf. *confuse.* Körting, § 7897. **Der.** *réfuse,* sb. (Levins), ME. *refuce,* Prompt. Parv., from MF. *refus,* 'refuse, outcasts, leavings,' Cot.; from the vb. Cf. OF. *mettre en refus, faire refus à,* to abandon, reject (Godefroy). Also *refus-al* (Levins), in which the suffix was added by analogy with *propos-al,* &c.

REFUTE, to oppose, dispose. (F.—L.) In Minsheu, ed. 1627.—MF. *refuter,* 'to refute, confute,' Cot.—L. *refūtāre,* to repel, repress, rebut, refute. The orig. sense was probably 'to pour back.' See **Re-** and **Confute;** also **Futile. Der.** *refut-able; refut-at-ion,* from MF. *refutation,* 'a refutation,' Cot.; *refut-at-or-y,* from L. adj. *refūtātōrius.*

REGAIN, to gain back. (F.—L. *and* Teut.) The sb. *regainyng* is in Hall's Chron. Hen. VI, an. 15. § 5.—MF. *regaigner,* 'to regaine;' Cot.; F. *regagner.*—F. *re-* (=L. *re-,* again); and MF. *gaigner* (F. *gagner*), to gain, a word of German origin, as shown under **Gain** (2).

REGAL, royal, kingly. (F.—L.) *Regall* occurs as a sb. in The Plowman's Tale, st. 19, l. 202; and as an adj. in Levins, ed. 1570.—MF. *regal,* 'regall, royal,' Cot.—L. *rēgālis,* royal, kingly.—L. *rēg-,* stem of *rex,* a king, with suffix *-ālis.*—L. *regere,* to rule.—√REG, to stretch, to govern; whence Skt. *rāj,* to govern. Cf. Skt. *rājan-,* a king; OIrish *rī,* a king. Brugmann, i. §§ 135, 549 c. **Der.** *regal-ly, regal-i-ty;* also *regal-ia,* q. v. From the same root are numerous words, such as *cor-rect, di-rect, e-rect, rectangle, rect-itude, rect-ify, rect-or; rajah; reach, right, rack* (1); *rig-id, reg-ent, regi-cide, regi-men, regi-ment, reg-ion, reg-ular, regnant, reign, rule;* also *dress, address, adroit, alert, dirge, escort, insurgent, insurrection, inter-regnum, real* (2), *realm, resource, resurrection, rule, sortie, source, surge, unruly;* cf. *rajah, rich, right.* **Doublet,** *royal.*

REGALE, to entertain, refresh. (F.—Ital.?) In Blount's Gloss., ed. 1674.—F. *régaler,* to entertain; see Littré. Cotgrave only gives *se regaler,* 'to make as much account of himself as if he were a king;' evidently in order to connect the word with F. *régal,* regal, royal; but this can hardly be right. Godefroy has OF. *regallir,* to feast. β. The word offers great difficulties. Minsheu's Span. Dict. gives *regalar,* 'to cocker, to make much of, to melt.' Diez takes the sense 'to melt' to be the orig. one; whence to warm, cherish, entertain. He makes the Span. *regalar=*L. *regelāre,* to thaw, to melt, supposing that it was a very old word, adopted at a time when *g* had the same sound before both *a* and *e.* The L. *regelāre* is from *re-,* again, back, and *gelāre,* to freeze; the orig. sense being 'to unfreeze,' i.e. to thaw. See **Re-** and **Gelatine.** γ. But Hatzfeld connects F. *régaler* with Ital. *regalare,* to give presents to, from *gala,* mirth; cf. Span. *gala,* parade. See **Gala.** See further in Diez, Körting, and Littré. **Der.** *regale-ment.*

REGALIA, insignia of a king. (L.) In Blount (1656). Merely L. *rēgālia,* lit. royal things, neut. pl. of *rēgālis,* royal; see **Regal.**

REGARD, to observe, respect, consider. (F.—L. *and* OHG.) In Palsgrave, spelt *regarde.* The sb. *regard* seems to be in earlier use in E., occurring in Chaucer, in the phr. *at regard of,* Pers. Tale, (Six-text, Group I, 788); but the verb is the orig. word in French.—F. *regarder,* 'to look, eye, see, view;' Cot.—F. *re-,* again; and *garder,* 'to keep, heed, mark;' Cot. See **Re-** and **Guard. Der.** *regard,* sb., as above; *regard-er; regard-ful; regard-ful-ly,* Timon, iv. 3. 81; *regard-less, regard-less-ly, -ness.* **Doublet,** *reward,* vb.

REGATTA, a rowing or sailing match. (Ital.) Properly a rowing match; a Venetian word, as explained in the quotation from Drummond's Travels, p. 84, in Todd's Johnson; a book which Todd dates A.D. 1744, but Lowndes in 1754.—Ital. *regatta, rigatta,* 'a strife or contention for the maistrie;' Florio. Cf. MItal. *rigattare,* 'to wrangle, sell by retail as hucksters do, to contend, to cope or fight;' Florio. This is allied to Span. *regatear,* to haggle, retail provisions, **also** to rival in sailing (Neuman); Span. *regateo,* a haggling, a regatta. Of unknown origin.

REGENERATE, to renew, produce anew. (L.) In Caxton, G. Legend, St. Genevefe, § 2.—L. *regenerātus,* pp. of *regenerāre,* to generate again.—L. *re-,* again; and *generāre;* see **Re-** and **Generate. Der.** *regenerat-ion,* ME. *regeneracioun,* Wyclif, Matt. xix. 28, from OF. *regeneration* (14th cent., Littré)<L. acc. *regenerātiōnem; regenerat-ive.*

REGENT, invested with authority for an interim period. (F.—L.) In Skelton, Against the Scottes, l. 114.—MF. *regent,* 'a regent, protector, vice-gerent;' Cot.—L. *regent-,* stem of pres. part. of *regere,* to rule. See **Regal. Der.** *regent-ship;* also *regenc-y,* formed with suffix *-y* from F. *regence,* 'the regency,' Cot.

REGICIDE, the slayer of a king; or, the slaying of a king. (F.—L.) 1. The former is the older sense. '*Regicide,* a king-killer;' Minsheu.—F. *regicide,* omitted by Cotgrave, but cited by Minsheu. Coined from L. *rēgi-,* from *rex,* a king; and *-cīda,* a slayer, as in *fratri-cīda, matri-cīda.* See **Fratricide, Matricide, Parricide.** 2. The latter answers to a word coined from L. *rēgi-* and *-cīdium,* a slaying. **Der.** *regicid-al.*

REGIMEN, a prescribed rule, rule of diet. (L.) In Phillips, ed. 1706; ME. *regimen,* Lanfrank, Cirurgie, p. 60.—L. *regimen,* guidance; formed with suffix *-men* from *regere,* to rule; see **Regal.**

REGIMENT, a body of soldiers commanded by a colonel. (F.—L.) Shak. has it in this sense, All's Well, ii. 1. 42; and also in the sense of 'government,' or sway; Antony, iii. 6. 95. In the latter sense, the word is old, and occurs in Gower, C. A. i. 218; bk. ii. 1751.—MF. *regiment,* 'a regiment of souldiers,' Cot. In older F., it meant 'government;' see Littré.—L. *regimentum,* rule, government; formed with suffixes *-men-to-* from *regere,* to rule; see **Regimen, Regal. Der.** *regiment-al.*

REGION, a district, country. (F.—L.) ME. *regioun,* King Alisaunder, l. 82.—MF. *region,* 'a region,' Cot.—L. *regiōnem,* acc. of *regio,* a direction, quarter, district (Bréal).—L. *regere,* to rule, direct. See **Regal.**

REGISTER, a written record of past events. (F.—L.) ME. *registre,* P. Plowman, B. xx. 269.—F. *registre,* 'a record, register;' Cot. Cf. Ital. and Span. *registro,* Port. *registro, registo,* the last being the best form.—Late L. *registrum,* more correctly *regestum,* a book in which things are recorded (*regeruntur*); see Ducange.—L. *regestum,* neut. of *regestus,* pp. of *regerere,* to record, lit. to bring back.—L. *re-,* back; and *gerere,* to bring; see **Re-** and **Jest. Der.** *register,* verb, L.L.L. i. 1. 2, and in Palsgrave; *registr-ar,* ME. *registrere,* P. Plowman, B. xix. 254; *registr-ar-ship; registr-ar-y* (Late L. *registrār-ius*); *registr-y; registr-at-ion.*

REGLET, a strip of wood, less than type-high, used in printing for making blanks between lines. (F.—L.) F. *réglet* (Hatzfeld); dimin. of *règle,* a rule.—L. *rēgula,* a rule; see **Rule.**

REGNANT, reigning. (L.) Mere Latin.—L. *regnant-,* stem of pres. pt. of *regnāre,* to reign.—L. *regnum,* a kingdom; see **Reign. Der.** *regnanc-y.*

REGRESS, return. (L.) In Shak. Merry Wives, ii. 1. 226; and in Minsheu, ed. 1627.—L. *regressus,* a return.—L. *regressus,* pp. of *regredi,* to go back.—L. *re-,* back; and *gradī,* to go. See **Re-** and **Grade. Der.** *regress,* verb; *regress-ion* (L. *regressio*); *regress-ive.*

REGRET, sorrow, grief. (F.—L. *and* Scand.?) The verb is in Pope, Epitaph on Fenton, l. 8. ME. *regretten,* The Pearl, 243. The sb. is in Spenser, F. Q. i. 7. 20. 'Hie *regrate* And still mourning;' Henrysoun, Test. of Creseide, st. 57, l. 397.—F. *regret,* 'desire, wille, also griefe, sorrow;' Cot. He also gives: *à regret,* 'loathly, unwillingly, with an ill stomach, hardly, mauger his head, full sore against his will;' Cot. Cf. *regretter,* 'to desire, affect, wish for, bewaile, bemoane, lament;' id. The F. *regretter* corresponds to an OF. *regrater,* of which Scheler cites two examples; cf. AF. *regretant,* pres. pt., bewailing, in Wace, St. Nicholas, l. 187. β. The etymology is much disputed; but, as the word occurs in no other Romance language, it is prob. of Teut. origin, the prefix *re-* being, of course, Latin. Perhaps from the Scand. verb which appears in Icel. *grāta,* to weep, bewail, mourn, Swed. *grāta,* Dan. *græde,* allied to Goth. *grētan,* AS. *grētan,* ME. *greten,* Lowland Sc. *greit.* See **Greet** (2). Wedgwood well cites from Palsgrave: 'I mone as a chylde doth for the wantyng of his nourse or mother, *je regrete.*' Others suggest L. *requiritāri,* but *quiritāri* became F. *crier;* see **Cry.** See the whole discussion in Scheler; and Körting, § 7989. **Der.** *regret,* verb, as above; *regret-ful, regret-ful-ly.*

REGULAR, according to rule. (L.) 'And as these chanouns *regulers,*' i.e. regular canons; Rom. of the Rose, 6694. Rather directly from L. *regulāris* than from OF. *regulier.*—L. *rēgula,* a rule. L. *reg-ere,* to rule, govern; see **Regal. Der.** *regular-ly; regular-i-ty,* from OF. *regularité* (14th cent., Littré); *regul-ate,* from L. *regulātus,* pp. of *regulāre; regul-at-ion, regulat-ive, regulat-or.*

REHEARSE, to repeat what has been said. (F.—L.) ME. *rehercen, rehersen;* P. Plowman, C. xviii. 25; A. i. 22.—OF. *reherser,* 'to harrow over again,' Cot.; better spelt *rehercer,* as in AF. *rehercier,* to repeat, in A Nominale, ed. Skeat, l. 405. From the sense of harrowing again we easily pass to the sense of 'going again over the same ground,' and hence to that of repetition. Cf. the phrase 'to *rake* up an old story.'—F. *re-* (=L. *re-*), again; and *hercer,* 'to harrow,' Cot., from *herce,* a harrow. The sb. *herce,* whence E. *hearse,* changed its meaning far more than the present word did; see **Re-** and **Hearse. Der.** *rehears-al,* spelt *rehersall* in Palsgrave; ME. *rehersaille,* Chaucer, C. T., G 852.

REIGN, rule, dominion. (F.—L.) ME. *regne,* Chaucer, C. T. 1638; spelt *rengne,* King Horn, ed. Lumby, 901, 908.—OF. *regne,* 'a realme,' Cot.—L. *regnum,* a kingdom.—L. *reg-ere,* to rule; see **Regal. Der.** *reign,* verb, ME. *regnen,* Havelok, 2586, from OF. *regner,* from L. *regnāre,* to reign. And see *regn-ant.*

REIMBURSE, to refund, repay for a loss. (F.—L. *and* Gk.) In Cotgrave; and in Phillips, ed. 1706. An adaptation of F. *rembourser*, made more full in order to be more explicit; the F. prefix *rem-* answering to L. *re-im-*, where *im-* stands for *in* before *b* following. 'Rembourser, to re-imburse, to restore money spent;' Cot. For the rest of the word, see **Purse.** Der. *reimburse-ment*, from F. *remboursement*, 'a re-imbursement;' Cot.

REIN, the strap of a bridle. (F.—L.) ME. *reine, reyne*, King Alisaunder, 786. — OF. *reine*, 'the reigne of a bridle;' Cot. Mod. F. *rêne.* The OF. also has *resne, redne*, corresponding to Ital. *redina*, and to Span. *rienda* (a transposed form, for *redina*); and these further correspond to a Late L. type *retina* (MItal. *retina*), easily evolved from L. *retinēre*, to hold back, restrain, whence was formed the classical L. *retināculum*, a tether, halter, rein. See **Retain.** Der. *rein*, verb, *rein-less.*

REINDEER, RAINDEER, a kind of deer. (Scand. *and* E.) Spelt *raynedere*, Morte Arthure, ed. Brock, 922. Perhaps the obscure word *ron*, in An Old Eng. Miscellany, ed. Morris, p. 92, l. 71, means a reindeer, as suggested by Stratmann. Formed by adding *deer* (an E. word) to Icel. *hreinn*, a reindeer, answering to MSwed. *ren*, and to AS. *hrān*, in Ælfred's tr. of Orosius, i. 1. § 15. [The AS. *hrān* accounts for ME. *ron* (above).] We find also Dan. *rensdyr*, Du. *rendier*, G. *rennthier*, all borrowed forms. A genuine Teut. word, as the forms show. Teut. type *hrainoz.* β. Diez refers us to the Lapp and Finnish word *raingo*, but this is a mere misspelling of Swed. *renko*, lit. 'rein-cow,' the female of the reindeer. The true Lapp word for reindeer is *pâtso*, and the word *reino*, pasturage or herding of cattle, does not help us.

REINS, the lower part of the back. (F.—L.) ME. *reines*; spelt *reynes* in Wyclif, Wisdom, i. 6, later version; *reenus*, earlier version. — OF. *reins*, 'the reines;' Cot. — L. *rēnēs*, s. pl., the kidneys, reins, loins. Hardly allied to Gk. φρήν, the midriff; pl. φρένες, the parts about the heart or liver. See **Frenzy.** Der. *ren-al.*

REINSTATE, REINVEST, REINVIGORATE, RE-ISSUE, REITERATE; see **Instate, Invest,** &c.

REJECT, to throw away or aside. (F.—L.) 'I *rejecte*, I caste awaye, *je rejecte*;' Palsgrave, ed. 1530. — MF. *rejecter*; mod. F. *rejeter.* The F. word was spelt *rejecter* in the 16th century, and our word seems to have been borrowed from it rather than from Latin directly; the still older spelling in OF. was *regeter.* — OF. *re-* (= L. *re-*), back; and OF. *geter, getter*, mod. F. *jeter*, to throw, from L. *iactāre.* See **Re-** and **Jet** (1). Cf. L. *rejectus*, pp. of *reicere*, to reject, compounded of *re-* and *iacere*, to throw. Der. *reject-ion*, from MF. *rejection*, 'a rejection;' Cot.

REJOICE, to feel glad, exult. (F.—L.) ME. *reioisen, reioicen* (with *i* = *j*), to rejoice; Chaucer, C. T. 9867 (E 1993); P. Plowman, C. xviii. 198. — OF. *resjoïs-*, stem of pres. part. of *resjoïr*, mod. F. *réjouir*, to gladden, rejoice. — OF. *re-* (= L. *re-*), again; and *esjoïr* (mod. F. *éjouir*), to rejoice, used reflexively. β. Again, the OF. *esjoïr* is from L. *ex-*, and the vb. *joïr* (mod. F. *jouir*), derived, like Ital. *godere*, from L. *gaudēre*, to rejoice. See **Re-, Ex-,** and **Joy.** Der. *rejoic-ing, rejoic-ing-ly.*

REJOIN, to join again. (F.—L.) Esp. used in the legal sense 'to answer to a reply.' 'I *rejoyne*, as men do that answere to the lawe and make answere to the byll that is put up agaynst them;' Palsgrave. — F. *rejoign-*, a stem of *rejoindre*, 'to rejoine;' Cot. See **Re-** and **Join.** Der. *rejoinder*, Sir T. Elyot, The Governour, b. i. c. 14. § 8, which is the F. infin. mood used substantively, like *attainder, remainder.*

REJUVENATE, to make young again. (L.) From L. *re-*, again; and *iuuen-*, for *iuuenis*, young; with pp. suffix *-ātus.* See **Juvenile.**

RELAPSE, to slide back into a former state. (L.) As sb. in Minsheu, ed. 1627, and in Shak. Per. iii. 2. 110. Cotgrave translates the MF. *relaps* by 'relapsed.' [There is no classical L. sb. *relapsus.*] — L. *relapsus*, pp. of *relābī*, to slide back. See **Re-** and **Lapse.** Der. *relapse*, sb.

RELATE, to describe, tell. (F.—L.) In Spenser, F. Q. iii. 8. 51; and in Palsgrave. — F. *relater*, 'to relate;' Cot. — Late L. *relātāre*, to relate. — L. *relātum*, used as supine of *referre*, to relate; which is, however, from a different root. — L. *re-*, back; and *lātum*, supine, *lātus*, pp., for *tlātus*, pp. of *tollere*, to lift, bear. See **Re-;** and **Elate.** Der. *relat-ed; relat-ion*, P. Plowman, C. iv. 363, from F. *relation*, 'a relation,' Cot.; *relat-ive*, ME. *relatif*, P. Plowman, C. iv. 391, from F. *relatif; relat-ive-ly.*

RELAX, to slacken, loosen. (L.) In Milton, P. L. vi. 599. [Bacon has *relax* as an adj., Nat. Hist. § 381.] — L. *relaxāre*, to relax. — L. *re-*, back; and *laxāre*, to loosen, from *laxus*, loose; see **Re-** and **Lax.** Der. *relax-at-ion*, in Minsheu, from F. *relaxation*, 'a relaxation,' Cot. Doublet, *release.*

RELAY (1), a set of fresh dogs or horses, a fresh supply. (F.—L.) Orig. used of dogs. 'What *relays* set you? None at all, we laid not In one fresh dog;' Ben Jonson, Sad Shepherd, Act i. sc. 2. ME. *relaye*, in the same sense, Chaucer, Book of the Duchess, 362. — F. *relais*, a relay; *par relais*, 'by turnes,' i.e. by relays, Cot. He also gives: '*chiens de relais*, dogs layd for a backset,' i.e. kept in reserve; '*chevaux de relais*, horses layed in certain places on the highway, for the more haste making.' He explains *relais* as 'a seat or standing for such as hold *chiens de relais*,' i.e. a station. See OF. *relais*, that which remains, in Godefroy. β. The word presents some difficulty. Mr. Wedgwood quotes from Torriano: '*Cani di rilasso*, fresh hounds laid for a supply set upon a deer already hunted by other dogs.' Also spelt *rilascio*, and allied to Ital. *rilasciare* (from L. *relaxāre*), OF. *relaissier*, to relinquish, and E. **Relax, Release,** q.v. Körting, § 7930. Cf. '*à relais*, spared, at rest, that is not used,' Cot. γ. It will be seen that *relay* was a new singular, due to a mistaken notion that the F. *relais* was a plural. So also in French, an OF. verb *relayer* was made out of a false sing. *relai.* The OF. *relais*, though usually sing., is sometimes treated as a plural, preceded by *les* instead of *le.* See **Relish.**

RELAY (2), to lay again. (Hybrid; L. *and* E.) Simply compounded of **Re-** and **Lay;** and distinct from the word above.

RELEASE, to set free, relieve, let go. (F.—L.) ME. *relessen*, P. Plowman, B. iii. 58; *relesen*, Chaucer, C. T. 8029 (E 153). — OF. *relessier*, MF. *relaisser*, 'to release,' Cot. — L. *relaxāre*, to relax; see **Relax.** Der. *release*, sb., OF. *reles*, for *relais.* Doublet, **Relax.**

RELEGATE, to consign to exile. (L.) 'To *relegate*, or exile;' Minsheu, ed. 1627. — L. *relegātus*, pp. of *relegāre*, to send away, dispatch, remove. — L. *re-*, back, away; and *legāre*, to send. See **Re-** and **Legate.** Der. *relegat-ion*, from MF. *relegation*, 'a relegation,' Cot.

RELENT, to grow tender, feel compassion. (F.—L.) In The Lamentacion of Mary Magdalene, st. 70, l. 489. Altered from F. *ralentir*, 'to slacken, .. to relent in;' Cot. Cf. L. *relentescere*, to slacken. — F. *re-* and *a* (shortened to *ra-*), from L. *re-* and *ad-*; and *lentus*, slack, slow, also tenacious, pliant, akin to E. *lithe*; see **Lithe.** The L. *relentescere* is simply from *re-* and *lentus*, omitting *ad.* Der. *relent-less, -ly, -ness.*

RELEVANT, relating to the matter in hand. (F.—L.) 'To make our probations and arguments *relevant*;' King Chas. I, Letter to A. Henderson, p. 55 (R.). It means 'assisting' or helpful. — F. *relevant*, pres. part. of *relever*, 'to raise up, also to assist;' Cot. — L. *releuāre*, to lift up again. — L. *re-*, again; and *leuāre*, to lift, from *leuis*, light; see **Re-** and **Levity.** Der. *relevance, relevanc-y; ir-relevant.*

RELIC, a memorial, remnant, esp. a memorial of a saint. (F.—L.) Chiefly in the plural; ME. *relykes*, s. pl., Rob. of Glouc. p. 177, l. 3688; Chaucer, C. T. 703 (A 701). — F. *reliques*, s. pl., 'reliques;' Cot. — L. *reliquiās*, acc. of *reliquiæ*, pl., remains, relics. — L. *relinquere* (pt. t. *relīquī*, pp. *relictus*), to leave behind. — L. *re-*, back, behind; and *linquere*, to leave, allied to E. *loan.* See **Re-** and **Loan.** And see **Relinquish, Relict.** Der. *reliqu-ar-y*, q. v.

RELICT, a widow. (F.—L.) In Phillips, ed. 1658. First in 1545 (N.E.D.). — OF. *relicte*, f., a widow (Godefroy). — L. *relicta*, fem. of *relictus*, left behind, pp. of *relinquere*; see **Relic, Relinquish.**

RELIEVE, to ease, help, free from oppression. (F.—L.) ME. *releuen* (with *u* = *v*), P. Plowman, B. vii. 32; Chaucer, C. T. 4180 (A 4182). — F. *relever*, 'to raise up, relieve,' Cot. — L. *releuāre*, to lift up. — L. *re-*, again; and *leuāre*, to lift, from *leuis*, light. See **Re-** and **Lever.** Der. *relief*, ME. *relief*, Gower, C. A. iii. 23, bk. vi. 640; from OF. *relef*, mod. F. *relief*, a sb. due to the verb *relever*; hence *bas-relief*; also *rilievo*, from Ital. *rilievo*, the relief or projection of a sculptured figure. And see *relev-ant.*

RELIGION, piety, the performance of duties to God and man. (F.—L.) In early use. Spelt *religiun*, O. Eng. Homilies, ed. Morris, ii. 49, l. 13; Ancren Riwle, p. 8. — F. *religion.* — L. *religiōnem*, acc. of *religio*, piety. Allied to *religens*, fearing the gods, pious. [And therefore not derived from *religāre*, to bind.] The opposite of *negligens*, negligent; see **Neglect.** Allied also to *dī-ligens*, diligent. β. 'It is clear that ἀλέγω is the opposite of L. *nec-lego* [*neglego*, *negligo*], and θεῶν ὅπιν οὐκ ἀλέγοντες (Homer, Il. xvi. 388) is the exact counterpart of L. *religens* and *religio*;' Curtius, i. 454. Thus *religion* and *neglect* are from the same root LEG, which appears also in Gk. ἀλέγειν, to have a care for, to heed; cf. also Gk. ἄλγος, care, sorrow. Der. *religion-ist; religi-ous*, from F. *religieux*, 'religious,' Cot., which from L. *religiōsus; religi-ous-ly.*

RELINQUISH, to leave, abandon. (F.—L.) In Levins, ed. 1570. — MF. *relinquiss-*, stem of pres. part. of *relinquir* (Burguy); cf. Norm. dial. *relenquir* (Moisy). — L. *relinquere*, to leave; by a change of conjugation, of which there are several other examples. See **Relic.** Der. *relinquish-ment.*

RELIQUARY, a casket for holding relics. (F.—L.) In

Blount's Gloss., ed. 1674.—F. *reliquaire*, 'a casket wherein reliques be kept;' Cot.—Late L. *reliquiāre*, neut. sb., or *reliquiārium*, a reliquary; Ducange.—L. *reliquiā-*, stem of *reliquiæ*, relics. See **Relic.**

RELIQUE, the same as **Relic**, q. v.

RELISH, orig. an after-taste; hence, as verb, to have a pleasing taste, to taste with pleasure. (F.—L.) The verb is in Shak. Temp. v. 23; Wint. Tale, v. 2. 132. The sb. is in Tw. Nt. iv. 1. 64; and in Palsgrave. ME. *reles*, an after-taste, Sir Cleges, 208; *reles*, 'tast or odowre,' Prompt. Parv.—OF. *reles*, *relais*, that which is left behind; also a relay; see **Relay** (1). Cf. mod. Prov. *relais*, a slight return of a disease. See Notes on Eng. Etym. p. 246.

RELUCTANT, striving against, unwilling. (L.) In Milton, P. L. iv. 311.—L. *reluctant-*, stem of pres. part. of *reluctāre*, *reluctāri*, to struggle against.—L. *re-*, back, against; and *luctāri*, to struggle, wrestle, from *lucta*, a wrestling. β. *Luc-ta* stands for **lug-ta*; cf. Gk. λυγ-ίζειν, to bend, twist, writhe in wrestling, overmaster; Lith. *lugnas*, flexible. (√LEUG.) **Der.** *reluctant-ly*, *reluctance*, Milton, P. L. ii. 337; *reluctanc-y*.

RELY, to rest or repose on, trust fully. (F.—L.; *influenced by* E.) The mod. sense suggests that it is a barbarous word, compounded of L. *re-* and E. *lie*, verb, to rest; but if this were so, the pt. t. would be *relay*, and the pp. *relain*. Shakespeare is an early authority for it, and he always uses it with the prep. *on* (five times) or *upon* (once). He also has *reliance*, followed by *on*, Timon, ii. 1. 22. So also *rely on*, Drayton, Miseries of Q. Margaret, st. 123; Dryden, Epistle to J. Dryden, 139; *relying in*, P. Fletcher, Eliza, an Elegy, l. 34; *reliers on*, Beaum. and Fletcher, Woman's Prize, i. 3 (Petruchio's 24th speech). Thus to *rely on* often suggests the notion of to lie back on, to lean on. β. But the right origin is rather the OF. *relier*, from the L. *religāre*, lit. to bind again.—L. *re-*, again; and *ligāre*, to bind; see **Ligament.** The E. verb signified at first 'to rally,' whence the sense of to trust to, depend upon, &c. F. Hall, in his work on Eng. adjs. in *-able*, gives examples. Thus we find: 'Therefore [they] must needs *relye* their faithe *upon* the sillie ministers;' H. T.; in Anth. Wotton's Answer to a Popish Pamphlet, 1605, p. 19. '*Whereon* these [men] . . . rest and *relye* themselves;' A World of Wonders, 1607; p. 21. **Der.** *reli-able*, a compound adj. which has completely established itself, and is by no means a new word, to which many frivolous and ignorant objections have been made; it was used by Coleridge in 1800, in the Morning Post of Feb. 18; see F. Hall, On Eng. Adjectives in *-able*, with special reference to Reliable, p. 29. Hence *reli-abil-i-ty*, used by Coleridge in 1816; *reli-able-ness*, also used by the same writer. Also *reli-ance*, in Shak., as above, from OF. *reliance* (<L. *religantia*), in Godefroy. Also *reli-er*, as above.

REMAIN, to stay or be left behind. (F.—L.) Spelt *remayne* in Palsgrave. Due to the OF. 1 p. pres. sing. *je remain*; cf. the impers. verb *il remaint*, as in the proverb '*beaucoup remaint de ce que fol pense*, much is behind of that a fool accounts of, a foole comes ever short of his intentions,' Cot. The infin. *remaindre* is preserved in our sb. *remainder*; cf. E. *rejoinder* from F. *rejoindre*, E. *attainder* from F. *attaindre*. Cf. L. *remanet*, it remains; *remanēre*, to remain.—L. *re-*, behind; and *manēre*, to remain; see **Re-** and **Manor.** **Der.** *remains*, s. pl., Titus Andron., i. 81; *remain-der*, Temp. v. 13, see above. And see *remnant*.

REMAND, to send back. (F.—L.) 'Whervpon he was *remaunded*;' Berners, tr. of Froissart, v. ii. c. 206 (R.).—OF. *remander*, 'to send for back again;' Cot.—L. *remandāre*, to send back word.—L. *re-*, back; and *mandāre*, to enjoin, send word; see **Re-** and **Mandate.**

REMARK, to take notice of. (F.—L. *and* Teut.) Shak. has *remark'd*, Hen. VIII, v. 1. 33; and *remarkable*, Antony, iv. 15. 67.—F. *remarquer*, 'to mark, note, heed;' Cot.—L. *re-*, again; and *marquer*, to mark, allied to *marque*, sb., a mark, OF. *merc* (Hatzfeld); which is from G. *marke*, cognate with E. *mark*; see **Re-** and **Mark** (1). **Der.** *remark-able*, from F. *remarquable*, 'remarkable,' Cot.; *remark-abl-y*; *remark-able-ness*.

REMEDY, that which restores, repairs, or heals. (F.—L.) ME. *remedie*, Chaucer, C. T. 1276 (A 1274); Ancren Riwle, p. 124, l. 22.—AF. *remedie*, Stat. Realm, i. 28 (1275); cf. MF. *remede*, mod. F. *remède*, a remedy. [Cf. OF. *remedier*, verb, to remedy.]—L. *remedium*, a remedy; lit. that which heals again.—L. *re-*, again; and *medēri*, to heal; see **Re-** and **Medical.** **Der.** *remedy*, verb (Levins, Palsgrave), from F. *remedier*; *remedi-able* (Levins); *remedi-al*, a coined word; *remedi-al-ly*.

REMEMBER, to recall to mind. (F.—L.) ME. *remembren*, Chaucer, C. T. 1503 (A 1501).—OF. *remembrer*, used reflexively, 'to remember;' Cot. Formed, with excrescent *b* after *m*, due to stress, from L. *rememorāri*, to remember; which gave rise to **rememem'rer* in OF.—L. *re-*, again; and *memorāre*, to make mention of,

from *memor*, mindful. See **Re-** and **Memory.** **Der.** *remembrance*, Chaucer, C. T. 8799 (E 923), from F. *remembrance*; *remembranc-er*, Macb. iii. 4. 37.

REMIND, to bring to the mind again. (Hybrid; L. *and* E.) A barbarous compound; from L. *re-*, again; and E. *mind*. Rather a late word; in Bailey's Dict. vol. ii. ed. 1731. See **Re-** and **Mind.**

REMINISCENCE, recollection. (F.—L.) In Blount's Gloss., ed. 1674. Spelt *reminiscens*, Puttenham, E. Poesie, ed. Arber, b. iii. c. 25; p. 312.—MF. *reminiscence*, 'remembrance of things;' Cot.—L. *reminiscentia*, remembrance.—L. *reminiscent-*, stem of pres. part. of *reminisci*, to remember, an inceptive verb, with suffix *-sci*.—L. *re-*, again; and *min-*, as in *me-min-ī*, I remember, think over again, from √MEN, to think. Allied to Gk. μέ-μον-α, I yearn, Skt. *man*, to think. Brugmann, i. § 431 (2). See **Re-** and **Mental.**

REMIT, to pardon, abate. (L.) 'Whether the consayle be good, I *remytte* [leave] it to the wyse reders;' Sir T. Elyot, The Governour, b. iii. c. 27 (near the end). '*Remyttinge* [referring] them . . . to the workes of Galene;' id., Castel of Helth, b. iii. c. 1.—L. *remittere*, to send back, slacken, abate.—L. *re-*, back; and *mittere*, to send; see **Re-** and **Mission.** **Der.** *remitt-er*, *remitt-ance*, *remitt-ent*; *remiss*, adj. (spelt *remysse*, Barclay, Ship of Fools, ii. 243), from L. *remissus*, pp. of *remittere*; *remiss-ly*, *remiss-ness*; *remiss-ible*, from L. *remissibilis*; *remiss-ibil-i-ty*; *remiss-ive*. Also *remiss-ion*, ME. *remission*, Ancren Riwle, p. 346, l. 21, from MF. *remission* (Cot.).<L. acc. *remissiōnem*, from nom. *remissio*.

REMNANT, a remainder, fragment. (F.—L.) ME. *remenant*, *remenaunt*, King Alisaunder, 5707.—OF. *remanant*, MF. *remenant*, *remanent*, 'a remnant, residue;' Cot.—L. *remanent-*, stem of pres. part. of *remanēre*, to remain; see **Remain.**

REMONSTRATE, to adduce strong reasons against. (L.) See Trench, Select Glossary. See Milton, Animadversions upon the *Remonstrant*'s Defence. The sb. *remonstrance* is in Shak. Meas. v. 397.—Late L. *remonstrātus*, pp. of *remonstrāre*, to expose, exhibit; used A.D. 1482 (Ducange); hence, to produce arguments.—L. *re-*, again; and *monstrāre*, to show, exhibit; see **Re-** and **Monster.** **Der.** *remonstrant*, from the stem of the pres. part.; *remonstrance*, from MF. *remonstrance*, 'a remonstrance,' Cot., Late L. *remonstrantia*.

REMORA, the sucking-fish. (L.) 'A little fish, that men call *remora*;' Spenser, Visions of the World's Vanitie, l. 108. Cf. MF. *remore*, 'the suck-stone; a little fish, which cleaving to the keele of a ship, hinders the course of it;' Cot. Such was the old belief.—L. *remora*, a hindrance, delay; afterwards used as the name of the fish.—L. *re-*, back; and *mora*, delay.

REMORSE, pain or anguish for guilt. (F.—L.) ME. *remors*. 'But for she had a maner *remors*;' Lydgate, Storie of Thebes, pt. iii (Of the wife of Amphiorax). 'Som *remors* of conscience;' Chaucer, Troil. i. 554.—OF. *remors*, 'remorse;' Cot.—Late L. *remorsus* (also *remorsio*), remorse; Ducange.—L. *remorsus*, pp. of *remordēre*, to bite again, vex.—L. *re-*, again; and *mordēre*, to bite; see **Re-** and **Mordacious.** ¶ Chaucer has the verb *remord* (<OF. *remordre*), tr. of Boethius, b. 4, pr. 6, l. 182. **Der.** *remorse-ful*, Rich. III, i. 2. 156; *remorse-ful-ly*; *remorse-less*, Hamlet, ii. 2. 609; *remorse-less-ly*, *-ness*.

REMOTE, distant. (L.) In Spenser, F. Q. iii. 4. 6. [Cf. MF. *remot*, m., *remote*, f., 'remote, removed;' Cot.] Directly, from L. *remōtus*, pp. of *remouēre*, to remove; see **Remove.** **Der.** *remote-ly*, *-ness*; also *remot-ion* = removal, Timon, iv. 3. 346.

REMOUNT, to mount again. (F.—L.) Also transitively, to cause to rise again, as in ME. *remounten*, Chaucer, tr. of Boethius, b. iii. pr. 1, l. 6.—F. *remonter*, 'to remount,' Cot.—F. *re-*, again; and *monter*, to mount; see **Re-** and **Mount** (2).

REMOVE, to move away, withdraw. (F.—L.) ME. *remeuen* (*remeven*), Chaucer, Troil. i. 691, where *remeve* rimes with *preve*, a proof. Just as we find ME. *remeven* for mod. E. *remove*, so we find ME. *preven* for mod. E. *prove*, *preve* for *proof*. Palsgrave uses *remeve* and *remove* convertibly: 'I *remeve*, as an armye . . . *removeth* from one place to another.'—OF. *removoir*, 'to remove, retire;' Cot.—F. *re-*, again; and OF. *movoir*, to move; see **Re-** and **Move.** ¶ The ME. *remewen*, to remove, Chaucer, C. T. 10495 (F 181), has nearly the same sense, but is quite a different word, answering to OF. *remuër*, 'to move, stir,' Cot., from L. *re-* and *mūtāre*, to change. **Der.** *remov-able* (Levins), *remov-abil-i-ty*; *remov-al*, a coined word; *remov-er*, Shak. Sonn. 116, *remov-ed-ness*, Wint. Tale, iv. 2. 41. Also *remote*, q. v.

REMUNERATE, to recompense. (L.) In Shak. Titus, i. 398.—L. *remūnerātus*, pp. of *remūnerāre*, *remūnerāri*, to reward.—L. *re-*, again; and *mūnerāre*, *mūnerāri*, to discharge an office, also to give, from *mūner-*, decl. stem of *mūnus*, a gift. See **Re-** and **Munificent.** **Der.** *remuner-able*, *remunerat-ion*, L. L. L. iii. 133, ME. *remuneracion*, Dictes, pr. by Caxton, fol. 6, from MF. *remuneration*, 'a remuneration,' Cot.<L. *remūnerātiōnem*, acc. of *remūnerātio*; *remunerat-ive*.

RENAISSANCE, a revival; esp. used of the revival of the classical art and letters, chiefly at the end of the fifteenth century. (F. – L.) Also called *renascence*, which is the L. form. – F. *renaissance*, a new birth; Cot. – L. *re-*, again; and *nascentia*, birth (Vitruvius), from *nascent-*, pres. pt. stem of *nasci*, to be born; see **Nascent.**

RENAL, pertaining to the reins. (F. – L.) Medical. – MF. *renal*, 'belonging to the kidneyes;' Cot. – L. *rēnālis*, adj., formed from *rēn-ēs*, the reins: see **Reins.**

RENARD, a fox; see **Reynard.**

RENASCENT; from **Re-** and **Nascent.**

RENCOUNTER, RENCONTRE, a meeting, collision, chance combat. (F. – L.) Now commonly *rencontre*; formerly *rencounter*, used as a verb by Spenser, F. Q. i. 4. 39; and as a sb., iii. 1. 9. – F. *rencontre*, 'a meeting, or incounter . . by chance;' Cot. Cf. *rencontrer*, verb, 'to incounter, meet;' id. Contracted forms for *reëncontre, *reëncontrer. – F. *re-* (= L. *re-*), again; and *encontrer*, to meet; see **Re-** and **Encounter.** ¶ Hence the spelling *reencounter* in Berners, tr. of Froissart, v. ii. c. 29 (R.).

REND, to tear, split. (E.) ME. *renden*, pt. t. *rente*, pp. *rent*; Chaucer, C. T. 6217 (D 635). AS. *hrendan*, *rendan*, not common. In the ONorthumb. versions of Luke, xiii. 7, *succidite* [cut it down] is glossed by *hrendas vel scearfaδ* in the Lindisfarne MS., and by *ceorfas vel rendas* in the Rushworth MS. Again, in Mark, xi. 8, the L. *cædebant* [they cut down] is glossed by *gebugun vel rendon*. Thus the orig. sense seems to be to cut or tear down. **+**OFries. *renda*, *randa*, to tear, break. **β.** The AS. *hrendan* answers to a theoretical form *hrandian, which may be connected with *hrand*, the pt. t. of *hrindan*, to push (Grein), Icel. *hrinda*, to push, kick, throw, which may be referred to √QERT, to cut. Cf. Skt. *kṛt*, to cut down (base of the present tense, *kṛnta*); Lithuan. *kirsti*, to cut, hew (see *kertu* in Nesselmann). Cf. also Skt. *kṛntana-m*, neut. sb., a cutting. Der. *rent*, sb., Jul. Cæsar, iii. 2. 179; *rent*, vb., ME. *renten*, Chaucer, Leg. Good Women, 843; both formed from the pp. *rent*.

RENDER, to restore, give up. (F. – L.) ME. *rendren*, P. Plowman, B. xv. 601. – F. *rendre*, 'to render, yield;' Cot. – Late L. *rendere*, nasalised form of L. *reddere*, to restore, give back. – L. *red-*, back; and *dare*, to give. See **Re-, Red-,** and **Date** (1). Der. *render-ing.* Also *rent* (2), q.v.; *redd-it-ion*; *rendez-vous*, q.v.

RENDEZVOUS, an appointed place of meeting. (F. – L.) In Hamlet, iv. 4. 4. – F. *rendezvous*, 'a rendevous, a place appointed for the assemblie of souldiers;' Cot. A substantival use of the phrase *rendez vous*, i. e. render yourselves, or assemble yourselves, viz. at the place appointed. **β.** *Rendez* is the imperative plural, 2nd person, of *rendre*, to render; and *vous* (< L. *uōs*) is the pl. of the 2nd pers. pronoun. See **Render.**

RENEGADE, RENEGADO, an apostate, vagabond. (Span. – L.) Massinger's play called *The Renegado* was first acted in 1624. In Shak. Tw. Nt. iii. 2. 74, the first folio has 'a verie *Renegatho*;' a spelling which represents the sound of the Spanish *d*. The word was at first *renegado*, and afterwards *renegade* by loss of the final syllable. – Span. *renegado*, 'an apostata,' Minsheu; lit. one who has denied the faith; pp. of *renegar*, 'to forsake the faith,' id. – Late L. *renegāre*, to deny again. – L. *re-*, again; and *negāre*, to deny; see **Re-** and **Negative.** ¶ 1. The word was not really new to the language, as it appears in ME. as *renegat*; but the ME. *renegat* having been altered to *runagate*, the way was cleared for introducing the word over again; see **Runagate.** 2. The odd word *renege* (with *g* hard), in King Lear, ii. 2. 84, = Late L. *renegāre*; cf. ME. *reneye*, P. Plowman, B. xi. 120; from OF. *reneier*. Doublet, *runagate*.

RENEW, to make new again. (Hybrid; L. *and* E.) ME. *renewen*, Wyclif, 2 Cor. iv. 16; where the L. *renouātur* is translated by *is renewid*. From **Re-** and **New.** Der. *renew-al*, a coined word; *renew-able*, also coined. Doublet, *renovate.*

RENNET (1), the prepared inner membrane of a calf's stomach, used to make milk coagulate. (E.) 'Renet, for chese, *coagulum*;' Levins. ME. *rennet*; 'Lactis, *rennet*, or *rennynge*;' Voc. 591. 19; cf. 574. 13. The word is found with various suffixes, but is in each case formed from ME. *rennen*, to cause to run, because *rennet* causes milk to *run*, i. e. to coagulate or congeal. This singular use of E. *run* in the sense 'to coagulate' is not always noticed in the Dictionaries. Pegge, in his Kenticisms (E. D. S. Gloss. C. 3) uses it; he says: '*Runnet*, the herb *gallium* [*Galium verum*], called in Derbyshire *erning*, Anglicè cheese-runnet; it *runs* the milk together, i. e. makes it curdle.' '*Earn*, *Yearn*, to coagulate milk; *earning*, *yearning*, cheese-rennet, or that which curdles milk;' Brockett. Here *earn* (better *ern*) is put, by shifting of *r*, for *ren*; just as AS. *yrnan* (*irnan*) is a causal form of *rinnan*, to run. Cf. Gloucestersh. *running*, rennet (E. D. S. Gloss. B. 4). '*Renlys*, or *rendlys*, for mylke, [also] *renels*, Coagulum;' Prompt. Parv. 'As nourishing milk, when *runnet* is put in, *Runs all in heaps* of tough thick curd, though in his nature

thin;' Chapman, tr. of Homer, Il. v, near the end. So also AS. '*rynning*, coagulum; *gerunnen*, coagulatus;' Wright's Vocab. i. 27, last line, i. 28, first line. All from AS. *rinnan*, to run. See **Run.** **+**MDu. *rinsel*, *runsel*, or *renninge*, 'curds, or milk-runnet,' Hexham; from *rinnen*, 'to presse, curdle;' id. Cf. *geronnen melck*, 'curded or rennet milke;' id. Cf. G. *rinnen*, to run, curdle, coagulate.

RENNET (2), a sweet kind of apple. (F. – L.) Formerly spelt *renat* or *renate*, from a mistaken notion that it was derived from L. *renātus*, renewed or born again. 'The *renat*, which though first it from the pippin came, Grown through his pureness nice, assumes that curious name;' Drayton, Polyolbion, song 18; l. 671. – F. *reinette*, *rainette*, a pippin, rennet; Hamilton. Scheler and Littré agree to connect it with MF. *rainette*, 'a little frog' (Cot.), the dimin. of *raine*, a frog, because the apple is speckled like the skin of a frog. (So also Hatzfeld.) From L. *rāna*, a frog. See **Ranunculus.**

RENOUNCE, to give up, reject, disown. (F. – L.) ME. *renouncen*, Gower, C. A. i. 258; bk. ii. 2931. – F. *renoncer*, 'to renounce;' Cot. – L. *renunciāre*, better *renuntiāre*, to bring back a report, also, to disclaim, renounce. – L. *re-*, back; and *nuntiāre*, to bring a message, from *nuntius*, a messenger; see **Re-** and **Nuncio.** Der. *renounce-ment*, Meas. for Meas. i. 4. 35; *renunciation*, q. v.

RENOVATE, to renew. (L.) In Thomson's Seasons, Winter, 704; Hakluyt, Voy. ii. 1. 37. The sb. *renovation* is in Bacon, Life of Henry VII, ed. Lumby, p. 203, l. 33. – L. *renouātus*, pp. of *renouāre*, to renew. – L. *re-*, again; and *nouus*, new, cognate with E. *new*; see **Re-** and **New.** Der. *renovat-ion*, from MF. *renovation*, 'a renovation,' Cot.; *renovat-or.* Doublet, *renew.*

RENOWN, celebrity, fame. (F. – L.) ME. *renoun*, Chaucer, C. T. 14553 (B 3825); Rob. of Brunne, tr. of Langtoft, p. 131, l. 5; King Alisaunder, 1448. [But also *renomé*, *renommé*, in three syllables, with final *e* as F. *é*; Gower, C. A. ii. 43; bk. iv. 1250; Barbour's Bruce, iv. 774; *renownee*, Barbour's Bruce, viii. 290.] In Bruce, ix. 503, one MS. has the pp. *renownit*, spelt *renommyt* in the other. – AF. *renoun*, Lib. Custum. p. 23; OF. *renon*; MF. *renom* [also *renommée*], 'renowne, fame;' Cot. Cf. *renommé*, 'renowned, famous;' Cot. [Cf. Port. *renome*, renown; Span. *renombre*, renown, also a surname; and Span. *renombrar*, to renown.] – F. *re-* (= L. *re-*), again; and AF. *noun*, F. *nom*, a name; hence *renown* = a renaming, repetition or celebration of a name. See **Re-** and **Noun.** Der. *renown*, verb, in Barbour, as above.

RENT (1), a tear, fissure, breach. (E.) See **Rend.**

RENT (2), annual payment for land, &c. (F. – L.) In early use; occurring, spelt *rente*, in the A. S. Chron. an. 1137; see Thorpe's edition, p. 383, l. 12. – F. *rente*, 'rent, revenue;' Cot. Cf. Ital. *rendita*, rent; which shows the full form of the word. From a nasalised form (*rendita*) of L. *reddita*, i. e. *reddita pecūnia*, money paid; fem. of *redditus*, pp. of *reddere*, to give back, whence F. *rendre*, and E. *render*. *Rent* = that which is rendered; see **Render.** Der. *rent-er*, *rent-roll*; also *rent-al*, P. Plowman, B. vi. 92.

RENUNCIATION, a renouncing. (F. – L.) In Cotgrave. It is neither true F. nor true L., but prob. taken from F., and modified by a knowledge of the L. word. – F. *renonciation*, 'a renunciation;' Cot. – L. *renuntiātiōnem*, acc. of *renuntiātio*, a renouncing; cf. *renuntiātus*, pp. of *renuntiāre*; see **Renounce.**

REPAIR (1), to restore, fill up anew, amend. (F. – L.) 'The fishes flete with new *repaired* scale;' Lord Surrey, Description of Spring, l. 8. – OF. *reparer*, 'to repaire, mend;' Cot. – L. *reparāre*, to get again, recover, repair. – L. *re-*, again; and *parāre*, to get, prepare; see **Re-** and **Parade.** Der. *repair*, sb., *repair-er*; *repar-able*, in Levins, from MF. *reparable*, 'repairable,' Cot., from L. *reparābilis*; *repar-abl-y*; *repar-at-ion*, Palsgrave, from MF. *reparation*, 'a reparation,' Cot.; *repar-at-ive.*

REPAIR (2), to resort, go to. (F. – L.) ME. *repairen*, Chaucer, C. T. 5387 (B 967). – F. *repairer*, 'to haunt, frequent, lodge in;' Cot. Older form *repairier* (Burguy); cf. Span. *repatriar*, Ital. *ripatriare*, to return to one's country. – L. *repatriāre*, to return to one's country. – L. *re-*, back; and *patria*, one's native land, from *patri-*, decl. stem of *pater*, a father, cognate with E. *father*. See **Re-** and **Father.** Der. *repair*, sb., Hamlet, v. 2. 228.

REPARTEE, a witty reply. (F. – L.) A misspelling for *repartie* or *reparty*. 'Some *reparty*, some witty strain;' Howell, Famil. Letters, b. i. sect. 1. let. 18. – F. *repartie*, 'a reply;' Cot. Orig. fem. of *reparti*, pp. of MF. *repartir*, 'to redivide, to answer a thrust with a thrust, to reply;' Cot. – F. *re-* (= L. *re-*), again; and *partir*, to part, divide, also to dart off, rush, burst out laughing, from L. *partīre*, *partīrī*, to share, from *part-*, stem of *pars*, a part. See **Re-** and **Part.**

REPAST, a taking of food; the food taken. (F. – L.) ME. *repast*, P. Plowman, C. x. 148; Gower, C. A. iii. 25; bk. vi. 698. – OF. *repast* (Littré), later *repas*, 'a repast, meale;' Cot. – F. *re-* (= L. *re-*), again; and OF. *past*, 'a meale, repast,' Cot., from L. *pastum*, acc. of *pastus*, food; cf. *pastus*, pp. of *pascere*, to feed. See **Re-** and **Pasture**. Der. *repast*, vb., Hamlet, iv. 5. 157.

REPAY, to pay back, recompense. (F.–L.) Spelt *repaye* in Palsgrave. – OF. *repayer*, to pay back; given in Palsgrave and in use in the 15th cent. (Littré); obsolete. See **Re-** and **Pay**. Der. *repay-able*, *repay-ment*.

REPEAL, to abrogate, revoke. (F.–L.) ME. *repele(n)*, Hoccleve, Reg. of Princes, 2960. AF. *repeler*, Langtoft, ii. 352. Altered (by putting *re-* for F. *ra-*) from OF. *rapeler*, F. *rappeler*, 'to repeale, revoke,' Cot. – F. *r-*, for *re-* (= L. *re-*), again, back; and OF. *apeler*, later *appeler*, to appeal. Thus *repeal* is a substitution for *re-appeal*; see **Re-** and **Appeal**. Der. *repeal*, sb., Cor. iv. 1. 41; spelt *rapeell*, i. e. recall, Caxton, Troy-book, fol. 294, bk.; *repeal-er*, *repeal-able*.

REPEAT, to say or do again, rehearse. (F.–L.) 'I repete, I reherce my lesson, *je repete*;' Palsgrave. – MF. *repeter*, 'to repeat;' Cot. – L. *repetere*, to attack again, reseek, resume, repeat; pp. *repetitus*. – L. *re-*, again; and *petere*, to seek; see **Re-** and **Petition**. Der. *repeat-ed-ly*, *repeat-er*; *repet-it-ion*, from MF. *repetition*, 'a repetition,' Cot., from L. acc. *repetitiōnem*.

REPEL, to drive back, check. (L.) 'I repelle, I put backe (Lydgat);' Palsgrave, who thus refers us to Lydgate. – L. *repellere*, to drive back; pp. *repulsus*. – L. *re-*, back; and *pellere*, to drive; see **Re-** and **Pulse**. Der. *repell-ent*, from the stem of the pres. part.; *repell-er*; and see *repulse*.

REPENT, to feel sorrow for what one has done, to rue. (F.–L.) ME. *repenten*, King Alisaunder, 4224. – F. *repentir*, reflexive verb, 'to repent;' Cot. – L. *re-*, again; and Folk-L. **penitere*, for L. *pœnitēre*, used impersonally in the sense 'repent;' see **Re-** and **Penitent**. Der. *repent-ant*, ME. *repentant*, Rob. of Glouc., p. 291, l. 5917, from F. *repentant*, pres. part. of *repentir*; *repent-ance*, Rob. of Brunne, tr. of Langtoft, p. 55, from F. *repentance*.

REPERCUSSION, reverberation. (F.–L.) 'That, with the *repercussion* of the air;' Drayton, The Owl; l. 1137. 'Salute me with thy *repercussive* voice;' Ben Jonson, Cynthia's Revels, Act i. sc. 1 (Mercury). – MF. *repercussion*, 'repercussion;' Cot. – L. acc. *repercussiōnem*; see **Re-** and **Percussion**. Der. *repercuss-ive*, from MF. *repercussif*, 'repercussive,' Cot.

REPERTORY, a treasury, magazine. (F.–L.) Formerly also a list, index. 'A *repertorie* or index;' Holland, tr. of Pliny, b. xxx. c. 1 (Of Hermippus). Altered from MF. *repertoire*, 'a repertory, list, roll;' Cot. – L. *repertōrium*, an inventory. – L. *repertor*, a discoverer, inventor; cf. *repertus*, pp. of *reperīre*, to find out, invent. – L. *re-*, again; and *parīre* (Ennius), usually *parere*, to produce; see **Re-** and **Parent**.

REPETITION; see under **Repeat**.

REPINE, to be discontented. (L.) Spelt *repyne* in Palsgrave; compounded of *re-* (again) and *pine*, to fret. No doubt *pine* was, at the time, supposed to be a true E. word, its derivation from the Latin having been forgotten. But, by a fortunate accident, the word is not hybrid, but wholly Latin. See **Re-** and **Pine** (2).

REPLACE, to put back. (F.–L.) 'To chase th'usurper, and *replace* their king;' Daniel, Civil War, b. iii. st. 30. From **Re-** and **Place**. Suggested by F. *remplacer*, 'to re-implace;' Cot. Der. *replace-ment*.

REPLENISH, to fill completely, stock. (F.–L.) ME. *replenissen*. 'Replenissed and fulfillid;' Chaucer, tr. of Boethius, b. i. pr. 4, l. 197. – OF. *repleniss-*, stem of pres. part. of *replenir*, to fill up again (Burguy); now obsolete. – L. *re-*, again; and a L. type **plēnīre*, formed as a verb from *plēnus*, full. See **Re-** and **Plenitude**. Der. *replenish-ment*. And see *replete*.

REPLETE, quite full. (F.–L.) Chaucer has *replete*, C. T. 14963 (B 4147); *repletion*, id. 14929 (B 4113). – MF. *replet*, m., *replete*, f., 'replete;' Cot. – L. *replētum*, acc. of *replētus*, filled up, pp. of *replēre*, to fill again. – L. *re-*, again; and *plēre*, to fill; see **Plenary**. Der. *replet-ion*, from MF. *repletion*, 'a repletion,' Cot.

REPLEVY, to get back, or return, goods detained for debt, on a pledge to try the right in a law-suit. (F.–L. *and* Teut.) 'Replevie, to redeliver to the owner upon pledges or surety; it is also used for the bailing a man;' Blount, Nomolexicon, ed. 1691. Spelt *replevie*, Spenser, F. Q., iv. 12. 31. Butler has *replevin* as a verb, Hudibras, The Lady's Answer, l. 4. – F. *re-* (= L. *re-*), again; and *plevir*, 'to warrant, be surety, give pledges,' Cot. The E. word follows the form of the pp. *plevi*. Cf. AF. *replevi*, pp., replevied, Stat. Realm, i. 361 (1311). See **Re-** and **Pledge**. Der. *replev-in*, properly a sb., from F. *re-* and OF. *plevine*, 'a warranty,' Cot.

REPLY, to answer. (F.–L.) ME. *replien*, *replyen*; Chaucer, Prol. to Legend of Good Women, 343. – OF. *replier*, the old form which was afterwards replaced by the 'learned' form *repliquer*, to reply. – L. *replicāre* (pp. *replicātus*), to fold back; as a law term, to reply. – L. *re-*, back; and *plicāre*, to fold. See **Re-** and **Ply**.

Der. *reply*, sb., Hamlet, i. 2. 121; *replic-at-ion*, Chaucer, C. T. 1848 (A 1846); < L. acc. *replicātiōnem*, from nom. *replicātio*, a reply, a law-term, as at first introduced. Also *replica*, a copy, lit. a repetition, from Ital. *replica*, a sb. due to *replicare*, to repeat, reply.

REPORT, to relate, recount. (F.–L.) ME. *reporten*, Chaucer, C. T. 4572 (B 152). – F. *reporter*, 'to recarrie, bear back;' Cot. – L. *reportāre*, to carry back. See **Re-** and **Port** (1). Der. *report*, sb., Chaucer, Troilus, i. 593; *report-er*.

REPOSE, to lay at rest, to rest. (F.–L. *and* Gk.) 'A mynde With vertue fraught, *reposed*, voyd of gile;' Surrey, Epitaph on Sir T. W., l. 24; Tottell's Misc., ed. Arber, p. 29. – F. *reposer*, 'to repose, pawse, rest, or stay,' Cot. Cf. Ital. *riposare*, Span. *reposar*, Port. *repousar*, Prov. *repausar* (Bartsch); all answering to Late L. *repausāre*, whence *repausātio*, a pausing, pause (White). – L. *re-*, again; and *pausāre*, to pause, from *pausa*, a pause, of Greek origin; see **Re-** and **Pause**. ¶ This word is of much importance, as it appears to be the oldest compound of *pausāre*, and gave rise to the later confusion between L. *pausāre* (of Gk. origin), and the pp. *positus* of L. *pōnere*. See **Pose**. Der. *repose*, sb., Spenser, F. Q. iii. 4. 6, from F. *repos*, 'repose,' Cot.; *repos-al*, King Lear, ii. 1. 70.

REPOSITORY, a place in which things are stored up, store-house. (F.–L.) Spelt *repositorie* in Levins and Minsheu. Altered from MF. *repositoire*, 'a store-house,' Cot. – L. *repositōrium*, a repository. Formed with suffix *-ōr-i-um* from *reposit-us*, pp. of *repōnere*, to lay up. See **Re-** and **Position**.

REPOUSSÉ, raised in relief by being beaten up from the under side; said of metal-work. (F.–L.) F. *repoussé*, lit. pushed back; pp. of *repousser*. – F. *re-*, back; and *pousser*, to push; see **Push**.

REPREHEND, to blame, reprove. (L.) ME. *reprehenden*, Chaucer, Troilus, i. 510. It must have been taken from L., as the OF. form was *reprendre* in the 12th century. – L. *reprehendere* (pp. *reprehensus*), to hold back, check, blame. – L. *re-*, back; and *prehendere*, to hold, seize. See **Re-** and **Comprehend**. Der. *reprehension*, Chaucer, Troil. i. 684, prob. direct from L. acc. *reprehensiōnem*, though the OF. *reprehension* occurs in the 12th century (Hatzfeld); *reprehens-ive*; *reprehens-ible*, from L. *reprehensibilis*; *reprehens-ibl-y*. And see *reprisal*.

REPRESENT, to describe, express, exhibit the image of, act the part of. (F.–L.) ME. *representen*, Rom. of the Rose, 7402. – OF. *representer*, 'to represent, express;' Cot. – L. *repraesentāre*, to bring before one again, exhibit. – L. *re-*, again; and *praesentāre*, to present, hold out, from *praesent-*, stem of *praesens*, present. See **Re-** and **Present** (1). Der. *represent-able*, *represent-at-ion*, *represent-at-ive*.

REPRESS, to restrain, check. (F.–L.) ME. *repressen*, Gower, C. A. iii. 166; bk. vii. 2410. Coined from **Re-** and **Press** (1), with the sense of L. *reprimere*, pp. *repressus*. Der. *repress-ion*, *repress-ive*. And see *reprimand*.

REPRIEVE, to delay the execution of a criminal. (F.–L.) In Spenser, F. Q. iv. 12. 31. It is formally the same word as *reprove*, of which the ME. form was commonly *repreuen* (= *repreven*), with the sense to reject. Palsgrave has *repreve* for *reprove*. 'The stoon which men bildynge *repreueden*' = the stone which the builders *rejected*; Wyclif, Luke, xx. 17. Cf. OF. *repreuve*, 3rd pers. sing. indic. of *reprover* (F. *réprouver*), to reprove. Cf. Schwan, § 348 (4). β. But the sense is really due to the obs. verb *to repry*, as in 'they were *repryed*,' lit. 'taken back,' but used to mean 'reprieved;' Fabyan, Chron., ed. Ellis, p. 389. And again, 'the sayd Turbiruyle was *repryed* to pryson;' id. p. 672. – OF. *repris*, pp. of *reprendre*, 'to resume, receive, take back; also to reprehend;' Cot. See **Reprehend**, **Reprisal**. Der. *reprieve*, sb., Cor. v. 2. 53. Doublet, *reprove*.

REPRIMAND, a reproof, rebuke. (F.–L.) In the Spectator, no. 112. – F. *réprimande*, formerly *reprimende*, 'a check, reprehension, reproof,' Cot. – L. *reprimenda*, a thing that ought to be repressed; fem. of fut. part. pass. of *reprimere*, to repress; see **Re-** and **Press** (1). Der. *reprimand*, verb.

REPRINT, to print again. (F.–L.) Prynne refers to a book 'printed 1599, and now *reprinted* 1629;' Histrio-mastix, part i. p. 358 (R.). From **Re-** and **Print**. Der. *reprint*, sb.

REPRISAL, anything seized in return, retaliation. (F.–Ital.–L.) It means 'a prize' in Shak. 1 Hen. IV, iv. 1. 118. Spelt *reprisels*, pl., in Minsheu, ed. 1627. – MF. *represaille*, 'a taking or seising on, a prise, or a reprisall;' Cot. [The modern vowel is due to the obsolete verb *reprise*, to seize in return, Spenser, F. Q. iv. 4. 8, from the pp. *repris* of OF. *reprendre* < L. *reprehendere*.] – MItal. *ripresaglia*, 'booties, preyes, prisals, or anything gotten by prize, bribing, or bootie;' Florio. – Ital. *ripresa*, 'a reprisall or taking again;' id. Fem. of *ripreso*, pp. of *riprendere*, 'to reprehend, also to take again, retake;' id. – L. *reprehendere*; see **Reprehend**, **Reprieve**. And see **Prize** (1).

REPROACH, to upbraid, revile, rebuke. (F.—L.) In Shak. Meas. for Meas. v. 426. The sb. is spelt *reproche* in Skelton, Bowge of Courte, l. 26. We find ME. *reproce*, sb., Early E. Psalter, xxx (xxxi). 14; and *reprocen*, vb., id., xxxiv (xxxv). 8.—F. *reprocher*, 'to reproach, . . . object or impute unto,' Cot.; whence the sb. *reproche*, 'a reproach, imputation, or casting in the teeth;' id. Cf. Span. *reprochar*, vb., *reproche*, sb.; Prov. *repropchar*, to reproach (cited by Diez). We also find Prov. *repropchiers*, *reprojers*, sb., a proverb (Bartsch). β. The etymology is disputed, yet is hardly doubtful; the Late L. *appropiare* became OF. *aprocher* and E. *approach*, so that *reproach* answers to a L. type *repropiāre, not found, to bring near to, hence to cast in one's teeth, impute, object. From L. *re-*, again; and *propi-us*, adv., nearer, comp. of *prope*, near; see **Propinquity.** See Diez, who shows that other proposed solutions of the word are phonetically impossible. γ. Scheler well explains the matter, when he suggests that *repropiāre is, in fact, a mere translation or equivalent of L. *obicere* (*objicere*), to cast before one, to bring under one's notice, to reproach. So also the G. *vorwerfen*, to cast before, to reproach. δ. And hence we can explain the Prov. *repropchiers*, lit. a bringing under one's notice, a hint, a proverb. **Der.** *reproach*, sb.; *reproach-able*, *reproach-abl-y*; *reproach-ful*, Titus Andron., i. 308; *reproach-ful-ly.*

REPROBATE, depraved, vile, base. (L.) Properly a pp. used as an adj., Trevisa, tr. of Higden, vi. 407; also in L. L. L. i. 2. 64; also as sb., Meas. iv. 3. 78.—L. *reprobātus*, censured, reproved, pp. of *reprobāre*; see **Reprove. Der.** *reprobat-ion*, a reading in the quarto editions for *reprobance*, Oth. v. 2. 209, from MF. *reprobation*, omitted by Cotgrave, but in use in the 14th cent. (Hatzfeld)<L. acc. *reprobātiōnem.*

REPRODUCE, to produce again. (L.) In Cotgrave, to translate F. *reproduire*. From **Re-** and **Produce. Der.** *reproduct-ion*, *reproduct-ive.*

REPROVE, to condemn, chide. (F.—L.) ME. *reprouen* (*reproven*), P. Plowman, C. iv. 389. [Also spelt *repreuen*; see **Reprieve.**]—OF. *reprover*, mod. F. *réprouver*, to reprove; Littré.—L. *reprobāre*, to disapprove, condemn.—L. *re-*, again; and *probāre*, to test, prove; hence 'to reprove' is to reject on a second trial, to condemn. See **Re-** and **Prove. Der.** *reprov-er*; *reprov-able*, *reprov-abl-y.* Also *reproof*, ME. *reprove*, *reproef*, Gower, C. A. iii. 230, bk. vii. 4108; see **Proof.** And see *reprob-ate.* Doublet, *reprieve.*

REPTILE, crawling, creeping. (F.—L.) In Cotgrave. ME. *reptil*, Gower, Conf. Amant. iii. 118; bk. vii. 1011.—F. *reptile*, 'reptile, creeping, crawling;' Cot.—L. *reptīlem*, acc. of *reptilis*, creeping; formed with suffix *-ilis* from *rept-us*, pp. of *rēpere*, to creep. +Lithuan. *reploti*, to creep (Nesselmann). **Der.** *reptil-i-an.*

REPUBLIC, a commonwealth. (F.—L.) Spelt *republique* in Minsheu, ed. 1627.—MF. *republique*, 'the commonwealth;' Cot.—L. *rēspublica*, a commonwealth; for *rēs publica*, lit. a public affair. See **Real** and **Public. Der.** *republic-an*, *republic-an-ism.*

REPUDIATE, to reject, disavow. (L.) In Levins. Used as a pp. or adj. in Harding's Chron. ch. 90, st. 4.—L. *repudiātus*, pp. of *repudiāre*, to put away, reject.—L. *repudium*, a casting off, divorce, lit. a rejection of what one is ashamed of.—L. *re-*, away, back; and *pud-*, base of *pudēre*, to feel shame, *pudor*, shame; cf. *prō-pudium*, a shameful action. **Der.** *repudiat-or*; *repudiat-ion*, from MF. *repudiation*, 'a refusall,' Cot.

REPUGNANT, hostile, adverse. (F.—L.) In Minsheu, ed. 1627; and in Sir T. Elyot, The Governour, b. ii. c. 11. § 4. The word is rather F. than L.; the sb. *repugnance* is in Levins, ed. 1570, and occurs, spelt *repungnaunce*, in Skelton, Garland of Laurell, 211. The verb *to repugn* was in rather early use, occurring in Wyclif, Acts, v. 39; also in Palsgrave.—MF. *repugnant*, pres. part. of *repugner*, 'to repugne, crosse, thwart;' Cot.—L. *repugnāre*, lit. to fight against.—L. *re-*, back, hence against; and *pugnāre*, to fight; see **Re-** and **Pugnacious. Der.** *repugnance*, from MF. *repugnance*, 'repugnancy,' Cot.

REPULSE, to repel, beat off. (L.) Surrey translates L. *repulsi* in Virgil, Æn. ii. 13, by *repulst.* 'Oftentymes the *repulse* from promocyon is cause of dyscomforte;' Sir T. Elyot, Castel of Helth, b. iii. c. 12.—L. *repulsus*, pp. of *repellere*, to repel; see **Repel.** β. The sb. answers to L. *repulsa*, a refusal, repulse; orig. fem. of the pp. *repulsus.* **Der.** *repulse*, sb., as above; *repuls-ive*, *-ly*, *-ness*; *repuls-ion.*

REPUTE, to estimate, account. (F.—L.) 'I *repute*, I estyme, or judge, *Ie repute*;' Palsgrave. The sb. *reputation* is in Chaucer, C. T. 12536 (C 602).—OF. *reputer*, 'to repute;' Cot. (And in Godefroy.)—L. *reputāre*, to repute, esteem.—L. *re-*, again; and *putāre*, to think; see **Re-** and **Putative. Der.** *reput-able*, *reput-abl-y*, *reput-able-ness*; *reput-ed-ly*; *reput-at-ion*, from MF. *reputation*, 'reputation, esteem,' Cot. Also *repute*, sb., Troil. i. 3. 337.

REQUEST, an entreaty, petition. (F.—L.) ME. *requeste*, Chaucer, C. T. 2687 (A 2685).—OF. *requeste*, 'a request;' Cot.—L. *requisīta*, a thing asked, fem. of pp. of *requīrere*, to ask; see **Re-** and **Quest;** and see **Require. Der.** *request*, verb, Two Gent. i. 3. 13.

REQUIEM, a mass for the repose of the dead. (L.) 'The *requiem-masse* to synge;' Skelton, Phylyp Sparowe, 401. The Mass for the Dead was so called, because the anthem or *officium* began with '*Requiem* æternam dona eis, Domine,' &c.; Procter, On the Common Prayer.—L. *requiem*, acc. of *requiēs*, rest.—L. *re-*, again; and *quiēs*, rest; see **Re-** and **Quiet.** And see **Dirge.**

REQUIESCENCE, repose, quiet. (L.) From L. *re-*, again; and *quiescentia*, quietness, from *quiescent-*, stem of pres. part. of *quiescere*, to rest; see **Quiescent.**

REQUIRE, to ask, demand. (F.—L.) Spelt *requyre* in Palsgrave. ME. *requiren*, Chaucer, C. T. 8306 (E 430); in l. 6634 (D 1052), we find *requere*, riming with *there.* The word was taken from F., but influenced by the L. spelling.—MF. *requerir*, 'to request, intreat,' Cot.; OF. *requerre*, with 1 pers. sing. ind. *requier.*—L. *requīrere*, lit. to seek again (pp. *requisītus*).—L. *re-*, again; and *quærere*, to seek; see **Re-** and **Quest. Der.** *requir-able*; *require-ment*, a coined word; *requis-ite*, adj., Wint. Tale, iv. 4. 687, from L. pp. *requisītus*; *requis-ite*, sb., Oth. ii. 1. 251; *requis-it-ion*, from MF. *requisition*, 'a requisition,' Cot.; *requis-it-ion-ist.*

REQUITE, to repay. (F.—L.) In Shak. Temp. v. 169. Surrey (Æn. ii. 205) translates *si magna rependam* (Æn. ii. 161) by 'requite thee large amendes.' The word ought rather to be *requit*; cf. 'hath *requit* it,' Temp. iii. 3. 71. But just as *quite* occurs as a variant of *quit*, so *requite* is used for *requit*; see **Re-** and **Quit. Der.** *requit-al*, Merry Wives, iv. 2. 3.

REREDOS, a screen at the back of an altar. (F.—L.) 'A *reredosse* in the hall;' Harrison, Desc. of Eng. b. ii. c. 12; ed. Furnivall, p. 240. Hall, in his Chronicle (Henry VIII, an. 12. § 22), enumerates 'harths, *reredorses*, chimnays, ranges;' Richardson. Spelt *reredos*, Earl of Derby's Expeditions in 1390-3 (Camd. Soc.), p. 219, l. 8. Compounded of *rear*, ME. *rere*, i. e. at the back, and F. *dos* (<L. *dorsum*), the back; so that the sense is repeated. See **Rear** (2) and **Dorsal.**

REREMOUSE, REARMOUSE, a bat. (E.) Still in use in the South and West of England; E. D. D. The pl. *reremys* occurs in Rich. the Redeles, ed. Skeat, iii. 272. AS. *hrēremūs*, a bat; Wright's Vocab., p. 77, col. 1, last line. β. Apparently due to a popular etymology (like prov. E. *flitter-mouse*, a bat) from the flapping of the wings; from AS. *hrēran*, to agitate, a derivative of *hrōr*, motion (with the usual change from *ō* to *ē*), allied to *hrōr*, adj., active, quick; see Grein, ii. 102, 108. Cf. Icel. *hræra*, G. *rühren*, to stir; Icel. *hræra tungu*, to wag the tongue. β. But the early form is *hrēatha-mūs*, a bat; Epinal Gloss., 978; spelt *hraeðemuus*, Corpus Gloss., 2103; *hreadaemus*, *hreadamus*, Ep. Gl. 1098. Cognate with OLow G. *hrōða-mūs*, a bat (Gallée).

REREWARD, the same as **Rearward,** q. v.

RESCIND, to repeal, annul. (F.—L.) In Blount's Gloss., ed. 1674.—F. *rescinder*, 'to cut or pare off, to cancell;' Cot.—L. *rescindere*, to cut off, annul.—L. *re-*, back; and *scindere* (pp. *scissus*), to cut; see **Re-** and **Schism. Der.** *resciss-ion*, from MF. *rescision*, 'a rescision, a cancelling,' Cot., from L. acc. *rescissiōnem.*

RESCRIPT, an official answer, edict. (F.—L.) In Cotgrave.—MF. *rescript*, 'a rescript, a writing back, an answer given in writing;' Cot.—L. *rescriptum*, a rescript, reply; neut. of *rescriptus*, pp. of *rescrībere*, to write back; see **Re-** and **Scribe.**

RESCUE, to free from danger, deliver from violence. (F.—L.) ME. *rescouen*, *rescowen*, Chaucer, tr. of Boethius, b. iv. met. 5, l. 15.—OF. *rescourre*, 'to rescue;' Cot. [The same word as Ital. *ri-scuotere*.]—Late L. *rescutere*, which occurs A.D. 1308 (Ducange); it stands for *reëxcutere.* So also the OF. *rescousse*, a rescue, answers to Late L. *rescussa*<L. *reëxcussa*, fem. pp. of the same verb; and mod. F. *recousse* is from *recussa*, the same sb. with the omission of *ex.* β. From L. *re-*, again; and *excutere* (pp. *excussus*), to shake off, drive away, comp. of *ex*, off, and *quatere*, to shake; see **Re-**, **Ex-**, and **Quash. Der.** *rescue*, sb., ME. *rescous*, Chaucer, C. T. 2645 (A 2643), from the OF. *rescousse*, 'rescue,' Cot. ¶ We find AF. *rescure*, vb., Vie de St. Auban, and *rescusse*, id. In the Coventry Myst., p. 114, is the sb. *rescu.* Either this sb. was formed anew from the vb., or the AF. *rescusse* (ME. *rescous*) was supposed to be a pl. form. Mrs. Quickley says: 'bring *a rescue or two*;' 2 Hen. IV, ii. 1. 62.

RESEARCH, a careful search. (F.—L.) 'Research, a strict inquiry;' Phillips, ed. 1706. From **Re-** and **Search.** Cf. MF. *recerche*, 'a diligent search,' Cot.; Norm. dial. *recerche*; mod. F. *recherche.*

RESEMBLE, to be like. (F.—L.) ME. *resemblen*, Gower, C. A.

iii. 117; bk. vii. 982.—OF. *resembler*, 'to resemble;' Cot. Mod. F. *ressembler.*—F. *re-*, again; and *sembler*, 'to seem, also to resemble,' id.—L. *re-*, again; and *similare*, more generally *simulāre*, to imitate, copy, make like, from *similis*, like; see **Re-** and **Similar**. Der. *resembl-ance*, ME. *resemblaunce*, Gower, C. A. ii. 83, bk. iv. 2424, from OF. *resemblance*, 'a resemblance;' Cot.

RESENT, to take ill, be indignant at. (F.—L.) Orig. merely to be sensible of a thing done to one; see Trench, Select Glossary. In Joseph Beaumont, Psyche, canto iv. st. 156. Used in the modern sense, Milton, P. L. ix. 300. ' *To resent*, to be sensible of, or to stomach an affront;' Phillips, ed. 1706. Blount's Gloss. has only the sb. *resentment*, also spelt *ressentiment.*—MF. *resentir, ressentir.* ' *Se ressentir*, to taste fully, have a sensible apprehension of; *se ressentir de iniure*, to remember, to be sensible or desire a revenge of, to find himself aggrieved at a thing;' Cot. Thus the orig. sense was merely 'to be fully sensible of,' without any sinister meaning.—F. *re-*, again; and *sentir*, to feel, from L. *sentīre*, to feel; see **Re-** and **Sense**. Der. *resent-ment*, from F. *ressentiment*; *re-sent-ful, -ly.*

RESERVE, to keep back, retain. (F.—L.) ME. *reseruen* (with *u=v*), Chaucer, C. T. 188.—OF. *reserver*, 'to reserve,' Cot.—L. *reseruāre*, to keep back.—L. *re-*, back; and *seruāre*, to keep; see **Re-** and **Serve**. Der. *reserve*, sb., from OF. *reserve*, 'store, a reservation,' Cot.; *reserv-ed, reserv-ed-ly, -ness*; *reserv-at-ion*; also *reserv-oir*, a place where any thing (esp. water) is stored up, Evelyn's Diary, 17 Oct., 1644, from F. *reservoir*, 'a store-house,' Cot., which from Late L. *reseruātōrium* (Ducange).

RESIDE, to dwell, abide, inhere. (F.—L.) See Trench, Select Glossary. In Shak. Temp. iii. 1. 65. [The sb. *residence* is much earlier, in Chaucer, C. T. 16128 (G 660).]—MF. *resider*, 'to reside, stay,' Cot.—L. *residēre*, to remain behind, reside.—L. *re-*, back; and *sedēre*, to sit, cognate with E. *sit*; see **Re-** and **Sit**. Der. *resid-ence*, as above, from F. *residence*, 'a residence, abode,' Cot.; *resid-ent*, Berners, tr. of Froissart, vol. ii. c. 210, and c. 129 (R.); *resid-ent-i-al, resid-enc-y*; *resid-ent-i-ar-y*. And see *resid-ue*.

RESIDUE, the remainder. (F.—L.) ME. *residue*, P. Plowman, B. vi. 102.—AF. *residue*, fem., Royal Wills, p. 39 (1360); cf. MF. *residu*, 'the residue, overplus,' Cot.—L. *residuum*, a remainder; neut. of *residuus*, remaining; the AF. *residue* answers to the fem. *residua.*—L. *resid-ēre*, to remain, also to reside; see **Reside**. Der. *residu-al, residu-ar-y.* Doublet, *residuum*, which is the L. form.

RESIGN, to yield up. (F.—L.) ME. *resignen*, Chaucer, C. T. 5200 (B 780).—OF. and MF. *resigner*, 'to resigne, surrender;' Cot.—L. *resignāre*, to unseal, annul, assign back, resign. Lit. 'to sign back or again.' See **Re-** and **Sign**. Der. *resign-at-ion*, from MF. *resignation*, 'a resignation;' Cot.

RESILIENT, rebounding. (L.) 'Whether there be any such *resilience* in Eccho's;' Bacon, Nat. Hist. § 245.—L. *resilient-*, stem of pres. part. of *resilīre*, to leap back, rebound.—L. *re-*, back; and *salire*, to leap; see **Re-** and **Salient**. Der. *resilience*. Also *result*, q. v.

RESIN, ROSIN, an inflammable substance, which flows from trees. (F.—L.—Gk.) *Resin* is the better form. ' Great aboundance of *rosin*;' Holland, tr. of Plutarch, b. xvi. c. 10. ME. *roseyne*, Earl of Derby's Expeditions, 1390–3 (Camden Soc.), p. 64, l. 6; *recyn, recyne*, Wyclif, Jer. li. 8.—OF. *resine*, 'rosin;' Cot. Mod. F. *résine*; Norman dial. *rousine* (Moisy).—L. *rēsīna*, Jer. li. 8 (Vulgate); Late L. *rosīna*, Voc. 714. 32. β. Borrowed from Gk. ῥητίνη (with long *i*), resin, gum from trees. For the change from τ to *s*, cf. Doric φατί as compared with Attic φησί, he says, and Gk. σύ for L. *tu*, thou. Moreover, there is a place called *Retina*, of which the mod. name is *Resina* (White). γ. Perhaps allied to Gk. ῥέειν, to flow; see Prellwitz. Der. *resin-ous*, from MF. *resineux*, 'full of rosin,' Cot.; *resin-y.*

RESIST, to stand against, oppose. (F.—L.) Spelt *resyste* in Palsgrave; *resyst* in Skelton, On the death of Edw. IV, l. 11; *resyste* in Caxton, G. Legend, St. Peter, § 4.—OF. *resister*, 'to resist;' Cot.—L. *resistere*, to stand back, stand still, withstand.—L. *re-*, back; and *sistere*, to make to stand, set, also to stand fast, a causal verb formed from *stāre*, to stand, cognate with E. *stand*. See **Re-** and **State**. Der. *resist-ance*, ME. *resistence*, Chaucer, C. T. 16377 (G 909), from OF. *resistence* (later *resistance*, as in Cotgrave, mod. F. *résistance*), which from L. *resistent-*, stem of pres. part. of *resistere*; *resist-ible, resist-ibil-i-ty, resist-less, resist-less-ly, resist-less-ness.*

RESOLVE, to separate into parts, analyse, decide. (L.) Chaucer has *resolued* (with *u=v*) in the sense of 'thawed;' tr. of Boethius, b. iv. met. 5, l. 20.—L. *resoluere*, to untie, loosen, melt, thaw.—L. *re-*, again; and *soluere*, to loosen; see **Re-** and **Solve**. Der. *resolv-able; resolv-ed, resolv-ed-ly*, All's Well, v. 3. 332; *resolv-ed-ness.* Also *resolute*, L. L. L. v. 2. 705, from the pp. *resolūtus*; *resolute-ly, resolute-ness*; *resolut-ion*, Macb. v. 5. 42, from MF. *resolution*, 'a resolution,' Cot.

RESONANT, resounding. (L.) In Milton, P. L. xi. 563.—L. *resonant-*, stem of pres. part. of *resonāre*, to resound. Cf. MF. *resonnant*, 'resounding;' Cot. See **Resound**. Der. *resonance*, suggested by MF. *resonnance*, 'a resounding;' Cot.

RESORT, to go to, betake oneself, have recourse to. (F.—L.) ' Al I refuse, but that I might *resorte* Unto my loue;' Lamentation of Mary Magdalene, st. 43, l. 299; Hoccleve, Reg. of Princes, 1397. The sb. *resort* is in Chaucer, Troilus, iii. 134.—OF. *resortir*, later *ressortir*, 'to issue, goe forth againe, resort, recourse, repaire, be referred unto, for a full tryal, .. to appeale unto; and to be removeable out of an inferior into a superior court;' Cot. (It was thus a law term.) Hence the sb. *resort*, later *ressort*, 'the authority, prerogative, or jurisdiction of a sovereign court,' Cot. Cf. Late L. *resortire*, to be subject to a tribunal. It looks like a compound of L. *re-*, again; and *sortīrī*, to obtain; as if to re-obtain, gain by appeal; and this may have affected the sense. The L. *sortīrī* is lit. ' to obtain by lot;' from *sorti-*, decl. stem of *sors*, a lot. See **Re-** and **Sort**. β. But this does not well account for the development of the senses; and it is probable that the Ital. *risorto*, jurisdiction, is allied to Ital. *risorto*, pp. of *risorgere* (L. *resurgere*), to rise again; see **Resurrection**. So also MF. *ressort* means 'the spring of a lock,' Cot.; and F. *sortir* means 'to go out.' The latter is from *surtus*, short for *surrectus*, pp. of *surgere*, to rise. Cf. MSpan. *surtir*, 'to rise, to rebound;' Minsheu. See *sortire* in Diez, *Sortir* (1) and (2) in Hatzfeld, and Körting, § 8018. See **Source**. Der. *resort*, sb., as above.

RESOUND, to echo, sound again. (F.—L.) The final *d* is excrescent after *n*, as in the sb. *sound*, a noise. ME. *resounen*, Chaucer, C. T. 1280 (A 1278).—OF. *resonner, resoner*, omitted by Cotgrave, but in use in the 12th cent. (Littré); mod. F. *résonner*.—L. *resonāre*.—L. *re-*; and *sonāre*, to sound, from *sonus*, a sound; see **Re-** and **Sound** (3). Der. *reson-ant*, q.v.

RESOURCE, a supply, support, expedient. (F.—L.) In Cotgrave, to translate F. *ressource*; he also gives the older form *resource*, 'a new source, or spring, a recovery.' The sense is 'new source, fresh spring;' hence, a new supply or fresh expedient. Compounded of **Re-** and **Source**.

RESPECT, regard, esteem. (F.—L.) In The Court of Love (not earlier than A.D. 1500), l. 155.—F. *respect*, 'respect, regard;' Cot.—L. *respectum*, acc. of *respectus*, a looking at, respect, regard.—L. *respectus*, pp. of *respicere*, to look at, look back upon.—L. *re-*, back; and *specere*, to see, spy. See **Re-** and **Spy**. Der. *respect*, verb, Cor. iii. 1. 307, and very common in Shak.; *respect-able*, from F. *respectable*, 'respectable,' Cot.; *respect-abl-y, respect-abil-i-ty*; *respect-ful, respect-ful-ly*; *respect-ive*, from F. *respectif*, 'respective,' Cot.; *respect-ive-ly.* Doublet, *respite*.

RESPIRE, to breathe, take rest. (F.—L.) In Spenser, F. Q. iii. 3. 36.—F. *respirer*, 'to breathe, vent, gaspe;' Cot.—L. *respīrāre*, to breathe.—L. *re-*, again; and *spīrāre*, to blow; see **Re-** and **Spirit**. Der. *respir-able, respir-abil-i-ty; respir-at-ion*, from F. *respiration*, 'a respiration,' Cot.; *respir-at-or, respir-at-or-y.*

RESPITE, a delay, pause, temporary reprieve. (F.—L.) 'Thre dayes haf *respite*;' Rob. of Brunne, tr. of Langtoft, p. 275, l. 2. Better spelt *respit* (with short *i*).—OF. *respit* (12th cent.), 'a respit, a delay, a time or term of forbearance; a protection of one, three, or five yeares granted by the prince unto a debtor,' &c.; Cot. Mod. F. *répit.* The true orig. sense is regard, respect had to a suit on the part of a prince or judge, and it is a mere doublet of *respect*.—L. acc. *respectum*; see **Respect**. Der. *respite*, verb, Chaucer, C. T. 11886 (F 1582). Doublet, *respect*.

RESPLENDENT, very bright. (L.) (Not from OF., which has the form *resplendissant*; see Cotgrave.) '*Resplendent* with glory;' Craft of Lovers, st. 5, l. 3; in Chaucer's Works, ed. 1561, fol. 341.—L. *resplendent-*, stem of pres. part. of *resplendēre*, to shine brightly, lit. to shine again.—L. *re-*, again; and *splendēre*, to shine; see **Re-** and **Splendour**. Der. *resplendent-ly, resplendence.*

RESPOND, to answer, reply. (F.—L.) 'For his great deeds *respond* his speeches great,' i.e. answer to them; Fairfax, tr. of Tasso, b. x. c. 40.—OF. *respondre*, 'to answer; also, to match, hold correspondency with;' Cot.—L. *respondēre* (pp. *responsus*), to answer.—L. *re-*, back, in return; and *spondēre*, to promise; see **Re-** and **Sponsor**. Der. *respond-ent*, Tyndall, Works, p. 171, col. 2, l. 47, from L. *respondent-*, stem of pres. part. of *respondēre*; *response*, ME. *response*, spelt *respons* in Rob. of Brunne, tr. of Langtoft, p. 98, l. 14, from OF. *response*, 'an answer,' Cot., from L. *responsum*, neut. of pp. *responsus*; *respons-ible, respons-ibl-y, respons-ibil-i-ty*; *respons-ive*, Hamlet, v. 2. 159, from MF. *responsif*, 'responsive, answerable,' Cot.; *respons-ive-ly.* Also *cor-respond*, q. v.

REST (1), repose, quiet, pause. (E.) ME. *reste* (dissyllabic), Chaucer, C. T. 9729 (E 1855). The final *e* is here due to the form of the oblique cases of the AS. sb. AS. *rest, ræst*, fem. sb., rest, quiet; but the gen., dat., and acc. sing. take final *-e*, making *reste*, *ræste*; see Grein, ii. 372.+Du. *rust*; Dan. and Swed. *rast*; Icel. *röst*, the distance between two resting-places, a mile; Goth. *rasta*, a stage of a journey, a mile; OHG. *rasta*, rest; also, a measure of distance. β. From the Teut. type *rast-jā, fem., 'a halting-place;' from Teut. base *ras, to dwell, as seen in Goth. *raz-ns*, a house. See **Ransack**. Brugmann, i. § 903 c. Cf. W. *aros*, to tarry; Stokes-Fick, p. 235. Der. *rest*, verb, AS. *restan*, Grein, ii. 373; *rest-less*, *rest-less-ly*, *rest-less-ness*.

REST (2), to remain, be left over. (F.—L.) Perhaps obsolete; but common in Shak. 'Nought *rests* for me but to make open proclamation;' 1 Hen. VI, i. 3. 70. The sb. *rest*, remainder, is still common; it occurs in Surrey, tr. of Virgil, Æn. ii. 856 (651 of the L. text).—F. *rester*, 'to rest, remaine;' Cot.—L. *restāre*, to stop behind, stand still, remain.—L. *re-*, behind, back; and *stāre*, to stand, cognate with E. *stand*; see **Re-** and **Stand**. Der. *rest*, sb., as above, from F. *reste*, 'a rest, residue, remnant;' Cot. And see *rest-ive*, *ar-rest*. *Rest-harrow* (Baret) = *arrest-harrow* (F. *arrête-bœuf*). And see *reasty*.

RESTAURANT, a place for refreshment. (F.—L.) Borrowed from mod. F. *restaurant*, lit. 'restoring;' pres. part. of *restaurer*, to restore, refresh; see **Restore**. Cot. has: 'restaurant, a restorative.'

REST-HARROW; see under Rest (2).

RESTITUTION, the act of restoring. (F.—L.) ME. *restitucion*, P. Plowman, B. v. 235, 238.—OF. *restitution*, 'a restitution.' L. *restitūtiōnem*, acc. of *restitūtio*, a restoring; cf. *restitūtus*, pp. of *restituere*, to restore.—L. *re-*, back; and *statuere*, to place; see **Re-** and **Statute**. Der. *restitue*, verb, in P. Plowman, B. v. 281 (obsolete); from F. *restituer*.

RESTIVE, unwilling to go forward, obstinate. (F.—L.) Sometimes confused with *restless*, though the orig. sense is very different. In old authors, it is sometimes confused with *resty*, adj., as if from *rest* (1); but properly *resty* or *restie* stands for OF. *restif* (F. *rétif*). 'The *restiff* world;' Dryden, Hind and Panther, iii. 1026. 'Grow *restie*, nor go on;' Chapman, tr. of Homer, Iliad, v. 234. 'When there be not stonds, nor *restiveness* in a man's nature;' Bacon, Essay 40, Of Fortune. See further in Trench, Select Glossary.—OF. and MF. *restif*, 'restie, stubborn, drawing backward, that will not go forward;' Cot.—F. *rester*, 'to rest, remain;' Cot. See **Rest** (2). ¶ Thus the true sense of *restive* is stubborn in keeping one's place; a *restive* horse is, properly, one that will not move for whipping; the shorter form *resty* is preserved in prov. E. *rusty*, restive, unruly (Halliwell); to *turn rusty* is to be stubborn. Der. *restive-ness*.

RESTORE, to repair, replace, return. (F.—L.) ME. *restoren*, Rob. of Glouc., p. 500, l. 10287.—OF. *restorer* (Burguy), also MF. *restaurer*, 'to restore,' Cot.—L. *restaurāre*, to restore.—L. *re-*, again; and *staurāre (not used), to set up, establish, make firm, a verb derived from an adj. *staurus = Gk. σταυρός, that which is firmly fixed, a stake. Cf. Skt. *sthāvara-s*, fixed, stable. Idg. root *steu, allied to √STĀ, to stand. Brugmann, i. § 198. See **Re-** and **Store**. Der. *restor-at-ion*, ME. *restauracion*, Gower, C. A. iii. 23, bk. vi. 637, from F. *restauration*, from L. acc. *restaurātiōnem*; *restor-at-ive*, ME. *restauratif*, Gower, C. A. iii. 30, bk. vi. 859. Also *restaur-ant*, q.v.

RESTRAIN, to hold back, check, limit. (F.—L.) ME. *restreinen*, *restreignen*, Gower, C. A. iii. 206, bk. vii. 3396; Chaucer, C. T. 14505 (B 3777).—OF. stem *restraign-*, as in *restraign-ant*, pres. pt. of *restraindre*, 'to restrain,' Cot.; mod. F. *restreindre*.—L. *stringere*, to draw back tightly, bind back.—L. *re-*, back; and *stringere*, to draw tight; see **Re-** and **Stringent**. Der. *restraint*, Surrey, Prisoned in Windsor, l. 52, from MF. *restraincte*, 'a restraint,' Cot., fem. of *restrainct*, old pp. of *restraindre*. Also *restrict*, in Foxe's Acts and Monuments, p. 1173 (R.), from L. *restrictus*, pp. of *restringere*; *restrict-ion*, tr. of More's Utopia, ed. Arber, b. ii (Of their iourneyng), p. 105, l. 9, from F. *restriction*, 'a restriction,' Cot.; *restrict-ive*, *restrict-ive-ly*.

RESULT, to ensue, follow as a consequence. (F.—L.) In Levins, ed. 1570.—MF. *resulter*, 'to rebound, or leap back; also, to rise of, come out of;' Cot.—L. *resultāre*, to spring back, rebound; frequentative of *resilīre*, to leap back; formed from a pp. *resultus*, not in use. See **Resilient**. Der. *result*, sb., a late word; *result-ant*, a mathematical term, from the stem of the pres. part.

RESUME, to take up again after interruption. (F.—L.) 'I *resume*, I take agayne;' Palsgrave.—MF. *resumer*, 'to resume;' Cot.—L. *resūmere*, to take again.—L. *re-*, again; and *sūmere*, to take. See **Assume**. Der. *resum-able*, *resumpt-ion*, formed from L. *resumptio*, which is from the pp. *resumptus*.

RESURRECTION, a rising again from the dead. (F.—L.) ME. *resurreccioun*, *resurexioun*; P. Plowman, B. xviii. 425.—OF. *resurrection*, 'a resurrection,' Cot.—L. acc. *resurrectiōnem*, from nom.

resurrectio; cf. *resurrectus*, pp. of *resurgere*, to rise again.—L. *re-*, again; and *surgere*, to rise; see **Re-** and **Source**.

RESUSCITATE, to revive. (L.) Orig. a pp. as adj., as in : 'our mortall bodies shal be *resuscitate*;' Bp. Gardner, Exposicion, On the Presence, p. 65 (R.). '*Resuscitate* from death to lyfe;' Hall, Chron., Hen. VII, an. vii. § 9.—L. *resuscitātus*, pp. of *resuscitāre*, to raise up again.—L. *re-*, again; and *suscitāre*, to raise up, for *sub-citāre, compounded of *sub*, up, under, and *citāre*, to summon, rouse. See **Re-**, **Sub-**, and **Cite**. Der. *resuscitat-ion*; *resuscitat-ive*, from MF. *resuscitatif*, 'resuscitative,' Cot.

RET, to steep flax-stems in water. (MDu.) Also *rait*; E. D. D.—Du. *reten*, to ret, break, soak hemp; MDu. *reten*, *reeten*. Cf. Pomeran. *röten*, Swed. *röta*, Norw. *röyta*, to ret; Dan. dial. *röde*. Lit. 'to make rotten;' formed by mutation from Teut. **raut-*, second grade of Teut. **reut-an-*, to rot. See **Rotten**.

RETAIL, to sell in small portions. (F.—L.) In Shak. L. L. L. v. 2. 317. Due to the phrase to *sell by retail*. 'Sell by whole-sale and not *by retaile*;' Hakluyt, Voyages, vol. i. p. 506, l. 34. To sell *by retail* is to sell by 'the shred,' or small portion.—OF. *retaille* (Hatzfeld); MF. *retail*, 'a shred, paring, or small peece cut from a thing;' Cot.—OF. *retailler*, 'to shred, pare, clip;' id.—F. *re-* (= L. *re-*), again; and *tailler*, to cut; see **Re-** and **Tailor**. Der. *retail*, sb. (which is really the more orig. word); cf. AF. *a retail*, by retail; Stat. Realm, i. 178 (1318). Cf. *de-tail*.

RETAIN, to hold back, detain. (F.—L.) In Skelton, Phylyp Sparrow, l. 1126. 'Of them that list all nice for to *retaine*;' Wyatt, Sat. ii. l. 21. Spelt *retayne* in Palsgrave; *reteyne*, Caxton, Godfrey of Bologne, p. 88, l. 28.—OF. *reteing*, *retien*, as in 1 p. s. pres. of *retenir*, 'to retaine, withholde;' Cot.—L. *retinēre*, to hold back.—L. *re-*, back; and *tenēre*, to hold; see **Re-** and **Tenable**. Der. *retainable*; *retain-er*, Hen. VIII, ii. 4. 113; *retent-ion*, q. v., *retin-ue*, q. v.

RETALIATE, to repay. (L.) In Blount's Gloss., ed. 1674.—L. *retāliātus*, pp. of *retāliāre*, to requite, allied to *tālio*, retaliation in kind. Cf. L. *lex tāliōnis*, the law of retaliation. β. It is usual to connect these words with L. *tālis*, such, like; but they are obviously allied to W. *tāl*, payment, Irish *taille*, wages, Gael. *taileas*, wages ; Corn. *taly*, to pay. Hence *retaliate* = repay. Der. *retaliat-ion*, a coined word; *retaliat-ive*, *retaliat-or-y*.

RETARD, to make slow, delay, defer. (F.—L.) In Minsheu, ed. 1627, 'To *retarde* you;' A.D. 1467; Excerpta Historica, p. 187.—MF. *retarder*, 'to foreslow, hinder;' Cot.—L. *retardāre*, to delay.—L. *re-*, back; and *tardāre*, to make slow, from *tardus*, slow. See **Re-** and **Tardy**. Der. *retard-at-ion*.

RETCH, REACH, to try to vomit. (E.) Sometimes spelt *reach*, but quite distinct from the ordinary verb to *reach*. In Todd's Johnson; without an example. '*Reach*, to retch, to strive to vomit;' Peacock, Gloss. of words used in Manley and Corringham (Lincoln). AS. *hrǣcan*, to try to vomit; whence: '*Phtisis*, wyrs-hrǣcing,' Voc. 113. 8; also *hrǣc-gebrǣc*, Voc. 112. 30. From AS. *hrāca*, spittle, A. S. Leechdoms, ii. 260.+Icel. *hrajka*, to retch; from *hrāki*, spittle. Prob. of imitative origin.

RETENTION, power to retain, or act of retaining. (F.—L.) In Shak. Tw. Nt. ii. 4. 99; v. 84.—MF. *retention*, 'a retention;' Cot.—L. *retentionem*, acc. of *retentio*, a retaining; cf. *retentus*, pp. of *retinēre*; see **Retain**. Der. *retent-ive*, *retent-ive-ly*, *-ness*.

RETICENT, very silent. (L.) Modern; the sb. *reticence* is in Holland, tr. of Plutarch, p. 841 (R.).—L. *reticent-*, stem of pres. part. of *reticēre*, to be very silent.—L. *re-*, again, hence, very much; and *tacēre*, to be silent; see **Re-** and **Tacit**. Der. *reticence*, from MF. *reticence*, 'silence,' Cot., from L. *reticentia*.

RETICULE, a little bag to be carried in the hand. (F.—L.) Modern; not in Todd's Johnson. Borrowed from F. *réticule*, a net for the hair, a reticule; Littré.—L. *rēticulum*, a little net, a reticule; double dimin. (with suffix *-cu-lu*) from *rēti-*, decl. stem of *rēte*, a net. ¶ Formerly also *ridicule*, both in F. and E., by confusion with *ridicule* (Littré). Cf. prov. F. *rédicule*, a reticule, dial. of Verdun (Fertiault); and Rouchi (Hécart). Der. *reticul-ar*, *reticul-ate*, *reticul-at-ed*; also *reti-ar-y*, i.e. net-like; *reti-form*, in the form of a net; also *reti-na*, q. v.

RETINA, the innermost coating of the eye. (L.) Called '*Retiformis tunica*, or *Retina*,' in Phillips, ed. 1706. So called because it resembles a fine network. A coined word; from *rēti-*, decl. stem of *rēte*, a net; see **Reticule**.

RETINUE, a suite or body of retainers. (F.—L.) ME. *retenue*, Chaucer, C. T. 2504 (A 2502).—OF. *retenue*, 'a retinue;' Cot.; fem. of *retenu*, pp. of *retenir*, to retain; see **Retain**.

RETIRE, to retreat, recede, draw back. (F.—L. *and* Teut.) In Shak. Temp. iv. 161.—OF. *retirer*, 'to retire, withdraw;' Cot.—F. *re-*, back; and *tirer*, to draw, pull, pluck, a word of Teut. origin. See **Re-** and **Tirade**. Der. *retire-ment*, Meas. for Meas. v. 130, from F. *retirement*, 'a retiring,' Cot.

RETORT, a censure returned; a tube used in distillation. (F. − L.) In both senses, it is the same word. The chemical *retort* is so called from its 'twisted' or bent tube; a *retort* is a sharp reply 'twisted' back or returned to an assailant. 'The *retort* courteous;' As You Like It, v. 4. 76. 'She wolde *retorte* in me and my mother;' Henrysoun, Test. of Creseide, st. 41, l. 286.−F. *retorte*, 'a retort, or crooked body,' Cot.; fem. of *retort*, 'twisted, twined, .. retorted, violently returned,' id.; pp. of *retordre*, 'to wrest back, retort;' id. −L. *retorquēre* (pp. *retortus*), to twist back.−L. *re-*, back; and *torquēre*, to twist; see **Re-** and **Torsion.**

RETOUCH, RETRACE; from **Re-** and **Touch, Trace.**

RETRACT, to revoke. (F.−L.) In Levins, ed. 1570. [The remark in Trench, Study of Words, lect. iii, that the primary meaning is 'to reconsider,' is not borne out by the etymology; 'to draw back' is the older sense.]−MF. *retracter*, 'to recant, revoke,' Cot. −L. *retractāre*, to retract; frequentative of *retrahere* (pp. *retractus*), to draw back.−L. *re-*, back; and *trahere*, to draw; see **Re-** and **Trace.** Der. *retract-ion*, from MF. *retraction*, 'a retraction,' Cot.; *retract-ive*, *retract-ive-ly*; also *retract-ile*, i.e. that can be drawn back, a coined word. And see *retreat*.

RETREAT, a drawing back, a place of retirement. (F.−L.) Spelt *retreit* in Levins. 'Betre is to make a *beau retret*' = it is better to make a good retreat; Gower, C. A. iii. 356; bk. viii. 2416.−OF. *retrete* (Littré), later *retraite*, spelt *retraicte* in Cotgrave, 'a retrait, a place of refuge;' fem. of *retret*, *retrait*, pp. of *retraire*, 'to withdraw;' Cot.−L. *retrahere*, to draw back; see **Retract.** Der. *retreat*, verb, Milton, P. L. ii. 547.

RETRENCH, to curtail expenses. (F.−L.) In Phillips, ed. 1706.−MF. *retrencher*, 'to cut, strike, or chop off, to curtall, diminish;' Cot. Mod. F. *retrancher*.−F. *re-* (= L. *re-*), back; and OF. *trencher*, 'to cut;' Cot. See **Re-** and **Trench.** Der. *retrench-ment*, Phillips.

RETRIBUTION, requital, reward or punishment. (F.−L.) In Minsheu, ed. 1627. Spelt *retrybucion*, Caxton, G. Legend, Pentecost, § 3.−MF. *retribution*, 'a retribution, requitall;' Cot. −L. *retribūtiōnem*, acc. of *retribūtio*, recompense; cf. *retribūtus*, pp. of *retribuere*, to restore, repay.−L. *re-*, back; and *tribuere*, to assign, give; see **Re-** and **Tribute.** Der. *retribut-ive*.

RETRIEVE, to recover, bring back to a former state. (F.−L. and Gk.) 'I retreve, I fynde agayne, as houndes do their game, *je retrouue*;' Palsgrave. Levins has: '*retrive*, retrudere;' he must mean the same word. Spelt *retriue*, Book of St. Albans, fol. b 4; cf. *retriuer*, a retriever (dog), id. fol. b 3, back. Just as in the case of *contrive*, the spelling has been altered; probably *retreve* was meant to represent OF. *retreuve*, a stem of the OF. *retrover*, later *retrouver*.−F. *retrouver*, 'to find again;' Cot.−F. *re-*, again; and *trouver*, to find. See **Contrive** and **Trover.** Thus the successive spellings are *retreve* (for *retreuve*), *retrive*, *retrieve*. Der. *retriev-er*, *retrievable*.

RETRO-, backwards, *prefix*. (L.; or F.−L.) L. *retrō-*, backwards. A comparative form, with comp. suffix *-trō*, as in *ul-trō*, *ci-trō*, *in-trō*; from *red-* or *re-*, back. Thus the sense is 'more backward.' See **Re-.** Cf. Goth. *-þrō* in *þa-þrō*, thence; Brugmann, ii. § 75.

RETROCESSION, a going back. (L.) A coined word, and not common; see an example in Richardson. As a math. term, in Phillips, ed. 1706. Formed with suffix *-ion* (= F. *-ion*, L. *-iōnem*) like *retrocess-us*, pp. of *retrōcēdere*, to go backwards; see **Retro-** and **Cede.** ¶ The classical L. sb. is *retrōcessus*.

RETROGRADE, going backwards, from better to worse. (L.) In early astronomical use, with respect to a planet's apparent backward motion. ME. *retrograd*, Chaucer, On the Astrolabe, ed. Skeat, pt. ii. § 4, l. 33; § 35, l. 12.−L. *retrōgradus*, going backward; used of a planet.−L. *retrōgradi*, to go backward.−L. *retrō-*, backward; and *gradi*, to go; see **Retro-** and **Grade.** Der. *retrograde*, verb, from MF. *retrograder*, 'to recoyle, retire,' Cot.; *retrogress-ion*, in Sir T. Browne, Vulg. Errors, b. vi. c. 3, last section, as if from L. **retrōgressio* (but the classical form is *retrōgressus*), like *retrōgressus*, pp. of *retrōgradi*. Hence *retrogress-ive*, *-ly*. Also *retrograd-at-ion*, Holland, tr. of Pliny, b. ii. c. 17, from MF. *retrogradation*, 'a retrogradation,' Cot., formed from *retrōgradātus*, pp. of *retrōgradāre*, collateral form of *retrōgradi*.

RETROSPECT, a contemplation of the past. (L.) Used by Steele in The Spectator, no. 374, § 1. Pope has *retrospective*, adj., Moral Essays, Ep. i. l. 99. Swift has *retrospection* (Todd; no reference). '*Retrospect*, or *Retrospection*, looking back;' Phillips, ed. 1706. Coined from L. *retrospectus*, unused pp. of *retrospicere*, to look back.−L. *retrō-*, backward; and *specere*, to look; see **Retro-** and **Spy.**

RETROUSSÉ, turned up at the end, as a nose. (F.) Modern. −F. *retroussé*, pp. of *retrousser*, to turn up; lit. to truss up.−F. *re-*, again; and *trousser*, to pack; see **Truss.**

RETURN, to come back to the same place, answer, retort. (F.−L.) ME. *returnen*, *retournen*, Chaucer, C. T. 2097 (A 2095); Rom. of the Rose, 382, 384.−F. *retourner*, 'to return;' Cot.−F. *re-*, back; and *tourner*, to turn: see **Re-** and **Turn.** Der. *return*, sb., King Alisaunder, l. 600. Der. *return-able*.

REUNION, REUNITE; see **Re-** and **Unit.**

REVEAL, to unveil, make known. (F.−L.) Spelt *revele*, Spenser, F. Q. iii. 2. 48.−MF. *reveler*, 'to reveale;' Cot.−L. *reuēlāre*, to unveil, draw back a veil.−L. *re-*, back; and *uēlāre*, to veil, from *uēlum*, a veil; see **Re-** and **Veil.** Der. *revel-at-ion*, ME. *reuelacioun*, Wyclif, Rom. xvi. 25, from MF. *revelation*, 'a revelation,' Cot., from *reuēlātiōnem*, acc. of *reuēlātio*, allied to *reuēlātus*, pp. of *reuēlāre*.

REVEILLE, an alarum at break of day. (F.−L.) 'Sound a *reveillé*, sound, sound;' Dryden, The Secular Masque, 61. 'Save where the fife its shrill *reveillé* screams;' Campbell, Gertrude, pt. iii. st. 7. 'So soon love beats *revellies* in her breast;' Davenant, Gondibert, b. iii. c. 5. st. 1. A trisyllabic word. The true F. word is *réveil*, an awaking, reveille; as in *battre le réveil*, *sonner le réveil*, to beat, to sound the reveille (Hamilton). But the E. word was originally *reveillez*; see Brand's Antiq. ed. Ellis, ii. 176. This was taken as a pl. form, and the final z was dropped.−MF. *resveillez vous*, awake ye; imper. pl. of *resveiller*, to awake, arouse. Cf. MF. *resveil*, 'a hunt's-up or morning-song for a new married wife, the day after the marriage.'−F. *re-* (= L. *re-*), again; and OF. *esveiller*, to waken (Cot.), from Late L. **exuigilāre*, not found, but a mere compound of *ex*, out, and *uigilāre*, to wake, watch, from *uigil*, wakeful. See **Re-, Ex-,** and **Vigil.** ¶ See the full account in Notes on E. Etym., p. 247. The F. *reveillez* is used as a sb., in the E. sense, in the dialect of Forez, near Lyons (Graz).

REVEL, to carouse, indulge in boisterous festivities, to frolic. (F.−L.) ME. *revelen*; Poems and Lives of Saints, ed. Furnivall, xxx. 15.−OF. *reveler*, to rebel, revolt, also to rejoice noisily, rejoice greatly (Godefroy).−L. *rebellāre*, to rebel; see **Rebel.** Der. *revel*, sb., ME. *reuel* (= *revel*), Chaucer, C. T. 2719 (A 2717), Legend of Good Women, 2255; P. Plowman, B. xiii. 442; Will. of Palerne, 1953. [On the strength of Chaucer's expression, 'And made *revel* al the longe night' (C. T. 2719), Tyrwhitt explained *revel* as 'an entertainment, properly *during the night*.' This is an attempt at forcing an etymology from F. *réveiller*, to wake, which is wrong. In Will. of Palerne, 1953, the *revels* are distinctly said to have taken place *in the forenoon*; and in Chaucer, Legend of Good Women, 2255, we read that 'This *revel*, full of songe and ful of daunce, Lasteth a *fourtenight*, or litel lasse,' which quite precludes a special reference to the night.]−OF. *revel*, which Godefroy explains by 'rebellion, revolt, pride, also great rejoicing, joy, amusement.' 'Plains est de joie et de *revel*' = is full of joy and revelry; Le Vair Palefroy, l. 760; Roquefort. 'La douçors de tens novel Fait changier ire en *revel*' = the sweetness of the fresh season changes anger into sport; Bartsch, Chrestomathie, col. 323, l. 28. Also *revell-er*, ME. *revelour*, Chaucer, C. T. 4389 (A 4391); *revel-ry*. ¶ Note also ME. *revelous*, full of revelry, full of jest, Chaucer, C. T. 12934 (B 1194) = OF. *reveleux*, *revelos*, riotous. Körting, § 7826.

REVENGE, to injure in return, avenge. (F.−L.) In Palsgrave. 'To *revenge* the dethe of our fathers;' Berners, tr. of Froissart, vol. ii. c. 240 (R.).−OF. *revengier* (Supp. to Godefroy, s.v. *revancher*); MF. *revenger* (Palsgrave), later *revencher*, 'to wreak, or revenge himselfe,' Cot., who gives the form *revengé* for the pp.; mod. F. *revancher*; whence the phrase *en revanche*, in return, to make amends; by a bettering of the sense.−F. *re-*, again; and *venger*, older from *vengier*, to take vengeance, from L. *uindicāre*. See **Re-** and **Vengeance;** also **Avenge, Vindicate.** Der. *revenge*, sb., Spenser, F. Q. i. 6. 44; *revenge-ful*, Hamlet, iii. 1. 126; *revenge-ful-ly*; *revenge-ment*, 1 Hen. IV, iii. 2. 7. Doublet, *revindicate*.

REVENUE, income. (F.−L.) Lit. 'that which comes back or is returned to one.' Often accented *revénue*; Temp. i. 2. 98.−OF. *revenuë*, 'revenue, rent;' Cot. Fem. of *revenu*, pp. of *revenir*, to return, come back.−F. *re-*, back; and *venir*, to come.−L. *re-*, back; and *uenire*, to come, cognate with E. *come*. See **Re-** and **Come.**

REVERBERATE, to re-echo, reflect sound. (L.) In Levins, ed. 1570.−L. *reuerberātus*, pp. of *reuerberāre*, to beat back.−L. *re-*, back; and *uerberāre*, to beat, from *uerber*, a scourge, lash, whip; cf. Gk. ῥάβδος, a rod. Der. *reverberat-ion*, ME. *reuerberacioun*, Chaucer, C. T. 7816 (D 2234), from F. *reverberation*, 'a reverberation,' Cot., from L. acc. *reuerberātiōnem*. Also *reverberat-or-y*; and *reverb* (a coined word, by contraction), K. Lear, i. 1. 156.

REVERE, to venerate, regard with awe. (F.−L.) Not an early word, *to reverence* being used instead. In Blount's Gloss., ed. 1674. −MF. *reverer* (mod. *révérer*), 'to reverence,' Cot.−L. *reuerēri*, to revere, stand in awe of.−L. *re-*, again (here intensive); and *uerēri*, to fear, feel awe (corresponding to the E. phrase *to be wary, to* *beware*), from the same root as *wary*. See **Re-** and **Wary**. Der. *rever-ence*, in early use, ME. *reuerence*, Rob. of Glouc., p. 553, l. 11547, King Alisaunder, 793, from OF. *reuerence*, 'reverence,' Cot., from L. *reuerentia*, respect. Hence *reverence*, vb., Minsheu, ed. 1627, P. Plowman, C. xiv. 248, from OF. *reuerencer*, 'to reverence,' Cot.; *reverenti-al*, from MF. *reuerential*, 'reverent,' Cot. Also *rever-ent*, Chaucer, C. T. 8063 (E 187), from OF. *reuerent* (14th century, see Littré, s. v. *révérend*), which from L. *reuerendus*, fut. pass. part. of *reuerērī*: later form *rever-end*, Frith's Works, p. 105, col. 2, l. 40.

REVERIE, REVERY, a dreaming, irregular train of thought. (F. – L. ?) 'When ideas float in our mind without any reflection or regard of the understanding, it is that which the French call *resvery*; our language has scarce a name for it;' Locke, Human Understanding, b. ii. c. 19 (R.). 'In a *reuerrye*;' Godfrey of Boloyne, ch. 116; p. 174. AF. *reverye*, raving; Langtoft, ii. 168. – F. *rêverie*, formerly *resverie*, 'a raving, idle talking, dotage, vain fancy, fond imagination;' Cot. – F. *rêver*, formerly *resver*, 'to rave, dote, speak idly, talke like an asse;' id. β. The F. *rêver* has the same sense as the Lorraine *râver*, whence E. *rave*; see **Rave**. Hence the form *ravery*, raving, rage, as a variant of *revery* (N. E. D.). Körting, § 7697.

REVERSE, opposite, contrary, having an opposite direction. (F. – L.) The adj. use seems to be the oldest in E.; it precedes the other uses etymologically. ME. *reuers* (= *revers*). 'A vice *reuers* unto this' = a vice opposite this; Gower, C. A. i. 167; bk. ii. 222. 'Al the *reuers* seyn' = say just the contrary; Chaucer, C. T. 14983 (B 4167). – OF. *revers*, 'strange, uncoth, crosse;' Cot. – L. *reuersus*, lit. turned back, reversed, pp. of *reuertere*, to turn backward, return. – L. *re-*, back; and *uertere*, to turn; see **Re-** and **Verse**. Der. *reverse*, verb, Gower, C. A. i. 3; prol. 30; *reverse*, sb., Merry Wives, ii. 3. 27, from F. *revers*, 'a back blow,' Cot. Cf. F. *les revers de fortune*, 'the crosses [reverses] of fortune;' id. Also *revers-ion*, Levins, from MF. *reversion*, 'a reverting,' Cot.; hence *revers-ion-ar-y*. Also *revers-al*, Bacon, Life of Hen. VII, ed. Lumby, p. 15, l. 26; *revers-ible*. And see *revert*.

REVERT, to return, fall back, reverse. (F. – L.) In Spenser, F. Q. iv. 6. 43. Also in Caxton; see gloss. to Eneydos. – MF. *revertir*, 'to revert, returne;' Cot. – L. type *revertīre*, for L. *reuertere*, to return; see **Reverse**. Der. *revert-ible*.

REVIEW, to view again, look back on, examine carefully. (F. – L.) 'To *reuiew*, to recognise, or revise;' Minsheu, ed. 1627. And see Shak. Sonn. 74; Wint. Tale, iv. 4. 680. From **Re-** and **View**. Der. *review*, sb., *review-er*, *review-al*.

REVILE, to calumniate, reproach. (F. – L.) ME. *reuilen* (with *u* = *v*), Gower, C. A. iii. 247, bk. vii. 4635; Rob. of Brunne, tr. of Langtoft, p. 161, l. 11. AF. *reviler* (Gower); OF. *reviler*, to revile (Godefroy). – F. *re-* (L. *re-*), again; and F. *vil*, from L. *uilis*, cheap, of small value. Cf. OF. *aviler* (mod. F. *avilir*), 'to disprise, disesteeme, imbase, make vile or cheap,' &c.; Cot.; where the prefix is F. *à*, L. *ad*. See **Vile**. Der. *revil-er*.

REVISE, to review and amend. (F. – L.) In Minsheu, ed. 1627. – MF. *reviser*, to revise; omitted by Cotgrave, but in early use (Littré). – L. *reuisere*, to look back on, to revisit. – L. *re-*, again; and *uisere*, to survey, frequent. form of *uidēre* (supine *uisum*), to see. See **Re-** and **Vision**. Der. *revise*, sb., *revis-al*, *revis-er*; *revis-ion*, from F. *revision*, 'a revision, revise, review,' Cot.

REVISIT, to visit again. (F. – L.) In Hamlet, i. 4. 53. From **Re-** and **Visit**.

REVIVE, to return to life, consciousness, or vigour, recover. (F. – L.) In Palsgrave; and in K. Lear, iv. 6. 47. 'His spyrite *reuyued*;' Caxton, G. Legend, Joseph, § 14. Also used actively, as: 'to *revive* the ded' = to reanimate the dead; Spenser, F. Q. ii. 3. 22. – F. *revivre*, 'to revive, recover, return unto life,'. Cot. – L. *reuiuere*, to live again. – L. *re-*, again; and *uiuere*, to live; see **Re-** and **Vivid**. Der. *reviv-al*, *revival-ist*, *reviv-er*. Also *reviv-ify*, from *re-* and *vivify*; *reviv-i-fic-at-ion*.

REVOKE, to repeal, recall, reverse. (F. – L.) Levins, ed. 1570, has both *revoke* and *revocate*. 'I revoke, je reuocque;' Palsgrave. Spelt *reuoke*, Dictes, pr. by Caxton, fol. 24, l. 11. – MF. *revocquer* (omitted by Cotgrave), to revoke; mod. F. *révoquer*. – L. *reuocāre*, to call back. – L. *re-*, back; and *uocāre*, to call. See **Re-** and **Voice**. Der. *revoc-at-ion*, from MF. *revocation*, 'a revocation,' Cot., from L. acc. *reuocātiōnem*; *revoc-able*, from MF. *revocable*, 'revokable,' Cot., from L. *reuocābilis*; *revoc-abl-y*; *ir-revoc-able*.

REVOLT, a turning away, rebellion. (F. – Ital. – L.) In Shak. Merry Wives, i. 3. 111. – MF. *revolte*, 'a revolt, a rebellion,' Cot. – MItal. *revolta* (mod. *rivolta*), 'a reuolt, turning, an ouerthrow;' Florio. Fem. of *revolto*, 'turned, revolted, ouerthrowne, ouerturned,' &c.; Florio. This is the pp. of *revolvere*, 'to revolve, ponder, turne, ouerwhelme;' id. See **Revolve**. Der. *revolt*, verb, K. John, iii.

l. 257, from MF. *revolter*, MItal. *revoltare*; *revolt-er*; *revolt-ing*, *revolt-ing-ly*.

REVOLVE, to roll round, move round a centre. (L.) 'This meditacion by no waie *reuolue*;' Test. of Love, b. i, ch. 8, l. 4. – L. *reuoluere*, to roll back, revolve. – L. *re-*, back; and *uoluere* (pp. *uolūtus*), to roll. See **Re-** and **Voluble**. Der. *revolv-er*; *revolut-ion*, ME. *reuolucion*, Gower, C. A. ii. 61, bk. iv. 1783, from OF. *revolution*, from L. acc. *reuolūtiōnem*, nom. *reuolūtio*, a revolving, allied to *reuolūtus*, pp. of *reuoluere*. Hence *revolution-ar-y*, *-ise*, *-ist*. And see *revolt*.

REVULSION, a tearing away, sudden forcing back. (F. – L.) Used by Bacon, Nat. Hist. § 66, to mean the withdrawal of blood from one part to another in the body. – MF. *revulsion*, 'a revulsion, plucking away; also, the drawing or forcing of humours from one part of the body into another;' Cot. – L. *reuulsiōnem*, acc. of *reuulsio*, a tearing away; cf. *reuulsus*, pp. of *reuellere*, to pluck back. – L. *re-*, back; and *uellere*, to pluck. Der. *revuls-ive*. And see *con-vulse*.

REWARD, to requite, recompense, give in return. (F. – L. and Teut.) ME. *rewarden*, verb, P. Plowman, B. xi. 129, Wyclif, Heb. xi. 26. Also *reward*, sb., used exactly in the sense of *regard*, of which it is a mere doublet. 'Took *reward* of no man' = paid regard to no one, P. Plowman, C. v. 40; see Chaucer, Legend of Good Women, prol. 399; Hampole, Pricke of Conscience, 1881; Will. of Palerne, 3339. – AF. *rewarder*, Langtoft, i. 176; OF. *rewarder*, the same as *regarder*, to regard (Burguy). – OF. *re-* (= L. *re-*), back; and *warder*, the same as *garder*, a word of Teut. origin. See **Re-gard**, **Guard**, **Ward**. The orig. sense was to mark or heed, as a lord who observes a vassal, and regards him as worthy of honour or punishment; hence, to requite. Der. *reward*, sb., OF. *reward*, the same as *regard*. ☞ Not connected with *guerdon*, as suggested in Richardson. **Doublet**, *regard*.

REYNARD, RENARD, a fox. (F. – Teut.) In Dryden, The Cock and the Fox, 581, 662, 721, 768, 794, 805. 'Hyer [here] begynneth thystorye [the history] of *reynard the foxe*;' Caxton, tr. of Reynard the Fox, A. D. 1481. See the Introductory Sketch to The History of Reynard the Fox, ed. Arber. – MF. *renard*, *regnard* (mod. F. *rénard*), 'a fox;' Cot. β. Of Teut. origin; the famous epic is of Low G. origin, and was composed in Flanders in the 12th century; see the edition, by Herr Ernst Martin, Paderborn, 1874, of Willems, *Gedicht von den vos Reinaerde* (poem of the fox Reynard). Thus the E. and F. words are due to the Flemish name *reinaerd* or *reinaert*. This is the same as the OHG. *reginhart*, used as a Christian name, meaning literally 'strong in counsel,' an excellent name for the animal. γ. The OHG. *regin*, *ragin*, counsel, is the same as Goth. *ragin*, an opinion, judgement, advice, decree. This is not to be connected with L. *regere*, to rule, but with Skt. *rachanā*, orderly arrangement, from *rach*, to arrange; see Uhlenbeck. δ. The OHG. *hart*, strong, lit. hard, is cognate with E. **Hard**, q. v. The OHG. *reginhart* became later *reinhart*, a reynard, fox. We also meet with the mod. G. *reinecke*, a fox; this is a dimin. of *Rein-*.

RHAPSODY, a wild, disconnected composition. (F. – L. – Gk.) Ben Jonson uses 'a *rhapsody* Of Homer's' to translate *Iliacum carmen*, Horace, Ars Poetica, l. 129. Spelt *rapsodie* in Minsheu, ed. 1627. – F. *rapsodie*, 'a rapsodie,' Cot. – L. *rhapsōdia*. – Gk. ῥαψῳδία, the reciting of epic poetry, a portion of an epic poem recited at a time, also, a rhapsody, tirade. – Gk. ῥαψῳδός, one who stitches or strings songs together, a reciter of epic poetry, a bard who recites his own poetry. The term merely means 'one who strings odes or songs together,' without any necessary reference to the actual stitching together of leaves. – Gk. ῥαψ-, stem of fut. tense of ῥάπτειν, to stitch together, fasten together; and ᾠδή, an ode, for which see **Ode**. Der. *rhapsodi-c*, Gk. ῥαψῳδικός, adj., *rhapsodi-c-al*, *rhapsodi-c-al-ly*; *rhapsodi-st*, sb.

RHETORIC, the art of speaking with propriety and elegance. (F. – L. – Gk.) ME. *retorykè* (4 syllables), Chaucer, C. T. 7908 (E 32). – OF. *rhetorique*, 'rhetorick,' Cot. – L. *rhētorica*, for *rhētorica ars*, i. e. rhetorical art; fem. of *rhētoricus*, rhetorical. – Gk. ῥητορική, for ῥητορικὴ τέχνη, i. e. rhetorical art; fem. of ῥητορικός, rhetorical. – Gk. ῥήτορι-, decl. stem of ῥήτωρ, an orator. For *ῥρή-τωρ, related by gradation to εἴρειν (for *ϝέρ-yειν), to say, of which the pt. t. is εἴ-ρη-κα. Formed with the suffix -τωρ (= L. -*tor*) of the agent; the sense being 'speaker.' β. The base of εἴρειν is ϝερ = √WER, to speak; whence also the E. *verb* and *word*; see **Verb**, **Word**. See Curtius, i. 428. Der. *rhetoric-al*, *-al-ly*; *rhetoric-ian*.

RHEUM, discharge from the lungs or nostrils caused by a cold. (F. – L. – Gk.) Frequent in Shak. Meas. iii. 1. 31; &c. '*Reumes* and moystures do increase;' Sir T. Elyot, Castel of Helth, b. ii. c. 24. Spelt *rewme*, Palsgrave. – OF. *reume*, MF. *rheume*, 'a rheume, catarrh;' Cot. (F. *rhume*). – L. *rheuma*. – Gk. ῥεῦμα (stem ῥευματ-), a flow, flood, flux, rheum. – Gk. ῥευ-, occurring in ῥεύ-σομαι, fut. t.

of ῥέειν, to flow, which stands for *σρέϜειν ; the base of the verb being *σρευ-, to flow, cognate with Skt. sru, to flow. — √SREU, to flow ; see **Stream**. Brugmann, i. § 462 ; Fick, i. 837 ; Curtius, i. 439. Der. rheum-y, Jul. Cæsar, ii. 1. 266 ; rheumat-ic, Mids. Nt. Dr. ii. 1. 105, from L. rheumaticus, from Gk. ῥευματικός, adj. ; rheumat-ic-al ; rheumat-ism, from L. rheumatismus, from Gk. ῥευματισμός, liability to rheum.

RHINOCEROS, a large quadruped. (L. – Gk.) In Shak. Macb. iii. 4. 101. Named from the remarkable horn (sometimes double) on the nose. — L. rhinoceros (Pliny). — Gk. ῥινόκερως, a rhinoceros, lit. 'nose-horned.' — Gk. ῥινο-, decl. stem of ῥίς (gen. ῥινός), the nose ; and κέρ-ας, a horn, allied to E. horn ; see **Horn**. ☞ See the description of the rinocertis and monoceros, supposed to be different animals, in K. Alisaunder, 6529, 6539 ; cf. Wright, Popular Treatises on Science, p. 81.

RHIZOME, a root-like stem. (F. – Gk.) Modern ; in botany. – F. rhizome. — Gk. ῥίζωμα, root. — Gk. ῥιζοῦν, to cause to take root. — Gk. ῥίζα, root ; see **Root**.

RHODODENDRON, a genus of plants with evergreen leaves. (L. – Gk.) Lit. 'rose-tree.' In Phillips, ed. 1706. — L. rhododendron (Pliny). — Gk. ῥοδόδενδρον, lit. 'rose-tree.' — Gk. ῥοδο-, for ῥόδον, a rose ; and δένδρον, a tree. β. As to ῥόδον, see **Rose**. Δέν-δρον appears to be a reduplicated form, connected with δρῦς, a tree, and therefore with E. tree ; see **Tree**.

RHODOMONTADE ; the same as **Rodomontade**, q. v.

RHOMB, RHOMBUS, a quadrilateral figure, having all its sides equal, but not all its angles right angles. (F. – L. – Gk. ; or L. – Gk.) The F. form rhomb is now less common than the L. form rhombus ; but it appears in Blount's Gloss., ed. 1674, and in Milton, P. R. iii. 309. — F. rhombe, 'a spinning wheel ; also, a figure that hath equall sides and unequall angles, as a quarry of glass,' &c. ; Cot. — L. rhombus. — Gk. ῥόμβος, anything that may be spun or twirled round, a spinning-wheel ; also a rhomb, or rhombus, from a certain likeness to a whirling spindle, when the adjacent angles are very unequal. — Gk. ῥέμβειν, to revolve, totter. Allied to **Wrinkle** (Prellwitz). See also **Rumb**. Der. rhomb-ic ; rhombo-id, i. e. rhomb-shaped, from ῥόμβο-, for ῥόμβος, and εἶδ-ος, form, shape ; rhombo-id-al. **Doublet**, rumb, q. v.

RHUBARB, the name of an edible plant. (F. – Late L. – Gk.) Spelt reubarbe by Sir T. Elyot, Castel of Helth, b. iv. c. 1 ; also Reubarbarum, id. b. iii. c. 6 ; rubarbe, Skelton, Magnificence, 2385 ; rubarb, Libell of E. Policy, l. 362. — OF. reubarbe, MF. rheubarbe, 'rewbarb ;' Cot. Mod. F. rhubarbe. Cf. Ital. reobarbaro, rhubarb ; spelt rabbarbaro in Florio. The botanical name is rhēum. — Late L. rheubarbarum (= rhēum barbarum), used by Isidore of Seville (Brachet). — Gk. ῥῆον βάρβαρον, rhubarb ; lit. 'the Rhēum from the barbarian country.' β. Gk. ῥῆον is an adjectival form, from ῥᾶ, the Rha-plant, i. e. reubarb, which was also called Rha Ponticum ; and Rha took its name from the Rha or Volga, the name of a river in Pontus. Cf. the Linnæan name Rhēum Rhăponticum, which is tautological. 'Huic Rha uicinus est amnis, in cujus superciliis quædam uegetabilis eiusdem nominis gignitur radix, proficiens ad usus multiplices medelarum ;' Ammianus Marcellinus, xxii. 8. 28 ; a passage which Holland translates by : 'Neere unto this is the river Rha, on the sides whereof groweth a comfortable and holsom root, so named, good for many uses in physick.' See Taylor's Words and Places, Lewis's Lat. Dict (s. v. rha), and Richardson.

RHUMB, the same as **Rumb**, q. v.

RHYME, the same as **Rime** (1), q. v.

RHYTHM, flowing metre, true cadence of verse, harmony. (F. – L. – Gk.) Formerly spelt rithme, as in Minsheu, ed. 1627. — F. rithme, 'rime, or meeter ;' Cot. — L. rhythmum, acc. of rhythmus. — Gk. ῥυθμός, measured motion, time, measure, proportion ; Ionic form, ῥυσμός. Cf. Gk. ῥύσις, a stream, ῥύμα, a stream, ῥυτός, flowing ; all from the base ῥυ- ; cf. ῥέειν (for *σρέϜειν), to flow. — √SREU, to flow ; see **Rheum**. Brugmann, ii. § 72, iii. § 691. ¶ See also **Rime** (1). Der. rhythm-ic, Gk. ῥυθμικός ; rhythm-ic-al.

RIATA ; see **Reata**.

RIB, one of the bones from the back-bone encircling the chest. (E.) ME. ribbe, Rob. of Glouc., p. 22, l. 518 ; P. Plowman, B. vi. 180. AS. ribb, Gen. ii. 21. + Du. rib ; Icel. rif ; Swed. ref-been, a rib-bone ; Dan. rib-been ; Pomeran. ribbe ; OHG. rippi, G. rippe. + Russ. rebro. β. The AS. ribb answers to a Teut. type *reb-jom, neut. Perhaps allied to G. reb-e, a tendril ; from the notion of winding round (Kluge). Cf. OHG. hirni-reba, the brain-pan, skull. Der. rib, verb ; ribb-ing ; spare-rib ; rib-wort, Palsgrave, a plantain, called simply ribbe (rib) in AS. ; see A. S. Leechdoms, Glossary.

RIBALD, a low, licentious fellow. (F. – Teut.) ME. ribald, but almost always spelt ribaud, P. Plowman, B. xvi. 151, v. 512 ; King Alisaunder, 1578 ; pl. ribauz, O. Eng. Homilies, ed. Morris, i. 279, last line but one. — OF. ribald, ribaud (ribauld in Cot.), a ribald,

ruffian ; mod. F. ribaut. The Late L. form is ribaldus ; see Ducange. And see a long note in Polit. Songs, ed. Wright, 1839, p. 369. We also find Late L. ribalda, fem., a prostitute. β. The suffix -ald shows the word to be Teutonic ; it answers to OHG. walt, power, and was (1) a common suffix in Frankish proper names, and (2) a common suffix in F. words, where it is used as a masc. termination denoting character, and commonly has a depreciatory sense, as in the present instance. γ. Diez connects ribald with OHG. hripā, MHG. ribe, a prostitute, and cites from Matthew Paris : 'fures, exules, fugitiui, excommunicati, quos omnes ribaldos Francia uulgariter consueuit appellare.' Hence also OF. riber, to be wanton ; which fully explains the sense. Cf. Körting, § 4019. Der. ribaldry, ME. ribaldrie, commonly written ribaudie, P. Plowman, C. vii. 435.

RIBAND, RIBBAND, RIBBON, a narrow strip, esp. of silk. (F.) Spelt riband from a fancied connexion with band, with which it may possibly be connected ; also ribband, Spenser, F. Q. iv. 10. 8. But the d is excrescent and is not always found in the ME. period, though occurring in the Prompt. Parv. ME. riban, P. Plowman, B. ii. 16 ; 'with ribanes of red golde' = with golden threads. 'Ragges ribaned with gold' = rags adorned with gold thread ; Rom. of the Rose, 4752. Again, in Rom. of the Rose, 1077, Riches wears a purple robe, adorned with orfreis (gold-embroidery) and ribaninges. [Irish ribin, a ribbon ; ribe, a flake, a hair, a ribbon ; Gael. ribean, a riband, fillet, rib, ribe, a hair, rag, clout, tatter, gin, snare, whence also ribeag, a hair, little hair, small rag, tassel, fringe, bunch of anything hairy ; W. rhibin, a streak, rhib, a streak, are all from W. riban.] β. From F. ruban, spelt riban in 1394 (Supp. to Godefroy), ruben in Cotgrave, rubant in Palsgrave. The form riban occurs also in mod. Prov., and in the Norman and Guernsey dialects (Mistral, Moisy, Métivier). Ducange also gives the form reband ; see Voc. 792. 20. γ. The suffix seems to be Du. and G. band, a band ; see **Band** (1). The ri- or re- perhaps occurs in EFries. rif-band, ref-band, a reef-band (Koolman). The old sense of reef (in a sail) was 'strip ;' cf. MSwed. rif, 'fascia ;' Swed. dial. rejv, Norw. reiv, a swaddling-band, lit. 'strip.'

RIBIBE, the same as **Rebeck**, q. v.

RICE, a kind of edible grain. (F. – Ital. – L. – Gk. – OPers.) In Shak. Wint. Tale, iv. 3. 41 ; spelt rize in Bacon, Nat. Hist. § 49 ; rice in Levins ; ryce in Palsgrave. ME. ryz, Mandeville, ch. 31, p. 310. — OF. ris, 'rice,' Cot. ; mod. F. riz. — Ital. riso. — L. orȳza, rice. — Gk. ὄρυζα, also ὄρυζον, rice ; both the plant and grain. β. Doubtless borrowed from an OPers. form, preserved in the Pushto (Afghan) wrijzey, wrijey, rice (Raverty). Hence also Arab. uruzz, ruzz, whence Span. arroz, rice. Allied forms are Pers. birinj, Armenian brinj, rice ; Skt. vrīhi-, rice. (Horn, § 208 ; Yule.)

RICH, wealthy, abounding in possessions. (E.) ME. riche (12th cent.), O. Eng. Homilies, i. 53, l. 10 ; Ancren Riwle, p. 66 ; Layamon, 128. (Not borrowed from F., but an E. word.) AS. rīce, rich, powerful ; Luke, i. 52 ; Mark, x. 25. The change from final c to ch is just as in Norwich from Norðwīc, pitch from AS. pic, &c. ; see Mätzner, i. 145. + Du. rijk ; Icel. rīkr ; Swed. rik ; Dan. rig ; Goth. reiks ; G. reich. β. All from a Teut. type *rīkjoz, lit. powerful, ruling ; from the base *rīk- as seen in Goth. reiks, a ruler. This is cognate with the Celtic base *rīg-, as in Gaulish rīx, a king (cf. OIrish rī (gen. rīg), a king, W. rhi, a chief) ; unless the Teut. reiks is merely borrowed from the Celtic rix (for *rēx), as Uhlenbeck suggests. All from √REG, to rule ; see **Regent**. Brugmann, i. §§ 135, 549 c. ¶ The fact that the word might have come into the language from F. riche, which is from MHG. rīche (G. reich), does not do away with the fact that it has always existed in our language. But the deriv. riches is really of F. origin ; see **Riches**. Der. richly, AS. rīclīce, Luke. xvi. 19 ; rich-ness, ME. richnesse, Rob. of Brunne, tr. of Langtoft, p. 155, l. 14. Also -ric in bishop-ric, where -ric = AS. rīce, a kingdom, dominion ; cf. Icel. riki, Goth. reiki, G. reich, sb., dominion, allied to L. reg-num and E. realm.

RICHES, wealth. (F. – OHG.) Now often regarded as a pl. sb. Shak. has it as a pl. sb., Timon, iv. 2. 32, Per. i. 1. 52 ; but usually as a sing sb., Oth. ii. 1. 83, iii. 3. 173, Sonnet 87. ME. richesse, a sing. sb. ; 'Mykel was the richesse,' Rob. of Brunne, tr. of Langtoft, p. 30, l. 24. The pl. is richesses, Ayenbite of Inwyt, p. 24, l. 21 ; Ancren Riwle, p. 168, l. 13. The word first appears (spelt riches) in Layamon, 8091. — F. richesse, 'riches, wealth ;' Cot. Formed with suffix -esse (cf. Port. and Span. riqu-eza, Ital. ricch-ezza) from the adj. riche, rich. — MHG. rīche, OHG. rīhhi (G. reich), rich ; cognate with E. **Rich**, q. v.

RICK, a heap or pile of hay or wheat. (E.) The mod. E. rick is from AS. hryce, as in corn-hryce, a corn-rick ; Ælfric's Hom. ii. 178. It also occurs as reek. ME. reek, Prompt. Parv. p. 428, col. 1, last line ; AS. hrēac, to translate L. aceruus, a heap ; Voc. 313. 33. + Icel. hraukr, a rick, small stack. Teut. types *hruk-jon-, *hraukoz, m. Cf. OIrish cruach, a heap ; and see **Ridge**. Brugmann, i.

§ 637. Doublet, prov. E. *ruck*, a heap, the Scand. form; see **Ruck** (2).

RICKETS, a disease of children, accompanied with softness of the bones and great weakness. (E.) The name was first given to this disease, about 1620, by the country-people in Dorsetshire and Somersetshire. This we learn from a treatise by Dr. Glisson, De Rachitide, cap. 1. He used the form *rachitis* (it should have been *rhachitis*) to denote the fact that it is sometimes accompanied by spinal disease, or, in Greek, ῥαχῖτις, founded on Gk. ῥόχις, the spine. This was easily confused with the prov. E. *rick, wrick*, to sprain, twist, wrench; whence the form *rickets*. ' *Cavil 7.* Hospitals generally have the *rickets*. . . . *Answer.* Surely there is some other cure for a *ricketish* body than to kill it;' Fuller, Worthies of England, 1662; repr. 1840, vol. i. p. 47. A still earlier notice of *rickets* is in Fuller, Meditations on the Times (first pub. 1647), xx. p. 163, in Good Thoughts, &c., Oxford, 1810; see N. and Q. 6 S. ii. 219. The prov. E. '*rickety* (unsteady) table' is well known. β. Formed, with pl. suffix *-ets*, from E. *wrick*, ME. *wrikken*, to twist, used in the phr. 'to *wrick* (i. e. to twist) one's ancle.' Thus the word denotes a disease accompanied with distortion. 'The deuel *wrikked* her and ther,' i. e. the devil (when seized by St. Dunstan) twisted hither and thither; Spec. of Eng., ed. Morris and Skeat, p. 22, l. 82. Allied to AS. *wringan*, to wring; see **Wring.**+Du. *wrikken*, to stir to and fro; *de bank wrikt nog*, 'the bench stands totteringly still' (i. e. is rickety); Sewel. See **Wriggle.**

RICOCHET, the rebound of a cannon-ball fired at a slight elevation. (F.—Prov.—L.) Not in Todd's Johnson.—F. *ricochet*, 'the sport of skimming a thin stone on the water, called a Duck and a Drake;' Cot. Rabelais (Pantagruel, iii. 10) has *chanson du ricochet*, which Cot. explains: 'an idle or endlesse tale or song;' and Hatzfeld as: 'a song with much repetition.' Littré quotes from a writer of the 15th century: 'Mais que il cede je cederai, et semblablement respond l'autre, et ainsi est *la fable du ricochet*.' β. There is also a F. verb *ricocher*, to ricochet, make ducks and drakes; and Scheler and Littré derive *ricochet* from *ricocher*. But Hatzfeld says that the derivation runs the other way. γ. However, mod. Prov. has the F. sb. *ricouchet*, and the vb. *ricouca, recauca*, to skip, to repeat; from L. *re-* and Prov. *couca, cauca*, to tread upon, from L. *calcāre*; and, as L. *recalcāre* means to tread upon again, to retrace, and also to repeat, the sense of 'repetition' is easily explained from the L. source. Thus *ricocher* is from Prov. *ricouca*; cf. MF. *caucher*, to tread (L. *calcāre*). **Der.** *ricochet*, verb.

RID (1), to free, deliver. (E.) ME. *ridden*, to separate two combatants, Gawain and the Grene Knight, 2246; also to deliver, O. Eng. Homilies, i. 273; also spelt *redden*, id. ii. 19, l. 20. (*Rid* stands for *red*, and that for *hred*). AS. *hreddan*, to snatch away, deliver; Grein, ii. 101.+OFriesic *hredda*; Du. *redden*; Dan. *redde*; Swed. *rädda*; G. *retten.* Teut. type *hrad-jan-*, a causal form. Cf. Skt. *çrath*, to untie, loose. **Der.** *ridd-ance*, Spenser, Daphnaida, 364; a hybrid word, with F. suffix *-ance* (L. *-antia*).

RID (2), to clear, esp. land. (Scand.). Prov. E. *rid*, to remove litter, to grub up. ME. *ruden* (pt. t. *rid*). 'The schal *ruden* thine weie to-fore the,' who shall clear thy way before thee; O. E. Homilies, ii. 133.—Icel. *ryðja*, to clear out; Dan. *rydde*, to clear, grub up land. EFries. and Low G. *rüden.* Teut. type *rud-jan-*; from *rud-*, weak grade of *reud-an-* (G. *reuten*), to clear out. Confused with **Rid** (1).

RIDDLE (1), a puzzling question, enigma. (E.) The word has lost a final *s*, and stands for *riddles*, with a plural *riddles-es*, if it were rightly formed. The loss of *s* was easy and natural, as it must have appeared like the sign of the plural number. ME. *redels*; we find F. *un devinal* explained by a *redels* in Wright's Vocab. i. 160. 'The kynge putte forth a *rydels*,' other MSS. *redels*; Trevisa, iii. 181; and see P. Plowman, B. xiii. 184. AS. *rǣdels*, also *rǣdelse*, pl. *rǣdelsan*, Ælfred, tr. of Boethius, c. xxvii. § 3 (bk. iii. pr. 4), c. xxxv. § 5 (bk. iii. pr. 12), where it means 'ambiguity.' The pl. *rǣdelsas* also occurs, Numb. xii. 8, where the A. V. has 'dark speeches.' The lit. sense is 'something requiring explanation.' Formed with suffixes *-el-s* (for *-isloz*) from AS. *rǣd-an*, to read, interpret; we still use the phr. 'to read a riddle.' See **Read.**+Du. *raadsel* (for *raad-is-lo-*), from *raden*, to counsel, to guess; G. *räthsel* (for *rath-is-lo-*), from *rathen.* Also O. Low G. *rādislo* (Gallée). **Der.** *riddle*, verb.

RIDDLE (2), a large sieve. (E.) For *hriddle*, by loss of initial *h.* ME. *ridil*, Prompt. Parv. p. 433. The suffixes *-il* (or *-el*) and *-er* being of equal force, we find the corresponding word in the AS. *hridder*, a vessel for winnowing corn; Voc. 141. 12; older form *hrider*, Voc. 1. 12. Cognate forms appear in Irish *creathair*, Gael. *criathar*, Corn. *croider*; L. *cribrum*, a sieve. Lit. sense 'separater.' All from the Idg. √QREI, to separate; cf. Gk. κρί-νειν. See **Critic.** **Der.** *riddle*, verb; cf. AS. *hridian*, to sift, Luke xxii. 31.

RIDE, to be borne along, esp. on a horse. (E.) ME. *ryden*, pt. t.

rood, pp. *riden* (with short *i*); Chaucer, C. T. 94, 169, &c. AS. *rīdan*, pt. t. *rād*, pp. *riden*, Grein, ii. 378. + Du. *rijden*; Icel. *rīða*; Dan. *ride*; Swed. *rida*; G. *reiten*; OHG. *rītan.* Teut. type *reidan-*. Cf. also OIrish *riad-aim*, I drive, ride; also L. *rēda* (a Celtic word), a four-wheeled carriage. From √REIDH. Brugmann, i. § 210. **Der.** *ride*, sb., *rid-er, rid-ing*; also *bed-ridden*, q. v., *raid*, q. v., *ready*, q. v., *road*, q. v. And see **Palfrey.**

RIDGE, anything resembling the top of a quadruped's back, an extended protuberance. (E.) ME. *rigge*, a back, esp. a quadruped's back, King Alisaunder, 5722; whence mod. E. *ridge.* The Northern form is *rig.* We find 'upon his *rig*'=upon his back, Havelok, 1755. We also find *rug*, Ancren Riwle, p. 264; pl. *rugges*, Layamon, 540. The double form is due to the AS. *y*. AS. *hrycg*, the back of a man or beast; Grein, ii. 109. + Du. *rug*, back, ridge; Dan. *ryg*; Swed. *rygg*; Icel. *hryggr*; G. *rücken*; OHG. *hrukki.* The Teut. type answering to AS. *hrycg* is *hrug-joz*, m. Cf. OIrish *croccenn*, (1) hide, (2) the back; Skt. *kruñch*, to be crooked. **Der.** *ridg-y.* Doublet, *rig* (3).

RIDICULOUS, laughable, droll. (L.) In Shak. Temp. ii. 2. 169. Englished (by the common change from *-us* to *-ous*) from L. *rīdiculus*, laughable.—L. *rīdēre*, to laugh; see **Risible.** **Der.** *ridiculous-ly, -ness.* Also *ridicule*, orig. *ridicle*, as in Foxe, Acts and Monuments, pp. 132, 747 (R.), from L. *rīdiculum*, a jest, neut. of *rīdiculus*, but changed to *ridicule* by confusion with F. *ridicule*, ridiculous, which is not a sb. but an adj.

RIDING, one of the three divisions of the county of York. (Scand.) For *thriding*; the loss of the *th* being due to the mis-division of the compound word *North-thriding*; cf. *East-thriding*, and *West-thriding.* Blackstone explains the *thridings*; Comment.; Introd. § 4. And note that the word *thriding* was Latinised as *tridingum*, Liber Custumarum, p. 353. Cf. *Estriding* (for *Est-triding*) in Birch, Cartul. Saxon. iii. 676.—Icel. *þriðjungr*, the third part of a thing, the third part of a shire; see Cleasby and Vigfusson.—Icel. *þriði*, third, cognate with E. **Third**, q. v. Cf. Norweg. *tridjung*, a third part, from *tridje*, third; Aasen.

RIFE, abundant, prevalent. (Scand.) ME. *rif* (with long *i*), also *rife, rive, ryfe, ryue*; adv. *riue, ryue.* 'þere was sorwe *riue*'=there was abundant sorrow, Will. of Palerne, 5414. 'Balu þer wes *riue*' =evil was abundant there; Layamon, 20079. Late AS. *rȳfe*, Leechdoms, iii. 164.—Icel. *rīfr*, munificent, abundant; cf. *rīfligr*, large, munificent; MSwed. *rif*, rife. β. Allied to MDu. *rijf, rijve*, 'abundant, copious, or large,' Hexham; Low G. *rive*, abundant, munificent, extravagant. Cf. Icel. *reifa*, to bestow, *reifir*, a giver; *reifr*, glad. **Der.** *rife-ly, rife-ness.*

RIFF-RAFF, refuse, rubbish, the off-scourings of the populace. (F.—Teut.) 'Lines, and circles, and triangles, and rhombus, and *rifferaffe*;' Gosson, School of Abuse, 1579, ed. Arber, p. 49, l. 26. Due to ME. *rif and raf*, every particle, things of small value. 'The Sarazins, ilk man, he slouh, *alle rif and raf*' = He slew the Saracens, every man of them, every particle of them; Rob. of Brunne, tr. of Langtoft, p. 151. And again: 'That neither he no hise suld chalange *rif no raf*'=That neither he nor his should claim a single bit of it; id. p. 111, l. 2.—F. *rif et raf*; as, 'Il ne luy lairra *rif ny raf*, he will strip him of all;' Cot. Cf. Walloon *rif, raf*; WFlem. *rifraf.* So also: 'On n'y a laissé *ne rifle, ne rafle*, they have swept all away, they have left no manner of thing behind them;' id. The lit. sense of *rif* is 'a piece of plunder of small value;' it is closely related to F. *rifler*, 'to rifle, ransack, spoile, make havock or clean work, sweep all away before him;' id. So also MF. *raffler*, 'to rifle, ravage, to sweep all away,' id. The connected E. words are **Rifle** (1) and **Raffle**, q. v. Cf. MItal. *raffola ruffola*, 'by riffraffe, by hooke or crooke, by pinching or scraping;' Florio.

RIFLE (1), to carry off as plunder, spoil, strip, rob. (F.—Teut.) ME. *riflen*, P. Plowman, B. v. 234.—OF. and MF. *rifler*, 'to rifle, ransack, spoile, make havock,' Cot. Norm. dial. *rifler* (Duméril). A word prob. due to the Norse sea-kings. Formed as a frequentative from Icel. *hrīfa*, to catch, to grapple, seize, *rifa* (usu. spelt *hrīfa*), to pull up, scratch, grasp; related to which are *hrifsa*, to rob, pillage, *hrifs*, sb., plunder. ¶ The F. *rifler* (from Icel. *hrīfa*) and *rafler* (from G. *raffen*) were not connected in the first instance, but the similarity of sound drew them together, as recorded in the E. *riff-raff*, q. v. **Der.** *rifl-er.*

RIFLE (2), a musket with a barrel spirally grooved to give the bullet a rotary motion. (Low G.) A modern word; *rifle* and *rifle-man* appear in Todd's Johnson, ed. 1827. 'Rifled arms were known on the continent about the middle of the 17th century; they do not appear to have been introduced into the British service till the time of the American revolutionary war;' Engl. Cycl. β. The sb. *rifle* is a short form for *rifled gun*, and is due to the technical word *rifle*, to groove; particularly, to groove in a spiral manner.—Low G. *rifeln*; EFries. *riffeln*, to furrow, chamfer; EFries. *riffel*, a grove; cf. Dan.

rifle, to rifle, *rifle*, a groove; Swed. *reffla*, to rifle; cf. *reffelbössa*, a rifled gun. — Low G. (EFries.) *rifen*, to scratch; Swed. *rifva*, to scratch, tear, grate, grind; Icel. *rifa*, to rive; see **Rive**. So also G. *riefe*, a furrow, *riefen* (from Low G.). ¶ The AS. *geriflian* does not correspond to E. *rifle*, but to the old verb *rivel*, to wrinkle; see **Rivel**. It is, however, a related word. Der. *rifle-man*.

RIFT, a fissure. (Scand.) In Spenser, F. Q. i. 2. 30. ME. *reft*, Rom. of the Rose, 2661; *ryfte*, Prompt. Parv. p. 433. — Dan. *rift*, a rift, rent, crevice, from *rive*, to rive; Norw. *rift*, a rift; Icel. *ript*, a breach of contract, from *rifa*, to rive. Cf. Swed. *refva*, a rift, strip, cleft, gap; from Swed. *rifva*, to tear, rive. See **Rive**. Der. *rift*, verb, Temp. v. 45, spelt *ryft* in Palsgrave.

RIG (1), to fit up a ship with tackle. (Scand. — Low G.) Also to dress up a person, but this is the jocular use of the word, and not the old sense, as supposed by Johnson. In Shak., only in the nautical sense; Temp. i. 2. 146, v. 224, &c. 'High *rigged* ships;' Surrey, tr. of Virgil, iv. 525; L. text, *celsas naues, Æn.* iv. 397. 'I *rygge* a shyppe, I make it redye;' Palsgrave. Of Scand. origin; the traces of the word are slight. — Norweg. *rigga*, to bind up, wrap round; in some districts, to rig a ship; *rigg*, sb., rigging of a ship; Aasen. Cf. Swed. dial. *rigga på*, to harness a horse, put harness on him. Allied to Pomeran. *rigen*, Westphal. *riggen*, to tack together; Du. *rijgen*, to tack together, reef sails, from *rij*, a row; G. *reihen*, to tack together, to arrange, from *reihe*, a row. Cf. Low G. *rige*, a row, rank, arrangement. See **Row** (1). Der. *rig*, sb., *rigg-ing*.

RIG (2), a frolic, prank. (E. ?) 'Of running such a *rig*;' Cowper, John Gilpin. '*Rig*, a frolic;' Halliwell. *Riggish*, wanton; Shak. Antony, ii. 2. 245. The verb *rigge*, to be wanton, occurs in Levins, col. 119, l. 6. Certainly connected with **Wriggle**. Cf. Norw. *rigga*, to rock; EFries. *wriggen*, to wriggle; Du. *wrikken*, to stir to and fro, *wriggelen*, to wriggle. And see **Rickets**.

RIG (3), a ridge. (E.) 'Amang the *rigs* o' barley;' Burns. ME. (Northern) *rig*, a ridge; see **Ridge**.

RIGADOON, a lively dance for a single couple. (F. — Prov.) 'Irish jig, and ancient *rigadoon*;' Byron, The Waltz, 110. In Bailey (1735). — F. *rigaudon*, *rigodon*; spelt *rigodon* in 1696 (Hatzfeld). Said to be from *Rigaud*, the name of a dancing-master (Hatzfeld). *Rigaud* is a Prov. name, and Mistral, s. v. *Rigaudoun*, a rigadoon, says that Rigaud, the dancing-master, lived at Marseilles, and that the dance was prohibited by the parliament of Provence in 1664 (April 3).

RIGHT, erect, straight, correct, true, just, proper, exact. (E.) ME. *right*, Wyclif, Matt. iii. 3; &c. AS. *riht*, adj., Grein, ii. 378. + Du. *regt*; Icel. *rēttr* (for **rehtr*); Dan. *ret*; Swed. *rät*; G. *recht*, OHG. *reht*; Goth. *raihts*. β. All from Teut. type **rehtoz*, Idg. type **rektos*, as in L. *rectus*. Cf. also W. *rhaith*, sb., right, OIrish *recht*, law. The Idg. **rektos* is for **reg-tos*, from √REG, to rule. See **Regent**. See **Rectitude**. Der. *right*, adv., AS. *rihte*; *right*, sb., AS. *riht*; *right-ly*, *right-ness*, AS. *rihtnes*; *right*, verb, AS. *rihtan*; *right-ful*, P. Plowman, B. prol. 127; *right-ful-ly*, *right-ful-ness*. Also *right-eous*, well known to be a corruption of ME. *rightwis*, Pricke of Conscience, 9154, AS. *rihtwis*, Grein, ii. 381, a compound of *riht* and *wīs* = wise, i. e. wise as to what is right. Palsgrave has the curious intermediate form *ryghtuous*. Hence *right-eous-ly*, AS. *rihtwislice* (Grein); *right-eous-ness*, ME. *rightwisnesse*, Wyclif, Matt. vi. 1, Luke, i. 75, AS. *rihtwisnes* (Grein). From the same root are *rect-i-tude*, *rect-i-fy*, *rect-or*, *rect-angle*, *rect-i-lineal*, as well as *reg-al*, *reg-ent*, &c.; also *cor-rect*, *di-rect*, *e-rect*. Also *regent*.

RIGID, stiff, severe, strict. (L.) In Ben Jonson, Epistle to a Friend, Underwoods, lv. 17. — L. *rigidus*, stiff. — L. *rigēre*, to be stiff. Brugmann, i. § 875. Der. *rigid-ly*, *-ness*, *rigid-i-ty*. Also *rig-our*, Chaucer, C. T. 11087 (F 775), from OF. *rigour* (mod. F. *rigueur*) < L. *rigōrem*, acc. of *rigor*, harshness; *rigor-ous*, Cor. iii. 1. 267, from F. *rigoreux*, 'rigorous,' Cot.; *rigor-ous-ly*, *-ness*.

RIGMAROLE, a long unintelligible story. (Hybrid: E. and F. — L.) The word is certainly a corruption of *ragman-roll*, once a very common expression for a long list of names, hence a long unconnected story. See my note to P. Plowman, C. i. 73, where it occurs as *rageman*; Anecdota Literaria, by T. Wright, 1844, p. 83, where a poem called *Ragman-roll* is printed; Wright's Homes of Other Days, p. 247; Jamieson's Dict., where we learn that the Scottish nobles gave the name of *ragman-rolls* to the collection of deeds by which they were constrained to subscribe allegiance to Edw. I, A.D. 1296; Towneley Mysteries, p. 311, where a catalogue of sins is called *a rolle of ragman*; Skelton, Garl. of Laurell, l. 1490, and Dyce's note; P. Plowman's Crede, l. 180; Cowel's Law Dict., and Todd's Johnson, s. v. *rigmarole*. Also the long note on *ragman-roll* in Halliwell. β. The precise meaning of *ragman* (oldest spelling *rageman*, but apparently with hard *g*) is not known. It first occurs as 'the name given to a statute of 4 Edw. I (appointing justices to hear and determine complaints of injuries done within 25

years previous), and to certain articles of inquisition associated with proceedings of *Quo Warranto* under this statute;' N. E. D., q. v. We also find *rageman* used to mean the devil; see P. Plowman, C. xix. 122, and the note. γ. The word *roll* is F.; see **Roll**. With *raggeman* we may perhaps compare Icel. *ragmenni*, a craven person, coward, *ragmennska*, cowardice; from Icel. *ragr*, a coward, and *maðr* (= *mannr*), a man. Cf. Swed. *raggen*, the devil; Rietz cites ON. *ragvættr*, an evil spirit, lit. 'a cowardly wight,' where *vættr* is our E. *wight* = G. *wicht* in *bösewicht*, a bad spirit. To call a person *ragr* was to offer him the greatest possible insult. ¶ The word *roll* was sometimes pronounced *row* (see Jamieson); hence we find in Levins. ed. 1570: '*Ragmanrew*, series,' where *rew* = *row*.

RIGOL, a circlet. (Ital. — G.) In Shak. 2 Hen. IV, iv. 5. 36. — Ital. *rigolo*, 'a little wheel under a sledge;' Torriano. Dimin. from Ital. *rigo*, *riga*, a line. — OHG. *riga*, a line, also, a circumference of a circle (G. *reihe*). Allied to E. *row*; see **Row** (1). See Notes on E. Etym., p. 249.

RILE, to vex; see **Roil**.

RILL, a streamlet, small brook. (Low G.) 'The bourns, the brooks, the becks, the *rills*, the rivulets;' Drayton, Polyolbion, Song i. 78. (He also has the dimin. *rill-et* in the same Song, l. 264.) — Low G. *rille*, used in the sense of a small channel made by rain-water running off meadows, also, a rill; see Bremen Wörterbuch. So also EFries. and Dan. dial. *rille*, a streamlet. β. *Rille* would appear to be a contraction from Teut. **riðele*, a dimin. of AS. *riðe* or *riðe*, a stream, a common word; cognate with O. Low G. *ride*, a water-course, NFries. *ride* or *ride*, a stream or rill. γ. The AS. *i* in *riðe* was probably long, as there are numerous streams in N. Germany with the name *reide* (Leo); and Halliwell gives South E. *rithe*, a small stream. Robin (p. 432) gives the Norm. dialect *risle*, *rille*, as the name of a small stream, which appears in old charters as *Ridula*, *Risila*, *Risla*. See my Notes on E. Etym., p. 249. Cf. L. *ri-uus*, a stream. Der. *rill-et*, *rill*, verb.

RIM, a border, edge, verge. (E.) 1. ME. *rim*, *rym*. '*Rym* of a whele;' Prompt. Parv. AS. *rima*, rim; in the comp. *sǣ-rima*, sea-shore, lit. sea-rim; A. S. Chron. an. 897; see Sweet, A. S. Reader. Cf. W. *rhim*, *rhimp*, *rhimyn*, a rim, edge. + Icel. *rimi*, a strip of land. Perhaps allied to G. *rand*, a rim; and to **Rind** (Kluge). Brugmann, i. § 421. 2. We also find *rim* used in the sense of peritoneum or inner membrane of the belly, as in Shak. Hen. V, iv. 4. 15; and see Pricke of Conscience, l. 520, Sir Gawain and the Green Knight, 1343; the sense may be 'border,' hence envelope or integument. Cf. EFries. *rim*, *rīm*, margin, border.

RIME (1), verse, poetry; the correspondence of sounds at the ends of verses. (F. — L. — Gk.) Usually spelt *rhyme*, by confusion with *rhythm*, which is a later form of the same word. But the ME. form was *rime*; and I have not found an instance of the spelling *rhyme* before A. D. 1550; or hardly so soon. Dr. Schmidt omits to state that the first folio of Shak. has the spelling *rime*, Two Gent. of Verona, iii. 2. 69, Merry Wives, v. 5. 95, L. L. L. i. 2. 190; &c. It is *rime* in Minsheu, ed. 1627, and in Cotgrave; *ryme* in Palsgrave. ME. *rime*, *ryme*, Chaucer, C. T. 13639 (B 1899). — OF. *rime*, F. *rime*, found in the 12th cent. (Hatzfeld). From L. acc. *rhythmum*, which became fem.; from nom. *rhythmus*. — Gk. ῥυθμός, measured motion, time, measure; see **Rhythm**. From the same classical source was derived MHG. *rim*, in the sense of verse; which is quite a distinct word from OHG. *rim*, a number, cognate with AS. *rim*, number, which is of true Teutonic origin, and cognate with W. *rhif*, number. The OF. *rime*, in very early use, was the source of Ital., Span., Port. *rima*; and even of Du. *rijm*, G. *reim*, Icel. *rīma*. Der. *rime*, verb (usually *rhyme*), ME. *rymen*, *rimen*, Chaucer, C. T. 1461 (A 1459); *rimeless* (usually *rhyme-less*); *rim-er* (usually *rhymer*), spelt *rimer* in the first folio ed. of Shak. Antony, v. 2. 215; *rime-ster* (usually *rhyme-ster*), the suffix of which is discussed under **Spinster**.

RIME (2), hoarfrost, frozen dew. (E.) The word has lost initial *h*, and stands for *hrime*. ME. *rime*, *ryme*. '*Ryme*, frost, *pruina*;' Prompt. Parv. AS. *hrim*, to translate L. *pruina*; Ps. cxviii. 83, ed. Spelman (margin). + Du. *rijm*; Icel. *hrīm*; Dan. *riim*; Swed. *rim*. Cf. also G. *reif*, MHG. *rife*, OHG. *hrifo*, hoar-frost; Du. *rijp*, hoar-frost. Der. *rim-y*.

RIMER, a tool for enlarging holes in metal. (E.) From AS. *rȳman*, to enlarge, make room. — AS. *rūm*, room; see **Room**.

RIMPLE, to ripple, as the surface of water. (E.) 'The *rimpling* of the brook;' Crabbe, Parish Register, pt. 1 (ed. 1802). Cf. ME. *rimpled*, wrinkled; Rom. Rose, 4495. From AS. *hrymp-*, mutated form of *hrump-*, weak grade of *hrimpan*, to wrinkle; cf. the gloss: '*rugosa*, þære gehrumpnan;' Voc. 521. 10. See **Ripple** (2).

RIND, the external covering, as the bark of trees, skin of fruit. (E.) ME. *rind*, *rinde*; Ancren Riwle, p. 150, ll. 4, 8. AS. *rinde*, the bark of a tree, Voc. 216. 5; also, a crust (of bread), Ælfric's Hom. ii. 114, last line but one. + MDu. *rinde*, 'the barke of a tree;'

Hexham; G. *rinde*, OHG. *rinta*, f. Prob. allied to G. *rand*, a rim, and to **Rim** (Kluge).

RINDERPEST, an infectious disease of cattle. (G. *and* L.) Modern. – G. *rinderpest*, cattle-disease. – G. *rinder*, pl. of *rind*, an ox; and *pest*, a pest, plague, from L. *pestis*. *Rind* is allied to E. *rother*; see **Rother** and **Pest**.

RING (1), a circle. (E.) Fo *hring*, initial *h* being lost. ME. *ring*, Chaucer, C. T. 10561 (F 247). AS. *hring*; Grein, ii. 106.+ Du. *ring*; Low G. *ring*, *rink*, Bremen Wörterbuch; Icel. *hringr*; Swed. and Dan. *ring*; G. *ring*, OHG. *hrinc*. Teut. type **hrengoz*; Idg. type **krenghos*. Allied by gradation to the Idg. type **khronghos*, as in OBulg. *krągŭ*, Russ. *krug(e)*, a ring, circle. See also **Rank, Harangue**. Note that the *e* of Teut. **hrengoz* is preserved in Finn. *rengas*, a ring, an early loan-word from Teutonic (Streitberg). Der. *ring*, verb, K. John, iii. 4. 31; *ring-dove*, so named from the ring on its neck; *ring-ed*; *ring-lead-er*, 2 Hen. VI, ii. 1. 170; *ring-let*, used to mean 'a small circle,' Temp. v. 37; *ring-straked*, i.e. streaked with rings, Gen. xxx. 35; *ring-worm*, a skin disease in which rings appear, as if formed by a worm, Levins, ed. 1570. **Doublet**, *rink*.

RING (2), to sound a bell, tinkle. (E.) ME. *ringen*, Chaucer, C. T. 3894. AS. *hringan*, to clash, ring; *byrnan hringdon*, breastplates clashed, Beowulf, 327, ed. Grein; *ringden þa belle*, they rang the bells, A. S. Chron. an. 1131. The verb is weak, as in Scand., but mod. E. has pt. t. *rang*, pp. *rung* (by analogy with *sing*); we also find pp. *rongen, rungen*, in Allit. Morte Arthure, ll. 462, 976, 1587. +Du. *ringen*; Icel. *hringja*; cf. *hrang*, sb., a din; Dan. *ringe*; Swed. *ringa*. Imitative. Der. *ring*, sb., *ring-er*.

RINK, a space for skating on wheels, a course for the game of curling. (E.) The former use is modern; the latter is mentioned in Jamieson's Dict. It appears to be a dialectal variant of *ring*; compare the use of *ring* in the compound *prize-ring*. As to the form, we may compare the Low G. *rink* used as a variant of *ring*; see the Bremen Wörterbuch; NFries. *rink*, variant of *ring*; and vulgar E. *anythink = anything*. See **Ring** (1).

RINSE, to cleanse with clean water, make quite clean. (F. – L. ?) Prov. E. *rinch, rench*; E. D. D. 'He may *rynse* a pycher;' Skelton, Magnificence, 2194. '*Rynce* this cuppe;' Rel. Antiq. i. 7, col. 1. '*Rense* thyn teyth;' Medical Works of 14th cent., ed. Henslow, p. 35, l. 13. – OF. *raincer* (Littré), MF. *rinser*, 'to reinse linnen clothes;' Cot.; mod. F. *rincer*. β. Of doubtful origin. The forms *rincer, raincer*, seem to be contractions of OF. *recincier*, to rinse (Godefroy); cf. Picard *rechincher*, to rinse. Körting (§ 7988) derives this OF. verb from a L. type **requinquiāre*, due to L. *quinquāre*, to cleanse, purify, a verb cited in the 4th century (Lewis). Cf. mod. Prov. *rinsar* (Mistral); OProv. *rezensar* (Bartsch).

RIOT, tumult, uproar. (F.) ME. *riote*, Chaucer, C. T. 4390; Ancren Riwle, p. 198, last line. – F. *riote*, 'a brabbling, brawling;' Cot. Cf. Prov. *riota*, dispute, strife (Bartsch); Ital. *riotta*, quarrel, dispute, riot, uproar. β. The orig. sense seems to be 'dispute;' of uncertain origin. See Diez and Körting. Der. *riot*, verb, ME. *rioten*, Chaucer, C. T. 4412 (A 4414), from F. *rioter*, 'to chide,' Cot.; *riot-er*, ME. *riotour*, Chaucer, C. T. 12595 (C 661); *riot-ous*, id. 4414, from F. *rioteux*; *riot-ous-ly*, *-ness*.

RIP, to divide by tearing open, cut open, tear open for searching into. (Scand.) '*Rip up* griefe;' Spenser, F. Q. i. 7. 39. [It does not seem to be the same word as ME. *rippen*, used in the Ormulum in the sense of 'seize;' this is a variant of ME. *ruppen*, to rob, Layamon, 10584, and allied rather to G. *rupfen*, to pluck, than to the present word.] It corresponds to ME. *ripen*, used in the secondary sense of to grope, probe, search into, also used occasionally (like the mod. word) with the prep. *up*. '*Rypande* . . the reynes and hert' = searching the reins and heart (said of God), Allit. Poems, B. 592. 'To *rype vpe* the Romaynes' = to search out the Romans, Morte Arthure, 1877. 'The riche kinge *ransakes* . . and *vp rypes* the renkes' = the rich king seeks for and searches out the men, id. 3940. 'To *ripe* thair war' = to search their ware (where two MSS. have *ransake*), Cursor Mundi, 4893. 'I *rype* in olde maters, *je fouble*;' also, 'I *ryppe* a seame that is sowed;' Palsgrave. A Northern word, of Scand. origin. – Norweg. *ripa*, to scratch, score with the point of a knife (Aasen); Swed. dial. *ripa*, to scratch, also to pluck asunder (cf. E. *rip open*), Rietz; Swed. *repa*, to scratch, to ripple flax; *repa upp*, to rip up; *repa*, sb., a scratch; Dan. *oprippe*, to rip up; WFlem. *open-rippen*, to rip up; Low G. *repen*, to ripple flax (Lübben). Allied to **Ripple** (1), and **Ripple** (3). Der. *rip*, sb.; *ripp-le* (1), q. v., *ripple* (3), q. v.

RIPE, developed, mature, arrived at perfection. (E.) ME. *ripe, rype*, Chaucer, C. T. 17032 (H 83). AS. *ripe*; and *swā swā ripe yrð fortreddon* ' = and trod [all] down like ripe corn; Ælfred, tr. of Beda, i. 12. This adj. signifies 'fit for reaping,' and (like the sb. *rip*, harvest) is derived from the strong verb *rīpan*, to reap; see

Reap. +Du. *rijp*; whence *rijpen*, to ripen; G. *reif*, OHG. *rīfi*; whence *reifen*, to ripen. **Der.** *ripe-ly*, *-ness*; also *ripen*, verb, from AS. *rīpian*, Gen. xviii. 12.

RIPPLE (1), to pluck the seeds from stalks of flax by drawing an iron comb through them. (E.) A Northern word; see Jamieson. ME. *ripplen, ripelen*. '*Rypelynge* of flax, or other lyke, *Avulsio*;' Prompt. Parv. 'Hoc *rupeste*, a *repylle-stok*,' i.e. an implement for cleaning flax; Voc. 795. 16. An early example is *ripling-combe*, in A Nominale, ed. Skeat, l. 545. The cleaning of flax was also termed *ribbing* (a weakened form of *ripping*); see Prompt. Parv., p. 432, note 2. β. *Ripple* is not to be taken as the frequentative form of *rip*, but as formed from the sb. *ripple*, a flax-comb (Jamieson); and this sb. is derived from *rip-* (weak grade of the strong AS. verb *rīp-an*, to reap, cut) by help of the suffix *-le*, sometimes used to express the instrument by which a thing is done, as in *beet-le* = a beat-er; *stopp-le*, used for stopping, *lad-le*, used for lading out, *gird-le*, used for girding. So *ripple* = an instrument for ripping off the flax-seeds; cf. Swed. *repa*, to ripple flax; see **Rip.** +Du. *repel*, a ripple, from *repen*, to beat flax (Hexham); whence *repelen*, to ripple; Low G. *repe*, a ripple, in the dialect of Brunswick called *repel, reppel*, Bremen Wörterbuch; Pomeran. *räpeln*, to ripple flax. The Du. *repel* is from the 2nd grade **raip-* (Franck) of Teut. **reipan-*, to reap; see **Ripe.** Cf. G. *riffel*, a ripple; whence *riffeln*, to strip flax. See **Ripple** (3).

RIPPLE (2), to cause or show wrinkles on the surface, like running water. (E.) The essential idea in the rippling of water is that it shows wrinkles on the surface. The earliest quotation in Richardson and Johnson is the following: 'Left the Keswick road, and turned to the left through shady lanes along the vale of Eeman, which runs *rippling* over the stones;' Gray, to Dr. Wharton, Oct. 18, 1769. But Dampier has: 'a great *ripling*;' A New Voyage (1699); ii. pt. 2. p. 10. As pointed out by Richardson, it is a by-form or contraction of the older verb *to rimple*; 'As gilds the moon the *rimpling* of the brook,' Crabbe, Parish Register, part 1, ed. 1807; where the edition of 1834 has *rippling*. ME. *rimplen*, to wrinkle, whence the pp. *rymplyd*, explained by 'Rugatus' in Prompt. Parv.; cf. 'a *rimpled* vecke' = a wrinkled old woman, Rom. of the Rose, 4495. This verb is from the sb. *rimple* or *rimpil*; '*Rympyl*, or *rymple*, or wrynkly, Ruga;' Prompt. Parv. – AS. *hrympel*, to translate L. *rūga*, a wrinkle, in a gloss; Voc. 531. 4 (where it is miswritten *hrypel*). See **Rumple.** +MDu. *rimpel*, 'a wrinckle, or a folde,' Hexham; *rimpelen*, 'to wrinckle;' id. β. The AS. *hrympel* is from the weak grade (*hrump-*) of *hrimpan*, to wrinkle, of which the pp. *ge-hrumpen* occurs in a gloss; Voc. 521. 10.+OHG. *hrimfan*, MHG. *rimpfen*, to bend together, crook, wrinkle; cf. mod. G. *rümpfen*, to crook, bend, wrinkle. From Teut. base **hremp-*. Cf. the similar base **kremp-*, as in **Crimp**, q. v. Der. *ripple*, sb.

RIPPLE (3), to scratch slightly. (Scand.) In the Whitby Glossary, by F. K. Robinson (E. D. S.). 'Having slightly *rippled* the skin of his left arm;' Holland, tr. of Ammianus, p. 264; see Trench, Select Glossary (where it is wrongly connected with the word above). '*Ripple*, rescindere;' Levins. This is merely a frequentative (or diminutive) form of **Rip**, q. v.

RISE, to ascend, go upward. (E.) ME. *risen*, pt. t. *roos* (pl. *risen*), pp. *risen*; Chaucer, C. T. 825, 1501 (A 823, 1499). AS. *rīsan*, pt. t. *rās* (pl. *rison*), pp. *risen*; Grein, ii. 382.+Du. *rijzen*, orig. 'to move,' and in MDu. 'to fall,' contrary to the E. sense; Icel. *rísa*; OHG. *rīsan*, to move up, rise; also to move down, fall; Goth. *reisan*, pt. t. *rais* (pl. *risum*), pp. *risans* , only in the comp. *ur-reisan*. β. All from Teut. type **reisan-* (pt. t. *rais*, pp. *risenoz*), to slip away, orig. expressive of motion only; cf. Skt. *ri*, to distil, ooze (we speak of the *rise* of a river); see **Rivulet.** The MDu. *rijzen* also means 'to fall;' *het loof rijst*, the leaves fall (Hexham). Der. *rise*, sb., Hen. V, iv. 1. 289; *a-rise*, q. v.; *ris-ing*, a tumult, also a tumour, Levit. xiii. 2; also *raise*, q. v., *rear*, q. v.

RISIBLE, laughable, amusing. (F. – L.) In Minsheu, ed. 1627. – F. *risible*, 'fit or worthy to be laughed at;' Cot. – L. *risibilis*, laughable. – L. *risi-*, from *ris-um*, supine of *rīdēre*, to laugh; with suffix *-bilis*. See **Ridiculous.** Der. *risibl-y*, *risibil-i-ty*. From the same L. verb (pp. *rīsus*) are *ar-ride* (rare, = L. *arrīdēre*, to laugh at), *de-ride, de-ris-ion, de-ris-ive, ir-ris-ion, rid-ic-ul-ous.*

RISK, hazard, danger, peril. (F. – Ital. – L.) Spelt *risque* in Blount's Gloss., ed. 1674. – F. *risque*, 'perill;' Cot. [Cf. Ital. *risico*, (in Ariosto, *risco*), formerly *risigo*, as in Florio; Span. *riesgo*, risk; Late L. *risigus, riscus*, risk.] Borrowed from Ital. *risico* (*rischio, risigo*), hazard, peril (Torriano). This seems to be the same word as Span. *risco*, a steep abrupt rock; from whence the sense of 'danger' may easily have arisen among sailors. Hence Span. *arriesgar* (*arriscar* in Minsheu), to venture into danger, lit. 'to go against a rock,' where the prefix *ar-* stands for L. *ad-* before *r* following, as usual; also *arriscado*, bold, forward (lit. venturesome); Ital. *arrischiarsi*, to venture oneself, *arrischiato*, hazardous. ‒ L. *resecāre*, to cut back, to cut off short or abruptly; whence the Span. sb. *risco* (Ital. *risico*) was formed in the same way as E. *scar*, an abrupt rock, is formed from the root of the verb to *shear* or cut off. ‒ L. *re-*, back; and *secāre*, to cut; see **Re-** and **Section**. β. This suggestion is due to Diez; he supports it by citing mod. Prov. *rezegue*, risk, *rezegá*, to cut off; *resega*, risk, also a saw, in the dialect of Como; Port. *risco*, risk, also a rock, crag, also a dash with the pen, *riscar*, to raze out with the pen (< L. *resecāre*, i. e. to cut out). And cf. Ital. *risico*, risk, with *risega*, a jutting out, *risegare*, *risecare*, to cast off; &c. ¶ Devic suggests a connexion with Arab. *rizq*, riches, good fortune, Rich. Dict. p. 731, but a risk is *bad* fortune; and, when he cites the Span. *arriesgar* as showing a prefix *ar-*=Arab. def. article *al-*, he forgets that the verbal prefix better represents the L. *ad*. Besides, the Ital. word is *risico*, spelt *risigo* in Florio. Mistral has mod. Prov. *risque*, *risco*, risk; Gascon *arrisque*. See Körting, § 7995. **Der.** *risk*, verb, *risk-y*.

RISSOLE, a dish of minced meat or fish with bread-crumbs, &c., fried. (F. ‒ L.) AF. *russole*, Chron. Monasterii de Abingdon, ed. Stevenson, ii. 308. Mod. F. *rissole*; OF. *roissole* (Godefroy), *roussole*. ‒ L. type *russeola; from L. *russeus*, reddish, or rather brownish; from the colour. ‒ L. *russus*, red; see **Russet**.

RITE, a religious ceremony. (L.) 'With sacred *rites*;' Spenser, F. Q. i. 12. 36. ‒ L. *rītus*, a custom, esp. a religious custom. Cf. Skt. *rīti-*, a going, also way, usage, manner; from *rī*, to go, flow. ‒ √REI, to go, run, let flow. Cf. Brugmann, ii. § 498. ¶ The F. *rit* or *rite* seems to have been little used; though found as *rit* in the 14th cent. (Hatzfeld). **Der.** *ritu-al*, from F. *ritual*, 'rituall,' Cot., from L. *ritū-ālis*, from *rītū-*, stem of *rītus*; *ritu-al-ly*; *ritu-al-ism*, *ritu-al-ist*.

RIVAL, a competitor. (F. ‒ L.) For the sense, see Trench, On the Study of Words. In Shak. Two Gent. ii. 4. 174. ‒ F. *rival*, sb., 'a rival, corrival, competitor in love;' Cot. ‒ L. *riuālis*, sb., one who uses the same brook as another, a near neighbour, a rival. ‒ L. *riuālis*, adj., belonging to a brook. ‒ L. *riu-us*, a brook, stream; with suffix *-ālis*. See **Rivulet**. **Der.** *rival*, adj., *rival*, verb, K. Lear, i. 1. 194; *rival-ry*, a coined word.

RIVE, to split, tear, slit, rend. (Scand.) ME. *riuen*, *ryuen* (with *u*=*v*), Chaucer, C. T. 12762 (C 828). ‒ Icel. *rifa*, pt. t. *reif*, pp. *rifinn* (=E. *riven*), to rive, tear; Dan. *rive*; Swed. *rifva*, to scratch, tear. β. Allied to Gk. ἐρείπειν, to throw or dash down, tear down; L. *rīpa*, a bank, a shore. Teut. base **reif-*; Idg. base **reip-*. **Der.** *rif-t*, q. v. And see *rifle* (2), *rivel*; also *riv-er*.

RIVEL, to wrinkle. (E.) 'Praise from the *rivell'd* lips of toothless, bald Decrepitude;' Cowper, Task, b. ii. l. 488. 'And *rivell'd* up with heat;' Dryden, Flower and the Leaf, 378. ME. *riuelen* (with *u* for *v*); 'Al my face . . . So *riueled*;' Gower, C. A. iii. 370; bk. viii. 2829. AS. *ge-riflian*, to wrinkle (Napier's Glosses); *rifelede*, gloss on L. *rugosus* (id.). A frequentative form; from **rif-*, weak grade of Teut. **reif-an-*, as seen in Icel. *rifa*, to rive; see above. Cf. AS. *gerifod*, wrinkled, Ælfric's Hom. i. 614.

RIVER, a large stream of running water. (F. ‒ L.) ME. *riuer* (with *u*=*v*); Chaucer, C. T. 3026 (A 3024); Rob. of Glouc., p. 1, l. 14. ‒ AF. *rivere*, OF. *riviere*, mod. F. *rivière*, a river, stream. It is the same word as Span. *ribera*, a shore, strand, sea-coast, Port. *ribeira*, a meadow near the bank of a river (whence *ribeiro*, a brook), Ital. *riviera*, a shore, a bank, also a river. ‒ Late L. *rīpāria*, (1) sea-shore or river-bank, (2) a river (Ducange); fem. of *rīpārius*, adj., formed from *rīpa*, a bank. Allied to Gk. ἐριπ-νη, a broken cliff, scaur (hence, a steep edge or bank), from the base REIP, to rive, rend, tear off, seen in Gk. ἐρείπειν, to tear down, and in E. *rive*; see **Rive**. Cf. E. *rift*, a fissure, from the same source. **Der.** *river-horse*, the hippopotamus, Holland, tr. of Pliny, b. viii. c. 25. Also (from L. *rīpa*) *ar-rive*, q. v. ☞ *Not* allied to *rivulet*.

RIVET, an iron pin for fastening armour, &c. together. (F. ‒ Scand.) 'The armourers, With busy hammers closing *rivets* up;' Hen. V, iv. chor. 13. 'With a palsy-fumbling at his gorget Shake in and out the *rivet*;' Troil. i. 3. 175. *Ryvet*, *revet*, Palsgrave. ME. *ryvette*; Voc. 573. 37. ‒ F. *rivet*, 'the welt of a shooe,' Cot. It also meant a rivet, as in the Supp. to Godefroy. Cf. Walloon *rivet*, a running noose (Sigart). In Hamilton's F. Dict. *rivet* is explained by 'rivet,' and marked as a farrier's term. ‒ F. *river*, 'to rivet, or clench, to fasten or turne back the point of a naile, &c.; also, to thrust the clothes of a bed in at the sides;' Cot. β. The word is Scand., as shown by the Aberdeen word *riv*, to rivet, clench, Shetland *riv*, to sew coarsely and slightly; which see in Jamieson. ‒ Icel. *rifa*, to tack together, sew loosely together; *rifa saman*, to stitch together, an expression which occurs in the Edda, i. 346. + O. Low G. *ribilon*, *rebolon*, to patch, sew together (Gallée). Perhaps allied to Icel. *reifa*, to swaddle. **Der.** *rivet*, verb, Hamlet, iii. 2. 90; Palsgrave.

has: 'I *revet* a nayle, *Je riue*;' also: '*Ryvet* this nayle, and then it wyll holde faste.'

RIVULET, a small stream. (L.) In Milton, P. L. ix. 420; Drayton, Muses' Elysium, Nymph. 6. l. 90. Not F., but an E. dimin., formed with suffix *-et* from L. *riuul-us*, a small stream, dimin. of *rīuus*, a stream, river. Cf. Ital. *rivoletto* (Torriano). See **Rival**. **Der.** (from L. *riu-us*) *riv-al*, q. v., *de-rive*, q. v. And see *rite*.

RIX-DOLLAR, the name of a coin. (Du. ‒ G.) 'He accepted of a *rix-dollar*;' Evelyn's Diary, Aug. 28, 1641; Evelyn was then at Leyden. ‒ Du. *rijks-daalder*, a rix-dollar. Hexham gives *rijcksdaelder*, 'a rix-daller, a peece of money of five schillings, or 50 stivers.' ‒ G. *reichsthaler*, 'a dollar of the empire.' ‒ G. *reichs*, gen. case of *reich*, empire, allied to *reich*, rich, powerful; and *thaler*, a dollar; see **Rich** and **Dollar**.

ROACH, a kind of fish. (F. ‒ Teut.) Allied to the carp, but confused with the ray and the skate; fish-names being very vaguely used. ME. *roche*. 'Roche, fysche, Rocha, Rochia;' Prompt. Parv. ‒ ONorth F. and Walloon *roche*, OF. *roce*, MF. *rosse* (Cot.). ‒ MDu. *roch*, 'a fish called a scait;' Hexham; Du. *rog*. + Dan. *rokke*, a ray; Swed. *rocka*, a ray, thorn-back; Low G. *ruche*, whence G. *roche*, a roach, ray, thorn-back; cf. AS. *reohhe*, a kind of fish. Teut. base **ruhh-*; Franck. Cf. AS. *rūh*, rough.

ROAD, a way for passengers. (E.) Also used of a place where ships *ride* at anchor; this is the same word, the F. *rade* being borrowed from Teutonic. Also used in the sense of *raid* or foray; 1 Sam. xxvii. 10. Shak. has the word in all three senses; (1) Much Ado, v. 2. 33; (2) Two Gent. i. 1. 53; (3) Cor. iii. 1. 5. ME. *roode* (for ships), Prompt. Parv.; *rode* (for horses); Cursor Mundi, 11427. AS. *rād*, a journey, riding expedition, road; Grein, ii. 362. [The sense of 'road' only appears in compounds; as *swan-rād*, swan-road, i. e. the sea; Beowulf, 200.] From the 2nd grade of Teut. **reid-an-*, to ride; cf. AS. *rād*, pt. t. of *rīdan*, to ride; see **Ride**. **Der.** *road-stead*, *road-way*, *road-ster* (for the suffix, see **Spinster**); also *in-road*. Doublet, *raid*.

ROAM, to rove about, to ramble, wander. (F. ‒ L.) ME. *romen*, P. Plowman, B. xi. 124; K. Alisaunder, 7207; Seven Sages, 1429 (in Weber's Met. Romances, vol. iii); Havelok, 64; Will. of Palerne, 1608. Prob. coined from F. *Rome*, Rome; from L. *Rōma*. Due to the frequent pilgrimages to that great city. Cf. OF. *romier*, a pilgrim to Rome; OF. *romel*, a pilgrim, *romeree*, a pilgrimage; Span. *romero*, a pilgrim. So also not only the Ital. *romeo*, a pilgrim, is derived from *Roma*, Rome, and denoted a pilgrim to Rome; but even in P. Plowman we have *religious romares*=religious pilgrims, B. iv. 120, which the author probably himself regarded as an equivalent to *Rome-renneres*=runners to Rome, B. iv. 128 (only 8 lines below). Cf. OFries. *rumera*, *rumfara*, a pilgrim to Rome. **Der.** *roam-er*.

ROAN, the name of a mixed colour, bay, sorrel, or chestnut, with grey hairs interspersed. (F. ‒ Span. ‒ L.) 'Roen, colour of an horse, *roven*;' Palsgrave. In Shak. Rich. II, v. 5. 78; 1 Hen. IV, ii. 4. 120. Explained by Schmidt as 'dark dappled-bay.' ‒ OF. *roan*; as in *ung destrier roan*, a roan horse, Supp. to Godefroy; MF. *rouën*; 'Cheval *rouën*, a roane horse,' Cot.; mod. F. *rouan*. ‒ Span. *roano*, sorrel-coloured, roan; OSpan. *raudano*. ‒ L. type *rāuidānum; from Late L. *rāuidus*, grey (Ducange). ‒ L. *rāuus*, gray-yellow, tawny.

ROAN-TREE, **ROWAN-TREE**, the mountain ash. (Scand.) A Northern term, and of Scand. origin. Spelt *roun-tree*, *roan-tree*, *rowan-tree* in Jamieson. ‒ Swed. *rönn*, MSwed. *rönn*, *runn* (Ihre), the mountain-ash; Dan. *rön*, the service, sorb, mountain-ash; Icel. *reynir*, the same. Also Norw. *rogn*, *raagn*, *raun*; Swed. dial. *rägna*, the roan-tree. The Icel. *reynir* is for *reyðnir, from *rauðnir, a deriv. of *rauðr*, red (Noreen, § 232). From the colour of the berries. See **Red**.

ROAR, to cry alowd, bellow. (E.) ME. *roren*, Wyclif, Rev. x. 3. AS. *rārian*, Ælfric's Homilies, i. 66, l. 18; and in Sweet's A. S. Reader. + MDu. *reeren*, Hexham; MHG. *rēren*. Cf. Lithuan. *rė-ju*, I scold, chide; Brugmann, ii. §§ 465, 741. Imitative. **Der.** *roar*, sb.; *roar-ing*. But not *up-roar*.

ROAST, to cook meat before a fire. (F. ‒ G.) ME. *rosten*, Legends of the Holy Rood, ed. Morris, p. 58, l. 504; Legend of St. Christopher, l. 203; Chaucer, C. T. 385 (A 383). ‒ OF. *rostir*, 'to rost, broile, tost,' Cot. Mod. F. *rôtir*. Prob. from OHG. *rōstan*, to roast, a weak verb formed from *rōst*, a grate, gridiron. β. We also find Irish *roistin*, a gridiron, *rosdaim*, I roast, *rost*, roast meat; Gael. *rost*, *roist*, W. *rhostio*; all borrowed from E.; and Bret. *rosta*, from F. **Der.** *roast*, sb.; *roast-meat* (=*roast-ed meat*).

ROB (1), to plunder, steal, spoil. (F. ‒ OHG.) In early use. ME. *robben*, Havelok, 1958; Ancren Riwle, p. 86, l. 13. ‒ OF. *robber*, 'to rob,' Cot. Usually spelt *rober*. The orig. sense was to despoil the slain in battle, to strip, disrobe; so that the verb is merely formed from the sb. *robe*, spelt *robbe* in Cotgrave, a robe. See **Robe**. ¶ The E. verb *reave* (usually *bereave*) is formed, in a precisely similar way, from the AS. sb. *rēaf*, clothing. Der. *robb-er*, ME. *robbour*, Rob. of Glouc., p. 94, l. 2091, from OF. *robbeur*, 'a robber,' Cot. ; *robb-er-y*, ME. *roberie*, O. Eng. Homilies, ii. 61, l. 27, from OF. *roberie*, F. *robberie*, 'robbery,' Cot. Doublet, *reave*.

ROB (2), a conserve of fruit. (F. – Span. – Arab. – Pers.) In Phillips (1706). – F. *rob*, 'the juice of black whortleberries preserved ;' Cot. – Span. *rob*, juice of fruit thickened with honey. – Arab. *rubb*, 'a decoction of the juice of citrons and other fruits, inspissated juice, *rob* ;' Rich. Dict.; p. 719. – Pers. *rub* (the same) ; Devic.

ROBBINS, ROBINS, ropes for fastening sails. (E.) Lowl. Sc. *raibandis*, pl., Complaint of Scotland, ed. Murray, p. 40, l. 30. EFries. *rā-band*, where *rā* = yard of a ship. Cf. Icel. *rā*, Dan. *raa*, Swed. *rå*, G. *rahe*, yard ; and see **Band** (1). Cf. G. *ragen*, to project. See my Notes on Eng. Etym., p. 252.

ROBE, a garment, dress. (F. – OHG.) ME. *robe*, Rob. of Glouc., p. 313, l. 6390; P. Plowman, B. ii. 15. – F. *robe*, a robe ; spelt *robbe* in Cotgrave. – MHG. *roub*, *roup*, OHG. *raup* (G. *raub*), booty, spoil ; hence, a garment, because the spoils of the slain consisted chiefly of clothing. **+**AS. *rēaf*, spoil, clothing ; Icel. *rauf*, spoil. Teut. type **rauðom*, neut. ; from **raub*, 2nd grade of Teut. **reuð-an-*, to reave ; see **Reave**. Der. *robe*, verb ; *rob-ed*, K. Lear, iii. 6. 38. Also *rob* (1), q. v.

ROBIN, a singing-bird, the red-breast. (F. – OHG.) 'Robyn redbrest ;' Skelton, Phyllyp Sparowe, 399; Holland's Howlat, l. 647. 'The most familiar of our wild birds, called *Robin red-breast*, from *Robin* (the familiar version of *Robert*), on the same principle that the pie and the daw are christened *Mag* (for *Margery*) and *Jack*. In the same way the parrot takes its name from *Pierrot*, the familiar version of *Pierre* ;' Wedgwood. *Robin Hood* is mentioned in P. Plowman, B. v. 402. – F. *Robin*, a proper name (Cotgrave) ; a pet name for *Robert*, which was early known in England, because it was the name of the eldest son of Will. I. β. *Robert* is a Frankish name, from OHG. *Ruodperht* (G. *Ruprecht*, whence our *Rupert*), meaning 'fame-bright,' i. e. illustrious in fame. γ. The syllable *perht* is cognate with E. **Bright**, q. v. The syllable *Ruod-* is cognate with Icel. *hrōðr*, praise, fame ; it occurs also in *Rud-olf*, *Rud-iger*, *Ro-ger*. Cf. Goth. *hrōtheigs*, victorious, triumphant, 2 Cor. ii. 14. And see **Hobgoblin**.

ROBUST, vigorous, in sound health. (F. – L.) 'A robust boysterous rogue knockt him down ;' Howell, Famil. Letters, b. i. sect. 3. let. 21 ; dated 1623. – F. *robuste*, 'strong, tough ;' Cot. – L. *rōbustus*, strong ; formed by adding *-tus* (Idg. *-to-*) to OL. *rōbus* (later *rōbur*), strength. Der. *robust-ly*, *robust-ness*. Also (obsolete) *robust-i-ous*, Shak. Haml. iii. 2. 10, better spelt *robusteous*, as in Blount, directly from L. *rōbusteus*, oaken (hence, strong), by the change of *-us* into *-ous*, as in numerous other words.

ROC, a huge bird. (F. – Pers.) In the Arabian Nights' Entertainment. – F. *rock* (Littré). – Pers. *rukh*, the name of a huge bird ; perhaps of Assyrian origin (Devic). Cf. *Nis-roch*, 2 Kings, xix. 37.

ROCHET, a surplice worn by bishops. (F. – OHG.) In the Rom. of the Rose, 4754. – F. *rochet*, 'a frock, loose gaberdine ; . . also, a prelates rochet ;' Cot. – MHG. *roc* (G. *rock*), a coat, frock.**+**Du. *rok*, OFries. *rokk*, AS. *rocc*, Icel. *rokkr*. Teut. type **rukkoz*, masc., a coat, frock.

ROCK (1), a large mass of stone. (F.) The pl. *rockes* or *rokkes* occurs in Chaucer, C. T. 11305 (F 993). – OF. *roke* (13th cent. Littré) ; also *roque*, commonly *roche*, a rock ; the masc. form *roc* is later, and only dates from the 16th century. Cf. Guernsey *roque*, Walloon *roc*, Languedoc *roquo* (D'Hombres), Prov. *roca*, Span. *roca*, Port. *roca*, *rocha*, Ital. *rocca*, *roccia*, a rock. Also Late L. *rocca* ; Ducange. (The Celtic forms are borrowed from E. or F.) We also find late AS. *stān-rocc* (Napier's Glosses). Of unknown origin. ¶ The ME. *roche*, in Gower, C. A. i. 314 (bk. iii. 1048), is from F. *roche*. Der. *rock-pigeon*, *-salt*, *-work* ; *rock-y*, *rock-i-ness*.

ROCK (2), to move backward and forward, to cause to totter, to totter. (E.) ME. *rokken*, Chaucer, C. T. 4155 (A 4157) ; Ancren Riwle, p. 82, l. 19. AS. *roccian* (Clark Hall) ; NFries. *rocke* ; O. Low G. *rukkian* (Gallée).**+**Dan. *rokke*, to rock, shake ; allied to Dan. *rykke*, to pull, tug, from *ryk*, a pull, a tug ; Swed. dial. *rukka*, to wag, to rock, allied to *rycka*, to pull, *ryck*, a pull, jerk. Cf. Icel. *rykkja*, to pull roughly and hastily, *rykkr*, a hasty pull, also a spasm. Also G. *rücken*, to move by pushing ; from *ruck*, a pull, jolt, jerk, Du. *ruk*, a jerk. Teut. types **rukkōjan-*, **rukkjan-*, to jolt, jerk (Franck). The base **rukk* (for **runk* ?) may be related to **renkan-*, to shake, as seen in Swed. dial. *rinka*, to shake (pt. *rank*, supine *runkit*), Rietz ; Swed. *runka*, to shake, *rankig*, rickety (Widegren). Der. *rock-er*, *rock-ing-chair*.

ROCK (3), a distaff. (Scand.) In Dryden, tr. of Ovid, Metam. b. viii., Meleager, l. 257. ME. *rokke*. 'Rokke, of spynnyng, Colus ;' Prompt. Parv. – Icel. *rokkr*, a distaff ; Swed. *rock* ; Dan. *rok*.**+**G.

rocken, MHG. *rocke*, OHG. *roccho*, a distaff ; Du. *rok*, *rokken*. Teut. type **rukkon-*, m. Der. *rock-et* (1), q. v.

ROCKET (1), a kind of fire-work. (Ital. – G.) In Skinner's Dict., ed. 1671. Dekker has the pl. *rockets* ; London Triumphant, speech of Envy (1612). – MItal. *rocchetto*, 'a bobbin to winde silke upon ; also, any kinde of squib of wilde fier ;' Florio. The *rocket* seems to have been named from its long thin shape, bearing some resemblance to a quill or bobbin for winding silk, and so to a distaff. The Ital. *rocchetto* is the dimin. of *rocca*, 'a distaffe or rocke to spinne with ;' Florio. – MHG. *rocke*, a distaff ; see **Rock** (3).

ROCKET (2), a plant of the genus *Eruca*. (F. – Ital. – L.) In Levins. Spelt *rokat* in Sir T. Elyot, Castle of Helth, b. ii. c. 9. – F. *roquette*, 'the herb rocket ;' Cot. – Ital. *ruchetta*, 'the herb called rocket ;' Florio. Dimin. of *ruca*, *eruca*, rocket, Baretti ; (only the pl. *eruche* appears in Florio). – L. *ērūca*, a sort of cole-wort ; whence also the G. *ranke*, rocket.

ROCOCO, a variety of ornamentation, characterized by meaningless scrolls and shell-work. (F.) F. *rococo*; of the time of Louis XIV. Playful variant from the base of F. *roc-aille*, rockiness, rock-work (Hatzfeld). – F. *roc*, rock ; see **Rock**.

ROD, a slender stick. (E.) ME. *rod*, Gower, C. A. i. 310; bk. iii. 910. Chaucer has *lym-rod*, a rod covered with bird-lime, C. T., B 3574. The word is a mere variant of *rood*, by a shortening of the vowel-sound of which we have a few other examples, viz. in *gosling* from AS. *gōsling*, *blossom* from AS. *blōstma*, *fodder* from AS. *fōdor*; not very dissimilar are *blood*, *mother*, from AS. *blōd*, *mōdor*. In the Owl and Nightingale, l. 1644 (or 1646), we have *rod* used in the sense of *rood* or gallows. 'Thou seist that gromes the i-foð, An heie on *rodde* the an-hoð' = thou (the owl) sayest that men take thee, and hang thee high on a rod (rood). See further under **Rood**. Cf. Pomeran. *rode*, a rod ; MDu. *roede*, a rod. Doublet, *rood*.

RODENT, gnawing. (L.) A scientific term. – L. *rōdent-*, stem of pres. part. of *rōdere*, to gnaw. Akin to *rādere*, to scratch ; see **Rase**. Cf. Skt. *rada-s*, a tooth. Der. (from L. *rōdere*) *cor-rode*, *e-rode*. And see *rostrum*, *rat*.

RODOMONTADE, vain boasting. (F. – Ital.) 'Crites. And most terribly he comes off, like your *rodomontado* ;' Ben Jonson, Cynthia's Revels, Act v. sc. 2. 'And triumph'd our whole nation In his *rodomant* fashion ;' id., Masque of Owls, Owl 5. – F. *rodomontade*, 'a brag, boast ;' Cot. – Ital. *rodomontada*, 'a boaste, brag ;' Florio. A proverbial expression, due to the boastful character of *Rodomonte*, in the Orlando Furioso of Ariosto, bk. xiv ; called *Rodamonte* by Bojardo, Orlando Innamorato, ii. 1. 56. Said to be coined from Lombard *rodare* (= Ital. *rotare*), to turn about, and *monte*, a mountain. See **Rotary** and **Mount** (1).

ROE (1), a female deer. (E.) ME. *ro*; Chaucer, C. T. 4084 (A 4086), purposely gives the Northern E. *raa*. AS. *rāha*, *rā*, m. ; *rǣge*, f. (so that ME. *ro* was masc.). See Voc. 11. 33.**+**Icel. *rā*; whence *rābukkr*, a roe-buck ; Dan. *raa*; whence *raabuk*, a roe-buck, *raadyr*, roe-deer ; Swed. *rå*; whence *råbock*, roe-buck ; Du. *ree*; *reebok*, roe-buck ; O. Low G. *rēho*, m. (Gallée) ; G. *reh*; *rehbock*. Teut. base **raihon-*, m. ; of unknown origin. Der. *roe-buck*, ME. *roobukke*, Trevisa, i. 337; see **Buck**.

ROE (2), the eggs or spawn of fishes. (Scand.) The form *roe* is in Shak. Rom. ii. 4. 39. But it is due to a curious mistake. The true form is *roan* (with *oa* as in *oak*), but it seems to have been regarded as a *plural*, like *oxen*, *eyne* (eyes), *shoon* (shoes), so that the *n* was dropped. This is unusual (perhaps unique) in the case of apparent plurals in *-en* or *-n*, but common with plurals (or rather *supposed* plurals) in *-s*; as shown under *cherry*, *sherry*, *pea*. 'Roan, the roe of a fish ;' Peacock's Glossary (Lincoln). 'Rownd, roe,' Whitby Glossary ; where the word has actually acquired an excrescent *d*. ME. *rowne*, Prompt. Parv. – Icel. *hrogn*, Dan. *rogn*, Swed. *rom*, roe, spawn.**+**G. *rogen*, roe (whence F. *rogue*, roe). β. Teut. type **hrug-on-*, or **hrugno-*, masc.

ROGATION, supplication. (F. – L.) Particularly used in the phr. *Rogation-days*; see the Prayer-book ; Hooker, Eccl. Polity, b. v. s. 41, Foxe, Acts and Monuments, p. 914, Hen. VIII (R.). Also 'Rogation weke ;' Palsgrave. – F. *rogation*; pl. *rogations*, 'rogation-daies ;' Cot. – L. *rōgātiōnem*, acc. of *rogātio*, a supplication, an asking. – L. *rogāre*, to ask. Der. *rogation-days*. Also (from *rogāre*) *ab-rogate*, *ar-rogate*, *ar-rogant*, *de-rogate*, *inter-rogate*, *pre-rogat-ive*, *pro-rogue*, *super-e-rogat-ion*, *sur-rogate*.

ROGUE, a knave, vagabond. (F. – Low G.) The word sometimes meant merely a wandering mendicant ; see K. Lear, iv. 7. 39, and Trench's Select Glossary. Shak. also has *roguing*, *roguish*, vagrant ; Per. iv. 1. 97 ; K. Lear, iii. 7. 104. Cotgrave has : '*Roder*, to roam, wander, vagabondize it, *rogue* abroad.' But the E. *roguish* also has the sense of arch, pert, and this can only be due to F. *rogue*, 'arrogant, proud, presumptuous, malapert, saucie, rude, surly ;' Cot. Thus the sense of 'surly fellow' would seem to be the original one, easily transferred to beggars as a cant term; and then the verb *to rogue abroad* would mean 'to go about as a beggar.' **β.** That a *rogue* was a common cant term may be seen in Harman's Caueat, ed. Furnivall; he devotes cap. iv (pp. 36–41) to the description of 'a roge,' and cap. v to the description of 'a wylde roge.' He concludes by saying: 'I once rebuking a wyld roge because he went idelly about, he shewed me that he was a beggar by inheritance; his grandfather was a begger, his father was one, and he must nedes be one by good reason.' **γ.** The F. *rogue* is referred by Diez to Icel. *hrōkr*, but this word means lit. 'a rook,' and secondarily, a croaker, long-winded talker; which does not suit the sense. It answers rather to Low G. *rook*, which not only means the bird, but also an arch-thief (Brem. Wört.). Cf. E. *rook*, to cheat; and Dan. *raage*, a rook. See **Rook** (1). Der. *rogu-ish, -ly, -ness*; *rogu-er-y*.

ROIL, RILE, to vex. (F.?–L.?) *Rile* seems to be the same word as *roil*, to vex; similarly *toil*, *soil*, are occasionally pronounced *tile*, *sile*. But the old word *roil* seems to show two distinct meanings: (1) to disturb, vex, trouble, and (2) to wander about, to romp. I have given examples in my note to P. Plowman, C. vi. 151; and five occur in Davies, Suppl. Glossary. 'The lamb down stream *roiled* the wolf's water above;' North, Examen, p. 359 (1740). Prov. E. *roil*, *rile*, to make turbid, to scold; E. D. D. Evidently of F. origin. Perhaps from OF. *roeiller*, *roelier*, *roillier*, to roll about, to roll the eyes, to beat (Godefroy); mod. F. *rouiller*, to roll the eyes; MF. *rouiller*, to pummel (Cot.). From a Lat. type *rotelliāre*, to roll.—L. *rotella*, dimin. of *rota*, a wheel; see **Rotary.**

ROISTERING, turbulent, blustering. (F.–L.) Todd cites from Swift (no reference): 'Among a crew of *roist'ring* fellows.' Shak. has *roisting*, Troil. ii. 2. 208; and Levins has *royst*, vb. We have Udall's play of *Roister Doister*, written before 1553; and the sb. *roister* is in the Mirror for Magistrates (Nares). *Roister*, a bully, a ruffian or turbulent fellow, seems to be the orig. word which gave rise to the verb *roist* on the one hand, and the adj. *roistering*, i. e. ruffianly, on the other.—F. *rustre*, 'a ruffin, *royster*, hackster, swaggerer, sawcie fellow;' Cot. This Littré explains as being another form of OF. *ruste*, a rustic, the *r* being 'epenthetic.'—L. *rusticum*, acc. of *rusticus*, rustic, hence clownish. See **Rustic.**

ROLL, to turn on an axis, revolve, move round and round. (F.–L.) In early use; ME. *rollen*, Layamon, 22287, later text; Chaucer, C. T. 12772 (C 838). Partly (see Hatzfeld) from OF. *roler*, *roller*, later *rouler*, to roll.—Late L. *rotulāre*, to roll, revolve.—L. *rotula*, a little wheel; dimin. of *rota*, a wheel. And partly from OF. *roeler*, to roll, from the sb. *roele*, a little wheel.—L. *rotella*, dimin. of the same L. *rota*. See **Rotary.** Der. *roll*, sb., ME. *rolle*, Ancren Riwle, p. 344, l. 11, from OF. *rolle*, later *roule*, 'a rowle,' Cot., which from Late L. *rotulum*, acc. of *rotulus*, a roll (preserved in the phrase *custos rotulōrum*). Also *roll-er*, *roll-ing*, *roll-ing-pin*, *rolling-press*. Also (from F. *roule*) *roul-eau*, *roul-ette*. Also *cont-rol*, q. v.

ROMANCE, a fictitious narrative. (F.–L.) The French originals from which some E. poems were translated or imitated are often referred to by the name of *the romance*. Rob. of Glouc. (p. 487, l. 9987), in treating of the history of Rich. I, says there is more about him 'in *romance*;' and, in fact, the Romance of Richard Cuer de Lion is extant in E. verse; see Weber's Met. Romances.—OF. *romanz*, *romans*, a romance (Godefroy). This peculiar form is believed to have arisen from the Late L. adv. *rōmānicē*, so that *rōmānicē loqui* was translated into OF. by *parler romans*. It then became a sb., and passed into common use. The Prov. *romans* occurs (1) as an adj.=L. *Rōmānus*, (2) as a sb., the 'Roman' language, and (3) as a sb., a romance. **β.** By the 'Roman' language was meant the vulgar tongue used by the people in everyday life, as distinguished from the 'Latin' of books. We now give the name of Romance Languages to the languages which are chiefly founded on Latin, or, as they are also called, the Neo-Latin languages. **γ.** The Late L. *Rōmānicē*, i. e. Roman-like, is formed from the adj. *Rōmānus*, Roman.—L. *Rōma*, Rome. Der. *romance*, verb, *romanc-er*. Also (from *Rōmānus*) *Roman*, *Roman-ist*, *Roman-ism*, *Roman-ise*; also *roman-esque*, from F. *romanesque*, 'Romish, Roman,' Cot., from Ital. *Romanesco*, Romanish. Also (from *Roma*) *Rom-ish*. And see **Romaunt.**

ROMAUNT, a romance. (F.–L.) *The Romaunt of the Rose*, usually attributed to Chaucer, though only 1705 lines of it are really his, is a well-known poem. It is a translation of the French poem *Le Roman de la Rose*. Thus *romaunt* answers to F. *roman*. The final *t* is found in F. as well as E.; the OF. form was (in the oblique case) *romant*, or even *roumant*. Another OF. form of the same word was *romanz* (whence E. *romance*), so that *romanz*, *roman*, *romant* are three forms of the same word. See further under **Romance.** Der. *romant-ic*, spelt *romantick* in Phillips, ed. 1706, from mod. F. *romantique*, romantic, an adj. formed from *romant*, another form of *roman*, as explained above; *romant-ic-al-ly*.

ROMMANY, gipsy; a gipsy; see **Rum** (2).

ROMP, to play noisily. (F.–Teut.) In the Spectator, no. 187, we find 'a *romping* girl,' and *rompishness*. The older spelling was **Ramp,** q.v. The intermediate form *raumpe* occurs in Caxton's print of Malory's Morte Arthure, bk. ix. c. 1, with reference to a '*raumpynge* lyon.' Der. *romp*, sb., Tatler, no. 15, *romp-ish*, *romp-ish-ly*, *romp-ish-ness*.

RONDEAU, a kind of poem. (F.–L.) Borrowed from mod. F. *rondeau*. The ME. word was **Roundel**, q. v. Doublet, *roundel*.

RONYON, a mangy person. (F.) In Shak. Merry Wives, iv. 2. 195; Macb. i. 3. 6. Prob. formed (with suffix *-on*) from MF. *rongne*, F. *rogne*, 'scurf, scabbiness, the mange;' Cot. Cf. Ital. *rogna*, scab; Span. *roña*, scab, dirt, fraud; Port. *ronha*, scab, craftiness; mod. Prov. *rougno*, scab; *meichanto rougno*, 'mauvais drôle,' Mistral. From a Late L. type *rōnea*; Körting, § 8141.

ROOD, the holy cross; a measure of land. (E.) The same word as *rod*, as shown under **Rod.** Hence its use as a measure of land, because measured with a measuring-rod or 'pole,' of the length of 5½ yards, giving a *square rod* of 30¼ square yards, and a *square rood* of 40 square rods, or a quarter of an acre. For the sense of 'cross,' see Legends of the Holy Rood, ed. Morris. AS. *rōd*, a gallows, cross, properly a rod or pole; Matt. xxvii. 40, John, xix. 17.+ OFries. *rōde*, OSax. *rōda*, gallows, cross; Du. *roede*, a rod, perch, wand, yard; G. *ruthe*, OHG. *ruota*, a rod, a rod of land. Teut. type *rōdā*, fem., a rod, a pole. The prime grade is *rad-*. Der. *rood-loft* (Nares).

ROOF, the covering of a house. (E.) For *hroof*, initial *h* being lost. ME. *rof*, Havelok, 2082; *rhof*, Ormulum, 11351. AS. *hrōf*, a roof, Mark, ii. 4; OFries. *hrōf*.+Du. *roef*, a cabin; Icel. *hrōf*, a shed under which ships are built or kept. Teut. type *hrōfo-*, Idg. type *krāpo-*. Cf. Irish *crō*, a hovel; W. *craw*, a pig-sty; Bret. *crou*, a stable; Stokes-Fick, p. 96. Der. *roof*, verb; *roof-ing*, *roof-less*.

ROOK (1), a kind of crow. (E.) ME. *rook*, Prompt. Parv. AS. *hrōc*; Ps. 146, 10; ed. Spelman.+Icel. *hrōkr*; Dan. *raage*; Swed. *råka*; MHG. *ruoch*, OHG. *hruoh*; cf. G. *ruchert*, a jackdaw (Flügel). Teut. type *hrōkoz*, m. **β.** The word means 'croaker;' cf. Goth. *hrūkjan*, to crow as a cock; Gk. κρώζειν (for *κρώγ-γειν), to caw. A word of imitative origin. Der. *rook-er-y*.

ROOK (2), a castle, at chess. (F.–Pers.) '*Roke* of the chesse, *roc*;' Palsgrave. ME. *rook*, Prompt. Parv.—F. *roc*, 'a rook at chesse,' Cot. [Cf. Span. *roque*, Ital. *rocco*.]—Pers. *rokh*, 'the rook or tower at chess;' Rich. Dict. p. 727. The remoter origin of this word is unknown; Devic cites d'Herbelot as saying that in the language of the ancient Persians, it signified 'a warrior' who sought warlike adventures, a sort of knight-errant. The piece was orig. denoted by an elephant carrying a castle on his back; we have suppressed the elephant. There seems to be nothing to connect this with the famous bird called the *roc* or *rukh*; except that the same form *rukh*, in Persian, means 'a hero, a knight-errant (as in d'Herbelot), a rhinoceros, the name of a bird of mighty wing, a beast resembling the camel, but very fierce,' &c.; Rich. (as above).

ROOM, space, a chamber. (E.) The older meaning is simply 'space;' hence a place at table, Luke, xiv. 7. ME. *roum*; 'and hath *roum* and eek space,' Chaucer, Legend of Good Women, 1999. AS. *rūm*; 'næfdon *rūm*'=they had no room, Luke ii. 7. We also find AS. *rūm*, adj., spacious; 'se weg is swiðe *rūm*'=the way is very broad or spacious, Matt. vii. 13.+Du. *ruim*, adj., spacious; sb., room; Icel. *rūmr*, spacious; *rūm*, space; Dan. and Swed. *rum*, space and sb.; Goth. *rūms*, adj. and sb., Matt. vii. 13; Luke, ii. 7; G. *raum*, OHG. *rūm*, space. **β.** All from the Teut. type *rūmoz*, adj., spacious; whence the sb. forms are derived. Allied to L. *rūs*, open country, Russ. *raviina*, a plain, Zend *ravanh*, wide, free, open, *ravan*, a plain; Fick, i. 197; OIrish *roe*, a plain. See **Rural.** Der. *room-y*, Dryden, Annus Mirabilis, st. 153, l. 609, a late word, substituted for the ME. adj. *roum* (room); *room-i-ly*, *room-i-ness*. Also *room-th* (Nares), obsolete. Also *rumm-age*, q.v.

ROOST, a place where fowls rest at night. (E.) Frequently applied to the perch on which fowls rest; as to which see below. Most common in the phr. *to go to roost*, i.e. to seek a sleeping-place. 'They go to *roost*;' Skelton, Elynour Rummyng, 191. '*Roost* for capons or hennes;' Palsgrave. AS. *hrōst*; Lye gives *henna hrōst*, a hen-roost; Gerēfa, § 11 (in Anglia, ix. 262); and *hrōst* appears again (in composition) in an obscure passage in the Exeter-book; see Grein. **β.** We also have OS. *hrōst* in the Heliand, 2316, where the palsied man healed by Christ is let down through the roof; or, as in the original, *thurh thes hūses hrōst*, through the wood-work of the house-top.+MDu. *roest*, or *hinnen-kot*, 'a hen-roest;' *roesten*, 'to goe to roost, as hens;' Hexham. **γ.** In the Heliand, the sense of *hrōst* comes close to that of 'roof;' and it is certainly related to Goth. *hrōt*, Icel. *hrōt*, a roof; cf. also Lowl. Scotch *roost*, the inner roof of a cottage, composed of spars reaching from one wall to the other (Jamieson). The orig. roosting-place for fowls was on the rafters of the inner roof. This is how *roost* acquired the sense of perch. Der. *roost*, verb.

ROOT (1), the part of a plant in the earth, which draws up sap from the soil, a source, cause of a matter. (Scand.) ME. *rote*, Chaucer, C. T. 2; Ancren Riwle, p. 54, l. 12.—Icel. *rōt*, a root; Swed. *rot*; Dan. *rod*. β. Hence Icel. *rōta*, to root up, rout up, as a swine, corresponding to prov. E. *wrout*, to dig up like a hog (E. D. S. Gloss. B. 7), ME. *wroten*, a word used by Chaucer of a sow, Persones Tale (Six-text, Group I, 157), AS. *wrōtan*; see **Root** (2). This proves that the Icel. *rōt* stands for *wrōt*, it being a characteristic of that language to drop *w* in the (initial) combination *wr*. γ. Further, *rōt* is allied to Goth. *waurts*, a root, AS. *wyrt*, a wort, a root; see **Wort**. It is also cognate with L. *rād-ix*, a root; the Teut. base *wrōt*- answering to L. *(w)rād-*. See **Radix, Rhizome**. Brugmann, i. § 350 (2). Der. *root*, verb, Wint. Tale, i. 1. 25; also *root*, vb., in the sense 'to grub up,' see **Root** (2); *root-less*, *root-let*. Doublets, *radix*, *wort*.

ROOT (2), **ROUT**, to grub up, as a hog. (E.) In Shak. Rich. III, i. 3. 228. AS. *wrōtan*, to grub up, Ælfric's Grammar, ed. Zupitza, p. 176, l. 12.+MDu. *wroeten*, 'to grub or root in the earth as hogs doe;' Hexham; Icel. *rōta*, to grub up, from *rōt*, a root; Dan. *rode*, to root up, from *rod*, a root. See **Root** (1).

ROPE, a thick twisted cord. (E.) ME. *rope*, *roop*; spelt *rop*, Rob. of Glouc., p. 448, l. 9212. AS. *rāp*, Judges, xv. 14, xvi. 9. Du. *reep*; Icel. *reip*; Swed. *rep*; Dan. *reb*; G. *reif*, a circle, hoop (of a barrel), ring, wheel, ferrule; occasionally, a rope; Goth. *skauda-raip*, shoe-latchet. β. All from the Teut. base *raip-*, prob. with the sense of 'strip,' whence 'string.' Perhaps from the 2nd grade of Teut. *reip-an-*, to cut (pt. t. *raip*); see **Reap** (Franck). And cf. **Ripe, Rip**. Der. *rope*, vb., *rop-er*, a rope-maker, P. Plowman, B. v. 336, *rop-er-y*, *rope-maker*, *rope-walk*; also *rop-y*, adj., stringy, glutinous, adhesive, lit. rope-like, Skelton, Elinour Rummyng, 24; *rop-ing*, Hen. V, iii. 5. 23; *stirrup*, q. v.

ROQUELAURE, a kind of cloak. (F.) In Gay's Trivia, i. 51. Named after the duke of *Roquelaure* (ab. 1715); Todd's Johnson.

RORQUAL, a kind of large whale. (F.—Scand.) F. *rorqual* (Littré).—Norw. *röyrkval* (Aasen); prob. short for *röyder-kval*, 'reddish whale;' from Norw. *raud*, red, and *kval*, a whale. Cf. Icel. *reyðr-hvalr*; from *rauðr*, red, and *hvalr*, whale.

ROSE, the name of a flower. (L.—Gk.—OPersian.) ME. *rose*; the old plural was *rosen*, as in Ancren Riwle, p. 276, l. 12. AS. *rose*, pl. *rosan*; Grein, ii. 384.—L. *rosa*, a rose. β. This is not a true L. word, but borrowed from Gk. *ῥόδον*, a rose, whence a form *ῥοδία* (not found), Æolic *ῥοζα*>L. *rosa*; cf. L. *Clausus* with *Claudius*. γ. Again, the Gk. *ῥόδον*, Æolic form *βρόδον* (for *Ϝρόδον*), is not a Gk. word, but borrowed from OPers. *vartā*, a rose; whence also the Armen. and Arab. *ward*. Rich. Dict. 1638; altered in mod. Persian to the form *gūl*; for which see **Julep**. (Horn, § 927; Brugmann, i. 772 b.) Der. *ros-ac-e-ous*, from L. *rosāceus* (Pliny); *ros-ar-y*, ME. *rosarie*, Chaucer, C. T. 16897 (G 1429), from OF. *rosarie* (not recorded), later form *rosaire*, from Late L. *rosārium*, a chaplet, also the title of a treatise on alchemy by Arnoldus de Villa Nova and of other treatises; *ros-e-ate*, a coined word; *ros-ette*, from F. *rosette*, 'a little rose,' Cot.; *rose-water*, *rose-wood*, *ros-y*, *ros-i-ness*.

ROSEMARY, a small evergreen shrub. (F.—L.) In Skelton, Garl. of Laurel, 980; and in Sir T. Elyot, Castel of Helth, b. ii. c. 9. Gower has the form *rosmarine*, C. A. iii. 132 (bk. vii. 1407), where the L. marginal note has *rosa marina*.—OF. *rosmarin*, 'rosemary,' Cot. (and in Hatzfeld); mod. F. *romarin*.—L. *rōsmarīnus*, *rōsmarīnum*, rosemary; lit. marine dew, or sea-dew; called in Ovid *rōs maris*, Metam. xii. 410.—L. *rōs*, dew; and *marīnus*, marine.+Russ. *rosa*, dew; Lithuan. *rasa*, dew (Nesselmann).+Skt. *rasa-s*, juice, essence; cf. *ras*, to taste. And see **Marine**. ¶ Named from some fancied connexion with 'sea-spray;' in English, it seems to have been altered to *rosemary* from a popular etymology connecting *rose* with *Mary*.

ROSIN, the same as **Resin**, q. v.

ROSTER, a military register. (Du.) The *o* is properly long; pron. *roaster*.—Du. *rooster*, a gridiron; also, 'a list, roll, table' (Calisch); said to be from the resemblance of the lines in a list to the bars of a gridiron.—Du. *roosten*, to roast; see **Roast**.

ROSTRUM, a platform for an orator to speak from. (L.) 'Before the *Rostra*;' P. Holland, tr. of Suetonius, Nero, ch. 13. '*Rostrum*, the beak of a bird, prow of a ship, nose of an alembic;' Phillips, ed. 1706.—L. *rostrum*, a beak, prow; pl. *rostra*, the Rostra, an erection for speakers in the forum, so called because adorned with the beaks of ships taken from the Antiates, A. U. C. 416; Livy, viii. 14 (White). For *rōd-trum*, as being the organ wherewith the bird pecks.—L. *rōdere*, to gnaw, peck; see **Rodent**. Der. *rostr-ate*, *rostri-form*.

ROT, to putrefy. (E.) A weak verb; pt. t. *rotted*; pp. *rotted*, as in Shak. Mid. Nt. Dream, ii. 1. 95. This pp. is little used, its place being supplied by *rotten*, a Scand. form; see **Rotten**. ME. *roten*, *rotien*, Chaucer, C. T. 4405 (A 4407); pt. t. *rotede*, Genesis and Exod., ed. Morris, 3342; pp. *roted*, Will. of Palerne, 4124. AS. *rotian*, pt. t. *rotode*, pp. *rotod*; Exod. xvi. 24.+Du. *rotten*; OHG. *rozēn*. β. Further allied to Icel. *rotna*, Swed. *ruttna*, Dan. *raadne*, to become rotten, verbs which are allied to the old strong pp. appearing in Icel. *rotinn*, Swed. *rutten*, Dan. *raaden*, rotten. See **Rotten**, which belongs to a more original type. Der. *rot*, sb., *dry-rot*.

ROTARY, turning like a wheel. (L.) A modern coined word; in Bailey's Dict., vol. ii. ed. 1731. As if from a L. type *rotārius*, from *rota*, a wheel.+Gael. and Irish *roth*, W. *rhod*, a wheel; Lithuan. *ratas*, a wheel; pl. *ratai*, a cart, wheeled vehicle; G. *rad*, a wheel. Cf. Skt. *ratha-s*, a car, chariot, vehicle. All from √RET, to run along; as in OIrish *rith-im*, I run; Lith. *ritù*, I roll, turn round; Brugmann, i. § 159. Der. *rot-ate*, from L. *rotātus*, pp. of *rotāre*, to revolve like a wheel; *rot-at-ion*, from L. acc. *rotātiōnem*; *rot-at-or-y*, formed with suffix -*y* from L. *rotātor*, a whirler round. And see *rotund-i-ty*, *rond-eau*, *round*, *round-el*, *rund-let*, *roué*, *roll*, *row-el*, *rouleau*, *roulette*.

ROTE (1), routine, repetition of the same words. (F.—L.) 'And euery statute coude he plaine *bi rote*' = and he knew the whole of every statute by rote; Chaucer, C. T. 329. '[He] can nouȝt wel reden His rewle . . . but *be* pure *rote*' = he cannot well read the rule of his order except merely by rote; P. Plowman's Crede, 377.—OF. *rote* (Godefroy), mod. F. *route*, a road, way, beaten track; Norm. dial. *rote*, a little path (Duméril). Hence the dimin. OF. *rotine*, mod. F. *routine*, as in the proverbial expression *par rotine*, 'by rote;' Cot. Hence *by rote*=along a beaten track, or with constant repetition; see **Rut** (1). β. The orig. sense of OF. *rote* is 'a great highway in a forest,' Cot., cognate with Ital. *rotta*, which, however, means a breaking up, a rout, defeat. The OF. *rote* is really the fem. of *rot*, old pp. of *rompre*, to break, and thus *rote*=L. *rupta*, lit. broken. As Diez says, the F. *route*, a street, way=*uia rupta*, a way broken through, just as the OF. *brisée* (lit. broken) means a way. Orig. applied to a way broken or cut through a forest.—L. *rupta*, fem. of *ruptus*, pp. of *rumpere*, to break; see **Rupture**. ¶ *By rote* has nothing to do with OF. *rote*, a musical instrument, as some suppose; see **Rote** (2). By way of further illustration, we may note that the Dict. of the French Academy (1813) gives: '*Router*, habituer quelqu'un à une chose, l'y exercer. *Les cartes se routent*, pour dire qu'on a beau les mêler, les mêmes combinaisons, les mêmes suites de cartes reviennent souvent.' And again : ' Il ne sait point de musique, mais il chante *par routine* ;' id. The latter passage expressly shows that to sing by rote is to sing *without* a musical instrument. Der. *rot-ed*, Cor. iii. 2. 55 ; cf. ' I *roote* in custome, *je habitue*,' Palsgrave. Doublets, *route*, *rout* (1), *rut* (1).

ROTE (2), the name of an old musical instrument. (F.—G.—C.) 'Wel coude he singe and plaien on a *rote* ;' Chaucer, C. T. 236. 'Playing on a *rote* ;' Spenser, F. Q. iv. 9. 6.—OF. *rote*, a musical instrument mentioned in Le Roman de la Rose, as cited by Roquefort. Burguy explains that there were two kinds of *rotes*, one a sort of psaltery or harp played with a *plectrum* or quill, the other much the same as the F. *vielle*, which Cotgrave calls 'a rude instrument of music, usually played by fidlers and blind men,' i. e. a kind of fiddle. [Roquefort absurdly connects *rote* with the L. *rota*, as if it were a kind of hurdy-gurdy, which it never was, and this has probably helped on the notion that E. *rote* in the phr. *by rote* must also have to do with the turning of a wheel, which is certainly not the case.]—OHG. *hrota*, *rota*, MHG. *rotte*, a rote; spelt *chrotta* in Low Lat. (Ducange). Of Celtic origin; OIrish *crot*, W. *crwth*, Gael. *cruit*, a harp, violin; see **Crowd** (2). Stokes-Fick, p. 99. ☞ See Lacroix, Arts of the Middle Ages, p. 217 of E. translation.

ROTHER, an ox. (E.) In Shak. Timon, iv. 3. 12. ME. *rotheren*, pl., P. Ploughman's Crede, 431; *ruðeren*, pl., Layamon, 8106. Late AS. *hrūðeru*, pl., Kemble, Cod. Dipl. iv. 275. Earlier AS. *hriðer*, *hryðer* (Bosworth); and in comp., *hrīð-*. The base *hrīð-* is for *hrinth-*, cognate with G. *rind*, ox. Teut. type *hrinthis*, n., ox (Kluge). The ME. *rother*, Du. *rund*, are (more probably) connected with Teut. type *hrunthis*, n.; see Kluge and Franck. Perhaps allied to AS. *hrindan* (pp. *hrunden*), Icel. *hrinda*, to push, to thrust; see **Rend**. And see **Runt**. See my Notes on Eng. Etym., p. 253.

ROTTEN, putrid. (Scand.) ME. *roten*, Chaucer, C. T. 4404 (A 4406); Ancren Riwle, p. 84, note *d*, where the text has *roted*.—Icel. *rotinn*, rotten; Swed. *rutten*; Dan. *raaden*. β. Apparently Icel. *rotinn* is the pp. of a lost verb *rjōta*, pr. t. *raut*, to wet, to decay, allied to AS. *rēotan*, OHG. *riuzan*, to weep, shed tears. Teut. type *reutan-*, pt. t. *raut*, pp. *rutanoz*. From √REUD;

whence also Lith. *raudóti*, Skt. *rud*, to weep, L. *rudere*, to bellow. See **Ret.** And see **Rot.** Der. *rotten-ness*.

ROTUNDITY, roundness. (F.–L.) In K. Lear, iii. 2. 7. Adapted from F. *rotondité*, Cot.–L. *rotunditātem*, acc. of *rotunditās*, roundness.–L. *rotundus*, round; see **Round.** Der. (from L. *rotundus*), rotund; *rotund-a*, a round building.

ROUBLE, RUBLE, a Russian coin. (Russ.) Spelt *rubble*, Hakluyt's Voyages, vol. i. p. 256; *roble*, id. i. 280, under the date Aug. 1, 1556.–Russ. *ruble*, a ruble, 100 copeks; worth about 3*s*. 4*d*. Perhaps from Pers. *rūpiya*, a rupee (Miklosich). See **Rupee.**

ROUÉ, a profligate. (F.–L.) Merely F. *roué*, lit. broken on the wheel; a name given, under the regency (A. D. 1715-1723), to the companions of the duke of Orleans, men worthy of being broken on the wheel; a punishment for the greatest criminals. Pp. of *rouer*, lit. to turn round (L. *rotāre*).–F. *roue*, a wheel.–L. *rota*, a wheel. See **Rotary.**

ROUGE, red paint. (F.–L.) Modern; added by Todd to Johnson.–F. *rouge*, red.–L. *rubeum*, acc. of *rubeus*, red; whence *rouge* is formed like *rage* from L. *rabiem* (Littré). Allied to *ruber*, red; see **Red, Ruby.** Der. *rouge*, verb.

ROUGH, shaggy, not smooth, uneven, violent, harsh, coarse, rugged. (E.) In Chaucer, C. T. 3736 (A 3738), the MSS. have *rough, rogh, row*. Other spellings are *ruh, rugh, ru, rou, ruȝ*; see Stratmann, s. v. *ruh*. AS. *rūh*, rough, hairy; Gen. xxvii. 11; also *rūg*. Cf. AS. *rūwan*, pl.; Gen. xxvii. 23.+Du. *ruig*, hairy, rough, harsh, rude; MDu. *ru* (Oudemans); Dan. *ru*; Low G. *ruug* (Bremen Wörterbuch); OHG. *rūh*, MHG. *rūch*, hairy; G. *rauh*, rough. Also Skt. *rūksha-*, rough. β. Cf. also Lithuan. *raukas*, a fold, wrinkle, *rùkti*, to wrinkle; the orig. sense may have been uneven, like something wrinkled. ¶ Distinct from *raw*. Der. *rough-ly*, -*ness*; *rough*, verb, *rough-en*; *rough-hew* (*rougheheawe* in Palsgrave); *rough-ish, rough-rider*. And see *rug*.

ROULEAU, a roll of coins in paper. (F.–L.) See Stanford Dict. In Pope, The Basset-table, l. 81. From F. *rouleau*, 'a roll of paper;' Cot. *Rouleau* stands for an OF. **roulel, *rolel*, in Froissart *roliel* (Hatzfeld), a diminutive from OF. *role*, later *roule*, a roll; see **Roll.**

ROULETTE, a game of chance. (F.–L.) See Sandford Dict. From F. *roulette*; named from the ball which rolls on a turning table. For **rouelette*, OF. *ruelete* (Hatzfeld); dimin. of *rouelle*, a little wheel, dimin. of *roue*, a wheel (L. *rota*). See **Rowel.**

ROUN, ROWN, ROUND, to whisper. (E.) Shak. has *rounded*, whispered, K. John, ii. 566; but the *d* is excrescent. ME. *rounen*, Chaucer, C. T. 5823 (D 241); P. Plowman, B. iv. 13. AS. *rūnian*, to whisper; *rūnedon* = L. *susurrabant*, Ps. xl. 8, ed. Spelman.–AS. *rūn*, a rune, mystery, secret colloquy, whisper; see **Rune.**

ROUND, circular, globular. (F.–L.) ME. *round*, Chaucer, C. T. 3932 (A 3934).–OF. *roònd*, mod. F. *rond*, round.–L. *rotundus*, round; formed, with suffix -*undus*, from *rot-a*, a wheel; see **Rotary.** Der. *round*, sb., *round*, verb; *round-about*, in Levins; *round-head*, from the Puritan fashion of having the hair cut close to the head; *round-house*; *round-ish, round-ly, round-ness*. Also *round-el*, q. v., *rond-eau*, q. v., *rund-let*, q. v.

ROUNDEL, a kind of ballad. (F.–L.) The mod. F. form is *rondeau*; see **Rondeau.** ME. *roundel*, Chaucer, C. T. 1531 (A 1529); Legend of Good Women, 423.–OF. *rondel*, later *rondeau*, which Cotgrave explains as 'a rime or sonnet that ends as it begins.' For a specimen of a *roundel*, in which the first two lines recur after the fifth, see Chaucer's poem of Merciless Beauty. So called from the first line coming *round* again. Dimin. from F. *rond*, round; see **Round.** Der. *roundel-ay*, Spenser, Shep. Kalendar, June, 49, from F. *rondelet*, dimin. of OF. *rondel* (Cot.); the E. spelling is prob. due to confusion with *lay*, a song.

ROUSE (1), to raise up, excite, awaken, rise up. (Scand.) 'To *rouse* a deare' [deer]; Levins. It was a term of the chase; cf. Rich. II, ii. 3. 128. 'Some like wilde bores, late *rouz'd* out of the brakes;' Spenser, F. Q. ii. 11. 10. But it was orig. intransitive. 'I *rowse*, I stretche myselfe;' Palsgrave.–Swed. *rusa*, to rush; *rusa fram*, to rush forward; *rusa upp*, to start up; MSwed. *rusa*, to rush, go hastily (Ihre); Dan. *ruse*, to rush. Allied to AS. *hrēosan*, to rush, also to fall down, 'to come down with a rush;' Grein, ii. 104. β. Teut. base **hreus-*; the orig. sense was prob. to start forward suddenly, to burst out. See further under **Rush** (1), which is not quite the same word as the present, but allied to it. Hence also *rouse* is to wake a sleeper, viz. by a sudden movement. Der. *a-rouse*, with a prefix suggested by *a-rise*.

ROUSE (2), a drinking-bout. (Scand.) In Shak. Hamlet, i. 2. 127; i. 4. 8; ii. 1. 58; Oth. ii. 3. 66.–Swed. *rus*, a drunken fit, drunkenness; *rusa*, to fuddle; Dan. *rus*, intoxication, *sove rusen ud* (to sleep out one's rouse), to sleep oneself sober. We find also Du.

---

roes, drunkenness; *eenen roes drinken* (to drink a rouse), 'to drink till one is fuddled' (Sewel); but it does not seem to be an old word in Dutch, being omitted by Hexham. Cf. EFries. *rūse*, noise, uproar, 'row;' *rūsen*, to make a noise; Low G. *rūse*, noise. ¶ That we got the word from *Denmark* is shown by a curious quotation in Todd's Johnson: 'Thou noblest drunkard Bacchus, teach me how to take the Danish *rowza*;' Brand's Pop. Antiq. ii. 228 (ed. Bohn, ii. 330). See **Row** (3).

ROUT, (1) a defeat, (2) a troop or crowd of people. (F.–L.) Notwithstanding the wide difference of sense, the word is but one. More than that, it is the same word as **Route,** q. v. 1. Shak. has *rout*, i. e. disordered flight, 2 Hen. VI, v. 2. 31; Cymb. v. 3. 41; and *rout*, verb, to defeat and put to disorderly flight, Cymb. v. 2. 12. This does not seem to occur much earlier. 2. ME. *route*, a number of people, troop, Chaucer, C. T. 624 (A 622), Will. of Palerne, 1213; Layamon, 2598, later text.–F. *route*, 'a rowt, over-throw, defeature; . . also, a rowt, heard, flock, troope, company, multitude of men or beasts; . . also, a rutt, way, path, street, course;' Cot.–L. *rupta*, fem. of *ruptus*, broken. β. The different senses may be thus explained. 1. A defeat is a breaking up of a host, a broken mass of flying men. 2. A small troop of men is a fragment or broken piece of an army; and the word is generally used in contempt, of a company in broken ranks or disorderly array. 3. A route was, originally, a way broken or cut out through a wood or forest. See **Route.** ¶ The G. *rotte*, a troop, is merely borrowed from the Romance languages. Cf. Ital. *rotta*, Span. *rota*, a rout, defeat. It is remarkable that the mod. F. *route* has lost the senses both of 'defeat' and 'troop.' Der. *rout*, verb, as above.

ROUTE, a way, course, line of march. (F.–L.) Not much used in later authors, but it occurs very early. ME. *route*, spelt *rute*, Ancren Riwle, p. 350, l. 1.–F. *route*, 'a way, path, street, course . . also, a glade in a wood;' Cot. β. The sense of 'glade' is the earliest; it meant a way *broken* or cut through a forest.–L. *rupta*, fem. of *ruptus*, pp. of *rumpere*, to break. See **Rote** (1), **Rout, Rupture.** Der. *rout-ine*. Doublets, *rote* (1), *rout, rut* (1).

ROUTINE, a beaten track, a regular course of action. (F.–L.) Modern.–F. *routine*, a usual course of action; lit. a small path, pathway; dimin. of *route*, a route, way; see **Route.**

ROVER, a pirate, wanderer. (Du.) ME. *rover, rovare*. 'Robare, or robbar yn the see, *rovare*, or thef of the se, *Pirata*;' Prompt. Parv. p. 437. 'A *rovere* of the see;' Gower, C. A. i. 359; bk. iii. 2369.–Du. *roover*, 'a rober, a pyrate, or a theef;' Hexham.–Du. *rooven*, to rob.–Du. *roof*, 'spoile;' id. β. The Du. *roof* is cognate with AS. *rēaf*, spoil, plunder. See **Reave, Rob.** Der. *rove*, verb; 'To *roue*, robbe, Rapere; to *roue* about, Errare, vagari;' Levins. The second sense was easily developed; the sb. *rover* is the older word in English though etymologically due to the verb. The Icel. *rāfa*, to rove, stray, is prob. not related.

ROW (1), a line, rank, series. (E.) ME. *rowe*, Amis and Amiloun, 1900 (Weber's Met. Rom. vol. ii); *rewe*, Chaucer, C. T. 2868 (A 2866); *raw*, Barbour's Bruce, v. 590. AS. *rāw, rǣw*, a row; a scarce word. 'þanon on þā rǣwe;' Kemble, Cod. Diplom. v. 275; 'on . . hege-rǣwe,' to the hedge-row, id. ii. 54. Allied to Du. *rij*, MDu. *rijg, rijge* (Oudemans), Low G. *rige, rege*, G. *reihe*, a row. The G. *reihe* is from OHG. *rīhan*, to string together, to arrange things (as beads) by passing a string or rod through them; a strong verb, of which the Teut. type is **reihwan-*, pt. t. **raihw*, whence the sb. **rai(g)wā*, f., Teut. type of AS. *rāw*, a form which occurs in A. S. Leechdoms, ii. 238. Further allied to Skt. *rēkhā*, a line; from root **reikh*, with labio-velar *kh*.

ROW (2), to propel a boat with oars. (E.) ME. *rowen*, Polit. Songs, ed. Wright, p. 254; Wyclif, Luke, viii. 26. AS. *rōwan*, to row, sail, Luke, viii. 23, 26.+Du. *roeijen*; Icel. *rōa*; Swed. *ro*; Dan. *roe*; MHG. *rüejen*. Allied to OIrish *rām*, L. *rēmus*, an oar; and further, to Skt. *aritra-*, a rudder, orig. a paddle; Lithuan. *irti*, to row; Gk. ἐρετμός, a paddle, oar. √ERE. Der. *row*, sb., *row-er*. Also *rudder*, q. v.

ROW (3), an uproar. (Scand.) Shortened from *rouse*, drunkenness, uproar, the older form being obsolete; see Todd's Johnson. The loss of *s* is as in *pea, cherry, sherry*, &c. See **Rouse** (2).

ROWAN-TREE, the same as *Roan-tree*, q. v.

ROWEL, a little wheel with sharp points at the end of a spur. (F.–L.) 'A payre of spurres, with a poynte without a *rowell*;' Berners, tr. of Froissart, vol. ii. c. 245. (R.) '*Rowell* of a spurre;' Palsgrave.–F. *rouelle*, 'a little flat ring, a wheele of plate or iron, in horses bitts;' Cot. [He gives *mollette* as the MF. word for a rowel; on the other hand, Spenser uses *rowel* for a part of a horse's bit; F. Q. i. 7. 37.]–Late L. *rotella*, a little wheel, dimin. of *rota*, a wheel; see **Rotary.**

ROWLOCK, ROLLOCK, RULLOCK. (E.) The history of this word is imperfectly known; in Ashe's Dict. (1775) it is oddly spelt *rowlack*. It is an alteration of *oar-lock*, due to confusion with the vb. *to row*. See **Oarlock** in N. E. D. The true AS. word was *ārloc* (Ettmüller); we find '*columbaria*, ār-locu,' Voc. 288. 6. Hence ME. *orlok*, Liber Albus, pp. 235, 237, 239. This word is compounded of AS. *ār*, an oar, and *loc*, cognate with G. *loch*, a hole, as is evident from comparing G. *ruderloch* or *rudergat*, a rowlock, rullock, or oar-hole. The AS. *loc* is also allied to AS. *loca* = the modern E. *lock*, in the sense of 'fastening;' and is derived from *loc-*, weak grade of the strong verb *lūcan*, to lock, fasten; see **Lock** (1). The orig. oar-fastenings or rullocks were, at least in some cases, actual holes; and hence at a later period we find them called *oar-holes*. In a Nominale pr. in Voc. 737. 32, we find: '*Hoc columber*, are-hole,' whereupon the editor notes that it means 'an air-hole, a small unglazed window.' This is wrong; *are* is the Northern form of *oar*, and *columber* is for L. *columbāre*. In Hexham's Du. Dict. the MDu. *riemgaten* and *roeygaten* are explained by 'the *oare-holes* to put out the oares.' Hence, in the word *rullock*, we know that *-lock* signifies 'hole.' And, as to the whole word, I believe it to be nothing but another form of ME. *orlok*, i. e. *oarlock*. The shifting of *r* is common in English; and, in this instance, it was assisted by confusion with the verb *to row* and (possibly) with the MDu. *roeygat*. If so, the spelling *rowlock* is merely due to popular etymology; it does not express the pronunciation. Worcester's Dict. gives the form *rollock*.

ROYAL, kingly. (F.—L.) ME. *real*, Chaucer, C. T. 1020 (A 1018), where some MSS. have *roial*.—OF. *real*, *roial*; spelt *royal* in Cotgrave, and explained as 'royall, regall, kingly.'—L. *rēgālis*, regal, royal; see **Regal**. Der. *royal-ty*; *royal-ty*, Gower, C. A. iii. 220; bk. vii. 3810, from OF. *realte*, *reialte*, spelt *royaulté* in Cotgrave, from L. acc. *rēgālitātem*. And see *real* (2). Doublet, *regal*.

RUB, to move over a surface with pressure, scour, wipe. (E.) ME. *rubben*, Chaucer, C. T. 3745 (A 3747); P. Plowman, B. xiii. 99. Not in AS. Cf. EFries. *rubben*, Dan. *rubbe*, Norw. *rubba*, to rub, to scrub. Also Norw. *rubben*, rough, uneven; EFries. *rubberig*, rough; Du. *robbelig*, 'rugged,' Sewel. Also W. Flem. *wrobbelen*, *wrubbelen*, to scrub, wash clothes by rubbing. The Teut. base is apparently *wreuᵬ*. Der. *rub*, sb., Macb. iii. 1. 134; *rubb-er*. ☞ Not connected with G. *reiben*, which is from a Teut. base *wreib*; cf. Du. *wrijven*, to rub. But they may be parallel formations.

RUBASSE, a variety of rock-crystal, with a red tinge. (F.—L.) F. *rubace*; from the base of L. *rub-eus*, reddish; see **Ruby**.

RUBBISH, broken stones, waste matter, refuse; nonsense. (AF.—Scand.) Prov. E. *rubbage*, as in Norfolk (Forby). Palsgrave has '*robrisshe* of stones, *plastras*;' and Cotgrave explains the F. *plastras* by '*rubbish*, clods or pieces of old and dry plaister.' Horman, in his Vulgaria (as cited by Way, note to Prompt. Parv., p. 435) says that '*Battz* [brick-bats] and great *rubbrysshe* serueth to fyl up in the myddell of the wall.' These quotations show that *rubbrish* was used in the exact sense of what we now usually call *rubble*; and the two words, *rubble* and *rubbish*, are closely connected. β. In the form *rubbrish*, the latter *r* is intrusive, since it disappears in earlier, as well as in later English. The ME. form is *robows*, or *robeux*; as, '*Robows*, or coldyr, *Petrosa*, *petro*,' where *coldyr* is an old word for rubble; Prompt. Parv. Way adds: in the Wardrobe Account of Piers Courteys, Keeper of the Wardrobe 20 Edw. IV (1480), occurs a payment to 'John Carter, for cariage away of a grete loode of *robeux*, that was left in the strete after the reparacyone made uppon a hous apperteigning unto the same Warderobe;' Harl. MS. 4780. γ. The spelling *robeux* furnishes the key to the solution of the word. It is an AF. plural form, from a sing. **robel*, i. e. rubble. Here **robel* is exactly the ME. *robel* (see **Rubble**), and the pl. *robeux* (or *robeaux*) became *robows*, as in the Prompt. Parv., and was easily corrupted into *rubbage* and *rubbish*, and even into *rubbrish* (with intrusive *r*). In this view, *rubbish* is the pl. of *rubble*, and was accordingly at first used in the same sense. δ. At what time the word *robeux* first appeared in English I have no exact means of knowing, but I find an earlier trace of it in the fact that an allied word was Latinised as *rubbōsa* (as if it were a neuter plural), in accordance with its plural form, as early as A. D. 1392 or 1393. Blount, in his Nomolexicon, s. v. *lastage*, cites an act against throwing rubbish into the Thames, in which are the words 'aut fimos, fimaria, sterquilinia, sordes, mucos, *rubbosa*, lastagium, aut alia sordida;' Claus. 16 Rich. II. dors. 11. And this *rubbōsa* answers to the AF. *robous*, *robouse*, rubbish, in the Liber Albus, pp. 579, 581. See further below.

RUBBLE, broken stones, rubbish. (Scand.) '*Rubble*, or rubbish;' Minsheu, ed. 1627. '*Rubble*, or rubbish of old houses;' also, 'carrie out *rubble*, as morter, and broken stones of old buildings;' Baret's Alvearie, ed. 1580. ME. *robell*; 'Oon parte of lyme and tweyn of *robell* have;' Palladius, bk. i. 340. Grammatically, *rubble* seems to be the singular of *robeux*, the old form of *rubbish*; see

above. The traces of the word are slight, but it seems to be of Scand. origin.—Norw. *rubl* (Ross), with the same sense as *rubb* (below); cf. Du. *robbelig*, rugged (Sewel) = prov. E. *rubbly*, lumpy, gritty.—Norw. *rubb* (Aasen), in the phr. *rubb og stubb*; Dan. *rub*, in the phr. *rub og stub*, 'bag and baggage;' including even articles of the least value; Icel. *rubbi*, *rubb*, rubbish, refuse. *Stub* = a stub, bit, piece. So prov. E. *stoup and roup*, 'entirely,' or 'every bit.' Prob. Dan. *rub* orig. meant 'a broken bit,' a lump.

RUBRIC, a direction printed in red. (F.—L.) ME. *rubryke*, St. Cuthbert, 1318 (Surtees Soc.). The *rubrics* in the Book of Common Prayer, and (earlier) in the Missal, &c., were so called from being usually written or printed in red letters. [ME. *rubriche*, Chaucer, C. T. 5928 (D 346); this is an OF. form; cf. *rubriche*, 'rudle, oaker;' Cot.]—F. *rubrique*, 'a rubrick; a speciall title or sentence of the law, written or printed in red;' Cot.—L. *rubrīca*, red earth; also a rubric, a title of law written in red. Formed as if from an adj. **rubricus*, extended from *rubri-*, from *ruber*, red; see **Ruby**.

RUBY, a red gem. (F.—L.) ME. *ruby*, P. Plowman, B. ii. 12. —OF. *rubi* (13th cent., Littré), also *rubis*, 'a ruby,' Cot. [The *s* is the old sign of the nom. case, and is still preserved in writing, though not pronounced.] Cf. Span. *rubi*, *rubin*, Port. *rubim*, Ital. *rubino*, a ruby; Late L. *rubīnus*. Allied to L. *rubeus*, red, *ruber*, red; cf. *rubēre*, to be red. Allied to Gk. ἐρυθρός, red; see **Rouge, Red**. Der. (from L. *rub-ēre*) *rub-esc-ent*, growing red, from the pres. part. of inceptive vb. *rubescere*, from F. *rubicunde*, very red (Cot.), which from L. *rubicundus*, very red, with suffixes *-c-* and *-undus*; *rub-r-ic*, q. v. Also *e-rub-esc-ent*.

RUCK (1), a fold, plait, crease. (Scand.) '*Ruck*, a fold or plait, made in cloth by crushing it;' Yorksh. Gloss., A. D. 1811 (E. D. S. Glos. B. 7).—Icel. *hrukka*, a wrinkle on the skin, or in cloth; cf. *hrokkinn*, curled, wrinkled, pp. of *hrökkva*, to recoil, give way, also to curl; Norw. *rukka*, a wrinkle. Cf. Swed. *rynka*, Dan. *rynke*, a wrinkle, also to gather, wrinkle. From Teut. base **hrenk* (Noreen). Der. *ruck-le*, to rumple (Halliwell).

RUCK (2), a heap. (Scand.) Cf. Norw. and MSwed. *ruka*, a heap; also Icel. *hraukr*, a rick. See **Rick**.

RUDD, a fish like a roach. (E.) 'A kind of bastard small Roach . . men call them *Ruds*;' I. Walton, Angler, ch. 17. Named from the deep red colour of the lower fins. Cf. AS. *rud-u*, redness; see **Ruddy**. MDan. *rude*, a rudd; Dan. *rudskalle*.

RUDDER, the instrument whereby a ship is steered. (E.) Orig. a paddle, for *rowing* as well as steering; hence the etymology. ME. *roder*, or (more usually) *rother*, Gower, C. A. i. 243; bk. ii. 2494; Allit. Poems, ed. Morris, B. 419. AS. *rōðer*, a paddle; 'Palmula, *rōðres blæd*' = blade of a paddle; 'Remus, *stēor-rōþer*,' lit. a steering-paddle; Voc. 167. 1, 166. 13. β. Here *rō-ðer* = rowing-implement; from AS. *rōw-an*, to row, with suffix *-ðer* (Idg. *-ter-*), denoting the agent or implement.✛Du. *roer* (for **roder*), an oar, rudder; Swed. *roder*, also contr. to *ror*; Dan. *ror* (for **roder*); G. *ruder*. See **Row** (2).

RUDDOCK, a red-breast. (E.) ME. *ruddok*, Chaucer, Parl. of Foules, l. 349. AS. *rudduc*; Voc. 131. 26; allied to *rud-ig*, ruddy. Hence W. *rhuddog*, Corn. *ruddoc*, a red-breast. See **Ruddy**.

RUDDY, reddish. (E.) ME. *rody*, P. Plowman, B. xiii. 99; *rodi*, Wyclif, Matt. xvi. 2. AS. *rudig*, in Napier's Glosses; formed with suffix *-ig* from *rud-*, weak grade of *rēodan*, to redden. Allied to AS. *rēad*, red; see **Red**. Cf. Icel. *roði*, redness, allied to *rauðr*, red. ¶ We also find AS. *rudu*, i. e. redness, applied to the complexion (of the face), Voc. 156. 19; this is ME. *rode*, complexion, Chaucer, C. T. 3317. Der. *ruddi-ly*; *ruddi-ness*, Wint. Tale, v. 3. 81. Also *ruddle*, a kind of red earth; spelt *ruddel* in Holland, tr. of Pliny, bk. xxxv. ch. 6. § 1.

RUDE, rough, uncivil, harsh. (F.—L.) ME. *rude*, Chaucer, C. T. 14814 (B 3998); Cursor Mundi, 23911.—F. *rude*, 'rude;' Cot.—L. *rudem*, acc. of *rudis*, rough, raw, rude, wild, untilled. Allied to L. *raudus*, rough ore; Russ. *ruda*, ore; Icel. *rauði*, red iron ore (from *rauðr*, red); Skt. *lōha-s*, iron. Allied to **Red**. Der. *rude-ly*, *rude-ness*; also *rudi-ment*, As You Like It, v. 4. 31 = F. *rudiment* (omitted by Cot., but in use in the 16th century, Littré), from L. *rudimentum*, a thing in the rough state, a first attempt; *rudiment-al*, *rudiment-ar-y*. Also *e-rud-ite*, *e-rud-it-ion*.

RUE (1), to be sorry for. (E.) For **hrue*, initial *h* being lost. ME. *rewen*, Chaucer, C. T. 1865 (A 1863); Havelok, 967. AS. *hrēowan*, Grein, ii. 104. ✛ OSax. *hrewan*; OHG. *hriuwan*, G. *reuen*. β. AS. *hrēowan* is a strong verb, with pt. t. *hrēaw*; so also OSax. *hrewan*, pt. t. *hrau*; Teut. type **hrewwan-*; pt. t. **hraw(w)*, to pity; whence also Icel. *hryggr*, grieved, afflicted, *hrygð*, ruth, grief, sorrow. Der. *rue-ful*, P. Plowman, B. xiv. 148; *rue-ful-ly*; *rue-ful-ness*, ME. *reoufulnesse*, Ancren Riwle, p. 368, l. 13. And see *ruth*.

RUE (2), a plant with bitter taste. (F.—L.—Gk.) ME. *rue*, Wyclif, Luke, xi. 42.—F. *rue*, 'rue, herb grace;' Cot.—L. *rūta*, rue; Luke, xi. 42.—Gk. ῥυτή, rue; a Peloponnesian word. ¶ The AS. *rūde* (Luke, xi. 42) is merely borrowed from L. *rūta*.

RUFF (1), a kind of frill, formerly much worn by both sexes. (E.) In Shak. Tam. of the Shrew, iv. 3. 56; Spenser, F. Q. i. 4. 14. Also as a verb: 'Whilst the proud bird, *ruffing* [ruffling] his fethers wyde;' F. Q. iii. 11. 32. '*Ruffe* of a shirt;' Levins. Pl. *ruffes*; Gascoigne, Steel Glas, l. 373. β. So called from its uneven surface; perhaps a shortened form of **Ruffle** (1). **Der.** *ruff* (2).

RUFF (2), the name of a bird. (E. ?) Said to be so named from the male having a *ruff* round its neck in the breeding season; see **Ruff** (1); which I doubt. The female is called a *reeve*, apparently formed by vowel-change; this is a very remarkable form, but has not been explained. Cf. 'The pheasant, partridge, godwit, *reeve*, *ruffe*, raile;' Herrick, A Panegyric to Sir L. Pemberton, l. 65. The AS. form should be **rōf*, fem. **rēfe*.

RUFF (3), a fish. (E.) ME. *ruffe*, Prompt. Parv., p. 438. Lit. 'rough;' from the spines on the back. Cf. Ital. *aspredo* (< L. *asper*, rough), 'a fish called a *ruffe*;' Florio.

RUFF (4), a game at cards. (F.) Mentioned in Cotgrave, and in Florio (1598); and see Nares. Now applied to the act of trumping instead of following suit, but orig. the name of a game (called also *trump*) like whist. Evidently a modification of F. *ronfle*, 'hand-ruffe, at cards;' *jouer à la ronfle*, 'to play at hand-ruffe, also to snore;' Cot. So also Ital. *ronfa*, 'a game at cards called ruffe or trumpe;' *ronfare*, 'to snort, snarle; also, to ruff or trump at cards;' Florio. Prob. of jocular origin, the trumping (when perhaps unexpected) being likened to a snarl, or the spitting of a cat; cf. *ronfamenti*, 'snortings, snarlings, or tuffings of a cat;' Florio. Of imitative origin; cf. Ital. *ronzare*, 'to humme or buzze,' Florio; Span. *roncar*, 'to snore, also, to threaten, boast, brag,' Cf. *brag* as the name of a game, *slam*, also a game, and *trump*, i. e. triumph.

RUFFIAN, a bully, violent, brutal fellow. (F.—Ital.—Teut.) 'A commune and notable *rufian* or *thefe*;' Sir T. Elyot, The Governour, b. ii. c. 12. § 7.—MF. *rufien*, *ruffien*, 'a bawd, a pandar,' Cot.—Ital. *ruffiano*, *roffiano*, 'a pandar, a ruffian, a swaggrer,' Florio.—Late L. type **rufflānus*; formed with L. suffix -*ānus* from Low G. *ruffel-n*, to act as pandar; see **Ruffle** (2). Cf. MDu. *roffen*, to pandar (Oudemans). **Der.** *ruffian-ly*, *ruffian-ism*.

RUFFLE (1), to wrinkle, disorder a dress. (E.) , I *ruffle* clothe or sylke, I bring them out of their playne foldynge, *Je plionne*;' Palsgrave. ME. *ruffelen*; '*Ruffelyn*, or snarlyn [i. e. to entangle or run into knots], *Innodo*, *illaqueo*;' Prompt. Parv. The pp. *ruffeld* occurs in the Cursor Mundi, 26391. The word is probably E.; it is parallel to MDu. *ruyffelen*, 'to ruffle, wrinckle, or crumple,' Hexham; cf. *ruyffel*, 'a wrinckle, a crumple, or a ruffle,' id. Also EFries. *ruffeln*, to pleat. The verb may be from the sb. *ruffle*; and both from Teut. **ruf-*, weak grade of Teut. **reufan-*, to break, tear; see **Reave**. β. The Lithuan. *ruple*, the rough bark on old trees, is a cognate word; so also is *rauple*, a rough scab or blister; both of which are allied to Lithuan. *rupas*, rough, uneven. See **Ruff** (1). **Der.** *ruffle*, sb., a wrinkle, a ruff (unless the vb. is from the sb.).

RUFFLE (2), to be noisy and turbulent, to bluster. (MDu.) 'To *ruffle* in the commonwealth of Rome;' Titus Andron. i. 313. Cf. 'the *ruffle* [bustle] . . . of court;' Shak. Lover's Complaint, 58. 'Twenty or more persons were sleyne in the *ruffle*;' Hall's Chron. Hen. VIII, an. 19. § 18. Nares has: 'A *ruffler*, a cheating bully, so termed in several acts of parliament,' particularly in one of the 27th year of Hen. VIII, as explained in Harman's Caveat, ed. Furnivall, p. 29. They were highway robbers, ready to use violence; any lawless or violent person was so named. It seems to have been a cant term, not in very early use; and borrowed, like several other cant terms, from the Low Countries.—MDu. *roffelen*, to pandar, of which the shorter form *roffen* is also found (Oudemans); so also Low G. *ruffeln*, to pandar, to reproach, *ruffeler*, a pimp, a person who carries on secret intrigues (Bremen Wörterbuch); prov. G. *ruffeln*, to pimp (Flügel); Dan. *ruffer*, a pandar, from Low G. *roffen*, *ruffen*, to be lewd (Lübben). β. The words *ruff-ler* and *ruff-ian* are closely related and mean much the same thing; see **Ruffian**. **Der.** *ruffl-er*, as above.

RUG, a coarse, rough woollen covering, a mat. (Scand.) 'Apparelled in diuers coloured *rugs*;' Hakluyt's Voyages, vol. ii. pt. ii. p. 87, last line but one. 'Irish *rug*,' Baret (1580).—Swed. *rugg*, rough entangled hair; cf. MSwed. *rugg-ig*, rough, hairy; Icel. *rögg*, shagginess. See Noreen, § 246. 2. The orig. sense of Swed. *rugg* was, doubtless, simply 'rough,' as it is cognate with Low G. *ruug*, Du. *ruig*, rough; EFries. *rüg*, rough, *ruge*, roughness, a rough side of a skin, *ruger*, a furry animal (as a cat). Allied to AS. *rūh* (gen. *rūwes*), rough; Skt. *rūksha-*, rough. And see **Rough**. **Der.** *rugg-ed*; also *rug-headed*, Rich. II, ii. 1. 156.

RUGGED, rough, shaggy. (Scand.) ME. *rugged*, Prompt. Parv. Chaucer has *ruggy*, C. T. 2885 (A 2883). The latter form

is from Swed. *ruggig*, rugged, rough, hairy; cf. *rugga*, to raise the nap on cloth, i. e. to roughen it.—Swed. *rugg*, rough entangled hair; orig. 'rough,' cognate with E. **Rough**, q. v. See also **Rug**. **Der.** *rugged-ly*, *rugged-ness*.

RUGOSE, full of wrinkles. (L.) The form *rugosous* is in Blount's Gloss., ed. 1674; Phillips has the sb. *rugosity*.—L. *rūgōsus*, wrinkled. —L. *rūga*, a wrinkle. Cf. Lith. *raukas*, a wrinkle, *runk-ù*, I grow wrinkled. Brugmann, ii. § 628. **Der.** *rugos-i-ty*.

RUIN, destruction, overthrow. (F.—L.) ME. *ruine*, Chaucer, C. T. 2465 (A 2463).—F. *ruine*, 'ruine;' Cot.—L. *ruina*, overthrow. —L. *ruere*, to fall down, tumble, sink in ruin, rush. Cf. Gk. ἐ-ρύειν, to drag, pull down; Brugmann, ii. § 529. **Der.** *ruin*, verb, Rich. II, iii. 4. 45; *ruin-ous*, Timon, iv. 3. 465, from F. *ruineux*, 'ruinous,' Cot.; *ruin-ous-ly*. Also *ruin-ate* (obsolete), Titus Andron. v. 3. 204.

RULE, a maxim, state, order, government. (F.—L.) ME. *reule*, Chaucer, C. T. 173. Earlier *riwle*, as in the *Ancren Riwle* = Rule of (female) Anchorites.—AF. *reule*, OF. *riule*, *reule*; mod. F. *règle*, a rule.—L. *regula*, a rule (whence also was borrowed AS. *regol*, a rule).—L. *regere*, to govern; see **Regent**. **Der.** *rule*, verb, ME. *reulen*, earlier *riwlen*, Ancren Riwle, p. 4; *rul-er*, *rul-ing*.

RUM (1), a kind of spirituous liquor. (E.) In Dampier's Voyages; Voyage to Campeachy, an. 1675; see quotation in R. [We find also Port. *rom*, Span. *ron*, Ital. *rum*, F. *rhum*; all from E.] Formerly *rumbo*, as in Smollett, Peregrine Pickle, ch. ii and ch. ix (1751). The earliest form was *rumbullion*. A MS. 'Description of Barbados' in Trin. Coll., Dublin, written ab. 1651, says:—'The chief fudling they make in the island is *Rumbullion*, alias *Kill-devil*, . . made of sugar-canes distilled, a hot, hellish, and terrible liquor.' Later, it was called *rumbowling* (Cent. Dict.), and then shortened to *rumbo*, and to *rum*. *Rumbullion* is a Devon. word meaning 'great tumult,' or disturbance; perhaps allied to prov. E. *rumpus*, an uproar, *rampage*, and *romp*; or else allied to E. *rumble*. See my Notes on E. Etym., p. 253; and N. Darnell Davis, in The Academy, Sept. 5, 1885. ¶ The F. name is *guildive*, a modification of E. *Kill-devil* (above).

RUM (2), strange, queer. (Hindi.) '*Rum*, gallant; a cant word;' Bailey's Dict., vol. i. ed. 1735. I suppose that *rum* means no more than 'Gypsy;' and hence would mean 'good' or 'gallant' from a Gypsy point of view, and 'strange' and 'suspicious' from an outsider's point of view. Hence *rome bouse*, wine, Harman's Caveat, ed. Furnivall, p. 83, spelt *rambooz* in Phillips; *rome mort*, the queen, id. p. 84 (where *mort* = a female). Cf. *rom*, a husband, a Gypsy, *róm-mani*, adj. Gypsy. The Gypsy word *rom* answers to the Hindi word *ḍom* (with initial cerebral *ḍ*); see English-Gipsy Songs, by Leland, Palmer, and Tuckey, pp. 2, 269. Cf. Skt. *ḍomba-* (with cerebral *ḍ*), 'a man of a low caste, who gains his livelihood by singing and dancing;' Benfey. Also Hindustāni *dom*, 'the name of a low caste, apparently one of the aboriginal races;' H. H. Wilson, Gloss. of Indian Terms, p. 147.

RUMB, RHUMB, a line for directing a ship's course on a map; a point of the compass. (F.—Span.—L.—Gk.) This is a very difficult word, both to explain and derive. The view which I here present runs counter to that in Littré and Scheler, but is recognized as possible by Diez. '*Rumb* or *Rhumb*, the course of a ship . . . also, one point of the mariner's compass, or 11¼ degrees . . . *Rumb-line*, a line described by the ship's motion on the surface of the sea, steering by the compass, so as to make the same, or equal angles with every meridian. These *rumbs* are spiral lines proceeding from the point where we stand, and winding about the globe of the earth, till they come to the pole, where at last they lose themselves; but in Mercator's charts, and the plain ones, they are represented by straight lines,' &c.; Phillips, ed. 1706. These lines are called *rumb-lines*. See *Rumb* in the Engl. Encyc. (Div. Arts and Sciences), where it is said to be a Portuguese word, and where we find: 'a *rumb* certainly came to mean any vertical circle, meridian or not, and hence any point of the compass. . . . To sail on a *rumb* is to sail continually on one course. Hence a *rumb-line* is a line drawn in [on?] the sphere, such as would be described by a moving point which always keeps one course; it is therefore the spiral of Mercator's projection, and is that which is also called the loxodromic course.' It is spelt *roomb*, *roumb*, and *roumbe* in Minsheu, ed. 1627.—F. *rumb*, 'a roomb, or point of the compass, a line drawn directly from wind to wind in a compasse, travers-boord, or sea-card;' Cot. He adds the phr. *voguer de rumb en rumb*, 'to saile by travers.'—Span. (and Port.) *rumbo*, 'a course, a way; *rumbo derecho*, the right course;' Minsheu's Span. Dict., ed. 1623; also, a point of the compass, intersection of the plane of the horizon, represented by the card of a compass, the course of a ship; Neuman. Cf. Port. *rumbo*, *rumo*, a ship's course; *quarto do rumo*, a point of the compass; Ital. *rombo*.—L. *rhombum*, acc. of *rhombus*, a magician's circle, a rhombus (Lewis).—Gk. ῥόμβος, a top, a magic wheel, whirling motion of a top, swoop of an eagle; also, a rhombus; see **Rhomb**.   β. In this view, the sense of circular or spiral motion comes first; then the delineation of such motion on a chart; and lastly, the sense of a point of a compass; which is the simple and natural order. Milton has the very word *rhomb* in the sense of the revolution of the sphere; see Paradise Lost, viii. 134, and uses *wheel* as a synonym. That the word arose among the early Spanish and Portuguese navigators, is in the highest degree probable. The view taken by Scheler and Littré seems to me obviously wrong; they refer F. *rumb* (also spelt *rum*) to the Du. *ruim*, E. *room*, on the ground that a *rumb* is the 'room' or space between two winds; thus taking the last sense first. I cannot find that the Du. *ruim* ever had this sense; indeed Sewel, as late as 1754, can only render *rumb* into Dutch by *een punt van't kompas*; and Hexham mentions no such use of the MDu. *ruym*. Perhaps Littré and Scheler are thinking of quite another matter, viz. the MF. *rum*, 'the hold of a ship,' Cot. This is certainly the Du. *ruim*, since Sewel gives the very phrase *ruim van een schip*, the hold of a ship, i.e. its room, capacity for stowage. Körting, § 8063. **Der.** *rumb-line*. **Doublet**, *rhomb*.

RUMBLE, to make a low and heavy sound. (E.) ME. *romblen*, to mutter, Chaucer, C. T. 14453 (B 3725); to rumble like thunder, Legend of Good Women, 1218. Cf. prov. E. *rommle*, to speak low or secretly (Halliwell); *rummle*, to rumble; id. The word *romblen* likewise stands for *romlen*, the *b* being excrescent, as usual after *m*; and the suffix *-len* has the usual frequentative force. Thus the word signifies 'to repeat the sound *rom* or *rum*;' from the base RUM, significant of a low sound; which is from √REU, to make a humming or lowing noise. Cf. Skt. *ru*, to hum, to bray; L. *ad-rūm-āre*, to make a murmuring noise (Festus); see **Rumour**.+Du. *rommelen*, to rumble, buzz; Low G. *rummeln, rumpeln*, to rumble; Dan. *rumle*, to rumble. And cf. Swed. *ramla*, to rattle, Ital. *rombare*, to rumble, hum, buzz; MDu. *rammelen*, 'to make a noise, or to rumble,' Hexham. **Der.** *rumble*, sb., *rumbl-ing*.

RUMINATE, to chew the cud, meditate. (L.) 'Let hym . . . *ruminate* it in his mynde a good space after;' Sir T. Elyot, Castel of Helth, b. iii. ch. 11.—L. *rūminātus*, pp. of *rūmināre* or *rūmināri*, to chew the cud, ruminate.—L. *rūmin-*, decl. stem of *rūmen*, the throat, gullet; cf. *rūmāre*, used (according to Festus) in the same sense as *rūmināre*. Cf. also L. *rūgire*, to roar, bray. From √REU, to hum, bray. See **Rumble, Rumour**. **Der.** *ruminat-ion*, As You Like It, iv. 1. 19, from L. acc. *rūminātiōnem*; also *rumin-ant*, from the stem of the pres. part. of *rūmināre*.

RUMMAGE, to search thoroughly among things stowed away. (E.; with F. *suffix*.) 'Searcheth his pockets, and takes his keyes, and so *rummageth* all his closets and trunks;' Howell, Famil. Letters, vol. i. sect. 5. let. last. This is altogether a secondary sense; the word is merely due to the sb. *room-age*, formed by suffix *-age* (of F. origin) from E. *room*, space. *Roomage* is a similar formation to *stowage*, and means much the same thing. It is an old nautical term for the close packing of things in a ship; hence was formed the verb to *roomage* or *romage*, i. e. to find room for or stow away packages; and the mariner who attended to this business was called the *roomager* or *romager*. β. The history of the word is in Hakluyt's Voyages. 'To looke and foresee substantially to the *roomaging* of the shippe;' vol. i. p. 274. 'They might bring away [in their ships] a great deale more then they doe, if they would take paine in the *romaging*;' vol. i. p. 308. 'The master must prouide a perfect mariner called a *romager*, to raunge and bestow all merchandize in such place as is conuenient;' vol. iii. p. 862. 'To *rummage* (sea-term) to remove any goods or luggage from one place to another, esp. to clear the ship's hold of any goods or lading, in order to their being handsomely stowed and placed; whence the word is us'd upon other occasions, for to rake into, or to search narrowly;' Phillips, ed. 1706. Spelt *rumidge* in ed. 1658. See further under **Room**. Cf. Du. *ruim*, room, also the hold of a ship; *ruimen*, to empty, clear, lit. to make room. **Der.** prov. E. *rummage*, litter, lumber, rubbish, as after a clearance.

RUMMER, a sort of drinking-glass. (W.Flem.—Du.) '*Rummer*, a sort of drinking-glass, such as Rhenish wine is usually drunk in; also, a brimmer, or glass of any liquor filled to the top;' Phillips, ed. 1706. 'Rhenish *rummers* walk the round;' Dryden, Ep. to Sir G. Etherege, l. 45.—W. Flem. *rummer, rommer* (De Bo); Du. *roemer, romer*, a wine-glass (Sewel); spelt *roomer* in Hexham; Low G. *römer*, a sort of large wine-glass (Brem. Wörterbuch). So also G. *römer*; Swed. *remmare*. [The G. *römer* also means 'Roman;' and some say that the glasses were so called because used in former times in the *Römersaal* at Frankfort, when they drank the new emperor's health; but this is an error; see Franck.] From Du. *roem*, boasting, praise; hence 'a glass to drink in praise of a toast;' Franck. Cf. G. *ruhm*, praise; OSax. *hröm*; also Icel. *hróðr*, praise; *hrós*, praise; Gk. κῆρυξ, a herald. And note O. Low G. *hrōmian*, to

praise (Gallée). **Der.** *rumkin, romekin*, W. Flem. *rummerken*, dimin. of *rummer* (above).

RUMOUR, report, current story. (F.—L.) ME. *rumour*, Chaucer, tr. of Boethius, b. ii. pr. 7, l. 81.—AF. *rumour*, Liber Albus, p. 462; F. *rumeur*, 'a rumor;' Cot.—L. acc. *rūmōrem*, from nom. *rūmor*, a noise, rumour, murmur. Cf. L. *rūmificāre*, to proclaim; *rūmitāre*, to spread reports; all from the base *rū-m-*, significant of a buzzing sound. = √REU, to make a humming or braying noise. See **Rumble**. **Der.** *rumour*, verb, Rich. III, iv. 2. 51.

RUMP, the end of the backbone of an animal with the parts adjacent. (Scand.) ME. *rumpe*, Prompt. Parv.—Icel. *rumpr*; Swed. *rumpa*; Dan. *rumpe*.+MDu. *rompe*, 'the bulke of a body or corps, or a body without a head;' Hexham; Du. *romp*; Low G. *rump*, trunk (of the body); G. *rumpf*. The orig. sense was 'stump;' cf. Norw. *ramp*, an old tree-stem. **Der.** *rump-steak*.

RUMPLE, to wrinkle, crease. (E.) Cotgrave explains F. *foupir* by 'to rumple, or crumple.' The ME. form is *rimplen*; *rimple* and *rumple* are allied forms, like *wrinkle* and prov. E. *runkle*. Of these, *rimple* is derived from the AS. *hrimpan*, to wrinkle, and *rumple* from *hrump-*, weak grade of the same; see further under **Ripple** (2). +MDu. *rompelen*, or *rompen*, 'to wrinckle,' Hexham; *rompel*, or *rimpel*, 'a wrinckle;' id. And cf. G. *rümpfen*, to crook, bend, wrinkle; OHG. *hrimfan*, strong vb. Teut. base **hremp-*; cf. OIrish *cromm*, W. *crwm*, bent. **Der.** *rumple*, sb.

RUN, to move swiftly, flee, flow, dart. (E.) ME. *rinnen, rennen*, pt. t. *ran*, pp. *runnen, ronnen*; Chaucer, C. T. 4098, 4103 (A 4100, 4105). The mod. E. verb has usurped the vowel of the pp. throughout, except in the pt. t. *ran*. By the transposition of *r*, we also find ME. *ernen, eornen*, to run; Ancren Riwle, pp. 42, 74, 80, 86, 332, 360. AS. *rinnan*, pt. t. *rann*, pp. *gerunnen*; Grein, ii. 382; also found in the transposed form *irnan, yrnan*, pt. t. *arn*; id. 146.+Du. *rennen*; Icel. *renna, rinna*; Dan. *rinde* (for **rinne*); Swed. *rinna*; Goth. *rinnan*; G. *rennen*. Teut. type **rennan-*, pt. t. **rann*, pp. **runnanoz*. See Brugmann, i. § 993; ii. § 654. **Der.** *run*, sb., Tam. Shrew, iv. 1. 16; *run-away*, Mids. Nt. Dr. iii. 2. 405; *runn-er*, *running*. Also *runn-el*, a small stream, Collins, Ode on the Passions, l. 63 (AS. *rynel*); *run*, a small stream. Also *renn-et* (1); old form also *runn-et*.

RUNAGATE, a vagabond. (F.—L.) In Ps. lxviii. 6, Prayer-Book version; Shak. Rich. III, iv. 4. 465. 'The A. V. has *rebellious*, as in Isaiah xxx. 1, which is quoted by Latimer (Remains, p. 434) in this form: "Wo be unto you, *runagate* children;" Bible Word-book. In the Coventry Mysteries, p. 384, it is written *renogat*: "Ys there ony *renogat* among us;"' id.   β. It so happens that *gate* in many E. dialects signifies *a way*; whilst at the same time the ME. verb *rennen* passed into the form *run*, as at present. Hence the ME. *renegat*, a renegade, was popularly supposed to stand for *renne a gate*, i. e. to run on the way, and was turned into *runagate* accordingly; esp. as we also have the word *runaway*. But it is certain that the orig. sense of ME. *renegat* was 'apostate' or 'villain;' see Chaucer, C. T. 5353 (B 934).—OF. *renegat*, 'a renegadoe, one that abjures his religion;' Cot.—Late L. *renegātus*, pp. of *renegāre*, to deny again, to deny the faith. See **Renegade**.   ¶ It is remarkable that when *renegate* had been corrupted into *runagate*, we borrowed the word over again, in the form *renegade*, from Span. *renegado*.

RUNDLET, RUNLET, a small barrel. (F.—L.) *Runlet* is a later form, corrupted from the older *rundelet* or *runlet*; spelt *rundlet* in Levins, ed. 1570. '*Rundelet*, or lytle pot, *orcula*.' Huloet (cited by Wheatley). ME. *rondelet* (1393); in Wylie, Hist. Hen. IV. iv. 179. '*Roundlet*, a certaine measure of wine, oyle, &c., containing 18½ gallons; An. 1. Rich. III. cap. 13; so called of his roundness;' Minsheu. Formed with dimin. suffix *-et* from OF. *rondelle, rondele*, a little tun (Godefroy); cf. *rondelle*, a buckler or round target (shield), in Cotgrave. This is again formed, with dimin. suffix *-ele, -elle*, from *ronde*, a circle, or from *rond*, round; see **Round**.

RUNE, one of the old characters used for inscriptions cut upon stone. (E.) ME. *rune*, counsel, a letter, Layamon, 25332, 25340, 32000; later *roun*, whence *roun* or *round* in Shakespeare; see **Roun**. AS. *rūn*, a rune, mystery, secret colloquy, whisper; Grein, ii. 385. The orig. sense seems to be 'whisper' or 'buzz;' hence, a low talk, secret colloquy, a mystery, and lastly a writing, because written characters were regarded as a mystery known to the few.+Icel. *rún*, a secret, a rune; Goth. *rūna*, a mystery, counsel; OHG. *rūna*, a secret, counsel, whence G. *raunen*, to whisper; OIrish *rūn*, W. *rhin*, a secret. Idg. type **rūnā*, fem. Cf. Gk. ἐρευνάω, I search out; ἔρευνα, f., an inquiry. **Der.** *run-ic, roun*.

RUNG, one of the rounds of a ladder. (E.) Also a staff (Halliwell); one of the stakes of a cart, a spar (Webster). ME. *ronge*, P. Plowman, B. xvi. 44; Chaucer, C. T. 3625 (where Tyrwhitt's edition wrongly has *renges* for *ronges*). AS. *hrung*, apparently a pole supporting the tilt of a cart; Grein, ii. 109.✚MDu. *ronge*, 'the beam upon which the coulter of a plough, or of a wagon rests;' Hexham; G. *runge*, a short thick piece of iron or wood, a pin, bolt; Goth. *hrugga* (=*hrunga*), a staff, Mark, vi. 8. [We find also Irish *ronga*, a rung, joining spar, Gael. *rong*, a joining spar, rib of a boat, staff; borrowed from English.] Cf. also Icel. *röng*, a rib in a ship. The sense seems to have been 'rounded staff.' Prob. connected by gradation with AS. *hring*, a ring; see **Ring**.

RUNNEL, a small stream; see **Run**.

RUNT, a bullock, heifer. (Du.) Florio (1598) has 'a *runt*, a bullocke;' s. v. *Giouenco*.—MDu. *rund*, 'a runt, a bullock,' Hexham; Du. *rund*. From Teut. base *hrunth*-, weak grade of *hrinth*-, *hrenth*-; see **Rother**. See my Notes on Eng. Etym., p. 255.

RUPEE, an Indian coin, worth about two shillings. (Hind.—Skt.) 'In silver, 14 *roopees* make a masse;' Sir T. Herbert, Travels, ed. 1665, p. 46; cf. p. 67. The *gold rupee* is worth about 29*s.*—Hindustāni *rūpiyah*, a rupee; Rich. Arab. and Pers. Dict. p. 753.—Skt. *rūpya-m*, neut. sb., silver, wrought silver, or wrought gold; orig. neut. of *rūpya-s*, adj., handsome.—Skt. *rūpa-m*, n., natural state, form, beauty. Allied by gradation to Skt. *varpas*, form, figure (Uhlenbeck).

RUPTURE, a bursting, breach, breakage. (F.—L.) 'No peryll of obstruction or *rupture*;' Sir T. Elyot, Castel of Helth, b. ii. c. 32.—F. *rupture*, 'a rupture, breach;' Cot.—L. *ruptura*, fem. of fut. part. of *rumpere* (pt. t. *rūpi*), to break, burst.—√REUP, to break, violate, rob; cf. Lithuan. *rupas*, rough, AS. *rēofan*, to reave, Skt. *rup*, to confound, *lup*, to break, destroy, spoil. Brugmann, i. § 466. See **Reave**. **Der.** *rupture*, verb. From the same root are *ab-rupt*, *bank-rupt*, *cor-rupt*, *dis-ruption*, *e-ruption*, *inter-rupt*, *ir-ruption*, *pro-ruption*, *rote* (1), *route*, *rout*, *rut*. Also *loot*; and perhaps *ruff*, *ruffle* (1).

RURAL, belonging to the country. (F.—L.) 'In a person *rurall* or of a very base lynage;' Sir T. Elyot, The Governour, b. i. c. 3. § 3. ME. *rurall*, Lydgate, Assembly of Gods, 1724.—F. *rural*, 'rurall;' Cot.—L. *rūrālis*, rural.—L. *rūr*-, for *rūs* (gen. *rūris*), the country; see **Rustic**. **Der.** *rural-ly*, *rural-ise*.

RUSA, a kind of deer. (Malay.) Malay *rūsa*, a deer; see **Babirusa**.

RUSE, a trick. (F.—L.) Used by Ray; Works of Creation, p. 137 (Cent. Dict.). Phillips, ed. 1706, gives the adj. *rusy*, full of tricks.—F. *ruse*, a stratagem.—F. *ruser*, 'to beguile, use tricks;' Cot. β. This F. *ruser* is a contraction of OF. *reüser*, to refuse, recoil, retreat, escape; hence, to use tricks for escaping (Burguy).—Late L. type *refūsāre*, to refuse (Hatzfeld, Körting, § 7897). See **Refuse**. ¶ But Scheler derives it from L. *recūsāre*, to refuse, with loss of *c* as in OF. *seür*, F. *sûr*, from L. *secūrus*. See **Recusant**.

RUSH (1), to move forward violently. (E.) ME. *ruschen*, *rushen*, Chaucer, C. T. 1641; Allit. Poems, ed. Morris, B. 368; Sir Gawayn and the Grene Knight, 2204. Partly from AS. *hryscan*, to rustle shrilly, roar (as wind); Napier's Glosses, i. 3740, 5006.✚MSwed. *ruska*, to rush; Ihre gives the example: 'Tha kommo the alle *ruskande* inn,' then they all came rushing in; Chron. Rhythm. p. 40. This is clearly connected with MSwed. *rusa*, to rush; whence E. **Rouse** (1), q. v. Another sense of MSwed. *ruska* (like G. *rauschen*) is to rustle. So also Low G. *rusken*, (1) to rustle, (2) to rush about, Bremen Wörterbuch; cf. Du. *ruischen*, to murmur as water, to rustle; Pomeran. *ruuschen*, to make a noise in running about. **Der.** *rush*, sb.

RUSH (2), a round-stemmed plant of grass-like aspect, common in wet ground. (E.) Prov. E. *rish*, *resh*, *rash*, ME. *rusche*, *rische*, *resche*, P. Plowman, B. iii. 141. AS. *risce*, *resce*, *ræsc*, Gloss. to A. S. Leechdoms; oldest form *risc* (O. E. Texts). Cf. Low G. *rusk*, *risch*, a rush, Brem. Wörterbuch; Du. *rusch*, rush; EFries. *rüske*; NFries. *rusken*, pl. rushes. β. Some think these are non-Teutonic words, and perhaps merely borrowed from L. *ruscum*, butcher's broom; yet the sense is very different, and *rash*, *resh*, cannot come from *ruscum*. γ. Rather cf. OHG. *rasc*, rash, quick, MHG. *resch*, quick, MHG. *risch*, quick, *rosc*, quick, lively; EFries. *rask*, rash, quick, *risk*, quick, upright, slender; Low G. *rusch*, quick (Lübben). I take *rush* to be a native name for a plant of quick, upright, slender growth. See **Rash**. ¶ Not connected with Goth. *raus*, G. *rohr*, a reed. **Der.** *rush-y*. Also *bul-rush*, ME. *bulrysche*, Prompt. Parv. p. 244; in which word the first part is prob. Icel. *bolr*, *bulr*, a stem, trunk, Dan. *bul*, trunk, stem, shaft of a column, Swed. *bål*, a trunk, so that the sense is 'stem-rush,' from its long stem; see **Bulwark**, **Bole**; cf. *bull-weed* (=*bole-weed*, *ball-weed*), knapweed; *bulrush* often means the reed-mace. Also *rush-candle*, Tam. Shrew, iv. 5. 14; *rush-light*.

RUSK, a kind of light, hard cake or bread. (Span.) 'The lady sent me divers presents of fruit, sugar, and *rusk*;' Ralegh, cited by Todd (no reference). 'A basket-full of white *ruske*;' Hakluyt, Voy. ii. pt. 1. p. 186.—Span. *rosca de mar*, sea-rusks, a kind of

---

biscuit, Meadows; *rosca*, a roll of bread, Minsheu, ed. 1623. Minsheu also has *rosquete*, a pancake, *rosquilla*, 'a clue of threed, a little roll of bread, also lying round like a snake.' Cf. Port. *rosca*, the winding of a serpent, a screw; *fazer roscas*, to wriggle. Thus the *rusk* was orig. a twist, a twisted roll of bread. Origin unknown (Diez).

RUSSET, reddish-brown; a coarse country dress. (F.—L.) ME. *russet*, P. Plowman, A. ix. 1; B. viii. 1.—AF. *russet*, Stat. Realm, i. 381 (1363); 'ma robe de *russet*,' Royal Wills, p. 30 (1360); OF. *rosset*, *rousset* (Godefroy); MF. *rousset*, 'russet, brown, ruddy;' Cot. Hence applied to a coarse brown rustic dress. Dimin. of F. *roux* (fem. *rousse*), 'reddish;' Cot.—L. *russus*, reddish. β. L. *russus* is from a type *rudzho*- (Brugmann, i. § 759); from the base *rudh* appearing in Gk. ἐ-ρυθ-ρός, red; see **Red, Ruddy**. **Der.** *russet-ing*, a russet apple.

RUST, a reddish-brown coating on iron exposed to moisture. (E.) Prov. E. *roust* (Yks.). ME. *rust*, Wyclif, Matt. vi. 19, 20; *roust*, Trevisa, tr. of Higden, iii. 445. AS. *rūst*, rust; whence *rūstig*, rusty, Ælfred, tr. of Orosius, b. v. c. 15. § 4.✚Du. *roest*; Dan. *rust*; Swed. *rost*; G. *rost*. Teut. type *rūsto*-; for Idg. *rudhs-to*-, from Teut. base *rud*-, Idg. base *rudh*-; see **Ruddy**. Brugmann, i. § 759 (note). Allied to AS. *rud-u*, ruddiness, and to E. *ruddy* and *red*; cf. Icel. *ryð*, rust, lit. redness; MHG. *rot*, rust, allied to G. *roth*, red. So also Lithuan. *rudis*, rust, *rūdas*, reddish; W. *rhwd*, rust. See **Red**. **Der.** *rust*, verb; *rust-y*, AS. *rūstig*, as above; *rust-i-ly*, *rust-i-ness*.

RUSTIC, belonging to the country. (F.—L.) Spelt *rusticke*, Spenser, F. Q. introd. to b. iii. st. 5.—F. *rustique*, 'rusticall;' Cot.—L. *rusticus*, belonging to the country; formed with double suffix *-ti-cus* from *rūs*, the country. β. The L. *rūs* is thought to be allied to Russ. *raviina*, a plain, Zend *ravan*, a plain, and to E. *room*; see **Room**. **Der.** *rustic-al-ly*, *rustic-ate*, *rustic-at-ion*; *rustic-i-ty*, from F. *rusticité*, 'rusticity,' Cot. And see *rur-al*, *roister-ing*.

RUSTLE, to make a low whispering sound. (Low G.) In Shak. Meas. for Meas. iv. 3. 38. The form is frequentative; and it seems best to connect it with the base *rus*-; see **Rouse**. Du. dial. *russeln*, to rustle as clothes do (Molema); Low G. and Pomeran. *russeln*, to rustle. Also MDu. *ruyselen*, 'to rustle,' Hexham; also spelt *reuselen*. **Der.** *rustle*, sb.; *rustl-ing*.

RUT (1), a track left by a wheel. (F.—L.) 'And as from hills rain-waters headlong fall, That all ways eat huge *ruts*;' Chapman, tr. of Homer, Iliad, iv. 480. The word is merely a less correct spelling of *route*, i. e. a track.—F. *route*, 'a rutt, way, path, street, . . trace, tract, or footing,' Cot. See **Route**. **Der.** *rut*, verb.

RUT (2), to copulate, as deer. (F.—L.) ME. *rutyen*, *rutien*; P. Plowman, C. xiv. 146; cf. *in rotey tyme*=in rut-time, id. B. xi. 329. Like other terms of the chase, it is of Norman-French origin. The ME. *rotey* answers to OF. *ruté*, spelt *ruité* in Cotgrave; he gives *venaison ruiteé*, venison that's killed in rut-time. The verb *rutien* is formed from the sb. *rut*.—F. *rut* (so spelt even in the 14th century, Littré), also *ruit*, as in Cotgrave, who explains it by 'the rut of deer or boars, their lust, and the season wherein they ingender.'—L. type *rugitum*, for L. *rūgītum*, acc. of *rūgītus*, the roaring of lions; hence, the noise of deer in rut-time. Cf. F. *ruir*, 'to roar,' Cot., from L. *rūgīre*, to roar.—√REU, to make a noise, whence also Lithuan. *rùja*, rutting-time; see **Rumour**.

RUTH, pity, compassion. (Scand.) ME. *reuthe*, *rewthe*, Chaucer, C. T. 916 (A 914); *reouthe*, Ancren Riwle, p. 32, l. 8; p. 54, l. 12. Formed like the Scand. sb., but with a vowel borrowed from the E. verb *to rue*.—Icel. *hryggð*, *hrygð*, affliction, sorrow. Cf. Icel. *hryggr*, grieved, sorrowful.—Teut. base HREU, to grieve, appearing in AS. *hrēowan*, to rue; see **Rue** (1). **Der.** *ruth-less*, Meas. for Meas. iii. 2. 121; *ruth-ful*, Troilus V. 3. 48.

RYE, a kind of grain. (E.) ME. *reye*, Chaucer, C. T. 7328 (D 1746); *ruȝe*, Polit. Songs, ed. Wright, p. 152. AS. *ryge*, Voc. 47·4.✚Du. *rogge*; Icel. *rûgr*; Dan. *rug*; Swed. *råg*; G. *roggen*, OHG. *rocco*. Further allied to Lithuan. pl. sb. *ruggei*, rye; OPruss. *rugis*; Russ. *roj(e)*, rye. Streitberg, § 131. **Der.** *rye-grass*.

RYOT, a Hindoo cultivator or peasant. (Hind.—Arab.) Hind. *rāiyat*, H. H. Wilson; p. 433. From Arabic. See Yule. The same word as **Rayah**, q. v.

SA—SE

SABAOTH, hosts, armies. (Heb.) In phr. 'the Lord of *Sabaoth*;' Rom. ix. 29; James, v. 4.—Heb. *tsebāōth*, armies; pl. of *tsābā*, an army.—Heb. *tsābā*, to go forth as a soldier.

SABBATH, the day of rest. (L.—Gk.—Heb.) ME. *sabat*, Wyclif, Mark, ii. 27; Cursor Mundi, 11997.—L. *sabbatum*.—Gk.

σάββατον.—Heb. *shabbāth*, rest, sabbath, sabbath-day.—Heb. *shabbath*, to rest from labour. ¶ The mod. E. word is a compromise between *sabbat* (the L. form) and *shabbath* (the Heb. form). Der. *Sabbat-ar-i-an*, *sabbat-ic-al*.

SABLE, an animal of the weasel kind, with dark or black fur; also, the fur. (F.—Slavonic.) ME. *sable*, Chaucer, Compl. of Mars, 284; the adj. *sabeline* occurs much earlier, O. Eng. Homilies, ed. Morris, i. 181, l. 362.—OF. *sable*, the sable (Burguy); 'the colour sables, or black, in blazon;' Cot. Cf. Low L. *sabelum*, the sable; *sabelinus*, sable-fur, whence the OF. *sebelin*, ME. *sabeline*; the mod. F. *zibeline* (from Ital.), properly an adj., is also used for the animal itself. Of Slavonic origin.—Russ. *sobol(e)*, the sable, also a boa or fur tippet; Pol. *sobol*. Cf. Turk. *samūr*, sable; Rich. Dict. p. 943. **Der.** *sable*, sb. and adj. The best fur being black, *sable* also means black; in heraldry; see Hamlet, ii. 2. 474, iii. 2. 137, iv. 7. 81. So 'sable and asure;' Caxton, tr. of Reynard, c. 32, ed. Arber, p. 81 (1481). ¶ It is sometimes said that the name of the sable is taken from *Siberia*, where it is found. The Russ. *sobole*, a sable, does not resemble *Sibire*, Siberia; nor does the adj. form *sabeline* (in OF.) approach *Sibirskii* or *Sibiriak'*, Siberian.

SABOT, a wooden shoe. (F.) From F. *sabot*, a word of unknown origin.

SABRE, SABER, a kind of sword. (F.—G.—MGk. ?) A late word. '*Sable* or *Sabre*, a kind of simetar, hanger, or broad sword;' Phillips, ed. 1706; MDu. *sabel*, 'a sable, or short broad sword;' Hexham.—F. *sabre*, a sabre.—G. *säbel* (formerly also *sabel*), a sabre, falchion. β. Thus Diez, who says that at least the F. form was borrowed from German; cf. Ital. *sciabla*, *sciabola*, Span. *sable*. γ. He adds that the G. word was also borrowed; and compares Hungarian *száblya*, Servian *sablja*, Wallachian *sabie*, a sabre. All (according to Diez) from MGk. ζαβός, crooked. I find Hung. *szablya*, a sabre, *szabni*, to cut, *szabo*, a cutter, in Dankovsky, Magyar Lexicon, 1833, p. 327; at p. 862, Dankovsky considers *szabni*, to cut, to be of Wallachian origin. **Der.** *sabre-tash*, F. *sabretache*, from G. *säbeltasche*, a sabretash, loose pouch hanging near the sabre, worn by hussars (Flügel); from G. *säbel*, a sabre, and *tasche*, a pocket.

SACCHARINE, sugar-like. (F.—L.—Gk.—Skt.) In Todd's Johnson.—F. *saccharin*, 'of sugar;' Cot. Formed with suffix *-in* (=L. *-inus*) from L. *sacchar-on*, sugar (Pliny).—Gk. σάκχαρον, sugar.—Pāli *sakkharā*, for Skt. *çarkarā*, candied sugar; see **Sugar**.

SACERDOTAL, priestly. (F.—L.) In Minsheu, ed. 1627.—F. *sacerdotal*, 'sacerdotall;' Cot.—L. *sacerdōtālis*, belonging to a priest.—L. *sacerdōt-*, stem of *sacerdōs*, a priest; lit. 'presenter of offerings or sacred gifts' (Corssen).—L. *sacer*, sacred; and *dare*, to give (Bréal); cf. L. *dōs* (gen. *dōtis*), a dowry, from the same verb. The fem. form *sacerdōta*, a priestess, occurs in an inscription. See **Sacred** and **Date** (1). Brugmann, i. § 241 (a). **Der.** *sacerdotal-ly, -ism*.

SACHEM, a W. Indian chief. (Amer. Indian.) In Phillips (1658). 'The Massachusets call .. their kings *sachemes*;' Capt. Smith, Works, ed. Arber, p. 939. See **Sagamore**.

SACK (1), a bag. (L.—Gk.—Heb.—Egyptian.) ME. *sak*, Chaucer, C. T. 4019 (A 4021). AS. *sacc*, Gen. xlii. 25, 28.—L. *saccus*.—Gk. σάκκος.—Heb. *saq*, stuff made of hair-cloth, sack-cloth; also, a sack for corn. β. A borrowed word in Hebrew, and prob. of Egyptian origin; cf. Coptic *sok*, sack-cloth, Gen. xxxvii. 34, Matt. xi. 21; see Peyron's Coptic Lexicon. E. Müller cites *sak* as being the Æthiopic form. γ. This remarkable word has travelled everywhere, together (as I suppose) with the story of Joseph; the reason why it is the same in so many languages is because it is, in them all, a borrowed word from Hebrew. We find Du. *zak*, G. *sack*, Icel. *sekkr*, Swed. *säkk*, Dan. *sæk*, Goth. *sakkus* (sack-cloth, Matt. xi. 21), Ital. *sacco*, Span. and Port. *saco*, F. *sac*, Irish and Gael. *sac*, W. *sach*. And see **Sack** (2). **Der.** *sack-cloth*, Gen. xxxvii. 34; ME. *sakcloth*, Lydgate, Assembly of Gods, 290; *sack-ing*, cloth of which sacks are made, coarse stuff; *sack-full*. Also *sack* (2), q.v.; *satch-el*, q.v. **Doublet**, *sac*, a bag or receptacle for a liquid, borrowed from F. *sac*.

SACK (2), plunder; as a verb, to plunder. (F.—L.—Gk.—Heb.—Egyptian.) 'The plenteous houses *sackt*;' Surrey, Ecclesiastes, c. v.; l. 45. Formed from the sb. *sack*, pillage. 'And Helen, that to utter *sack* both Greece and Troïe brought;' Turbervile, Disprayse of Women, st. 34.—F. *sac*, 'a sack, waste, ruine, havock, spoile;' Cot. Cf. F. *saccager*, 'to sack, pillage;' Cot.; also MF. *sacquer*, 'to draw hastily, to pull out speedily or apace;' Cot. We also find Low L. *saccāre*, to put into a bag; a common word; and Low L. *saccus*, a garment, robe, treasure, purse. β. There seems to be little doubt that the F. *sac*, pillage, is connected with, and due to, the F. *sac*, a sack, from L. *saccus*; see **Sack** (1). The simplest solution is that in Wedgwood, 'from the use of a sack in removing plunder;' though the sense is probably rather metaphorical

than exact. In the same way we talk of *bagging*, i.e. pilfering a thing, or of *pocketing* it, and of *baggage* as a general term, whether bags be actually used or not. Thus Hexham gives MDu. *zacken*, 'to put in a sack, or fill a sack;' *zacken ende packen*, 'to put up bagg and baggage, or to trusse up.' Cotgrave has: '*à sac, à sac*, the word whereby a commander authorizeth his souldiers to sack a place.' γ. The use of MF. *sacquer* (OF. *sachier*) is remarkable, as it seems to express, at first sight, just the opposite to packing up; but perhaps it meant, originally, to search in a sack, to pull out of a purse; for the sacking of a town involves the two processes: (1) that of taking them out of their old receptacles, and (2) that of putting them into new ones; note the Low L. *saccus* in the senses of 'treasure' and 'purse.' Burguy notes that the OF. *desacher*, lit. to draw out of a sack, was used in the same way as the simple verb. δ. It deserves to be added that Cotgrave gives 17 proverbs involving the word *sac*, clearly proving its common use in phrases. One of them is: '*On luy a donné son sac et ses quilles*, he hath his passport given him, he is turned out to grazing, said of a servant whom his master hath put away;' hence the E. phrase, 'to give one the sack.' And again: '*Acheter un chat en sac*, to buy a pig in a poak.'

SACK (3), the name of an old Spanish wine. (F.—L.) See the account in Nares. He notices that it was also called *seck*, a better form: 'It is even called *seck*, in an article cited by bp. Percy from an old account-book of the city of Worcester: "Anno Eliz. xxxiiij. Item, for a gallon of claret wine, and seck, and a pound of sugar."' Spelt *secke*, A. Borde, Dyetary, ch. x. ed. Furnivall, p. 255 (1542). By *Sherris sack*, Falstaff meant 'sack from Xeres,' our sherry; see **Sherry**. *Sack* was a Spanish wine made from grapes dried by the sun, and so *sweet* rather than *dry* in the mod. E. sense. See Minsheu; and note to Tw. Night, ed. W. A. Wright; A. ii. sc. 3. 178.—F. *sec*, dry; in the phrase *vin sec*; Sherwood (in his index to Cotgrave) has: '*Sack* (wine), vin d'Espagne, vin sec.' Cf. Span. *seco*, dry.—L. *siccum*, acc. of *siccus*, dry. ¶ We may note Du. *sek*, sack, a sort of wine (Sewel), as illustrating the fact that *sack* stands for *seck*; this also is from F. *sec*. So also G. *sekt*, sack; Swed. *seck* (Widegren).

SACKBUT, a kind of wind instrument. (F.—L.—Gk.—Chaldee.) In Dan. iii. 5. The *sack-but* resembled the modern trombone, and was a wind instrument; but the word is used to translate the Chald. *sabbekā* (with initial *samech*), Gk. σαμβύκη, L. *sambūca*, which was a stringed instrument. And these forms must be regarded as giving the real origin of the E. word, which was borrowed from French. Thus Ascham has: 'lutes, harpes, all maner of pypes, barbitons, *sambukes*;' Toxophilus, ed. Arber, p. 39. And in Dan. iii. 5, Wyclif has *sambukes*.—OF. *sambuque* (Roquefort).—L. *sambūca*.—Gk. σαμβύκη.—Chald. *sabbekā* (as above); Dan. iii. 5. β. Sir T. Elyot mentions *sackbottes* as wind instruments, Castel of Helth, b. ii. ch. 33.—F. *saquebute*, a sackbut, trombone, Littré; a popular perversion, due to confusion with OF. *saqueboute*, which was really a lance with a hook, for pulling a man off his horse (Godefroy), and then applied to a trombone from its being drawn in and thrust out (F. *sacquer*, to pull, *bouter*, to push). γ. A similar perversion occurs in Span. *sacabuche* (nautical word), a tube or pipe which serves as a pump; also, a sackbut (Neuman); as if from Span. *sacar*, to draw out, with reference to the tube of the instrument; and *buche*, the maw, crop, or stomach of an animal, and, colloquially, the human stomach. Hence the suggestion in Webster, that *sacabuche* means 'that which exhausts the stomach or chest;' a name possibly given (in popular etymology) from the exertion used in playing it.

SACRAMENT, a solemn religious rite, the eucharist. (L.) ME. *sacrament*, Chaucer, C. T. 9576 (E 1702).—L. *sacrāmentum*, an engagement, military oath; in ecclesiastical writers, a mystery, sacrament. Formed with suffix *-mentum* from *sacrāre*, to dedicate, consecrate, render sacred or solemn.—L. *sacr-*, for *sacer*, sacred; see **Sacred**. **Der.** *sacrament-al, sacrament-al-ly*.

SACRED, made holy, religious. (F.—L.) *Sacred* is the pp. of ME. *sacren*, to render holy, consecrate, a verb now obsolete. We find *sacreth* = consecrates, in Ancren Riwle, p. 268, l. 5. The pp. *i-sacred*, consecrated, occurs in Rob. of Glouc. p. 330 (l. 6762), where the prefix *i-* (=AS. *ge-*) is merely due to the Southern dialect. 'He was ... *sacryd* or enoynted emperour of Rome;' Fabyan's Chron. cap. 155, last line. [Hence too *sacring-bell*, Hen. VIII, iii. 2. 295.]—OF. *sacrer*, 'to consecrate;' Cot.—L. *sacrāre*, to consecrate.—L. *sacr-*, for *sacer*, sacred, holy.—L. base *sac-*, appearing in a nasalised form in *sancire*, to render inviolable, establish, confirm; see **Saint**. Brugmann, ii. § 744. **Der.** *sacred-ly, sacred-ness*; and see *sacra-ment, sacri-fice, sacri-lege, sacrist-an, sext-on*; *sacer-dotal*; *con-secrate, de-secrate, ex-ecrate, ob-secrate*; *sanct-ify*.

SACRIFICE, an offering to a deity. (F.—L.) ME. *sacrifise*, Ancren Riwle, p. 138, ll. 9, 11; also *sacrifice*.—F. *sacrifice*, 'a sacrifice;' Cot.—L. *sacrificium*, a sacrifice, lit. a rendering sacred; cf. *sacrificāre*, to sacrifice.—L. *sacri-*, for *sacro-*, from *sacer*, sacred; and *facere*, to make; see **Sacred** and **Fact**. **Der.** *sacrifice*, vb., *sacrific-er*; *sacrific-er*; *sacrifici-al*.

SACRILEGE, profanation of what is holy. (F.—L.) ME. *sacrilege*, Gower, C. A. ii. 374, ll. 5, 14; bk. v. 7165, 7174.—MF. *sacrilege*, 'a sacriledge, or church-robbing;' Cot.—L. *sacrilegium*, the robbing of a temple, stealing of sacred things.—L. *sacrilegus*, a sacrilegious person, one who steals from a temple.—L. *sacri-*, for *sacro-*, from *sacer*, sacred; and *legere*, to gather, steal, purloin; see **Sacred** and **Legend**. **Der.** *sacrileg-i-ous*, Macb. ii. 3. 72, a coined word; *sacrileg-i-ous-ly*, *-ness*.

SACRISTAN, SEXTON, an officer in a church who has charge of the sacred vessels and vestments. (F.—L.) The corruption of *sacristan* into *sexton* took place so early that it is not easy to find the spelling *sacristan*, though it appears in Blount's Glossographia, ed. 1674. Cf. ME. *sekesteyn* in Rob. of Brunne, Handlyng Synne, l. 11100. The duties of the *sacristan* have suffered alteration; he is now the grave-digger rather than the keeper of the vestments. The form *sexteyn* is in Chaucer, C. T. 13942 (B 3126); the collateral form *Saxton* survives as a proper name; I find it in the Clergy List for 1873.—F. *sacristain*, 'a sexton, or vestry-keeper, in a church;' Cot. Formed as if from Late L. **sacristānus*, but the usual word is simply *sacrista*, without the suffix; cf. '*Sexteyne*, Sacrista,' Prompt. Parv.; and see Ducange. Formed with suffix *-ista* (= Gk. *-ιστης*) from L. *sacr-*, from *sacer*, sacred; see **Sacred**. **Der.** *sacrist-y*, from F. *sacristie*, 'a vestry, or sextry in a church,' Cot.; cf. '*Sextrye*, Sacristia,' Prompt. Parv.

SAD, heavy, serious, sorrowful. (E.) '*Sadde*, tristis;' Levins. ME. *sad*, with very various meanings; Halliwell explains it by ' serious, discreet, sober, heavy (said of bread), dark (of colour), heavy, solid, close, firm (said of iron and stone).' The W. *sad* means ' firm, steady, discreet;' and may have been borrowed from E. during the ME. period. β. But the oldest meaning is ' sated.' Thus, in Layamon, 20830, we have ' *sad* of mine londe ' = sated, or tired, of my land. Hence seem to have resulted the senses of satisfied, fixed, firm, steadfast, &c.; see examples in Stratmann and in the Glossary to Will. of Palerne, &c. The mod. E. *sad* is from the sense of sated, tired, weary. AS. *sæd*, sated, satiated; Grein, ii. 394.+OSax. *sad*, sated; Icel. *saðr*, old form *saðr*, sated, having got one's fill; Goth. *saths*, full, filled, sated; G. *satt*, satiated, full, satisfied, weary. γ. All from the Teut. pp. type **sa-doz*, sated, Fick, iii. 318. Cognate words are found in Lithuan. *sotus*, satiated; Russ. *suitost'*, satiety; L. *satur*, sated, also deep-coloured (like E. *sad*-coloured), well filled, full; OIrish *sā-ith*, satiety, *sa-thech*, sated; Gk. *ā-μεναι*, to satiate. From √SA, SA, to satiate; Brugmann, i. § 196. See **Satiate, Satisfy**. ¶ In no way connected with *set*, which is quite a different word; nor with L. *sēdāre*, which is allied to E. *set*. **Der.** *sad-ly*, *-ness*. Also *sadd-en*, verb, from ME. *sadden*, to settle, confirm, P. Plowman, B. x. 242; cf. AS. *gesadian*, to fill (Grein), AS. *sadian*, to feel weary or sad, Ælfred, tr. of Boethius, cap. xxxix. § 4.

SADDLE, a leathern seat, put on a horse's back. (E.) ME. *sadel* (with one *d*), Chaucer, C. T. 2164 (A 2162). AS. *sadol*; Grein, ii. 387.+Du. *zadel*; Icel. *söðull*; Swed. and Dan. *sadel*; G. *sattel*; OHG. *satul*. Cf. also Russ. *siedlo*; L. *sella* (for **sed-la*). β. Teut. type **saduloz*. The form of the word is abnormal; some suppose it not to be Teutonic, but borrowed from some other Idg. language, probably Slavonic. Cf. Lower Sorbian *sodlo*, a saddle; OSlav. *sedlo*, a saddle. We may safely refer it, and all its cognates (or borrowed forms), to √SED, to sit; cf. (Vedic) Skt. *sad*, to sit down, Skt. *sadas*, a seat, abode. **Der.** *saddle*, verb, AS. *sadelian*, Ælfric's Grammar, ed. Zupitza, p. 165, l. 10; *saddl-er*, *saddl-er-y*; *saddle-bow*, ME. *sadel-bowe*, Proverbs of Alfred, l. 229.

SADDUCEE, the name of a Jewish sect. (L.—Gk.—Heb.) The ME. pl. *Saduceis* is in Wyclif, Deeds [Acts], xxiii. 8; &c.—L. pl. *Sadducæi*.—Gk. pl. Σαδδουκαῖοι.—Heb. pl. *tsedūqīm*, in the Mishna; see Smith, Concise Dict. of the Bible. Supposed to mean 'the righteous.' From the Heb. root *tsādaq*, to be just.

SAFE, unharmed, secure, free from danger. (F.—L.) ME. *sauf*, Will. of Palerne, 868, 1329; we also find the phr. *sauf and sound*, id. 868, 2816.—F. *sauf*, 'safe;' Cot.—L. *saluum*, acc. of *saluus*, whole, safe. Brugmann, i. § 860 c. **Der.** *safe-ly*, *safe-ness*; *safe*, sb.; *safe-conduct*, Hen. V, i. 2. 297, ME. *sauf conduit*, Gower, C. A. iii. 160; bk. v. 994; *safe-guard*, Rich. III, v. 3. 259. ME. *sauf-garde*, Caxton, tr. of Reynard, ch. 3; *vouch-safe*, q. v. Also *safe-ty*, K. John, iii. 3. 16, suggested by F. *sauvete*, 'safety,' Cot., from Late L. acc. *salutātem*. And see **Salvation, Sage** (2), **Salute, Save**.

SAFFRON, the name of a plant. (F.—Arab.) 'Maked geleu mid *saffran*' = made yellow with saffron; O. Eng. Homilies, ed. Morris, ii. 163, l. 32.—AF. *saffran*, Liber Albus, p. 224; F. *safran*,

saffran, saffron; Cot.—Arab. *za'farān*, saffron; Palmer's Pers. Dict. col. 321.

SAG, to droop, be depressed. (Scand.) Prov. E. *sag*, *seg*. ME. *saggen*, Prompt. Parv. p. 440.—Norw. *sakka*, *sekka*, to sink; Swed. *sacka*, to settle, sink down; Dan. *sakke* (as a nautical term), to have stern-way; Jutland *sakke*, to sink, settle down (Kok); whence Du. *zacken*, to sink. β. The MSwed. *sacka* is used of the settling of dregs; so also Low G. *sakken*, in the Bremen Wörterbuch. Rietz gives Swed. dial. *sakka*, to sink; *säkka*, to sag, droop. Cf. Icel. *sakka*, a plummet. All from the Scand. base **sakk-*, a form allied to **sank-*, 2nd grade of Teut. **senkan-*, to sink; see **Sink**.

SAGA, a tale, story. (Scand.) The E. word is saw. *Saga* is merely borrowed from Icel. *saga*, a story, tale; cognate with E. *saw*; see **Saw** (2).

SAGACIOUS. (L.) In Milton, P. L. x. 281. Coined, as if from L. **sagāciōsus*, from *sagāci-*, decl. stem of *sagax*, of quick perception, keen, sagacious; from a base SAG, to perceive clearly, perhaps to scent. Cf. *sāgīre*, to perceive by the senses. Allied to **Seek**, q. v. Brugmann, i. § 187. ¶ Not allied to **Sage** (1). **Der.** *sagacious-ly*, *sagacious-ness*. Also *sagac-i-ty*, in Minsheu, ed. 1627, formed (by analogy) from L. *sagācitās*, sagacity. And see *pre-sage*.

SAGAMORE, a W. Indian chief. (Amer. Indian.) In Phillips (1658). 'A tall savage .. He was a *sagama*;' Capt. Smith, Works, ed. Arber, p. 754. The name of a chief among some American Indian tribes. Micmac *sakamow*, a chief (S. T. Rand). See **Sachem**.

SAGE (1), discerning, wise. (F.—L.) In Shak. Tw. Nt. iii. 4. 413.—F. *sage*, 'sage, wise;' Cot. [Cf. Span. *sabio*, Ital. *saggio*, wise.]—Late L. **sabium*, not found, for L. *sapium*, acc. of *sapius*, wise; only found in comp. *ne-sapius*, unwise (Petronius).—L. *sapere*, to be wise; see **Sapience**. ¶ Not allied to **Sagacious**. **Der.** *sage*, sb., *sage-ly*, *sage-ness*.

SAGE (2), the name of a plant. (F.—L.) ME. *sauge*, *sawge*; Prompt. Parv.—AF. *sauge*, Voc. 555. 13: spelt *saulge* in Cot.—L. *saluia*, sage; so called from its supposed healing virtues.—L. *saluus*, sound, in good health; see **Safe**.

SAGITTARIUS, the archer. (L.) The name of a zodiacal sign. In Phillips (1658).—L. *sagittārius*, an archer.—L. *sagitta*, an arrow.

SAGO, a starch prepared from the pith of certain palms. (Malay.) See Yule. Mentioned in the Annual Register, 1766, Chronicle, p. 110; see Notes and Queries, 3. Ser. viii. 18. Spelt *sagu*, and called a Javanese word; Hakluyt, Voy. iii. 742.—Malay *sāgu*, *sāgŭ*, ' sago, the farinaceous and glutinous pith of a tree of the palm kind named *rumbiya*;' Marsden's Malay Dict. p. 158.

SAHIB, sir, master; a title. (Hind.—Arab.) Spelt *sahab* in Fryer's New Acct. of E. India (1673); p. 417 (Yule).—Hind. *sāḥib*, lord, master, companion (Forbes).—Arab. *ṣāḥib*, lord, master; orig. ' companion;' Rich. Dict. p. 924.

SAIL, a sheet of canvas, for propelling a ship by the means of the wind. (E.) ME. *seil*, *seyl*, Chaucer, C. T. 698 (A 696); Havelok, 711. AS. *segel*, *segl* (Grein).+Du. *zeil*; Icel. *segl*; Dan. *seil*; Swed. *segel*; G. *segel*. β. All from Teut. type **seglom*, n., a sail (Fick, iii. 316); which Fick ingeniously connects with Teut. base SEG = √SEGH, to bear up against, resist; so that the sail is that which resists or endures the force of the wind. Cf. Skt. *sah*, to bear, undergo, endure, be able to resist; Gk. *ἔχειν*, to hold, *ἔχειν νῆας*, to urge on ships, Od. ix. 279; from the same root. **Der.** *sail*, verb; *sail-cloth*, *sail-er*, *sail-or* (spelt *saylor* in Temp. i. 2. 270, doubtless by analogy with *tail-or*, though even the ending in *-or* is justifiable, whilst in *sail-or* it is not); *sail-ing*; also *sail-yard*, AS. *seglgyrd*, Voc. 288. 10.

SAINFOIN, a perennial herb, cultivated as a forage plant. (F.—L.) In Phillips, ed. 1706.—F. *sain foin*, *sainct foin*, 'Spanish trefoly;' Cot.; s. v. **Foin**.—L. *sānum* *fœnum*, lit. healthful hay.—L. *sānum*, n. of *sānus*, sane, healthful; *fœnum*, hay. ¶ Turned into *saint foin*, 'holy hay,' by popular etymology. See Hatzfeld.

SAINT, a holy man. (F.—L.) ME. *seint*, *saint*, *seinte*; '*seinte paul*' = Saint Paul, O. Eng. Homilies, ed. Morris, i. 131, l. 15.—AF. *seint*; F. *saint*.—L. *sanctum*, acc. of *sanctus*, holy, consecrated.—L. *sanctus*, pp. of *sancire*, to render sacred, make holy. Allied to L. *sac-er*, sacred; whence **Sacred, Sacerdotal**. **Der.** *saint-ed*, *saint-like*.

SAKE, purpose, account, cause, end. (E.) ME. *sake*, purpose, cause; 'for hire *sake*' = for her (its) sake; Ancren Riwle, p. 4, l. 16. It also means dispute, contention, law-suit, fault. 'For desert of sum *sake*' = on account of some fault; Allit. Poems, ed. Morris, C. 84. AS. *sacu*, strife, dispute, crime, law-suit, accusation (Bosworth). +Du. *zaak*, matter, case, cause, business, affair; Icel. *sök*, a charge, guilt, crime; Dan. *sag*; Swed. *sak*; G. *sache*. β. All from Teut. type **sakā*, f., a contention, suit at law (Fick, iii. 314), from the base SAK, appearing in Goth. *sakan* (a strong verb, pt. t. *sōk*), to contend, rebuke. Hence also Goth. *sakjō*, strife. Perhaps allied to OIrish *saig-im*, I say, I speak. Der. *seek*, q. v.

SAKER, a kind of falcon; a small piece of artillery. (F.–Span.–Arab.) 'Sacres, wherewith they shot;' Hakluyt, Voy. ii. 1. 79. The gun was named after the falcon. 'Sacre, a hauke;' Palsgrave.–MF. *sacre*, 'a saker; the hawk, and the artillery so called;' Cot.–Span. *sacre*; in both senses.–Arab. *ṣaqr*, a hawk; Rich. Dict. p. 938. Not of L. origin (Engelmann). See Devic; and Körting, § 1914.

SALAAM, SALAM, peace; a salutation. (Arab.) 'This low *salam*;' Byron, Giaour, see note 29; and in Herbert's Travels, ed. 1665, p. 142.–Arab. *salām*, 'saluting, wishing health or peace; a salutation; peace;' Rich. Dict. p. 842.–Arab. *salm*, saluting; id. p. 845. Cf. Heb. *shelōm*, peace; from the root *shālam*, to be safe.

SALAD, raw herbs cut up and seasoned. (F.–Ital.–L.) ME. *salade*, Flower and the Leaf, l. 412.–F. *salade*, 'a sallet of herbs;' Cot.–MItal. *salata*, 'a salad of herbes;' Florio. Fem. of Ital. *salato*, 'salt, powdred, sowsed, pickled, salted;' Florio. This is the pp. of *salare*, 'to salt;' id.–Ital. *sal*, *sale*, salt.–L. *sāl*, salt. See **Salt**.

SALAMANDER, a reptile. (F.–L.–Gk.) In Shak. 1 Hen. IV, iii. 3. 53.–F. *salamandre*, 'a salamander;' Cot.–L. *salamandra*.–Gk. σαλαμάνδρα, a kind of lizard, supposed to be an extinguisher of fire. An Eastern word; cf. Pers. *samandar*, a salamander; Rich. Dict. p. 850.

SALARY, stipend. (F.–L.) ME. *salarye*, P. Plowman, B. v. 433.–AF. *salarie*, Liber Albus, p. 48; F. *salaire*, 'a salary, stipend;' Cot.–L. *salārium*, orig. salt-money, or money given to the soldiers for salt.–L. *salārium*, neut. of *salārius*, belonging to salt; adj. from *sāl*, salt. See **Salt**. Der. *salari-ed*.

SALE, a selling for money. (E.) ME. *sale*, Prompt. Parv. AS. *sala*, a sale; Voc. 180. 16.+Icel. *sala*, fem., *sal*, neut., a sale, bargain: Swed. *salu*; Dan. *salg*. OHG. *sala*. Orig. 'a handing over,' or 'delivery.' Hence *sell*, v.; see **Sell**. Der. *sale-able*, *sales-man*; *hand-sel* or *han-sel*.

SALIC, SALIQUE, pertaining to the Salic tribe of the Franks. (F.–OHG.) In Shak. Hen. V, i. 2. 11.–F. *Salique*, belonging to the Salic tribe (Littré). The Salic tribe was a Frankish (High German) tribe, prob. named from the river *Sala* (now the Yssel, flowing into the Zuyder Zee). There are several rivers called *Saale* or *Saar*; cf. Skt. *salila-m*, *sarira-m*, flood, water.

SALIENT, springing forward. (L.) In Pope, Dunciad, ii. 162. But the older form was *saliant* (Skinner, Phillips), which was an heraldic term for animals represented as springing forward; and this was due to F. *saillant*, pres. part. of *saillir*, to leap; corresponding to L. *salient-*, pres. part. of L. *salire*, to leap, sometimes used of water.–√SAL, to leap; whence Gk. ἅλλομαι, I leap. Brugmann, i. § 514 (3). Der. *salient-ly*. From the same root are *as-sail*, *as-sault*, *de-sult-or-y*, *ex-ult* (for *ex-sult*), *in-sult*, *re-sili-ent*, *re-sult*, *sally*, *sal-mon*, *salt-at-ion*; *salt-ire*, q. v.

SALINE, containing salt. (F.–L.) In Phillips, ed. 1706; and see Blount's Gloss., ed. 1674.–F. *salin*, fem. *saline*, saline; Littré.–L. *salīnus*, only found in neut. *salinum*, a salt-cellar, and pl. *salīnæ*, salt-pits.–L. *sāl*, salt. See **Salt**.

SALIVA, spittle. (L.) In Phillips, ed. 1706.–L. *salīua*, spittle; whence also OIrish *saile*, W. *haliw*, saliva. Der. *saliv-ate*, *saliv-at-ion*; *saliv-al*, *saliv-ar-y*.

SALLET, a kind of helmet. (F.–Ital.–L.) In Shak. 2 Hen. VI, iv. 10. 12; and in Baret (1580). Palsgrave has: 'Salet of harnesse, *salade*.' 'A *salett* with a vysour;' York Wills, iii. 205 (1472); *salet*, Paston Letters, i. 265 (1454). Sallet is a corruption of *salade*, due to the fact that a salad of herbs was also called *sallet*.–MF. *salade*, 'a salade, helmet, headpiece; also a sallet of herbs;' Cot. [Here the spellings *salade* and *sallet* are interchanged; however, the two words are of different origin.]–L. *celata*, a helmet.–L. *cælāta*, that which is engraved or ornamented; Diez cites *cassis cælāta*, an ornamented helmet, from Cicero. [Cf. Span. *celar*, to engrave, *celadura*, enamel, inlaying, *celada*, a helmet.] L. *cælāta* is the fem. of the pp. of *cælāre*, to engrave, ornament.–L. *cælum*, a chisel, graver; allied to *cædere*, to cut. Brugmann, i. § 944. See **Cæsura**.

SALLOW (1), **SALLY**, a kind of willow. (E.) ME. *salwe*, Chaucer, C. T. 6237 (D 655). 'Salwhe, tree, Salix;' Prompt. Parv. OMerc. *salh*; AS. *sealh*; we find 'Amera, *sealh*; Salix, *welig*' mentioned together in Voc. 269. 35, 36. The suffix *-ow* = ME. *-we* = AS. *-ge*, suffix of the dat. case from nom. in *-h*, just as E. *farrow* is from AS. *fearh*, and the prov. E. *barrow-pig* from AS. *bearh*. In Lowland Sc. the word became *sauch*, *saugh*, by loss of *l*.+Icel. *selja*; Swed. *sälg*, *sälj*; Dan. *selje*; G. *sahlweide* (OHG. *salahá*, whence F. *saule*), the round-leaved willow; see Fick, iii. 320.+L. *salix*, a

willow; Gael. *seileach*, a willow; Irish *sail*, *saileach*; W. *helyg*, pl., willows; Gk. ἑλίκη, a willow.

SALLOW (2), of a pale, yellowish colour. (E.) ME. *salow* (with one *l*); we find: 'Saluhe, salowe, of colour, Croceus;' Prompt. Parv. p. 441. AS. *salu*, sallow, Grein, ii. 388; whence the compounds *saloneb*, with pale beak, *salupād*, with pale garment, *sealobrūn*, sallow-brown; id.+Du. *zaluw*, tawny, sallow; Icel. *sölr*, yellowish; MHG. *sal*, OHG. *salo*, dusky (whence F. *sale*, dirty). Teut. type **salwoz*. Brugmann, i. § 375 (9). Der. *sallow-ness*.

SALLY, to rush out suddenly. (F.–L.) 'Guyon *salied* forth to land;' Spenser, F. Q. ii. 6. 38. ME. *salien*, to dance, is the same word; Prompt. Parv. p. 441; P. Plowman, B. xiii. 233.–F. *saillir*, 'to go out, issue, issue forth; also to leap, jump, bound;' Cot.–L. *salire*, to leap; see **Salient**. Der. *sally*, sb., with which cf. F. *saillie*, 'a sally,' Cot.; from the fem. of the pp. *sailli*. Also *sally-port*, a gate whence a sally may be made.

SALMAGUNDI, a seasoned hodge-podge or mixture. (F.–Ital.–L.) 'Salmagundi, or Salmigund, an Italian dish made of cold turkey, anchovies, lemmons, oil, and other ingredients; also, a kind of hotch-potch or ragoo,' &c.; Phillips, ed. 1706. But the form is French.–F. *salmigondis*; spelt *salmigondin* in Cotgrave, who describes the dish. β. Etym. disputed; but probably of Ital. origin, as stated by Phillips. We may fairly explain it from Ital. *salami*, pl. of *salame*, salt meat, and *condito*, seasoned. This is the more likely, because the pl. *salami* was once the term in use. Thus Florio has: 'Salámi, any kinde of salt, pickled, or powdred meats or souse,' &c. γ. This also explains the F. *salmis* (not in Cotgrave), which has proved a puzzle to etymologists; I think we may take *salmis* (= salted meats) to be a *double* plural, the *s* being the F. plural, and the *i* the Ital. plural; that is, the Ital. *salami* became F. *salmi*, and then the *s* was added. δ. The derivation of Ital. *salami* is clearly from L. *sāl*, salt, though the suffix is obscure; cf. L. *salgama*, pl., pickles. The F. *-gondi*, for Ital. *condito* (or pl. *conditi*), is from L. *condītus*, seasoned, savoury, pp. of *condīre*, to preserve, pickle, season. Thus the sense is 'savoury salt meats.'

SALMON, a fish. (F.–L.) ME. *saumoun*, King Alisaunder, l. 5446; *salmon*, *salmond*, Barbour's Bruce, ii. 576, xix. 664; *samon*, Trevisa, i. 335. [The introduction of the *l* is due to our knowledge of the L. form; we do not *pronounce* it.]–OF. *saumon*, spelt *saulmon* in Cot.–L. *salmōnem*, acc. of *salmo*, a salmon. β. It has been conjectured that *salmo* means 'leaper;' from *salīre*, to leap; which well accords with the fish's habits. See **Salient**. (Otherwise in Walde.) Der. *salmon-leap*, ME. *samoun-lepe*, Trevisa, i. 369.

SALOON, a large apartment. (F.–OHG.) A late word; added by Todd to Johnson.–F. *salon*, a large room.–F. *salle*, a room, chamber.–OHG. *sal* (G. *saal*), a dwelling, house, hall, room.+Icel. *salr*, a hall; AS. *sæl*, *sele*, a house, hall. The orig. sense is 'abode;' cf. Goth. *saljan*, to dwell.

SALT, a well-known substance. (E.) ME. *salt*, P. Plowman, B. xv. 423. OMerc. *salt*; O. E. Texts; AS. *sealt*, Grein, ii. 434.+Du. *zout* (with *u* for *l*); Icel. *salt*; Dan. and Swed. *salt*; G. *salz*; Goth. *salt*. β. All from Teut. adj. type **sal-toz*, salt; Fick, iii. 321. On comparing this with L. *sāl*, salt, we see that the Teut. word is **sal-toz*, where *-toz* is the usual Idg. pp. suffix, of extreme antiquity. Accordingly we find that AS. *sealt* (E. *salt*) is also used as an adj., in the sense of 'salted' or 'full of salt,' as in *sealt wæter* = salt water; Grein, ii. 434. So also Icel. *saltr*, adj., salt; Du. *zout*, adj.; Dan. and Swed. *salt*, adj.; W. *hall-t*, L. *sal-sus*. γ. Removing the suffix, we find cognate words in L. *sāl*, salt, Gk. ἅλς, Russ. *sol(e)*, W. *halan*, OIrish *salann*, salt. Brugmann, i. § 182. Der. *salt-ly*, *salt-ness*; *salt-cellar*, q. v.; *salt*, vb., *salt-er*, *salt-ish*, *salt-less*, *salt-mine*, *salt-pan*; *salt-petre*, q. v. Also (from L. *sāl*) *sal-ine*, *sal-ary*, *sal-ad*, *sauce*, *sausage*, *salmagundi*.

SALTATION, dancing. (L.) Rare; in Sir T. Browne, Vulgar Errors, bk. v. c. 3. § 2. Formed (by analogy with F. words in *-ion*) from L. *saltātio*, a dance, a dancing.–L. *saltāre*, to dance, frequent. of *salīre*, to leap; see **Salient**. Der. *saltat-or-y*, from L. *saltātōrius*, adj. Cf. *saltire*.

SALT-CELLAR, a vessel for holding salt. (E.; *and* F.–L.) The word *salt* is explained above. *Cellar* is an absurd corruption of AF. *saler*, Lib. Custumarum, p. 461; equivalent to F. *salière*. Thus we find: 'Saliere, a salt-seller;' Cot. Cf. Ital. *saliera*, a salt-cellar. 'Hoc selarium, celare;' Voc. 658. 16. 'A *saltsaler* of sylver;' A.D. 1463, in Bury Wills, ed. Tymms, p. 23, l. 8. Formed from L. *sāl*, salt; see **Salary** and **Salt**. ¶ Hence *salt-cellar* = salt-salt-holder; a tautological expression.

SALTIER, SALTIRE, in heraldry, a St. Andrew's cross. (F.–L.) Spelt *sawtyre*, Caxton, Golden Legend, St. Alban, § 1. St. Andrew's cross is one in this position ✗; when charged on a shield, it is called a *saltier*. The ME. *sawtyre* is due to an AF. **sautier*, representing Late L. *saltārium*, a piece of wood placed transversely, which men (but not cattle) could get over; from L. *saltāre*, to dance (hence, to jump over); see below. In the Roll of Caerlaverock (1300), l. 13, the form is *sautour*, variant of *sauteur* (Godefroy), a saltire, also used like Late L. *saltārium*. Still commoner is the OF. *sautoir*, a saltire; MF. *saultoir*, 'Saint Andrew's crosse, tearmed so by heralds;' Cot. The old sense of OF. *sautoir* was stirrup (Littré, s. v. *sautoir*); the cross seems to have been named from the position of the side-pieces of a stirrup, formerly made in a triangle △; or it may have been suggested by the *saltārium*, a stirrup, a common word; Ducange. ─ L. *saltātōrius*, belonging to dancing or leaping, suitable for mounting a horse. ─ L. *saltātor*, a dancer, leaper. ─ L. *saltāre*, to dance, leap; frequentative of *salīre*; see **Salient.** ¶ In the Book of St. Alban's, pt. ii. fol. f 5, we find ME. *sawtre*, OF. *saultier*, and Late L. *saltātōrium*, all meaning 'saltire.'

SALT-PETRE, nitre. (F. ─ L. *and* Gk.) In Shak. 1 Hen. IV, i. 3. 60. For the former part of the word, see **Salt.** The E. word is a modification of ME. *salpeter*, Chaucer, C. T., G 808. ─ OF. *salpetre* (Supp. to Godefroy). ─ Late L. *salpetra*, salt-petre, which represents L. *sāl petræ*, lit. 'salt of the rock.' Lastly, L. *petra* is from Gk. πέτρα, a rock; see **Petrify.**

SALUBRIOUS, healthful. (L.) A late word. In Phillips, ed. 1706. Coined as if from a L. **salūbriōsus*, extended from L. *salūbris*, healthful. β. The suffix -*bris* is explained in Brugmann, ii. § 77. γ. *Salū*- is the base of *salū-ti*-, stem of *salūs*, health; and is allied to *saluus*, sound, in good health, whence E. *safe*; see **Safe.** Der. *salubrious-ly.* Also *salubri-ty*, Minsheu, from F. *salubrité* (Cot.), from L. acc. *salūbritātem*.

SALUTARY, healthful, wholesome. (F. ─ L.) In Blount's Gloss., ed. 1674. ─ F. *salutaire*, 'healthful;' Cot. ─ L. *salūtāris*, healthful. ─ L. *salūt*-, stem of *salūs*, health (above).

SALUTE, to wish health to, to greet. (L.) In Spenser, F. Q. i. 1. 30; and in Palsgrave. ─ L. *salūtāre* to wish health to, greet. ─ L. *salūt*-, stem of *salūs*, health (above). Der. *salutat-ion*, ME. *salutacioun*, Wyclif, Luke, i. 41, from F. *salutation* (Cot.), from L. acc. *salūtātiōnem*. And see **Salutary.**

SALVAGE, money paid for saving ships. (F. ─ L.) In Blount's Gloss., ed. 1674. ─ OF. and MF. *salvage*; 'droict de *salvage*, a tenth part of goods which were like to perish by shipwrack, due unto him who saves them;' Cot. ─ OF. *salver*, F. *sauver*, to save. ─ L. *saluāre*, to save; see **Save.**

SALVATION, preservation. (F. ─ L.) ME. *sauacioun*, Chaucer, C. T. 7080 (D 1498); spelt *sauuacion*, Ancren Riwle, p. 242, l. 26. ─ OF. *sauuacion*; F. *salvation*. ─ L. *saluātiōnem*, acc. of *saluātio*, a saving. ─ L. *saluāre*, to save; see **Save.**

SALVE, ointment. (E.) ME. *salue* (= *salve*), Chaucer, C. T. 2714 (A 2712); older form *salfe*, Ormulum, 6477. OMerc. *salf*, *salb*, O. E. Texts; AS. *sealf*, Mark, xiv. 5; John, xii. 3.+Du. *zalf*; G. *salbe*. β. AS. *sealf* is from the Teut. type **salbā*, f., Fick, iii. 321. The orig. sense was prob. 'oil' or 'grease;' it answers in form to Gk. ὄλπη, an oil-flask, related by gradation to the rare Gk. word ἔλπος, oil, in Hesychius; cf. also Skt. *sarpis*, clarified butter. ¶ The -*ve* is due to AS. *sealf-e*, gen., dat., and acc. of *sealf*. Der. *salve*, verb, from AS. *sealfian*, cognate with Goth. *salbōn*.

SALVER, a plate on which anything is presented. (Span. ─ L.) Properly *salva*, but misspelt *salver* by confusion with the old word *salver* in the sense of 'preserver,' or one who claims *salvage* for shipping. This is shown by the following. '*Salver*, from *salvo*, to save, is a *new fashioned* piece of wrought plate, broad and flat, with a foot underneath, and is used in giving beer, or other liquid thing, to *save* or *preserve* the carpit or clothes from drops;' Blount's Gloss., ed. 1674. This invented explanation does not affect the etymology. ─ Span. *salva*, a salver, a plate on which anything is presented; it also means 'pregustation, the previous tasting of viands before they are served up.' There is also the phrase *hacer salva*, 'to taste meat or drinke, . . as they do to princes;' Minsheu's Span. Dict. (1623). We also find the dimin. *salvilla*, a salver. ─ Span. *salvar*, 'to save, free from risk; to taste, to prove the food or drink of nobles;' Neuman. ─ L. *saluāre*, to save; see **Save, Safe.** ¶ Mr. Wedgwood says: 'as *salva* was the tasting of meat at a great man's table, *salvar*, to guarantee, to taste or make the essay of meat served at table, the name of *salver* is in all probability from the article having been used in connexion with the essay. The Ital. name of the essay was *credenza*, and the same term was used for a cupboard or sideboard; *credentiere*, *credenzere*, a prince's taster, cup-bearer, butler, or cupboard-keeper (Florio). F. *credence d'argent*, silver plate, or a cupboard of silver plate; Cot.' Thus a *salver* was the name of the plate or tray on which drink was presented to the taster, or to the drinker of a health.

SALVO, a general discharge of guns, intended as a salute. (Ital. ─ L.) So spelt in 1733 (Stanford Dict.); but more correctly *salva*, in 1591. ─ Ital. *salva*, 'a sauing, keeping; a volie or tire of

ordinance;' Florio. ─ L. *saluāre*, to save, keep; *salue*, hail! ─ L. *saluus*, safe. See **Safe.**

SAMBO, the offspring of a negro and a mulatto. (Span. ─ L. ─ Gk.) In An Eng. Garner, ed. Arber, v. 95, the men of a certain tribe are called *samboses*. And see Stedman's Surinam, i. 89. ─ Span. *zambo*, formerly *çambo* (Pineda), bandy-legged; used as a sb. as a term of contempt. ─ Late L. *scambus*. ─ Gk. σκαμβός, crooked; said of the legs (Diez).

SAME, of the like kind, identical. (E.) ME. *same*, Chaucer, C. T. 16923 (G 1455). AS. *same*, only as adv., as in *swā same swā men*, the same as men, just like men; Ælfred, tr. of Boethius, c. xxxiii. § 4 (bk. iii. met. 9). The adjectival use is Scand.; cf. Icel. *samr*, Dan. and Swed. *samme*, the same.+OHG. *sam*, adj., *sama*, adv.; Goth. *sama*, the same; cf. *samana*, together.+Russ. *samuii*, the same; Gk. ὁμός; Skt. *sama-*, even, the same. From the same base is the Skt. *sam*, with (Vedic); also the L. *simul*, together, *similis*, like (whence E. **Simultaneous, Similar**); also Gk. ὁμοῖος, like (whence E. **Homœopathy**). See Curtius, i. 400. Der. *same-ness*; and see *semi-*, *similar*, *simulate*, *semblance*, *as-semble*, *dis-semble*, *re-semble*. Also *some*, *-some*.

SAMITE, a rich silk stuff. (F. ─ L. ─ Gk.) ME. *samit*, spelt *samyte*, Ly beaus Disconus, 833 (ed. Ritson, vol. ii); King Alisaunder, 1027. And see two examples in Halliwell, who explains it by 'a very rich silk stuff, sometimes interwoven with gold or silver thread.' ─ OF. *samit*, a silk stuff; Burguy. See *samy* in Cotgrave. ─ Late L. *examitum*, samite; Ducange. ─ Late Gk. ἑξάμιτον, cited by Burguy, supposed to have been a stuff woven with six threads or different kinds of thread; from Gk. ἑξ, six (cognate with E. *six*), and μίτος, a thread of the woof. See **Dimity,** which is a word of similar origin. The mod. G. *sammet*, *sammt*, velvet, is the same word.

SAMOVAR, a kind of tea-urn. (Russ.) It occurs in 1884. ─ Russ. *samovar'*, a tea-urn; see Stanford Dict. Said to be of Tatar origin (Cent. Dict.).

SAMPAN, a kind of skiff, used in the East. (Malay ─ Chinese.) Spelt *champana* in 1516 (Yule). The Stanford Dict. quotes *sampan*, as occurring in 1622. ─ Malay *sampan*. ─ Chin. *sanpan*, lit. 'three boards.' Yule notes that another boat is called in Chinese *wupan*, i. e. 'five boards.'

SAMPHIRE, the name of a herb. (F. ─ L. *and* Gk.) Spelt *sampire* in K. Lear, iv. 6. 15; and in Minsheu, ed. 1627; and this is a more correct spelling, representing a former pronunciation. So also Sherwood, in his index to Cotgrave, who gives *herbe de S. Pierre* as a F. equivalent. Spelt *sampier* in Baret (1580), which is still better. ─ F. *Saint Pierre*, St. Peter; Cotgrave, s. v. *herbe*, gives: '*Herbe de S. Pierre*, sampire.' ─ L. *sanctum*, acc. of *sanctus*, holy; and *Petrum*, acc. of *Petrus*, Peter, named from Gk. πέτρος, a stone, πέτρα, a rock.

SAMPLE, an example, pattern, specimen. (F. ─ L.) ME. *sample*, Cursor Mundi, 9514; spelt *asaumple* (for *esaumple*), Ancren Riwle, p. 112, l. 16. ─ OF. *essemple*, *example*. ─ L. *exemplum*. See **Example.** Doublets, *ensample*, *example.* Der. *sampler*, Mids. Nt. Dr. iii. 2. 205, from OF. *examplaire* (14th cent., Littré), another form of OF. *exemplaire*, 'a pattern, sample, or sampler,' Cot., from L. *exemplar.* See **Exemplar,** which is a doublet.

SANATORY, healthful. (L.) Not in Todd's Johnson. [Phillips has the allied word *sanative*, used of medicinal waters, now nearly obsolete; it occurs in Bacon, Nat. Hist. § 787.] Coined as if from a L. **sānātōrius*, extended from *sānātor*, healer. We find also L. *sānātiuus*, healing. ─ L. *sānāre*, to heal. ─ L. *sānus*, in good health; see **Sane.**

SANCTIFY, to consecrate. (F. ─ L.) Spelt *sanctifie*, Tyndall's Works, p. 11, col. 2, l. 6; *seintefie*, Gower, C. A. iii. 234; bk. vii. 4247. ─ F. *sanctifier*, 'to sanctifie;' Cot. ─ L. *sanctificāre*, to make holy. ─ L. *sancti-*, for *sanctus*, holy; and -*fic-*, for *facere*, to make. See **Saint** and **Fact.** Der. *sanctific-at-ion*, from F. *sanctification* (Cot.); *sanctifi-er.*

SANCTIMONY, devoutness. (F. ─ L.) In Shak. Troil. v. 2. 139. ─ MF. *sanctimonie*; Cot. ─ L. *sanctimōnia*, sanctity. ─ L. *sancti-*, for *sanctus*, holy; with Idg. suffixes -*mōn-*, -*yā*. See **Saint.** Der. *sanctimoni-ous*, -*ly*, -*ness*.

SANCTION, ratification. (F. ─ L.) In Cotgrave. ─ F. *sanction*, 'sanction;' Cot. ─ L. *sanctiōnem*, acc. of *sanctio*, a sanction; cf. *sanctus*, pp. of *sancire*, to render sacred. See **Saint.**

SANCTITY, holiness. (L.) As You Like It, iii. 4. 14. Formed (by analogy) from L. *sanctitātem*, acc. of *sanctitās*, holiness. ─ L. *sancti-*, for *sanctus*, holy; see **Saint.**

SANCTUARY, a sacred place. (F. ─ L.) ME. *seintuarie*, a shrine; Chaucer, C. T. 12887 (C 953). ─ AF. *saintuarie*, Stat. Realm, i. 298 (F. *sanctuaire*), a sanctuary. ─ L. *sanctuārium*, a shrine. ─ L. *sanctu-s*, holy; see **Saint.**

SAND, fine particles of stone. (E.) ME. *sand*, *sond*, Chaucer,

C. T. 4929 (B 509). AS. *sand*; Grein, ii. 390.**+**Du. *zand*; Icel. *sandr*; Swed. and Dan. *sand*; G. *sand*; Bavarian *sambd*. β. All from the Teut. types **sam(a)doz*, m.; **sam(a)don*, n. Idg. type *samədhos; cf. Gk. ἄμαθος, sand. Brugmann, i. § 421. **Der.** *sand-eel*, *-glass*, *-heat*, *-martin*, *-paper*, *-piper*, *-pit* (Palsgrave), *-stone*; *sand-y*, AS. *sandig*; *sand-i-ness*.

SANDAL, a kind of shoe. (F.–L.–Gk.–Pers.) ME. *sandalies*, pl., Wyclif, Mark, vi. 9.–F. *sandale*, 'a sandall, or sendall;' Cot.–L. *sandalia*, pl. of *sandalium*.–Gk. σανδάλιον, dimin. of σάνδαλον (Æolic σαμβάλον), a wooden sole bound on to the foot with straps, a sandal. Supposed to be of Pers. origin; cf. Pers. *sandal*, a sandal, sort of slipper, Rich. Dict. p. 853.

SANDAL-WOOD, a fragrant wood. (F.–L.–Gk.–Pers.–Skt.) 'Sandal or Saunders, a precious wood brought out of India;' Blount's Gloss., ed. 1674. Spelt *sanders* in Cotgrave, and in Baret (1580); this form seems to be an E. corruption.–F. *sandal*, 'sanders, a sweet-smelling wood brought out of the Indies;' Cot. Also *santal* (Hatzfeld).–Late L. *santalum*.–Gk. σάνταλον, σάνδαλον.–Pers. *sandal*; also *chandal*, 'sandal-wood;' Rich. Dict., p. 544. Also spelt *chandan*, id.–Skt. *chandana*, sandal, the tree; which Benfey derives from *chand*, to shine, allied to L. *candēre*.

SAND-BLIND, semi-blind, half blind. (E.) In Shak., Merch. Ven. ii. 2. 37. A corruption of *sam-blind*, i.e. half-blind. ME. *sam-*, as in *sam-rede*, half red, *sam-ripe*, half ripe, P. Plowman, C. ix. 311, and footnote. AS. *sam-*, as in *sam-cucu*, half alive, Luke, x. 30. The AS. *sam-* is cognate with L. *sēmi-*, Gk. ἡμι-; see **Semi-, Hemi-**.

SANDWICH, two slices of bread with ham between them. (E.) So called from John Montague, 4th Earl of *Sandwich* (born 1718, died 1792), who used to have *sandwiches* brought to him at the gaming-table, to enable him to go on playing without cessation. *Sandwich* is a town in Kent; AS. *Sandwic* = sand-village.

SANE, of sound mind. (L.) A late word. In Todd's Johnson. –L. *sānus*, of sound mind, whole. Prob. allied to Icel. *sōn*, G. *sühne*, atonement (Kluge). **Der.** *sane-ness*; *san-at-ive, san-at-or-y* (see **Sanatory**); *san-i-ty*, Hamlet, ii. 2. 214, formed (by analogy) from L. acc. *sānitātem*; *san-i-ta-ry*, a coined word; *san-icle*, q. v.

SANGUINE, ardent, hopeful. (F.–L.) The use of the word is due to the old belief in the 'four humours,' of which *blood* was one; the excess of this humour rendered people of a hopeful 'temperament' or 'complexion.' ME. *sanguin*; 'Of his complexion he was *sanguin*;' Chaucer, C. T. 335 (A 333).–F. *sanguin*, 'sanguine, bloody, of a sanguine complexion;' Cot.–L. *sanguineum*, acc. of *sanguineus*, bloody.–L. *sanguin-*, stem of *sanguis*, blood. Root uncertain. **Der.** *sanguine-ly*, *-ness*; *sanguin-e-ous*, Englished from L. *sanguineus*; *sanguin-ar-y*, Dryden, Hind and Panther, pt. iii. l. 679, from F. *sanguinaire*, 'bloudy,' Cot. from L. *sanguinārius*.

SANHEDRIM, the highest council of the Jews. (Heb.–Gk.) In Todd's Johnson, who cites from Patrick's Commentary on Judges, iv. 5. Spelt *sanhedrin*, Purchas's Pilgrimage, bk. ii. ch. 12. § 3. –Late Heb. *sanhedrīn*, not a true Heb. word.–Gk. συνέδριον, a council; lit. a sitting together, sitting in council.–Gk. σύν, together; and ἕδρα, a seat, from ἕζομαι (fut. ἑδ-οῦμαι), I sit, cognate with E. *sit*. See **Syn-** and **Sit**.

SANICLE, a plant of the genus *Sanicula*. (F.–L.) ME. *sanycle*, Voc. 613. 33.–OF. *sanicle* (Hatzfeld).–Late L. *sānicula*, named from healing wounds.–L. *sānus*, whole; see **Sane**.

SANITARY, SANITY; see **Sane**.

SANS, without. (F.–L.) In Shak. As You Like It, ii. 7. 166.– F. *sans* (OF. *sens*), without; the final *s* is unoriginal (see Diez).– L. *sine*. without.–L. *si ne*, if not, unless, except.

SANSKRIT, lit. 'symmetrical language.' (Skt.) 'The word *Sanskrit* (Skt. *saṁskṛta*) is made up of the preposition *sam*, "together," and the pp. *kṛta-*, "made," an euphonic *s* being inserted. The compound means "carefully constructed," "symmetrically formed" (*confectus, constructus*). In this sense, it is opposed to the *Prakrit* (Skt. *prākṛta-*), "common," "natural," the name given to the vulgar dialects which gradually arose out of it, and from which most of the languages now spoken in upper India are more or less directly derived;' Monier Williams, Skt. Grammar, p. xix. *Sam* is allied to E. *same*; and *kṛ*, to make, to L. *creāre*; see **Same** and **Create**.

SAP (1), the juice of plants. (E.) ME. *sap*, Kentish *zep*, Ayenbite of Inwyt, p. 96, l. 5. AS. *sæp*, sap; Grein, ii. 397.**+**MDu. *sap*, 'sap, juice, or liquor;' Hexham; OHG. *saf*; G. *saft* (with added *t*). Not connected with Gk. ὀπός, juice; but perhaps borrowed from L. *sapa*, new wine boiled thick. **Der.** *sap-less, sapp-y, sapp-i-ness*; *sap-ling*, a young succulent tree, Rich. III, iii. 4. 71; *sap-green*.

SAP (2), to undermine. (F.–Late L.) 'Sapping or mining;' Howell, Famil. Letters, vol. ii. let. 4.–MF. *sapper* (F. *saper*), 'to undermine, dig into;' Cot.–OF. *sappe* (15th cent., Littré), a kind of hoe; mod. F. *sape*, an instrument for mining. Cf. Span. *zapa*, a spade; Ital. *zappa*, 'a mattocke to dig and delue with, a sappe;'

Florio; Late L. *sapa*, a hoe, mentioned A.D. 1183 (Ducange). β. Diez proposes to refer these words to Gk. σκαπάνη, a digging-tool, a hoe; from σκάπτειν, to dig. He instances Ital. *zolla*, which he derives from OHG. *skolla* (with z from *sk*). **Der.** *sapp-er*.

SAPAJOU, a spider-monkey. (F.–Brazil.) F. *sapajou*; of Brazil. origin (Hatzfeld). It occurs in French in 1614.

SAPID, savoury. (L.) Sir T. Browne has *sapidity*, Vulg. Errors, b. iii. c. 21. § 6; and *sapor*, id. § 8. All the words are rare.–L. *sapidus*, savoury.–L. *sapere*, to taste, also, to be wise. See **Sapience**. **Der.** *sapid-i-ty*; also *sap-or*, from L. *sapor*, taste. – And see *savour*, *in-sipid*.

SAPIENCE, wisdom. (F.–L.) [The adj. *sapient* is a later word.] ME. *sapience*, P. Plowman, B. iii. 330; Gower, C. A. ii. 167; bk. v. 1205.–F. *sapience*, 'sapience;' Cot.–L. *sapientia*, wisdom.– L. *sapient-*, decl. stem of pres. part. of *sapere*, to be wise, orig. to taste, discern. **Der.** (from L. *sapere*) *sapi-ent*, K. Lear, iii. 6. 24; *sapi-ent-ly*, *sage* (1); and see *sapid*.

SAPONACEOUS, soapy. (L.–Teut.) In Bailey's Dict., vol. ii. ed. 1731. Coined as if from L. *sāpōnāceus, soapy, from L. *sāpōn-*, stem of *sāpo*, soap (Pliny). β. It is doubtful whether *sāpo* (Gk. σάπων) is a L. word; it is the same as E. *soap*, and was probably borrowed from Teutonic (not Celtic, as Pliny inadvertently says); see **Soap**. See Pliny, Nat. Hist. bk. xxviii. c. 12.

SAPPHIC, a kind of metre. (L.–Gk.) 'Meter *saphik*;' G. Douglas, Palace of Honour, pt. ii. st. 4.–L. *Sapphicus*, Sapphic, belonging to Sappho, the poetess.–Gk. Σαπφώ, a poetess born at Mitylene in Lesbos, died about 592 B.C.

SAPPHIRE, a precious stone. (F.–L.–Gk.–Heb.–Skt.) ME. *saphir*, Old Eng. Miscellany, ed. Morris, p. 96, l. 115.–F. *saphir*, 'a saphir stone;' Cot.–L. *sapphīrus*.–Gk. σάπφειρος, a sapphire. –Heb. *sappīr*, a sapphire (with initial *samech*).–Skt. *çanipriyam*, a sapphire; lit. 'beloved of Saturn;' gems being often connected with names of planets.–Skt. *çani-s*, Saturn; and *priya-s*, dear, from *prī*, to love. (Uhlenbeck.) Cf. Pers. *saffīr*, a sapphire; Rich. Dict. p. 836. See the note in Schade, O. H. G. Dict., p. 1412.

SARABAND, a kind of dance. (F.–Span.–Pers.) In Ben Jonson, The Devil is an Ass, iv. 1 (Wittipol). Explained as 'a Spanish dance' in Johnson.–F. *sarabande* (Littré).–Span. *zarabanda*, a dance; of Moorish origin. Supposed to be from Pers. *sarband*, of which the lit. sense is 'a fillet for fastening the ladies' head-dress;' Rich. Dict. p. 822.–Pers. *sar*, head, cognate with Gk. κάρα; and *band*, a band. See **Cheer** and **Band** (1).

SARACEN, one of an Eastern people. (L.–Gk.–Arab.) ME. *saracen*, Rich. Coer de Lion, 2436; *sarezyn*, 2461.–L. *saracēnus*, a saracen; from Late Gk. Σαρακηνός; lit. 'one of the eastern people.' –Arab. *sharqīy*, oriental, eastern; sunny; Rich. Dict. p. 889. Cf. Arab. *sharq*, the east, the rising sun; id. From Arab. root *sharaqa*, it rose. (Doubtful; see note in Gibbon, Rom. Empire, c. 50.) **Der.** *Saracen-ic*; also *sarcen-et*, q. v.; *sirocco*, q. v.

SARCASM, a sneer. (F.–L.–Gk.) In Blount's Gloss., ed. 1674.–F. *sarcasme*, 'a biting taunt;' Cot.–L. *sarcasmus, sarcasmos*. –Gk. σαρκασμός, a sneer.–Gk. σαρκάζειν, to tear flesh like dogs, to bite the lips in rage, to sneer.–Gk. σαρκ-, stem of σάρξ, flesh. **Der.** *sarcas-t-ic*, Gk. σαρκαστικός, sneering; *sarcas-t-ic-al-ly*.

SARCENET, SARSNET, a fine thin silk. (F.–L.–Arab.) In Shak. 1 Hen. IV, iii. 1. 256. Spelt *sarzinett* in 1373; Wardrobe Acct. 47 Edw. III; N. and Q. 8 S. i. 129.–OF. *sarcenet*, a stuff made by the Saracens (Roquefort). Formed from Low L. *saracēnicum*, sarcenet (Ducange).–Low L. *Saracēni*, the Saracens; see **Saracen**.

SARCOPHAGUS, a stone receptacle for a corpse. (L.–Gk.) In Holland, tr. of Plinie, b. xxxvi. c. 17; it was the name of a kind of lime-stone, so called 'because that, within the space of forty daies it is knowne for certaine to consume the bodies of the dead which are bestowed therein.'–L. *sarcophagus*.–Gk. σαρκοφάγος, carnivorous, flesh-consuming; hence a name for a species of lime-stone, as above.–Gk. σαρκο-, from σάρξ, flesh (see **Sarcasm**); and φαγεῖν, to eat, from √BHAG, to eat.

SARDINE (1), a small fish. (F.–L.–Gk.) In Cotgrave. ME. *sardyn*, Earl of Derby's Exped. (C. S.), p. 228, l. 31.–F. *sardine*, also spelt *sardaine* in Cotgrave, and explained as 'a pilchard, or sardine.'–L. *sardīna*, also *sarda*, a sardine.–Gk. σαρδίνη, σάρδα, a kind of fish; explained as 'a kind of tunny caught near Sardinia' (Liddell). Perhaps named from Gk. Σαρδώ, Sardinia.

SARDINE (2), a precious stone. (L.–Gk.) ME. *sardyn*, Wyclif, Rev. iv. 3; AF. *sardine*, Gaimar, l. 4888.–L. *sardinus, the L. equivalent of Gk. σαρδῖνος. The Vulgate has *sardinis* in Rev. iv. 3 as a gen. case, from a nom. *sardo*.–Gk. σαρδῖνος, a sardine stone, Rev. iv. 3. Also σάρδιος; also σάρδιον. So called from Sardis, capital of Lydia in Asia Minor, where it was first found; Pliny, b. xxxvii. c. 7. **Der.** *sard-onyx*, q. v.

SARDIUS, a gem. (L.—Gk.) In Rev. xxi. 20.—L. *sardius* (Vulgate).—Gk. σάρδιος, Rev. xxi. 20 : the same as σάρδιον, a gem of Sardis (above). See the note in Schade, O. H. G. Dict., p. 1418.

SARDONIC, sneering, said of a laugh or smile. (F.—L.—Gk.) Only in the phr. ' *Sardonic* laugh ' or ' *Sardonic* smile.' In Blount's Gloss., ed. 1674, it is a ' *Sardonian* laughter.' So also ' *Sardonian* smile ; ' Spenser, F. Q. v. 9. 12. — F. *sardonique*, used in the 16th cent. (Littré) ; but usually MF. *sardonien*. Cotgrave has : ' *ris sardonien*, a forced or causelesse mirth.'—L. *Sardonicus*, for the more usual *Sardonius*, Sardinian. — Gk. σαρδόνιος, also σαρδάνιος ; hence σαρδάνιον γελᾶν, to laugh bitterly, grimly. ' Prob. from σαίρειν (to draw back the lips and show the teeth, grin) ; others write σαρδόνιος, deriving it from σαρδόνιον, a plant of Sardinia (Σαρδώ), which was said to screw up the face of the eater, Servius, on Virg. Ecl. vii. 41, and in Latin certainly the form *Sardonius* has prevailed ; ' Liddell. ' Immo ego *Sardois* uidear tibi amarior herbis ; ' Virgil (as above).

SARDONYX, a precious stone. (L.—Gk.) In Holland, tr. of Plinie, b. xxxvii. c. 6.—L. *sardonyx*.—Gk. σαρδόνυξ, the sard-onyx, i.e. Sardian onyx.—Gk. σαρδ-, for Σάρδεις, Sardis, the capital of Lydia ; and ὄνυξ, the finger-nail, also an onyx. See **Sardine** (2) and **Onyx**. See the note in Schade, O. H. G. Dict., p. 1420.

SARGASSO, gulf-weed, a kind of sea-weed. (Port.) ' *Sargasso*, for many miles floating upon the western ocean ; ' Sir T. Browne, Garden of Cyrus, ch. iv. § 13.—Port. *sargaço*, sea-weed, sea-wrack.—Port. *sarga*, a sort of grapes. The gulf-weed has berry-like air-vessels, and is also called the *sea-grape*.

SARK, a shirt. (Scand.—Slavonic.) ME. *serke*, P. Plowman, B. v. 66 ; *serk*, Havelok, 603.—Icel. *serkr*, a shirt ; Swed. *särk* ; Dan. *særk*. [Also AS. *serc, serce* (Bosworth) ; but *sark* is from Norse.]—Slav. type *sorka ; whence OSlav. *sraka*, a garment, Russ. *sorochka*, a shirt (Miklosich).

SARONG, a kind of body-cloth or kilt. (Malay.—Skt.) Modern. —Malay *sārung*.—Skt. *sāraṅga-s, çāraṅga-s*, adj. variegated ; sb. a garment.—Skt. *çāra-s*, variegated. See Yule.

SARSAPARILLA, the name of a plant. (Span.) ' *Sarsa-parilla*, a plant growing in Peru and Virginia . . commonly called prickly bind-weed ; ' Phillips, ed. 1706. Spelt *sassaparilla* in Capt. Smith, Works, ed. Arber, p. 582.—Span. *zarzaparilla*. β. The Span. *zarza* means ' bramble,' and is of Basque origin, from Basque *sartzia*, a bramble ; see Larramendi's Dict., p. 506. γ. The origin of the latter part of the name is unknown ; it has been supposed that *parilla* stands for *parrilla*, a possible dimin. of *parra*, a vine trained against stakes or against a wall. Others ascribe the name to a physician surnamed *Parillo*.

SARSNET : see **Sarcenet**.

SASH (1), a case or frame for panes of glass. (F.—L.) ' A Jezebel . . appears constantly dressed at her *sash* ; ' Spectator, no. 175 (A.D. 1711). ' *Sash*, or *Sash-window*, a kind of window framed with large squares, and corruptly so called from the French word *chassis*, a frame ; ' Phillips, ed. 1706.—MF. *chassis*, ' a frame of wood for a window ; ' Cot. ; F. *châssis*. Extended from OF. *chasse* (F. *châsse*), a shrine, case.—L. *capsa*, a box, case ; see **Chase** (3), **Case** (2). ¶ The F. *châssis* was formerly represented by E. *chassis*, a window-sash (N. E. D.) ; and the F. *châsse* by Lowl. Sc. *chess*, a sash (E. D. D.).

SASH (2), a scarf, band. (Pers.) Formerly spelt *shash*, with the sense of turban. ' His head was wreathed with a huge *shash* or tulipant [turban] of silk and gold ; ' Sir T. Herbert, Travels, 1638, p. 191 ; cited in Trench, Select Glossary. See also Sandys, Trav. (1632), p. 63. ' All these Tulbents [turbans of Turks] be of pure white ; but the . . Christians . . weare *Shasses*, that is, striped linnen . . wound about the skirts of a little cap ; ' Fynes Moryson, Itin. (1617), pt. iii. bk. 4, ch. 2, p. 174. ' So much for the silk in Judæa, called *shesh* in Hebrew, whence haply that fine linen or silk is called *shashes*, worn at this day about the heads of Eastern people ; ' Fuller, Pisgah Sight of Palestine, b. ii. c. 14, § 24. But it does not seem to be a Hebrew word. Trench, in his Eng. Past and Present, calls it a Turkish word ; which is also not the case. The solution is, that the word is Persian.—Pers. *shast*, ' a thumb-stall worn by archers, . . a girdle worn by the Magi,' &c., Rich. Dict. p. 891. In Vullers' Pers. Dict. ii. 425, 426, we find : *shest*, a thumb, archer's thumb-ring (to guard the thumb in shooting), a fish-hook, plectrum, fiddle-string, scalpel ; also ' cingulum idolatorum et ignisculorum,' i.e. a girdle worn by idolaters and fire-worshippers, thus accounting for our *sash*.

SASSAFRAS, a kind of laurel. (F.—Span.—L.) In Phillips, ed. 1706. ' The tree that is brought from the Florida, whiche is called *sassafras* ; ' J. Frampton, Joyfull Newes (1577), fol. 46.—F. *sassafras*.—Span. *sasafras*, sassafras ; from MSpan. *sassafragia*, the herb saxifrage (Minsheu) ; we find also Span. *salsafras, salsifrax, salsifragia*, saxifrage (Neuman), all various corruptions of *sassi-*

fragia. ' The same virtue was attributed to *sassafras* as to *saxifrage*, of breaking up the stone in the bladder ; ' Wedgwood. See **Saxifrage**.

SATAN, the devil. (Heb.) Lit. ' the enemy.' Called *Sathanas* in Wyclif, Rev. xii. 9 ; spelt *Satanas* in the Vulgate ; and Σαταυᾶς in the Greek.—Heb. *sātān*, an enemy, Satan ; from the root *sātan* (with *sin* and *teth*), to be an enemy, persecute. Der. *Satan-ic, Satan-ic-al*.

SATCHEL, a small bag. (F.—L.—Gk.—Heb.—Egyptian.) ME. *sachel*, Wyclif, Luke, x. 4.—AF. *sachel* (Bozon) ; OF. *sachel*, a little bag (Roquefort, with a citation).—L. *saccellum*, acc. of *saccellus*, dimin. of *saccus*, a sack, bag ; see **Sack**.

SATE, SATIATE, to glut, fill full, satisfy. (F.—L.) In Hamlet, i. 5. 56 ; we find *sated*, Oth. i. 3. 356. *Sate* is for *satie*.—OF. *satier*, to satiate (Godefroy).—L. *satiāre*, to satiate. *Sated* was used like *satiate* in a participial sense, i.e. with the sense of *satiated*. β. We find *saciate* thus used in Du Wes, Sup. to Palsgrave, p. 1077, l. 21. Cf. ' That *satiate* yet unsatisfied desire ; ' Cymb. i. 6. 48.—L. *satiātus*, pp. of *satiāre*, to sate, satiate, fill full. Cf. L. *satur*, full ; *sat, satis*, sufficient. Allied to E. *sad* ; see **Sad**. Der. *satiat-ion* ; *sat-i-e-ty*, from F. *satieté*, ' satiety, fulnesse,' Cot., from L. *satietātem*, acc. of *satietās*. Also *sat-is-fy*, q. v. ; *sat-ire*, q. v., *sat-ur-ate*, q. v., *soil* (3), q. v.

SATELLITE, a follower, attendant moon. (F.—L.) ' *Satellite*, one retained to guard a man's person, a yeoman of the guard, sergeant, catchpoll ; ' Blount, ed. 1674.—F. *satellite*, ' a sergeant, catch-pole, or yeoman of the guard ; ' Cot.—L. *satellitem*, acc. of *satelles*, an attendant, life-guard. Pope uses the L. pl. *satellites* (four syllables), Essay on Man, i. 42.

SATIN, a glossy silk. (F.—L.) ME. *satin*, Chaucer, C. T. 4557 (B 137).—F. *satin*, ' satin ; ' Cot. [Cf. Ital. *setino*, ' a kind of thin silke stuffe ; ' Florio. Also Port. *setim*, satin.]—Late L. *sātinus, sētinus*, satin (Ducange). Extended from L. *sēta*, a bristle ; we find the Late L. *sēta* in the sense of silk (Ducange) ; also Ital. *seta*, ' any kind of silke,' Florio. β. Similarly Span. *pelo*, hair, also means fibre of plants, thread of wool or silk, &c. ; and the L. *sēta* or *saeta* was used of the human hair as well as of the bristles of an animal ; see Diez. Allied to AS. *sāda*, a cord, a snare ; see Brugmann, i. § 209. Der. *satin-et, satin-y, satin-wood*.

SATIRE, a ridiculing of vice or folly. (F.—L.) In Shak. Much Ado, v. 4. 103.—F. *satire* ; Cotgrave has : ' *Satyre*, a satyr, an invective or vice-rebuking poem.'—L. *satira*, also *satura*, satire, a species of poetry orig. dramatic and afterwards didactic, peculiar to the Romans (White). β. It is said that the word meant ' a medley,' and is derived from *satura lanx*, a full dish, a dish filled with mixed ingredients ; *satura* being the fem. of *satur*, full, akin to *satis*, enough, and to *satiāre*, to satiate ; see **Sate**. Der. *satir-ic-al*, spelt *saturicall*, Skelton, ed. Dyce, i. 130, l. 139 ; *satir-ise*, *satir-ist*.

SATISFY, to supply or please fully. (F.—L.) ' Not al so *satisfide* ; ' Spenser, F. Q. i. 5. 15. ' I *satysfye*, I content, or suffyce, Ie *satisfie* ; ' Palsgrave.—OF. *satisfier*, to satisfy (as in Palsgrave) ; afterwards displaced by *satisfaire* ; see Littré. Formed as if from a Late L. *satisficāre*, substituted for L. *satisfacere*, to satisfy.—L. *satis*, enough ; and *facere*, to make. See **Sate** and **Fact**. Der. *satisfact-ion*, ME. *satisfaccioun*, Wyclif, 1 Pet. iii. 15, from F. *satisfaction*, ' satisfaction,' Cot. ; *satisfact-or-y*, from F. *satisfactoire*, ' satisfactory,' Cot. ; *satisfact-or-i-ly, -ness*.

SATRAP, a Persian viceroy. (F.—L.—Gk.—Pers.) In Blount's Gloss., ed. 1674. We find ME. *satraper*, Allit. Romance of Alexander, 1913, 1937.—F. *satrape*, ' a great ruler ; ' Cot.—L. *satrapam*, acc. of *satrapēs* ; we also find nom. *satraps* (acc. *satrapem*).—Gk. σατράπης, the title of a Persian viceroy or governor of a province. β. Certainly an OPers. word. Littré, citing Burnouf (Yaçna, p. 545), compares the Gk. pl. ἐξαιθραπεύοντες, found in inscriptions (Liddell and Scott give the form ἐξατράπης), and the Heb. pl. *achashdarpnīm*, satraps.—OPers. *khsatra-pāvā*, guardian of a province ; from *khsatra*, province, and *pā*, to protect ; F. Spiegel, Die altpersischen Keilin-schriften, p. 26. Cf. Skt. *kshatra-*, dominion, allied to *kshaya*, to rule ; and *pā*, to protect.

SATURATE, to fill to excess. (L.) In Minsheu, ed. 1627.—L. *saturātus*, pp. of *saturāre*, to fill full.—L. *satur*, full ; allied to *satis*, enough ; see **Sate**. Der. *satur-at-ion* ; *satur-able*.

SATURDAY, the seventh day of the week. (L. and E.) ME. *Saterday*, P. Plowman, B. v. 14, 367. AS. *Sæter-dæg*, Luke, xxiii. 54 ; also spelt *Sætern-dæg*, Exod. xvi. 23 ; *Sæternes dæg*, rubric to Matt. xvi. 28, xx. 29. The name *Sæter* or *Sætern* is borrowed from L. *Saturnus*, Saturn ; cf. L. *Sāturnī diēs*, Saturday ; Du. *zaturdag*, Saturday. See **Saturnine**.

SATURNINE, gloomy of temperament. (F.—L.) ' *Saturnine*, of the nature of Saturn, i.e. sterne, sad, melancholy ; ' Minsheu.—MF. *Saturnin*, a form noticed by Minsheu ; and Littré has *saturnin* as a medical term, with the sense of ' relating to lead ; ' lead being a symbol of Saturn. The more usual form is F. *Saturnien*, ' sad, sowre, lumpish, melancholy;' Cot. Both adjectives are from L. *Sāturnus*, the god Saturn, also the planet Saturn. β. The peculiar sense is due to the supposed evil influence of the planet Saturn in astrology; see Chaucer, C. T. 2455-2471. γ. *Sāturnus* (OL. *Saeturnus*) is said to mean 'the sower;' cf. *sē-men*, seed; from the root *sē-*, to sow; see **Seed**. Der. (from *Saturnus*) *Saturn-alia*, s. pl., the festival of Saturn, a time of licence and unrestrained enjoyment; *Saturn-ian*, pertaining to the golden age of Saturn, Pope, Dunciad, i. 28. iii. 320, iv. 16. Also *Satur-day*, q. v.

SATYR, a sylvan god. (F.—L.—Gk.) In Shak. Hamlet, i. 2. 140.—F. *satyre*, 'a satyr, a monster, halfe man halfe goat;' Cot.—L. *satyrus*.—Gk. σάτυρος, a Satyr, sylvan god, companion of Bacchus. Der. *satyr-ic*.

SAUCE, a liquid seasoning for food. (F.—L.) ME. *sauce*, Chaucer, C. T. 353; P. Plowman, B. xiii. 43.—F. *sauce*, 'a sauce, condiment;' Cot.—L. *salsa*, a salted thing; fem. of *salsus*, salted, salt, pp. of *salire*, to salt.—L. *sāl*, salt; see **Salt**. Der. *sauce-pan*; *sauc-er*, a shallow vessel orig. intended to hold sauce, L. L. L. iv. 3. 98; we find Late L. *salsārium*, glossed by ME. *sauser*, in Alex. Neckam, in Wright's Vocab. i. 98, l. 5; *sauce*, verb, to give a relish to, often used ironically, as in As You Like It, iii. 5. 69; *sauc-y*, i.e. full of salt, pungent, Twelfth Nt. iii. 4. 159; *sauc-i-ly*, K. Lear, i. 1. 22, ii. 4. 41; *sauc-i-ness*, Com. Errors, ii. 2. 28. Also *saus-age*, q. v.

SAUNTER, to lounge. (F.—L.) 'By *sauntering* still on some adventure;' Hudibras, pt. iii. c. 1. l. 1343 (ed. Bell, ii. 111). Not in early use. We find however, in the Romance of Partenay, ed. Skeat, l. 4653, that Geoffrey '*santred* and doubted,' i.e. hesitated and doubted as to whether he was of the lineage of Presine. And see gloss. to York Mystery Plays. In the dialect of Cumberland the word is *santer*. '*Santer*, saunter; [also], an oald wife *santer* = an unauthenticated tradition;' Dickinson's Cumberland Glossary. β. From AF. *sauntrer*, to venture forth, to go forth. It occurs in the Year-book of Edw. III, of the 11-12 year of his reign, p. 619 (Rolls Series); where we find mention of a man ' qe *saunter* en ewe,' who ventures upon the water, or who puts to sea. It represents a Late L. form *ex-adventurāre*, to venture out. See **Ex-** and **Adventure**. The ME. *aunter*, adventure, is not uncommon. See Notes on E. Etym., p. 256. Der. *saunter-er*.

SAURIAN, one of the lizard tribe. (Gk.) A modern geological term; formed from Gk. σαύρ-α or σαῦρ-ος, a lizard; with suffix *-ian* (=L. *-i-ānus*).

SAUSAGE, an intestine of an animal, stuffed with meat salted and seasoned. (F.—L.) Better *sausige*. Spelt *saulsage*, Gascoigne, Art of Venerie; Works, ed. Hazlitt, ii. 308, l. 3 from bottom; *sausedge* in Palsgrave.—AF. *sauciche* (Guernsey *sauciche*); F. *saucisse* (also *saulcisse* in Cotgrave), 'a saucidge;' Cot.—Late L. *salsicia*, fem. of *salsicius*, adj. (Georges), made of seasoned meat; a sausage. Cf. '*Salcice*, Gallice *sauchises*;' Wright's Vocab. i. 128, l. 1.—L. *salsi-*, for *salsus*, salted; with suffix *-ci-a*. See **Sauce**. See Notes on E. Etym., p. 257.

SAUTERNE, a kind of wine. (F.) From *Sauterne*, a place in France, in the department of Gironde.

SAVAGE, wild, fierce, cruel. (F.—L.) Lit. it merely means 'living in the woods,' rustic; hence, wild, fierce; spelt *salvage*, Spenser, F. Q. iv. 4. 39; &c. ME. *sauage* (with *u=v*), King Alisaunder, l. 869; spelt *salvage*, Gower, ii. 77; bk. iv. 2202.—OF. *salvage*, *savaige*, mod. F. *sauvage*, 'savage, wild;' Cot. And see Burguy.—L. *siluāticus*, belonging to a wood, wild.—L. *silua*, a wood. See **Silvan**. Der. *savage-ly*, *-ness*.

SAVANNA, SAVANNAH, a meadow-plain of America. (Span.—Carib.) '*Savannahs* are clear pieces of land without woods;' Dampier, Voyages, an. 1683; ed. 1699, i. 87; R. Eden, ed. Arber, p. 148.—Span. *sabana* (with *b* sounded as bi-labial *v*), a large plain; said to be of Caribbean origin (Oviedo). ¶ The Span. is *sabána* (whence F. *savane*); distinct from *sábana*, a sheet for a bed, an altar-cloth, which is from L. *sabana*, orig. pl. of *sabanum*, a linen cloth, towel.—Gk. σάβανον, a linen cloth, towel.

SAVE, to rescue, make safe. (F.—L.) ME. *sauuen* (=*sauven*), Ancren Riwle, p. 98, l. 10; *sauen* (=*saven*), Chaucer, C. T. 3534.—F. *sauver*, 'to save;' Cot.—L. *saluāre*, to secure, make safe.—L. *saluus*, safe; see **Safe**. Der. *sav-er*, *save-all*, *sav-ing*, sb., *sav-ings-bank*, a bank for money saved; *sav-i-our*, ME. *saveoure* (=*saveour*), P. Plowman, B. v. 486, from OF. *saveor*, *salveor* (Burguy), from L. acc. *saluātōrem*, a saviour. Also *save*, prep., ME. *saue* (=*save*), P. Plowman, B. xvii. 100, from F. *sauf*, in such phrases as *sauf mon droit*, my right being reserved; see Cotgrave. Also *sav-ing*, prep., K. John, i. 201.

SAVELOY, CERVELAS, a kind of sausage. (F.—Ital.—L.) Now corruptly spelt *saveloy*, but formerly *cervelas* or *cervelat*. The spelling *cervelas* is in Phillips, Kersey, and Ashe; Bailey, ed. 1735, has: '*Cervelas, Cervelat*, a large kind of Bolonia sausage, eaten cold

in slices.'—MF. *cervelat* (now *cervelas*), 'an excellent kind of drie saucidge,' &c.; Cot.—Ital. *cervelata*, a thick short sausage. So called because it contained pigs' brains (Zambaldi).—Ital. *cervello*, brain.—L. *cerebellum*, dimin. of *cerebrum*, brain; see **Cerebral**.

SAVIN, SAVINE, SABINE, an ever-green shrub. (L.) ME. *saveine*, Gower, C. A. iii. 130; bk. vii. 1353. AS. *safinæ*, *sauine*, savine; A. S. Leechdoms, ed. Cockayne, i. 34.—L. *sabīna*, or *Sabina herba*, savin; lit. Sabine herb (F. *sabine*). Fem. of *Sabinus*, Sabine. The Sabines were a people of central Italy.

SAVORY, a plant of the genus *Satureia*. (F.—L.) ME. *sauereye*; '*Satureia, sauereye*'; Voc. 609. 32.—OF. *savereie* (Godefroy).—L. *satureia*, savory. β. We find also MF. *savorée*, 'the herb savory;' Cot. App. due to confusion with MF. *savourée*, fem. of *savouré*, 'savoury, that hath a good smack or taste;' Cot.; orig. fem. pp. of MF. *savorer*, 'to savor;' Cot.—OF. *savour*, savour; see **Savour**.

SAVOUR, odour, scent, taste. (F.—L.) ME. *sauour* (*savour*), Chaucer, C. T. 15697, 15711 (G 229, 243).—OF. *savour* (Burguy); *saveur*, 'savour;' Cot.—L. *sapōrem*, acc. of *sapor*, taste.—L. *sapere*, to taste; see **Sapid**. Der. *savour*, vb., ME. *saueren*, Wyclif, Rom. xii. 3; *savour-y*, ME. *sauery*, Wyclif, Mark, ix. 49; *savour-i-ness*; *savour-less*.

SAVOY, a kind of cabbage. (F.) '*Savoys*, a sort of fine cabbage, first brought from the territories of the dukedom of *Savoy*;' Phillips, ed. 1706.

SAW (1), an instrument for cutting, with a toothed edge. (E.) ME. *sawe*, P. Plowm. Crede, l. 753; Voc. 628. 12. AS. *saga*; '*Serra, saga*;' Voc. 151. 2.+Du. *zaag*; Icel. *sög*; Dan. *sav*; Swed. *såg*; G. *säge*. β. All from Teut. type **sagā*, f., lit. 'a cutter;' from Teut. base **sag*, 2nd grade of Teut. root **seg*, to cut.—√SEQ, to cut; cf. L. *secāre*, to cut; see **Secant**. Der. *saw*, verb, ME. *sawen*, *sawyn*, Prompt. Parv.; *saw-dust*, *saw-fish*, *saw-mill*, *saw-pit*; also *saw-y-er* (formed like *bow-y-er* from *bow*, the *y* being due to a ME. verb **saw-i-en* = *saw-en*), spelt *sawer*, Wright's Vocab. i. 212, col. 2; *sawyer*, Caxton, Godfrey of Boloyne, ch. 57. Also *see-saw*, q. v.

SAW (2), a saying, maxim. (E.) In As You Like It, ii. 7. 156. ME. *sawe*, Chaucer, C. T. 1165 (A 1163). AS. *sagu*, a saying; Grein, ii. 387. Allied to AS. *secgan*, to say.+Icel. *saga*, a saga, tale; Dan. and Swed. *saga*; G. *sage*. See **Say**. Doublet, *saga*.

SAXHORN, a kind of horn. (F. *and* E.) Named after the inventor, Adolphe *Sax*, a Frenchman; ab. 1840.

SAXIFRAGE, a genus of plants. (F.—L.) In Cotgrave and Minsheu and Palsgrave.—F. *saxifrage*, 'the herb saxifrage, or stone-break;' Cot.—L. *saxifraga*, spleen-wort (White). The *adiantum* or 'maiden-hair' was also called *saxifragus*, lit. stone-breaking, because it was supposed to break stones in the bladder. 'They have a wonderful faculty ... to break the stone, and to expel it out of the body; for which cause, rather than for growing on stones and rocks, I believe verily it was .. called in L. *saxifrage*;' Pliny, b. xxii. c. 21 (Holland's translation).—L. *saxi-* = *saxo-*, for *saxum*, a stone, rock; and *frag-*, base of *frangere*, to break, cognate with E. *break*. Doublet, *sassafras*.

SAXON, the name of one of a certain Teutonic race. (L.—Teut.) Late L. *Saxonēs*, pl. Saxons; also *Saxo*, sing., a Saxon.—AS. *Seaxan*, pl., Saxons; so called because armed with a short sword.—AS. *seax*, OFries. *sax*, a knife; lit. 'cutter;' cf. L. *saxum*, a stone implement.—√SEQ, to cut; see **Secant**. Brugmann, i. § 549 c.

SAY (1), to speak, tell. (E.) ME. *seggen*, P. Plowman, B. v. 617; also *siggen*; and often *seien*, *sein*, *seyn*, *sain*, Chaucer, C. T. 1153 (A 1151); *saye*, *seie*, id. 781. AS. *secgan*, *secgean*, to say (pt. t. *sægde*, *sæde*, pp. *gesægd*, *sæd*), Grein, ii. 421.+Icel. *segja*; Dan. *sige*; Swed. *säga*; G. *sagen*; OHG. *sagēn*. β. All these are weak verbs, from a Teut. base **sag*, allied to Idg. √SEQ, to say. Cf. Lithuan. *sakýti*, to say, *sakau*, I say; Gk. ἔννεπε (for **έν-σεπ-ε*); OL. *in-sec-e*, imp. s., tell, say. And see Sweet, N. E. Gram., § 1293. From the same root is W. *heb*, an utterance; see Stokes-Fick, p. 296. Der. *say-ing*, L. L. L. i. 2. 21; *sooth-say-er*; and see *saga*, *saw* (2).

SAY (2), a kind of serge. (F.—L.—Gk.) '*Say*, a delicate serge or woollen cloth;' Halliwell. '*Saye* clothe, serge;' Palsgrave. ME. *saie*; in Wyclif, Exod. xxvi. 9, the later version has *say* where the earlier has *sarge*, i. e. serge.—OF. *saie*; Cotgrave has *saye*, 'a long-skirted jacket, coat, or cassock;' also *sayete*, 'the stuffe sey.' [Florio has Ital. *saio*, 'a long side coate,' and *saietta*, 'a kind of fine serge or cloth for coates; it is also called *rash*.' Neuman has Span. *saya*, *sayo*, a tunic; *sayete*, a thin light stuff.] β. The stuff *say* was so called because used for making a kind of mantle called in L. *sagum* (pl. *saga*, as f. sing.>F. *saie*); cf. Late L. *sagum* (1), a mantle, (2) a kind of cloth (Ducange).—Gk. σάγος, a coarse cloak, a soldier's mantle; cf. σαγή or σάγη, harness, armour, σάγμα, a pack-saddle, also a covering, a large cloak. These Gk. words are not of Celtic origin, as has been said, but allied to Gk. σάττειν (fut. σάξω), to pack, to load. See Prellwitz. See **Sumpter**.

SAY (3), to try, assay. (F.–L.) In Pericles, i. 1. 59; as a sb., in K. Lear, v. 3. 143. Merely an abbreviation of **Assay** or **Essay**; see **Essay**.

SBIRRO, an Italian police-officer. (Ital.–L.–Gk.) Modern. Byron has the pl. *sbirri*; The Two Foscari, A. ii. sc. 1 (Marina). –Ital. *sbirro* (with unoriginal *s*); formerly *birro*, 'a catchpoale,' Florio. So called from wearing a cloak.–L. *birrus*, a cloak to keep off rain; by-form of *burrus*, 'reddish' (because of its colour).– Gk. πυρρός, reddish.–Gk. πῦρ, fire. See **Bureau**. (Pl. *sbirri*.)

SCAB, a crust over a sore. (Scand.) ME. *scab*, Chaucer, C. T. 12292 (C 358). Of Scand. origin; as shown by the *sc* = *sk*.– Dan. and Swed. *skabb*.✛AS. *sceab*, *scæb* (whence E. *shabby*). β. The lit. sense is 'itch;' something that is scratched; cf. L. *scabiēs*, scab, itch, from *scabere*, to scratch. From the Teut. base **skaƀ-*, to scratch, whence mod. E. *shave*; see **Shave**. Der. *scabb-ed*, *scabb-y*, *scabb-i-ness*. Also *shabb-y*, q.v.

SCABBARD, a sword-sheath. (F.–Teut.) Spelt *scabberd* in Baret (1580). *Scabbard* is a corruption of ME. *scaubert* (v. r. *scauberc*), Rob. of Glouc. p. 273, l. 5538. In Prompt. Parv. p. 443, we find all three forms, *scawberk*, *scawbert*, *scauberd*. The form *scauberk* also appears as *scaberke*, Trevisa, v. 373; and is palatalised to *scaberge*, Romance of Partenay, 2790. β. *Scauberk* is obviously, like *hauberk*, a French word of Teutonic origin; but it does not appear in O. French texts; except that Wedgwood cites *vaginas*, glossed by AF. *escaubers*, from Johannes de Garlandiâ. Godefroy quotes the same; from a sing. form *escauberc*; where -*berc* (as in OF. *hau-berc*) means 'protection.' [Note that the OF. *halberc* or *hauberc*, a hauberk, is also spelt *haubert*, just as *scauberk* is also *scaubert*; and corresponding to the form *scaberge* we have *haberge-on*.] γ. The prefix appears to answer to OF. *escale*, mod. F. *écale*, a scale, husk, derived from OHG. *scala*, G. *schale*. G. *schale* means a shell, peel, husk, rind, scale, outside, skull, cover of a book, haft (of a knife), bowl, vase. In composition *schal* means cover or outside; as in *schalbrett*, outside plank (of a tree), *schalholz*, outside of a tree cut into planks, *schalwerk*, a lining of planks. Cf. *schalen*, to plank, inlay; *messer schalen*, to haft knives. δ. The prob. sense is 'scale-protection,' or 'cover-cover;' it is one of those numerous redupli-cated words in which the latter half repeats the sense of the former. The notion of putting a knife into a haft is much the same as that of putting a sword into a sheath. I conclude that *scabbard* = *scale-berk*, with the reduplicated sense of 'cover-cover.' See **Scale** (1) and **Hauberk**. ¶ Distinct from *scabbard*, variant of *scale-board*, a very thin board. See Notes on E. Etym., p. 257.

SCABIOUS, a plant. (F.–L.) ME. *scabiose*; Voc. 609. 36.– MF. and F. *scabieuse*, f.–L. *scabiōsa* (*herba*), a plant supposed to be good for skin-eruptions.–L. *scabiēs*, an itch.–L. *scabere*, to scrape, scratch. Cf. E. *scabrous*, rough, F. *scabreux*, from L. *scabrōsus*, rough, from *scaber*, rough.

SCAFFOLD, a temporary platform. (F.–Gk. *and* Teut.) ME. *scaffold*, *scafold*, Chaucer, C. T. 2533, 3384.–ONorth F. **escafalt*, found as *escafaut*, mod. F. *échafaud*. A still older form was *escadaf-fault* (Ducange), for **escadafalt*; with which cf. Span. *catafalco*, a funeral canopy over a bier, Ital. *catafalco*, a funeral canopy, stage, scaffold (whence mod. F. *catafalque*); showing that the form arose from prefixing *es-* (from L. *ex*, prep.) to the form *cadafalt*, the equivalent of Span. and Ital. *catafalco*. β. The word *catafalco* is a hybrid one; the orig. sense was 'a wooden erection crowning walls, and projecting from them on both sides; thence the besieged com-manded assailants beneath;' N. E. D., s.v. *catafalque*. Perhaps from Gk. κατά, down; and OHG. *balcho*, OSax. *balko*, a balk, a beam. γ. But Hatzfeld derives F. *chafaud* (the equivalent of Ital. *catafalco*) from Gk. κατά, down, and a Late L. type **falicum*, from L. *fala*, a kind of scaffold. (Doubtful.) Der. *scaffold*, verb; *scaffold-ing*.

SCALD (1), to burn with a hot liquid, to burn. (F.–L.) ME. *scalden*, pp. *yscalded*, Chaucer, C. T. Six-text, A 2020; Tyrwhitt (l. 2022) reads *yskalled*, but the 6 best MSS. have *yscalded*. '*Schaldinde water*, scalding water;' Ancren Riwle, p. 246, l. 3.–ONorth F. *escalder*, corresponding to OF. *eschalder* (Marie de France, Equitan, 261), later form *eschauder*, 'to scald;' Cot. Norm. dial. *écauder* (Moisy); mod. F. *échauder*.–L. *excaldāre*, to wash in hot water.– L. *ex*, out, very; and *caldus*, hot, contracted form of *calidus*, hot; cf. *calēre*, to be hot. See **Ex-** and **Caldron**. Der. *scald*, sb.

SCALD (2), scabby. (Scand.) In Shak. Hen. V, v. 1. 5. Con-tracted form of *scalled*, i.e. afflicted with the *scall*; see **Scall**. ME. *scalled*, Chaucer, C. T. 629 (A 627). Cf. Dan. *skaldet*, bald.

SCALD (3), a Scandinavian poet. (Scand.) ME. *scald*, Ormulum, 2192.–Icel. *skald*, a poet; older form *skåld* (Noreen). Perhaps allied to *scold*; but the long vowel is against this.

SCALE (1), a shell, small thin plate or flake on a fish, husk. (F.–OHG.) ME. *scale*; 'fisshes *scales*,' Gower, C. A. i. 275; bk. ii.

3456; *scale* (or *shale*), the shell of a nut, P. Plowman, C. xiii. 145, and footnote.–OF. *escale* (F. *écale*).–OHG. *scala* (G. *schale*), a scale, husk.✛AS. *scealu*, a shell or husk; Dan. and Swed. *skal*, a shell, pod, husk. Cf. Goth. *skalja*, a tile. [The AS. form gave the ME. form *skale*; with *sk*.] β. All from Teut. type **skalā*, f., lit. 'a flake,' that which can be peeled off; from Teut. base **skal*, 2nd grade of strong verb **skel-an-*, to cleave, divide; see **Skill**. Der. *scale*, verb; *scal-ed*, *scal-y*, *scal-i-ness*. Allied to **Scale** (2), **Shell**, **Scall**, **Scull**, **Skill**. And see *scall-op*, *scal-p*. Doublet, *shale*.

SCALE (2), a bowl or dish of a balance. (F.–Teut.) ME. *skale*, *schale* (also *scoale*), a bowl, Ancren Riwle, p. 214, note *i*; *scale*, Layamon, 5368. [The form *scoale* is from Icel. *skál*, scale.] –OF. *escale*, a cup (Godefroy).–Icel. *skål*, Dan. *skaal*, Swed. *skål*, a bowl; cf. Du. *schaal*, scale, bowl. Allied to **Scale** (1); being from Teut. base **skěl-*, 3rd grade of Teut. **skelan-*, to cleave (above). Der. *scole* (obsolete); as in 'Lanx, the *scole* of a balance,' Nomenclator, 1585 (Nares, ed. Wright and Halliwell); 'Then Jove his golden *scoles* weighed up;' Chapman, tr. of Homer, Iliad, b. xxii. l. 180; answering to the ME. form *scoale* above.

SCALE (3), a ladder, series of steps, graduated measure, gra-dation. (L.) ME. *scale*, Chaucer, On the Astrolabe, pt. i. § 12. Borrowed immediately from L. *scāla*, usually in pl. *scālæ*, a flight of steps, ladder. (Hence also F. *échelle*.) β. L. *scā-la* represents **scan(t)slā*, i.e. **scand-slā*, that by which one ascends or descends; cf. L. *scandere*, to climb; see **Scan**. Brugmann, i. § 414. Der. *scale*, verb, to climb by a ladder; Surrey translates 'Hærent parietibus *scalæ*, postesque sub ipsos Nituntur *gradibus*' (Æneid, ii. 442) by 'And rered vp ladders against the walles, Under the win-dowes *scaling* by their steppes;' clearly borrowed from Ital. *scalare*, to scale. See **Escalade**.

SCALENE, having three unequal sides, said of a triangle. (L.– Gk.) Phillips, ed. 1706, has: '*Scalenum*, or *Scalenous Triangle*.'– L. *scalēnus*, adj.–Gk. σκαληνός, scalene, uneven. Perhaps allied to σκολιός, crooked.

SCALL, a scab, scabbiness, eruption on the skin. (Scand.) In Levit. xiii. 30. 'Thou most haue the *skalle*;' Chaucer, Lines to Adam Scrivener. Gen. used with ref. to the head. 'On his heued he has the *skalle*;' Cursor Mundi, 11819.–Icel. *skalli*, a bare head. The lit. sense may be 'having a peeled head;' cf. Swed. *skallig*, bald, *skala*, to peel. If so, it is nearly related to Dan. and Swed. *skal*, a husk; see **Scale** (1). Der. *scald* (2), q.v.

SCALLION, a plant allied to the garlic and onion. (F.–L.– Gk.–Phœnician.) Phillips, ed. 1706, gives both *scallion* and *shalot*. ME. *scalone*, P. Plowman, C. ix. 310.–ONorth F. *escalogne*, a scallion; see further under **Shallot**.

SCALLOP, SCOLLOP, a bi-valvular shell-fish, with the edge of its shell in a waved form. (F.–Teut.) Holland's Pliny, b. ix. c. 33, treats 'Of *Scallops*.' ME. *scalop* (with one *l*), Prompt. Parv., p. 442.–OF. *escalope*, a shell; a word used by Rutebuef; see quota-tions in Godefroy; and cf. F. *escalope* in Littré. β. Of Teut. origin; cf. MDu. *schelpe* (Du. *schelp*), a shell; Hexham. Hexham has also: 'S. Iacobs *schelpe*, S. James his shell;' and the shell worn by pilgrims who had been to St. James's shrine was of the kind which we call 'a *scalloppe*-shell;' Chambers, Book of Days, ii. 121. Thus Palsgrave has: '*scaloppe*-shell, quocquille de saint Iacques.' Cf. G. *schelfe*, a husk. γ. The forms *schel-pe*, *schel-fe* are extensions from the form which appears in E. as *shell*; see **Scale** (1), **Shell**. Der. *scallop*, verb, to cut an edge into convex lobes or scallop-like curves. And see **Scalp**.

SCALP, the skin of the head on which the hair grows. (Scand.) 'Her *scalpe*, taken out of the charnel-house;' Sir T. More, p. 57 a. ME. *scalp*. 'And his wiknes in his *scalp* doune falle;' Early Eng. Psalter, ed. Stevenson, vii. 17; where *scalp* means the top of the head, Lat. *uertex*. Evidently a Scand. word, due to a form allied to that whence we also have MDu. *schelpe*, a shell, and OF. *escalope*, a shell; see **Scallop**. β. We may compare MSwed. *skalp*, a sheath, Icel. *skålpr*, a sheath; Dan. dial. *skalp*, a husk, pod. γ. The orig. sense is *shell* or *scull* (head-shell); and the word is allied to *scale*; see **Scale** (1). Florio has Ital. *scalpo della testa*, 'the skalp of ones head;' but this is merely borrowed from Teutonic. Der. *scalp*, verb; which may have been confused with L. *scalpere* (see **Scalpel**).

SCALPEL, a small surgeon's knife for dissecting. (L.) Phillips, ed. 1706, has *scalper* or *scalping-iron*; Todd's Johnson has *scalpel*. *Scalpel* is from L. *scalpellum*, a scalpel; dimin. of *scalprum*, a knife.– L. *scalpere*, to cut, carve, scratch, engrave; (whence E. *scalping-iron*). Allied to L. *sculpere*; see **Sculpture**.

SCAMBLE; see **Scamper**, **Scramble**, **Shamble**.

SCAMMONY, a cathartic gum-resin. (F.–L.–Gk.) Spelt *scamony* in Arnold's Chron. (1502), ed. 1811, p. 164, l. 16; *skamonye*,

Libell of Eng. Policy, l. 360.—OF. *scammonie, scammonée,* 'scammony, purging bind-weed;' Cot.—L. *scammōnia.*—Gk. σκαμμωνία, or rather σκαμωνία, scammony, a kind of bind-weed. It grows in Mysia, Colophon, and Priene, in Asia Minor; Pliny, b. xxvi, c. 8.

SCAMP; see **Scamper.**

SCAMPER, to run with speed, flee away. (F.—L.) 'We were forc'd to ... *scamper* away as well as we could;' Dampier's Voyages, an. 1685 (R.). The suffix *-er* is, as usual, frequentative, so that the orig. form is *scamp*; but this is only found as a sb. in the sense of 'worthless fellow,' or 'cheat,' though the orig. meaning is merely 'fugitive' or 'vagabond,' one given to frequent shifts or *decampings.*—ONorth F. *escamper,* or rather *s'escamper,* 'to scape, flie;' Cot.; OF. *eschamper* (Godefroy).—L. *ex,* out; and *campus,* a field, esp. a field of battle. A parallel formation to *decamp,* q. v. See **Ex-** and **Camp.** Der. *scamper,* sb.

SCAN, to count the measures in a poem, to scrutinise. (L.) In Shak. Oth. iii. 3. 245; Skelton, Bowge of Court, 245. In common use in the pp., which was frequently spelt *scand,* as in Spenser, F. Q. vii. 6. 8, where it is used in the sense of 'climbed.' The verb should rather have been *scand,* but the pp. was formed as *scand* (for *scanded*), and then the final *d* was taken to be the pp. termination, and was accordingly dropped.—L. *scandere,* to climb; also, to scan a verse. Cf. Skt. *skand,* to spring, ascend. Der. *scans-ion,* formed (by analogy) from L. *scansio,* a scanning, like the pp. *scansus.* Also *scans-or-i-al,* formed for climbing, from *scansōrius,* belonging to climbing. From the same root, *a-scend, a-scent, de-scend, de-scent, con-de-scend, transcend; scale* (3), *e-sca-lade.* See notes on E. Etym., p. 259.

SCANDAL, opprobrious censure, disgrace, offence. (F.—L.—Gk.) ME. *scandal;* spelt *scandle,* Ancren Riwle, p. 12, l. 12.—F. *scandale,* 'a scandall, offence;' Cot. We also find OF. *escandle* (Burguy); whence ME. *scandle.*—L. *scandalum.*—Gk. σκάνδαλον, a snare; also scandal, offence, stumbling-block. The orig. sense seems to be that of σκανδάληθρον also, viz. the spring of a trap, the stick on a trap on which the bait was placed, which sprang up and shut the trap. Prob. from √SQAND, to spring up; see **Scan.** Der. *scandal-ise,* from F. *scandaliser,* formerly *scandalizer,* 'to scandalize,' Cot. Also *scandal-ous,* from F. *scandaleux,* 'scandalous, offensive,' Cot.; *scandal-ous-ly, -ness.* Doublet, *slander.*

SCANSION, SCANSORIAL; see **Scan.**

SCANT, insufficient, sparing, very little. (Scand.) ME. *scant,* Prompt. Parv. Chaucer speaks of 'the inordinate *scantnesse*' of clothing; Pers. Tale, De Superbia (Six-text, I 414). *Scant* has been substituted for *scamt.*—Icel. *skamt,* neut. of *skammr,* short, brief; whence *skamta,* to dole out, apportion meals (and so, to scant or stint). Cf. also Icel. *skamtr,* sb., a dole, share, portion (hence, short or scant measure). In Norwegian, the *mt* changes to *nt,* so that we find *skantad,* pp. measured or doled out, *skanta,* to measure narrowly, reckon closely; *skant,* a portion, dole, piece measured off (Aasen). The *m* is preserved in the phrase 'to *scamp* work,' i. e. to do it insufficiently, and in the prov. E. *skimping,* scanty (Halliwell). Der. *scant,* adv., Romeo, i. 2. 104; *scant,* verb, Merch. Ven. ii. 1. 17; *scant-ly,* Antony, iii. 4. 6; *scant-y, scant-i-ly, scant-i-ness.*

SCANTLING, a piece of timber cut of a small size, sample, pattern. (F.—L.—Gk.; *with L. prefix.*) Here *-ing* is for *-on.* Palsgrave has *scantlon.* ME. *scantilone,* Rom. Rose, 7064; *skantulon,* Voc. 606. 16. The word has doubtless been confused with *scant* and *scanty;* but the old sense is 'pattern,' or 'sample,' or a small piece; with reference to the old word *cantle.* As used in Shak. (Troil. i. 3. 341) and in Cotgrave, it is certainly allied to OF. *eschanteler,* and answers to ONorth F. *escantillon,* corresponding to OF. *eschantillon,* 'a small cantle or corner-piece, also a *scantling,* sample, pattern, proof of any sort of merchandise;' Cot. Cf. also F. *eschanteler,* 'to break into cantles,' to cut up into small pieces; Cotgrave, Burguy.—OF. *es-,* prefix, from L. *ex,* out; and ONorth F. *cantel* (Burguy), a cantle, corner, piece, OF. *chantel, chanteau,* 'a cornerpeece, or piece broken off from the corner;' Cot. Hence E. *cantle, scantle,* 1 Hen. IV, iii. 1. 100. See **Cantle.** ¶ Cf. ME. *scantilon,* a measure, Cursor Mundi, 2231.

SCAPE (1), a leafless stalk bearing the fructification. (L.) Modern.—L. *scāpus,* a shaft, stalk, stem; allied to **Sceptre.**

SCAPE (2), short for *escape.* 'Help us to *scape;*' Chaucer, C. T., A 3608. See **Escape.**

SCAPEGOAT, a goat allowed to escape into the wilderness. (F.—L.; *and* E.) Levit. xvi. 8. From *scape* and *goat; scape* being a mutilated form of *escape,* in common use; see Temp. ii. 2. 117, &c. See **Escape** and **Goat.** So also *scape-grace,* one who has escaped grace or is out of favour, a graceless fellow.

SCAPULAR, belonging to the shoulder-blades. (L.) In Blount's Gloss., ed. 1674. [He also gives it as a sb., equivalent to the word generally spelt *scapulary;* see below.]—Late L. *scapulāris,* adj. formed from L. pl. *scapulæ,* the shoulder-blades, from a sing. *scapula,*

not in use. Der. *scapular-y,* spelt *scapularie* in Minsheu, a kind of scarf worn by friars and others, so called from passing over the shoulders; ME. *scaplorye, scapelary,* Prompt. Parv., *chapolory,* P. Plowman's Crede, l. 550; from F. *scapulaire,* Late L. *scapulāre.*

SCAR (1), the mark of a wound, blemish. (F.—L.—Gk.) '*Scarre* of a wounde, *covsture;*' Palsgrave. Spelt *skarre,* Gascoigne, Fruites of Warre, st. 40, and st. 90; ME. *scar,* Wyclif, Lev. xxii. 22. —MF. *escare,* 'a skar or scab;' Cot. [Cf. Span. and Ital. *escara, scar, scurf, crust.*]—L. *eschara,* a scar, esp. one produced by a burn. —Gk. ἐσχάρα, a hearth, fire-place, grate for a fire, brazier, scar of a burn. Der. *scar,* verb, Rich. III, v. 5. 23.

SCAR (2), **SCAUR,** a rock. (Scand.) ME. *scarre,* Wyclif, 1 Kings, xiv. 5; *skerre* (Halliwell); Lowland Sc. *scar, scaur* (Jamieson); Orkney *skerry,* a rock in the sea (id.).—Icel. *sker,* a skerry, isolated rock in the sea; Dan. *skjær,* Swed. *skär.* Cf. Icel. *skor,* a rift in a rock. So called because 'cut off' from the main land or 'cut down;' see **Shear.** Doublet, *share;* and cf. *score.*

SCARAB, a beetle. (F.—L.) 'They are the moths and *scarabs* of a state;' Ben Jonson, Poetaster, iv. 6. 16.—MF. *scarabee* (Hatzfeld).—L. *scarabæum,* acc. of *scarabæus,* a beetle. Der. *scarab-ee* (F.); *scarab-æus* (L.).

SCARAMOUCH, a buffoon. (F.—Ital.—Teut.) '*Scaramouch* and Harlequin at Paris;' Dryden, Kind Keeper, A. i. sc. 1. 'Th' Italian merry-andrews took their place ... Stout *Scaramoucha* with rush lance rode in;' Dryden, Epilogue to Silent Woman, spoken by Mr. Hart, ll. 11–15. '*Scaramoche,* a famous Italian zani, or mountebank, who acted here in England 1673;' Blount's Gloss., ed. 1674. Blount, writing at the time, is certainly right. The name was taken from a famous Italian buffoon, mentioned again in the Spectator, no. 283. He died at Paris in 1694; Chambers, Book of Days, ii. 671. His name was (rightly) *Scaramuccia,* altered by Dryden to *Scaramoucha,* and in French to *Scaramouche* (Littré).—F. *scaramouche.*— Ital. *Scaramuccia,* proper name; lit. 'a skirmish,' a word derived from Teutonic; see **Skirmish.**

SCARCE, rare, not plentiful. (F.—L.) ME. *scars,* Rob. of Glouc. p. 334, l. 6862. Chaucer has the adv. *scarsly,* C. T. 585 (A 583).—ONorth F. *escars* (Burguy), OF. *eschars,* 'scarce, needy, scanty, saving, niggard;' Cot. Cf. Ital. *scarso,* scarce; mod. F. *échars* (Littré). β. Derived by Diez from Late L. *scarpsus,* shorter form of *excarpsus,* used A. D. 805 as a substitute for L. *excerptus,* pp. of *excerpere,* (prob. also *excarpere* in Low Latin), to pick out, select, extract. The lit. sense is selected, extracted, or picked out, hence 'select,' and so scarce; and Diez remarks that *excarpsus* is found just with the sense of Ital. *scarso.*—L. *ex,* out; and *carpere,* to pluck, allied to E. *harvest.* See **Excerpt**; also **Ex-** and **Harvest.** Der. *scarce-ly,* ME. *scarse-liche,* K. Alisaunder, 3552; *scarce-ness,* Deut. viii. 9, ME. *skarsnesse,* Gower, C. A. ii. 284; bk. v. 4674; *scarc-i-ty,* ME. *scarseté,* K. Alisaunder, 5495, from OF. *escarsete* (escharsete in Burguy). ¶ Cf. AF. *escars,* niggard, Philip de Thaun, Bestiary, 602; and AF. *escarseté,* scarcity, Political Songs, ed. Wright, p. 186.

SCARE, to frighten away. (Scand.) ME. *skerren, skeren,* Prompt. Parv. p. 457; Destruction of Troy, 13404. Cf. 'the *skerre* hors' = the scared horse, Ancren Riwle, p. 242, note *d.* The ME. verb appears to be formed from the adj. *skerre,* scared, timid.—Icel. *skjarr,* shy, timid; *skjarrt hross,* a shy horse, just like ME. *skerre hors,* and Sc. *skair,* timorous (Jamieson). Cf. Icel. *skirra,* to bar, prevent; reflexive, *skirrask,* to shun, shrink from; *skirrast við,* to shrink from; Norw. *skjerr,* shy, *skjerra,* to scare; Swed. dial. *skjarra,* to scare. Further connexions doubtful. Der. *scare-crow,* something to scare crows away, Meas. for Meas. ii. 1. 1.

SCARF (1), a light piece of dress worn on the shoulders or about the neck. (Du.—Low G.) Spenser has *scarfe,* F. Q. v. 2. 3; and so in Baret.—Du. *scherf,* a shard, a shred; the sense being supplied from Low G. *scherf,* a military scarf, girdle (Brem. Wört.); or we may say that the Low G. word was influenced by Du. pronunciation. β. We also find the form *skarp;* as in 'with a *skarpe* about her neke;' Machyn's Diary (C.S.), p. 180 (1558). This is borrowed from ONorth F. *eskarpe* (Godefroy), MF. *escharpe,* 'a scarf, baudrick;' Cot. It also meant a scrip for a pilgrim, and is derived from MDu. *scharpe, schaerpe, scerpe,* a scrip, pilgrim's wallet (Oudemans); Low G. *schrap,* a scrip (Bremen Wörterbuch); and see **Scrip, Scrap.** γ. With Du. *scherf,* a shard, shiver, fragment; cf. G. *scherbe,* a fragment, also 'a scarf' in the sense of *scarf* (2) below. This suggests that the form *skarp* was influenced by *scarf* (2). ¶ The G. *schärpe,* a scarf, sash, Swed. *skärp,* Dan. *skjerf, skjærf,* are not true Teut. words, but borrowed from French. Der. *scarf,* verb, Hamlet, v. 2. 13; *scarf-skin,* the epidermis or outer skin (Phillips). Doublets, *scrip, scrap.*

SCARF (2), to join pieces of timber together. (Scand.) 'In the joining of the stern, where it was *scarfed;*' Anson's Voyage, b. ii. c. 7 (R.). The pp. *skarvyd* occurs in 1531–2; Strutt, Manners and

Customs, iii. 53. And in Phillips, ed. 1706. The word is Swedish. — Swed. *skarfva*, to join together, piece out. — Swed. *skarf*, a scarf, seam, joint; cf. *skarfyxa*, a chip-axe. + Bavarian *scharben*, to cut a notch in timber, G. *scharben*, OHG. *scarbōn*, to cut small. From Teut. **skarb*, 2nd grade of **skerban-*, to cut; as in AS. *sceorfan* (pt. t. *scearf*), to scrape. Cf. Du. *scherf*, a shard; see **Scarf** (1).

SCARF (3), a cormorant. (Icel.) A local name; also, corruptly, *scarth*, *scart*. — Icel. *skarfr*, Swed. *skarf*, Dan. *skarv*, a cormorant. + G. *scharbe*, OHG. *scarba*.

SCARIFY, to cut the skin slightly. (F. — L. — Gk.) ' Of *Scarifying*, called boxyng or cuppyng;' Sir T. Elyot, Castel of Helth, b. iii. c. 7. — F. *scarifier*, 'to scarifie;' Cot. — L. *scarificāre*, to scarify, scratch open; longer form of *scarifāre*, which also occurs (Lewis). β. Not cognate with, but absolutely borrowed from Gk. σκαρῑφάομαι, I scratch or scrape up. — Gk. σκάρῑφος, a style for drawing outlines (a sharp-pointed instrument). — L. *scribere*, to write; see **Scribe**. Der. *scarific-at-ion*, from F. *scarification* (Cot.).

SCARLET, a bright-red colour. (F. — Pers.) ME. *scarlat*, O. Eng. Miscellany, p. 92, l. 69; *skarlet*, p. 168, l. 10; *scarlet*, P. Plowman, B. ii. 15. — OF. *escarlate*, 'scarlet;' Cot. [Mod. F. *écarlate*; Span. *escarlata*; Ital. *scarlatto*.] — Pers. *saqalāt*, *siqalāt*, or *suqlāt*, scarlet cloth. Cf. Pers. *saqlātūn*, *saqlātīn*, scarlet cloth, *saqlān*, cloth; Rich. Dict. p. 837. β. The Pers. *saqlatūn* is clearly the origin of ME. *ciclatoun*, Chaucer, C. T. Group B, 1924, on which see my note, and Col. Yule's note to his edition of Marco Polo, i. 249. He remarks that *suqlāt* is applied, in the Punjab trade returns, to broad-cloth; it was used for banners, ladies' robes, quilts, leggings, housings and pavilions. We find also Arab. *saqarlāt*, a warm woollen cloth; Rich. Dict. p. 836; also Arab. *siqlāt*, a fine painted or figured cloth, a canopy over a litter. It seems to have been the name of a stuff, which was frequently of a scarlet colour; and hence to have become the name of the colour. Cf. 'scarlet reed;' Chaucer, Prol. 456. So also Telugu *sakalāti*, *sakalātu*, woollen or broad-cloth; Wilson, Gloss. of Indian Terms, p. 455. This can hardly be from English, as Wilson suggests, but corresponds to the Pers. and Ital. forms. ¶ The Turkish *iskerlat*, scarlet, is merely a loan-word from Italian; Zenker, p. 49. Der. *scarlet-runner*, a climbing plant with scarlet flowers; *scarlat-ina*, a disease named from the scarlet rash which accompanies it, Ital. *scarlattina*, from Ital. *scarlatto*, scarlet.

SCARP, part of a fortification. (F. — Ital. — Teut.) Formerly written *scarf*, as in Cotgrave, but this is an E. adaptation, by confusion with *scarf*. ' *Scarp*, the inward slope of the moat or ditch of a place;' Phillips, ed. 1706. — F. *escarpe*, 'a scarf, or little wall without the main rampire of a fort;' Cot. — Ital. *scarpa*, 'a counterscarfe or curtein of a wall;' Florio. β. Perhaps from OHG. *scarpōn*, to cut; with regard to the steep face presented. Or from Du. *scherp*, Low G. *scharp*, sharp; cognate with E. **Sharp**, q. v. Der. *counterscarp*, *escarp-ment*.

SCATCHES, stilts. (F. — Low G.) See **Skate** (2).

SCATHE, to harm, injure. (Scand.) In Romeo, i. 5. 86. ME. *scaþen*, Prompt. Parv. [The sb. *scathe*, harm, is in Chaucer, C. T. 448 (A 446); Havelok, 2006.] The *sc* (= *sk*) shows that the word is Scand., not E. — Icel. *skaða*; Swed. *skada*; Dan. *skade*. + AS. *sceaðan*, pp. *scōd*; G. and Du. *schaden*; Goth. *gaskathjan*, str. vb., pt. t. *gaskōth*, pp. *gaskathans*. β. All from Teut. base **skath*, to harm; Fick, iii. 330. Cf. Gk. ἀ-σκηθής, unharmed. Brugmann, i. § 791. Der. *scathe*, harm, injury, also spelt *scath*, Rich. III, i. 3. 3^17, from Icel. *skaði*; *scath-ful*, Tw. Nt. v. 59; *scathe-less*, or *scath-less*, ME. *scatheles*, Rom. of the Rose, 1550.

SCATTER, to disperse, sprinkle. (E.) ME. *scateren* (with one *t*), Chaucer, C. T. 16382 (G 914); *skatered*, pt. t., Early E. Psalter, xvii. 15. The frequentative of prov. E. *scat*, (1) to scatter, (2) to break to pieces, to shatter. *Scatter* is the Northern form corresponding to E. **Shatter**, q. v. Cf. Gk. σκεδάννυμι, I sprinkle, scatter, σκέδασις, a scattering, L. *scandula*, a shingle for a roof, Skt. *kshad*, *skhad*, to cut. Der. *scatter-ling*, a vagrant, one of a scattered race, Spenser, F. Q. ii. 10. 63. Doublet, *shatter*, q. v.

SCAUP-DUCK, a duck so named because she frequents *mussel-scaups* or *mussel-scalps*, i. e. beds of rock or sand on which mussels collect; see Newton, Dict. of Birds. (Scand. *and* E.) *Scalp* (see E. D. D.) means (1) skull, head . . (4) a bank of sand or mud uncovered at low tide, esp. a mussel-bed. *Scaup* is a dialectal variant of **Scalp**, q. v.

SCAUR; see **Scar** (2).

SCAVENGER, one who cleans the streets. (ONorth F. — Teut.) Spelt *scavengere*, Bp. Hall, Satires, b. iv. sat. 7. l. 48. The word appears in the Act of 14 Ch. II, cap. 2 (Blount). As in the case of *messenger* (for *messager*) and *passenger* (for *passager*), the *n* before *g* is intrusive, and *scavenger* stands for *scavager*. β. The *scavager* was an officer who had formerly very different duties; see Riley's tr. of Liber Albus, p. 34, which mentions 'the *scavagers*, ale-con-

ners, bedel, and other officials.' Riley says: ' *scavagers*, officers whose duty it was originally to take custom upon the *scavage*, i. e. inspection of the opening out, of imported goods. At a later date, part of their duty to see that the streets were kept clean; and hence the modern word *scavenger*, whose office corresponds with that of the *rakyer* (raker) of former times.' As a fact, the old word for scavenger is always *rakyer*; see P. Plowman, v. 322, and note. That the *scavagers* had to see to the cleansing of the streets, is shown in the Liber Albus, p. 313. Wedgwood cites the orig. French, which has the spelling *scawageour*. γ. *Scavage* or *scawage* is an AF. derivative, signifying ' inspection;' formed, with the suffix *-age* (< L. *-āticum*), from ONorth F. *escauwer*, to look, inspect. — OSax. *skawōn*, to behold; cognate with AS. *sceáwian*, to look at, and E. *show*. See Blount's Nomolexicon, where the various spellings *scavage*, *schevage*, *schewage*, and *scheawing* (showing) are cited; he says: ' In a charter of Hen. II it is written *scewinga* and (in Mon. Ang. 2 par. fol. 890 *b*.) *sceawing*, and elsewhere I find it in Latin *tributum ostensorium*.' Some of these forms are due to confusion with ME. *schewen*, to show. See further in Riley, p. 196, ' Oi *scavage*;' again, ' *Scavage* is the shewe,' &c., Arnold's Chron. (1502), ed. 1811, p. 99, l. 1; and see *Scawing* in the Glossary to Diplomatarium Ævi Saxonici, ed. Thorpe. See **Show**. And see Notes on E. Etym., p. 259.

SCENE, stage of a theatre, view, spectacle, place of action. (L. — Gk.) Common in the dramatists. ' A *scene*, or theater;' Minsheu. The old plays, as, e. g., that of Roister Doister, have the acts and scenes marked in Latin, by *Actus* and *Scæna* or *Scena*; and we certainly Anglicised the Latin word, instead of borrowing the F. one, which Cotgrave actually omits. — L. *scēna*. — Gk. σκηνή, a sheltered place, tent, stage, scene; cf. Skt. *chhāyā* (for **skāyā*), shade. Der. *scen-ic*, Gk. σκηνικός; *scen-er-y*, written *scenary* by Dryden (R.), from L. *scēnārius*, belonging to a play.

SCENT, to discern by the smell. (F. — L.) The spelling is false; it ought to be *sent*, as when first introduced. A similar false spelling occurs in *scythe*; so also we find *scite* for *site*, *scituation* for *situation*, in the 17th century. ' To *sent*, to smell;' Minsheu, ed. 1627. ' I *sent* the mornings ayre;' Hamlet, i. 5. 58 (ed. 1623). ' Delycious of *sent*;' Barclay, Ship of Fools, i. 100. — F. *sentir*, 'to feel, also to sent, smell;' Cot. — L. *sentīre*, to feel, perceive. See **Sense**. Der. *scent*, sb., spelt *sent*, i. e. discernment, Spenser, F. Q. i. 1. 43, last line; and in Barclay (above).

SCEPTIC, doubting, hesitating; often as sb. (F. — L. — Gk.) ' The Philosophers, called *Scepticks*;' Blount's Gloss., ed. 1674, s. v. *Sceptical*. — F. *sceptique*, ' one that is ever seeking, and never finds; the fortune, or humour of a Pyrrhonian philosopher;' Cot. — L. *scepticus*. — Gk. σκεπτικός, thoughtful, inquiring; σκεπτικοί, pl., the Sceptics, followers of Pyrrho (died abt. B.C. 285). — Gk. root **skep-*, as in σκέπτομαι, I consider. Allied to **Scope**. Der. *sceptic-al* (Blount); *sceptic-ism*.

SCEPTRE, a staff, as a mark of royal authority. (F. — L. — Gk.) ME. *ceptre*, Chaucer, C. T. 14379 (B 3563). — F. *sceptre*, 'a royall scepter;' Cot. — L. *scēptrum*. — Gk. σκῆπτρον, a staff to lean on; also, a sceptre. — Gk. σκήπτειν, to prop; also, to lean on. Cf. σκηπτός, a gust or squall of wind; σκήπτειν is also used in the sense to hurl, throw, shoot, dart. Allied to L. *scāpus*, a shaft, stem. Der. *sceptr-ed*, Rich. II, ii. 1. 40.

SCHEDULE, an inventory, list. (F. — L. — Gk.) In Shak. L. L. L. i. 1. 18; spelt *scedule* in the first folio. — MF. *schedule*, or *cedule*, ' a schedule, scroll, note, bill;' Cot. — L. *schedula*, a small leaf of paper; dimin. of *scheda*, also *scida* (Cicero, Att. i. 20 *fin*.), a strip of papyrus-bark. β. The Gk. σχέδη, a tablet, leaf, may have been borrowed from L. *scheda* (see Liddell); but we find also Gk. σχίδη, a cleft piece of wood, a splint, which is the true original of L. *scida*. (*Ch* is not a Latin symbol.) From Gk. σχίζειν (= **σχίδ-γειν*), to cleave; from √SKHEID, to cleave; cf. Skt. *chhid*, to cut. See **Schism**.

SCHEME, a plan, purpose, plot. (L. — Gk.) ' *Scheme* (*schema*), the outward fashion or habit of anything, the adorning a speech with rhetorical figures;' Blount's Gloss., ed. 1674. Borrowed directly, as a term in rhetoric, from L. *schēma*. — Gk. σχῆμα, form, appearance; also, a term in rhetoric. — Gk. σχη-, base of σχή-σω, future of ἔχειν, to hold, haye. The orig. base is σεχ-; from √SEGH, to hold; whence also Skt. *sah*, to bear, endure. Der. *scheme*, vb.; *schem-er*, *schem-ing*. And see *sail*, *hectic*.

SCHERZO, a playful movement in music. (Ital. — Teut.) Modern. — Ital. *scherzo*, play, sport. — MHG. (and G.) *scherz*, sport. Der. *scherz-ando*, playfully.

SCHIEDAM, Holland gin. (Du.) Made at *Schiedam*, near Rotterdam.

SCHISM, a division, due to opinion. (F. — L. — Gk.) Tyndall has ' *schismes* that were among our clergy;' Works, p. 176, col. 1.

ME. *scisme*, Gower, C. A. i. 15 ; prol. 348. – F. *schisme*, MF. *scisme*, 'a scisme, a division in, or from, the church ;' Cot. – L. *schisma*. – Gk. σχίσμα, a rent, split, schism. – Gk. σχίζειν (fut. σχίσ-ω, base σχιδ-), to cleave. – √SKHEID, to cleave ; Skt. *chhid*, L. *scindere*, to cut. **Der.** *schism-at-ic*, from MF. *scismatique*, 'scismaticall,' Cot., L. *schismaticus*, Gk. σχισματικός, from σχισματ-, stem of σχίσμα ; hence *schism-at-ic-al*, *-ly*. And see *schist*, *schedule*, *ab-scind*, *re-scind*.

SCHIST, rock easily cleft, slate-rock. (Gk.) In geology. – Gk. σχιστός, easily cleft. – Gk. σχίζειν, to cleave. See **Schism**.

SCHNAPPS, a name for spirit, esp. gin. (G. – Du.) G. *schnapps*. – Du. *snaps*, a dram, lit. mouthful. – Du. *snappen*, to snap up. See **Snap**.

SCHOOL (1), a place for instruction. (F. – L. – Gk.) ME. *scole*, Chaucer, C. T. 125 ; Layamon, 9897. The *sch* = ME. *sc* (= *sk*) shows that this form is of F. origin, not from Latin before the Conquest. – AF. *escole*, Stat. Realm, i. 103 (1285) ; OF. *escole*. – L. *schola*, a school. – Gk. σχολή, rest, leisure, spare time, employment of leisure, disputation, philosophy, a place where lectures are given, a school. The orig. sense is a resting or pausing ; from the base σχο-, a grade of σχε- (in σχέ-σις), allied to ἔχειν, to hold, check, stop. – √SEGH, to hold ; see **Scheme**. **Der.** *school*, verb, As You Like It, i. 1. 173 ; *schol-ar*, ME. *scoler*, Chaucer, C. T., A 260, from AF. *escoler*, altered to *scholar* to agree with L. adj. *scholāris* ; *scholar-ly*, *scholar-ship* ; *schol-ast-ic*, from L. *scholasticus* = Gk. σχολαστικός ; *schol-i-um*, a Latinised form of Gk. σχόλιον, an interpretation, comment, from σχολή in the sense of 'discussion ;' *scholi-ast*, from Gk. σχολιαστής, a commentator ; *scholi-ast-ic*. Also *school-man*, *school-master*, *school-mistress*.

SCHOOL (2), a shoal of fish. (Du.) 'A *scole* of Dolphins ;' Sandys, Trav., p. 100. – Du. *school visschen*, 'a shole of fishes ;' Sewel. See **Scull** (3), **Shoal** (1).

SCHOONER, SCOONER, a two-masted vessel. (Scand.) The spelling *schooner* is a false one ; it should be *scooner*. The mistake is due to a supposed derivation from the Du. *schooner*, a schooner, but, on the contrary, the Du. word (like G. *schoner*) is borrowed from E. There is no mention of Du. *schooner* in Sewel's Du. Dict., ed. 1754. The E. *schooner* occurs in Ash's Dict., ed. 1775 ; and earlier in the following: 'Went to see Captain Robinson's lady . . . This gentleman was first contriver of *schooners*, and built the first of that sort about 8 years since ;' extract from a letter written in 1721, in Babson's Hist. of Gloucester, Massachusetts ; cited in Webster's Dict., whence all the information here given is copied. 'The first *schooner* . . . is said to have been built in Gloucester, Mass., about the year 1713, by a Captain Andrew Robinson, and to have received its name from the following trivial circumstance: When the vessel went off the stocks into the water, a bystander cried out, "O how she *scoons!*" [i.e. glides, skims along]. Robinson instantly replied, "A *scooner* let her be ;" and from that time, vessels thus masted and rigged have gone by this name. The word *scoon* is popularly used in some parts of New England to denote the act of making stones skip along the surface of water. . . . According to the New England records, the word appears to have been originally written *scooner* ;' Webster. The New England *scoon* was imported from Clydesdale, Scotland ; being the same as Lowland Sc. *scon*, 'to make flat stones skip along the surface of water ; also, to skip in the above manner, applied to flat bodies ; Clydesdale ;' Jamieson. So also *scun* in E. D. D. – Icel. *skunda* (trans.), to speed, to hasten. Allied to **Shunt**, q. v. ☞ As a rule, derivations which require a story to be told turn out to be false ; in the present case, there seems to be no doubt that the story is true.

SCHORL, black tourmaline. (F. – G.) F. *schorl* (Littré). – G. *schörl*, schorl.

SCIATIC, pertaining to the hip-joint. (F. – L. – Gk.) 'Sciatick vein ;' Blount's Gloss., ed. 1674. 'Veyne that is clepid *sciatica* ;' Lanfrank, Cirurgie, p. 177. [The sb. *sciatica* is in Minsheu, ed. 1627.] – F. *sciatique*, 'of the sciatica ; *veine sciatique*, the sciatica vein, seated above the outward ankle ;' Cot. – Late L. *sciaticus*, corruption of L. *ischiadicus*, subject to gout in the hip (White). – Gk. ἰσχιαδικός, subject to pains in the loins. – Gk. ἰσχιαδ-, stem of ἰσχιάς, pain in the loins. – Gk. ἰσχίον, the socket in which the thigh-bone turns. **Der.** *sciatica*, fem. of L. *sciaticus*.

SCIENCE, knowledge. (F. – L.) ME. *science*, Chaucer, C. T. 11434 (F 1122) ; P. Plowman, B. x. 214. – F. *science*, 'science ;' Cot. – L. *scientia*, science, knowledge. – L. *scient-*, stem of pres. part. of *scire*, to know, orig. to discern. **Der.** *scienti-fic*, from F. *scientifique*, 'scientificall,' Cot., from L. *scientificus*, made by science, where the suffix *-ficus* is from *facere*, to make ; *scientific-al*, *-ly*. Also *a-scit-it-i-ous*, *scio-l-ist*.

SCIMETAR, CIMETER, a curved sword. (F. or Ital. – Pers.?) Spelt *semitar*, used of a *pointed* sword ; Titus Andron. iv. 2. 91. – F. *cimeterre*, 'a scymitar, or smyter, a kind of short and crooked sword,

much in use among the Turks ;' Cot. This accounts for the spelling *cimeter*. Also Ital. *scimitarra*, *scimitara*, 'a turkish or persian crooked sword, a simitar ;' Florio. This accounts for the spelling *scimetar*. β. It was fully believed to be of Eastern origin. If so, it can hardly be other than a corruption of Pers. *shimshīr*, *shamshīr*, 'a cimeter, a sabre, a sword, a blade ;' Rich. Dict. p. 909. Lit. 'lion's claw.' – Pers. *sham*, a nail ; and *shēr*, a lion ; id. pp. 907, 921 ; Vullers, ii. 464. γ. The Span. is *cimitarra*, explained by Larramendi from Basque *cimea*, a fine point, and *tarra*, belonging to ; prob. a mere invention, like his Basque etymology of *cigar*.

SCINTILLATION, a throwing out of sparks. (F. – L.) In Minsheu, ed. 1627. [The verb *scintillate* is much later.] – F. *scintillation*, 'a sparkling ;' Cot. – L. *scintillātiōnem*, acc. of *scintillātio*. – L. *scintillāre*, to throw out sparks. – L. *scintilla*, a spark ; a dimin. form, as if from **scinta*. Perhaps allied to AS. *scin-an*, to shine ; see **Shine**. **Der.** *stencil*, *tinsel*.

SCIOLIST, one whose knowledge is superficial. (L.) 'Though they be but smatterers and meer *sciolists* ;' Howell, Famil. Letters, b. iii. let. 8 (about A.D. 1646). Formed with suffix *-ist* (L. *-ista*, Gk. -ιστης) from L. *sciolus*, a smatterer. Here the suffix (in *scio-lus*) has a dimin. force, so that the sense is 'knowing little.' – L. *scius*, knowing. – L. *scīre*, to know ; see **Science**.

SCION, a cutting or twig for grafting ; a young shoot, young member of a family. (F. – L.) Spelt *scion*, Minsheu, ed. 1627. Also spelt *sion*, *syon*, *cion*. 'Syon, a yong sette,' i. e. slip or graft ; Palsgrave. 'Cyun of a tre, Surculus, vitulamen ;' Prompt. Parv. Spelt *sioun*, Poems and Lives of Saints, ed. Furnivall, xxxv. 74. – F. *scion*, 'a scion, a shoot, sprig, or twig ;' Cot. Spelt *cion* in the 13th cent. (Littré) ; Picard *chion*. Diez connects it with F. *scier*, MF. *sier*, to cut, to saw, which is from L. *secāre*, to cut. If so *sci-on* means 'a cutting,' just as a slip or graft is called in E. *a cutting*, and in G. *schnittling*, from *schnitt*, a cut. See **Section**. (Doubtful.)

SCIRRHOUS, pertaining to a hard swelling. (L. – Gk.) In Blount's Gloss., ed. 1674. Englished as if from a L. **scirrhōsus*, adj. formed from *scirrhus*, a Late L. medical term given in Blount and Phillips, used in place of L. *scirrhōma*, a hard swelling. – Gk. σκίρρος, better σκίρος, a hardened swelling, a 'scirrhus ;' also called σκίρρωμα, or σκίρωμα ; from the adj. σκιρός, hard.

SCISSORS, a cutting instrument with two blades fastened together at the middle. (F. – L.) Spelt *cissers* in Levins ; *sycers* in Palsgrave. 'Cysowre, forpex ;' Prompt. Parv. ME. *sisoures* (riming to *houres*), Chaucer, House of Fame, 690. – OF. *cisoires*, shears, scissors (Roquefort). [The more usual F. form is *ciseaux*, 'sizars or little sheers ;' Cot. The latter is the pl. of *ciseau*, older form *cisel*, a chisel, cutting instrument. See **Chisel**.] – L. *cisōrium*, a cutting instrument (Vegetius). – L. *cīs-*, for *cæs*, as in *cæsus*, pp. of *cædere*, to cut. β. It is clear that the mod. E. spelling of *scissors* is due to a supposed etymology (historically false) from L. *scissor*, a cutter, allied to *scissus*, pp. of *scindere*, to cleave. It is remarkable, however, that the L. *scissor* meant 'a person who cuts,' a carver, a kind of gladiator (White) ; whilst the Late L. *scissor* meant a carver, a butcher, and *scisor* meant a coin-engraver, a tailor. γ. There is absolutely not the slightest evidence for the use of *scissor* for a cutting instrument, and still less for the use of a plural *scissores*, which could only mean a couple of carvers, or butchers, or tailors. But popular etymology has triumphed, and the spelling *scissors* is the result. ¶ With L. *scindere* we may connect *ab-scind*, *ab-scissa*, *re-scind* ; and see *schism*. With L. *cædere* we may connect *circum-cise*, *con-cise*, *de-cide*, *de-cis-ion*, *ex-cis-ion*, *fratri-cide*, *homi-cide*, *in-cise*, *infanti-cide*, *matri-cide*, *parri-cide*, *pre-cise*, *regi-cide*, *sui-cide* ; *cæs-ura* ; *chisel*, *scissors*. For the derivatives of *secare*, see **Section**.

SCOFF, an expression of scorn, a taunt. (Scand.) ME. *scof*, *skof*, Ayenbite of Inwyt, p. 128, l. 3 from bottom ; 'nom *a skof*' = took it in scorn, K. Alisaunder, 6986 ; *skof*, id., 667. Cf. OFries. *schof*, a scoff, taunt (Richtofen). – MDan. *skof*, *skuf*, a scoff ; *skuffe*, to scoff, mock (Kalkar) ; Swed. dial. *skoff-*, as in *skoffs-ord*, words of abuse, *skoffsera*, to abuse (Rietz) ; cf. Icel. *skaup*, later *skop*, mockery, ridicule. Cf. also MDu. *schobben*, *schoppen*, to scoff, mock (Hexham) ; Icel. *skeypa*, *skopa*, to scoff. β. The orig. sense was probably 'a shove' or 'a push ;' cf. Swed. *skuff*, a push ; MHG. *schupfen*, to push, allied to E. *shove*. See **Shove**. Or allied to Gk. σκώπ-τειν, to mock. **Der.** *scoff*, verb, Rich. II, iii. 2. 163 ; *scoff-er*, As You Like It, iii. 5. 62.

SCOLD, to chide, rail at. (E. ?) ME. *scolden*, P. Plowman, B. ii. 81 ; *scolde*, sb., a scold, id. xix. 279. Not in AS. Hardly an E. word ; perhaps Frisian. From the weak grade **skəld* of the Teut. strong verb **skeldan-*, to scold (pt. t. **skald*, pp. **skəld-anoz*). It appears as OFries. *skelda*, Du. *schelden*, G. *schelten*, to scold ; cf. Dan. weak verb *skjelde*, *skælde*, to scold. · Perhaps allied to OSax. *scaldan*, to push off a boat (Kluge) ; OHG. *scaltan*, the same. **Der.** *scold*, *sb.*, Tam. Shrew, i. 2. 188, and in Palsgrave and P. Pl. (as above); *scold-er.* And see *scald* (3).

SCOLLOP, the same as **Scallop**, q.v.

SCONCE (1), a small fort, bulwark. (F.—L.) In Shak. Hen. V, iii. 6. 76; also applied to a helmet, Com. Errors, ii. 2. 37; and to the head itself, Com. Errors, i. 2. 79. [Cf. MDu. *schantse* (Du. *schans*), 'a fortresse, or a sconce;' Hexham; Swed. *skans*, fort, sconce, steerage; Dan. *skandse*, fort, quarter-deck; G. *schanze*, a sconce, fort, redoubt, bulwark; but none of these words are original.] β. All from OF. *esconse*, a hiding-place, sconce; orig. fem. of *escons*, pp.—L. *absconsa*, fem. of *absconsus*, used (as well as *absconditus*) as pp. of *abscondere*, to hide; see **Abscond**. The Span. *esconder*, Ital. *ascondere*, to hide, are directly from the infin. *abscondere*; with the reflexive sense, we find Span. *esconderse*, to hide oneself; and the E. to *ensconce oneself* simply means to lie hid in a corner, or to get into a secure nook. γ. Diez derives the Ital. *scancia*, a book-case, from Bavarian *schanz*=G. *schanze*, which is doubtless right; but the G. *schanze* may be none the less a borrowed word. It is singular that we also find G. *schanz* in the sense of 'chance;' and there can be no doubt as to its being borrowed from F. when used in that sense; for it is then from OF. or E. *chance*, chance. And see **Sconce** (2). Der. *ensconce*, coined by prefixing *en-*; see **En-**.

SCONCE (2), a candle-stick. (F.—L.) Palsgrave has: '*Scons*, to sette a candell in, *lanterne a mayn*.' ME. *sconce*. 'Sconce, Sconsa, vel absconsa, lanternula;' Prompt. Parv. p. 450. 'Hec absconsa, a scons;' Voc. 721. 12. This clearly shows that the word was used to mean a concealed or closely covered light; as we also find from Roquefort.—OF. *esconse*, a dark lantern, L. *absconsa*; Roquefort.—L. *absconsus*, pp. of *abscondere*; see **Abscond**. And see **Sconce** (1).

SCONE, SCON, a thin soft cake of wheat or barley-meal. (Dan.—Low G.) The pl. *sconnis* is in Douglas, tr. of Virgil, Æn. vii. 109.—MDan. *skon-roggen*, a muffin of bolted rye-flour (Kalkar).—Low G. *schön-roggen*, in Hamburg, a three-cornered loaf or bun.—Low G. *schön*, *schoon*, fine; *roggen*, rye.

SCOOP, a hollow vessel for ladling out water, a large ladle. (F.—Scand.) ME. *scope*. '*Scope*, instrument, Vatila, Alveolus;' Prompt. Parv. The pl. *scopes*, and the verb *scopen*, to ladle out water, occur in Manning's Hist. of England, ed. Furnivall, 8164, 8168 (Stratmann).—OF. *escope* (F. *écope*), a scoop (Hatzfeld).—Swed. *skopa*, a scoop; MSwed. *skopa*, with sense of L. *haustrum* (Ihre).+MDu. *schoepe*, a scoop, Hexham; MHG. *schuofe*. Cf. G. *schöpfen*, to draw water.—Teut. *skōp*, 2nd grade of Teut. *skap-*, as in OSax. *skeppian* (for *skap-jan*), Du. *scheppen*, OHG. *schephan* (pt. t. *scuof*), to draw up water. Der. *scoop*, vb., ME. *scopen*, as above; *coal-scoop*.

SCOPE, view, space surveyed, space for action, intention. (Ital.—Gk.) In Spenser, F. Q. iii. 4. 52. 'Wherein . . . we haue giuen ouer large a *skope*;' Gascoigne's Works, ed. Hazlitt, i. 460. Florio has Ital. *scopo*, 'a marke or but to shoote at, a *scope*, purpose, intent.' We seem to have taken it from Ital., as it is not a F. word, and has a more limited sense in Gk.—Gk. σκοπός, a watcher, spy; also a mark to shoot at.—Gk. *skop-*, second grade of *skep-*, as in σκέπτομαι, I consider, see, spy. Cf. **Sceptic**.

SCORBUTIC, pertaining to, or afflicted with scurvy. (Low L.—Scand.?) In Blount's Gloss., ed. 1674, we find: '*Scorbute* (*scorbutus*), the disease called the scurvy; *scorbutical*, pertaining, or subject to that disease.' Cf. 'the *Scuruie* or *Scorbute*;' Purchas's Pilgrimage, bk. iic. 13. § ii (1617); p. 1086. Formed with suffix *-ic* from Low L. *scorbūtus*, a Latinized form which some think was derived from MDu. *scheuren*, to break, and *bot*, a bone (Weigand); which is very unlikely. β. It appears rather to have been formed with L. suffix *-ūtus* (cf. *ac-ūtus*) from Swed. *skorf* (Dan. *skurv*, ME. *scurf*), i.e. 'scurf;' so that *scorbūtus* would express (1) *scurvy*, adj., and (2) *scurvy*, sb. This L. form was further debased so as to give Low G. *schorbock*, scurvy, also spelt *schärbuuk*, *scharbock*; see Bremen Wörterbuch, s.v. *schärbuuk*. Cf. MDu. *scheur-buyck*, 'the scurvie in the gumms,' Hexham; Du. *scheurbuik*. Also G. *scharbock*, scurvy, tartar on the teeth. γ. The Low G. *schärbuuk* is due to a popular etymology; viz. from *scheren*, to separate, part aside, tear, rupture, and *buuk*, the belly; so also Du. *scheur-buik*, from *scheuren*, to tear, rend, crack, and *buik*, the belly. The verbs are allied to E. **Shear**. The Low G. *buuk*, Du. *buik*, G. *bauch*, are the same as Icel. *būkr*, the trunk of the body, for which see **Bulk** (2). But see **Scurvy**. Der. *scorbutic-al*.

SCORCH, to burn slightly, burn the surface of a thing. (F.—L.) ME. *scorchen*, Chaucer, tr. of Boethius, bk. ii. met. 6, l. 18 (footnote), as a variant of *scorklen*; Romans of Partenay, 3678.—OF. *escorcher*, *escorcer*, 'to flay or pluck off the skin;' Cot. Cf. Span. *escorchar*, Ital. *scorticare*, to flay. β. These are due to Late L. *excorticāre*, to take off the skin; Ducange.—L. *ex*, off; and *cortic-*,

stem of *cortex*, bark, rind, husk. But the peculiar sense was prob. due to confusion with ME. *scorklen*, to scorch (above), and ME. *scorcned*, dried up, parched, Ormulum, 8626. These words seem to be of Scand. origin, and allied to Norw. *skrokkna*, to shrivel, *skrokken*, shrunken; which are further allied to **Shrink**. Perhaps further confused with ME. *scorch* (*scortch*), to score, scratch; see Notes on E. Etym., p. 259. Cf. prov. E. *scorch*, to shrivel up, and *scorch*, to scratch. See **Scotch**.

SCORE, a notch or line cut; a reckoning; twenty. (Scand.) ME. *score*; 'ten *score* tymes;' P. Plowman, B. x. 180. It is supposed that, in counting numbers by notches on a stick, every twentieth number was denoted by a longer and deeper cut or *score*. At Lowestoft, narrow passages cut in the side of the slope towards the sea are called *scores*. AS. *scoru*, twenty; which occurs, according to Napier, in a MS. of the AS. version of the Rule of St. Bennet, but is borrowed from Scandinavian.—Icel. *skor*, *skora*, a score, notch, incision; Swed. *skåra*, Dan. *skaar*, the same. From Teut. *skor-*, weak grade of *skeran-*, to shear, cut; see **Shear**. Der. *score*, to cut, Spenser, F. Q. i. 1. 2; also to count by scoring, Chaucer, C. T. 13346 (B 1606).

SCORIA, dross, slag from burnt metal. (L.—Gk.) In Holland, tr. of Pliny, b. xxxiii. c. 4.—L. *scōria*.—Gk. σκωρία, filthy refuse, dross, scum.—Gk. σκῶρ, dung, ordure.+AS. *scearn*, dung.

SCORN, disdain, contempt. (F.—OHG.) ME. *scorn* (dat. *scorne*), O. Eng. Homilies, ii. 169, l. 1; *schorn* (*scharn*), Ancren Riwle, p. 126, l. 24; (*skarn*), Ormulum, 4402; (*scarn*), scorn, Layamon, 17307.—OF. *escorne*, scorn; Cot.—OF. *escorner*, to humiliate, mock at; orig. 'to deprive of horns;' from L. *ex*, out (of), and *cornu*, a horn. β. But the ME. *scarn* in the same sense is from the OF. *escarn*, scorn, derision, Burguy; whence OF. *escarnir*, *escharnir*, to deride. We find OF. pp. pl. *escharnys*, glossed by E. *scornid*, in Wright's Vocab. i. 144, l. 8. Cf. Ital. *scherno*, derision.—OHG. *skern*, mockery, scurrility; whence OHG. *scernōn*, to deride. Der. *scorn*, verb, ME. *scornen*, P. Plowman, B. ii. 81; *skarnen*, Ormulum, 7397, from OF. *escarnir*, *escharnir*; also *scorn-ful*, K. Lear, ii. 4. 168; *scorn-ful-ly*; *scorn-er*, P. Plowman, B. xix. 279.

SCORPION, a stinging insect, a sign of the zodiac. (F.—L.—Gk.) ME. *scorpion*, K. Alisaunder, 5263.—F. *scorpion*, 'a scorpion;' Cot.—L. *scorpiōnem*, acc. of *scorpio*, another form of *scorpius*, a scorpion.—Gk. σκορπίος, a scorpion, a prickly sea-fish, a prickly plant.

SCOTCH, to cut with narrow incisions. (Scand.) In Shak. Cor. iv. 5. 198; Macb. iii. 2. 13; cf. *scotch*, sb., a slight cut, Antony, iv. 7. 10. ME. *scocchen*; as in '*scocched* it with knyues,' cut it about with knives; Hoccleve, De Regim. Princ., p. 134, l. 3727. In the Babees Book, p. 80, we find: 'With knyfe *scortche* not the boorde,' do not score the table with your knife. It seems to be an extension from *scor-en*, to score, affected by the verb *scorch*, to flay; perhaps even by the verb *scutch*. See Notes on E. Etym., p. 259. See **Score**. Cf. prov. E. *scorch*, to scotch; in E.D.D.

SCOT-FREE, free from payment. (Hybrid; F.—Teut. *and* E.) *Scot* means 'payment;' we frequently find *scot and lot*, as in Shak. 1 Hen. IV, v. 4. 115; Ben Jonson, Every Man, ed. Wheatley, iii. 7. 11; see a paper by D. P. Fry on *scot and lot*, Phil. Soc. Trans. 1867, p. 167. The phrase occurs in Thorpe, Ancient Laws, i. 491, in the Laws of Will. I. § v; 'omnis Francigena, qui tempore Eadwardi propinqui nostri fuit in Anglia particeps consuetudinum Anglorum, quod ipsi dicunt *an hlote* et *an scote*, persolvat secundum legem Anglorum.' Here *an*=on, in, by. See also Liber Albus, ed. Riley, pp. 128, 269. *Scot* is a F. form.—AF. and OF. *escot* (F. *écot*), a payment, esp. a payment into a common fund, into which it is shot; whence *escotter*, 'every one to pay his shot, or to contribute somewhat towards it,' Cot.; *disner à escot*, 'a dinner at an ordinary, or whereat every guest pays his part,' id.; so that *scot*=a tavern-score, is certainly the same word; cf. 'Simbolum, *escot de taverne*,' Wright's Voc. i. 134.—Icel. *skot*, a shot, a contribution.+Du. *schot*; G. *schoss*, a scot, shot; AS. *sceot*, which gave the form *shot*.—Teut. *skut-*, weak grade of *skeut-an-*, to shoot. See **Shoot**. ¶ The phrase *scot and lot*, as a whole, presents some difficulty, and has been variously interpreted; the lit. sense is 'contribution and share;' I suppose that originally *scot* meant a contribution towards some object to which others contributed equally, and that *lot* meant the privilege and liability thereby incurred; mod. E. *subscription* and *membership*. See Mr. Fry's paper, which is full of information. Doublet, *shot*.

SCOUNDREL, a rascal, worthless fellow. (E.) In Shak. Tw. Nt. i. 3. 36; and in Blount's Gloss., ed. 1674. Not common in old authors; used by Cotgrave to translate F. *maraud*. Formed, with agential suffix *-el*, from prov. E. and Scottish *skunner* or *scowner*, to loathe, shun; also, to cause loathing; with excrescent *d* after *n*. This word *scunner* was also used as a sb., to express an object of dislike.

β. Thus Brockett gives: '*Scunner*, to nauseate, feel disgust, to loathe, to shy, as a horse in harness. It is also applied, figuratively, to a man whose courage is not at the sticking place, one who shrinks through fear.' So also Jamieson has: '*Scunner, Scouner*, to loathe, shudder, hesitate, shrink back through fear; *Scunner, Skonner*, sb., loathing, a surfeit; also, any *person* or thing which excites disgust.' Also: '*Scunner*, vb. trans., to disgust, cause loathing.' To which the suffix *-el* has been added; cf. *cocker-el*. **γ.** The verb *scunner* is the frequentative form from a verb = AS. *scunian*, to shun; the *sk* sound being preserved (as usual) in the North of England. Hence *scoun-d-r-el* = *scun-er-el*, one whom one constantly shuns, or merely 'a shunner,' a coward. The word is rather Scand. than E.; having *sc*, not *sh*. In Barbour's Bruce, xvii. 651, we have: 'And *skunnyrrit* tharfor na kyn thing' = and did not shrink through fear one bit on that account; where the Edinb. MS. has *scounryt*; showing that *skunnyr* = *scouner*. And again, in the same, v. 211, where one MS. has *schonand* (shunning), the other has *skownrand* (scunnering), both words meaning 'dreading;' showing that *skowner* is the frequentative of *scun* = *shun*. Cf. Icel. *skunda*, to speed, to hasten, Swed. dial. *skunna sig*, to hasten away. See **Shun.**

SCOUR (1), to cleanse by hard rubbing, to make bright. (L.) ME. *scouren*; '*scowryn* awey ruste;' Prompt. Parv. 'As any bason *scoured* newe;' Rom. of the Rose, 540. Cf. OF. *escurer*, 'to scowre;' Cot.; also Span. *escurare*, MItal. *scurare*, 'to skoure dishes, to rub or cleanse harnesse,' Florio. [Hence also Swed. *skura*, Dan. *skure*, to scour: the word not occurring in Icelandic.]—L. *excūrāre*, to take great care of, of which the pp. *excūrātus* occurs in Plautus; see Diez.—L. *ex*, here used as an intensive prefix; and *cūrāre*, to take care, from *cūra*, care. See **Ex-** and **Cure.** ¶ The *ou* in ME. *scouren* is much better explained by supposing a derivation from L. *excūrāre* directly; or rather, from Late L. *scūrāre*, to scour (Duc.), a monkish form of the same. Der. *scour-er*.

SCOUR (2), to run hastily over. (F.—L.) 'When swift Camilla *scours* the plain;' Pope, Ess. on Criticism, 372. 'Apon the moss a *scurrour* sone fand he; To *scour* the land Makfadȝane had him send;' Blind Harry, Wallace, vii. 796.—OF. *escourre, escorre*, to run, run out.—L. *excurrere*, to run out, make excursions.—L. *ex*, out; *currere*, to run. See **Excursion.** Der. ME. *scurr-our* (= *scour-er*); cf. Ital. *scorridore*, a scout. See Notes on Eng. Etym., p. 261; and p. 264 (s. v. *Scur*).

SCOURGE, a whip, instrument of punishment. (F.—L.) ME. *scourge*, Wyclif, John, ii. 15; *schurge*, O. E. Homilies, i. 283, l. 11; Ancren Riwle, p. 418.—AF. *escorge*, Langtoft, ii. 430; OF. *escorgie* (see Littré), mod. F. *escourgée, écourgée*, a scourge. Cot. has *escourgée*, 'a thong, latchet, scourge, or whip.' Cf. MItal. *scoria*, 'a whip, scourge,' *scoriare*, 'to whip,' *scoriata, scoriada*, 'a whipping; also, the same as *scoria*,' i.e. a whip; Florio. **β.** The MItal. *scoriata* answers to L. *excoriāta*, lit. flayed off, hence a strip of skin or shred of leather for a whip; pp. of *excoriāre*, to strip off skin.—L. *ex*, off; and *corium*, skin; see **Ex-** and **Cuirass.** **γ.** We might explain the MItal. verb *scoriare* directly from L. *excoriāre*, to excoriate, to flay by scourging. Der. *scourge*, ME. *scourgen*, Rob. of Glouc. p. 263, l. 5304.

SCOUT (1), a spy. (F.—L.) ME. *scoute* (spelt *scout*, but riming with *oute*), Seven Sages, ed. Wright, l. 2218.—OF. *escoute*, 'a spie, eave-dropper, also, a scout, scout-watch;' Cot. Verbal sb. from *escouter*, 'to hearken;' id.—L. *auscultāre*, to hearken; see **Auscultation.** **β.** The transfer in sense, from listening to spying, causes no difficulty; the OF. *escoute* means both listener and spy.

SCOUT (2), to ridicule, reject an idea. (Scand.) In Todd's Johnson; noted as a vulgar word. Cf. Lowland Scotch *scout*, 'to pour forth any liquid forcibly;' Jamieson. The latter sense is closely related to *shoot*.—Icel. *skúta, skúti*, a taunt; cf. *skúta*, to jut out, allied to *skota, skotra*, to shove, *skot-yrði*, scoffs, taunts, and to the strong verb *skjóta* (pt. t. *skaut*, pl. *skutu*, pp. *skotinn*), to shoot. Cf. Swed. *skjuta*, (1) to shoot, (2) to shove, push; *skjuta skulden på*, to thrust the blame on; Dan. *skyde*, (1) to shoot, (2) to shove; *skyde skylden paa*, to thrust the blame on; *skyde vand*, to repel water. Thus the sense is to shoot, push away, reject. See **Shoot.**

SCOUT (3), a projecting rock. (Scand.) In place-names, as *Raven-Scout*. 'The steep ridges of rocks on Beetham-fell (Westmoreland) are called *scouts*;' A Bran New Wark (E. D. S.), l. 193, footnote.—Icel. *skúta*, to jut out; see **Scout** (2).

SCOWL, to look angry, to lower or look gloomy. (Scand.) ME. *scoulen*; spelt *scowle*, Prompt. Parv. 'The devils who gather round a dying man are said to '*skoul* and stare;' Pricke of Conscience, 2225.—Dan. *skule*, to scowl, cast down the eyes. Cf. Icel. *skolla*, to skulk, keep aloof, *skolli*, a skulker, a fox, the devil; Du. *schuilen*, to skulk, lurk, lie hid. That these are connected words is shown by Low G. *schulen*, to hide oneself, not to let oneself be seen, and the

prov. G. (Ditmarsch) *schulen*, to hide the eyes, to look slily as if peeping out of a hiding-place, look out. **β.** From the sb. seen in EFries. *schül*, Du. *schuil*, Dan. *skjul*, shelter (whence Dan. *skjule*, to hide), Icel. *skjól*, a shelter, cover. Teut. base *skeul-, *skūl-; from √SKEU, to cover. Thus the sense is 'to peep out of a hiding-place,' or to look from under the covert of lowering brows. Der. *scowl*, sb.; also *scul-k*, q. v.

SCRABBLE, to scrawl. (Scand.) In 1 Sam. xxi. 13; where the marginal note has 'made marks.' Cf. prov. E. *scrabble*, to scratch, frequentative of *scrab*, to scratch, i.e. to scrape (Halliwell).—Norw. *skrabba*, to scrape (Ross); Dan. *skrabe*, to scrape; Du. *schrabben*. Variant of prov. E. *scrapple*, to scrape (E. D. D.); which is a frequentative of **Scrape**, q. v. Cf. *scrabble*, to scribble; E. D. D.

SCRAGGY, lean, rough. (Scand.) Cotgrave translates F. *escharde* by 'a little, lean, or *skraggie* girle, that looks as if she were starved.' Cf. Prov. E. *scrag*, a crooked, forked branch, also, a lean thin person (Halliwell); *shrags*, the ends of sticks. Allied to prov. E. *scrog*, a stunted bush, *scroggy*, abounding in underwood, *scrogs*, blackthorn, *scroggy*, twisted, stunted, *scrog-legs*, bandy-legs (id.). ME. *scroggy*, covered with underwood, or straggling bushes. 'The wey toward the Cite was strong, thorny, and *scroggy*;' Gesta Romanorum, ed. Herrtage, p. 19, l. 19.—Swed. dial. *skragger*, a weak old man, *skragga*, to walk with difficulty; Norw. *skragg*, a poor weak creature, *skraggen*, scraggy (Ross). Cf. Icel. *skröggsligr*, scraggy; North Fries. *skrog*, a lean man; Dan. *skrog*, a carcase, a poor creature. See **Shrug, Shrink.** Der. *scraggi-ness*.

SCRAMBLE, to catch at or strive for rudely, struggle after, struggle. (E.) 'And then she'll *scramble* too;' Beaum. and Fletcher, Mons. Thomas, i. 3. 'I'll *scramble* yet amongst them;' id. Captain, ii. 1 (Jacomo). 'The cowardly wretch fell down, crying for succour, and *scrambling* through the legs of them that were about him;' Sidney, Arcadia, b. ii. (R.). Not found in ME. A frequentative form of prov. E. *scramb*, to pull, or rake together with the hands, *scramp*, to catch at, to snatch at; E. D. D. It may also be regarded as a nasalised form of prov. E. *scrabble*, to scramble (Somersets.), allied to *scraffle*, to scramble, and *scrapple*, to grub about, which is the frequentative of prov. E. *scrap*, to scratch. Halliwell cites 'to *scrappe* as a henne dose' from a MS. Dict. of A.D. 1540; which is merely E. *scrape*. And see **Scrabble.** Der. *scramble*, sb.; *scrambl-er*.

SCRANNEL, thin, poor, wretched. (Scand.) In Milton, Lycidas, 124. Cf. prov. E. *scrannel*, lean, wretched, weak (of the voice); *scranny*, meagre.—Swed. dial. *skran*, weak; Norw. *skran*, thin, lean, dry; *skranaleg*, lean (Ross); Dan. *skranten*, sickly, weakly. Cf. Swed. dial. and Norw. *skrinn*, thin, lean, weak, dry. And cf. AS. *scrimman* (pt. *scramm*), to shrink.

SCRAP, a small piece, shred. (Scand.) ME. *scrappe*. 'And also ȝif I myȝt gadre eny *scrappes* of the releef of the twelf cupes,' i.e. any bits of the leavings of the twelve baskets (in the miracle of the loaves); Trevisa, tr. of Higden, i. 15. (Rather Scand. than E.)—Icel. *skrap*, scraps, trifles, from *skrapa*, to scrape, scratch; Dan. *skrab*, scrapings, trash, from *skrabe*, to scrape; Swed. *afskrap*, scrapings, refuse, dregs, from *skrapa*, to scrape. See **Scrape.**

SCRAPE, to remove a surface with a sharp instrument, shave, scratch, save up. (Scand.) ME. *scrapien, scrapen*, also *shrapien, shrapen* (Stratmann). 'But ho so *schrape* my mawe' = unless one were to scrape my maw; P. Plowman, B. v. 124. Spelt *shreapien*, Ancren Riwle, p. 116, l. 15. (Rather Scand. than E.)—Icel. *skrapa*, to scrape; Swed. *skrapa*; Dan. *skrabe*.+Du. *schrapen*, to scrape. From Teut. *skrap-*, 2nd grade of the strong vb. *skrep-an-*, to scrape, as in AS. *screpan*, pt. t. *scræp*, to scratch; O. E. Texts. Der. *scrap-ing, scrap-er*; also *scrap*, q. v., *scrabb-le*, q. v., *scramb-le*, q. v.

SCRATCH, to scrape with a pointed instrument or with the nails. (1. Scand.; 2. MDu.—MHG.) *Scratch* has resulted from the confusion of ME. *scratten*, to scratch, with ME. *cracchen*, with the same sense. 1. ME. *scratten*, to scratch, Prompt. Parv.; Pricke of Conscience, 7378; Ancren Riwle, p. 186, note *b*. This form *scratten* appears to be for *s-kratten*, made by prefixing AF. *es-* (for L. *ex*), intensive prefix, to the Swed. *kratta*, to scrape (see below). 2. ME. *cracchen*, P. Plowman, B. prol. 154, 186. Apparently for *cratsen*.—MDu. *kratsen*, to scratch (Hexham); whence Du. *krassen*, Swed. *kratsa*, and Dan. *kradse*, to scrape.—MHG. *kratzen*, OHG. *chrazzôn*, to scratch.+Swed. *kratta*, to rake, scrape, scratch, cf. *kratta*, sb., a rake. All from a Teut. base *krat*, perhaps from a Teut. str. vb. *kret-an-* (pt. t. *krat*, pp. *krot-anoz*); cf. Icel. *krot-a*, to engrave. ¶ Hence *scratten* and *cracchen* are from the same base and mean much the same thing, so that confusion between them was easy enough. Der. *scratch*, sb., *scratch-er*. Doublet, *grate* (2).

SCRAWL, to write hastily or irregularly. (E.) A late word, used by Swift and Pope (Rich., and Todd). The *aw* (= *au*) denotes a long vowel or diphthong; better spelt *scrall*, with *a* as in *all*.

'To *scrall*, or *scrawl*, to scribble, to write after a sorry careless manner;' Phillips, ed. 1706. It appears to be a contraction of **Scrabble**, q. v. Cf. also E. *scribble*, and prov. E. *scribble-scrobble*, scribbling (North); and North Fries. *skrawe*, by-form of *skrape*, to scrape. Or perhaps prov. E., from Dan. *skrolle*, a poor worthless book (Larsen); MDan. *skrold*, a diffuse, poor letter (Kalkar). β. The form seems due to confusion with prov. E. *scrawl*, to crawl (West) in Halliwell; he cites 'To *scrall*, stir, *motito*' from Coles, Lat. Dict. To which add: 'The ryuer shall *scraule* [swarm] with frogges,' Exod. viii. 3; in Coverdale's version. This word is merely E. *crawl*, with prefixed *s* (AF. *es-*, L. *ex*) added in some cases with the idea of giving greater emphasis; see **Crawl**. Der. *scrawl*, sb., *scrawl-er*.

SCREAM, to cry out shrilly. (Scand.) ME. *scremen*, Polit. Songs, p. 158, l. 9; *screamen*, Hali Meidenhad, p. 37, last line but one.—Icel. *skræma*, to scare, terrify; Swed. *skrämma*, Dan. *skræmme*, to scare. β. Hence it appears that the E. word has preserved what was doubtless another sense of these Scand. words, viz. 'to cry aloud,' as the means of imposing or of expressing terror; we still commonly use *scream* with especial reference to the effects of sudden fright. Cf. Swed. *skrän*, a scream, *skräna*, to scream, to whimper, which is merely a parallel form; Jutland *skreme*, to whine, to speak hoarsely (Kok). Cf. **Screech**, **Shriek**. Der. *scream*, sb.

SCREECH, to shriek, cry aloud. (Scand.) 'Whilst the *screech-owl*, *screeching* loud;' Mids. Nt. Dr. v. 383; where the first folio has *scritch-owle*, *scritching*. Also spelt *scrike*, Spenser, F. Q. vi. 4. 18. Baret (1580) has *scriek*. ME. *scriken*, *skryken*, *schrichen*, *schriken*, Chaucer, C. T. 15406 (B 4590); spelt *shriken*, O. E. Homilies, ii. 181, l. 2. Also *skriche*, Seven Sages, ed. Weber, 1290. Cf. Lowl. Sc. *scraik*.—Icel. *skrækja*, to shriek; cf. *skrikja*, to titter (said of suppressed laughter); Swed. *skrika*, to shriek; Dan. *skrige*, to shriek; *skrige af Skræk*, to shriek with terror. Cf. Gael. *sgriach*, *sgreuch*, to screech, scream. See **Shriek**.+Gk. κρίζειν (for *κρίγ-γειν), to shriek; κριγ-ή, κριγ-μός, a shrieking. Der. *screech*, sb., answering to Swed. *skrik*, Dan. *skrig*, Irish *sgreach*, Gael. *sgreuch*; also *screech-owl*. And see *shrike*. Doublet, *shriek*, which is merely a variant, due to the alteration of *sc* to *sh* at the beginning and the preservation of *k* at the end.

SCREED, a shred, a harangue. (E.) The Northern form of **Shred**, q. v.

SCREEN, that which shelters from observation, a partition; also, a coarse riddle or sieve. (F.—Teut.) 1. ME. *scren*; spelt *screne*, Prompt. Parv., p. 450; Wright's Vocab. i. 197, col. 2.—OF. *escren* (Littré); MF. *escran*, 'a skreen to set between one and the fire, a tester for a bed;' Cot. Mod. F. *écran*. Also found as OF. *escranne* (Godefroy). Prob. from OHG. *skrank*, G. *schranke*, a barrier, rail, fence, limit, place railed off. In the sense of coarse sieve, it is spelt *skreine* in Tusser's Husbandry, sect. 17, st. 16 (E. D. S.), and is the same word as the above. 'A screen for gravel or corn is a grating which wards off the coarser particles and prevents them from coming through;' Wedgwood. Der. *screen*, verb, Hamlet, iii. 4. 3.

SCREES, the loose *débris* on the side of a mountain. (Scand.) For *screethes*, the *th* being lost as in *clothes*.—Icel. *skriða*, a land-slip on a hill-side.—Icel. *skrið-*, weak grade of *skriða*, to creep, glide; cognate with Dan. *skride* and G. *schreiten*. See E. D. D., s. v. *scree*, and s. v. *scriddan*; and Notes on E. Etym., pp. 262, 263.

SCREW (1), a cylinder with a spiral groove or ridge on its surface, used as a fastening or as a mechanical power. (F.—L.?) Better spelt *scrue*, as in Cotgrave; the spelling *screw* is due to association with *dew*, *flew*, &c. Spelt *screw* in Minsheu, ed. 1627. ME. *screu*; 'unum *screu* ferreum;' York Wills, i. 194 (1393).—OF. *escroe*, Godefroy; MF. *escroue*, 'a scrue, the hole or hollow thing wherein the vice of a presse, &c. doth turn;' Cot. Mod. F. *écrou*. β. Of uncertain origin. Diez derives it from L. *scrobem*, acc. of *scrobs*, a ditch, trench, also a hole; but the derivation (in Kluge) from L. *scrōfa*, a sow, is far more likely; from the action of sows in rooting things up. Cf. '*scrobs*: fossa quam *scrofe* maxime faciunt . . *Hic scrobs*, a swyn-wroting;' Cathol. Anglicum, p. 99, note 11. The Teut. words (G. *schraube*, Du. *schroef*, Low G. *skruve*) seem to be late and unoriginal. See **Scrofula**. ¶ For the loss of *f*, see **Scroyles**. The E. word is certainly from the F., as Scheler rightly remarks. Der. *screw*, verb, Macb. i. 7. 60; *screw-driv-er*, *screw-propell-er*, *screw-steamer*.

SCREW (2), a vicious horse. (E.) A well-known term in modern E., not noticed in Johnson or Halliwell. The same word as *shrew*, a vicious or scolding woman, spelt *screwe* in Political Songs, ed. Wright, p. 153, l. 13; and cf. prov. E. *screw-mouse*, a shrew-mouse. See **Shrew**. The *sc* (for *sh*) is due to Scand. influence. **Doublet**, *shrew*.

SCRIBBLE, to write carelessly. (L.; with E. suffix.) 'Scribled

forth in hast at aduenture;' Sir T. More, Works, p. 56 e. Formed with the frequentative suffix *-le* from *scribe*, sb., or from L. *scribere*, to write. Similarly, we find G. *schreibler*, a scribbler, from *schreiben*, to write. See **Scribe**. Der. *scribble*, sb., *scribbl-er*.

SCRIBE, a writer, a clerk, an expounder of the Jewish law. (L.) First in use as a scriptural term, and taken directly from Latin; Littré does not trace the F. *scribe* beyond the 16th century. ME. *scribe*, Wyclif, Matt. viii. 19.—L. *scrība*, a writer, Matt. viii. 19 (Vulgate).—L. *scribere*, to write (pp. *scriptus*), orig. to scratch marks on a soft surface, to cut slightly. Cf. **Scarify**. Der. *scribb-le*, q. v.; and see *scrip* (2), *script*, *script-ure*, *scriv-en-er*. Also (from L. *scribere*), *a-scribe*, *circum-scribe*, *de-scribe*, *in-scribe*, *pre-scribe*, *pro-scribe*, *sub-scribe*, *tran-scribe* (for *trans-scribe*); also (from pp. *scriptus*) *a-script-ion*, *circum-script-ion*, *con-script*, *de-script-ion*, *in-script-ion*, *manu-script*, *non-de-script*, *pre-script-ion*, *pre-script-ive*, *pro-script-ion*, *post-script*, *re-script*, *sub-script-ion*, *super-script-ion*, *tran-script*, *tran-script-ion*, &c. Also *shrive*, *shrift*, *Shrove-tide*.

SCRIMMAGE, the same as **Skirmish**, q. v.

SCRIP (1), a small bag or wallet. (E.) ME. *scrippe*, King Horn, ed. Lumby, 1061; Chaucer, C. T. 7319 (D 1737). AS. *scripp*, Ælfric, Hom. i. 394.+Icel. *skreppa*, a scrip, bag; Norweg. *skreppa*, a knapsack (Aasen); Swed. dial. *skräppa*, a bag (Rietz), Swed. *skräppa*, a scrip; MSwed. *skreppa* (Ihre); Low G. *schrap*, a scrip (Brem. Wört.); NFries. *skrap*. The orig. sense is 'scrap,' because made of a scrap or shred of skin or other material. See **Scrap**, **Scarf** (1). The sound of the AS. *sc* was affected by the Norse *sk*.

SCRIP (2), a piece of writing, a schedule. (F.—L.) In Shak. Mids. Nt. Dr. i. 2. 3. The same word as *script*, the *t* dropping off in common talk; see **Script**.

SCRIPT, a piece of writing. (F.—L.) 'This loving *script*;' Beaum. and Fletcher, A Wife for a Month, i. 2.—MF. *escript*, 'a writing;' Cot.—L. *scriptum*, a thing written, neut. of *scriptus*, pp. of *scribere*, to write; see **Scribe**. Der. *manu-script*, *re-script*, *tran-script*.

SCRIPTURE, writing, the Bible. (F.—L.) *Scripture*, in the sense of 'bible,' is short for *holy scripture*, or rather, *The Holy Scriptures*. ME. *scripture*; the pl. *scripturis* is in Wyclif, Luke, xxiv. 27. —OF. *escripture*, 'writ, scripture, writing;' Cot.—L. *scriptūra*, a writing; cf. L. *scriptūrus*, fut. part. of *scribere*, to write; see **Scribe**. Der. *scriptur-al*.

SCRIVENER, a scribe, copyist, notary. (F.—L.) Properly a *scriven*; the suffix *-er* (of the agent) is an E. addition. ME. *skrivenere*, Lydgate, Complaint of Black Knight, st. 28, l. 194; formed with suffix *-ere* from ME. *scriueyn*, Ayenbite of Inwyt, p. 44, l. 30.—OF. *escrivain*, 'a scrivener;' Cot. [Cf. mod. F. *écrivain*, Span. *escribano*, Ital. *scrivano*.]—Late L. *scribānum*, acc. of *scribānus*, a notary; extended from *scriba*, a scribe; see **Scribe**.

SCROFULA, a disease characterised by chronic swellings of the glands. (L.) Called 'the king's evil,' because it was supposed the touch of a king could cure it; see Phillips, Dict., &c. In Phillips, ed. 1706; Blount (1674) has the adj. *scrofulous*.—L. *scrōfula*; usually in pl. *scrōfulæ*, scrofulous swellings. The lit. signification of *scrōfula* is a little pig; dimin. of *scrōfa*, a breeding sow. The reason for the name is not certainly known, but perhaps it is from the swollen appearance of the glands. It is remarkable that the Gk. name (χοιράδες) for swollen or scrofulous glands appears to be similarly connected with χοῖρος, a pig. β. The L. *scrōfa* has been explained as 'a digger,' from the habit of swine, who are fond of 'rooting' or turning up the earth; allied to *scrobis*, a ditch. But we can hardly connect *-ōf-* with *-ob-*. Der. *scroful-ous*; and see *screw* (1).

SCROLL, a roll of paper or parchment, a schedule. (F.—Teut.) *Scroll*, formerly also *scrowl*, is a contraction of *scrow-el*, a dimin. form (with suffix *-el*) of *scrowe* or *scroue*, the earlier form of the word. ME. *scrowle*, Voc. 682. 26; but the ME. *scroue*, *scrowe*, is older. Palsgrave (A. D. 1530) gives both *scrolle* and *scrowe*, and equates both to F. *rolle*. Fabyan also has both forms: 'He [Rich. II.] therfore redde the *scrowle* of resygnacyon hymselfe,' an. 1398 (ed. Ellis, p. 547); 'wherefore, knowynge that the sayd Baylly vsed to bere *scrowys* and prophecye aboute hym,' an. 1449 (id. p. 624). ME. *scrowe*, Havelok; spelt *scrow*, Prompt. Parv.; pl. *scrowis*, Wyclif, Matt. xxiii. 5 (earlier version only); *scrowe*, Ancren Riwle, p. 282, last line.—OF. *escroue*, 'a scrowle;' Cot. Spelt *escroe* in the 14th cent. (Littré); mod. F. *écrou*; the Low L. *escrōa* occurs A. D. 1386 (Ducange). To which must be added that the dimin. form *escroele* actually occurs, in the sense of strip, as cited by Littré, s. v. *écrou*; thus proving the origin of E. *scroll* beyond all doubt. β. Of Teut. origin.—MDu. *schroode*, a strip, shred, slip of paper (Oudemans); allied to *schroden*, to cut off (id.). Cf. OHG. *scrōt*, the same; and E. *screed*. See **Shred**, **Shard**.

SCROYLES, scabby fellows, rascals. (F.—L.) In King John, ii. 1. 373; and see Nares.—OF. pl. *escroelles* (see *écrouelle* in Hatzfeld),

MF. *escrouelles*, 'the king's evil,' Cot.; i.e. scrofula; hence, men afflicted with scrofula. — Late L. type *scrōfellas, acc. pl.; for L. scrōfulas, acc. pl. of *scrōfula*. See **Scrofula**. See Notes on Eng. Etym., p. 263.

SCRUB (1), brushwood. (Scand.) Prov. E. *scrub*; and cf. Wormwood *Scrubbs*. The Scand. equivalent of E. *shrub*. — MDan. *skrubbe*, Dan. dial. *skrub*, brushwood; Norw. *skrubba*, dwarf cornel. See **Shrub**. Der. *scrubb-y*, dwarfed, mean; *scrub-bed*, insignificant, Merch. Ven. v. 162. And note Lowl. Sc. *scrubber*, 'a handful of heath tied tightly together for cleaning culinary utensils;' Jamieson. Prob. allied to *scrub* (2), as *broom* is to the plant so called. Cf. *scrublanda*, i.e. scrub-land; Liber Custumarum, p. 658.

SCRUB (2), to rub hard. (Scand.) ME. *scrobben*, to rub down a horse; King Alisaunder, 4310. Not found in AS. — MDan. *skrubbe*; Swed. *skrubba*, to scrub; cf. Dan. *skrubbet*, rough, 'scrubby.' + Du. *schrobben*, to scrub, wash, rub, chide; Low G. *schrubben*; NFries. *skrobbe*. According to Franck, it is allied, by gradation, to Du. and EFries. *schrabben*, to scratch; see **Scrabble, Scrape**. And see **Scrub** (1).

SCRUFF, SCRUFT, the nape of the neck. More correctly *scuff, scuft*. See **Scuft**.

SCRUPLE, a small weight, a doubt, perplexity, reluctance to act. (F. — L.) 'A *scrupil* weieth a peny; iii. *scrupilis* maken a dragme;' Medical Workes, ed. Henslow, p. 131. 'It is no consience, but a foolish *scruple*;' Sir T. More, Works, p. 1435 c. 'Would not haue bene too *scrupulous*;' Frith, Works, p. 143, col. 2. — F. *scrupule*, 'a little sharp stone falling into a mans shooe, and hindering him in his gate [gait]; also, a scruple, doubt, fear, difficulty, care, trouble of conscience; also, a scruple, a weight amounting unto the third part of a dram;' Cot. — L. *scrūpulum*, acc. of *scrūpulus*, a small sharp stone; hence, a small stone used as a weight, a small weight; also, a stone in one's shoe, an uneasiness, difficulty, small trouble, doubt. Dimin. of *scrūpus*, a sharp stone. *Scrū-pus* is allied to *scrū-ta*; see **Scrutiny**. Der. *scruple*, vb., to make a scruple of; *scrupul-ous*, from F. *scrupu-leux*, 'scrupulous,' Cot., from L. *scrūpulōsus*; *scrupul-ous-ly*, *-ness*.

SCRUTINY, a strict examination, careful inquiry. (L.) Spelt *scruteny*, Skelton, Garl. of Laurel, 782; cf. MF. *scrutine*, 'a scrutiny;' Cot. Englished from L. *scrūtinium*, a careful inquiry. — L. *scrūtāri*, to search into carefully, lit. to search among broken pieces. — L. *scrūta*, broken pieces, old trash; allied to AS. *scrēade*, a shred; see **Shred**. Der. *scrutin-ise, scrutin-eer*. And see *in-scrut-able*.

SCUD, to run quickly, run before the wind in a gale. (Scand.) In Shak. Venus, 301. '*Scuddyng* from place to place;' Udall, tr. of Erasmus' Apophthegmes, Pompeius, § 2. We also have prov. E. *scud*, a slight rapid or flying shower of rain (*Shropshire*, and elsewhere); Lowland Sc. *scuddin-stanes*, thin stones made to skim the surface of water, as an amusement, answering exactly to Dan. *skudsteen*, a stone quoit. A frequentative of *scud* is prov. E. *scuttle*, to walk fast, to hurry along, often used with precisely the same force as *scud*; also *scuddle*, to run away quickly, is given in Bailey, vol. i. ed. 1735. Hence *scud* is a weakened form of *scut* or *scoot*; cf. prov. E. 'to go like *scooter*, i.e. very quick, *East*' (Halliwell); and *scoot* is only a Scand. equivalent of *shoot*. Precisely the same voicing of *t* to *d* occurs in Danish, and the nautical use *to scud* is of Danish origin. — Norw. *skudda*, to push, shove; cf. Dan. *skyde*, to shoot, to push, to shove; *skyde i frō*, to run to seed; *skyde vand*, to repel water; *skyde over stevn* (lit. to shoot over the stem), to shoot ahead, i.e. scud along, as a nautical term; Dan. *skud-*, a shooting, used in compounds, as in *skud-aar*, leap-year, *skud-steen*, a 'scudding-stane.' Cf. Swed. dial. *skudda*, to shoot the bolt of a door; Swed. *skutta*, to leap, Swed. dial. *skuta*, a sledge (Rietz), allied to Swed. *skjuta*, to shoot, and to Icel. *skjōta*, to shoot, also to slip or scud away, abscond. See **Shoot**. Der. *scutt-le* (3), q.v.

SCUFFLE, to struggle, fight confusedly. (Scand.) In Beaum. and Fletcher, Philaster, v. 1. The frequentative form of *scuff*, preserved in prov. E. *scuff*, to shuffle in walking, *West*; Halliwell. — Swed. *skuffa*, to push, shove, jog; allied to E. *shove*. + MDu. *schuffelen*, to drive on, also, to run away, i.e. to shuffle off; allied to Du. *schuiven*, to shove. Thus *to scuffle* is 'to keep shoving about.' See **Shuffle, Shove**. Der. *scuffle*, sb., Antony, i. 1. 7.

SCUFT, SCUFF, SCRUFT, SCRUFF, the nape of the neck. (Scand.) The orig. form seems to have been *scuft*; a form which occurs even in Gothic. '*Scuft* of the neck;' Grose's Gloss. (1790). — ONorse *skopt* (pron. *skoft*), hair of the head; mod. Icel. *skott*, a fox's tail; NFries. *skuft*, nape of a horse's neck. + G. *schopf*, a tuft of hair; OHG. *scuft*, hair; Goth. *skuft*, hair of the head. Allied to **Sheaf**; cf. Icel. *skauf*, a fox's brush.

SCULK, SKULK, to hide oneself, lurk. (Scand.) ME. *sculken, skulken*, Pricke of Conscience, 1788; Gower, C. A. ii. 93; bk. iv. 2720; whence the sb. *scolkynge*, Rob. of Glouc. p. 256, l. 5130. — Dan. *skulke*, to sculk, slink, sneak; Norw. *skulka*; Swed. *skolka*, to

play the truant. Allied to Icel. *skolla*, to sculk, keep aloof. Extended from the Teut. base seen in Du. *schuilen*, Low G. *schulen*, to sculk, to lurk in a hiding-place; allied to Dan. *skjul*, Icel. *skjōl*, a place of shelter; see further under **Scowl**, which exhibits the shorter form.

SCULL (1), the cranium; see **Skull**.

SCULL (2), a small, light oar. (Scand.) '*Scull*, a little oar, to row with; *Sculler*, a boat rowed with sculls, or the waterman that manages it;' Phillips, ed. 1706. Also in the phrase 'rowing *scull*,' Hudibras, pt. i. c. 3, l. 351. We also find 'the old *sculler*,' i.e. Charon; Ben Jonson, Cynthia's Revels, i. 1 (Cupid's 7th speech). Dryden oddly uses *sculler* with the sense of 'boat;' tr. of Virgil, Georg. b. iv. l. 735. '*Scull* to rowe with, *auiron*; Scullar, *batellier*;' Palsgrave. 'To rowe .. with a *skulle*;' Piers of Fulham, l. 275; in Hazlitt's Early E. Pop. Poetry, ii. 12. β. Prob. named from the slightly hollowed blades. G. Douglas has *scull* in the sense of 'cup;' tr. of Virgil, bk. iii. ch. 1. l. 125. Cf. Swed. *skål*, a basin, bowl; *hufuud-skål*, scull (of the head); *våg-skål*, the scale of a balance; *skålig*, concave. Also Norw. *skul*, a husk, shell of fruit. Larsen gives Dan. *skullermand*, a waterman. Der. *scull*, verb; *scull-er* as above. See **Skull**.

SCULL (3), a shoal of fish. (Du.) In Shak. Troilus, v. 5. 22. ME. *sculle*, Prompt. Parv. A variant of **School** (2), q.v.

SCULLERY, a room for washing dishes, and the like. (F. — L.) Sherwood's Index to Cotgrave has: 'The scullery, *escueillerie*.' Spelt *scollery*; Cavendish, Life of Wolsey, ed. F. S. Ellis, p. 23. Formed with suffix *-ie* (cf. *pantr-y*) from OF. *esculier*, one who has charge of the dishes and plates (Godefroy); cf. *esculerie*, the office of keeping the dishes (id.). — Late L. *scutellārius*, the same (Ducange). — L. *scutella*, a dish (whence OF. *escuelle*, F. *écuelle*); dimin. of *scutra*, a tray. ¶ Godefroy also has *esquelier* (= *esculier*); hence ME. '*sqwyllare*, dysche wescheare,' i.e. dish-washer; in Prompt. Parv. Cf. 'The *squyler* of the kechyn;' Rob. of Brunne, Handlyng Synne, l. 5913. 'The pourvayours of the buttlarye [buttery] and .. of the *squylerey*;' Ordinances and Regulations of the Royal Household, 4to, 1790, p. 77; '*Sergeaunt-squylloure*,' in the same, p. 81. And see Halliwell. *Scullion* is of different origin; see below.

SCULLION, a kitchen menial. (F. — L.) In Shak. Haml. ii. 2. 616. 'Their smooked *scolions* faces, handes, and feete;' Barnes, Works, p. 341, col. 2. '*Scoulyon* of the kechyn, *souillon*;' Palsgrave. This word has undoubtedly been long understood as if it were connected with *scullery*, and the connexion between the two words in the popular mind may have influenced its form and use. But it is impossible to connect them etymologically; and Wedgwood well says that 'it has a totally different origin,' which he points out. — MF. *escouillon*, 'a wispe, or dishclout, a maukin or drag, to cleanse or sweepe an oven;' Cot. 'In the same way *malkin, mawkin*, is used both for a kitchen-wench and for the clout which she plies;' Wedgwood. β. The MF. *escouillon* is the same as *escouvillon*, Cot. The latter form answers to Span. *escobillon*, a sponge for a cannon; formed with suffix *-on* (L. *-iōnem*) from *escobilla*, a small brush, dimin. of *escoba* (OF. *escouve*), a brush, broom, which is cognate with Ital. *scopa*, a broom, a birch-tree. — L. *scōpa*, used in pl. *scōpæ*, thin twigs, a broom of twigs. Allied to L. *scāpus*, a stem, stalk; and to **Sceptre**.

SCULPTURE, the art of carving figures. (F. — L.) ME. *sculpture*, Gower, C. A. ii. 83; bk. iv. 2422. — F. *sculpture*, for which Littré cites nothing earlier than the 16th century; but it must have been in earlier use; see Hatzfeld. — L. *sculptūra*, sculpture; cf. L. *sculptūrus*, fut. part. of *sculpere*, to cut out, carve in stone; allied to *scalpere*, to scratch, grave, carve, cut; whence E. *scalp-el*. Der. *sculpture*, verb; *sculpt-or*, from L. *sculptor*; *sculptur-al*.

SCUM, froth, refuse on the surface of liquids. (Scand.) '*Scome* or *scum* of fletynge [floating], Spuma;' Prompt. Parv. '*Scummyn lycurys*, Despumo;' id. Dat. *scome*, Ayenbite of Inwyt, p. 44, l. 23. — Dan. *skum*, scum, froth, foam; Icel. *skúm*, foam (in Egillson's Dict.); Swed. *skum*. + OHG. *scūm*, G. *schaum* (whence F. *écume*); Du. *schuim*. β. Lit. 'a covering.' — √SKEU, to cover; Fick, iii. 336. ¶ The L. *spūma* is related to E. *foam*, not to *scum*. Der. *scum*, verb; *scumm-er*; *skim*.

SCUPPER, a hole in the side of a ship to carry off water from the deck. (F. — Scand.) '*Scuppers*, the holes through which the water runs off the deck;' Coles, ed. 1684. Called *scoper-holes*; Phillips (1706). 'Our galley's *scupper-holes*;' Marston, Antonio and Mellida, i. 1. 13. '*Skopper-lethers* and *skopper-nayles*;' Naval Accounts (1497); p. 298. The sense is '*scooper-hole*.' — OF. *escope, escoppe*, a scoop for baling out water (Supp. to Godefroy). — Swed. *skopa*, a scoop. Cf. MDu. *schoepe*, a shovel; Hexham. See **Scoop**. Cf. Prov. E. *scupper*, a scooper, a scoop; *scuppit*, a small shovel or scoop.

SCUR, to run rapidly over. (F. — L.) '*Scur* o'er the fields of corn;' Beaum. and Fletcher, Bonduca, i. 1. The same word as *skirr* and *scour*; see **Scour** (2). Der. *scur-ry*.

SCURF, small flakes of skin; flaky matter on the skin. (Scand.) ME. *scurf.* 'Scurf of scabbys, Squama;' Prompt. Parv.; Cursor Mundi, 11823.—Swed. *skorf*; Dan. *skurv*, scurf; Icel. *skurfur*, pl.+ AS. *scurf*, scurf (from Norse), A. S. Leechdoms, i. 116. Cf. 'mycel *sceorfa* on his heafde hæfde' = he had much scurf on his head; Ælfred, tr. of Beda, b. v. c. 2. Du. *schurft*, scurf; G. *schorf*. β. From Teut. *skurf-, weak grade of *skerfan-, as in AS. *sceorfan* (pt. t. *scearf*, pt. t. pl. *scurfon*), to scarify, gnaw. Der. *scur-fy*, *scurf-i-ness.* Also *scurv-y*, q.v.

SCURRILE, buffoon-like. (L.) In Shak. Troil. i. 3. 148.—L. *scurrilis*, buffoon-like.—L. *scurra*, a buffoon. Allied to OHG. *scern*, derision; see **Scorn**. Der. *scurril-i-ty*, L. L. L. iv. 2. 55, from L. acc. *scurrilitātem*; *scurril-ous*, Wint. Tale, iv. 4. 215; *scurril-ous-ly.*

SCURVY, afflicted with scurf, mean. (Scand.) 'All *scuruy* with scabbes;' Skelton, Elinour Rumming, 140. The same word as *scurfy*, with change from *f* to *v*; cf. Swed. *skorfvig*, scurfy, from *skorf*, scurf. See **Scurf.** Hence, as a term of contempt, vile, mean, Temp. ii. 2. 46, and very common in Shak. Cf. Low G. *schorfig*, *schorvig*, adj.; from *schorf*, scurf; Dan. *skurvet*, scurfy. Der. *scurvy*, Phillips, ed. 1706, the name of a disease, from the pitiful condition of those afflicted with it; and hence, probably, the Low L. medical term *scorbūtus*; see **Scorbutic.** Also *scurvi-ly*, *-ness.*

SCUTAGE, a tax on a knight's fee. (Late L.—L.) See Cowel's Interpreter and Blount's Nomolexicon.—Med. Latin *scūtāgium*, a form of *scūtāticum*, due to OF. *escuage*, with the same sense.—L. *scūtum*, a shield. See **Esquire.**

SCUTCH, to dress flax. (F.—Scand.) From the sb. *scutch*, an instrument for beating flax; Cent. Dict.—OF. *escouche, eschuche*, a swingle (Godefroy); Norm. dial. *écouche, écoche* (Moisy). Cf. *escucher*, vb.; Wright, Voc. i. 156.—Norw. *skuku, skoka*, a swingle. Otherwise in Hatzfeld; s. v. *écouche.*

SCUTCHEON, a painted shield. (F.—L.) ME. *scotchyne, scochone*, Prompt. Parv. The same as **Escutcheon**, q.v.

SCUTIFORM, shield-shaped. (F.—L.) In Blount, ed. 1674. 'Scutiforme *os*, the whirl-bone of the knee;' Phillips, ed. 1706.—MF. *scutiforme*, 'fashioned like a scutcheon, shield-fashion;' Cot.—L. *scūti-*, for *scūtum*, a shield; and *form-a*, form, shape: see **Escutcheon** and **Form.**

SCUTTLE (1), a shallow basket, a vessel for holding coal. (L.) ME. *scotille.* 'Hec scutella, a *scotylle*;' Wright's Vocab. i. 257, col. 1. A Northern form. Cf. Icel. *skutill*; AS. *scutel*, a dish, bowl. 'Catinus, *scutel*;' Wright's Voc. i. 290, col. 1.—L. *scutella*, a salver or waiter; dimin. of *scutra*, a tray, dish, or platter, also spelt *scuta.* Der. *coal-scuttle.* Doublet, *skillet.*

SCUTTLE (2), an opening in the hatchway of a ship. (F.—Span.—Teut.) 'Scuttles, square holes, capable for the body of a man to pass thorough at any hatch-way, or part of the deck, into any room below; also, those little windows and long holes which are cut out in cabbins to let in light;' Phillips, ed. 1706. And in Cotgrave. 'The *skottelles* of the haches;' Naval Accounts (1497); p. 323.— MF. *escoutilles*, pl., 'the scuttles, or hatches of a ship; th'overtures or trap-doors, whereat things are let down into the hold;' Cot. Mod. F. *écoutille.*—Span. *escotilla, escotillon*, 'a hole in the hatch of a ship, also the hatch itselfe,' Minsheu. β. The word appears to be Spanish; and we find another form in *escotadura*, the large trap-door of a theatre or stage (Neuman). Another sense of *escotadura* is the sloping of a jacket or pair of stays; and the form of the word is such as to be due to the verb *escotar*, to cut out a thing so as to make it fit, to slope, to hollow out a garment about the neck (a different word from Span. *escotar*, to pay one's reckoning, for which see **Scot-free**). The orig. sense is 'to cut a hole in a garment to admit the neck,' from the sb. *escote*, the sloping of a jacket, a tucker such as women wear above the bosom. This sb. is derived, as Diez points out, from the Teutonic; cf. Goth. *skauts*, the hem of a garment, Du. *schoot*, the lap, the bosom, G. *schooss*, the same; so that the orig. sense of Span. *escote* is 'a slope to fit the bosom,' a hole for the neck. ¶ So in Diez; see **Sheet.** Der. *scuttle*, verb, to sink a ship by cutting *scuttles* or holes in it.

SCUTTLE (3), to hurry along, scud away. (Scand.) Cf. Swed. *skutta*, to leap; Swed. dial. *skutta*, to take a long jump; allied to *scuddle* (Bailey), which is the frequentative of **Scud**, q.v. 'How the misses did huddle, and *scuddle*, and run;' Anstey's New Bath Guide, letter 13 (Davies). Davies also gives *scutter*, a hasty run.

SCYTHE, a cutting instrument for mowing grass. (E.) The intrusion of the letter *c* is due to false spelling; it should be *sythe* or *sithe.* Spelt *sythe* in L. L. L. i. 1. 6 (first folio, ed. 1623). ME. *sithe*, P. Plowman, C. iv. 464; *syþe*, Havelok, 2553. AS. *síðe, síþe*, a scythe; 'Falcastrum, *síþe*,' Wright's Vocab. i. 85, l. 3. The AS. *síðe* is for *sigðe* (a form actually found in the Epinal gloss), and the long *i* shows the loss of *g*; it means 'the cutting instrument.' From

the Teut. base SEG, to cut = √SEQ, to cut. See **Saw** (1), **Section.** Fick, iii. 314.+Du. *zeis*; Icel. *sigðr, sigð*, a sickle; Low G. *seged, segd*, also *seed, seid*, a kind of sickle; Brem. Wörterbuch. From the same root we have OHG. *segansa*, MHG. *segense*, G. *sense*, a scythe; OHG. *seh*, MHG. *sech*, a ploughshare; as well as E. *saw, sickle.* Der. *scythe*, verb, Shak. Complaint, l. 12; *scythe-tusked*, Two Noble Kinsmen, i. 1. 79.

SE-, away, apart, *prefix.* (L.) From L. *sē-*, short for *sēd*, without, which is retained as a prefix in *sed-ition. Sēd* is mentioned by Festus as having been used with the sense 'without.' Der. *se-cede, se-clude, se-cret, se-cure, sed-ition, se-duce, se-gregate, se-lect, se-parate*; and see *sever.*

SEA, a large lake, ocean. (E.) ME. *see*, Chaucer, C. T. 3033 (A 3031). AS. *sǣ*, sea, lake.+Du. *zee*; Icel. *sær*; Dan. *sö*; Swed. *sjö*; G. *see*; Goth. *saiws.* β. All from a Teut. type *saiwiz*, sea. Der. *sea-board*, from F. *bord*, the shore = Du. *boord*, edge, brim (see **Border**); *sea-coast, sea-faring, sea-girt, -green, -horse, -kale, -king, -level, -man, -man-ship, -mark, -room, -serpent, -shore, -sick, -side, -unicorn, -urchin, -ward, -weed, -worthy*; &c.

SEAL (1), a stamp for impressing wax, impressed wax, that which authenticates. (F.—L.) ME. *seel* (better than *sele*), Chaucer, C. T. 10445 (F 131). 'Seled with his *seale*,' Rob. of Brunne, tr. of Langtoft, i. 29, l. 12.—OF. *seel*, 'a seal, or signet;' Cot. Mod. F. *sceau*; Span. *sello, sigilo*; Ital. *sigillo.*—L. *sigillum*, a seal, mark; lit. 'a little sign;' allied to *signum*, a sign, mark; see **Sign.** Der. *seal*, verb, ME. *selen*, as above; *seal-engraving, seal-ing-wax.*

SEAL (2), a sea-calf, marine animal. (E.) ME. *sele*, Havelok, 755; which represents AS. *seole*, dat. of AS. *seolh*, a seal; Grein, ii. 438.+Icel. *selr*; Dan. *sæl*; also *sælhund* (seal-hound); Swed. *själ, själhund*; OHG. *selah.* Teut. type *selhoz.*

SEAM (1), a suture, a line formed by joining together two pieces, a line of union. (E.) ME. *seem*, Wyclif, John, xix. 23. AS. *sēam*, Ælfric's Hom. i. 20, l. 4 from bottom.+Du. *zoom*; Icel. *saumr*; Dan. and Swed. *söm*; G. *saum.* β. All from a Teut. type *saumoz*, m., a sewing, suture (Fick, iii. 325); formed, with suffix *-moz*, from *sau*, 2nd grade of root *seu, *siw*; Idg. root SIW, to sew. Cf. L. *su-ere*, to sow, Skt. *sū-tra-*, a thread; see **Sew.** Der. *seam-less, seam-y*; also *seam-str-ess*, q.v.

SEAM (2), a horse-load. (Late L.—Gk.) ME. *seem*; dat. *seme*, P. Plowman, B. iii. 40. AS. *sēam.* Borrowed (like G. *saum*) from Late L. *sauma*, late form of *sagma*, a horse-load.—Gk. σάγμα, a pack-saddle. See **Sumpter.**

SEAMSTRESS, SEMPSTRESS, a woman who sews seams. (E.; with F. *suffix.*) 'Seamster, and *Seamstress*, a man or woman that sows, makes up, or deals in linnen-clothes;' Phillips, ed. 1706. Only *seamster* is given in Minsheu, ed. 1627. The suffix *-ess* is a F. fem. suffix, F. *-esse* (from L. *-issa*, Gk. *-ισσα*), as in *princ-ess, marchion-ess.* ME. *semster*, Destruction of Troy, ed. Panton and Donaldson, l. 1585. AS. *sēamestre.* We find: 'Sartor, seamere,' and 'Sartrix, seamestre;' Wright's Vocab. i. 74. [Whence *sǣmestres*, Diplomatarium Ævi Saxonici, ed. Thorpe, p. 568, l. 10.] Formed from AS. *sēam*, a seam, by the addition of the AS. suffix *-estre*, explained under **Spinster.** See **Seam** (1).

SÉANCE, a sitting, session. (F.—L.) Modern.—F. *séance*, a session.—F. *séant*, pres. pt. of *seoir*, to sit.—L. *sedēre*, to sit. See **Sit.**

SEAR, SERE, withered. (E.) Spelt *sere*, Spenser, Shep. Kal. Jan. 37. ME. *seer*; spelt *seere*, Rob. of Brunne, tr. of Langtoft, p. 18, l. 25; *seer*, Rom. Rose, 4749. AS. *séar*, sere; best preserved in the derived verb; see below.+ODu. *sore*, dry (Oudemans); *zoor*, 'dry, withered, or seare;' Hexham; Low G. *soor*, dry; Brem. Wört. β. Teut. type *sauzoz*; Idg. type *sausos.* Allied to Russ. *suxoi*, dry; Lith. *sausas*, dry; Gk. αὖος (for *σαυσος), dry; Skt. *çush* (for *sush), to become dry. (√SEUS.) From the same root is Gk. αὖειν, to parch, αὐστηρός, dry, rough, whence E. *austere.* The Zend *hush*, to dry, proves that SEUS is the root; Curtius, i. 490. Brugmann, i. § 213. Der. *sear*, verb, to dry up, cauterise, render callous, Rich. III, iv. 1. 61, ME. *seeren*, Prompt. Parv., AS. *sēarian*, to dry up, to wither or pine away, Ælfred, tr. of Orosius, iv. 6. 15. See **Austere**; and **Sorrel** (2).

SEARCH, to seek, examine, explore. (F.—L.) ME. *serchen*, Rob. of Brunne, tr. of Langtoft, p. 268, last line but one; better spelt *cerchen*, as in Lydgate, Minor Poems, p. 159, Mandeville's Travels, p. 315.—AF. *cercher*, Stat. Realm, i. 219; *sercher*, id. 274. —OF. *cercher* (Burg uy); mod. F. *chercher*, to seek. Cf. Norm. dial. *sercher, cercher.* Ital. *cercare*, to seek, to search; Prov. *cercar, cerquar, sercar*, to search (Bartsch); Span. *cercar*, to encircle, surround.—L. *circāre*, to go round; hence, to go about, explore.—L. *circus*, a circle, ring; *circum*, round about. See **Circum-, Circus, Ring.** Note AF. *sercher*, ME. *serchen*; A Nominale, ed. Skeat, ll. 434, 435. Der. *search*, sb., Temp. iii. 3. 10; *search-ing, search-er, search-warrant.* Also *re-search, shark.*

SEASON, proper time, fit opportunity. (F.–L.) ME. *sesoun*, Chaucer, C. T. 1045 (A 1043); P. Plowman, B. prol. 1; *seysoun*, King Alisaunder, 5251.–OF. *seson, seison, saison*; mod. F. *saison*, 'season, due time;' Cot. Cf. Span. *sazon*, Port. *sazāo, sezāo*; OProv. *sadons, sasos, sazos* (Bartsch).–Late L. *satiōnem*, acc. of *satio*, a season, time of year, occurring A.D. 1028 (Ducange). The same as L. *satio*, a sowing, planting, Verg. Georg. i. 215, ii. 319 (hence, the time of sowing or spring-time, which seems to have been regarded as *the* season, *par excellence*). Allied to L. *satus*, pp. of *serere*, to sow. From √SE, to cast, sow; whence also *seminal, seed, sow*. See **Sow** (1). ¶ Besides the word *season*, we also find Span. *estacion*, used in the sense of 'season' or time as well as 'station;' and Ital. *stagione*, 'a season or time of the yeere,' Florio. These are, of course, from L. *statiōnem*, acc. of *statio*, a station, hence applied, we must suppose, to the four stations, stages, or seasons of the year; see **Station**. And it is probable that the use of this word affected and extended the senses of *season*. I have been informed that the prov. E. *season* is still occasionally used in Kent in the sense of 'sowing-time.' Moreover, AF. *seson* occurs with the sense 'sowing-time;' see Royal Wills, ed. Nichols, pp. 34, 35. Der. *season*, verb, Merch. Ven. v. 107, Ascham, Toxophilus, b. ii., ed. Arber, p. 124; *season-able, season-abl-y, season-able-ness*; also *season-ing*, that which 'seasons,' or makes food more suitable and palatable.

SEAT, a chair, bench, &c., to sit on. (Scand.) ME. *sete*; spelt *seete*, Wyclif, Rev. ii. 13.–Icel. *sæti*, a seat; Swed. *säte*; Dan. *sæde*. –Icel. *sāt-*, 3rd grade of *sitja*, to sit; see **Sit**. [The usual AS. word is *setl*, for which see **Settle**.]+MDu. *saet, sate*; MHG. *sāze*. Der. *seat*, verb, Macb. i. 3. 136; *dis-seat*, Macb. v. 3. 21; *un-seat*.

SEBACEOUS, pertaining to tallow, fatty. (L.) From L. *sēbāce-us*, fatty.–L. *sēbum*, tallow, fat. Prob. allied to E. *soap*. See **Soap**.

SECANT, a line that cuts another, or that cuts a circle. (L.) In Blount's Gloss., ed. 1674.–L. *secant-*, stem of pres. part. of *secāre*, to cut; see **Section**. (√SEQ.) Brugmann, i. § 635. See **Saw, Scythe, Sickle, Sedge**.

SECEDE, to withdraw oneself from others, go apart. (L.) A late word; in Todd's Johnson.–L. *sēcēdere*, pp. *sēcessus*, to go away, withdraw.–L. *sē-*, apart; and *cēdere*, to go, go away. See **Se-** and **Cede**. Der. *seced-er*; also *secess-ion*, in Minsheu, ed. 1627, from L. acc. *sēcessiōnem*, nom. *sēcessio*, formed from pp. *sēcessus*.

SECLUDE, to keep apart. (L.) '*Secluded* from the Scriptures;' Frith's Works, p. 3, col. 2.–L. *sēclūdere*, to shut off.–L. *sē-*, apart; and *claudere*, to shut; see **Se-** and **Clause, Close** (1). Der. *seclus-ion*, formed like *sēclūsus*, pp. of *sēclūdere*.

SECOND, next after the first, the ordinal number corresponding to two. (F.–L.) ME. *second*; spelt *secounde*, Wyclif, John, iv. 54; *secunde*, Rob. of Glouc. p. 282, l. 5724. Not a very common word, as *other* was usually employed instead, in early times; *second* being the only ordinal number of F. origin. (See **Other**.)–F. *second*, masc., *seconde*, fem., 'second;' Cot.–L. *secundus*, following, second; so called because it follows the first. Formed from *sec-*, from the base of *sequī*, to follow, with gerundive suffix, with the force of a pres. part. Brugmann, ii. § 69 (2). See **Sequence**. Der. *second*, sb., used with reference to *minutes*, or *first* small subdivisions of an hour, &c., from F. *seconde*, 'the 24 part of a prime, a very small weight used by goldsmiths and jewellers,' Cot. Also *second*, verb, Merry Wives, i. 3. 114; *second-er*; *second-ar-y, second-ar-i-ly*, Tyndall, Works, p. 120, col. 1; *second-ly*; *second-hand*, i.e. at second hand; *second-sight*.

SECRET, hidden, concealed, unknown. (F.–L.) Spelt *secrette* in Palsgrave. The ME. form is almost invariably *secree*, Chaucer, C. T. 12077 (C 143); spelt *secre*, P. Plowman, A. iii. 141; but we find *secret* in P. Plowman, B. iii. 145, C. iv. 183.–OF. *secret* (fem. *secreie*, Burguy), 'secret;' Cot.–L. *sēcrētus*, secret; orig. pp. of *sēcernere*, to separate, set apart.–L. *sē-*, apart; and *cernere*, to separate, sift; see **Se-** and **Concern**. Der. *secret*, sb., ME. *secree*, Chaucer, C. T. 16915 (G 1447), from L. *sēcrētum*, orig. neuter of *sēcrētus*; *secret-ly*, *secret-ness*; *secrec-y*, Hamlet, i. 2. 207, a coined word, by analogy with *constancy*, &c.; *secrete*, verb, formed from L. *sēcrētus*, considered as pp. of *sēcernere*, from MF. *secretion*, 'a separating, also a thing separated or set apart,' Cot.; *secret-ive, secret-ive-ly, secret-ive-ness, secret-or-y*; also *secret-ar-y*, q. v.

SECRETARY, orig. a private amanuensis, confidant. (F.– L.) The sense of the word is now much widened; it is frequently used where little privacy is intended. In Shak. Hen. VIII, ii. 2. 116, iv. 1, 102. Palsgrave has: '*Secretarye*, secretayre;' *secretarye* also occurs in a 15th-century poem called The Assemble of Ladies, l. 337. –F. *secretaire*, 'a secretary, clerk;' Cot.–Late L. *sēcrētārium*, acc. of *sēcrētārius*, a confidential officer; cf. L. *sēcrētārium*, a secret place,

consistory, conclave.–L. *sēcrēt-us*, secret; with suffix *-ārius*; see **Secret**. Der. *secretary-ship*; *secretari-al*.

SECT, a party who follow a particular teacher, or hold particular principles, a faction. (F.–L.) It is tolerably certain that the sense of the word has been obscured by a false popular etymology which has connected the word with L. *secāre*, to cut; and it is not uncommon for authors to declare, with theological intolerance and in contempt of history, that a *sect* is so called from its being 'cut off' from the church. But the etymology from *secāre* is baseless. Palsgrave well defines *secte* as 'a company of one opynion.' ME. *secte*, used convertibly with *sute* (=*suite*) in P. Plowman, C. viii. 130, B. v. 495; see my note on the line. Both *secte* and *sute* are here used in the sense of 'suit of clothes.'–F. *secte*, 'a sect or faction; a rout or troup; a company of one (most commonly bad) opinion;' Cot.–Late L. *secta*, a set of people, a following, suite; also, a quality of cloth, a suit of clothes; also, a suit or action at law; L. *secta*, a party, faction, sect, lit. 'a following.'–L. *sec-* (as in *sec-undus*), base of *sequī*, to follow, with suffix *-ta*. Cf. Gk. ἑπέτης, a follower, attendant, from ἕπομαι, I follow; see *secta* in Bréal, s. v. *sequor*. See **Sequence**. Der. *sect-ar-y*, Hen. VIII, v. 3. 70, from F. *sectaire*, 'a sectary, the ringleader, professor, or follower of a sect,' Cot.; *sect-ar-i-an, sect-ar-i-an-ism*. Doublets, *sept, set*.

SECTION, a cutting, division, parting, portion. (F.–L.) In Minsheu, ed. 1627, and Cotgrave.–F. *section*, 'a section, cutting.'– L. *sectiōnem*, acc. of *sectio*, a cutting; cf. *sectus*, pp. of *secāre*, to cut. –√SEQ, to cut; whence also Russ. *sieche*, to hew, Lithuan. *sykis*, a stroke, cut, and E. *saw, sickle, scythe, sedge*. Brugmann, i. § 635. Der. *section-al, section-al-ly*; also *sec-tor*, from L. *sector*, a cutter, used in Late L. to mean a sector (part) of a circle; *seg-ment*, q. v. From the same root are *sec-ant, co-sec-ant*; *bi-sect, dis-sect, inter-sect, tri-sect*; *in-sect*; also *saw, sickle, sedge, scythe, risk*.

SECULAR, pertaining to the present world, not bound by monastic rules. (F.–L.) In Levins. ME. *secular, seculer, seculere*; Chaucer, C. T. 9127, 15456 (E 1251, B 4640).–AF. *seculer*, Year-books of Edw. I, i. 59, 133; MF. *seculier*, 'secular, lay, temporall;' Cot.–L. *sæculāris*, secular, worldly, belonging to the age.–L. *sæculum*, a generation, age. β. Better written *sēculum*; from √SE, to sow (Bréal); see **Sow**. Der. *secular-ly, -ise, -is-at-ion, -ism*.

SECURE, free from care or anxiety, safe, sure. (L.) In Levins; accented *secúre* in Hamlet, i. 5. 61.–L. *sēcūrus*, free from care.–L. *sē-*, free from; and *cūra*, anxiety; see **Se-** and **Cure**. Der. *secure-ly, -ness*; *secur-able*; *secur-i-ty*, from MF. *securité*, 'security,' Cot., from L. acc. *sēcūritātem*. Doublets, *sicker, sure*.

SEDAN, SEDAN-CHAIR, a portable vehicle, carried by two men. (F.) In Dryden, tr. of Juvenal, sat. i. 186. Named from *Sedan*, a town in France, N. E. of Paris; first seen in England, A.D. 1581; regularly used in London, A.D. 1634 (Haydn). Evelyn speaks of '*sedans*, from hence [Naples] brought first into England by Sir Sanders Duncomb;' Diary, Feb. 8, 1645. Cf. F. *sedan*, cloth made at Sedan (Littré).

SEDATE, quiet, serious. (L.) In Phillips, ed. 1706; Blount (ed. 1674) has *sedateness* and *sedation*, of which the latter is obsolete.– L. *sēdātus*, composed, calm; pp. of *sēdāre*, to settle, causal of *sedēre*, to sit, cognate with E. *sit*; see **Sit**. Der. *sedate-ly, -ness*. Also *sedat-ive*, i.e. composing, from F. *sédatif*, 'quieting, asswaging;' Cot. And see *sedentary, sediment*, see (2).

SEDENTARY, sitting much, inactive. (F.–L.) Spelt *sedentarie*, Minsheu, ed. 1627; and occurring in Cotgrave.–F. *sédentaire*, 'sedentary, ever-sitting;' Cot.–L. *sedentārius*, sedentary.–L. *sedent-*, pres. part. of *sedēre*, to sit, cognate with E. *sit*; with suffix *-ārius*; see **Sit**. Der. *sedentari-ly, -ness*.

SEDGE, a kind of flag or coarse grass in swamps. (E.) ME. *segge*, Prompt. Parv.; Voc. 570. 48. The pl. *segges* occurs as late as in Baret (1580). *Segge* represents AS. *secge*, g., dat., and acc. of *secg*, sedge; Gloss. to A.S. Leechdoms, vol. iii.+Low G. *segge*, sedge; in the dialect of Oldenburg; Bremen Wörterbuch. And cf. Irish *seasg, seisg*, sedge; W. *hesg*. β. The AS. *cg* = *gg*; Teut. type *sag-jā*, f.; lit. sense, 'cutter,' i.e. sword-grass, from the sharp edge or sword-like appearance; cf. L. *gladiolus*, a small sword, sword-lily, flag. From the Teut. base *saχ-*, 2nd grade of Teut. root *seχ*, to cut = √SEQ, to cut; see **Saw** (1), **Section**. Der. *sedg-ed*, Temp. iv. 129; *sedg-y*.

SEDIMENT, dregs, that which settles at the bottom of a liquid. (F.–L.) In Minsheu, ed. 1627.–MF. *sediment*, 'a sitting or setling of dregs;' Cot.–L. *sedimentum*, a settling, subsidence.–L. *sedēre*, to sit, settle; with suffix *-mentum*. See **Sit**. Der. *sediment-ar-y*.

SEDITION, insurrection, rebellious conduct against the state. (F.–L.) ME. *sedicioun*, Wyclif, Mark, xv. 7, in some MSS.; others have *seducioun*.–OF. *sedition*, 'a sedition, mutiny;' Cot.–L. *sēditiōnem*, acc. of *sēditio*, dissension, civil discord, sedition. β. Lit. 'a going apart,' hence dissension; just as *amb-ition* is 'a going about.'—L. *sĕd-*, apart; and *it-um*, supine of *īre*, to go, from √EI, to go. See **Se-** and **Ambition**. Der. *sediti-ous*, Com. Errors, i. 1. 12, from MF. *seditieux*, 'seditious,' Cot.; *sediti-ous-ly*.

SEDUCE, to lead astray, entice, corrupt. (L.) In Levins, ed. 1570; Fryth's Works, p. 95, l. 16; Surrey, Ps. 73, l. 5 from end.—L. *sēdūcere*, to lead apart or astray; pp. *sēductus*.—L. *sē-*, apart; and *dūcere*, to lead; see **Se-** and **Duct**. Der. *seduc-er*; *seduce-ment*, a coined word; *seduct-ion*, from MF. *seduction*, 'seduction,' Cot., from L. acc. *sēductiōnem*, allied to the pp. *sēductus*. Also *seduct-ive*, a coined word, from the pp. *sēductus*; *seduct-ive-ly*.

SEDULOUS, diligent, attentive. (L.) Used by Bp. Taylor, vol. iii. ser. 4 (R.). [The sb. *sedulity* is in Minsheu and Cotgrave.] Englished from L. *sēdulus*, diligent, by change of *-us* into *-ous*, as in *arduous*, &c. Cf. *sēdulō*, adv. busily; from *sē*, apart from, and *dolō*, abl. of *dolus*, fraud. Brugmann, i. § 244. Der. *sedulous-ly*, *-ness*; also *sedul-it-y*, from MF. *sedulité*, 'sedulity,' Cot., from L. acc. *sēdulitātem*.

SEE (1), to perceive by the eye. (E.) ME. *seen, sen, se*; pt. t. *sei, sey, say, seigh, sigh, seiȝ, saugh, sauh, saw*; pp. *sein, seȝen, sen, seien, seie*; Chaucer, C. T. 193, &c. AS. *sēon*; pt. t. *sēah*, pl. *sāwon*; pp. *gesegen, gesewen*; Grein.✚Du. *zien*, pt. t. *zag*, pp. *gezien*; Icel. *sjā*, pt. t. *sā*, pp. *sēnn*; Dan. *se*; Swed. *se*; OHG. *sehan*; G. *sehen*; Goth. *saihwan*, pt. t. *sahw*, pl. *sēhwum*, pp. *saihwans*. β. All from a Teut. type *sehwan-* (pt. t. *sahw*); Fick, iii. 315; Brugmann, i. § 665. Der. *se-er*, lit. one who sees, hence, a prophet, 1 Sam. ix. 9, spelt *sear* in the edit. of 1551; *see-ing*. And see *sight*.

SEE (2), the seat of a bishop. (F.—L.) Used by Spenser in the sense of 'seat' or throne; F. Q. iv. 10. 30. ME. *se*, Chron. of England, 363, in Ritson, Met. Rom. vol. ii; Trevisa, tr. of Higden, ii. 119; P. Pl. Crede, 558.—OF. *sed, se*, a seat, see (Burguy).—L. *sēdem*, acc. of *sēdes*, a seat.—L. *sēd-*, as in *sēd-ī*, pt. of *sedēre*, to sit; cognate with E. **Sit**, q. v.

SEED, a thing sown, germ, first original or principle, descendants. (E.) ME. *seed*, Chaucer, C. T. 598 (A 596). AS. *sǣd*, seed; Grein, ii. 394.✚Du. *zaad*; Icel. *sæði, sāð*; Dan. *sæd*; Swed. *säd*; G. *saat*. Cf. Goth. *mana-sēths*, the world, lit. 'man-seed;' L. *sē-men*, seed. The AS. *sǣd* answers to the Teut. type *sǣ-dom*, neut.; from Teut. *sǣ-* = Idg. SĒ, to sow. See **Sow**. Der. *seed-bud, -ling, -lobe, -s-man, -time*; also *seed-y*, looking as if run to seed, hence shabby.

SEEK, to go in search of, look for, try to find. (E.) ME. *seken*, Chaucer, C. T. 17. AS. *sēcan*, to seek, pt. t. *sōhte*, pp. *gesōht*; Grein, ii. 418.✚Du. *zoeken*; Icel. *sækja*, written for *soekja*; Dan. *søge*; Swed. *söka*; OHG. *suohhan*, MHG. *suochen*, G. *suchen*; Goth. *sōkjan*; Teut. type *sōk-jan-*; from *sōk-* = Idg. *sāg-*, as in L. *sāg-īre*, to perceive, Gk. ἡγέομαι, I consider. Cf. OIrish *sagim*, I seek for. *Seek* is a weak verb, with mutation from *ō* to *ē* in the infin. mood. Der. *seek-er*, *be-seech*.

SEEL, to close up the eyes. (F.—L.) 'Come, *seeling* night;' Macb. iii. 2. 46. Spelt *cele* in Palsgrave. Orig. a term in falconry, to close up the eyelids of a hawk (or other bird) by sewing up the eyelids; see *Sealed-dove* in Halliwell, and *seel* in Nares.—MF. *siller*; *siller les yeux*, 'to seel, or sow up, the eie-lids, thence also, to hoodwink, blind;' Cot. Also spelt *ciller*, 'to seele or sow up the eie-lids;' id. The latter is the better spelling.—OF. *cil*, 'the brimme of an eie-lid, or the single ranke of haire that growes on the brim;' id.—L. *cilium*, an eye-lid, an eye-lash; perhaps allied to Gk. τὰ κύλα, the parts under the eyes. See **Supercilious**.

SEEM, to appear, look. (E.) The old sense 'to be fitting' is preserved in the derivative *seemly*. ME. *semen*, Chaucer, C. T. 10283 (E 2409). AS. *sēman, gesēman*, to satisfy, conciliate; Grein. Hence the idea of 'suit,' whence that of 'appear suitable,' or simply 'appear.' These senses are probably borrowed from the related adj. *seemly*, which is rather Scand. than E.; see **Seemly**.✚Icel. *sæma*, for *soema*, to honour, bear with, conform to; closely related to *sæmr*, adj., becoming, fit, and to *sōma*, to beseem, become, befit. β. Here *ē* is (as usual) the mutation of *ō*, and the Teut. type is *sōm-jan*; from *sōm*, 2nd grade of *sam-*, as in E. *same*; cf. Icel. *sōma*, to beseem, and Icel. *sama*, to beseem, *samr*, same; see further under **Seemly**. Der. *seem-ing*; also *seem-ly*, q. v.; *be-seem*, q. v.

SEEMLY, becoming, fit. (Scand.) ME. *semlich*, Ancren Riwle, p. 94, note *i*; *semli, semely*, Chaucer, C. T. 753 (A 751).—Icel. *sæmiligr*, seemly, becoming; a longer form of *sæmr*, becoming, fit, with suffix *-ligr* answering to AS. *-lic*, like, and E. *-ly*; where *sæm-* is the mutated form of *sōm-* (as in Icel. *sōma*, to befit), 2nd grade of *sam-*, as in Icel. *sama*, to beseem, befit, become; cognate with Goth. *samjan*, to please, lit. 'to be the same,' hence to be like, to fit, suit, be congruent with.—Icel. *samr*, the same, cognate with E. **Same**, q. v. ¶ Thus *seemly* = same-like, agreeing with, fit; and *seem* is to agree with, appear like, or simply, to appear; the AS. *sēman*, to conciliate, is the same, with the act. sense 'to make

like,' make to agree. Der. *seemly*, adv. (for *seem-li-ly*); *seemli-ness*, Prompt. Parv.

SEER, a prophet, lit. 'one who sees.' (E.) See **See**.

SEESAW, motion to and fro, or up and down. (E.) In Pope, Prol. to Satires, 323. A reduplicated form of *saw*; from the action of two men sawing wood (where the motion is up and down), or sawing stone (where the motion is to and fro). See **Saw** (1). It is used as adj., verb, and sb.; the orig. use was perhaps adjectival, as in Pope.

SEETHE, to boil. (E.) The pt. t. *sod* occurs in Gen. xxv. 29; the pp. *sodden* in Exod. xii. 9. ME. *sethen*, Chaucer, C. T. 385 (A 383); pt. t. sing. *seeth*, id. 8103 (E 227), pl. *sothen, soden*, P. Plowman, B. xv. 288, C. xviii. 20; pp. *soden, sothen*, id. B. xv. 425. AS. *sēoðan*, pt. t. *sēað*, pp. *soden*; Grein, ii. 437.✚Du. *zieden*; Icel. *sjōða*, pt. t. *sauð*, pl. *suðu*, pp. *soðinn*; Dan. *syde*; Swed. *sjuda*; OHG. *siodan*; G. *sieden*. Teut. type *seuthan-*, pt. t. *sauth*, pp. *sud-anoz*. Allied to Goth. *sauths, sauds*, a burnt-offering, sacrifice, Mark, xii. 33. Der. *sod, suds*.

SEGMENT, a portion, part cut off. (L.) In Minsheu, ed. 1627.—L. *segmentum*, a piece cut off; for *sec-mentum*.—L. *sec-āre*, to cut; with suffix *-mentum*; see **Section**.

SEGREGATE, to separate from others. (L.) Not common. In Sir T. More, Works, p. 428 d; where it occurs as a pp., meaning 'separated.'—L. *sēgregātus*, pp. of *sēgregāre*, to set apart, lit. 'to set apart from a flock.'—L. *sē-*, apart; and *greg-*, stem of *grex*, a flock; see **Se-** and **Gregarious**. Der. *segregat-ion*, from MF. *segregation*, 'a segregation,' Cot., from L. acc. *sēgregātiōnem*.

SEGUIDILLA, a lively Spanish dance. (Span.—L.) Moore has the F. form *seguadille*; Remember the Time, l. 5.—Span. *seguidilla*, a merry Spanish tune and dance, with a refrain. Dimin. of *seguida*, a continuation, succession (of the refrain).—Span. *seguir*, to follow.—L. *sequi*, to follow. See **Sequence**.

SEIGNIOR, a title of honour. (F.—L.) ME. *seignour*, King Alisaunder, 1458; the derived word *seignory* is much commoner, as in Rob. of Brunne, p. 24, l. 18, Rob. of Glouc. p. 186, l. 3858.—OF. *seignour*, MF. *seigneur*, 'a lord, sir, seignior;' Cot.—L. *seniōrem*, acc. of *senior*, elder, hence, an elder, a lord; see **Senior**. Der. *seignior-y*, as above, from OF. *seignorie*, MF. *seigneurie*, 'seigniory,' Cot.

SEINE, a large fishing-net. (F.—L.—Gk.) ME. *seyne*; Wright's Vocab. i. 159.—F. *seine*.—L. *sagēna*.—Gk. σαγήνη, a large fishing-net.

SEIZE, to lay hold of, grasp, comprehend. (F.—OHG.) ME. *saysen, seysen*, orig. a law term, to give seisin or livery of land, to put one in possession of, also to take possession of; hence, to grasp; see Havelok, 251, 2513, 2518, 2931.—OF. *seisir, saisir*, to put one in possession of, take possession of (Burguy).—Low L. *sacīre*, to take possession of. Usually referred to Teut. *satjan-*, OHG. *sazzan* (Goth. *satjan*, AS. *settan*), to set, put, place, cognate with E. **Set**. This may have given the Low L. form, though it would not give the OF. form directly. Der. *seiz-er*, *seiz-able*, a coined word; *seiz-ure*, Troil. i. 1. 57, a coined word, answering to the F. infin. *saisir* just as *pleasure* does to *plaisir*. Also *seis-in*, *seiz-in*, possession of an estate, a law term, ME. *seisine*, spelt *seysyne* in Rob. of Glouc. p. 382, l. 7851, from OF. *seisine*, the same as *saisine*, 'seisin, possession,' Cot.; where the suffix *-ine* answers to L. *-īna*; cf. Ital. *sagina*, seisin, possession.

SEJANT, sitting; a term in heraldry. (F.—L.) AF. *seiant*, pres. pt. of AF. *seier*, variant of OF. *seoir*, to sit (Godefroy).—L. *sedēre*, to sit. See **Séance, Sit**.

SELAH, a pause. (Heb.) In Ps. iii. 2; and elsewhere in the psalms. The meaning of the word is unknown, and cannot be certainly explained. Usually taken to indicate 'a pause.' See Smith, Dict. of the Bible.

SELDOM, rarely, not often. (E.) ME. *seldom*, P. Plowman, A. viii. 124; *selden*, B. vii. 137; *selde*, Chaucer, C. T. 1541 (A 1539). AS. *seldan, seldon, seldum*, seldom; Grein, ii. 426. β. The AS. *seldum* is formed with an adverbial suffix *-um* which was orig. the inflectional ending of the dat. plural; just as in *hwil-um*. E. *whil-om*, lit. 'at whiles' or at times, *wundr-um*, wondrously, *lytl-um*, little, *micl-um*, much, and the like; see March, A. S. Gram. § 251. This form easily passed into *seldon* or *seldan*, just as AS. *onsundr-on*, asunder, stands for *on sundrum*. γ. This takes us back to an adj. *seld*, rare, only found as an adverb. 'Þæt folc wundraþ þæs þe hit *seldost* gesihð' = the people wonder at that which it most seldom sees; Ælfred, tr. of Boethius, cap. xxxix. § 3; where *seldost* is the superl. form of the adverb. We also find such compounds as *seld-cūð*, rare, *seld-sine*, seldom seen; Sweet, A. S. Reader.✚Du. *zelden*, adv.; Icel. *sjaldan*, adv., seldom; Dan. *sjelden*, adv.; Swed. *sällan* (for *säldan*), adv.; G. *selten*; OHG. *seltan*. δ. All these are adverbial forms from a Teut. adj. *seldoz*, rare, strange, appearing in Goth. *silda-* in comp. *silda-leiks*, wonderful, orig. perhaps 'of strange form.'

SELECT, choice. (L.) In Shak. Haml. i. 3. 74.—L. *sēlectus,* select, chosen ; pp. of *sēligere,* to choose.—L. *sē-,* apart ; and *legere,* to choose. See **Se-** and **Legend.** Der. *select-ness* ; also *select,* verb, Cor. i. 6. 81 ; *select-ion,* sb., from L. acc. *sēlectiōnem.*

SELF, one's own person. (E.) ME. *self,* sometimes used in the sense of ' same ' or ' very ;' dat. *selue* ; ' right in the *selue* place ' = just in the very place, Chaucer, C. T. 11706 (F 1394). AS. *self,* also *seolf, silf, siolf, sylf,* self ; Grein, ii. 427, where numerous examples are given.+Du. *zelf* ; Icel. *sjálfr* ; old form *sjælfr* ; Dan. *selv* ; Swed. *sjelf* ; Goth. *silba* ; G. *selbe, selb-st.* The origin is unknown. Der. *self-denial, self-evident, self-existent, self-possession, self-righteous, self-same, self-sufficient, self-willed.* Also *self-ish,* in Hacket's Life of Archbp. Williams, pt. ii. p. 144 (Trench, Eng. Past and Present); *self-ish-ness,* Butler, Hudibras, pt. i. c. 2. l. 1052. Also *my-self,* AS. *min self,* where *min* is the possessive pron. of the 1st person ; *thy-self,* AS. *þin self,* where *þin* is the possessive pron. of the second person ; *him-self,* where the AS. phrase is *hē self,* nom., *his selfes,* gen., *him selfum,* dat., *hine selfne,* acc. (see Grein) ; *her-self,* due to AS. *hyre selfre,* dat. fem. ; &c. For the use of these forms in ME. and AS., see examples in Stratmann and Grein. Also *selv-age,* q. v.

SELL (1), to hand over or deliver in exchange for money or some other valuable. (E.) ME. *sellen,* Wyclif, Luke, xii. 33 ; *sillen,* Matt. xix. 21. AS. *sellan, sillan, syllan,* to give, hand over, deliver ; Grein, ii. 429.+Icel. *selja,* to hand over to another ; Dan. *sælge* ; Swed. *sälja* ; MHG. *sellen* ; OHG. *saljan.*+Goth. *saljan,* to bring an offering, to offer a sacrifice. β. All from a Teut. type **saljan-,* to offer, deliver, hand over. This is a causal form, allied to the sb. which appears in E. as **Sale,** q. v. Der. *seller.*

SELL (2), a saddle. (F.—L.) In Spenser, F. Q. ii. 2. 11, 3. 12. ME. *selle,* a seat, Wyclif, 2 Macc. xiv. 21.—OF. *selle,* ' a stool, a seat, also, a saddle ;' Cot.—L. *sella,* a seat. For **sed-la,* from *sedēre,* to sit ; see **Settle** (1), and **Sit.** Brugmann, i. § 475.

SELVAGE, SELVEDGE, a border of cloth, forming an edge that needs no hem. (Du.) In Exod. xxvi. 4, xxxvi. 11 ; spelt *seluege* in the edit. of 1551 ; *selvage* in G. Douglas, Prol. to Aen. xii. l. 16. It merely means *self-edge,* but it was borrowed from Dutch. ' The *self-edge* makes show of the cloth ;' Ray's Proverbs, ed. 1737.— MDu. *selfegge,* the selvage, spelt *self-egghe* in Kilian ; from *self,* self, and *egge,* edge. [The more usual Du. word is *zelfkant,* for *selfkant.*] ' *Egge,* an edge, or a selvage ; *kant,* the edge, brinke, or seame of anything ; *de zelfkant,* the selvage of cloath ;' Hexham. See **Self** and **Edge.**

SEMAPHORE, a kind of telegraph. (F.—Gk.) A late word, not in Todd's Johnson. A F. name (ab. 1803) for a telegraph worked with arms projecting from a post, the positions of the arms giving the signals. Coined from Gk. σῆμα, a sign ; and φορά, a carrying, from φέρειν, to bear, carry, cognate with E. **Bear,** vb.

SEMBLANCE, an appearance. (F.—L.) ME. *semblaunce,* Rom. of the Rose, 425.—OF. *semblance,* ' a semblance, shew, seeming ;' Cot. Formed, with suffix *-ance* (= L. *-antia*) from *sembl-er,* ' to seem, or make shew of ;' also, to resemble ;' Cot.—L. *simulāre,* to assume the appearance of, simulate ; see **Simulate.** Cf. *re-semblance.*

SEMI-, half. (L.) L. *sēmi-,* half ; reduced to *sēm-* in L. *sēmēsus.* +Gk. ἡμι-, half ; AS. *sam-,* half ; as in *sam-wis,* half wise, not very wise ; Grein, ii. 388, 390 ; Skt. *sāmi,* half ; which Benfey connects with *sāmya-,* equality, from *sama-,* even, same, equal, like, cognate with E. **Same.** Thus *semi-* denotes ' in an equal manner,' referring to an exact halving or equitable division ; and is a mere derivative of *same.* Doublet, *hemi-.*

SEMIBREVE, half a breve, a musical note. (Ital.—L.) From Ital. *semibreve,* ' a semibriefe in musike ;' Florio, ed. 1598.— Ital. *semi-,* half ; and *breve,* a short note. See **Semi-** and **Breve.** ¶ Similar formations are seen in *semi-circle, semi-circumference, semi-colon, semi-diameter, semi-fluid, semi-quaver, semi-tone, semi-transparent, semi-vocal, semi-vowel* ; all coined words, made by prefixing *semi-,* and presenting no difficulty.

SEMINAL, relating to seed. (F.—L.) Sir T. Browne has *seminality,* sb., Vul. Errors, b. vi. c. 1. § 3.—MF. *seminal,* adj. ' of seed ;' Cot.—L. *sēminālis,* relating to seed.—L. *sēmin-,* stem of *sēmen,* seed.—L. base *sē-,* appearing in *sē-ui,* pt. t. of *serere,* to sow ; and suffix *-men. Serere* is cognate with E. **Sow,** q. v. Der. *semin-ar-y,* q. v. Also *semin-at-ion* (rare), from L. *sēmin-ātio,* a sowing, which from *sēmināre,* to sow, derived from *sēmen.*

SEMINARY, a place of education. (L.) The old sense was a seed-garden. ' As concerning *seminaries* and nourse-gardens ;' Holland, tr. of Pliny, b. xvii. c. 10.—L. *sēminārium,* a seed-garden, nursery garden, seed-plot ; neut. of *sēminārius,* belonging to seed.— L. *sēmin-,* stem of *sēmen,* seed ; and suffix *-ārius.* See **Seminal.**

SEMOLINA, large grains left after the finer flour has passed through the sieve. (Ital.—L.) Modern ; for *semolino.*—Ital. *semolino,*

m., small seed, paste for soups, dimin. of *semola,* bran.—L. *simila,* fine wheaten flower.+Gk. σεμίδαλις, the same. See **Simnel.**

SEMPITERNAL, everlasting. (F.—L.) In Minsheu and Cotgrave. Altered from F. *sempiternel,* ' sempiternall ;' Cot. L. *sempitern-us,* everlasting ; with suffix *-ālis.*—L. *sempi-,* for *semper,* ever ; with suffixes *-ter-* and *-nus* ; cf. *noc-tur-nus* (for **noct-tur-nus*) from the stem *noct-.* β. L. *sem-per* is perhaps for **sem-perti,* ' in one (continuous) part, in one sequence, ever ;' from *sem-* ' one,' as in *semel,* once, and **perti,* allied to ' part.' Brugmann, i. § 1023 (12) ; ii. § 160 (1).

SEMPSTER, SEMPSTRESS, the same as **Seamstress,** q.v.

SENARY, belonging to six. (L.) The *senary* scale (scale by sixes) is a mathematical term.—L. *sēnārius,* consisting of six each. —L. *sēni,* six each ; for **sex-ni.*—L. *sex,* six, cognate with E. *six* ; see **Six.**

SENATE, a council of elders. (F.—L.) ME. *senat* ; spelt *senaht,* Layamon, 25388.—OF. *senat,* ' a senat ;' Cot.—L. *senātum,* acc. of *senātus,* the council of elders.—L. *sen-,* base of *sen-ex,* old, *sen-ium,* old age ; with pp. suffix *-ātus* ; so that *sen-ātus* = grown old. Cf. Vedic Skt. *sana-,* old (Benfey), OGk. *ἕνος,* old ; Goth. *sin-eigs,* old, *sin-ista,* eldest ; OIrish *sen,* Irish and Gael. *sean,* W. *hen,* old. See **Senior.** Der. *senat-or,* ME. *senat-our,* Chaucer, C. T. 5430 (B 1010), from OF. *senatour* (Littré), from L. acc. *senātōrem* ; altered to *senator* to make it like the L. nom. case. Hence *senator-ship, senator-i-al, senator-i-al-ly.* Brugmann, i. § 117.

SEND, to cause to go, despatch. (E.) ME. *senden,* pt. t. *sende, sente* ; pp. *sent* ; Chaucer, C. T. 5511 (B 1091), AS. *sendan,* pt. t. *sende,* pp. *sended,* Grein, ii. 431.+Du. *zenden* ; Icel. *senda* ; Dan. *sende* ; Swed. *sända* ; Goth. *sandjan* ; MHG. *senten,* G. *senden.* Teut. type **sandjan,* for **santhján-,* by Verner's Law ; from **santh,* 2nd grade of **senthan-,* to go. Hence *send* is a causal verb ; lit. ' to make to go.' β. The Teut. **senthan-,* to go, pt. t. **santh,* is a lost str. vb. of which the prime grade appears in Goth. *sinths* (for **senthoz*), AS. *sið* (for **sinð*), a journey, way ; Teut. type **senthoz,* m. ; Idg. **sentos,* a way, as seen in OIrish *sēt* (for **sent*), W. *hynt,* Bret. *hent* (for **sent*), a way. Cf. G. *gesinde,* followers ; Goth. *gasinthja,* a travelling companion. See **Sense.**

SENDAL, CENDAL, a kind of rich thin silken stuff. (F.— Low L.—Skt.) See *Sendall* and *Cendal* in Halliwell. ME. *sendal,* P. Plowman, B. vi. 11 ; Chaucer, C. T. 442 (440).—OF. *sendal* (Roquefort) ; also *cendal* (Burguy). Cf. Port. *cendal,* fine linen or silk ; Span. *cendal,* light thin stuff ; Ital. *zendalo, zendado,* ' a kind of fine thin silken stuffe, called taffeta, sarcenett, or sendall,' Florio.— Low L. *cendalum* ; also spelt *cendāle, cendātum, sendātum, sendādum, cindādus, cindātus.* Cf. also Gk. σινδών, fine linen. So called because brought from India.—Skt. *sindhu-,* the river Indus, the country along the Indus, Scinde. See **Indigo.**

SENESCHAL, a steward. (F.—Teut.) In Spenser, F. Q. iv. 1. 12. ME. *seneschal,* P. Plowman, C. i. 93.—OF. *seneschal,* ' a seneschall, the president of a precinct ;' Cot. Cf. Span. *senescal,* Ital. *siniscalco,* a seneschal, steward. The orig. signification must have been ' old (i. e. chief) servant,' as the etymology is undoubtedly from the Goth. *sins,* old (only recorded in the superl. *sin-ista,* eldest), and *skalks,* a servant. The Goth. *sins* is cognate with L. *sen-ex,* old. The word *mar-shal* is a similar compound. See **Senior** and **Marshal.**

SENILE, old. (L.) A late word ; in Todd's Johnson.—L. *senīlis,* old.—L. *sen-,* base of *sen-ex,* old, with suffix *-ilis.* See **Senior.** Der. *senil-i-ty.*

SENIOR, elder, older. (L.) In Shak. L. L. L. i. 2. 10 ; cf. *senior-junior,* L. L. L. iii. 182 ; spelt *seniour,* Tyndale, Mark, vii. 3 (1526) ; *senyor,* Monk of Evesham (ab. 1412), c. x. ed. Arber, p. 31. —L. *senior,* older ; comparative from the base *sen-,* old, found in *sen-ex,* old, *sen-ium,* old age. From the Idg. type **senos,* old ; see **Senate.** Der. *senior-i-ty.* Doublets, *signor, señor, seignior, sire, sir.*

SENNA, the dried leaflets of some kinds of cassia. (Ital.—Arab.) Spelt *sena* in Phillips, ed. 1706 ; the older name is *seny* or *senie,* ME. *senee,* Libell of E. Policy, l. 362, which is a F. form, from OF. *senné* (Cot.). Minsheu's Span. Dict. has ' *sen, seny ;*' ed. 1623.—Ital. *sena* (Florio).—Arab. *sanā,* senna ; Palmer's Pers. Dict., col. 361 ; Rich. Dict. p. 851.

SENNET, a signal-call on a trumpet. (F.—L.) In stage-directions ; see King Lear, i. 1. 33, and Wright's note. And see Nares. Also spelt *cynet, sinet, synnet, signate.*—OF. *sinet, senet, segnet* (Godefroy, s. v. *segnet*), lit. a signet, a little sign (hence, signal) ; dimin. of F. *seing, signe.*—L. *signum,* a sign ; see **Sign.** See Notes on Eng. Etym., p. 264.

SENNIGHT, a week. (E.) Spelt *senyght* in Palsgrave ; *synyght,* Sir Amadas, 590 (Weber) ; a contraction of *seven night* ; see **Seven** and **Night.**

SENSE, a faculty by which objects are perceived, perception, discernment. (F.—L.) It does not appear to be in early use; Palsgrave gives *sensualness* and *sensualyte*, but not *sense*. Levins has *sensible* and *sensual*, but also omits *sense*. Yet it is very common in Shakespeare. ' And shall *sensiue* things be so *sencelesse* as to resist *sence?*' Sir P. Sidney, Arcadia, poem ix. l. 137; ed. Grosart, ii. 25.— F. *sens*, 'sence, wit;' Cot.—L. *sensum*, acc. of *sensus*, feeling, sense; cf. *sensus*, pp. of *sentīre*, to feel, perceive. β. From the Idg. base *sent-*, to direct oneself towards, whence also not only G. *sinn*, sense, G. *sinnen*, to think over, reflect upon, but also Idg. *sentos*, a way, and E. *send*; see **Send**. Der. *sense-less*, *sense-less-ly*, *sense-less-ness*; *sens-ible*, Gower, C. A. iii. 88; bk. vii. 127, from F. *sensible*, 'sensible,' Cot., from L. *sensibilis*; *sens-ibl-y*, *sensible-ness*, *sensibil-i-ty*. Also *sens-it-ive*, from F. *sensitif*, ' sensitive,' Cot.; *sens-it-ive-ly*, *sens-it-ive-ness*; *sens-at-ion*, Phillips, from L. *sensātio*, a coined word from L. *sensātus*, endued with sense; *sens-at-ion-al*, *sens-at-ion-al-ism*. Also *sens-or-i-um*, from Late L. *sensōrium*, the seat of the senses (White); *sens-or-i-al*. And see *sens-u-al*, *sent-ence*, *sent-i-ment*. From the same source we also have *as-sent*, *con-sent*, *dis-sent*, *re-sent*; *in-sens-ate*, *non-sense*, *pre-sent-i-ment*, *scent*.

SENSUAL, affecting the senses, given to the pleasures of sense. (L.) In Levins; Palsgrave has *sensualness* and *sensualyte* (sensuality) in his list of sbs.; and *sensuall* in his list of adjectives. From Late L. *sensuālis*, endowed with feeling; whence *sensuālitās*, sensibility (White). Formed (with suffix *-ālis*), from *sensu-*, for *sensus*, sense; see **Sense**. Der. *sensual-ly*; *sensual-i-ty*, from F. *sensualité*, 'sensuality,' Cot.; *sensual-ness*, *sensual-ise*, *sensual-ism*, *sensual-ist*. Also *sensu-ous*, a coined word, used by Milton; see Rich. and Todd's Johnson.

SENTENCE, an opinion, maxim, decree, series of words containing a complete thought. (F.—L.) ME. *sentence*, Ancren Riwle, p. 348, l. 14.—F. *sentence*, 'a sentence,' Cot.—L. *sententia*, a way of thinking, opinion, sentiment. For *sentientia*, from the stem of the pres. part. of *sentīre*, to feel, think; see **Sense**. Der. *sentence*, vb., Meas. for Meas. ii. 2. 55; *sententi-ous*, As You Like It, v. 4. 66, from F. *sententieux*, 'sententious,' Cot., from L. *sententiōsus*; *sententi-ous-ly*, *-ness*. Also *sentient*, feeling, from stem of pres. part. of *sentīre*, to feel.

SENTIMENT, thought, judgement, feeling, opinion. (F.—L.) ME. *sentement*, Chaucer, Prol. to Legend of Good Women, l. 69. [Afterwards conformed to a supposed L. form *sentimentum*, not used.]—OF. *sentement*, 'a feeling;' Cot.; F. *sentiment*. Formed as if from L. *sentī-mentum*, a word made up of the suffix *-mentum* and the verb *sentī-re*, to feel. See **Sense**. Der. *sentiment-al*, *sentiment-al-ly*, *sentiment-al-ism*, *-ist*.

SENTINEL, one who keeps watch, a soldier on guard. (F.—Ital.—L.) Spelt *centonell*, Spenser, F. Q. i. 9. 41; *centronel*, Marlowe, Dido, ii. 1. 323; *sentinel*, Macb. ii. 1. 53.—MF. *sentinelle*, ' a sentinell, or sentry;' Cot.—Ital. *sentinella*, ' a watch, a sentinell, a souldier which is set to watch at a station;' Florio. Cf. Span. *centinela*, a sentinel; MF. *sentinelle*, a watch-tower (Godefroy). Usually explained from L. *sentīre*, to perceive; as if a *sentinel* meant a watcher, scout; but this does not account for the *-in-*. See Körting, §§ 8597, 8611. β. Derived by Wedgwood from OF. *sentine*, a path (Roquefort), due to L. *sēmita*, a path; this does not help us; for the word is Italian, not French. At the same time, it would be possible to derive the form *centronel* (in Marlowe) from OF. *sentron*, a path (Godefroy). See **Sentry**. γ. Perhaps from Ital. *sentina*, in the sense of 'rascal rout of camp-followers,' or ' a place where such used to congregate;' if the sentinel had to watch them; see Florio and Lewis.

SENTRY, a sentinel, soldier on guard. (F.—L.) Spelt *sentrie*, in Minsheu, ed. 1627; *senteries*, pl., Milton, P. L. ii. 412; *sentry* in Cotgrave, s. v. *sentinelle*. Perhaps from MF. *sentier*, adj., ' of, or in, a path;' Cot. Or from OF. *senteret*, a path; with reference to the sentinel's beat, or his guarding the approaches. The former answers to Late L. *sēmitārius*, adj. (Lewis); whence the neuter *sēmitārium* (F. *sentier*), a path (Ducange).—L. *sēmita* (whence OF. *sente*), a path. Der. *sentry-box*.

SEPAL, a calyx-leaf, division of a calyx; in botany. (F.—L.) F. *sépale*, a sepal. Coined (to pair with *pet-al*, F. *pétale*) by taking part of L. *sēp-ar*, separate, and adding *-ale*. Thus *sepal* is (practically) short for *sēpar-al*, where *sēpar-* was regarded as a part of L. *sēpar-āre*, to separate. See **Separate**.

SEPARATE, to part, divide, sever. (L.) We should have expected to find *separate* first used as a pp., in the sense ' set apart;' but I find no very early example. Levins, Shakespeare, and Minsheu recognize only the verb, which occurs as early as in Tyndale, Workes, p. 116, col. 2; see Richardson.—L. *sēparātus*, pp. of *sēparāre*, to separate.—L. *sē-*, apart; and *parāre*, to provide, arrange. See **Se-** and **Parade, Pare**. Der. *separate*, adj., from pp. *sēparātus*;

separate-ly; *separat-ion*, from MF. *separation*, 'separation,' Cot.; *separat-ism*, *separat-ist*. Also *separ-able*, from L. *sēparābilis*; *separabl-y*. Doublet, *sever*.

SEPIA, ink from the cuttlefish. (L.—Gk.) L. *sēpia*.—Gk. σηπία, cuttlefish, sepia.

SEPOY, one of the native troops in India. (Pers.) ' *Sepoys* (a corruption of *sipāhī*, Hindostanee for a soldier), the term applied to the native troops in India;' Haydn, Dict. of Dates. The word is, however, a Persian one.—Pers. *sipāhī*, ' a horseman, one soldier;' properly an adj., ' military, belonging to an army;' Rich. Dict. p. 807.—Pers. *sipāh*, *supāh*, an army; *sipah*, *supah*, *sapah*, an army; id. pp. 807, 808; Horn, § 699. ¶ The Pers. *ā* being sounded nearly as E. *au* in *maul*, the spelling *sepoy* gives the right sound very nearly.

SEPT, a clan. (F.—L.) It is chiefly used of the Irish clans. Spenser has ' the head of that *sept*;' and again, ' whole nations and *septs* of the Irish;' View of the State of Ireland, Globe ed., p. 611, col. 1. 'The Irish man .. termeth anie one of the English *sept*,' &c.; Holinshed, Descr. of Ireland, cap. 8. ' Five of the best persons of every *sept* ' [of the Irish]; Fuller's Worthies; Kent (R.). ' All of the old Irish *septs* of Ulster;' Clarendon, Civil Wars, iii. 430 (R.). Wedgwood says : ' a clan or following, a corruption of the synonymous *sect*.' He cites from Notes and Queries (2nd Series, iii. 361, May 9, 1857), two quotations from the State Papers, one dated A.D. 1537, which speaks of 'M'Morgho and his kinsmen, O'Byrne and his *septe*,' and another dated A.D. 1536, which says 'there are another *secte* of the Berkes and divers of the Irishry towards Sligo.'—OF. *septe*, variant of *secte*, a sect; Supp. to Godefroy. See **Sect**. Wedgwood adds : ' The same corruption is found in Prov. *cepte*. "Vist que lo dit visconte non era eretge ni de lor *cepte*"= seeing that the said viscount was not heretic nor of their sect; Sismondi, Litt. Provenç. 215.' Ducange has Late L. *septa* for Ital. *setta* (< L. *secta*). ¶ Perhaps influenced by L. *septum*, an enclosure; from *sēpīre*, *sæpīre*, to hedge in, from *sēpes*, *sæpes*, a hedge. Doublet, *sect*.

SEPTEMBER, the ninth month. (L.) ME. *Septembre*, Chaucer, On the Astrolabe, pt. i. § 10. l. 3. It seems to be meant for the Latin, not the French form; the other months being mostly named in Latin. —L. *September*, the name of the seventh month of the Roman year.— L. *septem*, seven, cognate with E. *seven*; and the suffix *-ber*, of uncertain origin. See **Seven**.

SEPTENARY, consisting of seven. (L.) In Sir T. Browne, Vulg. Errors, iv. 12. 12. A mathematical term.—L. *septēnārius*, consisting of seven.—L. *septēni*, pl., seven apiece, by sevens; for *septem-ni*.—L. *septem*, seven. See **Seven**.

SEPTENNIAL, happening every seven years, lasting seven years. (L.) Used by Burke; see Todd's Johnson. Formed, with suffix *-al*, from L. *septenni-um*, a period of seven years.—L. *septenni-s*, adj., of seven years.—L. *sept-*, for *septem*, seven; and *annus*, a year. See **Seven** and **Annual**. Der. *septennial-ly*.

SEPTIC, putrefying. (Gk.) Modern.—Gk. σηπτικός, characterised by putridity.—Gk. σηπτός, rotten; from σήπειν, to cause to rot.

SEPTUAGENARY, belonging to seventy years. (L.) In Sir T. Browne, Vulg. Errors, b. iii. c. 9, § 4, last line.—L. *septuāgēnārius*, belonging to the number seventy.—L. *septuāgēni*, seventy each; distributive form of *septuāgintā*, seventy.—L. *septuā-*, due to *septem*, seven; and *-ginta = -cinta*, short for *decinta*, tenth, from *decem*, ten. See **Seven** and **Ten**. Der. *septuagenari-an*. So also *septuagesima*, lit. seventieth, applied to the Third Sunday before Lent, about 70 days before Easter; from L. *septuāgēsima (diēs)*, fem. of *septuāgēsimus*, seventieth, ordinal of *septuāgintā*, seventy. Also *septua-gint*, the Greek version of the Old Testament, said to have been made by 70 translators; used by Burnet (Johnson).

SEPULCHRE, a tomb. (F.—L.) ME. *sepulcre*, in early use; O. Eng. Homilies, ed. Morris, ii. 95, l. 11.—OF. *sepulcre*, MF. *sepulchre*, ' a sepulcher, tomb;' Cot.—L. *sepulcrum* (also ill-spelt *sepulchrum*), a tomb.—L. *sepul-*, appearing in *sepul-tus*, pp. of *sepelīre*, to bury; with suffix *-crum*. Der. *sepulchr-al*, from F. *sepulchral*, ' sepulchral,' Cot.; also *sepult-ure*, Rob. of Glouc. p. 166, l. 3466, from MF. *sepulture*, 'sepulture, a burying,' Cot., from L. *sepultūra*, burial, due to pp. *sepultus*.

SEQUEL, consequence, result. (F.—L.) Spelt *sequele* in Levins, and by Surrey; see Tottell's Miscellany, ed. Arber, p. 218, l. 8; and in Dictes and Sayings, pr. by Caxton, fol. 3 b, l. 10.—OF. *sequele*, ' a sequell;' Cot.—L. *sequēla*, that which follows, a result. —L. *sequi*, to follow; see **Sequence**.

SEQUENCE, order of succession, succession. (F.—L.) In Shak. K. John, ii. 96; Gascoigne, Works, ed. Hazlitt, i. 422, l. 5.— OF. *sequence*, ' a sequence at cards;' *sequences*, pl., ' answering verses,' Cot.; with which cf. the passage in Gascoigne.—L. *sequentia*, sb., a following.—L. *sequent-*, stem of pres. part. of *sequi*, to follow.

—✓SEQ, to follow; whence Skt. *sach*, to follow; Lith. *sek-ti*, to follow, Irish *seich-im*, I follow; Gk. ἕπομαι, I follow. **Der.** *sequent*, following, from ᵗhe pres. part. of *sequi*. Also (from *sequī*) *con-sec-ut-ive*, *con-sequ-ence*, *ex-ec-ute* (for *ex-sec-ute*), *ex-equ-ies* (for *ex-sequ'es*), *ob-sequ-ies*, *per-sec-ute*, *pro-sec-ute*, *sequ-el*, *sequ-ester*, *sub-sequ-ent*. Also *as-soc-iate*, *dis-soc-iate*, *soc-iable*, *soc-ial*, *soc-iety*; *intrin-sic*. Also *sect*, *sec-ond*, *sue*, *en-sue*, *pur-sue*, *pur-suiv-ant*; *suit*, *suit-a-ble*, *suit-or*, *suite*, *pur-suit*. See **Sue**. Brugmann, i. § 118.

SEQUESTER, to set aside or apart. (F.—L.) 'Him hath God the father specially *sequestred* and seuered and set aside;' Sir T. More, Works, p. 1046 f. And see *sequestration* in Blount's Nomolexicon. We find also: ' *Hic sequestarius*, a sequesterer,' in the 15th century; Wright's Vocab. i. 210, col. 2 ; and see Wyclif, 1 Macc. xi. 34.—MF. *sequestrer*, 'to sequestrer (*sic*), or lay aside;' Cot.—L. *sequestrāre*, to surrender, remove, lay aside; cf. L. *sequester*, a mediator, agent or go-between, also a depositary or trustee. Allied to *sequi*, to follow (Bréal). **Der.** *sequester-ed*, set apart, retired; *sequester*, sb., seclusion, Oth. iii. 4. 40 ; also *sequestr-ate*, *sequestr-at-or*, *sequestr-at-ion*.

SEQUIN, a gold coin of Italy. (F.—Ital.—Arab.) Also spelt *chequin*, Shak. Pericles, iv. 2. 28 ; also *zechin*, which is the Ital. form. —F. *sequin*, 'a small Italian coin;' Cot.—Ital. *zecchino*, 'a coin of gold currant in Venice;' Florio.—Ital. *zecca*, 'a mint or place of coyning;' id.—Arab. *sikka*(*t*), pronounced *sikkah*, 'a die for coins;' Rich. Dict. p. 838. Hence *sicca rupee* (Yule).

SERAGLIO, a place of confinement, esp. for Turkish women. (Ital.—L.) **A.** The peculiar use of this word, in mod. E., is due to a mistake. The orig. sense is merely an enclosure, and it was sometimes so used. 'I went to the Ghetto [in Rome], where the Jewes dwell as in a suburbe by themselves . . I passed by the Piazza Judea, where their *seraglio* begins; for, being inviron'd with walls, they are lock'd up every night;' Evelyn, Diary, Jan. 15, 1645. We find it in the modern sense also: 'to pull the Ottoman Tyrant out of his *seraglio*, from between the very armes of his 1500 concubines;' Howell, Foreign Travel (1642), sect. ix; ed. Arber, p. 45.—Ital. *serraglio*, 'an inclosure, a close, a padocke, a parke, a cloister or secluse;' Florio, ed. 1598. **β.** There was at that date no such restricted use of the Ital. word as our modern sense indicates. Cotgrave, indeed, translates MF. *serrail* by 'the palace wherein the great Turk mueth up his concubines;' yet he also gives *serrail d'un huis*, the bolt of a door, which is the older sense. **γ.** The Ital. *serraglio* is formed with suffix -*aglio* (L. -*āculum*) from the verb *serrare*, 'to shut, lock, inclose;' Florio. Cf. Late L. *serācula*, a small bolt.—Late L. *serāre*, to bar, bolt, shut in.—L. *sera*, a bar, bolt.—L. *serere*, to join or bind together; see **Series**. **B.** It is clear that the modern use of *seraglio* was due to confusion with Pers. (and Turkish) *sarāy* or *serāi*, 'a palace, a grand edifice, a king's court, a seraglio;' Rich. Dict. p. 821. See Horn, § 727. It is equally clear that the Pers. word is not the real source of the Italian one. See **Serried**.

SERAI, a court for the accommodation of travellers, a caravan-seray. (Pers.) Also used to mean 'seraglio,' as in Byron, The Giaour: 'When Leila dwelt in his *Serai*.' From Pers. *serāi*, lit. a palace. Horn, § 727. See **Seraglio, B.**

SERAPH, an angel of the highest rank. (Heb.) Spenser has *seraphins*, Hymn of Heavenlie Beautie, l. 94. The A. V. has *seraphims*, Isa. vi. 2 ; *seraphim* being the Hebrew plural, out of which has been evolved the E. sing. *seraph*.—Heb. *serāphīm*, seraphs, exalted ones. 'Gesenius connects it with an Arabic term meaning *high* or exalted; and this may be regarded as the generally received etymology;' Smith, Dict. of the Bible. Cf. Arab. *sharaf*, 'being high or noble;' Rich. p. 888. **Der.** *seraph-ic*, *seraph-ic-al*, *seraph-ic-al-ly*.

SERASKIER, a Turkish general. (F.—Turk.—Pers. *and* Arab.) In Byron, Don Juan, viii. 98.—F. *sérasquier* (Littré).—Turk. *ser'ask*(*i*)*er*, general (where the *i* is slight).—Pers. *ser*, head; and Arab. *'asker*, army (Devic); i.e. 'head of the army.'

SERE (1), withered; the same as **Sear**, q. v.

SERE (2), a bird's claw; the catch of a gunlock. (F.—L.) For 'bird's claw,' see *sere* in Nares. 'Tickled [*read* tickle, i.e. ticklish] o' the *sere*;' Hamlet, ii. 2. 337 (see Wright's note); i.e. like a gunlock of which the catch is easily released.—MF. *serre*, 'a hawkes talon,' Cot.; because it holds fast.—F. *serrer*, 'to bind fast, lock;' Cot.—L. *serrāre*, to lock; see **Serried**.

SERECLOTH, waxed cloth; see **Cerecloth, Cere.**

SERENE, calm. (L.) In Milton, P. L. iii. 25, v. 123, 734.—L. *serēnus*, bright, clear, calm (of weather). See Brugmann, i. § 920 (4). **Der.** *serene-ly*, -*ness*; *seren-i-ty*, from MF. *serenité*, 'serenity,' Cot., from L. acc. *serēnitātem*. Also *seren-ade*, in Blount's Gloss., ed. 1674, from MF. *serenade* (Cot.), which from Ital. *serenata*, 'music given under gentlewomens windowes in a morning or euening,' Florio; properly pp. of Ital. *serenare*, 'to make cleere, faire, and

lightsome, to looke cheerfullie and merrilie,' id. Milton uses the Ital. form *serenate*, P. L. iv. 769. Hence *serenade*, verb.

SERF, a slave attached to the soil. (F.—L.) Given in Ash's Dict., ed. 1775. It occurs in Caxton's Golden Legend, St. John Evang., § 5.—F. *serf*, 'a servant, thrall;' Cot.—L. *seruum*, acc. of *seruus*, a slave; see **Serve**. **Der.** *serf-dom*, a coined word, with E. suffix -*dom*.

SERGE, a cloth made of twilled worsted or silk. (F.—L.—Gk.—Chinese.) Now used of stuff made of worsted; when of silk, it is called *silk serge*, though the etymology shows that the stuff was orig. of silk only. In Shak. 2 Hen. VI, iv. 7. 27.—F. *serge*, 'the stuff called serge;' Cot.—L. *sērica*, fem. of *sēricus*, silken; we also find *sērica*, neut. pl., silken garments.—L. *Sēricus*, of or belonging to the *Sēres*, i.e. Chinese.—Gk. Σῆρες, pl. Chinese. Cf. σήρ, a silkworm. From the Chinese *se*, *sei*, silk. See **Silk**.

SERGEANT, SERJEANT, a lawyer of the highest rank; a non-commissioned officer next above a corporal. (F.—L.) Orig. a law-term, in early use. ME. *sergantes*, pl., officers, O. Eng. Homilies, ed. Morris, ii. 177, l. 2 ; *sergeant*, Chaucer, C. T. 311 (A 309). —OF. *sergant*, *serjant* (Burguy), later *sergent*, 'a sergeant, officer;' Cot.—Late L. *seruientem*, acc. of *seruiens*, a servant, vassal, soldier, apparitor; Ducange. The Late L. *seruiens ad legem* = sergeant-at-law.—L. *seruiens*, pres. part. of *seruīre*, to serve; see **Serve**. **Der.** *sergeant-major*, *sergeanc-y*, *sergeant-ship*. Doublet, *servant*.

SERIES, a row, order, succession, sequence. (L.) In Blount's Gloss., ed. 1674.—L. *seriēs*, a row, series.—L. *serere*, pp. *sertus*, to join together, bind.+Gk. εἴρειν, to fasten, bind (for *σέργειν; cf. Lith. *sèris*, thread; Icel. *sörvi*, a necklace; Skt. *sarit*, thread). **Der.** *seri-al*, arranged in a series; modern, not in Todd's Johnson; hence *serial-ly*. **Der.** (from same root) *ser-aglio*, *serr-i-ed*. Also (from pp. *sertus*) *as-sert*, *con-cert*, *de-sert* (1), *dis-sert-at-ion*, *exert* (for *ex-sert*), *in-sert*.

SERIF, the short cross-line at the end of a stroke of a printed letter. (Du.) Letters made without this cross-stroke are called *sans-serif* (from F. *sans*, without). Most probably, *ser*- represents the E. (or F.) equivalent of Du. *schr*- in *schreef*, a dash, a short line; MDu. *schreve*, a line. Allied to OHG. *screvōn*, to scratch, incise. Cf. Low G. *schreve*, a line to mark how far one goes; *aver'n schreve*, over (beyond) the stroke, too far.

SERIOUS, weighty, solemn, in earnest. (F.—L.) 'So *serious* and ernest remembrance;' Sir T. More, p. 480 g. 'Seryouse, ernest, *serieux*;' Palsgrave.—OF. *serieux* (mod. F. *sérieux*), omitted by Cotgrave, but recorded by Palsgrave, and in use in the 14th cent. (Littré).—Late L. *sēriōsus*, serious; Ducange.—L. *sērius*, grave, earnest. **β.** Root uncertain; the long *e* in *sērius* induces Fick to compare it with G. *schwer* ᶜOHG. *swāri*), weighty, heavy; cf. Lith. *swarùs*, heavy; see Fick, i. 842. **Der.** *serious-ly*, -*ness*.

SERMON, a discourse on a Scripture text. (F.—L.) ME. *sermoun*, *sermun*; in early use; see Old Eng. Miscellany, ed. Morris, p. 186, title. The verb *sermonen*, to preach, occurs in O. E. Homilies, i. 81, l. 14.—F. *sermon*, 'a sermon;' Cot.—L. *sermōnem*, acc. of *sermo*, a speech, discourse. For **swer-mo*; and allied to E. **Swear**. See Walde, Et. Dict.

SEROUS, adj.; see **Serum.**

SERPENT, a reptile without feet, snake. (F.—L.) ME. *serpent*, Chaucer, C. T. 10826 (F 512).—F. *serpent*, 'a serpent;' Cot.—L. *serpentem*, acc. of *serpens*, a serpent, lit. a creeping thing; pres. part. of *serpere*, to creep.—✓SERP, to creep; whence Skt. *srp*, to creep, Gk. ἕρπειν, to creep, Skt. *sarpa*-, a snake. Brugmann, i. § 477. **Der.** *serpent-ine*, adj., Minsheu, from F. *serpentin*, L. *serpentīnus*; *serpent-ine*, a name for a kind of gun, Skelton, ed. Dyce, i. 124, l. 159.

SERRATED, notched like a saw. (L.) A botanical term; see examples in R.—L. *serrātus*, notched like a saw.—L. *serra*, a saw. **Der.** *serrat-ion*.

SERRIED, crowded, pressed together. (F.—L.) 'Their *serried* files,' Milton, P. L. vi. 599. Spelt *serred* in Blount.—F. *serrer*, 'to close, compact, presse neer together, to lock;' Cot.—Late L. *serāre*, to bolt.—L. *sera*, a bar, bolt.—L. *serere*, to join or bind together; see **Series**; and cf. **Seraglio**.

SERUM, whey, the thin fluid which separates from the blood when it coagulates. (L.) In Phillips, ed. 1706.—L. *serum*, whey, serum.+Gk. ὀρός, whey; Skt. *sara*(*s*), adj. flowing; sb. whey. (But see Brugmann, i. § 466.) **Der.** *ser-ous*.

SERVAL, the S. African tiger-cat. (F.—Port.—L.) A name now applied to the tiger-cat of S. Africa. But in a tr. of Buffon (1792), ch. xx, we read :—' The *maraputia*, which the Portuguese in India call *serval* (says Vincent Maria) is a wild and ferocious animal, much larger than the wild cat.' The word is therefore Portuguese. Vieyra gives *lobo cerval*, 'the lynx;' where *lobo* means wolf (L. *lupus*), and *cerval* (like Span. *cerval*) is said to be an adj., from *cerva*, a hind.

—L. *cerua*, a hind. Cf. L. *lupus ceruārius* (F. *loup cervier*), a lynx (Pliny) ; because it hunts deer. See **Hart.**

SERVE, to attend on another, wait upon obediently. (F.—L.) ME. *seruen*, Havelok, 1230 ; *seruien*, Ancren Riwle, p. 12, l. 4 from bottom.—F. *servir*, to serve.—L. *seruīre*, to serve. Cf. L. *seruus*, a servant, slave, *seruāre*, to keep, protect. **Der.** *serv-ant*, ME. *seruaunt*, *seruant*, Chaucer, C. T. 11104 (F 792) ; Ancren Riwle, p. 428, l. 9, from F. *servant*, serving, pres. part. of *servir*, to serve ; *serv-er* ; *serv-ice*, ME. *seruise*, Layamon, 8071, from OF. *servise*, *service*, from L. *seruitium*, service, servitude ; *service-able*, Levins ; *dis-service*. Also *serv-ile*, Levins, from L. *seruīlis* ; *servil-ly*, *servil-i-ty* ; *serv-it-or*, prob. suggested by F. *serviteur*, 'a servant, servitor' (Cot.), rather than borrowed directly from L. *seruitor* ; *serv-it-ude*, spelt *servitute*, Chaucer, C. T. 8674 (E 798), from F. *servitude*, from L. acc. *seruitūdinem*. Also *serf*, *sergeant* ; *con-serve*, *dis-serve*, *mis-serve*, *ob-serve*, *pre-serve*, *re-serve*, *sub-serve* ; *de-sert* (2), *un-de-serv-ing*, *un-de-serv-ed*, &c.

SERVICE-TREE, a kind of wild pear-tree. (L. *and* E.) Here *service* is a curious substitution for ME. *serves* (in Northern dialect *servis*), which is the pl. of a form *serf or *serve (not used) representing the AS. *syrfe*, a service-tree, also called in AS. *syrf-trēow*. Here *syrf* is not an E. word, but adapted from L. *sorbus*, a service-tree. The ME. *serves* = L. *sorba*, berries of the same. For details see Notes on Eng. Etym., p. 266.

SESSION, the sitting or assembly of a court. (F.—L.) In Shak. Oth. i. 2. 86.—F. *session*, not noticed by Cotgrave, though in use in the 12th cent. (Littré).—L. *sessiōnem*, acc. of *sessio*, a sitting, session ; cf. *sessus*, pp. of *sedēre*, to sit, cognate with E. **Sit**, q.v.

SET (1), to place, fix, plant, assign. (E.) ME. *setten*, pt. t. *sette*, pp. *set*. 'Thei *setten* Jhesu on hym ;' Wyclif, Luke, xix. 35. AS. *settan*, to set ; Grein, ii. 432. Causal of AS. *sittan*, to sit ; for *satian, from *sat*, oldest form of pt. t. of *sittan*. See **Sit.** ✛Du. *zetten* ; Icel. *setja* ; Dan. *sætte* ; Swed. *sätte* ; G. *setzen* ; Goth. *satjan*. Teut. type *satjan- ; from *sat, 2nd grade of *setjan-, to sit. **Der.** *set*, sb., Rich. III, v. 3. 19 ; *set-off*, sb., *sett-er*, sb., *sett-ing*. Also *sett-ee*, a seat with a long back (Todd's Johnson), of which the origin is by no means clear ; it seems to be an arbitrary variation of the prov. E. *settle*, used in the same sense, with a substitution of the suffix -*ee* for -*le* ; this suffix (= F. -*é*, L. -*ātus*) is freely used in English, as in *refer-ee*, *trust-ee* ; but it makes no good sense here. See **Settle** (1).

SET (2), a number of like things. (F.—L.) 'A *set* of beads ;' Rich. II, iii. 3. 147. When we speak of 'a *set* of things,' this is a peculiar use of **Sect**, q.v. (Not allied to the verb *to set*.)—OF. *sette*, variant of OF. *secte*, a sect ; Supp. to Godefroy.—L. *secta*, which often had the sense of 'set' in old wills. Cf. Ital. *setta*. See my Notes on E. Etym., p. 269. A *set* = a *suit* ; see **Suit.**

SETON, an artificial irritation under the skin. (F.—L.) '*Seton*, is when the skin of the neck, or other part, is taken up and run thro' with a kind of pack-needle, and the wound afterwards kept open with bristles, or a skean of thread, silk, or cotton,' &c. ; Phillips, ed. 1706.—F. *séton*, in use in the 16th cent. ; Littré cites 'une aiguille à *seton* enfilée d'un fort fil' = a needle with a seton, threaded with a strong thread ; where *seton* is a thick thread. Formed from a Late L. type *sēto (acc. *sētōnem*) ; derived from L. *sēta*, a bristle, thick stiff hair, which in Late L. also meant silk (Ducange). See **Satin.**

SETTEE, a kind of seat. (E.) 'The soft *settee*'; Cowper, The Task, i. 75 ; see under **Set** (1).

SETTLE (1), a long bench with a high back. (E.) Also used generally in the sense of 'seat' or 'bench ;' see Ezek. xliii. 14, 17, 20, xlv. 19. '*Setle*, a seat ;' E. D. S. Gloss. B. 17. ME. *setel*, *setil*. 'Opon the *setil* of his magesté' = upon the seat of His majesty, i. e. upon His royal seat ; Pricke of Conscience, 6122. 'On þe *setle* of unhele' = in the seat of ill-health ; O. Eng. Hom. ii. 59. AS. *setl*, a seat, Grein, ii. 432. ✛Goth. *sitls*, a seat, throne ; OHG. *sezzal* ; G. *sessel* ; Du. *zetel*. **β.** All from Teut. root *set, Idg. ✓SED, to sit ; cf. L. *sel-la* (for *sed-la), whence E. *sell*, a saddle ; see **Sell** (2) and **Sit.** **Der.** *settle* (2). **Doublet,** *sell* (2).

SETTLE (2), to fix, become fixed, adjust. (E.) Two distinct words have been confused ; in the peculiar sense 'to compose or adjust a quarrel,' the source is different from that of the commoner verb, and more remote. **A.** ME. *setlen*, trans. to cause to rest, intrans. to sink to rest, subside. 'Til þe semli sunne was *setled* to reste' = till the seemly sun had sunk to rest, Will. of Palerne, 2452. 'Him thoughte a goshauk . . . *Setlith* on his beryng' = it seemed to him that a goshawk settles down on his cognisance (?), King Alisaunder, 484 ; and see l. 488. AS. *setlan*, to settle down, to fix. '*Setlaþ* sæmearas' = the mariners fix (or anchor) their vessels (Grein). Cf. AS. *setl-gang*, the going to rest of the sun, sunset ; from AS. *setel*, a seat ; Grein, ii. 432. Thus the lit. sense of *settle* is 'to take a seat' or 'to set as in a fixed seat.' See **Settle** (1). **B.** At the same time, the

peculiar sense 'to settle a quarrel' appears to have been borrowed from ME. *saȝtlen*, *sahtlen*, *sauȝtlen*, to reconcile, make peace, P. Plowman, B. iv. 2 (footnote). 'Now *saghtel*, now strife' = now we make peace, now we strive ; Pricke of Conscience, 1470. *Saȝtled* = appeased, reconciled, Allit. Poems, ed. Morris, B. 230, 1139. AS. *sahtlian*, to reconcile ; 'gōde men . . . *sahtloden* heom' = good men reconciled them ; A. S. Chron. an. 1066 ; MS. Laud 636, ed. Thorpe, i. 337 ; see also p. 384, l. 19.—AS. *saht*, reconciliation ; A. S. Chron. ed. Thorpe, i. 385, l. 2 ; a word borrowed from Icel. *sātt*, *sætt*, reconciliation, peace ; which Noreen (§ 73) connects with L. *sanctus*, holy. Also sometimes spelt *seht*, the verb occurring as *sehtlian* (Toller). **β.** That these two verbs were actually confused, we have evidence in the fact that, conversely, the ME. *saȝtlen*, to reconcile, was also used in the sense of subside or become calm. 'þe sea *saȝtled* therwith' = the sea subsided ; Allit. Poems, ed. Morris, C. 232. We even find the intermediate form *sattle* ; 'Muche sorȝe þenne *satteled* vpon segge Ionas' = much sorrow then settled on the man Jonah ; id. C. 409. **Der.** *settl-er* ; *settle-ment*, with F. suffix -*ment*.

SEVEN, a cardinal number, six and one. (E.) ME. *seuen*, *seuene* ; P. Plowman, B. iv. 86. The final -*e* is prob. the mark of a pl. form ; both forms occur. AS. *seofon*, also *seofone*, seven ; Grein, ii. 437 ; the final -*e* marks the plural, and is unoriginal ; early form, *sibun*.✛Du. *zeven* ; Icel. *sjö*, *sjau* ; Dan. *syv* ; Swed. *sju* ; OHG. *sibun*, G. *sieben* ; Goth. *sibun*.✛L. *septem* ; Gk. ἑπτά ; W. *saith* ; Gael. *seachd* ; Irish *seacht* ; Russ. *sem(e)* ; Lithuan. *septyni* ; Skt. *saptan*. **β.** All from Idg. type **septm̥*, seven ; origin unknown. **Der.** *seven-fold*, AS. *seofon-feald* ; *seven-teen*, AS. *seofon-tȳne*, from *seofon*, seven, and *tȳn*, ten ; *seven-teen-th*, AS. *seofon-tēoða*, but formed by analogy, by adding -*th* to *seventeen* ; *seven-ty*, AS. *hundseofontig* (by dropping *hund*, for which see **Hundred**) ; *seven-ti-eth*. Also *seven-th*, formed by adding -*th* ; AS. *seofoða*.

SEVER, to separate, cut apart. (F.—L.) 'I *sever*, I departe thynges asonder, Ie *separe* ;' Palsgrave. ME. *seueren*, Gawain and the Grene Knight, 1797.—OF. *severer* (Burguy). Cf. Ital. *severare*, *sevrare*.—L. *sēparāre*, to separate ; see **Separate.** **Der.** *sever-al*, *sever-al-ly*, of which Sir T. More has *seuerally*, Works, p. 209 h ; from OF. *several*, Late L. *sēparāle*, a thing separate or a thing that separates (Ducange) ; as if from a L. adj. *sēparālis. Also *severance* ; *dis-sever* ; *dis-sever-ance* ; cf. OF. *dessevrance* (Burguy). **Doublet,** *separate*.

SEVERE, austere, serious, strict. (F.—L.) In Shak. Oth. ii. 3. 301.—OF. *severe*, 'severe,' Cot. ; mod. F. *sévère*.—L. *seuērus*, severe ; orig. reverenced, respected (of persons), hence serious, grave (in demeanour). **Der.** *severe-ly* ; *sever-i-ty*, from MF. *severité*, 'severity ;' Cot.

SEW (1), to fasten together with thread. (E.) Pronounced *so*. ME. *sowen*, P. Plowman, B. vi. 9 ; more commonly *sewen*, id. C. ix. 8 ; Wyclif, Mark, ii. 21. AS. *siwian*, Mark, ii. 21 ; Gen. iii. 7.✛ Icel. *sȳja* ; Dan. *sye* ; Swed. *sy* ; OHG. *siuwan*, *siwan* ; Goth. *siujan*. ✛L. *suere* ; Lithuan. *suti* ; Russ. *shit(e)* ; Skt. *siv*, to sew, whence *sūtra-*, thread. Cf. Gk. κασ-σύειν, to sew together. And see **Hymen.** **β.** All from the ✓SIW, to sew ; Fick, i. 229. **Der.** *sew-er*, *sew-ing* ; also *seam*, q.v.

SEW (2), to follow ; the same as **Sue**, q.v.

SEWER (1), an underground passage for water, large drain. (F.—L.) Frequently spelt *shore*, which represented a common pronunciation ; still preserved in *Shore-ditch* = sewer-ditch, in London. Spelt *sure*, Troil. v. 1. 83, ed. 1623. [To be kept distinct from the verb *sew*, to drain, to dry. '*Sewe* ponds' = drain ponds, Tusser's Husbandry, cap. 15. § 17 (E. D. S.) ; p. 32. Note also *sew*, sb., as in 'the towne sinke, the common *sew*,' Nomenclator, ed. 1585, p. 391 ; cited in Halliwell, s. v. *seugh*. These are prob. from OF. *essuier*, *esuer*, to dry (Burguy) ; gen. used in the sense 'to wipe dry,' but the true etym. sense is to drain dry, deprive of moisture, as in English. Cot. has *essuier*, 'to dry up.'—L. *exsūcāre*, *exsuccāre*, to deprive of moisture, suck the juice from.—L. *ex*, out, away ; and *sūcus*, juice, moisture, from the same root as L. *sūgere*, to suck, and E. *suck* ; see **Suck.**] **β.** But *sewer*, sb., is really an adaptation of OF. *seuwiere*, a sluice of a fishpond, for letting off water ; also spelt *sewiere* ; see examples in Godefroy, s. v. *sewiere*, and in Ducange, s. v. *seweria*.—L. *ex-aquāria ; like E. *ewer* from L. *aquāria*. Cf. Late L. *exaquātōrium*, a channel for draining ; from *ex* out, and *aqua*, water. **Der.** *sewer-age* ; also *sew-age*, formed directly from the verb *sew*. ¶ The F. suffix -*age* in these words is an indication of the F. origin of *sew* and *sewer*.

SEWER (2), the officer who formerly set and removed dishes, tasted them, &c. (F.—L.) In Halliwell. Baret (1580) has : '*The Sewer of the kitchin*, Anteambulo fercularius ; *The Sewer which tasteth the meate*, Escuyer de cuisine.' '*Seware, at mete*, Depositor, dapifer, sepulator ;' Prompt. Parv., p. 454. On the same page we have :

'*Sewyn*, or sette mete, Ferculo, sepulo;' and: '*Sew*, cepulatum.' A. It is therefore clear, that, in the 15th century, the word *sew-er* was regarded as being formed from a verb to *sewe*, that had really been evolved from *sewer*, sb. But we find, in the N. E. Dict., s. v. *asseour*, that the two forms *asseour* and *sewer* were used to denote 'one who sets meat on a table;' evidently allied to *sewyn*, to set meat, above. Of these *asseour* is the fuller form.—OF. *asseour*, used in speaking of the service of a table; '*qui fait asseoir*;' Godefroy.—OF. *asseoir*, to seat, set.—L. *assidēre*, to sit beside, to attend upon; cf. **Assiduous.**—L. *ad*, near; and *sedēre*, to sit, cognate with E. *sit*. Hence *sewer* is 'one who sets a table;' of F. origin; possibly confused with the native sb. *sew*, pottage, from AS. *sēaw*, juice.

SEX, the distinction between male and female, characteristics of such a distinction. (F.—L.) In Shak. Temp. iii. 1. 49.—F. *sexe*, 'a sex, or kind;' Cot.—L. *sexum*, acc. of *sexus*, sex. Cf. *secus*, n., sex. Perhaps orig. 'a division;' from *secāre*, to cut. Der. *sex-u-al*, a late word, from L. *sexu-ālis*, formed with suffix -*ālis* from *sexu*-, decl. stem of *sexus*; *sex-u-al-ly*, *sex-u-al-i-ty*.

SEXAGENARY, belonging to sixty. (L.) In Phillips, ed. 1706. —L. *sexāgēnārius*, belonging to sixty.—L. *sexāgēnī*, sixty each; distributive form from *sexāgintā*, sixty.—L. *sex*, six; and -*ginta*, for -*cinta*, short for **decinta*, tenth, from *decem*, ten. See **Six** and **Ten.** Der. *sexagenari-an*, Phillips.

SEXAGESIMA, the second Sunday before Lent. (L.) So called because about the sixtieth day before Easter. In Blount's Gloss., ed. 1674; and earlier, in Prayer-books.—L. *sexāgēsima*, lit. sixtieth; agreeing with *diēs*, day, understood. Fem. of *sexāgēsimus*, sixtieth. Allied to *sexāgintā*, sixty. See **Sexagenary.** Der. *sexagesim-al*.

SEXENNIAL, happening every six years, lasting six years. (L.) In Blount's Gloss., ed. 1674. Formed, with suffix -*al*, from L. *sexenni-um*, a period of six years.—L. *sex*, six; and *annus*, a year (becoming *enni*- in composition). See **Six** and **Annals.** Der. *sexennial-ly*.

SEXTANT, the sixth part of a circle. (L.) Chiefly used to mean an optical instrument, furnished with an arc extending to a sixth part of a circle. But in earlier use in other senses. '*Sextant*, a coin less than that called *quadrant* by the third part . . the sixth part of any measure;' Blount's Gloss., ed. 1674.—L. *sextant*-, stem of *sextans*, the sixth part of an as, a coin, weight. Formed with suffix -*ans* (like that of a pres. part. of a verb in -*āre*) from *sext*-, stem of *sextus*, sixth, ordinal of *sex*, six. See **Six.** Der. (from *sext-us*) *sext-ile*, Milton, P. L. x. 659; also *sextuple*, q. v.

SEXTON, a sacristan; see **Sacristan.**

SEXTUPLE, sixfold, having six parts. (L.) 'Whose length . . is *sextuple* unto his breadth;' Sir T. Browne, Vulg. Errors, b. iv. c. 5. § 12. Coined from *sextu-s*, sixth, just as *quadru-ple* is from *quadru*- (used for *quartus*) with the sense of fourth. The suffix -*ple* answers to L. -*plic*-, stem of -*plex*, as in *du-plex*, *com-plex*. See **Quadruple** and **Sextant.**

SFORZANDO, with special emphasis; in music. (Ital.—L.) Ital. *sforzando*, lit. 'constraining' or 'forcing;' pres. part. of *sforzare*, to force, lit. 'to force out.'—L. *ex*, out, strongly (whence Ital. *s*-); and Late L. *fortia*, force (Ital. *forza*), from L. *fortis*, strong. See **Force.**

SH

SHABBY, mean, paltry. (E.) Merely a doublet of *scabby*, by the usual change of AS. *sc* to E. *sh*. *Shabby* is the native E. equivalent of the Scand. *scabby*. 'They were very *shabby* fellows, pitifully mounted, and worse armed;' Lord Clarendon, Diary, Dec. 7, 1688. Cf. 'They mostly had short hair, and went in a *shabbed* condition;' A. Wood, Athen. Oxon. Fast. ii. 743 (Todd). We find *shabbyd* for *scabbed* in P. Plowman, C. x. 264. From AS. *sceab*, *scæb*, a scab, itch. See **Scab.** Der. *shabbi-ly*, *shabbi-ness*.

SHACKLE, a fetter, chain to confine the limbs, clog. (E.) ME. *schakkyl*, *schakle*, Prompt. Parv.; pl. *scheakeles*, Ancren Riwle, p. 94, l. 25. AS. *sceacul*, a bond; Voc. 107. 10. For an older form **seacul*. +Icel. *skökull*, the pole of a carriage; Swed. *skakel*, the loose shaft of a carriage; Dan. *skagle*, a trace (for a carriage); MDu. *schakel*, 'the links or ringes [*read* link or ring] of a chaine;' *schakelen van een net*, 'the masches [meshes] of a net;' Hexham. β. The orig. sense is a loose band or bond, hence a trace, single link of a chain, loose-hanging fetter. Perhaps named from its shaking about, as distinct from a firm bond; cf. Low G. *schake*, shank. From AS. *sceacan*, *scacan*, to shake. See **Shake.** Cf. Icel. *skökull*, from *skaka*; Dan. *skagle*, from *skage*, to shift, orig. to shake; Swed. dial. *skak*,

a chain, link (Rietz). Der. *shackle*, verb, ME. *schaklen*, Prompt. Parv.

SHAD, a fish. (E.) 'Like bleeding *shads*;' Beaum. and Fletcher, Love's Cure, Act ii. sc. 2 (Clara). 'And there the eel and *shad* sometimes are caught;' John Dennys, Secrets of Angling (before A. D. 1613); in Eng. Garner, ed. Arber, i. 171. 'A *shadde*, a fishe, *acon*;' Levins. AS. *sceadd*, a shad; Thorpe, Diplom. Ævi Saxonici, p. 544. Cf. prov. G. *schade*, a shad (Flügel). We also find Irish and Gael. *sgadan*, OIrish *scatán*, with the sense of 'herring;' W. *ysgadan*, pl. herrings.

SHADDOCK, a tree of the orange genus; also its fruit. (E.) Sir H. Sloane mentions the *shaddock-tree* in his Catalogus Plantarum (1696). In Stedman's Surinam (1796), i. 22, he tells us that it was brought to the W. Indies by a Captain *Shaddock*; this was in the 17th century (before 1696).

SHADE, SHADOW, obscurity, partial darkness. (E.) These are but two forms of one word; the latter form representing the dat. case. ME. *schade*, Will. of Palerne, 22; *schadue*, id. 754. From AS. *sceadu*, shadow, fem. (Grein, ii. 398, 401), we have the ME. *schade*, E. *shade*. From AS. dat. *sceadwe* we have ME. *schadwe*, E. *shadow*; cf. also ME. *scheadewe*, Ancren Riwle, p. 190, l. 24.+Du. *schaduw*, shadow; G. *schatten*, shade; OHG. *scato* (gen. *scatewes*), shade; Goth. *skadus*.+Irish and Gael. *sgath*, shadow, shade, shelter; OIrish *scáth*, Corn. *scod*, shade; Gk. σκότος, σκοτία, darkness, gloom. β. All from Idg. base **skot*-. Der. *shade*, verb, Court of Love, l. 1272; *shad-er*; *shad-y*, Spenser, F. Q. i. 1. 7; *shad-i-ly*, -*ness*; *shadow*, verb, ME. *schadowen*, Allit. Poems, ed. Morris, A. 42, AS. *sceadwian*, *scadwian*, Ps. xc. 4 (ed. Spelman); *over-shadow*, AS. *ofersceadwian*, Mark, ix. 7; *shadow-y*, ME. *shadewy*, Chaucer, tr. of Boethius, b. iii. pr. 4, l. 40. Doublet, *shed* (2).

SHADOOF, a contrivance for raising water. (Arab.) From Arab. *shādūf* (not in Rich. Dict.); an Egyptian-Arabic word; see Lane's Modern Egyptians.

SHAFT, an arrow, smoothed pole, column, cylindrical entrance to a mine. (E.) The orig. sense is 'shaven' rod, a stick smoothed into the shape of a spear-pole or an arrow. ME. *shaft*, *schaft*, an arrow, Chaucer, C. T. 1364 (A 1362); Parl. of Foules, 180. AS. *sceaft*, a shaft of a spear, dart; Grein, ii. 403. For *scaf-t*, formed with suffix -*t* (Idg. -*to*-) from *scaf*-, stem of pp. of *scafan*, to shave; see **Shave.**+Du. *schacht* (for *schaft*, like Du. *lucht* for *luft*, air); from *schaven*, to smooth, plane; Icel. *skapt*, better *skaft*, a shaved stick, shaft, missile; Dan. *skaft*, a handle, haft; Swed. *skaft*, a handle; G. *schaft*. Teut. types **skaf-toz*, m., **skaf-tom*, n. Prob. further allied to Gk. σκῆπ-τρον, a sceptre, Dor. σκᾶπ-τον, a staff, sceptre; L. *scāp-us*, a shaft, stem, stalk. √SQAP; as in Lith. *skap-oti*, to shave, cut. ¶ The ME. *schaft*, in the sense of 'creature,' is from AS. *sceppan*, to shape, make; see **Shape.** Der. *shaft-ed*.

SHAG, rough hair, rough cloth. (E.) 'Of the same kind is the goat-hart, and differing only in the beard and long *shag* about the shoulders;' Holland, tr. of Pliny, b. viii. c. 33 (Of the *shag-haired* and bearded stagge like to a goat). 'With rugged beard, and hoarie *shagged* heare;' Spenser, F. Q. iv. 5. 34. Shak. has *shag* for *shaggy*, Venus, 295; also *shag-haired*, 2 Hen. VI, iii. 1. 367. I know of no instance in ME. AS. *sceacga*; 'Coma, *feax*, *sceacga*; Comosus, *sceacgede*;' Voc. 379. 41; 380. 14.+Icel. *skegg*, Swed. *skägg*, a beard; Dan. *skjæg*, a beard, barb, awn, wattle; cf. Icel. *skaga*, to jut out, project; whence also Icel. *skagi*, a low cape or head-land (Shetland *skaw*). The orig. sense is 'roughness.' See **Shaw.** Der. *shagg-y*, *shagg-i-ness*; also *shagg-ed*, as above. *Shag* tobacco is rough tobacco; cf. Shakespeare's 'fetlocks *shag* and long;' Venus, 295.

SHAGREEN, a rough-grained leather, shark's skin. (F.—Turkish.) '*Shagreen*, a sort of rough-grained leather;' Phillips, ed. 1706. He also spells it *chagrin*.—F. *chagrin*, shagreen. It was orig. made of the skin (of the *back* only) of the horse, wild ass, or mule; afterwards, from the skin of the shark. See the full account in Devic, Supp. to Littré.—Turk. *sāghrī*, *saghrī*, the back of a horse; also, shagreen, Zenker, Turk. Dict. p. 561; and Devic. Cf. Pers. *saghrī*, shagreen; Palmer's Pers. Dict. col. 354. See **Chagrin.**

SHAH, a king of Persia. (Pers.) Spelt *shaw* in Blount's Gloss., ed. 1674, and in Herbert's Travels, ed. 1665.—Pers. *shāh*, a king; Palmer, Pers. Dict. col. 374. Remarkably shortened from OPers. *khsāyathiya*, a king; prob. orig. an adj., signifying 'mighty;' and formed (with lengthened *ā*) from *khsayathi*, might, sb.; allied to Skt. *kshatra-m*, dominion.—OPers. *khsi* (Skt. *kshi*), to rule, have power. Cf. Gk. κτάομαι, I possess. Horn, § 772; Brugmann, i. § 920. Der. *check*, *check-er*, *check-ers*, *check-mate*, *chess*; also *pa-sha* or *pa-cha*. Doublet, *check*, sb.

SHAKE, to agitate, jolt, keep moving, make to tremble; also to shiver, tremble. (E.) ME. *schaken*, *shaken*; pt. t. *schook*, *shook*, Chaucer, C. T. 2267 (A 2265); pp. *schaken*, *shaken*, *shakē*, id. 408.

AS. *sceacan, scacan,* pt. t. *scōc,* pp. *sceacen, scacen* ; Grein, ii. 401. **+**Icel. *skaka,* pt. t. *skōk,* pp. *skakinn* ; Swed. *skaka* ; Dan. *skage,* to shift, veer. Teut. type *skakan-.* Cf. also Skt. *khaj,* to move to and fro, hence, to churn ; from √SKAG, to move to and fro. Fick, iii. 329, i. 804. **Der.** *shake,* sb., a late word, Herbert, Church Porch, st. 38 ; *shak-y, shak-i-ness* ; *shack-le.* Also *Shake-speare.* Also *shock,* q. v., *shog,* q. v., *jog,* q. v., *shank,* q. v.

SHAKO, a kind of military cap. (F.—Hung.—Slav.) Modern ; F. *shako* or *schako* (Littré).—Hungarian *csako* (pron. *chaako*), a cap, shako ; see Littré and Mahn's Webster. Spelt *tsākō,* and explained as a Hungarian cap, in Dankovsky's Magyar Lexicon, ed. 1833, p. 900. He supposes it to be of Slavonic origin, not a real Magyar word. Miklosich (p. 27) gives the OSlav. form as *cakoninŭ.*

SHALE, a rock of a slaty structure. (G.) A term of geology, borrowed (like *gneiss, quartz,* and other geological terms) from German.—G. *schale,* a shell, peel, husk, rind, scale ; whence *schalgebirge,* a mountain formed of thin strata. Cognate with E. *shale,* a shell, Shak. Hen. V, iv. 2. 18 ; prov. E. *shale,* thin strata (E. D. D.) ; also with *scale* ; see **Scale** (1). **Der.** *shal-y.* Doublet, *scale* (1).

SHALL, I am bound to, I must. (E.) ME. *shal, schal,* often with the sense of 'is to ;' Chaucer, C. T. 733 (A 731) ; pt. t. *sholde, scholde, shulde* (mod. E. *should*), id. 964 (A 962). AS. *sceal,* an old past tense used as a present, and thus conjugated ; *ic sceal, þū scealt, hē sceal* ; pl. *sculon, sculun,* or *sceolun.* Hence was formed a pt. t. *scolde,* or *sceolde,* pl. *sceoldon.* The form of the infin. is *sculan,* to owe, to be under an obligation to do a thing ; Grein, ii. 413. Hence mod. E. *I shall* properly means 'I am to,' I must, as distinguished from *I will,* properly 'I am ready to,' I am willing to ; but the orig. sense of compulsion is much weakened in the case of the *first* person, though its force is retained in *thou shalt, he shall, they shall.* The verb following it is put in the infin. mood ; as, *ic sceal gān* = I must go ; hence the mod. use as an auxiliary verb.**+**Du. *ik zal,* I shall ; *ik zoude,* I should ; infin. *zullen* ; Icel. *skal,* pl. *skulum* ; pt. t. *skyldi, skyldu* ; infin. *skulu* ; Swed. *skall* ; pt. t. *skulle* ; infin. *skola* ; Dan. *skal* ; pt. t. *skulde* ; infin. *skulle* ; G. *soll,* pt. t. *sollte* ; infin. *sollen* (the *k* being lost, as in Dutch) ; Goth. *skal,* pl. *skulum* ; pt. t. *skulda* ; infin. *skulan.* **β.** All from Teut. type *skal,* I owe, am in debt, am liable ; a sense which is clearly preserved in AS. *scyld,* guilt, i.e. desert of punishment, G. *schuld,* guilt, fault, debt. We also find Lithuan. *skelù,* I am indebted, *skelėti,* to owe, be liable. See Fick, iii. 334. **γ.** Probably further allied to L. *scelus,* guilt, and Skt. *skhal,* to stumble, err, fail.

SHALLOON, a light woollen stuff. (F.) 'Shalloon, a sort of woollen stuff, chiefly used for the linings of coats, and so call'd from *Chalons,* a city of France, where it was first made ;' Phillips, ed. 1706. We find *chalons,* i. e. a coverlet made at Chalons, even in Chaucer, C. T. 4138 (A 4140).—F. *Chalons,* or *Chalons-sur-Marne,* a town in France, 100 miles E. of Paris. 'Sa seule robe . . était de ras de Chalons ;' Scarron, Virg. iv. (Littré, s. v. *ras,* § 9). Cf. AF. *Chalouns,* cloth of Chalons, Liber Albus, pp. 225, 231. *Chalons* takes its name from the tribe of the *Catalauni,* who lived in that neighbourhood.

SHALLOP, a light boat. (F.—Du.) In Spenser, F. Q. iii. 7. 27. —F. *chaloupe,* 'a shallop, or small boat ;' Cot.—Du. *sloep,* a sloop ; MDu. *sloepe,* 'a sloope ;' Hexham. ¶Hence also Span. *chalupa* (also Port. *chalupa*), 'a small light vessel, a long boat,' Neuman. Minsheu's Span. Dict., ed. 1623, has *chalupa,* 'a flat-bottomed boat.' The occurrence of *shallop* in Spenser's F. Q. shows that it is rather an old word in our own language. The Ital. form is *scialuppa.* Doublet, *sloop,* q. v.

SHALLOT, SHALOT, a kind of onion. (F.—L.—Gk.—Heb.) Added by Todd to Johnson ; it is also spelt *eschalot.*—MF. *eschalote, eschalotte,* 'a cive or chive,' i. e. a kind of onion ; Cot. Mod. F. *échalote.* The form *eschalote* is a variant, or corruption, of OF. *escalogne,* a shallot ; Roquefort.—L. *ascalōnia,* a shallot ; fem. of *ascalōnius,* adj., belonging to Ascalon. '*Ascalonia,* little onions or scalions, taking that name of Ascalon, a city in Jury ;' Holland, tr. of Pliny, b. xix. c. 6.—Gk. Ἀσκάλων, Ascalon, one of the chief cities of the Philistines, on the W. coast of Palestine ; Smith, Class. Dict.—Heb. *Ashqelōn.* See Joshua, xiii. 3 ; &c.

SHALLOW, not deep. (E.) ME. *schalowe.* 'Schold, or shalowe, noȝte depe ;' Prompt. Parv. p. 447 ; Trevisa, iii. 131, l. 7 ; *shald,* Barbour, Bruce, ix. 354. Not found in AS. ; but evidently from a base *seeal-,* which occurs again in ME. *schol-d, schal-d* (above), of which the AS. form was *sceald,* shallow. This AS. *sceald* is not in the Dict., but frequently occurs in A.S. Charters ; as shown by Mr. Stevenson, Phil. Soc. Trans., 1895-8, p. 532. Thus, in Birch, Cart. Saxon. ii. 485, we find : ' on *scealdan* ford ;' and in the same, i. 593, we have : ' æt *scealdan flēote.* AS. *sceald* represents a Teut. type *skal-þóz* (Idg. type *skaltós*). Cf. also prov. E. *shall, shaul,* shallow. Perhaps allied to Low G. *schaal, schalig,* G. *schal,*

insipid, stale, said of liquids when little is left in the vessel. **Der.** *shallow-ness.* And see *shoal* (2).

SHALM, the same as **Shawm,** q. v.

SHAM, to trick, verb ; a pretence, sb. (E.) 'Sham, pretended, false ; also, a flam, cheat, or trick ; *To sham one,* to put a cheat or trick on him ;' Phillips, ed. 1706. 'A meer *sham* and disguise ;' Stillingfleet, vol. iv. ser. 9 (R.). 'They . . found all this a *sham* ;' Dampier's Voyages, an. 1688 (R.). Earlier, in 1677, we find : '*Shamming* is telling you an insipid, dull lye with a dull face, which the sly wag the author only laughs at himself ; and making himself believe 'tis a good jest, puts the *sham* only upon himself ;' Wycherley, The Plain Dealer, iii. 1. We find also the slang expression 'to *sham* Abraham' = to pretend to be an Abraham-man, or a man from Bedlam hospital ; see *Abraham-men* in Nares, and in Hotten's Slang Dictionary. *To sham* appears to be merely the Northern E. form of *to shame,* to put to shame, to disgrace, whence the sense 'to trick' may easily have arisen. *Sham* for *shame* is very common in the North, and appears in Brockett, and in the Whitby, Mid-Yorkshire, Swaledale, and Holderness Glossaries (E. D. S.). 'Wheea's *sham* is it ' = whose fault is it ? Whitby Gloss. Cf. Icel. *skömm,* a shame, outrage, disgrace. See **Shame.** ¶ The explanation in North's Examen, 1740, p. 256, is neither clear nor helpful ; he confuses *sham* with *ashamed.*

SHAMBLE, to walk awkwardly. (E.) A weakened form of *scamble,* to scramble ; cf. prov. E. *scambling,* sprawling, Hereford (Hall.). 'By that *shambling* in his walk, it should be my rich old banker, Gomez ;' Dryden, Span. Friar, Act i. sc. 2. *Scamble,* to scramble, struggle, is in Shak. Much Ado, v. 1. 94 ; K. John, iv. 3. 146 ; Hen. V, i. 1. 4. It seems to be an E. word ; see *Shamble* and *Scamble* in the E. D. D. But it is difficult to find cognate words in other languages. Cf. *skimble-skamble,* wandering, wild, confused, I Hen. IV, iii. 1. 154.

SHAMBLES, stalls on which butchers expose meat for sale ; hence, a slaughter-house. (L.) 'As summer-flies are in the *shambles* ;' Oth. iv. 2. 66. *Shambles* is the pl. of *shamble,* a butcher's bench or stall, lit. a bench ; and *shamble* is formed, with excrescent *b,* from ME. *schamel,* a bench, orig. a stool ; see Ancren Riwle, p. 166, note *e.* AS. *scamel,* a stool ; *fōt-scamel,* a foot-stool ; Matt. v. 35.—L. *scamellum,* a little bench or stool (White) ; allied to *scamnum,* a step, bench, *scabellum,* a foot-stool. The orig. sense is 'prop.' Cf. L. *scāpus,* a shaft, stem, stalk ; Gk. σκήπτειν, to prop, also to throw. Brugmann, i. § 241 (a).

SHAME, consciousness of guilt, disgrace, dishonour. (E.) ME. *schame, shame,* Wyclif, Luke, xiv. 9. AS. *sceamu, scamu,* shame ; Grein, ii. 403.**+**Icel. *skömm* (stem *skamm-*) a wound, shame ; Dan. *skam* ; Swed. *skam* ; G. *scham.* **β.** Teut. type *skamā,* f., shame ; Fick, iii. 332. Allied to Goth. *skanda,* shame, G. *schande.* **Der.** *shame,* verb, AS. *sceamian, scamian,* Grein ; *shame-ful,* spelt *scheomeful,* Ancren Riwle, p. 302, l. 23 ; *shame-ful-ly, shame-ful-ness* ; *shameless,* AS. *scam-lēas,* Ælfred, tr. of Gregory's Past. Care, c. xxxi (ed. Sweet, p. 204) ; *shame-less-ly, shame-less-ness* ; also *shame-faced,* q. v. And see *sham.*

SHAMEFACED, modest. (E.) A corruption of *shamefast,* by a singular confusion with *face,* due to the fact that *shame* is commonly expressed by the appearance of the *face* ; see **Face.** We find *shamefastness* in Spenser, F. Q. iv. 10. 50 ; *shame-faced* in Shak. Rich. III, i. 4. 142, where the quarto ed. has *shamefast* (Schmidt). ME. *schamefast, shamefast,* Chaucer, C. T. 2057 (A 2055). AS. *scamfæst,* Ælfred, tr. of Gregory's Past. Care, c. xxxi (ed. Sweet, p. 204).—AS. *scamu,* shame ; and *fæst,* fast, firm ; see **Shame** and **Fast.** **Der.** *shamefaced-ness.*

SHAMMY, SHAMOY, a kind of leather. (F.—G.) So called because formerly made from the chamois. '*Shamois,* or *Chamois,* a kind of wild goat, whose skin, being rightly dressed, makes our true *Shamois* leather ;' Blount's Gloss., ed. 1674. '*Shamoy,* or *Shamoyleather,* a sort of leather made of the skin of the *Shamoys* ;' Phillips, ed. 1706.—F. *chamois,* 'a wilde goat, or shamois ; also the skin thereof dressed, and called ordinarily *shamois leather* ;' Cot. Cf. F. *chamoiser,* to prepare chamois leather ; Littré. See **Chamois.** ¶ Taylor professes to correct this etymology, and, without a word of proof, derives it ' from *Samland,* a district on the Baltic,' with which it has but two letters, *a* and *m,* in common. There is no difficulty, when it is remembered that *shamoy-leather* could only have been prepared from the chamois *at first* ; other skins were soon substituted, as being cheaper, when a larger demand set in. I see no force in Wedgwood's objection, that chamois skins were too scarce for general use. Imitations are always common. Cf. G. *gemsenleder,* chamois leather ; from *gemse,* a chamois !

SHAMPOO, to squeeze and rub the body of another after a hot bath ; to wash the head thoroughly with soap and water. (Hindustani.) A modern word ; the operation takes its name from the squeezing or kneading of the body with the knuckles, which forms a part of it, as properly performed. — Hind. *chāmpnā*, '(1) to join, (2) to stuff, thrust in, press, to shampoo or champoo;' Shakespear, Hind. Dict. ed. 1849, p. 846. The initial letter is rightly *ch*, as in *church.* Yule notes that E. *shampoo* may represent Hind. *chāmpo*, the imperative of the above verb.

SHAMROCK, a species of clover. (C.) 'Yf they founde a plotte of water-cresses or *shamrokes*;' Spenser, View of the State of Ireland, Globe ed., p. 654, col. 2. — Irish *seamrog*, trefoil, dimin. of *seamar*, trefoil ; Gael. *seamrag*, shamrock, trefoil, clover.

SHANK, the lower part of the leg, a stem. (E.) ME. *shanke*, *schanke*, Havelok, 1903. AS. *sceanca*, *scanca* ; John, xix. 31, 32. Esp. used of the bone of the leg.+Du. *schonk*, a bone ; Dan. *skank*, the shank ; Swed. *skank*, leg. Allied to G. *schinken*, the ham, *schenkel*, the shank, leg ; Low G. *schake*, shank. Perhaps ultimately related to **Shake**. **Der.** *skink-er*, *nun-cheon*.

SHANTY, a hut. (Irish.) From Irish *sean*, old, and *toigh*, a house. Similar compounds, beginning with *sean*, are common in Irish ; and the compound *seantoigh*, an old ruinous hut, is in actual use (Archiv f. n. Sprachen, cvii. 112).

SHAPE, to form, fashion, adapt. (E.) Formerly a strong verb. ME. *shapen*, *schapen* ; pt. t. *shoop*, Chaucer, C. T. 16690 (G 1222) ; pp. *shapen*, *shape*, id. 1227 (A 1225). A new formation from the ME. sb. *schap* (AS. *ge-sceap*) ; or from the pp., on the analogy of *sceacan*, to shake. The AS. verb is *scieppan*, *sceppan*, which has a weak infin. (= Goth. *skapjan* or *ga-skapjan*). But the verb is strong, with pt. t. *scōp*, *sceōp*, and pp. *scapen*, *sceapen*.+Icel. *skapa*, pt. t. *skōp* ; Swed. *skapa* ; Dan. *skabe* ; G. *schaffen*, to create ; pt. t. *schuf*, pp. *geschaffen* ; cf. Goth. *gaskapjan*. Teut. type *skapan-* (also *skapjan-*), pt. t. *skōp*. Cf. Lith. *skabéti*, to cut, hew. Brugmann, i. § 701. **Der.** *shape*, sb., AS. *gesceap*, a creature, beauty, Grein ; *shap-able* ; *shap-er* ; *shapely*, ME. *schaply*, Chaucer, C. T. 374 (A 372) ; *shape-li-ness* ; *shape-less*, *shape-less-ness*. Hence also the suffix *-ship*, AS. *-scipe* (as in *friend-ship*, i. e. *friend-shape*), cf. G. *freund-schaft* ; and the suffix *-scape* in *land-scape*, q. v.

SHARD, SHERD, a fragment. (E.) Commonly in the comp. *pot-shard*. 'Shardes of stones, Fragmentum lapidis ; a *shard* of an earthen pot ;' Baret (1580). The pl. *shards* is in Hamlet, v. 1. 254. ME. *scherd*, Prompt. Parv. p. 445. AS. *sceard*, a fragment ; Ælfred, tr. of Boethius, c. xviii. § 1 (bk. ii. pr. 7) ; cf. *sceard*, cut, notched. Lit. 'cut thing ;' from Teut. *skar*, 2nd grade of *sker-an-*, to cut. See **Shear**. Cf. Icel. *skarð*, a notch, *skarðr*, sheared, diminished.

SHARE (1), a portion, part, division. (E.) Spelt *schare* in Palsgrave ; very rare in ME. in this sense ; *schar*, i. e. the groin, Wyclif, 2 Kings, ii. 23, is the same word. AS. *scearu*, a rare word ; occurring in the comp. *land-scearu*, a share of land ; Grein. From Teut. *skar*, 2nd grade of *sker-an-*, to shear ; see **Shear**. And see below. **Der.** *share*, verb, Spenser, F. Q. iv. 8. 5 ; *shar-er*, *share-holder*.

SHARE (2), a plough-share. (E.) ME. *schare*, *share* ; P. Plowman, B. iii. 306. AS. *scear*, a plough-share ; Ælfric's Gloss., 1st word. From Teut. *skar*, 2nd grade of *sker-an-*, to shear ; see **Shear**.

SHARK, a voracious fish, hound-fish. (F.–L.) The name of the fish is from the Tudor E. verb *shark*, to prowl ; to *shark* for a dinner, to try to get one ; to *shark* for a living. 'Because they should not think I came to *sharke* Only for vittailes ;' Times' Whistle (E. E. T. S.), p. 85. 'They *shark* for a hungry diet ;' Ben Jonson, Mercury Vindicated. Prob. from North F. (Picard) *cherquier*, equivalent to OF. *cercher* (E. *search*), mod. F. *chercher*. Cf. *chercher le broust*, 'to hunt after feasts ;' Cot. Godefroy has two exx. of the spelling *cherquier*. Cf. also Ital. *cercare del pane*, 'to shift for how to live,' i. e. to shark (Torriano). — L. *circāre*, to go round, go about. — L. *circus*, a ring ; see **Circus**. And see **Search**. Thus *shark* is only a variant of *search*, but was used in a special sense. Hence *shark* (1), a greedy fellow, one who lives by his wits, described in ch. 14 of Earle's Micro-cosmographie (1628) ; (2) a greedy fish (in Florio, s. v. *Citaro*). **Der.** *shark-ing*, voracious, greedy, prowling ; one of the Dramatis Personæ of Love's Cure (by Beaum. and Fletcher) is 'Alguazeir, a *sharking* panderly constable ;' *shark up* = to snap up, Hamlet, i. 1. 98. And hence *shark* = a sharper, as a slang term. ☞ Some connect the last word with G. *schurke*, a rogue ; but without any attempt to explain the difference of vowels. Sewel's Du. Dict. has : 'schurk, a shark, a rascal ;' but this is merely a translation, not an identification.

SHARP, cutting, trenchant, keen, severe, biting, shrewd. (E.) ME. *sharp*, *scharp*, Chaucer, C. T. 1653. AS. *scearp* ; Grein, ii. 404. +Du. *scherp* ; Icel. *skarpr* ; Swed. and Dan. *skarp* ; G. *scharf*. Teut. type *skarpoz*. Perhaps allied to *scrape*. See **Scrape**. **Der.** *sharp-ly*, *sharp-ness* ; *sharp-er*, one who acts sharply, a cheat ; *sharp-set*, *-sighted*, *-witted* ; *sharp-en*, to make sharp, Antony, ii. 1. 25.

SHATTER, to break in pieces. (E.) The Southern E. form of

scatter ; with a difference of meaning. ME. *schateren*, to scatter, to dash, said of a falling stream ; Gawayn and Grene Knight, 2083. AS. *scateran*, to scatter, squander ; A. S. Chron. an. 1137. Milton uses *shatter* with the sense of *scatter* at least twice ; P. L. x. 1066, Lycidas, 5 ; so also prov. E. *shatter*, to scatter (Kent). See **Scatter**. Doublet, *scatter*.

SHAVE, to pare, strip, cut off in slices, cut off hair. (E.) ME. *shaven*, *schaven*, formerly a strong verb ; pt. t. *schoof* (misspelt *schoofe*), Wyclif, 1 Chron. xix. 4, earlier text ; the later text has *shauyde*. The strong pp. *shaven* is still in use. AS. *sceafan*, *scafan* ; pt. t. *scōf*, pp. *scafen* ; the pt. t. *scōf* occurs in Ælfred, tr. of Beda, b. i. c. 1, near the end.+Du. *schaven*, to scrape, plane wood ; Icel. *skafa* ; Swed. *skafva*, to scrape ; Dan. *skave*, to scrape ; Goth. *skaban*, 1 Cor. xi. 6 ; G. *schaben*. β. All from Teut. base SKAB, answering to √SQAP, to cut, dig, whence Lithuan. *skapoti*, to shave, cut, Russ. *skopite*, to castrate, Gk. σκάπτειν, to dig. Brugmann, i. §§ 569, 701. **Der.** *shav-er*, *shav-ing* ; also *shave-l-ing*, with double dimin. suffix, expressive of contempt, applied to a priest with shaven crown, in Bale, King John, ed. Collier, p. 17, l. 16. Also *scab*, *shab-by*, *shaf-t*.

SHAW, a thicket, small wood. (E.) ME. *schawe*, *shawe*, Chaucer, C. T. 4365 (A 4367). AS. *scaga*, a shaw ; Diplomatarium Ævi Saxonici, ed. Thorpe, p. 161, l. 5.+Icel. *skōgr*, a shaw, wood ; Swed. *skog* ; Dan. *skov*. Allied to Icel. *skagi*, a ness (Noreen) ; NFries. *skage*, a nook of land ; cf. Icel. *skaga*, to jut out. Allied to **Shag**.

SHAWL, a covering for the shoulders. (Pers.) Added by Todd to Johnson's Dict. — Pers. *shāl*, 'a shawl or mantle, made of very fine wool of a species of goat common in Tibet ;' Rich. Dict. p. 872. See Yule. The Pers. *ā* resembles E. *aw*, showing that we borrowed the word immediately from Persian, not from F. *châle*.

SHAWM, SHALM, a musical instrument resembling the clarionet. (F.–L.–Gk.) It was a reed-instrument. In Prayer-Book version of Ps. xcviii. 7. 'With *shaumes* and trompets, and with clarions sweet ;' Spenser, F. Q. i. 12. 13. The pl. form *shalmyes* occurs in Chaucer, House of Fame, iii. 128. *Shalmye* appears to have been abbreviated to *shalme*, *shaume*. — OF. *chalemie*, 'a little pipe made of a reed, or of a wheaten or oaten straw ;' Cot. Also *chalemelle*, *chalumeau* ; Cot. All allied to F. *chaume* (for *chalme*), straw, a straw. — L. *calamus*, a reed ; borrowed from Gk., the true Lat. word being *culmus*. — Gk. κάλαμος, a reed ; καλάμη, a stalk or straw of corn. Cognate with E. **Haulm**, q. v. ¶ The G. *schalmei* is also from French. Doublet, *haulm*.

SHE, the fem. of the 3rd pers. pronoun. (E.) ME. *she*, *sche*, *sheo* ; Chaucer, C. T. 121 ; *sho*, Havelok, 125 ; *scho*, id. 126 ; also *scæ*, A. S. Chron. an. 1140. In the Northumbrian dialect, we find ME. *scho* used as a dem. pronoun, though the AS. *sēo* is the fem. of the def. article. β. The AS. *sēo* should have become *see*, but this form never occurs ; rather it became *siō* (John iv. 23, Lindisfarne MS.) ; whence (perhaps influenced by the Icel. dem. pron. *sjā*, that) came Northumb. ME. *scho*, *sho* ; and this seems to have suggested the Midland *sche*, *she*, the true Southern forms being *heo*, *he*, which actually occur, and were easily confused with *he*, masc. γ. The AS. *sēo*, fem. of *se*, used as def. article, was orig. a demonstrative pronoun, meaning 'that.'+Du. *zij*, she ; Icel. *sū*, *sjā*, fem. of *sā*, dem. pron. ; G. *sie*, she ; Goth. *sō*, fem. of *sa*, dem. pron. used as def. article ; Gk. ἡ, fem. of ὁ, def. art. ; Skt. *sā*, she, fem. of *sas*, he. For Icel. *sjā*, see Noreen, § 399. And see Sweet, E. Gr. § 1068.

SHEAF, a bundle of things collected together, esp. used of grain. (E.) ME. *scheef*, *shef* (with long *e*), Chaucer, C. T. 104. AS. *scēaf*, Gen. xxxvii. 7 ; spelt *scēab* in the 8th cent., Corpus Gloss., 197.+Du. *schoof* ; Icel. *skauf* ; G. *schaub*. The sense of 'sheaf' is a bundle of things 'shoved' together. Teut. type *skauƀoz*, m. From *skauƀ*, 2nd grade of *skūƀan-*, to shove ; see **Shove**. ¶ The pl. *sheaves* answers to AS. pl. *scēafas*. **Der.** *sheaf*, verb, As You Like It, iii. 2. 113 ; *sheaf-y*.

SHEAL, a temporary summer hut. (Scand.) In Halliwell ; Jamieson has also *sheil*, *shielling*, *sheelin* ; spelt *shieling* in Campbell, O'Connor's Child, st. 3. Spelt *scheill*, Henrysoun, Upland Mouse, st. 6. Connected in the Icel. Dict. with Icel. *skáli*, Norweg. *skaale*, a hut ; but rather from Icel. *skjōl*, a shelter, cover, Dan. *skjul*, a shelter, Swed. *skjul*, a shed, shelter ; cf. Icel. *skýli*, a shed, shelter, *skýla*, to screen, shelter, *skýling*, a screening. These words are from the √SKEU, to cover ; cf. Skt. *sku*, to cover ; Fick, iii. 337. See **Sky**. ¶ For the form, cf. Icel. *skjōla*, a pail or bucket, called in Scotland a *skiel* or *skeel*.

SHEAR, to cut, clip, shave off. (E.) ME. *scheren*, *sheren*, pt. t. *schar*, *shar*, pp. *schoren*, now contracted to *shorn* ; Chaucer, C. T. 13958 (B 3142). AS. *sceran*, *sciran*, pt. t. *scær*, pl. *scǣron*, pp. *scoren* ; Gen. xxxviii. 13 ; Diplomatarium Ævi Saxonici, ed. Thorpe, p. 145, l. 14.+Du. *scheren* ; Icel. *skera* ; Dan. *skære* ; G. *scheren*. Teut. type *skeran-*, pt. t. *skar*, pp. *skor-anoz*. Allied to OIrish *scar-aim*,

I separate; Gael. *sgar*, to sever; W. *ysgar*, to part; Gk. κείρειν (for σκερχειν).—√SQER, to cut. Brugmann, i. § 631. Der. *shear-er*; **shears**, ME. *sheres*, P. Plowman, C. vii. 75, pl. of *shear* = AS. *sceara*, used to translate L. *forfex*, Voc. 336. 27; *shear-ling*, a sheep only once sheared, formed with double dimin. suffix -*l-ing*. Allied words are **Scar** (2), **Share**, **Sheer** (2), **Shard**, **Shore**, **Short**, **Score**, **Skerry**, and others.

SHEATH, a case for a sword or other implement, case, scabbard. (E.) ME. *schethe*, Wyclif, John, xviii. 11. AS. *scǣþ*, *scēþ*, *scēaþ*, a sheath; Grein, ii. 399.+Du. *scheede*; Icel. *skeiðir*, fem. pl.; Dan. *skede*; [Swed. *skida*]; G. *scheide*. Teut. type *skaithā*, f., orig. 'that which separates,' applied to the husk of a bean, as in Swed. *skida*, which also means 'a husk.' Since such a husk has two sides, we see why the Icel. *skeiðir* is only used in the plural; and these sides of a case must be *separated* before a knife or sword can be introduced, if the material of the scabbard is at all loose. All from Teut. base *skaith-* [except Swed. *skid-a* < weak grade *skith-*]; for which see **Shed** (1). Der. *sheathe*, verb, Macb. v. 7. 20; spelt *shethe* in Palsgrave; *sheath-ing*.

SHEAVE, a wheel of a pulley. (E.) A technical term; see Webster. A variant of prov. E. *shive*, a slice (Halliwell); see E. D. D., and see further under **Shive, Shiver** (2).

SHEBEEN, a liquor-shop. (Irish.—E.) Apparently a dimin. (with suffix -*in*) of Irish *seapa*, a shop.—E. *shop*; see **Shop**.

SHED (1), to part, scatter, cast abroad, pour, spill. (E.) The old sense 'to part' is nearly obsolete, except in *water-shed*, the ridge which parts river-systems. '*Shed*, to distinguish,' Ray, Gloss. B. 15 (E. D. S.). Spelt *shead* in Baret (1580). ME. *scheden*, Rob. of Glouc. p. 57, l. 1332; P. Plowman, B. vi. 9; pt. t. *shadde*, *shedde*, P. Plowman, B. xvii. 288; pp. *shad*, Gen. and Exodus, ed. Morris, 148; also *shed*. AS. *sceadan*, *scādan*, to part, separate, distinguish (hence, to scatter); pt. t. *scēd*, *scēad*, pp. *sceáden*, *scáden*; a strong verb; Grein, ii. 398; but we find the weak pt. t. *shadde* and the pp. *shad* as early as in the Ormulum, ll. 3200, 4939. The vowel of the mod. E. word has been shortened, as in *red* from AS. *rēad*, *bread* from *brēad*, and *head* from *hēafod*; this shortening began in the weak pt. t. *shedde* and the pp. *shed*.+OSax. *skēdan*, OFries. *skētha*, *scēda*, to part; G. *scheiden*; Goth. *skaidan*. Cf. Lithuan. *skēdziu*, I separate; L. *scindere*, Gk. σχίζειν, to cleave, split, part. All from Teut. base *skaith-*, varying to *skaid* (see **Shide**); allied to Idg. base *skhid*, to cleave. See Brugmann, i. §§ 201, 599. Der. *shedd-er*.

SHED (2), a slight shelter, hut. (E.) Allied to *shade*. '*Sheds* stuffed with lambs and goats;' Chapman, tr. of Odyssey, ix. 314; cf. prov. E. *cow-shade*, a cow-shed (Leic.). It appears to be a Kentish form, like OKentish *bend* for *band*, *mere* for *mare*, *leddre* for *ladder*, &c.; see Introd. to Ayenbite of Inwyt, ed. Morris, pp. v, vi. In the same work, p. 95, l. 28, we find *ssed* (= *shed*) for *shade*; *ssede*, dat. p. 97, l. 1; and *ssed* in the sense of 'shadow,' p. 137, l. 15. AS. *scead*, *sced*, shade; fig. shelter (Toller); allied to AS. *sceadu*, shade. See **Shade**. β. Or *shed* may be a Kentish form of prov. E. *shud*, a shed (E. D. D.), ME. *schudde*, a shed, Prompt. Parv., which answers to an AS. form *scydd*.

SHEEN, fairness, splendour. (E.) 'The *sheen* of their spears;' Byron, Destruction of Sennacherib. And in Hamlet, iii. 2. 167. But properly an adj., signifying 'fair,' as in Spenser, F. Q. ii. 1. 10, ii. 2. 40. ME. *schene*, adj., fair, beautiful, Chaucer, C. T. 974 (A 972). AS. *scēne*, *scēone*, *scīone*, *scȳne*, fair; Grein, ii. 416. Lit. 'showy,' 'fair to sight, and allied to **Show**, q. v. (But doubtless frequently supposed to be allied to *shine*, which the vowel-sound shows to be impossible; observe the cognate forms.)+OSax. *scōni*, adj.; Du. *schoon*, adj.; G. *schön*, adj.; Goth. *skauns*, beautiful. Teut. type *skau-niz* (Kluge); or *skau-n-joz* (Streitberg). See Fick, iii. 336.

SHEEP, a well-known animal. (E.) ME. *scheep*, *sheep*, pl. *scheep*, *sheep*; Chaucer, C. T. 498 (A 496). AS. *scēap*, *scēp*, pl. *scēap*, *scēp*, a neuter sb., which is unchanged in the plural, like *deer*; Grein, ii. 404. +OSax. *skāp*; Du. *schaap*, a sheep, a simpleton; G. *schaf*; OHG. *scāf*. Teut. type *skǣpom*, n. Origin unknown; the Pol. *skop*, Lith. *skapas*, sheep, are borrowed from Teutonic. Der. *sheep-cote*, *sheep-fold*; *sheep-ish*, -*ly*, -*ness*; *sheep-master*, *shearer*, -*shearing*, -*walk*. Also *shep-herd*.

SHEER (1), bright, clear, pure, simple, perpendicular. (Scand.) 'A *sheer* descent' is an unbroken one, orig. a clear one; the old meaning being 'bright.' And see Trench, Select Glossary. '*Sheer*, immaculate, and silver fountain;' Rich. II, v. 3. 61. ME. *scheere*, *shere*. 'The *shere* sonne;' Lydgate, Storie of Thebes, pt. i (How Edipus expouned the probleme). [Rather Scand. than E. The initial *sh* is due to AS. *scīr* (below).]—Icel. *skærr*, bright, clear; Swed. *skär*; Dan. *skær*, bright, pure; Teut. type *skairiz*. Allied to Icel. *skírr*, clear, bright (which is cognate with AS. *scīr*, bright (Grein), Goth. *skeirs*, G. *schier*) Teut. type *skeiroz*. β. Here *skai-riz* is from *skai-*, the 2nd grade, and *skei-roz* from *skei-*, the prime grade,

of Idg. root SKEI, to shine. Cf. Icel. * skí-na* (= AS. *scí-nan*), to shine; so that the orig. sense is 'shining.' See **Shine**. Der. *sheer*, adv.; also *Sheer-Thursday*, the old name of Maundy Thursday, lit. 'pure Thursday;' cf. Icel. *skíra*, to cleanse, baptize, *Skírdagr* or *Skíriþorsdagr*, Sheer-day or Sheer-Thursday, Dan. *Skærtorsdag*. See my note on P. Plowman, B. xvi. 140; p. 379 of 'Notes.'

SHEER (2), to deviate from one's course. (Du.) A nautical term. 'Among sea-men, a ship is said to *sheer*, or go *sheering*, when in her sailing she is not steadily steered, &c.;' Phillips, ed. 1706.—Du. *scheren*, to shear, cut, barter, jest; to withdraw, or go away; to warp, stretch. '*Scheerje van hier*, away, get you gone;' Sewel. This answers to mod. E. *sheer off*! Thus *sheer* is only a particular use of Du. *scheren*, cognate with E. **Shear**. So also G. *schere dich weg*, get you gone; *schier dich aus dem Wege*, out of the way! (Flügel).

SHEET, a large piece of linen cloth; a large piece of paper; a sail; a rope fastened to a sail. (E.) ME. *schete*, *shete*, Chaucer, C. T. 4138 (A 4140). AS. *scēte*, *scȳte*; 'Sindo, *scȳte*,' Voc. 124. 24; 'Sindonem, *scētan*' (Kentish Glosses), Voc. 86. 35; 'Sandalium, *scēte*,' Corpus gloss., 1776. 'On *scēte mīnum*,' in my bosom (L. *in sinu meo*); Ps. lxxxviii. 49, ed. Spelman. 'On clǣnre *scȳtan* befeold' = enfolded in a clean sheet; Gospel of Nicodemus, c. xiii. ed. Thwaites, p. 6. 'On *scētan bewunden*,' wound in a sheet; The Shrine, p. 69. *Sheet* answers to the Kentish and OMerc. form *scēte*, not to Wessex *scȳte*. The sense of 'bosom' is due to the use of *scȳte* to signify the fold of a garment. It is closely allied to AS. *scēat*, a much commoner word, meaning (1) a projecting corner, angle, nook of ground, (2) fold of a garment; Grein, ii. 405. β. The orig. sense is 'projection,' or 'that which shoots out,' then a corner, esp. of a garment or of a cloth; after which it was extended to mean a whole cloth or sheet. The nautical senses are found in AS. *scēáta*, explained '*pes veli*;' *scēat-line*, explained 'propes,' Voc. 288. 24, 25. γ. The vowels *ē*, *ȳ*, are due to a mutation from *ēa*; and all may be compared with AS. *scēat*, pt. t. of *scēotan*, to shoot; see **Shoot**. Cognate with the form *scēat-* are Icel. *skaut*, a sheet, corner of a square cloth, corner, sheet or rope attached to the corner of a sail, skirt or sleeve of a garment, a hood; Swed. *skot*, the sheet of a sail; Du. *schoot*, a shoot, sprig, sheet, bosom, lap; G. *schoosz*, flap of a coat, lap, bosom; Goth. *skauts*, the hem of a garment; all from Teut. *skaut*, 2nd grade of *skeutan-*, to shoot; see **Shoot**. Der. *sheet*, verb, Hamlet, i. 1. 115, Antony, i. 4. 65; *sheet-ing*; *sheet-lightning*, lightning which spreads out like a sheet. Also *sheet-anchor*, the same as *shoot-anchor*, an anchor to be shot out or lowered in case of great danger; 'This saying they make their *shoot-anker*,' Abp. Cranmer, Ans. to Bp. Gardiner, p. 117 (cited by Todd); also in Roister Doister, i. 1. 28. The form *sheet-anchor* is due to ME. *schēten*, to shoot; see **Shoot**.

SHEIK, a chief. (Arab.) In books of travel.—Arab. *sheikh*, an elder, a chief; Palmer's Pers. Dict. col. 394; *shaykh*, a venerable old man, a chief; Rich. Dict. p. 920. The orig. sense is 'old.'

SHEKEL, a Jewish weight and coin. (Heb.) See Exod. xxx. 13. The weight is about half an ounce; the value about half a crown.—Heb. *sheqel*, a shekel (weight).—Heb. *shāqal*, to weigh. [Both *ees* are short.]

SHEKINAH, SHECHINAH, the visible glory of the Divine presence. (Heb.) Not in the Bible, but in the targums; it signifies the 'dwelling' of God among His people. — Heb. *shek(h)īnāh*, dwelling, the presence of God.—Heb. *shāk(h)an*, to dwell.

SHELDRAKE, a kind of drake. (E.) ME. *scheldrak*; 'Hic umnis, *scheldrak*;' Voc. 762. 39. For *sheld-drake*, i.e. variegated or spotted drake; hence the ME. form *shelde-drake*, Rel. Antiq. ii. 82, col. 2. '*Sheldapple* [prob. for *sheld-dapple*], the chaffinch;' Halliwell. '*Sheld*, flecked, party-coloured;' Coles' Dict., ed. 1684. *Sheld* in this case is just the same as ME. *sheld*, a shield; and the allusion is, probably, to the ornamentation of shields, which is doubtless of great antiquity. The AS. *scyld* or *scild* is a shield; but is also used, in a curious passage, to denote a part of a bird's plumage. 'Is se *scyld* ufan frætwum gefēged ofer þæs fūgles bæc' = the shield above is curiously arranged over the bird's back; Poem on the Phœnix, l. 308 (Grein). So also Icel. *skjöldungr*, a sheldrake, allied to *skjöldóttr*, dappled, from *skjöldr*, a shield, spot, patch; Dan. *en skjoldet ko*, a brindled cow, from *skjold*, a shield; G. *schildern*, to paint, depict, from G. *schild*, a shield, escutcheon. See **Shield**.

SHELF, a ledge, flat layer of rock. (E.) ME. *schelfe*, *shelfe*; pl. *shelves*, Chaucer, C. T. 3211. AS. *scylfe* (for *scilfe*), a plank or shelf; Grein, ii. 416.+Low G. *schelf*, a shelf, Bremen Wörterbuch; allied to *schelfern*, to scale off, peel. Cf. Lowland Sc. *skelve*, a thin slice, *skelve*, to separate in laminæ (Jamieson); Du. *schilfer*, a scale; prov. G. *schelfe*, a husk, shell, paring; *schelfen*, *schelfern*, to peel off. Closely allied to *shell* and *scale*; the orig. sense is 'a husk,' thence a flake, slice, thin board, flat ledge, layer. See **Shell**. The Gael.

sgealb, a splinter, or (as a verb) to split, is from the same root. ¶ We occasionally find *shelf*, not only in the sense of a layer of rock, but in the sense of 'sand-bank' or 'shoal.' Dryden speaks of 'a *shelfy* coast' as equivalent to 'shoaly ground;' tr. of Virgil, Æn. v. 1125, 1130. He adds that Æneas 'steers aloof, and shuns the *shelf*,' l. 1132. There is confusion here with the verb to **Shelve**, q. v. Cf. '*shelvy* and shallow,' Merry Wives, iii. 5. 15.

SHELL, a scale, husk, outer covering, a bomb. (E.) ME. *schelle*, *shelle*; P. Plowman, B. v. 528; Gower, C. A. iii. 76; bk. vi. 2228. AS. *scell*, *scyll*; Grein, ii. 399. +Du. *schel*; Icel. *skel*; Goth. *skalja*, a tile; Luke, v. 19. Teut. type *skaljā*, f. The sense is 'thin flake;' cf. Swed. *skala*, to peel off; see **Skill**. And see **Scale** (1). **Der.** *shell-fish*, -*work*; *shell*, verb; *shell-y*.

SHELTER, a place of protection, refuge, retreat, protection. (E.) This curious word is perhaps due to a corruption of ME. *sheld-trume*, a body of troops used to protect anything, a guard, squadron. The corruption took place early, possibly owing to some confusion with the word *squadron* (of F. origin), with which it seems to have been assimilated, at least in its termination. Thus *sheld-trume* soon became *scheldtrome*, *sheltrome*, *sheltrone*, *sheltroun*, the force of the latter part of the word being utterly lost, so that at last -*roun* was confused with the common suffix -*er*, and the word *shelter* was the result. β. See examples in Stratmann, s. v. *schild*. To which add: *schiltrum*, Barbour's Bruce, xii. 429; *scheltrone*, *sheltron*, *sheltrun*, Allit. version of Destruction of Troy, 3239, 5249, 5804, 10047; Morte Arthure, ed. Brock, 1813, 1856, 1992, 2106, 2210, 2922. It occurs also in Trevisa's description of the battle of Hastings, and was quite a common word, known from Aberdeen to Cornwall. Loss of the true form caused loss of the true sense, so that it came to mean only *a place* of protection, instead of a body-guard or squadron. Note the use in P. Plowman, B. xiv. 81: 'make owre faithe owre *scheltroun*,' make our faith our *defence*. Also: '*scheltrun* schouris to shelde,' shelter to keep off showers (Halliwell). A sense of its derivation from *shield* survives in modern use. From AS. *scild-truma*, lit. a shield-troop, troop of men with shields or selected for defence; compounded of AS. *scild*, a shield, and *truma*, a band of men, Jos. xi. 10. The word *truma* does not appear to be a mere modification of the L. *turma*, but is allied to AS. *trum*, firm, *getrum*, a cohort, band of men (Grein); and to E. *trim*. See **Shield** and **Trim**.

SHELVE, to slope down, incline downwards gradually. (E.) We speak of a *shelving* shore, i. e. a shallow or sloping shore, where the water's depth increases gradually. 'The shore was *shelvy* and shallow;' Merry Wives, iii. 5. 15. We have *shelving* in Two Gent. of Verona, iii. 1. 115, which is explained by Schmidt as 'projecting like a shelf.' It seems to be from *shelf*, sb., but the connexion is not clear. A *shelf* sometimes meant a sand-bank; and the sense of 'slope' may refer to the sloping sides of the same. Cf. 'tawny sands and *shelves*;' Milton, Comus, 117. 'What bark beares sayle in tempeste on the *shelues*?' Higgins, Mirror for Magistrates; Severus, st. 8. In Lowl. Sc. we find *skelf*, a shelf, a ledge in a cliff, and *skelve*, vb., to shelve, to tilt; also *skelvy*, adj., applied to rocks that form a shelf or ledge. β. Torriano explains MItal. *stralare* by 'to *shelve* or go aside, aslope, awry;' a sense which may have been suggested by MDu. *scheel*, awry, G. *schel*, *scheel*, Bavar. *schelb*, awry. See **Shelf**.

SHEPHERD, a sheep-herd, pastor. (E.) ME. *schepherd*, *shepherd*, Chaucer, C. T. 506 (A 504). AS. *scēaphyrde*, a keeper of sheep, Gen. iv. 2.—AS. *scēap*, a sheep; and *hyrde*, a herd, i.e. guardian. See **Sheep** and **Herd** (2). **Der.** *shepherd-ess*, with F. suffix.

SHERBET, a kind of sweet drink. (Arab.) In Herbert's Travels, ed. 1665, pp. 203, 327; Sandys, Trav., p. 136.—Arab. *sharbat*, a drink, draught, sherbet, syrup; Rich. Dict. p. 887.—Arab. root *shariba*, he drank; id. Allied to *syrup*, q. v. Also to *shrub*, in the term '*rum-shrub*;' see **shrub** (2).

SHERD, **SHARD**, a fragment. (E.) See **Shard**.

SHERE-THURSDAY; see **Sheer** (1).

SHERIFF, an officer in a county who executes the law. (E.) ME. *shirreve*, Chaucer, C. T. 361 (A 359). AS. *scīr-gerēfa*, a shire-reeve. In Ælfric's Glossary we find: 'Consul, *gerēfa*;' also 'Pro-consul, *under-gerēfa*;' also 'Prætor, *burh-gerēfa*;' and 'Preses, *scīr-gerēfa*;' Voc. col. 110.—AS. *scīr*, a shire; and *ge-rēfa*, a reeve, officer; see **Shire** and **Reeve**. **Der.** *sheriff-ship*, *sheriff-dom*. Also *sheriff-al-ty*, generally written *shrievalty*, spelt *shrevalty* in Fuller, Worthies of England (R.); the suffix is F., as in *common-al-ty*. Dryden has the extraordinary adj. *shriev-al*, The Medal, 14.

SHERRY, a wine of Spain. (Span.—L.) Formerly *sherris*, 2 Hen. IV, iv. 3. 111. The final *s* was dropped, from a fancy that it was the pl. ending, just as in the case of *pea* for *pease*, &c. So called from the town of *Xeres*, in Spain, whence it was brought. There

are two towns of that name; but the famous one is *Xeres de la Frontera*, in the province of Sevilla, not far from Cadiz. The Spanish *x* is now a guttural letter (like G. *ch*); but formerly was like the E. *sh*. β. Dozy shows that *Xeres*=L. *Cæsaris*, by loss of the syllable -*ar*-, much as *Cæsar Augusta* became, by contraction, *Saragossa*; see Dozy, Recherches sur l'histoire et la littérature de l'Espagne, Leyden, 1860, i. 314. *Cæsaris* is the gen. case of L. *Cæsar*. **Der.** *sherris-sack*, i.e. dry sherry, 2 Hen. IV, iv. 3. 104; see **Sack** (3).

SHEW, the same as **Show**, q. v.

SHIBBOLETH, the criterion or test-word of a party. (Heb.) In Milton, Samson Agonistes, 289. See the story in Judges, xii. 6. —Heb. *shibbōleth*, (1) an ear of corn, (2) a river. From the obsolete root *shābhal*, to increase, grow, flow. ¶ Any word beginning with *sh* would have done as well to detect an Ephraimite.

SHIDE, a thin piece of board. (E.) '*Shide*, a billet of wood, a thin board, a block of wood; still in use;' Halliwell. Spelt *shyde* in Palsgrave. ME. *shide*, *schide*, Gower, C. A. i. 314; bk. iii. 1033; P. Plowman, B. ix. 131. AS. *scid*, a billet of wood, in a gloss; Voc. 266. 33; whence *scid-weall*, a fence made of palings; Voc. 146. 28. +Icel. *skíð*, a billet of wood; G. *scheit*, the same. Cf. OIrish *sciath*, a shield. From the same root as **Sheath** and **Shed**. Fick, iii. 335. Thus the orig. sense is 'a piece of cleft wood, a log, billet.' Doublet, *skid*.

SHIELD, a piece of defensive armour held on the left arm. (E.) ME. *schelde*, *sheelde*, Chaucer, C. T. 2506 (A 2504). AS. *scild*, *sceld*, a shield; Grein, ii. 407.+Du. *schild*; Icel. *skjöldr*, pl. *skildir*; Dan. *skjold*; Swed. *sköld*; Goth. *skildus*; G. *schild*. β. All from a Teut. type *skelduz*, a shield; Fick, iii. 334. The root is doubtful; it is usual to connect it with *shell* and *scale*, as denoting a thin piece of wood; cf. Lith. *skelti*, to split. Fick suggests a connexion with Icel. *skella*, *skjalla*, to clash, rattle, from the 'clashing of shields' so often mentioned; cf. G. *schelle*, a bell, allied to *schallen*, to resound. This seems unlikely. **Der.** *shield*, verb, K. Lear, iv. 2. 67; *shield-bearer*, *shield-less*. Also *shel-ter*, q. v., *shill-ing*, q. v.

SHIELING, the same as **Sheal**, q. v.

SHIFT, to change, change clothes, remove. (E.) The old sense was 'to divide,' now lost. ME. *schiften*, *shiften*, to divide, change, remove. In the Prompt. Parv. p. 446, it is explained by 'part asunder,' or 'deal,' i.e. divide, as well as by 'change.' 'Hastilich he *schifte* him'=hastily he removed himself, changed his place, P. Plowman, B. xx. 166. And see Chaucer, C. T. 5686 (D 104). AS. *sciftan*, *scyftan*, to divide; 'bēo his æht *gescyft* swiðe rihte'= let his property be divided very justly; Laws of Cnut (Secular), § 71; in Thorpe, Ancient Laws, i. 414, l. 1.+Du. *schiften*, to divide, separate, turn; Icel. *skipta* (for *skifta*), to part, share, divide; also to shift, change; so that the mod. use of *shift* is prob. Scandinavian; Swed. *skifta*, to divide, to change, shift; Dan. *skifte* (the same). β. The sense of 'divide' or 'part' is the orig. one. Allied to Icel. *skífa*, to cut into slices, Icel. *skífa*, a slice, and prov. E. *shive*, a slice. See **Shiver** (2). Cf. also Icel. *skipa*, to arrange, appoint; which may have influenced the sense. **Der.** *shift*, sb., a change, Timon, i. 1. 84; esp. a change of linen, and commonly restricted to the sense of chemise; *shift-less*; *shift-y*.

SHILLELAGH, an oaken stick used as a cudgel. (Irish.) In The Rejected Addresses (Living Lustres, st. 9). Named from *Shillelagh*, a barony in Wicklow famous for oaks. The Irish name *Siol-Elaigh* means 'the descendants of Elach.'—Irish *siol*, seed, descendants; and *Elach*, proper name. See Joyce, Irish Local Names. The OIrish *sil*, seed, is from √SE, to sow.

SHILLING, a silver coin worth 12 pence. (E.) ME. *shilling*, *shillyng*; P. Plowman, B. xii. 146. AS. *scilling*, *scylling*, Luke, xv. 9. +Du. *schelling*; Icel. *skillingr*; Dan. and Swed. *skilling*; Goth. *skilliggs* (for *skillings*); G. *schilling*. β. The suffix -*l-ing* is a double diminutive, the same as in AS. *feorð-ling* (or *feorð-ing*), a farthing. The base is perhaps SKEL, to divide, as in Lith. *skel-ti*, to split, Icel. *skilja*, to divide; see **Skill**. γ. The reason for the name is not certain; Ihre suggests that the old coins were marked with a cross, for the convenience of *dividing them* into four parts, as suggested by the AS. name *feorðling*, a fourth part or farthing. It is more likely that the word merely meant 'small piece,' as AS. *stycce*, a mite (Mark, xii. 42), merely means a 'bit' or 'small piece.' δ. The derivation from SKEL is strongly supported by the occurrence of Swed. *skiljemynt*, Dan. *skillemynt*, in the sense of 'small change' or 'small money;' and by the occurrence of numerous other derivatives from the same base. Cf. Gk. κέρ-μα, small coin, from κείρειν, to cut.

SHILLYSHALLY, to act irresolutely. (E.) Coined from the phr. *shill I*, *shall I*, which is a reduplicated form of *shall I*, used interrogatively. 'I thought it would be foolish to stand *shilli shalli* any longer;' Macklin, Love à la Mode, Act i; Sir Callaghan (reads a letter). And in Congreve, Way of the World, iii. 3 (Sir Wilfull).

SHIMMER, to glitter, shine faintly. (E.) ME. *shimeren*; whence *shimeryng*, Chaucer, C. T. 4295 (A 4297); spelt *shemering* in Tyrwhitt. It is the frequentative form of *scimian*, to shine, Luke, xvii. 24 (Lindisfarne MS.), and Grein, ii. 408.—AS. *scíma*, a light, brightness, Grein, ii. 408. From the base *sci-* of *sci-nan*, to shine; see **Shine.**+Du. *schemeren*, to glimmer; Swed. *skimra*, to glitter; G. *schimmern*, to glimmer; from OHG. *sciman*, to shine, *scímo*, a bright light. And cf. Icel. *skími*, *skíma*, a gleam of light, Goth. *skeima*, a torch or lantern; Irish *sgeimh*, *sgiamh*, beauty, OIrish *scíam*.

SHIN, the large bone of the leg, front of the lower part of the leg. (E.) ME. *shine*; dat. *shinne*, Chaucer, C. T. 388; pl. *shinnes*, id. 1281 (A 386, 1279). AS. *scinu*, Voc. 216. 3; 'Tibiae, *scina*, oððe *scin-bán*' [shin-bones]; id. 160. 19. Allied to AS. *scía*, shin, O. E. Texts, p. 54; so that the Teut. base is **skei-.*+Du. *scheen*; Swed. *sken-ben*, shin-bone; Dan. *skinne-been*, shin-bone; G. *schiene*; OHG. *scina*, *scena*. β. Origin uncertain; but note the use of G. *schiene*, a splint, an iron band, Dan. *skinne*, the same, Dan. *hiulskinne*, the tire of a wheel. It is probable that *shin* and *skin* are allied; the orig. sense may have been 'thin slice;' from √SQEI, to cleave, split; cf. L. *dé-sci-scere*, to separate oneself from. 'The *shin-bone* [is] so called from its sharp edge, like a splint of wood. The analogous bone in a horse is called the *splint-bone*;' Wedgwood. See **Skin.**

SHINE, to gleam, beam, glow, be bright. (E.) ME. *schinen*, *shinen*; pt. t. *schone* (better *schoon*), Wyclif, Matt. xvii. 2, pl. *shinen* (with short *i*), Gower, C. A. iii. 68; bk. vi. 1985; pp. *shinen* (rare). AS. *scínan*, pt. t. *scán*, pp. *scinen*, to shine, Grein, ii. 408.+Du. *schijnen*; Icel. *skína*; Dan. *skinne*; Swed. *skina*; Goth. *skeinan*; G. *scheinen*. Teut. type **skeinan-.* β. All from Teut. base SKEI, to shine; cf. Skt. *chháya-*, faint light. **Der.** *shine*, sb., Timon, iii. 5. 101; *shin-y*, Antony, iv. 9. 3. Also *sheer* (1), *shimmer*.

SHINGLE (1), a wooden tile. (L.) Formerly a common word; a *shingle* was a piece of wood, split thin, and cut into a square shape; used like modern tiles and slates, esp. for the fronts of houses. ME. *shingle*; spelt *shyngil*, K. Alisaunder, 2210; hence 'shyngled shippe,' P. Plowman, B. ix. 141. 'Scindula, *shyngul*;' Voc. 610. 13. A corrupt pronunciation for *shindle* or *shindel*, as shown by the corresponding G. *schindel*, a shingle, splint. [Both E. *shingle* and G. *schindel* are non-Teutonic words.]—L. *scindula* (as if from *scindere*, to cleave); but really a later spelling of *scandula*, a shingle, wooden tile. Minsheu (1627) has the form *shindle*; and see Holland, tr. of Pliny, bk. xvi. c. 10: Of *Shindles*.

SHINGLE (2), coarse round gravel on the sea-shore. (E.) I find no early use of the word. Phillips, ed. 1706, notes that *shingles* is 'the name of a shelf or sand-bank in the sea, about the Isle of Wight;' which is a confused statement. But the older spelling was *chingle* (with *ch*). G. Douglas has 'a dry *chyngill* or bed of sand,' tr. of Virgil, Æn. bk. x. ch. 6. 34. Cf. prov. E. *chingle*, shingle; Lowl. Sc. *chingle*, sometimes pronounced *channel*. Prob. from the vb. to *chink*, from the sound made when one walks on it. β. Perhaps influenced (as to sound) by the synonymous Norw. *singl* or *singling*, coarse gravel, small round stones (Aasen); named from the crunching noise made in walking along it. Cf. Norw. *singla*, to make a ringing sound, like that of falling glass or a piece of money (Aasen); Swed. dial. *singla*, to ring, rattle; *singel-skälla*, a bell on a horse's neck, *singel*, the clapper of a bell (Rietz). The verb *singla* is merely the frequentative of Swed. dial. *singa*, Swed. *sjunga*, Icel. *syngja*, to sing; see **Sing.**

SHINGLES, an eruptive disease. (F.—L.) 'Shingles, how to be cured;' Index to vol. ii of Holland's tr. of Pliny, with numerous references. It is a peculiarity of the disease that the eruption often encircles the body like a belt, for which reason it was sometimes called in Latin *zóna*, i. e. a zone, belt. A form of *sengles*, pl. of the old word *sengle*, a girth.—ONorth F. *chengle*, *chingle*; OF. *cengle*, 'a girth;' also spelt *sangle*, 'a girth, a sengle;' Cot. See *cengle* in Godefroy. Mod. F. *sangle*.—L. *cingula*, a belt, girdle.—L. *cingere*, to surround; see **Cincture.** Cf. the old word *surcingle*, a long upper girth (Halliwell).

SHIP, a vessel, barge, large boat. (E.) ME. *schip*, *ship*; pl. *shippes*, Chaucer, C. T. 2019 (A 2017). AS. *scip*, *scyp*, pl. *scipu*; Grein, ii. 409.+Du. *schip*; Icel. *skip*; Dan. *skib*; Swed. *skepp*; Goth. *skip*; G. *schiff*; OHG. *scif*. β. All from Teut. type **skipom*, n. Root unknown. **Der.** *ship*, verb, Rich. II, ii. 2. 42; *shipp-er*; *ship-board*, *ship-broker*, *-chandler*, *-man*, *-master*, *-mate*, *-ment* (with F. suffix *-ment*); *ship-money*, *-wreck*, *-wright*, *-yard*; *shipp-ing*. And see *equip*. **Doublet,** *skiff*, (of *shipper*), *skipp-er*, q. v.

SHIRE, a county, division of land. (E.) ME. *schire*, *shire*; Chaucer, C. T. 586 (A 584). AS. *scír*, A. S. Chron. an. 1010; older sense, office, charge, administration; see Bosw. and Toller,

A. S. Dict. 'Procuratio, *sciir*;' Voc. 40. 32 (8th century). Allied to OHG. *scira*, business; see Schade. Root unknown. The vowel-sound shows that it is in no way allied to **Shear** or **Share**, as has been repeatedly alleged. Note that the oldest sense is 'business.' Cf. AS. *scírian*, to distribute, assign, appoint, allot; G. *schirrmeister*, a steward; *anschirren*, to harness a horse. See Notes on E. Etym., p. 270. **Der.** *sher-iff*, for *shire-reeve*, see *sheriff*; also *shire-mote*, for which see *meet*.

SHIRK, to avoid, get off, slink from. (F.—L.) Formerly spelt *sherk*, which appears to be merely the same word as *shark*, to cheat, swindle; see Nares. Abp. Laud was accused of fraud in contracting for licences to sell tobacco; and it was said of him, 'that he might have spent his time much better . . . than thus *sherking* and raking in the tobacco-shops;' State-Trials, 1640, Harbottle Grimstone (R.). See **Shark.** So also *clerk* as compared with *Clark*, a proper name; ME. *derk*=mod. E. *dark*; ME. *berken*, to *bark*, &c.; also mod. E. *shirt* from ME. *sherte*. **Shirk** = *sherk*, *shark*; E. D. D.

SHIRT, a man's garment, worn next the body. (E.) ME. *schirte*, *shirte*, also *sherte*, *shurte*. Spelt *shirte*, Havelok, 768; *sherte*, Chaucer, C. T. 1566; *shurte*, O. Eng. Homilies, ed. Morris, ii. 139, l. 16. AS. *scyrte* (Toller).—AS. *scort*, short.+Icel. *skyrta*, a shirt, kirtle; Swed. *skjorta*; Dan. *skjorte*; G. *schurz*, *schürze*, an apron; cf. *schürzen*, to tuck up. β. So called from its being orig. a *short* garment; see **Short. Der.** *shirt-ing*, stuff for making shirts. **Doublet,** *skirt.*

SHITTAH-TREE, SHITTIM-WOOD. (Heb.—Egyptian.) *Shittim* is a plural form, referring to the clusters of groups of the trees; we find *shittim-wood* in Exod. xxv. 10, &c. The sing. *shittah-tree* only occurs once, Isaiah, xli. 19.—Heb. *shittáh*, pl. *shittím*, a kind of acacia. [The medial letter is *teth*, not *tau*.] For **shintáh*; cf. Arab. *sanṭ*, a thorn, acacia; Rich. Dict., p. 853. Of Egypt. origin.—Egypt. *shonte*, *shonti*; Gesenius, ed. 8, p. 830.

SHIVE, a slice; **SHEAVE,** a pulley; see **Shiver** (2).

SHIVER (1), to tremble, shudder, quiver. (E.) Spelt *sheuer* (=*shever*) in Baret (1580). This word seems to have been assimilated to the word below by confusion. It is remarkable that the ME. forms are distinct, viz. (1) *cheueren* or *chiueren* (*chiveren*), to tremble, and (2) *sheueren* or *shiueren*, to splinter. Whereas the latter word truly begins with *sh*, the present word is alliterated with words beginning with *ch*, and is spelt with *ch*, appearing as *chiueren*, *cheueren*, and *chiuelen*. 'Lolled his chekes; Wel sydder than his chyn, þei chiueled for elde '=his cheeks lolled about, (hanging down) even lower than his chin; and they *shivered* through old age;' P. Plowman, B. v. 193 (where other MSS. have *chyueleden*, *cheuerid*). 'Achilles at tho choise men *cheuert* for anger'=Achilles shivered (shook) with anger at those choice men; Destruction of Troy, 9370. 'And I haue *cheueride* for chele '=and I have shivered with cold; Morte Arthure, 3391. 'The temple-walles gan *chiuere* and schake;' Legends of the Holy Rood, p. 144, l. 386. '*Chyueren* in yse '=to shiver in ice; O. Eng. Miscellany, p. 177, l. 142. 'Heo quakeden and *chyuereden* faste,' they quaked and shivered fast; South E. Legendary, p. 210, l. 1. β. The persistence of the initial *ch* is remarkable; and takes us back to an earlier form **keveren*, **kiveren*, to shake continually, the suffix *-er* being frequentative. From an AS. base **cef-* or **cíf-* (Teut. **keƀ* or **kíƀ*), of which we have no clear trace; perhaps cf. Du. *kevelen*, to move the jaw continually. Prob. an imitative word, like *quiver*. Perhaps cf. also Norw. and Swed. dial. *kippa*, to snatch, twitch with the limbs, quiver convulsively (Aasen, Rietz). ¶ The resemblance to MDu. *schoeveren*, 'to shiver, or to shake' (Hexham), appears to be accidental.

SHIVER (2), a splinter, small piece, esp. of wood. (E.) The verb *to shiver* means to break into *shivers* or small pieces; the sb. being the older word. A *shiver* is a small piece, or small slice; gen. now applied to wood, but formerly also to bread. ME. *shiuer* (with *u=v*); 'And of your softe breed [bread] nat but a *shiuere*;' Chaucer, C. T. 7422 (D 1840). The pl. *scifren*, shivers, pieces of wood, is in Layamon, 4537; spelt *sciuren* (=*scivren*), id. 27785. β. *Shiver* is the dimin. of *shive*, a slice; 'Easy it is of a cut loaf to steal a *shive*,' Titus Andron. ii. 1. 87. Spelt 'a *sheeve* of bread;' Warner's Albion's England (R.). 'A *shive*, or *shiuer*, Segmen, segmentum;' Baret (1580). This *shive* is the same as the technical E. word *sheave*, a pulley, orig. a slice of a tree, disc of wood. Not in AS. Cf. EFries. *schife*, *schive*, *schíf*, NFries. *skiv*, *skeev*.+Icel. *skifa*, a slice; cf. *skifa*, to cut into slices; Du. *schiif*, Dan. *skive*, Swed. *skifva*, G. *scheibe*, a slice. γ. Teut. base **skeib*; Idg. root **skeip*; whence Gk. σκοῖπ-ος, a potter's disc (Hesychius). The G. *schiefer*, a slate, a splinter, is a related word, from the same base; and note OHG. *scivero*, a shiver. **Der.** *shiver*, verb, ME. *schiueren*, *shiueren*, Chaucer, C. T. 2607 (2605); *shiver-y*, easily falling into fragments. And see **Shift.**

SHOAL (1), a multitude of fishes, a troop, crowd. (E.) Gen.

applied to fishes, but also to people. 'A *shole* of shepeheardes;' Spenser, Shep. Kalendar, May, l. 20. The same word as AS. *scolu*, or *sceolu*, a troop, throng, crowd. [Distinct from AS. *scōl*, school; see **School**.] β. A Germanic word; cf. OSax. *skola*, a troop. Cf. 'a *scoll* of fysh;' Book of St. Alban's, f 7, col. 1. So also Du. *school*, a shoal; and the sailors' phrase 'a *school* of fishes,' given by Halliwell as a Lincolnshire word. So also Irish *sgol*, 'a scull or great quantity of fish.' See **Scull** (3). Teut. type **skulā*, f., prob. 'a division;' from **skul-*, weak grade of **skel-an-*, to divide. **Der.** *shoal*, verb, Chapman, tr. of Homer's Iliad, b. xxi. l. 191.

SHOAL (2), shallow; a sandbank. (E.) Properly an adj. meaning 'shallow;' and, indeed, it is from the same base as *shallow*. Spelt *shole*, adj., Spenser, On Mutability, c. vi. st. 40. Spelt *schold* (an older form), in the Prompt. Parv., which has: '*Schold*, or *schalowe*, *noȝte depe*.' The orig. final *d* is also found in Lowland Sc. *schald*, shallow, also spelt *schawd*. '*Quhar* of the dik the *schawdest* was' = where was the shallowest part of the dike, Barbour's Bruce, ix. 354; where the Edinb. MS. has *shaldest*. Another Sc. form is *shaul*; as '*shaul* water maks mickle din,' Sc. proverb, in Jamieson. The forms *shaul*, *shoal* result from the loss of the final *d*. AS. *sceald*, shallow; found in place-names. 'On *scealdan* ford,' to the shallow ford; Birch, Cart. Sax. ii. 485; whence *Shalford*, Surrey. See **Shallow**. Cf. Pomeran. *scholl*, shallow water. Hence the use of *shoal* as a sb., meaning (1) a shallow place; (2) a sandbank, from its sloping. It has the former sense in Hen. VIII, iii. 2. 437; the latter in Macb. i. 7. 6. Cf. *shold*, a sandbank; Hakluyt, Voy. iii. 547. **Der.** *shoal*, verb, to grow shallow; *shoal-y*, adj., Dryden, tr. of Virgil, Æn. v. 1130; *shoal-i-ness*.

SHOAR, a prop; the same as **Shore** (2).

SHOCK (1), a violent shake, concussion, onset, offence. (E.) We find only ME. *schokken*, verb, to shock, jog, move or throw with violence, Morte Arthure, ed. Brock, 1759, 3816, 3852, 4114, 4235. Not found in AS.; but the form is English. Cf. EFries. *schokken*, to shock, jolt. Also Du. *schok*, a shock, jolt; *schokken*, to jolt, agitate, shake; Icel. *skykkr*, a jolt, only used in dat. pl. *skykkjum*, tremulously; Low G. *schokken*, *schukken* ; OHG. *scoc*, sb. (whence F. *choc*, sb., *choquer*, vb.); Low G. *schocken*, to swing (Lübben), whence G. *schaukel*, a swing. See Du. *schok* in Franck. **Der.** *shock*, sb., *shock-ing*. Doublet, *shog*, q.v.

SHOCK (2), a pile of sheaves of corn. (E.) 'A *shocke* of *corne* in the field;' Baret (1580). ME. *schokke*, Prompt. Parv.; pl. *schockes*, Nominale, ed. Skeat, l. 314. Not found in AS. However, it is found in MDu. *schocke*, 'a shock, a cock, or a heape,' Hexham; whence *schocken*, 'to shock, to cock, or heape up.' So also Swed. *skock*, a crowd, heap, herd. The orig. sense must have been a heap violently pushed or tossed together, from MDu. *schocken*, Du. *schokken*, to jolt, move, agitate; and the word is doubtless allied to **Shock** (1). Similarly *sheaf* is formed from the verb *shove*. β. A *shock* (cf. Dan. dial. *shok*, NFries. *skock*, a set of 6 sheaves) generally means 12 sheaves; but G. *schock*, Dan. *skok*, Swed. *skock* mean threescore or 60.

SHOCK (3), a rough, shaggy-coated dog. (E.) A not uncommon name for a dog. Spelt *shough* in Macb. iii. 1. 94. 'My little *shock*;' Nabbes' Bride, 1640, sig. H (Halliwell). *Shock-headed* is roughheaded, with shaggy or rough hair. Perhaps from *shock*, a heap, pile (above).

SHODDY, a material obtained by tearing into fibres refuse woollen goods. (E.) Prob. so called from being, at first, the waste stuff *shed* or thrown off in spinning wool (Chambers). Cf. Devon *shod*, shed, spilt; ME. *schode*, division of the hair, Chaucer, C. T. 2009 (A 2007); Lowland Sc. *shoad*, a portion of land. See **Shed**. ¶ Another similar material is called *mungo*; perhaps 'mixture,' from AS. *ge-mang*, a crowd, lit. a mixture; allied to *mingle*.

SHOE, a covering for the foot. (E.) ME. *scho*, *shoo*, Chaucer, C. T. 255 (A 253); pl. *shoon*, *schon*, *shon*, Will. of Palerne, 14, Havelok, 860; also *sceos*, O. Eng. Homilies, i. 37, l. 4 from bottom. AS. *sceō*, pl. *sceōs*, Ælfric's Gloss., in Wright's Vocab. i. 26, col. 1. We also find pl. *gescȳ*, Matt. iii. 11; and *gescȳgian*, verb, to shoe, Diplomatarium, p. 616.+Du. *schoen*; Icel. *skōr*, pl. *skūar*, *skōr*; Swed. and Dan. *sko*; Goth. *skōhs*; G. *schuh*, OHG. *scōh*, *scuoch*. The Teut. type is **skōhoz*, m. **Der.** *shoe*, verb, K. Lear, iv. 6. 188; *shod* (for *shoe-d*); *shoe-black*, *-horn*.

SHOG, to shake, jog, move off or away. (E.) 'Will you *shog* off?' Hen. V, ii. 1. 47. 'I *shogge*, as a carte dothe,' i. e. jolt; Palsgrave. 'The boot .. was *schoggid* with wawis;' Wyclif, Matt. xiv. 24. A variant of ME. *schokken*, to shock, jolt. See **Shock** (1).

SHOOT, to dart, let fly, thrust forward. (E.) Palsgrave has *shote*; but ME. has the by-form *shēten*, *schēten* ; spelt *shete*, Chaucer, C. T. 3936 (A 3938). Just as ME. *chesen*, to choose, is from AS. *cēosan*, whilst E. *choose* represents *ceōsan* (with *eō* for *ēo*), so here. The mod. E. *shoot* is from AS. *sceōtan*, but ME. *scheten* is from AS.

scēotan, to shoot, dart, rush; pt. t. *scēat*, pp. *scoten*. (The pp. *scoten* is preserved in *shotten herring*, a herring that has spent its roe, 1 Hen. IV, ii. 4. 143.)+Du. *schieten*, pt. t. *schoot*, pp. *geschoten* ; Icel. *skjōta*, pt. t. *skaut*, pp. *skotinn* ; Dan. *skyde* ; Swed. *skjuta* ; G. *schiessen*. All from a Teut. type **skeutan-*, pt. t. **skaut*, pp. **skutanoz*. Brugmann, i. § 623. **Der.** *shoot*, sb., ME. *schote*, Morte Arthure, 3627; *off-shoot*, q. v.; *shoot-er*, L. L. L. iv. 1. 116; *shoot-ing* ; and see *shot*, *shut*, *shutt-le*, *sheet*, *scot*, *scud*, *skitt-ish*, *skitt-les*.

SHOP, a stall, a place where goods are sold. (E.) ME. *schoppe*, *shoppe*, Chaucer, C. T. 4420 (A 4422). AS. *sceoppa*, a stall or booth; but used to translate L. *gazophilacium*, a treasury, Luke, xxi. 1. Allied to AS. *scypen*, a shed for cattle; 'ne *scypene* his nēatum ne timbreþ' = nor builds sheds for his cattle, Ælfred, tr. of Beda, b. i. c. 1.+Low G. *schup*, a shed; Brem. Wörterb.; G. *schuppen*, a shed, cart-house; OHG. *scopf*, whence OF. *eschoppe*, *eschope*, 'a little low shop,' Cot. **Der.** *shop*, verb; *shop-lift-ing*, stealing from shops, for which see **Lift** (2); *shop-walker*.

SHORE (1), the boundary of land adjoining the sea or a lake, a strand. (E.) ME. *schore*, Allit. Poems, A. 230; Gawain and the Grene Knight, 2161. Not in AS. The orig. sense is 'edge,' or part shorn off; from *scor-en*, pp. of *sceran*, to shear. Cf. *scoren clif* (= shorn cliff), a precipice, Ælfred, tr. of Gregory's Past. Care, c. 33, l. 4; mod. E. *Shorncliff* (Kent). See **Shear**, **Score**. **Der.** *shore*, verb, to set on shore, Wint. Tale, iv. 4. 869.

SHORE (2), **SHOAR**, a prop, support. (E.) ME. *schore*. '*Schore*, under-settynge of a thynge þat wolde falle, Suppositorium;' Prompt. Parv. 'Hit hadde *shories* to shoue hit vp' = it (a tree) had props to keep it up; P. Plowman, C. xix. 20. *Shorier* is a sb. formed from *schorien*, verb, to under-prop, which (by its form) is a denominative verb from the sb. *schore*. Not found in AS.; but an E. word. Cf. EFries. *schōr*, *schore*, a prop. Cf. AS. *scorian*, to project, jut out.+Du. *schoor*, a prop; MDu. *schooren*, to underprop. Cf. also Icel. *skorða*, a stay, prop, esp. under a ship or boat when ashore; whence *skorða*, verb, to under-prop, shore up; Norw. *skorda*, *skora*, a prop (Aasen). **Der.** *shore*, verb.

SHORE (3), a corruption of **Sewer**, q. v.

SHORT, curt, scanty, not long, cut down, insufficient. (L.) ME. *schort*, *short*, Chaucer, C. T. 748 (A 746). AS. *sceort*, short, Grein, ii. 407. Cf. Icel. *skorta*, to be short of, to lack, *skortr*, shortness, want; OHG. *scurz*, short. Teut. type **skurtoz* ; which looks like a derivative (with suffix *-toz*) from the weak grade of Teut. base **sker-*, to shear; see **Shear**. Cf. also Icel. *skarðr*, diminished, cut down. ¶ But as the G. *kurz*, short, is from L. *curt-us*, short, it is usual to explain E. *short* as if from a Late L. type **ex-curtus* ; from the same Idg. √SQER. **Der.** *short-ly*, adv., ME. *shortly*, Chaucer, C. T. 717 (A 715), from AS. *sceortlīce* ; *short-ness*; *short-coming*, *-hand*, *-sight-ed*, *-wind-ed*. Also *short-en*, verb, cf. ME. *shorten*, Chaucer, C. T. 793 (A 791), AS. *sceortian* (Bosworth); where, however, the mod. final *-en* does not really represent the ME. suffix *-en*, but is added by analogy with ME. verbs in *-nen*, such as *waknen*, to waken; this suffix *-en* was at first the mark of an *intransitive* verb, but was afterwards made to take an active force.

SHOT, a missile, aim, act of shooting. (E.) ME. *schot*, *shot*, a missile, Chaucer, C. T. 2546 (A 2544). AS. *ge-sceot* ; 'nim þin *gesceot*' = take thy implements for shooting; Gen. xxvii. 3. Cf. AS. *scot-*, stem of pp. of *scēotan*, to shoot; see **Shoot**.+OFries. *skot*, a shot; Icel. *skot*, a shot, a shooting; Du. *schot*, a shot, shoot; G. *schoss*, *schuss*, a shot. All from Teut. **skut-*, weak grade of **skeutan-*, to shoot. A doublet of *scot*, a contribution; see **Scot-free**. **Der.** *shot*, verb, to load with shot; *shott-ed*.

SHOULDER, the arm-joint, joint in which the arm plays. (E.) ME. *shulder*, *shuldre*, Havelok, 604. AS. *sculder*, *sculdor*, Gen. ix. 23.+Du. *schouder* ; Swed. *skuldra* ; Dan. *skulder* ; G. *schulter*. Perhaps allied to OHG. *skerti*, the shoulder. Root unknown. **Der.** *shoulder*, verb, Rich. III, iii. 7. 128 ; *shoulder-blade*, *-belt*, *-knot*.

SHOUT, a loud outcry. (E.) Spelt *shoute*, *showte* in Palsgrave. ME. *shouten*, Chaucer, Troil. ii. 614. The AS. form **scūtian* does not occur. Perhaps we may compare it with Icel. *skūta*, *skūti*, a taunt. (The Icel. *skūta*, vb., means to jut out.) See **Scout** (2). **Der.** *shout*, sb. *shout-er*.

SHOVE, to push, thrust, drive along. (E.) ME. *shouen*, *schouen* ; 'to *shoue* hit vp' = to prop it up; P. Plowman, C. xix. 20. The usual strong form is *schouuen*, *showuen* (with latter *u* = *v*), Chaucer, C. T. 3910 (A 3912), pt. t. *shoof* (printed *shove* in some editions), id. Parl. of Foules, 154; pp. *shouen* (*shoven*), *shoue*, id. C. T. 11593 (F 1281). AS. *scūfan*, pt. t. *scēaf*, pl. *scufon*, pp. *scofen*, Grein, ii. 412.+Du. *schuiven* ; Icel. *skūfa*, *skȳfa* ; Dan. *skuffe* ; Swed. *skuffa* ; G. *schieben*, pt. t. *schob*, pp. *geschoben* ; OHG. *sciupan* ; Goth. *skiuban*. Teut. type **skeuban-*, or **skūban*, pt. t. **skaub*, pp. **skubanoz*. Allied to Lith. *skubùs*, quick, hasty, industrious; Skt. *kshubh*, to become agitated; the causal form signifies to agitate, shake, impel; hence *kshobha-*, agitation. Thus the primary sense was 'to shake' or 'push.' **Der.** *shove*, sb.; *shove-groat*, a game in which a *groat* (piece of money) was *shoved* or pushed about on a board; also *shov-el*, q. v.; *sheaf*, q. v.

SHOVEL, an instrument with a broad blade and a handle, for shoving and lifting; a sort of spade. (E.) ME. *schouel* (with *u*= *v*). 'With spades and with *schoueles*;' P. Plowman, B. vi. 192. AS. *scofl*; 'Trulla, *scofl*,' Wright's Voc. i. 289. Cf. AS. *scof-*, base of pp. of *scūfan*, to shove; with suffix -*l*.+Du. *schoffel*; Westphal. *schufel*; cf. G. *schaufel*. See **Shove. Der.** *shovel*, verb, Wint. Tale, iv. 4. 469. Also *shovel-er*, a kind of duck, Holland, tr. of Pliny, b. x. c. 40; *shouelar*, Skelton, i. 63; named from its broad beak.

SHOW, SHEW, to exhibit, present to view, teach, guide, prove, explain. (E.) *Shew* is the older spelling; sometimes *shew* is used to denote the verb, and *show* for the sb., but without any difference of pronunciation in mod. English. ME. *schewen*, *shewen*; Chaucer, C. T. 9380 (E 1506); P. Plowman, B. i. 2. AS. *scēawian*, to look, see, behold; the later sense is to make to look, point out. '*Scēawiaδ þā lilian*' = behold the lilies; Luke, xii. 27.+Du. *schouwen*, to inspect, view; Dan. *skue*, to behold; G. *schauen*, to behold, see. Cf. Goth. *us-skaws*, cautious, wakeful. Teut. base **skaw-*; Idg. base **sqou*; cf. Gk. θυο-σκόος, an inspector of an offering; L. *cau-ēre*, to take heed, *cau-tus*, watchful; Gk. κοέω, I observe; Skt. *kav-i-*, wise. From the same root we have *cau-tious*. Brugmann, i. §§ 163, 639. **Der.** *show*, sb., ME. *schewe*, Prompt. Parv.; *show-bill*; *shew-bread*, Exod. xxv. 30; *show-y*, Spectator, no. 434; *show-i-ly*; *show-i-ness*; *shee-n*; *scav-enger*.

SHOWER, a fall of rain. (E.) Orig. a monosyllable, like *flower*. ME. *shour*, *schour*, Chaucer, C. T. 1. AS. *scūr*, Grein, ii. 414.+Du. *schoer*; Icel. *skúr*; Swed. *skur*; Goth. *skūra*, a storm; *skūra windis*, a storm of wind, Mark, iv. 37; G. *schauer*; OHG. *scūr*. Teut. type **skū-roz*, m. Perhaps allied to Lith. *szau-ti*, to shoot. Brugmann, i. § 627 (1). Cf. Lith. *szaurys*, north wind. **Der.** *shower*, verb, Hen. VIII. i. 4. 63; *shower-y*.

SHRAPNEL, a bursting shell charged with bullets. (E.) Named after the inventor, Gen. *Shrapnel*, who died in 1842. See Dict. Eng. Biog. The date of the invention is about 1803; it was used in 1804.

SHRED, a strip, fragment, piece torn or cut off. (E.) The vowel was once long, as in the variant *screed* (Halliwell). ME. *shrēde*, Havelok, 99. AS. *scrēade*, a piece, strip. 'Sceda, *screade*;' also 'Presegmina, præcisiones, *screadan*' (plural); Voc. 164. 6; 151. 20; whence AS. *screadian*, to shred.+MDu. *schroode* (Kilian); whence *schrooder*, 'a lopper or pruner of trees,' Hexham; G. *schrot*, a piece, shred, block; whence *schroten*, to grind, cut, saw. β. All from a Teut. base **skraud*, 2nd grade of **skreud-*; for which see **Shroud**. Allied to L. *scrūta*, broken pieces; see **Scrutiny. Der.** *shred*, verb, ME. *shredden*, Chaucer, C. T. 8013 (E 227), AS. *screadian*; also *scroll*, q. v. **Doublet**, *screed*.

SHREW, a scold, scolding woman. (E.) ME. *shrewe*, *schrewe*, adj., wicked, bad; applied to both sexes. The Wife of Bath said her fifth husband was 'the moste *shrewe*,' the most churlish of all; Chaucer, C. T. 6087 (D 505). Cf. P. Plowman, B. x. 437; Prompt. Parv. Spelt *shrewe*, Polit. Songs, ed. Wright, p. 154, l. 4. AS. *scrēawa*, a shrew-mouse; 'Mus araneus, *scrēawa*;' Voc. 122. 20. Somner explains *scrēawa* as 'a shrew-mouse, which, by biting cattle, so envenoms them that they die,' which is, of course, a fable. But the fable is very old; the L. name *arāneus* means 'poisonous as a spider;' and Aristotle says the bite of the shrew-mouse is dangerous to horses, and causes boils; Hist. Anim. viii. 24. 'In Italy the hardy shrews are venomous in their biting;' Holland, tr. of Pliny, b. viii. c. 58. β. The ME. *schrewen*, to curse, whence E. *be-shrew*, is merely a derivative from the sb., with reference to the language used by a *shrew*. ¶ Wedgwood refers to a curious passage in Higden's Polychronicon, i. 334. The L. text has *mures nocentissimos*, which Trevisa translates by *wel schrewed mys* = very harmful mice. **Der.** *shrew-d*, *be-shrew*; also *shrew-ish*, Com. Errors, iii. 1. 2; *shrew-ish-ly*, -*ness*; also *screw* (2).

SHREWD, malicious, wicked; cunning, acute. (E.) The older sense is malicious, mischievous, scolding or shrew-like, as in Mids. Nt. Dr. iii. 2. 323, &c. ME. *schrewed*, *shrewed*, accursed, depraved, wicked; '*schrewede* folk' = wicked people, Chaucer, tr. of Boethius, bk. i. pr. 4. l. 136; cf. *schrewednesse*, wickedness, id. l. 139. *Schrewed* is lit. 'accursed,' pp. of *schrewen*, to curse, beshrew; Chaucer, C. T. 15432 (B 4616); and the verb is formed from the ME. adj. *schrewe*, evil, malicious; see **Shrew. Der.** *shrewd-ly*, -*ness*.

SHREW-MOUSE, an animal like a mouse; see **Shrew**.

SHRIEK, to screech, cry aloud, scream. (E.) A doublet of *screech*. Spenser has *shriek*, F. Q. vi. 4. 8; but also *scrike*, vi. 4. 18. Baret (1580) has *scriek*. ME. *skriken*, Chaucer, C. T. 15406 (B 4590); where other spellings are *schrichen*, *schriken*; also *shryke*, Polit.

Songs, p. 158. An E. form. See **Screech. Der.** *shriek*, sb., Macb. iv. 3. 168. Also *shrike*, q. v. **Doublet**, *screech*.

SHRIEVALTY, sheriffalty; see **Sheriff**.

SHRIFT, SHRIVE; see **Shrove-tide**.

SHRIKE, the butcher-bird. (E.) Named from its shrill cry. A native form; AS. *scric*, Voc. 52. 13. Cf. Westphal. *schrik*, a shrike; Icel. *skrikja*, a shrieker, also, the shrike or butcher-bird, from *skrikja*, to titter, but properly to shriek, and allied to Icel. *skrækja*, to screech. See **Shriek, Screech**.

SHRILL, acute in sound, piercing, loud. (E.) ME. *shril*, *schril*; pl. *shrille*, Chaucer, C. T. 15401 (B 4585); also *shirle*, in Levins and Palsgrave. The Southern form of Lowland Sc. *skirl*, a shrill cry; *skirl*, to cry shrilly. Cf. AS. *scralletan*, to make a loud outcry (Grein). Also Low G. *schrell*, shrill, Bremen Wörterbuch; prov. G. *schrill*, shrill, *schrillen*, to sound shrill (Flügel). β. The form *skirl* is Scand.; cf. Norw. *skryla*, *skrœla*, to cry shrilly. γ. From Teut. root **skrel*, to cry loudly; AS. *scrall-etan* is from the second grade **skral*. δ. We also find a Teut. str. vb. **skell-an-*, to resound (OHG. *scellan*), pt. t. **skall*; whence not only G. *schallen*, to resound, *schall*, an echo, but also ME. *schil*, *shil*, shrill. We find the adv. *shulle*, shrilly (with various readings *schille*, *schrille*), in P. Plowman, C. vii. 46. The base SKEL is also represented by the Icel. strong verb *skjalla*, *skella*, pt. t. *skall*, pp. *skolinn*. Cf. Lithuan. *skaliti*, to bark, give tongue, said of a hound. **Der.** *shrill-y*, *shrill-ness*.

SHRIMP, a small shell-fish. (E.) ME. *shrimp*, Chaucer, C. T. 13961 (B 3145). Cf. Lowland Sc. *scrimp*, to straiten, pinch; *scrimp*, scanty; '*scrimpit* stature' = dwarfish stature, Burns, To Jas. Smith, l. 14. It is an E. word; but, instead of **scrimpan*, we find AS. *scrimman*, used as equivalent to *scrincan*, to shrink, A. S. Leechdoms, ii. 6, l. 15. *Shrimp* is just a parallel form to *shrink*. β. Rietz makes no doubt that there was an OSwed. *skrimpa*, to contract, a strong verb, as well as a shorter form *skrina*. Traces of OSwed. *skrimpa* occur in Swed. *skrumpen*, Dan. *skrumpen*, shrivelled. Dan. dial. *skrimpe*, a lean cow; Norw. *skrampen*, lean, *skrampa*, *skrumpa*, an old lean animal (Ross). See **Shrink**. γ. Even in English we have clear traces of the same strong verb, since (besides *shrimp*) we find prov. E. *shrammed*, benumbed with cold, prov. E. *shrump*, to shrug, shrink, and *scrump*, to shrivel. So also G. *schrumpel*, a wrinkle, *schrumpfen*, to shrink; MHG. *schrimpfen*, to shrink; Westphal. *schrempen*, to shrivel. Cf. Westphal. *krimpe*, a shrimp.

SHRINE, a place in which sacred things are deposited, an altar. (L.) ME. *schrin*; dat. *schryne*, K. Alisaunder, 4670. AS. *scrin*, the ark (of the covenant), Jos. iii. 8, iv. 7. − L. *scrinium*, a chest, box, case. **Der.** *en-shrine*.

SHRINK, to wither, contract; to recoil. (E.) ME. *shrinken*, to contract, draw together; pt. t. *shronk*, Chaucer, tr. of Boethius, b. i. pr. 1, l. 9; pp. *shrunken*, Gower, C. A. i. 98; bk. i. 1683. AS. *scrincan*, pt. t. *scranc*, pp. *scruncen*, to contract, shrivel up; chiefly in comp. *for-scrincan*, pt. t. *forscranc*, Mark, iv. 6.+MDu. *schrinken*, 'to grow lesser or to shrinke,' Hexham. And cf. Swed. *skrynka*, a wrinkle; *skrynkla*, to wrinkle, to rumple; Norw. *skrökka*, to shrink. Teut. type **skrinkan-*, pt. t. **skrank*, pp. **skrunkanoz*, to shrivel, wrinkle, draw together; parallel to the base appearing in **Shrimp**, q. v., and see **Scraggy**. Further allied to **Shrug**.

SHRIVE, to confess; see **Shrove-tide**.

SHRIVEL, to wrinkle, crumple up. (E.) Shak. has *shrivel up*, Per. ii. 4. 9. It does not seem to appear in Middle English. It is a frequentative form, with the usual suffix -*el*, from an AS. base **scruf-*; as shown by the cognate Swed. dial. *skryvla*, to shrivel up, to wrinkle; and *skryvla*, a wrinkle. Allied to Swed. *skrof*, Swed. dial. and Norw. *skrov*, a carcase; prov. E. *scriff*, *scruff*, to shrink together. Possibly allied to **Shrub** (1). Cf. *scrubby*.

SHROUD, a garment, the dress of the dead. (E.) The word had formerly the general sense of garment, clothing, or covering. ME. *shroud*, *schroud*, P. Plowman, B. prol. 2; *shrud*, Havelok, 303. AS. *scrūd*, a garment, clothing, Grein, ii. 412.+Icel. *skrūð*, the shrouds of a ship, furniture of a church; Norweg. *skrud*, dress, ornament; Dan. and Swed. *skrud*, dress, attire. β. Closely allied to *shred*; and the orig. sense was a shred or piece of cloth or stuff, a sense nearly retained in that of winding-sheet. Chapman has *shroud* in the very sense of shred or scrap of stuff, tr. of Homer's Odyssey, b. vi. l. 274. Moreover, a *shred* is a piece roughly cut off; cf. G. *schrot*, a cut, a piece, *schroten*, to cut. The Teut. base is **skraud*, to cut; the 2nd grade **skraud* appears in **Shred. Der.** *shroud*, verb, AS. *scrȳdan*, Matt. vi. 30; *en-shroud*. Also *shrouds*, s. pl., K. John, v. 7. 53, part of the *rigging* of a vessel.

SHROVE-TIDE, SHROVE-TUESDAY, a time or day (Tuesday) on which shrift or confession was formerly made. (L. and E.) *Shrove-tide* is the tide or season for shrift; *Shrove-Tuesday* is the day preceding Ash Wednesday or the first day of Lent. *Shrove* is here used as a sb., conformed to *shrove*, the pt. t. of the verb *to shrive*; except in the two above compounds, the sb. invariably takes the form *shrift*. β. The verb *to shrive* (pt. t. *shrove*, pp. *shriven*) is ME. *schriven*, *shriven*, of which we find the pt. t. *shrof*, *shroof* in P. Plowman, B. iii. 44 (footnote), and the pp. *shriuen* in Chaucer, C. T. 7677 (D 2095). AS. *scrífan*, to shrive, to impose a penance or compensation, to judge; pt. t. *scráf*, pp. *scrifen*; Grein, ii. 411. Teut. type **skreiban-*, pt. t. **skraib*, pp. **skribanoz*. γ. But although it thus appears as a strong verb, it does not appear to be a true Teut. word. It was rather borrowed (at a very early period) from L. *scribere*, to write, to draw up a law (hence, prescribe); whence also G. *schreiben* (also conjugated as a strong verb), to write. See **Scribe.** B. The sb. *shrift* is ME. *shrift* (dat. *shrifte*), P. Plowman, C. xvii. 30; AS. *scrift*, confession, Laws of Æthelred, pt. v. § 22, pt. vi. § 27, in Thorpe, Anc. Laws, i. 310, 322; and just as the AS. verb *scrífan* is due to L. *scribere*, so AS. *scrift* may be due to the L. pp. *scriptus*. The Icel. *skript* or *skrift*, Swed. *skrift*, Dan. *skrifte*, shrift, are all borrowed from AS.

SHRUB (1), a low dwarf tree. (E.) ME. *schrob*, *schrub*, P. Plowman, C. i. 2. AS. *scrybb*, a shrub; see Bosworth-Toller, and Mr. Stevenson's remarks in Phil. Soc. Trans. 1895-8, p. 536. (Cf. E. *shut*, from AS. *scyttan*.) We also have the place-name *Wormwood-scrubbs*, near London.+Norweg. *skrubba*, the dwarf cornel (Aasen). Dan. dial. *skrub*, brushwood; MDan. *skrubbe*, a thicket (Kalkar). β. Cf. also prov. E. *shruff*, light rubbish wood, *scroff*, refuse of wood. Possibly related to **Shrivel.** Der. *shrubb-y*; *shrubb-er-y*, a coined word, by the analogy of *vin-er-y*, *pin-er-y*, and the like. Also *scrub*, q.v.

SHRUB (2), a drink made of lemon-juice, spirit, sugar, and water. (Arab.) Chiefly made with rum. In Johnson's Dict.—Arab. *shirb*, *shurb*, a drink, a beverage.—Arab. root *shariba*, he drank; Rich. Dict. p. 887. **Doublet,** *syrup.* And see *sherbet*.

SHRUG, to draw up, contract. (Scand.) In Temp. i. 2. 367; Cor. i. 9. 4. Generally used of drawing up the shoulders, but the true sense is to shrink. 'The touch of the cold water made a pretty kinde of *shrugging* come over her body;' Sidney's Arcadia, b. ii. ed. 1638, p. 138. '*Shruggyn*, Frigulo;' Prompt. Parv. An adaptation (with *sh* for *sk*) from the Scand., as shown by *gg*<*kk*<*nk*. Cf. Dan. *skrugge*, *skrukke*, to stoop; *skruk-rygget*, humpbacked; Swed. dial. *skrukka*, *skruga*, to huddle oneself up, to sit in a crouching position, allied to *skrinka*, to shrink (Rietz); see **Shrink.** Cf. Icel. *skrukka*, an old shrimp; Norw. *skrukken*, shrunken.

SHUDDER, to tremble with fear or horror. (OLow G.) 'Alas! they make me *shoder*;' Skelton, Colin Clout, 68. ME. *shoderen*, *schuderen*; pt. t. *schoderide*, Morte Arthure, 2106; pres. part. *schud-rinde*, Seint Margaret, ed. Cockayne, p. 15, l. 12. Not found in AS. It is a frequentative verb, formed with the usual suffix *-er* from the Teut. base **skud-*, to shake, appearing in OSaxon *skuddian.* '*Skuddiat* it fan iuwun skóhun'=shake it [the dust] from your shoes; Heliand, 1948. MDu. *schudden*, 'to shake or to tremble,' Hexham; he also gives '*schudden een boom*, to shake a tree, *schudden van koude*, to quake for colde; *schudden het hooft*, to shake or nod ones head; *schudderen*, to laugh with an open throate that his head shakes;' Dan. dial. *skuddre*, to shake (one) violently; EFries. *schüdden*, to shake, *schüddern*, to tremble, shudder.+OHG. *scuttan*, G. *schütten*, to shoot corn, pour, shed, discharge; *schüttern*, to shake, tremble, quake. The G. *schaudern* is borrowed from Low G. *schuddern.* Der. *shudder*, sb.

SHUFFLE, to push about, practise shifts. (Scand.) 'When we have *shuffled off* [pushed or shoved aside] this mortal coil;' Hamlet, iii. 1. 67. Merely a doublet of **Scuffle,** and the frequenta-tive of *shove*; but of Scand., not E. origin, as shown by the double *f*. The *sh* is modified from Scand. *sk.* Cf. EFries. *schuffeln*, to shuffle along, from *schufen*, to shove, push. The sense is 'to keep pushing about,' as in '*shuffle* the cards.' [It seems to have taken up some-thing of the sense of *shiftiness*, with which it has no etymological connexion.] See **Scuffle, Shove.** Der. *shuffle*, sb.; *shuffl-er.*

SHUN, to avoid, keep clear of, neglect. (E.) ME. *shunien*, *shonien*, P. Plowman, B. prol. 174. AS. *scunian*, not common except in the comp. *on-scunian*, to detest, refuse, reject, Gen. xxxix. 10. In Ps. lxix. 2, ed. Spelman, the L. *revereantur* is translated by *anðracian*, with the various readings *sconnyn*, *forwandian*, and *scunian*. The pp. *gescunned* is in Diplomatarium Ævi Saxonici, ed. Thorpe, p. 318, last line. Cf. prov. E. *scun*, to shun; *scunner*, to loathe; see **Scoundrel.** Der. *shun-less*, Cor. ii. 2. 116; *schoon-er*; *scoundrel.*

SHUNT, to turn off upon a side-rail. (E.) As a word used on railways, it was borrowed from prov. E. *shunt*, to turn aside. But the word itself is old. ME. *shunten*, to start aside, Gawayn and the Grene Knight, 1902; *schounten*, *schownten*, *schonten*, *schunten*, Morte Arthur, 736, 1055, 1324, 1759, 2106, 2428, 3715, 3816, 3842; *shunt*, Destruction of Troy, 600, 729, 10377, 10998. 'If at ʒe

shap ʒow to *shount*'=if ye intend to escape; Wars of Alexander, 2143; and see Ancren Riwle, p. 242, note *d*. β. *Shunten* seems to be a modification of *shunden*, being easier to pronounce quickly. The orig. sense is to speed, hasten, flee, escape. AS. *scyndan*, to hasten (Beowulf, 2570), also to urge, incite.+Icel. *skunda*, to speed. It seems to be a nasalised form of **Scud.**

SHUT, to fasten a door, close. (E.) ME. *shutten*, *shitten.* 'To close and to *shutte*;' P. Plowman, B. prol. 105. 'The ʒatis weren *schit*'=the gates were shut; Wyclif, John, xx. 19. AS. *scyttan*, to shut; 'sero, ic *scytte* sum loc oððe hæpsige,' i.e. I shut a lock or hasp it; Ælfric's Grammar, ed. Zupitza, p. 220. To shut a door was to fasten it with a bolt or sliding bar, called a *shuttle* or *shittle* (see **Shuttle,** which took its name from being *shot* across. We still say 'to *shoot* a bolt.' The AS. *scyttan* stands for **scut-ian* (by the usual change from *u* to *y*); derived from Teut. **skut-*, weak grade of **skeutan-*, to shoot. See **Shoot.**+Du. *schutten*, to shut in, lock up; *schut*, a fence, screen, partition, MDu. *schut*, an arrow, dart (Hexham), from *schieten*, to shoot; G. *schützen*, to protect, guard, shut off water; *schutz*, a guard, sluice, flood-gate, OHG. *scuz*, a quick movement, from *sciessen*, OHG. *sciozan*, to shoot. Der. *shutt-er*; *shutt-le*, q. v.

SHUTTLE, an instrument for shooting the thread of the woof between the threads of the warp in weaving. (E.) In Job, vii. 6. So called from its being *shot* between the threads. 'An honest weaver . . As e'er *shot shuttle*;' Beaum. and Fletcher, The Coxcomb, Act v. sc. 1. Also spelt *shittle*; in Palsgrave, '*shyttell* for a wevar.' ME. *schitel*; spelt *scytyl*, Prompt. Parv. p. 447, also *schetyl*, id. p. 470, l. 2. The same word as ME. *schitel*, a bolt of a door, similarly named from its being *shot* across. '*Schyttyl*, of sperynge [sparring, barring], Pessulum;' Prompt. Parv. The AS. form was *scyttel* (also *scytel*), in the sense of bar, bolt; also found in the longer form *scyttels*, pl. *scyttelsas*. See Toller. β. The word *scyttel* or *scytel* (for **skut-il-*) is from Teut. **skut-*, weak grade of **skeut-an*, AS. *sceótan*, to shoot; see **Shut, Shoot.**+Dan. *skytte*, *skyttel*, a shuttle; Swed. dial. *skyttel*, *sköttel*; cf. Du. *schiet-spoel*, a shuttle, lit. 'shoot-spool,' Swed. *skottspole*, a shuttle, 'shoot-spool.' Der. *shuttle-cock*, q. v.

SHUTTLE-COCK, a piece of wood or cork stuck with feathers, used as a plaything. (E.) Spelt *shyttelcocke* in Palsgrave; *shuttelcock*, Spenser, Mother Hubbard's Tale, 804. Prob. called *cock* from being stuck with feathers and flying through the air. [Not *shuttle-cork*, as Todd fancies, contrary to evidence and pro-bability; for they were most likely at first made of wood, and struck with a wooden battledore. See Strutt, Sports and Pastimes, bk. iv. ch. 1. § 22.] Called *shuttle* from being *shot* backwards and forwards like a weaver's shuttle. '*Schytle*, chyldys game, Sagitella;' Prompt. Parv. See **Shuttle;** and see **Skittles.**

SHY, timid, cautious, suspicious. (Scand.) In Shak. Meas. iii. 2. 138; v. 54. ME. *skyg*, scrupulous, careful to shun (evil), Allit. Poems, B. 21. It is rather a Scand. than an E. word, with *sh* for *sk*; we also find ME. *schey*, *skey*, shy (said of a horse), Prompt. Parv. p. 444; spelt *scheouh* (also of a horse), Ancren Riwle, p. 242, l. 9; answering to the rare AS. *sceóh*, timid, Grein, ii. 405.—Dan. *sky*, shy, skittish; Swed. *skygg*, skittish, starting, shy, coy; Swed. dial. *sky*, the same (Rietz).+EFries. *schöi*; Du. *schuw*; G. *scheu*, shy, timid, MHG. *schiech*. Teut. types **skeuh-joz*, **skeuh-oz*. β. Hence OHG. *sciuhan* to frighten, or (intransitively) to fear, shy at, whence (through the French) we have E. *eschew.* Der. *shy-ly*, *shy-ness*; *shy*, verb (cf. Swed. *sky*, to shun); and see *eschew*, *skew*.

SI—SY

SIAMANG, a large ape. (Malay.) Malay *siāmang.*

SIB, related. (E.) In Spenser, F. Q. iii. 3. 26. See further under **Gossip.** Der. *gos-sip.*

SIBILANT, making a hissing sound. (L.) We call *s* and *z* 'sibilant' letters. Bacon has 'sibilation or hissing sound;' Nat. Hist. § 176.—L. *sibilant-*, stem of pres. part. of *sibilāre*, to hiss.—L. *sibilus*, adj. hissing; formed from a base **sib-*, which is probably imitative of a whistling sound. Der. *sibil-at-ion.*

SIBYL, a pagan prophetess. (L.—Gk.) Shak. has both *Sibyl* and *Sybilla*; Oth. iii. 4. 70; Merch. Ven. i. 2. 116. Cotgrave has: '*Sybille*, Sybill, one of the 10 Sybillæ, a prophetesse.' Trevisa translates L. *Sibylla* by *Sibil*; ii. 399. The word was rather borrowed directly from L. than through the F., being known from Virgil.—L. *Sibylla*, a Sibyl; Virgil, Æn. vi. 10.—Gk. Σίβυλλα, a Sibyl. Origin uncertain; see Max Müller, Lectures, 8th ed. i. 109. Postgate compares it with L. *per-sibus*, very wise (Festus) and L. *sap-ere*, to be wise; so that σίβ-υλλα would mean 'wise woman.' **Der.** *sibyll-ine*, adj.; from L. *Sibyllīnus*.

SICCA, in phr. *sicca rupee*, newly coined rupee. (Hind.—Pers.—Arab.) Hind. *sikka*, a die for coining.—Pers. *sikka(h)*, the same.—Arab. *sikka(h)*, the same. Rich. Dict. p. 839. See **Sequin**.

SICK, affected with disease, ill, inclined to vomit. (E.) ME. *sik*, *sek*; pl. *seke*, Chaucer, C. T. 18. AS. *sēoc*; John, xi. 1.+Du. *ziek*; Icel. *sjúkr*; Dan. *syg*; Swed. *sjuk*; G. *siech*; Goth. *siuks*. β. All from a Teut. type **seukoz*, ill; from the Teut. base **seuk-*, to be sick or ill, appearing in the Goth. strong verb *siukan*, to be ill, pt. t. *sauk*, pp. *sukans*. Fick, iii. 325. **Der.** *sick-ness*, AS. *sēocnes*, Matt. viii. 28; *sick-en*, verb (intrans.), Macb. iv. 3. 173, (trans.) Hen. VIII, i. 1. 82; *sick-ish*, *-ly*, *-ness*; *sick-ly*, adj., ME. *sekly*, Will. of Palerne, 1505; *sick-li-ness*, Rich. II, ii. 1. 142.

SICKER, SIKER, certain, secure. (L.) *Siker* is a well-known Lowland Sc. word. ME. *siker*, Chaucer, C. T. 11451 (F 1139); Layamon, 15092. AS. *sicor*. Not a Teut. word, but borrowed from a Late L. *sēcurus*, for L. *sēcūrus*; see **Secure**. The OFries. *siker*, *sikur*, Du. *zeker*, OHG. *sichur*), Swed. *säker*, Dan. *sikker*, W. *sicr*, are all borrowed from the Latin, which accounts for their strong likeness in form to one another. **Doublets**, *secure*, *sure*.

SICKLE, a hooked instrument for cutting grain. (L.) ME. *sikil*, Wyclif, Mark, iv. 29. AS. *sicol*, Mark, iv. 29.—L. *secula*, a sickle (White); formed, with suffix *-u-lā* of the agent, from *sec-āre*, to cut; see **Secant**. ¶ The G. *sichel* is also from Latin; the native words from the same root are *saw* (1), *scythe*, and *side*.

SIDE, the edge or border of a thing, region, part, party. (E.) ME. *side*, *syde*, P. Plowman, B. prol. 8; Chaucer, C. T. 560 (A 558). AS. *sīde*, John, xix. 34, xx. 20.+Du. *zijde*; Icel. *sīða*; Dan. *side*; Swed. *sida*; G. *seite*, OHG. *sīta*. Teut. type **sidōn-*, f. It is probable that the orig. sense was 'that which is extended,' as it certainly seems to be closely connected with AS. *sīd*, long, wide, spacious, ME. *siid*, spelt *syyd* in the Prompt. Parv., but now obsolete; Icel. *siðr*, long, hanging down. **Der.** *side-board*, Milton, P. R. ii. 350; *side-box*, *one-sid-ed*, *many-sid-ed*, *side-saddle*, *side-ways*, *side-wise*, *sid-ing*. Also *side*, verb, Cor. i. 1. 197, iv. 2. 2; *side-ling*, *side-long*, adv., Milton, P. L. vi. 197, ME. *sideling*, *sidlinges*, spelt *sydlyngs*, Morte Arthur, 1039, where the suffix *-ling* or *-long* is adverbial, as explained under **Headlong**. Hence *sidelong*, adj. Also *a-side*, q. v., *beside*, q. v. Also *side-s-men*, officers chosen to assist a churchwarden, Blount, Nomolexicon, where a ridiculous explanation from *synodsmen* (!) is attempted, quite unnecessarily; see Notes and Queries, 5 S. xi. 504. They were also called *side-men* or *quest-men*; Halliwell. Cf. L. *assessor*, one who sits beside another.

SIDEREAL, starry, relating to the stars. (L.) Milton has *sideral*, P. L. x. 693. Phillips, ed. 1706, has *sidereal*, *siderean*. *Sideral* is from L. *sīderālis*, and is a correct form; *sidere-al* is coined from L. *sidere-us*, adj. All from *sīder-*, for **sīdes-*, stem of *sīdus*, a constellation, also, a star. **Der.** (from L. *sīdus*) *con-sider*.

SIEGE, a sitting down, with an army, before a fortified place, in order to take it. (F.—L.) The lit. sense is merely 'seat;' see Trench, Select Glossary. We find it in this sense in Shak. Meas. iv. 2. 101; Spenser, F. Q. ii. 2. 39. ME. *sege*, (1) a seat, Wyclif, Matt. xxv. 31; (2) a siege, Barbour's Bruce, iv. 45, ix. 332. In Ancren Riwle, p. 238, l. 1, *sege* means 'a throne.'—AF. *sege*, Gaimar, 3110, also *siege*; OF. *siege*, masc., a seat, throne; mod. F. *siège*. Cf. Ital. *sedia*, fem., *seggio*, masc., a chair, seat. Not *immediately* from L. *sedes*, but from a verb answering to a L. type **sedicāre*; we find also Late L. *assedium*, a siege, which (like L. *obsidium*, a siege) is from L. *sedēre*, to sit, cognate with E. **Sit**, q. v. **Der.** *be-siege*.

SIENNA, a pigment used in painting. (Ital.) *Raw sienna* and *burnt sienna* are the names of two pigments, made from earth, and properly from earth of *Sienna*, which is the name of a place in Tuscany, due S. of Florence.

SIERRA, a chain of hills. (Span.—L.) Span. *sierra*, a saw, ridge of hills.—L. *serra*, a saw. See **Serrated**.

SIESTA, orig. a noon-day nap. (Span.—L.) 'What, sister, at your *siesta* already?' Elvira, A. i; Dodsley's Old Plays, ed. Hazlitt, xv. 22. Now usually applied to a nap in the afternoon.—Span. *siesta*, 'the hottest part of the day, the time for taking a nap after dinner, generally from 1 to 3 o'clock;' Neuman.—L. *sexta*, i. e. *sexta hora*, sixth hour, noon; reckoning from 6 A. M.; so that the orig. sense was 'noonday nap.' *Sexta* is fem. of L. *sextus*, sixth.—L. *sex*, six; see **Six**. For a shifting of time in the reverse direction, see **Noon**.

SIEVE, a strainer for separating coarse particles from fine ones. (E.) ME. *sive*, Chaucer, C. T. 16408 (G 940); *her-seve*, a hair-sieve, Liber Cure Cocorum, ed. Morris, p. 7. AS. *sife*; 'Cribra, vel cribellum, *sife*,' Voc. 330. 32; spelt *sibi* in the 8th cent., id. 16. 3.+Du. *zeef*; G. *sieb*, MHG. *sip*. Teut. types **siðes*, **siðos*, n. Cf. Lith.

sijoti, to sift. Perhaps allied to AS. *sīhan*, *sēon*, G. *seihen*, to filter. See Kluge. **Der.** *sif-t*, q. v.

SIFT, to separate particles as with a sieve. (E.) ME. *siften*, Chaucer, C. T. 16409 (G 941); *sive* (=sieve) being in the line above. AS. *siftan*, *syftan*, Exod. xii. 34.—AS. *sif-e*, a sieve.+Du. *ziften*, to sift, *zift*, a sieve; from *zeef*, a sieve. See **Sieve**. β. We also find Dan. *sigte*, to sift, *sigte*, sb., a sieve or riddle; Swed. *sikta*, to sift, *sikt*, a sieve; Icel. *sikta*, *sigta*, to sift; all from G. *sichten*, to sift; which again is from Du. *ziften*.

SIGH, to inhale and respire with a long deep breadth. (E.) ME. *sighen*, *siȝen*, *siken*; in P. Plowman, B. xviii. 263, we have *syked*, with various readings *siȝede*, *siȝhede*; also *syhede*, *siȝte*, id. C. xxi. 276; *sighte*, Chaucer, Troil. iii. 1080. The ME. *sīken* thus made *sigh-te* as one form of the pt. t., whence a new infin. *sigh-en* was evolved by back-formation. From AS. *sīcan*, to sigh; Ælfred, tr. of Orosius, ii. 8; ed. Sweet, p. 92, l. 35. It is a strong verb; pt. t. *sāc*, pp. *sicen*; with a frequentative form *siccettan*, to sigh, sob. β. Prob. of imitative origin; cf. Swed. *sucka*, Dan. *sukke*, to sigh, groan. **Der.** *sigh*, sb., ME. *sike*, Chaucer, C. T. 11176 (F 864).

SIGH-CLOUT; see Notes on E. Etym., p. 271.

SIGHT, act of seeing, that which is seen, view, spectacle. (E.) ME. *sight*, Chaucer, C. T. 4982 (B 562). AS. *siht*, or rather *ge-siht*, Ælfred, tr. of Boethius, b. v. pr. 4; cap. xli. § 4. But it is almost always spelt *gesihð*, *gesiehð*, *gesyhð*; Grein, i. 454. From Teut. type **seh-iþā*, fem. (Sievers); allied to *sēon* (Goth. *saihwan*, for **sehwan*), to see; see **See**.+Du. *gezigt*; Dan. *sigte*; Swed. *sigt*; G. *sicht*; OHG. *siht*. **Der.** *sight*, verb; *sight-ed*, Wint. Tale, i. 2. 388; *sight-hole*, 1 Hen. IV, IV, i. 71; *sight-less*, Macb. i. 5. 50; *sight-ly*, K. John, ii. 143; *sight-li-ness*.

SIGN, a mark, proof, token, omen, notice. (F.—L.) ME. *signe*, Chaucer, C. T. 10365 (F 51); Ancren Riwle, p. 70, l. 1.—OF. *signe*, 'a signe, mark;' Cot.—L. *signum*, a mark, token. Brugmann, i. § 762 (3). **Der.** *sign*, verb, K. John, iv. 2. 222; *sign-board*, *sign-manual*, *sign-post*. Also *sign-at-ure*, from F. *signature*, 'a signature,' Cot.; from L. *signātūra*, from *signāre*, to sign, from *signum*. And see *sign-al*, *sign-et*, *sign-i-fy*, *re-sign*.

SIGNAL, a token, sign for giving notice. (F.—L.) ME. *signal*, Gower, C. A. iii. 57; bk. vi. 1668.—F. *signal*, 'a signall;' Cot.—Late L. *signāle*, neut. of L. *signālis*, belonging to a sign.—L. *signum*, a sign; see **Sign**. **Der.** *signal*, verb; *signal-ly*, *signal-ise*.

SIGNET, a seal, privy-seal. (F.—L.) In Hamlet, v. 2. 49; and in Palsgrave. ME. *signett*, Mandeville, Trav. c. viii. p. 82.—F. *signet*, 'a signet, seal, stamp;' Cot. Dimin. of F. *signe*; see **Sign**.

SIGNIFY, to indicate, mean. (F.—L.) ME. *signifien*; spelt *signefye*, Rob. of Glouc. p. 345, l. 7075. And see O. Eng. Miscellany, ed. Morris, p. 28, ll. 3, 8, 11, 12.—F. *signifier*, 'to signifie, betoken;' Cot.—L. *significāre*, to show by signs.—L. *signi-*, for *signum*, a sign; and *-fic-*, for *facere*, to make; see **Sign** and **Fact**. **Der.** *signific-ant*, from L. *significant-*, stem of pres. part. of *significāre*; hence *significant*, sb., 1 Hen. VI, ii. 4. 26; *significance*, from F. *significance* (Cot.), a false form which supplanted the true OF. *signifiance* (Cot.), whence ME. *signefiance*, O. Eng. Miscellany, ed. Morris, p. 28, l. 20, all from L. *significantia*; *significat-ion*, ME. *significacioun*, Chaucer, C. T. 14985 (B 4169), from F. *signification* < L. acc. *significātiōnem*; *signific-at-ive*, from L. *significātiuus*.

SIGNOR, SIGNIOR, sir. (Ital.—L.) Spelt *signior*, Two Gent. iii. 1. 279; &c.—Ital. *signore*, sir, a lord.—L. *seniōrem*, acc. of *senior*, an elder; see **Senior**. ¶ Cf. ME. *seignour*, King Alisaunder, 1458; from French. Span. *señor*, fem. *señora*. **Der.** *signor-a*, from Ital. *signora*, a lady, fem. of *signore*. **Doublets**, *sir*, *sire*, *señor*, *senior*, *seignior*.

SILENCE, stillness, muteness. (F.—L.) In early use. ME. *silence*, Ancren Riwle, p. 22, l. 6.—F. *silence*, 'silence,' Cot.—L. *silentium*, silence, a being silent.—L. *silent-*, stem of pres. part. of *silēre*, to be still.+Goth. *silan*, only in the compound *ana-silan*, to become silent, Mark, iv. 39. Thus the base is SIL. **Der.** *silent* (in later use, though etymologically a more orig. word), L. L. L. ii. 24, from L. *silent-*, stem of pres. part. of *silēre*; *silent-ly*.

SILEX, flint, quartz. (L.) Merely L. *silex*, flint (stem *silic-*). Brugmann, i. § 980. **Der.** *silic-a*, *silic-i-ous*, coined from the stem.

SILHOUETTE, a shadow-outline or profile filled in with a dark colour. (F.) This cheap and meagre form of portrait, orig. made by tracing the outline of a shadow thrown on to a sheet of paper, was named, in derision, after Etienne de *Silhouette*, minister of finance in 1759, who introduced several reforms which were considered unduly parsimonious. See Trench, Eng. Past and Present; Sismondi, Histoire des Français, tom. xix. pp. 94, 95.

SILK, the delicate, soft thread produced by certain caterpillars, and the stuff woven from it. (L.—Gk.—Chinese.) ME. *silk*, Chaucer, C. T. 10927 (F 613). AS. *seolc* (for **siluc*, as *meolc* for **miluc*), silk. 'Bombix, *seolc-wyrm*; Sericum, *seolc*;' Wright's Vocab. i. 40, col. 1.

Cf. Icel. *silki*, Swed. *silke*, Dan. *silke*; all of which, like AS. *seolc*, are adaptations of L. *sēricum*, silk, by the common change of *r* into *l*. β. L. *sēricum* is the neut. of *Sēricus*, of or belonging to the *Sēres*. — Gk. Σῆρες, pl., the name of the people from whom the ancients first obtained silk; gen. supposed to be the Chinese. Professor Douglas writes: 'The L. *Sēres* and *Sēricum* are probably derived from the Chinese word for *silk*, which is variously pronounced *se* (English *e*), *sei, sai, sat, sz*', &c.; see Williams, Chin. Dict. p. 835.' Cf. Max Müller, Lectures, ii. 182. γ. Kluge derives Icel. *silki* from Slavonic; but Miklosich derives OSlav. *shelkŭ*, Russ. *shelk'*, from the Scandinavian. The true source is L. *sēricum*, whence also OIrish *sīric*, silk. Der. *silk-mercer*, *silk-weaver*; *silk-worm*, AS. *seolc-wyrm*, as above; *silk-en*, AS. *seolcen*, Voc. 151. 9; *silk-y*, *silk-i-ness*. Also *serge*, q. v.

SILL, the timber or stone at the foot of a door or window. (E.) The true sense seems to be 'base' or 'basis;' sometimes 'floor.' ME. *sille*, *sylle*. '*Sylle* of an howse, *Silla*, *soliva*;' Prompt. Parv. Spelt *selle*, Chaucer, C. T. 3820 (A 3822), which is a Kentish form. AS. *syll*, a base, support. 'Basis, *syl*;' Voc. 8. 27; in a later gloss: 'Bassis, *sulle*;' Voc. 552. 12.+Icel. *syll*, *svill*, a sill, door-sill; Swed. *syll*; Swed. dial. *svill* (Rietz); Dan. *syld*, the base of a frame-work building; G. *schwelle*, OHG. *swelli*, a sill, threshold, beam. Cf. Goth. *gasuljan*, to found, lay a foundation for, Matt. vii. 25; Luke, vi. 48. β. The OHG. *swelli* is from a Teut. base *swal*, but AS. *syll* from a weak grade *swul*; implying a strong verb *swel-an-*, to found (?), pt. t. *swal*, pp. *swulanoz*. AS. *syll* represents *swul-jā*, fem. γ. The connexion with L. *solea*, the sole of the foot, is doubtful. ¶ Not to be confused with AS. *sȳl*, a pillar, column, in Ælfred, tr. of Orosius, b. i. c. 1. § 4; this is a different word, with a different sense, though possibly connected; it answers to G. *säule*, a pillar. Der. *ground-sill*, q. v.

SILLABUB, SYLLABUB, a mixture of wine with milk and sugar. (E.) Spelt *sillibub* in Minsheu, ed. 1627, who derives it from *swilling bubbles*. But the form is corrupt, a better form being *sillibouk*. '*Sillibouke* or *sillibub*, Laict aigre;' Sherwood, index to Cotgrave. Cotgrave gives: 'Laict aigre, whay; also, a *sillibub* or *merribowke*.' Halliwell gives '*sillybauk*, a sillabub,' as a Lincolnshire word. It is obvious that a corruption from *bouk* to *bub* is easy, whereas a change from *bub* to *bouk* is unlikely. We may therefore assume *sillibouk* as the older form, at the same time noting that another name for it is *merribouk*. Cf. '*merrybauks*, a cold posset, *Derbyshire*;' Halliwell. β. The prov. E. *bouk* is a well-known word for 'belly;' Mr. Peacock notes *bowk* as the Lincolnshire form; so that *merri-bouk* = 'merry belly,' and perhaps *silli-bouk* = 'happy belly,' from an old sense of *silly* (below). It is evidently a jocose name.

SILLY, simple, harmless, foolish. (E.) The word has much changed its meaning. It meant 'timely;' then lucky, happy, blessed, innocent, simple, foolish. ME. *sely*, Chaucer, C. T. 3601, 4088 (A 4090), 5952 (D 370); Havelok, 477; P. Plowman's Crede, 442; and see *sely*, *seely*, *seilye* in Gloss. to Spec. of English, ed. Skeat. AS. *sǣlig*, more usually *gesǣlig* (the prefix *ge-* making no difference), happy, prosperous, fortunate; see Sweet, A. S. Reader. Formed with the common adj. suffix *-ig* (E. *-y*) from AS. *sǣl*, a time, season, occasion, happiness (very common); Grein, ii. 395.+Du. *zalig*, blessed; Icel. *sǣll*, blest, happy; *sǣla*, bliss; Swed. *säll*, blest, happy; G. *selig*, OHG. *sālik*, good, excellent, blest, happy; Goth. *sēls*, good, kind. β. All from a Teut. base *sǣl-*; of unknown origin. Der. *silli-ly*, *-ness*.

SILO, a pit for storing grain or fodder. (Span. — L. — Gk.) Span. *silo*, 'a granier to lay up corne in;' Minsheu (1623). — L. *sīrum*, acc. of *sīrus*. — Gk. σῑρός, a pit for keeping corn in. Der. *en-sil-age*.

SILT, sediment, sand left by water that has overflowed. (Scand.) ME. *silte*, badly spelt *cilte*. 'Cilte, soonde [sand], *Glarea*;' Prompt. Parv. p. 77. It can hardly be other than the MSwed. *sylta*, mud, also a marshy place (Ihre); Dan. *sylt*, a salt marsh (Larsen); Dan. dial. *sylt*, a stretch of low coast-land, over which the sea sometimes flows; Norw. *sylta*, the same (Ross). Cf. Low G. *sulte*, a brine-pit; G. *sülze*, brine, also brine-pit. All from a Teut. base *sult-*, which is a weakened form of *salt-*, i. e. salt. See Kluge. So also we find Du. *zilt*, adj. salt, related to Du. *zout*, salt; and AS. *syltan*, to salt, from *sealt*, salt. Cf. prov. E. *silt*, a salting-tub. It must have referred orig. to salt deposited as a sediment by sea-water in brine-pits or very shallow pools.

SILVAN, SYLVAN, pertaining to woods. (L.) 'All *sylvan* offsprings round;' Chapman, tr. of Homer, Od. xix. 599. [The spelling with *y* is false, and due to the habit of spelling L. *silva* with *y*, in order to *derive* it from Gk. ὕλη, a wood, with which it is (at most) only cognate.] — L. *siluānus*, belonging to a wood, chiefly used of the wood-god Silvanus. — L. *silua*, a wood.+Gk. ὕλη, a wood (?). The relationship of the L. and Gk. words is doubted by some, and the root is uncertain; see Brugmann, i. § 102 (1), note. Der. (from L. *silua*) *savage*, q. v.

SILVER, a well-known white metal. (E.) ME. *siluer*, Chaucer, C. T. 16707 (G 1239). OMerc. *sylfur*, Matt. x. 9 (Rushworth MS.); AS. *seolfor*; early form *siolofr*.+Du. *zilver*; Icel. *silfr*; Dan. *sølv*; Swed. *silfver*; G. *silber*; Goth. *silubr*.+Russ. *serebro*. The origin is wholly unknown; Uhlenbeck thinks the Teut. forms are from Slavonic. Miklosich (p. 336) gives the Slav. type as *sĭrebro*, with varying forms in all the Slav. languages. Der. *silver*, verb; *silver-ing*; *silver-ling*, a small piece of silver, with double dimin. *-l-ing* (as in *duck-l-ing*), Isaiah, vii. 23, also in Tyndale's version of Acts, xix. 19, and Coverdale's of Judges, ix. 4, xvi. 5, the AS. form being *sylfring*, Gen. xlv. 22; *silver-smith*; *silver-y*. Also *silver-n*, adj., in some MSS. of Wyclif, Acts, xix. 24, AS. *sylfren*, Gen. xliv. 2. ¶ A possible guess is that which derives silver from Gk. *Σαλύβη, old form of Ἀλύβη, a town on the S. coast of the Black Sea, which, according to Homer (Iliad, ii. 857), was the home of silver.

SIMILAR, like. (F. — L.) In Minsheu, ed. 1627, and in Cotgrave. — F. *similaire*, 'similar;' Cot. As if from L. *similāris*, extended from *simil-is*, like, by the suffix *-āris*. Allied to *simul*, together, Gk. ἅμα, together, and E. *same*; from the Idg. base *samo-*, the same; see **Same**. Cf. OIrish *samail*, W. *hafal*, like; Gk. ὁμαλός, even. Also L. *sem-el*, once, Goth. *sim-lē*, once; Gk. ἅπαξ, once, ἕν, neut., one; &c. Der. *similar-ly*, *similar-i-ty*; also *simile*, q. v., *simili-tude*, q. v. And see *simul-ate*, *simul-ta-ne-ous*, *semblance*, *assemble*, *dis-semble*.

SIMILE, a comparison. (L.) In Shak. As You Like It, ii. 1. 45. — L. *simile*, a like thing; neut. of *similis*, like; see **Similar**.

SIMILITUDE, a comparison, parable. (F. — L.) ME. *similitude*, Chaucer, C. T. 10794 (F 480); Wyclif, Luke, viii. 4. — F. *similitude*, 'a similitude;' Cot. — L. *similitūdinem*, acc. of *similitūdo*, likeness. — L. *similis*, like; see **Similar**.

SIMIOUS, monkey-like. (L.) Coined from L. *sīmia*, an ape. — L. *sīmus* (Gk. σιμός), flat-nosed.

SIMMER, to boil gently. (E.) Formerly also *simber* (see Richardson) and *simper*. Halliwell cites: '*Simper*, to simmer, *East*;' also 'the creame of *simpering* milke, Florio, p. 189,' which is wrong as regards the edit. of 1598, which has: '*Cremore*, the creme or *simpring* of milke when it seethes.' 'I *symper*, as lycour dothe on the fyre byfore it begynneth to boyle;' Palsgrave. A frequentative form, with the usual suffix *-er*, and with excrescent *p* or *b* in some authors, from a base *simm* or *symm*, imitative of the sound of gentle boiling. Cf. Dan. *summe*, G. *summen*, Swed. dial. *summa*, to hum, to buzz; Bavar. *semmern*, to whimper.

SIMNEL, a kind of rich cake. (F. — L.) See Simnel in Halliwell. ME. *simnel*, Prompt. Parv.; *simenel*, Havelok, 779. — OF. *simenel*, bread or cake of fine wheat flour; Roquefort. — Late L. *siminellus*, bread of fine flour; also called *simella*; Ducange. β. Here *siminellus* stands for *similellus*, as being easier to pronounce; both *simil-ellus* and *simel-la* being derived from L. *simila*, wheat flour of the finest quality. Allied to Gk. σεμίδαλις, fine flour. And cf. G. *semmel*, wheat-bread.

SIMONY, the crime of trafficking in ecclesiastical preferment. (F. — L. — Gk. — Heb.) In early use; spelt *symonye*, O. Eng. Miscellany, ed. Morris, p. 89, l. 7. — F. *simonie*, 'simony, the buying or selling of spirituall functions or preferments;' Cot. — Late L. *simōnia*; Ducange. Named from *Simon Magus* (Gk. Σίμων), because he wished to purchase the gift of the Holy Ghost with money; Acts, viii. 18. — Heb. *Shim'ōn*, Simeon, Simon, lit. hearing, obedience; one who hears. — Heb. root *shāma‘*, to hear. Der. *simoni-ac*, *simonī-ac-al*.

SIMOOM, a hot, poisonous wind. (Arab.) See Southey, Thalaba, b. ii, last stanza, and the note. — Arab. *samūm*, a sultry pestilential wind, which destroys travellers; Rich. Dict. p. 850. So called from its poisonous nature. — Arab. root *samma*, he poisoned; id. p. 847.

SIMPER, to smile sillily or affectedly, to smirk. (Scand.) 'Yond *simpering* dame;' K. Lear, iv. 6. 120. 'With a made countenance about her mouth, between *simpering* and smiling;' Sidney, Arcadia, b. i. (R.) Cotgrave explains F. *coquine* by 'a begger woman, also a cockney, *simperdecockit*, nice thing.' We find traces of it in Norweg. *semper*, fine, smart (Aasen); Dan. dial. *semper*, *simper*, 'affected, coy, prudish, esp. of one who requires pressing to eat: as, she is as *semper* as a bride;' Wedgwood. Also MSwed. *semper*, one who affectedly refrains from eating. β. All these are formed (with a suffix *-er* which appears to be the same as the E. suffix *-er* of the agent) from a base *simp-*, which is a nasalized form of *sip-*. Without the nasal, we find MSwed. *sipp* (also *simp*), a woman who affectedly refuses to eat (Ihre); Swed. *sipp*, adj., finical, prim; Dan. *sippe*, a woman who is affectedly coy (Molbech). And note particularly Low G. *sipp*, explained in the Bremen Wörterbuch as a word expressing the gesture of a compressed mouth, and affected pronunciation; a woman who acts thus affectedly is called *Junfer Sipp*, Miss Sipp, and they say of her, 'She cannot say *sipp*.' Also Low G. *den Mund sipp trekken*, to make a small mouth; *De Bruut sitt so* sipp, the bride sits so prim. Of imitative origin. ¶ We find also prov. G. *zimpern*, to be affectedly coy, *zipp*, prudish, coy (Flügel); but these are most likely borrowed from Low German, as the true High G. z answers to E. *t*. **Der.** *simper, sb.*

SIMPLE, single, elementary, clear, guileless, silly. (F.—L.) In early use. ME. *simple*, The Bestiary, l. 790; in O. Eng. Miscellany, ed. Morris.—F. *simple*, 'simple;' Cot.—L. *simplicem*, acc. of *simplex* (stem *simplic-*), simple; lit. 'one-fold,' as opposed to *duplex*, two-fold, double.—L. *sim-*, appearing also in L. *sin-gŭlī*, one by one, *sem-per*, always alike, *sem-el*, once, *sim-ul*, together; and *-plic-*, as in *plic-āre*, to fold. See **Simulate** and **Ply.** **Der.** *simple-ness*, *simpl-y.* Also *simples*, s. pl., simple herbs; whence *simpl-er*, *simpl-ist*, both in Minsheu, ed. 1627. Also *simplic-i-ty*, Mids. Nt. Dr. i. 1. 171, from F. *simplicité*, from L. acc. *simplicitātem*; *simpli-fy*, in Barrow's Sermons, vol. ii. ser. 34 (Todd), a coined word, answering to late F. *simplifier* (Littré), where the suffix *-fier* = L. *-ficāre*, from *facere*, to make; see **Fact.** Hence *simplific-at-ion.* Also *simple-ton*, q. v. Brugmann, i. § 431 (1).

SIMPLETON, a foolish fellow. (F.—L.) 'A country farmer sent his man to look after an ox; the *simpleton* went hunting up and down;' L'Estrange (Todd's Johnson). 'O ye pitiful *simpletons*;' Lady Alimony (1659), A. v. sc. 2. Formed with the F. suffix *-on* (<L. acc. *-ōnem*) from F. *simplet*, masc., *simplette*, fem., a simple person (Littré). Cotgrave only gives the fem. *simplette*, 'a little, simple wench, one that is apt to believe, and thereby soon deceived;' but Godefroy has OF. *simplet*, simple, credulous; and Corblet has Picard *simplet*, a foolish person. Cf. Span. *simplon*, a simpleton. These are formed from *simple*, simple, with the dimin. suffix *-et* or *-ette.* Thus *simple-t-on* exhibits a double suffix *-t-on*, which is very rare; yet there is at least one more example in the old word *musk-et-oon*, a kind of musket, F. *mousqu-et-on.* β. There is also a phrase *simple tony*, with the same sense, as in Falstaff's Wedding, by Kenrick, A. iv. sc. 4 (near the end); A.D. 1766. But this seems to be later. We also find *Tony* (for *Anthony*) used in the same sense of 'foolish fellow;' as in Middleton, The Changeling, i. 2. Cf. prov. E. *idle-ton*, in E. D. D.

SIMULATE, to pretend, feign. (L.) Shak. has *simulation*, Tw. Nt. ii. 5. 151. *Simulate* first occurs with the force of a pp.; 'because they had vowed a *simulate* chastyte;' Bale, Eng. Votaries, pt. ii (R.). —L. *simulātus*, pp. of *simulāre*, also *similāre*, to feign, pretend, make like.—L. *similis*, like. See **Similar.** **Der.** *simulat-ion*, from F. *simulation*, 'simulation,' Cot., from L. acc. *simulātiōnem*, a feigning; *simulat-or.* Also *dis-simulat-ion.* And see *semblance, as-semble, dis-semble.* Also *simultaneous.*

SIMULTANEOUS, happening at the same moment. (L.) 'Whether previous or *simultaneous*;' Hammond's Works, vol. iv. ser. 2 (R.); p. 570 (Todd). Englished directly from Late L. *simul-tāneus*, by change of *-us* to *-ous*, as in *ardu-ous*, *strenu-ous*, &c. Formed from Late L. *simult-im*, at the same time, by analogy with L. *mōment-āneus*; and cf. E. *instantaneous.* β. The Late L. *simultim* is extended from L. *simul*, together, with adv. suffix *-tim*, as in *minūtā-tim.* See **Simulate, Similar.** **Der.** *simul-taneous-ly.*

SIN, wickedness, crime, iniquity. (E.) ME. *sinne, synne*; pl. *synnes*, Wyclif, Matt. ix. 2, 5, 6. AS. *synn, sinn*; gen., dat., and acc. *synne*; Grein, ii. 518.+Du. *zonde*; Icel. *synd*, older form *synð*; Dan. and Swed. *synd*; G. *sünde*, OHG. *suntea.* β. Thus the AS. *synn* represents a Teut. type **sundjā*, fem., or rather an Idg. type **səntjā*; where **sənt* is the weak grade of *sent* : *sont.* It is the abstract sb. allied to L. *sons* (stem *sonti-*), sinful, guilty, orig. 'being,' real; and Curtius refers this (along with Icel. *sannr*, true, very, Goth. *sunja*, the truth, sooth) to the √ES; by remarking that 'the connection of *son(t)s* and *sonticus* with this root has been recognized by Clemm, and established (Studien, iii. 328), while Bugge (iv. 205) confirms it by Northern analogies. Language regards the *guil*ty man as the man *who it was*;' Gk. Etym. i. 470. Cf. Ion. Gk. ἐ-όντ-, stem of ἐών (for **ἐσ-ών*), being; pres. pt. of εἰμί, I am. See **Sooth.** **Der.** *sin*, verb, ME. *sinnen*, but also *singen, sungen, sinegen* (see P. Plowman, A. ix. 17, B. viii. 22, C. xi. 23), from AS. *syngian, gesyngian*, Grein, ii. 519. Also *sin-ful*, AS. *synfull* (Grein); *sin-ful-ly, sin-ful-ness*; *sin-less*, AS. *synlēas*; *sin-less-ly, sin-less-ness*; *sinn-er, sin-offering.*

SINCE, after that, from the time that, past, ago. (E.) *Since* is written for *sins*, to keep the final *s* sharp (voiceless); just as we write *pence* for *pens, mice* for *mys, twice* for *twies*, and the like. Again, *sins* is an abbreviation of ME. *sithens*, also spelt *sithence* in later English, with the same intention of showing that the final *s* was voiceless. *Sithence* is in Shak. Cor. iii. 1. 47; All's Well, i. 3. 124; *sithens* in Spenser, F. Q. i. 4. 51. β. Next, the word *sithen-s* arose from the addition of *-s* or *-es* (common as an adverbial ending, as in *need-s, twi-es, thri-es*) to the older form *sithen*, which was

sometimes contracted to *sin.* We find *siþen*, Havelok, 399; *sithen*, Wyclif, Luke, xiii. 7; *sith*, Chaucer, C. T. 5234 (B 814); and see numerous examples in Stratmann, s. v. *siþþan.* γ. Lastly, *sithen* or *siþen* is for *siþþen*, the oldest ME. form, whence were made *siþen, sitthen, sithen-es, sithen-s*, as well as (by loss of *-n* or *-en*) *sithe, seþþe, sith*, and (by contraction) *sin* or *sen.*—AS. *siððan, siððon, syððan, seoððan, sioððan*, after that, since (very common), Grein, ii. 445. This *siððan* is a contraction from *sīð ðan*, for *sīð ðon*, after that; where *ðon*, that, is the instrumental case masc. of the demonstrative pronoun, also used as a def. article, for which see **That.** The AS. *sīð*, after, used as a prep., was orig. an adj., meaning 'late,' but here represents a comparative adv., meaning 'later, after.' We find *sīð*, after, later, both as adj. and adv., Grein, ii. 444. [Not the same word as AS. *sīð*, journey, time (Grein, ii. 443), which is cognate with Goth. *sinth*, discussed under **Send.**] This AS. *sīð* is cognate with Goth. *seithus*, late, whence the adv. *seithu*, late, Matt. xxvii. 57, John, vi. 16; also with G. *seit*, OHG. *sīt*, after. The G. *seit-dem*, since, is exactly the AS. *sīð-ðan*; in Gothic we find a somewhat similar compound in the expression *ni thana-seiths*, no longer, Mark, ix. 8. Other allied words are OIrish *sīr*, long, W. *hir*, long, tedious; L. *sēro*, late, Skt. *sāyam*, adv. in the evening. Stokes-Fick, p. 294; Sievers, §§ 323, 337.

SINCERE, true, pure, honest, frank. (F.—L.) 'Of a very *sincere* life;' Frith's Works, p. 117, last line.—OF. *sincere, syncere*, 'sincere;' Cot. Mod. F. *sincère.*—L. *sincērus*, pure, sincere. If, as some have thought, *sincērus* means *sine cēra*, 'without wax,' it was orig. applied to honey (Bréal). **Der.** *sincere-ly*; *sincer-i-ty*, from F. *sincerité*, 'sincerity,' Cot., from L. acc. *sincēritātem.*

SINCIPUT, the fore-part of the head, from the forehead to the top. (L.) In Phillips, ed. 1706. Used as distinct from *occiput*, the back part of the head. The lit. sense is 'half-head.'—L. *sinciput*, half a head; contracted from *sēmi-*, half; and *caput*, the head. Brugmann, i. § 121. See **Semi-** and **Capital.** Compare **Megrim.**

SINDER, the correct spelling of **Cinder,** q.v. 'Thus all in flames I *sinder-like* consume;' Gascoigne, Dan Bartholomew; Works, i. 117. 'Synders of the fyre;' Palsgrave. Note that the AS. *sinder* is cognate with Gk. ἄνθραξ, coal; from the common base **sendhro-* (Prellwitz).

SINE, a straight line drawn from one extremity of an arc or sector perpendicular to the radius at the other extremity. (L.) In Phillips, ed. 1658. Englished from L. *sinus*, a bosom, properly a curve, fold, coil, curl, esp. the hanging fold of the upper part of a toga. The use of the word in the math. sense is peculiar. We may note the Arab. *jayb*, 'cutting, traversing,' as also having (like L. *sinus*) the two meanings of 'breast of a garment' and 'sine' in geometry. The L. *sinus* may have translated the Arabic. Doublet, *sinus*, q.v.

SINECURE, an ecclesiastical benefice without the cure of souls, salary without work. (L.) 'One of them is in danger to be made a *sine cure*;' Dryden, Kind Keeper, Act ii. sc. 2. Englished from L. *sine cūrā*, without cure of souls.—L. *sine*, prep. without, lit. 'if not,' compounded of *si*, if, and *ne*, not; and *cūrā*, abl. case of *cūra*, cure; see **Cure.** **Der.** *sinecur-ist*, one who holds a sinecure.

SINEW, a tendon, that which joins a muscle to a bone. (E.) ME. *sinewe*; spelt *synewe*, Prompt. Parv. AS. *sinu, seonu, sionu* (dat. *sinwe*), a sinew; Grein, ii. 439.+Du. *zenuw*; Dan. *sene*; Swed. *sena*; G. *sehne*; OHG. *senawa, senewa, senuwa.* And cf. Icel. *sin*, a sinew, pl. *sinar.* β. The Teut. type is **sinawā*, f. Perhaps allied to Skt. *snāva(s)*, a tendon, which (however) answers better to G. *schnur*, a string. **Der.** *sinew*, verb, 3 Hen. VI, ii. 6. 91; *sinew-y*, L. L. L. iv. 3. 308.

SING, to resound, to utter melodious sounds, relate musically or in verse. (E.) The orig. sense is simply to ring or resound. 'We hear this fearful tempest *sing*;' Rich. II, ii. 1. 263. ME. *singen*, pt. t. *sang, song*, pl. *sungen*, pp. *sungen, songen*; Chaucer, C. T. 268, 1511 (A 266, 1509). AS. *singan*, pt. t. *sang*, pl. *sungon*, pp. *sungen*; Grein, ii. 452.+Du. *zingen*, pt. t. *zong*, pp. *gezongen*; Icel. *syngja*, pt. t. *saung, söng*, pp. *sunginn*; Dan. *synge*; Swed. *sjunga*; Goth. *siggwan* (written for **singwan*); G. *singen.* β. All from Idg. root **sengh(w)*, with labio-velar *gh*; so that the Gk. ὀμφή, voice, may be related. Brugmann, i. §§ 676, 797. **Der.** *sing-er*, in place of the AS. *sangere* (which would have given a mod. E. *songer*); see **Song-stress.** *Songer, Sanger, Songster, Sangster* occur as surnames. Also *sing-ing, sing-ing-master, sing-song*; *singe.* And see **Song.**

SINGE, to scorch, burn on the surface. (E.) For *senge.* ME. *sengen*; spelt *seengyn*, Prompt. Parv.; *senge*, Chaucer, C. T. 5931 (D 439). The curious pp. *seind* occurs as a substitute for *senged*; Chaucer, C. T. 14851 (B 4035). AS. *sengan*, to singe, burn; occurring in the comp. *besengan*, Ælfred, tr. of Orosius, ii. 8. § 4; A.S. Leechdoms, ed. Cockayne, ii. 124, l. 18. In Matt. xiii. 6, the Lindisfarne MS. has *besenced* (for *besenged*), scorched, burnt or dried up. The AS. *sengan* stands for *sang-ian, causal of *singan* (pt. t. *sang*), to sing. Thus the lit. sense is 'to make to sing,' with reference to the singing or hissing noise made by singed hair, and the sound given out by a burning log; see **Sing.**+Du. *zengen*, to singe, scorch, causal of *zingen*, to sing; G. *sengen*, to singe, scorch, parch, burn, causal of *singen*, to sing. Cf. Icel. *sangr*, singed, burnt.

SINGLE, sole, separate, alone. (L.) 'So that our eye be *single*;' Tyndale's Works, p. 75, col. 1. He refers to Matt. vi. 22, where the Vulgate has *simplex*, and Wyclif has *simple*.—L. *singulus*, single, separate, in Late Latin; in classical Latin we have only the pl. *singuli*, one by one. β. *Singulī* stands for *sin-culi or *sin-clī, where **sin-* corresponds to *sim-* in *sim-plex*, and is allied to *sem-el*, once, and to E. *same*; see **Simple, Same.** Der. *single*, verb, L. L. L. v. 1. 85; *singl-y*; *single-ness*, Acts, ii. 46; *single-heart-ed*, *single-mind-ed*; also *single-stick*, prob. so called because wielded by one hand only, as distinguished from the old *quarter-staff*, which was held in both hands. And see **singul-ar.** ¶ Spelt *sengle* in ME. and OF.

SINGULAR, single, alone, uncommon, strange. (F.—L.) ME. *singuler*; Gower, C. A. iii. 184; bk. vii. 2931. 'A *singuler* persone'=an individual, Chaucer, Tale of Melibee, Group B, 2625. —F. *singulier*, 'singular, excellent;' Cot.—L. *singulāris*, single, separate. Formed with suffix -*āris* from *singul-ī*, one by one; see **Single.** Der. *singular-ly*, *singular-i-ty*, from F. *singularité*, 'singularity, excellence,' Cot., from L. acc. *singulāritātem*.

SINISTER, on the left hand, inauspicious, evil. (F.—L.) Common as an heraldic term. 'Some secret *sinister* informacion;' Sir T. More, Works, p. 1447 b. 'By eny *sinistre* or euil temptacion;' Dictes of Philosophers, pr. by Caxton,*ₗ* fol. 7, l. 27.—F. *sinistre*, 'sinister, unlucky;' Cot.—L. *sinistrum*, acc. of *sinister*, left, on the left hand, inauspicious or ill-omened, as omens on the left hand were supposed to be. Cf. **Dexter.** Der. *sinistr-ous*, *sinistr-al*.

SINK, to fall down, descend, be overwhelmed; also, to depress. (E.) We have merged the transitive and intransitive forms in one; properly, we ought to use *sink* intransitively, and the trans. form should be *sench* or *senk*; cf. *drink*, *drench*. 1. ME. *sinken*, intrans., pt. t. *sank*, pp. *sunken*, *sonken*. The pt. t. *sank* is in P. Plowman, B. xviii. 67. This is the original and strong verb. AS. *sincan*, pt. t. *sanc*, pl. *suncon*, pp. *suncen*; Grein, ii. 451.+Du. *zinken*; Icel. *sökkva* (for *sinkva), pt. t. *sökk* (for *sank), pp. *sokkinn*; Dan. *synke*; Swed. *sjunka*; G. *sinken*; Goth. *sigkwan*, *siggkwan* (written for *sinkwan, *singkwan). Teut. type **senkwan-*. Brugmann, i. § 421 (3). 2. The trans. form appears in the weak ME. *senchen*, not common, and now obsolete. 'Hi *bisencheð* us on helle'=they will sink us into hell; O. Eng. Homilies, i. 107, l. 18. AS. *sencan*, to cause to sink; '*bisenced* on sǣs grund'=caused to sink (drowned) in the bottom of the sea, Matt. xviii. 6. For *sancian, formed from the 2nd grade *sanc*, as in the pt. t. of *sincan*, to sink. Cf. Goth. *saggkwan*, causal form of *siggkwan*. This verb still exists in Swed. *sänka*, Dan. *sænke*, G. *senken*, to immerse.+Lith. *sekti* (pres. *senkù*), to be drained away; cf. Skt. *sich*, to sprinkle. Brugmann, i. § 677; Streitberg, § 203. Der. *sink-er*. Also *sink*, sb., a place where refuse water *sinks* away, but orig. a place into which filth *sinks* or in which it collects, Cor. i. 1. 126.

SINOPLE, green, in heraldry. (F.—L.—Gk.) English heralds call 'green' *vert*; the term *sinople* is rather F. than E. It occurs in Caxton, tr. of Reynard the Fox: 'of gold, of sable, of siluer, of yelow, asure, and *cynope*, thyse sixe colowrs;' ed. Arber, p. 85; and, spelt *cinople* and distinguished from *grene*, in Lydgate, Siege of Troy, b. ii. c. 11; fol. G 1.—F. *sinople*, 'sinople, green colour in blazon;' Cot.—Late L. *sinōpis*, signifying both reddish and greenish (Littré).—L. *sinōpis*, a kind of red ochre, used for çolouring.—Gk. σινωπίς, σινωπική, a red earth found in Cappadocia, and imported into Greece from Sinope.—Gk. Σινώπη, Sinope, a port on the S. coast of the Black Sea.

SINUS, a bay of the sea, &c. (L.) Phillips, ed. 1706, gives: '*Sinus*, . . a gulph or great bay of the sea. . . . In anatomy, *sinus* is taken for any cavity in or between the vessels of an animal body. In surgery, it is when the beginning of an imposthume or ulcer is narrow, and the bottom large,' &c.—L. *sinus*, the fold of a garment, a bay, the bosom, a curve; &c. Der. *sinu-ous*; 'a scarfing of silver, that ran *sinuously* in works over the whole caparison,' Chapman, Mask of the Middle Temple, § 5; from F. *sinuëux*, 'intricate, crooked, full of hollow turnings, windings, or crinkle-crankles,' Cot.; from L. *sinuōsus*, winding, full of curves. Hence *sinuos-i-ty*, from F. *sinuosité*, a hollow turning or winding; Cot. Also *sinu-ate*, with a waved margin (botanical); *sinu-at-ion*; *in-sinu-ate*, *in-sinu-at-ion*. Doublet, *sine*.

SIP, to sup or drink in small quantities, to taste a liquid. (E.) ME. *sippen*, Chaucer, C. T. 5758 (D 176). It answers to AS. *sypian*, to absorb moisture (Toller), derived from *sup-*, weak grade of

sūpan, to sup; see **Sup.** And cf. **Sop.**+MDu. *sippen*, 'to sip, to sup, to tast little by little,' Hexham; from MDu. *zuypen*, Du. *zuipen*, to sup; Swed. dial. *syppa*, to sup. Der. *sip*, sb.; *sipp-er*. And see *sipp-et*.

SIPHON, a bent tube for drawing off liquids. (F.—L.—Gk.) In Phillips, ed. 1706.—F. *siphon*, 'the cock or pipe of a conduit,' &c.; Cot. (He notes its use by Rabelais.)—L. *sīphōnem*, acc. of *sīphō*, a siphon.—Gk. σίφων, a small pipe or reed.

SIPPET, a little sip, a little sop. (E.) Properly, there are two separate words. 1. A little sip. 'And ye wyll gyue me a *syppet* Of your stale ale;' Skelton, Elinour Rummyng, 367. This is the dimin. of *sip*; with suffix -*et*, of F. origin. 2. A little sop, a piece of sopped toast. 'Green goose! you're now in *sippets*;' Beaum. and Fletcher, Rule A Wife, iv. 1, last line. This seems to be more immediately from AS. *sypian*, to absorb moisture; and allied to *sop*. Palsgrave has: '*Syppet*, a litell soppe.'

SIR, SIRE, a respectful title of address. (F.—L.) *Sire* is the older form. ME. *sire*, as in 'Sire Arthure,' Layamon, 22485.—AF. *sire*, Polit. Songs, p. 232 (before 1307); F. *sire*, 'sir, or master;' Cot. Formed from L. *senior*, nom., lit. older; the F. *seigneur* being due to the accus. *seniōrem* of the same word. It is now well established that the L. *senior* produced an OF. *senre*, of which *sire* is an attenuated form; the same word appears in the curious form *sendra* in the famous Oaths of Strasburg, A. D. 842; see Bartsch, Chrest. Française, col. 4, l. 17. See Littré, Scheler, and Diez. β. The last remarks that the word is prob. of Picard or Northern origin, since Picard sometimes puts *r* for *ndr* or *nr*, as in *terons* for *tiendrons*, *tere* for *tendre*. ¶ It may be added that this word gave the old French etymologists a great deal of trouble; the word was even written *cyre* to make it look like the Gk. κύριος, a lord! The Prov. *sira*, *sire*, Span. *ser*, Ital. *ser*, are merely borrowed from French; and Icel. *sira*, from Prov. or E.; see **Sirrah.** Doublets, *senior*, *seignior*, *señor*, *signor*; though these really answer only to the acc. form *seniōrem*.

SIRDAR, a military commander. (Hind.—Pers.) Used in 1808 (Yule).—Hind. *sardār* (Forbes).—Pers. *sardār*, a chief.—Pers. *sar*, head (cf. Gk. κάρα, Skt. *çiras*); -*dār* (suffix), possessing, holding.

SIREN, a fabulous nymph who, by singing, lured mariners to death. (L.—Gk.) ME. *serein*, which is from OF. *sereine*, 'a mermaid,' Cot. 'Men clepen hem *sereins* in Fraunce;' Rom. of the Rose, 684. But we took the mod. E. word immediately from the Latin. Spelt *siren*, Com. of Errors, iii. 2. 47.—L. *sīrēn*.—Gk. σειρήν, a nymph on the S. coast of Italy, who enticed seamen by the magic sweetness of her song, and then slew them. At first the sirens were but two in number; Homer, Od. xii. 39, 167. It also means a wild bee, a singing-bird. β. Usually derived from σειρά, a cord, rope, as if they enticed mariners by pulling them; this is more likely to be a bad pun than an etymology. The orig. sense was probably 'bird;' see an article on 'Sirens,' by J. P. Postgate, in the Journal of Philology (Cambridge), vol. ix. Cf. G. *schwirren*, to chirp.

SIRLOIN, an inferior spelling of **Surloin**, q. v.

SIRNAME, a corruption of **Surname**, q. v.

SIROCCO, a hot, oppressive wind. (Ital.—Arab.) In Milton, P. L. x. 706. Spelt *xirocque* by E. G., tr. of Acosta, bk. iii. ch. 5 (1604).—Ital. *sirocco*, 'the south-east wind;' Florio. Cf. Span. *siroco*.—Arab. *sharq*, the east; Rich. Dict. p. 889. The etymology is well discussed in Devic, Supp. to Littré, who remarks that the introduction of a vowel between *r* and *q*, when the Arabic word was borrowed by European languages, presents no difficulty. Or there may have been some confusion with the closely-allied word *shurūq*, rising (said of the sun). The Eastern wind in the Mediterranean is hot and oppressive.—Arab. root *sharaqa*, (the sun) arose; Rich. Dict. p. 889. See **Saracen.**

SIRRAH, a term of address, used in anger or contempt. (Prov. —F.—L.) Common in Shak. Temp. v. 287; &c. Schmidt remarks that it is never used in the plural, is used towards comparatively inferior persons, and (when forming part of a soliloquy) is preceded by *ah*; as '*ah, sirrah*;' As You Like It, iv. 3. 166; '*ah, sirrah, quoth-a*,' 2 Hen. IV, v. 3. 17; cf. Romeo, i. 5. 31, 128. Minsheu has: '*Sirra*, a contemptuous word, ironically compounded of *Sir* and *a, ha*, as much as to say *ah, sir, ah, boy*.' Minsheu is not quite right; for the form *sira* is Provençal. It is also spelt *sirrha* in Holland, tr. of Pliny, b. xxxv. c. 10 (in a story of Apelles), ed. 1634, vol. ii. p. 538, l. 7 from bottom.—Prov. *sira*, sirrah, a term of contempt; formerly sir, in a good sense; borrowed from F. in the 15th cent., or earlier. Not the true OProv. form (which was *senher*, with variants), but borrowed from F. *sire*.—L. *senior*; see **Sir.** β. The fact that it was used contemptuously is the very thing that shows its Prov. origin; for Mistral (s. v. *sire*) quotes from Thierry to show that *sire* (formerly *sira*) was a term of contempt applied by the men of Provence to the lords and governors from Paris. When St. Louis

(Louis IX) was taken prisoner in the 13th century, the men of Marseilles sang a Te Deum for their deliverance (for the time) from the government of these *sires*. For two good examples of the offensive use of Prov. *sira* by two men who are disputing, see Bartsch, Chrest. Prov. (1875), 397. 34, 398. 13.

SIR-REVERENCE, save your reverence. (L.) In Shak. Com. Errors, iii. 2. 93. See *Save-reverence* in Nares, who shows that it was used also in the form *save-reverence* and *save-your-reverence*; the latter is in Romeo, i. 4. 42. ' This word was considered a sufficient apology for anything indecorous;' Nares. A translation of L. *saluā reuerentiā*, reverence to you being duly regarded.—L. *saluā*, fem. abl. of *saluus*, safe; and *reuerentiā*, abl. of *reuerentia*, reverence; see **Safe** and **Reverence**.

SIRUP, another spelling of **Syrup**, q. v.

SISKIN, a migratory song-bird. (Du.—Low G.—Slavonic.) Mentioned in a tr. of Buffon, Nat. Hist., London, 1792, ii. 90; and in Kilian. Spelt *sisken* in Phillips (1658). The *Carduelis spinus*; better *Spinus viridis* (Newton); also called *aberduvine*; also *Fringilla spinus*.—MDu. *cijsken, sijsken*, Anglice *siskin* (Kilian); later Du. *cysje* (Sewel), with dimin. suffix *-je* for the older dimin. suffix *-ken*; Du. *sijsje* (Calisch).—Low G. *zieske, zieseke* (Bremen).—Polish *czyżik*, dimin. form of *czyż*, a siskin; cf. Sloven. *chizhek*, Russ. *chij'*. See Miklosich, p. 36. ¶ Thus the Du. form should have been *cijske*; it was a mistake to turn *-ke* into the dimin. suffix *-ken*; and a greater one to substitute *-je*.

SISTER, a girl born of the same parents with another. (E.) ME. *suster*, Chaucer, C. T. 873 (A 871); rarely *sister, syster*, as in Prompt. Parv., and in Genesis and Exodus, ed. Morris, 766. It is extremely remarkable how the Scand. form *sister* has modified the E. form *suster*. AS. *sweostor, swuster* (whence ME. *suster*); Grein, ii. 509; modified by Icel. *systir*, Swed. *syster* (Dan. *söster*).+Du. *zuster*; Goth. *swistar*; G. *schwester*; OHG. *swester, swister*. β. The Teut. forms are all from the base *swestr-*, answering to an Idg. base *swesr- (without the *t*). Further related to Lithuan. *sessŭ* (gen. *sesseres*); L. *soror* (for older *swesor); Skt. *svasā*, nom.; OIrish *siur*; W. *chwaer*. **Der.** *sister-hood, -like, -ly*; *sister-in-law*. Also *cou-sin*, q. v.

SIT, to rest on the haunches, rest, perch, brood. (E.) ME. *sitten*, pt. t. *sat*; pl. *seten*, Chaucer, C. T. 10406 (F 92; where Tyrwhitt prints *saten*); pp. *seten, siten*, id. 1454 (where Tyrwhitt prints *sitten*). AS. *sittan*, pt. t. *sæt*, pl. *sǣton*, pp. *seten*; Grein, ii. 454.+Du. *zitten*; Icel. *sitja*, pt. t. *sat*, pp. *setinn*; Dan. *sidde*; Swed. *sitta*; Goth. *sitan*; G. *sitzen*; OHG. *sizzan*. Teut. type *setjan-, pt. t. *sat, pp. *setanoz. From Idg. √SED, to sit, whence Skt. *sad*, Gk. ἕζομαι (for ἕδ-γομαι), L. *sedēre*, Lithuan. *sēdėti*, Russ. *sidiet(e)*, to sit. **Der.** *sitt-er, sitt-ing*. Also (from L. *sedēre*) *as-sess, as-sid-uous, as-size, dis-pos-sess, dis-sid-ent, in-sid-ious, pos-sess, pre-side, re-side, re-sid-ue, sed-ate, sed-entary, sed-iment, sess-ile, sess-ion, sub-side, sub-sid-y; super-sede*; also *siege, be-siege, seize, size* (1), *size* (2), *siz-ar*. Also (from Gk. ἕζομαι) *octa-hedron, tetra-hedron, poly-hedron, cath-(h)edral; chair, chaise*. Also (from Teut. SET) *set, settle* (1); *settle* (2), in some senses; also *seat, dis-seat, un-seat, soot*; and see *saddle*.

SITE, a locality, situation, place where a thing is set down or fixed. (F.—L.) ' After the *site*, north or south;' Chaucer, On the Astrolabe, pt. ii. c. 17.—F. *site*, MF. *sit*. ' *Sit*, a site, or seat;' Cot. —L. *situm*, acc. of *situs*, a site. Perhaps allied to L. *situs*, pp. of *sinere*, to permit, of which an older meaning may have been to put, place. So Bréal. But see Brugmann, i. §§ 761, 920; where *situs*, sb., is compared with Gk. κτίσις, a foundation, and Skt. *kshiti-*, an abode, from *kshi*, to dwell. The L. *pōnere* (=*po-sinere) is certainly a derivative of *sinere*. **Der.** *situ-ate, situ-ation* (see below); also the derivatives of *pōnere*, for which see **Position.** ¶ We frequently find the odd spelling *scite*.

SITH, since. (E.) In Ezek. xxxv. 6. See **Since**.

SITHE, the correct spelling of **Scythe**, q. v.

SITUATE, placed. (L.) In Shak. L. L. L. i. 2. 142.—Late L. *situātus*, pp. of *situāre*, to locate, place; a barbarous word, found A.D. 1317 (Ducange).—L. *situ-*, stem of *situs*, a site; see **Site**. **Der.** *situat-ion*, 2 Hen. IV, i. 3. 51, from F. *situation*, ' a situation,' Cot.

SIX, five and one. (E.) ME. *six, sixe*, P. Plowman, B. v. 431. AS. *six, syx, siex*; Grein, ii. 454.+Du. *zes*; Icel., Dan., and Swed. *sex*; G. *sechs*; OHG. *sehs*; Goth. *saihs*.+Russ. *shest(e)*; W. *chwech*; Gael. and Irish *se*; L. *sex*; Gk. ἕξ (for *σϝέξ); Lithuan. *szeszi*; Pers. *shash*; Palmer's Dict. col. 382; Skt. *shash*. Idg. type *sweks. See Brugmann, ii. § 170. **Der.** *six-fold, six-pence*. Also *six-teen*, AS. *six-tíne, six-týne* (see **Ten**); *six-teen-th*; *six-ty*, AS. *six-tig* (see **Forty**); *six-ti-eth*; *six-th*, AS. *six-ta*, whence ME. *sixte, sexte*, Gower, C. A. iii. 121, bk. vii. 1082; P. Plowman, B. xiv. 300, now altered to *sixth* by analogy with *four-th, seven-th, eigh-th,*

nin-th, ten-th, just as *fif-th* is altered from AS. *fíf-ta*. Also (from L. *sex*) *sex-agenarian, sex-agesima, sex-ennial, sex-tant, sex-tuple*.

SIZAR, a scholar of a college in Cambridge, who pays lower fees than a *pensioner* or ordinary student. (F.—L.) Spelt *sizer* in Todd's Johnson. There was formerly a considerable difference in the social rank of a *sizar*, who once had to perform certain menial offices. At Oxford the corresponding term was *servitor*, defined by Phillips as ' a poor university scholar that attends others for his maintenance.' Formed from the sb. *size*. ' *Size* is a farthings worth of bread or drink, which scholars in Cambridge have at the buttery, noted with the letter *S.*, as in Oxford with the letter *Q.* for half a farthing, and Qa. [*Quadrans*] for a farthing. And whereas they say in Oxford, to *battel in the buttery-book*, i.e. to set down on their names what they take in bread, drink, butter, cheese, &c., in Cambridge they call it *sizing*;' Blount's Gloss., ed. 1674. The word *size* is also in Minsheu, and is a mere abbreviation of *assize*, i.e. quantity or ration of bread, &c. ' *Assise* of bread, i.e. setting downe the price and quantitie of bread;' Minsheu, ed. 1627. See **Assize**, and **Size** (1).

SIZE (1), an allowance or ration of food; hence, generally, magnitude. (F.—L.) ' To scant my *sizes*,' K. Lear, ii. 4. 178; see **Sizar**. ' *Syse* of bredde and ale;' Palsgrave. *Size* is merely short for *assize*, ME. *assise*, the usual old word for an allowance, or settled portion of bread, &c., doled out for a particular price or given to a dependent. We even find it used, at a very early period, almost as a general word for provisions. ' Whan ther comes marchaundise, With corn, wyn, and steil, othir [*or*] other *assise*;' K. Alisaunder, 7074. Hence *size* came to mean dimension, magnitude, &c., as at present; also bulk, as in Merry Wives, iii. 5. 12. For the etymology, see **Assize**. **Der.** *siz-ar*, q.v.

SIZE (2), weak glue, a stiffening gluey substance. (Ital.—L.) In Minsheu, ed. 1627. ' *Syse* for colours;' Palsgrave. Hence *blood-sized*, rendered sticky with gore; Two Noble Kinsmen, i. 1. 99; ' o'er-sized with coagulate gore,' Hamlet, ii. 2. 484. Cotgrave has: ' *assiette à dorer*, size to gild with, gold size.' It is not a F. word, but borrowed, like some other painters' terms, from Italian.—Ital. *sisa*, ' a kind of syse or glew that painters vse;' Florio, ed. 1598. And Ital. *sisa* is an abbreviation of *assisa*, ' size that painters vse;' also, an assise or manner; also, a liuerie, a guise or fashion, an assise or session;' id. He also gives *assisare*, ' to sise, to sesse, to assise, to sute well;' and *assiso*, ' seated, situated.' *Assisa* is the verbal sb. from *assisare*, which in its turn is from *assiso*, pp. of *assidere*, to situate. The sense is ' that which makes the colours lie flat,' so that, in Florio's phrase, they ' sute well.' The Ital. *assidere* is from L. *assidēre*, to sit at or near.—L. *ad*, near; and *sedēre*, to sit, cognate with E. **Sit**. We speak of ' making a thing *sit*,' which is just the idea here required. ¶ Thus *sise* (2), *size* (1), and *assize* are all, really, the same word. See **Size** (1), and **Assize**.

SJAMBOK, a whip. (Cape Du.—Malay.—Pers.) Modern. The Cape Du. *sjambok* seems to have been adopted from Malay *chābok* (Port. *chabuco*).—Pers. *chābuk*, alert, active; as sb., a horse-whip. See N. and Q., 9 S. iv. 456; *Chawbuck* in Yule, and *Chabouk, Chawbuck* in N. E. D.

SKAIN, SKENE, SKEIN, a dagger, knife. (Irish.) ' *Skain*, a crooked sword, or scimetar, used formerly by the Irish;' Halliwell. He cites the expression ' Iryshmen, armed . . with dartes and *skaynes*' from Hall, Hen. V, an. vi. § 3. ' Carrying his head-peece, his *skeane*, or pistoll;' Spenser, State of Ireland; Globe ed., p. 631, col. 2. ' *Skeyne*, a knyfe;' Palsgrave. ' j. baslard vocatum Iresch *skene*;' (1472), York Wills, iii. 202.—Irish (and Gael.) *sgian*, a knife; OIrish *scían*.+W. *ysgien*, a slicer, scimetar; cf. *ysgi*, a cutting off, a parer. β. Apparently from a base *skē; cf. Gk. σχάω, I scratch. See Stokes-Fick, p. 309. **Der.** (possibly) *skains-mate*, a companion in arms, comrade, Romeo, ii. 4. 162; but see **Skein**.

SKATE (1), a large flat fish of the ray family. (Scand.) Spelt *scate* in Levins, ed. 1570. ME. *scate*, Prompt. Parv.—Icel. *skata*, a skate; Norweg. *skata* (Aasen); Dan. *skade*. We find also Irish and Gael. *sgat*, a skate (from E.). ¶ The AS. *sceadd* is a *shad*, not a skate.

SKATE (2), **SCATE**, a frame of wood (or iron) with a steel ridge beneath it, for sliding on ice. (Du.—F.—Low G.) The word should be *skates*, with a pl. suffix; the final *s* has been mistaken for the pl. suffix, and so has dropped off, just as in other words; see **Pea, Sherry, Cherry**. Nares quotes the pl. *scatzes* in 1695. Spelt *scheets* in Evelyn's Diary, Dec. 1, 1662; *skeates* in Pepys' Diary, same date. ' *Scate*, a sort of pattern, to slide upon ice;' Phillips, ed. 1706. Cotgrave explains OF. *eschasses* by ' stilts, or *scatches* to go on;' here *scatches* is merely another form of *skateses*; ' the point in which stilts and skates agree is that they are both contrivances for increasing the length of stride,' Wedgwood.—Du. *schaatsen*, ' skates,' Sewel; where *-en* is the pl. suffix, so that the word itself is *schaats*, as in '*schaatsryder*, a skates-slider;' Sewel [misprinted *schaarsryder* by an obvious error]. MDu. *schaetsen*, 'skates [with] which they slide upon the yce in Holland;' Hexham, ed. 1658.—OF. *eschace* (with *ce* pron. as *tse*), a stilt (12th cent.); whence F. *échasse*.—Low G. type *skak-jā (Latinised as *scacia* in Ducange), a shank, leg; Low G. *schake*, the same. Compare E. *shank*, which inserts the nasal sound *n*; see **Shank.** Note the Low G. phrase *de schaken voort teen*, to go swiftly, lit. 'to pull one's shanks out;' and AS. *sceacan, scacan*, to shake, to go swiftly, to flee; see **Shake,** with which E. *shank* is allied. As to the sense, the words *scatches* and *skates* merely mean 'shanks,' i. e. contrivances for lengthening the leg. ¶ The Dan. *sköite*, a skate, older form *skejte* (Kalkar) is from E.; the Swed. word is *skridsko* or *skid* (see **Skid**).

SKEIN, SKAIN, a knot of thread or silk. (F.—C.?) Generally defined as 'a knot of thread or silk,' where probably 'knot' means a quantity collected together; a *skein* is a quantity of yarn, folded and doubled together. 'Layde downe a *skeyne* of threde, And some a *skeyne* of yarne;' Skelton, Elinor Rumming, 310. ME. *skeyne*, Prompt. Parv.—OF. *escaigne* (Godefroy), a skein (1354); MF. *escaigne*, 'a skain;' Cot. Prob. of Celtic origin; cf. Irish *sgainne*, 'a skein or clue of thread.' Cf. Gael. *sgeinnidh*, flax or hemp thread, small twine. If these are true Celtic words, they may be allied to Gk. σχοῖνος, a rope, a cord (Macbain). **Der.** (perhaps) *skains-mates*, companions in winding thread, companions, Romeo, ii. 4. 162; but see **Skain.** This solution is advocated in Todd's Johnson, which see; and cf. the phrase 'as thick [intimate] as *inkle-weavers*,' i. e. weavers of tape.

SKELETON, the bony frame-work of an animal. (Gk.) '*Skelitons* of ev'ry kinde;' Davenant, Gondibert, ii. 5. st. 32. See Trench, Select Glossary. Spelt *skeleton, sceleton* in Blount's Gloss., ed. 1674.—Gk. σκελετόν, a dried body, a mummy; neut. of σκελετός, dried up, parched.—Gk. σκέλλειν (for σκέλ-γειν), to dry, dry up, parch. **Der.** *skeleton-key.*

SKELLUM, a cheat. (Du.—G.) 'A Dutch *skelum*;' Coryat's Crudities; in Addit. to Nares.—Du. *schelm*, 'a rogue, a villaine;' Hexham.—G. *schelm*, a rogue; OHG. *scelmo, scalmo*, a pestilence, carrion; hence a rogue (as a term of abuse). See Notes to Eng. Etym., p. 271.

SKEPTIC, the same as **Sceptic,** q. v.

SKERRY, an insulated rock. (Scand.) In Scott, The Pirate; song in ch. xii.—Icel. *sker* (dat. *skeri*), a skerry; see **Scar** (2).

SKETCH, a rough draught of an object, outline. (Du.—Ital.—L.—Gk.) In Phillips, ed. 1706. 'To make a *sketch*;' Dryden, Parallel between Painting and Poetry (R.). Not used much earlier.—Du. *schets*, 'a draught, scheme, model, sketch;' Sewel. [The E. *sketch* is a mere corruption of the Du. word, and stands for *skets*.] The same word as G. *skizze*, a sketch; which was prob. borrowed from the Dutch, who, as being fond of painting, introduced the term from the Italian. At any rate, both Du. *schets* and G. *skizze* are from Ital. *schizzo*, 'an ingrosement or first rough draught of anything;' Florio.—L. *schedium*, an extemporaneous poem, anything hastily made.—L. *schedius*, adj., made hastily.—Gk. σχέδιος, sudden, offhand on the spur of the moment; also near, close to. Cf. Gk. σχεδόν, near, hard by, lit. 'holding to.' These words, like σχέ-σις, habit, state, σχε-τι-κός, retentive, are from the Gk. base σχε-, to hold, appearing in Gk. σχεῖν (= σχέ-ειν), 2 aorist infin. of ἔχειν, to hold, and in E. *sche-me.* See **Scheme.** β. Thus *scheme* and *sketch*, the meanings of which are by no means remote, are from the same root, but by different paths. **Der.** *sketch*, verb; *sketch-y; sketch-i-ness.*

SKEW, oblique, wry. (MDu.) 'To look *skew*, or *a-skew*, to squint or leer;' Phillips, ed. 1706. It seems first to have been used chiefly as a verb. 'To *skue*, or *walk skuing*, to waddle, to go sideling along;' Phillips. '*To skewe*, linis oculis spectare;' Levins, ed. 1570. 'Our service Neglected and look'd lamely on, and *skew'd* at;' Beaum. and Fletcher, Loyal Subject, A. ii. sc. 1 (Putskie). 'This *skew'd-eyed* carrion;' id., Wild-goose Chase, iv. 1 (Mirabel). ME. *skewen*, to turn aside, slip away, escape; Morte Arthure, ed. Brock, 1562. Prob. of MDu. origin; not from Icel. *skeifr*, awry.—MDu. *schouwen*, 'to avoid or to shunne,' also as Du. *schuwen*, Hexham; Low G. *schonen, schuwen*, to avoid.+OHG. *sciuhen*, MHG. *schiuhen*, to avoid, get out of the way, G. *scheuen*, to shun, avoid (whence G. *scheu*, shy); derived from the adj. appearing as MHG. *schiech*, timid. Thus ME. *skewen*, to escape, is really the verb corresponding to the adj. *shy*; to *skew* or *skue* is to shy as a horse, to start aside from. Cf. WFlem. *schui, schu*, shy; *schuien, schuen*, to avoid. See further under **Shy, Eschew. Der.** *a-skew*, q. v. Also *skew-bald.*

SKEWBALD, piebald. (Hybrid; MDu. *and* C.) In Halliwell. It means marked or spotted in a *skew* or irregular manner. From **Skew** and **Bald,** q. v. And cf. *pie-bald.* ¶ We find, however, ME. *skewed*, piebald (see Stratmann); perhaps from *skew*, ME.

variant of *skie*, a cloud, sky. If this is right, then *skew-bald* is connected with **Sky** rather than **Skew.**

SKEWER, a pin of wood or iron for holding meat together. (Scand.) In Dryden, tr. of Homer, Iliad, i. 633. Spelt *skuer* in 1411; Nottingham Records, vol. ii. *Skewer* is a by-form of prov. E. *skiver*, a skewer, E.D.D.; cf. *skiver-wood*, dogwood, of which skewers are made; Halliwell. And *skiver* is the Northern form of *shiver*, a splinter of wood, dimin. of Icel. *skifa*, Swed. *skifva*, a slice, a shive; see **Shiver** (2). The form *skiver* corresponds to Dan. *skifer*, Swed. *skiffer*, a slate, MDan. *skever*; MDu. *scheversteen*, 'a slate or a slate-stone,' Hexham; similarly named from its being sliced into thin flakes. Cf. Dan. dial. *skivrt*, small sticks; Norw. *skivra*, to cut into splinters (Ross). ¶ The spelling *skiver* occurs in W. Dampier, A New Voyage (1699); vol. ii. pt. 1, p. 31. Doublet, *shiver* (2). **Der.** *skewer*, verb.

SKID, a contrivance for locking the wheel of a carriage. (Scand.) Halliwell gives: '*skid-pan*, the shoe with which the wheel of a carriage is locked.' Ray has: 'To *skid a wheel*, rotam sufflaminare, with an iron hook fastned to the axis to keep it from turning round upon the descent of a steep hill; *Kent*.' The latter sense is merely secondary, and refers to a later contrivance; the orig. *skid* was a kind of shoe placed under the wheel, and in the first instance made of wood. [The word *skid* is merely the Scand. form corresponding to the ME. *schide*, a thin piece of wood; see **Shide.**]—Icel. *skið*, a billet of wood; also, a kind of snow-shoe; Norw. *skid*, a snow-shoe (Aasen); MSwed. *skid*, a thin flat piece of wood (Ihre); Swed. *skid*, 'a kind of scate or wooden shoe on which they slide on the ice,' Widegren.

SKIFF, a small light boat. (F.—Ital.—OHG.) 'Olauus fled in a litle *skiffe*;' Hakluyt's Voyages, vol. i. p. 14. And in Minsheu.—MF. *esquif*, 'a skiffe, or little boat,' Cot.—Ital. *schifo*, 'a skiffe;' Florio.—OHG. *skif, schif*, G. *schiff*, a ship; cognate with E. **Ship,** q.v. **Der.** *skiff*, verb, to cross in a skiff, Two Noble Kinsmen, i. 3. 37. Doublet, *scuttle* (1).

SKILL, discernment, discrimination, tact. (Scand.) ME. *skil*, gen. in the sense of 'reason,' Ancren Riwle, p. 204, l. 22; *skile*, id. p. 306, l. 17.—Icel. *skil*, a distinction, discernment; cf. *skilja*, to part, separate, divide, distinguish; Dan. *skjel*, a separation, boundary, limit; cf. *skille*, to separate; Swed. *skäl*, reason; cf. *skilja*, to separate. β. From √SQEL, to separate, divide, orig. to cleave, as appears by Lithuan. *skelti*, to cleave. Cf. Swed. *skala*, to peel. See **Shell, Scale. Der.** *skil-ful*, ME. *skilfulle*, Rob. of Brunne, tr. of Langtoft, p. 311, l. 17; *skil-ful-ly, skil-ful-ness; skil-less*, Ormulum, 3715; *skill-ed*, i. e. endowed with skill, Rich. III, iv. 4. 116. Also *skill*, verb, in the phr. *it skills not* = it makes no difference, Tam. Shrew, iii. 2. 134; from Icel. *skilja*, to separate, which is frequently used impersonally, with the sense 'it differs.'

SKILLET, a small pot. (F.—L.) In Othello, i. 3. 273. Spelt *skellet*, Skelton, Elinour Rumming, 250. Halliwell explains it as a small iron or brass pot, with a long handle.—OF. *escuellette*, 'a little dish;' Cot. Dimin. of OF. *escuelle*, a dish.—L. *scutella*, a salver; dimin. of *scutra, scuta*, a tray, dish, platter. Hardly allied to *scūtum*, a shield. Doublet, *scuttle* (1). ☞ The Suffolk word *skillet*, meaning a thin brass perforated implement used for skimming milk (Moor, Nall), perhaps acquired its peculiar sense from confusion with the Icel. *skilja*, to separate; but the sense of 'dish' will suffice, as the orig. skimmer must have been a simple dish. The fancy in Phillips, that a skillet [except when it means 'a bell'] is derived from Late L. *skeletta*, a little bell [from Du. *schel*, a bell], on the ground that *skillets* are made of bell-metal, is to be rejected. Othello's helmet can hardly have been made of bell-metal, and a *skillet* is usually of brass or iron.

SKIM, to clear of scum, to pass lightly over a surface. (Scand.) '*Skim* milk;' Mids. Nt. Dr. ii. 1. 36. A derivative of *scum*; the change of vowel from *u* to *i* (*y*) is precisely what we should expect; but we only find a change of this character in the cognate EFries. *schümen*, to skim; and G. *schäumen*, to skim, from *schaum*, scum. Of Scand. origin; cf. Dan. *skumme*, to skim, from *skum*, scum; Swed. *skumma mjölk*, to skim milk, from *skum*, scum. The right form appears in MSwed. *skymma*, to overshadow, from *skumm*, obscurity; which seems to be from the same root as *skum*, scum. Note also Dan. dial. *skimmel*, a thin film on milk; and even Irish *sgem-im*, I skim, from *sgeim*, foam, scum. See **Scum.** ¶ We find a similar vowel-change in *dint*, ME. *dunt*; in *fill*, derived from *full*; in *list*, verb, from *lust*, sb.; in *trim*, verb, from AS. *trum*; &c. **Der.** *skimmer; skim-milk*, i. e. skimmed milk.

SKIMP, to curtail, stint. (Scand.) See E.D.D.; and cf. *scrimp*, which may have affected it. It seems to be founded on Icel. *skemma*, to shorten; from *skamr*, short. See **Scant.** So also Eng. dial. *skimp*, to joke, is from NFries. *skempe*, Icel. *skemta*, to amuse.

SKIN, the natural covering of the body, hide, bark, rind. (Scand.)

ME. *skin*, Chaucer, C. T. 3809 (A 3811); *bere-skin* or *beres skin*, a bear-skin, id. 2144 (A 2142). Spelt *skine*, Rel. Ant. ii. 79, col. 1.— Icel. *skinn*, a skin; Swed. *skinn*; Dan. *skind*.   β. The Icel. *skinn* stands for **skinþ-*, by the assimilation common in that language; so also the Swed. *skinn*.   Teut. type **skinþom*, neut.; Idg. type **skéntom*. Hence also G. *schinden*, to skin, flay; OHG. *scintan*, *scindan*, sometimes a strong verb, with pt. t. *schant*, pp. *geschunden*. Cf. also W. *cen*, skin, peel, scales; *ysgen*, dandriff. **Der.** *skin*, verb, Hamlet, iii. 4. 147; *skin-deep*; *skinn-er*; *skin-flint*, a miser who would even *skin a flint*, if possible; *skinn-y*, Macb. i. 3. 45; *skinn-i-ness*.

SKINK (1), to draw or serve out wine. (Scand.) Obsolete. Shak. has *under-skinker*, 1 Hen. IV, ii. 4. 26. Dryden has *skinker*, tr. of Homer, Iliad, i. 803.—Icel. *skenkja*, to serve drink; cognate with AS. *scencan*. The latter verb is fully explained under **Nunchion**, q.v.

SKINK (2), a kind of lizard. (Gk.) 'Th' Alexandrian *skink*;' Sylvester, tr. of Du Bartas, i. 6 (C. D.).—Gk. σκίγκος, a kind of lizard; whence L. *scincus* (Pliny, viii. 25); written *scinke* in Holland's translation; spelt *scinc*, *scinque* in Cotgrave.

SKIP, to leap lightly, pass over quickly. (Scand.) ME. *skippen*, Chaucer, C. T. 3259; King Alisaunder, 768; pt. t. *skipte*, P. Plowman, B. xi. 103; *scep*, *skyp*, *scope*, Cursor Mundi, 19080. Of Scand. origin. Cf. Swed. dial. *skopa*, to skip, leap (as an animal), dance (Rietz); who cites MSwed. *skuppa*, *skoppa*, in the same sense; Norw. *skopa*, to skipaway (Ross); MDan. *skobe*, to dance, skip (Kalkar). Icel. *skoppa*, to spin like a top, whence *skoppara-kringla*, a top, North E. *scopperil spinner*, a teetotum (Whitby Glossary), named from its skipping about. And cf. MHG. *schüften*, to gallop. (The E. *i* is for *y*, mutation of *u*.) Perhaps MSwed. *pp* represents *mp*; cf. Swed. dial. *skimpa*, *skumpa*, to jump about. **Der.** *skip*, sb., *skipp-ing-rope*.

SKIPPER, the master of a merchant-ship. (Du.) 'In ages pass'd, as the *skipper* told me, there grew a fair forrest in that channel where the *Texel* makes now her bed;' Howell, Famil. Letters, vol. i. let. 5, dated from Amsterdam, April 1, 1617. Thus Howell picked up the word in Holland. Found much earlier, spelt *skypper*; Earl of Derby's Expeditions (1390); Camden Soc., p. 37.—Du. *schipper*, 'a marriner, a shipper, a saylour, a navigatour;' Hexham. Formed, with suffix *-er* (=E. *-er*) of the agent, from Du. *schip*, cognate with E. **Ship**, q.v. So also Swed. *skeppare*, from *skepp*, a ship (Ihre).

SKIRMISH, an irregular fight, contest. (F.—OHG.) Also spelt *scrimmage*; and even *scaramouch* is but the Ital. form of the ME. sb. This sb. appears as ME. *scarmuch*, a slight battle, Chaucer, Troil. ii. 934. Spelt *scarmoge*, Spenser, F. Q. ii. 6. 34.— OF. *escarmouche*, 'a skirmish, bickering;' Cot.   β. But the mod. form of the sb. is due to the ME. verb *skirmishen*, spelt *skirmysshe* in Trevisa, tr. of Higden, iv. 399.—OF. *eskermiss-*, a stem of *eskermir*, to fence, to fight; whence also the ME. *skirmen*, to fence or skirmish; the pt. t. *skirmden* occurs very early, in Layamon, 8406. Cf. MF. *escrimer*, 'to fence, or play at fence, also, to lay hard about him;' Cot.—OHG. *scirman*, MHG. *schirmen*, to defend, fight; especially, to fight, to defend oneself with a shield.—OHG. *scirm*, *schirm*, G. *schirm*, a shield, screen, shelter, guard, defence.   γ. It thus appears that the orig. sense of *skirmish* is 'to fight behind cover,' hence to take advantage of cover or slight shelter in advancing to fight.   δ. Diez and Scheler show clearly that the F. *escarmouche*, Ital. *scaramuccia*, are due to OHG. *skerman*, which is a mere variant of *scirman*. The ending of Ital. *scaramuccia* is a mere suffix; we find also Ital. *scherm-ugio*, a skirmish, fencing, *scherm-ita*, fencing, *schermire*, *schermare*, to fence, *schermo*, a defence, arms; also OF. *escarm-ie*, answering to Ital. *scherm-ita*. **Der.** *skirmish-er*. Doublets, *scrimmage*, *scaramouch*.

SKIRR, the same as **Scur**, q.v.

SKIRRET, SKERRET, a plant like the water-parsnep. (F.— Span.—Arab.) ME. *skyrwyt*; Voc. 567. 31; 580. 38. Also *skirwhit*, *skirwhite*; Sinonima Bartolomei, ed. Mowat, p. 20, l. 4; p. 33, l. 25. Spelt as if from Icel. *skir hvitr*, pure white. But this is probably a popular etymology; prob. adapted from OF. *eschervis* (Godefroy); MF. *chervis*, 'the root skirret or skirwicke;' Cot. The OF. *eschervis* is from Span. *chirivia*; from Arab. *karawia* (Devic); which is also the origin of our word *caraway*. See Notes on E. Etym., p. 271. And see **Caraway**.

SKIRT, the part of a garment below the waist, edge, border, margin. (Scand.) This is a doublet of *shirt*, but restricted to the sense of the *lower part* of the shirt or garment. Spelt *skort*, Hall's Satires, b. iv. sat. i. l. 28. ME. *skyrt*. 'Skyrt of a garment, Trames;' Prompt. Parv.—Icel. *skyrta*, a shirt, a kind of kirtle; Swed. *skjorta*, MDan. *skyrt*, Dan. *skjorte*, a shirt.   β. The cognate G. *schurz* has the sense of 'apron;' and special attention was called to the *lower part* of the shirt by the etymological sense, which signifies 'a short garment;' see **Shirt**. And see remarks on **Kirtle**. The general

sense of 'edge' comes from that of 'lower edge,' or place where the garment is cut *short*. **Der.** *skirt*, verb, Milton, P. L. v. 282.

SKIT, a taunt, a lampoon; see **Skittish** (below).

SKITTISH, frisking, full of frisks, said of a horse or unsteady person, fickle. (Scand.) 'Unstaid and *skittish* in all motions else;' Tw. Nt. ii. 4. 18. 'Some of theyr *skyttyshe* condycyons;' Fabyan's Chronicle, an. 1255-6, ed. Ellis, p. 339. 'Thy *skittish* youthe;' Hoccleve, de Regim. Principum, 590. Formed from the verb *to skit*, a Lowland Sc. word, meaning 'to flounce, caper like a *skittish* horse,' Jamieson. Of Scand. origin. We find nearly related words in Swed. *skutta*, to leap, Swed. dial. *skutta*, *skötta*, to leap, Swed. dial. *skytta*, to go a-hunting, to be idle, *skyttla*, to run to and fro; all of which (as Rietz says) are mere derivatives from Swed. *skjuta*, to shoot. To *skit* is a secondary verb, of Scand. origin, from the verb to *shoot*; and means to be full of shootings or quick darts, to jerk or jump about; hence the adj. *skittish*, full of frisks or capers. Cf. 'If she *skit* and recoil,' i. e. is shy; Chapman, May Day, ii. 3. See further under **Shoot**.   β. We may also note Swed. *skytt*, Icel. *skyti*, *skytja*, *skytta*, Dan. *skytte*, an archer, marksman (lit. 'a shooter'), whence the verb *to skit* also means 'to aim at' or reflect upon a person. '*Skit*, verb, to reflect on;' E. D. S. Gloss. B. 1; A.D. 1781. We even find MDan. *skytte-vers*, a jeering verse (Kalkar). This explains the sb. *skit*, 'an oblique taunt,' Jamieson. Cf. Dan. *skotte til*, to cast a sly look at (Larsen); AS. *on-scyte*, an attack, a calumny. Vigfusson notices E. *skit* with reference to Icel. *skúti*, *skúta*, *skæting*, a scoff, taunt; perhaps these also may be referred to the same prolific Teut. base **skeut-*.   ¶ The surname *Skeat*, ME. *skeet*, swift, in King Alisaunder, 5637, Icel. *skjótr*, swift, fleet, is likewise from Icel. *skjóta* to shoot; and is closely related.

SKITTLES, a game in which wooden pins are knocked down by a ball. (Scand.) Formerly *keels* or *kayles* or *kails*; see **Kails**. Also *kettle-pins* or *skittle-pins*. Todd cites: 'When shall our *kittle-pins* return again into the Grecian *skyttals*?' Sadler, Rights of the Kingdom, 1649, p. 43. Halliwell gives *kettle-pins*, skittles. 'The Grecian *skyttals*' is an invention, evidently suggested by Gk. σκυτάλη, a stick, staff, from which Sadler probably imagined that *skittles* was 'derived,' in the old-fashioned way of 'deriving' all English words from Latin and Greek. As *kittle-pins* never came from Greek, there is no reason why it should be expected to 'return' to it.   β. From comparison of *skittles* with *kittle-pins*, we may infer that the old name was *skittle-pins*, i.e. pins to be knocked down by a *skittle* or projectile. *Skittle* is, in fact, a doublet of *shuttle*, signifying, originally, anything that could be *shot* or thrown; thus the ME. *schitel* meant the bolt of a door. Cf. ME. *schytle*, a child's game, L. *sagitella*, Prompt. Parv.; though there is a doubt whether this refers to *skittles* or to *shuttle-cock*.   γ. *Shuttle* is the English, but *skittle* the Scand. form. —Dan. *skyttel*, a shuttle, Swed. dial. *skyttel*, *sköttel*, an earthen ball for a child's game (Rietz); MDan. *skyttel*, a shuttle, an earthen or stone ball to play with; *skyttelleg*, the game of skittles, *skyttelbane*, a skittle-track; Icel. *skutill*, an implement shot forth, a harpoon, a bolt or bar of a door.—Teut. and Icel. *skut-*, weak grade of the strong verb *skjóta*, to shoot, cognate with E. **Shoot**, q.v. And see **Shuttle**. Also see **Skittish**.   ¶ It follows that the *skittle* was orig. the ball which was aimed at the pins or 'skittle-pins;' and the *skittle-alley* was the course along which the ball ran.

SKUA, a bird, a kind of gull. (Scand.) '*Lestris cataractes*, the common skua;' Engl. Encycl. s. v. *Laridæ*. Shetland *skooi*; Faroese *skúir* (1604); see Newton, Dict. of Birds; Dan. *skua* (Larsen). Apparently a corruption of Icel. *skúfr*, a skua; also called *skúmr*, 'the skua, or brown gull;' Icel. Dict. I suppose the reference is to the colour; cf. Icel. *skúmi*, shade, dusk; Swed. *skum*, dusky; Norweg. *skum*, dull, dusky, chiefly used of the weather, but sometimes of colour. Perhaps allied to **Sky**.

SKUE, old spelling of **Skew**, q.v.

SKULK, the same as **Sculk**, q.v.

SKULL, SCULL, the bony casing of the brain, the head, cranium. (Scand.) ME. *skulle*, *sculle*, Chaucer, C. T. 3933 (A 3935); spelt *schulle*, Ancren Riwle, p. 296, l. 4; *scolle*, Rob. of Glouc. p. 16, l. 374. Named from its shell-like shape.—Swed. dial. *skulle*, variant of *sköllt*, scull; Norw. *skult*, scull. From Teut. **skul*, weak grade of **skelan-* (pt. t. **skal*), to cleave, divide. From the base **skal* we have Swed. *hufvud-skalle*, the skull, Dan. *hjerne-skal*, skull. See further under **Scale** (2). **Der.** *scull* (2), q.v.; also *skull-cap*.

SKUNK, a N. American quadruped. (N. American Indian.) Modern; imported from N. American. 'Contracted from the Abenaki *seganku*;' Webster. But this is an incorrect form of *segongw*; see N. and Q., 10 S. iii. 386. Abenaki is a dialect of the Algonquin race of N. American Indians, spoken in Lower Canada and Maine.

SKY, the clouds, the heavens. (Scand.) ME. *skie*, *skye*, in the sense of 'cloud;' Chaucer, Ho. of Fame, iii. 510. Used in the mod. general sense, King Alisaunder, 318.—Icel. *ský*, a cloud; Dan. and

Swed. *sky*, a cloud. Allied to AS. *scēo*, OSax. *scio*, a cloud ; AS. *scúa*, *scúwa*, a shade, Grein, ii. 412 ; Icel. *skuggi*, shade, shadow. All from the √SQEU, to cover ; whence also *scu-m*, *show-er*, *hide*, and *ob-scu-re* ; Fick, iii. 337. Cf. Skt. *sku*, to cover ; L. *ob-scū-rus*. Der. *sky-blue*, *-lark*, *-light*, *-rocket*, *-sail* ; *sky-ward*, toward the sky. Also *sky-ey*, adj., Meas. for Meas. iii. 1. 9.

SLAB (1), a thin slip or flat piece of stone or wood. (F.—Teut.) Now gen. used of stone ; but formerly also of timber. ‘ *Slab*, the outside plank of a piece of timber, when sawn into boards ;’ Ray, North-Country Words, ed. 1691 ; also written *slap* (Halliwell). Also used of pieces of tin ; Ray, Account of Preparing Tin. ‘ Saue *slab* of thy timber for stable and stie ;’ Tusser, Husbandry, sect. 16, st. 35. (E. D. S.) ME. *slab*, rare ; but we find the expression ‘ a *slab* of ire,’ i.e. a piece of iron, in Popular Treatises on Science, ed. Wright, p. 135, l. 141. Cf. also Prov. E. *slappel*, a piece, part, or portion, given as a Sussex word in Ray’s South-Country Words ; also *slape*, a flag-shaped slate (E. D. S.). The form *slape* was prob. the original one.—OF. *esclape*, ‘ éclat ; de menus *esclapes* de bois,’ i.e. thin slabs of wood (Godefroy). Hence Low L. *sclapa*, a shingle (Ducange). Cf. Prov. *esclapo*, a piece of cut wood, *esclapa-bos*, a wood-cutter, and *esclapa*, vb., to split wood (Mistral) ; Ital. *schiappare*, to cleave wood (Florio). Perhaps from the prefix *es-* (= L. *ex*), an intensive ; and Low G. *klappen*, to clap, to make an explosive sound (hence, to cleave noisily) ; cf. G. *klaffen*, to split. See Körting, § 5282. Cf. **Éclat**.

SLAB (2), viscous, slimy. (Scand.) ‘ Make the gruel thick and *slab* ;’ Macb. iv. 1. 32. ‘ *Slabby*, sloppy, dirty ;’ Halliwell. From prov. E. *slab*, a puddle ; whence, probably, Irish *slab*, *slaib*, Gael. *slaib*, mire, mud left on the strand of a river ; Gael. *slaibeach*, miry. — Icel. *slabb*, dirt from sleet and rain ; Swed. dial. and Norw. *slabb*, MDan. *slab*, mire (whence *slab*, slippery). Cf. ME. *slabben*, to wallow ; EFries. *slabben*, Du. *slabben*, to lap up ; Swed. dial. *slabba*, to splash, to soil. And see **Slabber** (below).

SLABBER, to slaver, to let the saliva fall from the mouth, to make wet and dirty. (E.) The forms *slabber*, *slobber*, *slubber*, are mixed up. *Slubber* (q.v.) is the Scand. form. Again, we have also the form *slaver* ; also of Scand. origin ; see **Slaver**. ‘ Her milke-pan and creame-pot so *slabbered* and sost ’ [dirtied] ; Tusser’s Husbandry, April, sect. 48, st. 20. (E. D. S.) ME. *slaberen*. ‘ Then come sleuthe al *bislabered* ’ = then came Sloth, all be-slabbered ; P. Plowman, B. v. 392 ; where another MS. has *byslobred*. Not found in AS. A frequentative form, with the usual suffix *-er*, from ME. *slabben*: ‘ hy ine helle *slabbeth*,’ they wallow in hell ; Shoreham’s Poems, p. 151 ; see **Slab** (above). Cf. MDan. *slabre*, to slabber ; Swed. dial. *slabbra i seg*, to eat greedily and carelessly ; EFries. and Westphal. *slabbern*, to lap, sup, or lick up ; Low G. *slabbern*, *slubbern*, to slabber, lap, sip, frequent. of *slabben*, to lap ; G. *schlabbern*, *schlabben*, to lap, to slabber. Also MDu. *slabben*, *be-slabben*, to slaver ; *een slabbe*, or *slab-doeck*, a child’s bib, or slavering clout [where *doeck* = G. *tuch*, cloth] ; Hexham. Hexham also gives *slabben*, ‘ to lappe as dogges doe in drinking, to sup, or to licke ;’ with the frequentative *slabberen*, ‘ to sup up hot broath.’ So also prov. E. *slap*, to slop ; Dan. dial. *slabbe*, *slappe*, to lap up. Of imitative origin ; cf. *slobber*, *slubber*, *slaver*.

SLACK, lax, loose. (E.) ME. *slak*. ‘ With *slakke* paas ’ = with slow pace ; Chaucer, C. T. 2903 (A 2901). AS. *sleac*, slack, slow, Grein, ii. 455. ‘ Lentus, vel piger, *sleac* ;’ Voc. 170. 1.+Icel. *slakr*, slack ; whence *slakna*, to slacken, become slack ; Swed. and Dan. *slak* ; Provincial G. *schlack*, slack (Flügel) ; MHG. *slach*, OHG. *slah*. β. All from a Teut. type *slakoz*. Allied to **Lag** and to **Lax**. Brugmann, i. § 193. Der. *slack-ly*, *slack-ness*. Also *slack*, verb, Oth. iv. 3. 88, spelt *slacke* in Palsgrave ; of which *slake* is a doublet ; see **Slake**. Also *slack-en*, properly ‘ to become slack,’ though often used in the trans. sense ; the ME. form is *slekken* (Stratmann). Also *slag*, q. v., *slug*. q. v.

SLADE, a dell, glade, valley. (E.) Common in prov. E. ; also in the form *slad*. ‘ My smoother *slades* ;’ Drayton, Polyolbion, Song i. l. 28 from end. Gower has the pl. *slades* ; Conf. Amant. ii. 93 ; bk. iv. 2727. AS. *slæd* (dat. *slade*), a strath, a valley.+ Westphal. *slade*, a ravine ; Dan. dial. *slade*, a flat piece of land ; Norw. *slade*, a slope, *sladna*, to slope down ; Aasen says there is evidence of a strong verb with the stems *sled*, *slad*, *slod*, to slope ; parallel to **Slide**. See **Sled**.

SLAG, the dross of metal, scoria. (Swed.) ‘ Another furnace they have, . . . in which they melt the *slags*, or refuse of the litharge ;’ Ray, On the Smelting of Silver (1674) ; in reprint of Ray’s Glossaries, Glos. B. 15, p. 10. (E. D. S.) It also occurs in Stanyhurst, tr. of Virgil (1582), Æn. iii. 576 ; ed. Arber, p. 89, l. 4. The word is Swedish.—Swed. *slagg*, dross, dross of metal, slag ; *järnslagg*, dross of iron ; *slaggvarp*, a heap of dross and cinders (Widegren) ; allied to Norw. *slagga*, to flow over. So called from its flowing

over when the metal is fused ; cf. Icel. *slagna*, to flow over, be spilt ; *slag*, *slagi*, wet, dampness, water penetrating walls. Cf. Dan. *slakker*, slag (Larsen) ; Low G. *slakke*, G. *schlacke*, scoria. These suggest a connexion with **Slack**. ¶ Not allied to Swed. *slag*, a blow. Der. *slagg-y*.

SLAKE, to slacken, quench, mix with water. (E.) To *slake* or *slack* lime is to put water to it, and so disintegrate or loosen it. ‘ Quick-lime, taken as it leaves the kiln, and thrown into a proper quantity of water, splits with noise, puffs up, produces a large disengagement of vapour, and falls into a thick paste ;’ Weale, Dict. of Terms in Architecture, &c. *Slake* is an older spelling than *slack* (verb), of which it is a doublet. ME. *slaken*, to render slack, to slake. ‘ His wraþþe for to *slake* ;’ Will. of Palerne, 728 ; spelt *slakie*, Layamon, 23345, later text. AS. *sleacian*, to grow slack or remiss ; found in the comp. *āsleacian*, Ælfric’s Homilies, i. 610, l. 16, ii. 98, l. 15.—AS. *sleac*, slack ; see **Slack**. Perhaps affected by the cognate MDu. *slaken*, ‘ to slack, let slip, soften, become liquid.’ β. There is also a ME. *slekken*, to quench, extinguish, Prompt. Parv. This is from AS. *sleccan*, Grein, ii. 455, which is a causal form. Cf. Icel. *slökva*, to slake ; which, however, was orig. a strong verb, with pp. *slokinn* ; still it is from the same Teut. base *slak-*. Also Swed. *släcka*, to quench, put out, allay, slack ; a causal form, from *slak*, slack.

SLAM, to shut with violence and noise. (Scand.) ‘ To *slam* one, to beat or cuff one strenuously, to push violently ; he *slamm’d-to* the door ; North ;’ Grose’s Provincial Glossary, ed. 1790. — Norweg. *slemba*, to smack, bang, bang or slam a door quickly ; also spelt *slemma*, *slamra* ; Swed. dial. *slämma*, to slam, strike or push hastily, to slam a door (Aasen, Rietz) ; Icel. *slamra*, *slambra*, to slam. Cf. Swed. *slamra*, to prate, chatter, jingle ; *slammer*, a clank, noise. To *slam* is to strike smartly, and is related to *Slap* ; see **Slap**. Of imitative origin ; note prov. E. *slam-bang*, *slap-bang*, violently ; Halliwell.

SLANDER, scandal, calumny, false report, defamation. (F.—L.—Gk.) A doublet of *scandal*, as will appear. ME. *sclaundre*, Chaucer, C. T. 8598 (E 722) ; *sclaundre*, Wyclif, Matt. xiii. 41 ; K. Alisaunder, 757.—OF. *esclandre*, ‘ a slander ;’ Cot. (We find the OF. forms *escandele*, *escandle*, *escandre* (Burguy) ; and lastly, by insertion of *l*, the form *esclandre*.)—L. *scandalum* ; see **Scandal**. Der. *slander*, verb, ME. *sclaundren*, Wyclif, Matt. xiii. 21 ; *slander-er* ; *slander-ous*, from OF. *esclandreux* (Cot.) ; *slander-ous-ly*. Doublet, *scandal*.

SLANG, low, vulgar language, a colloquial and familiar mode of expression. (Scand.) Not in early use. In the Slang Dict., the earliest known instance is given as follows. ‘ Let proper nurses be assigned, to take care of these babes of grace [young thieves] . . . The master who teaches them should be a man well versed in the cant language commonly called the *slang patter*, in which they should by all means excel ;’ Jonathan Wild’s Advice to his Successor ; London, J. Scott, 1758. The same Dict. gives : ‘ *Slang*, to cheat, abuse in foul language ; *Slang-whanger*, a long-winded speaker ; also, *out on the slang*, to travel with a hawker’s licence ; *slang*, a watch-chain, a travelling-show.’ [But the existence of this book (of 1758) is doubted. In 1762, Foote has : ‘ ay, but that’s all *slang* [pretence], I suppose ;’ The Orators, A. i. sc. 1.] Probably derived from *slang*, 2nd grade of the verb to sling, i. e. to throw, cast. This is shown by Wedgwood, following Aasen. β. We find, for example, Norweg. *sleng*, a slinging, also an invention, device, stratagem ; also, a little addition, or burthen of a song, in verse and melody ; *ettersleng* (lit. after-slang), a burthen at the end of a verse of a ballad ; *slenga*, to dangle (which shows why *slang* sometimes means a watch-chain) ; *slengja*, to sling, cast, *slengja kjeften* (lit. to sling the jaw), to use abusive language, to slang ; *slengjenamn*, a nickname (lit. a slang-name) ; also, a name that has no just reason ; *slengjeord* (lit. a slang-word), an insulting word or allusion, a new word that has no just reason, or, as Aasen puts it, *fornærmelige Ord eller Hentydninger*, *nye Ord som ikke have nogen rigtig Grund*. The use of *slang* in the sense ‘ to cheat ’ reminds us of Icel. *slyngr*, *slunginn*, versed in a thing, cunning. And that all the above Norweg. and Icel. words are derivatives from *sling* is quite clear ; see **Sling**. I see no objection to this explanation. Note also Swed. *slanger*, gossip. ¶ Taylor, in his Words and Places, gives, without any proof or reference, the following explanation. ‘ A *slang* is a narrow strip of waste land by the road-side, such as those which are chosen by the gipsies for their encampments. [This is amplified from Halliwell, who merely says : ‘ *Slang*, a narrow piece of land, sometimes called *slanket*.’] To be *out on the slang*, in the lingo used by thieves and gipsies, means to travel about the country as a hawker, encamping by night on the roadside slangs. [Amplified from the Slang Dict., which says not a word about these night-encampments. A travelling-show was also called a *slang*. It is easy to see how the term *slang* was transferred to the language spoken by hawkers and itinerant showmen.' To this I take exception; it is not 'easy to see.' On the other hand, it is likely that *a slang* (from the verb *sling*, to cast) may have meant 'a cast' or 'a pitch;' for both *cast* and *pitch* are used to mean a camping-place, or a place where a travelling-show is exhibited; and, indeed, 'a narrow slip of ground' is also called a *slinget* or *slanget*; E. D. D.

SLANT, to slope. (Scand.) 'Fortune beginneth so to *slant*,' i. e. fail; Libell of E. Policie, l. 757. We also have *slant*, adj. sloping; the verb should rather take the form *to slent*. Lowland Sc. *sclent*, *sklent*, *sklint*, to give a slanting direction, to dart askance (in relation to the eyes), to pass obliquely, to render sloping (Jamieson). ME. *slenten*, to slope, to glide; 'it [a blow] *slented* doune to the erthe,' Malory, Morte Arthure, bk. xvii. c. 1; leaf 345. 'A fote ynto the erthe hyt *sclente*;' MS. Camb. Ff. ii. 38, fol. 113; cited in Halliwell, p. 711. [The insertion of *c*, as in *sclenten*, occurs again in ME. *sclendre* for mod. E. *slender*.]—Norw. *slenta*, to fall aside, or fall slanting (Ross); Swed. dial. *slenta*, *slänta*, lit. 'to cause to slide;' causal form of the strong verb *slinta* (pt. t. *slant*, pp. *sluntit*), to slide, slip with the foot (Rietz). Cf. MSwed. *slinta*, to slip with the foot (Ihre); Swed. *slinta*, to slip, miss one's step, to glance (as a chisel on a stone), to slip or glance (as a knife); Widegren. Also MDan. *slanten*, slack; *slente*, to slip aside, be slack; Swed. *slutta* (= *slunta*), to slant, slope. β. The E. adj. *slant*, sloping, answers to the Swed. dial. *slant*, adj. slippery, esp. used of a path; the connexion between *sloping* and *slippery*, in this case, is obvious. **Der.** *slant-ly*, *slant-wise*; also *a-slant*, q. v.

SLAP, to smack, to strike with the flat open hand. (E.) Rare in literature; but we find ME. *slappe*, sb., a smart blow; Palladius on Husbandry, b. iv. l. 763. It seems to be an E. word; it occurs both in Low and High German.+Low G. *slapp*, the sound of a blow, a sounding box on the ears. '*Slapp! sloog ik em an de snute*, I hit him on the snout, *slap!*' Bremen Wörterbuch; G. *schlapp*, interj., slap! *schlappe*, sb., a slap; *schlappen*, verb, to slap. [Quite a different word from Swed. *slapp*, lax, loose, Dan. *slap*, slack, &c.] β. An imitative word, to express the sound of a blow; allied to *slam*; cf. prov. E. *slam-bang*, *slap-bang*, violently (Halliwell). **Der.** *slap*, sb., ME. *slappe*, as above; *slap*, adv., *slap-bang*, violently.

SLASH, to cut with a violent sweep, cut at random or violently. (F.—Teut.) ME. *slashen*; rare. In Wyclif, 3 Kings, v. 18, the L. *dolāuērunt* is translated by *han ouerscorchide* in the earlier text, with the various reading *han slascht*; the later text has *hewiden*. 'Hewing and *slashing*;' Spenser, F. Q. ii. 9. 15. 'Here's snip, and nip, and cut, and *slish*, and *slash*;' Tam. Shrew, iv. 3. 90. 'But presently *slash* off his traitorous head;' Green, Alphonsus, Act ii; ed. Dyce, vol. ii. p. 23. '*Slash*, a cut or gash, *Yorksh*.;' Halliwell. *Slashed* sleeves are sleeves with *gashes* in them, as is well known. OF. *esclachier*, to break in pieces (Godefroy).—OF. *es-* (<L. *ex*), very; and Teut. type **klakjan*, MHG. *klecken*, to break with a 'clack;' cf. F. *claque*, a clack, from MHG. *klac*, a clack, sudden noise. See Körting, § 5280. β. Perhaps confused with OF. *escleschier*, *esclicier*, to slice; see **Slice.** ¶ The Swed. *slaska*, to splash, accounts only for prov. E. *slashy*, wet, Lowland Sc. *slash*, to work in wet, *slatch*, to dabble in mire, *sclatch*, to bedaub; which are words unrelated to the present one, but allied to prov. E. *slosh* and *slush*. **Der.** *slash*, sb. *Slash*, to whip, is perhaps an intensive form of **Lash**, q. v.

SLAT, a long, narrow strip of wood, a lath. (F.—Teut.) The same word as **Slate** (below). Cf. prov. E. *slat*, a slate; ME. *slat*, a slate, Prompt. Parv.

SLATE (1), a well-known stone that is easily split, a piece of such stone. (F.—Teut.) ME. *slat*, usually *sclat*, Wyclif, Luke, v. 19. So called from its fissile nature.—OF. *esclat*, 'a shiver, splinter, or little piece of wood broken off with violence; also a small thin lath or shingle,' Cot. [A *shingle* is a sort of wooden tile.]—OF. *esclater*; whence *s'esclater*, 'to split, burst, shiver into splinters;' Cot. This answers to a Late L. type **ex-clapitāre*, to break with a clap; from L. *ex*, very, and Low G. *klapp*, a clap, *klappen*, to clap. Körting, § 5282. See **Slab** (1). The OF. *esclat* = mod. F. *éclat*; hence *éclat* is the same word. **Der.** *slate-pencil*, *slat-er*, *slat-ing*, *slat-y*. Doublets, *éclat*, *slat*.

SLATE (2), to set on a dog, to bait, damage, abuse. (E.) 'Of bole *slating*,' bull-baiting; King Alisaunder, 200. AS. *slǣtan*, to cause to rend.—AS. *slāt*, 2nd grade of *slītan*, to slit, tear; see **Slit.**

SLATTERN, a sluttish, untidy woman. (Scand.) It is used both by Butler and Dryden; Todd's Johnson (no reference). The final *-n* is difficult to account for; it is either a mere addition, as in *bitter-n*, or *slattern* is short for *slatterin'* = *slattering*; unless it was borrowed directly from MDan. *slatten*, untidy, dirty; *slatten-spaad*, a slattern (Kalkar). Ray, in his North-Country Words, has: 'Dawgos, or Dawkin, a dirty *slatternly* woman.' Kersey

(1721) has: *Slattern*, a slattering woman.' Grose's Supp. (1790) has *slatterkin*. The word is formed from the verb *to slatter*, to waste, use wastefully, be untidy. '*Slatter*, to waste; or rather, perhaps, not to make a proper and due use of anything; thus they say, take care, or you'll *slatter* it all away; also, to be negligent and slovenly;' Halliwell. '*Slatter*, to wash in a careless way, throwing the water about;' Forby. *Slatter* is the frequentative (with the usual suffix *-er*) of prov. E. *slat*, to splash, to dash; cf. Icel. *sletta*, to slap, dab (liquids). Perhaps from *slatt-*, as seen in Norw. *sletta*, str. verb (pt. t. *slatt*), to dangle, to hang loose (as clothes do); also, to be idle (Aasen); by-form of *slenta*, to slip, fall aside; see **Slant.** Allied words are Dan. *slat*, a slop; *slat*, *slatten*, *slattet*, loose, flabby; *slattes*, to become slack; *slatte*, a slattern; Low G. *slatje*, a slattern. Also Icel. *slattari*, a tramp. **Der.** *slattern-ly*. ☞ Distinct from *slut*, but perhaps allied to it.

SLAUGHTER, a slaying, carnage, butchery. (Scand.) ME. *slaghter*, Pricke of Conscience, 3367; also *slautir*, spelt *slawtyr* in Prompt. Parv. The word is strictly Scand., from Icel. *slātr*, a slaughtering, butcher's meat, whence *slātra*, verb, to slaughter cattle. See Noreen, § 224. If the E. word had been uninfluenced by the Icel. word, it would have taken the form *slaght* or *slaught*; in fact, the commonest forms in ME. are *slaȝt*, Rob. of Glouc. p. 56, l. 1286; *slawhte*, Gower, C. A. i. 348; directly from AS. *sleaht*, Grein, ii. 455. β. The AS. *sleaht* is cognate with Du. and Swed. *slagt*, G. *schlacht*. Teut. types **slah-toz*, m., **slah-tā*, f., a slaying (Fick, iii. 358); the Icel. *slātr* is a neut. sb., closely related, with the same sense. γ. All from the base SLAH, whence E. *slay*; see **Slay.** **Der.** *slaughter*, verb, K. John, iii. 1. 302; *slaughter-man*, *-house*; *slaughter-ous*, Macb. v. 5. 14; *slaughter-er*.

SLAVE, a serf, one in bondage. (F.—L.—Gk.—Slavonic.) In Chaucer, Troil. iii. 391. In A Deuise of a Maske for the right honourable Viscount Mountacute, Gascoigne introduces the words *slaue* and *slaueries*; see Works, ed. Hazlitt, i. 82, ll. 15, 20; i. 81, l. 13.—F. *esclave*, 'a slave;' Cot.—Late L. *sclavus*, a Slavonian captive, a slave.—Late Gk. Σκλάβος, Ἐσκλαβηνός, a Slavonian, one of Slavonic race captured and made a bondman. 'From the Euxine to the Adriatic, in the state of captives or subjects . . . they [the Slavonians] overspread the land; and the national appellation of the *Slaves* has been degraded by chance or malice from the signification of glory to that of servitude;' Gibbon, Decline of the Roman Empire, c. 55. β. Gibbon here supposes *slave* to be allied to Russ. *slava*, glory, fame; but the true origin of *Slavonian* is unknown; Miklosich, p. 308. **Der.** *slave*, verb, K. Lear, iv. 1. 71; *slav-er-y*, *slav-ish*, *-ly*, *-ness*; *slave-trade*; also *en-slave*.

SLAVER, to slabber. (Scand.) 'His mouthe *slavers*;' Pricke of Conscience, 784. *Slaveryt* [for *slaveryth*] is used to translate F. *bave*; Walter de Bibbesworth, l. 12, in Wright's Vocab. i. 143.—Icel. *slafra*, to slaver; cognate with Low G. *slabbern*, to slaver, slabber; see **Slabber.** **Der.** *slaver*, sb., from Icel. *slafr* (also *slefa*), sb.; *slaver-er*. **Doublet,** *slabber*.

SLAY (1), to kill. (E.) Orig. to strike, smite. ME. *sleen*, *slee*, Chaucer, C. T. 663 (A 661); pt. t. *slouh*, *slou* (*slew* in Tyrwhitt), id. 989 (A 987); pp. *slain*, id. 994 (A 992). AS. *slēan* (contracted form of **slahan*), to smite, slay; pt. t. *slōh*, *slōg*, pl. *slōgon*; pp. *slegen*; Grein, ii. 455, 456.+Du. *slaan*, pt. t. *sloeg*, pp. *geslagen*; Icel. *slā*; Dan. *slaae*; Swed. *slå*; Goth. *slahan*; G. *schlagen*; OHG. *slahan*. β. All from Teut. type **slah-an-*, to smite; Fick, iii. 358. Cf. OIrish *slig-im*, I strike. **Der.** *slay-er*, ME. *sle-er*, Chaucer, C. T. 2007 (A 2005); also *slaugh-t-er*, q. v.; *slay* (2), q. v.; *sledge-hammer*, q. v.

SLAY (2), **SLEY,** a weaver's reed. (E.) '*Slay*, an instrument belonging to a weaver's loom that has teeth like a comb;' Phillips. '*Slay*, a wevers tole;' Palsgrave.—AS. *slǣ*; 'Pe[c]tica, *slǣ*;' Voc. 262. 21; also *slege*, Voc. 188. 5; also (in the 8th century) 'Pectica, *slahae*,' id. 30. 19. So called from its striking or pressing the web tightly together.—AS. **slah-*, base of *slēan*, to strike, smite; see **Slay** (1). 'Percusso feriunt insecti pectine dentes;' Ovid, Metam. vi. 58. Cf. Icel. *slā*, a bar, bolt. See Camb. Phil. Trans. 1899, p. 139 (231).

SLEAVE, SLEAVE-SILK, soft floss silk. (Scand.—G.) 'Ravell'd *sleave*,' i. e. tangled loose silk, Macb. ii. 2. 37. See Nares and Halliwell.—Dan. dial. *slöve*, a knot, twist, tangle (in thread); Dan. dial. *slöfgarn*, yarn that runs into knots; Dan. *slöife*, a bow, a knot; EFries. *slöve*, *slöfe*, a slip-knot.—G. (dial.) *schläufe*, a slip-knot; with the same sense as G. *schleife* (Kluge). Cf. OHG. *sloufan*, causal of *sliofan*, to slip. See **Slip.**

SLEAZY, poor, light, said of a material. (Silesia.) 'Such *sleazy* stuff;' Howell's Letters, vol. i. let. 1. '*Sleazie Holland*, common people take to be all forrain linnen, which is sleight [slight] or ill wrought; whenas that only is properly *Slesia* or *Silesia* linnen cloth, which is made in, and comes from the Countrey *Silesia* in Germany;'

Blount's Gloss., ed. 1681. In fact, it is called *Silesia* still; see *Silesia* in C. D., where the name is said to be used in the United States; but it is used in England also.

SLED, SLEDGE, SLEIGH, a carriage made for sliding over snow or ice. (Du.) ME. *slede*, Prompt. Parv. Pl. *sledis*, Wyclif, 1 Chron. xx. 3; spelt *sleddis* in the later text. — MDu. *sledde*, a sledge; Du. *slede*. We also find Icel. *sleði*, Swed. *släde*, Dan. *slæde*. These forms are evidently from a Teut. root *sled*, whence would be formed the 2nd grade *slad*, and a weak grade *slud*, giving the strong verb *sledan-*, pt. t. *slad*, pp. *sludanoz*; quite distinct from E. *slide*, though a parallel formation and having a similar sense. Franck connects Du. *slede* with E. *slide*, without explaining the vowel. But it is obvious that the Norw. *slodde*, a kind of rude sledge (Larsen), cannot be related to the form *slide*. Cf. Irish and Gael. *slaod*, a sledge, from *slaod*, to slide. β. The different spellings may be thus explained. 1. The right form is *sled*. 2. The form *sledge* (perhaps from the pl. *sleds*) appears to be due to confusion with the commoner word *sledge* in the sense of 'hammer;' see *Sledge-hammer*. 3. The form *sleigh* is due to contraction by the loss of *d*. Thus the Norwegian and Low G. have both *slede* and *slee*; so also Du. *sleekoets*, a sleigh-coach, stands for *sledekoets*. The final *gh* is unmeaning.

SLEDGE-HAMMER, a mallet or heavy hammer. (E.) Properly *sledge*; *sledge-hammer* means 'hammer-hammer,' and shows reduplication. *Sledge* represents ME. *slegge*, Romans of Partenay, 3000; Trevisa, tr. of Higden, vi. 199. AS. *slecg* (dat. *slecge*), a heavy hammer; Voc. 448. 1. Lit. 'a smiter;' for *slag-jā*, fem.; from *slag-*, for *slah-*, base of AS. *slēan*, to smite, slay; see **Slay** (1).+Du. *slegge, slei*, a mallet; Swed. *slägga*, a sledge; Icel. *sleggja*. Cf. also G. *schlägel*, Du. *slegel*, a mallet; from the same verb. We even find G. *schlag-hammer*, with *hammer* suffixed, as in English.

SLEEK, SLICK, smooth, glossy, soft. (Scand.) 'I *slecke*, I make paper smothe with a *sleke-stone*, Je fais glissant;' Palsgrave. 'And if the cattes skyn be *slyk* and gay;' Chaucer, C. T. (D 351), Ellesmere MS.; other readings *slike, sclyke*. Tyrwhitt prints *sleke*, l. 5933. Spelt *slike*, adv., smoothly, Havelok, 1157. There is no AS. *slíc* (see Napier); only AS. *slician*, to make smooth.—Icel. *slíkr*, sleek, smooth; whence *slíki-steinn*, a fine whetstone (for polishing). Cf. MDu. *sleyck*, 'plaine, or even;' Hexham. β. The Du. *slijk*, Low G. *slikk*, G. *schlick*, grease, slime, mud, are closely related words; so also is the strong verb which appears in Low G. *sliken* (pt. t. *sleek*, pp. *sleken*), G. *schleichen* (pt. t. *schlich*, pp. *geschlichen*), OHG. *slíhhan*, to slink, crawl, sneak, move slowly (as if through mire); see **Slink**. The Teut. type of the verb is *sleikan-*, pt. t. *slaik*, pp. *slikanoz*. The orig. sense of *sleek* is 'greasy,' like soft mud. In exactly the same way, from the base *slíp*, we have Icel. *sleipr*, slippery (North E. *slape*), and *slípa*, to make smooth, to whet, Du. *slijpen*, to polish, G. *schleifen*, to glide, to whet, polish.

SLEEP, to slumber, repose. (E.) ME. *slepen*, Chaucer, C. T. 10. Properly a strong verb, with pt. t. *slēp*, which has become *slep* in Prov. E., and occurs in Chaucer, C. T. 98. AS. *slǽpan, slēpan*, pt. t. *slēp*; Grein, ii. 455.+Du. *slapen*; Goth. *slēpan*, pt. t. *sai-slēp* (with reduplication); G. *schlafen*; OHG. *slāfan*. In connexion with these is the sb. which appears as E. *sleep*, AS. *slǽp*, Du. *slaap*, Goth. *slēps*, G. *schlaf*, OHG. *slāf*; of which the orig. sense is drowsiness, numbness, lethargy; as shown more clearly by the related adjective in Low G. *slapp*, G. *schlaff*, lax, loose, unbent, remiss, flabby. Cf. Russ. *slabuii*, weak, feeble, faint, slack, loose; also L. *lābi*, to glide; *labāre*, to totter. The Teut. type of the sb. is *slǽpoz*, m.; and of the verb, *slǽpan-*. Brugmann, i. §§ 200, 567. Der. *a-sleep*, q.v.; *sleep-er, sleep-less, sleep-less-ly, sleep-less-ness; sleep-walk-er, sleep-walk-ing; sleep-y, sleep-i-ly, -ness*.

SLEEPER, a block of wood on which rails rest. (E.) From the verb above. Cf. F. *dormant*, a sleeper, from *dormir*, to sleep. And see Coles.

SLEET, rain mingled with snow or hail. (E.) ME. *sleet*, Chaucer, C. T. 11562 (F 1250). The word is English; answering to OMerc. *slēte*, AS. *sliete*, *slyte*, not found. Cf. EFries. *slaite*, hail; Norw. *sloten*, pl., hailstones (Lübben); G. *schlosse*, hailstone. The E. word would result regularly from the Teut. type *slautjā*, orig. sense unknown. Cf. Norw. *slūtr*, sleet (Ross); from the related Teut. base *slūt-* (appearing in the Du. *sluiten*, to close, shut; so that the orig. sense may have been 'blinding,' or closing the eyes).

SLEEVE, part of a garment, covering the arm. (E.) ME. *sleeue*, *sleue* (with *u* = *v*); Chaucer, C. T. 193. OMerc. *slēf*; AS. *slȳf* (for earlier *slīef*). 'On his twā *slēfan*,' in his two sleeves; Blickling Hom., p. 181, l. 17. 'On his twām *slȳfum*' = in his two sleeves; Ælfric's Homilies, i. 376. *Slēf-lēas*, sleeveless; Voc. 151. 35. 'Manica, *slȳf*;' id. 328. 13; pl. *slȳfa*, id. 125. 5. We also find the verb *slēfan*, to put on, to clothe; Life of St. Guthlac, c. 16. The long *e* (*ē*) results from a mutation of AS. *ēa* = Teut. *au*, pointing back to a Teut. type *slaubjā*, f., from Teut. root *sleub-*, variant of *sleup-*,

whence MHG. *sloufe*, a cover, allied to MHG. *sloufen*, to let slip, to cover. Cf. Goth. *sliupan* (pt. t. *slaup*), to slip, creep into. It is thus allied to *slip*; from the slipping off and on of the sleeve, in dressing and undressing; compare the history of **Smock**. See **Slip**, and **Slop** (2).+MDu. *sloove*, 'a vaile, or a skinne; the turning up of anything;' whence *slooven*, 'to turne up ones sleeves, to cover ones head;' Hexham. Also MDu. *sleve*, 'a sleeve,' id.; G. *schlaube*, a husk, shell (Flügel). **Der.** *sleeve-less*, AS. *slēflēas*, as above. Horne Tooke explains *a sleeveless errand* (Troil. v. 4. 9) as meaning 'without a cover or pretence,' which is hardly intelligible; I suspect it to mean simply 'imperfect,' hence 'poor,' like a garment without sleeves; cf. AS. *slēflēas*, said of a garment. We find: '*slevelesse wordes*,' Usk, Test. of Love, ii. 8. 77; '*sleeveless rhymes*,' Hall, Sat. iv. 1. 34; 'a *sleveles reson*,' Rel. Antiq. i. 83; 'any *sleeuelesse excuse*;' Lyly's Euphues, p. 114. In each instance it means 'imperfect, poor.'

SLEIGH, the same as **Sled**, q.v. Modern; Du. *slee*, for *slede*. The *gh* is unmeaning. See Notes on E. Etym., p. 273.

SLEIGHT, cunning, dexterity. (Scand.) ME. *sleighte*, Chaucer, C. T. 606 (A 604); *sleiʒte, sleithe*, P. Plowman, C. xxii. 98; *sleiʒþe*, Will. of Palerne, 2151; *slehþe*, Layamon, 17212 (later text, where the first text has *liste*, the E. word).—Icel. *slægð* (for *slægð*), slyness, cunning. Formed, with suffix -ð, from *slægr* (for *slægr*), sly; see **Sly**. Swed. *slögd*, mechanical art, dexterity (which is one sense of E. *sleight*); from *slög*, handy, dexterous, expert; Widegren. β. Thus *sleight* (formerly *sleighth*) is equivalent to *sly-th*, i. e. slyness. **Der.** *sleight-of-hand*. See **Sloid**.

SLENDER, thin, narrow, slight, feeble. (F.—OLow G.) ME. *slendre*, Chaucer, C. T. 589 (A 587), Richard Cuer de Lion, 3530.— OF. *esclendre*, 'sklendre,' Palsgrave, p. 323.—MDu. *slinder*, 'slender, or thinne;' Hexham. The same word is also used as a sb., meaning 'a water-snake;' whilst *slinderen* or *slidderen* means 'to dragge or to traine.' Allied to G. *schlender*, the train of a gown, an easy lounging walk; *schlendern*, to saunter, loiter; also to Low G. *slender*, a long, easy, trailing gown, *slindern*, to slide on the ice, as children do in sport. β. Prob. nasalised derivatives from the base of the verb *to slide*; see **Slide**. But to some extent confused with Du. *slenteren*, to saunter along, and Swed. *slinta*, to slip, glance; see **Slant** and **Slim**. **Der.** *slender-ly, -ness*.

SLEUTH-HOUND. Explained under **Slot** (2).

SLICE, a thin, broad piece. (F.—OHG.) The sb. *slice* seems to be older than the verb. ME. *slice, sclice*, a thin piece, shiver, splinter. 'They braken speres to *sclyces*;' King Alisaunder, 3833.—OF. *esclice*, a shiver, splinter, broken piece of wood; from the verb *esclicier*, to slit, split, break (Godefroy).—OHG. *slizjan, slizzen*, related to *slizan*, to slit; cognate with E. **Slit**, q.v. **Der.** *slice*, verb; 'sliced into pieces,' Chapman, tr. of Homer's Iliad, b. xxii. l. 298; *slic-er*.

SLICK, the same as **Sleek**, q.v.

SLIDE, to glide, slip along, fall. (E.) ME. *sliden, slyden*, Chaucer, C. T. 7958 (E 82); pt. t. *slood*, Wyclif, Lament. iii. 53, later text; pp. *sliden*, spelt *slyden*, ibid., earlier text. AS. *slidan*, pt. t. *slād*, pp. *sliden*; only found in compounds. The pt. t. *æt-slād* is in Ælfric's Homilies, ii. 512, l. 10; the pp. *ā-sliden* in the same, i. 492, l. 11. From the Teut. base SLEID, to slide (Fick, iii. 359); whence also AS. *slide*, a slip, *slidor*, slippery, Icel. *sliðrar*, fem. pl., a scabbard (into which a sword slides); G. *schlitten*, a sledge, *schlittschuh*, a skate (lit. slide-shoe); MDu. *slinder*, a water-snake, *slinderen, slidderen*, 'to dragge or to traine,' Hexham; &c. See **Slender**. β. Further related to Irish and Gael. *slaod*, to trail, Lithuan. *slidus*, slippery. **Der.** *slide, sb., slid-er*; also *sled, sledge*, or *sleigh* (under **Sled**); also *slender*, q. v.

SLIGHT, trifling, small, weak, slender. (OLow G.) ME. *sliʒt, slyʒt*. 'So smoþe, so smal, so seme *slyʒt*,' said of a fair young girl; Allit. Poems, A. 190. The orig. sense is even, flat, as a thing made smooth.—MDu. *slicht*, 'even, or plaine;' *slecht*, 'slight, simple, single, vile, or of little account;' *slecht ende recht*, 'simple and right, without deceit or guile;' Hexham. Thus the successive senses are flat or even, smooth, simple, guileless, vile; by a depreciation similar to that which changed the sense of *silly* from that of 'guileless' to that of 'half-witted.' The verb *to slight* was actually once used in the sense of 'to make smooth;' thus Hexham explains MDu. *slichten* by 'to slight, to make even or plaine.'+OLow G. *sligt*, even, smooth, simple, silly, poor, bad; Icel. *slēttr*, flat, smooth, slight, trivial, common; Dan. *slet*, flat, level, bad; Swed. *slät*, smooth, level, plain, wretched, worthless, slight; Goth. *slaihts*, smooth; Luke, iii. 5; G. *schlecht*, bad; OHG. *sleht*, smooth; G. *schlicht*, smooth, sleek, plain, homely. β. All from Teut. type *sleh-toz*, smooth. Of doubtful origin. **Der.** *slight-ly, slight-ness*; *slight*, verb, to consider as worthless.

SLIM, weak, slender, thin, slight. (Du.) Not in early use. Noticed in Skinner's Dict., ed. 1671, as being in common use in

Lincolnshire. Halliwell has : 'Slim, distorted or worthless, sly, cunning, crafty, slender, thin, slight ;' also slam, tall and lean, the slope of a hill. The orig. sense was 'lax' or 'bending,' hence 'oblique,' or 'transverse ;' then sly, crafty, slight, slender (in the metaphorical sense of unsubstantial) ; and hence slender or slight in the common sense of those words. Thus Barrow, On the Pope's Supremacy, says : 'that was a slim [slight, weak] excuse ;' Todd. Perhaps the earliest instance in which it approaches the modern sense is : 'A thin slim-gutted fox made a hard shift to wriggle his body into a henroost ;' L'Estrange [in Todd]. Perhaps the use of the word has been influenced by confusion with the (unrelated) word slender, which sounds somewhat like it. 'Slim, naughty, crafty, Lincolnsh.; also, slender ;' Bailey, vol. i. ed. 1735.—MDu. slim, 'awry, or byas-wise ; craftie,' Hexham ; [Dan. and Swed. slem, bad, vile, worthless ; from German] ; G. schlimm, bad, evil, sad, unwell, arch, cunning. Der. slim-ness.

SLIME, any glutinous substance, viscous mire, mucus. (E.) ME. slime, slyme, or slim (with long i) ; Gower, C. A. iii. 96 ; bk. vii. 338 ; spelt slim, Ancren Riwle, p. 276, l. 18. AS. slim ; as a various reading in Ps. lxviii. 2 (Spelman).+Du. slijm, phlegm, slime ; Icel. slīm ; Swed. slem ; Dan. sliim, mucus ; G. schleim. Cf. L. lima, a file ; limāre, to file smooth ; and limus, mud. Brugmann, i. § 877. Allied to **Lime** (1) and **Loam**. Der. slim-y, slim-i-ness.

SLING, to fling, cast with a jerk, let swing. (Scand.) ME. slingen ; pt. t. slang, Shoreham's Poems, ed. Wright, p. 132, l. 2 ; pp. slongen ; Sir Percival, 672, in the Thornton Romances, ed. Halliwell.—Icel. slyngva, slöngva, pt. t. slöng, slaung, pp. slunginn, to sling, fling, throw ; MDan. slinge, to sling, cast, twist ; Swed. dial. slinga (pt. t. slang), to sling. Cf. Dan. slynge, weak verb ; Swed. slunga, weak verb.+G. schlingen, pt. t. schlang, pp. geschlungen, to wind, twist, entwine, sling. Teut. type *slengwan- ; pt. t. *slang. Allied, formally, to Lith. slinkti, to creep. Brugmann, i. § 424 (4). ¶ AS. slingan (rare), to creep, seems to be a variant of slincan (below). Der. sling, sb., King Alisaunder, 1191 ; sling-er. Also slang, q. v.

SLINK, to sneak, crawl away. (E.) 'That som of ȝew shall be riȝt feyn to sclynk awey and hyde ;' Tale of Beryn, 3334. AS. slincan, Gen. vi. 7. A nasalised form of an AS. *slīcan, to creep, not found, but cognate with the strong Low G. verb sliken (pt. t. sleek, pp.sleken) and the G. schleichen (pt. t. schlich, pp. geschlichen), to slink, crawl, creep, move slowly ; see **Sleek**. Cf. Swed. dial. slinka (pt. t. slank), to hang loose, to slip. β. The AS. slincan was a strong verb ; we still use slunk as the past tense ; see Titus Andron. iv. 1. 63. Allied to Skt. lang, to limp, L. languēre, to be languid. Perhaps allied to **Sling**.

SLIP, to creep or glide along, to slink, move out of place, escape ; also, to cause to slide, omit, let loose. (E.) We have confused the strong (intransitive) and weak (transitive) forms ; or rather, we have preserved only the weak verb, with pt. t. slipped, pp. slipped or slipt. The strong verb would have become *slipe, pt. t. *slope, pp. *slippen, long disused ; but Gower has him slipeth (used reflexively), riming with wipeth, C. A. ii. 347 ; bk. v. 6530. Gower also has he slipte (wrongly used intransitively), from the weak verb slippen ; C. A. ii. 72 ; bk. iv. 2109 ; the pp. slipped (correctly used) is in Sir Gawayn and the Grene Knight, 244. ME. slippen, transitive weak verb, derived from an AS. strong verb *slīpan (not found ; pt. t. *slāp, pp. *slipen), to slip, glide. The AS. adj. sliper, slippery, is from the weak grade of the pp. ; it occurs in Ælfric's Homilies, ii. 92, l. 16. [It must further be remarked that there is another form of the verb, with a different root-vowel, occurring as AS. slūpan (pt. t. slēap, pp. slopen) ; Grein, ii. 457.]+Du. slippen (weak), to slip, escape ; Dan. slippe (weak), to let go, also to escape ; Swed. slippa (weak), to get rid of, also to escape ; OHG. slipfan, MHG. slipfen, to glide away ; a weak verb, from OHG. slīfan, G. schleifen, to slide, glance, also to grind, whet, polish (i. e. make slippery or smooth). In the last sense, to polish, we find also Du. slijpen, Swed. slipa, Dan. slibe, Icel. slīpa ; the forms require careful arrangement. β. All these are from a Teut. base *sleip-, to slip, glide. But the usual form of the base is *sleup ; whence Goth. sliupan (pt. t. slaup, pp. slupans), to slip or creep into, 2 Tim. iii. 6 ; AS. slūpan, as above ; Du. sluipen, to sneak ; G. schlüpfen, to slip, glide. The base *sleup corresponds to an Idg. base SLEUB, whence L. lūb-ricus, slippery ; see **Lubricate**. Cf. Brugmann, i. §§ 553, 563. Der. slip, sb. ; slip-knot, slip-shod ; also slipp-er, a loose shoe easily slipped on, K. John, iv. 2. 197, called in AS. slype-scōh, a slip-shoe ; Voc. 277. 29. Also slipp-er-y, adj., formed by adding -y (= AS. -ig) to ME. sliper (AS. sliper), slippery, which occurs, spelt slipper, as late as in Shak. Oth. ii. 1. 246, and Spenser, Shep. Kal., Nov. 153 ; slipper-i-ness. Also slope, q. v., sleeve, q. v., slops, q. v.

SLIT, to split, tear, rend, cut into strips. (E.) Just as we make slip do duty for two forms slip and slipe (see **Slip**), so we use slit in place of both slit and slite. ME. slitten, weak verb, Chaucer, C. T.

14402 (B 3674) ; from slīten, strong verb, whence the pp. slityn (with short i), Prompt. Parv. The latter is derived from AS. slītan, pt. t. slāt, pp. sliten (short i) ; Grein, ii. 456.+Icel. slīta, pt. t. sleit, pp. slitinn, to slit, rend ; Dan. slide ; Swed. slita, to tear, pull, wear ; Du. slijten, to wear out, consume ; OHG. slizan, G. schleissen, to slit, split ; whence the weak verb schlitzen, to slit, slash, cleave. β. All from Teut. type *sleitan-, pt. t. *slait, pp. slitanoz. Der. slit, sb., AS. slite, Matt. ix. 16. Also slice, q. v.

SLIVER, a splinter, twig, small branch broken off, slice. (E.) In Hamlet, iv. 7. 174. ME. sliver, Chaucer, Troil. iii. 1013. Sliver is the dimin. of slive, just as shiver is of shive, and splinter of splint. Prov. E. slive, a slice, chip, from the verb slive, to cut or slice off ; Halliwell. 'I slyve a .. floure from his braunche ;' Palsgrave. The verb slive is ME. sliuen, to cleave, spelt ʒlyvyn in Prompt. Parv.—AS. slīfan (pt. t. slāf, pp. slifen), to cleave ; as in tō-slāf, Voc. 406. 29. This verb appears to be exactly parallel to AS. slītan (pt. t. slāt, pp. sliten) ; see **Slit**.

SLOBBER, to slabber, drivel, do carelessly. (E.) ME. sloberen (Stratmann). A variant of **Slubber**, q. v.

SLOE, a small sour wild plum. (E.) ME. slo, pl. slon (with long o), King Alisaunder, 4983. AS. slā, pl. slān. 'Moros, slān ;' Voc. 269. 7. Also slāh, sing.; A. S. Leechdoms, iii. 2.+Du. slee, formerly sleeu ; Dan. slaaen ; Swed. slān ; G. schlehe ; OHG. slēha. Teut. type*slaihā. Fick compares it with Lithuan. slywa,a plum ; Russ. sliva, a plum ; the suffixes do not correspond. β. Sloe is ' the small astringent wild plum, so named from what we call setting the teeth on edge, which in other languages is conceived as blunting them ; see Adelung ;' Wedgwood. Cf. MDu. sleeuw, 'sharpe or tart ;' slee or sleeuw, 'tender, slender, thinne or blunt ;' de sleeuwigheydt der tanden, 'the edgnesse or sowrenesse of the teeth ;' Hexham. The Du. sleeuw is the same word as E. slow ; as if the sloe is the slow (i. e. tart) fruit. But the forms do not correspond (except in Dutch) ; and it can hardly be right. γ. The Russ. seems to be related to L. līu-idus, blue ; with reference to the colour ; and sloe may be connected with livid likewise.

SLOGAN, a Highland war-cry. (Gaelic.) Englished from Gael. sluagh-ghairm, ' the signal for battle among the Highland clans.' —Gael. sluagh, a host, army (W. llu, OIrish slúag) ; and gairm, a call, outcry, from gairm, to call, cry out, crow as a cock. Cf. Irish gairm, W. garm, outcry ; OIrish gáir, W. gawr, clamour, allied to L. garrire, to prate. See Stokes-Fick, pp. 106, 320. The sense is ' cry of the host.'

SLOID, SLOYD, mechanical skill, esp. in wood-carving. (Swed.) Modern. —Swed. slöjd, sleight, skill ; cognate with E. sleight, q. v.

SLOOP, a one-masted ship. (Du.—Low G.) 'Sloop, a small sea-vessel ;' Phillips, ed. 1706. Mentioned in Dampier, Voyages, an. 1680 (R.) ; and in Hexham.—Du. sloep ; MDu. sloepe, sloepken, ' a sloope, or a boate,' Hexham, ed. 1658. From Low G. sluup, slupe, a sloop ; whence also F. chaloupe, whence E. shallop ; see **Shallop**. The Low G. sb. is derived (as in the Bremen Wört.) from Low G. slupen, to glide along, orig. to slip ; see **Slip**. Shallop seems to be older than sloop, as far as English usage is concerned. Doublet, shallop.

SLOP (1), a puddle, water or liquid carelessly spilt. (E.) ME. sloppe, a pool, Morte Arthure, ed. Brock, 3923. AS. -sloppe, -slyppe, the sloppy droppings of a cow ; occurring in cū-sloppe, a cow-slop (now cowslip), and oxan-slyppe, an ox-slop (now oxlip) ; Voc. 135. 26. We also find AS. slype, a viscid substance, A. S. Leechdoms, ed. Cockayne, ii. 18, l. 27, spelt slipe in the next line. β. From Teut. *slup, AS. slop-, weaker grade of slūpan, to slip ; see **Slip**. ' þā wearð heora heorte tō-slopen ' =then was their heart dissolved, made faint ; Joshua, v. 1. γ. Similarly, slop (2) is from a closely related verb. Perhaps slop, a pool, merely meant ' a slippery place,' a place slippery with wet and mire. Der. slop, verb, to spill water, esp. dirty water ; slopp-y, slopp-i-ness. Also cow-slip, q. v., ox-(s)lip, q. v.

SLOP (2), a loose garment. (Scand.) Usually in the pl. slops, large loose trousers, 2 Hen. IV, i.,2. 34. ME. sloppe, Chaucer, C. T. 16101 (G 633). We find ' in stolum vel on oferslopum' = in stoles or over-slops, as a gloss to in stolis in the Northumbrian version of Luke, xx. 46. The word is Scand. rather than E., the AS. word being oferslype (dative case), Ælfric's Homilies, i. 456, l. 19.—Icel. sloppr, a slop, gown, loose trailing garment ; whence yfirsloppr, an outer gown or over-slop.—Icel. slup-, weak grade of sleppa, to slip, a strong verb ; so called from its looseness or its trailing on the ground. Cf. Du. slepen, to trail on the ground. Related to the AS. type *slūpan (?) ; see **Slip**. Cf. Streitberg, § 203.

SLOPE, an incline. (E.) ' Slope, or oblique ;' Minsheu. ME. slope. ' For many times I have it seen That many have begiled been For trust that they have set in hope Which fell hem afterward *a-slope;*' Rom. of the Rose, 4464. Here *a-slope,* lit. on the slope, means 'contrary to expectation,' or 'in a disappointing way.' It is the same idiom as when we talk of 'giving one the *slip.*' It is a derivative of the verb *to slip;* formed from the Teut. **slup-* (in AS. *slop-en,* pp.), weaker grade of the verb appearing as AS. *slūpan;* see **Slip.** Thus *a-slope* is 'ready to slip;' and *slope* means an 'incline.' **Der.** *slope,* verb, Macb. iv. 1. 57; *a-slope.*

SLOT (1), a broad, flat wooden bar which holds together larger pieces, bolt of a door. (Du.) 'Still in use in the North, and applied to a bolt of almost any kind;' Halliwell. '*Slotte* of a dore, *locquet;*' Palsgrave. Spelt *slot, sloot;* Prompt. Parv. — Du. *slot,* a lock (Sewel); *de sloten van kisten,* 'the locks of chests;' *de sloten van huysen,* 'the closures of houses;' Hexham. The Du. *slot* also means a castle. From Teut. **slut-* (Du. *slot-*), weak stem of the *slūtan-* (Du. *sluiten*), to shut (pt. t. *sloot,* pp. *gesloten*). So also OFries. *slot,* from *slūta,* to shut; Low G. *slot,* from *slūten.* β. The Teut. type **slūtan-,* to shut, appears in Du. *sluiten;* OFries. *sluta;* Low G. *sluten;* Swed. *sluta* (pt. t. *slöt,* pp. *sluten*); G. *schliessen,* MHG. *sliezen,* OHG. *sliozan.* γ. Cognate with L. *claudere,* to shut; from √SKLEUD; Brugmann, i. § 795 (2). See **Close** (1). ¶ *Slot,* with the sense of groove or slit, appears to be from Du. *sloot,* Low G. *sloot,* a ditch, trench, furrow; perhaps so called from its use as enclosing a field or piece of land; from *sloot,* 2nd grade of the same verb. Or perhaps the sense was affected by ME. *slīten* (pt. t. *sloot*), to slit.

SLOT (2), the track of a deer. (AF. — Scand.) In Blount's Gloss., ed. 1674. — AF. *esclot,* the track of a deer (Godefroy). Modified from ME. *slooth, slōth;* also spelt *sleuth,* as in the derivative Lowland Sc. *sleuth-hound* (Jamieson). ME. *sleuth,* a track, Barbour's Bruce, vii. 21; whence *slewth-hund, sleuth-hund, slooth-hund,* a hound for tracking deer, id. vi. 36, 484, 669. Also *sloth,* Cursor Mundi, 1254; Ormulum, 1194. — Icel. *slōð,* a track or trail in snow or the like; cf. *slæða,* to trail, *slæður,* a gown that trails on the ground. Swed. dial. *slo,* a track; prov. E. *slood,* a cart-rut.

SLOTH (1), laziness, sluggishness. (E.) Lit. 'slowness.' ME. *slouthe,* Chaucer, C. T. 15726 (G 258). For **slow-th;* formed directly from the adj. *slow.* In P. Plowman, B. v. 392, we find the form *sleuthe,* from AS. *slǽwð,* sloth; from AS. *slāw,* slow (with mutation). **Der.** *sloth,* sb., an animal (below); *sloth-ful,* 1 Hen. VI, iii. 2. 7; *sloth-ful-ly; sloth-ful-ness.*

SLOTH (2), a name sometimes given to the glutton (*Gulo luscus*); but usually to a S. American tardigrade edentate mammal that moves with difficulty on the ground. (E.) The same word as *sloth* (1) above. Prob. suggested by Span. *perezoso,* (1) slothful, (2) a sloth (Neuman, s. v. *Sloth*). Phillips (1706) has: '*Pigritia,* slothfulness; also an American beast call'd a *Sloth.*'

SLOUCH, to have a clownish look or gait. (Scand.) Now a verb; but formerly also a sb. '*Slouch,* a great, vnwieldie, ill-fashioned man;' Minsheu, ed. 1627. '*Slouch,* a great lubberly fellow, a meer country-bumpkin;' Phillips. The *ch* is for *k;* Levins has: '*Slouke,* *iners, ignarus.*' Cf. also Lowl. Sc. *sloatch, slotch,* a lazy fellow. — Icel. *slōkr,* a slouching fellow; Norw. *slōk,* a lazy fellow; cf. *sloka,* to be sluggish (Aasen); also *slōkje,* the same as *slōk* (Ross); Swed. *sloka,* to hang down, droop, flag, *slokig,* hanging, slouching. — Icel. **slōk-,* 2nd grade of **slak-,* as in *slakr,* slack. See **Slack.** ¶ Perhaps influenced by OF. *eslocher, eslochier,* to loosen, also, to become loose (Godefroy); from L. *ex,* and G. *locker,* loose.

SLOUGH (1), a hollow place filled with mud, a mire. (E.) ME. *slogh, slough,* Chaucer, C. T. 7147, 14804 (D 1565, B 3988). AS. *slōh* (stem *slōg*); Kemble's A. S. Charters, 59, 123, 354, 554 (Leo). The formation of *slough* is precisely parallel to that of *clough,* which is related to the OHG. *klingo,* with the same sense. In like manner, the AS. *slōh* is due to an older form **slonh,* corresponding to a Teut. base **slonχ-,* for **slanχ-,* from the strong verb which appears in the G. *schling-en,* to devour; so that the original sense was 'that which swallows up.' β. Similarly, G. *schlund,* a chasm, gulf, is derived from MHG. *slinden,* to devour, with a like sense; and Schmeller gives Bavar. *schlung,* with the same sense as G. *schlund,* i. e. a chasm; so also Bavar. *schlunk* = G. *schlund;* cf. Westphal. *slenke,* a ravine. The long *o* in *slōh* shows the loss of *n.* See **Clough.** And see *schlingen* in Kluge; where it appears to be doubtful if the sense 'to devour' is of early date.

SLOUGH (2), the cast-off skin of a snake; the dead part which separates from a sore. (Scand.) Pronounced *sluf.* Spelt *slough,* Stanyhurst, tr. of Virgil, Æn. ii. 483; ed. Arber, p. 58. ME. *slouh, slow,* Pricke of Conscience, 520 (footnote), where it is used in the sense of caul or integument. '*Slughe,* squama; *slughes of eddyrs* (snakes), exemie;' Cathol. Anglicum, p. 345; see the note. Spelt *slughe, slohu, slouȝe,* in the sense of skin of a snake; Cursor Mundi, 745. From its occurrence in these Northern poems we may presume that the word is Scandinavian. It answers in form to MDan. *slug,* a gap, opening, mouth, swallow; Dan. dial. *slug,* slough on an animal's horn. The Swed. dial. *sluv,* slough, is a different word. β. [With the latter form *sluv* we may compare Low G. *slu, sluwe,* a husk, covering, the pod of a bean or pea, husk of a nut; answering to the Cleveland word *slough,* the skin of a gooseberry (Atkinson); MDu. *sloove,* 'a vaile or a skinne;' Hexham; cf. *slooven,* 'to cover ones head;' id.; G. *schlaube* (provincial), 'a shell, husk, slough.' The etymology of the latter set of forms is from the Teut. base **sleuð,* noticed under **Sleeve,** q. v. The sense is 'that out of which a snake slips,' or a loose covering.] γ. But the E. *slough* and Jutland *slug* are allied to Dan. *slug,* gullet, *sluge,* to swallow; Norw. *sluka,* Low G. *sluken,* G. *schlucken,* to swallow, and, further, to G. *schlauch,* a skin, bag; MHG. *slūch,* a skin, bag. Cf. OIrish *slucc-im,* I swallow.

SLOVEN, a careless, lazy fellow. (Du.) Spelt *sloven, slovyn,* in Palsgrave. 'Some sluggysh *slouyns,* that slepe day and nyght;' Skelton, Garland of Laurel, 191. ME. *sloveyn,* Coventry Myst. p. 218. The suffix *-eyn* = F. *-ain,* from L. *-ānus,* as in ME. *scriv-ein* = OF. *escriv-ain,* from Late L. *scrib-ānus;* see **Scrivener.** This OF. suffix may have been added at first to give the word an adjectival force, which would soon be lost. — MDu. *slof, sloef,* 'a careless man, a sloven, or a nastie fellow,' Hexham; whence *sloefachtiglick,* 'negligent, or slovenly,' id. We also find the verb *sloeven,* 'to play the sloven;' id. Sewel gives Du. *slof,* careless; *slof,* sb., an old slipper, *slof,* sb., neglect, *sloffen,* to draggle with slippers. + Low G. *sluf,* slovenly; *sluffen, sluffern,* to be careless; *sluffen,* to go about in slippers, *sluffen,* slippers. **Der.** *sloven-ly, sloven-li-ness.*

SLOW, tardy, late, not ready. (E.) ME. *slow,* Wyclif, Matt. xxv. 26; *slaw,* Prompt. Parv. (where it has the sense of blunt, or dull of edge). AS. *slāw,* Matt. xxv. 26. + Du. *sleeuw;* Icel. *slær, sljōr;* OSax. *slēu;* OHG. *slēo,* blunt, dull, lukewarm. Teut. type **slaiwoz,* blunt, weak, slow; Fick, iii. 358. Some think it allied to L. *lævus,* Russ. *lievuii,* Gk. λαιός, left (of the hand); which is doubtful. **Der.** *slow-ly, slow-ness.* Also *slo-th* (for *slow-th*), q. v.

SLOW-WORM, a kind of snake. (E.) The allied words show that it cannot mean 'slow worm,' but the sense is rather 'slayer' or 'striker,' from its (supposed) deadly sting. Indeed, the Swedish word is equivalent to an E. form *worm-slow,* i.e. 'worm-striker' or stinging serpent, showing clearly that the word is compounded of two substantives. It was (and still is) supposed to be very poisonous. I remember an old rime: 'If the adder could hear, and the blind-worm see, Neither man nor beast would ever go free.' But it is quite harmless. Lowl. Sc. *slayworm.* ME. *slowerme,* Voc. 571. 33; *slowurme,* id. 766. 15. AS. *slā-wyrm.* We find: 'Stellio, *slā-wyrm;*' Voc. 122. 15; 321. 26. Here *slā* is (I suppose) contracted from *slah-,* from **slahan,* usually *slēan,* to smite; the sb. *slag-a,* a striker, occurs in Exod. xxii. 2; see **Slay.** + Swed. *slå,* usually *ormslå,* a blindworm (where *orm* = E. *worm*); from *slå,* to strike (Rietz, p. 618, where the dialectal form *slo* is given); Norweg. *slo,* a blindworm; also called *ormslo* (Aasen); from *slaa,* to strike. Cf. Icel. *slægr,* kicking, vicious (as a horse); from *slā,* to strike. (Doubtful.) ¶ Quite distinct from Swed. *slö,* blunt, dull, the cognate form with *slow.*

SLOYD, the same as **Sloid,** q. v.

SLUBBER, to do carelessly, to sully. (Scand.) 'I *slubber,* I fyle [defile] a thyng;' Palsgrave. And see Shak. Merch. Ven. ii. 8. 39; Oth. i. 3. 227. — Dan. *slubbre,* to slabber; Swed. dial. *slubbra,* to be disorderly, to slubber, slobber with the lips, a frequentative verb with suffix *-ra* (for *-era*) from *slubba,* to mix up liquids in a slovenly way, to be careless (Rietz). + Du. *slobberen,* 'to slap, to sup up;' Sewel; Low G. *slubbern,* to lap, sip. From the weak grade (**slub-*) of **slab-* in *slabber;* see **Slabber.**

SLUDGE, soft, greasy mud. (E.) ME. *sluche;* Destr. of Troy, l. 12529; apparently a corrupt form of *sliche,* with the same sense, spelt *slicche,* id., l. 13547; prov. E. *slutch,* also *sleech, sletch, slitch.* North E. *slik,* Barbour, Bruce, xiii. 352. An E. word; cognate with North E. Fries. *slick,* EFries. *slik,* slime. + Du. *slijk,* prov. G. *schlick,* grease, Westphal. *slick.* See **Sleek.** ¶ The *u* may be due to prov. E. *slud,* mud, mire, Icel. *sludda,* a clot of mucus.

SLUG, to be inactive. (Scand.) 'To *slug* in slouth;' Spenser, F. Q. ii. 1. 23. ME. *sluggen,* Prompt. Parv.; where we also find *slugge,* adj., slothful; *sluggy,* adj., the same; *sluggydnesse, slugnes,* sloth. *Sluggi,* adj., Ancren Riwle, p. 258. 'I *slogge,* I waxe slowe, or draw behind;' Palsgrave. The *verb* is now obsolete. — Dan. *slug,* voiced form of *sluk,* appearing in *slugöret, sluköret,* with drooping ears; Swed. dial. *slogga,* to be sluggish; allied to Norweg. *sloka,* to go heavily, to slouch, Swed. *sloka,* to hang down, droop. Cf. Icel. *slōkr,* a slouching fellow; and see **Slouch.** Note also Low G. *slukkern, slakkern,* to totter, *slukk,* melancholy, downcast; from the weak grade of *slakk,* slack. See **Slack.** **Der.** *slugg-ish,* Spenser, F. Q. i. 5. 10; *slugg-ish-ly, slugg-ish-ness.* Also *slugg-ard,* Rich. III,

v. 3. 225, with the F. suffix *-ard* (=OHG. *-hart*, cognate with E. *hard*); *slugg-ard-y*, ME. *slogardie*, Chaucer, C. T. 1044 (A 1042). Also *slug*, sb.

SLUG-HORN. (C.) An absurd perversion, by Chatterton (Battle of Hastings, pt. ii. st. 10) and Browning (Childe Roland) of Lowl. Sc. *slogorne*, in G. Douglas, tr. of Æneid, bk. vii. c. xi. l. 87. And *slogorne* is a bad spelling of *slogan*, a battle-cry; see **Slogan.** Hence a 'slug-horn' is not a horn, but a cry; L. 'tessera.'

SLUICE, a sliding gate in a frame for shutting off, or letting out, water; a floodgate. (F.—L.) In Shak. Venus, 956; Lucrece, 1076. ME. *scluse*, Ayenbite of Inwyt, p. 255.—OF. *escluse*, 'a sluice, floudgate;' Cot. Cf. Span. *esclusa*, a sluice, floodgate.—Late L. *exclūsa*, a floodgate; lit. 'shut off (water);' Hist. Mon. de Abingdon, ii. 92.—L. *exclūsa*, fem. of *exclūsus*, pp. of *exclūdere*, to shut out; see **Exclude.**

SLUMBER, to sleep lightly, repose. (E.) The *b* (after *m*) is excrescent. ME. *slumeren*, Bestiary, 576; *slumberen*, *slombren*, P. Plowman, A. prol. 10, B. prol. 10. Frequentative form of ME. *slumen*, to slumber, Layamon, 17995, 18408, 32058. And this verb is from the sb. *slume*, slumber, spelt *sloumbe* in Allit. Poems, C. 186. AS. *slūma*, sb., slumber; Grein, ii. 457. This is formed, with the substantival suffix *-ma*, from a Teut. base *sleu-*, to be silent; cf. Goth. *slawan*, to be silent, from the 2nd grade *slau-*.+Du. *sluimeren*; Dan. *slumre*, frequentative of *slumme*, to slumber; Swed. *slumra*, verb; *slummer*, sb.; G. *schlummern*, verb; *schlummer*, sb. **Der.** *slumber*, sb., *slumber-er*, *slumber-ous*.

SLUMP, a sudden fall, failure in stocks. (E.) From prov. E. *slump*, to fall suddenly, esp. into a ditch. Cf. Swed. and Dan. *slump*, a chance, an accident, Low G. *slump*. Of imitative origin; cf. Norw. *slump*, the noise made by plumping into water. See **Slip.**

SLUMS, dirty back-streets. (E.) Prob. allied to prov. E. *slump*, a muddy place, and (by gradation) to prov. E. *slamp*, wet, Low G. *slam*, mire (Lübben); Dan. and Swed. *slam*, from G. *schlamm*, mire. Cf. Bavarian *schlumpen*, to be dirty; prov. E. *slammock*, a slattern; Low G. *slummerke*, a slattern (Schambach).

SLUR, to soil, contaminate, reproach, pass over lightly with slight notice. (MDu.) 'With periods, points, and tropes he *slurs* his crimes;' Dryden (in Todd). 'They impudently *slur* the gospel;' Cudworth, Sermons, p. 73 (Todd). 'Without some fingering trick or *slur*;' Butler, Misc. Thoughts; Works, ed. Bell, iii. 176. Cf. ME. *sloor*, *slore*, mud, clay, Prompt. Parv.; whence *slooryyd*, muddy, id. Prov. E. *slur*, thin washy mud; Halliwell, Forby. The orig. sense is 'to trail,' or draggle; hence, to pass over in a sliding or slight way, also, to trail in dirt, to contaminate.—MDu. *sleuren*, *slooren*, to drag, trail, Du. *sleuren*, to trail; cf. MDu. *sloorigh*, 'filthie,' Hexham. Also Low G. *slüren*, *slören*, to draggle, Swed. dial. *slöra*, to be negligent; Norw. *slöra*, to be negligent, to sully; EFries. *sluren*, *slüren*, to go about carelessly and noisily. From a base *sleu-*; perhaps the same as that in **Slumber** (Franck). **Der.** *slur*, sb.

SLUSH, mire, mud. (Scand.) Perhaps from MDan. *slus*, (1) sleet; (2) mud (Kalkar); Dan. dial. *sluus*, sleet. Or rather from Norw. *slusk*, mud, dirty roads or weather (Ross); related by gradation to Swed. *slask*, sloppiness, wet weather, *slaska*, to splash, to dabble in water; cf. prov. E. *slosh*, slush; *slash*, to splash.

SLUT, a slovenly woman, slattern. (Scand.) ME. *slutte*, Coventry Plays, 218 (Stratmann); and in Palsgrave. 'Slutte, Cenosus, Cenosa;' Prompt. Parv. *Slutte* occurs also in Hoccleve, Letter of Cupide, st. 34; l. 237. Hence *sluttish*, Chaucer, C. T. 16104 (G 636).—Swed. dial. *slåta*, an idle woman, slut, *slåter*, an idler; Norweg. *slott*, an idler. Cf. Icel. *slota*, to droop, Swed. dial. *slota*, to be lazy, Norweg. *sluta*, to droop; allied to Dan. *slat*, loose, flabby, *slatte*, a slattern (Ferrall). β. The root-verb appears in Norweg. *sletta* (pt. t. *slatt*, pp. *slottet*), to dangle, hang loose like clothes, to drift, to idle about, be lazy (Aasen); and *tt* represents *nt*. Cf. Swed. dial. *slinta* (pt. t. *slant*, pp. *sluntit*), to slide, glide, slip aside, with its derivatives *slanta*, to be idle, and *slunt*, 'a lubber, lazy sturdy fellow,' Widegren. γ. Thus E. *slattern* and Dan. *slatte* may be referred to *slatt*, *slant*, 2nd grade of *sletta*, *slenta* (whence also Icel. *slentr*, sloth); while E. *slut*, Norw. *slott*, may be referred to *slott-*, *slunt-*, weak grade of the same; cf. Low G. *sluntje*, a slut. All from the Teut. str. vb. *slentan-*, to slip aside, pt. t. *slant*, pp. *sluntanoz*. See **Slant.** **Der.** *slutt-ish*, *-ly*, *-ness*.

SLY, cunning, wily. (Scand.) ME. *sleigh*, Chaucer, C. T. 3201; *sley*, Havelok, 1084; *sleh*, Ormulum, 13498.—Icel. *slægr* (for *slœgr*), sly, cunning; Swed. *slög*, cunning, dexterous. The Icel. *slægr* is from a Teut. type *slôg-joz* (Noreen, § 360), where *slôg-* may represent the 2nd grade of Teut. *slahan-*, to strike; see **Slay.** 'From the use of a hammer being taken as the type of a handicraft;' Wedgwood; and see Fick, iii. 358, who adduces G. *verschlagen*, cunning, crafty, subtle, sly, from the same root. ¶ But Swed. *slug*,

cunning, Dan. *slu*, Du. *sluw*, G. *schlau*, sly, are unrelated. **Der.** *sli-ly*, *sly-ness*. Also *sleight* (i. e. *sly-th*), q. v.

SMACK (1), taste, flavour, savour. (E.) ME. *smak*, a taste; Prompt. Parv. AS. *smæc*, taste; Grein, ii. 457; whence the verb *smecgan*, *smæccan*, to taste. 'Gusto, *ic gesmecge*,' Voc. 109. 11; *ic smæcce*, Ælfric's Grammar, ed. Zupitza, p. 166, l. 6.+MDu. *smaeck*, 'tast, smaek, or savour;' *smaecken*, 'to savour,' Hexham; Du. *smaken*, to taste; [Dan. *smag*, taste, *smage*, to taste, Swed. *smak*, taste, *smaka*, to taste, from Low G. *smakk*, taste;] G. *geschmack*, taste, *schmecken*, to taste. **Der.** *smack*, verb.

SMACK (2), a sounding blow. (Scand.) We find *smack*, sb., a loud kiss, Tam. Shrew, iii. 2. 180. But the word does not seem to be at all old, and its supposed connexion with **Smack** (1) is disproved by the forms found. It has been *confused* with it, but is quite distinct. It seems to be of imitative origin, and may be an E. word, unless borrowed from Scandinavian. β. The related words are Swed. *smacka*, to smack [distinct from *smaka*, to taste]; Swed. dial. *smakka*, to throw down noisily, *smäkk*, a light quick blow with the flat hand, *smäkka*, to hit smartly; Dan. *smække*, to slam, bang [distinct from *smage*, to taste], *smæk*, a smack, rap [distinct from *smag*, taste]. Also Low G. *smakken*, to smack the lips [distinct from *smekken*, to taste]; MDu. *smacken*, Du. *smakken*, to cast on the ground, fling, throw [distinct from Du. *smaken*, to taste]; Du. *smak*, a loud noise. And see **Smash.** Apparently of imitative origin, as seen in Du. *smak*, Dan. *smæk*; allied to Lith. *smog-ti*, to strike, smack; *smag-óti*, to strike with a whip. Cf. *knack*, *crack*. **Der.** *smack*, verb; cf. *smatt-er*, q. v., *smash*, q. v.

SMACK (3), a fishing-boat. (Du.) In Sewell's Du. Dict. Doubtless borrowed from Dutch, like *hoy*, *skipper*, *boom*, *yacht*, &c. —MDu. *smacke*, 'a kind of a long ship or boate,' Hexham; smack, 'a hoy, smack,' Sewel, ed. 1754.+Low G. *smakk*, a smack. β. Generally supposed to be a corruption for *snack*, allied to *snake*; cf. AS. *snacc*, a smack, small vessel, A. S. Chron. an. 1066, in the Laud MS., ed. Thorpe, p. 337; Icel. *snekkja*, a kind of sailing-ship, so called from its *snake*-like movement in the water. So also Swed. *snäcka*, Dan. *snekke* (or *snække*). ¶ For the interchange of *sm-* and *sn-*, see **Smatter.**

SMALL, little, unimportant. (E.) ME. *smal*; pl. *smale*, Chaucer, C. T. 9. AS. *smæl*, small, thin; Grein, ii. 457.+Du., Dan., and Swed. *smal*, narrow, thin; Goth. *smals*, small; G. *schmal*, narrow, thin, slim. Teut. type *smaloz*. Further allied to Icel. *smali*, small cattle, sheep; Gk. μῆλον, a sheep; Russ. *maluii*, small. ¶ We also find Icel. *smár*, Dan. *smaa*, Swed. *små*, OHG. *smāhi*, small. **Der.** *small-ness*; *small-pox* (see **Pox**); *small-age*, q. v.

SMALLAGE, celery. (Hybrid; E. *and* F.—L.) In Minsheu, ed. 1627. 'Smallage, a former name of the celery, meaning the *small ache* or parsley, as compared with the great parsley, *olus atrum*. See Turner's Nomenclator, A. D. 1548, and Gerarde's Herbal;' Prior, Popular Names of British Plants. ME. *smalege*, Voc. 711. 15; *smalache*, Lanfrank, Cirurgie, p. 94.—AS. *smæl*, small (see above); and F. *ache*, parsley, from L. *apium*, parsley.

SMALT, glass tinged of a deep blue, used as a pigment. (Ital.—OHG.) 'Smalt, a kind of blew powder-colour, us'd in painting; blue enamel;' Phillips, ed. 1706. Also in Blount's Gloss., ed. 1674.—Ital. *smalto*, 'amell [enamel] for goldsmiths,' Florio; allied to *smalzo*, butter.—Low G. *smalt* (Lübben), dial. form of G. *schmalz*, fat, butter; OHG. *smalzi*, *smelzi*, butter. From the 2nd grade (*smalz*) of OHG. *smelzan*, str. vb., to become liquid; whence also OHG. *smelzen*, G. *schmeltzen*, weak vb., to smelt. See **Smelt** (1). ¶ The Du. *smalt* (in the present sense) is borrowed from Italian. See Weigand.

SMARAGDUS, a precious stone, emerald. (L.—Gk.—Skt.—Semitic.) Also *smaragd*; ME. *smaragde*, An O. E. Miscellany, p. 98, l. 174.—L. *smaragdus*.—Gk. σμάραγδος, an emerald; also found in the form μάραγδος, which is from Skt. *marakata(m)*, *marakta(m)*, an emerald. Hence (says Uhlenbek) a Prakrit *açmā maragadō*, lit. emerald stone (from Skt. *açmā*, a stone); whence Gk. *σμαμάραγδος*, shortened to σμάραγδος by loss of -μα- (repeated). Further, the Skt. *marakata(m)* is from Semitic *bāraqt*, as in Heb. *bāreqet*, an emerald, from *bāraq*, to flash. See Schade, OHG. Dict., p. 1430. See **Emerald.** **Doublet,** *emerald*.

SMART, to feel a pain, to be punished. (E.) ME. *smerten*, Havelok, 2647; spelt *smeorten*, Ancren Riwle, p. 238, last line. Once a strong verb; the pt. t. *smeart* occurs in O. Eng. Homilies, ii. 21, l. 27. AS. *smeortan* (Toller). The AS. pt. t. would be *smeart*, and the pp. *smorten*.+Du. *smarten*, to give pain; *smart*, pain; Dan. *smerte*, vb. and sb.; Swed. *smärta*, vb. and sb.; OHG. *smerzan*, sometimes used as a strong verb (pt. t. *smarz*), G. *schmerzen*, to smart; OHG. *smerza*, G. *schmerz*, smart, pain.+L. *mordēre* (with lost initial *s*), to bite, pain, sting; Skt. *mṛd*, to rub, grind, crush. β. All from √SMERD; see Fick, i. 836. Whence also Gk.

σμερδαλέος, terrible. See **Mordacity.** Der. *smart*, sb., ME. *smert*, Chaucer, C. T. 3811 (A 3813); also *smart*, adj., ME. *smerte*, i. e. painful, Havelok, 2055. The use of the adjective has been extended to mean pungent, brisk, acute, lively, witty. Hence *smart-ly*, *smart-ness.*

SMASH, to crush, break in pieces. (E.) A late word, added by Todd to Johnson. According to Webster, it is used by Burke. It is well known in the North (see Brockett and Jamieson), and is clearly a dialectal word transferred to more polite speech. Prob. due to E. *mash*, to mix up; by prefixing *s-*, intensive prefix, from OF. *es-*, L. *ex.* And prob. influenced by prov. E. *smatter*, in the sense ' to smash.' See **Smattering.** ¶ We may perhaps also notice the prov. Swed. *smiska*, to slap, occurring in the very sense of ' to smash glass ' or to smash a window-pane, which is the commonest use of the word in ordinary E. conversation. Still nearer is the Norw. *smaska*, to smash; *sla i smask*, to break to bits (Ross). Cf. **Smack** (2).

SMATTERING, a superficial knowledge. (Scand.) From the old verb *to smatter*, to have a slight knowledge of; the orig. sense was ' to make a noise;' also, ' to prate.' ' I *smatter* of a thyng, I have lytell knowledge in it;' Palsgrave. ' For I abhore to *smatter* Of one so deuyllyshe a matter;' Skelton, Why Come Ye Nat to Courte, 711. ME. *smateren*, to make a noise; Songs and Carols, ed. Wright, no. lxxii (Stratmann).—Swed. *smattra*, to clatter, to crackle. +G. *schmettern*, to smash, to resound. From a repetition of the imitative sound *smat*; cf. **Smack** (2). Cf. MHG. *smetzen*, to prattle. [Parallel to *prat-tle*, *chat-ter*. Note also Swed. *snattra*, Dan. *snadre*, to prattle; Swed. *snakka*, Dan. *snakke*, to prate, G. *schnacken*.]

SMEAR, to daub with something greasy or sticky. (E.) ME. *smerien*, *smeren*, Ormulum, 994; also *smirien*; also *smurien*, Ancren Riwle, p. 372, l. 6. AS. *smerian*, Ps. xliv. 9; *smyrian*, Mark, xvi. 1. A weak verb, from the sb. *smeru*, fat, Levit. viii. 25, whence ME. *smere*, fat, fatness, Genesis and Exodus, 1573.+Du. *smeren*, to grease, from *smeer*, fat; Icel. *smyrja*, to anoint, from *smjör*, *smör*, grease; Dan. *smöre*, from *smör*, sb.; Swed. *smörja*, from *smör*, sb.; G. *schmieren*, from *schmeer*, sb., OHG. *smero*. β. The general Teut. form of the sb. is *smerwom*, n., fat, grease; Fick, iii. 356; allied to which are Goth. *smairthr*, fatness, *smarna*, dung. All from a base SMER; cf. Lithuan. *smarsas*, fat; Gk. μύρον, an unguent; OIrish *smir*, marrow; W. *mêr*, marrow. Der. *smear*, sb., at present signifying the result of smearing, and a derivative of the verb; not in the old sense of ' grease.' And see *smir-ch*.

SMELL, an odour. (E.) ME. *smel*, Chaucer, C. T. 2429 (A 2427), Ancren Riwle, p. 104, l. 16; also *smul*, O. Eng. Homilies, ii. 99, l. 1. Not found in AS., but prob. a true Eng. word. Allied to Du. *smeulen*, ' to smoke hiddenly,' i. e. to smoulder; EFries. *smälen*, Low G. *smelen*, to smoulder. β. The idea is evidently taken from the vapour given off by smouldering wood. See further under **Smoulder.** Der. *smell*, verb, ME. *smellen*, Chaucer, C. T. 3691, *smullen*, O. Eng. Hom. ii. 35, l. 3.

SMELT (1), to fuse ore. (Scand.) In Phillips, ed. 1706; but not noticed by Skinner, ed. 1671. I have little doubt that the word is really *Swedish*, as Sweden was the chief place for smelting iron ore, and a great deal of iron is still found there; (cf. **Slag**).—Dan. *smelte*, to fuse, smelt; Swed. *smälta*, to smelt, run, liquefy; *smälta malm*, to smelt ore; Widegren.+MDu. *smilten*, *smelten*, ' to melt, mollifie, make liquid, or to found;' Hexham. (Note here the use of *found* where we should now say *smelt*). G. *schmelzen*, OHG. *smalzjan*, to smelt. β. All these are secondary or weak verbs, connected with an older strong verb appearing in the Swed. *smälta*, to melt, i. e. to become liquid, for which Rietz gives the pt. t. *smalt* and supine *smultið*, and cites OSwed. *smälta* (pt. t. *smalt*, pp. *smultin*). It also appears in G. *schmelzen* (pt. t. *schmolz*), to melt, dissolve, become liquid; Westphal. *smelten* (pt. t. *smalt*). γ. From the Teut. str. vb. *smeltan-* (pt. t. *smalt*, pp. *smultanoz*); whence also MDu. *smalt*, ' grease or melted butter;' *smalts*, *smalsch*, ' liquid, soft, or fatt' (Hexham); OHG. *smalz*, fat, grease; see **Smalt.** δ. We may also compare Gk. μέλδομαι, I become liquid; Gk. μέλδειν, to melt, render fluid. Brugmann, i. § 475. See **Melt.** Der. *smalt*, q. v.; *enamel*, q. v. And see *mute* (2).

SMELT (2), a kind of fish. (E.) ME. *smelt*, Prompt. Parv. AS. *smelt*. ' Sardina, *smelt*,' in a list of fish; Voc. 262. 4; ' Sardas, *smeltas*,' id. 45. 3.+Dan. *smelt*; Norweg. *smelta* (1), a mass, lump; (2) the name of various kinds of small fish, as *Gadus minutus*, also a small whiting. β. The name prob. means ' smooth;' cf. AS. *smeolt*, *smylt*, serene, smooth (of the sea), orig. liquid; from the verb to *smelt*; see **Smelt** (1). Also prov. E. *smelt*, a smooth spot on water (as caused by oil); *smolt*, smooth, shining, polished; *smout* (for *smolt*), the fry of salmon. The *sand-smelt* is also called *silver-sides* (C. D.). See **Smolt.**

SMEW, a small diving-bird. (E.) Also called *smee* (E. D. D.), and *smeeth* or *smeath.* Drayton has ' the *smeath*;' Polyolbion, song 25, l. 67. [We find also EFries. *smënt*, Du. *smient*, smew. The Du. *smient* is explained as ' small duck,' from ODu. *smehi anud*, small duck; where *smëhi* is cognate with OHG. *smähi*, Icel. *smār*, small; and *anud* (*anid*) is cognate with AS. *ened*, G. *ente*, duck. Cf. G. *schmalente*, small wild-duck.] But *smeeth* resembles AS. *smëðe*, smooth; and *smee* may be the prov. E. *smee*, smooth.

SMILE, to laugh slightly, express joy by the countenance. (Scand.) ME. *smilen*, Chaucer, C. T. 4044 (A 4046); Will. of Palerne, 991. Not a very old word in E.—Swed. *smila*, to smirk, smile, fawn, simper; Dan. *smile*.+MHG. *smielen*, *smieren*, *smiren*, to smile; L. *mirāri*, to wonder at; *mirus*, wonderful; cf. also Gk. μειδάω, I smile; Skt. *smi*, to smile; Russ. *smiekh'*, a laugh. (√SMEI.) Der. *smil-er*, Chaucer, C. T. 2001 (A 1999); *smile*, sb., St. Brandan, l. 80: see *smir-k.*

SMIRCH, to besmear, dirty. (E.) ' And with a kind of umber *smirch* my face;' As You Like It, i. 3. 114. Allied to the old word *smore.* ' I *smore* ones face with any grease or soute [soot], or such lyke, *Ie barbouille*;' Palsgrave. And since *smore* is related to *smear*, it is clear that *smirch* (palatalised form of *smer-k*) is an extension from ME. *smeren*, to smear; see **Smear.**

SMIRK, to smile affectedly, smile, simper. (E.) ME. *smirken*, St. Katharine, 356. AS. *smercian*, Ælfred, tr. of Boethius, cap. xxxiv. § 12 (lib. iii. pr. 11). Cf. ONorthumb. *smerdon*, ' deridebant;' Matt. ix. 24; MHG. *smieren*, to smile; see **Smile.** Der. *smirk*, sb., also obsolete adj. *smirk*, trim, neat, Spenser, Shep. Kal., Feb. l. 72.

SMITE, to strike, beat, kill. (E.) ME. *smiten*, pt. t. *smat*, *smot*, pp. *smiten.* The pt. t. is spelt *smoot*, Wyclif, Luke, xxii. 50; with pl. *smyten* (= *smüten*), id. xxiii. 48. AS. *smītan*, pt. t. *smāt*, pp. *smiten*; Grein, ii. 458.+Du. *smijten*; MSwed. *smīta*, to smite; Dan. *smide*, to fling; G. *schmeissen*, to smite, fling, cast; OHG. *smīzan*, to throw, to stroke, to smear. Cf. Goth. *bismeitan*, to anoint, besmear, John, ix. 11. β. The orig. sense would appear to be ' to rub ' or smear over, a sense which actually appears in the OHG. and Gothic; and even in AS. this sense is the usual one; note MSwed. *smeta*, to smear (Ihre), Icel. *smita*, to steam from being fat or oiled. The connexion between ' to rub ' and ' to smite ' is curious, but the former sense is satirical; we had the phrase ' *to rub down with an oaken towel*,' i. e. to cudgel; and, in the Romance of Partenay, l. 5653, a certain king is said to have been ' so well *anoynted*' that he had not a whole piece of clothing left upon him; the orig. French text says that he was *bien oingt*. Der. *smit-er.*

SMITH, a worker in metals. (E.) ME. *smith*, Chaucer, C. T. 2027. AS. *smið*; Grein, ii. 457.+Du. *smid*; Icel. *smiðr*; Dan. and Swed. *smed*; G. *schmied*; MHG. *smit*, *smid*; Goth. *-smitha*, in comp. *aiza-smitha*, copper-smith. β. All from the Teut. type *smithoz*, a smith; Fick, iii. 357. [It was once usual to explain this (after the method of Horne Tooke, which is known to be wrong) as *he that smiteth*, from ' the sturdy blows that he smites upon the anvil;' Trench, Study of Words. But there is no support for this notion to be had from comparative philology.] γ. Cf. further Icel. *smið*, smith's work; Du. *smijdig*, G. *ge-schmeidig*, malleable (with *i*). From the obs. Teut. str. vb. *smeithan-*, pt. t. *smaith*, pp. *smidanoz*, to forge, only preserved in Swed. dial. *smida*, to forge (pt. t. *smed*, pp. *smiden*), Rietz; and in OSwed. *smiþa*, to forge (Noreen). Hence, as weak verbs, Swed. *smida*, Dan. *smede*, to forge. Cf. also OHG. *smīda*, metal, Gk. σμί-λη, a graver's tool. (√SMEI.) Brugmann, i. § 849. Der. *smith-y*, ME. *smiððe*, Ancren Riwle, p. 284, l. 24, AS. *smiððe*, Voc. 141. 22; Icel. *smiðja.* Also *gold-smith*, *silver-smith*; &c.

SMOCK, a shirt for a woman. (E.) ME. *smok*, Chaucer, C. T. 3238. AS. *smoc.* ' Colobium, *smoc* vel *syrc*' [sark]; Voc. 125. 1. For *smocc*; Teut. type *smuguoz*; and so called because ' crept into;' from *smug*, weak grade of *smeug*, to creep; cf. *smogen*, pp. of the strong verb *smūgan*, occurring in Ælfred, tr. of Boethius, cap. xxiv. § 1 (lib. iii. pr. 2). Cf. Shetland *smook*, ' to draw on, as a glove or a stocking;' Edmondston.+Icel. *smokkr*, a smock; allied to *smoginn*, pp. of *smjúga*, ' to creep through a hole, to put on a garment which has only a round hole to put the head through.' Cf. MSwed. *smog*, a round hole for the head; Ihre. Also Icel. *smeygja*, to slip off one's neck, causal of *smjúga*; OFries. *in-smuge*, sb., a creeping into. See further under **Smug** and **Smuggle.** Brugmann, i. § 899 (1).

SMOKE, vapour from a burning body, esp. wood or coal. (E.) ME. *smoke*, Chaucer, C. T. 5860 (D 278). AS. *smoca* (rare). ' Þone wlacan smocan wāces flæsces '=the warm smoke of weak flax; Be Dōmes Dæge, ed. Lumby, l. 51. Cf. AS. *smoc-*, stem of *smocen*, pp. of the strong verb *smēocan* (pt. t. *smēac*), to smoke, reek, Matt. xii. 20. [Hence also the various forms of the sb., such as *smēac*, *smȳc*; the latter occurs in Ælfric's Homilies, ii. 202, l. 4 from bottom. The secondary verb *smocigan* (derived from the sb. *smoca*) occurs on the same page, l. 24.]+Du. *smook*, sb.; Dan. *smög*, sb.; G. *smöge*, weak verb, to smoke; G. *schmauch*, smoke. β. All from a Teut. str. vb. *smeuk-an-*, pt. t. *smauk*, pp. *smukanoz.* Cf. Lith. *smaug-iu*,

I choke; allied to Gk. σμύχειν (2 aor. ἐ-σμύγ-ην), to burn slowly in a smouldering fire. Brugmann, i. § 849. **Der.** smoke, vb., AS. smocigan, as above; smok-er, smok-y, smok-i-ness.

SMOLT, a salmon in its second year, when it has assumed its silvery scales. (E.) From AS. smolt, serene, gentle; the prov. E. smolt not only means fair, serene, but also smooth, shining, and polished. See **Smelt**.

SMOOTH, having an even surface. (E.) ME. smothe, Rom. of the Rose, 542; also common in the form smethe, due to vowel-change from ō to œ (= ē), Rob. of Glouc. p. 424, l. 8781; Pricke of Conscience, 6349. AS. smēðe, Luke, iii. 5, where the Northumb. versions have smoeðe; cf. 'Aspera, unsmēag,' Voc. 350. 29; un-smōði, Corpus Gloss., 232. The preservation of the (older) vowel ō in mod. E. is remarkable. β. The form smōðe, with long o, shows that (as in other, tooth, goose) an n has been lost; the form of the base is *smonth-, for an older form *smanth-, corresponding to an Idg. base *smant-. γ. This Idg. base is remarkably exemplified in the G. Schmant (Bavar. schmand), a dialectal word corresponding to late MHG. smant, cream; allied to Bohem. smetana, cream; Miklosich, p. 189. Cf. Skt. manthaya-, butter; from manth, math, to churn. The Hamburgh smöden, to smoothe (Richey) may be related. **Der.** smooth, verb, from the adj.; cf. AS. smēðian, Voc. 130. 36; smooth-ly; smooth-ness, AS. smēðnys, Voc. 177. 5.

SMOTHER, a suffocating smoke, thick stifling dust. (E.) Smother stands for smorther, having lost an r, which was retained even in the 14th century. ME. smorther; spelt smorþre, smorþur, P. Plowman, C. xx. 303, 305 (some MSS. have smolder, id. B. xvii. 321). Smor-ther is 'that which stifles;' formed, with the suffix -ther (Idg. -ter) of the agent, from AS. smor-ian, to choke, stifle, Matt. xiii. 7 (Rushworth MS.), preserved in Lowland Sc. smoor, to stifle; see Burns, Brigs of Ayr, l. 33. β. Cognate with AS. smorian are Du. smoren, to suffocate, stifle, stew, and G. schmoren, to stew. Cf. MDu. smoor, 'smoother, vapour, or fume' (Hexham); Du. smeuren, to smother. Apparently from a root *smeur, from an older root SMEU; see **Smoulder, Smoke**. **Der.** smother, verb, ME. smortheren, O. Eng. Homilies, i. 251, l. 7. And see smoulder.

SMOULDER, to burn with a stifling smoke. (E.) 'I smolder, as wete wood doth; I smolder one, or I stoppe his brethe with smoke;' Palsgrave. ME. smolderen, Allit. Poems, B. 955; from the sb. smolder, a stifling smoke. 'Smoke and smolder,' P. Plowman, B. xvii. 321; where the later text has 'smoke and smorþer' (= E. smother), id. C. xx. 303; and see Palladius on Husbandry, i. 929. [The Dan. smuldre, to crumble, moulder, from smul, dust, may be ultimately related, but is not the original of the E. word, being too remote in sense.] β. The E. smoulder (for *smol-ther) is closely connected with Low G. smölen, smelen, to smoulder, as in dat holt smelet weg = the wood smoulders away (Bremen Wörterbuch); Du. smeulen, 'to smoak hiddenly,' Sewel; Low G. smöln, to give out fumes (Danneil). See **Smell**. From a root *smeul, from an older root SMEU; see **Smother** (above).

SMUDGE, to sully, to smear with dirt. (Scand.) ME. smogen, in Halliwell; a voiced form of smutch. Cf. Dan. smuds, smut, dirt, smudse, to soil; from G. schmutz, smut, dirt; MHG. smuz. Also ME. smod, dirt, Allit. Poems, ii. 711; EFries. and Low G. smudden, to soil; Du. smoddig, dirty. See **Smut**.

SMUG, neat, trim, spruce. (Low G.) In Shak. Merch. Ven. iii. 1. 49; &c. 'I could have brought a noble regiment Of smug-skinnde Nunnes into my countrey soyle;' Gascoigne, Voyage into Holland, A. D. 1572; Works, i. 393. Spelt smoog, Stanyhurst, tr. of Virgil, Æn. ii. 484; ed. Arber, p. 59. A voiced form of smuk. — MDan. smug, smooth, pliable (Kalkar); and Outzen (s. v. smock) notices a South Dan. form smugg; from Low G. smuk, neat, trim; cf. MDu. smucken, 'to be smugg,' Hexham. Hence also G. schmuck, trim, spruce. β. The MHG. smucken meant not only to clothe, adorn, but also to withdraw oneself into a place of security, and is an intensive form from the older strong verb smiegen, to creep into (G. schmiegen, to wind, bend, ply, cling to). This MHG. smiegen is cognate with AS. smūgan, to creep. γ. This links smug with smock, which has the same change from g to k, as shown under that word. A smock, orig. so named from the hole for the neck into which one crept, became a general term for dress, clothes, or attire, as in the case of G. schmuck, attire, dress, ornament, adornment, &c.; and smug is merely the corresponding adjective, meaning 'dressed,' hence spruce, neat, &c. See further under **Smock** and **Smuggle**.

SMUGGLE, to import or export secretly, without paying legal duty. (Low G.) Phillips, ed. 1706, gives the phrase 'to smuggle goods.' Blount's Gloss., ed. 1674, has: 'Smuglers, stealers of customs, well known upon the Thames.' Sewel's Du. Dict., ed. 1749, gives: 'Sluyken, to smuckle; sluyker, a smuckler.' [The word is not Dutch, the Du. smokkelen, to smuggle, being modern, and unnoticed by Sewel and Hexham. It is, however, plainly a sailor's word, and

of Low G. origin.] — Low G. smuggeln (whence also Dan. smugle), to smuggle; a frequentative form (with usual suffix -le) from the weak grade of the old strong verb found in Norweg. smjuga (pt. t. smaug), to creep; whence also Dan. i smug, adv., secretly, privately, and smughandel, contraband trade. Closely allied to Dan. smöge, a narrow (secret) passage, Swed. smuga, a lurking-hole (Widegren), Icel. smuga, a hole to creep through, smugall, smugligr, penetrating. β. All from the weak grade of the strong verb found in Icel. smjúga (pt. t. smaug, pl. smugu, pp. smoginn), to creep, creep through a hole, put on a garment which has only a round hole to put the head through; cf. Swed. smyga, to sneak, to smuggle. Cognate with AS. smūgan, to creep (pt. t. smēag, pl. smugon, pp. smogen); MHG. smiegen, strong verb, to press into (Fick, iii. 357); all from Teut. base SMEUG, to creep. Cf. Lithuan. smukti, to glide (pr. t. smunkù, I glide), i-smukti, to creep in. See Streitberg, § 203, note 1. **Der.** smuggl-er; see smock, smug.

SMUT, a spot of dirt, esp. of soot. (E.) From the base smut-, ME. smot-, as in i-smotted, smutted, Trevisa, tr. of Higden, i. 359; bi-smot-ered, besmutted, Chaucer, C. T. 76. Cf. G. schmutz, dirt. β. Hence the form smutch. 'Smutche on ones face, barboyllement;' Palsgrave. 'Hast smutched thy nose;' Winter's Tale, i. 2. 121. — Swed. smuts, smut, dirt, filth, soil; whence smutsa, verb, to dirt, to sully. Cf. Dan. smuds, filth; whence smudse, to soil, dirty, sully. The Dan. form (not old) resembles E. smudge, to smear, to soil (Halliwell), and ME. smoge, with the same sense (id.); see **Smudge**. γ. The Swed. smuts, Dan. smuds, were borrowed from G. schmutz (above). ¶ Perhaps allied to Du. smet, a spot, and to ME. smitten, to contaminate; from a base *smet. **Der.** smut, verb; smutt-y, smutt-i-ly, smutt-i-ness.

SNACK, a part, portion, share; see **Snatch**.

SNAFFLE, a bridle with a piece confining the nose, and with a slender mouth-piece. (Du.) 'A bitte or a snaffle;' Baret (1580). Short for snaffle-piece = nose-piece. 'With a snaffle and a brydle;' Sir T. More, Works, p. 1366 e. And in Shak. Antony, ii. 2. 63. 'A snaffle, Camus; to snaffle, rudere;' Levins. — Du. snavel, a horse's muzzle; MDu. snabel, snavel, 'the nose or snout of a beast or a fish;' Hexham. Dimin. of MDu. snabbe, snebbe, 'the bill or neb of a bird;' id. + G. schnabel, bill, snout; Lith. snapas, a bill. Allied to **Neb**, q. v. And see **Snap**.

SNAG, an abrupt projection, as on a tree where a branch has been cut off, a short branch, knot, projecting tooth. (Scand.) 'Which with a staffe, all full of litle snags;' Spenser, F. Q. ii. 11. 23; cf. iv. 7. 7. [The word knag, which has much the same sense, occurs as knagg in Swedish; see **Knag**.] Hence the prov. E. verb snag, to trim, to cut off the twigs and small branches from a tree; the tool used (a kind of bill-hook) is called a snagger; hence also the Kentish snaggle, to nibble (Halliwell). — Norw. snag, a projecting point or end, a spike; cf. Norw. snage, a projecting tongue of land; Icel. snag-hyrndr, with spiky horns; Icel. snagi, a clothes-peg; Norw. snaga, to stick out (Ross).

SNAIL, a slimy creeping gastropod. (E.) ME. snayle, Prompt. Parv. The i (y) is due to an earlier g, precisely as in hail (1), nail. AS. snægl, snegel; Voc. 121. 31, 321. 29; snegl, Voc. 30. 18. Snægl (= snag-il) is a diminutive, with g for c, from AS. snaca, a snake, a creeping thing; see **Snake**. The lit. sense is 'a small creeping thing,' or little reptile. Cf. ME. snegge (prov. E. snag), a snail, Ayenbite of Inwyt, p. 32; and G. schnecke, a snail, Swed. snäcka. + Icel. snigill, a snail; Dan. snegl, a snail; Swed. snigel, a slug; Westphal. snäel, a snail; Low G. snigge, a snail; NFries. snegge. Teut. types *snagiloz, snegiloz, masc. See Noreen, § 252.

SNAKE, a kind of serpent. (E.) The lit. sense is 'a creeping thing,' which is also the sense of serpent and of reptile. ME. snake, Wyclif, Rom. iii. 13. AS. snaca, to translate L. scorpio, Luke, x. 19. The sense is 'creeper,' but the related verb is only found in OHG. snahhan, pt. t. snuoh, which presupposes a Teut. type *snak-an-, to creep, pt. t. *snōk. + Icel. snākr; also snōkr, Dan. snog, Swed. snok (from the base *snōk); MDu. snake, a snake. And cf. Skt. nāga-s, a serpent. See **Sneak**. **Der.** snail.

SNAP, to bite suddenly, snatch up. (Du.) In Shak. Much Ado, v. 1. 116. 'A snapper-up of unconsidered trifles;' Wint. Tale, iv. 3. 26. 'I snappe at a thing to catche it with my tethe;' Palsgrave. Not an old word. — Du. snappen, to snap, snatch; 'to snap up, or to intercept,' Hexham. + Dan. snappe, Swed. snappa, from Low G. snappen; G. schnappen, MHG. snappen, to snap, snatch. β. All from Teut. base *snap; see **Snaffle**. **Der.** snapp-ish, i.e. ready to bite or snap; snapp-ish-ly, -ness. Also snap-dragon, a plant, so called because the lips of the corolla, when parted, snap together like a dragon's mouth; also a game in which raisins are snapped out of a flame, as if from a fiery dragon. Also snap-hance, a fire-lock (Nares), from Du. snaphaan, a fire-lock, MDu. snaphaen, 'a robber that snaps upon one in the highway, or a snap-haunce' (Hexham); from Du.

snappen, to snap, and *haan*, a cock, also a cock of a gun, allied to E. **Hen**, q.v. Also *snaff-le*, q. v. And see *snip*. ☞ It may be added that there may have been an old strong Teut. vb. **sneð-an*, pt. t. **snað*, pp. **snubanoz*. Rietz, indeed, gives a similar verb as still found in Swed. dialects, viz. infin. *snippa*, pt. t. *snapp*, old pp. *snuppit*, with the sense to snap, to snatch. This at once accounts for E. *snip*; cf. also *snub*, and *snuff* (2), to snap or snip off the end of the wick of a candle. And cf. **Snip, Snatch.**

SNARE, a noose, trap. (E.) Properly a noose, a trap formed with a looped string. 'Hongide himself with a *snare*;' Wyclif, Matt. xxvii. 5. AS. *snear*, a cord, string; Grein, ii. 459.+Du. *snaar*, a string; Icel. *snara*, a snare, halter; Dan. *snare*; Swed. *snara*; OHG. *snarahha*, a noose; cited by Fick, iii. 350, Curtius, i. 392. β. From the Teut. base **snarh-* (the *h* being preserved in OHG.); and this is from the 2nd grade of the Teut. strong verb **snerhan-*, appearing in OHG. *snerhan*, to bind tightly, to twist tightly; whence also Icel. *snara*, to turn quickly, twist, wring (though this is a weak verb). γ. The Teut. SNERH answers to Idg. SNERK, to draw together, contract, whence Gk. νάρκη, cramp, numbness; see **Narcissus.** δ. The Idg. SNERK is an extension from √SNER, to twist, wind; whence Lithuan. *ner-ti*, to thread a needle, draw into a chain. ε. And we may further note the OIrish *snäthe*, thread; from the √SNĒ, to wind, spin, whence L. *nēre*, to spin, G. *schnur*, a string. Cf. Skt. *snāva*(*s*), a tendon, sinew. **Der.** *snare*, verb, Temp. ii. 2. 174, ME. *snaren*, Prompt. Parv.; *snar-er*, *en-snare*. Also (obsolete) *snar-l*, a noose, Trevisa, ii. 385.

SNARL, to growl as a surly dog. (E.) In Shak. K. John, iv. 3. 150. The *-l* is a frequentative suffix; the sense is 'to keep on *snarring*.' 'I *snarre*, as a dogge doth under a door whan he sheweth his tethe,' Palsgrave; spelt *snar*, Spenser, F. Q. vi. 12. 27. Of OLow G. origin; perhaps E., though not found in AS. Cf. MDu. *snarren*, 'to brawl, to scould, or to snarle;' Hexham; G. *schnarren*, to rattle the letter *R*, to snarl, speak in the throat; MHG. *snar*, a growling. Cf. also Icel. *snörgla*, to rattle in the throat; *snörgl* (pronounced *snörl*), a rattling sound in the throat. Evidently related to **Sneer**; and see **Snort.**

SNATCH, to seize quickly, snap up. (E.) ME. *snacchen*, Wars of Alisaunder, 6559; spelt *snecchen*, Ancren Riwle, p. 324, l. 27. *Snacchen* is a palatalised form of **snakken*, and may be considered as an E. word, though not found in AS. The *k* is preserved in the sb. *snack*, a portion, lit. a snatch or thing snatched up; Lowland Scotch *snak*, a snatch made by a dog at a hart, a snap of the jaws, Douglas, tr. of Virgil, xii. 754 (L. text). 'Snack, a share; as, to go *snacks* with one;' Phillips, ed. 1706.+Du. *snakken*, to gasp, desire, long, aspire; '*de Visch snackt na het water*,' the fish gasps for water;' Hexham. β. From a Teut. base **snak-*, to catch at with the mouth, move the jaws, parallel to **snap-* (as in E. *snap*). These bases are imitative, with the notion of a movement of the jaws. **Der.** *snatch*, sb.; *body-snatcher*. Also *snack*, sb., as above. Also prov. E. *sneck*, the 'snap' or latch of a door.

SNEAK, to creep or steal away slily, to behave meanly. (E.) In Shak. Troil. i. 2. 246. Variant of ME. *sniken*. 'Sniked in ant ut neddren' = adders creep in and out; O. Eng. Homilies, i. 251; which is from AS. *snican*, to creep; Grein, ii. 459. Supposed to be a strong verb (pt. t. **snāc*, pp. **snicen*); the Icel. pp. *snikinn* occurs, from an obsolete verb **snika*, with the sense of covetous, hankering after. We also find Icel. *snikja* (weak verb), to hanker after, to beg for food silently, as a dog does; Dan. *snige sig*, to sneak, slink. Also Swed. dial. *sniga*, to creep, strong verb (pt. t. *sneg*); *snika*, to hanker after, strong verb (pt. t. *snek*). β. All from a Teut. verb **sneikan-* (pt. t. **snāk*, pp. *snikanoz*), to creep. Cf. Irish and Gael. *snaigh*, *snaig*, to creep, crawl, sneak (from E.). The mod. E. *sneak* would result from an AS. **snǣcan*, a derivative from the second grade **snāc*; whence also ME. *snoken*, to creep about; Wyclif, Works, ed. Arnold, ii. 83. **Der.** *snake*, q.v., *snail*, q. v.

SNEAP, to pinch, check. (Scand.) See **Snub.**

SNEER, to express contempt. (Scand.) 'Sneer, to laugh foolishly or scornfully;' Phillips, ed. 1706; prov. E. *sneering-match*, a grinning match (Forby). Rare. ME. *sneren*, to deride. 'Þai *snered* me with *snering* swa, Bot gnaisted over me with thaire tethe tha' = they derided me so with sneering, also they gnashed upon me with their teeth; Early Eng. Psalter, ed. Stevenson (Surtees Soc.), Ps. xxxiv. 16; and see Ps. ii. 4.—Dan. *snærre*, to grin like a dog; *Hunden snærrede ad hem*, the dog showed its teeth at him (Molbech); cf. MDan. *snarre*, the same. Closely allied to the obsolete E. *snar*; for which see **Snarl.**

SNEEZE, to eject air rapidly and audibly through the nose. (E.) 'Looking against the sunne doth induce *sneezing*;' Bacon, Nat. Hist. § 687. ME. *snesen*, Trevisa, v. 389 (Stratmann). In Chaucer, Group H, l. 62 (l. 17011, ed. Tyrwhitt), the right reading is *fneseth*,

not *sneseth*. But *snesen* is doubtless either a modification of *fnesen*, or a parallel form to it; the initial *s* is perhaps due to Dan. *snuse*, to sniff, for which see **Snout.** β. We find also *fnesynge*, violent blowing, Wyclif, Job, xli. 9. — AS. *fnēosan*, to sneeze; whence *fnēosung*, sternutatio; Voc. 162. 40. Allied to AS. *fnast*, a puff, blast, Grein, i. 307; Icel. *fnasa*, to sneeze, snort.+Du. *fniezen*, to sneeze; Swed. *fnysa*, Dan. *fnyse*, to snort. γ. We thus arrive at a Teut. base **fneus-*, Idg. PNEUS, evidently a mere variant of HNEUS, to sneeze, Fick, iii. 82; for which see **Neese.** Cf. Gk. πνέω, I breathe; see **Pneumatic.** **Der.** *sneeze*, sb. And see *neese*.

SNIFF, to scent, draw in air sharply through the nose. (Scand.) Not common in old books. Johnson defines *snuff*, sb., as 'resentment expressed by *snifting*.' ME. *sneuien* or *sneuen* (with *u=v*), O. Eng. Homilies, ii. 37, l. 25; ii. 207, l. 16; this would give a later E. **sneeve*, whence was formed *sneevle*, to snivel, given in Minsheu. — Icel. **snefja*, a lost verb; whence the pp. *snafðr*, sharp-scented, (Acts, xvii. 21); *snefill*, a slight scent; Dan. *snive*, to sniff, snuff. Note MDan. *snifte* (Kalkar), Dan. *snöfte*, to sniff (whence E. *snift*, above), from MDan. *snift*, air, breath. And cf. Icel. *snippa*, to sniff with the nose, *snapa*, to sniff. **Der.** *sniff*, sb.; *sniv-el*, q.v.

SNIP, to cut off, esp. with shears or scissors. (Du.) Shak. has *snip*, sb., L. L. L. iii. 22; also *snipt*, pp., All's Well, iv. 5. 2. He connects it with *snap*, L. L. L. v. 1. 63.—Du. *snippen*, to snip, clip. Allied to Du. *snappen*, 'to snap up, or to intercept,' Hexham; see **Snap.** + EFries. *snippen*; Low G. *snippeln*, to cut small; G. *schnippen*, to snap; *schnappen*, to snap, to catch. Cf. also EFries. *snip*, sharp; *snip*, *snippe*, a small piece of land; Hamburg *schnippen*, to cut into small bits (Richey). ¶ It has probably been influenced in use by the similar word *nip*. **Der.** *snip*, sb.; *snipp-et*, a small piece, dimin. of *snip*, sb., Butler's Hudibras, pt. ii. c. 3. l. 824. Also *snip-snap*, Pope, Dunciad, ii. 240.

SNIPE, a bird with a long bill, frequenting marshy places. (Scand.) ME. *snype*. 'Snype, or *snyte*, byrde, Ibex;' Prompt. Parv. 'Hic ibis, *or* hic ibex, a *snype*;' Voc. 701. 39. 'Snipe, or *snite*;' Baret (1580). [*Snipe* and *snite* are parallel names for the same bird; it is possible that the vowel of *snipe* has been affected by that of *snite*, which is the older word, found as AS. *snite*, Voc. 3. 28.] — Icel. *snipa*, a snipe, found in the comp. *mȳri-snipa*, a moor-snipe. Cf. Dan. *sneppe*, a snipe, Swed. *snäppa*, a sandpiper; from Du. *snip*, *snep*, MDu. *snippe*, *sneppe*, snipe (Hexham); G. *schnepfe*, snipe. β. The word means 'a snipper' or 'a snapper;' the standard form appears in MDu. *sneppe*, formed by the addition of a suffix *-pe* (for *-yā*) and vowel-change, from the Teut. base SNAP, to snap up; see **Snap.** Cf. MDu. *snabbe*, *snebbe*, 'the bill of a bird,' Hexham; a word with the same sense of 'snapper.' See **Snaffle.**

SNITE (1), to wipe the nose. (E.) See **Snout.**

SNITE (2), a snipe. (E.) See under **Snipe.**

SNIVEL, to sniff continually, to have a running at the nose, to whimper. (Scand.) Formerly *snevil*; spelt *sneuyll*, Skelton, Colin Clout, 1223. ME. *sneuelen* (with *u=v*), P. Plowman, B. v. 135, footnote; other MSS. have *nyuelynge*, *neuelynge*. Also *snuuelen* (Stratmann); answering to an AS. form **snyflan*; whence the derived sb. *snyflung*, in Napier's additions. — AS. *snofl*, mucus; A. S. Leechdoms, ii. 24. Cf. Low G. *snuven*, to sniff; Swed. *snöfla*, Dan. *snövle*, to snuffle, which is a parallel form; see **Snuffle.** And cf. **Snuff.** **Der.** *snivell-er*, *snivel*, sb.

SNOB, a vulgar person. (Scand.) 'That old *snob*;' Howard, The Committee (1665); A. iv. sc. 1 (Song). Prov. E. *snob*, a vulgar ignorant person; orig. a journeyman-shoemaker (Suffolk); see E. D. D. 'Snap, a lad or servant, now mostly used ludicrously;' Thoresby's letter to Ray, 1703 (E. D. S. Gloss. B. 17); 'Snape, a pert youth, *North*,' Halliwell. Lowland Sc. *snab*, a shoemaker's or cobbler's boy (Jamieson). Of Scand. origin.—Dan. dial. *snopp*, *snupp*, bashful, silly; MDan. *snåb*, foolish (Kalkar); Icel. *snápr*, a dolt, idiot, with the notion of impostor or charlatan, a boaster, used as a by-word; Swed. dial. *snöpp*, a boy, anything stumpy. The same Icel. word means the pointed end of a pencil; both senses may be explained from Swed. dial. *snöppa*, to cut off, make stumpy, hence to snub. Cf. Swed. *snopen*, out of countenance, ashamed. See **Snub, Snubnosed.**

SNOOD, a fillet, ribbon. (E.) 'Her satin *snood*;' Sir W. Scott, Lady of the Lake, c. i. st. 19; and see note 25 (31). ME. *snöd* (12th century); Voc. 540. 39. AS. *snöd*. 'Vitta, *snöd*;' Voc. 107. 35. The orig. sense is 'a twist;' cf. OIrish *snäthe*, thread; from the Idg. root **snē*, **snā*, to spin, to twist; whence also G. *schnur*, a string. Cf. Skt. *snāva-s*, a tendon, a muscle; Gk. νέω, I spin, νῆμα, thread, L. *nēre*, to spin. Note W. *noden*, a thread; *ysnoden*, a fillet. See **Snare.**

SNOOZE, to doze, to nap. (Scand.) Rietz gives Swed. dial. *snusa*, (1) to take snuff; (2) to draw breath loudly in sleep, like a child. Cf. Dan. *snuse*, to snuff, to sniff, to poke one's nose into a thing ; just as the prov. E. *snoozle* not only means ' to doze,' but also ' to sniff and poke with the nose,' like a dog. Cf. also Low G. *snuss*, with the same sense as *snute*, a snout ; *snusseln*, to poke with the nose ; W. Flem. *snuisteren*, *snoesteren*, to sniff after, like a dog. Allied to Dan. and Swed. *snus*, snuff ; and prob. of imitative origin, like **Sniff, Snuff.**

SNORE, to breathe hoarsely in sleep. (E.) ME. *snoren*, Chaucer, C. T. 5210 (B 790). Substituted for **fnoren*. Cf. AS. *fnora*, as in ' *Sternutatio*, fnora ;' Wright's Voc. 48. 14. The change from *fn* to *sn* occurs again in the case of the allied word *sneeze* (AS. *fnēosan*). In Chaucer (as above), MS. E. has *snoreth*, MS. C. has *snortith*, and MSS. Hn. Cp. have *fnorteth*. β. Formed from the weak grade *fnor-* (<**fnus*), as seen in *fnor-en*, pp. of *fnēosan*, to sneeze ; precisely as the word *frore*, frozen (Milton, P. L. ii. 595) is the pp. of *frēosan*, to freeze. See further under **Sneeze** ; and Notes on E. Etym., p. 273. Influenced by **Snort.** Der. *snore*, sb., *snor-er*.

SNORT, to force air violently through the nose, as a horse. (Scand.) ME. *snorten*, to snore, Chaucer, C. T. 4161 (A 4163). Cf. Low G. *snurten*, *snarten*, to make an explosive noise. From the base **snur-* ; as in Low G. *snurren*, to hum ; MDu. *snorren*, to murmur. Cf. also (with *k* for *t*) Dan. *snorke*, to snort ; Swed. *snorka*, to threaten (orig. to snort, fume, be angry) ; Du. *snorken*, to snore, snort ; G. *schnarchen*, to snore, snort, bluster ; Swed. *snarka*, to snore ; prov. E. *snork*, to snort. And see **Snarl.** Der. *snort-er* ; *snort*, sb.

SNOT, mucus from the nose. (E.) ME. *snotte*, *snothe*, Prompt. Parv. AS. *ge-snot* ; A. S. Leechdoms, ii. 54. OFries. *snotte*.+Du. *snot* ; Low G. *snotte* ; Dan. *snot*. Supposed to be allied to the pp. *snoten* of a lost strong verb, which would appear as AS. **snūtan* ; see further under **Snout.**

SNOUT, the nose of an animal. (E.) ME. *snoute*, Chaucer, C. T. 14911 (B 4095) ; *snute*, King Horn, ed. Lumby, 1082. AS. **snūt* ; whence *snȳtan*, vb., to snite, was formed by vowel-change ; see **Snite.** EFries. *snūte*.+Swed. *snut*, a snout, muzzle ; Dan. *snude* ; Low G. *snute* ; Westphal. *snūte* ; Du. *snuit*, G. *schnauze*. β. From a Teut. str. vb. **snūtan-*, to sniff, pt. t. **snaut*, pp. **snutanoz*. From the prime grade **snūt-* we have E. *snout* ; also Icel. *snȳta*, to wipe the nose, Swed. *snyta*, Dan. *snyde*, the same, AS. *snȳtan*, whence E. *snite*, to blow the nose (Halliwell). From the 2nd grade we have G. *schnauze* ; and from the weak grade E. *snot*, mucus. γ. We find shorter forms in Dan. *snue*, to sniff, snuff, snort, Low G. *snau*, prov. G. *schnau*, a snout, beak ; all from a base SNEU. And it is clear that prov. G. *schnuff*, a snout, E. *snuff*, *sniff*, *snivel*, Dan. *snuse*, to snuff or sniff, go back to the same base, which seems to have indicated a sudden inspiration of the breath through the nose. Cf. Lithuan. *snukkis*, a snout.

SNOW, a form of frozen vapour. (E.) ME. *snow* ; hence *snow-white*, Chaucer, C. T. 8264 (E 388). AS. *snāw* ; Grein, ii. 458.+Du. *sneeuw* ; Icel. *snær*, *snjár*, *snjór* ; Dan. *snee* ; Swed. *snö* ; Goth. *snaiws* ; G. *schnee*.+Lithuan. *snēgas* ; Russ. *snieg'* ; L. *nix* (gen. *niuis*) ; Gk. acc. *νίφα*, whence *νιφάς*, a snow-flake ; Irish and Gael. *sneachd* ; W. *nyf*. β. All from the √SNEIGwH, to snow, whence L. *ningit*, it snows (with inserted *n*), Lithuan. *snigti*, *sningti*, to snow, Greek *νείφει*, *νίφει*, it snows, Zend. *çnizh*, to snow ; Fick, i. 828. Brugmann, i. § 394. Der. *snow*, verb ; *snow-blind*, *-drift*, *-drop*, *-plough*, *-shoe*, *-slip* ; also *snow-y*, *snow-i-ness*.

SNUB, to check, scold, reprimand. (Scand.) ' To snub one, to take one up sharply ;' Phillips, ed. 1706 ; spelt *snubbe* in Levins, ed. 1570. Another form is *sneb* or *snib* ; spelt *snebbe*, Spenser, Shep. Kal. Feb. l. 126 ; *snib*, id. Mother Hubberd's Tale, 372. ME. *snibben*, Chaucer, C. T. 523. – Dan. *snubbe*, to nip off, to snub (Larsen) ; also *snibbe*, ' to set down, blow up,' i. e. reprimand (whence E. *snib*) ; Swed. *snubba*, to snub, to check ; NFries. *snubbe*, Icel. *snubba*, to snub, chide. The orig. sense was to snip off the end of a thing ; cf. Icel. *snubbōttr*, snubbed, nipped, the pointed end being cut off ; Swed. dial. *snubba*, to snip or clip off ; EFries. *snubbeln*, to snatch away, to snap. β. A form allied to *snub* appears in *sneap*, to check, pinch, nip, L. L. L. i. 1. 100 ; Wint. Tale, i. 2. 13. This is from Icel. *sneypa*, orig. to castrate, then used as a law-term, to outrage, dishonour, and in mod. usage to chide or snub a child ; whence *sneypa*, a disgrace. This is a related word, and cognate with Swed. *snöpa*, to castrate, Swed. dial. *snöppa*, to cut off, to snuff a candle ; Icel. *snupra*, to snub, chide. Der. *snub*, sb. ; also *snub-nosed*, q. v.

SNUB-NOSED, having a short nose. (Scand. *and* E.) Added by Todd to Johnson. It means, literally, with a short or stumpy nose, as if cut off short. Cf. *snubbes*, s. pl., the short stumpy projections on a staff that has been roughly cut and trimmed, Spenser, F. Q. i. 8. 7. *Snub* is from the Swed. dial. *snubba*, to clip, snip ; whence Swed. dial. *snubba*, a cow without horns or with cut horns, Icel. *snubbōttr*, snipped, clipped, with the end cut off. See **Snub** above. And see **Nose.**

SNUFF (1), to sniff, draw in air violently through the nose, to smell. (Du.) ' As if you *snuffed* up love by smelling love ;' L. L. L. iii. 16. Spelt *snuffe* in Levins, ed. 1570 ; *snoffe* and *snuffe* in Palsgrave. – MDu. *snuffen*, ' to snuffe out the filth out of one's nose' (Hexham) ; cf. Du. *snuf*, smelling, scent, *snuffelen*, to smell out ; allied to MDu. *snuyven*, Du. *snuiven*, to snort.+Swed. *snufva*, a cold, catarrh ; *snufven*, a sniff or scent of a thing ; Swed. dial. *snavla*, *snöfla*, *snuffla*, to snuffle (which is the frequent. form) ; Dan. *snövle*, to snuffle ; G. *schnauben*, *schnaufen*, *schnieben*, to snuff, snort ; from a Teut. base **sneuð-* ; Idg. base **sneup-*. To these we also find G. *schnupfen*, a catarrh, *schnupfen*, to take snuff ; prov. G. *schnuffeln*, *schnüffeln*, to snuffle, to smell (Flügel). Der. *snuff-le*, the frequentative form ; *snuff*, sb., powdered tobacco ; *snuff-box*, *snuff-y*.

SNUFF (2), to snip the top of a candle-wick. (E.) ME. *snuffen*, to snuff out a candle, Wyclif, Exod. xxv. 38, note *y* (later version) ; the earlier version has : ' where the *snoffes* ben quenchid ' = where the candle-snuffs are extinguished. β. This form *snuffen* is a parallel form to **snuppen*, **snoppen*, which agrees with prov. E. *snop*, to eat off, as cattle do young shoots (Halliwell). – Swed. dial. *snoppa*, to snip or cut off, esp. to snuff a candle (Rietz) ; cf. Norw. *snuppa*, *snubba*, to dock, cut off a top (Ross) ; *snupp*, a stump (Aasen) ; Hamburg *snüffe*, the peak of a shoe (Richey) ; Dan. *snubbe*, to nip off, the same word as E. *snub* ; see **Snub.** Der. *snuff* (of a candle), sb., ME. *snoffe*, as above ; *snuff-dishes*, Exod. xxv. 38 ; *snuff-ers*, Exod. xxxvii. 23.

SNUG, comfortable, lying close and warm. (Scand.) ' Where you lay *snug* ;' Dryden, tr. of Virgil, Past. iii. 24. Shak. has ' *Snug* the joiner ;' Mids. Nt. Dr. i. 2. 66. Cf. prov. E. *snug*, tight, handsome, Lancashire (Halliwell) ; *snog*, tidy, trimmed, in perfect order (Cleveland Glossary). Of Scand. origin ; cf. Icel. *snöggr*, smooth, said of wool or hair ; MSwed. *snygg*, short-haired, smooth, trimmed, neat, Swed. *snygg*, cleanly, neat, genteel ; Norweg. *snögg*, short, trim ; Dan. *snög* (also *snyg*), neat, smart, tidy (Molbech) ; EFries. *snügge*, *snigge*, smooth, neat. Cf. Norw. *snugga*, to arrange, get ready. β. The orig. sense was 'trimmed' or 'cropped ;' cf. prov. E. *snag*, to trim ; South E. *snig*, to cut or chop off, whence Devon. *snig*, close and private (i. e. snug) ; see Halliwell. See **Snag.** Der. *snug-ly*, *snug-ness*.

SO, thus, in such a manner or degree. (E.) ME. *so*, Chaucer, C. T. 11 ; Northern *sa*, Barbour's Bruce (*passim*) ; also *swa*, Chaucer, C. T. 4028 (A 4030), where the Northern dialect is imitated. AS. *swā*, so ; Grein, ii. 497.+Du. *zoo* ; Icel. *svā*, later *svö*, *svo*, so ; Dan. *saa* ; Swed. *så* ; G. *so* ; Goth. *:wa*, so ; *swē*, just as ; *swa-swē*, just as. Teut. types **swē*, *swō*, *swa*. Cf. Gk. *ὡς*. β. From an oblique case of the Teut. **swaz*, Idg. **swos*, one's own (a reflexive pronominal base) ; whence Skt. *:va-*, one's own self, own, L. *suus*, one's own. Thus *so* = ' in one's own way.' See Prellwitz (s. v. *ὡς*) ; Brugmann, i. § 362.

SOAK, to steep in a fluid. (E.) It also means to suck up, imbibe. ' A sponge, that *soaks* up the king's countenance ;' Hamlet, iv. 2. 16. This is the orig. sense ; the word is a derivative of *to suck*. ME. *soken*, (1) to suck, (2) to soak ; ' *Sokere*, or he that sokythe, sugens ;' Prompt. Parv. ' *Sokyn* yn lycure, as thyng to be made softe,' id. From AS. *socian*, to soak, tr. and intr. ; see Bosworth-Toller. Allied to AS. *soc-*, weak grade of *sūcan*, to suck. Cf. AS. *āsūcan*, *āsūgan*, to suck dry, whence the pp. *āsocene*, *āsogene* ; Grein, i. 43. β. There is also the sb. *soc*, or *ge:oc*, a sucking, Gen. xxi. 7, 8. See Notes on E. Etym., p. 273. See **Suck.** Der. *soak-er*.

SOAM, a horse-load. (Late L. – Gk.) The Western E equivalent of E. *seam*, AS. *sēam* ; see **Seam** (2).

SOAP, a compound of oil or fat with soda or potash, used for washing. (E.) ME. *sope*, Rob. of Glouc. p. 6, l. 143. [The long *o* is due to AS. *ā*, as in *stone* from AS. *stān*, &c.] AS. *sāpe*, soap ; Ælfric's Homilies, i. 472, l. 6.+Du. *zeep* ; [Icel. *sāpa*, Dan. *sæbe*, Swed. *sāpa* ; borrowed from AS.] G. *seife*, OHG. *seifa*. β. Teut. type **saipōn*, f. ; from **saip*, 2nd grade of Teut. **seipan*, to trickle (MHG. *sifen*, Low G. *sipen*, to be moist, OFries. *sipa*) ; see *Seife* in Kluge. γ. The L. *sāpo* (see Pliny, xxviii. 12. 51) was borrowed from the Teutonic, not (as Pliny says) from Celtic. (From the L. acc. *sāpōnem* came F. *savon*, Ital. *sapone*, Span. *xabon*, &c.) The truly *cognate* L. word would appear to be *sēbum*, tallow, grease. The W. *sebon*, Gael. *siopunn*, Irish *siabunn*, seem to be borrowed from the L. acc. *sāpōnem*. Der. *soap*, verb ; *soap-y*.

SOAR, to fly aloft. (F. – L.) ME. *soren*. ' As doth an egle, whan him list to *sore* ;' Chaucer, C. T. 10437 (F 123). A term of hawking, and accordingly of F. origin. – F. *essorer*, ' to expose unto, or lay out in, the weather ; also, to mount or sore up ;' Cot. Cf. Ital. *sorare*, ' to soare in the aire ;' Florio. – Late L. **exaurāre* (not found), to expose to the air ; regularly formed from *ex*, out ; and *aura*, a breeze, the air. β. The Lat. *aura* was probably borrowed from Gk. *αὔρα*, a breeze ; it is formed with the suffix *-ra*, from √AW, to blow. The √AW is allied to √WĒ, to blow ; see **Air.**

SOB, to sigh convulsively, with tears. (E.) ME. *sobben.* 'Swowed and *sobbed* and syked' [sighed]; P. Plowman, B. xiv. 326. Related to AS. *siofian, séofian,* to lament; Ælfred, tr. of Boethius, c. xxxvi. § 1, lib. iv. pr. 1; from **suð,* weak grade of **seuð,* variant of Teut. **seup,* to sup, suck in. The word represents the convulsive sucking in of air. β. This is clearly shown by the allied G. *seufzen,* MHG. *siuften, süften,* OHG. *súftôn,* to sigh, formed from the OHG. sb. *sûft,* a sigh, sob; this sb. being again related to OHG. *súfan,* to sup, sip, cognate with E. *sup;* see **Sup.** So also Icel. *syptir* (= *syftir*), a sobbing. Der. *sob,* sb.

SOBER, temperate, sedate, grave. (F. – L.) ME. *sobre,* Chaucer, C. T. 94 7. – F. *sobre,* 'sober;' Cot. – L. *sôbrium,* acc. of *sôbrius,* sober. Compounded of *sô-,* prefix; and *-brius,* as in *ê-brius,* drunken; both possibly related to the rare L. *bria,* a wine-vessel. The prefix *sô-,* as in *sô-cors,* signifies apart from, or without; and *sôbrius,* not drunken, is thus opposed to * êbrius.* Sô- is related to *sê-,* which before a vowel appears as *sêd-,* as in *sêd-itio,* lit. 'a going apart.' See **Se-,** prefix, and **Ebriety.** Der. *sober-ly, sober-ness;* also *sobrie-ty,* from F. *sobrieté,* 'sobriety,' Cot., from L. acc. *sôbrietâtem.*

SOBRIQUET, a nickname, assumed name. (F. – L. *and* C.) Sometimes spelt *soubriquet,* but *sobriquet* is the mod. F. form. Modern, not in Todd's Johnson. Borrowed from F. *sobriquet,* 'a surname, nickname, a quip or cut given, a mock or flowt bestowed, a jeast broken on a man;' Cot. Another form is *sotbriquet,* also in Cotgrave. β. Etym. disputed and uncertain. Cotgrave also spells the word *soubriquet,* and Littré and Scheler note the occurrence of *soubzbriquet* in a text of the 14th century with the sense of 'a chuck under the chin.' Here *soubz* (mod. F. *sous*) answers to L. *subtus,* below; and *briquet* is the Norm. dial. form of F. *brechet,* brisket; see Moisy. Hence *sobriquet,* properly a knock on the breast, hence, a chuck under the chin, and then 'a quip or cut given, a mock or flout, a jeast broken on a man,' [finally] 'a nickname;' Cotgrave. 'Percussit super mentonem faciendo dictum *le soubriquet;*' Act A.D. 1355 in Archives du Nord de la France, iii. 35. 'Donna deux petits coups appeléz *soubzbriquez* des dois de la main soubz le menton;' Act A.D. 1398, ibid. in Ducange, s. v. *Barba.* In the same way *soubarbe,* 'the part between the chin and the throat, also a check, twitch, jerk given to a horse with his bridle, *endurer une soubarbe,* to indure an affront;' Cot. If so, the sense is 'chuck under the chin,' hence an affront, nickname. At the same time, Cotgrave's *sotbriquet* must be due to some popular etymology (prob. from *sot,* foolish).

SOC, SOCAGE, law-terms. (E.) See **Soke.**

SOCIABLE, companionable. (F. – L.) In Shak. K. John, i. 188. – F. *sociable,* 'sociable;' Cot. – L. *sociâbilis,* sociable; formed with suffix *-bilis* from *sociâ-re,* to accompany. – L. *socius,* a companion, lit. 'a follower.' – L. base *soc-,* second grade of *seq-,* appearing in *sequî,* to follow; all from √SEQ, to follow; see **Sequence.** Der. *sociabl-y, sociable-ness, sociabili-ty.* From L. *socius* is also formed the adj. *sociâlis,* whence E. *social,* with the adv. *social-ly,* also *social-i-ty, social-ise, social-ist, social-ism.* Also *socie-ty,* L. L. L., iv. 2. 166, from MF. *societé,* 'society,' Cot., which from L. acc. *societâtem.* Also *dis-sociate, as-sociate.*

SOCK, a sort of half stocking, buskin. (L.) ME. *socke,* Prompt. Parv.; see Way's note. AS. *socc;* 'Soccus, *socc;*' Voc. 47. 22. – L. *soccus,* a light shoe, slipper, sock, worn by comic actors, and so taken as the symbol of comedy, as in Milton, L'Allegro, 132. Der. *sock-et.*

SOCKET, a hollow into which something is inserted. (F. – Du.) 'S*oket* of a candylstykke or other lyke;' Prompt. Parv. ME. *soket,* King Alisaunder, 4415. – OF. *soket,* given by Roquefort only as (1) a dimin. of F. *soc,* a ploughshare, and (2) a dimin. of F. *souche,* a stump or stock of a tree. β. [Of these, the F. *soc* is of Celtic origin; cf. W. *swch,* a (swine's) snout, a ploughshare (Thurneysen, p. 112), and with this word we have here nothing to do.] But *souche* appears in the Norman dial. as *chouque* (so Moisy), and is allied to the Ital. *ciocco,* a stump or stock of a tree; see Florio. Cf. Walloon *sokett,* a stump; F. dial. *soquette,* a stump of dead wood, patois de la Meuse (Labourasse); MF. *chouquet,* 'a block;' Cot.; OF. *chocquet,* a support (socket) for an arblast (Godefroy); F. dial. *chouquet,* a block on which one cuts wood, dimin. of *chouque,* a stump, patois du pays de Bray (Decorde); Picard *choke,* a block (Corblet); Walloon *choque,* stump of a tree (Sigart). Prob. of Teut. origin; perhaps from MDu. *schocke,* 'a shock, a cock, or a heape,' Hexham. See **Shock** (2). ¶ The Du. *sch-* may have caused difficulty; hence Ital. *zocco* = *ciocco.* Note 'une *souche* de fourment,' a shock of corn; Supp. to Godefroy.

SOD, turf, a surface of earth covered with growing grass. (E.) 'A *sod,* turfe, *cespes;*' Levins, ed. 1570. Perhaps so called because the turf was used as fuel for boiling (Weigand); or because sodden. Cf. AS. *ge-sod,* a cooking; *sod-en,* pp. of *séoðan,* to seethe. That the connexion with the verb to *seethe* is real is apparent from the cognate

terms. +Du. *zode,* sod, green turf; MDu. *zode,* 'seething or boiling,' also, 'a sodde or a turfe;' Hexham. Also contracted to *zoo* in both senses; 'zoo, a sod; *het water is aan de zoo,* the water begins to seeth;' Sewel. Note also MDu. *sood,* a well (Hexham); so named from the bubbling up of the water, and cognate with AS. *séað,* a well, a pit, from the same verb (*seethe*). +EFries. *sôd,* a well; *sode,* a cut turf, also boiling, cooking; Dan. dial. *sodd, saadd,* a sod; OFries. *sâtha, sâda,* sod, turf, allied to *sâth, sâd,* a well; Low G. *sode,* sod, allied to *sood,* a well; G. *sode,* sod, turf, allied to G. *sod,* broth, also, a bubbling up of boiling water. See **Seethe, Suds.**

SOD, SODDEN; see under **Seethe.**

SODA, oxide of sodium. (Ital. – L.) Modern; added by Todd to Johnson. – Ital. *soda,* soda; MItal. *soda,* 'a kind of fearne ashes wherof they make glasses:' Florio. Fem. of Ital. *sodo,* 'solide, tough, fast, hard, stiffe;' Florio. This is a contracted form of Ital. *solido,* solid; see **Solid.** So called, apparently, from the firmness or hardness of the products obtained from glass-wort; cf. OF. *soulde,* 'saltwort, glasswort,' from the L. *solida* (fem. of *solidus*), which Scheler supposes must have been the L. name of glass-wort. β. Note that the Span. name for soda is *sosa,* which also means glass-wort; but here the etymology is different, the name being given to the plant from its abounding in alkaline salt. *Sosa* is the fem. of Span. *soso,* insipid, orig. 'salt;' from L. *salsus,* salt; see **Sauce.** Der. *sod-ium,* a coined word.

SODER, the same as **Solder,** q. v.

SODOMY, an unnatural crime. (F. – L. – Gk. – Heb.) In Cot. Cf. ME. *sodomyte,* Lydgate, Assembly of Gods, 708; also *sodomite,* Cursor Mundi, l. 27950. – F. *sodomie,* 'sodomy;' Cot. So called because it was imputed to the inhabitants of Sodom; Gen. xix. 5. – F. *Sodome,* Sodom. – L. *Sodoma.* – Gk. Σόδομα. – Heb. *Secôm* (with initial *samech*); explained to mean 'burning' in Stanley's Sinai and Palestine, cap. vii; but this is quite uncertain. Gesenius gives the sense 'enclosure.'

SOFA, a long seat with stuffed bottom, back, and arms. (Arab.) 'He leaped off from the *sofa* in which he sat;' Guardian, no. 167 [not 198], Sept. 22, 1713. The story here given is said to be translated from an Arabian MS.; this may be a pretence, but the word is Arabic. – Arab. *suffa(t), suffah,* 'a sopha, a couch, a place for reclining upon before the doors of Eastern houses, made of wood or stone;' Rich. Dict., p. 936. – Arab. root *saffa,* to draw up in line, put a seat to a saddle; ibid.

SOFFIT, the under side of an architrave or arch, also a ceiling. (F. – Ital. – L.) F. *soffite* (Hatzfeld). – Ital. *soffitta,* a garret, a ceiling (Barretti). Orig. fem. of the pp. *soffitto,* fixed beneath; from *sof-* (from L. *sub,* under), and *fitto,* pp. of *figgere,* to fix, from L. *figere,* to fix. Thus it is (practically) a doublet of *suffix.*

SOFT, easily yielding to pressure, gentle, easy, smooth. (E.) ME. *softe,* Wyclif, Matt. xi. 8; Chaucer, C. T. 12035 (C 101). AS. *sôfte,* gen. used as an adv., Grein, ii. 464. The adj. form is commonly *séfte* (id. 423), where the *ô* is further modified to *ê* +OSax. *sâfto,* softly, only in the compar. *sâftur,* Heliand, 3302; G. *sanft,* soft; OHG. *samfto,* adv., softly, lightly, gently; Du. *zacht* (for *zaft), whence G. *sacht.* Teut. type **samftoz;* from **samjan-* (Goth. *samjan*), to please. Cf. OIrish *sâim,* mild, *sâm,* rest; Gk. ἥμερος, tame, mild; Skt. *sâman,* mildness. Der. *soft-ly,* ME. *softely* (three syllables), Chaucer, C. T. 4209 (A 4211); *soft-ness,* Layamon, 25549. Also *soft-en,* in which the final *-en* is added by analogy with *length-en,* &c.; the ME. *soften* would only have given a later E. verb to *soft;* cf. *softeð* in Ancren Riwle, p. 244, l. 27. The right use of *soften* is intransitive, as in Shak. Wint. Tale, ii. 2. 40.

SOHO, a cry of sportsmen, to call attention to the hunted animal. (F.) 'Soho! soho!' Two Gent. of Verona, iii. 3. 189. ME. *soho,* King Alisaunder, 3712. A better form is *sa ho,* as in Middleton, Trick to Catch the Old One; A. iv. sc. 4. 'Sohow is [as] moche to say as *sahow;* for because that it is short [i. e. easier] to say, we say alwey *sohow;*' Venery de Twety, in Reliq. Antiq. i. 154; 'sa, sa, cy, adesto, sohow,' id. 152. – F. *ça,* 'hither, .. follow hoe, come after,' Cot.; and *ho!* interj. The F. *ça* is from the popular L. *ecce hâc,* behold! this way! See Hatzfeld.

SOIL (1), ground, mould, country. (F. – L.) ME. *soile;* spelt *soyle,* Allit. Poems, ed. Morris, B. 1039. – AF. *soil,* Year-books of Edw. I (1304-5), p. 53; (1305), p. 9; (allied to OF. *soel, suel,* MF. *sueil,* 'the threshold of a door;' Cot., from L. *solium*). – L. *solea,* a covering for the foot, a sole, sandal, sole of the foot, timber on which wattled walls are built. The Late L. *solea* also means 'soil, or ground,' by confusion with L. *solum,* ground, whence F. *sol,* 'the soil, ground;' Cot. β. We cannot derive E. *soil* from F. *sol,* on account of the diphthong; but it makes little difference, since L. *solea,* sole of the foot, and *solum,* ground, are closely connected words. γ. The root of L. *sol-ea, sol-um* is uncertain; they may be allied to **Sill.** Doublets, *sole* (1), *sole* (2).

SOIL (2), to defile, contaminate. (F.—L.) ME. *soilen*, Ancren Riwle, p. 84, l. 23; P. Plowman, B. xiv. 2. The sense is to cover with mire; *to take soil*, lit. to betake oneself to muddy water, was a term of the chase; see Halliwell. 'To go to *soyle*' was said of the hart; Book of St. Albans, fol. e 4, back.—AF. *soyler*, Walter de Bibbesworth, in Wright's Vocab. i. 171; OF. *soillier* (12th cent., Littré), F. *souiller*, 'to soil,' Cot.; whence '*se souiller* (of a swine), to take soile, or wallow in the mire;' id.—OF. *soil*, *souil*; 'soil, or *souil de sanglier*, the soile of a wilde boare, the slough or mire wherein he hath wallowed;' Cot. Cf. MItal. *sogliare*, 'to sully, defile, or pollute,' Florio; also *sogliardo* (mod. Ital. *sugliardo*), 'slovenly, sluttish, or hoggish;' id. Diez also cites Prov. *solh*, m ire, *sulhar*, to soil; and *sul a*, a sow, which last is (as he says) plainly derived from L. *sucula*, a young sow, dimin. of *sus*, a sow. See **Sow**. β. Similarly, he explains the F. *souil* from the L. adj. *suillus*, belonging to swine, derived from the same sb.—L. *sūs*, a sow; see **Sow**. Körting, § 9247. γ. It will be observed that the difference in sense between *soil* (1) = ground, and *soil* (2), sb. = mire, is so slight that the words have doubtless frequently been confused, though really from quite different sources. There is yet a third word with the same spelling; see **Soil** (3). **Der.** *soil*, sb., a spot, stain, a new coinage from the verb; the old sb. *soil*, a wallowing-place (really the *original* of the verb), is obsolete. ☞ The AS. *sol*, mire, is not the orig. of E. *soil*, but of prov. E. *soal*, *sole*, a dirty pool, *Kent*; E. D. S. Gloss. C. 3. See **Sully**.

SOIL (3), to feed cattle with green grass, to fatten with feeding. (F.—L.) See Halliwell; the expression '*soiled* horse,' i. e. a horse high fed upon green food, is in King Lear, iv. 6. 124. [Quite distinct f om the words above.] Also spelt *soul*; Halliwell gives '*soul*, to satisfy with food.'—OF. *soeler*, *saoler* (Supp. to Godefroy, s. v. *saouler*); cf. AF. *sauler*, P. de Thaun, Bestiary, l. 527, later *saouler*, 'to glut, cloy, fill, satiate;' Cot. Mod. F. *soûler*.—AF. *saul*, satisfied, Vie de St. Auban; OF. *saol*, adj. (Burguy), later *saoul*, 'full, cloied, satiated,' Cot. Mod. F. *soûl*.—L. *satullum*, acc. of *satullus*, filled with food; a dimin. form from *satur*, full, satiated, akin to *satis*, enough. See **Sate, Satiate, Satisfy**.

SOIRÉE, an evening party. (F.—L.) Borrowed from French. 'A friendly *swarry*;' Pickwick Papers, c. 36; spelt *soiree* in the heading to the chapter.—F. *soirée*, 'the evening-tide,' Cot.; hence a party given in the evening. Cf. Ital. *serata*, evening-tide. Formed as a fem. pp. from a (supposed) Late L. verb **sērāre*, to become late; from L. *sērus*, late in the day, whence Ital. *sera*, F. *soir*, evening. Cf. OIrish *sír*, W. *hir*, long.

SOJOURN, to dwell, stay, reside. (F.—L.) ME. *soiornen*, Rob. of Brunne, tr. of Langtoft, p. 3, last line; *soiournen*, Chaucer, C. T. 4568 (B 148). (Here *i* = *j*.)—AF. *sojourner*, Stat. Realm. i. 277 (1336); OF. *sojorner*, *sojourner*, to sojourn; also spelt *sejorner*, *sejourner* (Burguy). Mod. F. *séjourner*; cf. Ital. *soggiornare*. This verb answers to a Late L. type **subdiurnāre*, composed of L. *sub*, under, and *diurnāre*, to stay, last long, derived from the adj. *diurnus*, daily; see **Sub-** and **Diurnal** or **Journal**. **Der.** *sojourn-er*; *sojourn*, sb., K. Lear, i. 1. 48, ME. *soiorne*, *soiorn*, Barbour's Bruce, ix. 369, vii. 385. The AF. sb. appears both as *sojourn* and *sojour*.

SOKE, SOC, a franchise, land held by socage. (E.) '*Soc*, signifies power, authority, or liberty to minister justice and execute laws; also the shire, circuit, or territory, wherein such power is exercised by him that is endued with such a priviledge or liberty;' Blount's Nomolexicon, ed. 1691. [Blount rightly notes the word as 'Saxon,' but under *socage* gives a wrong derivation from F. *soc*, a plough-share.] '*Sac* and *Sōc*; *sac* was the power and privilege of hearing and determining causes and disputes, levying of forfeitures and fines, executing laws, and administering justice within a certain precinct; see Ellis, Introduction to Domesday Book, i. 273. *Sōc* or *Sōcn* was strictly the right of investigating or seeking, or, as Spelman defines it, Cognitio quam dominus habet in curia sua, de causis litibusque inter vassallos suos exorientibus. It was also the territory or precinct in which the *sacu* and other privileges were exercised;' Gloss. to Thorpe's Diplomatarium, at p. 369 of which we find: 'ic ān heom þerofer saca and *sōcna*' = I grant them thereover the privileges of *sacu* and *sōcn*. See further in Schmidt, Die Gesetze der Angelsachsen, ed. 1858, p. 653. '*Soka*, sute of court; and therof cometh *Sokene*; but *Sokene* otherwhile is for to aske lawe in the gretter court;' Trevisa, tr. of Higden, ii. 95. β. Etymologically, *sac* (AS. *sacu*) is the same word as E. *sake*; the orig. sense is 'contention,' hence a law-suit; from AS. *sacan*, to contend; see **Sake**. *Soken* (AS. *sōcn*, *sōcen*) is 'an enquiry;' closely connected with mod. E. *seek*, to investigate, and derived from AS. *sōc*, 2nd grade of *sac-*, as seen in *sōc*, pt. t. of the same verb *sacan*; see **Seek**. Cf. Goth. *sōkns*, enquiry; *sōkjan*, to seek; *sakan*, to contend. Hence *Portsoken* (ward) in London, which Stow explains by 'franchise at the gate.' **Der.** *soc-*

age, a barbarous law-term, made by adding the F. suffix *-age* (L. *-āticum*) to AS. *sōc-*. (The *o* is long.)

SOLACE, a comfort, relief. (F.—L.) ME. *solas*, King Alisaunder, l. 15; Chaucer, C. T. 13712 (B 1972).—OF. *solaz*, solace; Burguy. (Here *z* = *ts*.)—L. *sōlācium*, a comfort; as if from an adj. **sōlax*; allied to the verb *sōlāri*, to console, to comfort. Allied to L. *sollus*, Gk. ὅλος, whole (Bréal, Prellwitz); Skt. *sarva(s)*, whole. **Der.** *solace*, verb, ME. *solacen*, P. Plowman, B. xix. 22, from OF. *solacier*, *solacer*, to solace (Burguy). And see **con-sole**.

SOLAN-GOOSE, the name of a bird. (Scand. *and* E.) The E. *goose* is an addition; the Lowland-Scotch form is *soland*, which occurs in Holland's poem of the Houlate (Owlet), about A. D. 1450; l. 700. [Here the *d* is excrescent, as is so common after *n*; cf. *sound* from F. *son*.]—Icel. *sūla*, also *haf-sūla*, a gannet, solan goose (see below); Norweg. *sula*, *havsula*, the same (Aasen). The Norweg. *hav* (Icel. *haf*) means 'sea.' β. As the Icel. *sūla* is feminine, the definite form is *sūlan* = the gannet; which accounts for the final *n* in the E. word. Similarly, Dan. *sol* = sun, but *solen* = the sun; whence the Shetland word *sooleen*, the sun (Edmonston).

SOLAR, belonging to the sun. (L.) 'The *solar* and lunary year;' Ralegh, Hist. of the World, b. ii. c. 3 (R.).—L. *sōlāris*, solar. —L. *sōl*, the sun.+Icel. *sól*; Goth. *sauil*; Lithuan. *sáulé*; Russ. *solntsé*; W. *haul* (for *saul*); Irish *súl*; Gk. ἥλιος, Homeric ἠέλιος, Doric ἀέλιος, Cretan ἀβέλιος (with long *a*); cf. Skt. *sura(s)*. Brugmann, i. § 481. **Der.** *sol-stice*, q. v.

SOLDER, a cement made of fusible metal, used to unite two metallic substances. (F.—L.) Sometimes spelt *soder*, and usually pronounced *sodder* [sod·ur]. Rich. spells it *soulder*. 'To *soder* such gold, there is a proper glue and *soder*;' Holland, tr. of Pliny, b. xxxiii. c. 5. 'I *sowder* a metall with *sowlder*, Ie soulde;' Palsgrave. ME. *sowdere*; sb. 'Soldatura, *sowdere*;' Voc. 612. 33.—OF. *soudure* (14th cent., Littré), later also *souldure*, 'a souldering, and particularly the knot of soulder which fastens the lead [lead] of a glasse window;' Cot. Mod. F. *soudure*, solder; Hamilton.—OF. *souder*, *soulder* (orig. *solder*), 'to soulder, consolidate, close or fasten together;' Cot. [Hence also ME. *souden*, *sowden*, to strengthen; 'anoon hise leggis and hise feet weren *sowdid togidere*;' Wyclif, Acts, iii. 7.]—L. *solidāre*, to make firm.—L. *solidus*, solid, firm; see **Solid**. And see **Soldier**. **Der.** *solder*, verb, formerly *soder*, as above. ☞ It is usual to derive, conversely, the sb. *solder* from the verb; this is futile, as it leaves the second syllable entirely unaccounted for. The OF. verb *souder* yielded the ME. verb *souden*, as shown above, which could only have produced a modern E. verb *sod* or *sud*. In no case can the E. suffix *-er* be due to the ending *-er* of the F. infinitive. The French for what we call *solder* (sb.) is *soudure*, and in this we find the obvious origin of the word. The pronunciation of final *-ure* as *-er* occurs in the common word *figure*, pronounced [fig·ər], which is likewise from the F. sb. *figure*, not from a verb.

SOLDIER, one who engages in military service for pay. (F.—L.) The common pronunciation of the word as *sodger* [soj·ər] is probably old, and may be defended, the *l* being frequently dropped in this word in old books. [Compare *soder* as the usual pronunciation of *solder*; see the word above.] ME. *soudiour*, Will. of Palerne, 3954; *souder*, Rob. of Brunne, tr. of Langtoft, p. 109, l. 14; *schavaldwr*, *sodiour*, *souldier*, Barbour's Bruce, v. 205, and various readings. So called from their receiving *soulde* (i. e. pay). 'He wolde paye them their *souldye* or wagis . . . [he] hadde goten many a *souldyour*;' Reynard the Fox (Caxton's translation), ed. Arber, p. 39.—OF. *soldier* (Burguy), also *soldoier*, *surdoier*; Cot. has *souldoyer*, 'a souldier, one that fights or serves for pay.' Cf. OF. *soulde*, 'pay or lendings for souldiers;' id. Also F. *soldat*, a soldier. β. Of these words, OF. *soldier* answers to Late L. *soldārius*, a soldier; cf. 'Soldarius, *a sowdeour*;' Voc. 612. 32. The OF. *soulde* is from Late L. *soldum*, pay; and F. *soldat* = Late L. *soldātus*, pp. of Late L. *soldāre*, to pay. All from Late L. *solidus*, a piece of money, whence is derived (by loss of the latter part of the word) the OF. *sol*, 'the French shilling,' Cot., and the mod. F. *sou*. We still use *L. s. d.* to signify *libræ*, *solidi*, and *denarii*, or pounds, shillings, and pence. The orig. sense was 'solid' money.—L. *solidus*, solid; see **Solid**. **Der.** *soldier-like*, *soldier-ship*, *soldier-y*.

SOLE (1), the under side of the foot, bottom of a boot or shoe. (L.) ME. *sole*. 'Sole of a foot, *Planta*; Sole of a schoo, *Solea*;' Prompt. Parv. AS. *sole*, pl. *solen* (for *solan*). 'Solen, soleæ;' Voc. 125. 25.—L. *solea*, the sole of the foot or of a shoe.—L. *solum*, the ground. See **Soil** (1). Doublet, *soil* (1), which is the F. form. **Der.** *sole*, verb.

SOLE (2), a kind of flat fish. (F.—L.) ME. *sole*. 'Sole, fysche, *Solia*;' Prompt. Parv.; cf. AF. *soel*, Liber Albus, p. 244.—F. *sole*, 'the sole-fish;' Cot.—L. *solea*, the sole of the foot, the fish called the sole. The sole of the foot is taken as the type of flatness. See **Sole** (1).

SOLE (3), alone, only, solitary, single. (F.–L.) ME. *sool*, Lydgate, Troy-book, bk. i. ch. i. l. 29; AF. *sole*, f., Liber Albus, p. 219.–OF. *sol*, mod. F. *seul*, sole.–L. *sōlum*, acc. of *sōlus*, alone. Perhaps the same word as OL. *sollus*, entire, complete in itself (hence alone); Bréal. Or allied to L. *sō-* (in *sō-brius*) and *sē-d-* in *sēd-itio* (Walde); see **Sober**. Der. *sole-ly*, *sole-ness*. From L. *sōlus* are also *de-sol-ate*, *soli-loquy*, *sol-it-ar-y*, *soli-tude*, *solo*.

SOLECISM, impropriety in speaking or writing. (F.–L.–Gk.) In Minsheu and Cotgrave.–MF. *soloecisme*, 'a solecisme, or incongruity;' Cot.–L. *solœcismum*, acc. of *solœcismus*.–Gk. σολοικισμός, sb.–Gk. σολοικίζειν, to speak incorrectly.–Gk. adj. σόλοικος, speaking incorrectly, like an inhabitant of Σόλοι (*Soloi*) in Cilicia, a place colonised by Athenian emigrants, who soon corrupted the Attic dialect which they at first spoke correctly. Others say it was colonised by Argives and Lydians from Rhodes, who spoke a corrupt dialect of Greek. See Diogenes Laertius, i. 51; and Smith, Class. Dict. Der. *solec-ist*, *solec-ist-ic-al*.

SOLEMN, attended with religious ceremony, devout, devotional, serious. (F.–L.) ME. *solempne*. 'In the *solempne* dai of pask;' Wyclif, Luke, ii. 41. Hence *solempnely*, adv., Chaucer, C. T. 276 (A 274).–OF. *solempne* (Roquefort); the mod. F. has only the derivative *solennel*.–L. *sōlemnem*, acc. of *sōlemnis*, later forms *sōlennis*, *sollennis*, as if it meant occurring annually like a religious rite, religious, festive, solemn; from *soll-us*, entire, complete, and *annus*, a year, which becomes *-ennus* in composition, as in E. *bi-ennial*, *tri-ennial*. But the latter part was orig. *-emnis*, perhaps from *amb-*, around. β. The OL. *sollus* is cognate with W. *holl*, entire, Gk. ὅλος (Ion. οὖλος), whole; Skt. *sarva(s)*, all, whole. Brugmann, i. § 417. Der. *solemn-ly*, *solemn-ness*; *solemn-ise*, spelt *solempnyse* in Palsgrave; *solemn-is-er*, *solemn-is-at-ion*; also *solemn-i-ty*, ME. *solemnitee*, Chaucer, C. T. 2704 (A 2702).

SOL-FA, to sing the notes of the gamut. (L.) ME. *solfye*, *solfe*; P. Plowman, B. v. 423; Reliquiæ Antiquæ, i. 292. 'They . . *solfa* so alamyre'=they sol-fa so a-la-mi-re; Skelton, Colin Clout, 107. To *sol-fa* is to practise singing the scale of notes in the gamut, which contained the notes named *ut*, *re*, *mi*, *sol*, *fa*, *la*, *si*. These names are of Latin origin; see **Gamut**. Der. *solfeggio*, from Ital. *solfeggio*, sb., the singing of the *sol-fa* or gamut. Also *sol-mi-s-at-ion*, a word coined from the names of the notes *sol* and *mi*.

SOLICIT, to petition, seek to obtain. (F.–L.) ME. *soliciten*; spelt *solycyte* in Caxton, tr. of Reynard the Fox, ed. Arber, p. 70, l. 24.–MF. *soliciter*, 'to solicit;' Cot.–L. *sollicitāre*, to agitate, arouse, excite, incite, urge, solicit.–L. *sollicitus*, lit. wholly agitated, aroused, anxious, solicitous.–L. *solli-*, for *sollus*, whole, entire; and *citus*, pp. of *ciēre*, to shake, excite, cite; see **Solemn** and **Cite**. Der. *solicit-at-ion*, Oth. iv. 2. 202, from MF. *solicitation*, 'a solicitation,' Cot. Also *solicit-or* (*solicitour* in Minsheu), substituted for MF. *soliciteur*, 'a solicitor, or follower of a cause for another,' Cot.; from L. acc. *sollicitātōrem*. And see **Solicitous**. (Spelt *solliciter* in F.)

SOLICITOUS, very desirous, anxious, eager. (L.) In Milton, P. L. x. 428. Englished from L. *sōlicitus*, better spelt *sollicitus*, by change of *-us* to *-ous*, as in *ardu-ous*, *strenu-ous*, &c. See **Solicit**. Der. *solicitous-ly*; *solicit-ude*, q.v.

SOLICITUDE, anxious care, trouble. (F.–L.) In Sir T. More, Works, p. 1266 h.–MF. *solicitude*, 'solicitude, care;' Cot.–L. *sōlicitūdinem*, acc. of *sōlicitūdo* (better *sollicitūdo*) anxiety.–L. *sollicitus*, solicitous; see **Solicitous**.

SOLID, firm, hard, compact, substantial, strong. (F.–L.) ME. *solide*, Chaucer, On the Astrolabe, pt. i. § 17, l. 15.–F. *solide*, 'solid;' Cot.–L. *solidum*, acc. of *solidus*, firm, solid. Allied to Gk. ὅλος, whole, entire, and Skt. *sarva(s)*, all, whole; see **Solemn**. Der. *solid-ly*, *solid-ness*. Also *solid-ar-i-ty*, 'a word which we owe to the F. Communists, and which signifies a fellowship in gain and loss, in honour and dishonour, . . a being, so to speak, all in the same bottom,' Trench, Eng. Past and Present; Cotgrave has the adj. *solidaire*, 'solid, whole, in for [or] liable to the whole.' Also *solid-i-fy*, from mod. F. *solidifier*, to render solid; *solid-i-fic-at-ion*. Also *solid-i-ty*, from F. *solidité*, which from L. acc. *soliditātem*. From L. *solidus* are also *con-solid-ate*, *con-sols*, *sold-er* (or *sod-er*), *sold-ier*, *soli-ped*. And cf. *catholic* (from Gk. ὅλος), *holo-caust*.

SOLILOQUY, a speaking to oneself. (L.) Spelt *soliloquie* in Minsheu, ed. 1627. Englished from L. *sōliloquium*, a talking to oneself, a word formed by St. Augustine; see Aug. Soliloq. ii. 7, near the end.–L. *sōli-*, for *sōlus*, alone; and *loqui*, to speak; see **Sole** (3) and **Loquacious**. Der. *soliloqu-ise*, a coined word.

SOLIPED, an animal with an uncloven hoof. (F.–L.) 'Solipeds or firm-hoofed animals;' Sir T. Browne, Vulgar Errors, b. vi. c. 6. § 9. A contraction for *solidiped*, which would be a more correct form.–OF. *solipede* (Godefroy); F. *solipède* (Hatzfeld).–L. *solidiped-*, stem of *solidipēs*, solid-hoofed, whole-hoofed; Pliny, x. 65; x. 73.–L.

solidi-, for *solidus*, solid; and *ɟēs*, a foot, cognate with E. *foot*; see **Solid** and **Foot**.

SOLITARY, lonely, alone, single. (F.–L.) ME. *solitarie*, P. Plowman, C. xviii. 7.–AF. *solitarie*, Langtoft's Chron. i. 176; usually *solitaire*, as in mod. F.–L. *sōlitārium*, acc. of *sōlitārius*, solitary. β. Formed as if contracted from *sōlitātārius*, from *sōlitāt-*, stem of *sōlitas*, loneliness; a sb. formed with suffix *-tāt-* from *sōli-*, for *sōlus*, alone; see **Sole** (3). Cf. *heredit-ary*, *milit-ary* from the stems *herēdit-*, *milit-*; also *propriet-ary*, similarly formed from the sb. *proprietās*. Der. *solitari-ly*, *-ness*. Also *solitaire*, from F. *solitaire*. And see *soli-tude*, *sol-o*.

SOLITUDE, loneliness. (F.–L.) In Minsheu, ed. 1627.–F. *solitude*, 'solitude;' Cot.–L. *sōlitūdo*, loneliness.–L. *sōli-*, for *sōlus*, sole; with suffix *-tūdo*. See **Sole** (3).

SOLO, a musical piece performed by one person. (Ital.–L.) 'Solos and sonatas;' Tatler, no. 222; Sept. 9, 1710.–Ital. *solo*, alone.–L. *sōlum*, acc. of *sōlus*, sole; see **Sole** (3).

SOLMISATION, a singing of *sol-mi*; see **Sol-fa**.

SOLSTICE, one of the two points in the ecliptic at which the sun is at his greatest distance from the equator; the time when the sun reaches that point. (F.–L.) In Minsheu, ed. 1627.–F. *solstice*, 'the solstice, sun-stead, or stay of the sun;' Cot.–L. *solstitium*, the solstice; lit. a point (in the ecliptic) at which the sun seems to stand still.–L. *sōl*, the sun; and **stit-um*, for *statum*, supine of *sistere*, to make to stand still, a reduplicated form from *stāre*, to stand, cognate with E. *stand*; see **Solar** and **Stand**. Der. *solstiti-al*, adj., from MF. *solstitial* or *solsticial* (Cot.); F. *solsticial*.

SOLUBLE, capable of being dissolved. (F.–L.) Spelt *soluble* and *solubil* in Levins, ed. 1570.–F. *soluble* (13th cent., Littré).–L. *solūbilem*, acc. of *solūbilis*, dissolvable. Formed, with suffix *-bilis*, from *solū-*, found in *solū-tus*, pp. of *soluere*, to solve, dissolve; see **Solve**. Der. *solubili-ty*, a coined word.

SOLUTION, a dissolving, resolving, explanation, discharge. (F.–L.) ME. *solucion*, Gower, C. A. ii. 86; bk. iv. 2515; it was a common term in alchemy.–F. *solution*, 'a discharge, resolution, dissolution;' Cot.–L. *solūtionem*, acc. of *solūtio*, lit. a loosing; cf. *solūt-us*, pp. of *soluere*, to loose, resolve, dissolve; see **Solve**.

SOLVE, to explain, resolve, remove. (L.) Not an early word. In Milton, P. L. viii. 55.–L. *soluere*, to loosen, relax, solve; pp. *solūtus*. A compound verb; compounded of *so-*, allied to *sē-*, apart; and *luere*, to loosen. For the prefix, see **Sober**. *Luere* is from *lu-*, weak grade of LEU, to set free, appearing also in Gk. λύ-ειν, to set free, release; see **Lose**. Brugmann, i. § 121. Der. *solv-able*, from F. *solvable*, orig. 'payable,' Cot. Also *solv-ent*, having power to dissolve or pay, from L. *soluent-*, stem of pres. part. of *soluere*; and hence *solv-enc-y*. Also *solv-er*; *ab-solve*, *ab-solute*, *as-soil*; *dis-solve*, *dis-solute*; *re-solve*, *re-solute*. And see *soluble*, *solution*.

SOMBRE, gloomy, dusky. (F.–L.) A late word; in Todd's Johnson.–F. *sombre*, 'close, dark, cloudy, muddy, shady, dusky, gloomy;' Cot. It answers to Span. adj. *sombrio*, adj., shady, gloomy, from the sb. *sombra*, shade, dark part of a picture, also a ghost. So also Port. *sombrio*, adj., from *sombra*, shade, protection, ghost. And cf. Span. *a-sombrar*, to frighten, terrify; mod. Prov. *souloumbrous*, dark. β. Diez refers these words to a L. form **sub-umbrāre*, to shadow or shade; a conjecture which is supported by the occurrence of Prov. *sotz-ombrar*, to shade (Scheler). There is also an OF. *essombre*, a dark place (Burguy), which is probably due to a L. form **ex-umbrāre*, and this suggests the same form as the original of the present word, a solution which is adopted by Littré. We may conclude that *sombre* is founded upon the L. *umbra*, a shadow, with a prefix due either to L. *ex* or to L. *sub*. See **Umbrage**. Der. *sombre-ness*.

SOMBRERO, a broad-brimmed hat. (Span.–L.) 'With a great *Sombrero* or shadow ouer their heads;' Hakluyt, Voy. ii. pt. 1. p. 258.–Span. *sombrero*.–Span. *sombra*, shade (above).

SOME, a certain number or quantity, moderate in degree. (E.) ME. *som*, *sum*; pl. *summe*, *somme*, *some*. 'Summe seedis'=some seeds; Wyclif, Matt. xiii. 4. 'Som in his bed, another in the depe see' =one man in his bed, another in the deep sea; Chaucer, C. T. 3033 (A 3031). AS. *sum*, some one, a certain one, one; pl. *sume*, some; Grein, ii. 493.+Icel. *sumr*; Dan. *somme*, pl.; Swed. *somlige*, pl. (=some-like). Goth. *sums*, some one; OHG. *sum*. β. All from a Teut. type **sumoz*, some one, a certain one; from **sum-*, weak grade of **sam-*, as in E. *same*; see **Same**. The like change from *a* to *u* (o) occurs in the suffix *-some*, which see. Der. *some-body*, Merry Wives, iv. 2. 121; *some-how*; *some-thing*=AS. *sum ðing*; *some-time*, ME. *somtime*, Chaucer, C. T. 1245 (A 1243); *some-times*, formed from *sometime* by the addition of the adverbial suffix *-s*, the sign of the gen. sing., not of the nom. pl. (cf. *need-s*, *whil-s-t*, *twi-ce*, &c.); *some-what*, ME. *somhwat*, Ancren Riwle, p. 44. l. 9=AS. *sum* *hwæt*; *some-where*, ME. *som-hwær*, Ormulum, 6929; *some-whither*, Titus Andron. iv. 1. 11.

-SOME, suffix. (E.) AS. *-sum*, as in *wyn-sum* (lit. love-some), E. *win-some*. A stronger grade of the same suffix appears in Icel. *frið-samr*, peaceful, G. *lang-sam*, slow. See **Some**, above; and see **Same**.

SOMERSAULT, SOMERSET, a leap in which a man turns heels over head. (F. – Prov. – L.) Commonly pronounced *summer-set*, where *-set* is an unaccented form of *-sault* or *-saut*. Spelt *summersaut* in Drayton's Polyolbion, song 6. l. 52; *somersault* in Palsgrave; *somersaut* in Harington's Ariosto, xxxv. 68 (Nares); see further in Rich. and Nares. – OF. *sombresaut* (in 1393, Supp. to Godefroy), MF. *soubresault*, 'a sobresault or summersault, an active trick in tumbling;' Cot.; F. *soubresaut*. – Prov. *sobresaut* (Hatzfeld); cf. Ital. *soprasalto*; where *sopra* = 'above, ouer, alo.t, on high,' and *salto* = 'a leape, a skip, a iumpe, a bound, a sault;' Florio. – L. *suprā*, above; and *saltum*, acc. of *saltus*, a leap, bound, formed like *saltus*, pp. of *salire*, to leap. See **Supra** and **Salient**.

SOMNAMBULIST, one who walks in his sleep. (L.; *with* Gk. suffix.) A coined word; an early example is given in Todd's Johnson, from Bp. Porteus' Sermons, A.D. 1789. The suffix *-ist* = F. *-iste*, from L. *-ista* = Gk. *-ιστης*; as in *bapt-ist*. – L. *somn-us*, sleep; and *ambul-āre*, to walk. See **Somniferous** and **Ambulation**. **Der.** *somnambul-ism*.

SOMNIFEROUS, causing sleep. (L.) 'Somniferous potions;' Burton, Anat. of Melancholy, pt. i. sect. 2. memb. 1, subsect. 5. Coined by adding suffix *-ous* (properly = F. *-eux*, from L. *-ōsus*) to L. *somnifer*, sleep-bringing. – L. *somni-*, for *somnus*, sleep; and *-fer*, bringing, from *ferre*, to bring, cognate with E. **Bear**, verb. β. The L. *somnus* represents an older form *swepnos*, cognate with Skt. *svapna-*, sleep, and allied to *sop-or*, sleep; from √SWEP, to sleep; see further under **Soporiferous**. Brugmann, i. § 121.

SOMNOLENCE, sleepiness. (F. – L.) ME. *somnolence*, spelt *sompnolence*, Gower, C. A. ii. 92; bk. iv. 2703. – F. *somnolence* (Littré); OF. *somnolence* (Hatzfeld). – L. *somnolentia*, also *somnulentia*, sleepiness. – L. *somnulentus*, sleepy; formed with suffix *-lentus* (as in *tēmu-lentus*, drunken) from *somnu-s*, sleep, allied to *sopor*, sleep; see **Somniferous, Soporiferous**. **Der.** *somnolent*, adj., from F. *somnolent*, L. *somnulentus*.

SON, a male child or descendant. (E.) ME. *sone* (properly a dissyllable); Chaucer, C. T. 79; older form *sune*, Ancren Riwle, p. 26, l. 1. AS. *sunu*, a son; Grein, ii. 496. ♦ Du. *zoon*; Dan. *sön*; Swed. *son*; G. *sohn*; OHG. *sunu*; Goth. *sunus*. Teut. type *sunuz*. Cf. Lithuan. *sūnus*; Russ. *suin'*; Gk. *υἱός* (*for* *συιός*); Skt. *sūnu-*, a son, from Skt. *sū*, *su*, to beget, bear, bring forth; cf. OIrish *suth*, birth. Brugmann, i. §§ 104, 292. Thus *son* = one who is begotten, a child. **Der.** *son-in-law*; *son-ship*; a coined word.

SONATA, a kind of musical composition. (Ital. – L.) 'An Italian *sonata*;' Addison, Spectator, no. 179. 'Of a *sonata*, on his viol;' Prior, Alma, iii. 436. – Ital. *sonata*, 'a sounding, or fit of mirth;' Florio. Hence used in the technical sense. – L. *sonāta*, fem. of *sonātus*, pp. of *sonāre*, to sound; see **Sound** (3), and **Sonnet**.

SONG, that which is sung, a short poem or ballad. (E.) ME. *song*, Chaucer, C. T. 95. AS. *sang*; varied to *song*; Grein, ii. 390. Cf. AS. *sang*, 2nd grade of *singan*, to sing; see **Sing**. ♦ Du. *zang*; Icel. *söngr*; Swed. *sång*; Dan. and G. *sang*; Goth. *saggws* (= *sangws*). Cf. Gk. *ὀμφή*, voice. **Der.** *song-ster*, used by Howell, L'Estrange, and Dryden (Todd, no references); from AS. *sangystre* (better *sangestre*), Voc. 308. 12, as a gloss to L. *cantrix*; formed with double suffix *-es-tre* from *sang*, a song: as to the force of the suffix, see **Spinster**. Hence *songstr-ess*, Thomson's Summer, 746; a coined word, made by needlessly affixing the F. suffix *-esse* (L. *-issa*, from Gk. *-ισσα*) to the E. *songster*, which was orig. used (as shown above) as a feminine sb. Also *sing-song*, Fuller's Worthies, Barkshire (R.); a reduplicated form.

SONNET, a rimed poem, of fourteen lines. (F. – Ital. – L.) In Shak. Two Gent. iii. 2. 69. See 'Songes and *Sonettes*' by the Earl of Surrey, in Tottell's Miscellany. – F. *sonnet*, 'a sonnet, or canzonet, a song (commonly) of 14 verses;' Cot. – Ital. *sonetto*, 'a sonnet, canzonet;' Florio. Dimin. of *sono*, 'a sound, a tune;' Florio. – L. *sonum*, acc. of *sonus*, a sound; see **Sound** (3). **Der.** *sonnet-eer*, from Ital. *sonettiere*, 'a composer of sonnets,' Florio; the suffix *-eer* (Ital. *-iere*) is due to L. *-ārius*.

SONOROUS, loud-sounding. (L.) Properly *sonórous*; it will probably, sooner or later, become *sónorous*. 'Sónorous metal;' Milton, P. L. i. 540; and in Cotgrave. Doubtless taken directly from the L. *sonōrus*, loud-sounding, by the change of *-us* to *-ous*, as in *arduous*, *strenuous*, and numerous other words. [The F. *sonoreux*, 'sonorous, loud,' is in Cotgrave; this would probably have produced an E. form *sónorous*, the length of the Latin penultimate being lost sight of.] – L. *sonor* (gen. *sonōr-is*), sound, noise; allied to *sonus*,

sound; see **Sound** (3). **Der.** *sonorous-ly, -ness*. The ME. form *sonowre* occurs in the Book of St. Albans, fol. d 3.

SOON, immediately, quickly, readily. (E.) ME. *sone* (dissyllabic); Chaucer, C. T. 13442 (B 1702). AS. *sōna*, soon; Grein, ii. 465. ♦ OSax. *sāna*, *sāno*; also OFries. *sān*, *sōn*; OSax. *sān*; OHG. *sān*. β. We find also Goth. *suns*, soon, at once, immediately, Matt. viii. 3.

SOOT, the black deposit due to smoke. (E.) ME. *sōt* (with long o); King Alisaunder, 6636. AS. *sōt*, soot; 'Fuligine, *soote*,' Voc. 404. 32; we also find *ge-sōtig*, adj. sooty (Toller). ♦ Icel. *sōt*; Swed. *sot*; Dan. *sod* (for *sot*). ♦ Lithuan. *sōdis*, soot; usually in the pl. form *sōdzei*; whence the adj. *sodzotas*, sooty, and the verb *apsōdinti*, to blacken with soot, besmut. β. The Lithuan. form is valuable as showing that the form *soot* is truly Teutonic; and suggests a derivation from Idg. *sōd-*, the ō-grade of √SED, to sit, rest upon. See **Sit**. (Noreen, § 146; Streitberg, § 95.) **Der.** *soot-y*, *soot-i-ness*.

SOOTH, adj., true; sb., truth. (E.) The adjectival sense is the older one. ME. *soth* (with long o), adj., true; Pricke of Conscience, 7687. Commoner as a sb., meaning 'the true thing,' hence 'the truth;' Chaucer, C. T. 847 (A 845). AS. *sōð*, adj., true (very common); Grein, ii. 460. Hence *sōð*, neuter sb., a true thing, truth; id. 462. The form *sōð* stands for **sanð*, the *n* being lost before the *th*, as in *tōð*, a tooth, which stands for **tanð*. ♦ Icel. *sannr* (for **sanðr*); Swed. *sann*; Dan. *sand*. β. All from Teut. type **santhoz*, true; Fick, iii. 318; Idg. type **sontos*, short for **es-ont-*, orig. signifying 'being,' or 'that which is,' hence that which is real, truth; a present participial form from the √ES, to be. The same loss of initial *e* occurs in the L. *-sens* as found in *præ-sens* (stem *præ-sent-*), preserved in E. *pre-sent*; and again in the Skt. *satya-*, true (for **es-ant-ya*); so also we have G. *sind* = L. *sunt* = Skt. *santi*, they are, all answering to Idg. **esanti*. The meaning 'true,' 'real,' appears already in the Skt. participle *sat*, a weaker form of *sont* = (*e*)*sont*. γ. Hence we conclude that the very interesting word *sooth* meant orig. no more than 'being,' and was at first the present participle of ES, to be. See **Are**, **Essence**, and **Suttee**. **Der.** *for-sooth*, = for a truth, AS. *for sōð*, as in 'wite þū *for sōð*' = know thou for a truth, Ælfred, tr. of Boethius, lib. ii. pr. 2, cap. vii. § 3. Also *sooth-fast*, true (obsolete), from AS. *sōðfæst*, Grein, ii. 463, where the suffix is the same as in *stead-fast* and *shame-fast* (now corrupted to *shame-faced*). And see *sooth-say*, and *soothe*.

SOOTHE, to please with gentle words or flattery, to flatter, appease. (E.) The orig. sense is 'to assent to as being true,' hence to say yes to, to humour by assenting, and generally to humour. 'Sooth, to flatter immoderatelie, or hold vp one in his talke, *and affirme it to be true*, which he speaketh;' Baret (1580). 'Is't good to *soothe* him in these contraries?' Com. of Errors, iv. 4. 82. '*Soothing* the humour of fantastic wits;' Venus and Adonis, 850. Cf. the expression 'words of *sooth*,' Rich. II, iii. 3. 136. 'I shall *sooth* it,' I must confirm it, Faire Em, A. iii. sc. 11. ME. *soðien*, to confirm, verify; whence *isoðet*, confirmed, O. Eng. Homilies, i. 261, l. 8. AS. *ge-sōðian* (where the prefix *ge-* makes no difference), to prove to be true, confirm; Dooms of Edward and Guthrum, sect. 6, in Thorpe's Ancient Laws, i. 170. Cf. AS. *gesōð*, a parasite, flatterer, in a gloss (Bosworth). – AS. *sōð*, true; see **Sooth**. Cognate verbs occur in the Icel. *sanna*, Dan. *sande*, to verify, confirm.

SOOTHSAY, to foretell, tell the truth beforehand. (E.) In Shak. Antony, i. 2. 52. Compounded of *sooth* and *say*; see **Sooth** and **Say**. We find the sb. *soothsayer*, spelt *zoþ-zigger* (in the OKentish dialect) in the Ayenbite of Inwyt, p. 256, l. 3 from bottom; spelt *sothsaier*, Gower, C. A. iii. 164; bk. vii. 2348. We also find the AS. sb. *sōðsegen*, a true saying, in Ælfric's Homilies, ii. 250, l. 11; and the adj. *sōðsagol*, truth-speaking, Voc. 316. 9. **Der.** *sooth-say-er*; *sooth- ay-ing*, Acts, xvi. 16.

SOP, anything soaked or dipped in liquid to be eaten. (E.) ME. *sop*, *soppe*; 'a sop in wyn,' Chaucer, C. T. 336 (A 334); spelt *soppe*, P. Plowman, B. xv. 175. AS. **soppe*, not found; but we find the strong form *sopp* (Napier's Glosses, 56. 10); the derived verb *soppigan*, to sop, A. S. Leechdoms, ii. 228, last line; and the compound sb. *sop-cuppe* (written *sóp-cuppe*), a sop-cup, in Thorpe's Diplomatarium Ævi Saxonici, pp. 553, 554; so that the word is certainly English. From Teut. **sup-*, weak grade of *sūpan*, to sup, as seen in AS. *sūpan*, to sup; see **Sup**. ♦ Icel. *soppa*, f., a sop; *soppa af vini* = a sop in wine; cf. *sopinn*, pp. of *sūpa*, to sup; cf. also *sopi*, a sup, sip, mouthful. Cf. MDu. *soppe*, 'a sop;' Hexham. ¶ Soup is a F. form from the same root, and has been borrowed back again into some Teutonic tongues, as e. g. in the case of G. *suppe*, soup, broth. **Der.** *sop*, verb, spelt *soppe* in Levins, from AS. *soppigan*, to sop, mentioned above. Also *sopp-y*, soaking, wet; *sops-in-wine* (see Nares). Also *milk-sop* = one who sups milk; see **Milksop**. And see **Soup**.

SOPHIST, a captious reasoner. (F. – L. – Gk.) Bacon refers to the *Sophists*; Adv. of Learning, bk. ii. c. xiv. § 6. But the form most in use in old authors was not *sophist*, but *sophister*. Frith has *sophisme*, *sophistry*, and *sophister* all in one sentence; Works, p. 44, col. 2. Shak. has *sophister*, 2 Hen. VI, v. 1. 191; Palsgrave has *sophyster*. The final *-er* is needlessly added, just as in *philosoph-er*, and was due to an OF. form *sophistre* (*sofistre* in Godefroy, x. 689), substituted for the true form *sophiste*. – F. *sophiste*, ' a sophister;' Cot. – Late L. *sophista*. – Gk. σοφιστής, a cunning or skilful man; also, a Sophist, a teacher of arts and sciences for money; see Liddell and Scott. – Gk. σοφίζειν, to instruct, lit. to make wise. – Gk. σοφός, wise. Brugmann, i. § 339. **Der.** *sophist-r-y*, ME. *sophistrie*, Chaucer, Leg. of Good Women, 137, from F. *sophisterie*, 'sophistry,' Cot. Also *sophist-ic*, from L. *sophisticus*, which from Gk. σοφιστικός; *sophist-ic-al*, *sophist-ic-al-ly*; *sophist-ic-ate*, used in the pp. *sophisticatid* by Skelton, Garland of Laurell, 110, from Late L. *sophisticātus*, pp. of *sophisticāre*, to corrupt, adulterate; cf. 'sophisticate and countrefeted;' Maundeville, Trav. ch. v. p. 52. Also *sophism* (used by Frith as above), from F. *sophisme*, 'a sophisme, fallacy, trick of philosophy,' Cot., which from L. *sophisma* = Gk. σόφισμα, a device, captious argument. Also *philo-sophy*; q. v.

SOPHY, a (former) title of the Shah of Persia. (Pers. – Arab.) In Shak. Merch. Ven. ii. 1. 25; Tw. Nt. ii. 5. 197. – Pers. *Safi*, used as a title, A. D. 1505–1736; ' so named from Ismael *Safi*, the first monarch of this house .. from a private ancestor of that prince, called *Safiyu'd'dīn* (the purity of religion), who was contemporary with Tamerlane;' Rich. Dict. p. 938. – Arab. *safiy*, pure. ¶ Not to be confused with *Sufi*, a Moslem mystic; from Arab. *sūfiy*, intelligent. See Devic; and Notes on E. Etym., p. 273. But see Yule, who says that *Safi* was also a *Sufi* (devotee).

SOPORIFEROUS, causing or inducing sleep. (L.) 'Soporiferous medicines;' Bacon, Nat. Hist. § 975. Coined by adding the suffix *-ous* (properly = F. *-eux*, from L. *-ōsus*) to L. *sopōrifer*, sleep-inducing. – L. *sopōri-*, decl. stem of *sopor*, sleep; and *-fer*, bringing, from *ferre*, cognate with E. **Bear**, verb. β. L. *sopor* is from √SWEP, to sleep, appearing in Skt. *svap*, to sleep, Gk. ὕπνος, sleep, AS. *swefen*, a dream; see Brugmann, i. § 551. See *soporific* and *somniferous*.

SOPORIFIC, inducing sleep. (L.) 'Soporific or anodyne virtues;' Locke, Human Understanding, b. ii. c. 23 (R.). A coined word, as if from L. **sopōrificus*; from *sopōri-*, decl. stem of *sopor*, sleep; and *-ficus*, causing, from *facere*, to make. See **Soporiferous** and **Fact**. And see **Somniferous**.

SOPRANO, the highest kind of female voice. (Ital. – L.) A musical term. – Ital. *soprano*, 'soveraigne, supreme, also, the treble in musicke;' Florio. – Late L. *superānus*, sovereign; see **Sovereign**. Doublet, *sovereign*.

SORB, the fruit of the service-tree. (F. – L.) Palsgrave has: ' *Sorbe*, a kynde of frute, [F.] *sorbe*.' – L. *sorbum*, the fruit of the service-tree; cf. *sorbus*, the service-tree. See **Service-tree**.

SORCERY, casting of lots, divination by the assistance of evil spirits, magic. (F. – L.) ME. *sorcerie*, Chaucer, C. T. 5175 (B 755); King Alisaunder, 478. – OF. *sorcerie*, casting of lots, magic. – OF. *sorcier*, a sorcerer. – Late L. *sortiārius*, a teller of fortunes by the casting of lots, a sorcerer; Late L. *sortiāre*, to cast lots, used A. D. 1350 (Ducange); cf. L. *sortīrī*, to obtain by lot. – L. *sorti-*, decl. stem of *sors*, a lot; see **Sort**. **Der.** *sorcer-er*, Shak. Temp. iii. 2. 49, where the final *-er* is needlessly repeated, just as in *poulter-er*, *upholster-er*; the form *sorcer* would have sufficed to represent the OF. *sorcier* mentioned above; cf. ME. *sorser* (for *sorcer*), a sorcerer; Allit. Poems, ed. Morris, B. 1579. Also *sorcer-ess*, coined as a fem. form of *sorcer-er* by the addition of *-ess* (F. *-esse*, Lat. *-issa*, Gk. *-ισσα*) to the short form *sorcer* as appearing in *sorcer-y*; the ME. *sorceresse* occurs in Gower, C. A. iii. 49; bk. vi. 1434; from AF. *sorceresse*, French Chron. of London (Camden Soc.), p. 3.

SORDID, dirty, mean, vile. (F. – L.) In Spenser, F. Q. v. 5. 23. – F. *sordide*, 'sordid;' Cot. – L. *sordidus*, vile, mean, orig. dirty. – L. *sordi-*, from *sordēs*, dirt, smuttiness, orig. blackness; allied to Russ. *sor'*, filth. See Brugmann, i. p. 1092. **Der.** *sordid-ly*, *-ness*.

SORE, wounded, tender or susceptible of pain, grieved, severe. (E.) ME. *sor* (with long o), grievous, Ancren Riwle, p. 208, l. 2; commoner as *sore* (dissyllabic), adverb, Chaucer, C. T. 7961 (E 85). AS. *sār*, painful; Grein, ii. 391; the change from *ā* to long *o* being regular, as in *stone*, *bone*, from AS. *stān*, *bān*. + Du. *zeer*, sore; also as adv. sorely, very much; Icel. *sárr*, sore, aching; Swed. *sår*; OHG. *sēr*, wounded, painful; cf. OHG. *sēro*, mod. G. *sehr*, sorely, extremely, very; G. *ver-sehren*, to wound, lit. to make sore. β. All from Teut. type **sairoz*, sore; Fick, iii. 313. Cf. OIrish *sáeth*, *sóeth*, tribulation. **Der.** *sore*, adv., ME. *sore*, AS. *sāre*, Grein; *sore-ly*, *sore-ness*. Also *sore*, sb., orig. a neuter sb., and merely the neuter of the adjective, occurring in AS. *sār* (Grein), cognate with Du. *zeer*, Icel. *sár*, Swed. *sår*, Goth. *sair*, OHG. *sēr*, all used as sbs. Also *sorr-y*, q. v.

SORREL (1), a plant allied to the dock. (F. – MHG.) ' *Sorell*,

an herbe;' Palsgrave. – OF. *sorel*, ' the herb sorrell or sour-dock;' Cot. Mod. F. *surelle* (Littré). So named from its sour taste; formed with the suffix *-el* (L. *-ellus*) from MHG. *sūr* (G. *sauer*), sour, cognate with E. **Sour**, q. v. Hence also we find AS. *sūre*, sorrel, Cockayne's Leechdoms, Gloss. to vol. ii; from AS. *sūr*, sour.

SORREL (2), of a reddish-brown colour. (F. – Teut.) ' *Sorrell*, colour of an horse, *sorrel*;' Palsgrave. He also gives: ' *Sorell*, a yonge bucke;' this is properly a buck of the third year, spelt *sorel*, L. L. L. iv. 2. 60, and doubtless named from its colour. ME. *sowrell*, Book of St. Albans, fol. e 4. – OF. *sorel*, a sorrel horse; Chanson de Roland, 1379. A dimin. form from OF. *sor*, a sorrel horse, id. 1943; F. *saur*, adj. 'sorrell of colour, whence *harenc saur*, a red herring,' Cot. Hence *saure*, sb. m., 'a sorrell colour, also, a sorrel horse;' id. Cf. Ital. *soro*, a sorrel horse, also spelt *sauro*; see Diez. – Low G. *soor*, sear, dried, dried or withered up; Du. *zoor*, 'dry, withered, or seare,' Hexham; cognate with E. **Sear**, adj., q. v. The reference is to the brown colour of withered leaves; cf. Shakespeare's ' the *sear*, the yellow leaf,' Macb. v. 3. 23. The F. *harenc saur*, explained by Cotgrave as a red herring, meant originally a *dried* herring; indeed Cot. also gives F. *sorer*, 'to dry in the smoak,' formed from Low G. *soor*. See *soures*, sorrels; Chaucer, Book of the Duchess, 429.

SORROW, grief, affliction. (E.) ME. *sorwe*, Chaucer, C. T. 1221 (A 1219); also *sorȝe*, Will. of Shoreham, p. 32, l. 7. AS. *sorg*, *sorh*, sorrow, anxiety; gen. dat. and acc. *sorge* (whence ME. *sorȝe*, *sorwe*); Grein, ii. 465. + Du. *zorg*, care, anxiety; Icel. *sorg*, care; Dan. and Swed. *sorg*; G. *sorge*; Goth. *saurga*, sorrow, grief; whence *saurgan*, to grieve. β. All from Teut. type **sorgā*, f., care, solicitude; Fick, iii. 329. Related to Lithuan. *sirgti* (1 p. s. pr. *sergu*), to be ill, to suffer; whence *sarginti*, to take care of a sick person, like G. *sorgen*, to take care of. And cf. OIrish *serg*, sickness. γ. It is quite clear that *sorrow* is entirely unconnected with *sore*, of which the orig. Teut. type was **sairoz*, from a √SEI (probably ' to wound'); but the two words were so confused in English at an early period that the word *sorry* owes its present sense to that confusion; see **Sorry**. **Der.** *sorrow-ful*, answering to AS. *sorgful*, Grein, ii. 466; *sorrow-ful-ly*, *sorrow-ful-ness*.

SORRY, sore in mind, afflicted, grieved. (E.) Now regarded as closely connected with *sorrow*, with which it has no etymological connexion at all, though doubtless the confusion between the words is of old standing. The spelling *sorry* with two *r*'s is etymologically wrong, and due to the shortening of the *o*; the *o* was orig. long; and the true form is *sor-y*, which is nothing but the sb. *sore* with the suffix *-y* (AS. *-ig*), formed exactly like *ston-y* from *stone*, *bon-y* from *bone*, and *gor-y* from *gore* (which has not yet been turned into *gorry*). We find the spelling *soarye* as late as in Stanyhurst, tr. of Virgil, Æn. ii. 651, ed. Arber, p. 64, l. 18. The orig. sense was wounded, afflicted, and hence miserable, sad, pitiable, as in the expression 'in a *sorry* plight.' Cf. 'a salt and *sorry* [painful] rheum;' Oth. iii. 4. 51. ME. *sory* (with long *o* and one *r*), often with the mod. sense of sorrowful; 'Sori for her synnes,' P. Plowman, B. x. 75. Also spelt *sary*, Pricke of Conscience, 3468. AS. *sārig*, sad; '*sārig* for his synnum' = sorry for his sins, Grein, ii. 392; *sār-nys*, sorrow, lit. soreness; Ælfric's Saints' Lives, vi. 321. Cf. *sār-līc*, lit. sore-like, used with the same sense of 'sad.' Formed with suffix *-ig* (as in *stān-ig* = *ston-y*) from AS. *sār*, a sore, neut. sb., due to the adj. *sār*, sore. See **Sore**. Cognate words appear in Du. *zeerig*, full of sores, Swed. *sårig*, sore; words which preserve the orig. sense. **Der.** *sorri-ly*, *sorri-ness*.

SORT, a lot, class, kind, species, order, manner. (F. – L.) ' *Sorte*, a state, *sorte*;' Palsgrave. A fem. sb., corresponding to which is the masc. sb. *sort*, a lot, in Chaucer, C. T. 846 (A 844). – OF. *sorte*, sb. fem. 'sort, manner, form, fashion, kind, quality, calling;' Cot. Related to F. *sort*, sb. masc. 'a lot, fate, luck,' &c.; id. Cf. Ital. *sorta*, sort, kind, *sorte*, fate, destiny; Florio gives only *sorte*, ' chance, fate, fortune, also the state, qualitie, function, calling, kinde, vocation or condition of any man,' whence the notion of *sort* (= kind) easily follows. ' *Sort* was frequently used in the sense of a company, assemblage (as in Spenser, F. Q. vi. 9. 5), as *lot* is in vulgar language;' Wedgwood. All the forms are ultimately due to L. *sortem*, acc. of *sors*, lot, destiny, chance, condition, state. Probably allied to *serere*, to connect, and to *seriēs*, order; see **Series**. Brugmann, i. § 516 (1). **Der.** *sort*, verb, L. L. L. i. 1. 261; *as-sort*, q. v.; *con-sort*, q. v. Also *sort-er*, sb.; *sort-ance*, 2 Hen. IV, iv. 1. 11; *sorc-er-y*, q. v.

SORTIE, a sally of troops. (F. – L.) A modern military term, and mere French. – F. *sortie*, ' an issue, going forth;' Cot. Fem. of *sorti*, 'issued, gone forth;' id.; which is the pp. of *sortir*, to issue, sally,' id. Cf. Span. *surtida*, a sally, sortie; from Span. *surtir*, ' to rise, rebound,' Minsheu, obsolete in this sense. Also Ital. *sortita*, a sally; from *sortire*, to make a sally, go out. β. According to

Diez and others, Ital. *sortire*, to sally, is quite a different word from *sortire*, to elect (the latter being plainly connected with L. *sortīrī*, to obtain by lot); whereas Ital. *sortire*, to sally, MSpan. *surtir*, to rise, answer to a L. type *surrectīre, to rouse or rise up, formed from *surrectum*, supine of *surgere*, to rise; see **Source**. We may further note Ital. *sorto*, used as the pp. of *sorgere*, to rise; showing that the contraction of *surrectīre to *sortire* presents no difficulty; cf. Span. *surto*, pp. of *surgir*, to rise; and see **Resort**.

SOT, a stupid fellow, a drunkard. (E.) ME. *sot*, in early use; Layamon, 1442; Ancren Riwle, p. 66, l. 1; in the sense of 'foolish.' We find *sot-cipe* = sot-ship, i. e. folly, in the A.S. Chron. an. 1131; ed. Earle, p. 260, l. 8. Spelt *sott*, Ælfric, Saints' Lives, 13. 132. The entry 'Sottus, *sot*,' is in an A. S. Glossary of the 11th century; in Voc. 316. 7; also 'Stolidos, *sot*,' in Napier's Glosses, 56. 173. Prob. a true Teut. word, though first appearing in the Late L. *sottus*, ab. A.D. 800 (Ducange); whence also F. *sot*. β. We also find MDu. *zot*, 'a foole or a sot,' Hexham; and MHG. *sote*. γ. Franck connects it with Du. *zwet-sen*, to tattle, to brag, G. *schwatzen*, to tattle; from **sot-*, weak grade of **swet-*. It is known that Theodulf, bishop of Orleans, punned upon the words *Scotus* and *sottus* (*Scot* and *sot*), in a letter to Charles the Great; see Ducange, s. v. *sottus*. ¶ Distinct from Span. *zote*, a blockhead, Ital. *zotico*, for which see Körting, § 4700. Der. *sott-ish, sott-ish-ly, sott-ish-ness*.

SOU, a French copper coin, five centimes. (F.—L.) Merely borrowed from F. *sou*; Cotgrave uses *sous* as an E. word.—OF. *sol*, later *sou*, 'the sous, or French shilling, whereof ten make one of ours;' Cot. The value varied.—L. *solidus*, adj. solid; also, as sb., the name of a coin, still preserved in the familiar symbols *l. s. d.* (= libræ, solidi, denarii). See **Solid** and **Soldier**. Der. *soldier*, q. v.

SOUBRETTE, a maid-servant, in French comedy. (F.—Prov.—L.) F. *soubrette* (see Hatzfeld).—Prov. *soubreto*, fem. of *soubret*, affected; allied to *soubra*, vb., to pass over, leave on one side, also to exceed, surpass.—L. *superāre*, to surpass, surmount.—L. *superus*, upper; allied to *super*, above; see **Super-** (prefix). Cf. the E. phr. 'a *superior* person.'

SOUBRIQUET, a nickname; see **Sobriquet**.

SOUCHONG, a kind of tea. (Chinese.) Yule (p. 691) explains it from Cantonese *siu-chung*, for Chin. *siao-chung*, 'little sort.' Douglas (Dict. of Amoy vernacular) gives it as *sió-chióng-tê*, souchong tea; and explains *chióng* as meaning, literally, 'seed.'

SOUGH, a sighing sound, as of wind in trees. (Scand.) Stanyhurst has *sowghing*, sb., tr. of Virgil, Æn. ii. 631, ed. Arber, p. 53. 'My heart, for fear, gae *sough* for *sough*;' Burns, Battle of Sheriffmuir, l. 7. We also find ME. *swough*, Chaucer, C. T. 1981 (A 1979), 3619; better *swogh*, as in Morte Arthure, ed. Brock, 759, where it has the sense of 'swaying motion;' formed as a sb. from the AS. verb *swōgan*, to sound, resound, make a noise, as in *swōgað windas* = the winds whistle; Grein, ii. 516. [The AS. sb. is *swēg*, with mutation of *ō* to *ē*.] Cf. OSax. *swōgan*, to rustle (Heliand); Icel. *-sūgr*, as in *arn-sūgr*, the rushing sound of an eagle's wings. Probably (like *sigh, sob*) of imitative origin. See **Surf**.

SOUL, the seat of life and intellect in man. (E.) ME. *soule*, Chaucer, C. T. 9010 (E 1134); also *saule*, Layamon, 27634; gen. sing. *soule*, Gower, C. A. i. 39; prol. 1052; pl. *soulen*, Ancren Riwle, p. 30, l. 16. AS. *sāwel, sāwol, sāwul*; also *sāwl, sāwle*; gen. sing. *sāwle*; Grein, ii. 392.+Du. *ziel*; Dan. *sjæl*; Swed. *själ*; G. *seele*; Goth. *saiwala*. β. All from Teut. type **saiwalōn-*, f., the soul. See Brugmann, i. § 200. Der. *soul-ed, high-soul-ed, soul-less*.

SOUND (1), adj., whole, perfect, healthy, strong. (E.) ME. *sound*, Chaucer, C. T. 5570 (B 1150). AS. *sund*, sound; Grein, ii. 494.+Du. *gezond* (with prefix *ge-*); Swed. and Dan. *sund*; G. *gesund* (with prefix *ge-*). By some connected with L. *sānus*, used with like meanings; see **Sane**. But it is rather for *swunðoz, from the weak grade *swunþ-* of Teut. **swenþ-*, whence Teut. *swenþoz, Goth. *swinths*, AS. *swiþ*, strong. Der. *sound-ly, sound-ness*.

SOUND (2), a strait of the sea, narrow passage of water. (E.) ME. *sound*, King Horn, 628, in Ritson's Met. Romances, ii. 117; spelt *sund*, Cursor Mundi, 621. AS. *sund*, (1) a swimming, (2) power to swim, (3) a strait of the sea, so called because it could be swum across; Grein, ii. 494. Hence AS. *sund-hengest*, a 'sound-horse,' i. e. a ship.+Icel., Dan., Swed., and G. *sund*. β. From the Teut. type *swum-ðoz; formed, with suffix -*ðoz*, from *swum-*, weak grade of AS. *swimman*, to swim; see **Swim**. Fick, iii. 362. Der. *sound*, the swimming-bladder of a fish; spelt *sounde*, Prompt. Parv. p. 466; this is merely another sense of the same word; Shetland *soond*; MDan. *sund*; cf. Icel. *sund-magi*, lit. sound-maw, the swimming-bladder of a fish.

SOUND (3), a noise. (F.—L.) The final *d* (after *n*) is excrescent, just as in the vulgar *gownd* for *gown*, in the nautical use of *bound* for ME. *boun* (ready), and in the obsolete *round*, to whisper, for *roun*. ME. *soun*, Chaucer, C. T. 4983 (B 563); King Alisaunder, 772; spelt *son*, Will. of Palerne, 39.—F. *son*, 'a sound;' Cot.—L. *sonum*, acc. of *sonus*, a sound.+Skt. *svana-*, sound; AS. *ge-swin* (<**swen-*), melody. From √SWEN, to sound, resound; cf. Skt. *svan*, to sound; Fick, i. 256. Brugmann, ii. § 519. Der. *sound*, verb, ME. *sounen*, Chaucer, C. T. 567 (A 565), from F. *sonner*, L. *sonāre*. Also see *son-ata, sonn-et, son-or-ous, per-son, par-son, as-son-ant, con-son-ant, dis-son-ant, re-son-ant, re-sound, uni-son*.

SOUND (4), to measure the depth of water with a plummet, to probe, test, try. (F.—Scand.) 'I *sownde*, as a schyppe-man *sowndeth* in the see with his plommet to knowe the deppeth of the see, *Je pilote*;' Palsgrave. ME. *sounden*, Chaucer, Troil. ii. 535.—F. *sonder*, 'to sound, prove, try, feel, search the depth of;' Cot., cf. *sonde*, 'a mariner's sounding-plummet,' id. β. Diez supposes that this answers to a L. form *subundare, to submerge; a similar contraction possibly occurs in the instance of *sombre* as connected with *sub umbrā*. If *s*, the etymology is from L. *sub*, under; and *unda*, a wave; see **Sub-** and **Undulate**. γ. But the Span. *sonda* means, not only a sounding-line, but also a sound or channel; and it is far more likely that the F. *sonder* was from the sb. *sonde*, and that this was taken from the Scand. word *sund*, a narrow strait or channel of water; see **Sound** (2). This seems to be corroborated by the following entries in Ælfric's Glossary, pr. in Voc. 182. 34, 35: 'Bolidis, *sundgyrd*;' and 'Cataprorates, *sund-line*.' So also: 'Bolidis, *sundgyrd in scipe, ōðde rāp*, i. *met-rāp*' = a sounding-rod in a ship, or a rope, i.e. a measuring rope; id. 358. 17. Here *bolidis* represents Gk. βολίς (gen. βολίδος), a missile, a sounding-lead; and *sund-gyrd* = sound-yard, i.e. sounding-rod. Similarly *sund-line* must mean a sounding-line, let down over the prow (κατὰ πρῷραν). Moreover *sund-gerd* is a very old word, as it occurs in the Corpus Gloss. 319 (8th cent.). There is always a probability in favour of a nautical term being of Scand. or E. origin. But it is remarkable that there is no trace of the verb except in French, Span., and Portuguese; so that we may have taken the verb from French; while this again was borrowed from the Scand. *sund* = AS. *sund*, a sound. Der. *sound-ing*.

SOUNDER, a herd of wild swine. (E.) 'Sownder, a term used by hunters for a company of wild Bores;' Phillips (1658). [Not a single boar, as sometimes erroneously said.] ME. *sounder*, Gawain and Grene Knight, 1440. AS. *sūnor*; ONorthumb. *sūnor*, Luke, viii. 32; OMerc. *sūner*, Matt. viii. 32 (Rushworth MS.). +OHG. *swaner*, a sounder. See Notes on E. Etym., p. 274.

SOUP, the juice or liquid obtained from boiling bones, &c., seasoned. (F.—Teut.) In Pope, Moral Essays, iv. 162.—F. *soupe*, 'a sop, potage or broth, brewis;' Cot.—F. *souper*, 'to sup;' Cot. —Low German *supen*, to sup; cf. Du. *zuipen*, AS. *sūpan*; see **Sup**.

SOUR, having an acid taste, bitter, acrid. (E.) 'Sour douз,' leaven; Wyclif, Matt. xiii. 33. AS. *sūr*; 'sūr meolc' = sour milk, Voc. 129. 1.+Du. *zuur*; Icel. *sūrr*; Dan. *suur*; Swed. *sur*; OHG. *sūr*; G. *sauer*. β. All from Teut. type *sūroz, sour; Fick, iii. 327. Further related to W. *sur*, sour; Russ. *surovuii*, raw, coarse, harsh, rough; Lithuan. *surus*, salt. Brugmann, i. § 114. Der. *sour-ly, sour-ness; sour*, verb, Cor. v. 4. 18; *sour-ish*. Also *sorr-el* (1).

SOURCE, rise, origin, spring. (F.—L.) ME. *sours*, Chaucer, C. T. 7925 (E 49); said of the 'rise' of a bird in flight, id. 7520 (D 1938).—OF. *sorse, surse, sorce, surce*, later *source*, 'a source,' Cot. Here *sorse* is the fem. of *sors*, the old pp. of *sordre* (mod. F. *sourdre*), to rise. The OF. *sordre* is contracted (with intercalated *d*) from L. *surgere*, to rise. See **Surge**. Der. *re-source*; and see *sortie, re-surrection, souse* (2).

SOUSE (1), pickle. (F.—L.) 'A *soused* [pickled] gurnet;' 1 Hen. IV, iv. 2. 13. ME. *sowse, souse*. 'Succidium, Anglice *souse*;' Voc. 614. 20. Hence also ME. *sowser*, another form of *saucer*; id. 661. 17. In fact, *souse* is a mere doublet of *sauce*.—OF. *sause*, later *sauce*, 'a sauce;' see **Sauce**. Der. *souse*, verb, to pickle, immerse in brine. 'I *sowse* fyshe, I laye it in *sowse* to preserve it;' Palsgrave.

SOUSE (2), **SOWSE**, to swoop down upon. (F.—L.) 'Spread thy broad wing, and *souse* on all mankind;' Pope, Epil. to Satires, Dial. ii. 15. See Shak. K. John, v. 2. 150; Spenser, F. Q. i. 5. 8. It was a term of falconry, and orig. applied, not to the downward, but the upward rapid flight of a bird of prey; see Chaucer, C. T. 7520 (D 1938); House of Fame, ii. 36; where it is spelt *sours*. But the *r* is lost in the Book of St. Albans, fol. d 1, back, where a hawk is said to take a bird 'at the mount or at the *souce*.' This E. *sours* is the same word as the mod. E. *source*. See **Source**. See Notes on E. Etym., p. 275. ¶ Quite distinct from Swed. *susa*, to rustle, G. *sausen*, &c.

SOUTH, the point of the compass where we see the sun at

mid-day. (E.) ME. *south*, Chaucer, C. T. 4913 (B 493). AS. *sūð*, Grein, ii. 492; also *sūða*, sb. masc., the south, southern region; *sūðan*, adv., from the south.+Du. *zuid*, south; *zuider*, southern (as in *Zuider Zee*, southern sea); *zuiden*, the south; Icel. *suðr*, old form also *sunnr*, south; *sunnan*, adv., from the south; cf. *suðrey*, southern island, pl. *Suðreyjar*, Sodor, the Hebrides.+Dan. *syd*, south, *sönden*, southern; Swed. *syd*, south, *söder*, the south, *sunnan*, the south; OHG. *sund*, south, mod. G. *süd*; OHG. *sundan*, the south, also, from the south, G. *süden*. β. All from the Teut. base **sunth-*; perhaps allied to Sun, q. v. ¶ The loss of *n* before *th* is regular in AS.; so that *sūð* is for **sunð*. Der. *south-east*, *south-east-ern*, *south-east-er-ly*; *south-west*, *so-uth-west-ern*, *south-west-er-ly*; *south-ward* (see Toward). Also *south-ern*, ME. *sothern*, Chaucer, C. T. 17353 (I 42), AS. *sūðerne* (Grein); cognate with Icel. *suðrænn* and OHG. *sundrōni*; see Northern. Hence *south-er-ly*, for *south-ern-ly*. Also *southernwood*, a kind of wormwood. AS. *sūðerne wudu*, as coming from southern Europe.

SOUVENIR, a remembrancer, memorial. (F.—L.) Modern.— F. *souvenir*, sb., 'a remembrance;' Cot. It is merely the infin. mood *souvenir*, 'to remember,' used substantively; cf. Leisure, Pleasure. —L. *subvenīre*, to come up to one's aid, to occur to one's mind.—L. *sub*, under, near; and *uenire*, cognate with E. *come*; see Sub- and Come.

SOVEREIGN, supreme, chief, principal. (F.—L.) The *g* is well known to be intrusive; as if from the notion that a *sovereign* must have to do with *reigning*. We find 'soueraigne power;' Hamlet, ii. 2. 27 (first folio); but the spelling with *g* does not seem to be much older than about A. D. 1570, when we find *soveraygne* in Levins. Palsgrave (A. D. 1530) has *soverayne*. ME. *souerein* (with *u*=*v*), Chaucer, C. T. 6630 (D 1048).—OF. *soverain* (Burguy); later *souverain*, 'soveraign, princely;' Cot.—Late L. acc. *superānum*, chief, principal; formed with suffix *-ānus* from L. *super*, above; see Super-. Der. *sovereign*, sb., a peculiar use of the adj.; *sovereign-ty*, ME. *souerainetee*, Chaucer, C. T. 6620 (D 1038), from OF. *soverainete*, later *souveraineté*, 'soveraignty,' Cot. See Soprano.

SOW (1), to scatter seed, plant. (E.) ME. *sowen*, Wyclif, Matt. xiii. 3; strong verb, pt. t. *sew*, id. xiii. 31; pp. *sowen*, *sowun*, id. xiii. 19. AS. *sāwan*, pt. t. *sēow*, pp. *sāwen*; Grein, ii. 392. The long *ā* becomes long *o* by rule; the pt. t. now in use is *sowed*, but the correct form is *sew* (in prov. E.); the like is true for the verb to *mow* (AS. *māwan*).+Du. *zaaijen*; Icel. *sā*; Dan. *saa*; Swed. *så*; OHG. *sāwen*, G. *säen*; Goth. *saian*. β. All from a Teut. root **sǣ-*=Idg. √SĒ, to sow. Further related to W. *hau*, to sow; Lithuan. *sėti* (pres. sing. *sėju*, I sow); Russ. *sieiat(e)*, to sow; L. *serere* (pt. t. *sē-uī*, pp. *sa-tum*); Gk. ἵημι (for **σί-ση-μι*), I send, throw. The orig. sense of the root was prob. 'to cast.' Brugmann, i. §§ 132, 310. Der. *see-d*, q. v.; and, from the same root, *se-min-al*, *dis-se-min-ate*.

SOW (2), a female pig; an oblong piece of metal in a lump larger than a pig of metal. (E.) ME. *sowe*, Chaucer, C. T. 2021 (A 2019); spelt *zoȝe* (for *soghe*), Ayenbite of Inwyt, p. 61; *suwe*, Ancren Riwle, p. 204. The *w* is substituted for an older *g*. AS. *sugu*, contracted form *sū*; Grein, ii. 492.+Du. *zog*; Icel. *sȳr*; Dan. so; Swed. *sugga*, so; OHG. *sū*; G. *sau*. Also W. *hwch*; Irish *suig*; L. *sūs*; Gk. ὖς or οὖς; Zend. *hu*, a boar (Fick, i. 801). All from the √SU, to produce; as in Skt. *su*, to generate, to produce, *sūsh*, to bring forth; from the prolific nature of the sow. 2. In the sense of 'a large mass of metal,' see explanation under Pig; we find 'sowe of leed' in Palsgrave. Der. *sow-thistle*, *sowethystell* (Palsgrave); AS. *sugepistel*, Gloss. to vol. iii. of A. S. Leechdoms, ed. Cockayne; also *soil* (2). And see *swine*.

SOWANS, SOWENS, flummery; made by steeping the husks of oatmeal in water. (C.) 'Sowens, with butter instead of milk to them, is always The Halloween Supper;' Burns, note to last st. of Halloween. Pronounced (suu·ǝnz).—Gael. *sùghan*, 'the juice of sowens;' Macleod.—Gael. *sùgh*, juice; allied to *sùgh*, vb., to drain, to suck in.+L. *sūgere*, to suck; AS. *sūcan*, to suck; cf. AS. *socian*, to soak. The sense is 'soakings.'

SOY, a kind of sauce. (Japanese.) 'Japan, from whence the true *soy* comes;' W. Dampier, A New Voyage, ed. 1699, ii. pt. 1. p. 28. And see tr. of Thunberg's Travels, vol. iv. p. 121, ed. 1795 (Todd). 'The Japanese . . . prepare with them [the seeds of the *Dolichos soja*, a kind of bean] the sauce termed *sooja*, which has been corrupted into *soy*;' English Cyclopædia. The Japanese word is properly *shōyu*, which is the name for the sauce made from a bean called *daidzu*. See Notes on E. Etym., p. 277; C. P. G. Scott, Malayan Words, p. 65.

SPA, a place where there is a spring of mineral water. (Belgium.) Called *spaw* in Johnson's Dict., and in Bailey, ed. 1735. The name, now generally used, is taken from that of *Spa*, in Belgium, S.W. of

Liège, where there is a mineral spring, famous even in the 17th century. 'The *spaw* in Germany;' Fuller's Worthies, Kent. 'Shaw, Spa, a town in Liege, famous for medicinal waters;' Coles' Dict., ed. 1684. 'The *Spawe*;' Gascoigne, Works, ed. Hazlitt, i. 376 (1572).

SPACE, room, interval, distance. (F.—L.) ME. *space* (dissyllabic), Assumption of Mary, ed. Lumby, 178; Chaucer, C. T. 35.—F. *espace*, 'space;' Cot.—L. *spatium*, a space; lit. 'that which is enlarged;' cf. Skt. *sphāy*, to swell, increase, *sphāta-*, enlarged. See Speed. Der. *space*, verb; *spac-i-ous*, from F. *spacieux* (for which Cot. has 'spatieux, spacious'), from L. *spatiōsus*, roomy; *spac-i-ous-ly*, *spac-i-ous-ness*. ¶ The prefixed *e* in F. *espace* is due to the difficulty of sounding words beginning with *sp* in French; in English, where there is no such difficulty, the *e* is dropped.

SPADE (1), an instrument to dig with. (E.) ME. *spade* (dissyllabic), Chaucer, C. T. 555 (A 553); Ancren Riwle, p. 384, l. 16. AS. *spædu*; 'Vanga, vel fossorium, *spædu*;' Voc. 333. 39; later *spade*, id. 550. 26. Also *spadu*, id. 106. 19.+Du. *spade*; Icel. *spaði*; Dan. and Swed. *spade*; G. *spate*, *spaten*; Gk. σπάθη, a broad blade, of wood or metal, a spatula, blade of an oar, blade of a sword, spathe or sheath of a flower (whence L. *spatha* was borrowed, which further gave rise to F. *épée*, OF. *espee*, a sword). Der. *spade* (at cards); *spaddle*, the same word as *paddle* (2), q. v.; *spat-u-la*, q. v.; *spad-ille*, spelt *spadillio* in Pope, Rape of the Lock, iii. 49, the ace of spades at the game of quadrille, F. *spadille*, borrowed from Span. *espadilla*, a small sword, the ace of spades, dimin. of *spada*, a sword, from L. *spatha*<Gk. σπάθη. And see *epaulet*.

SPADE (2), a suit at cards. (Span.—L.—Gk.) The name *spade* is really a substitution for the Spanish name *espada*, meaning (1) a sword, (2) a spade at cards; compare the etymology of *spadille*, given under Spade (1). The Spanish cards have swords for spades: see Strutt, Sports and Pastimes, b. iv. c. 2, § 20; Archæologia, viii. 135. ¶ Spade (1) and *spade* (2) are cognate, though one is E., and the other Gk.

SPALPEEN, a mean fellow. (Irish.) 'The poor harvest-men who now pass in troops from Ireland to England are now called *spalpeens*, with a show of contempt or disrespect;' MS. ab. 1740, in N. and Q. 3 S. viii. 307. And see under *Buckeen* in Davies, Suppl. Glossary. Sometimes introduced into novels relating to Ireland.— Irish *spailpin*, a mean fellow, rascal, stroller; from *spailp*, a beau, also pride, self-conceit.+Gael. *spailpean*, a beau, fop, mean fellow; from *spailp*, pride, self-conceit; cf. *spailp*, verb, to strut, walk affectedly.

SPAN, to measure, extend over, grasp, embrace. (E.) ME. *spannen*, very rare. 'Thenne the kinge *spanes* his spere'=then the king grasps his spear; Avowyng of Arthur, st. xiii. l. 1. AS. *spannan* (pt. t. *spēnn*), to bind; *gespannan*, to bind, connect; Grein, ii. 467, i. 456.+OHG. *spannan*, to extend, connect, a strong verb, pt. t. *spian*; hence G. *spannen*, weak verb. Further related words appear in the Du. *spannen*, pt. t. *spande* (weak), but pp. *gespannen* (strong), to stretch, span, put horses to; Dan. *spænde* (for *spænne*), to stretch, strain, span, buckle; Swed. *spänna*, to stretch, strain, draw, extend; Icel. *spenna* (=*spannja*, a causal form), to span, clasp. β. All from the Teut. verb **spannan-*, to extend, orig. a reduplicating verb with pt. t. **spespann*; Fick, iii. 352. The base SPAN is extended from √SPA, to span, extend; cf. Gk. σπάειν, to draw, draw out; Brugmann, ii. § 661. Perhaps allied to Spin. Der. *span*, sb., a space of about 9 inches, the space from the end of the thumb to the end of the little finger when the fingers are most extended, also, the stretch of an arch or a space of time, from AS. *span* (better *spann*); we find 'span, vel hand-bred'=span, or hand-breadth, in Voc. 158. 11; so also Du. *span*, Icel. *spönn*, Dan. *spand* (for *spann*), Swed. *spann*, G. *spanne*. Hence *span-long*, Ben Jonson, Sad Shepherd, Act ii. sc. 2, l. 23 from end; *span-counter*, a game, 2 Hen. VI, iv. 2. 166. ¶ For *span-new*, see that word, which is unconnected with the present one.

SPANCEL, a kind of fetter for a horse or cow. (E.) Ray has: 'Spancel, a rope to tye a cow's hinder legs;' as a N. Country Word. From ME. *spann-en*, to tie, fasten; and the equivalent of AS. *sāl*, ME. *sol*, prov. E. *sole*, a rope. The latter vowel is prob. due to AS. *sǣl-an*, vb., to tie (for **sāl-ian*), or to Icel. *seil*, a rope; cf. prov. E. *seal*, to bind with a rope.+Du. *spansel*, G. *spannseil*, a spancel. See Notes on E. Etym., p. 277.

SPANDREL, the triangular space included between the arch of a doorway, &c., and a part of a rectangle formed by the outer mouldings over and beside it. (F.—L.) History obscure; an architectural term. Older forms *spaundre* (Halliwell); *splaundrel* (Ogilvie's Dict.). Lit. 'level space.' From OF. *esplan-er*, to flatten, to level. —L. *ex*, out; and *planāre*, to make flat, from *plānus*, flat; see Plain and Esplanade. The F. sb. was prob. founded on Ital. *spianatura*, a levelling (Barretti).

SPANGLE, a small plate of shining metal. (E.) ME. *spangel*, of which the sense seems to have been a lozenge-shaped spangle used to ornament a bridle ; see Prompt. Parv., p. 313, note 3, and p. 467, note 1. It is the dimin. of *spang*, a metal fastening ; with suffix *-el* (which is commonly French, but occasionally English, as in *kernel* from *corn*). ' Our plumes, our *spangs* and al our queint aray ;' Gascoigne, Steel Glas, 377 ; 'With glittering *spangs* that did like starres appeare,' Spenser, F. Q. iv. 11. 45. AS. *spange*, a metal clasp or fastening, Grein, ii. 467 ; also *gespong*, id. i. 456.+MDu. *spange* ; ' een spange van *metael*, a thinne peece of mettle, or a spangle ;' Hexham ; ' een *spange-maecker*, a buckle-maker or a spangle-maker,' id. ; Icel. *spöng*, explained by ' spangle,' though it seems rather to mean a clasp ; G. *spange*, a brooch, clasp, buckle, ornament. β. Cf. Gk. σφηκ-οῦν, to bind tight, pinch in ; σφίγγειν, to bind tight. σφιγκτήρ, a lace, band.

SPANIEL, a Spanish dog. (F. – Span. – L.) ME. *spaniel*, Chaucer, C. T. 5849 ; spelt *spaynel* in five MSS., Group D, 267 ; *spaneʒeole*, Voc. 638. 10. Cf. ME. *Spaynyell*, a Spaniard, Trevisa, tr. of Higden, iv. 419. – OF. *espagneul*, ' a spaniel ;' Cot. – Span. *español*, Spanish. – Span. *España*, Spain. – L. *Hispania*, Spain. The origin of the name of the country is unknown.

SPANK, to beat or slap. (E.) ' *Spank*, a hard slap ; to move energetically ; *Spanker*, a man or animal very large, or excessively active ; *Spanking*, large, lusty, active,' &c. ; Halliwell. An E. word, though not found in old authors.+NFries. and Dan. *spanke*, to strut, to stalk ; Low G. *spakkern, spenkern*, to run and spring about quickly. β. From a Teut. base SPAK, significant of quick motion or violent action ; cf. EFries. *spaken*, to split, burst with heat. **Der.** *spank-er*, an after-sail in a barque.

SPAN-NEW, entirely new. (Scand.) ME. *spannewe*, Havelok, 968 ; Chaucer, Troilus, iii. 1665 ; *spon-neowe*, K. Alisaunder, 4055. (The term is prob. Scand., not E. ; otherwise we should rather have expected a form *spoon-new* or *spon-new*, ' spoon-new,' which is the corresponding E. form, as will appear.) – Icel. *spánnýr*, also *spánýr*, span-new ; compounded of *spánn*, a chip, shaving, made by a plane, knife, or axe ; and *nýr*, new, cognate with E. **New**, q. v. Another sense of Icel. *spánn* is a spoon ; see **Spoon**.+MHG. *spānnūwe* ; from MHG. *spān*, G. *span*, a chip, splinter, and *nūwe* or *neu*, new. β. We also use the phrase *spick and span new*, which is also of Scand. origin ; see the very numerous phrases of this character in Swed. dialects, as given by Rietz, who instances *spik-spängende ny*, completely new, answering to Swed. *till splint och spån ny*, with its varying forms *spingspångande ny*, *sprittspångande ny*, *splittspångande ny*, and 18 more of the same character. So also Du. *spikspeldernieuw*, lit. spick-and-spill-new ; since *speld* is a spill or splinter. So also Swed. *spillerny*, lit. spill-new. So also Dan. *splinterny*, lit. splinter-new. The Swed. and Du. *spik* are forms of **Spike** ; hence *spick and span new* = spike and chip new. All the terms ' signify fresh from the hands of the workman, fresh cut from the block, chip and splinter new ;' Wedgwood.

SPAR (1), a beam, bar, rafter ; a general term for yards, gaffs, &c. (E.) ME. *sparre* (dissyllabic), Chaucer, C. T. 992 (A 990). The AS. sb. is not found, but the word is doubtless E. ; we find the derived verb *sparrian*, to fasten with a bar, to bolt, as in ' *gesparrado dure*' = the door being fastened, Matt. vi. 6 (Lindisfarne MS.).+Du. *spar* ; Icel. *sparri* ; Dan. and Swed. *sparre* ; OHG. *sparro* ; MHG. *sparre* ; G. *sparren*. Cf. also Gael. and Irish *sparr*, a spar, joist, beam, rafter (from E.). β. The orig. sense seems to have been stick or pole ; perhaps related to **Spear**, q. v. **Der.** *spar*, verb, to fasten a door, bar it, P. Plowman, B. xix. 162 (footnote).

SPAR (2), a kind of mineral. (E.) An old prov. E. mining-term ; spelt *starr* in Manlove's Liberties and Customs of the Lead-mines, A.D. 1653, l. 265 (E. D. S. Gloss. B. 8). AS. *spær*, found in the compound *spær-stān* (spar-stone) ; ' Creta argentea, *spær-stān* ;' Voc. 146. 23 ; ' Gipsus, *spæren*,' id. 24. 20 (8th cent.). Cf. G. *sparkalk*, plaster. β. The true G. name is *spat* or *spath* ; which is a different word. **Der.** *sparr-y*.

SPAR (3), to box with the hands, dispute, wrangle. (F. – Teut.) ' To *sparre*, as cocks do, *confligere* ;' Levins (1570). It was thus a term in cock-fighting, and orig. used of striking with the spurs, as cocks do. – OF. *esparer*, ' to fling or yerk out with the heels, as a horse in high manage ;' Cot. Mod. F. *éparer*, little used (Littré) ; which Littré connects with Ital. *sparare*, of which one sense is ' to kick ;' but this must be a different word from Ital. *sparare* (=L. *exparare*), to unfurnish, to let off a gun. β. I suppose OF. *esparer* to be of Teut. origin ; cf. Low G. *sparre*, sb., a struggling, striving, Bremen Wörterbuch, iv. 945. Cf. G. *sich sperren*, to struggle against, resist, oppose. Perhaps allied to Lithuan. *spirti*, to stamp, kick, strike out with the feet, resist. See **Spur, Spurn**. **Der.** *sparr-er, sparr-ing*.

SPARABLE, a kind of headless nail used for boots. (E.) A contraction of *sparrow-bill* ; the old name. ' And *sparrowbils* to clout Pan's shoone ;' (1629) T. Dekker, London's Tempe (The Song).

SPARE, frugal, scanty, lean. (E.) ME. *spar* (rare) ; ' vpon *spare* wyse' = in a sparing manner, temperately ; Gawain and the Grene Knight, 901. AS. *spær*, spare, sparing, as a gloss to L. *parcus*, Liber Scintillarum, p. 52, l. 6 ; also found in the compounds *spærhynde*, sparing, *spær-līc*, frugal, *spærnis*, frugality, all in various glosses (Leo) ; the derived verb *sparian*, to spare, is not uncommon ; Grein, ii. 467.+Icel. *sparr*, sparing ; Dan. *spar-* in sparsom, thrifty ; Swed. *spar-* in sparsam ; G. *spär-* in spärlich. Cf. L. *parum*, little, *parcus*, sparing, *parcere*, to spare ; which seem to have lost initial *s*. **Der.** *spare*, verb, ME. *sparen*, Chaucer, C. T. 6919 (D 1337), from AS. *sparian* (Grein), as above ; cognate with Du. and G. *sparen*, Icel. and Swed. *spara*, Dan. *spare*, and perhaps allied to L. *parcere*. Also *spare-ness, spare-rib* ; *spar-ing, spar-ing-ly*.

SPARK (1), a small particle of fire. (E.) ME. *sparke*, Havelok, 91. OMerc. *spærca*, Voc. 46. 8 : AS. *spearca*, Ælfred, tr. of Boethius, lib. iii. c. 12 ; cap. xxxv. § 5.+MDu. *sparcke* (Hexham) ; Low G. *sparke* ; Brem. Wört. β. Perhaps so called from the crackling of a firebrand, which throws out sparks ; Icel. *spraka*, Dan. *sprage*, to crackle. Cf. Lithuan. *sprageti*, to crackle like burning fir-wood, Gk. σφάραγος, a cracking, crackling. Brugmann, i. § 531. **Der.** *spark-le*, a little spark, with dimin. suffix *-le* for *-el* (cf. *kern-el* from *corn*), ME. *sparcle*, Chaucer, C. T. 13833 (B 2095) ; also *spark-le*, verb, ME. *sparklen*, C. T. 2166 (A 2164).

SPARK (2), a gay young fellow. (Scand.) In Shak. All's Well, ii. 1. 25. The same word as prov. E. *sprack*, lively. ME. *sparklich*, adv., also spelt *sprackliche* ; P. Plowman, C. xxi. 10, and footnote. – Icel. *sparkr*, lively, sprightly ; also *sprækr*. Hence Icel. *sprækligr*, whence ME. *sprackliche*, adj.+Swed. dial. *spräker*, *sprāk*, *sprāg*, cheerful, talkative (Rietz) ; Norweg. *spræk*, ardent, cheerful, lively (Aasen). β. Perhaps the orig. sense was ' talkative,' or ' noisy ;' cf. **Speak**, and **Spark** (1). ¶ The prov. E. *sprack* is pronounced *s'rag* by Sir Hugh, Merry Wives, iv. 1. 84.

SPARROW, a small well-known bird. (E.) ME. *sparwe*, Chaucer, C. T. 628 (A 626) ; *sparewe*, Wyclif, Matt. x. 29. OMerc. *sparwa* ; AS. *spearwa*, Matt. x. 29.+Icel. *spörr* (rare) ; Dan. *spurv* ; Swed. *sparf* ; OHG. *sparo* (gen. sparwen), also *sparwe* ; MHG. *spar* ; whence G. *sper-ling*, a sparrow, with double dimin. suffix *-l-ing* ; Goth. *sparwa*. β. All from Teut. type *sparwon-*, m., a sparrow ; lit. ' a flutterer ;' from √SPER, to quiver, hence, to flutter ; see **Spar** (3). Cf. Lithuan. *sparnas*, a bird's wing, a fish's fin, the leaf of a folding door (from the movement to and fro). **Der.** *sparrow-hawk*, ME. *sperhauke*, P. Plowman, B. vi. 199, AS. *spearhafoc*, Voc. 132. 26 ; cf. Icel. *sparrhaukr* (where sparr- is the stem of spörr), Swed. *sparfhök* (from sparf), Dan. *spurvehög* (from spurv).

SPARVER, SPARVISE, the canopy or tester of a bed. (F.) In 1473 : ' j *sparvour* with j pelew' [pillow] ; York Wills, iii. 216. See Nares. – OF. *espervier, esprevier*, ' l'ensemble des pièces qui composent le coucher,' Godefroy ; but it may mean ' canopy.' Apparently the same as OF. *espervier*, a sparrow-hawk, also ' a sweep-net' (Cot.) ; hence, a canopy. Cf. Ital. *sparauiere*, ' any kinde of hauke ; also a sparvise of a bed ;' Florio.

SPARSE, thinly scattered. (L.) Modern ; yet the verb *sparse*, to scatter, occurs as early as 1536 (see Todd) : and Spenser has ' *spersed* ayre,' F. Q. i. 1. 39. – L. *sparsus* (for *sparg-sus*) ; pp. of *spargere*, to scatter, sprinkle. – √SPERG, to sprinkle ; an extension of √SPER, to scatter (Gk. σπείρειν, for *σπέρ-γειν) ; see **Sperm**. **Der.** *sparse-ly, -ness*. Also *a-sperse, di-sperse, inter-sperse*.

SPASM, a convulsive movement. (F. – L. – Gk.) ' Those who have their necks drawne backward . . with the *spasme* ;' Holland's Pliny, b. xx. c. 5 ; ed. 1634, ii. 41 d ; ME. *spasme*, Lanfrank, Cirurgie, p. 309, l. 19. – F. *spasme*, ' the cramp ;' Cot. – L. *spasmum*, acc. of *spasmus*. – Gk. σπασμός, a spasm, convulsion. – Gk. σπάειν, to draw, pluck. – √SPA, to draw. **Der.** *spasm-od-ic*, formed with suffix *-ic* from Gk. adj. σπασμώδ-ης, convulsive ; *spasm-od-ic-al*, *spasm-od-ic-al-ly*.

SPAT (1), a blow, a slap. (E.) In Cent. Dict. Of imitative origin ; cf. *slap, fat*.

SPAT (2), the young of shell-fish. (E.) In Cent. Dict. Formed from *spat-*, to eject, the base of *spatter* ; see **Spatter**. And compare **Spot** ; also Du. *spat*, a spot, speck, splash.

SPATE, a river-flood. (F. – Teut.) ' While crashing ice, borne on the roaring *spate* ;' Burns, Brigs of Ayr. And see Jamieson. Cf. Irish *speid* (borrowed from E. *spate*), a great river-flood. Also spelt *speit*. G. Douglas has *spait*, a torrent ; cf. Verg. Æn. ii. 496. – AF. *espeit* = OF. *espoit*, a spouting out (Godefroy). – EFries. *speiten*, *speuten*, *spoiten*, WFlem. *speeten*, Du. *spuiten*, to spout ; see **Spout**.

SPATS, gaiters. (E.) Shorter for *spatterdashes*, gaiters to keep off the *spatterings* of mud that are *dashed* against the wearer ; cf. *dash-board* or *splash-board* of a carriage.

SPATTER, to besprinkle, spit or throw out upon. (E.) 1. ' Which th' offended taste With *spattering* noise rejected ;' Milton, P. L. x.

567. Here Milton uses it for *sputter*, the frequentative of **Spit** (2), q. v.   **2.** The usual sense is *to be-spot*, and it is a frequentative form, with suffix *-er*, formed from a base *spat-*; cf. prov. E. *spat*, to spit; EFries. *spatten*, to burst, fly out, spirt.+Du. *spatten*, to throw, spatter, splash. Cf. Gk. σφενδόνη, a sling.

SPATULA, a broad-bladed knife for spreading plasters. (L.— Gk.) Spelt *spatule* in Holland's Pliny, b. xxiii. c. 7 [*not* 17], l. 24 from the end. This is F. *spatule*, as in Cot.—L. *spatula*, also *spathula*; dimin. of *spatha*, an instrument with a broad blade.—Gk. σπάθη, a broad blade, a spatula, a paddle; cognate with E. **Spade** (1), q.v.

SPAVIN, a swelling near the joints of horses, producing lameness. (F.— Teut.) In Shak. Hen. VIII, i. 3. 12. ME. *spaveyne*, 'horsys maledy;' Prompt. Parv.—OF. *esparvin* (13th cent., in Hatzfeld), MF. *esparvain*, 'a spavin in the leg of a horse,' Cot. Cf. MItal. *spavano*, 'a spavin,' Florio; Ital. *spavenio*; Span. *esparavan* (1) spavin, (2) a sparrow-hawk; Port. *esparavão*; mod. F. *éparvin*. β. A comparison of the forms (of which MItal. *spavano* is for *sparvano*) shows that they answer to a Late L. type **sparvānus*, parallel to Late L. *sparvārius*, a sparrow-hawk (F. *éparvier*). And just as *sparvārius* is formed with suffix *-ārius* from OHG. *sparwe*, a sparrow (or is Latinised from OHG. *sparwāri*, a sparrow-hawk, which comes to the same thing), so Late L. **sparvānus* is formed with suffix *-ānus* from the same base (*sparwe*). The lit. sense is, accordingly, 'sparrow-like,' from the hopping or bird-like motion of a horse afflicted with spavin. The OHG. *sparwe* is cognate with E. **Sparrow**, q.v. ¶ Ménage, who is followed by Diez and Littré, gives much the same explanation, but says that the disease is named from the *sparrow-hawk* (not the *sparrow*) because the horse lifts up his legs after the manner of sparrow-hawks. It is obvious that the sparrow is much more likely than the sparrow-hawk to have been the subject of a simile, and it is also clear that *sparvānus* may have been formed from *sparwe* directly. It makes better sense.

SPAW, the same as **Spa**, q. v.

SPAWL, spittle. (E.) 'In the *spawl* her middle finger dips;' Dryden, tr. of Persius, ii. 63. AS. *spāld*, Elene, 300 (*sic* in MS.); variant of OMerc. *spādl*, Matt. xxvii. 30; AS. *spātl*, spittle, allied to *spḿttan*, to spit. See **Spit** (2).

SPAWN, the eggs of fish or frogs. (F.—L.) 'Your multiplying *spawn*;' Cor. ii. 2. 82. 'Spawne of a fysshe;' Palsgrave. The verb occurs in Prompt. Parv., p. 467: '*Spawnyn*, *spanyn*, as fyschys, Pisciculo.' Short for **spaunden*, and certainly (as Wedgwood suggests), from OF. *espandre*, 'to shed, spill, poure out, to spread, cast, or scatter abroad in great abundance;' Cot. (So also Ital. *spandere*, to spill, shed, scatter.) β. The etymology is proved by a gloss in Wright's Voc. i. 164; cf. N. and Q. 6 S. v. 465. The AF. phrase 'Soffret le peysoun en ewe *espaundre*,' i. e. let the fish spawn in the water, occurs there; and *espaundre* is glossed by *scheden his roune*, i.e. shed his roe, in the MS.; though misprinted *scheden him frome*. From L. *ex-pandere*; see **Expand**. **Der.** *spawn-er*.

SPAY, to render sterile. (F.—L.— Gk.) See Todd's Johnson.— OF. **espeer*, not found; [but of the same form as OF. *espeer*, to pierce with a sword (Godefroy), from OF. *espee* (= Ital. *spada*), a sword]. Hence the OF. **espeer* would represent the Late L. *spadāre*, for *spadōnāre*, to geld.—L. *spad-o* (gen. *spadōnis*), a eunuch.—Gk. σπάδων, a eunuch.—Gk. σπά-ειν, to draw, tear, rend.

SPEAK, to utter words, say, talk. (E.) This word has lost an *r*, and stands for *spreak*. We can date the loss of the *r* as having taken place before A.D. 1100. The MSS. of the A.S. Gospels have sometimes *sprecan* and sometimes *specan*, so that the letter was frequently dropped as early as the 11th century, though it appears occasionally in the *latest* of them; the same is true for the sb. *sprḿc* or *spḿc*, mod. E. *speech* (for *spreech*); see John, iv. 26, &c. ME. *speken*, pt. t. *spak*, pp. *spoken*, *spoke*; Chaucer, C. T. 792, 914 (A 790, 912). AS. *sprecan* (later *specan*), pt. t. *spræc* (later *spæc*), pp. *sprecen*; Grein, ii. 472.+Du. *spreken*; OHG. *sprehhan*; G. *sprechen*, pt. t. *sprach*. β. All from Teut. base SPREK, to speak, of which the orig. sense was merely to make a noise, crackle, cry out, as seen in Icel. *spraka*, Dan. *sprage*, to crackle, Dan. *sprække*, to crack, burst; see **Spark** (1). Cf. Gk. σφάραγος, a cracking, crackling. Cf. Lowland Sc. *crack*, a talk. **Der.** *speak-er*; *speak-er-ship*; *speech*, q.v.; *spokes-man*, q.v.

SPEAR, a long weapon, spiked pole, lance. (E.) ME. *spere* (dissyllabic), Chaucer, C. T. 2551 (A 2549). AS. *spere*, John, xix. 34.+Du. *speer*; Icel. *spjör*; Dan. *spær*; G. *speer*; OHG. *sper*. Cf. L. *sparus*, a small missile weapon, dart, hunting-spear. Perhaps related to *spar*, a beam (hence, a pole). See **Spar** (1). **Der.** *spear-man*, Acts, xxiii. 23; *spear-grass*, 1 Hen. IV, ii. 4. 340; *spear-mint*; *spear-wort*, AS. *sperewyrt*, A. S. Leechdoms, Gloss. to vol. iii.

SPECIAL, particular, distinctive. (F.—L.) ME. *special*, *speciale*, Ancren Riwle, p. 56, l. 22. Short for *especial*; see **Especial**;

and **Species** (below).   **Der.** *special-ly*, *special-i-ty*, *special-ty*. **Doublet**, *especial*.

SPECIES, a group of individuals having common characteristics, subordinate to a genus, a kind. (L.) In Minsheu, ed. 1627; the ME. form was *spice* (see **Spice**).—L. *speciēs*, a look, appearance, kind, sort.—L. *specere*, to look, see.+OHG. *spehōn* (G. *spähen*), to spy. Cf. Skt. *paç*, *spaç*, to spy.—√SPEK, to see. Brugmann, i. § 551. See **Spy**. **Der.** *speci-al*, q.v. Also *specie*, money in gold or silver, a remarkable form, evolved as a sing. sb. from the old word *species* = 'money paid by tale,' as in Phillips, ed. 1706; probably by confusion with the L. ablative *speciē*, as if paid *in specie* = paid in visible coin. Also *speci-fy*, q.v., *speci-men*, q.v., *speci-ous*, q.v. Also *especi-al* (doublet of *special*); *fronti-spiece*, q.v. **Doublet**, *spice*.

SPECIFY, to particularise. (F.—L.) ME. *specifien*, Gower, C. A. i. 33; prol. 866.—OF. *specifier*, 'to specify, particularize;' Cot.—Late L. **specificāre*, to specify (Ducange); pp. *specificātus*.—L. adj. *specificus*, specific, particular.—L. *speci-*, for *speciēs*, a kind; and *-ficus*, i. e. making, from L. *facere*, to make; see **Species** and **Fact**. ¶ It thus appears that *specific* is a more orig. word, but *specify* is much the older word in English. Cf. *specific*, MF. *specifique*, 'speciall,' Cot., from L. *specificus*, special, as above; whence *specific-al*, *specific-al-ly*, *specific-ate*, *specific-at-ion*. And hence *specify*, verb (as above).

SPECIMEN, a pattern, model. (L.) '*Specimen*, an example, proof, trial, or pattern;' Blount's Gloss., ed. 1674.—L. *specimen*, an example, something shown by way of sample.—L. *speci-*, for *specere*, to see: with suffix *-men*. See **Species**.

SPECIOUS, showy, plausible. (F.—L.) ME. *specious*, sightly, beautiful; see Trench, Select Glossary.—MF. *specieux*, 'specious, fair;' Cot.—L. *speciōsus*, fair to see.—L. *speci-*, for *specere*, to behold; with suffix *-ōsus*. See **Species**. **Der.** *specious-ly*, *-ness*.

SPECK, a small spot, blemish. (E.) *Specke* in Levins, ed. 1570. '*Speckid* sheep,' i.e. spotted sheep; Wyclif, tr. of Gen. xxx. 32. '*Spekke*, clowte, Pictacium,' i.e. a patch; Prompt. Parv. AS. *specca*, a spot, mark, pl. *speccan*; 'Notæ, *speccan*,' Voc. 34. 25. Cf. Low G. *spaken*, to be spotted with wet, *spakig*, spotted with wet; Brem. Wört. iv. 931; MDu. *spickelen*, 'to speckle, or to spott,' Hexham. β. The MDu. *spickelen* is obviously the frequentative of MDu. *spicken*, to spit, and Wedgwood's suggestion that 'the origin lies in the figure of spattering with wet' is prob. correct. Cf. Du. *spikkel*, a speckle, spot. Hardly allied to L. *pingere*, to paint (Franck). **Der.** *speck*, verb, Milton, P. L. ix. 429. Also *speck-le*, a little spot, dimin. form, Spenser, tr. of Virgil's Gnat, 250; cf. Du. *spikkel*, a speckle. Hence *speckle*, verb.

SPECTACLE, a sight, show. (F.—L.) ME. *spectacle*, Wyclif, 1 Cor. iv. 9.—F. *spectacle*, 'a spectacle;' Cot.—L. *spectāculum*, a show. Formed with suffixes *-cu-lu-* (<*-cu-lo-*) from L. *spectā-re*, to see.—L. *spectum*, supine of *specere*, to see; see **Species**. **Der.** *spectacles*, pl. glasses for assisting the sight, pl. of ME. *spectacle*, a glass through which to view objects, Chaucer, C. T. 6785 (D 1203); hence *spectacl-ed*, Cor. ii. 1. 222. And see *spectator*, *spectre*, *speculate*.

SPECTATOR, a beholder. (L.; *or* F.—L.) In Hamlet, iii. 2. 46; spelt *spectatour*, Spenser, F. Q. ii. 4. 27. [Perhaps from F. *spectateur*, 'a spectator;' Cot.]—L. *spectātor*, a beholder; formed with suffix *-tor* from *spectā-re*, to behold.—L. *spectum*, supine of *specere*, to see; see **Spectacle**, **Spy**.

SPECTRE, a ghost. (F.—L.) In Milton, P. R. iv. 430.—F. *spectre*, 'an image, figure, ghost;' Cot.—L. *spectrum*, a vision. Formed with suffix *-trum* from *spec-ere*, to see; see **Spectacle**, **Spy**. **Der.** *spectr-al*. **Doublet**, *spectrum*, a mod. scientific term, directly from L. *spectrum*.

SPECULAR, suitable for seeing, having a smooth reflecting surface. (L.) 'This *specular* mount;' Milton, P. R. iv. 236.—L. *speculāris*, belonging to a mirror.—L. *speculum*, a mirror.—L. *spec-ere*, to see; see **Spy**. ¶ Milton's use of the word is due to L. *specula*, fem. sb., a watch-tower, a closely allied word. **Der.** *specul-ate*, from L. *speculātus*, pp. of *speculārī*, to behold, from *specula*, a watch-tower; hence *specul-at-ion*, Minsheu, ed. 1627, from F. *speculation*, 'speculation,' Cot., which from L. acc. *speculātiōnem*; *specul-at-or* = L. *speculātor*; *specul-at-ive*, Minsheu, from L. *speculātiuus*. We also use *specul-um* = L. *speculum*, a mirror.

SPEECH, talk, language. (E.) ME. *speche* (dissyllabic), Chaucer, C. T. 8729 (E 853). For *spreche*, by loss of *r*. AS. *spḿc*, later form of *sprḿc*; Grein, ii. 471.—AS. *spræc-*, 3rd grade of *sprecan*, to speak; see **Speak**.+Du. *spraak*, from *spreken*; G. *sprache*, from *sprechen*. **Der.** *speech-less*, Merch. Ven. i. 1. 164; *spee·h-less-ly*, *-ness*.

SPEED, success, velocity. (E.) The old sense is 'success' or 'help.' ME. *sped* (with long *e*); '*iuel sped*' = evil speed, ill success, Genesis and Exodus, ed. Morris, 310. AS. *spēd*, haste, success; Grein, ii. 467. Here *ē* is due to *ō*, by the usual change (as in *foot*, AS. *fōt*, pl. *feet*, AS. *fēt*), and *spēd* is due to a Teut. type *spōdiz.*+OSax. *spōd*, success (Heliand); Du. *spoed*, speed; OHG. *spuot*, *spōt*, success. **β.** All from Teut. type *spōdiz*, speed, success (Fick, iii. 355). Here the *-di-* is a suffix, answering to Idg. *-ti-* (by Verner's law). Allied to Skt. *sphā-ti-*, increase, growth; and *sphā-ta-s*, pp. of *sphāy*, to increase, enlarge; Benfey, p. 1087. **γ.** The AS. *spēd* is, accordingly, from the AS. strong verb *spōwan*, to succeed, Grein, ii. 471; and the OHG. *spuot* is allied to the verb *spuon*, to succeed, an impersonal weak verb. **δ.** Further allied to L. *spatium*, room, *spēs*, hope, *prosper*, prosperous, Lithuan. *spėtas*, leisure, opportunity. Brugmann, i. §§ 156, 223 (3, note). **Der.** *speed*, verb, AS. *spēdan*, weak verb, pt. t. *spēdde*, Grein, ii. 468; *speed-y*, AS. *spēdig*, id.; *speed-i-ly*, *speed-i-ness*.

SPEIR, to ask. (E.) See **Spur**.

SPELICANS, a game played with thin slips of wood. (Du.) Imported from Holland, which is famous for toys. Englished from MDu. *spelleken*, a small pin (Hexham); formed with the MDu. dimin. suffix *-ken* (= G. *-chen*, E. *-kin*) from MDu. *spelle*, a pin, splinter of wood, allied to E. **Spell** (4), q. v.

SPELL (1), a form of magic words, incantation. (E.) ME. *spel*, dat. *spelle*, Chaucer, C. T. 13821 (B 2083). AS. *spel*, *spell*, a saying, story, narrative; Grein, ii. 469.+Icel. *spjall*, a saying; OHG. *spel*, a narrative; Goth. *spill*, a fable, tale, myth. Teut. type *spellom*, n. **Der.** *spell* (2), q. v.; *go-spel*, q. v.

SPELL (2), to tell the names of the letters of a word. (F. − Teut.) ME. *spellen*; 'Spellyn letters, Sillabico; *Spellynge*, Sillabicacio; *Spellare* [speller], Sillabicator;' Prompt. Parv. 'Lere hem litlum and lytlum . . . Tyl þei couthe speke and *spelle*,' &c. = teach them by little and little till they could pronounce and spell; P. Plowman, B. xv. 599, 600. − OF. *espeler*, 'to spell, to speale, to join letters or syllables together;' Cot. Of Teut. origin. From Du. *spellen*, to spell; the same as AS. *spellian*, to relate, declare, tell, speak; MHG. *spellen*, to relate, Goth. *spillōn*, to narrate. All these are denominative verbs; thus Du. *spellen* is from OSax. *spel*, a word (see Heliand, 572); AS. *spellian* is from AS. *spell*, a tale; and Goth. *spillōn*, from *spill*, a fable; see **Spell** (1). ¶ E. *spell* does not appear to be directly from AS. *spellian*, but seems rather to have been borrowed from French. Certainly the word was sooner or later confused with the old and prov. E. *spell*, in the sense of a splinter of wood, as though to *spell* were to point out letters with a splinter of wood. Thus Palsgrave has 'festue to *spell* with;' where *festue* is F. *festu*, 'a straw, rush, little stalk or stick' (Cot.), from L. *festūca*; and Halliwell cites from a Dict. written about A.D. 1500 the entry 'To *speldyr*, Syllabicare,' agreeing with the form 'spelder of woode' in Palsgrave; indeed, *speldren*, to spell, occurs in the Ormulum, 16347, 16440. So even in Hexham's MDu. Dict. we have 'spelle, a pin,' with a striking resemblance to 'spellen, to spell letters or words.' See **Spell** (4). **Der.** *spell-er*, *spell-ing*, *spell-ing-book*.

SPELL (3), a turn of work. (E.) 'To Do a Spell, in sea-language, signifies to do any work by turns, for a short time, and then leave it. *A fresh spell*, is when fresh men come to work, esp. when the rowers are relieved with another gang; *to give a spell*, is to be ready to work in such a one's room;' Phillips, ed. 1706. Not found in ME., but it is almost certainly due to AS. *spelian*, to supply another's room, to act or be proxy for (Bosworth). Whelock, in his edition of Ælfred's tr. of Beda, p. 151, quotes the following sentence from a homily: 'Se cyning is Cristes sylfes *speligend*' = the king supplies the place of Christ himself. So also the following: 'Næs ðeah Isaac ofslegen, ac se ramm hine *spelode*' = Isaac, however, was not slain himself, but the ram supplied his place, or took his spell; Ælfric's Hom. ed. Thorpe, ii. 62. Cf. AS. *gespelia*, a vicar, deputy (Toller). **β.** The AS. *spelian* is perhaps allied to *spilian*, to play, to sport; and the latter is cognate with Du. *spelen*, G. *spielen*, to play, act a part; these being denominative verbs, formed from the sb. which appears as Du. *spel*, G. *spiel*, OHG. *spil*, a game.

SPELL (4), **SPILL**, a thin slip of wood, splinter; a slip of paper for lighting candles. (E.) This word has been assimilated to the verb *to spell*, from the use of a slip of wood, in schools of the olden times, to point out letters in a book. See remarks on **Spell** (2). The true form is rather *speld*. ME. *speld*, a splinter; pl. *speldes*, splinters of a broken spear, Will. of Palerne, 3392; hence the dimin. *spelder*, a splinter (Palsgrave), spelt *spildur*, Avowynge of Arthur, xiii. 6. AS. *speld*, a torch, spill used as a torch (Bosworth).+Du. *speld*, a pin (cf. *spil*, the pin of a bobbin, spindle, axis); Icel. *speld*, *speldi*, a square tablet, orig. a thin slice of board; *spilda*, a flake, a slice; Goth. *spilda*, a writing-tablet; MHG. *spelte*, a splinter. **β.** All from the Teut. verb *spaldan-* (G. *spalten*), to cleave; a reduplicating verb, like OHG. *spaltan*, to cleave, split. Cf. Shetland *speld*, to split (Edmonston); Skt. *sphaṭ* (for *sphalt*),

to burst open. See **Spelicans, Spill** (2). Thus the orig. sense is 'that which is split off,' a flake, slice, &c. **Der.** *spelicans*, q.v.

SPELT, a kind of corn. (L.) Called 'spelt corne' in Minsheu, ed. 1627. Not found in ME. AS. *spelt*. 'Faar [i.e. L. *far*], *spelt*;' Voc. 273. 20. Cf. Du. *spelt*; G. *spelz*, *spelt*. All from Late L. *spelta*, spelt (ab. A. D. 400); whence also Ital. *spelta*, *spelda*, F. *épeautre*, spelt.

SPELTER, pewter, zinc. (Low G.) 'Spelter, a kind of metall, not known to the antients, which the Germans call *zinc*;' Blount's Gloss., ed. 1674. I cannot find an early example of the word, but it is prob. Teutonic, in any case, and occurs again in Low G. *spialter*, pewter, Bremen Wörterbuch; cf. Du. *spiauter*, MDu. *speauter*, from OF. *espeautre* (Godefroy); which suggests an older form *espeltre*. It is obviously allied to Ital. *peltro*, pewter, and to E. *pewter*. See (in Ducange) Late L. *pestrum* (error for *peltrum*?) and *peutreum*. Hexham has: 'Peauter, or *Speauter*, Pewter, or fine Tinne.' Godefroy has OF. *pialtre* (12th cent.), s.v. *peautre*; and note that the earlier forms are without the initial *s-* or *es-*. See **Pewter**; where correct the note that initial *s* has been lost.

SPENCER, a short over-jacket. (F.−L.) Much worn about A.D. 1815; see Notes and Queries, 4 S. x. 356. 'Two noble earls, whom, if I quote, Some folks might call me sinner, The one invented *half a coat*, The other *half a dinner*;' Epigram quoted in Taylor, Words and Places. The reference is to Earl *Spencer* and Earl *Sandwich*. It thus appears that the *spencer* was named after the celebrated Earl Spencer, viz. John Charles Spencer, third earl, born 1782, died 1845. See further under **Spend**.

SPEND, to lay out (money), consume, waste. (L.) ME. *spenden*, Chaucer, C. T. 302 (A 300). AS. *spendan*; occurring in the compounds *ā-spendan* and *for-spendan*; see examples in Sweet's A.S. Reader. Not an AS. word, but merely borrowed from Late L. *dispendere*, to spend, waste, consume. Cf. Late L. *dispendium*, *dispensa*, expense, of which the shorter forms *spendium*, *spensa* are also found. We also find Late L. *spendibilis monēta*, spending money, i.e. money for current expenses, occurring as early as A.D. 922 (Ducange). So also Ital. *spendere*, to spend, *spendio*, expense, where *spendio* = L. *dispendium*. Observe also OF. *despendre*, 'to dispend, spend, expend, disburse,' Cot.; *despenser*, 'to dispend, spend,' id.; *despensier*, 'a spender, also a cater [caterer], or clarke of a kitchin,' id. **β.** In exactly the same way, the OF. *despensier* became ME. *spencere* or *spensere*, explained by *cellerarius* in the Prompt. Parv., and now preserved in the proper name *Spencer* or *Spenser*, formerly *Despenser*. Trevisa, tr. of Higden, iv. 33, translates L. *dispensator* by *spenser*. Hence even the buttery or cellar was called a *spence*, as being under the control of this officer; 'Spence, botery, or celere,' Prompt. Parv. **γ.** The L. *dispendere* is compounded of *dis-*, apart, and *pendere*, to weigh; see **Dis-** and **Pendant**. ¶ The etymology sometimes given, from L. *expendere*, is less likely; the *s* here represents *dis-*, not *ex-*; precisely the same loss occurs in *sport* for *disport*. **Der.** *spend-er*; *spend-thrift*, i.e. one who spends what has been accumulated by thrift, Temp. ii. 1. 24; *spencer* (above).

SPERM, animal seed, spawn, spermaceti. (F.−L.−Gk.) ME. *sperme*, Chaucer, C. T. 14015 (B 3199). − F. *sperme*, 'sperm, seed;' Cot.−L. *sperma*.−Gk. σπέρμα, seed.−Gk. σπείρειν (= σπέρ-γειν), to sow; orig. to scatter with a quick motion of the hand. (√SPER.) And see **Sparse**. **Der.** *spermat-ic*, Gk. σπερματ-ι-κός, from σπερματ-, stem of σπέρμα; *spermat-ic-al*. Also *sperm-oil*, *sperm-whale*; *spermaceti*, spelt *parmaceti* in 1 Hen. IV, i. 3. 58, from L. *sperma cētī*, sperm of the whale, where *cētī* is the gen. case of *cētus* = Gk. κῆτος, a large fish; see **Cetaceous**. And see *spor-ad-ic*, *spore*.

SPEW, SPUE, to vomit. (E.) ME. *spewen*, P. Plowman, B. x. 40. AS. *speowan*, *spiwian*, weak verbs; *spīwan*, strong verb, pt. t. *spāw*, pp. *spiwen*; Grein, ii. 470. Cf. MDu. *spouwen* (Hexham); Icel. *spýja*; Swed. *spy*; OHG. *spīwan*; G. *speien*; Goth. *speiwan*.+L. *spuere*; Lithuan. *spjauti*; Gk. πτύειν (for *σπιύειν*). **β.** All from √SPIW, to spit forth. Expressive of the sound of spitting out; cf. *puke* (1), *spit* (2). Brugmann, i. § 567.

SPHERE, a globe, orb, circuit of motion, province or duty. (F.−L.−Gk.) ME. *spere*, Chaucer, C. T. 11592 (F 1280). Later *sphere*, Spenser, F. Q. i. 10. 56.−OF. *espere*, a sphere (Littré); MF. *sphere*, 'a sphere;' Cot.−L. *sphæra*.−Gk. σφαῖρα, a ball, globe. **β.** Gk. σφαῖρα = *σφάρ-ya* = *σπάρ-ya*; perhaps 'that which is tossed about;' see **Spar** (3). **Der.** *spher-ic*, Gk. σφαιρικός, like a sphere; *spher-ic-al*, *spher-ic-al-ly*, *spher-ic-i-ty*; *spher-o-id*, that which is like a sphere, from σφαῖρο-ν for σφαῖρος, round, and εἶδος, form, shape, appearance (from √WEID); for σφαῖρος. Hence *spheroid-al*.

SPHINX, a monster with a woman's head and the body of a lioness, who destroyed travellers that could not solve her riddles. (L.−Gk.) 'Subtle as *Sphinx*;' L. L. L. iv. 3. 342. Spelt *Sfinx* by

Lydgate, Storie of Thebes, pt. i.—L. *sphinx* (gen. *sphingis*).—Gk. σφίγξ (gen. σφιγγός), lit. 'the strangler,' because she strangled the travellers who could not solve her riddles; from Gk. σφίγγειν, to throttle, strangle. ¶ But most likely, this is merely a popular etymology, and the word is foreign to Greek. In fact, the legend is Egyptian; Herodotus, ii. 175, iv. 79.

SPICE, an aromatic vegetable for seasoning food, a small quantity or sample. (F.—L.) A doublet of *species*. '*Spice*, the earlier form in which we made the word our own, is now limited to certain aromatic drugs, which, as consisting of various *kinds*, have this name of *spices*. But spice was once employed as *species* is now;' Trench, Select Glossary, q. v. '*Species*, used by the druggists of the Middle Ages for the four kinds of ingredients in which they traded—saffron, cloves, cinnamon, nutmegs;' Bréal, Semantics. ME. *spice*. 'Absteyne зou fro al yuel *spice*,' Wyclif, 1 Thess. v. 22; where the Vulgate has 'ab omni *specie* malā.' In early use. 'Hope is a swete *spice*;' Ancren Riwle, p. 78, last line.—OF. '*espice*, spice;' Cot.— L. *speciem*, acc. of *species*, a kind, species; in Late Latin, a spice, drug; see **Species.** Der. *spice*, verb; *spic-ed*, Chaucer, C. T. 528 (A 526); *spic-er*, an old word for spice-seller, answering to the mod. grocer, P. Plowman, B. ii. 225; *spic-er-y*, from OF. *espicerie*, 'a spicery, also spices,' Cot.; *spic-y*, *spic-i-ly*, *spic-i-ness*.

SPICK AND SPAN-NEW, quite new. (Scand.) In North's Plutarch, p. 213 (R.); Howell, Famil. Letters, vol. i. sect. 4, let. 2 (Jan. 20, 1624). Lit. 'spike and spoon new,' where *spike* means a point, and *spoon* a chip; new as a spike or nail just made and a chip just cut off. See further under **Span-new.** And see **Spike** and **Spoon.**

SPIDER, an insect that spins webs. (E.) ME. *spither*, spelt *spiþre*, Ayenbite of Inwyt, p. 164, l. 6 from bottom. Apparently this is the sense of AS. *spīder*, A. S. Leechdoms, iii. 42; with *-der* for *-þer*; from **spin-þer*; the loss of *n* before þ being of regular occurrence in AS. As *-þer* (Idg. *-ter*) is an agential suffix, the sense would be *spinner*, which is also a name for the spider; see E. D. D. From the verb to *spin*; see **Spin.**+Du. *spin*, a spider; Dan. *spinder* (for *spinner*), a spider, from *spinde* (for *spinne*), to spin; Swed. *spinnel*, a spider, from *spinna*, to spin; G. *spinne*, a spider, spinner.

SPIGOT, a pointed piece of wood for stopping a small hole in a cask. (Prov.—L.) ME. *spigot*, Wyclif, Job, xxxii. 19. Spelt *spygotte*, Voc 724. 10; *styket*, id. 573. 30. A term due to the Bourdeaux wine-trade. Apparently from an OProv. **espigote*; Mistral gives the mod. Prov. *espigoun, espigou*, the step of a ladder, the bar of a chair, also a spigot. Evidently derived from OProv. *espiga*, mod. Prov. *espigo*, an ear of corn. All from L. *spīca*, an ear of corn; see **Spike.** Cf. also OF. *espigeot*, a bad ear of corn (Godefroy); Walloon *spigot*, the peak of a shoe. Also Port. *espicho*, a spigot; from L. *spīculum*, a little spike, point, dart, dimin. of *spīca* (above). Torriano gives Ital. *spigo, spico*, the herb spikenard, also a spigot. ¶ The Irish *spiocaid*, W. *ysbigod*, are from E.

SPIKE (1), a sharp point, large nail. (Scand.) 'Iron for *spikes*;' Bacon, Advice to Sir G. Villiers (R.). '*Spykynge*, nayle;' Prompt. Parv. Somner gives an AS. *spicing*, a large nail; from A. S. Leechdoms, iii. 200. From Icel. *spík*, Swed. *spik*, a spike; cf. Low G. *spike*, a wooden peg (Schambach); Du. *spijker*, a nail. Thought to be distinct from **Spike** (2), and allied, by gradation, to **Spoke,** q. v. Der. *spike*, verb, *spiked*, *spik-y*.

SPIKE (2), an ear of corn. (L.) ME. *spik*, P. Plowman, C. xiii. 180.—L. *spīca*, an ear of corn. Der. *spike-nard*, q. v.; *spig-ot*, q. v.

SPIKENARD, an aromatic oil or balsam. (Hybrid; F.—L. and F.—L.—Gk.—Pers.) 'Precious oynement *spikenard*;' Wyclif, Mark, xiv. 3; where the Vulgate has 'alabastrum unguenti *nardi spicati* pretiosi.' [Thus *spike-nard* should rather be *spiked nard*; it signifies nard furnished with spikes, in allusion to the mode of growth. 'The head of Nardus spreads into certain *spikes* or eares, whereby it hath a twofold vse, both of *spike* and also of leaf; in which regard it is so famous;' Pliny, Nat. Hist. b. xii. c. 12 (in Holland's translation).] However, we borrowed it from OF. *spiquenard* (Godefroy).—L. *spīca*, an ear of corn; and *nardi*, gen. of *nardus*, nard; see **Nard.** The L. *spīcātus*, furnished with ears, is derived from *spīca*, an ear of corn; see **Spike** (2).

SPILE, a peg for a vent-hole. (E.) Not in Todd's Johnson; but in many E. dialects; see E. D. D. Cognate with Du. *spijl*, a spile, bar; Low G. *spile*, a bar, also a skewer (Schambach); cf. G. *speiler*, a skewer. Teut. types **spī-lā*, **spī-lo-* (Franck); allied to **Spire** (1).

SPILL (1), a splinter, thin slip of wood. (E.) '*Spills*, thin slips of wood or paper, used for lighting candles;' Halliwell. 'The *spill* of wood;' Holland's tr. of Pliny, bk. viii. c. 16; i. 203. ME. *spille*; Life of Beket, ed. W. H. Black, 1845, l. 850: 'hit nis noзt worþ a *spille* '=it is not worth a splinter or chip. The same word as **Spell** (4), q. v.

SPILL (2), to destroy, mar, shed. (Scand.) Often explained by

---

'spoil,' with which it has no etymological connexion. It stands for *spild*, the *ld* having passed into *ll* by assimilation. ME. *spillen*, commonly in the sense to destroy or mar; also, intransitively, to perish; see Chaucer, C. T. 6480. 5235 (D 898, B 815); Hamlet, iv. 5. 20. In mod. E., only to shed, pour out, effuse. Cf. AS. *spillan*, to destroy; Grein, ii. 470; apparently borrowed from Icel. *spilla*, to destroy; Swed. *spilla* (Dan. *spilde*, for **spille*), to spill. These are assimilated forms, with *ll* for *ld*; as shown by the (native) AS. *spildan*, to destroy, OSax. *spildian*. Teut. type **spelth-jan-*; allied to G. *spalten*, to split. Cf. Skt. *sphat, sphut*, to burst; Brugmann, i. § 530. See **Spell** (4). Der. *spill-er*; *spil-th* (=AS. *spild*), Timon, ii. 2. 169.

SPIN, to draw out into threads, cause to whirl rapidly. (E.) The second sense comes from the rapid motion of the spinning-wheel. The former sense is original. ME. *spinnen*, strong verb, pt. t. *span*, pp. *sponnen*; P. Plowman, B. v. 216. AS. *spinnan*, pt. t. *spann*, pp. *spunnen*; Matt. vi. 28.+Du. *spinnen*; Icel. and Swed. *spinna*; Dan. *spinde* (for *spinne*); G. *spinnen*; Goth. *spinnan* (pt. t. *spann*). β. All from Teut. base **spen-*, to draw out. Allied to Lith. *pin-ti*, to weave; OSlav. *peti*, to stretch out (span); Miklosich, p. 237. See **Span,** a related word. Der. *spinn-er*; *spinn-ing*; *spin-d-le*, q. v.; *spin-ster*, q. v.; *spi-der*, q. v.

SPINACH, SPINAGE, an esculent vegetable. (F.—Span.— Arab.—Pers.) '*Spinage* is a "voiced" form of *spinach*, as it was formerly written. Spelt *spinache* in Levins, ed. 1570. '*Spynnage*, an herbe, *espinars*;' Palsgrave. ME. *speneche*; MS. Harl. 2378, p. 247; in Henslow, p. 113.—OF. *espinache, espinage* (also *espinoche*); Godefroy. [Cf. Ital. *spinace*, 'the hearbe spinage,' Florio; mod. F. *épinard* (with excrescent *d*), OF. *espinars, espinar* (Cotgrave).]—Span. *espinaca*.—Arab. *aspanākh, isfanāj*; of Pers. origin (Devic). β. But referred, by popular etymology, to L. *spīna*, a thorn, a prickle; because 'the fruit is a small round nut, which is sometimes very prickly;' Eng. Cyclopædia. See **Spine.**

SPINDLE, the pin or stick from which a thread is spun. (E.) The *d* is excrescent, as is so common in English after *n*; cf. *soun-d, thun-d-er*; and *spindle* stands for *spin-le*. '*Spinnel*, a spindle; North;' Halliwell. In Walter de Bibbesworth (in Wright's Vocab. i. 157, l. 6) we meet with ME. *spinel*, where another MS. has *spindele*. AS. *spinl*; 'Fusus, *spinl*,' Wright's Voc. i. 82, col. 1; 281, col. 2. Formed, with suffix *-l*, denoting the agent, from AS. *spinnan*, to spin; see **Spin.**+MDu. *spille* (Hexham); by assimilation for **spinle*; OHG. *spinnila*, MHG. *spinnel*; whence G. *spindel* (with inserted *d*), as well as G. *spille* (by assimilation). Der. *spindle-shanks*, with shanks as thin as a spindle. *Spindle-tree* (Euonymus), because used for *spindles* or thin rods, named in German *spindelbaum* for a like reason; from its use for making skewers it was formerly called *prick-wood*, i. e. skewer-wood, or *prick-timber*; see **prickwood** and *spindle tree* in Phillips. Also *spindl-y*, thin (like a spindle or skewer).

SPINDRIFT, spray blown from the tops of waves by a strong wind. (Hybrid; L. and E.) A variant of *spoon-drift* (Worcester); and *spoon* (as in Bailey) is for *spoom*, before *d*. Hence it is really *spoom-drift*, i. e. spume-drift, from L. *spūma*, foam. See **Spoom.**

SPINE, a prickle, the backbone of an animal. (F.—L.) 'Roses, their sharp *spines* being gone;' Two Noble Kinsmen, first line.— MF. *espine*, 'a thorn, prick, prickle;' Cot.—L. *spīna*, a thorn, prickle; also, the spine, the backbone. Closely allied to L. *spīca*, an ear of corn; see **Spike** (2). ¶ Observe that, in the sense of 'backbone,' the word is Latin, rather than French; from the use of Latin in medical treatises. Der. *spin-al*; *spin-y*, *spin-i-ness*; *spin-ous*; *spin-ose*: also *spin-et*, q. v.; *spinn-ey*, q. v.

SPINET, a kind of musical instrument, like a harpsichord. (F.—Ital.—L.) Obsolete. It was so called because struck with a *spine* or pointed quill. In Phillips, ed. 1706.—MF. *espinette*, 'a paire of virginals;' Cot.—Ital. *spinetta*, 'a paire of virginals; also, a little tap, spigot, or gimblet, a prick, a thorne;' Florio. Dimin. of Ital. *spina*, a thorn.—L. *spīna*, a thorn; see **Spine.**

SPINK, a finch, small bird. (Scand.) Lowland Sc. and prov. E. *spink*, chiefly used of the goldfinch. ME. *spink*. 'Hic rostellus, Anglicè, *spynke*;' Voc. 640. 38.—Swed. dial. *spink*, a field-fare, sparrow; *gul-spink*, a goldfinch (Rietz); Dan. dial. *spinke*, Norweg. *spikke* (by assimilation for *spinke*), a small bird, sparrow, finch.+ Gk. σπίγγος, a finch; cf. σπίζειν, to pipe, chirp as a small bird. Also σπίζα, a small bird. **Doublet,** *finch*.

SPINNEY, a kind of thicket. (F.—L.) 'Or shelter'd in Yorkshire *spinneys*;' Hood, Miss Kilmansegg, Her Accident, st. 4. See *Spinet* in Nares. ME. *spenné*, Gawain and Grene Knight, 1709.— OF. *espenei, espinoi*, m., Godefroy; cf. MF. *espinoye*, 'a thicket, grove, or ground full of thorns, a thorny plot;' Cot.—L. *spīnētum*, a thicket of thorns.—L. *spīna*, a thorn; see **Spine.**

SPINSTER, a woman who spins, an unmarried female. (E.)

Formerly in the sense of a woman who spins. 'She spak to *spynne-steres* to *spynnen* it oute;' P. Plowman, B. v. 216. Formed from the verb to *spin* (AS. *spinnan*) by means of the suffix *-estre* (mod. E. *-ster*). ¶ This suffix (often imperfectly explained) presents no real difficulty; it is due to the conjunction of the Idg. suffixes *-es-* and *-ter*; cf. L. *min-is-ter*. β. This AS. suffix *-es-tre* was used to denote the agent, and was conventionally confined to the feminine gender only, a restriction which was gradually lost sight of, and remains only in the word *spinster* in mod. English. Traces of the restriction remain, however, in *semp-ster-ess* or *sempstress*, and *song-ster-ess* or *songstress*, where the F. fem. suffix *-ess* has been superadded to the E. fem. suffix *-ster*. The restriction was strictly observed in AS., and is retained in Dutch; cf. Du. *spin-ster*, a spinster, *zangster*, a female singer (fem. of *zanger*), *bedriegster*, a female impostor (fem. of *bedrieger*), *inwoonster*, a female inhabitant (fem. of *inwoner*); &c. γ. Examples in AS. are the following: 'Textrix, *webbestre*,' a webster, female weaver, fem. of 'Textor, *webba*,' answering to Chaucer's *webbe* (Prol. 364), and the name *Webb*. 'Citharista, *hear-pestre*,' a female harper, fem. of 'Citharedus, *hearpere*,' a harper; Voc. 190. 6. So also: 'Fidicen, *fiðelere*; Fidicina, *fiþelestre*; Saltator, *hleapere*; Saltatrix, *hleapestre*;' id. 311. 24, 32. A striking example is afforded by AS. *witegestre*, a prophetess, Luke, ii. 36, the word being almost always used in the masc. form *witega*, a prophet. See further under **Spin**.

SPIRACLE, a breathing-hole, minute passage for air. (F.—L.) ME. *spyrakle*, Allit. Poems, ed. Morris, B. 408.—F. *spiracle*, 'a breathing-hole;' Cot.—L. *spīrāculum*, an air-hole; formed with suffix *-cu-lum*, from *spīrāre*, to breathe; see **Spirit**.

SPIRE (1), a tapering body, sprout, point, steeple. (E.) ME. *spire*, used of a blade of grass or young shoot just springing out of the ground. 'Thilke *spire* that in-to a tree shulde wexe,' Test. of Love, bk. iii. ch. v. l. 9. 'Or as an ook comth of a litel *spyr* ;' Chaucer, Troilus, iii. 1335; spelt *spir*, P. Plowman, C. xiii. 180. AS. *spir* (rare); 'hrēodes *spir*,' a spike (or stalk) of a reed, A. S. Leechdoms, ii. 266, l. 10.+Icel. *spira*, a spar, a stilt; Dan. *spire*, a germ, sprout; Swed. *spira*, a sceptre, a pistil; G. *spiere*, a spar; Westphal. *spir*, a blade of grass. Distinct from **Spire** (2); but allied to **Spike** (1), **Spile**. Der. *spire*, verb, to germinate, spring up, Spenser, F. Q. iii. 5. 52, spelt *spyer* in Palsgrave; *spir-y*, spelt *spirie* in Bacon, Nat. Hist. § 592.

SPIRE (2), a coil, wreath. (F.—L.—Gk.) 'Amidst his circling *spires*;' Milton, P. L. ix. 502. [Perhaps directly from L. *spīra*.]—F. *spire*, 'a rundle, round, or circle, a turning or winding compasse ;' Cot.—L. *spīra*, a coil, twist, wreath.—Gk. σπεῖρα, a coil, wreath. For *σπέρ-ya*. From √SPER, to wind or twine round; whence also Gk. σπυρ-ίς, a basket, σπάρ-τον, a rope. Der. *spir-al*, from F. *spiral*, 'circling,' Cot., L. *spīrālis*; *spir-al-ly*; *spir-y*, Dryden, tr. of Virgil, Georgic i. l. 334.

SPIRIT, breath; the soul, a ghost, enthusiasm, liveliness, a spirituous liquor. (F.—L.) The lit. sense is 'breath,' but the word is hardly to be found with this sense in English. ME. *spirit*, Genesis and Exodus, ed. Morris, l. 203 ; pl. *spirites*, Chaucer, C. T. 1371 (A 1369).—OF. *espirit* (Littré), later *esprit*, 'the spirit, soul,' Cot.—L. *spiritum*, acc. of *spīritus*, breath, spirit.—L. *spīrāre*, to breathe. Der. *spirit-ed*, Hen. V, iii. 5. 21 ; *spirit-ed-ly*, *-ness* ; *spirit-less*, 2 Hen. IV, i. 1. 70; *spirit-stirring*, Oth. iii. 3. 352 ; *spirit-u-al*, from F. *spirituel*, 'spirituall,' Cot., from L. *spīritu-ālis*, formed with suffix *-ālis* from *spīritu-*, decl. stem of *spīritus*; *spiritu-al-ly*; *spiritu-al-i-ty*, ME. *spiritualte*, P. Plowman, B. v. 148; *spiritu-al-ise*, *spiritu-al-ism*, *spiritu-al-ist*; *spiritu-ous*. Also (from L. *spīrāre*) a-spire, con-spire, ex-pire (for *ex-spire*), in-spire, per-spire, re-in-spire, re-spire, su-spire, tran-spire; also di-spirit; and see spir-a-cle, spright-ly. Doublet, *sprite*.

SPIRT, the same as **Spurt**, q. v.

SPIT (1), a pointed piece of wood, skewer, iron prong on which meat is roasted. (E.) ME. *spite*, *spyte*. 'And *yspited* him thoru-out mid an yrene *spite*;' Rob. of Glouc. p. 207 ; l. 4213. See also Octovian Imperator, l. 122, in Weber, Met. Romances, vol. iii.— AS. *spitu*, a spit; 'Veru, *spitu*;' Voc. 127. 11 ; later *spite*, id. 548. 25.+Du. *spit*; Dan. *spid*; Swed. *spett*; MHG. *spiz*, G. *spiess*; a spit. Teut. type **spituz*, m. Cf. G. *spitze*, a point, top. Der. *spit*, verb, ME. *spiten*, *spyten*, as in Rob. of Glouc., above. Also prov. E. *spit*, the depth a spade goes in digging, about a foot (Halliwell), with reference to the point, i. e. blade of the spade; cf. AS. *spittan*, to dig, *spit-el*, a kind of spade, Du. *spitten* (lit. to spit); quite distinct from *spade*.

SPIT (2), to throw out from the mouth. (E.) Spelt *spet* in Baret (1580). ME. *spitten*, P. Plowman, B. x. 40; pt. t. *spette*, Wyclif, John, ix. 6. AS. *spittan*, Matt. xxvii. 30 (Rushworth MS.); akin to *spætan*, with the same sense, pt. t. *spætte*, Mark, xv. 19, John, ix. 6; as if from a Teut. root **speit-*. Apparently allied to Icel. *spȳta*,

Dan. *spytte*, to spit, to sputter; Swed. *spotta*; prov. G. *spützen* (with which cf. G. *spucken* in the same sense); though these are from a Teut. base **sput-*, allied to **Spout**. Perhaps both these Teut. bases are allied to an Idg. root **spyū*; whence E. *spew*. See Brugmann, §§ 279 (1), 299, 567. Der. *spitt-le*, *spyttell* in Palsgrave, formerly *spettle* (Baret), also *spattle*, spelt *spatyll* in Palsgrave, *spotil* in Wyclif, John, ix. 6; AS. *spātl*, John, ix. 6; *spitt-oon*, not in Todd's Johnson, an ill-coined word. ¶ Note that *spat* is not the orig. past tense of *spit*, but is due to AS. *spǣtte* above, used with the same sense as the true pt. t. *spit* (Meas. for Meas. ii. 1. 86).

SPITCH-COCK, orig. to split a fat eel, and broil it on a skewer. (G.) The pp. *spitch-cock'd* occurs in 1651, in T. Cartwright, The Ordinary ; in Dodsley's Old Plays, ed. Hazlitt, xii. 239. See exx. in Palmer, Folk-Etym., where it occurs also as *spits-cocked*. Here *spits-* is from MHG. *spiz*, a spit, as in MHG. *spiz-braten*, G. *spiess-braten*, meat roasted on a spit ; and G. *kochen*, to cook. It merely means 'spit-cooked ;' cf. Du. *spit-aal*, 'a spitch-eel ;' Kalisch.

SPITE, vexation, grudge, ill-will. (F.—L.) ME. *spyt* ; 'boute *spyt* more' = without further injury, Gawayn and Grene Knight, 1444. It is merely a contraction of ME. *despit*, mod. E. *despite*. This is best shown by the phrase *in spite of*, formerly *in despite of*, as in Shak. Merry Wives, v. 5. 132, Much Ado, ii. 1. 398, iii. 2. 68, iii. 4. 89, &c. So also we have *sport* for *disport*, *spend* for *dispend*, ME. *spenser* for *dispenser*. And observe ME. *spitous*, Rom. of the Rose, 979, as a form of *despitous*, Chaucer, C. T. 6343 (D 761). See further under **Despite**. Der. *spite*, verb, Much Ado, v. 2. 70 ; *spite-ful*, Macb. iii. 5. 12, short for *despiteful*, As You Like It, v. 2. 86 ; *spite-ful-ly*, *-ness*.

SPITTLE (1), saliva. (E.) See **Spit** (2).

SPITTLE (2), a hospital. (F.—L.) 'A *spittle*, hospitall, or lazarhouse;' Baret, 1580. ME. *spitel*. *Spitel-vuel* = hospital evil, i. e. leprosy ; Ancren Riwle, p. 148, l. 8.—OF. *ospital* (Burguy), the same as OF. *hospital*, a hospital ; see **Hospital**. ¶ The loss of initial *o* must have been due to an E. accent on the *i* ; cf. W. *yspytty*, a spittle (from E.). Icel. *spītal*. **Doublet**, *hospital*.

SPLASH, to splash about water or mud, to bespatter. (Low G.) 'To *splash*, to dash any liquid upon ; *Splashy*, wet, watry ;' Bailey's Dict., vol. i. ed. 1731. Coined by prefixing *s* (OF. *es-* = L. *ex*, used for emphasis, as in *squench* (Richardson) for *quench*), to *plash*, in the same sense. 'Plashy waies, wet under foot ; to *plash* in the dirt ; all *plash'd*, made wet and dirty ; to *plash* a traveller, to dash or strike up the dirt upon him ;' MS. Lansd. 1033, by Bp. White Kennett, died A. D. 1728. Stanyhurst (1582) has *plash* for 'a splashing noise ;' tr. of Virgil (Æn. ii. 115), ed. Arber, p. 21, l. 17. ME. *plassche*, a pool ; Allit. Morte Arthure, 2798. Cf. Low G. *plasken*, to splash ; short for **platsken*, as shown under **Plash** (1), q. v.; cf. MDu. *plasch*, a pool. Der. *splash*, sb. ; *splash-y* ; *splash-board*, a board (in a vehicle) to keep off splashes.

SPLAY, to slope or slant (in architecture) ; to dislocate a shoulder-bone. (F.—L.) A contraction of *display* ; cf. *sport* for *disport*, *spite* for *despite*, *spend* for *dispend*, &c. The sense 'to dislocate' is due to the fact that *display* formerly meant to carve or cut up a crane or other bird, by disjointing it and so *displaying* it upon the dish in several pieces. 'Dysplaye that crane ;' 'splaye that breme ;' The Boke of Keruynge, pr. in 1513, repr. in 1867; see The Babees Boke, ed. Furnivall, p. 265. In architecture, to *display* is to open out, hence to slope the side of a window, &c. 'And for to *splaye* out hir leves on brede ;' Lydgate, Complaint of Black Knight, l. 33. 'Here colere *splayed*,' her collar displayed ; Cov. Myst. p. 242. See further under **Display**. Der. *splay-foot-ed*, in Minsheu, and in Ford, The Broken Heart, Act v. sc. 1. l. 13, i. e. with the foot *displayed* or turned outward, as if dislocated at the knee-joint ; shortened to *splay-foot*, as in 'splay-foot rhymes,' Butler, Hudibras, pt. i. c. 3. l. 192 ; *splay-mouth*, a mouth opened wide in scorn, a grimace, Dryden, tr. of Persius, sat. 1, l. 116.

SPLEEN, a non-glandular, highly vascular organ situate in the abdomen, supposed by the ancients to be the seat of anger and ill-humoured melancholy. (L.—Gk.) ME. *splen*, Gower, C. A. iii. 99 ; bk. vii. 449.—L. *splēn*.—Gk. σπλήν, the spleen.+Skt. *plihan-*, *plihan-*, the spleen (with loss of initial s). The true L. word is *liēn* (with loss of initial *sp*). Brugmann, i. § 549 (c). Der. *splen-et-ic*, from L. *splēnēticus* ; *splen-et-ic-al*, *splen-et-ic-al-ly* ; *splen-ic*, from L. *splēnicus* ; *spleen-it-ive*, Hamlet, v. 1. 285 ; *spleen-ful*, 2 Hen. VI, iii. 2. 128 ; *spleen-y*, Hen. VIII, iii. 2. 99.

SPLENDOR, SPLENDOUR, magnificence, brilliance. (L.; or F.—L.) Spelt *splendor* in Minsheu, ed. 1627. According to Richardson, it is spelt *splendour* in Ben Jonson, Elegy on Lady Jane Pawlet, in Underwoods, no. 100, l. 32.—F. *splendeur*, 'splendor, light ;' Cot.—L. *splendōrem*, acc. of *splendor*, brightness. [Or directly from L. nom. *splendor*.]—L. *splendēre*, to shine. Root unknown. Der. *splend-id*, Milton, P. L. ii. 252, directly from L. *splendidus*, shining, bright; *splend-id-ly*. Also *splend-ent*, spelt *splendant* in Fairfax, tr. of Tasso, b. viii. st. 84, l. 3, but from L. *splendent-*, stem of pres. part. of *splendēre*. And see *re-splendent*.

SPLENT, the same as **Splint**, q. v.

SPLEUCHAN, a tobacco-pouch. (Gael.) In Burns, Death and Dr. Hornbook, st. 14.—Gael. *spliuchan*, a tobacco-pouch; Irish *spliuchan*, a bladder, pouch, purse.

SPLICE, to join two rope-ends by interweaving the strands. (Du.) In Phillips, ed. 1706. Like many sea-terms, borrowed from Dutch.—MDu. *splissen*, 'to wreathe or lace two ends together, as of a roape;' Hexham. So named from the *splitting* of the rope-ends into separate strands before the splicing is begun; from Du. *splitsen*, to splice (which is really the older form). Formed by the addition of *s* to *split-*, weak grade of Du. *splijten*, to split, MDu. *splijten* (Hexham). See **Split**. Cf. Dan. *splidse*, *spledse*, to splice (voiced form of Du. *splitsen*); *splitte*, to split. Cf. Swed. *splissa*, to splice; G. *splissen*, to splice, *spliss*, a cleft, *spleissen*, to split. Der. *splice*, sb., Phillips, ed. 1706.

SPLINT, SPLENT, a thin piece of split wood. (Scand.) Formerly usually *splent*. 'A little *splent* to staie a broken finger;' Baret (1580). '*Splent* for an house, *laite*;' Palsgrave. It also meant a thin steel plate, for armour. '*Splent*, harnesse for the arme, *garde de bras*;' Palsgrave. ME. *splent*, Lanfrank, Cirurgie, p. 63; Morte Arthure, ed. Brock, 2061; answering to OF. *esplente*, a thin steel plate (Godefroy).—Swed. *splint*, a kind of spike; esp. (in nautical language) a forelock, i. e. a flat piece of iron driven through the end of a bolt, to secure it. So also Dan. *splint*, a splinter; NFries. *splint*, *splenn*.+Low G. *splinte*, a forelock; G. *splint*, a thin piece of iron or steel, a forelock, perhaps borrowed. Cf. Swed. *splinta* to splinter; ultimately allied to Dan. *splitte*, Swed. *splitta*, to split. See **Split**. Der. *splint-er*, Beaum. and Fletcher, Maid in the Mill, Act i. sc. 3 (Ismenia), to split into shivers, a frequentative form (with the usual frequentative suffix *-er*) from Swed. *splinta*, to split, shiver; we actually find the frequentative form in Dan. *splintre*, to splinter, Du. *splinteren*, to splinter. Also *splint-er*, sb., a shiver, small piece or chip, Cor. iv. 5. 115, with which cf. Du. and EFries. *splinter*, a splinter, *splinterig*, full of splinters; *splint-er-y*, adj. Also *splint-armour*, armour made with long and narrow overlapping plates.

SPLIT, to cleave lengthwise, to tear asunder, rend apart. (Du.) Spelt *split* in Minsheu. ed. 1627; Shak. Winter's Tale, i. 2. 349. [Palsgrave has: 'I *splette* a fysshe a-sonder, *Je ouurs*;' but this is rather ME. *splatten*, to lay open, lay flat, as in Palladius on Husbandry, b. ii. l. 123.]—MDu. *splitten*, to split; cf. Dan. *splitte*, to split; Swed. dial. *splitta*, to disentangle or separate yarn (Rietz). From the weak grade *split-* of the Teut. strong verb **spleitan-*, as seen in OFries. *splita*, Westphal. *splitan*, Du. *splijten*, to split; G. *spleissen*. We also find Dan. *split*, Du. *spleet*, a slit, split, rent, Swed. *split*, discord (a sense not unknown to English), G. *spleisse*, a splinter, a shiver, MDu. *splete*, 'a split or a cleft' (Hexham). Compare also prov. E. *sprit*, to split, Swed. *spricka*, to split. Der. *split*, sb.; also *splint*, q. v., *splice*, q. v.

SPLUTTER, to speak hastily and confusedly. (E.) Added by Todd to Johnson; and see Halliwell. A by-form of *sputter*, which is the frequentative, with the usual suffix *-er*, of *spout*, to talk fluently, orig. to squirt out; see **Sputter** and **Spout**. In the sense 'to talk,' the latter word occurs in Beaum. and Fletcher, The Coxcomb, Act iv. sc. 4: 'Pray, *spout* some French, son.' To *splutter* is to talk so fast as to be unintelligible. The old Leicest. word *spirtle*, to sprinkle, used by Drayton (Evans) is similarly formed as the frequentative of **Spurt**. Cf. Low G. *sprutten*, to spout, spurt, sprinkle.

SPOIL, to plunder, pillage. (F.—L.) ME. *spoilen*, Wyclif, Mark, iii. 27. [The sb. *spoile* occurs even earlier, in King Alisaunder, 986.]—F. *spolier*, 'to spoile, despoile;' Cot.—L. *spoliāre*, to strip of spoil, despoil.—L. *spolium*, spoil, booty; the skin or hide of an animal stripped off, and hence the dress of a slain warrior stripped from him. Root uncertain. Some have connected it with Gk. σκῦλον, spoil. ¶ It is probable that *spoil* has been to some extent confused with its compound *de-spoil*, q. v. Cf. 'Dyspoylyn or Spoylyn, Spolio;' Prompt. Parv. Der. *spoil*, sb., ME. *spoile*, as above; *spoil-er*; *spoli-at-ion*, from F. *spoliation*, 'a spoiling,' Cot., from L. acc. *spoliātiōnem*; *spoli-ate* (rare), from pp. *spoliātus*.

SPOKE, one of the bars of a wheel, from the nave to the rim. (E.) ME. *spoke*, Chaucer, C. T. 7839 (D 2257). AS. *spāca*, pl. *spācan*; 'Radii, *spācan*,' Voc. 106. 28. [The change from *ā* to long *o* is perfectly regular; cf. *stān*, a stone, *bān*, a bone.]+Du. *speek*, a spoke; G. *speiche*, OHG. *speicha*. Teut. types **spaikon-*, **spaikōn-*; allied by gradation to *spike*; see **Spike** (1). Der. *spoke-shave* (Palsgrave).

SPOKESMAN, one who speaks in behalf of others. (E.) In Shak. Two Gent. ii. 1. 152; and in Exod. iv. 16 (A.V.). The form of the word is hardly explicable; we should rather have expected to meet with *speak-s-man*, formed by analogy with *hunt-s-man*, or else with *speech-man*. As it is, the pp. *spoke* (for *spoken*) has been substituted for the infin. *speak*; see **Speak** and **Man**.

SPOLIATION. (F.—L.) See under **Spoil**.

SPONDEE, in classical poetry, a foot containing two long syllables. (L.—Gk.) Called *spondeus* in Puttenham, Art of Eng. Poesie, ed. 1589, pt. ii. c. 3. Ben Jonson has: 'The steadie *spondæes*' to translate 'Spondæos stabiles' in his tr. of Horace's Art of Poetry, l. 266. Englished from L. *spondæus* or *spondēus*.—Gk. σπονδεῖος, in metre, a spondee, so called because slow solemn melodies, chiefly in this metre, were used at σπονδαί.—Gk. σπονδαί, a solemn treaty or truce; pl. of σπονδή, a drink-offering, libation to the gods (such as were made at a treaty).—Gk. σπονδ-, 2nd grade of σπένδειν, to pour out, make a libation. Perhaps allied to **Sponsor**. Brugmann, i. § 143, ii. § 802. Der. *spond-a-ic*, L. *spondāicus*, Gk. σπονδειακός.

SPONGE, the porous framework of an animal, remarkable for sucking up water. (F.—L.—Gk.) ME. *sponge*, Ancren Riwle, p. 262, l. 2.—OF. *esponge*, 'a spunge,' Cot. Mod. F. *éponge*.—L. *spongia*.—Gk. σπογγιά, a sponge; another form of σπόγγος (Attic σφόγγος), a sponge.+L. *fungus*, a fungus, from its spongy nature. ¶ Also AS. *sponge*, Matt. xxvii. 48, directly from Latin. Der. *sponge*, verb; *spong-y*, *spong-i-ness*; also *sponge-cake*; *spunk*, q. v. Allied to *fungus*.

SPONSOR, a surety, godfather or godmother. (L.) In Phillips, ed. 1706.—L. *sponsor*, a surety, one who promises for another; cf. *spons-us*, pp. of *spondēre*, to promise. Probably allied to Gk. σπονδαί, a treaty, truce, and σπένδειν, to pour a libation, as when making a solemn treaty; see **Spondee**. Der. *sponsor-i-al*, *sponsorship*. And see *spouse*. Also (from L. *spondēre*) *de-spond*, *re-spond*, *cor-re-spond*.

SPONTANEOUS, voluntary, acting on one's own impulse. (L.) In Blount's Gloss., ed. 1674. Englished from L. *spontāneus*, willing; by change of *-us* into *-ous*, as in *arduous*, *strenuous*, &c. Formed with suffix *-āneus* from *spont-*, appearing in the gen. *spontis* and abl. *sponte* of a lost sb. **spons*. *Sponte* is used to mean ' of one's own accord;' and *spontis* occurs in the phrase *suæ spontis esse*, to be at one's own disposal, to be one's own master. Der. *spontaneous-ly*; *spontane-i-ty*, a coined word.

SPONTOON, a half-pike formerly used by officers of infantry. (F.—Ital.—L.) 'You have never a *spontoon* in the house?' Foote, Mayor of Garrat, i. 1.—F. *sponton*, *esponton* (Hatzfeld).—Ital. *spontone*, 'a gleaue, a iauelin, a partisan;' Florio. It was orig. a blunted weapon.—Ital. *spontare*, 'to abate the edge or point of anie weapon;' Florio.—Late L. **expunctare*, to blunt a point (Körting).—L. *ex*, off, away; and *punctum*, a point. See **Ex-** and **Point**.

SPOOL, a reel for winding yarn on. (MDu.) ME. *spole*, Prompt. Parv. p. 470; also in W. de Bibbesworth, in Wright's Voc. i. 157. Imported from the Netherlands, with the Flemish weavers.—MDu. *spoeie* (Hexham); Du. *spoel*, a spool, quill; Low G. *spole* (Bremen Wörterbuch).+Swed. *spole*, a spool, spoke; Dan. *spole*; G. *spule*, a spool, bobbin, quill; OHG. *spuolo*, *spuola*. Perhaps allied to Icel. *spölr* (base *spal-*), a rail, a bar.

SPOOM, to run before the wind. (L.) An old sea-term; see examples in Nares. Lit. 'to throw up foam' by running through the water. As Nares remarks, it means to sail steadily rather than swiftly. From *spume*, foam (L. *spūma*); see **Spume**. Corruptly also *spoon*; 'spooning before the wind,' Capt. Smith, Works, p. 878. Hence *spoondrift* > *spindrift*. See **Spin-drift**.

SPOON, an instrument for supping liquids. (E.) The orig. sense was simply 'a chip,' then a thin slice of wood, lastly a spoon (at first wooden). ME. *spon* (with long *o*), Chaucer, C. T. 10916 (F 602). AS. *spōn*, a chip, a splinter of wood; see examples in Bosworth. In Voc. 149. 30, the L. *fomes*, a chip for firewood, is glossed by 'geswǣlud spoon, vel *tynder*,' i. e. a kindled chip, or tinder.+Du. *spaan*, a chip, splint; Icel. *spánn*, *spónn*, a chip, shaving, spoon; Dan. *spaan*, a chip; Swed. *spån*, a chip, splint; G. *spahn*, OHG. *spān*, a very thin board, chip, splint, shaving. β. The Teut. type is **spænuz*, a chip. Cf. Gk. σφήν, a wedge. Der. *spoon-bill*, a bird; *spoon-ful*, spelt *spoonefull* in Minsheu, ed. 1627, *sponeful* in Sir T. More, Works, p. 617 (R.). ME. *sponful*, in MS. Harl. 2378, p. 25 (see Henslow, Med. Wks., p. 78); the pl. is *spoonfuls* or see exx. in R.; *spoon-meat*, Com. of Errors, iv. 3. 61. Brugmann, i. § 552.

SPOOR, a trail. (Du.) Modern; not in Todd's Johnson. Introduced from the Cape of Good Hope.—Du. *spoor*, a spur; also a trace, track, trail. Cf. Low G. *spaor*, a spoor (Danneil). Allied to **Speir** and **Spur**.

SPORADIC, scattered here and there. (Gk.) '*Sporadici Morbi*, diseases that are rife in many places;' Phillips, ed. 1706. It thus arose as a medical term. The Late L. *sporadicus* is merely borrowed from Gk. σποραδικός, scattered.—Gk. σποραδ-, stem of σποράς, scattered. — Gk. σπορ-, 2nd grade of σπείρειν, to sow, to scatter abroad. See **Sperm**.

SPORE, a minute grain which serves as a seed in ferns, &c. (Gk.) Modern and botanical. — Gk. σπόρος, seed-time; also, a seed. — Gk. σπορ-, 2nd grade of σπείρειν, to sow. See above.

SPORRAN, a leathern pouch, worn with the kilt. (Gael. — L. — Gk.) In Scott's Rob Roy, c. xxxiv. — Gael. *sporan*, a purse, pouch worn with the kilt; Irish *sparan*, a purse, a pouch; MIrish *sboran*; for **s-burr<*burs*, from L. *bursa*, a purse, from Gk. βύρση, a hide; see **Purse** (Macbain).

SPORT, play, mirth, merriment, jest. (F. — L.) '*Sporte*, myrthe;' Palsgrave. Merely a contracted form of *disport*, *desport*, by loss of *di-* or *de-*; just as we have *splay* for *display*, *spend* for *dispend*. Strat-mann cites *sport* as occurring in the Coventry Plays, ed. Halliwell, p. 185. *Disport* is in Chaucer, C. T. 777 (A 775); see further under **Disport**. Der. *sport*, verb, spelt *sporte* (also *disporte*) in Palsgrave; *sport-ing*; *sport-ful*, Tw. Nt. v. 373; *sport-ful-ly*, *sport-ful-ness*; *sport-ive*, All's Well, iii. 2. 109, *sport-ive-ly*, *-ness*; *sport-s-man* (coined like *hunt-s-man*), *sport-s-man-ship*.

SPOT, a blot, mark made by wet, a discoloured place, small space, stain. (E.) ME. *spot*, Prompt. Parv.; pl. *spottes*, P. Plowman, B. xiii. 315. [I suspect that *spat* in Ancren Riwle, p. 104, note *e*, is a misprint for *swat*.] Prob. a native word; cf. EFries. *spot*, a spot, MDu. *spotten*, to spot, stain. Also Norw. *spott*, a spot, also a small piece of land, Icel. *spotti*, *spottr*, a small piece, bit. Perhaps also allied to Swed. *spott*, spittle, *spotta*, to spit. (Distinct from G. *spott*, mockery, derision.) Apparently from Teut. **sput-*, weaker grade of **spūtan*, to spout. See **Spout**. Der. *spot*, verb, chiefly in the pp. *spott-ed*, as in Spenser, F. Q. i. 6. 26, Wyclif, Gen. xxx. 35; *spott-y*, *spott-i-ness*; *spot-less*, Rich. II, i. 1. 178, *spot-less-ly*, *spot-less-ness*. And see *spatt-er*.

SPOUSE, a husband or wife. (F. — L.) One of the oldest words in the language of F. origin. ME. *spuse*, fem. sb., O. Eng. Homilies, ed. Morris, ii. 13, l. 5; the comp. sb. *spūshād*, spousehood, also occurs in the 11th century, O. Eng. Hom. i. 143, l. 24, having already acquired an E. suffix. The form is rather fem. than masc. — OF. *espous* (Burguy), later *espoux* (*époux*), 'a spouse, bridegroome,' Cot.; fem. form *espouse* (*épouse*), 'a spouse, a wife;' id. The former answers to L. *sponsum*, a betrothed, a bridegroom; the latter to *sponsa*, fem., a betrothed woman. — L. *sponsus*, pro-mised, pp. of *spondēre*, to promise; see **Sponsor**. Der. *espouse*, verb, q. v.; also *spous-al*, ME. *spousaile*, Gower, C. A. i. 181; bk. ii. 642; a doublet of *espousal*, ME. *espousaile*, Gower, C. A. ii. 322; bk. v. 5815; see under *espouse*.

SPOUT, to throw out a liquid violently, to rush out violently as a liquid from a pipe. (E.) ME. *spouten*, Chaucer, C. T. 4907 (B 487). Prob. from an AS. form **spūtan*, not found. But cf. Du. *uit-spuiten*, to spout out (with *ui* = AS. *ū*, by rule); also Swed. *sputa*, given by Widegren as equivalent to Swed. *spruta*, to squirt, spout, spurt; MDu. *spuyten*, 'to spout out water,' Hexham. Also Icel. *spȳta*, to spit, sputter. The Teut. type is **spūtan-*, to spit out, with a weaker grade **sput-*; see Franck. ¶ It is probable that *spout* is a by-form of *sprout*; compare D. *spuit*, a spout, squirt, syringe, fire-engine, with Swed. *spruta*, a squirt, syringe, fire-engine. See **Sprout**. For loss of *r* after *sp*, cf. *speak*. Der. *spout*, sb., ME. *spoute*, spelt *spowte* in Prompt. Parv. And see *sputter*.

SPRACK, SPRAG, quick, lively. (Scand.) See **Spark** (2).

SPRAIN, to overstrain the muscles of a joint. (F. — L.) A late word. Phillips, ed. 1706, gives it as a sb. The older word with much the same sense is *strain*; and *strain* is related to OF. *espreindre* just as *strain* is to OF. *estreindre*. — OF. *espreign-*, a stem of *espreindre*, 'to press, wring, strain, squeeze out, thrust together;' Cot. Mod. F. *épreindre*. — L. *exprimere*, to press out; whence *espreindre* is formed by analogy with F. forms from L. verbs in *-ingere*. — L. *ex*, out; and *premere*, to press: see **Ex-** and **Press**. And cf. **Express**. Der. *sprain*, sb.; cf. OF. *espreinte*, 'a pressing, straining,' Cot., from the pp. *espreint*.

SPRAT, a small sea-fish. (E.) ME. *sprot* or *sprotte*. 'Hec epimera, a *sprott*,' in a list of fishes; Voc. 704. 39; also 'Emiperus, *sprot*;' Voc. 580. 6. AS. *sprott* (Toller). Cf. AS. *sprot*, a sprout, twig. +Du. *sprot*, 'a sprat, a fish;' Hexham. He also gives 'sprot, a sprout, or a sprigg of a tree, or the younge of every thing;' which is the same word. '*Sprat*, a small fish, considered as the fry of the herring;' Wedgwood. Cf. prov. E. *sprats*, smallwood (Halliwell); lit. *sprouts*. All from Teut. **sprut-* (AS. *sprot-*), weak grade of **sprūtan-*, to sprout; with the sense of 'fry,' or young one. See **Sprout**.

SPRAWL, to toss about the limbs, stretch the body carelessly when lying. (E.) ME. *spraulen*, Gower, C. A. ii. 5; bk. iv. 111 (footnote); Havelok, 475. AS. *spreawlian*; Toller cites 'Spreawlige, palpitet.'+Norw. *sprala*, Dan. *sprælle*, *sprælde*, Swed. dial. *sprala*,

spralla, N Fries. *sprawle*. Perhaps allied to Swed. *sprattla*, to sprawl; or to Icel. *sprökla*, *spraukla*, to kick with the feet, to sprawl. If so, a dental or guttural has been lost before *l*.

SPRAY (1), foam tossed with the wind. (Low G.) 'Commonly written *spry*. "Winds raise some of the salt with the *spray*;" Arbuthnot;' Johnson's Dict. But no example of the spelling *spry* is given, and it is not easy to find one. Bailey has *spray* (1735). From Low G. *sprei*, a slight drizzle (Schambach); in Coburg, *sprē*; cf. Bavar. *spræen*, to drizzle (Schmeller), Thüringen *sprähen* (Hertel), MHG. *sprǣjen*, *sprǣwen*; allied to G. *sprühen*, to drizzle, to form spray, Du. *sproeien* (see Franck).

SPRAY (2), a sprig or small shoot of a tree. (E.) ME. *spray*, Chaucer, C. T. 13700 (B 1960); Floriz and Blancheflur, ed. Lumby, 275; answering to AS. **sprǣg*, allied to *sprǣc*, a shoot, spray; cf. Dan. *sprag*, a sprig, spray (Molbech); Swed. dial. *spragge*, *spragg*, a spray (Rietz). β. Allied to Icel. *sprek*, a stick (whence *smā-sprek*, small sticks, twigs, sprays); AS. *sprǣc*, a shoot; 'Sarmentum, spraec;' Voc. 44. 29. Cf. Lithuan. *sprogti*, to crackle, split, sprout or bud as a tree; whence *sproga*, a rift, a sprig or spray of a tree, *spurgas*, a knot or eye in a tree. Also Gk. ἀσπάραγος, asparagus, of which the orig. sense was perhaps merely 'sprout' or shoot. See Brug-mann, i. 523, 531. **Doublet**, *sprig* (and perhaps *asparagus*).

SPREAD, to scatter abroad, stretch, extend, overlay, emit, diffuse. (E.) ME. *spreden*, pt. t. *spradde*, *spredde*, pp. *sprad*, *spred*, P. Plow-man, B. iii. 308; pt. t. *spradde*, Gower, C. A. i. 182; bk. ii. 684. AS. *sprǣdan*, to spread out, extend, a rare word. It occurs as *gespraed*, imper. sing. = extend thou, stretch out, in the Northumb. version of Matt. xii. 13; and the comp. *ofer-sprǣdan*, to spread over, is in the Rule of St. Bennet, ed. Schröer, p. 109, l. 7.+Du. *spreiden*, to spread, scatter, strew; Low G. *spreden*, *spreën*, *spreien*; G. *spreiten*. Teut. type **spraidjan-*, a causal form, from the older base SPREID, to become extended, spread out. Der. *spread*, sb.; *over-spread*.

SPREE, a merry frolic. (Scand.?) Modern and colloquial. Sir W. Scott has *spree*, St. Ronan's Well, ch. xx. § 11; also *spray*, Introd. to Legend of Montrose. Cf. Irish *spre*, a spark, flash of fire, animation, spirit. Cf. Irish *sprac*, a spark, life, motion, *spraic*, strength, vigour, sprightliness, Gael. *spraic*, vigour, exertion, *spracadh*, sprightliness; not Celtic, but from Icel. *sprǣkr*, lively. See **Spry**. See Notes on E. Etym., p. 278.

SPRIG, a spray, twig, small shoot of a tree. (E.) ME. *sprigge*, a rod for beating children, stick; P. Plowman, C. vi. 139 (footnote). Allied to AS. *sprǣc*, a spray, twig; Voc. 44. 29.+Icel. *sprek*, a stick; Low G. *sprikk*, a sprig, twig, esp. a small dry twig or stick; EFries. *sprikke*, *sprik*, a stick, twig. Allied to Dan. *sprag*, a spray (Molbech); see further under **Spray** (2).

SPRIGHTLY, SPRITELY, lively. (F. — L.; *with E. suffix*.) The common spelling *sprightly* is wrong; *gh* is a purely E. com-bination, whereas the present word is French. The mistake was due to the very common false spelling *spright*, for *sprite*, a spirit; see **Sprite**. The suffix *-ly* is from AS. *-līc*, like; see **Like**. Der. *spright-li-ness*.

SPRING, to bound, leap, jump up, start up or forth, issue. (E.) ME. *springen*, strong verb, pt. t. *sprang*, pp. *sprungen*, *sprongen*; Chaucer, C. T. 13690 (B 1950). AS. *springan*, *sprincan*; pt. t. *sprang*, *spranc*, pp. *sprungen*. The spelling *springan* is the usual one, Matt. ix. 26. But we find *sprincð* = springs, Ælfred, tr. of Boethius, cap. xxv (lib. iii. met. 2). And in Matt. ix. 26, where the AS. version has 'þes hlisa *sprang* ofer eall þæt land' = this rumour spread abroad over all the land, the Northumbrian version has *spranc*.+Du. *springen*, pt. t. *sprong*, pp. *gesprongen*; Icel. *springa*, to burst, split; Swed. *springa*; Dan. *springe*; G. *springen*. β. All from the Teut. type **sprengan*, pt. t. **sprang*, pp. **sprunganoz*. Allied to Gk. σπέρχειν, to drive on; Brugmann, i. § 602. (√SPERGH.) γ. We still say of a cricket-bat that is cracked or split, that it is *sprung*; and cf. Prov. E. (Eastern) *sprinke*, a crack or flaw (Halliwell), where we even find the original E. final *k*; also Essex *sprunk*, to crack, split, E. Anglian *sprank*, a crack; E. D. D. The sense 'to split, burst' is that of Icel. *springa*. Der. *spring*, sb., a leap, also the time when young shoots spring or rise out of the ground, also a source of water that wells up, a crack in a mast, &c.; *spring-y*; *spring-bok*, a kind of antelope, from Du. *bok*, a he-goat, a buck; *spring-halt* (in horses), Hen. VIII, i. 3. 13; *spring-time*, As You Like It, v. 3. 20; *spring-flood*, ME. *spring-flod*, Chaucer, C. T. 11382 (F 1070); *spring-tide*; *day-spring*, *off-spring*, *well-spring*. Also *springe*, a snare that is provided with a flexible rod, called a *springe* in ME., as in P. Plowman, B. v. 41. And see *sprink-le*. ¶ To *spring* a mine is to cause it to burst; cf. Swed. *spränga*, to cause to burst, causal of *springa*, to burst.

SPRINGAL, a youngster. (E.; *with F. suffix*.) In Spenser, F. Q. v. 10. 6. Spelt *springall* in Minsheu; *spring-ald* in Levins

(1570). From *spring*, i. e. to be alert; with suffix *-ald*, of F. origin, from OHG. *-wald*, as in *her-ald*, &c.

SPRINKLE, to scatter in small drops. (Du. ?) In Spenser, F. Q. iii. 12. 13. A better form is *sprenkle*, written *sprenkyll* by Palsgrave, and *sprenkelyn* in the Prompt. Parv. Perhaps borrowed from Du. *sprenkelen*, to sprinkle. Cf. G. *sprenkeln*, to speckle, from MHG. *sprenkel*, a spot, allied to Icel. *sprekla*, Swed. *spräkla*, a little spot. See Kluge, s. v. *sprenkel* (who denies a connexion with *spring*). It seems to be allied to Skt. *pṛç-ni-*, speckled; see **Perch** (2). Brugmann, i. 509 (1). ¶ Distinct from ME. *sprengen*, to scatter, cast abroad, sprinkle. '*Sprengeð* ou mid hali water' = sprinkle yourselves with holy water, Ancren Riwle, p. 16, l. 9. From AS. *sprengan*, to sprinkle, scatter abroad, Matt. xxv. 24, Exod. xxiv. 8; A. S. Leechdoms, ed. Cockayne, i. 264, l. 15. This *sprengan* is the causal of AS. *sfringan*, to spring, leap abroad, regularly formed by the change of *a* (in the pt. t. *sprang*) to *e*, as if for *sprangjan. See **Spring**. Der. *sprinkle*, sb., a holy-water sprinkler, see Spenser, F. Q. iii. 12. 13; *sprinkl-er*.

SPRINT, to run at full speed; see **Spurt** (2).

SPRIT, a spar set diagonally to extend a fore-and-aft sail. (E.) The older sense is merely a pole or long rod, and an older spelling is found in ME. *spret*. 'A *spret* or an ore' = a sprit or an oar; Will. of Palerne, 2754; spelt *spreot*, King Alisaunder, 858. AS. *sprēot*, a pole. 'Contus, *sprēot*;' Voc. 139. 39; cf. 14. 22. 'Trudes, *sprēotas*,' in a list of things belonging to a ship; id. 166. 15. The orig. sense is 'a sprout,' or shoot, hence a branch, pole, &c. Allied to AS. *sprūtan*, to sprout; cognate with G. *spriessen*; see further under **Sprout**.✛Du. *spriet*, a sprit; MSwed. *spröte*; Dan. *spryd*, *spröd*. Der. *sprit-sail*, *bow-sprit*. Doublet, *sprout*.

SPRITE, **SPRIGHT**, a spirit. (F.—L.) The false spelling *spright* is common, and is still in use in the derived adj. *sprightly*. Spelt *sprite* in Spenser, F. Q. i. 1. 40, 43; but *spright*, id. i. 2. 2. 'Legions of *sfrights*,' id. i. 1. 38. ME. *sfrit*, *sprite*, *spryte*; 'the holy *spryte*,' Rich. Coer de Lion, 394.—F. *esprit*, 'the spirit,' Cot.—L. *spiritum*, acc. of *spiritus*. It is a doublet of **Spirit**, q. v. Der. *spright-ly* or *sprite-ly*; *spright-ed*, haunted, Cymb. ii. 3. 144; *spright-ful* or *sprite-ful*, K. John, iv. 2. 177; *spright-ful-ly*, Rich. II, i. 3. 3; *spright-ing*, Temp. i. 2. 298. Doublet, *spirit*.

SPROUT, to shoot out germs, burgeon, bud. (E.) Spelt *sprut* in Fitzherbert, Husbandry, § 13, l. 38 (E. D. S.). ME. *spruten*, Cursor Mundi, 11216; O. Eng. Homilies, ii. 217, l. 23. From AS. *sprūtan*, found in the pp. *ā-sproten*; OFris. *sprūta*, strong verb, pp. *spruten*, to sprout (Richtofen).✛Low G. *srūten*, to sprout; Du. *spruiten*; G. *spriessen*, to sprout, pt. t. *spross*, pp. *gesprossen*. The cognate Swed. *spruta* is only used in the sense to spout or squirt out water, and perhaps is the word whence E. *spout* is derived, by loss of *r*; see **Spout**, **Spurt** (1). β. All from a Teut. type **sprūtan-*, pt. t. *spraut, pp. *sprutanoz. We may also notice that E. *sprout* as a sb. is related to Du. *spruit*, Icel. *sproti*, G. *spross*, a sprout; cf. also AS. *sprot*, *sprota*, a sprout; and that E. *sprit*, q. v., is allied to the same words. Cf. Goth. *sprautō*, quickly. Der. *sprout*, sb. And see *spout*, *sprit*, *sprat*.

SPRUCE, fine, smart, gaily dressed. (F.—G.) In Shak. L. L. L. v. 1. 14; and in Minsheu, ed. 1627. 'It was the custom of our ancestors, on special occasions, to dress after the manner of particular countries. The gentlemen who adopted that of Prussia or *Spruce* seem, from the description of it, to have been arrayed in a style, to which the epithet *spruce*, according to our modern usage, might have been applied with perfect propriety. Prussian leather (*corium Pruscianum*) is called in Baret by the familiar name of *spruce*;' Richardson; see Baret, art. 781. Richardson then quotes from Hall's Chron. Hen. VIII, an. 1, § 25, as follows: 'And after them came syr Edward Haward, than Admyral, and wyth hym Syr Thomas Parre, in doblettes of crimosin veluet, voyded lowe on the backe, and before to the cannell-bone, lased on the breastes with chaynes of siluer, and ouer that shorte clokes of crimosyn satyne, and on their heades hattes after dauncers fashion, with feasauntes fethers in theim: They were appareyled after the fashion of Prusia or *Spruce*.' There may have been special reference to the leather worn; the name of *spruce* was especially given to the leather because it came from Prussia. Levins has: 'Corium pumicatum, *Spruce*;' col. 182, l. 14. '*Spruce leather*, corruptly so called for *Prussia* leather;' Phillips, ed. 1706. '*Spruce leather*, graauw leer, Pruysch leer,' i.e. gray leather, or *Prussian* leather; Sewel's Eng.-Du. Dict., 1749. [E. Müller objects that it is difficult to see why *Prussia* should always be called *Spruce*, not *Pruce*, in this particular instance; but the name, once associated with the leather, would easily remain the same, especially as the etymology may not have been very obvious to all. It is a greater difficulty to know why the *s* should ever have been prefixed, but it may be attributed to the English fondness for initial *s*; or it may have arisen from the G.

das Preussen.] It is sufficient to make sure that *Spruce* really did mean Prussia, and really *was* used instead of *Pruce*. Of this we have positive proof as early as the 14th century. 'And yf ich sente ouer see my seruaunt to brugges, Oþer in-to *prus* my prentys' = and if I sent my servant over the sea to Bruges, or sent my apprentice to Prussia; P. Plowman, C. vii. 279; where two MSS. read *spruce* for *prus*, and one MS. has *pruys-lond* = Prussian land, the land of Prussia. In the corresponding passage of P. Plowman, B. xiii. 393, three MSS. have *pruslonde*, *pruys londe*, and *pruce-lond* respectively; but a fourth has *spruce-land*. *Pruce* is the form in Chaucer, C. T. 53 (a well-known passage). β. Further, we find *Sprwys-chyst* (Spruce chest) in Paston Letters, iii. 407, but *prowce-kyst* in Records of Nottingham, ii. 86; *spruce hutche* in the Bury Wills (1493), p. 82, but *pruce hutche* (1448), p. 12. And Prussia is called *Sprucia* as late as 1614; see Eng. Garner, ed. Arber, iv. 329, 345. γ. We conclude that to dress *sprucely* was to dress after the *Prussian* manner; that *Spruce* was early used in place of *Pruce*, particularly with reference to Prussian leather; and consequently that *spruce* is due to OF. *Pruce*, mod. F. *Prusse*, Prussia.—G. *Preussen*, Prussia (or from an older form of the same). Der. *spruce-ly*, *spruce-ness*.

SPRUCE-BEER, a kind of beer. (G.; *confused with* F. *and* E.) '*Spruce-beer*, a kind of physical drink, good for inward bruises;' Phillips, ed. 1706. '*Spruce-beer*, and the beer of Hambur;' Colyn Blowbol's Testament, 332, in Hazlitt, E. Eng. Popular Poetry, i. 106. '*Essence of spruce* is obtained from the young shoots of the black spruce fir. . . . *Spruce beer* is brewed from this essence. . . . The black beer of Dantzig is similarly made from the young shoots of another variety of fir;' Eng. Cycl., Supp. to Arts and Sciences. 'A decoction of the young shoots of *spruce* and silver fir was much in use on the shores of the Baltic as a remedy in scorbutic, gouty, and rheumatic complaints. The sprouts from which it was made were called *sprossen* in German and *jopen* in Dutch, and the decoction itself *sprossen-bier* [in German] or *jopenbier* [in Dutch]. From the first of these is *spruce-beer*. See Beke in N. and Q. Aug. 3, 1860. And doubtless the *spruce-fir*, G. *sprossenfichte*, takes its name as the fir of which the sprouts are chiefly used for the foregoing purpose, and not from being brought from Prussia, as commonly supposed;' Wedgwood. β. The above explanation may be admitted; but with the addition that the *reason why* the G. word *sprossen-bier* was turned into *spruce-beer* in English is precisely because it was commonly known that it came from Prussia; and since *sprossen-bier* had no sense in English and was not translated into *sprouts-beer*, it was natural to call it *Spruce-beer*, i.e. Prussian beer. The facts, that *Spruce* meant Prussia as early as the 14th century, and that *spruce* or *spruce-leather* was already in use to signify Prussian leather, have been proved in the article above; see **Spruce**. Thus *spruce-beer* for *sprossen-bier* was no mere corruption, but a deliberate substitution. Accordingly, we find in Evelyn's Sylva, ch. 22, the remark: 'For masts, &c., those [firs] of *Prussia* which we call *Spruce*.' γ. With this understanding, we may admit that *spruce-beer* is one of the very few words in English which are derived immediately from German.—G. *sprossenbier*, spruce-beer, lit. 'sprouts-beer;' G. *sprossenfichte*, spruce-fir; *sprossenessenz*, spruce-wine.—G. *sprossen*, pl. of *sprosse*, a sprout, cognate with E. *sprout*; and *bier*, cognate with E. *beer*; see **Sprout** and **Beer**. Note also Du. *joopen-bier*, 'spruce-beer;' Sewel's Du. Dict. ed. 1754. The word *spruce* = Prussia, is French, from G. (*das*) *Preussen*, as shown above.

SPRY, active, nimble, lively. (E.) Added by Todd to Johnson. Given by Halliwell as a Somersetsh. word, but general; see E. D. D. Perhaps E. Cf. Swed. dial. *sprygg*, very lively, skittish (as a horse), Rietz; allied to Swed. dial. *spräg*, *sprák*, or *spräker*, spirited, mettlesome. Compare also prov. E. *sprag* (Halliwell); and *sprack*, active, a Wiltshire word. See **Spree** and **Spark** (2).

SPUD, an instrument for weeding. (Scand.) See E. D. D. It formerly also meant a knife or dagger; see Nares. ME. *spudde*, 'cultellus vilis;' Prompt. Parv. Prob. from Dan. *spyd*, MDan. *spyd*, *spjud*; cognate with Swed. *spjut*, Icel. *spjōt*, a spear, lance.✛G. *spiess*, a lance. ¶ Distinct from **Spit** (1).

SPUE, the same as **Spew**, q.v.

SPUME, foam. (L.) Not common. ME. *spume*, Gower, C. A. ii. 265; bk. v. 4122.—L. *spūma*, foam. For *spoima; Brugmann, i. § 791. Allied to Skt. *phēna-*, foam, Russ. *piena*, foam, AS. *fām*; see **Foam**. Der. *spoom*, verb, q. v.; *pum-ice*, q. v.; *pounce* (2), q. v. Doublet, *foam*.

SPUNK, tinder; hence, a match, spark, spirit, mettle. (C.—L. —Gk.) Also *sponk*; see examples in Jamieson and Halliwell. 'In *spunck* or tinder;' Stanyhurst, tr. of Virg. Æn. i. 175; ed. Arber, p. 23. The orig. sense is tinder or touchwood.—Irish *sponc*, Gael. *pong*, sponge, tinder, touchwood; applied to touchwood from its spongy nature.—L. *spongia*, a sponge; hence pumice-stone, or other porous material.—Gk. σπογγία, σπόγγος, a sponge; see **Sponge**.

SPUR, an instrument on a horseman's heels, for goading on a horse, a small goad. (E.) ME. *spure, spore,* Chaucer, C. T. 475 (A 473); P. Plowman, B. xviii. 12. AS. *spura, spora.* 'Calcar, *spura*;' Voc. 275. 33. Cf. *hand-spora,* a hand-spur, Beowulf, 986 (Grein). **+**Du. *spoor,* a spur; allied to *spoor,* a track; see **Spoor**; Icel. *spori*; Dan. *spore*; Swed. *sporre*; OHG. *sporo*; MHG. *spor*; G. *sporn.* β. All from **spor-,* weak grade of Teut. **sper-an-,* to kick. Brugmann, i. § 793 (2). From √SPER, to quiver, to jerk, which appears in G. *sich sperren,* to struggle against; one sense of this root is to kick, jerk out the feet, as in Lithuan. *spirti,* to resist, 'o kick out as a horse; cf. Skt. *sphur, sphar,* to throb, to struggle. Hence the sense of *spur* is 'kicker.' γ. A closely allied word occurs in AS. *spor,* a foot-trace, Du. *spoor,* Icel. *spor,* G. *spur* (see **Spoor**); whence was formed the verb appearing as AS. *spyrian,* Icel. *spyrja,* G. *spüren,* to trace a foot-track, to investigate, enquire into, represented by Lowland Sc. *speir,* to enquire, ask, search out. Der. *spur,* verb, ME. *spurien, sporien,* Layamon, 21354; Romance of Partenay, 4214. Also *spur-wheel;* and see *spoor, speir, spurn.*

SPURGE, a class of acrid plants. (F.—L.) 'Spurge, a plant, the juice of which is so hot and corroding that it is called *Devil's Milk,* which being dropped upon warts eats them away;' Bailey's Dict., vol. i. ed. 1735. And hence the name. ME. *sporge,* Prompt. Parv.; *spowrge,* Voc. 645. 15.—AF. *spurge,* a form given in Voc. 557. 7; more commonly OF. *espurge,* 'garden spurge;' Cot.—OF. *espurger,* 'to purge, cleer, cleanse, rid of; also, to prune, or pick off the noysome knobs or buds of trees;' Cot. Hence, to destroy warts.—L. *expurgāre,* to expurgate, purge thoroughly.—L. *ex,* out, thoroughly; and *purgāre,* to purge; see **Ex-** and **Purge**.

SPURIOUS, not genuine. (L.) In Milton, Samson, 391. Englished from L. *spurius,* false, spurious, by the common change of *-us* to *-ous,* as in *arduous,* &c. The orig. sense is 'of illegitimate birth;' perhaps allied to Gk. σπορά, seed, offspring, σπείρειν, to sow (Corssen); see **Sperm.** Der. *spurious-ly, -ness.*

SPURN, to reject with disdain. (E.) Properly 'to kick against,' hence to kick away, reject disdainfully. ME. *spurnen,* to kick against, stumble over, Ancren Riwle, p. 188, l. 2. 'Spornyng, or Spurnyng, Calcitracio;' Prompt. Parv. AS. *spornan, spurnan, gespornan,* to kick against; cf. also *æt-spornan,* Matt. iv. 6, John, xi. 9. A strong verb; pt. t. *spearn,* pl. *spurnon,* pp. *spornen.* **+**Icel. *sperna,* pt. t. *sparn,* to spurn, kick with the feet; L. *spurnere,* to spurn, despise (a cognate form, not one from which the E. word is borrowed, for the E. verb is a strong one). All from the Idg. base **spern,* to kick against, an extension from √SPER, to quiver, jerk, also to kick against; see **Spur** and **Spar** (3). Der. *spurn,* sb., Timon, i. 2. 146; Chevy Chase (oldest version), near the end.

SPURRY, the name of a herb. (F.—G.—Late L.) In Cotgrave. —MF. *spurrie,* 'spurry or frank, a Dutch herb, and an excellent fodder for cattle;' Cot. By 'Dutch' he prob. means 'German;' we find Du. *spurrie,* 'the herb spurge,' in Hexham; but this can hardly be other than the F. word borrowed. The etymology of the F. word is doubtful, but it may be German, as Cotgrave seems to suggest. We find in German the forms *spark, spergel, spörgel,* all meaning spurry.—Late L. *spergula;* A. D. 1482 (Weigand). It looks as if it might be connected with L. *spargere,* to scatter.

SPURT (1), **SPIRT,** to spout, jet out, as water. (E.) 'With toonge three-forcked furth *spirts* fyre;' Stanyhurst, tr. of Virgil, Æn. ii. ed. Arber, p. 59. The older meaning is to sprout or germinate, to grow fast; as in Hen. V, iii. 5. 8. We even find the sb. *spirt,* a sprout; 'These nuts . . . haue in their mids a little chit or *spirt*;' Holland, tr. of Pliny, b. xv. c. 22. Cf. 'from Troy blud *spirted*;' Stanyhurst, tr. of Virgil, Æn. i. ed. Arber, p. 35. By the common metathesis of *r* (as ME. *brid* for *bird*) *spurt* stands for *sprut;* as in ME. *sprutten;* 'þe wiði þet *sprutteð* ut' = the willow that sprouts or shoots out; Ancren Riwle, p. 86. AS. *spryttan, spritten;* 'spritte sēo eorðe grōwende gærs' = let the earth shoot out growing grass; Gen. i. 11. A causal verb, allied to the AS. strong verb *sprūtan,* to sprout; see **Sprout.** Cf. prov. E. *sprit,* to sprout; E. D. D.; and see **Spout.**

SPURT (2), a violent exertion. (Scand.) Used by Stanyhurst in the sense of 'space of time;' as, 'Heere for a *spirt* linger,' tr. of Virgil, Æn. iii. 453. Not the same word as the above, though perhaps confused with it.—Icel. *sprettr,* a spurt, spring, bound, run; from the strong verb *spretta* (pt. t. *spratt*), to start, to spring; also to spout out water; also to sprout. Cf. Swed. *spritta,* to start, startle; prov. E. *sprit,* to run quickly a short way (E. D. D.). The Teut. base is **sprent* (*tt < nt*); hence also E. *sprint,* to run a quick short race; which is the doublet of *spurt,* vb., to run fast. Cf. Swed. dial. *sprinnta,* to burst (as a bud); to run fast, to jump. The orig. *n* of the base SPRENT is also preserved in prov. E. *sprunt,* a convulsive struggle, *Warwickshire* (Halliwell).

SPUTTER, to keep spouting or jerking out liquid, to speak rapidly and indistinctly. (E.) 'And lick'd their hissing jaws, that *sputter'd* flame;' Dryden, tr. of Æneid, ii. 279 (ii. 211, Lat. text). The frequentative of **Spout,** q. v.; so that the sense is 'to keep on spouting.' From *sput-,* weaker grade of Teut. **spūtan-,* to spout. Cf. Du. dial. (Groningen) *spöttern,* to sputter; Low G. *sputtern;* Norw. *sputra,* to spout. ¶ Not to be confused with *spatter,* which is a different word, and allied to *spot.*

SPY, to see, discover. (F.—OHG.) Short for *espy.* ME. *spien,* Rob. of Brunne, tr. of Langtoft, p. 40, l. 14. [The ME. *spie,* sb., a spy, occurs in Floriz and Blancheflur, ed. Lumby, l. 332.] The same word as ME. *espien,* Chaucer, C. T. 4744 (B 324); House of Fame, l. 706.—OF. *espier,* to espy.—OHG. *spehôn,* MHG. *spehen* (mod. G. *spähen*), to watch, observe closely.**+**L. *specere,* to look; Skt. *pac, spac,* to spy; used to form some tenses of *dr̥ç,* to see.—√SPEK, to see; Brugmann, i. § 551. Der. *spy,* sb., as above; *spy-glass;* also (from *espy*) *espi-on-age, espi-al.* From L. *specere* we have *spice, spec-i-es, spec-i-al, espec-i-al, spec-i-men, spec-i-fy, spec-i-ous, spec-u-late; au-spice, con-spic-u-ous, de-spic-able, fronti-spiece, per-spic-u-ous, su-spic-i-ous, tran-spic-uous; de-spise, de-spite; a-spect, circum-spect, ex-pect, in-spect, intro-spect-ion, per-spect-ive, pro-spect, re-spect, dis-re-spect, ir-re-spect-ive, retro-spect, su-spect, spect-a-cle, spect-a-tor, spect-re, spect-rum;* also *spite, respite.*

SQUAB, 1. to fall plump; 2. a sofa; a young bird. (Scand.) 'Squab, an unfledged bird, the young of an animal before the hair appears (South); a long seat, a sofa; also, to squeeze, beat (Devon);' Halliwell. Halliwell also cites from Coles: 'A *squob* to sit on, *pulvinus mollicellus*;' this is not in the edition of 1684. *Squab,* a sofa, is in Pope, Imitation of Earl of Dorset, l. 10. Johnson also explains *squab* as 'unfeathered; fat, thick and stout;' and gives *squab,* adv., 'with a heavy, sudden fall, plump and flat,' with a quotation from Lestrange's Fables: 'The eagle took the tortoise up into the air, and dropt him down, *squab,* upon a rock;' also *squab,* verb, to fall down plump or flat; cf. prov. E. *squap,* to strike. In all senses, the word is of Scand. origin. 1. The Swed. dial. *sqvapp,* a word imitative of a splash (Rietz), explains Lestrange's *squab* and the verb 'to fall plump,' hence to knock, beat; cf. G. *schwapp,* a slap, E. *swap,* to strike; see **Swap** and **Squabble.** 2. The senses 'fat,' 'unfledged,' and 'soft' (as a sofa) are best explained by Swed. dial. *sqvabb,* loose or fat flesh, *sqvabba,* a fat woman, *sqvabbig,* flabby; from the verb appearing in Norweg. *sqvapa,* to tremble, shake (hence, to be flabby). Cf. also Norweg. *kveppa* (pt. t. *kvapp*), to slip suddenly, shake, shudder, and the ME. *quappen,* to throb, mentioned under **Quaver,** q. v. And note Icel. *kvap,* jelly, jelly-like things. See, in Rietz, the Swed. dial. str. vb. *skvimpa* (pt. t. *skvamp,* pp. *skvumpen*), to shake, agitate; and cf. Swed. *sqvalpa,* MDan. *skvalpe,* to shake.

SQUABBLE, to dispute noisily, wrangle. (Scand.) In Shak. Oth. ii. 3. 281.—Swed. dial. *skvabbel,* a dispute, a squabble (corresponding to a verb **skvabbla,* not given); Rietz. Allied to Swed. dial. *skvappa,* to chide, scold slightly, lit. make a splashing; from the sb. *skvapp,* a splash, an imitative word from the sound of dabbling in water; Rietz. Cf. Icel. *skvampa,* to paddle in water. We may also further compare Norweg. *svabba,* to dabble in water (Aasen), prov. E. *swap,* a blow, the noise of a fall, to strike swiftly, *swab,* to splash over, *swabble,* to squabble, *swobble,* to swagger in a low manner (East). 'Swablynge, swabbyng, or swaggynge;' Prompt. Parv. Also G. *schwabbeln,* to shake fluids about. See **Swap.** ¶ The interchange of initial *squ* and *sw* is common; Levins writes *squayne* for swain. Der. *squabble,* sb., *squabbl-er.*

SQUAD, a small troop. (F.—Ital.—L.) We speak of 'an awkward *squad.*'—MF. *esquadre, escadre,* 'a squadron of footmen;' Cot. —Ital. *squadra,* 'a squadron;' Florio. See **Square.** Der. *squadr-on.*

SQUADRON, a troop of soldiers, a body of cavalry, number of ships. (F.—Ital.—L.) In Oth. i. 1. 22; Spenser, F. Q. ii. 8. 2.— MF. *esquadron,* 'a squadron, a troope of souldiers ranged into a square body or battalion,' Cot.—Ital. *squadrone,* 'a squadrone, a troupe or band of men;' Florio. The augmentative form (with suffix *-one* < L. acc. *-ōnem*) of Ital. *squadra,* 'a squadron, also a square, squire, or carpenter's ruler, also a certain part of a company of souldiers of 20 or 25 [25 is a square number], whose chiefe is a corporall;' id. Doubtless so called, at first, from a formation into squares; see further under **Square.** And see *squad.*

SQUALID, filthy, dirty. (L.) In Spenser, F. Q. v. 1. 13.—L. *squālidus,* stiff, rough, dirty, foul.—L. *squālēre,* to be stiff, rough, or parched, to be dirty. Bréal connects it with *squā-ma,* a shell; but cf. Russ. *kal',* ordure. Der. *squalid-ly, -ness.* Also *squal-or* (rare), from *squāl-ēre.*

SQUALL, to cry out violently. (Scand.) 'The raven croaks, the carrion-crow doth *squall*;' Drayton, Noah's Flood, l. 150 from end.—Icel. *skvala,* to squeal, bawl out; *skval,* a squalling; Swed.

sqvala, to stream, gush out violently; *sqval*, an impetuous running of water; *sqval-regn*, a violent shower of rain (whence E. *squall*, sb., a burst of rain); Dan. *sqvaldre*, to clamour, bluster; *sqvalder*, clamour, noisy talk. Cf. Swed. dial. *skvala*, *skvåla*, to gush out with a violent noise, to prattle, chatter; Gael. *sgal*, a loud cry, sound of high wind, *sgal*, to howl; cf. W. *chwalu*, to babble. β. From a base **skwal*, expressive of the outburst of water; allied to Teut. base SKAL, to resound, as in G. *schallen*, Icel. *skjalla* (pt. t. *skall*). **Der.** *squall*, sb., as above; *squall-y*. And see *squeal*.

SQUANDER, to dissipate, waste. (Scand.) Now used only of profuse expenditure, but the orig. sense was to scatter or disperse simply, as still used in prov. E. 'His family are all grown up, and *squandered* [dispersed] about the country,' Warwicksh. (Halliwell). '*Squandered* [scattered] abroad;' Merch. of Ven. i. 3. 22. 'Spaine . . . hath many colonies to supply, which lye *squandered* up and down;' Howell, Foreign Travel, sect. ix, ed. Arber, p. 45. 'All along the sea They drive and *squander* the huge Belgian fleet;' Dryden, Annus Mirabilis, st. 67. Mr. Wedgwood's solution of this curious word is probably the right one, viz. that it is a nasalised form (as if for **squanter*) of Northumb. *squatter*, *squather*, to scatter, dissipate, or squander, to act with profusion (Jamieson). This is the same as prov. E. *swatter*, *swather*, to throw water about, as geese do in drinking, also, to squander, waste; also as prov. E. *swattle*, to drink as ducks do water, to waste; see E. D. D. These are frequentatives from Dan. *sqvatte*, to splash, spurt; figuratively, to dissipate, squander; cf. *sqvat*, sb., a splash. So also Swed. *sqvättra*, to squander, lavish one's money (Widegren); frequentative of *sqvätta*, to squirt (id.); Swed. dial. *skwätta*, a strong verb (pt. t. *skwatt*, supine *skwuttið*), to squirt. Note also Icel. *skvetta*, to squirt out water, properly of the sound of water thrown out of a jug, *skvettr*, a gush of water poured out. The *d* appears in MDu. *swadderen*, 'to dabble in the water as a goose or duck,' Hexham; and in Swed. dial. *skvadra*, verb, used of the noise of water gushing violently out of a hole (Rietz). The word is now used metaphorically, but the orig. sense was merely to splash water about somewhat noisily. The Icel. *skvetta* is for **skwenta* (Noreen); and may even be allied to Gk. σπένδειν, to pour out. A somewhat similar word is E. *scatter*. **Der.** *squander-er*.

SQUARE, having four equal sides and angles. (F. — L.) ME. *square* (dissyllabic), Chaucer, C. T. 1078 (A 1076); Cursor Mundi, 19843. — OF. *esquarré*, 'square, or squared,' Cot.; *esquarre*, sb., a square, or squareness. The sb. is the same as Ital. *squadra*, 'a squadron, also a square, squire, or carpenter's ruler;' cf. Ital. *squadrare*, 'to square,' id. All formed from a Late L. verb **exquadrāre*, not found, but a mere intensive of L. *quadrāre*, to square, make four-cornered, by prefixing the prep. *ex*. The verb *quadrāre* is from *quadrus*, four-cornered, related to *quatuor*, four, cognate with E. *four*. See **Ex-, Quarry, Quadrant,** and **Four.** **Der.** *square*, sb., *square*, verb, *square-ly*, *-ness*. Also *squire* (2), q. v., *squad*, *squadr-on*.

SQUASH, to crush, to squeeze flat. (F. — L.) *a*. No doubt commonly regarded as an intensive form of *quash*; the prefix *s-* answering to OF. *es-*=L. *ex-*. Cf. OF. *esquasser*, to break in pieces; from *es-* (L. *ex*), intensive prefix, and *quasser*, *casser*, to break; see **Quash.** β. But it commonly keeps the sense of ME. *squachen*, Barlaam and Josaphat, l. 663, pr. in Altenglische Legenden, ed. Horstmann, p. 224. — OF. *esquacher*, to crush (Roquefort, who gives a quotation); also spelt *escacher*, 'to squash, beat, batter, or crush flat;' Cot. Mod. F. *écacher*. This answers to Span. *acachar*, *agachar*, only used reflexively, in the sense to squat, to cower (Diez). The F. *cacher* answers to a Late L. type **co-act-icāre*, to press together (Körting, § 2272). The prefix *es-*=L. *ex-*, extremely; hence *es-cacher* is 'to press extremely,' crush flat, squash.—L. *ex-*; and *coact-us*, pp. of *cōgere* (=*co-agere*), lit. to drive together; see **Ex-, Cogent;** also **Con-** and **Agent.** And see **Squat,** a closely allied word. **Der.** *:quash*, a soft, unripe peascod, Tw. Nt. i. 5. 166.

SQUAT, to cower, sit down upon the hams. (F. — L.) 'To *squatte* as a hare doth;' Minsheu, ed. 1627. Here *squat* is to lie flat, as if pressed tightly down; and the old sense of *squat* is, occasionally, to press down, crush, much like the sense of **Squash,** which is a closely related word. [This is well exemplified in Spanish; see below.] 'His grief deepe *sq atting*,' where the L. text has *premit*; Stanyhurst, tr. of Virgil, Æn. i. 209. ME. *squatten*, to press or crush flat. 'The foundementis of hillis ben togidir smyten and *squat*'= the foundations of the hills are smitten together and crushed; Wyclif, 2 Kings, xxii. 8. '*Sqwat* sal he hevedes'= he shall crush the heads (L. *conquas abit capita*), Early Eng. Psalter, ed. Stevenson, Ps. cix. (or cx.) 6. This explains prov. E. *squat*, to make flat, and *squat*, adj., flat. It is important also to note that *quat* is used in the same sense as *squat*; indeed, in the Glossary to the Exmoor Scolding, the word *squat* is explained by 'to quat down;' which shows that

the *s-* in *squat* is a prefix. — OF. *esquatir*, to flatten, crush (Roquefort). — OF. *es-*, from L. *ex-*, extremely; and *quatir*, to press down, hence, reflexively, to press oneself down, to squat, cower. 'Ele *se quatist* deles lun de pilers'= she *squatted down* beside one of the pillars; Bartsch, Chrestomathie Française, col. 282, l. 16. The corresponding word is Span. *acachar*, *agachar*, whence *acacharse*, 'to crouch, lie squat' (Meadows), *agacharse*, 'to stoop, couch, squat, cower' (id.). Minsheu's M. Span. Dict. has: '*agachar*, to squat as a hare or conie.' Without the prefix, we find Span. *cacho*, *gacho*, bent, bent downward, lit. pressed down; Ital. *quatto*, 'squatte, husht, close, still, lurking' (Florio), *quattare*, 'to squat, to husht, to lye close' (id.). Diez shows that OF. *quatir* and Ital. *quatto* are due to L. *coact-us*, pressed close together (whence also F. *se cacher*, to squat, *cacher*, to hide). Thus the etymology of *squat* is from L. *ex-*, co-for *cum*, together, and *act-us*, pp. of *agere*, to drive. See **Ex-, Con-,** and **Agent;** and see **Squash. Der.** *squat-er*. ☞ Any connexion of *squat* with Dan. *sqvat.e*, to splash, is entirely out of the question; the E. word related to Dan. *sqvatte* is **Squander,** q. v.

SQUAW, a female, woman. (N. Amer. Indian.) It occurs in J. Mather, Remarkable Providences (1684); repr. by Offor, p. 33. '*Squaw*, a female, woman, in the language of the Indian tribes of the Algonkin family. — Massachusetts *squa*, *eshqua*; Narragansett *squâws*; Cree *iskwew*; Delaware *ochqueu* and *khqueu*; used also in compound words (as the names of animals) in the sense of *female*;' Webster; and Cent. Dict.

SQUEAK, to utter a shrill sharp cry. (Scand.) In Hamlet, i. 1. 116. 'The *squeaking*, or screeking of a rat;' Baret (1580). — MSwed. *sqwæka*, to squeake (Ihre); Swed. *sqväka*, to croak; cf. Norweg. *skvaka*, to cackle (Aasen); Icel. *skvakka*, to give a sound, as of water shaken in a bottle, *skak*, a noise. And cf. Swed. *sqväla*, to squeal. Allied to **Squeal, Quack, Cackle;** expressive of the sound made. So also G. *quaken*, to quack; *quäken*, *quieken*, to squeake. **Der.** *squeak*, sb.

SQUEAL, to utter a shrill prolonged sound. (Scand.) In Jul. Cæs. ii. 2. 24. ME. *squelen*, Cursor Mundi, l. 1344.—MSwed. *sqwæla*, to squeal (Ihre); Swed. *sqväla*, to squeal; Norweg. *skvella*, to squeal (Aasen). Used as a frequentative of *squeak*; the sense is 'to keep on squeaking;' see **Squeak.** ¶ Notwithstanding the close similarity, *squall* is not quite the same word, though the words are now confused. Both, however, are expressive of *continuous* sounds. See **Squall. Der.** *squeal*, sb.

SQUEAMISH, scrupulously fastidious, over-nice. (F.) 'To be *squamish*, or nice, Delicias facere;' Baret (1580). ME. *skeymous*, *sweymous*. '*Sweymous*, or *skeymouse*, Abhominativus;' Prompt. Parv., p. 482; also written *queymows*, p. 419. *Squaimous*, in Chaucer, C. T., A 3337, means fastidious, sparing, infrequent, with occasional violent exceptions; see l. 3805 (A 3807). '*Squaymose*, verecundus;' Catholicon Anglicum (1483); *squaymus*, Trevisa, tr. of Higden, vii. 461; *squeymous*, Lay Le Freine, 62. In a version of the Te Deum from a 14th-century primer given by Maskell (Mon. Rit. ii. 12) we have 'Thou were not *skoymus* of the maidens wombe;' see Notes and Queries, 4 S. iii. 181. — AF. **eskeimous* (with AF. *ei* for F. *oi*), spelt *escoymous* in Bozon, Contes Moralisés, p. 158, with the sense of 'sparing in eating, fastidious, nice as to food.' Of unknown origin. It might answer, as to form, to a Late L. type **schēmatōsus*, or **schēmōsus* (since L. *ē* gave AF. *ei*, F. *oi*; Schwan, §§ 39, 299); from Late L. *schēma*, fashion, manner; from Gk. σχῆμα, a scheme, figure, mien, air, fashion; the sense being 'full of airs or affectations.' See **Scheme. Der.** *squeamish-ly*, *-ness*.

SQUEEZE, to crush or press tightly, to crowd. (E.) 'To *squise*, or thrust together;' Baret (1580). The initial *s* is prefixed for emphasis, being due to the OF. *es-* < L. *ex-*, an intensive prefix; to *squeeze* = to *queeze* out. Late ME. *queisen*; '*queyse* out the jus' = squeeze out the juice, Reliq. Antiquæ, i. 302. It answers, in form, to OMerc. *cwēsan*, for AS. *cwiesan*, to squeeze, crush, generally written *cwȳsan*, and used in the compound *tōcwȳsan*, to crush to pieces, squeeze to death, Ælfric's Homilies, i. 60; ii. 26, 166, 294, 510. Also *cwēsan*; in Luke, xx. 18, where the earlier version has *tōcwȳst* (for *tō-cwȳsð*), the latter has *tōcwēst* (for *tōcwēsð*). β. Cognate with Low G. *qüösen* (Brem. Wörterbuch). From a Teut. root **kweus*. **Der.** *squeeze*, sb.

SQUIB, (1) a paper tube, filled with combustibles, like a small rocket; also (2) a lampoon. (Scand.) 1. 'Can he tie *squibs* i' their tails, and fire the truth out?' Beaum. and Fletcher, The Chances, v. 2. 6. 'A *squibbe*, a ball or darte of fire;' Minsheu, ed. 1627. Spenser has it in the curious sense of 'paltry fellow,' as a term of disdain; Mother Hubbard's Tale, 371. Squibs were sometimes fastened slightly to a rope, so as to run along it like a rocket; 'The *squib's* run to the end of the line, and now for the cracker' [explosion]; Dryden, Kind Keeper, Act v. sc. 1. 'Hung up by the heels like meteors, with *squibs* in their tails ; ' Ben Jonson, News from the New World (2nd Herald). β. *Squib* is a voiced form of *squip*, and prov. E. *squib*, to squirt, answers to Norw. *skvipa*, to squirt (Ross). It seems to be allied to *swip*, a word significant of swift smooth motion. Cf. ME. *squippen*, *swippen*, to move swiftly, fly, sweep, dash ; ' the *squyppand* water ' = the dashing or sweeping water, Anturs of Arthur (in Three Met. Romances), st. v. ' When the saul fra the body *:wippes*,' i.e. flies ; Prick of Conscience, l. 2196. ' Tharfor þai *swippe* [dart] þurgh purgatory, Als a foul [bird] that *flyes smertly* ;' id. l. 3322. ' I *swift* forð' = hurried away, snatched away, Ancren Riwle, p. 228, l. 4. *Swip* is from Icel. *svipa*, to flash, dart, of a sudden but noiseless motion ; *svipr*, a swift movement, twinkling, glimpse ; Norweg. *svipa*, to run swiftly (Aasen) ; cf. also Dan. *svip̃e*, to whisk, to run (Larsen). The Teut. base SWIP was also used to express the *swift* or *sweeping* motion of a whip ; as in AS. *swipe*, a whip (John, ii. 15), Du. *zweep*, a whip, G. *schwippe*, a whip-lash. Note also Dan. *swippe*, to crack a whip, *svip*, an instant, *i et svip*, in a trice, Swed. dial. *svipa*, *swepa*, to sweep, swing, lash with a whip. γ. All from Teut. base SWEIP, to move with a turning motion, move swiftly, sweep along (Fick, iii. 365) ; see further under **Swift.** Cf. '*swypyr*, agilis ' in Prompt. Parv. 2. A *squib* also means a political lampoon ; but it was formerly applied, not to the *lampoon itself*, but to the *writer* of it. ' The *squibs* are those who, in the common phrase of the world, are call'd libellers, lampooners, and pamphleteers ; their fireworks are made up in paper ; ' Tatler, no. 88 ; Nov. 1, 1709. It has been noted above that Spenser uses *squib* as a term of derision. 3. The sense of child's squirt is directly from Norw. *skvipa*, to squirt (above).

SQUID, a kind of cuttlefish. (Scand.) So named from its squirting out sepia ; cf. prov. E. *squiddle*, to squirt. A voiced form, with *d* for Scand. *t*; allied to Swed. dial. *squitta*, strong verb, to squirt ; Icel. *skvetta*, to squirt out. (Teut. base **skwet*.)

SQUILL, a genus of bulbous plants allied to the onion. (F.—L.— Gk.) ME. *squille*. ' *Squylle*, herba, Cepa maris, bulbus ; ' Prompt. Parv.—MF. *squille*, ' the squill, sea-onion ; also, a prawn, shrimp ; ' Cot.—L. *squilla*, also *scilla*, a sea-onion, sea-leek ; a kind of prawn. —Gk. σκίλλα, a squill ; cf. σχῖνος, a squill.

SQUINANCY, the old spelling of **Quinsey,** q.v.

SQUINT, to look askew. (E.?) Palsgrave has ' *a-squynte*, en lorgnant ;' p. 831. The earliest quotation is the following : ' Biholdeð o luft and *asquint* ' = looks leftwards and askew ; Ancren Riwle, p. 212, l. 4. Apparently due to *asquint* (above), with loss of *a* ; see *Asquint* in N. E. D. It is improbable that it is a native word, but it is difficult to say how we came by it. It seems to be allied to *askance* ; see *Askance* in N. E. D. β. Cf. Dan. *paa skøns*, aslant ; Swed. dial. *på skøns*, aslant ; Low G. *schiens*, *schüns*, obliquely ; Du. *schuin*, oblique, wry, *schuinen*, to slope ; *schuinte*, obliquity ; *in de schuinte*, aslant ; EFries. *schün*, oblique, *schünte*, obliquity.

SQUIRE (1), the same as **Esquire,** q.v. (F.—L.) It occurs, spelt *squiere*, as early as in King Horn, ed. Lumby, l. 360. **Doublet,** *esquire.*

SQUIRE (2), a square, a carpenter's rule. (F.—L.) In Shak. L. L. L. v. 2. 474. ME. *squire*, Floriz and Blancheflur, ed. Lumby, 325.—OF. *e.quire*, MF. *esquierre*, ' a rule, or square ; ' Cot. Mod. F. *équerre*. Merely another form of OF. *esquarre*, a square ; see **Square.** Doublet, *square*, sb.

SQUIRREL, a nimble, reddish-brown, rodent animal. (F.—L.— Gk.) ME. *squirel* (with one *r*), Seven Sages, ed. Weber, l. 2777. Also *scurel*. ' Hic scurellus, a *scurelle* ;' Voc. 759. 29.—OF. *escurel*, *escuirel* (Godefroy) ; spelt *escurieu* in Cotgrave. Mod. F. *écureuil*.— Late L. *scūrellus* (as above), also *scuriolus* (Ducange). For **sciūrel-lus*, **sciūriolus*, diminutives of *sciūrus*, a squirrel.—Gk. σκίουρος, a squirrel ; lit. ' shadow-tail,' from his bushy tail.—Gk. σκι-, for σκία, a shadow, and οὐρά, a tail. But this explanation of the Gk. word is prob. due to popular etymology. The AF. form was *esquirel* ; Liber Albus, pp. 225, 231.

SQUIRT, to jet, throw or jerk out water. (E.) ' I *squyrte* with a *squyrte*, an instrument ;' Palsgrave. The prov. E. *swirt*, to squirt, is the same word, with *sw* for *squ*; we even find *bilagged wit swirling* = dirtied with squirting, in Walter de Bibbesworth, Wright's Voc. i. 173, l. 1. Cf. Low G. *swirtjen*, to squirt ; orig. an extension of *swiren*, to whirr, turn about quickly, G. *schwirren* ; see **Swarm.** So also EFries. *kwirtjen*, to squirt out, to dart about, from *kwirt*, turning quickly about ; see **Whir.** Der. *squirt*, sb., in Palsgrave.

STAB, to pierce with a sharp instrument. (Scand.) ' I *stabbe* in with a dagger or any other sharpe wepyn ;' Palsgrave. ME. *stabbe*, sb. ; ' *Stabbe*, or wownde of smytynge, Stigma ;' Prompt. Parv. Apparently from Swed. dial. *stabbe*, a thick stick or stump ; Icel. *stabbi*, a stub, stump, allied to *stafr*, a staff ; Dan. dial. *stabb*, a short peg. Cf. Irish *stobaim*, I stab ; Gael. *stob*, to thrust or fix a stake in the ground, to stab, thrust, from *stob*, a stake, a pointed iron

or stick, a stub or stump. This Gael. *stob* is similarly borrowed from Icel. *stobbi*, a stub ; see **Staff, Stub.** Der. *stab*, sb., Temp. iii. 3. 63.

STABLE (1), a stall or building for horses. (F.—L.) ME. *stable*, King Alisaunder, 778.—OF. *estable*, ' a stable ; ' Cot. Mod. F. *étable*.—L. *stabulum*, a standing-place, abode, stall, stable. Idg. type **stadh-lom* ; cf. AS. *stað-ol*, a foundation, support, position. See **Stall.** Brugmann, §§ 483 (9), 573. Formed with suffix *-b(u)lum* (*b* < *dh*), from the weak grade of *stāre*, to stand, cognate with E. **Stand,** q.v. Der. *.stable*, verb, *stabl-ing*.

STABLE (2), firm, steady. (F.—L.) ME. *stable*, Rob. of Glouc. p. 54, l. 1245.—OF. *estable*, stable (Burguy).—L. *stabilem*, acc. of *stabilis*, stable, standing firmly ; formed with suffix *-bilis* from the weak grade of *stā-re*, to stand, cognate with E. **Stand,** q.v. Idg. type **stadhlis*. Der. *stabl-y*; *stable-ness*, Macb. iv. 3. 92 ; *stabili-ty*, spelt *stabilytye*, Wyatt, tr. of Ps. 38, coined from L. *stabilitās*, firmness. Also *stablish*, ME. *stablisen*, Chaucer, C. T. 2997 (A 2995), the same word as *establish*, q.v.

STACK, a large pile of wood, hay, corn, &c. (Scand.) ME. *stac*, *stak*. ' Stacke or heep, Agger ;' Prompt. Parv. *Stac* in Havelok, 814, is prob. merely our *stack*. [*Stacke*, Chaucer, Persones Tale, De Luxuria (Tyrwhitt), is an error for *stank*; see Group I, 841.]—Icel. *stakkr*, a stack of hay ; cf. Icel. *stakka*, a stump, as in our *chimney-stack*, and in *stack*, a columnar isolated rock ; Swed. *stack*, a rick, heap, stack ; Dan. *stak*. β. The Teut. type is **staknoz* (Noreen). The sense is ' a pile,' that which is set up ; the allied E. word is **Stake,** q.v. Cf. Russ. *stog'*, a heap, a hay-rick. Der. *stack*, verb, as in Swed. *stacka*, Dan. *stakke*, to stack ; *stack-yard*, answering to Icel. *stak-garðr*, a stack-garth (*garth* being the Norse form of *yard*) ; also *hay-stack*, *corn-stack*.

STAFF, a long piece of wood, stick, prop, pole, cudgel. (E.) ME. *staf*, pl. *staves* (where *u* = *v*). ' Ylyk a *staf*;' Chaucer, C. T. 594 (A 592). ' Two *staues* ;' P. Plowman, B. v. 28. AS. *stæf*, pl. *stafas*, Exod. xxi. 19, John, vii. 15. The pl. *stafas* also meant *letters of the alphabet* ; this meaning seems to have originated staves as a musical term.+Du. *staf*; Icel. *stafr*, a staff, also a written letter (see Icel. Dict.) ; Dan. *stav*, *stav*; Swed. *staf*; G. *stab*; Goth. *stafs*, a letter ; hence, an element, rudiment, Gal. iv. 3. β. The word is allied to O. Church Slav. *stoborŭ*, a pillar, Lith. *stobrys*, a stump of a tree ; from an Idg. root STEBH, whence Skt. *stambh*, to make firm, set fast. Cf. EFries. *staf*, unmoved. See **Stub, Stab.** Der. *distaff* (for *dis-staff*), q.v. **Doublet,** *stave*, sb., q.v.

STAG, a male deer. (Scand.) Late AS. *stagga*, from Norse ; as in ' regalem feram, quam Angli *staggon* appellant ;' Thorpe, Anc. Laws, i. 429. The word was also applied to the male of other animals. ' *Stagge*, ceruus ;' Levins. ' *Steggander* [= steg-gander, male gander], anser ;' id. Lowland Sc. *stag*, a young horse ; prov. E. *stag*, a gander, a wren, a cock-turkey.—Icel. *steggr*, *steggi*, a he-bird, a drake, a tom-cat. Teut. type **stagjoz*. Not allied to Icel. *stīga*. Der. *stag-hound*.

STAGE, a platform, theatre ; place of rest on a journey, the distance between two such resting-places. (F.—L.) ME. *stage*, Floriz and Blancheflur, ed. Lumby, 255 ; King Alisaunder, 7684.—OF. *estage*, ' a story, stage, loft, or height of a house ; also a lodging, dwelling-house ;' Cot. Mod. F. *étage* ; Ital. *staggio*, a prop ; Prov. *estatge*, a dwelling-place (Bartsch). Formed as if from a L. type **staticum* (not found), a dwelling-place ; allied to L. *stat-um*, supine of *stāre*, to stand, with suffix *-icum*. See **Stable** (1), **Stand.** Der. *stage-coach*, a coach that runs from stage to stage ; *stage-player* ; *stag-ing*, a scaffolding.

STAGGER, to reel from side to side, vacillate ; also, to cause to reel, to cause to hesitate. (Scand.) ' I *staggar*, I stande not stedfast ;' Palsgrave. *Stagger* is a weakened form of *stacker* (spelt *stakker* in Palsgrave), ME. *stakeren*. ' She rist her up, and *stakereth* heer and there ;' Chaucer, Legend of Good Women, l. 2687.—Icel. *stakra*, to push, to stagger ; frequentative of *staka*, to punt, to push, also, to stagger ; cf. Norw. *stakra*, *staka*, to stagger ; Swed. dial. *stagra* ; Dan. dial. *stagle*, *stagre*. Perhaps *staka*, to push, is allied to Swed. *stake*, a stake ; see **Stake.** Cf. Dan. *stage*, to punt with a pole, from *stage*, a pole, a stake. Thus the orig. sense was ' to keep pushing about,' to cause to vacillate or reel ; the intransitive sense, to reel, is later.+MDu. *staggeren*, to stagger as a drunken man (Hexham) ; frequent. of *staken*, *staecken*, to stop or dam up (with stakes), to set stakes, also ' to leave or give over worke,' id. In this latter view, to *stagger* might mean ' to be always coming to a stop,' or ' often to stick fast.' Either way, the etymology is the same. Der. *staggers*, s. pl., vertigo, Cymb. v. 5. 234.

STAGNATE, to cease to flow. (L.) A late word ; *stagnate* and *stagnant* are in Phillips, ed. 1706.—L. *stagnātus*, pp. of *stagnāre*, to be still, cease to flow, to form a still pool.—L. *stagnum*, a pool, a stank. See **Stank.** Der. *stagnat-ion*; also *stagnant*, from L. *stagnant-*, stem of pres. pt. of *stagnāre*. Also *stanch*, q.v.

STAID, steady, grave, sober. (F.—MDu.) It may be observed that the resemblance to *steady* is accidental, though both words are ultimately from the same root, and so have a similar sense. *Staid* stands for *stay'd*, pp. of *stay*, to make steady; and the actual spelling *stay'd* is by no means uncommon. 'The strongest man o' th' empire, Nay, the most *stay'd* . . . The most true;' Beaum. and Fletcher, Valentinian, v. 6. 11. 'The fruits of his *stay'd* faith;' Drayton, Polyolbion, song 24 (R.). Spenser even makes the word dissyllabic; 'Held on his course with *stayèd* stedfastnesse,' F. Q. ii. 12. 29. See **Stay** (1). Der. *staid-ly, staid-ness.*

STAIN, to tinge, dye, colour, sully. (F.—L.) An abbreviation of *distain*, like *sport* for *disport, spend* for *dispend*. ME. *steinen*, Gower, C. A. i. 225, bk. ii. 1963; short for *disteinen*, Chaucer, Legend of Good Women, 255.—OF. *destein-*, a stem of *desteindre*, 'to distain, to dead or take away the colour of;' Cot. 'I *stayne* a thynge, *Ie destayns*,' Palsgrave. Thus the orig. sense was 'to spoil the colour of,' or dim; as used by Chaucer.—L. *dis-*, away; and *tingere*, to dye. See **Dis-** and **Tinge.** Der. *stain*, sb.; *stain-less*, Tw. Nt. i. 5. 278.

STAIR, a step for ascending by. (E.) Usually in the plural. [The phrase 'a pair of stairs'=a set of stairs; the old sense of *pair* being a set of equal things; see **Pair.**] ME. *steir, steire, steyer.* 'Ne *steyers* to *steye* [mount] on;' Test. of Love, i. 1. 44. 'Heih is þe *steire*'=high is the stair; Ancren Riwle, p. 284, l. 8; the pl. *steiren* occurs in the line above. AS. *stæger*, a stair, step; 'Ascensorium, *stæger*,' Voc. 126. 9. [The *g* passes into *y* as usual, and just as AS. *dæg* became *day*, so AS. *stæger* became *stayer, steyer, steir*.] The lit. sense is 'a step to climb by,' 'a mounter;' formed (with mutation of *ā* to *æ*) from *stāg*, 2nd grade of *stīgan*, to climb. +Du. *steiger*, a stair; allied to *stegel*, a stirrup, *steg*, a narrow bridge; all from *stijgen*, to mount. Cf. also Icel. *stigi, stegi*, a step, ladder (whence prov. E. *stee*, a ladder), *stigr*, a path, foot-way (orig. an uphill path), from *stīga*, to mount; Swed. *steg*, a round of a ladder, *stege*, a ladder, from *stiga*, to mount; Dan. *stige*, a ladder, *sti*, a path, from *stige*, to mount; G. *steg*, a path, from *steigen*, to mount. β. All from Teut. str. vb. **steigan-*, to climb, pt. t. **staig*, pp. **stiganoz*; from Idg. √STEIGH, to climb, ascend, whence also Skt. *stigh*, to ascend, Gk. *στείχειν*, to ascend, march, go, Goth. *steigan*, to ascend; also E. *stile*, q.v., *stirrup*, q.v. Der. *stair-case*; *stairwork*, Wint. Tale, iii. 3. 75.

STAITHE, a landing-place. (E.) A provincial word; also spelt *staith, stathe* (Halliwell). AS. *stæð*, a bank, shore (Grein); also AS. *steð*, Thorpe, Diplomatarium Ævi Saxonici, p. 147, l. 5. Cf. Icel. *stöð*, a harbour, road-stead; MDu. *stade*, a haven. Allied to **Stead,** q.v.

STAKE, a post, strong stick, pale. (E.) ME. *stake*, Chaucer, C. T. 2620 (A 2618). AS. *staca*, a stake, Ælfred, tr. of Orosius, b. v. cap. 5; also a sharply pointed pin, Thorpe, Diplomatarium, p. 230, l. 14. The latter sense is important, as pointing to the etymology. From the Teut. base **stak*, 2nd grade of the strong verb **stekan-*, to pierce, stick into. See **Stick** (1). Thus, the orig. sense is 'a piercer,' the suffix *-a* marking the agent, as in AS. *hunt-a*, a hunter; hence a pin, a sharply pointed stick.+MDu. *stake, staeck*, 'a stake or a pale, a pile driven into water, a stake for which one playeth;' Hexham (Du. *staak*). Cf. *steken*, to stab, put, stick, prick, sting; id.+Icel. *stjaki*, a stake, punt-pole; Dan. *stage*, a stake; Swed. *stake*, a stake, a candle-stick. And cf. G. *stachel*, a prick, sting, goad. B. The sense of a sum of money to be played for may be borrowed from Dutch, being found in MDutch, as above. It occurs in Wint. Tale, i. 2. 248; and the phr. *at stake* or *at the stake* occurs five times in Shak. (Schmidt). In this sense, a stake is that which is 'put' or pledged; cf. MDu. *hemselven in schuldt steken*, 'to runne himself into debt;' Hexham. ¶ A closely allied word is *stack*, a pile, a thing stuck up; see **Stack.**

STALACTITE, an inverted cone of carbonate of lime, hanging like an icicle in some caverns. (F.—Gk.) Modern. Byron (wrongly) has *stylact-i-tes* (4 syllables); The Island, iv. 7. 23.—F. *stalactite* (A.D. 1752). So called because formed by the dripping of water. Formed, with suffix *-ite* (Gk. *-ιτης*), from *σταλακτ-ός*, trickling; cf. *σταλακτίς* (base *σταλακτιδ-*), that which drops.—Gk. *σταλάζειν* (=*σταλάγ-γειν*), to drop, drip; lengthened form of *σταλάειν*, to drip. See **Stalagmite.**

STALAGMITE, a cone of carbonate of lime on the floor of a cavern formed by dripping water. (F.—Gk.) Modern.—F. *stalagmite*. Formed with suffix *-ite* (Gk. *-ιτης*), from *σταλαγμ-α*, a drop; from *σταλάζειν* (=*σταλάγ-γειν*), to drip. See **Stalactite.**

STALE (1), too long kept, tainted, vapid, trite. (F.—Teut.) 1. *Stale* is also used as a sb., in the sense of urine. Palsgrave gives it in this sense; and see *escloy* in Cotgrave. Mares do not stop to *stale*; see Holland's Pliny, i. 222.—OF. *estaler*, to make water (in Godefroy, s. v. *estaler* (2), but wrongly explained). Of Teut. origin.

Cf. EFries. and Low G. *stallen*, Swed. *stalla*, to put into a stall, also to stale (as cattle and horses); Dan. *stalde*, to stale (as a horse), also to stall-feed. From **Stall,** sb. 2. *Stale*, adj., is in Chaucer, C. T. 13694 (B 1954), as applied to ale. We may explain *stale*, adj., as 'too long exposed for sale,' as in the case of provisions left unsold; cf. MF. *estaler*, 'to display, lay open wares on stalls' (Cot.), from *estal*, 'the stall of a shop, or booth, any place where wares are laid and shewed to be sold.' But since this F. *estal* is merely borrowed from the Teutonic word *stall*, it comes to much the same thing. Cf. MDu. *stel*, stale; *stel-bier*, stale beer; *stel-pisse*, urine (Hexham); Du. *stel*, a stall. See Körting, §§ 9014, 9015. ¶ Wedgwood, following Schmeller, explains *stale*, sb., from stopping the horse to let him stale; and cites Swed. *ställa en hest*, to stop a horse. But, here again, the Swed. *ställa* is derived from Swed. *stall*, orig. a stopping-place; while 'to stale' is Swed. *stalla*. Der. *stale*, verb, Antony, ii. 2. 240; *stale-ness*, Per. v. 1. 58.

STALE (2), a decoy, snare. (E.) 'Still as he went, he crafty *stales* did lay;' Spenser, F. Q. ii. 1. 4. Note AF. *estale*, a decoy-bird (Bozon). Adapted from AS. *stæl-*, as in *stæl-hrān*, a decoy reindeer, allied to ME. *stale*, theft; hence stealth, deceit, slyness, or a trap; it occurs in Ayenbite of Inwyt, p. 9, l. 24. Compare the phrase *cumen bi stale*=to come by stealth, to surprise; O. Eng. Homilies, i. 249, l. 20. From AS. *stalu*, theft, Matt. xv. 19.—Teut. **stal*, 2nd grade of **stelan-*, as in AS. *stelan*, to steal; see **Steal.**

STALE (3), **STEAL,** a handle. (E.) Chiefly applied to the long handle of a rake, hoe, &c.; spelt *Steale* in Halliwell. *Stale* also means a round of a ladder, or a stalk (id.). ME. *stale*. 'A ladel . . . with a long *stele*' (2 MSS. have *stale*); P. Plowman, C. xxii. 279. From AS. *stela, stæla, steola*; the dat. pl. *stælum* (in another MS. *stelum*) occurs in A. S. Leechdoms, ed. Cockayne, i. 154, in the sense of 'stalks.'+Du. *steel*, a stalk, stem, handle. [G. *stiel*, MHG. *stil*, a handle, seem distinct.] Allied to *still* and *stall*; the *stale* being the handle whereby the tool is firmly held. Cf. further Gk. *σταλίς*, a stake to which nets are fastened, *στελεόν*, *στειλειόν*, a handle or helve of an ax. See **Stalk.** Der. *stalk* (1) and (2), q.v.

STALK (1), a stem. (E.) ME. *stalke*, of which one sense is the stem or side-piece of a ladder. 'To climben by the ronges [rungs] and the *stalkes*;' Chaucer, C. T. 3625. A dimin. form, with suffixed *-ke*, of ME. *stale, stele*, a handle, AS. *stæla, stela*, a stalk; see **Stale** (3). [Icel. *stilkr*, a stalk, goes with G. *stiel*.] Cf. also Gk. *στέλεχος*, a trunk, stem (of a tree), allied to *στελεόν*, a handle. Der. *stalk* (2), q.v.

STALK (2), to stride, walk with slow steps. (E.) ME. *stalken*, to walk cautiously. '*Stalkeden* ful stilly;' Will. of Palerne, 2728. 'With dredful foot [timid step] then *stalketh* Palamoun;' Chaucer, C. T. 1481 (A 1479). AS. *stealcan*, to go warily; *stealcung*, a stalking. These forms are in Toller, with references for *bestealcian* and *stealcung*; Somner gives the forms *stælcan* and *stælcung*.+Dan. *stalke*, to stalk. Cf. AS. *stealc*, lofty, high (Grein). The notion is that of walking with lifted feet, so as to go noiselessly; the word is prob. connected with **Stilt,** q.v., and with **Stalk** (1) above. Halliwell has *Stalk*, the leg of a bird; *stalke*, to go slowly with, a quotation from Gower, C. A. i. 187; also *stilt*, the handle of a plough, which (like *stalk*) is an extension of *Steal*; see **Stale** (3). We may explain *stalk*, verb, as to walk on lengthened legs or *stalks*, to go on tiptoe or noiselessly. Der. *stalk-er*; *stalk-ing-horse*, a horse for stalking game, explained in Dictionarium Rusticum, 1726, quoted at length in Halliwell.

STALL, a standing-place for cattle, shed, division of a stable, a table on which things are exposed for sale, a seat in a choir or theatre. (E.) All the senses are from the notion of a fixed or settled place or station. Indeed, *station* is from the same root. ME. *stal*; dat. *stalle*, Chaucer, C. T. 8083 (E 207). AS. *steal, steall*, a place, station, stall; Grein, ii. 480; also *stæl*, id. 477.+Du. *stal*; Icel. *stallr*, a stall, pedestal, shelf; cf. *stalli*, an altar; Dan. *stald* (for *stall*), a stable; Swed. *stall*; G. *stall*; OHG. *stal*. Teut. type **stalloz*, perhaps for **stad-loz*; cf. E. *stead*, Gk. *σταθ-μός*, a stall; L. *stab-ulum* (for **stadh-lom*). See **Stead.** Brugmann, i. § 593 (4). Der. *stall-age*, from MF. *estallage*, 'stallage,' Cot., where *estal*, a stall, is borrowed from Teutonic, and the suffix *-age* answers to L. *-āticum*. Also *stall*, verb, Rich. III, i. 3. 206; *stall-ed*, fattened in a stall, Prov. xv. 17, from Swed. *stalla*, Dan. *stalle*, to stall-feed, feed in a stall. Also *stall-feed*, verb; *stall-fed*, Chapman, tr. of Homer, Odys. xiv. 161. Also *stall-i-on*, q.v. Doublet, *stable*.

STALLION, an entire horse. (F.—OHG.) Spelt *stalland* in Levins, with excrescent *d*; *stallant* in Palsgrave, with excrescent *t*. ME. *stalon*, Voc. 638. 3; Gower, C. A. iii. 280; bk. viii. 160.—OF. *estalon*, 'a stalion for mares;' Cot. Mod. F. *étalon*; cf. Ital. *stallone*, a stallion, also a stable-man, ostler. So called because kept in a stall and not made to work; Diez cites *equus ad stallum* from the Laws of the Visigoths.—OHG. *stal*, a stall, stable; cognate with E. **Stall** (above). **β.** The *i* may have been suggested by the Ital. *stallione*, given by Torriano as a variant of *stallone*, and explained by 'a horse long kept in the stable without being ridden or used; also, a stallion.'

STALWART, sturdy, stout, brave. (E.) A corruption of ME. *stalworth*, Will. of Palerne, 1950; Pricke of Conscience, 689; Havelok, 904. The intermediate form *stalward* occurs in Trevisa, tr. of Higden, iii. 439 (note). It is noticeable that *e* sometimes appears after the *l*, as in *stelewurðe*, O. Eng. Hom. i. 25, l. 12; *s'ealewurðe*, Juliana, p. 45, l. 11; *stalewurðe*, St. Margaret, p. 15, l. 3 from bottom. AS. *stælwyrðe* (plural), A. S. Chron. an. 896. **β.** In the A. S. Chron. it is applied to ships, and means 'serviceable;' we are told that the men of London went to fetch the ships, and they broke up all they could not remove, whilst those that were serviceable (*stælwyrðe*) they brought to London. Sievers shows that the *æ* was long (A. S. Grammar, § 202); and *stæl-* is contracted from *staþ l-*, just as *ge-stælan* is for *ge-staþol-ian*, and *stālian* for *staþolian*. The AS. *staþol* means 'foundation,' and *staþolwyrðe* means 'firm.' Cf. AS. *staðol-fæst*, stedfast. For the latter part of the word, see **Worth, Worthy.**

STAMEN, one of the male organs of a flower. (L.) The lit. sense is 'thread.' A botanical term. [The pl. *stamina*, lit. threads, fibres, is used in E. (almost as a sing. sb.) to denote firm texture, and hence strength or robustness.]—L. *stämen* (pl. *stämina*), the warp in an upright loom, a thread. Lit. 'that which stands up;' formed with suffix *-men* from *stäre*, to stand; see **Stand.** Cf. Gk. στῆμα, a stamen; also ἱστός, a warp, from the same root. Der. *stamin* or *tammy*.

STAMIN, TAMINE, TAMINY, TAMIS, TAMMY, a kind of stuff. (F.—L.) The correct form is *stamin* or *stamine*; Palsgrave has *stamyne*; the other forms are corruptions, with loss of initial *s*, as in *tank* (for *stank*). ME. *stamin*, Ancren Riwle, p. 418, l. 20.—OF. *estamine*, 'the stuffe tamine;' Cot.—L. *stämineus*, consisting of threads.—L. *stämin-*, decl. stem of *stämen*, a thread, stamen; see **Stamen.**

STAMMER, to stutter, to falter in speech. (E.) ME. *stameren*, in Reliquiæ Antiquæ, i. 65; Arthur and Merlin, 2864 (Stratmann). AS. *stomrian* (for *stamrian*), to stammer, The Shrine, p. 42. Formed as a verb from AS. *stamer* or *stamur*, adj., stammering. 'Balbus, *stamer*,' Voc. 161. 37; 'Balbus, *stamur*,' id. 314. 38; *stamor*, id. 275. 20. The suffix *-er*, *-ur*, or *-or* is adjectival, expressive of 'fitness or disposition for the act or state denoted by the theme;' cf. *bit-or*, bitter, from *bitan*, to bite; March, A. S. Grammar, § 242. Thus *stamer* signifies 'disposed to come to a stand-still,' such being the sense of the base *stam-*, which is an extension of the √STA, to stand; cf. prov. E. *stam*, to amaze, confound, related by gradation to G. *stumm*, dumb.✛Du. *stameren*, *stamelen*, to stammer; Icel. *stamr*, stammering; *stamma*, *stama*, to stammer; Dan. *stamme*, to stammer; Swed. *stamma* (the same); G. *stammern*, *stammeln* (the same), from OHG. *stam*, adj., stammering; Goth. *stamms*, adj. stammering, Mark, vii. 32. Der. *stammer-er*.

STAMP, to strike the foot firmly down, tread heavily and violently, to pound, impress, coin. (E.) ME. *stampen*, Chaucer, C. T. 12472 (C 538). 'And *stamped* heom in a mortar;' King Alisaunder, 332. AS. *stempen*, for *stampian*; A.S. Leechdoms, ed. Cockayne, i. 378, l. 18.✛Du. *stampen*; Icel. *stappa* (for *stampa*, by assimilation); Swed. *stampa*; Dan. *stampe*; G. *stampfen* (whence OF. *estamper*, F. *étamper*); cf. G. *stampfe*, OHG. *stamph*, a pestle for pounding.✛Gk. στέμβειν, to stamp. Der. *stamp*, sb., Cor. ii. 2. 111; *stamp-er*; also *stamp-ede*, q.v.

STAMPEDE, a panic, sudden flight. (Span.—Teut.) 'Stampede, a sudden fright seizing upon large bodies of cattle or horses, ... leading them to run for many miles; hence, any sudden flight in consequence of a panic;' Webster. The *e* represents the sound of Span. *i.*—Span. (and Port.) *estampido*, 'a crash, the sound of anything bursting or falling;' Neuman. Formed as if from a verb *estampir*, akin to *estampar*, to stamp. The reference appears to be to the sound caused by the blows of a pestle upon a mortar. The Span. *estampar* is of Teut. origin; see **Stamp.**

STANCE, a station, site; see **Stanza.**

STANCH, STAUNCH, to stop the flowing of blood. (F.—L.) ME. *staunchen*, to satisfy (hunger), Chaucer, tr. of Boethius, b. iii. pr. 3; b. iii. met. 3; to quench (flame), Gower, C. A. i. 15; prol. 345.—OF. *estancher*, 'to stanch, stop an issue of blood, to slake or quench hunger, thirst, &c.;' Cot. Cf. Walloon *stanchi* (Remacle), Span. *estancar*, to stop, check.—Late L. *stancāre*, to stop the flow of blood. The Late L. *stancāre* is a variant of a Late L. type *stagnicāre*, from L. *stagnāre*, also used in the same sense of to stop the flow of blood (Ducange). See **Stagnate.** Körting (§ 9009),

suggests that the sense may have been influenced by G. *stange*, a bar. Der. *stanch* or *staunch*, adj., firm, sound, spelt *stanche* in Palsgrave (p. 325); Phillips (ed. 1706) gives *stanch*, 'substantial, solid, good, sound;' this is derived from the verb, which Baret (1580) explains by 'to staie, or stanch blood, .. also to staie, to confirme, to make more strong;' it was suggested by the F. pp. *estanché*, 'stanched, stopped, stayed' (Cot.), or (as a nautical term) by OF. *estanche*, water-tight (Supp. to Godefroy), mod. F. *étanche*; cf. Span. *stanco*, water-tight, not leaky, said of a ship. Hence *stanch-ly* or *staunch-ly*; *stanch-ness* or *staunch-ness*. Also *stanch-less*, Macb. iv. 3. 78.

STANCHION, a support, an upright beam used as a support, a bar. (F.—L.) 'Stanchions (in a ship), certain pieces of timber which, being like pillars, support and strengthen those call'd waste-trees;' Phillips, ed. 1706. Spelt *stanchon*, *staunchon* in Palsgrave.—ONorth F. *estanchon*, Norm. dial. *étanchon*; MF. *estançon*, *estanson*, 'a prop, stay;' Cot. MF. *estançon* (mod. F. *étançon*) is not derived from OF. *estancher*, to stanch, also used (by confusion) in the sense 'to prop;' but is a dimin. of OF. *estance*, a situation, condition (Burguy), also used, according to Godefroy, in the sense of stanchion.—Late L. *stantia*, a house, chamber (Ducange); lit. 'that which stands firm.'—L. *stant-*, stem of pres. part. of *stäre*, to stand, cognate with E. **Stand.** See **Stanza.**

STAND, to be stationary or still, to rest, endure, remain, be firm, &c. (E.) ME. *standen*, pt. t. *stood, stod*, pp. *stonden, standen*. The pp. *stonden* is in Chaucer, C. T. 9368 (E 1494); and in the Earl of Tolouse, l. 322, in Ritson's Met. Romances, vol. iii. AS. *standan*, *stondan*, pt. t. *stōd*, pl. *stōdon*, pp. *standen*; Grein, i. 475.✛Icel. *standa*; Goth. *standan*, pt. t. *stōth*. Cf. Du. *staan*, pt. t. *stond*; G. *stehen*, pt. t. *stand*; Swed. *stå*, pt. t. *stod*. Teut. type *standan-*, pt. t. *stōth*; base *stadh*, *stad*, the *n* being orig. characteristic of the present tense. Allied to L. *stäre*; Gk. ἔστην (I stood); Russ. *stoiat(e)*, to stand; Skt. *sthā*, to stand. All from Idg. √STA, to stand; one of the most prolific roots. See **State.** Der. *stand*, sb., Merch. Ven. v. 77; *stand-er*, Troil. iii. 3. 84; *stand-er-by* (the same as *by-stand-er*), Troil. iv. 5. 190; *stand-ing*, Wint. Tale, i. 2. 431; *stand-ing-bed*, Merry Wives, iv. 5. 7; *standish* (for *stand-dish*), a standing dish for pen and ink, Pope, On receiving from Lady Shirley a Standish and two Pens; spelt *standysshe* in Cavendish, Life of Wolsey, ed. Ellis, p. 92. Also *under-stand*, *with-stand*. Also (from L. *stäre*) *sta-ble* (1), *sta-ble* (2), *sta-bl-ish*, *e-sta-bl-ish*, *stage*, *staid*, *sta-men*, *con-sta-ble*, *stay* (1); *ar-re-st*, *contra-st*, *ob-sta-cle*, *ob-ste-tric*, *re-st* (2); (from supine *stat-um*) *state*, *stat-us*, *stat-ion*, *stat-ist*, *stat-ue*, *stat-ute*, *estate*, *armi-stice*, *con-sti-tute*, *de-stit-ute*, *in-stit-ute*, *inter-stice*, *pro-stit-ute*, *re-in-state*, *re-stit-ut-ion*, *sol-stice*, *sub-stit-ute*, *super-stit-ion*; (from pres. part., base *stant-*) *circum-stance*, *con-stant*, *di-stant*, *ex-tant* (for *ex-stant*), *in-stant*, *in-stant-an-e-ous*, *in-stant-er*, *stanz-a*, *sub-stance*, *sub-stant-ive*. Also (from L. *sistere*, causal of *stäre*) *as-sist*, *con-sist*, *de-sist*, *ex-ist* (for *ex-sist*), *in-sist*, *per-sist*, *re-sist*, *sub-sist*. Words of Gk. origin are *sta-t-ics*, *apo-sta-sy*, *ec-sta-sy*, *meta-sta-sis*, *sy-st-em*.

STANDARD, an ensign, flag, model, rule, standing tree. (F.—L.) ME. *standard*, in early use; it occurs in the A. S. Chronicle, an. 1138, with reference to the battle of the *Standard*.—OF. *estandart*, 'a standard, a kind of ensigne for horsemen used in old time; also the measure ... which we call the Standard;' Cot. But also spelt *estendart*, Supp. to Godefroy, in the sense of 'flag, ensign.' The two forms represent two different ideas; but they were early confused; see *Standardum* in Ducange. 1. The former refers rather to the pole on which the flag was borne; and was formed with suffix *-art* (= G. *-hart*, suffix, the same word as *hart*, adj., cognate with E. *hard*, Brachet, Introd. § 196) from OHG. *stand-an*, to stand, now only used in the contracted form *stehen*. This OHG. *standan* is cognate with E. **Stand**, q.v. 2. The OF. *estendard* (also in Cotgrave) is from OF. *estendre* < L. *extendere*, to extend; see **Extend.** This is supported by the Ital. form *stendardo* and the Prov. *estendart-z* (Bartsch). On the other hand, we have E. *standard*, Span. *estandarte*; and the E. *standard of value* and *standard-tree* certainly owe their senses to the verb to *stand*. So also MDu. *standaert*, 'a standard, or a great ensigne, a pillar or a column, a mill-post;' Hexham.

STANG, a pole, stake. (Scand.) Spelt *stangue* in Levins (with added *-ue*, as in *tongue*). ME. *stange*, Gawain and Green Knight, 1614. [Rather from Scand. than from AS. *steng* (Grein).]—Icel. *stöng* (gen. *stangar*), a pole, stake; Dan. *stang*; Swed. *stång*.✛Du. *stang*; G. *stange*. From the 2nd grade of the verb *sting*; see **Sting.** Cf. Icel. *stanga*, to goad.

STANK, a pool, a tank. (F.—L.) A doublet of *tank*, of which it is a fuller form. Once a common word; see Halliwell. ME. *stank*; spelt *stanc*, Allit. Poems, ed. Morris, B. 1018; see Spec. of English, pt. ii. p. 162, l. 1018.—OF. *estanc* (Sup. to Godefroy), also *estang*, 'a great pond, pool, or standing water;' Cot. Cf.

Walloon *stank*, Prov. *estanc*, Span. *estanque*, Port. *tanque*. Indirectly from L. *stagnum*, a pool of stagnant or standing water; affected by the vb. *stagnicāre, to render stagnant, for which see **Stanch**. See **Stagnate**, **Stanch**, **Tank**. Der. *stagn-ate*, *stanch*, *stanch-ion*. Doublet, *tank*.

STANNARY, relating to tin-mines. (L.) 'The *Stannary courts* in Devonshire and Cornwall;' Blackstone, Comment. b. iii. c. 6 (R.). '*Stannaries* in Cornwall;' Minsheu, ed. 1627. — Late L. *stannāria*, a tin-mine (Ducange). — L. *stannum*, tin; also, an alloy of silver and lead; which seems to be the older sense, Pliny, b. xxxiv. c. 16. β. Also spelt *stagnum*, whence *stagneus*, adj.; and it is thought to be another sense of L. *stagnum*, a pool, applied perhaps to a mass of fused metal. Cf. Ital. *stagno*, tin, also, a pool. See **Stank**. Cf. Corn. *stean*, W. *ystaen*, Bret. *stean*, Irish *stan*, Gael. *staoin*, Manx *stainney*; all from L. *stannum*, tin. And see **Tin**.

STANZA, a division of a poem. (Ital. — L.) Used by Drayton in his Pref. to the Barons' Wars. We find *stanzo* (mod. editt. *stanza*) and *stanze* (now *stanza*) in Shak. As You Like It, ii. 5. 18, L. L. L. iv. 2. 107; Minsheu has *stanze*, ed. 1627. '*Staffe* in our vulgare poesie . . . the Italian called it *stanza*, as if we should say a resting-place;' Puttenham, Art of Eng. Poesie, ed. 1589, b. ii. c. 2. — Ital. *stanza*, MItal. *stantia*, 'a lodging, chamber, dwelling, also a *stance* or staffe of verses or songs;' Florio. So named from the stop or halt at the end of it. — Late L. *stantia*, an abode. — L. *stant-*, stem of pres. part. of *stāre*, to stand, cognate with E. **Stand**, q.v. And see **Stanchion**. Doublet, *stance*, a station, site; OF. *estance* < L. *stantia*.

STAPLE (1), a loop of iron for holding a pin or bolt. (E.) ME. *stapel*, *stapil*; spelt *stapylle* in the Prompt. Parv.; *stapil*, *stapul* in Cursor Mundi, 8288; *stapel*, a prop or support for a bed, Seven Sages, ed. Weber, 201. AS. *stapul*. 'Patronus, *stapul*;' Voc. 126. 8. (Here *patronus* = a defence; the gloss occurs amongst others having reference to parts of a house.) The orig. sense is a prop, support, something that furnishes a firm hold, and it is derived from the base **stap-* of the AS. strong verb *stæppan*, to step, to tread firmly. Cf. E. *stamp*; and see **Step**. And see **Staple** (2). +Du. *stapel*, a staple, stocks, a pile, allied to *stappen*, to step; MDu. *stapel*, 'the foot or trevet whereupon anything rests;' Hexham; Dan. *stabel*, a hinge, a pile; Swed. *stapel*, a pile, heap, stocks, staple or emporium; cf. *stappla*, to stumble (frequentative form); G. *staffel*, a step of a ladder, a step; provincially, a staple or emporium; *stapel*, a pile, heap, staple or emporium, stocks, a stake; cf. *stapfen*, *stappen*, to step, to strut.

STAPLE (2), a chief commodity, principal production of a country. (F. — Low G.) 'A curious change has come over this word; we should now say, Cotton is the great *staple*, i.e. the established merchandise, of Manchester; our ancestors would have reversed this and said, Manchester is the great *staple*, or established mart, of cotton;' Trench, Select Glossary. '*Staple* signifieth this or that towne, or citie, whether [whither] the Merchants of England by common order or commandement did carrie their woolles, wool-fels, cloathes, leade, and tinne, and such like commodities of our land, for the vtterance of them by the great' [wholesale]; Minsheu, ed. 1627. ME. *staple*, a market; Trevisa, tr. of Higden, viii. 488, 571. — OF. and MF. *estaple*, later *estape*, 'a staple, a mart or generall market, a publique store-house;' &c.; Cot. Mod. F. *étape*. — LowG. *stapel*, a heap, esp. one arranged in order, a store-house of certain wares in a town, where they are laid in order; whence such wares were called *stapel-waaren*; Brem. Wörterbuch, q.v. This is the same word as **Staple** (1), the meanings of which are very various; it has the sense of 'heap' in Du., Dan., Swed., and G., though not in English; showing that this particular use of the word was derived through the French. Prob. the word came into use, in the special sense, in the Netherlands, where were the great commercial cities. ¶ It is clear that the F. word was of *Low* G., not *High* G., origin. The word *stapel*, in mod. G., is clearly borrowed from Low G., the true G. form being *staffel*. As E. Müller well remarks, the successive senses were prop, foundation or support, stand for laying things on, heap, heaped wares, storehouse. The one sense of 'firmness' or 'fixedness' runs through all these.

STAR, a heavenly body, not including the sun and moon. (E.) ME. *sterre*, Chaucer, C. T. 2063 (A 2061). AS. *steorra*; Grein, ii. 482.+Du. *ster* (in composition, *sterre*); OHG. *sterro*. (There are also forms with final *-n-* (*-na*), viz. Icel. *stjarna*, Swed. *stjerna*, Dan. *stjerne*, Goth. *stairno*, G. *stern*.)+L. *stella* (for *ster-la, a diminform; the L. *astrum* is borrowed from Gk.); Gk. ἀστήρ, gen. ἀστέρ-os, with prosthetic α; Corn. and Bret. *steren*; W. *seren* (for *steren); Skt. *tārā* (for *stārā). Original sense uncertain: though some connect it with Skt. *str*, to spread, hence, to sprinkle (light); Max Müller, Lect. on Lang. ii. 237 (8th ed.). Cf. Brugmann,

i. § 473 (2). Der. *star*, verb; *star-fish*, *star-gaz-er*, *star-light*, *starr-ed*; *starr-y*; *day-star*, *lode-star*. And see *aster*, *stellar*.

STARBOARD, the right side of a ship, looking forward. (E.) Spelt *starboord* in Minsheu, ed. 1627. ME. *sterebourde*, Morte Arthur, 745; *stereburde*, id. 3665. AS. *stēorbord*, Ælfred, tr. of Orosius, b. i. c. 1, where it is opposed to *bæcbord*, i.e. larboard; see Sweet's A. S. Reader. There is no doubt that *stēorbord* = steer-bord, and that the steersman stood on the right side of the vessel to steer; in the first instance, he used a paddle, not a helm. The Icel. *stjórn* means steerage, and the phr. *ā stjórn*, lit. at the helm (or steering-paddle), means on the right or starboard side. Thus the derivation is from AS. *stēor*, a rudder (whence also *stēor-mann*, a steersman) and *bord*, a board, also the side of a ship; see **Steer** and **Board**.+Du. *stuurboord*, from *stuur*, helm, and *boord*, board, also border, edge; Icel. *stjórnborði*, starboard, from *stjórn*, steerage, and *borð*, a board, side of a ship; cf. *borði*, a border; Dan. *styrbord*, from *styr*, steerage, and *bord*; Swed. *styrbord* (the same).

STARCH, a gummy substance for stiffening cloth. (E.) 'Starche for kyrcheys,' i.e. starch for kerchiefs; Prompt. Parv. So named because starch or stiff; *starch* being properly an adjective, representing ME. *sterch*, strong, O. E. Misc., ed. Morris, p. 156, l. 11. AS. *sterce, adj., from *stercan*, to strengthen, stiffen; which appears in *sterced-ferhð*, strengthened in mind (Grein, ii. 480). The vb. *stercan* (for *starc-ian) is regularly formed from OMerc. *starc, AS. *stearc*, rigid; see **Stark**. Cf. G. *stärke*, (1) strength, (2) starch; from *stark*, strong. Der. *starch*, adj., in the sense of 'formal,' due rather to *starch*, sb., than to ME. *sterch*; rare; see an example in Todd's Johnson; hence *starch-ly*, formally, and *starch-ness*; also *starch-y*. Also *starch*, verb, to stiffen with starch, as in 'starched beard,' Ben Jonson, Every Man out of his Humour, A. iv. sc. 4 (Carlo).

STARE (1), to gaze fixedly. (E.) ME. *staren*, Chaucer, C. T. 13627 (B 1887). AS. *starian*, to stare; Grein, ii. 477. A weak verb, from a Teut. type *staroz, adj., fixed; appearing in AS. *stær-blind*, quite blind; cf. G. *starr* (for *star-roz), stiff, inflexible, fixed, staring; cf. Icel. *stara*, to stare; Low G. and Du. *staren*, OHG. *starēn*, to stare. Prob. allied to Gk. στερεός, στερρός, firm. ¶ Hence to *stare* is also 'to be stiff,' as in 'makest . . . my hair to *stare*,' Jul. Cæsar, iv. 3. 280. Der. *stare*, sb., Temp. iii. 3. 95. And see *sterile*, *stereoscope*.

STARE (2), to shine, glitter. (E.) ME. *staren*. '*Staryn*, or schynyn, and glyderyn, Niteo, rutilo;' Prompt. Parv. '*Starynge*, or schynynge, as gaye thyngys, Rutilans, rutulus;' id. We still speak of *staring*, i.e. very bright, colours. The same word as **Stare** (1). The Prompt. Parv. also has: '*Staryn* withe brode eyne, Patentibus oculis respicere.' From the notion of staring with fixed eyes we pass to that of the effect of the stare on the beholder, the sensation of the staring look. See **Stare** (1). ¶ No original connexion with *star*, of which the ME. form was *sterre*.

STARE (3), a starling; see **Starling**.

STARK, rigid, stiff; gross, absolute, entire. (E.) 'Stiff and *stark*;' Romeo, iv. 1. 103. ME. *stark*, stiff, strong, Chaucer, C. T. 9332 (E 1458). AS. *stearc* (for *starc), strong, and stiff; Grein, ii. 481. +Du. *sterk*; Icel. *sterkr*; Dan. *stærk*; Swed. and G. *stark*. β. In most of these languages, the usual sense is 'strong;' but the orig. sense may very well have been rigid or stiff, as in English; cf. Goth. *gastaurknith*, lit. becomes dried up, used to translate Gk. ξηραίνεται in Mark, ix. 18; and Lithuan. *strègti*, to stiffen, to freeze, become rigid; also Russ. *strogii*, severe, Pers. *suturg*, big, strong. The Idg. form of the root is STREG, extended from √STER, to be fixed; cf. Gk. στερ-εός, firm, MDu. *sterren*, 'to be stiffe or stubborne,' Hexham. See **Stare** (1). Der. *stark-ly*, Meas. for Meas. iv. 2. 70; *stark-ness*. Also *stark*, adv., wholly, as in *stark mad*. Also *starch*, q. v. ☞ But not *stark-naked*, q. v.

STARK-NAKED, quite naked. (E.) In Tw. Nt. iii. 4. 274; spelt *starke-naked*, Palsgrave, p. 842. This phrase is doubtless now used as if compounded of *stark*, wholly, and *naked*, just as in the case of *stark mad*, Com. of Err. ii. 1. 59, v. 281; but it is remarkable that the history of the expression proves that it had a very different origin, as regards the former part of the word. It is an ingenious substitution for *start-naked*, lit. tail-naked, i.e. with the hinder parts exposed. *Startnaked* occurs in The Castell of Love, ed. Weymouth, l. 431; also in the Ancren Riwle, pp. 148, 260, where the editor prints *sterc-naked*, *steorc-naked*, though the MS. must have *stert-naked*, *steort-naked*, since *stark* is never spelt *steorc*. The same remark applies to *steorc-naket* in St. Marharete, p. 5, l. 19, where the editor tells us (at p. 109) that the MS. may be read either way. In St. Juliana, pp. 16, 17, we have *steort-naket* in *both* MSS. β. The former element is, in fact, the ME. *stert*, a tail, Havelok, 2823, from AS. *steort*, a tail, Exod. iv. 4. It is still preserved in E. *redstart*, i.e. red tail, as the name of a bird.+Du. *stert*, a tail; Icel. *stertr*; Dan. *stjert*; Swed. *stjärt*; G. *sterz*. Cf. Gk. στόρθη, a spike. ¶ The phrase was early misunderstood; see Trevisa, iii. 97, where we have *streiʒt blynde* = wholly blind, with the various readings *start blynde* and *stark blynde*; here *start-blynde* is really nonsense. There is also *stareblind*, Owl and Nightingale, l. 241, AS. *stærblind*; Voc. 45. 22; but this answers to Dan. *stærblind*, from *stær*, a cataract in the eye. We may also note prov. G. *sterzvoll* (lit. tail-full), wholly drunk, cited by Schmeller, Bavar. Dict. col. 785, l. 48.

STARLING, the name of a bird. (E.) In Shak. 1 Hen. IV, i. 3. 224. ME. *sterlyng*, Voc. 640. 7; formed (with double dimin. suffix *-l-ing*) from ME. *stare*, a starling, Chaucer, Parl. of Foules, l. 348. AS. *stær*, a starling. 'Turdus, *stær*;' Voc. 132. 8; 'Sturnus, *stær*;' id. 48. 16. It also means a sparrow, Matt. x. 29 (Lind. MS.). We also find the forms *stærn, stearn*, meaning 'a tern.' 'Beatica, *stearn*,' Voc. 8. 36; 'Stronus [stornus?], *stærn*,' id. 132. 7.+Icel. *starri, stari*; Dan. *stær*; Swed. *stare*; G. *staar*. Cf. L. *sturnus*, a starling. See **Tern**.

START, to move suddenly, to wince, to rouse suddenly. (E.) ME. *sterten*, Chaucer, C. T. 1046 (A 1044). We also find *stert*, sb., a start, quick movement, Chaucer, C. T., A. 1705; Havelok, 1873. The verb does not appear in AS., but we find the pt. t. *stirte*, Havelok, 873; spelt *sturte, storte* in Layamon, 23951. We may call it an E. word; the AS. form may have been *styrtan (for *sturt-jan); from a Teut. base *stert. Stratmann cites an OIcel. *sterta*, but I cannot find it; there are traces of it in Icel. *stertimaðr*, a man who walks proudly and stiffly, and Icel. *uppstertr*, an upstart, both given in Egilsson. β. Allied words are Du. *storten*, to precipitate, plunge, spill, fall, rush; Dan. *styrte*, to fall, precipitate, hurl; Swed. *störta*, to cast down, ruin, fall dead; G. *stürzen*, to hurl, precipitate, ruin, overturn. Note also Swed. dial. *stjärta*, to run wildly about (Rietz); Low G. *steerten*, to flee; MDu. *steerten*, to flee, to run away. The G. *stürzen* is derived from the sb. *sturz*, a sudden fall, tumble, precipice, waterfall, from a Teut. base *stert; cf. Norw. *sterten*, adj., striving against. But the further history is obscure. Der. *start*, sb., ME. *stert*, as above; *start-er*; *start-up*, an upstart, Much Ado, i. 3. 69; *up-start*, q. v. Also *start-le*, the frequentative form, ME. *stertlen*, to stumble along, Debate of Body and Soul, l. 120, pr. in Alteng. Sprachproben, ed. Mätzner, i. 94, and in Mapes' Poems, ed. Wright, p. 335; from AS. *steartlian*, to stumble.

STARVE, to die of hunger or cold, to kill with hunger or cold. (E.) Orig. intransitive, and used in the *general* sense of 'to die,' without reference to the means. ME. *steruen* (with *u* = *v*), strong verb; pt. t. *starf*, Chaucer, C. T. 935 (A 933), pp. *storuen*, or *i-storuen*, id. 2016 (A 2014). AS. *steorfan*, to die, pt. t. *stearf*, pp. *storfen*; '*stearf* of hungor,' died of hunger, A. S. Chron. an. 1124. Hence was formed the AS. weak verb *sterfan*, to kill, weak vb., appearing in the pp. *astærfed*, Matt. xv. 13 (Rushworth gloss.). The mod. E. has confused the two forms, making them both weak.+Du. *sterven*, pt. t. *stierf, storf*; G. *sterben*, pt. t. *starb*. Teut. type **sterban-*, pt. t. *starð. Der. *starve-l-ing*, with double dimin. suffix, expressive of contempt, 1 Hen. IV, ii. 1. 76. Also *starv-ation*, a hybrid form, but now common, used by Mr. Dundas, the first Viscount Melville, in an American debate in 1775. 'That it then jarred strangely on English ears is evident from the nickname *Starvation Dundas*, which in consequence he obtained. See Letters of H. Walpole and Mann, vol. ii. p. 396, quoted in N. and Q. no. 225;' Trench, Eng. Past and Present.

STATE, a standing, position, condition, an estate, province, rank, dignity, pomp. (F.–L.) See Trench, Sel. Glossary. ME. *stat*, Ancren Riwle, p. 204.–OF. *estat*, 'estate, case, nature,' Cot.–L. *statum*, acc. of *status*, condition.–L. *statum*, supine of *stāre*, to stand; cognate with E. *stand*. From √STĀ, to stand. Der. *state*, verb (late); *stat-ed, stat-ed-ly, state-ment* (a coined word); *state-paper, state-room*, &c.; *state-s-man*, coined like *hunt-s-man, sport-s-man*; *states-man-like, states-man-ship*. Also *state-ly*, ME. *estat-lich*, C. T. 140, a hybrid compound; *state-li-ness*. And see *stat-ion, stat-ist, stat-ue, stat-ure, stat-ute*. Doublets, *estate, stat-us*.

STATICS, the science that treats of the properties of bodies at rest. (Gk.) Spelt *staticks* in Blount's Gloss., ed. 1674. Formed as a pl. from the adj. *statick*. 'The *statick* aphorisms of Sanetorius;' Sir T. Browne, Vulg. Errors, bk. iv. c. 7. § 2.–Gk. στατικός, at a standstill; ἡ στατική (sc. ἐπιστήμη), statics.–Gk. στατ-ός, placed, standing, verbal adj. from στα-, weak grade of the root of ἵστημι, I stand. –√STĀ, to stand; see **Stand**. Der. *hydro-statics*.

STATION, a standing, post, assigned place, situation, rank. (F.–L.) ME. *station*, Gower, C. A. iii. 91; bk. vii. 204.–F. *station*, 'a station;' Cot.–L. *stationem*, acc. of *statio*, a standing still.–L. *statum*, supine of *stāre*, to stand; see **State**. Der. *station-ary*, from MF. *stationnaire* (Cot.), L. adj. *statiōnārius*. Also *station-er*, a bookseller, Minsheu (1627), spelt *stacyoner* in Palsgrave, but orig. merely one who had a *station* or *stand* in a market-place for the sale of books; see Trench, Select Glossary; hence *stationer-y*.

STATIST, a statesman, politician. (F.–L.; *with* Gk. *suffix*.) So in Shak. Hamlet, v. 2. 33. A hybrid word, coined from the sb. *state* by adding *-ist* (F. *-iste* < L. *-ista* < Gk. *-ιστης*). See **State**. Der. *stat-ist-ic*, i. e. relating to the condition of a state or people; whence *statistic-s* (like *static-s* from *static*).

STATUE, an upright image. (F.–L.) Sometimes *statuë* (trisyllabic), in which case it is generally printed *statua* in mod. edd. of Shakespeare, as if from L. *statua* directly. But Cotgrave writes *statuë* for the MF. form. However, *statua* occurs in Bacon, Essays 27, 37, 45. ME. *statue*, Chaucer, C. T. 14165 (B 3349).–OF. *statuë*, a statue; Cot.–L. *statua*, a standing image.–L. *statu-*, decl. stem of *status*, a standing, position; see **State**. Der. *statu-ar-y*, from MF. *statuaire*, 'a statuary, stone-cutter,' Cot., from L. *statuārius*, a maker of statues (Pliny); *statu-ette*, from Ital. *statuetta*, dimin. of *statua*; *statu-esque*, formed with the F. suffix *-esque* = Ital. *-esco* < L. *-iscus*.

STATURE, height. (F.–L.) Used with special reference to the upright posture of a human being. ME. *stature*, Chaucer, C. T. 8133 (E 257).–F. *stature*, 'stature,' Cot.–L. *statūra*, an upright posture, height, growth.–L. *stat-um*, supine of *stāre*, to stand; see **State**.

STATUS, condition, rank. (L.) A late word; not in Todd's Johnson.–L. *status*, condition; see **State**. Doublets, *state, estate*.

STATUTE, an ordinance. (F.–L.) ME. *statute*, Gower, C. A. i. 217; bk. ii. 1741.–F. *statut*; Cot.–L. *statūtum*, a statute; neuter of *statūtus*, pp. of *statuere*, to set, establish.–L. *statu-*, decl. stem of *status*, state; see **State**. Der. *statut-able*, a coined word; *statut-abl-y*; *statut-ory*, a coined word. Here belong also *con-stitute, de-stitute, in-stitute, pro-stitute, sub-stitute*; *re-stitut-ion*.

STAUNCH, adj. and verb; see **Stanch**.

STAVE, one of the pieces of a cask, a part of a piece of music, a stanza. (E.) 1. Merely another form of *staff*, due to the dat. sing. *staue* (= stave), Owl and Night., 1165, and the pl. *staues* (= staves), Wyclif, Mark. xiv. 48. Perhaps the special sense is rather Scand. than E. Cf. Icel. *stafr*, a staff, also a stave; Dan. *stav*, a staff, stave, a stave. 2. A stanza was formerly called a *staff*, as forming a part of a poem; prob. suggested by the older use of AS. *stæf*, Icel. *stafr*, G. *buchstab*, in the sense of a letter or written character. Cf. Icel. *stef*, a stave in a song; Goth. *stafs*, a letter, element, rudiment, Gal. iv. 3. '*Staffe* in our vulgare poesie I know not why it should be so called, vnless it be for that we vnderstand it for a bearer or supporter of a song or ballad;' Puttenham, Art of Eng. Poesie, b. ii. c. 2. See **Staff**. Der. *stave*, verb; usually *to stave in*, to break into a cask, or *to stave off*, to ward off as with a staff; the verb readily puts *v* for *f*, as in *strive* from *strife*, *live* from *life*. Doublet, *staff*.

STAVESACRE, a species of larkspur; *Delphinium staphisagria*. (F.–L.–Gk.) Marlowe has *stavesaker*; Dr. Faustus, i. 4; see Nares. Englished from MF. *staphisaigre*, 'stavesaker, lice-bane;' Cot.–L. *staphisagria*.–Gk. σταφὶς ἄγρια; where ἄγρια is the fem. of ἄγριος, wild, from ἀγρός, a field (E. *acre*); and σταφίς is for ἀσταφίς, raisins.

STAY (1), to remain, abide, wait, prop, delay. (F.–MDu.) '*Steyyn* [= *stayen*], stoppyn, styntyn, or cesyn of gate, Restito, obsto;' Prompt. Parv. The pt. t. *stayd* occurs in London Lick-penny, st. 2.–OF. *estayer*, 'to prop, shore, stay, underset;' Cot. Mod. F. *étayer*.–OF. *estaye*, sb. fem., 'a prop, stay, supporter, shore, buttresse.' This is mod. F. *étai*, a prop; used as a masc. sb., by confusion with the nautical term *étai*; see **Stay** (2). Thus the orig. use was to support, whence the senses to hold, retain, delay, abide, were easily deduced. β. The OF. *estaye* is from MDu. *stade*, or *staeye*, 'a prop or a staye;' Hexham. He also gives *staey*, 'stay, or leisure;' *geen staey hebben*, 'to have noe time or leisure.' So also mod. Du. *stade*, in the phr. *te stade komen*, to come in due time (lit. 'to the right place').+OHG. *stata*, a fit place or time, opportunity. These words are closely allied to Du. *stad*, a town; Dan. *stad*, a town; Swed. *stad*, a town; G. *stadt*, a town, place, stead; Goth. *staths*, a place, stead. Also to E. *staithe* and *stead*; see **Stead**. γ. The loss of medial *d* is common in Dutch, and occurs in many words; e. g. *broêr* for *broeder*, a brother (Sewel), *teer* for *teder* or *teeder*, tender (id.). Der. *stay*, sb., spelt *staye* in Wyatt, tr. of Ps. 130 (R.), from OF. *estaye*, as above; this is really a more orig. word in F., though perhaps later introduced into English. Also *staid*, q. v.; for *stay'd* = *stayed*, pp. Also *stay-s*, pl., lit. supports; it is remarkable that *bodice* is also, properly, a plural form.

STAY (2), as a nautical term, a large rope supporting a mast. (E.) Rare in old books. Cotgrave uses it to translate MF. *estay*, which is the same word, the F. word being of Teut. origin. ME. *stey*; 'one *foresteye*, one couple of *baksteye*;' Riley, Memorials of London, p. 370 (1373). AS. *stæg*, a stay; in a list of the parts of a ship in

Voc. 288. 26. The change from AS. *stæg* to E. *stay* is just the same as that from AS. *dæg* to E. *day*.+Du. *stag*; Icel., Dan., and Swed. *stag*; G. *stag*. Perhaps from Teut. **stah-* = Idg. **stak-*, to resist; see **Steel**. ¶ It is difficult to say whether this E. *stay* is a survival of AS. *stæg*, or is from OF. *estaye*, a prop; see **Stay** (1). Der. *stay-sail*.

STEAD, a place, position, place which another person had or might have. (E.) ME. *stede*, in the general sense of place. 'In twenti *stedes*' = in twenty places; Havelok, 1846. AS. *stede*, a place; Grein, ii. 478. Closely allied to AS. *stæð*, *steð*, a bank, shore; see **Staithe**.+Du. *stede*, *stee*, a place; MDu. *stede*, a farm. Closely allied to Du. *stad*, a town; Icel. *staðr*, a stead, place, *staða*, a place; Dan. and Swed. *stad*, a town; Dan. *sted*, a place; G. *stadt*, *statt*, a town, place; OHG. *stat*; Goth. *staths*, a stead, place. Cf. L. *statio*, a station; Gk. στάσις; Skt. *sthiti-*, a standing, residence, abode, state. All allied to **Stand**, q. v. Der. *stead fast*, q.v., *stead-y*, q. v., *home-stead*, q.v.; *bed-stead*. And see *stay* (1), *staithe*, *station*.

STEADFAST, STEDFAST, firm in its place, firm, constant, resolute. (E.) ME. *stedẽfast*, appearing as a trisyllable in Gower, C. A. iii. 115; bk. vii. 906; and in the Ormulum, l. 1597. AS. *stedefæst*, firm in one's place, steadfast; Battle of Maldon, 127, 249; see Sweet's A. S. Reader. – AS. *stede*, a place; and *fæst*, fast. See **Stead** and **Fast**.+MDu. *stedevast*, 'steadfast,' Hexham; from MDu. *stede*, a farm (orig. a place), and *vast*, fast; Icel. *staðfastr*, from *staðr*, a stead, and *fastr*, fast; Dan. *stadfast*.

STEADY, firm, fixed, stable. (E.) Spelt *stedye* in Palsgrave. A new formation from ME. *sted-e*, a stead; with suffix *-y* (AS. *-ig*); suggested by *stead-fast*. The AS. word is *stæððig*, steady, appearing in *unstæððig*, unsteady, giddy, Ælfric's Homilies, i. 480, last line. Cf. MDu. *stedigh*, 'continuall, firme,' Hexham; from *stede*, a stead. Also Icel. *stöðugr*, steady, stable, from *staðr*, a place; Dan. *stadig*, steady, from *stade*, a stall, *stad*, a town, orig. a place; Swed. *stadig*, from *stad*, a place; G. *stätig*, continual, from *statt*, a place. Der. *steadi-ly*, *-ness*. Also *steady*, verb.

STEAK, a slice of meat, esp. beef, ready for cooking. (Scand.) ME. *steike*; spelt *steyke* in Prompt. Parv. – Icel. *steik*, a steak; so called from its being roasted, which was formerly done by placing it upon a wooden peg before the fire; cf. Icel. *steikja*, to roast, esp. on a spit or peg; cf. *stikna*, to be roasted or scorched. In the words *steikja*, *stikna*, the '*ei* and *i* indicate a lost strong verb.' The weak grade of this lost strong verb appears in the AS. *stic-ian*, to stick; see **Stick** (1). And cf. Icel. *stika*, a stick, *stika*, to drive piles. A *steak* is a piece of meat, *stuck* on a *stick* to be roasted.+Swed. *stek*, roast meat; *steka*, to roast; cf. *stick*, a stab, prick, *sticka*, to stick, stab; Dan. *steg* (for **stek*), a roast; *ad vende steg*, to turn the spit; *stege*, to roast; cf. *stik*, a stab, *stikke*, to pierce; *stikke* a stick. Der. *beef-steak*; whence F. *bifteck*.

STEAL, to take away by theft, to thieve. (E.) ME. *stelen*, Chaucer, C. T. 564 (A 562); pt. t. *stal*, id. 3993 (A 3995); pp. *stolen*. AS. *stelan*, pt. t. *stæl*, pl. *stǣlon*, pp. *stolen*; John, x. 10.+ Du. *stelen*; Icel. *stela*; Dan. *stjæle*; Swed. *stjäla*; G. *stehlen*; OHG. *stelan*; Goth. *stilan*. Teut. type **stelan-*, pt. t. **stal*, pp. **stulanoz*. β. Connexion with Gk. στέρομαι, I am deprived of, στερέω, I deprive, is doubtful, but is accepted by some. Der. *steal-th*, ME. *stalþe*, Rob. of Glouc. p. 197, l. 4057; cf. Icel. *stuldr*, Swed. *stöld*, theft. Hence *stealth-y*, *stealth-i-ly*, *-ness*. Also *stale* (2).

STEAM, vapour. (E.) ME. *steem*, which also meant a flame or blaze. '*Steem*, or lowe of fyre, Flamma; *Steem*, of hotte lycure, Vapor;' Prompt. Parv. [In Havelok, 591, *stem* is a ray of light, described as resembling a sun-beam. 'Two *stemynge* eyes' = two flaming eyes; Sir T. Wiat, Sat. i. 53.] AS. *stēam*, a vapour, smell, smoke; Grein, ii. 480.+Du. *stoom*, steam. Teut. type **staumoz*, m.; as if from a base **steu-*. Root unknown. Can it be allied to **Stove**? Der. *steam*, verb, ME. *stemen*, Chaucer, C. T. 202, AS. *stēman*, as in *be-stēman*, Grein, i. 94; *steam-boat*, *-engine*; *steam-er*; *steam-y*.

STEARINE, STEARIN, one of the ingredients of animal fats. (F. – Gk.) Modern; F. *stéarine*; formed, with suffix *-ine*, from Gk. στέαρ, tallow, hardened fat. Allied to Gk. στῆ-ναι, to stand, be firm. Brugmann, ii. § 82. See **Statics**.

STEATITE, soap-stone, a variety of talc. (F. – Gk.) Modern; F. *stéatite*; formed with suffix *-ite* (Gk. *-ιτης*) from Gk. στέατ-, as in στέατ-ος, gen. of στέαρ, fat (above).

STEED, a horse, esp. a spirited horse. (E.) ME. *stede*, Chaucer, C. T. 13831 (B 2093); Havelok, 1675. AS. *stēda*, masc., a stud-horse, stallion, war-horse; Ælfric's Homilies, i. 210, l. 14; also *gestēd-hors*, used as convertible with *stēda* in Ælfred's tr. of Beda, b. ii. c. 13, where it is also opposed to *myre*, a mare, as being of a different gender. Cf. AS. *stōdmyre*, a stud-mare, Laws of Ælfred (political), § 16, in Thorpe, Ancient Laws, i. 71. β. By the usual vowel change from ō to ē (as in *fōt*, a foot, pl. *fēt*, feet, and in a great

number of instances), *stēda* (for **stōd-jon-*) is derived from *stōd*, a stud; with the addition of the masc. nom. suffix *-a* (from *-jon*). Thus *stēd-a* = 'studder,' i. e. stud-horse or stallion, for breeding foals. See **Stud** (1). Allied to G. *stute*, a mare, Icel. *stedda*, a mare, *stōðhestr*, a stallion, *stōðmerr*, a stud-mare or brood-mare.

STEEL, iron combined with carbon, for tools, swords, &c. (E.) ME. *steel*, Chaucer, C. T. 10300 (E 2426). Also spelt *stiel*, Gower, C. A. vi. 1814; *style*, Sir Ferumbras, 4443. OMerc. *stēli*; Epinal Gloss. 49; AS. *stȳle*, Grein, ii. 490; and in the compounds *stȳl-ecg*, steel-edged, and *stȳlen*, made of steel; Grein, ii. 490. The OMerc. *stēli* is for **stehli*, from **stahli-*; see below.+Du. *staal*; Icel. *stāl*; Dan. *staal*; Swed. *stål*; G. *stahl*, contracted from OHG. *stahal*. β. The OHG. form furnishes the clue to the etymology; all the forms are due to Teut. types **stahlo-*, **stahli-*, formed from the Teut. base STAH, answering to an Idg. base STAK, to be firm or still, appearing in Skt. *stak*, to resist, Zend *staχ-ra-*, strong (Horn, § 714), and esp. in OPruss. *panu-stakla*, steel for kindling fire. Thus the long vowel in *steel* is due to loss of *h* before *l*. Der. *steel*, verb, from AS. *stylan*, to steel; cf. Icel. *stæla*, to steel (derived from *stāl* by the usual vowel-change), G. *stählen* (from *stahl*).

STEELYARD (1), a meeting-place, in London, for German merchants from the Hanse towns. (E.) 'Next to this lane [Cosin Lane], on the east, is the *Steelyard*, as they term it, a place for merchants of Almayne [Germany], that use to bring hither . . *steel*, and other profitable merchandises;' Stow's Chronicle, ed. Thoms, p. 67; see the whole passage. The Steelyard was a factory for the Hanse Merchants, and was in Dowgate ward. That the English really called this place the *steel-yard* appears from a document dated 1394, in which it is Latinised as *Curia Calibis* (= *Chalybis*); see N. and Q. 10 S. vi. 413. In 1475 it is 'called the *Stilehofe*, otherwise called the *Stileyerd*.' Here *stile* is a ME. variant of *steel*; see above. 'The marchauntes of the *styliarde*' are mentioned in Fabyan's Chron., an. 1527–8. And see *Stilyard* in Blount's Gloss., ed. 1674. β. But it is explained, in the Bremen Wörterbuch, that the Low G. name was *Staal-hof*, for which 'steel-yard' was a mistaken substitution; *hof* being correctly translated by 'yard.' The mistake obviously arose from the fact that both Low G. *staal* and MDu. *stael* had a double meaning, viz. (1) steel, and (2), sample, pattern; and the *latter* was really meant. Both Low G. *staal*, a sample, and MDu. *stael*, a sample, are from OF. *estaler*, to display wares on a stall (OF. *estal*).–Dan. *stal*, G. *stall*, a stall; see **Stall**. γ. Cf. Du. *staal-hof*, 'pattern-office, where the samples of cloth were stamped;' Calisch.

STEELYARD (2), a kind of balance, with unequal arms. (E.) The form is due to a popular etymology from *steel* and *yard*, as if 'a bar of steel.' But, as a fact, it was merely shortened from *stilyard-beme*, meaning the 'beam' or balance used in the *Steelyard* (as explained above). Hence the word *yard*, oddly enough, does not refer to the shape of the balance, but to the place wherein it was used; so that it is derived from *yard* (1), not from *yard* (2). 'The beam of *le Hanzes Hangis*, called the *Stilliarde Beme*;' Letters and Papers Foreign and Domestic, Henry VIII, vol. v. p. 104, col. 2; see N. and Q. 10 S. vi. 331. Later shortened to *stilliard*; Cotgrave, s. v. *Crochet*, calls it 'a Roman beame or *stelleere*;' Phillips (1706) has *stelleer*; and Torriano, s. v. *stadera*, has 'a pair of *stilliards*.' Hence prov. E. *stillur*, *stilliard*.

STEENBOK, a S. African antelope. (Du.) Du. *steenbok*, lit. 'rock-goat.' – Du. *steen*, stone, rock; and *bok*, he-goat. See **Stone** and **Buck** (1).

STEEP (1), precipitous. (E.) ME. *step*, *steep*. 'Theo path . . was narwe and *stepe*;' King Alisaunder, 7041. AS. *stēap*, steep, high, lofty; Grein, ii. 481. Cf. Icel. *steypðr*, steep, rising high. Both AS. *stēap* and Icel. *steypðr* are from a common Teut. base **staup*. β. The Icel. *steypðr* is allied to *steypa*, to overthrow, cast down, lit. to make to stoop, causal of the rare verb *stūpa*, to stoop, which is the same word as Swed. *stupa*, (1) to fall, (2) to tilt. Cf. Swed. *stupande*, sloping, *stupning*, a leaning forward; whence it appears that *steep* is allied to *stoop*, and meant, originally, tilted forward, sloping down. So also Norweg. *stupa*, to fall, tumble headlong, *stup*, a steep cliff. See **Stoop** (1), and **Stoup**. Der. *steep-ly*, *-ness*; *steep-le*, q. v.; *steep-y*, Timon, i. 1. 74; *steep* (2).

STEEP (2), to dip or soak in a liquid. (Scand.) ME. *stepen*. '*Stepyn* yn water or other licure, Infundo, illiqueo;' Prompt. Parv. Spelt *stepe*, Palladius, b. ii. l. 281. – Icel. *steypa*, to make to stoop, overturn, to pour out liquids, to cast metals; causal of *stūpa*, to stoop; see **Stoop** (1), and see **Steep** (1). So also Swed. *stöpa*, to cast (metals), to steep, to sink; *stöpa korn*, 'to steep barley in water' (Widegren); Dan. *stöbe*, to cast, mould (metals), to steep (corn), *stöb*, the steeping of grain, steeped corn. The succession of senses is: to make to stoop or overturn, to pour out or cast metals, to pour water over grain.

STEEPLE, a pointed tower of a church or building. (E.) ME. *stepel*, Rob. of Gloucester, p. 528, l. 10860. AS. *stypel*, a lofty tower, Luke, xiii. 4; the Hatton MS. has *stēpel*. So called from its 'steepness,' i.e. loftiness or height; from AS. *stēap*, lofty, high, mod. E. *steep*. The vowel-change from *ēa* to Merc. *ē*, Wessex *īe*, later *ȳ*, is regular; see **Steep** (1). Also spelt *stēapol*; OE. Texts, p. 616. **Der.** *steeple-chase*, modern, not in Todd's Johnson.

STEER (1), a young ox. (E.) ME. *steer*, Chaucer, C. T. 2151 (A 2149). AS. *stēor*; 'Juvencus, vel vitula, *steor*;' Voc. 120. 28.+Du. and G. *stier*, a bull; Icel. *stjörr*; Goth. *stiur*. Teut. type *steuroz*, m. Another Teut. type is *theuroz*, from Idg. *teuros*; as in Icel. *þjörr*, Swed. *tjur*, Dan. *tyr*, a steer; allied (by gradation) to L. *taurus*, Gk. ταῦρος, from Idg. *tauros*. β. The orig. sense is 'full-grown' or 'large,' as in Skt. *sthūla-* (for *sthūra-*), great, large, powerful, *sthūra-*, a man, *sthūrī*, a pack-horse; cf. Zend *staora-*, Pers. *sutūr*, a beast of burden. Brugmann, i. §§ 196, 230; Horn, § 720. γ. We even find the allied adj. in Teutonic, viz. AS. *stōr*, large, Icel. *störr*, Dan. and Swed. *stor*; Idg. type *sthār-os*, large. Thus a *steer* is a firm, full-grown animal, esp. a young bull. See also **Steer** (2). **Der.** *stir-k* (Jamieson); AS. *stȳric*, Luke, xv. 23, formed with dimin. suffix *-ic*, and consequent vowel-change from *ēo* to *ȳ*.

STEER (2), to direct, guide, govern. (E.) ME. *steren*, P. Plowman, B. viii. 47. AS. *stēoran*, *styran*, to direct, steer, Grein, ii. 481, 491.+Du. *sturen*; Icel. *stȳra*; Dan. *styre*; Swed. *styra*; G. *steuern*, OHG. *stiurjan*, *stiuran*; Goth. *stiurjan*, to establish, confirm. β. All from the Teut. weak verb *steur-jan-*, to steer (orig. to strengthen, confirm, hence, hold fast, direct). This is a denominative verb, from the sb. of which the base is *steur-*, a rudder (lit. that which holds fast). This sb. is now obsolete in E., but appears in Chaucer as *stere*, C. T. 4868 (B 448); AS. *stēor*, Du. *stuur*, a rudder, Icel. *styri*, a rudder, Dan. *styr*, steerage, G. *steuer*, a rudder, OHG. *stiura*, a prop, a staff, a paddle or rudder. It is still retained in E. in the comp. *star-board*, i.e. steer-board, AS. *stēor-bord* (rudder-side of a ship). γ. Closely allied to this sb. is Icel. *staurr*, a post, stake, Gk. σταυρός, an upright pole or stake. Noreen, § 143; Brugmann, i. § 198. The Teut. sb. meant, accordingly, a pole to punt with or a paddle to keep the ship's course right, then a rudder; whence the verb to *steer*, to use a stake or paddle, to use a helm. **Der.** *steer-age*, Romeo, i. 4. 112, with F. suffix; *steer-s-man*, Milton, P. L. ix. 513, formed like *hunt-s-man*, *sport-s-man*; also *star-board*, q.v., *stern*, q.v. And see **Store**.

STELLAR, belonging to the stars. (L.) 'Stellar vertue;' Milton, P. L. iv. 671.—L. *stellāris*, starry.—L. *stella*, a star; short for *ster-la*, a contracted dimin. from the same source as E. *star*; see **Star**. **Der.** (from *stella*) *stell-ate*, *stell-at-ed*; *stell-ul-ar*, from the dimin. *stellula*, a little star. Also *stell-i-fy*, obsolete; see Chaucer, Ho. of Fame, ii. 78.

STEM (1), the trunk or stalk of a tree or herb, a little branch. (E.) ME. *stem*, a trunk of a tree, Rob. of Brunne, tr. of Langtoft, p. 296, l. 8. AS. *stæfn*, *stefn*, (1) a stem of a tree, (2) the stem or prow of a vessel, (3) a stem or race of people, Grein, ii. 479. [The change from *fn* to *mn* is regular; so also AS. *hlāfmæsse* is now *Lammas*.] We also find a weak form *stefna*, *stæfna*, a stem or prow of a ship (Grein). Both these forms are apparently allied to AS. *stæf*, a staff; a stem of a tree is the *staff* or stock, or support of it; the stem of a vessel is the upright post in front of it. See further under **Staff**.+Du. *stam*, a trunk, stem, stock; *steven*, prow; Icel. *stafn*, later *stamn*, the stem of a vessel (from *stafr*, a staff), also written *stefni*, *stemni*, also *stofn*, *stomn*, the stem of a tree; Dan. *stamme*, the trunk of a tree; *stævn*, the prow of a vessel; Swed. *stam*, trunk; *stäf*, prow; *framstam*, fore-stem, prow, *bakstam*, back-stem, stern; G. *stamm*, a trunk; *steven* or *vorder steven*, the stem, prow-post; cf. *hinter steven*, stern-post.

STEM (2), the prow of a vessel. (E.) Spelt *stam* in Morte Arthure, l. 3664; but this is rather the Scand. form; the pl. *stemmes* is in Baret (1580). It is precisely the same word as when we speak of the *stem* of a tree; see further under **Stem** (1). ¶ As the orig. signification was merely 'post,' there was no particular reason (beyond usage) why it should have been used more of the prow-post than of the stern-post; accordingly, the Icel. *stafn* sometimes means 'prow,' and sometimes 'stern;' and in G. the distinction is made by saying *vorder steven* (fore-stem) for stem or prow-post, and *hinter steven* (hind-stem) for stern or stern-post.

STEM (3), to check, stop, resist. (E.) 'Stem, verb, to oppose (a current), to press forward through; *to stem the waves*, 3 Hen. VI, ii. 6. 36; *stemming it*, J. Cæsar, i. 2. 109;' Schmidt, Shak. Lexicon. Cf. Icel. *stemma*, to dam up; Dan. *stemme*, to stem; G. *stemmen*, to dam up water. Teut. type *stemjan-*; a verb derived (by vowel-change of *a* to *e*) from a base *stam-*, with the idea of 'obstruction;' see **Stammer**.

STENCH, a bad smell. (E.) ME. *stench*, Rob. of Glouc. p. 405, l. 8354. AS. *stenc*, dat. *stence*, a strong smell, common in the sense of sweet smell or fragrance; Grein, ii. 479.—AS. *stanc*, 2nd grade of *stincan*, to smell, to stink; see **Stink**. [Stench from *stink*, like *drench* from *drink*.]+G. *ge-stank*, a stench (from *stinken*).

STENCIL, to paint or colour in figures by means of a stencilling-plate. (F.—L.) In Webster; he defines a *stencil* (as a stencilling-plate is sometimes called) as 'a thin plate of metal, leather or other material, used in painting or marking; the pattern is cut out of the plate, which is then laid flat on the surface to be marked, and the colour brushed over it.' Various guesses have been made at the etymology of this word, all worthless. I think it probable that to *stencil* is from OF. *estenceler*, to sparkle, also to cover with stars, to adorn with bright colours (Godefroy), MF. *estinceller*, 'to sparkle, . . . to powder, or set thick with sparkles;' Cot. It was an old term in heraldry. Littré gives a quotation of the 15th century; 'L'aurmoire estoit tute par dedans de fin or *estincelee*' = the box (?) was all (covered) within with fine gold *scattered in stars*. This peculiar kind of ornamentation (star-work) is precisely what *stencilling* must first have been used for, and it is used for it still. Since the pattern is cut quite through the plate, it must all be in separate pieces, so that no better device can be used than that which, to quote Cotgrave, is *set thick with sparkles*. Cf. 'With his sternes [stars] of gold, *stanseld* on-stray,' i.e. stencilled at random; Aunters of Arthure, st. 31.—OF. *estencele*, a spark; in Walter de Bibbesworth, in Wright's Vocab. i. 171.—L. type *stincilla*, mistaken form of L. *scintilla*, a spark. See **Scintillation**; also **Tinsel**. ¶ The note to Aunters of Arthur, st. 31, quotes from the Wardrobe accounts of Edw. III: 'harnesium de bokeram albo, *extencellato* cum argento,' i. e. starred with silver.

STENOGRAPHY, short-hand writing. (Gk.) Not a very new word; spelt *stenographie* in Minsheu, ed. 1627. Coined from Gk. στενο-, for στενός, narrow, close; and -γραφία, writing (as occurring in ὀρθογραφία, orthography), from γράφειν, to write. **Der.** *stenograph-er*, *stenograph-ic*, *-ic-al*, *-ic-al-ly*.

STENTORIAN, extremely loud. (Gk.) See Ben Jonson, Staple of News, very near the end; and Blount's Gloss., ed. 1674; he rightly explains it with reference to the voice of *Stentor*.—Gk. Στέντωρ, Stentor, a Greek at Troy, famous for his loud voice, Homer, Iliad, v. 785.—Gk. στέν-ειν, to groan, make a noise; with suffix -τωρ of the agent, as in L. *ama-tor*, a lover.—√STEN, to make a noise; cf. Skt. *stan*, to sound, to thunder. Cf. E. *stun*. *Stentor* = *stunner*.

STEP, a pace, degree, round of a ladder, foot-print. (E.) ME. *steppe*, in the sense of foot-step, Ywaine and Gawin, 2889, in Ritson's Met. Romances, vol. i; Mandeville's Travels, ed. Halliwell, p. 81. OMerc. *stepe* (Sweet); AS. *stæpe*, a pace, Jos. x. 12.—AS. *steppan*, to go, advance, a strong verb with a weak infinitive, pt. t. *stōp*, pp. *stapen*. The pt. t. *stōp* occurs frequently; see Grein, ii. 476. β. The orig. sense is 'to set the foot down firmly;' from a Teut. base STAP; see further under **Stamp**, which is merely the nasalised form. Allied to Du. *stap*, G. *stapfe*, a footprint, footstep. **Der.** *foot-step*; *door-step*; *stepp-ing-stone*, in Wright's Voc. i. 159, where it is miswritten *seping-stone*, by an obvious error.

STEPCHILD, one who stands in the relation of child through the marriage of a parent. (E.) The pl. *step-childre* occurs in Early Eng. Psalter, ed. Stevenson, Ps. xciii. 6. *Stepmoder* is in Gower, C. A. i. 104; bk. i. 1844. AS. *stēopcild*, Exod. xxii. 22; John, xiv. 18, q. v. For *cild*, see **Child**. β. The prefix *stēop*- occurs also in *stēopbearn*, a stepbairn, stepchild, *stēopfæder*, stepfather, *stēopmōder*, stepmother, *stēopsunu*, stepson, and *stēopdohtor*, stepdaughter; see Voc. 9. 10; 34. 27; 22. 23; 88. 20. γ. The sense of *stēop* is 'orphaned,' or 'deprived of its parent;' so that it was first used in the compounds stepchild, stepbairn, stepson, stepdaughter, and afterwards extended, naturally enough, so as to form the compounds *stepfather*, *stepmother*, to denote the father or mother of the child who had lost one of its first parents. Thus the Lat. 'Fiant filii ejus *orfani*' is translated in the Vespasian Psalter by 'sien bearn his *āstēapte*;' Ps. cviii. 9, ed. Sweet. 'Astēpnes', orbatio,' occurs in a gloss (Bosworth). δ. The Teut. type is *steupoz*, adj., with the sense of 'orphaned' or 'deprived;' the root is unknown; Fick, iii. 347. We only know that it is wholly unconnected with *step* above; it may, however, be related to **Stoop** (1), q.v.+Du. *stiefkind*; so also *stiefzoon*, *stiefdochter*, *stiefvader*, *stiefmoeder*; Icel. *stjūpbarn*, a step-bairn; so also *stjūpson*, *-dóttir*, *-faðir*, *-mōðir*; Dan. *stedbarn*, a corrupt form; Swed. *styfbarn*; G. *stiefkind*; so also *stiefsohn*, *-tochter*, *-vater*, *-mutter*; cf. OHG. *stiuf->*G. *stief-*; and OHG. *stiufan*, to deprive of parents, also to deprive of children. See also **Steep** (1).

STEPPE, a large plain. (Russ.) In Webster. Perhaps in Mids. Nt. Dream, ii. 1. 69, such being the reading of the first quarto;

most edd. have *steep*. – Russ. *stepe* (with final *e* mute), a waste, heath, steppe.

STEREOSCOPE, an optical instrument for giving an appearance of solidity. (Gk.) Modern. First constructed in 1838. Coined from Gk. στερεό-, for στερεός, stiff, hard, firm, solid; and σκοπ-εῖν, to behold. β. Gk. στερεός is cognate with G. *starr*, stiff, and perhaps with Skt. *sthira-s*, firm; and σκοπεῖν is allied to σκέπτομαι, I look round; see **Stare** (1) and **Scope** or **Sceptic**. Der. *stereoscop-ic, -ic-al, -ic-al-ly*.

STEREOTYPE, a solid plate for printing. (Gk.) '*Stereotype* was invented (not the *thing*, but the *word*) by Didot not very long since;' Trench, Eng. Past and Present, 4th ed. 1859. – Gk. στερεο-, for στερεός, hard, stiff; and *type*. See **Stereoscope** and **Type**. Der. *stereotype*, verb.

STERILE, unfruitful, barren. (F. – L.) Spelt *steril* in Levins. – MF. *sterile*, 'sterile;' Cot. – L. *sterilem*, acc. of *sterilis*, barren. From the base STER appearing in Gk. στερεός, στερρός, hard, stiff, firm, sterile; cf. G. *starr*, rigid; for which see **Stare** (1). Cf. also Gk. στεῖρα (for *στέρ-ya), a barren cow; Goth. *stairō*, a barren woman. Brugmann, i. § 838. A *sterile* soil is a hard, stony, unproductive one. Der. *steril-i-ty*, from F. *sterilité*, 'sterility,' Cot., from L. acc. *sterilitātem*.

STERLING, genuine, applied to money. (E.) ME. *starling, sterling*, Chaucer, C. T. 12841 (C 907); P. Plowman, B. xv. 342; Rob. of Glouc. p. 294, l. 5949. In all these passages it is a sb., meaning 'a sterling coin,' a coin of true weight. Thus Rob. of Glouc. speaks of ' Four þousend pound of *sterlynges*.' Of E. origin; the MHG. *sterlinc*, cited by Stratmann, is borrowed from it. First applied to the E. penny, then to standard current coin in general. Wedgwood cites from Ducange a statute of Edw. I, in which we meet with ' Denarius Angliæ, qui vocatur *Sterlingus*;' also a Charter of Hen. III, where we have ' In centum marcis bonorum nouorum et legalium *sterlingorum*, tredecim solid. et 4 *sterling*. pro qualibet marca computatis.' That is, a mark is 13*s*. and 4*d*., a *sterling* being here a *penny*. β. Wedgwood adds : ' The hypothesis most generally approved is that the coin is named from the Easterlings or North Germans, who were the first moneyers in England. Walter de Pinchbeck, a monk of Bury in the time of Edw. I, says : "sed moneta Angliæ fertur dicta fuisse a nominibus opificum, ut Floreni a nominibus Florentinorum, ita *Sterlingi* a nominibus *Esterlingorum* nomina sua contraxerunt, qui hujusmodi monetam in Anglia primitus componebant."' This notable passage proves only that the name *Esterlingi*, as applied to a people, goes back to the 14th century; and it is difficult to prove that it is much older. γ. But Ducange quotes from a document dated 1184, which has : ' in Anglia unus *sterlingus* persolvetur.' Indeed, the E. *sterling* is even older than this, as Wace (d. ab. 1180) has : ' por ses *estérlins* recevoir;' Roman de Rou, 6873. δ. The word appears to be native English ; there are two theories as to its origin. (1) From AS. **steorling*, 'little star,' with reference to a very small star on some early coins, as, e. g. on some of Will. II ; or (2) from AS. *stærling*, a starling (Clarke Hall), ME. *sterling* (Voc. 640. 7, 761. 28 ; Cursor Mundi, 1789), dimin. of AS. *stær*, ME. *ster* (Voc. 542. 45), a starling ; see **Starling**. Ducange quotes from Lyndwode to the effect that the reference may be to the four birds conspicuous on most coins of Edward the Confessor.

STERN (1), severe, harsh, austere. (E.) ME. *sterne*, Wyclif, Luke, xix. 21, 22 ; also *sturne*, Rob. of Glouc. p. 27, l. 628. AS. *styrne*, stern, Grein, ii. 492 ; where we also find *styrn-mōd*, of stern mood, stern-minded, *styrnan*, to be severe. (The AS. *y* often becomes ME. *u*, as in AS. *wyrm*, ME. *wurm*, a worm; AS. *fyrs*, ME. *furs* or *firs*, furze. Certainly *stern* should rather be spelt *sturn*; it has been assimilated to the form below. Still we find the AS. *y* becoming mod. E. *e* in *kernel*<AS. *cyrnel*.] Teut. type **sturnjoz*. Perhaps allied to OHG. *stornēn*, to be astonished, *sturnī*, stupor. β. The suffix -*n*- is adjectival (Idg. -*no*-), as in L. *Africā-nus*; the base *stur*- seems to be the weak grade of the base STER, as seen in Gk. στερ-εός, solid, stiff. Cf. Goth. *and-staurran*, to murmur against, G. *störrig*, morose, stubborn, *starr*, stiff, rigid ; Du. *stuursch*, stern ; Icel. *stūra*, to mope. See **Stare** (1). The idea of *sternness* is closely allied to those of stiffness and austerity of manner. Der. *stern-ly, -ness*.

STERN (2), the hinder part of a vessel. (Scand.) ME. *sterne*, P. Plowman, B. viii. 35, footnote ; other MSS. have *stere, steere, stiere*, meaning a rudder. Spelt *steorne*, id. A. ix. 30. – Icel. *stjórn*, a steering, steerage ; hence the phr. *sitja við stjórn*, to sit at the helm ; whence *stern* became recognised as a name for the hinder part of the vessel. Extended from *stjór*- (occurring in *stjóri*, a steerer, ruler) which answers to ME. *stere*, a rudder. See **Steer** (2). Compare Icel. *stjórnborði* with E. *starboard* (= *steer-board*). Thus *stern* is allied to *steer*, in the obsolete sense of ' rudder.' Der. *stern-*

most ; *stern-sheets*, where *sheet* had once (I suppose) the nautical sense of ' rope.'

STERNUTATION, sneezing. (L.) In Sir T. Browne, Vulg. Errors, b. iv. c. 9, l. 1. – L. *sternū.ātiōnem*, acc. of *sternūtātio*, a sneezing. – L. *sternūtāre*, to sneeze, frequent. of *sternuere*, to sneeze. Allied to Gk. πτάρνυσθαι, to sneeze. β. The bases *ster-, πταρ-*, seem to be from an imitative base **pster-*, expressive of sneezing. Der. *sternutat-or-y*.

STERTOROUS, snoring. (L.) Modern. Coined (as if from L. **stertorōsus*) from *stertere*, to snore. Prob. of imitative origin ; cf. **Sternutation**. Der. *stertorous-ly*.

STETHOSCOPE, the tube used in auscultation, as applied to the chest. (Gk.) Added by Todd to Johnson. Modern ; lit. ' chest-examiner.' Coined from Gk. στηθο-, for στῆθος, the chest ; and σκοπ-εῖν, to consider, examine. β. The Gk. στῆθος is allied to Skt. *stana-s*, the female breast, a nipple. Cf. Gk. στηνίον = στῆθος (Hesychius). For -*scope*, see **Scope** or **Sceptic**. Der. *stethoscop-ic*.

STEVEDORE, one whose occupation it is to load and unload vessels in port. (Span. – L.) Webster has *stevedore*, which is a well-known word in the mercantile world, and *steve*, verb, to stow, as cotton or wool in a vessel's hold. The word is Spanish, Spain being a wool-producing country and once largely engaged in sea-traffic. – Span. *estivador*, 'a packer of wool at shearing ;' Neuman. It may also mean a stower of cargo, as will be seen. Formed with suffix -*dor* (<L. acc. -*tōrem*) from *estiva-r*, to stow, to lay up cargo in the hold, to compress wool. – L. *stīpāre*, to crowd together, press together ; allied to **Stiff**. The verb appears also in Ital. *stivare*, to press close, Port. *estivar*, to trim a ship. There is also a verbal sb., viz. Ital. *stiva*, ballast of a ship, Span. *estiva*, the stowage of goods in a ship's hold, MF. *estive*, ' the loading or lading of a ship ;' Cot. From the same root are *stip-end, stip-ul-at-ion, con-stip-ate, co-stive*.

STEW (1), to boil slowly with little moisture. (F. – Teut.) ME. *stuwen*. ' *Stuwyn*, or *stuyn mete*, Stupho ; *Stuwyn or bathyn*, or *stuyn in a stw*, Balneo ;' Prompt. Parv. The older sense was to bathe ; and the verb was formed from the old sb. *stew* in the sense of bath or hot-house (as it was called), which was chiefly used in the pl. *stews*, with the low sense of brothel-house. See Liber Albus, ed. Riley, p. 277 (242 in the translation). The old spelling of the pl. sb. was *stues, stuwes, stewes, stives, stuyves, stywes*, P. Plowman, B. vi. 72, A. vii. 65, all variously Anglicised forms of OF. *estuve*, of which Cotgrave explains the pl. *estuves* by ' stews, also stoves or hot-houses.' [Cf. Ital. *stufa*, Port. and Span. *estufa*, a stove, a hot-house ; mod. F. *étuve*.] β. Of Teut. origin. The OHG. form is *stupa*, a hot room for a bath ; the mod. G. *stube* merely means a room in general. The corresponding E. word is **Stove**, q. v. We may particularly note MDu. *stove*, ' a stewe, a hot-house, or a baine ' [bath], *een stove om te baden*, ' a stewe to bathe in ;' Hexham. The *stews* in Southwark were chiefly filled with Flemish women. Der. *stew*, sb., in the sense of stewed meat ; this is merely a derivative from the verb. The pl. sb. *stews* is treated of above ; cf. ' The bathes and the *stewes* bothe,' Gower, C. A. iii. 291 ; bk. viii. 484.

STEW (2), a fish-pond. (Du.) ME. *stewe*, Chaucer, C. T., A 350. – MDu. *stouwen*, to drive forward ; Du. *stouwen, stuwen*, to stow ; cf. Low G. *stau*, a dam, *stauen*, to keep water back. Allied to **Stow**.

STEWARD, one who superintends another's estate or farm. (E.) ME. *stiward*, Havelok, 666 ; Ancren Riwle, p. 386, l. 5 from bottom. AS. *stigweard*, in a will (Toller) ; also *stiweard*, Voc. 223. 7 ; spelt *stiward*, A. S. Chron. an. 1093, and an. 1120. ' Economus, *stiward*;' Voc. 129. 13 ; also in Thorpe, Diplomatarium, p. 570, l. 12. The full form of the word was *stigweard*, lit. a sty-ward ; from AS. *stig-o*, a sty, and *weard*, a guardian, warden, keeper. The orig. sense was one who looked after the domestic animals, and gave them their food ; hence, one who provides for his master's table, and generally, one who superintends household affairs for another. See **Sty** and **Ward**. β. For the change of sound, cf. the name *Seward*, formerly *Siward*, Macb. iii. 6. 31. The Icel. *stīvarðr*, gen. assigned as the origin of E. *steward*, occurs but rarely ; the Icel. Dict. gives but one reference, and adds the remark that it is ' from the English.' γ. Grein (ii. 484) draws especial attention to the parallel form *stigwita*, also *stīwita*, in the same sense of steward, the suffix being the AS. *wita*, a wise man, one who is skilled. Der. *steward-ship*, Luke, xvi. 2 ; *steward-ess*, with F. suffix.

STICK (1), to stab, pierce, thrust in, to fasten by piercing ; to adhere. (E.) The orig. sense is to stab or pierce (cf. *sting*), hence to fasten into a thing by thrusting it in ; hence, the intransitive use, to be thrust into a thing and there remain, to cling or adhere, to be set fast, stop, hesitate, &c. Two verbs are confused in mod. E., viz. (1) *stick*, to pierce, and (2) *stick*, to be fixed in. 1. STRONG FORM. ME. *steken*, strong verb, to pierce, fix, pt. t. *stak*, Rom. of the Rose, 458 ; pp. *steken, stiken, stoken* (see Stratmann), also *stoke*,

Gower, C. A. i. 60, bk. i. 538; which = mod. E. *stuck*. This answers to AS. **stecan*, not found; pt. t. **stac*, pp. **stecen*; a strong verb, which does not appear in AS., though found both in OFries. *steka*, and in OSaxon, where we find the pt. t. *stak*, Heliand, 5707. And compare **Sting**. Cognate words are Low G. *steken*, to pierce, stick, pt. t. *stak*, pp. *steken*; and G. *stechen*, to sting, pierce, stick, stab, pt. t. *stach*, pp. *gestochen*. Teut. type **stekan*-, pt. t. **stak*, pp. **stakanoz*; transferred to the *e*-series from the older type **steikan*-, pt. t. **staik*, pp. **stikanoz*. Cf. Goth. *staks*, a mark, stigma; *stiks*, a point, a moment of time. β. The latter strong verb is from the Idg. √STEIGw, to pierce (Brugmann, i. § 633); whence Gk. στίζειν (= στίγ-γειν), to prick, L. *instigāre*, to instigate, Skt. *tigma-*, sharp, *tij*, to be sharp, *tejaya*, to sharpen; see **Stigma, Instigate, Sting**. 2. WEAK FORM. ME. *stikien*, to be in-fixed, to stick into, cling to, adhere; a weak verb; also used in a trans. sense. ' And anoon he *stykede* faste ' = he stuck fast, Seven Sages, ed. Wright, 1246; pp. *ystiked*, Chaucer, C. T. 1565. AS. *stician*, pt. t. *sticode*, both trans. and intrans., Grein, ii. 482. Cognate words are Icel. *stika*, to drive piles, Dan. *stikke*, to stab, Swed. *sticka*, to stab, sting, stitch, prick, G. *stecken*, to stick, set, plant, fix, also, to stick fast, remain. Thus the sense of ' stick fast ' appears in G. as well as in E., but G. restricts the strong form *stechen* to the orig. sense, whilst *stecken* has both senses. Der. *stick* (2), q.v.; *stick-y*, spelt *stickie* in Bacon, Nat. Hist. § 583, *stick-i-ness*; *stick-le-back*, q.v.; *stitch*, q.v.; and see *sting, stang, stack, stake, steak*. From the same root are *di-sting-uish, di-stinct, ex-ting-uish, ex-tinct, in-stinct, pre-stige, in-stig-ate, sti-mu-late, style* (1), *stig-ma*.

STICK (2), a staff, small branch of a tree. (E.) ME. *stikke*, Chaucer, C. T. 16733 (G 1265). AS. *sticca*, a stick, also a peg or nail, Judges, iv. 21, 22. So called from its piercing or sticking into anything; the orig. sense was ' peg,' then any small bit of a branch of a tree. ' Se *teldsticca sticode* þurh his heafod ' = the tent-peg stuck through his head, Judges, iv. 22.+Icel. *stika*, a stick; EFries. *stikke, stik*; allied to Du. *stek*, G. *stecken*, a stick. See **Stick** (1), **Steak**, and **Stake**. Der. *stick-le-back*. And see *stitch*. Also *single-stick*; see under *quarterstaff*.

STICKLEBACK, a small fish. (E.) So called from the *stickles* or prickles on its back; cf. *thornback*. ME. *stykylbak*, Reliq. Antiquæ, i. 85. Corruptly *sticklebag*, Walton's Angler, p. i. c. 5 (R.); and still more corruptly *tittlebat* (Halliwell). In the Prompt. Parv., and in Voc. 610. 30, there is mention of a fish called a *stikling* or *stykelyng*. The sb. *stikel* or *stickle* is from AS. *sticel*, a prickle, sting, used of the sting of a gnat in Ælfred, tr. of Boethius, b. ii. pr. 6, cap. xvi. § 2.—AS. *stician*, to stick; just as *prickle* is from *prician*, to prick. See **Stick** (1) and **Stitch**. The suffix -*el* denotes the instrument; it is not (in this case) a diminutive, as is often imagined; see March, A. S. Grammar, § 228. For *back*, see **Back**. Cf. Du. *stekelvisch*, a stickleback; MDu. *stickel*, ' a prick or a sting;' Hexham; also EFries. *stikel*, a thorn.

STICKLER, (formerly) one who parts combatants or settles disputes between two men fighting. (E.) Nearly obsolete; once common; see Halliwell, Nares, and Trench, Select Glossary. ' Like *sticklers* of the war;' Dryden, Oliver Cromwell, 41. Now only used in the sense of a man who insists on etiquette or persists in an opinion. See Troil. v. 8. 18. The verb *to stickle* meant to part combatants, act as umpire. ' I *styckyll* betwene wrastellers, or any folkes that prove mastries [try conclusions] to that none do other wronge, or I parte folkes that be redy to fyght;' Palsgrave. It is common to explain this word (with profound disregard for the *l* in it) by saying that the umpire must have parted combatants by means of *sticks*, or else that the umpire arbitrated between men who fought with *single-sticks*. Both assertions are mere inventions; and a *stickle* is not a stick at all, but a prickle. If this were the etymology, the word would mean ' one who uses prickles.' β. It is probable that *stickle* represents the once common ME. *stightlen* or *stightilen*, to dispose, order, arrange, govern, subdue, &c. It was commonly used of a steward, who disposed of and arranged everything, and acted as a master of the ceremonies; see Will. of Palerne, 1199, 2899, 3281, 3841, 5379; Destruction of Troy, 117, 1997, 2193, 13282; Gawayn and Grene Knight, 2137; &c. ' When þay com to þe courte, keppte wern þay fayre, *Styȝtled* with þe steward, stad in þe halle;' Allit. Poems, B. 90. ' To *styȝtle* the peple ' = to keep order among the people;' P. Plowm. Crede, 315; and cf. P. Plowman, C. xvi. 40. We also find *stighill* (without *t*), York Myst. (glossary); and the sb. is *stiteler* in the Cov. Myst. p. 23. γ. This ME. *stiȝtlen* is the frequentative of AS. *stihtan, stihtian*. ' Willem weolde and *stihte* Engleland ' = William ruled and governed England, A. S. Chron. an. 1086 (Thorpe renders it by ' held despotic sway').+MDu. *stichten*, ' to build, edefie, bound, breed or make (a contention), impose or make (a lawe),' Hexham; mod. Du. *stichten*, to found, institute,

establish, excite, edify. Further allied to Dan. *stifte*, to found, institute, establish; *stifte forliȝ* = to reconcile, *stifte fred* = to make peace (just exactly *to stickle*); Swed. *stifta*, also *stikta*, similarly used; G. *stiften*, to found, institute, cause, excite; *Freundschaft stiften* = to make friendship. Cf. also Icel. *stētt* (from **stihti*-), a foundation, base. Kluge derives *stih-, stif-*, from a Teut. base **stihw* (= Idg. **stig*), to build, found; cf. OSax. *stihtan*, to build.

STIFF, rigid, obstinate, formal. (E.) The vowel was once long; and remains so in North E. *stive*, muscular, and in the derivative *stifle*. ME. *stif*, Chaucer, C. T. 7849 (D 2267); the superl. is spelt *styuest, steuest, steffest, stiffest*, P. Plowman, C. vii. 43. AS. *stif, stiff* (Toller); this form is verified by the derivatives *stifian* and *āstifian*. ' Heora hand *āstifedon*' = their hands became stiff; Ælfric's Homilies, i. 598, l. 11. ' Obrigesco, ic *stifie*,' Voc. 118. 20.+Du. *stijf*, stiff, hard, rigid, firm; Dan. *stiv*; Swed. *styf*; Low G. *stif* (Danneil); Westphal. *stif*. [The G. *steif* is supposed to be borrowed from Low G.] β. Allied to Lithuan. *stiprùs*, strong, *stipti*, to be stiff, L. *stipes*, a stem, trunk of a tree, *stipāre*, to pack tight; *stipulus*, firm. See **Stipulation**. Der. *stiff-ly, -ness, stiff-en* (Swed. *stifna*, Dan. *stivne*), Hen. V, iii. 1. 7, *stiff-neck-ed*, Acts, vii. 51; *stif-le*.

STIFLE, to suffocate. (Scand.) ' *Stifil, Stifle*, suffocare;' Levins. ' Smored [smothered] and *stifled*;' Sir T. More, Works, p. 68 f.—Icel. *stifla*, to dam up, prop. used of water; hence, to block up, choke; Norweg. *stivla*, to stop, hem in, check, lit. ' to stiffen;' cf. *stivra*, to stiffen; both are frequent. forms of *stiva* (Dan. *stive*), to stiffen. [Cf. also ME. *stiuen*, to stiffen, Will. of Palerne, 3033; Swed. *styfva*, Du. *stijven*; G. *steifen*, to stiffen.] All these words are derived from the adj. appearing as AS. *stif*, stiff; the vowel of which was once long, and is still so in prov. E. Halliwell gives ' *Stive*, strong, muscular, North:' which is nothing but ME. *styue*, an occasional spelling of *stiff*; see **Stiff**. The loss of the adj. ' stiff' in Icel. is remarkable, as it is preserved in Swed., Dan., and Norwegian; the OIcel. form was *stif*, cited by E. Müller. ¶ We cannot derive *stifle* from the verb *stive*, to pack close, the change from *v* to *f* being contrary to rule; but it is very probable that *stifle* has been frequently confused with *stive*, which, though it properly means to pack close, came to have much the same sense, as in prov. E. *stivy*, close, stifling (Worcestershire). *Stive* is a F. word, from OF. *estiver* < L. *stipāre*, to compress, pack tight, as explained under **Stevedore**. Note that E. *stiff* and L. *stipāre* are closely related words, from the same root.

STIGMATISE, to brand with infamy, defame publicly. (F.—Late L.—Gk.) ' *Stigmatised* with a hot iron;' Burton, Anat. of Melancholy, p. 470 (R.). [Shak. has *stigmatic*, naturally deformed, 2 Hen. VI, v. 1. 215; *stigmatical*, Com. Errors, iv. 2. 22.]—F. *stigmatiser*, in Cotgrave *stigmatizer*, ' to brand, burn, or mark with a red hot iron, to defame publicly.'—Late L. *stigmatizāre*, to mark; see Higden, ii. 146.—Gk. στιγματίζειν, to mark or brand.—Gk. στιγματ-, base of στίγμα, a prick, mark, brand. From the base στιγ-, as in στίζειν (= στίγ-γειν), to prick. From Idg. √STEIGw, to prick; whence also E. *stick*; see **Stick** (1). Der. (from Gk. στιγματ-) *stigmat-ic, stigmat-ic-al*. We also use now *stigma*, sb., from Gk. στίγμα.

STILE (1), a step or set of steps for climbing over a fence or hedge. (E.) ME. *stile, style*, Chaucer, C. T. 10420 (F 106). AS. *stigel*, a stile; Thorpe, Diplomatarium, p. 146, l. 6. Formed with suffix -*el*, denoting the means or instrument, from *stig-*, weak grade of AS. *stīgan*, to climb, mount. See **Sty** (1). The AS. *stigel* first became *stiȝel*, and then *stile*; so also AS. *tigul* became mod. E. *tile*.+OHG. *stigila*, a stile (obsolete), from OHG. *stīgan*, to climb; MDu. *stichel* (Hexham). And cf. Shetland *stiggy*, a stile (Edmonston); from the same root.

STILE (2), the correct spelling of **Style**, q. v.

STILETTO, a small dagger. (Ital.—L.) In Minsheu, ed. 1627; Heywood, Eng. Traveller, A. i. sc. 2.—Ital. *stiletto*, ' a little poyniard;' Florio. Dimin. of *stilo*, MItal. *stillo*, now a gnomon, formerly a dagger (Florio).—L. *stilum*, acc. of *stilus*, a style; see **Style** (1).

STILL (1), motionless, calm, silent. (E.) ME. *stille*, Chaucer, C. T. 11782 (F 1472). AS. *stille*, still, Grein, ii. 484. Allied to AS. *stillan*, verb, to rest, be still, id.; lit. ' to remain in a *stall* or place;' a sense well shown by the adv. *still* = continually. Teut. type **steljoz*; allied to AS. *stellan*, to place. From Teut. base **stal-*, as in AS. *steal, stæl*, a place, station, stall; see **Stall**.+Du. *stil*, still, *stillen*, to be still; *stellen*, to place, from *stal*, a stall; Dan. *stille*, still, hushed, *stille*, to still, also, to set, post, station, put in place, allied to *stald* (formerly *stall*), a stall; Swed. *stilla*, still, *stilla*, to quiet, allied to *stall*; G. *still*, still, *stillen*, to still, *stellen*, to place, from *stall*. The sense of *still* is ' brought to a stall or resting-place.' Der. *still*, adv., ME. *stille*, silently, Havelok, 2997, from AS. *stille* (Grein); this adverb has preserved the sense of ' continually' or ' abidingly,' and has come to mean always, ever, as in the strange compound *still-vexed* = always vexed, Temp. i. 2. 229. Also *still*, verb, AS. *stillan*; *stil-ly*, adj., ME. *stillich* (= still-like), Layamon, 2374; *stil-ly*, adv.; *still-ness*; *still-born*, 2 Hen. IV, i. 3. 64; *still-stand*, 2 Hen. IV, ii. 3. 64; *stand-still*.

STILL (2), to distil, to trickle down. (L.; *or* F. — L.) In some cases, *still* represents L. *stillāre*, to fall in drops; as, e. g., in Spenser, F. Q. iv. 7. 35. Cf. 'stille hem in a *stillatory*;' Medical Works of the 14th Century, ed. Henslow, p. 117. But it is more often a mere contraction for *distil*, just as *sport* is for *disport*, *spend* for *dispend*, and *spite* for *despite*. Thus Tusser writes: 'The knowledge of *stilling* is one pretie feat;' May's Husbandry, st. 33; where *stilling* plainly stands for *distilling*. See **Distil**. Der. *still*, sb., an apparatus for distilling, equivalent to ME. *stillatorie*, in the same sense, Chaucer, C. T. 16048 (G 580), answering to a Late L. **stillātōrium*, from *stillāre*. And see *di-stil*, *in-stil*.

STILT, a support of wood with a foot-rest, for lengthening the stride in walking. (Scand.) ME. *stilte*. 'S*tylte*, calepodium, lignipodium;' Prompt. Parv. — Swed. *stylta*, Dan. *stylte*; cf. Norweg. *styltra*, a stilt, Dan. *stylte*, to walk on stilts, also to stalk, walk slowly. We also find Swed. dial. *stylt*, a prop (Rietz).+Du. *stelt*, a stilt; Westphal. *stelte*; G. *stelze*, a stilt; OHG. *stelza*, a prop, a crutch. β. We may particularly note Lowl. Sc. *stult*, a crutch; this, like Swed. *stylta*, is from the Scand. base *stult-*, as in Swed. dial. *stullta*, to stagger about, S. Swed. *stulta*, the same (Möller). γ. I suppose this form to have arisen from the addition of *-t-* to the base *stull-*, as seen in Swed. dial. *stull-a*, *stul-a*, to stagger about. Cf. OHG. *stullan* (pt. t. *stulta*), to come to a halt, to stop, allied to OHG. *stulla*, a moment (whence Ital. *tra-stullo*, 'a pastime, quietnes,' Florio). From the weak grade **stull* of a lost Teut. strong verb **stillan*, pt. t. **stall*, pp. **stullanoz*; Grimm, Gram. ii. 57. Prob. the AS. *styltan*, to be amazed, hesitate (come to a stand), is closely allied. δ. We can then explain Du. *stelt*, G. *stelze*, as allied to G. *gestalt*, shape, form, allied to OHG. *stellan*, to place, fix, cause to halt (pp. *gestalt*). Der. *stilt-ed*.

STIMULATE, to instigate. (L.) In Blount's Gloss., ed. 1674. [The sb. *stimulation* is in Minsheu, ed. 1627.] — L. *stimulātus*, pp. of *stimulāre*, to prick forward. — L. *stimulus*, a goad; perhaps for **stimmulus*, for **stig-mulus*; and formed with suffixes *-mu-lo-*, from **stig-*, weak grade of √STEIG, to stick, to prick; see **Stick** (1). Der. *stimulat-ion*, from F. *stimulation*, 'a pricking forward,' Cot.; *stimulat-ive*; *stimulant*, from L. *stimulant-*, base of pres. part. of *stimulāre*. We also now use L. *stimulus* as an E. word.

STING, to prick severely, pain acutely. (E.) ME. *stingen*, strong verb; pt. t. *stang*, *stong*; pp. *stungen*, *stongen*, Chaucer, C. T. 1081 (A 1079). AS. *stingan*, pt. t. *stang*, pp. *stungen*; Grein, ii. 484.+ Dan. *stinge*; Swed. *stinga*; Icel. *stinga*, pt. t. *stakk* (for **stang*), pp. *stunginn*. Cf. Goth. *us-stiggan* (for *us-stingan*), to push out, put out, Matt. v. 29. Teut. type **stengan-*, pt. t. **stang*, pp. **stunganoz*. Perhaps allied, ultimately, to **Stick** (1); cf. prov. E. *stang*. a pole, with E. *stake*. See **Stang, Stake**. Der. *sting*, sb., AS., Dan., and Swed. *sting*. Also *sting-y*, q.v.

STINGY, mean, avaricious. (E.) Pronounced (stinji). 'Slingy, niggardly;' Phillips, ed. 1706. 'A *stingy*, narrow-hearted fellow;' L'Estrange (Todd). It is the same word as prov. E. *stingy* [pronounced *stinji*], common in Norfolk in the sense of 'nipping, unkindly,' and esp. used of a cold East wind. Forby defines it : (1) cross, ill-humoured, (2) churlish, biting, as applied to the state of the air. See *Stingy* in Ray's Glossary (E. D. S. B. 16), and my notes upon it, esp. at p. xix; see also E.D.D. It is merely the adj. formed from *sting*, sb., by the addition of *-y*, and means (1) stinging, keen, (2) churlish; by an easy transition of sense, which is exactly parallelled by the Swed. *sticken*, pettish, waspish, fretful, from *sticka*, to sting. Cf. MDan. *stinge*, adj., contrary to. β. The sounding of *g* as *j* causes no difficulty, as it is still common in Wiltshire, where a bee's *sting* is called a *stinge* [stinj]; cf. also Shropsh. *stinge*, a grudge; as 'I ow'd him a *stinge*.' See **Sting**. Der. *stingi-ly*, *-ness*.

STINK, to smell strongly. (E.) ME. *stinken*, strong verb; pt. t. *stank*, *stonk*, Chaucer, C. T. 14535 (B 3807); pp. *stonken*, AS. *stincan*, pt. t. *stanc*, *stonc*, pp. *stuncen*, Grein, ii. 484. This verb not only means to stink, or to be fragrant, but has the singular sense of to rise as dust or vapour. 'Dūst *stonc* tō heofonum' = dust rose up to heaven.+Du. *stinken*; Icel. *stökkva*, pt. t. *stökk* (for **stönk*), pp. *stokkinn* (for **stonkinn*), to spring up, take to flight; the pp. *stokkinn* means bedabbled, sprinkled; Dan. *stinke*; Swed. *stinka*; G. *stinken*. Cf. Goth. *stiggkwan* (= **stinkwan*), to strike, smite, thrust; whence *bistuggkw*, a cause of offence, 2 Cor. vi. 3. The form of the Teut. base is **stengq*. Possibly allied to L. *-stinguere*, as in *ex(s)tinguere*, to thrust out; and if so, allied further to √STEIGw, to pierce, as in L. *in-stig-are*, to instigate. ¶ There are difficulties as to the sense; and it is not certain that the Icel. and Goth. forms belong here. If

not, then the connexion with L. *-stinguere* fails. As to the possible connexion with Gk. ταγγός, rancid, see Prellwitz. Der. *stink*, sb., *stink-pot*; also *stench*, q.v.

STINT, to limit, restrain. (E.) Properly 'to shorten,' or 'curtail.' ME. *stinten*, *stynten*, gen. in the sense to stop, cause to cease, P. Plowman, B. i. 120; also, intransitively, to pause, id. v. 585. Allied to ME. *stenten*, to cease, Chaucer, C. T. 905 (A 903). AS. *styntan*, to make dull, Voc. 25. 28; *for-styntan* (= L. *contundere*), in a gloss (Bosworth). [Also *gestentan*, to warn, perhaps to restrain, Ælfric's Homilies, i. 6, l. 24.] The proper sense is rather 'to make dull,' as it is a causal verb, formed (by vowel-change from *u* to *y*) from the adj. *stunt*, dull, obtuse, stupid, Matt. v. 22; cf. *stuntscipe*, folly, Mark, vii. 22.+Icel. *stytta* by assimilation for **stynta*), to shorten, from the adj. *stuttr* (for **stuntr*), short, stunted; Swed. dial. *stynta*, to shorten, from *stunt*, small, short (Rietz); Norweg. *stytta*, *stutta*, to shorten, tuck up the clothes, from *stutt*, small, short (Aasen); cf. Dan. dial. *stynte*, to crop. β. The E. word comes nearer to the sense of the Icel. word; the AS. *stunt* is used metaphorically, in the sense of 'short of wit.' However, *to stint* is certainly formed from **Stunt** by vowel-change; see further under **Stunted**.

STIPEND, a salary, settled pay. (L.) 'Yearly *stipendes*;' Ascham, Toxophilus, b. ii. ed. Arber, p. 130. — L. *stipendium*, a tax, impost, tribute, stipend. For **stip-pendium* or **stipi-pendium*, a payment of money; from *stip-* or *stipi-*, base of *stips*, small coin or a contribution in small coin, and *-pendium*, a payment, from *pendere*, to weigh out, to pay. For *pendere*, see **Pendant**. Der. *stipendi-ar-y*, from L. *stipendiārius*, receiving pay.

STIPPLE, to engrave by means of dots. (Du.) Added by Todd to Johnson's Dict.; he calls it a modern term in art. — Du. *stippelen*, to speckle, cover with dots. — Du. *stippel*, a speckle, dimin. of *stip*, a point. Hexham gives *stip*, *stup*, or *stippelken*, 'a point, or a small point;' also *stippen*, 'to point, or to fixe;' *stippen* or *sticken met de naelde*, 'to stitch with the needle,' *stip-naelde*, 'a stitching-needle.' Allied to Low G. *stippelen*, to drip as raindrops (Danneil); *stippen*, to speckle; G. *stepten*, to stitch, G. *stift*, a peg, pin.

STIPULATION, a contract, agreement. (F. — L.) In Minsheu, ed. 1627. [The verb *to stipulate* is prob. later, but is used by Cotgrave to trans!ate F. *stipuler*.] — F. *stipulation*, 'a stipulation, a covenant;' Cot. — L. *stipulātiōnem*, acc. of *stipulātio*, a covenant, bargain. — L. *stipulārī*, to settle an agreement, bargain; lit. to make fast. — OL. *stipulus*, fast, firm; '*stipulum apud ueteres firmum* appellabatur,' Justiniani Institutiones, iii. 15 (Lewis). Allied to *stipes*, a post; and to E. **Stiff**. Der. (from L. *stipulātus*, pp. of *stipulārī*) *stipulate*, verb. ☞ The story about *stipula*, a straw, noticed in Trench, Study of Words, is needless; *stipulate* simply keeps the sense of the root. It may be noted that L. *stipula* = E. **stubble**.

STIR, to rouse, instigate, move about. (E.) ME. *stiren*, *sturen* (and even *steren*, but properly always with one *r*), Chaucer, C. T. 12280, 16746 (C 346, G 1278). AS. *styrian*, to move, to stir, Gen. vii. 21, ix. 3; Grein, ii. 491. [Various forms are given in Ettmüller, which seem to have been altered and accented in order to bring the word into connexion with *steer*; but its true connexion is rather with *storm*. Grein keeps *styrian*, to stir, and *styran*, *stieran*, to steer, quite distinct.] Allied to Icel. *styrr*, a stir, disturbance, Du. *storen*, to disturb, interrupt, vex, Swed. *störa*, G. *stören*, to disturb, OHG. *stœren*, *stōren*, to scatter, destroy, disturb. Teut. types **sturjan-*, **staurjan-* (Franck). See **Storm**. Der. *stur-geon*; and see *stor-m*.

STIRK, dimin. of **Steer** (1), q.v.

STIRRUP, a ring or hoop suspended from a saddle. (E.) For *sty-rope*, i.e. a rope to climb by; the orig. *stirrup* was a looped rope for mounting into the saddle. Spelt *styrop* in Palsgrave. ME. *stirop*, Chaucer, C. T. 7247 (D 1665). AS. *stirāp*. 'Scansile, *stirāp*;' Voc. 120. 2; fuller form *stigrāp*, id. 332. 11. — AS. *stig-*, weak grade of *stīgan*, to climb, mount; and *rāp*, a rope. See **Stile** (1) or **Sty** (1), and **Rope**.+MDu. *stegel-reep*, or *steegh-reep*, 'a stirrope-leather,' Hexham. [This is another use of the word; that which we now call: stirrup is called in Du. *stijbeugel*, i.e. 'the little bow or loop whereby to mount.'] Similarly formed from Du. *stijgen*, to mount, and *reep*, a rope. Also Icel. *stig-reip*, from *stiga* and *reip*; G. *stegreif*, a stirrup, from *steigen* and *reif*; cf. *steigbügel*, a stirrup.

STITCH, a pain in the side, a passing through stuff of a needle and thread. (E.) The sense of 'pain in the side,' lit. 'pricking sensation,' is old. ME. *stiche*. 'Styche, peyne on þe syde;' Prompt. Parv. AS. *stice*, a pricking sensation; A. S. Leechdoms, i. 370. § 10. — AS. *stician*, to prick, pierce; see **Stick** (1). So also G. *stich*, a prick, stitch, from *stechen*, to prick; also *sticken*, to stitch, from the same. Der. *stitch*, verb; also *stich-wort*, a herb good for the stitch, spelt *stichworte* in Palsgrave; *stitch-er*, *stitch-er-y*, Cor. i. 3. 75.

STITH, an anvil. (Scand.) 'Vulcan's *stith*;' Hamlet, iii. 2. 89;

some edd. have *stithy*. ME. *stith*, Chaucer, C. T. 2028 (A 2026); Havelok, 1877. — Icel. *steði*, an anvil. Allied to *staðr*, a place, i.e. fixed stead; and so named from its firmness. + Swed. *städ*, an anvil; MDu. *stiet*. From the same root as **Stead**, q. v. Der. *stith-y*, also used with the sense of anvil, like ME. *stethi*, Cursor Mundi, 23237.

STIVER, a Dutch penny. (Du.) In Evelyn's Diary, Oct. 2, 1641. Also in Arber's Eng. Garner, iii. 404 (ab. 1594). — Du. *stuiver*, formerly *stuyver*, 'a stiver, a Low-Countrie peece of coine, of the value of an English penny;' Hexham. β. Hence G. *stüber*, a stiver. Perhaps the orig. sense was 'bit' or small piece. Franck connects it with Low G. *stuuf*, stumpy; Icel. *stúfr*, a stump, *stýfa*, to cut off.

STOAT, an animal of the weasel kind. (E.) 'Stoat, a stallion-horse, also, a kind of rat;' Bailey's Dict., vol. i. ed. 1735. Spelt *stote*, Phillips, 1706; Levins, 1570. Cf. prov. E. *stoot* (Suffolk); *stot* (Hants.), a weasel (E. D. D.); also *stot*, *stote*, a young bull, a young horse (E. D. D.). ME. *stot*; in the Coventry Mysteries, ed. Halliwell, p. 218, l. 14, a scribe says to the woman taken in adultery: 'Therfore come forthe, thou stynkynge *stott*;' and in l. 19: 'To save suche *stottys*, it xal [shall] not be.' Here the sense is probably *stoat*. The ME. *stot* means (1) a stoat, (2) a horse or stallion, (3) a bullock; see Chaucer, C. T. 617 (A 615); and my note to P. Plowman, C. xxii. 267. The reason is that the word is a general name for a male animal, and not confined to any one kind; the word *stag* is in the same case, meaning a hart, a gander, and a drake; see **Stag**. The pl. *stottes*, stallions, occurs in the Owl and Nightingale, 495; AS. *stottas*, 'equi uiles' (Napier). Allied to Icel. *stútr*, a bull; Swed. *stut*, a bull, also a hard blow with a rod; Dan. *stud*, a bullock; Swed. dial. *stut*. (1) a young ox, (2) a young man; Norweg. *stut*, (1) a bullock, (2) an ox-horn. From **stut-*, weak grade allied to Teut. **stautan-*, to push, strike. Cf. Du. *stooten*, to push, thrust, whence Du. *stooter*, sb., a thruster, also a stallion, *stootig*, adj., butting, goring; Swed. *stöta*, to push, Dan. *stöde*, G. *stossen* (strong verb), Goth. *stautan*, to strike. See **Stutter.**

STOCCADO, STOCCATA, a thrust in fencing. (Ital. – Teut.) *Stoccado*, Merry Wives, ii. 1. 234. *Stoccata*, Romeo, iii. 1. 77. *Stoccado* is an accommodated form, prob. from MF. *estoccade*, with the same sense, with a final *o* to imitate Spanish; cf. Shakespeare's *barricado* with E. *barricade*. [The true Span. form was *estocada*, 'a stocada or thrust with a weapon;' Minsheu.] *Stoccata* is the better form. — Ital. *stoccata*, 'a foyne, a thrust, a stoccado given in fence;' Florio. Formed as if from a fem. pp. of a verb **stoccare*, which is made from the sb. *stocco*, 'a truncheon, a tuck, a short sword, an arming sword;' Florio. — G. *stock*, a stick, staff, trunk, stump; cognate with E. **Stock**, q. v. And see **Stoke.** Cf. MDu. *stock*, 'a stock-rapier;' Hexham.

STOCK, a post, stump, stem, &c. (E.) In all its senses, it is the same word. The sense is 'a stump;' hence a post, trunk, stem (metaphorically a race or family), a fixed store or fund, capital, cattle, trunk or butt-end of a gun; the pl. *stocks* signify a place where a criminal is set fast, or a frame for holding ships fast, or public capital. See Trench, Study of Words, which partly follows Horne Tooke's Diversions of Purley, pt. ii. c. 4. ME. *stok*, trunk of a tree, Pricke of Conscience, 676; pl. *stokkes*, the stocks, P. Plowman, B. iv. 108. AS. *stocc*, a post, trunk; Deut. xxviii. 36, 64. + Du. *stok*, stick, handle, stocks; MDu. *stock*; whence MDu. *stockduyue*, a stock-dove, *stockvisch*, stock-fish; *stockroo*e, 'a rose so called beyond the sea,' i.e. *stocks*; Hexham; Icel. *stokkr*, trunk, log, stocks, stocks for ships; Dan. *stok*, a stick; Swed. *stock*, a beam, log; G. *stock*; OHG. *stoch*. Teut. type **stukkoz*, m. The orig. sense may have been 'stump of a cut tree;' cf. AS. *stycce*, G. *stück*, a bit, fragment; also Low G. *stuke*, a stump, Norw. *stauka*, to strike, hack. Some connect it with Skt. *tuj*, to strike; just as Icel. *stauta*, to push, is allied to Skt. *tud*, to strike. Der. *stock*, verb, ME. *stokken*, Chaucer, Troilus, b. iii. l. 380; *stock-broker*; *stock-dove*, Skelton, Philip Sparowe, l. 429; *stock-exchange*, *stock-holder*, *stock-jobbing*; *stock-fish* (prob. from Du. *stokvisch*), Prompt. Parv., and Temp. iii. 2. 79; *stock-ish*, i.e. log-like, Merch. Ven. v. 81; *stock-still*, i.e. still as a post (cf. MDu. *stock-stille*, 'stone-still, or immoveable,' Hexham); *stock*, a flower, called *stocke-gyllofer* (stock-gilliflower) in Palsgrave; *stock-ing*, q. v., *stoke*, q. v. Also *stocc-ado*, *stocc-ata*.

STOCKADE, a breast-work formed of stakes stuck in the ground. (Span. – Teut.) A modern word; it occurs in Mason's Eng. Garden, b. ii. l. 293, spelt *stoccade* (A.D. 1777). The pl. *stockadoes* occurs ab. 1602; see Arber, Eng. Garner, vii. 175. A mistaken form, due to association with *stock*. — Span. *estacada*, 'a place palisadoed, or hemm'd in with stakes;' see Don Quixote, pt. ii. c. 66 (Pineda). — Span. *estaca*, a stake. — MDu. *stake*, a stake; see **Stake.** See Notes on E. Etym. p. 283.

STOCKING, a close covering for the foot and leg. (E.) 'A *stocking*, or paire of *stockings*;' Minsheu, ed. 1627. Formerly called *stocks*; 'Our knit silke *stockes*, and Spanish lether shoes;' Gascoigne, Stele Glas, l. 375. 'He rose to draw on his strait *stockings*, and, as the deuill would, he hit vpon the letter, bare it away in the heele of his *stocke*,' &c.; Holinshed, Chron. of Ireland, an. 1532 (R.). 'Un bas de chausses, a *stocking*, or nether-stock;' Cot. He also has: 'Un bas de manches, a *stocking*;' which we may compare with 'Manche Lombarde, a *stock-sleeve*, or fashion of halfe sleeve;' id. β. 'The clothing of the legs and lower part of the body formerly consisted of a single garment, called *hose*, in F. *chausses*. It was afterwards cut in two at the knees, leaving two pieces of dress, viz. knee-breeches, or, as they were then called, *upper-stocks*, or in F. *haut de chausses*, and the *netherstocks* or *stockings*, in F. *bas de chausses*, and then simply *bas*. In these terms, the element *stock* is to be understood in the sense of stump or trunk, the part of a body left when the limbs are cut off. In the same way G. *strumpf*, a stocking, properly signifies a stump;' Wedgwood. Similarly, a *stock-sleeve* is a truncated sleeve, a half-sleeve. γ. To this I may add that *stock-ing* is a dimin. form; the *nether-stock* being the smaller portion of the cut hose; it was sometimes called *stock* simply, but also *nether-stock* or *stock-ing* (= little stock); and the last name has alone survived. See **Stock.**

STOIC, a disciple of Zeno. (L. – Gk.) Spelt *Stoick*, Milton, P. R. iv. 280; cf. *Stoa*, id. 253. From L. *Stoicus*. — Gk. Στωϊκός, a Stoic; lit. belonging to a colonnade, because Zeno taught under a colonnade at Athens, named the Pœcilē (ποικίλη). — Gk. στοά (Ionic στοιά, Attic στωά), a colonnade, place enclosed by pillars. The Ionic στοιά is for **στοϝ-yά*; allied to στῦ-λος, a pillar. See **Style** (2). Der. *stoic-al*, *stoic-al-ly*, *stoic-ism*.

STOKER, one who tends a fire. (Du.) We have now coined the verb to *stoke*, but only the sb. appears in Phillips, Bailey, &c. '*Stoaker*, one that looks after a fire and some other concerns in a brew-house;' Phillips, ed. 1706. The word is Dutch, and came in as a term in brewing. — Du. *stoker*, 'a kindler, or a setter on fire;' Hexham. — Du. *stoken*, 'to make or kindle a fire, to instigate, or to stirre up;' id. [This is the same word as OF. *estoquer*, ME. *stoken*, to stab; see Chaucer, C. T., Group A, 2546 (Six-text), altered in Tyrwhitt to *stike*, l. 2548.] Allied to MDu. *stock*, a stick, stock, also a stock-rapier (stabbing rapier); no doubt from the use by the *stoker* of a *stock* (thick stick) to stir the fire with and arrange the logs. The MDu. *stock* (Du. *stok*) is cognate with E. **Stock**, q. v. Der. *stoke*, in the mod. sense (as distinct from ME. *stoken*, to stab, which is from OF. *estoquer*).

STOLE, a long robe, a long scarf for a priest. (L. – Gk.) In very early use. AS. *stole*; 'Stola, *stole*;' Voc. 327. 23. — L. *stola*. — Gk. στολή, equipment, a robe, a stole. — Gk. στολ-, 2nd grade of στέλλειν, to equip, lit. to set in order.

STOLID, dull, heavy, stupid. (L.) A late word. '*Stolid*, foolish;' Bailey, vol. i. ed. 1735. — L. *stolidus*, firm, stock-like; hence, dull, stupid. Prob. allied to L. *stul-tus*, foolish; see **Stultify.** And see **Stout.** Der. *stolid-i-ty*, coined from L. *stoliditās*.

STOMACH, a more or less sac-like portion of the body, wherein food is digested. (F. – L. – Gk.) ME. *stomak*, Prompt. Parv. [Now accommodated to the Gk. spelling.] — F. *estomac*, spelt *estomach* in Cotgrave. — L. *stomachum*, acc. of *stomachus*. — Gk. στόμαχος, a mouth, opening, the gullet, the stomach; dimin. of στόμα, the mouth. Brugmann, i. § 421 (5). Der. *stomach*, verb, to resent, Antony, iii. 4. 12, from the use of *stomach* in the sense of anger, 1 Hen. VI, iv. 1. 141; *stomach-er*, an ornament for the breast, Wint. Tale, iv. 4. 226; Paston Letters, iii. 325; *stomach-ic*.

STONE, a hard mass of mineral matter, piece of rock, a gem. (E.) ME. *ston*, *stoon*, Chaucer, C. T. 7997 (E 121). AS. *stān* (common); the change from *ā* to long *o* is usual, as in *bān*, a bone, *bār*, a boar. + Du. *steen*; Icel. *steinn*; Dan. and Swed. *sten*; G. *stein*; Goth. *stains*. β. All from Teut. type **stainoz*, m. Cf. Russ. *stiena*, a wall; Gk. στία, a stone, pebble. Curtius, i. 264. Der. *stone*, verb; *stone-blind*, as blind as a stone; *stone-bow*, used for shooting stones, Tw. Nt. ii. 5. 51; *stone-chat*, a chattering bird; *stone-crop*, Baret (1580), ME. *ston-croppe*, Voc. 712. 35; *stone-cutter*, K. Lear, ii. 2. 63; *stone-fruit*; *stone-still*, K. John, iv. 1. 77; *stone-ware*; *stone's cast* or *stone's throw*, the distance to which a stone can be cast or thrown; *ston-y*, AS. *stānig*, stony; *ston-y-heart-ed*, 1 Hen. IV, ii. 2. 28. Also *stan-iel*, q. v.

STOOK, a number of corn-sheaves; usually twelve. (Scand.) Also *stouk*, in Prov. E.; see E. D. D. Spelt *stowke* in Cathol. Anglicum (1483), q. v. — Swed. dial. *stuke*, a shock of sheaves; Dan. dial. *stuke* (Kok). + Low G. *stuke*, a heap, a shock. Allied to E. **Stake, Stock,** q. v. See Notes on E. Etym., p. 284.

STOOL, a seat without a back. (E.) ME. *stool*, Prompt. Parv.;

dat. *stole*, P. Plowman, B. v. 394. AS. *stōl*, a seat, a throne; Grein, ii. 485.+Du. *stoel*, a chair, seat, stool; Icel. *stōll*; Dan. and Swed. *stol*, a chair; Goth. *stōls*, a seat; G. *stuhl*, OHG. *stuol*, *stual*. Teut. type *stōlöz*, m Teut. *ō* = ldg. *ā*. From √STĀ, to stand, stand firm. Brugmann, i. § 191; Streitberg, § 153 (5). Cf. **Stow, Stand.** **Der.** *stool-ball*, a game played with a ball and one or two stools, Two Noble Kinsmen, v. 2; see *stool-ball* in Halliwell.

STOOP (1), to bend the body, lean forward, condescend. (E.) ME. *stoupen*, Wyclif, John, xx. 5. AS. *stūpian*, Ælfred, tr. of Orosius, b. vi. c. 24. § 1.+MDu. *stuypen*, 'to bowe;' Hexham; Icel. *stūpa* (obsolete); Swed. *stupa*, to fall, to tilt; cf. *stupande*, sloping, *stupning*, a leaning forward. β. From a Teut. base *stū*?, apparently meaning to lean forward; see *steep* (1) and *steep* (2), the latter of which is the causal of *stoop*. And perhaps the *step*- in *step-child* is from the same root. **Der.** *steep* (1); *steep* (2).

STOOP (2), a beaker; see **Stoup.**

STOP, to obstruct, hinder, restrain, intercept, to cease. (L.) ME. *stoppen*, Ancren Riwle, p. 72, l. 19. AS. *stoppian*, in the comp. *for-stoppian*, to stop up; A. S. Leechdoms, ii. 42. So also Du. *stoppen*, to fill, stuff, stop; Swed. *stoppa*, to fill, stuff, cram, stop up; Dan. *stoppe*, to fill, stuff, cram, &c.; G. *stopfen*; OSax. *stuppōn*, Ps. 57. 5. Not a Teut. word, but the same as Ital. *stoppare*, to stop up with tow, Late L. *stuppāre*, to stop up with tow, also used in the general sense of cram, stop. β. All from L. *stūpa*, *stuppa*, the coarse part of flax, hards, oakum, tow; cognate with Gk. στύπη, στύππη, with the same sense. Hence also E. **Stuff.** **Der.** *stop*, sb., K. John, iv. 2. 239; *stop-cock*; *stopp-age* (with F. suffix), *stopp-er*; also *stopp-le*, ME. *stoppel*, Prompt. Parv. (with E. suffix, signifying the instrument). **Doublets,** *estop*, to impede, bar, a law term, borrowed from AF. *estoper* (mod. F. *étouper*), from Late L. *stuppāre*, as above; also *stuff*, verb.

STORAX, a resinous gum. (L.—Gk.) In Holland, tr. of Pliny, b. xii. c. 25, heading.—L. *storax*, *styrax*.—Gk. στύραξ, a sweet-smelling gum produced by the tree called στύραξ; Herodotus, iii. 107.

STORE, provision, abundance, stock. (F.—L.) ME. *stor*, *stoor*, Chaucer, C. T. 600 (A 598); Rob. of Glouc. p. 395, l. 8138; the derived verb *storen* occurs as early as in Layamon, l. 13412, later text. ' *Stoor*, or purvyaunce, *Staurum*;' Prompt. Parv.—OF. *estor*, store, provision (Godefroy).—Late L. *staurum*, the same as *instaurum*, store.—L. *instaurāre*, to construct, build, restore, renew; Late L. *instaurāre*, to provide necessaries. Cf. OF. *estorer*, 'to build, make, edifie; also to store;' Cot.—L. *in*, prep. as prefix; and *staurāre*, to set up, place, found also in the comp. *restaurāre*, to restore. β. This form *staurāre*, orig. 'to erect,' is due to a lost adj. *staurus*, allied to Skt. *sthāvara-s*, fixed, stable, and Gk. σταυρός, an upright pole or stake, orig. 'upright.' See **Steer** (2). Brugmann, i. § 198. **Der.** *store*, verb, ME. *storen*, OF. *estorer*, as above; *stor-age*, with F. suffix *-age* < L. *-āticum*; *store-house*; also *re-store*, q. v.; *stor-y* (2), q. v.

STORK, a wading bird. (E.) ME. *stork*, Chaucer, Parl. of Foules, 361. AS. *storc*, Voc. 13. 7.+Du. *stork*; Icel. *storkr*; Dan. and Swed. *stork*; G. *storch*, OHG. *storah*, *stork*. β. Root uncertain; but almost certainly the same word as Gk. τόργος, a large bird (vulture, swan); Fick, iii. 346; which Fick considers as allied to E. *stark*, as if the orig. sense were 'the strong one.' Cf. Pers. *suturg*, large. See **Stark.** **Der.** *stork's-bill*, a kind of geranium, from the shape of the fruit.

STORM, a violent commotion, tempest. (E.) ME. *storm*, Chaucer, C. T. 1982 (A 1980). AS. *storm*, Grein, ii. 485.+Icel. *stormr*; Du., Swed., Dan., *storm*; G. *sturm*. Teut. type *stur-moz*, m. Allied to **Stir**, q. v. We also find Gael. and Irish *stoirm*, Bret. *stourm*, a storm (borrowed forms). **Der.** *storm*, verb, AS. *styrman*, with vowel-change; *storm-y*, *storm-i-ness*.

STORY (1), a history, narrative. (F.—L.—Gk.) ME. *storie*, Chaucer, C. T. 1203, 15503 (A 1201, G 35); Havelok, 1641; Ancren Riwle, p. 154, l. 24.—AF. *storie* (Bartsch); OF. *estoire*, a history, a tale; F. *histoire*, history.—L. *historia*, history; see **History.** **Der.** *stori-ed*, i. e. painted with stories, representing tales, Milton, Il Pens. 159; cf. MF. *historié*, 'beautified with story-work,' Cot. **Doublet,** *history*.

STORY (2), the height of one floor in a building, a set of rooms at one level. (F.—L.) Bacon, in his Essay 45 (On Building), speaks of 'the first *story*,' 'the under *story*,' 'the second *story*,' &c. 'A floure [floor] or *stuorie*;' R. Eden, First Three Books on America (1526); ed. Arber, p. 257. In Rob. of Gloucester, p. 181, l. 3756 (footnote), the word *storys* seems to mean 'buildings;' but other MSS. have a verb here. Orig. 'a thing built;' it represents OF. *estorée*, a thing built. ' *Estorée*, built, made, erected, edified; also furnished, stored;' Cot. This is the pp. of *estorer*, to build, to store; see **Store.** ¶ Wedgwood adds: 'I cannot find that

estorée was ever used in the sense of E. *story*.' This is prob. right; the sense in E. seems to have been at first simply a thing built, a building; the restriction of the word to one floor only is peculiar to English. Just in the same way, a *floor* is properly only a boarded (or other) covering of the ground, but was used, by an easy extension of meaning, as synonymous with *story*. Cf. Picard *chambre étorée*, a furnished room (Corblet). There can be little doubt as to the derivation. **Der.** *clear-story* or *clere-story*, Skelton, Garland of Laurel, 479, a story lighted with windows, as distinct from the *blind-story*, as the triforium was sometimes called (Lee, Gloss. of Liturgical Terms (Oxford), Glossary, p. 57).

STOT, (1) a stallion; (2) a bullock. (E.) See **Stoat.**

STOUP, STOOP, a vessel or flagon. (Scand.) In Hamlet, v. 1. 68. ME. *stope*. 'Hec cupa, a *stope*;' Voc. 728. 28. Lowl. Sc. *stowp*, Dunbar, ed. Small, p. 161.—Icel. *staup*, a knobby lump, also a stoup, beaker, cup.+Du. *stoop*; Low G. *stoop*; AS. *stēap*, a beaker, cup; MHG. *stouf*, G. *stauf*, a cup. [Or else, from the MDu. *stoop*.] The Teut. base is *staup*-; cf. Icel. *steypa*, to cast metals, pour out, &c. See **Steep** (1) and **Stoop.** ¶ The Latinised form *stopa* occurs in 1390, in the Earl of Derby's Accounts (Camden Soc.), p. 9, l. 23. This looks more like the Du. form. For the form *stoop*, cf. E. *loose* < Icel. *laus*.

STOUT, bold, strong, robust. (F.—OLow G.) ME. *stout*, Chaucer, C. T. 547 (A 545).—OF. *estout*, stout, furious, also rash, stupid (Burguy).—MDu. *stolt*, *stout*, 'stout, bolde, rash;' Hexham. Low G. *stolt*, the same; cognate with G. *stolz*, proud. β. Perhaps a Teut. word; or else early borrowed from L. *stultus*, foolish. It answers better, in sense, to L. *stolidus*, firm. **Der.** *stout*, sb., a strong kind of beer; *stout-ly*, *-ness*.

STOVE, a hot-house, an apparatus for warming a room. (E.) 'This word has much narrowed its meaning; [a] bath, hot-house .. was a *stove* once;' Trench, Select Glossary. 'A *stoue*, or hot-house;' Minsheu, ed. 1627. AS. *stofa*; 'Balneum, *stofa*,' Voc. 8. 33. +MDu. *stove*, 'a stewe, a hot-house, or a baine;' Hexham; Low G. *stove*, *stave*, the same; Icel. *stofa*, *stufa*, a bathing-room with a stove, a room; G. *stube*, a room; OHG. *stupa*, a heated room. β. Root unknown; supposed to be a Teut. word, but even this is doubtful. Cf. Ital. *stufa*, Span. *estufa*, F. *étuve*. See **Stew.** ¶ Perhaps lost in ME., and re-introduced from Dutch.

STOVER, fodder for cattle. (F.—L.?) In Shak. Temp. iv. 63. ME. *stouer* (with *v* = *u*), Seven Sages, ed. Weber, 2606.—OF. *estover*, *estovoir*, necessaries, provisions; orig. the infin. mood of a verb which was used impersonally with the sense 'it is necessary;' Burguy, Diez. On the difficult etymology see Diez, who refers it to L. *studēre*, to study, endeavour, desire; see **Student.** Or perhaps from L. *est opus*, there is need (Tobler).

STOW, to arrange, pack away. (E.) ME. *stowen*, Allit. Poems, B 113. Lit. 'to put in a place;' cf. ME. *stowe*, a place, Layamon, 1174. AS. *stōwigan*, Voc. 43. 12. From AS. *stōw*, a place, Mark, i. 45; OFries. *sto*, a place. We also find Icel. *stō*, in the comp. *eldstō*, a fire-place, hearth. Cognate with Lithuan. *stowa*, the place in which one stands; from *stōti*, to stand. β. All from the √STĀ, to stand; see **Stand.** **Der.** *stow-age*, with F. suffix, Cymb. i. 6. 192; whence Low L. *stowagium*, Earl of Derby's Accounts (1394); Camden Soc. p. 155. l. 32. Also *be-stow*, q. v.

STRADDLE, to stand or walk with the legs wide apart. (E.) In Baret, ed. 1580. Spelt *striddil* and *stridle* in Levins, ed. 1570. The frequentative of *stride*, used in place of *striddle*. See **Stride.** Cf. prov. E. *striddle*, to straddle; Halliwell.

STRAGGLE, to stray, ramble away. (Scand.) Formerly *stragle*, with one *g*, Chapman, tr. of Homer, Iliad, b. x. l. 158; and in Minsheu, ed. 1627; and in Baret (1580). Palsgrave has *stragler*, sb. Cf. Norw. *stragla*, to walk unsteadily and with difficulty; frequent. of MDan. *strage*, to rove, wander. Allied to *strackle*; cf. prov. E. *strackling*, a loose wild fellow (North); *strackle-brained*, dissolute, thoughtless; Halliwell. Apparently the frequentative of ME. *straken*, to go, proceed, roam; 'þey ouer lond *strakeþ*' = they roam over the land; P. Plowman's Creed, l. 82; and cf. Cursor Mundi, l. 1845, Trin. MS. 'To *strake* about, circumire;' MS. Devonsh. Gloss., cited in Halliwell. Cf. also prov. E. *strag*, a vagabond; Icel. *strākr*, a vagabond. ¶ Not allied to *stray*. **Der.** *straggl-er*.

STRAIGHT, direct, upright. (E.) Spelt *strayght* in Palsgrave. It is identical with ME. *streiʒt*, the pp. of *strecchen*, to stretch. 'Sithe thi flesche, lord, was furst perceyued And, for oure sake, laide *streiʒt* in stalle;' Political, Religious, and Love Poems, ed. Furnivall, p. 252, l. 46. AS. *streht*, pp. of *streccan*, to stretch; see **Stretch.** 2. The adverbial use is early; 'William *streiʒt* went hem to;' Will. of Palerne, l. 3328; spelt *straght*, Gower, C. A. iii. 36; bk. vi. 1030. **Der.** *straight-ly*, *straight-ness*; *straight-forward*, *-ly*; *straight-way* = in a straight way, directly, spelt *streightway*, Spenser, F. Q. i. 10. 63; *straight-en*, verb, a late coinage. ☞ Distinct from *strait*.

STRAIN (1), to stretch tight, draw with force, overtask, constrain, filter (F.—L.) ME. *streinen*, Chaucer, C. T. 9627 (E 1753).—OF. *estraign-, estreign-*, a stem of *estraindre, estreindre*, MF. *estraindre*, 'to straine, wring hard;' Cot.—L. *stringere*, to draw tight; pt. t. *strinxi*, pp. *strictus*. See **Stringent**. Der. *strain*, sb., *strain-er*; *con-strain, di-strain, re-strain*; and see *strait, stringent, strict*.

STRAIN (2), a race, stock, breed. (E.) 'The noblest of thy *strain*;' Shak. J. Cæsar, v. 1. 59. ME. *streen*; Chaucer, C. T., E 157. AS. *strēon*, gain, product, whence, in ME., lineage, progeny, as in Layamon, 2737; whence *strīenan, strȳnan*, to beget. Cf. OHG. *striunan*, to acquire.

STRAIT, strict, narrow, rigid. (F.—L.) ME. *streit*, Chaucer, C. T. 174; Layamon, 22270.—AF. *estreit*, Bozon, p. 124; OF. *estroict*, 'strait, narrow, close, strict;' Cot. Mod. F. *étroit*.—L. *strictum*, acc. of *strictus*, strict, strait. See **Strict**. Der. *strait*, sb., used to translate MF. *estroict*, sb., in Cotgrave; *strait-ly, -ness*; *strait-laced*; *strait-en*, a coined word, Luke, xii. 50. Doublet, *strict*.

STRAND (1), the beach of the sea or of a lake. (E.) ME. *strand*, often *strond*, Chaucer, C. T. 5245 (B 825). AS. *strand*, Matt. xiii. 48.+Du. *strand*; Icel. *strönd* (gen. *strandar*), margin, edge; Dan., Swed., and G. *strand*. Root unknown. Der. *strand*, verb; cf. Du. *stranden*, 'to arrive on the sea-shoare,' Hexham.

STRAND (2), one of the smaller strings that compose a rope. (F.—OHG.) 'Strand, in sea-language, the twist of a rope;' Phillips, ed. 1706. The *d* is excrescent, as commonly in E. after *n* final. Spelt *strain*, Hakluyt, Voy. iii. 108.—ONorman F. *estran*, a strand; Wace, Rom. de Brut, 11486; see Moisy.—OHG. *streno* (G. *strähne*), a cord. Cf. MDu. *strene*, a string (Kilian); Du. *streen*, 'a skain,' Sewel. Parallel to Du. *striem*, OHG. *strimo*, a stripe.

STRANGE, foreign, odd. (F.—L.) ME. *strange*, Rob. of Glouc. p. 16, l. 379; Chaucer, C. T. l. 13.—OF. *estrange*, 'strange;' Cot. [Mod. F. *étrange*;] Span. *extraño*, Ital. *estranio, estraneo*.]—L. *extrāneum*, acc. of *extrāneus*, foreign; lit. 'that which is without.'—L. *extrā*, without, outside; see **Extra**. Der. *strange-ly, -ness*; *strang-er*, from OF. *estrangier*, 'a stranger,' Cot. Also *estrange*, q. v. Doublet, *extraneous*.

STRANGLE, to choke. (F.—L.—Gk.) ME. *stranglen*, Havelok, 640.—OF. *estrangler*, 'to strangle, choake;' Cot.—L. *strangulāre*, to throttle, choke.—Gk. στραγγαλόειν, to strangle; also στραγγαλίζειν.—Gk. στραγγάλη, a halter.—Gk. στραγγός, twisted. Allied to **Strict**; and see below. Der. *strangl-er*; *strangulat-ion*, from F. *strangulation*, 'a strangling,' Cot., from L. acc. *strangulātiōnem*.

STRANGURY, extreme difficulty in discharging urine. (L.—Gk.) In Ben Jonson, The Fox, A. ii. sc. 1.—L. *strangūria*.—Gk. στραγγουρία, retention of the urine, when it falls by drops.—Gk. στραγγ-, base of στραγξ, that which oozes out, a drop; and οὖρ-ον, urine. The Gk. στραγξ is allied to στραγγός, twisted, compressed. See **Strangle** and **Urine**.

STRAP, a narrow strip of leather. (L.) Frequently called a *strop* in prov. E., and this is the better form. ME. *strope*, a noose, loop; 'a rydynge-knotte or a *strope*,' Caxton, tr. of Reynard the Fox, ed. Arber, p. 33. 'A thonge, . . a *strope*, or a loupe,' Elyot, 1559; cited in Halliwell. AS. *stropp*. 'Struppus, strop, *vel* ārwiðõe;' Voc. 181. 42.—L. *struppus*, a strap, thong, fillet. From the same L. word are borrowed Du. *strop*, a halter, F. *étrope*, &c. Doublet, *strop*.

STRAPPADO, a species of torture. (Ital.—Teut.) In 1 Hen. IV, ii. 4. 262. The word has been turned into a Spanish-looking form, but it is rather Italian. In exactly the same way, the Ital. *stoccata* also appears as *stoccado*; see **Stoccado**.—Ital. *strappata*, a pulling, wringing; the strappado.—Ital. *strappare*, to pull, wring.—High-German (Swiss) *strapfen*, to pull tight, allied to G. *straff*, tight (Diez). From Low G. or Du.; cf. Du. *straffen*, to punish, from *straf*, severe. Cf. EFries. *strabben*, to be stiff; *strabbig, strappig*, severe.

STRATAGEM, an artifice, esp. in war. (F.—L.—Gk.) Spelt *stratageme*, Sir P. Sidney, Apology for Poetry, ed. Arber, p. 37.—MF. *stratageme*, 'a stratagem;' Cot.—L. *stratēgēma*.—Gk. στρατήγημα, the device or act of a general.—Gk. στρατηγός, a general, leader of an army.—Gk. στρατ-ός, an army; and ἄγ-ειν, to lead. β. The Gk. στρατός means properly an encamped army, from its being spread out over ground, and is allied to Gk. στόρνυμι, I spread out, and L. *sternere*; see **Stratum**. The Gk. ἄγειν is cognate with L. *agere*; see **Agent**. Der. *strateg-y*, from Gk. στρατηγία, generalship, from στρατηγός, a general; *strateg-ic*, Gk. στρατηγικός; *strateg-ic-al, -ly*; *strateg-ist*.

STRATH, a flat valley. (C.) In Leslie, Hist. Scotland (1595), p. 12. Common in Scot. place-names, as *Strath-spey*, valley of the Spey.—Gael. *srath*, a flat valley, low-lying country beside a river; Irish *srath, sratha*, fields beside a river, bottom of a valley; W. *ystrad*. Allied to **Stratum**.

STRATUM, a layer, esp. of earth or rock. (L.) In Thomson, Autumn, 745.—L. *strātum*, that which is laid flat or spread out, neut. of *strātus*, pp. of *sternere*. Allied to Gk. στόρνυμι, I spread out.—Skt. *str̥*, to spread.—√STER, to scatter, spread out. Der. *strati-fic-at-ion, strat-i-fy*, coined words. And see *street, con-ster-nat-ion, pro-strate, strat-agem*; also *strew, straw*.

STRAW, a stalk of corn when thrashed. (E.) ME. *straw*, Chaucer, C. T. 11007 (F 695); also *stre, stree*, id. 2920 (A 2918). AS. *streaw, streow*; see Toller; it also occurs in *streawberige*, a strawberry, Voc. 298. 11, and in the derivative *streaw-ian, streow-ian*, to strew, as below.+Du. *stroo*; Icel. *strā*; Dan. *straa*; Swed. *strå*; G. *stroh*, OHG. *strou, strau*. Allied to Goth. *straujan*, to strew. From Teut. base **strau-* (cf. Lat. pt. t. *strāui*), extended from √STER, to spread out, scatter. Der. *straw-y*; *strew*, verb, q. v.; *straw-berry*, AS. *streawberige*, as above, from its propagation (or strewing) by runners. See **Stratum**.

STRAY, to wander, rove, err. (F.—L.) ME. *straien*: the derivative *a-straied*, pp., is in Gower, C. A. ii. 132; bk. v. 145; and see the Prompt. Parv.—OF. *estraier*, to stray. See Diez, who compares Prov. *estradier*, one who roves about the streets or ways, one who strays, from Prov. *estrada*, a street; also OF. *estree*, a street. This is confirmed by MItal. *stradiotto*, 'a wandrer, gadder, traueller, earth-planet, a highwaie-keeper,' Florio; from Ital. *strada*, a street. β. Thus the lit. sense is 'to rove the streets.' All from L. *strāta*, a street; see **Street**. Cf. mod. F. *batteur d'estrade*, a loiterer (Hamilton). Der. *stray*, sb., oddly spelt *streyue, strayue*, in P. Plowm. B. prol. 94, C. i. 92, old form also *estray* (Blount, Nomolexicon), AF. *estray* (Britton), from OF. *estraier*, to stray, as above.

STREAK, a line or long mark on a differently coloured ground. (Scand.) ME. *streke*, Prompt. Parv.; prob. of Scand. or Low G. origin.—Swed. *streck*, MSwed. *strek*, a stroke, streak, line; Norw. *strek, streek* (cf. EFries. *streke*, Du. *streek*); Dan. *streg*. From Teut. **strik*, weak grade of **streikan-*, to strike; see **Strike**. β. We also find the (native) ME. *strike*, a stroke, Chaucer, On the Astrolabe, pt. i. § 7; AS. *strica* (cognate with G. *strich*, Goth. *striks*, a stroke with the pen); from **strik-*, weak grade of Teut. **streikan-*; see **Strike**. Further allied to L. *striga*, a line, furrow, and to L. *stringere*; see **Stringent**. ¶ It may be noted that ME. *striken* sometimes means to go or come forward, to proceed, advance; see Gloss. to Spec. of Eng., ed. Morris and Skeat, and P. Plowman, B. prol. 183. A *streak* is properly a stroke made by sweeping anything along. Der. *streak*, verb, Mids. Nt. Dr. ii. 1. 257; *streak-y*.

STREAM, a current or flow. (E.) ME. *streem*, Chaucer, C. T. 466, 3893 (A 464, 3895). AS. *strēam*, Grein, ii. 488.+Du. *stroom*; Icel. *straumr*; Swed. and Dan. *ström*; G. *strom*; OHG. *straum, stroum*. β. All from the Teut. type **strau-moz*, m. The word means 'that which flows,' from the Teut. base STREU, to flow. The Idg. root is √SREU, to flow; cf. Skt. *sru*, to flow, Gk. ῥέειν (for σρέϝειν), to flow, Irish *sruaim*, a stream. The *t* seems to have been inserted, for greater ease of pronunciation, not only in Teutonic, but in Slavonic; cf. Russ. *struia*, a stream. See **Rheum**. Brugmann, i. §§ 462, 816. From the same root we have *rheum, rhythm, ruminate, catarrh*. Der. *stream*, verb, ME. *stremen, streamen*, Ancren Riwle, p. 188, note *e*; *stream-er*, Hen. V, iii. chor. 6; *stream-l-et*, a double diminutive; *stream-y*.

STREET, a paved way, a road in a town. (L.) ME. *strete*, Wyclif, Matt. xii. 19. AS. *strǣt*, Grein, ii. 487.—L. *strāta*, for *strāta uia*, a paved way; *strāta* is fem. of *strātus*, pp. of *sternere*, to strew, scatter, pave.—√STER, to spread out; see **Stratum**. ¶ The G. *strass* is likewise borrowed from Latin; so also Ital. *strada*, &c. Der. *stray*, q. v.

STRENGTH, might. (E.) ME. *strengthe*, Chaucer, C. T. 84. AS. *strengðu*, Grein, ii. 487; for **strang-i-ðu*.—AS. *strang*, strong; see **Strong**. Der. *strength-en*.

STRENUOUS, vigorous, active, zealous. (L.) In Minsheu, ed. 1627. Englished from L. *strēnuus*, vigorous, active. Allied to Gk. στρηνής, strong, στηρίζειν, to make firm, στερεός, firm; see **Stereoscope**. Der. *strenuous-ly, -ness*.

STRESS, strain, force, pressure. (F.—L.) 1. Used in the sense of *distress*, Rob. of Brunne, tr. of Langtoft, p. 321, last line. 'Stresse, or wed take [pledge taken] by strengthe and vyolence, Vadimonium;' Prompt. Parv. Here *stresse* is obviously short for ME. *destresse*, in the sense 'distress for rent;' and *stress* may sometimes be taken as a short form of *distress*; see **Distress**. 2. 'Stresse, or streytynge, Constrictio;' Prompt. Parv. 'I stresse, I straught one of his liberty or thrust his body to-guyther, *Ie estroysse*;' Palsgrave. This is from OF. *estrecier* (later *estrecir, estroissir*), 'to straiten, pinch, contract, bring into a narrow compass,' Cot. This answers to a Folk.-L. type **strictiāre*, not found, a derivative of *strictus*, drawn together; see **Strict**. We may regard *stress* as due, in general, to this verb, or else to *di-strictiāre*; it comes to much the same thing. ¶ The loss of the initial *di-* occurs also in *sport*, *splay*, *spend*, &c.; and is therefore merely what we should expect.

STRETCH, to draw out, extend. (E.) ME. *strecchen*, Chaucer, C. T. 15937 (G 469); pt. t. *straughte*, id. 2918 (A 2916); pp. *straught* or *streight*, whence mod. E. *straight*. AS. *streccan*, John, xxi. 18; pt. t. *strehte*, Matt. xxi. 8; pp. *streht*. Formed as a causal verb from AS. *stræc*, *stree*, strong, violent, of which the pl. *strece* occurs in Matt. xi. 12, and the form *stræc*, severe, in Gregory's Past. Care, c. xvii (heading), ed. Sweet, p. 107. The sense of *stretch* is, accordingly, to make stiff or hard, as in tightening a cord.+Du. *strekken*; Dan. *strække*, to stretch; *stræk*, a stretch; Swed. *sträcka*; G. *strecken*, from *strack*, adj., tight, straight; cf. *stracks*, straightway, immediately. Cf. also L. *stringere*, to draw tight, which is related; Gk. στραγγός, twisted tight. Other nearly related words are *string* and *strong*; also *strain*, *strait*, *stringent*, *strangle*, *strict*. **Der.** *stretch*, sb., *stretch-er*, *stra ght*.

STREW, **STRAW**, to spread, scatter loosely. (E.) Spelt *straw*, Matt. xxi. 8. ME. *strawen*, *strewen*, Chaucer, C. T. 10927 (F 613). AS. *streawian*, *streowian*, Matt. xxi. 8; Mark, xi. 8; *streaw*, straw; see **Straw**.+Du. *strooijen*, to scatter; allied to *stroo*, straw. Cf. Icel. *strá*, Swed. *strö*, Dan. *ströe*, G. *streuen*, to strew; also Goth. *straujan*, to strew (pt. t. *strawida*). The last of these is from a Teut. base *stráu*, extended from √STER, to strew, spread; as in L. *ster-n-ere* (pt. t. *stráui*); Gk. στόρ-ν-υμι, I spread; Skt. *str*, to spread. See **Stratum**. Brugmann, i. § 570. **Der.** *be-strew*.

STRIATED, streaked, marked with streaks. (L.) Scientific and modern. — L. *striātus*, pp. of *striāre*, to furrow or channel. — L. *stria*, a furrow, channel, groove.+G. *strieme*, a stripe.

STRICKEN, advanced (in years); see **Strike**.

STRICT, strait, exact, severe, accurate. (L.) In Meas. for Meas. i. 3. 19. — L. *strictus*, pp. of *stringere*, to tighten, draw together; see **Stringent**. **Der.** *strict-ly*, -*ness*; *strict-ure*, from L. *strictūra*, verbal sb. allied to *strict-us*, pp. of *stringere*. **Der.** *stress*. Doublet, *strait*, adj.

STRIDE, to walk with long steps. (E.) ME. *striden*, Cursor Mundi, 10235; Layamon, 17982; pt. t. *strade*, Ywaine and Gawin, 3193, in Ritson's Met. Rom. vol. i; cf. *bestrode*, *bestrood*, in Chaucer, C. T. 13831 (B 2093). AS. *strīdan*, to stride; rare, but in Epinal Glos. 1086; the pt. t. *be-strād* is in Ælfric's Hom. ii. 136. Pt. t. *strād*, pp. *striden*, as shown by mod. E. *strode*, and the derivative *striddle*, cited under **Straddle**. β. That the word should have meant both to *strive* and to *stride* is curious; but is certified by the cognate Low G. *strīden* (pt. t. *streed*, pp. *s'reden*), meaning (1) to strive, (2) to stride; with the still more remarkable derivative *be-striden*, also meaning (1) to combat, (2) to bestride, as in *dat Peerd bestriden*, to bestride the horse; Bremen Wörterbuch, pp. 1063, 1064. [Precisely the same double meaning reappears in Low G. *streven*, (1) to strive, (2) to stride, and the sb. *streve*, (1) a striving, (2) a stride. Hexham notes MDu. *streven*, 'to force or to strive, to walke together;' which points to the meaning of *stride* as originating from the contention of two men who, in walking side by side, strive to outpace one another, and so take long steps.] γ. Other cognate words are Du. *strijden* (pt. t. *streed*, pp. *gestreden*), G. *streiten* (pt. t. *stritt*, pp. *gestritten*), Dan. *stride* (pt. t. *stred*), only in the sense to strive, to contend; cf. also the weak verbs, Icel. *stríða*, Swed. *strida*, to strive. Teut. type *streidan-*, pt. t. *straid*, pp. *stridanoz*. Cf. Skt. *sridh*, to assail. **Der.** *stradd-le*, q. v.; *stride*, sb.; *a-stride*, adv., King Alisaunder, 4445; *be-stride*.

STRIDENT, grating, harsh. (L.) Dryden has: 'And *stridor* of her wings;' tr. of Virgil, xii. 1258. Chapman has: 'grasshoppers are *stridulous*;' tr. of Homer's Iliad, iii. commentary, note 2. *Strident* seems to be modern.—L. *strīdent-*, stem of pres. part. of *strīdēre*, also *stridere*, to creak, rattle, grate; of imitative origin. Cf. Gk. τρίζειν, to creak. **Der.** *stridor*, sb., from L. *strīdor*, a creaking; *strid-ulous*, adj., from L. *strid-ulus*, creaking, harsh.

STRIFE, contention, dispute, contest. (F.—Scand.) In early use; Layamon, 24966, later text; Ancren Riwle, p. 200, last line but one. — OF. *estrif*, 'strife, debate;' Cot. — Icel. *stríð*, strife, contention; by the change of *th* to *f*, as in Shakespeare's *fill-horse* for *thill-horse*; *stríða*, to strive; weak verb allied to Du. *strijden*, to strive, AS. *strīdan*, to stride; see **Stride** (above).+OSax. and OFries. *strid*, strife; Du. *strijd*; Dan. and Swed. *strid*; G. *streit*; OHG. *strīt*. **Der.** *strive*, q. v.

STRIGIL, a flesh-scraper. (L.) L. *strigilis*; allied to *stringere*, to graze; see **Strike**.

STRIKE, to hit, dash, stamp, coin, give a blow to. (E.) ME. *striken*, orig. to proceed, advance, esp. with a *smooth* motion, to flow; hence used of smooth swift motion, to strike with a rod or sword. 'Ase strem þat *strikeþ* stille' = like a stream that *flows* gently; Spec. of Eng., ed. Morris and Skeat, p. 48, l. 21. 'Strek into a studie' =

fell into a study; Will. of Palerne, 4038. 'A mous . . . *Stroke* forth sternly' = a mouse advanced boldly; P. Plowman, prol. 183. Strong verb, pt. t. *strak*, *strek*, *strok*, mod. E. *struck*; pp. *striken*, later *stricken*, mod. E. *struck*. The phr. '*stricken* in years' = advanced in years; Luke, i. 7. AS. *strican*, to go, proceed, advance, pt. t. *strāc*, pp. *stricen*. 'Rodor *stríceð* ymbūtan' = the firmament goes round, i. e. revolves; Grein, ii. 489.+Du. *strijken*, to smooth, rub, stroke, spread, strike; G. *streichen*, pt. t. *strich*, pp. *gestrichen*, to stroke, rub, smooth, spread, strike. β. Teut. type *streikan-*, pt. t. *straik*, pp. *strikanoz*. Cf. Goth. *striks*, a stroke, dash with a pen, cognate with L. *striga*, a row, a furrow. [We also find Icel. *strjúka*, pt. t. *strauk*, pp. *strokinn*, to stroke, rub, wipe, to strike, flog; Swed. *stryka*, to stroke, wipe, strike, rove; Dan. *stryge*, the same; from a related type *streukan-* (with a different gradation).] γ. The Idg. root is STREIG, related to L. *stringere*, which is equivalent to AS. *strican*, when used in the sense to graze, or touch slightly with a swift motion. But L. *stringere*, to draw tight, seems to be a different word; see **Stringent**. **Der.** *strik-er*, *strik-ing*; also *stroke*, q. v.; *streak*, q. v. Also *strike*, sb., the name of a measure. orig. an instrument with a straight edge for levelling (striking off) a measure of grain; ME. *strik*, Liber Albus, p. 243.

STRING, thin cord. (E.) ME. *string*, *streng*, Chaucer, C. T. 7649 (D 2067). AS. *streng*, John, ii. 15. From its being strongly or tightly twisted; allied to AS. *strang*, strong, violent.+Du. *streng*; cf. *streng*, adj., severe, rigid; Icel. *strengr*, string; *strangr*, strong; Dan. *stræng*, Swed. *sträng*, G. *strang*, string. Cf. Gk. στραγγάλη, a halter; from στραγγός, hard twisted. See **Strong**. **Der.** *string*, verb, properly a weak verb, being formed from the sb., but the pp. *strung* also occurs, L. L. L. iv. 3. 343, formed by analogy with *flung* from *fling*, and *sung* from *sing*. And Dryden has the pt. t. *strung*, Epist. to J. Dryden, l. 89. Also *string-ed*; *string-y*; *bow-string*; *heart-string*.

STRINGENT, urgent, strict. (L.) In Phillips, ed. 1706.—L. *stringent-*, stem of pres. part. of *stringere*, to draw tight, compress, urge, &c.; pp. *strictus*. From the Idg. root STREIG, to draw or twist tight. See **Strong**. **Der.** *stringent-ly*, *stringenc-y*; and see *strict*, *strait*, *a-stringent*, *a-striction*, *strain*, *con-strain*, *di-strain*, *re-strain*, *stress*, *di-stress*.

STRIP, to tear off, skin, render bare, deprive, plunder. (E.) ME. *stripen*, *strepen*, Chaucer, C. T. 1008, 8739 (A 1006, E 863); pt. t. *strepte*, spelt *strupte*, Juliana, p. 63, l. 16; pp. *strept*, spelt *i-struped*, Ancren Riwle, p. 148, note *g*. AS. *strīepan*, *strȳpan*, in comp. *bestrȳpan*, to plunder, A. S. Chron. an. 1065.+Du. *stroopen*, to plunder, strip; EFries. *stropen*; MDu. *stroopen*, 'to flea [flay], to skin, or to pill,' Hexham; OHG. *stroufen*. Teut. type *straupjan-*; from *straup*, 2nd grade of the strong verb *streupan-*; for which cf. Norw. *strūpa*, to grip, to throttle (pt. t. *straup*). **Der.** The sb. *strip*, a piece, is often understood as being 'a piece stripped off;' but it seems to belong rather to *stripe* (below).

STRIPE, a streak, a blow with a whip. (Du.) Not a very old word, and apparently borrowed from Dutch; prob. because connected with the trade of weaving. ME. *stripe*, Prompt. Parv.—MDu. *strijpe*, as in *strijp-kleedt*, 'a parti-coloured sute,' Hexham; cf. Du. *streep*, a stripe, streak.+Norw. *strípa*, Dan. *stribe*, a stripe, streak; Low G. *stripe*, a stripe, strip; *stripen*, to stripe; *striped Tüg*, striped cloth; G. *streifen*, MHG. *streif*, a stripe, streak, strip. Cf. also OIrish *sriab*, a stripe. ¶ Similarly E. *streak* is connected with E. *strike*; from the mark of a blow. **Der.** *stripe*, verb. Also *strip*, which is rather a variant of *stripe* than allied to *strip*, vb. Cf. Low G. *stripe*, (1) a stripe, (2) a strip of cloth; Prov. E. *stripe*, a strip; *stripe*, a stream, of which *strippet* (noted under **Stripling**) is a diminutive.

STRIPLING, a youth, lad. (E.) In Shak. Tam. Shrew, i. 2. 144. 'He is but an yongling, A stalworthy *striplyng*;' Skelton, Why Come Ye Nat to Courte, 345. Also ME. *striplynge*, Mandeville, Trav. ch. 27, p. 278. A double dimin. from *stripe*; the sense is 'one as thin as a stripe,' a growing lad not yet filled out. Cf. 'you tailor's yard, you sheath, you bow-case;' 1 Hen. IV, ii. 4. 273. Similarly a *strippet* is a very narrow stream; 'a little brooke or strippet;' Holinshed's Descr. of Scotland, c. 10. § 2. See **Stripe**.

STRIVE, to struggle, contend. (F.—Scand.) ME. *striuen*, a weak verb, pt. t. *striued*, Will. of Palerne, 4099. Made into a strong verb, with pt. t. *strof*, Chaucer, C. T. 1040 (A 1038); mod. E. *strove*, pp. *striven*; by analogy with *drive* (*drove*, *driven*).—OF. *estriver*, 'to strive,' Cot.—OF. *estrif*, strife. See **Strife**.

STROKE (1), a blow. (E.) ME. *strok*, *strook*, Chaucer, C. T. 1709. From AS. *strāc*, 2nd grade of *strican*, to strike; with the usual change of *a* to long *o*. See **Strike**. So also G. *streich*, a stroke, from G. *streichen*, to stroke, to whip.

STROKE (2), to rub gently. (E.) ME. *stroken*, Chaucer. C. T. 10479 (F 165). AS. *strācian*, to stroke; Ælfred, tr. of

Gregory's Past. Care, ed. Sweet, p. 303, l. 10. A causal verb; from *strắc*, 2nd grade of AS. *strīcan*, to go, pass swiftly over, mod. E. **strike**. See **Strike**. So also G. *streicheln*, to stroke, from *streichen*, to rub, strike.

STROLL, to rove, wander. (F. – Teut.) A late word. 'When *stroulers* durst presume to pick your purse;' Dryden, 5th prol. to Univ. of Oxford, l. 33. 'Knowing that rest, quiet, and sleep, with lesser meat, will sooner feed any creature than your meat with liberty to run and *stroyle* about;' Blith's Husbandry, 1652; cited by Wedgwood. Formed by prefixing s- (for OF. *es-*, L. *ex*) to *troll*, in the sense to range, rove. Cotgrave has MF. *troller* (F. *trôler*), 'to trowle, raunge, or hunt out of order,' of hounds; cf. Norm. dial. *treuler*, to wander; dial. of Verdun *trôler*, *trauler*, to rove; Guernsey *étreulaǐ* (= *estreulé*), adj., idle, vagabond (Métivier); Picard *troleuse*, a wandering woman (Corblet); see **Troll**. Schmeller gives the forms *strālen*, *strolen*, to stroll, as Bavarian; and Wedgwood quotes Swiss *strielen*, *strollen*, *strolchen*, to rove about. Ross has Norw. *strolla*, to go about wilfully and idly. Der. *stroll*, sb.; *stroll-er*.

STRONG, forcible, vigorous, energetic. (E.) ME. *strong*, Chaucer, C. T. 2137 (A 2135), &c. '*Strong* and *stark*;' Havelok, 608. AS. *strang*, *strong*; Grein, ii. 485.╋Du. *streng*; Icel. *strangr*; Dan. *streng*; Swed. *sträng*; OHG. *strang*, *strangi*, G. *streng*, strict. β. All from Teut. types **strangoz*, **strangjoz*, adj., strong. Cf. Gk. στραγγός, tightly twisted, whence στραγγάλη, a halter (E. *string*), and L. *stringere*, in the sense 'to draw tight;' hence the identity in meaning between L. *strictus* and G. *streng*. Der. *strong-ly*, *strong-hold*; *string*, q. v.; *streng-th*, q. v.; *strength-en*. Related words are *stringent*, *strain*, *strict*, *strait*, *stretch*, *straight*, *strangle*, &c.

STROP, a piece of leather, &c. for sharpening razors. (L.) Merely the old form of *strap*; from L. *struppus*; see **Strap**.

STROPHE, part of a song, poem, or dance. (Gk.) Formerly used also as a rhetorical term; '*Strophes*, wily deceits, subtilties in arguing, conversions, or turnings;' Blount's Gloss., ed. 1674. – Gk. στροφή, a turning, twist, trick; esp. the turning of the chorus, dancing to one side of the orchestra; hence, the strain sung during this evolution; the strophé, to which the antistrophe answers. – Gk. στροφ-, 2nd grade of στρέφειν, to turn. Der. *anti-strophe*, *apo-strophe*, *cata-strophe*, *epi-strophe*.

STROW, the same as **Strew**, vb., q. v.

STRUCTURE, a building, construction, arrangement. (F. – L.) In Minsheu, ed. 1627. – F. *structure*, 'a structure;' Cot. – L. *structūra*, a building; allied to *structus*, pp. of *struere*, to build, orig. to heap together, arrange. From the base STREU, allied to Goth. *straujan*, G. *streuen*, to strew, lay; allied to √STER, to spread out. Der. (from *struere*) con-*strue*, con-*struct*, de-*stroy*, de-*struction*, in-*struct*, in-*stru-ment*, mis-con-*strue*, ob-*struct*, super-*structure*.

STRUGGLE, to make great bodily efforts. (Scand.) ME. *strogelen*, Chaucer, C. T. 10248 (E 2374). Palsgrave not only gives: 'I *stroggell* with my bodye,' but also: 'I *strogell*, I murmure with wordes secretly, *je grommelle*.' The latter, however, is merely a metaphorical sense, i.e. to oppose with words instead of deeds. ME. *strogelen* is a frequentative verb formed from the Scand. base *strug-*, appearing in Swed. dial. *strug*, contention, strife, dispute; Rietz notes that *draga i strug*, to draw with difficulty, is used of horses. Related words are Swed. dial. *struug*, revengeful, Norw. *stru*, refractory, Dan. dial. *struende*, reluctantly. β. The Idg. form of the root is STREUGH; or with loss of *s*, TREUGH; the latter appears in Icel. *þrúga*, Swed. *truga*, to force, compel, AS. *þryccan*, to force, G. *drucken*, to print; and in EFries. *trüggeln*, to struggle against, as a restive horse; cf. MDu. *truggelen*, Du. *troggelen*, to beg persistently. Der. *struggle*, sb.

STRUM, to thrum on a piano. (Scand.) 'The *strum-strum* [a musical instrument] is made like a cittern;' Dampier's Voyages, an. 1684; see A New Voyage (1699), i. 127. The word is imitative, and made by prefixing s- (F. *es-*, from L. *ex*), intensive prefix, to the imitative word *thrum*, variant of *thrum*, as in Low G. *trummen*, Du. *trommen*, to drum. Cf. Norw. *strumla*, to rumble, rattle. See **Thrum** and **Drum**. So also s-*plash* for *plash*.

STRUMPET, a prostitute. (F. – L.; or F. – Teut.) ME. *strompet*, P. Plowman, C. xv. 42; also spelt *strumpet*, Polit. Songs, p. 153 (temp. Edw. II). 1. If the *m* in this word be an E. addition, it is a strengthened form of **strup-et*, in which the -*et* is a F. dimin. suffix; and the derivation is from OF. *strupe*, noted by Roquefort as a variant of OF. *stupre*, concubinage. – L. *stuprum*, dishonour, violation. β. The curious position of the *r* causes no difficulty, as there must have been a Late L. form **strupāre*, used convertibly with L. *stuprāre*. This is clear from Ital. *strupare*, variant of *stuprare*, Span. *estrupar*, variant of *estuprar*, to ravish, and from the OF. *strupe* quoted above. Perhaps the E. word was

formed directly from an OF. **strupée*, from Late L. **strupāta* = *stuprāta*, fem. of the pp. of *stuprāre*. The verb *stuprāre* is from the sb. *stuprum*. γ. We find also Irish and Gael. *striopach*, a strumpet; this is to be referred to the same Late L. **strupāre*. The history is unknown. 2. The form of the word answers better to MDu. *strompe*, Low G. *strump*, a stocking (but there is no connexion); or to Norw. *strumpen*, adj., stumbling (Ross), Low G. *strumpen*, *strumpeln*, to stumble; *strumpelig*, staggering, tottery in gait; MDu. *strompelen*, 'to stagger, to trip, or to reele,' Hexham. We might perhaps then explain *strumpet* as 'one who trips,' or makes a false step. The above words are allied to G. *strampeln*, to kick. It is remarkable that the prov. E. (Hants.) *strumpet* means a fat, hearty child, esp. a baby; where the sense 'little kicker' is appropriate. A Germanic origin seems probable.

STRUT (1), to walk about pompously. (Scand.) ME. *strouten*, to spread out, swell out. 'His here [hair] *strouted* as a fanne large and brode;' Chaucer, C. T. 3315. '*Strowtyn*, or bocyn owt [to boss out, swell out],' Turgere;' Prompt. Parv. In Havelok, 1779, to *stroute* is to make a disturbance or to brag. – Dan. *strutte*, *strude*, to strut, Swed. dial. *strutta*, to walk with a jolting step (Rietz). The Norweg. *strut* means a spout that sticks out, a nozzle; the Icel. *strútr* is a sort of hood sticking out like a horn; the Swed. *strut* is a cone-shaped piece of paper, such as grocers put sugar in. The orig. notion of *strut* seems to be 'to stick out stiffly;' cf. prov. E. *strut*, rigid. Note further Low G. *strutt*, rigid, stiff, G. *strauss*, a tuft, bunch, *strotzen*, to be puffed up, to strut. The prov. E. *strunt*, to strut (Halliwell), is a nasalised form of *strut*. Der. *strut*, sb.

STRUT (2), a support for a rafter, &c. (Scand.) '*Strut*, with carpenters, the brace which is framed into the ring-piece and principal rafters;' Bailey, vol. ii. ed. 1731. The orig. sense is a stiff piece of wood; cf. Low G. *strutt*, rigid; prov. E. *strut*, rigid. It is, accordingly, closely allied to **Strut** (1).

STRYCHNINE, a violent poison. (Gk.) Modern. Formed with suffix -*ine* (F. -*ine*, L. -*īna*, -*īnus*) from Gk. στρύχνος, nightshade, poison.

STUB, the stump of a tree left after it is cut down. (E.) 'Old stockes and *stubs* of trees;' Spenser, F. Q. i. 9. 34. ME. *stubbe*, Chaucer, C. T. 1980 (A 1978). AS. *stybb*, *stubb* (Toller); spelt *stub* in Birch, Cart. Saxon. i. 316, iii. 353; EFries. *stubbe*. From a base **stuf-*.╋Du. *stobbe*; Icel. *stubbi*, *stubbr*; Dan. *stub*; Swed. *stubbe*. β. Allied to Icel. *stúfr*, a stump; and Gk. στύπος, a stub, stump; Skt. *stupa-s*, m., a heap. Allied to **Stump**. Der. *stub*, verb, to root out stubs; *stubb-y*, *stubb-ed*, *stubb-ed-ness*; and see *stubb-orn*, *stump*.

STUBBLE, the stalks of cut corn. (F. – L.) ME. *stobil*, Wyclif, Job, xiii. 25; Chaucer has *stubbel-goos*, C. T. 4351. – OF. *estouble*, 'stubble,' Cot.; also *estuble* (Littré, s. v. *éteule*). – Late L. *stupula*, *stupla*, stubble, a variant of L. *stipula*, stubble, due to the influence of Low G. *stoppel*, stubble (Lübben); Du. and EFries. *stoppel*, cognate with MHG. *stupfel*, OHG. *stupfila*, stubble.

STUBBORN, obstinate, persistent. (E.) ME. *stoburn*, also *stiborn*. '*Styburne*, or *stoburne*, Austerus, ferox,' Prompt. Parv.; *stiborn*, Chaucer, C. T. 6038 (D 456). Cf. *styburnesse*, sb., Prompt. Parv. As the AS. *y* is represented in later English both by *i* and *u* (as in AS. *cyssan* = E. *kiss*, AS. *fyrs* = E. *furze*) we at once refer *stibborn* or *stubborn* to AS. *stybb*, a stub, with the sense of stub-like, hence immovable, stiff, steady, &c. β. The suffix -*orn* is to be regarded as adjectival, and stands for -*or*, the -*n* being merely added afterwards, by taking *stubor-ness* as *stubborn-ness*; -*or* being the same adj. suffix as in AS. *bit-or*, E. *bitt-er*. We should thus have, from AS. *styb*, an adj. **stybor* = stub-like, stubborn, and the sb. **stybornes*. γ. This is verified by the forms in Palsgrave; he gives the adj. as *stoburne*, but the sb. as *stubbernesse* and *stubblenesse*, the latter of which could have arisen from an AS. form **stybol*, with suffix -*ol* as in *wac-ol*, vigilant. ¶ The suffix -*ern* in *north-ern* admits of a different explanation. Der. *stubborn-ly*, -*ness*.

STUCCO, a kind of plaster. (Ital. – OHG.) In Pope, Imit. of Horace, ii. 192. – Ital. *stucco*, 'glutted, gorged, .. dride, stiffe, or hardned; also, a kind of stuffe or matter to build statue or image-worke with, made of paper, sand, and lyme, with other mixtures; the imagerie-work at Nonesuch in England in the inner court is built of such;' Florio. – OHG. *stucchi*, a crust; Graff, vi. 631 (Diez), the same as G. *stück*, AS. *stycce*, a piece (hence, a patch). Allied to **Stock**.

STUD (1), a collection of breeding-horses and mares. (E.) ME. *stod*, Gower, C. A. iii. 204; bk. vii. 3345; cf. *stod-mere*, a stud-mare, Ancren Riwle, p. 316, l. 15. AS. *stōd*, a stud; spelt *stood*, Voc. 119. 39; *stōd*, Thorpe, Diplomatarium, p. 574, l. 20.╋Icel. *stōð*; Dan. *stod*; G. *gestüt*; MHG. *stuot*. Cf. Russ. *stado*, a herd or drove; Lith. *stodas*, a drove of horses. β. All from Teut. base *stō-d-* ; the orig. sense is 'an establishment,' as we should call it ; from √STĀ, to stand. Der. *stud-horse* ; also *steed*, q. v.

STUD (2), a nail with a large head, large rivet, double-headed button. (E.) A *stud* is also a stout post ; 'the upright in a lath and plaster wall,' Halliwell. Also, a stiff projection, a boss, &c. ME. *stode* ; L. *bulla* is glossed 'a *stode*,' also 'nodus in cingulo,' Voc. 623. 3 ; '*stode*, or stake, *Palus*;' Voc. 600. 4. AS. *studu*, a post, Ælfred, tr. of Beda, l. iii. c. 10 ; written *stupu* in one MS.+ Dan. *stöd*, in the sense of stub, stump ; Swed. *stöd*, a prop, post ; Icel. *stoð*, a post ; whence *stoða*, *styðja*, to prop ; G. *stütze*, a prop. β. The Teut. base is *stu-, weak grade of *steu-, Idg. √STEU ; cf. Gk. στῦ-λος, a pillar, σταυ-ρός, a stake, Skt. *sthūṇā*, a post ; Gk. στύ-ειν, to erect. Der. *stud*, verb ; *studd-ed*, Shak. Venus, 37.

STUDENT, a scholar, learner. (L.) In Shak. Merry Wives, iii. 1. 38.—L. *student-*, stem of pres. part. of *studēre*, to be eager about, to study. β. Some have thought that *studēre* is allied to Gk. σπεύδειν, to hasten, to be eager about ; but this is very doubtful, though the senses of L. *studium* and Gk. σπουδή are curiously similar ; see Curtius, ii. 360. See **Study**.

STUDY, application to a subject, careful attention, with the wish to learn. (F.—L.) ME. *studie*, Will. of Palerne, 2981, 4038, 4056.—AF. *estudie* ; OF. *estudie*, later *estude*, mod. F. *étude*, study (Littré).—L. *studium*, eagerness, zeal, application, study. Der. *study*, verb, ME. *studien*, Chaucer, C. T. 184 ; *studi-ed* ; *studi-ous*, from F. *studieux*, 'studious,' from L. *studiōsus* ; *studi-ous-ly*, *-ness*. Also *studio*, Ital. *studio*, study, also a school, from L. *studium*.

STUFF, materials, household furniture. (F.—L.) 1. See Luke, xvii. 31 (A. V.). 'The sayd treasoure and *stuffe*;' Fabyan's Chron. c. 123, § 2. ME. *stuf* ; '*Stuf*, for a chapman ;' Lydgate, Minor Poems, p. 166.—OF. *estuffe*, 'stuffe, matter ;' Cot. [Mod. F. *étoffe* ; Ital. *stoffa* ; Span. *estofa*, quilted stuff ; Walloon *stoff* (Rémacle).] Derived from L. *stūpa*, *stuppa*, the coarse part of flax, hards, oakum, tow (used as material for *stuffing* things or for *stopping* them up) ; but, instead of being derived directly, the pronunciation of the L. word was Germanised before it passed into French. See Diez. Hence also G. *stoff*, stuff ; but English retains the L. *p* in the verb to *stop* ; see **Stop**. 2. The sense of the L. word is better shown by the verb to *stuff*, i.e. to cram. Skelton has the pp. *stuffed*, Bowge of Court, 180 ; pres. t. *stuffeth*, Trevisa, tr. of Higden, vii. 401.—OF. *estoffer*, 'to stuffe, to make with stuffe, to furnish or store with all necessaries ;' Cot. This answers to G. *stopfen*, to fill, to stuff, to quilt (note the Span. *estofa*, quilted stuff, above), which is a Germanised pronunciation of Late L. *stūpare*, *stuppāre*, to stop up with tow, to cram, to stop ; see **Stop**. 3. We also use E. *stuff-y* in the sense of 'close, stifling ;' this sense is due to OF. *estouffer*, 'to stifle, smother, choake, stop the breath,' Cot. Mod. F. *étouffer*. The etymology of this last word is disputed ; Diez derives it from OF. *es-* (< L. *ex-*) prefix, and Gk. τῦφος, smoke, mist, cloud, which certainly appears in Span. *tufo*, warm vapour from the earth. Scheler disputes this view, and supposes OF. *estouffer* to be all one with OF. *estoffer* ; which seems reasonable. In E., we talk of '*stopping* the breath' with the notion of suffocating. Littré says that the spelling *étouffer* is in Diez's favour, because the F. word for *stop* is *étouper*, with *p*, not *f* ; but this is invalidated by his own derivation of F. *étoffe* from L. *stūpa*. In E., we seem to regard all the senses of *stuff* as belonging to but one word ; 'I *stuffe* one up, I stoppe his breathe ;' Palsgrave. See Körting, §§ 3538, 9136.

STULTIFY, to cause to seem foolish. (L.) A mod. word ; coined (as if with F. suffix *-fy*, F. *-fier*) from a L. form *stultificāre*, to make foolish.—L. *stulti-*, for *stultus*, foolish ; and *-ficāre*, for *facere*, to make. β. The L. *stultus* is closely allied to *stolidus*, with the like sense of fixed, immovable ; hence, stupid, dull, foolish. See **Stolid**. Der. *stultific-at-ion*, also a coined word.

STUMBLE, to strike the feet against obstacles, to trip in walking. (Scand.) ME. *stumblen*, Wright's Voc. i. 143, l. 20 ; *stomblen*, Chaucer, C. T. 2615 (A 2613). The *b* is excrescent, as usual after *m*, and the better form is *stomelen* or *stumlen*. In the Prompt. Parv. pp. 476, 481, we have *stomelyn*, *stummelyn*, with the sbs. *stomelare* or *stumlere*, and *stomelynge* or *stumlynge*. The form *stomeren* also occurs, in the same sense, in Reliquiæ Antiquæ, ii. 211 (Stratmann). β. The forms *stomelen*, *stomeren* (*stumlen*, *stumren*), are frequentatives from a base *stum-*, which is a weak grade allied to the base *stam-*, as seen in Goth. *stamms*, stammering, and E. *stammer*. The word seems to be of Scand. origin.—Dan. dial. *stumle*, Icel. *stumra*, to stumble ; Norweg. *stumra*, the same (Aasen) ; cf. Swed. dial. *stambla*, *stammla*, *stomla*, *stammra*, to stumble, to falter, go with uncertain steps (Rietz). γ. Thus the word is related to *stammer*, with reference to hesitation of the step instead of the speech ; cf. E. *falter*, which expresses both. Cf. OSax., Mid. Dan., OHG. *stum*, mute. See **Stammer**. ¶ The G. *stümmeln*, to mutilate, is not the same thing,

though it is an allied word ; it means to reduce to a stump, from G. *stummel*, a stump, dimin. of a word not now found in G., but represented by Norweg. *stumme*, a stump, allied to G. *stamm*, a stock, trunk ; we are thus led back to the base of *stem* (1). Der. *stumble*, sb., *stumbl-er*, *stumbl-ing-block*, 1 Cor. i. 23.

STUMP, the stock of a tree, after it is cut down, a stub. (Scand.) ME. *stumpe*, Prompt. Parv. ; *stompe*, Joseph of Arimathea, 681. Not found in AS.—Icel. *stumpr*, Swed. and Dan. *stump*, a stump, end, bit.+EFries. *stump* ; MDu. *stompe*, Du. *stomp* ; G. *stumpf*, a stump, trunk, stem. Allied to G. *stumpf*, blunt, stumpy ; Du. *stomp*, blunt, dull ; Skt. *stambha-s*, m., a post. Allied to **Stamp** and **Staple** and **Stub**. Der. *stump*, verb, to put down one's stumps, in cricket.

STUN, to make a loud din, to amaze with a blow. (E.) ME. *stonien*, Romance of Partenay, 2940 ; *stownien*, Gawayn and Grene Knight, 301. AS. *stunian*, to make a din, resound, Grein, ii. 490. Cf. AS. *gestun* (the prefix *ge-* making no difference), a din, Grein, i. 459. Cf. pt. t. *ā-sten* (rugiebam) in the Blickling Glosses.+Icel. *stynja*, to groan ; *stynr*, a groan ; G. *stöhnen*, to groan. From Teut. *stun-*, weak grade of Idg. √STEN, as in Lithuan. *stenéti*, Russ. *stenat(e)*, Gk. στένειν, to groan, Skt. *stan*, to sound, to thunder. Brugmann, i. § 818 (2). See **Stentorian**.

STUNTED, hindered in growth. (Scand.) 'Like *stunted* hidebound trees ;' Pope, Misc. Poems, Macer, l. 11. Allied to the AS. adj. *stunt*, dull, obtuse, stupid, hence, metaphorically, short of wit ; also, not well grown ; but this sense seems to be Scandinavian. The proper form of the verb is *stint*, made from *stunt* by vowel-change ; see **Stint**. Cf. Icel. *stuttr* (for *stuntr* by assimilation), short, stunted ; MSwed. *stunt*, cut short (Ihre) ; showing that the peculiar sense is rather Scand. than E. See E. D. D.

STUPEFY, to deaden the perception, deprive of sensibility. (F.—L.) Less correctly *stupify*. Spenser has *stupefide*, F. Q. v. 3. 17.—F. *stupéfier*, to stupefy, found in the 16th cent., but omitted by Cotgrave (Littré). This verb is due to the F. pp. *stupéfait*, formed from L. *stupefactus*, stupefied ; there being no such L. word as *stupeficāre*, but only *stupefacere*, and even the latter is rarely found except in the pp. and in the pass. form.—L. *stupe-*, allied to *stupēre*, to be amazed ; and *facere* (pp. *factus*), to make. See **Stupendous** and **Fact**. Der. *stupefact-ion*, from F. *stupéfaction*, from L. acc. *stupefactiōnem* ; also *stupefact-ive*.

STUPENDOUS, amazing. (L.) In Milton, P. L. x. 351. Englished from L. *stupendus*, amazing, to be wondered at, fut. pass. part. of *stupēre*, to be amazed, to be struck still with amazement. Note Skt. *stubh*, *stumbh*, to stupefy (Benfey). Der. *stupendous-ly*, *-ness* ; also *stup-or*, sb., Phillips, ed. 1706, from L. *stupor*, sb., amazement ; and see *stup-id*, *stupe-fact-ion*.

STUPID, insensible, senseless, dull. (F.—L.) In Wint. Tale, iv. 4. 409.—F. *stupide*, 'stupid ;' Cot.—L. *stupidus*, senseless.—L. *stupēre*, to be amazed ; see **Stupendous**. Der. *stupid-ly*, *stupid-ness* ; also *stupid-i-ty*, from F. *stupidité*, 'stupidity,' Cot., from L. acc. *stupiditātem*.

STURDY, resolute, stout, firm. (F.—Teut. ?) The sense of the word has suffered considerable change ; it seems to have been influenced by some notion of relationship with *stout*, with which it is not connected. The true sense is rash or reckless. ME. *sturdy*, inconsiderate, Chaucer, C. T. 8574 (E 698) ; *stordy*, *stourdi*, Rob. of Glouc. p. 157, l. 3287 ; *stourdy*, p. 186, l. 3842.—OF. *estourdi*, 'dulled, amazed, astonished .. heedless, inconsiderate, unadvised, .. rash, retchless, or careless ;' Cot. Pp. of *estourdir*, 'to astonish, amaze ;' id. Mod. F. *étourdir* ; Span. *aturdir*, Ital. *stordire*, to stun, amaze, surprise. β. Of unknown origin ; Körting mentions the suggestion of a derivation from OHG. *sturzan* (for *sturtjan*), to overthrow, a verb allied to OHG. *sturz*, a fall ; Du. *storten*, to spill, shed, hurl down, ruin. This is allied to E. *start-le*, to astonish. See **Start**. Cf. ME. *sturt*, impetuosity. Der. *sturdi-ly*, *-ness*.

STURGEON, a large fish. (F.—OHG.) ME. *sturgiun*, Havelok, 753.—OF. *esturgeon*, *estourgeon*, 'a sturgeon ;' Cot. ; Low L. *sturiōnem*, acc. of *sturio*, a sturgeon. β. Of Teut. origin ; the lit. sense is 'stirrer,' from its habits. 'From the quality of floundering at the bottom it has received its name ; which comes from the G. verb *stören*, signifying to wallow in the mud ;' E. tr. of Buffon, pub. at London, 1792.—OHG. *sturo*, *sturjo*, MHG. *stür*, G. *stör*, a sturgeon ; cf. OHG. *stören*, to spread, stir, G. *stören*, to trouble, disturb, rake, rummage, poke about. So also Swed. and Dan. *stör*, a sturgeon ; Swed. *störa*, to stir. This etymology is favoured by the AS. form of the word, viz. *styria*, a sturgeon, also spelt *styriga*, Voc. 16. 13 ; 261. 31. This word seems to mean 'stirrer,' from AS. *styrian*, to stir, agitate ; see **Stir**. The AS. *styria* is the oldest known name of the fish ; it occurs in the Epinal Glos., no. 809.

STUTTER, to stammer. (E.) In Minsheu, ed. 1627. It is the frequentative of *stut*, which was once commonly used in the same sense. 'Her felow did stammer and *stut* ;' Elynour Rummyng, l. 339. 'I *stutte*, I can nat speake my wordes redyly ;' Palsgrave. ME. *stoten* ; the F. *s'yl ne bue* is glossed 'bote he *stote*' = unless he stutter ; Wright's Voc. i. 173, l. 6. Cf. EFries. *stuttern*, to stutter ; Du. *stotteren*. From Teut. **stut-*, weak grade of Teut. root **steut-* ; cf. Du. *stuiten*, to stop. The second grade *staut-* occurs in Icel. *stauta*, to beat, strike, also, to read stutteringly ; Swed. *stöta*, to strike, push, hit against ; Dan. *stöde*, to push, jolt, jog, trip against, stumble on ; G. *stossen*, to strike ; Goth. *stautan*, to strike. β. Thus the orig. sense of *stut* is to strike, strike against, trip ; and *stutter* = to keep on tripping up. From √STEUD, to strike ; whence also L. *tundere*, to beat (pt. t. *tu-tud-i*) ; Skt. *tud*, to strike, the initial s being lost in Skt. and L. See Brugmann, i. § 818 (2). **Der.** *stutter-er*, *stutter-ing*. From the same root are *con-tuse*, *ob-tuse* ; also *stoat*, q. v., *stot*.

STY (1), an enclosure for swine. (E.) ME. *stie*, *stye*, Chaucer, C. T. 7411 (D 1829). *Sti*, Ancren Riwle, p. 128, l. 1. AS. *stigo*, a sty. In a glossary printed in Voc. 271, we find : 'Incipit de suibus,' followed by : 'Vistrina, *stigo* ;' where a *sty* is doubtless meant. Older form *stigu*, a pen for cattle ; Voc. 7. 35. +Icel. *stia*, *sti*, a sty, a kennel ; *svinsti*, a swine-sty ; *stia*, to pen ; Dan. *sti*, a path, also, a sty, pen ; Swed. *stia*, 'a sty, cabbin to keep hogs or geese in ;' whence *gåsstia* (a goose-pen), *svinstia* (a swinesty),' Widegren ; MSwed. *stia*, *stiga* (Ihre) ; Swed. dial. *sti*, *steg*, a pen for swine, goats, or sheep (Rietz). Rietz also cites Du. *svijn-stijge*.+G. *steige*, a stair, steps, stile, stair-case ; also a hen-roost, chicken-coop ; OHG. *stiga*, a pen for small cattle. β. Teut. types **stīgā*, *stigā*, a pen for cattle ; Fick, i. 348. Ihre notes that the word was used to mean a pen for any kind of domestic animal ; and its application to pigs is prob. later than its other uses. The reason for the name is not clear, though it may have been from the ladder-like arrangement of the laths of a hen-coop, or the use of laths or sticks placed in rows ; cf. Gk. στοῖχος below. Just as Ettmüller derives AS. *stigo* from *stigan*, to climb, so Rietz derives Swed. *stia* from *stiga*, to climb, and Fick (iii. 348) derives G. *steige* from G. *steigen*, to climb. γ. The verb to *sty*, ME. *stiȝen*, to climb, was once common in E., but is now obsolete ; the forms of it are AS. *stigan*, Du. *stijen*, Icel. *stiga*, Swed. *stiga*, Dan. *stige*, G. *steigen*, Goth. *steigan*, and it is a strong verb. Further cognate with Gk. στείχειν, to climb, to go ; from the second grade is the sb. στοῖχος, a row, a file of soldiers, also (in Xenophon) a row of poles with hunting-nets into which the game was driven (i. e. a pen or *sty*).—√STEIGᴡH, to climb ; Fick, i. 826 ; Brugmann, i. § 632. **Der.** (from same root) *sty* (2), *stile* (1), *stirrup*, *stair*, *acro-stic*, *di-stich*, *ve-stige*.

STY (2), a small inflamed tumour on the edge of the eye-lid. (E.) The AS. name was *stigend*. This is shown by the entry 'Ordeolus, *stigend*' in Voc. 114. 10 ; where *ordeolus* = L. *hordeolus*, a sty in the eye. This *stigend* was orig. the pres. part. of *stigan*, to climb, rise, and signifies 'rising,' i. e. swelling up. For the verb *stigan*, see **Sty** (1). β. We also meet with '*styanye*, or a perle in the eye,' Prompt. Parv. ; 'the *styonie*, sycosis,' Levins, ed. 1570 (which is a very late example) ; also '*Styony*, disease growyng within the eye-liddes, sycosis,' Huloet (cited in Wheatley's ed. of Levins). Cf. prov. E. *stine*, *styon*, a sty ; also *stiony*, which seems to have been resolved into *sty-on-eye* in some dialects ; see E. D. D. γ. Cognate words are Low G. *stieg*, *stige*, a sty in the eye, from *stigen*, to rise ; EFries. *stiger* ; Norweg. *stig*, *stigje*, sty, also called *stigköyna* (where *köyna* = a pustule), from the verb *stiga*, to rise.

STYLE (1), a pointed tool for engraving or writing, mode of writing, manner of expression, way, mode. (F.—L.) ME. *stile*, Chaucer, C. T. 10419 (F 105), where it rimes with *stile* in the sense of way over a hedge.—MF. *stile*, *style*, 'a stile, form or manner of indicting, the pin of a pair of writing tables ;' Cot.—L. *stilus*, an iron-pointed peg used for writing on wax tablets ; also, a manner of writing. Perhaps allied to L. *sti-mulus*. ¶ The spelling *style* is false ; it ought to be *stile*. The mistake is due to the common error of writing the L. word as *stylus*. This error was due to some late writers who imagined that the Gk. στῦλος, a pillar, must be the original of L. *stilus*. β. But note, that when the E. *style* is used, as it sometimes is, in botany or dialling, it then represents the Gk. στῦλος ; see **Style** (2). **Der.** *style*, verb, *styl-ish*, *-ly*, *-ness*.

STYLE (2), in botany, the middle part of a pistil of a flower. (Gk.) 1. '*Style*, or *stylus*, among herbalists, that middle bunching out part of the flower of a plant, which sticks to the fruit or seed ;' Phillips, ed. 1706.—Gk. στῦλος, a pillar, a long upright body like a pillar ; cf. Skt. *sthūnā*, a pillar, post ; from √STEU, to erect ; cf. Gk. στύειν, to erect. Not connected with L. *stilus*, as is often imagined. 2. Another sense may be noted ; 'in dialling, *style* is a line whose shadow on the plane of the dial shows the true hour-line, and it is the upper edge of the gnomon, cock, or needle ;' Phillips, ed. 1706. Here *style* orig. meant the gnomon itself, and answers rather to Gk. στῦλος than to L. *stilus*. Some difficulty has resulted from the need-

less confusion of these two unrelated words. **Der.** *styl-ar*, pertaining to the pin of a dial.

STYPTIC, astringent, that stops bleeding. (F.—L.—Gk.) Spelt *styptick* in Holland, tr. of Pliny, b. xxiv. c. 13, and in Cotgrave. ME. *stiptik*, Lanfrank, Cirurgie, p. 98, l. 16.—F. *styptique*, 'styptick,' Cot.—L. *stypticus*.—Gk. στυπτικός, astringent.—Gk. στύφειν, to contract, draw together, also, to be astringent ; allied to στῦψις, contraction ; and prob. to E. **Stop**.

SUASION, advice. (F.—L.) In Sir T. More's Works, p. 157 a, l. 5.—F. *suasion*, 'persuasion,' Cot.—L. *suāsiōnem*, acc. of *suāsio*, persuasion ; allied to L. *suāsus*, pp. of *suādēre*, to persuade ; allied to L. *suāuis* (for **suad-vis*), sweet. See **Suave**. **Der.** *suas-ive*, a coined word ; *suas-ive-ly*, *suav-ish-ness* ; see also *dis-suade*, *per-suade*.

SUAVE, pleasant, agreeable. (F.—L.) Not common ; the derived word *suavity* is in earlier use, in Cotgrave. F. *suave*, 'sweet, pleasant,' Cot.—L. *suāuis*, sweet ; for **suad-vis*, and allied to E. **Sweet**, q. v. Brugmann, i. § 187. **Der.** *suav-ity*, from F. *suavité*, 'suavity,' Cot., from L. acc. *suāuitātem*.

SUB-, a common prefix. (L. ; or F.—L.) L. *sub-*, prefix (whence F. *sub-*) : L. *sub*, prep., under. The L. *sup-er*, above, is certainly a comparative form from *sub* (orig. **sup*), and corresponds, in some measure, to Skt. *upari*, above. As to the connexion of *super* with *upari* there can be no doubt, but the prefixed *s* in L. *s-uper* is difficult ; perhaps it resulted from a prefixed *ex*, prep. ; cf. Gk. ἐξ-ὑπερθε ; Brugmann, i. § 761. Certainly L. *super* is allied to E. *over*. See further under **Over**. β. '*Sub*, it is true, means generally below, under ; but, like the Gk. *hypó* (ὑπό), it is used in the sense of 'from below,' and thus may seem to have two meanings diametrically opposed to each other, *below* and *upward*. *Submittere* means to place below, to lay down, to submit ; *sublevare*, to lift from below, to raise up. *Summus*, a superl. of *sub*, *hýpatos* (ὕπατος), a superl. of *hypó* (ὑπό), do not mean the lowest, but the highest ;' Max Müller, Lectures, ii. 310, ed. 1875. And see **Hypo-, Hyper-**. γ. *Sub-*, prefix, becomes *suc-* before *c* following, *suf-* before *f*, *sug-* before *g*, *sum-* before *m*, *sup-* before *p* (though *sup* is rather the orig. form), *sur-* before *r*. And see **Sus-**. **Der.** *sub-ter-*, prefix ; *sup-er-*, prefix ; *sup-ra-*, prefix ; *sur-*, prefix (French) ; and see *sum*, *supreme*, *soprano*, *sovereign*, *sup-ine*. Doublet, *hypo-*, prefix.

SUBACID, somewhat acid. (L.) Richardson gives an example from Arbuthnot, Of Aliments, c. 3.—L. *subacidus*, somewhat acid, lit. 'under acid.' See **Sub-** and **Acid**.

SUBALTERN, subordinate, inferior to another. (F.—L.) '*Subaltern* magistrates and officers of the crown ;' Sidney, Arcadia, b. iii. (R.). '*Subalterne*, vnder another ;' Minsheu, ed. 1627.—F. *subalterne*, adj., 'subalterne, secondary ;' Cot.—L. *subalternus*, subordinate.—L. *sub*, under, and *alter*, another ; with adj. suffix *-nus* (Idg. *-no-*). See **Sub-** and **Alter**. **Der.** *subaltern*, sb., a subordinate ; for *subaltern officer*.

SUBAQUEOUS, under water. (L.) In Pennant's Brit. Zoology, on swallows (R.). A coined word ; from L. *sub*, under, and *aqua*, water ; see **Sub-** and **Aquatic**. The true L. word is *subaquāneus*.

SUBDIVIDE, to divide again into smaller parts. (L.) '*Subdivided* into verses ;' Fuller's Worthies, Kent (R.).—L. *subdividere*, lit. to divide under. See **Sub-** and **Divide**. **Der.** *subdivis-ion*.

SUBDUE, to reduce, conquer, tame, soften. (F.—L.) In Palsgrave ; and in Sir T. More, Works, p. 962 a, l. 4. The ME. form was *soduen*, and this was afterwards altered to *subduen* for the greater clearness, by analogy with the numerous words beginning with *sub-*. We find 'schal be *sodued*' in Trevisa, iii. 123, l. 7, where two other MSS. have *soduwed*, *sudewide*, but Caxton's (later) edition has *subdued*. So also the same, iii. 153, 407 ; iii. 19 ; &c. The pt. t. *sodu-ed* was adapted from AF. **subdut*, occurring in the pl. *subduz* (=*subduts*), 'subdued ;' Stat. Realm, i. 339 (A.D. 1353).—Late L. **subdutus*, for L. *subditus*, subdued, pp. of *subdere*, to subdue, subjugate.—L. *sub*, under ; and *-dere*, to put, from the weak grade of √DHĒ, to put. ¶ For the form **subdutus*, cf. Late L. **perdutus* (Ital. *perduto*, F. *perdu*), and such Ital. past participles as *cad-uto* (from *cad-ere*), *ved-uto* (from *ved-ere*), *ten-uto*, *sap-uto*, *bev-uto*, &c. ¶ It is impossible to derive *subdue* from L. *subdūcere*, with an alien sense. **Der.** *subdu-er*, *subdu-al*, *subdu-able*.

SUB-EDITOR ; from **Sub-** and **Editor**.

SUBJACENT, lying beneath. (L.) In Boyle's Works, vol. i. p. 177 (R.).—L. *subiacent-*, stem of pres. part. of *subiacēre*, to lie under.—L. *sub*, under ; and *iacēre*, to lie. *Iacēre* is allied to *iacere*, to cast, throw. See **Sub-** and **Jet** (1) ; and see **Subject**.

SUBJECT, laid or situate under, under the power of another, liable, disposed, subservient. (F.—L.) The spelling has been brought nearer to Latin, but the word was taken from French. The OF. word was also, at one time, re-spelt, to bring it nearer to Latin. ME. *suget*, adj., Wyclif, Rom. xiii. 1 ; *suget*, *subget*, sb., Chaucer, C. T. 8358 (E 482).—OF. *suget* (Hatzfeld), later *subiect*, 'a subject, vassall;' Cot. Mod. F. *sujet.*—L. *subiectus*, subject; pp. of *subicere*, to place under, put under, subject.—L. *sub*, under; and *iacere*, to cast, throw, put. See **Sub-** and **Jet** (1). Der. *subject*, sb., ME. *subget*, as above; *subject*, verb, spelt *subiecte* in Palsgrave; *subject-ion*, ME. *subiectioun*, Chaucer, C. T. 14384 (B 3656), from OF. *subiection*, 'subjection,' Cot., from L. acc. *subiectiōnem*; *subject-ive*, from L. *subiectīuus*; *subject-ive-ly*; *subject-ive-ness*; *subject-iv-i-ty*, a late coinage.

SUBJOIN, to join on at the end, annex, affix. (F.—L.) In Cotgrave.—MF. *subioign-* (*subjoign-*), a stem of MF. *subioindre*, 'to subjoin;' Cot.—L. *subiungere*, to subjoin. See **Sub-** and **Join.** And see *subjunct-ive.*

SUBJUGATE, to bring under the yoke. (L.) In Palsgrave.—L. *subiugātus*, pp. of *subiugāre*, to bring under the yoke.—L. *sub-*, under; and *iugum*, a yoke, cognate with E. *yoke*, and allied to *iungere*, to join (above); see **Sub-** and **Yoke.** Der. *subjugat-or*, from L. *subiugātor*; *subjugat-ion*, from F. *subjugation*, 'a subduing,' Cot., from L. acc. *subiugātiōnem*, not used.

SUBJUNCTIVE, denoting that mood of a verb which expresses contingency. (L.) Spelt *subiunctiue*, Minsheu, ed. 1627; Palsgrave, p. 380.—L. *subiunctīuus*, subjunctive, lit. joining on at the end, from its use in dependent clauses.—L. *subiunct-us*, pp. of *subiungere*, to subjoin; see **Subjoin.**

SUBLEASE, an under-lease. (F.—L.; *with* L. *prefix.*) From **Sub-** and **Lease.**

SUBLET, to let, as a tenant, to another. (Hybrid; L. *and* E.) From **Sub-** and **Let** (1).

SUBLIME, lofty, majestic. (F.—L.) In Spenser, F. Q. v. 8. 30. [As a term of alchemy, the verb *to sublime* is much older; Chaucer has *subliming*, C. T. 16238 (G 770); also *sublimatorie*, id. 16261 (G 793); these are rather taken directly from L. *sublimāre* and *sublimātōrium* than through the F., as it was usual to write on alchemy in Latin.]—F. *sublime*, 'sublime,' Cot.—L. *sublīmis*, lofty, raised on high. β. A difficult word; prob. it means passing under the lintel or cross-piece of a door, hence reaching up to the lintel, tall, high; if so, the part *-līmis* is connected with *līmen*, a lintel, or a threshold. See Brugmann, ii. § 12 (stems in *-n-*). See **Sub-** and **Limit.** Der. *sublime-ly*; *sublim-i-ty*, from F. *sublimité*, 'sublimity,' Cot., from L. acc. *sublimitātem.* Also *sublime*, verb, in alchemy = L. *sublimāre*, lit. to elevate; *sublim-ate*, verb and sb., *sublim-at-ion*, *sublim-at-or-y*.

SUBLUNAR, under the moon, earthly. (L.) In Milton, P. L. iv. 777. Coined from **Sub-** and **Lunar.** Der. *sublunar-y*, Howell, Instructions for Foreign Travel (1642), sect. vi. parag. 7.

SUBMARINE, under or in the sea. (Hybrid; L. *and* F.—L.) Rich. gives a quotation from Boyle's Works, vol. iii. p. 342. It occurs in Blount's Gloss., ed. 1674, where it is said to have been used by Bacon. Coined from **Sub-** and **Marine.**

SUBMERGE, to plunge under water, overflow with water. (F.—L.) In Shak. Antony, ii. 5. 94.—F. *submerger*, 'to submerge;' Cot.—L. *submergere* (pp. *submersus*); see **Sub-** and **Merge.** Der. *submerg-ence*; *submers-ion*, from F. *submersion*, 'a submersion,' Cot., from L. acc. *submersiōnem*; also *submerse*, from the pp. *submersus*; *submers-ed.*

SUBMIT, to refer to the judgment of another, yield, surrender. (L.) 'I *submyt* myselfe, Ie me submets;' Palsgrave. 'Ye been *submitted*;' Chaucer, C. T. 4455 (B 35). It may have been taken from F. in the first instance, but, if so, was early conformed to the L. spelling.—L. *submittere*, to let down, submit, bow to.—L. *sub-*, under, down; and *mittere*, to send (pp. *missus*); see **Sub-** and **Missile.** Der. *submission*, AF. *submission*, MF. *soubmission*, 'submission,' Cot., from L. acc. *submissiōnem*; *submiss-ive*, *-ly*, *-ness*; *submiss*, Spenser, F. Q. iv. 10. 51, from L. pp. *submissus.*

SUBORDINATE, lower in order or rank. (L.) 'Inferior and *subordinate* sorts;' Cowley, Essay 6, Of Greatness (R.). 'His next *subordinate*;' Milton, P. L. v. 671. Coined from Late L. *subordinātus*, pp. of *subordināre*, coined from *sub ordinem*, under the order or rank. *Ordinem* is the acc. of *ordo*, order, rank. See **Sub-** and **Order.** Der. *subordinate*, as sb., *subordinate-ly*; *subordinat-ion*, Howell, Instructions for Foreign Travel (1642), sect. vi. parag. 8; whence *in-subordinat-ion.*

SUBORN, to procure privately, instigate secretly, to cause to commit perjury. (F.—L.) In Spenser, F. Q. i. 12. 34. Sir T. More has *subornacion*, Works, p. 211 h.—F. *suborner*, 'to suborn,' Cot.—L. *subornāre*, to furnish or supply in an underhand way or secretly.—l. *sub*, under, secretly; and *ornāre*, to furnish, adorn. See **Sub-** and **Ornament.** Der. *suborn-er*; *subornat-ion*, from F. *subornation*, 'a subornation,' Cot.

SUBPŒNA, a writ commanding a person to attend in court under a penalty. (L.) Explained in Minsheu, ed. 1627; and much older.—L. *sub pœnā*, under a penalty.—L. *sub*, under; and *pœnā*, abl. of *pœna*, a pain or penalty. See **Sub-** and **Pain.** Der. *sub-pœna*, verb, to serve a subpœna.

SUBSCRIBE, to write underneath, to sign one's name to. (L.) 'And *subscribed* their names vndre them;' Sir T. More, Works, p. 3 h. 'My lettre *subscribed*;' Will of Hen. V; Royal Wills, p. 238.—L. *subscribere*, to write under, sign one's name to.—L. *sub*, under; and *scribere*, to write. See **Sub-** and **Scribe.** Der. *sub-scrib-er*; *subscript*, from the pp. *subscriptus*; *subscript-ion*, from MF. *soubscription*, 'a subscription or subscribing,' Cot., from L. acc. *subscriptiōnem.*

SUBSECTION, an under-section, subdivision of a subject. (Hybrid; L. *and* F.—L.) From **Sub-** and **Section.**

SUBSEQUENT, following after. (L.) In Shak. Troil. i. 3. 334, and Milton, Samson, 325.—L. *subsequent-*, stem of pres. part. of *subsequī*, to follow close after.—L. *sub*, under, close after; and *sequī*, to follow. See **Sub-** and **Sequel.** Der. *subsequent-ly.*

SUBSERVE, to serve subordinately. (L.) In Milton, Samson, 57. Englished from L. *subseruīre*, to serve under a person.—L. *sub*, under; and *seruīre*, to serve; see **Sub-** and **Serve.** Der. *subservi-ent*, from L. *subseruient-*, stem of pres. part. of *subseruīre*; *subservient-ly*, *subservience.*

SUBSIDE, to settle down. (L.) Dryden has *subsides*, tr. of Virgil, Æn. i. 212; Phillips, ed. 1706, has *subside*, *subsidence.*—L. *subsīdere*, to settle down.—L. *sub*, under; and *sīdere*, to settle, allied to *sedēre*, to sit, which latter is cognate with E. *sit*. For **si-zd-ere*, where *zd-* is the weak grade of the root SED, to sit. See **Sub-** and **Sit.** Der. *subsid-ence*, from L. *subsīdentia*, a settling down. And see *subsidy.*

SUBSIDY, assistance, aid in money. (F.—L.) In Shak. 2 Hen. VI, iv. 7. 25; 3 Hen. VI, iv. 8. 45. ME. *subsidie*, The Crowned King, l. 36, in App. to P. Plowman, C-text, p. 525; the date of the poem is ab. A.D. 1415.—AF. *subsidie* (in Godefroy); though the usual F. form is *subside*, as in Cotgrave and Palsgrave.—L. *subsidium*, a body of troops in reserve, aid, assistance. The lit. sense is 'that which sits [remains] behind or in reserve;' from L. *sub*, under, behind, and *sedēre*, to sit, cognate with E. *sit*; see **Sub-** and **Sit**; and see **Subside.** Cf. L. *præ-sidium*, *ob-sidium*, from the same verb. Der. *subsidi-ar-y*, from L. *subsidiārius*, belonging to a reserve; *subsid-ise*, a coined verb.

SUBSIST, to live, continue. (F.—L.) In Shak. Cor. v. 6. 73.—F. *subsister*, 'to subsist, abide;' Cot.—L. *subsistere*, to stand still, stay, abide.—L. *sub*, under, but here used with very slight force; and *sistere*, orig. to set, make to stand, but also used in the sense to stand. *Sistere* is the causal of *stāre*, to stand (cf. Gk. ἵστημι, for **σί-στημι*); and *stāre* is from √STĀ, to stand; see **Sub-** and **Stand.** Der. *subsist-ence*, from F. *subsistence*, 'subsistence, continuance,' Cot., from L. *subsistentia*; *subsist-ent*, from the stem of the pres. part. of *subsistere.*

SUBSOIL, the under-soil. (Hybrid; L. *and* F.—L.) From **Sub-** and **Soil.**

SUBSTANCE, essential part, matter, body. (F.—L.) ME. *substance*, *substaunce*, Chaucer, C. T. 14809 (B 3993).—F. *substance*, 'substance;' Cot.—L. *substantia*, essence, material, substance.—L. *substant-*, stem of pres. part. of *substāre*, to be present, exist, lit. to stand beneath.—L. *sub*, beneath; and *stāre*, to stand, from √STĀ, to stand. See **Sub-** and **Stand.** Der. *substanti-al*, ME. *substancial*, Gower, C. A. iii. 92; bk. vii. 226; from F. *substantiel*, from L. adj. *substantiālis*; *substanti-al-ly*; *substanti-ate*, a coined word. Also *substant-ive*, ME. *substantif*, P. Plowman, C. iv. 345, from F. *substantif* (Littré), from L. *substantīuus*, self-existent, that which denotes existence, used of the 'substantive' verb *esse*, and afterwards extended, as a grammatical term, to nouns substantive as distinct from nouns adjective.

SUBSTITUTE, one person put in place of another. (F.—L.) Orig. used as a pp. 'This pope may be deposed, and another *substitute* in his rome;' Sir T. More, Works, p. 1427 f. Hence used as a verb. 'They dyd also *substytute* other;' id. p. 821 d.—F. *substitut*, 'a substitute;' Cot.—L. *substitūtus*, one substituted; pp. of *substituere*, to lay under, put in stead of.—L. *sub*, under, in place of; and *statuere*, to place, pp. *statūtus*; see **Sub-** and **Statute.** Der. *substitute*, verb, as above; *substitut-ion*, Gower, C. A. iii. 178, bk. vii. 2769, F. *substitution* (Cot.), from L. acc. *substitūtiōnem.*

SUBSTRATUM, an under stratum. (L.) L. *substrātum*, neut. of *substrātus*, pp. of *substernere*, to spread under. See **Sub-** and **Stratum.**

SUBTEND, to extend under or be opposite to. (L.) Phillips, ed. 1706, gives *subtended* and *subtense* as mathematical terms; *subtense* is in Blount, ed. 1674.—L. *subtendere* (pp. *subtensus*), to stretch beneath.—L. *sub*, under; and *tendere*, to stretch; see **Sub-** and **Tend.** Der. *subtense*, from pp. *subtensus*. And see *hypotenuse.*

SUBTER-, under, secretly. (L.) Formed from L. *sub*, under, by help of the suffix *-ter*, which is properly a comparative suffix, as in *in-ter*; see **Inter-**, **Other.**

SUBTERFUGE, an evasion, artifice to escape censure. (F. − L.) In Bacon, Life of Hen. VII, ed. Lumby, p. 182, l. 18. − F. *subterfuge*, 'a subterfuge, a shift;' Cot. − Late L. *subterfugium*, a subterfuge (Ducange). − L. *subterfugere*, to escape secretly. − L. *subter*, secretly; and *fugere*, to flee; see **Subter-** and **Fugitive**.

SUBTERRANEAN, SUBTERRANEOUS, underground. (L.) Both forms are in Phillips, ed. 1706. Blount, ed. 1674, has *subterrany* and *subterraneous*. Bacon has *subterrany*, Nat. Hist. § 603. Both are formed from L. *subterrāneus*, underground; the former by adding *-an* (= L. *-ānus*) after *-e-*, the latter by changing *-us* to *-ous*. − L. *sub*, under; and *terr-a*, the earth; with suffix *-ān-eus*. See **Sub-** and **Terrace**.

SUBTLE, fine, rare, insinuating, sly, artful. (F. − L.) Pronounced [sət·l]. The word was formerly spelt without *b*, but this was sometimes inserted to bring it nearer to the L. form. We also meet with the spellings *subtil*, *subtile*. ME. *sotil*, *sotel*, Chaucer, C. T. 1056, 2051; the Six-text edition has the spellings *sotil*, *sotyl*, *subtil*, *subtile*, *sotel*, *soutil*, Group A, 1054, 2049. − OF. *sutil*, *soutil* (Burguy), later *subtil*, 'subtill,' Cot. − L. *subtīlem*, acc. of *subtīlis*, fine, thin, slender, precise, accurate, subtle. β. It is gen. thought that the orig. sense of *subtīlis* was 'finely woven;' cf. *sub*, beneath (= closely?), and *tēla*, a web. See **Sub-** and **Toil** (2). Der. *subtl-y* (sometimes *subtile-ly*), *subtle-ness* (sometimes *subtile-ness*); also *subtle-ty* or *subtil-ty*, ME. *soteltee*, *sotelte*, P. Plowman, C. xv. 76, from OF. *sotilleté* (Littré), also *subtilité*, from L. acc. *subtīlitātem*. ¶ Note that the pronunciation without *b* agrees with the orig. ME. form.

SUBTRACT, to take away a part from the whole. (L.) In Minsheu, ed. 1627. − L. *subtract-us*, pp. of *subtrahere*, to draw away underneath, to subtract. − L. *sub*, under; and *trahere* (pp. *tractus*), to draw. See **Sub-** and **Trace**. Der. *subtract-ion* (as if from F. *subtraction*, not used), from L. acc. *subtractiōnem*; *subtract-ive*; also *subtrahend*, in Minsheu, a number to be subtracted, from L. *subtrahend-us*, fut. pass. part. of *subtrahere*.

SUBURB, SUBURBS, the confines of a city. (F. − L.) Commonly used in the pl. form. 'The *suburbes* of the towne;' Fabyan's Chron. c. 219; Chaucer, C. T., G 657. − AF. *suburbe*, Stat. Realm, i. 97 (1285). − L. *suburbium*, the suburb of a town. − L. *sub*, under (here, near); and *urbi-*, decl. stem of *urbs*, a town, city; see **Sub-** and **Urban**. Der. *suburb-an*, from L. *suburbānus*.

SUBVENTION, a subsidy, a pecuniary grant in aid. (F. − L.) In Cotgrave. − F. *subvention*, 'subvention, help, aid; also, a subsidy;' Cot. − L. *subuentiōnem*, acc. of *subuentio*, assistance; cf. *subuentus*, pp. of *subuenire*, to come to one's aid, assist, relieve, succour. − L. *sub*, under (by way of help); *uenire*, to come. See **Sub-** and **Venture**. Der. We also find *subvene*, vb., from *subuenire*; and the adj. *subvent-itious*.

SUBVERT, to overthrow, ruin, corrupt. (F. − L.; *or* L.) ME. *subuerten*, Wyclif, Titus, iii. 11. − F. *subvertir*, 'to subvert;' Cot. − L. *subuertere* (pp. *subuersus*), to turn upside down, overthrow, lit. to turn from beneath. − L. *sub*, from under; and *uertere*, to turn. See **Sub-** and **Verse**. Der. *subvers-ion*, AF. *subversion*, Stat. Realm, i. 300, F. *subversion*, 'a subversion,' Cot., from L. acc. *subuersiōnem*; *subvers-ive*.

SUCCEED, to follow next in order, take the place of, to prosper. (F. − L.) Better spelt *succede*. ME. *succeden*, Chaucer, C. T. 8508 (E 632). − F. *succeder*, 'to succeed;' Cot. − L. *succēdere* (pp. *successus*), to go beneath or under, follow after. − L. *suc-* (for *sub* before *c*), under; and *cēdere*, to go; see **Sub-** and **Cede**. Der. *success*, an issue or result, whether good or bad (now chiefly only of a *good* result), as in 'good or ill *successe*,' Ascham, Schoolmaster, pt. i, ed. Arber, p. 35, from MF. *succes*, 'success,' Cot., from L. *successum*, acc. of *successus*, result, event; *success-ful*, *success-ful-ly*. Also *success-or*, ME. *successour*, Rob. of Glouc. p. 507, l. 10440, F. *successeur*, from L. acc. *successōrem*, one who succeeds; *success-ion*, F. *succession*, 'succession,' Cot., from L. acc. *successiōnem*; *success-ion-al*; *success-ive*, F. *successif*, 'successive,' from L. *successiuus*; *success-ive-ly*. Also *succed-an-e-ous*, explained by Phillips, ed. 1706, as 'succeding, or coming in the room of another,' from L. *succēdāneus*, that which supplies the place of another; *succed-an-e-um*, sb., neut. of *succēdāneus*.

SUCCINCT, concise. (L.) In Minsheu, ed. 1627. − L. *succinctus*, prepared, short, small, contracted; pp. of *succingere*, to gird below, tuck up, gird up, furnish. − L. *suc-* (for *sub* before *c*), under; and *cingere*, to gird; see **Sub-** and **Cincture**. Der. *succinct-ly*, *succinct-ness*.

SUCCORY, chicory. (F. − L. − Gk.) 'Of *cykorie* or *suckorie*,' Sir T. Elyot, Castle of Helth, b. ii. c. 8. Minsheu gives *succory*, *cichory*, and *chicory*. *Succory* is a corruption of *cichory*, now usually called *chicory*; see **Chicory**.

SUCCOUR, to assist, relieve. (F. − L.) ME. *socouren*, Will. of Palerne, 1186. − OF. *sucurre*, *sosoorre* (Burguy), MF. *secourir*, as in Cotgrave; this change to *e* is no improvement. − L. *subcurrere*, *succurrere*, to run under, run up to, run to the aid of, aid, succour. − L. *sub*, under, up to; and *currere*, to run; see **Sub-** and **Current**. Der. *succour-er*. Also *succour*, sb., ME. *sucurs*, Ancren Riwle, p. 244, l. 9, from OF. *socors*, later *secours*, as in Cotgrave, from L. *subcursus*, *succursus*, pp. of *succurrere*. ¶ The spelling is prob. due to that of the AF. *succour*, sb., in Langtoft's Chron. i. 302, also spelt *soccours*, i. 16; and not from AF. *sucure*, vb., as used in the Vie de St. Auban.

SUCCUBA, a wanton female demon. (L.) In Beaum. and Fletcher, Knight of Malta, v. 2 (Norandine). − L. *succuba*. − L. *succubāre*, to lie under. − L. *suc-* (for *sub*), under; *cubāre*, to lie down. See **Sub-** and **Covey**. Der. *succubus*, a masc. form; Webster, Westward Ho, iv. 2.

SUCCULENT, juicy. (F. − L.) In Minsheu, ed. 1627. − F. *succulent*, 'succulent;' Cot. − L. *succulentus*, *sūculentus*, full of juice; formed with suffix *-lentus* from *succu-s*, *sūcu-s*, juice (the gen. is *succī*, but there is a collateral form with *u*-stem, found in the gen. pl. *sucuum*). Allied to E. **Suck**.

SUCCUMB, to yield. (L.) In Butler, Hudibras, pt. i. c. 3, l. 459. − L. *succumbere*, to lie or fall under, yield. − L. *suc-* (for *sub* before *c*), under; and **cumbere*, to lie, a nasalised form allied to *cubāre*, to lie. See **Sub-** and **Incubus, Incumbent, Covey**.

SUCH, of a like kind. (E.) ME. *swulc*, *swilc*, *swilch*, *swich*, *such* (with numerous other forms, for which see Stratmann). We find *swulc*, *swilc* in Layamon, 31585, 1375; *swilch*, Reliquiæ Antiquæ, i. 131; *swich*, *such*, Chaucer, C. T. 3 (see Six-text). It will thus be seen that the orig. *l* was lost, and the final *c* palatalised to *ch*. The forms *swulc*, *swilc* are from AS. *swylc*, *swilc*, *swelc*, such, Grein, ii. 513.+OSax. *selic*, *selk*, *sullik*, *sulch*, *suk*; Du. *zulk*; Icel. *slíkr*; Dan. *slig*; Swed. *slik*; MSwed. *salik* (Ihre); G. *solch*; OHG. *solich*; Goth. *swaleiks*. β. The Goth. *swaleiks* is simply compounded of *swa*, so, and *leiks*, like; and all the Teut. forms admit of a similar explanation. Thus *such* is for *so-like*, of which it is a corruption. See **So** and **Like**; and cf. **Which**.

SUCK, to draw in with the mouth, imbibe, esp. milk. (E.) ME. *souken*, Chaucer, C. T. 8326 (E 450); once a strong verb, with pt. t. *sek* or *sec*, Ancren Riwle, p. 330, l. 6, pp. *i-soke* (for *i-soken*), Trevisa, iii. 267, l. 12. AS. *sūcan*, strong verb, pt. t. *sēac*, pp. *socen*; Grein, ii. 492; Deut. xxxii. 13; Luke, xi. 27. [There is also a form *sūgan*, and there is a double form of the Teut. base, viz. SEUK and SEUG. Of the former, we find examples in AS. *sūcan*, E. *suck*, cognate with L. *sūgere*. Of the latter, we have examples in AS. *sūgan*, Icel. *sjūga*, *sūga* (pt. t. *saug*, pp. *soginn*), Dan. *suge*, Swed. *suga*, G. *saugen*, OHG. *sūgan*; which is the prevailing type in Teutonic.] We find also W. *sugno*, to suck, *sug*, juice; Irish *sughaim*, I suck in, *sugh*, juice; Gael. *sug*, to suck, *sugh*, juice; cf. L. *sūcus*, *succus*, juice. β. The Idg. root of E. *suck* is SEUG. See Brugmann, i. § 112. The word *succulent* is related. Der. *suck*, verb, *suck-er*, sb.; *suck-le*, Cor. i. 3. 44, a frequentative form, with the usual suffix *-le*; *suck-l-ing*, ME. *sokling* or *sokeling*, spelt *sokelynge* in Prompt. Parv., formed with dimin. suffix *-ing* from the form *sokel* = one who sucks, where the *-el* is the suffix of the agent (so that it is hardly a parallel form to *duck-l-ing*, which is merely a double dimin. from *duck*). Also *honey-suckle*, q.v.; *suc-t-ion*, q.v.; *soak*, q.v.

SUCTION, the act or power of sucking. (F. − L.) In Bacon, Nat. Hist., § 191. − F. *suction*, 'a sucking;' Cot. Formed, as if from L. **suctio*; cf. *suctus*, pp. of *sūgere*, to suck; see **Suck**.

SUDATORY, a sweating bath. (L.) In Blount's Gloss., ed. 1674. Rare. Rich. gives an example from Holyday, Juvenal, p. 224. − L. *sūdātōrium*, a sweating-bath; neut. of *sūdātōrius*, serving for sweating. − L. *sūdātōri-*, decl. stem of *sūdātor*, a sweater. − L. *sūdāre*, to sweat, allied to E. **Sweat**, q.v.; with suffix *-tor* of the agent. See *sudorific*.

SUDDEN, unexpected, abrupt, hasty. (F. − L.) ME. *sodain*, *sodein*, *soden*, Chaucer, C. T. 4841 (B 421); *sodeynliche*, suddenly, King Alisaunder, 3568. − OF. *sodain*, *sudain*, mod. F. *soudain*, sudden. − F. Prov. *soptanej*, suddenly (Bartsch); Ital. *subitano* (also *subitaneo*). − Late L. **subitānus*, for L. *subitāneus*, sudden; extended from *subitus*, sudden, lit. 'that which has come stealthily,' orig. pp. of *subīre*, to go or come stealthily. − L. *sub*, under, stealthily; and *īre*, to go, from √EI, to go. See **Sub-** and **Itinerant**. Der. *sudden-ly*, *-ness*.

SUDORIFIC, causing sweat. (F. − L.) '*Sudorifick* herbs;' Bacon, Nat. Hist. § 706. − F. *sudorifique*, causing sweat, Cot. − L. *sūdōrificus*, the same. − L. *sūdōri-*, decl. stem of *sūdor*, sweat; and *-ficus*, making, from *facere*, to make. See **Sweat** and **Fact**. Der. *sudorific*, sb.; and see *sudatory*.

SUDS, boiling water mixed with soap. (E.) 'Sprinkled With *suds* and dish-water;' Beaum. and Fletcher, Wit without Money,

A. iii. sc. 1. *Suds* means 'things sodden;' and is formed as a pl. from *sud*, derived from Teut. **sud-*, the weak grade of Teut. **seuthan-*, to seethe; see **Seethe**. Hence Gascoigne uses *suddes* metaphorically, in the sense of 'worthless things;' see Gascoigne's Works, ed. Hazlitt, ii. 310, l. 9. *In the suds*=in the middle of a wash, is a proverbial expression for being in a sulky temper; cf. prov. E. *sudded*, flooded. Cf. MDu. *zode*, a seething, boiling, Hexham; Icel. *soð*, water in which meat has been sodden; and see **Sod**.

SUE, to prosecute at law. (F. – L.) The orig. sense is merely to follow; it was technically used as a law-term. Spelt *sewe* in Palsgrave. ME. *suen*, Wyclif, Matt. viii. 19, 22; also *sewen, suwen*, P. Plowman, B. xi. 21; *suwen*, Ancren Riwle, p. 208, l. 5. – OF. *su-* (as in pr. pl. *su-ent*, pres. pt. *su-ant*), a stem of OF. *sivir, siuwir, suivir* (Godefroy, with several other forms), mod. F. *suivre*, to follow. Cf. Prov. *segre, seguir* (Bartsch), Ital. *seguire*, to follow. – Late L. *sequere*, to follow, substituted for L. *sequi*, to follow; see the changes traced in Brachet. See **Sequence**. Der. *en-sue*, q.v., *pur-sue; suit, suite*, q.v.

SUET, the fat of an animal about the kidneys. (F. – L.) ME. *suet*. ' *Swëte* [where *w=uu*], *suët* (due sillabe), of flesche or fysche or oþer lyke, *Liquamen, sumen*;' Prompt. Parv. Formed with dimin. suffix *-et* from OF. *seu*, Norman *sieu*, Walloon *sew* (Littré), mod. F. *suif*, suet, fat. Cf. Span. *sebo*; Ital. *sevo*, 'tallow, fat, *sewet*,' Florio. – L. *sēbum*, also *sēuum*, tallow, suet, grease. Prob. allied to L. *sāpo*, soap; see **Soap**.

SUFFER, to undergo, endure, permit. (F. – L.) ME. *soffren, suffren*, in early use; Chaucer, C. T. 11089 (F 777); Layamon, 24854 (later text). – OF. *soffrir, suffrir*, mod. F. *souffrir*. – Folk-L. **sufferīre*, for L. *sufferre*, to undergo, endure. – L. *suf-* (for *sub* before *f*), under; and *ferre*, to bear, cognate with E. *bear*. See **Sub-** and **Bear** (1). Der. *suffer-er, suffer-ing; suffer-able*; also *suffer-ance* or *suff-rance*, ME. *suffrance*, Chaucer, C. T. 11100 (F 788), OF. *soffrance*, later *souffrance*, 'sufferance,' Cot., from Late L. *sufferentia* (Ducange).

SUFFICE, to be enough. (F. – L.) ME. *suffisen*, Chaucer, C. T. 9908 (E 2034). – F. *suffis-*, occurring in *suffis-ant*, stem of pres. part. of *suffire*, to suffice; cf. ME. *suffisaunce*, sufficiency, Chaucer, C. T. 492 (A 490), from F. *suffisance*, sufficiency. – L. *sufficere*, lit. to make or put under, hence to substitute, provide, supply, suffice. – L. *suf-* (for *sub* before *f*), and *facere*, to make; see **Sub-** and **Fact**. Der. *suffici-ent*, Merch. Ven. i. 3. 17, from L. *sufficient-*, stem of pres. part. of *sufficere; suffici-ent-ly; sufficienc-y*, Meas. for Meas. i. 1. 8.

SUFFIX, a letter or syllable added to a word. (L.) Modern; used in philology. – L. *suffixus*, pp. of *suffigere*, to fasten on beneath. – L. *suf-* (for *sub* before *f*), and *figere*, to fix; see **Sub-** and **Fix**. Der. *suffix*, verb.

SUFFOCATE, to smother. (L.) Orig. used as a pp. ' May he be *suffocate*,' 2 Hen. VI, i. 1. 124. – L. *suffōcātus*, pp. of *suffōcāre*, to choke. Lit. ' to put something under the gullet, to throttle.' – L. *suf-* (for *sub-* before *p*), and *fauc-*, stem of *faucēs*, s. pl., the gullet, throat. [The same change from *au* to *ō* occurs in *fōcale*, a neckcloth.] Der. *suffocat-ion*, from F. *suffocation*, 'suffocation,' Cot., from L. acc. *suffocātiōnem*.

SUFFRAGE, a vote, united prayer. (F. – L.) In Shak. Cor. ii. 2. 142; Caxton, Siege of Troy, fol. 51 b, l. 10; *sofragys*, pl., Monk of Evesham (ab. 1482), c. 44, ed. Arber, p. 92. – F. *suffrage*, 'a suffrage, voice;' Cot. – L. *suffrāgium*, a vote, voice, suffrage. *Suffrāgium* has been ingeniously explained as 'a broken piece' such as a pot-sherd, &c., whereby the ancients recorded their votes (Vaniček, Bréal). If this be right, *suf-* is the usual prefix (=*sub*), and *-frāgium* is connected with *frangere*, to break, cognate with E. **Break**. Cf. L. *nau-frāgium*, a ship-wreck. β. But Walde connects it with L. *frag-or*, noise, din, i.e. outcry; and further, with AS. *sprǣc*, E. *speech*; see **Speech**. Der. *suffrag-an*, ME. *suffragan*, Trevisa, ii. 115, l. 9, from F. *suffragant*, 'a suffragant, or suffragan, a bishop's deputy,' Cot., from L. *suffrāgant-*, stem of pres. part. of *suffrāgārī*, to vote for, support, assist; but *suffragan* may also represent the Late L. *suffrāgāneus*, a suffragan bishop.

SUFFUSE, to overspread or cover, as with a fluid. (L.) 'Her *suffused* eyes;' Spenser, F. Q. iii. 7. 10. – L. *suffūsus*, pp. of *suffundere*, to pour beneath, diffuse beneath or upon. – L. *suf-* (for *sub* before *f*), and *fundere*, to pour; see **Sub-** and **Fuse**. Der. *suffus-ion*, from F. *suffusion*, 'a suffusion, or powring upon,' Cot., from L. acc. *suffūsiōnem*.

SUFI, a Moslem mystic; see under **Sophy**.

SUGAR, a sweet substance, esp. that obtained from a kind of cane. (F. – Span. – Arab. – Pers. – Skt.) ME. *sugre*, Chaucer, C. T.

10928 (F 614); in P. Plowman, B. v. 122, two MSS. read *sucre*, of which *sugre* is a 'voiced' form. – F. *sucre*, 'sugar;' Cot. – Span. *azucar*, sugar. – Arab. *sakkar, sokkar*, sugar; Palmer's Pers. Dict., col. 357, Freytag's Arab. Dict. ii. 334 a; whence, by prefixing the article *al*, the form *assokkar*, accounting for the prefixed *a* in the Span. form. – Pers. *shakar*, sugar; Palmer's Pers. Dict., col. 385. – Skt. *çarkarā*, gravel, a soil abounding in stony fragments, clayed or candied sugar; Benfey, p. 936. Prob. allied to Gk. κρόκαλη, a pebble on the sea-shore. β. From the Pāli form *sakkharā* are derived Gk. σάκχαρ, σάκχαρον, and L. *saccharum*. It is a mistake to derive F. *sucre* (as Brachet does) from L. *saccharum*. See **Saccharine**. Der. *sugar*, verb, Palsgrave; *sugar-y, sugar-cane, sugar-candy* (see *candy*); *sugar-loaf*, Paston Letters, iii. 37.

SUGGEST, to introduce indirectly, hint. (L.) In Shak. Rich. II, i. 1. 101, iii. 4. 75. – L. *suggestus*, pp. of *suggerere*, to carry or lay under, furnish, supply, suggest. – L. *sug-* (for *sub* before *g*); and *gerere*, to carry; see **Sub-** and **Jest**. Der. *suggest-ion*, Chaucer, C. T. 14727 (B 3607), from F. *suggestion*, 'a suggestion,' from L. acc. *suggestiōnem; suggest-ive*, a coined word; *suggest-ive-ly*.

SUICIDE, self-murder; one who dies by his own hand. (F. – L.) The word was really coined *in England*, but on a F. model. See note at the end of the article. In Blackstone's Commentaries, b. iv. c. 14 (R.); in the latter sense. Rich. gives a quotation for it, in the former sense, from a tr. of Montesquieu, The Spirit of Laws, b. xiv. c. 13; the first E. translation appeared in 1749, immediately after its appearance in France. Littré says that *suicide* is in Richelet's Dict. in 1759, and is said to have been first used in French by Desfontaines not much earlier (1738). As remarked under **Homicide**, the same form has two senses, and two sources. 1. F. *suicide*, a coined word, from L. *sui*, of oneself, gen. case of *sē*, self; and *-cīdium*, a slaying (as in *homi-cīdium*), from *cædere*, to slay. 2. F. *suicide*, coined from L. *sui*, of oneself, and *-cīda*, a slayer (as in *homi-cīda*), from *cædere*, to slay. Der. *suicid-al, -ly*. ¶ Trench, in his English Past and Present, observes that Phillips notices the word, as a monstrous formation, in 1671, long before its appearance in French; and it is given by Blount, ed. 1674. It seems to have been suggested by the queer words *suist*, a selfish man, and *suicism*, selfishness, which had been coined at an earlier date, and were used by Whitlock in an essay entitled The Grand Schismatic, or *Suist* Anatomised; cf. his Zootomia, 1654. The word is clumsy enough, but we may rightly claim it. Littré's objection, that the form of the word is plainly French, is of no force. We had the words *homicide, patri-cide, matri-cide, fratri-cide*, already in use; and *sui-cide* was coined *by analogy with these*, which accounts for the whole matter simply enough. It may be added that, though the translator of Montesquieu uses the word, the *original* has only *l'homicide de soi-même*.

SUIT, an action at law, a petition, a set, as of clothes. (F. – L.) ME. *suite*, Chaucer, C. T. 2875 (A 2873). – F. *suite* (also *suitte* in Cotgrave), 'a chase, pursuit, suit against, also the train, attendants, or followers of a great person;' Cot. – Late L. type **sequita*, variant of *secta* (L. *secūta*), a following, a sect (whence the sense of *suite* or train); in Late L. extended to mean a suit at law, a series, order, set, a suit of clothes, &c.; see Ducange. From the base of *sequ-ī*, to follow, as noted under **Sect**, q.v. Cf. 'secta vestium,' a suit of clothes; Liber Albus, p. 29. 'Sex cochliaria eiusdem *sectæ*,' six spoons of the same set; York Wills, iii. 3 (1395). Der. *suit*, verb, to clothe, As You Like It, i. 3. 118, also to fit, adapt, agree, accord, id. ii. 7. 81, Macb. ii. 1. 60; 'to *suit* to agree together, as things made on a common plan,' Wedgwood. Also *suit-or*, L. L. L. ii. 34; *suit-able*, Timon, iii. 6. 92, *suit-abl-y, suit-able-ness*. Doublets, *suite*, q.v., *sect, sept, set* (2).

SUITE, a train of followers. (F. – L.) 'With fifty in their *suite* to his defence;' Sidney (in Todd's Johnson; no reference). – F. *suite*; see further under **Suit**, of which *suite* is a doublet.

SULCATED, furrowed, grooved. (L.) 'Sulcate, to cast up in furrows, to till;' Blount, ed. 1674. Chiefly scientific. – L. *sulcātus*, pp. of *sulcāre*, to furrow. – L. *sulcus*, a furrow. + Gk. ὁλκός, a furrow, from ἕλκειν, to draw along; cf. AS. *sulh*, a plough.

SULKY, obstinate, silently sullen. (E.) The word is rare in old books, and the Dictionaries omit it, till we come to Todd's Johnson, where 'the *sulkiness* of my disposition' is quoted from a Letter of Gray to Dr. Clarke, A.D. 1760. It is an incorrect form, and should rather be *sulken*; it arose from misdividing the sb. *sulken-ness* as *sulke-nness*, by analogy with *happi-ness* from *happy*, &c. The sb. appears as *a-swolkenesse*, i.e. sloth, O. Eng. Hom. i. 83, l. 25; and is not uncommon in AS., which also has the true old form of the adj. – AS. *solcen*, orig. slothful, remiss; in the comp. *āsolcen*, slothful, remiss, lazy, Ælfric's Homilies, ed. Thorpe, vol. i. p. 306, l. 11, p. 340, last line; also ii. 220, l. 23, where it means 'disgusted.' The sb. *āsolcennes* is quite a common word; see Ælf. Hom. i. 602, l. 8, ii. 46, l. 11,

ii. 218, l. 22, ii. 220, l. 21 ; Thorpe, Diplomatarium, p. 240, l. 12 ; the sense comes very near to that of mod. E. *sulkiness.* ' Accidiosus, vel tediosus, *āsolcen ;*' Voc. 190. 14. Another trace of AS. *solcen* occurs in the comp. *besolcen,* used as a pp., with the sense of ' stupefied ;' Ælfred, tr. of Gregory's Past. Care, c. 35, ed. Sweet, p. 238, l. 3. **β.** We further know that *solcen* was the pp. of a strong verb *seolcan* (pt. t. *sealc,* pp. *solcen*), appearing in the comp. *āseolcan* (pt. t. *āsealc,* pp. *āsolcen*), for which Leo refers to Ælf. Hom. ii. 592, the reference, unluckily, being wrong. We find the verb again, spelt *āsealcan* in Cædmon, (d. Grein, 2167 ; see Grein, i. 41. **γ.** There is even a cognate OHigh G. word, viz. the verb *arselhan,* Graff, vi. 216, where the prefix *ar-* = AS. *á-.* Thus the Teut. type is **selkan-,* from a base **selk-,* answering to an Idg. base SELG. **δ.** It is remarkable that the Skt. *srj* means ' to let loose, abandon,' and the pp. *srshta* is ' abandoned,' which comes very near the sense of AS. *solcen.* Der. *sulk:-ness,* really for *sulken-ness,* as explained above. ☞ Ettmüller, p. 753, gives a form *āswolcen,* but the MS. has *āsolcen,* Liber Scint. § 16, p. 79, l. 5 ; also *āsolcenysse,* id. § 24, p. 98, l. 1.

SULLEN, gloomily angry, morose. (F.–L.) ME. *solein, solain,* orig. merely ' solitary,' then ' hating company,' or morose, as explained in the Prompt. Parv. ' *Soleyne* of maners, or he that lovythe no cumpany, Solitarius ;' Pr. Parv. A mess of meat *for one person* was also called *soleyne,* as explained on the same page. ' By hymself as a *soleyne,*' i. e. a lonely person ; P. Plowman, B. xii. 205. In the Rom. of the Rose, 3896, *solein* means ' sullen,' but in Chaucer, Book of the Duchess, 982, and Parl. of Foules, 607, it means ' solitary ' or ' lonely.' – OF. *solain,* lonely, solitary, of which the only trace I find is in Roquefort, where *solain* is explained as ' a portion served out to a religious person,' a pittance, doubtless a portion *for one* ; so also in Ducange, s. v. *solatium* (5). E. Müller and Mahn cite Prov. *solan,* solitary. These Romance forms presuppose a Late L. **sōlānus,* solitary, but it does not occur ; however, it is a mere extension from L. *sōlus,* sole, alone ; see **Sole.** Cf. OF. *soltain,* solitary (Burguy), which answers, similarly, to a Late L. **solitānus.* Der. *sullen-ly, -ness.*

SULLY, to tarnish, spot, make dirty. (F.–L.) Shak. has *sullied,* Sonnet 15 ; also the infinitive form *sully* ; Merry Wives, iv. 1. 102. [We also find the ME. *solwed,* soiled, Cursor Mundi, l. 22491, spelt *sullowed* in 1608 (Nares). From ME. *solwen,* spelt *solwyn, solowyn* in Prompt. Parv., to soil, bemire ; from AS. *solw-e,* g., d., and acc. of *solu,* f., mire, by-form of AS. *sol,* mire (below). And also ME. *sulien* ; whence *sulieþ* = sullieth, Owl and Nightingale, 1238 ; pp. *ysuled* = sullied, P. Plowman's Creed, 752, Ancren Riwle, p. 396, l. 1. AS. *sylian,* to sully, defile with dirt or mud. ' Sio sugu hi wile *sylian* on hire *sole* æfter ðæm ðe hio āðwægen bið ' = the sow will wallow [lit. sully herself] in her mire after she is washed ; Ælfred, tr. of Gregory's Past. Care, ed. Sweet, c. liv. p. 419, l. 27. This form is from AS. *sol,* mire, mud, for which see the quotation above. ✚ Swed. *sōla,* to bemire ; Dan. *sōle,* to bemire, *sōle, sōl,* mire ; Goth. *bisauljan,* to sully, render impure ; G. *sühlen,* to sully, *sich herum sühlen,* to wallow, from *suhle,* slough, mire, MHG. *sol,* mire. Cf. Norw. *saula,* mire.] **β.** Nevertheless, the modern verb *to sully* is a doublet of the earlier verb *to soil.* – MF. *souiller,* ' to soil, slurry, durty, smutch ; *se souiller,* (of a swine) to wallow in the mire ;' Cot. – OF. *souil,* for which see **Soil** (2). Doublet, *soil* (2).

SULPHUR, brimstone. (L.) [ME. *soulfre* (an OF. form, cf. F. *soufre*) ; Chaucer, Ho. of Fame, iii. 418.] In Spenser, F. Q. i. 5. 31. A term in alchemy, from L. *sulphur,* also spelt *sulfur.* Der. *sulphur-e-ous,* from L. *sulphureus* or *sulfureus,* adj. ; *sulphur-ous,* from F. *sulphureux,* ' sulphurous,' Cot., from L. adj. *sulphurōsus* or *sulfurōsus* ; also the coined words *sulphur-ic, sulphur-et, sulphur-ett-ed,* and *sulphate* (used for **sulphur-ate*).

SULTAN, an Eastern ruler, head of the Ottoman empire. (F.–Arab.) In Shak. Merch. Ven. ii. 1. 26. – F. *sultan,* ' a sultan or souldan,' Cot. – Arab. *sultān,* victorious, also a ruler, prince ; cf. *sultat,* dominion ; Rich. Dict. pp. 843, 844. **β.** The word occurs early, in the ME. form *soudan,* Chaucer, C. T. 4597 (B 177) ; this is from OF. *soudan, souldan,* both in Cotgrave, which are derived from the same Arab. word. Der. *sultan-ess,* with F. suffix ; *sultan-a,* Dryden, Kind Keeper, i. 1, from Ital. *sultana,* fem. of *sultano,* a sultan, from Arab. *sultān.*

SULTRY, SWELTRY, very hot and oppressive. (E.) *Sultry* and *sweltry,* both in Phillips, ed. 1706, are the same word ; the latter being the fuller and older form. Shak. has *sultry,* Hamlet, v. 2. 101 ; also *swelter'd* = caused to exude by heat, Macb. iv. 1. 8. The *we* has passed into *u* ; cf. so from AS. *swā,* and mod. E. *sword,* where the *w* is entirely lost. The *-y* (= AS. *-ig*) is an adjectival suffix, and *sweltr-y* is short for *swelter-y,* formed from the verb to *swelter.* ' *Sweltrynge* or *swalterynge,* or *swonynge,* Sincopa,' Prompt. Parv. ; where the sense is ' a swooning with heat.' ' *Swalteryn* for hete, or febylnesse, or other cawsys, or swownyn, Exalo, sincopizo,' id. p. 481. **β.** Again,

swelter is a frequent. form (with the usual suffix *-er*) from ME. *swelten,* to die, also to swoon away or faint. ' Swowe or swelte ' = swoon or faint, P. Plowman, B. v. 154. From AS. *sweltan,* to die, Grein, ii. 505.✚Icel. *svelta,* to die, starve (pt. t. *svalt,* pl. *sultu,* pp. *soltinn* ; Dan. *sulte* ; Swed. *svälta* ; Goth. *swiltan,* to die. Cf. Icel. *sultr,* Dan. *sult,* hunger, famine ; from the weak grade **swult>*sult.* Also OHG. *schwelzan,* to burn, to be consumed by fire or love. **γ.** All from Teut. base **swelt-,* to die ; prob. an extension of the base **swel-,* to burn, glow, be hot, from which the E. word has undoubtedly received its present sense ; this appears in AS. *swelan,* to burn, ME. *swelen, swalen,* prov. E. *sweal,* to waste away under the action of fire, allied to G. *schwelen,* to burn slowly, *schwül,* sultry, with the extended forms OHG. *swilizo,* heat, *swilizōn,* to burn slowly ; Lith. *swil-ti,* to shine, burn. Der. *sultri-ness.*

SUM, the amount, whole of a thing, substance, total, summary, fulness. (F.–L.) ME. *somme,* Chaucer, C. T. 11537 (F 1225). – AF. *summe,* a sum, Vie de St. Auban, ed. Atkinson ; F. *somme,* ' a summe of money,' Cot. – L. *summa,* sum, chief part, amount ; orig. fem. of *summus,* highest, chief, principal. *Summus* stands for **supmus,* uppermost, superl. form from **sup,* old form of *sub* (cf. *super-*) ; the sense of ' under ' and ' over ' are curiously mixed ; see **Sub-.** Allied to Gk. ὕπα-τος, highest, with a different suffix. Brugmann, i. § 762. Der. *sum,* verb, ME. *sommen,* Trevisa, iii. 261, l. 15, F. *sommer,* from L. *summāre* ; *summ-at-ion,* from F. *sommation,* ' the summing of money,' Cot., due to L. *summāre* ; *summ-ar-y,* sb., answering to F. *sommaire,* ' a summary,' Cot., from L. *summārium,* a summary, epitome, which presupposes an adj. **summārius* ; *summary,* adj., answering to F. *sommaire,* adj., ' summary,' Cot. ; *summ-ar-i-ly, summ-ar-i-ness ; summ-ar-ise,* a coined word. Also *summ-it,* q.v. And see *supreme, sovereign, soprano.*

SUMACH, a tree. (F.–Span.–Arab.) ' *Sumach* or *Sumack,* a kind of rank-smelling shrub that bears a black berry made use of by curriers to dress their leather ;' Phillips, ed. 1706. Spelt *sumack, sumake, sumaque* in Blount's Gloss., ed. 1674, with a similar definition. ME. *sumac,* Lanfrank, Cirurgie, p. 218, l. 19. – F. *sumac,* formerly spelt *sumach* ; Littré. – Span. *zumaque.* – Arab. *summāq,* a species of shrub ; Rich. Dict. p. 847. Another Arab. name is *samāqil* (id.) ; this will account for another F. form *sommail,* noticed by Littré.

SUMMER (1), the warmest season of the year. (E.) ME. *somer, sumer* (with one *m*), Chaucer, C. T. 396 (A 394). AS. *sumor, sumer,* Matt. xxiv. 32.✚Du. *zomer* ; Icel. *sumar* ; Dan. *sommer* ; Swed. *sommar* ; G. *sommer* ; OHG. *sumar.* **β.** From a Teut. type **sum-rus,* m. (Franck) ; connected with Irish and OWelsh *ham,* W. *haf,* summer (the initial *h* standing, as usual, for *s*), Skt. *samā,* a year, Zend *hama,* summer. Brugmann, i. § 436. Der. *summer,* verb, to pass the summer, Isaiah, xviii. 6 ; *summer-house,* Amos, iii. 15.

SUMMER (2), a beam. (F.–Low L.–Gk.) See **Sumpter.**

SUMMERSET, the same as **Somersault,** q. v.

SUMMIT, highest point, top. (F.–L.) In Shak. Haml. i. 4. 70, iii. 3. 18 ; K. Lear, iv. 6. 57. Caxton has *sommete,* Godfrey of Boloyne, p. 251, l. 21. – F. *sommet,* ' the top,' Cot. Dimin., with suffix *-et,* of OF. *som,* the top, esp. of a hill ; see Burguy, Littré. – L. *summum,* highest point, neut. of *summus,* highest ; see **Sum.**

SUMMON, to cite to appear, call with authority. (F.–L.) The examples in the Glossary to Layamon, s. v. *somnien,* show that two distinct words were early confused, viz. AS. *samnian, somnian,* to collect together (a derivative verb from *saman,* together, from *sam,* together) and OF. *somoner, semoner,* mod. F. *semondre.* But since *summons,* sb., and *summoner* are both F. words, and the word to *summon* properly belongs to the law-courts, we need only here consider the F. form. We find *let somony* = caused to attend, in Rob. of Glouc. p. 377, l. 7739 ; and the word *somne* in Chaucer, C. T. 6943 (D 1361), clearly refers to the mod. E. sense of summon, though its form would suit the AS. *somnian* equally well. – OF. *somoner* (Roquefort), in which form it is rare, having been early corrupted to *semoner* or *semondre.* Cotgrave gives F. *semondre,* ' to bid, invite, summon, warn, cite.' Littré gives an 11th-cent. example of the form *sumoner* ; and Roquefort gives an excellent example in which the OF. *somoner* is used with the orig. sense of ' to admonish,' the word *somonoit* being used to translate L. *admonēret* ; Dial. de Saint Grégoire, liv. 2. chap. 5. Cf. Prov. *somonre,* to summon, a common word (Bartsch). – L. *summonēre,* to remind privily. – L. *sum-* (for *sub* before *m*) ; and *monēre,* to advise ; see **Sub-** and **Monition.** Der. *summon-er,* ME. *sompnour,* Chaucer, C. T. 625 (represented by mod. E. *Sumner* as a proper name), also *somonour,* P. Plowman, B. iii. 133 (footnote), from the AF. *sumenour,* Laws of Will. I. § 47, MF. *semonneur,* ' a summoner, citer, apparitor,' Cot. Also *summon-s,* ME. *somouns,* Allit. Morte Arthure, 91, from the AF. *somonse,* f. Stat. Realm, i. 29 (1295), MF. *semonce,* ' a warning, citation, summons,' Cot. ; Littré explains that the F. *semonce,* formerly *semonse* (*somonse*), is the fem. of *semons* (*somons*), the pp. of *semondre* (*so-*

mondre), to summon. Cf. Prov. *somonsa*, a summons, cited by Littré; we also find Prov. *somos, somosta, semosta* used in the same sense. ☞ Thus the *s* at the end of *summons* is *not* due to the L. *summoneūs*, as some have supposed.

SUMPITAN, a blow-pipe. (Malay.) Malay *sumpitan.* – Malay *sumpit* (also *menyumpit*), to blow; with suffix -*an.*

SUMPTER, a horse for carrying burdens, a pack-horse. (F. – Late L. – Gk.) Two forms of the word were once in use, viz. ME. *somer*, King Alisaunder, 850, and *sumpter*, id. 6023. The former, once the commoner form, is now lost; but it is necessary to explain it first. 1. From OF. *somier, sommier* (Burguy), a pack-horse; formed, with suffix -*ier* of the agent, from OF. *somme, some, saume, sume*, a pack, burden. [Cotgrave gives OF. *sommier*, ' a sumpter-horse, also the piece of timber called a summer.'] – Late L. *salma*, corrupt form of *sagma*, a pack, burden; whence *sagmārius, salmārius*, a pack-horse (>F. *sommier*). – Gk. σάγμα, a pack-saddle. – Gk. σάττειν (=*σάκ-γειν, fut. σάξω), to pack, put a burden on a horse, fasten on a load, orig. to fasten. Allied to Gk. σάγη, housings, σάγος, a soldier's cloak. 2. The etymology of *sumpter* is similar; it orig. meant, not the horse, but the horse's driver; and such is the sense in King Alisaunder, 6023, where the *sumpters* are reckoned among the squires and guides belonging to an army. Hence, also, the mod. E. *sumpter-horse*, i. e. a baggage-carrier's horse, the addition of *horse* being necessary to the sense, whereas the ME. *somer* was used alone, in the same sense. *Sumpter* is, accordingly, from OF. *sommetier*, a packhorse-driver (Roquefort). This answers to a Low L. **sagmatārius*, not found, but formed from the Gk. σαγματ-, the true stem of σάγμα, just as *sagmārius* is formed from σάγμα. 3. The E. word *summer*, noticed by Cotgrave (above) as meaning ' a beam,' is worth notice. It occurs in Barbour's Bruce, xvii. 696, and is given in Halliwell; being so called from its bearing a great burden or weight; cf. Norman dial. *sommier*, a summer (Duméril). Hence also the E. *breast-summer* (gen. pronounced *bressomer*), defined in Webster as ' a summer or beam placed breast-wise to support a superincumbent wall.' ☞ Note that *sumpter* in K. Lear, ii. 4. 219, does not mean ' a packhorse,' but a packhorse-driver.

SUMPTUARY, relating to expenses. (L.) In Cotgrave, to translate E. *somptuaire.* It is rather Englished from L. *sumptuārius*, belonging to expenses, than borrowed from French. Formed, with suffix -*ārius*, from *sumptu-*, decl. stem of *sumptus*, expense, cost; see **Sumptuous.**

SUMPTUOUS, expensive, costly. (F. – L.) ' *Sumptuous* expenses of the meane people;' Sir T. Elyot, Castel of Helth, b. ii. c. 28. – F. *somptueux*, 'sumptuous,' Cot. – L. *sumptuōsus*, costly. – L. *sumptu-*, decl. stem of *sumptus*, expense, cost. – L. *sumptus*, pp. of *sūmere*, to take, spend, consume. β. *Sūmere* (**sups-emere*) is a derivative of *emere*, to buy, orig. to take. Brugmann, i. § 240. See **Sus-** and **Example.** Der. *sumptuous-ly, -ness.*

SUN, the celestial body which is the source of light and heat. (E.) ME. *sonne*, two syllables, Chaucer, C. T. 7. AS. *sunne*, a *fem.* sb., Exod. xvi. 21, xvii. 12 (common). + Du. *zon*, fem. sb.; Icel. *sunna*, fem., only in poetry, the common word being *sól*; G. *sonne*, fem., OHG. *sunna*; Goth. *sunna*, masc., *sunnō*, fem. β. The Teut. type is **sunnōn-*, fem. Here -*nōn* is a suffix (as in Teut. **ster-non-*, a star); and the base **sun-* is the weak grade of a root **swen*, which is prob. allied to the root **sāu, *sū*, ' to shine,' whence Goth. *sau-il*, L. *sō-l*, the sun, Icel. *sō-l*, the sun. See **Solar.** Der. *sun*, verb; *sun-beam*, AS. *sunnebēam*; *sun-burnt*; *sun-rise*, spelt *sonne ryse* in Palsgrave; *sun-set*, spelt *sonne sette* in Palsgrave, ONorthumb. *sun-set*, Matt. xxiv. 27 (Lindisfarne MS.). Also *Sun-day*, AS. *sunnan dæg*, lit. ' day of the sun,' where *sunnan* is the gen. case. Other compounds are *sun-fish, -flower, -shine, -stroke, sunn-y, sun-less, sun-ward*; and see *south.*

SUNDER, to part, divide. (E.) ME. *sundren*, Ancren Riwle, p. 270, last line. AS. *sundrian, gesundrian*, Grein, i. 459; also *syndrian*, in comp. *āsyndrian*, Matt. x. 35; lit. 'to put asunder.' – AS. *sundor*, adv., asunder, Grein, ii. 495. + Icel. *sundra*, to sunder, from *sundr*, adv., asunder; Dan. *söndre*, to sunder from *sönder*, adv.; Swed. *söndra*, from *sönder*, adv.; G. *sondern*, from *sonder*, adj., separate. And cf. Goth. *sundrō*, adv., separately; Du. *zonder*, conj., but. β. All allied to Gk. ἄ-τερ (for **sənter*), without, Skt. *san-utar*, aside, far from (Macdonell); so that -*der* in *sun-der*, adv., is a suffix. Further allied to OIrish *sain*, separate, L. *sin-e*, without. Brugmann, i. § 500. Der. *a-sunder*, q. v.; *sundr-y*, adj., separate, hence several, divers, ME. *sundry, sondry*, Chaucer, C. T. 4601 (B 181), from AS. *syndrig*, Luke, iv. 40, for **sunderig*, and formed with suffix -*ig* (mod. E. -*y*) from *sundor*, adv., as above.

SUP, to imbibe, as a liquid, gradually; also, to eat a supper. (E.) Once a strong verb; the short *u* is prob. due to association with *supper*, q. v. ME. *soupen*, P. Plowman, B. ii. 96, vi. 220. AS. *sūpan* (strong verb, pt. t. *sēap*, pl. *supon*, pp. *sopen*), Ælfred, tr. of Gregory's

Past. Care, c. 58, ed. Sweet, p. 447, l. 1. + Du. *zuipen*; Low G. *supen*; Icel. *sūpa* (pt. t. *saup*, pp. *sopinn*); Swed. *supa*; OHG. *sūfan*. β. All from Teut. type **sūpan-* (pt. t. *saup*, pp. *supanoz*), to drink in, sup up. ¶ Partly from OF. *souper*, to sup; it makes but slight difference. Der. *sup*, sb., *sop, sip*; also *soup*, q. v., *supp-er*, q. v.

SUPER-, *prefix*, above. (L.) L. *super*, above, prep.; orig. a comparative form of *sub*; see **Sub-.** Orig. a locative case of *superus*, adj., upper (for *s-uperus*, where *s-* is a weak form of *ex*); whence **Superior.** + Gk. ὑπέρ, above; orig. a locative case of ὑπερος, upper, comparative from ὑπό (E. *hypo-*); see **Hyper-, Hypo-;** allied to Skt. *upari*, above, locative of Vedic *upara-*, compar. of *upa*, near, close to, under. See **Over.** Der. *super-ior, supreme, in-super-able; super-b; super-n-al.* Doublet, *hyper-*, prefix. And see *supra-*, prefix.

SUPERABOUND, to be more than enough. (F. – L.) In Cotgrave; and Howell, Famil. Letters, b. iv. let. 39, § 3. – F. *superabonder*, 'to superabound,' Cot. – L. *superabundāre*, to be very abundant. – L. *super* and *abundāre*; see **Super-** and **Abound.** Der. *superabundance*, from F. *superabondance*, 'superabundance,' Cot., L. *superabundantia*; also *superabundant*, adj., from the stem of the L. pres. part.; *superabundant-ly.*

SUPERADD, to add over and above. (L.) In Phillips, ed. 1706; and earlier, see Richardson. – L. *superaddere*; see **Super-** and **Add.** Der. *superaddit-ion* (not in Cotgrave).

SUPERANNUATE, to disqualify by length of years. (L.) Bacon has *superannuate* = to live beyond the year, used of annual plants; Nat. Hist. § 448. This is cited by Richardson, who misspells it. Howell has ' *superannuated* virgin;' Famil. Letters, vol. i. let. 12; A. D. 1619. Blount, ed. 1674, has both *superannate* and *superannuate.* An ill-coined word, prob. suggested by *annu-al, annu-ity*; Bacon's *superannate* is countenanced by Late L. *superannātus*, that has lived beyond a year; hence F. *suranner*, ' to passe or exceed the compass of a year; also, to wax very old;' Cot. Thus *superannuate* is for *superannate*; coined from *super*, above, and *annus*, a year. See **Super-** and **Annual.** Der. *superannuat-ion.*

SUPERB, proud, magnificent. (F. – L.) ◦Quite a late word; in Prior, Alma, c. i. l. 383. – F. *superbe*, 'proud;' Cot. – L. *superbum*, acc. of *superbus*, proud. β. Lit. ' one who thinks himself (or is) above others;' for **super-fu-os*, ' being above,' from *super*, above, and *fu-*, as in L. *fu-ī*, I was. Brugmann, ii. § 4. See **Super-,** Der. *superb-ly.*

SUPERCARGO, an officer in a merchant-ship. (L.; *and* Span. – C.) ' *Supercargo*, a person employed by the owners of a ship to go a voyage, to oversee the cargo,' &c.; Phillips, ed. 1706. Partially translated from Span. *sobrecargo*, a supercargo, by substituting L. *super* for Span. *sobre*, which is the Span. form of the same word. See **Super-** and **Cargo.**

SUPERCILIOUS, disdainful. (L.) ' *Supercilious* air;' Ben Jonson, Underwoods, xxxii (Epistle to a Friend, Master Colby), l. 19. Coined with suffix -*ous* (F. -*eux*, L. -*ōsus*) from L. *supercili-um*, (1) an eyebrow, (2) pride, haughtiness, as expressed by raising the eyebrows. – L. *super*, above; and *cilium*, an eyelid, perhaps allied to Gk. τὰ κύλα, the parts under the eyes (Prellwitz). Der. *supercilious-ly, -ness.*

SUPEREMINENT, excellent above others. (L.) In Chapman, tr. of Homer, Odys. b. vi. l. 305. – L. *superēminent-*, stem of pres. part. of *superēminēre*, to be eminent above others. See **Super-** and **Eminent.** Der. *supereminence*, from MF. *supereminence*, 'supereminence,' Cot., from L. *superēminentia.*

SUPEREROGATION, doing more than duty requires. (L.) ' Works of *supererogation*;' Articles of Religion, Art. 14 (1562). From Late L. *superērogātio*, that which is done beyond what is due. – L. *superērogāre*, to pay out beyond what is expected. – L. *super*, above, beyond; *ē*, out; and *rogāre*, to ask. The L. *ērogāre* = to lay out, expend money (lit. to ask out, require). See **Super-, E-,** and **Rogation.**

SUPEREXCELLENT, very excellent. (L.; *and* F. – L.) Used by Spenser in a postscript to a letter to G. Harvey (R.). – L. *super*, above; and MF. *excellent*; see **Super-** and **Excellent.**

SUPERFICIES, the surface of a thing. (L.) In Minsheu, ed. 1627; and in Cotgrave, to translate F. *superficie* and *surface.* – L. *superficiēs*, upper face, surface. – L. *super-*, above; and *faciēs*, a face; see **Super-** and **Face.** Der. *superfici-al*, in Lydgate, Assembly of the Gods, l. 538, from F. *superficiel*, 'superficiall,' Cot., from L. *superficiālis; superfici-al-ly, -ness*; also *superfici-al-i-ty*, spelt *superficialyte* in Palsgrave, from MF. *superficialité*, recorded by Palsgrave. Doublet, *surface.*

SUPERFINE, extremely fine. (L.; *and* F. – L.) 'Many inuentions are so *superfine*;' Gascoigne, Works, ed. Hazlitt, i. 500; also in Steel Glas, &c., ed. Arber, p. 31. Coined from *super* and *fine*; see **Super-** and **Fine** (1).

SUPERFLUOUS, excessive. (L.) 'A *superfluous* abundaunce;' Sir T. Elyot, Castel of Helth, b. iii. c. 1. [Palsgrave gives *superflue* as an E. word, from F. *superflu*, superfluous.] Englished from L. *superfluus*, overflowing. ‒ L. *super*, over; and *fluere*, to flow; see **Super-** and **Fluent.** Der. *superfluous-ly*; *superflu-i-ty*, ME. *superfluite*, Gower, C. A. ii. 201, bk. v. 2217, from F. *superfluité*, 'superfluity,' Cot., from L. acc. *superfluitātem*.

SUPERHUMAN, more than human. (L.; *and* F. ‒ L.) Spelt *superhumane* in Phillips, ed. 1706. Coined from **Super-** and **Human.**

SUPERIMPOSE, SUPERINCUMBENT, SUPERINDUCE; see **Super-** and **Impose, Incumbent, Induce.**

SUPERINTENDENT, an overseer. (F. ‒ L.) In Minsheu, ed. 1627. ‒ MF. *superintendant*, 'a superintendent,' Cot. ‒ L. *superintendent-*, stem of pres. part. of *superintendere*, to superintend. ‒ L. *super*, over, above; and *intendere*, to attend to, apply the mind. See **Super-** and **Intend.** [The verb *superintend* is directly from the Latin.] Der. *superintendence*, from MF. *superintendance*, 'a superintendency,' Cot.

SUPERIOR, higher in rank, &c. (F. ‒ L.) Now spelt so as to resemble Latin; spelt *superyour* in Palsgrave; *superior* in Caxton, Golden Legend, Adam, § 6. ‒ MF. *superieur*, 'superiour,' Cot. ‒ L. *superiōrem*, acc. of *superior*, higher, comp. of *superus*, high, which is itself an old comp. form from *sub* (orig. *sup). Hence *sup-er-ior* is a *double* comparative; see **Super-** and **Sub-.** Der. *superior-i-ty*, from MF. *superiorité*, 'superiority,' Cot., from Late L. acc. *superiōritātem*.

SUPERLATIVE, superior, extreme, supreme. (F. ‒ L.) In Minsheu, ed. 1627; and in Palsgrave, p. xxviii. ‒ F. *superlatif*, 'superlative,' Cot. ‒ L. *superlātiuus*, superlative, as a gram. term. ‒ L. *superlāt-us*, excessive; with suffix *-iuus*, lit. ' carried beyond,' exaggerated. ‒ L. *super*, beyond; and *lātus*, carried, or borne. *Lātus*< *tlātus; see **Super-** and **Tolerate.** Der. *superlative-ly*.

SUPERNAL, placed above, heavenly. (F. ‒ L.) 'Supernal judge;' K. John, ii. 112. ‒ MF. *supernel*, 'supernall,' Cot. As if from Late L. *supernālis, not in use; formed with suffix *-ālis* from *supern-us*, upper, extended by help of suffix *-nus* from *super*, above; see **Super-.**

SUPERNATURAL, miraculous. (F. ‒ L.) In Macb. i. 3. 130; and in Palsgrave. ‒ MF. *supernaturel*, 'supernaturall;' Cot. See **Super-** and **Natural.** Der. *supernatural-ly.*

SUPERNUMERARY, above the necessary number. (F. ‒ L.) In Cotgrave. ‒ MF. *supernumeraire*, 'supernumerary,' Cot. ‒ L. *supernumerārius*, excessive in number. ‒ L. *super*, beyond; and *numer-us*, number; see **Super-** and **Number.**

SUPERSCRIPTION, something written above or without. (F. ‒ L.) ME. *superscriptioun*, Henrysoun, Test. of Creseide, l. 604. ‒ MF. *superscription*, 'a superscription;' Cot. ‒ Late L. *superscriptiōnem*, acc. of *superscriptio*, a writing above, Luke, xxiii. 38 (Vulg.); cf. *superscriptus*, pp. of *superscribere*, to write above. ‒ L. *super*, above; and *scribere*, to write; see **Super-** and **Scribe.** ¶ The verb *superscribe* is coined directly from L. *superscribere.*

SUPERSEDE, to displace by something else, to come in place of something else. (F. ‒ L.) The word has much changed its meaning, both in L. and E. *Supersede* in old authors means to desist, forbear, stay proceedings, &c. Thus Rich. quotes from the State Trials, 19 Hen. VIII, an. 1528: 'He [Hen. VIII] desired the bishop of Paris to certify Francis, that if the Pope would *supersede* from executing his sentence, until he had indifferent [impartial] judges sent who might hear the business, he would also *supersede* from the execution of what he was deliberated to do in withdrawing his obedience from the Roman see.' '*Supersede*, to suspend, demurr, put off or stop an affair or proceeding, to countermand;' Phillips. Thus, the sense was to stay a proceeding, whence, by an easy transition, to substitute some other proceeding for it. A writ of *supersedeas* is, in some cases, a writ to stay proceedings, and is mentioned in P. Plowman, C. iii. 187, on which see my note. ‒ OF. *superseder*, *superceder* (mod. F. *superséder*), 'to surcease, leave off, give over;' Cot. ‒ L. *supersedēre*, pp. *supersessus*, lit. to sit upon, also to preside over, to forbear, refrain, desist from. ‒ L. *super*, above; and *sedēre*, cognate with E. *sit*. See **Super-** and **Sit.** Der. *supersession*, from MF. *supersession*, 'a surceasing, giving over, the suspension of an accompt upon the accomptant's humble suit;' Cot. ‒ L. *supersessiōnem, acc. of *supersessio, not used, but regularly formed like *supersession*, pp. of *supersedēre.* Doublet, *surcease*, q. v.

SUPERSTITION, excessiveness in religious worship or belief. (F. ‒ L.) Skelton has *supersticyons*, s. pl., Philip Sparowe, l. 1350; the adj. *superstitious* occurs in Acts, xvii. 22, in the Bible of 1551 and in the A. V.; also, spelt *supersticious*, in Lydgate, Storie of Thebes, pt. iii, How the bishop Amphiorax, &c. ‒ F. *superstition*, 'superstition;' Cot. ‒ L. *superstitiōnem*, acc. of *superstitio*, a standing still over or near a thing, amazement, wonder, dread, religious scruple. ‒

L. *superstit-*, stem of *superstes*, one who stands near, a witness. ‒ L. *super*, near, above; and *statum*, supine of *stāre*, to stand, which is cognate with E. *stand*. See **Super-** and **Stand.** Der. *superstitious*, as above, from F. *superstitieux*, 'superstitious,' Cot., from L. adj. *superstitiōsus*; *superstiti-ous-ly.*

SUPERSTRUCTURE, the upper part of a building. (L.) 'In som places, as in Amsterdam, the foundation costs more than the *superstructure*;' Howell, Famil. Letters, vol. i. sect. 2. let. 15, May 1, 1622. From **Super-** and **Structure.**

SUPERVENE, to occur or happen in consequence of, to occur, happen. (L.) '*Supervening* follies;' Bp. Taylor, vol. i. ser. 12 (R.). ‒ L. *superuenīre*, to come upon or over, to come upon, to follow; pp. *superuentus*. ‒ L. *super*, over, upon, near; and *uenīre*, to come, cognate with E. *come*. See **Super-** and **Venture or Come.** Der. *supervent-ion*, regularly formed like the pp. *superuentus.*

SUPERVISE, to inspect, oversee. (L.) In Shak. L. L. L. iv. 2. 135. ‒ L. *super*, above; and *uīsere*, to survey, formed from *uīs-um*, supine of *uidēre*, to see. See **Super-** and **Visit or Vision.** Der. *supervise*, sb., Hamlet, v. 2. 23; *supervis-or*, Oth. iii. 3. 395 (First Quarto); *supervis-ion*, ibid. (Folio editions); *supervis-al.*

SUPINE, lying on one's back, lazy. (L.) Sir T. Browne has *supinity*, Vulg. Errors, b. i. c. 5, § 3. '*Supine* felicity;' Dryden, Astræa, 107. As a term in grammar; Palsgrave, p. xxxvii. ‒ L. *supīnus*, backward, lying on one's back; extended, with suffix *-īnus*, from *sup, orig. form of *sub*, under, below; hence, downward. Cf. *sup-er*, from the same source. So also Gk. ὕπτιος, bent backwards, backward, lying on one's back, from ὑπό, under. See **Sub-.** Der. *supine*, sb., as a grammatical term, L. *supīnum*, of which the applied sense is not very obvious (perhaps positive, absolute, like Gk. θετικόν, absolute, as applied to verbal forms); *supine-ly*, *supine-ness*; also *supin-i-ty*, as above, prob. obsolete.

SUPPER, a meal at the close of a day. (F. ‒ Teut.) ME. *soper*, *super*; spelt *super*, Havelok, 1762. ‒ OF. *soper*, *super*, later *souper*, 'a supper;' Cot. It is the infin. mood used as a substantive, exactly as in the case of *dinner*. ‒ OF. *soper*, *super*, later *souper*, to sup, to eat a meal of bread *sopped* in gravy, &c. [Cf. OF. *sope*, *soupe*, later *soupe*, 'a sop, a piece of bread in broth, also pottage or broth, wherein there is store of sops or sippets,' Cot.] ‒ Low G. *supen*, to sup or sip up; Icel. *súpa*, Swed. *supa*, to sup; cognate with E. **Sup**, q. v.

SUPPLANT, to take the place of, displace, undermine. (F. ‒ L.) ME. *supplanten*, Gower, C. A. i. 239, bk. ii. 2369. ‒ F. *supplanter*, 'to supplant, root or trip up;' Cot. ‒ L. *supplantāre*, to put something under the sole of the foot, to trip up the heels, overthrow. ‒ L. *sup-* (*sub*); and *planta*, the sole of the foot, also a plant. See **Sub-** and **Plant.** Der. *supplant-er*, spelt *supplantour*, in Gower, C. A. i. 261, bk. ii. 3024.

SUPPLE, pliant, lithe, fawning. (F. ‒ L.) ME. *souple*, Chaucer, C. T. 203; Rob. of Glouc. p. 223, l. 4577. ‒ F. *souple*, spelt *soupple* in Cotgrave, who explains it by ' supple, limber, tender, pliant.' ‒ L. *supplicem*, acc. of *supplex*, in the old orig. sense of ' bending under,' hence submissive, which is the usual sense in Latin. The OF. *soplier*, vb., also kept the orig. sense, though the classical L. *supplicāre* only means to beseech; hence Cotgrave has ' *souplié*, bent or bowed underneath, subject unto.' β. The formation of *souple* from *supplicem* is precisely like that of E. *double* from *duplicem*, *treble* from *triplicem*, *simple* from *simplicem*. γ. The L. *supplex* is from *sup-* (*sub*) and the base *plic-*, as seen in *plic-āre*, to fold. See **Sub-** and **Ply;** also **Supplicate.** Der. *supple-ness.*

SUPPLEMENT, that which supplies, an addition. (F. ‒ L.) In Skelton, Garl. of Laurell, 415. ‒ F. *supplément*, 'a supplement;' Cot. ‒ L. *supplēmentum*, a supplement, filling up. ‒ L. *supplē-re*, to fill up; with suffix *-men-tum*. ‒ L. *sup-* (*sub*), up; and *plēre*, to fill; see **Supply.** Der. *supplement-al*, *supplement-ar-y.*

SUPPLIANT, entreating earnestly. (F. ‒ L.) In Rich. II, v. 3. 75. ‒ F. *suppliant*, 'suppliant;' Cot.; pres. pt. of *supplier*, 'humbly to pray,' id. ‒ L. *supplicāre*, to supplicate; see **Supplicate.** Doublet, *supplicant.*

SUPPLICATE, to entreat. (L.) In Blount, ed. 1674; it seems to be quite a late word, though *supplication*, spelt *supplicacion*, is in Gower, C. A. iii. 348, bk. viii. 2184, and *supplicant* in Shak. Complaint, 276. ‒ L. *supplicāt-us*, pp. of *supplicāre*, to supplicate. ‒ L. *supplic-*, stem of *supplex*, bending under or down, hence beseeching, suppliant; see **Supple.** Der. *supplic-ant*, from the stem of the pres. pt. of *supplicāre*; *supplicat-or-y*; *supplicat-ion* (as above), from F. *supplication*, 'a supplication,' Cot., from L. acc. *supplicātiōnem*. Also *suppliant*, q. v.

SUPPLY, to fill up a deficiency. (F. ‒ L.) In Shak. Tw. Nt. i. 1. 38. Levins (1570) spells it *supploy*, and Huloet has *supploye*; Palsgrave has *supplye*. ‒ OF. *supploier*; F. *suppléer*, 'to supply;'

Cot. — L. *supplēre*, to fill up. — L. *sup-* (*sub*), up; and *plēre*, to fill; see **Sub-** and **Plenary.** Der. *supply*, sb., Hamlet, ii. 2. 24; and see *supple-ment*.

SUPPORT, to endure, sustain. (F. — L.) ME. *supporten*, Wyclif, 2 Cor. xi. 1. — F. *supporter*, 'to support;' Cot. — L. *supportāre*, to carry, bring, or convey to a place; in Late L., to endure, sustain. — L. *sup-* (*sub*), near; and *portāre*, to carry; see **Sub-** and **Port** (1). Der. *support*, sb., ME. *support*, Gower, C. A. iii. 193, bk. vii. 3207, from F. *support*, 'a support,' Cot.; *support-er*, *support-able*, *support-abl-y*.

SUPPOSE, to assume as true, imagine. (F. — L. *and* Gk.) ME. *supposen*, Chaucer, C. T. 6368 (D 786). — F. *supposer*, 'to suppone, to put, lay, or set under, to suborn, forge; also to suppose, imagine;' Cot. — F. *sup-*, prefix < L. *sup-* (*sub*), prefix, under; and F. *poser*, to place, put. Thus the orig. sense is 'to lay under, put under,' hence to substitute, forge, counterfeit; all of which are senses of L. *suppōnere*. β. The F. *poser* is not from L. *pōnere*, but from Gk., though it (with all its compounds) took up the senses of L. *pōnere*. See further under **Pose**; and note Cotgrave's use of the verb to *suppone*, now obsolete. Der. *suppos-er*, *suppos-able*; but not *supposition*, q. v.

SUPPOSITION, an assumption, thing supposed. (F. — L.) In Shak. Merch. Ven. i. 3. 18. — F. *supposition*, omitted by Cotgrave, but in use in the 14th cent. (Littré). — L. *suppositiōnem*, acc. of *suppositio*, properly 'a substitution,' but extended in meaning according to the extension of meaning of the verb *suppōnere* (pp. *suppositus*) from which it is derived. — L. *sup-* (*sub*), under, near; and *pōnere*, to place; see **Sub-** and **Position.** Der. *supposit-it-i-ous*, spurious, substituted, from L. *supposītīcius*, formed with suffix *-īc-i-us* from *supposit-*, stem of pp. of *suppōnere*, of which one sense was 'to substitute.' Also *supposit-or-y*, as in 'suppositoryes are used where the pacyent is weake,' Sir T. Elyot, Castel of Helth, b. iii. c. 5, from L. *supposītōrius*, that which is placed underneath. (See note on **Suppose.**)

SUPPRESS, to crush, keep in, retain, conceal. (L.) The instance of *suppressed*, cited by Rich. from Lydgate, Storie of Thebes, pt. ii, The Answer of Ethiocles, is not to the point; it is clearly an error for *surprised*. For the verb *suppress*, see Palsgrave. — L. *suppressus*, pp. of *supprimere*, to press under, suppress. — L. *sup-* (*sub*), under; and *premere*, to press; see **Sub-** and **Press.** Der. *suppress-or*, L. *suppressor*; *suppress-ion*, printed *supression* in Sir T. More, p. 250 f, from F. *suppression*, 'suppression,' Cot., from L. acc. *suppressiōnem*. Also *suppress-ive*, a coined word.

SUPPURATE, to gather pus or matter underneath. (L.) In Minsheu, ed. 1627. — L. *suppūrātus*, pp. of *suppūrāre*, to gather pus underneath. — L. *sup-* (*sub*), beneath; and *pūr-*, decl. stem of *pūs*, matter; see **Sub-** and **Pus.** Der. *suppurat-ion*, from F. *suppuration*, 'a suppuration,' Cot., from L. acc. *suppūrātiōnem*; *suppurat-ive*, adj., from F. *suppuratif*, 'suppurative,' Cot., a coined word.

SUPRA-, prefix, above. (L.) L. *suprā-*, prefix; from *suprā*, adv. and prep., short for *superā*, the orig. form, Lucretius, iv. 674; orig. abl. fem. of *superus*, adj., above. — L. *super*, above; see **Super-, Sub-.**

SUPRAMUNDANE, situate above the world. (L.) 'Supramundane deities;' Waterland, Works, i. 86 (R.); and in Blount, ed. 1674. A coined word; from **Supra-** and **Mundane.** ¶ Similarly formed is *supralapsarian*, antecedent to the fall, from *suprā*, above, and *laps-um*, acc. of *laps-us*, a fall; with suffix *-arian*; see **Lapse.**

SUPREME, greatest, most excellent. (F. — L.) Accented *súpreme*, Cor. iii. 1. 110; usually *suprême*, K. John, iii. 1. 155. — F. *supreme*, omitted by Cotgrave, but in use in the 16th cent. (Littré); now written *suprême*. — L. *suprēmus*, supreme, highest. Formed with superl. suffix *-mus* from **suprē-*, an adverb allied to L. *super*, above. Brugmann, ii. § 75. See **Super-.** Der. *supreme-ly*; also *suprem-a-cy*, K. John, iii. 1. 156 (cf. F. *suprématie*, Littré, not in Cotgrave), a word arbitrarily formed on the model of *primacy* (OF. *primacie*, Late L. *primatia*) from *primate*.

SUR- (1), *prefix.* (L.) For *sub-* before *r* following; see **Sub-.** Only in *sur-reptitious* and *sur-rogate*.

SUR- (2), *prefix.* (F. — L.) F. *sur*, prep., contr. from L. *super*, upon, above. Exx. *sur-cease*, *sur-charge*, *sur-face*, &c.

SURCEASE, to cease, to cause to cease. (F. — L.) It is obvious, from the usual spelling, that this word is popularly supposed to be allied to *cease*, with which it has no etymological connexion. It is a corruption of *sursis* or *sursise*, and is etymologically allied to *supersede*. It was very likely misunderstood from the first, yet Fabyan spells the word with *s* for *c*, correctly. 'By whiche reason the kyngdome of Mercia *surseased*, that had contynued from their firste kynge;' Fabyan, Chron. c. 171, § 5. 'To *sursese* and leve of' [leave off]; Paston Letters, i. 390. β. But the verb is really due

to the sb. *surcease*, a delay, cessation, which was in use as a law-term, and prob. of some antiquity in this use, though I do not know where to find an early E. example. It occurs in Shak. Macb. i. 7. 4, and (according to Richardson) in Bacon, Of Church Controversies; Nares cites an example from Danett's tr. of Comines (published in 1596 and 1600). — AF. *sursise*, a surcease, 'Ki le cri orat e sursera, la *sursise* enuers li rei amend;' in Latin, 'qui, clamore audito, insequi supersederit, de *sursisa* erga regem emendet;' Laws of Will. I, § 50; F. *sursis*, masc., *sursise*, fem., 'surceased, intermitted;' Cot. Littré quotes 'pendant ce *sursis*' = during this delay, from Ségur, Hist. de Nap. x. 2. *Sursis* is the pp. of AF. *surseer* (pr. pl. subj. *surseis-ent*), Stat. Realm, i. 49, 300; MF. *surseoir*, 'to surcease, pawse, intermit, leave off, give over, delay or stay for a time,' Cot. — L. *supersedēre*, to preside over, also to forbear, refrain, desist from, omit; see **Supersede.** The word also appears in F. as *superséder*, spelt also *superceder* in Cotgrave, and explained by 'to surcease, leave off, give over.' This shows that not only was *surcease* wrongly connected in the popular mind with *cease*, but that, even in F., *superséder* was similarly connected with L. *cēdere*, from which *cease* is derived. Der. *surcease*, sb., really the older word, as shown above.

SURCHARGE, an over-load. (F. — L.) 'A *surcharge*, or greater charge;' Bacon, Nat. Hist. § 228. — AF. *surcharge*, Year-books of Edw. I. 1304-5, p. 45; F. *surcharge*, 'a surcharge, or a new charge;' Cot. — F. *sur*, from L. *super*, over; and *charge*, a load; see **Sur-** (2) and **Charge.** Der. *surcharge*, vb., from F. *surcharger*, 'to surcharge;' Cot.

SURCINGLE, a girth for a horse, a girdle. (F. — L.) 'Sursenglys and crowpers' [cruppers]; Malory, Morte Arthure, bk. vii. ch. 16; leaf 119, back. — OF. *sourcengle*, *surcengle* (Godefroy), MF. *sursangle*, 'a sursengle, or long girth;' Cot. — F. *sur-*, above; and OF. *cengle*, 'a girth,' Cot. — L. *super*, above; and *cingula*, a belt. See **Sur-** and **Shingles.**

SURCOAT, an outer garment. (F. — L. *and* G.) ME. *surcote*, Chaucer, C. T. A 617. — AF. *surcote*, Liber Custumarum, p. 226. See **Sur-** (2) and **Coat.**

SURD, inexpressible by a rational number or having no rational root. (L.) Cotgrave translates *nombre sourd* by 'a surd number.' A term in mathematics, equivalent to *irrational*, in the math. sense. — L. *surdus*, deaf; hence, deaf to reason, irrational. The word is frequently applied to colours, when it means dim, indistinct, dull; thus *surdus color* = a dim colour, Pliny. Nat. Hist. b. xxxvii. c. 5. So likewise L. *sordēre* = to be dirty. See **Sordid.** Brugmann, i. § 362. Der. *surd*, adj., irrational; *absurd*, q. v.

SURE, certain, secure. (F. — L.) See Trench, Select Glossary. ME. *sur*, Will. of Palerne, 973; *seur*, Seven Sages, ed. Weber, 2033. — OF. *sur*, *seür*, oldest form *segur* (Burguy); mod. F. *sûr*. — L. *sēcūrus*, secure, sure; see **Secure.** Der. *sure*, adv., *sure-ly*; *sure-ty*, ME. *seurte*, Will. of Palerne, 1463, also *seurtee*, Chaucer, C. T. 4663 (B 243), from OF. *seürte*, *segurtet*, from L. acc. *sēcūritātem.* Hence *sure-ti-ship*, Prov. xi. 15. Doublets, *secure*, *sicker*.

SURF, the foam made by the rush of waves on the shore. (E.) This is a difficult word, being disguised by a false spelling; the *r* is unoriginal, just as in the word *hoarse*, which is similarly disguised. The spelling *surf* is in Defoe, Robinson Crusoe, ed. 1719, pt. i, in the description of the making of the raft. 'My Raft was now strong enough . . . my next care was . . . how to preserve what I laid upon it from the *Surf* of the Sea.' But the earlier spelling is *suffe*, with the sense of 'rush,' in a remarkable passage in Hakluyt's Voyages, ed. 1598, vol. ii. pt. i. p. 227, where we are told that certain small ra'ts are carried to the shore by the force of the in-rushing wave; 'the *Suffe* of the Sea setteth her [the raft's] lading dry on land.' So also: 'so neere the shore, that the *counter-suffe* of the sea would rebound against the shippes side;' id. iii. 848. β. This *suffe* is, I believe, a phonetic spelling of the word usually spelt *sough*, i. e. 'rush' or 'rushing noise;' see *sough o' the sea* in Jamieson, who also spells it *souf* and *souch*. And see *sough*, *souff*, *suff*, in E. D. D. The word *sough* has lost a *w* after the *s*; the Middle-English spelling is *swough* or *swow*, in the sense of 'rush,' or 'rushing sound.' 'For *swoughe* of his dynttez' = for the rushing sound of his blows; Morte Arthure, 1127. But it was particularly used of the swaying or rushing of the sea; 'with the *swoghe* of the see' = with the swaying motion [surf] of the sea; id. 759. Halliwell notes prov. E. *swowe*, 'to make a noise, as water does in rushing down a precipice; also, to foam or boil up,' &c. Cf. 'swowynge of watyre,' rushing of water, accompanied by noise; Morte Arthure, 931. γ. The ME. verb *swowen* or *swoȝen* answers to AS. *swōgan*, to make a rushing noise, &c., treated of under **Swoon,** q. v. The derived sb. in AS. took the form *swēg* (with vowel-change from *ō* to *ē*), and this word answers in force, though not in form, to E. *sough*. Hence a secondary form *swēgan*, with much the same sense as the primary

verb *swōgan*. In Luke, xxi. 25, we might almost translate *swēg* by *surf*; ' for gedréfednesse sǽs *swēges* and y̌þa ' = for confusion of the sound [surf] of the sea and waves ; L. præ confusione *sonitus* maris. In Ælfric's Hom. i. 566, l. 7, we have : ' com séo sǽ fǽrlíce *swē-gende*,' which Thorpe translates by ' the sea came suddenly *sounding* ;' but it rather means *rushing in*, as appears by the context. In Ælfric's Hom. i. 562, l. 14, we read that a spring or well of water ' *swēgde ūt*,' i.e. rushed out, or gushed forth, rather than ' sounded out,' as Thorpe translates it. δ. There is thus plenty of authority for the use of ME. *soṇgh* with the sense of ' rush ' or ' noisy gush,' which will well explain both Hakluyt's *suffe* and mod. E. *surf*. I believe this will be found to be the right explanation. ε. We may connect *surf* with Norweg. *sog* in *some* of its senses, viz. (1) a noise, tumult, rushing sound ; and (2) a current in a river, the inclination of a river-bed, where the stream is swift, i.e. a rapid. [This is distinct from Norweg. *sog* in the sense of ' sucking.']
¶ The usual explanation of *surf* from F. *surflot* [L. *super-fluctus*], ' the rising of billow upon billow, or the interchanged swelling of severall waves,' as in Cotgrave, is unlikely ; for (1) it interprets *f* as equivalent to a whole word, viz. F. *flot*, and (2) it is contradicted by the form *suffe*, which involves no *r* at all.

SURFACE, the upper face of anything. (F. – L.) In Minsheu, ed. 1627. – F. *surface*, ' the surface, the superficies ;' Cot. Not directly derived from L. *superficies*, but compounded of F. *sur* (from L. *super*, above), and *face* (from L. *faciem*, acc. of *faciēs*, the face) ; see **Sur-** (2) and **Face**. However, it exactly corresponds to L. *superficiēs*, which is compounded in like manner of *super* and *faciēs*. Hence the words are doublets. Doublet, *superficies*.

SURFEIT, excess in eating and drinking. (F. – L.) ME. *surfet*, P. Plowman, A. vii. 252 ; *surfait*, id. B. vi. 267. – AF. *surfet*, a surfeit, A Nominale, ed. Skeat, l. 343 ; OF. *sorfait*, excess (Burguy) ; orig. pp. of *sorfaire*, later *surfaire*, ' to overprise, to hold at an overdeer rate ;' Cot. – OF. *sor*, F. *sur*, from L. *super*, above ; and F. *fait* (pp. of *faire*), from L. *factus* (pp. of *facere*), to make, hence, to hold, deem. See **Sur-** (2) and **Fact**. Der. *surfeit*, verb, spelt *surfet* in Palsgrave ; *surfeit-ing*, sb.

SURGE, the swell of waves, a billow. (F. – L.) The orig. sense was ' a rising ' or rise, or source. ' All great ryuers are gurged and assemblede of diuers *surges* and springes of water ;' Berners, tr. of Froissart, vol. i. c. 1 (R.). ' Wyndes and *sourges* ;' Sir T. Elyot, Castel of Helth, bk. ii. c. 14. ' Thus with a *surge* of teares bedewde ;' Turbervile, The Louer to his carefull Bed. ' *Surge* of the see, *vague* ;' Palsgrave. Coined from OF. stem *sourge-*, as in *sourge-ant*, pres. pt. of *sourdre*, to rise. – L. *surgere*, to rise. Cf. MF. *sourgeon*, ' the spring of a fountain, or the rising, boyling, or sprouting out of water in a spring,' Cot., which is likewise derived from the same L. verb. The proper F. sb. is *source*, E. *source* ; see **Source**. β. The L. *surgere* makes pt. t. *surrexi*, showing that it is contracted from *surrigere* ; from L. *sur-* (for *sub* before *r*), and *regere*, to rule, direct ; thus the orig. sense was ' to direct or take one's way from under,' hence to rise up. See **Sub-** and **Regent**. Der. *surge*, verb, *surg-y*. Also (from *surgere*) *in-surgent*, *re-surrect-ion*, *source*, *re-source*, *sortie*.

SURGEON, a chirurgeon, one who cures diseases by operating upon the patient. (F. – L. – Gk.) A very early contraction of *chirurgeon*. ME. *surgien*, P. Plowman, B. xx. 308 ; *surgeyn*, *surgen*, id. C. xxiii. 310, 313 ; spelt *cirurgian*, Rob. of Glouc. p. 566, l. 11925. – OF. *surgien* (Godefroy) ; variant of *cirurgien*, *serurgien*, a surgeon ; see Littré, s.v. *chirurgien* ; the AF. forms *surigien*, *surrigien*, *sirogen*, *cyrogen*, all occur in Langtoft, Chron. ii. 104, 158 ; and *surgion* is in Britton, i. 34. – OF. *cirurgie*, later *chirurgie*, surgery ; with suffix *-en* < L. *-ānus*. See further under **Surgery**.

SURGERY, the art practised by a surgeon, operation on a patient. (F. – L. – Gk.) ME. *surgerie*, Chaucer, C. T. 415 (A 413). A variation of OF. *cirurgie*, *sirurgie*, later form *chirurgie*, surgery. We have, in fact, turned *cirurgy* or *sirurgy* into *surgery* ; perhaps through a form *surgeon-ry* ; for the spelling *surgenry* occurs as a reading in P. Plowman, B. xvi. 106. – Late L. *chirurgia*. – Gk. χειρουργία, a working with the hands, handicraft, skill with the hands. – Gk. χειρο-, from χείρ, the hand ; and ἔργειν, to work, allied to E. *work* ; see **Chirurgeon** and **Work**. Der. *surgeon*, short for *chirurgeon*, old form of *chirurgeon*. Der. *surgi-c-al*, short for *chirurgical*, formed with suffix *-al* (F. *-el*, L. *-ālis*) from Late L. *chirurgic-us*, an extended form of *chirurgus* = Gk. χειρουργός, working with the hand, skilful ; hence *surgi-c-al-ly*.

SURLOIN, the upper part of a loin of beef. (F. – L.) Frequently spelt *sirloin*, owing to a fable that the loin of beef was knighted ' by one of our kings in a fit of good humour ;' see Johnson. The ' king ' was naturally imagined to be the merry monarch Charles II, though Richardson says (on no authority) that it was ' so entitled by King James the First.' Both stories are discredited by

the use of the orig. F. word *surlonge* in the *fourteenth* century ; see Littré. Indeed, Wedgwood cites ' A *surloyn* beeff, vii. *d*.' from an account of expenses of the Ironmongers' Company, temp. Henry VI ; with a reference to the Athenæum, Dec. 28, 1867 (p. 902). Cotgrave explains MF. *haut coste* by ' a *surloine*.' – F. *surlonge*, ' a sirloin,' Hamilton ; see Littré for its use in the 14th cent. – F. *sur*, from L. *super*, above, upon ; and *longe*, a loin ; see **Super-** and **Loin**.

SURLY, morose, uncivil. (E.) In Shak. K. John, iii. 3. 42 ; &c. ' The orig. meaning [or rather, the meaning due to popular etymology] seems to have been *sir-like*, magisterial, arrogant. " For shepherds, said he, there doen leade As *Lordes* done other-where . . . Sike *syrlye* shepheards han we none ;" Spenser, Sheph. Kal. July, 185–203. Ital. *signoreggiare*, to have the mastery, to domineer ; *signoreggevole*, magisterial, haughty, stately, *surly* ; Altieri. *Faire du grobis*, to be proud or surly, to take much state upon him ; Cotgrave :'—Wedgwood. I give the quotation from Cotgrave slightly altered to the form in which it stands in ed. 1660. As to the spelling, it is remarkable that while Spenser has *syrlye*, the Glosse to the Sheph. Kal. by E. K. has ' *surly*, stately and prowde.' Drant (1566) has ' His *surly* corps in rytche array ;' tr. of Horace, Sat. 3. Minsheu has *surlie*. Cotgrave has : ' Sourcilleux, . . . *surly*, or proud of countenance.' It answers to prov. E. *soorlike*, ill-tempered, cross, surly, lit. ' sour-like ' (E. D. D.) ; and the *u* has been shortened before *rl*, as in *burly* from an AS. form *bûr-lîc ; see **Burly**. Cf. prov. E. *sour*, ill-tempered, surly, cross (E. D. D.) ; and Baret has ' *sowre*, morose.' See **Sour**. Cf. G. *sauer*, sour, surly ; MSwed. *sur* (the same) ; Swed., Dan. *syrlig*, sourish. And note ME. *surdagh*, sour dough ; Voc. 663. 22. Der. *surli-ly*, *surli-ness*.

SURMISE, an imagination, suspicion, guess. (F. – L.) Levins has *surmise* both as sb. and vb. ; so has Baret (1580). Caxton has : ' xxxm li. that he had *surmysed* on hym to haue stolen ;' Golden Legend, Th. Becket, § 4. Halliwell gives the obs. verb *surmit*, with an example. – OF. *surmise*, an accusation, charge (Roquefort) ; properly fem. of *surmis*, pp. of *surmettre*, to charge, accuse, lit. ' to put upon,' hence to lay to one's charge, make one to be suspected of. – F. *sur*, from L. *super*, upon, above ; and F. *mettre*, to put, from L. *mittere*, to send ; see **Super-** and **Mission**. Der. *surmise*, verb ; *surmis-al*, Milton, Church Government, ii., Int.

SURMOUNT, to surpass. (F. – L.) ME. *surmounten*, spelt *sormounten*, Chaucer, tr. of Boethius, b. iii. pr. 8, l. 19. – F. *surmonter*, ' to surmount ;' Cot. From **Sur-** (2) and **Mount** (2). Der. *surmount-able*, *in-surmount-able*.

SURNAME, a name added to the Christian name. (Hybrid ; F. – L. ; *and* E.) In Trevisa, iii. 265, l. 10. See Trench, Study of Words. A partial translation of ME. *surnom*, spelt *sournoun* in Chron. of Eng. 982 (in Ritson, Met. Romances, ii. p. 311), from F. *surnom*, ' a surname ;' Cot. – F. *sur*, from L. *super*, over, above ; and E. *name*. See **Super-** and **Name** ; and see **Noun**. So also Span. *sobrenombre*, Ital. *soprannome*. Der. *surname*, verb.

SURPASS, to go beyond, excel. (F. – L.) In Spenser, F. Q. i. 10. 58. – F. *surpasser*, ' to surpasse,' Cot. From **Sur-** (2) and **Pass**. Der. *surpass-ing*, *surpass-able*, *un-surpass-able*.

SURPLICE, a white garment worn by the clergy. (F. – L.) Spelt *surplise*, *surplys*, in Chaucer, C. T., A 3323. – F. *surplis*, ' a surplis ;' Cot. – Late L. *superpelliceum*, a surplice. – L. *super*, above ; and *pelliceum*, neut. of *pelliceus*, *pellicius*, made of skins ; see **Super-** and **Pelisse**. Cf. ' *surplyce*, superpellicium ;' Prompt. Parv. So also Span. *sobrepelliz*.

SURPLUS, overplus, excess of what is required. (F. – L.) ME. *surplus*, Gower, C. A. iii. 24 ; bk. vi. 682. – F. *surplus*, ' a surplusage, overplus ;' Cot. – L. *super*, above ; and *plūs*, more ; see **Super-** and **Plural**. Der. *surplus-age*, Spenser, F. Q. ii. 7. 18 ; Lydgate, Storie of Thebes, pt. iii. Of a tame tiger, &c. ; see Richardson.

SURPRISE, a taking unawares. (F. – L.) In Shak. Mer. Wives, v. 5. 131. The verb (though from the F. sb.) occurs earlier, Rom. of the Rose, 3235. – OF. *sorprise*, *surprise* (Burguy), MF. *surprinse*, ' a surprisall, or sudden taking ;' Cot. Properly fem. of *sorpris*, *surpris* (*surprins* in Cot.), pp. of *sorprendre*, *surprendre*, ' to surprise, to take napping,' Cot. – F. *sur*, from L. *super*, above. upon ; and *prendre*, from L. *prehendere*, to take ; see **Super-** and **Prehensile**. Cf. Ital. *sorprendere*, to surprise. Der. *surprise*, verb, *surpris-al* (in Cotgrave, as above), *surpris-ing*, *-ing-ly*.

SURREBUTTER ; see Surrejoinder.

SURREJOINDER, a rejoinder upon, or in answer to, a rejoinder. (F. – L.) ' The plaintiff may answer the *rejoinder* by a *surrejoinder* ; upon which the defendant may *rebut* ; and the plaintiff answer him by a *surrebutter* ;' Blackstone, Comment., b. iii. c. 20 (R.). And in Blount's Gloss., ed. 1674. The prefix F. *sur*, upon, hence, in answer to ; see **Sur-** (2) and **Rejoin**. And see **Rebut**.

SURRENDER, to render up, resign, yield. (F. – L.) ' I *surrender* ie surrenders ' Palsgrave. – OF. *surrendre*, to deliver up into the hands of justice, Roquefort, Palsgrave ; not in Cotgrave. — F. *sur*, upon, up ; and *rendre*, to render ; see **Sur-** (2) and **Render**. Der. *surrender*, sb., Hamlet, i. 2. 23.

SURREPTITIOUS, done by stealth or fraud. (L.) ' A soden *surrepticious delyte* ;' Sir T. More, Works, p. 1278 (miscalled 1276) g. — L. *surreptītius*, better *surreptīcius*, stolen, done stealthily. — L. *surrept-um*, supine of *surripere*, to pilfer, purloin. — L. *sur-* (for *sub* before *r*), under, secretly ; and *rapere*, to seize. See **Sur-** (1) and **Rapid**. Der. *surreptitious-ly*.

SURROGATE, a substitute, deputy of an ecclesiastical judge. (L.) In Blount's Gloss., ed. 1674. — L. *surrogātus*, pp. of *surrogāre*, to substitute, elect in place of another. — L. *sur-* (for *sub* before *r*), under, in place of ; and *rogāre*, to ask, elect. See **Sur-** (1) and **Rogation**.

SURROUND, to encompass. (F. — L.) In Minsheu, ed. 1627. Altered in sense by association with *round* ; but the orig. sense was ' to overflow.' ' The waters more abounded, And . . all abroad *surrounded* ;' Marlowe, tr. of Ovid, bk. iii. Elegy 6. ' *Oultrecouler*, to surround or overflow ;' Cot. Orig. *suround* (with one *r*) : ' by then-crease of waters dyuers londes and tenementes in grete quantite ben *surounded* and destroyed ;' Stat. of Hen. VII (1489) ; pr. by Caxton, fol. c 7. — OF. *souronder*, *soronder*, *surunder*, to overflow (Godefroy). — L. *super*, over ; and *undāre*, to flow, from *unda*, a wave. So also *red-ound*, *ab-ound*, from OF. *red-onder*, *ab-onder*. See Notes on E. Etym., p. 286.

SURTOUT, an overcoat, close frock-coat. (F. — L.) In Dryden, tr. of Juvenal, Sat. iii. 250. ' *Surtoot*, *Surtout*, a great upper coat ;' Phillips, ed. 1706. Worn over all. — F. *sur tout*, over all. — L. *super tōtum*, over the whole ; see **Super-** and **Total**.

SURVEILLANCE, inspection. (F. — L.) Modern ; not in Todd's Johnson. — F. *surveillance*, superintendence ; Hamilton. — F. *surveillant*, pres. part. of *surveiller*, to superintend. — F. *sur*, from L. *super*, over ; and *veiller*, from L. *uigilāre*, to watch ; see **Sur-** (2) and **Vigil**. F. *veillance* < L. *uigilantia*.

SURVEY, to look over, inspect. (F. — L.) ' To *suruey*, or *ouersee* ;' Minsheu, ed. 1627. The obs. sb. *surveance*, *surveyaunce*, is in Chaucer, C. T. 12029 (C 95). — AF. *surveier*, Liber Albus, 512. — F. *sur*, over ; and OF. *veeir*, *veĕr*, later *veoir*, ' to see,' Cot. — L. *super*, over ; and *uidēre*, to see ; see **Super-** and **Vision**. And see **Supervise**. Der. *survey*, sb., All's Well, v. 3. 16 ; *survey-or* (*survyowre* in Prompt. Parv.), AF. *surveour*, Stat. Realm, i. 289 (1340), *survey-or-ship*.

SURVIVE, to overlive, outlive. (F. — L.) Spelt *survyve* in Palsgrave. — F. *survivre*, ' to survive ;' Cot. — L. *superuīuere*, to outlive. — L. *super*, above ; and *uiuere*, to live ; see **Super-** and **Victual**. Der. *surviv-al*, a coined word, Chapman, tr. of Homer, Odys. b. i. 638 ; *surviv-or*, Hamlet, i. 2. 90 ; *surviv-or-ship*.

SUS-, prefix. (L.) L. *sus-*, prefix ; for **sups*, an extended form of **sup*, old form of *sub*, under ; so also Gk. ὑψ-ί, aloft, ὑψ-os, height, from ὑπ-ό ; see **Sub-**. Der. *sus-ceptible*, *sus-pend*, *sus-pect*, *sus-tain*.

SUSCEPTIBLE, readily receiving anything, impressible. (F. — L.) In Cotgrave. — F. *susceptible*, ' susceptible, capable ;' Cot. — L. **susceptibilis*, ready to undertake. — L. *suscepti-*, for *susceptus*, pp. of *suscipere*, to undertake ; with suffix *-bilis*. — L. *sus-*, for **sups*, extension of **sup*, orig. form of *sub*, under ; and *capere*, to take ; see **Sus-** and **Captive**. Der. *susceptibili-ty*, a coined word ; *susceptive*, from L. **susceptīuus*, capable of receiving or admitting.

SUSPECT, to mistrust, conjecture. (F. — L.) See Trench, Select Glossary. The word was orig. a pp., as in Chaucer, where it is used adjectivally, with the sense of ' suspicious,' C. T. 8417 (E 541). — F. *suspect*, ' suspected, mistrusted ;' Cot. — L. *suspectus*, pp. of *suspicere*, to look under, look up to, admire, also to mistrust. — L. *su-*, for *sus-*, **sups-*, extension of **sup*, orig. form of *sub*, under ; and *specere*, to look ; see **Sub-** and **Spy**. Der. *suspic-i-on*, ME. *suspecioun*, K. Alisaunder, 453, OF. *suspezion* (Burguy), later *souspeçon*, ' suspition,' Cot. (mod. F. *soupçon*), from L. *suspiciōnem*, acc. of *suspicio*, suspicion ; hence *suspic-i-ous*, ME. *suspecious*, Chaucer, C. T. 8416 (E 540) ; *suspic-i-ous-ly*, *-ness*. ☞ Observe that the old spellings *suspecion*, *suspecious*, have been modified so as to accord more closely with the L. originals.

SUSPEND, to hang beneath or from, to make to depend on, delay. (F. — L.) ME. *suspenden*, Rob. of Glouc., p. 563, l. 11818. — F. *suspendre*, ' to suspend ;' Cot. — L. *suspendere* (pp. *suspensus*), to hang up, suspend. — L. *sus-*, for **sups*, extension of **sup*, orig. form of *sub*, under ; and *pendere*, to hang ; see **Sus-** and **Pendant**. Der. *suspend-er*. Also *suspense*, properly an adj. or pp., as in Spenser, F. Q. iv. 6. 34, from F. *suspens*, ' doubtful, uncertain,' Cot., from L. pp. *suspensus*, suspended, wavering, hesitating ; *suspens-ion*, from F. acc. *suspensiōnem* ; *suspens-or-y*, from MF. *suspensoire*, ' hanging, suspensory, in suspence,' Cot. ; *suspens-or-y*, sb., a hanging bandage, &c.

SUSPICION ; see under **Suspect**.

SUSTAIN, to hold up, bear, support. (F. — L.) ME. *susteinen*, *susteynen*, Rob. of Glouc., p. 111, l. 2412. — AF. *sustein-*, a stem of OF. *sustenir*, *sostenir*, spelt *soustenir* in Cot. ; mod. F. *soutenir*. — L. *sustinēre*, to uphold. — L. *sus-*, for **sups-*, extension of **sup*, orig. form of *sub*, up ; and *tenēre*, to hold ; see **Sus-** and **Tenable**. Der. *sustain-er*, *sustain-able* ; also *sustenance*, ME. *sustenaunce*, Rob. of Glouc., p. 41, l. 975, from OF. *sustenance*, spelt *soustenance* in Cotgrave, from L. *sustinentia* ; also *sustent-at-ion*, Bacon, Essay 58, from L. acc. *sustentātiōnem*, maintenance, from *sustentāre*, frequent. form of *sustinēre* (pp. *sustentus*).

SUTLER, one who sells provisions in a camp. (Du.) In Shak. Hen. V, ii. 1. 116. — Du. *soetelaar* (Sewel), usually *zoetelaar* ; in Hexham *zoetelaer*, ' a scullion, or he that doth the druggerie in a house, a sutler, or a victualler.' Formed with suffix *-aar* of the agent (cf. L. *-ārius*) from *zoetelen*, ' to sullie, to suttle, or to victuall ;' Hexham. β. This frequent. verb is cognate with Low G. *suddeln*, to sully, whence *suddeler*, a dirty fellow, scullion, and sometimes a sutler (Brem. Wört.) ; Dan. *sudle*, *besudle*, to sully, G. *sudeln*, to sully, daub. All these are frequent. forms, with the usual frequent. suffix *-el-* ; the simple form appears in Swed. *sudda*, to daub, stain, soil ; whence Swed. dial. *sudda*, sb., a dirty woman (Rietz). These are obviously connected with Icel. *suddi*, steam from cooking, drizzling rain, *suddaligr*, wet and dank ; all from Teut. **sud-*, weak grade of Teut. verb **seuthan-*, to seethe (Icel. *sjóða*). Further allied to E. *suds*, a derivative of *seethe* ; with which cf. G. *sud*, a seething, brewing, *sudel*, a puddle, *sudeln*, to daub, dabble, sully, *sudelkoch*, a sluttish cook ; all from the same weak grade. The *t* (for *d*) is abnormal, and due to High G. influence. Cf. Bavarian *suttern*, *sottern*, to boil over, MHG. *sut*, boiling liquid.

SUTTEE, a widow who immolates herself on the funeral pile of her husband ; also the sacrifice of burning a widow. (Skt.) The E. *u* represents Skt. short *a*, which is pronounced like *u* in *mud*. The word is properly an epithet of the widow herself, who is reckoned as ' true ' or ' virtuous ' if she thus immolates herself. — Skt. *satī*, a virtuous wife (Benfey, p. 63, col. 2) ; fem. of *sant-*, being, existing, true, right, virtuous. *Sant-* is short for **as-ant-*, pres. part. of *as*, to be. — √ES, to be ; see **Sooth** and **Is**.

SUTURE, a seam. (F. — L.) In Minsheu, ed. 1627. — F. *suture*, ' a suture or seam ;' Cot. — L. *sūtūra*, a suture ; cf. *sūtus*, pp. of *suere*, to sow ; cognate with E. **Sew**.

SUZERAIN, a feudal lord. (F. — L.) Not in Johnson ; used by Scott, Quentin Durward, ch. 35. — F. *suzerain*, ' sovereign, yet subaltern, superior, but not supreme ;' Cot. A coined word ; from F. *sus* (L. *sūsum* or *sursum*, above), in the same way as *sovereign* is made from L. *super* ; it corresponds to a Late L. type **sūserānus*, for **surserānus*. β. The L. *sursum* is contracted from **su-uorsum*, where *su-* is for *sub*, up, and *uorsum* (E. *-ward*) means ' turned,' from L. *uertere*, to turn ; see **Sub-** and **-Ward**, suffix. Der. *suzerain-ty*, from F. *suzeraineté*, ' soveraigne, but subaltern, jurisdiction,' Cot.

SWAB, to clean the deck of a vessel. (Du.) Shak. has *swabber*, Temp. ii. 2. 48 ; whence the verb to *swab* has been evolved. The sb. is borrowed directly from Du. *zwabber*, ' a swabber, the drudge of a ship ;' Sewel. Cf. Du. *zwabberen*, to swab, do dirty work. ✚ Swed. *svabb*, a fire-brush, *svabla*, to swab ; Dan. *svabre*, to swab ; G. *schwabber*, a swabber, *schwabber-stock*, a mop-stick ; *schwabbern*, to swab. Cf. also Norw. *svabba*, to splash about, Pomeran. *swabbeln*, to splash about ; Low G. *swappen*, to shake about (said of liquids ; Danneil) ; G. *schwabbeln*, to shake to and fro. Allied to Lith. *sup-ti*, to rock ; Slovenian *svep-ati*, to totter (Miklosich, p. 330). Of imitative origin. Cf. ME. *quappen*, to palpitate ; E. *swap*, *swash*. Der. *swabb er*.

SWADDLE, to swathe an infant. (E.) ' I *swadell* a chylde ;' Palsgrave. Also spelt *swadil*, *swadle* in Levins. *Swadel* stands for *swathel*, and means to wrap in a *swathel* or swaddling-band. ME. *sweþelband*, a swaddling-band ; spelt *sueþelband*, *suadiling-band*, *swaþeling-bonde* in Cursor Mundi, 1343 ; whence the pp. *suedeld*, *swetheled* = swaddled, id. 11236. — AS. *sweðel*, a swaddling-band ; spelt *suaeðil* in the Corpus Gloss., 833. The sense is ' that which swathes ;' formed with suffix *-el*, *-il* (Idg. *-lo-*), representing the agent, from the verb to *swathe* ; see **Swathe**. Der. *swaddl-ing-band* ; *swaddl-ing-clothes*, Luke, ii. 7.

SWAGGER, to hector, to be boisterous. (Scand.) In Shaks. Mids. Nt. Dr. iii. 1. 79. ' To *swagger* in gait is to walk in an affected manner, swaying from one side to the other ;' Wedgwood. It is the frequentative of *swag*, now almost disused. ' I *swagge*, as a fatte persons belly *swaggeth* as he goth ;' Palsgrave. ' *Swag*, to hang loose and heavy, to sag, to swing about ;' Halliwell. — Norweg. *svagga* (Ross), allied to *svaga*, to sway. Cf. Icel. *sveggja*, to cause to sway ; Norw. *svagg* (Ross), Dan. *sugg*, a big, thumping fellow (Larsen). Allied to **Sway**. Der. *swagger-er*.

SWAIN, a young man, peasant. (Scand.) ME. *swain,* Chaucer, C. T. 4025 (A 4027); *swein,* Havelok, 273. [The form is Scand., not E.; the AS. form was *swān,* Grein, ii. 500, which would have given a mod. E. *swone,* like *stone* from *stān.* We do, indeed, find *swein* in the A.S. Chron. an. 1128, but this is borrowed from Scand.] — Icel. *sveinn,* a boy, lad, servant; Dan. *svend,* a swain, journeyman, servant; Swed. *sven,* a young man, a page.+Low G. *sween,* a swineherd, Hannover (Brem. Wört.); OHG. *swein,* a servant. β. The Teut. type is *swainoz;* which may (formally) be allied by gradation to AS. *swīn,* a swine, with the sense of 'swine-herd;' as in Low G. *sween.* But if it be allied to Lith. *swaine,* a sister-in-law, it is from another source. **Der.** *boat-swain, cox-swain.*

SWALLOW (1), a migratory bird. (E.) ME. *swalowe,* Prompt. Parv.; Chaucer, C. T. 3258. AS. *swalewe,* a swallow; Voc. 132. 28.+Du. *zwaluw;* Icel. *svala,* for **svalva,* gen. *svölu;* Dan. *svale;* Swed. *svala;* G. *schwalbe;* OHG. *swalawa.* β. The Teut. type is **swalwōn,* f. Cf. EFries. *swälke,* Low G. *swaalke,* a swallow. The prob. sense is 'tosser about,' or 'mover to and fro;' allied to Gk. σαλεύειν, to shake, to move to and fro, to toss like a ship at sea; σάλος, the tossing rolling swell of the sea. See **Swell.** Fick, i. 842. Cf. MDu. *swalpen,* 'to flote, to tosse, beate against with waves,' *swalpe,* a tossing, *swalcke,* a swallow; Hexham.

SWALLOW (2), to absorb, ingulf, receive into the stomach. (E.) ME. *swolowen, swolwen,* Chaucer, C. T. 16985 (H 36); also *swolhen,* Juliana, p. 74, l. 4; *swolȝhen,* Ormulum, 10224 (written *swollȝhenn* in the MS.). Thus the final *w* stands for an older guttural. It is a secondary form, modified from the AS. strong verb *swelgan,* to swallow, pt. t. *swealg,* pp. *swolgen;* Grein, ii. 505.+Du. *zwelgen;* Icel. *svelgja,* pt. t. *svalg,* pp. *solginn;* also as a weak verb; Dan. *svelge;* Swed. *svälja;* G. *schwelgen,* to eat or drink immoderately. The strong and weak forms are confused. The strong verb is of the Teut. type **swelgan-;* pt. t. **swalg,* pp. **swulganoz.* **Der.** *ground-sel,* q. v.

SWAMP, wet spongy land, boggy ground. (E.) Not found in old books. ' *Swamp, Swomp,* a bog or marshy place, in Virginia or New England;' Phillips, ed. 1706. This points to its being a prov. E. word. According to Rich., it occurs in Dampier's Voyages, an. 1685. Prob. a native word.+Du. *zwamp,* a swamp (Calisch). With a change to a weak grade, we have prov. E. *sump* (for *swump), a puddle, G. *sumpf,* a swamp (whence Du. *somp*). We also find prov. E. *swank, swang,* a swamp; Norw. and Swed. dial. *swank.* Connexion with Dan. and Swed. *svamp,* a sponge, fungus, AS. *swamm,* G. *schwamm,* Goth. *swamms,* sponge, is not clear. Cf. Gk. σομφός, spongy. **Der.** *swamp,* vb., *swamp-y, swamp-i-ness.*

SWAN, a large bird. (E.) ME. *swan,* Chaucer, C. T. 206. AS. *swan,* Grein, ii. 500.+Du. *zwaan;* Icel. *svanr;* Dan. *svane;* Swed. *svan;* G. *schwan.* The Teut. types are **swanoz,* **swanon-.* The form suggests connexion with Skt. *swan,* to resound, sound, sing; cf. L. *sonāre,* to sound. ' Argutos .. olores;' Vergil, Ecl. ix. 36.

SWAN-HOPPING, taking up swans to mark them. (E.) A mistaken form of *swan-upping* (Halliwell). Swans, esp. on the Thames, are annually taken up for the purpose of marking them by certain nicks made upon their bills. That the old word was really *upping* is shown by a tract dated 1570, printed in Hone's Every-day Book, vol. ii. col. 958–962. In sect. 8 there is mention of 'the *vpping-daies.*' In sect. 15—'the swan-herdes .. shall *vp* no swannes,' &c. In sect. 14—'that no person *take vp* any cignet unmarked;' and in sect. 28—'the maister of the swannes is to have for every white swanne and gray *vpping,* a penny.'

SWAP, to strike. (E.) ME. *swappen;* ' *Swap* of his heed' = strike off his head; Chaucer, C. T. 15834 (G 366). ' Beofs to him *swapte*' = Beofs went swiftly to him; Layamon, 26775 (later text). An E. word.+EFries. *swappen,* to strike noisily, from *swap,* the sound of a blow; prov. G. (dial. of Thüringen, by L. Hertel) *schwappen,* to make swinging movements, to cut; G. *schwapp, schwapps,* Low G. *swaps,* interj. slap, smack! crack! said of a blow. Imitative; cf. E. *slap, whap,* prov. E. *swack,* a blow. Cf. **Swoop.**

SWARD, green turf, grassy surface of land. (E.) It formerly meant also skin or covering; the *green-sward* is the turfy surface of the land; the prov. E. *sward-pork* is bacon cured in large flitches or flakes (Halliwell, Forby). ' *Swarde,* or *sworde* of flesch, *Coriana; Swarde* of þe erþe, turfeflag, or *sward* of erth, *Cespes;*' Prompt. Parv. pp. 482, 506. AS. *sweard,* skin; Voc. 265. 9.+Du. *zwoord,* skin of bacon; Icel. *svörðr,* skin, hide of the walrus, sward or surface of the earth; *jarðar-svörðr,* earth-sward, *grassvördr,* grass-sward; Dan. *flesksvær,* flesh-sward, skin of bacon; *grönsvær,* green-sward; G. *schwarte,* rind, bark, skin, outside-plank. β. The Teut. type perhaps is **swarduz,* with the sense of 'rind.' Root unknown. **Der.** *sward-ed, green-sward.*

SWARM, a cluster of bees or insects. (E.) ME. *swarm,* Chaucer, C. T. 15398 (B 4582); AS. *swearm* (Bosworth).+Du. *zwerm;* Icel.

svarmr; Dan. *sværm;* Swed. *svärm;* G. *schwarm;* MHG. *swarm.* β. Teut. type **swarmoz,* where *-moz* is a noun-suffix, as in *bloo-m, doo-m.* The sense is 'that which hums,' from the buzzing made by a swarm of bees. Cf. Lithuan. *surma,* a pipe or fife, from the sound it makes; Russ. *sviriele,* a pipe, G. *schwirren,* to buzz, whiz, *surren,* to hum, buzz. —√SWER, to hum, buzz; whence Skt. *svr,* to sound, *svara-,* a sound, voice; L. *susurrus,* a hum, whisper. Brugmann, i. § 375 (8). **Der.** *swarm,* verb, AS. *swierman, swyrman,* A. S. Leechdoms, i. 384, l. 21. And see *swear.*

SWART, SWARTHY, black, tawny. (E.) The proper form is *swart;* thence a less correct form *swarth* was made, occurring in Chapman, tr. of Homer, Odyss. b. xix. l. 343; and hence *swarth-y* (=*swart-y*) by the help of suffix *-y* (AS. *-ig*) occasionally added to adjectives (as in *murk-y*). Shak. has *swarth,* Titus, ii. 3. 72; *swarthy,* Two Gent. ii. 6. 26; *swarty,* Titus, iii. 3. 72, in the quarto editions. ME. *swart,* spelt *suart* in Rob. of Glouc., p. 490, l. 10049. AS. *sweart,* black; Grein, ii. 507.+Du. *zwart;* Icel. *svartr;* Dan. *sort;* Swed. *svart;* G. *schwarz;* OHG. *swarz, suarz;* Goth. *swarts.* β. The Teut. type is **swartoz;* allied to L. *sordes,* dirt, *sordidus,* dirty, and prob. to L. *surdus,* dim-coloured. The Norse god *Surtr,* i. e. Swart, is the god of fire; this suggests a connexion with Skt. *svar,* the sun. Perhaps *swar-t* meant 'blackened by fire.' **Der.** *swarth-y* or *swart-y,* as above; *swarth-i-ly, swarth-i-ness.* And see *serene, solar.*

SWASH, to strike with force. (E.) ' Thy *swashing* blow,' Romeo, i. 1. 70. *Swashing* is also swaggering, and a *swasher* is a swaggerer, a bully; As You Like It, i. 3. 122, Hen. V, iii. 2. 30. Of imitative origin; cf. Swed. dial. *svasska,* to make a 'squashing' or 'swashing' noise, as when one walks with water in the shoes (Rietz). β. By the interchange of *ks* and *sk* (as in prov. E. *axe* = to ask), *svasska* stands for **svak-sa,* an extension from a base SWAK. Norweg. *svakka,* to make a noise like water under the feet; Aasen. Cf. prov. E. *swack,* a blow or fall, *swacking,* crushing, huge; *swag,* the noise of a heavy fall (Halliwell). **Der.** *swash-buckler,* in Fuller, Worthies of England, iii. 347 (Cent. Dict.); one who strikes his buckler with a swashing blow, hence, a noisy ruffian.

SWATH, a row of mown grass. (E.) ME. *swathe.* ' A mede . . . In *swathes* sweppen down' = a meadow, mown (lit. swept) down in swaths; Allit. Morte Arthure, 2508. ' Cam him no fieres *swaðe* ner' = no track (or trace) of fire came near him; Genesis and Exodus, ed. Morris, 3786. AS. *swæð, swaðu,* a track, trace, Grein, ii. 500, 501. EFries. *swad.*+Du. *zwaad,* a swathe; also *zwad, zwade,* 'a swath, a row of grass mowed down,' Sewel; G. *schwad,* a row of mown grass. β. The sense 'row of *mown* grass' is the orig. one, whence that of track or foot-track easily follows. This appears by comparing Low G. *swad,* a swath, with *swade,* a scythe; see Brem. Wörterbuch, pt. iv. 1107, where the EFriesic *swade, swae, swah,* a scythe, is also cited. γ. The earliest meaning may have been a 'shred' or 'slice;' cf. Norw. *swada,* vb. act. and neut., to shred or slice off, to flake off. See Du. *zwad* in Franck.

SWATHE, to bind in swaddling-cloths, to bandage. (E.) Shak. has *swath,* (1) that which the mower cuts down with one sweep of the scythe, Troil. v. 5. 25; (2) a swaddling-cloth, Timon, iv. 3. 252; also *swathing-clothes,* 1 Hen. IV, iii. 2. 112; *swathing-clouts,* Haml. ii. 2. 401; *enswathed,* Complaint, 49. ME. *swathen,* pt. t. *swathed,* Cursor Mundi, 11236. From a base *swað-;* whence also AS. *sweðian,* in comp. *besweðian,* to enwrap, John, xix. 40 (Lindisfarne MS.); A. S. Leechdoms, ii. 18, l. 8; and AS. *sweð-el, swæð-il,* a swaddling band; see **Swaddle.** ¶ Perhaps (see **Swath**) the AS. *swað-u* meant orig. a shred; hence (1) as much grass as is mown at once, (2) a shred of cloth used as a bandage. **Der.** *swadd-le* (for *swath-le*).

SWAY, to swing, incline to one side, influence, rule over. (E.) ME. *sweyen,* Gawain and Green Knight, 1429; Allit. Poems, ed. Morris, C. 151. It also means to go, walk, come, Allit. Poems, B. 788, C. 429; spelt *sweȝe,* id. C. 72, 236. Cf. Swed. *svaja,* to jerk; Dan. *svaie,* to swing to and fro, to sway; Du. *zwaaijen,* to sway, swing; EFries. *swäien,* Low G. *swajen.* β. All from the Teut. base SWAG, to sway, swing, well preserved in Norweg. *svaga,* to sway, swing, reel, stagger (Aasen). Allied to **Swagger;** and perhaps even to **Swing.** **Der.** *sway,* sb., Jul. Cæsar, i. 3. 3, ME. *sweigh,* Chaucer, C. T. 4716 (B 296).

SWEAL, to singe, scorch slightly. (E.) See under **Sultry.**

SWEAR, to affirm to be true, to affirm with an oath, to use oaths freely. (E.) ME. *sweren,* strong verb, pt. t. *swor, swoor,* Rob. of Glouc. p. 33, l. 776; pp. *sworen, sworn,* Havelok, 439. AS. *swerian,* pt. t. *swōr,* pp. *sworen,* to swear, Grein, ii. 506. We also find AS. *swerian,* with the simple sense of speak or declare, conjugated as a weak verb, particularly in the comp. *andswerian,* to declare in return, to answer. The orig. sense was simply to speak aloud, declare.+Du. *zweren,* pt. t. *zwoor,* pp. *gezworen;* Icel. *sverja,* pt. t. *sōr,* pp.

svarinn; Dan. *sværge*; Swed. *svärja*; G. *schwören*. And cf. Goth. *swaran*, Icel. *svara*, Dan. *svare*, Swed. *svara*, to answer, reply. **β.** All from √SWER, to hum, buzz, make a sound; whence also Skt. *svṛ*, to sound, to praise, *svara-*, sound, a voice, tone, accent, L. *susurrus*, a humming, and E. *swarm*; see **Swarm.** Brugmann, i. § 121. **Der.** *swear-ing*, *for-sworn*; *an-swer*.

SWEAT, moisture from the skin. (E.) ME. *swoot* (Tyrwhitt prints *swete*), Chaucer, C. T. 16046 (G 578); whence the verb *sweten*, id. 16047 (G 579). AS. *swāt*, Grein, ii. 501. (By the usual change from *ā* to long *o*, AS. *swāt* became ME. *swoot*, and should have been *swote* in mod. E.; but the word has been altered in order to make the sb. accord with the derived verb, viz. AS. *swǣtan*, ME. *sweten*, mod. E. *sweat*, with the *ea* shortened to the sound of *e* in *let* (ME. *lēten*<AS. *lǣtan*). The spelling *swet* would, consequently, be better than *sweat*, and would also be phonetic.)+Du. *zweet*; Icel. *sveiti*; Dan. *sved*; Swed. *svett*; G. *schweiss*; OHG. *sweiz*. **β.** The Teut. stem is **swaito-*, sweat, cognate with Skt. *svēda-*, sweat; from Teut. base SWEIT, to sweat, of which we find (weak-grade) traces in Icel. *sviti*, sweat, G. *schwitzen*. This answers to Idg. √SWEID, to sweat, whence Skt. *svid*, to sweat, L. *sūdor* (for **swoidor*), sweat, Gk. ἰδ-ρώς, sweat, W. *chwys*, sweat. Brugmann, i. § 331 c. **Der.** *sweat*, verb, AS. *swǣtan*, as above; *sweat-y*, *sweat-i-ness*; and see *sud-at-or-y*, *sud-or-i-fi-c*.

SWEEP, to brush, strike with a long stroke, pass rapidly over. (E.) ME. *swepen*, Chaucer, C. T. 16404 (G 936); pp. *sweped*, Pricke of Conscience, 4947. A weak secondary verb from the base *swēp-*, as in *swēþð*, 3rd p. s. pres. t. of AS. *swāpan*, to sweep, a strong verb with pt. t. *sweóp*, Grein, ii. 500. Cf. *ge-swēþa*, pl. sweepings, Voc. 464. 20. [This AS. *swāpan* is represented in mod. E. by the verb to **Swoop,** q.v.] Cf. also OFries. *swēþa*, to sweep; EFries. *swepen* (pt. t. *swep-de*), to swing, sway, vibrate. Also MSwed. *swepa*, Swed. *sopa*, Icel. *sópa*. From Teut. base **swaip*, 2nd grade of Teut. root **sweip*. See **Swipe.** Cf. Icel. *sveipa*, to sweep along, a wk. vb., from an old verb *svipa* (pt. t. *sveip*); also OHG. *sweifan* (pt. t. *swief*), whence G. *schweifen*, to rove, stray, sweep along. Brugmann, i. § 701. **Der.** *sweep*, sb., Timon, i. 2. 137; *sweep-er*, *chimney-sweep-er* (often used in the forms *sweep*, *chimney-sweep*, cf. AS. *hunta*, ME. *hunte*, a hunter); *sweep-ings*; *sweep-stake*, the same as *swoop-stake*, sweeping off all the stakes at once, Hamlet, iv. 5. 142, whence *sweep-stakes*, sb., the whole money staked at a horse-race that can be won or swept up at once.

SWEET, pleasing to the senses, esp. to the taste. (E.) ME. *swete*, Chaucer, C. T. 3206; with the by-forms *swote*, *sote*, id. 3205. AS. *swēte*, Grein, ii. 506.+OSax. *swōti*; Du. *zoet*; Icel. *sœtr*, *sætr*; Dan. *söd*; Swed. *söt*; G. *süsz*; OHG. *suozi*; Goth. *sūts*. **β.** The AS. *ē* is a modified *ō*; cf. the *ö* in Dan. *söd*, Swed. *söt*. The AS. *swēte* is for **swōtjoz*, adj.; where **swōt-* is the 2nd grade of **swat*, answering to Idg. √SWAD, to please, to taste nice, whence also Skt. *svad*, *svād*, to taste, to eat, to please, *svādu-*, sweet, Gk. ἡδύς, sweet, L. *suāuis* (for **suaduis*), pleasant, L. *suadere*, to persuade. **Der.** *sweet-ly*, *sweet-ness*; *sweet-bread*, the pancreas of an animal, so called because *sweet* and resembling *bread*; *sweet-briar*, Milton, L'Allegro, 47; *sweets*, pl. sb., Cor. iii. 1. 157; *sweet-ish*, *sweet-ish-ness*; *sweet-en*, to make sweet, Rich. II, ii. 3. 13; *sweet-en-er*, *sweet-en-ing*; *sweet-ing*, formed with a dimin. suffix *-ing*, a term of endearment, Oth. ii. 3. 252, also a kind of sweet apple, Romeo, ii. 4. 83; *sweet-pea*, *sweet-potato*; *sweet-william*, Bacon, Essay 46, § 6 (from the name William). Also *sweet-meat*, lit. sweet food, chiefly in the pl., ME. *swete metes*, Henrysoun, Test. of Creseide, l. 420; see **Meat.** And see *sweet-heart*, below.

SWEETHEART, a lover or mistress. (E.) Used as a term of endearment. The derivation is simply from *sweet* and *heart*; it is not an absurd hybrid word with the F. suffix *-ard* (=OHG. *-hart*), as has been supposed. Creseide calls Troilus her '*dere herte*' and her '*swete herte*' both; Chaucer, Troil. iii. 1181-1183. Again, he calls her *my swetĕ hertĕ derĕ*, id. iii. 1210; and in the last line of bk. iii we read: '*Is with Creseide his owĕn hertĕ swetĕ*.' Further examples are needless, but may easily be found in the same poem and elsewhere.

SWELL, to grow larger, expand, rise into waves, heave, bulge out. (E.) ME. *swellen*, strong verb, pt. t. *swal*, Chaucer, C. T. 6549 (D 967), pp. *swollen*, id. 8826 (E 950). AS. *swellan*, pt. t. *sweall*, pp. *swollen*, Exod. ix. 10; Grein, ii. 505.+Du. *zwellen*, pt. t. *zwoll*, pp. *gezwollen*; Icel. *svella*, pt. t. *sval*, pp. *sollinn*; Swed. *svälla*; G. *schwellen*. **β.** All from Teut. type **swellan-*, pt. t. **swall*, pp. **swullanoz*. Cf. Goth. *uf-swalleins*, a swelling up. Brugmann, i. § 903. Perhaps allied to Gk. σαλεύειν, to toss, wave. **Der.** *swell*, sb., Antony, iii. 2. 49; *swell-ing*. Also *sill*, q.v., *ground-sill*.

SWELTER, to be faint with heat, also, to cause to exude by excess of heat. (E.) See further under **Sultry.**

SWERVE, to depart from a right line, turn aside. (E.) Palsgrave has *swarve*. ME. *sweruen* (*swerven*), Gower, C. A. iii. 7, 92; bk. vi. 168, bk. vii. 232. Once a strong verb, with pt. t. *swarf*, *swerf* (Stratmann). AS. *sweorfan*, to rub, to file, to polish, pt. t. *swearf*, pp. *sworfen*, Grein, ii. 509; whence the sb. *geswearf*, *geswyrf*, filings, A. S. Leechdoms, i. 336, note 15.+Du. *zwerven*, to swerve, wander, rove, riot, revel; OSax. *swerban*, pt. t. *swarf*, to wipe; OFries. *swerva*, to rove; Icel. *sverfa*, to file; pt. t. *svarf*, pp. *sorfinn*; Goth. *bi-swairban*, to wipe, *af-swairban*, to wipe off. **β.** Teut. type **swerban-*, to wipe, pt. t. **swarð*, pp. **swurðanoz*. Cf. EFries. *swarven*, to wander, Swed. *svarfva*, to turn; also prov. E. *swarve* in the sense of 'to climb a tree devoid of side-boughs,' by swarming up it.

SWIFT, extremely rapid. (E.) ME. *swift*, Chaucer, C. T. 190. AS. *swift*, Grein, ii. 513. From *swif-*, weak grade of AS. *swīfan*, to move quickly, with suffixed *-t* (Idg. *-tos*, participial). Cf. Icel. *svīfa*, to rove, turn, sweep; OHG. *sweibōn*, to move or turn quickly. Teut. base **sweið*. Cf. Teut. base **sweip*; see **Sweep.** **Der.** *swift*, sb., *swift-ly*, *-ness*. And see *swivel*.

SWILL, to wash dishes; to drink greedily. (E.) The proper sense is to wash dishes. ME. *swilien*, *swilen*; 'dishes *swilen*' = wash dishes, Havelok, 919. AS. *swilian*, to wash, in the Lambeth Psalter, Ps. vi. 6 (Bosworth). **Der.** *swill*, hog's-wash, whence *swilling-tub*, Skelton, Elinor Rummyng, 173. Hence the verb to *swill*, to drink like a pig, as in 'the *boar* that . . . *swills* your warm blood like *wash*,' Rich. III, v. 2. 9; there is no reason for connecting *swill* with *swallow*, as is sometimes done. Hence *swill-er*.

SWIM (1), to move to and fro on or in water, to float. (E.) ME. *swimmen*, Chaucer, C. T. 3575. AS. *swimman*, pt. t. *swamm*, *swomm*, Grein, ii. 515.+Du. *zwemmen*; Icel. *svima*, pt. t. *svamm*, pp. *summit*; Dan. *svömme*; Swed. *simma*; G. *schwimmen*, pt. t. *schwamm*. **β.** All from Teut. type **swemman-*, pt. t. **swamm*, pp. **swummanoz*. **Der.** *swim*, sb., *swimm-er*, *swimm-ing*, *swimm-ing-ly*.

SWIM (2), to be dizzy. (E.) 'My head *swims*' = my head is dizzy. The verb is from the ME. *swime*, sb., dizziness, vertigo, a swoon; spelt *swyme*, *suime*, Cursor Mundi, 14201; *swym*, Allit. Morte Arthure, 4246. AS. *swima*, a swoon, swimming in the head, Grein, ii. 515; whence *āswāmian*, verb, to fail, be quenched, and *āswēman*, verb, to wander, id. i. 43, 44.+Du. *zwijm*, EFries. *swim*, a swoon; cf. Icel. *svimi*, a swimming in the head; whence *sveima*, verb, to wander about; Dan. *svimle*, to be giddy, *svimmel*, giddiness, *besvime*, to swoon; Swed. *svimma*, to be dizzy. **β.** The AS. *swīma* probably stands for *swi-ma*; the base is *swī-* (Teut. **swei-*) whence also OHG. *swinan*, to decrease, disappear; to which are allied Swed. *svindel*, dizziness, G. *schwindel*, dizziness, *schwinden*, to disappear, dwindle, decay, fail, *schwindsucht*, consumption; Swed. *försvinna*, to disappear, Icel. *svina*, to subside (said of a swelling). The primary sense is that of failing, giving way. **Der.** *swin-dler*, q.v.

SWINDLER, a cheat. (G.) 'The dignity of the British merchant is sunk in the scandalous appellation of a *swindler*;' V. Knox, Essay 8 (first appeared in 1778); cited in R. One of our few loanwords from High-German. — G. *schwindler*, an extravagant projector, a swindler. — G. *schwindeln*, to be dizzy, to act thoughtlessly, to cheat. — G. *schwindel*, dizziness. — G. *schwinden*, to decay, sink, vanish, fail; cognate with AS. *swindan* (pt. t. *swand*), to languish. **Der.** **Swim** (2). **Der.** *swindle*, verb and sb., evolved from the sb. *swindler* rather than borrowed from G.

SWINE, a sow, pig; pigs. (E.) ME. *swin*, with long *i*, pl. *swin* (unchanged). 'He sleep as a *swyn*' (riming with *wyn*, wine); Chaucer, C. T. 5165 (B 745). 'A flocke of many *swyne*;' Wyclif, Matt. viii. 30. AS. *swīn*, pl. *swīn*, Grein, ii. 515. The AS. *swīn* is a neuter sb. with a long stem, and therefore unchanged in the plural, by rule.+Du. *zwijn*, a swine, hog; Icel. *svin*, pl. *svín*, neuter sb.; Dan. *sviin*, neut., pl. *sviin*; Swed. *svin*, neut.; G. *schwein*, OHG. *swin*; Goth. *swein*, neut. Teut. type **swinom*, neut. Cf. Russ. *svin(e)ya*, a swine, dimin. *svinka*, a pig, *svinoi*, adj., belonging to swine, *svinina*, pork. **β.** Fick conjectures that the form was orig. adjectival, like that of L. *suīnus*, belonging to swine, an adj. noted by Varro (Vaniček, p. 1048); this adj. is regularly formed from *sus*, a sow. See **Sow** (2). Brugmann, i. § 95. **Der.** *swine-ish*, *-ly*, *-ness*; *swine-herd*, ME. *swyyne-herd*, Prompt. Parv.; *swine-cote*, ME. *swyyne-kote*, id.; *swine-sty*, ME. *swinysty*, id., spelt *swynsty*, Pricke of Conscience, 9002.

SWING, to sway or move to and fro. (E.) ME. *swingen*, strong verb, pt. t. *swang*, *swong*, pp. *swungen*; Allit. Poems, ed. Morris, A. 1058 (or 1059), Havelok, 226. AS. *swingan*, pt. t. *swang*, pp. *swungen*, to scourge, also, to fly, flutter, flap with the wings; Grein, ii. 515.+Swed. *svinga*, to swing, to whirl; Dan. *svinge*, to swing, whirl; G. *schwingen*, to swing, soar, brandish; also, to swingle or beat flax; pt. t. *schwang*. Cf. also Goth. *afswaggwjan*, to cause to doubt or despair. **β.** All from Teut. base **swengw-*, Idg. **swenq*. **Der.** *swing*, sb.; *swinge*, q.v.; *swingle*, q.v.

SWINGE, to beat, whip. (E.) In Shak. Two Gent. ii. 1. 88, &c. ME. *swengen*, to beat; see Prompt. Parv. AS. *swengan*, to shake, toss; cf. *sweng*, a stroke, blow; see Bosworth. AS. *swengan* is the causal form of *swingan*, to swing, to flourish a whip, to beat. See **Swing.**

SWINGLE, a staff for beating flax. (MDu.) 'To *swingle*, to beat, a term among flax-dressers;' Phillips. The verb is ME. *swinglen*, Reliquiæ Antiquæ, ii. 197; formed from the sb. *swingle.* In Wright's Voc. i. 156, near the bottom, we find *swingle*, sb., *swinglestok*, sb., and the phrase 'to *swingle* thi flax.' From MDu. *swingelen*, or *swingen*, 'to beate flax;' Hexham. Cf. Du. *zwingel*, a swingle for flax, a flail; *zwingelen*, to swingle; also AS. *swingele*, a scourging; Laws of Ine, § 48, in Thorpe, Anc. Laws, i. 132; from AS. *swing-an*, to beat, to swing. A *swingle* is 'a swinger,' a beater; and *swingle*, verb, is 'to use a swingle.' See **Swing.** Der. *swingle*, verb. Also *swingle-tree*, q.v.

SWINGLETREE, the bar that swings at the heels of the horses when drawing a harrow, &c. (E.) See Halliwell. Also applied to the swinging bar to which traces are fastened when a horse draws a coach. [Corruptly called *single-tree*, whence the term *double-tree* has arisen, to keep it company. 'A *single-tree* is fixed upon each end of another cross-piece called the *double-tree*, when 2 horses draw abreast,' Haldeman (in Webster).] ME. *swingle-tre*, spelt *swyngletre* in Fitzherbert, On Husbandry, § 15 (E.D.S.). The word *tree* here means a piece of timber, as in *axle-tree.* The word *swingle* means 'a swing-er,' a thing that swings; so named from the swinging motion, which all must have observed who have sat behind horses drawing a coach. See **Swingle, Swing.**

SWINK, to toil; obsolescent. (E.) Once an extremely common word; Milton has '*swink'd* hedger'=hedger overcome with toil, Comus, 293. ME. *swinken*, pt. t. *swank*, Havelok, 788; pp. *swunken*, Ormulum, 6103. AS. *swincan*, pt. t. *swanc*, pp. *swuncen*, to toil, labour, work hard. This form, so curiously like AS. *swingan*, pt. t. *swang*, pp. *swungen*, is perhaps a parallel form to it. Cf. Du. *zwenk*, a swing, a turn; G. *schwanken*, to totter, stagger, falter.

SWIPE, to strike with a sweeping stroke. (E.) Cf. prov. E. *swipple*, the striking part of a flail. The *i* has prob. been lengthened; cf. ME. *swipe, swip*, a stroke, Layamon, 7648; *swippen*, vb., to swipe, strike, Layamon, 878. AS. *swipian, swippan*, to beat (Grein); *swipe*, a whip. From **swip-*, weak grade of Teut. **sweipan-*; see **Sweep.** Cf. Icel. *svipa*, to whip; *svipa*, a whip.

SWIRL, to whirl in an eddy. (Scand.) '*Swirl*, a whirling wavy motion, *East*;' Halliwell. A prov. E. word, now used by good writers, as C. Kingsley, E. B. Browning, &c.; see Webster and Worcester. — Norweg. *svirla*, to wave round, swing, whirl (Aasen), frequent. of *sverra* (Dan. *svirre*), to whirl, turn round, orig. to make a humming noise. Cf. Swed. *svirra*, to murmur; G. *schwirren*, to whir; Skt. *svṛ*, to sound. Formed from the Idg. root SWER, to hum, just as *whir-l* is from *whir*; see further under **Swarm.**

SWITCH, a small flexible twig. (Du.—G.) In Romeo, ii. 4. 73; Dr. Schmidt notes that old editions have *swits* for the pl. *switches*. Not found in ME., and perhaps borrowed from Du. in the 16th cent. *Switch* or *swich* is a palatalised form of *swick*.—MDu. *swick*, 'a scourge, a *swich*, or a whip;' Hexham. It also means a wooden vent-peg (Hexham); Low G. *swikk, zwikk*, a twig, a vent-peg. Not a Low G. word, but borrowed from High G. — Bavarian *zwick*, the lash of a whip, or a stroke with the same; variant of G. *zwecke*, a tack, a small wooden peg; Bavar. *zweck*, a splinter, a tapering piece of wood. From MHG. *zwec*, a nail, bolt, peg, esp. a peg in the centre of a target, called in E. the *prick* or the *pin*, which explains why G. *zweck* means 'an aim.' Further allied to G. *zwicken*, to pinch, to tweak; which is allied to E. *twitch*; see Kluge. The fact that the MDu. *s* in this word answers to High G. *z* = Low G. *t*, is pointed out by Franck. No other E. word has initial *s* from *t*. ¶ Icel. *svigi*, a switch, seems to be unrelated. Der. *switch*, verb.

SWIVEL, a ring or link that turns round on a pin or neck. (E.) Spelt *swiuell* in Minsheu, ed. 1627. Not found in ME.; it corresponds to an AS. form **swifel*, not found, but regularly formed, with the suffix *-el* of the agent, from the weak grade (*swif-*) of AS. *swifan*, to move quickly, revolve; for which see **Swift.** Related words are Icel. *sveifla*, to swing or spin in a circle, like a top, *svif*, a swinging round, from *svifa*, to ramble, to turn. The sense is 'that which readily revolves.' Cf. Brugmann, i. § 818 (2).

SWOON, to faint. (E.) ME. *swownen*, Chaucer, C. T. 5478 (B 1058); also *swoghenen*, King Alisaunder, 5857; also *swowenen* (Stratmann). A comparison of the forms shows, as Stratmann points out, that the standard ME. form is **swoȝnen*, the *ȝ* being represented either by *gh, w*, or *u*; and this is a mere extension of a form **swoȝen*, with the same sense. The *n* is the same formative element as is seen in Goth. verbs ending in *-nan*; cf. E. *awaken* from *awake*, &c. β. The form **swoȝen* appears, slightly altered, as *swowen* (with *w* for *ȝ*), to swoon, P. Plowman, B. v. 154, xiv. 326; also as *sowghen, soghen*, to sigh deeply, Romans of Partenay, 1944, 2890. This is a weak verb, closely allied to the ME. strong verb *swoȝen*, to make a loud or deep sound, to sigh deeply, droop, swoon, pt. t. *sweȝ*, pp. *iswoȝen* or *iswowen.* 'Sykande ho *sweȝe* doun'= sighing, she drooped down; Gawain and Green Knight, 1796. 'Adun he feol *iswoȝ*?'=down she fell in a swoon, King Horn, ed. Lumby, 428. From AS. *swōgan*, to move or sweep along noisily, to sough, to sigh, orig. used esp. of the wind. '*Swōgað* windas'= the winds sough, Grein, ii. 516; cf. *āswōgen*, pp. choked, Ælfred, tr. of Gregory's Past. Care, § 52, ed. Sweet, p. 411, l. 17. Mr. Cockayne points out that the form *geswowung*, a swooning, occurs in A. S. Leechdoms, ii. 176, l. 13; and that in Ælfric's Hom. ii. 356, we find: 'Se læg . . *geswōgen* betwux ðām ofslegenum'= he lay *in a swoon* amongst the slain. Here AS. *geswōgen* > ME. *iswoȝen*, as cited above. This AS. *swōgan* is represented by mod. E. **Sough,** q. v. It will thus be seen that the final *n* is a mere formative element, and unoriginal. Cf. Low G. *swögen*, to sigh, *swugten*, to sigh, also to swoon; Brem. Wört. Der. *swoon*, sb. Also *swoun-d*, with excrescent *d*, and *soun-d*, with loss of *w*. Palsgrave has 'I *swounde*,' i. e. I swoon.

SWOOP, to sweep along, to descend with a swift motion, like a bird of prey. (E.) Shak. has *swoop*, sb., Macb. iv. 3. 219. ME. *swopen*, usually in the sense to sweep. In Chaucer, C. T. 16404, where Tyrwhitt prints *swepe*, the Corpus MS. has *swope* (Group G, l. 936); two lines lower, in place of *ysweped*, the Lichfield MS. has *yswopen.* The ME. *swopen* was orig. a strong verb, with pt. t. *swep*, and pp. *yswopen* (as above). AS. *swāpan*, to sweep along, rush; also, to sweep; a strong verb, pt. t. *swēop*, pp. *swāpen*; Grein, ii. 500. '*Swāpendum* windum'=with swooping (rushing) winds; Ælfred, tr. of Beda, iii. 16, ed. Smith, p. 542, l. 37. 'Swift wind *swāpeð*'=a swift wind swoops; Ælfred, tr. of Boethius, met. vii (b. ii. met. 4). (The AS. *ā* became ME. open *ō*, but this became close *ō* under the influence of the *w*.)+Icel. *sveipa*, to sweep, swoop; cf. *sveip*, pt. t. of an obsolete strong verb *svipa*; *sveipinn*, pp. of the same. Also Icel. *sōpa*, weak verb, to sweep. And cf. G. *schweifen*, to rove, ramble; Goth. *sweipains*, in the comp. *midja-sweipains*, a deluge, Luke, xvii. 27. β. The AS. *swāpan* answers to a Teut. **swaipan-*, from the Teut. root **sweip*, for which see **Swipe.** Der. *swoop*, sb.; also *sweep*, q. v.; and see *swift, swiv-el.*

SWORD, an offensive weapon with a long blade. (E.) ME. *swerd*, Chaucer, C. T., A 1700. AS. *sweord*, Matt. xxvi. 47.+Du. *zwaard*; Icel. *sverð*; Dan. *sværd*; Swed. *svärd*; G. *schwert.* The Teut. type is **swerdom*, neut. Of unknown origin. Der. *sword-cane, -fish, -stick*; *sword-s-man*, formed like *hunt-s-man, sport-s-man*; *sword-s-man-ship.*

SYBARITE, an effeminate person. (L.—Gk.) In Blount's Gloss., ed. 1674; he also has the adj. *Sybaritical*, dainty, effeminate. — L. *Sybarīta.* — Gk. Συβαρίτης, a Sybarite, an inhabitant of Sybaris, a luxurious liver, voluptuary; because the inhabitants of this town were noted for voluptuousness. The town was named from the river *Sybaris* (Gk. Σύβαρις), on which it was situated. This river flows through the district of Lower Italy formerly called Lucania. Der. *Sybarit-ic, Sybarit-ic-al.*

SYCAMINE, the name of a tree. (L.—Gk.—Heb.?) In Luke, xvii. 6 (A.V.). — L. *sȳcamīnus.* — Gk. συκάμινος; Luke, xvii. 6. It is gen. believed to be the mulberry-tree, and distinct from the *sycamore*; Thomson, in The Land and the Book, pt. i. c. 1, thinks the trees were one and the same. β. That the word has been confused with *sycamore* is obvious, but the suffix *-ine* (*-ινος*) is difficult to explain. Thomson's explanation is worth notice; he supposes it to be nothing more than a Gk. adaptation of the Heb. plural. The Heb. name for the sycamore is *shiqmāh*, with the plural forms *shiqmōth* and *shiqmim*; from the latter of these the Gk. συκάμινος may easily have been formed, by partial confusion with Gk. συκόμορος, a sycamore; see **Sycamore.**

SYCAMORE, the name of a tree. (L.—Gk.—Heb.?) The trees so called in Europe and America are different from the Oriental sycamore (*Ficus sycomorus*). The spelling should rather be *sycomore*; Cotgrave gives *sycomore* both as an E. and a F. spelling. Spelt *sicomoure* in Wyclif, Luke, xix. 4.—L. *sȳcomorus.* — Gk. συκόμορος, as if it meant 'fig-mulberry' tree. As if from Gk. συκο-, decl. stem of σῦκον, a fig; and μόρον, a mulberry, blackberry; but it seems to have been a popular adaptation of Heb. *shiqmāh*, sycamore. See **Sycamine.**

SYCOPHANT, a servile flatterer. (L.—Gk.) See Trench, Select Glossary; he shows that it was formerly also used to mean 'an informer.' 'That *sicophants* are counted iolly guests;' Gascoigne, Steel Glas, 207. Cotgrave gives the F. form as *sycophantin.* — L. *sycophanta*, an informer, tale-bearer, flatterer, sycophant.—Gk.

συκοφάντης, lit. 'a fig-shower,' said to mean one who informs against persons exporting figs from Attica, or plundering sacred fig-trees; hence, a common informer, slanderer, also, a false adviser. 'The lit. signification is not found in any ancient writer, and is perhaps altogether an invention;' Liddell and Scott. That is, the early history of the word is lost, but this does not affect its obvious [perhaps only a popular] etymology.—Gk. σῦκο-, decl. stem of σῦκον, a fig; and -φαντης, lit. a shower (appearing also in ἱεροφάντης, one who shows or teaches religious rites), from φαίνειν, to show. See Sycamore and Phantom. Der. sycophant-ic, -ic-al, -ism; sycophanc-y.

SYLLABLE, part of a word, uttered by a single effort of voice. (F.—L.—Gk.) ME. *sillable*, Chaucer, C. T. 10415 (F 101).—OF. *sillabe* (Littré), later *syllabe* and *syllable*, with an inserted unoriginal *l*.—L. *syllaba*.—Gk. συλλαβή, lit. 'that which holds together,' hence a syllable, so much of a word as forms a single sound.—Gk. συλ- (for συν before following λ), together; and λαβ-, base of λαμβάνειν, to take, seize (aorist infin. λαβεῖν). See **Syn-** and **Cataleptic.** Der. *syllab-ic*, from Gk. συλλαβικός, adj.; *syllab-ic-al*, *syllab-i-fy.* Also *syllabus*, a compendium, from Late L. *syllabus*, a list, syllabus (White), from Late Gk. σύλλαβος, allied to συλλαβή.

SYLLOGISM, a reasoning from premises, a process in formal logic. (F.—L.—Gk.) ME. *silogime*, Gower, C. A. iii. 366; bk. viii. 2708.—OF. *silogime* (Littré), later *sillogisme*, spelt *syllogisme* in Cotgrave.—L. *syllogismum*, acc. of *syllogismus*.—Gk. συλλογισμός, a reckoning all together, reckoning up, reasoning, syllogism.—Gk. συλλογ-ίζομαι, I reckon together, sum up, reason.—Gk. συλ- (for συν before λ following), together; and λογίζομαι, I reckon, from λόγ-ος, a word, reason, reasoning. See **Syn-** and **Logic.** Der. *syllogise*, spelt *sylogyse* in Lydgate, Assembly of the Gods, 19. From συλλογίζ-ομαι; *syllogis-t-ic*, from L. *syllogisticus*<Gk. συλλογιστικός; *syllogis-t-ic-al*, -ly.

SYLPH, an imaginary being inhabiting the air. (F.—Gk.) 'Ye *sylphs* and *sylphids*;' Pope, Rape of the Lock, ii. 73; and see Pope's Introduction to that poem (A.D. 1712). Pope tells us that he took the account of the Rosicrucian philosophy and theory of spirits from a French book called Le Comte de Gabalis.—F. *sylphe*, the name given to one of the pretended genii of the air; Hatzfeld quotes *les sylfes* from a work of the 16th or 17th century.—Gk. σίλφη, used by Aristotle, Hist. Anim. 8. 17. 8, to signify a kind of beetle or grub. β. It is usually supposed that this word suggested the name *sylph*, which is used by Paracelsus. The other names of genii are *gnomes*, *salamanders*, and *nymphs*, dwelling in the earth, fire, and water respectively; and, as all these names are Greek, it is likely that *sylph* was meant to be Greek also. The spelling with *y* causes no difficulty, and is, indeed, an additional sign that the word is meant to be Greek. It is not uncommon to find *y* (called in F. *y Grec*) used in words derived from Gk., not only where it represents Gk. *v*, but even (mistakenly) where it represents Gk. *ι*; thus *syphon* occurs instead of *siphon* both in F. and E. γ. Littré (followed by Hatzfeld) accounts for the word quite differently. He says that F. *sylphe* is a Gaulish (Celtic) word signifying genius, and that it is found in various inscriptions as *sulfi*, *sylfi*, *sylphi*, or, in the feminine, as *suleuæ*, *suleviæ* (which are, of course, Latinised and plural forms); he cites '*Sulfis* suis qui nostram curam agunt,' Orel. Helvet. 117. And he supposes that Paracelsus revived these names. Scheler, on the contrary, has no doubt that the word is Greek. Der. *sylph-id*, from F. *sylphide*, a false form, but only explicable on the supposition that the word *sylph* was thought to be Gk., and declined as if the nom. was σίλφις (stem σίλφιδ-).

SYLVAN, a common mis-spelling of **Silvan,** q. v.

SYMBOL, a sign, emblem, figurative representation. (F.—L.—Gk.) See Trench, Select Glossary. In Shak. Oth. ii. 3. 350.—F. *symbole*, 'a token,' &c.; Cot.—L. *symbolum*.—Gk. σύμβολον, a token, pledge, a sign by which one infers a thing.—Gk. συμβάλλειν (aor. infin. συμβαλεῖν), to throw together, bring together, compare, infer. —Gk. συμ- (for συν before β), together; and βάλλειν, to throw. See **Syn-.** Der. *symbol-ic*, from Gk. συμβολικός, adj.; *symbol-ic-al*, -ly; *symbol-ise*, from F. *symboliser*, spelt *symbolizer* in Cot., and explained by 'to symbolize;' *symbol-is-er*; *symbol-ism*, *symbol-ist*.

SYMMETRY, due proportion, harmony. (F.—L.—Gk.) Spelt *simmetrie* in Minsheu, ed. 1627.—F. *symmetrie*, 'symmetry,' Cot.— L. *symmetria*.—Gk. συμμετρία, due proportion.—Gk. σύμμετρος, adj., measured with, of like measure with.—Gk. συμ- (for συν before μ), together; and μέτρον, a measure. See **Syn-** and **Metre.** Der. *symmetr-ic-al*, a coined word; *symmetr-ic-al-ly*; *symmetr-ise*, a coined word.

SYMPATHY, a feeling with another, like feeling. (F.—L.— Gk.) Spenser has *sympathie* and *sympathize*, Hymn in Honour of Beautie, ll. 199 and 192.—F. *sympathie*, 'sympathy;' Cot.—L. *sympathīa*.—Gk. συμπάθεια, like feeling, fellow-feeling.—Gk. συμπαθής,

adj., of like feelings.—Gk. συμ- (for συν before π), together; and παθ-, base of παθ-εῖν, aor. infin. of πάσχειν, to suffer, experience, feel. See **Syn-** and **Pathos.** Der. *sympath-et-ic*, a coined word, suggested by *pathetic*; *sympath-et-ic-al*, -ly; *sympath-ise*, from F. *sympathiser*, 'to sympathize,' Cot.; *sympath-is-er*.

SYMPHONY, concert, unison, harmony of sound. (F.—L.— Gk.) There was a musical instrument called a *symphony*, ME. *simphonie* or *symphonye*; see my note to Chaucer, C. T. Group B, l. 2005. And see Wyclif, Luke, xv. 25.—F. *symphonie*, 'harmony;' Cot.—L. *symphōnia*, Luke, xv. 25 (Vulgate).—Gk. συμφωνία, music, Luke, xv. 25.—Gk. σύμφωνος, agreeing in sound, harmonious.— Gk. συμ- (for συν before φ), together; and φωνεῖν, to sound, φωνή, sound. See **Syn-** and **Phonetic.** Der. *symphoni-ous*; *symphon-ist*, a chorister, Blount's Gloss., ed. 1674.

SYMPOSIUM, a merry feast. (L.—Gk.) Blount, Gloss., ed. 1674, has *symposiast*, 'a feast-master,' and *symposiaques*, 'books treating of feasts.' *Symposium* is in Sidney, Apol. for Poetrie, p. 57. —L. *symposium*.—Gk. συμπόσιον, a drinking-party, banquet.—Gk. συμ- (for σύν before π), together; and the base πο-, to drink, appearing in pt. t. πέ-πω-κα, I drank, aor. ἐ-πό-θην, I drank, and in the sb. πό-σις, drink. See **Syn-** and **Potable.**

SYMPTOM, an indication of disease, an indication. (F.—L.— Gk.) Properly a medical term. In Cotgrave, to translate MF. *symptome*.—L. *symptōma*.—Gk. σύμπτωμα, anything that has befallen one, a casualty, usu. in a bad sense.—Gk. συμπίπτειν, pt. t. συμ-πέ-πτωκα, to fall together, to fall in with, meet with.—Gk. σύμ- (for σύν before π), together, with; and πίπτειν (πί-πτ-ειν) to fall, from √PET, to fall. See **Syn-** and **Asymptote.** Der. *symptomat-ic*, from Gk. συμπτωματικός, adj., from συμπτωματ-, stem of σύμπτω-μα; *symptomat-ic-al*, -ly.

SYN-, prefix, together. (L.—Gk.; *or* F.—L.—Gk.) A Latinised spelling of Gk. σύν, together. Cf. Gk. ξύν, together; a form not clearly explained. β. The prefix σύν becomes συλ- (*syl-*) before *l*, συμ- (*sym-*) before *b*, *m*, *p*, and *ph*, and συ- (*sy-*) before *s* or *z*; as in *syllogism*, *symbol*, *symmetry*, *sympathy*, *symphony*, *system*, *syzygy*.

SYNÆRESIS, the taking of two vowels together, whereby they coalesce into a diphthong. (L.—Gk.) A grammatical term. Spelt *sineresis* in Minsheu.—L. *synæresis.*—Gk. συναίρεσις, lit. a taking together.—Gk. σύν, together; and αἵρεσις, a taking, from αἱρεῖν, to take. See **Syn-** and **Heresy.** Cf. **Diæresis.**

SYNAGOGUE, a congregation of Jews. (F.—L.—Gk.) ME. *synagoge*, Wyclif, Matt. iv. 23.—F. *synagogue*, 'a synagogue;' Cot. —L. *synagōga.*—Gk. συναγωγή, a bringing together, assembly, congregation.—Gk. σύν, together; and ἀγωγή (=ἀγ-ωγ-ή), a bringing, from ἄγειν, to bring, drive; a reduplicated form, from √AG, to drive.

SYNALŒPHA, a coalescence of two syllables into one. (L.—Gk.) A grammatical term; in Blount's Gloss., ed. 1674.—L. *synalæpha.*—Gk. συναλοιφή, lit. a melting together.—Gk. σύν, together; and ἀλείφειν, to anoint with oil, to daub, blot out, efface, whence ἀλοιφή, fat. The Gk. ἀλείφειν is allied to λίπ-ος, fat; cf. Skt. *lip*, to besmear, anoint.

SYNCHRONISM, concurrence in time. (Gk.) Blount, ed. 1674, says the word is used by Sir W. Raleigh.—Gk. συγχρονισμός, agreement of time.—Gk. σύγχρονο-ος, contemporaneous; with suffix -ισμος, from -ίζειν.—Gk. σύγ- (written for σύν before χ), together; and χρόνος, time. See **Syn-** and **Chronicle.** Der. *synchronous* adapted from Gk. σύγχρονος, adj.

SYNCOPATE, to contract a word. (L.—Gk.) In Blount's Gloss., ed. 1674.—L. *syncopātus*, pp. of *syncopāre*, of which the usual sense is 'to swoon.'—L. *syncopē*, *syncopa*, a swooning; also *syncope*, as a gram. term.—Gk. συγκοπή, a cutting short, syncope in grammar, a loss of strength, a swoon.—Gk. συγ- (written for σύν before κ), together; and κοπ-, base of κόπτειν, to cut. See **Syn-** and **Apocope.** Der. *syncopat-ion*, a musical term, which Blount says is in Playford's Introd. to Music, p. 28. Also *syncope*, as a grammat. term, also a swoon, spelt *sincopin* (acc.), Lanfrank, p. 205, from L. *syncopē*<Gk. συγκοπή, as above.

SYNDIC, a government official, one who assists in the transaction of business. (F.—L.—Gk.) Spelt *sindick* in Minsheu, ed. 1627.—F. *syndic*, 'a syndick, censor, controller of manners;' Cot.— L. *syndicus.*—Gk. σύνδικος, adj., helping in a court of justice; as sb., a syndic.—Gk. σύν, with; and δίκη, justice. The orig. sense of δίκ-η is a showing, hence a course, custom, use, justice; from δικ-, weak grade of √DEIK, to show. See **Syn-** and **Diction.** Der. *syndic-ate*, a coined word.

SYNECDOCHE, a figure of speech whereby a part is put for the whole. (L.—Gk.) Spelt *sinecdoche* in Minsheu, ed. 1627; but *synecdoche*, Caxton, Golden Legend, The Resurrection, § 1.—L. *synecdochē.*—Gk. συνεκδοχή, lit. a receiving together.—Gk. συνεκδέχομαι, I join in receiving.—Gk. σύν, together; and ἐκδέχομαι, I receive, compounded of ἐκ, out, and δέχομαι (Ionic δέκομαι), I receive, from √DEK, to take. See **Syn-, Ex-**.

SYNOD, a meeting, ecclesiastical council. (F.–L.–Gk.) *Synodes* and counsayles;' Sir T. More, Works, p. 406 h.–F. *synode*, a synod;' Cot.–L. *synodum*, acc. of *synodus*.–Gk. σύνοδος, a meeting, lit. a coming together.–Gk. σύν, together; and ὁδός, a way, here, a coming, from √SED, to go. See **Method**. Der. *synod-ic*, from Gk. συνοδικός, adj.; *synod-ic-al, synod-ic-al-ly*.

SYNONYM, a word having the same sense with another. (F.–L.–Gk.) The form is French; in old books it was usual to write *synonima*, which, by a curious blunder, was taken to be a fem. sing. instead of a neut. pl., doubtless because the L. *synonyma* was only used in the plural; and, indeed, the sing. is seldom required, since we can only speak of *synonyms* when we are considering more words than one. *Synonima* is used as a sing. by Cotgrave and Blount.–F. *synonime*, 'a synonima, a word having the same signification which another hath;' Cot.–L. *synonyma*, neut. pl., synonyms; from the adj. *synonymus*, synonymous.–Gk. συνώνυμος, of like meaning or like name.–Gk. σύν, with; and ὄνομα, a name, cognate with E. *name*; see **Syn-** and **Name**. Der. *synonymous*, Englished from L. adj. *synonymus*, as above; *synonymous-ly*; *synonym-y*, L. *synonymia*, from Gk. συνωνυμία, likeness of name.

SYNOPSIS, a general view of a subject. (L.–Gk.) Spelt *sinopsis* in Minsheu, ed. 1627.–L. *synopsis*.–Gk. σύνοψις, a seeing all together.–Gk. σύν, together; and ὄψις, a seeing, sight; cf. ὄψ-ομαι, fut. from base ὀπ-, to see. See **Syn-** and **Optics**. Der. *synopt-ic*, from Gk. adj. συνοπτικός, seeing all together; *synopt-ic-al, -ly*.

SYNTAX, the arrangement of words in sentences. (L.–Gk.) In Ben Jonson, Eng. Grammar, b. ii. c. 1; spelt *sintaxis* in Minsheu, ed. 1627.–L. *syntaxis*.–Gk. σύνταξις, an arrangement, arranging.–Gk. σύν, together; and τάξις, order, from τάσσειν (for *τάκ-γειν), to arrange. See **Syn-** and **Tactics**. Der. *syntact-ic-al*, due to Gk. συντακτός, adj., put in order; *syntact-ic-al-ly*.

SYNTHESIS, composition, combination. (L.–Gk.) In Blount's Gloss., ed. 1674, s.v. *Synthetical*.–L. *synthesis*.–Gk. σύνθεσις, a putting together.–Gk. σύν, together; and θέσις, a putting; see **Syn-** and **Thesis**. Der. *synthet-ic-al*, due to Gk. adj. συνθετικός, skilled in putting together, from συνθέτης, a putter together, where θε- is the weak grade of θη-, to put, and -της is the suffix denoting the agent (Idg. -τᾱ-); *synthet-ic-al-ly*.

SYPHON, SYREN, inferior spellings of **Siphon, Siren**, q.v. Cot. has the F. spelling *syphon*; also *siphon*.

SYRINGE, a tube with a piston, for ejecting fluids. (F.–L. –Gk.) The *g* was prob. once hard, not as *j*. Cot., however, already has *siringe*.–MF. *syringue*, 'a siringe, a squirt;' Cot.–L. *syringem*, acc. of *syrinx*, a reed, pipe, tube.–Gk. σύριγξ, a reed, pipe, tube, shepherd's pipe, whistle. From the Gk. base συρ-, to perforate; with suffix -ιγξ as in φόρμ-ιγξ, πλάστ-ιγξ. Brugmann, i. § 230. Der. *syring-a*, a flowering shrub so named because the stems were used for the manufacture of Turkish pipes; see Eng. Cycl., s.v. *Syringa*.

SYRUP, SIRUP, a kind of sweetened drink. (F.–Span.–Arab.) 'Spicery, sawces, and *siropes*;' Fryth's Works, p. 99, col. 1. –MF. *syrop*, 'sirrop;' Cot. Mod. F. *sirop*; OF. *ysserop* (Littré).–MSpan. *xarope*, a medicinal drink (Span. *jarope*); the OF. *ysserop* is due to a Span. form *axarope*, where *a* represents *al*, the Arab. article.–Arab. *sharāb, shurāb*, wine or any beverage, syrup; lit. a beverage; Rich. Dict. p. 886.–Arab. root *shariba*, he drank; id. p. 887. See **Sherbet**.

SYSTEM, method. (L.–Gk.) It is not an old word in F., and seems to have been borrowed from Latin directly. Spelt *systeme* in Blount's Gloss., ed. 1674.–L. *systēma*.–Gk. σύστημα (stem συστηματ-), a complex whole, put together; a system.–Gk. συ- (for σύν before σ), together; and the base στη-, to stand; with suffix -ματ- (Idg. -mənt-). The base στη- occurs in στῆναι, to stand; from √STA, to stand; see **Stand**. Der. *system-at-ic*, from Gk. adj. συστηματικός, adj., formed from συστηματ-, stem of σύστημα; *system-at-ic-al, -ly*; *system-at-ise*, a coined word · *system-at-is-er*.

SYSTOLE, contraction of the heart, shortening of a syllable. (Gk.) In Blount's Gloss., ed. 1674. Englished (with *y* for *v*) from Gk. συστολή, a contracting, drawing together.–Gk. συστολ-, 2nd grade of συστέλλειν, to draw together, contract.–Gk. συ- (for σύν before σ), together; and στέλλειν, to equip, set in order. See **Syn-** and **Stole**.

SYZYGY, conjunction. (Gk.) A modern term in astronomy.–Gk. συζυγία, union, conjunction.–Gk. σύζυγος, conjoined.–Gk. συ- (for σύν before ζ), together; and ζυγ-, weak grade of ζεύγνυμι, I join (cf. ζύγον, a yoke), from √YEUG, to join. See **Syn-** and **Yoke**; and compare **Conjunction**.

TA–TE

TAB, a small flap or strip, usually attached at one end. (E.) Prob. allied to *tape*; cf. AS. *tæppe*, a tape, fillet. See **Tape**.

TABARD, a sleeveless coat, formerly worn by ploughmen, noblemen, and heralds, now by heralds only. (F.–L.?) ME. *tabard*, Rob. of Brunne, tr. of Langtoft, p. 280, l. 2; Chaucer, C. T. 543 (A 541).–OF. *tabart, tabard*; see a quotation in Roquefort with the spelling *tabart*; mod. F. *tabard* (Hamilton, omitted in Littré). Ducange gives an OF. form *tribart*. Cf. Span. and Port. *tabardo*; Ital. *tabarro*. The last form (like MF. *tabarre* in Cotgrave) has lost a final *d* or *t*. [The W. *tabar* is borrowed from English.] We also find a MHG. *tapfart, taphart*; and even a mod. Gk. ταμπάριον. β. Etym. unknown; Diez suggests L. *tapēt-*, stem of *tapēte*, hangings, painted cloths; but this is unlikely. Cf. MItal. and L. *trabea*, a robe of state.

TABBY, a kind of waved silk. (F.–Span.–Arab.) Chiefly retained in the expression ' a *tabby* cat,' i. e. a cat brindled or diversified in colour, like the markings on *tabby*. ' Tabby, a kind of waved silk;' Phillips, ed. 1706.–F. *tabis*, in use in the 15th century (Littré); also OF. *atabis*, Godefroy.–Span. *tabi*, a silken stuff; Low L. (or rather OSpan.) *attabi*, where *at* was supposed (but wrongly) to represent the Arab. article *al*, and so came to be dropped. Cf. 'j panno *Attaby*' (mispr. *Accaby*) ' Earl of Derby's Expeditions, Camden Soc., p. 283, l. 24.–Arab. 'utābī, a kind of rich undulated silk; Rich. Dict. p. 992. See Devic, who calls it an Arab. word (Rich. marks it Pers.). He adds that it was the name of a quarter of Bagdad where this silk was made (Defrémery, *Journal Asiatique*, Jan. 1862, p. 94); and that this quarter took its name from prince Attab, great-grandson of Omeyya (Dozy, Gloss. p. 343). ¶ Hence perhaps *tabin-et*, spelt *tabbinet* in Webster, and explained, as 'a more delicate kind of tabby;' from Ital. *tabin-o*, tabine, tabby (Torriano). But Trench, Eng. Past and Present, tells us that it was named from M. Tabinet, a French Protestant refugee, who introduced the making of *tabinet* in Dublin; for which statement he adduces no reference or authority. Cf. *tabine*, in ' Cloth of tissue or *tabine*,' Middleton, Anything for a Quiet Life, ii. 2 (C. D.).

TABERNACLE, a tent used as a temple, a tent. (F.–L.) ME. *tabernacle*, Rob. of Glouc. p. 20, l. 466.–F. *tabernacle*, 'a tabernacle,' Cot.–L. *tabernāculum*, double dimin. of *taberna*, a hut, shed; see **Tavern**.

TABID, wasted by disease. (F.–L.) Rare; in Phillips, ed. 1706. –F. *tabide*, consuming, wasting; Cot.–L. *tābidus*, wasting away, decaying, languishing.–L. *tābēs*, a wasting away; *tābēre*, to waste away, languish. Allied to Gk. τήκειν, in the same sense; and to E. *thaw*. See **Thaw**. Der. *tabe-fy*, to cause to melt, Blount's Gloss., from MF. *tabifier*, to waste (Cot.), due to L. *tābefacere*, to cause to melt.

TABLE, a smooth board, usually supported on legs. (F.–L.) ME. *table*, Chaucer, C. T. 355 (A 353).–F. *table*.–L. *tabula*, a plank, flat board, table. Der. *table-s*, pl. sb., a kind of game like backgammon, played on flat boards, Rob. of Glouc. p. 192, l. 3965; *table*, verb, Cymb. i. 4. 6; *table-book*, Hamlet, ii. 2. 136; *table-talk*, Merch. Ven. iii. 5. 93; *table-land*, land flat like a table; *tabl-et*, Cymb. v. 4. 109, from F. *tablette*, 'a little table,' Cot., dimin. of F. *table*. Also *tabul-ar, tabul-ate*, from L. *tabula*. Also *tabl-eau*, borrowed from F. *tableau*, dimin. of *table*. Also *taffer-el*, q. v.; *en tabla-ture*.

TABOO, TABU, to forbid approach to, forbid the use of. (Polynesian.) ' *Taboo*, a political prohibition and religious consecration interdict, formerly of great force among the inhabitants of the islands of the Pacific; hence, a total prohibition of intercourse with, or approach to anything;' Webster. ' South-Sea-Isle *taboo*;' Tennyson, Princess, iii. 261. Kotzebue mentions the ' *Tabu*, or interdict;' New Voyage round the World, 1830, ii. 178. The E. pron. of New Zealand (Maori) *tapu*, consecrated or forbidden; pron. *tambu* in the Solomon Isles. See E. E. Morris, Austral. Dict.

TABOUR, TABOR, a small drum. (F.–Span.–Arab.) ME. *tabour*, Havelok, 2329.–OF. and MF. *tabour*, 'a drum, a tabor;' Cot. Mod. F. *tambour*; Littré gives the spellings *tabur*, 11th cent.; *tabour*, 13th to 16th century. Cf. Prov. *tabor, tanbor* (cited by Littré); Span. *tambor*, MSpan. *atambor* (Minsheu); Ital. *tamburo*. The F. word was most likely borrowed from Span. *tambor*, also called *atambor*, where the prefix *a-* stands for the Arab. def. art. *al*, showing that the word was borrowed from the Moors.–Arab. *ṭambūr*, 'a kind of lute or guitar with a long neck, and six brass strings; also, a drum;' Rich. Dict., p. 976. He gives it also as a Pers. word, and

Devic seems to think that the word was borrowed from Persian. The initial letter is the 19th of the Pers. alphabet, sometimes written *th*, not the ordinary *t*. On the same page of Rich. Dict. we also find Pers. *ṭumbuk*, a trumpet, clarion, bagpipe, *ṭambal*, a small drum ; also Arab. *ṭabl*, a drum, a tambourin, Pers. *ṭablak*, a small drum, p. 964. Also Pers. *tabir* (with the ordinary *t*), a drum, kettle-drum, a large pipe, flute, or hautboy, p. 365 ; *tabūrāk*, a drum, tabour, tambourin, a drum beaten to scare away birds, p. 364. See the account in Devic, who considers the form *ṭambūr* as derived from Pers. *tabir* ; and the form *tabūrāk* to be dimin. of Pers. **tabūr*, a form not found. β. It will be observed that the sense comprises various instruments that make a din, and we may note Port. *atabale*, a kettle-drum, from *a* for *al*, the Arab. article, and Pers. *ṭambal*, a drum. All the above words contain a base *tab*, which we may regard, with Mr. Wedgwood, as being of imitative origin, like the English *dub-a-dub* and *tap*. This is rendered likely by the occurrence of Arab. *ṭabṭabat*, the sound made by the dashing of waterfalls ; Rich. Dict. 963 ; cf. Arab. *ṭabbāl*, a drummer, ibid. **Der.** *tabor-er*, Temp. iii. 2. 160 ; *tabour-ine*, Antony, iv. 8. 37, from F. *tabourin*, ‘a little drum,’ Cot. ; *tabour-et*, Bp. Hall, Sat. iv. 1. 78, a dimin. form ; shortened to *tabret*, Gen. xxxi. 27. And see *tambourine*.

TABULAR, TABULATE; see **Table**.

TACHE (1), a fastening. (F.—Teut.) In Exod. xxvi. 6. ‘A *tache*, a buckle, a claspe, a bracelet, *Spinter* ;’ Baret, s. v. *Claspe*. A palatalised form of *tack* ; cf. *beseech* for *beseek*, *church* for *kirk*, &c. ; esp. the derived words *att-ach*, *de-tach*. Minsheu, ed. 1627, gives : ‘To *tache*, or *tacke*.’ ME. *tache*, Voc. 564. 2. We find AF. *taches*, pl., pegs, Year-books of Edw. I., 1304–5, p. 53.—OF. *tache*, a nail, fastening (Godefroy).—EFries. (Low G.) *take*, a point, prick, thorn, allied to *tak*, *takke*, a pointed thing, a twig ; Low G. *takk*, a pointed thing. See **Tack**.

TACHE (2), a blot, blemish ; see **Tetchy**.

TACIT, silent. (L.) In Milton, Samson, 430. No doubt directly from L., though Cot. gives F. *tacite*, ‘silent.’—L. *tacitus*, silent.—L. *tacēre*, to be silent. Cognate with Goth. *thahan*, to be silent, Icel. *þegja*, Swed. *tiga*, to be silent. **Der.** *tacit-urn*, from F. *taciturne*, ‘silent,’ Cot. ; *tacit-urn-i-ty*, Troilus, iv. 2. 75, from F. *taciturnité*, ‘taciturnity,’ Cot. ; from L. acc. *taciturnitātem*. Also *re-ticent*.

TACK, a small nail, a fastening ; to fasten. (F.—Teut.) ME. *takke*. ‘*Takke*, or *botun*, *Fibula*,’ Prompt. Parv. ; where we also find : ‘*Takkyn*, or *festyn to-gedur*, or *some-what sowyn to-gedur*.’ The sb. is spelt *tak*, Legends of Holy Rood, ed. Morris, p. 145, l. 419. [The Irish *taca*, a peg, pin, nail, fastening ; Gael. *tacaid*, a tack, peg, stab ; Breton *tach*, a nail, *tacha*, to fasten with a nail, are borrowed words.] —O. North F. *taque* (OF. *tache*), a fastening, nail (Godefroy) ; a peg, clothes-peg (Moisy, s. v. *taque*).—EFries. and Dan. *takke*, Low G. *takk*, a tine, a pointed thing ; Westphal. *tacke*, a tack ; G. *zacke*, a tooth, tine, prong, twig. Allied to EFries. *tak*, a twig, a bough, Du. *tak*, a twig. 2. The nautical use of *tack* is from the same source. ‘In nautical language a *tack* is the rope which draws forward the lower corner of a square sail, and *fastens* it to the windward side of the ship in sailing transversely to the wind, the ship being on the *starboard* or *larboard tack* according as it presents its *right* or *left* side to the wind ; the ship is said to *tack* when it turns towards the wind, and changes the *tack* on which it is sailing ;’ Wedgwood. See **Tache** (1) and **Zigzag**. Cf. *to tack*, to sew slightly, fasten slightly. **Der.** *tache*, q. v. ; and see *tack-le*. Also *tack-et*, a small nail (Levins).

TACKLE, equipment, implements, gear, tools. (Low G.) ME. *takel*, Chaucer, C. T. 106 ; Gen. and Exodus, ed. Morris, 883 ; *takil*, the tackle of a ship, Gower, C. A. iii., bk. viii. 470.—Low G. *takel*, tackle ; *takeln*, to equip ; MDu. *taeckelen*, the tackling of ships, *taeckel*, ‘munition, riggings,’ Hexham ; Du. *takel*, tackle, *takelen*, to rig ; whence Swed. and MSwed. *tackel*, tackle of a ship (Ihre), *tackla*, to rig ; Dan. *takkel*, tackle, *takle*, to rig. β. The suffix *-el* is used to form substantives from verbs, as in E. *sett-le*, sb., a thing to sit on, from *sit*, *stopp-le* from *stop*, *shov-el* from *shove*, *shutt-le* from *shoot*, *gird-le* from *gird*, and denotes the implement. *Tack-le* is that which *takes* or grasps, holding the masts, &c. firmly in their places ; from Icel. *taka*, MSwed. *taka* (mod. Swed. *taga*), to take, seize, grasp, hold, which had a much stronger sense than the mod. E. *take* ; cf. Icel. *tak*, a grasp in wrestling, *taka*, a seizing, capture ; and observe the wide application of *tackle* in the sense of implements or gear. Cf. MDu. *taeckel*, ‘a rope to drawe a boate ;’ Hexham. γ. Often derived from W. *tacl*, an instrument, tool, tackle ; but the W. word was borrowed from E. **Der.** *tackl-ing*, Rich. III, iv. 4. 233.

TACT, peculiar skill, delicate handling. (L.) Modern ; Webster gives examples from Macaulay. Todd says : ‘*Tact*, touch, an old word, long disused, but of late revived in the secondary senses of *touch*, as a masterly or eminent effort, and the power of exciting the affections.’ He then cites a passage containing ‘ sense of *tact*,’ i. e. touch, from Ross, Arcana Microcosmi (1652), p. 66.—L. *tactus*, touch.—L. *tactus*, pp. of *tangere*, to touch ; see **Tangent**. **Der.** *tact-able*, that may be touched, Massinger, Parl. of Love, ii. 1. 8, a coined word, made to rime with *tractable* ; *tact-ile*, from L. *tactilis*, tangible ; *tact-ion*, a touching, Blount.

TACTICS, the art of arranging or manœuvring forces. (Gk.) ‘ And teaches all the *tactics* ;’ Ben Jonson, Staple of News, iv. 1 (Lickfinger).—Gk. τακτικά, sb. pl., military tactics.—Gk. τακτικός, adj., fit for arranging, belonging to tactics.—Gk. τακτός, ordered, arranged ; verbal adj. from τάσσειν (<τάκ-γειν), to arrange, order. Of uncertain origin ; Curtius, ii. 328. The base is either TAK, Fick, i. 588 ; or TAG (Prellwitz). **Der.** *tactic*, adj., from Gk. τακτικός ; *tactic-i-an*, a coined word.

TADPOLE, a young frog in its first stage, having a tail. (E.) ‘ Young frogs, . . . whiles they be *tadpoles* and have little wriggling tailes ;’ Holland, tr. of Pliny, b. xxxii. c. 10. ME. *tadpolle*, Voc. 766. 20 ; *taddepol*, 569. 7. Called *bull-head* in Cotgrave ; he has : ‘*Chabot*, the little fish called a gull, bull-head, or miller's thumbe ; also the little water-vermine called a *bull-head*.’ Also : ‘ *Testard*, the pollard, or chevin fish, also the little black water-vermine called a *bull-head*.’ Observe that F. *chabot* is from L. *caput*, a head (cf. L. *capito*, a fish with a large head) ; that *testard* is from OF. *teste*, a head ; that *chevin* is from F. *chef*, a head ; and that *bull-head* contains the E. *head* ; the striking feature about the *tadpole* is that it appears nearly all head, with a little tail attached which is afterwards dropped. See Wedgwood, who adduces also E. dial. *poll-head*, Lowl. Sc. *pow-head*, a tadpole (which merely *repeat* the notion of head), E. dial. *polwiggle*, *pollywig*, a tadpole, with which we may compare *wiggle* or *waggle*, to wag the tail. β. Hence *tad-pole* = toad-poll, the *toad* that seems all *poll* ; see **Toad** and **Poll**. The former part is from AS. *tād-ige*, a toad, with loss of suffix, and shortening of *ā* before *dᵏ*.

TAEL, a Chinese weight, about 1⅓ oz. ; the chief Chinese money of account. (Malay.) Called *liang* in Chinese ; see Yule. A Malay word.—Malay *tahil*, a certain weight.

TÆNIA, a fillet, a tape-worm. (L.—Gk.) L. *taenia*.—Gk. ταινία, a band, fillet, strip.—Gk. τείνειν, to stretch. Allied to **Thin**.

TAFFEREL, TAFFRAIL, the upper part of the stern of a ship. (Du.—L.) ‘ *Tefferel*, the uppermost part, frame, or rail of a ship behind, over the poop ;’ Phillips, ed. 1706.—Du. *tafereel*, a pannel, a picture ; Hexham explains it by ‘ a painter's table or board,’ and adds the dimin. *tafereelken*, ‘ a tablet, or a small board.’ The *taffrail* is so called because it is flat like a table on the top, and sometimes ornamented with carved work ; cf. G. *täfelei*, boarded work, flooring, wainscoting. β. The Du. *tafer-eel* stands for **tafel-eel*, a dimin. from Du. *tafel*, a table ; just as G. *täfelei* is from G. *tafel*, a table. The Du. and G. *tafel* are not to be considered as Teut. words ; the MHG. form is *tavele*, OHG. *tavela*, borrowed from L. *tabula*, a table. See **Table**. ¶ The spelling *taffrail* is prob. due to confusion with E. *rail*.

TAFFETA, TAFFETY, a thin glossy silk stuff, with a wavy lustre. (F.—Ital.—Pers.) ‘ *Tafata*, a maner of sylke, *taffetas* ;’ Palsgrave. ME. *taffata*, Chaucer, C. T. 442 (A 440). *Taffata* occurs in 1324 ; Wardrobe Acct. 18 Edw. II. 24. 17, Q. R. ; see N. and Q. 8 S. i. 129.—F. *taffetas*, ‘taffata ;’ Cot.—Ital. *taffetà*, ‘ taffeta ;’ Florio.—Pers. *tāftah*, ‘ twisted, woven, a kind of silken cloth, taffeta ;’ Rich. Dict. p. 356.—Pers. *tāftan*, to twist, to spin, curl, &c. ; see Horn, § 372. See **Tapestry**.

TAG, a point of metal at the end of a lace, anything tacked on at the end of a thing. (Scand.) ‘ An aglet or *tag* of a poynt ;’ Baret, ed. 1580. ‘ Are all thy points so voide of Reasons *taggs* ?’ Gascoigne, Fruites of War, st. 61. A ‘ point ’ was a tagged lace ; cf. ‘ *Tag* of a poynt, Ferretum ;’ Levins.—Swed. *tagg*, a prickle, point, tooth ; Norw. *tagge*, a tooth, cog.+Pomeran. *tagᵧ*, a point, tack ; Low G. *takk*, a point, tooth. β. The Low G. *takk* is the same word as E. *tack*, a small nail, and G. *zacke*, a tooth, tine, prong. See **Tack**, **Tache**. **Der.** *tag*, verb ; *tag-rag*, used by Stanyhurst (tr. of Virgil, ed. Arber, p. 21) to mean ‘ to small pieces,’ but usual in the sense of ‘ every appendage and shred,’ a shortened form of *tag and rag*, as in ‘ they all came in, both *tagge and ragge*,’ Spenser, State of Ireland, Globe ed., p. 662, col. 2. So also *tag and rag*, Whitgift's Works, i. 315 (Parker Soc.). So also *tag-rag-and-bobtail*, where *bobtail* = short or bunchy tail, from *bob*, a bunch ; see **Bob**.

TAIL (1), the end of the back-bone of an animal, a hairy appendage, appendage. (E.) ME. *tail*, *tayl*, Chaucer, C. T. 3876 (A 3878). AS. *tægl*, *tægel*, a tail, Grein, ii. 523.+Icel. *tagl*, Swed. *tagel*, hair of the tail or mane ; Goth. *tagl*, hair, Mark, i. 6 ; G. *zagel*, a tail. β. Root uncertain ; it has been compared with Skt. *daçā*, the fringe of a garment. **Der.** *tail-piece*, a piece or small drawing at the tail or end of a chapter or book. Also *tail-ed*, Rich. Coer de Lion, l. 1868.

TAIL (2), the term applied to an estate which is limited to certain heirs. (F. – L.) Better spelt *taille*. 'This limitation, or *taille*, is either general or special;' Cowel, in Todd's Johnson; see the whole article. – F. *taille*, 'a cutting,' &c.; Cot.; see **Tally**.

TAILOR, one who cuts out and makes cloth garments. (F. –L.) Properly 'a cutter.' ME. *tailor, taylor*, Rob. of Glouc. p. 313, l. 6394. – OF. *tailleor*, later *tailleur*, 'a cutter;' Cot. – F. *tailler*, to cut; cf. F. *taille*, an incision, a slitting. – Late L. *tāleāre*, to cut; cf. *tālea*, a thin rod, stick, also a cutting, slip, layer (an agricultural word). See Diez, who cites from Nonius, 4. 473; '*taleas* scissiones lignorum vel præsegmina Varro dicit de re rust. lib. I.; nam etiam nunc rustica voce *intertaleare* dicitur dividere vel exscindere ramum.' This verb *intertaleare* is preserved in the Span. *entre.allar*, to slash. Der. *tailor-ing*. And see *tally, de-tail, en-tail, re-tail*.

TAINT, a tinge, dye, stain, blemish. (F. – L.) In Shak. Macb. iv. 3. 124. Cf. ME. *taint, taynt*, a disease in hawks; Book of St. Albans, fol. b 2, back. – F. *teint*; MF. *teinct*, 'a tincture, die, stain;' Cot. – F. *teint*, pp. of *teindre*, 'to stain,' id. – L. *tingere*; see **Tinge**. Der. *taint*, vb., Romeo, i. 4. 76. ¶ Perhaps confused with *attaint*, from *tangere*.

TAKE, to lay hold of, seize, grasp, get. (Scand.) ME. *taken*, pt. t. *tok*, pp. *taken*, Chaucer, C. T. 572 (A 570); pp. *takē*, id. 2649 (A 2647). Late AS. *taken*, A. S. Chron. an. 1127. Not a true AS. word, but borrowed from Norse. – Icel. *taka*, pt. t. *tōk*, pp. *tekinn*, to lay hold of, seize, grasp (a very common word); Swed. *taga*, MSwed. *taka*; Dan. *tage*.✝Goth. *tēkan*, pt. t. *taitōk*, pp. *tēkans*, to touch. Der. *tak-ing, tak-ing-ly*. Allied words are *tack, tache, tag, tack-le, attach, at-tack, de-tach*.

TALC, a mineral occurring in thin flakes. (F. – Span. – Arab.) 'Oil of *talc*;' Ben Jonson, Epigram to the Small-pox; Underwoods, ii. 11. And see Nares. – F. *talc* (Cot.). – Span. *talco*. – Arab. *ṭalq*, 'talc, mica;' Rich. Dict. p. 974.

TALE, a number, reckoning, narrative. (E.) ME. *tale*; see Chaucer, Cant. *Tales*. AS. *tæl*, a number, *talu*, a narrative; Grein, ii. 521.✝Du. *taal*, language, tongue, speech; Icel. *tal*, talk, a tale; *tala*, a number, a speech; Dan. *tale*, speech; Swed. *tal*, speech, number; G. *zahl*, number; OHG. *zala*. It is probable that Goth. *untals*, uninstructed, *talzjan*, to instruct, are related words. Der. *tale-bear-ing, tale-bear-er, tell-tale* (Sherwood's Index to Cotgrave has 'a *tale-bearer* or *tell-tale*'); *tale-tell-er*, P. Plowman, B. xx. 297. Also *tell*, q.v., *talk*, q.v.

TALENT, a weight or sum of money, natural gift or ability, inclination. (F. – L. – Gk.) See Trench, Study of Words, and Select Glossary. We derive the sense of ability from the parable in Matt. xxv. our *talents* being gifts of God. The ME. *talent* occurs in the sense of will or inclination, from the figure of the inclination or tilting of a balance. ME. *talent*; whence *mal-talent*, ill-will, Rom. of the Rose, 273, 330; and see Wyclif, Matt. xxv. 15; King Alisaunder, 1280. – F. *talent*, 'a talent in mony; also will, desire, an earnest humour unto;' Cot. – L. *talentum*. – Gk. τάλαντον, a balance; a weight, weight or sum of money, talent. Named from the notion of lifting and weighing; allied to τάλας (stem ταλαντ-), bearing, enduring, L. *toll-ere*, to lift, sustain, Skt. *tul*, to lift, weigh, *tulana-*, lifting, *tulā*, a balance, weight. All from √TEL, to lift. See **Tolerate**. Der. *talent-ed*, endued with talent, added by Todd to Johnson, with the remark that the word is old; he gives a quotation from Archbp. Abbot, in Rushworth's Collections, p. 449; which book first appeared between 1659 and 1701, and treats of matters from 1618-1648; see an excellent note on *talented* in Modern English, by F. Hall, p. 70. Brugmann, i. § 580.

TALISMAN, a spell. (Span. – Arab. – Gk.) 'In magic, *talisman*, and cabal;' Butler, Hudibras, pt. i. c. 1. l. 530. The F. is also *talisman*, but is a late word; both F. and E. words were prob. taken directly from Spanish. – Span. *talisman*, a magical character; also a doctor of the Mohammedan law, in which sense Littré notes its use in French also. – Arab. *ṭilsamān*, properly the pl. of *ṭilsam*, or *ṭilism*, 'a talisman or magical image, upon which, under a certain horoscope, are engraved mystical characters, as charms against enchantment;' Rich. Dict. p. 974. – Gk. τέλεσμα, a payment; used in Late Gk. to mean initiation or mystery (Devic); cf. τελεσμός, an accomplishment or completion. – Gk. τελέειν, to accomplish, fulfil, complete, end; also, to pay. – Gk. τέλος, end, completion; also, initiation into a mystery; whence the sense of the derived sb. τέλεσμα. Der. *talisman-ic*.

TALK, to discourse. (E.) ME. *talken*, Wyclif, Luke, xxiv. 15; and much earlier, in St. Marharete, p. 13, Ancren Riwle, p. 422. Cf. EFries. *talken*, to talk; *talke*, a short tale. We may note that the Harl. MS. actually has *talken* in Chaucer, C. T., where the Six-text (A 772) has *talen* in all the MSS. And we may compare the Low G. *taalke*, (1) a jackdaw, (2) a talkative woman. β. Apparently

extended (like *wal-k*, q.v.) from AS. *tal-*, as in *tal-u*, a tale, *tal-ian*, to account, with suffix *-k*, which seems to give a frequentative force. Cf. Icel. *tal-a*, Swed. *tal-a*, Dan. *tal-e*, to talk. See **Tale**. So also AS. *tam-c-ian*, to tame (Napier); from *tam*, tame. Der. *talk-er*; *talk-at-ive*, a strangely coined word, spelt *talcatife* in The Craft of Lovers, st. 4, pr. in Chaucer's Works, ed. 1561, fol. 341. Hence *talk-at-ive-ly*, *-ness*.

TALL, high in stature, lofty. (E. *or* C.) Two distinct words appear with this spelling: (1) *tall*, in the sense of 'serviceable,' or 'valiant,' which is obsolescent; and (2) *tall*, in the sense of 'high in stature.' 1. The former is English; see Trench, Select Glossary. ME. *tal*. '*Tal*, or semely, *Decens, elegans*;' Prompt. Parv. 'So humble and *talle*;' Chaucer, Compl. of Mars, l. 38, where the sense appears to be 'obedient or docile, or obsequious.' In old plays it means 'valiant, fine, bold, great;' Halliwell. In the Plowman's Tale, st. 3, *untall* seems to mean 'poorly clad.' Allied to AS. *ge-tal*, quick, prompt; AS. *-tæl*, as in *lēof-tæl*, friendly. Also to OHG. *gi-zal*, quick; and further, to Goth. *tals*, only used in the comp. *un-tals*, indocile, uninstructed. Note also the forms *un-tala*, *un-tale*, bad, used to gloss *mali* in the Northumb. Gospels, Matt. xxvii. 23. 2. Perhaps, in the sense of 'lofty,' the word may be Celtic. We find *tal*, tall, high, both in W. and Cornish; Williams instances *tal carn*, the high rock, in St. Allen. It is remarkable that the Irish *talla* means 'meet, fit, proper, just.' Further light is desired as to this difficult word. Der. *tall-ness*.

TALLAGE, a tribute; see **Tally**.

TALLOW, fat of animals melted. (E.) ME. *talgh*, Reliquiæ Antiq. i. 53; *talwȝ*, Eng. Gilds, p. 359, l. 11; *talwgh*, Rich. Coer de Lion, 1552. Cf. EFries. *talg, tallig*, tallow.✝MDu. *talgh, talch*, tallow, Hexham; mod. Du. *talk*, Low G. *talg*; Dan. and Swed. *talg*; Icel. *tōlgr*, also *tōlg, tōlk*. The G. *talg* is borrowed from Low G. β. There is an AS. *telg, tælg*, a stain, dye, but its connexion with *tallow* is very doubtful. If *tallow* meant 'hardened' fat, cf. Goth. *tulgus*, steadfast, firm. See **Stearine**.

TALLY, a stick cut or notched so as to match another stick, used for keeping accounts; an exact match. (F. – L.) ME. *taille*, Chaucer, C. T. 572 (A 570); whence *taillen*, verb, to score on a tally, P. Plowman, B. v. 429. – F. *taille*, 'a notch, nick, incision, notching, nicking; . . . also, a tally, or score kept on a piece of wood;' Cot. – F. *tailler*, to cut. – Late L. *tāleāre*, to cut; cf. L. *tālea*, a slip of wood; see **Tailor**. It is probable that the final *-y* in *tall-y* is due to the frequent use of the F. pp. *taillé*, 'cut, nicked, notched,' as applied to the piece of wood scored, in place of the sb. *taille*. The final *-y* in *lev-y, jur-y, pun-y* is likewise due to the F. pp. suffix. Der. *tally*, verb; *tally-shop*. Also *tallage*, a tribute; ME. *taylage*, Chaucer, The Former Age, 54; OF. *taillage* (Godefroy); from F. *tailler*, to cut, 'also, to levy tributes on,' Cot. And see *en-tail, de-tail, tail-or*.

TALMUD, the body of Hebrew laws, with comments. (Chaldee.) See *Talmud* in Index to Parker Society. Spelt *talmud, thalmud* in Blount's Gloss., ed. 1674; *talmud* in Minsheu, ed. 1627; *thalmud* in Cotgrave. – Chaldee *talmūd*, instruction, doctrine; cf. Heb. *talmīd*, a disciple, scholar; from *lāmad*, to learn, *limmad*, to teach.

TALON, the claw of a bird of prey. (F. – L.) Spelt *talant* in Palsgrave (with excrescent *t* after *n*). He gives: '*Talant* of a byrde, the hynder clawe, *talon*.' Thus the *talon* was particularly used of the bird's hind claw. ME. *talon*, Allit. Romance of Alexander, 5454; *taloun*, Mandeville's Travels, in Spec. of Early English, part II., p. 174, l. 130. – F. *talon*, 'a heel;' Cot. – Late L. *tālōnem*, acc. of *tālo*, a heel. – L. *tālus*, heel.

TAMANDUA, an ant-eater. (Brazil.) From Guarani *tamàn-duá* (where *à* is nasal); see Granada, Vocabulario Rioplatense.

TAMARIND, the fruit of an E. Indian tree. (F. – Span. – Arab. *and* Pers.) Spelt *tamarinde* in Sir T. Elyot, Castel of Helth, b. iii. c. 6. – MF. *tamarind*, 'a small, soft, and dark-red Indian date;' Cot. Also *tamarinde*, 'the Indian date-tree;' id. – Span. *tamarindo*. (Cf. Ital. *tamarindo*; Florio gives the Ital. pl. *tamarindi*, and Minsheu the Span. pl. *tamarindos*, without mention of the sing. form.) – Arab. *tamr*, a ripe date, a dry or preserved date; and *Hind*, India; whence *tamr'ul Hind*, a tamarind, lit. date of India; Rich. Dict. pp. 446, 1691. The Arab. *tamr* is allied to Heb. *tāmār*, a palm-tree, occurring in the Bible as *Tamar*, a proper name. The word *Hind* is borrowed from Persian (which turns initial *s* into *h*), and is derived from Skt. *sindhu-*, the river Indus; see **Indigo**.

TAMARISK, the name of a tree. (L.) Spelt *tamariske* in Minsheu, ed. 1627. Cf. MF. *tamaris*, 'tamarisk,' in Cot.; but the E. word keeps the *k*. – L. *tamariscus*, also *tamarix, tamaricē*, a tamarisk. (The Gk. name is μυρίκη.) Hardly a L. word; perhaps due to, or connected with Skt. *tamālaka-s, tamāla-s*, a tree with a dark bark; allied to *tamas*, darkness; Fick, i. 593. See **Dim**.

TAMBOUR, a small drum-like circular frame, for embroidering.

(F.—Span.—Arab.—Pers.?) In Todd's Johnson.—F. *tambour*, a drum, a tambour; *broder au tambour*, to do tambour-work; Hamilton. See further under **Tabour.** Der. *tambour-ine*, spelt *tamburin* in Spenser, Shep. Kalendar, June, l. 59, from F. *tambourin*, a tabor (Hamilton), dimin. of F. *tambour*.

TAME, subdued, made gentle, domesticated. (E.) ME. *tame*, Wyclif, Mark, v. 4. AS. *tam*, Matt. xxi. 5; whence *temian*, vb., to tame, in Ælfric's Colloquy (section on the Fowler), in Voc. p. 95. +Du. *tam*; Icel. *tamr*; Swed. and Dan. *tam*; G. *zahm*. Cf. Goth. *gatamjan*, to tame; a causal verb. β. All from Teut. type **tamoz*, tame. Allied to Skt. *dam*, to be tame, also to tame, Gk. δαμάειν, L. *domāre*, to tame. Der. *tame*, vb.; *tame-ly, -ness*; *tam-er*, *tam-able*; also (from same root) *daunt*, q.v., *in-dom-it-able*.

TAMMY, the same as **Stamin,** q.v. See *Tamine* in Nares.

TAMPER, to meddle, practise upon, play with. (F.—L.) 'You have been *tampering*, any time these three days Thus to disgrace me;' Beaum. and Fletcher, The Captain, iv. 2 (Jacomo). The same word as *temper*, but used in a bad sense; to *temper* is to moderate, allay by influence, but is here made to mean to interfere with, to influence in a bad way. Prob. Southern F. Mistral gives *tampera* as the Limousin form of mod. Prov. *tempera*, vb., to temper. Godefroy has *tamprure* as a variant of OF. *tempreure*, moderation. See **Temper.** Doublet, *temper*.

TAMPION, a kind of plug. (F.—Teut.) '*Tampyon* for a gon [gun], *tampon*;' Palsgrave.—F. *tampon*, 'a bung or stopple;' Cot. A nasalised form of *tapon*, 'a bung or stopple;' id. Formed with suffix *-on* (L. *-ōnem*) from OF. *tampe, tape*, a bung. Cotgr. gives the Picard vb. *taper* (or *tapper*), 'to bung, or stop with a bung.'—Du. *tap*, 'a bunge or a stopple,' Hexham; Low G. *tappe*, a tap, bung. See **Tap** (2).

TAN, oak-bark or other bark used for converting hides into leather. (F.—G.) The sb. is, etymologically, the orig. word, but is rarely seen in books; Levins has only *tan* as a verb. Rich. quotes 'skinnes in *tan-tubs*' from Hakluyt's Voyages, vol. iii. p. 104. The ME. *tannen*, verb, to tan, occurs in Eng. Gilds, p. 358, l. 16, and the sb. *tanner* is common, as in P. Plowman, C. i. 223, &c.—F. *tan*, 'the bark of a young oak, wherewith leather is tanned;' Cot. Cf. Bret. *tann*, an oak, occasionally used (but rarely) with the sense of tan; Legonidec.—G. *tanne*, a fir-tree; the names of *oak* and *fir* seem to have been confused; the OHG. *tanna* meant both 'fir' and 'oak' (Kluge). A High G. form; cf. Du. *den*, a fir-tree, MDu. *dan*, 'abies,' in Mone, Quellen, p. 302; Low G. *danne*, a fir-tree (Lübben). Cf. Skt. *dhanva*, a bow. Der. *tan*, verb, as above; *tann-er*; *tann-er-y*, from F. *tannerie*, 'tanning, also a tan-house,' Cot. Also *tann-ic*, a coined word; *tann-in*, F. *tanin* (Hamilton), a coined word; *tan-ling*, one scorched by the sun, Cymb. iv. 4. 29. Also *tawn-y*, q.v. Also *tan*, to beat; Norm. dial. *tanner la peau*, to tan one's skin; Dubois.

TANDEM, applied to two horses harnessed one before the other instead of side by side. (L.) So called because harnessed *at length*, by a pun upon the word in university slang Latin.—L. *tandem*, at length.—L. *tam*, so, so far; and suffix *-dem*, allied to *-dam* in *qui-dam*.

TANG (1), a strong or offensive taste, esp. of something extraneous. (Scand.) 'It is said of the best oyl that it hath no tast, that is, no *tang*, but the natural gust of oyl therein;' Fuller, Worthies, England (R.). ME. *tang*, a sting; Cath. Angl. (1483). See **Tang** (2). So also ME. *tongge*, 'scharpenesse of lycure in tastynge;' Prompt. Parv. Cf. MDu. *tanger*, 'sharpe, or tart upon the tongue;' *tangere kaese*, tart or byting cheese;' Hexham. The lit. sense of *tanger* is 'pinching;' from Du. *tang*, a pair of tóngs, pincers, nippers; cognate with E. *tongs*. See E. D. D. Cf. MHG. *zanger*, sharp, sharp-tasted; AS. *ge-tingan*, to press hard upon (pt. t. *ge-tang*).

TANG (2), the part of a knife which goes into the haft, the tongue of a buckle, the prong of a fork. (Scand.) See Halliwell; who cites: 'A *tange* of a knyfe, *piramus*;' see Cath. Angl. (1483). It also means a bee's sting. '*Pugio*, a tange;' Voc. 703. 27. '*Tongge* of a bee, *Aculeus*; *Tongge* of a knyfe, *Pirasmus*;' Prompt. Parv.— Icel. *tangi*, a spit or projection of land; the pointed end by which the blade of a knife is driven into the handle, allied to *töng* (gen. *tangar*), a smith's tongs; *tengja*, to fasten. So called because it is the part *nipped* and held fast by the handle; so the *tongue* of a buckle (corrupted from *tang* of a buckle) *nips* and holds fast the strap; the bee's sting *nips* or stings. The form *tong* in the Prompt. Parv. answers to the sing. of E. *tongs*. See **Tongs.**

TANG (3), to make a shrill sound. (E.) Shak. has it both as sb. and verb. 'A tongue with a *tang*,' i. e. with a shrill sound, Temp. ii. 2. 52. 'Let thy tongue *tang*,' i. e. ring out; Tw. Nt. ii. 5. 163, iii. 4. 78. An imitative word, allied to *ting*, whence the frequentative *tingle*; also to *tink*, whence the frequent. *tinkle*. Cf. Prov. E. *ting-tang*, the saints-bell; *tingle-tangle*, a small bell, which

occurs in Randolph's Amintas (1640); Halliwell. So also MDu. *tinge-tangen*, to tinkle; Hexham. Cf. MF. *tantan* (= *tang-tang*), 'the bell that hangs about the neck of a cow;' Cot. See **Tingle, Tinker, Twang.**

TANG (4), sea-weed; see **Tangle.**

TANGENT, a line which meets a circle, and, being produced, does not cut it. (L.) In Blount's Gloss., ed. 1674.—L. *tangent-*, touching, stem of pres. part. of *tangere* (base *tag-*), to touch; pp. *tactus*.+Gk. base ταγ-, to touch, seen in τεταγών, taking. Der. *tangent-i-al*, in the direction of the tangent, Tatler, no. 43; *tangenc-y*; also (from pp. *tactus*) *tact*. And see *tang-ible, task, taste, tax*. Also *attain, attainder, attaint, con-tact, con-tagion, con-taminate, con-tiguous, con-tingent, entire, in-teger, redintegration.*

TANGIBLE, perceptible by the touch, that can be realised. (F.—L.) In Cotgrave.—F. *tangible*, 'tangible;' Cot.—L. *tangibilis*, touchable; formed with suffix *-bilis* from *tangere*, to touch; see **Tangent.** Der. *tangibl-y, tangibili-ty.*

TANGLE, to interweave, knot together confusedly, ensnare. (Scand.) 'I *tangell* thynges so togyther that they can nat well be parted asonder, *Jembrouille*;' Palsgrave. Levins has the comp. *entangle*. To *tangle* is 'to keep twisting together like sea-weed;' a frequentative verb from *tang*, sb. (also *tangle*, sb.), sea-weed, a Northern word. Cf. *tangle*, a stalk of sea-weed; in Leslie's Hist. of Scotland, i. 62 (1596; S. T. S.).—Dan. *tang*, Swed. *tång*, Icel. *þang*, kelp or bladder-wrack, a kind of sea-weed; whence the idea of confused heap. We also find the dimin. Icel. *þöngull*, sea-weed; Norw. *tongul*, a tangle-stalk. Cf. Norman dialect *tangon* (a Norse word), explained by Métivier as *Fucus flagelliformis*. (The G. *tang*, sea-weed, was borrowed from Scand.; for it begins with *t*, not *d*.) All from Teut. base **thang-*; see **Tight.** β. We also find *tangle* in the sense of sea-weed (Halliwell); and the verb to *tangle* may have been made directly from it. It makes no great difference; cf. Icel. *þöngull*, as above; Norw. *tengel*, a stalk of sea-weed. Der. *tangle*, sb., which seems to be a later word than the verb, Milton, P. L. ix. 632; *en-tangle*, q. v.

TANIST, a presumptive heir to a prince. (Irish.) Spelt *tanistih* in Spenser, View of Ireland, Globe ed., p. 611.—Irish *tanaiste*, the presumptive or apparent heir to a prince.—OIrish *tanaise*, second in rank. See Macbain. Der. *tanist-ry*, a coined word, to signify the custom of electing a *tanist*; also in Spenser, as above.

TANK, a large cistern. (Port.—L.) In Sir T. Herbert, Travels, ed. 1665, p. 66; and at p. 43 in another edition (Todd). Also in Dryden, Don Sebastian, ii. 2. The same word as **Stank,** q. v. The form *tank* is Portuguese, which is the only Romance language that drops the initial *s*.—Port. *tanque*, a tank, pond; the same word as Span. *estanque*, OF. *estanc*, Prov. *estanc*, *stanc*, a pond, dam of water; from Port. and Span. *estancar*, to stanch, stop.—Late L. *stancāre*, to stanch. Ultimately from L. *stagnum*, a pool; see **Stank, Stanch, Stagnant.** ¶ See *Tank* in Yule.

TANKARD, a large vessel for holding drink. (F.—Teut.) ME. *tankard*, used to translate L. *amphora*, Voc. 563. 28; also in Lydgate, Ballad of Jack Hare, st. 2; and in Prompt. Parv.—MF. *tanquard*, 'a tankard, in Rabelais;' Cot. Cf. MDu. *tanckaert*, 'a wodden [wooden] tankard,' Hexham; a word borrowed from F. β. The suffix *-ard* is common in OF., showing that the word was really, at some time, French. [Irish *tancard* must have been borrowed from E.] Prob. from Swed. *stånka*, 'a large wooden can' (Widegren), 'a tankard' (Öman); with F. suffix *-ard*. The Swed. *stånka* is a dimin. of *stånna*, *stånda*, a vat (Rietz); note the *aa* in Norw. *taankar* (also *tankar*), an oil-can. Cf. also Westphal. *stande*, *stanne*, a vessel broader at the bottom (Woeste); Low G. *stande* (corruptly, *stanne*), the same; whence E. *standard*, a tankard, a standing bowl. 'Frolic, my lords, and let the *standards* walk;' Greene, A Looking-glass, ed. Dyce, p. 141. See Notes on E. Etym., p. 290. All from the vb. *to stand*.

TANSY, a tall plant, with small yellow flowers. (F.—Late L. —Gk.) ME. *tansaye*, a tansy-bed; 'Hoc tansetum, *tansaye*,' Voc. 712. 33. 'Tansey, an herbe, *tanasie*,' Palsgrave.—OF. *tanasie*, as in Palsgrave, later *tanaisie*, 'the herb tansie;' Cot. Other forms are OF. *athanasie*, Cot.; MItal. *atanasia*, 'the herb tansie,' Florio; Port. *atanasia, athanasia.* [Late L. *tanacetum* (spelt *tansetum* above) means properly 'a bed of tansy;' as remarked in Prior, Popular Names of British Plants.] The OF. *athanasie*, MItal. *atanasia*, and Port. *atanasia, athanasia*, answer to a L. form *athanasia*, which is only the Gk. ἀθανασία, immortality, in Latin spelling. β. Prior says that *athanasia* was 'the name under which it was sold in the shops in Lyte's time.' The plant is bitter and aromatic, and was (and is) used in medicine, whence, probably, the name. Prior thinks there is a reference to 'Lucian's Dialogues of the Gods, no. iv, where Jupiter, speaking of Ganymede, says to Mercury, ἄπαγε αὐτὸν, ὦ Ἑρμῆ, καὶ πιόντα τῆς ἀθανασίας ἄγε οἰνοχοήσοντα ἡμῖν, take him away, and when he has drunk of immortality, bring him back as cupbearer to us : the ἀθανασία here has been misunderstood, like ἀμβροσία in other passages, for some special plant.' Cf. MItal. *atanato*, 'the rose campion,' Florio; lit. 'the immortal.' γ. The Gk. ἀθανασία is allied to ἀθάνατος, immortal; from ά, negative prefix, and θανεῖν, 2 aor. of θνήσκειν, to die. See Lyte's Dodoens, bk. i. c. 10.

TANTALISE, to tease or torment, by offering something that is just out of reach and is kept so. (Gk.) 'What greater plague can hell itself devise, Than to be willing thus to *tantalize*?' Answer to Ben Jonson's Ode (*Come leave the loathed Stage*), by T. Randolph, st. 2; printed in Jonson's Works, after the play of The New Inn. Formed with the suffix -*ise* (F. -*iser*, L. -*izāre*, Gk. -ιζειν) from the proper name *Tantal-us*, Gk. Τάνταλος, in allusion to his story. The fable was that he was placed up to his chin in water, which fled from his lips whenever he desired to drink. This myth perhaps relates to the sun, which evaporates water, but remains, as it were, unsated. Allied to τανταλεύειν, to sway to and fro, and to τάλ-αντον, a balance; see **Talent. Der.** *tantal-ism* (with F. suffix -*isme*<L. -*isma*<Gk. -ισμα), Beaum. and Fletcher, Wit at Several Weapons, act ii. sc. 2, l. 10 from end.

TANTAMOUNT, amounting to as much, equal. (F. — L.) Rich. points out, by 2 quotations from Bp. Taylor, Episcopacy Asserted, §§ 9 and 31, that it was first used as a *verb*; which agrees with the fact that *amount* was properly at first a verb. It meant 'to amount to as much.' — AF. *tant amunter*, to amount to as much, Yearbooks of Edw. I., 1292-3, p. 31; cf. F. *tant*, so much, as much; and E. **Amount**, q. v. β. The F. *tant* is from L. *tantum*, neut. of *tantus*, so great; formed from pronominal base *to*-, he, the, so as to answer to *quantus*, from the base *quo*-, who. See **The**.

TAP (1), to strike or knock gently. (F. — Teut.) ME. *tappen*, to tap; the imperative appears as *tep* (for *tap*), Ancren Riwle, p. 296, l. 4; cf. *tappe*, sb., a tap, Gawain and the Grene Knight, 2357. — F. *taper, tapper*, 'to tap, strike, hit, bob, clap;' Cot. Of Teut. origin; Low G. (and G.) *tappen*, to grope, to fumble, EFries. *tappen*, to tap, *tap*, a light blow. So also Icel. *tapsa*, to tap. Prob. of imitative origin; cf. Russ. *topate*, to stamp with the foot; Malay *tabah*, to beat out corn, *tapuk*, to slap, pat, dab (Marsden's Dict. pp. 69, 77); Arab. *tabl*, a drum; E. *dub-a-dub*, noise of a drum, E. *dab*, a pat. **Der.** *tap*, sb. And see *tip* (2).

TAP (2), a short pipe through which liquor is drawn from a cask, a plug to stop a hole in a cask. (E.) ME. *tappe*, Chaucer, C. T. 3890. AS. *tæppa*, a tap (Toller); whence *tæppere*, one who taps casks; 'Caupo, tabernarius, *tæppere*,' Voc. 129. 9.+Du. *tap*, sb., whence *tappen*, verb; Icel. *tappi*, sb., *tappa*, vb.; Dan. *tap*, sb., *tappe*, vb.; Swed. *tapp*, a tap, handful, wisp, whence *tappa*, vb.; G. *zapfen*, sb. and vb.; OHG. *zapho*, sb. β. Teut. type *tappon-*. The Swed. *tapp* means a wisp, handful, and G. *zapfen* is bung, stopple. Prob. the orig. idea (as Wedgwood suggests) was a bunch of some material to stop a hole with, a tuft of something. We may connect it, as Fick does, with E. *top*, G. *zopf*; the G. *zopf* means a top of a tree, a weft or tuft of hair, a 'pig-tail;' and the Icel. *toppr* means, first of all, a tuft or lock of hair. **Der.** *tap*, vb., Merry Wives, i. 3. 11; *tap-room*; *tap-root*, a root like a tap, i. e. conical, cf. G. *zapfen*, a tap, cone of a fir, *zapfenwurzel*, a tap-root. Also *tapster*, ME. *tapstere*, Chaucer, C. T. 241, AS. *tæppestre*, Ælfric's Grammar, ed. Zupitza, p. 36, l. 13, a fem. form of AS. *tæppere*, a tapper, as above; for the suffix -*ster*, see **Spinster**. Also *tampion*, q. v. And see **Tip** (1).

TAPE, a narrow band or fillet of woven work, used for strings, &c. (L. — Gk.) ME. *tape*, Chaucer, C. T. 3241; also *tappe*. 'Hec tenea, *tappe*;' in a list of ornaments, Voc. 655. 15. AS. *tæppe*, a tape, fillet. 'Tenia, *tæppan vel dol-smeltas*,' where *tæppan* is a pl. form; Voc. 107. 33. The orig. sense may have been 'a strip of stuff;' it is closely allied to AS. *tæppet*, a tippet, ME. *tapet*, a piece of tapestry; and the use of the pl. *tæppan* is suggestive of strips of stuff or cloth. Not an E. word, but borrowed from L. *tapēte*, cloth, hangings, tapestry, a word borrowed from Greek. See **Tapestry, Tippet**. In like manner we find OHG. *tepih, teppi* (mod. G. *teppich*) tapestry, with the same sense as OHG. *tepid*, from the same L. word. **Der.** *tape-worm*.

TAPER (1), a small wax-candle. (E.) ME. *taper*, Rob. of Glouc., p. 456, l. 9350. AS. *tapor, taper*, a taper; Voc. 267. 12; 202. 35. Cf. Irish *tapar*, a taper; W. *tampr*, a taper, torch.

TAPER (2), long and slender. (E.) 'Her *taper* fingers;' Dryden, tr. of Ovid, Metam. bk. i. l. 676. Here the fingers are likened to *tapers* or small wax-candles; and the word is nothing but a substitution for *taper-like*. This appears more clearly from the use of *taper-wise*, i. e. in the form of a taper, in Holland's tr. of Pliny, b. xvi. c. 16: 'the French box [box-tree] . . . groweth *taper-wise*, sharp pointed in the top, and runneth vp to more than ordinarie height.' As wax tapers were sometimes made smaller towards the top, the

word *taper* meant growing smaller towards the top, not truly cylindrical; whence the adj. *tapering* with the sense of *taper-like*, and finally the verb to *taper*. Note also '*tapering* top' in Pitt, tr. of Virgil, Æn. bk. v. l. 489 of L. text. **Der.** *taper-ing, taper*, vb.

TAPESTRY, a kind of carpet-work, with wrought figures, esp. used for decorating walls. (F. — L. — Gk.) 'A faire and pleasaunt lodginge, hanged with riche Aresse or *tapestrie*;' Sir T. Elyot, The Governour, b. iii. c. 2. § 3. Lydgate has *tapcery*; Minor Poems, p. 6. *Tapestrye* is a contraction of *tapisserye*; Palsgrave gives: '*Tappysserye* worke, *tapisserie*.' — F. *tapisserie*, 'tapistry;' Cot. — F. *tapisser*, 'to furnish with tapistry;' id. — F. *tapis*, 'tapistry hangings;' id. (Cf. Span. *tapiz*, tapestry, *tapete*, small floor-carpet; Ital. *tappeto*, a carpet, *tappezzare*, to hang with tapestry; *tappezzeria*, tapestry.) — Late L. *tapētium*, tapestry (Körting); cf. *tapēte*, cloth, hangings. — Gk. ταπήτιον, dimin. of τάπης, a carpet, woollen rug. Cf. Pers. *tabastah*, a fringed carpet or cushion, Rich. Dict., p. 362; *tābīdan*, to spin; *tāftah*, taffeta; see **Taffeta**. Horn, § 372. Thus the Gk. word is prob. of Pers. origin. See also **Tape, Tippet. Der.** We say 'on the *tapis*;' from F. *tapis*, carpet.

TAPIOCA, the glutinous and granular substance obtained from the roots of the Cassava plant of Brazil. (Port. — Brazilian.) Not in Todd's Johnson. 'The fecula or flour [of the cassava] . . is termed *mouchaco* in Brazil. . . . When it is prepared by drying on hot plates, it becomes granular, and is called *tapioca*;' Eng. Cyclopædia, art. *Tapioca.* — Port. *tapioca.* — Brazilian *tipioka*, 'the Tupi-Guarani [Brazilian] name of the poisonous juice which issues from the root of the *manioc* [cassava] when pressed;' Littré. [He refers to Burton, ii. 39, who follows The Voyage to Brazil of the Prince de Wied-Neuwied, i. 116.] β. The Tupi (native Brazilian) *tipi-ōka* means 'dregs squeezed out;' from *tipi*, 'residue, dregs,' and the verbal root *og*, *ōk*, to take by force, pluck, pull, hence also, to squeeze (Cavalcanti). See Notes on E. Etym., p. 340.

TAPIR, an animal with a short proboscis, found in S. America. (Brazilian.) Called the *tapir* or *anta* in a tr. of Buffon's Nat. Hist., London, 1792, i. 250; where the animal is said to be a native of Brazil, Paraguay, and Guiana. — Brazilian *tapira, tapȳra*, a tapir. See Notes on E. Etym., p. 340.

TAR, a resinous substance of a dark colour, obtained from pine-trees. (E.) ME. *terre*, Prompt. Parv.; spelt *tarre*, P. Plowman, C. x. 262. AS. *teoru*, tar; the dat. *teorwe* occurs in A. S. Leechdoms, ii. 132, l. 5; also spelt *teru* in a gloss (Bosworth); also *tyrwa*, Gen. vi. 14; Exod. ii. 3. We also find the comp. *scip-teora, -teara, -tara, -tera*, ship-tar (Toller).+Du. *teer*; Icel. *tjara*; Dan. *tjære*; Swed. *tjära*. And cf. G. *theer*, prob. borrowed from Low G. *tär* or Du. *teer*. [We find also Irish *tearr*, borrowed from E.; as the word is certainly Teutonic.] β. We also find Icel. *tyri, tyrfi*, a resinous fir-tree; whence *tyrviðr, tyrvitrē*, with the sense of 'tar-wood.' Allied to Lithuan. *darwa, derwa*, resinous wood, particularly the resinous parts of the fir-tree that easily burn (Nesselmann); and this is allied to Russ. *drevo*, a tree, *derevo*, a tree, wood, timber, W. *derw*, an oak-tree, and E. **Tree**, q. v. γ. Thus the orig. sense was simply 'tree' or 'wood,' esp. resinous wood, as most in request for firing; hence the resin or tar itself. **Der.** *tarr-y*; also *tar-pauling*, q. v.

TAR (2), a sailor; in Swift's Poems, To the Earl of Peterborow, st. 11. It is simply short for **Tarpauling**, q. v.

TARANTELLA, the name of a dance. (Ital.) Both Ital. *tarantella*, the dance, and Ital. *tarantola*, a tarantula or large spider, derive their names from *Taranto*, a town in S. Italy (L. *Tarentum*).

TARAXACUM, the dandelion. (Arab.) '*Taraxacum* or *Taraxacon*, the herb dandelion or sow-thistle;' Phillips, ed. 1706. The common dandelion is *Leontodon taraxacum*. The etymology of this strange word is given by Devic, Supp. to Littré. He shows that it is not Greek, but Arabic or Persian. We find Pers. *tarkhashgūn*, wild endive; Rich. Dict. p. 967; but Devic says he can only find, in Razi, the statement that 'the *tarashaqūq* is like succory but more efficacious,' where he thinks we evidently ought to read *tarashaqūn*, and to explain it by dandelion or wild succory. In Gerard of Cremona he finds Arab. *tarasacon*, explained as a kind of succory; and a chapter on *taraxacon* in a Latin edition of Avicenna, Basle, 1563, p. 312.

TARBOOSH, a round cap much worn by Arabs and Turks. (Arab. — Pers.) Arab. *tarbūsh*, a kind of red cap (Devic). Devic takes it to be of Pers. origin. — Pers. *sar-pōsh*, a head-dress; properly, for women. — Pers. *sar*, head; *pōsh*, a cover; see Rich. Dict., pp. 340, 818, 822.

TARDY, slow, sluggish, late. (F. — L.) In Shak. As You Like It, iv. 1. 51. — F. *tardif*, 'tardy,' Cot. Cf. Ital. *tardivo*, tardy. These forms correspond to Late L. *tardīuus*, formed with suffix -*īuus* from L. *tard-us*, slow. **Der.** *tardi-ly, -ness*; (from L. *tardus*) *re-tard*.

TARE (1), a plant like the vetch. (E.) ME. *tare*, Chaucer, C. T.

3998 (A 4000); pl. *taris*, i. e. darnel, Wyclif, Matt. xiii. 25. Palsgrave has: '*taare*, a corne lyke a pease, *lupins*;' also: '*tarefytche* [=tare-vetch], a corne, *lupyn*.' The mod. E. *tare* is, in fact, short for *tare-vetch*, lit. 'wheat-vetch,' or 'darnel-vetch.'+MDu. *terwe*, Du. *tarwe*, Low G. *tarve*, wheat. Cf. Lithuan. *dirwa*, a corn-field, Skt. *dūrvā*, a kind of grass. See Notes on E. Etym., p. 291.

TARE (2), an allowance made for the weight of the package in which goods are contained, or for other detriment. (F.—Span.—Arab.) A mercantile term; explained in Phillips, ed. 1706.—F. *tare*, 'losse, diminution, . . waste in merchandise by the exchange or use thereof;' Cot.—Span. *tara*, tare, allowance in weight. (Cf. Ital. and Port. *tara*, the same.)—Arab. *tarha* (given by Devic); from *ṭarh*, throwing, casting, flinging. Richardson, Pers. Dict. p. 967, gives Arab. *ṭirh*, *ṭurrah*, thrown away, from *ṭarh*. The orig. sense is 'that which is thrown away,' hence loss, detriment. From the Arab. root *ṭaraha*, he threw prostrate, threw down; Rich., as above.

TARGET, a small shield, buckler, a mark to fire at. (F.—Scand.) The mark to fire at is named from its resemblance to a round shield. It is remarkable that the *g* is hard; indeed, the pl. is spelt *targattes* in Ascham, Toxophilus, bk. i. ed. Arber, p. 69, l. 28; and we find *tergate* in Sir T. Elyot, The Governour, bk. i. c. 18, § 2. This may be accounted for by derivation from OF. *targuete*, a small shield (Godefroy); dimin. of OF. *targue*, as in Cot. [The mod. F. *targe* is from OF. *targe* (with *g* = E. *j*); but cf. mod. Prov. *targueto*, dimin. of *targo*, OProv. *targa*.] We also had *targe* as a F. word, Rob. of Glouc., p. 361, l. 7462; and see Chaucer, C. T. 473 (A 471). The dimin. suffix -*et* is the usual F. dimin. so common in E.—Icel. *targa*, a target, small round shield; OHG. *zarga*, a frame, side of a vessel, wall; G. *zarge*, a frame, case, side, border. Cf. also AS. *targe*, a round shield, pl. *targan*, A.D. 970; Thorpe, Diplomatarium, p. 516. [We find also F. *targe*, 'a kind of target or shield,' Cot.; Port. *tarja*, an escutcheon on a target, a border; Span. *tarja*, a shield; Ital. *targa*, a buckler; words which Diez explains to be of Teut. origin.] The Irish and Gael. *targaid*, a target, shield, must have been taken from ME. *targat*; cf. Rhys, Lect. ii. ¶ Among the words of Teut. origin Diez includes the Port. and Span. *adarga*; the Port. *adarga* is a short square target, and the Span. *adarga* is explained by Minsheu to be 'a short and light target or buckler, which the Africans and Spaniards doe vse.' But this word is plainly Moorish, the *a* being for *al*, the Arab. article, and the etymology is from Arab. *darqa*(*t*), *daraqa*(*t*), 'a shield or buckler of solid leather;' Rich. Dict., p. 664. Note the Late L. *adarca*, a shield (1099) in Ducange; and the Late L. *tarcheta*, a target (1443). It is remarkable that Cotgrave explains F. *targe* as 'a kind of target or shield, almost square, and much in use along the Spanish coast, lying over against Africk, from whence it seems the fashion of it came.' He seems to be thinking *only* of the Moorish square shield; but the OF. *targe* is as old as the 11th cent., and the AS. *targe* as old as the 10th; so that the Teut. and Moorish words would seem to be distinct. But if the AS. *targe* can be of Moorish origin, the G. *zarge* is prob. unrelated.

TARGUM, a Chaldee paraphrase of the Old Testament. (Chaldee.) See *Targums* in Index to Parker Society. In Phillips, ed. 1706. 'The *Thargum* or paraphrase of Jonathan;' Sir T. Browne, Vulg. Errors, b. i. c. 1. § 4.—Chaldee *targūm*, an interpretation; from *targēm*, to interpret (Webster). Cf. Arab. *tarjumān*, an interpreter; for which see **Dragoman**.

TARIFF, a list or table of duties upon merchandise. (F.—Span.—Arab.) '*Tariff*, a table made to show . . . any multiple or product . . . a proportional table . . . a book of rates agreed upon for duties,' &c.; Phillips, ed. 1706.—MF. *tariffe*, 'arithmetick, or the casting of accompts;' Cot.—Span. *tarifa*, a list of prices, book of rates.—Arab. *ta'rif*, giving information, notification (because a *tariff* does this); Rich. Dict. p. 416.—Arab. *'irf*, knowing, knowledge; from Arab. root *'arafa*, he knew; Rich. Dict. p. 1003. See further in Devic, Supp. to Littré.

TARLATAN, a kind of thin muslin. (F.) F. *tarlatane*, formerly spelt *tarnatane*, in 1723 (Hatzfeld). Of unknown origin.

TARN, a small lake, a pool. (Scand.) In Levins. ME. *terne*, Allit. Poems; see Morris, B. 1041.—Icel. *tjörn* (gen. *tjarnar*), a tarn, pool; Swed. dial. *tjärn*, *tärn*, a tarn, pool without inlet or outlet (Rietz); Norweg. *tjörn*, *tjönn*, *kjönn*, *tjödn*, *kjödn*, a tarn (Aasen). Cf. Skt. *dara-*, a cavity.

TARNISH, to soil, diminish the lustre of, to dim. (F.—OHG.) Also to grow dim, as in Dryden, Absalom and Achitophel, 249; this appears to be the orig. sense in E.—F. *terniss-*, stem of pres. part. of *se ternir*, 'to wax pale, wan, discoloured, to lose its former luster;' Cot. Cf. *terni*, pp. 'wan, discoloured, whose luster is lost;' id.—MHG. *ternen*, OHG. *tarnan*, to obscure, darken; cf. *tarnhut*, *tarnkappe*, a hat or cap which rendered the wearer invisible. From OHG. *tarni*, secret (whence F. *terne*, dim).+AS. *dernan*, *dyrnan*, to

hide, Gen. xlv. 1; causal verb from *derne*, *dyrne*, hidden, secret, Grein, i. 214; and this adj. is cognate with OSax. *derni*, OFries. *dern*, hidden, secret. See **Darn**.

TARPAULING, TARPAULIN, a cover of coarse canvas, tarred to keep out wet. (Hybrid; E. *and* L.) *Tarpawling* is in Dryden, Annus Mirabilis, st. 148. It was once oddly used to denote also a sailor, whence our modern *tar*, in the same sense, rather than from an extension of *tar* to mean a man daubed with tar; though it makes little ultimate difference. '*Tarpawling*, or *Tarpaulin*, a piece of convass tar'd all over, to lay upon the deck of a ship, to keep the rain from soaking through; also a general name for a common seaman, because usually cloathed in such canvass;' Blount's Gloss., ed. 1674; Phillips, ed. 1706. And see Trench, Select Gloss., who gives two quotations for *tarpaulin* = sailor, viz. from Smollett, Rod. Random, vol. i. c. 3, and Turkish Spy, letter 2. The pl. *tarpaulins* occurs in Lady Alimony, Act iii. sc. 1; in Hazlitt's Old Plays, xiv. 325 (1659). Compounded of *tar* and *palling*. β. A *palling* is a covering, from *pall*, verb, to cover, which from *pall*, sb., L. *palla*; see **Pall**. 'Come, thick night, And *pall* thee in the dunnest smoke of hell;' Macb. i. 5. 52. '*Pauling*, a covering for a cart or waggon, *Lincolnshire*;' Halliwell.

TARRAGON, the name of a plant. (Span.—Arab.—Gk.) '*Tarragon*, a certaine hearbe, good to be eaten in sallads with lettuce;' Baret (1580); *Tarragon* in Levins.—Span. *taragona* (Diez); usually *taragontia*; Minsheu also gives the form *taragoncia*, which he explains by 'an herbe called dragons.' [Hence also F. *targon*, 'the herb tarragon;' Cot.]—Arab. *tarkhūn*, 'dragon-wort;' Rich. Dict. p. 389.—Gk. δράκων, a dragon; see **Dragon**. See Devic, s.v. *estragon*. Thus the strange form *tarragon* is nothing but *dragon* in a form changed by passing through an Oriental language, and decked in Spanish with a Latin suffix (viz. -*tia*). The botanical name is *Artemisia dracunculus*, where *dracunculus* is a double dimin. from L. acc. *draconem*.

TARRE, to incite, set on. (E.) In Shak. Hamlet, ii. 2. 37. ME. *tarien*, *terien*, to provoke; see **Tarry** (below).

TARRY, to linger, loiter, delay. (E.) The present form is due to ME. *tarien*, to irritate, provoke, worry, vex; later, to hinder, delay; affected by ME. *targen*, to delay. The mod. sense goes with the latter form. 1. ME. *tarien*, *terien*, to irritate, vex, provoke. 'I wol nat *tarien* you, for it is pryme;' Chaucer, C. T. 10387 (F 73), where it may fairly be explained by 'delay.' In the Prompt. Parv. we have: '*teryyn*, or longe abydyn, Moror, pigritor;' but also '*teryyn*, or ertyn, Irrito.' AS. *tergan*, to vex; a rare word. Trevisa has *tarry*, to provoke, annoy; tr. of Higden, v. 355. 'Tredað þec and tergað and heora torn wrecað' = they will tread on thee and vex thee and wreak their anger; Gúthlác, l. 259. Usually *tirgan*.+MDu. *tergen*, 'to vexe' (Hexham); Low G. *targen*, *tarren*, to provoke. So also prov. G. *zergen*, Dan. *tærge*, to irritate; answering to a Teut. type *targjan-*; to which Russ. *dergat*(*e*), to pluck, pull, draw, may be related. 2. ME. *targen*, to delay, tarry. 'That time thought the king to *targe* no lenger;' Alexander, fragment A, l. 211, pr. with Will. of Palerne.—OF. *targer*, to tarry, delay; allied to *tarder*, with the same sense; Cot.—Late L. *tardicāre*, an extension of L. *tardāre* (= F. *tarder*), to delay.—L. *tardus*, slow; see **Tardy**.

TART (1), acrid, sour, sharp, severe. (E.) 'Very *tarte* vinegar;' Sir T. Elyot, The Governour, b. iii. c. 22. § 11. Spelt *tarte* also in Palsgrave. '*Poudre-marchant tart*' = a sharp (tart) kind of flavouring powder; Chaucer, C. T. 381 (A 383). AS. *teart*, tart, sharp, severe; Ælfric's Hom. ii. 344, l. 4 from bottom; ii. 590, l. 4 from bottom. Perhaps lit. 'tearing,' just as *bitter* is from the notion of biting.—AS. *tar* (*tær*), pt. t. of *teran*, to tear; see **Tear** (1). Der. *tart-ly*, -*ness*.

TART (2), a small pie. (F.—L.) ME. *tarte*; pl. *tartes*, Rom. of Rose, 7041.—OF. *tarte*, 'a tart;' Cot. Perhaps so called from the paste being twisted together; it seems to be the same word as F. *tourte*, a tart, OF. *torte*, a kind of bread; whence the dimin. forms *tortel*, a cake (Roquefort), *torteau*, a pancake (Cotgrave). Godefroy gives also OF. *tarteau*, a little tart, with the same sense as *torteau*. [So also Ital. *tartera*, 'a tarte,' Florio, *torta*, a pie, tart, Span. *torta*, a round cake; Du. *taart*, Dan. *tærte*, G. *torte*, not Teutonic words.]—L. *torta*, fem. of *tortus*, twisted, pp. of *torquēre*, to twist; see **Torture**. Der. *tart-let*, from F. *tartelette*, 'a little tart;' Cot.

TARTAN, a woollen stuff, chequered, much worn in the Highlands of Scotland. (F.—L.—Tatar.) In Jamieson; spelt *tartane* in 1474; also *blew tartane*; at first all of one colour; the chequered patterns are comparatively modern. Spelt *tartar* in 1488. Borrowed from French. At first applied to various cloths from the East, and also to fine silk; see my note to Piers Plowman, C. xvii. 299.—AF. *tartayn*; as in 'un vestiment de blank *tartayn*;' Will of Lady Clare (1355), in Royal Wills, p. 31.—Late L. *Tartānus*, by-form of *Tartēnus*, as in ' de pannis *Tartenis*;' Liber Custumarum, p. 209. β. More commonly *Tartarinus* (OF. *Tartarin*), Tatar [Tartar] cloth; a general term for various Eastern cloths, including such as came through Tartary from China ; see Marco Polo, ed. Yule. Cf. ' the third [standard] was of yelowe *tarterne* ;' Hall's Chron., Hen. VII, an. 1. § 3. ' Corteyns of grene *tartren*,' in 1453 ; Cambridge Antiq. Soc., vol. iv. p. 357 ; ' aulter clothes of grene *tartren* ;' ibid. ' Blue *tartourne* ;' Cambridge Churchwardens' Accounts, ed. J. E. Foster, p. 7 (1504). ' Hec linostema, *tarteryne* ;' Voc. 655. 6. γ. The form *tartar* is from OF. *Tartaire*, Late L. *Tartara* ; with the same meaning. All from the name of the country ; see **Tartar** (2).

TARTAR (1), an acid salt which forms on the sides of casks containing wine ; a concretion which forms on the teeth. (F.—Low L.—Arab.) This is one of the terms due to the alchemists. Called *sal tartre* in Chaucer, C. T. 16278 (G 810); and simply *tartre*, id. 16281 (G 813).—F. *tartre*, ' tartar, or argall, the lees or dregs that stick to the sides of wine-vessels, hard and dry like a crust;' Cot.—Low L. *tartarum* (perhaps confused with *Tartarus*, whence the mod. E. spelling *tartar*).—Arab. *durd*, ' dregs, sediment, the tartar of wine, the mother of oil ;' Rich. Dict. p. 662 ; where it is marked as a Pers. word, though, according to Devic, of Arab. origin. Rich. also gives Pers. *durdī*, Arab. *durdiy*, ' sediment, dregs ;' p. 663. Note also Arab. *darad*, a shedding of the teeth, *dardā*, a toothless woman ; which Devic explains with reference to the tartar on teeth. Der. *tartar-ic*, *tartar-ous*.

TARTAR (2), a native of Tartary. (Tatar.) Chiefly used in the phr. ' to catch a *Tartar*,' to be caught in one's own trap. ' The phrase is prob. owing to some particular story ;' Todd's Johnson, with the following quotation. ' In this defeat they lost about 5000 men, besides those that were taken prisoners :—so that, instead of *catching the Tartar*, they were catched themselves ;' Life of the Duke of Tyrconnel, 1689. ' *Tartar*, a native of Tartary, . . . the people of which are of a savage disposition : whence the proverbial expression to *catch a Tartar*, i.e. to meet with one's match, to be disappointed, balked, or cowed ;' Phillips, ed. 1706. Shak. has ' the *Tartar's* bow,' Mids. Nt. Dr. iii. 2. 101. Sir J. Mandeville professed to have travelled in *Tartarye* ; see prol. to his Travels. See Trench, Eng. Past and Present, where he explains that the true spelling is *Tatar*, but the spelling *Tartar* was adopted from a false etymology, because their multitudes were supposed to have proceeded out of *Tartarus* or hell.—Pers. *Tātār*, ' a Tartar, or Scythian ;' Rich. Dict. p. 351 ; a word of Tatar origin.

TARTAR (3), Tartarus, hell. (L.—Gk.) ' To the gates of *Tartar* ;' Tw. Nt. ii. 5. 225.—L. *Tartarus*.—Gk. Τάρταρος, Tartarus, the infernal regions ; apparently conceived to be a place of extreme cold. Cf. Gk. ταρταρίζειν, to shiver with cold. Der. *tartar-e-ous*, ' the black *tartareous* cold ;' Milton, P.L. vii. 238; *tartar-e-an*, id.ii. 69.

TASK, a set amount of work imposed upon any one, work. (F.— L.) Lit. a *tax*. ME. *task*, *taske*, Cursor Mundi, 5872.—ONorth F. *tasque*, Norm. dial. *tasque*, OF. *tasche*, ' a task ;' Cot. Mod. F. *tâche*.—Late L. *tasca*, a tax ; the same word as *taxa*, a tax. (For a similar metathesis cf. E. *ask* with prov. E. *ax*.)—L. *taxāre*, to rate, value ; see **Tax**. Der. *task*, vb., *task-er*, sb. ; ' to *task* the *tasker*,' L. L. L. ii. 20 ; *task-master*, Milton, Sonnet i. 14. **Doublet**, *tax*.

TASSEL (1), a hanging ornament consisting of a bunch of silk or other material. (F.—L.) ME. *tassel*, a fastening of a mantle, consisting of a cord ending in a tassel, Cursor Mundi, 4389. Cf. ' a Mantle of Estate, . . . with strings dependant, and *tasselled* ;' Guillim, Display of Heraldry (1664), p. 271 ; a wood-cut on p. 272 shows the *tassel*, ornamented with strings and dots, that divide it into *squares like the ace on a die*.—OF. *tassel*, a fastening, clasp ; mod. F. *tasseau*, only in the sense of bracket. We also find Late L. *tassellus*, used in the Prompt. Parv. as equivalent to E. *tassel*. The OF. *tassel* also meant a piece of square stuff, used by ladies as an ornament ; see Godefroy. Cf. Ital. *tassello*, a collar of a cloak, a square.—L. *taxillum*, acc. of *taxillus*, a small die ; dimin. of *tālus*, a knuckle-bone, also a die orig. made of the knuckle-bone of an animal. We may conclude that the *tassel* was a sort of button made of a piece of squared bone, and afterwards of other materials. β. The curious form *taxillus* shows that *tālus* is a contraction for **taxlus*; origin unknown. *Taxillus* may have been confused with L. *tessella*, dimin. of *tessera*, a die ; cf. the entry : ' Tessera, *tasol*,' Epinal Gloss. 998. See Notes on E. Etym., p. 292. Der. *tassell-ed*, ME. *tasseled*, Chaucer, C. T. 3251.

TASSEL (2), the male of the goshawk. In Shak. Romeo, ii. 2. 160. The same as **Tercel**, q.v.

TASTE, to handle to try, to try or perceive by the touch of the tongue or palate, to eat a little of, to experience. (F.—L.) The sense of feel or handle is obsolete, but the ME. *tasten* meant both to feel and to taste. ' I rede thee lat thyn *hand* upon it falle, And *taste* it

wel, and ston thou shalt it finde ;' Chaucer, C. T. 15970 (G 502). ' Every thyng Himseolf schewith in *tastyng* ;' King Alisaunder, 4042. —OF. *taster*, ' to taste or take an assay of; also, to handle, feele, touch ;' Cot. Mod. F. *tâter* ; Ital. *tastare*, ' to taste, to assaie, to feele, to grope, to trye, to prooffe, to touch ;' Florio. We find also Late L. *taxta*, a tent or probe for wounds ; whence Ital. *tasta*, ' a tent that is put into a sore or wound, also a taste, a proofe, a tryall, a feeling, a touch ;' Florio. β. The Late L. *taxta* is short for **taxita*, and prob. points, as Diez says, to a Late L. verb **taxitāre*, not found, but a mere iterative of L. *taxāre*, to feel, to handle (Gellius). This *taxāre* (<**tagsāre*) is an intensive form of *tangere* (pp. *tactus*), to touch ; see **Tax, Tangent**. Hence the orig. sense of *taste* was to keep on touching, to feel carefully. Der. *taste*, sb., ME. *taste*, Gower, C. A. iii. 32; bk. vi. 925 ; *tast-er*, *tast-able*, *taste-ful*, *taste-ful-ly* ; *taste-ful-ness*, *taste-less*, *-less-ly*, *-less-ness*; *tast-y*, *tast-i-ly*.

TAT, to make trimming. (Scand.) North E. *tat*, to entangle. Cf. MSwed. *tätte*, Dan. dial. *tat* ; Norw. *taait*, a thread, a strand of a rope, whence Norw. *tätta*, to interweave. Also Icel. *þáttr*, Swed. *tåt*, Dan. *tot*, a filament ; G. *docht*, a wick.

TATTER, a shred, loose hanging rag. (Scand.) ' Tear a passion to *tatters* ;' Hamlet, iii. 2. 11 ; spelt *totters* in quarto edd. So also *totters* in Ford, Sun's Darling, i. 1, 2nd Song ; and see *tottered* in Nares. It is remarkable that the derived word *tattered* occurs earlier, spelt *tatered*, P. Plowman's Crede, 753, where it means ' jagged ;' *tatird*, ragged, Pricke of Conscience, 1537.—Icel. *töturr*, pl. *tötrar*, better spelt *tötturr*, pl. *töttrar* ; the pl. signifies tatters, rags ; Norweg. *totra*, pl. *totror*, *tottrur*, also *taltra*, *tultre*, pl. *taltrar*, *tultrer*, tatters, rags.+Low G. *taltern*, tatters, rags ; *to taltren riten*, to tear to tatters ; *taltrig*, tattered ; EFries. *talte*, a rag. β. It will be seen that an *l* has been lost ; and this is why the Icel. word should be spelt with double *t*, for *töttürr* = **töltürr*, by assimilation. Hence *tatter* stands for **talter* ; the assimilation of *lt* to *tt* being due to Scand. influence. I suppose *tatter* to be closely allied to *totter* = to wag, vacillate, shake about ; and that *totter* meant orig. a shaking strip, a fluttering strip. At any rate, *totter* is in the like case as regards letter-change, since it stands for *tolter*. See **Totter**. ¶ We find also AS. *tættec*, *tættic*, a rag ; the relationship of which is not clear. Der. *tatter-ed*, as above ; *tatter-demallion*, Massinger, Virgin Martyr, iii. 3 (Hircius) ; see my Notes on E. Etym., p. 292.

TATTLE, to talk idly, prattle. (E.) In Shak. Much Ado, ii. 1. 11. ' Every *tattling* fable ;' Spenser, Mother Hubbard's Tale, 724. ME. *totelen*, variant of *tateren*, to tattle, Prompt. Parv. ; pp. 498, 487. We may consider it E. ; it is closely allied to *tittle*, to tell tales, talk idly, which is equivalent to ME. *titeren*, whence *titerere* (also *titelere*), a tatler, teller of tales, P. Plowman, B. xx. 297. The verbs *tatt-le*, *titt-le*, and ME. *tat-eren*, *tit-eren*, are all frequentatives, from a base TAT, expressive of the sound of talking or repeating the syllables *ta ta ta* (Wedgwood). Allied words are Du. *tateren*, to stammer, MDu. *tateren*, ' to speake with a shrill noise, or to sound *taratantara* with a trumpet ;' Hexham ; Low G. *tateln*, to gabble as a goose, to tattle ; *titeltateln*, to tittle-tattle, *täteler*, a tattler ; *taat-goos*, a gabbling goose, chatterer ; *täterletät*, an interjection, the noise of a child's trumpet ; and even Ital. *tattamella*, chat, prattle, *tattamelare*, to prattle, which clearly show the imitative origin of the word. Allied to **Titter**, q.v. Der. *tattle*, sb. ; *tittle-tattle*, sb. and vb., see Wint. Tale, iv. 4. 248; *tiddle-taddle* (Fluellen's pronunciation), Hen. V, iv. 1. 71. And see *twadd-le* (formerly *twattle*).

TATTOO (1), the beat of drum recalling soldiers to their quarters. (Du.) ' If they hear but the *tattoo* ;' Prior, Alma, c. i. 454. ' Tattoo, Taptoo (also Taptow), the beat of drum at night for all soldiers to repair to their tents in a field, or to their quarters ; also called *The Retreat* ;' Phillips, ed. 1706. ' To beat the *taptow*, de Aftogt slaan ;' Sewel, Eng.-Du. Dict., 1754. A later edition (in 1766) has : *de taptoe slaan*, ' to beat the tap-tow.' ' The *tattoo* is used in garrisons and quarters by the beat of the drum ;' Silas Taylor, On Gavelkind, ed. 1663, p. 74.—Du. *taptoe*, tattoo (Calisch) ; whence *de taptoe slaan*, to beat the tattoo.—Du. *tap*, a tap ; and *toe*, put to, shut, closed. The sense is ' the tap is closed ;' cf. Du. *Is de deur toe* = is the door closed ? *doe het boek toe* = shut the book ; *haal't venster toe* = shut the window (Sewel). Hexham has *toe slaen*, to shut, conclude. The *tattoo* was thus the signal for closing the taps of the public-houses. β. So also G. *zapfenstreich*, the tattoo (lit. tap-stroke), where *zapfen* is a tap of a cask ; and Low G. *tappenslag*, the tattoo (lit. a tap-shutting). Cf. Low G. *tappen to slaan* = to close a tap, an expression used proverbially in the phrase *Wi wilt den Tappen to slaan* = we will shut the tap, put the tap to, i. e. we will talk no more of this matter. This last expression clearly shows that ' a tap-to ' was a conclusion, a time for shutting-up. ¶ I do not think that Span. *tapatan*, the sound of a drum, has anything to do with the present matter.

TATTOO (2), to mark the skin with figures, by pricking in colouring matter. (Tahitian.) 'They have a custom . . . which they call *tattowing*. They prick the skin so as just not to fetch blood,' &c.; Cook, First Voyage, b. i. c. 17; id. ib. b. iii. c. 9 (R.). Cook is speaking of the inhabitants of Tahiti. — Tahitian *tatau*, signifying tattoo-marks on the human skin; derived from *ta*, a mark, design; see Littré, who refers us to Berchon, Recherches sur le Tatouage. See E. E. Morris, Australasian Dict.; Notes on E. Etym., p. 293.

TAUNT, to scoff, mock, tease. (F.—L.) 'I *tawnte* one, I check hym, *Je farde*;' Palsgrave. '*Smacco*, . . . a check or *tant* in a woord or deede;' Florio. The old sense had less of mockery in it, and sometimes meant merely to tease. 'For a proper wit had she, . . . sometime *taunting* without displesure and not without disport;' Sir T. More, Works, p. 57 b. Perhaps the vb. is due to the sb. 'Which liberall *taunte* that most gentill emperour toke in so good part;' Sir T. Elyot, The Governour, b. ii. c. 5. § 17. 'Gave me a *taunte*, and sayde I was to blame;' Skelton, Bowge of Courte, 70. α. The verb answers in form, but hardly in sense, to OF. *tanter* (Burguy), occasional form of *tenter*, 'to tempt, to prove, try, sound, essay, attempt; also to suggest, provoke, or move unto evill;' Cot. From L. *tentāre*, to try, prove, test, attack, assail, agitate, disquiet, &c. See **Tempt**. β. We may rather, perhaps, look upon the sb. as the original; it may have arisen from the phrase *taunt pour taunt*, i. e. tit for tat. This occurs in : 'Geuyng vnto the same *taunt pour taunte*, or one for another;' Udall, tr. of Erasmus' Apophthegmes, Diogenes, § 68. Cf. also : 'Mery conceipted and full of pretie *tauntes*;' id., Philippus, § 29. If this is right, *taunt* arose from F. *tant*, so much. — L. *tantum*, neut. of *tantus*, so much. Cf. ME. *ataunt*, as much as (F. *autant*); N. E. D. Godefroy has OF. *tante donner*, to give such great blows. Der. *taunt-er*, *taunt-ing-ly*.

TAURUS, the bull; the 2nd zodiacal sign. (L.) In Chaucer, On the Astrolabe, pt. i. § 8, l. 2. — L. *taurus*, a bull. + Gk. ταῦρος, a bull. + AS. *stéor*, a young ox, a steer; see **Steer** (1). Der. *taur-ine*, from L. *taurinus*, adj., belonging to bulls.

TAUT, tight, firm. (E.) ME. *togt, toght*. 'Made it *toght*,' i. e. made it sure; Allit. Poems, A. 522. 'With bely stif and *toght* As any tabour;' Chaucer, C. T., D 2267. It seems to be the weak pp. of ME. *toȝen*, to pull, tow, tug; so that the orig. sense was 'pulled tight.' See **Tow** (1). See Notes on E. Etym., p. 294.

TAUTOLOGY, needless repetition, in the same words. (L.—Gk.) 'With ungratefull *tautologies*;' Fuller's Worthies, Kent (R.). — L. *tautologia* (White). — Gk. ταυτολογία, a saying over again of the same thing. — Gk. ταυτολόγος, repeating what has been said. — Gk. ταὐτό, contracted from τὸ αὐτό, or τὸ αὐτόν, the same; and -λογος, speaking, allied to λέγειν, to speak, for which see **Legend**. Der. *tautolog-ic*, *tautolog-ic-al*, *-ly*; *tautolog-ise*.

TAVERN, an inn, house for accommodating travellers and selling liquors. (F.—L.) ME. *tauerne* (with *u=v*), Rob. of Glouc. p. 195, l. 4024. — F. *taverne*, 'a tavern;' Cot. — L. *taberna*, a hut, orig. a hut made of boards, a shed, booth, tavern. Usually said to be allied to L. *tab-ula*, a plank, board; see **Table**. But Walde takes it to stand for *traberna*; from *trabs*, a beam; see **Trave**.

TAW (1), **TEW**, to prepare skins, so as to dress them into leather, to curry, to toil. (E.) Spelt *tawe* and *tewe*; Levins. Palsgrave has both 'I *tawe* leather' and 'I *tewe* leather.' ME. *tewen*, to prepare leather, Prompt. Parv.; *tawen*, Ormulum, 15908. AS. *tawian*, to prepare, dress, get ready, also, to maltreat. 'Séo deoful éow *tawode*,'=the devil maltreated you; Ælfric's Hom. ii. 486, l. 4 from bottom. 'Tó yrmðe *getawode*'=reduced to poverty; S. Veronica, p. 34, l. 18. Cf. *getawe*, implements; Grein, i. 462. + Du. *touwen*, to curry leather; OHG. *zouwan*, to make, prepare; Goth. *ga-tēwjan*, to appoint, *taujan*, to do, cause. See **Tool**. Der. *taw-yer*, ME. *tawier, tawer*, Wyclif, Deeds, ix. 43, early version, where the later version has *curiour*, i. e. currier; cf. *bow-yer, law-yer*.

TAW (2), a game at marbles. (Gk.) 'A game of marbles not unlike our modern *taw*;' The Tatler, no. 112, Dec. 27, 1709. In the United States, *taw* means 'a line or mark from which the players begin a game of marbles;' Webster. A similar mark is also called a *tee*. The easiest way of marking an exact spot on the ground is to draw the letter T, which defines the point where a stroke meets a cross-stroke. The T is named *tee* in English, and *tau* in Greek. Hence '*tau* and chuck-farthing' in Additions to Nares. See Notes on E. Etym., p. 294.

TAWDRY, showy, but without taste, gaudy. (E.) 'A *tawdrie* lace;' Spenser, Shep. Kal., April, 135; 'a *tawdry* lace,' Wint. Tale, iv. 4. 253; '*tawdry-lace*,' Beaum. and Fletcher, Faithful Shepherdess, Act iv. sc. 1 (Amarillis). 'Seynt Audries lace, cordon;' Palsgrave. Thus it was first used in the phr. *tawdry lace*=a rustic necklace; explained in Skinner (following Dr. Hickes) as being a necklace bought at *St. Awdry's* fair, held in the Isle of Ely (and elsewhere) on St. Awdry's day, Oct. 17. (See Palsgrave, as above.)

Wedgwood doubts the ancient celebrity of this fair (which I do not), and accepts in preference the alternative account in Nares, that St. Audry 'died of a swelling in the throat, which she considered as a particular judgment, for having been in her youth much addicted to wearing fine necklaces;' see Nich. Harpsfield, Hist. Eccl. Anglicana, Sæc. Sept. p. 86; Brady, Clavis Calendaria, Oct. 17. β. In any case, *Tawdry* is a contraction from *St. Audry*; and *Audry* is a corruption of *Etheldrida*, the famous saint who founded Ely Cathedral. γ. Again, *Etheldrida* is the Latinised form of the AS. name *Æþel-þrȳð*; see Sweet, O. E. Texts, p. 638. From AS. *æþel*, noble; and *þrȳð* or *þrȳþ*, strength. The latter element is allied to the OHG. word which appears in the name *Ger-trude*. See *Thrúdhr* in Schade. In the Latin text of Beda, Hist. Eccl. iv. 3, it is spelt *Aedilthryd*. See Notes on E. Etym., p. 295.

TAWNY, a yellowish brown. (F.—Teut.) Merely another spelling of *tanny*, i. e. resembling that which is tanned by the sun, sunburnt. By heraldic writers it is spelt *tenny* or *tenné*. 'Tawny . . in blazon, is known by the name of *tenne*;' Guillim, Display of Heraldry, sect. i. cap. 3. ME. *tanny*. 'Tanny colowre, or *tawny*;' Prompt. Parv. 'Unum goun de *tawnè*;' Excerpta Historica, p. 24 (1375). — F. *tanné*, 'tawny;' Cot. It is the pp. of F. *tanner, taner*, to tan. — F. *tan*, tan; see **Tan**. Der. *tawni-ness*. Doublet, *tenné* or *tenny*.

TAX, a rate imposed on property, anything imposed, a task. (F.—L.) ME. *tax*, Polit. Songs, ed. Wright, p. 151, l. 4 (temp. Edw. II). — F. *taxe*, 'a taxation;' Cot. — F. *taxer*, 'to tax, rate, assess;' Cot. — L. *taxāre*, to handle; also to rate, value, appraise; whence Late L. *taxa*, a rating, a taxation. For *tagsāre; from *tag-*, the base of *tangere*, to touch; see **Tangent, Tact**. Der. *tax*, verb, F. *taxer; tax-able, tax-abl-y; tax-at-ion*, from F. *taxation*, 'a taxation,' from L. acc. *taxātiōnem*. Doublet, *task*.

TAXIDERMY, the art of preparing and stuffing the skins of animals. (Gk.) Modern; coined from Gk. ταξι-, decl. stem of τάξις, order, arrangement; and δέρμα, a skin. β. Τάξις (<*τάκ-γις) is from τάσσειν (<*τάκ-γειν), to arrange; see **Tactics**. Gk. δέρμα, a skin, is that which is *torn* or flayed off; formed with suffix -μα from δέρ-ειν, to flay, cognate with E. *tear*; see **Tear** (1). Der. *taxiderm-ist*.

TAZZA, a cup, bowl. (Ital.—Arab.—Pers.) Ital. *tazza*, a cup, bowl (F. *tasse*). — Arab. *ṭass, ṭassa(t)*, a cup, bason; Rich. Dict., p. 970. Derived by Devic from Pers. *tast*, a cup; Rich. gives Pers. *tasht*, a bason; p. 403. So Horn, § 389. Cf. also Pers. *tās*, a cup; p. 355.

TEA, an infusion made from the dried leaves of the *tea-tree*, a shrub found in China and Japan. (Chinese.) Formerly pronounced *tay* [tei], just as *sea* was called *say*; it rimes with *obey*, Pope, Rape of the Lock, iii. 8, and with *away*, id. i. 62. 'I did send for a cup of *tee* (a China drink) of which I never had drank before;' Pepys, Diary, Sept. 28, 1660. Also spelt *cha* in Blount's Gloss., ed. 1674, with a reference to Hist. of China, fol. 19; also *chau*, Dampier's Voyages, an. 1687 (R.). 'That excellent . . China drink called by the Chineans *tcha*, by other nations *Tay*, alias *tee*;' The Gazette, Sept. 9, 1658; qu. in N. and Q. 8 S. vi. 266. Prof. Douglas writes: 'The E. word *tea* is derived from the Amoy pronunciation of the name of the plant, which is *té*. In the other parts of the empire it is called *ch'a, ts'a*, &c.; see Williams, Chinese Dict., p. 5.' Cf. *té*, tea; Chinese Dict. of the Amoy Vernacular, by Rev. C. Douglas, 1873, p. 481. This accounts for the old spelling *cha*, and for the Ital. *cia*, tea. Cf. F. *thé*, G. *thee*, pronounced as *tea* was in Pope's time. So also Malay *téh*, tea; Marsden, Malay Dict., p. 97. Der. *tea-caddy*; see **Caddy**.

TEACH, to impart knowledge, show how to do. (E.) ME. *techen*, weak verb, pt. t. *taughte* (properly dissyllabic), Chaucer, C. T. 499 (A 497); pp. *taught*. AS. *tǽcan, tǽcean*, to show, teach, pt. t. *tǽhte*, pp. *tǽht, getǽht*; Grein, ii. 522. Formed (with change of *ā* to *ǽ* before *j*, as in Teut. *taikjan-*) from *tác-* (Teut. *taik-*) base of AS. *tácen*, a token. From √DEIK, to show; cf. G. *zeigen*, to show; see further under **Token**. Der. *teach-able, teach-able-ness, teach-er*.

TEAK, an E. Indian and African tree, with very hard wood. (Malayālam.) Modern; not in Todd's Johnson. — Malayālam *tēkka*, the teak tree; Tamil *tēkku*; H. H. Wilson, Gloss. of Indian Terms, p. 516. The best *teak* is from the mountains of the Malabar Ghauts; also found on the Coromandel coast; Eng. Cycl.

TEAL, a web-footed water-fowl. (E.) *Teale*; Levins. ME. *tele*, Prompt. Parv.; Squire of Low Degree, l. 320, in Ritson, Met. Rom. vol. iii. p. 158; used to translate OF. *cercele* in Walter de Bibbesworth, pr. in Wright's Voc. i. 151, l. 12; i. 165, l. 15. This takes us back to the close of the 13th cent., and the word is prob. E.; certainly Low German, in any case. + Du. *taling, teling*, a generation, production, also, teal; derived from *telen*, to breed, produce; i. e. if *teling* is the same word in both senses. MDu. *teelingh*, a teal (Kilian). Cf. MDu. *teelen*, to propagate, to till; Low G. *teling*, a progeny, *telen*, to breed. The AS. base would be **tǣl-*; see Du. *taling* in Franck. Perhaps connected with the verb to *till*; see **Till** (1). Der. *atteal*, a kind of teal, N. E. D.; Prof. Newton, Dict. of Birds, cites a 'Scandinavian' form *atteling-and*; s. v. **Teal**.

TEAM, a family; a set; a number of animals harnessed in a row. (E.) ME. *tem*, *teem*, *team*; 'a *teme* [of] foure gret oxen,' P. Plowman, B. xix. 257; *tem*=a family, Rob. of Glouc. p. 261, l. 5241. AS. *tēam*, a family, offspring, Genesis, 1613; Grein, ii. 526.+Du. *toom*, the rein of a bridle; the same word, from the notion of guiding; Icel. *taumr*, a rein; Low G. *toom*, a progeny, team, also, a rein; Dan. *tömme*, Swed. *töm*, a rein; G. *zaum*, a bridle, MHG. *zoum*. Teut. type **tau-moz* for **taug-moz* (Noreen); from **tauh*, 2nd grade of **teuh-an-*, to draw, lead. See **Tow** (1). From Idg. √DEUK. But see Brugmann, i. § 630. In the sense of 'team of horses,' the AS. form is *ge-týme*; Luke, xiv. 19. Der. *teem*, verb, q. v. Also *team-ster* (Webster, not in Johnson), with suffix *-ster*; for which see **Spinster**.

TEAPOY, a small tripod table. (Hybrid; Hind. *and* Pers.) Also *tepoy*, *tinpoy* (1844); see Yule.— Hind. *tin*, three (Forbes); and Pers. *pāi*, foot (Palmer).

TEAR (1), to rend, lacerate. (E.) ME. *teren*, strong verb, pt. t. *tar*, Seven Sages, ed. Weber, l. 472, pp. *toren*, id. 782. AS. *teran*, pt. t. *tær*, pp. *toren*, Grein, ii. 525.+Goth. *ga-tairan*, to break, destroy, pt. t. *ga-tar*; Lithuan. *dirti*, to flay; Gk. δέρειν, to flay; Russ. *drat(e)*, to tear; cf. *dira*, a rent, a hole; Zend *dar*, to cut; Pers. *daridan*, to tear; Skt. *dāraya*, to tear; cf. W. *dar-n*, a fragment. Teut. type **teran-*, pt. t. **tar*, pp. **taranoz*. Idg. √DER, to burst, tear open. The G. *zehren*, Low G. *teren*, Icel. *tæra*, to consume, are *weak* verbs, from the same root. Brugmann, i. § 594. Der. *tear*, sb. (Goth. *gataura*), Chevy Chase, l. 134, in Spec. of Eng. ed. Skeat, p. 75. Also *tar-t* (1); and (from same root) *epi-der-mis*, *taxi-der-my*.

TEAR (2), a drop of the fluid from the eyes. (E.) ME. *tere*, Chaucer, C. T. 8960 (E 1084). AS. *tēar*, *tǣr*, Grein, ii. 526; also *teagor*; ONorthumb. *tæher*.+Icel. *tár*; Dan. *taar*, *taare*; Swed. *tår*; Goth. *tagr*; OHG. *zahar*, pl. *zaheri*, whence G. *zähre*. β. All from a Teut. base **tah-r-*, **tak-r-*. Further allied to OL. *dacrima*, usually *lacrima*, *lacruma* (whence F. *larme*), a tear; Gk. δάκρυ, δάκρυον, δάκρυμα, a tear; W. *dagr*, a tear; OIrish *dēr*. Brugmann, i. § 178. Der. *tear-ful*, 3 Hen. VI, v. 4. 8; *tear-ful-iy*, *tear-ful-ness*; *tear-less*. And see *train-oil*.

TEASE, to comb or card wool, scratch or raise the nap of cloth; to vex, plague. (E.) ME. *tesen*, Cathol. Anglicum; also *taisen*, of which the pp. *taysed* is in Gawain and the Grene Knight, 1169. But the more common form is *tosen* or *toosen*. 'They *toose* and pulle;' Gower, C. A. i. 17; Prol. 400. '*Tosyn*, or *tose* wul' [tease wool]; Prompt. Parv. We also find *to-tosen*, to tease or pull to pieces, Owl and Nightingale, l. 70. AS. *tǣsan*, to pluck, pull, Ælfric's Grammar, ed. Zupitza, p. 170, l. 13. The ME. *tosen* would answer to a by-form **tāsan*, not recorded.+MDu. *teesen*, to pluck; *wolle teesen*, 'to pluck wooll,' Hexham; Dan. *tæse*, *tæsse*, to tease wool; Bavarian *zaisen*, to tease wool, Schmeller; he also cites MHG. *zeisen*, to tease, a strong verb, with pt. t. *zies*, pp. *gezeisen*. β. The form of the base is Teut. **teis*. Der. *teas-el*, q. v.

TEASEL, a plant with large heads covered with crooked awns which are used for teasing cloth. (E.) ME. *tesel*, Voc. 559. 7; also *tasel*, P. Plowman, B. xv. 446. AS. *tǣsl*, *tǣsel*, a teasel, A. S. Leechdoms, i. 282, note 26. Formed with suffix *-l* (*-il-*) from *tǣs-an*, to tease; the sense is 'an instrument to tease with.' See **Tease**.

TEAT, the nipple of the female breast. (F.— Low G.) [Also called *tit*, which is the native word.] ME. *tete*, Chaucer, C. T. 3704; also *tette*, Genesis and Exodus, ed. Morris, 2621.— OF. *tete*, teat; F. *tette*, teat.— Low G. *titte*, MDu. *titte*, a teat; Hexham.+ G. *zitze*. [Cf. also Span. *teta*, Ital. *tetta*, words of Teut. origin.] Also W. *did*, *didi*, a teat. These words have much the appearance of being reduplicated from a base TI (Idg. DI). β. Besides these, there is a second form represented by Gk. τίτθη, τιτθός; of these the Gk. τίτθη, τιτθός, have been explained from √DHEI, to suck; cf. Skt. *dhē*, to suck, Goth. *daddjan*, to suckle. See **Tit** (2).

TEAZLE, the same as **Teasel**, q.v.

TECHNICAL, artificial, pertaining to the arts. (Gk.; *with* L. *suffix*.) In Blount's Gloss., ed. 1674. Formed with suffix *-al* (<L. *-ālis*), from Gk. τεχνικ-ός, belonging to the arts.— Gk. τέχνη, art; allied to τέκτων, a carpenter.— √TEK, to prepare, get ready; cf. Skt. *taksh*, to prepare, form, cut wood, *takshan-*, a carpenter; see **Text**. Der. *technical-ly*, *technical-i-ty*; *techno-logy*, with suffix = Gk. -λογία, from λέγειν, to speak. Also (from the same source) *archi-tect*, *pyro-technic*; and see *text*, *text-ure*.

TECHY, the same as **Tetchy**, q.v.

TED, to spread new-mown grass. (Scand.) 'I *teede* hey, I tourne it afore it is made in cockes;' Palsgrave. 'To *tedde* and make hay;'

Fitzherbert, Book of Husbandry, § 25. 'Gras .. *unteddid*;' Wyclif's Works, ed. Arnold, ii. 301.— Icel. *teðja* (pp. *taddr*), to spread manure; from *tað*, manure. Cf. Icel. *taða*, hay grown in a well-manured field, a home-field; *töðu-verk*, making hay in the in-field. Also Norw. *tedja*, to spread manure; from *tad*, manure; Aasen. So also Swed. dial. *täda*, vb., from *tad*.+Bavarian *zetten*, to strew, to let fall in a scattered way, Schmeller, p. 1159; cf. G. *verzetteln*, to scatter, spill, disperse. Cf. also MHG. *zetten*, to scatter, derived from OHG. *zata*, allied to *zota* (mod. G. *zotte*, a rag); see Schade. β. All these words can be derived from a sb. of which the Teut. base is **tad-*. Cf. Gk. δατ-έομαι, I distribute. Cf. **Tod**.

TEDIOUS, tiresome, from length or slowness, irksome. (L.) Spelt *tedyouse* in Palsgrave. Coined immediately from L. *tædiōsus*, irksome.— L. *tædium*, irksomeness.— L. *tædet*, it irks one. Der. *tedious-ly*, *-ness*. We also use *tedium*, the sb.

TEE, a mark, a starting-point. (E.) From the use of a T to mark an exact spot. Cf. *tee-totum*; and see **Taw** (2).

TEEM (1), to bring forth, bear, or be fruitful; be pregnant, full, or prolific. (E.) 'Hyndre [her] of *teming*;' Sir T. More, Works, p. 644 g. ME. *temen*, to produce, Ancren Riwle, p. 220, l. 15. Obviously from ME. *teme*, a team, a progeny; see **Team**. The AS. verb is *tieman*, *týman*, to teem, Gen. xxx. 9; formed (with the usual vowel-change from *ēa* to *ie*, later *ȳ*) from AS. *tēam*, a team, a progeny. Teut. type **taumjan-*, vb., from **taumoz*, sb.

TEEM (2), to think fit. (OLow G.) Rare, and obsolete; but Shak. has the comp. *beteem*, to be explained presently. 'I coulde *teeme* it [think fit] to rend thee in pieces;' Gifford's Dialogue on Witches, A.D. 1603. 'Alas, man, I could *teeme* it to go;' id. See both quotations in full, in Halliwell, s. v. **Teem**.— Low G. *tämen*, *temen*, to fit; also, to allow; as, '*He tämet sik een good Glas Wien*, he allows himself a good glass of wine;' allied to *betamen*, to be fit, and to *tämen*, to tame; EFries. *temen*, to find fitting, to allow oneself. β. Related words are easily found, viz. in Goth. *gatēmiba*, fitly, from the strong verb *gatiman* (pt. t. *gatam*), to suit, agree with; Luke, v. 36; Du. *tamen*, 'to be comely, convenient, or seemely,' Hexham; *tamelick*, or *tamigh*, 'comely, convenient,' id.; whence *het betaemt*, 'it is convenient, requisite, meete, or fitting,' id.; mod. Du. *betamen*, to beseem; G. *ziemen*, to be fit; *ziemlich*, passable, lit. suitable; OHG. *zeman*, to fit, closely related to *zeman*, *zamjam*, to tame. Allied to **Tame**, q.v. 2. We can now explain *beteem* in Shak. Mids. Nt. Dr. i. 1. 131; Hamlet, i. 2. 141. It means to make or consider as fitting, hence to permit, allow; a slightly forced use of the word. In Golding's translation of Ovid's Metamorphoses, A.D. 1587, we have 'could he not *beteeme*' = he did not think fit, would not deign; the L. text has *dignatur*, Metam. x. 158. Spenser uses it still more loosely: 'So woulde I ... *Beteeme* to you this sword' = permit, grant, allow you the use of this sword; F. Q. ii. 8. 19.

TEEM (3), to empty, pour out. (Scand.) See Halliwell.— Icel. *tæma*, to empty, from *tómr*, empty; Dan. *tömme*, to empty, from *tom*, empty; Swed. *tömma*, from *tom*; see **Toom**.

TEEN, vexation, grief. (E.) In Shak. Temp. i. 2. 64; &c. ME. *tene*, Chaucer, C. T. 3108 (A 3106). AS. *tēona*, accusation, injury, vexation, Grein, ii. 528.— AS. *tēon*, contracted from *tihan*, to accuse; see Grein, ii. 532, s. v. *tīhan*. [To be distinguished from *tēon* (= *tēohan*), to draw.]+Goth. *gateihan*, to tell, announce, make known to, point out (as distinct from *gatiuhan*, to lead); G. *zeihen*, to accuse (as distinct from *ziehen*, to draw).+L. *dicāre*, to make known.— √DEIK, to show. See **Token**. ¶ The successive senses of *teen* are making known, public accusation, reproach, injury, vexation. We have *indication* and *inditement* from the same root. The word *teen* also occurs as Old Saxon *tiono*, injury; Icel. *tjón*, loss.

TEETOTALLER, a total abstainer. (F.—L.; *with* E. *prefix and suffix*.) A teetotaller is one who professes *total* abstinence from all spirituous liquors; the orig. name was *total abstainer*. The adj. *teetotal* is an emphasized form of *total*, made on the principle of reduplication, just as we have L. *te-tigi* as the perfect of *tangere*. The word 'originated with Richard Turner, an artisan of Preston, who, contending for the principle at a temperance meeting about 1833, asserted that "nothing but *te-te-total* will do." The word was immediately adopted. He died 27 Oct., 1846. These facts are taken from the *Staunch Teetotaller*, edited by Joseph Livesey, of Preston (an originator of the movement in August, 1832), Jan. 1867;' Haydn, Dict. of Dates. And see **Teetotum**. ¶ *Teetotal* may have been suggested by *teetotum*. In N. and Q. 5 S. v. 18, it is asserted that *teetotal* was in use, as an intensive of *total*, before 1832.

TEETOTUM, TOTUM, a spinning toy. (L.) Not in Todd's Johnson. I had a *teetotum* (about A.D. 1840) with four sides only, marked P (*Put down*), N (*Nothing*), H (*Half*), T (*Take all*). These were very common, and the letters decided whether one was to put into the pool or to take the stakes. (Strutt gives the same account, in his Sports and Pastimes, bk. iv. c. 4. § 6.) I suppose that these letters took the place of others with Latin explanations, such as P (*Pone*), N (*Nil*), D (*Dimidium*), T (*Totum*). The toy was named, accordingly, from the most interesting mark upon it ; and was called either a *totum* or a *T-totum*. Ash's Dict., ed. 1775, has : ' *Totum*, from the Latin, a kind of die that turns round, so called because the appearance of one lucky side [*that marked* T] entitles the player that turned it to the whole stake.' ' *Totum*, a whirl-bone, a kind of die that is turned about ;' Phillips, ed. 1706. Dunbar alludes to this game : ' He playis with *totum*, and I with *nichil* ;' Works, ed. Small, p. 106, l. 74. *Teetotums* are now made with the thickest part polygonal, not square, which entirely destroys the original notion of them ; and they are marked with numbers instead of letters. − L. *tōtum*, the whole (stake) ; neut. of *tōtus* ; see **Total**.

TEG, a young sheep of the first year, a ewe. (Scand.) Pl. *teggys* ; Skelton, Against Garnesche, 31. Cf. Swed. *tacka*, a ewe (Widegren, Ihre).

TEGUMENT, a covering. (L.) Rare ; commoner in deriv. *integument*. In Sir T. Browne, Vulg. Errors, b. ii. c. 6. § 5. − L. *tegumentum* (also *tegimentum*, *tegmentum*), a covering. − L. *tegere* (for **stegere*), to cover. +Gk. στέγειν, to cover. −√STEG, to cover ; whence also Skt. *sthag*, to cover, Lithuan. *stégti*, to thatch ; OIrish *tech*, W. *tŷ*, a house. Brugmann, i. § 632. And see **Thatch**. Der. *in-tegument* ; also (from *tectus*, pp. of *tegere*), *de-tect*, *pro-tect* ; and see *tile*, *toga*, *thatch*, *deck*.

TEIL-TREE, a linden tree. (F. − L. ; *and* E.) ' A *teil-tree* ;' Isaiah, vi. 13 (A.V.). − OF. *teil*, the bark of a lime-tree (Roquefort) ; cf. mod. F. *tille*, bast. [The added word *tree* is E.] − L. *tilia*, a lime-tree ; also, the inner bark of a lime-tree.+Irish *teile*.

TEIND, a tithe. (Scand.) A Lowl. Sc. form. ' Bot tak his *teind* ;' Sir D. Lyndesay, The Monarche, bk. iii. 4690. − Icel. *tíund*, a tenth, tithe. − Icel. *tíu*, ten ; see **Ten**.

TELEGRAPH, an apparatus for giving signals at a distance, or conveying information rapidly. (Gk.) Modern ; in Richardson's Dict. M. Chappe's telegraph was first used in France in 1793 ; see Haydn, Dict. of Dates. Coined from Gk. τῆλε, afar off ; and γράφειν, to write. The Gk. τῆλε, τηλοῦ, afar, are from an adj. form **τῆ-λος*, not in use. Gk. γράφειν is cognate with **Carve**. Der. *telegraph-ic*, *telegraph-y*, *telegraph-ist*. Also *tele-gram*, a short coined expression for 'telegraphic message,' from γράμμα, a letter of the alphabet, a written character. So also *tele-phone* ; from Gk. φωνή, voice, sound.

TELESCOPE, an optical instrument for viewing objects at a distance. (Gk.) Galileo's telescopes were first made in 1609. Milton alludes to the *telescope*, P. R. iv. 42. Coined from Gk. τῆλε, afar ; and σκοπεῖν, to behold ; see **Telegraph** and **Scope**. Der. *tele-scop-ic*. So also *tele-pathy*, sympathy at a distance ; from Gk. -παθεία, from πάθος, suffering, feeling.

TELL, to count, narrate, discern, inform. (E.) ME. *tellen*, pt. t. *tolde*, pp. *told* ; often in the sense ' to count,' as in P. Plowman, B. prol. 92. 'Shal *telle tales* tweye ;' Chaucer, C. T. 794 (A 792). AS. *tellan*, to count, narrate ; pt. t. *tealde*, pp. *teald* ; Grein, ii. 524. A weak verb, formed from the sb. *talu*, a tale, number ; so that *tellan* is for **taljan*, with mutation of *a* to *e*. See **Tale**.+Du. *tellen*, from *tal*, sb. ; Icel. *telja*, from *tala*, sb. ; Dan. *tælle*, from *tal* ; Swed. *tälja*, from *tal* ; G. *zählen*, from *zahl*. Der. *tell-er* ; *tell-tale*, Merch. Ven. v. 123.

TELLURIC, belonging to the earth. (L.) Rare, and scientific. Coined with suffix -*c* (L. -*cus*), from L. *tellūri-*, decl. stem of *tellus*, earth. Allied to Irish *talamh*, OIrish *talam*, earth, Skt. *tala-m*, surface. Der. *telluri-um*, a rare metal, discovered in 1782 (Haydn).

TEMERITY, rashness. (F. − L.) Spelt *temeritie* in Minsheu, ed. 1623. − MF. *temerité*, 'temerity,' Cot. − L. *temeritātem*, acc. of *temeritās*, rashness. − L. *temeri-* for **temerus*, rash, only used in the adv. *temere*, rashly. − L. *temere*, rashly ; cf. Skt. *tamas*, dimness, darkness, gloom. The orig. sense of *temere* is 'in the dark,' hence blindly, rashly ; cf. Skt. *tamas*, dimness, darkness, gloom.

TEMPER, to moderate, modify, control, qualify, bring to a proper degree of hardness. (L.) ME. *temprien*, *tempren*, Rob. of Glouc., p. 72, l. 1684 ; Gower, C. A. i. 266 ; bk. ii. 3178. AS. *temprian*, for which see Toller. − L. *temperāre*, to apportion, moderate, regulate, qualify ; allied to *temperi* or *tempori*, adv., seasonably, and to *tempus*, fit season, time. See **Temporal**. (Perhaps modified by MF. *temperer* to temper ; also from L. *temperāre*. Brugmann, ii. § 132. Der. *temper*, sb., Oth. v. 2. 253, Merch. Ven. i. 2. 20 (see Trench, Study of Words, and cf. L. *temperiēs*, a tempering, right admixture) ; *temper-ance*, ME. *temperaunce*, Wyclif, Col. iii. 12 ; from F. *temperance*<L. *temperantia* ; *temper-ate*, Wyclif, 1 Tim. iii. 3, from L. *temperātus*, pp. of *temperāre* ; *temper-ate-ly*, *temper-ate-ness* ; *temper-at-ure*, from F. *temperature*, 'a temper, temperature,' Cot, from L. *temperātūra*, due to *temperāre* ; *temper-a-ment*, in Trench, Select Glossary, from L. *temperāmentum*. Also *dis-temper*, q. v., *at-temper*. **Doublet**, *tamper*.

TEMPEST, bad weather, violent storm, great commotion. (F. − L.) ME. *tempest*, Rob. of Glouc. p. 50, l. 1151. − OF. *tempeste*, 'a tempest, storm, bluster ;' Cot. Mod. F. *tempête*. − Late L. **tempesta*, not found (though *tempestus*, adj., and *tempestāre*, verb, both appear) ; for L. *tempestās*, season, fit time, weather, good weather ; also bad weather, storm ; allied to *tempus*, season, time ; see **Temporal**. Brugmann, ii. §§ 102, 132. Der. *tempest*, verb, Milton, P. L. vii. 412, from MF. *tempester*, 'to storm ;' Cot. Also *tempest-u-ous*, 1 Hen. VI, v. 5. 5, from MF. *tempestuĕux*, 'tempestuous,' Cot., from L. *tempestuōsus* ; *tempestuous-ly*, -*ness*.

TEMPLE (1), a fane, edifice in honour of a deity or for religious worship. (L.) ME. *temple*, Chaucer, C. T. 10167, 10169 (E 2293, 2295). AS. *templ*, *tempel* (common), John, ii. 20. − L. *templum*, a temple. Formed (with excrescent *p* after *m*) from an older form **tem-lum* (Walde).+Gk. τέμενος, a sacred enclosure, piece of ground cut off and set apart for religious purposes ; allied to Gk. τέμ-ν-ειν (fut. τεμῶ), to cut. Der. *templ-ar*, one of a religious order for the protection of the *temple* and Holy Sepulchre, founded in 1118, suppressed in 1312 (Haydn), ME. *templere*, P. Plowman, B. xv. 509, from Late L. *templārius* (Ducange). Also *templet*, a pattern or model indicating the outline of a baluster, &c., from F. *templet*, the same (Littré), dimin. of F. *temple*, in the same sense, from L. *templum*, a small timber, the same word as *templum*, a temple. Also *con-templ-ate*, q. v.

TEMPLE (2), the flat portion of either side of the head above the cheek-bone. (F. − L.) Gen. used in the plural. ME. *templys*, pl., Voc. 626. 16. Gower has *temples*, C. A. iii. 370 ; bk. viii. l. 2819. − OF. *temples*, 'the temples ;' Cot. ; Norm. dial. *temples* ; Mod. F. *tempe*, sing. Formed, with the common change from *r* to *l*, from L. *tempora*, pl., the temples. Der. *tempor-al*, adj., from F. *temporal*, ' of or in the temples,' Cot., from L. *temporālis*, (1) temporal, (2) belonging to the temples.

TEMPORAL (1), pertaining to this world only, worldly, secular. (F. − L.) ME. *temporal*, Wyclif, Matt. xiii. 21. − OF. *temporal*, usually *temporel*, 'temporall ;' Cot. − L. *temporālis*, temporal. − L. *tempor-*, for *tempus*, season, time, opportunity. Der. *temporal-ly* ; *temporal-i-ty*, spelt *temporalitie*, Sir T. More, Works, p. 232 e, from Late L. *temporālitās*, revenues of the church (Ducange). Also *tempor-ar-y*, Meas. for Meas. v. 145 (where it seems to mean respecting things not spiritual), from L. *temporārius*, lasting for a time ; *tempor-ar-i-ly*, *tempor-ar-i-ness*. Also *tempor-ise*, Much Ado, i. 1. 276, from F. *temporiser*, 'to temporise it, to observe the time,' Cot. ; *tempor-is-er*, Wint. Tale, i. 2. 302. Also *con-tempor-an-e-ous*, *con-tempor-ar-y*, *ex-tempore*. And see *temper*, *tempest*, *tense* (1).

TEMPORAL (2) ; for which see **Temple** (2).

TEMPT, to put to trial, test, entice to evil. (F. − L.) ME. *tempten*, Ancren Riwle, p. 178. − OF. *tempter*, later *tenter*, 'to tempt, prove, try, sound, provoke unto evill ;' Cot. − L. *temptāre*, occasional spelling of *tentāre*, to handle, touch, feel, try the strength of, assail, tempt. Frequentative of *tendere*, to stretch (pp. *tentus*) ; Bréal. [But *temptāre* may have been written as *tentāre* by error ; if so, the words are unconnected.] Der. *tempt-er*, Wyclif, Matt. iv. 3 ; *tempt-r-ess*, Ford, The Broken Heart, v. 1, from MF. *tenteresse*, 'a tempteresse, a woman that tempts,' Cot. ; *tempt-ing*, *tempt-ing-ly* ; *tempt-at-ion*, ME. *temptacioun*, Wyclif, Matt. xxvi. 41, from OF. *temptation*, usually *tentation*, 'a temptation,' Cot., from L. acc. *tentātiōnem*. Also *at-tempt*. **Doublet**, *tent* (2), vb.

TEMULENT, drunken. (L.) Rare. − L. *tēmulentus*, drunken. Allied to *tēmētum*, intoxicating drink. See **Abstemious**. Cf. Skt. *tāmya*, to be exhausted.

TEN, twice five. (E.) ME. *ten*, Wyclif, Matt. xxv. 1. OMerc. *tēn* ; AS. *tien*, *tŷn*. Usually *tŷn*, Matt. xxv. 1.+Du. *tien* ; Icel. *tíu*, ten, *tigr*, a decade ; Dan. *ti* ; Swed. *tio* ; Goth. *taihun* ; G. *zehn*, OHG. *zehan*.+L. *decem* (whence F. *dix*, Ital. *dieci*, Span. *diez*) ; Gk. δέκα ; Lithuan. *deszimtis* ; Russ. *desiat(e)* ; W. *deg* ; Irish and Gael. *deich* ; Pers. *dah* (Palmer's Dict. col. 278) ; Skt. *daça*. β. All from Teut. type **tehun* ; Idg. type **dekəm*. Brugmann, ii. § 174. Origin unknown. Der. *ten-fold*, O. Eng. Homilies, ii. 135, l. 19 (see **Fold**) ; *ten-th*, ME. *tenþe*, Will. of Palerne, 4715, also *teonþe*, O. Eng. Homilies, i. 219, l. 17 ; also *tende*, Ormulum, 2715, due to a confusion of AS. *tēoða*, tenth, with Icel. *tíundi*, tenth ; the true E. word is *tithe*, q. v. Hence *tenth-ly*. From the same base we have *decim-al*, *decim-ate*, *duo-decim-al*, *deca-de*, *deca-gon*, *deca-hedron*, *deca-logue*, *deca-syllabic*, *decem-vir*, *dec-ennial*, *do-deca-gon*, *do-deca-hedron*, *dime*. ¶ The suffix -*teen*, ME. -*tenĕ* (dissyllabic), answers to OMerc. -*tēne*, AS. -*tiĕne*, -*tŷne*, as in *eahta-tŷne*, eighteen, Judg. iii. 14 ; formed by adding the pl. suffix -*e* to *tēn* or *tŷn*, ten. Hence *thir-teen* (AS. *þrēotŷne*) ; *four-teen* (AS. *fēower-tŷne*) ; *fif-teen* (AS. *fíf-tŷne*) ; *six-teen* (AS. *six-tŷne*) ; *seven-teen* (AS. *seofon-tŷne*) ; *eigh-teen*, miswritten for *eight-teen* (AS. *eahta-tŷne*) ; *nine-teen* (AS. *nigon-tŷne*). ¶ The suffix -*ty*, ME. -*ty*=

AS. *-tig*, as in *twen-ty* (AS. *twĕn-tig*), &c. This suffix appears also in Icel. *sex-tigir*, *sex-tugr*, *sex-tögr*, sixty, and in Goth. *saihs-tigjus*, G. *sech-zig*, sixty, &c.; all from a Teut. base **tegu-*, allied to **Ten.**

TENABLE, that can be held, kept, or defended. (F.—L.) In Hamlet, i. 2. 248.—F. *tenable*, 'holdable;' Cot. Coined from F. *tenir*, to hold.—L. *tenēre*, to hold, keep, retain, reach, orig. to stretch or extend, a sense retained in *per-tinēre*, to extend through to. —√TEN, to stretch, extend; see **Thin.** Cf. Gk. τείνειν (for **τέν-γειν*), to stretch, Skt. *tan*, to stretch. **Der.** (from L. *tenēre*) *abs-tain*, *abs-tin-ence*, *ap-per-tain*, *ap-pur-ten-ance*, *attempt*, *con-tain*, *con-tent*, *con-tin-ent*, *con-tin-ue*, *coun-ten-ance*, *de-tain*, *de-tent-ion*, *dis-con-tin-ue*, *dis-con-tent*, *dis-coun-ten-ance*, *enter-tain*, *im-per-tin-ent*, *in-con-tin-ent*, *lieu-ten-ant*, *main-tain*, *main-ten-ance*, *mal-con-tent*, *ob-tain*, *per-tain*, *per-tin-ac-i-ous*, *per-tin-ent*, *pur-ten-ance*, *rein*, *re-tain*, *re-tent-ion*, *re-tin-ue*, *sus-tain*, *sus-ten-ance*, *sus-tent-at-ion*; and see *ten-ac-i-ous*, *ten-ac-i-ty*, *ten-ant*, *tend* (with its derivatives), *tend-er*, *tend-on*, *ten-dril*, *ten-e-ment*, *ten-et*, *ten-on*, *ten-or*, *tent* (2), *ten-u-ity*, *ex-ten-u-ate*, *ten-ure*, *tempt*, *tent-acle*, *tent-at-ive*. And see *tone*.

TENACIOUS, holding fast, stubborn. (L.) 'So *tenacious* of his bite;' Howell, Famil. Letters, b. ii. let. 2, July 3, 1635. Coined as if from L. **tenaciōsus*, from *tenāci-*, decl. stem of *tenax*, holding fast.—L. *tenēre*, to hold. See **Tenable. Der.** *tenacious-ly*, *-ness*.

TENACITY, the quality of sticking fast to. (F.—L.) Spelt *tenacitie* in Minsheu, ed. 1627.—MF. *tenacité*, 'tenacity;' Cot.—L. *tenācitātem*, acc. of *tenācitās*.—L. *tenāci-*, decl. stem of *tenax*; see **Tenacious.**

TENANT, one who holds land under another. (F.—L.) ME. *tenant*, Rob. of Brunne, tr. of Langtoft, p. 19, l. 10.—F. *tenant*, holding; pres. part. of *tenir*, to hold; see **Tenable. Der.** *tenanc-y*, Bp. Hall, Satires, b. iv. sat. 2, l. 25 from end; *tenant-able*, *tenant-less*, *tenant-ry* (a coined word). Also *lieu-tenant*, q.v. And see *tenement*.

TENCH, a fish of the carp kind. (F.—L.) ME. *tenche*, Prompt. Parv.—OF. *tenche*, 'a tench;' Cot. Mod. F. *tanche*.—L. *tinca*, a tench. Cf. Gascon *tenco*, a tench.

TEND (1), to aim at, or move towards, to incline, bend, to contribute to a purpose. (F.—L.) In Hamlet, iii. 1. 170.—F. *tendre*, 'to tend, bend;' Cot.—L. *tendere*, to stretch, extend, direct, tender. Allied to *tenēre*, to hold; see **Tenable.** From √TEN, to stretch; see **Thin.** Brugmann, ii. § 696 (3). **Der.** *tend-enc-y*, formed by adding *-y* to the obsolete sb. *tendence*, signifying 'inclination,' for which see Richardson; and the sb. *tendence* was coined from L. *tendent-*, stem of the pres. part. of *tendere*. Also *tense* (2); *tend-er* (2). Also (from L. *tendere*, pp. *tensus* and *tentus*), *at-tend*, *tend* (2), *at-tent-ion*, *co-ex-tend*, *con-tend*, *dis-tend*, *ex-tend*, *ex-tens-ion*, *ex-tent*, *in-tend*, *in-tense*, *in-tent*, *ob-tend*, *os-tens-ible*, *os-tent-at-ion*, *por-tend*, *pre-tend*, *pro-tend*, *sub-tend*, *super-in-tend*; and see *tense* (2), *tens-ile*, *tender* (3), *tend-on*, *tent* (1), *tent-er*, *toise*. **Doublet,** *tender* (2).

TEND (2), to attend, take care of. (F.—L.) In Hamlet, i. 3. 83, Much Ado, i. 3. 17. Coined by dropping the initial *a* of OF. *atendre*, to wait, attend. It is, in fact, short for **Attend,** q.v. **Der.** *tend-ing*, sb. (for *attending*), Macb. i. 5. 36; *tend-ance* (for *attendance*), Timon, i. 1. 57. And see *tender* (3).

TENDER (1), soft, delicate, fragile, weak, feeble, compassionate. (F.—L.) ME. *tendre*, Ancren Riwle, p. 112, l. 11.—F. *tendre*, 'tender;' Cot. Formed (with excrescent *d* after *n*) from L. *tenerum*, acc. of *tener*, tender; orig. thin, fine, allied to *tenuis*, thin. —√TEN, to stretch; see **Thin. Der.** *tender-ly*, *-ness*; *tender-heart-ed*, Rich. II, iii. 3. 160; *tender-heft-ed*, K. Lear, ii. 4. 176 (Folio edd.), where *heft* = *haft*, a handle; so that *tender-hefted* = tender-handled, tender-hilted, gentle to the touch, impressible; see **Haft.** Also *tender*, vb., to regard fondly, cherish, Rich. II, i. 1. 32, and in Palsgrave; a word which seems to be more or less confused with *tender* (2), q.v. Hence *tender*, sb., regard, care, K. Lear, i. 4. 230. And see *tendr-il*.

TENDER (2), to offer, proffer for acceptance, show. (F.—L.) In Shak. Temp. iv. 5.—F. *tendre*, 'to tend, bend, . . . spread, or display . . also, to tender or offer unto;' Cot.—L. *tendere*, to stretch, &c. See **Tend** (1), of which *tender* is a later form, retaining the *r* of the F. infinitive; cf. *attainder* = F. *attaindre*. **Der.** *tender*, sb., an offer, proposal. **Doublet,** *tend* (1).

TENDER (3), a small vessel that attends a larger one with stores; a carriage carrying coals, attached to a locomotive engine. (F.—L.) 'A fireship and three *tenders*;' Dampier's Voyages, an. 1685 (R.). Merely short for *attender* = attendant or subsidiary vessel; see **Tend** (2).

TENDON, a hard strong cord by which a muscle is attached to a bone. (F.—L.) In Cotgrave.—F. *tendon*, 'a tendon, or taile of a muscle;' Cot. Cf. Span. *tendon*, Port. *tendão*, Ital. *tendine*, a tendon.

From a Late L. type **tendo*, with gen. case both *tendōnis* and *tendinis*; formed from L. *tendere*, to stretch, from its contractile force. See **Tend** (1). **Der.** *tendin-ous* (R.), from F. *tendineux*, 'of a tendon;' Cot.

TENDRIL, the slender clasper of a plant, whereby it clings to a support. (F.—L.) Spelt *tendrell* in Minsheu, ed. 1627; and in Drant, tr. of Horace, Bk. ii. Sat. 4, fol. G 8, back (1566). In Milton, P. L. iv. 307. Shortened from MF. *tendrillons*, s. pl. 'tendrells, little gristles;' Cot. Or from an OF. **tendrille* or **tendrelle*, not recorded. Cot. also gives F. *tendron*, 'a tender fellow, a cartilage, or gristle; also a *tendrell*, or the tender branch or sprig of a plant.' All these forms are from F. *tendre*, tender; see **Tender** (1). So also Ital. *tenerume*, a tendril, from *tenero*, tender. ¶ Not from *tenēre*, to hold, nor from *tendere*, to stretch.

TENEBROUS, TENEBRIOUS, gloomy, dark. (F.—L.) *Tenebrous* is in Cotgrave, and in Hawes, History of Grand Amour (1555), ch. 3 (Todd). '*Tenebrious* light' is in Young, Night Thoughts, Night 9, l. 966. The latter is a false form.—F. *tenebreux*, 'tenebrous;' Cot.—L. *tenebrōsus*, gloomy.—L. *tenebræ*, s. pl., darkness. Allied to Skt. *tamisra-*, darkness, *tamas*, gloom. √TEM, to choke. Brugmann, i. §§ 413, 590.

TENEMENT, a holding, a dwelling inhabited by a tenant. (F.—L.) ME. *tenement*, Rob. of Brunne, tr. of Langtoft, p. 34, last line.—F. *tenement*, 'a tenement, inheritance,' &c.; Cot.—Late L. *tenementum*, a holding, fief; Ducange.—L. *tenēre*, to hold; see **Tenable** and **Tenant. Der.** *tenement-al*, adj.

TENET, a principle which a person holds or maintains. (L.) 'The *tenet* must be this;' Hooker, Eccl. Polity, b. viii. (R.).—L. *tenet*, he holds; 3 p. s. pres. tense of *tenēre*, to hold; see **Tenable.** Cf. *audit*, *habitat*, *exit*, and other similar formations.

TENNIS, a game in which a ball is driven against a wall (or over a cord) by rackets, and kept continually in motion. (F.—L.) First mentioned in Gower's Balade to King Henry IV, st. 43, l. 295; printed in Chaucer's Works, ed. 1532, fol. 377, col. 2; ed. 1561, fol. 332, col. 1, where it is spelt *tennes*; but the Trentham MS. has *tenetz*. Other spellings are *teneis*, *tenyse*. '*Teneys*, pley, Teniludus, manupilatus, tenisia. *Teneys-pleyer*, Teniludius;' Prompt. Parv. Spelt *tenyse*, Sir T. Elyot, The Governour, b. i. c. 27, § 7. '*Tenyse-ball*, pelote: *Tennys-play*, jeu de la paulme;' Palsgrave. Turbervile has a poem 'to his friend P., Of Courting, Trauailing, and *Tenys.*' It is spelt *tenes* in 1494; Excerpta Historica, p. 98. β. The AF. *tenetz*, F. *tenez* (<L. *tenētis*, 2 p. pl. indic. of *tenēre*, to hold) was also used for L. *tenēte*, 2 p. pl. imperative; with the sense 'take this;' and we may conjecture that it was used by the player who served, like our 'play!' ¶ This seems the only possible explanation of the form *tenetz*, which was accented on the 2nd syllable, as the rhythm shows:—'Of the *tenétz* to winne or lese a chace.' The word (as a sb.) is AF., not OF. In N. and Q. 9 S. ix. 27, is the following note. 'M. Jusserand quotes from Lusus Puerilis, Paris, 1555, and deduces that the *excipe* of Cordier and the *accipe* of Erasmus were the Latin version[s] of the French *tenez*, an exclamation used in commencing play.' The AF. *tenez*, 'take or receive this,' is addressed to one person only in the Chanson de Roland, 387.

TENNY, the colour of orange, in heraldry. (F.—G.) Also spelt *tenney*, *tawney*; see Boutell's Heraldry.—OF. *tenné*, variant of *tané*, *tanné*, tawny, tan-coloured (Godefroy). The same word as **Tawny,** q.v.

TENON, the end of a piece of wood inserted into the socket or mortice of another, to hold the two together. (F.—L.) In Levins. ME. *tenown*, *tenon*; Prompt. Parv.—F. *tenon*, 'a tenon; the end of a rafter put into a morteise; *tenons*, pl. the vice-nailes wherewith the barrel of a piece is fastened unto the stock; also the (leathern) handles of a target;' Cot. All these senses involve the notion of *holding fast.* Formed, with suffix *-on* (L. acc. *-ōnem*), from *ten-ir*, to hold.—L. *tenēre*; see **Tenable.**

TENOR, the general course of a thought or saying, purport; the highest kind of adult male voice. (F.—L.) ME. *tenour*. '*Tenour*, Tenor;' Prompt. Parv. 'Anothir lettre . . of a more bitter *tenour*;' King Alisaunder, 2977. 'Many . . ordenauncis were made, wherof the *tenoure* is sette out in the ende of this boke;' Fabyan's Chron. an. 1257, ed. Ellis, p. 343. '*Tenour*, a parte in pricke-songe, *teneur*;' Palsgrave.—F. *teneur*, 'the tenor part in musick; the tenor, content, stuffe, or substance of a matter;' Cot.—L. *tenōrem*, acc. of *tenor*, a holding on, uninterrupted course, tenor, sense or tenor of a law, tone, accent.—L. *tenēre*, to hold; see **Tenable.** ¶ The old (and proper etymological) spelling is *tenour*, like *honour*, *colour*, &c. The *tenor* in music (Ital. *tenore*) is due to the notion of holding or continuing the dominant note (Scheler).

TENSE (1), the form of a verb used to indicate the time and state of the action. (F.—L.) In Levins. Spelt *tence* and *tense* by

Palsgrave, On the Verb. Shoreham has *tense*, in the sense of 'time;' p. 39. In Chaucer, C. T. 16343 (G 875), the expression 'that futur *temps*' ought to be explained rather as 'that future *tense*' than 'that future time;' see my note on the line. — F. *temps*, time, season; OF. *tens* (Burguy). — L. *tempus*, time; also a tense of a verb; see **Temporal**.

TENSE (2), tightly strained, rigid. (L.) 'Her forehead was *tense*;' Goldsmith, Vicar of Wakefield, ch. 28, § 1. — L. *tensus*, stretched, pp. of *tendere*; see **Tend** (1). Der. *tense-ly*, *-ness*; *tension*, in Phillips, ed. 1706, from L. *tensiōnem*, acc. of *tensio*, a stretching; *tensor*, in Phillips, used as a variant of *extensor*; *tens-ile*, in Blount, ed. 1674, a coined word; *tens-i-ty*, a coined word. Also *in-tense*, *toise*.

TENT (1), a pavilion, a portable shelter of canvas stretched out with ropes. (F. — L.) ME. *tente*, Rob. of Glouc., p. 203, l. 4156. — F. *tente*, 'a tent or pavillion;' Cot. — Late L. *tenta*, a tent; Ducange. Properly fem. of *tentus*, pp. of *tendere*, to stretch; see **Tend** (1). Obviously suggested by L. *tentōrium*, a tent, a derivative from the same verb. Der. *tent-ed*, Oth. i. 3. 85.

TENT (2), a roll of lint used to dilate a wound. (F. — L.) See **Nares**. Properly a probe; the verb *to tent* is used for to probe, Hamlet, ii. 2. 626. ME. *tente*. '*Tente* of a wownde or a soore, *Tenta*;' Prompt. Parv. — F. *tente*, 'a tent for a wound;' Cot. Due to the L. verb *tentāre*, to handle, touch, feel, test; cf. F. *tenter*, 'to tempt, to prove, try, sound, essay;' Cot. See **Tempt**. Cf. Span. *tienta*, a probe, *tiento*, a touch. Der. *tent*, verb, as above.

TENT (3), a kind of wine. (Span. — L.) '*Tent* or *Tent-wine*, is a kind of Alicant, . . . and is a general name for all wines in Spain except white; from the Span. *vino tinto*, i.e. a deep red wine;' Blount, ed. 1674. — Span. *vino tinto*, red wine; *tinto*, deep-coloured, said of wine. — L. *tinctus*, pp. of *tingere*, to dye; see **Tinge**.

TENT (4), care, heed. (F. — L.) 'Took *tent*;' Burns, Death and Doctor Hornbook, st. 3. Short for *attent* or *attention*; see **Attend**. Der. *tent*, verb.

TENTACLE, a feeler of an insect. (L.) Modern. Englished from Late L. *tentāculum, which is also a coined word, formed from *tentāre*, to feel; see **Tempt**. Cf. L. *spirāculum*, from *spirāre*. Der. *tentacul-ar*.

TENTATIVE, experimental. (L.) 'Falsehood, though it be but *tentative*;' Bp. Hall, Contemplations, b. xx. cont. 3. § 21. — L. *tentātiuus*, trying, tentative. — L. *tentātus*, pp. of *tentāre*, to try; see **Tempt**.

TENTER, a frame for stretching cloth by means of hooks. (F. — L.) Properly *tenture*; but a verb *tent* was coined, and from it a sb. *tenter*, which took the place of *tenture*. The verb occurs in P. Plowman, B. xv. 447; or rather the pp. *ytented*, suggested by L. *tentus*. ME. *tenture*. '*Tenture*, *Tentowre*, for clothe, Tensorium, extensorium, tentura;' Prompt. Parv. '*Tentar* for clothe, tend, tende; *Tenterhoke*, houet;' Palsgrave. — F. *tenture*, 'a stretching, spreading, extending;' Cot. — L. *tentūra*, a stretching; cf. *tentus*, pp. of *tendere*, to stretch; see **Tend** (1). Der. *tenter-hook*, spelt *tenterhoke* in Palsgrave, a hook orig. used for stretching cloth.

TENUITY, slenderness, thinness, rarity. (F. — L.) Spelt *tenuitie* in Minsheu, ed. 1627. — MF. *tenuité*, 'tenuity, thinness;' Cot. — L. *tenuitātem*, acc. of. *tenuitās*, thinness. — L. *tenuis*, thin. — √TEN, to stretch; see **Thin**. Der. (from L. *tenuis*) *ex-tenu-ate*.

TENURE, a holding of a tenement. (F. — L.) In Hamlet, v. 1. 108. — F. *tenure*, 'a tenure, a hold or estate in land;' Cot. — Late L. *tenūra* (in common use); Ducange. — L. *tenēre*, to hold; see **Tenable**.

TEOCALLI, a Mexican temple. (Mexican.) Mex. *teocalli*. — Mex. *teotl*, a god (which loses *tl* in composition); and *calli*, a house.

TEPID, moderately warm. (L.) In Milton, P. L. vii. 417. — L. *tepidus*, warm. — L. *tepēre*, to be warm. — √TEP, to be warm, to glow; whence Skt. *tap*, to be warm, to warm, to shine, *tapas*, fire; Russ. *topit(e)*, to heat; Irish *tē*, hot. Der. *tepid-i-ty*, from MF. *tepidité*, luke-warmnesse,' Cot., as if from L. acc. *tepiditātem; *tepid-ness*.

TERAPHIM, idols, images, or household gods, consulted as oracles. (Heb.) See Judges, xvii. 5, xviii. 14; Hosea, iii. 4 (A.V.). — Heb. *terāphim*, s. pl., images connected with magical rites.

TERCE, the same as **Tierce**, q. v.

TERCEL, the male of any kind of hawk. (F. — L.) Corruptly spelt *tassel*, Romeo, ii. 2. 160; rightly *tercel*, Troilus, iii. 2. 56. See *Tassel* in Nares. ME. *tercel*; 'the *tercel* egle,' Chaucer, Assembly of Fowls, 393. Also *tercelet*, a dimin. form; Chaucer, C. T. 10818 (F 504). — OF. *tercel*, *tiercel* (Godefroy), whence MF. dimin. *tiercelet*, 'the tassell, or male of any kind of hawk, so tearmed because he is commonly, a third part lesse then the female;' Cot. Cf. Ital. *terzolo* (now spelt *terzuolo*), 'a tassell-gentle of a hauke;' Florio. Derived (with dimin. suffix *-el*) from OF. *tiers*, *tierce*, third; just as Ital. *terzolo* is from Ital. *terzo*, third. — L. *tertius*, third; see **Tierce** and **Three**. ¶ Burguy gives a different reason, viz. that, in popular opinion,

every third bird hatched was a male; he refers to Raynouard's Provençal Dict., v. 412. Either way, the etymology is the same.

TEREBINTH, the turpentine-tree. (L. — Gk.) *Teribinth*; in Spenser, Shep. Kal., July, 86. — L. *terebinthus*. — Gk. τερέβινθος, the turpentine-tree. Der. *turpent-ine*.

TEREDO, a wood-worm. (L. — Gk.) L. *terēdo*. — Gk. τερηδών, a wood-worm; so named from boring into wood. — Gk. τερ-, base of τείρειν (for *τέρ-γειν), to bore. See **Trite**, **Termite**.

TERGIVERSATION, a subterfuge, fickleness of conduct. (F. — L.) In Cotgrave. — F. *tergiversation*, 'tergiversation, a flinching, withdrawing;' Cot. Lit. a turning of one's back. — L. *tergiuersātiōnem*, acc. of *tergiuersātio*, a subterfuge. — L. *tergiuersāri*, to turn one's back, decline, refuse, shuffle, shift. — L. *tergi-*, for *tergum*, the back; and *uersāri*, to turn oneself about, pass. of *uersāre*, to turn about, frequentative of *uertere* (pp. *uersus*), to turn; see **Verse**.

TERM, a limited period, a word or expression. (F. — L.) ME. *terme*, Rob. of Brunne, tr. of Langtoft, p. 316, l. 21. — F. *terme*, 'a term, time, or day; also, a tearm, word, speech;' Cot. — L. *terminum*, acc. of *terminus*, a boundary-line, bound, limit (whence also Ital. *termine*, *termino*, Span. *termino*). Cf. OL. *termen*, with the same sense; Gk. τέρμα, a limit. — √TER, to pass over, cross, fulfil; cf. Skt. *tāraya*, to cause to pass over. Der. *term*, vb., Temp. v. 15; and see *termination*. Also (from L. *terminus*) *termin-al*, adj., from L. *terminālis*; *con-termin-ous*, *ex-termin-ate*, *pre-de-termine*. And (from the same root) *en-ter*; *thrum* (1).

TERMAGANT, a boisterous, noisy woman. (F. — Ital. — L.) ME. *Termagant*, *Termagaunt*, Chaucer, C. T. 13739 (B 2000). *Termagant* was one of the idols whom (in the medieval romances) the Saracens are supposed to worship; see King of Tars, in Ritson's Metrical Romances, ii. 174-182; Lybeaus Disconus, in the same, ii. 55. See Nares, who explains that the personage of *Termagant* was introduced into the old moralities, and represented as of a violent character. In Ram Alley, we have the expression : 'that swears, God bless us, Like a very *termagant*;' Dodsley's Old Plays, ed. Hazlitt, x. 322; and see Hamlet, iii. 2. 15. So also: 'this hot *termagant* Scot;' 1 Hen. IV, v. 4. 114. It has now subsided into the signification of a scolding woman. 'So must all our tavern *tarmagons* be used, or they'll trepan you;' Lady Alimony, Act i. sc. 4 (1659). The name is a corruption of OF. *Tervagant*, *Tervagan*, or *Tarvagan*; spelt *Teruagant* in Layamon's Brut, l. 5353, where he is a Roman (!) god; and *Tervagan* in the Chanson de Roland, l. 611, where it signifies a Saracen idol. — Ital. *Trivigante*, the same, Ariosto, xii. 59 (see Nares, s. v. *Trivigant*); more correctly, *Trivagante*. It has been suggested that *Trivagante* or *Tervagante* is the moon, wandering under the three names of *Selene* (or *Luna*) in heaven, *Artemis* (or *Diana*) in earth, and *Persephone* (*Proserpine*) in the lower world. Cf. *dea trivia* as an epithet of Diana. — L. *ter*, thrice, or *tri-*, thrice; and *uagant-*, stem of pres. part. of *uagāri*, to wander. See **Ternary** and **Triform**, and **Vagabond**. ¶ See also my note to the line in Chaucer and Tyrwhitt's note; Ritson, Met. Rom. iii. 260; Quarterly Review, xxi. 515; Wheeler, Noted Names of Fiction; Trench, Select Glossary; &c. Perhaps Ital. *Trivigante* is of Eastern origin.

TERMINATION, end, limit, result. (F. — L.) In Much Ado, ii. 1. 256, where it is used with the sense of *term*, i. e. word or expression. — F. *termination*, 'a determining, limiting;' Cot. — L. *terminātiōnem*, acc. of *terminātio*, a bounding, fixing, determining. — L. *termināre*, to limit. — L. *terminus*, a bound, limit; see **Term**. Der. *termination-al*. Also (from L. *termināre*) *termin-ate*, *termin-able*, *termin-at-ive*, *terminat-ive-ly*. We also use L. *terminus*, sb., as an E. word; Marlowe, Dr. Faustus, A. ii. sc. 2.

TERMITE, a white ant. (F. — L.) F. *termite*, used in 1812 (Hatzfeld). — L. *termitem*, acc. of *termes*, more commonly *tarmes*, a wood-worm. Allied to *terēdo*, a wood-worm; from the same root. See **Teredo**.

TERN, an aquatic fowl. (Scand.) Not in the old dictionaries. I find it in a translation of Buffon's Nat. Hist., London, 1792; and it was, doubtless, in much earlier use. — Dan. *terne*, *tærne*, a tern; Swed. *tärna*; Icel. *þerna*, a tern, occurring in the local name *þerney* (tern-island), near Rejkjavik in Iceland. Widegren's Swed. Dict. (ed. 1788) has *tärna*, 'tern.' β. It is remarkable that Dan. *terne*, Swed. *tärna*, Icel. *þerna*, also mean a hand-maid, maid-servant; cf. G. *dirne*; but the words are unrelated (see *dirne* in Kluge). ¶ The scientific L. name *Sterna* was taken from E. *stern*, a name for the black tern used by Turner (1544). 'The field is Azure, a Cheuron betweene three *Sternes*,' the said birds being figured in the accompanying wood-cut; Guillim, Display of Heraldry, ed. 1664, p. 216. Evidently from AS. *stearn*; 'Beacita, vel sturnus, *stearn*,' in a list of birds, Voc. 131, 11; 'Beacita, *stearn*;' Corpus Gloss., 284. The forms *stern*, *stare* (for starling), and L. *sturnus*, are related; and so also (with loss of initial *s*) Icel. *þerna*, Dan. *terne*, Swed. *tärna*. The form *tern* is Scand., because the cognate E. form would be *thern or *stern*. Cf. Norfolk *starn*, a tern; E. D. D.

TERNARY, proceeding by, or consisting of threes. (L.) ' A senary, and a *ternary*;' Holland, tr. of Plutarch, p. 652 (R.).—L. *ternārius*, consisting of threes.—L. *ternī*, pl., by threes. Allied to *ter*, thrice, and to *trēs*, three; the latter being cognate with E. *three*. See **Three**. Der. (from L. *ternī*), *tern-ate*, arranged in threes, a coined word.

TERRA-COTTA, a kind of hard pottery. (Ital.—L.) From Ital. *terra cotta*, baked (lit. cooked) earth.—L. *terra*, earth (see **Terrace**); *cocta*, fem. of *coctus*, cooked, pp. of *coquere*, to cook; see **Cook**.

TERRACE, a raised level bank of earth, elevated flat space. (F.—Ital.—L.) Frequently spelt *tarras*, as in Spenser, F. Q. v. 9. 21; here *ar* is put for *er*, as in *parson* for *person*, *Clark* for *clerk*; &c. —MF. *terrace*, F. *terrasse*, 'a plat, platform, hillock of earth, a terrace, or high and open gallery;' Cot.—Ital. *terraccia, terrazza*, 'a terrace;' Florio. Formed with suffix *-accia*, usually with an augmentative force, from Ital. *terr-a*, earth.—L. *terra*, earth. **β.** L. *terra* stands for an older form *tersa, and signifies dry ground or land, as opposed to sea. Allied to Gk. ταρσός (Attic ταρρός), a stand or frame for drying things upon, any broad flat surface; τέρσεσθαι, to become dry, dry up. Also to Irish *tir*, land, *tirmen*, main land, *tirim*, dry; W. *tir*, land; Gael. *tir*, land (whence *ceanntire*, headland, land's end, Cantire). Cf. also L. *torrere*, to parch.—√TERS, to be dry; whence Skt. *trsh*, to thirst, Goth. *thaursus*, dry, G. *dürr*, dry. See **Thirst** and **Torrid**. Brugmann, i. § 881. Der. *terra-cotta*, q. v. Also *terr-aqueous*, consisting of land and water; see **Aqueous**. And see *terr-een, terr-ene, terr-estri-al, terr-i-er, terr-it-or-y*. Also *fumi-tory, in-ter, medi-terr-an-e-an, tur-meric*.

TERREEN, TUREEN, a large dish or vessel, esp. for soup. (F.—L.) Both spellings are poor; it should rather be *terrine*; *tureen* is the commoner, and the worse, spelling. So called because orig. made of earthenware. Spelt *tureen*, Goldsmith, The Haunch of Venison; *terrine* in Phillips, ed. 1706.—F. *terrine*, 'an earthen pan;' Cot. Formed, as if from a L. adj. *terrīnus, earthen, from *terra*, earth; see **Terrace**.

TERRENE, earthly. (L.) In Shak. Antony, iii. 13. 153.—L. *terrēnus*, earthly.—L. *terra*, earth; see **Terrace**.

TERRESTRIAL, earthly. (L.) Spelt *terestryall*, Skelton, Of the Death of Edw. IV, l. 15. Coined by adding *-al* (L. *-ālis*) to L. *terrestri-*, decl. stem of *terrestris*, earthly.—L. *terra*, earth · with suffix *-st-tri-*; see **Terrace**.

TERRIBLE, awful, dreadful. (F.—L.) Spelt *terryble* in Palsgrave.—F. *terrible*, 'terrible;' Cot.—L. *terribilis*, causing terror.—L. *terrēre*, to terrify; with suffix *-bilis*. Allied to L. *terror*, terror : see **Terror**. Der. *terribl-y, terrible-ness*.

TERRIER, a kind of dog; also a register of landed property. (F.—L.) In both senses, the word has the same etymology. 1. ME. *terrere, terryare*, hownde; Terrarius;' Prompt. Parv. The dog was so called because it pursues rabbits, &c., into their burrows. *Terrier* is short for *terrier-dog*, i. e. burrow-dog.—F. *terrier*, as in *chien terrier*, 'a terrier;' Cot.—Late L. *terrārius*, belonging to earth. —L. *terra*, earth. Cf. MF. *terrier*, 'the hole, berry, or earth of a conny or fox, also, a little hillock;' Cot.—Late L. *terrārium*, a little hillock; hence, a mound thrown up in making a burrow, a burrow. 2. A legal term; spelt *terrar* in Blount's Nomolexicon; *terrere*, Bury Wills, p. 78 (1478).—F. *papier terrier*, 'the court-roll or catalogue of all the names of a lord's tenants,' &c.; Cot.—Late L. *terrārius*, as in *terrārius liber*, a book in which landed property is described. Formed with suffix *-ārius* from L. *terr-a*, as above. See **Terrace**.

TERRIFIC, terrible, inspiring dread. (L.) Spelt *terrifick*, Milton, P. L. vii. 497.—L. *terrificus*, causing terror.—L. *terri-*, appearing in *terri-tus*, pp. of *terrēre*, to frighten; and *-ficus*, causing, from *facere*, to make; see **Terror** and **Fact**. Der. *terrific-ly*. Also *terrify*, formed as if from a F. *terrifier (given in Littré as a new coinage), from L. *terrificāre*, to terrify.

TERRINE, the same as **Terreen**, q. v.

TERRITORY, domain, extent of land round a city. (F.—L.) In As You Like It, iii. 1. 8; *terrytorie* in Caxton, Siege of Troy, lf. 68, back. Adapted from F. *territoire*, 'a territory;' Cot.—L. *territōrium*, a domain, the land round a town. Formed from L. *terra*, land; as if from a sb. with decl. stem *territōri-*, which may be explained as possessor of land. See **Terrace**. Der. *territori-al*, adj.

TERROR, dread, great fear. (F.—L.) Formerly written *terrour*, All's Well, ii. 3. 4 (first folio); but also *terror*, Meas. for Meas. i. 1. 10; ii. 1. 4 (id.). ME. *terrour*, Libell of E. Policy, l. 935.—F. *terreur*, 'terror;' Cot.—L. *terrōrem*, acc. of *terror*, dread. Allied to *terrēre*, to frighten, to scare; orig. to tremble. **β.** *Terrēre* stands for *tersēre (like *terra* for *tersa); cognate with Skt. *tras*, to

tremble, be afraid, whence *trāsa-*, terror; Gk. τρέειν (for *τρέσ-ειν), to tremble; Lithuan. *triszēti*, to tremble, Russ. *triast(e)*, to shake, shiver. Allied to **Tremble**. Brugmann, ii. § 657. Der. *terror-ism*. And (from same root) *terri-ble, terri-fic, de-ter*.

TERSE, concise, compact, neat. (L.) ' So *terse* and elegant were his conceipts and expressions;' Fuller, Worthies, Devonshire (R.). Used also in the sense of smooth : ' many stones also, . . although *terse* and smooth;' Sir T. Browne, Vulg. Errors, b. ii. c. 4. § 3.—L. *tersus*, wiped off, clean, neat, pure, nice, terse. *Tersus* is pp. of *tergere*, also *tergĕre*, to wipe, rub off, wipe dry, polish a stone (whence Sir T. Browne's use of *terse*). Der. *terse-ly, -ness*.

TERTIAN, occurring every third day. (F.—L.) Chiefly in the phr. *tertian fever* or *tertian ague*. ' A feuer *terciane*;' Chaucer, C. T. 14965 (B 4149).—F. *tertiane*, 'a tertian ague;' Cot.—L. *tertiāna*, a tertian fever; fem. of *tertiānus*, tertian, belonging to the third.—L. *tertius*, third.—L. *ter*, thrice; *trēs*, three, cognate with E. **Three**, q. v. And see **Tierce**.

TERTIARY, of the third formation. (L.) Modern.—L. *tertiārius*, properly containing a third part; but accepted to mean belonging to the third.—L. *terti-us*, third; with suffix *-ārius*; see **Tertian**.

TESSELATE, to form into squares or lay with checker-work. (L.) Chiefly used in the pp. *tesselated*, which is given in Bailey's Dict. vol. ii. ed. 1731. ' *Tesseled* worke;' Knolles, Hist. of the Turks, 1603 (Nares).—L. *tessellātus*, furnished with small square stones, checkered.—L. *tessella*, a small squared piece of stone, a little cube, dimin. of *tessera*, a squared piece, squared block, most commonly in the sense of a die for playing with. **β.** Root uncertain; sometimes referred to Gk. τέσσαρες, four, from its square shape; but such a borrowing is very unlikely, and a *tessera* was cubical, having *six* sides.

TEST, a pot in which metals are tried, a critical examination, trial, proof. (F.—L.) The *test* was a vessel used in alchemy, and also in testing gold. ' *Test*, is a broad instrument made of maribone ashes, hooped about with iron, on which refiners do fine, refine, and part silver and gold from other metals, or as we use to say, *put them to the test* or trial;' Blount's Gloss., ed. 1674. ME. *test*, Chaucer, C. T. 16286 (G 818).—OF. *test*, mod. F. *têt*, a test, in chemistry and metallurgy (Hamilton). Cf. OF. *teste*, sometimes used in the sense of skull, from its likeness to a potsherd; mod. F. *tête*. It is probable that OF. *test* and *teste* were sometimes confused; they merely differ in gender; otherwise, they are the same word. *Test* answers to a L. *testŭ, testum*, an earthen pot (Lewis); whilst *teste* answers to Late L. *testa*, used to denote a certain vessel in treatises on alchemy; a vessel called a *testa* is figured in Theatrum Chemicum, iii. 326. In Italian we find the same words, viz. *testo*, ' the test of silver or gold, a kind of melting-pot that goldsmiths vse,' Florio; also *testa*, 'a head, pate, . . a test, an earthen pot or gallie-cup, burnt tile or brick, a piece of a broken bone, a shard of a pot or tile.' **β.** All allied to L. *testa*, a brick, a piece of baked earthenware, pitcher, also a potsherd, piece of bone, shell of a fish, skull. Some make it an abbreviation of *tersta, i. e. dried or baked, with reference to clay or earthenware; allied to *terra* (<*tersa), dry ground.— √TERS, to be dry; see **Terrace**. Or perhaps cognate with Pers. *tasht*, a bason; see **Tazza**. Der. *test*, verb; cf. ' *tested* gold,' Meas. for Meas. ii. 2. 149. Also *test-ac-e-ous, test-er, test-y*, q. v.

TESTACEOUS, having a hard shell. (L.) In Blount's Gloss., ed. 1674. Englished from L. *testaceus*, consisting of tiles, having a shell, testaceous.—L. *testa*, a piece of dried clay, tile, brick. See **Test**.

TESTAMENT, a solemn declaration in writing, a will, part of the bible. (F.—L.) ME. *testament*, Rob. of Brunne, tr. of Langtoft, p. 20, l. 9; Ancren Riwle, p. 388.—F. *testament*, 'a testament or will;' Cot.—L. *testāmentum*, a thing declared, last will.—L. *testā-ri*, to be a witness, depose to, testify; with suffix *-mentum*.—L. *testis*, a witness. Root uncertain. Der. *testament-ar-y*; *in-test-ate*, q. v.; *test-at-or*, Heb. ix. 16, from L. *testātor*, one who makes a will; *testatr-ix*, L. *testātrix*, fem. form of *testātor*. And see *testify, testimony*. (From L. *testis*) *at-test, con-test, de-test, pro-test*.

TESTER, a sixpence; a flat canopy over a bed or pulpit. (F.—L.) 1. The sense 'sixpence' is obsolete, except as corrupted to *tizzy*; see Shak. 2 Henry IV, iii. 2. 296. The *tester* was so called from the *head* upon it; it is a short form of *testerne*, as in Latimer's Sermons, 1584, fol. 94 (Todd). Again, *testern* is, apparently, a corruption of *teston* (sometimes *testoon*), which was ' a brass coin covered with silver, first struck in the reign of Hen. VIII. The name was given to shillings and sixpences, and Latimer got into trouble by referring to the newly coined shilling or *teston*; see Latimer, Seven Sermons, ed. Arber, p. 85, where it is spelt *testyon*. In 1560 the *teston* of 6*d*. was reduced to 4½*d*. The name *teston* was given to the new coins of Louis XII. of France because they bore the head of that prince; but Ruding observes that the name must have been applied to the E. coin by mere caprice, as all money of this country bore the head of the sovereign;' H. B. Wheatley, note to Ben Jonson, Every Man in his Humour, iv. 2. 104, where *teston* occurs. — F. *teston*, 'a testoon, a piece of silver coin worth xviij*d*. sterling;' Cot. — OF. *teste*, a head; mod. F. *tête*. — L. *testa*, of which one sense was 'skull;' see further under **Test**. 2. '*Testar* for a bedde;' Palsgrave. [Allied to ME. *tester*, a head-piece, helmet, Chaucer, C. T. 2501 (A 2499).] Cf. '*Teester* of a bed;' Prompt. Parv. — OF. *testre*, tester of a bed (Godefroy); cf. MF. *testiere*, 'any kind of head-piece;' Cot. — OF. *teste*, a head; as above.

TESTICLE, a gland in males, secreting seminal fluid. (F. — L.) In Cotgrave. — F. *testicule*, 'a testicle;' Cot. — L. *testiculum*, acc. of *testiculus*, dimin. of *testis*, a testicle.

TESTIFY, to bear witness, protest or declare. (F. — L.) ME. *testifien*, P. Plowman, C. xiii. 172. — F. *testifier*, 'to testify;' Cot. — L. *testificārī*, to bear witness. — L. *testi-*, decl. stem of *testis*, a witness; and *-fic-*, for *facere*, to make; see **Testament** and **Fact**. Der. *testifi-er*.

TESTIMONY, evidence, witness. (L.) In K. Lear, i. 2. 88. Englished from L. *testimonium*, evidence. — L. *testi-*, decl. stem of *testis*, a witness; see **Testament**. The suffix *-monium* = Idg. *-mon-yo-*. ¶ The F. word is *témoin*, OF. *tesmoing*. Der. *testimoni-al*, in Minsheu, from F. *testimonial*, 'a testimoniall,' Cot.; from L. *testimoniālis*, adj.

TESTY, heady, fretful. (F. — L.) In Palsgrave; and in Jul. Cæs. iv. 3. 46. ME. *testif*, Chaucer, C. T., A 4004. — OF. **testif* (not found); allied to MF. *testu*, 'testy, heady, headstrong;' Cot. — OF. *teste*, the head; mod. F. *tête*. See **Test**. Der. *testi-ly*; *testi-ness*, Cymb. iv. 1. 23.

TETANUS, a disease characterised by rigid spasms. (L. — Gk.) Late L. *tetanus*. — Gk. τέτανος, a strain, convulsive spasm; allied to τετανός, adj., stretched. Reduplicated forms (with prefix τε-) allied to τείνειν (for **τέν-γειν*), to stretch. — √TEN, to stretch. See **Thin**.

TETCHY, TECHY, touchy, fretful, peevish. (F. — Low G.) In Rich. III, iv. 4. 168; Troil. i. 1. 99; Rom. i. 3. 32. The sense of *tetchy* (better *techy*) is full of *tetches* or *teches*, i. e. bad habits, freaks, whims, vices. The adj. is formed from ME. *tecche* or *tache*, a habit, esp. a bad habit, vice, freak, caprice, behaviour. '*Tetche, tecche, teche*, or maner of condycyone, Mos, condicio;' Prompt. Parv. 'A chyldis *tatches* in playe, *mores pueri inter ludendum*;' Horman, Vulgaria; cited by Way. '*Offritiæ*, crafty and deceytfull *taches*;' Elyot's Dict. 'Of the maners, *tacches*, and condycyons of houndes;' MS. Sloane 3501, c. xi; cited by Way. 'Þe sires *tacches*' = the father's habits; P. Plowman, B. ix. 146. *Techches*, vices; Ayenbite of Inwyt, p. 32, l. 15. — OF. *tache*, 'a spot, staine, blemish; also, a reproach, disgrace, blot unto a man's good 'name;' Cot. Also spelt *taiche, teche, teque, tek*, a natural quality, disposition, esp. a bad disposition, vice, ill habit, defect, stain (Burguy). Mod. F. *tache*, only in the sense of stain, mark. [Cf. Ital. *tacca*, a notch, cut, defect, stain, Port. and Span. *tacha*, a defect, flaw, crack, small nail or tack.] Of Low G. origin. See **Tache** (2) and **Tack**. Cf. *at-tach* and *de-tach*, from the same source. We even find the E. form *tack*, a spot, stain; Whitgift's Works, ii. 84 (Parker Soc.). ¶ Now corrupted to *touch-y*, from the notion of being sensitive to the *touch*. This is a mere adaptation, not an original expression; see **Touchy**. (The double form in OF., viz. *tache, teche*, causes difficulty and doubt; two or more sources may have been confused together. See Körting, §§ 9331, 9346, 9420.)

TETHER, a rope or chain for tying up a beast. (E.) Formerly written *tedder*. 'Live within thy *tedder*,' i. e. within your income's bounds; Tusser, Husbandry, sect. 10, st. 9 (sidenote). '*Teddered* cattle,' id. sect. 16, st. 33 (E. D. S. p. 42). ME. *tedir*; 'Hoc ligatorium, a *tedyre*;' Wright's Voc. i. 234, col. 2. Not found earlier than the 15th century. The corresponding AS. form would be **teoder*, as shown by OFries. *tiader, tieder*, NFries. *tjödder, tjüdder*, EFries. *tüdder*; cf. also Mid. Du. *tuyer*, 'a line, a shackle, or roape to tye beasts in a pasture;' Hexham. β. We might explain the AS. **teoder* as standing for **teoh-der*; from the base *teoh-* = G. *zieh-*, to draw; cf. Goth. *tiuhan*, to pull, cognate with L. *dūc-ere*. If this be right, the original sense was 'puller;' from its restraint. Cf. OHG. *zeotar*, MHG. *zieter*, a thill, shaft (of a cart). γ. We also find Icel. *tjóðr*, a tether, Low G. *tider, tier*, a tether, Norw. *tjoder* (Aasen), Swed. *tjuder*, Dan. *töir*; all similarly formed. See **Tie**. The suffix *-der* answers to Gk. *-τρον*, L. *-trum*, and denotes the agent. Cf. Bahder, p. 147; Brugmann, ii. § 62. Der. *tether*, verb.

TETRAGON, a figure with four angles. (F. — L. — Gk.) '*Tetragonal*, that is, four-square, as a *tetragon* or quadrangle;' Blount's Gloss., ed. 1674. — MF. *tetragone*, adj., 'of four corners;' Cot. — L. *tetragōnus*. — Gk. τετράγων-ος, four-angled, rectangular, square. — Gk.

τέτρα-, for τετάρα-, prefix allied to τέτταρες, Attic form of τέσσαρες, four, which is cognate with E. **Four**, q. v.; and γωνία, an angle, corner, allied to Gk. γόνυ, a knee, cognate with E. **Knee**. Cf. L. prefix *quadri-*, similarly related to *quatuor*, four. Der. *tetragon-al*, adj., as above.

TETRAHEDRON, a pyramid, a solid figure contained by four equilateral triangles. (Gk.) Spelt *tetraedron* and *tetrahedron* in Phillips, ed. 1706. — Gk. τετρα-, prefix allied to τέσσαρες, four; and -ἑδρον, from ἑδρα, a base, which from ἑδ-, cognate with E. *sit*. See **Tetragon**; and see **Four** and **Sit**. Der. *tetrahedr-al*, adj.

TETRARCH, a governor of a fourth part of a province. (L. — Gk.) ME. *tetrark* (ill spelt *tetrak*), Wyclif, Luke, ix. 7. — L. *tetrarcha*, Luke, ix. 7. — Gk. τετράρχης, a tetrarch. — Gk. τετρ-, prefix allied to τέσσαρες, four; and ἀρχ-ειν, to be first. Cf. Skt. *arh*, to be worthy. See **Tetragon**; also **Four** and **Arch-**. Der. *tetrarch-ate*; *tetrarch-y*, Gk. τετραρχία.

TETRASYLLABLE, a word of four syllables. (F. — L. — Gk.) A coined word; from MF. *tetrasyllabe*, 'of four syllables;' Cot. — Late L. *tetrasyllabus* (not in Ducange). — Gk. τετρασύλλαβος, of four syllables. — Gk. τέτρα-, prefix allied to τέσσαρες, four; and συλλαβή, a syllable. See **Tetragon**; also **Four** and **Syllable**. Der. *tetrasyllab-ic*.

TETTER, a cutaneous disease. (E.) In Hamlet, i. 5. 71; and in Baret (1580). ME. *teter*, Trevisa, ii. 61. 'Hec serpedo, a *tetere*;' Voc. 791. 14. AS. *teter*. 'Impetigo, *teter*;' Voc. 26. 12. Cf. G. *zittermal*, a tetter, ring-worm, serpigo; OHG. *zitaroch* (Bavar. *zitteroch*). Allied to L. *derbiōsus*, scabby; Skt. *dadru-*, a tetter.

TEUTONIC, pertaining to the Teutons or ancient Germans. (L. — Teut.) Spelt *Teutonick* in Blount, ed. 1674. — L. *Teutonicus*, adj., formed from *Teutones*, the Teutons, a people of Germany. The word *Teutones* means no more than 'men of the nation;' or 'the people,' being formed with L. suffix *-ones* (pl.) from **teutā*, pre-Teutonic form of Goth. *thiuda*, a people, nation; cf. Irish *tuath*, a people. See further under **Dutch**. Brugmann, i. § 218.

TEW, to taw, to scourge. (E.) A variant of **Taw**, q. v.

TEXT, the original words of an author; a passage of scripture. (F. — L.) ME. *texte*, Chaucer, C. T. 17185 (H 236). — F. *texte*, 'a text, the originall words or subject of a book;' Cot. — L. *textum*, that which is woven, a fabric, also the style of an author; hence, a text. Orig. neut. of *textus*, pp. of *texere*, to weave. ✛ Skt. *taksh*, to cut wood, prepare, form. Further allied to **Technical**, q. v. Der. *text-book*; *text-hand*, a large hand in writing, suitable for the *text* of a book as distinct from the notes; *text-u-al*, ME. *textuel*, Chaucer, C. T. 17184 (H 235), from F. *textuel*, 'of, or in, a text,' Cot., coined as if from a Late L. **textuālis*, adj.; *textu-al-ly*, *textu-al-ist*. And see *text-ile*, *text-ure* below. From the same root are *technic-al*, q. v.; *con-text*, *pre-text*. Also *sub-tle*, *toil* (2), *tissue*; and cf. *toxicology*.

TEXTILE, woven, that can be woven. (L.) 'The warp and the woofe of *textiles*;' Bacon, Nat. Historie, § 846. — L. *textilis*, woven, textile. — L. *textus*, woven, pp. of *texere*; see **Text**. See also *texture*, *tissue*.

TEXTURE, anything woven, a web, disposition of the parts. (F. — L.) In Cotgrave. — F. *texture*, 'a texture, contexture, web;' Cot. — L. *textūra*, a web; cf. *textus*, pp. of *texere*, to weave; see **Text**. And see *textile* above.

TH

TH. This is a distinct letter from *t*, and ought to have a distinct symbol. Formerly, we find AS. þ and ð used (indiscriminately) to denote *both* the sounds now represented by *th*; in Middle-English, ð soon went out of use (it occurs in Genesis and Exodus, ed. Morris), whilst þ and *th* were both used by the scribes. The letter þ was assimilated in shape to *y*, till at last both were written alike; hence *ye*, *yt* (really *the*, *that*) are not unfrequently pronounced by modern Englishmen like *ye* and *yat*; it is needless to remark that *ye man* was never pronounced as *ye man* in the middle ages.

For greater distinctness, the symbol ð will be used for AS. words (and *th* for ME. words) corresponding to mod. E. words with the 'voiced' *th*, as in *thou*; and the symbol þ for AS. and ME. words corresponding to mod. E. words with the 'voiceless' *th*, as in *thin*. It is useful to note these three facts following. 1. When *th* is initial, it is *always* voiceless, *except* in two sets of words, (*a*) words etymologically connected with *that*; and (*b*) words etymologically connected with *thou*. 2. When *th* is in the *middle* of a word or is *final*, it is almost always 'voiced' when the letter *e* follows, and not otherwise; cf. *breathe*, with *breath*. A remarkable exception occurs in *smooth*. 3. No word beginning with *th* (except *thurible*, the base of which is Greek) is of Latin origin; most of them are E., but some (easily known) are Greek; *thummim* is Hebrew. In the G. *thaler* (below), the *th* is sounded as *t*.

THALER, a dollar. (G.) G. *thaler*, a dollar; see **Dollar.**

THAN, a conjunction placed, after the comparative of an adjective or adverb, between things compared. (E.) Frequently written *then* in old books; extremely common in Shakespeare (1st folio). ME. *thanne*, *thonne*, *thenne*; also *than*, *thon*, *then*. AS. ðonne, than; ' betera ðonne ðæt réaf '= better than the garment; Matt. vi. 25. Closely allied to the demonst. pronoun; see **That.** See March, A. S. Grammar, § 252.+Du. *dan*, than, then; Goth. *than*, then, when, allied to the demonst. pron. with neut. *thata*; G. *dann*, then, *denn*, for, then, than, allied to *der*. Cf. L. *tum*, then; *-tud* in L. *is-tud*. ¶ The same word as *then*; but differentiated by usage.

THANE, a dignitary among the English. (E.) In Macb. i. 2. 45. ME. *þein*, Havelok, 2466. AS. *þegen*, *þegn*, often *þén* (by contraction), a thane; Grein, ii. 578.+Icel. *þegn*; G. *degen*, a warrior. Teut. type *thegnóz*, m. Allied to Gk. τέκνον, a child, which is from τεκ-, as in τεκ-εῖν, 2nd aorist infin. of τίκτειν, to beget. (√TEK.) Brugmann, ii. § 66.

THANK, an expression of good will; commonly used in the pl. *thanks*. (E.) Chaucer uses it in the sing. number. ' And haue a *þank* ;' C. T. 614 (A 612). So also Gower: ' Althogh I may no *þonk* deserve ;' C. A. i. 66; bk. i. 738. AS. *þanc*, often also *þonc*, thought, grace or favour, content, thanks. The primary sense of ' thought ' shows that it is closely allied to **Think**, q. v. The verb *þancian*, to thank (Mark, viii. 6), is a derivative from the sb.+Du. *dank*, sb., whence *danken*, vb.; Icel. *þökk* (<*þonk*), gen. *þakkar*, whence *þakka*, vb.; Dan. *tak*, sb., whence *takke*, vb.; cf. *tanke*, a thought, idea; Swed. *tack*, sb., whence *tacka*, vb.; Goth. *thagks* (for *thanks*), thank, Luke, xvii. 9, where the *s* is the usual suffix of the nom. sing.; cf. *thagkjan*, to think; G. *dank*, sb., whence *danken*, verb. Teut. type *thankoz*, m.; from *thank*, 2nd grade of *thenkan-*, to think; see **Think.** Der. *thank*, verb, as above; *thank-ful*, AS. *þancful*, spelt *ðoncful* and glossed ' gratiosus,' Voc. 191. 15; *thank-ful-ly*, *thank-ful-ness*; *thank-less*, Cor. iv. 5. 76, *thank-less-ly*, *thank-less-ness*, *thank-offer-ing*, *thank-worthy*, 1 Pet. ii. 19. Also *thanks-giving*, i.e. a giving of thanks, L.L.L. ii. 193; *thanks-giver*.

THAT, demonst. and rel. pronoun and conjunction. (E.) ME. *that*. AS. ðæt, orig. neut. of demonstrative pronoun, frequently used as neut. of the def. article, which is merely a peculiar use of the demonst. pronoun. [The masc. *sē*, and fem. *sēo*, are from a different base; see **She.**] In late MSS., we meet with a corresponding masc. form ðe, as in ' ðe hearpere '= the harper, Ælfred, tr. of Boethius, c. xxxv. § 6, lib. iii. met. 12, where the Cotton MS. has ' *se* hearpere.' Also with a corresponding late fem. form ðéo, as in ' ðā ðéo sáwul hæbban sceal '= which the soul is to have; Adrianus and Ritheus, in Ettmüller's A. S. Selections, p. 40, l. 43. The neut. ðæt is from the Teut. pronominal base THA=Idg. TO, meaning ' he ' or ' that.' The suffix *-t* in *tha-t* is merely the mark of the neut. gender, as in *wha-t* from *who*, *i-t* (formerly *hi-t*) from *he*; it answers to L. *-d* as seen in *is-tu-d*, *qui-d*, *i-d*, *illu-d*. β. From Idg. TO are Skt. *tat*, it, that, and numerous cases, such as *tam*, him (acc. masc.), *tām*, her (acc. fem.), *tē*, they, &c. Also Gk. τό, neut. of def. art., and the gen. τοῦ, τῆς, dat. τῷ, τῇ, acc. τόν, τήν, τό, &c. Also the latter part of L. *is-te*, *is-ta*, *is-tud*. So also Lithuan. *tas*, m., *ta*, f., *tai*, n., that; Russ. *tot*, masc., *ta*, fem., *to*, neut., that; Du. *de*, masc. and fem., *het*, neut., the; Icel. *þat*, neut., the; Dan. *den*, masc. and fem., *det*, neut., the; Swed. *den*, masc. and fem., *det*, neut., this; G. *der*, masc., *die*, fem., *das*, neut., the; *dass*, conj., that; Goth. *thata*, neut. of def. article.

For the purposes of E. etymology it is necessary to give the AS. def. art. in full. It is as follows, if we put *sē* and *sēo* (the usual forms) in place of ðe, ðéo. SING. NOM. *sē*, *sēo*, ðæt; GEN. ðæs, ðǽre, ðæs; DAT. ðǽm, ðǽre, ðǽm; ACC. ðone, ðá, ðæt; INSTRUMENTAL, ðȳ (*for all genders*). PLUR. NOM. AND ACC. ðá; GEN. ðára; DAT. ðǽm. ¶ Allied words all begin with ' voiced' *th*; as *there*, *than*, *then*, *the* (1), *the* (2), *they*, *their*, *them*; *thence*, *thither*; *these*, *those*, *thus*.

THATCH, a covering for a roof. (E.) A palatalised form of *thak*. Cf. prov. E. *thack*, a thatch, *thacker*, a thatcher; ME. *þak*, Prompt. Parv. AS. *þæc* (dat. *þæce*), thatch, Grein, ii. 564; whence *þeccan* (for *þac-ian*), to thatch, cover, Grein, ii. 577.+Du. *dak*, sb., whence *dekken*, verb (whence E. *deck* is borrowed); Icel. *þak*, sb., *þekja*, v.; Dan. *tag*, sb., *tække*, v.; Swed. *tak*, sb., *täkke*, v.; G. *dach*, s., *decken*, v. β. Teut. type *þak-om*, neut. From *þak*, 2nd grade of Teut. *þek*, to cover=Idg. √TEGw, STEGw; cf. Gk. τέγος, variant of στέγος, a roof. From the same root we have Skt. *sthag*, to cover, Gk. στέγειν, to cover, L. *tegere*, to cover, Lithuan. *stégti*, to cover, OIrish *tech*, Irish *teagh*, a house, Gael. *teach*, *tigh*,

a house, Gael. *a stigh*, within (i.e. under cover), W. *tŷ*, a house. Der. *thatch*, vb., as above; *thatch-er*, spelt *thacker*, Pilkington's Works, p. 381 (Parker Soc.). Also (from L. *tegere*) *teg-u-ment*, tile. Also (from Du. *decken*) *deck*. Brugmann, i. § 632.

THAUMATURGY, magic. (Gk.) Cf. F. *thaumaturgie* (1878); Hatzfeld.—Gk. θαυματουργία, a working of wonders.—Gk. θαυματ-, stem of θαῦμα, a wonder, marvel; and ἔργ-ον, a work, cognate with E. **Work**, q. v.

THAW, to melt, as ice, to grow warm after frost. (E.) Prov. E. *thow*, rhyming with *snow*. ME. *þowen*, in comp. *of-þowed*, pp. thawed away, Chaucer, House of Fame, iii. 53. Spelt *þowyn*, Prompt. Parv. AS. *þāwian*; ' se wind tō-wyrpð and þāwað '=the [south] wind disperses and thaws; Popular Treatises on Science, ed. Wright, p. 17, last line. A weak verb.+Du. *dooi en*, to thaw; cf. *dooi*, thaw; Icel. *þeyja*, to thaw; *þá*, a thaw, thawed ground; cf. *þeyr*, a thaw; Dan. *töe*, to thaw; *tö*, a thaw; Swed. *töa*, to thaw; *tö*, a thaw. Cf. MHG. *douwen*, G. *verdauen*, to concoct, digest. β. Prob. allied to L. *tābēs*, a melting, *tābescere*, to dissolve, Gk. τήκειν, to melt; Skt. *tōya-*, water; W. *tawdd*, melted, *toddi*, to melt. ☞ In no way connected with *dew*.

THE (1), def. article. (E.) ME. *the*. AS. ðe, substituted in Late AS. for *sē*, the nom. masc. of the def. article; the m. *sē*, f. *sēo*, being replaced by m. ðe, f. ðeo, by the influence of neut. ðæt, and the forms of the oblique cases. Thus we find ðe *hearpere* = the harper; see quotation under **That.** The real use of AS. ðe was as an indeclinable relative pronoun, in extremely common use for all genders and cases; see several hundred examples in Grein, ii. 573-577. See further under **That.**

THE (2), in what degree, in that degree. (E.) When we say ' *the* more, *the* merrier ' we mean ' in what degree they are more numerous, in that degree are they merrier.' This is not the usual def. article, but the *instrumental case* of it. ME. *the*; as in ' neuer *the* bet '= none the better, Chaucer, C. T. 7533 (D 1951). AS. ðȳ, ðȳ, as in ðȳ *bet* = the better; see numerous examples in Grein, ii. 568. This is the instrumental case of the def. article, and means ' on that account ' or ' on what account,' or ' in that degree ' or ' in what degree.' Common in the phrase *for* ðȳ, on that account; cf. *for* hwȳ, on what account. See **That**; and see **Why.**+Goth. *thē*, instrumental case of def. article; Icel. *þvī*, *þí*, dat. (or inst.) case of *þat*. Cf. Skt. *tēna*, instr. case of *tad*, sometimes used with the sense of ' therefore ;' Benfey, p. 349, s. v. *tad*, sect. iv.

THEATRE, a place for dramatic representations. (F.—L.—Gk.) ME. *theatre*, Chaucer, C. T. 1887 (A 1885); spelt *teatre*, Wyclif, Deeds [Acts], xix. 31.—MF. *theatre*, ' a theatre ;' Cot.—L. *theātrum*.—Gk. θέατρον, a place for seeing shows, &c.; formed with suffix *-τρον* (agential) from θεά-ομαι, I see. Cf. θέα, a view, sight, spectacle; see Prellwitz. Der. *theatr-ic-al*, adj., *theatr-ic-al-ly*; *theatr-ic-al-s*, s. pl.; *amphi-theatre*. And see *theorem*, *theo-ry*.

THEE (1), acc. of **Thou**, pers. pron., which see.

THEE (2), to prosper, flourish, thrive. (E.) Obsolete; ME. *þeon*, usually *þe* or *þee*, Chaucer, C. T. 7789 (D 2207). ' Theen, or thryvyn, Vigeo ;' Prompt. Parv. AS. *þéon*, *þíon* (for *þíhan*), pt. t. *þāh*, *þéah*, pp. *þigen*, *þogen*, also *ge-þungen*, to thrive.+Goth. *theihan*, to thrive, increase, advance; Du. *gedijen*, to thrive, prosper, succeed ; G. *gedeihen*, OHG. *dîhan*, to increase, thrive. Another allied form is OSax. *ge-þengian*, to fulfil. The old AS. pp. *geþungen* shows that the AS. *þíhan* resulted from an earlier Idg. *þinhan*; from the Teut. root *þinχ*, *þenχ*, answering to √TENK; which appears in Lith. *tenka*, it suffices; whence also OIrish *tocad*, prosperity, W. *tynged*, luck; cf. Lith. *tekti*, to suffice (pres. t. *tenkù*, I have enough). Brugmann, i. § 421 (3). See **Tight.**

THEFT, an act of thieving, stealing. (E.) ME. *þefte*, Chaucer, C. T. 4393 (A 4395). *Theft* is for *thefth*, as being easier to pronounce. AS. *þiefðe*, *þéofðe*, *þȳfðe* (with *f* sounded as *v*, and ð voiced), theft; Laws of Ine, §§ 7 and 46; Thorpe, Ancient Laws, i. 106, 130. Formed with suffix *-(i)ðe* (Idg. *-itā*) from AS. *þéof*, *þíof*, or *þéf*, a thief, or from *þéofian*, to steal; see **Thief.**+OFries. *thiufthe*, theft; cf. *thiaf*, a thief : Icel. *þýfð*, sometimes *þýft*; cf. *þjófr*, a thief.

THEIR, belonging to them. (Scand.) The word *their* belongs to the Northern dialect rather than the Southern, and is rather a Scand. than an AS. form. Chaucer uses *hire* or *here* in this sense (<AS. *hira*, of them); C. T. 32. ME. *thair*, Pricke of Conscience, 52, 1862, &c. ; *thar*, Barbour, Bruce, i. 22, 23 ; *þeȝȝre*, Ormulum, 127. The word was orig. not a possess. pron., but a gen. plural; moreover, it was not orig. the gen. pl. of *he* (he), but of the def. article.—Icel. *þeirra*, OIcel. *þeira*, of them; used as gen. pl. of *hann*, *hon*, *þat* (he, she, it), by confusion; it was really the gen. pl. of the def. article, as shown by the AS. forms. (The use of *that* for *it* is a Scand. peculiarity, very common in Norfolk, Suffolk, and Cambs.)+AS. ðǽra, also ðára, gen. pl. of def. art.; see Grein, ii. 565; G. *der*, gen.

pl. of def. art. ; Goth. *thizē*, fem. *thizō*, gen. pl. of *sa, so, thata*. See further under **They** and **That**. Der. *their-s*, Temp. i. 1. 58 ; spelt *þeȝȝress*, Ormulum, 2506 ; cf. Dan. *deres*, Swed. *deras*, theirs ; formed by analogy with *our-s, your-s*.

THEISM, belief in the existence of a God. (Gk.) ' All religion and *theism* ;' Pref. to Cudworth, Intellectual System (R.). Coined, with suffix *-ism* (Gk. *-ισμος*), from Gk. θε-ός, a god. Prob. for *θεσ-ός ; cf. OIrish *dess*, God (Stokes-Fick, p. 151) ; also Gk. θέσ-φατος, spoken by a god. See Prellwitz. ¶ Not related to L. *deus*. Der. *the-ist* (from Gk. θεός) ; *the-ist-ic, the-ist-ic-al* ; *a-the-ist*, q. v. ; *apo-the-os-is*, q. v. And see *theo-crac-y, theo-gon-y, theo-log-y, the-urg-y*.

THEM, objective case of **They**, q.v. Der. *them-selves*.

THEME, a subject for discussion. (F. – L. – Gk.) ME. *teme*, P. Plowman, B. iii. 95, v. 61, vi. 23. At a later period spelt *theme*, Mids. Nt. Dr. v. 434. – OF. *teme*, MF. *theme*, ' a theam,' Cot. – L. *thema*. – Gk. θέμα, that which is laid down, the subject of an argument. – Gk. base θε-, to place, weak grade of θη-, as in τίθημι, I place. – √DHĒ, to place, put ; whence Skt. *dhā*, to put ; &c. See **Thesis**.

THEN, at that time, afterward, therefore. (E.) Frequently spelt *than* in old books, as in Shak. Merch. Ven. ii. 2. 200 (First folio) ; it rimes with *began*, Lucrece, 1440. Orig. the same word as *than*, but afterwards differentiated. ME. *thenne*, P. Plowman, A. i. 56 ; *thanne*, B. i. 58. AS. *ðænne* ; also *ðanne, ðonne*, then, than ; Grein, ii. 562, 563. See **Than**.

THENCE, from that place or time. (E.) ME. *thennës* (dissyllabic), Chaucer, C. T. 4930 (B 510) ; whence (by contraction) *thens*, written *thence* in order to represent that the final *s* was voiceless, and not sounded as *z*. Older forms *thonne, thenne, thanne*, Owl and Nightingale, 132, 508, 1724 ; also *thanene*, Rob. of Glouc. p. 377, l. 7743. Here *thanne* is a shorter form of *thanene* (or *thanen*) by the loss of *n*. AS. *ðanan, ðanon*, thence ; also *ðananne, ðanonne*, thence, Grein, ii. 560, 561. It thus appears that the fullest form was *ðananne*, which became successively *thanene, thanne, thenne*, and (by addition of *s*) *thennes, thens, thence*. *S* was added because *-es* was a favourite ME. adverbial suffix, orig. due to the genitive suffix of sbs. Again, *ða-nan, ða-nan-ne*, is from the Teut. base THA = Idg. TO, he, that ; see **That**. March (A. S. Grammar, § 252) explains *-nan, -nanne*, as an oblique case of the (repeated) adj. suffix *-na*, with the orig. sense of ' belonging to ;' cf. L. *super-no-*, belonging (*super*) above, whence the ablative adverb *super-ne*, from above. He remarks that *belonging to* and *coming from* are near akin, but the lost case-ending inclines the sense to *from*. ' The Goth. *in-nana*, within, *ut-ana*, without, *hind-ana*, behind, do not have the plain sense *from*. Pott suggests comparison with a preposition (Lettish *no*, from). Here belong *ēast-an*, from the east ; *æft-an*, aft ; *feorr-an*, from far ; &c.' Compare also **Hence**, **Whence**. + G. *dannen*, OHG. *dannana*, thence ; from G. base *da-*. Der. *thence-forth, thence-forward*, not in early use.

THEOCRACY, the government of a state immediately by God ; the state so governed. (Gk.) In Blount's Gloss., ed. 1674. – Gk. θεοκρατία, the rule of God ; Josephus, Against Apion, ii. 16 (Trench, Study of Words). Formed (by analogy with *demo-cracy, aristo-cracy*, &c.), from Gk. θεο-, for θεός, a god ; and *-κρατια, -κρατεια* (as in δημο-κρατία, δημο-κράτεια), i. e. government, power, from κρατύς, strong, allied to E. *hard*. See **Theism** and **Hard**; and see **Democracy**. Der. *theocrat-ic, theocrat-ic-al*.

THEODOLITE, an instrument used in surveying for observing angles and distances. (Gk.) In Blount, ed. 1674. Certainly of Gk. origin. The original *theodolite* was not quite like the present one. Hopton, in his Topographicall Glasse (1611) defines it as ' an instrument consisting of a planisphere and an alhidada,' i.e. a revolving rule with sights, and spells it *Theodelitus* ; N. and Q. 3 S. iv. 51. In Pantometria, by T. Digges, 1571, ch. 27 of book i is headed ' The composition of the instrument called *Theodelitus*,' and begins : ' It is but a circle divided into 360 grades or degrees,' &c. Prof. Adams informs me that the method of subdividing the degrees of the circle was known to the Greeks, and is well explained in Rathbone's Surveying, ed. 1616. Also spelt *theodolet, theodelet, theodolit* ; the last occurs in 1784 ; N. and Q. 9 S. vii. 412. It seems to be taken (we know not why) from the OF. *Theodolet, Theodelet*, the name of a treatise, lit. ' a work by Theodulus.' Godefroy quotes ' Cathonnet, *Theodelet*, bien gloses,' i.e. a work by Cato, a work by Theodulus, well glossed (1408). It was usual to add *-et* in this manner ; thus *Esop-et* meant a work by Æsop, viz. his ' Fables.' One *Theodolet*, viz. the *Ecloga Theoduli*, is mentioned by Rabelais (I. xiv) ; when Gargantua was instructed in Latin literature, he read ' Donat, le Facet, *Theodolet*,' &c. This *Ecloga Theoduli* was a poem in Latin hexameters, containing a dispute between Truth and Falsehood. But it is more likely that the reference in this instance is to a mathematician named Theodulus ;

see N. and Q. 3 S. vii. 337, 428, &c. The name *Theodūlus* meant ' servant of God ;' from θεο-, for θεός, God ; and δοῦλος, a servant. For the suffix *-et*, cf. **Pamphlet**.

THEOGONY, the part of mythology which taught of the origin of the gods. (L. – Gk.) In Blount's Gloss., ed. 1674. ' The *theogony* in Hesiod ;' Selden, Illustrations to Drayton's Polyolbion, song 11 (R.). Englished from L. *theogonia*. – Gk. θεογονία, the origin of the gods ; the title of a poem by Hesiod. – Gk. θεο-, for θεός, a god ; and *-γονία*, origin, from γον-, 2nd grade of the Gk. base γεν-, to beget, from √GEN, to beget. Cf. Gk. γένος, race, ἐγενόμην, I became. See **Theism** and **Genus**. Der. *theogon-ist*, a writer on theogony.

THEOLOGY, the science which treats of the relations between God and man. (F. – L. – Gk.) ME. *theologie*, Chaucer, Persones Tale, 3rd pt. of Penitence (Group I, 1043). – MF. *theologie*, ' theology ;' Cot. – L. *theologia*. – Gk. θεολογία, a speaking about God. – Gk. θεολόγος, adj., speaking about God. – Gk. θεο-, for θεός, a god ; and λογ-, 2nd grade of λέγειν, to speak. See **Theism** and **Logic**. Der. *theologi-c, theologi-c-al, theologi-c-al-ly* ; *theolog-ise, ist* ; *theologi-an*.

THEORBO, a kind of lute. (Ital.) Formerly also *theorba* : *theorbo* in Drayton, Polyolbion, song iv. 363. – Ital. *tiorba* ; the *th* being due to the occasional F. spelling *théorbe*, for *téorbe*. Named after its inventor (Zambaldi).

THEOREM, a proposition to be proved. (L. – Gk.) In Phillips, ed. 1706. ' More *theoremes* ;' Marston, What You Will, A. iv. sc. 1. – L. *theōrēma*. – Gk. θεώρημα, a spectacle ; hence, a subject for contemplation, principle, theorem. Formed with suffix *-μα* (*-ματ-*) from θεωρεῖν, to look at, behold, view. – Gk. θεωρός, a spectator. – Gk. θεῶ-μαι, θεάο-μαι, I see ; with suffix *-ρος* (Idg. *-ρο-*). See **Theatre**. And see **Theory**.

THEORY, an exposition, speculation. (F. – L. – Gk.) Spelt *theorie* in Minsheu. [The ME. word was *theorike*, as in Chaucer, On the Astrolabe, prol. 59 ; Gower, C. A. iii. 86 ; bk. vii. 61. This is F. *theorique*, sb. fem. = L. *theōrica*, adj. fem., the sb. *ars*, art, being understood. See Nares.] – MF. *theorie*, ' theory ;' Cot. – L. *theōria*. – Gk. θεωρία, a beholding, contemplation, speculation. – Gk. θεωρός, a spectator ; see **Theorem**. Der. *theor-ise, theor-ist* ; also *theor-et-ic*, Gk. θεωρητικός, adj. ; *theor-et-ic-al, -ly*.

THERAPEUTIC, pertaining to the healing art. (F. – L. – Gk.) Spelt *therapeutick*, Blount's Gloss., ed. 1674 ; and see Sir T. Browne, Vulg. Errors, b. iv. c. 13. § 26. – MF. *therapeutique*, ' curing, healing ;' Cot. – L. *therapeutica*, fem. sing. of adj. *therapeuticus*, healing ; the sb. *ars*, art, being understood. – Gk. θεραπευτικός, inclined to take care of, tending. – Gk. θεραπευτής, one who waits on a great man, one who attends to anything. – Gk. θεραπεύειν, to wait on, attend, serve. – Gk. θεραπ-, stem of θέραψ, a rare sb., for which the more usual form θεράπων, a servant, is used. The stem θερ-απ- means, literally, one who supports or assists ; from base θερ- = Idg. DHER, to support ; cf. Skt. *dhṛ*, to bear, maintain, support, *dharitṛī*, a supporter. Der. *therapeutic-s*, s. pl.

THERE (1), in that place. (E.) ME. *ther*, Chaucer, C. T. 43 ; written *thar* in Barbour's Bruce. AS. *ðær, ðer*, Grein, ii. 564 ; better written *ðǣr, ðēr*, with long vowel. The base is Teut. THA = Idg. TO, he, that ; see **That**. March, A. S. Gram. § 252, explains the suffix *-r* as the locative case of the comparative suffix *-ro-* ; cf. Skt. *upa-ri*, Gk. ὑπέ-ρ, L. *supe-r*, Goth. *ufa-r*, AS. *ofe-r*, E. *ove-r*. + Du. *daar*. + Icel. *þar* ; Dan. and Swed. *der* ; Goth. *thar* ; G. *da*, OHG. *dār*. Cf. **Here** and **Where**.

THERE- (2), *as a prefix*. (E.) In *there-fore, there-by*, &c. It will suffice to explain *there-fore*. This is ME. *therforē*, with final *-e*, as in Ormulum, 2431, where we find : ' *þærforē* seȝȝdë ȝho þiss word.' For AS. *ðær-*, see above. For the prep. *fore* (allied to *for*), see Grein, ii. 320. It thus appears that the final *e* in *therefore* is not wrong, but *therefore* and *therefor* are equivalent. β. Similar compounds are *there-about* or (with added adverbial suffix *-s*) *there-about-s, there-after, there-at, there-by, there-from, there-in, there-of, there-on, there-through, there-to, there-unto, there-upon, there-with*. The construction with *ðær* before a preposition occurs even in AS. ' When a thing is referred to, *ðær* is generally substituted for *hit* with a prep., the prep. being joined on to the *ðær*; e. g. *on hit* becomes *ðæron* ; Curfon hie ðæt of beorhtum stāne, gesetton hie ðæron sigora Wealdend = they cut it [the tomb] out of the bright rock, they placed in it the Lord of victories ;' Sweet, A. S. Grammar, 2nd ed. p. xci.

THERMOMETER, an instrument for measuring the variations of temperature. (Gk.) In Blount's Gloss., ed. 1674 ; and in Evelyn's Diary, July 13, 1654. First invented about 1597 (Haydn). Coined from Gk. θερμο-, for θερμός, hot, warm ; and μέτρον, a measure, a measurer, for which see **Metre**. β. The Gk. θερμός is allied to L. *formus*, warm, and to Skt. *gharma-*, heat. Der. *thermometr-ic, -ic-al, -ic-al-ly* ; and see *iso-therm-al*.

THESAURUS, a treasury of knowledge, esp. a dictionary. (L.—Gk.) A doublet of **Treasure,** q. v.

THESE, pl. of **This,** q. v. ME. *thise, these,* a new pl. of *this.* The old pl. (AS. *þās*) has become the mod. E. *those.* See **Those.**

THESIS, a statement laid down to be argued about, an essay on a theme. (L.—Gk.) In Minsheu, ed. 1627.—L. *thesis.*—Gk. θέσις, a proposition, statement, thing laid down. For *θε-τι-s,* allied to θε-τός, placed, verbal adj. from the base θε-, weaker form of θη-, as in τί-θη-μι, I put, place. See **Theme.** Der. *anti-thesis, apo-thesis, epen-thesis, hypo-thesis, meta-thesis, para-thesis, paren-thesis, pros-thesis, pro-thesis, syn-thesis.* From the same root are *apo-the-c-ar-y, ana-the-ma, epi-the-t, the-me, the-s-au-rus, treasure.*

THEURGY, supernatural agency. (L.—Gk.) Rare. A name applied to a kind of magic said to be performed by the operation of gods and demons. Rich. gives an example from Hallywell's Melampronvea (1682), p. 51. Englished from L. *theurgia,* Latinised form of Gk. θεουργία, divine work, magic.—Gk. θεο-, for θεός, a god; and ἔργ-ον, work, cognate with E. *work.* See **Theism** and **Work.** Der. *theurgi-c, theurgi-c-al.*

THEWS, pl. sb., sinews, strength, habits, manners. (E.) 'Thews and limbs;' Jul. Cæs. i. 3. 81; cf. Haml. i. 3. 12. AS. *þewès,* i. e. habits, manners, Chaucer, C. T. 9416 (E 1542). 'Alle gode *þeawes,*' all good virtues; Ancren Riwle, p. 240, l. 16. The sing. *þeauwe* (dat. case) occurs in Layamon, l. 6361, with the sense of sinew or strength; on which Sir F. Madden remarks: 'This is the only instance in the poem of the word being applied to bodily qualities. Cf. Scotch *thowles,* feeble.' In other passages it occurs in the pl. *þeauwes, þewes,* ll. 2147, 6899, 7161, with the usual sense of mental qualities. Of course, as in all metaphorical expressions, the sense of ' bodily strength' is the orig. one, and that of ' mental excellence' is secondary. AS. *þeaw,* habit, custom, behaviour; the pl. *þeawas* signifies manners; Grein, ii. 584.+OSax. *thau,* custom, habit.+OHG. *dau,* discipline. β. The Teut. base is *thau-,* allied to Skt. *tavas,* strong; *tu,* to be strong. The sense of bulk, strength, survives in Scotch *thowless, thewless, thieveless,* for which Jamieson gives a wrong etymology (from AS. *þeow,* a servant). The remarks in Trench, Select Glossary, are due to a misapprehension of the facts. From the Idg. √TEU, to be strong; see **Thigh, Tumid.**

THEY, used as pl. of *he, she, it.* (Scand.) The word *they* (in ME.) is chiefly found in the Northern dialect; Barbour uses nom. *thai,* gen. *thair,* dat. and acc. *thaim* or *tham,* where Chaucer uses nom. *they,* C. T. 18, gen. *here, hire, hir,* id. 588 (A 586), dat. and acc. *hem,* id. 18. The Ormulum has *þeȝȝ,* they, *þeȝȝre,* their, of them, *þeȝȝm,* dat. and acc., them. Of these forms, *hem* survives only in the mod. prov. E. *'em,* as in 'I saw *'em* go;' whilst the gen. *here* is lost. Again, *here* and *hem* (AS. *hira* or *heora, heom* or *him*) are the true forms, properly used as the pl. of *he,* from the same base; whilst *they, their, them* are really cases of the pl. of the def. article. β. The use is Scand., not E.; the AS. usage confines these forms to the def. article, but Icelandic usage allows them to be used for the personal pronoun.—Icel. *þeir,* nom.; *þeirra,* gen.; *þeim,* dat.; used to mean *they, their, them,* as the pl. of *hann, hon,* he, she. The extension of the use of dat. *them* to its use as an accusative is precisely parallel to that of *him,* properly a dat. form only. The Icel. acc. is *þā,* but Danish and Swedish confuse dat. and acc. together. Cf. Dan. and Swed. *de,* they; *dem* (dat. and acc.), them. Also Dan. *deres,* their, theirs; Swed. *deras,* their, theirs.+AS. *þā,* nom.; *þāra, þæra,* gen.; *þām, þæm,* dat.; Grein, ii. 568. [The AS. acc. was *þā,* like the nom.; cf. prov. E. 'I saw *they* horses,' i. e. those horses.] These forms *þā, þāra, þām,* are cases of the plural of the def. art.; from Teut. THA =Idg. TO, pronom. base of the 3rd person. See **That.** ¶ This explains *they, their, them; their* was orig. only the gen. pl., just like *our, your.* Their-*s* occurs as *þeȝȝress,* in the Ormulum, 2506, and may be compared with Dan. *deres,* Swed. *deras,* theirs.

THICK, dense, compact, closely set. (E.) ME. *þikke,* Chaucer, C. T. 1058 (A 1056). AS. *þicce,* thick, Grein, ii. 590.+OSax. *thikki;* Du. *dik;* Icel. *þykkr;* Dan. *tyk;* Swed. *tjok, tjock;* G. *dick,* OHG. *dicchi.* β. The Teut. type is **thikwuz* (Kluge). Further allied to Gael. and Irish *tiugh,* thick, fat, dense, W. *tew,* thick, plump; from Celtic type **tegus.* Further connexions doubtful. Der. *thick-ly, thick-ness,* AS. *þicnes,* Mark, iv. 5; *thick-ish, thick-en,* Macb. iii. 2. 50, properly intransitive, but Goth. verbs in *-nan,* formed by analogy with other verbs in *-en,* or borrowed from Icel. *þykkna,* to become thick (cf. AS. *þiccian,* to make thick, Ælfric's Gram. ed. Zupitza, p. 220); *thick-et,* L.L.L. iv. 2. 60, AS. *þiccet,* of which the pl. *þiccetu* occurs in Ps. xxviii. (xxix.) 8 to translate L. *condensa; thick-head-ed; thick-skin,* sb., Mids. Nt. Dr. iii. 2. 13.

THIEF, one who steals. (E.) Pl. *thieves.* ME. *þeef,* Wyclif, Matt. xxvi. 55; pl. *þeues,* id. Mark, xv. 27. AS. *þeof,* pl. *þeofas,* Grein, ii. 588.+Du. *dief;* Icel. *þjófr;* Dan. *tyv;* Swed. *tjuf;* G. *dieb,* OHG. *diub;* Goth. *thiubs.* β. All from Teut. type **theufoz;*

perhaps related to Lithuan. *tupėti,* to squat or crouch down (i.e. to hide oneself); see Kluge. Der. *theft,* q. v.; *thieve,* AS. *ge-þeofian,* Laws of Ine, § 48, in Thorpe, Ancient Laws, i. 133; *thiev-ish,* Romeo, iv. 1. 79; *thiev-er-y,* Timon, iv. 3. 438, a coined word (with F. suffix *-erie*)

THIGH, the thick upper part of the leg. (E.) ME. *þih,* Layamon, 26071; *þeiȝ,* Trevisa, iv. 185; but the guttural is often dropped, and a common form is *þi* or *þy,* Prompt. Parv., or *þe,* Havelok, 1950. AS. *þeóh,* or *þeó,* Grein, ii. 588.+Du. *dij;* Icel. *þjō,* thigh, rump; OHG. *deoh, dioh.* β. The Teut. type is **theuhom,* n. The orig. sense is 'the fat, thick, plump part;' cf. Icel. *þjō,* the rump. Closely allied to Lithuan. *taukas,* fat of animals, *tùkti,* to become fat, *tùkinti,* to fatten; Russ. *tuk',* fat of animals, *tuchnit(e),* to fatten. From an Idg. base TEUK, extension of √TEU, to increase, be strong, swell; see **Thews, Thumb, Tumid.**

THILL, the shaft of a cart. (E.) 'Thill, the beam or draughttree of a cart or waggon, upon which the yoke hangs; *Thiller* or *Thill-horse,* the horse that is put under the thill;' Phillips, ed. 1706. Hence *fill-horse,* for *thill-horse,* Merch. Ven. ii. 2. 100; *fill* for *thill,* Troil. iii. 2. 48. ME. *þille.* 'Thylle,' of a carte, Temo; *Thylle-horse,* Veredus;' Prompt. Parv. AS. *þille,* glossed by *tabulamen,* Voc. 282. 2, where the sense seems to be ' board' or ' trencher;' *þille* meant a thin slip of wood, whether used for a thill or for a wooden platter. We also find: 'Tabulatorium, *wāh-þyling,*' id. 147. 31; also: 'Area, *breda þiling,* vel *flōr on tō perscenne,*' i. e. a thilling of boards, or floor to thrash on, id. 14.+Icel. *þilja,* a plank, planking, esp. in a ship, a bench for rowers, deck; Swed. *tilja,* a plank, floor; MHG. *dille,* OHG. *dilla, thili,* G. *diele,* a board, plank; Du. *deel,* a plank. Teut. types **theljōn-,* f., **thelom,* n. Allied to OIrish *talam,* earth, L. *tellus,* earth, Lith. *tille,* a little plank in the bottom of a boat, Skt. *tala-m,* bottom, floor, surface. See **Deal** (2). Der. *thill-horse,* as above.

THIMBLE, a metal cover for the finger, used in sewing. (E.) Though now worn on the finger, similar protections were once worn on the *thumb,* and the name was given accordingly. ME. *þimbil.* 'Thymbyl, Theca;' Prompt. Parv. Formed (with excrescent *b,* as in *thumb* itself) from AS. *þymel,* a thumb-stall; A. S. Leechdoms, ii. 150, l. 6. Teut. type **thūmiloz.* Formed with suffix *-(i)lo-,* indicative of the agent, or in this case of the protector, from AS. *þūma,* a thumb; see **Thumb.** *Thimble=thumb-er;* formed by vowel-change.

THIN, extended, slender, lean, fine. (E.) ME. *þinne,* Chaucer, C. T. 9556 (E 1682); *þunne,* Ancren Riwle, p. 144, l. 13. AS. *þynne,* Grein, ii. 613.+Du. *dun;* Icel. *þunnr;* Dan. *tynd* (for **tynn*); Swed. *tunn;* G. *dünn;* OHG. *dunni.*+W. *teneu;* Gael. and Irish *tana;* Russ. *tonkii;* L. *tenuis;* Gk. ταναός, slim; Skt. *tanu-,* thin; Pers. *tanak,* slender (Horn, § 397). β. All from the sense ' outstretched,' as in Gk. ταναός. From √TEN, to stretch; cf. Skt. *tan,* to stretch, Goth. *uf-thanjan,* AS. *āþenian,* to stretch out, L. *ten-d-ere.* Der. *thin-ly, thin-ness; thinn-ish; thin,* verb. From same root are *ten-uity, at-ten-uate, ex-ten-uate; tena-ble,* q. v.; *tend* (1), q. v.

THINE, THY, poss. pron. belonging to 'thee.' (E.) ME. *þin,* with long *i,* and without final *e;* gen. *thines,* dat. *thine,* nom. and acc. pl. *thine;* by loss of *n,* we also have ME. *thi*=mod. E. *thy.* The *n* was commonly retained before a vowel; 'This was *thin* ooth, and *min* also certeyn;' Chaucer, C. T. 1141 (A 1139). 'To me, that am *thy* cosin and *thy* brother,' id. 1133 (A 1131). AS. *ðīn,* poss. pron., declined like an adjective; derived from *ðīn,* gen. case of *ðū,* thou; see **Thou.**+Icel. *þinn, þín, þitt,* poss. pron.; from *þín,* gen. of *þū;* Dan. and Swed. *din,* poss. pron.; G. *dein,* from *deiner,* gen. of *du;* Goth. *theins,* from *theina,* gen. of *thu.* Der. *thy-self* (=*thine self*), lit. ' self of thee.'

THING, an inanimate object. (E.) ME. *þing,* Chaucer, C. T. 13865 (B 2127). AS. *þing,* a thing; also, a cause, sake, office, reason, council; also written *þincg, þinc,* Grein, ii. 592.+Du. *ding;* Icel. *þing,* a thing; also, an assembly, meeting, council; Dan. and Swed. *ting,* a thing; also, an assize; G. *ding,* OHG. *dinc.* Teut. type **thingom,* n. Prob. allied to Goth. *theihs,* season, time (hence, time for meeting). And further, to AS. *þeon,* pt. t. *þāh,* to prosper, succeed, thrive. See **Thee** (2). Der. *any-thing,* ME. *any þing; no-thing,* ME. *no thing;* also *hus-tings,* q. v.

THINK, to exercise the mind, judge, consider, suppose, purpose, opine. (E.) ME. *þenken,* to think, suppose, also *þenchen,* as in Chaucer, C. T. 3253. Orig. distinct from the impers. verb. *þinken,* explained under **Methinks;** but confusion between the two was easy and common. Thus, in P. Plowman, A. vi. 90, we have *I þenke,* written *I þinke* in the parallel passage, B. v. 609. [The pt. t. of both verbs often appears as *þoughte,* pp. *þought.* Strictly, the pt. t. of *think* should have become *thoght,* and of *me-thinks* should have become *me-thught,* but the spellings *ogh* and *ugh* are confused in modern E. under the form *ough.*] AS. *þencan, þencean,* to think, pt. t. *þōhte;*

Grein, ii. 579. A weak verb, allied to *þanc*, sb., (1) a thought, (2) a thank; see **Thank.**+Icel. *þekkja*, old pt. t. *þátti*, to perceive, know; Dan. *tænke*; Swed. *tänka*; G. *denken*, pt. t. *dachte.*+Goth. *thagkjan* (=*thankjan*), pt. t. *tháhta.* Teut. type **thankjan*; from **thank*, 2nd grade of the root **thenk*, Idg. **teng*; whence also OL. *tongēre*, to think (from the 2nd grade **tong*). See **Thank.** Der. *thought*, sb., q. v. Also *be-think*, vb. Allied to *thank.*

THIRD, the ordinal of the number *three.* (E.) For *thrid.* ME. *þridde*, Chaucer, C. T. 12770 (C 836); spelt *þirde*, Seven Sages, ed. Wright, l. 49. AS. *þridda*, third; Grein, ii. 499.—AS. *þrēo*, *þrí*, three; see **Three.**+Du. *derde*; Icel. *þriði*; Dan. *tredje*; Swed. *tredje*; G. *dritte*; Goth. *thridja.*+W. *tryde*, *trydydd*; Gael. and Irish *treas*; Russ. *tretii*; Lithuan. *trēczias*; L. *tertius*; Gk. τρίτος; Skt. *tṛtīya-.* Der. *third-ly*; and see *riding.*

THIRL, to pierce. (E.) See **Thrill.**

THIRST, dryness, eager desire for drink, eager desire. (E.) ME. *þurst*, P. Plowman, B. xviii. 366; various readings *þruste*, *þrist*, *þrest.* AS. *þurst*, Grein, ii. 611; also *þyrst*, *þirst*, id. 613; whence *þyrstan*, verb, id. 614.+Du. *dorst*, whence *dorsten*, verb; Icel. *þorsti*, whence *þyrsta*, vb.; Dan. *törst*, whence *törste*, vb.; Swed. *törst*, whence *törsta*, vb.; G. *durst*, whence *dürsten*, vb.; Goth. *þaurstei*, sb. β. The Goth. *thaurstei* (= *thorstei*) is from the Goth. weak stem *thaurs-*, as seen in -*thaurs-ans*, pp. of (*ga*)*thairsan* (pt. t. *thars*), to be dry (with Goth. *ai* for Teut. *e*); the suffix -*tei*=-*ti.* The Teut. **thers-an-*, vb., is cognate with Gk. τέρσ-εσθαι, to become dry, τερσαίνειν, to dry up, wipe up, L. *torrēre* (for **torsēre*), to parch, *terra* (for **tersa*), dry ground; cf. Skt. *tṛsh*, to thirst; *tarsha-*, thirst. (√TERS). Allied to **Terrace** and **Torrid.** Der. *thirst*, vb., as above; *thirst-y*, AS. *þurstig*, Grein, ii. 611; *thirst-i-ly*, *thirst-i-ness.* And (from the same root) *terr-ace*, *torr-id*, *test*, *toast*, *tur-een.*

THIRTEEN, three and ten. (E.) ME. *þrettene*, P. Plowman, B. v. 214. AS. *þrē̆tēne*, *þrēotȳne*, Grein, ii. 599.—AS. *þrēo*, three; and *tēn*, *tȳn*, ten; with pl. suffix -*e.* See **Three** and **Ten.**+Du. *dertien*; Dan. *tretten*; Swed. *tretton*; G. *dreizehn.* All similar compounds. Der. *thirteen-th*, AS. *þrēotēoða* (Grein), Icel. *þrettándi*; but the *n*, dropped in AS., has been restored.

THIRTY, three times ten. (E.) ME. *þritti*, Wyclif, Luke, iii. 23; *þretty*, *þirty*, Prompt. Parv., p. 492. AS. *þritig*, *þrittig*, Grein, ii. 601; the change of long *i* to short *i* caused the doubling of the *t.* —AS. *þri*, variant of *þ-ēo*, three; and -*tig*, suffix denoting 'ten;' see further under **Three** and **Ten.**+Du. *dertig*; Icel. *þrjátiu*; Dan. *tredive*; Swed. *trettio*; G. *dreiszig.* All similar compounds. Der. *thirti-eth*, AS. *þritigoða.*

THIS, *demonst. pron.* denoting a thing near at hand. (E.) 1. SINGULAR FORM. ME. *this*, Chaucer, C. T. 1576 (A 1574); older form *thes*, Ancren Riwle, p. 170, l. 12. AS. *ðes*, masc.; *ðēos*, fem.; *ðis*, neuter; see Grein, ii. 581.+Du. *deze*; Icel. *þessi*, masc. and fem.; *þetta*, neuter; G. *dieser*; MHG. *diser*; OHG. *deser.* β. *This* is most likely an *emphatic* form, due to suffixing an emphatic particle to the pronominal base THA. 2. PLURAL FORMS. The mod. E. pl. form is *these*; *those* being only used as the plural of *that.* This distinction is unoriginal; both *these* and *those* are varying forms of the plural of *this*, as will appear by observing the numerous examples supplied by Stratmann. β. The ME. word for 'those' was *tho* or *thoo*, due to AS. *ðā*, nom. pl. of the def. article; in accordance with this idiom, we still have the common prov. E. 'they horses'=*those* horses; it will be easily seen that the restriction of the form *those* (with *o*) to its modern use was due to the influence of this older word *tho.* For examples of *tho*=those, see Wyclif, Matt. iii. 1, xiii. 17. γ. It remains to give examples of the ME. pl. forms of *this.* Layamon has *þas*, *þæs*, *þes*, *þeos*, *þus*, ll. 476, 1038, 2219, 3816; *alle þos*=all these, Ayenbite of Inwyt, p. 10, l. 17; *þos word*=these words, Owl and Nightingale, 139; *þese wordes*=these words, P. Plowman, B. prol. 184; *þuse wordes*=these wordes, id. C. i. 198. Cf. AS. *ðās*, *ðæs*, these, pl. of *ðes*, this, Grein, ii. 581. Of these forms, *ðās* became *those*, while *ðēs* assisted in forming *these*; we also find ME. *this-e*, i. e. *this*, with the pl. suffix -*e.*

THISTLE, a prickly plant. (E.) ME. *þistil*, spelt *thystylle* in Prompt. Parv.; where we also find *sowthystylle*=sow-thistle. AS. *þistel*; 'Cardu[u]s, *þistel*,' Voc. 11. 13.+Du. *distel*; Icel. *þistill*; Dan. *tidsel*; Swed. *tistel*; G. *distel*; OHG. *distil*, *distula.* β. The *i* was once long, as in some E. and G. dialects; cf. Somersets. *daash-l*, a thistle, EFries. *dîssel.* Teut. types **þistiloz*, m.; **þistilā*, f. Perhaps allied to Goth. *at-thinsan*, to pull towards one; from its catching the clothes of the passer-by. Cf. **Tonsil.** Der. *thistl-y.*

THITHER, to that place. (E.) ME. *thider* (cf. ME. *fader*, *moder* for mod. E. *father*, *mother*); Chaucer, C. T. 1265 (A 1263). AS. *ðider*, *ðyder*, thither; Grein, ii. 590. Cf. Icel. *þaðra*, there; Goth. *thathrō*, thence. Skt. *tatra*, there, thither. Formed from Teut. THA=Idg. TO, demonst. pronom. base, for which see **That**;

with a suffix like L. -*tro* in *ul-tro.* Compare **Hither** and **Whither** Der. *thither-ward*, AS. *þiderweard*, Grein, ii. 591.

THOLE (1), **THOWL,** a pin or peg in the side of a boat to keep the oars in place. (E.) Commonly called a *thole-pin*, though the addition of *pin* is needless. ME. *thol*, *tol.* 'Tholle, carte-pynne, or tol-pyn, Cavilla;' Prompt. Parv. 'Tholle, a cartpynne;' Palsgrave. AS. *þol*; 'Scalmus, *thol*,' Corpus gloss., 1820 (8th cent.)+ Du. *dol*, 'a thowl;' Sewel; Icel. *þollr*, a fir-tree, a young fir, also a tree in general, as *ask-þollr*, ash-tree, *ālm-þollr*, elm-tree; also a wooden peg, the thole of a row-boat. Cf. Icel. *þöll* (gen. *þallar*), a young fir-tree; Dan. *tol*, a stopple, stopper, thole, pin; Swed. *tall*, a pine-tree; Swed. dial. *tåll*, the same (Rietz); Swed. *tull*, a thole. And cf. Norweg. *tall*, *toll*, a fir-tree, esp. a *young* fir-tree; *toll*, a thole (Aasen). β. Teut. base **thul-*, weak grade allied to **þal-*, as in *þal-lar*, gen. of Icel. *þöll* (above); and perhaps to **thel-*; see **Thill.** Der. *thole-pin.*

THOLE (2), to endure, suffer. (E.) In Levins. Obsolete in books, but a good word; it still occurs in prov. E. 'He that has a good crop may *thole* some thistles;' North-Country Proverb, in Brockett. ME. *þolien*, *þolen*, Chaucer, C. T. 7128 (D 1546). AS. *þolian*, to suffer, endure, tolerate; Grein, ii. 594.+Icel. *þola*, the same; Dan. *taale*; Swed. *tåla*; MHG. *dolen*, *doln*; OHG. *dolēn*, whence MHG. *duld*, G. *geduld*, patience; Goth. *thulan.* β. All from a Teut. base **þul-*, weak grade of Idg. √TEL, to bear; allied to Skt. *tul*, to lift, Gk. τλῆναι, to suffer; L. *tollere*, *tolerāre*; see further under **Tolerate.**

THONG, a strip or strap of leather. (E.) Spelt *thwangue* in Levins. For *thwong*; the *w* is now lost. ME. *þwong*, Wyclif, John, i. 27; we also find *þuong*, *þong*, Rob. of Glouc. p. 116, l. 2497. AS. *þwang*; in *sceō-þwang*=shoe-thong, John, i. 27. The change from *a* to *o* before *n* is common, as *song*<AS. *sang*; *strong*<AS. *strang.* +Icel. *þvengr*, a thong, latchet; esp. of a shoe. From **thwang*, 2nd grade of Teut. **thwengan-*, to constrain. The verb from which it is derived will be found under **Twinge**, q. v.

THORAX, the chest of the body. (L.—Gk.) A medical term. In Phillips, ed. 1706; Blount gives the adj. *thorachique.*—L. *thōrax* (gen. *thōrācis*), the breast, chest, a breast-plate.—Gk. θώραξ (gen. θώρακος), a breast-plate; also, the part of the body covered by the breast-plate. β. The orig. sense is 'protector' or 'defender;' the Gk. θωρακ- answers to Skt. *dhāraka-*, a trunk or box for keeping clothes, lit. a protector or preserver; √DHER, to bear, hold; see **Firm.** Der. *thoraci-c*, from the decl. stem *thōrāci-.*

THORN, a spine, sharp woody spine on the stem of a plant, a spiny plant. (E.) ME. *þorn*, Wyclif, Matt. xxvii. 29. AS. *þorn*, Matt. xxvii. 29.+Du. *doorn*; Icel. *þorn*; Dan. *tjörn*; Swed. *törne*; G. *dorn*; Goth. *thaurnus.* And cf. Russ. *tern'*, the black-thorn, *térnie*, thorns; Polish *tarn*, a thorn. Also Skt. *tṛna-*, a grass-blade. Teut. type **thurnuz*, m.; from the base THER=Idg. √TER, to bore, pierce, so that the sense is 'piercer.' See further under **Trite.** Der. *thorn-y*, cf. AS. *þorniht*, thorny, Voc. 139.18; *thorn-less.* Also *thorn-back*, the name of a fish which has spines on its back, ME. *þornebake.* Havelok, 759.

THOROUGH, going through and through, complete, entire. (E.) It is merely a later form of the prep. *through*, which was spelt *þoru* as early as in Havelok, 631, and *þuruh* in the Ancren Riwle, p. 92, l. 17. Shak. has *thorough* as a prep., Merry Wives, iv. 5. 32, Mids. Nt. Dr. ii. 1. 3 (where the folios and 2nd quarto have *through*); also as an adv., 'it pierced me *thorough*,' Pericles, iv. 3. 35; and even as an adj., L. L. L. ii. 235. The use of it as an adj. probably arose from the use of *throughly* or *thoroughly* as an adv. in place of the adverbial use of *through* or *thorough.* Cf. 'the feast was *throughly* ended;' Spenser, F. Q. iv. 12. 18. We find *thorough* as a sb., in the sense of 'passage,' J. Bradford's Works, i. 303 (Parker Society). The old sense of *through* is still preserved in *thorough-fare*, i. e. *through fare.* See **Through.** Der. *thorough-ly*, *thorough-ness*; *thorough-bred*, *thorough-going*, *thorough-paced.* Also *thorough-bass*, which prob. means *through-bass*, the bass being marked throughout by figures placed below the notes; and *thorough-fare*, i. e. *through-fare*, Cymb. i. 2. 11, Milton, P. L. x. 393.

THORP, THORPE, a village. (E.) Best spelt *thorp.* In Fairfax, tr. of Tasso, b. xii. st. 32. ME. *þorp*, Chaucer, C. T. 8075 (E 199). AS. *þorp*, as a place-name, A. S. Chron. an. 963. It means a village.+Du. *dorp*, a village; Icel. *þorp*; Dan. *torp*, a hamlet; Swed. *torp*, a little farm, cottage; G. *dorf*; Goth. *þaurp*, a field, Nehem. v. 16. β. The Teut. type is **thurpo-.* Allied to Lithuan. *trŏba*, a building, house. Also to Irish *treabh*, 'a farmed village [meaning, I suppose, a village round a farm], a tribe, family, clan;' Gael. *treabhair*, s. pl. (used collectively), houses; W. *tref*, a homestead, hamlet, town; Idg. type **trebo-.* Brugmann, i. § 553.

THOSE, now used as the pl. of *that*, but etymologically one of the forms of the pl. of *this.* (E.) See **This.**

THOU, the second pers. pronoun. (E.) ME. *thou.* AS. *ðū.*+ Icel. *þū*; Goth. *þu*; Dan., Swed., and G. *du*; (lost in Dutch); Irish and Gael. *tu*; W. *ti*; Russ. *tu*; L. *tu*; Gk. σύ, τύ; Pers. *tū*; Palmer's Pers. Dict. col. 152; Skt. *tvam* (nom. case). Brugmann, ii. § 440. Der. *thine,* q. v., often shortened to *thy.*

THOUGH, on that condition, even if, notwithstanding. (Scand.) It would be better to spell it *thogh,* in closer accordance with the pronunciation; but it seems to have become a fashion in E. always to write *ough* for *ogh,* and not to suffer *ogh* to appear. ME. *thogh,* Chaucer, C. T. 727 (A 729); the Ellesmere MS. has *thogh,* the Camb. MS. has *thow,* and the Petworth MS. has *þoo*; the rest, *though, thoughe.* [Older spellings, given by Stratmann, are *þah, þaih, þeah, þæh, þeʒ, þaʒ, þauh, þau, þei, þeiʒ, þeiʒh,* where some of the forms, as *þæh, þeʒ, þei, þeiʒh* are from AS. *ðēah, ðēh,* Grein, ii. 582.] The later ME. *thogh* answers to Icel. *þō.*+Du. *doch,* yet, but; Dan. *dog*; Swed. *dock*; G. *doch,* OHG. *doh*; Goth. *thauh.* β. All from the Teut. type **thau-h,* in which *-h* is an enclitic, answering to L. *-que,* Idg. **que.* **Thau-* is probably related to the Skt. *tu,* 'but.' In the D. and G. *doch,* the short *o* is due to loss of emphasis. **Der.** *al-though,* q. v.

THOUGHT, the act or result of thinking, an idea, opinion, notion. (E.) Better spelt *thoght*; the introduction of *u* is due to the prevalence of forms with *ough.* ME. *þoght, þouʒt*; the pl. *þouʒtis* is in Wyclif, 1 Cor. iii. 20. AS. *þōht,* also *geþōht,* as in Luke, ii. 35. Lit. ' a thing *thought* of, or *thought upon*;' cf. AS. *geþōht* or *þōht,* pp. of *þencan,* to think; Grein, ii. 579. See **Think.**+Icel. *þōtti, þōttr,* thought; allied to *þekkja,* to know, pt. t. *þātti,* the pp. not being used; G. *ge-dacht,* cf. *gedacht,* pp. of *denken,* to think; Goth. *thūhtus,* thought, allied to *thugkjan,* to seem, and *thagkjan,* to think; where *thugk-* (=*thunk-*) is the weak grade of *thagk-* (=*thank-*). **Der.** *thought-ful,* ME. *þohtful,* Ormulum, 3423; *thought-ful-ly, thought-ful-ness; thought-less, -less-ly, -less-ness.*

THOUSAND, ten hundred. (E.) ME. *þousand,* Chaucer, C. T. 1956 (A 1954). AS. *þūsend,* Grein, ii. 611.+Du. *duizend*; Icel. *þūsund*; also *þūshund, þūshundrað*; Dan. *tusind*; Swed. *tusen* (for *tusend*); G. *tausend*; Goth. *thūsundi.* We also find Lithuan. *tuk-stantis,* a thousand; Russ. *tuisiacha,* a thousand. β. The word is not yet explained; in Icel. *þūs-hund,* the syllable *hund*=AS. *hund,* a hundred, and is due to popular etymology; which may, however, prove to be correct. See the long discussion of Goth. *thūsundi* in Schade, OHG. Dictionary. It is suggested that the sense was ' great hundred;' the prefix *þūs-* being allied to Skt. *tavas,* strong; Streitberg, § 129 (5). Cf. also OPruss. *tūsimtons,* a thousand. **Der.** *thousand-th,* a late word, formed by analogy with *four-th,* &c.; *thousand-fold,* ME. *þusendfald,* St. Katherine, 2323.

THOWL, the same as **Thole** (1), q. v.

THRALL, a slave. (Scand.) ME. *þral,* Chaucer, C. T. 12123 (C 189). ONorthumb. *ðrǽl,* Mark, x. 44; not an AS. word, but borrowed from Norse. — Icel. *þrǽll,* a thrall, serf, slave; Dan. *trǽl*; Swed. *trǽl.* Teut. type **thrǽhiloz,* m. (base **thrǽh-*); and allied to OHG. *drigil, drëgil,* a slave, a thrall; lit. ' a runner,' i.e. one who runs on messages. Formed from the Teut. base THREG, to run, whence also Goth. *thragjan,* AS. *þrǽgan,* to run. Cf. AS. *þrag, þrah,* a running, course. Further connexions uncertain; perhaps allied to L. *trahere,* to draw, or to Celto-L. *vertraga,* a greyhound; see **Feuterer.** The Gk. τρέχ-ειν, to run, is of uncertain origin. **Der.** *thral-dom,* ME. *þraldom,* Layamon, 29156; from Icel. *þrǽldōmr,* thraldom; the Icel. suffix *-dōmr* being the same as the AS. suffix *-dōm.*

THRASH, THRESH, to beat out grain from the straw. (E.) The spelling with *e* is the older. ME. *þreschen, þreshen,* Chaucer, C. T. 538 (A 536). For *þerschen,* by metathesis of *r.* AS. *þerscan, þirscan,* Grein, ii. 581. A strong verb, pt. t. *þærsc,* pp. *þorscen.* The ME. pp. *þroschen* occurs in the Ormulum, l. 1530; and *iðrosschen* in the Ancren Riwle, p. 186, l. 18.+MDu. *derschen* (Hexham); Du. *dorschen*; Icel. *þreskja*; Dan. *tærske*; Swed. *tröska*; G. *dreschen*; Goth. *thriskan,* pt. t. *thrask,* pp. *thruskans.* β. All from Teut. type **threskan,* pt. t. **thrask,* pp. **thruskanoz*; to beat noisily. Allied to Lithuan. *tarszkéti,* to rattle, clap; *traszkéti,* to rattle, make a cracking noise; Russ. *treskat(e),* to burst, crack, crackle, *tresk*', a crash. From an Idg. base **tresk-,* to crack, burst, crackle; then to strike, thrash. Fick cites OSlavonic *troska,* Lat. ' *fulmen*;' which suggests the rattling of thunder; whence, perhaps, the noise of the flail. **Der.** *thrash-er* or *thresh-er,* ME. *þreschare,* Prompt. Parv.; *thrash-ing* or *thresh-ing*; *thrashing-floor* or *threshing-floor,* Ruth, iii. 2. Also *thresh-old,* q. v.

THRASONICAL, vain-glorious. (L.—Gk.) In Shak. L. L. L. v. 1. 14; As You Like It, v. 2. 34. A coined word, as if with suffix *-al* (L. *-ālis*) from a L. adj. **Thrasōnicus*; but the adj. really in use was *Thrasōniānus,* whence MF. *Thrasonien,* ' boasting, Thraso-like:' Cot. Formed, with suffix *-cus* (or *-ānus*), from *Thrasōni-,*

decl. stem of *Thraso,* the name of a bragging soldier in Terence's Eunuchus. Evidently coined from Gk. θρασ-ύς, bold, spirited. — √DHERS, to be bold; cf. Skt. *dharsha-,* arrogance, *dhṛsh,* to be bold: see **Dare** (1).

THRAVE, a number of sheaves of wheat. (Scand.) See Nares. Generally 12 or 24 sheaves. The pl. *threaves*=clusters or handfuls of rushes, is in Chapman, Gent. Usher, ii. 1 (Bassiolo). ME. *þraue, þreue,* P. Plowman, B. xvi. 55. The late AS. pl. *þreues* occurs in Birch, Cart. Saxon. iii. 367.—Icel. *þrefi,* a thrave, number of sheaves; Dan. *trave,* a score of sheaves; Swed. *trafve,* a pile of wood. Cf. Swed. dial. *trave,* a thrave; *trafve,* 24 or 30 sheaves in a shock (F. Möller); NFries. *trav.*

THREAD, a thin twisted line or cord, filament. (E.) ME. *þreed, þred,* Chaucer, C. T. 14393 (B 3665). The *e* was once long; the Ellesmere and Hengwrt MSS. have the spelling *threed.* AS. *þrǽd,* a thread; Ælfred, tr. of Boethius, c. xxix. § 1 (b. iii. pr. 5). Lit. ' that which is twisted.'—AS. *þrāwan,* to twist, also to throw; see **Throw.**+Du. *draad,* thread; cf. *draaijen,* to twist, turn; Icel. *þrāðr*; Dan. *traad*; Swed. *tråd*; G. *draht, drath,* wire, thread; OHG. *drāt,* wire. Teut. type **þrǽ-duz*; cf. Gk. τρῆ-σις, a boring through, a hole. **Der.** *thread,* verb, Rich. II, v. 5. 17; *thread-y,* i.e. thread-like. Also *thread-bare,* so bare that the component threads of the garment can be traced, ME. *þredbar* (*þreedbare* in the Hengwrt MS.), Chaucer, C. T. 262 (A 260). **Doublet,** *thrid.*

THREAT, a menace. (E.) ME. *þret*; the dat. *þrete* occurs in The Owl and Nightingale, l. 58; hence the verb *þreten,* Chaucer, Legend of Good Women, 754; also the verb *þretenen,* Wyclif, Mark, i. 25. [The latter is mod. E. *threaten.*] AS. *þrēat,* (1) a crowd, crush, or throng of people, which is the usual meaning, Grein, ii. 598; also (2) a great pressure, calamity, trouble, and hence, a threat, rebuke, Grein, ii. 598, l. 1. The orig. sense was a push as of a crowd, hence pressure put upon any one. Cf. AS. *þrēat,* pt. t. of the strong verb *þrēotan,* appearing only in the impersonal comp. *āþrēotan,* to afflict, vex, lit. to press extremely, urge.+Icel. *þrjōta,* pt. t. *þraut,* pp. *þrotinn,* to fail, lack, come short; used impersonally. (The orig. sense was perhaps to urge, trouble, whence the sb. *þraut,* a hard task, struggle); Goth. *thriutan,* only in the comp. *usthriutan,* to use despitefully, trouble, vex greatly; OHG. *driozan,* in the comp. *ardriozan,* MHG. *erdriezen,* impers. verb, to tire, vex; also appearing in G. *verdriessen* (pt. t. *verdross*), to vex, trouble. β. Hence AS. *þrēat,* a crush, Teut. type **thrautoz,* m., is from Teut. **thraut,* 2nd grade of **threutan-,* to crowd. Allied to L. *trūdere,* to push, shove, crowd, urge, press upon (cf. *trudis,* a pole to push with); also to Russ. *trudit(e),* to make a man work, to trouble, disturb, vex. (√TREUD, to push, urge.) **Der.** *threat,* verb, K. John, iii. 1. 347; ME. *þreten* (as above), AS. *þrēatian* (weak verb), Grein, ii. 598; also *threat-en,* ME. *þretenen* (as above), AS. *þrēatnian*; *threat-en-ing, threat-en-ing-ly.* From the same base, *abs-truse, de-trude, ex-trude, in-trude, ob-trude, pro-trude.* Cf. *thrust.*

THREE, two and one. (E.) ME. *þre,* Wyclif, Matt. xviii. 20. AS. *þrēo,* Matt. xviii. 20; other forms *þrio, þrī, þrȳ,* Grein, ii. 599. +Du. *drie*; Icel. *þrir* (fem. *þrjar,* neut. *þriu*); Dan. *tre*; Swed. *tre*; Goth. *threis*; G. *drei.*+Irish, Gael., and W. *tri*; Russ. *tri*; L. *trēs,* neut. *tria*; Gk. τρεῖς, neut. τρία; Lithuan. *trys* (stem *tri-*); Skt. masc. nom. pl. *trayas.* Idg. masc. nom. pl. **treyes.* Brugmann, ii. § 167. **Der.** *three-fold,* AS. *þrifeald, þriefeald,* Ælfred, tr. of Boethius, c. xxxiii. § 4 (b. iii. met. 9); *three-score,* Much Ado, i. 1. 201; also *thri-ce,* q. v.; and see *thir-d, thir-teen, thir-ty.* From the same source are *tri-ad, tri-angle, tri-nity, tri-pos,* &c. See **Tri-.** Also *tierce, terc-el, ter-t-ian, ter-t-i-ar-y.*

THRENODY, a lament, song of lamentation. (Gk.) Shak. even ventures upon *threne,* Phœnix, l. 49. Blount's Gloss., ed. 1674, has both *threne* and *threnody.* Englished from Gk. θρηνῳδία, a lamenting. — Gk. θρῆν-ος, a wailing, lamenting, sound of wailing, funeral dirge (cf. θρέ-ομαι, I cry aloud); and ᾠδή, an ode, from ἀείδειν, to sing. See **Drone** (1) and **Ode.**

THRESH, the same as **Thrash,** q. v.

THRESHOLD, a piece of wood or stone under the door or at the entrance of a house. (E.) The word is to be divided *thresh-old,* where *-old* was (by popular etymology) supposed to stand for *wold* (wood). (Shak. has *old*=*wold,* K. Lear, iii. 4. 125.) ME. *þreshwold, þreswold,* Chaucer, C. T. 3482; *þresshewold,* P. Plowman, B. v. 357; *þriswald,* Voc. 667. 14. AS. *þerscold,* Deut. vi. 9 (where the *w* does not appear; later form *þerscwald,* as in ' Limen, *þerscwald*;' Voc. 280. 15. Supposed to mean ' the piece of wood which is beaten' by the feet of those who enter the house, the *thrash-wood.*—AS. *þersc-an,* to thresh, thrash; and *wald, weald,* a wood, hence a piece of wood. β. But this was a popular etymology; King Alfred has *þerscold* simply; tr. of Gregory's Pastoral Care, p. 77, l. 22. This form represents Teut. **þresko-ðlo* (Sievers); cf. OHG. *drisc-ū-fli,* a threshold. Here **þresko-* is from Teut. **þreskan-,* to thrash;

but -ðlo- represents the Idg. suffix -tro-. See my Principles of Eng. Etymology, i. § 228 (h). The Icel. þreskjöldr, a threshold, is spelt in various ways; cf. Swed. tröskel.

THRICE, three times. (E.) The final -ce is for s; it is a mere device for showing that the final sound is voiceless, i. e. sounded as s and not as z. So also the pl. of mous(e) is written mice; &c. Thrice stands for thris, contracted form of ME. þriës or þryës, a word which was formerly dissyllabic: 'And þryës with hir speres clateringe,' Chaucer, C. T. 2956 (A 2954). β. Again, þrie-s was formed (with adverbial suffix -s, orig. the suffix of the gen. case) from an older form þrië, also dissyllabic; the words on-ce, twi-ce originating in a similar manner. The form þrie is in Layamon, 17432, earlier text; and þries in the same, 26066, later text.—AS. þriwa, thrice, Exod. xxiii. 14; Grein, ii. 601.—AS. þri, three. See **Three**.

THRID, a thread. (E.) In Dryden, Hind and Panther, iii. 278. The same as **Thread**, q.v. Der. thrid, verb, Dryden, Palamon and Arcite, l. 495.

THRIFT, frugality. (Scand.) ME. þrift, Chaucer, C. T. 16893. —Icel. þrift, thrift, where the t is added to the stem; we also find þrif, thriving condition, prosperity.—Icel. þrif-, weak grade, as seen in þrif-inn, pp. of þrifa, only used in the reflex. þrifask, to thrive; see **Thrive**. Cf. Dan. triv-else, prosperity, with a different suffix. The suffix -t is from the Idg. suffix -to-. Cf. thef-t.

THRILL, THIRL, to pierce. (E.) Spenser uses thrill in the unmetaphorical sense, to pierce with an arrow; F. Q. iii. 5. 20, iv. 7. 31; hence the metaphorical use, as in F. Q. iv. 1. 49. Thirl is an older spelling of the same word. 'Thyrlyn, thryllyn, or peercyn, Penetro, terebro, perforo;' Prompt. Parv. ME. þirlen, Chaucer, C. T. 2712 (A 2710); þrullen, Trevisa, tr. of Higden, i. 339; þurlen, Ancren Riwle, p. 392, l. 24. AS. þyrlian, to pierce through, spelt þirlian, Exod. xxi. 6, Levit. xxv. 10. Again, þyrlian is a shorter form for þyrelian; we find the sb. þyrel-ung, a piercing, in Ælfred, tr. of Gregory's Past. Care, c. xxi, ed. Sweet, p. 153, last line, and the verb ðurh-ðyrelian, to pierce through (through-thirl), two lines further on. The verb þyrelian is a causal verb, from the sb. þyrel, a hole (caused by boring), Ælfred, tr. of Boethius, c. xxxiv. § 11 (b. iii. pr. 11). β. Lastly, þyrel is also found as an adj., with the sense of bored or pierced. 'Gif monnes þeoh bið þyrel' (various reading þyrl) = if a man's thigh be pierced; Laws of Ælfred, § 62, in Thorpe, Ancient Laws, i. 96. This is equivalent to the cognate MHG. durchel, pierced, an adj. derived from durch, prep., through; similarly, AS. þyrel stands for *þyrhel (from *þurh-il-), derived (with the usual vowel-change from u to y) from AS. þurh, through. γ. We thus see that AS. þyrl meant 'going through,' and hence, 'a hole;' whence the verb was formed. See **Through**. Cf. Irish tar, through. ¶ The Du. drillen is from dril (MDu. drille), a hole; and drille must have been a derivative from the old form of Du. door, through; cf. OSaxon thurh, through. Der. thrill, sb., a late word; thrill-ing, pres. part. as adj. Also nos-tril, q.v. Doublet, drill (from Dutch).

THRIVE, to prosper, flourish, be successful. (Scand.) ME. þriuen (with u = v), Chaucer, C. T. 3677 (A 3675); Havelok, 280; Ormulum, 10868. A strong verb; pt. t. þraf, Ormulum, 3182, þrof, Rob. of Glouc. p. 11, l. 240; pp. þriuen.—Icel. þrifa, to clutch, grasp, grip, seize; hence þrifask (with suffixed -sk = sik, self), lit. to seize for oneself, to thrive. [It is suggested in the Icel. Dict. that þrifask is not connected with þrifa, but the transition from 'seizing to oneself' to 'thriving' is easy, and, as both are strong verbs, conjugated alike, it is hardly possible to separate them. Cf. Norw. triva, to seize, trivast, to thrive; and Widegren has Swed. trifven, thrifty, active, diligent, coinciding with the Icel. pp. þrifinn, from þrifa; and even Icel. þrifinn also means 'thrifty.'] The pt. t. is þreif, and the pp. þrifinn; hence the sb. þrif, prosperity, and E. thrif-t.+Dan. trives, reflex. verb, to thrive; whence trivelse, prosperity; Swed. trifvas, reflex. verb, to thrive; cf. trefnad, prosperity. Der. thriv-ing-ly; thrif-t, q.v.; thrif-ty, ME. þrifty, Chaucer, C. T. 12905 (B 1165); thrift-i-ly, thrift-i-ness; thrift-less, thrift-less-ly, thrift-less, -ness.

THROAT, the forepart of the neck with the gullet and windpipe, the gullet. (E.) ME. þrote, Ancren Riwle, p. 216, l. 4. AS. þrote, throat, Ælfred, tr. of Boethius, c. xxii, § 1 (bk. iii. pr. 1); also þrotu, 'Guttur, þrotu,' Voc. 157. 41; 'Guttur, þrota,' id. 306. 13.+OHG. drozza, MHG. drozze, the throat; whence G. drossel, throat, throttle. β. Referred in Ettmüller to AS. þreotan (pp. þroten), to press; a verb treated of s. v. **Threat**. But it is more likely that an initial s has been lost, and that AS. þrote is allied to Du. strot, the throat, MDu. stroot, strot, 'the throat or the gullet,' Hexham, stroote, 'the wesen [weasand] or the wind-pipe,' id. So also OFries. strotbolla = AS. þrotbolla, the gullet or windpipe; and cf. Ital. strozza, the gullet, a word of Teut. origin. We must therefore refer it to a Teut. base *strut-; and a connexion with E. strut

is possible. The reference may be to the 'prominence' or swelling in the throat below the chin. Cf. Icel. þroti, a swelling; þrutna, to swell. See **Thropple**. Der. þrott-le, the wind-pipe, dimin. of þroat; þrott-le, verb, to press on the windpipe, ME. þrotlen, Destruction of Troy, 12752. Also þropple, q.v.

THROB, to beat forcibly, as the heart. (E.) ME. þrobben, rare. 'With þrobbant herte' = with throbbing heart; P. Plowman, A. xii. 48. The word must be either E. or Scand., as it begins with þ; but it appears neither in AS. nor in the Scand. languages. We must call it E. β. Allied to Russ. trepet(e), palpitation, throbbing, trembling, fear; trepetat(e), to throb, palpitate with joy; and prob. to trepat(e), to beat hemp, also to knock softly. Also to L. trepidus; see **Trepidation**. Der. throb, sb., Spenser, Shep. Kal. May, 208.

THROE, pang, pain, agony. (Scand.) ME. þrowe. 'Throwe, Erumpna;' Prompt. Parv. And see þrowes, pl., pangs, O. Eng. Homilies, ed. Morris, ii. 181, l. 2.—Icel. þra, a throe, pang, longing; Norw. traa, longing, traa, to long for; MSwed. trå, longing, trå, to long for, to pine away (Swed. tråna). Cf. OHG. dróa, burden, suffering, druoēn, dróēn, to suffer; AS. þrowian, to suffer. Base *thraw-, from Idg. root *treu; cf. L. trux, fierce. See **Truculent**. Cf. also Icel. þreyja, endurance, þreyja, to long for.

THRONE, a royal seat, chair of state. (F.—L.—Gk.) Now conformed to the Gk. spelling. ME. trone, Wyclif, Matt. v. 34.—OF. trone (13th cent.), spelt throne in Cot.; mod. F. trône.—L. thronum, acc. of thronus, Matt. v. 34.—Gk. θρόνος, a seat, chair; lit. a support.—√DHER, to hold, support; whence also Gk. θρᾶνος, a bench, Ion. θρῆνυς, a stool.

THRONG, a great crowd of people. (E.) ME. þrong, Allit. Poems, ed. Morris, B. 135; þrang, Pricke of Conscience, 4704. AS. ge-þrang, a throng, Grein, i. 473; where the common prefix ge- makes no difference.—AS. þrang, 2nd grade of the strong vb. þringan, to crowd, to press (pp. þrungen), Mark, v. 24.+Du. drang, a crowd, from dringen, to crowd; Icel. þröng, a throng; G. drang, a throng, from drang, 2nd grade of dringen (pp. drungen), to crowd, press. Cf. Dan. trang, Swed. trång, adj., pressed close, tight, prov. E. throng, adj., busy; Goth. threihan (pp. thraihans), to throng, press round (for *thrinhan). β. All from the Teut. strong verb *threnχan-, to throng, from Idg. root *trenk; whence Lithuan. trenkti, to jolt, to push, tranksmas, a tumult; and even L. truncus, maimed, mutilated. Brugmann, i. § 144 (1). Der. throng, verb, ME. þrongen, Morte Arthure, ed. Brock, 3755.

THROPPLE, THRAPPLE, the wind-pipe. (E.) Spelt thrapple by Johnson, who gives it as a Lowland Sc. word; better thropple, see Halliwell and Jamieson. Halliwell gives also thropple, to throttle; a derived sense. Thropple is usually said to be a corruption of AS. þrotbolla, the wind-pipe, also the gullet; which requires rather violent treatment to reduce it to the required form. The AS. þrotbolla survived for a long time; Palsgrave gives: 'Throtegole or throtebole, neu de la gorge, gosier.' The usual sense of AS. bolla is 'bowl;' see **Throat** and **Bowl** (2), **Bole**.

THROSTLE, the song-thrush. (E.) ME. þrustel, Chaucer, C. T. 13703 (B 1963). 'Mavis' is glossed by 'a throstel-kok' in Walter de Bibbesworth; Wright's Voc. i. 164, l. 1. AS. þrostle; 'Merula, þrostle,' Voc. 286. 20; spelt þrosle (by loss of t), id. 132. 25. +MHG. trostel. Teut. type *thrustlā, fem.; Idg. type *tǝrzd-lā, f. Allied to L. turdus, a thrush; also to Icel. þröstr (gen. þrastar), Swed. and Norw. trast, a thrush (from *þrast, 2nd grade of a Teut. root *þrest); cf. OPruss. tresde, a thrush. Also, with initial s, Lith. strazdas, m., strazda, f., a thrush. See further under **Thrush** (1). Throstle has a variant throshel, ME. thrusshil, Prompt. Parv. Brugmann, i. §§ 818 (2), 882.

THROTTLE, the wind-pipe. (E.) See **Throat**.

THROUGH, from beginning to end, from one side to the other, from end to end. (E.) For the form thorough, see **Thorough**. ME. þurh, þuruh, Ancren Riwle, p. 92, ll. 12, 17. Other forms are þurʒ, þurw, þurch, þurgh, þorw, þoruh, þoru, &c.; see Stratmann. Also þruh, Reliquiæ Antiquæ, i. 102, by metathesis of r; and hence mod. E. through. AS. þurh, prep. and adv., through, Grein, ii. 607, 610; ONorthumb. þerh, Matt. xxvii. 18 (Lindisfarne MS.).+Du. door; G. durch, OHG. durh, duruh. Teut. type *þurh. Allied to Goth. thairh (for *þerh), through. β. The Goth. thairkō, a hole, is prob. connected with thairh; and the AS. þyrel, a hole, is a derivative from þurh, through; as shown under **Thrill**. The fundamental notion is that of boring or piercing; and we may refer through to the √TER, to bore, as in L. terere, to bore, Gk. τείρειν (for *τέρ-yειν). See **Trite**. Cf. through with Irish tar, beyond, over, through, tri, through, tair, beyond; L. tr-ans, across; Skt. tiras, through, over. Brugmann, i. § 527. Der. through-ly, thoroughly (see **Thorough**); through-out, ME. þuruhut, Ancren Riwle, p. 212, l. 23, with which cf. G. durchaus, a similar compound. And see **Throw**.

THROW, to cast, to hurl. (E.) One sense of the word was to twist or wind silk or thread; hence *throwster*, a silk-winder; ' *Throwster*, devideresse de soye;' Palsgrave. The orig. sense was to turn, twist, whirl; hence a turner's lathe is still called a *throw* (Halliwell). ME. *þrowen*, pt. t. *þrew*, P. Plowman, B. xx. 163; pp. *þrowen*, Wyclif, Matt. xiv. 24 (earlier version), now contracted to *thrown*. AS. *þráwan*, to twist, whirl, hurl; pt. t. *þréow*, pp. *þráwen*; a verb which, strangely enough, is rare. 'Contorqueo, ic samod þráwe,' i. e. I twist together, occurs in Ælfric's Grammar, ed. Zupitza, p. 155, l. 16. The pt. t. *þréow* = turned itself, occurs in Ælfric's Homilies, ii. 510, l. 8. Leo quotes, from various glossaries: ' *ge-þráwan*, torquere; *á-þráwan*, crispare; *ed-þráwan*, to twist double; *þráwing-spinl*, a throwing (or winding) spindle.' The orig. sense is still preserved in the derived word *thread* = that which is twisted. β. Allied to G. *drehen*, OHG. *drájan*, to turn, whirl, Du. *draaijen*, to turn, twist, whirl; all from Teut. base *þræ-* = Idg. base *trē-*, as in Gk. τρη-τός, bored through, τρῆ-μα, a hole, τρή-σω, fut. of τε-τραίνειν, to bore through. The grade *ter* occurs in L. *ter-ere*, Gk. τείρειν (for *τέρ-γειν), to bore. (√TER). **Der.** throw, sb., throw-er; and see thread.

THRUM (1), the tufted end of a weaver's thread; coarse yarn. (E.) See *Thrum* in Nares. In Shak. Mids. Nt. Dr. v. 291. ME. *þrum*. 'Thrumm, of a clothe, Filamen;' Prompt. Parv. 'Hoc licium, a *throm*;' Voc. 728. 17. AS. *þrum*, found in *tunge-þrum*, a ligament of the tongue; A. S. Leechdoms, i. p. lxxiv. l. 9; p. lxx. l. 9. Allied to Icel. *þrömr* (gen. *þramar*), the edge, verge, brim of a thing (hence the rough edge of a web); Norweg. *tröm*, *tram*, *trumm*, edge, brim (Aasen); Swed. dial. *tromm*, *trumm*, *tröm*, a stump, the end of a log (Rietz); MDu. *drom*, or *drom-garen* [thrum-yarn], 'thred on the shittle of a weaver;' Hexham; Du. *dreum*; G. *trumm*, end, thrum, stump of a tree. β. Allied to Gk. τέρ-μα, end, L. *ter-minus*, end, limit; see **Term**. **Der.** thrumm-ed, Merry Wives, iv. 2. 80.

THRUM (2), to strum, play noisy music. (Scand.) 'This single *thrumming* of a fiddle;' Beaum. and Fletcher, Woman's Prize, i. 1 (Jaques). — Icel. *þruma*, to rattle, to thunder; cf. *þrymr*, an alarm, a noise; Dan. *tromme*, a drum; Swed. *trumma*, to beat, to drum. See **Trumpet** and **Drum**.

THRUSH (1), a small singing-bird. (E.) ME. *þrusch*. 'Boþe þe *þrusche* and þe *þrustele*' = both the thrush and throstle, Will. of Palerne, 820. AS. *þrysce*, spelt *þryssce* in Voc. 286. 23; *þrisce*, id. 260. 30.+OHG. *drosca*, a thrush; whence G. *drossel*. β. The AS. word answers to the Teut. type *thruskjōn-*, f. Allied to **Throstle**, q. v.

THRUSH (2), a disease marked by small ulcerations in the mouth. (Scand.) 'Thrush, a disease in the mouth, esp. of young children;' Phillips, ed. 1706. The form shows that the word is English or Norse, as it begins with *th*. From ONorse *þruskr*, thrush; whence MDan. *torsk*, Dan. *tröske*, the thrush on the tongue, Swed. *torsk*, Swed. dial. *trösk* (Rietz); Norw. *trausk*, *trosk*, *trösk*, thrush (Ross). Prob. the same as Norw. *trausk*, variant of *frausk*, *frosk*, a frog; *frosk*, the thrush. In the same way, Gk. βάτραχος and L. *rāna* meant (1) a frog, (2) a disease of the tongue (Falk).

THRUST, to push forcibly. (Scand.) ME. *þrusten*, but more commonly *þristen*, as in Havelok, 2019, and sometimes *þresten*, as in Chaucer, C. T. 2614 (A 2612). The form *thrust* is properly of Scand. origin. — Icel. *þrýsta*, to thrust, compress, press, force, compel; Norw. *trysta*, to thrust. The Teut. base is *þrūst*, perhaps for *þrūt-st*; prob. allied to Icel. *þraut*, a struggle, and to L. *trūd-ere*, to thrust, to push. See **Threat**. **Der.** thrust, sb., Oth. v. 1. 24.

THUD, a dull sound resulting from a blow. (E.) In Burns, Battle of Sheriffmuir, l. 8. Also used by G. Douglas and others (Jamieson); and see Notes and Queries, 4 S. i. 34, 115, 163, 231, 275. Allied to AS. *þyddan*, to strike, thrust, push.

THUG, an assassin. (Hindustani.) Modern. — Hind. *thag*, *thug* (with cerebral *th*), a cheat, knave, imposter, a robber who strangles travellers; Marāthī *thak*, *thag*, the same; H. H. Wilson, Gloss. of Indian Terms; p. 517. And see Yule.

THUMB, the short, thick finger of the hand. (E.) ME. *þombe*, Chaucer, C. T. 565 (A 563); formed with excrescent *b* (after *m*) from the earlier *þume*, Ancren Riwle, p. 18, l. 14. AS. *þúma*, the thumb; 'Pollex, *þuma*,' Voc. 40. 22.+Du. *duim*; Swed. *tumme*; OHG. *dūmo*, G. *daumen*. Cf. Icel. *þumall*, the thumb of a glove; Dan. *tommel-finger*, thumb. β. Teut. type *þū-mon-*, m., thumb, lit. 'the *thick* finger;' Fick, iii. 135. From Teut. base THEU = √TEU, to swell, grow large; see **Tumid**. Cf. **Tuber**. **Der.** thumb-kin, a dimin. of *thumb*, but used as equivalent to *thumb-screw*, an instrument of torture for compressing the thumb (Webster); *thumb-ring*, 1 Hen. IV, ii. 4. 365; also *thimb-le*, q. v.

THUMMIM, perfection. (Heb.) We have *urim and thummim*, Exod. xxviii. 30, Ezra, ii. 63, &c. The *literal* sense of these difficult words is, probably, 'fires (or lights) and perfections,' but the Heb. pl. need not be exactly kept to in English; 'light and perfection' would probably be the best E. equivalent; Smith, Dict. of the Bible. — Heb. *tummim*, pl. of *tóm*, perfection, truth (with initial *tau*). — Heb. root *támam*, to be perfect. See **Urim**.

THUMP, to beat heavily. (E.) In Rich. III, v. 3. 334; and in Spenser, F. Q. vi. 2. 10. 'Thomp! thomp!' Bale, Kynge Johan, p. 53 (C. S.). An imitative word; from the sound of a blow. Cf. EFries. *dump*, a thump; also Icel. *dumpa*, to thump, Swed. dial. *dompa*, to thump, *dumpa*, to make a noise. Of imitative origin. **Der.** thump, sb., thump-er.

THUNDER, the loud noise accompanying lightning. (E.) For *thuner*; the *d* after *n* is excrescent. ME. *þoner*, Iwain and Gawain, l. 370, in Ritson, Met. Romances, i. 16; more commonly *þonder* or *þunder*, Chaucer, C. T. 494, 6314 (A 492, D 732). AS. *þunor*, thunder, Grein, ii. 606. Allied to AS. *þunian*, to rattle, thunder; Grein, ii. 606. Cf. AS. *ge-þun*, a loud noise, in a gloss (Bosworth). +Du. *donder*; Icel. *þórr* (for *þonr*), Thor, the god of thunder; with which cf. Dan. *torden*, Swed. *tordön*, thunder; G. *donner*, OHG. *thonar*, thunder. β. All from Teut. base *thun-*, to thunder (Fick, iii. 130) = Idg. *tun-*. We have further allied words in L. *tonāre*, to thunder, *tonitru*, thunder, Skt. *tan*, to sound; from Idg. √TEN, to sound, by-form of √STEN, to thunder, make a noise, appearing in Skt. *stan*, to sound, sigh, thunder, *stanita-*, thunder, *stanana-*, sound, groaning, Gk. στέν-ειν, to groan, Lithuan. *stenéti*, to groan, Russ. *stenat(e)*, *stonat(e)*, to groan, moan; see **Stun** and **Stentor**. **Der.** thunder, verb, AS. *þunrian*, Grein; *thunder-bolt*, Temp. ii. 2. 38 (see **Bolt**); *thunder-stone*, J. Cæs. i. 3. 49; *thunder-stroke*, Temp. ii. 1. 204; *thunder-struck*, Milton, P. L. vi. 858; *thunder-ous*, id. P. L. x. 702; *thunder-er*, id. P. L. vi. 491. Also *Thurs-day*, q. v. See Brugmann, i. § 818(2).

THURIBLE, a censer for burning frankincense. (L. — Gk.) 'A pot of manna, or *thurible*;' Bp. Taylor, Rule of Conscience, b. ii. c. 2 (R.). Phillips, ed. 1706, has only the L. form *thúribulum*. Englished from L. *thúribulum*, also spelt *túribulum*, a vessel for holding frankincense. — L. *thúri-*, *túri-*, decl. stem of *thus* or *tús*, frankincense; with suffix *-bulum*, as in *fundi-bulum* (from *fundere*). This sb. *thús* is not a true L. word, but borrowed from Gk. θύ-ός, incense. — Gk. θύ-ειν, to offer part of a meal to the gods, by burning it, to sacrifice. Cf. Skt. *dhúma-*, smoke; L. *fúmus*, smoke, which is the native L. word from the same root as Gk. θυός. — √DHEU, to shake, blow, fan a flame. See **Fume**. **Der.** (from L. *thúri-*), *thuri-fer*, one who carries incense; where the suffix *-fer* = bearing, from *ferre*, to bear. From the same root as *thyme* and *fume*.

THURSDAY, the fifth day of the week. (Scand.) The day of the god of thunder, the Scand. Thor. ME. *þurs-dei*, Ancren Riwle, p. 40, l. 7; *þorsday*, *þoresday*, *þursday*, P. Plowman, B. xvi. 140, and footnotes; (spelt *þunres-dæi*, Layamon, 13929). — AS. *þúres dæg*, Thursday. — AS. *þúres*, gen. of *þúr*, Thor; and *dæg*, day. Borrowed from Icel. *þórs-dagr*, Thursday; from *þórs*, gen. case of *þórr*, Thor, thunder; *dagr*, a day. So also are compounded Du. *Donderdag*, Swed. and Dan. *Torsdag*, G. *Donnerstag* and the (native) AS. *þunres dæg*. All are translations of L. *diēs Iouis*, Jupiter's day. See **Sweet**, Hist. E. Sounds, § 578. And see **Thunder**.

THUS, in this manner. (E.) ME. *thus*, Chaucer, C. T. 1880 (A 1878). AS. *ðus*, thus, so, Grein, ii. 611.+OFries. and OSax. *thus*, thus; Du. *dus*. Of obscure origin; prob. allied to **That**; and perhaps to **This**.

THWACK, WHACK, to beat severely. (E.) In Levins, and in Shak. Cor. iv. 5. 189. 'If it be a *thwack*' [blow]; Beaum. and Fletcher, Nice Valour, iii. 2 (Lapet). Tusser has *thwack* as a verb; Husbandry, § 18, st. 3 (E.D.S.). Prob. of imitative origin. Cf. Icel. *þjökka*, to thwack, thump; *þjaka*, the same; prov. G. *wackeln*, to cudgel. β. For the change from *thwack* to *whack*, see **Whittle**. ¶ It does not agree, in form or sense, with ME. *thakken*, to stroke, as in: 'When Nicholas had doon thus euery del, And *thakked* her about the lendes wel;' Chaucer, C. T. 3304; AS. *þaccian*, to stroke, said of stroking a horse; Ælfred, tr. of Gregory's Past. Care, c. 41, ed. Sweet, p. 303, l. 10.

THWAITE, a clearing. (Scand.) Common in place-names, in Cumberland, as in *Esthwaite*, *Legberthwaite*, &c.; see Taylor's Words and Places, c. 8; Gent. Maga. Nov. 1856, p. 530. In N. and Q. 3 S. x. 68, an example of *thwayt* is given, as occurring in the 16th century. — Icel. *þveit*, a paddock, &c., orig. a 'cutting,' i. e. a clearing in a wood. As if from *þveit*, 2nd grade of a strong verb *þvíta*, to cut; not found, but the same word as AS. *þwítan*, to cut; for which see **Whittle** (1). Cf. Norw. *tveit*, a cut, also a small clear space (Aasen); prov. Sw. *tveit*, a chip, *-tveta*, a suffix in place-names (Rietz); Dan. dial. *tved*. And see **Doit**.

THWART, transversely, transverse. (Scand.) Properly an adv., as used by Spenser: 'Yet whether *thwart* or flatly it did lyte' [light, alight]; F. Q. vi. 6. 30. He also has it as a prep.: 'thwart her horse' = across her horse, F. Q. iii. 7. 43. The ME. use shows clearly that the word was used adverbially, esp. in certain phrases, and then as an adj. ; the verbal use was the latest of all. ME. *þwert, þwart.* 'Andelong, nouht *ouer-þwert*' = endlong, not across ; Havelok, 2822. 'Ouerthwart and endelong' = across and endlong, Chaucer, C. T. 1993; *þwertouer,* Ancren Riwle, p. 82, l. 12; *þwert ouer þe ilond,* Trevisa, v. 225; 'His herte ðo wurð ðwert' = his heart then became perverse, Genesis and Exodus, 3099. The word is of Scand. origin, as it is only thus that the final *-t* can be explained. The AS. for 'perverse' is *þweorh,* Grein, ii. 612, cognate with which is Icel. *þverr,* masc., the neut. *þvert.* The sense of *þverr* is across, transverse, whence *um þvert* = across, athwart ; *taka þvert,* to take athwart, to deny flatly ; *storm mikinn ok veðr þvert* = a great storm and adverse winds. + Dan. *tvær,* adj., transverse ; *tvært,* adv., across ; Swed. *tvär,* adj., cross, unfriendly, *tvärt,* adv., rudely. Allied to Du. *dwars,* adj. and adv., cross, crossly ; AS. *þweorh,* perverse, transverse (as above) ; MHG. *dwerch, twerch,* G. *zwerch,* adv., across, awry, askance, obliquely ; Goth. *thwairhs,* cross, angry. β. All from Teut. base **þwerh,* transverse, also cross, angry ; answering to Idg. base **twerq.* Allied to L. *torquēre,* to twist ; Skt. *tarku-,* a spindle. Brugmann, i. § 593 (3). Allied to **Twirl**; and see **Torsion**. Der. *thwart,* verb, ME. *þwerten,* Genesis and Exodus, 1324 ; also *a-t wart,* q. v. And see **Queer**.

THWITE, to cut. (E.) Obsolete. AS. *þwitan,* to cut. See **Thwaite** and **Whittle**.

THY, shorter form of **Thine**, q. v. (E.) Der. *thy-self,* AS. *þin self,* where both *þin* and *self* are declined, the gen. being *þines selfes* ; see Grein, ii. 427, s. v. *self.*

THYME, a fragrant plant. (F. — L. — Gk.) The *th* is pronounced as *t,* because the word was borrowed from F. at an early period. ME. *tyme,* Prompt. Parv., p. 494. — OF. *tym,* F. *thym,* 'the herb time;' Cot. — L. *thymum,* acc. of *thymus,* thyme. — Gk. θύμος, θύμον, thyme ; from its sweet smell ; cf. Gk. θύος, incense, and L. *fūmus,* smoke. See **Thurible**. (√DHEU.) Der. *thym-y,* Gay, Fable 22, l. 11.

THYROID, a term in anatomy. (Gk.) Lit. 'shield-shaped.' For *thyreoid.* — Gk. θυρεοειδής, shield-shaped (Galen). — Gk. θυρεο-, for θυρεός, a stone against a door ; also, a shield, from θύρα, a door ; and εἶδος, form. See **Door** and **Idyll**.

THYRSUS, a long wand, an attribute or emblem of Dionysus or Bacchus. (L. — Gk.) Herrick has *thyrse:* 'Shake the *thyrse,*' A Lyric to Mirth, l. 8. — L. *thyrsus,* a stalk, stem. — Gk. θύρσος, the same. See **Torso**.

TI–TY

TIARA, a round wreathed ornament for the head. (L. — Gk. — Pers. ?) In Dryden, tr. of Virgil, vii. 337 ; and used by Tyndale ; see Index to Parker Soc. publications. [The form *tiar* in Milton, P. L. iii. 625, is from F. *tiare,* given in Cotgrave.] — L. *tiara,* Virg. Æn. vii. 247. — Gk. τιάρα, τιάρας, the Persian head-dress, esp. on great occasions ; see Herodotus, i. 132, vii. 61, viii. 120 ; Xenophon, Anab. ii. 5. 23. And see Smith's Dict. of Antiquities. β. Clearly not a Gk. word, and presumably of Persian origin. The modern name is Pers. *tāj,* 'a crown, a diadem, a crest ;' see Rich. Pers. Dict. p. 351, where the tiara is described. Cf. *tājwar,* 'wearing a crown, crowned ;' id. p. 352.

TIBERT, a name for a cat. (F. — Teut.) Alluded to as *Tybalt* in Shak. Romeo, iii. 1. 80. See Nares. ' *Tybert* the catte ;' Caxton, tr. of Reynard the Fox, ch. iii. — Low G. *Tibeert* (Willem, author of Reynard). This answers to AS. *Thēod-beorht,* from *thēod,* people, and *beorht,* bright. β. But *Tybalt* is rather from OF. *Thibaut,* a form of *Theobald,* answering to AS. *Thēod-beald,* from *beald,* bold. See **Teutonic**; and **Bright, Bold**.

TIBIA, the large bone of the leg. (L.) In Phillips, ed. 1706. A medical term. — L. *tibia,* the shin-bone. Der. *tibi-al.*

TIC, a convulsive motion of certain muscles, esp. of the face, a twitching. (F. — Teut.) Borrowed from F. *tic,* a twitching ; and chiefly used of the *tic douloureux,* painful twitching, the name of a nervous disease ; where *douloureux* = L. *dolorōsus,* painful, from *dolor,* pain. The F. *tic* was formerly esp. used with respect to a twitching of the muscles of horses (see Littré), and is the same word as MF. *ticq,* or *tiquet,* 'a disease which, on a sudden stopping a horses breath, makes him to stop and stand still ;' Cot. Cf. *près du tiquet de la mort,* 'near his last gasp ;' id. The F. *tic* also means a vicious habit ; cf. Ital. *ticchio,* a ridiculous habit, whim, caprice. β. Of Teutonic origin ; guided by the etymology of *caprice,* Diez suggests a prob. origin from OHG. *zikin,* a kid, dimin. of OHG. *ziga,* G.

ziege, a goat, cognate with AS. *ticcen,* a goat, Gen. xxxviii. 19. γ. But rather from MHG. *tuc,* a quick movement, or Low G. *tukken,* to twitch ; perhaps allied to Low G. *twikken,* to twitch. And see **Tick** (4).

TICK (1), a small insect infesting dogs, &c. (E.) 'A *tick* in a sheep ;' Troil. iii. 3. 315. ME. *tyke* (dat. case), in Polit. Songs, p. 238, l. 4, in a poem of the time of Edw. II. Spelt *teke,* Voc. 565. 47. AS. *ticia,* Erfurt Glossary, 1130. Hence the F. *tique* was borrowed. + MDu. *teke,* 'a tike, or a doggs-lowse ;' Hexham ; Low G. *teke, täke* ; G. *zäcke, zecke,* a tick (whence Ital. *zecca*). Allied to Lith. *dygus,* sharp, *dėg-ti,* to sting (Franck).

TICK (2), the cover into which feathers are put, to serve for a bed. (L. — Gk.) 'Quilts, *ticks,* and mattrasses ;' Holland. tr. of Pliny, b. xix, c. 1. § 2. ' And of federbeddes rypped the *tekys* & helde theym in the wynde, that the fethers myght be blowyn away ;' Fabyan's Chron., an. 1305–6, fol. lxxx ; ed. Ellis, p. 414. Spelt *ticke* in Palsgrave. The spelling *teke* used by Fabyan is Englished from L. *thēca,* a case, which became Late L. *tēcha,* a linen case, a tick (Ducange) ; also *tēca,* as in Prompt. Parv., s. v. *teye.* ' The *teke* of a bed, *Teca culcitaria,*' Levins ; the L. *th* being sounded as *t.* [From the same L. *thēca* was derived the F. *taie,* spelt *taye* in Cotgrave, and explained as 'any filme or thin skin,' whence *vne taye d'oreiller,* 'a pillowbeer,' i. e. a pillow-case.] — Gk. θήκη, a case to put anything into ; derived from the base θη- as seen in τί-θη-μι, I place, put. — √DHĒ, to put ; see **Theme**. ¶ The Du. *tijk,* a tick, is likewise from L. *thēca.* Der. *tick-ing.*

TICK (3), to make a slight recurring noise, to beat as a watch. (E.) Todd cites from Ray, Remains, p. 324, 'the leisurely and constant *tick* of the death-watch.' The word is prob. imitative, to express the clicking sound, cf. *click* ; or it may have been suggested by **Tick** (4), q. v. Cf. G. *ticktack,* pit-a-pat ; F. *tictac,* the ticking of a clock.

TICK (4) to touch lightly. (E.) There is a game called *tig,* in which children endeavour to *touch* each other ; see Halliwell. This was formerly called *tick.* 'At hood-wink, barley-break, at *tick,* or prison-base ;' Drayton, Polyolbion, song 30, l. 132. ME. *tek,* a light touch. ' *Tek,* or lytylle towche, Tactulus ;' Prompt. Parv. Not found earlier, except in the frequentative form *tikelen* ; see **Tickle**. + Du. *tik,* a touch, pat, tick ; *tikken,* to pat, to tick ; Norw. *tikka,* to touch lightly ; Low G. *tikk,* a light touch with the tip of the finger ; metaphorically, a moment of time. ' *Ik quam up den Tikk daar,* I came there just in the nick of time ;' Bremen Wörterbuch. β. Apparently a lighter form of the Teut. base **tak-,* to touch, just as *tip* (in *tip* and *run*) is a weakened form of *tap,* made by the substitution of a lighter vowel. See **Take**. Der. *tick-le,* q. v.

TICK (5), credit. (E.) See **Ticket**.

TICKET, a bill stuck up, a marked card, a token. (F. — G.) In Minsheu, ed. 1627, and in Cotgrave. — MF. *etiquet,* 'a little note, breviate, bill or ticket ; especially such a one as is *stuck up* on the gate of a court, &c., signifying the seizure, &c. of an inheritance by order of justice ;' Cot. This is the masc. form of *étiquette* (formerly *estiquete,* Littré), a ticket. — G. *stecken,* to stick, put, set, fix ; allied to E. **Stick**, q. v. And see **Etiquette**. Der. *tick-et,* vb. Also *tick,* credit, by contraction for *ticket* ; 'taking things to be put into a bill, was taking them *on ticket,* since corrupted into *tick,*' Nares gives examples, showing that *tick* occurs as early as 1668, and that the phrases *upon ticket* and *on ticket* were in use.

TICKLE, to touch slightly so as to cause to laugh. (E.) ME. *tikelen, tiklen,* Chaucer, C. T. 6053 (D 471). Not found earlier, but the frequentative from the base *tik-,* to touch lightly ; see **Tick** (4). We also find ME. *tikel,* adj., unstable, ticklish, easily moved by a touch, Chaucer, C. T. 3428 ; from the same source. Cf. Icel. *kitla,* to tickle ; similarly formed from a base **kit-.* Der. *tickl-er* ; *tickl-ish,* Troil. iv. 5. 61, formed by adding *-ish* to ME. *tikel* above ; *tickl-ish-ly, -ness.*

TIDE, season, time, hour ; flux or reflux of the sea. (E.) ME. *tide,* Chaucer, C. T. 4930 (B 510) ; the usual sense is 'season' or hour ; hence the time between flux and reflux of the sea, and, finally, the flux or reflux itself. AS. *tīd,* time, hour, Mark, xiii. 33. + Du. *tijd* ; Icel. *tīð* ; Dan. and Swed. *tid* ; G. *zeit* ; OHG. *zīt.* β. All from Teut. type **ti-di-,* time, division of time, portion of time. Allied to **Time**, q. v. Der. *tide,* vb., to happen, Mids. Nt. Dr. v. 205, ME. *tiden,* Chaucer, C. T. 4757 (B 337), AS. *ge-tīdan,* to happen, John, v. 14 ; hence *be-tide,* q. v. Also *morning-tide, morrow-tide, even-tide, harvest-tide,* &c. ; *tide-mill, tide-table* ; *tide-waiter,* an officer who *waits* for the arrival of vessels with the *tide,* to secure payment of duties ; *tide-way* ; *tid-al,* adj., *tide-less* ; *tid-ings, tid-y.*

TIDINGS, things that happen ; usually, information respecting things that happen. (Scand.) Not an E. word, but adapted from Norse. ME. *tidinde,* Layamon, 2052, altered in the later text to *tidinge* ; spelt *tiþennde* (for *tiþende*), Ormulum, dedication, l. 158.

AS. *tídung*, tidings; A. S. Chron. an. 995.—Icel. *tíðindi*, neut. pl., tidings, news; also spelt *tíðenda*. The word may have originated from a pres. part. **tíðandi* of a verb **tíða*, to happen, with the same sense as AS. *tídan*; and this verb is from Icel. *tíð*, sb., tide, time, cognate with AS. *tíd*; see **Tide**. The final *s* is an E. addition, to show that the word is a pl. form; the ME. *tiding* or *tithing* (without *s*) is not uncommon; see Chaucer, C. T. 5146 (B 726). Cf. Dan. *tidende*, tidings, news; Du. *tijding*; G. *zeitung*. Noreen, § 150 (2).

TIDY, seasonable, hence, appropriate, neat. (E.) ME. *tidy*. 'Tidy men;' P. Plowman, B. ix. 104; '*þe tidy* child;' Will. of Palerne, 160. Formed with suffix -*y* (<AS. -*ig*) from ME. *tid* (AS. *tíd*), time; see **Tide**.+Du. *tijdig*, timely, from *tijd*; Dan. and Swed. *tidig*, timely, from *tid*; G. *zeitig*. Der. *tidi*-*ness*.

TIE, a fastening, band; to fasten, bind. (E.) 1. ME. *tiȝen*, verb, Allit. Poems, ed. Morris, A. 464; *tyen*, P. Plowman, B. i. 96; *teiȝen*, *teyen*, id. A. 94. The ME. forms *tiȝen*, *tyen* answer to AS. *tíegan*, to tie, fasten, spelt *tígan*, Matt. xxi. 2. The forms *teiȝen*, *teyen* answer to an Anglian form *tégan*. 2. The verb is an unoriginal form, due to the sb. *teȝe*. 'And *teien* heom to-gadere mid guldene *teȝen*' = and tie them together with golden ties; Layamon, 20997, 20998. The corresponding AS. word is *téag*, or rather *téah* (stem *téag*-), a rope; see Grein. Again, we read: 'habbað langne *tige* to geléafan trimminge' = they have a long-lasting *tie* for the establishment of the faith; Ælfric, Of the New Test., ed. De L'Isle, p. 27, last line; here *tige* = *týge* (with mutation). Cf. Icel. *taug*, a tie, string; *tygill*, a string. β. The form *téah* corresponds to *téah*, pt. s. of *téohan*, to tow, pull, draw, drag; so that a *tie* means that which draws things together. For the strong verb *téohan* or *téon* (pt. t. *téah*, pl. *tugon*, pp. *togen*), see Grein, ii. 527. It is cognate with Goth. *tiuhan* (pt. t. *tauh*. pp. *tauhans*), to tow, tug, pull, and G. *ziehen*. See further under **Tow** (1). γ. Thus *tie*, vb., is from *tie*, sb.; and the latter is ultimately from Teut. **tauh*, 2nd grade of the Teut. base TEUH = Idg. √DEUK, as in L. *dūcere*, to draw. Cf. **Tether**.

TIER, a rank, row. (F.—Teut. ?) 'Tire (or *teer* of ordnance, as the seamen pronounce it), a set of great guns on both sides of a ship, lying in a rank,' &c.; Phillips, ed. 1706. Spelt *tire*, with the same sense of 'row of guns,' in Milton, P. L. vi. 605. We find 'tyres of batterie,' i. e. rounds of shot, Life of Lord Grey (ab. 1575), p. 20 (Camden Soc.). Also '*tyre* of ordinance,' Florio, s. v. *tiro*.—OF. *tire*, *tiere*, a rank, row, series (Godefroy); cf. Prov. *tieira*, mod. Prov. *tiero*, *tieiro*, a row, series. Perhaps of Teut. origin; see Körting, § 9464. And cf. *attire*, q. v. ¶ Distinct from Late L. *tirāre*, to draw, pull, extend, hurl; whence also Ital. *tirare*, Span. Port. Prov. *tirar*.

TIERCE, TERCE, one of the canonical hours, a cask holding a third of a pipe; a sequence of three cards of a colour; a thrust in fencing. (F.—L.) In all its senses, it meant orig. 'third;' as the third hour, third of a pipe, third card, third sort of thrust. ME. *tierce*; 'At howre of *tyerse*,' Myrour of Our Lady, ed. Blunt, p. 13, l. 21; spelt *tierce*, Wyclif's Works, ed. Matthew, p. 41.—F. *tiers*, masc., *tierce*, fem., 'third;' *tiers*, m., 'a tierce, third, third part;' Cot.—L. *tertius*, masc., *tertia*, fem., third; the ordinal corresponding to *trēs*, three, which is cognate with E. **Three**, q. v.

TIERCEL, the same as **Tercel**, q. v.

TIFF (1), to deck, dress out. (F.—O. Low G.) ME. *tiffen*; Will. of Palerne, l. 1725; *tiffung*, finery, Ancren Riwle, p. 420, note *a*. —OF. and MF. *tiffer*, *tifer* (more commonly *atiffer*, *attiffer*), 'to deck, prancke, trick, trim, adorn;' Cot. Of Low G. origin; cf. Du. *tippen*, to cut, clip (lit. to cut off the *tip* of the hair, to trim); Low G. *tippen*, to touch lightly, as with the tips of the fingers. These verbs are from Du. *tip*, Low G. *tipp*, sb. a tip. See **Tip** (1). Cf. prov. E. *tippy*, smart, fine (Brockett, Halliwell). So also Swed. *tippa*, to touch gently, from *tipp*, sb. See F. *attiffer* in Scheler.

TIFF (2), a pet, fit of ill-humour; also, liquor, drink. (Scand.) 'My lord and I have had another little—*tiff*, shall I call it? it came not up to a quarrel;' Richardson, Grandison, iv. 291 (1754, ed. 1812). Spelt *tift* in Jamieson and Brockett. 'Small acid *tiff*;' J. Phillips, The Splendid Shilling; where it means 'drink.' Spelt *tiffe* in Brome, To his University Friend, 1661, where it means 'thin small beer' (Halliwell, Richardson). The orig. sense is 'a sniff;' hence (1) an expression of indignation; (2) a sup or draught of beer (see Halliwell), or the beer itself.—Norweg. *tev*, a drawing in of the breath, scent, smell, esp. a bad smell; *teva*, to puff, sniff, smell; Swed. dial. *täv*, smell, scent, taste; Icel. *þefr*, a smell, *þefa*, to sniff. Hence *tiff* really stands for *thiff*, the old Scand. *th* being turned into *t*, as in *tight*. β. This etymology is at once verified by the Norweg. derivatives *teft*, sb. a scent, and *tefta*, verb, to scent, which explain the North E. *tift*. Wedgwood well remarks: 'a *tiff* or fit of ill humour must be explained from snuffing or sniffing the air.' Cf. AS. *þefian*, to pant. See **Tiffin**.

TIFFANY, a kind of thin silk, gauze. (F.—Late L.—Gk.) 'Velvets, *tiffinies*, jewels, pearls;' Fletcher, The Noble Gentleman,

A. i. sc. 1. Lit. 'a dress for Twelfth Night,' i. e. a holiday dress, gay dress. *Tiffany* was formerly a Christian name, esp. for a woman born on Twelfth Day; see Bardsley, Dict. of Surnames.—OF. *Tiffanie* (and numerous other forms, as *Theophanie*); see Godefroy, s. v. *Tifaigne*, a name for Twelfth Day.—Late L. *Theophania*, lit. 'manifestation of God;' another name for Epiphany.—Gk. θεό-s, God; φάνεια, appearance, from φαίνειν, to show. See **Epiphany**.

TIFFIN, luncheon. (Scand.) An Anglo-Indian word, but originally provincial English. Wedgwood says it 'is the North-country *tiffing* (properly sipping), eating or drinking out of due season.' This is quoted from Grose, Lexicon Balatronicum (1785); see *Tiffin* in Yule, and *Tiff* in Davies, Supplementary Glossary. The latter has 'a *tiff* [draught] of punch;' Fielding, Amelia, bk. viii. ch. 10. Lowland-Scotch has the verb *tift*, to quaff, from the sb. *tift*, a drink; corresponding to which we have prov. E. *tiff*, to quaff; whence the sb. *tiffin* = *tiffing*, a quaffing, a drinking; hence, a luncheon. See **Tiff** (2).

TIGER, a fierce beast of prey. (F.—L.—Gk.—Pers.) ME. *tigre*, Chaucer, C. T. 1657.—F. *tigre*, 'a tiger;' Cot.—L. *tigrem*, acc. of *tigris*.—Gk. τίγρις. β. Said to be of Pers. origin; according to Littré, named from its 'swiftness,' the tiger being compared to an arrow. So also Mandeville (Trav. ch. xxx. p. 305) has: '*tigris*, that is, faste rennynge.'—Zend. *tighri*, an arrow; from *tighra*, sharp, pointed; words cited by Fick, i. 333. Hence mod. Pers. *tir*, 'an arrow, also the river *Tigris*, so named from its rapidity;' Rich. Dict. p. 473. Horn, § 406. Allied to Skt. *tigma*-, sharp, *tigmaga*-, flying swiftly, from *tij*, to be sharp. All these words have lost initial *s*; *tij* being allied to Gk. στίζειν (= στίγ-γειν), to prick.—√STEIG, to stick, prick; see **Stigma**. Der. *tigr*-*ess*, *tiger*-*ish*.

TIGHT, close, compact, not leaky. (Scand.) It should rather be *thight*, as in the dialect of Orkney; the change from *th* to *t* is common in Scandinavian, since neither Danish nor Swedish admits of initial *th*, which is only preserved in Icelandic. The *th* still exists also in prov. E. *thite*, 'tight, close, compact, East;' Halliwell. ME. *tiȝt*; whence *tiȝtli*, closely, Will. of Palerne, 66; also *þiȝt*, spelt *thyht*, in the Prompt. Parv., which has: 'Thyht, bool, not brokyn, Integer, solidus;' also: 'Thyhtyn, or make thyht, Integro, consolido.' Hence prov. E. *theat*, firm, close, staunch, spoken of barrels when they do not run (Halliwell). So also: 'as some *tight* vessel that holds against wind and water;' Bp. Hall, Contemplations, Ruth; bk. xi. cont. 3. § 11. It is spelt *tith* four times in Beaum. and Fletcher; see Nares.—Icel. *þéttr* (for **þihtr*), tight, esp. not leaking, water-tight, whence *þétta*, to make tight; Swed. *tät*, close, tight, solid, thick, hard, compact, whence *täta*, to make tight, *tätna*, to become tight (E. *tighten* used intransitively); Dan. *tæt*, tight, close, dense, compact, water-tight, used as a naut. term in *tæt til Vinden*, close to the wind; *tætte*, to tighten; NFries. *tacht* (variant *ticht*), tight. β. The substitution of ME. *iȝ* for Icel. *é* is curious; the E. has preserved the old guttural, which in the Icelandic is no longer apparent. Teut. type **þihtoz*, for **þinχtoz*, **þenχtoz*; whence also G. *dicht*, tight, compact, Du. *digt*, tight, compact (where the guttural is also preserved). Allied to Lith. *tenku*, I have enough, *tankus*, close, tight; Pers. *tang*, tight. See **Thee** (2). Der. *tight*-*ly*, *tight*-*ness*; *tight*-*en*, properly intransitive like Swed. *tätna*, but used, by analogy, in the sense 'to make tight.' Brugmann, i. § 577.

TIKE, a dog; contemptuously, a low fellow. (Scand.) ME. *tike*, *tyke*; P. Plowman, B. xix. 37; Morte Arthure, ed. Brock, 3642. —Icel. and Norw. *tík*, Swed. *tik*, a bitch; Dan. dial. *tiig*, a male dog.

TILE, a piece of baked clay for covering roofs, &c. (L.) ME. *tile*, Chaucer, C. T. 7687 (D 2105). A contracted form of *tigel*, the long *i* being due to loss of *g*. Spelt *tigel*, Genesis and Exodus, 2552; *teȝele*, Ayenbite of Inwyt, p. 167, l. 13. AS. *tigele*; pl. *tygelan*, Gen. xi. 3; hence *tigel-wyrhta*, a tile-wright, a potter, Matt. xxvii. 7. —L. *tēgula*, a tile, lit. 'that which covers;' formed with suffix -*lā* from *tegere*, to cover.—√STEG, to cover; see **Teguement**. Der. *tile*, verb, *til-er*, *til-ing*; also *til-er*-*y*, imitated from F. *tuilerie*, which is from F. *tuile*, L. *tēgula*, a tile.

TILL (1), to cultivate. (E.) ME. *tilien*, Rob. of Glouc. p. 21, l. 488. AS. *tilian*, *teolian*, to labour, endeavour, strive after, to till land; Grein, ii. 533. The orig. sense is to strive after, or aim at excellence.—AS. *til*, good, excellent, profitable; Grein, ii. 532; cf. *til*, sb., goodness. Allied to *till*, prep.; see **Till** (2).+Du. *telen*, to breed, raise, till, cultivate; G. *zielen*, to aim at, from *ziel*, OHG. *zil*, an aim, mark; cf. Goth. *ga-tils*, fit, convenient. Further allied to OIrish *dil*, pleasant. Der. *till-er*, *till-age*; also *til-th*, Temp. ii. 1. 152, from AS. *til-ð*, cultivation, crop, A. S. Chron. an. 1098; cf. Du. *teelt*, a crop.

TILL (2), to the time of, to the time when. (Scand.) A Norse word; orig. used as a preposition, then as a conjunction. ME. *til*, prep., to, occurring (rarely) even in Chaucer, where it seems to be put for *to* because it is accented and comes before a vowel. ' Hoom *til* Athénès whan the play is doon;' C. T. 2964 (A 2966). As a rule, it is a distinguishing mark of works in the Northumbrian dialect, such as Barbour's Bruce, where *til* occurs for *to* throughout. Somner cites ' cweð *til* him hælend '=the Saviour said to them, without a reference; but he really found ' cueð *til* him ðe hælend,' Matt. xxvi. 31, in the ONorthumb. (not the AS.) version.— Icel. *til*, till, to, prep. governing the genitive; Dan. *til*; Swed. *till*; in very common use; it even answers to E. *too* in phrases such as *til ungr*, too young; *til gamall*, too old. β. Quite distinct from *to*, and orig. a case of *tili* or *tili*, sb., in the sense of ' aim ' or ' bent,' whence the notion of ' towards ' was easily developed. The Icel. *til* frequently expresses ' purpose,' as in *til hvārs* =for what purpose. The sb. is rare in Icel., though it occurs in *ū-tili*, a mischance; but OHG. *zil*, G. *ziel*, aim, purpose, is a common word; so also is the closely allied AS. adj. *til*, suitable, fit (cognate with Goth. *ga-tils*, fit, convenient), as well as the AS. adv. *tela*, *teala*, excellently, Grein, ii. 524. See **Till** (1). **Der.** *un-til*, q.v.

TILL (3), a money-box or drawer in a tradesman's counter. (E.) The proper sense is ' drawer,' something that can be ' pulled ' in and out. Dryden uses *tiller* in this sense, tr. of Juvenal, Sat. vi. 384, where *till-er* is just parallel to *draw-er*. Cotgrave explains F. *layette* by ' a till or drawer;' also, ' a box with *tills* or drawers.' Palsgrave has: ' *Tyll* of an almery, lyette' [*sic*]; an *almery* being a kind of cupboard or cabinet. Cf. also prov. E. *tiller*, a till, a place for money; E. D. D. Thus the word is by no means modern; and, just as *drawer* is from the verb *to draw*, so *tiller* is from ME. *tillen*, to draw, pull, allure, now obsolete, but once not uncommon. ' To the scole him for to *tille* ' =to draw (or allure) him to school, Cursor Mundi, 12175. ' The world . . tyl him *drawes* And *tilles* ' =the world draws and allures to itself, Pricke of Conscience, 1183; and see Seven Sages, ed. Wright, 1563, and esp. Rob. of Glouc. p. 115, l. 2492, where it occurs in a literal, not a metaphorical sense. Spelt also *tullen*; the pt. t. *tulde* =drew, is in Ancren Riwle, p. 320, l. 13. AS. *tyllan*, appearing only in the comp. *for-tyllan*, with the apparent sense of draw aside, lead astray, Grein, i. 332. AS. *tyllan* answers to Teut. type *tul-jan-*; but the root does not appear. Allied to **Toll** (2). See **Tiller**.

TILLER, the handle or lever for turning a rudder. (E.) Cf. prov. E. *tiller*, the stalk of a cross-bow, the handle of any implement (Halliwell). Phillips has it in the usual sense. ' *Tiller*, in a boat, is the same as helme in a ship;' Coles, ed. 1684. ' The *tiller* of their helme was burst;' Hakluyt, Voy. iii. 111. The word means ' pull-er ' or handle; from ME. *tillen*, to pull, draw; see further under **Till** (3).

TILT (1), the canvas covering of a cart or waggon. (E.) ME. *teld*, a covering, tent, Layamon, 31384; a later form was *telt*. ' *Telte* or tente;' Prompt. Parv.; hence our *tilt*. AS. *teld*; whence *geteld*, a tent, Gen. xviii. 1; the prefix *ge-* making no difference.+ MDu. *telde*, *telte*, a tent; Hexham; Icel. *tjald*; Low G. *telt* (whence Dan. *telt*; Swed. *tält*); G. *zelt*. β. It thus appears that the form *tilt* (with final *t* for *d*) may have been due to Dutch influence. From the Teut. strong verb *teldan-*, to cover, spread over (pt. t. *tald*); found in AS. *be-teldan*, *ofer-teldan*, both strong verbs. If the reference is to covering over with boards, connexion with Gk. δέλτ-ος, a writing-tablet, is possible (Prellwitz).

TILT (2), to ride in a tourney, thrust with a lance; to cause to heel over. (E.) In 1 Hen. IV, ii. 3. 95. But the verb was orig. intransitive, meaning ' to totter, toss about unsteadily;' whence the active use of ' cause to totter, upset,' was evolved. The intrans. sense occurs at least as late as Milton, and is still in use when we say ' that table will *tilt* over.' ' The floating vessel . . Rode *tilting* o'er the waves;' Milton, P. L. xi. 747. ME. *tilten*, to totter, fall; ' þis ilk toun schal *tylte* to grounde,' Allit. Poems, C. 361. β. The lit. sense is ' to be unsteady,' formed from AS. *tealt*, adj., unsteady, tottering, unstable; see Sweet's A. S. Reader, § xv. 74. Hence the verb *tieltan*, *tyltan*, to totter, would be regularly formed, with the usual vowel-change from *ea* to *ie* (y).+Icel. *tölta*, to amble as a horse; cf. Milton's use of *tilting* above; Norw. *tylta*, to walk on tiptoe; Swed. *tulta*, to waddle. Cf. **Totter**. **Der.** *tilt*, sb., *tilt-ing*; *tilt-hammer*, a hammer which, being tilted up, falls by its own weight. Also *tott-er*, q.v.

TILTH, sb. (E.) See **Till** (1).

TIMBER, wood for building. (E.) The *b* is excrescent, as usual after *m*, but occurs very early. ME. *timber*, Chaucer, C. T. 3666. AS. *timber*, stuff or material to build with; Grein, ii. 534.+Du. *timmer*, ' timber or structure;' Hexham; Icel. *timbr*; Dan. *tömmer*; Swed. *timmer*; G. *zimmer*, a room; also timber. Cf. also Goth. *timrjan*, to build, *timrja*, a builder. β. All from Teut. type *tim-rom*<*tem-rom*, n., timber; formed with agential suffix *-ro* from Teut. base TEM=√DEM, to build, as seen in Gk. δέμ-ειν, to

build; see **Dome**. Brugmann, i. § 421 (8). **Der.** (from same root) *dome*, *dom-icile*, *dom-estic*, *major-domo*.

TIMBREL, a kind of tambourine. (F.—L.—Gk.) In Spenser, F. Q. i. 12. 7. Dimin., with suffix *-l* (= *-el*), from ME. *timber*, used in the same sense, Gower, C. A. iii. 63; bk. vi. 1844.—F. *timbre*, ' the bell of a little clock;' Cot.; OF. *tymbre*, a timbrel, as shown by a quotation in Diez.—L. *tympanum*, a drum.—Gk. τύμπανον, a kettle-drum; see **Tympanum**. Cf. ' Hoc timpanum, a *tymbre*;' Voc. 616. 28.

TIME, season, period, duration of life, &c. (E.) ME. *time*, Chaucer, C. T. 35, 44. AS. *tīma*, time, Grein, ii. 534.+Icel. *tīmi*; Dan. *time*; Swed. *timme*, an hour. β. The Teut. type is *tī-man-*, closely allied to *tī-di-*, tide, time, from which it only differs in the suffix. See **Tide**. **Der.** *time*, verb, cf. ME. *timen*, to happen, AS. *getīman*; *time-ly*, adj., Macb. iii. 3. 7; *time-ly*, adv., Macb. ii. 3. 51; *time-li-ness*; *time-honoured*, *-keeper*, *-piece*, *-server*, *-table*, *-worn*.

TIMID, afraid, fearful. (F.—L.) ' The *timid* friend;' Pope, Prol. to Satires, 343. [The sb. *timidity* is earlier, occurring in Cotgrave.]—F. *timide*, ' timorous;' Cot.—L. *timidus*, full of fear.— L. *timēre*, to fear; see **Timorous**. **Der.** *timid-ly*, *-ness*; *timid-i-ty*, from F. *timidité*, ' timidity,' Cot., from L. acc. *timiditātem*.

TIMOROUS, full of fear. (L.) The Court of Love begins: ' With *timerous* herte;' but this is quite a late poem. Fabyan has *timerousnesse*, Chron. cap. 175; Sir T. Elyot has *timerositie*, The Governour, b. i. c. xviii. § 4. [There is no F. *timoreux*.] Coined, as if from L. adj. *timorōsus*, fearful, a word not used.—L. *timor*, fear; *timēre*, to fear. β. Prob. allied to Skt. *tam*, to become breathless, to be distressed, to be exhausted. **Der.** *timorous-ly*, *timorous-ness*; (from same root) *tim-id*, *in-tim-id-ate*.

TIN, a silvery-white metal. (E.) ME. *tin*, Chaucer, C. T. 16296 (G 828). AS. *tin*; ' stagnum, *tin*,' Ælfric's Gram. (ed. Zupitza), p. 15, l. 11; whence ' stagneus, *tinen* ' as an adj., ibid.+Du. *tin*; Icel. *tin*; Dan. *tin*; Swed. *tenn*; G. *zinn*. β. All from Teut. type *tino-*, tin. Possibly connected with Teut. *taino-*, a rod, for which see **Mistletoe**; cf. G. *zain*, an ingot, a bar of metal. γ. Quite distinct from L. *stagnum*, *stannum*, tin, whence W. *ystaen*, Corn. *stean*, Bret. *stéan*, Irish *stan*, F. *étain*, are all borrowed; see Rhys, Lectures on Welsh, Appendix C. **Der.** *tin-foil*, spelt *tynfoyle* in Levins, i.e. tin-leaf; see **Foil** (2).

TINCTURE, a shade of colour, a solution. (L.) In Shak. Two Gent. iv. 4. 160. ME. *tincture*, Lanfrank, Cirurgie, p. 180, l. 6. Englished from L. *tinctūra*, a dyeing; cf. *tinctus*, pp. of *tingere*, to tinge; see **Tinge**. **Der.** *tincture*, verb. Shak. also has *tinct*, sb., a dye, Hamlet, iii. 4. 91, from pp. *tinctus*.

TIND, to light or kindle. (E.) Also spelt *tine*. Now obsolete, except in prov. E. Spelt *tinde* in Minsheu, ed. 1627. ME. *tenden*, Wyclif, Luke, xi. 33. AS. *tendan*, to kindle; chiefly in comp. *on-tendan*, Exod. xxii. 6.+Dan. *tænde*; Swed. *tända*; Goth. *tandjan*. β. These are verbs of the weak form, from the base of a Teut. lost strong verb *tendan-*, making *tand* in the pt. t., and *tundanoz* in the pp. γ. From the weak grade of the same strong verb was formed E. *tinder*, q.v.

TINDER, anything used for kindling fires from a spark. (E.) ME. *tinder*, Layamon, 29267; more often *tunder*, *tondre*, P. Plowman, B. xvii. 245. AS. *tyndre*, Voc. 266. 39; *tynder*, id. 33. 41. Cf. OHG. *zuntira*, tinder. Teut. type *tund-ir-ōn-*, f.; from *tund-*, weak grade of a lost strong verb *tendan-*, to kindle, whence the weak verb *tendan*, to kindle; see **Tind**.+Icel. *tundr*, tinder; cf. *tendra*, to light a fire, *tandri*, fire; Dan. *tönder*; Swed. *tunder*; G. *zunder*; cf. *anzünden*, to kindle.

TINE (1), the tooth or spike of a fork or harrow. (E.) Formerly *tind*; cf. *wood-bine* for *wood-bind*. ME. *tind*, spelt *tynde*, Allit. Poems, ed. Morris, A. 78; ' *tyndis* of harowis,' Allit. Romance of Alexander, 3907, 3925. AS. *tind*, pl. *tindas*, Salomon and Saturn, ed. Kemble, p. 150, l. 25.+Icel. *tindr*, a spike, tooth of a rake or harrow; Swed. *tinne*, Dan. dial. *tind*, the tooth of a rake; MHG. *zint*. Teut. type *tendoz*, m.; allied to L. *dens* (acc. *dent-em*), a tooth; see **Tooth**. Cf. Skt. *danta-*, a tooth; *hasti-danta-*, a peg to hang clothes on. **Der.** *tin-ed*.

TINE (2), to kindle; see **Tind**.

TINE (3), to lose. (Scand.) ' His blisse gan he *tyne*;' P. Plowman, B. i. 112.—Icel. *tȳna*, to lose.—Icel. *tjōn*, loss, damage; cognate with AS. *tēona*, harm, loss; see **Teen**.

TINGE, to colour, dye. (L.) ' *Tinged* with saffron;' Holinshed, Desc. of Scotland, c. 7. The pp. form *tinct* is in Spenser, Shep. Kal. November, 107.—L. *tingere* (pp. *tinctus*), to dye, stain.+Gk. τέγγειν, to wet, moisten, dye, stain. Cf. OHG. *thuncōn*, G. *tunken*, to dip, steep; from the weak grade (*tung-*) of √TENG. **Der.** *tinge*, sb., *tinct-ure*, q.v.; also *taint*, *tent* (3), *tint*, *stain*, *mezzo-tinto*.

TINGLE, to thrill, feel a thrilling sensation. (E.) Spelt *tingil* in Levins. ME. *tinglen*. In Wyclif, 1 Cor. xiii. 1, we have : ' a cymbal *tynkynge*,' where other readings are *tynclynge* and *tinglinge*. *Tingle* is merely a weakened form of *tinkle*, being the frequentative of *ting*, a weakened form of *tink*. ' Cupyde the kynge *tynkyng* a syluer bel ; ' Test. of Creseide, st. 21 (Thynne). ' To *ting*, tinnire ; to *tingil*, tinnire ; ' Levins. Cf. *ting-tang*, the saint's-bell (Halliwell) ; ' *Sonner* to sound, . . to *ting*, as a bell,' Cot. To make one's ears *tinkle* or *tingle* is to make them seem to ring ; hence, to *tingle*, to vibrate, to feel a sense of vibration as when a bell is rung. Hence ' bothe his eeris shulen *tynclen* ; ' Wyclif, 1 Sam. iii. 11. See **Tinkle, Tinker.** β. But prob. affected by prov. E. *ting*, to sting, a by-form of *sting*. Cf. prov. E. *tingling*, sharp ; MDu. *tingel*, a nettle : *tingelen*, ' to sting with nettles ; ' Hexham.

TINKER, a mender of kettles and pans. (E.) ME. *tinkere*, P. Plowman, A. v. 160 ; B. v. 317. So called because he makes a *tinking* sound ; from ME. *tinken*, to ring or tinkle. ' A cymbal *tynkynge* ; ' Wyclif, 1 Cor. xiii. 1. Of imitative origin ; cf. MDu. *tinge-tangen*, to tingle (Hexham) ; also MDu. *tintelen*, ' to ring, tingle, or make a noise like brasse ' (id.), where mod. Du. has *tintelen* only in the sense to tingle or sparkle. Cf. EFries. *tinken*, *tingen*, *tengen*, to make a bell ring ; L. *tinnīre*, to tinkle, ring, *tintinnum*, a tinkling ; F. *tinter*, ' to ting, ring, tinkle.' Cot., whence *les oreilles me tintent*, ' mine eares tingle or glow,' id. ; F. *tintin*, *tinton*, ' the ting of a bell,' id. Cf. Tudor E. *tinkler*, a tinker (Levins). ¶ Grimm's law does not necessarily apply to words so directly imitative as this.

TINKLE, to jingle. (E.) ME. *tinklen*, whence ' a cymbal *tynclynge*,' in some MSS. of Wyclif, 1 Cor. xiii. 1 ; frequentative of ME. *tinken*, to ring. See further under **Tinker** and **Tingle.**

TINSEL, gaudy ornament, showy lustre. (F.—L.) ' *Tinsill* clothe,' Baret, ed. 1580 ; cf. Much Ado, iii. 4. 22. ' Under a duke, no man to wear cloth of gold *tinsel* ; ' Literary Remains of K. Edw. VI, an. 1551–2 ; cited in Trench, Select Glossary, q.v. ' A gowne of silver *tyncell* ; ' Excerpta Historica, p. 288 (ab. 1516). ' *Tinsell* (dictum a Gall. *estincelle*, i. *scintella*, a sparke). It signifieth with vs, a stuffe or cloth made partly of silke, and partly of gold or siluer, so called because it glistereth or sparkleth like starres ; ' Minsheu, ed. 1627. [Minsheu's etymology is correct ; the OF. *estincelle*, later *étincelle*, lost its initial syllable just as did the F. *estiquet* or *étiquet*, which became *ticket* in English.]—MF. *estincelle*, *étincelle*, ' a sparke or sparckle of fire, a twinkle, a flash ; ' Cot.—L. *scintilla*, a spark ; which seems to have been mispronounced as **stincilla*. *Scintilla* is dimin. from a form **scinta*, a spark, not used. Allied to AS. *scīnan*, to shine ; see **Shine**. Der. *tinsel*, adj., i.e. tinsel-like ; *tinsel-slippered*, Milton, Comus, 877. And see *stencil*.

TINT, a slight tinge of colour. (L.) 1. For *tinct*, which was the older form of the word ; Hamlet, iii. 4. 91. ' The first scent of a vessel lasts, and the *tinct* the wool first receives ; ' Ben Jonson, Discoveries, Præcipiendi Modi. ' A rosy-*tincted* feature is heav'n's gold ; ' Drayton, K. John to Matilda, l. 57. Cf. *tinct* = dyed ; Spenser, Shep. Kal. Nov. 107.—L. *tinctus*, pp. of *tingere*, to tinge ; see **Tinge**. 2. But the mod. *tint*, as a term in painting, was prob. borrowed directly from Ital. *tinta*, a tint.—L. *tincta*, fem. of *tinctus*, pp. (as before). Der. *tint*, verb.

TINTINNABULATION, the ringing of bells. (L.) See E. A. Poe, The Bells. Formed from L. *tintinnābulum*, a bell.—L. *tintinnāre*, to clink, to ring ; reduplicated form, from *tinnīre*, to ring, to tinkle. Of imitative origin ; cf. *tink-le*, *ting-le*.

TINY, very small. (F.—L. ?) In Shak. Tw. Nt. v. 398, 2 Hen. IV, v. 1. 29, v. 3. 60, K. Lear, iii. 2. 74, where it is always preceded by *little* ; the old editions have *tine* or *tyne*. He speaks of ' a little *tine* boy ' (twice), ' my little *tyne* thief,' and ' pretty little *tine* kickshaws.' The word was formerly spelt *tine* or *tyne* ; we find ' littel *tyne* child,' in a Coventry pageant pr. by Sharp ; see note to Cov. Myst., ed. Halliwell, p. 414. ' A litill *tyne* egg,' Wars of Alexander, 507. It is almost always preceded by *little*, and was once a sb. ' He was constreynd . . . A *lytyll tyne* abak to make a bew retret,' Lydgate, Assembly of Gods, 1063 ; ' A *lytyll tyne* his ey castyng hym besyde, id. 1283. ' Sir, I pray you a *lytyll tyne* stande backe ; ' Skelton, Garl. of Laurel, 505. And later, we find : ' Thou hast striken the Lord of Learne A *litile tinye* above the knee ; ' Percy Folio MS., i. 192. The sense seems to be ' a little bit ; ' and the form corresponds to OF. *tinee*, lit. ' a tub-full,' from OF. *tine*, a vat, tub, basin, bowl.—Late L. *tīna*, a wine-vessel (Lewis). See Notes on E. Etym., p. 300.

TIP (1), the extreme top, the end. (E.) ' The *tippe* of a staffe ; ' Levins. ME. *typ*, Prompt. Parv. ' Uort þe nede *tippe* ' = until the extremity of need, i. e. until [there be] extreme need, Ancren Riwle, p. 338, l. 19. Prob. E., though not found in AS. ✚ Du. *tip*, tip, end point ; Low G. *tipp*, tip, point ; *up den Tipp van ter Tied*, in the very nick of time, Brem. Wört. ; NFries. *tipp*, *tippken*, a tip ; Dan. *tip*,

tip ; Swed. *tij*, end, point, extremity ; G. *zipfel*, a dimin. form. Allied to Du. and EFries. *tepel*, a teat, EFries. *tippel*, a point. Cf. MDu. *tip-ken*, a teat. Der. *tip*, verb, to place on the tip of, chiefly in the pp. *tipped*, as in Chaucer, C. T. 14909 (B 4093) ; hence the sb. *tipped-staf*, i. e. spiked or piked staff, Chaucer, C. T. 7319 (D 1737) ; and hence (just as *piked-staff* became *pike-staff*) *tip-staff*, a term afterwards applied to ' certain officers that wait on the judge bearing a rod tipt with silver,' Phillips ; also to other officers who took men into custody. Cf. ' I *typpe* a staffe with yron ; ' Palsgrave. Also *tip-toe* ; cf. *on tiptoon* = on tip-toes, Chaucer, C. T. 15313 (B 4497) ; *tipp-le*.

TIP (2), to tilt, cause to slant or lean over. (E.) Gen. in the phr. *to tip up* = to tilt up, or *tip over* = to overturn. It is a weakened form of *tap*, as in *tip* (i. e. *tap*) *and run*, a game. Thus *tip up* is to tilt up by giving a slight tap, or by the exercise of a slight force ; cf. *tip for tap* (blow for blow), Bullinger's Works, i. 283, now *tit for tat*. From the sense of slight movement we can explain the phrase *to tip the wink* = to make a slight movement of the eye-lid, sufficient to warn a person ; it occurs in Dryden, tr. of Juvenal, Sat. vi. 202. Johnson gives : ' *tip*, to strike lightly, to tap ; ' with an illustration from Swift : ' he *tips* me by the elbow.' Palsgrave has : ' I *type* ouer, I ouerthrowe or ouerwhelme, *Je renuerse*.' ' *Tip*, a fall ; ' Bradford's Works, ii. 104 (Parker Soc.). Not in AS. ME. *tippen*, *tipen*. ' *Tipe* doun 3onder toun ; ' Allit. Poems, C. 506. Cf. EFries. *tippen*, to tap lightly. ✚ Swed. *tippa*, ' to tap, to tip, to strike gently, to touch lightly ; see Johnson's E. Dict. ; ' Widegren. Der. *tip*, sb., a slight tap, wink, hint ; *tip-cat*.

TIPPET, a cape, a cape of a cloak. (L.—Gk.) Also *tepet*, as in Babees Book, ed. Furnivall, p. 301, l. 92. ' *Teppet* of velvet ; ' Paston Letters, iii. 325. ME. *tipet*, *tepet*, Chaucer, C. T. 233. AS. *tæppet*. ' *Sipla*, ān healf hruh *tæppet*,' i. e. a half rough tippet ; Voc. 152. 14 ; (*Vestium nomina*). [We also find AS. *tæppe*, a fillet or band ; ' *Tenia*, *tæppan*, *vel* dol-smeltas,' Voc. 107. 33 ; where *tæppan* is the nom. plural. Not E. words, but borrowed.]—L. *tapēte*, cloth, hangings.—Gk. ταπητ-, stem of τάπης, a carpet, woollen rug. See **Tape, Tapestry.**

TIPPLE, to drink in small quantities, and habitually. (Scand.) Shak. has *tippling*, Antony, i. 4. 19. ' To *tipple*, potitare ; ' Levins, ed. 1570. A Scand. word ; still preserved in Norweg. *tipla*, to drink little and often, to tipple (Aasen). It is the frequent. of Norw. *tippa*, to drip from a point or tip ; Swed. dial. *tippa*, to drip, from *tipp*, a tip ; cf. Du. *tefel*, a nipple, teat. See **Tip** (1). Der. *tippl-er*, *tippl-ing*.

TIPSY, intoxicated. (Scand.) In Shak. Mid. Nt. Dr. v. 48. The formation of the word is difficult to explain, but it is clearly related to **Tip** (2), q. v. It means ' likely to tip over,' or ' unsteady ; ' ready to fall. Cf. ME. *tipen*, to upset. Cf. *trick-sy*, and other words with suffix -*sy*, in F. Hall, Modern English, p. 272. β. Wedgwood cites Swiss *tips*, a fuddling with drink, *tipseln*, to fuddle oneself, *betipst*, tipsy. These words present a remarkable likeness, especially as the E. and Swiss words can only be cognate, and neither language can easily have borrowed from the other ; moreover, the Swiss words seem to be allied rather to *tipple* and to *tip* (1), than to *tip* (2). Cf. prov. E. *tipty*, *tippity*, easily upset. Der. *tipsi-ly*, -*ness*.

TIRADE, a strain of censure or reproof. (F.—Ital.) Modern. —F. *tirade*, ' a draught, pull, . . a shooting ; ' Cot. Hamilton explains F. *tirade* by ' a passage, a tirade or long speech (in a play).' The lit. sense is a drawing out, a lengthening out.—Ital. *tirata*, a drawing, a pulling.—Ital. *tirare*, to pull, draw, pluck, snatch. From Late L. *tīrāre*, to pull, draw ; of unknown origin ; whence also F. *tirer*.

TIRE (1), to exhaust, weary, fatigue, become exhausted. (E.) ME. *tiren*, *teorian*, not a very common word. Stratmann refers us to the Towneley Mysteries, p. 126 ; and to p. 5 of a Fragment printed by Sir Thos. Phillips, where occur the words *him teoreþ his miht* = his might is exhausted. It occurs also in the compound *atieren*, as : ' gief mihte þe ne atiereð ' = if might (or power) fail thee not, i. e. if thy power be not tired out ; O. Eng. Homilies, ed. Morris, ii. 29, l. 25. AS. *tyrigan* ; as in ' ðeah þu ge-*tyrige*,' though thou grow weary ; Alfred's tr. of Boethius, ch. xl (bk. v. pr. 1). The ȳ is a mutation from ēo, as in *tēorian*, (1) to be tired, be weary, (2) to tire, fatigue ; Grein, ii. 529. β. It is remarkable that the dictionaries frequently refer *tire* (in the sense to be weary) to AS. *tirigan*, which is not the same thing, but related rather to **Tarre**, q. v. That *tēorian* is the real equivalent of E. *tire* may be seen by examining the uses of *tēorian*, *getēorian*, and *ātēorian*. One example may suffice. ' *Tēorode* hwæþre . . strong . . wērig þæs weorces ' = nevertheless the strong one *tired*, being *weary of the work* ; Exeter Book, ed. Thorpe, p. 436, Riddle lv, l. 16. ' Fatigatus, *atered* ; ' Voc. 170, 30. Further connexions doubtful ; it can hardly be allied to E. *tear*, vb., or to G. *zehren*. Sweet marks the *e* long (*tēoran*) ; cf. OLow G.

tiurung, lassitude (Gallée). Der. *tir-ed*, *tir-ed-ness*, *tire-some*, *tire-some-ness*.

TIRE (2), a head-dress; as a verb, to adorn or dress the head. (F. — Teut. ?) 'She .. *tired* her head;' 2 Kings, ix. 30. The examples show that this is an abbreviation for *attire*. See esp. Prompt. Parv. p. 494: '*Tyre*, or *a-tyre* of wemmene, Mundum muliebris.' Again, in Will. of Palerne, 1147, we have *atir*, but in l. 1725 we have *tyr*; cf. 'in no gay *tyr*,' Alexander and Dindimus, 883; 'tidi *a-tir*,' id. 599. β. We have also the verb *to tire*, 2 Kings, ix. 30; cf. 'Attouré, *tired*, dressed, *attired*, decked,' Cot. The ME. verb was *atiren*, whence *atired*, pp., Will. of Palerne, 1228. However, the sb. appears earlier than the verb, being spelt *atyr*, with the sense 'apparel;' Layamon, 3275, later text. See **Attire**.

TIRE (3), a hoop of iron that binds the fellies of wheels together. (F. — Teut. ?) '*Tire*, the ornament or dress of womens heads; also, the iron band of a cart-wheel;' Phillips, ed. 1706. 'The mettall [a kind of iron] is brittle and short .. such as will not serue one whit for stroke and nail to bind cart-wheels withall, which *tire* indeed would [should] be made of the other that is gentle and pliable;' Holland, tr. of Pliny, b. xxxiv. c. 14. [Here *stroke* = *strake*, rim of a wheel; see Halliwell.] β. The history of the word is obscure; it seems to me that the word is identical with **Tire** (2), the wheel-band being likened to a woman's *tire*. *Tire* meant to dress or arrange; 'I *tyer* an egge, Ie accoustre; I *tyer* with garmentes,' &c.; Palsgrave. To *attire* once meant to equip, or to furnish (N. E. D.). ¶ I have no belief in Richardson's jest-like suggestion, that a *tire* is a *ti-er*, because it *ties* the wheel together. The ME. *teȝere* or *tyere* nowhere occurs in connexion with a wheel.

TIRE (4), to tear a prey, as is done by predatory birds. (F. — Late L.) In Shak. Venus, 56; 1 Hen. VI, i. 1. 269. ME. *tiren* to tear a prey, only used of vultures, &c.; see Chaucer, Troilus, i. 787; tr. of Boethius, b. iii. met. 12, l. 30. — F. *tirer*, 'to draw, drag, .. pull, pluck, tug, twitch;' Cot. — Late L. *tīrāre*, to draw, extract; Ducange. See **Tirade**.

TIRE (5), a train. (F. — Late L.) Only in Spenser, F. Q. i. 4. 35. — F. *tire*, 'a draught, pull, .. stretch .. reach, gate, course, or length and continuance of a course;' Cot. — F. *tirer*, to draw; see **Tirade**.

TIRO, TYRO, a novice. (L.) Usually misspelt *tyro*. '*Tyro*, a new fresh-water soldier, a novice, apprentice;' Phillips, ed. 1706. 'That timorous *tyro* should dare;' Blennerhasset, Introd. in Mirror for Magistrates (1578). In Blount's Gloss., ed. 1674, it appears as *tyrone*, evidently from Ital. *tirone*, 'a milkesop,' Florio, answering to L. acc. *tīrōnem*. — L. *tīro*, a recruit, novice, tiro. Root uncertain. Der. *tiro-cinium*, a first campaign, school, apprenticeship; the title of a poem by Cowper.

TISIC, phthisis. (F. — Gk.) Spelt *tysyke*, Skelton, Magnificence, 561. See **Phthisis**.

TISSUE, cloth interwoven with gold or silver. (F. — L.) ME. *tissew*, a ribband, Chaucer, Troil. ii. 639. — F. *tissu*, 'a bawdrick, ribbon, fillet, or head-band of woven stuffe;' Cot. Also *tissu*, m., *tissue*, f., 'woven, plaited, interlaced;' id. *Tissu* was the old pp. of *ti tre* (mod. F. *tisser*), to weave. — L. *texere*, to weave; see **Text**.

TIT (1), a small horse or child. (Scand.) 'The *tits* are little worth;' Dryden, tr. of Ovid, Metam. ix. 14; where *tit* means 'a little girl.' 'A little *tit*,' a small horse; Holinshed, Desc. of Ireland, c. ii (R.). — Icel. *tittr*, a tit, bird (now obsolete); the dimin. *titlingr*, a sparrow, is still in use; Norweg. *tita*, a little bird, small trout (Aasen). The orig. sense is merely something small; cf. prov. E. *titty*, small; *tiddy-wren*, a wren (Halliwell). Der. *tit-ling*, a sparrow, from Icel. *titlingr*, as above, with double dimin. suffix *-l-ing*. Also *ti -lark*, q. v., *tit-mouse*, q. v.

TIT (2), a teat. (E.) ME. *titte*; pl. *tittes*, Ancren Riwle, p. 330, l. 5. AS. *tit*, *titt*, Voc. 88. 24; pl. *tittas* (Toller). + Low G. *titte*, MDu. *ti te*, G. *zitze*; cf. Welsh *did*, *didi*, a teat. See **Teat**.

TIT FOR TAT, blow for blow. (E.) In Holinshed, Chron., ed. 1808, vi. 298. Perhaps a corruption of *tip for tap*, where *tip* is a slight tap; Bullinger's Works, i. 283 (Parker Society). 'That which requireth *tip for tap*;' Gascoigne, Works, i. 463. See **Tip** (2). β. Or it may be from the proverb — 'To give one *tint for tant*,' in Walker's Proverbs (1672); see Hazlitt's Proverbs. And *tint for tant* seems to be an E. version of F. *tant pour tant*, lit. 'so much for so much. *Tit for tat* is in Heywood's Prov. (1546); repr. 1874, p. 109.

TITAN, the sun-god. (L. — Gk.) In Shak. Rom. ii. 3. 4; &c. Spelt *Tytan*, Lydgate, Compl. of Black Knight, l. 28. — L. *Tītān*, *Tītānus*; whence *Tītāni*, descendants of Titan, giants. — Gk. Τιτάν, the sun-god, brother of Helios. + Skt. *tithā*, fire; in the dict. by Böhtlingk and Roth, iii. 327. — √TEITH, to burn. Der. *titan-ic*, i. e. gigantic. Also *titan-ium*, a metal.

TITHE, a tenth part, the tenth of the produce as offered to the clergy. (E.) ME. *tithe*, Chaucer, C. T. 541 (A 539). The proper sense is 'tenth;' hence tenth part. [Another spelling is *tethe*, as in 'the *tethe* hest' = the tenth commandment, Will. of Shoreham, p. 101, l. 1; AS. *teoða*, tenth.] β. The form *tithe* answers to AS. suffix *-tigoða*, as in *twen-tigoða*, twentieth. Also spelt *-teogoða*, OMerc. *-tegða*; allied to Gk. δέκατος, tenth, from δέκα, ten, see **Ten**. We also have *ten-th*, in which *n* is retained; so that tenth and tithe are doublets. Cf. Icel. *tiund*, tenth, tithe; see **Decimal**. Der. tithe, verb, ME. *tithen*, *tethen*, P. Plowman, C. xiv. 73, AS. *tēoðian*, Matt. xxiii. 23; *tith-er*, Chaucer, C. T. 6896; *tith-ing*, ME. *tething*, a district containing ten families, Rob. of Glouc. p. 267, l. 5402.

TITILLATION, a tickling. (F. — L.) [The verb *titillate* is in later use; cf. '*titilating* dust,' Pope, Rape of the Lock, v. 84.] The sb. is in Bacon, Nat. Hist. § 766. — F. *titillation*, a tickling; Cot. — L. *titillātiōnem*, acc. of *titillātio*, a tickling. — L. *titillāre*, to tickle.

TITLARK, a kind of lark. (Scand. *and* E.) Lit. 'small lark;' see **Tit** and **Lark**.

TITLE, an inscription set over or at the beginning of a book, a name of distinction. (F. — L.) ME. *title*, Chaucer, C. T. 14328 (B 3512); Wyclif, John, xix. 19. — OF. *title*; mod. F. *titre*, by change from *l* to *r*. — L. *titulum*, acc. of *titulus*, a superscription on a tomb, altar, &c.; an honourable designation. Der. *title*, verb; *titl-ed*, All's Well, iv. 2. 2; *title-deed*; *title-page*, Per. ii. 3. 4; *titul-ar*, from F. *titulaire*, 'titular, having a title,' Cot., as if from L. *titulāris, from L. *titulāre*, verb, to give a title to. Hence *titular-ly*, *titular-y*. See also **Tittle**.

TITLING, a small bird. (Scand.) See **Tit**.

TITMOUSE, a kind of small bird. (Scand. *and* E.) Not connected with *mouse*; the true pl. should be *titmouses*, yet *titmice* is usual, owing to confusion with *mouse*. In Spenser, Shep. Kal., Nov. 26, it is spelt *titmose*. ME. *titmose*; spelt *tytemose*, Prompt. Parv.; *titmase*, Voc. 640. 28. Compounded of *tit*, small, or a small bird, Icel. *tittr* (see **Tit**); and AS. *māse*, a name for several kinds of small birds. β. The AS. *māse* occurs in: 'Sigatula, *fræc-māse*; Parra, *col-māse*; Parrula, *spic-māse*,' all names of birds; see Voc. 286. 13–15. The *a* is long, as shown by the ME. *-mose*. + Du. *mees* (for *mese*); G. *meise*, a titmouse; OHG. *meisa*; Icel. *meisingr* (F. *mésange*). Teut. type **maisōn-*, f. The sense was prob. 'twitterer;' cf. L. *maerēre* (for *maesēre, cf. pp. *maes-tus*), to lament, mourn (Franck). Cf. also L. *merula* (for *mis-ula), from the weak grade *mis; see **Merle**.

TITTER, to giggle, laugh restrainedly. (E.) Cf. *twitter*. In Pope, Dunciad, iv. 276. The same as ME. *titeren*, to chatter, prattle, tell idle tales, whence *titerere*, a teller of tales, P. Plowman, B. xx. 297. A frequentative form from a base TIT, expressive of repeating the sound *ti*, just as *tattle* expresses the repetition of *ta*. See further under **Tattle**. C. **Twitter**. Der. *titter*, sb.

TITTLE, a jot, small particle. (F. — L.) ME. *titel*, *titil*, used by Wyclif to translate L. *apex*; Matt. v. 18; Luke, xvi. 17. [Really a doublet of *title*.] — OF. *title*, a title; (F. *titre*, a title); MF. *titre*, 'a t.ttle, a small line drawn over an abridged word, to supply letters wanting; also a title,' &c.; Cot. — L. *titulum*, acc. of *titulus*, a title, used by Petronius in the sense of sign or token. β. In Late L. *titulus* must have meant a mark over a word in writing, as this sense appears again in Span. *tilde*, Port. *til*, a stroke over a letter such as the mark over Span. *ñ*; also in the Catalan *titlla*, Wallachian *title*, a mark of an accent, cited by Diez, s. v. *tilde*. The latter forms are unmistakably Latin. See **Title**. ¶ Not allied to *tit*.

TITTLE-TATTLE, prattle. (E.) See Wint. Tale, iv. 4. 248. A reduplicated form of *tattle*. Note the use of *titelere*, also spelt *titerere*, a prattler, P. Plowman, B. xx. 297. See **Tattle** and **Twaddle**; and see **Titter**.

TO, in the direction of, as far as. (E.) ME. *to*, Chaucer, C. T. 16; and, as sign of the gerund, 13, 17; now considered as the sign of the infin. mood, the gerundial use being nearly lost. AS. *tō*, prep.; also a sign of the gerund as distinct from the infin. mood; Grein, ii. 536–542. + Du. *toe*; G. *zu*; MHG. *zuo*, *ze*; OHG. *za*, *ze*, *zi*, *zuo*. + Russ. *do*, to, up to. Supposed to be further related to Gk. -δε, towards, as in οἰκόν-δε, homewards; see Curtius, i. 289. Perhaps also to OIrish *do*, to; OWelsh *di* (mod. W. *i*), to; W. *dy*- as a prefix; see Rhys, Lectures on W. Philology. Doublet, *too*, q. v. And see *to-* (2), *to-ward*, *to-day*, *to-night*.

TO- (1), *prefix*, in twain, asunder, to pieces. (E.) Retained in the phr. *all to-brake* = utterly broke asunder, Judges, ix. 53. With regard to the dispute as to whether it should be printed *all to-brake* or *all-to brake*, it is certain that only the former is *etymologically* correct; but the phrase was already so ill understood in the Tudor period that such a mistaken use as *all-to brake* was possible, though it is charitable to give our translators the benefit of the doubt. It is purely a question of chronology. At first the prefix *to-* was used without *all*; later, *all* was often added as well, not only before the prefix *to-*, but before the prefixes *for-* and *bi-* also; next, *all* was considered as in some way belonging to *to*, as if *all-to* were short for *altogether* (which it is not), and consequently *all-to* appeared as a sort of adverb, and was considered as such, apparently, by Surrey and Latimer. It would be difficult to find any clear example of this latest use *before* A.D. 1530. It began with AS. *tō-*, prefix; appearing in *tō-beran*, to bear apart, remove; *tō-berstan*, to burst asunder; *tō-blāwan*, to blow asunder, dissipate; *tō-brecan*, to break asunder; and in nearly *fifty* other verbs, for which see Grein, ii. 542-549. We may particularly note '*hyra setlu he tō-brǣc*' = he brake in pieces their seats, Matt. xxi. 12. **2.** ME. *to-*, prefix; appearing in *tobeatan*, to beat in pieces, *tobiten*, to bite in pieces, *tobreken*, to break in pieces; and in nearly *a hundred* other verbs; for which see Stratmann's Dict., 3rd ed., pp. 565-568. We may particularly note '*al his bondes he to-brak* for ioye' = all his bonds he brake in twain for joy; Will. of Palerne, 3237. **β.** It should also be observed that most verbal prefixes (such as *for-*, *be-*) were usually written *apart* from the verb in old MSS.; ignorance of this fact has misled many. Good examples of the addition of *al* as an intensive, meaning 'wholly,' are the following. '[He] *al to-tare* his a-tir þat he *to-tere* miȝt;' Will. of Palerne, 3884; '*al for-waked*' = entirely worn out with lying awake, id. 790; '*al bi-weped* for wo' = all covered with tears for wo, id. 661; '*al is to-brosten* thilke regioun,' Chaucer, C. T. 2759 (A 2757); 'he suld be soyne *to-fruschit al*' = he would soon be dashed in pieces, Barbour, Bruce, x. 597. The last instance is particularly instructive, as *al* follows the pp. instead of preceding it. **3.** *All-to* or *al-to*, when (perhaps) misunderstood. 'To-day redy ripe, to-morowe *all-to-shaken*;' Surrey, Sonnet 9, last line. 'We be fallen into the dirt, and be *all-to-dirtied*;' Latimer, Remains, p. 397 (Parker Soc.). 'Smiling speakers ∴ love and *all-to* love him;' Latimer, Sermons, p. 289. The last instance is a clear one. Spenser has *all to-torne*, F. Q. v. 9. 10, and *all to-worne* in the same stanza; *all to-rent*, F. Q. iv. 7. 8. Milton has *all-to-ruffled*, Comus, 380; this is a very late example. **B.** Etymologically, the AS. *tō-* is cognate with OFries. *to-*, *te-*; OHG. *zar-*, *zer-*, mod. G. *zer-*, as in *zerbrechen*, to break in pieces, pt. t. *zerbrach* (=*to-brake*). The sense of this prefix is 'in twain,' or 'asunder;' but it is difficult to connect it with AS. *twā*, two, or even with L. *dis-*.

TO- (2), *prefix*, to. (E.) Besides the prefix *to-* (=in twain) discussed above, we also have the prep. *to* in composition in some verbs, &c. Of these compounds, we still use *to-ward*, q. v. Others are obsolete; the chief are the sbs. *tocume*, advent, *toflight*, a refuge, *tohope*, hope, *toname*, a nick-name; and the verb *toneȝhen*, to approach, Wyclif, Judith, xiv. 14. See Stratmann. And see **Today**.

TOAD, an amphibious animal. (E.) ME. *tode*; spelt *toode*, Prompt. Parv., p. 495; *tade*, Pricke of Conscience, 6900. AS. *tádige*; '*Buffo*, *tádige*,' Voc. 122. 11. Also *tádie*, id. 321. 23. Root unknown. The Dan. *tudse*, Swed. *tåssa*, a toad, must be from a different root. Der. *tad-pole*, q. v.; also *toad-stool*, spelt *todestoole*, Spenser, Shep. Kal., Dec. 69, and in Palsgrave; *toad-flax*; *toad-eater*, formerly an assistant to a mountebank (see Wedgwood, and N. and Q. 3rd S. i. 128, 176, 236, 276, v. 142), now shortened to *toady*; *toad-stone*, Sir T. Browne, Vulg. Errors, b. iii. c. 13, § 3.

TOAST (1), bread scorched before the fire. (F. — L.) ME. *tost*, *toost*, whence the verb *tosten*, to toast; see Prompt. Parv. p. 497. — OF. *toster*, to toast (Godefroy); the usual OF. sb. was *tostée*, 'a toast of bread;' marked as a Picard word in Cotgrave. — L. *tostus*, pp. of *torrēre*, to parch; see **Torrid**. Cf. Span. *tostar*, *torrar*, to toast, *tostada*, a toast, slice of toasted bread; Port. *tostado*, toasted, *tostar*, *torrar*, to toast. Der. *toast*, verb; *toast-er*, *toast-ing-iron*, K. John, iv. 3. 99.

TOAST (2), a person whose health is drunk. (F. — L.) It was formerly usual to put toasted bread in liquor; see Shak. Merry Wives, iii. 5. 3. The story of the origin of the present use of the word is given in the Tatler, no. 24, June 4, 1709. 'Many wits of the last age will assert that the word, in its present sense, was known among them in their youth, and had its rise from an accident at the town of Bath, in the reign of king Charles the Second. It happened that, on a public day, a celebrated beauty of those times was in the Cross Bath, and one of the crowd of her admirers took a glass of the water in which the fair one stood, and drank her health to the company. There was in the place a gay fellow half fuddled, who offered to jump in, and swore, though he liked not the *liquor*, he would have the *toast*. He was opposed in his resolution; yet this whim gave foundation to the present honour which is done to the lady we mention in our liquors, who has ever since been called a *toast*.' Whether the story be true or not, it may be seen that a *toast*, i. e. a toast, easily took its name from being the usual accompaniment to liquor, esp. in loving-cups, &c. As to this putting of toast into drinks, see Brand's Pop. Antiq. ii. 340. Der. *toast*, vb.; *toast-master*, the announcer of toasts at a public dinner.

TOBACCO, a narcotic plant. (Span. — Hayti.) Formerly spelt *tabacco*, Ben Jonson, Every Man, i. 4 (last speech). See remarks in Wheatley's Introduction to Ben Jonson, Every Man in his Humour. Harrison fixes on 1573 as the date when the smoking of tobacco became general in England. Spelt *tabacco* in Hakluyt, Voy. ii. 2. 158. Cotgrave mentions *tobacco*, s. v. *Nicotiane*. — Span. *tabaco*, tobacco. Las Casas (Hist. of the Indies) says that *tabaco* was the name of the tube or pipe in which the Indians or Caribs smoked the plant, transferred by the Spaniards to the herb itself. Oviedo (1535) says *tabaco* is a Hayti word; see Oviedo, ed. 1851, Madrid, iv. 96. So also Clavigero, in his Conquest of Mexico (E. transl. i. 430), says: '*tabaco* is a word taken from the Haitine language,' i. e. the language spoken in the island of Hayti or St. Domingo. Der. *tobacco-n-ist*, a coined word, orig. used, not of the *seller* (as now), but of the *smoker* of tobacco; see examples in Trench, Select Glossary; *tobacco-pipe*.

TOBOGGAN, a kind of snow-sledge. (Amer. Indian.) Said to be a Canadian perversion of an American Indian *odabagan*, a sledge. S. T. Rand, in his Micmac Vocabulary, gives the Micmac form as *tobaakun* (= *tobākun*), a sled. Micmac is a language belonging to the Algonkin family.

TOCHER, a dowry. (Gaelic.) 'Hey for a lass wi' a *tocher*;' Burns (Song). — Gael. and Irish *tochar*, a dowry, assigned portion. — OIrish *tochur*, a putting, assigning; *tochurim*, I put. — OIrish *to-*, *do-*, to, prep. and verbal prefix; *cuir-im*, I put, assign.

TOCSIN, an alarm-bell, or the sound of it. (F. — Teut. *and* L.) Added by Todd to Johnson. He quotes: 'The priests went up into the steeple, and rang the bells backward, which they call *tocksaine*, whereupon the people .. flocked together;' Fulke, Answer to P. Frarine (1580), p. 52. — MF. *toquesing*, 'an allarum bell, or the ringing thereof;' Cot. Mod. F. *tocsin* (see Littré). — OF. *toquer*, 'to clap, knock, hit,' Cot.; and OF. *sing* (Norm. dial. *sin*), 'a sign, mark, .. also a bell or the sound of a bell, whence *tocsing*, an alarum bell;' id. Thus it means 'a striking of the signal-bell.' **β.** The Norm. dial. *toquer*, Picard *toker*, are variants of F. *toucher*, to touch; see **Touch**. The OF. *sing*, mod. F. *signe*, is from L. *signum*, a mark, hence a signal, signal-bell; see **Sign**. Cf. AF. *sein*, a bell; Liber Albus, p. 119. Thus *toc-sin* = *touch-sign*. See **Tucket**.

TOD, a bush; a certain measure of wool; a fox. (Scand.) 'An yuie *todde*,' an ivy-bush; Spenser, Shep. Kal., March, 67. 'Wulle is bought by the sacke, by the *tod*, by the stone;' Arnold's Chron. ed. 1811, p. 191. Palsgrave has '*Todde* of woll' = tod of wool; and '*tode* of chese' = tod of cheese. See Nares. *Tod*, a fox, occurs in Ben Jonson, Pan's Anniversary, hymn 4; and see Jamieson's Sc. Dict. The fox is supposed to be so named from his *bushy* tail. — Icel. *toddi* (nearly obsolete), a tod of wool; a bit, a piece. + Du. *todde*, a rag; EFries. *todde*, a bundle; G. *zotte*, *zote*, a tuft of hair hanging together, a rag, anything shaggy. Allied to EFries. *todden*, to trail, to draw along, drag after one. Perhaps allied to **Ted**.

TODAY, this day. (E.) Compounded of *to*, prep., and *day*. The etymology is obscured by the disuse of the prep. *to* in the old sense of 'for;' thus *to day* = for the day; *to night* = for the night; &c. Stratmann cites *me ches him to kinge* = people chose him for king, Rob. of Glouc. p. 302; *yeuen to wyue* = to give to wife, Chaucer, C. T. 1862 (A 1860). See particularly the article on AS. *tō* in Grein, p. 540: he gives examples of *tō dæge*, for the day, today; *tō dæge ðissum*, for this day, today; *tō midre nihte*, to or at midnight; *tō morgene* = for the morn, to-morrow. Hence our *to-day*, *to-morrow*, *to-night*, and prov. E. *to-year*, i. e. for the present year, this year; ME. *toyere*, Chaucer, C. T., 5750 (D 168).

TODDLE, to walk unsteadily, as a child. (E.) Given as a Northern word by Todd, in his additions to Johnson. The same as Lowl. Sc. *tottle*, to walk with short steps; Jamieson. Further, *tottle* is equivalent to *totter*, the frequentative suffixes *-le* and *-er* being equivalent; see **Totter**. + Swed. *tulta*, to toddle; the spelling with *l* is duly explained s. v. *totter*. And cf. G. (Bavar.) *zotteln*, to toddle, though probably formed in another way.

TODDY, a mixture of spirits. (Hindustani. — Pers.) 'The *toddy-tree* is not unlike the date or palm;' Sir T. Herbert, Travels, p. 29 (R.). — Hindustani *tāri*, *tādi*, 'vulgarly *toddy*, the juice or sap of the palmyra-tree and of the cocoa-nut [which] when allowed to stand .. becomes a fiery and highly intoxicating spirit;' H. H. Wilson, Glossary of Indian Terms, p. 510. — Hind. *tār*, 'a palm-tree, .. most appropriate to the Palmyra, from the stem of which the juice is extracted which becomes *toddy*;' id. — Pers. *tār*, 'a species of palm-tree from which an intoxicating liquor, *toddy*, is extracted;' Rich. Dict. p. 353. The *r* in the Hind. word has a peculiar (cerebral) sound, which has come to be represented by *d* in English. Cf. Skt. *tāla*, the palmyra tree.

TO-DO, stir, bustle. (E.) 'What a *to-do* is here!' Evelyn, Diary, Mar. 22, 1675. Compounded of *to*, prep., and *do*, verb. See **Ado**.

TOE, one of the five small members at the end of the foot. (E.) ME. *too*, pl. *toon*, Chaucer, C. T. 14868 (B 4052). AS. *tā*, pl. *tān* or *taan*, Laws of Æthelbirht, §§ 70, 71, 72, in Thorpe, Ancient Laws, i. 20. This is a contracted form, standing for *tāhe*, Corpus Gloss. 141.+Du. *teen*; Icel. *tā*, pl. *tær*; Dan. *taa*, pl. *taaer*; Swed. *tå*; G. *zehe*; OHG. *zēha*, a toe, also a finger. We also find OLow G. *tēwa*, a toe (Gallee); with *w* (< *gw*) for *h* (< *hw*). β. All from Teut. type **taihwōn-*, f. Possibly allied to L. *digitus* (< **dicitus*), a finger (Walde). See **Digit** and **Token**. ¶ Distinct from *toe* in mistletoe. **Der.** *to-ed*, having toes.

TOFFEE, TOFFY, a coarse kind of candy, made of sugar or molasses, &c. (F.—Malay.) In the United States, it is usually *taffy*. — F. *tafia*, a spirit made from molasses; in use in 1722 (Hatzfeld). — Malay *tāfia*, the same. See **Ratafia**.

TOFT, a green knoll, open ground, homestead. (Scand.) ME. *toft*, a knoll, P. Plowm. B. prol. 14. Late AS. *toft* (Toller).—Icel. *topt* (pron. *toft*), also *tupt* (pron. *tuft*), *toft*, *tomt* (the oldest spelling), a place to build on; Swed. *tomt*, the site of a building. Perhaps for **tumft-*< **tum-f(e)t-*, cognate with Gk. δά-πεδον, soil, floor; lit. ‘site for building.’ From the weak grade of **dem*, to build (Gk. δέμ-ειν); and **pedom*, as in Gk. πέδον, ground, earth. See Dan. *tomt* in Falk.

TOGA, the mantle of a Roman citizen. (L.) Whether *toge* = toga really occurs in Shakespeare is doubtful. Phillips gives it in his Dict. — L. *toga*, a kind of mantle, lit. a covering. — L. *tog-*, 2nd grade of *tegere*, to cover; see **Tegument**.

TOGETHER, in the same place, at the same time. (E.) ME. *to-gedere*, *to-gedre*, *to-gidere*, P. Plowman, B. prol. 46; *togideres*, id. xvi. 80. We even find the compound *altogedere* as early as in the Ancren Riwle, p. 320, l. 25. For the spelling with *d*, cf. ME. *fader*, a father, *moder*, a mother. AS. *tō-gædere*, *tō-gædre*; together, Grein, ii. 544.— AS. *tō*, to; and *gador*, together, Grein, i. 491; see further under **Gather**. **Der.** *al-together*.

TOIL (1), labour, fatigue; as a verb, to labour. (F.—L.) ME. *toil*; the dat. *toile*, in Morte Arthure, ed. Brock, 1802, means a tussle or struggle. ‘And whan these com on ther was so grete *toile* and romour of noyse that wonder it was to heere, and therwith aroos so grete a duste;’ Merlin, ed. Wheatley, p. 393, l. 1. Lowl. Sc. *tuyll*, disturbance; Bernardus, &c., ed. Lumby, p. 24, l. 45 (E. E. T. S.); *tuyll*, vb., to trouble, id. p. 27, l. 123. Thus the old sense was rather turmoil or disturbance than labour. Cf. AF. *toyl*, glossed ‘strif,’ Walter de Bibbesworth; in Wright, Vocab. 147, l. 3. Also AF. *toiler*, to strive; A Nominale, ed. Skeat, l. 131. β. As to the verb *toilen*, its meaning was also different from that of mod. E. *toil*. We find: ‘reuliche *toyled* to and fro’ = ruefully pulled or tugged to and fro, Debate between Body and Soul, l. 368, in Mätzner, Sprachproben, i. 100. Also: ‘tore and *toyled*’ = torn and pulled about or spoilt, Legends of the Holy Rood, ed. Morris, p. 143, l. 372. We may also note Lowland Sc. *tuill*, toil (Jamieson); and perhaps Sc. *tuilȝie*, *tuilyie*, a quarrel, broil, struggle, is closely related, as well as *tulȝe*, to harass, occurring in Barbour’s Bruce, iv. 152, where the Edinb. MS. has the pp. *toilȝit*. γ. The origin seems to be found in OF. *toillier*, MF. *touiller*, ‘filthily to mix or mingle, confound or shuffle together; to intangle, trouble, or pester by scurvy medling, also to bedirt, begrime, besmear, smeech, beray;’ Cot. The origin of this F. word is obscure; but Hatzfeld derives it from L. *tudiculāre*, to stir up (correctly, as it seems). — L. *tudicula*, a machine for bruising olives, dimin. of *tudes*, a mallet. — L. *tud-*, as in *tu-tud-ī*, pt. t. of *tundere*, to beat. ¶ Sometimes derived from MDu. *tuylen*, ‘to till, or to manure lands,’ Hexham; cf. *tuyl*, sb., ‘tilling or manuring of lands,’ id.; but it seems impossible to explain the senses of ME. *toilen* from this source only. **Der.** *toil-some*, Spenser, F. Q. ii. 12. 29; *toil-some-ness*.

TOIL (2), a net or snare. (F.—L.) In Hamlet, iii. 2. 362. The pl. *toyles* is in Spenser, Astrophel, 97.— F. *toile*, ‘cloth, linen cloth, also, a staulking-horse of cloth; *toile de araigne*, a cob-web; pl. *toiles*, toils, or a hay to inclose or intangle wild beasts in;’ Cot.— L. *tēla*, a web, thing woven; for **tex-la*.— L. *texere*, to weave; see **Text**. Der. *toil-et* (below).

TOILET, TOILETTE, a small cloth on a dressing-table; hence, a dressing-table, or the operation of dressing. (F.—L.) ‘Toilet, a kind of table-cloth, .. made of fine linnen, &c. spread upon a table .. where persons of quality dress themselves; a dressing-cloth;’ Phillips, ed. 1706. Spelt *toylet* in Cotgrave.—F. *toilette*, ‘a toylet, the stuff which drapers lap about their cloths, also a bag to put nightcloths in;’ Cot. Dimin. of *toile*, cloth; see **Toil** (2).

TOISE, a French measure of length. (F.—L.) It contains 6 feet, and a little over 4½ inches. — F. *toise*, ‘a fadome, a measure containing six feet in length;’ Cot. Cf. Ital. *tesa*, a stretching. — L. *tensa*, sc. *brāchia*, the [length of the] outstretched arms, neut. pl. of pp. of *tendere*, to stretch. See **Tense** (2).

TOKAY, a white wine. (Hungary.) Mentioned in Townson’s Travels in Hungary (1797); see quotation in Todd’s Johnson. Also in Fielding, The Miser (1732), A. iii. Sc. 3. So named from *Tokay*, a town in Hungary, at some distance E.N.E. from Pesth.

TOKEN, a mark, sign, memorial, coin. (E.) ME. *token*, Chaucer, C. T. 13289 (B 1549). The *o* answers to AS. *ā*, as usual. AS. *tācen*, *tācn*, a very common word; Grein, ii. 520.+Du. *teeken*, a sign, mark, token, miracle; Icel. *tākn*, *teikn*; Dan. *tegn*; Swed. *tecken*; G. *zeichen*; Goth. *taikns*. Teut. types **taiknom*, n., **taikniz*, fem.; allied to **Teach**. The base **taik* answers to Idg. **doig*, 2nd grade of **deig*, which seems to be a variant of Idg. √DEIK, to show, indicate; cf. L. *dig-nus*, worthy. Brugmann, i. § 762 (3). Cf. **Index**, **Diction**. Cf. L. *in-dic-āre*, to point out, AS. *tīhan*, Goth. *gateihan*, to show, G. *zeigen*, to show. **Der.** *be-token*.

TOLERATE, to bear, endure, put up with. (L.) ‘To *tollerate* those thinges;’ Sir T. Elyot, The Governour, b. iii. c. 14, § 2.—L. *tolerātus*, pp. of *tolerāre*, to endure; allied to *tollere*, to lift, bear. — √TEL, to lift, bear; cf. Skt. *tul*, to lift, Gk. τλῆναι, to suffer, AS. *þolian*, to endure, L. *lātus*, pp. (for *tlātus*). See **Thole** (2). **Der.** *tolera-ble*, from F. *tolerable*, ‘tollerable,’ Cot., from L. *tolerābilis*, that can be endured; *toler-abl-y*, *toler-able-ness*; *toler-at-ion*, from F. *toleration*, omitted by Cotgrave, but in use in the 16th cent. (Littré), from L. acc. *tolerātiōnem*, endurance; *toler-ance*, from MF. *tolerance*, ‘tolleration, sufferance,’ Cot., from L. *tolerantia*, sufferance; *toler-ant*, from the stem of the pres. part. of *tolerāre*. From the same root are *a-tlas*, *tal-ent*, *ex-tol*; *e-late*, *col-late*, *di-late*, *ob-late*, *pre-late*, *pro-late*, *re-late*, *trans-late*, *legis-late*, *ab-lat-ive*, *super-lat-ive*.

TOLL (1), a tax for the privilege to use a road or sell goods in a market. (L.—Gk.) ME. *tol*, tribute, Wyclif, Rom. xiii. 7. AS. *toll*, Matt. xvii. 25.+Du. *tol*; Icel. *tollr*; Dan. *told* (for **toll*); Swed. *tull*; G. *zoll*. β. All from Teut. type **tulloz*, m.; which might be explained as < **tulnoz*, from the weak grade **tul-* (with suffix *-noz*) of Teut. **tel-*, the root of **Tale**. But the existence of by-forms, as AS. *toln*, a toll (whence *toln-ere*, a toller), OSax. *tolna*, toll, OFries. *tolne*, OHG. *zollan-tuom*, as well as OHG. *zolanari*, MDu. *tollenaer*, a toller, suggest that all these were borrowed from Late L. *tollōnium*, for L. *telōnium*; from Gk. τελώνιον, a toll-house, Matt. ix. 9. Cf. also F. *tonlieu*, a toll; from Late L. *tonleium*, *toleneum*, for L. *telōnium*. γ. The Gk. τελώνιον is from τέλος, a tax, toll, allied to L. *tollere*, to take, and Gk. τάλαντον (see **Talent**); a distinct word from τέλος, with the sense of ‘end.’ **Der.** *toll*, verb, ME. *tollen*, Chaucer, C. T. 564 (A 562); *toll-er*, ME. *tollere*, P. Plowman, B. prol. 220; *tol-booth*, ME. *tolbothe*, Wyclif, Matt. ix. 9; *toll-bar*, *-gate*, *-house*.

TOLL (2), to pull a large bell; to sound as a bell. (E.) We now say ‘a bell *tolls*,’ i.e. sounds, but the old usage was ‘to *toll* a bell,’ i.e. to pull it, set it ringing, as in Minsheu, Skinner, and Phillips. The latter explains *to toll a bell* by ‘to ring a bell after a particular manner.’ It is remarkable that the sense of ‘sound’ occurs as early as in Shakespeare, who has, ‘the clocks do *toll*;’ Hen. V, chorus to act iv. l. 15. Yet we may be satisfied that the present word, which has given some trouble to etymologists, is rightly explained by Nares, Todd, and Wedgwood, who take *toll* to be the ME. *tollen*, to pull, entice, draw, and Wedgwood adds: ‘To *toll* the bells is when they ring slowly to invite the people into church.’ The double sense of *toll* is remarkably shown by two quotations given by Richardson from Dryden, Duke of Guise, Act iv: ‘Some crowd the spires, but most the hallow’d bells And softly *toll* for souls departing knells:’ and again: ‘When hollow murmurs of their evening-bells Dismiss the sleepy swains, and *toll* them [invite them] to their cells.’ Minsheu has: ‘To *toll* a bell,’ and ‘to *tolle*, draw on or entice.’ See examples in Nares and Todd. β. ME. *tollen*. ‘*Tollyn*, or *mevyn*, or *steryn* to doon, Incito, provoco, excito;’ Prompt. Parv. ‘*Tollare*, or *styrare* to do goode or badde, Excitator, instigator;’ id. ‘[He] *tollyd* [drew] hys oune wyf away;’ Seven Sages, ed. Wright, 3052. ‘This *tolleth* him toward thee’ = this draws him towards you; Ancren Riwle, p. 290, l. 5. There is a long note on this curious word, with numerous examples, in St. Marharete, ed. Cockayne, p. 110; the oldest sense seems to be to coax or fondle, entice, draw towards one. γ. All is clear so far; but the origin of ME. *tollen* is obscure; we may suppose it to be nearly related to AS. *fortyllan*, to allure, Grein, i. 332; cf. ME. *tullen*, to entice, lure, Chaucer, C. T. 4132 (A 4134). See **Till** (3).

TOLU, a kind of resin. (S. America.) Also called *Tolu balsam* or *balsam of Tolu*. ‘Balme .. from .. *Tollu*, not farre from Carthagene;’ E. G., tr. of Acosta, Hist. Indies (1604), bk. iv. ch. 28. Named from *Tolu*, a place on the N. W. coast of New Granada, in S. America.

TOM, a pet name for Thomas. (L.—Gk.—Heb.) Spelt *Thomme*, P. Plowman, B. v. 28.—L. *Thōmas*.—Gk. Θωμᾶς, Matt. x. 3. Lit.

'twin;' cf. Heb. *tōmim*, pl., twins. This is why Thomas was also called *Didymus*; from Gk. δίδυμος, a twin. **Der.** *tom-boy, tom-cat, tom-tit.*

TOMAHAWK, a light war-hatchet of the N. American Indians. (W. Indian.) Capt. J. Smith has : '*Tomahacks*, axes;' in his Vocabulary of Indian words; Works, p. 44. From the Algonkin *tomehagen*, Mohegan *tumnahegan*, Delaware *tamoihecan*, a war-hatchet (Webster); Micmac *tumīgun* (S. T. Rand). 'Explained by Lacombe from the Cree dialect; *otamahuk*, knock him down; *otǎmahwaw*, he is knocked down;' Cent. Dict.

TOMATO, a kind of fruit, a love-apple. (Span.—Mexican.) '*Tomates*, which are . . very wholesome;' E. G., tr. of Acosta, Hist. Indies (1604); bk. iv. ch. 20. From Span. (and Port.) *tomate*, a tomato; we probably used final *o* for *e* because *o* is so common an ending in Spanish. Borrowed from Mexican *tomatl*.

TOMAUN, a Persian gold coin. (Pers.—Mongol.) Worth about 7*s.* 6*d.* 'A *Toman* is five markes sterlin;' Sir T. Herbert, Trav. (1638), p. 225 (Yule).—Pers. *tūmān*, 'a gold coin worth about 10*s.*;' Palmer. From a Mongol word meaning 'ten thousand;' spelt *toman* by Marco Polo, bk. i. ch. 54 (Yule).

TOMB, a grave, vault for the dead. (F.—L.—Gk.) ME. *toumbe, tombe*, Chaucer, C. T. 10832 (F 518); *tumbe*, Layamon, 6080, later text.—OF. *tumbe*; F. *tombe*, 'a tombe;' Cot.—L. *tumba*, a tomb (White).—Gk. τύμβα, for the common form τύμβος, a tomb, sepulchre; properly a burial-mound.+Irish *tomm*, a little hill; Skt. *tuṅga-*, prominent, a height. Brugmann, i. § 103. Prob. allied to L. *tumulus* (Curtius, ii. 139); see **Tumulus**. **Der.** *tomb-less*, Hen. V, i. 2. 229: *tomb-stone*; *en-tomb*.

TOMBAC, TOMBACK, a variety of brass. (F.—Port.—Malay.—Skt.) F. *tombac* (Hatzfeld).—Port. *tambaca*, 'tambac,' Vieyra; (and see Yule).—Malay *tambaga*, copper.—Skt. *tāmraka-m*, copper (Benfey).

TOMBOY, a rude girl. (L.—Gk.—Heb.; *and* E.) In Shak. Cymb. i. 6. 122. From **Tom** and **Boy**. ¶ So also *tom-cat, tom-tit, tom-fool.*

TOME, a volume of a book. (F.—L.—Gk.) In Blount's Gloss., ed. 1674; and in Cotgrave.—F. *tome*, 'a tome, or volume;' Cot.—L. *tomum*, acc. of *tonus*, a volume.—Gk. τόμος, a section; hence, a volume. From τομ-, 2nd grade of τεμ-, as in τέμ-νειν, to cut.—√TEM, to cut, whence L. *tondere*, to shear; see **Tonsure**. **Der.** (from same root) *ana-tom-y, a-tom, en-tom-o-logy, epi-tom-e, litho-tom-y, phlebo-tom-y, zoo-tom-y.*

TOMORROW, on the morrow, on the morn succeeding this one. (E.) ME. *to morwe*, P. Plowman. B. ii. 43. From *to*, prep., with the sense of 'for' or 'on;' and *morwe*, morrow. So also AS. *tō morgen*; Luke xiii. 32 (MS. A.). See **Today** and **Morrow**.

TOMTIT, a small bird. (L.—Gk.—Heb.; *and* Scand.) In the Tatler, no. 112; Dec. 27, 1709. From **Tom** and **Tit**, q. v.

TOMTOM, a kind of drum. (Bengali.) From Bengāli *ṭanṭan*, vulgarly *tom-tom*, a small drum, esp. one beaten to bespeak notice to a public proclamation; laxly applied to any kind of drum; H. H. Wilson, Gloss. of Indian Terms, p. 509.

TON, TUN, a large barrel; 4 hogsheads; 20 hundredweight. (C.) We use *ton* for a weight; and *tun* for a cask; but the word is all one. Properly a large barrel, hence, the contents of a large barrel; and hence, a heavy weight. ME. *tonne*, Chaucer, C. T. 3892. AS. *tunne*, a barrel; 'Cupa, *tunne*,' Voc. 123. 9; 'Cuba, *tunne*,' id. 16. 21 (8th cent.); the pl. *tunnan* is in the A. S. Chron. an. 852. We find also Du. *ton*, a tun; Icel. and Swed. *tunna*, Dan. *tönde*, a tun, cask; G. *tonne*, a cask, also a heavy weight; Low L. *tunna*, *tonna*, whence F. *tonneau*, 'a tun,' Cot., Irish, and Gael. *tunna*, Irish *tonna*, W. *tynell*, a tun, barrel. β. The Low L. *tunna*, a cask, written *tunne*, occurs in the Cassel Glossary of the 9th century; see Bartsch, Chrest. Franc. col. 2, l. 15. It is supposed to be of Celtic origin; from the OIrish *tonn*, a skin, a hide, hence 'a wine-skin;' cognate with OGael. *tonn*, W. *tonn*, skin, hide. Celtic type *tunnā*, f. (Macbain; Stokes-Fick, p. 135). ¶ This explains AS. *tyncen*, a small wine-skin, used to support a swimmer; Ælfred's Orosius, ii. 4; ed. Sweet, p. 72, l. 30. **Der.** *tonn-age*, a coined word; *tunn-el*, q. v. Doublet, *tun*, q. v.

TONE, the sound emitted by a stretched string, the character of a sound, quality of voice. (F.—L.—Gk.) Spelt *toone* in Levins. In Bacon, Nat. Hist. § 112. ME. *ton*, Reliquiæ Antiquæ, i. 292 (riming with *nōn*, noon).—F. *ton*, 'a tune or sound;' Cot.—L. *tonum*, acc. of *tonus*, a sound.—Gk. τόνος, a thing stretched, a rope, sinew, tone, note; from the sound of a stretched string.—Gk. τον-, 2nd grade of τεν-, Idg. √TEN, to stretch; Skt. *tan*, to stretch, Gk. τείνειν, to stretch; see **Tend** (1). **Der.** *ton-ed*; *ton-ic*, increasing the tone or giving vigour, a late word, from Gk. τονικός, relating to stretching. Also *a-ton-ic, bary-tone, mono-tone, oxy-tone, semi-tone; in-tone.* Doublet, *tune*, q. v.

TONGS, an instrument consisting of two jointed bars of metal, used for holding and lifting. (E.) In Spenser, F. Q. iv. 5. 44. But earlier, the singular form *tonge* or *tange* is usual. ME. *tange, tonge*. 'Thu tuengst þarmid so doþ a *tonge*'=thou twingest therewith as doth a tong; Owl and Nightingale, 156. AS. *tange*; 'Forceps, *tange*,' Voc. 336. 25. Also spelt *tang*, Ælfric's Grammar, ed. Zupitza, p. 67, l. 3.+Du. *tang*, a pair of tongs or pincers; Icel. *töng* (pl. *tangir*); Dan. *tang*; Swed. *tång*; G. *zange*. β. All from Teut. type *tangā*, f., with the sense 'a biter' or 'nipper;' cf. E. *nippers, pincers* (Fick, iii. 116). From the base *tang-*, nasalised form of *tah-* (Idg. *dak-*), to bite.—√DENK, to bite; cf. Gk. δάκ-νειν, to bite (from the weak grade), Skt. *daṃṣ, daṣ*, to bite, *daṃça-*, a bite, *daṃçaka-*, a crab (a pincher). In particular, cf. OHG. *zanga*, a pair of tongs, with OHG. *zanger*, biting, pinching. See **Tang** (1), **Tough**. Brugmann, i. § 420, 431 (3).

TONGUE, the fleshy organ in the mouth, used in tasting, swallowing, and speech. (E.) The spelling with final *-ue* is of Norman origin, to show that the *ng* was not palatalised; cf. F. *langue*; a better spelling is *tong*, as in Spenser, F. Q., introd. to b. i. st. 2. ME. *tunge, tonge*, Chaucer, C. T. 267 (A 265). AS. *tunge*, a tongue, Luke, i. 64.+Du. *tong*; Icel. and Swed. *tunga*; Dan. *tunge*; G. *zunge*, OHG. *zunga*; Goth. *tuggō* (=*tungō*). β. All from Teut. type *tungōn-*, f. Further related to OL. *dingua*, L. *lingua* (whence F. *langue*), the tongue. Allied to **Lingual**. Brugmann, i. § 441. **Der.** *tongue*, vb., Cymb. v. 4. 148; *tongu-ed*; *tongue-less*, Rich. II, i. 1. 105; *tongue-tied*, Mids. Nt. Dr. v. 104. From the same root are *lingu-al, ling-o, langu-age*.

TONIC, strengthening. (Gk.) See **Tone**.

TONIGHT, this night. (E.) See **Today**.

TONSIL, one of two glands at the root of the tongue. (F.—L.) '*Tonsils* or almonds in the mouth;' Holland, tr. of Pliny, b. xxiv. c. 7. § 1.—F. *tonsille*; *tonsilles*, pl., 'certain kernels at the root of the tongue;' Cot.—L. *tonsilla*, a sharp pointed pole stuck in the ground to fasten vessels to the shore; pl. *tonsillæ*, the tonsils. 'There is one [Latin] sb. in *-li-*, viz. L. *tōlēs*, pl. m. "wen on the neck;" for *tons-li-*, from *tens-*, "to stretch," Goth. *at-thins-an*, to draw towards one, Lith. *tęs-ti*, to stretch by pulling; *tonsillæ*, "tonsils," points to an older form *tons-lo-* or *tons-lā*;' Brugmann, ii. § 98. Cf. **Thistle**.

TONSURE, a clipping of the hair, esp. the corona of hair worn by Romish priests. (F.—L.) ME. *tonsure*, Gower, C. A. iii. 291; bk. viii. 482.—F. *tonsure*, 'a sheering, clipping, the shaven crown of a priest;' Cot.—L. *tonsūra*, a clipping; cf. *tonsus*, pp. of *tondēre*, to shear, clip. Cf. Gk. τένδειν, to gnaw; for *tém-d-ein*; ultimately allied to Gk. τέμνειν, to cut; see **Tome**.

TONTINE, a certain financial scheme, the gain of which falls to the longest liver. (F.—Ital.) See Haydn's Dict. of Dates, and Littré. First started at Paris, about A.D. 1653.—F. *tontine*, a tontine. Named from Lorenzo *Tonti*, a Neapolitan, who originated the scheme.

TOO, more than enough, likewise. (E.) The emphatic form of *to*, prep. ME. *to*; '*to* badde'=too bad; Will. of Palerne, 5024.—AS. *tō*, too; Grein, ii. 542, q. v. The same word as *tō*, prep., but differently used. See **To**.

TOOL, an instrument used by workmen. (E.) ME. *tol, tool*; pl. *toles, tooles*, P. Plowman, A. xi. 133; B. x. 177. AS. *tōl*, a tool; Ælfric's Hom. ii. 162, l. 12; spelt *tool*, Voc. 116. 35; *tohl*, id. 429. 15.+Icel. *tōl*, neut. pl., tools. β. Teut. type *tōlom*, n.; for *tōu-lom*; where *tōu-* is related to *tau-*, *taw-*, as in AS. *tawian*, to prepare, dress, get ready; so that *tool* is the instrument by which this is done. Cf. Goth. *taujan*, to make, cause, and E. *taw*, *tew*, to work hard, to dress leather; see **Taw**. The Teut. base *tau-* seems to be connected with a Skt. root *du* or *dū*, to work. γ. 'This root is not recognized by Skt. grammarians, but it has to be admitted by comparative philologists. There is the verb *duvasyati* in the Veda, meaning to worship, a denominative verb derived from *dúvas*. *Dúvas* meant, originally, any *opus operatum*, and presupposes a root *du* or *dū*, in the sense of actively or sedulously working. It exists in Zend as *du*, to do. With it we may connect Goth. *taujan*, the G. *zauen* (Grimm, Gram. i. 1041), Goth. *tawi*, work, &c. See my remarks on this root and its derivatives in the Veda in my Translation of the Rig-Veda, i. 63, 191;' Max Müller, letter to The Academy, July, 1874. As to the *duvās* in Uhlenbeck, p. 128. As to the connexion of *tool* with Goth. *taujan*, see Streitberg, § 85.

TOOM, empty. (Scand.) Common in Lowland Scotch; '*toom* dish'=empty dish; Burns, Hallowe'en, l. 12 from end. ME. *tom, toom*. '*Toom*, or voyde, Vacuus;' Prompt. Parv. Not an AS. word, though the adv. *tōme* occurs once (Grein).—Icel. *tōmr*, empty; Swed. and Dan. *tom*. Cf. OHG. *zuomig*, empty. The Teut. type is *tōmoz*, adj., empty. **Der.** *teem* (3), q. v.

TOOT (1), to peep about, spy. (E.) A form of **Tout**, q. v.

TOOT (2), to blow a horn. (Scand.) ' To *tute* in a horn, cornucinere;' Levins. Not an AS. form, which would have given *theet* or *thout*; but borrowed from a dialect which sounded *th* as *t*.—MSwed. and Norw. *tuta*, to blow a horn. Cf. EFries. and Low G. *tuten*, to toot, MDu. *tuyten*, ' to sound or winde a cornet,' Hexham; Du. *toet-hren*, a bugle-horn; Swed. *tjuta*, to howl; Dan. *tude*, to howl, blow a horn; Icel. *þjóta*, strong verb, pt. t. *þaut*, to whistle as wind, sough, resound; also, to blow a horn; AS. *þéotan*, to howl, make a noise; Grein, ii. 5⁸9; also AS. *þútan* (Toller); MHG. *diezen*, OHG. *diozan*, to make a loud noise; Goth. *thut-haurn*, a trumpet.　β. All from Teut. base **theut*, to make a noise, resound; of imitative origin. The Idg. form of the root agrees with that of L. *tundere* (<**teud*), to strike; but this may be accidental.

TOOTH, one of the small bones in the jaws, used in eating; a prong. (E.) ME. *toth*, *tooth*; pl. *teth*, *teeth*, spelt *teð*, Ancren Riwle, p. 288, l. 3 from bottom. AS. *tóð*, pl. *téð* and *tóðas*, Grein, ii. 543. Here a short *o* has been lengthened, with ultimate loss of *n* before *th* following; *tóð* stands for **tonð*, for **tanð*; cf. OSax. *tand*.+Du. *tand*; Icel. *tönn*, gen. sing. *tann-ar*; Dan. *tand*; Swed. *tand*; G. *zahn*; MHG. *zan*, OHG. *zand*.　β. All from Teut. type **tanth-us*, m.; cf. (from the weak stem) Goth. *tunthus*, a tooth. From the Idg. bases **dent-*, **dont-*, we have L. *dens* (stem *dent-*), W. *dant*, Gk. ὀδούς (stem ὀδόντ-), Lithuan. *dantis*, Skt. *danta-*, a tooth. And cf. Pers. *dandān*, a tooth.　γ. The Idg. **dont-*, for **ed-ónt-*, is a pres. participial form from √ED, to eat; see **Eat**. Der. *tooth*, verb, spelt *tothe*, Fitzherbert, Husbandry, § 24, l. 7; *tooth-ed*; *tooth-ache*, Much Ado, iii. 2. 21; *tooth-less*, Prompt. Parv.; *tooth-drawer*, Prompt. Parv.; *tooth-pick*, All's Well, i. 1. 171; *tooth-some*, i. e. dainty, nice, not an early word. Brugmann, ii. § 126. See **Tine** (1).

TOP (1), the highest part of anything, the summit. (E.) ME. *top*; *top ouer tail* = head over heels, Will. of Palerne, 2776. AS. *top*; ' Apex, summitas galeæ, *helmes top*,' Voc. 143. 26.+Du. *top*; Icel. *toppr*, a tuft, lock of hair, crest, top; Dan. *top*, a tuft, crest, top; Swed. *topp*, a summit; G. *zopf*, a tuft of hair, pigtail, top of a tree; OHG. *zoph*.　β. All from Teut. type **tuppoz*, m., a peak, top; allied to E. *tap*, a spike for a cask. Cf. G. *zapfen*, a peg, tap, also a fir-cone; Norweg. *topp*, a top, a bung (Aasen). Der. *top*, verb, Macb. iv. 3. 57; *top-dressing*; *top-gallant-mast*, for which Shak. has *top-gallant*, Romeo, ii. 4. 202; *top-full*, K. John, iii. 4. 180; *top-less*, Troil. i. 3. 152; *top-mast*, Temp. i. 1. 37; *top-sail*, Temp. i. 1. 7; *top-m-ost*, really a *double* superl. form, see **Aftermost**; *topp-le*, to tumble, be top-heavy, and so fall headlong, Macb. iv. 1. 56. Also *top-sy-turvy*, q. v.

TOP (2), a child's toy. (F.—G.) In Shak. Merry Wives, v. 1. 27. ME. *top*, a child's toy; King Alisaunder, 1727. Late AS. *topp*; Anglia, i. 465.—AF. **top* or **tope*; only found in the OF. dimin. *topet*, *tupet*. ' Trocus, *topet*;' Glasgow MS., in Godefroy; he also gives *tupet*, a top, and *topier*, to spin like a top, like MF. *toupier*, Cot.; cf. F. *toupie*, a top, and MF. *tupin*, a pipkin, Cot.—MHG. *topf*, a top; also, a pot, a scull (the humming-top being like a round pot).+Low G. *dop*, a shell; MDu. *dop*, *doppe*, a top (also *top*, from HG.); MDu. *dop*, a shell, *doppe*, a little pot, pipkin; EFries. *dop*, *doppe*, a shell. Allied to ME. *doppen*, to dive, to dip (a water-pot), WFlem. *doppen*, to dip, to plunge in (De Bo). Cf. **Dip**. ¶ Or from OLow G. *top*; from the same MHG. *topf*.

TOPAZ, a precious stone. (F.—L.—Gk.) ME. *topas*, whence Chaucer's *Sir Topas*; spelt *tupace*, O. Eng. Miscellany, ed. Morris, p. 98, l. 172.—OF. *topase*, ' topase, a stone;' Cot.—L. *topazus*, *topazon*, *topazion*, a topaz.—Gk. τόπαζος, τοπάζιον, the yellow or oriental topaz.　β. According to Pliny, b. xxxvii. c. 8, named from an island in the Red Sea called *Topazos*, the position of which was ' conjectural;' from Gk. τοπάζειν, to conjecture! But this is a popular etymology. It is probable that the name is of Eastern origin; cf. Skt. *tapas*, fire, *tap*, to shine. See Schade, OHG. Dict., p. 1432.

TOPER, a great drinker. (F. or Ital.—Teut.) ' *Tope*, to drink briskly or lustily;' Phillips, ed. 1706. ' The jolly members of a *toping* club;' Butler, Epigram on a Club of Sots, l. 1. ' *Tope*! here pledge me! (*drinks*);' Etheredge, The Comical Revenge, A. ii. sc. 3. Certainly connected, as Wedgwood shows, with F. *tôper*, to cover a stake, a term used in playing at dice; whence *tôpe*! interj. (short for *je tôpe*, lit. I accept your offer), used in the sense of good! agreed! well done! It came to be used as a term in drinking, though this only appears in Italian. ' According to Florio [i. e. in ed. 1688] the same exclamation was used for the acceptance of a pledge in drinking. [He gives]: *topa*, a word among dicers, as much as to say, I hold it, done, throw! also by good fellows when they are drinking; I'll pledge you;' Wedgwood.　β. Of Teut. origin; from the *striking together* of hands or glasses; cf. Picard *toper*, to strike hands in bargaining, Ital. *in-toppare*, to strike against an obstacle. Originally from the act of placing together the *tops* of the

thumbs, at the same time crying *topp*! See *topp* in Ihre, Outzen, and the Bremen Wörterbuch. Cf. **Top** (1).

TOPIARY, adj. (L.—Gk.) *Topiary* work is a term applied to clipped trees and shrubs, in landscape gardening.—L. *topiārius*, belonging to landscape gardening.—L. *topia*, fancy gardening.—Gk. τόπος, a place, a district.

TOPIC, a subject of discourse or argument. (F.—L.—Gk.) Properly an adj.; Milton has ' a *topic* folio ' = a common-place book; Areopagitica, ed. Hales, p. 40, l. 27, on which see the note. ' *Topicks* (*topica*), books that speak of *places* of invention, or that part of logick which treats of the invention of arguments;' Blount's Gloss., ed. 1674. Spelt *topickes* in Minsheu, ed. 1627.—F. *topiques*, 'topicks, books or places of logicall invention;' Cot.—L. *topica*, s. pl., the title of a work of Aristotle, of which a compendium is given by Cicero (White).—Gk. τοπικός, adj., local; also concerning τόποι or common-places. Aristotle wrote a treatise on the subject (τὰ τοπικά).—Gk. τόπος, a place. Der. *topic-al* (Blount), *topic-al-ly*; and see *topo-graphy*.

TOPOGRAPHY, the art of describing places. (F.—L.—Gk.) Spelt *topographie* in Minsheu, ed. 1627.—F. *topographie*, the description of a place;' Cot.—L. *topographia*.—Gk. τοπογραφία, a description of a place; Strabo.—Gk. τοπο-, for τόπος, a place; and γράφειν, to describe. See **Topic** and **Graphic**. Der. *topograph-er*, formed with E. suffix *-er* from Gk. τοπογράφ-ος, a topographer, describer of places: *topograph-ic*, *topograph-ic-al*, *-ly*.

TOPPLE, to fall over. (E.) See **Top** (1).

TOPSYTURVY, upside down. (E.) Examples show that *-sy* does *not* stand for *side*, as the word is sometimes written; for *topsytervy* is the older form. In Stanyhurst's tr. of Virgil, ed. Arber, we have *top-turuye*, p. 33, l. 13; *topsy-turuye*, p. 63, l. 25; and *top-syd-turuye*, p. 59, l. 23. *Topside-turvey* occurs twice (at least) in the play of Cornelia, printed in 1594, in Act i. and Act v; see Dodsley's Old Plays, ed. Hazlitt, vol. v. p. 186, l. 1, p. 250, l. 15. Much earlier, we find ' He tourneth all thynge *topsy tervy*;' Roy, Rede Me and Be Not Wroth, ed. Arber, p. 51, l. 25 (printed in 1528). And Palsgrave (1530) has *topsy tyrvy*, p. 843, col. 1.　β. In Trench, Eng. Past and Present, we are told that *topsy turvy* is a corruption from *topside the other way*; to which the author adds: ' There is no doubt of the fact; see Stanihurst's Ireland, p. 33, in Holinshed's Chronicles.' After searching in three editions of Holinshed, I find, in the reprint of 1808, at p. 33, that Stanihurst has the equivalent expression *topside the other waie*; to which may be added that Richardson quotes *topside tother way* from Search's Light of Nature, vol. ii. pt. ii. c. 23.　γ. But this only proves that such was a current explanation of the phrase in the time of Stanihurst and later. It can hardly be doubted that *topsy tervy* stood for *top-so-tervy*; just as *upside-down* was originally *up-so-down*, i. e. ' up as (if) down.' Hence the derivation is from *top*, *so*, and the old verb *terve*, to overturn, orig. ' to roll back;' see *Terve* in my Gloss. to Chaucer, and *topsy-turvy* in my Notes on E. Etym., p. 303. Cf. Lowl. Sc. *our-tyrve*, to turn upside down (Jamieson); *ourtirvit*, upset, turned over, Book of the Houlate, 837; *ouer-terue*, to overthrow; Hoccleve, De Regim. Princ., st. 259, l. 1811. G. Douglas has *tirvit*, stripped, despoiled, to translate L. *detraxerat*, Æn. v. 260. Allied to AS. *tearflian*, to turn, roll over; Low G. *tarven*, to roll or turn up a cuff; OHG. *zerben*, *umbi-zerben*, to turn oneself round.

TORCH, a light formed of twisted tow dipped in pitch, a large candle. (F.—L.) ME. *torche*, Floriz and Blancheflur, l. 238.—F. *torche*, ' a link; also, the wreathed clowt, wisp, or wad of straw, layed by wenches between their heads and the things which they carry on them;' Cot. [Cf. Ital. *torcia*, a torch, *torciare*, to twist; Span. *entorchar*, to twist, *antorcha*, a torch.]—Late L. *tortica*, a torch; cf. also *tortisius*, occurring A.D. 1287; also *tortius*, &c. All various derivatives from L. *tort-us*, pp. of *torquēre*, to twist; see **Torture**. A torch is simply ' a twist.' Der. *torch-light*.

TOREADOR, a bull-fighter. (Span.—L.) In use in 1618 (Stanford Dict.).—Span. *toreador*.—Span. *torear*, to fight bulls.—Span. *toro*, a bull.—L. *taurus*, a bull; see **Taurus**.

TORMENT, anguish, great pain. (F.—L.) ME. *torment*, Rob. of Brunne, tr. of Langtoft, p. 148, l. 6, where it means ' a tempest;' also *tourment*, K. Alisaunder, 5869.—OF. *torment*, ' torment;' Cot. Mod. F. *tourment*.—L. *tormentum*, an instrument for hurling stones, an instrument of torture, torture. Formed with suffix *-men-tum* from *tor-* (for *torc-*), base of *torquēre*, to twist, hurl, throw; see **Torture**. Der. *torment*, verb, ME. *tormenten*, Rob. of Glouc. p. 240, l. 14 (ed. Wright, p. 349, l. 36); *torment-ing-ly*; *torment-or*, ME. *tormentour*, Chaucer. C. T. 1:995 (G 527); also *torment-er*. And see *tormentil*.

TORMENTIL, the name of a herb. (F.—L.) In Levins. Spelt *turmentyll*; Palsgrave.—F. *tormentille*, ' tormentile;' Cot.—Late L. *tormentilla*; Voc. 713. 6. Cf. Ital. *tormentilla*, ' tormentill,' Florio. Said to be so called because it relieved tooth-ache, an idea which is at least as old as the 16th century; see Littré. — OF. *torment*, great pain, an ache; see **Torment.**

TORNADO, a violent hurricane. (Span. — L.) 'Tornado (Span. *tornada*, i. e. return, or turning about) is a sudden, violent, and forcible storm . . . at sea, so termed by the marriners;' Blount's Gloss., ed. 1674. But this is only a popular etymology; due to misapprehension of the form of the word. 'Ternados, that is, thundrings and lightnings;' Hakluyt, Voy. iii. 719. — Span. *tronada*, a thunder-storm. — Span. *tronar*, to thunder. — L. *tonāre*, to thunder. See **Thunder.**

TORPEDO, the cramp-fish; a kind of eel that produces numbness by communicating an electric shock. (L.) 'Like one whom a *torpedo* stupefies;' Drummond, sonnet 53; and see Gosson, School of Abuse, p. 56. — L. *torpēdo*, numbness; also, a torpedo, cramp-fish. — L. *torpēre*, to be numb; see **Torpid.**

TORPID, sluggish, lit. numb. (L.) In Blount's Gloss., ed. 1674. — L. *torpidus*, benumbed, torpid. — L. *torpēre*, to be numb, to be stiff. Cf. Lith. *tirpti*, to grow stiff; Russ. *terpnute*, to grow numb. Der. *torpid-ly*, *torpid-ness*, *torpid-i-ty*; *torp-or*, L. *torpor*, numbness, inactivity; also *torp-esc-ent*, from the stem of pres. part. of *torpescere*, to grow torpid, inceptive form of *torpēre*; *torp-esc-ence*.

TORQUE, a twisted metal ornament, esp. for the neck. (L.) Englished from L. *torques*, a torque. — L. *torquēre*, to twist; see **Torsion.** Or from OF. *torque*, the same (Supp. to Godefroy). See **Tort.**

TORRENT, a boiling, rushing stream. (F. — L.) In Shak. J. Cæs. i. 2. 107. — F. *torrent*, 'a torrent, land-flood.' — L. *torrentem*, acc. of *torrens*, hot, boiling, raging, impetuous; and as a sb. a torrent. raging stream. Orig. pres. part. of *torrēre*, to parch, dry up; see **Torrid.** Der. (obs.) *torrent-yne*, a trout; Babees Book, p. 173, note 4.

TORRID, parching, violently hot. (F. — L.) In Cotgrave. — F. *torride*, 'torrid, scorched, parched;' Cot. — L. *torridus*, parched. — L. *torrēre*, to parch, dry up. β. *Torrēre* stands for *torsēre*, like *terra* for *tersa*; from √TERS, to be dry; see **Terrace** and **Thirst.** Cf. Gk. τέρσεσθαι, to become dry. Der. *torr-ent*, *torre-fy*, to make dry, from F. *torrefier*, 'to scorch,' Cot.; *torre-fact-ion*, from L. *torrefactus*, pp. of *torrefacere*, to make dry, dry up.

TORSION, a violent twisting, twisting force. (F. — L.) A late word. In Johnson. — F. *torsion*, 'a winding, wrying, wresting;' Cot. — L. *torsionem*, acc. of *torsio*, a wringing. — L. *torquēre* (pt. t. *torsī*), to twist; see **Torture.**

TORSK, a fish of the cod family. (Scand.) From Dan. and Swed. *torsk*; Icel. *þorskr*, a cod-fish; whence also G. *dorsch*. Perhaps named from its being dried; cf. Swed. *torr*, Dan. *tör*, Icel. *þurr*, dry. Cf. **Torrid.**

TORSO, the trunk of a statue. (Ital. — L. — Gk.) A late word; not in Todd's Johnson. — Ital. *torso*, a stump, stalk, core, trunk. — L. *thyrsum*, acc. of *thyrsus*, a stalk, stem of a plant; a thyrsus. — Gk. θύρσος, a straight stem, stalk, rod. See **Thyrsus.**

TORT, a wrong. (F. — L.) 'Fraud or tort;' Spenser, F. Q. iv. 8. 31. — F. *tort*, a wrong, harm; also pp. of F. *tordre*, to twist. — L. *tortus*, pp. of L. *torquēre*, to twist. Cf. Irish *torc*, W. *torch*, a wreath; Russ. *trok'*, a girth; Gk. ἄτρικτος, a spindle; Skt. *tarku-*, a spindle. — √TERQ, to twist. See **Torture.**

TORTOISE, a reptile. (F. — L.) ME. *tortuce*, Prompt. Parv.; *tortoise*, in Temp. i. 2. 3 6. We also find ME. *tortu*, Knight de la Tour, ch. xi. l. 2. 1. The latter form is immediately from MF. *tortue*, a tortoise (now *tortue*); with which cf. Span. *tortuga*, a tortoise; both from Late L. *tortūca*, *tartūca*, a tortoise, for which Diez gives a reference. So also MItal. *tartuga* (Florio); now corrupted to *tartaruga*. 2. The E. *tortoise* answers to an OF. form, not recorded, but cognate with Prov. *tortesa*, a tortoise (Diez). In all these instances the animal is named from its crooked or twisted feet, which are very remarkable; cf. OF. *tortis* (fem. *tortisse*), 'crooked;' Cot. Both Late L. *tort-ūca* and Prov. *tort-esa* are formed as if from L. *tort-us*, pp. of *torquēre*, to twist; see **Torture.**

TORTUOUS, crooked. (F. — L.) ME. *tortuos*, Chaucer, On the Astrolabe, pt. ii. c. 28, l. 19. — F. *tortueux*, 'full of crookedness or crookings;' Cot. — L. *tortuōsus*, twisting about, crooked. — L. *tort-us*, pp. of *torquēre*, to twist; see **Torture.** Der. *tortuous-ly*, -ness.

TORTURE, a wringing pain, torment, anguish. (F. — L.) In Shak. All's Well, ii. 1. 177, &c. — F. *torture*, 'torture;' Cot. — L. *tortūra*, torture; allied to L. *tortus*, pp. of *torquēre*, to twist, whirl. See **Tort.** Der. (from L. *torquēre*) *torch*, *tor-ment*, *tor-s-ion*, *tort-oise*, *tort-u-ous*; *con-tort*, *de-tort*, *dis-tort*, *ex-tort*, *re-tort*; also *tart* (2), *tormentil*.

TORY, a Conservative in English politics. (Irish.) 'Tory, an Irish robber, or bog-trotter; also a nick-name given to the stanch Royalists, or High-flyers, in the times of King Charles II. and James II.;' Phillips, ed. 1706. As to the use of the name, see Trench, Select Glossary, and Todd's Johnson. First used about 1680. Dryden even reduplicates the word into *tory-rory*. 'Before George, I grew tory-rory, as they say,' Kind Keeper, i. 1; 'Your tory-rory jades,' id. iv. 1. By this adj. he appears to mean 'wild.' 'Tories was a name properly belonging to the Irish bogtrotters, who during our Civil War robbed and plundered, professing to be in arms for the royal cause; and from them transferred, about 1680, those who sought to maintain the extreme prerogatives of the Crown;' Trench, Select Glossary. Trench cites 'the increase of tories and other lawless persons' from the Irish State Papers, Jan. 24, 1656. In Irish the word means 'pursuer;' hence, I suppose, it was easily transferred to bogtrotters and plunderers. — Irish *toiridhe*, also *toruighe*, a pursuer; cf. *torachd*, pursuit, search, *toir*, a pursuit, diligent search, also pursuers; *toireacht*, pursuit, search; *toirighim*, I fancy, I think, I pursue, follow closely. Cf. Gael. *toir*, a pursuit, diligent search, also pursuers; *torachd*, a pursuit with hostile intention, strict search. From OIrish *toracht* (for **do-fo-racht*), pursuit; where *do* (to) and *fo* (under) are prefixes; and *racht* is from √REG, as in L. *reg-ere*, to direct, Irish *rig-im*, I stretch out (Macbain). Der. *Tory-ism.*

TOSE, to pull, or pluck; see **Tease, Touse.**

TOSS, to jerk, throw violently, agitate, move up and down violently. (Scand.) 'I tosse a balle;' Palsgrave. — Norw. *tossa*, to sprinkle, strew, spread out; hence, 'to toss hay.' Allied to Dan. dial. *tusse*, to stir, move, shake; also to E. **Touse**, q. v.; and to Low G. *teusen*, to toss (hay). ¶ W. *tosio*, to toss, is from E.; not a Celtic word. Der. *toss*, sb.; *toss-pot*, Tw. Nt. v. 412.

TOTAL, complete, undivided. (F. — L.) 'Thei toteth [look] on her summe *totall*;' Plowman's Tale, pt. i. st. 46. We still use *sum total* for *total sum*, putting the adj. *after* the sb., according to the F. idiom. — F. *total*, 'the totall, or whole sum;' Cot. — Late L. *tōtālis*, extended from L. *tōtus*, entire. Der. *total-i-ty*, from F. *totalité*, 'a totality;' Cot. Also *sur-tout*.

TOTEM, a natural object, usually an animal, used as a badge or token of a clan, among N. American Indians. (Amer. Indian.) 'Each his own ancestral *totem*;' Longfellow, Hiawatha, xiv. Said to be from the Algonquin *otem*, with a prefixed poss. pron.; giving *nt'otem*, 'my totem;' Cent. Dict.

TOTTER, to be unsteady, stagger. (E.) For *tolter*, by assimilation; it is related to *tilt* (ME. *tulten*, *tilten*); and means to be always tilting over, to be ready to fall at any minute. 'Where home the cart-horse *tolters* with the wain;' Clare, Village Minstrel, Rural Evening, l. 20. 'The *toltering* [jolting] bustle of a blundering trot;' id., Rural Morning, 37. Cf. prov. E. *tolter*, to struggle, flounder about (Halliwell). Trevisa, ii. 387, has: 'men *totrede* þeron [swung on ropes] and meued hider and þider;' here the *l* is dropped. The form *tolter* occurs twice in the King's Quhair, by James I of Scotland; but not as a verb, as Jamieson wrongly says. 'On her *tolter* quhele' = on her [Fortune's] tottering wheel, st. 9; where *tolter* is an adj. 'So *tolter* quhilum did she it to wrye' = so totteringly (unsteadily) did She (Fortune) cause it (her wheel) to go aside, st. 164; where *tolter* is an adverb. The suffix -*er* is here adjectival; *tolter* means 'ready to tilt.' Precisely the same loss of *l* occurs in *tatter* (also spelt *totter*), a rag; see **Tatter.** β. Again, *tolter* is a frequent. related to ME. *tulten*, to totter or tilt over; 'Feole temples þer-inne *tulten* to þe eorþe' = many temples therein tottered (fell) to the earth; Joseph of Arithmathie, ed. Skeat, 100. *Tulten* is another form of *tilten*; see **Tilt** (2). But it is important to remark that the word *totter* itself is allied to AS. *tealtrian*, to totter, vacillate, Grein, ii. 526; formed from the adj. *tealt*, tottery, unstable; id. Add, that we have the cognate MDu. *touteren*, 'to tremble,' Hexham; for **tolteren*, like Du. *goud* for *gold*. Hence Du. *touter*, a swing; like the Norfolk *teeter-cum-tauter*, a see-saw; cf. *tytter-totter*, a see-saw (Palsgrave, p. 282). Further allied to Bavar. *zelter-n*, to hobble along. Der. *totter-er*. Note also *tott-y* (i. e. *tolty*, *tilty*), unsteady, Chaucer, C. T. 4251 (A 4253); Spenser, F. Q. vii. 7. 39. And see *toddle*.

TOUCAN, a large-beaked tropical bird. (F. — Brazilian.) Littré gives a quotation of the 16th century. 'Il a veu aux terres neufves un oiseau que les sauvages appellant en leur gergon [jargon] *toucan*,' &c.; Paré, Monstr. app. 2. The form *toucan* is F., as above. — Brazil. *tucana*, *toucan*, Hist. Nat. Brasiliæ (1648), p. 217. According to Burton, Highlands of Brazil, i. 40, the bird is named from its cry. The Guarani form is said to be *tucā* (whence Port. *tucano*); Granada gives the Guarani form as *tùcà* (with *ù* and *à* both nasal).

TOUCH, to perceive by feeling, handle, move influence. (F. — Teut.) ME. *touchen*, King Alisaunder, ed. Weber, 1195. — F. *toucher*, to touch. [Cf. Ital. *toccare*, Span., Port., and Prov. *tocar*, to touch; also OF. *toquer*, 'to clap, knock, or hit against;' Cot. To touch a lyre is to strike the strings, or rather to twitch them; so also Ital. *toccare il liuto*, to twang the lute; Florio gives 'to strike, to smite, to hit,' as senses of *toccare*.]—Teut. type *tukkōn, represented by Low G. *tukken*, and OHG. *zucchen*, mod. G. *zucken*, to draw with a quick motion, to twitch; cf. MDu. *tocken, tucken*, to touch (Hexham). This is an intensive form, from the weak grade (*tuh-) of Teut. *teuhan-, as seen in Goth. *tiuhan*, AS. *tēon* (<*tēohan), to pull, to draw, cognate with OHG. *ziohan*, G. *ziehen*, and therefore with L. *dūcere*, to draw; see **Tuck** (1), **Tow** (1), and **Duke**. The Teut. base *tukk- arose from the Idg. *duk-n-; Brugmann, i. § 421 (7). Der. *touch*, sb., As You Like It, iii. 4. 15; *touch-ing*, i. e. relating to, orig. pres. part. of the verb *touchen*, Chaucer, C. T. 7872 (D 2290), spelt *touchende* (which is a pres. part. form) in Gower C. A. p. 249, l. 2 of Macaulay's edition, but spelt *touchinge* in Pauli's edition, i. 307, bk. iii. 842; *touch-ing*, adj., *touch-ing-ly*, *touch-stone*, a stone for testing gold, Palsgrave; *touch-hole*, Beaum. and Fletcher, Custom of the Country, iii. 3. 8. Also *toc-sin*, q. v., *tuck-et*.

TOUCH-WOOD, wood used (like tinder) for taking fire from a spark. (F.—Teut.; and E.) We find 'Peace, *Touchwood!*' in Beaum. and Fletcher, Little French Lawyer, Act ii (Cleremont). Capt. Smith has: 'smal peeces of *touchwood*;' Works, p. 74. Apparently, *wood* that catches fire at the *touch* of a spark; cf. *touch-box*, box for priming, *touch-pan*, pan of a flint-lock musket, *touch-hole* of a gun. Probably influenced by ME. *tache*, in the sense of touchwood or tinder; Piers Plowman, C. xx. 211.

TOUCHY, apt to take offence. (F.—Low G.) 'You're *touchy* without all cause;' Beaum. and Fletcher, Maid's Tragedy, iii. 2 (Melantius). Doubtless often used as if derived from *touch*; but really a corruption of **Tetchy**, q. v.

TOUGH, firm, not easily broken, stiff, tenacious. (E.) ME. *tough*, Chaucer, Book of the Duchess, 531. AS. *tōh*, tough; Voc. 29. 39.+Du. *taai*, flexible, pliant, tough, viscous, clammy; Low G. *taa, tage, tau*, tough; G. *zähe, zäh*, tough, tenacious, viscous, MHG. *zæhe*, OHG. *zāhi*. β. Teut. type *tanχuz, later *tāhuz; allied to AS. *ge-teng-e*, close to, oppressive, OSax. *bi-teng-i*. oppressive. The orig. sense is 'holding tight' or 'tenacious;' cf. **Tongs**. ¶ The Teut. type regularly becomes *tanh, *tonh, *tōh* in AS.: cf. **Tooth**. Der. *tough-ly, tough-ness, tough-ish*; also *tough-en*, formed like *heighten*, &c.

TOUR, a going round, circuit, ramble. (F.—L.—Gk.) 'Tour, a travel or journey about a country;' Phillips, ed. 1706.—F. *tour*, 'a turn, round, compasse, .. a bout or walk;' Cot. Cf. Prov. *tors*, also *torns*, a turn; Bartsch, Chrest. Provençale. *Tour* is a verbal sb. from *tourner*, to turn; it is a short form of *tourn* (as the Prov. form shows), in the sense of 'a turn;' the final *n* being lost.—L. *tornum*, acc. of *tornus*.—Gk. τόρνος, a lathe. See **Turn**. Der. *tour-ist*.

TOURMALINE, the name of a certain mineral. (F.—Cingalese.) First brought from Ceylon by the Dutch in 1703; see tr. of Beckmann, Hist. of Inventions, ed. 1846, vol. i. 89.—F. *tourmaline*; formed from the native name in Ceylon, where it was called *tōramalli*. This name is explained (vaguely) as 'a general name for the cornelian;' Clough, Singhalese Dict. (1830), ii. 246.

TOURNAMENT, TOURNEY, a mock fight. (F.—L.—Gk.) So named from the swift *turning* of the horses in the combat. Cotgrave has F. *tournay*, 'a tourney;' Chaucer has *turneyinge*, sb., C. T. 2559 (A 2557). ME. *turnement*, Ancren Riwle, p. 390, l. 5 from bottom.—OF. *tornoiement*, a tournament (Burguy). Formed with suffix -*ment* (L. -*mentum*) from OF. *tornoier*, to joust.—OF. *tornoi*, a tourney, joust; properly, a turning about.—OF. *torner*, to turn; see **Turn**. 2. *Tourney* is from AF. *torney* = OF. *tornoi*, a tourney (above); see *torney* in Stat. Realm, i. 230.

TOURNIQUET, a bandage which is tightened by turning a stick round to check a flow of blood. (F.—L.—Gk.) Properly the stick itself. 'Tourniquet, a turn-still (*sic*); also the gripe-stick us'd by surgeons in cutting off an arm;' Phillips, ed. 1706.—F. *tourniquet*, 'the pin of a kind of fiddle, that which the fiddler turns with his hand as he plays;' Cot. He refers, apparently, to a sort of hurdygurdy, of which the F. name was *vielle*. 'Tourni-qu-et is formed, with dimin. suffixes, from *tourner*, to turn; see **Turn**. [N.B. turn-still = turn-stile, a sense of F. *tourniquet*.]

TOUSE, to pull about, tear or rend. (E.) In Shak. Meas. v. 313. Spenser has *touse* in the sense to worry, to tease; F. Q. ii. 11. 33. ME. *tūsen*, in comp. *tō-tūsen*, to pull about (Stratmann). It answers to EFries. *tūsen*, NFries. *tuse*, to tear, pull, rend. Cf. Low G. *tuseln*, G. *zausen*, to touse. Der. *tous-er*; spelt also *Towzer*, as a dog's name; also *tous-le, tuss-le*; and cf. *toss*.

TOUT, to look about, solicit custom. (E.) 'A *touter* is one who looks out for custom;' Wedgwood. We often shorten the sb. to *tout*. But *tout* is properly a verb, the same as prov. E. *toot*, ME. *toten*, to peep, look about, P. Plowman's Crede, 142, 168, 339, 425. 'Totehylle, Specula;' Prompt. Parv.; whence *Tothill*, a look-out hill

(W. *Twthill*, at Carnarvon). Also *toot*, to look, search, pry; Index to Parker Soc. publications; Tusser's Husbandry, § 94, st. 2; Peele, Arraignment of Paris, i. 2. See *Toot* in E.D.D., and in Nares. The latter has: 'The tradesmen of Tunbridge Wells were used formerly to hunt out customers on the road, at their arrival; and hence they were called *tooters*.' AS. *tōtian*, to project, stick out; hence, to peep out; 'þā heafdu *tōtodun* ūt' = the heads projected out; Ælfred, tr. of Gregory's Past. Care, c. xvi, ed. Sweet, p. 104, l. 5. The orig. sense was 'to project;' hence, to put out one's head, peep about, look all round; and finally, to *tout* for custom. Der. *tout-er*. ☞ '*Tout* and *touter* are found in no dictionaries but those of very recent date; yet these words were in use before 1754.' See S. Richardson, Correspondence, &c., vol. iii. p. 316;' F. Hall, Mod. English, p. 134. Distinct from *toot*, verb, to blow a horn.

TOW (1), to tug or pull a vessel along. (E.) ME. *towen, toȝen*; Allit. Poems, ed. Morris, C. 100; Layamon, 7536 (later text). AS. *togian*, to tug, draw (Toller); whence the sb. *toh-line*, a tow-line, tow-rope, Voc. 182. 32. Cf. OFries. *toga*, to pull about.+Icel. *toga*, to draw, pull; *tog*, a cord, a tow-rope; MHG. *zogen*, OHG. *zogōn*, to tear, pluck, pull. β. Derived from Teut. *tuh- (>*tug-), weak grade of *teuhan-, to draw; as seen in AS. *togen*, pp. of the strong verb *tēohan, tēon*, to pull, draw, which is cognate with G. *ziehen*, OHG. *ziohan*, Goth. *tiuhan*, to draw. All from the Teut. base TEUH, to draw (Fick, iii. 122); answering to √DEUK, as seen in L. *dūcere*, to draw. ¶ F. *touer*, to tow, is of Teut. origin. Der. *tow-boat, -line, -rope*; *tow-age*, Blount's Nomolexicon, 1691. And see *tie, tug*.

TOW (2), the coarse part of flax or hemp. (E.) ME. *tow* or *towe*, P. Plowman, B. xvii. 245; Tyrwhitt prints *tawe* in Chaucer, C. T. 3772 (A 3774). AS. *tow* (*tōw*?); it occurs in *tow-lic*, tow-like, fit for spinning. 'Textrinum opus, *towlic weorc*;' Voc. 125. 20; the next entries being 'Colus, *distæf*,' and 'Fusus, *spinl*,' i. e. distaff and spindle. Again, we find: '*tow-hūs* of wulle' = a tow-house or spinning-house for wool, id. 186. 29; see the footnote. And see *tow-cræft*, skill in spinning (Toller). *Tow* was, in fact, orig. the working or spinning itself, the operation of spinning; whence it came to be applied to the material wrought upon. Hence we find *getawa*, implements (Grein); and the word is brought into close connexion with E. *taw* and *tew*. See further under **Tool, Taw**.+ MDu. *touw*, or *werck*, 'towe;' Hexham; *touwe*, 'the instrument of a weaver,' *touwen*, 'to tanne leather,' i. e. to taw; id., Icel. *tō*, a tuft of wool for spinning; *vinna tō*, to dress wool. (Quite distinct from Icel. *tog*, goat's hair.) Cf. Low G. *tou, touw*, implements; also Goth. *taui*, a work, a thing made, *taujan*, to make. Similarly G. *werg* or *werk*, tow, is merely the same word as *werk*, a work.

TOWARD, TOWARDS, in the direction of. (E.) As in other cases, *towards* is a later form, due to adding the adverbial suffix -*es* (orig. the mark of a gen. case) to the shorter *toward*. In Layamon, 566, we have '*toward* Brutun' = toward Brutus; in l. 515, we have 'him *towardes* com' = he came towards him. The AS. *tōweard* is used as an adj. with the sense of 'future,' as in: 'on *tōweardre* worulde' = in the future world, in the life to come; Mark, x. 30. Hence was formed *tōweardes*, towards, used as a prep. with a dat. case, and commonly occurring *after* its case, as 'ēow *tōweardes*' = towards you, Ælfred, tr. of Boethius, c. xxxix. § 1 (b. iv. met. 4). β. Compounded of *tō*, to (see **To**); and *weard* in the sense of 'becoming' or 'tending to.' *Weard* only occurs as the latter element of several adjectives, such as *afweard* (lit. off-ward), absent; *æfterweard*, afterward; *andweard*, present; *foreweard*, forward, in front; *innanweard*, inward; *niðerweard*, netherward; *ufanweard*, upward, upward; *ūtanweard*, outward; *wiðerweard*, contrary; and in the adverbs *hiderweard*, hitherward, *þiderweard*, thitherward; see Ettmüller's Dict., p. 107. γ. Cognate with Icel. -*verðr*, similarly used in the adj. *ūtanverðr*, outward, and in other adjectives; also with MHG. -*wert*, whence G. *vorwärts*, forwards, and the like; also with Goth. -*wairths*, as in *andwairths*, present, 1 Cor. vii. 26; also allied to L. *uersus*, towards, which is often used after its case. δ. And just as L. *uersus* is from *uertere*, to turn, so AS. *weard* is from the cognate verb *weorþan* (pt. t. *wearð*), to become. See further under **Worth** (2), verb. ε. We may note that *ward* can be separated from *to*, as in *to you-ward* = toward you, 2 Cor. xiii. 3; see *Ward* in The Bible Word-book, ed. Eastwood and Wright. Also that *toward* is properly an adj. in AS., and commonly so used in later E., as opposed to *froward*; it is common in Shakespeare. Der. *toward-ly*, Timon, iii. 1. 37; *toward-ness, toward-li-ness*. And (with the suffix -*ward*) *after-ward, back-ward, east-ward, for-ward, fro-ward, home-ward, hither-ward, in-ward, nether-ward, north-ward, out-ward, south-ward, to-ward* (as above), *thither-ward, up-ward, west-ward, whither-ward*.

TOWEL, a cloth for wiping the skin after washing. (F.—OHG.) ME. *towaille*, Floriz and Blancheflur, 563; *towaille*, Chaucer, C. T.

14663 (B 3935).—F. *touaille*, 'a towel,' Cot.; OF. *toaille*. [Cf. Low L. *toacula*; Span. *toalla*; Ital. *tovaglia*. All of Teut. origin.] —OHG. *twahila, dwahila*, MHG. *dwehele*, G. *zwehle*, a towel.—OHG. *twahan*, MHG. *dwahen*, to wash.+Icel. *þvá* (pp. *þveginn*), to wash; Dan. *toe*; AS. *þwēan* (contr. for *þwahan*), to wash; Goth. *thwahan*, to wash. And cf. AS. *þwæle*, a towel (O. E. Texts); *þwēal*, a bath; Du. *dwaal*, a towel; *dweil*, a clout, whence prov. E. *dwile*, a clout, coarse rag for rubbing. β. All from Teut. base THWAH, to wash. N.B. The AF. form *towayle* occurs in A Nominale, ed. Skeat, l. 498. Der. *towell-ing*, stuff for making towels.

TOWER, a lofty building, fort, or part of a fort. (F.—L.—Gk.) Spelt *tur* in the A. S. Chron. an. 1097.—OF. *tur*, later *tour*, 'a tower;' Cot.—L. *turrem*, acc. of *turris*, a tower.—Gk. τύρσις, τύρρις, a tower, bastion. We also find Gael. *torr*, a hill or mountain of an abrupt or conical form, a lofty hill, eminence, mound, tower, castle; Irish *tor*, a castle; cf. prov. E. (Devon.) *tor*, a conical hill, a word of Celtic origin. 'Scopulum, *torr*;' Voc. 147. 38. Cf. Skt. *tōraṇa-*, an arch. Der. *tower*, verb; *tower-ed, tower-ing, tower-y*.

TOWN, a large village. (E.) The old sense is simply 'enclosure;' it was often applied (like Lowland Sc. *toon*) to a single farmhouse with its outbuildings, &c. ME. *toun*, Wyclif, Matt. xxii. 5. AS. *tūn*, Matt. xxii. 5; where the L. text has *uillam*. The orig. sense is 'fence;' whence the derived verb *tȳnan*, to enclose.+Du. *tuin*, a fence, hedge; Icel. *tūn*, an enclosure, a homestead, a dwelling-house; G. *zaun*, OHG. *zūn*, a hedge. β. All from Teut. type *tūnoz*, m., a hedge, enclosure. Cognate words appear in Irish and Gael. *dun*, a fortress, W. *din*, a hill-fort (whence *dinas*, a town); this Celtic word is conspicuous in many old place-names, such as *Augustodūnum, Camalo-dūnum*, &c. Lit. 'fastness;' allied to Irish *dur*, firm, strong, L. *dūrus*, hard, lasting; Gk. δύ-ναμις, strength. See **Dure**. Brugmann, i. § 112; ii. § 66. Der. *town-clerk, -crier, -hall, -house, -ship, -talk*; also *towns-man* (= *town's man*), *towns-folk* (= *town's-folk*). Also *town-ish*, Sir T. Wyat, Sat. i. 4.

TOXICOLOGY, the science which investigates poisons. (Gk.) Modern; not in Johnson. Coined from Gk. τοξικό-ν, poison for smearing arrows with; and -λογία, from λόγος, a discourse, λέγειν, to say (see **Logic**). Τοξικόν is neut. of τοξικός, adj., belonging to arrows or archery; from τόξον, a bow, lit. a piece of shaped wood. Perhaps from √TEKS, to cut; hew, shape; cf. Skt. *takṣh*, to cut. See **Technical**. Or allied to L. *taxus*, a yew. Der. *toxicologi-c-al, toxicolog-ist*.

TOXOPHILITE, a lover of archery. (Gk.) Coined from Gk. τόξο-ν, a bow, and φιλ-εῖν, to love; with suffix -*ite*, Gk. -ιτης. See above.

TOY, a plaything; also, as a verb, to trifle, dally. (Du.) 'Any silk, any thread, any *toys* for your head;' Wint. Tale, iv. 4. 326. 'On my head no *toy* But was her pattern;' Two Noble Kinsmen, i. 3. This is only a special sense. 'Any folysshe *toy*;' Barclay, Ship of Fools, i. 176. Palsgrave has: '*Toy*, a tryfell;' also, 'I *toye*, or tryfell with one, I deale nat substancyally with hym; I *toye*, I playe with one; He doth but *toye* with you, *Il ne fait que se jouer auecques vous*.' Not in ME.—Du. *tuig*, tools, utensils, implements, stuff, refuse, trash; which answers to Palsgrave's definition as 'a trifle.' The sense of plaything occurs in the comp. *speeltuig*, playthings, child's toys; lit. 'stuff to play with.' Sewel gives: '*Speeltuyg*, playtools, toys;' also: '*Op de tuy houden*, to amuse,' lit. to hold in trifling, toy with one; also: '*een tuyg op zy*, silver chains with a knife, cissars, pincushion, &c. as women wear,' which explains the Shakespearian usage.+Low G. *tüg*, used in all the senses of G. *zeug*; Icel. *tygi*, gear; Dan. *töi*, stuff, things, gear; *dumt töi*, stuff and nonsense, trash; whence *legetöi*, a plaything, a toy, from *lege* (= prov. E. *laik*), to play; Swed. *tyg*, gear, stuff, trash.+G. *zeug*, stuff, matter, materials, lumber, trash; whence *spielzeug*, toys; MHG. *ziuc*, stuff, materials. β. Connected by some with the strong Teut. verb *teuhan-* (Goth. *tiuhan*, AS. *téon*, OHG. *ziohan*, G. *ziehen*), to draw, cognate with L. *dūcere*, to lead (√DEUK); which may be correct. ¶ The pronunciation of *oy* in *toy* is an attempt at imitating the pronunciation of Du. *tuig*, just as *hoy*, a sloop, answers to the Flemish *hui*; see **Hoy** (1). Der. *toy-ish*.

TRACE (1), a track left by drawing anything along, a mark left, a footprint. (F.—L.) ME. *trace*, King Alisaunder, ed. Weber, 7771; Pricke of Conscience, 4349.—F. *trace*, 'a trace, footing, print of the foot; also, a path or tract;' Cot. [Cf. Ital. *traccia*, a trace, track; Span. *traza*, a first sketch, outline.] A verbal sb., from MF. *tracer*, verb, 'to trace, follow, pursue;' of which another form was MF. *trasser*, 'to delineate, score, trace out;' Cot. Cf. Ital. *tracciare*, to trace, devise; Span. *trazar*, to plan, sketch. These verbs are all formed (as if from a Late L. **trāctiare*) from *tract-us*, pp. of *trahere*, to draw, orig. to drag with violence. See **Trait**. Der. *trace*, verb, ME. *tracen*, Chaucer, Parl. of Foules, 54 (less common than the sb.), directly from F. *tracer*. to trace. as above: *trac-er*.

trace-able, trac-ing; *trac-er-y*, a coined word, in rather late use. Also (from L. *trahere*) *trace* (2), *tract* (1), *tract* (2), *tract-able, tract-ile, tract-ion, tract-ate, trail, train, trait, treat, treat-ise, treat-y*; also *abs-tract, at-tract, con-tract, de-tract, dis-tract, ex-tract, pro-tract, re-tract, sub-tract*; *en-treat, es-treat, mal-treat, por-trait, por-tray* or *pour-tray, re-treat*.

TRACE (2), one of the straps by which a vehicle is drawn. (F.—L.) 'Trace, horse harnesse, *trays*;' Palsgrave. MF. *traice*: 'Trayce, horsys harneys, Tenda, traxus, restis, trahale;' Prompt. Parv. Evidently from the OF. *trays*, cited by Palsgrave, which is a pl. form equivalent to F. *traits*, pl. of *trait*. In Walter de Bibbesworth, we find: '*Les trays* si unt braceroles,' and *braceroles* is glossed by 'henekes (?) of *trays*;' Wright, Vocab. i. 168. Golding has *trace* as a plural; tr. of Ovid, Met. ii.; fol. 16 b (1603). Cf. 'for v pair *trays*,' for the king's car; Privy Purse Exp. of Eliz. of York (1480), p. 123. Cotgrave gives as one sense of *trait* (which he spells *traict*) that of 'a teame-trace or trait, the cord or chain that runs between the horses, also the draught-tree of a caroch.' Thus *trace* = F. *traits*; so that *traces* is a double plural. See **Trait**.

TRACHEA, the wind-pipe. (L.—Gk.) In Phillips, ed. 1607.—L. *trachēa*; also *trachīa*. The latter form is given in White.—Gk. τραχεῖα, lit. 'the rough,' from the rings of gristle of which it is composed; τραχεῖα is the fem. of τραχύς, rough, rugged, harsh. Allied to τέ-τρηχ-α, perf. tense of θράσσειν, ταράσσειν, to disturb. Der. *trache-al*.

TRACK, a path, course. (F.—Teut.) Confused with *tract* in old authors; also with *trace* both in old and modern authors. Minsheu has: 'A *trace*, or *tracke*;' Cotgrave explains F. *trac* by 'a track, tract, or trace.' In Shak. Rich. II, iii. 3. 66, Rich. III, v. 3. 20, the folios have *tract* for *track*; and in Timon, i. 1. 50, the word *tract* is used in the sense of *trace*. 'The *trak* of his hors;' Malory, Morte Arthure, bk. x. c. 14. These words require peculiar care, because *trace* and *tract* are really connected, but *track* is not of L. origin, and quite distinct from the other two words.—F. *trac*, 'a track, tract, or trace, a beaten way or path, a trade or course.' Cf. Norm. dial. *trac*, a track; Walloon *trak*, a stage, or distance along a road. The sense of 'beaten track' is the right one; we still use that very phrase. Of Teut. origin.—MDu. *treck*, Du. *trek*, a draught; from *trekken*, to draw, pull, tow, travel, march, &c., MDu. *trecken*, 'to drawe, pull, or hale,' Hexham; also MHG. *trecken*, to draw, a secondary verb formed from the OHG. strong verb *trehhan*, to scrape, shove, draw. As the last is a strong verb, we see that *track* is quite independent of the L. *trahere*. Note that NFries. has *tracke* for Du. *trekken*. Der. *track*, verb; *track-less*, Cowley, The Muse, l. 25.

TRACT (1), continued duration, a region. (L.) Often confused both with *trace* and *track*; it is related to the former *only*; see **Trace** (1). 'This in *tracte* of tyme made hym welthy:' Fabyan, Chron. c. 56.—L. *tractus*, a drawing out; the course of a river, a tract or region.—L. *tractus*, pp. of *trahere*, to draw; see **Trace** (1). And see **Tractable**.

TRACT (2), a short treatise. (L.) An abbreviation for *tractate*, which is now little used. 'Tractate, a treatise;' Blount's Gloss., ed. 1674.—L. *tractātum*, acc. of *tractātus*, a handling, also a treatise, tractate, or tract. See **Tractable**. Der. *tract-ar-i-an*, one who holds opinions such as were propounded in 'Tracts for the Times,' of which 90 numbers were published, A. D. 1833–1841; see Haydn, Dict. of Dates.

TRACTABLE, easily managed, docile. (L.) In Shak. 1 Hen. IV, iii. 3. 194.—L. *tractābilis*, manageable, easily wrought.—L. *tractāre*, to handle, frequent. of *trahere* (pp. *tractus*), to draw. See **Trace** (1). Der. *tractabl-y, tractable-ness, tractabili-ty*. Also (like L. pp. *tractus*) *tract-ile*, that may be drawn out; *tract-ion*, from F. *traction*, 'a draught or extraction,' Cot.; *tract-ive*, drawing or pulling; *tract-or* (see Webster). Also *tract-ate*, for which see **Tract** (2).

TRADE, way of life, occupation, commerce. (E.) 'Properly that path which we *tread*, and thus the ever recurring habit and manner of our life;' Trench, Select Glossary. It once meant, literally, a *path*; 'A common *trade*, to passe through Priams house;' Surrey, tr. of Virgil, Æn. ii. 593. Not common; the usual ME. words are *tred* and *trod*, both in the sense of footmark, Ancren Riwle, p. 380, note *g*. But we find the exact form in the ME. *trade*, Sir Guy (Caius MS.), 4731, the prov. E. *trade* (E. D. D.), and Low G. *trade*, Swed. dial. *trad*, a beaten track; from the 2nd grade of the vb. All from AS. *tredan*, to tread; see **Tread**. Der. *trades-man*, i. e. *trade's-man*, one who follows a trade; *trades-woman*; *trades-union* (= either *trade's* union or *trades'* union). Also *trade*, vb., *trad-ed*, K. John, iv. 3. 109; *trad-er*, 1 Hen. IV, i. 2. 141. Also *trade-wind*, a wind blowing in a constant direction, formed from the phr. *to blow trade* = to blow always in the same course; 'the wind *blowing trade*,' Hakluyt's Voyages, iii. 849; the word *trade-wind* is in Dryden, Annus Mirabilis, last line but one.

TRADITION, the handing down to posterity of unwritten practices or opinions. (L.) ME. *tradicioun,* Wyclif, Col. ii. 8. Formed directly from L. *trāditio,* a surrender, delivery, tradition (Col. ii. 8). [The F. form of the word gave us our word *treason.*] Cf. L. *trādit-us,* pp. of *trādere,* to deliver; see **Traitor.** Der. *tradition-al.* Doublet, *treason.*

TRADUCE, to defame. (L.) In Shak. All's Well, ii. 1. 175. In the Prologue to the Golden Boke, *traduce* occurs in the sense of *translate,* and *traduction* is *translation.*—L. *trādūcere,* to lead across, transfer, derive; also, to divulge, convict, prove guilty (whence our use to defame).—L. *trā-,* for *trans,* across; and *dūcere,* to lead; see **Trans-** and **Duke.** Der. *traduc-er.*

TRAFFIC, to trade, exchange, barter. (F.—Ital.) In Shak. Timon, i. 1. 158; Macb. iii. 5. 4; we have also the sb. *traffic,* spelt *trafficke* in Spenser, F. Q. vi. 11. 9.—F. *trafiquer,* 'to traffick, trade;' Cot. We find also F. *trafique,* sb. 'traffick;' id.—Ital. *trafficare,* to traffick, manage (*traficare* in Florio). Cf. Span. *traficare, trafagar;* Port. *traficar, trafeguear,* to traffic, to cheat. Also Ital. *traffico* (*trafico* in Florio), Span. *trafico, trafago,* traffic, careful management; Port. *trafico, trafego,* traffic. β. Origin unknown. It has been proposed to derive it from Heb. *traffik,* a late Heb. rendering of late Gk. τροπαϊκός; which again is a Gk. rendering of L. *uictoriātus,* the name of a silver coin bearing the figure of Victory (Lewis). See Athenæum, Apr. 7, 1900. Der. *traffic,* sb.; *traffick-er,* Merch. Ven. i. 1. 12.

TRAGACANTH, a gum obtained from several shrubs of the genus *Astragalus.* (F.—L.—Gk.) In Bailey, vol. ii (1731), who explains it by 'gum dragon;' where *dragon* is due to the old name *dragagant,* from MF. *dragagant* in Cotgrave.—F. *tragacanthe* (Hatzfeld), the name of a shrub.—L. *tragacantha,* the tragacanth-shrub; cf. *tragacanthum,* also *dragantum,* gum tragacanth.—Gk. *tragacantha,* astragalus, lit. 'goat-thorn.'—Gk. τράγ-ος, a goat; and ἄκανθα, a thorn, from ἀκ-ίς, a sharp point.

TRAGEDY, a species of drama of a lofty and mournful cast. (F.—L.—Gk.) ME. *tragédie;* see Chaucer's definition of it, C. T. 13979 (B 3163).—MF. *tragedie,* 'a tragedy;' Cot.—L. *tragœdia.*—Gk. τραγῳδία, a tragedy. 'There is no question that *tragedy* is *the song of the goat;* but *why* the song of the goat, whether because a goat was the prize for the best performance of that song in which the germs of the future tragedy lay, or because the first actors were dressed, like satyrs, in goat-skins, is a question which has stirred abundant discussion, and will remain unsettled to the end;' Trench, Study of Words, lect. v. The latter theory now finds most favour. A third theory is that a goat was sacrificed at the singing of the song; a goat, as being the spoiler of vines, was a fitting sacrifice at the feasts of Dionysus. In any case, the etymology is certain.—Gk. τραγῳδός, lit. 'a goat-singer,' a tragic poet and singer.—Gk. τράγ-ος, a he-goat; and ῳδός, a singer, contracted from ἀοιδός; see **Ode.** Der. *tragedi-an,* All's Well, iv. 3. 299, apparently a coined word, not borrowed from French. Also *trag-ic,* 2 Hen. IV, i. 1. 61, from F. *tragique,* 'tragicall, tragick,' Cot., L. *tragicus,* Gk. τραγικός, goatish, tragic, from τράγ-ος, a goat. Hence *tragic-al, -al-ly, -al-ness.*

TRAIL, to draw along the ground, to hunt by tracking. (F.—L.) ME. *trailen.* In Wyclif, Esther, xv. 7, later version, we find: 'but the tother of the seruauntessis suede the ladi, and bar vp the clothis *fletinge* doun in-to the erthe;' where, for *fletinge,* some MSS. have *trailinge,* and the earlier version has *flowende* = flowing. Cf. 'Braunches doo *traile;*' Palladius, iii. 289, p. 71. '*Traylyn* as cloþys, Segmento;' Prompt. Parv. We have also ME. *traile,* sb. '*Trayle,* or trayne of a clothe;' Prompt. Parv. So also: '*Trayle,* sledde [sledge], traha; to *Trayle,* trahere,' Levins, ed. 1570. John de Garlande, in the 13th cent., gives a list of 'instrumenta mulieribus convenientia;' one of these is *trahale,* of which he says: '*Trahale* dicitur a traho, Gallice *traail;*' Wright's Voc. i. 134. Palsgrave has: 'I *trayle,* lyke as a gowne dothe behynde on the grounde;' also 'I *trayle,* as one *trayleth* an other behynde or at a horse-tayle.' —OF. *trailler,* to tow a boat (Supp. to Godefroy); MF. *trailler,* to wind a yarn; also, to traile a deer, or hunt him upon a cold sent;' Cot.—OF. *traille,* a tow-rope (Supp. to Godefroy); also, a ferry-boat with a cord.—L. *trāgula,* a drag-net, sledge; cf. *traha,* a sledge.—L. *trahere,* to draw; see **Trait.** And cf. **Train.** Cf. MDu. *treylen,* 'to drawe, or dragge a boate with a cord,' Hexham; borrowed (like MDu. *treyn,* a train) from French.

TRAILBASTON, a law-term. (F.—L.) See Blount's Nomo-lexicon, ed. 1691, and Spelman. There were *justices of traylbaston,* appointed by Edw. I. [' The common people in those days called them *tray-baston,* quod sonat *trahe baculum;*' Bl unt. Roquefort divides the word as *tray-le-baston.* It would seem that the word was considered as a compound of OF. *tray* (=L. *trahe*), give up, and *baston,* a wand of office, because many unjust officers were deprived of their offices.] But this view is proved to be wrong by the passage from Langtoft's Chronicle printed in Polit. Songs, ed. Wright, p. 318; on which see Wright's note, p. 383. The Anglo-F. word was *traylbastoun, traylebastoun* or *trayllebastoun,* meaning 'trail-stick' or 'stick-carrier;' (id. pp. 231, 233, 319); and the name was given to a particular set of lawless men, who carried sticks, and committed acts of violence. Against these the *articles of trailbaston* were directed; and the *justices of trailbaston* tried them. The Outlaw's Song (Polit. Songs, p. 231) is explicit; he says that these *articles* were unreasonable; for if he merely gives his servant a buffet or two, the servant will have him arrested, and he will be heavily fined. Mr. Wright notes that some have supposed (quite wrongly) that the name was given, not to the outlaws, but the judges. For the form of the word, compare MDu. *kolf-drager,* a sergeant, lit. 'club-bearer.' See **Trail** and **Baton.**

TRAIN, the hinder part of a trailing dress, a retinue, series, line of gun-powder, line of carriages; as a verb, to trail, to allure, educate, discipline. (F.—L.) ME. *train,* sb., spelt *trayn,* with the sense of plot, Rob. of Brunne, tr. of Langtoft, p. 295, l. 22; *trayne,* id. p. 263, l. 23; 'treson and *trayne,*' Morte Arthure, ed. Brock, 4192; ME. *traynen,* verb, to entice, id. 1683.—F. *train,* m., 'a great man's retinue, the train or hinder part of a beast; .. work, dealing, trade, practise;' Cot. Also *traine,* f., 'a sled, a drag or dray without wheels, a drag-net,' id. Also *trainer,* verb, 'to traile, drag, draw;' id. OF. *trahin, train,* a train of men; *trahiner, traïner,* verb; cf. Late L. *trahināre,* to drag; occurring A.D. 1268. —Late L. *tragināre,* to draw along (Schwan); evidently founded upon L. *trahere,* to draw; see **Trace, Trail.** Cf. AF. *treine,* pp. dragged along, Liber Custumarum, p. 284. Der. *train-er; train-band,* i.e. *train'd band,* a band of trained men, Cowper, John Gilpin, st. 1, and used by Dryden and Clarendon (Todd); *train-bear-er.* ¶ But not *train-oil.*

TRAIN-OIL, oil procured from the blubber or fat of whales by boiling. (Hybrid; Du.; *and* F.—L.—Gk.) Spelt *trane-oyle,* Hakluyt's Voyages, i. 477, last line; *trayne oyle,* Arnold's Chron. p. 236. In Hexham's Du. Dict., ed. 1658, we find: '*Traen,* trayne-oile made of the fat of whales.' Also: '*traen,* a tear; liquor pressed out by the fire.' Cf. mod. Du. *traan,* a tear; *traan,* train-oil. We thus see that the lit. sense of *train* is 'tear,' then, a drop of liquor forced out by fire; and lastly, we have *train-oil,* or oil forced out by boiling. Cf. Dan. and Swed. *tran,* train-oil, blubber, G. *thran,* all borrowed from Dutch; cf. G. *thräne,* a tear, also a drop exuding from a vine when cut. So also Low G. *traan,* train-oil; *trane,* a tear; very well explained in the Bremen Wörterbuch. Similarly, we use E. *tear* in the sense of 'a drop' of some balsams and resins, &c. β. The Du. *traan* (equivalent to OHG. *trahan* below) is the only form for 'tear' used in Dutch; the G. *thräne* is really a pl. form, due to MHG. *trähene,* pl. of *trahen,* OHG. *trahan,* a tear. It has been thought that the OHG. *trahan* is allied to E. *tear;* but the connexion is not clear. ¶ It thus appears that *train-oil* is a tautological expression; accordingly, we find *trane,* train-oil, in Ash's Dict., ed. 1775.

TRAIT, a feature. (F.—L.) Given in Johnson, with the remark 'scarcely English.'—F. *trait,* 'a draught, line, streak, stroak,' Cot. He also gives the MF. spelling *traict.*—F. *trait,* formerly also *traict,* pp. of *traire,* to draw.—L. *tractus,* pp. of *trahere,* to draw; see **Trace** (1).

TRAITOR, one who betrays, a deceiver. (F.—L.) ME. *traitour,* spelt *traitoure,* Rob. of Brunne, tr. of Langtoft, p. 61, l. 12; *treitur,* O. Eng. Homilies, i. 279, l. 22.—OF. *traitor, traiteur,* a traitor.—L. *trāditōrem,* acc. of *trāditor,* one who betrays.—L. *trādere,* to hand over, deliver, betray.—L. *trā-,* for *trans,* across, over; and *-dere,* for *dare,* to give; (hence *trā-didī,* pt. t., is due to *dedī,* I gave). See **Trans-** and **Date.** Der. *traitor-ous,* 1 Hen. VI, iv. 1. 173; *traitor-ous-ly; traitr-ess,* All's Well, i. 1. 184. From the same source are *tradit-ion, treason, be-tray.*

TRAJECTORY, the curve which a body describes when projected. (F.—L.) In Phillips, ed. 1706. ⌐Suggested by MF. *trajec-toire,* 'casting, thrusting, sending, transporting;' Cot. Formed as if from a L. **trāiectorius,* belonging to projection; formed from *trā-iectus,* pp. of *trāicere* (*trājicere*), to throw, cast, or fling over or across.—L. *trā-,* for *trans,* across; and *iacere,* to cast. See **Trans-** and **Jet.** Der. *traject,* which is perhaps the right reading for *tranect* in Merch. of Ven. iii. 4. 53; from MF. *traject,* 'a ferry, a passage over,' Cot., which from L. *trāiectus,* a passage over. Shakespeare would have written *traiect,* which was made into *tranect,* a false form.

TRAM, a coal-waggon, a carriage for passengers running on iron rails. (Scand.) There have been frequent inquiries about this word; see Notes and Queries, 2 Ser. v. 128, xii. 229, 276, 358; 4 Ser. xii. 299, 420; 6 Ser. ii. 225, 356. A tram is an old Northern word for a coal-waggon, esp. such a one as ran upon rails. In N. and Q., 2 Ser. xii. 276, J. N. quoted an Act of Parliament for the year 1794, for the construction of 'an iron *dram-road, tram-road*, or railway' between Cardiff and Merthyr Tydvil; but the date 1794 should have been 1820. In N. and Q., 6 S. ii. 356, A. Wallis stated that 'tramways were in use in Derbyshire before 1790; one of planks and log-sleepers was laid between Shipley coal-pit and the wharf near Newmansleys, a distance of 1½ miles, and was discontinued in the above year.' [About A.D. 1800, a Mr. Benjamin Outram made certain improvements in connexion with railways for common vehicles, which gave rise to the fiction (ever since industriously circulated) that *tram-road* is short for *Outram road*, in ignorance of the fact that the accent alone is sufficient to show that *Outram*, if shortened to *one* syllable, must become *Out* rather than *ram* or *tram*.] Brockett's Glossary (3rd ed. 1846) explains that a *tram* is the Northern word for 'a small carriage *on four wheels*, so distinguished from a sledge. It is used in coal-mines to bring the coals from the hewers to the crane.' β. The word is clearly the same as Lowland Scotch *tram*, '(1) the shaft of a cart or carriage of any kind, (2) a beam or bar,' Jamieson. Dunbar has *barrow-tram*; Of the same James Dog, l. 19. Cf. prov. E. *tram*, a small milk-bench (Halliwell); which was orig. a plank of wood. It was prob. used first of the shaft of a small carriage, and then applied to the small carriage itself, esp. such a one as was pushed or drawn by men or boys in coal-pits. This notion is borne out by the cognate Low G. *traam*, a word particularly used of the handles of a wheel-barrow or the handles by which a kind of sledge was pushed; Bremen Wörterbuch, ed. 1771. In N. and Q., 6 S. ii. 498, J. H. Clark notes that 'the amendinge of the higheway or *tram* from the Weste ende of Bridgegait, in Barnard Castle' occurs in a will dated 1555; see Surtees Soc. Publications, vol. xxxviii. p. 37. Here a *tram* prob. means a log-road. The word is Scandinavian.—Norw. *tram*, a doorstep (of wood); *traam*, a frame; Swed. dial. *tromm*, a log, stock of a tree; also a summer-sledge (*sommarsläde*); also *trömm, trumm* (Rietz); MSwed. *trām, trum*, a piece of a large tree, cut up into logs. The orig. sense is clearly a beam or bar of cut wood, hence a shaft of a sledge or cart, or even the sledge itself. Cf. EFries. *trame*, a step of a ladder, handle of a barrow; Low G. *traam*, a balk, beam, esp. one of the handles of a wheel-barrow, as above; also MDu. *drom*, a beam (obsolete); Hexham. Also OHG. *drām, trām*, a beam, once a common word; see Grimm's Dict. ii. 1331, 1332. The last form may account for the variation *dram-road*, in the Act of Parliament cited above; and it has been already observed that a *dramroad* or *tramroad* might also be explained as a *log-road*. γ. The comparison of Swed. *tromm* with Du. *drom* shows that the original Low G. initial letter must have been *th*; which is proved by the Icel. *þram-valr*, lit. 'a beam-hawk,' a poet. word for a ship. δ. The Swed. dial. *trumm* (above) further resembles G. *trumm*, lump, stump, end, thrum, fragment, and suggests a connexion with **Thrum** (1), to which Icel. *þram-* is related by gradation. Hence, the orig. sense was 'end;' then fragment, bit, lump, log, plank, shaft, &c. **Der.** *tram-road, -way*.

TRAMMEL, a net, shackle, anything that confines or restrains. (F.—L.) ME. *tramayle*, 'grete nette for fyschynge;' Prompt. Parv. Spenser has *tramels*, nets for the hair, F. Q. ii. 2. 15.—MF. *tramail*, 'a tramell, or a net for partridges;' Cot. Cf. F. *trameau* (answering to an older form **tramel*), 'a kind of drag-net for fish, a trammell net for fowle;' this comes still nearer to Spenser's *tramel*. Cf. Ital. *tramaglio*, a drag-net, trammel; Port. *trasmalho*, Span. *trasmallo*, a trammel or net; Gascon *tramail*; mod. F. *trémail*.—Late L. *tramacula, tramagula*, a trammel, occurring in the Lex Salica, ed. Hessels and Kern, xxvii. 20, col. 154; cf. coll. 158, 161. The word has numerous other forms, such as *tremacle, tremale, trimacle*, &c., in other texts of the Lex Salica. Kern remarks: '*tremacle*, &c. is a diminutive, more or less Latinised. The Frankish word must have differed but slightly, if at all, from the Drenthian (N. Saxon) *treemke* (for *tremike, tramke*), a trammel. Both the English and Drenthian word point to a simplex *trami* or *tramia*;' col. 501. β. This assumes the word to be Teutonic, yet brings us back to no intelligible Teut. base; nor does it account for the Ital. form. Diez takes it to be Latin, and explains *tremacula* from L. *tri-*, thrice, three times, and *macula*, a mesh or net, as if it meant treble-mesh or treble-net. He remarks that a similar explanation applies to **Trellis**, q.v. [This account is accepted, without question, by Scheler, Littré, and Hatzfeld.] It is to be further noted that, according to Diez, the Piedmontese *trimaj* is explained by Zalli to mean a fish-net or bird-net made of *three layers* of net of different-sized meshes; and that Cherubini and Patriarchi make similar remarks concerning the Milanese *tremagg* and Venetian *tramagio*. γ. As to L. *tri-*, see **Three**; as to L. *macula*, see **Mail** (1). The Span. *trasmallo* is an altered form, as if from *trans maculam*, across the net, which is not very intelligible. See Körting, § 9739.

TRAMONTANE, foreign. (F.—Ital.—L.) The word is pro-

perly Italian, and only intelligible from an Italian point of view; it was applied to men who lived *beyond the mountains*, i. e. in France, Switzerland, Spain, &c. It came to us through the French, and was at first spelt *tramountain*. 'The Italians account all *tramountain* doctors but apothecaries in comparison of themselves;' Fuller, Worthies, Hertfordshire (R.).—MF. *tramontain*, 'northerly;' Cot. —Ital. *tramontano*, pl. *tramontani*, 'those folkes that dwell beyond the mountaines;' Florio.—L. *transmontānus*, beyond the mountains. —L. *trans*, beyond; and *mont-*, stem of *mons*, a mountain; see **Trans-** and **Mountain**. Cf. **Ultramontane**.

TRAMP, to tread, stamp. (E.) ME. *trampen*. '*Trampelyn, trampyn*, Tero;' Prompt. Parv. 'He *trampith* with the foot;' Wyclif, Prov. vi. 13. Not in AS., but prob. E.; it is found in G. and Low G., whence the Scand. forms. Cf. Low G. and G. *trampen, trampeln*, to stamp; Dan. *trampe*, Swed. *trampa*, to tread, trample on. From the Teut. base TRAMP, to tread, occurring as the 2nd grade of the Goth. strong verb *ana-trimpan*. 'Managei *ana-tramp* ina' = the multitude pressed upon him, lit. trampled on him, Luke, v. 1. β. This is a nasalised form of the Teut. base TRAP, to tread; see **Trap** (1). **Der.** *tramp*, sb., a journey on foot; *tramp-er*, a vagrant (see Johnson); also *tramp*, a shortened familiar form of *tramper*, both forms being given in Grose's Dict. of the Vulgar Tongue, 1790. And see *tramᵇ-le*.

TRAMPLE, to tread under foot. (E.) ME. *trampelen*; Prompt. Parv. The frequentative of **Tramp**, q.v. The sense is, accordingly, 'to keep on treading upon.' Cf. Low G. *trampeln*, G. *trampeln*, to trample, stamp; from Low G. and G. *trampen*, to tramp or stamp.

TRAM-ROAD, TRAM-WAY; see **Tram**.

TRANCE, catalepsy, ecstasy, loss of self-consciousness. (F.—L.) ME. *trance*, Chaucer, C. T., A 1572.—F. *transe*, 'extreme fear, dread, ... a trance or swoon;' Cot. A verbal sb. from the OF. *transir*, of which Cot. gives the pp. *transi*, 'fallen into a trance or sown, astonied, amazed, half dead.'—L. *transire*, to go or pass over; whence Ital. *transire*, 'to goe foorth, passe ouer; .. also to fall in a swoune, to dye or gaspe the last;' Florio. [This shows that *transire* came to have the sense of 'die' or 'swoon;' similarly the OF. *trespasser* (our *trespass*) commonly means 'to die.']—L. *trans*, across; and *ire*, to go; see **Transit**. **Der.** *en-trance* (2). Also *tranc-ed*, K. Lear, v. 3. 218.

TRANQUIL, quiet, peaceful. (F.—L.) In Shak. Oth. iii. 3. 348. [The sb. *tranquillity* is in much earlier use; we find ME. *tranquillitee*, Chaucer, tr. of Boethius, b. ii. pr. 4, l. 99.]—F. *tranquille*, 'calm;' Cot.—L. *tranquillus*, calm, quiet, still. Prob. associated with *qui-ēs*, rest; compare *-quillus* with E. *while*. **Der.** *tranquil-ly*; *tranquill-i-ty*, from F. *tranquilité*, 'tranquillity,' Cot., from L. acc. *tranquillitātem*. Also *tranquill-ise*, Thomson, Castle of Indolence, c. ii. st. 19.

TRANS-, beyond, across, over. (L.) L. *trans-*, prefix; also as prep. *trans*, beyond. *Trans* is the pres. part. of a verb **trāre*, to cross, go beyond, only occurring in *in-trāre, ex-trāre, pene-trāre*. Cf. Skt. *tara-*, a crossing over. Brugmann, ii. § 579. Allied to **Term**. β. The comp. suffix *-ter* (in Latin) is prob. from the same root; cf. *præ-ter, sub-ter, in-ter-ior*, &c. In composition, *trans-* becomes *tran-* in *tran-quil, tran-scend, tran-scribe, tran-sept, tran-spire, tran-substantiate*; and *tra-* in *tra-dition, tra-duce, tra-jectory, tramontane* (though the last is only an Ital., not a Latin spelling); also in *tra-verse, tra-vesty*.

TRANSACTION, the management of an affair. (F.—L.) In Cotgrave.—F. *transaction*, 'a transaction, accord, agreement;' Cot. —L. *transactiōnem*, acc. of *transactio*, a completion, an agreement; cf. L. *transactus*, pp. of *transigere*, to drive or thrust through, also to settle a matter, complete a business.—L. *trans*, across, through; and *agere*, to drive; see **Trans-** and **Act**. **Der.** *transact-or*, in Cot., to translate F. *transacteur*, but perhaps directly from L. *transactor*, a manager. Hence was evolved the verb *transact*, Milton, P. L. vi. 286.

TRANS-ALPINE, beyond the Alps. (F.—L.) '*Transalpine* garbs;' Beaum. and Fletcher, The Coxcomb, i. 1.—F. *transalpin*, 'forraign;' Cot.—L. *transalpīnus*, beyond the Alps.—L. *trans*, beyond; and *Alp-*, stem of *Alpēs*, the Alps; with suffix *-īnus*. See **Trans-** and **Alp**. ¶ So also *trans-atlantic*, a coined word, 'used by Sir W. Jones in 1782; see Memoirs, &c., p. 217;' F. Hall, Mod. English, p. 275.

TRANSCEND, to surmount, surpass. (L.) In Gawain Douglas, Palace of Honour, pt. ii. st. 18.—L. *transcendere*, to climb over, surpass.—L. *trans*, beyond; and *scandere*, to climb. **Der.** *transcend-ent*, used by Cot. to translate F. *transcendant*; *transcend-ent-ly*, *transcendence*, All's Well, ii. 3. 40, from L. sb. *transcendentia*; *transcend-ent-al*, given as a mathematical term in Phillips, ed. 1706; *transcend-ent-al-ly, -ism, -ist*.

TRANSCRIBE, to copy out. (L.) In Minsheu, ed. 1627; and in Cot., to translate F. *transcrire.* — L. *transcrĭbere* (pp. *transcriptus*), to transfer in writing, copy from one book into another. — L. *trans,* across, over; and *scrĭbere,* to write; see **Trans-** and **Scribe**. Der. *transcrib-er,* Tatler, no. 271, § 3; *transcript,* in Minsheu, from L. pp. *transcriptus; transcript-ion.*

TRANSEPT, the part of a church at right angles to the nave. (L.) Lit. 'a cross-enclosure.' Not an old word; and coined. Oddly spelt *transcept* in Wood's Fasti Oxonienses, vol. ii. (R.); of which the first edition appeared in 1691–2. — L. *tran-,* for *trans,* across; and *septum,* an enclosure. *Septum* is from *septus,* pp. of *sēpīre* or *sæpīre,* to enclose; from *sæpēs,* a hedge.

TRANSFER, to transport, convey to another place. (L.) In Shak. Sonnet 137. Cot. gives F. pp. *transferé,* 'transferred;' but the E. word was prob. directly from L. *transferre,* to transport, transfer. — L. *trans,* across; and *ferre,* to carry, cognate with E. *bear.* See **Trans-** and **Bear** (1). Der. *transfer-able,* also spelt *transferr-ible* (quite needless); *transfer-ence, transfer-ee.*

TRANSFIGURE, to change the appearance of. (F.–L.) ME. *transfiguren,* Chaucer, C. T. 1107 (A 1105). — F. *transfigurer,* 'to transfigure;' Cot. — L. *transfĭgūrāre,* to change the figure of. — L. *trans,* across (hence implying change); and *figūra,* figure, outward appearance. See **Trans-** and **Figure**. Der. *transfigurat-ion,* from F. *transfiguration,* 'a transfiguration,' Cot., from L. acc. *transfigūrātiōnem.*

TRANSFIX, to fix by piercing through. (L.) 'Quite through *transfixed* with a deadly dart;' Spenser, F. Q. iii. 12. 21. — L. *transfixus,* pp. of *transfĭgere,* to thrust through. See **Trans-** and **Fix**.

TRANSFORM, to change the form of. (F.–L.) ME. *transformen,* Wyclif, 2 Cor. iii. 18. — F. *transformer,* 'to transform;' Cot. — L. *transfōrmāre,* to change the form of. — L. *trans,* across (implying change); and *forma,* form. See **Trans-** and **Form**. Der. *transformat-ion,* from F. *transformation,* 'a transformation,' Cot., from L. acc. *transformātiōnem.*

TRANSFUSE, to cause to pass from one person or part into another, to make to imbibe. (L.) In Milton, P. L. iii. 389, vi. 704. — L. *transfūsus,* pp. of *transfundere,* to pour out of one vessel into another, to decant, transfuse. — L. *trans,* across; and *fundere,* to pour; see **Trans-** and **Fuse**. Der. *transfus-ion.*

TRANSGRESSION, violation of a law, sin. (F.–L.) 'For the rage of my *transgression;*' Lydgate, Storie of Thebes, pt. iii (How the Child was slain by a serpent). — F. *transgression,* 'a transgression, trespasse;' Cot. — L. *transgressiōnem,* acc. of *transgressio,* a passing over, transposition, also a transgression of the law; cf. *transgressus,* pp. of *transgredī,* to step over, pass over. — L. *trans,* across; and *gradī,* to step, walk; see **Trans-** and **Grade**. Der. *transgress-or,* formerly *transgressour,* Rom. of Partenay, Chaucer. an. 1180, ed. Ellis, p. 299, from F. *transgresseur,* 'a transgressor,' Cot., from L. acc. *transgressōrem.* Hence was made *transgress,* verb, used by Tyndall, Works, p. 224, col. 1, l. 3 from bottom. ☞ Observe *trespass,* a similar formation to *trans-gress.*

TRANSIENT, passing away, not lasting. (L.) In Milton, P. L. xii. 554. Suggested by L. *transiens,* of which the oblique-case stem is *transeunt-,* not *transient-.* [Cf. *ambient,* from *ambire,* which is conjugated regularly.] *Transiens* is the pres. part. of *transīre,* to go across, to pass away. — L. *trans,* across; and *īre,* to go, from √EI, to go. See **Trans-** and **Itinerant**. Der. *transient-ly, -ness.* Also (like pp. *transitus*) *transit,* in Phillips, ed. 1706, shortened from L. *transĭtus,* a passing over; *transit-ion,* Phillips, from L. acc. *transitiōnem,* a passing over, a transition; *transit-ion-al; transit-ive,* from L. *transĭtīuus,* a term applied to a transitive or active verb; *transit-ive-ly, -ness; transit-or-y,* Lydgate, Minor Poems, p. 128, suggested by F. *transitoire,* 'transitory,' Cot., from L. *transĭtōrius,* liable to pass away, passing away; *transit-or-i-ly, -ness.* And see *trance.*

TRANSLATE, to transfer, move to another place, to render into another language. (F.–L.) ME. *translaten,* to remove, Gower, C. A. i. 261; bk. ii. 3044. — F. *translater,* 'to translate, .. reduce, or remove;' Cot. — Late L. *translātāre,* to translate, in use in the 12th century. — L. *translātus,* transferred; used as the pp. of *transferre,* but really from a different root. — L. *trans,* across; and *lātus,* carried, borne, for **tlātus,* from √TEL, to lift, bear, whence L. *tollere,* to lift. See **Trans-** and **Tolerate**. Der. *translat-ion,* ME. *translacioun,* Chaucer, C. T. 15493 (G 25), from F. *translation,* 'a translation,' Cot., from L. acc. *translātio,* a transference, transferring.

TRANSLUCENT, clear, allowing light to pass through. (L.) In Milton, Comus, 861. — L. *translūcent-,* stem of pres. part. of *translūcēre,* to shine through. — L. *trans,* through; and *lūcēre,* to shine; see **Trans-** and **Lucid**. Der. *translucent-ly, translucence.*

TRANSMARINE, beyond the sea. (L.) In Blount's Gloss., ed. 1674. — L. *transmarīnus,* beyond sea. — L. *trans,* beyond; and *mar-e,* sea; with suffix *-īnus.* See **Trans-** and **Marine**.

TRANSMIGRATION, the passing into another country or state of existence. (F.–L.) Spelt *transmygracioun,* Trevisa, i. 33, l. 20. — F. *transmigration,* 'a transmigration, a flitting or shifting of aboad;' Cot. — L. *transmigrātiōnem,* acc. of *transmigrātio,* a removing from one country to another. — L. *transmigrāre,* to migrate across, from one place to another. See **Trans-** and **Migrate**. Der. (from L. pp. *transmigrātus*) *transmigrate,* Antony, ii. 7. 51; *transmigrat-or, transmigrat-or-y.*

TRANSMIT, to cause or suffer to pass through, to deliver. (L.) In Holland, tr. of Plutarch, p. 576 (R.). — L. *transmittere,* to cause to go across, send over, dispatch, transmit. — L. *trans,* across; and *mittere,* to send; see **Trans-** and **Mission**. Der. *transmitt-al, transmitt-er; transmiss-ion,* Bacon, Nat. Hist. § 2, from L. acc. *transmissiōnem; transmiss-ible,* from F. *transmissible,* 'transmittable,' Cot.; *transmiss-ibil-i-ty.*

TRANSMUTE, to change to another form or substance. (L.) '[He] *transmutyd* the sentence of deth vnto perpetuyte of pryson;' Fabyan, Chron. c. 159. [The ME. form was *transmuen,* or *transmewen,* Chaucer, C. T. 8261 (E 385), from F. *transmuer,* 'to change or alter over,' Cot., from L. *transmūtāre.*] — L. *transmūtāre,* to change into another form. — L. *trans,* across (implying change); and *mūtāre,* to change; see **Trans-** and **Mutable**. Der. *transmut-able; transmut-at-ion,* spelt *transmutacioun,* Chaucer, C. T. 2841 (A 2839), from F. *trans-mutation,* 'a transmutation, alteration,' Cot., from L. acc. *trans-mūtātiōnem.*

TRANSOM, a thwart-piece across a double window; the lintel over a door; in ships, a beam across the stern-post to strengthen the after-part. (L.) '*Transome,* or lintell ouer a dore;' Baret, ed. 1580. 'The *transome* of a bed, *trabula;*' Levins. '*Meneau de fenestre,* the *transome,* or cross-bar of a window;' Cot. 'Beames, prickeposts, groundsels, summers or dormants, *transoms,* and such principals;' Harrison, Desc. of England, b. ii. c. 12, ed. Furnivall, p. 233. Spelt *trampsom,* meaning the part of the bedstead between the two headposts, Bury Wills, p. 23 (1463); spelt *traunsom,* Paston Letters, iii. 407. [Halliwell notes the spelling *transumpt,* but this is a corrupt form; the real meaning of *transumpt* is a copy of a record; see *Transumpt* in Cot. Webster says it is sometimes spelt *transummer,* but I can nowhere find it, and such a spelling is obviously due to confusion with *summer,* a beam, as used in the above quotation from Harrison.] β. It is a corruption of L. *transtrum,* used as an architectural and nautical term. It means precisely a *transom,* in all its senses. '*Transtra* et tabulæ nauium dicuntur et tigna, quæ ex pariete in parietem porriguntur;' Festus (White). '*Transoms* est vox Architectonica et transversas trabes notat, Vitruvio *transtra;*' Skinner, 1671. Cooper's Thesaurus (1565) explains L. *transtrum* by 'a *transome* going ouerthwarte an house.' Florio explains MItal. *transtri* as 'crosse or overthwart beames, *transtroms;*' and *trasto* as 'a *transome* or beame going crosse a house.' γ. The L. *transtrum* is derived from L. *trans,* orig. 'going across' (see **Trans-**); *-trum* is a suffix, denoting the agent, as in *arā-trum,* that which ploughs. Hence *trans-trum*=that which goes across; cf. *in-trans,* going in.

TRANSPARENT, clear, allowing objects to be seen through. (F.–L.) In Shak. L. L. L. iv. 3. 31. — F. *transparent,* 'transparent, clear-shining;' Cot. — L. *trans,* through; and *pārent-,* stem of pres. part. of *pārēre,* to appear; see **Trans-** and **Appear**. Der. *transparent-ly, -ness; transparenc-y.*

TRANSPICUOUS, transparent, translucent. (L.) In Milton, P. L. viii. 141. Coined, as if from L. **transpicuus,* from L. *transpicere,* to see or look through; see **Conspicuous, Perspicuous**. — L. *trans,* through; and *specere,* to look; see **Trans-** and **Spy**.

TRANSPIERCE, to pierce through. (F.–L.) Used by Drayton; Civil War, bk. vi. last stanza. — F. *transpercer,* 'to pierce through;' Cot. See **Trans-** and **Pierce**.

TRANSPIRE, to pass through the pores of the skin, to become public, or ooze out. (L.) In Milton, P. L. v. 438. — L. *tran-,* for *trans,* through; and *spīrāre,* to breathe, respire. See **Trans-** and **Spirit**. Der. *transpir-at-ion,* from F. *transpiration,* 'a transpiration, evaporation,' Cot. This sb. prob. really suggested Milton's verb.

TRANSPLANT, to plant in a new place. (F.–L.) In Cotgrave. — F. *transplanter,* 'to transplant;' Cot. — L. *transplantāre.* — L. *trans,* across, implying change; and *plantāre,* to plant. See **Trans-** and **Plant**. Der. *transplant-at-ion,* from F. *transplantation,* 'a transplantation,' Cot.

TRANSPORT, to carry to another place, carry away by passion or pleasure, to banish. (F.–L.) In Spenser, Hymn 4, Of Heavenly Beauty, l. 18. — F. *transporter,* 'to transport, transfer;' Cot. — L. *transportāre,* to carry across. — L. *trans,* across; and *portāre,* to carry.

See **Trans-** and **Port** (1). **Der.** *tránsport*, sb., Pope, Windsor Forest, 90; *transport-able*; *transport-ance*, Troil. iii. 2. 12; *transport-at-ion*.

TRANSPOSE, to change the position of, change the order of. (F.—L. *and* Gk.) ME. *transposen*, Gower, C. A. ii. 90; bk. iv. 2656.—F. *transposer*, 'to transpose, translate, remove;' Cot. See **Trans-** and **Pose**. **Der.** *transpos-al*.

TRANSPOSITION, a change in the order of words, &c. (F.—L.) In Cotgrave.—F. *transposition*, 'a transposition, removall out of one place into another;' Cot. See **Trans-** and **Position**. ¶ Not *ultimately* connected with *transpose*, which is from a different source.

TRANSUBSTANTIATION, the doctrine that the bread and wine in the Eucharist are changed into Christ's body and blood. (F.—L.) In Tyndall, Works, p. 447, col. 2; he also has *transubstantiated*, id. p. 445, col. 2.—F. *transubstantiation*; Cot.—Late L. *transubstantiātiōnem*, acc. of *transubstantiātio*; see Hildebert, Bp. of Tours, Sermon 93. Hildebert died in 1134 (Trench, Study of Words). Cf. Late L. *transubstantiātus*, pp. of *transubstantiāre*, coined from *trans*, across (implying change), and *substantia*, substance. See **Trans-** and **Substance**.

TRANSVERSE, lying across or cross-wise. (L.) 'But all things tost and turned by *transverse*,' Spenser, F. Q. vii. 7. 56; where *by transverse* = in a confused manner, or reversedly.—L. *transuersus*, turned across; hence, athwart. Orig. pp. of *transuertere*, to turn across. See **Trans-** and **Verse**. And see **Traverse**. **Der.** *transverse-ly*.

TRAP (1), an instrument or device for ensnaring animals. (E.) ME. *trappe*, Chaucer, C. T. 145. AS. *treppe*, a trap; Ælfric's Colloquy (Fowler); for **træppe*; cf. *be-træppan*, to entrap; A. S. Chron. an. 992. But the pronunciation has perhaps been affected by F. *trappe*, a trap, a word of Teut. origin.+MDu. *trappe*, 'a trap to catch mice in;' Hexham; OHG. *trapa*, *trappa*, a snare, trap [whence Low L. *trappa*, Ital. *trappa*, F. *trappe*, Span. *trampa*, a trap (Diez)]. β. Orig. sense 'step;' the *trap* is that on which an animal steps, or puts its foot, and is so caught. Cf. Westphal. *trappe*, a step; Du. *trap*, a stair, step, kick; G. *treppe*, a flight of steps; Swed. *trappa*, a stair; allied to Du. *trappen*, to tread on, EFries. and Low G. *trappen*, Norw. *trappa*, to tread on, trample. Allied to **Tramp**. The nasalised form *tramp* appears in Span. *trampa*, a trap. **Der.** *trap*, verb, spelt *trappe* in Palsgrave; *trap-door*, a door falling and shutting with a catch; also *en-trap*, q. v. Also *trap-ball* or *trap-bat*, a game played with a ball, bat, and a *trap* which, when lightly tapped, throws the ball into the air. And see *trap* (3).

TRAP (2), to adorn, or ornament with gay dress or clothing. (F.—Teut.) The pp. *trapped* occurs in Chaucer: 'Upon a stede bay, *trapped* in stele,' C. T. 2159 (A 2157); and see l. 2892 (A 2890). This is formed from a sb. *trappe*, meaning the trappings or ornaments of a horse. 'Mony *trappe*, mony croper' = many a trapping, many a crupper; King Alisaunder, 3421. 'Upon a stede whyt so milke; His *trappys* wer off tuely sylke;' Rich. Cuer de Lion, 1515; where *tuely* means 'scarlet.' Coined, with unusual change from *dr* to *tr* (by sound association with *trap* (1)), from F. *drap*, cloth; as shown by Chaucer's use of *trappure*, trappings of a horse, C. T., A 2499, from OF. *drapure*, trappings of a horse (Godefroy). We also find Late L. *trapus*, cloth (usually *drappus*), Span. and Port. *trapo*, cloth; Late L. *trappātūra*, a horse's trappings. See **Drape**. β. Cf. F. *draper*, 'to dress, to or full cloath; to beat, or thicken, as cloath, in the fulling.' Possibly for **traper*; in which case it may come from Low G. and Du. *trappen*, to tread upon, trample on (hence, to full cloth). See **Trap** (1). **Der.** *trapp-ings*, s. pl., ornaments for a horse, Shak. Venus, 286, hence, any ornaments, Hamlet, i. 2. 86. Also *rattle-traps*, q. v.

TRAP (3), a kind of igneous rock. (Swed.) Modern. So called because such rocks often appear in large tabular masses, rising above each other like steps (Webster).—Swed. *trappa*, a stair, or flight of stairs, *trapp*, trap (rock); Dan. *trappe*, a stair, *trap*, trap.+Du. *trap*, a stair, step; G. *treppe*, a stair. See **Trap** (1) and **Tramp**.

TRAPAN, the same as **Trepan** (2), q. v.

TRAPEZIUM, a plane four-sided figure with unequal sides. (L.—Gk.) In Phillips, ed. 1706. Also in M. Blundevile's Exercises, 1594, fol. 36 b (wrongly marked 39 b).—L. *trapezium*.—Gk. τραπέζιον, a small table or counter; a trapezium, because four-sided, like such a table. Dimin. of τράπεζα, a table, esp. a dining-table. Cf. ἀργυρόπεζα, i. e. silver-footed, as an epithet of Thetis.—Gk. τρα-, allied to τετρα-, prefix signifying 'four,' as in τετρά-γωνος, four-cornered, from τέτταρες, Attic for τέσσαρες, four; and πέζα, a foot, for **πέδ-ya*, an allied word to πούς (stem ποδ-), a foot, which is cognate with E. *foot*. See **Tetragon** and **Foot**. **Der.** *trapezo-id*, lit. 'trapezium-like,' from τράπεζο-, for τράπεζα, and εἶδ-ος, form; *trapezo-id-al*.

Also *trapeze*, from F. *trapèze*, the name of a kind of swing for athletic exercise, so called from being sometimes made in the shape of a trapezium, as thus: △. The F. *trapèze* is from L. *trapezium*.

TRAPPINGS, horse-ornaments; see **Trap** (2).

TRAPPIST, a member of a certain monastic body. (F.) 'Named from the village of *Soligny-la-Trappe*, in the department of Orne, France, where the abbey of *la Trappe* was founded in 1140;' Cent. Dict.

TRASH, refuse, worthless stuff. (Scand.) In Shak. Temp. iv. 223; Oth. iii. 3. 157; hence used of a worthless person, Oth. ii. 1. 312, v. 1. 85. The orig. sense is clippings of trees, as stated by Wedgwood, or (yet more exactly) the bits of broken sticks found under trees in a wood, and collected for fire-wood. Wedgwood quotes from Evelyn as follows, with a reference to Notes and Queries, June 11, 1853: 'Faggots to be every stick of three foot in length—this to prevent the abuse of filling the middle part and ends with *trash* and short sticks.' Hence it came to mean refuse generally; Cotgrave explains *menüailles* by 'small ware, small *trash*, small offals.' Of Scand. origin. Cf. Icel. *tros*, rubbish, leaves and twigs from a tree picked up and used for fuel, whence *trosna*, to become worn out, to split up as a seam does; cf. *trassi*, a slovenly fellow, *trassa*, to be slovenly. Norweg. *trask*, trash, scraps (Ross); *tras*, small pieces (Ross); *trasa*, a rag, tatter (Ross); *trase*, the same; also *tros*, fallen twigs, half-rotten branches easily broken, allied to *trysja*, to break into small pieces, to crackle. Swed. *trasa*, a rag, a tatter; Swed. dial. *trase*, a rag; *trås*, a heap of sticks, a worthless fellow (which is one sense of Cleveland *trash*), oid useless bits of fencing. β. Rietz points out the true origin; he adduces Swed. dial. *slå i tras*, to break in pieces, which is obviously the same phrase as Swed. *slå i kras*, to break in pieces; the substitution of *tr* for *kr* being a Scan. peculiarity, of which we have an undoubted example in Icel. *trani*, Swed. *trana*, Dan. *trane*, all variants of the word which we spell *crane*; see **Crane**. Hence the etym. is from Swed. *krasa*, Dan. *krase*, to crash, as a thing does when broken; see **Crash**. The Icel. form *tros* answers to Swed. *krossa*, to bruise, crush, crash, a collateral form of *krasa*; cf. Orkney *truss*, refuse, also prov. E. *trous*, the trimmings of a hedge (Halliwell). γ. Thus *trash* means 'crashings,' i. e. pieces that break off short with a snap or *crash*, dry twigs; hence also a bit of torn stuff, a rag, &c. ¶ This throws no light on *trash*, as in Shak. Temp. i. 2. 81; which has prob. a different origin, perhaps *trace* (2). **Der.** *trash-y*.

TRAVAIL, toil, labour in child-birth. (F.—L.) ME. *trauail* (with *u* for *v*), Ayenbite of Inwyt, p. 130, l. 32.—F. *travail*, 'travell, toile, labour, business, pains-taking;' Cot. [Cf. Ital. *travaglio*, Span. *trabajo*, Port. *trabalho*, Prov. *trabalhs* (Bartsch), toil, labour; orig. an obstacle or impediment, which is still a sense of Span. *trabajo*.] According to P. Meyer (Romania, xvii. 421) it answers to Late L. *trepālium*, a kind of rack for torturing martyrs (Ducange); perhaps made of three beams (*tres pāli*). Others equate it to Late L. **trabāculum*, which might have been formed from L. *trab-*, base of L. *trabs*, *trabes*, a beam. Cf. L. *trabāle*, an axle-tree; and see **Trave**. ¶ The W. *trafael*, travail, is borrowed from English. **Der.** *travail*, verb, ME. *trauaillen*, King Alisaunder, 1612, Old Eng. Miscellany, p. 34, l. 3, from F. *travailler*, 'to travell, toile, also to harry, weary, vex, infest;' Cot. **Doublet**, *travel*.

TRAVE, a beam, a shackle. (F.—L.) '*Trave*, a frame into which farriers put unruly horses;' Halliwell. '*Trave, Travise*, a place enclosed with rails for shooing an unruly horse;' Bailey, vol. i. ed. 1735. '*Trave*, a trevise or little room made purposely to shoo unbroken horses in;' Blount's Gloss., ed. 1674. '*Treuys*, to shoe a wylde horse in, *trauayl a cheual*;' Palsgrave. ME. *traue* (with *u* for *v*); 'And she sprong as a colt doth in the *traue*;' Chaucer, C. T. 3282.—OF. *trave*, a beam, Godefroy; *traf*, a beam, given in the Supp. to Roquefort; usually *tref*, 'the beam of a house;' Cot. [Cf. MItal. *traue*, 'any kinde of beame;' Florio.]—L. *trabem*, acc. of *trabes* or *trabs*, a beam. **Der.** *archi-trave*, q. v.

TRAVEL, to journey, walk. (F.—L.) Merely the same word as *travail*; the two forms are used indiscriminately in old editions of Shakespeare (Schmidt). So also *travail*, to travel; in Ben Jonson, Every Man, ii. 5. 32. The word forcibly recalls the toil of travel in former days. See **Travail**. **Der.** *travel*, verb; *travell-er*, L. L. L. iv. 3. 308. **Doublet**, *travail*.

TRAVERSE, laid across; as sb., a cross, obstruction, a thing built across; as a verb, to cross, obstruct, deny an argument, also to pass over a country. (F.—L.) 'Trees .. hewen downe, and laid *trauers*, one ouer another;' Berners, tr. of Froissart, vol. ii. c. 186 (R.). 'Smote his hors *trauerse*;' Malory, Morte Arthure, bk. x. c. 65. Gower has *trauers* as a sb., meaning 'cross' or impediments, in the last line but 14 of his Conf. Amantis.—F. *travers*, m., *traverse*, f., 'crosse-wise, overthwart;' Cot. (Hence the sb. *traverse*, 'a cross-way, also .. a thwart, .. let, bar, hinderance;' id.; also the verb *traverser*, 'to thwart or go overthwart, to crosse or passe over,' id.) —L. *transuersus*, turned across, laid athwart; pp. of *transuertere*, to turn across; see **Transverse**. Der. *traverse*, verb, in Malory, M. A. bk. x. c. 30, from F. *traverser*, as above; *travers-er*.

TRAVERTINE, TRAVERTIN, a kind of white lime-stone. (Ital.—L.) Used for building. Spelt *Treuertino*, R. Eden, Three Books on America, ed. Arber, p. 367.—Ital. *travertino*, MItal. *tivertino*, 'a kind of stone to build withall' (Florio).—L. *Tibertinus*, belonging to *Tibur*, the modern Tivoli.

TRAVESTY, a parody. (F.—Ital.—L.) 'Scarronides, or Virgile *Travestie*, being the first book of Virgils Æneis in English Burlesque; London, 1664;' by Charles Cotton. Probably *travestie* is here used in the lit. sense of 'disguised,' or as we should now say, *travestied*. It is properly a pp., being borrowed from F. *travesti*, pp. of *se travestir*, 'to disguise or shift his apparell, to play the counterfeit;' Cot.—Ital. *travestire*, 'to disguise or shift in apparel, to maske;' Florio.—L. *trans*, prefix, lit. across, but implying change; and *uestire*, to clothe. The verb *uestire* is from the sb. *uestis*, clothing. See **Trans-** and **Vest**. Der. *travesty*, verb.

TRAWL, to fish with a drag-net. (F.—Teut.) 'Trawler-men, a sort of fishermen that us'd unlawful arts and engines, to destroy the fish upon the river Thames; among whom some were styl'd *hebbermen*, others *tinckermen*, *Petermen*, &c.;' Phillips, ed. 1706.—OF. *trauler*, to go hither and thither (Roquefort); Walloon *trauler*, the same (Sigart); mod. Prov. *traula*; also OF. *troller*, mod. F. *trôler*, to drag about; Hamilton. See **Troll**.   ¶ Quite distinct from *trail*.

TRAY, a shallow vessel, a salver. (E.) 'A *treie*, or such hollowe vessel .. that laborers carrie morter in to serue tilers or plasterers;' Baret, ed. 1580. ME. *treye* 'Bolles, *treyes*, and platers,' i. e. bowls, trays, and platters; Rich. Cuer de Lion, l. 1490. AS. *tryg*, written *trig*; A. S. Leechdoms, ii. 340. Derived, by mutation, from AS. *trog*, a trough; see **Trough**. Cf. Low G. *trügge* (Stratmann); deriv. of *trog*, trough; Icel. *trygill*, a little trough, tray; Swed. dial. *trygel*, Norw. *trygel*.   ¶ The alleged AS. *treg* is an error for *trog*; but *treg* might be a Kentish form of *tryg*, and would give ME. *trey*.

TREACHERY, faithlessness, trickery of a gross kind. (F.—L.) ME. *trecherie*, spelt *treccherye*, P. Plowman, B. i. 196; older spelling *tricherie*, id. A. i. 172; Ancren Riwle, p. 202, l. 18.—OF. *trecherie*, *tricherie*, Godefroy; MF. *tricherie*, 'whence, as it seems, our *trechery*, cousenage, deceit, a cheating, a beguiling;' Cot.—OF. *trechier*, *trichier*, MF. *tricher*, 'to cousen, cheat, beguile, deceive;' id. Cf. Ital. *treccare*, to cheat; Prov. *tricharia*, treachery, *trichaire*, a traitor.— Late L. *tricāre*, for *tricāri*, to dally (Ecclus. xxxii. 15), L. *tricāri*, to make difficulties.—L. *tricæ*, pl., difficulties, wiles; see **Intricate**. See Körting, § 9727. But prob. confused with Du. *trek*, a stroke; see further under **Trickery**. Der. *treacher-ous*, Spenser, F. Q. i. 6. 41, spelt *trecherous*, Pricke of Conscience, 4232, coined by adding the suffix *-ous* to the old word *trecher*, a traitor, spelt *trichour* in Rob. of Glouc. p. 455, l. 9329, *trecchour* in Wyclif's Works, ed. Matthew, p. 239, l. 6; *treacherous-ly*, *-ness*. Körting, § 9727.

TREACLE, the syrup drained from sugar in making it. (F.—L. —Gk.) ME. *triacle*, a medicament, a sovereign remedy (very common), P. Plowman, C. ii. 147, B. i. 146; see my note on it, explaining the matter. It had some resemblance to the *treacle* which has inherited its name.—OF. *triacle*, 'treacle,' Cot. The *l* is unoriginal; *triacle* is only another spelling of OF. *theriaque*, 'treacle;' Cot.—L. *thēriaca*, an antidote against the bite of serpents, or against poison; also spelt *thēriacē*.—Gk. θηριακός, belonging to wild or venomous beasts; hence θηριακὰ φάρμακα, antidotes against the bite of venomous animals; and (no doubt) *θηριακή, sb. sing. fem., in the same sense, whence L. *thēriacē*.—Gk. θηρίον, a wild animal, poisonous animal; dimin. of θήρ, a wild beast, Æolic φήρ; cf. Russ. *zvier(e)*, a wild beast; Lith. *żwèris*, a wild beast; L. *ferus*. Brugmann, i. § 319.

TREAD, to set down the foot, tramp, walk. (E.) ME. *treden*; pt. t. *trad*, Ormulum, 2561; pp. *troden*, *treden*, Chaucer, C. T. 12646 (C 712). AS. *tredan*, pt. t. *træd*, pp. *treden*, Grein, ii. 550.+Du. *treden*; G. *treten*, pt. t. *trat*, pp. *getreten*. We find also Icel. *troða*, pt. t. *trað*, pp. *troðinn*; which accounts for our pp. *trodden*; Dan. *træde*; Swed. *tråda*; Goth. *trudan*, to tread, pt. t. *trath*. Teut. type *tredan-*, pt. t. *trad*, pp. *trudanoz*. Der. *tread-le* or *tredd-le*, the same as ME. *tredyl*, a step, AS. *tredel*; 'Bases, *tredelas* vel *stæpas*,' i. e. steps, Voc. 117. 6. Also *tread-mill*; *trade*, q. v.

TREASON, a betrayal of the government, or an attempt to over-throw it. (F.—L.) ME. *traison*, *treison*; spelt *trayson*, Havelok, 444; *treisun*, Ancren Riwle, p. 56, l. 17.—OF. *traïson*, mod. F. *trahison*, treason, betrayal.—L. acc. *trāditiōnem*, betrayal.—L. *trādere*, to deliver, betray; see **Traitor**. Der. *treason-able*, *treason-abl-y*. Doublet, *tradition*.

TREASURE, wealth stored up, a hoard. (F.—L.—Gk.) ME. *tresor*, occurring very early, in the A. S. Chron. an. 1137.—OF.

tresor, mod. F. *trésor*, treasure. [Cf. Ital. *tesoro*, Span. *tesoro*, Port. *thesouro*, spelt without *r* after *t*.]—L. *thēsaurum*, acc. of *thēsaurus*, a treasure.—Gk. θησαυρός, a treasure, a store, hoard; formed (it is not very clear with what suffixes) from the base θη-, to lay up, as seen in τίθημι, I place, lay up; or from θησ-. as in the future θήσ-ω. See **Theme, Thesis**. Der. *treasure*, verb, Shak. Sonnet 6; *treasur-er*, from F. *tresorier*, spelt *thesorier* in Cot., and explained by 'a threasurer;' *treasur-y*, ME. *tresorie*, *tresorye*, Rob. of Glouc. p. 274, l. 5540, contracted from OF. *tresorerie*, spelt *thresorerie* in Cotgrave, so that *treasury* is short for *treasurery*. Also *treasure-trove*, i. e. treasure found; see **Trover**. Doublet, *thesaurus*.

TREAT, to handle in a particular manner, to entertain, manage by applying remedies, discourse of. (F.—L.) ME. *treten*, Wyclif, Mark, ix. 32; Chaucer, C. T. 12455 (C 521).—F. *traiter*, to treat.— L. *tractāre*, to handle; frequent. form of *trahere* (pp. *tractus*), to draw; see **Trace**. Der. *treat-ment*, from F. *traitement*; *treat-ise*, ME. *tretis*, Chaucer, On the Astrolabe, prol. l. 8, from OF. *tretis*, *treitis*, *traictis* (see *traictis* in Roquefort), meaning (a thing) well handled or nicely made, attractive, admirable, an adj. which was even applied by Chaucer to the Prioress's nose, C. T. 152, and answering to a Late L. form *tractitius*. Also *treat-y*, ME. *tretee*, Chaucer, C. T. 1290 (A 1288), from F. *traité* (*traicté* in Cotgrave), 'a treaty,' properly the pp. of *traiter*, to treat, and therefore 'a thing treated of.'

TREBLE, threefold; the highest part in music. (F.—L.) Why the highest part in music is called *treble* is not clear; it is usually explained as being the third part, after the tenor and alto. In this sense, it is the same word as when it means *triple*. Indeed, we find *triple* used by Fairfax in the musical sense of *treble*. 'The human voices sung a *triple* hie;' Fairfax, tr. of Tasso, b. xviii. st. 24. Palsgrave has: 'Treble of a song, *le dessus*; Treble-stryng of an instrument, *chanterelle*.' Reginald atte Pette, in 1456, bequeathed 6s. 8d. towards the making of a new bell called *trebyll*; Testamenta Vetusta, ed. Nicholas, p. 286. ME. *treble*, threefold, Gower, C. A. iii. 159; bk. vii. 2202.—OF. *treble*, triple (Burguy).—L. *triplum*, acc. of *triplus*, triple. See **Triple**. For the change from *p* to *b*, cf. E. *double*, due to L. *duplus*. Der. *treble*, verb, Temp. iii. 1. 221; *trebl-y*. Doublet, *triple*.

TREDDLE, the same as **Treadle**; see **Tread**.

TREE, a woody plant, of a large size. (E.) ME. *tree*, *tre*; also used in the sense of *timber*. 'Not oneli vessels of gold and of siluer, but also of *tree* and of erthe;' Wyclif, 2 Tim. ii. 20. AS. *trēo*, *trēow*, a tree, also dead wood or timber; Grein, ii. 551.+Icel. *trē*; Dan. *træ*; Swed. *trä*, timber; *träd*, a tree, a corruption of *träet*, lit. 'the wood,' with the post-positive article; Goth. *triu* (gen. *triwis*), a tree, piece of wood.   β. All from Teut. type *trewom*, n., a tree, Fick, iii. 118; further allied to Russ. *drevo*, a tree, W. *derw*, an oak, Irish. *darag*, *darog*, an oak, Gk. δρῦς, an oak, Skt. *dru-*, wood; cf. Gk. δόρυ, a spear-shaft, Skt. *dāru*, wood, a species of pine.   γ. Benfey connects Skt. *dru-* and *dāru* with the root √DER, to tear, rend, whence E. *tear*; see **Tear** (1); so also Fick, i. 615, 616. The explanation is that it meant a piece of cleft wood; cf. Gk. δέρειν, to flay, E. *tear*, to rend. But this is improbable. Brugmann, i. § 486. Der. *tre-ën*, adj., made of wood, or belonging to a tree, Spenser, F. Q. i. 7. 26, Cursor Mundi, 12392; with suffix *-en* as in *gold-en*, *wood-en*. Also *tree-nail*, a peg, a pin or nail made of wood, a nautical term. And see *rhodo-den-dron*, *dryad*.

TREFOIL, a three-leaved plant such as the white and red clover. (F.—L.) Given by Cot. as the tr. of F. *treffle*.—AF. *trifoil*; in a Vocabulary pr. in Voc. 556. 33, we find AF. *trifoil* answering to L. *trifolium* and E. *wite clouere* [white clover].—L. *trifolium*, a three-leaved plant, as above.—L. *tri-*, prefix allied to *trēs*, three; and *folium*, a leaf; see **Tri-** and **Foil**.

TRELLIS, a structure of lattice-work. (F.—L.) ME. *trelis*. 'Trelys, of a wyndow or other lyke, Cancellus;' Prompt. Parv.—F. *treillis*, 'a trellis;' Cot.—F. *treiller*, 'to grate or lattice, to support or underset by, or hold in with, crossed bars or latticed frames;' Cot.; F. *treille*, 'an arbor or walk set on both sides with vines, &c. twining about a latticed frame;' id.—Late L. *trichila*, *tricla*, a bower, arbour, or summer-house. Origin doubtful.   ☞ Quite distinct from F. *treillis*, sackcloth, OF. *treilis*, *treslis*, adj., applied to armour covered with a sort of lattice-work, Late L. *trislicium*, a covering of sackcloth.—L. *trēs*, three; *licium*, a thread. But the suffix *-is* in the former OF. *treillis* seems to have been due to association with this latter word. Der. *trellis-ed*.

TREMBLE, to shiver, shake, quiver. (F.—L.) ME. *tremblen*, P. Plowman, B. ii. 235.—F. *trembler*, 'to tremble;' Cot. The *b* is excrescent, as is common after *m*.—Late L. *tremulāre*, to hesitate, lit. to tremble.—L. *tremulus*, trembling.—L. *trem-ere*, to tremble, with adj. suffix *-ul-us*.+Lithuan. *trim-ti*, to tremble; Gk. τρέμ-ειν, to tremble.—√TREM, to tremble; Fick, i. 604; Brugmann, i. § 474. Der. *trembl-er*, *trembl-ing-ly*. From L. *tremere* are also *trem-or*, in

Phillips, borrowed from L. *tremor*, a trembling; *trem-end-ous*, also in Phillips, from L. *tremendus*, that ought to be feared, fut. pass. part. of *tremere*; *trem-end-ous-ly*; *trem-ul-ous*, Englished from L. *tremulus*, as above; *trem-ul-ous-ly*, *-ness*.

TRENCH, a kind of ditch or furrow. (F. – L. ?) ME. *trenche*, Chaucer, C. T. 10706; (F 392). Shortened from F. *trenchée*, 'a trench,' Cot., lit. a thing cut. – F. *trencher* (now spelt *trancher*), 'to cut, carve, slice, hack, hew;' Cot. Cf. Span. *trinchea*, a trench, *trinchar*, to carve, *trincar*, to chop; Port. *trinchar*, to carve, *trincar*, to crack asunder, break; Ital. *trincea*, a trench, *trinciare*, to cut, carve. β. There is no satisfactory solution of this word; see Littré, Scheler, and Diez. Prob. Latin; apparently from Late L. *trencāre*, to cut, substituted for L. *truncāre*, to lop, from *truncus*, the trunk of a tree. We may notice, in Florio, Ital. *trincare*, 'to trim or smug up,' *trinci*, 'gardings, fringings, lacings, iaggings, also cuts, iags, or snips in garments.' Der. *trench*, verb, Macb. iii. 4. 27, from *trencher*, to cut; *trench-ant*, cutting, Timon, iv. 3. 115, from F. *trenchant*, pres. part. of *trencher*; *trench-er*, a wooden plate for cutting things on, ME. *trenchere*, Voc. 610. 17, from F. *trencheoir*, 'a trencher,' Cot., OF. *trencheor*. Cf. **Trinket** (1).

TREND, to turn or bend away, said of direction or course. (E.) See Nares. 'The shoare *trended* to the southwestward;' Hakluyt, Voyages, i. 276, § 7. 'By the *trending* of the land [you] come backe;' id. i. 383. ME. *trenden*, to roll or turn about. 'Lat hym rollen and *trenden*,' &c.; Chaucer, tr. of Boethius, b. iii. met. 11. l. 2. The word is E., being formed from the same source as AS. *trendel*, a circle, a ring, esp. a ring seen round the sun, A. S. Chron. an. 806; cf. AS. *tryndel*, a ring. Allied words are Dan. *trind*, adj. round, *trindt*, adv. around, *trindes*, to grow round; Swed. *trind*, round, cylindrical; OFriesic *trind*, *trund*, round; see **Trundle**. Cf. *trendil*, a hoop, mill-wheel, *trendle*, to trundle, in Levins, ed. 1570; *trindals*, rolls of wax, Cranmer's Works, ii. 155, 503 (Parker Soc.). All from the Teut. str. vb. **trend-an*, to roll; whence AS. *trendan*, to roll (Napier), and *ā-trend-lian*, to roll.

TRENTAL, a set of thirty masses for the dead. (F. – L.) See the poem of St. Gregory's *Trental*, in Polit. Relig. and Love Poems, ed. Furnivall, p. 83, and my note on P. Plowman, C. x. 320. See Spenser, Mother Hubbard's Tale, 453; and see Nares. – OF. *trentel*, *trental*, a trental, set of thirty masses; Roquefort. Cf. Low L. *trentāle*, a trental. – F. *trente*, thirty. – L. *triginta*, thirty. – L. *tri-*, thrice, allied to *trēs*, three; and *-ginta*, i. e. *-cinta*, short for **decinta* = **decenta*, tenth, from *decem*, ten. See **Three** and **Ten**.

TREPAN (1), a small cylindrical saw used in removing a piece of a fractured skull. (F. – L. – Gk.) ME. *trepane*, Lanfrank, Cirurgie, p. 127. Spelt *trepane* in Cot. – MF. *trepan*, 'a trepane, an instrument having a round and indented edge,' &c.; Cot. – Late L. *trepanum* (for **trypanum*). – Gk. τρύπανον, a carpenter's tool, a borer, augur; also a surgical instrument, a trepan (Galen). – Gk. τρυπᾶν, to bore. – Gk. τρῦπα, τρύπη, a hole. Ultimately from √TER, to pierce; as in L. *terere*, to bore, Gk. τείρειν (for **τέρ-yειν*).

TREPAN (2), **TRAPAN**, to ensnare. (F. – Teut.) In Butler, Hudibras, pt. ii. c. 3. l. 617. Usually spelt *trepan*, as in Phillips, by a ridiculous confusion with the word above. Rightly spelt *trapan* in South's Sermons, vol. v. ser. 3 (R.), and in Anson's Voyages, b. i. c. 9 (R.). 'Forthwith alights the innocent *trapann'd*;' Cotton, Wonders of the Peak, 1681, p. 38 (Todd). 'For fear his words they should *trapan*;' Tom Thumb (1630); in E. Eng. Pop. Poetry, ii. 247. Not an old word. – OF. *trappan*, a snare or trap for animals (Roquefort); he also gives *trapant*, a kind of trap-door; OF. *trapan*, *trapant*, a plank (Godefroy). – Late L. *trapentum*, a plank for a trap-door. – F. *trappe*, a trap. – OHG. *trappa*, a trap; see **Trap** (1). ¶ The E. word is now only used as a verb, but it must have come in as a sb. in the first instance, as it is used by South: 'It is indeed a real *trapan*,' i. e. stratagem, Serm. ii. 377; 'Nothing but gins, and snares, and *trapans* for souls,' Serm. iii. 166 (Todd). The last quotation puts the matter in a very clear light. Cotgrave has the verb *attrapper*, and the sbs. *trape*, *trapelle*, *attrapoire*.

TREPANG; see **Tripang**.

TREPHINE, an improved form of the trepan. (F. – L. – Gk.) F. *tréphine*; in Littré; not in Hatzfeld. An arbitrary variant of *trépan*; see **Trepan** (1).

TREPIDATION, terror, trembling, fright. (F. – L.) In Milton, P. L. iii. 483, where it is used in an astronomical sense. 'A continual *trepidation*,' i. e. trembling motion, Bacon, Nat. Hist. § 137. – F. *trepidation*, 'trembling, terrour;' Cot. – L. *trepidātiōnem*, acc. of *trepidātio*, alarm, a trembling. – L. *trepidāre*, to tremble. – L. *trepidus*, agitated, disturbed, alarmed. Allied to OSlav. *trepetu*, to tremble, Russ. *trepetat(e)*, Skt. *tarala-s*, trembling. See Brugmann, ii. § 797 (note). Der. (from L. *trepidus*) *in-trepid*.

TRESPASS, a passing over a boundary, the act of entering another man's land unlawfully, a crime, sin, offence, injury. (F. – L.) ME. *trespas*, Rob. of Glouc. p. 505, l. 10403, where it means 'sin.' – OF. *trespas*, a crime (Burguy); also 'a decease, departure out of this world, also a passage;' Cot. (The lit. sense is 'a step beyond or across,' so that it has direct reference to the mod. use of *trespass* in the sense of intrusion on another man's land. Cf. Span. *trespaso*, a conveyance across, also a trespass; Ital. *trapasso*, a passage, digression.) The sb. is from *trespass*, verb, ME. *trespassen*, Wyclif, Acts, i. 25. – OF. *trespasser*, 'to passe over,' Cot., also to trespass (Burguy). – L. *trans*, across; and Late L. *passāre*, to pass, from *pass-us*, a step; see **Trans-** and **Pass**. Der. *trespass-er*, ME. *trespassour*, P. Plowman, C. ii. 92; also *trespass-offering*.

TRESS, a curl or lock of hair, a ringlet. (F. – Late L. – Gk.) ME. *tresse*, Chaucer, C. T. 1051 (A 1049); the pp. *tressed*, adorned with tresses, is in King Alisaunder, l. 5409. – F. *tresse*, 'a tresse or lock of haire;' Cot. He also gives *tresser*, 'to plait, weave, or make into tresses.' (Cf. Ital. *treccia*, a braid, knot, curl; pl. *treccie*, 'plaites, tresses, tramels, or roules of womens haires;' Span. *trenza*, a braid of hair, plaited silk.) β. The orig. sense is 'a plait.' – Late L. *tricia*, variant of *trica*, a plait. – Gk. τρίχα, in three parts, threefold (Diez); from the usual method of plaiting the hair in three folds. – Gk. τρι-, thrice; allied to τρεῖς, three, cognate with E. **Three**, q. v. γ. This is borne out by the Ital. *trina*, a lace, loop, allied to *trino*, threefold, from L. *trinus*, threefold. Der. *tress-ed*, as above. Also *tress-ure*, q. v.

TRESSURE, a kind of border, in heraldry. (F. – Late L. – Gk.) In Phillips, ed. 1706, and in works on heraldry. – MF. *trescheur*, 'a tresseur, in blazon;' Cot. – F. *tresser*, 'to plait, weave;' Cot. – F. *tresse*, 'a tress or plait of hair; see **Tress**. ¶ I find 'Hoc tricatorium, Anglice, *tressure*;' and again, 'Hec *trjcatura*, Anglice, *tresewyr*,' Voc. 656. 17, 792. 18. Here *tricātūra* is merely a Latinised form of the F. word, the F. *tresser* being Latinised as *tricāre*.

TRESTLE, TRESSEL, a movable support for a table, frame for supporting. (F. – L.) '*Trestyll* for a table, *tresteau*;' Palsgrave. 'Hic *tristellus*, Anglice, *treste*;' Voc. 656. 28. '*Hic tristellus*, a *trestylle*;' id. 723. 33. The pl. *trestelys*, i. e. trestles, occurs in Bury Wills, ed. Tymms, p. 23, l. 6, in a will dated 1463; and ME. pl. *tresteles* is in Rich. Coer de Lion, 102. – OF. *trestel*, spelt *tresteau*, *treteau* in Cot., and explained 'a tresle for a table, &c., also a kind of rack, or stretching torture.' Mod. F. *tréteau* (see Littré). – Late L. **transtellum*, for L. *transtillum*, dimin. of *transtrum*, a little cross-beam. See **Transom**. ¶ This Late L. form should rather have given OF. *trastel*; but we find F. *tres-* for L. *trans-* in our *tres-pass*. We must by no means neglect Lowland Sc. *traist*, *trast*, a trestle, *trast*, a beam, North E. *tress*, a trestle (Brockett), Lanc. *trest*, a strong large stool (Halliwell), and ME. *treste*, a trestle, above. These are from OF. *traste*, a cross-beam (Roquefort), the same word as MItal. *trasto*, 'a bench of a gallie, a transome or beame going cross a house,' which is obviously from L. *transtrum*. See **Transom**. Scheler takes the same view, proposing a Late L. **transtellum*, as a parallel form to *transtillum*, in order to give the exact OF. form. Cotgrave's explanation of the word as meaning a *rack* is much to the point; a rack requires two cross-beams (*transtilla*) to work it, these beams being turned round with levers, thus pulling the victim by means of ropes wound round the beams. And note *trestelli fortes*, strong trestles, in John de Garlande; in Wright, Vocab. i. 132.

TRET, an allowance to purchasers on consideration of waste. (F. – L.) '*Tret*, an allowance made for the waste, . . which is always 4 in every 104 pounds;' Phillips, ed. 1706. Also in Blount's Nomolexicon, ed. 1691. It appears much earlier. 'For the *tret* of the same peper,' i. e. pepper; Arnold's Chron. (1502), repr. 1811, p. 128. – AF. **trete*, f., answering to F. *traite* just as AF. *tret* (Gloss. to Britton) answers to F. *trait*; cf. F. *traite*, 'a draught, . . also, a transportation, vent outward, shipping over, and an imposition upon commodities;' Cot. This F. *traite* answers to L. *tracta*, fem. of *tractus*, pp. of *trahere*, to draw; see **Trace**. Cf. MItal. *tratta*, 'leaue to transport merchandise, also a trade or trading;' Florio. Also Late L. *tracta*, a payment on exports (Ducange).

TREWS, an old form of **Trousers**, q. v.

TREY, three, at cards or dice. (F. – L.) 'Two *treys*;' L. L. L. v. 2. 232. And in Chaucer, C. T. 12587 (C 653). – AF. *treis*; OF. *trei*, *treis* (mod. F. *trois*), three. – L. *trēs*, three; see **Three**.

TRI-, relating to three, threefold. (L. or Gk.; or F. – L. or Gk.) F. and L. *tri-*, three times, prefix related to L. *tri-a*, neut. of *trēs*, three, cognate with E. **Three**, q. v. So also Gk. τρι-, allied to τρί-α, neut., or τρεῖς, m., three.

TRIAD, the union of three. (F. – L. – Gk.) 'This is the famous Platonical *triad*;' More, Song of the Soul (1647), preface (Todd). – F. *triade*, 'three;' Cot. – L. *triad-*, stem of *trias*, a triad. – Gk. τριάς, a triad. – Gk. τρι-, from τρεῖς, three; see **Tri-**.

TRIAL, a test; see **Try**.

TRIANGLE, a plane, three-sided figure. (F. – L.) ME. *triangle*; Lanfrank, Cirurgie, p. 215. '*Tryangle*, triangle;' Palsgrave. – F. *triangle*, 'a triangle;' Cot. – L. *triangulum*, a triangle; neut. of *triangulus*, adj., having three angles. – L. *tri-*, three; and *angulus*, an angle; see **Tri-** and **Angle**. Der. *triangl-ed*; *triangul-ar*, used by Spenser (Todd), from F. *triangulaire*, 'triangular,' Cot., from L. *triangulāris*; *triangul-ate*, a coined word; *triangul-at-ion*.

TRIBE, a race, family, kindred. (F. – L.) Gower, C. A. iii. 230 (bk. vii. 4118), has the pl. *tribes*. – F. *tribu* (a tribe,' Cot. – L. *tribu-*, decl. stem of *tribus*, a tribe; cf. Umbrian *trifo*. β. A *tribus* is supposed to have been, in the first instance, one of the three families of people in Rome, their names being the Ramnes, Tities, and Luceres. The etymology is thought to be from L. *tri-* (akin to *trēs*, three), and *-bus*, family, from √BHEU, to be; cf. Gk. φυ-λή, a tribe, family, from the same root. See **Tri-** and **Be**. But Brugmann thinks this unlikely; ii. § 104. Rather, allied to W. *tref*, a homestead; see **Thorpe**. Der. *trib-une*, q. v.; *tri-bute*, q. v.

TRIBRACH, a metrical foot consisting of three short syllables. (L. – Gk.) Written *tribrachus* or *tribrachys* in Phillips, ed. 1706; and *tribrachus* in Puttenham, Art of Poetry, b. ii. c. 3. – L. *tribrachys*. – Gk. τρίβραχυς, a tribrach. – Gk. τρι-, akin to τρεῖς, three; and βραχύς, short. See **Brief**.

TRIBULATION, great affliction, distress. (F. – L.) ME. *tribulacioun*, spelt *tribulaciun*, Ancren Riwle, p. 402, l. 24. – F. *tribulation*, 'tribulation;' Cot. – L. *tribulātiōnem*, acc. of *tribulātio*, tribulation, affliction; lit. a rubbing out of corn by a sledge. – L. *tribulāre*, to rub out corn, to oppress, afflict. – L. *tribulum*, a sledge for rubbing out corn, consisting of a wooden platform studded underneath with sharp flints or iron teeth. – L. *tri-*, base of *trī-uī*, *trī-tum*, pt. t. and pp. of *terere*, to rub; with suffix *-bulum* denoting the agent (as in *uerti-bulum*, that which turns about, a joint). See further under **Trite**.

TRIBUNE, a Roman magistrate elected by the plebeians. (F. – L.) ME. *tribun*; pl. *tribunes*, Wyclif, Mark, vi. 21. – F. *tribun*. – L. *tribūnum*, acc. of *tribūnus*, a tribune, properly the chief of (or elected by) a *tribe*; also a chieftain, Mark, vi. 21. – L. *tribu-*, decl. stem of *tribus*, a tribe; with suffix *-nus* (Idg. *-no-*). See **Tribe**. Der. *tribune-ship*. Also *tribun-al*, Antony, iii. 6. 3, from L. *tribūnal*, a raised platform on which the seats of *tribunes*, or magistrates, were placed.

TRIBUTE, homage, contribution paid to secure protection. (F. – L.) ME. *tribut*, Wyclif, Luke, xxiii. 2; Gower, C. A. ii. 74, l. 7. – F. *tribut*, 'tribute;' Cot. – L. *tribūtum*, tribute; lit. a thing contributed or paid; neut. of *tribūtus*, pp. of *tribuere*, to assign, impart, allot, bestow, pay; orig. to allot or assign (to a tribe?). Perhaps (says Bréal) from L. *tribu-*, decl. stem of *tribus*, a tribe; see **Tribe**. Der. *tribut-ar-y*, ME. *tributairie*, Chaucer, C. T. 14594 (B 3866), from AF. **tributarie*, F. *tributaire*, 'tributary,' Cot., from L. *tribūtārius*, paying tribute. Also *at-tribute*, *con-tribute*, *dis-tribute*, *re-tribut-ion*.

TRICE (1), a short space of time. (Low G.) In the phrases *in a trice*, Twelfth Nt. iv. 2. 133; *on a trice*, Temp. v. 238; *in this trice of time*, K. Lear, i. 1. 219. 'And wasteth *with a trice*;' Turbervile, To his Friend, &c., st. 5. Now only in the phr. *in a trice*, i.e. suddenly. '*Subitement*, swiftly, quickly, speedily, *in a trice*, out of hand;' Cot. ME. *at a tryse*, at a (single) pull. 'The howndis that were of gret prise Pluckid down dere all *at a tryse*;' Ipomydon with his houndis thoo Drew downe bothe buk and doo;' Ipomydon (ed. Weber), 392. Here *tryce* (*tryce*) is a verbal sb. from the verb *trysen, trycen*, to pull, haul; Chaucer, C. T. 14443 (B 3715). See further under **Trice** (2). ¶ The later phrase *in a trice* bears a remarkable resemblance to the Span. *en un tris*. We find Span. *tris*, noise made by the breaking of glass; also, a trice, a short time, an instant; *venir en un tris*, to come in an instant; *estar en un tris*, to be on the verge of (Neuman). So also Port. *triz*, a word to express the sound of glass when it cracks; *estar por hum triz*, to be within a hair's breadth, to have a narrow escape; *en hum triz*, in a trice. But it does not appear that we could have borrowed such a phrase from Spain. It occurs as early as in Skelton, Philip Sparowe, 1131.

TRICE (2), **TRISE**, to haul up or hoist. (Low G.) '*Trise* (sea-word), to hale up anything into the ship by hand with a dead rope, or one that does not run in a block or pulley;' Phillips, ed. 1706. ME. *tricen, trisen*, to pull, haul; Chaucer, C. T. 14443 (B 3715). 'They *trisen* vpe thaire saillez;' Morte Arthure, ed. Brock, 832. A nautical term; of Low G. origin; and the sense noted by Phillips is unoriginal, as it must once have meant to haul by help of a pulley, and not only *without* it. Cf. ME. *tryys*, (and, with a final *t*) *tryyste*, 'troclea,' Prompt. Parv. – Low G. *trissen*, *trītsen*, to trice up; from *trisse, trītse*, a hauling-rope (which explains the sense given by Phillips), also a pulley (Lübben). Cf. also (from Low G.)

Swed. *trissa*, a sheave, pulley, truckle, *triss*, a spritsail-brace; Dan. *tridse*, a pulley, whence *tridse*, verb, to haul by means of a pulley, to trice; Norweg. *triss*, *trissel*, a pulley, or sheave in a block; Swed. dial. *trissa*, a roller, also a shoemaker's implement, a little round wheel with teeth on it. Note also Low G. *trisel*, a whirling round, giddiness, in the Bremen Wörterbuch; where also are cited OG. *tryssen*, to wind, and Hamburg *drysen*, *up drysen*, to wind up, *dryseblok*, the block of a pulley, like Dan. *tridseblok*.

TRICENTENARY, a space of 300 years. (L.) Modern. From **Tri-** and **Centenary**.

TRICK (1), a stratagem, clever contrivance, fraud, parcel of cards won at once. (F. – L.) Common in Shakespeare. 'A *trick*, facinus;' Levins, ed. 1570. 'It were but a schoole-*trick*,' Spenser, Mother Hubbard's Tale, 512. 'Suche unknyghtly *trikkes*;' Hoccleve, De Reg. Princ. 2286. – ONorth F. *trique* (for OF. *triche*); cf. Norm. dial. *trique*, a trick (Moisy, ed. 1895). Godefroy gives the vb. *triquier*, and Moisy has Norm. dial. *triquier*, for OF. *trichier*, to trick, deceive. Cf. ME. *trichen*, to deceive, cozen, trick, occurring early in the 14th century, Polit. Songs, p. 69, l. 7. This ME. *trichen* is from OF. *trichier*, *trechier*, explained under **Treachery**. β. Some of the senses are due to Du. *trek*. Thus Shakespeare has *trick* in the sense of lineament, K. John, i. 85; this is precisely the Du. *trek*. '*De trekken van't gelaat*, the lineaments of the face;' Sewel. Cf. Du. '*een slimme trek*, a cunning trick; *Iemand eenen trek speelen*, to play one a trick; *de kap trekken*, to play tricks, play the fool;' Sewel. γ. The Du. *trek* (*treek*), a trick (borrowed from, or suggested by the ONorthF. *trique*) is properly distinct from, but was easily confused with Du. *trek*, a pull, draught, tug; from the verb *trekken*, to draw, pull. We find also OFries. *trekka* or *tregga*, NFries. *trecke*, *tracke* (Outzen), Low G. *trekken*, Dan. *trække*, MHG. *trecken*, to draw, drag, pull. The MHG. *trecken* is a causal form, from the strong verb found as MHG. *trechen*, OHG. *trehhan*, to push, shove, also to pull. Der. *trick-er*, *trick-ster*; *trick-er-y* (doublet of *treachery*, q. v.); *trick-ish*, *trick-ish-ly*, *trick-ish-ness*; also *tricks-y*, full of tricks (formed by adding *-y* to the pl. *tricks*), Temp. v. 226. And see *trigger*, *trick* (2), *trick* (3).

TRICK (2), to dress out, adorn. (F. – L.) 'Which they *trick up* with new-tuned oaths;' Hen. V, iii. 6. 80. 'To *trick*, or trim, Concinnare;' Levins, ed. 1570. Minsheu also has the word, but it is not a little strange that Blount, Phillips, Coles, and Kersey ignore *trick*, in whatever sense. [It is remarkable that *trick* appears early as an *adjective*, synonymous with *neat* or *trim*. 'The same reason I finde true in two bowes that I haue, wherof the one is quicke of caste, *tricke*, and trimme both for pleasure and profyte;' Ascham, Toxophilus, ed. Arber, p. 28. So also in Levins. But this is prob. a different word; cf. Lowl. Sc. *trig*, neat, trim.] The verb is a derivative from the sb. *trick*, above, which obtained many meanings, for which see Schmidt's Shak. Lexicon. For example, a *trick* meant a knack, neat contrivance, custom, particular habit, peculiarity, a trait of character or feature, a prank, also a toy or trifle, as in 'a knack, a toy, a *trick*, a baby's cap,' Tam. Shrew, iv. 3. 67. Cf. MF. *trique-nisques*, 'trifles;' Cot. Hence to *trick*, to use a neat contrivance, to exhibit a trait of character, to have a habit in dress. Compare **Trick** (3), below. Der. *trick-ing*, ornament, Merry Wives, iv. 4. 79.

TRICK (3), to delineate arms, to blazon; an heraldic term. (Du.) This is the true sense in Hamlet, ii. 2. 479. It is much clearer in the following. 'There they are *trick'd*, they and their pedigrees; they need no other heralds;' Ben Jonson, The Poetaster, i. 1 (Tucca). – Du. *trekken*, formerly *trecken*, 'to delineate, to make a draught or modell, to purtray;' Hexham. *Tricking* is a kind of sketching. This is only a particular use of Du. *trekken*, to pull or draw; cf. our double use of *draw*. See **Trick** (1), § γ.

TRICKLE, to flow in drops or in a small stream. (E.) ME. *triklen*. In Chaucer, C. T. 13604 (B 1864), two MSS. have *trikled*, two have *striked* or *stryked*, and one has *strikled*; Tyrwhitt prints *trilled*. 'With teris *trikland* on hir chekes;' Ywaine and Gawain, 1558; in Ritson, Met. Romances, i. 66. 'The teeris *trikilen* downe;' Polit., Religious, and Love Poems, ed. Furnivall, p. 207, l. 47. 'Teres *trekyl* downe be my face;' Cov. Mysteries, p. 72. In all these passages the word is preceded by the sb. *teres*, pronounced as a dissyllable, and such must often have been the case; this caused a corruption of *strikelen* by the loss of initial *s*; the phrases *the teres strikelen* and *the teres trikelen* being confused by the hearer. *Trickle* is clearly a corruption of *strikelen*, to flow frequently or to keep on flowing, the frequent. of ME. *striken*, to flow. 'Ase strem that *strikeþ* stille' = as a stream that flows quietly; Specimens of English, ed. Morris and Skeat, p. 48, l. 21. – AS. *strican*, to move or sweep along, to hold one's course, Grein, ii. 489. This is the same word as AS. *strican*, to strike; see **Strike**. Cf. mod. E. *streak*; to *trickle* or *strickle* is to flow in a course, leaving a *streak* behind; G. *streichen*, to move onward, rove, sweep on. The loss of *s* was facilitated by association with *trill* (Dan. *trille*), to roll.

TRICOLOR, the national flag of France, having three colours, red, white, and blue. (F.—L.) The flag dates from 1789.—F. *tricolore*, short for *drapeau tricolore*, the three-coloured flag.—F. *tricolor*, the three-coloured amaranth (Hamilton).—L. *tri-*, prefix, three; and *colōrem*, acc. of *color*, colour. See **Tri-** and **Colour.** Der. *tri-colour-ed.*

TRIDENT, a three-pronged spear. (F.—L.) In Temp. i. 2. 206.—F. *trident*, 'Neptune's three-forked mace;' Cot.—L. *tridentem*, acc. of *tridens*, an implement with three teeth, esp. the three-pronged spear of Neptune.—L. *tri-*, three; and *dens*, a tooth, prong. See **Tri-** and **Tooth.**

TRIENNIAL, happening every third year, lasting for three years. (L.) A coined word, made by adding *-al* (L. *-ālis*) to L. *trienni-um*, a period of three years. It supplanted the older word *triennal*, of F. origin, which occurs early, in P. Plowman, B. vii. 179; this is from F. *triennal*, 'triennal,' Cot., formed by adding *-al* to L. adj. *trienn-is*, lasting for three years. β. Both *triennium* and *triennis* are from L. *tri-*, three, and *annus*, a year; see **Tri-** and **Annual.** Der. *triennial-ly.*

TRIFLE, anything of small value. (F.—L.) The spelling with *i* is remarkable, as the usual ME. spelling was *trufle*. Spelt *tryfyl*, Rob. of Brunne, Handl. Synne, 5031; but *trufle*, Rob. of Glouc. p. 417, l. 8613; *trufle* (one MS. has *trefle*), P. Plowman, B. xii. 140; also id. B. xviii. 147 (other MSS. have *tryfule, truyfle*); also id. C. xv. 83 (other MSS. *trefele, trifle*). Spelt *trofle* (also *trefle*), P. Plowman's Crede, 352. There is the same variation of spelling in the verb; the proper ME. form is *truflen*, spelt *trufly*, Ayenbite of Inwyt, p. 214; *trofle*, Morte Arthure, ed. Brock, 2932, *trifelyn*, Prompt. Parv. '*Trufa*, a trefele; *Trufo*, to trefele;' Voc. 617. 42, 43. The sb. is the more orig. word; we find 'þeos ant oðre *trufles* þet he *bitrufleð* monie men mide'=these and other delusions that he beguiles many men with, Ancren Riwle, p. 106, l. 7. The old sense was a delusion or trick, a sense still partly apparent in the phr. ' to *trifle* with.'—OF. *trufle, truffle*, mockery, raillery (Godefroy; who quotes 'Nuga, *truffle*' from a glossary); variant of *truffe*, 'a gibe, mock, flout, jeast, gullery; also, a most dainty kind of round and russet root, which grows in forrests or dry and sandy grounds,' &c.; Cot. He refers to a *truffle*. That *truffle* and *trifle* are the same word, or rather that both senses of F. *truffe* arose from one form, is admitted by Burguy, Diez, and Littré. It is supposed that a *truffle* became a name for a small or worthless object, or a subject for jesting. Similarly, in English, the phrases *not worth a straw, not worth a bean, not worth a cress* (now turned into *curse*) were proverbial; so also ' a *fico* for the phrase,' or ' a *fig* for it.' See further under **Truffle.** Cf. WFlem. *truffel, trijfel*, false news (De Bo). Note also: 'Mantiglia, a kinde of clouted creame called a *foole* or a *trifle*, in English;' Florio. Der. *trifle*, verb, ME. *truflen*, as above; *trifl-er, trifl-ing, trifl-ing-ly.*

TRIFOLIATE, three-leaved. (L.) Modern.—L. *tri-*, three; and *foliātus*, leaved, from *folium*, a leaf; see **Trefoil.**

TRIFORIUM, a gallery above the arches of the nave and choir of a church. (L.) From L. *tri-*, for *trēs*, three; and *fori-s*, a door, an opening. ¶ Now usually built with but *two* arches or openings (within a third); but some early examples had *three* such. See wood-cut in Cent. Dict.

TRIFORM, having a triple form. (L.) In Milton, P. L. iii. 730.—L. *triformis*; often applied to the moon or Diana.—L. *tri-*, three; and *form-a*, form; see **Tri-** and **Form.**

TRIGGER, a catch which, when pulled, lets fall the hammer or cock of a gun. (Du.) A weakened or ' voiced' form of *tricker*. In Butler, Hudibras, pt. i. c. 3, l. 528, Bell's edition, we find: ' The *trigger* of his pistol draw.' Here the editor, without any hint and free from any conscience in the matter, has put *trigger* in the place of *tricker*; see the quotation as it stands in Richardson and Todd's Johnson. Spelt *tricker* in Farquhar, Recruiting Officer, i. 1 (1706). —Du. *trekker*, a trigger; formerly *trecker*, 'a drawer, a haler, or a puller,' Hexham.—Du. *trekken*, to pull, draw; see **Trick** (3). Der. *trig*, vb., to skid a wheel (Phillips).

TRIGLYPH, a three-grooved tablet. (L.—Gk.) A term in Doric architecture. In Blount's Gloss., ed. 1674.—L. *triglyphus*; Vitruvius, iv. 2 (White).—Gk. τρίγλυφος, thrice-cloven; also, a tri-glyph, three-grooved tablet.—Gk. τρι-, three; and γλύφειν, to carve, hollow out, groove, which is allied to E. *cleave*; see **Cleave** (1). Der. *triglyph-ic.*

TRIGON, a combination of three zodiacal signs, so as to form an equilateral triangle. (L.—Gk.) ' The fiery *trigon*;' Shak. 2 Hen. IV, ii. 4. 288. The combination of Aries, Leo, and Sagittarius was the ' fiery' trigon.—L. *trigōnum*, a triangle, trigon.—Gk. τρίγωνον, a triangle, neut. of τρίγωνος, three-cornered.—Gk. τρι-, for τρεῖς, three; γων-ία, an angle, akin to γόνυ, a knee. Cf. **Trine.**

TRIGONOMETRY, the measurement of triangles. (Gk.) Shak. has *trigon*, i.e. triangle, 2 Hen. IV, ii. 4. 288. In Phillips, ed. 1706. Coined from Gk. τρίγωνο-, for τρίγωνον, a triangle; and -μετρια, measurement (as in *geo-metry*, &c.), from μέτρον, a measure. β. Τρίγωνον is properly neut. of τρίγωνος, three-cornered; from τρι-, three, and γων-ία, an angle, akin to γόνυ, a knee. See **Tri-**, **Knee**, and **Metre.** Der. *trigonometri-c-al, -ly.*

TRILATERAL, having three sides. (L.) In Phillips, ed. 1706. Coined with suffix *-al* (L. *-ālis*) from L. *trilater-us*, three-sided.—L. *tri-*, three; and *later-*, decl. stem of *latus*, a side; see **Tri-** and **Lateral.**

TRILINGUAL, consisting of three languages. (L.) Coined with suffix *-al* (L. *-ālis*) from L. *trilingu-is*, triple-tongued, speaking three languages.—L. *tri-*, three; and *lingua*, a tongue. See **Tri-** and **Lingual.**

TRILITERAL, consisting of three letters. (L.) A term applied to Hebrew roots. From **Tri-** and **Literal.**

TRILL (1), to shake, to quaver. (Ital.) ' The sober-suited song-stress *trills* her lay;' Thomson, Summer, 746. ' His *trills* and quavers;' Tatler, no. 222, Sept. 9, 1710. Phillips, ed. 1706, gives: ' *Trill*, a quavering in musick,' and rightly notes that it is an Ital. word, like many other musical terms.—Ital. *trillare*, to trill, shake, quaver; *trillo*, sb., a trill, shake. A word of imitative origin, meaning ' to say *tril*.' Cf. Span. *trinar*, to trill. Hence are derived E. *trill*, Du. *trillen*, G. *trillern*, &c. Der. *trill*, sb.

TRILL (2), to turn round and round. (Scand.) Perhaps obsolete, but once common. ' As fortune *trills* the ball;' Gascoigne, Fruits of War, st. 67.' ' To *tril*, circumuertere;' Levins. ' I *tryll* a whirlygig rounde aboute, *Je pirouette*;' Palsgrave. ME. *trillen*, Chaucer, C. T. 10630 (F 316).—Swed. *trilla*, to roll, whence *trilla*, a roller; Dan. *trille*, to roll, trundle, whence *trille*, a disc, *trillebör*, a wheel-barrow. Perhaps allied to E. *drill*; but this is by no means certain. It may be allied to Low G. *triseln*, to turn round; see **Trice** (2).

TRILL (3), to trickle, to roll. (Scand.) In Spenser, F. Q. ii. 12. 78; K. Lear, iv. 3. 13. ' With many a teere *trillyng* on my cheeke;' Chaucer, C. T. 7246, D 1864 (Corpus MS.).—Dan. *trille*, to roll, to trickle (as tears), Larsen; Swed. *trilla ned*, to roll down. This is merely a particular use of **Trill** (2).

TRILLION, a million raised to the third power. (F.—L.) A coined word, said in Todd's Johnson to have been invented by Locke. Composed of *tr-*, for *tri-*, three; and *-illion*, the latter part of the word *million*. See **Tri-** and **Million**; and see **Billion.**

TRILOBITE, a kind of fossil. (Gk.) Named from its three lobes.—Gk. τρι-, for τρεῖς, three; λοβ-ός, a lobe; -ιτ-ης, suffix.

TRILOGY, a series of three tragedies or poems. (F.—Gk.) F. *trilogie* (1812); Hatzfeld.—Gk. τριλογία.—Gk. τρι-, for τρεῖς, three; -λογία, from λόγ-ος, a tale, story; see **Logic.**

TRIM, to put in due order, to adjust, to deck, dress, arrange. (E.) ' I *trymme*, as a man doth his heare [hair];' Palsgrave. ME. *trumen, trimen*, a rare word. ' Ich iseo godd seolf mid his eadi engles *bitrumen* þe abuten '=I see God Himself with His blessed angels be-trim [surround] thee about; St. Marharete, p. 20, l. 3. ' Helle hundes habbeð *bitrumet* me '=hounds of hell have surrounded me; id. p. 6, l. 4 from bottom. AS. *trymian, trymman*, to make firm, strengthen (a common word), Grein, ii. 554; also, to set in order, array, prepare, Blickling Homilies, p. 91, l. 31; p. 201, l. 35. The orig. sense is preserved in our phrase ' to *trim* a boat,' i.e. to make it steady; hence to put in perfect order. Formed (by the regular vowel-change from *u* to *y*) from the Teut. type of AS. *trum*, adj., firm, strong, Grein, ii. 553.+Low G. *trim*; only in the derivative *betrimmen, betrimmd*, decked, trimmed, adorned; *trimmke*, an affected or over-dressed person. Root uncertain. Der. *trim*, sb., Cor. i. 9. 62; *trim*, adj. (with the vowel *i* of the derived verb), Much Ado, iv. 1. 323; *trim-ly, trim-ness*; *trimm-er, trimm-ing*; also *be-trim*, verb, Temp. iv. 65.

TRIMETER, a division of a verse consisting of three measures. (L.—Gk.) In Ben Jonson, tr. of Horace, Art of Poetry, l. 333.—L. *trimetrus*, Horace, Art of Poetry, ll. 252, 259.—Gk. τρίμετρος, con-sisting of three measures.—Gk. τρι-, three; and μέτρον, a measure, metre. See **Tri-** and **Metre.**

TRINE, a certain aspect of the planets. (L.) In Milton, P. L. x. 659. ' *Tryne* in trone;' Cov. Myst., p. 88. ' *Trine*, belonging to the number three; as, *a trine aspect*, which is when 2 plants are distant from each other [by] a third part of the circle, i.e. 120 degrees. It is noted thus △, and accounted by astrologers an aspect of amity and friendship;' Phillips.—L. *trinus*, more common in pl. *trini*, three by three. For *tris-nus*, allied to *trēs*, three. Brugmann, ii. § 66. See **Tri-** and **Three.** Der. *trin-al*, Spenser, F. Q. i. 12. 39. Also *trin-i-ty*, q.v.

TRINITY, the union of Three in One Godhead. (F.—L.) ME. *trinitee*, Chaucer, C. T. 7406 (D 1824); Ancren Riwle, p. 26,

l. 10.—OF. *trinite*, later *trinité*.—L. *trīnitātem*, acc. of *trīnitās*, a triad.—L. *trīnus*, threefold; see **Trine.** Der. *Trinity-Sunday*; *Trinit-ar-i-an, Trinit-ar-i-an-ism.*

TRINKET (1), a small ornament. (F.—L. ?) We find ME. '*trenket*, sowtarys knyfe,' i.e. a shoemaker's knife, Prompt. Parv. '*Trenket*, an instrument for a cordwayner, *batton a torner* [*soulies*];' Palsgrave. Way, in his note to Prompt. Parv., says: 'In a *Nominale* by Nich. de Minshull, Harl. MS. 1002, under *pertinentia allutarii*, occur:—*Anserium*, a schavyng-knyfe; *Galla*, idem est, *trynket*; also, under *pertinentia rustico*, occur:—*Sarculum*, a wedehoke; *Sarpa*, idem est, *trynket*.' This shows that a *trynket* was a general name for a sort of knife, whether for shoemaking or weeding. Palsgrave gives the spelling *trynket* as well as *trenket*. We may fairly assume that *trinket* was also used to denote a toy-knife, such as could be worn about the person, and that for three reasons. These are: (1) the sense of something worn about the person still clings to *trinket* at this day; (2) *trinket*, as used by old authors, means sometimes a tool or implement, sometimes a knife; and (3) toy-knives were very commonly given as presents to ladies, and were doubtless of an ornamental character, and worn on the person. As early as Chaucer's time, the Friar had his tippet 'farsed [stuffed] ful of *kniues* And pinnes, *for to giuen faire wiues*.' A few examples of the use of the word may be added. 'The poorer sort of common souldiers haue euery man his leather bag or sachell well sowen together, wherin he packs up all his *trinkets*;' Hakluyt's Voyages, i. 62. 'What husbandlie husbands, except they be fooles, But handsome have storehouse for *trinkets* and tooles?' Tusser, Husb. § 53. 13. Todd cites from Arbuthnot: 'She was not *hung about* with toys and *trinkets*, tweezer-cases, pocket-glasses.' More extracts would probably make this matter clearer. β. The etymology of *trinket*, formerly *trenket*, in the sense of 'knife,' is from ONorth F. *trenquet*, variant of OF. *tranchet*, a small knife (see Supp. to Godefroy).—ONorth F. *trenquer*, occurring in *trenquefile*, variant of *tranchefile* (Godefroy), so that *trenquer* is a variant of OF. *tranchier*, *trenchier*, to cut. Cf. Span. *trinchete*, a shoemaker's paring-knife, *tranchete*, a broad curvated knife, used for pruning, a shoemaker's heel-knife; mod. F. *tranchet*, a shoemaker's knife; OF. *trinchet*, supp. to Godefroy, s.v. *tranchet*. And cf. Span. *trinchar*, to cut. See further under **Trench.** γ. Perhaps we may also note MItal. *trincare*, 'to trim or smug up,' whence *trincato*, 'fine, neat, trim,' Florio. This seems allied to *trinci*, 'fringings, lacings, cuts, or snips in garments,' id.; and to *trinciare*, to cut, allied to Span. *trinchar*, as above.

TRINKET (2), **TRINQUET**, the highest sail of a ship. (F.—Ital.—L.) In Hakluyt, Voy. iii. 411. Spelt *trinkette* in Minsheu, ed. 1627. '*Trinquet*, is properly the top or top-gallant on any mast, the highest sail of a ship;' Blount's Gloss., ed. 1674.— F. *trinquet*, 'the top or top-gallant,' &c. (as in Blount); Cot.—Ital. *trinchetto*, 'a small saile in a ship called a trinket;' Florio. [Or from Span. *trinquete*, a trinket.] Prob. from L. *triquetrum*, acc. of *triquetrus*, three-cornered (with reference to lateen sails). Prob. from L. *tri-*, allied to *tres*, three; and **quatrus, quadrus*, square, hence 'cornered.' Cf. L. *quater*, four times, *quatuor*, four. ¶ The *n* may have been due to association with Span. *trinca*, a rope for lashing fast; *trincar*, to keep close to the wind; *poner la vela a la trinca*, 'to put a ship that the edges of the sailes may be to the wind;' Minsheu.

TRINOMIAL, in mathematics, an expression consisting of three terms. (L.) Not a good form; it should rather have been *trinominal*. Coined, in imitation of *binomial*, from *tri-*, three; and *nōmi-*, for *nōmini-*, decl. stem of *nōmen*, a name. See **Tri-** and **Nominal;** and **Binomial.**

TRIO, in music, a piece for three performers. (Ital.—L.) Modern; added by Todd to Johnson.—Ital. *trio*, a trio, three parts together.—L. *tri-*, three, allied to *tres*, three; see **Tri-** and **Three.**

TRIP, to move with short, light steps, to stumble, err; also, to cause to stumble. (F.—Teut.) ME. *trippen*; 'This hors anon gan for to *trippe* and daunce;' Chaucer, C. T. 10626 (F 1312).—OF. *treper* (Wace), *triper, tripper*, to dance; Norm. dial. *triper*.—MDu. *trippen*, 'to tread under foot;' *trippelen*, 'to trip or to daunce;' Hexham. Cf. Low G. *trippeln*, to trip; Swed. *trippa*, to trip; Dan. *trippe*, to trip, *trip*, a short step; Icel. *trippi*, a young colt (from its tripping gait). The base *trip-* is a lighter form of *trap-*, as in MDu. *trappen*, to tread under foot; the nasalised form appears in **Tramp,** q.v. Der. *trip*, sb., Tw. Nt. v. 170; *tripp-ing-ly*, Hamlet, iii. 2. 2.

TRIPANG, TREPANG, an edible sea-slug. (Malay.) Malay *tripang.*

TRIPARTITE, divided into three parts, having three corresponding parts, existing in three copies. (L.) In Shak. 1 Hen. IV, iii. 1. 80. 'Indentures *trypartyte* indented;' Bury Wills, ed. Tymms,

p. 57, in a will dated 1480.—L. *tri-*, three; and *partīt-us*, pp. of *partīri*, to part, divide, from *parti-*, decl. stem of *pars*, a part. See **Tri-** and **Part.**

TRIPE, the stomach of ruminating animals, prepared for food. (F.) ME. *tripe*, Prompt. Parv.; King Alisaunder, l. 1578.—F. *tripe*, tripe. Cf. Span. and Port. *tripa*, Ital. *trippa*. Of unknown origin. We also find Irish *triopas*, s. pl., tripes, entrails; W. *tripa*, the intestines; Bret. *stripen*, tripe, more commonly used in the pl. *stripennou, stripou*, the intestines.

TRIPHTHONG, three vowel characters representing a single sound. (Gk.) Little used; coined in imitation of *diphthong*, with prefix *tri-* (Gk. τρι-), three, instead of *di-* (Gk. δι-), double. See **Tri-** and **Diphthong.** Der. *triphthong-al.*

TRIPLE, threefold, three times repeated. (F.—L.) In Shak. Mid. Nt. Dr. v. 391. [Rich. refers us to Chaucer, tr. of Boethius, b. iv. met. 7, l. 26, but the reading there is *treble*, a much older form.]—F. *triple*, 'triple, threefold;' Cot.—L. *triplus*, triple.—L. *tri-*, three; and *-plus*, related to L. *plēnus*, full. See **Tri-** and **Double.** Der. *tripl-y*; *tripl-et*, formed in imitation of *doubl-et*. **Doublet,** *treble.*

TRIPLICATE, threefold. (L.) In mathematics, a *triplicate* ratio is not the ratio of 3 to 1, but the ratio of two cubical numbers, just as the duplicate ratio is a ratio of squares. In Phillips, ed. 1706.— L. *triplicātus*, pp. of *triplicāre*, to treble.—L. *tri-*, three; and *plic-āre*, to fold, weave. See **Tri-** and **Ply.** Der. *triplicat-ion*, from L. acc. *triplicātiōnem*. Also *triplex*, from L. *triplex*, threefold, Tw. Nt. v. 41; *tri-lic-i-ty*, Spenser, F. Q. i. 12. 39.

TRIPOD, anything supported on three feet, as a stool. (L.—Gk.; or Gk.) In Chapman, tr. of Homer, Iliad, b. ix. l. 127; where it was taken directly from Gk. Also in Holland, tr. of Plutarch, 1102, where we find '*tripode* or three-footed table' (R.). ME. *tripod*, Trevisa, tr. of Higden, i. 179.—L. *tripod-*, stem of *tripūs*.—Gk. τρίπους (stem τριποδ-), three-footed; or, as sb., a tripod, a three-footed brass kettle, a three-legged table.—Gk. τρι-, three; and πούς (stem ποδ-), a foot, cognate with E. *foot*; see **Tri-** and **Foot.** Der. *tripos* (for L. nom. *tripūs*, Gk. τρίπους), an honour examination at Cambridge, so called at present because the successful candidates are arranged in *three* classes; but we must not forget that a *tripos* sometimes meant an oracle (see Johnson), and that there was formerly a certain scholar who went by the name of *tripos*, being otherwise called *prevaricator* at Cambridge or *terræ filius* at Oxford; he was a master of arts chosen at a commencement to make an ingenious satirical speech reflecting on the misdemeanours of members of the university, a practice which gave rise to the so-called *tripos-verses*, i.e. facetious Latin verses printed on the back of the tripos-lists (after 1798). The orig. reference was to the *Tripus* on which the M.A. sat; and the lists were named from the verses which took the place of his speech. See Phillips, ed. 1706. 'Wits, . . who never . . were at all inspired from a *Tripus's, Terræ-filius's*, or *Prævaricator's* speech;' Eng. Garner, vii. 267 (1670). **Doublet,** *trivet.*

TRIPTYCH, a picture in three compartments. (Gk.) Frequently, the two side-pictures can be folded over the central one, which is of double their breadth.—Gk. τρίπτυχον, neut. of τρίπτυχος, threefold, or consisting of three layers.—Gk. τρι-, for τρεῖς, three; πτυχή, a fold, from πτύσσειν (for **πτύχ-γειν*), to fold.

TRIREME, a galley with three ranks of oars. (L.) 'Thucydides writeth that Aminocles the Corinthian built the first *trireme* with thre rowes of oars to a side;' Holland, tr. of Pliny, b. vii. c. 56.—L. *trirēmis*, a trireme.—L. *trirēmis*, having three banks of oars.—L. *tri-*, three; and *rēmus*, an oar. β. The L. *trirēmis* corresponds to Gk. τριήρης, a trireme; Thucydides, i. 13. γ. The L. *rēmus* = OL. *resmos*, is allied to Gk. ἐρετμός, a rudder, orig. a paddle. The Gk. ἐρ-ετμός, like *-ηρ-ης* in τριήρης, is allied to E. *rudder* and *row*. See **Row** (1).

TRISE, the same as **Trice** (2); q.v.

TRISECT, to divide into three equal parts. (L.) Coined (in imitation of *bi-sect*) from L. *tri-*, three; and *sect-um*, supine of *secāre*, to cut. See **Tri-**, **Section, Bisect.** Der. *trisect-ion.*

TRIST, the same as **Tryst**, q.v.

TRISYLLABLE, a word of three syllables. (F.—L.—Gk.) From **Tri-** and **Syllable;** see **Dissyllable.** Cotgrave gives F. *trisyllabe*, adj., of three syllables. Der. *trisyllab-ic, trisyllab-ic-al, -ly.*

TRITE, worn out by use, hackneyed. (L.) In Blount's Gloss., ed. 1674.—L. *trītus*, worn, pp. of *terere*, to rub, to wear.+Russ. *teret(e)*, to rub; Lithuan. *triti*, to rub; Gk. τείρειν (for **τέρ-γειν*), to rub. √TER, to rub. Der. *trite-ly, -ness*. Also *trit-ur-ate, tri-bul-at-ion*, q.v. And see *try*. From the same root, *con-trite, de-tri-ment.*

TRITON, a marine demi-god. (L.—Gk.) In Shak. Cor. iii. 1. 89.—L. *Trītōn*.—Gk. Τρίτων, a Triton. Cf. Irish *triath*, the sea; Skt. *trita-*, the name of a deity.

TRITURATE, to rub or grind to powder. (L.) Blount, ed. 1674, has *triturable* and *trituration.* Perhaps the sb. *trituration* was first introduced from the F. sb. *trituration,* 'a crumming, crumbling,' Cot. — L. *triturātus,* pp. of *trītūrāre,* to thrash, hence to grind. — L. *trītūra,* a rubbing, chafing; formed like the fut. part. of *terere,* to rub; see **Trite.** Der. *triturat-ion, tritur-able.*

TRIUMPH, joy for success, rejoicing for victory. (F. — L. — Gk.) ME. *triumphe,* Chaucer, C.T. 14369 (B 3553). — OF. *triumphe, triomphe,* 'a triumph;' Cot. — L. *triumphum,* acc. of *triumphus,* a triumph, or public rejoicing for a victory. — Gk. θρίαμβος, a hymn to Bacchus, sung in festal processions to his honour; also used as a name for Bacchus. Der. *triumph,* verb, L.L.L. iv. 3. 35; *triumph-er,* Titus Andron. i. 170; *triumph-ant,* Rich. III, iii. 2. 84, from the stem of the pres. part. of L. *triumphāre,* to triumph; *triumph-ant-ly;* also *triumph-al,* from L. *triumphālis,* belonging to a triumph. **Doublet,** *trump* (2). (Perhaps L. *triumphus* is a native word.)

TRIUMVIR, one of three men in the same office or government. (L.) Shak. has *triumvirate,* Antony, iii. 6. 28; and even *triumviry,* L.L.L. iv. 3. 53. — L. *triumuir,* one of three men associated in an office. A curious form, evolved from the pl. *triumuirī,* three men, which again was evolved from the gen. pl. *trium uirōrum,* so that *trium* is the gen. pl. of *trēs,* three; whilst *uir,* a man, is a nom. sing. See **Three** and **Virile.** Der. *triumvir-ate,* from L. *triumuirātus,* the office of a triumvir.

TRIUNE, the being Three in One. (L.) In Phillips, ed. 1706. Coined from L. *tri-,* three; and *ūnus,* one, cognate with E. *one.* See **Tri-** and **One.**

TRIVET, TREVET, a three-legged support. (L.) 'A *triuette,* tripes;' Levins. In the Bury Wills, ed. Tymms, p. 82, we find *trevid* under the date 1493, and the pl. *treuettis* at p. 100, under the date 1504. AS. *trefet,* Cart. Saxon., ed. Birch, iii. 367. — L. *tripedem,* acc. of *tripēs,* having three feet. — L. *tri-,* three, and *pēs,* a foot, cognate with E. *foot.* **Doublet,** *tripod,* which is a Greek form.

TRIVIAL, common, slight, of small worth. (F. — L.) In Shak. All's Well, v. 3. 61. It also meant trite or well-known; see Trench, Select Glossary. — F. *trivial,* 'triviall, common;' Cot. — L. *triuiālis,* that which belongs to the cross-roads, that which may be picked up anywhere, ordinary, common-place. — L. *triuia,* a place where three roads meet. — L. *tri-,* three; and *uia,* a way; see **Tri-** and **Voyage.** Der. *trivial-ly, -ness.*

TROCHEE, a metrical foot of two syllables, a long one followed by a short one. (L. — Gk.) Spelt *trocheus* in Puttenham, Art of Poetry, b. ii. c. 3; now shortened to *trochee.* — L. *trochæus.* — Gk. τροχαῖος, running; also a trochee, from its tripping measure. — Gk. τροχός, a running. — Gk. τρέχειν, to run. The form of the root appears to be DHREGH. Der. *trocha-ic,* from Gk. τροχαϊκός. And see *truck* (2).

TROGLODYTE, a dweller in a cave. (F. — L. — Gk.) 'These savages . . . flew away at last into their caves, for they were *troglodites;*' Howell, Foreign Travel, sect. x; ed. Arber, p. 51. And see Trevisa, tr. of Higden, i. 159. — F. *troglodyte,* used by Montesquieu, and doubtless somewhat older than his time. — L. *trōglodyta.* — Gk. τρωγλοδύτης, one who creeps into holes, a cave-dweller; Herod. iv. 183. — Gk. τρωγλο- for τρώγλη, a hole, a cave; and δύ-ειν, to enter, creep into; with suffix -της, of the agent. β. Τρώγλη is from Gk. τρώγ-ειν, to gnaw, to bite, hence to gnaw a hole; whence also **Trout.**

TROLL, to roll, to sing a catch, to fish for pike with a rod of which the line runs on a reel. (F. — Teut.) ME. *trollen,* to roll; Prompt. Parv. To *troll the bowl,* to send it round, circulate it; see *Troul* in Nares. To *troll a catch* is, probably, to sing it irregularly (see below); to *troll,* in fishing, is prob. rather to draw the line hither and thither than to use a reel; see **Trawl.** — MF. *troller,* which Cot. explains by 'hounds to *trowle,* raunge, or hunt out of order;' to which he subjoins the sb. *trollerie,* 'a trowling or disordered ranging, a hunting out of order;' this shows it was a term of the chase. Roquefort gives OF. *trauler, troller,* to run hither and thither; cf. mod. F. *trôler,* to lead, drag about, also to stroll about, to ramble. — G. *trollen,* to roll, to troll; cognate with MDu. *drollen,* 'to troole,' Hexham; Low G. *drulen,* to roll, troll, Bremen Wörterbuch. Prob. allied to EFries. *drallen,* to turn, to roll; and to **Drill** (1). ¶ Distinct from *trail.* Der. *troll-er;* also *troll-op,* a stroller, slattern, loitering person, where the suffix is obscure; perhaps suggested by *gallop.* Phillips gives *troll about,* 'to ramble up and down in a careless or sluttish dress;' also *trollop,* 'an idle, nasty slut.' And see *trull.*

TROMBONE, a deep-toned bass instrument of music. (Ital. — G. — Slav.) Not in Todd's Johnson. — Ital. *trombone,* a trombone, trumpet, sackbut; augmentative form of *tromba,* a trumpet; see **Trump** (1).

TRON, a weighing-machine. (F. — L.) See Riley, tr. of Liber Albus, pp. 124, 199, 548; hence *tronage,* pp. 199, 215. The *tron* was gen. used for weighing wool. The *Tron Church* in Edinburgh is so called from being situate near the site of the old weighing-machine. We read of 'Tronage and Poundage' in Arnold's Chronicle, ed. 1811, p. 100; where we also find: 'To *tronage* perteinen thoos thing*is* that shal be weyen by the *trone* of the kynge.' — AF. *trone,* a weighing-machine, Liber Albus, p. 246; and Latinised as Low L. *trona* (in Ducange); cf. OF. *trosnel,* a dimin. form in Godefroy. — L. *trutina,* a pair of scales. Cf. Gk. τρυτάνη, a tongue of a balance, a pair of scales. Der. *tron-age;* with F. suffix *-age* < L. *-āticum.*

TROOP, a company, especially of soldiers, a crew. (F.) In Shak. Temp. i. 2. 220. — F. *troupe,* 'a troop, crue;' Cot. OF. *trope,* in use in the 13th cent., Littré; cf. Span. *tropa,* MItal. *troppa,* 'a troupe,' Florio; mod. Ital. *truppa;* Late L. *troppus.* β. Origin doubtful; perhaps from Norw. *torp,* a flock, a crowd, Icel. *þorp;* cf. Icel. *þyrpast,* to throng. Körting, § 9520. Der. *troop,* verb, Romeo, i. 5. 50; hence *troop-er, moss-troop-er.*

TROPE, a figure of speech. (L. — Gk.) In Levins; and in Sir T. More, Works, p. 1340 a. — L. *tropus,* a figure of speech, a trope. — Gk. τρόπος, a turning, a turn, a turn or figure of speech. — Gk. τροπ-, 2nd grade of τρέπειν, to turn. + OL. *trepere,* to turn. Der. *trop-ic,* q.v. Also *trop-ic-al,* i. e. figurative; *tropo-log-ic-al,* expressed in tropes, Tyndall, Works, p. 166, col. 1 (see **Logic**). Also *helio-trope.* And see *trophy, troubadour, trover.*

TROPHY, a memorial of the defeat of an enemy, something taken from an enemy. (F. — L. — Gk.) Formerly spelt *trophee,* as in Cotgrave, and in Spenser, F. Q. vii. 7. 56. — F. *trophée,* 'a trophee, a sign or mark of victory;' Cot. — L. *tropæum,* a sign of victory. — Gk. τρόπαιον, τροπαῖον, a trophy, a monument of an enemy's *defeat,* consisting of shields, &c., displayed on a frame. Neut. of τροπαῖος, adj., belonging to a defeat. — Gk. τροπή, a return, a putting to flight of an enemy by causing them to *turn.* — Gk. τροπ-, 2nd grade of τρέπειν, to turn; see **Trope.** Der. *trophi-ed.*

TROPIC, one of the two small circles on the celestial sphere, where the sun appears to *turn,* after reaching its greatest declination north or south; also one of two corresponding circles on the terrestrial sphere. (F. — L. — Gk.) ME. *tropik,* Chaucer, On the Astrolabe, pt. i. c. 17, l. 8. — F. *tropique,* 'a tropick;' Cot. — L. *tropicum,* acc. of *tropicus,* tropical. — Gk. τροπικός, belonging to a turn; ὁ τροπικός κύκλος, the tropic circle. — Gk. τρόπος, a turn; see **Trope.** Der. *tropic,* adj.; *tropic-al, tropic-al-ly.*

TROT, to move or walk fast, run as a horse when not going at full pace. (F. — L.?) ME. *trotten,* Chaucer, C. T. 9412 (E 1538); P. Plowman, B. ii. 164. — F. *trotter,* 'to trot;' Cot. OF. *troter,* 13th cent.; Littré. We also find OF. *trotier,* a trotter, messenger, Late L. *trotārius;* and this answers so nearly to L. *tolūtārius,* going at a trot, that it is usual to suppose OF. *troter* to result from a Late L. **tolūtāre,* to trot, by the common change of *l* into *r,* and loss of *o.* β. *Tolūtārius* is derived from *tolūtim,* adv., at a trot, used of horses. The lit. sense is 'with a lifting up of the feet.' — L. *tollere,* to lift; see **Tolerate.** γ. This etymology is accepted by Diez, Scheler, and Littré; but some compare MHG. *trotten,* to run, perhaps allied to G. *treten,* to tread; MDu. *tratten,* 'to goe, to pace, or to trot;' Hexham. G. *treten* is cognate with E. *tread.* Der. *trot,* sb., *trott-er.*

TROTH, truth, fidelity. (E.) In Shak. Mids. Nt. Dr. ii. 2. 36. ME. *trowþe,* Ormulum, i. 44. Formed from the verb **Trow,** q. v. Der. *troth-ed,* Much Ado, iii. 1. 38; *troth-plight,* a plighting of troth, Wint. Tale, i. 2. 278; *troth-plight = troth-plighted,* Wint. Tale, v. 3. 151. Also *be-troth,* q. v.

TROUBADOUR, a Provençal poet. (Prov. — L. — Gk.) See Warton, Hist. of Eng. Poetry, sect. iii. And see Littré, Roquefort, and Raynouard. *Troubadour* does not seem to be the right Prov. word, but a F. modification of it. The Prov. word is *trobador* (Littré), or (very commonly) *trobaire;* see Bartsch, Chrest. Provençale. From a L. type **tropātōrem,* acc. of **tropātor;* from a verb **tropāre,* formed from L. *tropus,* which was used by Venantius Fortunatus (about A.D. 600) with the sense of 'a kind of singing, a song,' White; and see Ducange. This is only a peculiar use of L. *tropus,* which usually means a trope; see **Trope.** β. The Late L. **tropāre* would have the exact sense 'to make or write, or sing a song' which is so conspicuous in OF. *trover* (F. *trouver*), Prov. *trobar,* Port. and Span. *trovar,* Ital. *trovare;* for, though the mod. F. *trouver* means 'to find' in a general sense, this is merely generalised from the particular sense of 'to find out' or 'devise' poetry; cf. Port. *trova,* a rime, *trovar,* to make rimes, *trovador,* a rimer; Span. *trova,* verse, *trovar,* to versify, also to find; *trovador,* a versifier, finder; *trovista,* a poet; Ital. *trovare,* 'to finde, to deuise, to inuent, to imagine, get, obtain, procure, seeke out,' Florio. It may be added that, even in Gk., τρόπος was used with reference to music, to signify a particular mode, such as τρόπος Λύδιος, the Lydian mode, &c. **γ.** As regards the letter-changes, a L. *p* rightly gives Ital. *v* and Prov. *b*, as in Ital. *arrivare* = Prov. *arribar* < L. *adripare* (see **Arrive**). Cf. also Prov. *trobaire*, a troubadour; from L. nom. **tropātor*. See **Trover**.

TROUBLE, to agitate, disturb, confuse, vex. (F. – L.) ME. *troublen*, Wyclif, Mark, ix. 19; *trublen*, Ancren Riwle, p. 268, l. 20. – OF. *trubler, trobler*, later *troubler*, 'to trouble, disturb;' Cot. Formed as if from a Late L. **turbulāre*, a verb made from L. *turbula*, a disorderly group, a little crowd of people (White), dimin. of *turba*, a crowd. In fact, we find OF. *torbleur*, one who troubles. [From the L. *turba* we have also the verb *turbāre*, to disturb, with much the same sense as F. *troubler*.] **β.** The L. *turba*, a crowd, confused mass of people, is cognate with Gk. τύρβη, also written σύρβη, disorder, throng, bustle; whence τυρβάζειν, to disturb. See **Turbid**. Der. *trouble*, sb., spelt *torble, turble* in Prompt. Parv.; from OF. *troble, truble*, later *trouble*, 'trouble,' Cot.; *trouble-some*, Mer. Wives, i. 1. 325; *troubl-ous*, 2 Hen. VI, i. 2. 22. Also *turb-id, turb-ul-ent*, q. v. Also (from L. *turbāre*) *dis-turb, per-turb*.

TROUGH, a long hollow vessel for water. (E.) ME. *trogh, trough*, Chaucer, C. T. 3627. AS. *troh* or *trog* (gen. *troges*), a trough or hollow vessel; used by Ælfred in the sense of a little boat, tr. of Orosius, b. ii. c. 5. § 7 (end). 'Littoraria, *troh-scip*,' i.e. a little boat, Voc. 166. 4; 'Canthera, *trog*,' id. 12. 12.+Du. *trog*; Icel. *trog*; Dan. *trug*; Swed. *tråg*; G. *trog*, MHG. *troc*. We find also G. *truhe*, OHG. *truha*, a chest or trunk. Teut. type **trugóz*, Idg. type **drukós*, m.; from **Idg. dru-*, as in Skt. *dru*, a tree; with adj. suffix. Thus the sense is 'wooden;' see **Tree**. Der. *tray*.

TROUNCE, to beat, castigate. (F. – L.) 'But the Lord *trounsed* Sisara and all his charettes;' Bible, 1551, Judges, iv. 15. Lit. 'to beat with a truncheon.' – OF. *trons*, m. a truncheon; *tronce*, f., variant of OF. *tronche*, 'a great piece of timber,' Cot., allied to F. *tronc*, a trunk; cf. also F. *tronson*, mod. F. *tronçon*, 'a truncheon or little trunk, a thick slice,' id. See **Truncheon** and **Trunk**. Cf. also F. *troncir*, 'to cut or break off in two,' Cot.; Span. *tronzar*, to shatter.

TROUSERS, TROWSERS, a garment worn by males on the lower limbs. (F. – L. – Gk.) The form *trousers* does not seem to be old; Richardson quotes 'by laced stockings and *trowzers*' from Wiseman's Surgery, b. i. c. 18; Wiseman died in 1676. In older books the word appears without the latter *r*, in the forms *troozes, trouses*, &c., and even *trooze*; cf. Lowland Sc. *trews*. We find, however, the curious and corrupt form *strossers* in Shak. Hen. V, iii. 7. 57, where most mod. editions have *trossers*, though the same form occurs also in Dekker and Middleton; see Dyce's Glossary to Shakespeare. **β.** The word was particularly used of the nether garments of the Irish; Nares cites, from Ware's Antiquities of Ireland, 'their little coats, and strait breeches called *trouses*.' 'Their breeches, like the Irish *trooze*, have hose and stockings sewed together;' Sir T. Herbert, Travels, p. 297 (Todd); or p. 313, ed. 1665. Hence Irish *trius, triubhas*, trousers; MIrish *tribus*; Gael. *triubhas*. Herbert also has the spelling *troozes*, p. 325, ed. 1665. 'The poor *trowz'd* Irish there;' Drayton, Polyolbion, song 22. Cf. also: 'And leaving me to stalk here in my *trowses*,' Ben Jonson, Staple of News, i. 1 (Pennyboy junior). 'Four wild Irish in *trowses*;' Ford, Perkin Warbeck, iii. 1; stage direction. – F. *trousses*, s. pl., trunk-hose, breeches (Hamilton; see also Littré). *Trousses* is the pl. of *trousse*, a bundle, a 'truss,' formerly also a case, such as 'a quiver for arrows;' Cot. Hence *trousses* became a jocular term, used esp. of the breeches of a page (Littré), and was so applied by the English to the Irish garments. – F. *trousser*, 'to trusse, pack, tuck, bind or girt in, pluck or twitch up;' Cot. These senses help to explain the sb. See further under **Truss**. Der. *trosseau*, q. v.

TROUSSEAU, a package; esp. the lighter articles of a bride's outfit. (F. – L. – Gk.) Modern; yet it is not a little remarkable that *trusseaus*, i.e. packages, occurs in the Ancren Riwle, p. 168, l. 1. – F. *trousseau*, 'a little trusse or bundle;' Cot.; OF. *troussel*, dimin. of F. *trousse*, a truss, bundle; see **Truss**.

TROUT, a fresh-water fish. (L. – Gk.) ME. *troute*, spelt *trowte* in the Prompt. Parv. AS. *truht*: 'Tructa, *truht*,' Voc. 180. 37. – L. *tructa* (whence also F. *truite*); also *tructus*. – Gk. τρώκτης, a gnawer, lover of dainties; also a sea-fish with sharp teeth. – Gk. τρώγ-ειν, to gnaw; with suffix -της of the agent. As the sense is 'gnawer' or 'nibbler,' it was easily applied to fish of various kinds. Cf. **Troglodyte**.

TROVER, the gaining possession of goods, by finding or otherwise. (F. – L. – Gk.) 'Trover is the name of an action, which a man hath against one who, having found any of his goods, refuseth to deliver them upon demand;' Blount's Nomolexicon, ed. 1691. In Butler, Hudibras, pt. iii. c. 3, l. 648. An old law-term, in early use, as shown by the spelling. – OF. *trover*, later *trouver*, to find. It answers in form to the Late L. **tropāre*, orig. used in the sense to find out poetry, to invent, devise, which was a sense of OF. *trover*, and prob. the orig. one. See further under **Troubadour**. Hence *treasure-trove*, treasure found, where *trove* is now barbarously pronounced as a monosyllable, though it stands for OF. *trove* (*trové*), pp. of *trover*, to find; see Blackstone, Commentaries, b. i. c. 8. Der. *con-trive, re-trieve*.

TROW, to believe, think, suppose to be true. (E.) In Luke, xvii. 9 (A. V.). ME. *trowen*, Chaucer, C. T. 693 (A 691). OFries. *trouwa*, EFries. *trōen*, to believe. AS. *trūwian*, to trow, trust; from Teut. base **trū-*. We also find AS. *trēowian*, to believe, allied to *trēow*, sb., faith, and to *trēowe*, adj., true; from the Teut. base **trew(w)*. Cf. Icel. *trúa*, to trow, *trúr*, true; Dan. *troe*, to trow, *tro*, true; Swed. *tro*, to trow; Low G. *trouen*, to trow, *trou*, true; Du. *trouwen*, to marry, *trouw*, true; G. *trauen*, OHG. *trūwēn*, to trust; Goth. *trauan*, to believe. See **True**.

TROWEL, a tool used in spreading mortar and in gardening. (F. – L.) ME. *truel* : 'a *truel* of [a] masoun;' Wyclif, Amos, vii. 7, earlier version; the later version has *trulle*. 'Hec trolla, a *trowylle*;' Voc. 728. 29. Spelt *trowell* in Palsgrave. – F. *truelle*, a trowel, spelt *truele* in the 13th cent. (Littré). – Late L. *truella*, a trowel, in use A.D. 1163 (Ducange); cf. L. *trulla*, a small ladle, scoop, fire-pan, trowel. A dimin. of L. *trua*, a stirring-spoon, skimmer, ladle. See **Twirl**.

TROWSERS, the same as **Trousers**, q. v.

TROY-WEIGHT, the weight used by goldsmiths. (F.; *and* E.) Spelt *troie-weight* in Minsheu, ed. 1627. *Troy weyt*; Paston Letters, iii. 297. 'The received opinion is that it took its name from a weight used at the fair of *Troyes*; this is likely enough; we have the pound of Cologne, of Toulouse, and perhaps also of Troyes. That there was a very old English pound of 12 oz. is a well-determined fact, and also that this pound existed long before the name *Troy* was given to it, [is] another .. The *troy-pound* was mentioned as a known weight in 2 Hen. V. cap. 4 (1414), and 2 Hen. VI. cap. 13 (1423),' &c.; Eng. Cyclopædia. And see Haydn, Dict. of Dates. This explanation is verified by the expression 'a Paris pece of syluer weyng *bee the weyght off troye* viij. vuncis;' Arnold's Chronicle, ed. 1811, p. 108; at p. 191, it appears simply as 'troy weyght.' As early as 1392-3, we find 'ponderis .. *de Troye*;' Earl of Derby's Expeditions (C. S.), p. 100, l. 28. *Troyes* is a town in France, to the S.E. of Paris. Cotgrave, s.v. *livre*, mentions the pounds of Spain, Florence, Lyons, and Milan; and explains *la livre des apothecaires* as belonging to 'Troy weight.'

TRUANT, an idler, a boy who absents himself from school without leave. (F. – C.) ME. *truant*, Gower, C. A. ii. 13; bk. iv. 342. The derived sb. *trewandise* occurs as early as in the Ancren Riwle, p. 330, l. 2. – AF. *truaunt*, Boeve de Haumtone, ed. Stimming, l. 281; Vie de St. Auban; F. *truand*, 'a common beggar, vagabond, a rogue, a lazie rascall;' Cot. He also gives the adj. *truand*, 'beggarly, rascally, roguish.' [We find also Span. *truhan*, Port. *truhão*, a buffoon, jester.] Of Celtic origin. – W. *truan*, wretched, *truan*, a wretch; cf. *truedd*, wretchedness, *trueni*, pity, *trugar*, compassionate, *truenus*, piteous. Corn. *tru*, interj. alas! woe! *troc*, wretched; Breton *truez, truhez*, pity, *trueza*, to pity; *truant*, a vagabond, beggar, of which Legonidec says that, though this particular form is borrowed from French, it is none the less of Celtic origin, and that, in the dialect of Vannes, a beggar is called *truek*. Irish *trogha*, miserable, unhappy; *troighe*, grief; *tru*, lean, piteous; *truadh*, a poor, miserable creature; *truagh*, pity, also poor, lean, meagre; &c. Gael. *truaghan*, a poor, distressed creature; *truaghanta*, lamentable, from *truagh*, wretched; cf. *truas*, pity, *trocair*, mercy. **β.** Thus the F. *truand* is formed, with excrescent *d*, from the sb. which appears as W. *truan*, Gael. *truaghan*, a wretched creature; which sb. was orig. an adj. extended from the shorter form seen in W. *tru*, Corn. *troc*, Irish *trogha*, Gael. *truagh*, wretched; OIrish *trúag*; Celtic type **trougos*, wretched (Stokes-Fick, p. 138). Allied to Gk. στρεύγ-ομαι, I am wretched, I feel distress.

TRUCE, a temporary cessation of hostilities, temporary agreement. (E.) The etymology is much obscured by the curious modern spelling; it is really a plural form, and might be spelt *trews*, i.e. pledges, pl. of *trew*, a pledge of truth, derived from the adj. *true*. This comes out clearly in tracing the ME. forms. ME. *triwes*, R. of Glouc. p. 488, l. 10005; *treowes*, K. Alisaunder, 2808; *trewes*, Rich. Coer de Lion, 3207. '*Truwys, trwys*, or *truce* of pees;' Prompt. Parv. All these are pl. forms; the sing. *trewe*, a truce, pledge of reconciliation, occurs in P. Plowman, B. vi. 332, Morte Arthure, ed. Brock, 879. – AS. *trēow*, a compact, promise, pledge, faith (Grein); cf. AS. *trēowa*, by-form *trúwa*, used in the sense of compact in Gen. xvii. 19; it also means faith, Mark, xi. 22. Allied to AS. *tréowe*, true; see **True**. Cf. AF. *trues*, truce, Gaimar, 567; *triwes*, id. 3046; *trewe*, sing., Stat. Realm, i. 300 (1344).

TRUCK (1), to barter, exchange. (F. – Teut.) 'All goods, wares, and merchandises so *trucked*, bought, or otherwise dispended;' Hakluyt's Voyages, i. 228. Just above, on the same page, we have: 'by way of marchandise, *trucke*, or any other respect.' ME. *trukken*, Prompt. Parv.; and even in Ancren Riwle, p. 408, l. 15. – AF. *troquier*, La Clef d'Amors, l. 1067; F. *troquer*, 'to truck, chop, swab, scorce, barter;' Cot. Cf. Span. (and Port.) *trocar*, to barter; Ital. *truccare*, 'to truck, barter;' Florio. β. From OF. *troque*, sb., barter (1537), Godefroy; MF. *troc*, *troq*, 'a bartering;' Cot. And the Vocab. du Haut Maine has *tric pour troc*, a simple exchange; and we find Norm. dial. *faire la troque*, to barter; Walloon *trouk po trouk*, a simple exchange (Rémacle). A North F. form; the Central F. *trocher* occurs in 1434 (Ducange, s. v. *Trocare*). – WFlem. *trok*, *truk*, sale; used with regard to the (good or bad) 'sale' of goods, *trokken*, to procure goods. The WFlem. *trok* and *trokken* are used in *all* the senses of Du. *trek*, *trekken* (De Bo). Cf. Du. *trek*, demand, quick sale; *in trek zijn*, to be in vogue; from *trekken*, vb., to draw. See **Trigger**. Der. *truck*, sb., as above, from F. *troq*, 'a truck, or trucking,' Cot.; cf. Span. *trueca*, *trueque*, barter, Port. *troco*, the change of a piece of gold or silver, *troca*, barter. Also *truck-age*. See Notes on E. Etym., p. 307.

TRUCK (2), a small wheel, a low-wheeled vehicle for heavy articles. (L. – Gk.) 'In gunnery, *trucks* are entire round pieces of wood like wheels fixed on the axle-trees of the carriages, to move the ordinaunce at sea;' Phillips, ed. 1706. He also gives: '*trochus*, a wheel, a top for children to play with.' *Truck* is an English adaptation of L. *trochus*, now disused in its L. form. – Gk. τροχός, a runner, a wheel, disc. – Gk. τροχ-, 2nd grade of τρέχειν, to run; see **Trochee**. Der. *truck-le*, a little wheel, answering to L. *trochlea*; Phillips gives: '*trochlea*, a truckle or pulley, .. which is one of the six mechanical powers or principles;' showing that the L. form *trochlea* was once in use. Baret has: '*Pullie*, trochlea; a *truckle*, or *pullie*.' Cotgrave explains F. *jabot* by 'a truckle or pully;' and the word occurs rather early, as shown under **Truckle**, verb. Hence *truckle-bed*, a bed that runs on small wheels and can be pushed under another bed, Romeo, ii. 1. 39; see Nares. And see *truckle* below.

TRUCKLE, to submit servilely to another. (L. – Gk.) '*Truckle*, to submit, to yield or buckle to;' Phillips, ed. 1706. Not an old word; Todd's Johnson has: 'Shall our nation be in bondage thus Unto a nation that *truckles under* us?' Cleaveland (no reference). Also: 'For which so many a legal cuckold Has been run down in courts and *truckled*;' Butler's Hudibras, Part iii. c. 1. l. 613. To *truckle under* is a phrase having reference to the old *truckle-bed*, which could be pushed under another larger one; and the force of the phrase is in the fact that a pupil or scholar slept *under* his tutor on a *truckle-bed*. See Hall's Satires, b. ii. sat. 6, where he intentionally *reverses* the order of things, saying that a complaisant tutor would submit 'to lie upon the *truckle-bed*, Whiles his young maister lieth *o'er his head*.' Warton, in his Hist. of Eng. Poetry, ed. 1840, iii. 419, has a note upon this passage in which he proves that such was the usual practice both at Oxford and Cambridge, citing: 'When I was in Cambridge, and lay in a *trundle-bed under my tutor*,' Return from Parnassus (1606), Act ii. sc. 6 (Amoretto). He quotes from the statutes of Magdalen College, Oxford, 1459, the statute: 'Sint duo lecti principales, et duo lecti rotales, *trookyll-beddys* vulgariter nuncupati;' cap. xlv. He adds: 'And in the statutes of Trinity College, Oxford, given [in] 1556, *troccle-bed*, the old spelling, ascertains the etymology from *troclea*, a wheel.' In fact, this shows how the words *truckle* and *truck* (2) came to be taken *immediately* from the Latin; they originated at the universities. ¶ No connexion with AS. *trucian*, to fail, which does not in any way explain the word or its use.

TRUCULENT, fierce, barbarous, cruel. (F. – L.) In Cotgrave. – MF. *truculent*, 'truculent, cruell;' Cot. – L. *truculentum*, acc. of *truculentus*, cruel; extended from *trux* (gen. *truc-is*), fierce, wild. Perhaps the orig. sense was 'threatening;' cf. G. *drohen*, MHG. *drouwen*, OHG. *drauwen*, to threaten, AS. *þréagan*, to threaten. Der. *truculent-ly*, *truculence*.

TRUDGE, to travel on foot slowly, march heavily. (F. – Teut.?) In Shak. it means to run heavily, trot along or away; Merry Wives, i. 3. 91; iii. 3. 13; Romeo, i. 2. 34; i. 3. 34. 'May from the prison *trudge*;' Turbervile, That Lovers must not despair, st. 6. 'And let them *trudge* hence apace;' Bale, Apologie, fol. 6 (R.). 'I *trudge* about from gate to gate;' Mirror for Magistrates (Alurede). Perhaps it meant to go about like a vagabond or idle beggar. – F. *trucher*, to beg idly (16th cent.), Littré; Picard *trucher*, to beg; Norm. dial. *trucher*, to sponge upon. Of Teut. origin; cf.

Low G. *truggeln*, to beg fawningly; Du. *troggelen*, to beg, to wheedle; MDu. *truggelen*, 'to trugge up and downe a begging,' Hexham; WFlem. *troggelen*, to walk with difficulty, De Bo (who notices that in Limburg it is pronounced *truggelen* or *trukkelen*); EFries. *trüggeln*, to press back, also to beg with importunity. From Teut. base *þrūg-*, to press; as in Icel. *þrúga*, Swed. *truga*, Dan. *true*, to press. ¶ Florio has Ital. *truccare*, 'to trudge, to skud, or pack away.' Cf. *grudge*<OF. *groucher*. (Doubtful.)

TRUE, firm, established, certain, honest, faithful. (E.) ME. *trewe* (properly dissyllabic), P. Plowman, B. i. 88. AS. *tréowe*, true, also spelt *trýwe*, Grein, ii. 552. Cf. AS. *tréow*, *trýw*, truth, preservation of a compact.+Du. *trouw*, true, faithful; *trouw*, fidelity; Icel. *tryggr*, *trúr*, true; Dan. *tro*, true; *tro*, truth; Swed. *trogen*, true; *tro*, fidelity; G. *treu*, OHG. *triuwi*, true; *treue*, OHG. *triuwa*, fidelity; Goth. *triggws*, true; *triggwa*, a covenant; cf. *trauan*, to trow, trust, be persuaded. β. The Teut. type appears to be **trewwoz*, adj., 'believed in, relied upon;' from Idg. √DREU, to rely upon, trust in; whence also Lith. *drú-tas*, firm, OPrussian *druwis*, *druwi*, belief, *druwit*, to believe. Der. *tru-ly*, *tru-ism* (a coined word); also *tru-th*, ME. *trewthe*, *trouthe*, Chaucer, C. T. 10877 (F 563), AS. *tréowðu*, Exod. xix. 5, cognate with Icel. *tryggð*; hence *truth-ful*, *-ly*, *-ness*. Also *troth* (doublet of *truth*), *trow*, *tru-st*.

TRUFFLE, a round underground edible fungus. (F. – L.) In Phillips, ed. 1706. 'A dish of *trufles*;' Evelyn, Diary, Sept. 30, 1644. – MF. *trufle*, another spelling of *truffe*, 'a most dainty kind of round and russet root;' Cot. Cf. Span. *trufa*, a truffle; also a cheat (see **Trifle**). We also find F. *tartoufle* in the same sense; Ital. *tartufo*, a trúffle; *tartufi bianchi*, white esculent roots, i. e. potatoes. β. The F. *truffe*, Span. *trufa*, is supposed to be derived from L. *tuber*, a tuber, esculent root, a truffle (Juv. v. 116); the neut. pl. *tubera* would give a nom. fem. **tufre* (whence *trufe* by shifting of *r*) as in other instances; e. g. the L. fem. sing. *antiphōna*=Gk. neut. pl. ἀντίφωνα. γ. That this is the right explanation (for which see Diez and Scheler) is rendered almost certain by the Ital. form *tartufo* (also *tartufola*), where *tar-* stands for L. *terræ* (of the earth), and *tartufo* is from *terræ tuber*. Florio gives Ital. *tartuffo*, *tartuffola*, 'a kinde of meate, fruite, or roote of the nature of potatoes called *traffles* [*truffles*?]; also, a kind of artichock.' Brugmann derives Ital. *-tufo* (in *tar-tufo*) from an Oscan-Umbrian dialect; i. § 413 (8). δ. From the Ital. *tartufola* is derived (by dissimilation of the double *t*) the curious G. *kartoffel*, a potato; of which an earlier form was *tartuffel*. See further under **Tuber**. Doublet, *trifle*, q. v.

TRULL, a drab, worthless woman. (G.) In Shak. Antony, iii. 6. 95; and in Levins. 'The Governour [of Brill, in Holland] was all bedewed with drinke, His *truls* and he were all layde downe to sleepe;' Gascoigne, Voyage into Holland, A. D. 1572; Works, ed. Hazlitt, i. 391. We should expect to find it a Du. word, but it is German, imported, perhaps, by way of Holland, though not in Hexham's or Sewel's dictionaries. – G. *trolle*, *trulle*, a trull (whence Walloon *trouille* (Sigart), Picard *troule*, the same. It is a fem. form, allied to MDu. *drol*, m., 'a pleasant or a merrie man, or a gester,' Hexham, and to Dan. *trold*, Swed. and Icel. *troll*, a merry elf; see **Droll**. The orig. sense was merely a merry or droll companion.

TRUMP (1), a trumpet, kind of wind instrument. (F. – G. – Slav.) ME. *trumpe*, *trompe*, Chaucer, C. T. 676 (A 674); Rob. of Brunne, tr. of Langtoft, p. 30, l. 13. – F. *trompe*, 'a trump, or trumpet;' Cot. [Cf. Span., Port., and Prov. *trompa*, Ital. *tromba*.] – OHG. *trumpa*, *trumba*, a trumpet (Hatzfeld). Of Slavonic origin. – OSlav. type **tromba* (Miklosich); evidenced by OSlav. and Polish *tra(m)ba*, with the former *a* nasal, Slovenian *tromba*, *trôba*, a trumpet; Russ. *truba*, a pipe, a tube, a trumpet. Der. *trump-et*, ME. *trompette*, Gower, C. A. iii. 217; bk. vii. 3744; from F. *trompette*, 'a trumpet,' Cot., dimin. of F. *trompe*; *trump-et-er*, from F. *trompeteur*, 'a trumpeter,' Cot. Also *trumpet-fish*; *trumpet-tongued*, Macb. i. 7. 19. And see *trumpery*.

TRUMP (2), one of the suit of cards that takes any other suit. (F. – L.) Well known to be a corruption of *triumph*; see Latimer's Sermons (Parker Society), i. 1, 8, 13, and Foxe's remarks on them, id. vol. ii. p. xi. *Triumph* in Shak. Antony, iv. 14. 20, prob. means a trump-card; see Nares. – F. *triomphe*, 'the card-game called ruffe, or trump; also the ruffe or trump at it;' Cot. See **Triumph**. Der. *trump*, verb; *trump-card*.

TRUMPERY, falsehood, idle talk, trash. (F. – L.) In Temp. iv. 186; and in Levins. Caxton has *tromperye*, meaning 'deception;' Godfrey of Bulloigne, p. 238. The proper sense is deceit, or something deceptive, hence imposture, &c. – F. *tromperie*, 'a craft, wile, fraud;' Cot. – F. *tromper*, 'to cousen, deceive,' id. β. Littré says that the orig. sense was to play on the trump or trumpet; thence arose the phrase *se tromper de quelqu'un*, to play with any one, to amuse oneself at his expense; hence the sense to beguile, cheat.

This seems to be the right and simple solution; and Littré also quotes, s. v. *trompette* (1), the [15th cent.] phrase *me joues tu de la trompete?* are you playing the trumpet with me, i. e. are you playing with me, which confirms it. See further under **Trump** (1).

TRUMPET, the dimin. of **Trump** (1), q. v.

TRUNCATE, to cut off short. (L.) Phillips has '*truncated* pyramid or cone.'—L. *truncātus*, pp. of *truncāre*, to cut off, reduce to a trunk.—L. *truncus*, a trunk, stock; see **Trunk**. Der. *truncat-ion*, from F. *troncation*, 'a truncation, trunking, mutilation, cutting off,' Cot. from L. acc. *truncātiōnem*.

TRUNCHEON, a cudgel, short staff. (F.—L.) ME. *tronchoun*, Chaucer, C. T. 2617 (A 2615), where it means the shaft of a broken spear; so also *tronchon*, King Alisaunder, 3745.—ONorth F. *tronchon* (Norm. dial.); see Moisy and Godefroy; OF. *tronçon*; MF. *tronson*, 'a truncheon, or little trunk, a thick slice, luncheon, or piece cut off;' Cot. Mod. F. *tronçon*. Dimin. of F. *tronc*, 'trunck, stock, stemme;' Cot.; see **Trunk**. Der. *truncheon-er*, Hen. VIII, v. 4. 54.

TRUNDLE, a wheel, anything round; to roll. (F.—Low G.) Now chiefly used only as a verb, to roll round; the sb. occurs in *trundle-bed*, a bed running on wheels, *trundle-tail*, a round tail of a dog; cf. AS. *tryndled*, rounded; Voc. 152. 5. [We also find: '*Trendyll*, sb., tournouer;' Palsgrave. 'I *tryndell*, as a boule or a stone dothe, *Je roulle*;' id. ME. *trendil*, sb., *trendelen*, verb. '*Trendyl*, troclea;' '*Trendelyn* a rownd thynge, Trocleo, volvo;' Prompt. Parv.; from AS. *trendel*, a circle; see further under **Trend**.] β. The vowel is due to borrowing from MF. (Picard) *trondeler*, 'to trundle,' Cot.; Walloon *trondeler*, to roll (Sigart). Of Low G. origin; cf. Low G. *tröndeln*, Pomeran. *tründeln*, to trundle a hoop.—Teut. *trund-*, weak grade of a lost str. vb. *trendan*, to roll (pt. t. *trand*); whence also AS. *sin-tryndel*, a large round shield; OFries. *trund*, round. Cf. NFries., Swed., Dan. *trind*, round. The ME. *trenden*, to turn, roll, is a secondary verb from *trand*, 2nd grade of *trendan-*. See **Trend**. Der. *trundle-bed*, see quotation s. v. *truckle*; *trundle bedstead* occurs in Bury Wills, ed. Tymms, p. 220, l. 11, in a will dated 1649; *trundle-tail*, a cur, Beaum. and Fletcher, Love's Cure, iii. 3. 16, according to Richardson, but Darley's ed. has *trindle-tail*; see, however, K. Lear, iii. 6. 73.

TRUNK (1), the stem of a tree, proboscis of an elephant, shaft of a column, chest for clothes. (F.—L.) 'A cheste, or *trunke* of clene syluer;' Fabyan, Chron. cap. 131, fol. lxvii. ed. Ellis, p. 113. ME. *tronke*, a body without limbs; Caxton, Golden Legend, Saul, § 3. —F. *tronc*, 'the truncke, stock, stemme, or body of a tree; also a trunk, or headlesse body; also, the poor man's box in churches' [whence E. *trunk* = box]; Cot.—L. *truncum*, acc. of *truncus*, a trunk, stem, trunk of the body, piece cut off. Spelt *troncus* in Lucretius, i. 354; cf. *truncus*, adj., maimed, mutilated. See Brugmann, i. § 144. ☞ The elephant's *trunk* owes its name to an error (see below). The AF. *trunk*, a trunk of a tree, is in Wm. of Wadington's Manuel, l. 11090. Der. *trunk-ed*, having a trunk; *trunk-line* (of a railway); *trunk-hose*, *trunk-breeches* (see Nares), short wide breeches, reaching a little above or sometimes below the knee, and striped, meaning (I suppose) *trunked hose*, i. e. cut short (cf. *trunked* = truncated, Spenser, F. Q. ii. 5. 4). Also *trunc-ate*, q. v., *trunch-eon*, q. v., *trunn-ion*, q. v., *trounce*, q. v.

TRUNK (2), the proboscis of an elephant. (F.—G.—Slav.) In Holland, tr. of Pliny, bk. viii. c. 7. A mistaken form of *trump*; which was confused with *trunk*, because the latter was sometimes used with the notion of a (hollow) stem or a 'tube,' which was also a sense of *trump* (Palsgrave). Cf. F. *trompe*, 'a trump, or trumpet; . . also, the snowt of an elephant,' Cot. See **Trump** (1). For *trunk*, a speaking-tube, see Ben Jonson, Epicœne, i. 1. Halliwell gives both *trunk* and *trump*, as meaning 'a pea-shooter;' and notes the corrupt use of *trunk* to mean a trumpet at cards. See **Trunk** (1).

TRUNNION, one of the stumps or round projections on each side of a cannon, on which it rests in the carriage. (F.—L.) In Phillips, ed. 1706.—F. *trognon*, 'the stock, stump, or trunk of a branchless tree;' Cot. Dimin. of *tron*, 'a piece of anything, a trunk, stem,' &c.; Cot. This is a shortened form of *tronc*, due perhaps (as Diez suggests) to misdividing the derived word *tronçon* as *tron-çon*; in any case *tron* and *tronc* meant the same thing, as Cotgrave tells us. Cf. Ital. *troncone*, from *tronco*. See **Trunk**.

TRUSS, to pack, bind up, fasten as in a package or in bundles. (F.—L.—Gk.) ME. *trussen*, P. Plowman, B. ii. 218; Ancren Riwle, p. 322, l. 6. [The sb. *trusse*, a package, is in the Prompt. Parv., p. 504.]—OF. *trusser*, *trosser* (also *tourser*, *torser*), MF. *trousser*, 'to trusse, pack, bind or girt in;' Cot. The old spelling *torser* (*tourser*, *torser* in Godefroy) is supposed to be due to Late L. *tursus*, L. *thyrsus*, a stalk.—Gk. θύρσος, a stalk, stem; see **Thyrsus**. § 9606. Hence OF. *tourse*, a bundle, *toursel*, *trousel*, a little bundle, F. *trousseau*. ¶ The idea seems to be that of 'gathering stalks

together,' as in making up a bunch of flowers, &c. Cf. Ital. *torso*, 'a stem or stalke of any herbe;' Florio. Der. *truss*, sb., ME. *trusse*, as above. Also *trous-ers*, q. v., *trouss-eau*, q. v.

TRUST, confidence, belief, credit, ground of confidence. (E.) ME. *trust*, Ancren Riwle, p. 202, l. 7. AS. *trūst*, not found; cf. *trēows-ian*, to pledge oneself, *trūw-ian*, to trust.+OFries. *trāst*; Icel. *traust*, trust, protection, firmness; Dan. and Swed. *tröst*, comfort, consolation.+G. *trost*, consolation, help, protection; Goth. *trausti*, a covenant; Eph. ii. 12. β. The Teut. base of the Icel. form is *trausto-*, formed with Idg. suffix *-to-* from *trau-s-*, extended from *trau-*, as seen in Goth. *trau-an*, to believe, to trust; see **True**, **Trow**. Der. *trust*, verb, ME. *trusten*, O. Eng. Homilies, i. 213, l. 7; *trust-er*; *trust-ee*, one who is trusted, a coined word, with the suffix *-ee* = F. *é* (L. *-ātus*); *trust-ful*, 1 Hen. IV, ii. 4. 434, *trust-ful-ly*, *trust-ful-ness*; *trust-less*, Shak. Lucrece, 2; *trust-y*, ME. *trusti*, Ancren Riwle, p. 334, l. 21; *trust-i-ly*, *trust-i-ness*; *trust-worthy* (not in Todd's Johnson), *trust-worthi-ly*, *trust-worthi-ness*. Also *mis-trust*, q. v., *tryst*, q. v.

TRUTH, sb.; see **True**. Doublet, *troth*.

TRY, to test, sift, select, examine judicially, examine experimentally; also, to endeavour. (F.—L.) The old sense is usually to sift, select, pick out. ME. *trien*, *tryen*, P. Plowman, B. i. 205. '*Tryin*, *tryyn*, Eligo, preēligo, discerno;' Prompt. Parv.—F. *trier*, 'to pick, chuse, cull out from among others;' Cot. Cf. Prov. *triar*, to choose, *tria*, choice (Bartsch). —Late L. *tritāre*, to triturate; cf. Ital. *tritare*, 'to bruze, to weare, . . . also to grinde or thresh corne,' Florio.—L. *tritus*, pp. of *terere*, to rub, to thresh corn; see **Trite**. β. Diez explains it thus: L. *terere grānum* is to thresh corn; the Prov. *triar lo gra de la palha* is to separate the corn from the stalk; to which he adds other arguments. It would appear that the meaning passed over from the threshing of corn to the separation of the grain from the straw, and thence to the notion of selecting, culling, purifying. Cf. Ital. *tritare*, 'to crumble, grind; to ponder, consider, sift, scan, examine;' Baretti. To *try* gold is to purify it; cf. 'tried gold,' Merch. Ven. ii. 7. 53; 'the fire seven times *tried* this;' id. ii. 9. 63. Der. *try*, sb., Timon, v. 1. 11. Also *try-ing*; *try-sail*, a small sail *tried* when the wind is very high. Also *tri-al*, a coined word, spelt *triall* in Frith's Works, p. 81, col. 1.

TRYST, **TRIST**, an appointment to meet, an appointed meeting. (F.—Scand.) See Jamieson's Scottish Dictionary. A *trist* (ME. *trist*, *trister*) was an appointed station in hunting, a place where a man was stationed to watch. 'Lo, holde thee at thy *triste* cloos, and I Shal wel the deer vnto thy bowe dryue;' Chaucer, Troil. ii. 1534. 'To *triste* was he set, forto waite the chance;' Rob. of Brunne, tr. of Langtoft, p. 94. Spelt *tryster*, Gawain and Grene Knight, 1712; *tristre*, Ancren Riwle, p. 332. Hence the phr. *to hold trist*, *to keep trist*, *to bide trist*, to stay where placed, or to come to an appointed place. 'Halden *triste*,' O. Eng. Met. Hom., ed. Small, p. 82.—OF. *triste*, *tristre*, station to watch (in hunting), ambush (Godefroy); Low L. *trista*. Prob. of Scand. origin; cf. Icel. *treysta*(*st*), to trust to, rely upon; Swed. *trösta*, Dan. *tröste*, to trust; see **Trust**. Hence ME. *trist*, trust. 'Lady, in yow is all my *tryste*;' Erl of Tolous, 550, in Ritson, Met. Romances, vol. iii.

TSAR, a better spelling of **Czar**, q. v.

TUB, a kind of vessel, a small cask. (O. Low G.) ME. *tubbe*, Chaucer, C. T. 3621. Not improbably a term introduced by Flemish brewers.—MDu. *tobbe*, *dobbe*, 'a tubbe;' Hexham; mod. Du. *tobbe*. EFries. *tubbe*; Low G. *tubbe*, a tub, esp. a tub in which orange-trees are planted. ¶ The G. *zuber*, cognate with Low G. *töver*, means a two-handled vessel, and is the same as OHG. *zupar*, *zubar*; this is derived from *zwi*, later *zwei*, two, and the suffix *-bar* (as in *frucht-bar*, fruit-bearing) from OHG. *beran*, *peran*, to bear. Thus G. *zu-ber* = Low G. *tö-ver*, (= two-bearing), i. e. a vessel borne or carried by two handles. But this throws no light on *tub*, since *tubbe* and *töver* are a long way apart. Der. *tubb-y*, tub-like.

TUBE, a pipe, long hollow cylinder. (F.—L.) In Milton, P. L. iii. 590.—F. *tube*, 'a conduit-pipe;' Cot.—L. *tubum*, acc. of *tubus*, a pipe, tube; akin to L. *tuba*, a trumpet. Der. *tub-ing*, a length of tube; *tubul-ar*, from L. *tubul-us*, dimin. of *tubus*; *tubul-at-ed*, from L. *tubulātus*, formed like a pipe.

TUBER, a knob on a root, a rounded root. (L.) '*Tuber*, a truffle, a knot in a tree,' &c.; Phillips, ed. 1617.—L. *tūber*, a bump, swelling, tumour, knob on plants, a truffle. To be divided as *tū-b-er* (cf. L. *plu-u-ia*, rain, with *plu-it*, it rains); allied to *tu-m-ēre*, to swell; so that *tūber* is lit. 'a swelling.' See **Tumid**. Brugmann, i. § 413 (8). Der. *tuber-cle*, from F. *tubercle*, 'the small rising or swelling of a pimple,' Cot., from L. *tūber-cu-lum*, double dimin. of *tūber*; whence *tubercul-ar*, *tubercul-ous* < F. *tuberculeux*, 'swelling,' Cot. Also *tuber-ous* (Phillips), from F. *tubereux*, 'swelling, bunchy,' Cot., from L. *tūberōsus*, full of swellings; also *tuber-ose* (Phillips), directly from L. *tūberōsus*. Also *tuberosa* (Phillips), fem. of L. *tūberōsus*, as the name of a flower: now *tuberose* (often absurdly pronounced as *tube-rose* !). Also *truffle*, q. v. ; *trifle*, q. v. ; *pro-tuber-ant.*

TUCK (1), to draw close together, fold or gather in a dress. (OLow G.) ME. *tukken.* ' *Tukkyn vp*, or stykkyn vp, trukkyn vp or stakkyn vp, *Suffarcino*;' Prompt. Parv. Chaucer has *tukked*, i. e. with the frock drawn up under the girdle, C. T. 623 ; also *y-tukked*, 7319 (D 1737). Not an E. word, but borrowed from abroad.—Low G. *tukken, tokken*, to pull up, draw up, tuck up ; also to entice ; allied to Low G. *tuken*, to ruck up, lie in folds, as a badly made garment. The same word as MDu. *tocken*, ' to entise,' Hexham ; MSwed. *tocka*, to draw towards one.+G. *zucken*, OHG. *zucchen*, to draw or twitch up, to shrug. β. Teut. base *tukk-*; intensive form from the weak grade (**tuh*) of **teuhan-*, the strong verb appearing as Goth. *tiuhan*, AS. *teön*, G. *ziehen*, to draw ; see **Touch**. Allied to **Tug**. The verb means ' to draw up with a *tug* or twitch,' to hitch up. **Der.** *tuck*, sb., a fold ; *tuck-er*, a piece of cloth tucked in over the bosom. ☞ ME. *trukken*, in Prompt. Parv. as above, is a Scand. word ; Swed. *trycka*, Dan. *trykke*, to press, squeeze ; cf. G. *drücken.*

TUCK (2), a rapier. (F.—Ital.—G.) ' Dismount thy *tuck* ;' Tw. Nt. iii. 4. 244. A fencing term, and, like other such terms, an Ital. word, but borrowed through French. Just as E. *ticket* is from F. *estiquet* or *étiquet*, so *tuck* is short for *étoc*, occasional form of MF. *estoc*, ' the stock of a tree ; . . . also a rapier, or tuck ; also a thrust ;' Cot.—Ital. *stocco*, ' a truncheon, a tuck, a short sword ;' Florio.—G. *stock*, a stump, stock, stick, staff ; cognate with E. **Stock**, q. v.

TUCK (3), beat of drum, blow, stroke. (F.—Teut.) ' Hercules it smyttis with a mighty *touk* ;' G. Douglas, tr. of Virgil, Æn. viii. ch. iv. 119.—Picard (or Walloon) *toquer, toker*, ONorth F. *touquer*, to touch, strike ; variant of F. *toucher*, to touch ; see below.

TUCKER, a fuller. (F.—Teut.) ME. *tokker*, lit. ' beater ;' though the cloth was worked up with the feet ; P. Plowman, A. prol. 100.—ONorth F. *touquer* (above).—Low G. *tukken*, to beat, to touch. See Notes on E. Etym., p. 308.

TUCKET, a flourish on a trumpet. (F.—Teut.) In Hen. V, iv. 2. 35. The form answers to ONorth F. **touket*, for OF. *touchet*, a blow ; given in Godefroy. The sense answers to that of Ital. *toccata*, a prelude to a piece of music (Torriano) ; Florio only gives *toccata*, ' a touch, a touching ;' but he notes *tocco di campana* (lit. a touch of the bell), ' a knock, a stroke, a knell or peale, or toule upon the bells.' *Toccata* is properly the fem. of the pp. of *toccare*, to touch ; of Teut. origin. See **Touch**. And compare **Tocsin.**

TUESDAY, the third day of the week. (E.) ME. *Tewesday* ; spelt *Tewisday* in Wyclif's Select Works, ed. Arnold, ii. 75, l. 14. AS. *Tiwes dæg*, Mark, xiv. 1, *rubric*. Lit. the day of Tiw, of which *Tiwes* is the gen. case.+Icel. *Tȳs dagr*, the day of *Tȳr* ; where *Tȳs* is the gen. of *Tȳr*, the god of war ; Dan. *Tirsdag* ; Swed. *Tisdag* ; G. *Dienstag*, MHG. *Zistag*, OHG. *Zies tac*, the day of *Ziu*, god of war. β. The AS. *Tiw* (Icel. *Tȳr*, OHG. *Ziu*) answers to the L. *Mars* as far as the sense goes ; but the *name itself* answers to Skt. *dēva-s*, god ; allied to L. *deus*, and to L. *Iu-* in *Iu-piter*, Gk. Ζεύς, Skt. *Dyaus*, and means ' the shining one.' ¶ A translation of L. *diēs Martis.*

TUFA, a soft stone, usually calcareous. (Ital.—L.) Not from Ital. *tufa*, ' volcanic earth ;' Baretti. But an error for *tufo*, ' a kind of porous stone ;' id.—L. *tōfus, tōphus.* Cf. Gk. τόφος, tufa. ¶ Also written *tuff*, from MF. *tuf, tuffe* (from Ital. *tufo*), ' a kind of soft and brittle stone ;' Cotgrave.

TUFT (1), a small cluster or knot, crest. (F.—Teut.) ' With a knoppe, othir-wyse callyd a *tufft* ;' Bury Wills, ed. Tymms, p. 36, in a will dated 1463. ' A *tuft* (or *toft*) of heres'= a tuft of hairs ; Chaucer, C. T. 557 (A 555). The proper form should rather be *tuff*, as in prov. E. *tuff*, a lock of hair (Halliwell), Lowland Sc. *tuff*, a tuft of feathers (Jamieson). Howell has *tuffs*, pl. ; Famil. Letters, i. let. 27. Cf. W. *twff* (from E.). The final *t* was due to confusion with **Tuft** (2), q. v. ; or it may have been excrescent.—F. *touffe* ; ' *touffe de cheveux*, a tuft or lock of curled hair ;' Cot. [He also gives *touffe de bois*, ' a hoult, a tuft of trees growing near a house ;' which was easily altered to *tuft* (2) below.] Of Teut. origin ; cf. Swed. dial. *tuppa*, a tuft, fringe ; Icel. *toppr*, a top, tuft or lock of hair, horse's crest ; MDu. *top*, ' a tuft of haire, a top,' Hexham ; G. *zopf.* If so, *tuft* is a doublet of *top* (1). 2. Otherwise, F. *touffe* may be from Late L. *tūfa*, a kind of standard, perhaps a tuft ; said to be from AS. *þūf*, a tuft (see Toller). Cf. Swed. *tofva*, a tuft, matted hair ; EFries. *tūf-ke*, a little tuft ; Swed. *tofs*, a tuft. Perhaps also MDu. *tuyf*, a Turkish turban (Hexham) ; called in E. a *tuff* (Nares). **Der.** *tuff-et*, Norm. dial. *touffette*, a little tuft, a bow of ribbon (Moisy) ; dimin. of *touffe* (above).

TUFT (2), a plantation, clump of trees. (F.—Teut.) ' The *tuft* of olives ;' Shak. As You Like It, iii. 5. 75. Halliwell gives : ' *Tuft*, a plantation.' It seems to be the same as *tuft* (1) ; and is sufficiently

explained by Cotgrave's ' *touffe de bois*, a hoult or tuft of trees growing near a house ;' see **Tuft** (1). Perhaps sometimes confused with **Toft**, q. v.

TUG, to pull, drag along. (Scand.) ME. *toggen*, Prompt. Parv. ; Ancren Riwle, p. 424, last line but one, where it means to sport or dally. A verb formed from Icel. *tog*, MSwed. *tog*, a rope to pull by ; or, as a secondary verb, from the weak grade (**tuh, *tug*) of the strong verb which appears as Icel. *tjūga* (pp. *tog-inn*), AS. *teón*, G. *ziehen*, Goth. *tiuhan*, to draw, whence a great number of derivatives have arisen. One of these derivatives, *to tow*, comes very near to *tug* in sense. See **Tow** (1). Allied to EFries. *tokken*, to pull, tug ; Low G. *tukken*, to pull up, draw up ; cf. Low G. *togg*, a pull, a tug (Danneil). Cf. also MDu. *toge*, ' a draught of beere,' Hexham ; G. *zug*, a pull, tug, draught ; Icel. *töggla*, to tug. **Der.** *tug*, sb. Allied to *tuck* (1).

TUITION, care and instruction of the young. (F.—L.) ' *Tuicyon* and gouernaunce ;' Sir T. Elyot, The Governour, b. i. c. 6 ; ME. *tuicion*, Libell of Eng. Policy, l. 1138.—F. *tuition*, ' tuition, protection ;' Cot.—L. *tuitiōnem*, acc. of *tuitio*, protection ; cf. *tuit-us*, pp. of *tuērī*, to watch, protect. **Der.** *in-tuition* ; and see *tu-tel-age, tu-tor.*

TULIP, the name of a flower. (F.—Ital.—Turk.—Pers.) In Ben Jonson, Pan's Anniversary (Shepherd).—MF. *tulippe*, also *tulipan*, ' the delicate flower called a *tulipa*, or *tulipie*, or Dalmatian Cap ;' Cot. So called from its likeness to a *turban.*—Ital. *tulipa, tulipano*, a tulip.—Turk. *tulbend*, vulgar pronunciation of *dulbend*, a turban ; Zenker's Turk. Dict. p. 433.—Pers. *dulband*, a turban. (See *Turban* in Yule.) See **Turban**. Doublet, *turban.*

TULLE, a kind of silk open-work or lace. (F.) Named from *Tulle*, in the department of Corrèze, France ; where it was first made (Littré).

TULWAR, an Indian sabre. (Hind.) From Hind. *talwār, tar-wār*, a sword (Forbes).

TULY, red or scarlet. (F.—L.) ' Off *tuely* silk ;' Rich. Coer de Lion, 67, 1516 ; and see Halliwell.—OF. *tieulé*, of the colour of a tile ; i.e. red (Godefroy).—OF. *tieule*, F. *tuile*, a tile.—L. *tēgula*, a tile. See **Tile.**

TUMBLE, to fall over, fall suddenly, roll over. (E.) ME. *tumblen*, Wyclif, Matt. xiv. 6, in one MS. of the later version ; *tomblen*, King Alisaunder, 2465. Frequentative form (with the usual -*l-* for -*el-*) of *tumben* or *tomben* ; in Trevisa, iv. 365, we have *þe wenche þat tombede* (various reading *tomblede*) ; Stratmann.—AS. *tumbian*, to tumble, turn heels over head, Matt. xiv. 6 ; in some old pictures of this scene, Herodias' daughter is represented as standing on her head.+Du. *tuimelen*, to tumble ; MDu. *tumelen* (Hexham), also *tommelen, tummelen*, id. ; G. *taumelen, tummeln*, to reel, to stagger ; OHG. *tūmōn*, to turn round and round, whence *tūmari*, a tumbler, acrobat (an OLow G. form, acc. to Gallée) ; Dan. *tumle*, Swed. *tumla*, to tumble, toss about. The F. *tomber* is of Teut. origin. β. It will be observed that, contrary to Grimm's law, the word begins with *t* both in German and English ; this points to borrowing, and suggests that the G. word is of Low G. origin. **Der.** *tumble*, sb. ; *tumbl-er*, an acrobat, L. L. L. iii. 190, which took the place of AS. *tumbere* ; ' *Saltator, tumbere*,' Voc. 150. 20 ; cf. ' *Saltator*, a *tumbler*,' in a Nominale of the 15th century, id. 696. 35 ; also *tumbl-er*, a kind of drinking-glass, orig. without a foot, so that it could not be set down except when empty. Also *tumb-r-el* (see Nares), spelt *tumrell-cart* in Palsgrave (for which he gives *tumbreau* as the F. equivalent), from OF. *tumbrel, tumberel*, later *tumbereau*, ' a tumbrell,' Cot., also spelt *tomberel, tombereau* (Cot.), lit. a *tumble*-cart, or two-wheeled cart which could be tumbled over or upturned to deposit the manure with which it was usually laden ; derived from F. *tomber*, to fall, a word of Teut. origin, as above. Cf. AF. *tumberel*, a tumbrel, Stat. Realm, i. 218.

TUMEFY, to cause to swell, also to swell. (F.—L.) Spelt *tumify* in Phillips, who also has the sb. *tumefaction.*—F. *tumefier*, ' to make to swelle, or puffe up ;' Cot.—Late L. **tumeficāre*, for L. *tume-facere*, to tumefy, make to swell.—L. *tume-*, for *tumēre*, to swell ; and *facere*, to make ; see **Tumid** and **Fact**. **Der.** *tumefaction*, as if from L. **tumefactio* (not used), like *tumefactus*, pp. of *tume-facere.*

TUMID, inflated, bombastic. (L.) In Milton, P. L. vii. 288. —L. *tumidus*, swelling.—L. *tumēre*, to swell.—√TEU, to swell, increase ; whence also Gk. τύ-λη, τύ-λος, a swelling. Cf. Skt. *tu*, to be powerful, to increase. Brugmann, i. § 413 (8). **Der.** *tumid-ly*, -*ness*. Also (from *tumēre*) *tum-our*, a swelling, Milton, Samson, 185, from F. *tumeur*, ' a tumor, swelling,' Cot., from L. acc. *tumōrem.* And see *tum-ult, tum-ul-us.* From the same root are *tu-ber, pro-tuber-ant, truffle, trifle, thumb.*

TUMP, a hillock. (C.) The W. *twmp*, a tump, may be from E. But the word is prob. Celtic ; from W. *tom*, Gael. and Irish *tom*, a hillock ; allied to Gk. τύμβος, L. *tumulus*, a mound. See **Tumulus, Tomb.**

TUMULT, excitement, uproar, agitation. (F.–L.) In K. John, IV. 2. 247 ; *tumulte* in Levins.–F. *tumulte*, ' a tumult, uprore ; ' Cot. –L. *tumultum*, acc. of *tumultus*, a restless swelling or surging up, a tumult.–L. *tum-ēre*, to swell ; cf. *tumulus*, of which *tumultus* seems to be an extended form ; cf. Skt. *tumula-m*, n., tumult ; *tumula-*, adj., noisy, tumultuous. See **Tumulus, Tumid. Der.** *tumult*, verb, Milton, tr. of Ps. ii. 1 ; *tumult-u-ar-y*, from F. *tumultuaire*, ' tumultuary,' Cot., from L. *tumultuārius*, hurried. Also *tumult-u-ous*, Rich. II, iv. 140, from F. *tumultueux*, ' tumultuous,' Cot., from L. *tumultuōsus*, full of tumult, which from *tumultu-*, decl. stem of *tumultus*, with suffix *-ōsus* ; *tumultuous-ly, -ness.*

TUMULUS, a mound of earth over a grave. (L.) A late word ; not in Todd's Johnson.–L. *tumulus*, a mound ; lit. a swelling. –L. *tum-ēre*, to swell ; see **Tumid.** And see **Tump.**

TUN, a large cask ; see **Ton.**

TUNE, tone, sound, melody, a melodious air. (F.–L.–Gk.) ' With many a *tun* and many a note ; ' Gower, C. A. iii. 303 ; bk. viii. 830.–AF. *tun*, Life of Edw. Conf. p. 18 ; F. *ton*, ' a tune, or sound ; ' Cot.–L. *tonum*, acc. of *tonus*, a sound.–Gk. τόνος, a tone ; see **Tone.** ¶ The old word *tune* was afterwards re-introduced as *tone*, which is a later form. **Der.** *tune*, verb, Two Gent. iv. 2. 25 ; *tune-able*, Mids. Nt. Dr. i. 1. 184 ; *tun-er*, Romeo, ii. 4. 30 ; *tune-ful*, Spenser, Tears of the Muses, 27 ; *tune-ful-ly* ; *tune-less*, Spenser, Sonnet 44.

TUNGSTEN, a very heavy metal. (Swedish.) Also called *wolfram*, and *scheelium* (from the discoverer). ' From tungstate of lead, Scheele in 1781 obtained tungstic acid, whence the brothers De Luyart in 1786 obtained the metal ; ' Haydn, Dict. of Dates. ' The name indicates *heavy stone*, in consequence of the high specific gravity of its Swedish ore ; ' Engl. Cycl. The word is Swedish.– Swed. *tungsten*, compounded of *tung*, heavy ; and *sten*, a stone. Ferrall and Repp's Dan. Dict. gives the very word *tungsteen*, tungsten, from similar Danish elements, viz. *tung*, heavy, and *steen*. β. Swed. *sten*, Dan. *steen*, are cognate with E. **Stone.** Swed. and Dan. *tung* are the same as Icel. *þungr*, heavy ; whence *þungi*, a load, *þunga*, to load. Cf. Lithuan. *tunku*, I become fat, infin. *tùkti*.

TUNIC, an under-garment, loose frock. (L.) Introduced directly from the Latin, before the Norman conquest. AS. *tunice, tunece*. ' Tunica, *tunice* ; ' also ' Tonica, *tunece* ; ' Voc. 151. 8 ; 268. 1.–L. *tunica*, an under-garment of the Romans, worn by both sexes ; whence also F. *tunique* (Cot.). Perhaps of Semitic origin ; see Gk. χιτών in Prellwitz. **Der.** *tunic-le*, P. Plowman, B. xv. 163, from OF. *tunicle* (Roquefort) < L. *tunicula*, dimin. of *tunica*. Also *tunic-at-ed*, a botanical term, from L. *tunicātus*, provided with a coating ; from *tunica* in the sense of coating, membrane, or husk.

TUNNEL, a hollow vessel for conveying liquors into bottles, a funnel, a passage cut through a hill. (F.–C.) Formerly, when a *chimney* meant a fireplace, a *tunnel* often meant a chimney, or flue. ' Tonnell to fyll wyne with, *antonnoyr* ; ' Palsgrave. ' Tonnell of a chymney, *tuyau* ; ' id. Hence the sense of flue, shaft, railway-tunnel. –OF. *tonnel* (Burguy), later *tonneau*, ' a tun, or (generally) any great vessel, or piece of cask for wine, &c., as a tun, hogshead, &c., also a tunnell for partridges ; ' Cot. The tunnel for partridges was a long tunnel or covered passage made of light wire, strengthened with hoops, into which partridges were decoyed, and could not afterwards escape. Cf. prov. E. *tunnel*, a funnel, an arched drain ; OF. *tonnelle*, with like senses (Godefroy). The word evidently once meant a sort of cask, then a hooped pipe or funnel, then a flue, shaft, &c. In the Bury Wills, ed. Tymms, p. 20, we find (in 1463) ' my newe hous with the iij. *tunnys* of chemeneyis ; ' Mr. Tymms remarks (p. 241) : ' The passage of the chimney was called a *tunnel* till the beginning of the present century, and the chimney-shaft is still called a *tun*.' β. F. *tonneau* is the dimin. of F. *tonne*, ' a tun ; ' Cot. Ultimately of Celtic origin ; see **Ton.** Cf. AF. *tonel*, a tun ; Stat. Realm, i. 156 (1309) ; *tonel*, a tunnel (for birds), Bozon, p. 173. **Der.** *tunnel*, verb ; modern.

TUNNY, the name of a fish. (F.–Prov.–L.–Gk.) ' A *tuny* fish, *thunnus* ; ' Levins. Palsgrave gives ' *Tonny*, fyshe ' without any F. equivalent. The final *-y* is an E. addition.–F. *thon*, ' a tunny fish,' Cot.–Prov. *ton* (mod. Prov. *toun*) ; see Hatzfeld.–L. *thunnum*, acc. of *thunnus*, a tunny ; also spelt *thynnus*.–Gk. θύννος, a tunny ; also spelt θῦνος. Lit. ' the darter,' the fish that darts about (cf. E. *dart*). Cf. Gk. θύνειν, allied to θύειν, to rush along.–√DHEU, to shake, blow, rush ; see **Dust.**

TUP, a ram. (Scand.) ME. *tuppe* ; Palladius on Husbandrie, viii. 71 ; ' Vervex, *a tuppe* ; ' Voc. 698. 29. Prob. a transferred name ; cf. Swed. and Norw. *tupp*, a cock, allied to Dan. *top*, a cock's crest, Icel. *toppr*, a top, a crest. See **Top.**

TURBAN, a head-covering worn in the East. (F.–Ital.–

Turkish.–Pers.) Spelt *turbant*, Fairfax, tr. of Tasso, b. xvii. st. 10 ; *turribant*, Spenser, F. Q. iv. 11. 28 ; *turband*, Cymb. iii. 3. 6. ' Nash, in his Lenten Stuffe (1598) has *turbanto* ; ' F. Hall, Mod. English, p. 112. [Todd remarks that it is spelt *tulibant* in Puttenham, Art of Poesie (1589), and *tulipant* repeatedly in Sir T. Herbert's Travels. As a fact, Puttenham has *tolibant*, Art of Poesie, b. iii. c. 24 ; ed. Arber, p. 291. These forms with *l* are really more correct, as will be seen, and answer to the occasional F. form *tolopan*, given in Cotgrave as equivalent to *turbant*.]–MF. *turbant* (given by Cotgrave, s. v. *tolopan*), but usually *turban*, ' a turbant, a Turkish hat ; ' Cot.–Ital. *turbante*, ' a turbant,' &c. ; Florio.–Turkish *tulbend*, vulgar pronunciation of Turkish *dulbend*, a turban ; a word borrowed from Persian ; Zenker's Dict., p. 433, col. 3.–Pers. *dulband*, a turban ; Rich. Dict., p. 681. Vüllers, in his Etym. Pers. Dict. i. 893, col. 2, says that *dulband* seems to be of Hindustāni origin ; cf. Hind. *dulband*, a turban ; Shakespear, Hind. Dict. p. 1059. But this is doubtful. See *Turban* in Yule. See *tulip.*

TURBARY, a right of digging turf, or a place for digging it. (F.–Teut.) ' *Turbary* (*turbaria*) is a right or interest to dig turves on another man's ground ; ' Blount, Nomolexicon (1691).–OF. *torberie*, Low L. *turbāria*, the same.–OHG. *turba*, older form of *zurba*, turf ; see **Turf.** Cf. AF. *turberie*, Year-books, 1304-5, p. 485.

TURBID, disordered, muddy. (L.) ' Lees do make the liquor *turbide* ; ' Bacon, Nat. Hist. § 306.–L. *turbidus*, disturbed.–L. *turbāre*, to disturb.–L. *turba*, a crowd, confused mass of people ; see **Trouble. Der.** *turbid-ly, -ness.*

TURBINE, a hydraulic wheel, wheel driven by water. (F.–L.) Used in various ways.–F. *turbine*, a hydraulic wheel ; MF. *turbine*, a whirlwind (Cot.)–L. *turbinem*, acc. of *turbo*, a wheel, a top, a whirlwind ; cf. *turbāre*, to disturb.

TURBOT, a flat, round fish. (F.–L.) ME. *turbut*, Prompt. Parv. ; Havelok, 754 ; spelt *turbote*, Wright's Voc. i. 189.–F. *turbot*, ' the turbot-fish ; ' Cot. According to Diez, formed with suffix *-ot* from L. *turb-o*, a whipping-top, a spindle, a reel ; from its rhomboidal shape. This is verified by two facts : (1) the L. *rhombus*, a circle, a turbot, is merely borrowed from Gk. ῥόμβος, a top, wheel, spindle, having, in fact, just the same senses as L. *turbo* : and (2) the Late L. *turbo* was used to mean a turbot ; thus we have : ' *Turbut*, turtur, turbo,' Prompt. Parv. We also find Irish *turbit*, a turbot, a rhomboid, Gael. *turbaid*, W. *torbwt* ; but it is a borrowed word in Celtic. Cf. ' The Lozange .. Rombus .. the *Turbot* ; ' Puttenham, Arte of E. Poesie, bk. ii. c. 11 (12). Also AF. *turbut*, Liber Albus, p. 234.

TURBULENT, disorderly, restless as a crowd, producing commotion. (F.–L.) In Hamlet, iii. 1. 4.–F. *turbulent*, ' turbulent, blustering ; ' Cot.–L. *turbulentus*, full of commotion or disturbance. –L. *turb-āre*, to disturb.–L. *turba*, a crowd of people ; see **Trouble. Der.** *turbulent-ly* ; *turbulence*, Troil. v. 3. 11, from F. *turbulence* (which Cotgrave omits, but see Littré), which from L. *turbulentia* ; also *turbulenc-y*, from L. *turbulentia.*

TUREEN, the same as **Terreen,** q. v.

TURF, the surface of land matted with roots of grass, &c., sward, sod, peat. (E.) ME. *turf*, sometimes *torf* ; pl. *turues* (=*turves*), Havelok, 939 ; Chaucer, C. T. 10109 (E 2235). AS. *turf* (dat. *tyrf*), turf, A. S. Chron. an. 189 (Laud MS.). So also : ' Gleba, *turf*,' Voc. 146. 13 ; pl. *tyrf*, id. 236. 18.+Du. *turf*, peat ; Icel. *torf*, a turf, sod, peat ; Dan. *törv* ; Swed. *torf* ; OHG. *zurba*, turf (the mod. G. *torf* being borrowed from Low German). β. All from Teut. base *torb-* ; and allied to Skt. *darbha-*, a kind of grass, Benfey, p. 388 ; so called from its being twined or matted together, from Skt. *dṛbh*, to string, to bind.–√DERBH, to wind, twine, knit together. **Der.** *turf-y*, Temp. iv. 62.

TURGID, swollen, pompous, bombastic. (L.) In Blount's Gloss., ed. 1674.–L. *turgidus*, swollen, extended.–L. *turgēre*, to swell out. **Der.** *turgid-ly, -ness, turgid-i-ty.* Also *tugg-esc-ence*, Sir T. Browne, Vulg. Errors, b. ii. c. 7, part 5, formed as if from L. *turgescentia*, swelling up, from *turgescere*, inceptive form of *turgēre*.

TURKEY, the name of a bird. (F.–Tatar.) ' *Turky-cocke*, or *cocke of India*, auis ita dicta, quod ex Africa, et, ut nonnulli volunt alii, ex India vel Arabia ad nos illata sit ; Belg. *Indische haen*, Teut. *Indianisch hun*, Calekuttisch *hun*, i. e. Gallina Indica seu Calecuttensis, Ital. *gallo, o gallina d'India*, Hispan. *pauon de las Indias*, Gall. *poulle d'Inde*,' &c. ; Minsheu, ed. 1627. ' A *turkie*, or Ginnie henne, Belg. *Indisch hinne*, Teut. *Indianisch henn*, Ital. *gallina d'India*, Hispan. *gallina Morisca*,' &c. ; id. *Turkey* in Shak. means (1) the bird, 1 Hen. IV, ii. 1. 29 ; (2) adj. Turkish, Tam. Shrew, ii. 355 ; hence he also says *turkey-cock*, Tw. Nt. ii. 5. 36. ' Meliagrides, Birdes that we call *hennes of Ginnie* or *Turkey hennes* ; ' Cooper's Thesaurus, ed. 1565. Turkeys were ' unknown in Europe until introduced from the New World ; ' see Trench, Study of Words. The date of their introduction was about 1530 (Beckmann). As they were strange birds, they were hastily called *Turkey-cocks* and *Turkey-hens,* by which it was merely meant that they were foreign; it must be remembered that *Turkey* was at that time a vague term, and often meant Tartary. '*Turkie,* Tartaria;' Levins. Similarly, the French called the bird *poule d'Inde,* whence mod. F. *dinde,* a turkey; Cotgrave gives: '*Dindar, Indar,* a turkey-cock.' Minsheu, in his Span. Dict., gives '*gallina Morisca,* a hen of Guynie, *gallina de India,* a Turkie hen;' whilst in his Eng. Dict. (as quoted above) he calls *gallina Morisca,* the turkey-hen; showing that he was not particular. The German *Calecutische hahn,* a turkey-cock, means 'a cock of Calicut,' not ·Calcutta;' a name extremely wide of the mark. β. The E. *Turkey,* though here used as an adj. (since *turkey* is short for *turkey-cock* or *turkey-hen*) was also used as a sb., to denote the name of the country.—F. *Turquie,* 'Turkie,' Cot.—F. *Turc,* m., *Turque,* f., 'Turkish,' id.—Tatar *turk,* orig. meaning 'brave.' [The Turkish word for Turk is '*osmānlī*.] Cf. Pers. *Turk,* 'a Turk, comprehending likewise those numerous nations of Tartars . . . who claim descent from Turk, the son of Japhet. . . . Also a Scythian, barbarian, robber, plunderer, villain, vagabond;' Richardson's Dict., p. 392. Hence Pers. *Turki,* 'Turkish, Turk-like;' id. p. 393. (See *Turkey* in Yule.) ¶ So also maize was called Turkey wheat, F. *bled de Turquie;* Wedgwood. Der. *turq-uoise,* q. v.

TURMERIC, the root of an E. Indian plant, used as a yellow dye, and in curry-powder. (F.—L.—Arab.?) Spelt *turmerick* in Phillips, ed. 1706; also in Ben Jonson, Cynthia's Revels, v. 2 (Perfumer). A gross corruption of the F. name.—F. *terre-mérite,* turmeric; not given in Littré under *terre,* but under *Curcuma* he says that the root is called in commerce 'safran des Indes, et curcuma, dite *terre-mérite,* quand elle est réduite en poudre.'—L. *terra merita;* turmeric 'is likewise called by the French *terra merita;* Curcuma, hæc Gallis *terra merita* male dicitur,' see Royle, Antiquity of Hindoo Medicine, p. 87; (Eng. Cycl. Division Arts and Sciences). I suppose it means 'excellent earth;' as if from L. *terra,* earth, and *merita,* fem. of *meritus,* pp. of *merēri,* to deserve. But *terra merita* is hardly Latin, and is doubtless a barbarous corruption; perhaps of Arab. *karkam, kurkum,* saffron or curcuma (whence Span. and Port. *curcuma,* turmeric); Rich. Dict., p. 1181.

TURMOIL, excessive labour, tumult, bustle; as a verb, to harass. (F.—L.?) 'The *turmoyle* of his mind being refrained;' Udal, on St. John, c. 11 (R.). The pp. *turmóild* occurs in Spenser, F. Q. iv. 9. 39; and *turmóil-èd* in Shak. 2 Hen. VI, iv. 10. 18. 'At seas *turmóylde* fiue days with raging winde;' Mirror for Mag., Brennus, st. 9. The origin is somewhat doubtful; the form is prob. corrupt, the latter part of the word being perhaps due to E. *moil,* q. v., and the former part assimilated to *turn.* β. It has been suggested that it may have something to do with MF. *trameul, tremouille,* 'the hopper of a mill,' Cot., also called *tremie,* and prob. so called from being in continual movement, from L. *tremere,* to tremble, shake. But the old accent on the latter syllable suggests that *tur-* is a mere prefix, and may represent the OF. intensive prefix *tra-* or *tres-* (both from L. *trans*); as in OF. *tres-batre, tra-batre,* to beat extremely (Godefroy). If so, the sense is 'to moil (or harass) greatly.' See **Moil.**

TURN, to cause to revolve, transfer, convert, whirl round, change. (L.—Gk.) ME. *tournen, tornen, turnen;* Ormulum, 169; cf. F. *tourner,* OF. *torner, turner,* to turn. But it occurs in late AS. as *turnian, tyrnan* (Toller); so that it was taken directly from L. *tornāre,* to turn in a lathe, to turn.—L. *tornus,* a lathe, turner's wheel.—Gk. τόρνος, a carpenter's tool to draw circles with, compasses, whence τορνεύειν, to turn, work with a lathe. Allied to Gk. τορός, adj. piercing, τείρειν, to pierce, L. *terere,* to rub.—√TER, to rub, hence to bore a hole; see **Trite.** Der. *turn,* sb., *turn-er;* *turn-er-y,* from F. *tournerie,* 'a turning, turner's work;' *turn-ing, turn-ing-point;* *turn-coat,* Much Ado, i. 1. 125; *turn-key,* one who turns a prison-key, a warder; *turn-pike,* q. v.; *turn-sol,* a heliotrope, or flower that turns with the sun, OF. *torne-sol* (Supp. to Godefroy), from L. *söl,* the sun; *turn-spit,* one who turns a spit; *turn-stile,* a stile that turns, Butler's Hudibras, pt. i. c. 3, l. 23; *turn-stone,* a small bird that turns over stones to find food; *turn-table,* a table that turns. Also (from *tornāre*) *tour, tour-na-ment, tour-ni-quet.*

TURNIP, TURNEP, a plant with a round root, used for food. (F.—L.; *and* L.) The pl. *turneps* is in Holland, tr. of Pliny, b. xviii. c. 13; spelt *turnepes* in Sir T. Elyot, Castel of Helth, b. ii. c. 9. 1. The latter part of the word is *nep* or *nepe.* We find '*wild nepe,* Cucurbita, brionia' in Prompt. Parv. p. 528. 'Hoc bacar, *nepe;*' Voc. 645. 17. 'As a *nepe* white'=as white as a turnip; Destruction of Troy, 3076. This is from AS. *nǣp,* a turnip, borrowed from L. *nāpus,* a kind of turnip. 'Napus, *nǣp;* Rapa, *nǣp;*' Voc. 135. 30, 37. Hence the etymological spelling should rather be *turnep* than *turnip,* and we know that the latter part of the word is from Latin. Cf. Irish and Gael. *neip,* a turnip. 2. The former part of the word is less obvious; but it is most likely F. *tour* in the

sense of 'wheel,' to signify its round shape, as if it had been 'turned.' Cotgrave gives, among the senses of *tour,* these: 'also a spinning-wheel, a turn, or turner's wheel.' Or it might be the E. *turn,* used in a like sense; Cotgrave also gives: '*Tournoir,* a turn, turning-wheel, or turners wheel, called a lathe or lare.' It makes but little difference, since F. *tour* is the verbal sb. of *tourner,* to turn; see **Tour, Turn.** Cf. Ital. *torno,* 'a turne, a turners or spinners wheele,' Florio; W. *turn,* a turn, also round (from E.); Irish *turnapa,* a turnip, *turnoir,* a turner (from E.).

TURNPIKE, a gate set across a road to stop those liable to toll. (F.—L.) The name was given to the toll-gate, because it took the place of the old-fashioned *turn-pike,* which had three (or more) horizontal bars or pikes (sharp at one end) revolving on a central post. For the difference between a *turn-pike* and a *turn-stile,* see figs. 266, 267, in Boutell's Heraldry. Jamieson cites *turn-pyk* from Wyntoun, viii. 38. 74. The word occurs in Cotgrave, who translates F. *tour* by 'a turn, . . . also, a turn-pike or turning-stile.' So also: 'I move upon my axle like a *turnpike;*' Ben Jonson, Staple of News, iii. 1 (Picklock); see Nares. The word *turn-pike* was also used in the sense of *chevaux de Frise,* as in Phillips, ed. 1706. From **Turn** and **Pike.** Der. *turn-pike-gate, turn-pike-road.*

TURPENTINE, the resinous juice of the terebinth tree, &c. (F.—L.—Gk.) In Levins, ed. 1570. ME. *turbentine,* Mandeville's Trav. ch. v. p. 51.—MF. *turbentine,* 'turpentine;' Cot.—L. *terebinthus,* a terebinth-tree; whence the adj. *terebinthinus,* made from the terebinth-tree.—Gk. τερεβίνθινος, made from the tree called τερέβινθος; see **Terebinth.** Cf. Norm. dial. *turbentine* (Moisy).

TURPITUDE, baseness, depravity. (F.—L.) In Shak. Troil. v. 2. 112.—F. *turpitude,* 'turpitude;' Cot.—L. *turpitūdo,* baseness. —L. *turpi-,* decl. stem of *turpis,* base; with suffix *-tūdo.* β. The L. *turpis* is 'shameful;' cf. Skt. *trap,* to be embarrassed, be ashamed; causal, *trāpaya,* to make ashamed; *trapā,* shame.

TURQUOISE, TURQUOIS, TURKOISE, TURKIS, a precious stone. (F.—Low L.—Tatar.) In Cotgrave; also Palsgrave has: '*Tourques,* a precious stone, *tourquois.*' *Turcas,* a turquoise, Bale's Works, p. 607 (Parker Soc.).—F. *turquoise,* 'a turquois, or Turkish stone;' Cot. *Turquoise* is the fem. of *Turquois,* 'Turkish,' id.; cf. MItal. *Turchesa,* 'a blue precious stone called a Turkoise;' Florio. The sense is *Turkish;* the Late L. *turchesius* is found with the sense of turquoise in A.D. 1347 (Ducange). The F. *Turquois* is an adj. form, from Low L. *Turcus,* a Turk, which is from Tatar *turk,* a Turk; see **Turkey.**

TURRET, a small tower. (F.—L.) ME. *touret,* Chaucer, C. T. 1909 (A 1911); *toret,* Prompt. Parv.—F. *tourette,* 'a turret or small tower;' Cot. Dimin. of F. *tour* (OF. *tor, tur*), a tower.—L. *turrem,* acc. of *turris,* a tower; see **Tower.** Cf. AF. *turette,* French Chron. of London, p. 49. Der. *turret-ed.*

TURTLE (1), a turtle-dove, kind of pigeon. (L.) ME. *turtle,* Chaucer, C. T. 10013 (E 2139). AS. *turtle.* 'Turtur, *turtle;*' Voc. 132. 1.—L. *turtur,* a turtle; with the common change from *r* to *l.* Hence also G. *turtel-taube,* a turtle-dove; Ital. *tortora, tortola,* a turtle. β. The L. *tur-tur* is of imitative origin; due to a repetition of *tur,* imitative of the coo of a pigeon. Cf. Du. *kirren,* to coo.

TURTLE (2), the sea-tortoise. (L.) In Phillips, ed. 1706. This word is absolutely the same as the word above. It occurs, according to Richardson, in Dampier's Voyages, an. 1687; see ed. 1699, i. 395. The islands called *Tortugas* in Spanish were called *Tortles* in English, because turtles bred there; Eng. Garner, ed. Arber, v. 121; vii. 355, 357-8. The English sailors having a difficulty with the Portuguese *tartaruga,* a tortoise or turtle, and the Span. *tortuga,* tortoise, turtle, overcame that difficulty by substituting the E. *turtle,* with a grand disregard of the difference between the two creatures. The Span. and Port. names did not readily suggest the E. *tortoise;* whereas *tartaruga* could easily become **tortaluga,* and then **tortal* for short. See **Tortoise.**

TUSH, an exclamation of impatience. (E.) Common in Shak. Much Ado, iii. 3. 130; &c. Holinshed (or Stanihurst) gives the form *twish.* 'There is a .. disdainfull interiection vsed in Irish called *boagh,* which is as much in English as *twish;*' Holinshed, Desc. of Ireland, c. 8 (R.). *Twish* is expressive of disgust; cf. *pish;* also *tut.* Note also Low G. *tuss,* silence! Dan. *tysse,* to be silent; *tys,* hush! NFries. *tüss,* hush! *tüsse, tüsche,* to command silence. See **Tut.**

TUSK, a long pointed tooth. (E.) Shak. uses the pl. form *tushes,* Venus, 617, 624. ME. *tusk, tusch, tosch;* spelt *tosche,* Prompt. Parv.; we even find the pl. *tuskes* in K. Alisaunder, 6547. AS. *tusc,* almost always spelt *tux,* esp. in the pl. *tuxas,* just as AS. *fisc* is often spelt *fix;* here *x = cs,* by metathesis of *sc.* Spelt *tux,* translated 'grinder' by Thorpe, Ancient Laws, i. 95, § 49. 'Canini, vel colomelli, *mannes tuxas;*' Voc. 157. 31.+OFries. *tusk, tosch;* EFries.

tŭsk; Icel. *toskr*. Perhaps the AS. form was orig. *tûsk* (with long *u*). Hardly allied to **Tooth**; see Brugmann, i. § 795. **Der.** *tusk-ed*, *tusk-y*.

TUSSLE, to scuffle. (E.) Allied to *tousle*, to disorder, frequent. of **Touse**, q. v. Cf. Westphal. *tusseln*, to pull about; Dan. dial. *tusse.* to move about, to confuse. And cf. **Toss**.

TUSSOCK, a clump or tuft of growing grass. (Scand. ?) Latimer has : '*tussocks* nor tufts;' see Todd's Johnson. The suffix *-ock* is a diminutive, as in *hill-ock*. Cf. Swed. dial. *tuss*, a wisp of hay (Rietz); and cf. E. *touse.* Dryden has *tuzzes*, i. e. tufts or knots of hair; tr. of Persius, iv. 90.

TUT, an exclamation of impatience. (E.) Common in Shak. Merry Wives, i. 1. 117; &c. 'And that he said . . *Tut, tut, tut* ;' State Trials, Hen. VIII, an. 1536; Q. Anne Boleyn (R.). Cf. F. *trut*, 'an interjection importing indignation, tush, tut, fy man;' Cot. '*Ptrot*, skornefulle word, or *trut* ;' Prompt. Parv., p. 415. And cf. **Tush**.

TUTELAGE, guardianship. (L.; *with* F. *suffix.*) 'The *tutelage* whereof,' &c.; Drayton, Polyolbion, song 3; l. 218. Coined with F. suffix *-age* (< L. *-āticum*) from L. *tūtēla*, protection; see **Tutelar**.

TUTELAR, protecting, having in charge. (L.) '*Tutelar* god of the place ;' Ben Jonson, Love's Triumph through Callipolis, Introduction.—L. *tūtēlāris*, tutelar.—L. *tūtēla*, protection; allied to *tūtor*, a protector; see **Tutor**. **Der.** *tutelar-y*, from F. *tutelaire*, 'tutelary, garding ;' Cot.

TUTOR, an instructor, teacher, guardian. (F.—L.) For *tutour*, the older form. ME. *tutour*, P. Plowman, B. i. 56.—F. *tuteur*, 'a tutor ;' Cot.—L. *tūtōrem*, acc. of *tūtor*, a guardian; allied to L. *tūt-us* (short for *tuitus*), pp. of *tuēri*, to look after, guard; see **Tuition**. **Der.** *tutor*, verb, L. L. L. iv. 2. 77; *tutor-ship*, *tutor-age*, *tutor-i-al*.

TUTTY, a collyrium. (F.—Pers.) '*Tutie*, a medicinable stone or dust;' Blount (1681). ME. *tutie*, Lanfrank, Cirurgie, p. 95. —MF. *tuthie*, 'a medicinable stone or dust, said to be the heavier foile of brasse, cleaving to the upper sides and tops of brasse-melting houses ;' Cot. F. *tutie.*—Pers. *tūtiyā*, tutty; Rich. Dict. p. 461. Cf. Skt. *tuttha-m*, blue vitriol (Benfey).

TWADDLE, to tattle, talk unmeaningly. (E.) Formerly *twattle*. 'No gloasing fabil I *twattle* ;' Stanyhurst, tr. of Virgil, Æn. ii ; ed. Arber, p. 46. 'Vaynelye toe *twattle*,' id. Æn. iv ; p. 101. A collateral form of **Tattle**, q. v. So also *twittle-twattle*, sb., used by L'Estrange (Todd's Johnson) as equivalent to *tittle-tattle*. Cf. 'such fables *twitled*, such untrue reports *twatled* ;' Stanihurst, Desc. of Ireland, ed. 1808, p. 48. Cf. AS. *twædding*, adulation (Napier). **Der.** *twaddle*, sb., *twaddl-er*.

TWAIN, two; see under **Two**.

TWANG, to sound with a sharp noise. (E.) 'Sharply *twanged* off ;' Tw. Nt. iii. 4. 198. 'To *Twangue*, resonare ;' Levins. 'To *twang*, as the string of an instrument ;' Minsheu. A collateral form of *tang*, used with the same sense; see **Tang** (2), **Tingle**. It represents the ringing sound of a tense string. **Der.** *twang*, sb.

TWEAK, to twitch, pull sharply, pinch. (E.) In Hamlet, ii. 2. 601. A better form is *twick*; cf. prov. E. *twick*, a sudden jerk (Halliwell). ME. *twikken*, Prompt. Parv. p. 505. AS. *twiccian* (pt. t. *twicc-ode*), The Shrine, ed. Cockayne, p. 41. Besides which, we find AS. *angel-twicca* = a hook-twitcher, the name of a worm used as bait for fishing; Voc. 320. 32. *Twitch* is a palatalised form of it; see **Twitch**.+Low G. *twikken*, to tweak, nip ; G. *zwicken*, to pinch, nip ; whence *zwick*, a pinch, *zwick bei der Nase*, tweak by the nose ; also G. *zwacken*, to pinch, to twitch. Cf. **Twinge**. **Der.** *tweak*, sb.

TWEEZERS, nippers, small pincers for pulling out hairs. (F.— Teut. ; *with* E. *suffix.*) 'Handkerchers, rosaries, *tweezers* ;' Middleton, Span. Gipsy, ii. 1. The history of this word is remarkable ; it exhibits an unusual development. A *tweez-er* or *twees-er* is properly, an instrument contained in a *tweese*, or small case for instruments. And as the *tweese* contained *tweesers*, it was also called a *tweeser-case* ; hence it is that we find *tweese* and *tweeser-case* used as synonymous terms. '*Tweezers*, nippers or pincers, to pull hair up by the roots ;' Phillips, ed. 1706. 'Then his *tweezer-cases* are incomparable ; you shall have one not much bigger than your finger, with *seventeen several instruments* in it, all necessary every hour of the day ;' Tatler, no. 142 ; March 7, 1709-10. This shows that a *tweezer-case* was a case containing a great number of small instruments, of which what are *now* specifically called *tweezers* was but one. See another quotation under **Trinket** (1). B. Next, we observe that the proper name for such a case was a *tweese*, or a *pair of tweeses* ; probably a *pair of tweeses* means that the case was made double, folding up like a book, as some instrument cases are made still. 'Drawing a little penknife out of *a pair of tweeze* I then chanced to have about me ;' Boyle, Works, ii. 419 (R.). 'I have

sent you by Vacandary the post, the French bever [hat] and *tweeses* you writ for ;' Howell, Familiar Letters, vol. i. let. 17; May 1, 1620. 'A Surgeon's *tweese*, or box of instruments, *pannard a chirurgien* ;' Sherwood, index to Cotgrave. C. Lastly, the word *tweese* is a new pl. formed from *twee*, short for *etwee*, from MF. *estuy* (mod. F. *étui*). '*Estuy*, a sheath, case, or box to put things in, and more particularly, a case of *little instruments*, or *sizzers*, *bodkin*, *penknife*, &c., now commonly tearmed an *ettwee* ;' Cot. And again : '*Pennarol de Chirurgien*, a chirurgian's case or *ettuy* ; the box wherein he carries his instruments ;' id. Hence *twee* ; 'sure I have not dropt my *twee* ;' Hoadly, The Suspicious Husband, A. ii. sc. 2 (1747). Here we see that the F. *estuy* was pronounced *et-wee* ; then the initial *e* (for *es*) was dropped, just as in the case of **Ticket** and **Tuck** (2) ; then *twee* became *twees* or *tweese*, probably because the case was double ; then it was called a *pair of tweeses*, and a particular implement in it was called a *tweezer* or *tweezers*, prob. from some confusion with the obsolete *twich*, tweezers ; see additions to Nares, by Halliwell and Wright. The most remarkable point is the double addition of the pl. form, so that *twee-s-es* is from *twee* ; this can be explained by the common use of the plural for certain implements, such as *shears*, *scissors*, *pliers*, *snuffers*, *tongs*, *scales*, *nippers*, *pincers*, &c. So far, the history of the word is quite clear, and fully known. D. The etymology of OF. *estuy* or *estui* is difficult ; it is the same as Span. *estuche*, a scissors-case, also scissors (note this change of sense), Port. *estojo*, a case, a tweezer-case, Low Lat. *estugium*, a case, box, occurring A.D. 1231 (Ducange). We also find MItal. *stuccio*, *stucchio*, 'a little pocket-case with cisors, pen-knives, and such trifles in them,' (sic) Florio ; whence (with prefix *a-* < L. *ad*) Ital. *astuccio*, a small box, case, sheath. The form *stucchio* does not seem to have been observed before ; perhaps it helps the etymology, proposed by Diez, from MHG. *stûche*, OHG. *stûcha*, a cuff, a muff (prov. G. *stauche*, a short and narrow muff).+Icel. *stûka*, a sleeve. If so, the orig. case for small instruments was a muff, or a cuff, or a part of the sleeve. Körting, § 9128.

TWELVE, two and ten. (E.) ME. *twelf*; whence also *twelf-e*, *twel-ue* (= *twel-ve*), a pl. form and dissyllabic. It was not uncommon to use numerals in the pl. form of adjectives ; cf. E. *five* (= *fi-vĕ*), from AS. *fif*. '*Twelue winter*' = twelve years, P. Plowman, B. v. 196, where two MSS. have *twelf*. We have, in the Ormulum, the form *twellf*, 11069; but also *twellf-e* (dissyllabic), 537. AS. *twelf*, also *twelfe*, Grein, ii. 556.+OFris. *twelef*, *twilif*, *iwelf*, *tolef* ; Du. *twaalf* ; Icel. *tôlf* ; Dan. *tolv* ; Swed. *tolf* ; G. *zwölf* ; OHG. *zwelif* ; Goth. *twalif*. β. All from the Teut. type *twalif*, as in Gothic. Here *twa-* is *two* ; see **Two**. The suffix *-lif* is the Teut. equivalent (but from another root *leip*, to stick, remain, *leave*) to the Lithuan. *-lika* occurring in *dwy-lika*, twelve. The Lithuan. *-lika* is due to the adj. *lëkas*, signifying 'what is over,' or 'remaining over;' see Nesselmann, p. 365. In fact, the phr. *antras lëkas*, lit. 'second one over,' is used as an ordinal, meaning 'twelfth.' *Lëka* is from Lith. *lik-ti*, to leave, allied to L. *linquere*. See **Eleven**. Brugmann, ii. § 175. **Der.** *twelf-th*, used instead of *twelft* (ME. *twelfte*, AS. *twelfta*, Grein, ii. 556) by analogy with *seven-th*, *eigh-th*, *nin-th*, &c.; hence *twelfth-day*, *twelft-i-night* (often called *twelfday*, *twelfnight*, as in Shakespeare's play of '*Twelfe Night* '); *twelve-month*, ME. *twelf-monthe*, P. Plowman, C. vii. 80.

TWENTY, twice ten. (E.) ME. *twenty*, Chaucer, C. T. 17118 (H 169). AS. *twentig*, Grein, ii. 557. Prob. for *twěn-tig* = *twegen-tig* ; from AS. *twegen*, twain, and the suffix *-tig*, cognate with Goth. *tigjus*, Gk. δεκάς, a decade, a collection of ten things ; allied to E. *ten*, Goth. *taihun*, Gk. δέκα. See **Two** and **Ten**.+Du. *twintig* ; Icel. *tuttugu* ; Goth. *twaitigjus*, Luke, xiv. 31 ; G. *zwanzig*, MHG. *zweinzic*, OHG. *zueinzuc*. All similarly formed. β. So also L. *ui-ginti*, twenty ; from *ui-* (for **dui*, twice, related to *duo*, two), and *-ginti* (for **-centi*, short for *decenti*, tenth, from *decem*, ten) ; whence F. *vingt*, twenty, &c. **Der.** *twenti-eth*, AS. *twentigoða*, Exod. xii. 18.

TWIBILL, TWYBILL, a two-edged bill or mattock. (E.) Still in use provincially ; see Halliwell. In Becon's Works, ii. 449; Parker Society. ME. *twibil*; spelt *twybyl*, Prompt. Parv. 515. *twibille* or *twibill*. 'Bipennis, *twibille*, vel *stān-æx* [stone-axe] ; Falcastrum, *bill* ;' Voc. 141. 27, 28. Also: 'Bipinnis, *twibill* ;' id. 361. 6.—AS. *twi-*, double ; and *bill*, a bill. See **Twice** and **Bill**.

TWICE, two times. (E.) For ME. *twiĕs* or *twyĕs*, formerly dissyllabic ; the word has been reduced to a single syllable, and the final *-ce* is a mere orthographical device for representing the fact that the final *s* was voiceless, and not sounded as *z*. 'He *twyĕs* wan Jerusalem the citee ;' Chaucer, C. T. 14153 (B 3337). AS. *twiges* ; A. S. Chron. an. 1120 (Laud MS.). This is a genitive form, genitives being often used adverbially ; the more common AS. word is *tuwa*, Luke, xviii. 12, older form *twiwa*, twice, Ælfred, tr. of

Orosius, b. v. c. 2. § 7. Both *twi-ges* and *twi-wa* are from the base *twi-*, double, only used as a prefix, answering to Icel. *tvi-*, L. *bi-* (for **duis*), Gk. δι-, Skt. *dvi-*, and allied to *twā*, two; see **Two**. Cf. prov. E. *twi-bill*, a mattock (above), *twi-fallow*, to till ground a second time; and see **Twilight**.

TWIDDLE, to twirl idly. (Scand.) As in the phr. ' to *twiddle* one's thumbs.' From Norw. *tvidla*, variant of *tvilla*, to mix up by stirring round; and *tvilla* is a mere variant of *tvirla*, with the same sense; see Aasen and Ross. See **Twirl**. (Prob. *tvir-la*>*tvil-la*> **tvil-da* or *tvid-la*.) Cf. mod. Icel. *kalla*, to call; pronounced (kad-la).

TWIG (1), a thin branch, small shoot of a tree. (E.) ME. *twig*, spelt *tuyg* in Ayenbite of Inwyt, p. 22, l. 5; pl. *twigges*, Chaucer, Persones Tale, De Superbia (I 390). AS. *twig*, pl. *twigu*, a twig; Northumb. *twigge*, pl. *twiggo*, John, xv. 5.+Westphalian *twich*, *twick*; Du. *twijg*; G. *zweig*. β. From the AS. base *twi-*, double, because orig. applied to the fork of a branch, or the place where a small shoot branches off from a larger one. In fact *twi-g* is cognate with Skt. *dvi-ka-*, 'consisting of two,' Gk. δισσός, double, twofold. Brugmann, ii. § 166. A similar explanation applies to ME. *twist*, often used in the sense of twig or spray, as in Chaucer, C. T. 10223 (E 2349). Cf. G. *zwiesel*, a forked branch; and see **Twilight, Twice, Twist, Two**.

TWIG (2), to comprehend. (E.) Orig. to observe, mark, take note of; as in ' Now *twig* him; now mind him; ' Foote, Mayor of Garratt (1763), ii. 2. Cf. prov. E. *twig*, a glance; *twig*, to pull quickly; *twick*, to twitch; *twitch*, to snatch, pinch, also to hold tight, to nip. See E. D. D. β. Otherwise, *twig* may be from the Irish *tuicim*, I understand, discern; Stokes-Fick, p. 50.

TWILIGHT, the faint light after sunset or before sunrise. (E.) ME. *twilight*, spelt *twyelyghte* in Prompt. Parv. The AS. *twi-*, prefix, means ' double,' like Icel. *tvi-*, Du. *twee-*, G. *zwie-*; but it is here used rather in the sense of ' doubtful ' or ' half.' The ideas of double and half are liable to confusion; cf. AS. *twēo*, doubt, from the hovering between two opinions; see **Doubt** and **Between**. β. Precisely the same confusion appears in German; we there find *zwiefach*, double, *zwielicht*, twilight, *zwiesel*, a branch dividing into two ends, *zwietracht*, discord, all with the prefix *zwie-*=AS. *twi-*. The prefix is related to **Two**; cf. **Twice, Twig**. And see **Light**. By way of further illustration, I find MDu. *tweelicht*, *twylicht*, 'twilight,' Hexham; cf. Du. *twee*, two, *tweedubbel*, twice double, &c. Also Low G. *twe-lecht*; AS. *twēone-lēoht*, twilight, Voc. 175. 34. But this last would only give a mod. E. form *tweenlight*, and does not account for the form *twilight*.

TWILL, an appearance of diagonal lines in textile fabrics produced by causing the weft-threads to pass over one and under two warp-threads, instead of over one and under one. (E.) Added by Todd to Johnson; Lowland Sc. *tweel*, *tweil*, *tweal* (Jamieson). ' De i. mappa mensali de *twill*,' York Wills, iii. 14 (1400); ' panno vocato *twylled*,' id. iii. 71 (1423). The form is very old, and has reference to a peculiar method of doubling the warp-threads, or taking two of them together. From AS. *twilic* (Toller), OLowG. *twili*, adj., woven with double thread, twill (Gallée). Cognate with G. *zwillich*, 'ticking,' MHG. *zwilich*, *zwilch*, OHG. *zwi-lih*, 'two-threaded; ' a word suggested by L. *bilix*, two-threaded, from *bi-*, double, and *licium*, a thread. See EFries. *twillen*, to double, in Koolman. Formed, like *twig*, *twine*, *twist*, from the Teut. base *twi-*, double, appearing in AS. *twi-*, Du. *twee-*, G. *zwie-*, all allied to **Two**, q.v. We also find: ' *Trilicis*, þrylen hrægel,' i. e. a garment woven with *three* threads, corresponding to an E. form **thrill*; Voc. 151. 34. And see **Twilight, Twice**. Der. *twill*, verb. ☞ *Twilled* in Temp. iv. 64, is yet unexplained. Ray tells us that North E. *twill* means a spool, and is a corruption of *quill* (see E. D. D.). I doubt it as regards this passage; the Swed. dial. *tvill* is to turn round like a spindle, to become entangled, as thread (Rietz); Norweg. *tvilla* is to stir milk round and round, also to twist into knots, as a thread; *tvilla*, sb., is a twist or knot in a thread. And the Norw. verb *tvilla* is merely an assimilated form of Norw. *tvirla*, to twirl, to turn round; like prov. E. *twell*, to turn a spadeful over (E. D. D.). I explain *pioned* as ' dug out,' and *twilled* as ' turned over; ' said of excavated trenches with sloping sides, on which the mud is laid. See the context. Halliwell gives *twilly*, to turn reversedly.

TWIN, one of two born at a birth. (E.) ME. *twin*, adj., double. ' Iosep gaf ilc here *twinne* scrud '=Joseph gave each of them double raiment, ' changes of raiment,' cf. Gen. xlv. 22. ' Þiss *twinne* seollþe '=this double blessing, Ormulum, 8769. AS. *ge-twinn-as*, pl., twins (Bosworth); ' *bini*, *getwinne*; ' Ælfric's Grammar, ed. Zupitza, p. 13, l. 14; ' *gemellus*, *getwin*; ' Corpus Gloss., 12. +Icel. *tvinnr*, *tvennr*, two and two, twin, in pairs; cf. *tvinna*, to twine, twist two together. We also find Dan. *tvilling*, Swed. *tvilling*, a twin, perhaps for **tvinling*, by assimilation; cf. ME. *twinling*,

---

Bavar. *zwin-ling*, G. *zwil-ling*, a twin. Due to AS. *twi-*, double; see **Twibill**. + Lithuan. *dwyni*, twins, sing. *dwynys*; from *dwi*, two, The *n* seems to give a collective force, as in Goth. *tweihnai*, two apiece, Luke, ix. 3; L. *bini*, two at a time. Hence *twin*, by two at a time, orig. an adj., as above. Der. *twin*, verb, Wint. Tale, i. 2. 67.

TWINE, to double or twist together; as sb., a twisted thread. (E.) ME. *twinen*, to twine; pp. *twyned*, P. Plowman, B. xvii. 204. In Layamon, 14220, the later text has ' a *twined* þred,' where the earlier text has ' a *twines* þræd '=a thread of twine. The supposed AS. *twinan* is unauthorised, but the verb was early coined from the sb. *twin*, a twisted thread, curiously used to translate L. *bysso* in Luke, xvi. 19 (as if from L. *bis*, twice).+Du. *twijn*, twine, twist, whence *twijnen*, to twine; Icel. *tvinni*, twine, whence *tvinna*, to twine; Dan. *tvinde* (for **tvinne*), to twine; Swed. *tvinnträd*, twine-thread, *tvinna*, to twine; also Du. *tweern*, twine, G. *zwirn*. β. All from Teut. type **twis-no-*>**twiz-no-*, double; the *iz* becomes *ī* in AS. *twīn*, Du. *twijn*; the *zn* becomes *nn* in Icel. and Swed.; and the *z* becomes *r* in Du. and G. The base **twis-* occurs in Goth. *twis-*, prefix, and in E. *twis-t*; cf. L. *bis* (for **dwis*), Gk. δίς, Skt. *dvis*, twice. Brugmann, i. § 903 (c, note 2).

TWINGE, to affect with a sudden, sharp pain, to nip. (E.) ME. *twengen*, weak vb. (*ng*=*nj*), to twinge, tweak; Owl and Night., 156. Cf. ' Whil þat *twinges* me the foe '=while the foe afflicts me; E. Eng. Psalter, ed. Stevenson, Ps. xli. 10. Causal of ME. *twingen*, str. vb.; ' I am meked and *twungen* smert,' id. Ps. xxxvii. 9. AS. *twengan*, weak vb. (Toller); for earlier **þwengan*, causal of **þwingan*, whence the derived word **Thong**. For change of *thw-* to *tw-*, cf. *twirl* below, q. v. It is preserved in OFriesic *thwinga*, also *twinga*, *dwinga*, to constrain, pt. t. *twang*, *twong*, pp. *twongen*.+OSax. *thwingan*, in the pp. *bithwungan*, oppressed; Dan. *tvinge*, to force, compel, constrain; Swed. *tvinga*, to force, bridle, restrain, compel; Icel. *þvinga*, to oppress; Du. *dwingen*, to constrain, pt. t. *dwong*, pp. *gedwongen*; G. *zwingen*, pt. t. *zwang*, pp. *gezwungen*. β. All from the Teut. type **þwengan-* (pt. t. **þwang*), to constrain, compel; whence also the secondary verbs appearing in G. *zwängen*, to press tightly, constrain, and ME. *twengen*, to press tightly, tweak, or twinge (as above), and in the Life of St. Dunstan, l. 81: ' he *tuengde* and schok hir bi þe nose '=he twinged and shook her by the nose, Spec. of English, ed. Morris and Skeat, p. 22. The mod. E. *twinge* answers rather to this secondary or causal form than to the strong verb; just as in the case of *swinge*, due to the strong verb *swing*. γ. Cf. Lithuan. *twenkti*, to be hot, to smart; *twankas*, sultry. (√TWENK). Der. *twinge*, sb. Also *thong*, q. v.

TWINKLE, to shine with a quivering light. ME. *twinklen*, Chaucer, C. T. 269 (A 267). AS. *twinclian*, to twinkle, shine faintly, Ælfred, tr. of Boethius, c. xxxv. § 3; b. iii. pr. 12. *Twinkle* is a frequentative from a form *twink*, appearing in ME. *twinken*, to blink, wink; Prompt. Parv., p. 505. And again, *twink* is a nasalised form of AS. *twiccan*, to twitch; see **Tweak, Twitch**. The sense is to keep on twitching or quivering, hence to twinkle.+Bavar. *zwinkern*, frequentative of *zwinken*, to blink. Der. *twinkle*, sb.; *twinkl-er*. Also *twinkl-ing*, sb., a twitch or wink with the eye, ME. *twinkeling*; ' And in the *twinkeling* of a loke ' [look, glance], Gower, C. A. i. 144, bk. i. 3033; this is from ME. *twinkelen* in the sense to wink, as : ' he *twincleþ* with the eзen '=he winks with the eyes, Wyclif, Prov. vi. 13 (earlier version); see *twink*, sb., a twinkling, in Shak. Temp. iv. 43.

TWINTER, a beast two winters old. (E.) ' Five *twinteris* britnit he; ' G. Douglas, tr. of Virgil, bk. v. ch. ii. 105. AS. *twiwintre*, adj., of two years.—AS. *twi-*, double (see **Twibill**); and *winter*, a winter, a year.

TWIRE, to peep out. (E.) In Shak. Son. 28. Recorded in the cognate Bavarian *zwiren*, *zwieren*, to peep out (Schmeller); MHG. *zwieren*, to peep out (Schade). Not in Chaucer, as Nares asserts; but known in prov. E. (E. D. D.).

TWIRL, to whirl, turn round rapidly. (Scand.) *Twirl* stands for *thwirl*, as *twinge* (q. v.) for *thwinge*. ' Leave *twirling* of your hat; ' Beaum. and Fletcher, Rule a Wife, Act ii. sc. 3 (Altea); *twyrle*, Fitzherbert, Husb., § 55, l. 1.—Norw. *tvirla*, to twirl (Ross). *Twir-l* is a frequentative form, from Teut. **þwer-an-*, AS. *þwer-an*, to agitate, turn; it means ' to keep on turning,' and is used of rather violent motion. The AS. *þweran* only occurs in the *āþweran*, to stir round, to churn, and *ge-þweran* to churn (Toller). We have also the derived sb. *þwiril*, supposed to mean the handle of a churn, which was steadily turned round. We find : ' *Lac*, *meolc* [milk]; *Lac coagolatum*, *molcen* [curdled milk]; *Verberaturium*, *þwiril*; *Caseum*, *cyse* [cheese],' &c.; Voc. 280. 27–33. Slight as these traces are, they are made quite certain by the cognate words; it may be necessary to observe that, in AS. *þwir-il*, the final *-il* denotes the implement, and is an agential suffix, distinct from the frequentative *-l* in *twirl*. Cf. Du. *dwarlen*, to whirl; whence *dwarlwind*, a whirlwind (the Du. *d*=AS. þ). That the *l* is frequentative, appears at once from the Low G.

dweerwind, a whirlwind, as well as from MHG. *dwer(e)n*, OHG. *dweran*, *tweran*, strong verb, to turn round swiftly, to whirl, to mix up. From the Teut. type **thweran-*, to stir round (pt. t. **thwar*); whence also Icel. *þvara*, Norw. *tvare*, AS. *þwǣre*, OHG. *thwiril*, MHG. *twirl*, G. *quirl*, a stirring-stick. Note also EFries. *dwireln*, *dwirlen*, to twirl, *dwarrel*, a whirl, from *dweren*, to turn. From Idg. √TWER, whence also Gk. τορ-ύνη, L. *trua*, a stirrer. See **Trowel.**

TWIST, to twine together, wreathe, turn forcibly. (E.) ME. *twisten*, Chaucer, C. T. 10880 (F 566); O. Eng. Homilies, ed. Morris, ii. 213. Not found in AS., but regularly formed from a sb. *twist*, a rope, occurring in the comp. *mæst-twist*, a stay, a rope used to stay a mast. 'Parastates, *mæst-twist*,' Voc. 182. 8; one sense of Gk. παραστάτης is a stay. Again, *twis-t* is formed, with suffix *-t*, from AS. **twis-*, double, explained under **Twine.** The suffix *-t* is the very common Idg. suffix *-to-*. We should also notice ME. *twist*, a twig, i. e. forked branch, branch dividing into two; see under **Twig.**+Du. *twisten*, to quarrel; from *twist*, a quarrel. This is the same form, but used in quite a different sense, from the notion of *two* persons contending; cf. Du. *tweespalt*, discord, *tweedragt*, discord, *tweestrijd*, a duel; Dan. *tviste*, to strive, from *tvist*, strife; the Dan. *tvist* also means a twist; Swed. *tvista*, to strive, from *tvist*, strife; G. *zwist*, a twist, also discord, whence *zwistig*, discordant. And cf. Icel. *tvistr*, the two or 'deuce' in card-playing. Der. *twist*, sb. (really an older word, as appears above); *twist-er*. Cf. obsol. *twiss-el*, a double fruit (Nares), from AS. *twisel*, double.

TWIT, to remind of a fault, reproach. (E.) For *twite*; the *i* was certainly once long, which accounts for the extraordinary form *twight* (miswritten for *twite*, like *delight* for *delite*) in Spenser, F. Q. v. 6. 12, where it rimes with *light* and *plight*. Palsgrave has the queer spelling *twhyte*, prob. a misprint for *twyte*, as it occurs immediately before *twyne* and under the heading 'T before W: I *twhyte* one, I caste hym in the tethe or in the nose, *Je luy reproche*; this terme is also northren.' The orig. length of the vowel leaves no doubt that *twite* is due to ME. *atwiten*, to twit, reproach, by loss of initial *a*; this verb is used in much the same way as the mod. E. word, and was once common; Stratmann gives more than 12 examples. 'Imputo, to *a-twyte*,' Voc. 589. 17. Spelt *attwyte*, Ayenbite of Inwyt, p. 198, l. 16; whence *atuytinges*, twittings, reproaches, id. p. 194, l. 6. '*Þat atwytede* hym' = that twitted him, Rob. of Glouc. p. 33, l. 782. AS. *ætwitan*, to twit, reproach; see Sweet, AS. Reader, and Grein. [We also find AS. *ed-witan* with the same sense, but the prefix differs.]—AS. *æt*, at, prep. often used as a prefix; and *witan*, to blame, the more orig. sense being to behold, observe, hence to observe what is wrong, take notice of what is amiss; Grein, ii. 724. For the prefix, see **At.** The AS. *witan* is cognate with Goth. *weitjan*, occurring in *idweitjan*, to reproach (= AS.*edwitan*), and in *fairweitjan*, to observe intently. AS. *witan*, Goth. *weitjan*, are allied to AS. and Goth. *witan*, to know, and to L. *uid-ēre*, to see.— √WEID, to see; see **Wit** and **Vision.** Cf. Du. *wijten*, to reproach, G. *ver-weisen*.

TWITCH, to pluck, snatch, move suddenly. (E.) ME. *twicchen*, a palatalised form of *twikken*, to tweak. ' *Twikkyn*, *twychyn*, or somwhat drawyn*, Tractulo;' Prompt. Parv. We find also the comp. verb *to-twicchen*, to pull to pieces, O. Eng. Homilies, i. 53, l. 4; with the pt. t. *to-twiʒte*, spelt *to-twiʒt*, Will. of Palerne, 2097. Similarly the simple verb *twicchen* makes the pt. t. *twiʒte*, and pp. *twiʒt*. This explains *twight* = twitched, pulled, Chaucer, C. T. 7145 (D 1563). For the form, cf. AS. *angel-twicce*, prov. E. *angletwitch*, an earth-worm (for fishing). See **Tweak.** Der. *twitch*, sb.; *twitch-er*.

TWITTER, to chirp as a bird, to feel a slight trembling of the nerves. (E.) ME. *twiteren*; whence ' þilke brid . . *twitereth*' = that bird twitters, Chaucer, tr. of Boethius, b. iii. met. 2, l. 21. *Twitter* is a frequentative from a base *twit*, and means 'to keep on saying *twit*;' and *twit* is a lighter or weakened form of *twat*, appearing in the old word *twatt-le*, now *twaddle*; see **Twaddle.** Again, *twaddle* is related to *tattle*; and as *twitter* : *twattle* : : *titter* : *tattle*. All these words are of imitative origin.+G. *zwitschern*, to twitter; Bavar. *zwitzern*. And cf. Du. *kwetteren*, to twitter, warble, chatter; Dan. *kvidre*, Swed. *quittra*, to chirp, twitter. Der. *twitter*, sb. ☞ The sense of trembling may follow from that of tremulous sound; but a *twitter* of the nerves may be due to the influence of ME. *twikken*, to tweak or twitch.

TWO, TWAIN, one and one. (E.) The difference between *two* and *twain* is one of *gender* only, as appears from the AS. forms. *Twain* is masc., whilst *two* is fem. and neuter; but this distinction was early disregarded. ME. *tweien*, *tweiʒe*, *twein*, *tweie*, *twei*, *twey*, &c.; also *twa*, *two*, in which the *w* was pronounced; the pronunciation of *two* as *too* being of rather late date. ' Us *tweyne*' = us twain, us two, Chaucer, C. T. 1136 (A 1134). 'Sustren *two*' = sisters two, id. 1021 (A 1019). Our poets seem to use *twain* and *two* indiffer-

ently. AS. *twegen*, masc. nom. and acc.; *twā*, fem. nom. and acc.; *twā*, *tu*, neut. nom. and acc.; *twegra*, gen. (all genders); *twām*, dat. (all genders). The neut. *tu* already shows an occasional loss of *w*; and even in AS. *twā* was used instead of *twegen* when nouns of different genders were conjoined; see Grein, ii. 556.+Du. *twee*; Icel. *tveir*, acc. *tvā*, *tvo*; Dan. *to*; Norw. *tvo*; Swed. *två*, *tu*; Goth. *twai*, masc., *twōs*, fem., *twā*, neut.; gen. *twaddje*, dat. *twaim*; acc. *twans*, *twōs*, *twā*; G. *zwei*; also *zween*, only in the masc. gender; also *zwo*, fem. (rare); OHG. *zwēnē*, *zwa*, *zwo*, *zwei*.+Irish *da*; Gael. *da*, *do*; W. *dau*, *dwy*; Russ. *dva*; Lithuan. *dù*, *dwi*, f.; L. *duo* (whence F. *deux*, Ital. *due*, Span. *dos*, Port. *dous*, E. *deuce*); Gk. δύο; Skt. *dvāu*, *dvā*. β. All from the Idg. type **dwo-*, **duwo-*; Brugmann, ii. § 166. γ. In composition, we find, as a prefix, AS. *twi-* (E. *twi-* in *twi-ce*, *twi-light*), Icel. *tví-*, Du. *twee-*, Dan. and Swed. *tve-*, G. *zwie-*, L. *bi-* (for **dui-*), Gk. δι- (for **δϝι-*), Skt. *dvi-*, *dvā-*; also E. *twis-* (L. *bis*), as in *twis-t*; see **Twine.** Der. *two-edged*; *two-fold*, a modern substitution for ME. *twifold*, Early Eng. Psalter, ed. Stevenson, Ps. cviii. 29. AS. *twifeald*, spelt *twigfeald* in Gen. xliii. 15, so that *two-fold* should rather be *twy-fold*. Also *a-two*, ME. *a two*, Chaucer, C. T. 3569, AS. *on tu*, Grein, ii. 556, so that the prefix *a- = on*; see **A-** (2). Also *twain* (as above), *twe-lve*, *twen-ty*, *twi-bill*, *twi-ce*, *twi-light*, *twill*, *twig*, *twin*, *twine*, *twist*; *bi-*, prefix; *bis-*, prefix, in *bis-sextile*; *di-*, prefix, *dia-*, prefix, *dis-*, prefix. Also *deuce* (1).

TYBALT, the 'prince of cats.' (AF.—Low G.) See Shak. Romeo, iii. 1. 80.—AF. *Tebalt*, *Tebaud*.—OSax. *Thiod-bald*, Theobald.—OSax. *thiod*, people, *bald*, bold. See **Tibert.**

TYMPANUM, the hollow part of the ear, &c. (L.—Gk.) In Phillips, ed. 1706. [He also gives: '*Tympan*, the drum of the ear, a frame belonging to a printing-press covered with parchment. . . . pannel of a door,' &c.; this is from F. *tympan*, 'a timpan, or timbrell, also a taber; . . also, a printer's timpane,' &c.; Cot.]—L. *tympanum*, a drum; area of a pediment (in architecture); panel of a door.—Gk. τύμπανον, a drum, roller, area of a pediment, panel of a door. Formed with inserted μ from the rarer τύπανον, a drum.—Gk. τυπ-, base of τύπτειν, to strike, beat, beat a drum; see **Type.** And see **Timbrel.** Der. *tympan-y*, a flatulent distension of the belly, Dryden, Mac-Flecknoe, 194, from Gk. τυμπανίας, a kind of dropsy in which the belly is stretched tight like a drum; the F. form *tympanie* is given in Sherwood's index to Cotgrave; Palsgrave has E. *tympan*.

TYPE, a mark or figure, emblem, model, a raised letter in printing. (F.—L.—Gk.) In Shak. Rich. III, iv. 4. 244; and in Spenser, F. Q. Introd. to b. i. st. 4.—F. *type*, a type; in Sherwood's index to Cotgrave.—L. *typum*, acc. of *typus*, a figure, image, type.—Gk. τύπος, a blow, the mark of a blow, stamp, impress, mark, mould, outline, sketch, figure, type, character of a disease.—Gk. τυπ-, base of τύπτειν, to strike, beat. Allied to Skt. *tup*, *tump*, to hurt; and to Gk. στυφ-ελίζειν, to strike. (√STEU). β. We also find Skt. *tud*, L. *tundere* (pt. t. *tu-tud-i*), to strike. These are from a base **steud-*, to strike; whence Goth. *stautan*, to strike. Cf. Brugmann, i. § 818 (2). Der. *typ-ic*, from Gk. τυπικός, typical, figurative; *typ-ic-al*, *typ-ic-al-ly*; *typi-fy*, a coined word, Sir T. Browne, Vulg. Errors, b. ii. c. 5, § 1; *type-founder*, *type-metal*; also *typo-graphy*, orig. in the sense of 'figurative description,' Sir T. Browne, Vulg. Errors, b. i. c. 8. § 15, where the suffix is from Gk. γράφειν, to write; *typo-graph-ic*, *typo-graph-ic-al*, *-ly*; *typo-graph-er*. And see *tympanum*, *thump*.

TYPHOON, a violent whirlwind or hurricane. (Arab.—Gk.) [The word has been claimed as Chinese, from the Chinese *ta*, 'great,' and *fang* (Cantonese *fung*), 'wind;' as if 'great wind.' But this seems to be a late mystification, and unhistorical.] In old authors, the forms are *tuffon*, *tuffoon*, *tiphon*, &c. Spelt *touffon*, and explained as ' an extraordinary storme at sea;' Hakluyt, Voy., ii. 1. 239; *tuffoons*, pl., W. Dampier, New Voyage (1699), ii. 1. 35. (See *Typhoon* in Yule).—Arab. *tūfān*, a hurricane, storm; Rich. Dict. p. 466.—Gk. τυφών, better τυφώς, a whirlwind. Allied to τῦφος, smoke, cloud; see **Typhus.**

TYPHUS, a kind of continued fever. (L.—Gk.) Added by Todd to Johnson. Todd says it is 'one of the modern names given to low fever.'—L. *typhus*; a Latinised form from the Gk.—Gk. τῦφος, smoke, cloud, mist, stupor, esp. stupor arising from fever; so that ' typhus fever' = stupor-fever.—Gk. τύφειν, to raise a smoke, to smoke. Allied to θυ-μός, vigour, courage, θύ-ειν, to rush along; from √DHEU, to blow, fan a flame, shake; see **Fume.** Der. *typhous*, adj.; *typho-id*, resembling typhus, from Gk. τῦφο-, for τῦφος, and εἶδ-ος, resemblance, from εἴδομαι, I seem; see **Idol.**

TYRANT, a despotic ruler, oppressive master. (F.—L.—Gk.) The word was not originally used in a bad sense; see Trench, Study of Words. The spelling with *y* is modern, and due to our knowledge of Gk.; the word was really derived from French, and might as well have *i*. ME. *tirant*, but spelt *tyrant* in Rob. of Glouc. p. 374, l. 7689; *tiraunt* in Chaucer, prol. to Legend of Good Women,

l. 374.—OF. *tiran*, also *tiranz*, whence an oblique case *tirant*; also spelt *tyran, tyrant*; see Littré. Cotgrave gives: '*Tyran*, a tirant.'—L. *tyrannum*, acc. of *tyrannus*.—Gk. τύραννος, a lord, master, an absolute sovereign; later, a tyrant, usurper. Prob. orig. an adj. signifying kingly, lordly, in a good sense; as in the tragedians. Der. *tyrann-y*, ME. *tyrannie* or *tirannye*, Chaucer, C. T. 943 (A 941), from F. *tyrannie*, 'tyranny,' Cot., L. *tyrannia*, Gk. τυραννία, sovereign sway; also *tyrann-ic*, F. *tyrannique*, L. *tyrannicus*, Gk. τυραννικός; *tyrann-ic-al*, Cor. iii. 3. 2; *tyrann-ic-al-ly, tyrann-ous*, Meas. for Meas. iv. 2. 87, a coined word; *tyrann-ous-ly*; *tyrann-ise*, K. John, v. 7. 47, from F. *tyranniser*, 'to tyrannize, to play the tirant,' Cot., as if from L. *tyrannizāre=Gk. τυραννίζειν, to take the part of a tyrant (hence to act as one).

TYRO, a gross misspelling of **Tiro**, q. v.

U

UBIQUITY, omnipresence. (F.—L.) In Becon's Works, iii. 450, 524 (Parker Soc.); and in Cotgrave.—F. *ubiquité*, 'an ubiquity;' Cot. It answers to L. *ubiquitātem, acc. of *ubiquitās, a coined word, coined to signify 'a being everywhere,' i.e. omnipresence.—L. *ubique*, wherever, also, everywhere.—L. *ubi*, where; with suffix *-que*, answering to Gk. τε, and allied to L. *quis*, Gk. τίς, and E. *who*. β. *Ubi* is short for *cubi*, appearing in *ali-cubi*, anywhere, *nē-cubi*, nowhere; and *cubi stands for *quu-bi, where *-bi* is a suffix as in *i-bi*, there. Cf. Skt. *ku-*, as in *ku-ha*, where; also Oscan *pu-fe*, Umbrian *pu-fe*, where. Brugmann, i. § 667. Der. *ubiquit-ous, -ous-ly*.

UDDER, the breast of a female mammal. (E.) ME. *vddir* (=*uddir*); '*Iddyr*, or *vddyr* of a beeste;' Prompt. Parv. AS. *ūder*, in a Gloss. to Prov. vii. (Bosworth); cf. L. *ūberibus* in Prov. vii. 18 (Vulgate); see Kentish Glosses, 203.+MDu. *uder, uyder* (Hexham); Du. *uijer*; Low G. *üder* (Danneil); Icel. *jūgr* (an abnormal form; for *jūdr); Swed. *jufver, jur*; Dan. *yver* (cf. North E. *yure*, a Scand. form); G. *euter*, OHG. *ūtar*. Teut. type **ūdro-*; Idg. type **ūdhro-*. Further cognate with L. *ūber* (for *ūdher), Gk. οὖθαρ (gen. οὖθατος), Skt. *ūdhar*, an udder. Der. (from L. *ūber*) *ex-uber-ant*.

UGLY, frightful, hateful. (Scand.) ME. *ugly*, Chaucer, C. T. 8549 (E 673); spelt *uglike*, Genesis and Exodus, ed. Morris, 2805. We also find *ugsom*, frightful, Destruction of Troy, 877.—Icel. *uggligr*, fearful, dreadful, to be feared.—Icel. *ugg-r*, fear; with suffix *-ligr*=AS. *-lic*=E. *-like*, *-ly*. Cf. Icel. *ugga*, to fear. Apparently allied to Icel. *agi*, whence E. *awe*. Also to Goth. *ōgan*, to fear, *ōgjan*, to terrify. See **Awe**. Der. *ugli-ness*, spelt *uglynes*, Pricke of Conscience, 917, where it is used to translate L. *horror*.

UHLAN, ULAN, a lancer. (G.—Polish—Turkish.) Modern. 'Each *Hulan* forward with his lance!' Scott, Field of Waterloo, x. 5.—G. *uhlan*, a lancer.—Pol. *ulan*, an uhlan; not of Polish origin. β. According to Heyse, *uhlans* were a kind of light cavalry of Tataric origin, first introduced into European armies in Poland; the Polish *ulan*, a lancer, having been borrowed from Turkish *oglān*, also *ōlan*, a youth, lad. Of Tataric origin. From Tatar *oglān*, a son, child; formerly also a Mogul title. See Zenker, Turk. Dict., p. 124; Pavet de Courteille, Dict. Turk-Oriental, p. 68.

UKASE, an edict of the Czar. (F.—Russ.) Modern.—F. *ukase*. —Russ. *ykaz'*, an ordinance, edict; cf. *ykazuivat(e), ykazat(e)*, to indicate, show, order, prescribe.—Russ. *y-*, prefix; *kazat(e)*, to show. The Russ. *y-*, Church Slav. *u-*, is allied to Skt. *ava*, away, off; and *kazat(e)* is the Ch. Slav. *kazati*, to show. Brugmann, i. § 163 (note), § 616.

ULCER, a dangerous sore. (F.—L.) In Hamlet, iv. 7. 124.— MF. *ulcere* (Cot.), mod. F. *ulcère*, 'an ulcer, a raw scab.'—L. *ulcer-*, decl. stem of *ulcus*, a sore; cf. Span. and Ital. *ulcera*, an ulcer.+Gk. ἕλκος, a wound, sore, abscess; Skt. *arças*, hemorrhoids. Der. *ulcer-ion*, from F. *ulceration*, 'an ulceration,' Cot., from L. acc. *ulcerātiōnem*; *ulcer-ate*, from L. *ulcerātus*, pp. of *ulcerāre*, to make sore; *ulcer-ous*, Hamlet, iii. 4. 147, from L. adj. *ulcerōsus*, full of sores.

ULLAGE, the unfilled part of a cask. (Prov.—L.) '*Ullage of a Cask*, is what a cask wants of being full;' Phillips, ed. 1706. A Prov. word; due to the wine trade.—Prov. *ulhage* (given by Mistral s. v. *uiage*), a filling up of a cask; OF. *eullage* (Roquefort); *ouillage* (Godefroy).—Prov. *ulha*, OProv. *ulhar* (in Mistral, s. v. *ria*) to fill up; OF. *eullier, ouillier*; MF. *oeiller*, to fill up wine vessels, Cot. The Late L. type is *oculāre, to fill up to the *oculus*, the eye, or orifice.—L. *oculus*, the eye; see **Ocular**. We also find OF. *aouillier*, as if for *adoculāre. Cf. MF. *oeillade*, an amorous look, *oeil*, the eye (Cot.).

ULTERIOR, further, more remote. (L.) A late word; added by Todd to Johnson.—L. *ulterior*, further; comp. of *ulter*, beyond, on that side, an old adj. only occurring in the abl. *ulter* (=*ultrā parte*) and *ultrō*, which are used as adverbs with the sense of beyond; *ultrā* is also used as a preposition. β. *Ul-ter* is also a comparative form (*ul-ter-ior* being a double comparative, like *ex-ter-ior* from *ex*); cf. OL. *uls*, beyond, allied to OL. *ollus*, that, yon, *olle* (=*ille*), he. Hence *ul-ter*=more that way, more in that direction. γ. OL. *ollus* is for *olnus; cf. Skt. *araṇa-s*, foreign, far, yon. Brugmann, i. § 163. Der. *ultra-*, prefix, q. v.; *ultim-ate*, q. v. Also *outrage*, *utterance* (2).

ULTIMATE, furthest, last. (L.) 'The *ultimate* end of his presence;' Bp. Taylor, Of the Real Presence, s. 1. (R.).—L. *ultimātus*, pp. of *ultimāre*, to come to an end, to be at the last.—L. *ultimus*, last. *Ul-ti-mus* is a superl. form (like *op-ti-mus, in-ti-mus*), formed from the base *ul-* appearing in *ul-ter, ul-ter-ior*; see **Ulterior**. Der. *ultimate-ly*; also *ultimat-um*, from L. *ultimātum*, neut. of pp. *ultimātus*. Der. *pen-ultimate, ante-pen-ultimate*.

ULTRA-, beyond. (L.) L. *ultrā-*, prefix; *ultrā*, beyond, adv. and prep., orig. abl. fem. of OL. *ulter*, adj; see **Ulterior**. ¶ The F. form is *outre*, Ital. *oltra*, Span. *ultra*.

ULTRAMARINE, beyond sea; as sb., sky-blue. (Ital.—L.) '*Ultramarine*, that comes or is brought from beyond sea; also, the finest sort of blew colour used in painting;' Phillips, ed. 1706; spelt *ultramarin* in ed. 1658. And used by Dryden, On Painting, § 354 (R.), who talks of '*ultramarine* or azure.' 'Asure, .. such as the paynters caule *Azurro Oltramarino*, that is, Asure of beyonde the sea;' Eden, Three E. Books on America, ed. Arber, p. 366 (1555). The word is Ital. (the Ital. *oltra* being altered to L. *ultrā*).—Ital. *oltra marino*, of beyond the seas (Florio). Cf. Span. *ultramarino*, beyond sea, foreign; also as sb. '*ultramarine*, the finest blue colour, produced by calcination from lapis lazuli;' Neuman.—L. *ultrā*, beyond; *mar-e*, sea; and suffix *-inus*. See **Ultra-** and **Marine**. ☞ So called because *lapis lazuli* was a foreign production; see **Azure**.

ULTRAMONTANE, beyond the Alps. (F.—Ital.—L.) '*Ultramontanes*, a name given by the Italians to all people living on the hither side of the Alps, who, with respect to their country, are beyond those mountains;' Phillips, ed. 1706. He is an *ultramontane*;' Bacon, Observations on a Libel (R.).—F. *ultramontain*, applied by the French to the Italians themselves, as being beyond the Alps from the *French* side, and in use as early as the 14th cent. (Littré). This is also the E. view of the word, which is used with reference to the Italians, esp. to those who hold extreme views as to the Pope's supremacy.—Ital. *oltramontano*, beyond the mountains; Late L. *ultrāmontānus*, coined in imitation of classical L. *trāmontānus*.—L. *ultrā*, beyond; and *mont-*, stem of *mons*, a mountain; with suffix *-ānus*. See **Ultra-** and **Mountain**; and see **Tramontane**. Der. *ultramontan-ist, -ism* (F. *ultramontanisme*).

ULTRAMUNDANE, beyond the limits of our solar system, beyond the world. (L.) 'Imaginary *ultramundane* spaces;' Boyle's Works, vol. v, p. 140 (R.). And in Blount's Gloss., ed. 1674.—L. *ultrāmundānus*, beyond the world.—L. *ultrā*, beyond; and *mundānus*, worldly, from *mundus*, world. See **Ultra-** and **Mundane**.

UMBEL, a form of flower in which a number of stalks, each bearing a flower, radiate from a centre. (L.) Phillips, ed. 1706, gives it in the form *umbella*; it has since been shortened to *umbel*. Florio gives Ital. *umbella*, 'a little shadow, .. also the round tuft or head of fenell or dill.' So called from its likeness in form to an umbrella.—L. *umbella*, a parasol; Juvenal, ix. 50. Dimin. of *umbra*, a shade. See **Umbrella**. Der. *umbell-fer-ous*, bearing umbels (Phillips), coined with suffix *-fer-ous*, as in *cruci-ferou*-, from L. suffix *-fer*, bearing, and E. *-ous* (F. *-eux*, L. *-ōsus*). Doublet, *umbrella*.

UMBER, a species of brown ochre. (F.—Ital.—L.) In Shak. As You Like It, i. 3. 114.—F. *ombre*, used shortly for *terre d'ombre*, 'beyond-sea azur, an earth found in silver mines, and used by painters for shadowings;' Cot. [As 'beyond-sea azur' is properly ultramarine, it must here be differently applied.]—Ital. *ombra*, used shortly for *terra d'ombra*, umber. Torriano has '*terra d'ombra*, a kind of earth found in silver-mines used by painters for shadowings.' Lit. 'earth of shadow,' i.e. earth used for shadowing; cf. Ital. *ombreggiare*, to shadow. The Ital. *ombra* is from L. *umbra*, shadow; see **Umbrage**. ¶ See Wedgwood (p. 746), who notes that 'the fable of the pigment taking its name from *Umbria* [which is only a guess by Malone] is completely disproved by the Span. name *sombra* (shade); *sombra di Venecia*, Venetian umber; *sombra de hueso*, bone-umber.' Some paintings of the *Venetian* school in the Fitzwilliam Museum, Cambridge, are remarkable for their *umbered* or *sombre* appearance. Cf. also F. *ombré*, 'umbered or shadowed,' Cot.; and see **Sombre**.

UMBILICAL, pertaining to the navel. (F.—L.) In Cotgrave. —MF. *umbilical*, 'umbilicall, belonging to the navell;' Cot. —MF. *umbilic*, 'the navell or middle of;' id. —L. *umbilīcum*, acc. of *umbilīcus*, the navel, middle, centre. Allied to Gk. ὀμφαλός, the navel; *umbilicus* being really an adjectival form, from a sb. **umbilus=ὀμφαλός*. Cf. L. *umbo*, a boss. Allied to Skt. *nābhi-*, navel; and E. **Navel**, q.v. All from a common root **enebh* (Uhlenbeck).

UMBLE-PIE, pie containing the *umbles* or *numbles* (entrails) of deer. (F.—L.) 'The *vmblis* of venyson;' Skelton, Garland of Laurell, 1240. See further under **Numbles**. And see **Umbles** in Nares.

UMBRAGE, a shade or screen of trees, suspicion of injury, offence. (F.—L.) The proper sense is 'shadow,' as in Hamlet, v. 2. 125; thence it came to mean a shadow of suspicion cast upon a person, suspicion of injury, &c. 'It is also evident that St. Peter did not carry himself so as to give the least overture or *umbrage* to make any one suspect he had any such preëminence;' Bp. Taylor, A Dissuasive from Popery, p. i. § 8 (R.); and see Trench, Select Glossary. —F. *ombrage* (also *umbrage*), 'an umbrage, shade, shadow; also jealousie, suspition, an incling of;' whence *donner ombrage à*, to discontent, make jealous of;' Cot. —F. *ombre*, a shadow; with suffix *-age* (<L. *-āticum*); cf. L. *umbrāticus*, belonging to shade. —L. *umbra*, a shadow. **Der.** *umbrage-ous*, shadowy, from F. *ombrageux*, 'shady, ... umbragious,' Cot.; *umbrageous-ly, -ness.* And see *umb-el, umber, umbr-ella, sombre.*

UMBRELLA, a screen carried in the hand to protect from sunshine or rain. (Ital.—L.) Now used to protect from rain, in contradistinction to a *parasol*; but formerly used to protect from sunshine, and rather an old word. Cotgrave translates F. *ombraire* by 'an umbrello, or shadow,' and F. *ombrelle* by 'an umbrello.' 'Now you have got a *shadow*, an *umbrella*, To keep the *scorching* world's opinion From your fair credit;' Beaum. and Fletcher, Rule a Wife, iii. 1. 2.—Ital. *umbrella* (see below); better spelt *ombrella*, 'a fan, a canopie, .. also a kind of round fan or shadowing that they vse to ride with in sommer in Italy, a little shade;' Florio. Dimin. of Ital. *ombra*, a shade.—L. *umbra*, a shade; see **Umbrage.** ¶ The true classical L. form is *umbella*; *umbrella* is an Ital. diminutive, regularly formed from *ombra*; the spelling with *u* is found even in Italian. Florio has *umbella*, *umbrella*, 'a little shadow, a little round thing that women bare in their hands to shadow them; also, a broad brimd hat to keepe off heate and rayne; also, a kind of round thing like a round skreene that gentlemen vse in Italie in time of sommer.' This account of the word, in the edition of Florio of 1598, clearly implies that the word *umbrella* was not, in that year, much used in English; for he does not employ the word. **Doublet,** *umbel.*

UMPIRE, a third person called in to decide a dispute between two others. (F.—L.) This curious word has lost initial *n*, and stands for *numpire*, once a common form. See remarks under the letter **N**. Spelt *umpire* in L. L. L. i. 1. 170. ME. *nompere* or *noumpere*. '*N*(*o*)*wmpere*, or *owmpere*, Arbiter;' Prompt. Parv. Spelt *noumpere, nounpere, nounpier*, P. Plowman, B. v. 337; *nompeyr*, id. C. vii. 388; and id. A. v. 181. In Wyclif, Prologue to Romans, ed. Forshall and Madden, p. 302, l. 24, we have *noumpere*, where six MSS. read *vmpere*. It also occurs, spelt *nompere*, in the Testament of Love, bk. i. ch. 2. l. 96. Tyrwhitt shows (in his Glossary to Chaucer) that the L. *impar* was sometimes used in the sense of arbitrator, and rightly suggests a connexion with mod. F. *nonpair*, odd. β. The ME. *nompere* exactly represents the OF. form *nomper*, peerless (Godefroy). Later, it occurs in Cotgrave as *nompair*, 'peerless, also odde;' and an earlier spelling *nonper* is given by Roquefort, with the sense of peerless. It is simply a compound of F. *non*, not, and OF. *per*, a peer, an equal; from L. *non*, not, and *par*, equal; see **Non-** and **Peer** (1). γ. The OF. *nonper* became *nomper* regularly, since *n* before *p* becomes *m*, as in *hamper<hanaper*; see **Hamper** (2). It may also be noted that it is not the only ME. word in which the same F. prefix occurs, since we also have ME. *nonpower*, i.e. lack of power, in P. Plowman, C. xx. 292, spelt *nounpower, noumpower*, and even *vnpower*. The last form suggests that the loss of initial *n* was due to some confusion between the F. *non* and E. *un-*, with much the same negative sense. Hence *a numpire* or *an umpire* was *a non-peer* or *an un-peer*, orig. the former. δ. The sense is curious; but the use of L. *impar*, lit. odd, in the sense of arbitrator or umpire sufficiently explains it; the *umpire* is the *odd* man, the *third* man, called in to settle a dispute between two others. It may also be noted that *pair* and *peer* are doublets.

UN- (1), negative prefix. (E.) Prefixed to substantives, adjectives, and adverbs; distinct from the verbal prefix *un-* below. ME. *un-*, AS. *un-*; very common as a neg. prefix.+Du. *on-*; Icel. *ū-* or *ō-* (for *un-*); Dan. *u-*; Swed. *o-*; Goth. *un-*; G. *un-*.+W. *an-*; Irish *an-, in-*; L. *in-*; Gk. ἀν-, ἀ-; Zend. *an-, a-*; Skt. *an-, a-*.

β. All from Idg. **ən*, negative prefix; cf. Brugmann, i. § 432. Allied to Skt. *na*, not; Goth. *ni*, not, Lith. *nè*; also to L. *nē*, not, Gk. νη-, neg. prefix.

B. It is unnecessary to give all the words in which this prefix occurs; it is used before words of various origin, both English and French. The following may be noted in particular. **1.** It occurs in words purely English, and appears in many of these in Anglo-Saxon; Grein gives AS. words, for example, answering to *un-clean, un-even, un-fair, un-whole, un-smooth, un-soft, un-still, un-wise.* Some compounds are now disused, or nearly so; such as *un-bold, un-blithe, un-little, un-right, un-sad, un-slow* (all in Grein). In the case of *past participles*, the prefix is *ambiguous*; thus *un-bound* may either mean 'not bound,' like AS. *unbunden*; or it may mean 'opened' or 're-leased,' being taken as the pp. of *unbind*, verb. **2.** *Un-* is frequently prefixed to words of F. origin; examples such as *un-feyned* (unfeigned) and *un-stable* occur in Chaucer; we even find *un-famous* in House of Fame, iii. 56, where we should now say *not famous*. Palsgrave has *un-able, un-certayne, un-cortoyse* (uncourteous), *un-gentyll, un-gracyous, un-honest, un-maryed, un-parfyte* (imperfect), *un-profytable, un-raysonable* (unreasonable). **3.** In some cases, such as *un-couth*, the simple word (without the prefix) is obsolete; such cases are discussed below.

UN- (2), verbal prefix, expressing the reversal of an action. (E.) In the verb to *un-lock*, we have an example of this; it expresses the reversal of the action expressed by *lock*; i.e. it means to open again that which was closed by locking. This is quite distinct from the mere negative prefix, with which many, no doubt, confound it. ME. *un-*, AS. *un-*; only used as a prefix in *verbs*.+Du. *ont-*; as in *ont-laden*, to unload, from *laden*, to load; G. *ent-*, as in *ent-laden*, to unload; OHG. *ant-*, as in *ant-lūhhan*, to unlock; Goth. *and-*, as in *and-bindan*, to unbind. β. It is precisely the same prefix as that which appears as *an-* in E. *an-swer*, and as *and-* in AS. *and-swarian*; and it is cognate with Gk. ἀντι-, used only in the not very different sense of 'in opposition to;' thus, whilst E. *un-say* is to reverse what is said, to deny it, the Gk. ἀντι-λέγειν is to *with-say* or *gain-say*, to deny what is said by others. See **Answer** and **Anti-.** B. It is unnecessary to give all the words with this prefix; I may note that Grein gives the AS. verb corresponding to E. *un-do*, viz. *undōn*, with which cf. EFries. *und-dōn, unt-dōn*, Du. *ontdoen*; also *un-tynan*, to unfasten, open, now obsolete; Bosworth gives *unbindan*, to unbind, *unfealdan*, to unfold, *unlūcan*, to unlock, and a few others, but verbs with this prefix are not very numerous in AS. γ. However, it was so freely employed before verbs of French origin, that we have now many such words in use; Palsgrave has *un-arm, un-bend, un-bind, un-boukell* (unbuckle), *un-bridle, un-clasp*, &c., with others that are obsolete, such as *un-custume*, to disuse a custom. δ. The most common and remarkable of the mod. E. verbs with this prefix are: *un-bar, -bend, -bind, -bolt, -bosom, -brace, -buckle, -burden, -button, -case, -chain, -clasp, -close, -clothe, -coil, -couple, -cover, -curl, -deceive, -do, -dress, -earth, -fasten, -fetter, -fix, -fold, -furl, -gird, -hand, -harness, -hinge, -hook, -horse, -house, -kennel, -knit, -knot, -lace, -lade, -learn, -limber, -load, -lock, -loose, -make, -man, -mask, -moor, -muffle, -muzzle, -nerve, -pack, -people, -ravel, -rig, -robe, -roll, -roof, -root, -saddle, -say, -screw, -seal, -seat, -settle, -sex, -shackle, -ship, -stop, -string, -thread, -tie, -tune, -twine, -twist, -warp, -weave, -wind, -wrap, -yoke.* See further under the simple words. ¶ Note the ambiguity in the case of *past participles*; for which see under **Un-** (1).

UN- (3), prefix. (E.) See **Unto, Until.**

UNANELED, without having received extreme unction. (E.; and L.—Gk.) In Hamlet, i. 5. 77. Lit. 'not on-oiled.'—AS. *un-*, not; and ME. *an-eled*, pp. of *anelien, anelen*, to give extreme unction to; Rob. of Brunne, Handlyng Synne, 11269 (1303). The verb is from ME. *an* (AS. *on*), on, upon; and *elien*, to oil, regularly formed from AS. *ele*, sb., oil. The AS. *ele* is not a Teut. word, but borrowed from L. *oleum*, oil, Gk. ἔλαιον. See **Un-** (1), **On**, and **Oil.** Cf. also *anoil*, v., which see in N. E. D. 'I *aneele*, .. I *anoynt* .. with holy oyle;' Palsgrave.

UNANIMOUS, of one mind. (L.) 'The universall and *unanimous* belief;' Camden, Hist. of Q. Elizabeth, an. 1588 (R.). Englished (by change of *-us* to *-ous*, as in *arduous*, &c.), from L. *ūnanimus*, of one mind. —L. *ūn-us*, one; and *animus*, mind; see **Unit** and **Animosity. Der.** *unanimous-ly*; also *unanim-i-ty*, spelt *unanimitee* in The Libell of Englishe Policye (A. D. 1436), l. 1068 (quoted in Hakluyt's Voyages, i. 206), from F. *unanimité*, omitted by Cotgrave, but in use in the 14th century (Littré), from L. acc. *ūnanimitātem*, due to the adj. *ūnanimis*, by-form of *ūnanimus*.

UNCIAL, pertaining to a certain style of writing. (L.) 'Uncial, belonging to an ounce or inch;' Blount, ed. 1674. Applied to a particular form of letters in MSS. from the 4th to the 9th centuries. The letters are of large size, and the word signifies 'of the size of an inch.' Phillips gives *uncial* only in its other sense, viz. 'belonging to an ounce.' Cotgrave gives F. *oncial*, 'weighing as much as an ounce;' but he also gives *lettres onciales*, 'huge letters, great letters.' — L. *unciālis*, belonging to an inch, or to an ounce. — L. *uncia*, an inch, an ounce. See **Inch** and **Ounce** (1). ¶ 'The term *uncial* was orig. a misapplication of St. Jerome's expression *litterae unciāles*, "inch-high," i. e. large, handsome letters;' Cent. Dict. See Jerome's Prologue to the book of Job (near the end).

UNCLE, the brother of one's father or mother. (F.—L.) ME. *vncle*, *uncle*; Rob. of Glouc. p. 58, l. 1337. — AF. *uncle*, Gaimar, 188; F. *oncle*, 'an uncle;' Cot. — L. *auunculum*, acc. of *auunculus*, a mother's brother; *auunculum* was shortened to *unculum*, whence F. *oncle*. The lit. sense is 'little grandfather;' it is a double dimin. (with suffixes *-cu-lu-*) from *auus*, a grandfather. Allied to Goth. *awō*, a grandmother, Lith. *avynas*, an uncle, W. *ewythr*, an uncle. Brugmann, i. § 330. ¶ The G. *onkel* is also from Latin. The E. *nuncle*, K. Lear, i. 4. 117, is due to the phrase *my nuncle*, corrupted from *mine uncle*.

UNCOMEATABLE, unapproachable. (E.; *with F. suffix*.) In the Tatler, no. 12. A strange compound, with prefix *un-* (1) and suffix *-able*, from **Come** and **At**.

UNCOUTH, unfamiliar, odd, awkward, strange. (E.) The lit. sense is simply 'unknown;' hence strange, &c. ME. *uncouth*, strange, Chaucer, C. T. 10598 (F. 284). A common word; see Stratmann. AS. *uncūð*, unknown, strange (common); Grein, ii. 616. — AS. *un-*, not; and *cūð*, known, pp. of *cunnan*, to know, but used as an adj.; Grein, i. 172. See further under **Can** (1); and see **Un-** (1). ¶ The Lowland Sc. *unco* is the same word; and, again, the prov. E. *unked* or *unkid* (spelt *unkard* in Halliwell), strange, unusual, odd, also lonely, solitary, corresponds to ME. *unkid*, 'not made known,' where *kid* (= AS. *cȳðed*) is the pp. of the causal verb *cȳðan*, to make known, a derivative from *cūð* by vowel-change from *ū* to *ȳ*; Grein, i. 181.

UNCTION, an anointing, a salve; also, warmth of address, sanctifying grace. (F.—L.) In Shak. Hamlet, iii. 4. 145, iv. 7. 142. 'His inwarde *vnccion* wyl worke with our diligence;' Sir T. More, Works, p. 763 a. ME. *vncioun*; spelt *vnccioun*, Trevisa, i. 113. — F. *onction*, 'unction, an anointing;' Cot. — L. *unctiōnem*, acc. of *unctio*, an anointing; cf. *unctus*, pp. of *ungere*, to anoint; see **Unguent**. Der. *unctu-ous*, Holinshed, Desc. of Britain, c. 24 (R.), Trevisa, i. 113, also spelt *vnctious*, Timon of Athens, iv. 3. 195 (first folio), and even *vncteous*, Holland, tr. of Pliny, b. xxxiv. c. 12, p. 510, from F. *onctueux*, 'oily, fatty,' Cot., from Late L. *unctuōsus* (Ducange); due to L. *unctu-*, decl. stem of *unctus* (gen. *unctūs*), an anointing. Hence *unctu-os-i-ty*, from F. *onctuosité*, 'unctuositie;' Cot.

UNDER, beneath, below. (E.) ME. *vnder*, *under*, Chaucer, C. T. 1697. AS. *under*; Grein, ii. 617.+Du. *onder*; Icel. *undir*; Swed. and Dan. *under*; Goth. *undar*; G. *unter*; OHG. *untar*. β. Further allied to Skt. *adharas*, lower; and to *adhas*, prep. under, adv. below; L. *infrā*, beneath. Brugmann, i. § 446; ii. § 75. ¶ For the phrase *under way*, see **Way**.

UNDER-, *prefix*, beneath. (E.) The same word as the above. Very common; the chief words with this prefix are *under-bred*, *-current*, *-done*, *-gird* (Acts, xxvii. 17), *under-go* (AS. *undergān*, Bosworth), *under-graduate*, i. e. a student who is under a graduate, one who has not taken his degree, *under-ground*, *-growth*, *under-hand*, adv., secretly, Spenser, F. Q. iv. 11. 34, also as adj., As You Like It, i. 1. 146, *under-lay* (AS. *underlecgan*, Ælfric's Grammar, ed. Zupitza, p. 190, l. 5), *under-lie* (AS. *underlicgan*, Bosworth), *under-line*. Also *under-ling*, Gower, C. A. iii. 80 (bk. vi. 2350), Layamon, 19116, with double dimin. suffix *-l-ing*. Also *under-mine*, Wyclif, Matt. vi. 20, early version; with double superl. suffix, as explained under **Aftermost**; *under-neath*, ME. *vndirneþ*, Chaucer, tr. of Boethius, b. iii. pr. 5, l. 15, compounded like **Beneath**, q. v. Also *under-plot*, sb., *-prop*, vb., *-rate*, *-sell*; *-set*, Ancren Riwle, p. 254, l. 5; *under-sign*; *under-stand*, q. v.; *under-state*; *under-take*, q. v.; *under-tone*, *-value*, *-wood* (Ben Jonson), *-write*, *-writer*.

UNDERN, a certain period of the day. (E.) The time denoted by *undern* differed at different periods. In Chaucer, C. T. 15228 (B 4412), it denotes some hour of the fore-noon, perhaps about 11 o'clock. 'At *undren* and at midday,' O. Eng. Miscellany, p. 33; with reference to the parable of the Labourers in the Vineyard. 'Abuten *undern* deies'=about the undern-tide of the day, Ancren Riwle, p. 24; where perhaps an earlier hour is meant, about 9 A. M. AS. *undern*; whence *undern-tīd*, undern-tide, Matt. xx. 3; here it means the third hour, i.e. 9 A.M.+Icel. *undorn*, mid-afternoon; also mid-forenoon; MHG. *undern*, OHG. *untorn*, a time of the day; Goth. *undaurni*; only in the compound *undaurni-mats*, a morning-meal, Luke, xiv. 12. β. The true sense is merely 'intervening period,' which accounts for its vagueness; this sense does not appear in *under*, prep., but suggests a connexion with L. *inter*, between,

Skt. *antar*, within. Cf. L. *internus*, inward. ¶ The word is by no means obsolete, but appears in various forms in prov. E., such as *aandorn*, *aunder*, *orndorns*, *doundrins*, *dondinner*, all in Ray, *aunder*, in Halliwell, &c. (Here Nares is wrong.)

UNDERSTAND, to comprehend. (E.) ME. *vnderstanden*, *understanden*, a strong verb; the pp. appears as *understanden*, Pricke of Conscience, l. 1681. The weak pp. *understanded* occurs in the Prayer-book. AS. *understandan*, lit. to stand under or among, hence to comprehend (cf. L. *intel-ligere*); Ælfred, tr. of Boethius, b. iv. pr. 6, c. xxxiv. § 8. — AS. *under*, under; and *standan*, to stand; see **Under** and **Stand**. So also MSwed. *understå*, from *under* and *stå*, to stand; see Ihre. Another AS. word, with the same prefix and the same sense, is *undergitan* (lit. to underget), John, viii. 27, xii. 16. Der. *understand-ing*, spelt *onderstondinge*, Ayenbite of Inwyt, p. 24, l. 8.

UNDERTAKE, to take upon oneself, attempt. (*Hybrid*; E. and Scand.) ME. *vndertaken*, strong verb; pt. t. *vndertok*, see Havelok, 377. It first appears in the Ormulum, l. 10314. The latter part of the word is of Scand. origin; see **Under** and **Take**. β. The word is a sort of translation of (and was suggested by) the AS. *underniman*, to understand, receive, Matt. xix. 12, and AS. *underfōn*, to receive, Matt. x. 40, John, xviii. 3. Neither of these words have *precisely* the same sense, but both *niman* and *fōn* have the sense of E. take (Icel. *taka*). Der. *undertak-ing*, Haml. ii. 1. 104; *undertak-er*, orig. one who takes a business in hand, Oth. iv. 1. 224, Tw. Nt. iii. 4. 349.

UNDULATE, to wave, move in waves. (L.) In Thomson, Summer, 982. Phillips, ed. 1706, has *undulate* only as a pp. Blount, ed. 1674, gives *undulated* and *undulation*. — L. *undulātus*, undulated, wavy. — L. **undula*, a little wave; not used, but a regular dimin. of *unda*, a wave, properly 'water.' β. *Unda* is a nasalised form, like OPruss. *unds*, water, allied to Gk. ὕδωρ, water, and to E. *water*. Cf. Skt. *udan*, water, *und*, to wet; Lithuan. *wancu*, water; Russ. *voda*, water. — √WED, to wet; see **Water**. Brugmann, i. §§ 102, 594. Der. *undulat-ion* (Phillips); *undulat-or-y*. Also (from *unda*) *ab-ound*, *ab-und-ant*, *in-und-ate*, *red-ound*, *red-und-ant*, *super-ab-ound*, *surr-ound*.

UNEATH, scarcely, with difficulty. (E.) Obsolete; in Spenser, F. Q. i. 9. 38; misused, with the sense 'almost,' id. i. 12. 4. ME. *vneþe*, Gawain and the Grene Knight, 134. AS. *unēaðe*, with difficulty, Gen. xxvii. 30; adv. from adj. *unēaðe*, difficult, Grein, ii. 620. — AS. *un-*, not; and *ēaðe*, easy, smooth, common also in the adv. form *ēaðe*, easily, Grein, i. 254; we also find *ēðe*, *ȳðe*, easy, id. i. 230, ii. 767.+OSax. *ōði*, easy. Some further compare it with the OHG. *ōdi*, desert, empty, G. *öde*, deserted, desolate; Icel. *auðr*, empty; Goth. *auths*, *authis*, desert, waste. But it is probable that these words, though similar in form, are of independent origin.

UNGAINLY, awkward. (Hybrid; E. and Scand.) ME. *ungeinliche*, used as an adv., awkwardly, horribly, St. Marharete, ed. Cockayne, p. 9, l. 14. Formed by adding *-liche* (*-ly*) to the adj. *ungein*, inconvenient, spelt *ungayne* in Le Bone Florence, l. 1421, in Ritson, Met. Romances, iii. 60. — AS. *un-*, not, see **Un-** (1); and Icel. *gegn*, ready, serviceable, convenient, allied to *gegna*, to meet, to suit, *gegn*, against, and E. *again*; see **Again**. Cf. Icel. *geigniligr*, meet; *ōgegn* (ungain), ungainly, ungentle. Der. *ungainli-ness*. ¶ We also find AS. *gægne* in a gloss: 'Compendiose, breuiter, *gægne*;' Voc. 207. 17. Perhaps the word is of native origin.

UNGUENT, ointment. (L.) In Blount's Gloss., ed. 1674. — L. *unguentum*, ointment. — L. *unguent-*, stem of pres. part. of *unguere*, *ungere*, to anoint.+Skt. *añj*, to anoint, smear. Brugmann, i. § 398. Der. (from *ungere*, pp. *unctus*) *unct-ion*, q. v.; also *oint-ment*, *an-oint*.

UNICORN, a fabulous animal with one horn. (F.—L.) ME. *unicorne*, Ancren Riwle, p. 120, l. 9. — AF. *unicorne*, Psalm xxi. 22; F. *unicorne*, 'an unicorn;' Cot. — L. *unicornem*, acc. of *unicornis*, adj., one-horned. — L. *ūni-*, for *ūno-*, decl. stem of *ūnus*, one; and *corn-u*, a horn, cognate with E. *horn*. See **Unity** and **Horn**.

UNIFORM, consistent, having throughout the same form or character. (F.—L.) Spelt *uniforme* in Minsheu, ed. 1627; *uniform* in Cotgrave. — F. *uniforme*, 'uniform,' Cot. — L. *ūniformem*, acc. of *ūniformis*, having one form. — L. *ūni-*, for *ūno-*, decl. stem of *ūnus*, one; and *form-a*, a form; see **Unity** and **Form**. Der. *uniform*, sb., a like dress for persons who belong to the same body; *uniform-ly*; *uniform-i-ty*, from F. *uniformité*, 'uniformity,' Cot., from L. acc. *ūniformitātem*.

UNILITERAL, consisting of one letter. (L.) The only such words in E. are *a*, *I*, and *O*. Coined from L. *ūni-*, for *ūno-*, decl. stem of *ūnus*, one; and *litter-a*, a letter; with suffix *-al*; cf. *bi-literal*, *tri-literal*.

UNION (1), concord, harmony, confederation in one. (F.—L.) Spelt *vnyon*, Berners, tr. of Froissart, vol. ii. c. 233 (R.). — F. *union*, 'an union;' Cot.—L. *uniōnem*, acc. of *unio*, oneness.—L. *ŭn-us*, one, cognate with E. **One**, q. v. And see **Unity**.

UNION (2), a large pearl. (F.—L.) In Hamlet, v. 2. 283.—AF. *union*; Bestiary, 1482. Really the same word as the above; the L. *ŭnio* means (1) oneness, (2) a single pearl of a large size. *Onion* is also the same word. See above; and see **Onion**. Doublet, *onion*.

UNIQUE, single, without a like. (F.—L.) Modern; added by Todd to Johnson.—F. *unique*, 'single,' Cot.—L. *ŭnicum*, acc. of *ŭnicus*, single.—L. *ŭni-*, for *uno-*, decl. stem of *ŭnus*, one; with suffix *-cus* (Idg. *-ko-*). See **Unity**.

UNISON, concord, harmony. (F.—L.) 'In concordes, discordes, notes and cliffes in tunes of *vnisonne*;' Gascoigne, Grene Knight's Farewell to Fansie, st. 7; Works, i. 413. Spelt *vnysoune*, York Plays, p. 209, l. 262.—MF. *unisson*, 'an unison;' Cot. [The spelling with *ss* is remarkable, as it is not etymological.]—L. *ŭnisonum*, acc. of *ŭnisonus*, having the same sound as something else.—L. *ŭni-*, for *ŭno-*, decl. stem of *ŭnus*, one; and *sonus*, a sound. See **Unity** and **Sound** (3). Der. *unison-ous*; *uni-son-ant* (from *sonant-*, stem of pres. part. of *sonāre*, to sound); *uni-son-ance*.

UNIT, a single thing, person, or number. (F.—L.) Not derived from L. *ŭnitum*, which would mean 'united,' but a purely E. formation, made by dropping the final letter of *unit-y*. 'Unit, Unite, or Unity, in arithmetic, the first significant figure or number 1; in *Notation*, if a number consist of 4 or 5 places, that which is outermost towards the right hand is called the *Place of Unites*;' Phillips, ed. 1706. The number 1 is still called *unity*. See **Unity**.

UNITE, to make one, join. (L.) 'I *vnyte*, I bringe diverse thynges togyther in one;' Palsgrave.—L. *ŭnit-us*, pp. of *ŭnīre*, to unite.—L. *ŭn-us*, one; see **Unity**.

UNITY, oneness, union in one, concord. (F.—L.) ME. *vnitee*, *vnite*, *unite*, Gower, C. A. iii. 181 (bk. vii. 2836); P. Plowman, C. vi. 10.—AF. *unitè*, Stat. Realm, i. 186 (1322); F. *unité*, 'an unity;' Cot.—L. *ŭnitātem*, acc. of *ŭnitās*, oneness.—L. *ŭni-*, for *ŭno-*, decl. stem of *ŭnus*, one; with suffix *-tās*. The L. *ŭnus* is cognate with E. **One**, q. v. Der. *unit-ari-an*, a coined word, added by Todd to Johnson; hence *unit-ari-an-ism*. Doublet, *unit*, q. v. We also have (from L. *ŭn-us*) *un-ite*, *un-ion*, *uni-que*, *uni-son*, *uni-vers-al*, *uni-corn*, *uni-form*, *uni-literal*, *uni-vocal*; also *un-animous*, *dis-un-ite*, *dis-un-ion*, *re-un-ite*, *re-un-ion*, *tri-une*, *onion*. Also *null*, q. v.; *an-nul*, q. v.

UNIVERSAL, comprehending the whole, extending to the whole. (F.—L.) ME. *vniuersal*; spelt *vniuersal*, Gower, C. A. iii. 91; (bk. vii. 215).—F. *universel* (sometimes *universal* in the 14th century), 'vniversall,' Cot.—L. *ŭniuersālis*, belonging to the whole.—L. *ŭniuersum*, the whole; neut. of *ŭniuersus*, turned into one, combined into a whole.—L. *ŭni-*, for *ŭno-*, decl. stem of *ŭnus*, one; and *uersus*, pp. of *uertere*, to turn; see **Unity** and **Verse**. Der. *universal-ly*, *universal-i-ty*, *universal-ism*. Also (from F. *univers*<L. *ŭniuersum*) *universe*, Henry V, iv. chor. 3; also *univers-i-ty*, a school for universal knowledge, ME. *vniuersite*, used in the sense of 'world' in Wyclif, James, iii. 6, AF. *universitè*, Yearbooks of Edw. I, 1304-5, p. 429, from F. *université*, 'university, also an university,' Cot., from L. acc. *ŭniuersitātem*.

UNIVOCAL, having one voice, having but one meaning. (L.) Now little used; it is the antithesis of *equi-vocal*, i. e. having a variable meaning. In Bp. Taylor, Rule of Conscience, b. ii. c. 3 (R.). Cf. F. *univoque*, 'of one onely sence;' Cot.—L. *ŭniuoc-us*, univocal; with suffix *-ālis*.—L. *ŭni-*, for *ŭno-*, decl. stem of *ŭnus*, one; and *uoc-*, allied to *uōx*, voice, sound. See **Unity** and **Voice**.

UNKEMPT, not combed. (E.) In Spenser, F. Q. iii. 10, 29; and Shep. Kal. November, 51; in both places in the metaphorical sense of rough or rude. A contracted form of *unkembed*. From *un-*, not; and ME. *kembed*, *kempt*, combed, Chaucer, C. T. 2145 (A 2143). *Kembed* is the pp. of *kemben*, to comb, P. Plowman, B. x. 18.—AS. *cemban*, to comb; Ælfric's Grammar, ed. Zupitza, p. 168, l. 6; formed (by vowel-change of *a* to *e*) from AS. *camb*, a comb; see **Comb**.

UNLESS, if not, except. (E.) Formerly written *onless*, *onlesse*, with *o*; Horne Tooke remarks: 'I believe that William Tyndall . . was one of the first who wrote this word with a *u*;' and he cites: 'The scripture was geven, that we may applye the medicine of the scripture, every man to his own sores, *unlesse* then we entend to be idle disputers;' Tyndal, Prol. to the 5 books of Moses. Horne Tooke gives 16 quotations with the spellings *onles* and *onlesse*; the earliest appears to be: 'It was not possible for them to make whole Cristes cote without seme, *onlesse* certeyn grete men were brought out of the way;' Trial of Sir John Oldcastle, an. 1413. We may also note: 'That, *lesse than* synne the soner swage, God wyl be vengyd,' &c.; Coventry Myst. p. 40. Also: 'Charitie is not perfect *onles that* it be burninge,' T. Lupset, Treatise of Charitie, p. 8. '*Onles that* ye tary ouer longe;' Malory, Morte Arthur, bk. x. c. 20. [But Horne Tooke's

own explanation of the phrase is utterly wrong.] Palsgrave, in his list of conjunctions, gives *onlesse* and *onlesse that*. β. Thus the full phrase was *on lesse that*; but *that* was soon dropped. Here *on* is the preposition; and *lesse* is mod. E. *less*; see **On** and **Less**. The sense is 'in less than,' or 'on a less supposition.' Thus, if charity be (fully) burning, it is perfect; *in a less case*, it is imperfect. The use of *on* in the sense of *in* is extremely common in ME., as in *on liue* = in life (see **Alive**), *on sleep* = in sleep (see **Asleep**); and see numerous examples in Stratmann. *On less* or *in less* is similar to *at least*, *at most*. ¶ Mätzner, and Mahn (in Webster, 1864) wrongly explain *un-* in *unless* as a negative prefix; this is contrary to all the evidence, and makes nonsense of the phrase. Morris (Hist. Outlines of Eng. Accidence, p. 332) rightly gives *on lesse* as the orig. form, but does not explain it.

UNRULY, disregarding restraint. (Hybrid; E. and F.—L.; with E. suffix.) In James, iii. 8 (A.V.), where Wyclif has *vnpesible*; here the E. version translates the Gk. ἀκατάσχετον, i. e. that cannot be ruled. Thus *unruly* is for *unrule-ly*; it does not seem to be a very old word, though going back to 1483; the Cathol. Anglicum has: '*Reuly*, tranquillus;' and '*unrewely*, inquietus;' also '*reule*, regula; *reule*, regulare.' Cf. 'Ye . . *vnrulilye* haue *ruled*;' Sir J. Cheke, Hurt of Sedition (R.) Cotgrave translates F. *moderé* by 'moderate, quiet, *ruly*, temperate, orderly.' From **Un-** and **Rule**; with suffix *-ly*. ¶ It is remarkable that the ME. *unro*, unrest, might have produced a somewhat similar adj., viz. *unroly*, *unrouly*, restless. [But Stratmann gives no example of the word, and the vowel-sound does not accord; so that any idea of such a connexion may be rejected. This ME. *unro* is from AS. *un-*, not, and *rōw*, rest (Grein, ii. 384), cognate with Icel. *ró*, G. *ruhe*, rest.] We must also note that *unruled* occurs as equivalent to *unruly*, as in 'theyse *vnrulyd* company,' Fabyan, Chron. an. 1380-1. Der. *unruli-ly*, *-ness*.

UNTIL, till, to. (E. and Scand.) ME. *until*, P. Plowman, B. prol. 227; Pricke of Conscience, 555; spelt *ontil*, Havelok, 761. A substituted form of *unto*, due to the use of the Northern E. *til* for *to*; the two latter words being equivalent in sense. ME. *til* (E. *till*) is of Scand. origin, as distinguished from *to* (= AS. *tō*). See **Till** (2), and see further under **Unto**.

UNTO, even to, to. (E.) Not found in AS. ME. *unto*, Chaucer, C. T. 490 (A 488); earlier in Rob. of Brunne, tr. of Langtoft, p. 1, l. 7. It stands for **und-to*; where *to* is the usual E. prep. (AS. *tō*), and *und* is the OFries. *und* (also *ont*), unto, OSax. *und*, unto (whence OSax. *unt*, shortened from *und-te*, unto, where *te* = AS. *tō*, as well as *untō*, unto, shortened from *und-tō*). 'Fōrun folk *untō* = folk went unto him; Heliand, 2814. So also Goth. *und*, unto, until, as far as, up to; '*und* Bethlahaim' = unto Bethlehem, Luke, ii. 15; whence *untē* (= *und tē*), until. [It is remarkable that a closely related word is common in AS. in a different form, viz. *ōð*, for an older **anth*.] β. The Goth. *und* is the weak-grade form answering to the Goth. *and-*, prefix, cognate with Gk. ἀντί, so that the *un-* in *un-to* is allied to the verbal prefix *un-*; see **Un-** (2). And see **Until**.

UP, towards a higher place, aloft. (E.) ME. *vp*, *up*; common. AS. *up*, *upp*, up, adv.; Grein, ii. 630.+Du. *op*; Icel. *upp*; Dan. *op*; Swed. *upp*; Goth. *iup*; OHG. *ûf*. β. AS. *upp*<the Teut. type **uppo-*, from Idg. **up-n-*; and thus allied to Teut. **uf*, as seen in Goth. *uf*, under, *uf-ar*, over (comparative form), and in E. *over*; further allied to Gk. ὑπό, under, Skt. *upa*, near, on, under. See the account under **Over**. Der. *upp-er*, ME. *vpper*, King Alisaunder, 5691; Chaucer uses *over* in the same sense, as in *ouer lippe* = upper lip, C. T. 133. Hence *upper-most* (not an old form), as in 'euen vpon the *vppermoste* pinnacle of the temple,' Udall, On St. Luke, iv. 9; this is not a correct form, but made on the model of **Aftermost**, q. v. Also *up-most*, Jul. Cæs. ii. 1. 24, which appears to be simply a contraction for *uppermost*, though really a better form. And see **Up-below**, and **Upon**; also **Open**.

UP-, prefix. (E.) The same word as the above. The chief words in which it occurs are: *up-bear*, *up-bind*, *up-braid*, q. v.; *up-heave*, Shak. Venus, 482; *up-hill*; *up-hoard*, Hamlet, i. 1. 136; *up-hold*, *up-holsterer*, q. v.; *up-land*, *up-land-ish* = ME. *vplondysche* in Prompt. Parv.; *up-lift*, Temp. iii. 3. 68; *up-right*, AS. *upriht*, *uppriht*, Grein, ii. 632; *up-ris-ing*, L. L. L. iv. 1. 2, with which cf. ME. *vprysynge*, resurrection, Rob. of Glouc. p. 379, l. 7792; *up-roar*, q. v.; *up-root*, Dryden, St. Cecilia's Day, 49; *up-set* = set up, Gower, C. A. i. 53 (bk. i. 339), also to overset, id. iii. 283 (bk. viii. 244); *up-shot*, Hamlet, v. 2. 395; *up-side*, *up-side-down*, q. v.; *up-start*, q. v.; *up-ward*, AS. *upweard*, Grein, ii. 632; *up-ward-s*, AS. *upweardes*, adv., ibid.

UPAS, the poison-tree of Java. (Malay.) Not in Todd's Johnson; the deadly effects of the tree have been grossly exaggerated.—Malay *ūpas*, 'a milky juice extracted from certain vegetables, operating, when mixed with the blood, as a most deadly poison, concerning the effects of which many exaggerated stories have been related; see Hist. of Sumatra, ed. 3, p. 110. *Pūhn ūpas*, the poison-tree, arbor toxicaria Macassariensis ;' Marsden, Malay Dict. p. 24. The Malay *pūhun* or *pūhn* means ' tree ;' id. p. 239. Now commonly pronounced *pŏhun ípoh,* 'upas tree.'

UPBRAID, to reproach. (E.) ME. *upbreiden,* to upbraid ; we also find *upbreid,* sb., a reproach. ' The deuyls ranne to me with grete scornes and *vpbraydys* ;' and again, 'wykyd angelles of the deuylle *vpbreydyn* me ;' Monk of Evesham, c. 27 ; ed. Arber, p. 67. *Up-breiding,* sb., a reproach, occurs in Layamon, 19117 ; also *vpbreid, upbræid,* sb., id. 26036. AS. *up-bregdan ;* found in the equivalent form *up-gebrēdan,* to upbraid, in Wulfstan's Homilies, ed. Napier, p. 249. — AS. *upp,* up ; and *bregdan, brēdan,* to braid, weave, also to lay hold of, pull, draw, used (like Icel. *bregða*) in a variety of senses ; so that *up-braid* is simply compounded of **Up** and **Braid** (1), q. v. The orig. sense of *upbraid* was prob. to lay hands on, lay hold of, hence to attack, lay to one's charge. Cf. ' *Bregdeð* sōna fēond be ðām feaxe '= he shall soon seize the fiend by the hair, Salomon and Saturn, ed. Grein, 99 ; and see *bregdan* in Grein, i. 138. Cf. Dan. *bebreide,* to upbraid, which only differs in the prefix (Dan. *be-*= E. *be-*). Der. *upbraid-ing,* sb., as above.

UPHOLSTERER, one who supplies beds and furniture. (E.) Formerly called an *upholder.* An equivalent form was *upholdster,* used by Caxton (see Prompt. Parv., p. 512, note 2), with suffix *-ster* for *-er ;* see **-ster.** Hence, by a needless addition of *-er* (as in *poult-er-er*), was made *upholdster-er,* whence the corrupt form *upholsterer,* by loss of *d* after *l.* ' *Upholdster* or *upholsterer,* a tradesman that deals in all sorts of chamber-furniture ;' Phillips, ed. 1706. Already spelt *upholstar* in Palsgrave. ME. *vpholder,* a broker, a tradesman, P. Plowman, B. v. 325 ; C. xiii. 218. At the latter reference we read : ' *Vpholderes* on the hul shullen haue hit to selle '= upholders on the hill [Cornhill] shall haue it to sell. It is clear from this and from my note to P. Plowman, C. vii. 377, that the *upholder* was a broker or auctioneer ; so that the name may have arisen from his *holding up* wares for inspection while trying to sell them. The derivation is from **Up** and **Hold.** Cf. ' *Vpholdere,* þat sellythe smal thyngys ;' Prompt. Parv. Der. *upholster-y,* a coined word, from the form *upholster.*

UPON, on, on the top of. (E.) ME. *vpon, upon,* prep., Chaucer, C. T. 111. AS. *uppon,* upon, Gen. xxii. 2 ; also *uppan,* Matt. xxi. 44. — AS. *upp,* up, above, adv. ; and *on, an, on.* See **Up** and **On.** +Icel. *up ā, upp ā,* upon ; where *upp*= AS. *upp,* and *ā* (for *an*) = AS. *on ;* Swed. *på,* upon, clearly a shortened form of *upp å,* where *å*= E. *on ;* Dan. *paa,* upon.

UPROAR, a tumult, clamour, disturbance. (Du.) In Acts, xvii. 5, xix. 40, xx. 1, xxi. 31, 38 ; in Shak. Lucrece, 427, we have : ' his eye . . . Unto a greater *uproar* tempts his veins ;' where there is no notion of *noise,* but only of *excitement* or *disturbance.* ' To haue all the worlde in an *vprore,* and *vnquieted* with warres ;' Udall, on St. Mark, preface, fol. vi, l. 9. Spelt *uprore* in Levins. It is a corrupt form, due to confusion with E. *roar,* with which it has no real connexion ; it is not an E. word at all, but borrowed from Dutch. — Du. *oproer,* 'uprore, tumult, commotion, mutiny, or sedition ;' *oproer maken,* to make a vprore ; *oproerigh,* seditious, or tumultuous ;' Hexham. — Du. *op,* up ; and *roeren,* to stir, move, touch ; so that *uproer*= a stirring up, commotion, excitement. [Formerly also spelt *rueren* (Hexham) ; the Du. *oe* is pronounced as E. *oo ;* Du. *boer*= E. *boor.*]+Swed. *uppror,* revolt, sedition ; allied to *upp,* up, and *röra,* to stir ; Dan. *oprör,* revolt ; *oprøre,* to stir up, from *op,* up, and *röre,* to stir ; G. *aufruhr,* tumult ; *aufrühren,* to stir up, from G. *auf,* up, and *rühren,* to stir. β. The verb appears as Du. *roeren,* Swed. *röra,* Dan. *röre,* Icel. *hrœra,* G. *rühren,* AS. *hrēran,* OSax. *hrōrian,* to stir ; and is the same word as *rear-* or *rere-* in E. *rearmouse, reremouse,* a bat ; see **Reremouse.** γ. The AS. *hrēran,* to stir, agitate, is from *hrōr,* motion, allied to *hrōr,* adj., active (with the usual change from ō to ē) ; the Swed. *uppror* preserves the orig. unmodified *ō.* Perhaps allied to Skt. *çrā,* to boil. See **Crater.** Der. *uproar-i-ous,* an ill-coined word ; *uproar-i-ous-ly, -ness.*

UPSIDE-DOWN, topsyturvy. (E.) ' Turn'd *upside-down* to me ;' Beaum. and Fletcher, Wit at Several Weapons, v. 1 (Gregory). ' I torne *upsyde downe* ;' Palsgrave, p. 760. From *up, side,* and *down.* But it is remarkable that this expression took the place of ME. *vp so doun,* once a common phrase, as in Wyclif, Matt. xxi. 12, Luke xv. 8 ; Chaucer, tr. of Boethius, b. ii. pr. 5. l. 91, b. v. pr. 3. l. 60 ; this is composed of *up, so,* and *down,* where *so* has (as often) the force of *as,* or as it were, i. e. *up as it were down.*

UPSTART, one who has suddenly started up from low life to wealth or honour. (E.) In Shak. 1 Hen. VI, v. 7. 87. A sb. coined from the verb *upstart,* to start up ; the pt. t. *upstart* is in Spenser, F. Q. i. 1. 16. From **Up** and **Start ;** see note to **Start,** § γ.

UPWARD, UPWARDS ; see **Up** and **-ward,** suffix.

URBANE, pertaining to a city, refined, courteous. (L.) Spelt *vrbane* in Levins, ed. 1570. — L. *urbānus,* belonging to a city. — L.

urb-s, a city. Der. *urban,* belonging to a city (which is only another spelling of the same word) ; *sub-urban,* q. v. And see below.

URBANITY, courteousness. (F. — L.) Spelt *vrbanitie* in Levins, ed. 1570. — F. *urbanité,* ' urbanity, civility ;' Cot. — L. *urbāni-tātem,* acc. of *urbānitās,* city-manners, refinement. — L. *urbāni-,* from *urbānus,* urbane ; with suffix *-tās ;* see **Urbane.**

URCHIN, a hedgehog, a goblin, imp, a small child. (North F. — L.) In Shak. it means (1) a hedgehog, Temp. i. 2. 326, Titus, ii. 3. 101 ; (2) a goblin, Merry Wives, iv. 4. 49. Spelt *urchone* in Palsgrave. ME. *vrchon, vrchone,* Prompt. Parv., see the note ; also spelt *irchon,* Early E. Psalter, Ps. ciii. 18 (l. 42) ; see Specimens of English, ed. Morris and Skeat (Glossary). — ONorth F. *herichun,* Marie (Fable 62) ; cf. Picard *irechon ;* Walloon *urechon, irchon* (Sigart) ; Rouchi *urchon* (Hécart) ; Norm. dial. *hérichon ;* also OF. *ireçon,* a hedgehog ; also spelt *heriçon, eriçon* (Burguy) ; mod. F. *hérisson.* Formed, with dimin. suffix *-on* (as if from a L. acc. **ērici-ōnem*), from L. *ēricius,* a hedgehog. β. *Ericius* is a lengthened form from *ēr* (gen. *ēris*), a hedgehog ; for **hēr,* and cognate with Gk. χήρ, a hedgehog. The Gk. χήρ is allied to χάρ-αξ, a pointed stake, χαρ-άσσειν, to scratch (see **Character**) ; and further, to L. *horrēre,* to be bristly, *hirsūtus,* bristly, Skt. *hṛsh,* to bristle. Named from its sharp prickles.

URE, practice, use. (F. — L.) Obsolete, except in the derivative *in-ure ;* and cf. *man-ure.* The real sense is work, practice ; and, as it often has the sense of *use,* Richardson and others confuse it with *use* or *usage ;* but it has no connexion with those words. It was once a common word ; see examples in Nares. ' To put in *vre,* in usum trahere ;' Levins, 193. 17. ' I *vre* one, I accustume hym to a thyng ;' Palsgrave. ME. *vre ;* ' Moche like thyng I haue had in *vre* ;' Remedie of Loue, st. 23, pr. in Chaucer's Works, ed. 1561, fol. 323. [Distinct from ME. *vre*= good luck.] — OF. *eure, uevre, ovre,* work, action, operation. — L. *opera,* work. See further under **Inure, Manure,** and **Operate.** Doublet, *opera.*

URGE, to press earnestly, drive, provoke. (L.) Levins, ed. 1570, has both *urge* and *urgent.* — L. *urgēre,* to urge, drive. β. For **uurg-ēre,* where *uurg-* is the weak grade of **uerg-.* Allied to Gk. εἴργειν (for **ἐϝέργειν*), to repress, constrain, Lithuan. *werž-iù,* I press tight, Goth. *wrikan,* to persecute. — √WERG, to compel ; see **Wreak.** Brugmann, i. § 350. Der. *urg-ent,* from L. *urgent-,* stem of pres. part. of *urgēre ; urgent-ly, urgenc-y.*

URIM, lit. lights. (Heb.) Only in the phr. *urim and thummim ;* see **Thummim.** The lit. sense is ' lights,' though the word may be used in the sing. sense ' light.' — Heb. *ūrim,* lights, pl. of *ūr,* light. — Heb. root *ūr,* to shine.

URINE, the water separated by the kidneys from the blood. (F. — L.) In Macb. ii. 3. 32 ; and in Chaucer, C. T. 5703 (D 121). — F. *urine,* ' urine ;' Cot. — L. *ūrīna,* urine ; where *-ina* is a suffix.+ Gk. οὖρον, urine ; Skt. *vāri,* water ; *vār,* water. Allied to Icel. *ūr,* drizzling rain ; *ver,* the sea ; AS. *wær,* the sea. β. Orig. sense ' water.' Der. *urin-al,* ME. *urinal,* Chaucer, C. T. 12239 (C 305), Layamon, 17724, from F. *urinal* (Cot.) ; *urin-ar-y,* from F. *urinaire* (Cot.).

URN, a vase for ashes of the dead. (F. — L.) ME. *vrne, urne,* Chaucer, Troil. v. 311. — F. *urne,* ' a narrow necked pot, or pitcher of earth ;' Cot. — L. *urna,* an urn. For **urc-na ;* and allied to L. *urc-eus,* a pitcher. Brugmann, i. § 756.

URSINE, of or belonging to a bear. (L.) Modern ; not in Todd's Johnson. — L. *ursīnus,* bear-like. — L. *ursus,* a bear. Allied to Gk. ἄρκτος, a bear ; W. *arth,* Skt. *ṛksha-s,* a bear ; see **Arctic.** Brugmann, i. § 598.

US, the objective case of *we.* (E.) ME. *vs, ous, us ;* used both as acc. and dat. AS. *ūs,* dat. ; *ūs, ūsic, ussic,* acc. pl., us (Grein).+Du. *ons ;* Icel. *oss,* dat. and acc. pl. ; Swed. *oss ;* Dan. *os ;* G. *uns ;* Goth. *uns, unsis,* dat. and acc. pl. β. All from a Teut. base **uns-.* Cf. L. *nōs,* us ; also Gk. ἡμᾶς, Skt. *asmān,* us. Brugmann, i. § 437 (2) ; ii. § 436.

USE (1), sb., employment, custom. (F. — L.) ME. *vse, use ;* properly *us,* as in Ancren Riwle, p. 16, l. 7 ; the word being monosyllabic. — AF. *us* (Havelok, 860), OF. (and F.) *us,* use, usage (Burguy) ; spelt *uz* in Cotgrave. — L. *ūsum,* acc. of *ūsus,* use ; cf. *ūsus,* pp. of *ūti,* to use. Der. *use,* vb., ME. *vsen, usen,* Layamon, 24293, from F. *user,* to use, from Late L. *ūsāre,* to use, for **ūsāri,* frequentative form of *ūti,* to use. Also *us-able,* from the verb *to use ; us-age,* ME. *vsage, usage,* King Alisaunder, l. 1286, from AF. *usage* (Stat. Realm, i. 100), F. *usage,* ' usage,' Cot. Also *use-ful, use-ful-ly, use-ful-ness ; use-less, use-less-ly, use-less-ness ;* all from the sb. *use.* Also *us-u-al,* Hamlet, ii. 1. 22, from L. *ūsuālis,* from *ūsu-,* decl. stem of *ūsus ; us-u-al-ly.* And see *usurp, usury, utensil, utility.* Also *ab-use, dis-use, mis-use, ill-use, per-use.*

USE (2), profit, benefit. (F. — L.) When *use* is employed, in legal documents, in the special sense of ' benefit,' it is a modernised spelling of the Anglo-F. form of the L. *opus*, employment, need. Cf. Anglo-F. *oes*, use, profit, Annals of Burton, pp. 474, 482, A.D. 1258; *oeps*, Liber Custumarum, p. 202; Statutes of the Realm, i. 144, A.D. 1299; *uoes*, service, Vie de St. Auban, 1554. A good example is the following: 'Que il feist a sun *oes* guarder,' which he caused to be kept for his own *use*; Roman de Rou, 2336. See *oes*, *ues*, *eus*, *obs*, in Bartsch.

USHER, a door-keeper, one who introduced strangers. (F. – L.) ME. *vschere*; 'Vschere, Hostiarius' [i.e. ostiarius]; Prompt. Parv. 'That dorë can non *huissher* schette' [shut]; Gower, C. A. i. 231 (bk. ii. 2130).–AF. *usser*, Gaimar, 5995; OF. *ussier*, *uissier* (Burguy); also *huissier*, 'an usher, or door-keeper of a court, or of a chamber in court;' Cot.–L. *ostiārium*, acc. of *ostiārius*, belonging to a door, or (as sb.) a door-keeper.–L. *ostium*, a door, an entrance; extended from *ōs*, a mouth; see **Oral.** Cf. OPruss. *austo*, a mouth. **Der.** *usher*, verb, L. L. L. v. 2. 328; *usher-ship*.

USQUEBAUGH, whiskey. (Irish.) In Ben Jonson, The Irish Masque; Beaum. and Fletcher, Scornful Lady, ii. 3 (Savil); Ford, Perkin Warbeck, iii. 3.–Irish *uisge beatha*, usquebaugh, whiskey, lit. 'water of life;' cf. L. *aqua uītæ*, F. *eau-de-vie*.–Irish *uisge*, water, whiskey (see **Whiskey**); and *beatha*, life, OIrish *bethu*, allied to Gk. *βίος*, L. *uīta*, life, and E. *quick* (see **Quick**). Brugmann, i. §§ 85, 368.

USURP, to seize to one's own use, take possession of forcibly. (F. – L.) Spelt *usurpe* in Palsgrave; ME. *usurpen*, Chaucer, Astrolabe, prol. 42.–F. *usurper*, 'to usurpe,' Cot.–L. *ūsurpāre*, to employ, acquire; and, in a bad sense, to assume, usurp. β. Bréal suggests a formation from a sb. *ūsu-rapus* (*ūsu-ripus?*), one who seizes for his own use. Cf. L. *surpere* for *surripere*. **Der.** *usurp-er*; *usurp-at-ion*, from F. *usurpation*, 'a usurpation,' Cot., from L. acc. *ūsurpātiōnem*.

USURY, large interest for the use of money. (F. – L.) 'Userer, usurier; Usery, usure;' Palsgrave. ME. *vsure*, of which *vsury* was another form. 'Ocur, or *vsure* of gowle, Usura;' Prompt. Parv. p. 362; *vsurye*, id. p. 513. Spelt *vsurie*, P. Plowman, B. v. 240; *v.erie*, id. C. vii. 239. Here *vsurie* seems to be a by-form of *vsure*. –F. *usure*, 'the occupation of a thing, usury;' Cot.–L. *ūsūra*, use, enjoyment; also, interest, usury.–L. *ūs-um*, supine of *ūtī*, to use; see **Use.** **Der.** *usur-er*, ME. *vsurere*, Prompt. Parv., F. *usurier*, from L. *ūsūrārius*.

UT, the first note of the musical scale. (L.) In Shak. L. L. L. iv. 2. 102. Cf. F. and L. *ut*, the same. See **Solfa.**

UTAS, the octave of a feast. (F. – L.) Also *utis*, 2 Hen. IV, ii. 4. 22; where it means 'the time between a festival and the eighth day after it, merriment;' Schmidt. 'Utas of a feest, octaues;' Palsgrave. ME. *utas*, Trevisa, vii. 259. *Utas* is shortened from AF. *utaves*, *utavs*, Yearbooks of Edw. I., 1302-3, p. 407; 1292-3, p. 75; corresponding to OF. *oitauves* (Burguy), *oitieves* (Roquefort), the pl. of *oitauve*, octave, or eighth (day). *Utas* occurs in the statute concerning General Days in the Bench, 51 Hen. III, i.e. A.D. 1266-7 (Minsheu). 'El dyemanche des *oitieves* de la Resurrection' = on the Sunday of the octaves of the resurrection; Miracles de S. Louis, c. 39 (Roquefort). The OF. *oitauve* is from the L. *octāva* (*diēs*), eighth day; cf. OF. *oit*, *oyt*, *uit* (mod. F. *huit*), from L. *octo*, eight. Thus *utas* is, as it were, a pl. of *octave*; see **Octave.**

UTENSIL, an instrument or vessel in common use. (F. – L.) 'All myn hostilmentis, *vtensiles*,' &c.; Bury Wills, ed. Tymms, p. 94; in a will dated 1504. 'Alle the *vtensyl* of myn hows;' Early E. Wills, ed. Furnivall, p. 18 (1411).–MF. *utensile*, 'an utensile;' Cot.–L. *ūtensilis*, adj., fit for use; whence *ūtensilia*, neut. pl., utensils. β. L. *ūtensilis* is for *ūtent-tilis*, formed with suffix -*tilis* (as in *fer-tilis*, *fic-tilis*) from *ūtent-*, stem of pres. part. of *ūtī*, to use; see **Use.** The mod. F. is *ustensile* (corruptly).

UTERINE, born of the same mother by a different father. (F. – L.) In Blount's Gloss., ed. 1674. ME. *uterynes*, pl. Trevisa, v. 29. –MF. *uterin*, 'of the womb, born of one mother or damme;' Cot. –L. *uterinus*, born of the same mother.–L. *uterus*, the womb. Cf. Gk. *ὑστέρα*, the womb; Skt. *udara-*, belly. Brugmann, i. § 706.

UTILISE, to put to good use. (F. – L.) Not in Todd's Johnson; quite modern.–F. *utiliser*, to utilise; a modern word (Littré). Coined, with suffix -*iser* (< L. -*izāre* = Gk. -*ιζειν*), from L. *util-is*, useful; see **Utility.**

UTILITY, usefulness. (F. – L.) ME. *vtilitē*, Chaucer, On the Astrolabe, pt. ii. § 26. l. 16.–F. *utilité*, 'utility;' Cot.–L. *ūtilitātem*, acc. of *ūtilitās*, usefulness.–L. *ūtili-*, decl. stem of *ūtilis*, useful; with suffix -*tās*.–L. *ūtī*, to use; see **Use.** **Der.** *utilit-ar-i-an*, a modern coined word.

UTMOST, outmost, most distant, extreme. (E.) ME. *utemest*, orig. trisyllabic; spelt *utemæste* in Layamon, 11023; *outemeste* in Rich. Coer de Lion, 2931; *utmeste*, Trevisa, vi. 359. From AS. *ūte-m-est*, double superl. from *ūt*, out, also found as *ūte*, adv. out.

[We also find the mutated forms *ȳtemest*, *ȳtmest*, Grein, fi. 777.] This word is therefore a doublet of *outmost*; see **Out.** On the double suffix, see **Aftermost;** *utmest* became *utmost* by confusion with *most*. We also find *utt-er-most*; see **Utter** (1).

UTOPIAN, imaginary, chimerical. (Gk.) An adj. due to Sir T. More's description of *Utopia*, an imaginary island situate *nowhere*, as the name implies. Coined (by Sir T. More, A.D. 1516) from Gk. *oὐ*, not; and *τόπ-os*, a place; see **Topic.**

UTTER (1), outer, further out. (E.) ME. *vtter*, *utter*; whence was formed a superlative *vtter-est*, used in the def. form *vttereste* by Chaucer, C. T. 8663 (E 787). AS. *uttera* (which occurs as well as *ūtera*), compar. adj. formed from *ūt*, adv., out; see **Out.** Thus *utter* is a doublet of *outer*. **Der.** *utter-ly*; *utter-most* (see **Utmost**). And see *utter* (2).

UTTER (2), to put forth, send out, circulate. (E.; *perhaps confused with* F. – L.) ME. *uttren*, attributed to Chaucer, C. T. 16302, in Thynne's edition (1532), but every one of the MSS. in the Six-text edition has *outen*, Group G, l. 834; so also the Harl. MS. Hence there is really no authority for supposing that Chaucer used the word. The verb *outen*, which he really uses, is to put out, to 'out with,' as we say; answering to AS. *ūtian*, vb., to put out, expel; from *ūt*, out; see **Out.** β. The verb *outre*, to utter, speak, occurs frequently in the Romance of Partenay, ll. 1024, 1437, 1563, 2816, 3156, &c. It is possible that the *r* was suggested by OF. *outrer*, to go beyond, surpass, finish (Godefroy); cf. F. *outre*, beyond; see **Utterance** (2). And this last partly owed its form to **Utter** (1). Cf. AS. *ūtian*, to put out, eject; Laws of the Northumb. Priests, § 22, in Thorpe's Ancient Laws, ii. 294. **Der.** *utter-able*; *utter-ance*, Hamlet, iii. 2. 378.

UTTERANCE (1), an uttering; see **Utter** (2); as above.

UTTERANCE (2), extremity. (F. – L.) Only in the phrases *to the utterance*, Macb. iii. 1. 72; *at utterance*, Cymb. iii. 1. 73. ME. *oultrance*; in Lydgate, Siege of Troy, bk. i. ch. 2; fol. b 4, back, col. 1: 'Unto *oultrance* with these bulles to fyght.'–F. *outrance*, MF. *oultrance*, 'extremity;' Cot. 'Combatre à *oultrance*, to fight it out, or to the uttermost;' id.–F. *outre* (*oultre* in Cotgrave), beyond; with suffix -*ance*.–L. *ultrā*, beyond; see **Outrage.**

UVULA, the fleshy conical body suspended from the soft palate. (L.) In Cotgrave, to translate F. *uvule*.–Late L. *ūvula*, dimin. of *ūua*, a cluster, grape, also the uvula.+Lith. *ûga*, a berry. Brugmann, i. § 223(2).

UXORIOUS, excessively fond of a wife. (L.) In Ben Jonson, Silent Woman, iv. 1 (Otter).–L. *uxōrius*, belonging to a wife; also, fond of a wife.–L. *uxōri-*, decl. stem of *uxor*, a wife. **Der.** *uxorious-ly*, -*ness*.

V

V. In Middle-English, *v* is commonly written *u* in the MSS., though many editors needlessly falsify the spellings of the originals to suit a supposed popular taste. Conversely, *u* sometimes appears as *v*, most often at the beginnings of words, especially in the words *vs*, *vse*, *vp*, *vn-to*, *vnder*, and *vn-* used as a prefix. The use of *v* for *u*, and conversely, is also found in early printed books, and occurs occasionally down to rather a late date. Cotgrave ranges all F. words beginning with *v* and *u* under the common symbol *V*. We may also note that a very large proportion of the words which begin with *V* are of French or Latin origin; only *vane*, *vat*, *vinewed*, *vixen*, are English.

VACATION, leisure, cessation from labour. (F. – L.) In Palsgrave, spelt *vacacion*. ME. *vacacioun*, Chaucer, C. T., D 683.–F. *vacation*, 'a vacation, vacancy, leisure;' Cot.–L. *uacātionem*, acc. of *uacātio*, leisure; cf. *uacātus*, pp. of *uacāre*, to be empty, to be free from; to be unoccupied. See **Vacuum.** **Der.** *vacant*, in early use, in Rob. of Brunne, tr. of Langtoft, p. 110, l. 15, from F. *vacant*, 'vacant,' Cot., from the stem of the pres. part. of L. *uacāre*; hence *vacanc-y*, Hamlet, iii. 4. 117; *vacate*, vb., a late word, from *uacātus*, pp. of *uacāre*. And see *vac-uum*.

VACCINATE, to inoculate with the cow-pox. (L.) 'Of modern formation, from the inoculation of human beings with the *variolæ vaccinæ*, or cow-pox. . . . Dr. Jenner's *Inquiry* was first published in 1798;' Richardson. Coined, as if from the pp. of *uaccināre*, to inoculate, from L. *uaccinus*, belonging to cows.–L. *uacca*, a cow. Cf. Skt. *vaçā*, a cow. It prob. means 'the lowing animal;' cf. Skt. *vāç*, to cry, to howl, to low. **Der.** *vaccinat-ion*; also *vaccine*, from L. *uaccinus*.

VACILLATION, wavering, unsteadfastness. (F. – L.) 'No remainders of doubt, no *vacilation*;' Bp. Hall, The Peace-maker, § 15 (R.). And in Blount.–F. *vacillation*, 'a reeling, staggering, wagging;' Cot.—**L.** *uacillātiōnem*, acc. of *uacillātio*, a reeling, wavering; cf. *uacillātus*, pp. of *uacillāre*, to sway to and fro, waver, vacillate. Formed as if from an adj. *nacillus, from a base *uac*-. — √WAQ, to bend, sway to one side; cf. Skt. *vaṅk*, to go tortuously, to be crooked, *vakra*-, bent; AS. *wōh*, crooked. **Der.** vacillate, from **L.** pp. *uacillātus*; a late word. Cf. *woo.*

VACUUM, an empty space. (L.) It was supposed that nature abhorred a *vacuum*; see Cranmer's Works, i. 250, 330 (Parker Society).—**L.** *uacuum*, an empty space; neut. of *uacuus*, empty. Allied to **L.** *uacāre*, to be empty; see **Vacation.**+W. *gwag*, empty. **Der.** *vacu-i-ty*, in Cotgrave, from F. *vacuité*, 'vacuity,' Cot., from **L.** acc. *uacuitātem.*

VADE, to wither. (Du.—F.—L.) In Shak. Pass. Pilgrim, 131, 170, 174, 176; Spenser, F. Q. v. 2. 40.—MDu. *vadden*, 'to fade;' Hexham.—OF. *fader*, to fade; see **Fade.**

VAGABOND, adj., wandering; as sb., a wandering, idle fellow. (F.—L.) Spelt *vacabonde* in Palsgrave; he gives the MF. form as *uacabond*; so also 'Vacabonds, vagabonds,' Cot. Rich. cites *vaga-bunde* from the Bible (1534), Gen. iv. 12; spelt *vacabund* in the edit. of 1551. Also *vacabonde*, Caxton, Siege of Troy, fol. 334, back.—F. *vagabond*, 'a vagabond,' Cot. We also find OF. *vacabond* (Gode-froy).—**L.** *uagābundus*, adj., strolling about. Formed, with suffix *-b-undus* (a gerundive form), from *uagā-ri*, to wander.—**L.** *uagus*, wandering; see **Vague.**

VAGARY, a wild freak, a whim. (L.) In The Two Noble Kinsmen, iv. 3. 54 (82); *figaries*, pl., Ford, Fancies Chaste and Noble, iii. 3. Also *vagare*, sing., a trisyllabic word, in Stanyhurst, tr. of Virgil, Æn. b. ii, ed. Arber, p. 44, l. 10. Perhaps orig. a *verb*; see below. Apparently borrowed directly from L. *uagāri*, to wander; and, in any case, due to this verb. Cf. F. *vaguer*, 'to wander, *vagary*, gad, range, roam,' Cot.; also Ital. *vagare*, 'to wander, to *vagarie*, or range,' Florio. We have instances of F. in-finitives used as sbs. in *attainder, remainder, leisure, pleasure.* See above.

VAGRANT, wandering, unsettled. (F.—OHG.) 'A *vagarant* and wilde kinde of life;' Hakluyt's Voyages, i. 490; quoted by Richard-son, who alters *vagarant* to *vagrant*; but *vagarant* is, I think, quite right. Cf. *vagarantes*, vagrants, Harman's Caveat, p. 19. It corre-sponds to Anglo-F. *wakerant*, a vagrant, vagabond; see Liber Albus, p. 275. Also found an AF. and OF. *waucrant*, pres. pt. of OF. *walcrer*, to wander about. Spelt *wacrant*, Tristan, ii. 75, 80; Bozon, p. 72; *walcrant*, Horn, fol. 8, back, col. 2. See *walcrer, wacrer, vacrer*, in Godefroy. Of Germanic origin; cf. MLow G. *welkern*, MHG. *walgern*, to walk about; allied to OHG. *walkan, walchan*, to move oneself about, to full cloth; cognate with E. *walk*, AS. *wealcian*. See **Walk. Der.** *vagrant*, sb., *vagranc-y.* ¶ Doubtless confused with L. *uagāri*, to wander; but not derived from it. Roque-fort notes the use of OF. *wakerant* to translate L. *uaga* in Prov. vii. 10. See Notes on E. Etym., p. 311.

VAGUE, unsettled, uncertain. (F.—L.) It seems to have been first in use as a verb, parallel in use to *vagary*, q. v. 'Doth *vague* and wander;' Holland, tr. of Plutarch, p. 231 (R.); 'To *vague* and range abroad;' id. p. 630 (R.). As an adj. it is later. '*Vague* and insignificant forms of speech;' Locke, Human Understanding, To the Reader (R.).—F. *vaguer*, 'to wander; *vague*, wandering;' Cot.—**L.** *uagāri*, to wander; from *uagus*, adj., wandering. β. Con-nected by Fick, iii. 761, with AS. *wancol*, unsteady; from √WAG, a by-form of √WAQ, to swerve, for which see **Vacillate. Der.** *vague-ly, -ness*; and see *vag-abond, vag-ar-y.* From the same L. *uagāri* we have *extra-vagant.*

VAIL (1), the same as **Veil,** q. v.

VAIL (2), to lower. (F.—L.) In Merch. Ven. i. 1. 28, &c.; and not uncommon. A headless form of *avail* or *avale*, in the same sense. 'I *avale*, as the water dothe whan it goeth downewardes or ebbeth, *Jauale*;' Palsgrave.—F. *avaler* (in Cot. *avaller*), 'to let, put, lay, cast, fell down,' Cot. See further under **Avalanche. Der.** *vail*, sb., Troil. v. 8. 7.

VAIL (3), a gift to a servant. (F.—L.) Dryden has the pl. *vails*; tr. of Juvenal, Sat. iii. l. 311. '*Vails*, profits that arise to servants, besides their salary or wages;' Phillips, ed. 1706. A headless form of *avail*, sb., in the sense of profit, help. '*Avayle*, sb., prouffit;' Palsgrave. '*Vaile* my preȝeres' = let my prayers avail, Wyclif, Jer. xxxvii. 19, earlier version. See **Avail.**

VAIN, empty, fruitless, unreal, worthless; also, conceited. (F.—L.) ME. *vain, vein, veyn*, Chaucer, C. T. 15965 (G 497).—F. *vain*, 'vain;' Cot.—**L.** *uānum*, acc. of *uānus*, empty, vain. Brugmann, i. § 414 (3). **Der.** *vain-ly, -ness*; also the phr. *in vain*, a translation of F. *en vain* (Cot.). Also *vain-g'ory*, ME. *veingloire*, Gower, C. A. i. 132, b. i. 2677; *vain-glori-ous, -ly, -ness*. Also *van-i-ty*, q. v., *vaunt*, q. v., *van-ish*, q. v.

VAIR, a kind of fur. (F.—L.) A common term in heraldry; whence the adj. *vairy* or *verry*, given in Phillips, ed. 1706, and spelt *varry* in Blount. ME. *veir*, Reliquiæ Antiquæ, i. 121; Rob. Man-ning, ed. Furnivall, l. 615.—F. *vair*, 'a rich fur of ermines,' &c.; Cot.—**L.** *varius*, variegated. See **Minever** and **Various.** Cf. Late **L.** *varium*, vair; Gloss. to Liber Custumarum. **Der.** *vair-y*, adj., from F. *vairé*, 'verry, diversified with argent and azure;' Cot. Also *mine-ver.*

VALANCE, a fringe of drapery, now applied to a part of the bed-hangings. (F.—L.) In Shak. Tam. Shrew, ii. 356; he also has *valanced* = fringed, Haml. ii. 2. 442. 'Rich cloth of tissue, and *vallance* of black silk;' Strype, Eccles. Mem., Funeral Solemnities of Henry VIII. Cf. 'A subtil kerchef of *Valence*;' Chaucer, Assembly of Foules, 272. Florio (1598) has Ital. '*Valenzana*, a kind of saye, serge, or stuffe to make curteins for beds with; *Valenzana del letto*, the valances of a bed.' Torriano (1688) has *Valenza* as well as *Valenzana* in the former sense, and *Valenzane* for *Valenzana* in the latter one. Prob. named from *Valence* in France, not far to the S. of Lyons, where silk is made even to this day; Lyons silks are well-known. Sir Aymer de *Valence*, whose widow founded Pembroke College, Cambridge, may have taken his name from the same place. *Valence* = L. *Valentia*, a name given to more towns than one, and clearly a derivative of *ualēre* (pres. part. *ualent*-), to be strong; whence also the names *Valens* and *Valentinian*; see **Valiant.** ¶ See Todd; Johnson derives *Valence* from *Valencia* in Spain, which was also famous for silk. Mahn (in Webster) derives *valance* (without evi-dence) from a supposed Norm. F. *valaunt*, answering to F. *avalant*, pres. part. of *avaler*, to let fall; for which see **Avalanche.**

VALE, a valley. (F.—L.) ME. *val*, as a various reading for *ualeie* (valley), in Legends of the Holy Rood, p. 22, l. 47.—F. *val*, 'a vale;' Cot.—**L.** *uallem*, acc. of *uallis*, a vale. **Der.** *vall-ey*, q. v.; also *a-val-anche, vail* (2).

VALEDICTION, a farewell. (L.) 'He alwayes took this solemn *valediction* of the fellowes;' Fuller, Worthies; Shropshire (R.). Englished from a supposed L. *ualēdictio, coined like *ualē-dictus*, pp. of *ualēdicere*, to say farewell.—**L.** *ualē*, farewell; and *dicere*, to say. β. L. *ualē*, lit. 'be strong, be of good health,' is the 2 pers. sing. imp. of *ualēre*, to be strong. See **Valiant** and **Diction. Der.** *valedict-or-y.*

VALENTINE, a sweetheart; also a love-letter sent on Feb. 14. (F.—L.) In Nares and Brand. See Hamlet, iv. 5. 48, 51. Named from *St. Valentine's* day, when birds were supposed to pair; see Chaucer, Assembly of Foules, 309, 322, 683; Spenser, F. Q. vi. 7. 32.—F. *Valentin*.—**L.** *Valentīnus*.—**L.** *ualent*-, stem of pres. part. of *ualēre*, to be strong; see **Valiant.**

VALERIAN, the name of a flower. (F.—L.) '*Valeryan*, an herbe;' Palsgrave. And in Chaucer, C. T., G 800.—F. *valeriane*, 'garden valerian;' Cot.—Late L. *ualeriāna*, valerian. β. Orig. unknown; *ualeriāna* is the fem. of *Valeriānus*, which must mean either 'belonging to *Valerius*' or 'belonging to *Valeria*,' a province of Pannonia. Both names are doubtless due to L. *ualēre*, to be strong, whence many names were derived; see **Valance, Valentine,** and **Valiant.**

VALET, a man-servant. (F.—C.) In Blount. 'The king made him his *valett*;' Fuller, Worthies, Yorkshire. *Valet-de-chambre* occurs in Vanbrugh, The Provoked Wife, Act v. 3.—F. *valet*, 'a groom, yeoman, &c.,' Cot.; *valet de chambre*, 'a chamberlain,' id. The same word as **Varlet,** q. v.

VALETUDINARY, sickly, in weak health. (F.—L.) In Sir T. Brown, Vulg. Errors, b. iv. c. 13, § 26.—F. *valétudinaire*, 'sickly;' Cot.—**L.** *ualētūdinārius*, sickly.—L. *ualētūdin*-, stem of *ualētūdo*, health, whether good or bad, but esp. bad health, feebleness; with suffix *-ārius*.—L. *ualē-re*, to be in good health; with suffix *-tūdo*. See **Valiant. Der.** *valetudinari-an*, adj. and sb.; as sb. in Spec-tator, no. 25; *valetudinari-an-ism.*

VALHALLA, the hall of the slain. (Scand.) In Scand. mytho-logy, the place of immortality for the souls of heroes slain in battle. The spelling *Valhalla* is hardly correct; it is probably due to Bp. Percy, who translated M. Mallet's work on Northern Antiquities; see chap. v of the translation.—Icel. *valhöll* (gen. *valhallar*), lit. the hall of the slain.—Icel. *valr*, the slain, slaughter; and *höll* or *hall*, a hall, cognate with E. **Hall.** β. The Icel. *valr* is cognate with AS. *wæl*, slaughter, the slain, also a single corpse; prob. allied to OHG. *wuol*, slaughter, AS. *wōl*, disease. It was thought that the dead were selected from the field of battle by the deities called in Icelandic *Valkyrjur* and in AS. *Wælcyrigan*, lit. 'choosers of the slain.' See **Valkyria.**

VALIANT, brave. (F.—L.) ME. *valiant*, Rob. of Brunne, tr. of Langtoft, p. 9, l. 4; p. 177, l. 3.—F. *vaillant*, 'valiant;' Cot. Also spelt *valant* in OF., and the pres. part. of the verb *valoir*, 'to profit, serve, be good for;' id.—**L.** *ualēre*, to be strong, to be worth. Allied to E. **Wield,** q. v. **Der.** *valiant-ly, -ness*; and see *vale-*

diction, *Val-ent-ine*, *vale-tu-di-nar-y*, *val-id*, *val-our*, *val-ue*; also *a-vail*, *counter-vail*, *pre-vail*, *con-val-esce*; *equi-val-ent*, *pre-val-ent*, *in-val-id*.

VALID, having force, well-founded, conclusive. (F.—L.) In Cotgrave.—F. *valide*, 'valid, strong, weighty;' Cot.—L. *ualidus*, strong.—L. *ualēre*, to be strong; see **Valiant**. **Der.** *valid-ly*; *valid-i-ty*, Hamlet, iii. 2. 199, from F. *validité*, 'validity,' Cot., from L. acc. *ualiditātem*.

VALISE, a travelling-bag, small portmanteau. (F.—Late L.) 'Seal'd up In the *vallies* of my trust, lock'd close for ever;' Ben Jonson, Tale of a Tub, A. ii. sc. 1 (Metaphor).—F. *valise*, 'a male, cloak-bag, budget, wallet;' Cot. The same word as Span. *balija*, Ital. *valigia* (Florio), with the same sense. Corrupted in G. into *felleisen* (Diez).—Late L. *valisia* (1401), Ducange; also spelt *valixia* (id.). β. Etym. unknown. Diez imagines a Late L. form **uidul-itia*, made from L. *uidulus*, a leathern travelling-trunk; which at any rate gives the right sense. Devic (Supp. to Littré) suggests Pers. *walīchah*, 'a large sack;' or Arab. *waliha(t)*, 'a corn-sack;' Rich. Dict. p. 1657.

VALKYRIA, one of the handmaidens of Odin. (Scand.) Icel. *ualkyrja*, a goddess; lit. 'chooser of the slain;' pl. *valkyrjur*.—Icel. *val*, acc. of *valr*, the slain (AS. *wæl*); and *-kyrja*, f., a chooser, from *kur-* (<**kuz-*), weak grade of *kjōsa*, to choose, cognate with E. *choose*. Cf. AS. *walcyrge*, Corpus gloss., 2017.

VALLEY, a vale, dale. (F.—L.) ME. *valē*, Assumption of St. Mary, ed. Lumby, l. 590; *ualeie*, Legends of the Holy Rood, p. 22, l. 47.—OF. *valee* (F. *vallée*), a valley; Burguy. This is parallel to Ital. *vallata*, a valley, and appears to mean, literally, 'formed like a vale,' or 'vale-like.' Formed, with suffix *-ee* (<L. *-āta*), from F. *val*, a vale; see **Vale**.

VALOUR, courage, bravery. (F.—L.) Spelt *valoure*, King Alisaunder, 2530.—OF. *valor*, *valur*, F. *valeur*, 'value, worth, worthinesse;' Cot.—L. *ualōrem*, acc. of *ualor*, worth; hence, worthiness, courage.—L. *ualēre*, to be strong, to be worth; see **Valiant**. **Der.** *valor-ous*, 2 Hen. IV, ii. 4. 236, from F. *valeureux*, 'valorous, valiant,' Cot.; *valor-ous-ly*.

VALUE, worth. (F.—L.) 'All is to him of o [one] *value*,' Gower, C. A. iii. 346 (bk. viii. 2121).—F. *valuë*, fem., 'value;' Cot. Fem. of *valu*, pp. of *valoir*, to be worth.—L. *ualēre*, to be worth. **Der.** *value*, verb, in Palsgrave; *valu-able*; *value-less*, K. John, iii. 1. 101; *valu-at-ion*, a coined word.

VALVE, one of the leaves of a folding-door, a lid which opens only one way, one of the pieces of a (bivalve) shell. (F.—L.) '*Valves*, folding-doors or windows;' Blount's Gloss., ed. 1674. *Valves*, pl., doors, Trevisa, iv. 499.—F. *valve*, 'a foulding, or two-leaved door, or window;' Cot.—L. *ualua*, sing. of *ualuæ*, the leaves of a folding-door. Allied to L. *uoluere*, to roll, turn round about; from the revolving of the leaves on their hinges. See **Voluble**. **Der.** *valv-ed*, *valv-ul-ar*; *bi-valve*, *uni-valve*.

VAMBRACE, **VANTBRACE**, armour for the fore-arm. (F.—L.) 'Plate, cum *vambrace* et *rerebrace*;' York Wills, i. 171 (1392). The word properly signifies 'fore-arm.' It is short for *avant-brace*.—MF. *avant-bras*, 'a vambrace, armour for an arm;' also, the part of the arm which extends from the elbow to the wrist;' Cot.—F. *avant*, before; *bras*, the arm.—L. *ab ante*, from before, in front; *brachium*, arm (of which the pl. *brachia* gave OF. *brace*, arm; see Scheler. See **Van** (1), **Vamp**, **Vamplate**. ¶ The armour for the upper arm was called a *rere-brace*, i.e. rear-brace.

VAMP, the fore-part or upper leather of a boot or shoe. (F.—L.) ME. *uaumpé* (dissyllabic). 'Hosen wiðuten *uampez*' = hose without vamps; Ancren Riwle, p. 420, l. 3. [Another copy has *uampeð*; Reliq. Antiquæ, ii. 3.] '*Vampe*, or *naumpe* of an hoose, Pedana;' Prompt. Parv. 'Hoc antepedale, Anglice *wampe*' [for *vampé*]; Wright's Voc. i. 197, col. 1. 'Hec pedana, Anglice *wampay*,' id. 201, col. 2.—MF. *avant-pied*, 'the part of the foot that's next to the toes, and consisteth of five bones;' Cot. (Hence E. *vampé*, *vamp*; by loss of initial *a*, change of *ntp* to *mp*, and suppression of the un-stressed termination.—F. *avant*, before; and *pied*, the foot. For F. *avant*, see **Advance** or **Van** (1). The F. *pied* is from L. *pedem*, acc. of *pēs*, a foot; see **Foot**. ☞ This etymology is verified by the fact that the word also appears as *vauntpe*. '*Vauntpe* of a hose, *uantpie*;' Palsgrave (where the final *d* is dropped, as well as the initial *a*, in the F. form). So also ME. *vampay*, above, and later *vampay* (Phillips). Godefroy has OF. *avantpied*, a kind of sandal. **Der.** *vamp*, verb, to mend with a new vamp, Beaum. and Fletcher, Bonduca, Act i. sc. 2' (Petillius); hence *vamp up* = to patch up, *vamp*, to improvise a musical accompaniment.

VAMPIRE, a ghost which sucks the blood of men, a blood-sucker. (F.—G.—Servian.) In Todd's Johnson. 'Of these beings many imaginary stories are told in Hungary; Ricaut, in his State of the Greek and Armenian Churches (1679), gives a curious account of this superstitious persuasion, p. 278;' Todd. Todd also cites:

'These are the *vampires* of the publick, and riflers of the kingdom;' Forman, Obs. on the Revolution in 1688 (1741), p. 11.—F. *vampire*. —G. *vampyr* (Flügel).—Servian *vampir*, a werwolf, blood-sucker, Popović, Servian Dict.; cf. Polish *upior*, *upir*, a vampire. Prob. of Turkish origin; from N. Turk. *uber*, a witch (Miklosich). **Der.** *vampire-bat*; so named by Linnæus.

VAMPLATE, an iron plate protecting a lance. (F.—L.) 'Pro uno pare de schynbaldes, aliter *vamplattes*;' York Wills, iii. 73 (1423). From F. *avant*, in front, fore; and *plate*. See **Vam-brace**.

VAN (1), the front of an army. (F.—L.) In Shak. Antony, iv. 6. 9. An abbreviated form of *van-guard*, *vant-guard*, or *avant-garde*, also spelt *van-ward*, *vaunt-warde*. 'And when our *vauntgard* was passed the toune;' Holinshed, Chron. Edw. III, an. 1346. 'And her *vantwarde* was to-broke;' Rob. of Glouc. p. 362, l. 7478; the pl. *vantwardes* occurs, id. p. 437, l. 9006. Spelt *vaunt-warde*, *vaun-warde*, *auaunt-warde*, P. Plowman, C. xxiii. 94.—OF. *avant-warde*, later *avant-garde*, 'the vanguard of an army;' Cot. Here *avant* is from L. *ab ante*, 'from front;' see **Advance**. And see **Guard**, **Ward**.

VAN (2), a fan for winnowing, &c. (F.—L.) 'His sail-broad *vans*,' i.e. wings; Milton, P. L. ii. 927.—F. *van*, 'a vanne, or winnowing sieve;' Cot.—L. *uannum*, acc. of *uannus*, a fan; see **Fan**. L. *uannus* is for **cuannus*; cf. OHG. *hwennen* (for **hwanjan*), to swing, vibrate. Brugmann, i. § 357. (Doubtful; it may be allied to L. *uentus*, wind.) **Der.** *van*, v., to winnow, spelt *vanne* in Levins, from F. *vanner*, 'to vanne;' Cot. **Doublet**, *fan*.

VAN (3), a caravan or large covered wagon for goods. (F.—Pers.) A modern abbreviation for *caravan*, just as we now use *bus* for *omnibus*, and *wig* for *periwig*. See **Caravan**. 'The little man will now walk three times round the *cairawan*;' Dickens, Going into Society. 'Carry me into the *wan*;' ibid.

VANDAL, a barbarian. (L.—Teut.) See *Vandalick* and *Vandal-ism* in Todd's Johnson.—L. *Vandalus*, a Vandal, one of the tribe of the *Vandali*, whose name means, literally, 'the wanderers;' see Pliny. *Vandali* answers to AS. pl. *Wendlas* (sing. *Wendil*-). Cf. Icel. *Vendill* (also *Vandill*), a proper name. Cf. G. *wandeln*, to wander; a frequentative verb cognate with E. **Wander**, q. v. **Der.** *Vandal*, adj.; *Vandal-ic*, *Vandal-ism*.

VANE, a weather-cock. (E.) Also spelt *fane* (cf. *vat*, *vetch*); it formerly meant a small flag, pennon, or streamer; hence applied to the weather-cock, from its likeness to a small pennon. '*Fane* of a stepylle;' Prompt. Parv. p. 148; and see Way's note. 'Chaungynge as a *vane*' (other MSS. *fane*); Chaucer, C. T., Group E, 996; in the Ellesmere and Hengwrt MSS. AS. *fana*, a small flag; Grein, i. 263.+Du. *vaan*; Icel. *fāni*; Dan. *fane*; Swed. and Goth. *fana*; G. *fahne*; MHG. *fano*. β. Teut. type **fanon-*, m. Orig. 'a bit of cloth;' cognate with L. *pannus*, a cloth, piece of cloth; see **Pane**. **Der.** *gon-fan-on* or *gon-fal-on*, q. v. **Doublet**, *pane*.

VANGUARD; see under **Van** (1).

VANILLA, the name of a plant. (Span.—L.) In Todd's Johnson; Johnson says: 'the fruit of those plants is used to scent chocolate.' Misspelt for *vainilla*, by confusion with F. *vanille*, which is merely borrowed from Spanish, like the E. word.—Span. *vainilla*, a small pod, husk, or capsule; which is the true sense of the word. Dimin. of *vaina*, a scabbard, case, pod, sheath.—L. *uagina*, a scabbard, sheath, husk, pod.

VANISH, to disappear. (F.—L.) ME. *vanissen*, Chaucer, tr. of Boethius, b. iii. pr. 4, l. 53. The pt. t. appears as *vanisshide*, *vanysched*, *vansched*, *vanshede*, in P. Plowman, C. xv. 217. Certainly derived from OFrench, but the F. word is not recorded as commencing with *v*. Prob. shortened from the pres. pt. stem (*evaniss-*) of AF. *evanir*, OF. *esvanir*, to vanish away; cf. Ital. *svanire*, to vanish (where *s* is from L. *ex*).—Late L. type **exvānīre*, for L. *ēuānescere*, to vanish away.—L. *ē*, *ex*, away; and *nānescere*, to vanish; lit. to become empty, from *uānus*, empty; see **Vain**. **Der.** *e-van-esc-ent*.

VANITY, empty pride, conceit, worthlessness. (F.—L.) ME. *uanité* (= *uanitee*), Hali Meidenhad, p. 27, l. 25.—F. *vanité*, 'vanity;' Cot.—L. *uānitātem*, acc. of *uānitās*, emptiness, worthlessness.—L. *uānus*, empty, vain; see **Vain**.

VANQUISH, to conquer, defeat. (F.—L.) ME. *venkisen*, P. Plowman, C. xxi. 106; *venkusen*, Wyclif, 1 Kings, xiv. 47, earlier version; *venquishen*, Chaucer, C. T. 4711 (B 291).—AF. *venquiss-*, OF. *veinquiss-*, stem of pres. pt. of AF. *venquir*, OF. *veinquir*, occurring in the 14th century as a collateral form of OF. *veincre* (mod. F. *vaincre*); cf. F. *vainquis*, still used as the pt. t. of *vaincre*, and the form *que je vainquisse*.—L. *uincere*, to conquer; pt. t. *uici*, pp. *uictus* (stem *uic-*).—√WEIQ, to fight, strive; whence also Goth. *weihan*, *weigan* (pp. *wig-ans*), OHG. and AS. *wīgan*, to strive, fight, contend. Brugmann, i. §§ 85, 367. **Der.** *vanquish-er*; and see *victor*.

VANTAGE, advantage. (F.—L.) Common in Shak.; in K.

John, ii. 550, &c.; spelt *vauntage* in Palsgrave; who also gives: 'I *vauntage* one, I profyte him, *je vantaige*; What dothe it *vauntage* you, *quest ce quil vous vantage*, or *aduantage.*'—AF. *vantage*, advantage; Year-books of Edw. I., 1302–3, p. 209; F. *avantage*, 'an advantage'; *avantager*, to advantage;' Cot. See **Advantage**. Thus *vantage* is a headless form of F. *avantage*; and it is clear from Palsgrave (as above) that the loss of initial *a* occurred in F. as well as in E.

VANWARD; see **Vaward** and **Van** (1).

VAPID, spiritless, flat, insipid. (L.) In Blount's Gloss., ed. 1674. Prob. directly from L. *uapidus*, vapid, spoiled, flat, rather than from F. *vapide*, 'that sends up an ill fume,' marked by Cotgrave as a scarce or old word. Allied to L. *uappa*, wine that has emitted its vapour, vapid or palled wine; closely allied to L. *uapor*, vapour. β. The L. *uap-or* is allied to Gk. καπνός, smoke, καπνειν, to breathe forth; Lithuan. *kwápas*, breath, fragrance, evaporation, *kwépti*, to breathe, smell, *kwépalas*, perfume. Brugmann, i. § 193.—√QwEP, to reek, breathe out; cf. Fick, i. 542. Der. *vapid-ly*, *-ness*. And see *vapour*.

VAPOUR, water in the atmosphere, steam, fume, fine mist, gas. (F.—L.) ME. *vapour*, Chaucer, C. T. 10707 (F 393).—F. *vapeur*, 'a vapor, fume;' Cot.—L. *uaporem*, acc. of *uapor*, vapour; see **Vapid**. Der. *vapour*, verb; *vapor-ous*, Macb. iii. 5. 24; *vapour-y*; *vapor-ise*, a coined word; *vapor-is-at-ion*, *e-vapor-ate*.

VARICOSE, permanently dilated, as a vein. (L.) A late word. [Phillips, ed. 1706, has: '*Varix*, a crooked vein.']—L. *uaricōsus*, varicose.—L. *uaric-*, stem of *uarix*, a dilated vein. Perhaps allied to L. *uarus*, a blotch, a pimple.

VARIEGATE, to diversify. (L.) '*Variegated* tulips;' Pope, Moral Essays, ii. 41.—L. *uariegātus*, pp. of *uariegāre*, to make of various colours.—L. *uari(o)-*, for *uarius*, of divers colours; and *-igāre*, due to *agere*, to drive, cause, make; *agere* being used to form verbs expressive of an object (see **Agent**). See **Various**. Der. *variegat-ion*, in Blount's Gloss., ed. 1674.

VARIETY, difference, diversification, change, diversity. (F.—L.) In Shak., Antony, ii. 2. 241.—F. *varieté*, 'variety;' Cot.—L. *uarietātem*, acc. of *uarietās*, variety.—L. *uarius*, various; see **Various**.

VARIOUS, different, several. (L.) 'A man so *various*;' Dryden, Absalom and Achitophel, 545. Englished from L. *uarius*, variegated, diverse, manifold; with suffix *-ous*. Der. *various-ly*; *varie-gate*, *varie-ty*; also, *vary*, q. v.; *vair*, q. v.

VARLET, a groom, footman, low fellow, scoundrel. (F.—C.) In Spenser, F. Q. ii. 4. 40. 'Not sparyng maisters nor *varlettis*;' Berners, tr. of Froissart, vol. i. c. 16 (R.).—OF. *varlet*, 'a groom;' also, a yonker, stripling, youth;' Cot. He notes that 'in old time it was a more honourable title; for all young gentlemen, untill they come to be 18 years of age, were tearmed so.' β. An older spelling was *vaslet* (Godefroy), which became *varlet*, *vallet*, *valet*. We also find the AF. spelling *vadlet* in the Liber Albus, ed. Riley, p. 46, where *d* stands for an older *sd*, as in *medlar. medley*; which again proves that *vaslet* was the orig. form. γ. *Vaslet* is for **vasalet*, the regular diminutive of OF. *vasal*, *vassal*, a vassal; so that a *varlet* was orig. a young vassal, a youth, stripling; hence, a servant, &c.; and finally a *valet*, and a *varlet* as a term of reproach. OF. *vaslet* became **vasdlet*, *vadlet* in AF.; also *varlet*, *vallet*, *valet*. See **Vassal**. Doublet, *valet*.

VARNISH, a kind of size or glaze, a liquid employed to give a glossy surface. (F.) ME. *vernisch*. 'Vernysche, Vernicium;' Prompt. Parv. In P. Plowman, A. v. 70, the Vernon MS. wrongly reads *vernisch* for *vergeous* (verjuice); still, this shows that the word was already known before A. D. 1400.—F. *vernis*, 'varnish, made of linseed oyle and the gumme of the juniper-tree;' Cot. Hence the verb *vernisser*, 'to sleeke or glaze over with varnish;' Cot. Cf. Span. *berniz*, *barniz*, varnish, lacquer; *barnizar*, to varnish, lacquer; Ital. *vernice*, varnish; *vernicare*, *verniciare*, to varnish. β. Of doubtful origin; but compare the MGk. βερνίκη; see Schade, O. H. G. Dict., p. 1439. Wedgwood says: 'It seems to me probable that it is from Gk. βερονίκη, βερνίκη, amber, applied by Agapias to *sandarach*, a gum rosin similar in appearance to amber, of which varnish was made; Gk. βερνικιάζειν, to varnish;' Ducange, Greek Glossary. Cf. mod. Gk. βερνίκι, varnish.' But the MGk. βερνίκη seems to be merely a Gk. form of Ital. *vernice*. Ducange gives a Late L. form *vernicium* (A. D. 1243). Der. *varnish*, verb; Palsgrave has: 'I *vernysshe* a spurre, or any yron with vernysshe, *je vernis*;' which exemplifies the MF. verb *vernir*, late by-form of *vernisser*.

VARSOVIENNE, a dance in imitation of a Polish dance. (F.—Polish.) F. *Varsovienne*, a dance (about 1853); lit. 'belonging to Warsaw.'—F. *Varsovie*, Warsaw.—Pol. *Warszawa*, Warsaw.

VARY, to alter, change. (F.—L.) ME. *varien*, Prompt. Parv.; pres. part. *variande*, Pricke of Conscience, 1447.—F. *varier*, 'to vary;' Cot.—L. *uariāre*, to diversify, vary.—L. *uarius*, various; see

Various. Der. *vari-able*, spelt *varyable* in Palsgrave, from F. *variable*, 'variable,' Cot., from L. *uariābilis*; *variable-ness*, *vari-abil-i-ty*; *vari-at-ion*, ME. *variacioun*, Chaucer, C. T. 2590 (A 2588), from F. *variation*, 'a variation,' from L. acc. *uariātiōnem*; *vari-ance*, Chaucer, C. T. 8586 (E 710), as if from L. **uariantia*. And see *vair*, *mine-ver*.

VASCULAR, consisting of vessels, as arteries, veins, &c. (L.) In Todd's Johnson. Formed, with suffix *-ar* (from L. *-āris*) from L. *uascul-um*, a small vessel; formed with the double dimin. suffix *-cu-lu-*, from *uās*, a vessel; see **Vase**. Der. *vascular-i-ty*.

VASE, a vessel, particularly an ornamented one. (F.—L.) In Pope, Rape of the Lock, i. 122.—F. *vase*, 'a vessel;' Cot.—L. *uāsum*, a vase, vessel; a collateral form of *uās* (gen. *uās-is*), a vessel; the pl. *uāsa* is common, though the sing. *uāsum* is hardly used. β. L. *uāsum* resembles Skt. *vāsana-*, a receptacle, box, basket, water-jar; also, an envelope, cover, cloth; the orig. sense being perhaps 'case' or protecting cover. Perhaps allied to **Vest**. Der. *vas-cu-lar*; *vessel*.

VASELINE, a semi-fluid greasy substance, used in ointments, &c. A fanciful name; given by the maker. Said to have been suggested by G. *wass(er)*, water, and Gk. ἔλ(αιον), oil; with F. suffix *-ine*. (Cent. Dict.)

VASSAL, a dependent. (F.—C.) In Spenser, Daphnaida, 181. Certainly in early use; the ME. *vassal*, however, is rare, though the derivative *vasselage* (*vassalage*) is in Chaucer, C. T. 3056 (A 3054), where it means 'good service' or prowess in arms; it has the same sense in Rob. of Brunne, tr. of Langtoft, p. 86, l. 21, and in Gower (as cited in Richardson). [The word *vassayl*, cited by Richardson from Rob. of Glouc., means *wassail*.]—AF. *vassal*, Philip de Thaun, Livre des Creatures, l. 698; F. *vassal*, 'a vassall, subject, tenant;' Cot. (Cotgrave well explains the word.) The orig. sense is 'servant;' and the word is of Celtic origin, Latinised (in Low Latin) as *vassallus*, in which form it is extremely common. We also find the shorter form *uassus* or *uasus*, a servant; which occurs in the Lex Salica, ed. Hessels and Kern, coll. 55, 56.—OBret. *uuas*=*was*, Bret. *gwaz*, a servant, vassal; W. and Corn. *gwas*, a youth, servant. Cf. OIrish *foss*, a servant. All from Celtic type **wassos*, a servant; Stokes-Fick, p. 278. Cf. L. *verna*, a home-born slave. See **Vernacular**. Der. *vassal-age*; also *varlet*, *valet*.

VAST, great, of great extent. (F.—L.) We possess this word in two forms, viz. *vast* and *waste*, both being from French; the latter being much the older. They are generally used with different senses, but in the Owl and Nightingale, l. 17, we have: 'in ore *waste* þikke hegge'=in a vast thick hedge, in a great thick hedge. We may, however, consider *vast* as belonging to the 16th century; it does not seem to be much older than the latter part of that century. 'That mightie and *vaste* sea;' Hakluyt's Voyages, vol. iii. p. 822.—F. *vaste*, 'vast;' Cot.—L. *uastum*, acc. of *uastus*, vast, of large extent. See further under **Waste**. Der. *vast*, sb., Temp. i. 2. 327, Wint. Tale, i. 1. 33; *vast-ly*, *vast-ness*; also *vast-y*, adj., Merch. Ven. ii. 7. 41. Also *de-vast-ate*.

VAT, a large vessel for liquors. (E.) ME. *fat*. 'Fate, vesselle;' Prompt. Parv. Palsgrave has *fatte*; and the A. V. of the Bible has *fats* (Joel, ii. 24) and *wine-fat* (Mark, xii. 1). The difference between the words *fat* and *vat* is one of dialect; *vat* is Southern English, prob. Kentish. The use of *v* for *f* is common in Devonshire, Somersetshire, and in Old Kentish; the connexion of the word with Kent may have been due to the brewing trade; cf. *vane*, *vetch*. AS. *fæt* (pl. *fatu*), a vessel, cask; Mark, iii. 27.+Du. *vat*; Icel. *fat*; Dan. *fad*; Swed. *fat*; G. *fass*; MHG. *vaz*. β. All from the Teut. type **fatom*, n., a vat, a barrel. From the Teut. base **fat-*, to catch, take, seize, comprehend, contain; cf. OFries. *fatia*, EFries. *faten*, Du. *vatten*, to catch, take, contain, G. *fassen*, to seize, also to contain; so that the sense is 'that which contains.' Der. *wine-fat* or *wine-vat*.

VATICAN, the palace of the pope. (F.—L.) F. *Vatican*.—L. *Vāticānus* (*mons*), the Vatican hill in Rome.

VATICINATION, a prediction, prophecy. (F.—L.) 'This so clear *vaticination*;' Jeremy Taylor, Works (1835); ii. 333.—MF. *vaticination*, 'a prophecying;' Cot.—L. acc. *uāticinātiōnem*.—L. *uāticinārī*, to prophesy; *uāticinium*, a prophecy.—L. *uāti-*, decl. stem of *uātes*, a prophet; and *-cin-*, weak grade of *can-ere*, to sing. Cf. **Wood** (2).

VAUDEVILLE, VAUDEVIL, a lively satirical song; a kind of drama. (F.) Spelt *vaudevil* in Blount's Gloss., ed. 1674.—F. *vaudeville*, 'a country ballade, or song; so tearmed of *Vaudevire*, a Norman town, wherein Olivier Bassel [or Basselin], the first inventor of them, lived;' Cot. Olivier de Basselin was a Norman poet of the 15th century, and his songs were called after his native valley, the *Vau* (or *Val*, i. e. valley) *de Vire*; see **Vale**. *Vire* is a town in Normandy, to the S. of Bayeux.

VAULT (1), an arched roof, a chamber with an arched roof, esp.

one underground, a cellar. (F.—L.) The spelling with *l* is comparatively modern; it has been inserted, precisely as in *fault*, from pedantic and ignorant notions concerning 'etymological' spelling. The ME. form is *voute*, also *vowte*; in King Alisaunder, 7210, it is spelt *vawte*. 'Vout under the ground, *uoute*;' Palsgrave. 'Vowte, lacunar; *Vowtyd*, arculatus; *Vowtyn*, or make a *vowte*, arcuo;' Prompt. Parv.—MF. *voute* (also *voulte*, with inserted *l* as in English), 'a vault, or arch, also, a vaulted or enbowed roof;' Cot. OF. *volte*, *voute*, *vaute*, a vault, cavern; Burguy (mod. F. *voûte*); where *volte* is a fem. form, from OF. *volt*, vaulted, lit. bent or bowed. *Volte* is the same word as Ital. *volta*, 'a time, a turn or course; a circuit, or a compasse; also, a vault, cellar, an arche, bow;' Florio. β. The OF. *volt* answers to L. *uol'tus*, and the OF. *volte*, Ital. *volta*, to L. *uol'ta*; these are abbreviated forms of *uolūtus* (fem. *uolūta*), pp. of *uoluere*, to roll, turn round; whence the later sense of bend round, bow, or arch. Similarly we have *volute*, in the sense of a spiral scroll. γ. Thus a *vault* means an arch, an arched roof; hence, a chamber with an arched roof, and finally a cellar, because it often has an arched roof, for the sake of strength. See **Voluble.** Der. *vault*, verb, to overarch, ME. *vouten*, as above; *vault-ed*, Cymb. i. 6. 33; *vault-y*, concave, Romeo, iii. 5. 22; *vault-age*, a vaulted room, Hen. V. ii. 4. 124.

VAULT (2), to bound, leap. (F.—Ital.—L.) 'Vaulting ambition;' Macb. i. 7. 27.—MF. *volter*, 'to vault;' Cot.—MF. *volte*, 'a round or turn; and thence, the bounding turn which cunning riders teach their horses; also a tumbler's gamboll;' id.—Ital. *volta*, 'the turn that cunning riders teach their horses;' Florio. The same word as Ital. *volta*, a vault; both from the orig. sense of 'turn;' see further under **Vault** (1). Der. *vault*, sb.; *vault-er*, *vault-ing-horse*.

VAUNT, to boast. (F.—L.) 'I *vaunte*, I boste, or crake, *Ie me vante*;' Palsgrave. [It is remarkable that the ME. form was *avaunten* or *auaunten*, from OF. *avanter*, to boast (Godefroy), in which the *a-* (from L. *ad*) was intensive, or may have been due to confusion with F. *avant*, before, and *avancer*, to advance. This ME. *auaunten* occurs in Chaucer, C. T. 5985 (D 403), and at least twice in Chaucer, tr. of Boethius, b. i. met. 1, l. 21, b. 1, pr. 4, l. 158; and hence the sb. *auaunt*, *avaunt*, *auant*, in Chaucer, C. T. 227. However, the prefix is to be neglected. Cf. *avauntour*, a vaunter, Chaucer, Troilus ii. 724.]—F. *vanter*; 'se *vanter*, to vaunt, brag, boast, glory, crack;' Cot.—Late L. *vānitāre*, to speak vanity, flatter (Ducange); so that *se vanter* = to speak vainly of oneself. (Diez remarks that *vānitāre*, to boast, occurs in S. Augustine, Opp. i. 437, 761.) This verb is a frequentative formed from L. *uānus*, vain. See **Vain;** and cf. L. *uānitās*, vanity. Der. *vaunt*, sb., ME. *auaunte*; *vaunt-er*, formerly *avauntour* (as above), or *avaunter*, Court of Love, 1219.

VAVASSOR, a vassal not holding immediately from the sovereign, but from a great lord, having inferior vassals under him. (F.—Late L.—C.) 'A worthy *vavasour*;' Chaucer, C. T., prol. 360.—OF. *vavassour*.—Late L. *vassus vassōrum*, lit. 'vassal of vassals.' The Late L. *vassus* is of Celtic origin; see **Vassal.**

VAWARD, another spelling of *vanward* or *vanguard*. (F.—L. and G.) In Berners, tr. of Froissart, vol. i. c. 209; and *vanward*, in Drayton, Battle of Agincourt, st. 218. Spelt *vaward*, in Lydgate, Assembly of Gods, l. 602. See **Van** (1).

VEAL, the flesh of a calf. (F.—L.) ME. *veel*, Chaucer, C. T. 9294 (E 1420).—OF. *veël*, later *veau*, 'a calfe, or veale;' Cot.—L. *uitellum*, acc. of *uitellus*, a little calf, allied to *uitulus*, a calf.＋Gk. ἶταλός, the same (little used). Allied to Skt. *vatsa-*, a calf, *vatsatara-*, a steer, *vatsalā*, a cow anxious for her calf. β. All from Idg. **wetos*, a year, as in Gk. ἔτος, a year. See **Wether.** Hence the sense of Skt. *vatsa-* was really 'a yearling calf;' and the same sense of 'yearling' was the orig. one of L. *uitulus*. γ. From the same sense of 'year,' differently applied, we have L. *uetus*, old in years, aged, *uetulus*, a little old man. See **Veteran.** Der. *vell-um*, q. v.

VEDA, knowledge; one of the ancient sacred books written in Skt. (Skt.) Skt. *vēda-*, 'knowledge;' the generic name for the sacred writings of the Hindus, esp. the 4 collections called *rig-vēda*, *yajur-vēda*, *sāma-vēda*, and *atharva-vēda*;' Benfey, p. 900. Formed by gradation (Skt. *ē* = Gk. *οι* = AS. *ā*) from *vid*, to know, cognate with E. **Wit,** q. v. The Skt. nom. case is *vēdas*.

VEDETTE, VIDETTE, a cavalry sentinel. (F.—Ital.—L.) Modern; not in Todd's Johnson.—MF. *vedette*, 'a sentry; any high place from which one may see afar off;' Cot.—Ital. *vedetta*, a horse-sentry; also a sentry-box; formerly a watch-tower, a beacon, a peeping-hole (Florio). An altered or dimin. form of Ital. *veduta*, 'a high prospect' (Florio); orig. fem. pp. of *vedere*, to see.—L. *uidēre*, to see; see **Vision.** See Körting, § 10156. ¶ Diez takes it to be an Ital. corruption of *veletta*, a sentry-box; due to confusion with *vedere*, to see (pp. *veduto*), from which *vedetta* cannot (he thinks) be derived. *Veletta* is a dimin. of *veglia*, a watch, watching, vigil; just as Span. *veleta*, a weather-cock (lit. a watcher),

is a dimin. of Span. *vela*, a watching, vigil (Diez).—L. *uigilia*; see **Vigil.** But, as Körting notes, the dimin. of *veglia* would have been *veglietta*, not *veletta*.

VEER, to turn round, change direction, swerve. (F.—L.) 'Vere the main shete;' Spenser, F. Q. i. 12. 1; 'and *vereth* his main sheat,' id. v. 12. 18. 'Vere the shete;' Reliquiæ Antiquæ, i. 2 (15th cent.). [The spelling with *e* or *ee* is hard to explain; but it may have been due to the confusion between the sound of *ee* in late ME. and that of F. *i*. Sir P. Sidney writes *vire*; see Nares.]—F. *virer*, 'to veer, turne round, wheele or whirle about;' Cot. β. The F. *virer* is the same word as Span. *virar*, *birar*, to wind, twist, tack, or veer, Port. *virar*, to turn, change, Prov. *virar*, to turn, to change (Bartsch). Allied words are Port. *viravolta*, a circular motion, Ital. *virolare*, 'to scrue,' i. e. twist round (Florio); &c. The orig. sense is to turn round, and it appears as Late L. *virāre*, which is rather an old word (Diez); it appears also in F. *en-vir-on*, round about, in a circle (whence E. *environs*), in F. *vir-ole* (whence E. *ferrule*), and in MF. *vir-ol-et*, 'a boy's windmill,' Cot. γ. The key to this difficult word lies in the sense of 'ring' or 'circle' as appearing in *environ* and *ferrule*; the Late L. *virola*, a ring to bind anything, answers to L. *uiriola*, a bracelet, dimin. of *uiria*, an armlet, large ring, gen. used in the pl. form *uiriæ*.—√WEI, to twist, wind round; see **Ferrule, Withy.** ¶ The Du. *vieren*, to veer, is merely borrowed (like our own word) from F. *virer*. The old derivation of *virer* from L. *gyrāre* cannot possibly be sustained; even the above solution is doubtful. See Diez; and Körting, § 10135. The latter refers (but obscurely) Late L. *virāre* to √WEI. Der. (from L. *uir-ia*), *en-vir-on*, *ferr-ule*.

VEGETABLE, a plant for the table. (F.—L.) Properly an adj., as used by Milton, P. L. iv. 220. The pl. *vegetables* is given (both as E. and F.) in Supp. to Palsgrave, p. 1053. [Instead of *vegetables*, Shak. has *vegetives*, Pericles, iii. 2. 36; and Ben Jonson has *vegetals*, Alchemist, i. 1. 40.]—MF. *vegetable*, 'vegetable, fit or able to live;' Cot.—L. *uegetābilis*, animating; hence, full of life. Formed, with suffix *-bilis*, from L. *uegetā-re*, to enliven, quicken.—L. *uegetus*, lively.—L. *uegēre*, to excite, quicken, arouse; allied to *uig-il*, wakeful, and *uig-ēre*, to flourish. See **Vigil, Vigorous.** Der. (from *uegetāre*) *veget-ate*; *veget-at-ion*, from F. *vegetation*, 'a giving of life,' Cot.; *veget-at-ive* (Palsgrave), from F. *vegetatif*, 'vegetative, lively,' Cot.; *veget-al* (as above), from MF. *vegetal*, 'vegetall,' Cot.; *veget-ar-i-an*, a modern coined word, to denote a *vegetable-arian*, or one who lives on vegetables (though it should rather mean 'vigorous'); *veget-ar-i-an-ism*.

VEHEMENT, passionate, very eager. (F.—L.) In Palsgrave. —MF. *vehement*, 'vehement;' Cot.—L. *uehementem*, acc. of *uehemens*, passionate, eager, vehement. *Vehe-* has been explained as equivalent to *uē-*, 'apart from,' as in *uē-cors*, senseless; cf. Skt. *vahis*, apart; cf. E. *de-ment-ed.* For *mens*, the mind, see **Mental.** Der. *vehement-ly*; *vehemence* (Levins), from MF. *vehemence*, 'vehemence,' from L. *uehementia.*

VEHICLE, a carriage, conveyance. (L.) 'Alms are but the *vehicles* of prayer;' Dryden, Hind and Panther, l. 1400. Englished from L. *uehiculum*, a carriage.—L. *ueh-ere*, to carry; with double dimin. suffix *-cu-lum.*—√WEGH, to carry; whence also Skt. *vah*, to carry, Gk. ὄχ-ος, a chariot. Brugmann, i. § 128. Der. *vehicul-ar*, from L. *uehiculāris*, adj. And see *veil*, *con-vex*, *in-veigh*, *vex*, *vein*, *via-duct*, *voy-age.*

VEIL, a curtain, covering, cover for the face, disguise. (F.—L.) ME. *veile*, Ancren Riwle, p. 420.—OF. *veile* (Burguy), later *voile*, 'a vayle;' Cot.—L. *uēlum*, a sail; also, a cloth, covering. The orig. sense was sail or 'propeller' of a ship; Curtius, i. 237.—*Vēlum* is for **uexlum* = **uec-slum*; cf. *uexillum*, a standard. Brugmann, i. § 883.—L. *ueh-ere* (pt. t. *uex-ī*), to carry, bear along; see **Vehicle.** But Walde derives it from √WEG, to weave; as seen in OIrish *fig-im*, I weave; cf. W. *gwe*, a web of cloth. Der. *veil*, verb.

VEIN, a tube conveying blood to the heart, a small rib on a leaf. (F.—L.) ME. *veine*, Gower, C. A. iii. 92 (bk. vii. 245); Chaucer has *veine-blood*, C. T. 2749 (A 2747).—F. *veine*, 'a vein;' Cot.—L. *uēna*, a vein. For **uecsna*; perhaps (like *uē-lum*, see **Veil**) from L. *ueh-ere*, to carry; a vein being the 'conveyer' of blood.—√WEGH, to carry; see **Vehicle.** Der. *vein-ed.*

VELDT, an open grassy tract of country. (Du.) A term used in S. Africa.—MDu. *veldt*, 'a field, or a campaine,' Hexham; Du. *veld*. The same word as AS. *feld*, a field; see **Field.**

VELLUM, prepared skin of calves, &c., for writing on. (F.—L.) ME. *velim*, Lydgate, Minor Poems, p. 204; spelt *velyme* in Prompt. Parv., and *velym* in Palsgrave.—F. *velin*, 'vellam;' Cot. Mod. F. *vélin*. (For the change of final *n* to *m*, compare *venom*.)—L. *uitulīnus*, adj., belonging to a calf.—L. *uitulus*, a calf; see **Veal.** Cf. Late L. *uitulīnium*, or *pellis uitulīna*, vellum.

VELOCIPEDE, a light carriage for one person, propelled by the feet. (L.) Modern; coined from L. *uēlōci-*, from *uēlox*, swift; and *ped-*, stem of *pēs*, the foot, cognate with E. **Foot**. Thus the sense is 'swift-foot,' or 'swift-footed.' See **Velocity**.

VELOCITY, great speed. (F.–L.) In Cotgrave. – MF. *velocité*, 'velocity;' Cot. – L. acc. *uēlōcitātem*, acc. of *uēlōcitās*, swiftness, speed. – L. *uēlōci-*, decl. stem of *uēlox*, swift; with suffix *-tās*. The lit. sense of *uēlox* is 'flying;' if it be allied to *uol-āre*, to fly; see **Volatile**.

VELVET, a cloth made from silk, with a close, shaggy pile; also made from cotton. (F.–L.) 'Velvet, or *velwet*, Velvetus;' Prompt. Parv. Chaucer has the pl. *veluëttes* (four syllables), C. T. 10958, F 644; whilst Spenser has *vellet*, Shep. Kal., May, 185. [Again, the form *vellure* occurs in Holinshed, Descr. of England, b. iii. c. 1 (R.); which is borrowed from F. *velours*, 'velvet,' Cot.] But *velvet, velwet, velouet, vellet* are from AF. *velwet, veluet*, Late L. *velluētum*; from a Romanic type **villutettum.* β. The Ital. *velluto* answers to a Late L. type *villūtus, shaggy, allied to L. *uillōsus*, shaggy; whilst F. *velours* (OF. *velous*, the *r* being unoriginal) answers to L. *uillōsus* directly. – L. *uillus*, shaggy hair, a tuft of hair; so that *velvet* means 'woolly' or shaggy stuff, from its nap. Allied to *uellus*, a fleece; see **Wool**. Der. *velvet-y, velvet-ing.*

VENAL, that can be bought, mercenary. (F.–L.) In Pope, Epistle to Jervas, l. 2. – MF. *venal*, 'vendible, saleable;' Cot. – L. *uēnālis*, saleable, for sale. – L. *uēn-us*, or *uēn-um*, sale. Allied to Gk. ὧνος, price, ὠνή, a buying; Brugmann, i. § 329. Der. *venal-i-ty*, from MF. *venalité*, 'venality,' Cot.; from L. acc. *uēnālitātem.*

VEND, to sell. (F.–L.) 'Twenty thousand pounds worth of this coarse commodity is yearly . . *vended* in the vicinage;' Fuller, Worthies, Yorkshire. – F. *vendre*, 'to sell;' Cot. – L. *uendere*, to sell; contracted from *uēnundare*, to sell, which again stands for *uēnum dare*, to offer for sale, a phrase which occurs in Claudian, &c. – L. *uēnum*, sale; and *dare*, to give, offer; see **Venal** and **Date** (1). Der. *vend-er* or *vend-or*; *vend-ible*, Merch. Ven. i. 1. 112, from F. *vendible*, 'vendible,' Cot., from L. *uendibilis*, saleable; we also find *vend-able*, a spelling due to MF. *vendable* (Cot.), formed from the F. verb *vendre*; *vend-ibl-y, vend-ible-ness.*

VENDETTA, a blood-feud; esp. in Corsica. (Ital.–L.) Ital. *vendetta*, lit. 'vengeance, revenge.' – L. *vindicta*, revenge; see **Vindictive**.

VENEER, to overlay or face with a thin slice of wood. (G.–F. –OHG.) This curious word, after being borrowed by French from Old German, was again borrowed back from French, as if it had been foreign to the G. language. It is not old in E., and the sense has changed. It was orig. used with reference to marquetry-work. '*Veneering*, a kind of inlaid work;' Phillips, ed. 1706. Johnson (quoting from Bailey) describes *to veneer* as signifying 'to make a kind of marquetry or inlaid work, whereby several thin slices of fine wood of different sorts are fastened or glued on a ground of some common wood.' Also formerly spelt *fanneer*, as in Old Farming Words (E. D. S.), Part I; and *fineer*, Smollett, France and Italy, let. 28 (Davies). The E. verb (older than the sb.) is borrowed from G. *furniren*, to inlay, to veneer, lit. 'to furnish' or provide small pieces of wood; from the careful arrangement of the pieces. – F. *fournir*, 'to furnish, supply, minister, find, provide of [i. e. with], accommodate with;' Cot. A word of OHG. origin; see **Furnish**. Der. *veneer*, sb., *veneer-ing*. Doublet, *furnish*.

VENERABLE, worthy of reverence. (F.–L.) In Shak. As You Like It, ii. 7. 167. – MF. *venerable*, 'venerable;' Cot. – L. *uenerābilis*, to be reverenced. – L. *uenerāri*, to reverence, worship, adore. – L. *uener-*, for **uenes-*, stem of *uenus*, love; allied to Skt. *van*, to serve, to honour. – √WEN, to love, to win; Fick, i. 768; Benfey, p. 812. See **Venereal**, and **Win**. Der. *venerabl-y, venerable-ness*; also (from pp. *uenerātus*) venerate, Geo. Herbert, The Church Porch, st. 45; *veneration*, from MF. *veneration*, 'veneration,' Cot., from L. acc. *uenerātiōnem.*

VENEREAL, pertaining to sexual intercourse. (L.) Spelt *veneriall* in Levins. Coined, with suffix *-al*, from L. *Venereus* (also *Venerius*), belonging to Venus. [The MF. word is *venerien* (Cotgrave), whence *venerean* in Chaucer, C. T. 6191 (D 609).] – L. *Vener-*, for **uenes-*, stem of *Venus*, Venus, love. Allied to Skt. *van*, to love. See **Venerable** and **Win**. Der. *venery*, sb., spelt *venerie* in Levins, from L. *Venerius.*

VENERY, hunting, the sport of the chase. (F.–L.) ME. *venerie*, Chaucer, C. T. 166. – MF. *venerie*, 'a hunt, or hunting;' Cot. – MF. *vener*, 'to hunt;' id. – L. *uēnāri*, to hunt; see **Venison**.

VENESECTION, blood-letting. (L.; *and* F.–L.) According to Richardson, it is spelt *venæsection* in Wiseman's Surgery, b. i. c. 3. – L. *uēnæ, uēnae*, gen. case of *uēna*, a vein; and F. *section*. See **Vein** and **Section**.

VENEW, VENUE, VENEY, a thrust received at playing with weapons; a turn or bout at fencing. (F.–L.) In Merry Wives, i. 1. 296; L. L. L. v. 1. 62. – MF. *venuë*, 'a coming, arrivall, also a *venny* in fencing, a turn, trick;' Cot. The sense is 'an arrival;' hence a thrust that attains the person aimed at, one that reaches home. *Venue* is the fem. of *venu*, pp. of *venir*, to come. – L. *uenīre*, to come, cognate with E. **Come**, q.v. Doublet, *venue*, q.v.

VENGEANCE, retribution, vindictive punishment. (F.–L.) ME. *vengeance, vengeaunce*; but spelt *vengaunce*, King Alisaunder, 4194. – F. *vengeance*, 'vengeance;' Cot. – F. *venger*, 'to avenge,' id.; with suffix *-ance* (<L. *-antia*). Cf. Span. *vengar*, Ital. *vengiare*. – L. *uindicāre*, to lay claim to, also to avenge; cf. F. *manger* <L. *mandūcāre*. See **Vindicate**. Der. *a-venge, re-venge* (from F. *venger*); also *venge-ful*, i. e. *avenge-ful*, Tit. Andron. v. 2. 51; *venge-ful-ly.*

VENIAL, excusable, that may be pardoned. (F.–L.) ME. *uenial* (= *venial*), Ayenbite of Inwyt, p. 16, l. 9; P. Plowman, B. xiv. 92. – OF. *venial* (Littré). – L. *ueniālis*, pardonable. – L. *uenia*, grace, favour, kindness; also, pardon. Allied to Skt. *van*, to love. – √WEN, to love, win; see **Venerable** and **Win**. Der. *venial-ly, venial-ness* or *venial-i-ty.*

VENISON, the flesh of animals taken in hunting, esp. flesh of deer. (F.–L.) ME. *veneison*; spelt *ueneysun*, Havelok, 1726, *veneson*, Rob. of Glouc. p. 243, l. 101. – OF. *veneisun* (Burguy), later *venaison*, 'venison, the flesh of (edible) beasts of chase, as the deer, wild boar,' &c., Cot. – L. *uēnātiōnem*, acc. of *uēnātio*, the chase; also, that which is hunted, game; cf. *uēnātus*, pp. of *uēnāri*, to hunt. See **Gain** (2). Der. (from L. *uēnāri*) *venery*, q.v.

VENOM, poison. (F.–L.) ME. *venim*; spelt *venyme*, King Alisaunder, 2860; *venym*, Rob. of Glouc. p. 43, l. 1010. – OF. *venim*, 'venome,' Cot. We also find OF. *velin*; mod. F. *venin.* – L. *uenēnum*, poison. (For change of *n* to *m*, cf. *vellum*.) Perhaps *uenēnum* is for *uenesmum, a love-potion; from **uenes-*, **uenos-*; cf. *uenus*, love. Der. *venom-ous*, ME. *venimous*, Ayenbite of Inwyt, p. 203, l. 17, from F. *venimeux*, 'venomous,' Cot., from L. *uenēnōsus*, poisonous: *venomous-ly, -ness.*

VENOUS, contained in a vein. (L.) Modern; not in Todd's Johnson. Englished from L. *uenōsus*, belonging to a vein. – L. *uēna*, a vein; see **Vein**.

VENT (1), an opening for air or smoke, an air-hole, flue. (F.–L.) 'A *vent*, meatus, porus; *To vent*, aperire, euacuare;' Levins. Halliwell gives Somerset *vent-hole*, a button-hole in a wristband. It is most likely that the word has been connected in popular etymology with F. *vent*, the wind, as if it were a hole to let wind or air in; but the senses of 'aperture' and 'wind' are widely different. The older spelling was *fent* or *fente*, used in the sense of slit in a garment, whence the notion of 'button-hole.' The Prompt. Parv. gives: '*Fente* of a clothe, fibulatorium,' on which Way notes that 'the *fent* or *vent*, in the 13th cent., appears at the collar of the robe, . . being a short *slit* closed by a brooch, which served for greater convenience in putting on a dress so fashioned as to fit closely round the throat;' see the whole note. 'The coller and the *vente*;' Assemblee of Ladies, 526. '*Fent* of a gowne, *fente*;' Palsgrave. The sense was easily extended to slits and apertures of all kinds, esp. as the F. original was unrestricted. – F. *fente*, 'a cleft, rift, chinke, slit, cranny;' Cot. A participial sb. from the verb *fendre*, to cleave. – L. *findere*, to cleave; see **Fissure**. Der. *vent*, verb, to emit from an orifice, as in 'can he *vent* [emit] Trinculos?' Temp. ii. 2. 111; but it is tolerably certain that the use of this verb was influenced by F. *vent*, wind; see **Vent** (3). And see **Vent** (2).

VENT (2), sale, utterance of commodities, and hence, generally, utterance, outlet, publication. (F.–L.) 'The merchant-adventurers likewise . . did hold out bravely; taking off the commodities . . though they lay dead upon their hands for want of *vent*;' Bacon, Life of Henry VII, ed. Lumby, p. 146, l. 6. '*Vent* of utterance of the same,' viz. of 'spices, drugges, and other commodities;' Hakluyt's Voyages, i. 347. 'Find the meanes to haue a *vent* to make sales;' id. i. 356. – F. *vente*, 'a sale, or selling, an alienation, or passing away for money,' &c.; Cot. *Vente* is a participial sb. from the F. *vendre*, 'to sell;' Cot. – L. *uendere*, to sell; see **Vend**. Der. *vent*, to utter, as in: 'when he found ill money had been put into his hands, he would never suffer it to be *vented* again,' Burnet, Life of Hale (R.); but it is tolerably certain that the use of *vent* as a verb has been largely influenced by confusion with **Vent** (1) and **Vent** (3), and it is extremely difficult to determine its complete history without very numerous examples of its use.

VENT (3), to snuff up air, breathe, or puff out, to expose to air. (F.–L.) 'See howe he [a bullock] *venteth* into the wynd;' Spenser, Sheph. Kal. Feb. 75. Explained by 'snuffeth in the wind' in the Glosse, but more likely it means to puff out or exhale. In Spenser,

F. Q. iii. 1. 42, we are told that Britomart 'vented up her umbriere, And so did let her goodly visage to appear.' Here the poet was probably thinking of F. *vent*, the wind, and of the part of the helmet called the *ventail* or *aventail*, which was the *lower* half of the movable front of a helmet as distinct from the upper half or *visor*, with which it is often confused; see my note on *auentaile* in Chaucer, C. T. Group E, 1204. If we had a large collection of quotations illustrative of the use of *vent* as a verb, I suspect it would appear that the connexion with the F. *vent*, wind, was due solely to a misunderstanding and misuse of the word, and that it is etymologically due to **Vent** (1) or **Vent** (2), or to confusion of both; and, in particular, to inability to account for **Vent** (1), shown above to be used in place of ME. *fente*. That writers used the word with reference to *air* is certain; we have: 'there's none [air] abroad so wholesome as that you *vent*;' Cymb. i. 2. 5; also: 'which have poisoned the very *air* of our church wherein they were *vented*;' Bp. Hall, Ser. Eccl. iii. 4 (R.); and hence the sbs. *ventage*, *venting-hole* (see below).—F. *venter*, '(the wind) to blow or puffe,' Cot.—F. *vent*, the wind.—L. *uentum*, acc. of *uentus*, wind, cognate with E. **Wind**, q.v. Der. *vent-age*, the air-hole of a flute (app. a coined word), Hamlet, iii. 2. 373; *vent-ing-hole*, an outlet for vapour, Holland, tr. of Pliny, b. xxxi. c. 3. § last. And see *vent-ail*, *vent-il-ate*.

VENTAIL, the lower half of the movable part of the front of a helmet. (F.—L.) In Spenser, F. Q. iii. 2. 24, iv. 6. 19. ME. *ventaile*, Early E. Wills, ed. Furnivall, p. 19, l. 4 (1411); also *auentaile*, Chaucer, C. T. 9080 (E 1204), which is the same word with the addition of F. prefix *a-* (< L. *ad-*).—AF. *ventaile*, Langtoft, ii. 428; MF. *ventaille*, 'the breathing-part of a helmet.'—F. *venter*, 'to blow or puffe,' Cot.; with suffix *-aile* < L. *-ā-cu-lum*.—F. *vent*, wind.—L. *uentum*, acc. of *uentus*, wind; see **Vent** (3), **Ventilate**, and **Wind**.

VENTILATE, to fan with wind, to open to air, expose to air or to the public view. (L.) Spelt *ventylate* in Palsgrave. *Ventilate* is used as a pp. by Sir T. Elyot, The Governour, b. i. c. 25, § 3; and in Trevisa, ii. 141, 299 (later text).—L. *uentilātus*, pp. of *uentilāre*, to blow, winnow, ventilate. From an adj. **uentilus* (not used), from *uentus*, wind, cognate with E. **Wind**. Der. *ventilat-or*, from L. *uentilātor*, a winnower; *ventilat-ion*, MF. *ventilation*, 'a ventilation, breathing,' Cot., from L. acc. *uentilātiōnem*.

VENTRAL, belonging to the belly. (L.) Added by Todd to Johnson.—L. *uentrālis*, belonging to the belly.—L. *uentr-*, for *uenter*, the belly. Der. *ventri-cle*, q. v.; *ventri-loquist*, q. v.

VENTRICLE, the stomach; a part of the heart. (F.—L.) In Cotgrave; and in Lanfrank, Cirurgie, p. 113.—F. *ventricule*, 'the ventricle, the place wherein the meat sent from the stomack is digested, some call so the stomack itselfe;' Cot.—L. *uentriculum*, acc. of *uentriculus*, the stomach, also a ventricle of the heart. A double dimin. (with suffix *-cu-lu-*) from *uentri-*, decl. stem of *uenter*, the belly; see **Ventral**. Der. *ventricul-ar*.

VENTRILOQUIST, one who speaks so that the voice seems to come from a distance or from some one else. (L.) 'Ventriloquium, a speaking in the belly;' Ady, Discovery of Witches (1661), p. 77. In Blount's Gloss., ed. 1674; but Phillips has *ventriloquus*, 'a person that speaks inwardly;' this is the true L. word, whence *ventriloqu-ist* has since been formed, by adding the suffix *-ist* (L. *-ista*, Gk. *-ιστης*). —L. *uentriloquus*, a ventriloquist, lit. one who speaks from (or in) the belly.—L. *uentri-*, decl. stem of *uenter*, the belly; and *loqu-ī*, to speak; see **Ventral** and **Loquacious**. Der. *ventriloqu-ism*.

VENTURE, chance, luck, hazard. (F.—L.) Common in Shak. both as sb. and vb.; as sb., Merch. Ven. i. 3. 92; as a verb, id. iii. 2. 10. It is a headless form of ME. *aventure* or *auenture*, which also took the form **Adventure**, q. v. Der. *venture*, Mids. Nt. Dr. iv. 1. 39, short for ME. *auenturous*, later *adventurous*; *ventur-ous-ly*, *-ness*. Also *venture-some*, in Strype, Eccles. Mem., Henry VIII, an. 1546 (R.), where the suffix *-some* is English.

VENUE, the same as **Venew**, q. v. (F.—L.) As a law-term, it is the place where the jury are summoned to come; from F. *venüe*, 'a coming, arrival, approach, a passage, accesse,' Cotgrave; which is merely another sense of *venew*, as above. β. Blackstone has: 'a change of the *venue*, or *visne* (that is, the *vicinia* or neighbourhood in which the injury is declared to be done);' Comment. b. iii. c. 20. His interpretation of *visne* as having the same sense as L. *uicīnia* is right; but that has nothing to do with the etymology of *venue*, which is, of course, a different word. Der. *a-venue*.

VENUS, the goddess of love. (L.) In Chaucer, C. T. 1538 (A 1536).—L. *Venus*; see **Venereal**.

VERACIOUS, truthful. (L.) A late word; Phillips, ed. 1706, has only the sb. *veracity*. Coined from L. *uērāci-*, decl. stem of *uērax*, truthful; with suffix *-ous*.—L. *uēr-us*, true. β. The orig. sense is 'credible;' see **Very**. Der. *verac-i-ty*, Englished from L. *uērācitās*, truthfulness.

VERANDA, VERANDAH, a kind of covered balcony. (Port.—L. ?) Modern; added by Todd to Johnson; it should be spelt *varanda*. 'The other gate leads to what in this country [India] is called a *veranda* or *feranda*, which is a kind of piazza or landing-place before you enter the hall or inner apartments;' Archæologia (1787), viii. 254.—Port. *varanda*, a balcony. Marsden, in his Malay Dict., 1812, p. 30, has: '*barandah* (Portuguese), a varánda, balcony, or open gallery to a house;' but the Malay word is, as Marsden says, adapted from the Portuguese. Cf. OSpan. *varanda*, in the sense of balustrade or stair-railing; as early as A.D. 1505; see the quotation from Port. and Span. *vara*, a rod; from L. *uāra*, a forked pole. Cf. Port. *varal*, the shaft of a post-chaise. Dryden has *vare*, a rod; Absalom, i. 595. ¶ Hence also mod. Skt. *varanda*, a portico; the Skt. (or Hind.) word being quite modern. Minsheu's Span. Dict. (1623) has '*Vara*, a rod;' and '*Varanda*, railes to leane the brest on.'

VERB, the word; in grammar, the chief word of a sentence. (F.—L.) ME. *verbe* (15th cent.), Reliq. Antiquæ, ii. 14. Palsgrave gives a 'Table of Verbes.'—F. *verbe*, 'a verbe;' Cot.—L. *uerbum*, a word, a verb. β. Here the L. *b* represents an Idg. *dh* (> Teut. *d*); and *uerbum* is cognate with E. **Word**, q.v.—√WER, to speak; cf. Gk. *εἴρ-ειν* (< *ϝέρ-γειν*), to speak; Fick, i. 772. Der. *verb-al* (Palsgrave), from F. *verbal*, 'verball,' Cot., from L. *uerbālis*, belonging to a word; *verbal-ly*; *verbal-ise*, to turn into a verb, a coined word; *verbal-ism*; *verb-i-age*, wordiness, not in Johnson's Dict., but used by him on April 9, 1778 (Boswell), from F. *verbiage*, a late F. word, coined (according to Littré) from OF. *verboier* (*verbier), to talk; *verb-ose*, wordy (Phillips), from L. *uerbōsus*; *verb-ose-ly*, *verbose-ness*, *verb-os-i-ty*. Also *verbatim*, 1 Hen. VI, iii. 1. 13, from L. *uerbātim*, adv. word by word.

VERBENA, vervain. (L.) See **Vervain**.

VERDANT, green, flourishing. (F.—L.) In Spenser, F. Q. i. 9. 13. Coined as if from a F. *verdant, substituted for F. *verdissant*, pres. part. of *verdir*, 'to flourish, to wax green;' Cot.—F. *verd*, green.—L. *uiridem*, acc. of *uiridis*, green. See **Vert**. Cf. also OF. *verdoyant*, becoming green (Supp. to Godefroy). Der. *verdant-ly*, *verdanc-y*; also *verd-ure*, Temp. i. 2. 87, from F. *verdure*, 'verdure,' Cot.; also *verdur-ous* (Nares). And see *farthingale*, *verdigris*, *verjuice*.

VERDERER, a wood-ward, forester. (F.—L.) 'Forresters, verderers;' Howell, Famil. Letters, vol. iv. let. 16. Formed by adding *-er* (needlessly) to AF. *verder*, which is glossed by 'wodeward' in W. de Bibbesworth; Wright's Voc. i. 164.—Late L. *viridārius*, a forester (Ducange).—L. *uirid-is*, green (above).

VERDICT, the decision of a jury, decision. (F.—L.) Lit. 'a true saying.' The true word is *verdit*, pedantically altered to the mongrel form *verdict*, to bring the latter half of it nearer to the L. spelling. ME. *verdit*, Chaucer, C. T. 789 (A 787).—OF. *verdit*, verdict; see *verdict* in Littré, the mod. F. form being borrowed again from English.—L. *uērē dictum*, truly said, which passed into Late L. *vērēdictum*, with the sense of true saying or verdict, occurring A.D. 1287 (Ducange). Formed similarly to *bene-diction*, *male-diction*. —L. *uērē*, truly, adv., from *uērus*, true; and *dictum*, a saying, orig. neut. of pp. of *dīcere*, to say; see **Very** and **Diction**.

VERDIGRIS, the rust of bronze, copper, or brass. (F.—L.) Spelt *verdgrese* in Arnold's Chronicle (1502), repr. 1811, p. 74; *verdegrees*, Chaucer, C. T. 16258 (G 790). Cf. MF. *verd de gris*, 'verdigrease, Spanish green,' Cot.; spelt *verte grez* in the 13th cent. (Littré). But the Prompt. Parv. has: '*Verte grece*, viride grecum, flos eris.' So also: '*Viride grecum*, *verdegrece*;' Wright's Voc. 619. 35. Hence the sense is 'Greek green,' or 'green of Greece'; and we may explain ME. *verte grece* as from AF. *vert de Grece*, for which see Vie de S. Gile, 853. See **Verdant**. See Academy, no. 1118, Oct. 1893.

VERDITER, a green pigment. (F.—L.) Adapted from MF. *verd de terre*, a green pigment; Cot.—L. acc. *uiridem*, green (see **Verdant**); *dē*, of; *terra*, earth.

VERGE (1), a wand of office, extent of jurisdiction, edge, brink. (F.—L.) In the sense of edge or brink it is quite a different word from *verge*, to incline (see below), though some late writers may have confused the words, as indeed is done in Johnson's Dict. The sense of 'edge' follows at once from the use of *verge* (as a lawterm) to mean a limit or circuit, hence a circle, Rich. II, ii. 1. 102; cf. i. 1. 93. In the sense of 'wand,' it is best known by the derivative *verger*, a wand-bearer. ME. *verge*. 'Verge, in a wrytys [wright's] werke, Virgata;' Prompt. Parv. Here it must mean a yard (in length); cf. *verge le roy*, a standard length; Liber Albus, p. 278.—F. *verge*, 'a rod, wand, sticke; also, a sergeant's *verge* or mace; also, a yard; . . a plaine hoope, or gimmal, ring; also, a rood of land;' Cot.—L. *uirga*, a twig, rod, wand. Der. *verg-er*, a wand-bearer, 'that bereth a rodde in the churche' (Palsgrave), from MF. *verger*, ' one that beares a verge before a magistrate, a verger,' Cot., from Late L. *uirgārius*, an apparitor, occurring A. D. 1370 (Ducange).

VERGE (2), to tend towards, tend, slope, border on. (L.) ' *Verging* more and more westward ;' Fuller, Worthies, Somersetshire (R.).—L. *uergere*, to bend, turn, incline, verge towards, incline. Allied to Skt. *vrjana-*, crooked, *vrj*, to exclude (of which the orig. sense seems to be to bend, Benfey).—√WERG, to bend, turn, force; Fick, i. 772. ¶ The phrase ' to be on the *verge* of ' is perhaps connected with this verb by many writers; but belongs to **Verge** (1). Der. *con-verge, di-verge*.

VERIFY, to show to be true, confirm by evidence. (F.—L.) ' *I verifye*, Je verifie;' Palsgrave.—MF. *verifier*, ' to verifie;' Cot.—L. *uērificāre*, to make true.—L. *uēri*, for *uērus*, true; and -*ficāre*, for *facere*, to make; see **Very** and **Fact**. Der. *verifi-er, verifi-able, verific-at-ion*, from MF. *verification*, ' a verification, verifying,' Cot.

VERILY, adv. ; see **Very**.

VERISIMILITUDE, likelihood. (F.—L.) In Holland, tr. of Plutarch, p. 845 (R.).—MF. *verisimilitude*, ' likelihood ;' Cot.— L. *uērisimilitūdo*, likelihood.—L. *uēri similis*, likely, like the truth. —L. *uēri*, gen. of *uērum*, the truth, orig. neut. of *uērus*, true; and *similis*, like; see **Very** and **Similar**.

VERITY, truth, a true assertion. (F.—L.) Spelt *verytie* in Levins.—MF. *verité*, ' verity ;' Cot.—L. *uēritātem*, acc. of *uēritās*, truth.—L. *uērus*, true; see **Very**. Der. *verit-able*, spelt *verytable* in Palsgrave, from MF. *veritable*, ' true,' Cot., a coined word.

VERJUICE, a kind of vinegar. (F.—L.) ME. *vergeous, verious*, P. Plowman, A. v. 70 (footnote).—F. *verjus*, ' verjuice, esp. that which is made of sowre, and unripe grapes ;' Cot. Lit. ' green juice.'—F. *vert* (spelt *verd* in Cotgrave), green; and *jus*, juice; see **Verdant** and **Juice**.

VERMEIL, vermilion. (F.—L.) ' A *vermeil*-tinctured lip ;' Milton, Comus, 752.—F. *vermeil*, vermilion; see **Vermilion**.

VERMICELLI, dough of wheat flour formed into thin wormlike rolls. (Ital.—L.) In Phillips, ed. 1706.—Ital. *vermicelli*, lit. ' little worms;' from the shape. It is the pl. of *vermicello*, a little worm, which is the dimin. of *verme*, a worm.—L. *uermem*, acc. of *uermis*, a worm, cognate with E. **Worm**.

VERMICULAR, pertaining to a worm. (L.) Phillips, ed. 1706, has: ' *Vermiculares*, certain muscles, &c.; *Vermicularis*, worm-grass, lesser house-leek; *Vermiculated*, inlaid, wrought with checker-work; *Vermiculation*, worm-eating;' &c. All are derivatives from L. *uermiculus*, a little worm, double dimin. of *uermis*, a worm; see **Worm**. Der. So also *vermi-form*, worm-shaped; from *uermi-*, decl. stem of *uermis*, and *form*; also *vermi-fuge*, a remedy that expels a worm, from L. *-fugus*, putting to flight, from *fugāre*, to put to flight; see **Fugitive**. And see *vermilion, vermin, vermicelli*.

VERMILION, a scarlet colouring substance obtained from cochineal, &c. (F.—L.) ' *Vermylyone*, minium;' Prompt. Parv.; spelt *vermyloun*, Wyclif, Exod. xxxix. 1 (later version).—F. *vermillon*, ' vermillion ;.. also, a little worm ;' Cot.—F. *vermeil*, ' vermillion ;' id.—L. *uermiculus*, a little worm; double dimin. of *uermis*, a worm; see **Vermicular** and **Worm**. ¶ For the reason of the name, see **Crimson** and **Cochineal**; but *vermilion* is now generally made of red lead, or various mineral substances, and must have been so made at an early date; it was perhaps named merely from its resemblance to *crimson*.

VERMIN, any small obnoxious insect or animal. (F.—L.) ME. *vermine*, Chaucer, C. T. 8971 (E 1095).—F. *vermine*, ' vermine; also little beasts ingendred of corruption and filth, as lice, fleas, ticks, mice, rats;' Cot. As if from a L. adj. **uerminus*, formed from *uermi-*, decl. stem of *uermis*, a worm; see **Vermicular** and **Worm**.

VERNACULAR, native. (L.) ' In the *vernacular* dialect ;' Fuller, Worthies, General (R.); and in Phillips, ed. 1706. Blount has *vernaculous*. Formed with suffix -*ar* (L. -*āris*) from L. *vernā-cul-us*, belonging to home-born slaves, domestic, native, indigenous; double dimin. of L. *uerna*, a home-born slave. β. *Verna* is for **ues-ina*, dwelling in one's house, from √WES, to dwell, live, be; see **Was**. Brugmann, ii. § 66. Der. *vernacular-ly*.

VERNAL, belonging to spring. (L.) Spelt *vernall* in Minsheu, ed. 1627.—L. *uernālis*, vernal; extended from L. *uernus*, belonging to spring.—L. *uer*, the spring.+Gk. ἔαρ (for **Ϝέσαρ*), the spring; Russ. *vesna*, the spring; Lithuan. *wasarà*, summer; Icel. *vár*; Dan. *vaar*; Swed. *vår*. β. All from √WES, to brighten, dawn; cf. Skt. *vasanta-*, spring, *ush*, to burn, L. *aurōra*, dawn; OIrish *fáir*, W. *gwawr*, dawn. Fick, i. 780.

VERNIER, a short scale made to slide along a graduated instrument for measuring intervals between its divisions. (F.) So named from its inventor (1631). ' Peter *Vernier*, of Franche Comté; in-

ventor of scale, born 1580, died Sept. 14, 1637;' Hole, Brief Biographical Dictionary.

VERSATILE, turning easily from one thing to another. (F.— L.) In Phillips, ed. 1706.—F. *versatil*, ' quickly turning ;' Cot.—L. *uersātilis*, that turns round, movable, versatile.—L. *uersāre*, to turn often, frequentative of *uertere*, to turn (pp. *uersus*); see **Verse**. Des. *versatil-i-ty*.

VERSE, a line of poetry, poetry, a stanza, short portion of the Bible or of a hymn. (L.) In very early use, and borrowed from Latin directly, not through the F. *vers*. ' *Veerce*, verse, Versus;' Prompt. Parv. Spelt *fers* in the Ormulum, 11943. AS. *fers*, a verse, a line of poetry; ' hū man tōdǣlð þā *fers* on rǣdinge '= how one divides the verse in reading; Ælfric's Grammar, ed. Zupitza, p. 291, l. 2.— Late L. *versus*, a verse; L. *uersus*, a turning, a line, row; so named from the turning to begin a new line. [Vaniček separates *uersus*, a furrow, which he connects with *uerrere*, to sweep.]—L. *uersus*, pp. of *uertere*, to turn.—√WERT, to turn; whence also E. *worth*, verb, to become; see **Worth** (1). Der. *vers-ed*, Milton, P. R. iv. 327, only in the phr. *versed in* = conversant with, and used (instead of *versate*) as a translation of L. *uersātus*, pp. of *uersāri*, to keep turning oneself about, passive form of the frequentative of *uertere*; and see *vers-i-fy, vers-ion*, &c. Also (from *uertere*), *ad-vert, ad-verse, ad-vert-ise, anim-ad-vert, anni-vers-ary, a-vert, a-verse, contro-vert, con-vert, con-verse, di-vert, di-vers, di-verse, di-vers-i-fy, di-vorce, e-vert, in-ad-vert-ent, intro-vert, in-vert, in-verse, mal-vers-at-ion, ob-verse, per-vert, per-verse, re-vert, re-verse, sub-vert, sub-vers-ion, tergi-vers-at-ion, trans-verse, tra-verse, uni-verse, vers-at-ile, vert-ebra, vert-ex, vert-ig-o, vort-ex*; and see *verst*.

VERSIFY, to make verses. (F.—L.) ME. *versifien*, P. Plowman, B. xv. 367.—F. *versifier*, ' to versifie,' Cot.—L. *uersificāre*, to versify.—L. *uersi-*, for *uersus*, a verse; and -*ficāre*, for *facere*, to make; see **Verse** and **Fact**. Der. *versific-at-ion*, in Holland, tr. of Plutarch, p. 977 (R.), from F. *versification* (omitted by Cotgrave), from L. acc. *uersificātiōnem*; *versifi-er*, Sidney, Apology for Poetrie, ed. Arber, p. 49.

VERSION, a translation, statement. (F.—L.) Formerly used in the sense of turning or change; Bacon's Essays, Ess. 58 (Of Vicissitude). —F. *version*, a version, a translation (not given in Cotgrave). —Late L. *uersiōnem*, acc. of *uersio*, regularly formed from *uers-*, as in *uers-us*, pp. of *uertere*, to turn.

VERST, a Russian measure of length. (Russ.) In Hakluyt's Voyages, i. 388, l. 30.—Russ. *versta*, a verst, 3,500 Eng. feet, a verst-post; also, age. For **vert-tā*; from √WERT, as in Russ. *vertiet(e)*, to turn. Brugmann, ii. § 79.

VERT, green, in heraldry. (F.—L.) In Blount, ed. 1674. From F. *vert*, green; formerly *verd*, Cot.—L. *uiridem*, acc. of *uiridis*, green. Cf. L. *uirēre*, to be green.+W. *gwyrdd*, green; Corn. *guirt*. Or (if these Celtic words are borrowed from L.) perhaps allied to *vivid*; cf. Skt. *jī-ra-*, active, *jī-va-*, living. Brugmann, ii. § 74.

VERTEBRA, one of the small bones of the spine. (L.) In Phillips, ed. 1706.—L. *uertebra*, a joint, a vertebra.—L. *uert-ere*, to turn; see **Verse**. Der. *vertebr-al*, a coined word; *vertebr-ate, vertebr-at-ed*, from L. *uertebrātus*, jointed.

VERTEX, the top, summit. (L.) In Phillips, ed. 1706; the adj. *vertical* is in Cotgrave.—L. *uertex*, the top, properly the turning-point, esp. the pole of the sky (which is the turning-point of the stars), but afterwards applied to the zenith.—L. *uertere*, to turn; see **Verse**. An older form of *uertex* was *uortex*. Brugmann, i. § 144. Der. *vertic-al*, from F. *vertical*, ' vertically,' Cot., from L. *uertic-ālis*, vertical, from *uertic-*, stem of *vertex*. Hence *vertical-ly*. Doublet, *vortex*.

VERTIGO, giddiness. (L.) In Phillips, ed. 1706.—L. *uertīgo* (gen. *uertīgin-is*), a turning or whirling round, giddiness.—L. *uertere*, to turn; see **Verse**.

VERVAIN, a plant of the genus verbena. (F.—L.) ME. *ver-veyne*, Gower, C. A. ii. 262 (bk. v. 4039).—F. *verveine*, ' verveine ;' Cot.—L. *uerbēna*, used in pl. *uerbēnæ*, sacred boughs, usually of olive, laurel, or myrtle. Allied to *uerber*, a rod, properly a twig, shoot.

VERVE, spirit, energy, enthusiasm. (F.—L.) ' If he . . . is resolved to follow his own *verve*, as the French call it ;' Dryden, Ded. of the Æneid.—F. *verve*, ' a brawling, jangling, jarring; also, an odd humour,in a man ;' Cot. Supposed to represent a Late L. **verva*, for L. *uerba*, lit. ' words,' i. e. talk, a neut. pl. treated as a fem. sing.; pl. of L. *uerbum*, a word; see **Verb**. (So Hatzfeld.)

VERY, true, real, actual. (F.—L.) ME. *verrai, verrei* ; ' *verrey* charite '= true charity, P. Plowman, B. xvii. 289; ' *verrei* man '= true man, id. C. xxii. 153. It occurs as *verray* in An Old Eng. Miscellany, p. 27, l. 26, in the O. Kentish Sermons (about A. D. 1240). —OF. *verai*, later *vrai* (in Cotgrave *vray*), true. Cf. Prov. *verai*, true. It answers to a Late L. type **vērācus*, not found; similarly, Scheler compares F. *Cambrai, Douai* from L. *Cameracum, Duacum*.

Cf. Schwan, § 56. This *vērăcus is a by-form of L. uĕrax (stem uĕrăc-), truthful, extended from uĕrus, true (represented in OF. by ver, veir, voir, true). β. The orig. sense of uĕrus is 'existing.' For *ues-ro-; from √WES, to be.**+**W. gwir, OIrish fīr, true; cf. Russ. viera, faith; G. wahr, true; AS. wær, true. Brugmann, i. § 367; § 818 (note 3). Der. very, adv., as in 'very wel,' i. e. truly well, Sir T. More, Works, p. 108 h; veri-ly, adv., ME. verraily, veraily, Chaucer, C. T. 13590 (B 1850). Also (from L. uĕrus) veri-fy, veri-similar, veri-ty, ver-ac-ious; ver-dict; a-ver.

VESICLE, a small tumour, bladder-like cell. (L.) Phillips, ed. 1706, has: 'Vesicula, a vesicle, or little bladder.' Englished from L. uĕsīcula, a little bladder; dimin. of uĕsīca, a bladder. Allied to Skt. vasti-, the bladder. Der. vesicul-ar, adj.; also vesic-at-ion, the raising of blisters on the skin.

VESPER, the evening star; the evening; pl. vespers, even-song. (L.) In the ecclesiastical sense, the word does not seem to be old, as the E. name for the service was eve-song or even-song. Vespers occurs in Bp. Taylor, vol. ii. ser. 7 (R.); and see the Index to Parker Soc. Publications. But we already find vesper, in the sense of evening-star, in Gower, C. A. ii. 109 (bk. iv. 3209).—L. uesper, the evening-star, the evening; cf. uespera, even-tide. Hence OF. vespre (F. vêpre), 'the evening,' Cot., and vespres, 'even-song,' id.**+**Gk. ἕσπερος, adj. and sb., evening, ἕσπερος ἀστήρ, the evening star; ἑσπέρα, even-tide; OIrish fescor, W. ucher, evening. Brugmann, i. §§ 329, 565 (3); Stokes-Fick, p. 278.

VESSEL, a utensil for holding liquids, &c., a ship. (F.–L.) ME. vessel, Chaucer, C. T. 5682 (D 100).—AF. vessel, a vessel, OF. vaissel, veissel, a ship (Burguy); later vaisseau, 'a vessel, of what kind soever;' Cot.—L. uascellum, a small vase or urn; dimin. of uās, a vase, whence also the dimin. uasculum; see **Vascular, Vase.**

VEST, a garment, waistcoat. (L.) In Milton, P. L. xi. 241.—L. uestis, a garment; orig. the act of putting on clothes (Bréal). Formed (with Idg. suffix -ti-) from √WES, to clothe, protect; cf. Skt. vas, to put on (clothes), Gk. ἕν-νυμι (<ϝέσ-νυμι), I clothe, ἐσ-θής, clothing, Goth. gawasjan, to clothe, wasti, clothes; Curtius, i. 470. Der. vest, vb., formerly used in such phrases as to vest one with supreme power, and (less properly) to vest supreme power in one; see Phillips, ed. 1706; hence vest-ed, fully possessed. And see vest-ment, vest-ry, vest-ure. Also di-vest, in-vest, tra-vest-y.

VESTAL, chaste, pure. (F.–L.) As adj. in Shak. Romeo, iii. 3. 38; as sb., a Vestal virgin, priestess of Vesta, Antony, iii. 12. 31. —F. vestal, a Vestal virgin; see Cotgrave.—L. Vestālis, belonging to a Vestal, al-o (for Vestālis uirgo), a priestess of Vesta.—L. Vesta, a Roman goddess; goddess of the flocks and household.**+**Gk. Ἑστία, daughter of Chronos and Rhea, goddess of the domestic hearth.— √WES, to dwell (Walde). See **Was.**

VESTIBULE, a porch. (L.) In Swinburne, Travels in Spain, p. 216. Phillips has only the L. form vestibulum. Englished from L. uestibulum, a fore-court, entrance-court, entrance. Lit. 'that which forms a part of the abode.' Perhaps from L. *ues-ti-, a dwelling; with suffix -bulum, as in sessi-bulum, a seat. Cf. Skt. vasta-, vāstu-, a house, OHG. wist, an abode; from √WES, to dwell (Walde).

VESTIGE, a foot-print, a trace. (F.–L.) In Blount's Gloss., ed. 1674.—F. vestige, 'a step, foot-step, track, trace;' Cot.—L. uestīgium, a foot-step, track. β. Of doubtful origin; see Walde.

VESTMENT, a garment, long robe. (F.–L.) ME. vestiment; pl. vestimenz, Ancren Riwle, p. 418. This form occurs as late as in Spenser, F. Q. iii. 12. 29; whilst the Prompt. Parv. has both vest-ment and vestymente.—OF. vestement, 'a vestment,' Cot. (Mod. F. vêtement).—L. uestimentum, a garment.—L. uestī-re, to clothe.—L. uesti-, decl. stem of uestis; see **Vest.**

VESTRY, a place for keeping vestments. (F.–L.) ME. vestrye, Prompt. Parv. Slightly altered from OF. vestiairie, whence MF. vestiaire, 'the vestry in a church;' Cot.—L. uestiārium, a wardrobe; orig. neut. of uestiārius, adj., belonging to a vest or robe.—L. uesti-, decl. stem of uestis, a garment; see **Vest.**

VESTURE, dress, a robe. (F.–L.) In P. Plowman, B. i. 23. —OF. vestūre, MF. vesture, 'a clothing, arraying;' Cot.—Late L. uestītūra, clothing.—L. uestīt-us, pp. of uestīre, to clothe.—L. uesti-, decl. stem of uestis; see **Vest.** Cf. E. in-vestiture.

VETCH, a genus of plants. (F.–L.) The same as fitch; pl. fitches, Isaiah xxviii. 25, Ezek. iv. 9 (A.V.). In the earlier of Wyclif's versions of Isaiah xxviii. 25, the word is written ficche, and in the later fetchis. Baret (Alvearie) gives: 'Fitches, Vicia . . Plin. Βίκιον; A vinciendo, vt Varroni placet;' Bible Word-book, ed. Eastwood and Wright. For the variation of the initial letter, cf. fane and vane, fat and vat; the variation is dialectal, and in the present case the right form is that with initial v. The correct ME. spelling would be veche; we actually find 'Orobus, vech' in Voc. 599. 26; also 'Hec uicia, Anglice feche' in Voc. 664. 24, in a vocabulary strongly marked

by Northern forms; feche being the Northern form corresponding to the Southern veche.—ONorth. F. veche (Walloon veche), OF. vece, MF. vesce, a vetch. Palsgrave has: 'Fetche, a lytell pease, uesse, ueche, lentille;' whilst Cotgrave has: 'Vesce, the pulse called fitch or vitch.'—L. uicia, a vetch; whence also G. wicke, Du. wikke. β. As the vetch has tendrils, Varro's derivation is perhaps to be accepted; viz. from the base WEIK, to bind, as appearing in uincīre, to bind, uinca, a plant (orig. a climbing one). Cf. √WEI, to wind, whence L. uī-tis, a vine, uī-men, a pliant twig. See **Withy.**

VETERAN, experienced, long exercised in military life. (L.) In Blount's Gloss., ed. 1674.—L. ueterānus, old, veteran, experienced; as sb., a veteran.—L. ueter-, for *uetes-, stem of uetus, old, aged; lit. 'advanced in years.' Cf. Gk. ἕτος (=ϝέτ-ος), a year, Skt. vatsa-, a year. See **Veal.** Der. veteran, sb. From the same base are veter-in-ar-y, in-veter-ate, veal, wether.

VETERINARY, pertaining to the art of treating diseases of domestic animals. (L.) 'Veterinarian, he that lets horses or mules to hire, a hackney-man, also a horse-leech or farrier;' Blount's Gloss., ed. 1674. Sir T. Browne has veterinarian as a sb., Vulg. Errors, b. iii. c. 2, § 1.—L. ueterinārius, of or belonging to beasts of burden; as sb., a cattle-doctor.—L. ueterīnus, belonging to beasts of burden; pl. ueterīnæ (sc. bestiæ), beasts of burden. β. The L. ueterina probably meant, originally, an old animal, one that was no longer fit for anything but carrying burdens; from the same base as that which occurs in uetus (gen. ueter-is), old; see **Veteran** and **Veal.** And see **Wether.** Der. veterinari-an, as above.

VETO, a prohibition. (L.) Not in Todd's Johnson.—L. ueto, I forbid; hence, the saying of 'I forbid,' i. e. a prohibition. OL. uoto. Der. veto, verb.

VEX, to harass, torment, irritate. (F.–L.) ME. vexen, Prompt. Parv.—F. vexer, 'to vex;' Cot.—L. uexāre, to vex, orig. to shake; of doubtful origin. Der. vex-at-ion, from F. vexation, 'vexation,' Cot., from L. acc. uexātiōnem; vex-at-i-ous, vex-at-i-ous-ly, vex-at-i-ous-ness.

VIADUCT, a road or railway carried across a valley or river. (L.) Not in Todd's Johnson. Englished from L. uia ducta, a way conducted across; from L. uia, a way, and ducta, fem. of ductus, pp. of dūcere, to lead, conduct; see **Duct, Duke.** Prob. coined in imitation of aqueduct. β. L. uia was formerly written uea, and some connect it with E. way; which can hardly be right. Der. uiaticum, a doublet of voyage, q. v.; also con-vey, con-voy, de-vi-ate, de-vi-ous, en-voy, im-per-vi-ous, in-voice, ob-vi-ate, ob-vi-ous, per-vi-ous, pre-vi-ous, tri-vi-al.

VIAL, PHIAL, a small glass vessel or bottle. (F.–L.–Gk.) Phial is a pedantic spelling; the spelling vial is historically more correct, as we took the word from French; another (French) spelling was viol. 'Vyole, a glasse, fiolle, uiole;' Palsgrave. ME. viole; pl. violis, Wyclif, Rev. v. 8, where the A. V. has vials.—OF. viole, fiole, fiolle (for which forms see Palsgrave above), later phiole, 'a violl, a small glass bottle;' Cot. Mod. F. fiole.—L. phiala, a saucer, a shallow drinking-vessel (the form of which must have been altered).—Gk. φιάλη, a shallow cup or bowl.

VIAND, food, provision. (F.–L.) Usually in pl. viands. (F.–L.) 'Deintie viande;' Sir T. More, Works, p. 6 b.—F. viande, 'meat, food, substance;' Cot. [The same as Ital. vivanda, victuals, food, eatables.]—L. uiuenda, neut. pl., things to live on, provisions; considered as a fem. sing., by a change common in Late L.—L. uiuendus, fut. pass. of uiuere, to live; see **Victuals.**

VIBRATE, to swing, move backwards and forwards. (L.) Phillips, ed. 1706, has vibration; the verb is perhaps a little later.—L. uibrātus, pp. of uibrāre, to shake, swing, brandish.—WEIB, variant of √WEIP, to shake, agitate; cf. Skt. vep, to tremble, Icel. veifa, to vibrate, wave. Brugmann, i. § 701. See **Sweep, Waive.** Der. vibrat-ion, vibrat-or-y.

VICAR, lit. a deputy; the incumbent of a benefice. (F.–L.) ME. vicar, a deputy, Chaucer, Parl. of Foules, 379; also vicary, a vicar, id. C. T. 17333 (I 22).—F. vicaire, 'a vicar, or vice-gerent, who the tenant or incumbent who, in the right of a corporation or church, is to pay duties, or do services, unto the lord of the land;' Cot.—L. uicārium, acc. of uicārius, a substitute, deputy; orig. an adj., substituted, deputed, said of one who supplies the turn or place of another.—L. uic-, stem of uicis (gen.), a turn, change, succession.— √WEIQ, to yield, give way; hence to succeed in another's turn: cf. Gk. εἴκ-ειν, to yield, G. wech-sel, a turn. Brugmann, i. § 701. Der. vicar-age, spelt vycarage in Palsgrave (prob. a misprint for vycarage); vicar-i-al; vicar-i-ate, sb., from F. vicariat, 'a vicarship,' Cot. Also vicar-i-ous, Englished from L. uicārius, substituted, delegated, vicarious (as above); vicar-i-ous-ly. And see vice-gerent, vic-iss-i-tude.

VICE (1), a blemish, fault, depravity. (F.–L.) ME. vice, vyce, Rob. of Glouc., p. 195, l. 4025.—F. vice, 'a vice, fault;' Cot.—L. uitium, a vice, fault. Der. vici-ous, from F. vicieux, 'vicious,' Cot., from L. *uitiōsus*, faulty ; *vici-ous-ly*, *vici-ous-ness*, spelt *vyciousnesse* in Palsgrave ; *viti-ate*, spelt *viciate* in Cot. (to translate F. *vicier*), from L. *uitiātus*, pp. of *uitiāre*, to injure ; *viti-at-ion*.

VICE (2), an instrument, tightened by a screw, for holding anything firmly. (F. – L.) ME. *vice*, *vyce*, in Wyclif, 3 Kings, vi. 8, where it means 'a winding-stair ' (see the A. V.), the orig. sense being 'a screw.' A *vice* is so called because tightened by a screw. – F. *vis*, 'the vice, or spindle of a presse, also a winding-staire ;' Cot. OF. *viz* ; Burguy. – L. *uītis*, a vine, bryony, the lit. sense being 'that which winds or twines ;' hence the OF. *viz* (= *vits*), where the suffixed *s* represents the termination *-is* of the L. nom. sing. or *-ēs* of the L. nom. pl. – √WEI, to wind, bind, or twine about ; cf. E. *withe*, *withy*, L. *uī-men*, a pliant twig, &c. Cf. Ital. *vite*, 'the vine, also a vice or a scrue,' Florio.

VICE-GERENT, having delegated authority, acting in place of another. (F. – L.) In Shak. L. L. L. i. 1. 222. – F. *vicegerent*, 'a vicegerent, or deputy ;' Cot. – L. *uice*, in place of ; and *gerent-*, stem of pres. part. of *gerere*, to carry on, perform, conduct, act, rule. Here *uice* is the abl. from the gen. *uicis*, a turn, change, stead (the nom. not being used) ; see **Vicar**. For *gerere*, see **Gesture**. ¶ With the same prefix *vice-* (F. *vice*, L. *uice*, in place of) we have *vice-admiral*, *vice-chancellor* ; also *vice-roy*, Temp. iii. 2. 116, where *roy* = F. *roi*, from L. *rēgem*, acc. of *rex*, a king ; *vice-regal* ; and see *vis-count*.

VICINAGE, neighbourhood. (F. – L.) *Vicinage* is a pedantic spelling of *voisinage*, due to an attempt to reduce the F. word to a L. spelling ; both forms are given in Blount's Gloss., ed. 1674. Bp. Taylor has the spelling *voisinage* more than once, in Episcopacy Asserted, § 21 (R.), and Rule of Conscience, b. i. c. 4 (R.). – F. *voisinage*, 'neighbourhood ;' Cot. – F. *voisin*, 'neighbouring,' id. – L. *uicīnum*, acc. of *uicīnus*, neighbouring, near, lit. belonging to the same street. – L. *uīc-us*, a village, street (whence the AS. E. *wick*, a town, is borrowed). +Gk. οἶκος, a house, dwelling-place ; Russ. *ves(e)*, a village ; Skt. *veça(s)*, a house, entrance. – √WEIK, to come to, enter, enter into ; Skt. *viç*, to enter. **Der.** *vicin-i-ty*, from MF. *vicinité*, 'vicinity,' Cot., from L. acc. *uīcinitātem*, neighbourhood. **Der.** (from Gk. οἶκος), *par-ish*, *par-och-i-al*.

VICISSITUDE, change. (L.) In Bacon, Essay On *Vicissitude of Things*. – L. *uicissitūdo*, change. Allied to *uicissi-m*, by turns ; where the suffix *-sim* may be compared with *pas-sim*, *reces-sim*, &c. – L. *uicis* (gen.), a change ; see **Vicar**.

VICTIM, a living being offered as a sacrifice, one who is persecuted. (F. – L.) In Dryden, tr. of Virgil, Æn. xii. l. 319. – F. *victime* (not in Cotgrave). – L. *uictima*, a victim. Allied to Goth. *weihan*, to consecrate, *weihs*, holy. Brugmann, i. § 606. **Der.** *victim-ise*, a coined word.

VICTOR, a conqueror. (L.) In K. John, ii. 324 ; and in Trevisa, i. 239. – L. *uictor*, a conqueror ; see below.

VICTORY, success in a contest. (F. – L.) ME. *victorie*. In King Alisaunder, 7663. – OF. *victorie* (Burguy), later *victoire*, 'victory,' Cot. – L. *uictōria*, conquest ; L. *uictor*, a conqueror ; cf. *uict-us*, pp. of *uincere*, to conquer (pt. t. *uīc-i*). – √WEIQ, to fight ; whence also Goth. *weigan*, *weihan* (pp. *wigans*), to strive, contend ; AS. *wig*, war. Brugmann, i. § 367. **Der.** *victori-ous* (Palsgrave), from F. *victorieux*, L. *uictōriōsus*, full of victory ; *victori-ous-ly*. Also (from *uincere*) *victor*, as above ; *vanquish*, *vinc-ible* ; *con-vince*, *con-vict*, *e-vince*, *e-vict*, *in-vinc-ible*.

VICTUALS, provisions, meat. (F. – L.) The sing. *victual* is little used now, but occurs in Exod. xii. 39 (A. V.), and in Much Ado, i. 1. 50. The word is misspelt, by a pedantry which ignores the F. origin ; yet the true orthography *vittle* fairly represents the pronunciation still commonly used by the best speakers. ME. *vitaille*, Chaucer, C. T. 248. – OF. *vitaille* (Burguy), later *victuaille* (with inserted *c*, due to pedantry) ; Cot. gives 'victuailles, victualls,' but Palsgrave has 'Vytaile, uitaille, uiures ; Vytaylles, mete and drinke, *toute maniere de uitailles*.' – L. *uictuālia*, neut. pl., provisions, victuals. – L. *uictuālis*, belonging to nourishment. – L. *uictu-*, for *uictus*, food, nourishment ; with suffix *-ālis*. – L. *uict-us*, pp. of *uīuere*, to live ; allied to *uīuus*, living. – √GwEI, to live ; cf. Skt. *jīv*, to live, Gk. βί-ος, life, Russ. *jit(e)*, to live ; and see **Quick**. Brugmann, ii. § 488. **Der.** *victual*, verb, As You Like It, v. 4. 198 ; *victuall-er*, spelt *vytailer* in Palsgrave. Also (from the same root) *vi-and*, *vi-tal*, *viv-ac-i-ous*, *viv-id*, *viv-i-fy*, *vivi-par-ous*, *vivi-section* ; *con-viv-i-al*, *re-vive*, *sur-vive* ; also *bio-graphy*, *bio-logy* ; *quick* ; but hardly *viper*, *wyvern*.

VICUNA, a quadruped of the camel tribe. (Span. – Peruv.) 'Those beastes, which at Peru they call . . *Vicunas* ;' E. G., tr. of Acosta's Nat. Hist. (1604) ; bk. i. c. 21 ; p. 70. – Span. *vicuña* ; Minsheu (1623). Of Peruvian origin ; Monlau gives the form as *vicunna* ; see Garcilasso de la Vega (bk. viii. c. 17).

VIDELICET, namely. (L.) In Mids. Nt. Dr. v. 330. In old MSS. and books, the abbreviation for L. *-et* (final) closely resembled a *z*. Hence the abbreviation *viz.* = *viet.*, short for *videlicet.* – L. *uidēlicet*, for *uidēre licet* (like *scilicet* = *scire licet*), it is easy to see, it is manifest, hence plainly, to wit, namely. – L. *uidēre*, to see ; and *licet*, it is allowable, hence, it is easy. See **Vision** and **License**.

VIDETTE, another spelling of **Vedette**, q. v.

VIE, to contend, strive for superiority. (F. – L.) ME. *vien*, a contracted form of ME. *envien*, due to the loss of the initial syllable, as in *story* for *history*, *fence* for *defence*, &c. In Chaucer, Death of Blaunche, l. 173, we have : 'To *vye* who might slepe best,' ed. Thynne (1532), and so also in the Tanner MS. 346 ; but MS. Fairfax 16 has : 'To *envye* who myght slepe best,' where To *envye* = T*envye* in pronunciation, just as Chaucer has *tabiden* = *to abiden*, &c. β. This ME. *envien* is quite a different word from *envien*, to envy ; it is really a doublet of *invite*, and is a term formerly used in gambling. – OF. *envier* (*au ieu*), to vie ;' Cot. – L. *inuītāre*, to invite ; see **Invite**. γ. This is proved by the Span. and Ital. forms ; cf. Span. *envidar*, 'among gamesters, to invite or to open the game by staking a certain sum,' Neuman ; Ital. *inuitare* (*al giuoco*), 'to vie or to reuie at any game, to drop vie ; *inuito*, a vie at play, a vie at any game ; also, an inviting, proffer, or bidding ;' Florio. See plentiful examples of *vie*, to wager, and *vie*, sb., a wager, in Nares ; and remember that the true sense of *with* is against, as in *with-stand*, *fight with*, &c., so that to *vie with* = to stake against, wager against, which fully explains the word. Much more might be added ; Scheler's excellent explanation of F. *à l'envi* is strictly to the point ; so also Wedgwood's remarks on E. *vie*. In particular, the latter shows that the OF. *envier* also meant 'to invite,' and he adds : 'From the verb was formed the adv. expression *à l'envi*, E. *a-vie*, as if for a wager: "They that write of these toads strive *a-vie* who shal write most wonders of them," Holland, tr. of Pliny ; [b. xxxii. c. 5].' Doublet, *invite*.

VIEW, a sight, reach of the sight, a scene, mental survey. (F. – L.) Very common in Shak.; see Mids. Nt. Dr. iii. 1. 144, iii. 2. 377, &c. Levins has the verb *to vewe*. – AF. *view*, Liber Albus, p. 182 ; *vewe*, Stat. Realm, i. 192 (1323) ; MF. *veuë*, 'the sense, act, or instrument of seeing, the eyes, a glance, a view, look, sight,' &c.; Cot. Properly the fem. of *veu*, 'viewed, seen,' pp. of *veoir* (mod. F. *voir*), 'to view, see ;' id. – L. *uidēre*, to see ; see **Vision**. **Der.** *view*, verb ; *view-er* ; *re-view* ; *view-less*, invisible, Meas. for Meas. iii. 1. 124.

VIGIL, the eve before a feast or fast-day. (F. – L.) Lit. 'a watching ;' so named because orig. kept by watching through the night. ME. *uigile*, Ancren Riwle, p. 412, l. 23 ; Chaucer, C. T. 379 (A 377). – F. *vigile*, 'a vigile, the eve of a holy or solemn day ;' Cot. – L. *uigilia*, a watch, watching. – L. *uigil*, awake, lively, vigilant, watchful. – L. *uigēre*, to be lively or vigorous, flourish, thrive ; allied to *uegēre*, to arouse. +Irish *feil*, W. *gwyl*, a festival (lit. vigil). – √WEG, to be strong, to wake ; see **Vegetable**. **Der.** *vigil-ant*, 1 Hen. IV, iv. 2. 64, from F. *vigilant*, 'vigilant,' Cot., from L. *uigilant-*, stem of pres. part. of *uigilāre*, to watch ; *vigil-ance*, Temp. iii. 3. 16, from F. *vigilance*, 'vigilancy,' Cot., from L. *uigilantia*. From the same root are *veg-etable*, *vig-our*, *in-vig-or-ate*, *re-veillé*, *sur-veill-ance* ; also *wake*, *watch*, *wait*.

VIGNETTE, a small engraving with ornamented borders. (F. – L.) So called because orig. applied to ornamented borders in which vine-leaves and tendrils were freely introduced. In the edition of Cotgrave's Dict. published in 1660, the English Index (by Sherwood) has a title-page with such a border, in which two pillars are represented on each side, wreathed with vines bearing leaves, tendrils, and bunches of grapes. ME. *vinettes*, vine-branches ; Lydgate, Siege of Troy, fol. F 5, col. 2. – F. *vignette*, 'a little vine ; *vignettes*, vignets, branches, or branchlike borders or flourishes, in painting or ingravery ;' Cot. Dimin. of F. *vigne*, a vine ; see **Vine**.

VIGOUR, vital strength, force, energy. (F. – L.) ME. *vigour* ; spelt *vigor*, King Alisaunder, l. 1431. – OF. *vigur*, *vigor*, later *vigueur*, 'vigor ;' Cot. – L. *uigōrem*, acc. of *uigor*, liveliness, activity, force. – L. *uigēre*, to be lively or vigorous ; see **Vigil**. **Der.** *vigor-ous*, spelt *vygorouse* in Palsgrave, from F. *vigoureux*, 'vigorous,' Cot. ; *vigor-ous-ly*, *vigor-ous-ness*.

VIKING, a Northern pirate. (Scand.) The form *wīcing* occurs in AS., but *viking* is borrowed from Scandinavian. – Icel. *vikingr*, a freebooter, rover, pirate, used in the Icel. Sagas esp. of the bands of Scand. warriors who, during the 9th and 10th centuries, harried the British Isles and Normandy. [Wrongly explained as 'a creek-dweller,' one of the men who haunted the bays, creeks, and fjords. – Icel. *vik*, a creek, inlet, bay ; with suffix *-ingr* (AS. *-ing*) in the sense of 'son of' or belonging to. Cf. also Swed. *vik*, Dan. *vig*, a creek, cove.] Explained also as 'a warrior' for **vigningr* (where *ign* > *ik*) ; allied to Icel. *vīg*, war, Goth. *weihan*, to fight, L. *uincere*, to conquer ; see **Victor**. (So Noreen, § 252 ; Sweet, Hist. E. Sounds, § 319.) +AS. *wīcing*, the same.

VILE, abject, base, worthless, wicked. (F.–L.) ME. *vil,* Rob. of Glouc. p. 488, l. 10003.–F. *vil* (fem. *vile*), ' vile, abject, base, low, meane, .. good cheape, of small price;' Cot.–L. *uilem,* acc. of *uilis,* of small price, cheap, worthless, base, vile.+W. *gwael,* vile; Stokes-Fick, p. 259. Der. *vile-ly, vile-ness; vil-i-fy,* a coined word, to account vile, defame, properly to make vile, as in Milton, P. L. xi. 516 ; *vil-i-fi-er, vil-i-fic-at-ion, re-vile.*

VILIPEND, to despise. (L.) Spelt *vilepende* in Skelton; i. 202.–L. *uilipendere,* to hold cheap.–L. *uili-,* for *uilis,* vile, cheap; and *pendere,* to weigh, esteem. See **Poise.**

VILLA, a country residence or seat, a house. (L.) In Dryden, tr. of Lucretius, b. iii. l. 283.–L. *uilla,* a farm-house; lit. ' a house in a village.' Perhaps for **uic-sla,* i. e. ' dwelling ; ' from *uic-us,* a village; see **Vicinage.** Der. *vill-age,* Chaucer, C. T. 12621 (C 687), from F. *village,* ' a village,' Cot., from L. adj. *uillāticus,* belonging to a villa ; *villag-er,* Jul. Cæsar, i. 2. 172; *villag-er-y,* a collection of villages, Mids. Nt. Dr. ii. 1. 35. And see *vill-ain.*

VILLAIN, a clownish or depraved person, a scoundrel. (F.–L.) ME. *vilein, vileyn,* Ayenbite of Inwyt, p. 18, l. 7. ' For *vilany* makith *vilein* ; ' Rom. of the Rose, 2181.–OF. *vilein,* ' servile, base, vile;' Cot. He also gives *vilain,* ' a villaine, slave, bondman, servile tenant.'–Late L. *uillānus,* a farm-servant, serf; the degradation by which it passed into a term of reproach is well stated by Cotgrave, who further explains *vilain* as meaning ' a farmer, yeoman, churle, carle, boore, clown, knave, rascall, varlet, filthie fellow.'–L. *uilla,* a farm; see **Villa.** Der. *villain-ous,* Merry Wives, ii. 2. 308; *villain-ous-ly;* also *villain-y,* ME. *vileinie,* Chaucer, C. T. 70, Ancren Riwle, p. 216, from OF. *vilenie* (or *vilanie*), ' villainy,' Cot.

VINCIBLE, that can be conquered. (L.) Rare. In Bp. Taylor, Of Repentance, c. 3. § 3 (R.).–L. *uincibilis,* easily overcome.–L. *uincere,* to conquer; see **Victor.** Der. *vincibil-i-ty; in-vincible.*

VINCULUM, a link. (L.) Modern; chiefly used as a mathematical term.–L. *uinculum,* a bond, fetter, link.–L. *uincīre,* to bind, fetter. Brugmann, ii. § 631. See **Vetch.**

VINDICATE, to lay claim to, defend, maintain by force. (L.) In Milton, P. R. ii. 47.–L. *uindicātus,* pp. of *uindicāre,* to lay legal claim to, arrogate, avenge.–L. *uindic-,* decl. stem of *uindex,* a claimant, maintainer. Orig. ' one who favours or protects a friend ; ' from *uen-* (as in *uen-ia,* favour, cf. AS. *win-e,* a friend), and *dic-āre,* to appoint, *dicere,* to say; cf. the suffix in *iū-dex,* a judge. See Walde. Der. *vindicat-or, vindic-able, vindic-at-ion; vindic-at-ive,* i. e. vindictive, Troil. iv. 5. 107 ; *vindic-at-or-y;* and see *vindic-tive, vengeance.*

VINDICTIVE, revengeful. (F.–L.) *Vindictive* is merely a shortened form of *vindicative,* obviously due to confusion with the related L. *uindicta,* revenge. Bp. Taylor, in his Rule of Conscience, b iii. c. 3, speaks of ' *vindicative* justice,' but in the same work, b. ii. c. 2, of ' *vindictive* justice;' if Richardson's quotations be correct. Shak. has *vindicative = vindictive,* Troil. iv. 5. 107.–F. *vindicatif,* ' vindicative, revenging,' Cot. Formed with suffix *-if* (L. *-iuus*) from *uindicāt-um,* supine of *uindicāre,* (1) to claim, (2) to avenge; see **Vindicate.** Der. *vindictive-ly, -ness.*

VINE, the plant from which wine is made. (F.–L.) ME. *vine, vyne;* Wyclif, John, xv. 1.–F. *vigne,* ' a vine;' Cot.–L. *uinea,* a vineyard, which in late L. (see Lewis) also had the sense of ' vine,' for which the true L. word is *uitis. Vinea* is properly the fem. of adj. *uineus,* of or belonging to wine.–L. *uinum,* wine.+Gk. οἶνος, wine; allied to οἴνη, the vine, οἰνάς, the vine, grape, wine. Cf. L. *uitis,* the vine.–√WEI, to twine; as seen in L. *uiēre,* to twist together, *uī-men,* a pliant twig, *uī-tis,* the vine, &c. Brugmann, ii. § 66. And see Curtius, i. 487, who notes that the Gk. words were used ' by no means exclusively of the drink, but just as much of the vine. Pott very appropriately compares the Lithuan. *ap-vy-nys,* a hop-tendril. . . . The fact is therefore that the Indo-Germans had indeed a common root for the idea of winding, twining, and hence derived the names of various pliant twining plants, but that it is only among the Græco-Italians that we find a common name for the grape and its juice. The Northern names (Goth. *wein,* &c.) are undoubtedly to be regarded (with Jac. Grimm, Gramm. iii. 466) as borrowed.' See the whole passage. To which we may add that the L. *uinum* also meant ' a vine,' and the E. *vine-yard =* AS. *wingeard =* wine-yard, which identified *wine* with the *vine* itself. Der. *vine-dress-er; vin-er-y,* occurring in ' the *vynery* of Ramer,' in Fabyan's Chronicle, John of France, an. 8 (ed. Ellis, p. 511), a word coined on the model of *butt-er-y, pant-ry, brew-er-y; vine-yard,* ME. *vyneyerd,* Trevisa, i. 337, AS. *win-geard,* Matt. xx. 1; *vin-ous,* a late word, from L. *uinōsus,* belonging to wine. Also *vin-egar, vin-t-age, vin-t-ner,* which see below. From the same root are *withe* or *withy,* *wine* ; cf. *vetch, vinculum.*

VINEGAR, an acid liquor made from fermented liquors. (F.–L.) ME. *vinegre, vynegre,* Wyclif, Mark, xv. 36. Lit. ' sour wine.'–F. *vinaigre,* ' vineger;' Cot.–F. *vin,* wine; and AF. *egre,* F. *aigre,* sharp, sour; see **Vine** or **Wine,** and **Eager.**

VINEWED, mouldy. (E.) In mod. edd. of Shak. Troil. ii. 1. 15, we generally find *vinewed'st,* where the folios have *whinid'st.* Minsheu, ed. 1627, has *finewed,* as equivalent to ' mustie ; ' and also the sb. *vinewedness;* and see *vinewed, finewed, fenowed* in Nares. Cf. prov. E. *vinewed* (West), Halliwell. The form *finewed* answers to the pp. of AS. *finegian, fynegian,* to become mouldy or musty, occurring in the Canons of Ælfric, § 36 ; in Thorpe, Ancient Laws, ii. 360, l. 7. It is a verb formed from an adj. *finig* or *fynig,* mouldy, occurring in the same passage. We also find the pl. *finie* (for *finige*) in Josh. ix. 5, where it is used of mouldy loaves. The true form is *fynig* (with *y,* mutation of *u*) ; the adj. is from the sb. *fyne,* mouldiness, Voc. 183. 19. From a Teut. base **fun-;* allied to Du. *vuns,* rank, ME. *vunstigh,* ' mustie (as hay);' Hexham. Cf. **Foul.**

VINTAGE, the gathering or produce of grapes, time of grape-gathering. (F.–L.) ' Tyll they had inned [gathered in] all their corne and *vyntage;*' Berners, tr. of Froissart, vol. ii. c. 22 (R.). *Vintage* is for ME. *vindage,* Wyclif, Levit. xxv. 5, or *vendage,* P. Plowman, B. xviii. 367, which was also pronounced as *ventage,* as shown by the various readings in P. Plowman, C. xxi. 414. And again, ME. *vendage* is for *vendange,* the unfamiliar ending *-ange* being turned into the common suffix *-age;* it is clear that the word was confused with *vint-ner, vint-ry;* see **Vintner.** AF. *vendenge,* Statutes of the Realm, i. 331 (1353); F. *vendange* (MF. *vendenge* in Cotgrave), ' a vintage;' Cot.–L. *uindēmia,* a vintage.–L. *uin-um,* (1) wine, (2) grapes; and *dēm-ere,* to take away; so that *uin-dēmia =* a taking away of grapes, grape-gathering. β. For L. *uinum,* see **Vine, Wine.** The L. *dēmere* is for **dē-imere,* to take away; from *dē,* prep., off, away, and *emere,* to take ; see **De-** and **Redeem.**

VINTNER, a wine-dealer, tavern-keeper. (F.–L.) ' *Vyntenere,* Vinarius;' Prompt. Parv. Thus *vin!ner* is short for *vintener;* and again, *vintener* is an altered form of *vineter* or *viniter,* which is the older form. It occurs, spelt *viniter,* in Rob. of Glouc., p. 542, l. 11226, in a passage where we also find *viniterie,* now shortened to *vintry,* and occurring as the name of a house in London (Stow, Survey of London, ed. Thoms, p. 90).–AF. *vineter,* Bozon, p. 19; MF. *vinetier,* ' a vintner, taverner, wine-seller;' Cot.–Late L. *vinētārius,* a wine-seller (occurring A.D. 1226). Really derived from L. *uinētum,* a vine-yard, but used with the sense of L. *uinārius,* a wine-seller.–L. *uinum,* grapes, wine; see **Vine** and **Wine.**

VIOL, a kind of fiddle, a musical instrument. (F.–Prov.–Late L.) In Shak. Rich. II, i. 3. 162.–MF. *viole* (also *violle*), ' a (musical) violl, or violin;' Cot.–Prov. *viula,* a viol; see Bartsch. Cf. Ital., Span., and Port. *viola* (Diez). Diez takes the Prov. *viula* (a trisyllabic word) to be the oldest form, derived from Late L. *vitula, vidula,* a viol, which was first transposed into the form **viudla* (cf. Prov. *veuza* from L. *uidua, teune* from L. *tenuis*), and then became **viulla, viula, viola.* ' *Vidulatores* dicuntur a *vidula,* Gallice, *vicle;*' John de Garlande, in Wright's Voc. i. 137, l. 4 from bottom. The AS. *fiðel,* OHG. *fidula,* E. *fiddle* appear to be the same as Late L. *vitula, vidula;* see **Fiddle,** which may be a doublet. [The *i* in *vitula* was short (Ducange); connexion with L. *uitulārī,* to rejoice, is doubtful.] Der. *viol-in,* Spenser, Shep. Kal. April, l. 103, from Ital. *violino,* dimin. of *viola,* a viol; *viol-in-ist,* a player on the violin; *viol-on-cell-o,* a bass violin, from Ital. *violoncello,* dimin. of *violone,* a bass-viol, augmentative form of *viola.* Also *bass-viol,* Comedy of Errors, iv. 3. 23. Doublet, *fiddle.*

VIOLATE, to injure, abuse, profane, ravish. (L.) In Shak. L. L. L. i. 1. 21.–L. *uiolātus,* pp. of *uiolāre,* to violate. Orig. ' to treat with force;' formed as if from an adj. **uiolus,* due to *uī-s,* force. β. Allied to Gk. ἴς, strength, force ; cf. Skt. *vayas,* youth. See Brugmann, i. § 91. Der. *violat-or,* from L. *uiolātor; viola-ble,* from L. *uiolābilis; violat-ion,* from F. *violation,* ' a violation,' Cot., from L. acc. *uiolātiōnem.* Also *viol-ent,* q. v.; (from the same root) *per-vi-cac-i-ous.*

VIOLENT, vehement, outrageous, very forcible. (F.–L.) In Chaucer, C. T. 12801 (C 867).–F. *violent,* ' violent,' Cot.–L. *uiolentus,* violent, full of might. Formed with suffix *-entus* from an adjectival form **uiolus,* due to *uis,* strength; see above. Der. *violent-ly; violence,* Chaucer, C. T. 16376 (G 908), from F. *violence,* ' violence,' Cot., from L. sb. *uiolentia.*

VIOLET, a flower ; a light purple colour. (F.–L.) ME. *violet, vyolet,* Prompt. Parv.; Trevisa, i. 261. ' Tunicam de *vyolet;*' York Wills, i. 23 (1346).–MF. *violet,* m., also *violette,* fem., ' a violet; also, violet-colour;' Cot. Dimin. of MF. *viole,* ' a gilliflower,' Cot.; it must also have meant a violet.–L. *uiola,* a violet. Formed with dimin. suffix *-la* from a base *uio-,* cognate with Gk. ἴο-, base of ἴον (for **ϝίον*), a violet. See **Iodine.** Der. *violet,* adj., violet-coloured.

VIOLIN, VIOLONCELLO; see under **Viol.**

VIPER, a poisonous snake. (F.–L.) In Levins, ed. 1570.–F. *vipère,* 'the serpent called a viper;' Cot.–L. *uīpera,* a viper. Usually explained as the serpent 'that produces living young;' Buffon says that the viper differs from most other serpents in being much slower, as also in excluding its young completely formed, and bringing them forth alive. As if *uīpera* were short for *uīuipara,* fem. of *uīuiparus,* producing live young; see **Viviparous.** β. Walde prefers a derivation from the √WEIP, to wind round, as in Goth. *biwaibjan,* to wind round; from the viper's coils. Der. *viper-ous,* Cor. iii. 1. 287; *viper-ine,* Blount, from L. *uīperīnus,* adj. Doublet, *wyvern.*

VIRAGO, a bold, impudent, manlike woman. (L.) In Stanyhurst, tr. of Virgil, Æn. b. i, ed. Arber, p. 34, l. 2. 'This [woman] schal be clepid *virago,*' Wyclif, Gen. ii. 23.–L. *uirāgo,* a manlike maiden, female warrior; extended from *uir,* a man. See **Virile.**

VIRELAY, an old French form of poem, running on two rimes. (F.) Chaucer has: 'roundels, *virelayes;*' C. T., F 948 (Frank. Ta. 220).–OF. *virelai,* MF. *virelay,* 'a virelay, round, freemans song;' Cot.–OF. *virer,* to turn, change the direction of (see **Veer**); and OF. *lai,* a lay, song (see **Lay**).

VIRGATE, an (old) measure of land. (L.) Also formerly called a *yardland;* see Blount, who says:–'This Yardland, Bracton (lib. 2. cap. 10 and 27) calls *virgatam terræ;* but expresseth no certainty what it contains. It is called a *verge of land,* anno 28 Edw. I.'–Late L. *virgāta,* a fem. pp. form, from L. *uirga,* a rod. See **Verge** (1).

VIRGIN, a maiden. (F.–L.) In early use; the pl. *virgines* occurs in St. Katharine, l. 2342.–OF. *virgine* (Burguy).–L. *uirginem,* acc. of *uirgo,* a virgin. Root uncertain (not allied to *uir,* a man, or *uirēre,* to flourish, as the base is *uirg-,* not *uir-*). Der. *virgin-i-ty,* ME. *uirginitee,* Chaucer, C. T. 5657 (D 75), from F. *virginité,* 'virginity,' Cot., from L. acc. *virginitātem.* Also *virgin-al,* spelt *virginall* in Levins, ed. 1570; an old musical instrument, also named *the virginals,* or a *pair* [set] *of virginals,* so called because played upon by virgins (Blount, Nares); cf. ME. *virginal,* adj., Hoccleve, Reg. Princes, 3584; from F. *virginal,* 'belonging to a virgin,' Cot., from L. adj. *uirginālis.* Also *Virgo* (L. *uirgo*), the Virgin, a zodiacal sign.

VIRIDITY, greenness. (L.) Little used; in Blount's Gloss., ed. 1674, and added to Johnson's Dict. by Todd, who gives an example from Evelyn. Englished from L. *uiriditās,* greenness.–L. *uiridis,* green. See **Verdant.**

VIRILE, male, masculine, manly. (F.–L.) In Cotgrave.–F. *viril,* 'virile, manly;' Cot.–L. *uirilis,* manly.–L. *uir,* a man, a hero.+W. *gwr,* OIrish *fer,* Irish *fear,* a man; Goth. *wair,* a man; AS. *wer;* Icel. *verr;* OHG. *wer.* See **Werwolf.** Further allied to Skt. *vīra-s,* sb., a hero; adj., strong, heroic; Zend *vīra,* a hero (Fick, i. 786). Der. *viril-i-ty* (Blount), from F. *virilité,* 'virility,' Cot., from L. acc. *uirīlitātem,* manhood. Also (from L. *uir*) *vir-ago,* q. v., *vir-tue,* q. v.; *decem-vir, trium-vir.*

VIRTUE, excellence, worth, efficacy. (F.–L.) ME. *vertu,* Ancren Riwle, p. 340, l. 9.–F. *vertu,* 'vertue, goodnesse;' Cot.–L. *uirtūtem,* acc. of *uirtūs,* manly excellence.–L. *uir,* a man; see **Virile.** ¶ The spelling has been changed from *vertu* to *virtue* to bring it nearer to Latin. Der. *virtu-ous,* ME. *vertuous,* Chaucer, C. T. 251, from F. *vertueux,* 'vertuous,' Cot., from Late L. *uirtuōsus,* full of virtue (Ducange); *virtu-ous-ly; virtu-al,* having effect, in Bp. Taylor, Dissuasive from Popery, § 3 (R.), from F. *virtuel* (Littré), as if from a L. form **uirtuālis; virtu-al-ly.* Also *virtu,* a love of the fine arts, a late word, borrowed from Ital. *virtù* (also *vertù*), shortened form of *virtute,* virtue, excellence, used in the particular sense of learning or excellence in a love of the fine arts, from L. acc. *uirtūtem;* whence *virtu-os-o,* Evelyn's Diary, Feb. 27, 1644, from Ital. *virtuoso,* lit. virtuous, learned, esp. a person skilled in the fine arts.

VIRULENT, very active in injuring, spiteful, bitter in animosity. (F.–L.) Lit. poisonous. 'The seed of dragon is hot and biting, and besides of a *virulent* and stinking smell;' Holland, tr. of Pliny, b. xxiv. c. 16. ME. *virulent,* Lanfrank, Cirurgie, p. 80.–F. *virulent,* omitted by Cotgrave, but in use in the 16th century (Littré); and prob. much earlier.–L. *uirulentus,* poisonous, virulent.–L. *uīru-,* for *uirus,* slime, poison; with suffix *-lentus.*+Gk. ἰός (for ϝισός), poison; Skt. *visha-m,* poison. Allied to Irish *fī,* poison, W. *gwy,* fluid; and to E. **Wizen.** Der. *virulent-ly; virulence,* from F. *virulence,* 'stench, ranknesse, poison,' Cot., from L. *uirulentia.* The sb. *virus,* borrowed immediately from Latin, is now also in use.

VISAGE, the face, mien, look. (F.–L.) ME. *visage,* King Alisaunder, 7652.–F. *visage,* 'the visage, face, look;' Cot. Formed with suffix *-age* (<L. *-āticum*) from MF. *vis,* 'the visage, face,' Cot.–L. *uīsum,* acc. of *uīsus,* the vision, sight; whence the sense was transferred to that of 'look' or mien, and finally to that of 'face;'

perhaps (as Scheler suggests) under the influence of G. *gesicht,* the face, lit. the sight.–L. *uīsus,* pp. of *uidēre,* to see; see **Vision.** Der. *visag-ed,* as in *tripe-visaged,* 2 Hen. IV, v. 4. 9.

VISARD, the same as **Visor,** q. v.

VIS-A-VIS, in a position (that is) face to face. (F.–L.) F. *vis à vis,* 'face to face, directly opposite;' Cot. The F. *vis* represents the L. acc. *uīsum;* see **Visage.** The F. *à* is from L. *ad,* to, towards.

VISCACHA, VIZCACHA, a South-American rodent mammal. (Span.–Peruv.) Span. *viscacha, vizcacha,* 'a creature like a hare;' Pineda.–Peruv. *viskacha,* 'conejo de la tierra;' Peruv. Dict.

VISCERA, the entrails. (L.) A medical term.–L. *uiscera,* neut. pl., the entrails; from nom. sing. *uiscus.* Perhaps allied to L. *uiēre,* to twist together. Der. *viscer-al* (Blount), *e-viscer-ate.*

VISCID, sticky, clammy. (F.–L.) '*Viscid,* or *Viscous,* clammy, fast as glue;' Blount's Gloss., ed. 1674.–F. *viscide,* 'clammy,' Cot.–L. *uiscidus,* clammy, like birdlime.–L. *uiscum,* the mistletoe, also birdlime.+Gk. ἰξός, ἰξία, mistletoe, the mistletoe-berry, from which birdlime was made. Der. *viscid-i-ty,* from F. *viscidité,* 'visciditie,' Cot. So also *visc-ous,* Lanfrank, Cirurgie, p. 178, from L. *uiscōsus,* clammy; *visc-os-i-ty,* from F. *viscosité,* 'viscositie,' Cot.

VISCOUNT, a title; an officer who formerly supplied the place of a count or earl. (F.–L.) The *s* (in the E. word) is not pronounced; the usual E. spelling was formerly *vicounte* (pronounced with *i* as in F., whence the mod. E. *vicount,* pronounced with *i* as in modern E.); spelt *vicounte* in Fabyan, Chron. c. 245. But we also find AF. *visconte,* a sheriff, Stat. Realm, i. 28 (1275).–F. *vicomte,* 'a vicount, was at the first the deputy or lieutenant of an earle,' &c.; Cot.; OF. *viscomte* (12th cent.).–L. *uice,* in place of; *comitem,* acc. of *comes,* count. In the 12th century the word was spelt *visconte* (Littré), a traditional spelling which we still retain, though the *s* was early lost in F., and ceased to be sounded in E. The prefix was also written *vice,* as in MF. *vice-admirall,* 'a viceadmirall,' *vice-conte,* 'a vicount,' Cot.; Roquefort notes the OF. *vis-admiral,* a vice-admiral. See **Vicegerent** and **Count** (1). Der. *viscount-ess,* from OF. *vis-,* prefix, 'vice,' and **Countess.**

VISE, another spelling (chiefly American) of **Vice** (2), q. v.

VISÉ, an endorsement made upon a pass-port. (F.–L.) Modern. –F. *visé,* i. e. 'examined,' pp. of *viser,* to view, inspect.–Late L. **visāre,* used for L. *uīsere,* to behold; from *uidēre* (pp. *uisus*), to see; see **Visit.** ¶ The true F. word is *visa,* sb.

VISIBLE, that can be seen. (F.–L.) Spelt *vysyble* in Palsgrave. F. *visible,* 'visible;' Cot.–L. *uīsibilis,* that may be seen.–L. *uīsus,* pp. of *uidēre,* to see. See **Vision.**

VISIER, the same as **Vizier,** q. v.

VISIGOTH, one of the West Goths. (Late L.–Teut.) The Goths were divided into Ostro-Goths and Visi-Goths, i. e. Eastern and Western Goths. See Gibbon, Roman Empire, cap. 36.–Late L. *Visigothī* or *Visigothæ,* pl., the Visigoths. Of Teut. origin; from Teut. *west,* West; and Teut. **Gutōs* or **Gutans,* pl.; only found in Gothic in the comp. *Gut-thiuda,* the Gothic people.

VISION, sight, a sight, dream. (F.–L.) ME. *visioun, visiun,* Cursor Mundi, 4454.–F. *vision,* 'a vision, sight;' Cot.–L. *uīsionem,* acc. of *uīsio,* sight; cf. *uīsus,* pp. of *uidēre,* to see.+Gk. ἰδεῖν (for ϝιδεῖν), to see, infin. of εἶδον, I saw, a 2nd aorist form; whence perf. t. οἶδα (I have seen), I know (=E. *wot*).+Skt. *vid,* to know; Goth. *witan,* to know; AS. *witan.* β. All from √WEID, to see, know; see **Wit,** verb. Der. *vision-ar-y,* adj., Dryden, Tyrannick Love, Act i. sc. 1 (R.), a coined word; also *vision-ar-y,* sb., one who sees visions, or forms impracticable schemes. Also (like L. *uīsus*) *vis-age,* q. v., *vis-ible,* q. v., *vis-or,* q. v., *vis-it,* q. v., *vis-ta,* q. v., *vis-u-al,* q. v.; also *ad-vice, ad-vise, de-vice, de-vise, im-pro-vise, pre-vis-ion, pro-vis-ion, pro-vis-o, pro-vis-or, re-vise, super-vise.* Also (from L. *uidēre*) *en-vy, e-vid-ence, in-vid-i-ous, juris-pr-ud-ence, pro-vide, pro-vid-ent, pr-ud-ent, pur-vey, re-view, sur-vey, vide-licet, view.* And see *veda.*

VISIT, to go to see or inspect, call upon. (F.–L.) ME. *visiten,* Ancren Riwle, p. 154, l. 8.–F. *visiter,* 'to visit, or go to see;' Cot. –L. *uīsitāre,* to go to see, visit; frequentative of *uīsere,* to behold, survey, intensive form of *uidēre* (pp. *uīsus*), to see; see **Vision.** Der. *visit,* sb.; *visit-at-ion,* from F. *visitation,* 'a visitation, visiting.' Cot., from L. acc. *uīsitātiōnem; visit-ant,* Milton, P. L. xi. 225, from L. *uīsitant,* stem of pres. part. of *uīsitāre; visit-or,* Timon, i. 1. 42 (for *visitour*), from F. *visiteur,* 'a visitor, searcher, overseer,' Cot., the true L. word being *uīsitātor; visit-or-i-al.*

VISOR, VIZOR, VISARD, VIZARD, a mask, part of a helmet. (F.–L.) In the forms *visard, vizard,* the final *d* is excrescent and unoriginal. It is variously spelt in Shak. Romeo, i. 4. 30, L. L. L. v. 2. 242, Macb. iii. 2. 34, &c. ME. *visere;* 'Vysere, larva,' Prompt. Parv.–AF. *visere* (A. Neckam), in Wright, Vocab. i. 113; MF. *visiere,* 'the viser, or sight of a helmet;' Cot. Formed from F. *vis,* the face; and so called from its protecting the face. In the same way, the vizard was named from its covering the face ; cf. *faux visage*, 'a maske, or vizard,' Cot. ; lit. a false face. — L. *uisum*, acc. of *uisus*, the sight ; see further under **Vision**. Der. *visor-ed*; spelt *vizard-ed*, Merry Wives, iv. 6. 40.

VISTA, a view or prospect, seen as through an avenue of trees. (Ital.—L.) In Pope, Moral Essays, iv. 93. — Ital. *vista*, 'the sence of sight, seeing, a looke, a prospect, a view;' Florio. — Ital. *vista*, fem. of *visto*, seen, one of the forms of the pp. of *vedere*, to see ; the other form being *veduto*. — L. *uidēre*, to see ; see **Vision**.

VISUAL, used in sight or for seeing. (F.—L.) 'Visual, belonging to, or carried by the sight; extending as far as the eye can carry it;' Blount's Gloss., ed. 1674. — F. *visual*, 'visuall,' Cot. — L. *uisuālis*, belonging to the sight. — L. *uisu-*, for *uisus*, the sight ; with suffix *-ālis*. — L. *uisus*, pp. of *uidēre*, to see ; see **Vision**.

VITAL, containing life, essential. (F.—L.) ME. *vital*, Chaucer, C. T. 2804 (A 2802). — F. *vital*, 'vitall;' Cot. — L. *uitālis*, belonging to life. — L. *uita*, life. Allied to *uiuere*, to live ; cf. *βίos*, life. — √GwEI, to live ; see **Victuals**. Der. *vital-ly*; *vital-i-ty*, in Blount, Englished from L. *uitālitās*, vital force ; *vitalise*, to give life to, a coined word. Also *vital-s*, parts essential to life, coined in imitation of L. *uitālia*, parts essential to life, neut. pl. of *uitālis*, vital.

VITIATE, see under **Vice**.

VITREOUS, pertaining to glass, glasslike. (L.) In Ray, On the Creation, pt. ii. § 11, where he speaks of 'the *vitreous* humor' of the eye (R.). Englished (by change of *-us* to *-ous*, as in *arduous*, &c.) from L. *uitreus* (also *uitrius*), glassy. — L. *uitri-*, for *uitrum*, glass. β. The *i* of *uitrum* is short in Horace (Odes, iii. 13. 1), but may have been orig. long, as in Propertius, iv. 8. 37 ; and *uī-trum* may be for **uid-trum*, i. e. an instrument or material for seeing with. — L. *uidēre*, to see ; see **Vision**. (But this is doubtful). Der. *vitri-fy*, from F. *vitrifier*, 'to turn or make into glasse,' formed as if from a L. verb **uitrificāre* ; hence also *vitrific-at-ed*, Bacon, New Atlantis, ed. 1631, p. 34 ; *vitrific-at-ion*, Sir T. Browne, Vulg. Errors, b. ii. c. 5, pt. 2 ; *vitrifi-able* ; also *vitri-ol*, q. v.

VITRIOL, the popular name of sulphuric acid. (F.—L.) ME. *vitriole*, Chaucer, C. T. 16276 (G 808). — F. *vitriol*, 'vitrioll, copperose;' Cot. Cf. MItal. *vitriolo*, 'vitrioll or coperasse,' Florio. Said to be so called from its glassy look. — Late L. **uitriolus*, answering to L. *uitreolus*, glassy, made of glass. — L. *uitreus*, glassy. — L. *uitrum*, glass ; see **Vitreous**. ¶ It is not improbable that *vitriol* was supposed to be made from glass ; from the popular belief that glass was poisonous ; see Sir T. Browne, Vulg. Errors, b. ii. c. 5. Der. *vitriol-ic*.

VITUPERATION, blame, censure, abuse. (F.—L.) Spelt *vituperacyon* in The Boke of Tulle of Old Age, c. 8 (Caxton) ; cited in the Appendix to Richardson's Dict. Also in Cotgrave. — F. *vituperation*, 'a vituperation, or dispraising;' Cot. Cf. L. *uituperātus*, pp. of *uituperāre*, to censure, abuse. The orig. sense is 'to get ready a blemish,' i. e. to find fault. — L. *uitu-*, for *uiti-*, base of *uitium*, a vice, fault, blemish ; and *parāre*, to get ready, furnish, provide. See **Vice** and **Parade**. Der. *vituperate* (from L. pp. *uituperātus*), used by Cot. to translate MF. *vituperer* ; *vituperat-ive*, *-ly*.

VIVACITY, liveliness. (F.—L.) In Cotgrave. Also formerly used to mean 'longevity;' see Trench, Select Glossary. — F. *vivacité*, 'vivacity, liveliness;' Cot. — L. *uiuācitātem*, acc. of *uiuācitās*, natural vigour. — L. *uiuāci-*, decl. stem of *uiuax*, tenacious of life, vigorous. — L. *uiuus*, lively ; see **Vivid**. Der. (from L. *uiuāci-*), *vivaci-ous*, *-ly*, *-ness*.

VIVANDIERE, a sutler, a woman attached to French and other continental regiments, who sells provisions and liquor. (F.—L.) F. *vivandière*, fem. form of *vivandier*, 'a victualler, sutler;' Cot. — L. *uiuenda*, viands, provisions ; see **Viands**.

VIVID, life-like, having the appearance of life, very clear to the imagination. (L.) In Blount's Gloss., ed. 1674. — L. *uiuidus*, animated, true to life, lively. — L. *uiuus*, living ; allied to *uiuere*, to live ; see **Victuals**, and **Quick**. Cf. Skt. *jīva*, living ; Lith. *gywas*, living : Russ. *jivoi*. Der. *vivid-ly*, *-ness*.

VIVIFY, to quicken, endue with life. (F.—L.) Bacon has *vivifie* and *vivification*, Nat. Hist. § 696. — F. *vivifier*, 'to quicken;' Cot. — L. *uiuificāre*, to vivify, make alive. — L. *uiui-*, for *uiuus*, living ; and *-ficāre*, for *facere*, to make ; see **Vivid** and **Fact**. Der. *vivific-at-ion*.

VIVIPAROUS, producing young alive. (L.) In Sir T. Browne, Vulg. Errors, b. iii. c. 21, part 2. Englished from L. *uiuiparus*, producing living young. — L. *uiui-*, for *uiuus*, alive ; and *parere*, to produce, bring forth. See **Vivid** or **Victuals**, and **Parent**.

VIVISECTION, dissection of a living animal. (L.) Modern. From *vivi-*, as seen in **Viviparous** ; and **Section**.

VIXEN, a she-fox, an ill-tempered woman. (E.) *Vixen* is the same as *fixen*, occurring as a proper name (spelt *Fixsen*) in the Clergy List, 1873. Spelt *vixen*, Mids. Nt. Dr. iii. 2. 324. That false

fixen;' Gammer Gurton, A. iii. sc. 2. Halliwell quotes ME. *fixene fox*, i. e. vixen-fox, from MS. Bodley 546. Cf. AS. *fixenhȳd*, vixen hide, AS. Leechdoms, i. 342 ; *fyxan dīc*, Kemble, Cod. Dipl. ii. 29, l. 1. It is the fem. form of *fox* ; and by the ordinary laws of vowel-change, the AS. fem. form is *fyx-en*; cf. AS. *gyd-en*, a goddess, from *god*, a god. From the Teut. type **fuhs-in-jā*, fem. ; cf. Teut. type **fuhs-*, a fox ; see **Fox**. The Southern E. form *vox* for *fox* is common, as in Ancren Riwle, p. 128, l. 5 ; so also *vane* for *fane*, and *vat* for *fat*. ╋G. *füchsin*, fem. of *fuchs*, a fox ; similarly formed. The fem. suffix occurs again in G. *königinn*, a queen, &c. Cf. L. *rēg-īna*, *Faust-īna*, &c.

VIZ., an abbreviation for **Videlicet**, q. v.

VIZARD, a mask; see **Vizor**.

VIZIER, VISIER, an oriental minister or councillor of state. (Arab.) 'The Gran Visiar;' Howell, Foreign Travel, Appendix; ed. Arber, p. 85. — Arab. *wazīr*, 'a vazir, counsellor of state, minister, a vicegerent, or lieutenant of a king ; also, a porter;' Rich. Dict. p. 1642. The sense of 'porter' is the orig. one ; hence it meant, the bearer of the burden of state affairs. — Arab. root *wazara*, to bear a burden, support, sustain; id. p. 1641. Doublet, *al-guazil*, q. v.

VOCABLE, a term, word. (F.—L.) 'This worde aungell is a *vocable* or worde synnifyinge a minyster;' Udall, on Hebrews, c. 1 ; fol. 206, back. — F. *vocable*, 'a word, a tearm;' Cot. — L. *uocābulum*, an appellation, designation, name. — L. *uocā-re*, to call ; allied to *uōx*, voice; see **Voice**. Der. *vocabul-ar-y*, from F. *vocabulaire*, 'a vocabulary, dictionary, world of words,' Cot., from Late L. *uocābulārium*.

VOCAL, belonging to the voice, uttering sound. (F.—L.) 'They'll sing like Memnon's statue, and be *vocal*;' Ben Jonson, Staple of News, Act iii. sc. 1 (Lickfinger). — F. *vocal*, 'vocall;' Cot. — L. *uōcālis*, sonorous, vocal. — L. *uōc-*, stem of *uōx*, the voice ; see **Voice**. Der. *vocal-ise*, from F. *vocaliser*; Cotgrave has *vocalizé*, 'vowelled, made a vowel;' *vocal-is-at-ion*, *vocal-ist*; *vowel*.

VOCATION, a calling, occupation. (F.—L.) In Levins, ed. 1570. — F. *vocation*, 'a vocation,' Cot. — L. *uocātiōnem*, acc. of *uocātio*, a bidding, invitation ; cf. *uocātus*, pp. of *uocāre*, to call, bid ; see **Vocable**. Der. *vocat-ive*, Merry Wives, iv. 1. 53, lit. the calling case, from L. *uocātiuus*, the vocative case.

VOCIFERATION, a loud calling, noisy outcry. (F.—L.) 'Of *Vociferation*;' Sir T. Elyot, Castel of Helth, b. ii. c. 35 (misprinted 25 in ed. 1561). — MF. *vociferation*, 'vociferation;' Cot. — L. *uōciferātiōnem*, acc. of *uōciferātio*, a loud outcry ; cf. *uōciferātus*, pp. of *uōciferāre*, commonly *uōciferārī*, to lift up the voice ; lit. 'to bear the voice afar.' — L. *uōci-*, for *uox*, the voice ; and *fer-re*, to bear, cognate with E. **Bear**. See **Voice**. Der. *vociferate*, from L. pp. *uōciferātus* ; *vocifer-ous*, *-ly*.

VODKA, a Russian strong liquor. (Russ.) Russ. *vodka*, brandy ; a dimin. of *voda*, water, which is cognate with E. *water* ; see **Water**.

VOGUE, mode, fashion, practice. (F.—Ital.—Teut.) We now say to be *in vogue*, i. e. in fashion. Formerly *vogue* meant sway, currency, prevalent use, power, or authority. 'The predominant constellations, which have the *vogue*;' Howell, Foreign Travel, sect. 6, ed. Arber, p. 34. 'Considering these sermons bore so great a *vogue* among the papists;' Strype, Eccl. Mem., 1 Mary, an. 1553. — F. *vogue*, 'vogue, sway, swindge, authority, power ; a cleer passage, as of a ship in a broad sea;' Cot. β. The orig. sense is 'the swaying motion of a ship,' hence its sway, swing, drift, or course ; or else the sway or stroke of an oar. It is the verbal sb. of F. *voguer*, 'to saile forth, set saile;' Cot. — Ital. *voga*, 'the stroke of an oare in the water when one roweth,' Florio ; verbal sb. of *vogare*, 'to rowe in a gallie or any bote,' id. (So also Span. *boga*, the act of rowing ; *estar en boga*, to be in vogue.) Of Teut. origin. — G. *wogen*, to fluctuate, be in motion ; MHG. *wāgen*. — MHG. *wāg*, OHG. *wāc*, a wave (G. *woge*). ╋AS. *wǣg*, Goth. *wēgs*, a wave ; Teut. type **wǣgoz*, m. ; from **wǣg*, 3rd stem of Teut. **wegan*, to move. See **Weigh**. ¶ Thus the idea of *vogue* goes back to that of 'movement,' as exhibited in the 'wave' or swaying of the sea.

VOICE, sound from the mouth, utterance, language. (F.—L.) The spelling with *ce* (for *s*) is adopted to keep the hard sound of *s*. ME. *vois*, *voys*, King Alisaunder, 3864. — OF. *vois* (Burguy), later *voix*, 'a voice, sound;' Cot. — L. *uōcem*, acc. of *uōx*, a voice. — √WEQ, to resound, speak ; cf. Skt. *vākya-m*, speech, also *vacha-s*, speech, cognate with Gk. *ἔπos*, a word. Brugmann, i. § 678. Der. *voice*, verb, Timon, iv. 3. 81 ; *voice-less*. From L. *uox* (stem *uōc-*) or from L. *uocāre* (stem *uoc-*) we also have *voc-al*, *voc-able*, *voc-at-ion*, *voci-fer-at-ion*, *ad-voc-ate*, *a-voc-at-ion*, *ad-vow-son*, *a-vouch*, *con-voc-at-ion*, *con-voke*, *equi-voc-al*, *e-voke*, *in-voc-ate*, *in-voke*, *ir-re-voc-able*, *pro-voke*, *re-voke*, *uni-voc-al*, *vouch*, *vouch-safe*, *vow-el*. And see *ep-ic*.

VOID, empty, unoccupied, unsubstantial. (F.—L.) ME. *voide*, Chaucer, tr. of Boethius, b. ii. pr. 5, l. 127. — OF. *voide* (Burguy), MF. *vuide*, 'void, empty,' Cot. Mod. F. *vide*. The OF. *voide* is a fem. form ; masc. *void*, *vuit*. Due to a supposed Romance **voc-i-tus*, related to L. *uac-uus*, empty, void. Körting, § 10280. **Der.** *void*, verb, ME. *voiden*, to empty, King Alisaunder, 373, from OF. *voider*, MF. *vuider*, 'to void,' Cot. Also *void-able*, *void-ance* (cf. MF. *vuidange*, 'a voidnesse,' Cot.) ; *void-ness*; *a-void*.

VOLANT, flying, nimble. (F.—L.) Rare. 'In manner of a star *volant* in the air ;' Holland, tr. of Plutarch, p. 525 (R.).—F. *volant*, pres. part. of *voler*, ' to flye,' Cot.—L. *uolāre*, to fly. Formed from the adj. **uolus*, flying, occurring only in *uēli-uolus*, flying on sails. Allied to Skt. *garut*, a wing, *garuḍa-*, a mythical bird ; Brugmann, i. § 663. **Der.** *vol-at-ile*, Ben Jonson, Alchemist, Act ii. sc. 1 (Subtle), from F. *volatil*, 'flying,' Cot., from L. *uolātilis*, flying, from *uolātus*, flight, which from *uolātus*, pp. of *uolāre*. Hence *volatile-ness*, *volatil-it-y*, *volatil-ise*, *volatil-is-at-ion*. Also *volley*, q. v.

VOLAPÜK, a kind of world-speech. (E.) An artificial language for international speech, invented about 1879 by J. M. Schleyer, of Constance, Baden. Properly written *Volupük*. This form was suggested by E. *world* (here turned into *vola*) and E. *speak* or *speech* (here turned into *pük*).

VOLCANO, a burning mountain. (Ital.—L.) 'A *vulcano* or *volcano*;' Skinner, ed. 1691. Spelt *volcan*, J. Frampton, Joyfull Newes, fol. 31 (1577). Borrowed from Italian, because the chief burning mountain known to sailors was that of Ætna.—Ital. *volcano*, 'a hill that continually burneth ;' Florio.—L. *Volcānum*, *Vulcānum*, acc. of *Volcānus* or *Vulcānus*, Vulcan, the god of fire, hence fire. β. The true form is *Volcānus* (with *o*). Allied to Skt. *ulkā*, a fire-brand, fire falling from heaven, a meteor. **Der.** *volcan-ic*; and see *vulcan-ise*.

VOLE, a field-mouse. (Scand.) A word that reached us from the Orkney Islands. A shortened form of *vole-mouse*; see Jamieson, who quotes from the Edin. Maga., July, 1819, p. 505 ; and from Barry's Orkney, p. 314 (ed. 1805), who says:—'*with us* it has the name of the *vole-mouse*.' So also *vole-mouse* is given in Edmondston's Shetland and Orkney Words. Of Norse origin ; from an unrecorded (prob. colloquial) Norw. **vollmus*, field-mouse; for the word is known in Iceland in the colloquial form *vallarmús* (E. Magnusson). The former element is the Norw. *voll*, Swed. *vall*, Icel. *völlr*, a plain, field ; which is cognate with E. *wold*; see **Wold**. There are many compounds with Norw. *voll* (and the like); cf. Norw. *voll-gras*, field-grass, *voll-höy*, meadow-hay, Icel. *vallar-garðr*, a paddock-fence, *vall-humall*, milfoil ; Swed. *vall-hund*, a shepherd's dog; Swed. dial. *vall-gås*, wild goose.

VOLITION, the exercise of the will. (F.—L.) 'Consequent to the mere internal *volition* ;' Bp. Taylor, Rule of Conscience, b. iv. c. i.—F. *volition*, found in the 16th century (Hatzfeld); we find cognate terms in Span. *volicion*, Ital. *volizione*, volition. All these answer to a Late L. *volitiōnem*, acc. of **volitio*, volition; a word not recorded by Ducange, but prob. a term of the schools. It is a pure coinage, from L. *uol-o*, I wish ; of which the infinitive is *uelle*; see **Voluntary**.

VOLLEY, a flight of shot, the discharge of many fire-arms at once. (F.—L.) In Hamlet, v. 2. 363. See Nares.—F. *volée*, 'a flight, or flying, also a whole flight of birds ;' Cot. [Cf. Ital. *volata*, a flight, volley.]—L. *uolāta*, orig. fem. of *uolātus*, pp. of *uolāre*, to fly; see **Volant**.

VOLT, a bound, a leap; the same as **Vault** (2), q. v.

VOLTAIC, originated by Volta. (Ital.) Applied to *Voltaic* electricity, or galvanism ; the *Voltaic* pile or battery, first set up about 1800, was discovered by Alessandro Volta, of Como, an experimental philosopher, born 1745, died March 6, 1826 ; see Haydn, Dict. of Dates, and Hole, Brief Biograph. Dict. **Der.** (from *Volta*) *volt*, a unit of electromotive force.

VOLUBLE, flowing smoothly, fluent in speech. (F.—L.) In Shak. Comedy of Errors, ii. 1. 92.—F. *voluble*, 'voluble, easily rolled, turned, or tumbled ; hence, fickle, . . glib ;' Cot.—L. *uolūbilem*, acc. of *uolūbilis*, easily turned about ; formed with suffix *-bilis* from *uolū-*, as seen in *uolūtus*, pp. of *uoluere*, to roll, turn about.+Goth. *walwjan*, to roll; Gk. εἰλύειν, to roll ; from a base **welu-* (**wolu-*). The shorter base WEL occurs in Lithuan. *welti*, to full, Russ. *valit(e)*, to roll, Skt. *val*, to move to and fro ; cf. AS. *weallan*, to boil, Icel. *valr*, round, Gk. ἕλιξ, a spiral, ἐλ-ίσσειν, to turn round. See **Helix**. **Der.** *volubl-y*, *volubil-i-ty*; also (from L. *uoluere*), *vault* (1), *vault* (2), *vol-ume*, *vol-ute*, *circum-volve*, *con-volv-ul-us*, *con-vol-ut-ion*, *de-volve*, *e-volve*, *e-volu-t-ion*, *in-volve*, *in-volu-t-ion*, *in-vol-ute*, *re-volt*, *re-volu-t-ion*, *re-volve*. From the same root are *valve*, *wale*, *helix*.

VOLUME, a roll, a book, tome. (F.—L.) ME. *volume*, Chaucer, C. T. 6263 (D 681).—F. *volume*, 'a volume, tome, book ;' Cot.—L. *uolūmen*, a roll, scroll ; hence, a book written on a parchment roll.—L. *uolū-*, as seen in *uolū-tus*, pp. of *uoluere*, to roll. See **Voluble**. **Der.** *volum-ed*; *volumin-ous*, Milton, P. R. iv. 384, from L. *uolūminōsus*, full of rolls or folds, from *uolūmin-*, decl. stem of *uolūmen*; *volumin-ous-ly*.

VOLUNTARY, willing, acting by choice. (F.—L.) Spelt *voluntarie* in Levins, ed. 1570.—MF. *voluntaire*, also spelt *volontaire*, 'voluntary, willing, free, of his owne accorde ;' Cot.—L. *uoluntārius*, voluntary.—L. *uoluntās*, free will. Formed, with suffix *-tās*, from a present participial stem **uolunt-*, a variant of *uolent-*, from *uolens*, willing, from *uolo*, I will ; infin. *uelle*.+Lithuan. *weliti*, Goth. *wiljan*; Skt. *vṛ*, to select, choose. Brugmann, ii. §§ 102, 493. See **Will**. **Der.** *voluntari-ly*, *voluntari-ness* ; also *volunteer*, Drayton, Miseries of Qu. Margaret, st. 177, from F. *voluntaire* (used as a sb.), 'a voluntary, one that serves without pay or compulsion,' Cot.; hence *volunteer*, verb. And see *vol-up-tu-ous*, *vol-it-ion*; *bene-volent*, *male-volent*.

VOLUPTUOUS, sensual, given up to pleasure. (F.—L.) ME. *voluptuous*, Chaucer, Troil. iv. 1573. [Gower has *voluptuosite*, sb., C. A. iii. 280; bk. viii. 156.]—F. *voluptuéux*, 'voluptuous,' Cot. —L. *uoluptuōsus*, full of pleasure.—L. *uoluptu-*, akin to *uoluptās*, pleasure.—L. *uolup*, *uolupe*, adv., agreeably.—L. *uol-o*, I wish ; *uelle*, to wish ; see **Voluntary**. Cf. Gk. ἐλπίς, hope. **Der.** *voluptuous-ly*, *-ness* (Palsgrave) ; *volup-tu-ar-y*, from L. *uoluptuārius*, *uoluptārius*, devoted to pleasure. Hence prob. the vulgar *goluptious*.

VOLUTE, a spiral scroll on a capital. (F.—L.) Spelt *voluta* in Phillips, which is the L. form.—F. *volute*, 'the rolling shell of a snail; also, the writhen circle that hangs over the chapter of a pillar ;' Cot.—L. *uolūta*, a volute (Vitruvius). Orig. fem. of *uolūtus*, pp. of *uoluere*, to roll ; see **Voluble**. **Der.** *volut-ed*.

VOMIT, matter rejected by, and thrown up from the stomach. (L.) ME. *vomite*, *vomyte*, sb. ; Prompt. Parv. Palsgrave has *vomyt*, verb.—L. *uomitus*, a vomiting, vomit; whence *uomitāre*, to vomit often.—L. *uomitus*, pp. of *uomere*, to vomit.+Gk. ἐμεῖν, to vomit; Skt. *vam*, to vomit, spit out; Lithuan. *wemti*.—√WEM, to spit out; Fick, i. 769. **Der.** *vomit*, vb. ; *vomit-or-y*, causing to vomit. And see *em-et-ic*.

VORACITY, eagerness to devour. (F.—L.) In Cotgrave.—F. *voracité*, 'voracity ;' Cot.—L. *uorācitātem*, acc. of *uorācitās*, hungriness.—L. *uorāci-*, decl. stem of *uorax*, greedy to devour.—L. *uor-āre*, to devour.—L. *-uorus*, adj., devouring ; only in compounds, such as *carni-uorus*, flesh-devouring. β. The L. *-uorus* stands for **guorus*, as shown by the allied Skt. *-gara-*, devouring, as seen in *aja-gara-*, a boa constrictor, lit. 'goat-devouring,' from *aja-*, a goat. Cf. also Gk. βορός, gluttonous, βορά, meat, βιβρώσκειν, to devour.—√GwER, to swallow down. Brugmann, i. § 653. **Der.** *voraci-ous*, from L. *uorāci-*, decl. stem of *uorax*, greedy to devour ; *voraci-ous-ly*. From the same root are *gramini-vorous*, *carni-vorous*, *omni-vorous*, &c., also *de-vour*.

VORTEX, a whirlpool, whirlwind. (L.) In Phillips, ed. 1706. —L. *uortex* (also *uertex*), a whirlpool, whirl, eddy.—L. *uertere*, to turn, whirl; see **Verse**. The pl. is *vortices*, as in Latin.

VOTE, an ardent wish, the expression of a decided wish or opinion, expressed decision. (L.) In Selden, Table-talk, Bishops in the Parliament, § 4.—L. *uōtum*, a wish ; orig. a vow.—L. *uōtum*, neut. of *uōtus*, pp. of *uouere*, to vow ; see **Vow**. **Der.** *vot-ive*, from L. *uōtiuus*, promised by a vow ; *votive-ly*. Also *vot-ar-y*, a coined word, L. L. L. ii. 37 ; *vot-ar-ess*, Pericles, iv. prol. 4 ; *vot-ress*, Mids. Nt. Dr. ii. 1. 123 ; *vot-ar-ist*, Timon, iv. 3. 27.

VOUCH, to warrant, attest, affirm strongly. (F.—L.) ME. *vouchen*, Gower, C. A. ii. 24 ; bk. iv. 668.—MF. *voucher*, 'to vouch, cite, pray in aid or call unto aid, in a suit,' Cot. Marked by Cotgrave as a Norman word ; cf. Norm. dial. *vocher*, to call (Moisy).—L. *uocāre*, to call, call upon, summon. See **Vocable**. **Der.** *vouch-er*; *vouch-safe*, q. v.

VOUCHSAFE, to vouch or warrant safe, sanction or allow without danger, condescend to grant. (F.—L.) Merely due to the phr. *vouch safe*, i. e. vouch or warrant as safe, guarantee, grant. The two words were run together into one. ME. *vouchen safe*, or *saue*. 'The kyng *vouches* it *saue* ;' Rob. of Brunne, tr. of Langtoft, p. 260. 'Vowche *sauf* þat his sone hire wedde ;' Will. of Palerne, 1449 ; '*sauf* wol I *fouche*,' id. 4152. See **Vouch** and **Safe**.

VOUSSOIR, a stone forming part of an arch, the key-stone being the central one. (F.—L.) F. *voussoir*, OF. *volsoir*, a stone for an arch (Godefroy).—Late L. type **volsōrium*; from **volsum*, equivalent to L. *uolūtum*, neut. pp. of *uoluere*, to roll. See **Volute**.

VOW, a solemn promise. (F.—L.) ME. *vow*, *vou* ; pl. *vowes*, P. Plowman, B. prol. 71. [The ME. *avow* is commoner ; it is a compound word, with prefix *a-* (<L. *ad*), but is frequently misprinted *a vow* ; Tyrwhitt rightly has 'min *avow*,' Chaucer, C. T. 2239 (A 2237) ; 'this *avow*,' id. 2416 (A 2414).]—OF. *vou*, *vo*, *veu* (mod. F. *vœu*), a vow.—L. *uōtum*, a vow, lit. 'a thing vowed,' neut. of *uōtus*, pp. of *uouere*, to promise, to vow. (N.B. Another *avow* answers to F. *avouer*, L. *aduocāre*, and is a doublet of *avouch*.) **Der.** *vow*, verb, ME. *vowen*, Prompt. Parv. Also (from L. *uōtum*), *vote*, q.v.

VOWEL, a simple vocal sound ; the letter representing it. (F. — L.) Spelt *vowell* in Levins, ed. 1570 ; and in Palsgrave, b. i. c. 2. — OF. *vouel, voiel* ; F. *voyelle*, 'a vowell ;' Cot. — L. *uŏcālem*, acc. of *uŏcālis* (sc. *littera*), a vowel. Fem. of *uŏcālis*, adj. sounding, vocal. — L. *uŏc-*, stem of *uŏx*, a voice ; see **Vocal, Voice.**

VOYAGE, a journey, passage by water. (F.—L.) ME. *viage*, Chaucer, C. T. 4679, 4720 (B 259, 300) ; *veiage*, Rob. of Glouc. p. 200, l. 4112. The later form *voyage* (as in Caxton, Siege of Troy, fol. 120) answers to the 15th cent. spelling of the F. word. — AF. *veiage* ; OF. *voiage*, later *voyage*, 'voyage ;' Cot. — L. *uiāticum*, provisions for a journey, money or other requisites for a journey ; whence also Ital. *viaggio*, Span. *viage*, Prov. *viatge* ; see Ducange. — L. *uiāticus*, belonging to a journey. — L. *uia*, a way, journey. Der. *voyage*, verb, from F. *voyager*, 'to travell, goe a voyage,' Cot. ; *voyag-er*. Also (from L. *uia*), *via-duct*, and related words given under **Viaduct.**

VULCANISE, to combine caoutchouc with sulphur, by heat. (F.—L.) Modern ; F. *vulcaniser* (1878). Formed with suffix *-ise* (F. *-iser*, from Gk. *-ιζειν*) from L. *Vulcān-us*, god of fire, hence fire ; see **Volcano.** Der. *vulcan-ite*, vulcanised caoutchouc.

VULGAR, used by the common people, native, common, mean, rude. (F.—L.) In Cor. i. 1. 219. — F. *vulgaire*, 'vulgar, common ;' Cot. — L. *uulgāris*, vulgar. — L. *uulgus*, the common people ; also spelt *uolgus*. The lit. sense is 'a throng, a crowd ;' allied to Skt. *varga-s*, a troop ; OIrish *folc*, abundance (Stokes) ; W. *gwala*, fulness ; Bret. *gwalch*, repletion. Stokes-Fick, p. 286. Der. *vulgar*, sb., L. L. L. i. 2. 51, from F. *vulgaire*, sb., Cot. ; *vulgar-ly*, *vulgar-ise*, *vulgar-ism*, *vulgar-i-ty*. Also *vulg-ate*, the E. name for the Latin version of the Bible known as the *Editio Vulgata* (see publications of the Parker Society, &c.) ; where *uulgāta* is the fem. of *uulgātus*, pp. of *uulgāre*, to make public, to publish.

VULNERABLE, liable to injury. (L.) In Macb. v. 8. 11. — L. *uulnerābilis*, wounding, likely to injure ; but also (taken in the pass. sense) vulnerable (in late Latin). — L. *uulnerāre*, to wound. — L. *uulner-*, stem of *uulnus*, a wound ; OL. *uolnus*. Allied to *uellere* (pt. t. *uul-sī*), to pluck, pull, tear. + Gk. οὐλή, W. *gweli*, Corn. *goly*, Skt. *vraṇa-*, a wound. Stokes-Fick, p. 285. Der. *vulner-ar-y*, from F. *vulneraire*, 'vulnerary, healing wounds,' Cot., from L. *uulnerārius*, suitable for wounds. And see *vul-ture.*

VULPINE, fox-like, cunning. (F.—L.) 'The slyness of a *vulpine* craft ;' Feltham, pt. i. Res. 10. Blount, ed. 1674, has : '*Vulpinate*, to play the fox.' — MF. *vulpin*, 'fox-like.' Cot. — L. *uulpīnus*, fox-like. — L. *uulp-*, base of *uulpes*, a fox ; with suffix *-īnus.* Allied to **Wolf** (see Darbishire, Reliquiæ Philologicæ, p. 92).

VULTURE, a large bird of prey. (L.) In Macb. iv. 3. 74. ME. *vultur*, Wyclif, Job, xxviii. 7, later version. — L. *uultur*, a vulture ; OL. *uolturus* ; lit. 'a plucker' or 'tearer.' — L. *uul-* (*uol-*), as seen in *uul-sī*, pt. t. of *uellere*, to pluck ; with suffix *-tur* denoting the agent. See **Vulnerable.** Der. *vultur-ine*, from L. *uulturīnus*, vulture-like.

WA–WE

WABBLE, WOBBLE, to reel, move unsteadily. (E.) '*Wabble*, to vacillate, reel, waver ;' Brockett. A voiced form of **wapple*, equivalent to prov. E. *wapper*, 'to move tremulously, Somerset ;' Halliwell. Both *wabble* and *wapper* are frequentatives of *wap* in the sense 'to flutter, beat the wings' (Halliwell), whence also *wapping*, quaking, used by Batman, 1582 (id.). There are several verbs which take the form *wap*, but the one now under consideration is properly *whap*, a by-form of ME. *quappen*, to palpitate ; see **Quaver.** Cf. *quabbe*, a bog, quagmire (Halliwell). So also Low G. *wabbeln* or *quabbeln*, to wabble ; EFries. *wabbeln, kwabbeln*, to wabble ; Swed. dial. *vabbla*, to move round to and fro in the mouth, which is given as a sense of *wobble* in the E. D. D. Cf. AS. *wapol*, foam. See **Whap.**

WACKE, a kind of soft rock. (G.) Modern ; geological. — G. *wacke*, 'a sort of stone, consisting of quartz, sand, and mica ;' Flügel. MHG. *wacke*, OHG. *waggo*, a kind of flint.

WAD, a small bundle of stuff, a little mass of tow, &c. (Scand.) Nares (ed. Halliwell) cites 'a *wadde* of hay,' a bundle of hay, from the poet Taylor's Works, 1630. 'Make it [lupines] into *wads* or bottles ;' Holland, tr. of Pliny, b. xvii. c. 9 ; cf. the phrase 'a *bottle* of hay.' — Swed. *vadd*, wadding ; MSwed. *wad*, clothing, cloth, stuff (Ihre) ; Icel. *vaðr*, stuff, only in the comp. *vaðmāl*, a plain woollen stuff, wadmal ; cf. MSwed. *wadmal*, Dan. *vadmel*. Cf. G. *watte*, wadding, wad, a large fishing-net ; *watten*, to dress cloth, to wad ; also *wat*, cloth (Flügel). Hence Dan. *vat*, F. *ouate*, wadding. β. The

stuff called *wadmal* was formerly well known in England ; in Arnold's Chronicle (repr. 1811), p. 236, we find, among imports, notice of ' Rollys of *wadmoll*' and 'curse [coarse] *wadmoll*.' 'Pann' grisei qui voca[n]tur *wadmal* ;' (1326), Wardrobe Acc. 20 Edw. II. 26. 3. Q. R. Halliwell gives : '*Wadmal*, a very thick coarse kind of woollen cloth ; coarse tow used by doctors for cattle is also so called.' It may be that our *wad* is nothing but a shortened form of *wadmal* in the sense of coarse tow, or coarse stuff ; it brings us, however, ultimately, to the same source. [The Icel. *vaðr* properly means 'a fishing-line,' just as the G. *watte* means a fishing-net.] The Icel. *vaðmāl* (from *māl*, a measure = E. *meal* (2)) is for *vāðmāl* ; from Icel. *vāð, vōð, voð*, a piece of stuff, cloth as it leaves the loom, which is again allied to E. *weed*, a garment, as used in the phr. 'a widow's *weeds.*' γ. From Teut. base **wǣd*, 3rd grade of Teut. root WED, as in Goth. *ga-widan*, OHG. *wetan*, to bind together. This base accounts for *wad*, stuff wound together < Icel. *vāð*, stuff bound or woven together, whilst the 2nd grade **wad* accounts for G. *watte*, a fishing-net (because twined together), and Icel. *vaðr*, a fishing-line (because twisted together). See further under **Weed** (2). δ. The Russ. *vata*, F. *ouate*, wadding, Span. *huata*, Ital. *ovata*, may be of Teut. origin, the last form being due to an attempt to give it a sense from Ital. *ovo*, an egg. It is quite unnecessary to suppose (as Diez, not very confidently, suggests) that the whole set of words allied to *wad* are derived from the L. *ōuum*, an egg. Der. *wadd-ing* ; *wad-mal*, as above. (The prov. E. *woadmel* shows that the OIcel. form was *vāðmāl*.)

WADDLE, to walk with short steps and unwieldy gait. (E.) In Shak. Romeo, i. 3. 37. The frequentative of **Wade**, q. v. Der. *waddl-er.*

WADE, to walk slowly, esp. through water. (E.) ME. *waden*, Chaucer, C. T. 9558 (E 1684). AS. *wadan*, pt. t. *wōd*, to wade, trudge, go ; '*wadan* ofer wealdas,' to trudge over the wolds, Genesis, ed. Grein, 2886 ; see Grein, ii. 636. + Du. *waden*, to wade, ford ; Icel. *vaða*, strong verb, pt. t. *vōð*, to wade, to rush through, whence *vað*, sb., a ford ; Dan. *vade* ; Swed. *vada* ; OHG. *watan*, pt. t. *wuot* ; the mod. G. *waten* is only a weak verb. β. All from the Teut. base WAD, to go, press through, make one's way ; Idg. √WADH, to go ; whence also L. *uādere*, to go, *uadum*, a ford. Der. *wadd-le*, q. v. ; *wad-er* ; and compare (from L. *uādere*) *e-vade*, *in-vade*, *per-vade.*

WADI, WADY, a water-course, river. (Arab.) From Arab. *wādī*, a water-course, channel, river-bed ; Rich. Dict., p. 1624.

WADMAL, WADMALL; see under **Wad.**

WAFER, a thin small cake, usually round, a thin leaf of paste. (F.—OLow G.) ME. *wafre*, pl. *wafres*, Chaucer, C. T. 3379 ; P. Plowman, B. xiii. 271. We find Low L. *gafras*, glossed by *wafurs*, in John de Garlande ; Wright's Voc. i. 126, l. 14. — AF. *wafre*, Liber Custum. p. 473 ; OF. *waufre*, mod. F. *gaufre*, a wafer. The form *waufre* occurs in a quotation, dated 1433, given by Roquefort in his Supplement, s. v. *Audier* ; cf. *waufret* in Godefroy. (The more usual OF. form was *gaufre*, or *goffre*, in which *g* is substituted for the orig. *w*.) In this quotation we have mention of *un fer a waufres*, an iron on which to bake wafers. Cf. Walloon *wâfe*, *wauffe*, a wafer. β. The word is of Low G. origin ; Hexham gives MDu. *waeffel*, 'a wafer ;' *waeffel-yser*, 'a wafer-yron to bake wafers in,' of which *fer a waufres* is a translation ; mod. Du. *wafel*, a wafer, *wafel-ijzer*, a wafer-iron. So also Low G. *wafeln*, pl. wafers ; *wafel-isern*, a wafer-iron. Webster's Dict. gives *waffle* and *waffle-iron* as E. words ; they are obviously borrowed from Dutch immediately, and seem to be modern. Cf. also G. *waffel*, a wafer, *waffel-eisen*, a wafer-iron ; Dan. *vaffel*, Swed. *våffla* ; from Low G. *wafel*. γ. The *wafer* (dotted regularly with small indentations) was named from its resemblance to a piece of honey-comb or cake of wax in a bee-hive ; from a Low G. form allied to G. *wabe*, a honey-comb, cake of wax, a derivative from the Teut. base **web* (2nd grade **wab*), to weave, Fick, iii. 289 ; the comb constructed by the bees being, as it were, *woven* together. The *f* appears in Icel. *vaf*, a weft, Swed. *väf*, a web, AS. *wefan*, to weave ; see **Weave.** The spelling with *ae* (in Hexham) of the MDu. word suggests a derivation from **wǣb*, the 3rd grade of the root. The form *waeffel* is a diminutive. Der. *wafer*, verb ; *wafer-er*, a wafer-seller, Chaucer, C. T. 12413 (C 479) ; ME. *wafr-estre*, a female wafer-seller, P. Plowman, B. v. 641.

WAFT, to bear along through air or water. (E.) 'Neither was it thought that they should get any passage at all, till the ships at *Middleborough* were returned, . . . by the force whereof they might be the more strongly *wafted* ouer ;' Hakluyt's Voyages, i. 175. Shak. has it in several senses ; (1) to beckon, as by a wave of the hand, Merch. Ven. v. 11 ; Timon, i. 1. 70 ; (2) to turn quickly, Wint. Tale, i. 2. 372 ; (3) to carry or send over the sea, K. John, ii. 73, 2 Hen. VI, iv. 1. 114, 116 ; 3 Hen. VI, iii. 3. 253 ; v. 7. 41. He also has *waftage*, passage by water, Com. Errors, iv. 1. 95 ; *wafture* (old edd. *wafter*), the waving of the hand, a gesture, Jul. Cæs. ii. 1. 246. We must also note, that Shak. has *waft* both for the pt. t. and pp. ; see

Merch. Ven. v. 11; K. John, ii. 73. [Rich. cites *waft* as a pt. t., occurring in Gamelyn, 785, but the best MSS. have *fast*; so that this is nothing to the point.] β. The word *waft* is not old, and does not occur in ME.; it seems to be nothing but a variant of *wave*, used as a verb, formed by taking the pp. and pt. t. *waved* (shortened to *waft* by rapid pronunciation), as the infinitive mood of a new verb. This is by no means an isolated case; by precisely the same process we have mod. E. *hoist*, due to *hoised*, pp. of Tudor Eng. *hoise*, and mod. E. *graft*, due to *graffed*, pp. of Tudor Eng. *graff*; while Spenser actually writes *waift* and *weft* instead of **Waif**, q. v. By way of proof, we should notice the exact equivalence of *waved* and *waft* in the following passages. 'Yet towardes night a great sort [number of people] came doune to the water-side, and *waued* us on shoare [beckoned us ashore] with a white flag;' Hakluyt's Voyages, vol. ii. pt. ii. p. 34 (also on p. 33). 'And *waft* [beckoned] her love To come again to Carthage;' Merch. Ven. v. 11. And again, we must particularly note Lowland Sc. *waff*, to wave, shake, fluctuate, and as a sb., a hasty motion, the act of waving, a signal made by waving (Jamieson); this is merely the Northern form of *wave*. 'And therfore schall y *waffe* it away;' York Plays, p. 301. In Gawain Douglas's translation of Virgil (Æneid, i. 319), we have, in the edition of 1839, 'With wynd *waving* hir haris lowsit of tres,' where another edition (cited by Wedgwood) has *waffing*. So also, in Barbour's Bruce, ix. 245, xi. 193, 513, we have the forms *vafand*, *vaffand*, *wawand*, all meaning 'waving,' with reference to banners waving in the wind. γ. We thus see that *waft* is due to *waft* or *waved*, pp. and pt. t. of *waff* or *wave*; cf. AS. *wafian*, to wave with the hand, and see further under **Wave** (1). Der. *waft-age*, *waft-ure*, as above; *waft*, sb., *waft-er*.

WAG, to move from side to side, shake to and fro. (Scand.) ME. *waggen*, introduced (probably) as a Northern word in Chaucer, C. T. 4037 (A 4039); cf. P. Plowman, B. viii. 31, xvi. 41. Earlier, in Havelok, 89.—MSwed. *wagga*, to wag, fluctuate; whence *wagga*, a cradle, *wagga*, to rock a cradle (Ihre); Swed. *vagga*, a cradle; or as verb, to rock a cradle; Norw. *vagga*, to wag. Cf. Icel. *vagga*, a cradle; Dan. *vugge*, a cradle, also, to rock a cradle; AS. *wecgan*, to wag, OHG. *weggen*, Goth. *wagjan*. Closely allied to AS. *wagian*, to move, vacillate, rock (Grein, ii. 637), which became ME. *wawen*, and could not have given the mod. form *wag*. In Wyclif, Luke, vii. 25, the later version has '*waggid* with the wynd,' where the earlier version has *wawid*. β. The AS. *wagian* is a secondary weak verb, from the strong verb *wegan* (pt. t. *wæg*, pp. *wegen*), to bear, move, carry (*weigh*), Grein, ii. 655; and similarly the MSwed. *wagga* is from the 2nd grade *wag* of Teut. *wegan-*, cognate with L. *ueh-ere*, to carry, from Idg. √WEGH, to carry; see **Weigh**, **Waggon**. Der. *wag*, sb., a droll fellow, L. L. L. v. 2. 108, as to which Wedgwood plausibly suggests that it is an abbreviation for *wag-halter*, once a common term for a rogue or gallows-bird, one who is likely to *wag in a halter* (or rather, to *wag* or *sway a halter*), see Nares; and cf. 'little young *wags* . . these are lackies;' Holinshed, Descr. of Ireland, ed. 1808, p. 68; also 'Oh! thou crafty *wag-string*!' Heywood, Eng. Traveller, Act iv (near end); 'a *wag-halter* page,' Ford, The Fancies, A. i. sc. 2. Hence *wagg-ish*, *wagg-ish-ly*, *wagg-er-y* (formed like *knav-er-y*). Also *wagg-le*, q. v.; *wag-tail*, q. v.; *wag-moire*, a quagmire, Spenser, Shep. Kal. Sept. 130. And see *wedge*.

WAGE, a gage, pledge, stake, pay for service; pl. **Wages**, pay for service. (F.—Teut.) ME. *wage*, usually in the sense of pay, Rob. of Brunne, p. 319, l. 19; for which the pl. *wages* occurs only two lines above. '*Wage*, or hyre, Stipendium, salarium;' Prompt. Parv. We now usually employ the word in the plural.—AF. *wage*, a prize, Langtoft, i. 222; *wages*, pl., Fr. Chron. of London, p. 83; OF. *wage*, also *gage*, a gage, pledge, guarantee (Burguy); hence it came to mean a stipulated payment. The change from initial *w* to *gu* (and even, as here, to *g*) is not uncommon in OF. A verbal sb. from OF. *wager*, *gager*, *gagier*, to pledge; cf. Walloon *wager*, to pledge. —Low L. *wadiāre*, to pledge.—Low L. *uadium*, a pledge.—Goth. *wadi*, a pledge; whence *gawadjōn*, to pledge. β. The Goth. *wadi* is cognate with AS. *wedd*, a pledge; see **Wed** (1). Der. *wage*, verb, ME. *wagen*, to engage or go bail, P. Plowman, B. iv. 97, from OF. *wager*, verb, as above. Also *wag-er*, q. v.; *en-gage*, q. v. Doublet, *gage* (1). ☞ To *wage war* was formerly to *declare* war, *engage* in it, not merely to *carry* it on, as now; cf. the phr. '*wager* of battle;' see Wedgwood.

WAGER, a pledge, bet, something staked upon a chance. (F.—Teut.) ME. *wageour*, Assembly of Ladies, st. 55, l. 383; spelt *waiour*, Polit. Songs, ed. Wright, p. 218, l. 19, in a song dated 1308. —OF. *wageure*, orig. form of OF. *gageure*, 'a wager,' Cot.—Low L. *wadiātūra*, sb. formed from the pp. of *wadiāre*, to pledge, also to wager (as shown in Ducange); see **Wage**. Der. *wager*, verb, Haml. iv. 7. 135; *wager-er*.

WAGGLE, to wag frequently. (Scand.) Shak. has *waggling*, Much Ado, ii. 1. 119. The frequentative of **Wag**, q. v. Another frequentative form (with *-er* instead of *-el* or *-le*) appears in ME. *wageren*, to tremble, in Wyclif, Eccles. xii. 3, early version; the later version has *tremble*. Cf. Swed. dial. *vagla*, to totter; also G. *wackeln* (whence Swed. *vackla*); Pomeran. *waggeln*, to waggle; Low G. *wigel-wageln*, to wiggle-waggle; Du. *waggelen*, to totter.

WAGON, WAGGON, a wain, a vehicle for goods. (Du.) The spelling with double *g* merely serves to show that the vowel *a* is short. We find the spelling *waggon* in Romeo. i. 4. 59 (ed. 1623); *wagon*, Spenser, F. Q. i. 5. 28. The word is not very old, and not E., being borrowed from Dutch. (The E. form is *wain*.) 'They trussed all their harnes in *waganes*;' Berners, tr. of Froissart, vol. i. c. 62 (R.); 'charyotts or *waggans*;' Cavendish, Life of Wolsey, p. 88.—Du. *wagen*, 'a wagon, or a waine,' Hexham.+AS. *wægn*, a wain; see **Wain**. ☞ The mod. F. *wagon* is borrowed from English. Doublet, *wain*. Der. *waggon-er*, Romeo, i. 4. 64.

WAGTAIL, the name of a bird. (Hybrid; Scand. *and* E.) In King Lear, ii. 2. 73; and in Palsgrave. Formerly called a *wag-start* (*start* meaning *tail*); ME. *wagstyrt*, Voc. 763. 2. From **Wag** and **Tail**. Cf. Swed. *vippstjert*, a wagstart or wagtail; from *vippa*, to wag.

WAIF, anything found astray without an owner. (F.—Scand.) ME. *waif*, *weif*; the pl. is *wayues* or *weyues* (with *u* = *v*), P. Plowman, B. prol. 94; C. i. 92. A Norman-French law-term.—AF. *wayf*, Lib. Custumarum, 434, 775; OF. *waif*, later *gaif*, pl. *waives*, *gaives*. Godefroy gives *gaif*, a thing lost and not claimed; *choses gaives*, things lost and not claimed; also *wayve*, a waif, which is a feminine form, evolved from a pl. form *wayves*, of which the sing. would be *wayf* or *waif*. Cotgrave has: '*Choses gayves*, weifes, things forsaken, miscarried, or lost,' &c. *Waif* is an old Norman-French term, and of Norse origin.—ONorse *weif*, Icel. *veif*, anything flapping about, applied, e. g. to the fin of a seal; *veifan*, a moving about uncertainly, whence *veifanar-orð*, 'a word of wafting,' a rumour; from *veifa*, to vibrate, move about, whence *veifi-skati*, a spendthrift, lit. one who squanders coin. β. The ONorse *v* was sounded as E. *w*, and thus *weifa* (Icel. *veifa*) is the source of E. *waive*, vb., whence *waif* seems to have been derived as a verbal sb. Cf. Norw. *veiva*, to swing about. A *waif* is a thing tossed loosely abroad, and then abandoned. See further under **Waive**. γ. We may also note that Spenser writes *waift*, F. Q. iv. 12. 31; *weft*, id. v. 3. 27, where the *t* is unoriginal (just as in *waft*), and due to the pp. *waived*. ¶ The E. *weft* (from weave) is a different word. So also is *wave*, though easily confused with *waive*, when used as a verb.

WAIL, to lament. (Scand.) ME. *weilen*, *wailen*, Chaucer, C. T. 1297 (A 1295); Wyclif, Matt. xxiv. 30.—Icel. *væla* (formerly *wæla*), to wail; also spelt *vála*, mod. Icel. *vola*; Swed. dial. *väla*, to wail; Dan. dial. *vælle*, to wail, *væl*, a wail; Norw. *væla*, to bleat. Orig. 'to cry woe;' from *væ*, *vei*, woe! used as an interjection; cf. the curious ME. *waymenten*, to lament, Prompt. Parv., formed from the same interjection with the F. suffix *-ment*, and apparently imitated from L. *lāmentare*.+Ital. *guajolare*, to wail, cry woe; from *guai*, woe! a word of Teut. origin; cf. Goth. *wai*, woe! whence Goth. *wajamērjan*, to lament. See **Wo**. Der. *wail-ing*.

WAIN, a waggon, vehicle for goods. (E.) ME. *wain*; written *wayn*, Rob. of Glouc. p. 416, l. 8596. AS. *wægn*, a wain; also used in the contracted form *wæn*, Grein, ii. 644.+Du. *wagen* (whence E. *wagon* was borrowed in the 15th or 16th century); OSax. *wagan*; Icel. *vagn*; Dan. *vogn*; Swed. *vagn*; G. *wagen*, OHG. *wagan*. β. The AS. *wægn* soon passed into the form *wæn* by the loss of *g* (sounded as *y*), just as AS. *regn* became *rēn*, mod. E. *rain*; cf. *hail*, *nail*, *tail*, in which *g* similarly disappears; so also E. *day* from AS. *dæg*, &c. Hence it is impossible to regard *wagon* as a true E. word. γ. All the above forms are from Teut. *wagnoz*, m., a wain, carriage; from the 2nd grade (*wag*) of Teut. *wegan-*, to carry; from Idg. √WEGH, to carry, whence E. *vehicle*. From the same root we have L. *ueh-iculum*, Skt. *vahana-*, a vehicle, Skt. *vah-ya-*, a car, OIrish *fēn*, a car, Russ. *voz'*, a load. See **Vehicle**. Doublet, *wagon* or *waggon*. And see *weigh*.

WAINSCOT, panelled boards on the walls of rooms. (Du.) In Shak. As You Like It, iii. 3. 88. Applied to any kind of panelled work. I find: 'a tabyll of *waynskott* with *to* [two] joynyd trestell*is*;' Bury Wills, ed. Tymms, p. 115, in a will dated 1522; also 'a rownde tabyll of *waynskott* with lok and key,' id., p. 116; also 'a brode cheste of *wayneskott*,' id. p. 117. Still earlier, I find *waynskot* in what appears to be a list of imports; Arnold's Chron. (1502), ed. 1811, p. 236, l. 4. And much earlier 'c du bord appelle *weynscott*,' Liber Albus, p. 238. Hakluyt even retains something of the Du. spelling, where he speaks of 'boords [boards] called *waghenscot*;' Voyages, i. 173.—Du. *wagen-schot*, 'wainscot;' Hexham. Low G. *wagenschot*, the best kind of oak-wood, well-grained and without knots. Cf. Low G. *bökenschot*, the best kind of beech-wood, without knots, in which the former part of the word is Low G. *böken, beechen*, adj. formed from *book*, a beech. (We may here remark that E. *wainscot*, in the building trade, is applied to the best kind of oak-timber only, used for panelling because it would not 'cast' or warp; see *Wainscot* in Trench, Select Glossary.) β. The Du. *schot* (like E. *shot*) has numerous senses, of which one is 'a closure of boards,' Hexham. It also meant 'a shott, a cast, or a throwe, the flowre of meale, revenue or rent, gaine or money, a shot or score to pay for any things,' id. Sewel also explains *schot* by 'a wainscot, partition, a stop put to anything, the pace (of a ship), a hogs-sty.' See **Shot**. γ. The mod. Du. *wagen-schot* is an altered form, due to popular etymology; as if the derivation were from Du. *wagen*, a wain or waggon; see **Wain**. But the older form is MDu. *waeghe-schot* (without *n*, Kilian); which some (see Ten Kate, Aenleiding, &c. (1723), ii. 507) wrongly take to be connected with MDu. *weech, weegh*, Du. *weeg*, a wall, cognate with AS. *wāh*, OFries. *wāch*, OSax. *wēg*, a wall, and allied to Icel. *veggr*, Goth. *waddjus*, a wall. See the article by J. B. Vinckers, in Taalstudie, dated Oct. 7, 1882, from which I quote: 'Dutch shipwrights still use a very remarkable term *wageren*, meaning "to cover the inside of a ship with boards," from which is derived the pl. noun *wageringen*, the inside boards.' δ. A better theory is that given in Kilian, which connects *waeghe-* with MDu. *waeghe* (G. *woge*, AS. *wǣg*, Goth. *wēgs*), a wave; with reference to the waving grain appearing upon the cleft wood. This suits the phonology better. ε. Hexham also has *want-schot*, wainscot, from *want*, a wall; and explains *wantschotten* by 'to wainscott walls.' Der. *wainscot*, verb.'

WAIST, the middle part of the human body, or of a ship. (E.) Spelt *wast* in Palsgrave. ME. *wast*, called *waste of a mannys myddel* or *wast of the medyl* in Prompt. Parv. The dat. *waste* is in Gower, C. A. ii. 373, l. 13. The right sense is 'growth,' hence the thick part or middle of the body, where the size of a man is developed; we find the spelling *wacste* (dat. case) with the sense of 'strength,' in O. Eng. Homilies, i. 77, l. 3. It answers to an AS. form **wæhst, *wæst*, not found, though the nearly related *wæstm*, growth, also fruit, produce, is a very common word; see Grein, ii. 650. Indeed, the AS. *wæstm* became *wastme, westme* in later English, and it is by no means improbable that the mod. E. *vaist* was suggested by it. In Genesis and Exodus, 1910, Joseph is described as being 'brictest of *waspene*,' certainly miswritten (in the MS.) for 'brictest of *wasteme*,' i.e. fairest of form or shape, 'well-waisted.'—AS. *weaxan*, to grow, to wax; from Teut. base **wahs-* (as in Goth. *wahsjan*, to wax); whence AS. **wæhs-t, *wæst*; cf. AS. *wæstm*, formed like *blō-stma* (E. *blossom*) from *blōwan*, to flourish. See **Wax** (1). So also Goth. *us-vahsts*, out-growth, *wahsjan*, to grow; OHG. *wahst, wast*, growth, *wahs-an*, to grow. Further allied to Goth. *wahstus*, growth; Icel. *vöxtr*, stature, also shape, *vaxa*, to grow; Dan. *væxt*, Swed. *växt*, growth, size. Der. *waist-band*; *waist-coat*, spelt *wast-coate* in Browne, Britannia's Pastorals, b. i. s. 5, l. 106 from the end; and see Nares.

WAIT, to watch, stay in expectation, abide, lie in ambush. (F.—Low L.—OHG.) ME. *waiten*, P. Plowman, B. v. 202; Havelok, 512.—AF. *wayter*, to watch, Langtoft, i. 448; OF. *waiter, waitier*, also *gaiter, gaitier* (Godefroy), later *guetter*, 'to watch, warde, mark, heed, note, dog, stalk after, lie in wait for;' Cot. Cf. Walloon *weitier*, to spy. A denominative verb.—AF. *wayte*, Liber Albus, p. 646; OF. *waite, gaite* (Godefroy), a guard, sentinel, watchman, or spy; later *guet*, 'watch, ward, heed, also the watch, or company appointed to watch;' Cot.—Low L. *wacta*, a guard; whence *wactāre*, to guard, Ducange (>OF. *waiter*).—OHG. *wahta*, MHG. *waht*, G. *wacht*, a guard, watch; whence was formed G. *wächter*, a watchman. (The Icel. *vakta*, to watch, is merely borrowed from G., not a true Scand. word.) β. The sb. *wah-ta* answers to a Teut. type **wah-ton-*, m., for **wak-ton-*, a watcher, one who is awake; from Teut. **wak-an-*, to wake; see **Wake** (1). Der. *wait-er*, ME. *waitere*, a watchman, Wyclif, 4 Kings ix. 17 (one MS. of later version). Also *wait*, sb., chiefly in the phr. 'to lie in wait,' Acts, xxiii. 21. The ME. *waite* properly signifies a watchman or spy, as in Cursor Mundi, 11541, from OF. *waite*, as above, and is really an older word than the verb, as above shown; it only remains to us in the phrase 'the Christmas *waits*,' where a *wait* is 'one who is awake,' for the purpose of playing music at night; cf. '*Wayte*, a spye; *Wayte*, waker, Vigil;' Prompt. Parv. 'Assint etiam excubiæ vigiles [glossed by OF. *veytes veliables*], cornibus suis strepitum et clangorem et sonitum facientes;' Wright's Voc. i. 106, l. 1. Also *wait-ing*, *wait-ing-woman*, K. Lear, iv. 1. 65; *a-wait*, vb., q. v.

WAIVE, to relinquish, abandon a claim. (F.—Scand.) Chiefly in the phr. 'to *waive* a claim,' as in Cotgrave (see below). ME. *waiuen, weiuen* (with *u*=*v*), a difficult and rather vague word, chiefly in the sense 'to set aside' or 'shun,' also 'to remove' or 'push aside;' see P. Plowman, B. v. 611 (where the MS. may be read

wayne); id. B. xx. 167; Chaucer, C. T. 4728, 9357, 10298, 17127, 17344 (B 308, E 1483, 2424, H 178, I 33), Troil. ii. 284; Gower, C. A. i. 276, bk. ii. 3469.—AF. *weiver*, to waive, Year-Books of Edw. I (1292–3), pp. 39, 53, 55, 205; OF. *gaiver* (Godefroy), to cede, abandon; later *guesver*, 'to waive, refuse, abandon, give over, surrender, resigne;' Cot. The AF. *waif*, sb., is in the Liber Custumarum, pp. 151, 434, 486; OF. *gaif* in Godefroy; see **Waif**. Ducange gives Low L. *waviāre*, to waive, abandon, *wayvium*, a waif, or a beast without an owner, *vayvus*, adj., abandoned as a waif, which are merely Latinised forms of the F. words; and he remarks that these words are of common occurrence. β. The sb. seems to be from the vb.—ONorse **weifa*, Icel. *veifa*, to vibrate, swing about, move to and fro in a loose way; Norw. *veiva*, to swing about, to turn a grindstone, Swed. *vefva*, to wind; cf. Low G. *weifen*, to swing about, to toss (Schambach). Hence the sense 'to cast loose.' + OHG. *weibōn*, MHG. *weiben, waiben*, to fluctuate, swing about; cf. Goth. *bi-weibjan*, to wind about; Skt. *vēp*, to shake. (√WEIP.) ☞ Distinct from *wave*, despite some similarity in the sense; but the words have been confused.

WAKE (1), to cease from sleep, be brisk. (E.) ME. *waken*, strong verb, pt. t. *wook*, Chaucer, C. T. Group A, 1393 (Six-text); where Tyrwhitt, l. 1395, prints *awook*; also *wakien*, weak verb, to keep awake, pp. *waked*, Havelok, 2999. Corresponding to these verbs, we should now say 'he *woke*,' and 'he was *waked*.' [They are both distinct from ME. *waknen*, to waken; which see under **Waken**.] AS. *wacan*, to arise, come to life, be born, pt. t. *wōc*, pp. *wacen*; also *wacian*, to wake, watch, pt. t. *wacode, wacede*; Grein, ii. 635. + Goth. *wakan*, pt. t. *wōk*, pp. *wakans*, to wake, watch; whence *wakjan*, weak verb, only in comp. *uswakjan*, to wake from sleep; Du. *waken* (weak verb); Icel. *vaka* (weak); Dan. *vaage*; Swed. *vaka*; G. *wachen*. β. All from Teut. base WAK, to be brisk, be awake, allied to Idg. √WEGw, to be vigorous, whence **Vigil, Vegetable**, q. v. Brugmann, ii. § 804. Der. *wake* (weak verb), to rouse, answering to AS. *wacian*, as above; *wake*, sb., a vigil, ME. *wake*, Ancren Riwle, p. 314, l. 2 from bottom, from AS. *wacu*, occurring in the comp. *niht-wacu*, a night-wake, Grein, ii. 286, l. 5. Also *wake-ful*, Spenser, F. Q. iii. 9. 7, substituted for AS. *wacol* or *wacul* (allied to L. *uigil*), Voc. 315. 26; hence *wake-ful-ly, wake-ful-ness*. Also *wak-en*, q. v., *watch*, q. v.

WAKE (2), the track of a ship. (Scand.) 'In the *wake* of the ship (as 'tis called), or the smoothness which the ship's passing has made on the sea;' Dampier's Voyages, an. 1699 (R.). 'Wake, (among seamen) is taken for that smooth water which a ship leaves astern when under sail, and is also called *the ship's way*;' Phillips, ed. 1706. 'In Norfolk, where the broads [large tarns] are mostly frozen over, the spaces of open water are called *wakes*;' Wedgwood. Like many other E. Anglian words, *wake* is of Scand. origin. It was originally applied to an open space in half-frozen water, and esp. to the passage cut for a ship in a frozen lake or sea; thence it was easily transferred to denote the smooth watery track left behind a ship that had made its way through ice, and at last (by a complete forgetfulness of its true use) was applied to the smooth track left behind a vessel when there is no ice at all. And even, in prov. E., rows of green damp grass are called *wakes* (Halliwell).—Icel. *vök* (stem *vak-*, gen. sing. and nom. pl. *vakar*), a hole, opening in ice; *draga þeir skipit milli vakanna* = to drag their ship between [or along] wakes (Vigfusson); Swed. *vak*, an opening in ice; Norw. *vok*, the same, whence *vekkja*, to cut a hole in ice, 'especially to hew out a passage for ships in frozen water' (Aasen); NFries. *wak*, Dan. *vaage*, the same. The mod. Du. *wak* (like E. *wake*) is merely borrowed from Scandinavian. The orig. sense is a 'moist' or wet place; and it is allied to Icel. *vökr*, moist, *vökva*, to moisten, to water, *vökva*, moisture, juice, whence Lowland Sc. *wak*, moist, watery; so also Du. *wak*, moist. Teut. type **wakwoz*, moist (Franck); Teut. base WEQ, to wet, answering to Idg. root WEGw, to wet, whence Gk. *ὑγ-ρός*, L. *ū-midus*, wet; see further under **Humid**. Brugmann, i. § 658 (b). β. The F. *ouaiche*, formerly also *ouage*, now usually *houache*, the wake of a ship, is clearly borrowed from English, as Littré says. γ. The connexion between *wake*, a wet track through ice, and prov. E. *wake*, a row of damp grass, is sufficiently clear. Cf. Homer's *ὑγρὰ κέλευθα*, Od. iii. 71. From the same root is *quaff*, q. v.

WAKEN, to awake. (E.) This verb is of considerable grammatical importance, and should be carefully studied, being one of a class not very common in mod. E., and peculiarly liable to be misunderstood. The point is, that it was orig. *intransitive*, whereas in Shak. it is *transitive only*, 3 Hen. VI, iv. 3. 19, Romeo, iii. 1. 28, iv. 4. 24, Oth. ii. 1. 188; &c. In mod. English, verbs in *-en*, by a singular change, are mostly transitive, such as *strengthen, embolden*, &c.; but this is just contrary to the older usage, not only in ME. and AS. but in the Teut. languages generally. The subject is discussed in Grimm's Grammar, ed. 1837, iv. 23, where he shows that Goth.

auk-a, I eke, or increase, answers to Gk. αὐξάνω, whereas *aukna* (= I eke-n) answers to Gk. αὐξάνομαι, in the *middle voice*; and there was even in Gothic a third form *aukada* = Gk. αὐξάνομαι in the *passive voice*. β. The ME. form is *waknen* or *wakenen*, intransitive. ' So þat he bigan to *wakne*' = so that he began to waken (or be aroused from sleep), Havelok, 2164. AS. *wæcnan*, to arise, be aroused, be born; Grein, ii. 642. The formative *-n-* in *wæc-n-an* is due to the pp. suffix *-en* (Teut. *-anoz*) seen in AS. *wacen*, pp. of *wac-an*, to wake; so that *wæc-n-an* orig. meant ' to become awake.' Allied to AS. *wacan*, to wake; see **Wake.**+Icel. *vakna*, to become awake; allied to *vaka*, to wake; Swed. *vakna*, allied to *vaka*; Dan. *vaagne*, allied to *vaage*; Goth. *gawaknan*, allied to *wakan*; whence pres. part. pl. *gawaknandans* = becoming awake, Luke, ix. 32. Der. *a-waken*.

WALE (1), **WEAL**, the mark of a stroke of a rod or whip upon the flesh, a streak, a ridge, a plank along a ship's side. (E.) Sometimes spelt *wheal*, but a *wheal* is properly a blister; see **Wheal** (1). ' The *wales*, marks, scars, and cicatrices;' Holland, tr. of Plutarch, p. 459 (R.). ' The *wales* or marks of stripes and lashes;' id. p. 547 (R.). ME. *wale*. ' *Wale*, or strype,' Prompt. Parv. ' Wyghtly on the *wale* [gunwale] thay wye vp thair ankers;' Morte Arthure, 740. AS. *walu* (pl. *wala*), a weal, mark of a blow, occurring 4 times in glosses; also, a ridge (Toller). We also find AS. *wyrt-wala* (-*walu*), properly the shoot or stem of a root, as when the root of a tree projects from the ground, hence used for ' root' simply; cf. ' ðū plantudest wyrttruman hys ' = thou plantedst his roots, Ps. lxxix. 10, ed. Spelman, where the Trinity MS. has ' ðū wyrtwalodes (sic) *wirt-waloda*,' the last word being corruptly written for *wyrtwala*. The orig. sense was ' rod,' hence the rounded half-buried side-shoot of a root (as above), or the raised stripe or ridge caused by the blow of a rod or whip. Hence also the sense of ridge or plank along the edge of a ship, as in the comp. *gun-wale*, q. v.+OFries. *walu*, a rod, wand; only in the comp. *walubera*, *walebera*, a rod-bearer, a pilgrim; EFries. *wale*, a weal; NFriesic *waal*, a staff, rod (Outzen); Icel. *völr* (gen. *valar*), a round stick, a staff; Swed. dial. *val*, a round stick, cudgel, flail-handle (Rietz); Goth. *walus*, a staff; Luke, ix. 3. β. All from the Teut. types *walou-*, *walā*, *waluz*, a round stick, so named from its roundness; the sense of ' rounded ridge' still lingers in mod. E. *wale*; cf. Icel. *valr*, round, EFries. *walen*, to turn round, Russ. *val'*, a cylinder, *valiat(e)*, to roll; allied to L. *uoluere*, to roll, Gk. ἑλίσσειν, to turn round. (√WEL). See **Volute. Der.** *gun-wale*.

WALE (2), choice; as a vb., to choose. (Scand.) Obsolete; except in N. dialects. ME. *walen*, to choose, Wars of Alexander, 4655; from *wale*, sb., choice, Allit. Troy-book, 11952.—Icel. **wal*, Icel. *val*, choice; Swed. *val*; MDan. *val*.+OHG. *wala*, choice; G. *wahl*. Hence Icel. *velja*, to choose, Swed. *välja*, Dan. *vælge*; cf. Goth. *waljan*, to choose, Skt. *varaya*, to choose, causal form of *vṛ*, to choose. From Teut. **wal*, Idg. **wol*, 2nd grade of √WEL, to desire. See **Will** (1).

WALK, to move along on foot without running. (E.) ME. *walken*, formerly a strong verb, pt. t. *welk*, pp. *walken*. The pt. t. *welk* occurs in the Pricke of Conscience, ll. 4248, 4390; the pp. is spelt *walke*, King Horn, ed. Lumby, 953. AS. *wealcan*, pt. *wēolc*, pp. *wealcen*, to roll, to toss oneself about, rove about, esp. used of the movement or flow of water; Grein, ii. 669. Thus the orig. sense was ' to roll,' much as in the proverb ' a *rolling* [moving] stone gathers no moss.' Hence the ME. *walker*, Wyclif, Mark, ix. 2 (earlier version), lit. a roller, a term applied to a fuller of cloth (from his stamping on or pressing it); AS. *wealcere* = L. *fullo*, Voc. 407. 29; *Walker* is still common as a proper name.+Du. *walken*, to work or make a hat.+MDu. *walcken*, ' to presse, to squeeze, or to straine;' *walcker*, ' a fuller;' Hexham; Icel. *valka*, *volka*, to roll, to stamp, to roll oneself, to wallow; *válk*, a tossing about; Swed. *valka*, to roll, to full, to work; Dan. *valke*, to full, to mill; G. *walken*, to full, OHG. *walchan*, to full, also to roll or turn oneself round, to move about; hence G. *walker*, a fuller. β. All from Teut. base WALK, to roll about, answering to Idg. WALG, whence Skt. *valg*, to go by leaps. Der. *walk*, sb., Tw. Nt. i. 3. 138; *walk-ing-staff*, Rich. II, iii. 3. 151; *walk-ing-stick*. Also *walk-er*, a fuller, P. Plowman, C. i. 222. And see *wallow*.

WALL, a stone fence, a fence of stone or brick, a rampart. (L.) ME. *wal*, appearing as *walle*, Chaucer, C. T. 8923 (E 1047). AS. *weal*, *wall*, a rampart of earth, a wall of stone; Grein, ii. 671. Not a Teut. word, but borrowed from the famous L. *uallum*, a rampart, whence also W. *gwal*, a rampart, as well as Du. *wal*, Swed. *vall*, G. *wall*, &c. β. The L. *uallum* is a collective sb., signifying a row or line of stakes.—L. *uallus*, a stake, pale, palisade; lit. a protection. Allied to OIrish *fál*, a hedge; Stokes-Fick, p. 276. ¶ The true AS. word for ' wall' was *wāh*, Grein, ii. 643 (where the accent is wrongly omitted), whence ME. *wowe*, P. Plowman, B. iii. 61 (obsolete). Der. *wall*, verb, ME. *wallen*, Rob. of Glouc. p. 51, l. 1169; *wall-flower*, *wall-fruit*; also *wall-newt*, K. Lear, iii. 4. 135. ☞ No connexion with *wall-eyed*.

WALLA, WALLAH, short for *Competition-walla*. (Hind.—Skt.) A *competition-walla* is an Anglo-Indian term, applied, after 1836, to one who entered the Civil Service by the competitive system then established. See Yule, who explains that the Hind. *-walā* is properly a Hindi adjectival suffix, with a similar value to that of Lat. *-ārius*, or E. *-er*; so that *competition-walla* = *competition-er*, i. e. competitor. Cf. Hind. *gwālā*, a cow-herd; for **gō-wālā*; from *gō*, a cow.—Skt. *-vala-*, suffix; as in *vid-vala-*, clever, from *vid*, to know; Brugmann, ii. § 76, note 1.

WALLABY, a small kangaroo. (Australian). ' *Wallaby*, a name used for the smaller kinds of kangaroos;' E. E. Morris, Austral. Dict.; q. v. From the native Austral. *walla*, to jump.

WALLET, a bag for carrying necessaries, a budget. (E. ?) ME. *walet* (with one *l*), Chaucer, C. T. 683 (A 681); P. Plowman, C. xi. 269, where for ' bag-full' some MSS. have *watel-ful* and others have *walet-ful*. In the latter passage we have the probable solution of the word; the ME. *walet* being apparently a corruption of *watel*. In the same way, *wallets*, used by Shakespeare for bags of flesh upon the neck (Temp. iii. 3. 46), may be the same as *wattles*, ' teat-like excrescences that hang from the cheeks of swine,' Brockett. That *wattle* should turn into *wallet* is not very surprising, for *l* is near akin to *r*, and a similar shifting of *r* is a common phenomenon in English, as in AS. *irnan* = *rinnan*, to run, ME. *brid* = a bird, ME. *burd* = a bride, &c.; so also *neeld*, a needle, *mould* = *model*; *wordle* for *worlde*, i. e. world, P. Plowm. C. i. 10, &c. We even find *fadock* for *fagot*, Old Plays, ed. Hazlitt, vi. 77; and *maddock* with the same sense as *maggot*. At any rate, the very special use of *wallets* = *wattles* = fleshy bags, is remarkable, as well as the equivalent use of *walet* and *watel* in the MSS. of P. Plowman. β. The E. *wattle* commonly means ' hurdle,' but ME. *watel* appears to have also meant a basket, and hence a bag. See further under **Wattle**. It is perhaps worth while to add that we find, in Voc. 656. 9, the entry ' Hic pero, *wolyng*,' which Mr. Wright explains as ' a leathern sack.' This ME. *wolyng*, having no obvious etymology, is perhaps a contraction of *watling* (the dimin. of *watel*), by loss of *t*. (Doubtful; some assume OF. **walet*, bag; as if from OHG. *wallōn*, to go on pilgrimage.)

WALL-EYED, with glaring eyes, diseased eyes. (Scand.) In Shak. K. John, iv. 3. 49, Titus, v. 1. 44. Spenser has *whally eyes*, F. Q. i. 4. 24. ' *Glauciolus*, An horse with a *waule eye*;' Cooper's Thesaurus, ed. 1565. Nares writes it *whally*, and explains it from *whaule* or *whall*, the disease of the eyes called *glaucoma*; and cites: ' *Glaucoma*, a disease in the eye; some think it to be a *whal eie*;' A. Fleming's Nomenclator, p. 428. Cotgrave has: ' *Oeil de chevre*, a *whall*, or over-white eye; an eie full of white spots, or whose apple seems divided by a streak of white.' But the spelling with *h* is wrong. ME. *wald-eyed*, Wars of Alexander, 608; *wolden-eighed*, King Alis. 5274. Also *wawil-eyed*, Wars of Alexander, 1706.—Icel. *vald-eygðr*, a corrupted form of *vagl-eygr*, wall-eyed, said of a horse. —Icel. *vagl*, a beam, also a beam in the eye, a disease of the eye (as in *vagl ā auga*, a wall in the eye); and *eygr*, *eygðr*, eyed, an adj. formed from *auga*, the eye, which is cognate with E. **Eye.** β. The Icel. *vagl* is the same as Swed. *vagel*, a roost, a perch, also a sty in the eye; *vagel på ögat*, ' a tumor on the eyelid, a stye on the eyelid,' Widegren. Cf. Norweg. *vagl*, a hen-roost, Aasen. The lit. sense is ' a perch,' or ' a small support;' closely allied to Icel. *vagn-a*, a wain.—√WEGH, to carry, as in Skt. *vah*, L. *uehere* (whence *uec-tis*, a pole); see **Wain.** See Notes on E. Etym., p. 316.

WALLOP, to boil; see **Potwalloper** and **Gallop.**

WALLOW, to roll oneself about, as in mire. (E.) ME. *walwen*, Chaucer, C. T. 6684 (D 1102). AS. *wealwian*, to roll round, Ælfred, tr. of Boethius, c. 6 (b. i. met. 7).+Goth. *walwjan*, to roll, in comp. *atwalwjan*, *afwalwjan*, *faurwalwjan*; L. *uoluere*, to roll. See **Volute.**

WALNUT, lit. a foreign nut. (E.) ME. *walnote*, spelt *walnot*, P. Plowman, B. xi. 251. OMerc. *walh-hnutu*, a walnut; Voc. 452. 34. Lit. ' foreign (i. e. Gaulish) nut.'—OMerc. *walh*, AS. *wealh*, foreign; and *hnutu*, a nut. The pl. *Wealas* means ' strangers,' i. e. the *Welsh*; but in mod. E. it has become *Wales*.+Du. *walnoot*, MDu. *walnote* (Hexham); Icel. *valhnot*; Dan. *valnöd*; Swed. *valnöt*; G. *wallnuss*; also *Wälsche nuss*, i. e. foreign nut. β. For the latter element, see **Nut.** The former element is AS. *wealh*, foreign, OHG. *walah*, a foreigner, whence G. *Wälsch*, Italian. The sense ' foreign' is inexact; the AS. *Wealh* meant a Celt, either of Wales or Gaul. It answers in form to ' one of the tribe of *Volcæ*,' who occupied Southern Gaul; Cæsar, Bellum Gallicum, vii. 7.

WALRUS, a kind of seal. (Du.—Scand.) In Ash's Dict., ed. 1775.—Du. *walrus*, ' a kind of great fish with tusks;' Sewel, ed. 1754. Hence also the modern Scand. forms; as Swed. *vallross*, a morse, walrus; Dan. *hvalros*. The name is very old, since the word *ross* (for *horse*) is no longer in use in Swedish and Danish, which languages now employ *häst*, *hest* in its stead; but we find the right word, in an inverted form, in Icel. *hross-hvalr*, a walrus, lit. a horse-whale; the name being given (it is suggested) from the noise made by the animal, somewhat resembling a neigh. So also AS. *hors-hwæl*, a horse-whale or walrus.   β. The Swed. *vall*, Dan. *hval*, Icel. *hvalr*, are cognate with E. **Whale**. The Swed. *ross*, Dan. *ros*, Icel. *hross* or *hors*, are cognate with AS. *hors* (the *r* in which has shifted); see **Horse**.   ¶ The name *morse*, q. v., is of Finnish origin.

WALTZ, the name of a dance. (G.) Introduced in 1812; see Byron's poem on 'The Waltz.' A shortened form of G. *walzer* (with z sounded as *ts*, whence the E. spelling), 'a jig, a waltz;' Flügel. – G. *walzen*, 'to roll, revolve, dance round about, waltz;' id.+AS. *wealtan*. to roll. twist: see further under **Welter**. Der. *waltz*, verb.

WAMPUM, small beads, used as money. (N. American Indian.) '*Wampum*, small beads made of shells [sometimes white], used by the N. American Indians as money, and also wrought into belts, &c. as an ornament;' Webster. Modern; not in Todd's Johnson. From the Narraganset *wompi*, white, and *-ompeag*, a suffix to denote a string of money; whence the compound *wampumpeag*, or briefly, *wampum*; Notes and Queries, 9 S. x. 226. Cf. Algonkin *wab*, white (Cuoq); Massachusetts *wómpi*. Delaware *wápi*, white (Mahn). See **Wapiti**.

WAN, colourless, languid, pale. (E.) ME. *wan*, Chaucer, C. T. 2458 (A 2456). AS. *wann*, *wonn*, dark, black, Grein, ii. 638. It occurs as an epithet of a raven, and of night; so that the sense of the word appears to have suffered a strange change; the sense, however, was probably 'dead' or 'colourless,' which is applicable to black and pallid alike. Hence Ettmüller derives it from AS. *wann*, 2nd grade of *winnan*, to strive, contend, toil (whence E. *win*); so that the orig. sense would have been 'worn out with toil, tired out,' from which we easily pass to the sense of 'worn out' or 'pallid with sleeplessness' in the mod. E. word. (Cf. Goth. *wunns*, affliction; from the weak grade *wunn-*.) So also in Stokes-Fick, p. 259, who takes it to be cognate with Irish *fann*, W. *gwan*, feeble, weak, faint. It seems to be distinct from **Wane**, confusion with which has affected its sense. See further under **Win**. Der. *wan-ly*, *wan-ness*.

WAND, a long slender rod. (Scand.) ME. *wand*, Pricke of Conscience, 5580; Ormulum, 16178. – Icel. *vöndr* (gen. *vandar*), a wand, a switch, whence *vandahús*, a wicker-house; MSwed. *wand* (Ihre); Dan. *vaand*.+Goth. *wandus*, a rod, 2 Cor. xi. 25.   β. The Teut. type is *wanduz*, m.   It was perhaps named from its pliancy and use in wicker-work, the orig. sense being a lithe twig, that could be wound into wicker-work. From Teut. *wand*, 2nd grade of *windan-*, to wind; see **Wind** (2). But some give it the sense of 'weapon,' and connect it with **Wound**.

WANDER, to ramble, rove. (E.)   ME. *wandrien*, *wandren*, P. Plowman, B. vi. 304. AS. *wandrian*, to wander, Ælfred, tr. of Boethius, lib. iv. met. 1 (cap. xxxvi. § 2). The frequentative form of *wend*, to go; hence it means 'to keep going about.' From *wand-*, base of *wand-jan*, the orig. form of *wend*. See **Wend**.+EFries. *wandern*, *wandeln*; Swed. *vandra*, Dan. *vandre* (from Low G.); Du. *wandelen*, 'to walke,' Hexham; G. *wandeln*, to wander, travel, walk. Der. *wander-er*. Also *Vandal*, q. v.

WANDEROO, a large Cingalese and Malabar monkey. (Cingalese. – Skt.) Spelt *wanderow* in 1681 (Yule). – Cing. *wanderu*; cf. Hind. *bandar*, an ape. – Skt. *vānara-*, *vanara-*, a monkey. Lit. 'forest-dweller.' – Skt. *vana-*, forest. Allied to Goth. *winja*, pasture; Icel. *vin*, meadow; orig. free space or 'pleasure-ground;' and allied to **Winsome** and **Win**. (√WEN.)

WANE, to decrease (as the moon), to fail. (E.) ME. *wanien*, *wanen*, Chaucer, C. T. 2080 (A 2078). AS. *wanian*, *wonien*, to decrease, grow less; Grein, ii. 639. – AS. *wan*, *won*, deficient, id. 638.+Icel. *vana*, to diminish, from *vanr*, lacking, wanting; also *van-*, in composition. Cf. OHG. and MHG. *wanōn*, *wanēn*, to wane, from *wan*, deficient, appearing in mod. G. compounds as *wahn-*. So also Du. *wan-*, prefix, in *wanhoop*, despair (lit. lacking hope). Also Goth. *wans*, lacking.   β. All from Teut. type *wa-noz*, adj., deficient; perhaps orig. a pp. Allied to the Gk. εὖνις, bereaved, Skt. *ūna-s*, wanting, lessened, inferior. Der. *want*, *wan-ton*; and prob. *wan-i-on*, q. v.

WANION, in the phrase *with a wanion*. (E.) In Shak. Per. ii. 1. 17; the phr. *with a wanion* means 'with a curse on you,' or 'with bad luck to you,' or 'to him,' as the case may be. Explained by Wedgwood, Phil. Soc. Trans. 1873-4, p. 328; the connexion with the verb *to wane* was pointed out by Nares. There is no doubt (1) that it stands for *waniand*, and (2) that *waniand* was taken to be a sb., instead of a pres. part. Rich. quotes from Sir T. More: 'He would of likelyhod binde them to cartes and beate them, and make theim wed *in the waniand*,' Works, p. 306 h; which means, I suppose,

he would flog them at the cart's tail (a common expression), and make them marry in the waning moon, i. e. at an unlucky time. So also: 'in woo to wonne [dwell], *in the wanyand*,' York Plays, p. 124. 'It was *in the waniand*' [in an unlucky time]; Minot, ed. T. Wright, i. 87. And even in AS. we have: 'Ealle eorðlīce līchaman bēoð fulran on weaxendum mōnan þonne *on wanigendum*;' i. e. all earthly things are fuller in the waxing than in the waning moon; Pop. Treatises on Science, ed. T. Wright, p. 15. Halliwell gives '*wani-and*, the wane of the moon,' without any authority; but compare the following. 'So myghte he wel say, that *in the crook* [crescent] *of the mone* com he thiderward, and *in the wylde wanyande* [i. e. waning] wente homward;' A Chronicle of London, ed. Sir H. Nicolas, 1827, p. 122; see note to Tale of Beryn, ed. Furnivall, l. 398. So that the first and last quarters of the moon were both unpropitious.   β. *Waniand* is the *Northern* form of the pres. part. of ME. *wanien*, to wane, also used actively in the sense to lessen, deprive (see below). The confusion of the pres. part. with the sb. in *-ing* is so common in English that many people cannot parse a word ending in *-ing*. Thus *in the waniand* came to mean 'in the waning,' and *with a wanion* means with a diminution, detriment, ill-luck. On 'the fatal influence of the waning moon, .. general in Scotland,' see Brand's Popular Antiquities, chapter on *The Moon*. The Icel. *vana*, to wane, is commonly transitive, with the senses 'to make to wane, disable, spoil, destroy,' which may have influenced the superstition in the North, though it is doubtless widely spread. Cf. 'wurreð uppe chirches, oðer *wanieð* hire rihtes, oðer letteð' = war upon churches, or *lessen* their rights, or hinder them; O. Eng. Homilies, ed. Morris, ii. 177, l. 6. See **Wane**.

WANT, lack, deficiency, indigence, need. (Scand.) ME. *want*, first in the Ormulum, 14398, where it is spelt *wannt*, and has the adj. sense of 'deficient;' spelt *wonte*, and used as a sb., Ancren Riwle, p. 284, l. 2. – Icel. *vant*, neuter of *vanr*, adj., lacking, deficient. This neuter form was used with a gen. case following; as, *var þeim vettugis vant* = there was lacking to them of nothing, i. e. they wanted nothing. [The Icel. sb. for *want* is *vansi*.]   β. Thus the final *t* was orig. merely the termination of the neut. gender (as in E. *i-t*, *tha-t*, *thwar-t*); but the word *vant* was in common use, and even the verb *vanta*, to want, to lack, was formed from it, which is the origin of E. *want* as a verb.   γ. The Icel. *vanr*, adj., is explained under **Wane**, q. v.   Der. *want*, verb, ME. *wanten*, spelt *wonten* in Ancren Riwle, p. 344, l. 14; from Icel. *vanta*, verb, as above. Also *wanting*, pres. part., sometimes used as adj.

WANTON, playful, sportive, unrestrained. (E.) The true sense is unrestrained, uneducated, not taken in hand by a master; hence, licentious. ME. *wantoun*, contracted form of *wantowen*; spelt *wantoun*, Chaucer, C. T. 208; spelt *wantowen*, *wantowne*, *wanton*, P. Plowman, C. iv. 143, where it is applied to women. Compounded of *wan-*, prefix, and *towen*, pp.   β. The prefix *wan-* signifies 'lacking, wanting,' and is explained under **Wane**. In composition it has sometimes the force of *un-* (to which it is *not* related), but also gives an ill sense, almost like Gk. δυς-.   γ. The pp. *towen* stands for AS. *togen*, pp. of *tēon*, to draw, to educate, bring up, Grein, ii. 527. The change from AS. *g* to ME. *w* (after *a*, *o*, or *u*) is seen again in AS. *mugan* = ME. *mowen*, to be able, and is regular. The AS. *togen* is cognate with G. *gezogen*, so that E. *wanton*, ill-bred, corresponds very nearly to G. *ungezogen*, 'ill-bred, unmannerly, rude, uncivil,' Flügel. For an account of AS. *tēon*, see **Tow** (1). Mr. Wedgwood well cites *wel i-towune*, well educated, modest, Ancren Riwle, p. 204, l. 17; *vntowune*, licentious, id. p. 342, l. 26. So also *fūl itowene*, foully (badly) educated; id. p. 140, l. 26. Der. *wanton-ly*; *wanton-ness*, ME. *wantounesse*, Chaucer, C. T. 266 (A 264). Also *wanton*, sb.

WAPENTAKE, an old name for a hundred or district. (Scand.) 'Fraunchises, hundredis, *wapentakes*;' Arnold's Chron. (1502), ed. 1811, p. 181. '*Candred* . . is a contray þat conteyneþ an hundred townes, and is also in Englische i-cleped *wepentake*;' Trevisa, ii. 87; spelt *wapentake*, Rob. of Brunne, tr. of Langtoft, p. 145, l. 16. The word occurs in the AS. Laws, but was merely adapted from Norse; the AS. *tǣcan* does not mean 'to touch,' but 'to teach,' and is altogether removed from the word under discussion. It is remarkable that various explanations of this word have been given, seeing that all the while the Laws of Edward the Confessor fully explain the orig. sense. AS. *wǣpengetǣce*, dat. case, a district, wapentake, Secular Laws of Edgar, § vi, in Thorpe, Ancient Laws, vol. i. p. 274; we also find *wǣpentake*, dat. case, id. p. 292. The nom. is *wǣpengetǣc* or *wǣpentac*, Latinised as *wapentac* or *wapentagium*, Laws of Edw. Conf. § xxx, in Thorpe, i. 455, where we also read: 'Quod alii vocant *hundredum*, supradicti comitatus vocant *wapentagium*, et hoc non sine causa; cum enim aliquis accipiebat prefecturam *wapentagii*, die constituto, conveniebant omnes majores contra eum in loco ubi soliti erant congregari, et, descendente eo de equo suo, omnes assurgebant contra eum, et ipse erigebat lanceam suam in altum, et omnes de lanceis suis tangebant hastam ejus, et sic confirmabant se sibi. Et de armis, quia arma vocant *wappa*, et *taccare*, quod est confirmare.' To which another MS. adds: ' Anglice vero arma vocantur *wapen*, et *taccare* confirmare, quasi armorum confirmaċio, vel ut magis expresse, secundum linguam Anglicam, dicamus *wapentac*, i. e. *armorum tactus*: *wapen* enim *arma* sonat, *tac tactus* est. Quamobrem potest cognosci quod hac de causa totus ille conventus dicitur *wapentac*, eo quod per *tactum armorum* suorum ad invicem confœderate (*sic*) sunt.' We may then dismiss other explanations, and accept the one above, that when a new chief of a *wapentake* was elected, he used to raise his *weapon* (a spear), and his men *touched* it with theirs in token of fealty. However the word (as above said) is Norse.—Icel. *vāpnatak*, lit. a weapon-taking or weapon-touching ; hence, a vote of consent so expressed, and lastly, a subdivision of a shire in the Danish part of England, answering (somewhat) to the hundred in other parts ; the reason for this being as above given.—Icel. *vāpna*, gen. pl. of *vāpn*, a weapon, cognate with E. *weapon* ; and *tak*, a taking hold, a grasp, esp. a grasp in wrestling (here used for the contact of weapons), from *taka*, to take, seize, grasp, also to touch. See **Weapon** and **Take**. ¶ As the Icel. *taka* means *to touch* as well as *to take*, it will be seen that the explanation ' weapon-grasping ' in the Icel. Dict. is insufficient ; it means more than that, viz. the *clashing* of one spear against another. ' Si placuit [sententia], frameas *concutiunt* ; honoratissimum assensus genus est *armis laudare*,' Tacitus, Germania, chap. 11 ; &c. Cf. Lowland Sc. *wapinschaw* (weapon-show), an exhibition of arms made at certain times in every district ; Jamieson.

WAPITI, the American elk. (Amer. Indian.) From the Cree *wapitik*, ' white deer ;' cf. Delaware *wāpi*, white. See **Wampum**. ¶ The name is misapplied, as the *wapiti* is not white ; it was first given to the Rocky Mountain goat (*Haplocerus montanus*) ; and then transferred to the wapiti, which does not much resemble it. See Century Dict.

WAR, hostility, a contest between states by force of arms. (F.—Teut.) ME. *werre* (dissyllabic), Chaucer, C. T. 47. It occurs in the A. S. Chron. an. 1119, where it is spelt *wyrre*, but a little further on, an. 1140, it is spelt *uuerre* (= *werre*). But we also find ' armorum oneribus, quod Angli *war-scot* dicunt' in the Laws of Cnut, De Foresta, § 9 ; Thorpe, Anc. Laws, i. 427 (evidently from a MS. of later date). The word is really French ; the usual AS. word is *wīg* ; we also find *hild, winn, gūð*, &c. The derivatives *warrior* and *warraye* (to make war on, Spenser, F. Q. i. 5. 48), respecting which see below, are also of F. origin.—OF. *werre*, war (Burguy, Roquefort), whence mod. F. *guerre*. Of Teut. origin. From the sb. seen in MDu. *werre*, ' warre,' Hexham ; OHG. *werra*, broil, confusion, strife.—OSax. and OHG. *werran*, str. vb., to confuse, embroil ; cf. mod. G. *verwirren*. The Teut. base is **werr-*, for older **werz-, *wers-*, meaning ' to confuse.' Prob. allied to *worse* ; see **Worse**. Der. *war*, verb, late AS. *werrien*, A. S. Chron. an. 1135, formed from the sb. *werre*. Also *war-fare*, properly ' a warlike expedition ;' ' he was nat in good poynt to ride *a warfare*,' i. e. on a warlike expedition, Berners, tr. of Froissart's Chron. vol. ii. c. 13 (R.) ; see **Fare**. Also *war-like*, K. John, v. 1. 71 ; *warr-i-or*, ME. *werreour*, Rob. of Brunne, tr. of Langtoft, p. 166, l. 5, from OF. **werreiur*, not recorded, old spelling of OF. *guerreiur* (Burguy), a warrior, one who makes war, formed with suffix *-ur* from OF. *werreier, guerreier* (spelt *werrier* in Supp. to Godefroy, s.v. *guerreier*), to make war, borrowed by E. and appearing as ME. *werreien* or *werreyen*, Chaucer, C. T. 1546, 10324 (A 1544, F 10), and in Spenser as *warray* or *warrey*, F. Q. i. 5. 48, ii. 10. 21 ; so that *warrior* is really a familiar form of *warrey-our* ; cf. *guerroyeur*, ' a martialist, or warrior.' Cot., from *guerroyer*, ' to warre,' id.

WARBLE, to sing as a bird, chirp, carol. (F.—MHG.) ME. *werblen*, spelt *werbelen*, Gawain and the Grene Knight, 2004 ; the sb. *werble* occurs in the same, 119.—OF. *werbler*, to quaver with the voice, speak in a high tone (Burguy).—MHG. **wirbeln* (not given), or **werbelen*, mod. G. *wirbeln*, to whirl, to run round, to warble, frequentative form of MHG. *werben*, OHG. *hwerban*, to be busy, to set in movement, urge on (whence mod. G. *be-werben*, to sue for, *er-werben*, to acquire), the orig. sense being to twirl oneself about, to twirl or whirl. See **Whirl**, which is, practically, a doublet. Der. *warble*, sb., ME. *werble*, as above ; *warbl-er*.

WARD, a guard, a watch, means of guarding, one who is under a guardian, &c. (E.) 1. ME. *ward*, dat. *warde*, P. Plowman, B. xviii. 320 ; pl. *wardes*, guards, King Alisaunder, 1977. AS. *weard*, a guard, watchman, Grein, ii. 673. This is a masc. sb. (gen. *weardes*) ; we also find AS. *weard*, fem. (gen. *wearde*), a guarding, watching, protection ; id. Both senses are still retained. Both sbs. are formed from the Teut. base WER, to watch ; see **Wary**. Thus the orig. sense of the masc. sb. is ' a watchman,' and of the fem. sb. is ' a watching.'+Icel. *vörðr*, gen. *varðar*, (1) a warder or watchman, (2) a watch ; G. *wart*, a warder, or keeper. Goth. *-wards*, masc. sb., a keeper, only

in the comp. *daurawards*, a door-keeper. All these are from the same root. 2. From this sb. was formed the verb to *ward*, AS. *weardian*, to keep, to watch, Grein, ii. 674 ; cognate with which are Icel. *varða*, to warrant, G. *warten*, and OSax. *wardōn*, to watch, from the last of which were derived the OF. (and AF.) *warder*, to guard, whence E. *ward-en*, and (through the French) E. *guard*. Der. *ward-er*, Spenser, F. Q. v. 2. 21 ; *ward-room, ward-ship*. Also *ward-en*, q. v., *ward-robe*, q. v. Also *bear-ward, door-ward, hay-ward* (= hedge-ward, from AS. *hege*, a hedge) ; *ste-ward*, q. v. Doublet, *guard*, sb. and verb.

-WARD, suffix. (E.) A common suffix, expressing the direction towards which one tends. AS. *-weard*, as in *tō-weard*, toward ; see **Toward**, where the suffix is fully explained. It occurs also as Icel. *-verðr*, Goth. *-wairths*, OHG. *-wert, -wart* ; and cf. L. *uersus*, towards, from the same root. We also have *-wards*, AS. *-weardes*, where *-es* is a genitival suffix giving an adverbial force. Der. *after-ward, back-ward, east-ward, for-ward, fro-ward, hind-ward, hither-ward, home-ward, in-ward, nether-ward, north-ward, out-ward, south-ward, thither-ward, to-ward, up-ward, west-ward*. To most of these *s* can be added, except to *froward*. See also *way-ward, wool-ward*, *verse, prose, suzerain*.

WARDEN, a guardian, keeper, one who keeps guard. (F.—OSax.) Though the verb to *ward* is English, and so is its derivative *warder*, yet the sb. *warden* is F., as shown by the suffix. ME. *wardein*, Ancren Riwle, p. 272, l. 4.—AF. *wardein*, Liber Albus, p.247 ; OF. *wardain* (Godefroy), old spelling of OF. *gardein, gardain*, a warden, guardian. Cf. Low L. *gardiānus*, a guardian ; showing that OF. *wardein* was formed from OF. *ward-er* by help of the L. suffix *-i-ānus*. See **Ward**.

WARDON, WARDEN, a pear. (E.) A *wardon* was ' a large coarse pear used for baking,' Voc. 717, note 1, where we find it spelt *wardun*, in a Nominale of the 15th century ; it is spelt *warden* in Voc. 629. 7, and in Shak. Wint. Tale, iv. 3. 48. By popular etymology, a *keeping* pear (see Nares) ; Cotgrave has ' *poire de garde*, a warden, or winter pear, a pear which may be kept very long ;' but the adj. *gardien*, ' keeping, warding, guarding,' answering to Low L. *gardiānus* (for **wardiānus*), had an active sense, and is therefore inappropriate. The better spelling is *wardon*, as in Palsgrave, the Prompt. Parv., and the Catholicon ; in Two Cookery Books, ed. Austin, we find *wardon, wardone, wardoun*. In Lydgate, Minor Poems, p. 15, the pl. *wardouns* rimes with two sbs. ending with *-ouns*, showing that the form *wardon* (*-oun, -un*) is right. Cf. ' medlers and *wardones* ;' Excerpta Historica, p. 115 (1498). So named from *Wardon* (<AS. *Weard-dūn*) in Beds. The arms of Wardon (or Warden) Abbey were argent, three wardon-pears, or ; see Privy Purse Expenses of Princess Mary, ed. Madden, p. 272.

WARDROBE, a place to keep clothes in. (F.—Teut.) ME. *warderobe* ; ' Jupiter hath in his *warderobe* bothe garmentes of ioye and of sorowe,' Test. of Love, b. ii. ch. ix. 140.—OF. *warderobe*, old spelling of *garderobe* ; see Godefroy. The spelling *garderobe* is in Palsgrave, s. v. *wardroppe*. Cotgrave spells it *garderobbe*, ' a wardrobe, also a house of office ' [see *wardrope* in Halliwell].—OF. *warder*, to ward, keep, preserve ; and *robe*, a robe ; both words being of G. origin. See **Ward** and **Robe**.

WARE (1), merchandise. (E.) ME. *ware* (dissyllabic), Chaucer, C. T. 4560 (B 140). AS. *waru*, ware ; ' Merx, *waru* ;' Voc. 311. 35. We also find AS. *waru*, protection, guard, care, custody, which is tolerably common ; Grein, ii. 641. These words are doubtless related ; the sense of *wares* appears to have been ' things kept in store ;' cf. Icel. *varnaðr*, (1) protection, (2) wares.+Du. *waar*, a ware, commodity ; pl. *waren*, wares. Cf. MDu. *waren*, ' to keepe or to garde,' Hexham ; Low G. *ware*, Icel. *vara*, pl. *vörur*, wares ; Dan. *vare*, pl. *varer* ; cf. *vare*, care ; Swed. *vara*, pl. *varor* ; cf. *vara*, care ; G. *waare*, pl. *waaren* ; cf. *wahre*, care, *wahren*, to guard. Teut. type **warā*, fem. ; from the Teut. base WER, to guard ; as distinct from the base WER, to watch. See **Weir** (1) and **Worth**. Der. *warehouse* (Palsgrave).

WARE (2), aware. (E.) ' They were *ware* of it,' Acts, xiv. 6 ; so also in Romeo, i. 1. 131, ii. 2. 103, &c. See further under **Wary**.

WARE (3), sea-weed. (E.) The Northern form ; see Jamieson, who quotes from G. Douglas, tr. of Virgil. Prov. E. *wore, waur*. AS. *wār*, sea-weed. ' Alga, *waar* ;' Voc. 5. 1.+MDu. *wier*, ' seagrasse ;' Hexham. Perhaps from √WEI, to twine ; see **Withy**.

WARE (4), pt. t. of **Wear**, q. v.

WARFARE, WARLIKE ; see under **War**.

WARILY, WARINESS ; see under **Wary**.

WARISON, protection, reward. (F.—Teut.) ME. *warisoun*, protection, Rob. of Brunne, p. 198, l. 1. This is the true sense ; but it is much more common in the sense of help or ' reward ;' see Will. of Palerne, 2259, 2379, Barbour, Bruce, ii. 206, x. 526, xx. 544. The usual sense of mod. F. *guérison* is ' recovery from illness,' which

is yet a third sense of what is really the same word. Cf. ME.
warisshen, to cure, P. Plowman, B. xvi. 105.—OF. *warison, garison*
(Godefroy), surety, safety, provision, also healing. Cot. has *guarison*,
'health, curing, recovery.'—OF. *warir, garir*, to keep, secure, also
to heal (Godefroy); mod. F. *guérir*. β. Of Teut. origin; from
the verb appearing as Goth. *warjan*, to defend, forbid, keep off from,
whence the sense 'secure;' and in OHG. *werjan*, to keep off, AS.
werian, to defend; Teut. type **warjan-*, to keep off. Allied to Gk.
ἔρυσθαι, to keep off; see **Weir**. γ. We may note that the OF.
garison corresponds to the mod. E. *garrison* in form; but the sense of
garrison is such as to link it more closely with OF. *garnison*, another
sb. from a different √WER, for which see **Ware** (1). And see
Garrison. ¶ Sir W. Scott, Lay of the Last Minstrel, iv. 24,
uses *warrison* in the sense of 'note of assault,' as if it were a *warry*
(warlike) *sound*. This is a singular blunder.

WARLOCK, a wizard. (E.) In Jamieson's Scot. Dict. '[Æneas]
was no *warluck*, as the Scots commonly call such men, who they
say are iron-free or lead-free;' Dryden, Dedication to tr. of Virgil's
Æneid; § 28. The final *ck* stands for an orig. guttural sound, just as
most Englishmen say *lock* for the Scottish *loch*; the suffix was prob.
confused with that of *hem-lock* or *wed-lock*. ME. *warloghe*, a wicked
one, a name for the devil, Destruction of Troy, 4439. Spelt *warlagh*,
a warlock, devil, Cursor Mundi, 8915; *warlau*, id. 725; *warlawe*,
a deceiver, P. Plowman's Crede, l. 783. AS. *wǣrloga*, a traitor,
deceiver, liar, truce-breaker, Grein, ii. 650. Lit. 'one who lies
against the truth.'—AS. *wǣr*, truth (as in *wǣrlēas*, false, lit.
'truthless,' Grein), cognate with L. *uērum*, truth; and *loga*, a liar,
from *log-* (Teut. **lug-*), weak grade of *lēogan* (pp. *log-en*), to lie,
Grein, ii. 176,194. See **Verity** and **Lie** (2).

WARM, moderately hot. (E.) ME. *warm*, Chaucer, C. T. 7409
(D 1827). AS. *wearm*, Grein, ii. 675.+Du. *warm*; Icel. *varmr*;
Dan. and Swed. *varm*; G. *warm*. Cf. Goth. *warmjan*, to warm; the
adj. *warms* does not occur. β. The Teut. is type **war-moz*, warm,
Fick, iii. 292. It is usual to connect this with L. *formus*, Gk. θερμός,
hot, Skt. *gharma-s*, heat, from the √GwHER, to glow; with labio-
velar *gh*. γ. But this is not very satisfactory. On this account,
Fick (ii. 465) connects *warm* with Russ. *varite*, to boil, brew, scorch,
burn, Lithuan. *werdu*, I cook, seethe, boil (infin. *wirti*), and hence
infers a √WER, to cook or boil, common to Teutonic and Slavonic.
So also Brugmann, i. § 680; cf. § 650. Der. *warm-ly, warm-ness*;
also *warm*, verb, AS. *wearmian*, Grein, ii. 675, whence *warm-er*,
warm-ing-pan; also *warm-th*, sb., ME. *wermþe*, O. Eng. Homilies, ed.
Morris, i. 37, l. 33 (not found in AS., which has *wearm-ness*).

WARN, to caution against, put on one's guard. (E.) ME.
warnien, warnen, Chaucer, C. T. 3535. AS. *wearnian, warnian*,
(1) to take heed, which is the usual sense, Luke, xi. 35; (2) to warn,
Gen. vi. 6; cf. *warnung*, a warning, Gen. xli. 32. Cognate with
OHG. *warnōn*, to provide for oneself against, used reflexively,
whence G. *warnen*, to warn against, to caution against. Further
allied to *beware* and *wary*; see **Wary**. ¶ Distinct from the AS. sb.
wearn, a refusal, denial (Grein), an obstacle, impediment (Bosworth);
the orig. sense being a guarding of oneself, a defence of a person on
trial, as in Icel. *vǫrn*, a defence; cf. Icel. *varna*, to warn off, refuse,
abstain from. Der. *warn-ing*. And see *garn-ish, garr-i-son* (for
garn-ison). Also *fore-warn, pre-warn*.

WARP, the thread stretched lengthwise in a loom, to be crossed
by the woof; a rope used in towing. (E.) Lit. 'that which is thrown
across;' see Nares. ME. *warp*; 'Warp, threde for webbynge;'
Prompt. Parv. AS. *wearp*, a warp; 'Stamen, *wearp*,' Voc. 48. 33.
+Low G. *warp* (Danneil); Icel. *varp*, a casting, throwing, also the
warping of anything; Dan. *varp*, only as a naut. term; Swed. *varp*,
a warp; OHG. *warf*, a warp. Teut. type **warpom*, n. β. All
from the Teut. base **warp*, 2nd grade of Teut. **werpan-*, to throw,
as seen in AS. *weorpan*, G. *werfen*, Goth. *wairpan*, to throw. If the
Teut. **werp* is for an older **werq*, from Idg. √WERGw, we may
compare Russ. *verg-at(e)*, to throw. ¶ The ME. *werpen*, to throw,
pt. t. *warp*, pp. *worpen*, occurring in Havelok, 1061, &c., is obsolete.
Der. *warp*, verb, to pervert, twist out of shape (cf. *cast* in the sense
of to twist timber out of shape); Palsgrave has: 'I *warpe*, as bordes
do.' This is not the ME. *werpen* (as above), but a derived weak
verb, and is of Scand. origin; ME. *warpen*, Prompt. Parv., from
Icel. *varpa*, to throw, cast; cf. *varp*, sb., a casting, also a warping.
Cf. Swed. *varpa*, Dan. *varpe*, to warp a ship, from Swed. *varp*, the
draught of a net, Dan. *varp*, a warp; Dan. *varpanker*, a warp-anchor
or kedge.

WARRANT, a voucher, guarantee, commission giving authority.
(F.—OHG.) ME. *warant*, Havelok, 2067, St. Marharete, ed.
Cockayne, p. 8, l. 10.—OF. *warant, guarant* (Burguy, Supp. to
Godefroy), later *garant*, 'a vouchee, warrant; also, a supporter,
defender, maintainer, protector;' Cot. Cotgrave also gives the
spelling *garent*, 'a warrenter.' In the Laws of Will. I, ꟁ Thorpe's

Ancient Laws, i. 476, 477, the AF. spelling is *guarant*, and the Low
L. *warantum* and *warrantum*. The suffix -*ant* is clearly due to the
-*ant*- used as the suffix of a present participle; so that the orig.
sense of OF. *war-ant* was 'certifying' or 'securing.'—OHG.
werēnt-, stem of pres. pt. of *werēn* (G. *gewähren*), to certify, to
warrant. Allied to OFries. *wera*, to warrant. Of uncertain origin;
Schade suggests connexion with OHG. and AS. *wer*, a man; as if
'to offer oneself as a surety.' Der. *warrant*, verb, ME. *warranten*,
K. Alisaunder, 2132 (cf. Walloon *waranti*, to warrant); *warrant-er*,
warrant-or, warrant-able, warrant-abl-y, warrant-able-ness. Also
warrant-y, from OF. *warantie*, later *garantie*, 'garrantie, warrantie,
or warrantise,' Cot., orig. fem. of pp. of *warantir*, later *garantir*,
to warrant, guarantee. Also *guarant-ee* (error for *guarant-ie*), q. v.

WARREN, a preserved piece of ground, now only used of a
place where rabbits abound, not always a preserved place. (F.—
OHG.) ME. *wareine*, P. Plowman, B. prol. 163.—OF. *warenne,
varenne, varene* (Roquefort); *warenne, garenne, garene* (Godefroy);
later *garenne*, 'a warren of connies [conies], also a certain, or limited
fishing in a river;' Cot. The orig. sense was 'a preserve.' Cf.
Low L. *warenna*, a preserve for rabbits, hares, or fish, occurring
A. D. 1186 (Ducange). Formed (with Low L. suffix -*enna*) from
OHG. *warjan* (>OF. *warir*), to protect, keep, preserve; see
Warison. Cf. Du. *warande*, a park; borrowed from OFrench.
Der. *warren-er*, contracted to *warner*, P. Plowman, B. v. 316; which
explains the name *Warner*.

WART, a small hard excrescence, on the skin, or on trees. (E.)
ME. *werte* (dissyllabic), Chaucer, C. T., A 555 (Six-text edition,
where one MS. has *wrete*); spelt *wert* in Tyrwhitt, l. 557. AS.
wearte, pl. *weartan*, Cockayne's A. S. Leechdoms, i. 130, l. 20.
'Papula, *wearte*;' Voc. 37. 9.+Du. *wrat*; MDu. *warte, wratte*
(Hexham); Pomeran. *wratte*; Icel. *varta*; Dan. *vorte*; Swed. *vårta*;
G. *warze*. β. All from Teut. type **wartōn-*, f. Perhaps the orig.
sense is 'growth,' hence out-growth or excrescence; and closely
allied to **Wort** (1), q. v. Some connect it with AS. *wearr*, a
callosity, L. *uerrūca*, a wart, from an allied root **wers*, to rise.
Brugmann, i. § 380. Der. *wart-y*.

WARY, WARE, guarding against deception or danger, cautious.
(E.) The ME. form is *war*; *war-y* is a comparatively late formation;
perhaps the -*y* was subjoined as in *murk-y* from ME. *mirke, merke*,
and *swarth-y* from *swart*. In Meas. for Meas. iv. 1. 38. ME. *war*,
Chaucer, C. T., A 309 (Six-text ed.), misspelt *ware* in Tyrwhitt,
l. 311. AS. *wær*, cautious, Grein, ii. 649.+Icel. *varr*; Dan. and
Swed. *var*; Goth. *wars*; G. *gewahr*, aware. β. All from Teut. type
*waroz, cautious. From Teut. base **war*, answering to Idg. **wor*,
as in Gk. ὁράω, I perceive, look out for, observe, 2nd grade of Idg.
√WER, to watch, regard, as in L. *uerēri*, to regard, respect, dread.
Der. *wari-ly, wari-ness*; *a-ware, be-ware*. And see *war-d, guar-d*;
ware (1); *re-vere*; *pan-or-a-ma, di-or-a-ma*.

WAS, WAST, WERE, WERT, used as parts of the verb *to
be*. (E.) ME. pt. t. sing. *was, wast, was*; pl. *weren* or *were*. AS.
wesan, infin. to be; whence pt. t. indic. sing. *wæs, wǣre, wæs*; pl.
wǣran, wǣron, or *wǣrun*; pt. t. subj. sing. *wǣre* (for all persons), pl.
wǣren or *wǣron* (for all persons). See Grein, ii. 664. β. As to
the use of *was* in the 1st and 3rd persons, there is no difficulty.
γ. As to the 2nd person, the AS. form was *wǣre*, whence ME. *were*,
as in 'thou *were* betraied,' Chaucer, C. T. 14690 (B 3570). In
Wyclif, Mark, xiv. 67, where 7 MSS. read *were*, one MS. has *was*,
and another has *wast*; no doubt *was-t* was formed (by analogy with
hast) from the dialectal *was*, which was prob. Northern. When *you*
came to be used for *thou*, the phrase *you was* took the place of *thou
was*, and is very common in writings of the 18th century. Cf. *I has*,
Barbour, Bruce, xiii. 652; *I is, ye is* (Northern dialect), Chaucer,
C. T. 4043; *thou is*, id. 4087 (A 4045, 4089). In the subj. mood, the
true form is *were*; hence *wer-t* (by analogy with *wast*), K. John, iii.
1. 43, ed. 1623. δ. In the first and third persons singular of the
subjunctive, and in the plural, the true form is *were*; but the use of
were in the singular is gradually becoming obsolete, except when
the conjunction *if* precedes. The forms *if I were, if he were, if I be,
if he be, if he have*, exhibit the clearest surviving traces of a (grammatically marked) subj. mood in mod. English; and of these, *if he have* is
almost gone. Some careful writers employ *if he do, if it make*, and
the like; but it is not improbable that the subjunctive mood will
disappear from the language; the particular phrase *if I were* will
probably linger the longest.+Du. infin. *wezen*; indic. sing. *was,
waart, was*; pl. *waren, waart, waren*; subj. sing. *ware, waret, ware*;
pl. *waren, waret, waren*; Icel. infin. *vera*; indic. sing. *var, vart, var*,
pl. *várum, várut, váru*; subj. sing. *væra, værir, væri*; pl. *værim,
værit, væri*; Dan. infin. and pl. *var*; subj. sing. and pl. *var*; Swed. infin. *vara*; indic. sing. *var*; pl. *voro, voren, voro*;
subj. sing. *vore*; pl. *vore, voren, voro*; Goth. *wisan*, to be, dwell, re-
main; pt. t. indic. sing. *was, wast, was*; dual, *wēsu, wēsuts*; pl.

wēsum, wēsuth, wēsun; subj. sing. *wēsjau, wēseis, wēsi*; dual, *wēseiwa, wēseits*; pl. *wēseima, wēseith, wēseina*; G. pt. t. sing. *war, warest* or *warst, war*; pl. *waren, waret, waren*; subj. sing. *wāre, wārest* or *wärst, wäre*; pl. *wären, wäret, wären*. **B.** All from √WES, to dwell; cf. Skt. *vas*, to dwell, remain, live; Gk. ἑσ-τία, a hearth, ἄσ-τυ, a dwelling-place, city; L. *uer-na* (for **ues-na*), a household slave; *Ves-ta*, goddess of the household; Irish *feis-im*, I remain. **Der.** *wass-ail*, q. v. And see *ver-na-c-ul-ar.*

WASH, to cleanse with water, overflow. (E.) Formerly a strong verb; hence *un-washen*, Mark, vii. 2. ME. *waschen, weschen*, pt. t. *wesch, wosch*, pp. *waschen*; *he is wessh* in Chaucer, C. T. 2285 (A 2283), misprinted *wesshe* by Tyrwhitt. AS. *wascan*, Grein, ii. 641. Just as we find *āxian* (=*ācsian*) as well as *āscian*, so also *wascan* appears as *waxan*; the pt. t. is *wōsc* or *wōx*; the pp. is *wascen* or *wæscen*. 'Hīg hira rēaf *wōxon*' = they washed their robes, Exod. xix. 14.✛Du. *wasschen*; Icel. and Swed. *vaska*; Dan. *vaske*; G. *waschen*, pt. t. *wusch*, pp. *gewaschen*. β. The Teut. type is **waskan-*, to wash, prob. for **wasskan-, *wat-skan-*, to rinse in wet or in water, where **wat* is allied to E. *wat-er, wet*. Brugmann, i. § 942. **Der.** *wash*, sb., as in *The Wash* (place-name); *wash-er, wash-er-woman, wash-y.*

WASP, a stinging insect. (E.) ME. *waspe*, P. Plowman's Crede, l. 648. Cf. prov. E. *waps, wops*. AS. *wæps*. ' Vespa, *wæps*;' Voc. 121. 14. In a very old AS. glossary of the 8th century, we find : ' Fespa, *wæfs*, Voc. 21. 42.✛OHG. *wefsa, wafsa*; G. *wespe*; Bavarian *webes*, a wasp ; OLow G. *uepsia* (Gallée). Contracted from a Teut. type **waƀis-*, answering to Idg. **wobhes-* (whence Russ. *osa*, a wasp, Lith. *wapsà*, a gadfly) ; from **wobh*, 2nd grade of √WEBH, to weave (whence L. *uespa*, a wasp, for **uepsa, *uebsa*), from the nests which they construct. See **Weave.** Brugmann, i. § 918. Cf. Skt. *ūrṇa-vābhi-*, a spider, lit. ' wool-weaver,' in Macdonell's Dict. **Der.** *wasp-ish*, As You Like It, iv. 3. 9 ; *wasp-ish-ly, -ness.*

WASSAIL, a festive occasion, a carouse. (AF. — Teut.) See Brand's *Popular Antiquities*, vol. i. p. 2, where also Verstegan's 'etymology' (from *wax hale*) and Selden's (from *wish-hail*) and other curiosities may be found. In Macb. i. 7.64; Hamlet, i. 4. 9, &c. ME. *wasseyl, washayl*, Rob. of Glouc. p. 117, 118, ll. 2514, 2522 ; and see Hearne's Glossary, p. 731, and Layamon. The story is that Rowena presented a cup to Vortigern with the words *was heil*, and that Vortigern, who knew no English, was told to reply by saying *drinc heil*. Whatever truth there be in this, we at any rate learn that *was heil* and *drinc heil* were phrases used at a drinking-bout. The former phrase is a salutation, meaning ' be of good health,' lit. ' be hale ;' the latter phrase is almost untranslateable, meaning literally ' drink, hale !' i. e. ' drink, and good luck be with you.' β. These forms are not AS., but Norman; Wace, describing the night before the battle of Hastings, gives the forms *weisseil* and *wesse heil* (error for *wes heil*). The latter represents the OSax. *wes hēl*, OIcel. **wes heill* (Icel. *ver heill*). The corresponding AS. (Wessex) form of salutation was *wæs þū hāl*, occurring in Beowulf, 407; or *hāl wes ðū*, Luke, i. 28. It occurs in the plural in Matt. xxviii. 9; ' *hāle wese gē* ' = whole be ye, or peace be unto you; from AS. *wes, wæs*, be thou, imperative sing., 2nd person, of *wesan*, to be; and *hāl*, whole. See **Was** and **Whole.** γ. In the Icel. Dict. we find similar phrases, such as *kom heill*, welcome, hail ! (lit. come, hale !) ; *far heill*, farewell ! (lit. fare, hale !), *sit heill*, sit hail ! (lit. sit, hale !) ; the last of these fully explains *drinc heill*. We may also notice Icel. *heill*, sb., good luck; and we even find AS. *hǣl* (as a sb.), health, salvation, Luke, xix. 9. See **Hail** (2). Explained by me in N. and Q. 10 S. iii. 455. Cf. ONorthumbrian *wes hāl*, whence mod. Yorks. *wessal*, a wassail.

WASTE, desert, desolate, unused. (F.—OHG.—L.) ME. *wast*, Rob. of Glouc. p. 372, l. 7667.—OF. *wast*, in the phr. *faire wast*, to make waste (preserved in E. as *lay waste*), Roquefort; later form *gast*. He also gives *waster*, to waste; see also *gast, gaster*, in Godefroy. We find AF. *wast*, adj., and *wastee*, pp. fem., in Stat. Realm. i. 48 (1278).—MHG. *waste*, sb., a waste, *wasten*, to lay waste; whence also Ital. *guastare*, to waste, F. *gâter*, to spoil. Not a Teut. word; but simply borrowed from L. *uastus*, waste, desolate, also vast, whence the verb *uastāre*, to waste, lay waste. Allied to OIrish *fās*, empty; Idg. types **wāstos, wāstios*; Brugmann, i. § 317. **B.** It is remarkable that we should have adopted this word from French, since we had the word already in an AS. form as *wēste*; but it is quite certain that we did so, since *wēste* would have been *weest* in mod. E. ; besides which, there are *two* ME. forms, viz. *wast* (from F.) and *weste* (from AS.), of which the latter soon died out, the latest example noted by Stratmann being from the Owl and Nightingale, l. 1528. And the result is remarkably confirmed by the ME. *wastour* for *waster* (see below). **C.** The history of the word in G. is equally curious. There also the OHG. has *wuosti*, adj., empty, *wuostī*, sb., a waste, and *wuostan*, to waste; yet, in

addition to these, we also find *waste*, sb., *wasten*, verb, borrowed from Latin, as shown above. But in G. the native form prevailed, as shown by mod. G. *wüst*, waste, *wüste*, a waste, *wüsten*, to waste. Cf. also OHG. *wuosti*, AS. *wēste*, OSax. *wōsti*, Du. *woest*, adj. waste, empty; Teut. type **wōstjoz*, Idg. type **wāstios* (as above). ¶ Hatzfeld derives OF. *waster* from L. *uastāre*, explaining the *w* as due to OHG. influence. It comes to much the same thing. See **Vast. Der.** *waste*, sb., ME. *waste*, Gawain and the Grene Knight, 2098 ; *waste*, verb, ME. *wasten*, Layamon, 22575, from OF. *waster* <OHG. *wasten*, from L. *uastāre*; *wast-er*, ME. *wastour*, P. Plowman, B. prol. 22, vi. 29, where the suffix *-our* is French. Also *waste-ful*, K. John, iv. 2. 16; *waste-ful-ly, -ness*; *waste-ness*, Zeph. i. 15. (A. V.) Doublet, *vast.*

WATCH, a keeping guard, observation. (E.) ME. *wacche*, P. Plowman, B. ix. 17. AS. *wæcce*, a watch, Grein, ii. 641.—AS. *wacian*, to watch; Matt. xxvi. 40; AS. *wacan*, to wake; see **Wake** (1). **Der.** *watch*, verb, ME. *wacchen*, Gower, C. A. i. 163; bk. ii. 110; *watch-er*; *watch-ful*, Two Gent. i. 1. 31, *watch-ful-ly, -ness*; *watch-case*, a sentry-box, 2 Hen. IV, iii. 1. 17; *watch-dog*, Temp. i. 2. 383; *watch-man* (Palsgrave); *watch-word*, 2 Hen. IV, iii. 2. 231.

WATCHET, light blue. (F.) Cotgrave has : ' *pers*, watchet, blunket, skie-coloured.' Nares gives exx. of *watchet* from Browne, Lily, Drayton, and Taylor; and Richardson from Beaum. and Fletcher, Hakluyt, Spenser, Ben Jonson, and Chaucer. ' *Watchet* eyes;' tr. of Juvenal, Sat. xiii. (not by Dryden). ' Al in a kertell of a liht *wachett* ;' Chaucer, C. T., A 3321 ; Lansdowne MS. The Camb. MS. has *vachet*, the Harl. MS. has *wachet* ; the rest *waget, wagett*.—OF. *wachet*, a sort of stuff (Godefroy); cf. *wache, wasce*, the same. Perhaps from OHG. *wāt*, clothing; see **Wadmal.** As with *blunket* (see N. E. D.), the difficulty is to know whether the stuff gave name to the colour or conversely.

WATER, the fluid in seas and rivers. (E.) ME. *water*, Chaucer, C. T. 402 (A 400). AS. *wæter*, Grein, ii. 651.✛Du. *water*; OSax. *watar*; G. *wasser*, OHG. *wazar, wazzar*. β. From the Teut. type **watrom*, n., water. There is also a Teut. type **waton-*, water, appearing in Icel. *vatn*, Dan. *vand*, Swed. *vatten*, Goth. *watō* (pl. *watna*), water. Allied words are Russ. *voda*, Gk. ὕδωρ, L. *unda*, Lithuan. *wandù*, Skt. *udan*, water; OIrish *fand*, a tear. All from the √WED, to wet; see **Wet. Der.** *water*, verb, AS. *wætrian*, Gen. ii. 6, 10 ; *water-ish*, K. Lear, i. 1. 261 ; *water-y*, AS. *wæterig*, Voc. 147. 6. Also *water-carriage, -clock, -closet; -colour*, 1 Hen. IV, v. 1. 80; *-course, -cress*, ME. *water-kyrs*, Voc. 643. 26 ; *-fowl; -gall*, a rainbow, Shak. Lucrece, 1588; *-level; -lily*, ME. *water-lylle*, Voc. 644. 1 ; *-line, -logged, -man, -mark, -mill* (Palsgrave) ; *-pipe ; -pot*, Chaucer, C. T. 8166 (E 290) ; *-power, -proof, -shed* (modern), *-spout, -tight, -wheel, -work*; &c., &c.

WATTLE, a twig, flexible rod, usually a hurdle; the fleshy part under the throat of a cock or turkey. (E.) In all senses, it is the same word. The orig. sense is something twined together; hence it came to mean a hurdle, woven with twigs, a basket; hence, a bag; also, the baggy flesh on a bird's neck. (It also appears in the corrupt form *wallet*; see **Wallet.**) ME. *watel*, a bag, P. Plowman, C. xi. 269; see further under **Wallet.** Hence ME. *watelen*, verb, to wattle, twist together or strengthen with hurdles, P. Plowman, B. xix. 323. AS. *watel*, a hurdle, covering; also *watul*. ' Teges, *watul* ;' Ælfric's Grammar, ed. Zupitza, p. 52, l. 13. *Watelas*, pl., coverings of a roof, tiles, Luke, v. 19; also in the sense of twigs or hurdles, Ælfred, tr. of Beda, b. iii. c. 16. Allied to AS. *wætla*, a bandage. There appear to be no cognate words, and the root is unknown. **Der.** *wattle*, verb, ME. *watelen*, as above. Doublet, *wallet.*

WAUL; see under **Wawl.**

WAVE (1), to fluctuate, to move or be moved about with an undulating motion or up and down. (E.) ME. *wauen*, Lydgate, Minor Poems, p. 256. The pres. part. is spelt *vafand, vaffand*, Barbour, Bruce, ix. 245, xi. 193, 513; the scribe constantly writes *v* for *w*. AS. *wafian*, to wave (with one's hand), Leechdoms, ii. 318; Ælfric's Saints' Lives, xxvii. 151. The sense also comes out in the derived adj. *wæfre*, wavering, restless, Grein, ii. 642; see **Waver.**✛OIcel. **vafa*, cited by E. Müller and Stratmann; the Dict. gives the derivatives *vafra, vafla*, to waver, *vafl*, hesitation (which presuppose an orig. verb **vafa*) ; also *vāfa, vōfa, vofa*, to swing, vibrate. Cf. also MHG. *waberen, wabelen*, to move about, to stir ; Bavarian *wabern*, to sway to and fro; see **Wabble. Der.** *wave*, sb., a late word, occurring in the Bible of 1551, James, i. 6 ; it is due to the verb, and took the place of ME. *wawe*, a wave, Wyclif, James, i. 6, which is not the same word, but allied to E. **Wag,** q. v. (cf. Icel. *vāgr*, Dan. *vove*, G. *woge*, a wave). Also *wave-less; wave-let*, a coined word, with double dimin. suffix; *wave-offering*, Exod. xxix. 24; *wave-worn*, Temp. ii. 1. 120; *wav-y*. Also *wav-er*, q. v.; and *waft*. ☞ Distinct from *waive, waif.*

WAVE (2), the same as **Waive**, q. v.

WAVER, to vacillate. (E.) ME. *waueren* (=*waveren*), Prompt. Parv. p. 518. Barbour has *waverand*, wandering about ; Bruce, vii. 112, xiii. 517, cf. vii. 41. ' *Wauerand* wynd ' = a changeable wind, Wallace, iv. 340 ; *waferyng*, wavering, York Plays, p. 39, l. 111. [Apparently a Northern and E. Anglian word ; and perhaps of Scand. origin ; cf. Icel. *vafra*, to waver, Norw. *vavra*.] If a native word, it was suggested by AS. *wæfre*, adj., wandering, restless, Grein, ii. 652.+Icel. *vafra*, to hover about ; Norw. *vavra*, to flap about ; OHG. *wabar-* (in compounds), wavering. β. It is the frequentative form of **Wave**, q. v. **Der.** *waver-er*.

WAWL, WAUL, to cry as a cat, cry, squall. (E.) Cotgrave has : ' *houaller*, to yawl, *wawl*, cry out aloud.' It is the frequent. form of *waw*, as in ME. *waw-en* ; see *a-eater-wawed* in Chaucer, C. T., D 354 ; and the note. A more usual old form is *wrawl*, frequent. of *wraw-en* ; cf. ' he [a cat] began to *wrawen*,' Caxton, Reynard the Fox, ch. x ; ed. Arber, p. 22. Of imitative origin ; see **Wail**. Cf. also Swed. *vråla*, to bellow, Dan. *vraale*, *vrælle*, to squall ; Norw. *raala*, to cry as a cat ; also Icel. *våla*, to wail.

WAX (1), to grow, increase, become. (E.) ME. *waxen, wexen*, a strong verb, pt. t. *wox, wex*, pp. *woxen, waxen, wexen* ; Wyclif, Matt. xiii. 30 ; Luke, ii. 40, xxiii. 5, 23 ; Matt. xiii. 32. AS. *weaxan*, pt. t. *wēox*, pp. *geweaxen*, Grein, ii. 676.+Du. *wassen*, pt. t. *wies*, pp. *gewassen* ; Icel. *vaxa*, pt. t. *ōx*, pp. *vaxinn* ; Dan. *væxe* ; Swed. *växa* ; G. *wachsen*, pt. t. *wuchs*, pp. *gewachsen* ; Goth. *wahsjan*, pt. t. *wōhs*, pp. *wahsans*. β. All from Teut. base *wahs-*, to grow ; from Idg. √WEKS, to grow ; whence Gk. ἀέξειν, αὔξειν, αὔξανειν, to wax, Skt. *vaksh*, to wax, grow. Extended from √WEG, to be strong, be lively and vigorous ; cf. Skt. *vaj*, to strengthen, L. *augēre*, to increase, *uigēre*, to flourish, &c. When extended by the addition of *s*, the form *wegs* became *weks*. Brugmann, i. § 635 ; ii. § 657. See **Eke** (1), **Vigour, Vegetable, Augment, Auction**. **Der.** *waist*, q. v.

WAX (2), a substance made by bees ; other substances resembling it. (E.) ME. *wax*, Chaucer, C. T. 677 (A 675). AS. *weax*, Grein, ii. 676.+Du. *was* ; Icel. and Swed. *vax* ; Dan. *vox* ; G. *wachs* ; Russ. *vosk'* ; Lithuan. *waszkas*. Root unknown. Some (wrongly) connect it with L. *uiscum*, birdlime ; see **Viscid**. **Der.** *wax*, verb ; *wax-cloth*, *wax-work* ; *wax-en*, Rich. II, i. 3. 75 ; *wax-y*.

WAY, a road, path, distance, direction, means, manner, will. (E.) ME. *wey, way*, Chaucer, C. T. 34. AS. *weg*, Grein, ii. 655.+Du. *weg* ; Icel. *vegr* ; Dan. *vei* ; Swed. *väg* ; G. *weg* ; OHG. *wec* ; Goth. *wigs*. β. All from Teut. type *wegoz*. Further allied to Lithuan. *weža*, the track of a cart, from *wèszti*, to drive, or draw, a waggon : L. *uia* (?), a way ; Skt. *vaha-*, a road, way, from *vah*, to carry. All from √WEGH, to carry ; see **Wain, Viaduct, Vehicle.** ¶ *Under way* is from the Du. *onderweeg*, on the way. **Der.** *al-way, al-ways*, q. v. ; *length-ways, side-ways*, &c. ; also *way-faring*, i. e. faring on the way, spelt *wayvaring*, Trevisa, v. 449 ; cf. AS. *weg-fērend*, Matt. xxvii. 39, where *fērend* is the pres. part. of *fēran*, to fare, travel, Grein, i. 285, a derivative of the more primitive verb *faran*, to go (see **Fare**) ; *way-far-er* ; *way-lay*, Tw. Night, iii. 4. 176 ; *way-mark*, Jer. xxxi. 21 (A. V.) ; *way-worn* ; *way-ward*, q. v.

WAYWARD, perverse. (E.) ME. *weiward* ; 'if thin iȝe be *weiward* [L. *nequam*], al thi bodi shal be derk,' Wyclif, Matt. vi. 23 ; used as an adj., but orig. a headless form of *awaiward*, adv., Owl and Nightingale, 376, Layamon, 8878, 21464 ; Reliq. Antiquæ, i. 292, ii. 9 ; cf. *aweiwardes*, in a direction away from, Layamon, 22352, Will. of Palerne, 2188. In Trevisa, iii. 215, we find : ' man is euere faillynge and *aweyward*,' where Caxton prints *wayward*. Thus *wayward* is *away-ward*, i. e. turned away, perverse. A parallel formation to *fro-ward*, q. v. It is now often *made* to mean *bent on one's way*. Cf. ' ouerthwartlie *waiwarded* ' = perversely turned away, Holinshed, Descr. of Ireland, ed. 1808, p. 274. **Der.** *wayward-ness*, ME. *weiwardnesse*, Wyclif, Rom. i. 29.

WE, pl. of the 1st pers. pronoun. (E.) ME. *we*, Chaucer, C. T. 29. AS. *wē* ; Grein, ii. 652.+Du. *wij* ; Icel. *vér, vær* ; Dan. and Swed. *vi* ; G. *wir* ; Goth. *weis*. Cf. Skt. *vay-am*, we.

WEAK, yielding, soft, feeble. (E.) [A. The verbal form has ousted the AS. *wāc*, which became ME. *wook*, spelt *wooc* in Genesis and Exodus, ed. Morris, l. 1874 ; and would have given a mod. E. *woak*, like *oak* from AS. *āc*. We also find ME. *weik, waik*, whence the pl. *weike*, for which Tyrwhitt prints *weke*, Chaucer, C. T. 889 ; but see Six-text ed., A 887 ; the pl. is spelt *wayke*, Havelok, l. 1012. This is a Scand. form ; from Icel. *veikr, veykr*, weak, Swed. *vek*.+AS. *wāc*, pliant, weak, easily bent, Grein, ii. 635 ; Du. *week*, tender, weak ; G. *weich*, pliant, soft. All from the Teut. type *waikoz*, weak ; from *waik*, 2nd grade of Teut. *weikan-*, as in AS. and OSax. *wīcan*, G. *weichen*, to yield, give way. From an Idg. base WEIGw, a by-form of √WEIQ, as in Gk. εἴκειν, to yield, Brugmann, i. § 701.] B. But the mod. E. *weak* is a back-formation from the verb *to weaken*, Chaucer, Troil. iv. 1144 (in Thynne's ed.), from AS. *wǣcan* ; for

wācian, formed by mutation from AS. *wāc*, weak, adj. (above). **Der.** *weak-ly, weak-ness*. Also *weak-en*, in which the suffix is added as in *length-en*, &c. ; cf. ME. *weken*, Chaucer, Troil. iv. 1144, AS. *wǣcan, wācian*, Grein, ii. 641, 636, Icel. *veikja-sk*, to grow ill ; as above. Also *weak-ly*, adj., used by Ralegh (Todd's Johnson, no reference) ; *weak-l-ing*, 3 Hen. VI, v. 1. 37, with double dimin. suffix, as in *gos-l-ing*. And see *wick* (3), *wicked, wick-er*.

WEAL, prosperity, welfare. (E.) ME. *wele*, Chaucer, C. T. 3103, 4595 (A 3101, B175). AS. *wela, weala, weola*, weal, opulence, prosperity ; Grein, ii. 656.+OHG. *wela, wolo*, G. *wohl*, welfare ; cf. Dan. *vel*, weal, welfare ; Swed. *väl*. β. The orig. sense is a ' well-being,' welfare, and (like the words *well-being, wel-fare, wel-come, fare-well*) it is allied to AS. *wel*, well, adv., the notion of condition being expressed by the nominal suffix *-a*. See **Well** (1). And see **Wealth**.

WEALD, a wooded region, an open country. (E.) The peculiar spelling of this word is not improbably due to Verstegan, who was anxious to spell it so as to connect it at once with the AS. form, forgetting that the diphthong *ea* was scarcely ever employed in the 13th and 14th centuries. Minsheu, in his Dict., ed. 1627, has : ' *Weald* of *Kent*, is the woodie part of the countrey. Verstegan saith that *wald, weald*, and *wold* signifie a wood or forrest ; à Teut. *Wald*, i. *sylua*, a wood.' This fashion, once set, has prevailed. β. It also appears that two words have been confused, viz. *wald* and *wild*. *Wald* (now also *wold*) was sometimes spelt *wæld*, as in Layamon, 21339 ; hence it passed into *weld* or *weeld*. Caxton, in the preface to his Recuyell of the Histories of Troye, tells us that he was born in Kent, ' in the *weeld*.' In the reprint of this book by Copland, this phrase appears as ' in the *wilde*.' Lyly, in his Euphues and his England, says : ' I was borne in the *wylde* of Kent ;' ed. Arber, p. 268. Shak. has ' *wilde* of Kent,' 1 Hen. IV, ii. 1. 60, ed. 1623. γ. For the further explanation of ME. *wald*, see **Wold**. For the further explanation of *wild*, see **Wild**. Both words are English. **Der.** *weald-en*, adj., belonging to the wealds of the S. of England ; a term in geology. For the suffix *-en*, cf. *gold-en*.

WEALTH, prosperity, riches. (E.) ME. *welthe* (dissyllabic), P. Plowman, B. i. 55. Spelt *welðe*, Genesis and Exodus, l. 796. Not in AS. A longer by-form of *weal* (ME. *wele*), made with the suffix *-th*, denoting condition or state ; cf. *heal-th* and *heal, dear-th* and *dear*, &c. See **Weal**.+Du. *weelde*, luxury ; from *wel*, adv., well ; OHG. *welida*, riches. **Der.** *wealth-y*, spelt *welthy* in Fabyan, Chron. c. 56 ; *wealth-i-ness*, spelt *welthines* in Fabyan, in the same passage.

WEAN, to accustom a child to bread, &c., to reconcile to a new custom. (E.) The proper sense is to ' accustom to ;' we also use it, less properly, in the sense of to ' disaccustom to.' These opposite senses are easily reconciled ; the child who is being accustomed to bread, &c. is at the same time disaccustomed to, or weaned from, the breast. Cf. G. *entwöhnen*, lit. to disaccustom, also *to wean* ; where *ent-* is equivalent to E. *un-* as a verbal prefix ; so that *ent-wöhnen* = *un-wean*. ME. *wenen*. ' *Wene* chylder fro sokynge [sucking], Ablacto, electo ;' Prompt. Parv. AS. *wenian*, to accustom, Grein. ii. 660. Hence *āwenian*, answering to G. *entwöhnen* ; ' ǣr þonne þæt acennede bearn fram meolcum *āwened* sī = before the child that is born be weaned from milk ; Ælfred, tr. of Beda, l. i. c. 27, ed. Wheloc, p. 88. ' Ablacto, *to awenye* ;' Voc. 560. 8.+Du. *wennen*, to accustom, inure ; *afwennen*, to wean ; Icel. *venja*, to accustom ; Dan. *vænne*, to accustom ; *vænne fra Brystet*, to wean ; Swed. *vänja*, to accustom ; *vänjaaf*, to wean ; G. *gewöhnen*, to accustom, OHG. *wenjan, wennan*, MHG. *wenen* ; whence *entwöhnen*, to wean. β. All from a Teut. weak verb *wanjan*, to make accustomed, accustom ; from the adj. *wanoz*, wont, accustomed, used to, as in Icel. *vanr*, Swed. *van*, accustomed, allied to Icel. *vani*, a usage. From Teut. *wan*, 2nd grade of √WEN, to desire, earn ; see **Win** and **Wont**.

WEAPON, an instrument for offence or defence. (E.) ME. *wepen*, Chaucer, C. T., A 1591. AS. *wǣpen*, a weapon, shield, or sword ; Grein, ii. 648.+Du. *wapen* ; Icel. *vāpn* ; Dan. *vaaben* ; Swed. *vapen* ; G. *waffe*, OHG. *wāfan* (also *wappen*, borrowed from Dutch or Low G.) ; Goth. *wēpna*, neut. pl., John, xviii. 3. β. All from the Teut. type *wǣpnom*, n., a weapon. A by-form (with *k* for *p*) is found in MSwed. *wåkn*, a weapon (Ihre). **Der.** *weapon-ed*, Oth. v. 2. 226 ; *weapon-less*. Also *wapen-shaw, wapen-take*.

WEAR (1), to carry on the body, as clothes ; to consume by use, rub away. (E.) The pt. t. *wore*, now in use, is due to analogy with *bore*, pt. t. of *bear* ; the word is not really a strong one, the ME. pt. t. being *wered*. We also find pt. t. *ware*, Luke, viii. 27. (A. V.) ME. *weren*, pt. t. *wered*, Chaucer, C. T. 75. AS. *werian* (pt. t. *wǝrode*), Exod. xxix. 29. (Quite distinct from AS. *werian*, to defend ; Grein.) +Icel. *verja*, to wear (quite distinct from *verja*, to defend) ; OHG. *werian* ; Goth. *wasjan*, to clothe ; pp. *wasids*, Matt. xi. 8. β. From the Teut. and Idg. √WES, to clothe ; the *r* standing for *s* (by Verner's law), as shown by the Gothic form. Hence also L. *uestis*, clothing ;

Gk. ἐσ-θής, clothing ; Skt. *vas*, to put on clothes. See **Vest**. Der. *wear*, sb., As You Like It, ii. 7. 34; *wear-able*; *wear-er*, Antony, ii. 2. 7. ☞ All the senses of *wear* can be deduced from the carrying of clothes on the body ; it hence means to bear, to carry; also to consume or use up by wear, destroy, tire, efface; also, to become old by wearing, to be wasted, pass away (as time); to *wear well* = to bear wear and tear, hence to last out, endure. There is no connexion with the sense of AS. *werian*, to defend.

WEAR (2), the same as **Weir**, q. v.

WEAR (3), in phr. ' to wear a ship ;' the same as **Veer**, q. v.

WEARISH, insipid, weakly. (E.) ' A wretched *wearish* [weak] elfe ;' Spenser, F. Q. iv. 5. 34. ' *Werysshe*, as meate is that is nat wel tastye ;' Palsgrave. Prov. E. *wairsh*, *wairish*, *weerish*, insipid, squeamish, weak. See *Wearish* in Nares, whose explanation is conjectural. The orig. sense may have been 'watery ;' from AS. *wær*, the sea; cf. Icel. *ver*, the sea, orig. 'water.' Cf. also Skt. *vār*, *vāri*, water ; Gk. οὖρον ; Swed. *var*, pus. See **Urine**.

WEARY, exhausted, tired, causing exhaustion. (E.) ME. *weri*, *wery*, Chaucer, C. T. 4232 (A 4234). (The *e* is long, as in mod. E.) AS. *wērig*, tired ; Grein, ii. 663 ; *wōerig*, O. E. Texts.+OSax. *wōrig*, weary ; in the comp. *sīð-wōrig*, fatigued with a journey; Heliand, 660, 670, 678, 698, 2238 ; cf. OHG. *wuorag*, intoxicated. β. The long *ē* is (as usual) due to a mutation of long *ō*, as shown by the cognate OSaxon form. It is, consequently, connected with AS. *wōrian*, to wander, travel, Gen. iv. 14; Numb. xiv. 33; Grein, ii. 736. γ. This verb is a weak one, formed from the sb. *wōr*, which probably meant a moor or swampy place ; so that *wōrian* was orig. 'to tramp over wet ground,' the most likely thing to cause weariness. Hence AS. *wōr-hana*, a moor-cock, O. E. Texts, p. 465. Not allied to **Wear** (1). δ. Prob. allied to Skt. *vār*, water; the prime grade appears in AS. *wær*, sea. Der. *weari-ly*, *-ness* ; *weary*, verb, Temp. iii. 1. 19 ; *weari-some*, Two Gent. ii. 7. 8 ; *weari-some-ly*, *-ness*.

WEASAND, WESAND, the wind-pipe. (E.) Spelt *wesand* in Spenser, F. Q. v. 2. 14; he also has *weasand-pipe*, id. iv. 3. 12. ME. *wesand* ; spelt *wesande*, Voc. 676. 24; *waysande*, id. 635. 19. AS. *wāsend*, Voc. 157. 45 ; 264. 19 ; used to translate L. *rūmen*, the gullet. The mod. E. *weasand* answers rather to a by-form *wēsend* ; whilst the AS. *wāsend* answers to prov. E. *wosen*, the wind-pipe (Halliwell).+OFries. *wāsende*, *wāsande*. Cf. Bavar. *waisel*, the gullet of animals that chew the cud ; MHG. *weisant*, OHG. *weisunt*, weasand, cited by E. Müller. The form is like that of a pres. part.

WEASEL, a small slender-bodied quadruped. (E.) ME. *wesele*, *wesel*, Chaucer, C. T. 3234. AS. *wesle*, Voc. 119. 6; oldest forms, *weosule*, *wesulae* ; O. E. Texts.+Du. *wezel* ; Icel. *vīsla* (given in the comp. *hreysivisla*) ; Dan. *væsel* ; MSwed. *wisla* ; Swed. *vessla* ; G. *wiesel* ; OHG. *wisala*, *wisela*, *wisula*. β. The Teut. type seems to be *wisalōn-* or *wisulōn-*, f. (Franck) ; evidently a dimin. form. Root uncertain ; cf. Gk. αἰέλουρος, αἴλουρος, a weasel ; perhaps allied to αἰόλος (for *ἀϝισόλος?), nimble.

WEATHER, the condition of the air, &c. as to sunshine or rain. (E.) ME. *weder*, P. Plowman, B. vi. 326 ; Chaucer, C. T. 10366, where Tyrwhitt prints *wether*, but the MSS. mostly have *weder*, as in all the six MSS. in the Six-text edition, Group F, l. 52. The mod. E. *th* for ME. *d* occurs again in ME. *fader*, *moder*, and is prob. due to dialectal influence. AS. *weder*, Grein, ii. 654.+Du. *weder* ; Icel. *veðr* ; Dan. *veir* (a contracted form) ; Swed. *väder*, wind, air, weather ; G. *wetter* ; OHG. *wetar* ; cf. G. *gewitter*, a storm. β. All from the Teut. type *wedrom*, n., weather, storm, wind ; allied words appear in G. *gewitter*, as above, and in Icel. *land-viðri*, a landwind, *heið-viðri*, bright weather. Further allied to Lithuan. *wėtra*, a storm, OPruss. *wetro*, wind ; Russ. *vieter'*, *vietr'*, wind, breeze ; Skt. *vātara-*, adj. windy. γ. To be divided as *we-drom*, where the suffix (as in *fa-ther*, *mo-ther*) answers to Idg. *-tró-*, denoting the agent ; and the base is *we*, weak grade of √WE, to blow, which occurs in Gothic *waian*, to blow, Skt. *vā*, to blow ; cf. Gk. ἄημι (for ἀϝη-μι), I blow ; whence also E. *wi-nd*; see **Wind** (1). δ. Thus *weather* and *wind* mean much the same, viz. ' that which blows,' and they are constantly associated in the E. phrase ' wind and weather.' ' *Wind* ligeð, *weder* bið fæger;' Phœnix, ed. Grein, l. 182. A *weather-cock* means a *wind-cock*. Der. *weather*, verb, Spenser, F. Q. v. 4. 42 ; *weather-board*, cf. Icel. *veðrborð*, the windward side ; *weather-bound*; *weather-cock*, ME. *wedercoc*, Ayenbite of Inwyt, p. 180, l. 27, and in Wright, Voc. i. 115 (12th cent.), so called because formerly often in the shape of a cock, as some are still made (cf. Du. *weerhaan*= *wederhaan*, from *haan*, a cock) ; *weather-fend*, i. e. to defend from the weather, Temp. v. 10, where *fend* is a clipped form of *defend* (see **Fence**) ; *weather-gage*, *weather-side* ; *weather-wise*, ME. *wederwis*, P. Plowman, B. xv. 350. And see *weather-beaten*, *wither*.

WEATHER-BEATEN, WEATHER-BITTEN, harassed by the weather. (E. *or* Scand.) *Weather-beaten*, lit. beaten by the weather, or beaten upon by the weather, makes such good sense that

I do not know that we can disallow it as being a genuine phrase ; it occurs in 1 Hen. IV, iii. 1. 67, in Spenser, F. Q. ii. 1. 2, and in Nich. Breton, ed. Grosart (see the Index). Cf. also prov. E. *weather-bet*, i. e. ' weather-beaten;' E. D. D. β. At the same time there can be little doubt that, in some cases, the right word is *weather-bitten*, i. e. bitten by the weather, as in Shak. Wint. Tale, v. 2. 60. The latter is a true Scand. idiom. We find Swed. *väderbiten*, lit. weather-bitten, but explained in Widegren as 'weather-beaten ;' so also Norweg. *vederbiten*, which Aasen explains by Dan. *veirbidt*, also as ' tanned in the face by exposure to the weather,' said of a man ; he also gives the expressive Norw. *vederslitten*, weather-worn (lit. weather-slit).

WEAVE, to twine threads together, work into a fabric. (E.) ME. *weuen* (for *weven*) ; pt. t. *waf*, Gower, C. A. ii. 320 ; bk. v. 5770 ; pp. *wouen* (= *woven*), spelt *wounun*, Wyclif, John, xix. 23. AS. *wefan*, pt. t. *wæf*, pp. *wefen* ; Grein, ii. 654.+Du. *weven* ; Icel. *vefa*, pt. t. *vaf*, pp. *ofinn* ; Dan. *væve* ; Swed. *vefva* ; G. *weben*, to weave, pt. t. *wob*, pp. *gewoben* ; also as a weak verb. β. All from Teut. type *weban-*, to weave ; from Idg. √WEBH, to weave, which further appears in Gk. ὑφ-ή, ὕφ-ος, a web, ὑφ-αίν-ειν, to weave, and Skt. *ūrṇa-vābhis*, a spider (lit. a wool-weaver), Brugmann, i. § 562. Der. *weav-er*, *weav-ing* ; also *web*, q. v., *wef-t*, q. v., *woof*, q. v., *waf-er*, *wasp*, *weevil*.

WEB, that which is woven ; a film over the eye, the skin between the toes of water-birds. (E.) ME. *web*, Wyclif, Job, vii. 6 ; also *webbe*, P. Plowman, B. v. 111. AS. *webb*, gen. written *web*, Voc. 50. 28.+Du. *web* ; Icel. *vefr* (gen. *vefjar*) ; Dan. *væv* ; Swed. *väf* ; G. *ge-webe*, OHG. *weppi*, *wappi*. β. All from the Teut. type *wabjom*, n., a web ; from *wab*, 2nd grade of *weban-*, from √WEBH, to weave ; see **Weave**. Der. *webb-ing*, *webb-ed*, *web-foot-ed*. Also ME. *webbe*, Chaucer, C. T. 364 (A 362), AS. *webba*, a weaver, Voc. 188. 10, where the suffix *-a* denotes the agent (obsolete, except in the name *Webb*); ME. *webster*, Wyclif, Job, vii. 6, AS. *webbestre*, a female weaver, used to translate L. *textrix*, Voc. 188. 11 (obsolete, except in the name *Webster*) ; for the suffix *-ster*, see **Spinster**.

WED, to engage by a pledge, to marry. (E.) ME. *wedden*, Chaucer, C. T. 870 (A 868). AS. *weddian*, lit. to pledge, engage, Luke xxii. 5.—AS. *wed*, sb., a pledge, Grein, ii. 653.+Du. *wedden*, to lay a wager, from MDu. *wedde*, ' a pledge, a pawne,' Hexham ; Icel. *veðja*, to wager, from *veð*, a pledge ; Dan. *vedde*, to wager ; Swed. *vädja*, to appeal, from *vad*. a bet, an appeal ; G. *wetten*, to wager, from *wette*, a wager ; Goth. *ga-wadjōn*, to pledge, betroth, from *wadi*, a pledge. β. All from the Teut. type *wad-jom*, n., a pledge. Further allied to Lithuan. *wadóti*, to redeem a pledge ; L. *uas* (gen. *uad-is*), a pledge.—√WEDH, to carry home, to marry, Fick, i. 767 ; cf. Lithuan. *wèsti*, pres. tense *wedù*, to marry, take home a bride, *wadas*, a conductor, guide, leader by the hand, Russ. *vesti*, to lead, conduct ; OIrish *fed-im*, I carry off, W. *dy-weddio*, to wed ; Skt. *vadhū-*, a bride. Der. *wedd-ed* ; *wedd-ing*, AS. *weddung*, Gospel of Nicodemus, c. 7 ; also *wed-lock*, q. v. Also see *wage*, *wager*, *gage* (1), *en-gage*.

WEDGE, a piece of metal or wood, thick at one end and sloping to a thin edge at the other. (E.) Also used to denote simply a mass of metal, as in Rich. III, i. 4. 26. ME. *wegge*, Chaucer, On the Astrolabe, pt. i. § 14, l. 3. AS. *wecg*, a mass of metal ; Sweet, A. S. Reader. ' Cuneus, *wecg* ;' Voc. 216. 12.+Du. *wig*, *wigge*, a wedge ; Icel. *veggr* ; Dan. *vægge* ; Swed. *vigg* ; OHG. *wekki*, MHG. *wecke*, a wedge ; G. *wecke*, a kind of loaf, from its shape (cf. prov. E. *wig*, a kind of cake). β. All from Teut. type *wag-joz*, m., a wedge ; from Teut. base *wag-* = Idg. *wogh*, with velar *gh*, as shown by the cognate Lithuan. *wagis*, a bent wooden peg for hanging things upon, also a spigot for a cask, also a wedge. See Brugmann, i. §§ 367, 654. Der. *wedge*, verb.

WEDLOCK, marriage. (E.) ME. *wedlok* (with long o), written *wedloke*, P. Plowman, B. ix. 113, 119 ; where some MSS. have *wedlok*. AS. *wedlāc*, in the sense of pledge ; ' Arrabo, *wedlāc*,' Voc. 115. 42. —AS. *wed*, a pledge ; and *lāc*, a sport, also a gift, in token of pleasure. Thus the sense is ' a gift given as a pledge, and in token of pleasure ;' hence, the gift given to a bride. It was usual to make a present to the bride on the morning after marriage ; cf. G. *morgengabe*, a nuptial (lit. morning) gift. However, *-lāc* is also used as a mere suffix, with but slight meaning. See **Wed**. And see **Knowledge**, which has a like suffix.

WEDNESDAY, the fourth day of the week. (E.) ME. *wednesday*, P. Plowman, B. xiii. 154, where one MS. has *wodnesday*. AS. *Wōdnes dæg*, rubric to Matt. v. 25. The change from *ō* to *ē* is the usual vowel-change, when the vowel *i* follows ; this vowel appears in the OFries. *Wernisdei*, for *Wēdnisdei* ; cf. OFries. *Wēda*, Woden (Weigand, s. v. *Wotan*), NFries. *Weensdi*, Outzen, p. 38 ; so that the *ē* for *ō* is Friesian. '*Wōdnes dæg*' means 'day of Wōden or Wōdin,' after whom it was named ; see **Day**. Cognate words are Du. *woensdag*, Icel. *ōðinsdagr*, Swed. Dan. *onsdag* (for *odensdag*). The

G. name is simply *mitwoch* (mid-week). β. The AS. *Wōden* is cognate with Icel. *Ōðinn*, OHG. *Wōtan*, *Wuotan*. The name signifies 'the furious,' or rather 'the divinely inspired;' being apparently c'osely related to L. *uātes* (stem *uāti*-), a prophet, a seer, and to OIrish *faith* (Celtic stem *wāti*-), a singer, minstrel. Also, to AS. *wōd*, raging, mad (cognate with Icel. *ōðr*, Goth. *wōds*), whence ME. *wood*, mad, a word which occurs as late as in Shakespeare, Mids. Nt. Dr. ii. 1. 192; see **Wood** (2). ¶ It is remarkable that the Romans, whilst looking upon Wōden as the chief divinity of the Teutonic races, nevertheless identified him with Mercury; hence *dies Mercurii* was translated into AS. by *Wōdnesdæg*. Cf. 'kölluðu þeir Pāl Ōðin, en Barnabas Þōr'=they called Paul Odinn, but Barnabas Thor; Icel. Bible, Acts, xiv. 12.

WEE, small, tiny. (E.) 'A little *wee* face;' Merry Wives, i. 4. 22. ME. *we*, only as a sb., a bit. 'A little *we*,' a little bit, for a short space; Barbour, Bruce, vii. 182, xiii. 217. 'And behynd hir a litill *we* It fell'=and it fell a little way behind her; id. xvii. 677. In all three passages it occurs in the same phrase, viz. 'a little *we*;' and in the last case we should now say 'a little way.' So also: 'a litill *wee*;' G. Douglas, tr. of Virgil, Æn. bk. x. ch. 6; cf. 'in a litel *wei*,' in a short time, Cursor Mundi, 12531; 'He ne es yitt bot a littel *wei*,' he is yet but young; id. 8419. And as it is a sb., I believe it is nothing but the Northern form of E. *way*. See **Way**. ¶ That the constant association of *little* with *we* (=way) should lead to the supposition that the words *little* and *wee* are synonymous, seems natural enough; and we have the evidence of Barbour that the word is Northern. The above solution is strongly corroborated by the fact that *way-bit* is still in use, in the North, in the sense of *wee bit* or little bit; see Halliwell, and *wee* in E. D. D.; also *Way-bit* in Davies, Supp. Glossary. 'In the North parts, wher ther is a *wea-bit* to every mile;' Howell, Letters, bk. iv. let. 28.

WEED (1), any useless and troublesome plant. (E.) ME. *weed*, Prompt. Parv. p. 519. AS. *wēod*, *wiod*; Grein, ii. 676.+OSax. *wiod*; whence Du. *wieden*, vb., to weed. Teut. type *weudom*, n. Root unknown. Der. *weed*, verb, ME. *weeden*, Palladius on Husbandry, ii. 289; cf. Du. *wieden*, Low G. *wēden*, to weed. Der. *weed-y*, Hamlet, iv. 7. 175.

WEED (2), a garment. (E.) Chiefly in the phr. 'a widow's *weeds*,' i. e. a widow's mourning apparel. Common in Shak. as a sing. sb., in the sense of garment, Mids. Nt. Dr. ii. 1. 256, &c. ME. *wede* (dissyllabic), Havelok, l. 94. AS. *wǣde*, neut., also *wǣd*, fem., a garment; Grein, ii. 642.+OFriesic *wēde*, *wēd*; OSax. *wādi*; MDu. *wade*, 'a garment, a habit, or a vesture,' Hexham; Icel. *vāð*, a piece of stuff, cloth; also, a garment; OHG. *wāt*, *wōt*, clothing, armour; O. Low G. *wād*, a coverlet (Gallée). β. All from the Teut. base *wǣd*-, a garment, perhaps 'something woven;' cf. Skt. *vē*, to weave. Others connect it with Goth. *ga-widan*, pt. t. *gawath*, Mark, x. 9, OHG. *wetan*, to bind, yoke together. Cf. Skt. *vi-vadha*-, a yoke for carrying a burden. See **Wad**.

WEEK, a period of seven days. (E.) The vowel, in ME., is very variable; we find *weke*, *wike*, on the one hand, and *wouke*, *woke*, *wuke* on the other. In Chaucer, Six-text, Group A, 1539, we have *weke*, *wike*, as well as *wouke*; Tyrwhitt, C. T. 1541, prints *weke*. 1. The forms *weke*, *wike* (together with mod. E. *week*) answer to AS. *wice*, *wicu*, of which the gen. *wican* occurs in Thorpe, Ancient Laws, ii. 438, l. 23 (Eccl. Institutes, § 41). 2. The forms *wouke*, *woke*, *wuke*, answer to AS. *wuce*, *wucu*, Grein, ii. 744. We find the same change in AS. *widu*, later form *wudu*, wood.+Du. *week*; Icel. *vika*; Swed. *vecka*; OHG. *wecha*, *wehha*; but the MHG. form is *woche*, which is also the mod. G. form. Cf. Dan. *uge* (=*vuge*), a week. β. The prevalent Teut. type is *wikōn*-, f. The Goth. *wikō* occurs only once, in Luke, i. 8, where the Gk. ἐν τῇ τάξει τῆς ἐφημερίας αὐτοῦ (L. in ordine uicis suæ) appears in Gothic as *in wikōn kunjis seinis*=in the *order* of his course. It is by no means clear what is the precise force of this Goth. *wikō* (which exactly answers in form to E. *week*), and some have (wrongly) supposed that it was borrowed from L. *uicis*, which is, however equivalent in this passage to *kunjis*, not to *wikō*. γ. It is usual to consider *week* as a true Teut. word, and allied to AS. *wice*, an office, duty, function; perhaps it meant 'succession' or 'change,' being related to Icel. *vikja*, to turn, return; from Teut. *wik*-, weak grade of *wīkan*-, to yield, give way, give place to. Cf. Icel. *vixl*, a change, *vixling*, a changeling, G. *wechsel*, a change; a week corresponds to a phase of the moon. Cf. also Skt. *vij*, to tremble; and see **Weak**. Der. *week-day*, Icel. *vikudagr*; *week-ly*.

WEEN, to suppose, imagine, think. (E.) ME. *wenen*, Chaucer, C. T. 1655. AS. *wēnan*, to imagine, hope, expect; Grein, ii. 658.—AS. *wēn*, expectation, supposition, hope; id.+Du. *wanen*, to fancy, from *waan*, conjecture; Icel. *vāna*, to hope, from *vān*, expectation; G. *wähnen*, from *wahn*, OHG. *wān*, sb.; Goth. *wēnjan*, to expect, from *wēns*, expectation. β. From the sb. of which the Teut. type

is *wǣniz*, f., expectation, hope. Perhaps it meant orig. 'a striving after,' and hence an expectation of obtaining. Some compare it with L. *uēnārī*, to hunt after; and with Teut. *wǣn*, 3rd grade of Teut. *wenan*-, to crave, desire; cf. L. *uen-us*, desire, Skt. *van*, to crave. See **Win**.

WEEP, to wail, lament, shed tears. (E.) ME. *wepen*, orig. a strong verb, pt. t. *weep*, *wep*, Chaucer, C. T. Six-text ed., Group D, l. 588, where only one MS. has *wepte* (dissyllabic), for which Tyrwhitt erroneously prints *wept*, C. T. 6170. AS. *wēpan*, pt. t. *wēop*; Grein, ii. 661. The lit. sense is to cry aloud, raise an outcry, lament loudly; *wēpan* (for *wōpian*) is regularly formed, with the usual vowel-change, from *wōp*, a clamour, outcry, lament, Grein, ii. 732.+OSax. *wōpian*, to raise an outcry; *wōp*, sb.; Goth. *wōpjan*, to cry out; OHG. *wuofan*, to lament, weep, str. vb.; also *wuoffan*, weak vb., *wuof*, *wuaf*, an outcry; Icel. *æpa*, to shout, cry; *ōp*, a shout. β. All from the Teut. base *wōp*-, appearing in *wōpoz*, m. (AS. *wōp*), an outcry, loud lament. ¶ This AS. *wōp* is quite distinct from E. *whoop*, in which the initial *w* is unoriginal, but the *h* essential. Der. *weet-er*, *weep-ing*.

WEET, to know; the same as **Wit** (1), q. v.

WEEVIL, a small kind of beetle very destructive to grain. (E.) ME. *weuel*, *wiuel* (with *u*=*v*), spelt *wevyl*, *wyvyl* in Prompt. Parv., pp. 523, 531. AS. *wifel*, to translate L. *scarebius* (sic), Voc. 261. 13; spelt *wibil* in a very early gloss of the 8th century, where it translates L. *cantarus*, i. e. *cantharis*, a beetle; Voc. 11. 28. We even find the older form *wibba*; 'Scarabeus, *scærn-wibba*,' Voc. 319. 2; where *scærn* means dung.+Icel. *-yfill*, in comp. *tordyfill*, a dung-beetle; MDu. *wevel*, 'a little worme eating corne or beanes, or a wevill,' Hexham; OHG. *wibil*, MHG. *wibel*; G. *wiebel*. β. The Teut. type is *webiloz*, m., a beetle; a dimin. form of Teut. *webjon*-, m., whence AS. *wibba*. From the Teut. *web-an*-, to weave; from the filaments spun for the larva-case. See **Weave**. γ. Further allied to Lithuan. *wábalas*, a chafer, winged insect.

WEFT, the threads woven into and crossing the warp. (E.) ME. *weft*, Wyclif, Exod. xxxix. 3, earlier version, where the later version has *warp*. AS. *weft*, *wefta*; 'Deponile, *weft*, vel *wefta*;' Voc. 187. 32; and again 'Deponile, *wefta*' in a gloss of the 8th century, id. 17. 6.+Icel. *veftr*; also *vipta*, *vifta*. β. The Teut. types are *weftoz*, m., *wefton*-, m., lit. 'a thing woven;' formed with participial suffix -*to*- from *web-an*-, to weave, whence AS. *wef-an*, to weave; see **Weave** and **Woof**.

WEIGH, to balance, ponder, to have weight, be heavy. (E.) ME. *weghen*, *weȝen*, *weyen*, *weien*, Chaucer, C. T. 456 (A 454). AS. *wegan*, str. vb., pt. t. *wæg*, to carry, bear; also, intrans., to move; Grein, ii. 655. From the sense of 'carry' we pass to that of 'raise' or 'lift,' as when we say 'to *weigh* anchor;' so also Cowper says: '*Weigh* the vessel up;' Loss of the Royal George, st. 7. From the sense of raising or lifting, we pass to that of weighing.+Du. *wegen*, to weigh; Icel. *vega*, to move, carry, lift, weigh; Dan. *veie*, to weigh; Swed. *väga*, to weigh; *väga upp*, to weigh up, to lift; G. *wegen*, to move, *wiegen*, to move gently, rock, *wägen*, to weigh; OHG. *wegan*, to move, bear, weigh. Cf. Goth. *gawigan*, to shake about. β. The AS. *wegan* is a strong verb; pt. t. *wæg*, pp. *wegen*; so also is the Icel. *vega*; pt. t. *vā*, pp. *veginn*. All from the Teut. type *wegan*-, pt. t. *wag*, pp. *weganoz*, to carry, move, weigh, answering to Idg. √WEGH, to carry, as in Skt. *vah*, L. *uehere*; see **Vehicle**. Der. *weigh-t*, ME. *weght*, P. Plowman, B. xiv. 292, also spelt *wight*, Chaucer, Troilus, ii. 1385; AS. *ge-wiht*, Gen. xxiii. 16, cognate with MDu. *wicht*, *gewicht* (Hexham), Du. *gewigt*, G. *gewicht*, Swed. *vigt*; cf. Icel. *vætt*, Dan. *vægt*. Teut. type *weg-tom*, n., which became *weh-tom*; and AS. *weht* became *wiht* by palatal mutation (Sievers); whence *weight*, spelt *wayghty* in Palsgrave; *weight-i-ly*, -*ness*. Also *wag*, q. v.; *wagg-on*, *wain*, *wey*, *wight*, *whit*.

WEIR, **WEAR**, a dam in a river. (E.) ME. *wer*; dat. *were*, Chaucer, Parlament of Foules, 138. AS. *wer*, a weir, dam, Ælfred, tr. of Gregory's Past. Care, c. 38, ed. Sweet, p. 278, l. 16; the pp. *gewered*, dammed up, occurs in the line above. The lit. sense is 'defence,' hence a fence, dam; closely allied to AS. *werian*, to defend, protect, also (as above) to dam up, Grein, ii. 662.+Icel. *vörr*, a fenced in landing-place, *ver*, a fishing-station; G. *wehr*, a defence; cf. *wehren*, to defend, also to check, constrain, control; *mühl-wehr*, a mill-dam; MDu. *weer*, 'a palissado, or a rampard,' Hexham. Cf. also Goth. *warjan*, to defend, Icel. *verja*; allied to Skt. *vṛ*, to cover, *vāraya*, to stop, hinder, keep off, *vartra*-, a dam, embankment (Macdonell); Gk. ἔρυσθαι, to ward off. From the √WER, to protect.

WEIRD, fate, destiny. (E.) As an adj. in Shak. Macb. i. 3. 32; i. 5. 8; ii. 1. 20; iii. 4. 133; iv. 1. 136, where it means 'subservient to destiny.' But it is properly a sb. ME. *wirde*, *wyrde*; 'And out of wo into wele ȝoure *wyrdes* shul chaunge'=and out of woe into weal your destinies shall change; P. Plowman, C. xiii. 209. AS. *wyrd*, also *wird*, fate, destiny, also one of the 'Norns' or Fates, an extremely common word in poetry, Grein, ii. 760. Teut. type *wurðiz*, f. Formed, by vowel-change from *u* to *y*, from Teut. *wurð-* (with *wurð-*<*wurþ*, by Verner's Law), weak grade of Teut. *werthan-*>AS. *weorþan*, to be, become, take place, happen, come to pass; see **Worth** (2). The lit. sense is 'that which happens,' or 'that which comes to pass;' hence fate, destiny.+Icel. *urðr*, fate, one of the three Norns or Fates; cf. *urð-*, stem of pt. t. pl. of *verða*, to become; OSax. *wurð*, fate; OHG. *wurt*. (✔WERT.)

WELCOME, received gladly, causing gladness by coming. (Scand.) Now used as an adj., and derived from *well*, adv., and the pp. *come* of the verb *to come*; and hence of Scand. origin.—Icel. *velkominn*, welcome; cf. Dan. *velkommen*, Swed. *välkommen*.—Icel. *vel*, well; and *kominn*, pp. of *koma*, to come. Hence also the AF. verb *welcomer*, to welcome (Godefroy). β. Substituted for AS. *wilcuma*, masc. sb., one who comes so as to please another, Grein, ii. 705.—AS. *wil-*, prefix, allied to *willa*, will, pleasure; and *cuma*, a comer, one who comes, formed, with suffix *-a* of the agent, from *cuman*, to come; Grein, ii. 706; i. 169. See **Will** and **Come**. Hence AS. *wilcumian*, to welcome.

WELD (1), to beat metal together. (Scand.) The final *d* is excrescent, like *d* after *l* in *alder*, a tree, *elder*, a tree, and Shakespeare's *alder-liefest* for *aller-liefest*, 2 Hen. VI, i. 1. 28. It is only a particular use of the word *well*, verb, to spring up as a fountain, lit. to boil up. It meant (1) to boil, (2) to heat to a high degree, (3) to beat heated iron. We find this particular use in Wyclif, Isaiah, ii. 4; where the earlier version has 'thei shul *bete* togidere their swerdes in-to shares,' the later version has 'thei schulen *welle* togidere her swerdes in-to scharris.' See further under **Well** (2). The word is apparently Scand., not E.; for (1) the Swed. *välla* (lit. to well) is only used in the sense 'to weld,' as in *välla järn*, to weld iron (Widegren); the sense 'to well' appearing in the comp. *uppvälla*, to boil up; (2) Sweden exports large quantities of iron and steel. Cf. Dan. *vælde* (with excrescent *d*), to well up; Pomeran. *wellen*, to weld iron; prov. E. *well*, to weld. In Icel. and Norw., a distinction is made between *vella*, intr., to well, pt. t. *vall* (str. vb.), and *vella*, tr., to cause to boil (wk. vb.); the Swed. *välla* to weld, answers to the latter. ¶ 'The process of welding iron is named, in many languages, from the word for boiling; cf. Illyrian *variti*, to boil, weld iron, Lettish *wárit*, to boil, *sawárit*, to weld,' &c.; Wedgwood.

WELD (2), dyer's weed; *Reseda luteola*. (E.) ME. *welde*; 'Madyr, *welde*, or *wood*'=madder, weld, or woad; Chaucer, Ætas Prima, l. 17. '*Welde*, or *wolde*;' Prompt. Parv. pp. 520, 532. According to Cockayne, A. S. Leechdoms, iii. 349, it is spelt *wolde* in MS. Harl. 3388. In Lowland Scotch, it is *wald*; see Jamieson. It appears to be an E. word. Cognate with Low G. *wolde*, weld (Lübben), Du. *wouw*, MDu. *wouwe* (for **wolde*); also G. *wau*, Swed. Dan. *vau* (from Du.). We also find Span. *gualda*, F. *gaude* (of Teut. origin). Prob. allied to AS. *weald*, a wood, as if 'belonging to the wood or wold;' see **Wold**. Cf. OSax. *sin-weldi*, a great wood. ¶ Quite distinct from **Woad**.

WELFARE, prosperity. (E.) Lit. a state of *faring* or going on *well*. ME. *welfare*, Chaucer, C. T. 11150 (F 838); compounded of *wel*, adv. well, and *fare*=AS. *faru*, sb., lit. a journey, from *faran*, to fare, go. See **Well** (1) and **Fare**. Cf. Icel. *velferð*, a welldoing.

WELKIN, the sky, the region of clouds. (E.) In Shak. Merry Wives, i. 3. 101, &c. ME. *welkin*, as printed in Tyrwhitt's edition of Chaucer, C. T. 9000, where the MSS. have *welkne*, *welken*, *welkine*, *walkyn*, Six-text, Group E, 1124. In P. Plowman, B. xvii. 160, we have *welkne*, *wolkne*, *þe welkene*, *welken* in the various MSS. It thus appears that *welkne* is a mutated form of *wolkne*, which is an older spelling; in Layamon, 4574, 23947, we have *wolkne*, *wolcne*, *weolcene*, prob. a pl. form, and signifying 'the clouds.' AS. *wolcnu*, clouds, pl. of *wolcen*, a cloud, Grein, ii. 731.+OSax. *wolkan*, a cloud. Du. *wolk*, Low G. *wulke*; G. *wolke*, OHG. *wolka*, f., *wolkan*, n., a cloud. Teut. base **wulk(e)no-*. β. Some have connected it with AS. *geweale*, a rolling about, as in *yða geweale*, the rolling of the waves, Grein, i. 477; from *wealcan*, to roll, walk; see **Walk**. There is no proof of this; if it were true, *wolcen* would mean 'that which rolls about;' cf. AS. *wealca*, a wave, billow. γ. Or else connected with OHG. *welk*, moist, damp; Russ. *vlaga*, moisture; Lith. *wilg-yti*, to wet, moisten; from an Idg. ✔WELG.

WELL (1), in a good state, excellently. (E.) ME. *wel*, Chaucer, C. T. 106; *weel*, 4728 (B 308). AS. *wel*, Grein, ii. 656; also spelt *well*.+Du. *wel*; Icel. *vel*; Dan. *vel*; Swed. *väl*; Goth. *waila*.+G. *wohl*, *wol*; OHG. *wela*, *wola*. β. The Goth. *waila* answers to a Teut. type **wela*. The orig. sense is 'agreeably,' or suitably to one's will or wish; from the Idg. ✔WEL, to wish; cf. L. *uol-o*, I wish, *uel-le*, to wish, Russ. *vol-ia*, sb., will, W. *gwell*, better, Skt. *vara-*,

better, *vara-*, a wish, *prati varam*, according to a wish; see **Will**. Der. *well-behaved*, Merry Wives, ii. 1. 59; *-beloved*, Jul. Cæs. iii. 2. 180; *-born*, *-bred*, *-disposed*; *-favoured*, Two Gent. ii. 1. 54; *-meaning*, Rich. II, ii. 1. 128; *-meant*, 3 Hen. VI, iii. 3. 67; *-nigh*; *-spoken*, Rich. III, i. 1. 29; *-won*, Merch. Ven. i. 3. 51; and numerous other compounds. And see *wel-come*, *wel-fare*; also *weal*, *weal-th*.

WELL (2), a spring, fountain of water. (E.) ME. *welle* (dissyllabic), Chaucer, C. T. 5689 (D 107). AS. *wella*, also *well*, Grein, ii. 657; also spelt *wylla*, *wylle*, *wyll*, id. 756. Teut. type **walljon-*, m.; allied to AS. *weallan* (strong verb, pt. t. *weoll*, pp. *weallen*), to well up, boil, id. 672; the mod. E. verb *to well* being derived, not from this strong verb, but from the sb.; so that the pt. t. in mod. E. is *welled*.+Icel. *vell*, ebullition; from *vella*, to well, boil, pt. t. *vall*, pp. *ollinn* (strong verb); whence also *vella*, weak verb, to make to boil; Du. *wel*, a spring; Dan. *væld* (for *væll*), a spring; G. *welle*, a wave, surge; cf. *wallen*, to undulate, boil, bubble up, of which the OHG. pt. t. was *wial*. β. All from the Teut. **wallan-*, str. vb., to boil up, undulate; from the Idg. ✔WEL, to turn round, roll, as in Skt. *val*, to move to and fro, Russ. *valiate*, to roll. See further under **Helix**. From the weak grade we have Goth. *wulan*, to boil; cf. also AS. *wielm*, *wylm*, a boiling, and Skt. *ūrmi-*, a wave. Der. *well*, verb, ME. *wellen*, verb, in P. Plowman, B. xix. 375, from AS. *wellan*, *wyllan*; we find 'Ferueo, ic *welle*,' Ælfric's Grammar, ed. Zupitza, p. 156, l. 14, in the Royal MS. (see the footnote), though most MSS. have ic *wealle*. Der. *wellspring*, ME. *wellespring*, Genesis and Exodus, l. 1243. And see *weld* (1).

WELLAWAY, an exclamation of great sorrow. (E.) In Spenser, F. Q. ii. 8. 46. ME. *weilawey*, Chaucer, C. T. 13048 (B 1308); the MSS. have *weylawey*, *weilaweie*, and (corruptly) *well awaye*, *wele away*, showing that some scribes mistook it to mean 'weal [is] away,' i. e. prosperity is over! '*Weilawei*, and *wolowo*'=alas! and alas! Ancren Riwle, p. 88, l. 7; *weilawei*, id. p. 274, l. 2. 'Wo is us þat we weren born! *Weilawei*!' Havelok, 462; cf. l. 570. Written *wæila wæi*, Layamon, 8031; *wala wa*, 7971; also *wela*, *wo la* (without *wei* or *wa* following), 3456. It stands for *wei la wei* or *wā lā wā* (*wo lo wo*). AS. *wā lā wā*, written *wālā wā*, alas! lit. 'woe! lo! woe!' Ælfred, tr. of Boethius, c. xxxix. § 1 (b. iv. met. 4); *wei lā wei*, id., c. xxxv. § 6 (b. iii. met. 12); we also find *wālā*, Mark, xv. 29, and simply *wā*, Mark, xiv. 21.—AS. *wā*, woe; *lā*, lo; *wā*, woe. See **Woe** and **Lo**. ¶ The expression was early misunderstood; and was even turned into *wella-day*, Merry Wives, iii. 3. 106; in which unmeaning expression, though intended as an exclamation of sorrow, we seem to have *well* in place of *wo*, and *day* introduced without any sense; perhaps *alas! the day* also owed its existence to this unmeaning corruption.

WELSH, pertaining to Wales. (E.) *Welsh* properly means 'foreign.' ME. *walsh*, P. Plowman, B. v. 324; *Walsh* is still in use as a proper name. AS. *wælisc*, *welisc*; 'þā *welisce* menn'=the foreigners, i. e. Normans, A. S. Chron. an. 1048; see Earle's edition, p. 178, l. 15; 'þā *wælisce* men,' ibid. l. 24; and see the note. Formed, with suffix *-isc* (>E. *-ish*) and vowel-change, from AS. *wealh*, a foreigner; orig. a Celt. (From the pl. *Wealas* we have mod. E. *Wales*, now the name of a country.) The Teut. form **Walh-* answers to L. *Volc-*, i. e. 'one of the tribe of *Volcæ*,' who occupied Southern Gaul. See **Walnut**. Der. *Welsh-rabbit*, a Welsh dainty, i. e. not a rabbit, but *toasted cheese*; this is a mild joke, just as a *Norfolk-capon* is not a capon at all, but a red-herring (Halliwell). There is no authority for the assertion that *rabbit* is a corruption of *rare bit*; which renders *Welsh* pointless.

WELT, a narrow strip of leather round a shoe. (E.) The old sense seems to be hem or border. Cotgrave explains F. *orlet* by 'a little hemme, selvidge, welt, border;' and the verb *orler* by 'to hemme, selvidge, border, welt the edges or sides of.' 'Take care of the skirts, fringes, and *welts* of their garments,' Holland, tr. of Pliny, b. vii. c. 51. '*Welt* of a garment, *ourelet* [F. *orlet*]; *Welte* of a shoe, *oureleure*;' Palsgrave. ME. *welte*. '*Welte* of a schoo, Incucium, vel intercucium;' Prompt. Parv. 'Hec pedana, Anglice *wampay* [a vamp]; Hoc intercucium, Anglice *weltte*;' Voc. 664. 34, 35. Palsgrave also has the verb; 'I *welte*, as a garment is, *je ourle*: This kyrtell is well welted, *ce corset icy est bien ourlé*.' Lowl. Sc. *waut*, ME. *walte*, a welt, *walte*, to welt; Cathol. Anglicum. The pl. *waltys* occurs as a gloss to *intercucia*, in John de Garlande; Wright's Vocab. i. 125. Lit. 'a hem,' or 'strip turned over;' cf. Norw. *vælt*, a card turned up as a trump; allied to AS. *wyltan*, *gewæltan*, to roll, Icel. *velta*, to roll over; see **Welter** and **Wale**. We also find W. *gwald*, a hem, welt, *gwaltes*, the welt of a shoe; *gwaldu*, to welt, hem; Gael. *balt*, a welt of a shoe, a border; Irish *balt*, a welt, border; all (apparently) borrowed from E. Der. *welt*, verb.

WELTER, to wallow, roll about. (Scand.) Surrey has '*waltring* tongs,' i. e. rolling or lolling tongues of snakes, tr. of Virgil's Æneid, bk. ii. l. 266. 'I *walter*, I tumble, *je me voystre*; Hye you, your horse is *walteringe* yonder, *hastez vous, vostre cheual se voystre la ;* ' Palsgrave. ' I *welter, je verse* ; Thou *welterest* in the myer, as thou were a sowe ;' Palsgrave. ME. *weltren*, to wallow ; Cursor Mundi, 4503 ; prob. of Scand. origin ; cf. Swed. *vältra*, to roll, to wallow. *Walter* and *welter* are frequentative forms, with the usual suffix -*er*, from ME. *walten*, to roll over, overturn, hence to totter, fall, throw, rouse, rush, &c. ; Destruction of Troy, 1956, 3810, 4627, 4633, 4891, pt. t. *welt*, id. 4418, 4891, &c. This ME. *walten* is from the AS. **wealtan, wæltan*, a strong verb, of which the pp. *gewælten* (for *gewealten*) occurs in the Lindisfarne MS., in the ONorthumb. translation of Matt. xvii. 14, where *cnêum gewælteno* occurs as a gloss on *genibus prouolutis* ; hence the secondary verb *wyltan*, to roll round, Grein, ii. 757, also the adj. *unwealt*, steady, lit. ' not tottering,' A. S. Chron. an. 897, ed. Earle, p. 95, l. 14, and the note. Cf. Low G. *weltern, wältern*, to roll over ; Icel. *veltask*, to rotate, to roll over, as a horse does, from *velta*, pt. t. *valt*, to roll ; Dan. *vælte*, to roll, overturn ; Swed. *vältra*, to roll, wallow, welter, frequentative of *välta*, to roll ; G. *wälzen*, to roll, wallow, welter, from *walzen*, to roll ; Goth. *us-waltjan*, to subvert. See **Waltz, Wallow**. From Idg. base **wel-d-*, extended from √WEL, to turn ; see **Well** (2).

WEN, a fleshy tumour. (E.) ME. *wenne* ; ' Wenne, *veruca, gibbus*,' Prompt. Parv. AS. *wenn* ; acc. pl. *wennas*, A. S. Leechdoms, iii. 12, l. 22 ; nom. pl. *wænnas*, id. 46, l. 21.+Du. *wen* ; Low G. *ween* ; *ween-bulen* [wen-boils] ; prov. G. *wenne, wehne, wähne*, cited by E. Müller ; Dan. dial. *van*, a wen, wart. β. The orig. sense was prob. 'pain,' or painful swelling ; Teut. type *wanjoz, m. Prob. from *wann, 2nd grade of the Teut. str. vb. seen in Goth. *winnan*, to suffer, as in *aglōns winnan*=to suffer afflictions, 1 Tim. v. 10 ; cf. *wunns*, affliction, suffering, 2 Tim. iii. 11. So also Icel. *vinna*, though cognate with E. *win*, means not only to work, labour, toil, but also to suffer, and *vinna ā* is to do bodily harm to another. See **Win**.

WENCH, a young girl, vulgar woman. (E.) Common in prov. E. without any depreciatory intention ; as, ' a fine young *wench*.' ' Temperance was a delicate *wench*,' Temp. ii. 1. 43. ME. *wenche*, Chaucer, C. T. 3254 ; P. Plowman, B. v. 364. We also find the form *wenchel*, Ancren Riwle, p. 334, note *k*. β. It is to be particularly noted that *wenchel* is the earlier form ; Stratmann gives no references for *wenche* earlier than Will. of Palerne, l. 1901, Wyclif, Matt. ix. 24, and Poems and Lives of the Saints, ed. Furnivall, xvi. 98, where, however, the form printed is *wenclen*. But *wenchel* (spelt *wennchell*) occurs in the Ormulum, 3356, where it is used of a *male* infant, viz. in the account of the annunciation of Christ's birth to the shepherds. The orig. sense was simply ' infant,' without respect of sex, but, as the word also implies ' weak ' or ' tender,' it was naturally soon restricted to the weaker sex. The ME. *wenche* resulted from *wenchel* by loss of *l*, which was doubtless thought to be a dimin. suffix ; yet in this particular instance, it is not so. The sb. *wenchel*, an infant, is closely allied to the ME. adj. *wankel*, tottery, unsteady, Reliquiæ Antiquæ, i. 221. AS. *wencel*, a child, a daughter (Toller) ; pl. *winclo*, children (of either sex), Exod. xxi. 4. Allied to *wencel, wencele*, weak, Grein, ii. 659 ; *wancol, woncol*, unstable, Ælfred, tr. of Boethius, c. vii. § 2 (b. ii. pr. 1). γ. The lit. sense of *wancol* is ' tottery,' whence the senses unstable, weak, infantine, easily followed. Formed, with AS. suffix -*ol*, from Teut. base **wank-*, to bend sideways, nod, totter, as in G. *wanken*, to totter, reel, stagger, waddle, flinch, shrink ; cf. MHG. *wenken* (causal form), to render unsteady.+MHG. *wankel*, OHG. *wanchal*, unstable ; mod. G. (provincial) *wankel*, ' tottering, unsteady,' Flügel. The base **wank-* is the 2nd grade of Teut. **wenkan-* ; see further under **Wink**.

WEND, to go, take one's way. (E.) Now little used, except in the pt. t. *went*, which is used in place of the pt. t. of *go*. When used, it is gen. in the phr. ' to *wend* one's way ;' but Shak. twice has simply *wend*, Com. of Errors, i. i. 158, Mids. Nt. Dr. iii. 2. 372. ME. *wenden*, Chaucer, C. T. 16. AS. *wendan*, (1) trans. to turn ; (2) intrans. to turn oneself, proceed, go ; common in both senses, Grein, ii. 659. The pt. t. was *wende*, which became *wente* in ME., and is now *went*. The lit. sense was orig. ' to make to wind,' and it is the causal of *wind* ; formed, by vowel-change of *a* to *e*, from Teut. *wand, 2nd grade of **wendan-, windan-*, to wind.+Du. *wenden*, to turn, to tack, causal of *winden* ; Icel. *venda*, to wend, turn, change, causal of *vinda* ; Dan. *vende*, caus. of *vinde* ; Swed. *vända*, caus. of *vinda* ; Goth. *wandjan*, caus. of *windan* ; G. *wenden*, caus. of *winden*. See **Wind** (2).

WERE, pl. of *was* ; also as subj. sing. and pl. See **Was**.

WERGILD, in AS. law, a fine paid for manslaughter or crime against the person. (E.) See Blount's Nomolexicon. AS. *wergild*, the price set upon a man according to his rank (Toller). — AS. *wer*, a man ; and *gild*, a payment, from *gildan, gieldan*, to pay. See **Werwolf** and **Yield**.

WERWOLF, a man-wolf. (E.) On the subject of *werwolves*, i. e. men supposed to be metamorphosed into wolves, see pref. to William of Palerne, otherwise called William and the Werwolf, p. xxvi ; where the etymology is discussed. Cf. Gk. λυκάνθρωπος, i. e. wolf-man. ME. *werwolf*, Will. of Palerne, 80, &c. AS. *were-wulf*, a werwolf ; as an epithet of the devil (meaning fierce despoiler). Laws of Cnut, § 26, in Thorpe, Ancient Laws, i. 374. Usually explained as from AS. *wer*, a man ; and *wulf*, a wolf.+G. *währwolf*, a werwolf ; MHG. *werwolf* ; as if from MHG. *wer*, a man, and *wolf*, a wolf. This was Latinised as *garulphus* or *gerulphus*, whence OF. *garoul* (Burguy), mod. F. *loup-garou*, i. e. wolf-man-wolf, the word *loup* being prefixed because the sense of the final -*ou* had been lost. For the latter syllable, see **Wolf**. For the AS. *wer*, see **Virile**. B. Kluge thinks this is uncertain ; for the AS. prefix *were-* (answering to OHG. *weri-* in *Weri-wolf*, a man's name) suggests connexion with AS. *weri-an*, to wear clothes ; cf. Icel. *ûlf-hamr*, lit. ' wolf-skin,' applied to the skin of a werwolf. But it is easy to reply that the AS. *wergild* (certainly derived from AS. *wer*, a man) is also spelt *weregild* ; the OHG. forms being *weragilt, werigelt*. Hence the usual explanation ' man-wolf ' may certainly be accepted. See **Wergild**. Cf. O. Low G. *weregild* (Gallée).

WEST, the quarter where the sun sets. (E.) ME. *west*, P. Plowman, B. xviii. 113. AS. *west*, Grein, ii. 667, where it occurs as an adv., with the sense ' westward ;' we also find *westan*, adv., from the west, id. 668 ; *west-dæl*, the west part, *west-ende*, the west end, *west-mest*, most in the west.+Du. *west*, adj. and adv. ; Icel. *vestr*, sb., the west ; Dan. and Swed. *vest*, sb. ; G. *west* (whence F. *ouest*) β. All from Teut. base **wes-t-*, west. Prob. allied to Gk. ἕσ-περος, L. *ues-per*, evening. See **Vesper**. Der. *west-ward*, AS. *weste-weard*, adj., Ælfred, tr. of Boethius, c. xvi. § 4 (b. ii. met. 6)· *west-ern* ; *west-er-ly* (short for *west-ern-ly*).

WET, very moist, rainy. (E.) ME. *wēt* (with long *e*), spelt *weet* in The Castle of Love, l. 1433 (Stratmann) ; whence pl. *wēte* (dissyllabic), Chaucer, C. T. 1282 (A 1280), riming with *grēte*, pl. of *grēt*, great. AS. *wǣt*, Grein, ii. 651.+Icel. *vātr* ; Dan. *vaad* ; Swed. *vāt* ; NFries. *weet*. β. All from Teut. type *wǣtoz, wet ; from the same root as E. *water*. From Teut. **wǣt-*, 3rd grade of *wet, Idg. √WED, to wet, or spring up (as water). See **Water**. Der. *wet*, verb, AS. *wǣtan* (Grein) ; *wet*, sb., AS. *wǣta* (Grein) ; *wett-ish*, *wet-ness* ; *wet-shod*, P. Plowman, B. xiv. 161. From the same root are *ott-er, und-ul-ate, hyd-ra, hyd-raul-ic, hyd-ro-gen*, &c.

WETHER, a castrated ram. (E.) ME. *wether*, Chaucer, C. T. 3249. AS. *weðer*, Ps. xxviii, 1, ed. Spelman (marginal reading).+OSax. *wethar, withar* ; Kleinere Altniederdeutsche Denkmäler, ed. Heyne, p. 186 ; Icel. *veðr* ; Dan. *væder, vædder* ; Swed. *vädur* ; G. *widder*, OHG. *widar* ; Goth. *withrus*, a lamb, John, i. 29. β. All from Teut. type *wethruz, m. The orig. sense was doubtless ' a yearling,' as the word corresponds very closely to L. *uitulus*, a calf, Skt. *vatsa-*, a calf, allied to Skt. *vatsara-*, Gk. ἔτος, a year. See **Veterinary** and **Veal**. ¶ We may note the distinction between *weather* and *wether* by observing that the former is *wea-ther* (with Idg. suffix -*tro-*), whilst the latter is *weth-er* (with suffix -*ro-*), the *th* answering to the *t* in *uit-ulus*.

WEY, a heavy weight. (E.) The weight varies considerably, from 2 cwt. to 3 cwt. ME. *weye*, P. Plowman, B. v. 93. The lit. sense is merely ' weight.' AS. *wǣge* ; ' Pondus, *byrðen oððe wǣge*,' i. e. burden or weight ; Ælfric's Grammar, ed. Zupitza, p. 58, l. 17. Allied to AS. *wǣg-*, stem of pl. of pt. t. of *wegan*, to bear, carry, weigh ; so that the sb. is from Teut. **wǣg-*, 3rd grade of **wegan-*, to carry. See **Weigh**.

WH

WH. This is distinct from *w*, just as *th* is from *t*. The mod E. *wh* is represented by *hw* in AS., and by *hv* in Icelandic ; it answers to L. *qu*, Gk. π, τ, κ ; Idg. *kw*.

WHACK, to beat. (E.) See **Thwack**, which is supposed to be the same word. But it is rather a variant, i. e. a similarly sounding imitative word. Cf. EFries. and Westphalian *wack-eln*, to beat, to cudgel ; prov. G. (Thüringen) *wackeln, walken*, to beat (Hertel).

WHALE, the largest of sea-animals. (E.) ME. *whal*, Chaucer, C. T. 7512 (D 1930) ; *qual*, Havelok, 753. AS. *hwæl*, Voc. 94. 15.+Du. *walvisch*, i. e. whale-fish ; Icel. *hvalr* ; Dan. and Swed. *hval* ; G. *wal, wallfisch*. β. The Teut. type is *hwaloz, m. The name was orig. applied to any large fish, including the walrus, grampus, porpoise, &c. Thus Ælfric explains *hwæl* by ' balena, vel cete, vel pistrix.' Cf. G. *wels*, a catfish ; OPruss. *kalis*, a catfish. Perhaps it meant 'roller,' from the rolling of porpoises; cf. Icel. *hvel*, a wheel, OPruss. *kelan*, a wheel; Gk. πέλωρ, a monster, πόλος, a pivot; see **Pole** (2), and **Wheel**. ¶ *Whale* and *balæna* have nothing in common but the letter *l*, and cannot be compared. **Der.** *whale-bone*, formerly *whales bone*, Spenser, F. Q. iii. 1. 15, where the reference is to the ivory of the walrus' tusk, ME. *whales bon*, Layamon, 23633; *whal-ing*, *whal-er*. Also *wal-rus*, q. v.

WHAP, to beat, flutter. (E.) Sometimes spelt *whop*; and *wap*. Halliwell has *wap*, 'to beat; to flutter, to beat the wings, to move in any violent manner;' also *wappeng* (for *whapping*), 'quaking, used by Batman, 1582.' 'A *whapp*,' a blow; York Plays, xxxii. 199. 'The waters *wappe*,' i.e. lap; Malory, Morte Arthur, bk. xxi. c. 5. A variant of *quap*; an imitative word. Cf. ME. *quappen*, to palpitate, Chaucer, Troil. iii. 57, Legend of Good Women, 865; Wyclif, Tobit, vi. 4, earlier version. From a base *kwap*, to throb; see **Quaver**. Allied to Low G. *quabbeln*, to palpitate, with which cf. E. *wabble*. Note also W. *chwap*, a sudden stroke, *chwapio*, to strike, to slap; EFries. *wappen*, to swing, to rock; *wip-wap*, a swing. **Der.** *wabb-le*. And see *whip*.

WHARF (1), a place on the shore for lading and unlading goods. (E.) Spelt *warf* in Fabyan's Chron. an. 1543, where we read that 'the maior wente to the *woode-warfes*, and solde to the poore people billet and faggot,' because of the severe frost. Palsgrave has *wharfe*. ME. *Wharfe*, in Liber Custumarum, p. 447 (1343); cf. pp. 62, 150. Blount, ed. 1694, explains *wharf* as meaning, not only a landing-place, but also 'a working-place for shipwrights;' see below. AS. *hwerf*, a dam or bank to keep out water; 'þa gyrnde hē þæt hē mōste macian foran gēn Mildryþe æker ænne *hwerf* wið þon wodan tō werianne,' which Thorpe translates by 'then desired he that he might make a wharf over against Mildred's field as a protection against the ford, where 'ford' is a conjectural translation of *wodan*; Diplomatarium Ævi Anglo-Saxonici (A. D. 1038), p. 384; and again, 'þat land and ðane *wearf* ðartō' = the land and the wharf thereto; id. (an. 1042), p. 361. The orig. sense seems to have been a bank of earth, used at first as a dam against a flood; the present use is prob. of Dutch or Scand. origin. The lit. sense is 'a turning,' whence it came to mean a dam, from its turning the course of water; the allied AS. *hwearf* not only means 'a returning,' but also 'a change,' and even 'a space or distance,' as in the ONorthumb. tr. of Luke, xxiv. 13; also 'a crowd,' Grein, ii. 118; cf. *hwearfan*, to turn about. A good example is seen in the comp. *mere-hwearf*, the sea-shore, Grein, ii. 233. It corresponds, as to form, with AS. *hwearf*, pt. of *hweorfan*, to turn, turn about, Grein, ii. 119.+Du. *werf*, a wharf, yard; also a turn, time; Hexham has *werf*, 'a wharfe, or a working-place for shipwrights or otherwise;' Icel. *hvarf*, a turning away, also, a shelter; cf. *hwarf*, pt. t. of *hverfa*, to turn; Dan. *værft*, a wharf, a dock-yard; Swed. *varf*, a shipbuilder's yard; MSwed. *hwarf*, *skeps-hwarf* (ship's wharf), the same (Ihre). The MSwed. *hwarf* also meant a turn or time, order, stratum, or layer; Ihre, i. 945; from *hwerfwa*, to turn, return. B. It thus appears that, even in AS., this difficult word, with a great range of senses, meant not only a turning, reversion, but also turning-place, dam, shore, space, distance. Cf. prov. E. *wharfstead*, a ford in a river (Halliwell). In Swedish and Dutch it had a narrower sense, that of 'ship-builder's yard,' so called from its being situate on a shore. And from this sense to that of 'landing-place' the step is not a long one. C. The AS. strong verb *hweorfan*, answering to Goth. *hwairban*, to turn oneself about (hence to walk), and to Icel. *hverfa*, answers to a Teut. type *hwerfan-*, pt. t. *hwarf*, to turn, turn about. Cf. Gk. καρπός, the wrist (from its turning). ¶ Not allied to G. *werfen*, to throw, which is allied to E. *warp*. **Der.** *wharf-age*, Hakluyt's Voyages, i. 135; *wharf-ing-er*, which occurs (according to Blount, ed. 1674) anno 7 Edw. VI, cap. 7, a corruption of *wharfager*, just as *messenger* is of *messager*.

WHARF (2), the bank of a river. (E.) In Shak. Hamlet, i. 5. 33; Antony, ii. 2. 218. The occurrence of *mere-hwearf*, the sea-shore (for which see Grein, ii. 233), justifies Shakespeare's spelling, and shows that the present word is only a peculiar sense of **Wharf** (1), q. v. Hence perhaps the river-name *Wharfe*.

WHAT, neuter of **Who**, q. v. (E.) We find the form *whatsom-euer* in Dictes and Sayings, pr. by Caxton, fol. 18, back, l. 2. **Der.** *what-ever*, *what-so-ever*; *what-not*, a piece of furniture for holding *anything*, whence the name.

WHAUP, the curlew. (E.) Prov. E. *whaup*; Lowl. Sc., *quhaip*, in 1551 (Jam.). Prob. the same as AS. *huilpa* (for *hwilpa*) in The Sea-farer, l. 21. Of imitative origin.

WHEAL (1), a pimple. (E.) Not to be confused with *weal*, another spelling of *wale*, the mark caused by a stripe; for which see **Wale**. A *wheal* is a swelling, pimple, caused by ill-health. It occurs frequently in Holland, tr. of Pliny, b. xxii. c. 25, where is mention of 'pushes, *wheals*, and blains,' and of 'pushes and angry

wheales,' &c.; **a** *push* being a pustule, still in use in Cambs. ME. *whele*; 'Whele, whelle, wheel, or whelke, qwelke, soore, Pustula;' Prompt. Parv. Cf. pl. *whelkes*, Chaucer, C. T. 634 (A 632). AS. *hwele*, a wheal; an unauthorised word, due to Somner. [Ettmüller cites AS. *hweal*, with a reference to Ælfric's Glossary; but Wright prints it *þweal*; 'Lotium, *þweal*,' Wright's Voc. i. 46, l. 7; and the word is very doubtful.] There is also a verb *hwelian*, to turn to pus or matter (Toller), also to pine away, as in sect. 15 of the Liber Scintillarum : 'Unde bonus proficit, inde inuidus *contabescit*,' glossed by 'þanon þe se goda framað, þanon se andiga hwelað.' The pp. is *gehweled*, inflamed. Cf. W. *chwiler*, a maggot, wheal, pimple. A ME. *whelke*, a pimple, is clearly a dimin. form; hence *whelk*, Hen. V; iii. 6. 108.

WHEAL (2), a mine. (C.) Still common in Cornwall.—Corn. *hwel*, a work, a mine; also written *wheal*, *whel*, *wheyl*; Williams, Corn. Dict. Williams compares it with W. *chwyl*, a turn, a course, a while, *chwylo*, to turn, revolve, run a course, bustle; cf. also W. *chwel*, a course, turn. Stokes-Fick, p. 324.

WHEAT, the name of a grain used for making bread. (E.) ME. *whete*, Chaucer, C. T. 3986 (A 3988). AS. *hwǣte*; Grein, ii. 117.+Du. *weite*, *weit*; Icel. *hveiti*; Dan. *hvede*; Swed. *hvete*; G. *weizen*; Goth. *hwaiteis*. (The Lithuan. *kwëtys*, wheat, is borrowed from Teutonic.) β. All from a Teut. type *hwaitjo-*, wheat; from *hwait*, 2nd grade of *hweit-*; so named from the whiteness of the meal. See **White**. **Der.** *wheat-en*, AS. *hwǣten*, John, xii. 24; *wheat-fly*; *buck-wheat*.

WHEAT-EAR, the name of a small bird. (E.) In Phillips; formerly *wheatears* (with final *s*), in T. Fuller, Worthies of England, ii. 382 (see Palmer, Folk-Etymology); as to which Smollett says: 'this is a pleasant corruption of *white-a—e*, the translation of their French name *cul blanc*, .. for they are actually white towards the tail;' Travels, letter iii. Swainson, in his Bird-names (E. D. S.), gives the name *white ass* [= *white-arse*] as in use in Cornwall, and *white-rump* in Norfolk; while Cotgrave has: '*Cul blanc*, the bird called a whittaile,' i. e. white tail. Hence the etymology is from *white* and *arse*. Cf. Du. *wit-staart*, 'a white-tail, white-ear;' Calisch; MDan. *hvid-stjært* (Kalkar).

WHEEDLE, to cajole, flatter. (E.?) In Butler, Hudibras, pt. iii. c. 1, l. 760. In Dryden, Kind Keeper, Act i. sc. 1, we find: 'I must *wheedle* her.' Blount, ed. 1674, notes it as a *new* word, saying; 'Wheadle in the British tongue signifies a story, whence probably *our late word of fancy*, and signifies to draw one in by fair words or subtil insinuation,' &c. He is referring to W. *chwedl*, a saying, sentence, fable, story, tale, *chwedla*, to gossip, *chwedlu*, to tell a fable; but this is not a satisfactory explanation, nor does it account for the long *e*. But we should note his spelling with *ea* (from an open *ē*). It seems more likely that the word should be *weadle*, and that it was a prov. E. word, answering to AS. *wǣdlian*, to beg. 'Mē sceamaþ þæt ic *wǣdlige*,' to beg I am ashamed, Luke, xvi. 3. The orig. sense of *wǣdlian* was 'to be poor;' from *wǣdl*, poverty, indigence, *wǣdla*, poor. Cf. ME. *wēdle*, poor; Ormulum, 5638. **Der.** *wheedl-er*.

WHEEL, a circular frame turning on an axle. (E.) ME. *wheel*, Wyclif, James, iii. 6. AS. *hwēol*, Grein, ii. 119. *Hwēol* is a shortened form of *hweowol*, Ps. lxxxii. 12, ed. Spelman; it is also spelt *hweogul* (Toller), and *hweohl*, Ælfred, tr. of Boethius, c. xxxix. § 7 (b. iv. pr. 6).+Icel. *hjōl*; Dan. *hiul*; Swed. *hjul*; MSwed. *hiughl* (Ihre). Teut. type *hwegwlóm*, n., for *hwehwlóm*, Idg. type *qeqló*, as in Skt. *chakrá-*, Gk. κύκλος, a wheel. The Idg. *qe-qlo-* is a reduplicated form, from √QwEL, to drive; whence Gk. πόλος, an axis, Russ. *koleso*, Icel. *hvel*, a wheel. See **Cycle** and **Pole** (2). Brugmann, i. § 658. Cf. **Calash**. **Der.** *wheel*, verb; *wheel-er*; *wheel-barrow*, spelt *whelebarowe* in Le Bone Florence, l. 2031, pr. in Ritson's Met. Romances, iii. 86; *wheel-wright* (see **Wright**).

WHEEZE, to breathe audibly and with difficulty. (E.) ME. *whesen*, Towneley Mysteries, 152 (Stratmann); rare. AS. *hwēsan*, to wheeze, A. S. Leechdoms, iii. 365 (glossary). [The 3rd pers. pres. sing. *hwēst* occurs in the same volume, p. 126, l. 9, according to Cockayne; but perhaps *hwēst* is here for *hwōstd*, from *hwōstan*, to cough, which is a related word, but not quite the same thing.] The only sure trace of the verb is in Ælfric's Homilies, i. 86, where we find the strong pt. t. *hwēos* = wheezed (mistranslated by Thorpe, but rightly explained by Cockayne). As *ē* is the mutation of *ō*, the Teut. base is *hwōs-*, whence also AS. *hwōs-ta*, a cough, prov. E. *hoast*, a cough, Du. *hoest*, G. *husten*. Teut. base *hwōs-* = Idg. *qūs-*, as in Skt. *kās*, to cough; 2nd grade of Idg. √QAS, to cough, as in Irish *cas-achdach*, W. *pas*, a cough; cf. Lith. *kosti*, to cough. See **Pose** (3). Brugmann, i. § 675. Connexion with Icel. *hvæsa*, to hiss. is doubtful.

WHELK (1), a mollusc with a spiral shell. (E.) The *h* is unoriginal, and due to confusion with the word below; the right (etymological) spelling is *welk* or *wilk*. Spenser has '*whelky* pearles' = shelly pearls, pearls in the shell; Virgil's Gnat, l. 105. ME. *wilk*; spelt *wylke*, Prompt. Parv.; and in Voc. 642. 6. Pl. *welkes*, Liber Albus, pp. 179, 244, &c. AS. *wiloc* (8th cent.), Voc. 13. 40; also *weoluc, weluc*, id. 261. 22, 181. 10.+Du. *wulk*, also spelt *welk, wilk, willok, wullok* (Franck). Cf. '*inuolucus, uulloc*,' Corpus Gloss. 1115; prov. E. *wulk, wullok*. Prob. named from its convoluted shell; cf. Gk. ἕλιξ (for ϝέλ-ιξ), a volute; see **Helix**. And cf. **Walk**. **Der.** Hence prob. *welk-ed*, K. Lear, iv. 6. 71, spelt *wealk'd*, i.e. convoluted, in the first folio; cf. '*welked* horns,' in Golding's Ovid, pp. 60 b, 107 b, 122 b.

WHELK (2), a small pimple. (E.) The dimin. of **Wheal** (1), q. v.

WHELM, to overturn, cover over by something that is turned over, overwhelm, submerge. (Scand.) 'Ocean *whelm* them all;' Merry Wives, ii. 2. 143. ME. *whelmen*, to turn over; Chaucer, Troilus, i. 139. '*Whelmyn*, a vessel, Suppino,' Prompt. Parv.; on which Way cites Palsgrave: 'I *whelme* an holowe thyng over an other thyng, *Je mets dessus*; Whelme a platter upon it, to save it from flyes.' He adds: 'in the E. Anglian dialect, to *whelm* signifies to turn a tub or other vessel upside down, whether to cover anything with it or not; see Forby.' '*Whelm*, to turn upside down, cover over,' E. D. D.; which see. The Lowland Sc. form is *quhemle, whemmle*, or *whommel*, to turn upside down; *ovir quhemlit* = did overturn, occurs in Bellenden's Chron., prol. st. 2 (Jamieson). Jamieson gives Sibbald's opinion (which is correct) that the Lowl. Sc. *whemmle* is due to E. *whelm*, the letters being transposed to make the word easier of utterance; but he afterwards assumes the Lowl. Sc. word as the older form, in order to deduce its etymology from MSwed. *hwimla*, to swarm (=G. *wimmeln*), which he explains wrongly. **β.** The word presents some difficulty; but it is obvious that *whelm* and *overwhelm* must be closely related to ME. *wheluen* (*whelven*) and *overwheluen* (*overwhelven*), which are used in almost precisely the same sense. *Wheluen* is also spelt *hwelfen*; 'He *hwelfde* at þare sepulchre-dure enne grete ston' = he rolled (or turned) over a great stone at the door of the sepulchre; O. Eng. Miscellany, p. 51, l. 513. 'And perchaunce the *overwhelve*' = and perchance overwhelm thee; Palladius on Husbandry, b. i. l. 161. Cf. AS. *ā-hwylfan*; as in: '*ā-hwylfte* Pharaones cratu,' (the sea) overwhelmed Pharaoh's chariots; Exod. xiv. 27. **γ.** The only difficulty is to explain the final *-m*; this is due to the fact that *whelm*, verb, is really formed from a substantive *whelm*; and the sb. *whel-m* stands for *whelf-m*, in which the *f* was dropped; the suffix *-m* being substantival, as in *doo-m, bloo-m*. This appears from MSwedish; Ihre gives the verb *hwalma*, to cock hay, derived from *hwalm*, a hay-cock; and he connects *hwalm* with *hwälfwa*, to arch over, make into a rounded shape, and *hwalf*, an arch, a vault. So also Rietz gives Swed. dial. *hvalm*, a hay-stack, from *hvälva* (pt. t. *hvalv*); cf. Swed. *vålma*, to cock hay, *vålm*, a hay-cock (which have lost the *h*); *hvälfva*, to arch, *hvalf*, an arch. Cf. Dan. *hvælve*, to arch, vault over. Thus the orig. sense of *whelm* was to arch over, vault, make of a convex form; hence, to turn a hollow dish over, which would then present such a form; hence, to upset, overturn, which is now the prevailing idea. **δ.** We conclude that *whelm* (for *whelf-m*) is from the strong verb appearing in Swed. dial. *hvälva* (for *hvelva*), pt. t. *hvalv*, Norw. *kvelva* (for *hvelva*), pt. t. *kvalv*, MHG. *welben* (pt. t. *walb*), to distend oneself into a convex form, swell out, become convex, answering to the Teut. base HWELF, to become convex. From the same base in AS. *hwealf*, adj. convex, sb. a vault (Grein, ii. 118); *ā-hwylfan*, to overwhelm; *be-hwylfan*, to vault over (Grein); Icel. *hválf, hólf*, a vault, *hválfa, hólfa*, to 'whelve' or turn upside down, overwhelm or capsize a ship, *hvelfa*, to arch, vault, to turn upside down, &c.; mod. G. *wölben*, to arch over. All from Idg. √QwELP; whence also OPruss. *po-quelb-ton*, kneeling, Gk. κόλπος, bosom, a hollow. See Prellwitz. **Der.** *over-whelm*.

WHELP, a puppy, young of the dog or lion. (E.) ME. *whelp*, Chaucer, C. T. 10805 (F 491). AS. *hwelp*, Matt. xv. 27.+Du. *welp*; Icel. *hvelpr*; Dan. *hvalp*; Swed. *valp*; MSwed. *hwalp* (Ihre); MHG. *welf*. **β.** The Teut. types are **hwelpoz, *hwalpoz*, m. Root unknown. **Der.** *whelp*, vb., J. Caesar, ii. 2. 17.

WHEN, at what time, at which time. (E.) ME. *whan*, Chaucer, C. T. 5, 169; *whanne*, Ormulum, 133. AS. *hwænne, hwonne*; Grein, ii. 115.+MDu. *wan* (Hexham); Goth. *hwan*; G. *wann*; OHG. *hwanne*. **β.** Evidently orig. a case of the interrogative pronoun; cf. Goth. *hwana*, acc. masc. of *hwas*, who; see **Who**. So also L. *quan-do*, when, *quis*, who; W. *pan*, when; OIrish *can*. **Der.** *when-ever, when-so-ever*; and see *when-ce*.

WHENCE, from what place. (E.) ME. *whennes* (dissyllabic), Chaucer, C. T. 12269 (C 335). This form *whenn-es*, in which the suffix imitates the adverbial *-es* (as in *twi-es*, twice, *ned-es*, of necessity), was substituted for the older form *whanene*, written *wonene* in Laya-

mon, l. 16. The suffix *-es* was orig. a genitive case-ending, as in *dæg-es*, of a day. **β.** The form *whanene* is from AS. *hwanan*, also *hwanon, hwonan*, whence, Grein, ii. 114. This is closely connected with AS. *hwænne*, when; the suffix *-an* being used to express direction, as in AS. *sūð-an*, from the south. See **When.**+G. *wannen*, whence; allied to *wann*, when. ¶ Compare *hen-ce*, similarly formed from ME. *henn-es*, AS. *heon-an*, hence; see **Hence**. Also **Thence**. **Der.** *whence-so-ever*.

WHERE, at which place. (E.) ME. *wher*, Chaucer, C. T. 4918 (B 498). AS. *hwār, hwǣr*, Grein, ii. 116.+Du. *waar*; Icel. *hvar*; Dan. *hvor*; Swed. *hvar*.+OHG. *hwār*, whence MHG. *wār, wā*, G. *wo*; cf. G. *war-* in *war-um*, why, lit. about what; Goth. *hwar*. Evidently allied to AS. *hwā*, who, and to *when*. Cf. Lithuan. *kur*, where? Skt. *kar-hi*, at what time? **Der.** *where-about, where-about-s, where-as, where-at*; *whereby*, ME. *whar-bi*, Will. of Palerne, 2256; *where-fore*, ME. *hwarfore*, Ancren Riwle, p. 158, note *g*; *where-in*; *where-of*, ME. *hwarof*, Ancren Riwle, p. 12, l. 12; *where-on*, ME. *whær-on*, Layamon, 15502; *where-so-ever*; *where-to*, ME. *hwerto*, St. Marharete, p. 16, l. 29; *where-unto*, Cymb. iii. 4. 109; *where-upon*, K. John, iv. 2. 65; *wher-ever*, As You Like It, ii. 2. 15; *where-with*, ME. *hwerwið*, Hali Meidenhad, p. 9, l. 19; *where-with-al*, Rich. II, v. 1. 55. ☞ These compounds were prob. suggested as correlative to the formations from *there*; see **There**.

WHERRY, a shallow, light boat. (E.) 'A *whyrry*, boate, *ponto*;' Levins, ed. 1570. The pl. is *wheries* in Hakluyt, Voyages, iii. 645. In use on the Thames in particular. Spelt *whirry* in Latimer, Seven Sermons, ed. Arber, p. 170. 'A *whery*, cymbe,' Du Wez, appendix to Palgrave, p. 916, col. 3. Cf. Lowl. Sc. *whirry*, to whir, to hurry; prov. E. *whirry*, dizzy; see **Whir**. Perhaps named from its lightness. Cf. Icel. *hverfr*, shifty, crank (said of a ship); Norw. *kverv*, crank, also swift of motion. See **Wharf**.

WHET, to sharpen, make keen. (E.) ME. *whetten*, Prompt. Parv. AS. *hwettan*, to sharpen, Grein, ii. 118. For **hwatjan*; from **hwat-*, as in AS. *hwæt*, keen, bold, brave; ibid.+Du. *wetten*, to sharpen; cf. OSax. *hwat*, sharp, keen; Icel. *hvetja*, to sharpen, to encourage; cf. *hvatr*, bold, active, vigorous; Swed. *vättja*, to whet; G. *wetzen*, OHG. *hwazan*; cf. OHG. *hwaz*, sharp. **β.** All from Teut. type **hwatoz*, sharp, keen; allied to Skt. *chōd-ana-m*, an inciting. ¶ Not allied to L. *cōs*, a whet-stone, which is related to E. *hone* and *cone*. **Der.** *whet*, sb.; *whett-er*; *whet-stone*, AS. *hwetstān*, Ælfred, tr. of Orosius, b. iv. c. 13. § 5.

WHETHER, which of two. (E.) 'Whether of the twain;' Matt. xxvii. 21. ME. *whether*, Chaucer, C. T. 1858 (A 1856). AS. *hwæðer*, which of two; Grein, ii. 114.+Icel. *hvárr* (a contracted form); MHG. *weder*, OHG. *hwedar*, adj., which of two; Goth. *hwathar*, adj. Formed, with comparative suffix *-ther* (Idg. *-tero-*), from the base of *who*; see **Who**. Cf. Lith. *katras*, Gk. πότερος, κότερος, Skt. *katara-*, which of two. **Der.** *whether*, conj., AS. *hwæðer*, Grein, ii. 115. Also *neither, nor*.

WHEY, the watery part of milk, separated from the curd. (E.) Lowland Sc. *whig*, see Jamieson; and see Nares. ME. *whey*, Prompt. Parv. AS. *hwæg*; 'Serum, *hwæg*,' Voc. 46. 28.+MDu. *wey*; Du. *wei*. Cf. W. *chwig*, 'whey fermented with sour herbs;' *chwig*, adj. fermented, sour. **β.** In the Bremen Wörterbuch, v. 161, we find various Low G. words for *whey*, which are not all related; the related forms are the Holstein *waje* and the Ditmarsch *hei, heu*, which (like Du. *hui*) are from a weaker grade (**hujo-*) of the base (**hwajo-*) of AS. *hwæg*. **Der.** *whey-ey, whey-ish*; *whey-face*, Macb. v. 3. 17.

WHICH, a relative and interrogative pronoun. (E.) ME. *which*, formerly used with relation to persons, as in Chaucer, C. T. 16482 (G 1014); spelt *quhilk* in Barbour, Bruce, i. 77. AS. *hwilc, hwelc, hwylc*, Grein, ii. 121. A contracted form of AS. *hwi-lic*, of what form.—AS. *hwi-*, allied to *hwā*, who; and *līc*, like. See **Who** and **Like.**+OSax. *hwilik*; OFriesic *hwelik, hwelk, hwek*; Du. *welk*; Icel. *hvílíkr*, of what kind; Dan. *hvilk-en*, masc., *hvilk-et*, neut.; Swed. *hvilk-en, hvilk-et*; G. *welcher*; OHG. *hwelih*; Goth. *hwileiks*. Also Goth. *hwēleiks*; from *hwē*, instrumental case of *hwas*, who, and *leiks*, like. Allied to L. *quā-lis*, of what sort, lit. 'what-like;' Gk. πηλίκος. Brugmann, ii. § 88. **Der.** *which-ever, which-so-ever*; also (from L. *quālis*) *quali-ty*, q. v.

WHIFF, a puff of wind or smoke. (E.) In Hamlet, ii. 2. 495. ME. *weffe*, vapour; Prompt. Parv. An imitative word; cf. *puff, pipe, fife*. Cf. W. *chwiff*, a whiff, puff; *chwiffio*, to puff; *chwaff*, a gust; Dan. *vift*, a puff, gust; Lowl. Sc. *wheef*, a fife. Cf. G. *piff-paff*, to denote a sudden explosive sound; also Icel. *hwiða*, a puff; AS. *hwiða*, a breeze; Voc. 175. 21. **Der.** *whiff*, verb, *whiff-le*, q. v.

WHIFFLE, to blow in gusts, veer about as the wind does. (E.) 'But if the winds *whiffle* about to the south;' Dampier, Discourse of Winds, c. 6 (R.). *Whiffle* is the frequentative of *whiff*, to puff, and was specially used of puffing in various directions; hence it came to mean to trifle, to trick (Phillips). See **Whiff**. Der. *whiffl-er*, Henry V, v. chor. 12, orig. a piper or fifer, as explained by Phillips, who says that 'it is also taken for a piper that plays on a fife in a company of foot-soldiers;' hence it meant one who goes first in a procession; see *Whiffle* in E. D. D., and *Whiffler* in Nares, whose account is sufficient.

WHIG, one of a political party. (North E.) First about 1678 (Haydn). 'Wit and fool are consequents of *Whig* and *Tory*;' Dryden, Pref. to Absalom and Achitophel (1681). See the full account in Todd's Johnson and Nares. The standard passage on the word is in b. i. of Burnet's Own Times, fully cited by Johnson; it is to the effect that *whig* is a shortened form of *whiggamor*, applied to certain Scotchmen who came from the west in the summer to buy corn at Leith; and that the term was given them from a word *whiggam*, which was employed by those men in driving their horses. A march to Edinburgh made by the Marquis of Argyle and 6,000 men (in 1648) was called 'the *whiggamor's* inroad,' and afterwards those who opposed the court came in contempt to be called *whigs*. The term had been applied previously (in 1667) to the Scottish Covenanters (Lingard). [There seems no reason to doubt this account, nor does there seem to be any foundation for an assertion made by Woodrow that *Whigs* were named from *whig*, sour whey, which is obviously a mere guess.] β. The Glossary to Sir W. Scott's novels has *whigamore*, a great whig; also *whigging*, jogging rudely, urging forward; Jamieson has '*whig*, to go quickly; *whig awa*', to move at an easy and steady pace, to jog (Liddesdale); *to whig awa*' *with a cart*, remarks Sir W. Scott, signifies to drive it briskly on.' I suspect that *whig* should be *wig*, and that these words are connected with Lowland Sc. *wiggle*, to wriggle (or rather to keep moving about) and with EFries. *wiggen*, Norw. *vigga*, to rock. Cf. Lowl. Sc. *wig*, to wag, shake, move (E. D. D.); and E. **Wag**. Der. *whigg-ish*, *-ish-ly*, *-ism*, *-ery*.

WHILE, a time, space of time. (E.) ME. *whil*, *while*, P. Plowman, B. xvii. 46. AS. *hwīl*, sb. a time, Grein, ii. 120.+Icel. *hvila*, only in the special sense of a place of rest, a bed; Dan. *hvile*, rest; Swed. *hvila*, rest; G. *weile*, OHG. *hwīla*+Goth. *hweila*, a time, season. β. The Teut. types are *hwīlā*, f., *hwīlōn-*, f., a time, rest, pause, time of repose. Prob. allied to L. *qui-es*, rest; see **Quiet**; and to Skt. *chi-ra-*, long-lasting. Idg. √QwEI. Brugmann, i. § 675. Der. *while*, adv., from some case of the sb., prob. from the acc. or dat. *hwīle*; *whil-es*, Matt. v. 25, ME. *whiles*, Chaucer, C. T. 35 (in the Harleian MS.), where *whiles* is the gen. case (m. or n.) used adverbially, as in *twi-es*, twice, *ned-es*, needs, &c. [but note that the AS. genitive was *hwīle*, the sb. being feminine]; hence *whil-s-t*, Spenser, F. Q. ii. 2. 16, with added excrescent *t* after *s* (as in *amongs-t*, *amids-t*). Also *whil-om*, spelt *whylome* in Spenser, F. Q. ii. 2. 13, from AS. *hwīlum*, instr. or dat. pl. of *hwīl*, signifying 'at times.' Also *mean-while*, see **Mean** (3); *while-ere*, Temp. iii. 2. 127. Also *whiling-time*, the 'waiting a little before dinner,' Spectator, no. 448, Aug. 4, 1712; whence 'to *while* away time;' prob. with some thought of confusion with *wile*.

WHIM, a sudden fancy, a crotchet. (Scand.) 'With a *whym-wham* Knyt with a trym-tram Upon her brayne-pan;' Skelton, Elinour Rummyng, 75.—Icel. *hvima*, to wander with the eyes, as a silly person; Norweg. *kvima*, to whisk or flutter about, to trifle, play the fool (Aasen); cf. Swed. dial. *hvimmer-kantig*, dizzy, giddy in the head; Icel. *vim*, Norw. *kvim* (Ross), giddiness, folly. β. This etymology is verified by the derived word *whimsey*, a whim, Ben Jonson, The Fox, iii. 1. 4, pl. *whimsies*, Beaum. and Fletcher, Women Pleased, iii. 2, last line; from the allied Norweg. *kvimsa*, Dan. *vimse*, to skip, whisk, bustle, Swed. dial. *hvimsa*, to be unsteady, giddy, dizzy. γ. All from a base *hwim*, to move briskly. Der. *whim-wham*, a reduplicated word, as above; *whims-ey*, as above; *whims-ic-al*, *whims-ic-al-ly*; *whim-ling* (Nares). Also *wim-ble* (2), q. v.

WHIMBREL, a bird, a sort of curlew. (E.) Willughby says the bird was described to him under this name by Mr. Johnson of Brignal (N. Riding of Yorkshire). See also Swainson, Provincial Bird-names, E. D. S., p. 199. It is easily analysed as standing for *whim-b-r-el*; where *-b-* is excrescent after *m*, *-r-* is frequentative, *-el* is the suffix of the agent, and *whim-* (allied to *whine*) is imitative. It means the bird that repeats the cry imitated by *whim*; cf. Lowl. Sc. *whimmer*, E. *whimper* and *whine*, G. *wimmern*. See **Whimper**.

WHIMPER, to cry in a low, whining voice. (E.) 'Liue in puling and *whimpering* and heuines of hert;' Sir T. More, p. 90 b. And in Palsgrave. A frequentative form, from *whimpe*. 'There shall be *intractabiles*, that will *whympe* and whine;' Latimer, Seven Sermons (March 22, 1549), ed. Arber, p. 77, last line. In both words the *p* is excrescent, as is so common after *m*; *whimper* and *whimpe* stand for *whimmer* and *whim*; cf. Scotch *whimmer*, to whimper. And further, *whim* is an imitative word allied to *whine*, so that Latimer

joins the words naturally enough. See **Whine.**+Low G. *wemern*, to whimper; G. *wimmern*. Der. *whimper-er*.

WHIN (1), gorse, furze. (Scand.) '*Whynnes* or hethe, *bruiere*;' Palsgrave. '*Whynne*, Saliunca;' Prompt. Parv. 'With thornes, breres, and moni a *quyn*;' Ywain and Gawain, 159; in Ritson, Met. Romances, i. 8. Prob. from Norw. *hvin*, *hven*, purple melic grass, *hvene*, bent-grass, coarse grass (Larsen); cf. Norw. *kvein*, thin and stalky, *kveinutt*, stunted (Ross); *kveina*, used of grass-stalks and trees that are thin and stand alone (Ross); Swed. *hven*, bent-grass; Norw. *kveinen*, adj., said of birch-trees and branches with long thin twigs. Hence also (probably) W. *chwyn*, weeds; cf. Bret. *chouenna* (with guttural *ch*), to weed. Der. *whin-bush*.

WHIN (2), a kind of hard rock. (E.) G. Douglas has 'ane cald hard *quhyn*,' Lat. *duris cautibus*, Virgil's Æn. iv. 366. ME. *quin*, hard stone, Cursor Mundi, 7531. [AS. form not recorded.]

WHINE, to utter a plaintive cry. (E.) ME. *whinen*, said of a horse, Chaucer, C. T. 5968 (D 386). AS. *hwīnan*, to whine, Grein, ii. 122.+Icel. *hvīna*, to whiz, whir; Dan. *hvine*, to whistle, to whine; Swed. *hvina*, to whistle. β. All from the Teut. base *hwein-*, *hwīn-*, to make a discordant noise. Cf. Icel. *kveina*, to wail; Goth. *kwainōn*, to mourn. And see **Whimper**. Der. *whine*, sb., *whin-er*, *whin-ing*; also *whinn-y*, Drayton, The Moon-calf, l. 119 from end, which is a sort of frequentative. And see *whimp-er*.

WHINYARD, a sword. (Scand.; with F. suffix.) Nares, following Minsheu, explains *whinyard* as a hanger, i.e. a kind of sword. Minsheu, in 1627, spells it *whinneard*; but it is usually *whinyard*, as in the play of Edw. III, i. 2. 33; and in Ram Alley (1611), pr. in Hazlitt's Dodsley, x. 363. Cotgrave explains MF. *braquemar* as 'a wood knife, hanger, *whineyard*;' but Skelton has simply *whynarde*, Bowge of Court, 363. From Icel. *hvīna*, to whizz, as an arrow or a gust of wind; Swed. *hvina*, Dan. *hvine*, to whistle, shriek; with a suffix which simulated E. *yard*, a rod. It really arose from the suffix *-ard* (as in *drunk-ard*), which is of F. origin. The sense is 'a thing that whizzes through the air,' or that cuts the air with a whizzing sound. Also called a *whinger*, from an imitative form *whinge*, which is a variant of *whine*; cf. *whinger*, a whining person; E. D. D. See **Whine**.

WHIP, to move suddenly and quickly, to flog. (E.) 'I *whipt* me behind the arras,' Much Ado, i. 3. 63; '*Whips* out his rapier,' Hamlet, iv. 1. 10. This seems to be the orig. sense, whence the notion of flogging (with a quick sudden stroke) seems to have been evolved. [The AS. *hweop*, a whip, and *hweopian*, to whip, scourge, are given by Somner, but are unauthorised; the AS. word for 'scourge' being *swipe*, John, ii. 15.] Another sense of *whip* is to overlay a cord by rapidly binding thin twine or silk thread round it, and this is the only sense of ME. *whippen* noticed in the Prompt. Parv., which has: '*Whyppyn*, or closyn threde in sylke, as sylkewomene [do], *Obvolvo*.' But G. Douglas has '*wyppit* with bendis,' to translate L. *uittā comptos* in Virgil, Æn. viii. 128. The sb. *whippe*, a scourge, occurs in Chaucer, 5757, 9545 (D 175, E 1671); it is spelt *quippe* in Voc. 811. 36; *wyppe*, Voc. 665. 16; *wippe*, Nominale, ed. Skeat, 194, 886. All from the notion of rapid movement. The word is presumably English, and is preserved in the nearest cognate languages. Cf. Du. *wippen*, to skip, to hasten, also to give the strappado, formerly 'to shake, to wagge,' Hexham; Du. *wip*, a moment, a swipe, the strappado, MDu. *wippe*, 'a whipe or a scourge,' Hexham; Low G. *wippen*, *wuppen*, to go up and down, as on a see-saw; *wips*! quickly; Mid. Dan. *hvip*, a jump, *hvippe*, to jump, to whip (Kalkar); Dan. *vippe*, to see-saw, rock, bob, *vips*! pop! *vipstiert*, a wag-tail, lit. 'whip-start,' where *start*=tail; Swed. *vippa*, to wag, to jerk or give the strappado; *vippgalge*, a gibbet, lit. 'whip-gallows,' *vips*! quick! G. *wippen*, to move up and down, balance, see-saw, rock, to draw up a malefactor at a gibbet, and drop him again, to give the strappado; *wipp-galgen*, a gibbet. β. The Du. *wippen*, to skip, also to wag, is regarded as being a secondary verb allied to OHG. *wifan*, to turn round, to reel (G. *weifen*), Goth. *weipan*, to crown, *wipja*, a crown; which may be connected with L. *uibrāre*, to vibrate, swing. Cf. also Goth. *bi-waibjan*, to wind round, which may be compared with Skt. *vēp*, to tremble, vibrate. Perhaps even the E. form ought to be *wip* (not *whip*). ¶ The Gael. *cuip*, a whip, W. *chwip*, a quick turn, *chwipio*, to move briskly or nimbly, are borrowed from English, and have taken up different senses of the E. word. Der. *whip*, sb., as above; *whip-cord*, *-hand*, *-lash*; *whipper*; *whipp-er-in*, one who keeps the hounds from wandering, and whips them in to the line of chase; *whipp-ing*, *-ing-post*; also *whip-ster*, Oth. v. 2. 244; *whip-stock*, i.e. whip-handle, Tw. Nt. ii. 3. 28, and in Palsgrave; and see *whipp-le-tree*. And see *wisp*, *wipe*. Cf. *whisk*, for *wisk*.

WHIPPLE-TREE, a swing-bar, to which traces are fastened for drawing a carriage, &c. (E.) In Forby's Norfolk Glossary

(1830). Spelt *whypple-tree* in Palsgrave, where it is left unexplained. As in the case of *swingle-tree*, the word means 'piece of swinging wood,' and is composed of *tree* in the sense of timber (as in *axle-tree*, &c.) and the verb *whipple*, frequentative of *whip*, to move about quickly, to see-saw. See **Whip** and **Tree**; and see **Swingletree**. ¶ ME. *whippeltree*, in Chaucer, C. T., A 2923, is the cornel-tree; cf. Mid. Low G. *wipel-bom*, the cornel-tree, Low G. *wepe* (Lübben).

WHIR, to buzz, whirl round with a noise. (Scand.) In Shak. Pericles, iv. 1. 21. ME. (Northern), *whirr*, *quirr*, to rush out, hurl; Wars of Alexander, 1556, 2226. Probably to some extent imitative, like *whiz*.—Dan. *hvirre*, to whirl, twirl; Swed. dial. *hwirra*, to whirl (Rietz). Cf. Icel. *hverfa*, to turn round; the frequentative is **Whirl**. And see **Whiz**.

WHIRL, to swing rapidly round, to cause to revolve rapidly, to rotate quickly. (Scand.) ME. *whirlen*, Chaucer, Parl. of Foules, l. 80. In Wyclif, Wisdom, v. 24, the earlier version has 'whirle-*puff* of wind,' and the later version '*whirlyng* of wind.' This word is not a mere extension of *whir* (which is not found till a later date), but is a contraction for *whirf-le*, frequentative of the verb equivalent to ME. *wherfen*, to turn (Stratmann); and it is of Scand. origin rather than directly from AS. *hweorfan*.—Icel. *hvirfla*, to whirl, frequent. of *hverfa* (pt. t. *hvarf*), to turn round; Mid. Dan. *hvirle*, the same as Dan. *hvirvle*, to whirl; Swed. *hvir/la*, to whirl; cf. *hvarf*, a turn; MDu. *wervelen*, 'to whirle,' Hexham; G. *wirbeln*, to whirl; also, to warble. β. But the verb is really a denominative one, from the sb. found as ME. *whirl*, as in the compounds *whirl-bone* (Prompt. Parv.), *whirl-wind* (below); cf. Icel. *hvirfill*, a ring, Dan. *hvirvel*, Mid. Dan. *hvirlen*, a whirl, a whirlpool, Swed. *hvirfvel* (the same), Du. *wervel*, a hasp, *wervel-wind*, whirlwind, G. *wirbel*, a turning round, OHG. *wirbil*; Teut. type *hwirfiloz*, m.; with *i*-mutation of *e* to *i*. From Teut. base *hwerf*, as in AS. *hweorfan*, Goth. *hwairban*, to turn; see **Wharf**. Der. *whirl-wind*, spelt *whyrle-wynde*, Prompt. Parv., from Icel. *hvirfilvindr*, a whirlwind, Dan. *hvirvelvind*, Mid. Dan. *hvirrelvind*; *whirl-pool*, spelt *whirl-pole* in Palsgrave, and applied to a large fish, from the commotion which it makes. Also *whirl-i-gig*, spelt *whirly-gigge* (toy to play with) in Palsgrave; see **Gig**. Doublet, *warble*.

WHISK, to sweep round rapidly, to brush, sweep quickly, move quickly. (Scand.) The proper sense is merely 'to brush or sweep,' esp. with a quick motion, then to flourish about as when using a light brush; then (as in our phrases *to brush along*, *to sweep along*) to *whisk* is to move quickly, esp. with a kind of flourish. The *h* is intrusive, and probably due to confusion with *whiz*, *whirl*, &c. It should rather be *wisk*. 'He winched [winced] still alwayes, and *whisked* with his taile;' Gascoigne, Complaint of the Grene Knight, Works, ed. Hazlitt, i. 403. 'The *whyskynge* rod;' Skelton, Why Come Ye Nat to Courte, l. 1161. '*Whisking* his riding-rod;' Beaum. and Fletcher, Noble Gentleman, Act ii (Gentleman). 'As she *whisked* it' [her tail]; Butler, Hudibras, pt. ii. c. 3. l. 897. Cf. prov. E. *whisk*, to switch, beat, *wisk*, to switch, move rapidly (Halliwell). G. Douglas translates Virgil's *bacchatur* (Æn. iv. 301) by 'She *wiskis* wild.' The verb is from ME. *wisk*, sb., a swift stroke, Barbour, Bruce, v. 641. The *sk* (as in many words) indicates a Scand. origin.—Dan. *viske*, to wipe, rub, sponge, from *visk*, sb., a wisp, a rubber; Swed. *viska*, to wipe, to sponge, also to wag (the tail), from *viska*, a whisk. Widegren's Swed. Dict. gives *viska*, 'a small broom, whisk;' and the example *hunden viskar med swansen*, 'the dog wags his tail,' which precisely shows the sense of the E. word in old authors. The sb. appears further in Icel. *visk*, a wisp of hay or the like, lit. something to wipe with.+G. *wischen*, 'to wipe, wisk (sic), rub,' Flügel; from the sb. *wisch*, 'a whisk, clout, wisp, malkin,' id. β. The sb. which thus appears as Icel. and Dan. *visk*, Swed. *viska*, G. *wisch*, meant orig. 'a wisp;' and perhaps *wis-k* is a related form to *wis-p*. See **Wisp**. Cf. also AS. *weoxian* (for *wiscian*), to wipe. Der. *whisk*, sb. (as above, really a more orig. word). Hence *whisk-er*, sb., from its likeness to a small brush; 'old Nestor put aside his gray beard and *brush'd* her with his *whiskers*,' Dryden, Troilus and Cressida, Act iv. sc. 2 (R.); *whisker-ed*. Also *whisk-y*, a kind of light gig, from its being easily *whisked* along; it occurs in Crabbe, Tales of the Hall, b. viii (R.). ¶ Note MDan. *hviske*, for Dan. *viske*.

WHISKEY, WHISKY, a spirit distilled from grain, &c. (Gaelic.) In Johnson's Dict. Spelt *whisquy-beath* in Sinclair's Statistical Acct. of Scotland (1791-9), iii. 525; Brand, Pop. Antiq. ii. 285.—Gael. *uisge-beatha*, water of life, whisky; the equivalent of F. *eau de vie*. We have dropped the latter element, retaining only *uisge*, water. See **Usquebaugh**.

WHISPER, to speak very softly, or under the breath. (E.) ME. *whisperen*; '*Whysperyn*, mussito;' Prompt. Parv. In Wyclif, Ecclus. xii. 19, 'whispering' is expressed by *whistrende* or *whistringe*. ONorthumbrian *hwisprian*; the L. *murmurābant* is glossed by

hwispredon in the Rushworth MS., and by *huuæstredon* in the Lindisfarne MS.; Luke, xix. 7. Again, the L. *murmur* is glossed by *hwisprunge* in the Rushworth MS. and by *huæstrung* in the Lind. MS.; John, vii. 12. We see, then, that *hwisprian* and *hwæstrian* were parallel forms, and *hwæstrian* is evidently closely allied to AS. *hwistlian*, to whistle. *Whisper* and *whistle* are allied words, both of an imitative character; further, they are frequentatives, from the bases *whisp-* and *whist-* respectively; and these are extended from an imitative Teut. root *hweis-* (weak grade *hwis-*). Cf. *wheeze*, which is likewise imitative; also *whiz*.+MDu. *wisperen*, *wispelen*, to whisper, Hexham; G. *wispeln*. So also (from the base *whisk* or *hwisk*) we have Icel. *hviskra*, Swed. *hviska*, Dan. *hviske*, to whisper. Der. *whisper*, sb., *whisper-er*.

WHIST, hush, silence; a game at cards. (1. Scand.; 2. E.) The game was at first called *whisk* by Taylor the Water-poet in 1630, who is said to be the earliest writer to mention it; see Nares. It was so named from the sweeping up or *whisking off* the cards from the table; see **Whisk**. β. But about 1709, *whisk* was corrupted into *whist* (Compleat Gamester, p. 86); and a new etymology was found for it, viz. that it was so named from the silence requisite to play it attentively. The old verb *whist*, to keep silence, also to silence, had *whisted* for its past tense, but *whist* for its pp. 'So was the Titanesse put down and *whist*,' i.e. silenced; Spencer, F.Q. vii. 7. 59. 'All the companie must be *whist*,' i.e. silent; Holinshed, Descr. of Ireland, ed. 1808, p. 67. 'They *whisted* all' =they all kept silence, Surrey, tr. of Virgil, Æn. ii. 1. ME. *whist*, interj., be silent! Wyclif, Judges, xviii. 19 (earlier version), where the later version has *Be thou stille*, and the Vulgate has *tace*. It is thus seen to have been orig. an interjection, commanding silence. See **Hist** and **Hush**. Cf. L. *st!* hist! G. *st! bst! pst!* hist, hush, stop! 'The orig. intention of the utterance is to represent a slight sound, such as that of something stirring, or the breathing or whispering of some one approaching. Something stirs; listen; be still;' Wedgwood. By way of further illustration may be quoted: 'I . . made a contenaunce [gesture] with my hande in maner to been *huisht*,' i.e. to enjoin silence; Test. of Love, b. ii. ch. vii. 122. ¶ *Whisk* occurs in Pope, 2nd Epist. to Mrs. Blount (1715), l. 24, and in Thomson's Autumn (1730), l. 524; modern editions have *whist*.

WHISTLE, to make a shrill sound by forcing the breath through the contracted lips. (E.) ME. *whistlen*, P. Plowman, B. xv. 467. AS. *hwistlian*, to make a hissing noise (Toller); also found in derivatives; as *hwistlere*, a whistler, piper, Matt. ix. 23; 'Sibilatio, *hwistlung*,' Voc. 162. 44; 'Fistula, *wistle*,' id. 406. 23. A frequentative verb, from a base *hwist-*, meant to imitate the hissing sound of whistling, and extended from the Teut. base *hwis-*, weak grade of *hweis-*; see **Whisper**.+Icel. *hvisla*, to whisper; *hviss*, whew! to imitate the sound of whistling; Dan. *hvisle*, to whistle, also to hiss; Swed. *hvissla*, to whistle. Der. *whistle*, sb.; *whistl-er*, AS. *hwistlere*, as above.

WHIT, a thing, a particle, a bit. (E.) The *h* is in the wrong place; *whit* stands for *wiht* = *wight*, and is the same word as *wight*, a person. We find 'neuer a *whyt*' in Palsgrave, p. 881, col. 1. ME. *wight*, a person; also a thing, a bit. 'For she was falle aslepe a little *wight*' = for she had fallen asleep a little whit; Chaucer, C. T. 4281 (A 4283). 'A *lutewiht*' = a little bit, for a short time, Ancren Riwle, p. 72, l. 24. AS. *wiht*, (1) a wight, person, (2) a whit, bit; see abundant examples in Grein, ii. 704. The latter sense is particularly conspicuous in *āwiht* = aught, i.e. 'one whit,' and *nāwiht* = naught, i.e. 'no whit.' See further under **Wight** (1). Der. *aught*, q.v.; *naught*, q.v.; *not*.

WHITE, of the colour of snow, very pale. (E.) ME. *whit* (with long *i*), *whyt*; pl. *white*, Chaucer, C. T. 90. AS. *hwīt*; Grein, ii. 122.+Du. *wit*; Icel. *hvītr*; Dan. *hvid*; Swed. *hvit*; Goth. *hweits*; G. *weiss*; OHG. *hwīz*. β. All from Teut. type *hweitoz*, *hwītoz*, white, shining; further allied to Skt. *çvēta-*, white, *çvit*, *çvind*, to be white, to shine. The Skt. *çvēta* is from √KWEIT, to shine, whence also Russ. *svietluii*, light, bright, *svietit(e)*, to shine, give light, OLithuan. *szweitu*, later form *szweicziu*, I make white, I cleanse. Brugmann, i. § 319; as to the final dental, cf. § 701, note 2. Der. *white-ly*; *white-ness*, spelt *whytnesse* in Prompt. Parv. Also *white*, verb, ME. *hwiten*, used intransitively, to become white, Ancren Riwle, p. 150, l. 7; *whit-en*, ME. *whitenen*, to make white, Early Eng. Psalter, Ps. l. 9, but properly intransitive, from Icel. *hvītna*, to become white (see note on **Waken**). Also *whit-ing*, a fish with delicate white flesh, spelt *whytynge* in Prompt. Parv.; it also means ground chalk. Also *whit-ish*, *whit-ish-ness*; *white-bait*, a fish; *white-faced*, K. John, ii. 23; *white-heat*; *white-lead*, spelt *whyte led* in Prompt. Parv.; *white-limed*, spelt *whitlymed*, P. Plowman, B. xv. 111; *white-livered*, i.e. cowardly, Hen. V, iii. 2. 34; *white-wash*. Also *whit-leather*, leather dressed with alum; Beaum. and Fletcher, Scornful Lady, v. 1; *whit-ster*, a bleacher, Prompt. Parv.; *whit-tawer*, a worker in white leather. And see *wheat, wheat-ear, Whit-sunday, whitt-le* (3). ☞ But not *whit-low.*

WHITHER, to what place. (E.) ME. *whider*; spelt *whidir*, Wyclif, Mark, xiv. 12, *whidur*, id. xiv. 14. (Cf. ME. *fader* for *father*, *moder* for *mother*.) AS. *hwider, hwyder*, Grein, ii. 120.+Goth. *hwadrē*, whither, John, vii. 35. Closely allied to *Whether*, and formed from the Teut. base **hwa-*, who, with a compar. suffix allied to Idg. **ter-*; see **Whether.** Cf. *hither, thither.* Der. *whither-ward*, ME. *whiderward*, Chaucer, C. T. 11814 (F 1510); *whither-so-ever.*

WHITLOW, a painful swelling on the fingers. (Scand.) Nothing but a careful tracing of the history of the word will explain it; it seems to be an alteration of *quick-flaw*, i.e. a *flaw* or flaking off of the skin in the neighbourhood of the *quick*, or sensitive part of the finger round the nail. The word is properly Northern, and of Scand. origin. It is still preserved in the North E. *whickflaw*, a whitlow (Halliwell). Here *whick* is the well-known (and very common) Northern form of *quick*, in the sense of 'alive' and 'quick' part of the finger. This is why the sore was called *paronychia.* 'Paronychia, a preternatural swelling or sore, *under the root of the nail*, in one's finger, a felon or *whitlow*;' Phillips, ed. 1706. [Der. from Gk. παρ-, for παρά, beside, and ὄνυχι-, from ὄνυξ, the nail.] And this is also why horses were subject to *whitlows*; in farriery, it is a disease of the feet, of an inflammatory kind, occurring round the hoof, where an acrid matter is collected (Webster); the hoof of the horse answering to the nail of a man. Cf. '*Quick-scab*, a distemper in horses,' Bailey, vol. i. (1735). β. If so, *quick* was replaced by *whit-*, understood as *white*; 'some doth say it is a *white flawe* under the nayle;' A. Boorde, Breviary of Health, c. 265 (Palmer). Cotgrave explains *poil de chat* by 'whitlow;' but Palsgrave has: '*Whitflowe* in ones fyngre, *poil de chat.*' The spelling *whitflaw* occurs repeatedly in Holland's tr. of Pliny (see the index), and is once spelt *white-flaw*, showing that the former syllable was already confused with the adj. *white.* '*Whitflawes* about the root of the nails,' Holland, tr. of Pliny, b. xxiii. c. 4. § 1; &c., &c. '*Paronychia* .. by the vulgar people amongst us it is generally called a *whitflaw*;' Wiseman, Surgery, b. i. c. 11 (R.). Both parts of the word are properly Scandinavian. — Icel. *kvika*, 'the quick under the nail or under a horse's hoof;' otherwise *kvikva*, 'the flesh under the nails, and in animals under the hoofs;' and Swed. *flaga*, a flaw, crack, breach, also a flake, Icel. *flagna*, 'to flake off, as skin or slough.' See **Quick** and **Flaw;** and see **White.** ¶ *Whick* easily turned to *whit*, which was naturally interpreted as *white* (from the words *whit-tawer, whitster*), the more so as the swelling is often of a white colour; the true sense of the word was thus lost, and a *whitlow* was applied to *any* similar sore on the finger, whether near the quick or not. *Low* may have been suggested by prov. E. *low*, 'fire;' with the idea of 'inflammation.'

WHITSUNDAY, the seventh Sunday after Easter, commemorating the day of Pentecost. (E.) Lit. *white Sunday*, as will appear. The word is old. In the Ancren Riwle, p. 412, l. 13, we have mention of *hwitesunedei* immediately after a mention of *holi þursdei.* Again, we find: 'þe holi goste, þet þu on *hwite sune dei* sendest' = the Holy Ghost, whom thou didst send on Whit-sunday; O. Eng. Homilies, i. 209, l. 16. In Layamon, l. 31524, we already have mention of *white sune tide* (= *whit-e sun-e tid-e*, in six syllables), i.e. Whitsun-tide, which in the later version appears in the form *Witson-time*, showing that even at that early period the word *White* was beginning to be confused with *wit*; hence the spelling *witsondai* in Wycliffe's Works, ed. Arnold, ii. 158, 159, &c., is not at all surprising. In the same, p. 161, we already find *witson-weke*, i.e. Whitsun week. In the Cursor Mundi, the word 'white' is written *wijt* (where the *ij* = *ī*); and, accordingly, we there find the form *wijt sundai*, 18914. Cf. *Wit-sonentid*, S. Legendary, p. 115, l. 297. AS. *hwita Sunnan-dæg*; only in the dat. case *hwitan sunnan dæg*, A. S. Chron. an. 1067. However, the AS. name is certified, beyond all question, by the fact that it was early transplanted into the Icelandic language, and appears there as *hvitasunnu-dagr.* In Icelandic we also find *hwita-daga*, lit. 'white days,' as a name for Whitsun week, which was also called *hvitadaga-vika* = whitedays week, and *hvita-sunnudags-vika* = Whitsunday's week. β. All these names are unmistakeable, and it is also tolerably certain that the E. name *White Sunday* is not older than the Norman conquest; for, before that time, the name was always *Pentecoste* (see **Pentecost**). We are therefore quite sure that, for some reason or other, the name *Pentecost* was then exchanged for that of *White Sunday*, which came into common use, and was early corrupted into *Wit-Sunday*, proving that *white* was soon misunderstood, and was wrongly supposed to refer to the *wit* or wisdom conferred by the Holy Ghost on the day of Pentecost, on which theme it was easy for the preacher (to whom etymology was no object) to expatiate. Nevertheless, the truer

spelling has been preserved to this day, not only in English and in modern Icelandic, but in the very plainly marked modern Norwegian dialects, wherein it is called *Kvitsunndag*, whilst Whitsun-week is called *Kvitsunn-vika*, obviously from *kvit*, white (Aasen). See, therefore, **White** and **Sunday.** B. But when we come to consider *why* this name was given to the day, room is at last opened for conjecture. Perhaps the best explanation is Mr. Vigfusson's, in the Icel. Dict., who very pertinently remarks that even Bingham gives no reference whatever to Icelandic writers, though, from the nature of the case, they know most about it, the word having been borrowed by Icelandic whilst it was still but new to English. He says: 'The great festivals, Yule, Easter, and Pentecost, but esp. the two latter, were the great seasons for christening: in the Roman Catholic church especially Easter, whence in Roman usage the Sunday after Easter was called *Dominica in Albis*; but in the Northern churches, perhaps owing to the cold weather at Easter-time, Pentecost, as the birth-day of the church, seems to have been esp. appointed for christening and for ordination; hence the following week was called the Holy Week (*Helga Vika*). Hence, Pentecost derived its name from the *white garments*,' &c. See the whole passage, and the authorities cited. The W. *sulgwyn*, Whitsuntide, is translated from English; cf. W. *sul*, sun, and *gwyn*, white. Hexham's MDu. Dict. has: '*Witten Donder-dagh*, Holy Thursday; *Witten Sondagh*, Palme Sunday; *Witte-brodt*, white bread;' ed. 1658. Kalkar's Mid. Dan. Dict. has: '*Hvideson-dag*, (1) the first Sunday after Easter; (2) the first Sunday in Lent; from *hvid*, white, and *söndag*, Sunday. It is clear that *white Sunday* was a name not confined to the day of Pentecost. ¶ It deserves to be recorded, as a specimen of English popular etymology, that many still prefer to consider AS. *hwita sunnan* (occurring in the A. S. Chronicle) as a corruption of the mod. G. *pfingsten* (which is acknowledged to be from the Gk. πεντηκοστή). Seeing that *pfingsten* is a modern form, and is an old dative case turned into a nominative, the MHG. word being *pfingeste*, we are asked to believe that *pfingeste* became *hwita su*, and that *nnan* was afterwards luckily added! Comment is needless. Der. *Whitsun-week*, a shortened form for *Whitsunday's week* (as shown by Icel. *hvitasunnudags-vika*); and similarly, *Whitsun-tide.* Also *Whit-Monday, Whit-Tuesday*, names coined to match *Whit-Sunday*; formerly called *Monday in Whitsun-week*, &c.; Wycliffe, Works, ii. 161. ¶ Cf. *Palmson, Lowson*, as contractions of *Palmsunday, Lowsunday.* See Oxford Dict.

WHITTLE (1), to pare or cut with a knife. (E.) In Johnson's Dict. A mere derivative from the sb. *whittle*, a knife, Timon, v. 1. 183. And *whittle* is the same as ME. *þwitel, thwitel*, a knife, Chaucer, C. T. 3931 (A 3933). Lit. 'a cutter;' formed, with suffix *-el* of the agent, from *þwit-*, weak grade of AS. *þwitan*, to thwite, to cut, to pare; whence the verb which is spelt by Palsgrave both *thwyte* and *whyte.* See Rom. of the Rose, l. 933. ¶ The alleged AS. *hwitel*, a knife, is a mere myth; see **Whittle** (3).

WHITTLE (2), to sharpen. (E.) Used as a slang term; 'well *whittled* and thoroughly drunk;' Holland, tr. of Plutarch, p. 387 (R.). 'Throughly *whitled*' = thoroughly drunk; Holland, tr. of Pliny, b. xiv. c. 22. The lit. sense is, sharpened like a *whittle* or knife; see **Whittle** (1). It may have been confused with *whet*, the frequentative of which, however, could only have been *whettle*, and does not occur.

WHITTLE (3), a blanket. (E.) ME. *whitel*, P. Plowman, C. xvii. 76. AS. *hwitel*, a blanket, Gen. ix. 23. Lit. 'a small white thing.' — AS. *hwit*, white. See **White.**+Icel. *hvítill*, a whittle, from *hvítr*, white; Norweg. *kvitel*, from *kvit*, white (Aasen). Cf. E. *blank-et*, from F. *blanc*, white. ¶ Somner gave 'knife' as one sense of AS. *hwitel*; he was clearly thinking of *whittle* (1), which happens to be a corruption of *thwitel*; see **Whittle** (1). His mistake has been carefully preserved in many dictionaries.

WHIZ, to make a hissing sound. (E.) 'The woods do *whiz*;' Surrey, tr. of Æneid, b. ii, l. 534. An imitative word, allied to **Whistle,** q.v. Cf. Icel. *hvissa*, to hiss, to run with a hissing sound, said, e.g., of a stream; and cf. E. *whis-per, hiss, whir.*

WHO, an interrogative and relative pronoun. (E.) 'Formerly *who, what, which*, were not relative, but interrogative pronouns; *which, whose, whom* occur as relatives [*misprinted* interrogatives] as early as the end of the twelfth century, but *who* not until the 14th century, and was not in common use before the 16th century;' Morris, Hist. Outlines of E. Accidence, § 188. AS. *hwā*, who (interrogatively), masc. and fem.; *hwæt*, neuter; gen. *hwæs*, for all genders; dat. *hwām, hwǣm*, for all genders; acc. masc. *hwone*, fem. *hwone*, neut. *hwæt*; instrumental *hwī, hwȳ* (mod. E. *why*); Grein, ii. 113; Sweet, A. S. Reader. We now have *who* = AS. *hwā*; *what* = *hwæt*; *whose* = *hwæs*, with a lengthening of the vowel, to agree with the vowel of other cases (seldom used in the neuter, though there is nothing against it); *whom* = dat. *hwām*, but also used for the accusative, the old acc. *hwone* being lost; *why* = inst. *hwī*; see **Why.**+Du. *wie*, who; *wat*, what; *wiens*, whose; *wien*, whom (dat. and acc.); Icel. *hverr, hver,* who; *hvat,* what; *hvers,* whose; *hverjum* (masc.), whom; pl. *hverir,* &c.; Dan. *hvo,* who; *hvad,* what; *hvis,* whose; *hvem,* whom (dat. and acc.); Swed. *hvem,* who, whom (nom. dat. and acc.); *hvad,* what; *hvems, hvars,* whose; G. *wer,* who; *was,* what; *wessen, wess,* whose; *wem,* to whom; *wen,* whom (acc.); Goth. nom. *hwas, hwō, hwa* (or *hwata*); gen. *hwis, hwizōs, hwis;* dat. *hwamma, hwizai, hwamma;* acc. *hwana, hwō, hwa* (or *hwata*); instr. *hwē;* pl. *hwai,* &c.; Irish and Gael. *co;* W. *pwy;* L. *quis, quæ, quid;* Russ. *kto, chto,* who, what; Lithuan. *kas,* who; Skt. *kas,* who (masc.), *kim,* what; *kam,* whom (acc.). β. All from the Idg. interrogative base QO (Teut. HWA), who? The neuter has the characteristic neut. suffix -*d* (L. *qui-d*), Teut. -*t* (E. *wha-t,* Goth. *hwa-ta*), as in the words *i-t, tha-t.* Brugmann, ii. § 411. **Der.** *who-ever, who-so, who-so-ever.* Also *whe-n, whe-re, whe-ther, whi-ch, whi-ther, why.* Also *quidd-i-ty, qua-li-ty, qua-nti-ty, quillet.*

WHOLE, hale, sound, entire, complete. (E.) The orig. sense is 'hale,' or in sound health; hence the senses entire, complete, &c., have been deduced. The spelling with initial *w* is curious, and points back to a period when a *w*-sound was initially prefixed in some dialect and afterwards became general; this pronunciation is now again lost. We have other examples in *whot = hot,* Spenser, F. Q. ii. 1. 58, ii. 9. 29, &c.; in *whore = hore;* in *whoop = ME. houpen,* where the *w* is still sounded; and in mod. E. *wun* as the pronunciation of *one,* where the *w* is not now written. I believe the spelling with *w* is hardly older than about A.D. 1500; Palsgrave, in 1530, still writes *hole.* 'A *wholle* man;' Golden Booke, c. 29; first printed in 1534. 'The *whole* neade not the visicion;' Tyndale, tr. of Matt. ix. 12 (1526). Richardson cites the adv. *wholly* from Gower; but Pauli's edition (vol. ii. p. 4, l. 21) has *holy* (for *holly*); so also in Macaulay's edition, i. 303, l. 91. ME. *hol, hool,* Wyclif, John, v. 6. AS. *hāl,* whole; whence ME. *hool* by the usual change from AS. *ā* to ME. long *o,* as in AS. *stān* > ME. *stoon,* a stone; Grein, ii. 6. + Du. *heel;* Icel. *heill;* Dan. *heel;* Swed. *hel;* G. *heil;* Goth. *hails.* β. All from Teut. type **hailoz,* Idg. type **koilos,* hale, whole; allied to W. *coel,* an omen; OSlav. *cêlu,* wholly, Russ. *tsiel-it(e),* to heal. See Stokes-Fick, p. 88. **Der.** *whol-ly,* ME. *holly, holy,* in Gower, as above, Chaucer, C. T. 601 (A 599); *whole-ness* (modern). Also *whole-some,* ME. *holsum, holsom,* Chaucer, Troilus, i. 947, spelt *halsumm* in the Ormulum, 2915, not in AS., but suggested by Icel. *heilsamr,* salutary, formed from *heill,* whole, with suffix -*samr* corresponding to E. -*some;* hence *whole-somely, whole-some-ness.* Also *whole-sale,* used by Addison (Todd), from the phrase *by whole sale,* for which see Hakluyt, Voy. i. 471 (l. 6 from bottom), as opposed to *retail.* Also *heal,* q.v.; *hol-y,* q.v. **Doublet,** *hale.* ☞ If we write *whole* for *hole,* we ought to write *wholy* for *holy:* 'For their *wholy* conversacion;' Roy, Rede Me and be not Wroth, ed. Arber, p. 75, l. 24.

WHOOP, to shout clearly and loudly. (F.—Teut.) Here, as in the case of *whole, whot* for *hot* (Spenser), and a few other words, the initial *w* is unoriginal, and the spelling should rather be *hoop.* The spelling with *w* dates from about A.D. 1500. Palsgrave, in 1530, has: 'I *whoope,* I call, *je huppe;*' yet Shakespeare (ed. 1623) has *hooping,* As You Like It, iii. 2. 203. [The derivative *whoobub* is, conversely, now spelt *hubbub;* see **Hubbub.**] ME. *houpen,* to call, shout, P. Plowman, B. vi. 174; Chaucer, C. T. 15406 (B 4590). — F. *houper,* 'to hoop unto, or call afar off;' Cot. From F. *houp!* an exclamatory interjection. Of Teut. origin; cf. EFries. *hup!* up! Pomeran. *hup-hei!* a cry of joy (Schambach); G. *hopsa,* heyday! (Flügel). **Der.** *whoop,* sb.; *whoop-ing-cough* or *hoop-ing-cough; hubb-ub.* **Doublet,** *hoop* (2), which is a mere variation of spelling, and exactly the same word.

WHORE, a harlot. (Scand.) As in the case of *whole,* q. v., the initial *w* is not older than about A.D. 1500. Palsgrave, in 1530, still has *hore.* 'The *whoores* beleved hym;' Tyndale, tr. of Matt. xxi. 32 (1526). In Bale's Kynge Johan, ed. Collier, p. 26, l. 21, we find *horson,* but on p. 76, l. 12, it is *whoreson.* [It is remarkable that the word *hoar,* white, as applied to hair, also occurs with initial *w* at perhaps an earlier period. 'The heere of his hedd was *whore*' = the hair of his head was hoar; Monk of Evesham, c. 12; ed. Arber, p. 33. Spelt also *whore* in Lydgate, Assembly of Gods, 400.] ME. *hore,* King Alisaunder, l. 1000; P. Plowman, B. iv. 166. The word is not AS., but Scandinavian. [The AS. word was *miltestre,* Matt. xxi 31.] In the Laws of Canute (Secular), § 4, we find *hōr-cwene,* an adulteress, where the Danish word has the AS. *cwene* (a quean) added to it; Thorpe, Ancient Laws, i. 378. — Icel. *hōra,* an adulteress, fem. of *hōrr,* an adulterer (we also find *hōr,* neut. adultery); Dan. *hore;* Swed. *hora.* + Du. *hoer,* G. *hure,* OHG. *huora;* Goth. *hōrs,* masc., an adulterer, Luke, xviii. 11. β. The Teut. types are **hōroz,* m., and **hōrā,* f.; Idg. types **qāros,* m., and *qārā,* f. [The Church-Slavonic *kuruva,* an adulteress, Polish *kurwa,* are from Teutonic.]

Cf. L. *cārus,* dear, orig. 'loving;' Irish *caraim,* I love, Skt. *chāru-,* agreeable, beautiful, &c. γ. If this be right, the word prob. meant at first no more than 'lover,' and afterwards descended in the scale, as so often happens. Brugmann, i. § 637. ¶ Not allied to the verb *to hire.* **Der.** *whore-dom,* ME. *hordom,* Ancren Riwle, p. 204, l. 20, from Icel. *hōrdōmr,* Swed. *hordom; whor-ish,* Troil. iv. 1. 63, *whor-ish-ly,* -*ness; -master,* K. Lear, i. 2. 137, spelt *horemaister* in Palsgrave; -*monger,* Meas. for Meas. iii. 2. 37; -*son,* in Bale, Kynge Johan (as above).

WHORL, a number of leaves disposed in a circle round the stem of a plant. (E.) It is closely allied to *wharl,* which is the name for a piece of wood or bone placed on a spindle to twist it by. The latter is also called a *wharrow,* a picture of which will be found in Guillim, Display of Heraldry, 1664, p. 289: 'The round ball [disc] at the lower end serveth to the fast twisting of the thread, and is called a *wharrow.*' The likeness between a *wharl* on a spindle and a *whorl* of leaves is sufficiently close. Palsgrave has: '*Wharle* for a spyndell, *peson.*' *Wharl, whorl* are contracted forms for *wharvel, whorvel.* '*Whorlwyl, whorwhil, whorle* of a spyndyl, *Vertebrum,*' Prompt. Parv.; where *whorlwyl* is clearly an error for *whorwyl* (= *whorvil*). The AS. name for a *wharrow* was *hweorfa;* we find '*Vertellum* [*sic*], hweorfa' in a list of spinning-implements, Voc. 294. 6; this is clearly an allied word, but without the suffix -*el,* and the etymology is from the strong verb *hweorfan,* to turn; see **Whirl** and **Wharf.** β. The particular form *whorl* may have been borrowed from MDu., and introduced by the Flemish weavers; cf. MDu. *worvel,* 'a spinning-whirle,' Hexham; also *worvelen,* 'to turne, to reele, to twine,' id.; these words are from the weak grade of the same root, and help to account for the vowel *o.* Cf. AS. *hworf-en,* pp. of *hweorfan.*

WHORTLE-BERRY, a bilberry. (E.) '*Airelles,* whurtleberries;' Cot. But the *w* seems to be unoriginal, as in *whole, whoop, whore* (above). Older form *hurtilberye,* J. Russell, Book of Nurture, l. 82 (ab. 1460). Again, *hurtil-berye* is an extension of *hurt-berye,* also (simply) *hurt.* 'Strawberyes or *hurtes;*' Boorde, Dyetary, xiii. (1542, ed. 1870) 267 (N. E. D.). The last form answers to AS. *horta,* a whortle-berry, pl. *hortan;* see Napier's Glosses, 2. 433 (note), and cf. '*Facinia* [i. e. vaccinia], *hortan,* Voc. 234. 37. ¶ In Dorsetsh., bilberries are called *hurt-berries,* which answers to AS. *heorot-bergan,* pl. of *heorot-berge;* cf. '*Mora, heorotberge,*' Corpus Gloss. 1333; but this is an unrelated name. The AS. form of ME. *hurtil* must have been **hyrtel.* In America, *hurtleberry* has become *huckleberry.*

WHY, on what account. (E.) *Why* is properly the instrumental case of *who,* and was, accordingly, frequently preceded by the prep. *for,* which (in AS.) sometimes governed that case. ME. *whi, why,* Wyclif, Matt. xxi. 26; *for whi* = on which account, because, id. viii. 9. AS. *hwī, hwȳ, hwig,* instr. case of *hwā,* who; *for hwig,* why; Grein, ii. 113 See **Who.** + Icel. *hvī,* why; allied to *hverr,* who, *hvat,* what; Dan. *hvi;* Swed. *hvi;* Goth. *hvē,* instr. case of *hvas,* who. β. The word *how* is closely related. See **How.**

WI—WY

WICK (1), the cluster of threads of cotton in a lamp or candle. (E.) Spelt *weeke,* in Spenser, F. Q. ii. 10. 30. ME. *wicke,* P. Plowman, C. xx. 205; *weyke,* id. B. xvii. 239; *wueke,* O. Eng. Homilies, ii. 47, l. 30. There seem to be at least two distinct forms. E. *wick* = ME. *wicke;* and ME. *weke,* Voc. 592. 30, whence Spenser's *weeke.* The ME. *wicke* answers to AS. *wice* (Sweet), and *weke* to AS. *weoce,* Voc. 126. 29, 439. 36; cf. '*Funalia, vel funes, candel-weoca;*' Voc. 154. 14; pl. *candel-weocan,* id. 404. 22. + MDu. *wiecke,* 'a weeke of a lampe, a tent to put into a wounde;' Hexham; Low G. *weke,* lint, to put to a wound; whence Dan. *væge,* a wick; Norw. *veik;* Swed. *veke,* a wick, Widegren. + Bavarian *wichengarn,* wickyarn, Schmeller, 835; he also gives various G. forms, viz. OHG. *wieche, weche,* with a reference to Graff, i. 728; Schade gives OHG. *wioh* and *wike.* The orig. sense was prob. 'twist,' or 'thing woven;' cf. Irish *fig-im,* I weave (base **weg-*); Stokes-Fick, p. 268; and Skt. *vāg-urā,* a net.

WICK (2), a town. (L.) AS. *wīc,* a village, town; Grein, ii. 688. Not E., but borrowed. — L. *uīcus,* a village; see **Vicinity.**

WICK (3), **WICH,** a creek, bay. (Scand.) In some placenames, as in *Green-wich,* &c. — Icel. *vīk,* a small creek, inlet, bay; OIcel. **wīk.* From *vīk-ja,* to recede; see **Weak.** ¶ It is not easy, in all cases, to distinguish between this and the word above. Ray, in his Account of Salt-making (E. D. S., Gloss. B. 15, p. 20), mentions *Nant-wich, North-wich, Middle-wich, Droit-wich*; here *wich* = brine-pit, apparently a peculiar use of Icel. *vik* above. See *Wych*, a salt-work, in Nares.

WICKED, evil, bad, sinful. (E.) The word *wicked* was orig. a past participle, with the sense 'rendered evil,' formed as if from a verb **wikken*, to make evil, from the obsolete adj. *wikke* (dissyllabic), evil, once common. Again, the adj. *wikke* is allied to AS. *wicca*, masc., a wizard [*wicce*, fem., a witch]. Hence the adj. *wikke* is allied to *Weak*, q. v. From the weak grade **wic-*, of AS. *wīcan* (Icel. *vikja*, G. *weichen*), to yield, give way. And see *Witch*. We also find ME. *wikked*, as in the adv. *wikked-ly*, Chaucer, C. T. 8599 (E 723); spelt *wickede*, def. form of *wicked*, Layamon, later text, 14983, where it takes the place of *swicfulle* (deceitful) in the earlier text. This is prob. the earliest instance of the word. β. The shorter form *wikke* is common; it occurs in Havelok, 688; P. Plowman, B. v. 229; Chaucer, C. T. 1089, 5448, 15429 (A 1087, B 1028, 4613); cf. 'wicci ræd,' i. e. wicked counsel, A. S. Chron. an. 1140; as if for **wicc-ig*, an adj. from *wicca*, a wizard. It became obsolete in the 15th century as an adj., but the *fem.* sb. is still in use in the form *witch*. Der. *wicked-ly*; *wicked-ness*, ME. *wikkednesse*, P. Plowm. B. v. 290.

WICKER, made of twigs. (Scand.) 'A *wicker* bottle,' Oth. ii. 3. 152 (folios, *twiggen bottle*). *Wicker* is properly a sb., meaning a pliant twig. ME. *wiker, wikir*; '*Wykyr*, to make wythe baskettys, or to bynde wythe thyngys [i. e. to make baskets with, or bind things with], *Vimen, vituligo*;' Prompt. Parv. '*Wycker*, osier;' Palsgrave. The AS. form does not appear; and perhaps E. *wicker* may have been borrowed from Scandinavian. We find MSwed. *wika*, to bend, whence *weck*, a fold, *wickla*, to fold, wrap round (Ihre); also Swed. dial. *vekare, vekker, vikker* (which is our very word), various names for the sweet bay-leaved willow, *Salix pentandra*, lit. 'the bender,' from *veka*, to bend, to soften, allied to Swed. *vika*, to fold, to double, to plait (Widegren). *Wicker-work* means, accordingly, 'plaited work,' esp. such as is made with pliant twigs, according to the common usage of the word. The word is closely allied, in the same way, to Dan. *veg*, pliant (with *g* for *k*, as usual in Danish), in connexion with which Wedgwood cites, from various Danish dialects, *vöge, vögger, vegre*, a pliant rod, a withy (lit. a *wicker*), *vögrekurv, vegrekurv*, a wicker-basket, *væger, vægger*, a willow (= Swed. dial. *vekare* above); cf. Skt. *vāg-urā*, a net. Cf. *Weak*, *Wick* (1), *Wick* (3). And see *Witch-elm*.

WICKET, a small gate. (F. — Teut.) ME. *wiket*, P. Plowman, B. v. 611; Rom. of the Rose, 528. — AF. *wiket*, Tristan, ed. Michel, ii. 101; cf. Supp. to Godefroy, s. v. *guichet*; he also has *guischet*, and Littré's quotations give us the forms *wisket* and *viquet*; mod. F. *guichet*, a wicket. Littré also cites the Walloon *wichet*, Norman *viquet*, Prov. *guisquet*, all of them deduced from the common form *wisket*. It is supposed that the *s* is radical; and it has been derived from OHG. *wisk-en*, to wipe, to whisk; and intr., to move quickly, to slip aside. Hence, perhaps, it meant a postern-door, to slip out at. It was esp. used of a small door easily opened and shut. Cf. MDu. *wicket*, a wicket, Hexham; also *wincket*, 'a wicket,' id.; prob. from OF. Cf. EFries. *wisken*, to wipe, also to move quickly; Norw. *viska* (the same); Swed. dial. *viska*, to throw, to swing; also Norw. *viskjen*, light and quick (Ross). See *Whisk*. Körting, § 10171. B. In the game of cricket, the *wicket* was at first (A. D. 1700) lit. 'a small gate,' being 2 feet wide by 1 foot high; but the shape has so greatly altered that there is no longer any resemblance. See the diagrams in the Eng. Cyclop. div. Arts and Sciences, Supplement; s. v. *Cricket*.

WIDE, broad, far extended. (E.) ME. *wid* (with long *i*); pl. *wide* (dissyllabic), Chaucer, C. T. 28. AS. *wīd*, wide; Grein, ii. 690. + Du. *wijd*; Icel. *vīðr*; Swed. and Dan. *vid*; G. *weit*, OHG. *wīt*. β. All from Teut. type **widoz*, wide; perhaps for **wi-ðoz*, orig. a pp. from √WEI; cf. Skt. *vi-taram*, farther (Macdonell). Der. *wide-ly*, *-ness*; *wid-en*, verb, Cor. i. 4. 44, with which cf. ME. *widen*, Prompt. Parv., imperative *wide*, Palladius on Husbandry, iii. 923, though the mod. suffix *-en* is not the same as the ending of the ME. infin. *widen* (see this explained under *Waken*). Also *wid-th*, not an old word, used in Drayton's Battle of Agincourt, st. 142, as equivalent to the older sb. *wideness*; formed by analogy with *leng-th*, *bread-th*, &c.; cf. Icel. *vidd*, width.

WIDGEON, the name of a kind of duck. (F. — L.) 'A *wigion*, bird, *glaucea*;' Levins, ed. 1570. Spelt *wygeon*, Sir T. Elyot, Castel of Health, b. ii. ch. 13. The suffix and form of the word show that it is certainly French; and it is clear that the E. word has preserved an older form (presumably **wigeon*) than can be found in French. Littré gives the three forms *vigeon, vingeon, gingeon*, as names of the 'whistling duck' (*canard siffleur*). Pr. b. from L. *uipionem*, acc. of *uipio*, used by Pliny, bk. x. c. 49, to mean a kind of small crane. Cf. Ital. *vipione*, a small crane (Torriano). There is a by-form *bibio*,

probably *bibio, uipio* are of imitative origin, like L. *pīpio*. (For the letter-changes, cf. E. *pigeon* from L. acc. *pipiōnem*.)

WIDOW, a woman whose husband is dead. (E.) ME. *widewe*, *widwe*, Chaucer, C. T. 255, 1173 (A 253, 1171). AS. *widwe, weoduwe*; also *wudwe, wuduwe, wydewe*, Grein, ii. 692. + Du. *weduwe*; G. *wittwe*, OHG. *wituwa, witewa, witiwa*; Goth. *widuwō, widowō*. β. The Teut. types are **widewā, *widowā*, fem. sb., a widow; Idg. types **widhewā, *widhowā*. Further cognate with L. *uidua*, fem. of *uiduus*, deprived of, bereft of (which gave rise to Ital. *vedova*, Span. *viuda*, F. *veuve*, a widow); also with Irish *feadhb*, OIrish *fedb*, W. *gweddw*, Russ. *vdova*, Skt. *vidhavā*, a widow. γ. Here the L. *d*, as in other cases, answers to Skt. *dh*, and the root is √WIDH, to lack, want, hence, to be bereft of. This root is preserved in the Skt. *vindh*, to lack (not in Benfey), for which see the St. Petersburg Dict. vol. vi. 1070. Brugmann, ii. § 64. Cf. also Gk. ἠίθεος (for **ἠ-ϝιθ-ε-ϝος*), a bachelor, one who is unmarried. Der. *widow*, verb, Cor. v. 6. 153; *widow-hood*, ME. *widewehad*, Holi Meidenhad, p. 23, l. 20; *widow-er*, ME. *widewer, widwer*, P. Plowman, A. 10. 194, B. 9. 174, formed by adding *-er*; cf. G. *wittwer*.

WIELD, to manage, to use. (E.) ME. *welden*, to govern, also to have power over, to possess, Wyclif, Matt. v. 4, Luke, xi. 21, xviii. 18. AS. *geweldan, gewyldan*, to have power over, Gen. iii. 16; Mark, v. 4. This is a weak verb, answering to ME. *welden*, and mod. E. *wield*, which are also weak verbs; all are derivatives from the strong verb *wealdan* (pt. t. *wēold*, pp. *wealden*), to have power over, govern, rule, possess. + Icel. *valda*, to govern (pt. t. *olli*); G. *walten*, OHG. *waltan*, to dispose, manage, rule; Goth. *waldan*, to govern. β. The Icel. pt. t. *olli* is for **wolþi* (Noreen, § 215), and the Idg. base was **walt*, whence Celtic **wlat-is*, OIrish *flaith*, dominion (Stokes-Fick, 262). Hence it is supposed that Russ. *vladiet(e)*, to reign, rule, possess, make use of, Lithuan. *waldyti*, to rule, govern, possess, are early loans from Teutonic. But W. *gwlad*, a region, is a cognate word. Some connect it with the √WAL, to be strong; cf. L. *ualēre*, to be strong. See *Valiant*. Der. *wield-er*, *un-wield-y*.

WIFE, a woman, a married woman. (E.) ME. *wif* (with long *i*), *wyf*, Chaucer, C. T. 447, 1173 (A 445, 1171); pl. *wyues* (*wyves*), id. 234. AS. *wīf*, a woman, wife, remarkable as being a neuter sb., with pl. *wīf* like the singular. + Du. *wijf*, woman, wife, fem.; Icel. *vīf*, neut. a woman; only used in poetry; Dan. *viv*, fem.; G. *weib*, neut. a woman; OHG. *wīp*. β. The Teut. type is **wībom*, n. The form of the root is **weib* = Idg. √WEIP; in accordance with which we find OHG. *weibōn, weipōn*, to waver, be irresolute, L. *uibrare*, to quiver, Skt. *vep*, to tremble; but the real origin of the word remains obscure. ¶ It cannot be allied to AS. *wefan*, to weave. Der. *wife-like*, Cymb. iii. 2. 8, *fish-wife*, i. e. fish-woman; *mid-wife*, q. v.; *house-wife* (see *House*); *wive*, v., AS. *wīfian*, Luke, xx. 34. Also *wo-man*, q. v.

WIG, a peruke. (Du. — F. — Ital. — L.) *Wig* occurs frequently in Pope; Moral Essays, iii. 65, 295, &c., and is merely a shortened form of *periwig*, which is much older, and occurs in Shakespeare. Cf. *bus* for *omnibus*. See further under *Periwig* and *Peruke*. Der. *wigg-ed*.

WIGHT (1), a person, creature. (E.) ME. *wiȝt, wight*, Chaucer, C. T. 848 (A 846). AS. *wiht* (very common), a creature, animal, person, thing; also spelt *wuht, wyht*, and used both as fem. and neut.; Grein, ii. 703. + Du. *wicht*, a child; Westphalian *wicht*, a girl; Icel. *vættr*, a wight; *vætta*, a whit; Dan. *vætte*, an elf; G. *wicht*; Goth. *waihts*, fem., *waiht*, neut., a whit, a thing. β. It is probable that the fem. and neut. sbs. were orig. distinct, but they were early confused. The Teut. base **weh-t-* may perhaps be connected with AS. *weg-an*, to move; if so, it may have meant a moving object; orig. 'a thing carried' (L. *uectum*); or (in the imagination of the spectator), an elf or demon. Cf. the Celtic type **wektā*, f., a movement, a course, a time; as in Irish *feachd*, OIrish *fecht*, a course, turn, time, W. *gwaith* (the same); Stokes-Fick, p. 266. *Whit* is nothing but another spelling of *wight*. Doublet, *whit*.

WIGHT (2), nimble, active, strong. (Scand.) 'He was so wimble and so *wight*;' Spenser, Shep. Kal. March, 91. ME. *wight*, *wiȝt*, valiant, P. Plowman, B. ix. 21; Layamon, 20588. — Icel. *vigr*, in fighting condition, serviceable for war; the final *t* seems to have been caught up from the neut. *vigt*, which was used in certain phrases; '*þeir drāpu karla þā er vigt var at*' = they smote the men that might be slain, i. e. the men who were serviceable for war; referring to the rule not to slay women, children, or helpless men. See Icel. Dict. For similar instances of final *t* from Icelandic, see *Want*, *Thwart*. The same word as Swed. *vig*, nimble, agile, active (whence *vigt*, nimbly), allied to AS. *wiglic*, warlike. β. From the sb. which appears as Icel. *vig*, AS. *wig*, war. The Icel. *vig*, war, is derived from Icel. *vega*, to fight, smite (quite distinct from *vega*, to move, weigh), allied to Goth. *weigan, weihan* (pt. t. *waih*, pp. *wigans*), to fight, strive, contend. — Teut. base WEIH, to fight; Fick, iii. 303. Allied to L. *uincere*, to fight, conquer; see *Victor*. Also to OIrish *fich-im*, I fight, Lith. *wik-rus*, active, **wight**, *wĕkà*, strength, OSlav. *vĕku*, strength, Russ. *viek'*, life.

WIGWAM, an Indian hut or cabin. (N. American Indian.) In books relating to N. America. 'They built a long *wigwam* ;' I. Mather, Remarkable Providences (1684); repr. by Offor, p. 31. In Eliot's Indian Grammar, 1666, p. 11, Eliot gives the pronominal forms of the Massachusetts word for 'house' as follows: '*Week*, his house; *Weekou*, their house; *weekit*, in his house, *wekuwomut*, in his [*read* their] house. Against *wekuwomut* he has a note—hence we corrupt this word *wigwam*.'—J. Platt (in N. and Q., 9 S. x. 446). S. T. Rand, in his Dict. of Micmac (a language of the Algonkin family) has: '*wigwom*, a house.' Cuoq gives Algonkin *mikiwam*, also *wikiwam*, a house (pp. 221, 438).

WILD, self-willed, violent, untamed, uncivilised, savage, desert. (E.) In Barbour's Bruce, we find *will of red* = wild of rede or counsel, at a loss what to do, i. 348, iii. 494, xiii. 478 ; *will of wane* = wild of weening or thought, at a loss, i. 323, ii. 471, vii. 225. The form *will*, here used as an adj., is simply due to the fact that the Icel. form for 'wild' is *villr*, which stands for *vilþr by the assimilation so common in Icelandic. By themselves, these passages would not by any means prove any connexion between *wild* and *will*; nevertheless, the connexion is real, as appears from a consideration of the words cognate with *wild*. (See further below.) ME. *wilde*, rarely *wielde*, though we find 'a *wielde* olyue-tre' in Wyclif, Rom. xi. 17 ; spelt *wyld*, Rob. of Glouc. p. 57, l. 1322. AS. *wilde* (Toller). Grein gives the examples : *se wilda fugel* = the wild bird ; *wilde dēor* = wild deer or animals.+Du. *wild*, proud, savage; Icel. *villr* (for *vilþr), wild ; also astray, bewildered, confused; Dan. and Swed. *vild* ; G. *wild*, OHG. *wildi*; Goth. *wiltheis*, wild, uncultivated, Mark, i. 6 ; Rom. xi. 17. β. All from Teut. type *welthjoz, astray, wild ; the Goth. form *wil-theis* is important, because the Goth. -*th*- answers to L. -*t*-, used as a suffix with pp. force (cf. L. *rectus*, right, orig. a pp. form). The orig. sense is perhaps indicated by the Icel. *villr* and by the common E. use of the word, viz. 'actuated by *will*;' to act *wildly* is to act *wilfully*. Cf. the Celtic type *wel-tos, as in W. *gwyllt*, wild ; Stokes-Fick, p. 277. Perhaps from √WEL, to will, to wish. See **Will** (1). Cf. W. *gwyllys*, the will. Others connect Goth. *wiltheis* with Russ. *vil-iat(e)*, to run hither and thither. **Der.** *wild*, sb., Merch. Ven. ii. 7. 41, ME. *wilde*, Rob. of Glouc. p. 553, l. 11539 ; *wild-ly* ; *wild-ness*, spelt *wyyldnesse* in the Prompt. Parv. ; *wild-fire*. ME. *wylde fur*, Rob. of Glouc. p. 410, l. 8485; *wild-ing*, a wild or crab-apple, Spenser, F. Q. iii. 7. 17. Also *be-wild-er*, q.v.; *wild-er-ness*, q. v.

WILDERNESS, a wild or waste place. (E.) ME. *wilder-nesse*, Ancren Riwle, p. 158, l. 18. *Wildernesse* first appears in Layamon, 30335 ; and stands for *wildern-nesse*. It is formed by adding the ME. suffix -*nesse* to the shorter word *wildern*, which was used in the same sense. Thus, in the Ancren Riwle, p. 160, l. 7, one MS. has *wilderne* in place of *wildernesse*. So also in Layamon, l. 1238 : 'þar is wode, þar is water, þar is *wilderne muchel* ' = there is wood, there is water, there is a great desert. This ME. *wilderne*, a desert, is formed with the adj. suffix -*n* (-*en*) from the AS. sb. *wilder*, *wildor*, a wild animal (Grein), a neuter sb. answering to Teut. type *wilthos, allied to *wild* (Teut. *welthjoz). See Sievers, § 289.+ MDu. *wildernisse*. And see *be-wilder*.

WILE, a trick, a sly artifice. (E.) ME. *wile* (dissyllabic), Chaucer, 3403. AS. *wil*, a wile, A. S. Chron. an. 1128. This AS. *wil* is late; it prob. represents AF. *wile, answering to OF. *guile*, guile ; see **Guile**. Modern E. *wile* is rather a shortened form of AS. *wigl*, 'divination,' in Napier (see the note on p. 159, l. 165). Cf. His [the devil's] *wiƷeles*, deceits, Ancren Riwle, p. 300. The AS. *wilung* (for *wiglung), divination, occurs in the Kentish Glosses, 554. Divination was regarded as heathen, and a deceit of the devil. The verb is AS. *wīglian*, to divine ; cf. MDu. *wichelen* (Hexham), Du. *wigchelen*, *wichelen*, to divine, practise augury ; whence OF. *guiler*. A primary form occurs in AS. *wīg*, a sanctuary, allied to Goth. *weihs*, holy. Cf. L. *uictima*. **Der.** *wil-y*, ME. *wili*, *wely*, Cursor Mundi, 11807 ; *wil-i-ness*. **Doublet,** *guile*; whence *be-guile*. ¶ Note the spelling *wyhyl* in the Play of Mary Magdalen, l. 377 (15th c.).

WILFUL, obstinate, self-willed. (E.) ME. *wilful*, Life of Beket, ed. Black, l. 1309 (Stratmann). Formed with suffix -*ful* (= *full*) from AS. *will*, will ; see **Will** (2). **Der.** *wilful-ly*, ME. *wilfulliche*, in the sense 'willingly,' O. Eng. Homilies, i. 279, l. 8 ; *wilful-ness*, ME. *wilfulnesse*, O. Eng. Homilies, ii. 73.

WILL (1), to desire, be willing. (E.) ME. *willen*, infin. ; pres. t. *wol*, Chaucer, C. T. 42 ; pt. t. *wolde* (whence mod. E. *would*), id. 257. AS. *willan*, *wyllan*, Grein, ii. 708. Pres. sing. 1 and 3 p. *wile*, *wyle* (whence ME. *wul*, *wol*), *wille*, *wylle* ; 2 p. *wilt* ; pl. *willaŏ*, *wyllaŏ* ; pt. t. *wolde*, 2 p. *woldest*, pl. *woldan*, *woldon*, or *woldun*.+ Du. *willen* ; Icel. *vilja*, pt.t. *vilda* ; Dan. *ville* ; Swed. *vilja* ; G. *wollen*, pr. t. *will*, pt. t. *wollte* ; Goth. *wiljan*, pt. t. *wilda*. Teut. type

*weljan-.+Lithuan. *weliti* ; L. *uelle*, pr. t. *uolo*, pt. t. *uolui* ; Skt. *vṛ*, to choose, select, prefer. β. All from √WEL, to choose ; whence also G. *wahl*, choice, E. *well*, adv., *will*, sb., &c. The Goth. *waljan*, to choose, is a causal form, from *wol, 2nd grade of √WEL. **Der.** *will-ing*, *will-ing-ly* ; *will-ing-ness*. Also *will* (2), q. v. Also *will-y-nill-y*, answering either to *will I*, *nill I*, i. e. whether I will or whether I nill (will not), or to *will he*, *nill he*, i. e. whether he will or whether he nill (will not), as in Hamlet, v. 1. 18; we also find *will we*, *nill we*, Udall, on 1 St. John, cap. 2; *will you*, *nill you*, Tam. Shrew, ii. 1. 273; cf. AS. *nillan* (short for *ne willan*), not to wish, Grein, ii. 296, cognate with L. *nolle* (short for *ne uelle*); and see **Hobnob**. From the same root are *well* (1), *wil-ful*, *weal*, *wild*, *vol-unt-ar-y*, *vol-upt-u-ous*.

WILL (2), sb., desire, wish. (E.) ME. *wille*, Wyclif, Luke, ii. 14. AS. *willa*, will, Grein, ii. 706. = AS. *willan*, verb, to wish ; see **Will** (1).+Du. *wil* ; Icel. *vili* ; Dan. *vilje* ; Swed. *vilja* ; G. *wille* ; Goth. *wilja*. Teut. type *weljon-, m.+Russ. *volia*. Cf. L. *uoluntās*. **Der.** *wil-ful*, q. v.

WILLOW, a tree, with pliant branches. (E.) ME. *wilow*, *wilwe*, Chaucer, C. T. 2924. AS. *welig* ; '*Salix*, *welig* ;' Voc. 269. 36.+ Du. *wilg* ; MDu. *wilge* (Hexham) ; Low G. *wilge* (another AS. name is *wichel*) ; MHG. *wilge* ; OLow G. *wilgia*. β. The Low G. *wichel* is clearly allied to E. *wicker* and to AS. *wican*, to give way, bend ; the tree being named from the pliancy of its boughs. Perhaps the name *willow* has a similar origin, as prov. E. *willy* not only means a willow, but also a wicker-basket, like the *weele* or fish-basket of which an illustration is given in Guillim, Display of Heraldry (1664), p. 316. The AS. *wel-ig* may be from the √WEL, to turn, wind, roll, appearing in G. *welle*, a wave (lit. that which rolls), and in Gk. ἑλ-ίσσειν, as the willow-twigs can be wound to form baskets ; cf. Gk. ἑλ-ένη, a wicker-basket. It may therefore have meant 'pliant.' See **Helix**. γ. A much commoner name for the tree in AS. is *wiŏig*, mod. E. *withy*, with a like sense. See **Withy**. And cf. **Wicker**.

WIMBERRY, the same as **Winberry**, q.v.

WIMBLE (1), a gimlet, an instrument for boring holes. (E.?) ME. *wimbil*, spelt *wymbyl* in the Prompt. Parv., where we also find the verb *wymbelyn*, or *wymmelyn*, to bore. 'A Frenssh *wymble*,' Palladius, xi. 85 ; spelt *wymbul*, Nominale, ed. Skeat, 517. Of E. or Low G. origin ; cf. MDu. *wemelen*, 'to pearce with a wimble,' from *weme*, 'a wimble,' Hexham ; Low G. *wemel*, *wemmel*, a wimble, whence *wemelen*, to bore (Lübben). Also Dan. *vimmel*, an augur, tool for boring ; borrowed from Low G. Apparently from a Teut. base *wem-, to turn ; see **Wimble** (2). Cf. Shropsh. *wim-wam*, a turn-stile. **Der.** *gimlet*.

WIMBLE (2), active, nimble. (Scand.) 'He was so *wimble* and so wight ;' Spenser, Shep. Kal. March, 91. Cf. North E. *wheamow*, nimble (Ray). The true sense is full of motion, skipping about. Spenser perhaps picked up the word in the North of England. The *b* (as often after *m*) is excrescent, and due to stress. = Swed. *vimmel-*, in comp. *vimmelkantig*, giddy, whimsical ; Swed. dial. *vimmla*, to be giddy or skittish ; cf. Swed. dial. *vimmra*, the same, whence *vimmrig*, skittish, said of horses. The verbs *vimmla*, *vimmra*, are frequentatives of Swed. dial. *vima*, to be giddy, allied to Icel. *vim*, giddiness, from *whim, by-form of *whim ; see **Whim**. So also Dan. *vimse*, to skip about, *vims*, brisk, quick.+Du. *wemelen*, to move about, or 'to remove often,' Hexham ; a frequentative verb from a Teut. base *wem-, perhaps meaning to turn. See **Wimble** (1). Cf. MG. *wimmen*, to stir oneself quickly (Schade).

WIMPLE, a covering for the neck. (E.) In Spenser, F. Q. i. 12. 22 ; hence *wimpled*, id. i. 1. 4 ; Shak. L. L. L. iii. 181. ME. *wimpel*, Chaucer, C. T. 151 ; Rob. of Glouc. p. 338, l. 6941 ; hence *ywimpled*, Chaucer, C. T. 472 (A 470). AS. *winpel*, the same. ' *Ricinum*, *winpel*, vel *orl*,' Voc. 107. 37 ; '*Anabola*, *winpel*,' id. 125. 8.+Du. *wimpel*, a streamer, a pendant ; Icel. *vimpill* ; Dan. and Swed. *vimpel*, a pennon, pendant, streamer ; G. *wimpel*, a pennon (whence F. *guimpe*, E. *gimp*). β. The AS. *win-pel* was doubtless a compound ; prob. for *wind-pel, where *wind- is from *windan*, to wind ; and perhaps -*pel* is for AS. *pell*, *pæll* (Latin *pallium*), a covering. Cf. OHG. *wim-pal*, a summer garment, head-dress, pennon. And see **Gimp**.

WIN, to gain by labour or contest, earn, obtain. (E.) The orig. sense was to fight, struggle ; hence to struggle for, gain by struggling. ME. *winnen*, pt. t. *wan*, won, Chaucer, C. T. 444 (A 442); pp. *wonnen*, id. 879 (A 877). AS. *winnan*, to fight, labour, endure, suffer ; pt. t. *wann*, pp. *wunnen*, Grein, ii. 715.+Du. *winnen*, pt. t. *won*, pp. *gewonnen* ; Icel. *vinna*, pt. t. *vann*, pp. *unninn*, to work, toil, win ; Dan. *vinde* (for *vinne*) ; Swed. *vinna* ; G. *gewinnen*, OHG. *winnan*, to fight, strive, earn, suffer ; Goth. *winnan*, pt. t. *wann*, pp. *wunnans*, to suffer. β. All from Teut. type *wennan- (pt. t. *wann), to work, suffer, strive. = √WEN, to desire, hence to strive for ; whence Skt. *van*, to ask, beg for, also to honour, L. *Ven-us*, desire, love, *uen-er-āri*, to honour; W. *gwên*, a smile. **Der.** *winn-er*, *winn-ing*; also *win-some*, q. v. From the same root are *wean*, *ween*, *won-t*, *wi-sh*; also *ven-er-e-al*, *ven-er-ate*.

WINBERRY, WIMBERRY, a whortleberry. (E.) Whortle-berries are called, in some parts, *wimberries* or *winberries*. The latter form, in Halliwell, is the more correct. ME. *winberis*, grapes, Cursor Mundi, 4468. AS. *win-berie*, *win-berige*, a grape; lit. a wine-berry, Matt. vii. 16; Luke, vi. 44. See **Wine** and **Berry**.

WINCE, WINCH, to shrink or start back. (F.—MHG.) ME. *wincen*, *winsen*, *winchen*. 'It is the wone of wil to *wynse* and to kyke' =it is the wont of Will (wilfulness) to wince and to kick, P. Plow-man, C. v. 22. '*Wyncyn*, Calcitro;' Prompt. Parv. Spelt *wynche*, Allit. Morte Arthure, 2104.—OF. **wencir*, not found, but necessarily the older form of OF. *guincir* (Godefroy); (note. AF. *guincer*, Toynbee, x. 96, to escape); North F. variant of OF. *guenchir*, to flinch, wince (Godefroy), MF. *guinchir*, 'to wrigle, writhe, winche a toe-side' [i.e. on the one side, aside]; Cot. Roquefort gives *guincher*, *guinchir*, to wince; also *guencher*, *guenchir*, *guencir*, the same; Burguy gives *ganchir*, *guenchir*, *guencir*.—OSax. *wenkian*; cf. MHG. *wenken*, *wenchen*, to wince, start aside; cf. also *wanken*, OHG. *wankōn*, weak verb, the same. Teut. type **wankjan-*, a causal form.—Teut. **wank*, 2nd grade of **wenkan-*, as in MHG. *winken*, to move aside, to nod, the same as G. *winken*, to nod; cognate with E. **Wink**, q.v. *Wince* is, in fact, merely the causal verb formed from *wink*. Cf. G. *wanken*, to totter, waver, stir, budge, flinch, shrink back.

WINCH, the crank of a wheel or axle. (E.) ME. *winche*; spelt *wynche*, Palladius on Husbandry, b. i. l. 426. [Cf. prov. E. *wink*, a periwinkle, also a winch; Halliwell. E. Cornwall *wink*, 'the wheel by which straw-rope is made;' E.D.S.] AS. *wince*. '*Gigrillus*, *wince*,' Voc. 416. 6; here *Gigrillus* is an error for *girgillus*, a winch; see Ducange. The connexion with *winkle* is obvious (see **Winkle**); and both *winch* and *winkle* are derivatives from Teut. base WENK, to bend sideways, nod, totter, &c.; see further under **Wink**. A *winch* was simply 'a bend,' hence a bent handle; cf. AS. *wincel*, a corner (Somner); MHG. *wenke*, a bending or crooking; Lithuan. *winge*, a bend or turn of a river or road. And cf. Norman dial. *vinche*, 'guindeau;' Le Héricher. And see **Winkle, Wench.**

WIND (1), air in motion, breath. (E.) ME. *wind*, *wynd*, Wyclif, Matt. xiv. 24. AS. *wind*, Grein, ii. 712.+Du. *wind*; Icel. *vindr*; Dan. and Swed. *vind*; G. *wind*, OHG. *wint*; Goth. *winds*, *winths*. β. All from the Teut. type **wenðoz*, m., wind. Cognate with L. *uentus*, W. *gwynt*, Breton *gwent*, wind. Orig. a pres. part., Idg. **wēnto-*, signifying 'blowing.' From √AWĒ, to blow. Hence also Skt. *vā*, to blow, *vāta-s*, wind, Goth. *waian*, to blow; Russ. *vieiat(e)*, to blow, *vieter'*, wind, Lithuan. *wėjas*, wind; as well as L *uentus* and E. *wind*. See Brugmann, i. § 420. And see **Weather**. **Der.** *wind*, to blow a horn, pp. *winded*, Much Ado, i. 1 243, oddly cor-rupted to *wound* (by confusion with the strong verb *to wind*), Scott, Lady of the Lake, i. 17. 1; &c.; *wind-age*, a coined word; *wind-bound*, Milton, Hist. of Britain, b. ii, ed. 1695, p. 44; *wind-fall*, that which falls from trees, &c., being blown down by the wind, hence, a piece of good fortune that costs nothing, Beaum. and Fletcher, The Captain, ii. 1 (Fabritio), also used in a bad sense (like *downfall*), Bacon, Essay 29, Of Kingdoms; *wind-mill*, Rob. of Glouc. p. 547, l. 11383; *wind-pipe*, spelt *wyndpype* in Palsgrave; *wind-row*, a row of cut grass exposed to the wind, Holland, tr. of Pliny, b. xviii. c. 28; *wind-ward*; *wind-y*, AS. *windig*, Grein, ii. 713; *wind-i-ness*. And see *wind-ow*, *winn-ow*, *vent-il-ate*.

WIND (2), to turn round, coil, encircle, twist round. (E.) ME. *winden*, pt. t. *wand*, *wond*, pl. *wonden*, P. Plowman, B. ii. 220, pp. *wunden*, spelt *wnden*, Havelok, 546. AS. *windan*, pt. t. *wand*, *wond*, pp. *wunden* (gen.); Grein, ii. 713.+Du. *winden*; Icel. *vinda*, pt. t. *vatt* (for *vand*), pp. *undinn*; Dan. *vinde*, Swed. *vinda*, to squint; G. *winden*, pt. t. *wand*, pp. *gewunden*; OHG. *wintan*; Goth. *-windan*, only in compounds such as *biwindan*, *dugawindan*, *uswindan*; pt. t. *-wand*, pp. *-wundans*. β. All from Teut. type **wendan-* (pt. t. **wand*, pp. **wundanoz*), to wind or bind round, hence to turn. Perhaps ulti-mately allied to √WEI, to twine; see **Withy**. Streitberg, §§ 68, 203, note 2. **Der.** *wind-ing*, sb.; also *wind-lass*, q.v.; *wend*, q. v.; *wand-er*, q. v.; *wond-er*, q.v.; *wand*, q. v.

WINDLASS (1), a machine with an axle, for raising heavy weights. (Scand.) The spelling *windlass* is a by-form, encouraged by popular etymology (as if the word were from *wind*, verb, and *lace*), of the shorter word below. ME. *windelas*, *windlas*, Prompt. Parv., p. 529.—Icel. *vindil-āss*, a windlass (still in use, see Notes on E. Etym., p. 321).—Icel. *vindill*, a winder; and *āss*, a beam. β. But the commoner ME. form was *windas*, Chaucer, C. T. 10498 (F 184); Rich. Cuer de Lion, l. 71; Allit. Poems, ed. Morris, C. 103. '*Wyndace* for an engyn, *guyndas*;' Palsgrave.—Icel. *vindāss*, a windlass; lit. a winding-pole, i.e. a rounded pole (like an axis) which can be wound round.—Icel. *vind-a*, to wind; and *āss*, a

pole, main rafter, yard of a sail, &c. γ. Here *vinda* is cognate with E. *wind*; see **Wind** (2). The Icel. *āss* is cognate with Goth. *ans*, a beam, Luke, vi. 41 (the long *ā* showing a loss of *n*). The root of *āss* is not known; it has nothing to do with *axis* or *axle*, as some suggest.+Du. *windas*, a windlass; MDu. *windaes*, 'a wind-lasse or an engine,' Hexham; where *aes* (Icel. *āss*, a beam) is distinct from MDu. *asse* (mod. Du. *as*), an axis.

WINDLASS (2), a circuit, circuitous way. (F.—Teut.?) Shak. has *windlasses*, Hamlet, ii. 1. 65. 'Bidding them fetch a *windlasse* a great way about;' Golding, tr. of Cæsar, fol. 206 (R.). 'And fetched a *windlasse* round about;' Golding, tr. of Ovid (see Wright's note on Hamlet). 'I now fetching a *windlesse*,' Lyly, Euphues, ed. Arber, p. 270. Apparently compounded of *wind* (verb) and *lace*; but it was prob. a popular alteration of ME. *wanlace*, a trick, subtlety, artifice. Golding has the form *winlas*, for L. *gyrum*, Ovid, Metam. vii. 784. *Wanlace* is used by Rob. of Brunne, Handlyng Synne, 4378, 12010.—OF. *wanelace*, perfidy, deceit (Godefroy); also spelt *wenelat* (id.). Hence the ME. *wanelasour*, *wandlessour*, one who drives game (Stratmann). Prob. a hunting term, of Teut. origin. See Gloss. to Toynbee's Specimens of Old French. Per-haps allied to MHG. *wandelāt*, change, alteration, OHG. *wantalōn*, G. *ver-wandeln*, to change, OHG. *wanta*, a turning, a small (green) path; all connected with **Wind**, verb, and **Wander**.

WINDOW, an opening for light and air. (Scand.) The orig. sense is 'wind-eye,' i.e. eye or hole for the wind to enter at, an opening for air and light. [The AS. word was *ēgþyrl* (=eye-thrill), Joshua, ii. 15; also *ēagdura* (=eye-door), according to Bosworth.] ME. *windou*, Cursor Mundi, 1683; *windoge*, Genesis and Exodus, ed. Morris, l. 602; *windohe*, Ancren Riwle, p. 50, note *a*; *windowe*, P. Plowman, B. iii. 48; Wyclif, Acts, xx. 9.—Icel. *vindauga*, a window; lit. 'wind-eye.'—Icel. *vindr*, wind; and *auga*, an eye, cognate with AS. *ēage*, an eye; Dan. *vindue*, a window; (cf. *vind*, wind, and *öie*, an eye); but Dan. *vindue* is from a Low G. **wind-ooge* (wind-eye). See **Wind** (1) and **Eye**. ¶ Butler has *windore*, Hudibras, pt. i. c. 2. l. 214, as if from *wind* and *door*; but this is nothing but a corruption.

WINE, the fermented juice of the vine. (L.) ME. *win* (with long *i*), Chaucer, C. T. 637 (A 635). AS. *win*, Grein, ii. 712.—L. *uinum*, wine (whence also Goth. *wein*, G. *wein*, OHG. *win*, Du. *wijn*, Icel. *vin*, Swed. *vin*, Dan. *viin*).+Gk. οἶνος, wine, allied to οἴνη, the vine.—√WEI, to twine; see **Withy**. β. 'The Northern names, Goth. *wein*, G. *win*, &c. are undoubtedly to be regarded (with Jac. Grimm, Gramm. iii. 466) as borrowed; so also OIrish *fīn*, wine, &c. Pott very appropriately compares the Lith. *apwynys*, hop-tendril, pl. *apwynei*, hops. The Skt. *vēṇi-*, a braid of hair, also belongs here. We cannot see why the fruit of the twining plant should not itself have been called originally 'twiner.' The Lith. word offers the most striking analogy. The fact is, therefore, that the Indo-Germans had indeed a common root for the idea of winding, twining, and hence derived the names of various twining plants, but that it is only among the Græco-Italians that we find a common name for the *grape* and its *juice*;' Curtius, i. 487. See Brugmann, i. § 204, ii. § 66. ¶ Not of Semitic origin; rather, the Heb. *yayin*, wine, Arab. *waynat*, black grape, are borrowed from the Idg. type **woino-*. The early L. *uinum* meant 'vine.' **Der.** *wine-bibber*, Matt. xi. 19; see **Bib**.

WING, the limb by which a bird flies, any side-piece, flank. (Scand.) ME. *winge* (dissyllabic), Chaucer, C. T. 1966 (A 1964); the pl. appears as *hwingen*, Ancren Riwle, p. 130, last line, Layamon, 29263; we also find *wenge*, *whenge* (dat. case), P. Plowman, B. xii. 263; '*wenge* of a fowle, Ala,' Prompt. Parv.; pl. *wenges*, Ormulum, 8024. It is clear that the form *wenge* is Scand.; and, as there does not seem to be any authority for an alleged AS. *winge*, it is simplest to suppose *winge* to result from *wenge*. [The AS. word for 'wing' is *feðer*.]—Norw. *vengja* (for ON. **wengja*); Icel. *vængr*, a wing; Dan. and Swed. *vinge*; North Fries. *winge*. Teut. type *wāingi-*, allied to Goth. *waian*, to blow (cf. Du. *waaijer*, a fan); Skt. *vā*, to blow, *vājin-*, winged (Macdonell); from √WĒ, to blow. **Der.** *wing*, verb, to fly, Cymb. iii. 3. 28; *wing-ed*, Chaucer, C. T. 1387 (A 1385); *wing-less*.

WINK, to move the eyelids quickly. (E.) 1. ME. *winken*, pt. t. *winked*, P. Plowman, B. iv. 154. AS. *wincian*, to wink. 'Conniveo, *ic wincige*;' Voc. 140. 17. 2. But *winken* also occurs as a strong verb, pt. t. *wank*, Ancient Met. Tales, ed. Hartshorne, p. 79 (Strat-mann); also *wonk*, Lancelot of the Laik, ed. Skeat, l. 1058; and we may certainly conclude that there was also a *strong* verb, viz. AS. **wincan*, with pt. t. **wanc*, pp. **wuncen*. This is verified by AS. *wancol*, wavering, and E. **wench**, q. v.; as well as by the cognate forms.+MDu. *wincken* (Hexham); also *wencken*, 'to winke, or to give a signe or token with the eyes;' id. Allied to MDu. *wanck*, 'a moment, an instant,' id. (lit. the twinkling of an eye); *wanckel*, unsteady; Icel. *vanka*, to wink, to rove; Dan. *vinke*, to beckon; cf. *vanke*, to rove, stroll; Swed. *vinka*, to beckon, wink; cf. *vanka*, to rove, *vankelmodig*, fickle-minded; G. *winken*, to nod, make a sign; OHG. *winkan*, strong vb., to move aside, stir, waver (see Schade). β. Teut. type *wenkan-, pt. t. *wank, pp. *wunkanoz. Further allied to Lithuan. *wengti*, to shirk work, to flinch, *wingis*, a bend of a river, *wangus*, idle. Der. *wink*, sb., Temp. ii. 1. 285. Also (from the same root) *wench, wince, winch, winkle, peri-winkle* (the sea-snail). Cf. *vacillate*.

WINKLE, a kind of sea-snail. (E.) Holland, tr. of Pliny, b. ix. c. 32, uses *winkles* to denote shell-fish and also snails. AS. *-wincla*, occurring in *wine-wincla*, a winkle; see A. S. Leechdoms, ii. 240; misprinted *pinewinclan*, as a gloss to *torniculi* in Ælfric's Colloquy; Voc. 94. 14. Named from the convoluted shell; allied to **Winch**, q. v., and to **Wink**. Der. *periwinkle* (2), q. v.

WINNOW, to fan grain, so as to separate the chaff from it. (E.) Winnow stands for *window*, if we may so write it; *nn* being put for *nd* (but without reference to the sb. *window*). ME. *windewen*, Wyclif, Jer. xlix. 36, to translate L. *uentilāre*; some MSS. have *wynewen*, showing that the *d* was being lost just at this time. AS. *windwian*, less correctly *wyndwian*, Ps. xliii. 7, ed. Spelman; to translate L. *uentilāre*.—AS. *wind*, wind; with formative suffix *-w-*. See **Wind**. Cf. Goth. *winthi-skaurō*, a winnowing-fan; *diswinthjan*, to disperse, grind to powder; from *winths, collateral form of *winds*, wind. So also OHG. *wintōn*, to winnow, from *wint*, wind; Icel. *vinza*, to winnow, from *vindr*, wind; L. *uentilāre* from *uentus*; see **Ventilate**. Der. *winnow-er, winnow-ing-fan.*

WINSOME, pleasant, lovely. (E.) ME. *winsom*, with the sense 'propitious,' Northumb. Psalter, Ps. lxxviii. 9; also 'pleasant,' id. Ps. lxxx. 3. AS. *wynsum*, delightful, Grein, ii. 759; formed with suffix *-sum* (E. *-some*) from *wynn*, joy, id. ii. 757. *Wynn* is formed (by vowel-change from *u* to *y*), from *wunn*, weak grade of *winnan*, to desire, win; see **Win**. Cf. OSax. *wunnia*, G. *wonne*, joy (from *winnen*) ; Icel. *unaðr*, joy, *unaðsamr*, winsome; Skt. *vani-*, desire.

WINTER, the cold season, fourth season of the year. (E.) ME. *winter*, orig. unchanged in the plural; 'a thousand *winter*' = a thousand winters, i.e. years; Chaucer, C. T. 7233 (D 1651). AS. *winter*, a winter, also a year; pl. *winter*, or *wintru*.+Du. *winter*; Icel. *vetr*; OIcel. *vettr*, *vittr*, assimilated form of *vintr*; Dan. and Swed. *vinter*; G. *winter*, OHG. *wintar*; Goth. *wintrus*. β. All from Teut. type *wintruz, for older *wentruz, winter, Fick, iii. 284; where *-ru-* is evidently a suffix. Origin doubtful, but the suggestion in Fick is a good one, viz. that it meant 'wet season,' and is a nasalised form allied to E. *wet*. This is made more probable by the fact that we find nasalised forms of this root in L. *unda*, a wave, Lithuan. *wandū*, water, Skt. *und*, to wet, moisten; whilst, on the other hand, we find E. *water* with a similar suffix, but without the nasal sound. See **Wet, Water**. Der. *winter*, verb, to pass the winter; *wintr-y* (for *winter-y*); *winter-ly*, Cymb. iii. 4. 13; *winter-quarters.*

WIPE, verb, to cleanse by rubbing, to rub. (E.) ME. *wipen*, Chaucer, C. T. 133. AS. *wīpian*, to wipe; Ælfric's Homilies, i. 426, l. 30; 'Tergo, ic *wīpige*,' Ælfric's Gram. ed. Zupitza, p. 172, l. 8. This is a weak verb, meaning to rub over with a wisp, or to use a wisp of straw; formed, with the usual casual suffix *-ian*, from a sb. *wīp, a wisp of straw, which does not occur in AS. But it is preserved in EFries. *wīp*, Pomeranian *wiip*, Hamburg *wype*, a twist or wisp of straw, and in Low G. *wiep*, a wisp of straw, or a rag to wipe anything with, Bremen Wörterbuch, v. 269; and the common E. *wisp* is related to it. Cf. Goth. *waip-s*, a wreath, from the strong verb *weipan*, to crown (orig. to twine); cf. OHG. *wifan*, to wind round. See **Wisp**. Der. *wipe*, sb., sometimes in the sense of sarcasm or taunt, Shak. Lucrece, 537; *wip-er.*

WIRE, a thread of metal. (E.) ME. *wir, wyr* (with long *i*); dat. *wyre*, P. Plowman, B. ii. 11. AS. *wīr*, a wire, Grein, ii. 717.+Low G. (Hamburg) *wyren*, pl., wires; Icel. *vīrr*, wire; cf. Swed. *vira*, to wind, twist. Cf. OHG. *wiara*, MHG. *wiere*, an ornament of refined gold. Orig. a thread of metal, properly a 'twisted' thread or an ornament of twisted metal-wire; cf. Icel. *vīravirki*, filagree-work, lit. 'wire-work;' L. *uiriæ*, armlets of gold. Formed with suffix *-ro-* from √WEI, to twist, twine; see **Withy**. Der. *wire-draw*, verb, to draw into wire; *wire-draw-ing*; *wire-work*; *wir-y.* And see *ferrule.*

WIS; for this fictitious verb, see **Ywis**.

WISE (1), having knowledge, discreet, learned. (E.) ME. *wis* (with long *i*), *wys*, Chaucer, C. T. 68. AS. *wīs*, wise; Grein, ii. 718. +Du. *wijs*; Icel. *vīss*; Dan. *viis*; Swed. *vis*; G. *weise*, OHG. *wīs*; Goth. *-weis*, in comp. *unweis*, unwise. β. All from Teut. type *wīsoz; for *witsoz; from Teut. base *wīt-, answering to Idg. √WEID, to know; see **Wit** (1). Thus *wise* = 'knowing;' cf. *cunning*, adj.; Brugmann, i. §§ 759, 794. ¶ Otherwise explained

as for *wissoz < *wittoz; formed from *wit-, Idg. *wid-, weak grade of √WEID (as above). Der. *wise-ly*; *wis-dom*, AS. *wīsdōm*, Grein, ii. 719 (where *dōm* = E. *doom*, i.e. judgement); *wiseman* (one word), As You Like It, i. 2. 93, &c.; *wise-ness*, Hamlet, v. 1. 286. Also *wise* (2). (But not *wiseacre*, q. v.)

WISE (2), way, manner, guise. (E.) ME. *wise* (dissyllabic), Chaucer, C. T. 1448 (A 1446). AS. *wīse*, Grein, ii. 719.+Du. *wijs*; Icel. *-vīs*, in the comp. *ōðruvīs*, otherwise; Dan. *viis*; Swed. *vis*; G. *weise*; OHG. *wīsa* (whence, through French, E. *guise*). β. All from Teut. type *wīsōn, f. Allied to AS. *wīsian*, to show the way, direct, orig. 'to make wise,' to instruct; from *wīs*, adj. wise. See **Wise** (1). Cf. L. *uīsus*, sb., appearance. Der. *like-wise, other-wise*. Doublet, *guise*.

WISEACRE, a wise fellow (ironically), a fool. (Du.—G.) In Blount's Gloss., ed. 1674.—MDu. *wijs-segger*, as if 'a wise-sayer,' whence *wijs-seggen* (Hexham), a verb wrongly used as if equivalent to the more usual MDu. *waerseggen*, 'to sooth-say,' id., whence *waersegger*, 'a diviner, or a soothsayer,' id. (from MDu. *waer*, true). But the MDu. word is merely borrowed from G. *weissager*, a soothsayer, as if it meant 'a wise-sayer;' cf. *weissagen*, to foretell, prophesy, soothsay. β. Not only is the E. form a travesty of the G. word, but the latter has itself suffered from the manipulation of popular etymology, and is a corrupt form, having originally nothing to do with the verb *to say*, nor even precisely containing the word *wise*. This appears from the older forms; the G. *weissager* is the MHG. *wīzagōn*, to prophesy, corrupted to *wīzsagen, wissagen*, by confusion with *sagen*, to say. This MHG. verb was unoriginal, being formed from the sb. *wīzago*, a prophet, which was itself afterwards corrupted into *weissager*. Now *wiz-ag-o* is exactly parallel to AS. *wit-eg-a* or *wit-ig-a*, a prophet (Grein, ii. 726); both words are formed (with adj. suffix *-ag* (*-ig*) and sb. suffix *-o* (*-a*), denoting the agent) from the verb which appears as OHG. *wizan*, AS. *wītan*, to see; from √WEID, to know; see **Wit**. δ. It follows that the *s* is for G. *z*, the equivalent of E. *t*; whilst the un-meaning suffix *-acre* is no worse than the corrupt G. suffix *-sager*. Moreover, the sense 'wise-sayer' is merely an erroneous popular interpretation; the true sense is simply *seer* (= *see-er*).

WISH, to have a desire, be inclined. (E.) ME. *wisshen, wischen*; P. Plowman, B. v. 111. AS. *wyscan*, to wish; Grein, ii. 766; less correctly *wiscan*, id. The long *ȳ* shows a loss of *n*, and *wyscan* represents Teut. type *wunskjan-, to wish; a verb formed from the Teut. sb. *wunsko-, a wish. Cf. Du. *wenschen*; Icel. *æskja*, with the usual loss of initial *v*, and written for *œskja*; Dan. *önske*; Swed. *önska*; G. *wünschen*; OHG. *wunscan*. β. The AS. sb. is *wūsc*, a wish, very rare, in Ælfred, tr. of Beda, b. v. c. 19, ed. Smith, p. 638, l. 40, where it is misprinted *wiisc*; whence *wȳscan*, vb., with the usual change from *ū* to *ȳ*. Cognate words to the sb. are found in MDu. *wunsch* (Hexham); Icel. *ōsk*; G. *wunsch*; OHG. *wunsc*; the Teut. types being *wunskoz, m., *wunskā, f. All from Teut. *wunsk-, weak grade of *wen-sk-, formed with verbal suffix *-sk-* (L. *-scō*) from √WEN, to desire, strive after, appearing in Skt. *van*, to ask, and in E. *win*; see **Win**. Cf. Skt. *vāñchh*, to desire, wish, from *van*, to ask. Der. *wish*, sb., merely from the verb, and not the same as the more orig. ME. *wusch*, Prompt. Parv. p. 535, which answers to AS. *wūsc*, as above. Also *wish-er, well-wish-er*; *well-wish-ed*, Meas. for Meas. ii. 4. 27; *wish-ful*, i.e. longing, 3 Hen. VI, iii. 1. 14; *wish-ful-ly, wish-ful-ness*. And see *wist-ful*.

WISP, a small bundle of straw or hay. (E.) ME. *wisp, wips*; spelt *wispe, wips*, P. Plowman, B. v. 351; *wysp, wesp,wips*, id. A. v. 195; the Vernon MS. has '*Iwipet* with a *wesp*' = wiped with a wisp. As in other cases where *sp* and *ps* are interchanged, the spelling with *ps* is the older; cf. *hasp, clasp*, &c. The AS. form would be *wips, but it does not occur; and the final *s* is formative, *wip-s* being closely connected with the verb to *wipe*. We find also Low G. *wiep*, a wisp; Norweg. *vippa*, a wisp to sprinkle or daub with (also a swape, or machine for raising water); Swed. dial. *vipp*, an ear of rye, also a little sheaf or bundle; Goth. *waips*, a crown, orig. a twisted wreath (where *-s* is merely the suffix of the Goth. nom. case). β. Thus the Teut. base is *wip-, weak grade of *weipan-, as seen in Goth. *weipan*, to crown, to wreathe, OHG. *wifan*, to wind round (hence, to twist). See **Wipe**. It has probably been confused with *whisk*, as in Dan. *visk*, a wisp, a rubber; but the two words are from different roots; see **Whisk**. Cf. MSwed. *wisp*, a wisp; mod. Swed. *visp*, a whisk, a twirling-stick.

WIST, knew, or known; see **Wit** (1).

WISTFUL, eager, earnest, attentive, pensive. (E.) The word appears to be not very old, and it has almost supplanted the word *wishful*, which was once common. The orig. sense seems to have been 'silent' or 'hushed;' as in 'the sweet dale and the *wistfull* hill,' W. Browne, Britannia's Pastorals, bk. ii. song 2. 544 (see Cent. Dict.). If so, it stands for *whist-ful*, from *whist*, silent, hushed; see

Whist. It would naturally be associated with the adv. *wistly*, attentively, earnestly, used 4 times by Shakespeare, which may likewise have arisen from *whist*, silent. The quartos read *wishtly* (*whistly*?) for *wistly* in Rich. II, v. 4. 7 ; see also Venus and Adonis, 343, Lucrece, 1355, Pass. Pilgrim, 82.   β. As regards *wishful*, &c., we find *wishful* in 3 Hen. VI, iii. 1. 14; 'There be certain Women that can kill with their eye-sight whom they look *wishfully* upon ;' Ady, Discovery of Witches (1661), p. 97. 'O. *Hoard.* I long to have a smack at her lips. *Hoard.* And most *wishfully*, brother, see where she comes ;' Middleton, Trick to Catch the Old One, A. v. sc. 2. 'I sat looking *wishfully* at the clock,' Idler, no. 67 (R.) ; 'We looked at the fruit very *wishfully*,' Cook, First Voyage, b. iii. c. 7 ; 'I was weary of this day, and began to think *wishfully* of being again in motion,' Boswell, Tour to the Hebrides, p. 98 (Todd) ; 'I looked at them *wishfully*,' Boswell, Life of Johnson, Sept. 1, 1773. γ. Examples of *wistful* occur in : 'Lifting up one of my sashes, [I] cast many a *wistful* melancholy look towards the sea,' Swift, Gulliver, bk. ii. ch. 8 ; 'Why, Grubbinol, dost thou so *wistful* seem ? There's sorrow in thy look,' Gay, Pastorals, Friday, l. 1.   δ. Note that *wishly* (= *wishfully*) occurs in the Mirror for Magistrates, p. 863 (Todd). Also, that Sir T. More seems to use *wishely* nearly in the sense of ME. *wisly*, certainly, which suggests a possibility that *wis(t)ly* arose from that form : 'To putte on his spectacles, and pore better and more *wishely* with his olde eyen vpon Saynt Iohns ghospell ;' Sir T. More, Workes, p. 1134 (R.).   Der. *wistful-ly*.

WIT (1), to know. (E.) This verb is ill understood and has suffered much at the hands of grammarians and compilers of dictionaries. *Wit* is the infin. mood; *to wit* (as in 'we do you to *wit* ') is the gerund ; *wot* is the 1st and 3 pers. of the *present* indicative, the 3rd person being often corruptly written *wotteth* ; *wost* (later form *wottest*) is the 2nd pers. sing. of the same tense ; *wiste*, later *wist*, is the pt. t. ; and *wist* is the pp. [The adv. *ywis* or *Iwis*, certainly, was often misunderstood, and a verb *wis*, to know, was evolved, which is wholly unsanctioned by grammar; see **Ywis**.] ME. *witen*, infin.; pres. t. *wot*, *wost*, *wot*, pl. *witen* ; pt. t. *wiste*, pp. *wist* ; see Chaucer, C. T. 1142, 1158, 1165, 8690, 9614 (A 1140, 1156, 1163, E 814, 1740), &c. [There was also ME. *witen*, to see (with long *i*); see Stratmann, who puts *wot* under this latter verb, as if *I have seen = I know*. It makes little difference, since AS. *witan*, to know, and *witan*, to see, are closely connected ; I follow the arrangement in Grein.] AS. *witan*, to know ; pres. t. *ic wāt*, *þū wāst*, *hē wāt*, pl. *witon* ; subj. sing. *wite*, pl. *witon* ; pt. t. *wiste* (sometimes *wisse*), 2 p. *wisses*, pl. *wiston* ; pp. *wist* ; Grein, ii. 722. Allied to AS. *witan*, to see ; pt. t. *wāt*, pl. *witon* ; id. ii. 724. It is clear that *ic wāt* is really an old past tense (of *witan*) used as a present; causing the necessity of creating a new past tense *wisse* or *wiste*, which is, however, of great antiquity. Similar anomalous verbs are found in E., viz. *can*, *may*, *shall*, &c. The gerund is *tō witanne*, whence mod. E. *to wit*. The form *weet*, in Spenser, F. Q. i. 3. 6, is nothing but a corruption of *wit*.+Du. *weten*, pt. t. *wist*, pp. *geweten* ; Icel. *vita*, pr. t. *veit*, pt. t. *vissa*, pp. *vitaðr* ; Dan. *vide*, pr. t. *veed*, pt. t. *vidste*, pp. *vidst* ; Swed. *veta*, pr. t. *vet*, pt. t. *visste*, pp. *veten* ; G. *wissen*, pr. t. *weiss*, pt. t. *wusste*, pp. *gewusst* ; Goth. *witan*, pr. t. *wait*, pt. t. *wissa*. β. All from Teut. type *witan-, to know, pr. t. *wait*, the base being *weit-, orig. 'to see.' Further allied to Lithuan. *weizdēti*, to see, Russ. *vidiet(e)*, to see, L. *uidēre*, to see, Gk. ἰδεῖν, to see, οἶδα, I know, Skt. *vēda*, I know, orig. I have seen (= E. *wot*), Skt. *vid*, to perceive, know, orig. to see.−√WEID, to see, perceive, know. Der. *wit* (2), *wit-ness*, q.v., *t-wit* (for *at-wit*) ; *witt-ing-ly*, knowingly, Haml. v. 1. 11. Also, from the same root, *wise*, *guise* ; *vis-ion*, *vis-ible*, &c. (see **Vision**) ; *id-ea*, *id-ol*, and the suffix *-id* in *rhombo-id*, &c. ; *ved-a*. And see *wiseacre*, *wizard*.

WIT (2), understanding, knowledge, the power of combining ideas with a happy or ludicrous effect. (E.) ME. *wit*, Chaucer, C. T. 748 (A 746). AS. *witt*, knowledge, Grein, ii. 722.−AS. *witan*, to know; see **Wit** (1).+Icel. *vit* ; Dan. *vid* ; Swed. *vett* ; Goth. *-witi*, in comp. *un-witi*, n., lack of wisdom ; allied to G. *witz*. Teut. type *witjom*, n. Der. *wit-less*, *wit-less-ly*, *wit-less-ness* ; *wit-l-ing*, a pretender to wit, with double dimin. suffix *-l-ing* ; *witt-ed*, as in *blunt-witted*, 2 Hen. VI, iii. 2. 210 ; *witt-y*, AS. *witig* or *wittig*, Grein, ii. 726 ; *witt-i-ly*, *witt-i-ness*. Also *witt-i-c-ism*, used by Dryden in his pref. to the State of Innocence, with the remark that he asks 'pardon for a new word' (R.); evidently put for *witty-ism*, the *c* being introduced to avoid the hiatus, and being suggested by *Galli-cism*, &c.

WIT (3), a wise man, a witty fellow. (E.) ME. *wite* ; AS. *wita*, lit. 'one who knows.'−AS. *witan*, to know. Der. *witena gemōt*, a meeting of 'wits,' a parliament.

WITCH, a woman regarded as having magical power. (E.) Formerly used also of a man, Comedy of Errors, iv. 4. 160, Antony,

i. 2. 40 ; but this is unusual. ME. *wicche*, applied to a man, P. Plowman, B. xviii. 69 ; also to a woman, Sir Percival, l. 826 (in the Thornton Romances). AS. *wicca*, masc. a wizard ; *wicce*, fem. a witch. 'Ariolus, *wicca* ;' Voc. 183. 31. 'Phytonyssa, *wycce*,' Voc. 313. 5. The pl. *wiccan*, occurring in the Laws of Edward and Guthrum, § 11, and Laws of Cnut, Secular, § 4 (Thorpe, Anc. Laws, i. 172, 378), may refer to either gender. β. *Wicce* is merely the fem. of *wicca* ; and *wicca* is a sb., denoting the agent, allied to *wiccian*, to practise sorcery, EFries. *wikken*.+MDu. *wicker*, 'a soothsayer,' Hexham ; Low G. *wikken*, to predict (see *wicken*, to practise sorcery, in Schade). Cf. Norw. *vikja* (1) to turn aside, to conjure away, exorcise. This links it with Icel. *vīkja* (pp. *vik-inn*), to move, turn, push aside ; Dan. *vige*, as in *vige bort, Satan!* 'get thee behind me, Satan !' Cf. AS. *wīcan*, to give way ; whence E. *weak*. Perhaps *wiccian* meant 'to avert ;' and *wicca*, 'an averter.' B. Also explained as a variant of AS. *witga*, shortened form of *witega*, a wise man, a prophet, a soothsayer ; cf. Icel. *vitki*, a wizard, allied to *vita*, to know. For AS. *witega*, see **Wiseacre**. Der. *witch-craft*, AS. *wiccecræft*, Levit. xx. 27, from *wicce*, a witch, and *cræft* craft, art. Also *witch*, verb, AS. *wiccian*, Thorpe, Ancient Laws, ii. 274, sect. 39 ; hence *witch-er-y*, a coined word, Browne, Britannia's Pastorals, b. ii. s. 1, l. 412. Also *be-witch*, q.v.

WITCH-ELM, WYCH-ELM, a kind of elm. (E.) Spelt *weech-elm*, Bacon, Nat. Hist. § 475. There is also a *witch-hasel*. ME. *wyche*, *wiche* ; 'Wyche, tre, Ulmus ;' Prompt. Parv. AS. *wice*, occurring in a list of trees. 'Virecta, *wice* ; Cariscus, *wice* ;' Voc. 269. 16, 19. The sense is 'drooping' or 'bending ;' and it is derived from AS. *wic-*, weak grade of *wīcan*, to bend ; see **Wicker**. The *t* in the word is superfluous, and due to confusion with the word *witch* above. 'Some varieties of the *wych-elm* have the branches quite pendulous, like the weeping-willow, thus producing a most graceful effect ;' Our Woodlands, by W. S. Coleman.

WITH, by, near, among. (E.) ME. *with*, Chaucer, C. T. 1. AS. *wið*, governing gen., dat., and acc. ; Grein, ii. 692. It often has the sense of 'against,' which is still preserved in *to fight with* = to fight against, and in *with-say*, *with-stand*.+Icel. *við*, against, by, at, with ; Dan. *ved*, by, at ; Swed. *vid*, near, at, by. β. From Teut. type *wi-th-, against, shortened from AS. *wi-ðer*, against ; see **Withers**. ¶ We must observe that *with* has to a great extent taken the place of AS. and ME. *mid*, with, which is now obsolete. Der. *with-al*, with it, with, Temp. iii. 1. 93, ME. *withalle*, Chaucer, C. T. 14130 (B 3314), compounded of *with*, prep., and *alle*, dat. case of *al*, all, and used in place of AS. *mid ealle*, with all, wholly, Grein, i. 238, l. 12. Also *with-in*, ME. *with-inne*, Wyclif, Matt. ii. 16, AS. *wiðinnan*, on the inside, Matt. xxiii. 26 ; *with-out*, ME. *with-uten*, *with-outen*, Chaucer, C. T. 463 (A 461), AS. *wiðūtan*, on the outside of, Matt. xxiii. 25 ; and note that AS. *innan* and *ūtan* are properly adverbial formations, extended from *in* and *ūt* respectively. And see *with-draw*, *with-hold*, *with-say*, *with-stand* ; also *with-ers*.

WITHDRAW, to draw back or away, to recall. (E.) ME. *withdrawen*, to draw back, take away, Ancren Riwle, p. 230, last line. Not found in AS. From **With** and **Draw** ; where *with* has the old sense of 'towards,' hence *towards oneself*, and *away from another*. Der. *with-draw-al*, *with-draw-ment*, late and coined words. Also *withdrawing-room*, a retiring-room, esp. for ladies (see example in Todd's Johnson, and in Scott, Fortunes of Nigel, ch. ix.), now unmeaningly shortened to *drawing-room* !

WITHE, WITH, a flexible twig ; see **Withy**.

WITHER, to fade. (E.) Palsgrave has : 'I *wydder*, as a floure dothe ;' and 'I *wydder*, I drie up.' ME. *widren*, not an old form. 'Now grene as leif, now *widderit* and ago ;' Test. of Creseide, l. 238. This ME. *widren* is nothing but a variant of ME. *wederen*, to expose to the weather, so that *widred = wedered*, exposed to weather. 'Wederyn, or leyn or hangyn yn the weder, Auro ;' Prompt. Parv. And the verb *wederen* is from ME. *weder*, weather ; see **Weather**. For the *i*, cf. AS. *ge-wider*, weather, temperature ; Icel. *haf-viðri*, a sea-breeze. Cf. G. *ver-wittern*, to decay by exposure to the atmosphere ; from *wetter*, weather, storm. ¶ It follows that *wither* is properly transitive, as in 'Age cannot *wither* her,' Antony, ii. 2. 240 ; but the intrans. use is much more common.

WITHERS, the ridge between the shoulder-blades of a horse. (E.) In Hamlet, iii. 2. 253. Skelton has : 'Ware gallyng in the *widders* ;' i. 24. So called because it is the part which the horse *opposes* to his load, or on which the stress of the collar comes in drawing. Cf. Cleveland *withers*, the barbs of an arrow-head, which oppose its being drawn backwards (Atkinson). The lit. sense is 'things which resist ;' formed from ME. *wider*, resistance. '*Wiðer* com to-ȝenes' = resistance (or an adverse wind) came against me ;' Layamon, 4678. Hence *wiðerful*, full of resistance, hostile, O. Eng. Homilies, ii. 51, l. 19 ; *wiðeren*, *wiðerien*, to resist, id. ii. 123, last line ; and see Stratmann. Cf. AS. *wiðer* (only in gen. *wiðres*), resistance ; Beowulf, 2953. — AS. *wiðer*, against, Grein, ii. 697 ; common in composition. Sometimes shortened to *wið*, against, also used in the sense of ' with ; ' see **With**. The AS. *wiðer*, also *widere*, is cognate with Du. *weder*, Icel. *viðr*, Dan. and Swed. *veder*, G. *wieder*, Goth. *withra*, signifying against, or again. This very prefix is represented by *guer-* in **Guerdon**, q. v. β. The Goth. *withra* is to be divided as *wi-thra*, a comparative form ; cf. Skt. *vi-taram*, away, further, from *vi*, away, apart. Brugmann, ii. § 75. The above etymology is verified by the similar word found in G. *widerrist*, the withers of a horse, from *wider*, old spelling of *wieder*, against, and *rist*, which not only means wrist or instep, but also an elevated part, the withers of a horse.

WITHHOLD, to hold back, keep back. (E.) ME. *withholden*, pp. *withholdë*, Chaucer, C. T. 513 (A 511) ; and see Ancren Riwle, p. 348, l. 22. From **With**, in the sense of ' back,' or ' towards' the agent, and **Hold**. Cf. *with-draw*.

WITHIN, WITHOUT; see under **With**.

WITHSAY, to contradict. (E.) ME. *withseien*, Chaucer, C. T. 807 (A 805) ; *withsiggen*, Ancren Riwle, p. 86, l. 7. — AS. *wið*, against ; and *secgan*, to say ; see **With** and **Say**.

WITHSTAND, to stand against, resist. (E.) ME. *withstonden*, Wyclif, Rom. ix. 19. AS. *wiðstandan*, to resist, Grein, ii. 699. — AS. *wið*, against ; and *standan*, to stand ; see **With** and **Stand**.

WITHY, WITHE, a flexible twig, esp. of willow. (E.) Spelt *withes* or *withs*, pl., Judg. xvi. 7. ME. *wiði*, *wiððe*, &c. ; spelt *wythe*, *witthe*, *wythth*, Prompt. Parv. p. 531 ; *withthe*, K. Alisaunder, 4714 ; *wiði*, Ancren Riwle, p. 86, l. 15. AS. *wiðig*, a willow, also a twig of a willow. ' Salix, *wiðig* ;' Voc. 139. 30. Also AS. *wiððe*, a thong ; Voc. 183. 16. + MDu. *wiede*, ' a twigge, a willowe,' Hexham ; Icel. *viðja*, a withy ; *við*, a with (showing the different forms) ; *viðir*, a willow ; Dan. *vidje*, a willow, osier ; Swed. *vide*, a willow, *vidja*, a willow-twig ; G. *weide*, a willow ; OHG. *wida*. β. All from a Teut. base *with-*, *weith-*, Idg. base *weit-*. We find allied words in Lithuan. *żil-wittis*, the gray willow (used for basket-work), Gk. *ἰτέα* (for *ϝιτέα*), a willow, a wicker-shield ; also in Russ. *vitsa*, a withe, Lith. *wytis*, a withe, W. *gwden*, a withe, L. *uītis*, a vine. The application is to plants that twine or are very flexible ; and all these words are from the √WEI, to twine, plait, as in Russ. *vit(e)*, to twine, plait, L. *ui-ēre*, L. *ui-men*, a twig, *ui-tis*, a vine, *ui-num*, wine (orig. vine). Brugmann, ii. §§ 685, 789. From the same root we have *vetch*, *wire*, *ferrule* (for *virole*), *wine*, *vine*.

WITNESS, testimony ; also, one who testifies. (E.) Properly an abstract sb., like all other sbs. in *-ness*. ME. *witnesse*, Ancren Riwle, p. 68, l. 3. AS. *witnes*, testimony, Luke, ix. 5 ; also *ge-witnes*, Mark, i. 44. [The use of the word in the sense of ' witnesser ' is unoriginal ; it occurs in Wyclif, Matt. xxvi. 60 ; so also ONorthumb. *gewitnes*, Mark, xiv. 63 ; and in AS.] — AS. *wit-*, as in *wit-an*, to know ; with suffix *-nes* ; see **Wit** (1) ; thus the orig. sense was ' knowledge ' or ' consciousness.' Cf. ME. *witnen*, to testify, Ancren Riwle, p. 384 ; for *witen-en*, from *witen*, pp. of *witan*, to know ; cf. Icel. *vitna*, Dan. *vidne*, to testify. Also Goth. *weit-wōds*, a witness. **Der.** *witness*, vb., ME. *witnessen*, P. Plowman, B. prol. 191.

WITTOL, a cuckold. (E.) In Merry Wives, ii. 1. 3. Not an old word in this sense. It occurs also in Ben Jonson, The Fox, Act v. sc. 1 (Mosca) ; and in Beaum. and Fletcher, Knight of Malta, iii. 2 (Gomera). ' *Jannin*, a wittall, one that knows and bears with, or winks at, his wife's dishonesty ;' Cotgrave. (It does not mean ' know-all.') It has been explained as equivalent to ME. *witele* knowing, a rare word, occurring once in Layamon, 18547. And this again has been supposed to represent the AS. *witol*, adj., wise, sapient ; formed with suffix *-ol* (as in *sprec-ol*, talkative), from *wit-an*, to know. In that case, the word would mean wise or knowing ; or, ironically, a simpleton, a gull. β. But all this is due to popular etymology ; the AS. *witol* is rare, occurring in the comp. *un-wittol*, Liber Scintillarum, p. 80, l. 12 ; *fore-witol*, A. S. Chron. an. 1067 ; and is hardly known in ME. Hence Wedgwood's suggestion is worth notice ; viz. that a *wittol* is the bird commonly called in olden times a *witwall*. Indeed, Bp. Hall uses this very form : ' Fond *wit-wal*, that wouldst load thy witless head With timely horns, before thy bridal bed ;' Satires, i. 7. 17. Florio explains Ital. *godano* by ' the bird called a *witwal* or *woodwall* ;' ed. 1598. In a later edition, according to Wedgwood, this appears as : ' Godano, a *wittal* or *woodwale* ;' and Torriano has ' *Wittal*, becco contento,' i. e. a cuckold. The corruption from *witwall* to *wittal* is easy and natural. γ. An older spelling is *wetewold* ; for which see Skelton, Garl. of Laurel, 187 ; Lydgate, Assembly of Gods, 710. With this form compare MDu. *weduwael*, ' a kinde of a yellow bird,' Hexham ; OHG. *witewal*, a woodwale. δ. *Witwall* itself is the same word as *wodewale*, an old name usually given to the green woodpecker, but also to the oriole ; in any case, it appears that the *witwall* (like the cuckoo and the Late L. *curruca*) were the subjects of ribald jests. ' *Curruca* est avis, vel ille qui, cum credat nutrire filios suos, nutrit alienos ; ' Supp. to Ducange, by Diefenbach. On which Wedgwood remarks : ' the origin of this name [*wittol*] is undoubtedly from the fact that the bird known under the name of *curruca* is one of those in the nest of which the cuckoo drops its egg.' See further under **Woodwale**. Cf. *gull*, (1) a bird, (2) one who is deceived.

WIVERN; see **Wyvern**.

WIZARD, WISARD, one who practises magic, a magician. (E. ; with F. suffix.) ME. *wisard* ; spelt *wysard*, *wysar*, Prompt. Parv. It was simply formed by adding the AF. suffix *-ard*, as in *cow-ard*, *lagg-ard*, to the ME. *wis*, wise. Thus it merely meant ' wise-like.' The F. suffix *-ard*, due to OHG. suffix *-hart*, is merely G. *hart*, i. e. strong, confirmed in (= E. *hard*).

WIZEN, to shrivel or dry up. (E.) Added by Todd to Johnson. ME. *wisenen*, to become shrivelled ; see quotation in Halliwell, s. v. *wisened*. AS. *wisnian*, to become dry, John, xv. 6 (in the Lindisfarne and Rushworth MSS., both Northumbrian). We find also AS. *for-wisnode*, to translate L. *emarcuit*, Voc. 394. 5. + Icel. *visna*, to wither. β. This is an intransitive verb, with formative *-n-*, giving it the sense ' to become ; ' so that the orig. sense was ' to become dry ; ' see this suffix explained under **Waken**. The Icel. *vis-n-a* is derived from *vis-inn*, wisened, withered, palsied, dried up, which, by its form, is the pp. of an old lost strong verb **vīsa* (pt. t. **veis*, pp. *visinn*) ; cf. *rīsa*, to rise (pt. t. *reis*, pp. *risinn*). The Icel. *visinn* is cognate with Dan. and Swed. *vissen*, withered ; cf. also Swed. *vissna*, to fade, OHG. *wësanēn*, to dry up. All from a lost Teut. strong verb **weisan-*, **wisan-*, pt. t. **wais*, pp.* *wisanoz* ; from Idg. √WEIS. Hence also L. *uīr-us* (for **uis-us*), poison, Gk. *ἰός*, Skt. *vish-a-*, poison ; see **Virulent**. Cf. also AS. *weornian*, to pine away ; from the same root ; answering to a Teut. type **wiznōn* (see **Learn**). **Der.** *wizen*, adj., dried up, orig. the pp. of the strong verb.

WO, WOE, grief, misery. (E.) ME. *wo*, Chaucer, C. T. 353, 1458 (A 351, 1456). AS. *wā*, *wo*, used as interj. and adv., sometimes with dat. case, Grein, ii. 635 ; *wēa*, wo, sb., id. 668. + Du. *wee*, interj. and sb. ; Icel. *vei*, interj., used with dat. case ; Dan. *vee*, interj. and sb. ; Swed. *ve*, interj. ; G. *weh*, interj. and sb. ; Goth. *wai*, interj. β. Further allied to L. *uae*, wo! W. *gwae*, wo. Orig. an exclamation ; hence, a cry of pain, a pain, &c. Idg. types **wai*, interj., **waiwa*, sb. (whence AS. *wēa*, *wāwa*, wo, OHG. *wēwa*, wo). **Der.** *wo-ful*, ME. *woful*, Chaucer, C. T. 2058 (A 2056) ; *wo-ful-ly*, *-ness*. Also *wo-begone*, spelt *woe-begon*, Spenser, F. Q. iii. 7. 20, i. e. surrounded with wo, from ME. *wo begon*, Chaucer, C. T. 5338 (B 918), where *begon* is the pp. of ME. *begon*, to go about, surround, equivalent to AS. *begān*, compounded of *be*, prep. (E. *by*) and *gān*, to go ; see further in Stratmann, s. v. *bigān*. Also *wo worth*, wo be to ; for which phrase see **Worth** (1). Also *wai-l*, q. v.

WOAD, a plant used as a blue dye-stuff. (E.) ME. *wōd* (with long o), Chaucer, Ætas Prima, l. 17, pr. in Chaucer's Works, ed. Skeat, vol. i. AS. *wād*, *waad* ; ' Sandix, *wād* ; Fucus, *waad* ;' Voc. 136. 25, 26. The OF. name is spelt *waisde* in a Vocab. of the 13th century ; id. 556. 14 ; cf. F. *guède*. + Du. *weede* ; [Dan. *vaid*, *veid*, Swed. *veide*, from German] ; G. *waid*, MHG. *weit* ; whence OF. *waide*, *waisde*, *gaide*, mod. F. *guède*. Root unknown ; allied to L. *uitrum*, woad, Gk. *ἰσάτις* (<*ϝισάτις*) woad. ¶ Distinct from *weld* (2).

WOLD, a down, plain open country. (E.) Spelt *old* in Shak. K. Lear, iii. 4. 125 ; *wolde*, *woulde* in Minsheu, ed. 1627. ME. *wold*, Genesis and Exodus, ed. Morris, 938 ; the dat. case is spelt *walde* in one text of Layamon, 20842, but *wolde* in the other ; it is thus seen to be the same word as ME. *wald*, a wood, which was, however, more commonly used in the sense of waste ground, wide open country (as in Norse) ; in Layamon, 21339, where one text has *wæld*, the other has *feld*, field, in the sense of open country. AS. *weald*, *wald*, a wood, forest, Grein, ii. 669. + OSax. and OFries. *wald*, a wood ; NFries. *wold* ; G. *wald*, OHG. *walt* ; Icel. *völlr*, gen. *vallar* (<*valthar*), a field, plain ; Du. *woud*. β. All from Teut. type **walthuz*, m., a wood. It has been compared with Skt. *vāṭā-s*, an enclosure ; and with E. *wild*. Neither connexion is at all certain. Doublet, *weald*, q. v. **Der.** *vole*.

WOLF, a rapacious beast of prey. (E.) ME. *wolf* ; pl. *wolues* (= *wolves*), Wyclif, Matt. x. 16. AS. *wulf*, pl. *wulfas*, Grein, ii. 750. + Du. and G. *wolf* ; Icel. *úlfr* (for *vulfr*) ; Dan. *ulv* ; Swed. *ulf* ; Goth. *wulfs*. β. All from Teut. type **wulfoz*, m. Further allied to Lith. *wilkas*, Russ. *volk', Gk. λύκος*, L. *lupus*, Skt. *vṛka-*, a wolf ; the common Idg. type being **wlqos*. γ. The sense is ' tearer,' or ' render,' from his ravenous nature. — √WELQ, to tear ; Lithuan. *wilkti*, to pull, &c. ¶ The suggested connexion with L. *uulpēs*, a fox, is doubtful. Brugmann, ii. § 60. **Der.** *wolf-ish*, *wolf-ish-ly* ; *wolf-dog*. Also *wolv-er-ene*, or *wolv-er-ine*, a coined word ; apparently suggested by MHG. *wölfelīn*, a little wolf ; spelt *wulverin* in

Hakluyt, Voy. i. 477, and in Cotgrave, s. v. *louviere*; a name given to an American animal resembling the *glutton*, a name sometimes incorrectly given to the wolverene also.

WOMAN, a grown female. (E.) That *woman* is an altered form of AS. *wífman*, lit. wife-man, is certain; and it must be remembered that the AS. *man* (like L. *homo*) was used of both sexes. To show this, it is best to trace the word *downwards*. The AS. form is *wífman*, a woman, Grein, ii. 700. By assimilation, this form became *wimman* in the 10th century. In Judges, iv. 17, we have the dat. sing. *wífmen*, but in the very next verse (and in verse 22) Jael is called *séo wimman* = the woman. [Similarly, the AS. *hláfmæsse* (loaf-mass) became *lammas*; see **Lammas**.] By way of further illustration, see Mark, x. 6, where the various MSS. have *wyfman, wifmon, wimman*. β. The pl. of *wífman* was *wífmen*, which was similarly reduced to *wimmen*, as in Gen. xx. 17, and this form has held its ground, in the *spoken* language, to the present day. γ. But the sing. form suffered further alteration; we still find *wifmon* (later text *wimmon*) in Layamon, l. 1869, *wimman*, Havelok, l. 1168, *wyfman*, Ayenbite of Inwyt, p. 11, l. 1 [as late as A. D. 1340; the pl. being both *wyfmen*, p. 10, last line but one, and *wymmen*, according to Morris]; but we also find *wummon*, Ancren Riwle, p. 12, l. 11, *wumman*, Rich. Cuer de Lion, 3863; *wommon*, Rob. of Glouc. p. 9, l. 211, P. Plowman, B. i. 71, ii. 8; so also in Chaucer, C. T. Group D, 66 [l. 5648], where 5 MSS. have *womman*, and one has *woman*; after which the spelling *woman* is common. Thus the successive spellings are *wifman* (*wifmon*), *wimman* (*wimmon*), *wumman* (*wummon*), *womman*; and lastly *woman*, as at present. In some dialects, the pronunciation *wumman* [glossic wum'un] is still heard. Some have thought that popular fancy connected the word with *womb*, as if the word were *womb-man*; but the change of vowel was due to the preceding *w*, just as in AS. *widu*, later form *wudu*, a wood; see **Wood**. For further discussion, see **Wife** and **Man**. ¶ Note also the word *leman*, which was successively *léof man, lemman, leman*; here we have a similar assimilation of *fm* to *mm*, and a considerable change in sense; see **Leman**. Der. *woman-hood*, ME. *womanhede, wommanhede*, Chaucer, C. T. 1750 (A 1748), the corresponding AS. word being *wífhád*, Gen. i. 27; *woman-ish*, K. John, iv. 1. 36; *woman-ish-ly, -ness; woman-kind*, Tam. Shrew, iv. 2. 14; *women-kind*, Pericles, iv. 6. 159; *woman-like, woman-ly*, ME. *wummonlich*, Ancren Riwle, p. 274, l. 9; *woman-li-ness*.

WOMB, the belly, the place of conception. (E.) Lowl. Sc. *wame*, the belly; Burns, Scotch Drink, st. 5. ME. *wombe*, Wyclif, Matt. xv. 17; *wambe*, Pricke of Conscience, 4161. AS. *wamb, womb*, the belly, Grein, ii. 637. 'Venter, *wamb*;' Voc. 306. 34.+Du. *wam*, the belly of a fish; Icel. *vömb*, the belly, esp. of a beast; Dan. *vom*; Swed. *våmb, våmm*; G. *wampe, wamme*, OHG. *wampa*; Goth. *wamba*. β. The Teut. type is **wambôn-*, f., the belly, paunch. Root unknown. ¶ Quite distinct from L. *uenter*.

WOMBAT, a marsupial mammal, found in Australia. (Australian.) In Webster. A corruption of the native Australian name *womback* or *wombach*. 'The *wombat*, or, as it is called by the natives of Port Jackson, the *womback*;' Collins, New South Wales (1802), quoted in the Penny Cyclopædia. 'The mountain natives call it *wombach*;' letter from Governor Hunter, dated Sydney, 1798; in Bewick's Quadrupeds. See E. E. Morris, Austral English.

WON, to dwell, remain. (E.) In Milton, P. L. vii. 457. Practically obsolete, though occurring in Sir Walter Scott, Lady of the Lake, iv. 13. ME. *wonen*, Chaucer, C. T. 7745 (D 2163). AS. *wunian*, to dwell.+Icel. *una*, to dwell; see further under **Wont**.

WONDER, a strange thing, a prodigy, portent, admiration. (E.) ME. *wonder*; pl. *wondris*, Wyclif, Mark, xiii. 22. AS. *wundor*, a portent, Grein, ii. 751.+Du. *wonder*; Icel. *undr* (for **wundr*); Dan. and Swed. *under*; G. *wunder*, OHG. *wuntar*. β. The Teut. type is **wundrom*, n., a wonderful thing. Perhaps allied to AS. *wandian*, lit. to turn aside from, but usually to turn from through a feeling of fear or awe, to respect, to revere. 'Þú ne *wandast* for nánum man' = thou respectest, or dreadest, no man; Matt. xxii. 16; Luke, xx. 21. Grein explains *wandian* by 'præ metu siue alicujus reuerentiâ omittere, cunctari;' ii. 638. Hence ME. *wonden*, to conceal through fear, to falter, &c.; Will. of Palerne, 4071; Gower, C. A. i. 332, bk. iii. 1569; Chaucer, Legend of Good Women, l. 1187. Perhaps further allied to **Wend** and **Wind** (2). Der. *wonder*, verb, AS. *wundrian*, Grein, ii. 753; *wonder-ful*, ME. *wonderfol*, Layamon, l. 280, later text, used in place of AS. *wunderlic*, lit. wonder-like, Grein, ii. 753; *wonder-ful-ly, -ness*. Also *wondr-ous*, q. v.

WONDROUS, wonderful. (E.) Spelt *wonderouse* in Palsgrave, and prob. not found much earlier; it is a corrupt form (like *righteous* for *rightwise*), and took the place of the older word *wonders*, properly an adj., but also used as an adj. 'Ye be *wonders* men' = ye are wondrous men; Skelton, Magnificence, 90. 'Where suche a solempne yerely myracle is wrought so *wonderly* in the face of the worlde;'

Sir T. More, Works, p. 133 h. Earlier as an adv., as '*wonders* dere,' i. e. wonderfully dear, Test. of Love, b. ii. ch. 3, l. 45. β. *Wonders* is formed by adding *s* (an adv. suffix, as in *need-s*) to *wonder* used as an adv. or adj.; Chaucer has '*wonder* diligent,' C. T. 485 (A 483); Gower has 'such a *wonder* syhte,' C. A. i. 121, bk. i. 235. *Wonder* became an adj. through the use of the AS. *wunderlic*, adj., wonderful, as an adverb; thus Chaucer has '*wonderly* deliver,' C. T. 84; so also 'so *wonderly* sore,' Tale of Gamelyn, 266 (late editions, *wondrously*). γ. Hence the history of the word is clear; the AS. *wunderlic*, adj., became ME. *wonderly*, adv., whence ME. *wonder*, adj. and adv., lengthened to *wonders*, adv. and adj., and to *wondersly*, adv.; the double use of *-ly*, both as an adjectival and adverbial suffix, being a lasting cause of confusion. ¶ The spurious poem called Chaucer's Dream has the word *wondrous*, l. 1898, but the MSS. are of late date. Hence *wondrous-ly, wondrous-ness*.

WONT, used or accustomed. (E.) In Anglia, xi. 493, Hupe suggests that the phr. *wont to* (accustomed to) arose from the ME. phr. *wone to*, where *wone* was properly an adj. (AS. *gewun*, adj., *gewuna*, adj.), with the sense of 'accustomed.' This ME. *wone* occurs (without *to*) in Genesis and Exodus, 1530, Havelok, 2297; but in Cursor Mundi, 3646, where 3 MSS. have *wont to*, the Cotton MS. has *wonto* (sic). At the same time, it is clear that ME. *wone*, adj., was confused with ME. *woned*, the pp. of *wonen*, to dwell, to be used to. We also find that *wont* came to be used as a sb.; and then, by way of distinction, a new form *wont-ed* was evolved, to keep up the pp. use. Hence *won-t-ed* (= *won-ed-ed*) has the suffix *-ed* twice over! [For *wont*, sb., and *wont-ed*, see the end of the article.] 'As they were *woont* [accustomed] to dooe;' Sir T. More, Works, p. 1195 g. 'She neuer was to swiche gestes *woned*' = she was never accustomed to such guests, Chaucer, C. T. 8215 (E 339). 'Thou were ay *wont* eche lover reprehende;' = thou wert ever wont to reprehend each lover, Chaucer, Troilus, i. 510. *Woned* is the pp. of ME. *wonen, wonien*, to dwell, to be accustomed to; in Chaucer, C. T. 7745 (D 2163), it means simply 'to dwell,' but the sense 'to be accustomed' was easily (in AS. times) introduced from the related adj. *wone* (above). Cf. AS. *wunod*, pp. of *wunian*, to dwell, remain, continue in, Grein, ii. 753; also *gewunian*, to dwell, to be accustomed to. 'Swá swá he *gewunade*' = as he was accustomed (lit. as he *wont*), Mark, x. 1; cf. 'whom we *wont* to fear,' 1 Hen. VI, i. 2. 14. A weak verb, allied to the sb. *wuna*, custom, use, wont, commonly spelt *gewuna*, Luke, i. 9, ii. 27. Allied to AS. *wunn-*, weak grade of *winnan*, to strive after, orig. to desire; see **Win**. *Wont*, sb., is 'a thing desired,' a habit due to acquiescence in what seems pleasant. β. Cf. Icel. *vanr*, adj., accustomed, used (to a thing), *vani*, a usage, whence *vandi*, a custom, habit, *venja*, to accustom (pt. t. *vanði, vandi*, pp. *vandr, vannin*) = E. *wean*; see **Wean**. So also (in connexion with MHG. *gewinnen*) we find MHG. *gewon*, OHG. *giwon*, adj., accustomed to, MHG. *gewon*, OHG. *giwona*, usage, MHG. *gewonen*, to be used to, *gewonlích*, customary; G. *gewohnen*, to be used to, pp. *gewohnt*, wont, *wohnen*, to dwell. See Fick, iii. 287. Der. *wont*, sb., Hamlet, i. 4. 6, employed in place of ME. *wone*, sb., by confusion with *wont* above. Also *wont-ed*, used as a pt. t. by Surrey instead of *wont*; 'Of me, that *wonted* to rejoice,' Complaint of the Absence of her Louer, l. 5, in Tottell's Misc., ed. Arber, p. 15; so also Palsgrave gives *wont* as a verb, 'I *wonte* or use; it is no wysdome to wont a thing that is nat honest;' and hence *wonted* as a pp. or adj., Mids. Nt. Dr. ii. 1. 113, iii. 2. 369.

WOO, to sue, court, ask in order to marriage. (E.) Spelt *wo* in Palsgrave; but Spenser retains the old spelling *wowe*, F. Q. vi. 11. 4. ME. *woȝen*, King Horn, ed. Lumby, 546; later *wowen* (by change of ȝ to *w*), P. Plowman, B. iv. 74. AS. *wógian*, to woo, occurring in the comp. *áwógian*, to woo, Ælfric's Saints' Lives, vii. 14 (E. E. T. S.). Hence the sb. *wógere*, a wooer; 'Procus, *wógere*,' Voc. 171. 6. The lit. sense is simply to bend, incline; hence to incline another towards oneself.—AS. *wóh* (declensional stem *wóg-*, pl. *wóge*), bent, curved, crooked; Grein, ii. 731. Cf. *wóh*, sb., a bending aside, turning aside, iniquity; *wóh-bogen*, bowed in a curve, bent; id. β. The AS. *wóh* (Teut. type **wanχoz*), bent, is cognate with Goth. *wáhs*, bent, only occurring in *un-wáhs*, straight, blameless, Luke, i. 6.—√WANK, to go tortuously, be crooked; whence also Skt. *vañk*, to go tortuously, be crooked; cf. also *vakra-*, crooked, L. *uacillare*, to vacillate, and perhaps OSax. *wáh*, evil, W. *gwaeth*, worse. See **Vacillate**. Der. *woo-er*, ME. *wowere*, P. Plowman, B. xi. 71, AS. *wógere*, as above.

WOOD (1), a collection of growing trees, timber. (E.) ME. *wode*, Chaucer, C. T. 1424 (A 1422). AS. *wudu*, Grein, ii. 745; but the orig. form was *widu*; id. 692.+Icel. *viðr*, a tree, wood; Dan. *ved*; Swed. *ved*; MHG. *wite*, OHG. *witu*. β. The Teut. type is **widuz*, wood. Cf. also OIrish *fid*, Irish *fiodh*, a wood, a tree; *fiodais*, shrubs, underwood; Gael. *fiodh*, timber, wood, a wilderness; *fiodhach*, shrubs, W. *gwŷdd*, trees, *gwyddeli*, bushes, brakes. See

Stokes-Fick, pp. 265, 280. **Der.** *wood-bine* or *wood-bynd*, spelt *wodbynde* in Palsgrave, *wodebynde* in Chaucer, C. T. Six-text, 1508 (1510 in Tyrwhitt), AS. *wudebinde*, used to translate *hedera nigra* in Voc. 137. 5; so called because it binds or winds round trees; cf. AS. *wuduwinde*, lit. wood-wind, used to tr. *vivorna*, id. 270. 16. Also *wood-coal*; *wood-cock*, AS. *wuducoc*, Voc. 258. 5 (note Guernsey *vidco*, a woodcock); *wood-craft*, ME. *wodecraft*, Chaucer, C. T. 110; *wood-cut*; *wood-dove*, ME. *wode-douue*, Chaucer, C. T. 13700 (B 1960); *wood-engraving*; *wood-land*, ME. *wodelond*, Layamon, 1699; *wood-lark*; *wood-man*, Cymb. iii. 6. 28, spelt *wodman* in Palsgrave; *wood-nymph*; *wood-pecker*, Palsgrave; *wood-pigeon*; *wood-ruff*, q.v. Also *wood-ed*; *wood-en*, i.e. made of wood, K. Lear, ii. 3. 16; *wood-y*, Spenser, F. Q. i. 6. 18.

WOOD (2), mad, furious. (E.) In Mids. Nt. Dr. ii. 1. 192. ME. *wood, wōd* (with long o), Chaucer, C. T. 184. AS. *wōd*, mad, raging, Grein, ii. 730; whence *wēdan* (<*wōdian*), to be mad, 653. +Icel. *ōðr*, raging, frantic; Goth. *wōds*, mad. And cf. Du. *woede*, G. *wuth*, MHG. *wuot*, madness. **β.** The Teut. type is *wōdoz*, adj., wood, frantic. Perhaps allied, as Fick suggests (iii. 308), to L. *uātes*, a prophet, poet, one who is filled with divine frenzy, OIrish *fáith*, a prophet. Hence (perhaps) the name *Wōden*, applied to the highest of the Teutonic divinities. **Der.** *Wed-nes-day*, q. v.

WOODRUFF, the name of a plant. (E.) Spelt *woodrofe* in Palsgrave. ME. *wodruffe*, Voc. 712. 28; *woderofe*, 566. 20. AS. *wuderōfe*, id. 133. 30; also *wudurōfe*. See Cockayne's Leechdoms, ii. 412, where it is shown that it was not only applied to the *Asperula odorata* (as at present), but also to *Asfodelus ramosus*; and it is also called *astula* (*hastula*) *regia* in glosses. The former part of the word is AS. *wudu*, a wood; the sense of *rōfe* is uncertain, but the ō was long; compare the sound of *blood* from AS. *blōd*, and note the form *woodroof* in Britten's Plant-names. As AS. ō answers to OHG. *uo*, the AS. *rōfe* is equivalent to OHG. *ruofe*, adj. fragrant. Hence the probable sense was 'fragrant wood-plant;' well answering to the L. name *Asperula odorata*, which alludes to its sweet scent. So does the F. name *muguet*.

WOODWALE, the name of a bird. (E.) Also called *witwall* and even *wittal*; see **Wittol**. Cotgrave explains F. *oriol* or *oriot* as 'a heighaw or *witwall*.' [The form *witwall* was not borrowed from G., but stands for *widwall*; the old form of AS. *wudu* being *widu*.] ME. *wodewale*, the same as *wodehake* (i.e. wood-hatch or wood-hack, a woodpecker), Prompt. Parv.; Rom. of the Rose, 658; used to translate OF. *oriol*, W. de Bibbesworth, in Wright, Voc. i. 166 (13th century); Owl and Nightingale, 1657. Not found in AS.+MDu. *weduwael*, 'a kinde of a yellow bird;' Hexham; G. *wittewal*, a yellow thrush; MHG. *witewal*, an oriole (Schade). **β.** The former element is certainly AS. *widu*, *wudu*, ME. *wode*, a wood; just as MHG. *witewal* is from MHG. *wite*, a wood. Cf. ME. *wodehake*, above, and E. *woodpecker*. But the sense of the latter element has not been explained; it may mean 'stranger,' from AS. *wealh*. Schade suggests the same sense of 'stranger in the wood from the South' for the OHG. name. The MDu. *wedu-wael* may be compared with MDu. *Wael*, a Celt, the same word as AS. *Wealh*, and therefore 'stranger.' **Doublet**, *wittol*, q. v.

WOOF, the weft, the threads crossing the warp in woven cloth. (E.) In Shak. Troil. v. 2. 152. A corruption of ME. *oof*, due to a supposed connexion (which happens to be right, but not in the way which popular etymology would suggest) with the vb. to *weave* and the sb. *weft*. 'Oof, threde for webbynge, Trama, stamen, subtegmen;' Prompt. Parv. So also in Wyclif, Levit. xiii. 47, earlier version (cited in Way's note). AS. *ōwef*, a woof; 'Cladica, *wefl*, vel *ōwef*;' Voc. 13. 23 (8th century). *Cladica* is the dimin. of Late L. *clada*, a woven hurdle, and *wefl* is clearly a variant of *weft*; so that there can be no doubt as to the sense of *ōwef*. Somewhat commoner is the parallel form *ōweb* or *āweb*, frequently contracted to *āb*; and this word has precisely the same sense. 'Subtimen, *āweb*' immediately follows 'Stamen, *wearp*,' i.e. the warp, in Voc 262. 20; 'Trama, vel subtemen, *ōweb*, vel *ōb* ;' id. 188. 12; 'Linostema, linen *wearp*, vel *wyllen* [woollen] *āb*,' id. 151. 18; where Mr. Wright adds the note: 'the yarn of a weaver's warp is, I believe, still called an *abb*.' [For *warp* we should doubtless read *woof*.] **β.** The words *ōwef*, and *ōweb* or *āweb* are compounds, containing the prefix *ā* (as in *ā-wefan*, to weave, see **A-** (4) and **Weave**) or *ō-*, short form of *on*, prep. Also *wef* and *web* are both sbs., meaning 'web,' from *wefan*, to weave. Thus the word *woof*, for *oof*, is short for *ō-wef* or *on-wef*, i.e. on-web, the *web* that is laid *on* or thrown across the first set of threads or *warp*. See **On** and **Weave**.

WOOL, the short thick hair of sheep and other animals. (E.) ME. *wolle*, P. Plowman, B. vi. 13. AS. *wull*, *wul*. 'Lana, *wul*;' Voc. 294. 19; *wull*, id. 190. 25.+Du. *wol* (for *vull*); Dan. *uld* (for *ull* or *wull*); Swed. *ull*; G. *wolle*, OHG. *wolla*; Goth. *wulla*. **β.** The Teut. type is *wollā*, f., which is certainly an assimilated

form for *wolnā*, with Idg. suffix *-nā*, as shown by the cognate words, viz. Lithuan. *wilna*, Russ. *volna*, Skt. *ūrnā*, wool; cf. also OIrish *olann*, W. *gwlan*; and perhaps Gk. λῆνος (for ϝλῆνος), L. *lāna*, wool. Brugmann, i. §§ 317, 524 (2); Stokes-Fick, p. 276. The same assimilation appears in L. *uillus*, shaggy hair, *uellus*, a fleece. **Der.** *wooll-en*, ME. *wollen*, P. Plowman, B. v. 215, AS. *wyllen* (with the usual vowel-change from *u* to *y*), Voc. 151. 17; *wooll-y*, Merch. Ven. i. 3. 84; *wool-monger*, ME. *wolmongere*, Rob. of Glouc. p. 539, l. 11173; *woolpack*, ME. *wolpak*, same page, l. 18; *wool-sack*, 1 Hen. IV, ii. 4. 148, ME. *wollesak*, Gower, C. A. i. 99; bk. i. 1692. Also *wool-gathering* (Halliwell), idly roving (said of the thoughts), as if gathering wool scattered on the hedges. Also *woolward*, q. v.

WOOLWARD, clothed in wool only. (E.) 'I have no shirt, I go *woolward* for penance;' L. L. L. v. 2. 717; on which Dr. Schmidt says: 'Woolward, in wool only, without linen, a dress often enjoined as a penance by the church of Rome.' ME. *wolward*, *wolleward*, P. Plowman, B. xviii. 1; Pricke of Conscience, 3514; P. Plowman's Crede, 788. See four more examples in Nares, and his note upon the word. 'To goo *wulward* and barfott;' Arnold's Chron. ed. 1811, p. 150. Palsgrave has, in his list of adverbs : 'Wolwarde, without any lynnen nexte ones body, *sans chemyse*.' I have elsewhere explained this as 'with the wool next one's skin;' I should rather have said 'with the skin against the wool,' though the result is practically much the same. This is Stratmann's explanation ; he gives: '*wolwarde*, cutis lanam uersus.' Cf. *home-ward*, *heaven-ward*. See **Wool** and **Ward**. A like phrase occurs in French. 'Assez sovent lessa le linge Et si frotta *le dos au lange* ;' i.e. Very often she left off her linen [chemise], and rubbed her back against her woollen garment; Rutebuef, ii. 157, cited by Littré, s. v. *lange*. ¶ To the above explanation, viz. that *wool-ward* = against the wool, with reference to the skin, which agrees with all that has been said by Nares and others, I adhere. In an edition of books iii and iv of Beda's Eccl. History, by Mayor and Lumby, Cambridge, 1878, p. 347, is a long note on this phrase, with references to Bp. Fisher's Works, ed. Mayor, pt. i. p. 181, l. 13; Burton, Anatomy of Melancholy, pt. iii. sect. 4. memb. 1. subsect. 2, and subsect. 3; Christ's Own Complaint, ed. Furnivall (E. E. T. S.), l. 502; Myrour of Our Lady (E. E. T. S.), p. lii, where we read of St. Bridget that 'she neuer vsed any lynen clothe though it weer in tyme of sykenes but only vpon hir hed, and next hir skyn she weer euer rough and sharpe *wolen* cloth.' The note further corrects my explanation 'with the wool towards the skin,' because this 'would only suit with a clothing made of the fleece as it came from the sheep's back ;' and I have amended my explanation accordingly. It then goes on : '*ward* is *wered*, the pp. of AS. *werian*, to wear, and *woolward* means "wool-clad," just as in Beowulf, 606, *sweglwered* means "clad in brightness;" *scirwered* and *ealdawered* may be cited as other examples of this pp. in composition. It has fared with *woolward*, when it became a solitary example of this compound, as it did with *rightwise* under similar circumstances. The love for uniform orthography made this latter word into *righteous*, and *woolwered* into *woolward* to conform to the shape of *forward*, &c. The use of *go* is the same as in *to go bare*, *naked*, *cold*,' &c. This is ingenious, but by no means proven, and I beg leave to reject it. The suffix *-wered* is extremely rare; *sweglwered* and *scīrwered* each occur only once, and only in poetry, and even Grein can only guess at the sense of them ; whilst *ealdāwered* has nothing to do with the matter, as it means 'worn out by old age,' Ettmüller, p. 4. There is no such word as *wullwered* in AS., or *wolwered* in ME.; and it is a long jump of many centuries from these doubtful compounds with *-wered* in AS. poetry to the first appearance of *wolwarde* (always so spelt) in the 14th century.

WOON, a governor, officer. (Burmese.) Burm. *wun*, a governor, or officer of administration; lit. 'a burden,' hence presumably the 'bearer of the burden' (Yule).

WORD, an oral utterance or written sign, expressing thought; talk, message, promise. (E.) ME. *word*, pl. *wordes*, Chaucer, C. T. 315 (A 313). AS. *word*, neut. sb., pl. *word*, Grein, ii. 732.+Du. *woord*; Icel. *orð* (for *word*); Dan. and Swed. *ord*; G. *wort*; Goth. *waurd*. **β.** The Teut. type is *wordom*, n. Cognate with Lithuan. *wardas*, a name, L. *uerbum* (base *uerdh*), a word, a verb; the Idg. type being *wardhom*, n. From √WER, to speak; whence Gk. εἴρειν, to speak; so that the lit. sense is 'a thing spoken.' Cf. Gk. ῥή-τωρ, a speaker, from the same root. **Der.** *word*, vb., to speak, Cymb. iv. 2. 240, ME. *worden*, P. Plowman, B. iv. 46; *word-less*, Lucrece, 112; *word-ing*; *word-y*, ME. *woordi*, Wyclif, Job, xvi. 21 (earlier version); *word-i-ness*. Also *word-book*, a dictionary, prob. imitated from Du. *woordenboek*, G. *wörterbuch*. And see *rhetoric*. Brugmann, i. § 589. **Doublet**, *verb*.

WORK, a labour, effort, thing done or written. (E.) ME. *werk*, Wyclif, Mark, xiv. 6; Chaucer, C. T. 481 (A 479). AS. *weorc*, *werc*, Grein, ii. 677.+Du. *werk*; Icel. *verk*; Dan. *værk*; Swed. *verk*; G. *werk*, OHG. *werch, werah*.   β. All from Teut. type **werkom*, n., work; which from Teut. base WERK, Idg. √WERG, to work. Hence also Gk. ἔ-οργ-α, I have wrought, ῥέζειν (= Ϝρέγ-γειν), to do, work, ἔργον, a work, ὄργανον, an instrument, organ, ὄργια, orgies; Zend *vareza*, a working, *varezāna*, a making (cited by Fick); cf. Pers. *warz*, gain, profit, acquisition, habit, *warzad*, he studies or labours, *warz-kār*, a ploughman (lit. work-doer), *warz-gāw*, an ox for ploughing (lit. work-cow), *warzah*, agriculture; Rich. Dict. p. 1638.   **Der.** *work*, verb, ME. *werchen, wirchen*, Chaucer, C. T. 2761 (A 2759), pt. t. *wroughte*, id. 499 (A 497), pp. *wrought*, id. 16800 (G 1332), from AS. *wiercan, wyrcan* (with the usual vowel-change to *ie* or *y*), pt. t. *worhte*, pp. *geworht*, Grein, ii. 759; cognate with Goth. *waurkjan*, Teut. type **work-jan-*, from Idg. **worg*, second grade of √WERG.   Also *work-able* (from the verb); and (from the sb.) *work-day*, ME. *werk-edei* (trisyllabic), Ancren Riwle, p. 20, l. 7, AS. *weorc-dæg*, Wright's Voc. i. 37; *work-house*, AS. *weorc-hūs* (L. *officina*), Voc. 185. 3; *work-man*, ONorthumb. *wercmonn*, Matt. x. 10 (Lindisfarne MS.); *work-man-like*; *work-man-ship*, ME. *werkemanship*, P. Plowman, B. x. 288; *work-shop*. Also *wright*, q. v. And see *en-erg-y*, *lit-urg-y*, *metall-urg-y*, *chir-urg-eon*, *s-urg-eon*, *organ*.

WORLD, the earth and its inhabitants, the system of things, present state of existence, a planet, society. (E.)   ME. *werld*, Genesis and Exodus, l. 42; *world, worlde*, P. Plowman, B. prol. 19; also spelt *wordle*, Ayenbite of Inwyt, p. 7, l. 10; *werd*, Havelok, 1290; *ward*, Lancelot of the Laik, 3184.   AS. *weoruld, weorold, woruld, worold, world*, Grein, ii. 684.+Du. *wereld*; Icel. *veröld* (gen. *veraldar*); Dan. *verden* (for *verld-en*, where *en* is really the postposed def. article); Swed. *verld*; G. *welt*, MHG. *werlt*, OHG. *weralt*.   β. The cognate forms show clearly that the word is a composite one. It is composed of AS. *wer*, cognate with Icel. *verr*, OHG. *wer*, Goth. *wair*, a man, L. *uir*, a man; and OMerc. *ældu* (AS. *ieldu*), cognate with Icel. *öld*, Goth. *alds*, an age; see **Virile** and **Eld**. Thus the sense is 'age of man' or 'course of man's life,' whence it came to mean lifetime, course of life, experience of life, usages of life, &c.; its sense being largely extended. The sb. *eld* is a derivative from the adj. *old*, as shown s. v.; and is well exhibited also in the curious Dan. *hedenold*, the heathen age, heathen times, from *heden*, a heathen.   γ. We may compare AS. *weoruld* with *wer* and *ældu*; Icel. *veröld* with *verr* and *öld*; OHG. *weralt* with *wer* and a sb. formed from *alt*, old; hence the word is a very old one, formed in times previous to all record of any Teutonic speech; really from a Teut. type **wer-aldi-*.   **Der.** *world-ly*, AS. *weoruld-lic*, Grein, ii. 687; *world-li-ness*; *world-ly-mind-ed*, *world-ly-mind-ed-ness*; *world-l-ing*, with double dimin. suffix, As You Like It, ii. 1. 48.

WORM, a small creeping animal. (E.)   Formerly applied to a snake of the largest size; cf. *blind-worm*. ME. *worm*; pl. *wormes*, Chaucer, C. T. 10931 (F 617). AS. *wyrm*, a worm, snake, dragon; Grein, ii. 763.+Du. *worm*; Icel. *ormr* (for **wormr*); Dan. and Swed. *orm* (for **worm*); G. *wurm*: Goth. *waurms*.   β. The Teut. type is **wurmiz*, Idg. type **wɔrmis*; cf. L. *uermis*, a worm. Brugmann, i. § 371; ii. § 97. Prob. allied to Gk. ῥόμος (for *Ϝρόμος*), an earthworm.   **Der.** *worm*, verb; *worm-y*. Allied words are *verm-ine, verm-icular, verm-icelli*. (But not *wormwood*.)

WORMWOOD, a very bitter plant. (E.)   The suffix *-wood* is corrupt, due to confusion with *wood*, in order to make it sound more intelligible. We find the spelling *wormwod* as early as the 15th century. 'Hoc absinthium, *wórmwod*;' Voc. 711. 24. But only a little earlier (early 15th century), we find *wermode*, id. 645. 35. AS. *wermōd*; 'Absinthium, *wermōd*,' in a glossary of the 8th century; Voc. 2. 15.+Du. *wermoet*, 'worm-wood;' Hexham; G. *wermuth*, MHG. *wermuote*, OHG. *werimuota, wermuota*.   β. It is thus evident that the word is doubly corrupt, and has no more to do with *worm* than it has with *wood*; the G. forms show clearly that the division of the AS. word is *wer-mōd*. [It is quite distinct from AS. *wyrmwyrt*, worm-wort, *Sedum album* or *villosum*; Cockayne's A. S. Leechdoms, ii. 411.] Mr. Cockayne, Leechdoms, i. 217, supposes AS. *wermōd* to mean 'ware-moth,' i. e. that which keeps off moths; but *mōd* is not 'a moth,' and words like 'ware-moth,' in which the *former* part is verbal, are not found in AS.   γ. The fullest forms are AS. *were-mōd*, Voc. 296. 24; OHG. *weri-muota, weri-muot*, as if the sense were 'manly courage;' see **Werwolf**. But the orig. sense remains unknown.

WORRY, to harass, tease. (E.)   The old sense was to seize by the throat, or strangle, as when a dog *worries* a rat or sheep. ME. *worowen, wirien*; also *wery*, Rom. of the Rose, 6264; also *wyrwyn* or *worowen*, and explained by 'strangulo, suffoco,' Prompt. Parv.; *worow*, used of lions and wolves that *worry* men, Pricke of Conscience, 1229; pp. *werewed, wirwed*, Havelok, 1915, 1921. The theoretical

ME. type is **wurȝen* (Stratmann), which passed, as usual, into *wurwen, worwen*, or *wirwen*, and other varieties; the second *w* is usually due (in such a position) to an older ȝ, and answers to AS. *g*. The various vowels point back to AS. *y*, so that the AS. form must have been *wyrgan*. AS. *wyrgan*, found in the gloss: 'strangulat, *wyrgeð*;' Corpus Gloss. 1926.+Du. *worgen*, to strangle, whence *worg*, quinsy; OFries. *wergia, wirgia*, to strangle; Low G. *worgen*; G. *würgen*, OHG. *wurgan*, to strangle, suffocate, choke; as in *Wölfe würgen die Schafe*, .wolves worry the sheep, Flügel.   β. These verbs are secondary forms, due to the Teut. str. verb **wergan-*, found in MHG. *wergen, ir-wergan*, to strangle. The Teut. base is **wergh-*, from Idg. √WERGH; as in Lithuan. *wersz-ti*, to strangle, to oppress; cf. Slav. base *verz-*, to bind fast, in Miklosich. Brugmann, i. § 624. Cf. **Wring**.

WORSE, comp. adj. and adv., more bad; **WORST**, superl. adj. and adv., most bad. (E.)   1. ME. *wurs, wors, wers*, adv.; *wurse, worse, werse* (properly dissyllabic), adj. 'Now is my prison *wersë* than before;' Chaucer, C. T. 1226 (A 1224). [Hence perhaps the suggestion of the double comp. *wors-er*, Temp. iv. 27.] 'Me is the *wrs*' = it is the worse for me; Owl and Nightingale, l. 34. We find also ME. *werre*, worse, spelt also *worre*, Gawayn and the Grene Knight, 1588; this is a Scand. form, due to assimilation. AS. *wyrs*, adv.; *wyrsa, wirsa*, adj.; Grein, ii. 765.+OSax. *wirs*, adv.; *wirsa*, adj.; OFries. *wirra, werra*, adj. (for **wirsa, *wersa*, by assimilation); Icel. *verr*, adv.; *verri*, adj. (for **vers, *versi*); Dan. *værre*, adj.; Swed. *värre*, adj.; MHG. *wirs*, adv.; *wirser*, adj.; Goth. *wairs*, adv.; *wairsiza*, adj.   β. In Gothic, *-iza* is a common suffix in comparatives, as in *hard-iza*, hard-er, from *hard*, hard; and it answers to mod. E. *-er*. The common Teut. type is **wersizon-*, adj., where *-izon-* is the comparative suffix. The base is **wers-*, perhaps to twist, entangle, confuse; whence also OHG. *werran*, G. *wirren*, to twist, entangle. See **War**.   γ. The same base **wers* (assimilated to **werr*) occurs perhaps in L. *uerrere*, pt. t. *uerri*, pp. *uersus*, to whirl, toss about, drive, sweep along, sweep; cf. Lucretius, v. 1226.   2. The superl. form presents no difficulty. ME. *worst, werst*, adv.; *worste, werste*, adj., Gower, C. A. i. 25; prol. 641. AS. *wyrst*, adv., *wyrsta*, adj. (Grein); this is a contracted form of *wyrsesta*, which appears as *wyrresta* (by assimilation) in Matt. xii. 45.+OSax. *wirsista*, adj.; Icel. *verst*, adv., *verstr*, adj.; Dan. *værst*; Swed. *värst*; OHG. *wirsist, wirsest*, contracted form *wirst*. The Teut. type is **wers-ist-oz*.   ¶ It is now seen that the *s* is part of the base or root; *worse* really does duty for *wors-er*, which was in actual use in the 16th century; and *wors-t* is short for *wors-est*. **Der.** *worse*, verb, Milton, P. L. vi. 440, ME. *wursien*, Ancren Riwle, p. 326, AS. *wyrsian*, properly intrans., to grow worse, A. S. Chron. an. 1085; *wors-en*, verb, to make worse, Milton, Of Reformation in England, b. i (R.); *wors-en*, to grow worse (Craven dialect). Also *worst*, verb, to defeat, Butler, Hudibras, pt. i. c. 2. l. 878; this answers to ME. *wursien* above (AS. *wyrsian*), and is a form due to the usual excrescent *t* after *s* (as in *among-st, whil-st*, &c.) rather than formed from the superlative.

WORSHIP, honour, respect, adoration. (E.)   Short for *worth-ship*; the *th* was not lost till the 14th century. Spelt *worschip*, P. Plowman, B. iii. 332; but *worþssipe* (= *worþshipe*), Ayenbite of Inwyt, p. 8, l. 8 (A.D. 1340). AS. *weorðscipe, wyrðscipe*, honour; Grein, ii. 683. Formed with suffix *-scipe* (E. *-ship*) from AS. *weorð, wurð*, adj., worthy, honourable; cf. L. *dignitās* from the adj. *dignus*. See **Worth** (1).   **Der.** *worship*, verb, ME. *worthschipen*, spelt *wurðschipen* in St. Katharine, l. 55 (so in the MS., but printed *wurð-schipen*); not found in AS. Also *worship-ful*, spelt *worþssipuol*, Ayenbite of Inwyt, p. 80, l. 22; *worship-ful-ly*.

WORST, adj. and verb; see under **Worse**.

WORSTED, twisted yarn spun out of long, combed wool. (E.) ME. *worsted*, Chaucer, C. T. 264 (A 262). So named from the town of *Worsted*, now *Worstead*, not far to the N. of Norwich, in Norfolk. Probably not older than the time of Edward III, who invited over Flemish weavers to improve our woollen manufactures. It is mentioned as early as 1348; see Archæologia, xxxi. 78. Chaucer is perhaps the earliest author who mentions it. '*Worsted*: these first took their name from *Worsted*, a village in this country;' Fuller, Worthies; Norfolk (R.).   β. *Worstead* stands for *Worthstead*; this we know from Charter no. 785 in Kemble, Codex Diplomaticus, iv. 111, where the name appears as *Wrðestede*, and *w* = *wu*, as in other instances. The AS. *wurð, weorð*, worth, value, was also used in the sense of 'estate' or 'manor,' and appears in place-names, such as *Sawbridge-worth, Rickmans-worth*; however, in the sense of 'estate,' the usual form is *weorðig*, and this may suit the AF. form *Wrðestede*, if the former *e* represents an earlier *-ig*. The AS. *stede* = mod. E. *stead*, or place. Hence *Worstead* means 'the place of an estate;' see **Worth** and **Stead**.

WORT (1), a plant. (E.)   Orig. the general E. name for 'plant;' *plant* being a Latin word. ME. *wort*; pl. *wortes*, Chaucer, C. T.

15227 (B 4411). AS. *wyrt*, a wort; Grein, ii. 765.+OSax. *wurt*; Icel. *urt* (for **wurt*); also spelt *jurt*, borrowed from Low G.; Dan. *urt*; Swed. *ört*; G. *wurz*; Goth. *waurts*. β. All from Teut. type **wurtiz*, f.; Idg. type **wardis*. Allied to W. *gwreiddyn*, a root; OIrish *frem*, a root; also to Icel. *rōt*, a root, L. *rādix*, Gk. *ῥίζα*, a root; *ῥάδ-αμνος*, a young shrub. Brugmann, i. §§ 350, 529; a plant, herb, Fick, iii. 294. See further under **Root** (1). Der. *mug-wort*, and other plant-names in which *wort* is suffixed; also *wort* (2). Allied to *radix*, *liquorice*, &c.

WORT (2), an infusion of malt, new beer unfermented or while being fermented. (E.) ME. *wort* or *worte*, Chaucer, C. T. 16281 (G 813). 'Hoc idromellum, Anglice *wurte*;' Voc. 772. 2. AS. *-wyrt*, in the comp. *mäx-wyrt*, lit. mash-wort, an infusion of worts; A. S. Leechdoms, ii. 216, 399. Here *wyrt* seems to be a peculiar use of the *wyrt* given under **Wort** (1); but the G. *würze* (below) is derived from *wurz*, a wort. Cf. also MDu. *wort*, 'wort, or new beere before it be clarified,' Hexham; *worte*, 'a root or a wort,' id.; Low G. *wört*. Also Icel. *virtr*; Norweg. *vyrt*, *vört*, Aasen; Swed. *vört*; G. *bier-würze*, beer-wort, allied to *wurz*, a wort, herb, whence *würze*, seasoning, spice, *würzsuppe*, spiced soup, &c. β. The Icel. *virtr*, MHG. *wirz*, which differ in the vowel, are from a Teut. base **werti-*, which differs in gradation from **wurtiz*, a wort, but is closely related to it.

WORTH (1), equal in value to, deserving of; as sb., desert, price. (E.) ME. *wurð*, *worþ*, worth, adj., worthy, honourable, Will. of Palerne, 2522, 2990; Rob. of Glouc. p. 364, l. 7547. Also *wurþ*, *worþ*, ill-spelt *worthe* in P. Plowman, B. iv. 170; but *wurþ* in Rob. of Glouc. p. 373, l. 3674. AS. *wyrðe*, adj., a mutated by-form of *weorþ*, adj., valuable; *wyrð*, by-form of *weorþ*, sb., value.+Du. *waard*, adj.; *waarde*, sb.; Icel. *verðr*, adj.; *verð*, sb.; Dan. *værd*, adj. and sb.; Swed. *värd*, adj.; *värde*, sb.; Dan. *werth*, MHG. *wert*, adj. and sb.; Goth. *wairths*, adj. and sb. β. All from Teut. type **werthoz*, adj., valuable. This word is probably to be divided as **wer-thoz*; note also Lith. *wer-tas*, worthy (probably borrowed from Teutonic). Also cf. W. *gwerth* (type **wer-tos*), value, price; allied to L. *uer-ērī*, to respect. Prob. from √WER, to guard, keep; see **Ware** (1). Der. *worth-y*, spelt *wurrþi*, Ormulum, 2705, *wurrþiȝ*, id. 4200, AS. *wyrðig*, adj., Alfred, tr. of Orosius, vi. 2 (the AS. *weorðig* or *worðig* only occurs as a sb. meaning an estate); hence *worthi-ly*, *worthi-ness*; *worth-less*, *worth-less-ly*, *-ness*. Also *wor-ship*.

WORTH (2), to become, to be. (E.) Now only in the phr. *wo worth the day!* = evil be to the day. ME. *worþen*, to become; formerly common. In P. Plowman's Crede, a short poem of 850 (long) lines, it occurs 8 times; as 'schent mote I *worþen*' = I must be blamed, l. 9; 'wo mote ȝou *worþen*' = may evil be (or happen) to you; and see P. Plowman, B. prol. 187, i. 186, ii. 43, iii. 33, v. 160, vi. 165, vii. 51. AS. *weorðan*, to become; also spelt *wurðan*, *wyrðan*; pt. t. *wearð*, pl. *wurdon*; Grein, ii. 678.+Du. *worden*, pt. t. *werd*, pp. *ge-worden*; Icel. *verða*, pt. t. *varð*, pp. *orðinn*, to become, happen, come to pass; Dan. *vorde*; Swed. *varda*; G. *werden*, OHG. *werdan*; Goth. *wairthan*, pt. t. *warth*, pp. *waurthans*. β. All from Teut. type **werthan-* (pt. t. **warth*, pp. **wurthanoz*), to become, turn to; allied to L. *uertere*, to turn, *uertī*, to turn to. – √WERT, to turn; see **Verse**. Der. *wierd*, q. v.

WOT, I know, or he knows; see **Wit** (1). Der. *not* (2).

WOULD; see **Will** (1).

WOUND, a hurt, injury, cut, bruise. (E.) ME. *wounde*, Chaucer, C. T. 1012 (A 1010). AS. *wund*, Grein, ii. 750.+Du. *wond*, or *wonde*; Icel. *und* (for **wund*); Dan. *vunde*; G. *wunde*; OHG. *wunta*. β. All from Teut. type **wundā*, f., a wound. We find also an older type in the Teut. adj. **wundoz*, wounded, appearing in G. *wund*, OHG. *wunt*, Goth. *wunds*, wounded. β. The type **wun-dóz* seems to answer to an Idg. type **wn-tós*, formed with a pp. suffix from **wun(n)-*, weak grade of Teut. **winnan-* (for **wennan-*), a verb signifying 'to fight' or 'suffer,' represented in AS. by *winnan*, to strive, fight, suffer, pp. *wunnen*. See **Win**. Der. *wound*, verb, AS. *wundian*, Grein, ii. 751. Cf. *wen*.

WOURALI, OURALI, OORALI, OURARI, CURARI, a resinous substance, extracted from the *Strychnos toxifera*, used for poisoning arrows, &c. (Guiana.) 'The hellish *oorali*;' Tennyson, In the Children's Hospital, l. 10. And see Waterton's Wanderings. From '*ourali*, written also *wourali*, *urali*, *urari*, *curare*, &c., according to the pronunciation of the various tribes;' W. H. Brett, Indian Tribes of Guiana, 1868, p. 140. It is spelt *wourara* in Stedman's Surinam (1796), i. 395; *ourari* in Hakluyt, Voy. iii. 689, last col.

WRACK, a kind of sea-weed; shipwreck, ruin. (E.) *Wrack*, as a name for sea-weed, merely means 'that which is cast ashore,' like things from a wrecked ship. This is well shewn by mod. F. *varech*, which has both senses, (1) sea-weed cast on shore, and (2) pieces of a wrecked ship cast on shore; this F. word being merely borrowed from English. Cotgrave has F. *varech*, 'a sea-wrack or wreck,

all that is cast aland by chance or tempest.' Shak. has *wrack*, shipwreck, destruction, ruin, Merch. Ven. iii. 1. 110; Macb. i. 3. 114, &c. ME. *wrak*, a wreck, Chaucer, C. T. (Six-text edition), Group B, l. 513; where Tyrwhitt prints *wrecke*, l. 4933. AS. *wræc*, 'what is driven,' Lat. 'actuārius;' O. E. Texts, p. 37; cf. *wræc*, banishment, exile, misery, Grein, ii. 738. From **wrak*, 2nd grade of Teut. **wrek-an-*; the sense is immediately due to the orig. verb, AS. *wrecan* (pt. t. *wræc*), to drive, expel, cast forth; so that *wræc* is here to be taken in the sense of 'that which is driven ashore.' The AS. *wrecan* also means to wreak, punish; see **Wreak**. And see **Wreck**.+Du. *wrak*, sb., a wreck; adj., cracked, broken; cf. *wraken*, to reject; cf. Icel. *rek* (for *vrek*), also *reki*, anything drifted or driven ashore, from *reka* (for *vreka*), to drive. Cf. Dan. *vrag*, wreck, *vrage*, to reject, Swed. *vrak*, wreck, refuse, trash; all from Dutch. Doublets, *wreck*, *rack* (4).

WRAITH, an apparition. (E.) '*Wraith*, an apparition in the likeness of a person, supposed to be seen soon before, or soon after death. . . . The apparition called a *wraith* was supposed to be that of one's guardian angel;' Jamieson. He adds that the word is used by King James I [Demonology; Works, p. 125). G. Douglas translates *figūras* (Æn. x. 641) by '*wraithis* of goistis;' and *umbræ* (Æn. x. 593) by *wrathis* (also written *wrethis*). Note that the *wraith* of Æneas was formed of a cloud (Æn. x. 636); and *wraith* or *wreth* may be the same word as *wreath*; cf. prov. E. *snow-wreath*, a mass of drifted snow. Cf. Milton, P. L. vi. 58. See **Wreath**. β. The Ayrshire *warth*, an apparition, may be a different word, and allied to the curious Norw. *vardyvle* [= ward-evil?], a guardian or attendant spirit, a fairy or sprite said to go before or follow a man, also considered as an omen or a boding spirit (Aasen); which seems to be allied to E. *ward*, to guard. But there is also a prov. E. *swarth*, with the same sense.

WRANGLE, to dispute, argue noisily. (E.) ME. *wranglen*, a various reading for *wraxlen* (to wrestle), in P. Plowman, C. xvii. 80. The sb. *wranglyng* is in P. Plowman, B. iv. 34. A frequentative formed from AS. *wrang*, 2nd grade of Teut. **wreng-*, as seen in AS. *wringan*, to press. Thus the orig. sense was to keep on pressing, to urge; hence to argue vehemently. Cf. Low G. *vrangeln*, to wrestle (Schambach); G. *ringen*, to wrestle; Dan. *vringle*, to twist, entangle; Norw. *rangla*, to begin to quarrel. See **Wring**. Der. *wrangle*, sb.; *wrangl-er*, a disputant in the schools (at Cambridge), now applied (till 1909) to a first-class man in the mathematical tripos; *wrangl-ing*.

WRAP, to fold, infold, cover by folding round. (E.) ME. *wrappen*, Chaucer, C. T. 10950; Will. of Palerne, 745. [We also find a form *wlappen*, Wyclif, Luke, ii. 7, John, xx. 7, now spelt *lap*; see **Lap** (3).] Cf. Prov. E. *warp*, to wrap up, Somersetshire (Halliwell), also to weave; also, to lace together the ends of a fishing-net (E. D. D.); *warple*, to entangle, id. Not found in AS. Cf. North Friesic *wrappe*, to press into, to stop up. β. The form of the word suggests a connexion with **Warp**, q. v. G. Douglas has *warpit about* (L. *cingit*) to translate Virgil, Æn. i. 112; *warpit* (L. *euinctus*), Æn. v. 774; *warpit* my head = wrapped up my head, Prol. to Æn. vii. 95. Perhaps the sense was due to the folding together of a fishing-net; cf. Icel. *varp*, the cast of a net, *varpa*, a cast, also the net itself; *skóvarp*, lit. 'a shoe-warp,' the binding of a shoe; Swed. dial. *varpa*, a fine herring-net (Rietz). Der. *wrapp-er*, sb.

WRATH, anger, indignation. (E.) ME. *wraþþe*, *wratthe*, P. Plowman, B. iv. 34; *wraththe*, Wyclif, Eph. iv. 31. Properly dissyllabic. AS. and ONorthumbrian *wrǣðo*, *wrǣððo*, Mark, iii. 21; Luke, xxi. 23; John, iii. 36 (both in the Lindisfarne and Rushworth MSS.). Teut. type **wraithithā*, f., from the adj. **wraithoz*, AS. *wrāð*. The sb. is somewhat rare, but the adj. *wrāð*, wroth, from which it is formed, is common; see **Wroth**.+Icel. *reiði* (for **wreiði*), wrath, from *reiðr*, adj., wroth; Dan. and Swed. *vrede*, from *vred*, adj. Der. *wrath-ful*, King John, ii. 87; *wrath-ful-ly*, *-ness*.

WREAK, to revenge, inflict (vengeance) on. (E.) ME. *wreken*, Chaucer, C. T. 963 (A 961); formerly a strong verb; pt. t. *wrak*, Tale of Gamelyn, l. 303; pp. *wroken*, *wroke*, *wreken*, P. Plowman, A. ii. 169, B. ii. 194. AS. *wrecan*, to wreak, revenge, punish, orig. to drive, urge, impel, Grein, ii. 741; pt. t. *wræc*, pp. *wrecen*.+Du. *wreken*, to avenge; Icel. *reka* (for **wreka*), pt. t. *rak*, pp. *rekinn*, to drive, thrust, repel, toss, also, to wreak vengeance; G. *rächen*, to avenge; OHG. *rechen*; Goth. *wrikan*, to wreak anger on, to persecute. β. All from Teut. type **wrekan-*, pt. t. **wrak*; orig. to press, urge, drive; Fick, iii. 308. Further allied to Lithuan. *wargti*, to suffer affliction, *wargas*, affliction; Russ. *vrag'*, an enemy, foe (persecutor); L. *urgēre*, to press, urge on, Gk. *εἴργειν*, for **ἐϝέργειν*, to shut in. All from √WERG, to press, urge; Fick, i. 773. Der. *wrack*, q. v.; *wretch*, q. v., *wretch*, q. v.

WREATH, a garland. (E.) ME. *wrethe*, Chaucer, C. T. 2147 (A 2145). AS. *wrǣð*, a twisted band, a bandage; *gewriðen mid wrǣðe* = bound with a bandage, Ælfred, tr. of Gregory's Pastoral

Care, ed. Sweet, cap. xvii. p. 122, l. 16. Formed (with vowel-change from *ā* to *æ*) from AS. *wrāð*, 2nd grade of *wriðan*, to writhe, twist; see **Writhe**. Der. *wreathe*, verb; 'together *wreathed* sure,' Surrey, Paraph. of Ecclesiastes, c. iv. l. 34.

WRECK, destruction, ruin, remains of what is wrecked. (E.) Formerly *wrack*, as in Shak. Temp. i. 2. 26. ME. *wrak*, Chaucer, C. T. 4933 (Group B, l. 513), where Tyrwhitt prints *wrecke*. In a glossary of E. Law-terms, written in the 13th c., and pr. in Reliq. Antiquæ, i. 33, we find: '*Wrec*, truvure de mer,' i.e. what is cast up by the sea; also *wrek*, Stat. Realm, i. 28 (anno 1275); also *ship-wrek*, Thorpe, Cod. Diplom. p. 382. AS. *wræc*, expulsion, banishment, misery; Grein, ii. 738. The peculiar use may be due to Scand. influence; see **Wrack**.+Du. *wrak*, wreck; cf. *wrak*, adj., broken; Icel. *rek* (for **wrek*), also *reki*, anything drifted or driven ashore, from *reka*, to drive; [Dan. *vrag*, wreck, Swed. *vrak*, refuse, trash, wreck, from] Low G. (Hamburg) *wrack*, a broken bit, a battered ship (Richey); Guernsey *vrec*. β. The lit. sense 'that which is drifted or driven ashore;' hence it properly meant pieces of ships drifted ashore, also *wrack* or sea-weed. Secondly, as the pieces thus driven ashore were from ships broken up by tempests, it came to mean fragments, refuse, also destruction, or ruin caused by *any* kind of violence, as in Shakespeare and Milton. The orig. sense of AS. *wrecan* was to impel, drive, persecute, expel, wreak; hence *wræc* in AS. poetry commonly means banishment or misery such as is endured by an exile. Der. *wreck*, verb; also *wrack*, Temp. i. 2. 236; *wrack-ful*, Shak. Sonnet 65; *wreck-ful*, Spenser, F. Q. vi. 8. 36; *wreck-er*, one who plunders wrecks. And see *wretch*.

WREN, a small bird. (E.) ME. *wrenne*, Gower, C. A. iii. 349; bk. viii. 2227. AS. *wrenna*, *wrænna*; Voc. 131. 33; 286. 16. Cf. Icel. *rindill*, a wren; OLow G. *wrendo*, *wrendil*, a wren (Gallée).

WRENCH, a twist, sprain, side-pull, jerk. (E.) 'I *wrenche* my foote, I put it out of joynt;' Palsgrave. He also spells it *wrinche*. ME. *wrench*, sb., in the metaphorical sense of perversion, guile, fraud, deceit. 'Withouten eny *wrenche*' = without any guile, Rob. of Glouc. l. 1264. Cf. *wrenk*, *wrench*, a trick, Cursor Mundi, 13336, 29307. AS. *wrenc* (dat. *wrence*), guile, fraud, deceit, Grein, ii. 742. β. It is obvious that mod. E. has preserved the orig. sense, and that the AS. and ME. uses are merely metaphorical. So also G. *rank* (pl. *ränke*), a cognate form, means an intrigue, trick, artifice, but provincially it means 'crookedness,' Flügel; hence MHG. *renken*, G. *verrenken*, to wrench. [On the other hand, mod. E. only uses the allied word *wrong* in the metaphorical sense of perverse, bad.] Teut. type **wrankiz*, lit. 'a twist.' From **wrank*, 2nd grade of **wrenk-*, for which see **Wrinkle**. Der. *wrench*, verb, AS. *wrencan*, to deceive, Grein, ii. 742; so also AS. *bewrencan*, to obtain by fraud, A. S. Apothegms, no. 34, pr. in Salomon and Saturn, ed. Kemble, p. 262.

WREST, to twist forcibly, distort. (E.) ME. *wresten*, in the sense to wrestle, struggle, Ancren Riwle, p. 374, l. 7; Cursor Mundi, 19353. AS. *wrǣstan*, to twist forcibly, Grein, ii. 740; cf. Salomon and Saturn, ed. Kemble, p. 140, l. 191. We also find AS. *wrǣst*, adj., firm, strong (Grein); the orig. sense of which is supposed to have been tightly twisted, or rather (as I should suppose) tightly strung, with reference to the strings of a harp when tightened by the instrument called a *wrest*; see Shak. Troil. iii. 3. 23; and note that the word *strong* itself merely means *strung*.+Icel. *reista*, to wrest; MDan. *vreste*, to wrest, Dan. *vriste*. β. The form *wrǣst* is closely allied to *wrǣð*, a wreath or twisted bandage, and stands (probably) for Teut. **wraith-t-joz*; from Teut. **wraith-*, as in AS. *wrāð*, 2nd grade of *wriðan*, to writhe or twist; see **Writhe**. And see **Wrist**. Der. *wrest*, sb. (as above); *wrest-le*, q.v.

WRESTLE, to struggle, contend by grappling together. (E.) ME. *wrestlen*, Gower, C. A. iii. 350, bk. viii. 2240; *wrastlen*, Ancren Riwle, p. 80, l. 7. The frequentative of **Wrest**, q.v. The AS. *wrǣstlian*, to wrestle, is rare; the form more commonly found is *wrāxlian*, Gen. xxxii. 24, whence ME. *wraxlen*, P. Plowman, C. xvii. 80, where we also find the various readings *wrastle*, *wraskle*. Still, we find: 'Luctatur [read Luctator], *wrǣstlere*; Luctatorum, *wrǣstliendra*;' Voc. 431. 25, 26.+MDu. *wrastelen*, *worstelen*, 'to wrestle or to struggle,' Hexham. Der. *wrestl-er*, *wrestl-ing*.

WRETCH, a miserable creature. (E.) Orig. an outcast or exile. ME. *wrecche*, Chaucer, C. T. 933 (A 931), where Tyrwhitt prints *wretched wight*, and omits *which*. AS. *wrecca*, an outcast, exile, lit. 'one driven out,' also spelt *wrǣcca*, *wreca*, Grein, ii. 739. Cf. AS. *wræc*, exile.—AS. *wrecan*, to drive out, also to persecute, wreak, avenge; see **Wreak**. Cf. Lithuan. *vargas*, affliction, misery. Der. *wretch-ed*, ME. *wrecched*, Chaucer, C. T. 923 (A 921), lit. 'made like a wretch;' *wretch-ed-ly*, *wretch-ed-ness*.

WRETCHLESSNESS, a misspelling of *rechlessness*, i.e. *reck-lessness*; see **Reck**.

WRIGGLE, to move along by twisting to and fro. (E.) 'With their much winding and *wrigling*;' Holland, tr. of Pliny, b. xxxii. c. 2. § 1. The frequentative of *wrig*, to move about; 'The bore his tayle *wrygges*,' Skelton, Elinour Rumming, l. 177. Allied to ME. *wrikken*, to twist to and fro, Life of St. Dunstan, l. 82; see Spec. of Eng., ed. Morris and Skeat, p. 22. Not found in AS., but a Low G. word as well as Scand., and preserved in mod. E. *wrick*, to twist. β. We find the closely related AS. *wrigian*, to impel, move towards, but this became ME. *wrien* (with loss of *g*), whence mod. E. *wry*, adj.; see further under **Wry** and **Wring**. ME. *wrikken* and AS. *wrigian* are closely related forms.+Du. *wriggelen*, to wriggle; frequentative of *wrikken*, 'to move or stir to and fro,' Sewel; whence *onwrikbaar*, immovable, steady; Low G. (Westphalian) *vriggeln*, to wriggle, to loosen by moving to and fro; (Hamburg) *wrickeln*, to wriggle; Low G. *wriggeln*, to wriggle (Danneil); *wrikken*, to turn, move to and fro, wriggle; Dan. *vrikke*, to wriggle; Swed. *vricka*, to turn to and fro, whence *vrickning*, distortion. γ. The orig. sense seems to have been 'to bend' or 'turn;' and we may deduce the orig. sense of E. *wriggle* as having been 'to keep on bending or twisting about.' See also **Rig** (2). Der. *wriggl-er*. Also *rick-ets*, q.v.

WRIGHT, a workman. (E.) ME. *wrighte*, Chaucer, C. T. 3145 (A 3143). AS. *wyrhta*, a worker, workman, maker, creator; Grein, ii. 763; with the common shifting of *r*.—AS. *wyrht*, a deed, work; formed, with suffix -*t*, from *wyrc-an*, to work. (The AS. *wyrht* occurs in *ge-wyrht*, a work, Grein, i. 489, where the prefix *ge-* makes no appreciable difference; and it stands for **wyrc-t*, with the usual substitution of *ht* for *ct*).+OSax. *wurhtio*, a wright, from *wurht*, a deed; OHG. *wurhto*, a wright, from OHG. *wuruht*, *wuraht*, a work, merit. β. The AS. *gewyrht*, OSax. *wurht*, OHG. *wuruht*, are all from Teut. **wurk-*, weak grade of **werk-*; see **Work**. Der. *cart-wright*, *ship-wright*, *wheel-wright*.

WRING, to twist, force by twisting, compress, pain, bend aside. (E.) ME. *wringen*; pt. t. *wrang*, *wrong*, Chaucer, C. T. 5026 (B 606); pp. *wrungen*, *wrongen*. AS. *wringan*, to press, compress, strain, pt. t. *wrang*, Gen. xl. 11, pp. *wrungon*.+Du. *wringen*; Low G. *wringen*, to twist together; G. *ringen*, to wring, wrest, turn, struggle, wrestle; a strong verb, pt. t. *rang*, pp. *gerungen*; OHG. *hringan* (for **wringan*), strong verb. β. All from Teut. type **wreng-an-*, pt. t. **wrang*, pp. **wrunganoz*; a nasalised form from a base **wreg* = **werg*; for which see **Worry**. And cf. **Wriggle**. Der. *wrang-le*, *wrong*; probably allied to *wrench*, *wrink-le*, *wrigg-le*, *wry*.

WRINKLE (1), a small ridge on a surface, unevenness. (E.) ME. *wrinkel* or *wrinkil*. 'Wrynkyl, or rymtyl, or wrympyl, Ruga; Wrynkyl, or playte [pleat] in clothe, Plica;' Prompt. Parv. [Here the spelling *wrympyl* stands for **hrympyl*; *wrinkle* and *rimple* are from different roots, as shown under *ripple* (2). Elsewhere, we find, in Prompt. Parv. p. 434, the spelling *rymtyl*, given under *R*.] The pl. *winclis* occurs, in the various readings of the later version, in Wyclif, Gen. xxxviii. 14. Somner gives AS. *winclian*, to wrinkle; the pp. *ge-wrinclod* occurs in Kemble, Cod. Dipl. iv. 34; l. 9. From a sb. **wrincel*. β. Evidently a dimin. form from a base **wrenk*, prob. allied to Teut. **wreng-an-*, to wring, to twist. See **Wring**; and see **Wrinkle** (2).+MDu. *wrinckel*, 'a wrinckle;' *wrinckelen*, 'to wrinckle, or to crispe;' prob. allied to *wringen*, 'to wreath [i.e. writhe, twist] or to wring;' Hexham. Perhaps further allied to Goth. *wraiqs*, crooked, Luke, iii. 5; L. *uerg-ere*, to bend; Skt. *vrjina-*, crooked; Gk. ῥαιβ-ός, crooked, ῥέμβ-ειν, to revolve. Brugmann, i. §§ 371, 677. See **Rhomb**. ¶ Dan. *rynke*, a wrinkle, pucker, gather, fold, *rynke*, to wrinkle, Swed. *rynka*, both sb. and vb., and Icel. *hrukka* (for **hrunka*), a wrinkle, are all forms due to the weak grade of an old str. vb. **hrenkan-*, and are related rather to **Ruck** (1). Der. *wrinkle*, vb.; *wrinkl-y*.

WRINKLE (2), a hint, small piece of advice. (E.) Prov. E. *wrinkle*, a new idea (Halliwell). It means 'a new idea' imparted by another, a hint; but the lit. sense is 'a small trick,' or 'little stratagem.' 'Having learned . . . euery *wrinckle*;' Lyly, Euphues, p. 389 (ed. Arber). And see Polit. Poems, ed. Wright, ii. 45; l. 7. It is the dimin. of AS. *wrenc*, a trick; for which see **Wrench**. Allied to **Wrinkle** (1).

WRIST, the joint which turns the hand. (E.) The pl. is spelt *wrestes* in Spenser, F. Q. i. 5. 6. ME. *wriste* or *wrist*; also *wirst*, by shifting of *r*. 'Wryst, or wyrste of an hande;' Prompt. Parv. AS. *wrist*. We find 'óð þā *wriste*' = up to the wrist; Laws of Æthelstān, pt. iv. § 7, in Thorpe, Ancient Laws, i. 226, l. 17. The full form was *hand-wrist*, i.e. that which turns the hand about. We find 'betwux elboga and *handwyrste*' = betwixt elbow and handwrist; Voc. 158. 10. Cf. 'geniculi, *cneow-wyrste*,' i.e. knee-joints, Voc. 160. 17. Prob. for **wrið-t*, and formed with suffix -*t* from *wrið-*, weak grade of *wriðan*, to writhe, to twist; see **Writhe**. Cf. **Wrest**, from the same verb.+OFries. *wriust*, *wrist*, *werst*; whence *hondwriust*, hand-wrist, *fotwriust*, foot-wrist or instep ; Low G. *wrist* ; Icel. *rist*, the instep ; cf. *rið-inn*, pp. of *riða*, to twist ; Dan. and Swed. *vrist*, the instep ; cf. *vride*, *vrida*, to twist ; G. *ri:t*, instep, wrist. Cf. also Westphal. *werste*, the instep, *vrist*, the ankle ; Low G. (Hamburg) *wristen*, pl., wrists, ankles. **Der.** *wrist-band*, the band of the sleeve at the wrist.

WRITE, to form letters with a pen or pencil, engrave, express in writing, compose, communicate a letter. (E.) The orig. sense was 'to score,' i. e. to cut slightly, as when one scores letters or marks on a piece of bark or soft wood with a knife ; it also meant to engrave runes on stone. ME. *writen*, pt. t. *wroot*, Chaucer, C. T. 5310 (B 890) ; pp. *writen* (with short *i*). AS. *writan*, pt. t. *wrāt*, pp. *writen*, to write, inscribe (orig. to score, engrave), Grein, ii. 743.+ OSax. *writan*, to cut, injure, also to write ; Du. *rijten*, to tear, split ; Icel. *rita*, pt. t. *reit*, pp. *ritinn*, to scratch, cut, write ; Swed. *rita*, to draw, delineate ; G. *reissen*, pt. t. *riss*, pp. *gerissen*, OHG. *rizan*, to cut, tear, split, draw or delineate. Cf. Goth. *writs*, a stroke made with a pen. β. All from the Teut. type **wreit-an-*, pt. t. *wrait, pp. *writ-anoz*, to cut, scratch, hence to engrave, write. **Der.** *writ*, sb., AS. *ge-writ*, also *writ*, a writing, Grein, i. 486, ii. 743, from *writ-*, weak grade of *writan*, to write. Also *writ-er*, AS. *writere*, Matt. ii. 4 ; *writ-er-ship*, *writ-ing*.

WRITHE, to twist to and fro. (E.) Spelt *wrethe* in Palsgrave. ME. *writhen*, spelt *wrythen* in Chaucer, tr. of Boethius, b. v. pr. 3, l. 15 ; pt. t. *wroth* (with long *o*), Gawain and the Grene Knight, l. 1200 ; pp. *writhen* (with short *i*), P. Plowman, B. xvii. 174. Cf. *writhing* in Chaucer, C. T. 10441 (F 127). AS. *wriðan*, to twist, wind about, pt. t. *wrāð*, pp. *wriðen*, Grein, ii. 743.+Icel. *riða* (for *wriða), pt. t. *reið*, pp. *riðinn* ; Dan. *vride* ; Swed. *vrida*, to wring, twist, turn, wrest ; OHG. *ridan*, MHG. *riden*, a strong verb, now lost. β. All from Teut. type **wreith-an-*, pt. t. *wraith, pp. *writh-anoz, to twist. **Der.** *wrath*, *wroth*, *wreath*, *wri-st*, *wre-st*.

WRONG, perverted, unjust, bad ; also as sb., that which is wrong or unjust. (Scand.) ME. *wrong*, adj., Will. of Palerne, 706 ; sb., P. Plowman, B. iii. 175. Late AS. *wrang* (*a* passing into *o* before *n*), occurs as a sb. in the A. S. Chron. an. 1124. Properly an adj. signifying ' a wrong thing,' a thing perverted or *wrung* aside ; compare the use of *wrong nose*, for ' crooked nose,' in Wyclif, Levit. xxi. 19 (later version). Not E., but Scand.—ONorse *wrangr ; as in Icel. *rangr*, awry, metaphorically, wrong, unjust ; Dan. *vrang*, wrong, adj. ; Swed. *vrång*, perverse. All from Teut. *wrang, 2nd grade of **wrengan-*, to wring, twist ; see **Wring**. **Der.** *wrong*, verb, to injure, as in ' to *wrong* the *wronger*,' Shak. Lucrece, 819 ; *wrong-er* (as above) ; *wrong-ly* ; *wrong-ful*, Wyclif, Luke, xii. 58 (earlier version) ; *wrong-ful-ly*, *-ness* ; *wrong-head-ed*, i. e. perverse. Also *wrong-wise*, ME. *wrongwis*, O. Eng. Homilies, ed. Morris, i. 175, l. 256 (Swed. *vrångvis*, iniquitous), now obsolete, but remarkable as being the converse of E. *righteous*, formerly *right-wise* ; Palsgrave actually spells it *wrongeous* !

WROTH, full of wrath, angry. (E.) ME. *wroth*, Chaucer, Parl. of Foules, l. 504. AS. *wrāð*, wroth, Grein, ii. 737.—AS. *wrāð*, 2nd grade of *wriðan*, to writhe ; so that the orig. sense was twisted or perverted in one's temper.+Du. *wreed*, cruel ; Icel. *reiðr* ; Dan. *vred* ; Swed. *vred* ; OHG. *reid*, *reidi*, only in the sense of twisted or curled. All from Teut. *wraith, 2nd grade of **wreithan-*. See **Writhe** and **Wrath**.

WRY, twisted or turned to one side. (E.) ' With visage *wry* ;' Court of Love, l. 1162 (a late poem, perhaps 16th century). But the verb *wrien*, to twist, bend, occurs in Chaucer, C. T. 17211 (H 262) ; and answers to AS. *wrigian*, to drive, impel, also to tend or bend towards. ' Hláford mīn ... *wrigað* on *wonge* '= my lord [i. e. master of a plough] pushes his way along the field ; Codex Exoniensis, ed. Thorpe, p. 403 (Riddle xxii, l. 9). Of a bough bent down, and then let go, it is said : ' *wrigað* wiþ his *gecyndes* '= it moves towards its kind, i. e. as it is naturally inclined ; Ælfred, tr. of Boethius, b. iii. met. 2 (cap. xxv). This AS. base *wrig-* is preserved in the frequentative **Wriggle**, q. v. See further under **Awry**. **Der.** *a-wry*, q. v. ; *wry-neck*, a small bird, allied to the woodpecker, so called from ' the writhing snake-like motion which it can impart to its neck without moving the rest of its body ;' Engl. Cycl. Also *wry-ness*.

WYCH-ELM ; see under **Witch-elm**.

WYVERN, WIVERN, in heraldry, a kind of flying serpent or two-legged dragon. (F.—L.) The final *n* is excrescent after *r*, as in *bitter-n*, q. v. ME. *wivere*, a serpent, Chaucer, Troilus, iii. 1010. —AF. *wyvre* (also *guivre*) ; see Notes on E. Etym. p. 470 ; OF. *wivre*, a serpent, viper, esp. in blazon ; see Roquefort and Burguy ; mod. F. *givre*, a viper. Burguy says it was also formerly spelt *vivre*, and that it is still spelt *voivre* in some F. dialects.—L. *uīpera*, a viper ; see **Viper**. ¶ The spelling with *w* in OF. was due to Germanic influence ; as if from an OHG. *wipera, borrowed from L. *uīpera*. **Doublet**, *viper*.

X

XEBEC, a small three-masted vessel used in the Mediterranean. (Span.—Turk.) In Ash's Dict. ed. 1775.—Span. *xabeque*, a xebec. So also Port. *zabeco*, F. *chebec*.—Turk. *sumbakí*, written *sunbakí*, ' a kind of Asiatic ship ;' Rich. Dict. p. 852. He also gives Pers. *sumbuk*, a small ship ; Arab. *sumbūk*, a small boat, a pinnace. See Devic, Supp. to Littré, s. v. *chebec*, which is the F. form ; he notes also Port. *xabeco*, Ital. *zambecco*, the latter form retaining the nasal *m*, which is lost in the other languages. He adds that the word *sumbekí* is given in the first ed. of Meninski's Thesaurus (1680) ; and that the mod. Arab. word is *shabbāk* ; see Dozy, Glossaire, p. 352.

XYLOBALSAM, the wood (or dried twigs) of the balm-of-Gilead tree. (L.—Gk.) ' The Indians doe call it *Xilo*, and we do call the same *Balsamo* ;' Frampton, tr. of Monardes, fol. 7, back. Evidently an error, as the word occurs in Pliny. Spelt *xylobalsamum* in Holland, tr. of Pliny.—L. *xylobalsamum* ; Pliny, Nat. Hist. b. xii. c. 25.—Gk. ξυλοβάλσαμον, the wood of the balsam tree.—Gk. ξυλο-, for ξύλον, wood ; and βάλσαμον, resin of the βάλσαμος, or balsam-tree, a word of Semitic origin ; see **Balsam**. From ξύλον we also have *xylo-graphy*, engraving on wood.

Y

Y-, *prefix*. (E.) This prefix is nearly obsolete, being only retained in the archaic words *y-clept* (called), *y-wis* (certainly). The ME. forms are *y-*, *i-* ; the latter being frequently written *I* (as a capital). —AS. *ge-*, an extremely common prefix, both of sbs. and verbs. [In verbs it was prefixed, not only to the pp. (as in mod. G. and in Middle-English), but also to the past tense, to the infinitive, or indeed occasionally to *any* part of the verb, without appreciably affecting the sense. In the word *y-wis*, certainly, many editors have ignorantly mistaken it for the pronoun *I* ; see **Ywis**. It appears as *e-* in the word *e-nough* ; and as *a-* in the word *a-ware*.]+Du. *ge-*, prefix ; G. *ge-* ; OHG. *ka-*, *ki-* ; Goth. *ga-*. As regards usage, it resembles L. *com-*, *con-*, for *cum*, with ; but the forms can hardly be reconciled.

YACHT, a swift pleasure-boat. (Du.) Pron. *yot*. ' One of his *yachts* ;' Evelyn's Diary, Oct. 1, 1661. In Phillips, ed. 1706 ; also in Blount's Gloss., ed. 1674, where it is badly spelt *yatcht* ; Bailey has *yatch*.—Du. *jagt*, formerly spelt *jacht* ; ' *een Iacht*, *ofte* [or] *See-roovers Schip*, a pinace, or a pirate's ship,' Hexham. ' *Jagt*, a yacht ;' Sewel. Named from its speed ; cf. Du. *jagten* (formerly *jachten*), to speed, to hunt ; *jagt* (formerly *jacht*), a hunting.—Du. *jagen*, ' to hunt or to chase deere, hares, &c. ;' Hexham.+G. *jagen*, to hunt. **Der.** *yacht-er*, *yacht-ing*.

YAK, the name of a bovine quadruped. (Thibet.) In a Thibetan Dict., by H. A. Jäschke, p. 668, we are told that the Thibet. word is γγag, a male yak, the female being called *po-γγag*. The symbol γ is used to denote a peculiar Thibetan sound.

YAM, a large esculent tuber, resembling the potato. (Port.—W. African.) Mentioned in Cook's Voyages (Todd) ; ed. 1777, i. 146 ; and by H. Pitman in 1689, in Arber's Eng. Garner, vii. 367. —Port. *inhame*, a yam ; not given in Vieyra, but noted in Webster and in Littré. Littré gives the F. form as *igname*, which he says is borrowed from the Port. *inhame* ; and adds : ' it was the Portuguese who first found the yam used as an object of culture, first on the coast of Africa, afterwards in India and Malacca, and gave it its name ; but the language whence it was taken is unknown.' It is really W. African ; see Hakluyt's Voyages (1599), v. ii. pt. 2. p. 129 ; where the African name is given as *inamia*, in Benin ; under the date 1588. Called *ñames* in Minsheu's Span. Dict. (1623). See Notes on E. Etym. p. 323. ' The country [Benin] abounds with *yams* ;' Voyages, 1745 ; ii. 707. The Malay name is *ūbi* ; Marsden, Malay Dict. p. 21.

YANKEE, a citizen of New England, or (later) of the United States. (Dutch ?) The word occurs as early as 1765. Webster cites : ' From meanness first this Portsmouth *Yankee* rose, And still to meanness all his conduct flows,' Oppression, A Poem by an American, Boston, 1765. We also find in the same : ' Commonly considered to be a corrupt pronunciation of the word *English*, or of the F. word *Anglais*, by the native Indians of America. According to Thierry, a corruption of *Jankin*, a dimin. of *John*, a nickname given to the English colonists of Connecticut by the Dutch settlers of New York,' [which may be partly correct]. Note that a Captain *Yanky*, commanding a Dutch ship, is mentioned several times in Dampier's Voyages, ed. 1699, i. 38, 39. Again, a Dutch boat seems to have been called a *yanky* by Smollett, Sir L. Greaves, ch. iii (Davies). β. Dr. Wm. Gordon, in his Hist. of the American War, ed. 1789, vol. i. pp. 324, 325, says it was a favourite cant word in Cambridge, Mass., as early as 1713, and that it meant 'excellent;' as, a *yankee* good horse, *yankee* good cider, &c. He supposes that it was adopted by the students there as a by-word, and, being carried by them from the college, obtained currency in the other New England colonies, until at length it was taken up in other parts of the country, and applied to New Englanders generally as a term of slight reproach. Cf. Lowland Sc. *yankie*, a sharp, clever, forward woman ; *yanker*, an agile girl, an incessant speaker ; *yanker*, a smart stroke, a great falsehood, a bounce ; *yank*, a sudden and severe blow, a sharp stroke ; *yanking*, active, pushing (Jamieson). Without the nasal, there is also Lowland Sc. *yack*, to talk precipitately and indistinctly, *yaike*, a stroke or blow. γ. The reference in 1765 may well be to Portsmouth in New Hampshire, not far to the N. of Boston ; and Thierry may be right in supposing it to be a Dutch nickname. I accept the suggestion made by Dr. H. Logeman, that *Yankee* was formed (like *Chinee* from *Chinese*, &c.) from the Du. *Jan Kees*, a familiar form of *John Cornelius*. Both *Jan* and *Kees* are very common Du. names, and both were familiarly used as terms of contempt ; see N. and Q. 10 S. iv. 509, v. 15. Cf. EFries. *Jan*, John, and *Kēs*, Cornelius (Koolman). The EFries. *kēs* also meant 'cheese;' and it is remarkable that Ascham uses *John Cheese* as a term of contempt; as in— 'Away, good Peek-goos! hens, *John Cheese!*' The Scholemaster, ed. Arber, bk. i. p. 54.

YAP, to yelp, bark. (E.) 'The *yapping* of a cur;' L'Estrange, tr. of Quevedo, p. 243 (Todd). *Yap* is imitative ; so also *yaup*, the Lowland Sc. equivalent of *yelp* (Jamieson). The Lowland Sc. *yaff* also occurs, which is a variant of *yap*. The F. *japper*, 'to bark, to yawle,' Cot., is of similar origin. Cf. EFries. and Low G. *jappen*, to gasp ; Norm. dial. *japer*, to yap (Duméril).

YARD (1), an enclosed space. (E.) ME. *yerd*, Chaucer, C. T. 15181 (B 4365). AS. *geard*, an enclosure, court ; Grein, i. 493.+ Du. *gaard*, a yard, garden ; Icel. *garðr* (whence prov. E. *garth*) ; Dan. *gaard* ; Swed. *gård* ; Goth. *gards*, a house ; allied to Goth. *garda*, a field, OHG. *gart*, *garto*, whence G. *garten*.+Russ. *gorod'*, a town ; L. *hortus* ; Gk. χόρτος, a court-yard, enclosure ; OIrish *gort*, a field. β. From the Teut. type **gardoz*, m.; Idg. type **ghortos*, a yard, court, enclosure. But the connexion with Gk. χόρτος is uncertain. See **Gird** (1). Der. *court-yard*, *orchard*. From the same root are *garden*, *gird* (1), *gird-le* ; *horti-culture* ; as well as *cohort*, *court*, *curt-ain*, &c. **Doublets**, *garden*, prov. E. *garth*.

YARD (2), a rod, an E. measure of 36 inches, a cross-beam on a mast for spreading square sails. (E.) ME. *jerde*, *yerde*, a stick, Chaucer, C. T. 149 ; also a yard in length, id. 1052 (A 1050). AS. *gyrd*, *gerd*, a stick, rod ; Grein, i. 536.+Du. *garde*, a twig, rod ; G. *gerte*, a rod, switch ; OHG. *gerta*, *kerta*. Teut. type **gardjā*, f. Allied to O. Bulgarian *žrŭdī* (Russ. *jerde*), a rod. But not to Goth. *gazds*, a goad. See Streitberg, § 125 (4). **Der.** *yard-arm*, the arm (i. e. the half) of a ship's yard, from the mast to the end of it.

YARE, ready. (E.) As adj. in Temp. v. 224; as adv., readily, quickly, Temp. i. 1. 7. ME. *jare*, Will. of Palerne, 895, 1963, 3265 ; *yare*, Rob. of Glouc. p. 52, l. 1213. AS. *gearu*, *gearo*, ready, quick, prompt; Grein, ii. 493.+Du. *gaar*, done, dressed (as meat) ; *gaar*, adv., wholly ; Icel. *görr*, adj., ready ; *görva*, *gerva*, *gjörva*, adj., quite, wholly ; OHG. *garo*, *karo*, prepared, ready ; G. *gar*, adj., wholly. β. Teut. type **garwoz*, adj., ready (Fick, iii. 102). Allied to **Gear**. **Der.** *yare-ly*, adv., Temp. i. 1. 4 ; also *gear*, *garb* (1), *gar* (2). Also (perhaps) *yarr-ow*, q. v.

YARN, spun thread, the thread of a rope. (E.) ME. *yarn*, *jarn* ; '*jarne*, threde, *Filum*;' Prompt. Parv. p. 536. AS. *gearn*, yarn, Voc. 238. 27.+Du. *garen*; Icel., Dan., and Swed. *garn* ; G. *garn*. β. All from the Teut. type **garnom*, n., yarn, string, Fick, iii. 101. Further allied to Gk. χορδή, a string, cord ; a string of gut ; cf. Icel. *görn*, or *garnir*, guts (i.e. strings or cords) ; Lith. *žarnos*, guts ; L. *haru-*, in *haru-spex*, inspector of entrails. See **Cord**, **Chord**. Cf. Brugmann, i. § 605.

YARROW, the plant milfoil. (E.) ME. *jarowe*, *jarwe* ; Prompt. Parv. p. 536. AS. *gæruwe*, explained by 'millefolium;' Voc. 133. 32; spelt *gearwe*, id. 32. 36.+Du. *gerw* ; G. *garbe* ; MHG. *garbe*, *garwe*, OHG. *garawa*. β. Perhaps there is a reference to the old belief in the curative properties of the yarrow, which was supposed to be a great remedy for wounds ; in Cockayne's A. S. Leechdoms, i. 195, we are told that Achilles was the first person who applied it to the cure of sword-wounds; hence, indeed, its botanical name of *Achillea millefolium*. If so, we might connect it with the verb *gearwian*, to make ready, from the adj. *gearo*, ready, yare; see **Yare**. Thus *yarrow* = that which makes *yare*, or restores. But this is uncertain.

YATAGHAN, ATAGHAN, a dagger-like sabre, with doubly curved blade. (Turk.) Spelt *ataghan* in Byron, Giaour; see note 27.

Spelt *yataghan* or *ataghan* in F. also.—Turk. *yātāghān*, a yataghan ; see Devic, and Pavet de Courteille, Dict. du Turc Oriental ; spelt *yātāghān*, *yatāghān*, Zenker's Dict. pp. 947, 958.

YAW, to go unsteadily, bend out of its course, said of a ship. (Scand.—Du.) In Hamlet, v. 2. 120. The sense is to go aside, swerve, bend out of the course; see Phillips.—Icel. *jaga*, properly, to hunt ; but used in the peculiarly specialised sense 'to move to and fro ;' see Vigfusson. For the sound *aw*, cf. the derivation of mod. E. *awe* from Icel. *agi*. Cf. Dan. *jage*, Swed. *jaga*, to hunt.— Du. *jagen*, to hunt, drive, chase. See further under **Yacht**.

YAWL (1), a small boat. (Du.) In Anson's Voyages, b. ii. c. 3 (R.). 'Barges or *yauls* of different kinds;' Drummond's Travels (Letter, dated 1744), p. 87 (Todd). 'Like our Deal *yalls*;' W. Dampier, A New Voyage, i. 429. The word is common at Lowestoft.—Du. *jol*, a yawl, skiff ; Sewel explains *jol* as 'a Jutland boat.' Cf. Dan. *jolle* ; Swed. *julle*, a yawl. Hexham records MDu. *iolleken*, 'a small barke or boate.' The mod. Icel. form is *jula*. β. Prob. of Low G. origin. The Low G. forms are *jelle*, *jolle*, *jülle* (Schambach); also *gelle*, *gölle*, *jölle* (Koolman, s. v. *jülle*) ; of which the forms *gelle*, *gölle* seem older than the rest. A borrowing from L. *galea* seems possible. See **Galley**.

YAWL (2), to howl. (E.) 'There howling Scyllas, *yawling* round about;' Fairfax, tr. of Tasso, b. iv. st. 5. Also spelt *yole*, *yowl* (Halliwell). ME. *goulen*, Havelok, 164; *joulen*, Chaucer, C. T. Group A, 1278 (Six-text ed.); Wyclif, Micah, i. 8 ; *jaulen*, Gawain and the Grene Knight, 1453. Of imitative origin. Cf. EFries. *jaueln*, Low G. *jaueln*, to yawl ; Du. *jolen*, to groan.+Icel. *gaula*, to low, bellow ; Norweg. *gaula*, to bellow, low, roar (Aasen) ; Swed. dial. *göla*, *gjöla*. Of imitative origin, like *yell*. See **Yell**.

YAWN, to gape. (E.) Spelt *yane* in Palsgrave. ME. *geonien*, Ancren Riwle, p. 242; whence E. *yawn*, by lengthening of *o* to open long *o* ; cf. E. *frost*, *broth*. [Cf. also ME. *ganien*, Chaucer, Six-text ed., Group H, l. 35; where Tyrwhitt (l. 11698a) has *galpeth*.] AS. *geonian* ; tr. of Beda, Hist. iv. 19 ; variant of *ginian*, tr. of Orosius, iii. 3. From *gin-*, weak grade of *-gīnan* (pt. t. *-gān*), in comp. *be-ginan*, to yawn (Grein). Cf. AS. *gānian*, to yawn ; Grein, i. 370. +OHG. *ginēn*, to yawn. Cf. Icel. *gina*, to gape, pt. t. *gein* ; MDu. *gienen*, 'to yawne,' Hexham ; Du. *geeuwen*, to yawn. From Idg. √GHEI, whence also L. *hi-āre*, to gape ; Slav. root *zi-*, to gape, in Miklosich. **Der.** *yawn-ing*. From the same root, *hi-at-us*.

YE, the nom. pl. of the 2nd personal pronoun. (E.) The nom. pl. is properly *ye*, whilst the dat. and acc. pl. is *you*; the gen. pl. is properly *your*, now only used as a possessive pronoun. But in mod. E. *ye* is almost disused, and *you* is constantly used in the nominative, not only in the plural, but in the singular, as a substitute for *thou*. 'Ye in me, and I in you;' John, xiv. 20 ; this shows the correct use. ME. *ye*, *je*, nom. ; *your*, *jour*, gen. ; *you*, *jou*, *yow*, dat. and acc. AS. *gē*, nom. ; *ēōwer*, gen. ; *ēōw*, dat. and acc. ; Grein, i. 263, 375.+Du. *gij*, ye ; *u*, you ; Icel. *ēr*, *ier*, ye ; *yðar*, *your* ; *yðr*, you ; Dan. and Swed. *i*, ye (also *you*) ; G. *ihr*; OHG. *īr*, ye, *iuwar*, *iuwer*, your, *iu*, you ; Goth. *jūs*, ye ; *izwara*, *your* ; *izwis*, you. We also have the AS. dual form *git*, ye two. β. The common Idg. base is *yū-*, whence also Lithuan. *jūs*, ye, Gk. ὑ-μεῖς, ye, Skt. *yū-yam*, ye. See Brugmann, ii. § 436.

YEA, an affirmative adverb; verily. (E.) The distinction between ME. *je*, *ja*, yea, and *jis*, *jes*, *jus*, yes, is commonly well marked ; the former is the simple affirmative, giving assent, whilst the latter is a strong asseveration, often accompanied by an oath; see Will. of Palerne, &c. Spelt *ye*, Chaucer, C. T. 9219 (E 1345). OFries. *jē*, AS. *gēa*, *geā*, yea ; John, xxi. 15.+Du., Dan., Swed., and G. *ja* ; Icel. *jā* ; Goth. *ja*, *jai* ; W. *ie* ; Gk. ῆ, truly. **Der.** *ye-s*, q.v.

YEAN, EAN, to bring forth lambs. (E.) 'The new-*yean*'d lamb;' Beaum. and Fletcher, Faithful Shepherdess, iii. 1. Spelt *ean* in Shak. Merch. Ven. i. 3. 88; Mer. E. *enen* ; 'Enyn, or brynge forthe kyndelyngys, Feto;' Prompt. Parv. p. 140. The difference between *ean* and *yean* is easily explained; in the latter, the prefixed *y* represents the very common AS. prefix *ge-*, readily added to any verb without affecting the sense; see **Y-**, prefix, above. AS. *ēanian*, to ean, Lambeth Psalter, Ps. lxvii. 70; *ge-ēanian*, to yean, of which the only clear trace appears to be in the expression *ge-ēane eowa* = the ewes great with young, Gen. xxxiii. 13. β. The AS. *ēa* answers to Germanic *au*, from Teut. type *-ōjan* (Sievers, Gr. § 411) ; so that the Germ. type is **aunōjan*; a type which also appears in Dutch dial. *oonen*, to ean; see Franck. This appears to be derived from a form **au-no-*, meaning 'lamb;' which some consider as being allied to Goth. *aw-is*, L. *ou-is*, a sheep, AS. *eowu*, a ewe. See **Ewe**. Scheller, in his Bavarian Dict. p. 1, cites the forms *äen*, *äuen*, *äuwen*, to yean, produce lambs, which are immediately derived from *ä*, *äu*, *äuw*, a ewe. Cf. Kluge, s. v. *Schaf*. γ. But Kluge and Lutz (Eng. Etym.) consider Teut. **auno-* as equivalent to **agwno-*, corresponding to L. *agnus*, a lamb, and to Celtic type **ognos*, a lamb, as seen in OIrish *ūan*, W. *oen*, Bret. *oan*, a lamb. So also Swed. dial. *åina*, *öna*, to yean; from *ön*, a lamb (Rietz, p. 114). Also Manx *eayney*, to yean, from *eayn*, a lamb. Thus the sense is merely 'to produce lambs.' Brugmann, i. §§ 671, 704. Der. *yean-ling*, a new-born lamb; with double dimin. suffix *-l-ing*.

YEAR, the time of the earth's revolution round the sun. (E.) ME. *зeer, yeer, зer, yer*; Chaucer, C. T. 601, where it appears as a plural. This sb. was formerly unaltered in the plural, like *sheep, deer*; hence the mod. phrase 'a *two-year* old colt.' The pl. *year* is common in Shak. Temp. i. 2. 53, &c. AS. *gēar, gēr*, a year; pl. *gēar*; Grein, i. 496.+Du. *jaar*; Icel. *ār*; Dan. *aar*, pl. *aar*; Swed. *år*; G. *jahr*; OHG. *jār*; Goth. *jēr*. β. All from Teut. type **jērom*, n., a year. Further allied to Gk. *ὧρος*, a season, a year; *ὧρα*, a season, an hour.—√YĒ, to go, pass; an extension from √EI, to go; whence also Skt. *yātu-*, time. See **Hour.** Brugmann, i. § 308, ii. § 587. Der. *year-ly*, adj. and adv.; *year-ling*, an animal a year old, with double dimin. suffix *-l-ing*. Allied to *hour*.

YEARN (1), to desire strongly, be eager for. (E.) ME. *зernen*, P. Plowman, B. i. 35. Cf. AS. *giernan*, to yearn, be desirous; later *gyrnan*, Grein, i. 537; formed (by the usual change of *eo* to *ie*) from AS. *georn*, adj., desirous, eager, id. i. 500. Cf. also *georndon*, desired; A. S. Chron. an. 1011; which better agrees with the ME. form.+Icel. *girna*, to desire; from *gjarn*, eager; Goth. *gairnjan*, to long for, from *-gairns*, desirous, only in the comp. *faihu-gairns*, covetous, lit. desirous of money. β. The verb answers to a Teut. type **gernjan-*, from the adj. **ger-noz*, desirous of. Again, the adj. is formed (with Idg. suffix *-no*) from the base GER, appearing in OHG. *gerōn, kerōn*, mod. G. *be-gehren*, to long for.—√GHER, to desire; whence also Gk. *χαίρειν*, to rejoice, *χαρά*, joy, L. *hor-ior*, I urge, Skt. *hary*, to desire. Der. *yearn-ing,-ly*. ☞ *Not* connected with *earnest* (1), but with *hor-tatory*.

YEARN (2), to grieve. (E.) This verb, not often well explained, occurs several times in Shak.; and it is remarkable that Shak. *never* uses *yearn* in the sense 'to long for,' i. e. he never uses it in the sense of the verb *yearn* (1) above. It is often spelt *earn* or *ern* in old editions. The proper sense is *intransitive*, to grieve, mourn, Hen. V, ii. 3. 3, ii. 3. 6; Jul. Cæs. ii. 2. 129; it is also *transitive*, to grieve, vex, Merry Wives, iii. 5. 45; Rich. II, v. 5. 76; Hen. V, iv. 3. 26. Other authors use it besides Shakespeare; as in the following examples. 'I must do that my heart-strings *yearn* [mourn] to do;' Beaum. and Fletcher, Bonduca, iv. 4 (Judas); and see Richardson. Nares gives *yernful*, grievous, melancholy; so also prov. E. *ernful* (Halliwell, Pegge). β. In the form *yern* or *yearn*, it is prob. the same as *yearn* (1) above; with a change of sense from 'desire' to 'regret.' γ. In the form *ern* or *earn* it answers to AS. *eorn-* as found in *eorn-igende*, murmuring, *eornfullnes*, anxiety, Matt. xiii. 22. From a verb *eornian*, which seems to be a mere variant of *geornian*, to yearn for, desire. If so, *yearn* (2) is merely *yearn* (1) with a change of sense. Cf. 'His heart did *earne* (i. e. yearn) To proue his puissance;' Spenser, F. Q. i. i. 3. ¶ Possibly influenced by ME. *ermen*, to grieve; see Gloss. to Chaucer.

YEAST, the froth of malt liquors in fermentation, a preparation which raises dough. (E.) ME. *зeest*. '*Зeest*, berme, Spuma;' Prompt. Parv. p. 537. AS. *gist*; spelt *gyst*, A. S. Leechdoms, ed. Cockayne, i. 118, l. 10.+Du. *gest*; Icel. *jast, jastr*; Swed. *jäst*; [Dan. *gjær*]; G. *gäscht, gischt*, MHG. *jest, gest, gist*. β. The Teut. type is **yes-t-*, formed (with suffix *-t-*) from the base YES, to ferment; appearing in MSwed. *gäsa*, OHG. *jesan*, MHG. *jesen, gesen, gern*, whence mod. G. *gähren* (causal).—√YES, to foam, ferment; whence Skt. *nir-yāsa-*, exudations of trees, Gk. *ζέειν*, to boil, *ζεστός*, fervent. Der. *yeast-y*, spelt *yesty* in Shak. Macb. iv. 1. 53, Hamlet, v. 2. 199, just as *yeast* is also written *yest*, Wint. Tale, iii. 3. 94; the sense is 'frothy.' [Not allied to AS. *ȳst*, a storm.]

YEDE, went. (E.) Obsolete. Also spelt *yode*, Spenser, F. Q. ii. 7. 2. Spenser, unaware that *yede* and *yode* are varying forms of the same past tense, and that the verb is only used in the past tense, wrongly uses *yede* or *yeed* as an infinitive mood (!); F. Q. i. 11. 5; ii. 4. 2. ME. *зede, yede*, Chaucer, C. T., G 1141, 1281; *yode*, Sir Eglamour (Thornton Romances), 531; *зeode*, King Horn, ed. Lumby, 381, 1025; *eode, зeode*, Rob. of Glouc. pp. 53, 79; ll. 1217, 1766. The proper form is *eode* (Stratmann); it is probable that the forms *yede* and *yode* answer rather to AS. *ge-ēode*, with prefixed *ge-*, as in the case of *yean* and *ean*, see **Yean.** AS. *ēode*, went, only in the past tense; pl. *ēodon*; Grein, i. 256. β. The pl. *ēodon* may be compared with the Goth. pl. *iddjēdun*, they went. The Goth. *iddja*, sing., answers to Skt. *ayāt*, he went; from the base *yā*, to go, allied to √EI, to go, as in Gk. *εἶ-μι*, I shall go. See *iddja* in Uhlenbeck; Streitberg, § 190; Brugmann, i. § 309 (2); ii. § 478. Cf. **Year.**

YELK, the same as **Yolk,** q. v.

YELL, to utter a loud noise, to howl. (E.) ME. *зellen, yellen*, Chaucer, C. T. 2674, 15395 (A 2672, B 4579). AS. *geāllan, giellan*,

gyllan, to yell, cry out, resound; Grein, i. 423.+Du. *gillen*; Icel. *gella*; also *gjalla* (pt. t. *gall*); Dan. *gjælle, gjalde* (for *gialle*); Swed. *gälla*, to ring, resound; G. *gellen*, to resound. β. All from the Teut. type **gellan-*, pt. t. **gall*; allied to Teut. type **galan-*, to sing, as seen in Icel. *gala*, to sing (pt. t. *gōl*, pp. *galinn*), AS. *galan* (pt. t. *gōl*), OHG. *galan*, to sing; see **Nightingale.** Der. *yell*, sb., Oth. i. 1. 75; also *stan-iel*, q. v.

YELLOW, of a bright golden colour. (E.) ME. *yelow*, Chaucer, C. T. 2168, 2172 (A 2166, 2170). Also spelt *зelu, зeoluh*, &c.; Stratmann. AS. *geolo, geolu* (acc. fem. *geolwe*), Grein, i. 497.+Du. *geel*; G. *gelb*, OHG. *gelo*. β. The Teut. type is **gelwoz*; Idg. type **ghelwos*, Fick, iii. 103. Further allied to L. *heluus*, light yellow; Russ. *zelenuii*, green, Gk. *χλόη*, young verdure of trees, *χλωρός*, green, Skt. *hari-*, green, yellow. Further allied to **Gall** (1). Der. *yellow-ness*; *yellow fever*, a malignant fever that often turns the skin yellow; *yellow-ish*, spelt *yelowysshe* in Palsgrave; *yellow-ish-ness*. Also *yellow-hammer*, q. v.; *yel-k, yol-k*.

YELLOW-HAMMER, YELLOW-AMMER, a song-bird, named from its yellow colour. (E.) In Ash's Dict., ed. 1775. Spelt *yellow-hamer*, Harrison, Desc. of England, bk. iii. ch. 2 (end). Beyond doubt, the *h* is an ignorant insertion, due to substitution of a known for an unknown word, irrespective of the sense. Yet the name is E., and very old. The former part of the word (*yellow*) is explained above; the latter part is the AS. *amore*. In a list of birds, we find: 'Scorellus, *amore*,' Voc. 260. 27. Much older forms are AS. *omer*, Corpus gloss., 1810; *emer*, Epinal gloss., 909. Cognate words occur both in Du. and G.+MDu. *emmerick, emmerlinck*, 'a kind of merlin or a hawke,' Hexham; Low G. *geel-emerken*, a yellow-ammer; G. *gelb-ammer, gold-ammer*, yellow-ammer, gold-ammer; also *emmerling*, a yellow-ammer; OHG. *amero*, an ammer.

YELP, to bark, bark shrilly. (E.) ME. *зelpen, gelpen*, only in the sense to boast, boast noisily; but it is the same word. 'I kepe not of armes for to *yelpe*;' Chaucer, C. T. 2240 (A 2238). AS. *gilpan, gielpan, gylpan*, to boast, exult; orig. to talk noisily; Grein, i. 509. A strong verb; pt. *gealp*, pp. *golpen*; whence *gilp, gielp, gelp, gylp*, boasting, arrogance, id.+Icel. *gjālpa*, to yelp; cf. *gjālfra*, to roar as the sea; MHG. *gelfen*. β. From a base GELP, to make a loud noise. allied to **Yell.** And cf. **Yap.** Der. *yelp*, sb.

YEOMAN, a man of small estate, an officer of the royal household. (E.) ME. *зeman, yeman, зoman*; in Chaucer, C. T. 101, the Lansdowne MS. has *зoman*, whilst the rest have *зeman* or *yeman*. In Sir Amadas (pr. in Weber's Met. Rom. vol. iii), l. 347, it is written *yomon*; but the usual spelling is *зeman*, as above, and as in Allit. Poems, ed. Morris, A. 534 (or 535). In Will. of Palerne, l. 3649, however, we have *зomen*, pl.; and *зoman, yoman*, sing., Cursor Mundi, 3077, 7822. I know not where to find an example earlier than the 13th century. β. The variation of the vowel in the ME. forms is curious, but we find other examples almost as remarkable; thus we find ME. *chēsen*, to choose, from AS. *cēosan*, and mod. E. *choose*, answering to AS. *cēosan*, with the stress on *ō*, instead of *ē*. So also AS. *gēar*, E. *year*, as compared with AS. *geāra*, E. *yore*. And the AS. *scēotan* gives both ME. *shēten* and mod. E. *shoot*. γ. The word does not appear in AS.; but it would (judging by the foregoing examples) take the form **gēa-man*, regularly corresponding to OFriesic *gā-man*, a villager; and, as the AS. *ēa* (OFr. *ā*) answers to G. *au*, the first syllable is cognate with G. *gau*, Goth. *gawi*. [The alleged AS. *gā* is incorrect. Kemble, Saxons in England, b. i. c. 3, treats of the *gā* or district, though he gives no reference to show where the word occurs; Leo (A. S. Glossar) gives *gā*, a district, as in *Ohtgagā, Noxgagā*, but we cannot draw such an inference from these examples.] It will be observed that the AS. assumed form **gēa* would produce ME. *yē-*, whilst the form **geā* would produce *yō-*; as in *year, yore*. δ. And in fact, we find AS. *Sūðri-gēa*, i. e. Southern district, in the A. S. Chron. an. 836, 855; as well as other examples, for which see H. M. Chadwick's Studies in O. English, p. 147, in Trans. Camb. Phil. Soc. 1899, vol. iv. pt. 2. Cf. OFriesic *gā, gō* (nom. pl. *gāe*), a district, village; whence *gāman*, a villager; *gāfolk*, people of a village. Also Du. *gouw, gouwe*, a province; MDu. *gouwe*, 'a hamlet where houses stand scattered, a countrie village, or a field; *goograve* or *gograef*, a field-judge; *goy-lieden* or *goy-mannen*, arbitrators, or men appointed to take up a businesse betwenee man and man;' Hexham. Also Low G. *goë, gohe*, a tract of country, *go-grāve*, a judge in one of the 4 districts of Bremen, Brem. Wörterbuch; Bavarian *gäu*, whence *gäumann*, a peasant. Cf. also G. *gau*, a province, OHG. *gowi, gewi*, Goth. *gawi*. Der. *yeoman-ry*, where *-ry* is used as a collective suffix; spelt *yomanry*, Dictes of the Philosophers, pr. by Caxton, fol. 42 b.

YERK, in Shak. Hen. V, iv. 7. 83; equivalent to **Jerk,** q. v.

YES, a word denoting affirmation. (E.) A much stronger form than *yea*, and often accompanied, in old authors, by an oath. ME.

ȝus, ȝis, P. Plowman, B. v. 125; 'ȝis, be marie,' Will. of Palerne, 1567; 'ȝis, bi crist,' id. 5149. AS. gise, gese; 'gise, lā gese' = yes, O, yes; Ælfred, tr. of Boethius, b. ii. met. 6; cap. xvi. § 4. Probably contracted from gēa swā, yea, so; cf. AS. nese, a form of denial. from ne swā, not so.

YESTERDAY, the day last past. (E.) ME. ȝistirdai, Wyclif, John, iv. 52. AS. geostra, giestra, gystra (yester-), Grein, i. 501; and dæg, a day; commonly in the acc. geostran dæg, yesterday.+ Du. gisteren, dag van gister; G. gestern; Goth. gistra-dagis, to-morrow. β. Cf. L. hester-nus, adj. belonging to yesterday, where the syllable hes- is cognate with Icel. gær, Dan. gaar, Swed. går, L. heri, Gk. χθές, Skt. hyas, yesterday. The suffix -ter- is a comparative form, as in in-ter-ior, ex-ter-ior, &c. Brugmann, i. §§ 624, 923. Der. Similarly, yester-night.

YET, moreover, besides, hitherto, still, nevertheless. (E.) ME. ȝit, ȝet, yet, Chaucer, C. T. 565 (A 563). AS. git, get, giet, gyt; Grein, i. 511.+OFries. ieta, eta, ita, yet; mod. Fries. jiette (Richtofen); MHG. iezuo, ieze; whence G. jelzt, now. Origin obscure.

YEW, an evergreen tree. (E.) Spelt yowe in Palsgrave. ME. ew, Chaucer, C. T. 2925 (A 2923). AS. īw, to translate L. taxus, Voc. 138. 14; spelt iuu, 49. 38.+Icel. ȳr; G. eibe; OHG. īwa. β. The Teut. type is *īwā, f., or *īwoz, m. The Celtic type is *īwo-, as in OIrish eo, W. yw, Corn. hiuin, Bret. ivin, yew (Stokes-Fick, p. 46). Of unknown origin. ¶ Distinct from ivy.

YEX, to hiccough. (E.) Prov. E. yex (Halliwell); spelt yeske in Palsgrave. ME. ȝexen, ȝesken, ȝoxen, Chaucer, C. T. 4149 (A 4151). 'ȝyxyn, yexen, Singulcio, Singulto;' Prompt. Parv., p. 539. AS. giscian, to sob, sigh; Ælfred, tr. of Boethius, b. i. met. 1. c. 2. Cf. OLow G. geskon, to yawn (Gallée). Probably an extension from the Teut. base *gi-, weak grade of *gei-, base of gī-nan, to gape; just as L. hiscere, to yawn, gape, is extended from L. hi-āre. See Yawn, Hiatus.

YIELD, to resign, grant, produce, submit, give way. (E.) The orig. sense was 'to pay.' ME. gelden, ȝelden, yelden; a strong verb; pt. t. yald, pp. yolden. Chaucer has un-yolden, C. T. 2644 (A 2642). In P. Plowman, B. xii. 193, we have both yald (strong) and ȝelte (weak), as forms of the pt. t. AS. gieldan, geldan, gildan, to pay, restore, give up; pt. t. geald, pl. guldon, pp. golden, Grein, i. 508. +Du. gelden; Icel. gjalda, pt. t. galt, pp. goldinn; Dan. gjelde; Swed. gälla (for *gälda), to be of consequence, be worth; G. gelten, to be worth, pt. t. galt, pp. gegolten; Goth. -gildan, only in the compounds fra-gildan, ūs-gildan, to pay back. β. All from Teut. type *geld-an-, to be worth, to pay for, repay. Allied to OIrish gell, a pledge; gell-aim, I promise, engage (Stokes-Fick, p. 113). Der. yield, sb.; yield-ing, -ly; also guild or gild; but hardly guilt.

YOKE, the frame of wood joining oxen for drawing, a similar frame for carrying pails, a mark of servitude, a pair. (E.) ME. ȝok, yok, Chaucer, C. T. 7989 (E 113). AS. geoc, gioc, ioc, a yoke; Grein, i. 497.+Du. juk; Icel. ok; Dan. aag; Swed. ok; Goth. juk; G. joch, OHG. joh. Teut. type *yokom, n.; Idg. type *yugom, n.+ W. iau; L. iugum (whence Ital. giogo, Span. yugo, F. joug); Russ. igo; Lithuan. jungas; Gk. ζυγόν; Skt. yuga-, a yoke, pair, couple. β. All from the Idg. type *yug-om, a yoke; lit. 'that which joins.' From *yug-, weak grade of √YEUG (Teut. YEUK), to join; see Join. Der. yoke, verb, Two Gent. i. 1. 40; yoke-fellow, companion, K. Lear, iii. 6. 39.

YOKEL, a country bumpkin. (E.) 'This was not done by a yokel;' Dickens, Oliver Twist, ch. 31. Lowl. Sc. yochel, a stupid, awkward person (E. D. D.); prov. E. yokel, the plough-boy who does the day's ploughing or yoking; W. Yksh. (id.); from yoke, the time during which a ploughman and his team work at a stretch (id.). Cf. ME. ȝok, to attach a team to a cart, Barbour's Bruce, x. 215. Note yokelet, an old name (in Kent) for a little farm or manor; noticed by Somner in his A. S. Dict., s. v. Iocle'.

YOLK, YELK, the yellow part of an egg. (E.) Spelt yelke in Palsgrave. ME. ȝolke, Morte Arthure, 3283; ȝelke, Prompt. Parv. p. 537. AS. geolca, gioleca, the yolk; Grein, i. 497. Lit. 'the yellow part.'—AS. geolu, yellow; see Yellow.

YON, at a distance. (E.) Properly an adj., as in prov. E., in which such phrases as 'yon house' and 'yon field' are common. Common in Shak., Mids. Nt. Dr. iii. 2. 188, &c. ME. ȝon, P. Plowman, C. xxi. 149 (also ȝeon, and even ȝond, ȝeond, see the footnote). AS. geon, yon; 'tō geonre byrg' = to yon city; Ælfred, tr. of Gregory's Past. Care, ed. Sweet, p. 443, l. 25; where geon-re is the dat. fem.+Icel. enn, the (orig. that), used as the def. art., and often miswritten hinn; see Vigfusson's remarks on hinn; Goth. jains, yon, that; G. jener, MHG. gener, yon, that. β. The Teut. types appear to be *yainoz, *yinoz; which render difficult a relation to Skt. yas, who, that; cf. Brugmann, i. § 308. Der. yond, adv., Temp. i. 2. 409 (also incorrectly used instead of yon, Temp. ii. 2. 20),

from AS. geond, adv., but often used as a prep., Grein, i. 497; cf. Goth. jaind, adv., there, John, xi. 8. Hence be-yond, q.v. Also yond-er (not in AS.), ME. yonder, adv., Chaucer, C. T. 5438 (B 1018); cf. Goth. jaindrē, adv., yonder, there, Luke, xi. 37.

YORE, in old time, long ago. (E.) ME. ȝore, yore, Chaucer, C. T. 4594 (B 174). AS. geāra, formerly (with the usual change from ā to long o, as in stān > stone); Grein, i. 496. Orig. gēara, gen. pl. of gēar, a year, so that the sense was 'of years,' i.e. in years past; the gen. case being often used to express the time when, as in dæges—by day, &c. See Year.

YOU, pl. of second pers. pronoun; see Ye. Der. you-r, q.v.

YOUNG, not long born, new to life. (E.) ME. ȝong, yong, yung. In Chaucer, C. T. 79, we have the indef. form yong (misprinted yonge in Tyrwhitt); whilst in l. 7 we have the def. form yongë (dissyllabic). AS. geong, giung, iung (and even geng, ging), young; Grein, i. 499.+Du. jong; Icel. ungr, jungr; Dan. and Swed. ung; G. jung; OHG. junc; Goth. juggs (written for jungs). β. All from a Teut. type *yungoz, a contracted form of *yuwungoz, answering to the cognate OIrish ōac, W. ieuanc, young, and to the L. form iuuencus, an extension (with Idg. suffix -kos) from iuuen-is, young. γ. The base *yuwen-, young, occurs in L. iuuenis, young, Skt. yuvan, young, Russ. iunuii, young, Lithuan. jaunas, young. [The lit. sense is perhaps 'protected,' from √YEU, to guard; cf. Skt. yu, to keep back, L. iuuāre, to aid, help; Fick, i. 732.] Brugmann, i. § 280. Der. young, sb.; young-ish; young-ling, Spenser, F. Q. i. 10. 57, ME. ȝonglyng, Wyclif, Mark, xvi. 5, with double dimin. suffix -l-ing; young-ster, as to which see Spinster. Also younker, Spenser, F. Q. iv. 1. 11, and in G. Douglas, tr. of Virgil, bk. viii. l. 11; borrowed from Du. jonker, also written jonkheer, compounded of jong, young, and heer, a lord, sir, gentleman; Hexham has MDu. jonck-heer or joncker, 'a young gentleman or a joncker' (sic). Also you-th, q.v.

YOUR, possess. pron. of 2nd person. (E.) Properly the possess. pron. of the 2nd person plural, but commonly used instead of thy, which was considered too familiar, and has almost passed out of use in speech. ME. ȝour, your, Chaucer, C. T. 2251 (A 2249). Orig. the gen. pl. of the 2nd pers. pronoun; a use which occurs even in ME., as: 'ich am ȝoure aller hefd' = I am head of you all, P. Plowman, C. xxii. 473; where aller = AS. ealra, gen. pl. of eall, all. AS. eōwer, your; orig. gen. of gē, ye; see Ye. Der. your-s, ME. youres, Chaucer, C. T. 13204 (B 1464), from AS. eōwres, gen. sing. masc. and neut. of eōwer, poss. pronoun; Grein, i. 263. Also yourself (see Self).

YOUTH, early life. (E.) ME. youthe, Chaucer, C. T. 463 (A 461); older forms ȝuweðe, Ancren Riwle, p. 156, l. 22; ȝuȝeðe, Layamon, 6566; ȝeoȝeðe, id. 19837. AS. geoguð, gioguð, youth, Grein, i. 502. [The middle g first turned to w or ȝ, and then disappeared.]+OSax. juguð; Du. jeugd; G. jugend, OHG. jugund; we also find OHG. jungedi. Cf. Goth. junda, youth. β. The AS. geoguð stands for *geoguð < *geogunð, Teut. type *yugunðiz, for *yuwunþiz, f.; from Idg. base *yuwan-ti-, which is from *yuwen-, young; see Young. Cf. L. iuuenta, Skt. yuvatā, youth. We also find a later ME. form ȝungthe, youth, Prompt. Parv. p. 539, ȝongthe, Wyclif, Mark, x. 20. Der. youth-ful, -ly, youth-ful-ness.

YOWL; a variant of Yawl (2); q.v.

YUCCA, a genus of American liliaceous plants. (Span.— Caribbean). 'They have also another kynde of rootes, whiche they call Iucca;' R. Eden, First Three E. Books on America, ed. Arber, p. 67; where they refers to the people of Hayti. Spelt yuca, tr. of Acosta, bk. iv. c. 17.—Span. yuca, yucca. From the old (Caribbean) language as spoken in Hayti. See Notes on E. Etym., p. 346.

YULE, Christmas. (E.) 'Yu-batch, Christmas batch; yu-block or yule-block, Christmas block; yu-gams or yule-gams, Christmas games;' Ray's Gloss. of N. Country Words. Here yu is short for yule. ME. ȝole; 'the feste of ȝole,' Rob. of Brunne, tr. of Langtoft, p. 65, l. 6; whence ȝole-stok, a yule-stock or yule-log, Voc. 657. 6. AS. iula, geōla. Spelt iula, Grein, i. 148. Spelt geōla in the following: 'Se mōnað is nemned on Leden Decembris, and on ūre geðeode se ærra geōla, forðan ðā mōnðas twegen syndon nemde ānum naman, ōðer se ærra geōla, ōðer se æftera, forþan ðe hyra ōðer gangeð beforan ðæra [read ðære] sunnan ærþon þe hēo cyrre hig tō ðæs dæges lenge, ōðer æfter,' i. e. This month is named Decembris in Latin, and in our tongue the former Yule, because two months are named with one name; one is the former Yule, the other the after Yule, because one of them comes before the sun, viz. before it turns itself about [at the winter solstice] to the lengthening of day, whilst the other [January] comes after; MS. Cotton, Tib. B. 1, quoted in Hickes, Thesaurus, i. 212. Beda, De Temporum Ratione, cap. 13, has the same account (but in Latin), and calls the Yule-months Menses Giuli; i.e. he Latinises Yule as Giulus. Spelt geol, *gehhol, gehhel*, Laws of Ælfred, § 5, and § 43; in Thorpe, Ancient Laws, i. 64, note 54; i. 92, note 4; *geohol*, tr. of Beda, bk. iv. c. 19. The AS. form appears to represent a Teut. type *yeh-ol-oz, or *yehw-loz, m.+Icel. *jōl*; Dan. *juul*; Swed. *jul*. We may also note that, in a fragment of a Gothic calendar (pr. in Massmann's Ulfilas, p. 590), November appears to be called *fruma Jiuleis*, which seems to mean 'the first Yule;' a name not necessarily inconsistent with the AS. use, since November may once have *also* been reckoned as a Yule-month. This Goth. form answers to Icel. *ȝlir*, December. ¶ Origin unknown; for guesses, see Uhlenbeck, Goth. Dict. The usual attempt to connect this word with E. *wheel*, AS. *hwēol*, Icel. *hjōl*, with the far-fetched explanation that the sun *turns* at the winter solstice, cannot be admitted, since an initial *h* or *hw* makes all the difference. Besides *Yule* did not denote the shortest day, but *a season*. Brugmann, i. § 681. **Der.** *jolly*.

YWIS, certainly. (E.) In Spenser, F. Q. ii. 1. 19. ME. *ywis*, Chaucer, C. T. 3277; *iwis*, Ancren Riwle, p. 270, l. 11. AS. *gewis*, adj., certain, *gewislice*, adv., certainly, Grein, i. 483. The adj. came to be used adverbially.+Du. *gewis*, adj. and adv., certain, certainly; Icel. *viss*, certain; Dan. *vis*, certain; *vist*, certainly; Swed. *viss*, certain; *visst*, certainly; G. *gewiss*, certainly. β. The *ge-* is a mere prefix; see **Y-**. The adj. answers to a Teut. type *wissoz, Idg. type *wid-tos, an old pp. signifying 'known,' hence 'sure;' from **wid-*, weak grade of √WEID, to know. See **Wit**, verb. Cf. Goth. *wissa*, I knew. Brugmann, i. § 794 e. ¶ It is particularly to be noted that the commonest form in MSS. is *iwis*, in which the prefix (like most other prefixes) is frequently written *apart* from the rest of the word, and not unfrequently the *i* is represented by a capital letter, so that it appears as *I wis*. Hence, by an extraordinary error, the *I* has often been mistaken for the 1st pers. pron., and the verb *wis*, to know, has been thus created, and is given in many dictionaries! But it is a pure fiction, and the more remarkable because there actually exists a ME. causal verb *wissien*, or *wissen*, but it means to teach, show, instruct. We should distinguish between the ME. words *wit*, *wot*, *wistë*, *wist*, *I wissë*, and *i-wis*.

Z

ZAMINDAR, ZEMINDAR, a land-holder, occupant of land. (Hind.—Pers.) Spelt *zemindar* in 1778 (Yule). Hind. *zamīndār*, vernacularly *jamīndār*, corruptly *zemīndār*, an occupant of land, a land-holder; Wilson, Ind. Terms, p. 562.—Pers. *zamīn*, earth, land, soil; *dār*, holding, possessing, Rich. Dict. pp. 782, 646. Here Pers. *zamīn* is allied to L. *humus*, ground; and Pers. *dār* to Skt. *dhṛ*, to hold; see **Homage** and **Firm**.

ZANANA, ZENANA, female apartments. (Hind.—Pers.) Spelt *zunana* in 1761 (Yule). Hindustāni *zanāna*, vernacularly *janāna*, incorrectly *zenana*, the female apartments; sometimes, the females of a family.—Pers. *zanān*, women; pl. of *zan*, a woman. Allied to Gk. γυνή, a woman, and E. *quean*. H. H. Wilson, Gloss. of Indian Terms, p. 564; Rich. Dict. p. 783; Horn, § 668.

ZANY, a buffoon, a mimic. (Ital.—Gk.—Heb.) In L. L. L. v. 2. 463; and in Beaum. and Fletcher, Cupid's Revenge, ii. 6 (Bacha).—MItal. *Zane*, 'the name of Iohn, also a sillie Iohn, a gull, a noddie; used also for a simple vice, clowne, foole, or simple fellowe in a plaie;' Florio. Mod. Ital. *Zanni*; cf. OF. *zani* (Godefroy). *Zane* and *Zanni* are familiar forms of *Giovanni*, John.—Gk. Ἰωάννης; John, i. 6.—Heb. *Yōkhānān*, i. e. the Lord graciously gave.—Heb. *Yō*, the Lord; and *khānan*, to show mercy. **Der.** *zany*, verb, Beaum. and Fletcher, Qu. of Corinth, i. 2 (Crates).

ZARIBA, ZAREEBA, ZEREBA, a temporary camp, fenced round with bushes, &c. (Arab.) Chiefly used in the Soudan.—Arab. *zarība(t)*, 'a fold, a pen; an enclosure for cattle; den, or haunt of wild beasts;' lurking-place of a hunter;' Rich. Dict. p. 775.

ZEAL, fervour, ardour. (F.—L.—Gk.) Spelt *zele* in Palsgrave; *zeele* in Caxton, Godfrey of Bologne, prol. p. 2, l. 8.—MF. *zele*, 'zeale,' Cot. Mod. F. *zèle*.—L. *zēlum*, acc. of *zēlus*, zeal.—Gk. ζῆλος, zeal, ardour. Doric ζᾶλος; Idg. type *yālos; perhaps from *yā*, to drive, as in Skt. *yā-tṛ*, a driver (Prellwitz). **Der.** *zeal-ous*, L. L. L. v. 2. 116; *zeal-ous-ly*. Also *zeal-ot*, Selden's Table-Talk, s. v. *Zealot*, from MF. *zelote*, 'jealous, or zealous,' Cot., from L. *zēlōtēs*, Gk. ζηλωτής. And see *jealous*.

ZEBRA, a striped animal of the horse kind. (Port.—W. African.) Added by Todd to Johnson. Described in Purchas's Pilgrimage (1617), bk. vi. ch. i. § 2.—Port. *zebra*. (Also Span. *zebra, cebra*.) The animal is a native of S. Africa, and the name originated in Congo; see N. and Q. 9 S. v. 480. According to Littré, it is Ethiopian; he

cites: 'Pecora, congensibus *zebra*, dicta,' Ludolph, Histor. Ethiop. i. 40. But Littré is mistaken as to the true source.

ZEBU, the humped domestic ox of India. (F.—Thibet.) See *Zebu* in Yule.—F. *zébu*, a name taken by Buffon from the exhibitors of such a beast at a French fair. A perversion of *zobo*, a name for a male hybrid between a yak-bull and a hill-cow (Yule).—Thibet. *mdzo-po*, the male of *madzo*, a mongrel bred of a yak-bull and a common cow; the female mongrel is called *mdzo-mo*.

ZECCHINO, a gold coin of Venice. (Ital.—Arab.) The pl. *zecchins* occurs in Sandys, Travels (1632), p. 3.—Ital. *zecchino*, a sequin.—Ital. *secca*, a mint (Florio).—Arab. *sikka(t)*, pron. *sikkah*, a die for coins. **Doublet**, *sequin*.

ZED, the name of the letter Z. (F.—L.—Gk.) In Shak. K. Lear, ii. 2. 69.—F. *zède*.—L. *zēta*.—Gk. ζῆτα. **Doublet**, *izzard*, q. v.

ZEDOARY, an East-Indian root resembling ginger. (F.—Low L.—Pers.) 'Zedoary, a spicy root, very like ginger, but of a sweeter scent, and nothing near so biting; it is a hot and dry plant, growing in the woods of Malabar in the E. Indies;' Phillips, ed. 1706. Spelt *zedoari*, Hakluyt, Voy. vol. ii. pt. 1. 277; col. 1. [In old F., the name was corrupted to *citoal, citoual, citouart* (Roquefort); whence the ME. *cetewale*, Chaucer, C. T. 13691 (B 1951), on which see my note.]—MF. *zedoaire*, 'an East-Indian root which resembleth ginger;' Cot.—Low L. *zedoāria*.—Pers. *zadwār, zidwār*, zedoary; Rich. Dict. p. 771; or *jadwār*, zedoary, id. p. 794. The initial letter is sometimes the 13th, sometimes the 14th letter of the Pers. alphabet; see Palmer, Pers. Dict., col. 314.

ZEMSTVO, a local elective assembly. (Russ.) Russ. *zemstvo*, collective sb., the county-courts (Reiff).

ZENITH, the point of the heavens directly overhead. (F.—Span.—Arab.) ME. *senith*, Chaucer, On the Astrolabe, i. 18. 4.—OF. *cenith* (Littré); mod. F. *zénith*.—Span. *zenit*, formerly written *zenith*, as in Minsheu's Span. Dict.—Arab. *samt*, a way, road, path, tract, quarter; whence *samt-ur-ras*, the zenith, vertical point of the heavens, also *as-samt*, an azimuth; Rich. Dict. p. 848. *Samt* was pronounced *semt*, of which Span. *zenith* or *zenit* is a corruption; in the sense of zenith, it is an abbreviation for *samt-ur-ras* or *semt-er-ras*, lit. the way overhead, from *ras*, the head, Rich. Dict. p. 715. The word *azimuth*, q. v., is from the same source. See Devic, Supp. to Littré.

ZEPHYR, a soft gentle breeze. (F.—L.—Gk.) In Shak. Cymb. iv. 2. 172. Chaucer has the form *Zephirus*, directly from the Latin, C. T. 5.—MF. *zephyre*, 'the west wind,' Cot.; F. *zéphyr*.—L. *zephyrum*, acc. of *zephyrus*, the west wind.—Gk. ζέφυρος, the west wind.

ZERO, a cipher, nothing, denoted by o. (F.—Ital.—Low L.—Arab.) A late word, added by Todd to Johnson.—MF. *zero*, 'a cypher in arithmetick, a thing that stands for nothing,' Cot.; F. *zéro*.—Ital. *zero*, 'a figure of nought in arithmetike;' Florio. A contracted form of *zefiro* or *zifro, parallel form to *zifra*, 'a cifre,' i. e. cipher; Florio. —Low L. *zephyrum* (Devic).—Arab. *sifr* (with initial *sad*), a cipher; Rich. Dict. p. 937. See **Cipher**. See Devic, Supp. to Littré; he explains that the old Latin treatises on arithmetic wrote *zephyrum* for Arab. *sifr*, which became, in Italian, *zefiro*, and (by contraction) *zero*. **Doublet**, *cipher*.

ZEST, something that gives a relish or a flavour. (F.—L.—Gk.) In Skinner's Dict., ed. 1671. Phillips explains *zest* as a chip of orange or lemon-peel, used for flavouring drinks.—MF. *zest*, 'the thick skinne or filme wherby the kernell of a wallnut is divided;' Cot. Mod. F. *zeste*, a piece of the skin of a citron or lemon, whence *zester*, 'to cut up lemon rind;' Hamilton. The E. sense is due to the use of lemon or citron-peel for flavouring.—L. *schistos* (*schistus*), cleft, divided, used by Pliny [bk. xix. c. 6]; according to Diez, who notes that L. *schedula* became, similarly, F. *cédule*; there must have been a transference of sense from 'divided' to 'division.' —Gk. σχιστός, divided.—Gk. σχίζειν, to cleave. See **Schism**. (Very doubtful; but no other solution has been proposed.)

ZIGZAG, having short, sharp turns. (F.—G.) In Pope, Dunciad, i. 124.—F. *zigzag*.—G. *zickzack*, a zigzag; whence *zickzack segeln*, to tack, in sailing. [We also find Swed. *sicksack*, zigzag (Widegren, 1788).] Reduplicated from *zacke*, a tooth, with reference to *zacken-werk*, notched work; so that *zickzack* means 'in an indented manner.' Cf. EFries. *takken*, to notch (whence *tack*, in sailing). See **Tack**. **Der.** *zigzagg-ery*, Sterne, Tristram Shandy, bk. iii. c. 3.

ZINC, a whitish metal. (G.) In Locke, Elements of Nat. Philosophy, c. 8 (R.).—G. *zink*, zinc; whence also F. *zinc*, &c. Origin uncertain; see Schade. The name *der Zinck* occurs in Paracelsus (died 1541); see Weigand.

ZIRCON, the name of a mineral. (Arab.—Pers.) The F. form is *jargon*. *Zircon* represents the Arab. *zarqūn*, not a true Arab. word, but from Pers. *zargūn*, of the colour of gold; Rich. Dict. p. 774.—Pers. *zar*, gold (allied to Skt. *hari-*, yellow, and E. *yellow*); and *gūn*, colour; id. pp. 771, 1247. See Devic.

ZITHER, a cittern, kind of guitar. (G. – L. – Gk.) A modern form; from G. *zither.* – L. *cithara.* – Gk. κιθάρα, a kind of lyre. See **Cithern, Cittern, Guitar, Kit** (2).

ZODIAC, an imaginary belt in the heavens, containing the twelve constellations called *signs.* (F. – L. – Gk.) ME. *zodiac, zodiak,* Chaucer, On the Astrolabe, prol. 70. – F. *zodiaque,* 'the zodiack,' Cot. – L. *zōdiacus.* – Gk. ζωδιακός, adj., of or belonging to animals, whence ὁ ζωδιακός, the zodiac circle; so called from containing the twelve constellations represented by animals. – Gk. ζῴδιον, a small animal; dimin. of ζῷον, a living creature, an animal. β. Gk. ζῷον is from ζωός, adj., living; allied to ζωή, life, and ζάειν, ζῆν (Ionic ζώειν), to live. Allied to Zend *ji,* to live; from √GwEI, to live. See **Victuals.** Brugmann, ii. § 488. **Der.** *zodiac-al,* adj.

ZONE, a belt, one of the great belts into which the earth is divided. (F. – L. – Gk.) In Hamlet, v. 1. 305. 'Their *zone* is milde;' Higgins, Mirror for Mag., Fulgentius, st. 4. – F. *zone,* 'a girdle, zone;' Cot. – L. *zōna,* a girdle, belt, zone. – Gk. ζώνη, a girdle. Put for *ζώσνη. – Gk. ζώννυμι (= *ζωσ-νυμι), I gird. – √YOS, to gird; whence also Lithuan. *jōsta,* a girdle, *jōsti,* to gird (Nesselmann). Brugmann, i. § 167. **Der.** *zon-ed.*

ZOOLOGY, the natural history of animals. (Gk.) See Pennant's British *Zoology,* London, 1766. Coined from Gk. ζωο-, for ζῷον, a living creature; and -λογία, allied to λόγος, a discourse, from λέγειν, to speak. See **Zodiac** and **Logic.** **Der.** *zoologi-c-al, zoolog-ist.* ¶ Pronounced zo-o-, the *o*'s being separate.

ZOOPHYTE, an animal plant, a term now applied to corals, &c. (F. – Gk.) In Johnson's Dict. – F. *zoophyte,* pl. *zoophytes,* 'such things as be partly plants, and partly living creatures, as spunges, &c.;' Cot. – Gk. ζωόφυτον, a living being; an animal-plant, the lowest of the animal tribe, Aristotle, Hist. Anim. xviii. 1. 6. – Gk. ζωό-, for ζωός, living; and φυτόν, a plant, that which has grown, from φύειν, to produce, also to grow, from √BHEU, to grow, exist, be. See **Zodiac** and **Be.**

ZOUAVE, one of a body of soldiers in the French service, orig. Arabs, but now Frenchmen in Arab. dress. (F. – N. African.) Modern; since the conquest of Algeria by the French in 1830; Haydn, Dict. of Dates. – F. *Zouave.* – N. African *Zuawa,* a tribe of Kabyles living among the Jurjura mountains in Algeria (Mahn, Littré).

ZYMOTIC, a term applied to diseases, in which a poison works through the body like a ferment. (Gk.) Modern. – Gk. ζυμωτικός, causing to ferment. – Gk. ζυμόω, I leaven, cause to ferment. – Gk. ζύμη, leaven. Allied to L. *iūs,* broth; see **Juice.**

APPENDIX

I. LIST OF PREFIXES

The following is a list of the principal Prefixes in English, showing their origin. It is not quite exhaustive, but contains all of any consequence. For further information, see the etymologies of *adown*, &c., in the Dictionary.

A- (1); in a-down, a-kin, a-new, a-thirst. (E.) See **Of-** (below).

A- (2); in a-back, a-baft, a-bed, a-blaze, a-board, a-bout, a-bove, a-broach, a-broad, a-cross, a-drift, a-far, a-float, a-foot, a-fore, a-gape, a-ground, a-head, a-jar, a-kimbo, a-like, a-live, a-loof, a-main, a-mid, a-miss, a-mong, a-round, a-skew, a-slant, a-sleep, a-slope, a-stern, a-stir, a-thwart, a-way, a-work, now-a-days; &c. (E.) See **On-** (below).

A- (3); in a-long. (E.) See **An-** (5).

A- (4); in a-bide (1), a-bide (2), a-ghast, a-go, a-light, a-maze, a-rise, a-rouse, a-wake, a-waken. (E.) AS. *ā-*, intensive prefix to verbs. See note on **Arise**. And see **Ac-** (3), **Af-** (3).

A- (5); in a-bandon, a-base, a-bate, a-bet, a-beyance, a-bridge, a-but, a-chieve, a-mass, a-merce, a-mort, a-mount, a-vail, a-valanche, a-venge, a-venue, a-ver, a-vouch, a-vow (1), a-vow (2), a-wait. (F.—L.) F. *à, a-*; from L. *ad*. See **Ad-**. So also L. *a-* for *ad* before *gn*, as in a-gnate; or before *sc, sp, st*; as in a-scend, a-spect, a-stringent.

A- (6); in a-vert, a-vocation. (L.) See **Ab-** (1).

A- (7); in a-bash, a-mend, a-void. (F.—L.) See **Ex-** (1).

A- (8); in a-las. (F.—L.) OF. *a*, interj.; from L. *ah!* interj. Cf. a-lack.

A- (9); in a-byss, a-catalectic, a-cephalous, a-chromatic, a-damant, a-gnostic, a-maranth, a-methyst, a-mnesty, a-neroid, a-orist, a-pathy, a-pepsia, a-pteryx, a-sbestos, a-sphyxia, a-sylum, a-symptote, a-taxy, a-theism, a-tom, a-tomy, a-trophy, a-zote. (Gk.) See **An-** (2).

A- (10); in a-do. (E.) For *at do*.

A- (11); in a-ware. (E.) ME. *i-, y-*, prefix; AS. *ge-*. See **Af-** (2), **Y-**.

A- (12); in a-pace, a-piece. (E.) For *a pace, a piece*; *a* for *an*, indef. article. See **An-** (6).

A- (13); in a-vast. (Du. or Span.) Du. *hou vast*, hold fast; or Span. *a-basto*. (Doubtful.)

A- (14); in a-pricot. (Arab.) Arab. *al*, the; def. article. See **Al-** (4).

A- (15); in a-colyte. (Gk.) Gk. *ă-*, with; cf. Skt. *sa-*, together with.

A- (16); in a-fraid. (F.—L.) For *af-frayed*; see **Af-** (4), **Ex-** (1).

Ab- (1); in ab-dicate, ab-duce, ab-erration, ab-hor, ab-ject, ab-jure, ab-lative, ab-lution, ab-negate, ab-normal, ab-olish (?), ab-ominate, ab-origines, ab-ortion, ab-ound, ab-rade, ab-rogate, ab-rupt, ab-scind, ab-solute, ab-solve, ab-sorb, ab-surd, ab-undance, ab-use. (L.; or F.—L.) L. *ab*, from, orig. form *ap*, for which see **Aperient**, p. 25; lengthened to *abs-* in abs-cond, &c.; cf. Gk. ἄψ.+E. *of*; Gk. ἀπό; Skt. *apa*, away from. This prefix also appears as *a-* (6), *adv-, av-, v-*; as in a-vert, a-vocation, adv-ance, av-aunt, v-anguard.

Ab- (2); in ab-breviate. (L.) Used for L. *ad*; see **Ad-**.

Abs-; in abs-cess, abs-cond, abs-ent, abs-tain, abs-temious, abs-tention, abs-tract, abs-truse. (L.; or F.—L.) L. *abs-* (F. *abs-*), extended form of *ab-*; see **Ab-** (1).

Ac- (1); in ac-cede, ac-celerate, &c. (L.; or F.—L.) The form assumed by L. *ad* before the following *c*; see **Ad-**. So also before *qu*; as in ac-quaint, ac-quiesce, ac-quire, ac-quit.

Ac- (2); in ac-knowledge. (E.) ME. *a-*; from AS. *on*. Used in place of **A-** (2).

Ac- (3); in ac-cursed. (E.) For ME. *a-*; AS. *ā-*; used in place of **A-** (4).

Ad-; in ad-age, ad-agio, ad-apt, &c. (L.; or F.—L.) L. *ad*, to, at, for.+Goth. *at*; AS. *æt*; E. *at*. This prefix appears also as

a- (5), *ab-* (2), *ac-* (1), *af-* (1), *ag-*, *al-* (2), *an-* (1), *ap-* (1), *ar-* (1), *as-* (1), *at-* (1); as in a-bandon, ab-breviate, ac-cede, af-fix, ag-gress, al-lude, an-nex, ap-pend, ar-rogate, as-sign, at-tract.

Adv-; in adv-ance, adv-antage. For *av-*; F. *av-* from L. *ab*; see **Ab-** (1).

Af- (1); in af-fable, af-fect, af-feer, af-fiance, &c. The form taken by L. *ad* before *f*; see **Ad-**. So also *af-* for ME. *a-* (F. *a-* <L. *ad*); as in af-fair.

Af- (2); in af-ford. (E.) ME. *a-*; for *i-, y-*, from AS. *ge-*. See **A-** (11) and **Y-**.

Af- (3); in af-fright. (E.) ME. *a-*; from AS. *ā-*; see **A-** (4).

Af- (4); in af-fray. (F.—L.) OF. *ef-*; from L. *ex*; see **Ex-** (1).

Af- (5); in af-fair. See **Af-** (1) above.

After-; in after-math, after-most, after-ward. (E.) ME. *after*; AS. *æfter*. See **After**, p. 9.

Ag-; in ag-glomerate, ag-glutinate, ag-grandise, &c. (L.; or F.—L.) The form taken by L. *ad* before *g*; see **Ad-**.

Al- (1); in al-mighty, al-most, al-one, &c. (E.) For *all*; see **All**, p. 14.

Al- (2); in al-lege, al-leviate, &c. (L.; or F.—L.) The form taken by L. *ad* before *l*; see **Ad-**. So also *al-* for ME. *a-* (F. *a-* <L. *ad*); as in al-legiance.

Al- (3); in al-ligator. (Span.—L.) Span. *el*, def. art.—L. *ille, he*.

Al- (4); in al-batross, al-cayde, al-chemy, al-cohol, al-coran, al-cove, al-embic, al-gebra, al-guazil, al-kali. (Arab.) Arab. *al*, def. art. This also appears as *a-, ar-, as-, el-, l-*. Ex.: a-pricot, ar-tichoke, as-sagai, el-ixir, l-ute. See **L-** (2).

Al- (5); in al-legiance; see **Al-** (2).

Am- (1); in am-bush. (F.—L.) F. *em-*.—L. *im-*, for *in*, prep.; see **In-** (2). Cf. am-buscade.

Am- (2); in am-brosia. (Gk.) See **An-** (2).

Amb-; in amb-assador. Of Celtic origin; see **Ambassador**, p. 17. And see **Ambi-** below, and **Emb-**.

Ambi-, Amb-; in ambi-dextrous, amb-ient, amb-iguous, amb-ition. (L.; or F.—L.) L. *ambi-*, on both sides, around.+Gk. ἀμφί. See below.

Amphi-. (Gk.) Gk. ἀμφί, on both sides, around.+L. *ambi-*; see Ambi-.

An- (1); for L. *ad* before *n*; see **Ad-**.

An- (2), **A-** (9), negative prefix; in an-æmia, an-æsthetic, an-archy, &c. (Gk.) Gk. ἀν-, ἀ-, neg. prefix. Hence *am-* in am-brosia; *a-* in a-byss.+L. *in-*, E. *un-*; see **In-** (3), **Un-** (1), **A-** (9).

An- (3); see **Ana-**.

An- (4); in an-oint. (F.—L.) For F. *en-*.—L. *in*, prep.; see **In-** (2). It appears as *ann-* in ann-oy.

An- (5); in an-swer. (E.) AS. *and-*, in reply to, opposite to.+Goth. *and-*; Du. *ent-*; G. *ent-*; Gk. ἀντί. Shortened to *a-* in a-long; allied to *un-* in verbs. See **A-** (3), **Anti-**, **Un-** (2).

An- (6); in an-other. (E.) E. *an*; AS. *ān*. The indef. article. See **A-** (12).

An- (7); in an-ent, an-on, an-vil. (E.) ME. *an*; for AS. *on*, prep. See **On-**, **A-** (2), **Ann-**.

An- (8); in an-cestor. (F.—L.) See **Ante-**.

Ana-, An- (3); in ana-baptist, ana-chronism, &c.; an-eurysm. (Gk.) Gk. ἀνά, upon, on, up.+AS. *on*, Goth. *ana*. See **On-**.

Anci-; in anci-ent. (F.—L.) See **Ante-**.

Ann- (1); in ann-eal. (E.) See **Anneal**, p. 22.

Ann- (2); in ann-oy; OF. *an-*, F. *en*; see **An-** (4).

Ant-; in ant-agonist, ant-arctic. (Gk.) See **Anti-**.

Ante-. (L.) L. *ante*, before. Also *anti-, ant-, anci-, an-*; as in anti-cipate, ant-erior, ant-ler (cf. antique, antic); anci-ent, an-cestor.

Anth-; in anth-em. (Gk.) See below.

Anti- (1), **Ant-**. (Gk.) Gk. ἀντί, against, opposite to. Also *ant-*, *anthe-*, as in ant-agonist, ant-arctic, anthe-m. See **An-** (5), **Un-** (2).

Anti- (2); see **Ante-**.

Ap- (1); in ap-paratus, ap-pend, ap-petite, &c. (L.; *or* F.—L.) The form taken by L. *ad* before *p*; see **Ad-**, and **Ap-** (2).

Ap- (2); in ap-pall, ap-panage, ap-parel, &c. (F.—L.) Substituted for OF. *a-*, when derived from L. *ad* followed by *p*.

Ap- (3); in ap-erient. (L.) L. *ap*, *ab*; see p. 25.

Aph-; in aph-æresis, aph-orism; cf. aph-elion; see below.

Apo-. (Gk.) Hence *aph-* in aph-æresis. Gk. ἀπό, from, off.+ L. *ab*; AS. *of*; see **Ab-** (1), **Of-** (1).

Ar- (1); in ar-rogate; the form taken by L. *ad-* before *r*. Often appearing as *a-* in OF., as in ar-raign (OF. *a-rainier*), &c.; see **Ad-**.

Ar- (2); in ar-tichoke; see **Al-** (4).

Arch-, Archi-, Arche-; in arch-bishop, arch-angel, archi-tect, arche-type. (Gk.) Gk. ἀρχί-, chief.—Gk. ἄρχειν, to be first.

As- (1); in as-severate, as-siduous, as-sign, &c. (L.; *or* F.—L.) The form taken by L. *ad-* before *s*; see **Ad-**. Cf. as-certain.

As- (2); in as-sagai; see **Al-** (4).

As- (3); in as-tonish. (F.—L.) ME. *as-*, for OF. *es-*; from L. *ex*; see **Ex-** (1). Cf. as-sart.

At- (1); in at-tempt, at-tend, &c. (L.; *or* F.—L.) The form taken by L. *ad-* before *t*. Often appearing as *a-* in OF.; as in at-tend (OF. *a-tendre*); see **Ad-**.

At- (2); in at-one. (E.) E. *at*, AS. *æt*.

Auto-, Auth-, self. (Gk.) Gk. αὐτός, self. Hence *auth-* in auth-entic; *eff-* in eff-endi.

Av-; in av-aunt. (F.—L.) F. *av-*; from L. *ab*; see **Ab-** (1).

Ba-; in ba-lance; see **Bi-**.

Be-. (E.) AS. *be-*, *bi-*, the same as *bī*, by, prep.; E. *by*.

Bi- (1), double. (L.) L. *bi-*, double, from an earlier form *dui-*, related to *duo*, two.+Gk. δι-, double, allied to δύο, two; Skt. *dvi-*, allied to *dva*, two; E. *twi-* in twi-bill. Hence F. *bi-* in bi-as, F. *ba-* in ba-lance; and see below.

Bi- (2); in bi-shop. (Gk.) AS. *bi-*, for Gk. ἐπί; see **Epi-**.

Bin-; in bin-ocular. (L.) L. *bin-ī*, collective form allied to *bi-* (1) above.

Bis-; in bis-cuit. (F.—L.) F. *bis*, L. *bis*, twice; extended from *bi-* (1). See **Dis-**. Also L.; in bis-sextile.

By-; in by-path, by-way, by-word. (E.) AS. *bī*; see **By**, p. 83.

Cat-; in cat-echism; see **Cata-**.

Cata-, down. (Gk.) Gk. κατά, down, downwards. Hence *cat-*, *cath-*, in cat-echism, cath-olic.

Cath-; in cath-olic; see below.

Circum-, round. (L.) L. *circum*, around, prep. Hence *circu-* in circu-it.

Co-; see **Com-**. Cf. co-gnate, co-gnisance, co-gnition.

Coi-; see **Com-**.

Col-; see **Com-**.

Com-. (L. *or* F.—L.) L. *com-*, together, used in composition for *cum*, prep. together. It appears as *co-*, *col-*, *com-*, *comb-*, *con-*, *cor-*, *coun-*; ex.: co-agulate, col-lect, comb-ustion, com-mute, con-nect, cor-rode, coun-cil. Also as *co-* in co-st, co-stive, co-venant, co-ver, co-vin; as *cou-* in cou-ch, cou-sin; as *coi-* in coi-l; as *cu-* in cu-rfew, cu-stom; as *cur-* in curry (1); and even as *ke-* in ke-rchief.

Con-; in con-nect; see **Com-**.

Contra-, against. (L.) L. *contrā*, against. It becomes *contro-* in contro-versy; and loses final *a* in Ital. contr-alto. Hence F. *contre*, against, as in contr-ol; but the F. form is usually written *counter* in English. Hence also *countr-y*.

Cor-; in cor-rode; see **Com-**.

Cou-; in cou-ch, cou-sin; see **Com-**.

Coun-; in coun-cil, coun-sel, coun-t (1), coun-t (2), coun-tenance; see **Com-**.

Counter-. (F.—L.) See **Contra-**.

Cu-; in cu-rfew, cu-stom; see **Com-**.

Cur-; in cur-ry (1); see **Com-**.

D-; in d-affodil; see **Daffodil**, p. 152.

De- (1); in de-scend, de-bate. (L.; *or* F.—L.) L. *dē*, down, downward. Used with an oppositive sense in de-cipher, de-merit, de-form; with an intensive sense in de-clare, &c. Changed to *di-* in di-stil. Distinct from the prefix below.

De- (2); in de-bar, de-bark, de-bauch, de-bouch, de-but, de-camp, &c. (F.—L.) F. *dé-*, OF. *des-*, from L. *dis-*, apart; see **Dis-**. Distinct from the prefix above.

De- (3); in de-luge. (F.—L.) OF. *de-*; L. *dī-*, for *dis-*; see **Dis-**. And see above.

De- (4); in de-vil; see **Dia-**.

Dea-; in dea-con; see **Dia-**.

Demi-, half. (F.—L.) F. *demi-*.—L. *dimidius*, half; see **Demi-**, p. 162.

Des-; in des-cant; see **Dis-**.

Di- (1), double. (Gk.) Gk. δι-, double, allied to δίς, twice, and δύο, two; see **Bi-**. Ex. di-lemma. And see **Dia-**.

Di- (2), apart, away; in di-lute. (L.) See **Dis-**.

Di- (3); in di-stil; see **De-** (1).

Dia-. (Gk.) Gk. διά, through, between, apart; allied to **Di-** (1). Shortened to *di-* in di-æresis, di-ocese, di-optrics, di-orama, di-uretic; appearing as *de-*, *dea-*, in de-vil, dea-con.

Dif-; see **Dis-**.

Dis-, apart, away. (L.; *or* F.—L.) L. *dis-*, apart, in two, another form of *bis-*, double; *dis-* and *bis-* are variants from an older form *duis-*, double, also used in the sense in two, apart; see **Bis-**. Dis- becomes *des-* in OFrench, also *dé-* in later F.; but the OF. *des-* is sometimes altered to *dis-*, as in dis-cover. The various forms are *di-*, *dif-*, *dis-*, *des-*, *de-*, and even *s-*; as in di-gest, di-ligent, di-lute, di-mension, di-minish, di-missory, di-varicate, di-verge, &c.; dif-fer, dif-ficulty, dif-fident, dif-fract, dif-fuse; dis-pel, &c.; des-cant, des-habille, des-patch; de-bar, de-bark, de-bauch, &c.; s-pend, s-tain. See **De-** (2), **De-** (3), **S-** (2).

Do-; in do-zen; see **Duo-**.

Dou-; in dou-ble; see **Duo-**.

Duo-, Du-, two, double. (L.) L. *duo*, two; cognate with E. *two*. Only in duo-decimo, duo-denum; shortened to *du-* in du-al, du-el, du-et, du-plicate, &c. Appearing as *dou-* in dou-ble, dou-bloon, dou-bt; and as *do-* in do-zen.

Dys-, badly. (Gk.) Gk. δύς, badly, with difficulty. Some connect it with **To-** (2).

E- (1); in e-ducate, e-lapse, e-normous, &c.; see **Ex-** (1).

E- (2); in e-nough; see **Y-**.

E- (3); in e-lope. (AF.—L.) AF. *a-*, for OF. *es-*; see **Es-**. See **Elope**, p. 191.

E- (4); in e-squire. (F.) This *e-* is a F. addition, of purely phonetic value, due to the difficulty which was experienced in pronouncing initial *sq-*, *sc-*, *st-*, *sp-*. So also in e-scalade, e-scarpment, e-scritoire, e-scrow, e-scuage, e-scutcheon; e-spalier, e-special, e-spouse, e-spy; e-stablish, e-state, e-stop, e-stovers; cf. e-paulette; to which add e-schew.

Ec-; in ec-centric, ec-clesiastic, ec-lectic, ec-lipse, ec-logue, ec-stasy, ec-zema. (Gk.) Gk. ἐκ, also ἐξ, out; see **Ex-** (2).+L. *ex*, Lithuan. *isz*, Russ. *iz'*, out; see **Ex-** (1). Also *el-*, *ex-*, as in el-lipse, ex-odus.

Ef-; see **Ex-** (1).

Eff-; in eff-endi; see **Auto-**.

El- (1); in el-lipse; see **Ec-**.

El- (2); in el-ixir; see **Al-** (4).

Em- (1); in em-balm, em-bank, &c. (before *b*; cf. em-bargo, from Spanish); also in em-pale, em-panel, em-ploy, &c. (before *p*). (F.—L.) F. *em-*; L. *im-*, for *in*; see **In-** (2).

Em- (2); in em-phasis (before *ph*); em-piric, em-porium, em-pyreal (before *p*); see **En-** (2).

Emb-; in emb-assy; see **Amb-**.

En- (1); in en-able, &c. (F.—L.) F. *en-*; L. *in-*; see **In-** (2).

En- (2); in en-ergy. (Gk.) Gk. ἐν, in.+L. *in*; AS. *in*. See **Em-** (2), **In-** (1), **In-** (2).

En- (3); in en-emy. (F.—L.) Negative prefix; see **In-** (3).

Endo-, within. (Gk.) Gk. ἔνδο-ν, within; extended from ἐν, in; see **En-** (2), and **Ind-**. E.: endo-gen.

Enter-; in enter-tain. (F.—L.) F. *entre-*.—L. *inter*, among; see **Inter-**. Shortened to *entr-* in entr-ails.

Ep-, Eph-; see below.

Epi-, upon. (Gk.) Gk. ἐπί, upon.+Skt. *api*; allied to L. *ob-*. See **Ob-**. It appears as *ep-*, *eph-*, in ep-och, eph-emeral, &c.

Es-; in es-cape, &c.; see **Ex-** (1).

Eso-, within. (Gk.) Gk. ἔσω, within; from ἐς, εἰς, into. Ex.: eso-teric.

Eu-, well. (Gk.) Gk. εὖ, well; neut. of ἐύς, good. Written *ev-* in ev-angelist.

Ev-; in ev-angelist; see above.

Ex- (1), out of, very. (L.; *or* F.—L.) L. *ex*, also *ē*, out of; also used intensively.+Gk. ἐξ, ἐκ, out. See **Ec-**, and see below. It appears as *a-*, *e-*, *ef-*, *es-*, *ex-*, *iss-*, *s-*, in a-mend, e-normous, ef-fect, es-cape, ex-tend, iss-ue, s-ample, &c. Also as *af-* (*a-*), in af-fray (a-fraid); see **Af-** (4), **A-** (16), **E-** (1). And see **As-** (3).

Ex- (2), out of, away. (Gk.) Gk. ἐξ, out; as in ex-arch, ex-egesis, ex-odus, ex-orcise; and (through F.) ex-ergue. See above.

Ex- (3); in ex-cise. (Du.–F.–L.) Du. *ak-*; for F. *ac-*; from L. *ac-*, for *ad*. See **Ad-**.

Exo-, without. (Gk.) Gk. ἔξω, outside, without; adv. from ἐξ, out; see **Ex-** (2).

Extra-, beyond. (L.) A comparative abl. form, from L. *ex*, out; see **Ex-** (1). Cf. *exter-* in exter-ior, exter-nal. It appears also as *stra-* in stra-nge; cf. estra-nge.

For- (1), in place of. (E.) E. *for*, prep.; in for-as-much, for-ever, which might just as well be written as separate words instead of compounds. Allied to **Para-** (1), **Per-**, **Pro-**.

For- (2); in for-give. (E.) AS. *for-*, intensive prefix. ✛ Icel. *for-*, Dan. *for-*, Swed. *för-*, Du. G. *ver-*, Goth. *fra-*, Skt. *parā*. See p. 221. See **Fore-** (2).

For- (3); in for-feit. (F.–L.) F. *for-*, prefix.—L. *forīs*, outside, out of doors. Also in *for-close*, sometimes spelt *fore-close*; and see *fore-judge* (2).

For- (4); in for-ward. AS. *fore-weard*; see below.

Fore- (1), before. (E.) AS. *fore*, for, before, prep.; *fore*, adv. Allied to **For-** (1).

Fore- (2); in fore-go. (E.) A bad spelling of *for-go*; see **For-** (2).

Forth-. (E.) Only in *forth-coming, forth-with*. AS. *forð*, forth.✛Gk. πρός, Skt. *prati*, to-wards; L. *por-*; see **Por-** (1).

Fro-; in fro-ward. (Scand.) Icel. *frā*, from. See p. 227.

Gain-, against. (Scand.) Icel. *gegn*, against. Ex.: gain-say.

Hemi-, half. (Gk.) Gk. ἡμι-, half.✛L. *sēmi-*, half; see **Semi-**. Shortened to *me-* in me-grim.

Hetero-, other. (Gk.) Gk. ἕτερο-s, other.

Holo-, entire. (Gk.) Gk. ὅλο-s, entire.

Homo-, same. (Gk.) Gk. ὁμό-s, same; cognate with E. *same*. Lengthened to *homœo-*, Gk. ὅμοιο-s, like, in homœo-pathy (homeo-pathy).

Hyper-, above, beyond. (Gk.) Gk. ὑπέρ, above; see **Super-**. Cf. **Over-**.

Hypo-, Hyph-, Hyp-. (Gk.) Gk. ὑπό, under. ✛ L. *sub*, under; see **Sub-**. Hence *hyph-* in hyph-en; *hyp-* in hyp-allage.

I-; in i-gnoble, i-gnominy, i-gnore. L. *i-*, for *in-*, not, before *gn*; see **In-** (3).

Il- (1); in il-lapse, il-lation, il-lision, il-lude, &c.; see **In-** (2).

Il- (2); in il-legal; see **In-** (3).

Im- (1); in im-brue, im-mure, im-pair. (F.–L.) Here *im-* is for *em-*, the OF. form derived from L. *in*, in. See **In-** (2).

Im- (2); in im-bed. For E. *in*, as if for *in-bed*. But really due to the influence of **Im-** (1).

Im- (3); in im-bue, im-merge, im-pel, &c. (L.) L. *im-*, for *in*, in; when *b, m,* or *p* follows.

Im- (4), negative prefix. (L.; *or* F.–L.) For L. *in-*, neg. prefix; when *m* or *p* follows. See **In-** (3).

In- (1); in in-born. (E.) AS. *in*, prep.

In- (2); in in-clude. (L.; *or* F.–L.) L. *in*, in.✛Gk. ἐν, in; AS. *in*. See **In-** (1), **En-** (2). It appears as *am-, an-, em-, en-, il-, im-, in-, ir-*, in am-bush, an-oint, em-brace, en-close, il-lude, im-mure, in-clude, ir-ritate, &c. Also as *ann-* in ann-oy.

In- (3), negative prefix. (L.) L. *in-*, neg. prefix.✛Gk. ἀν-, ἀ-, neg. prefix; E. *un-*, before nouns. See **An-** (2), **A-** (9), **Un-** (1). It appears as *en-, i-, il-, im-, in-, ir-*, in en-emy, i-gnoble, il-legal, im-mortal, in-firm, ir-regular, &c.

Indi-, Ind-, as in indi-genous, ind-igent. (L.) OLat. *ind-u*, within.✛Gk. ἔνδον, within; see **Endo-**.

Intel-; see below.

Inter-, between. (L.) L. *inter*, between. A comparative form, allied to L. *inter-ior*, within; cf. L. *inter-nus*, internal. It appears as *intel-* in intel-lect, *enter-* in enter-tain; and cf. entr-ails. Closely allied are L. *intrō-*, within, *intrā-*, within.

Intra-, within; see **Inter-**.

Intro-, within; see **Inter-**.

Ir- (1); in ir-radiate, ir-rigate, ir-rision, ir-ritate, ir-ruption; for L. *in*, prep. before *r*; see **In-** (2).

Ir- (2); in ir-rational, ir-reclaimable, &c.; for L. *in-*, negative prefix, before *r*; see **In-** (3).

Iss-; in iss-ue. (F.–L.) F. *iss-*, from L. *ex*; see **Ex-** (1).

Juxta-, near. (L.) L. *iuxtā*, near.

L- (1); in l-one. (E.) Short for *all*; l-one = al-one. See **Al-** (1).

L- (2); in l-ute. (Arab.) Short for Arab. *al*, the, def. art. See **Al-** (4).

Male-, Mal-, Mau-, badly. (L.; *or* F.–L.) L. *male*, badly, ill; whence F. *mal*, which becomes also *mau-* in mau-gre.

Me-; in me-grim; see **Hemi-**.

Meta-, Meth-, Met-, among, with, after; also used to imply change. (Gk.) Gk. μετά, among, with, after.✛AS. *mid*, G. *mit*, Goth. *mith*, with. It appears also as *meth-* in meth-od, *met-* in met-empsychosis, met-eor, met-onymy.

Min-; in min-ster; see **Mono-**.

Mis- (1); in mis-deed, mis-take, &c. (E. *and* Scand.) AS. *mis-*, wrongly, amiss.✛Icel. Dan. Du. *mis-*; Swed. *miss-*; Goth. *missa-*, wrongly. Allied to *miss*, vb.

Mis- (2), badly, ill. (F.–L.) OF. *mes-*, from L. *minus*, less; used in a depreciatory sense. Appearing in mis-adventure, mis-alliance, mis-chance, mis-chief, mis-count, mis-creant, mis-nomer, mis-prise, mis-prision. Quite distinct from **Mis-** (1).

Mono-, Mon-, single. (Gk.) Gk. μόνο-s, single, sole, alone. Hence *mon-k*, *min-ster*.

Multi-, Mult-, many. (L.; *or* F.–L.) From L. *multus*, much, many.

N- (1); in n-ewt, n-ickname, n-once, n-uncle. (E.) *A newt = an ewt*, where the prefixed *n* is due to the indef. article. *A n-ickname = an eke-name*. *My nuncle = mine uncle*, where the *n* is due to the possessive pronoun. In *n-once*, the prefixed *n* is due to the dat. case of the def. article, as shown.

N- (2), negative prefix. (E. or L.) In *n-aught, n-ay, n-either, n-ever, n-o, n-one, n-or, n-ot* (1), and in *hob-n-ob*, the prefixed *n* is due to AS. *ne*, not. In *n-ull*, it is due to the cognate L. *ne*, not. See **Ne-**.

Ne-, Neg-. (L.) L. *ne*, not; *neg-* as in *neg-ligere*, not. In ne-farious, neg-ation, neg-lect, neg-otiate, ne-scient, ne-uter. See **N-** (2).

Non-, not. (L.; *or* F.–L.) L. *non*, not; OLat. *noenum*, for *ne oinum*, i. e. *ne ūnum*, not one; see above. It appears as *um-* in um-pire, for *numpire*.

O-; in o-mit; see **Ob-**.

Ob-. (L.; *or* F.–L.) L. *ob*, near; allied to Gk. ἐπί, upon, near; Skt. *api*, moreover; Oscan *op*. See **Epi-**. The force of *ob-* is very variable; it appears as *o-, ob-, oc-, of-, op-*, also as extended to *os-* (for *ops*); as in o-mit, ob-long, oc-cur, of-fer, op-press, os-tensible.

Oc-; in oc-casion, oc-cident, oc-ciput, oc-cult, oc-cupy, oc-cur; see **Ob-**.

Of- (1); in of-fal. (E.) AS. *of*, of, off, away. This word is invariably written *off* in composition, except in the case of *offal*, where its use would have brought three *f*'s together.✛L. *ab*, Gk. ἀπό; see **Ab-** (1), **Apo-**. It appears as *a-* in a-down, a-kin, a-new, a-thirst; see **A-** (1).

Of- (2); in of-fend, of-fer; see **Ob-**.

Off-; see **Of-** (1).

On-, on, upon. (E.) AS. *on*, on.✛Gk. ἀνά. From a pronominal base. See **Ana-**. It often appears as *a-*, as in a-foot, a-sleep, &c. See **A-** (2).

Op-; in op-pilation, op-ponent, op-portune, op-pose, op-posite, op-press, op-probrious, op-pugn; see **Ob-**.

Or- (1); in or-deal, or-ts. (E.) AS. *or-*; cognate with Du. *oor-*, OSax. and G. *ur-*, Goth. *us*, away, out of.

Or- (2); in or-lop. (Du.) Short for Du. *over*, cognate with E. *over*; see **Over-**.

Os-; in os-tensible; see **Ob-**.

Out-. (E.) AS. *ūt*, E. *out*, prep.✛Goth. *ut*, G. *aus*, Skt. *ud*, out. Shortened to *utt-* in utt-er; and to *ut-* in ut-most.

Outr-; in outr-age. (F.–L.) F. *outre* = L. *ultrā*, beyond; see **Ultra-**.

Over-. (E.) AS. *ofer*, E. *over*, prep.✛Goth. *ufar*, L. *s-uper*, Gk. ὑπέρ, Skt. *upari*, above. A comparative form from **Up**, q.v. See **Hyper-, Super-, Or-** (2).

Pa-; in pa-lsy; see **Para-**.

Palin-, Palim-, again. (Gk.) Gk. πάλιν, back, again. It becomes *palim-* in palim-psest.

Pan-, Panto-, all. (Gk.) Gk. πᾶν, neut. of πᾶς, all; παντο-, declensional form of the same, occurring in panto-mime.

Par- (1); in par-amount, par-amour, par-boil, par-don, par-son, par-terre, par-venu; see **Per-**.

Par- (2); in par-agon, par-allel, par-egoric, &c.; see **Para-**.

Par- (3); in par-get. (F.–L.) OF. *par-*, *por-*; from L. *prō-*; see **Pro-** (1).

Para- (1), beside (Gk.) Gk. παρά, beside. Allied to E. *for*, L. *per*, also to Gk. περί. See **Per-, Peri-**, and **For-** (1). It becomes *pa-*

in pa-lsy; *par-* in par-ody, &c. ¶ Quite distinct from *para-* in para-chute, para-pet, para-sol, from F. *parer.*

Para- (2); in para-dise. Zend *pairi* = Gk. περί. Shortened to *par-* in par-vis·

Pel-; in pel-lucid; see **Per-**.

Pen-; in pen-insula, pen-ultimate, pen-umbra. (L.) L. *pæn-e,* almost.

Per-, through. (L.; *or* F.—L.) L. *per,* through. Allied to **Para-** and **For-** (1). It appears also as *par-* in par-son, par-don, &c.; as *pel-* in pel-lucid; and as *pil-* in pil-grim. See **Par-** (1).

Peri-, around. (Gk.) Gk. περί, around.+Skt. *pari,* round about. Allied to **Para-**, &c.

Pil-; in pil-grim; see **Per-**.

Po-, in po-sition, po-sitive. (L.) L. *po-,* short for **apo,* allied to L. **ap,* original form of *ab* (Walde). See **Ab-** (1).

Pol-; in pol-lute; see **Por-** (1).

Poly-, many. (Gk.) Written for Gk. πολύ-, decl. form of πολύ-s, much, many. Allied to E. *full.*

Por- (1); in por-tend. (L.) L. *por-,* allied to L. *per,* through (Walde). It appears as *pol-* in pol-lute. The origin of *pos-* in pos-sess is doubtful; but may be allied.

Por- (2); in por-trait; see **Pro-** (1).

Pos-; in pos-sess; see **Por-** (1).

Post-, after. (L.) L. *post,* after, behind. Hence F. *puis,* appearing as *pu-* in pu-ny.

Pour-; in pour-tray; see **Pro-** (1).

Pr- (1); in pr-ison, pr-ize (1); see **Pre-**.

Pr- (2); in pr-udent; see **Pro-** (1).

Pre-, Præ-, before. (L.) L. *pre-,* for *præ,* prep., before; for **prai,* an old locative case. Allied to **Pro-**. This prefix occurs also in pr-ison, pr-ize (1); and is curiously changed to *pro-* in pro-vost.

Preter-, beyond. (L.) L. *præter,* beyond; comparative form of *præ,* before. See above.

Pro- (1), before, instead of. (L.; *or* F.—L.) L. *prŏ-,* before, in front, used as a prefix; also L. *prō,* for *prŏd,* abl. case used as a preposition, which appears in prod-igal. Allied to Gk. πρό, before, Skt. *pra,* before, away; also to E. *for.* See below; and see **For-** (1). It appears also as *pour-, por-, pur-, pr-,* in pour-tray, por-trait, pur-vey, pr-offer, pr-udent; where *pour-, por-, pur-* are due to the F. form *pour.*

Pro- (2), before. (Gk.) Gk. πρό, before; cognate with **Pro-** (1). In pro-boscis, pro-blem, pro-em, pro-gnostic, pro-gramme, pro-lepsis, pro-logue, pro-phet, pro-scenium, pro-thalamium, &c.

Pro- (3); in pro-vost; see **Pre-**.

Prod-; in prod-igal; see **Pro-** (1).

Pros-, in addition, towards. (Gk.) Gk. πρός, towards. Allied to **Forth-**.

Proto-, Prot-, first. (Gk.) From Gk. πρῶτο-s, first; superl. form of πρό, before; see **Pro-** (2). Shortened to *prot-* in prot-oxide.

Pu-; in pu-ny; see **Post-**.

Pur-; in pur-chase, pur-loin, pur-port, pur-pose (1), pur-pose (2), pur-sue, pur-vey, pur-view. (F.—L.) See **Pro-** (1).

R-; in r-ally; see **Re-**.

Re-, Red-, again. (L.) L. *re-, red-* (only in composition), again, back. *Red-* occurs in red-eem, red-integrate, red-olent, red-ound, red-undant, red-dition; and is changed to *ren-* in ren-der, ren-t. In re-ly, re-mind, re-new, it is prefixed to purely E. words; and in re-call, re-cast, to words of Scand. origin. It appears as *r-* in r-ally (1); and as *ru-* in ru-nagate. 2. *Re-* is frequently prefixed to other prefixes, which sometimes coalesce with it, so that these words require care. For example, rampart = re-em-part; cf. also re-ad-apt, re-col-lect, re-con-cile, re-sur-rection, &c. Also ransom, rascal.

Rear-; see **Retro-**.

Red-, Ren-; see **Re-**.

Rere-; in rere-ward; see **Retro-**.

Retro-, backwards, behind. (L.) L. *retrō-,* backwards, back again; a comparative form from *re-,* back; see **Re-**. The prefixes *rear-, rere-,* in rear-guard. rere-dos, rere-ward, are due to L. *retrō,* and are of F. origin.

S- (1); in s-ure; see **Se-**.

S- (2); in s-pend, s-pite, s-play, s-tain; see **Dis-**.

S- (3); in s-ample; see **Ex-** (1).

S- (4); in s-ombre; see **Sub-**.

Sans-, without. (F.—L.) F. *sans,* without.—L. *sine,* without; see **Sine-**.

Se-, Sed-, away, apart. (L.) L. *sē-,* apart; OLat. *sēd-,* apart, which is probably retained in sed-ition. The orig. sense was probably ' by oneself.' It appears as *s-* in s-ure; cf. sober.

Semi-, half. (L.) L. *sēmi-,* half.+Gk. ἡμί-, half; see **Hemi-**. It appears as *sin-* in sin-ciput.

Sin-; in sin-ciput; see above.

Sine-, without. (L.) L. *sine,* without; lit. if not.—L. *si,* if; *ne,* not. Hence F. *sans,* without.

So- (1); in so-journ; see **Sub-**.

So- (2); in so-ber. (L.) L. *sō-,* apart, allied to *sē-,* apart; see **Se-**.

Sover-, Sopr-; see **Super-**.

Stra-; in stra-nge; see **Extra-**.

Su-; in su-dden, su-spect; see **Sub-**.

Sub-, under. (L.) L. *sub,* under, (sometimes) up. Allied to Gk. ὑπό, under; Skt. *upa,* near, under; also to E. *up* and *of.* See **Hypo-, Of-, Up-**. *Sub* also appears as *s-, so-, su-, suc-, suf-, sug-, sum-, sup-, sur-,* in s-ombre (?), so-journ, su-dden, su-spect, suc-ceed, suf-fuse, sug-gest, sum-mon, sup-press, sur-rogate. It is also extended to *sus-* (for *sups-*); as in sus-pend. And cf. suzerain.

Subter-, beneath. (L.) L. *subter,* beneath; comparative form from *sub,* under. See **Sub-**.

Suc-, Suf-, Sug-, Sum-, Sup-; see **Sub-**.

Super-, above, over. (L.) L. *super,* above; comparative form of L. *sub,* under, also up.+Gk. ὑπέρ, over, beyond; AS. *ofer,* E. *over.* See **Hyper-, Over-**; also **Sub-**. Hence *suprā,* beyond, orig. abl. feminine. Reduced to *supr-* in supr-eme. Note also *sover-* in sover-eign, which is a F. form; and *sopr-* in sopr-ano, which is an Ital. form. Also F. *sur-* < L. *super;* see **Sur-** (2).

Supra-, beyond; see above.

Sur- (1); in sur-reptitious, sur-rogate; see **Sub-**.

Sur- (2); in sur-cease, sur-charge, sur-face, sur-feit, &c.; see **Super-**.

Sus-; in sus-pend; see **Sub-**.

Sy-, Syl-, Sym-; see **Syn-**.

Syn-, with, together with. (Gk.) Gk. σύν, with. Allied to L. *cum,* with; see **Com-**. It appears as *sy-, syl-, sym-,* and *syn-,* in sy-stem, syl-logism, sym-metry, syn-tax, &c.

T- (1); t-wit. (E.) *Twit* is from AS. *æt-wītan,* to twit, reproach; thus *t-* is here put for E. *at.*

T- (2); t-awdry. (F.—L.) *Tawdry* is for *Saint Awdry;* thus *t-* is here the final letter of *sain-t.*

T- (3); t-autology. (Gk.) Here *t-* represents Gk. τό, neuter of the def. article.

Thorough-, through. (E.) Merely another form of E. *through.*

To- (1), in to-day, to-morrow. (E.) AS. *tō,* to.

To- (2), intensive prefix. (E.) Obsolete, except in *to-brake.* AS. *tō,* apart, asunder; prob. allied to L. *dis-,* apart. See **Dis-**. ¶ Some connect it with Gk. δυσ-; see **Dys-**.

Tra-, Tran-; see below.

Trans-, beyond. (L.) L. *trans,* beyond. Shortened to *tran-* in tran-scend: and to *tra-* in tra-duce, tra-verse, &c. Hence F. *tres-,* occurring in tres-pass; and *tre-* in tre-ason. And see tranc-e, trans-om, tres-tle.

Tre- (1), **Tres-**. (F.—L.) See above.

Tre- (2); in tre-ble. (F.—L.) See below.

Tri- (1), thrice. (L.) L. *tri-,* thrice; allied to *trēs,* three. Hence tri-ple, tre-ble, &c.; also (perhaps) *tra-* in tra-mmel.

Tri- (2), thrice. (Gk.) Gk. τρι-, thrice; allied to τρία, neut. of τρεῖs, three. Hence tri-gonometry, &c.

Twi-, double, doubtful. (E.) AS. *twi-,* double; allied to *twā,* two. Hence twi-bill, twi-light.

U-; in u-topian. (Gk.) Gk. οὐ, not; see p. 682.

Ultra-, beyond. (L.) L. *ultrā,* beyond; allied to OLat. *ulter,* adj., appearing in *ulter-ior,* which see in Dict. Hence F. *outre,* beyond, appearing in outr-age; also in E. utter-ance (2), corruption of F. *outr-ance.*

Um-; in umpire; see **Non-**.

Un- (1), negative prefix to nouns, &c. (E.) AS. *un-,* not; cognate with L. *in-,* not, Gk. ἀν-, not. See **An-** (2), **In-** (3).

Un- (2), verbal prefix, signifying the reversal of an action. (E.) AS. *un-,* verbal prefix; allied to Du. *ont-, ent-,* G. *ent-,* OHG. *ant-,* Goth. *and-,* and E. *an-* in an-swer; see **An-** (5), **Anti-**.

Un- (3); in un-til, un-to. (E.) See *un-to* in Dict., p. 680.

Un- (4), **Uni-**, one. (L.) L. *ūn-us,* one; whence uni-vocal, with one voice; un-animous, of one mind; &c. Cognate with E. *one.*

Under-. (E.) AS. *under,* E. *under,* prep.

Up-. (E.) AS. *up,* E. *up,* prep. Allied to **Of-, Sub-, Hypo-**.

Ut-, Utt-. (E.) See **Out-**.

Utter-. (F.—L.) Only in utter-ance (2). F. *outre,* L. *ultra;* see **Ultra-**.

V-; in v-an (1), v-anguard. (F.—L.) See **Ab-** (1).

Vice-, Vis-, in place of. (L.; or F.—L.) L. *uice*, in place of, whence OF. *vis*, the same. The latter appears only in vis-count.

Wan-, negative prefix; see *wan-ton* in Dict.

With-, against. (E.) A shortened form of AS. *wiðer*, against; see *withers* in Dict. The sense is preserved in with-stand. In with-hold, with-draw, it signifies 'back.'

Y-; in y-wis, y-clept. (E.) AS. *ge-*, prefix; ME. *i-*, *y-*. This prefix appears as *a-* in a-ware; as *i-* in i-wis (the same as y-wis); and as *e-* in enough. See **A-** (11), **E-** (2).

A. Summary. A few of the Prefixes given above, such as *al-* in *al-mighty*, are rather true words that can be used alone; for *al-* is merely a spelling of *all*. Omitting these and some forms that are mere variants, the list may be reduced to the following.

A- (with several values), ab-, abs- (see Abscond), ad-, al- (Arabic), ambi- or amb- (see Ambidextrous), amphi-, an-, ana-, ante-, anti- or ant-, aph- or apo-, be-, bi- or bis-, cata-, circum-, co- (com-, con-), contra-, counter-, de-, di-, dia-, dis-, dys- (see Dysentery), e-, em- (see Embark), en-, endo-, epi-, eso-, ex-, exo-, extra-, for- (2), fore- (2), fore-, forth, fro-.

Gain- (see Gainsay), hemi-, hyper-, hypo-, i-, il- (1), il- (2), im- (1), im- (2), im- (3), in- (1), in- (2), in- (3), indi-, inter-, intra-, intro- (see Introduce), ir- (1), ir- (2), juxta- (see Joust).

Meta-, mis- (1), mis- (2), ne- (see No (1)), non-, ob-, on-, or- (see Ordeal, Ort, Orlop), out-, over-, palin- (see Palindrome), pan- (panto-), para-, per-, peri-, pol- or po- (see Pollute, Position), por- (see Portend), post-, pre-, preter-, pro-, pros-, pur-, re-, red-, retro-.

Se- (sed-), semi-, sine- (see Sinecure), sub-, sub-ter, super-, supra-, sur- (1), sur- (2), sus-, syn-, to- (1), to- (2), trans-, ultra-, un- (1), un- (2), un- (3), under-, up-, with-, y-.

B. Some of these prefixes assume various shapes in accordance with phonetic laws. Of these, the most important are the following:—

(*a*) The Lat. prep. *ad* appears as *a-, ab-, ac-, ad-, af-, ag-, al-, an-, ap-, ar-, as-, at-.*

(*b*) The Lat. prep. *cum* appears as *co-, col-, com-, comb-, con-, cor-.* Also (through F.) as *co-, coi-, cou-, coun-, cu-, cur-.*

(*c*) The Lat. prefix *dis-* appears as *dē-, des-, di-, dif-, dis-,* and even *s-.*

(*d*) The Lat. prep. *ex* appears as *a-, as-, e-, ef-, es-, ex-,* and even *iss-* and *s-.*

(*e*) The Lat. prep. *in* appears as *am-, an-, em-, en-, il-* (1), im- (1, 3), *in-* (2), *ir-* (1).

(*f*) The Lat. negative prefix *in-* appears as *en-, i-, il-* (2), im- (4), *in-* (3), *ir-* (2).

(*g*) The Lat. prep. *ob* appears as *o-, ob-, oc-, of-, op-;* we even find *os-.*

(*h*) The Lat. prep. *sub* appears as *s-* (in s-ombre?), *so-* (in so-journ), *su-, sub-, suc-, suf-, sug-, sum-, sup-, sur-.*

(*i*) The Greek prefix *apo-* (ἀπό) also appears as *aph-*; *cata-* (κατά), also as *cat-, cath-*; *en-* (ἐν), also as *em-*; *epi-* (ἐπί), also as *ep-, eph-*; *hypo-* (ὑπό), also as *hyp-, hyph-*; *syn-* (σύν), also as *sy-, syl-, sym-.*

These very common variations should be observed and learnt For this purpose. I suggest a study of the following words:—

(*a*) A-chieve, ab-breviate, ac-cede, ad-mire, af-fix, ag-gress, al-lude, an-nex, ap-pend, ar-rogate, as-sign, at-tract.

(*b*) Co-agulate, col-lect, com-mute, comb-ustion, con-nect, cor-rode; also co-st, coi-l, cou-ch, coun-cil, cu-ll, cur-ry (1).

(*c*) De-feat, des-cant, di-verge, dif-fuse, dis-pel, s-pend.

(*d*) A-mend, as-tonish, e-normous, ef-fect, es-cape, ex-tend, iss-ue, s-ample.

(*e*) Am-bush, an-oint, em-bellish, en-close, il-lude, im-mure, im-merge, in-clude, ir-ritate.

(*f*) En-emy, i-gnoble, il-legal, im-mortal, in-firm, ir-regular.

(*g*) O-mit, ob-long, oc-cur, of-fer, op-press, os-tensible.

(*h*) S-ombre, so-journ, su-dden, sub-mit, suc-ceed, suf-fuse, sug-gest, sum-mon, sup-press, sur-rogate.

(*i*) Apo-logy, aph-æresis; cata-logue, cat-echism, cath-olic; en-ergy, em-phasis; epi-logue, ep-och, eph-emera; hypo-thesis, hyp-allage, hyph-en; syn-onymous, sy-stem, syl-logism, sym-metry.

It may be noted here that more than one prefix may be placed at the beginning of a word, as in *re-im-burse, ram-part* (= re-em-part), *in-ex-act,* &c.

C. Some prefixes exhibit such unusual forms in certain words that they can only be understood upon a perusal of the etymology of the word as given in the Dictionary. I note here a few curious examples.

A- replaces *e-* (Lat. *e,* for *ex*) in *a-mend.*

Al-, the Arabic definite article, appears at the beginning of *al-cohol, a-pricot, ar-tichoke, as-segai, el-ixir, l-ute.* But the *al-* in *al-ligator* is the Span. *el,* Lat. *ille.*

The Latin *ab* has actually become *adv-* in the word *adv-antage*; whilst in *v-an-guard* it appears as *v-.* But, in *ab-breviate,* the prefix is *ad-.* The Latin *cum-* appears in *co-st, co-stive, coi-l, cou-ch, cou-sin, cur-ry* (1), *cu-ll, cu-stom.*

The *dea-* in *dea-con* represents the Greek διά; so also *de-* in *de-vil.*

The *e-* in *e-lope* represents the AF. *a-,* OF. *es-,* L. *ex.*

The *e-* in *e-squire, e-scutcheon,* &c., is purely phonetic, as explained.

The *ev-* in *ev-angelist* is for Gk. *eu-,* as in *eu-logy.*

The *or-* in *or-deal* and *or-t* is a Teutonic prefix.

The *outr-* in *outr-age* represents the Latin *ultrā*; cf. *utter-ance* (2).

The *s-* in *s-ure* (Lat. *sē-cūrus*) represents the Latin *sē-.*

The *t-* in *t-wit* represents the AS. *æt*; but in *t-awdry* it is the last letter of *saint.*

D. Numerals are peculiarly liable to sink into apparent prefixes; such are Lat. *ūnus, duo* (adverbially, *bis*), *trēs,* &c.; hence un-animous, du-et, bin-ary, bi-sect, bis-cuit, ba-lance, dou-ble, tre-ble, tri-ple, &c.

Other noteworthy Latin words are *dimidium, male, pæne, sēmi-, vice*; whence demi-, mal-treat, mau-gre, pen-insula, semi-circle, vice-admiral, vis-count.

As in Latin, the Greek numerals are peculiarly liable to sink into apparent prefixes; hence *di-cotyledon,* from δίς, twice; *tri-gonometry, tetra-hedron, penta-gon, hex-agon, hepta-gon, octa-gon, nona-gon, deca-gon,* &c. Other noteworthy Greek words are ἀρχι-, chief (archi-pelago, arche-type, arch-bishop); αὐτός, self (auto-graph, auth-entic, eff-endi); ἥμι-, half (hemi-); ἕτερος, other (hetero-); ὅλος, entire (holo-); ὁμός, same (homo-); μόνος, single (mono-); πᾶν, all (pan-, panto-); πολύς much, many (poly-); πρῶτος, first (proto-).

II. SUFFIXES

The number of suffixes in modern English is so great, and the forms of several, especially in words derived through the French from Latin, are so variable that an attempt to exhibit them all would tend to confusion. The best account of their origin is to be found in Brugmann, Grundriss der Vergleichenden Grammatik der Indogermanischen Sprachen. An account of Anglo-Saxon suffixes is given at p. 119 of March, Comparative Grammar of the Anglo-Saxon Language. Lists of Anglo-Saxon words, arranged according to their suffixes, are given in Loth, Etymologische Angelsächsisch-englische Grammatik, Elberfeld, 1870. Simple accounts of English suffixes in general are given in Morris, Historical Outlines of English Accidence, pp. 212–221, 229–242; in Nesfield, Historical English and Derivation, pp. 185–252; and in the two series of my Principles of English Etymology; to which the reader is referred. See also

Koch, Historische Grammatik der Englischen Sprache, vol. iii. pt. 1, pp. 29–77. It is clearly established that the Indo-germanic languages abound in suffixes, each of which was originally intended slightly to modify the meaning of the root to which it was added, so as to express the radical idea in a new relation. The force of many of these must, even at an early period, have been slight, and in many instances it is difficult to trace it; but in some instances it is still clear, and the form of the suffix is then of great service. The difference between *lov-er, lov-ed,* and *lov-ing* is well marked, and readily understood. One of the most remarkable points is that most of the Indo-germanic languages delighted in adding suffix to suffix, so that words are not uncommon in which two or more suffixes occur, each repeating, it may be, the sense of that which preceded it. Double diminutives, such as *parti-c-le,* i. e. 'a little

little part,' are sufficiently common. The Lat. superl. suffix *-is-si-mus* is an example of the use of a treble suffix, which really expresses no more than is expressed by *-mus* alone in the word *prī-mus*. The principal Indo-germanic suffixes, omitting feminine forms, are these: *-o, -i, -u, -yo* (written *-jo*), *-wo, -mo, -mi, -men* (*-mon*), *-meno, -no, -tno, -ni, -nu, -en* (*-on*), *-ent* (*-ont*), *-lo, -li, -lu, -ro, -ri, -ru, -er* (*-or*), *-es* (*-os*), *-to, -men-to, -ti, -ti-ōn, -tā-ti, -tu, -tū-ti, -ter* (*-tor, -tr*), *-tŭro, -tro, -tlo, -id, -d, -d-en* (*-d-on*), *-tū-den, -qo, -go, -ko, -k, -sko, -bho*. But these can be readily compounded, so as to form new suffixes; so that from *-men-to* was formed *-mento* (as in E. *argument*).

One common error with regard to suffixes should be guarded against, viz. that of mis-dividing a word so as to give the suffix a false shape. This is extremely common in such words as *logi-c, civi-c, belli-c-ose*, where the suffix is commonly spoken of as being *-ic* or *-ic-ose*. This error occurs, for instance, in the elaborate book on English Affixes by S. S. Haldemann, published at Philadelphia in 1865; a work which is of considerable use as containing a very full account, with numerous examples, of suffixes and prefixes. The truth is that *civi-c* (Lat. *cīuicus*) is derived from Lat. *cīui-*, declensional stem of *cīuis*, a citizen, with the suffix *-cus* (Idg. *-ko*); and *logi-c* is from Gk. λογικός, from λογι-, for λογο-, declensional stem of λόγος, a discourse, with the suffix *-κος*, as before. Compare Lat.

cīui-tas, Gk. λογο-μαχία. Of course, words in *-ic* are so numerous that *-ic* has come to be regarded as a suffix at the present day, so that we do not hesitate to form *Volta-ic* as an adjective of *Volta*; but this is English misuse, not Latin etymology. Moreover, since both *-i-* and *-ko* are Indo-germanic suffixes, such a suffix as *-i-kos, -i-cus*, is *possible* both in Greek and Latin; but in the particular words above cited it is clearer to take the *-i-* as due to the declensional stem.

One more word of warning may perhaps suffice. If we wish to understand a suffix, we must employ comparative philology, and not consider English as an absolutely isolated language, with laws different from those of other languages of the Indo-germanic family. Thus the *-th* in *tru-th* is the *-δ* of AS. *trēow-δ*, gen. case *trēow-δe*, fem. sb. This suffix answers to that seen in Goth. *gabaur-ths*, birth, gen. case *gabaur-thais*, fem. sb., belonging to the *-i-* stem declension of Gothic strong substantives. The true suffix is therefore to be expressed as Teut. *-thi*, cognate with Idg. *-ti*, so extremely common in Latin; cf. *dō-ti-*, dowry, *men-ti-*, mind, *mor-ti-*, death, *mes-si-* (<*met-ti-*), harvest, that which is mown. Hence, when Horne Tooke gave his famous etymology of *truth* as being ' that which a man *troweth*,' he did in reality suggest that the *-ti-* in Lat. *mor-ti-* is identical with the *-t* in *mori-t-ur* or in *ama-t*; in other words, it was a mere whim.

III. LIST OF HOMONYMS

Homonyms are words spelt alike, but differing in use. In a few cases, I include different uses of what is either exactly, or nearly, the same word, at the same time noting that the forms are allied; but in most cases, the words are of different origin.

Abide (1), to wait for. (E.)
Abide (2), to suffer for a thing. (E.)
Air (1), the atmosphere. (F. – L. – Gk.)
Air (2), demeanour; tune. (F. – L. – Gk.) *From* Air (1).
Allow (1), to assign, grant. (F. – L.)
Allow (2), to approve of. (F. – L.)
Along (1), lengthwise of. (E.)
Along (2), *in* ' along of.' (E.) *Allied to* Along (1).
Amice (1), a piece of linen. (F. – L.)
Amice (2), a hood for pilgrims. (F. – Span. – Teut. ?)
An (1), the indef. article. (E.)
An (2), if. (E.) Shortened from *and*.
Ancient (1), old. (F. – L.)
Ancient (2), a banner, standard-bearer. (F. – L.)
Angle (1), a bend, corner. (F. – L.)
Angle (2), a fishing-hook. (E.)
Arch (1), a construction of stone or wood, &c., in a curved form. (F. – L.)
Arch (2), roguish, waggish, sly. (L. – Gk.) *From* Arch- below.
Arch-, chief; used as a prefix. (L. – Gk.)
Arm (1), s., the limb extending from the shoulder to the hand. (E.)
Arm (2), verb, to furnish with weapons. (F. – L.)
Art (1), 2 p. s. pres. of the verb substantive. (E.)
Art (2), skill, contrivance. (F. – L.)
Ay! interj. of surprise. (E.)
Ay, Aye, yea, yes. (E.)
Aye, adv., ever, always. (Scand.)

Baggage (1), travellers' luggage. (F. – Scand.)
Baggage (2), a worthless woman. (F. – Scand.) *From* Baggage (1).
Bail (1), security, to secure. (F. – L.)
Bail (2), a bucket. *See* Bale (3).
Bale (1), a package. (F. – MHG.)
Bale (2), evil. (E.)
Bale (3), to empty water out of a ship. (F. – Late L.)
Balk (1), a beam; a ridge, a division of land. (E.)
Balk (2), to hinder. (E.) *Allied to* Balk (1).
Ball (1), a dance. (F. – Late L.)
Ball (2), a spherical body. (Scand.)
Band (1), also Bond, a fastening. (Scand.)
Band (2), a company of men. (F. – G.) *Allied to* Band (1).
Bang (1), to beat violently. (Scand.)
Bang (2), a narcotic drug. (Port. – Hind. – Skt.)
Bank (1), a mound of earth. (Scand.)

Bank (2), a place for depositing money. (F. – Ital. – G.) *Allied to* Bank (1).
Barb (1), the hook on the point of an arrow. (F. – L.)
Barb (2), a Barbary horse. (F. – Barbary.)
Bard (1), a poet. (C.)
Bard (2), armour for a horse. (F. – Scand.)
Bark (1), Barque, a sort of ship. (F. – Ital. – Late L.)
Bark (2), the rind of a tree. (Scand.)
Bark (3), to yelp as a dog. (E.)
Barm (1), yeast. (E.)
Barm (2), the lap. (E.)
Barnacle (1), a species of goose. (F. – Late L.) *Hence* Barnacle (2).
Barnacle (2), a sort of small shell-fish. (F. – Late L.)
Barrow (1), a burial-mound. (E.)
Barrow (2), a wheelbarrow. (E.)
Base (1), low, humble. (F. – L.)
Base (2), a foundation. (F. – L. – Gk.)
Basil (1), a kind of plant. (F. – L. – Gk.)
Basil (2), Bezel, a bevelled edge. (F.)
Basil (3), a tanned sheep-hide. (F. – Span. – Arab.)
Bass (1), the lowest part in a musical composition. (F. – L.)
Bass (2), Barse, Brasse, a fish. (E.)
Baste (1), vb., to beat, strike. (Scand.)
Baste (2), to pour fat over meat. (F. – Prov. – Late L.)
Baste (3), to sew slightly. (F. – OHG.)
Bat (1), a short cudgel. (E.)
Bat (2), a winged mammal. (Scand.)
Bate (1), to abate, diminish. (F. – L.)
Bate (2), strife. (F. – L.) *Allied to* Bate (1).
Batten (1), to grow fat; to fatten. (Scand.)
Batten (2), a wooden rod. (F. – Late L.)
Batter (1), to beat. (F. – L.) *Whence* Batter (2).
Batter (2), a compound of eggs, flour, and milk. (F. – L.)
Bauble (1), a fool's mace. (F.)
Bauble (2), a plaything. (F.) *See* Bauble (1).
Bay (1), a reddish brown. (F. – L.)
Bay (2), a kind of laurel-tree. (F. – L.)
Bay (3), an inlet of the sea. (F. – L.)
Bay (4), a division in a barn. (F. – L.)
Bay (5), to bark as a dog. (F. – L.)
Bay (6), in phr. *at bay*. (F. – L.) *Allied to* Bay (5).
Beam (1), a piece of timber. (E.)
Beam (2), a ray of light. (E.) *The same as* Beam (1).
Bear (1), to carry. (E.)
Bear (2), an animal. (E.)
Beaver (1), an animal. (E.)
Beaver (2), the lower part of a helmet. (F.)
Beaver (3), Bever, a short repast. (F. – L.)
Beck (1), a nod or sign. (E.)
Beck (2), a stream. (Scand.)

Beetle (1), an insect. (E.) *Allied to* Beetle (3).
Beetle (2), a heavy mallet. (E.)
Beetle (3), to jut out and hang over. (E.)
Bend (1), to bow, to curve. (E.) *Hence* Bend (2).
Bend (2), a slanting band; in heraldry. (F.—G.)
Bestead (1), to assist, avail. (E.)
Bestead (2), situated, beset. (Scand.) *Allied to* Bestead (1).
Bid (1), to pray. (E.)
Bid (2), to command. (E.)
Bile (1), secretion from the liver. (F.—L.)
Bile (2), a boil. (E.)
Bill (1), a chopper, battle-axe, sword. (E.)
Bill (2), a bird's beak. (E.)
Bill (3), a writing, account. (F.—L.)
Billet (1), a note, ticket. (F.—L.)
Billet (2), a log of wood. (F.)
Bit (1), a small piece, a mouthful. (E.)
Bit (2), a curb for a horse. (E.) *Allied to* Bit (1).
Blanch (1), v., to whiten. (F.—OHG.)
Blanch (2), v., to blench. (E.)
Blaze (1), a flame; to flame. (E.)
Blaze (2), to proclaim. (Scand.)
Blazon (1), a proclamation; to proclaim. (Scand.) *See* Blazon (2).
Blazon (2), to pourtray armorial bearings. (F.—Teut.)
Bleak (1), pale, exposed. (Scand.)
Bleak (2), a kind of fish. (Scand.) *The same as* Bleak (1).
Blot (1), a spot, to spot. (F.—Teut.)
Blot (2), at backgammon. (Du.)
Blow (1), to puff. (E.)
Blow (2), to bloom, flourish as a flower. (E.)
Blow (3), a stroke, hit. (E.)
Bluff (1), downright, rude. (Dutch.)
Bluff (2), to cow by bragging. (Low G.)
Board (1), a table, a plank. (E.) *Hence* Board (2).
Board (2), to approach, to accost. (F.—Teut.)
Boil (1), to bubble up. (F.—L.)
Boil (2), a small tumour. (E.)
Boom (1), to hum, buzz. (E.)
Boom (2), a beam or pole. (Dutch.)
Boot (1), a covering for the leg and foot. (F.—Late L.)
Boot (2), advantage, profit. (E.)
Bore (1), to perforate. (E.)
Bore (2), to worry, vex. (E.) *The same as* Bore (1).
Bore (3), a tidal surge in a river. (Scand.)
Botch (1), to patch, a patch. (E.)
Botch (2), a swelling. (F.—G.)
Bottle (1), a hollow vessel. (F.—Late L.)
Bottle (2), a bundle of hay. (F.—OHG.)
Bound (1), to leap. (F.—L.—Gk.)
Bound (2), a boundary, limit. (F.—C.)
Bound (3), ready to go. (Scand.)
Bourn (1), a boundary. (F.)
Bourn (2), Burn, a stream. (E.)
Bow (1), vb., to bend. (E.)
Bow (2), a bend. (E.) *Allied to* Bow (1).
Bow (3), a weapon to shoot with. (E.) *Allied to* Bow (1).
Bow (4), the bow of a ship. (Scand.)
Bowl (1), a round wooden ball. (F.—L.)
Bowl (2), a drinking-vessel. (E.)
Box (1), the name of a tree. (L.—Gk.)
Box (2), a case to put things in. (L.—Gk.) *See* Box (1).
Box (3), in ' *box* the compass.' (L.—Gk.) *See* Box (2).
Box (4), to fight with fists; a blow. (E.)
Brake (1), a machine for breaking hemp, &c. (OLow G.)
Brake (2), a bush, thicket, fern. (E.)
Brat (1), a cloak, rough mantle. (C.)
Brat (2), a child. (C.) *From* Brat (1).
Brawl (1), to quarrel, roar. (E.)
Brawl (2), a sort of dance. (F.)
Bray (1), to bruise, pound. (F.—Teut.)
Bray (2), to make a loud noise, as an ass. (F.—C.)
Braze (1), to harden. (F.—Scand.)
Braze (2), to ornament with brass. (E.) *Allied to* Braze (1).
Breeze (1), a gadfly. (E.)
Breeze (2), a strong wind. (F.)
Breeze (3), cinders. (F.—Scand.)
Brief (1), short. (F.—L.)
Brief (2), a letter, &c. (F.—L.) *The same as* Brief (1).
Broil (1), to fry, roast over hot coals. (F.—Teut.)
Broil (2), a disturbance, tumult. (F.)
Brook (1), to endure, put up with. (E.)

Brook (2), a small stream. (E.)
Buck (1), a male deer or goat. (E.)
Buck (2), to steep clothes in lye. (E.)
Budge (1), to stir, move from one's place. (F.—L.)
Budge (2), a kind of fur. (F.)
Buff (1), in ' blindman's buff.' (F.—Teut.)
Buff (2), a pale yellow colour. (F.—L.—Gk.)
Buffer (1), a foolish fellow. (F.) *Allied to* Buffer (2).
Buffer (2), a cushion with springs used to deaden concussion. (F.)
Buffet (1), a blow; to strike. (F.)
Buffet (2), a side-board. (F.)
Bug (1), Bugbear, a terrifying spectre. (C.)
Bug (2), an insect. (E.)
Bugle (1), a wild ox; a horn. (F.—L.)
Bugle (2), a kind of ornament. (F.—L.) *See* Bugle (1).
Bugle (3), a plant. (F.—Late L.)
Bulk (1), magnitude, size. (Scand.)
Bulk (2), the trunk of the body. (Dutch.)
Bulk (3), a stall of a shop. (Scand.)
Bull (1), a male bovine quadruped. (E.)
Bull (2), a papal edict. (L.)
Bump (1), to thump, beat; a blow, knob. (E.)
Bump (2), to make a noise like a bittern. (E.)
Bunting (1), the name of a bird. (Scand. ?)
Bunting (2), a thin woollen stuff, of which ship's flags are made. (E. ?)
Burden (1), Burthen, a load carried. (E.)
Burden (2), the refrain of a song. (F.—Late L.)
Burn (1), to set on fire. (E.)
Burn (2), a brook. (E.) *See* Bourn (2).
Bury (1), to hide in the ground. (E.)
Bury (2), a town, as in *Canterbury.* (E.) *Allied to* Bury (1).
Bush (1), a thicket. (Late L.)
Bush (2), the metal box in which an axle works. (Du.—L.—Gk.)
Busk (1), to get oneself ready. (Scand.)
Busk (2), a support for a woman's stays. (F.)
Buss (1), a kiss, to kiss. (E.)
Buss (2), a herring-boat. (F.)
But (1), prep. and conj., except. (E.)
But (2), to strike; a but-end. *See below.*
Butt (1), an end; a thrust; to thrust. (F.—OLow G.)
Butt (2), a large barrel. (F.—Late L.)
Butt (3), a thick end. (E.)
Butt (4), a kind of flat fish. (E.)

Cab (1), an abbreviation of *cabriolet.* (F.—Ital.—L.)
Cab (2), a Hebrew measure, 2 Kings vi. 25. (Heb.)
Cabbage (1), a vegetable with a large head. (F.—L.)
Cabbage (2), to steal. (F.—Prov.—Late L.—L.)
Calender (1), a machine for pressing cloth. (F.—Late L.—Gk.)
Calender (2), a kind of wandering monk. (F.—Pers.)
Calf (1), the young of the cow. (E.)
Calf (2), a part of the leg. (Scand.) *See above.*
Can (1), I am able. (E.)
Can (2), a drinking vessel. (E.)
Cannon (1), a large gun. (F.—Ital.—L.—Gk.)
Cannon (2), a stroke at billiards.' (F.—Span.)
Canon (1), a rule, ordinance. (L.—Gk.) *Hence* Canon (2).
Canon (2), a dignitary of the church. (F.—L.—Gk.)
Cant (1), to talk hypocritically. (L.)
Cant (2), an edge, corner. (Dutch—L.—Gk.)
Cape (1), a covering for the shoulders. (F.—Span.—Late L.)
Cape (2), a headland. (F.—Ital.—L.)
Caper (1), to dance about. (Ital.—L.)
Caper (2), the flower-bud of the caper-bush. (F.—L.—Gk.)
Capital (1), relating to the head; chief. (F.—L.) ⎫
Capital (2), wealth, stock of money. (F.—L.) ⎬ *Allied.*
Capital (3), the head of a pillar. (F.—L.) ⎭
Card (1), a piece of paste-board. (F.—Ital.—Gk.)
Card (2), an instrument for combing wool. (F.—L.)
Carousal (1), a drinking-bout. (F.—G.)
Carousal (2), a kind of pageant. (F.—Ital.)
Carp (1), a fresh water fish. (F.—Late L.—Teut.)
Carp (2), to cavil at. (Scand.)
Case (1), that which happens; an event, &c. (F.—L.)
Case (2), a receptacle, cover. (F.—L.)
Cash (1), coin or money. (F.—Ital.—L.)
Cash (2), an Indian coin. (Tamil—Skt.)
Celt (1), a name given to the Gauls, &c. (C.)
Celt (2), a primitive chisel. (L.)
Chap (1), to cleave, crack; Chop, to cut. (E.)
Chap (2), a fellow; Chapman, a merchant. (E.)

Char (1), to turn to charcoal. (E.)
Char (2), a turn of work. (E.)
Char (3), a kind of fish. (C.)
Charm (1), a song, a spell. (F.—L.)
Charm (2), a blended noise of voices. (E.)
Chase (1), to hunt after, pursue. (F.—L.)
Chase (2), to enchase, emboss. (F.—L.) *Allied to* Chase (3).
Chase (3), a printer's frame for type. (F.—L.) *See* Case (2).
Chase (4), the cavity of a gun-barrel. (F.—L.) *See* Case (2).
CLink (1), a cleft, crevice. (E.)
Chink (2), to jingle. (E.)
Chit (1), a whelp, cub, brat. (E.)
Chit (2), a shoot, a sprout. (E.)
Chop (1), to cut suddenly, strike off. (E.)
Chop (2), to barter, exchange. (E.)
Chuck (1), to strike gently ; to toss. (F —OLow G.)
Chuck (2), to cluck as a hen. (E.)
Chuck (3), a chicken. (E.) *Allied to* Chicken.
Clam (1), to adhere, as something viscid. (E.)
Clam (2), a kind of clamp or vice. (E.)
Cleave (1), *strong verb*, to split asunder. (E.)
Cleave (2), *weak verb*, to stick, adhere. (E.)
Clip (1), to cut off, to shear. (Scand.)
Clip (2), to embrace, to grip. (E.)
Close (1), to shut in, shut, make close. (F.—L.) *Whence* Close (2).
Close (2), adj., shut up, confined, narrow. (F.—L.)
Clove (1), a kind of spice. (F.—L.)
Clove (2), a bulb or tuber. (E.)
Clove (3), a denomination of weight. (F.—L.)
Club (1), a heavy stick, a cudgel. (Scand.) ⎫
Club (2), an association of persons. (Scand.) ⎬ *Allied.*
Club (3), one of a suit at cards. (Scand.) ⎭
Clutter (1), to coagulate, clot. (E.) *Hence* Clutter (2).
Clutter (2), a confused heap ; to heap up. (E.)
Clutter (3), a noise, great din. (E.)
Cob (1), a round lump, or knob. (E.)
Cob (2), to beat, strike. (E.) *Allied to* Cob (1).
Cobble (1), to patch up. (E.)
Cobble (2), a small round lump. (E.)
Cock (1), the male of the domestic fowl. (E.)
Cock (2), to stick up abruptly. (E.)
Cock (3), part of the lock of a gun. (E.)
Cock (4), a small pile of hay. (Scand.)
Cock (5), Cockboat, a small boat. (F.—L.—Gk.)
Cockle (1), a sort of bivalve. (F.—L.—Gk.)
Cockle (2), a weed among corn; darnel. (E.)
Cockle (3), to be uneven, pucker up. (Scand.)
Cocoa (1), the cocoa-nut palm-tree. (Port.)
Cocoa (2), corrupt form of Cacao. (Span.—Mexican.)
Cod (1), a kind of fish. (E.)
Cod (2), a husk, shell, bag, bolster. (E.)
Codling (1), a young cod. (E.)
Codling (2), Codlin, a kind of apple. (C.; *with* E. *suffix.*)
Cog (1), a tooth on the rim of a wheel. (Scand.)
Cog (2), to trick, delude. (Scand.)
Coil (1), to gather together. (F.—L.)
Coil (2), a noise, bustle, confusion. (F.—L.) *From* Coil (1).
Colleague (1), a coadjutor, partner. (F.—L.)
Colleague (2), to join in an alliance. (F.—L.)
Colon (1), a mark printed thus (:). (Gk.)
Colon (2), part of the intestines. (Gk.)
Compact (1), close, firm. (F.—L.) *Allied to* Compact (2).
Compact (2), a bargain, agreement. (L.)
Compound (1), to compose, mix. (L.)
Compound (2), an enclosure of a factory. (Malay.)
Con (1), to enquire into, observe closely. (E.)
Con (2), used in the phrase *pro and con.* (L.)
Contract (1), to draw together, shorten. (L.) *Allied to* Contract (2).
Contract (2), a bargain, agreement. (F.—L.)
Cope (1), a cap, hood, cloak, cape. (Late L.)
Cope (2), to vie with, match. (F.—L.—Gk.)
Cope (3), to buy. (Dutch.)
Corn (1), grain. (E.)
Corn (2), an excrescence on the foot. (F.—L.)
Corporal (1), a subordinate officer. (F.—L.)
Corporal (2), belonging to the body. (F.—L.)
Cotton (1), a downy substance. (F.—Span.—Arabic.)
Cotton (2), to agree. (F.—Span.—Arab.) *From* Cotton (1).
Count (1), a title of rank. (F.—L.)
Count (2), to enumerate, compute. (F.—L.)
Counterpane (1), a coverlet for a bed. (F.—L.)

Counterpane (2), the counterpart of a deed. (F.—L.)
Court (1), a yard, enclosed space, tribunal, &c. (F.—L.)
Court (2), to woo, seek favour. (F.—L.) *From* Court (1).
Cow (1), the female of the bull. (E.)
Cow (2), to subdue, dishearten. (Scand.)
Cowl (1), a monk's hood, a cap, hood. (L.)
Cowl (2), a vessel carried on a pole. (F.—L.)
Coy (1), modest, bashful, retired. (F.—L.)
Coy (2), a decoy for wild duck. (Du.—L.)
Crab (1), a common shell-fish. (E.)
Crab (2), a kind of apple. (E.)
Crank (1), a bent arm, for turning an axis. (E.) ⎫
Crank (2), liable to be upset, said of a boat. (E.) ⎬ *Allied.*
Crank (3), lively, brisk. (E.) ⎭
Crease (1), a wrinkle, small fold. (F.—L.)
Crease (2), Creese, a Malay dagger. (Malay.)
Cricket (1), a shrill-voiced insect. (F.—Du.)
Cricket (2), a game with bat and ball. (F.—Du.)
Croup (1), an affection of the larynx. (E.)
Croup (2), the hinder parts of a horse. (F.—Teut.)
Crowd (1), to push, press, squeeze. (E.)
Crowd (2), a fiddle, violin. (W.)
Cue (1), a tail, a billiard-rod. (F.—L.)
Cue (2), a direction for an actor's appearance. (F.—L.)
Cuff (1), to strike with the open hand. (Scand.)
Cuff (2), part of the sleeve. (L. ?)
Culver (1), a dove. (E. *or* L.)
Culver (2), another form of Culverin. (F.—L.)
Cunning (1), skilful, knowing. (E.)
Cunning (2), knowledge, skill. (Scand.) *See* Cunning (1)
Curry (1), to dress leather. (F.—L. *and* Teut.)
Curry (2), a kind of seasoned dish. (Tamil.)
Cypress (1), a kind of tree. (F.—L.—Gk.)
Cypress (2), Cypress-lawn, crape. (F.—L.—Gk.)

Dab (1), to strike gently. (E.)
Dab (2), expert. (E.)
Dab (3), a fish. (E.)
Dam (1), an earth-bank for restraining water. (E.)
Dam (2), a mother, chiefly applied to animals. (F.—L.)
Dare (1), to be bold, to venture. (E.)
Dare (2), a dace. (F.—OLow G.)
Date (1), an epoch, given point of time. (F.—L.)
Date (2), the fruit of a palm. (F.—L.—Gk.—Semitic.)
Deal (1), a share, division ; a quantity. (E.)
Deal (2), to distribute, to traffic. (E.) *Allied to* Deal (1).
Deal (3), a thin plank of timber. (Du.)
Defer (1), to put off, delay. (F.—L.)
Defer (2), to submit, submit oneself. (F.—L.)
Defile (1), to make foul, pollute. (Hybrid ; L. *and* E.)
Defile (2), to pass along in a file. (F.—L.)
Demean (1), to conduct; *refl.* to behave. (F.—L.)
Demean (2), to debase, lower. (Hybrid ; L. *and* E.)
Desert (1), a waste, wilderness. (F.—L.)
Desert (2), merit. (F.—L.)
Deuce (1), a two, at cards or dice. (F.—L.)
Deuce (2), an evil spirit, devil. (F.—L.) *From* Deuce (1).
Die (1), to lose life, perish. (Scand.)
Die (2), a small cube, for gaming. (F.—L.)
Diet (1), a prescribed allowance of food. (F.—L.—Gk.)
Diet (2), an assembly, council. (F.—L.—Gk.) *See* Diet (1).
Distemper (1), to derange the temperament. (F.—L.)
Distemper (2), a kind of painting. (F.—L.) *From* Distemper (1).
Dock (1), to cut short, curtail. (E.)
Dock (2), a kind of plant. (E.)
Dock (3), a basin for ships. (Du.)
Don (1), to put on clothes. (E.)
Don (2), a Spanish title. (Span.—L.)
Down (1), soft plumage. (Scand.)
Down (2), a hill. (C.) *Whence* Down (3).
Down (3), adv. and prep., in a descending direction. (AS.; *from* C.)
Dowse (1), to strike in the face. (Scand.)
Dowse (2), to plunge into water. (Scand.)
Dowse (3), to extinguish. (E.)
Drab (1), a low, sluttish woman. (E.)
Drab (2), of a dull brown colour. (F.—Late L.)
Dredge (1), a drag-net. (E.)
Dredge (2), to sprinkle flour on meat, &c. (F.—Late L.—Gk.)
Drill (1), to pierce, to train soldiers. (Du.)
Drill (2), to sow corn in rows. (Low G.)
Drone (1), to make a murmuring sound. (E.)

Drone (2), a non-working bee. (E.) *Allied to* Drone (1).
Duck (1), a bird. (E.) *From* Duck (2).
Duck (2), to dive, bob the head. (E.)
Duck (3), a pet, darling. (E.) *From* Duck (1).
Duck (4), light canvas. (Du.)
Dudgeon (1), resentment. (F.?)
Dudgeon (2), the haft of a dagger. (Unknown.)
Dun (1), of a dull brown colour. (C.)
Dun (2), to urge for payment. (Scand.)

Ear (1), the organ of hearing. (E.)
Ear (2), a spike, or head, of corn. (E.)
Ear (3), to plough. (E.)
Earnest (1), eagerness, seriousness. (E.)
Earnest (2), a pledge, security. (F.–L.–Gk.–Heb.)
Egg (1), the oval body from which chickens are hatched. (Scand.)
Egg (2), to instigate. (Scand.)
Eke (1), to augment. (E.)
Eke (2), also. (E.) *From* Eke (1).
Elder (1), older. (E.)
Elder (2), the name of a tree. (E.)
Embattle (1), to furnish with battlements. (F.)
Embattle (2), to range in order of battle. (F.–L.)
Emboss (1), to adorn with raised work. (F.)
Emboss (2), to shelter in a wood. (F.)
Endue (1), to endow. (F.–L.)
Endue (2), to clothe. (L.) *For* Indue (1).
Entrance (1), ingress. (F.–L.)
Entrance (2), to put into a trance. (F.–L.)
Exact (1), precise, measured. (L.)
Exact (2), to demand, require. (F.–L.) *From* Exact (1).
Excise (1), a duty or tax. (Du.–F.–L.)
Excise (2), to cut out. (L.)

Fair (1), pleasing, beautiful. (E.)
Fair (2), a festival, market. (F.–L.)
Fallow (1), untilled; said of land. (E.)
Fallow (2), pale brown; said of deer. (E.)
Fast (1), firm, fixed. (E.)
Fast (2), to abstain from food. (E.) } *Allied.*
Fast (3), quick, speedy. (Scand.)
Fat (1), stout, gross. (E.)
Fat (2), a vat. (North E.)
Fawn (1), to cringe to. (E.)
Fawn (2), a young deer. (F.–L.)
Fell (1), to cause to fall, cut down. (E.)
Fell (2), a skin. (E.)
Fell (3), cruel, fierce. (F.–Late L.–L.)
Fell (4), a hill. (Scand.)
Ferret (1), an animal of the weasel tribe. (F.–Late L.–L.)
Ferret (2), a kind of silk tape. (Ital.–L.)
Feud (1), perpetual hostility, hatred. (E.)
Feud (2), a fief. (Low L.–F.–OHG.)
File (1), a string, line, list. (F.–L.)
File (2), a steel rasp. (E.)
File (3), to defile; in Shakespeare. (E.)
Fine (1), exquisite, complete, thin. (F.–L.)
Fine (2), a tax, forced payment. (Law L.) *Allied to* Fine (1).
Firm (1), steadfast, fixed. (F.–L.)
Firm (2), a partnership. (Span.–L.) *From* Firm (1).
Fit (1), to suit; as adj., suitable. (Scand.)
Fit (2), a part of a poem; a sudden attack of illness. (E.)
Flag (1), to droop, grow weary. (E.)
Flag (2), an ensign. (E.) } *Allied.*
Flag (3), a water-plant, reed. (E.)
Flag (4), Flagstone, a paving-stone. (Scand.)
Fleet (1), a number of ships. (E.)
Fleet (2), a creek, bay. (E.) } *Allied to* Fleet (4).
Fleet (3), swift. (E.)
Fleet (4), to move swiftly. (E.)
Flight (1), the act of flying. (E.)
Flight (2), the act of fleeing away. (E.)
Flip (1), to fillip, jerk lightly. (E.)
Flip (2), a mixture of beer with sugar, &c. (E.)
Flock (1), a company of birds or sheep. (E.)
Flock (2), a lock of wool. (F.–L.)
Flounce (1), to plunge about. (Scand.)
Flounce (2), a plaited border on a dress. (F.–L.)
Flounder (1), to flounce about. (Scand.)
Flounder (2), the name of a fish. (F.–Scand.)
Flue (1), an air-passage, chimney-pipe. (F.–L.)

Flue (2), light floating down. (E.?)
Fluke (1), a flounder, kind of fish. (E.)
Fluke (2), part of an anchor. (E.)
Flush (1), to flow swiftly. (E.)
Flush (2), to blush, to redden. (E.)
Flush (3), level, even. (E.) *Perhaps from* Flush (1).
Flush (4), a term in playing cards. (F.–L.)
Fly (1), to move or float in air. (E.)
Fly (2), a vehicle. (E.) *From* Fly (1).
Fob (1), a pocket for a watch. (OLow G.)
Fob (2), to cheat, deceive. (Low G.)
Foil (1), to disappoint, defeat. (F.–L.)
Foil (2), a set-off, in the setting of a gem. (F.–L.)
Fold (1), to double together, wrap up. (E.)
Fold (2), a sheep-pen. (E.)
Font (1), a basin for baptism. (L.) *Allied to* Font (2).
Font (2), Fount, an assortment of types. (F.–L.)
Fool (1), a silly person, a jester. (F.–L.) *Hence* Fool (2).
Fool (2), a dish of crushed fruit, &c. (F.–L.)
For (1), in the place of. (E.)
For- (2), only in composition. (E.)
For- (3), only in composition. (F.–L.)
Forbear (1), to hold away or abstain from. (E.)
Forbear (2), an ancestor, lit. 'fore-be-ër.' (E.)
Force (1), strength, power. (F.–L.)
Force (2), to stuff fowls, &c. (F.–L.)
Force (3), Foss, a waterfall. (Scand.)
Fore-arm (1), the fore part of the arm. (E.)
Fore-arm (2), to arm beforehand. (Hybrid; E. *and* F.)
Forego (1), to relinquish; better Forgo. (E.)
Forego (2), to go before. (E.)
Forejudge (1), to judge beforehand. (Hybrid; E. *and* F.)
Forejudge (2), to deprive by the judgement of a court. (F.–L.)
Foster (1), to nourish. (E.)
Foster (2), a forester. (F.–L.)
Found (1), to lay the foundation of. (F.–L.)
Found (2), to cast metals. (F.–L.)
Fount (1), a fountain. (F.–L.) *Allied to* Fount (2).
Fount (2), an assortment of types. (F.–L.) *See* Font (2).
Fratricide (1), a murderer of a brother. (F.–L.)
Fratricide (2), murder of a brother. (L.) *Allied to* Fratricide (1).
Fray (1), an affray. (F.–L.)
Fray (2), to terrify. (F.–L. *and* OHG.)
Fray (3), to wear away by rubbing. (F.–L.)
Freak (1), a whim, caprice. (E.)
Freak (2), to streak, variegate. (E.?)
Fret (1), to eat away. (E.)
Fret (2), to ornament, variegate. (F.)
Fret (3), a kind of grating. (F.–L.?) *See* Fret (4).
Fret (4), a stop on a musical instrument. (F.–L.)
Frieze (1), a coarse, woollen cloth. (F.–Du.)
Frieze (2), part of the entablature of a column. (F.–L.)
Frith (1), a forest, a wood. (E.)
Frith (2), Firth, an estuary. (Scand.)
Fritter (1), a kind of pancake. (F.–L.)
Fritter (2), a fragment. (F.–L.)
Frog (1), a small amphibious animal. (E.)
Frog (2), a substance in a horse's foot. (E.?)
Fry (1), to dress food over a fire. (F.–L.)
Fry (2), the spawn of fishes. (F.–L.)
Full (1), filled up, complete. (E.)
Full (2), to full cloth, to felt. (F.–L.)
Fuse (1), to melt by heat. (L.)
Fuse (2), a tube with combustible materials. (F.–L.)
Fusee (1), a fuse or match. (F.–L.) *See* Fuse (2).
Fusee (2), a spindle in a watch. (F.–L.) *From* Fusee (1).
Fusil (1), a light musket. (F.–L.)
Fusil (2), a spindle, in heraldry. (F.–L.)
Fusil (3), easily molten. (L.)
Fust (1), to become mouldy or rusty. (F.–L.) *From* Fust (2).
Fust (2), the shaft of a column. (F.–L.)

Gad (1), a wedge of steel, goad. (Scand.)
Gad (2), to ramble idly. (Scand.) *From* Gad (1)?
Gage (1), a pledge. (F.–Teut.)
Gage (2), to gauge. (F.–Low L.)
Gain (1), profit, advantage. (F.–Teut.)
Gain (2), to acquire, get, win. (F.–Teut.) *From* Gain (1).
Gale (1), a strong wind. (Scand.)
Gale (2), a plant; the bog-myrtle. (E.)
Gall (1), bile, bitterness. (E.)

Gall (2), to rub a sore place, to vex. (F.—L.)

Gall (3), Gall-nut, a vegetable excrescence produced by insects. (F.—L.)

Galt (1), a series of beds of clay and marl. (Scand.)

Galt (2), a boar-pig. (Scand.)

Gammon (1), the pickled thigh of a hog. (F.—L.)

Gammon (2), nonsense, a jest. (E.)

Gang (1), a crew. (Scand.) *From* Gang (2).

Gang (2), to go. (Scand.)

Gantlet (1), the same as Gauntlet, a glove. (F.—Scand.)

Gantlet (2), also Gantlope, a military punishment. (Swed.)

Gar (1), Garfish, a kind of pike. (E.)

Gar (2), to cause. (Scand.)

Garb (1), dress, manner, fashion. (F.—Ital.—OHG.)

Garb (2), a sheaf. (F.—OHG.)

Gate (1), a door, opening, way. (E.)

Gate (2), a street. (Scand.)

Gauntlet (1), the same as Gantlet (1).

Gauntlet (2), the same as Gantlet (2).

Gender (1), kind, breed, sex. (F.—L.)

Gender (2), to engender, produce. (F.—L.) *Allied to* Gender (1).

Gill (1), an organ of respiration in fishes. (Scand.)

Gill (2), a ravine, yawning chasm. (Scand.)

Gill (3), with *g* as *j*; a quarter of a pint. (F.—L.?)

Gill (4), with *g* as *j*; a woman's name; ground-ivy. (F.—L.)

Gin (1), to begin; pronounced with *g* hard. (E.)

Gin (2), a trap, snare. (F.—L.)

Gin (3), a kind of spirit. (F.—L.)

Gird (1), to enclose, bind round, surround, clothe. (E.)

Gird (2), to jest at, jibe. (E.)

Glede (1), the bird called a kite. (E.)

Glede (2), a glowing coal; *obsolete.* (E.)

Gleek (1), a scoff, jest. (F.—Du. ?)

Gleek (2), a game at cards. (F.—Du.)

Glib (1), smooth, slippery, voluble. (E.)

Glib (2), a lock of hair. (C.)

Glib (3), to castrate; *obsolete.* (E.)

Gloss (1), brightness, lustre. (Scand.)

Gloss (2), a commentary, explanation. (L.—Gk.)

Gore (1), clotted blood, blood. (E.)

Gore (2), to pierce, bore through. (E.)

Gore (3), a triangular piece let into a garment; a triangular slip of land. (E.) *Allied to* Gore (2).

Gout (1), a drop, a disease. (F.—L.)

Gout (2), taste. (F.—L.)

Grail (1), a gradual, or service-book. (F.—L.)

Grail (2), the Holy Dish at the Last Supper. (F.—L.)

Grail (3), fine sand. (F.)

Grate (1), a framework of iron bars. (Late L.—L.)

Grate (2), to rub, scrape, scratch, creak. (F.—Teut.)

Grave (1), to cut, engrave. (E.)

Grave (2), solemn, sad. (F.—L.)

Graze (1), to feed cattle. (E.)

Graze (2), to scrape slightly, rub lightly. (E.)

Greaves (1), Graves, the sediment of melted tallow. (E.)

Greaves (2), armour for the legs. (F.)

Greet (1), to salute. (E.)

Greet (2), to weep, cry, lament. (E.)

Grig (1), a small lively eel. (Scand.)

Grig (2), a cricket. (E.)

Grit (1), gravel, coarse sand. (E.)

Grit (2), coarse oatmeal. (E.) *Allied to* Grit (1).

Gull (1), a web-footed sea-bird. (C.)

Gull (2), a dupe. (Low G.)

Gum (1), the flesh of the jaws. (E.)

Gum (2), the hardened juice of certain trees. (F.—L.—Gk.—Egypt.)

Gust (1), a sudden blast or gush of wind. (Scand.)

Gust (2), relish, taste. (L.)

Guy (1), a hideous creature, a fright. (F.—Ital.—Teut.)

Guy (2), a rope used to steady a weight. (F.—Teut.)

Hack (1), to cut, chop, mangle. (E.)

Hack (2), a hackney. *See* Hackney. (E.)

Hackle (1), Hatchel, an instrument for dressing flax. (E.)

Hackle (2), long shining feathers on a cock's neck. (E.)

Haggard (1), wild, said of a hawk. (F.—G.)

Haggard (2), lean, hollow-eyed, meagre. (F.—G.) *See* above.

Haggle (1), to cut awkwardly, mangle. (Scand.)

Haggle (2), to be slow in making a bargain. (Scand.) *See* above.

Hail (1), frozen rain. (E.)

Hail (2), to greet, call to, address. (Scand.)

Hail! (3), an exclamation of greeting. (Scand.) *See* Hail (2).

Hale (1), whole, healthy, sound. (E.)

Hale (2), Haul, to drag, draw violently. (F.—OHG.)

Halt (1), lame. (E.)

Halt (2), a sudden stop. (F.—G.)

Hamper (1), to impede, hinder, harass. (E.)

Hamper (2), a kind of basket. (F.—G.)

Handy (1), dexterous, expert. (E.)

Handy (2), convenient, near. (E.) *Allied to* Handy (1).

Harrier (1), a hare-hound. (E.)

Harrier (2), a kind of falcon. (E.)

Hatch (1), a half-door, wicket. (E.)

Hatch (2), to produce a brood by incubation. (E.)

Hatch (3), to shade by minute lines. (F.—G.)

Hawk (1), a bird of prey. (E.)

Hawk (2), to carry about for sale. (OLow G.)

Hawk (3), to clear the throat. (E.)

Hay (1), grass cut and dried. (E.)

Hay (2), a hedge. (E.)

Heel (1), the part of the foot projecting behind. (E.)

Heel (2), to lean over, incline. (E.)

Helm (1), the instrument by which a ship is steered. (E.)

Helm (2), Helmet, armour for the head. (E.)

Hem (1), the border of a garment. (E.)

Hem (2), a slight cough to call attention. (E.)

Herd (1), a flock of beasts, group of animals. (E.)

Herd (2), one who tends a herd. (E.) *From* Herd (1).

Heyday (1), interjection. (G. or Du.)

Heyday (2), frolicsome wildness. (E.)

Hide (1), to cover, conceal. (E.)

Hide (2), a skin. (E.) } *Allied.*

Hide (3), to flog, castigate. (E.)

Hide (4), a measure of land. (E.)

Hind (1), the female of the stag. (E.)

Hind (2), a peasant. (E.)

Hind (3), adj., in the rear. (E.)

Hip (1), the haunch, upper part of the thigh. (E.)

Hip (2), also Hep, the fruit of the dog-rose. (E.)

Hob (1), Hub, the nave of a wheel, part of a grate. (E.)

Hob (2), a clown, a rustic, a fairy. (F.—OHG.)

Hobby (1), Hobby-horse, an ambling nag, a favourite pursuit (F.—OHG.)

Hobby (2), a small species of falcon. (F.—Du.)

Hock, (1), Hough, back of the knee-joint. (E.)

Hock (2), the name of a wine. (G.)

Hold (1), to keep, retain, defend, restrain. (E.)

Hold (2), the 'hold' of a ship. (Du.) *Allied to* Hole.

Homicide (1), manslaughter. (F.—L.)

Homicide (2), a man-slayer. (F.—L.) *Allied to* Homicide (1).

Hoop (1), a pliant strip of wood or metal bent into a band. (E.)

Hoop (2), to call out, shout. (F.—Teut.)

Hop (1), to leap on one leg. (E.)

Hop (2), the name of a plant. (Du.)

Hope (1), expectation; as a verb, to expect. (E.)

Hope (2), a troop; in the phr. 'forlorn hope.' (Du.)

Host (1), one who entertains guests. (F.—L.) *From* Host (2).

Host (2), an army. (F.—L.)

Host (3), the consecrated bread of the eucharist. (L.)

How (1), in what way. (E.)

How (2), a hill. (Scand.)

Hoy (1), a kind of sloop. (Du.)

Hoy (2), interj., stop! (Du.)

Hue (1), show, appearance, colour, tint. (E.)

Hue (2), clamour, outcry. (F.—Teut.)

Hull (1), the husk or outer shell of grain or of nuts. (E.)

Hull (2), the body of a ship. (Du.) *Cf.* Hull (1), Hold (2).

Hum (1), to make a low buzzing or droning sound. (E.)

Hum (2), to trick, to cajole. (E.) *From* Hum (1).

Il- (1), a form of the prefix *in-* = L. prep. *in.* (L.; or F.—L.)

Il- (2), a form of the prefix *in-* used negatively. (L.; or F.—L.)

Im- (1), prefix. (F.—L.) *Hence* Im- (2), prefix.

Im- (3), prefix. (L.)

Im- (4), negative prefix. (F.—L.; or L.)

In- (1), prefix, in. (E.)

In- (2), prefix, in. (L.; or F.—L.)

In- (3), prefix with negative force. (L.; or F.—L.)

Incense (1), to inflame. (L.) *Hence* Incense (2).

Incense (2), spices, odour of spices burned. (F.—L.)

Inch (1), the twelfth part of a foot. (L.)

Inch (2), an island. (Gaelic.)

Incontinent (1), unchaste. (F.—L.)
Incontinent (2), immediately. (F.—L.) *Due to the above.*
Indent (1), to notch. (Law L.)
Indent (2), to make a dint in. (E.)
Indue (1), to invest or clothe with, supply with. (L.)
Indue (2), a corruption of Endue, q.v. (F.—L.)
Ingle (1), fire. (C.)
Ingle (2), a darling, paramour. (Du.—L.—Gk.)
Interest (1), profit, premium for use of money. (F.—L.)
Interest (2), to engage the attention. (F.—L.) *Allied to* Interest (1).
Intimate (1), to announce, hint. (L.)
Intimate (2), familiar, close. (L.) *Allied to* Intimate (1).
Ir- (1), prefix; for *in* before *r*. (L.; or F.—L.)
Ir- (2), negative prefix. (L.; or F.—L.)

Jack (1), a saucy fellow, sailor. (F.—L.—Gk.—Heb.)
Jack (2), a coat of mail. (F.—L.—Gk.—Heb.) *From* Jack (1).
Jade (1), a sorry nag, an old woman. (Scand. ?)
Jade (2), a hard dark green stone. (F.—Span.—L.)
Jam (1), to press, squeeze tight. (E.) *Hence* Jam (2).
Jam (2), a conserve of fruit boiled with sugar. (E.)
Jar (1), to make a discordant noise, creak, clash, quarrel. (E.)
Jar (2), an earthen pot. (F.—Span.—Arab.)
Jet (1), to throw out, fling about, spout. (F.—L.)
Jet (2), a black mineral, used for ornaments. (F.—L.—Gk.)
Jib (1), the foremost sail of a ship. (Du.) ⎫
Jib (2), to shift a sail from side to side. (Du.) ⎬ *Allied.*
Jib (3), to move restively, as a horse. (F.—Scand.) ⎭
Job (1), to peck with the beak, as a bird. (E. ?)
Job (2), a small piece of work. (F.—C.)
Jump (1), to leap, spring, skip. (Scand.)
Jump (2), exactly, just, pat. (Scand.) *From* Jump (1).
Junk (1), a Chinese three-masted vessel. (Port.—Malay.)
Junk (2), pieces of old cordage. (Port.—L.)
Just (1), righteous, upright, true. (F.—L.)
Just (2), the same as Joust, to tilt. (F.—L.)

Kedge (1), to warp a ship. (F.—L.)
Kedge (2), Kidge, cheerful, lively. (E.)
Keel (1), the bottom of a ship. (Scand.)
Keel (2), to cool. (E.)
Kennel (1), a house for dogs, pack of hounds. (F.—L.)
Kennel (2), a gutter. (F.—L.)
Kern (1), Kerne, an Irish soldier. (Irish.)
Kern (2), the same as Quern, a hand-mill. (E.)
Kind (1), sb., nature, sort, character. (E.)
Kind (2), adj., natural, loving. (E.) *From* Kind (1).
Kindle (1), to set fire to, inflame. (Scand.)
Kindle (2), to bring forth young. (E.)
Kit (1), a vessel, milk-pail, tub; hence, an outfit. (Du.)
Kit (2), a small violin. (F.—L.—Gk.)
Kit (3), a brood, family, quantity. (Du.) *From* Kit (1).
Knoll (1), the top of a hill, a hillock, mound. (E.)
Knoll (2), Knell, to toll a bell. (E.)

Lac (1), a resinous substance. (Hind.—Skt.)
Lac (2), a hundred thousand. (Hind.—Skt.) *Allied to* Lac (1).
Lack (1), want. (E.)
Lack (2), to want, be destitute of. (E.) *From* Lack (1).
Lade (1), to load. (E.)
Lade (2), to lade out water, drain. (E.) *Same as* Lade (1).
Lake (1), a pool. (F.—L.)
Lake (2), a colour, a kind of crimson. (F.—Pers.—Skt.)
Lama (1), a high priest. (Thibetan.)
Lama (2), the same as Llama, a quadruped. (Peruvian.)
Lap (1), to lick up with the tongue. (E.)
Lap (2), the loose part of a coat, an apron, part of the body covered by an apron, a fold, flap. (E.)
Lap (3), to wrap, involve, fold. (E.) *From* Lap (2).
Lark (1), the name of a bird. (E.)
Lark (2), a game, sport, fun. (E.) *From* Lark (1).
Lash (1), to fasten firmly together. (F.—L.)
Lash (2), a thong, flexible part of a whip. (F.—L.) *From* Lash (1).
Last (1), latest, hindmost. (E.)
Last (2), a mould of the foot on which shoes are made. (E.)
Last (3), to endure, continue. (E.) *From* Last (2).
Last (4), a load, large weight, ship's cargo. (E.)
Lathe (1), a machine for 'turning' wood and metal. (Scand.)
Lathe (2), a division of a county. (E.)
Launch (1), to lance; to send into the water. (F.—L.)
Launch (2), a kind of long-boat. (Span.—Port.—Malay.)

Lawn (1), a smooth grassy space of ground. (F.—C.)
Lawn (2), a sort of fine linen. (F.—C.)
Lay (1), to cause to lie down, place, set. (E.)
Lay (2), a song, lyric poem. (F.—OHG.)
Lay (3), Laic, pertaining to the laity. (F.—L.—Gk.)
Lea (1), Ley, Lay, a tract of open ground. (E.)
Lea (2), Ley, Lay, fallow land, pasture-land. (E.)
Lead (1), to bring, conduct, guide, precede, direct. (E.)
Lead (2), a well-known metal. (E.)
League (1), a bond, alliance, confederacy. (F.—Ital.—L.)
League (2), a distance of about three miles. (Prov.—L.—C.)
Lean (1), to incline, bend, stoop. (E.)
Lean (2), slender, not fat, frail, thin. (E.) *From* Lean (1).
Lease (1), to let tenements for a term of years. (F.—L.)
Lease (2), to glean. (E.)
Leave (1), to quit, abandon, forsake. (E.)
Leave (2), permission, farewell. (E.)
Leech (1), a physician. (E.)
Leech (2), a blood-sucking worm. (E.) *Same as* Leech (1).
Leech (3), Leach, the edge of a sail at the sides. (Scand.)
Let (1), to allow, permit, suffer, grant. (E.)
Let (2), to hinder, prevent, obstruct. (E.) *Allied to* Let (1).
Lie (1), to rest, lean, lay oneself down, be situate. (E.)
Lie (2), to tell a lie, speak falsely. (E.)
Lift (1), to elevate, raise. (Scand.)
Lift (2), to steal. (E.) *From* Lift (1).
Light (1), illumination. (E.)
Light (2), active, not heavy, unimportant. (E.)
Light (3), to settle, alight, descend. (E.) *From* Light (2).
Lighten (1), to illuminate, flash. (E.)
Lighten (2), to make lighter, alleviate. (E.) *See* Light (2).
Lighten (3), to descend, settle, alight. (E.) *See* Light (3).
Like (1), similar, resembling. (E.)
Like (2), to approve, be pleased with. (E.) *From* Like (1).
Limb (1), a member of the body, branch. (E.)
Limb (2), the edge or border of a sextant, &c. (L.)
Limber (1), flexible, pliant. (E.)
Limber (2), part of a gun-carriage. (F.)
Lime (1), viscous substance, mortar, oxide of calcium. (E.)
Lime (2), the linden-tree. (E.)
Lime (3), a kind of citron. (F.—Span.—Arab.—Malay.)
Limp (1), flaccid, flexible, pliant, weak. (E.)
Limp (2), to walk lamely. (E.) *Compare* Limp (1).
Ling (1), a kind of fish. (E.)
Ling (2), heath. (Scand.)
Link (1), a ring of a chain, joint. (Scand.)
Link (2), a torch. (Scand.)
List (1), a stripe or border of cloth, selvage. (E.)
List (2), a catalogue. (F.—G.) *Allied to* List (1).
List (3), gen. in pl. Lists, space for a tournament. (E.) *See* List (1).
List (4), to choose, to desire, have pleasure in. (E.)
List (5), an inclination (of a ship) to one side. (E.) *Cf.* List (4).
List (6), to listen. (E.)
Litter (1), a portable bed. (F.—L.) *Hence* Litter (2), (3).
Litter (2), materials for a bed, a confused mass. (F.—L.)
Litter (3), a brood. (F.—L.)
Live (1), to continue in life, exist, dwell. (E.)
Live (2), adj., alive, active, burning. (E.) *Allied to* Live (1).
Lock (1), an instrument to fasten doors, &c. (E.)
Lock (2), a tuft of hair, flock of wool. (E.)
Log (1), a block, piece of wood. (E.)
Log (2), a thin quadrant of wood, loaded, and fastened to a line, for measuring the rate of a ship. (E.) *The same as* Log (1).
Log (3), a Hebrew liquid measure. (Heb.)
Long (1), extended, not short, tedious. (E.)
Long (2), to desire, yearn; to belong. (E.)
Loom (1), a machine for weaving cloth. (E.)
Loom (2), to appear faintly, or at a distance. (Scand.)
Loon (1), Lown, a base fellow. (E.)
Loon (2), a water-bird, diver. (Scand.)
Low (1), inferior, deep, mean, humble. (Scand.)
Low (2), to bellow as a cow or ox. (E.)
Low (3), a hill. (E.)
Low (4), flame. (Scand.)
Lower (1), to let down, abase, sink. (E.)
Lower (2), to frown, look sour. (E.)
Lumber (1), cumbersome or useless furniture. (F.—G.)
Lumber (2), to make a great noise, as a heavy rolling object. (Scand.)
Lurch (1), to lurk, dodge, steal, pilfer. (Scand.)
Lurch (2), the name of a game. (F.—G.)

Lurch (3), to devour; *obsolete.* (F.?—G.?)
Lurch (4), a sudden roll sideways. (Scand.) *See* Lurch (1).
Lustre (1), splendour, brightness. (F.—Ital.—L.)
Lustre (2), Lustrum, a period of five years. (F.—L.)
Lute (1), a stringed instrument of music. (F.—Prov.—Span.—Arab.)
Lute (2), a composition like clay, loam. (F.—L.)

Mace (1), a kind of club. (F.—L.)
Mace (2), a kind of spice. (F.—L.—Gk.)
Mail (1), steel network forming body-armour. (F.—L.)
Mail (2), a bag for carrying letters. (F.—OHG.)
Mail (3), Black, a forced tribute. (Scand.)
Main (1), sb., strength, might. (E.) *Allied to* Main (2).
Main (2), adj., strong, great. (Scand.)
Mall (1), a wooden hammer or beetle. (F.—L.) *Hence* Mall (2).
Mall (2), the name of a public walk. (F.—Ital.—OHG. *and* L.)
Mangle (1), to render maimed, tear, mutilate. (F.—G.)
Mangle (2), a roller for smoothing linen. (Du.—Late L.—Gk.)
March (1), a border, frontier. (F.—OHG.)
March (2), to walk with regular steps. (F.—L.? *or* G.?)
March (3), the name of the third month. (F.—L.)
Mark (1), a stroke, outline, trace, line, sign. (E.)
Mark (2), a march, limit, boundary. (E.) *Cf.* Mark (1).
Mark (3), the name of a coin. (Scand.) *From* Mark (1).
Maroon (1), brownish crimson. (F.—Ital.)
Maroon (2), to put ashore on a desolate island. (F.—Span.—L.—Gk.)
Marrow (1), soft matter within bones. (E.)
Marrow (2), a companion, partner. (Scand.)
Martlet (1), a kind of bird, a martin. (F.)
Martlet (2), a swift; in heraldry. (F.—L.)
Mass (1), a lump of matter, quantity, size. (F.—L.—Gk.)
Mass (2), the celebration of the Eucharist. (L.)
Mast (1), a pole to sustain the sails of a ship. (E.)
Mast (2), the fruit of beach and forest-trees. (E.)
Match (1), an equal, a contest, game, marriage. (E.)
Match (2), a prepared rope for firing a cannon. (F.—L.—Gk.)
Mate (1), a companion, comrade, equal. (Low G.)
Mate (2), to check-mate, confound. (F.—Pers.—Arab.)
Matricide (1), a slayer of his mother. (F.—L.) *See below.*
Matricide (2), a killing of one's mother. (F.—L.)
Matter (1), the material part of a thing, substance. (F.—L.)
Matter (2), pus, a fluid in abscesses. (F.—L.) *Same as* Matter (1).
May (1), I am able, I am free to act, I am allowed to. (E.)
May (2), the fifth month. (F.—L.)
Mead (1), a drink made from honey. (E.)
Mead (2), Meadow, a grass-field, pasture-ground. (E.)
Meal (1), ground grain. (E.)
Meal (2), a repast, share or time of food. (E.)
Mean (1), to have in the mind, intend, signify. (E.)
Mean (2), common, vile, base, sordid. (E.)
Mean (3), coming between, intermediate, moderate. (F.—L.)
Meet (1), fitting, according to measure, suitable. (E.)
Meet (2), to encounter, find, assemble. (E.)
Mere (1), a lake, pool. (E.)
Mere (2), pure, simple, absolute. (L.)
Mere (3), a boundary. (E.)
Mess (1), a dish of meat, portion of food. (F.—L.)
Mess (2), a mixture, disorder. (F.—L.) *Same as* Mess (1).
Mew (1), to cry as a cat. (E.)
Mew (2), a sea-fowl, gull. (E.)
Mew (3), a cage for hawks, &c. (F.—L.)
Might (1), power, strength. (E.)
Might (2), was able. (E.) *Allied to* Might (1)
Milt (1), the spleen. (E.)
Milt (2), soft roe of fishes. (MDu.)
Mine (1), belonging to me. (E.)
Mine (2), to excavate, dig for metals. (F.—C.)
Mint (1), a place where money is coined. (L.)
Mint (2), the name of an aromatic plant. (L.—Gk.)
Mis- (1), prefix. (E. *and* Scand.)
Mis- (2), prefix. (F.—L.)
Miss (1), to fail to hit, omit, feel the want of. (E.)
Miss (2), a young woman, a girl. (F.—L.)
Misty (1), nebulous, foggy. (E.)
Misty (2), used for Mystic. (F.—L.—Gk.)
Mite (1), a very small insect. (E.)
Mite (2), a very small portion. (F.—Du.) *Allied to* Mite (1).
Mob (1), a disorderly crowd. (L.)
Mob (2), a kind of cap. (Dutch.)
Mole (1), a spot or mark on the body. (E.)

Mole (2), a small animal that burrows. (E.)
Mole (3), a breakwater. (F.—Ital.—L.)
Mood (1), disposition of mind, temper. (E.)
Mood (2), manner, grammatical form. (F.—L.)
Moor (1), a heath, extensive waste ground. (E.)
Moor (2), to fasten a ship by cable and anchor. (E.)
Moor (3), a native of North Africa. (F.—L.)
Mop (1), a implement for washing floors, &c. (F.—L.)
Mop (2), a grimace; to grimace. (E.)
Mortar (1), Morter, a vessel in which substances are pounded. (L.)
Mortar (2), cement of lime, &c. (F.—L.) *Allied to* Mortar (1).
Mother (1), a female parent. (E.)
Mother (2), the hysterical passion. (E.) } *Allied.*
Mother (3), lees, sediment. (E.)
Mould (1), earth, soil, crumbling ground. (E.)
Mould (2), a model, pattern, form, fashion. (F.—L.)
Mould (3), rust, spot. (E.) *See* Mole (1).
Mount (1), a hill, rising ground. (L.)
Mount (2), to ascend. (F.—L.) *From* Mount (1).
Mow (1), to cut down with a scythe. (E.)
Mow (2), a heap, pile of hay or corn. (E.)
Mow (3), a grimace; *obsolete.* (F.—MDu.)
Muff (1), a warm cover for the hands. (Walloon—F.—Late L.)
Muff (2), a silly fellow, simpleton. (E.)
Mullet (1), a kind of fish. (F.—L.)
Mullet (2), a five-pointed star. (F.—L.)
Mum (1), an interjection, imposing silence. (E.)
Mum (2), a kind of beer. (Low G.)
Muscle (1), the fleshy part of the body. (F.—L.)
Muscle (2), Mussel, a shell-fish. (L.) *The same as* Muscle (1).
Muse (1), to meditate, be pensive. (F.—L.)
Muse (2), one of nine fabled goddesses. (F.—L.—Gk.)
Must (1), part of a verb implying 'obligation.' (E.)
Must (2), new wine. (L.)
Mute (1), dumb. (L.)
Mute (2), to dung; used of birds. (F.—MDu.)
Mystery (1), anything kept concealed, a secret rite. (L.—Gk.)
Mystery (2), Mistery, a trade, handicraft. (F.—L.)

Nag (1), a small horse. (MDu.)
Nag (2), to worry, tease. (Scand.)
Nap (1), a short sleep. (E.)
Nap (2), the roughish surface of cloth. (MDu.)
Nave (1), the central portion or hub of a wheel. (E.)
Nave (2), the middle or body of a church. (F.—L.)
Neat (1), black cattle, an ox, cow. (E.)
Neat (2), tidy, unadulterated. (F.—L.)
Negus (1), a beverage of wine, water, sugar, &c. (E.)
Negus (2), an Abyssinian title. (Abyssinian.)
Net (1), an implement for catching fish, &c. (E.)
Net (2), clear of all charges. (F.—L.)
Nick (1), a small notch, a cut. (E.)
Nick (2), the devil. (F.—L.—Gk.)
No (1), a word of refusal or denial. (E.)
No (2), none. (E.)
Not (1), a word expressing denial. (E.)
Not (2), I know not, or he knows not. (E.)
Not (3), to crop, to shear closely. (E.)

O (1), Oh, an interjection. (E.)
O (2), a circle. (E.)
One (1), single, undivided, sole. (E.) *Hence* One (2)
One (2), a person, spoken of indefinitely. (E.)
Or (1), conjunction, offering an alternative. (E.)
Or (2), ere. (E.)
Or (3), gold. (F.—L.)
Ought (1), past tense of Owe. (E.)
Ought (2), another spelling of Aught, anything. (E.)
Ounce (1), the twelfth part of a pound. (F.—L.)
Ounce (2), Once, a kind of lynx. (F.—L.—Gk.)
Own (1), possessed by any one, belonging to oneself. (E.)
Own (2), to possess. (E.) *From* Own (1).
Own (3), to grant, admit. (E.) *From* Own (2).

Pad (1), a soft cushion, &c. (E.)
Pad (2), a thief on the high road. (Du.)
Paddle (1), to finger; to dabble in water. (E.)
Paddle (2), a little spade, esp. for cleaning a plough. (E.)
Paddock (1), a toad. (Scand.)
Paddock (2), a small enclosure. (E.)
Page (1), a young male attendant. (F.—Low Lat.—Gk.?)

Page (2), one side of the leaf of a book. (F.—L.)
Pale (1), a stake, enclosure, limit, district. (F.—L.)
Pale (2), wan, dim. (F.—L.)
Pall (1), a cloak, mantle, archbishop's scarf, shroud. (L.)
Pall (2), to become vapid, lose taste or spirit. (F.—L.)
Pallet (1), a kind of mattress or couch. (F.—L.)
Pallet (2), an instrument used by potters, &c. (F.—Ital.—L.)
Pap (1), food for infants. (E.)
Pap (2), a teat, breast. (E.) *Allied to* Pap (1).
Parricide (1), the murderer of a father. (F.—L.)
Parricide (2), the murder of a father. (F.—L.) *See* above.
Partisan (1), an adherent of a party. (F.—Ital.—L.)
Partisan (2), Partizan, a kind of halberd. (F.—Ital.—L.?)
Pat (1), to strike lightly, tap. (E.)
Pat (2), a small lump of butter. (E.) *Allied to* Pat (1).
Pat (3), quite to the purpose. (E.) *Allied to* Pat (1).
Patch (1), a piece sewn on a garment, a plot of ground. (E.?)
Patch (2), a paltry fellow. (E.) *From* Patch (1).
Pawn (1), a pledge, security for repayment of money. (F.)
Pawn (2), one of the least valuable pieces in chess. (F.—L.)
Pay (1), to discharge a debt. (F.—L.)
Pay (2), to pitch the seam of a ship. (F.—L.)
Peach (1), a delicious fruit. (F.—L.—Pers.)
Peach (2), to inform against. (F.—L.) *For* Impeach.
Peck (1), to strike with something pointed, snap up. (E.?)
Peck (2), a dry measure, two gallons. (F.—Low G.?)
Peel (1), to strip off the skin or bark. (F.—L.)
Peel (2), to pillage. (F.—L.)
Peel (3), a fire-shovel. (F.—L.)
Peel (4), a small castle. (F.—L.)
Peep (1), to cry like a chicken. (F.—L.)
Peep (2), to look through a narrow aperture, look slily. (F.—L.)
Peer (1), an equal, a nobleman. (F.—L.)
Peer (2), to look narrowly, to pry. (E.?)
Peer (3), to appear. (F.—L.)
Pellitory (1), Paritory, a wild flower. (F.—L.)
Pellitory (2), Pelleter, the plant pyrethrum. (Span.—L.—Gk.)
Pelt (1), to throw or cast, to strike by throwing. (L.)
Pelt (2), a skin, esp. of a sheep. (F.—L.)
Pen (1), to shut up, enclose. (L.)
Pen (2), an instrument used for writing. (F.—L.)
Perch (1), a rod for a bird to sit on; a measure. (F.—L.)
Perch (2), a fish. (F.—L.—Gk.)
Periwinkle (1), a genus of evergreen plants. (L.)
Periwinkle (2), a small univalve mollusc. (E.; *with* Gk. *prefix*.)
Pet (1), a tame and fondled animal or child. (F.?)
Pet (2), a sudden fit of peevishness. (F.?) *From* Pet (1).
Pie (1), a magpie; mixed printer's type. (F.—L.) *Hence* Pie (2).
Pie (2), a book which regulated divine service. (F.—L.)
Pie (3), a pasty. (F.—L.?)
Pile (1), a tumour; in the pl. Piles. (L.)
Pile (2), a roundish mass, heap. (F.—L.)
Pile (3), a large stake to support foundations. (L.)
Pile (4), a hair, fibre of wool. (L.)
Pill (1), a little ball of medicine. (L.)
Pill (2), to rob, plunder. (F.—L.)
Pine (1), a cone-bearing, resinous tree. (L.)
Pine (2), to suffer pain, be consumed with sorrow. (L.)
Pink (1), to pierce, stab, prick. (E.)
Pink (2), half-shut, applied to the eyes. (Du.)
Pink (3), the name of a flower and of a colour. (E.) *See* Pink (1).
Pink (4), a kind of boat. (Du.)
Pip (1), a disease of fowls. (Du.—L.)
Pip (2), the seed of fruit. (F.—L.—Gk.)
Pip (3), a spot on cards. (F.—L.?)
Pitch (1), a black, sticky substance. (L.)
Pitch (2), to throw, fall headlong, fix a camp, &c. (E.)
Plane (1), a level surface. (F.—L.) *Hence* Plane (2).
Plane (2), a tool; also to render a surface level. (F.—L.)
Plane (3), Plane-tree, the name of a tree. (F.—L.—Gk.)
Plantain (1), the name of a plant. (F.—L.)
Plantain (2), a tree resembling the banana. (F.—Span.—L.)
Plash (1), a puddle, a shallow pool. (E.)
Plash (2), another form of Pleach, to intertwine. (F.—L.)
Plat (1), Plot, a patch of ground. (E.)
Plat (2), to plait. (F.—L.)
Plight (1), a condition, promise; as vb., to pledge. (E.)
Plight (2), to fold; as sb., a fold, condition, state. (F.—L.)
Plot (1), a conspiracy, stratagem. (F.—L.)
Plot (2), Plat, a small piece of ground. (E.)
Plump (1), full, round, fleshy. (E.)

Plump (2), straight downwards. (F.—L.)
Plump (3), to fall heavily down. (E.)
Poach (1), to dress eggs. (F.—OLow G.)
Poach (2), to intrude on another's preserves of game. (F.—OLow G.) *Allied to* Poach (1).
Point (1), a dot, a prick. (F.—L.)
Point (2), a sharp end. (F.—L.) *From* Point (1).
Poke (1), a bag, pouch. (Scand.)
Poke (2), to thrust or push, esp. with something pointed. (E.)
Pole (1), a stake, long thick rod. (L.)
Pole (2), a pivot, end of the earth's axis. (F.—L.—Gk.)
Pool (1), a pond, small body of water. (E.)
Pool (2), the receptacle for the stakes at cards. (F.—L.)
Pore (1), a minute hole in the skin. (F.—L.—Gk.)
Pore (2), to look steadily, gaze long. (E.?)
Port (1), demeanour, carriage of the body. (F.—L.)
Port (2), a harbour, haven. (L.) ⎫
Port (3), a gate, port-hole. (F.—L.) ⎬ *Allied to* Port (1).
Port (4), a dark purple wine. (Port.—L.) ⎭
Porter (1), a carrier. (F.—L.) ⎫
Porter (2), a gate-keeper. (F.—L.) ⎬ *Allied.*
Porter (3), a dark kind of beer. (F.—L.) ⎭
Pose (1), a position, attitude. (F.—L.—Gk.)
Pose (2), to puzzle, perplex by questions. (F.—L. *and* Gk.)
Pose (3), a cold in the head. (C.)
Post (1), a stake set in the ground, a pillar. (L.) *Allied to* Post (2).
Post (2), a military station, a stage on a road, &c. (F.—L.)
Pounce (1), to seize with the claws, as a bird, to dart upon. (F.—L.)
Pounce (2), fine powder. (F.—L.)
Pound (1), a weight, a sovereign. (L.)
Pound (2), an enclosure for strayed animals. (E.)
Pound (3), to beat, bruise in a mortar. (E.)
Pout (1), to look sulky or displeased. (E.)
Pout (2), a kind of fish. (E.) *Cf.* Pout (1).
Prank (1), to deck, adorn. (E.)
Prank (2), a trick, mischievous action. (E.) *From* Prank (1).
Pregnant (1), pressing, urgent, cogent. (F.—L.)
Pregnant (2), fruitful, with child. (F.—L.)
Present (1), near at hand, in view, at this time. (F.—L.)
Present (2), to give, offer, exhibit to view. (F.—L.) *From* Present (1).
Press (1), to crush strongly, squeeze, push. (F.—L.)
Press (2), to hire men for service. (F.—L.)
Prig (1), to steal. (E.)
Prig (2), a pert fellow. (E.) *Allied to* Prig (1).
Prime (1), first, chief, excellent. (F.—L.) *Hence* Prime (2).
Prime (2), to make a gun quite ready. (F.—L.)
Prior (1), former, coming before in time. (L.) *Hence* Prior (2).
Prior (2), the head of a priory or convent. (F.—L.)
Prize (1), a thing captured or won. (F.—L.)
Prize (2), to value highly. (F.—L.)
Prize (3), Prise, to open a box. (F.—L.) *From* Prize (1).
Prune (1), to trim trees, &c. (F.—L.)
Prune (2), a plum. (F.—L.—Gk.)
Puddle (1), a small pool of muddy water. (E.)
Puddle (2), to close with clay, to work iron. (E.) *From* Puddle (1).
Puke (1), to vomit. (E.?)
Puke (2), the name of a colour; *obsolete*. (MDu.)
Pulse (1), a throb, vibration. (F.—L.)
Pulse (2), grain or seed of beans, pease, &c. (L.)
Pump (1), a machine for raising water. (F.—Teut.)
Pump (2), a thin-soled shoe. (F.—L.—Gk.)
Punch (1), to pierce with a sharp instrument. (F.—L.)
Punch (2), to beat, bruise. (F.—L.)
Punch (3), a beverage. (Hindi—Skt.)
Punch (4), a hump-backed fellow in a puppet-show. (Ital.—L.)
Puncheon (1), a steel tool for stamping; a punch. (F.—L.)
Puncheon (2), a cask, a measure of 84 gallons. (F.—L.)
Punt (1), a ferry-boat, a flat-bottomed boat. (L.—C.)
Punt (2), to play at basset. (F.—Span.—L.)
Pupil (1), a scholar, a ward. (F.—L.) *Allied to* Pupil (2).
Pupil (2), the central spot of the eye. (F.—L.)
Puppy (1), a whelp. (F.—L.)
Puppy (2), a dandy. (F.—L.) *Allied to* Puppy (1).
Purl (1), to flow with a murmuring sound. (Scand.)
Purl (2), spiced or medicated beer or ale. (F.—L.?)
Purl (3), to form an edging on lace. (F.—L.)
Purl (4), to upset. (E.) *Allied to* Purl (1).
Purpose (1), to intend. (F.—L.—Gk.; *with* F. *prefix.*)
Purpose (2), intention. (F.—L.)

Quack (1), to make a noise like a duck. (E.)
Quack (2), to cry up pretended nostrums. (Du.) *From* Quack (1).
Quail (1), to cower, shrink, fail in spirit. (F.—L.)
Quail (2), a migratory bird. (F.—Low L.—Low G.)
Quarrel (1), a dispute, brawl. (F.—L.)
Quarrel (2), a square-headed cross-bow bolt. (F.—L.)
Quarry (1), a place where stones are dug for building. (F.—L.)
Quarry (2), a heap of slaughtered game. (F.—L.)
Quill (1), a feather of a bird, a pen. (E.)
Quill (2), to pleat a ruff. (F.—L.; *or* E.)
Quire (1), a collection of so many sheets of paper. (F.—L.)
Quire (2), a choir, a band of singers. (F.—L.—Gk.)
Quiver (1), to tremble, shiver. (E.)
Quiver (2), a case for arrows. (F.—OHG.)

Race (1), a trial of speed, swift course, swift current. (E.)
Race (2), a lineage, family, breed. (F.)
Race (3), a root. (F.—L.)
Rack (1), a grating above a manger, instrument of torture. (MDu.)
Rack (2), to torture on the rack. (MDu.) *From* Rack (1).
Rack (3), light vapoury clouds, the clouds generally. (Scand.)
Rack (4), to pour off liquor from the lees. (Prov.)
Rack (5), a short form of Arrack. (Arab.)
Rack (6), &c. We find (6) prov. E. *rack*, a neck of mutton; from AS. *hracca*, neck, according to Somner. Also (7) *rack*, for reck, to care; see Reck. Also (8) *rack*, a pace of a horse (Palsgrave); perhaps a rocking pace; see Rock (2). Also (9) *rack*, a track, cart-rut; cf. Icel. *reka*, to drive; see Rack (3).
Racket (1), Raquet, a bat with a blade of net-work. (F.—Span.—Arab.)
Racket (2), a noise. (E.)
Rail (1), a bar of timber, an iron bar for railways. (F.—L.)
Rail (2), to brawl, to use reviling language. (F.—L.)
Rail (3), a genus of wading birds. (F.)
Rail (4), a woman's wrap or night-dress. (E.)
Rake (1), an instrument for scraping things together. (E.)
Rake (2), a wild, dissolute fellow. (E.) *From* Rake-hell.
Rake (3), the projection of the extremities of a ship beyond the keel; the inclination of a mast from the perpendicular. (Scand.)
Rally (1), to gather together again, reassemble. (F.—L.)
Rally (2), to banter. (F.—Teut.)
Rank (1), a row or line of soldiers, class, grade. (F.—OHG.)
Rank (2), adj., coarse in growth, strong-scented. (E.)
Rap (1), to strike smartly, knock. (E. *or* Scand.)
Rap (2), to snatch, seize hastily. (Scand.)
Rape (1), a seizing by force, violation. (L.)
Rape (2), a plant nearly allied to the turnip. (L.)
Rape (3), a division of a county, in Sussex. (E.)
Rash (1), hasty, headstrong. (E.)
Rash (2), a slight eruption on the body. (F.—L.)
Rash (3), to pull, or tear violently. (F.—L.)
Rash (4), a kind of inferior silk. (F.—L.)
Rate (1), a proportion, allowance, price, tax. (F.—L.)
Rate (2), to scold, chide. (F.—L.)
Raven (1), a well-known bird. (E.)
Raven (2), to plunder with violence, devour. (F.—L.)
Ray (1), a beam of light or heat. (F.—L.)
Ray (2), a class of fishes, such as the skate. (F.—L.)
Ray (3), a dance. (MDu.)
Reach (1), to attain, extend to, arrive at, gain. (E.)
Reach (2), Retch, to try to vomit. (E.)
Real (1), actual, true, genuine. (F.—L.)
Real (2), a small Spanish coin. (Span.—L.)
Rear (1), to raise. (E.)
Rear (2), the back part, last part, esp. of an army. (F.—L.)
Rear (3), insufficiently cooked. (E.)
Reef (1), a ridge of rocks. (Du.)
Reef (2), portion of a sail. (Du.)
Reel (1), a small spindle for winding yarn. (E.)
Reel (2), a Highland dance. (Scand.?)
Reeve (1), to pass a rope through a ring. (Du.)
Reeve (2), a steward, governor. (E.)
Reeve (3), the female of the ruff. (E.)
Refrain (1), to restrain, forbear. (F.—L.)
Refrain (2), the burden of a song. (F.—L.)
Relay (1), a fresh supply. (F.—L.)
Relay (2), to lay again. (Hybrid; L. *and* E.)
Rennet (1), a substance for coagulating milk. (E.)
Rennet (2), a kind of apple. (F.—L.)
Rent (1), a tear. (E.)
Rent (2), annual payment. (F.—L.)

Repair (1), to restore, mend. (F.—L.)
Repair (2), to resort, go to. (F.—L.)
Rest (1), repose. (E.)
Rest (2), to remain; remainder. (F.—L.)
Rid (1), to free, to deliver. (E.)
Rid (2), to clear land. (Scand.)
Riddle (1), an enigma. (E.)
Riddle (2), a large sieve. (E.)
Rifle (1), to plunder, rob. (F.—Teut.)
Rifle (2), a kind of musket. (Low G.)
Rig (1), to fit up a ship. (Scand.—Low G.)
Rig (2), a frolic. (E.?)
Rig (3), a ridge. (E.)
Rime (1), Rhyme, verse. (F.—L.—Gk.)
Rime (2), hoar-frost. (E.)
Ring (1), a circle. (E.)
Ring (2), to tinkle, resound. (E.)
Ripple (1), to pluck the seeds from flax. (E.)
Ripple (2), to show wrinkles. (E.)
Ripple (3), to scratch slightly. (Scand.) *Allied to* Rip.
Rob (1), to plunder, steal, spoil. (F.—OHG.)
Rob (2), a conserve of fruit. (F.—Span.—Arab.—Pers.)
Rock (1), a mass of stone. (F.)
Rock (2), to cause to totter, to totter. (E.)
Rock (3), a distaff. (Scand.)
Rocket (1), a kind of fire-work. (Ital.—G.)
Rocket (2), a plant. (F.—Ital.—L.)
Roe (1), a female deer. (E.)
Roe (2), spawn of fishes. (Scand.)
Rook (1), a kind of crow. (E.)
Rook (2), a castle, at chess. (F.—Pers.)
Root (1), part of a plant. (Scand.)
Root (2), Rout, to grub up. (E.) *From* Root (1).
Rote (1), routine. (F.—L.)
Rote (2), an old musical instrument. (F.—G.—C.)
Rouse (1), to excite. (Scand.)
Rouse (2), a drinking-bout. (Scand.)
Row (1), a line, rank, series. (E.)
Row (2), to propel with oars. (E.)
Row (3), an uproar. (Scand.)
Ruck (1), a fold, crease. (Scand.)
Ruck (2), a heap. (Scand.)
Rue (1), to be sorry for. (E.)
Rue (2), a bitter plant. (F.—L.—Gk.)
Ruff (1), a kind of frill. (E.)
Ruff (2), a bird. (E.?)
Ruff (3), a fish. (E.)
Ruff (4), a game at cards. (F.)
Ruffle (1), to wrinkle, disorder a dress. (E.)
Ruffle (2), to be turbulent, to bluster. (MDu.)
Rum (1), a kind of spirit. (E.)
Rum (2), strange, queer. (Hindi.)
Rush (1), to move forward violently. (E.)
Rush (2), a plant. (E.)
Rut (1), a wheel-track. (F.—L.)
Rut (2), to copulate, as deer. (F.—L.)

Sack (1), a bag. (L.—Gk.—Heb.—Egypt.)
Sack (2), plunder; to plunder. (F.—L.—Gk.—Heb.—Egypt.) *From* Sack (1).
Sack (3), an old Spanish wine. (F.—L.)
Sage (1), discerning, wise. (F.—L.)
Sage (2), a plant. (F.—L.)
Sallow (1), Sally, a willow. (E.)
Sallow (2), of a wan colour. (E.)
Sap (1), juice of plants. (E.)
Sap (2), to undermine. (F.—Late L.)
Sardine (1), a small fish. (F.—L.—Gk.)
Sardine (2), a precious stone. (L.—Gk.)
Sash (1), a frame for glass. (F.—L.)
Sash (2), a scarf, band. (Pers.)
Saw (1), a cutting instrument. (E.)
Saw (2), a saying, maxim. (E.)
Say (1), to speak, tell. (E.)
Say (2), a kind of serge. (F.—L.—Gk.)
Say (3), to essay. (F.—L.)
Scald (1), to burn with hot liquid. (F.—L.)
Scald (2), scabby. (Scand.)
Scald (3), a poet. (Scand.)
Scale (1), a shell. (F.—OHG.)
Scale (2), a bowl of a balance. (F.—Teut.) *Allied to* Scale (1).

Scale (3), a ladder, gradation. (L.)
Scape (1), a leafless stalk. (L.)
Scape (2), *short for* Escape. (F.—L.)
Scar (1), mark of a wound. (F.—L.—Gk.)
Scar (2), Scaur, a rock. (Scand.)
Scarf (1), a light piece of dress. (Du.—Low G.)
Scarf (2), to join timbers together. (Scand.)
Scarf (3), a cormorant. (Icel.)
School (1), a place for instruction. (F.—L.—Gk.)
School (2), a shoal of fish. (Du.)
Sconce (1), a small fort. (F.—L.)
Sconce (2), a candle-stick. (F.—L.) *Allied to* Sconce (1).
Scour (1), to cleanse by hard rubbing. (L.)
Scour (2), to run hastily over. (F.—L.)
Scout (1), a spy. (F.—L.)
Scout (2), to ridicule an idea. (Scand.)
Scout (3), a projecting rock. (Scand.)
Screw (1), a mechanical contrivance. (F.—L. ?)
Screw (2), a vicious horse. (E.)
Scrip (1), a small wallet. (E.)
Scrip (2), a piece of writing. (F.—L.)
Scrub (1), brushwood. (Scand.)
Scrub (2), to rub hard. (Scand.) *From* Scrub (1).
Scull (1), Skull, the cranium. (Scand.)
Scull (2), a small, light oar. (Scand.) *Allied to* Scull (1).
Scull (3), a shoal of fish. (Du.)
Scuttle (1), a shallow vessel. (L.)
Scuttle (2), an opening in a ship's hatchway. (F.—Span.—Teut.)
Scuttle (3), to hurry along. (Scand.)
Seal (1), a stamp for impressing wax. (F.—L.)
Seal (2), a sea-calf. (E.)
Seam (1), a suture. (E.)
Seam (2), a horseload. (Late L.—Gk.)
See (1), to behold. (E.)
See (2), the seat of a bishop. (F.—L.)
Sell (1), to deliver for money. (E.)
Sell (2), a saddle. (F.—L.)
Sere (1), withered. (E.)
Sere (2), the catch of a gun-lock. (F.—L.)
Set (1), to place, fix, plant. (E.)
Set (2), a number of like things. (F.—L.)
Settle (1), a long bench. (E.)
Settle (2), to adjust a quarrel. (E.)
Sew (1), to fasten together with thread. (E.)
Sew (2), to follow. (F.—L.)
Sewer (1), a large drain. (F.—L.)
Sewer (2), an officer who arranged dishes. (F.—L.)
Share (1), a portion. (E.)
Share (2), a plough-share. (E.) *Allied to* Share (1).
Shed (1), to part, scatter, spill. (E.)
Shed (2), a slight shelter. (E.)
Sheer (1), bright, clear, perpendicular. (E.)
Sheer (2), to deviate from a course. (Du.)
Shingle (1), a wooden tile. (L.)
Shingle (2), coarse round gravel. (E.)
Shiver (1), to tremble, to shudder. (E.)
Shiver (2), a splinter, small piece of wood. (E.)
Shoal (1), a troop, crowd, multitude of fishes. (E.)
Shoal (2), shallow; a sand-bank. (E.)
Shock (1), a violent concussion. (E.)
Shock (2), a pile of sheaves. (E.)
Shock (3), a shaggy-coated dog. (E.)
Shore (1), the strand. (E.)
Shore (2), Shoar, a prop. (E.)
Shore (3), Sewer, a sewer. (F.—L.)
Shrew (1), a scolding woman. (E.) *The same as* Shrew (2).
Shrew (2), Shrewmouse, a quadruped. (E.)
Shrub (1), a low dwarf tree. (E.)
Shrub (2), a beverage. (Arab.)
Size (1), a ration; magnitude. (F.—L.)
Size (2), weak glue. (Ital.—L.) *Allied to* Size (1).
Skate (1), a large flat fish. (Scand.)
Skate (2), a contrivance for sliding on ice. (Du.—F.—Low G.)
Skink (1), to serve out wine. (Scand.)
Skink (2), a kind of lizard. (Gk.)
Slab (1), a thin slip of timber, &c. (F.—Teut.)
Slab (2), viscous, slimy. (Scand.)
Slate (1), a stone easily split. (F.—Teut.)
Slate (2), to set on a dog, to damage, abuse. (E.)
Slay (1), to kill. (E.)
Slay (2), Sley, a weaver's reed. (E.) *From* Slay (1).

Slop (1), a puddle. (E.)
Slop (2), a loose garment. (Scand.)
Slot (1), a broad, flat wooden bar. (Du.)
Slot (2), the track of a deer. (AF.—Scand.)
Slough (1), a muddy place, a mire. (E.)
Slough (2), the cast-off skin of a snake. (Scand.)
Smack (1), taste, savour. (E.)
Smack (2), a sounding blow. (Scand.)
Smack (3), a fishing-boat. (Du.)
Smelt (1), to fuse ore. (Scand.)
Smelt (2), a kind of fish. (E.)
Snite (1), to wipe the nose. (E.)
Snite (2), a snipe. (E.) *Allied to* Snipe.
Snuff (1), to sniff, draw in air. (Du.)
Snuff (2), to snip a candle-wick. (E.)
Soil (1), ground, mould, country. (F.—L.)
Soil (2), to defile. (F.—L.)
Soil (3), to feed cattle with green grass. (F.—L.)
Sole (1), the under side of the foot. (L.)
Sole (2), a flat fish. (F.—L.) *Allied to* Sole (1).
Sole (3), alone, only. (F.—L.)
Sorrel (1), a plant. (F.—MHG.)
Sorrel (2), of a reddish-brown colour. (F.—Teut.)
Sound (1), whole, perfect. (E.)
Sound (2), a strait of the sea. (E.)
Sound (3), a noise. (F.—L.)
Sound (4), to try the depth of. (F.—Scand.) *From* Sound (2).
Souse (1), pickle. (F.—L.)
Souse (2), Sowse, to swoop down upon. (F.—L.)
Sow (1), to scatter seed. (E.)
Sow (2), a female pig. (E.)
Spade (1), an instrument to dig with. (E.)
Spade (2), a suit at cards. (Span.—L.—Gk.)
Spar (1), a beam, rafter. (E.)
Spar (2), a kind of mineral. (E.)
Spar (3), to box with the hands; to wrangle. (F.—Teut.)
Spark (1), a small particle of fire. (E.)
Spark (2), a gay young fellow. (Scand.) *Allied to* Spark (1).
Spat (1), a blow, a slap. (E.)
Spat (2), the young of shellfish. (E.)
Spell (1), an incantation. (E.)
Spell (2), to tell the letters of a word. (F.—Teut.) *From* Spell (1).
Spell (3), a turn of work. (E.)
Spell (4), Spill, a splinter, slip. (E.)
Spike (1), a sharp point, a large nail. (Scand.)
Spike (2), an ear of corn. (L.)
Spill (1), Spell, a splinter, slip. (E.)
Spill (2), to destroy, shed. (Scand.)
Spire (1), a tapering sprout, a steeple. (E.)
Spire (2), a coil, wreath. (F.—L.—Gk.)
Spit (1), a pointed piece of wood or iron. (E.)
Spit (2), to eject from the mouth. (E.)
Spittle (1), saliva. (E.)
Spittle (2), a hospital. (F.—L.)
Spray (1), foam tossed by the wind. (Low G.)
Spray (2), a sprig of a tree. (E.)
Spurt (1), Spirt, to spout, jet out as water. (E.)
Spurt (2), a violent exertion. (Scand.)
Squire (1), an esquire. (F.—L.)
Squire (2), a carpenter's rule. (F.—L.)
Stable (1), a stall for horses. (F.—L.)
Stable (2), firm, steady. (F.—L.) *Allied to* Stable (1).
Stale (1), too long kept, vapid. (F.—Teut.)
Stale (2), a decoy, snare. (E.)
Stale (3), Steal, a handle. (E.)
Stalk (1), a stem. (E.)
Stalk (2), to stride along. (E.) *Allied to* Stalk (1).
Staple (1), a loop of iron. (E.)
Staple (2), a chief commodity. (F.—Low G.) *From* Staple (1).
Stare (1), to gaze fixedly. (E.)
Stare (2), to shine. (E.) *The same as* Stare (1).
Stay (1), to remain. (F.—MDu.)
Stay (2), a large rope to support a mast. (E.)
Steep (1), precipitous. (E.)
Steep (2), to soak in a liquid. (Scand.)
Steer (1), a young ox. (E.)
Steer (2), to direct, guide, govern. (E.)
Stem (1), a trunk of a tree. (E.)
Stem (2), prow of a vessel. (E.) *From* Stem (1).
Stem (3), to check, resist. (E.)
Stern (1), severe, harsh. (E.)

Stern (2), the hinder part of a ship. (Scand.)
Stew (1), to boil slowly. (F.—Teut.)
Stew (2), a fishpond. (Du.)
Stick (1), to stab, pierce; to adhere. (E.)
Stick (2), a small staff. (E.) *From* Stick (1).
Stile (1), a set of steps for passing a hedge. (E.)
Stile (2), the correct spelling of Style (1). (L.)
Still (1), motionless, silent. (E.)
Still (2), to distil; apparatus for distilling. (L.)
Stoop (1), to bend the body, condescend. (E.)
Stoop (2), a beaker, also Stoup. (Scand.)
Story (1), a history, narrative. (F.—L.—Gk.)
Story (2), the height of one floor in a building. (F.—L.)
Strain (1), to stretch tight. (F.—L.)
Strain (2), race, stock, breed. (E.)
Strand (1), the beach of a sea or lake. (E.)
Strand (2), part of a rope. (F.—OHG.)
Stroke (1), a blow. (E.)
Stroke (2), to rub gently. (E.) *Allied to* Stroke (1).
Strut (1), to walk about pompously. (Scand.)
Strut (2), a support for a rafter. (Scand.) *Allied to* Strut (1).
Stud (1), a collection of horses and mares. (E.)
Stud (2), a nail with a large head, rivet. (E.)
Sty (1), an enclosure for swine. (E.)
Sty (2), a small tumour on the eye-lid. (E.) *Allied to* Sty (1).
Style (1), a mode of writing. (F.—L.)
Style (2), the middle part of a flower's pistil. (Gk.)
Summer (1), a season of the year. (E.)
Summer (2), a cross-beam. (F.—Late L.—Gk.)
Sur- (1), *prefix*; for L. *sub*. (L.)
Sur- (2), *prefix*; for F. *sur*, L. *super*. (F.—L.)
Swallow (1), a migratory bird. (E.)
Swallow (2), to absorb, engulf. (E.)
Swim (1), to move about in water. (E.)
Swim (2), to be dizzy. (E.)

Tache (1), a fastening. (F.—Teut.)
Tache (2), a spot, blemish. (F.—Teut.) *Allied to* Tache (1).
Tail (1), a hairy appendage. (E.)
Tail (2), a law-term, applied to an estate. (F.—L.)
Tang (1), a strong taste. (Scand.)
Tang (2), part of a knife or fork. (Scand.) *Allied to* Tang (1).
Tang (3), to make a shrill sound. (E.)
Tang (4), sea-weed. (Scand.)
Tap (1), to knock gently. (F.—Teut.)
Tap (2), a plug to take liquor from a cask. (E.)
Taper (1), a small wax-candle. (E.)
Taper (2), long and slender. (E.) *From* Taper (1).
Tar (1), a resinous substance. (E.)
Tar (2), a sailor; short for Tarpauling. (E. *and* L.)
Tare (1), a vetch-like plant. (E.)
Tare (2), an allowance for loss. (F.—Span.—Arab.)
Tart (1), acrid, sour, sharp. (E.)
Tart (2), a small pie. (F.—L.)
Tartar (1), an acid salt; a concretion. (F.—Low L.—Arab.)
Tartar (2), a native of Tartary. (Tatar.)
Tartar (3), Tartarus, hell. (L.—Gk.)
Tassel (1), a hanging ornament. (F.—L.)
Tassel (2), the male of the goshawk. (F.—L.)
Tattoo (1), the beat of a drum. (Du.)
Tattoo (2), to mark the skin with figures. (Tahiti.)
Taw (1), Tew, to curry skins. (E.)
Taw (2), a game at marbles. (Gk.)
Tear (1), to rend, lacerate. (E.)
Tear (2), a drop of fluid from the eyes. (E.)
Teem (1), to be fruitful. (E.)
Teem (2), to think fit. (OLow G.)
Teem (3), to empty, pour out. (Scand.)
Temple (1), a fane, divine edifice. (L.)
Temple (2), the flat part above the cheek-bone. (F.—L.)
Temporal (1), pertaining to time. (F.—L.)
Temporal (2), belonging to the temples. (F.—L.)
Tend (1), to aim at, move towards. (F.—L.)
Tend (2), to attend to. (F.—L.) *Short for* Attend.
Tender (1), soft, delicate. (F.—L.)
Tender (2), to proffer. (F.—L.) *Allied to* Tend (1).
Tender (3), an attendant vessel or carriage. (F.—L.) *For* Attender.
Tense (1), a part of a verb. (F.—L.)
Tense (2), tightly strained. (L.)
Tent (1), a pavilion. (F.—L.)
Tent (2), a roll of lint. (F.—L.)

Tent (3), a kind of wine. (Span.—L.)
Tent (4), care, heed. (F.—L.) *Allied to* Tend (2).
Terrier (1), a kind of dog. (F.—L.) *Allied to* Terrier (2).
Terrier (2), a register of landed property. (F.—L.)
The (1), def. article. (E.)
The (2), in what (or that) degree. (E.) *From* The (1).
Thee (1), personal pronoun. (E.)
Thee (2), to thrive, prosper; *obsolete*. (E.)
There (1), in that place. (E.)
There- (2), as a prefix. (E.) *Allied to* There (1).
Thole (1), Thowl, an oar-pin. (E.)
Thole (2), to endure; *provincial*. (E.)
Thrum (1), the end of a weaver's thread. (E.)
Thrum (2), to play noisy music. (Scand.)
Thrush (1), a small singing-bird. (E.)
Thrush (2), a disease in the mouth. (Scand.)
Tick (1), an insect infesting dogs. (E.)
Tick (2), part of a bed. (L.—Gk.)
Tick (3), to beat as a watch. (E.)
Tick (4), to touch lightly. (E.)
Tick (5), credit. (F.—G.)
Tiff (1), to deck, to dress out. (F.—OLow G.)
Tiff (2), a fit of ill humour. (Scand.)
Till (1), to cultivate. (E.)
Till (2), to the time when. (E.) *Allied to* Till (1).
Till (3), a drawer for money. (E.)
Tilt (1), the cover of a cart. (E.)
Tilt (2), to ride in a tourney. (E.)
Tine (1), the tooth of a fork or harrow. (E.)
Tine (2), to light or kindle. (E.)
Tine (3), to lose. (Scand.)
Tip (1), the extreme top. (E.)
Tip (2), to tilt over. (E.)
Tire (1), to exhaust, fatigue. (E.)
Tire (2), a head-dress. (F.—Teut.) *Same as* Tire (3).
Tire (3), a hoop for a wheel. (F.—Teut.)
Tire (4), to tear a prey. (F.—Late L.)
Tire (5), a train. (F.—Late L.)
Tit (1), a small horse or child. (Scand.)
Tit (2), a teat. (E.)
To- (1), *prefix*, in twain. (E.)
To- (2), *prefix*, to. (E.)
Toast (1), roasted bread. (F.—L.) *Hence* Toast (2).
Toast (2), a person whose health is drunk. (F.—L.)
Toil (1), labour, fatigue. (F.—L.)
Toil (2), a net, a snare. (F.—L.)
Toll (1), a tax. (L.—Gk.)
Toll (2), to sound a bell. (E.)
Toot (1), to peep about. (E.)
Toot (2), to blow a horn. (Scand.)
Top (1), a summit. (E.)
Top (2), a child's toy. (F.—G.)
Tow (1), to pull a vessel along. (E.)
Tow (2), the coarse part of flax. (E.)
Trace (1), a mark left, footprint. (F.—L.) *Allied to* Trace (2).
Trace (2), a strap to draw a carriage. (F.—L.)
Tract (1), a region. (L.)
Tract (2), a short treatise. (L.) *Allied to* Tract (1).
Trap (1), a kind of snare. (E.)
Trap (2), to adorn, decorate. (F.—Teut.)
Trap (3), a kind of igneous rock. (Swed.) *Allied to* Trap (1).
Trepan (1), a small cylindrical saw. (F.—L.—Gk.)
Trepan (2), Trapan, to ensnare. (F.—Teut.)
Trice (1), a short space of time. (Low G.) *From* Trice (2).
Trice (2), Trise, to haul up, hoist. (Low G.)
Trick (1), a stratagem. (F.—L.) ⎫
Trick (2), to dress out. (F.—L.) ⎬ *Allied.*
Trick (3), to emblazon arms. (Du.) ⎭
Trill (1), to shake, to quaver. (Ital.)
Trill (2), to turn round. (Scand.)
Trill (3), to trickle. (Scand.)
Trinket (1), a small ornament. (F.—L.?)
Trinket (2), the highest sail of a ship. (F.—Ital.—L.)
Truck (1), to barter. (F.—WFlem.—Du.)
Truck (2), a small wheel. (L.—Gk.)
Trump (1), a trumpet. (F.—G.—Slav.)
Trump (2), one of the highest suit at cards. (F.—L.)
Trunk (1), the stem of a tree, box for clothes. (F.—L.)
Trunk (2), the proboscis of an elephant; *error for* Trump (1).
Tuck (1), to fold or gather in a dress. (OLow G.)
Tuck (2), a rapier. (F.—Ital.—G.)

Tuck (3), beat of a drum. (F. — Teut.)
Tuft (1), a small knot, crest. (F. — Teut.)
Tuft (2), Toft, a clump of trees. (F. — Teut.)
Turtle (1), a turtle-dove. (L.)
Turtle (2), a sea-tortoise. (L.) *Confused with* Turtle (1).
Twig (1), a small branch of a tree. (E.)
Twig (2), to comprehend. (E.)

Un- (1), negative prefix. (E.)
Un- (2), verbal prefix. (E.)
Un- (3), prefix in *un-to*. (E.)
Union (1), concord, harmony. (F. — L.)
Union (2), a large pearl. (F. — L.) *Allied to* Union (1).
Use (1), employment, custom. (F. — L.)
Use (2), profit, benefit. (F. — L.)
Utter (1), outer. (E.)
Utter (2), to put forth. (E.) *Allied to* Utter (1).
Utterance (1), a putting forth. (E.)
Utterance (2), extremity. (F. — L.)

Vail (1), Veil, a slight covering. (F. — L.)
Vail (2), to lower. (F. — L.)
Vail (3), a gift to a servant. (F. — L.)
Van (1), the front of an army. (F. — L.)
Van (2), a fan for winnowing. (F. — L.)
Van (3), a caravan. (F. — L. — Pers.)
Vault (1), an arched roof. (F. — L.)
Vault (2), to leap or bound. (F. — Ital. — L.) *Allied to* Vault (1).
Vent (1), an opening for air. (F. — L.)
Vent (2), sale, utterance, outlet. (F. — L.)
Vent (3), to snuff up air. (F. — L.)
Verge (1), a wand of office. (F. — L.)
Verge (2), to tend towards. (L.)
Vice (1), a blemish, fault. (F. — L.)
Vice (2), an instrument for holding fast. (F. — L.)

Wake (1), to cease from sleep. (E.)
Wake (2), the track of a ship. (Scand.)
Wale (1), Weal, the mark of a blow. (E.)
Wale (2), choice; to choose. (Scand.)
Ware (1), merchandise. (E.)
Ware (2), aware. (E.)
Ware (3), sea-weed; *provincial*. (E.)
Wave (1), to fluctuate, undulate. (E.)
Wave (2), *a form of* Waive. (F. — Scand.)
Wax (1), to grow, increase. (E.)
Wax (2), a substance in a honeycomb. (E.)
Wear (1), to carry on the body, to consume by use. (E.)
Wear (2). *A form of* Weir.

Wear (3). *A form of* Veer.
Weed (1), a useless plant. (E.)
Weed (2), a garment. (E.)
Weld (1), to beat (metal) together. (Scand.)
Weld (2), a plant; dyer's weed. (E.)
Well (1), in a good state. (E.)
Well (2), a spring of water. (E.)
Wharf (1), a place for lading and unlading vessels. (E.)
Wharf (2), the bank of a river; in Shakespeare. (E.) *The same as* Wharf (1).
Wheal (1), a swelling, a pimple. (E.)
Wheal (2), a mine. (C.)
Whelk (1), a mollusc with a spiral shell. (E.)
Whelk (2), a small pimple. (E.)
Whittle (1), to pare with a knife. (E.)
Whittle (2), to sharpen. (E.) *The same as* Whittle (1).
Whittle (3), a blanket. (E.)
Wick (1), the cotton of a lamp. (E.)
Wick (2), a town. (L.)
Wick (3), a bay. (Scand.)
Wight (1), a creature, person. (E.)
Wight (2), nimble. (Scand.)
Will (1), to desire, to be willing. (E.)
Will (2), desire, wish. (E.) *From* Will (1).
Wimble (1), a kind of auger. (E.)
Wimble (2), quick, active. (Scand.)
Wind (1), air in motion, breath. (E.)
Wind (2), to turn round, coil. (E.)
Windlass (1), a machine for raising weights. (Scand.)
Windlass (2), a circuitous way. (F. — Teut.)
Wise (1), having knowledge. (E.)
Wise (2), way, manner. (E.) *From* Wise (1).
Wit (1), to know. (E.)
Wit (2), insight, knowledge. (E.) *From* Wit (1).
Wit (3), a witty fellow. (E.) *From* Wit (1).
Wood (1), a collection of trees. (E.)
Wood (2), mad. (E.)
Wort (1), a plant, cabbage. (E.)
Wort (2), an infusion of malt. (E.) *From* Wort (1).
Worth (1), value. (E.)
Worth (2), to be, become. (E.)
Wrinkle (1), a slight ridge on a surface. (E.)
Wrinkle (2), a hint. (E.) *Allied to* Wrinkle (1).

Yard (1), an enclosed space. (E.)
Yard (2), a rod or stick. (E.)
Yawl (1), a small boat. (Du.)
Yawl (2), to howl, yell. (E.)
Yearn (1), to long for. (E.)
Yearn (2), to grieve. (E.) *The same as* Yearn (1).

IV. LIST OF DOUBLETS

Doublets are words which, though apparently differing in form, are nevertheless, from an etymological point of view, one and the same, or only differ in some unimportant suffix. Thus *aggrieve* is from L. *aggrauāre*; whilst *aggravate*, though really from the pp. *aggrauātus*, is nevertheless used as a verb, precisely as *aggrieve* is used, though the senses of the words have been differentiated. In the following list, each pair of doublets is entered only *once*, to save space, except in a few remarkable cases, such as *cipher, zero*. When a pair of doublets is mentioned *a second time*, it is enclosed within square brackets.

abbreviate—abridge.
abet—bet.
acajou—cashew.
adamant—diamond.
adventure—venture.
advocate—avouch, avow (1).
aggrieve—aggravate.
ait—eyot.
alarm—alarum.
allocate—allow (1).
ameer—emir (omrah).
amiable—amicable.
an—one.
ancient (2)—ensign.

announce—annunciate.
ant—emmet.
anthem—antiphon.
antic—antique.
appal—pall (2).
appeal, *sb.*—peal.
appear—peer (3).
appraise—appreciate.
apprentice—prentice.
aptitude—attitude.
arc—arch (1).
army—armada.
arrack—rack (5), raki.
asphodel—daffodil.

assay—essay.
assemble—assimilate.
assess—assize, *vb.*
assoil—absolve.
attach—attack.
attire—tire (2), tire (3).

bale (1)—ball (2).
balm—balsam.
band (1)—bond.
banjo—mandoline.
barb (1)—beard.
base—basis.
bashaw—pasha.

baton—batten (2).
bawd—bold.
beadle—bedell.
beaker—pitcher.
beef—cow.
beldam—belladonna.
bench—bank (1), bank (2).
benison—benediction.
blame—blaspheme.
boil (1)—bile (2).
boss—botch (2).
bough—bow (4).
bound (2)—bourn (1).
bower—byre.

bowl (1)—bull (2).
box (2)—pyx, bush (2).
brave—bravo.
breve—brief.
brother—friar.
brown—bruin.
buff (2), buffalo.

cadence—chance.
caitiff—captive.
caldron, cauldron—chaldron.
caliber—caliver.
calumny—challenge.
camera—chamber.
cancer—canker.
cannon (1)—canon.
caravan—van (3).
card (1)—chart, carte.
case (2)—chase (3), cash (1).
cask—casque.
castigate—chasten.
catch—chase (1).
cattle—chattels, capital (2).
cavalier—chevalier.
cavalry—chivalry.
cess—assess.
chaise—chair.
chalk—calx.
champaign—campaign.
[chance—cadence.]
channel—canal, kennel (2).
chant—cant (1).
chapiter—capital (3).
charge—cark, cargo.
chateau—castle.
cheat—escheat.
check, sb.—shah.
chicory—succory.
chief—cape (2).
chieftain—captain.
chirurgeon—surgeon.
choir—chorus, quire (2).
choler—cholera.
chord—cord.
chuck (1)—shock (1), shog.
church—kirk.
cipher—zero.
cist—chest.
cithern—guitar, gittern, kit (2).
cive—chive.
clause—close, sb.
climate—clime.
coffer—coffin.
coin—coign, quoin.
cole—kail.
collect—cull, coil, vb.
collocate—couch.
comfit—confect.
commend—command.
commodore—commander.
complacent—complaisant.
complete, vb.—comply.
compost—composite.
comprehend—comprise.
compute—count (2).
conduct, sb.—conduit.
confound—confuse.
construe—construct.
convey—convoy.
cool—gelid.
[cord—chord.]
corn (1)—grain.
corn (2)—horn.
coronation—carnation (2).
corral—kraal.
corsair—hussar.
costume—custom.
cot—cote.
[couch—collocate.]
couple, vb.—copulate.
[cow (1)—beef.]

coy (1)—quiet, quit, quite.
coy (2)—cage.
crape—crisp.
cream—chrism.
crease (1)—crest.
crevice—crevasse.
crib—cratch.
crimson—carmine.
crop—croup (2).
crowd (2)—rote (2).
crypt—grot.
cud—quid.
cue (1)—queue.
[cull—collect, coil, vb.]
curari—wourali.
curricle—curriculum.
curtle-axe—cutlass.
cycle—wheel.

dace—dart, dare (2).
dainty—dignity.
dame—dam (2), donna, duenna.
dan—don (2), domino.
dauphin—dolphin.
deck—thatch.
defence—fence.
defend—fend.
delay—dilate.
dell—dale.
demesne—domain.
dent—dint.
deploy—display, splay.
depot—deposit, sb.
descry—describe.
desiderate—desire, vb.
despite—spite.
deuce (1)—two.
devilish—diabolic.
[diamond—adamant.]
die (2)—dado.
direct, vb.—dress.
dish—disc, desk, daïs.
[display—deploy, splay.]
disport—sport.
distain—stain.
ditch—dike.
ditto—dictum.
diurnal—journal.
doge—duke.
doit—thwaite.
dole—deal, sb.
dominion—dungeon.
doom— -dom (suffix).
dragon—dragoon.
dropsy—hydropsy.
due—debt.
dune—down (2).

eatable—edible.
éclat—slate (1).
elf—oaf, ouphe.
élite—elect.
emerald—smaragdus.
emerods—hemorrhoids.
[emmet—ant.]
employ—imply, implicate.
endow—endue (1), indue (2).
engine—gin (2).
[ensign—ancient (2).]
entire—integer.
envious—invidious.
escape—scape.
eschew—shy, vb.
escutcheon—scutcheon
especial—special.
espy—spy.
esquire—squire (1).
[essay—assay.]
establish—stablish.
estate—state, status.
estimate—esteem.

estop—stop.
estreat—extract.
etiquette—ticket.
example—ensample, sample.
exemplar—sampler.
extraneous—strange.
[eyot—ait.]

fabric—forge, sb.
fact—feat.
faculty—facility.
fan—van (2).
fancy—fantasy, phantasy.
fashion—faction.
fat (2)—vat.
fauteuil—faldstool.
fealty—fidelity.
feeble—foible.
fell (2)—pell.
[fence—defence.]
[fend—defend.]
fester, sb.—fistula.
feud (2)—fief, fee.
feverfew—febrifuge.
fiddle—viol.
fife—pipe, peep (1).
finch—spink.
finite—fine (1).
fitch—vetch.
flag (4)—flake, flaw.
flower—flour.
flush (4)—flux.
foam—spume.
font (1)—fount.
force (2)—farce.
foremost—prime.
foster (2)—forester.
fragile—frail (1).
fray (1)—affray.
[friar—brother.]
fro—from.
frounce—flounce.
fungus—sponge.
furl—fardel.

gabble—jabber.
gad (1)—ged.
gaffer—grandfather.
gage (1)—wage.
gambado—gambol.
game—gammon (2).
gaol—jail.
garth—yard (1).
gear—garb (1).
[gelid—cool.]
genteel—gentle, gentile.
genus—kin.
germ—germen.
gig—jig.
[gin (2)—engine.]
gin (3)—juniper.
gird (2)—gride.
girdle—girth.
glamour—gramarye.
[grain—corn (1).]
granary—garner.
grece, grise—grade.
[grot—crypt.]
guarantee, sb.—warranty.
guard—ward.
guardian—warden.
guest—host (2).
guile—wile.
guise—wise (2).
[guitar—cithern, gittern, kit (2).]
gullet—gully.
gust (2)—gusto.
guy—guide, sb.
gypsy—Egyptian.

hackbut—arquebus.

hale (1)—whole.
hamper (2)—hanaper.
harangue—ring, rank (1), rink.
hash, vb.—hatch (3).
hatchment—achievement.
hautboy—oboe.
heap—hope (2).
heckle—hackle, hatchel.
hemi- —semi-.
[hemorrhoids—emerods.]
hent—hint.
history—story (1).
hock (1)—hough.
hoop (2)—whoop.
[horn—corn (2).]
hospital—hostel, hotel, spital,
   spittle (2).
[host (2)—guest.]
hub—hob (1).
human—humane.
[hussar—corsair.]
hyacinth—jacinth.
hydra—otter.
[hydropsy—dropsy.]
hyper- —super-.
hypo- —sub-.

illumine—limn.
[imply—implicate, employ.]
inapt—inept.
inch (1)—ounce (1).
indite—indict.
influence—influenza.
innocuous—innoxious.
[integer—entire.]
[invidious—envious.]
invite—vie.
invoke—invocate.
iota—jot.
isolate—insulate.

[jabber—gabble.]
[jacinth—hyacinth.]
jaggery—sugar.
[jail—gaol.]
jealous—zealous.
[jig—gig.]
jinn—genie.
joint—junta, junto.
jointure—juncture.
[jot—iota.]
[journal—diurnal.]
jut—jet (1).
jutty—jetty.

[kail—cole.]
[kennel (2)—channel, canal.]
ketch—catch.
[kin—genus.]
[kirk—church.]
[kraal—corral.]

label—lapel, lappet.
lac (1)—lake (2).
lace—lasso.
lair—leaguer.
lake (1)—loch, lough.
lateen—Latin.
launch, lanch—lance, verb.
leal—loyal, legal.
lection—lesson.
lib—glib (3).
lieu—locus.
limb (2)—limbo.
limbeck—alembic.
[limn—illumine.]
lineal—linear.
liquor—liqueur.
list (5)—lust.
load—lode.
lobby—lodge.

locust—lobster.
lone—alone.
losel—lorel.
lurch (1)—lurk.

madam—madonna.
major—mayor.
male—masculine.
malediction—malison.
mandate—maundy.
[mandoline—banjo.]
mangle (2)—mangonel.
manœuvre—manure.
march (1)—mark (2), marque.
margin—margent, marge.
marish—morass.
maul—mall (1).
mauve—mallow.
maxim—maximum.
mazer—mazzard.
mean (3)—mesne, mizen.
memory—memoir.
mentor—monitor.
metal—mettle.
milt (2)—milk.
minim—minimum.
minster—monastery.
mint (1)—money.
mister—master.
[mizen, mesne—mean (3).]
mob (1)—mobile, movable.
mode—mood (2).
mohair—moire.
moment—momentum, movement.
monster—muster.
morrow—morn.
moslem—mussulman.
mould (2)—module.
munnion—mullion.
musket—mosquito.

naive—native.
naked—nude.
name—noun.
natron—nitre.
naught, nought—not.
nausea—noise.
neat (2)—net (2).
nias—eyas.
noyau—newel.

[oaf, ouphe—elf.]
obedience—obeisance.
[oboe—hautboy.]
octave—utas.
of—off.
[one—an.]
onion—union (2).
oration—orison.
ordinance—ordnance.
orpiment—orpine.
osprey—ossifrage.
[otter—hydra.]
otto—attar.
ouch—nouch.
[ounce (1)—inch (1).]
outer—utter (1).
overplus—surplus.

paddle (2)—spatula.
paddock (2)—park.
pain, vb.—pine (2).
paladin—palatine.
pale (2)—pallid; cf. fallow (2).
palette—pallet (2).
paper—papyrus.
parade—parry.
paradise—parvis.
paralysis—palsy.
parole—parable, parle, palaver.
parson—person.

[pasha—bashaw.]
pass—pace.
pastel—pastille.
pasty—patty.
pate—plate.
patron—pattern.
pause—pose (1).
pawn (1)—pane, vane.
paynim—paganism.
[peal—appeal, sb.]
[peer (3)—appear.]
peise—poise.
pelisse—pilch.
[pell—fell (2).]
pellitory (1)—paritory.
penance—penitence.
peregrine—pilgrim.
peruke—periwig, wig.
pewter—spelter.
phantasm—phantom.
[phantasy—fancy.]
piazza—place.
pick—peck (1), pitch, verb.
picket—piquet.
piety—pity.
pigment—pimento.
pike—peak, pick, sb., pique, sb., spike.
[pipe—fife, peep (1).]
pippin—pip (2).
pistil—pestle.
pistol—pistole.
[pitcher—beaker.]
plaintiff—plaintive.
plait—pleat, plight (2).
plan—plain, plane (1), llano.
plateau—platter.
plum—prune (2).
poignant—pungent.
point—punt (2).
poison—potion.
poke (1)—pouch.
pole (1)—pale (1), pawl.
pomade, pommade—pomatum.
pomp—pump (2).
poor—pauper.
pope—papa.
porch—portico.
posy—poesy.
potent—puissant.
poult—pullet.
pounce (1)—punch (1).
pounce (2)—pumice.
pound (2)—pond.
pound (3)—pun, vb.
power—posse.
praise—price.
preach—predicate.
premier—primero.
[prentice—apprentice.]
priest—presbyter.
[prime—foremost.]
private—privy.
probe, sb.—proof.
proctor—procurator.
prolong—purloin.
prosecute—pursue.
provide—purvey.
provident—prudent.
punch (2)—punish.
puny—puisne.
purl (3)—profile.
purpose (1)—propose.
purview—proviso.
[pyx—box (2), bush (2).]

quartern—quadroon.
queen—quean.
[queue—cue.]
[quid—cud.]
[quiet, quit, quite—coy.]

[quoin—coin, coign.]
raceme—raisin.
rack (3)—wrack, wreck.
[rack (5)—arrack, raki.]
radix—radish, race (3), root (1), wort (1).
raid—road.
rail (2)—rally (2).
raise—rear (1).
ramp—romp.
ransom—redemption.
rapine—ravine, raven (2).
rase—raze.
ratio—ration, reason.
ray (1)—radius.
rayah—ryot.
rear-ward—rear-guard.
reave—rob.
reconnaissance—recognisance.
regal—royal, real (2).
relic—relique.
renegade—runagate.
renew—renovate.
reprieve—reprove.
residue—residuum.
respect—respite.
revenge—revindicate.
reward—regard.
rhomb, rhombus—rumb.
ridge—rig (3).
[ring, rank (1), rink—harangue.]
[road—raid.]
rod—rood.
rondeau—roundel.
[root (1)—radix, radish, race (3), wort (1).]
rote (1)—route, rout, rut (1).
[rote (2)—crowd (2).]
round—rotund.
rouse (2)—row (3).
rover—robber.

sack (1)—sac.
sacristan—sexton.
[sample—example, ensample.]
[sampler—exemplar.]
saw (2)—saga.
saxifrage—sassafras.
scabby—shabby.
scale (1)—shale.
scandal—slander.
[scape—escape.]
scar (2), scaur—share.
scarf (1)—scrip (1), scrap.
scatter—shatter.
school (2)—shoal (1), scull (3).
scot(free)—shot.
screech—shriek.
screed—shred.
screw (2)—shrew.
scur—scour (2).
[scutcheon—escutcheon.]
scuttle (1)—skillet.
sect, sept, set (2)—suite, suit.
[semi-—hemi-.]
sennet—signet.
separate—sever.
sequin—sicca.
sergeant, serjeant—servant.
settle (1)—sell (2), saddle.
[shah—check, sb.]
shammy—chamois.
shark—search.
shawm, shalm—haulm.
sheave—shive.
shed (2)—shade.
shirt—skirt.
[shock (1)—chuck (1), shog.]
[shot—scot.]
[shred—screed.]
[shrew—screw (2).]

shrub (2)—sherbet, syrup.
shuffle—scuffle.
sicker, siker—secure, sure.
sine—sinus.
sir, sire—senior, seignior, señor, signor.
size (1), size (2)—assise (2).
skewer—shiver (2).
skiff—ship.
skirmish — scrimmage, scaramouch.
slabber—slaver.
[slander—scandal.]
[slate (1)—éclat.]
sleight—sloid.
sleuth—slot (2).
slobber—slubber.
sloop—shallop.
[smaragdus—emerald.]
snivel—snuffle.
snub—snuff (2).
soil (1)—sole (1), sole (2).
soprano—sovereign.
sough—surf.
soup—sup.
souse—sauce.
spade (1)—spade (2).
[spatula—paddle (2).]
[special—especial.]
species—spice.
spell (4)—spill (1).
spend—dispend.
[spink—finch.]
spirit—sprite, spright.
[spite—despite.]
[spittle (2), spital — hospital, hostel, hotel.]
[splay—display, deploy.]
[sponge—fungus.]
spoor—spur.
[sport—disport.]
spray (2)—sprig (perhaps asparagus).
sprit—sprout, sb.
sprout, vb.—spout.
spry—spark (2).
[spume—foam.]
[spy—espy.]
squall—squeal.
squinancy—quinsy.
[squire (1)—esquire.]
squire—square.
[stablish—establish.]
[stain—distain.]
stank—tank.
[state—estate, status.]
stave—staff.
steer (1)—Taurus.
still (2)—distil.
stock—tuck (2).
[story (1)—history.]
stove—stew, sb.
strait—strict.
[strange—extraneous.]
strap—strop.
stress—distress.
[sub-, prefix—hypo-, prefix.]
[succory—chicory.]
[suit, suite—sect, sept, set (2).]
[super-, prefix—hyper-, prefix.]
superficies—surface.
supersede—surcease.
suppliant—supplicant.
[surgeon—chirurgeon.]
sweep—swoop.
[syrup—shrub (2), sherbet.]

tabor—tambour.
tache (1)—tack.
taint—attaint.
tamper—temper.

|tank—stank.]
tarpauling—tar (2).
task—tax.
taunt—tempt, tent (2).
tawny—tenny.
tease—tose.
tee—taw (2).
teind—tithe, tenth.
tend (1)—tender (2).
tense (2)—toise.
tercel—tassel (2).
[thatch—deck.]
thread—thrid.
thrill, thirl—drill.
[ticket—etiquette.]
tine (1)—tooth.
tippet—tape.
[tire (2), tire (3)—attire.]
tit (2)—teat.
[tithe—tenth, teind.]
title—tittle.
to—too.
ton—tun.
tone—tune.
tour—turn.
tow (1)—tug.

town—down.
track—trick (1).
tract (1)—trait.
tradition—treason.
travail—travel.
treble—triple.
trifle—truffle.
tripod—trivet.
triumph—trump (2).
troth—truth.
tuck (1)—tug.
[tuck (2)—stock.]
tuck (3)—touch.
tulip—turban.
tweak—twitch.
[two—deuce (1).]

umbel—umbrella.
[union (2)—onion.]
unity—unit.
ure—opera.
[utas—octave.]
[utter (1)—outer.]

vade—fade.
vair—various.

valet—varlet.
[van (2)—fan.]
[vane—pane, pawn (1).]
vantage—advantage.
vast—waste.
[vat—fat (2).]
vaward—vanguard.
veal—wether.
veldt—field.
veneer—furnish.
venew, veney—venue.
verb—word.
vermeil—vermilion.
vertex—vortex.
vervain—verbena.
[vetch—fitch.]
viaticum—voyage.
[vie—invite.]
[viol—fiddle.]
viper—wyvern, wivern.
visor—vizard.
vizier, visier—alguazil.
vocal—vowel.

[wage—gage (1).]
wain—wagon, waggon.

wale (1)—weal.
[ward—guard.]
[warden—guardian.]
[warranty—guarantee.]
[waste—vast.]
wattle—wallet.
weet—wit (1).
[wether—veal.]
whirl—warble.
[whole—hale (1).]
[whoop—hoop (2).]
[wig—peruke, periwig.]
wight (1)—whit.
[wile—guile.]
[wise (2)—guise.]
wold—weald.
[word—verb.]
[wort—root (1), radix, radish, race (3).]
[wrack—wreck, rack (3).]

yelp—yap.

[zealous—jealous.]
[zero—cipher.]

V. LIST OF INDOGERMANIC ROOTS

THE following is a brief list of the principal Indogermanic roots that have English derivatives. Those of which examples are either scanty or doubtful are not noticed. Many of the roots here given are of some importance and can be abundantly illustrated. I have added, at the end of the brief account of each root, several miscellaneous examples of derivatives; but these lists are by no means exhaustive, nor are they arranged in any particular order beyond the separation into groups of the words of Greek, Latin, and Teutonic origin.

Many of these roots (but given in forms which are no longer generally accepted) may be found in 'Fick, Vergleichendes Wörterbuch der indogermanischen Sprachen,' in Curtius, 'Greek Etymology, English edition, translated by Wilkins and England,' and in 'Vaniček, Griechisch-Lateinisches Etymologisches Wörterbuch, Leipzig, 1877.' More correct forms are frequently cited by Brugmann and Uhlenbeck, and are here adopted. The chief modern improvements are the substitution of *e* or *o* for *a* in many instances, of *ei* for *i* and of *eu* for *u* likewise in many instances, and in the treatment of the gutturals.

The account of each root is, in each case, very brief, and mentions only a few characteristic derivatives. Further information may be obtained in the above-mentioned authorities. The English examples are accounted for in the present work. Thus, under the word Agitate, a cross-reference is given to Agent; and under Agent is cited the √AG, to drive; with a reference to Brugmann, i. § 175.

Instead of giving Grimm's Law in the usual form, I omit the Old High German modifications, and use the word 'Teutonic' as inclusive of all other Germanic forms, tbus reducing the number of varying bases, as due to 'sound-shifting' of the consonants, from *three* to *two*. This being premised, I give a short and easy method for the conversion of 'Indogermanic' roots into the corresponding 'Teutonic' ones; though it must be remembered that each language has ways of its own for representing certain original sounds. Some of these modifications are noticed below.

Let the student learn by heart the following scheme.

Dentals; viz. dh, d, t, th.
Labials; viz. bh, b, p, f.
Gutturals; viz. gh, g, k, h.

This is all that need be remembered; it only remains to explain what the scheme means.

It is to be read in the following manner. When a dental sound occurs (especially at the *beginning* of a word, for in other positions the rule is liable to exception), an Idg. *dh* becomes a Teut. *d* [for dh is followed in the scheme by d]; an Idg. *d* becomes a Teut. *t*

[for a like reason]; and an Idg. *t* becomes a Teut. *th* (as in English).

In practice, inevitable modifications take place, some of the *principal* ones being these (I do not give them all).

For **dh**, as above, Skt. has *dh*; Gk. has θ; Latin has *f* (or if the **dh** be not initial, *d* or *b*).

For **bh**, as above, Skt. has *bh*; Gk. has φ; and Latin has *f* (or if the **bh** be not initial, *b*).

For **gh**, as above, Skt. has *gh* or *h*; Gk. has χ; and Latin has *f* or *h* (or if the **gh** be not initial, *g*, *gu*, *u*).

Note the threefold value of the Latin *f*, which may stand, initially, for *dh*, *bh*, or *gh*. Also, that Latin uses *c* for *k*, but the *c* is always hard, having the sound of *k* before *all* vowels.

A few selected examples are here noted.

Dentals. Lat. *facere*, to do, to put, is allied to Gk. τί-θη-μι, I place, and to E. *do*. From √dhē, to place, put; Sanskrit has *dhā*, to put. Skt. *dva*, Gk. δύω, Lat. *duo*, are cognate with E. *two*. Gk. τρεῖς, Lat. *trēs*, are cognate with E. *three*.

Labials. From the √bher, to bear, we have the Skt. *bhar*, to bear; Gk. φέρειν, Lat. *ferre*, to bear; E. *bear*. Examples of the change from the classical *p* to E. *b* are very scarce; compare the Lat. *labium* with the E. *lip*. Gk. πούς (stem ποδ-); Lat. *pēs* (stem *ped*-); E. *foot*.

Gutturals. From the √ghel, to be yellow, we have the Gk. χολή, gall; Lat. *fel*, gall, *heluus*, light yellow; E. *gall*. The Gk. γένος, Lat. *genus*, race, is allied to the E. *kin*; and the Gk. καρδία, Lat. *cor*, to the E. *heart*. It is now recognised, however, that there are really *three* series of gutturals, sometimes named the palatal gutturals, the middle gutturals, and the labialised velar gutturals. Some further information on the more elementary points of comparative philology will be found in my Primer of Classical and English Philology.

I denote the palatal gutturals by GH, G, K; the middle gutturals by G(w)H, G(w), Q; and the labialised velar gutturals by GwH, Gw, and Qw. They cannot always be distinguished, and I am not sure that I have always given them correctly.

The list of Roots given below is arranged in alphabetical order. They may be regarded as elementary bases (usually monosyllabic) which underlie all the various forms that are given by way of example. Each of them may be regarded, to use Brugmann's words, as 'the nucleus (so to speak) of a whole system of word-forms;' and are of much service in grouping words together. But they do not afford any very sure indications of what the primitive Indo-germanic was like; 'it must not (says Brugmann) be supposed that the roots, which we in ordinary practice abstract from words, are at all to be relied upon as representing the word-forms of the root-period.'

By way of further illustration, I give a fuller treatment of the first root on the list.

The form **AG** (AK) means that the Indogermanic root **AG** takes the form AK in Teutonic, by the 'sound-shifting' of *g* to *k* already noticed above. The sense of the root seems to have been 'to drive, urge, lead, conduct,' and the like. The Skt. form (originally *ag*) has been palatalised to *aj*, which is the base of the verb *ajami*, 'I drive;' the third person singular is *ajati*, 'he drives;' and the form *ajati* is taken in Uhlenbeck's Etymological Dictionary of Sanskrit to represent this verb. The Greek infinitive is ἄγειν, and the Latin infinitive is *agere*. (It is further represented by the Old Irish *agaim*, 'I drive.') The chief representative of this root in Teutonic occurs in the Icel. *aka*, to drive (pt. t. *ōk*); the corresponding AS. form *acan* (pt t. *ōc*) took up a new sense, viz. 'to give pain,' as in *mīne ēagan acaδ*, 'my eyes give pain,' or in modern English, *ache*. I give, as characteristic examples, the words *agony* and *axiom*, from Greek; *agent*, *agile*, and *axis*, from Latin; and *acre*, *acorn*, and *ache*, from Anglo-Saxon. How each of these words is connected with the root **AG**, is explained in the Dictionary.

But these are not the only English derivatives from this root. The Latin *agere* had the pp. *actus*, whence the E. *act*, *active*, *actor*, *actual*, *actuate*, *actuary*, *counteract*, *enact*, *exact*, *transact*; while from the base *ag-* we have also *agitate*, *cogitate*, *ambiguous*, *coagulate*, *cogent*, *exigent*, *examine*, *prodigal*. In connexion with the Gk. *agony* we may further cite *antagonist*. And it is very likely that another native English derivative is *axle*; for the addition of *s* to the base *ag* would give a base *ags*, which would necessarily become *aks*, accounting for the Gk. ἄξων and the Lat. *axis* (see **Axis**); and this new base *aks* would become *ahs* in Teutonic, by the usual 'sound-shifting' from Idg. *k* to E. *h*. But the Teutonic *hs* becomes *x* in Anglo-Saxon, so that there is no difficulty in connecting the AS. *eax*, an axle, with the Latin *axis*; see further under **Axle**.

Similarly, many other roots have often more derivatives than it seemed to me at all necessary to indicate.

AG (AK), to drive, urge, conduct. Skt. *aj*, to drive; Gk. ἄγ-ειν, L. *ag-ere*, to drive; Icel. *ak-a* (pt. t. *ōk*), to drive. Ex. *agony*, *axiom*, *synagogue*, *hegemony*; *agent*, *agile*, *axis*; *acre*, *acorn*, *ache*.

AGH (AG), to pull tight (?). Gk. ἄχ-ομαι, I am vexed, ἄχ-os, anguish; Goth. *ag-is*, fright, awe. Ex. *ail*, *awe*. Cf. ANGH.

AIDH (AID), to kindle. Skt. *indh*, to kindle; *ēdh-as*, fuel; Gk. αἴθ-ειν, to burn; αἰθ-ήρ, upper air; L. *aed-ēs*, orig. a hearth, *aestus*, heat; AS. *ād*, a funeral pile, *āst*, a kiln. Ex. *ether*; *edify*, *estuary*; *oast-house*.

AK (AH), to be sharp, to pierce. Gk. ἄκ-ρos, pointed; ἀκ-όνη whetstone; ἀκ-μή, edge; L. *ac-us*, needle, *ac-uere*, to sharpen, *ac-iēs*, edge; AS. *ecg*, edge. Ex. *acacia*, *acme*, *aconite*, *acrobat*, *acrostic*; *acid*, *acumen*, *acute*, *acrid*, *ague*, *aglet*, *eager*; *ear* (2), *edge*, *awn*, *egg* (2), and cf. *paragon*.

AL, to nourish, raise. L. *al-ere*, to nourish; *ad-ol-escere*, to grow up; *al-tus*, raised; Goth. *al-an*, to nourish; *al-ds*, an age. Ex. *aliment*, *altitude*, *adolescent*, *adult*, *exalt*; *old*.

AN, to breathe. Skt. *an*, to breathe; Gk. ἄν-εμos, wind; L. *animus*, spirit; Goth. *us-anan*, to breathe out, expire. Ex. *anemone*; *animal*, *animosity*, *animadvert*.

ANGH (ANG), to choke, strangle. Gk. ἄγχ-ειν, to strangle; L. *ang-ere*, to choke, *anx-ius*, anxious; Icel. *angr*, grief. Ex. *quinsy* (for *quin-anc-y*); *angina*, *anguish*, *anxious*; *anger*.

ANQ (ANH, ANG), to bend. Skt. *añch*, to bend, curve; Gk. ἄγκ-υρα, an anchor; Gk. ἀγκ-ών, a bend; L. *unc-us*, curved, *ang-ulus*, an angle; AS. *ang-el*, a hook. Ex. *anchor*; *angle* (1); *angle* (2).

AR, to plough. Gk. ἀρ-όειν, L. *ar-āre*, AS. *er-ian*, to plough. Ex. *arable*; *ear* (3).

AR, to fit. Skt. *ar-as*, spoke of a wheel; Gk. ἄρ-μενos, fitted, ἄρ-θρον, joint; ἀρ-μόs, joint, shoulder; L. *ar-mus*, *ar-tus*, a limb; *ar-ma*, arms, *ar-s*, art; Goth. *ar-ms*, an arm. Ex. *harmony*; *arms*, *art*, *article*; *arm* (1).

ARG, to shine. Skt. *arj-unas*, white (cf. *raj-atam*, silver); Gk. ἀργ-όs, white, ἄργ-υρos, silver, L. *arg-entum*, silver, *arg-illa*, white clay; *arg-uere*, to make clear. Ex. *argent*, *argillaceous*, *argument*. Also *Argonaut*.

ARQ, to protect, keep safe. Gk. ἀρκ-εῖν, to keep off; L. *arc-ēre*, to keep off, *arc-a*, a box. Ex. *arcana*, *ark*.

AUG(w) (AUK), to increase. Apparently allied to **AWEG**(w), **WEG**(w); see **WEG**(w). Skt. *ug-ra(s)*, very strong, *ōj-as*, strength (cf. *vaj*, to strengthen); L. *aug-ēre*, to increase; Goth. *auk-an*, to eke. Hence **AUG**(w)-**S**, **AUQ-S**, as in Gk. αὐξ-άνειν, to increase,

L. *aux-ilium*, help. Ex. *augment*, *august*, *auction*, *author*, also *auxiliary*; *eke* (1), *eke* (2).

AWES, to shine; see **EUS**, **WES**.

BHA [= bhā], to speak, declare. Gk. φη-μί, I say, φή-μη, report, φά-τις, a saying, φω-νή, clear voice; L. *fā-ri*, to speak, *fā-ma*, fame, *fā-bula*, a narrative, *fa-teor*, I confess. Ex. *antiphon*, *anthem*, *prophet*, *euphemism*, *euphony*, *phonetic*; *fate*, *fable*, *fairy*, *fame*, *affable*, *confess*. See **BHAN** (below).

BHAN (BAN), to speak, declare. Skt. *bhan*, to speak, declare; AS. *ban-nan*, to proclaim. Ex. *ban*, *banns*.

BHA [= bhā], to shine, to be clear. Skt. *bhā*, to shine. Hence the extended forms **BHAL**, **BHAN**, **BHAW**.

BHAL, to shine. Skt. *bhāl-am*, lustre, Lith. *bál-ti*, to be white, Gk. φαλ-ιός, white. Breton *bal*, a white streak in an animal's face, AS. *bǣl*, a blaze. Ex. *bald*, *bald-faced*; also *bale-fire*, *beltane*.

BHAN, to show, display clearly. Gk. φαίνειν (for *φάν-γειν), to show, φαν-τάζειν, to display, φά-σις, appearance, phase; Irish *bān*, white. Ex. *fancy*, *hierophant*, *sycophant*, *phantom*, *phenomenon*, *phase*. Also *pant*.

BHAW, to glow. Gk. φά-os (for *φαϝ-os), φῶs, light; φα-έθειν, to shine, glow. Ex. *phaeton*, *phosphorus*.

BHEID (BEIT), to cleave, bite. Skt. *bhid*, to cleave; L. *findere* (pt. t. *fid-ī*), to cleave; AS. *bīt-an*, to bite; Icel. *beita*, to make to bite, to bait. Ex. *fissure*; *bite*, *bitter*, *bait*, *abet*, *bet*. (Cf. *bill* (1), which Walde refers to an Idg. type *bhid-lom*.)

BHEIDH (BEID), to persuade, trust. Gk. πείθ-ω, I persuade; L. *fīd-ere*, to trust, *fid-es*, faith, *foed-us*, a treaty. Ex. *affiance*, *confide*, *defy*, *faith*, *fealty*, *fidelity*, *infidel*, *perfidious*, *federal*, *confederate*. Perhaps *bid* (1). Perhaps *bide* (disputed).

BHELGH (BELG), to bulge, swell out. Icel. *bolg-inn*, swollen, from a lost strong verb; Irish *bolg-aim*, I swell, *bolg*, a bag, budget, belly, pair of bellows; Goth. *balg-s*, a bag; AS. *belg-an*, to swell with anger. Ex. *bulge*, *bilge*, *budget*; *bag* (?), *belly*, *bellows*, *billow*, *bolled*. Cf. *bulk* (1).

BHELS (BELL), to resound. Lith. *bals-as*, voice, sound; AS. *bell-an*, to make a loud noise. Cf. Skt. *bhāsh* (for *bhals), to speak (Uhlenbeck). Ex. *bell*, *bellow*, *bull* (1).

BHENDH (BEND), to bind. Skt. *bandh* (for *bhendh*), to bind; Pers. *band*, a bond; Gk. πείσμα (for *πένθ-σμα), a cable; L. *of-fend-ix*, a knot, band; Goth. *bind-an*, to bind. Ex. *bind*, *bend*, *bond*, *bundle*.

BHER (BER), to bear, carry. Skt. *bhṛ*, to support, *bhrā-tar-*, a brother, friend; Gk. φέρ-ω, L. *fer-o*, I bear; *for-s*, chance (which brings things about); *fūr*, a thief (cf. Gk. φώρ). Ex. *fertile*, *fortune*, *fortuitous*, *furtive*; *bear* (1), *burden*, *bier*, *barrow*, *bairn*, *barm* (2), *birth*, *brother*; *bore* (3).

BHER (BER), to cut, bore. Zend *bar*, to cut, bore; Pers. *bur-enda*, sharp, cutting; Gk. φαρ-άω (for *φαρ-άω), I plough, φάρ-αγξ, a ravine, φάρ-υγξ, gullet; L. *for-āre*, AS. *bor-ian*, to bore. Ex. *pharynx*; *perforate*; *bore* (1), *bore* (2).

BHERG, **BHLEG** (BERK, BLEK), to shine, burn. Skt. *bhrāj*, to shine; Gk. φλέγ-ειν, to burn, L. *fulg-ēre*, to shine, *ful-men* (*fulg-men*), thunder-bolt, *flag-rāre*, to burn, *flam-ma* (*flag-ma*), flame; Goth. *bairh-ts*, bright. Ex. *phlox*; *refulgent*, *fulminate*, *flagrant*, *flame*; *bright*. Also *blink*, *blank*.

BHERS (BERS), to be stiff or bristling. Skt. *bhṛsh-ṭi-*, a point; Icel. *brod-dr* (*broz-dr*), a spike; AS. *byrs-t*, a bristle, *bears*, *bærs*, a perch (fish). Ex. *brad*, *bristle*, *bass* (2).

BHEU (BEU), to dwell, become, be. Skt. *bhū*, to be; *bhav-ana(m)*, a dwelling, house; Gk. ἔ-φυ, he was; L. *fu-ī*, I was; AS. *bēo-n*, to be; *bo-ld*, a house; Goth. *bau-an*, to dwell; Lith. *bu-ti*, to be. Ex. *physic*, *euphuism*, *imp*; *future*; *be*, *boor*, *booth*, *busk* (1), *bower*, *byre*, *by-law*, *burly*, *build*.

BHEUDH (BEUD), to awake, inform, bid, command. Skt. *budh* (*bhudh*), to awake, understand, *bōdh-aya*, to inform; Gk. πευθ-ομαι, I search, ask; AS. *bēod-an*, to bid. Ex. *bid* (2), *beadle*, *bode*.

BHEUQw, **BHEUGw**, (BEUHw), to bow, bend, turn about. Skt. *bhuj*, to bend, stoop; Gk. φεύγ-ειν, to flee; L. *fug-ere*, to flee; AS. *būg-an*, to bow, bend, *bog-a*, a bow. Ex. *fugitive*, *fugue*, *refuge*, *subterfuge*; *bow* (1), *bow* (2), *bow* (3), *bight*, *bout*, *buxom*. See Brugmann, i. § 658; who adds *boil* (2).

BHLE (= bhlē), Teut. BLE (= blē), to blow. L. *flā-re*, AS. *blā-wan*, to blow. Ex. *flatulent*; *blow* (1), *blaze* (2), *blast*, *bladder*.

BHLEG, to shine, burn; see **BHERG**.

BHLO (= bhlō), Teut. BLO (= blō), to blow as a flower, to flourish. L. *flō-s*, a flower, *flō-rēre*, to flourish; AS. *blō-wan*, to blow, *blō-ma*, bloom. Ex. *floral*, *flourish*; *blow* (2), *bloom*, *blossom*, *blood*, *bleed*, *bless*.

BHOG, *bhōg* (BAK, bōk), to bake or roast. Gk. φώγ-ειν, to roast, bake; AS. *bac-an* (pt. t. *bōc*), to bake. Ex. *bake*

BHREG (BREK), to break (with a cracking noise). L. *frang-ere* (pt. t. *frēg-i*), to break; *frag-ilis*, fragile; Goth. *brik-an*, AS. *brec-an*, to break. Ex. *fragile, fragment, frail; break, brake* (1), *brake* (2). Perhaps *brook* (2).

BHREQ, to crowd close, fence round, shut in. Gk. φράσσειν (*φράκ-γειν), to shut in, make fast, φράγ-μα, a fence; L. *frequ-ens*, crammed; *farc-īre*, to stuff full. Ex. *diaphragm; frequent, farce, force* (2).

BHREU (BREU), to decoct. L. *dē-fru-tum*, new wine boiled down; Thracian βρῦ-τον, beer; OIrish *bruith*, cooking; AS. *brēo-wan*, to brew. Ex. *brew, broth, brose, bread*. Allied to the above words are, further, Gk. φύρ-ειν, to mix up, mingle together, Skt. *bhuraṇya*, to be active, L. *fur-ere*, to rage. Ex. *fury*; also *purple*. Also L. *feru-ēre*, to boil, to be fervent, *fermentum*, leaven; AS. *beorma*, yeast. Ex. *fervent, ferment; barm* (1).

BHREUG (BREUK), to enjoy, use. L. *fru-or* (for *frūg-uor*), pp. *fruc-tus*, I enjoy, *frūg-ēs*, fruit, *frū-mentum* (*frūg-mentum*), corn; AS. *brūc-an*, to use. Ex. *fruit, frugal, furmity, fructify; brook* (1).

BUQ, to bellow, snort, puff; of imitative origin. Skt. *bukk*, to sound; L. *bucc-a*, the puffed cheek. Ex. *disembogue, debouch, embouchure*.

DAK (TAH), to bite, tear, hold fast. Skt. *daç*, to bite; Gk. δάκ-νειν, to bite; Goth. *tah-jan*, to rend; AS. *tang-e*, a pair of tongs. Ex. *tang* (1), *tang* (3), *tongs*.

DAM (TAM), to tame. Skt. *dam*, to tame; Gk. δαμ-άειν, to tame; L. *dom-āre*, to tame; Goth. *ga-tam-jan*, to tame. Ex. *adamant, diamond; daunt; tame*.

DE (=dē), to bind. Gk. δέ-ω, I bind, διά-δη-μα, fillet. Ex. *diadem*.

DEIK (TEIH), to show, point out. Skt. *diç*, to show; Gk. δείκ-νυμι, I show, δίκ-η, justice; L. *in-dic-āre*, to point out, *dīc-ere*, to tell; Goth. *ga-teih-an*, to teach, tell; AS. *tēon* (*tīh-an*), to accuse. Ex. *syndic; indicate, dedicate, diction*, &c.; *dight, index, judge, judicious*, &c.; *verdict, vindicate; teen, token, teach*.

DEIW (TEIW), to shine. Skt. *div*, to shine; *dēv-a(s)*, God, *div-ya(s)*, brilliant, divine; Gk. Ζεύς (stem Δί͜F-), Zeus, δῖ-ος, heavenly, L. *de-us*, God, *diu-us*, divine, *di-ēs*, day; AS. *Tīg* (gen. *Tiwes*), the god of war. Ex. *Zeus; Jupiter, deity, divine, dial, diary, meridian, jovial; Tuesday*.

DEK (KEK), to honour, think fit. Sk. *dāç*, to honour, worship; Gk. δοκ-εῖ, it seems fit, δόξ-α, opinion; L. *dec-et*, it is fit, *doc-ēre*, to teach, *discere* (*di-dc-scere*), to learn. Ex. *paradox, dogma, didactic; decent, decorum, docile, disciple*.

DEM (TIM), to build. Gk. δεμ-εῖν, to build, δόμ-ος, a building; L. *dom-us*, a house; Goth. *tim-rjan*, to build. Ex. *dome, major-domo, domestic, domicile* (also *despot*); *timber*. Perhaps L. *dom-inus*, a master, with its derivatives, is from the same root.

DER (TER), to tear, rive. Skt. *dṛ-ṇāmi*, I burst open, tear asunder; Gk. δέρ-ειν, to flay, δέρ-μα, skin; Goth. *ga-tairan*, to break, destroy, AS. *ter-an*, to rend. Ex. *epidermis, pachydermatous; tear* (1), *tire* (1), *tire* (4); perhaps *tree, tar, larch*.

DERBH (TERB), to knit together. Skt. *dṛbh*, to bind, *darbh-a(s)*, matted grass; AS. *turf*, turf. Ex. *turf*.

DEU (TEU), to work, prepare. Skt. *dū-ta(s)*, a messenger (?); Goth. *tau-jan*, to do; AS. *taw-ian*, to prepare, to scourge; *tō-l* (*tōu-l*), a tool. Ex. *taw, tew, tow* (2), *tool*. (Hence the final *-t* in *herio-t*.)

DEUK (TEUH), to lead, conduct. L. *dūc-ere*, to lead; Goth. *tiuh-an*, AS. *tēo-n*, to draw, pull. Ex. *duke, ad-duce*, &c., *conduit, doge, douche, ducal, redoubt, educate; tow* (1), *tug, tuck* (1), *tuck* (3), *tie, touch, tocsin, team*.

DHE (=dhē), weak grade dhə (Teut. *dē, *dō), to put, place, set, do. Skt. *dhā*, to place, put; Gk. τί-θη-μι, I place, set, θέ-μα, a thing proposed, θέ-σις, a placing, θέ-μις, law, θη-σαυρός, treasure; L. *fa-c-ere*, to do, *fa-c-ilis*, easy to do; AS. *dǣ-d*, a deed, *dō-m*, judgement, *dē-man*, to judge. Ex. *anathema, hypothec, theme, thesis, epithet, treasure, tick* (2); *fact*, suffix *-fy* in *magni-fy*, &c.; *-ficent*; *do* (1), *deed, doom, deem*. Also *creed*. See note to **DO** (above).

DHEGwH (DEG), to burn. Skt. *dah* (for *dhagh*), to burn; L. *fau-illa*, hot ashes; Lith. *deg-ù*, I burn; Goth. *dag-s*, day. Ex. *day*. Cf. *foment*, from L. *fou-ēre*.

DHEI (=dhēi), to suck. Skt. *dhē*, to suck; Gk. θη-λή, the breast; L. *fē-lare*, to suck, *fē-mina*, woman, *fī-lius*, son, OIrish *dī-nim*, I suck. Ex. *female, feminine, filial*.

DHEIGH (DEIG), to smear, knead, mould, form. Skt. *dih* (*dhigh*), to smear; Gk. τεῖχ-ος, a wall (orig. of earth); L. *fing-ere* (pp. *fic-tus*), to mould, form, feign, *fig-ulus*, a potter; Goth. *deig-an*, *dīg-an*, to knead, *daig-s*, a kneaded lump. Ex. *paradise; fiction, fictile, feign, figure; dough, dairy, lady*.

DHER, to support, hold, keep. Skt. *dhṛ*, to bear, support, maintain, keep, hold, retain; Gk. θρό-νος, a support, seat; θώρ-αξ,

a breast-plate (keeper); L. *frē-tus*, relying on, *fir-mus*, secure. Ex. *throne, thorax; firm, farm*.

DHERS (DERS), to dare. Skt. *dṛṣh*, to dare; Gk. θαρσ-εῖν, to be bold, θρασ-ύς, bold; Goth. *dars*, I dare, *daurs-ta*, I durst. Ex. *thrasonical; dare, durst*.

DHEU (DEU), to run, to flow. Skt. *dhav, dhāv*, to run, to flow; Gk. θέ-ειν, to run (fut. θεύ-σομαι); AS. *dēaw*, dew. Ex. *dew*.

DHEU (DEU), to agitate, fan into flame. Skt. *dhū*, to agitate, fan into flame; *dhū-ma(s)*, smoke; Gk. θύ-ειν, to rush, rage, sacrifice, θύ-ος, incense; θύ-μος, θύ-μον, thyme; L. *fū-mus*, smoke; AS. *dū-st*, dust. Ex. *tunny, thyme; thurible, fume; dust*.

DHEUB (DEUP), to be deep, to be hollow. Lith. *dub-ùs*, deep, *dub-ti*, to be hollow; Goth. *diup-s*, deep. Ex. *deep, depth, dip*. Variant **DHEUP** (DEUF). Russ. *dup-lo*, hollow, AS. *dȳf-an*, to dive into, AS. *dūfe-doppa*, a diving-bird. Ex. *dive, dove*.

DHEUBH (DEUB), to fill with smoke or mist. Skt. *dhūp-a(s)*, vapour; Gk. τῦφ-ός (*θύφ-ος), smoke, gloom, stupefaction; τυφ-λός, blinded, dark; Goth. *daub-s*, deaf, (perhaps) *dumb-s*, dumb. Ex. *typhoon, typhus; deaf, dumb*? Allied to **DHEU**, to agitate.

DHREN (DREN), to make a droning noise. Skt. *dhraṇ*, to sound; Gk. θρῆν-ος, lamentation, θρῶν-αξ, a drone-bee; Goth. *drun-jus*, a sound; OSax. *drān*, a drone. Ex. *threnody; drone* (1), *drone* (2).

DHWEL (DWEL), to be confused or troubled. Gk. θολ-ερός, troubled, thick, muddy (as water), θολ-ός, mud; Goth. *dwal-s*, foolish; Icel. *dwel-ja*, to hinder, delay, dwell; AS. *dol*, foolish. Ex. *dull, dwell, dwale*. Perhaps allied to **DHEU**, to agitate.

DHWES (DWES), to breathe, inspire. Gk. θέσ-φατος, spoken by God, inspired, θε-ός (*θἑF͜εσ-ός), God; Lith. *dwes-iù*, I breathe, *dwasê*, breath, spirit, ghost, *dus-éti*, to breathe hard; Goth. *dius*, a wild animal (cf. L. *animal* from *anima*); AS. *dēor*, a deer. Ex. *theism, theology; deer*.

DO (=dō), to give. Skt. *dā*, to give; Gk. δί-δω-μι, I give, δό-σις, a gift, dose; L. *dō-num*, a gift, *dō-s*, dowry, *da-re*, to give. Ex. *dose; donation, dower, dowry, date* (1), *dado, die* (2), *render, rent* (2), *traitor, treason*. ¶ The verbs *con-dere, crē-dere*, and some others ending in *-dere* are usually referred to the root *dhē*.

DRE (=drē), weak grade dər, to sleep. Skt. *drā*, to sleep. Gk. δαρ-θάνειν, L. *dor-mire*, to sleep. Ex. *dormitory, dormant, dormer-window*.

DREM, to run. Skt. *dram*, to run; Gk. ἔ-δραμ-ον, I ran, δρόμ-ος, a running. Ex. *dromedary*.

ED (ET), to eat. Skt. *ad*, to eat; Gk. ἔδ-ειν, L. *ed-ere*, AS. *et-an*, to eat. Ex. *edible, eat, fret, ort*. Perhaps *tooth, dental*.

EI, to go; whence yē, to go, to pass. Skt. *ī*, to go; *yā*, to go; Gk. εἶ-μι, I shall go, L. *ī-re*, to go; AS. *ē-ode*, I went. Ex. *proem; ambient, circuit, commence, count* (1), *exit, eyre, initial, issue, itinerant, obit, perish, prætor, preterite, sedition, sudden*, &c. Also *yede*.

EL, to drive. Gk. ἐλ-αύνειν, to drive; L. *al-acer*, brisk. Ex. *elastic; alacrity, allegro*.

ERE, erē (rō), to row. Skt. *ari-tra(s)*, a rudder, Gk. ἐρε-τμός, an oar; Lith. *ir-ti*, to row; L. *rē-mus*, an oar; AS. *rō-wan*, to row. Ex. *trireme; row* (2), *rudder*.

ES, to dwell, to be. Skt. *as*, to exist, be; Gk. ἐσ-μί, εἰ-μί, I am; L. *es-se*, to be, *s-um*, I am; *ab-s-ens*, being away; AS. *is*, is, *s-ōð*, true (orig. being). Ex. *suttee; palæontology; absent, present, essence, entity; am, art, is, are, sooth*.

GEN (KEN), to generate, produce. Skt. *jan*, to beget; Gk. γέν-ος, race, γί-γν-ομαι, I am born, L. *gi-gn-ere* (pt. t. *gen-ui*), to beget, *gen-itor*, father, *gn-ascor*, I am born, *gen-us*, kin; Goth. *kun-i*, kin. Ex. *Genesis, endogen, cosmogony; genus, genius, gentile, benign, cognate, indigenous, natal, native, nature; kin, kind* (1), *kind* (2), *kindred, kith*.

GEN (KEN), to know; also gnā, gnō (knā). Skt. *jnā*, to know; Gk. γι-γνώ-σκειν, to know; γνω-τός, known; L. *gnō-scere, nō-scere*, to know, *i-gnō-rāre*, not to know, *gnā-rus*, knowing (whence *narrāre*, to tell); Goth. *kann*, I know; AS. *cnā-wan*, to know. Ex. *gnostic, gnomon; ignorant, narrate, noble; can* (1), *ken, know, cunning, keen, uncouth*.

GER (KER), to grind, to crumble with age. Skt. *jīr-ṇa(s)*, decayed, pp. of *grī*, to wear out; *jar-as*, decrepitude; Gk. γέρ-ων, old man; L. *grā-num*, corn; AS. *cor-n*, corn. Ex. *grain; corn, kernel*.

GERPH (KERF), to carve, write. Gk. γράφ-ειν, to incise, write; AS. *ceorf-an*, to carve. Ex. *graphic, autograph*, &c., *diagram*, &c., *grammar, programme; carve*.

GEUS (KEUS), to choose, taste. Skt. *jush*, to like, enjoy; Gk. γεύ-ομαι, I taste, γευσ-τός, to be tasted; L. *gus-tāre*, to taste; Goth. *kius-an*, to choose, *kus-tus*, taste. Ex. *gust* (2), *disgust; choose; choice*.

GLEU (KLEU), to draw together, conglomerate. Skt. *glau*, a lump (Macdonell); L. *glu-ere*, to draw together, *glo-mus*, a clew, *glo-bus*, a ball; AS. *clēo-we*, a clew. Ex. *globe, conglomerate; clew* (*clue*).

GLEUBH (KLEUB), to cleave, to split asunder. Gk. γλύφ-ειν, to hollow out; L. *glūb-ere*, to peel, *glū-ma* (**glūb-ma*), a husk; AS. *clēof-an*, to cleave, split. Ex. *glyptic, hiero-glyphic; glume; cleave* (1), *cleft*.

G(w)EL (KEL), to be cold. L. *gel-u*, frost; *gel-idus*, cold; Goth. *kal-ds*, cold; AS. *cōl*, cool, *ceal-d*, cold. Ex. *gelid, jelly, congeal; cool, cold, keel* (2).

G(w)ER, to assemble. Gk. ἀ-γείρειν (**ἀ-γέρ-γειν*), to assemble, ἀ-γορ-ά, an assembly; L. *grex* (stem *gre-g*), a flock. Ex. *category, paregoric; gregarious, egregious.*

G(w)ER (KER), to cry out (perhaps imitative). Skt. *gir*, voice; Gk. γέρ-ανος, a crane, γῆρ-υς, speech; L. *gr-us*, a crane, *gar-rīre*, to talk; Gael. *gair*, a shout, *sluagh-ghairm*, a battle-cry, slogan; AS. *cear-u*, care, lament. Ex. *geranium, garrulous; pedigree; slogan; care, crane, jar* (1), *jargon.*

G(w)LEI (KLEI), to stick to. Gk. γλοι-ός, sticky substance, gum; L. *glū-ten*, glue; AS. *clǣ-g*, clay, *clī-fan*, to stick to. Ex. *glue; clay, cleave* (2).

GwEI (QEI), to live; also in the form **GwEIW** (QEIW). Skt. *jiv*, to live, *jiv-a(s)*, living, life; Gk. βί-ος, life, also ζά-ω (for **g(w)yē-yō*), I live, ζώ-ω, I live; L. *uīu-ere*, to live, *uī-ta*, life; Goth. *kwius*, quick, living, active, AS. *cwic*, alive, quick. Ex. *biology, zoology; vivid, vital, victuals; quick. Also usquebaugh, azote, zodiac.*

GwEM (QEM), to come, to go, walk. Skt. *gam*, to go; Gk. βαίνειν (**βάν-γειν*), to go, βά-σις, a going; L. *uen-ire*, to come; Goth. *kwim-an*, AS. *cum-an*, to come. Ex. *base* (2), *basis; venture, advent, avenue, convene, &c.; come.*

GwER, to devour, swallow greedily. Skt. *aja-gar-a(s)*, lit. goat-swallower; Gk. βορ-ά, food, βορ-ός, gluttonous; L. *uor-āre*, to devour. Further allied to Skt. *gal-a(s)*, throat; L. *gula*, gullet, throat, *gl-utire*, to gulp down. It seems to be reduplicated in Skt. *gar-gar-a(s)*, a whirlpool (which may be partly imitative); Gk. γαρ-γαρ-ίζειν, to gurgle; L. *gur-gēs*, a whirlpool. Ex. *voracious; also gullet, gully, glut, glutton; also gargle, gurgle, gorge, gorget, gorgeous.*

GHA (GA), to gape, yawn. Gk. χά-ος, χά-σμα, abyss, χαίνειν (for **χά-ν-γειν*), to yawn; χήν, a goose; L. *anser*, a goose; G. *gans*, AS. *gōs*, a goose. Ex. *chasm, chaos; goose, gannet, gander.* See **GHEI**.

Base **GHAID** (GAIT), to sport, skip. L. *haed-us*, a kid; Lith. *žaid-žiu*, I play, sport; AS. *gāt*, a goat. Ex. *goat.*

GHEI (GEI), to yawn. L. *hi-āre*, to gape, yawn; AS. *tō-gīn-an*, str. vb., to gape open. Ex. *hiatus; yawn.* Perhaps *gill* (2). See **GHA**.

Base **GHEI-M-** (GEI-M-), cold, winter. Skt. *him-a(s)*, cold, *him-a(m)*, frost, snow; Gk. χει-μ-ών, winter; L. *hi-em-s*, winter, *hi-bernus*, wintry. Ex. *hibernal, hibernate;* prov. E. *gimmer*, a one-year-old (winter-old) ewe (Icel. *gymbr*).

GHEIS (GEIS), to be hostile (?). Skt. *hēḍ*, to disregard, *hēḍ-a(s)* (for **hēzd-a(s)*), anger, wrath (of the gods); Lith. *žeid-žiu*, I wound; Goth. *us-gais-jan*, to terrify, Icel. *geis-a*, to rage; AS. *gās-t*, a spirit, ghost; *gǣs-tan*, to terrify. Ex. *ghost, aghast.*

GHEL (GEL), to be green or yellow. Skt. *har-it*, green; Gk. χόλ-ος, χολ-ή, gall, χλό-η, verdure, χλω-ρός, greenish, yellowish; L. *hel-uus*, light yellow; AS. *geol-o*, yellow, *gol-d*, gold. Cf. L. *fel*, gall. Ex. *chlorine, choler; yellow, yolk, gold, gall.*

GHEL (GEL), to yell, cry out, cry as a bird. Gk. χελ-ιδών, a swallow; AS. *gell-an*, to yell, sing; *stān-gella*, a staniel; *gal-an*, to sing. Ex. *nightingale, staniel, yell.*

Base **GHEM-** (GEM-), from GHZEM-, earth, the ground. Skt. *ksham-ā*, earth, Gk. χαμ-αί, on the ground; Russ. *zem-lia*, earth, land; L. *hum-ī*, on the ground, *hum-us*, earth, *hom-o*, man (son of earth), Goth. *gum-a*, man. Ex. *chameleon, chamomile; homage, humble, humane, exhume.* Cf. *bridegroom.*

GHENG(w)H (GENG), to go, stride along. Skt. *jangh-ā*, the leg; Lith. *ženg-iù*, I go, march; Icel. *gang-a*, to go. Ex. *gang.*

GHER (GER), to desire, to yearn. Skt. *har-y*, to desire; Gk. χαίρειν (**χάρ-γειν*), to rejoice, χαρ-ά, joy, χάρ-ις, favour, grace; L. *hor-tārī*, to exhort; AS. *geor-n*, desirous. Ex. *eucharist, chervil; hortatory, exhort; yearn.*

GHER (GER), to seize, grasp, hold, gird. Skt. *hṛ*, to seize, *har-aṇa(s)*, the hand; Gk. χείρ (gen. χειρ-ός, χερ-ός), hand; χορ-ός, a dance in a ring or enclosure, χόρ-τος, an enclosure, yard; L. *hor-tus*, yard, garden; AS. *gear-d*, yard. Further allied to χορ-δή, a cord, a string of guts, Lith. *žar-nos*, Icel. *gar-nir*, guts, AS. *gear-n*, yarn. Ex. *cheiromancy, surgeon, chorus, choir; horticulture, cohort,*

court; *yard* (1), *garth, gird* (1), *girth.* Perhaps also *chord, cord; yarn.*

GHERS (GERS), to bristle. Skt. *hṛsh*, to bristle; L. *horr-ēre* (**hors-ēre*), to bristle; cf. *hirs-ūtus*, bristling. Cf. Gk. χήρ, L. *ēr*, a hedgehog; Gk. χαρ-άσσειν, to scratch. Ex. *horrid, hirsute;* perhaps *gorse.* Cf. *urchin, character.*

GHEU (GEU), to pour. Whence also **GHEUD** (GEUT), to pour. Gk. χέ-ειν (fut. χεύ-σω), to pour, χυ-μός, χυ-λός, juice; L. *fū-tis*, a water-vessel, *re-fū-tāre*, to refute (pour back), *fū-tilis*, easily emptied, futile; also *fund-ere* (pt. t. *fūd-i*), to pour; AS. *gēot-an*, to pour; Icel. *gjō-sa*, *gū-sa*, to gush. Ex. *chyme, chyle* (cf. *alchemy*); *confute, refute, futile, refund, found* (2), *fuse* (1), *confuse, diffuse; ingot, gut; gush, geysir.*

GHREM (GRIM), to make an angry noise. Gk. χρεμ-ίζειν, χρεμ-ετίζειν, to neigh; AS. *grim*, fierce. Ex. *grim, grumble.*

G(w)HAIS, to stick, adhere. L. *haer-ēre* (pt. t. *haes-ī*), to stick; Lith. *gaisz-ti*, to delay, tarry. Ex. *adhere, cohere, hesitate.*

G(w)HEND (GET), to seize, get. Gk. χανδ-άνειν (2 aor. ἔ-χαδ-ον); L. *prae-hend-ere*, to grasp, seize, *hed-era*, ivy, *praeda* (for **prae-hed-a*), booty, prey; Goth. *bi-git-an*, to find, AS. *giet-an*, to get. Ex. *prehensile, apprehend, prey, predatory; get, beget, forget.*

G(w)HES (meaning unknown). L. *hos-tis*, orig. a stranger, a guest; also a stranger, an enemy; Goth. *gas-ts*, AS. *gæs-t*, *gies-t*, a guest. Ex. *host* (1), *host* (2), *ostler, hotel, hospice; guest.*

G(w)HLEU (GLEU), to rejoice (?). Gk. χλεύ-η, sport; Icel. *glau-mr*, glee; AS. *glēo*, glee. Ex. *glee.*

G(w)HRADH (GRAD), to step, walk, go. L. *grad-ī*, to step, go; *grad-us*, a step; Goth. *grid-s*, *grip-s*, a step. Ex. *grade, gradient, gradual, graduate.*

GwHEN, to strike. Skt. *han*, to strike, wound; Gk. θείνειν (**θεν-γειν*), to strike, slay (cf. pt. t. πέ-φα-ται), to strike against; cf. OHG. *gund*, Icel. *gunnr*, AS. *gūd*, war. Ex. *defend, offend, infest, fence, fend.* Also *gonfalon, gonfanon, gun.*

GwHER, to glow. Skt. *ghṛ*, to shine; *ghar-ma(s)*, heat, hot season; Gk. θερ-μός, warm, θέρ-ος, summer heat; L. *for-mus*, warm, *for-nax*, furnace. Ex. *thermometer; furnace, fornicate.* Perhaps *warm.*

☞ For forms not found under K, see under Q.

KAM (HAM), to cover over. Gk. καμ-άρα, a vaulted place (whence L. *camera*); κάμ-ινος, an oven; Goth. *ga-ham-ōn*, to cover with clothes; Icel. *ham-r*, a covering. Ex. *chamber, chimney;* cf. *chemise.*

KAN (HAN), to sing. Gk. καν-αχή, a ringing sound; L. *can-ere*, to sing; AS. *han-a*, a cock (singer). Ex. *chant, canto, accent, incentive, &c.; hen.*

KEI, to lie down, repose. Skt. *çī*, to recline, rest; Gk. κεῖ-μαι, I lie down. Hence also Skt. *çē-va(s)*, kind, friendly; L. *cī-uis*, fellow-citizen; OHG. *hī-wo*, husband; AS. *hī-wan*, household servants. Ex. *cemetery; civil, city; hind* (2).

KEL (HEL), to hide. OIrish *cel-im*, I hide; L. *cel-la*, a hut; AS. *hel-an*, to hide, *hel-m*, a covering; *heal-l*, a hall, *hell-e*, hell. L. *oc-cul-ere*, to hide; Gk. καλ-ιά, a hut, καλ-ύπτειν, to cover; Goth. *hul-jan*, to hide; AS. *hol*, a hole; L. *cēl-āre*, to hide. Ex. *eucalyptus; cell, conceal; helm, hall, hell, hole, hollow.* Or **QEL**, q.v.

KENQ (HENH), to waver, to hang. Skt. *çaṅk*, to hesitate; L. *cunc-tārī* (for **conc-itāri*), to delay; Goth. *hāhan* (**hanhan*), to hang, AS. *hang-ian*, to hang. Ex. *hang, hank, hanker, hinge.*

KER (HER), to project, stand up (?). Skt. *çir-as*, head; Pers. *sar*, head; Gk. κάρ-α, head; κέρ-as, a horn; L. *cer-ebrum*, brain. Closely allied to Skt. *çṛ-nga(m)*, a horn (Gk. κόρ-υμβος, highest point), L. *cor-nu*, horn, *cer-uus*, stag; AS. *hor-n*, horn, *heor-ut*, hart. Ex. *ginger; sirdar; corymb; cerebral, corner, cornet, cervine, serval; hart, horn, hornet.*

Base **KERD** (HERT), heart. Gk. καρδ-ία, κῆρ, heart; L. *cor* (gen. *cord-is*), heart; Lith. *szird-is*, Irish *cridhe*, W. *craidd*, Russ. *serdtse*, AS. *heort-e*, heart. Ex. *cardiac; cordial, accord, concord, discord, record, courage, quarry* (2); *heart.*

KERS (HERS), to run. L. *curr-ere* (pp. *curs-us*), to run; OIrish *carr*, a car; AS. *hors*, a horse; Icel. *hross*, a horse. Ex. *current, curricle, course, cursive, concur, &c.; car; horse.*

KEU (HEU), to swell out; also, to be hollow. Skt. *çū-na(s)*, swollen, *çū-nya(s)*, void, hollow; Gk. κύ-αρ, a cavity, κυ-εῖν, to be pregnant, κῦ-μα, a wave (swelling); L. *cau-us*, hollow. Ex. *cave, cavern, cage, gabion; maroon* (2).

KEUDH (HEUD), to hide. Gk. κεύθ-ειν, to hide; W. *cuddio*, to hide; AS. *hȳd-an*, to hide. Cf. L. *cus-tōs*, a custodian, Goth. *huz-d*, a hoard. Ex. *custody; hide* (1), *hoard.* Cf. *house, husk.*

KLEI (HLEI), to lean. Gk. κλί-νειν, to incline, lean, κλῖ-μαξ, a ladder, κλί-μα, situation, climate (slope); L. *in-clī-nāre*, to make to lean; AS. *hli-nian*, to lean, *hlǣ-ne*, frail, lean, *hlǣ-w*, a hill, declivity. Ex. *climax, climate, clinical; incline, decline, acclivity, declivity; lean* (1), *lean* (2), *low* (3), *ladder.*

KLEU (HLEU), to hear, listen to. Skt. *çru*, to hear; Gk. κλύ-ειν, L. *clu-ere*, to hear; AS. *hlū-d*, loud, *hly-st*, hearing. Ex. *loud, listen.* (The derivation of *client* from L. *cluere* is doubtful.)

KLEU(D), to wash, cleanse. Gk. κλύζειν (*κλυδ-γειν), to cleanse, κλυσ-τήρ, a clyster, syringe; cf. L. *clu-ere*, to cleanse. Ex. *clyster.*

KWEID (HWEIT), to gleam, to be white; allied to **KWEIT**, with the same sense. Skt. *çvind*, to be white; *çvit*, to be white; *çvet-a(s)*, white; Russ. *sviet-ite*, to shine; AS. *hwit*, white, *hwæt-e*, wheat. Ex. *white, wheat.*

KWERP (HWERF), to turn round. Gk. καρπ-ός, the wrist (that turns the hand); Goth. *hwairb-an*, to turn round. Ex. *whirl, wharf, warble.*

KWES (HWES), to pant, sigh, wheeze. Skt. *çvas*, to pant, snort, hiss; L. *quer-or* (pp. *ques-tus*), I complain; AS. *hwēsan* (not *hwæsan*), to wheeze. Ex. *querulous; wheeze.* (See Brugmann, i. § 355.)

LAB (LAP), to lap with the tongue. L. *lambere*, to lap; AS. *lap-ian*, to lap. (Root *lāb; Brugmann, ii. § 632.) Ex. *lambent, lap* (1).

LAS, to desire. Skt. *lā-las-a(s)*, ardent, desirous, *lash*, to desire; Gk. λι-λαίομαι (*λι-λάσ-γομαι), I desire; L. *las-c-iuus*, lascivious; AS. *lus-t*, desire. Ex. *lascivious; lust, lusty, list* (4).

LAU (= lāu), to acquire as spoil; see LEU.

LED (= lēd), Teutonic *lēt*, to let go, leave free. L. *las-sus* (for *lad-tus), tired, Gk. λη δ-ειν, to be tired (see Brugmann, i. § 478); Goth. *lēt-an*, to let, let go; AS. *læt*, slow, late. Ex. *lassitude; let* (1), *late, lass.*

LEG, to collect; hence, to put together, to read. Gk. λέγ-ειν, to collect, read; L. *leg-ere*, to read, *de-lec-tus*, choice, *lec-tus*, chosen. Ex. *logic, eclogue, syllogism,* and the suffix *-logy; legend, legion, elect, delight,* &c.

LEGH (LEG), to lie down. Gk. λέχ-ος, a bed; L. *lec-tus* (*leg-tus), a bed; Goth. *lig-an*, to lie down, *lig-rs*, a couch; Icel. *lāg-r*, lying low, *lag*, a stratum, *lög*, a law. Ex. *litter* (1), *lie* (1), *lay* (1), *low* (1), *law, lair, log* (1); *ledger, beleaguer.*

LEI; see **REI.**

LEIGH (LEIG), to lick. Skt. *lih, rih*, to lick. Gk. λείχ-ειν, to lick; L. *ling-ere*, to lick; Goth. *bi-laig-ōn*, to lick; AS. *licc-ian* (from **ligh-n-*), to lick. Ex. *lichen* (?); *electuary* (?); *lick.*

LEIP (LEIF), to smear, cleave, remain. Skt. *lip*, to smear, anoint; Gk. ἀ-λείφ-ειν, to smear, λίπ-ος, fatness; L. *lip-pus*, bleareyed; Lith. *lip-ti*, to stick, cleave; Goth. *bi-leib-an*, to remain behind, *bi-laib-jan*, to leave behind, *laib-a*, a remnant; Icel. *lif-a*, to remain, to live; AS. *libb-an* (for *lif-jan), to live. Ex. *synalæpha; life, live, leave* (1).

LEIQw (LEIHw), to leave, lend. Skt. *rich*, to leave; Gk. λείπ-ειν, to leave; L. *linqu-ere*, to leave, *re-liqu-us*, remaining; Goth. *leihw-an*, AS. *lih-an*, to lend. Ex. *relinquish, relic, relict; lend, loan.*

LEIS, to trace, follow a trace. L. *lir-a* (for *liz-a), a trace, furrow, *de-lir-āre*, to leave the furrow, become mad; Goth. *lais* (I have followed up the trace), I know, *lais-ts*, a trace, track, AS. *lær-an*, to teach, *leor-nian*, to learn, *lār*, lore. Ex. *delirious; last* (2), *last* (3), *lore, learn.*

LENGwH (LENG), to leap over (hence, to go lightly). Skt. *langh*, to leap over, *laghu(s)*, light; Gk. ἐ-λαχ-ύς, light, small; Lith. *lengw-as*, light; L. *leu-is*, light; Russ. *legk-ii*, light; *legk-oe*, lung; AS. *lung-en*, lung, *lung-re*, quickly. Ex. *levity, alleviate; light* (2), *lights, lungs.*

LEP, to peel. Gk. λέπ-ειν, to peel, λεπ-ίς, a scale, λέπ-ρα, leprosy; L. *lib-er*, bast of a tree (Brugmann, i. § 499), a book. Ex. *lepidoptera, leper; library.*

LEU, to cut off, separate, loosen. Skt. *lū*, to cut off; Gk. λύ-ειν, to loosen; L. *so-lu-ere*, pp. *so-lū-tus*, to loosen, solve; Goth. *laus*, Icel. *lauss*, AS. *lēas*, loose, free from; AS. *los-ian*, to become loose. Ex. *solve, solution, dissolve, resolve; loose, lose, leasing* (falsehood), and suffix *-less.*

LEU, to gain, acquire (as spoil). Prellwitz gives the form of the root as **lāw**. Gk. λεία, booty, Ion. ληίη (for *λᾱϝίᾱ); ἀπο-λαύ-ειν, to enjoy; L. *lū-crum*, profit, lucre; Goth. *lau-n*, OHG. *lō-n*, pay, reward. Ex. *lucre; guerdon.*

LEUBH (LEUB), to desire, love. Skt. *lubh*, to covet, desire; L. *lub-et, lib-et*, it pleases, *lub-ido, lib-ido*, lust; Goth. *liub-s*, dear, *ga-laub-jan*, to believe; AS. *lēof*, dear, *luf-u*, love. Ex. *libidinous; lief, love, leave* (2), *furlough, believe, leman.*

LEUQ (LEUH), to shine. Skt. *ruch*, to shine; Gk. λευκ-ός, white; L. *lūc-ēre*, to shine, *lux* (gen. *lūc-is*), light; *lū-men* (for *leuc-men), light, *lū-na* (for *louc-sna), moon; Goth. *liuh-ath*, light, AS. *lēoh-t*, light. Ex. *lucid, luminous, lunar, lustre* (1), *illustrate, illustrious; light* (1), *lea.* Also *lucubration.*

LOW (LAW), to wash. Gk. λού-ειν, to wash; L. *ab-lu-ere*, to wash off, *lau-āre*, to wash, *lu-strum*, a lustration; Icel. *lau-g*, a bath; AS. *lēah*, lye, *lēa-ðor*, lather. Ex. *ablution, alluvial, deluge, dilute, laundress, lave, lotion, lustre* (2), *lustration, lute* (2); *lye, lather.*

MAGH (= māgh), Teut. (MAG), to be strong; also in the form **MAG** (MAK). **1.** Skt. *mah-ant-*, great, large; Gk. μῆχ-ος, means, expedient, μηχ-ανή, a machine; Goth. *mag*, I may, *mah-ts*, might, AS. *mæg-en*, might, main. **2.** Skt. *majman*, strength; Gk. μέγ-ας, L. *mag-nus*, great; AS. *mic-el*, great. Ex. *Magi, magic; machine; maxim, May, major, mayor, main* (2), *master; may* (1), *maid, main* (1), *might, mickle, much.*

ME (= mē), to measure; also **MED** (MET). Skt. *mā*, to measure, Gk. μῆ-τις, counsel; L. *mē-tior*, I measure. Also L. *med-itārī*, to consider about, *mod-us*, a measure; AS. *met-an*, to mete. Ex. *metre; meditate, mode, moderate, modern, modest, measure, mensuration; mete, meal* (2), *moon, month;* also *firman.*

MEI, to diminish. Skt. *mi*, to hurt, diminish; Gk. μι-νύ-ειν, to diminish, μεί-ων, less; L. *mi-nuere*, to diminish; *mi-n-or*, less; Goth. *mi-n-s*, less. Ex. *minor, minute, minim, diminish, minister, minnow, mis-* (2), prefix. See below.

MEI, to change, exchange; also as **MEI-T** (MEITH), to exchange, to change for the worse, deprave. L. *com-mū-nis* (Old L. *com-moi-nis*), common, mutual, AS. *mā-n*, wickedness; Lith. *mai-nas*, barter; MHG. *mei-n*, false. Hence Gk. μοῖτ-ος, thanks (good return), L. *mūt-āre* (Old L. *moit-āre*), to exchange; Goth. *maid-jan*, to alter, deprave, *ge-maith-s*, maimed; AS. *ge-mæd*, troubled in mind, mad. Also Skt. *mith-ras*, mutually, *mith-yā*, falsely (hardly L. *mit-tere*, to send away, OHG. *mīd-an*, to avoid); Goth. *missa-* (prefix), *mis-*, wrongly. Ex. *common, mutable, mutual, community, moult; mean* (2), *mis-* (1), *miss* (1), *mad.* See above.

MEIGH (MEIG), to wet. Skt. *mih*, to sprinkle, *mēh-a(s)*, urine; Gk. ὀ-μιχ-έω, L. *ming-o*; AS. *mig-a*, I make water; Goth. *maih-stus*, dung, AS. *meox*, dung. Ex. *mistle-toe, missel-thrush, mixen.*

MEIK (MEIH); also **MEIG**, to mix. Skt. *miç-ra(s)*, mixed, *mik-sh*, to mix; Gk. μίγ-νυμι, I mix, μίσγ-ειν (*μίγ-σκ-ειν), to mix; L. *misc-ēre* (*mic-sc-ēre), to mix; AS. *mi-sc-an*, to mix. Ex. *miscellaneous, mix, mixture; mash.*

MEIT; see **MEI** (2) above. MEIT (Teutonic); see *mite* (1).

MEL (MEL), to stain. Skt. *mal-a*, dirty; Gk. μολ-ύνειν, to sully, μέλ-ας, black; L. *mul-lus*, red mullet. Ex. *melancholy; mullet.* (But not *mole* (1).)

MEL, to grind; whence **MEL-D** (MEL-T). Skt. *mlā*, to be worn down, *mr̥d-u(s)*, soft; Gk. μαλ-ακός, soft, μαλ-άχη, mallow; Gk. ἀ-μαλ-ός, soft, ἀ-μαλδ-ύνειν, to soften; L. *mol-ere*, to grind, *moll-is* (for *mold-uis), soft; OIrish *mel-im*, I grind; AS. *mel-u*, meal, *melt-an*, to melt. Also **MEL-DH** (MEL-D). Gk. μαλθ-ακός, soft, tender, mild; AS. *mild-e*, mild; Goth. *muld-a*, mould; AS. *mold-e*, mould. Ex. *malachite; molar, mill, mollify, mauve; meal* (1), *mellow; mallow; melt, malt; mild, mould* (1). Cf. *mole* (2), *s-melt* (1).

MELG (MELK), to milk. Skt. *mr̥j*, to rub, wipe, stroke; Gk. ἀ-μέλγ-ειν, to milk; L. *mulg-ēre*, to milk, AS. *melc-an*, to milk. Der. *milk*; cf. *milt* (2).

MEN, to remember, to think. Skt. *man*, to think, mind, understand, *man-as*, mind, *mnā*, to remember; Gk. μέν-ος, spirit, courage, μέ-μον-α, I wish, μαν-ία, madness, μέ-μη-μαι, I remember, μνή-μων, mindful; L. *me-min-i*, I remember, *men-s*, mind, *mon-ēre*, to remind; Goth. *mun-an*, to think, AS. *ge-myn-d*, memory. Ex. *automaton, amnesty, mania, mnemonic, mental, monition, monster, monument, comment, reminiscence; man, mind;* cf. *mean* (1).

MEN, to remain. Gk. μέν-ειν, to remain; L. *man-ēre*, to remain. Ex. *mansion, manor, manse, menial, menagerie, messuage, permanent, remain, remnant.*

MEN, to project. L. *ē-min-ēre*, to jut out, L. *men-tum*, the chin, *mon-s*, mountain, *min-æ*, things ready to fall, threats; (perhaps) Goth. *mun-th-s*, AS. *mūð*, mouth. Ex. *eminent, prominent, mountain, mount* (1), *mount* (2), *amount, promontory, menace, commination, amenable, demeanour, mound.* Perhaps *mouth.*

MER, to die. Skt. *mr̥-ta(s)*, dead; Gk. ἄμ-βρο-τος (for ἀ-μρο-τος), immortal; L. *mor-s*, death, *mor-ī*, to die, *mor-bus*, disease; AS. *mor-ð*, death, *morð-or*, murder. Ex. *amaranth, ambrosia, mortal, morbid; murder.*

MER, to remember; see **SMER.**

MEUK, to wipe away. Skt. *much*, to loosen, free, shed; Gk. ἀπο-μύσσειν (*μυκγειν), to wipe away, μυκ-τήρ, nose, snout, μύξα (*μυκ-σα), nozzle of a lamp; L. *mūc-us*, mucus, *ē-mung-ere*, to wipe away. Ex. *match* (2); *mucus.*

MU, to make a suppressed noise (imitative). Skt. *mū-kas*, dumb; Gk. μύ, μῦ, a sound of muttering, μύ-ειν, to close lips or eyes; L. *mu-ttum, mū-tum*, a slight sound, *mu-ttire, mū-tire*, to mutter, *mū-tus*, dumb; E. *moo*, to low; cf. *mum*, a slight sound. Similarly, Gk. μύ-σ-της, one who is initiated, μυ-σ-τήριον, a mystery, secret (thing muttered). Cf. L. *mur-mur-āre*, to murmur. Ex. *myth, mystic, mystery*; *mute, mutter, motto*. Cf. *mumble, murmur*.

MUS, or **MŪS**, to steal. Skt. *mush*, to steal; *mūsh-as*, a stealer, rat, mouse; Gk. μῦς, a mouse, L. and AS. *mūs*. Ex. *mouse, muscle, niche*. And see *musk*.

NE, to bind together, to spin; see **SNE**.

(E)NEBH (eNEB), to swell out, to burst (?) Skt. *nabh*, to burst, taken as the root of *nābh-i-*, the hub, nave of a wheel, *nābh-il-a(m)*, navel; Gk. ὀμφ-αλός, navel, boss of a shield; L. *umb-o*, boss of a shield, *umb-il-īcus*, navel; AS. *naf-u*, *nab-u*, nave, *naf-el-a*, *nab-ul-a*, navel. Ex. *umbilical*; *nave* (1), *navel*; *auger* (for *nauger*).

(E)NEBH, to burst forth (?), to spread (?). Perhaps the same as the above. Skt. *nabh-as*, cloud, mist, vapour; Gk. νέφ-ος, cloud; L. *neb-ula*, cloud; G. *neb-el*, cloud. Ex. *nebula, nimbus*.

NEDH, to bind, tie. Skt. *nah* (for *nadh*), to bind, pp. *naddha-s*, bound, tied; L. *nōd-us*, a knot. Ex. *node, nodule*.

NEK, to perish, die. Skt. *naç*, to perish; Gk. νέκ-υς, a corpse, νεκ-ρός, dead; L. *nec-āre*, to kill, *noc-ēre*, to hurt. Ex. *necromancy*; *internecine, pernicious, noxious, nuisance*.

(E)NEK, **(E)NENK**, to attain to. Skt. *naç*, to attain to; Gk. ἐ-νεγκ-εῖν, to bear, put up with; L. *nanc-iscī* (pp. *nac-tus*), to acquire; Goth. *ga-nah*, it suffices, *ga-nōh-s*, enough. Ex. *enough*.

NEM, to allot, share, take. Gk. νέμ-ειν, to portion out, νέμ-ος, pasture, νόμ-ος, custom, law; L. *nem-us*, grove, *num-erus*, number; Goth. *nim-an*, to take. And perhaps L. *em-ere*, to buy (orig. to take). Ex. *Nemesis, nomad, numismatic*; *number*; *nimble numb*. Perhaps *exempt, example, redeem, assume*, &c.

NEU, to nod. Gk. νεύ-ειν, to nod; L. *nu-ere*, to nod, *nū-tāre*, to nod. Ex. *nutation*.

NEUD (NEUT), to enjoy, profit by, use. Lith. *naud-à*, use; AS. *nēot-an*, to enjoy, use, employ, *nēat*, domestic cattle. Ex. *neat* (1).

oNOG(w)H (NAG); base of the sb. 'nail.' Skt. *nakh-a-*, nail, claw (an abnormal form); Gk. ὄνυξ (stem ὀνυχ-), nail, claw; L. *ung-uis*, nail; Lith. *nag-as*, nail; AS. *næg-el*, nail. Ex. *onyx*; *nail*.

NOGw (NAKW); base of the adj. 'naked.' Skt. *nag-na(s)*, naked; L. *nū-dus* (*nog(w)edos*), nude; Russ. *nag-oi*, naked; Goth. *nakw-aths*, AS. *nac-od*, naked. Ex. *nude*; *naked*.

OD (ōd, od), to smell. Gk. ὄζειν (for *ὄδ-γειν*), to smell, pt. t. ὄδ-ωδ-α; L. *od-or*, smell, *ol-ere* (*od-ere*), to smell. Ex. *ozone*; *odour, olfactory, redolent*.

OID (AIT), to swell. Gk. οἰδ-άνειν, to swell; AS. *āt-an*, pl. oats. Ex. *oats*.

OQw (AH), to see. Gk. ὄσ-σε (for ὄκ-γε), the two eyes; ὄψομαι (*ὄπ-σομαι*), fut. tense, I shall see, ὄπ-ωπ-α, pt. t., I have seen; ὀφ-θαλμός, eye, ὄψ-ις, sight; L. *oc-ulus*, eye; Russ. *ok-o*, eye. Perhaps Goth. *aug-ō*, AS. *ēag-e*, eye (it is suggested that the diphthong is due to association with Goth. *aus-ō*, AS. *ēar-e*, ear). See Brugmann, i. § 681 (c). Ex. *optics, ophthalmist, canopy*; *ocular, oculist, antler*; perhaps *eye*.

PA (pā), Teut. FA (fō), to feed, nourish. Gk. πα-τέομαι, I feed upon; L. *pā-scere* (pt. t. *pā-uī*), to feed, *pā-nis*, bread; Goth. *fō-djan*, to feed, AS. *fō-da*, food, *fō-dor*, fodder. Ex. *pastor, pastern, pester, pannier, pantry, pabulum, company*; *food, fodder, feed, foster*. Perhaps *father*.

PAK, PAG (= pāk, pāg) (FAH), to fasten, fix, hold, secure. Skt. *paç*, to bind; Gk. πάσσαλος (*πάκ-γαλος*), a peg; L. *pac-iscī* to stipulate, agree, *pax* (*pac-s*), peace; Goth. *fag-rs*, AS. *fæg-er*, fair. Also Gk. πήγ-νυμι, I secure, fasten, L. *pang-ere*, pp. *pac-tus*, to fasten, *pāg-ina*, a page (perhaps *pro-pāg-āre*, to peg down, propagate by layers); Gk. πηγ-ός, firm, strong (and perhaps L. *pāg-us*, a village). Ex. *pact, propagate* (?), *page* (2), *compact, pale* (1), *impinge, peace, pay* (1), &c.; *fair, fain, fang*.

PAU (FAU), to cease, leave off. Gk. παύ-ομαι, I cease, παύ-ειν, to make to cease, παῦ-σις, a pause, παῦ-ρος, small, L. *pau-cus*, small, *pau-per* (providing little), poor; Goth. *faw-ai*, pl., few. Ex. *pause, pose* (with re-pose, com-pose, &c.); *pauper, poor*; *few*.

PED (FET), to go, fetch. Skt. *pad*, to fall, go to, obtain, *pad-a(m*), a step, trace, place, abode; *pād-a(s)*, a foot; Gk. πέδ-ον, ground, πέδ-η, a fetter, πούς (gen. ποδ-ός), a foot; L. *pēs* (gen. *ped-is*), foot, *ped-ica*, a fetter; AS. *fōt*, foot, *fet-ian*, to fetch, *fet-or*, fetter. Ex. *tripod, parallelopiped*; *pedal, pedestal, pedestrian, pawn* (2), *pioneer, oppidan, impede, expedient*; *foot, fetter, fetch, fetlock*.

PEI (FEI), to hate. Skt. *pīy*, to revile, scoff; Goth. *fī-jands*, hating, *fai-an*, to blame. Ex. *fiend, foe, feud* (1).

PEI (FEI), to swell, to be fat. Skt. *pī-van*, swelling, full, fat; Gk. πί-ων, fat; Icel. *fei-tr*, fat, AS. *fǣ-tt*, fat. Ex. *fat*.

PEIK, PEIG, to scratch, cut, adorn, paint. Skt. *piç*, *piñç*, to cut, prepare, adorn; Gk. ποικ-ίλος, variegated, parti-coloured. Also L. *ping-ere* (pp. *pic-tus*), to paint. Ex. *picture, pigment, paint, orpiment, orpine*; *depict, pimento, pint*.

PEIS, to pound, stamp. Skt. *pish*, to pound, bruise; Gk. πίσ-ος, a pea (cf. πτίσ-μα, peeled grain); L. *pins-ere*, to pound, grind (pp. *pis-tus*), *pī-lum* (for *pins-lum*), a pestle; *pis-tillum*, a small pestle. Ex. *pea, pestle, piston, pistil*.

PEK (FEH), to comb. Gk. πέκ-ειν, to card wool; πόκ-ος, wool; L. *pec-tere*, to comb; OHG. *fah-s* (AS. *fex, feax*), hair. Ex. *pectinal*; and cf. *pax-wax*.

PEL (FEL), to flay, skin (?). Gk. -πελας, skin, in ἐρυσί-πελ-ας, inflammation of the skin; L. *pel-lis*, AS. *fel-l*, skin. Ex. *erysipelas*; *pell, pellicle, pelisse, pilch, surplice, peel* (1); *pillion*; *fell* (2), *film*.

PEL, to fill; see **PLE**.

PELT (FELTH), to fold. Gk. πλάσ-σειν (for *πλάτ-γειν*), to form, mould, shape; δι-πλάσ-ιος, two-fold; Goth. *falth-an*, AS. *feald-an*, to fold. Ex. *plastic, cataplasm*; *fold*.

PEQw, to cook, to ripen. Skt. *pach*, to cook; Gk. πέσσειν, to cook, πέπ-των, cooked, πέπ-ων, ripe; L. *coqu-ere* (for *pequ-ere*), to cook; Russ. *pech(e)*, to bake. Ex. *pepsine, dyspeptic, pip* (2), *pippin, pumpkin*; *cook, kitchen, precocious, apricot*.

PER (FER), to go through, experience, fare, travel. Skt. *pr*, to bring across, causal *pār-aya*, to conduct across; *par-as*, beyond, further, *par-ā*, away; Gk. περ-άω, I press through, pass through, πόρ-ος, a way, πορ-θμός, ferry, πορ-εύω, I convey, πορ-εύομαι, I travel, πεῖρα (*πέρ-γα*), an attempt; also πρό, before, πρῶ-τος, first, πέρ-αν, beyond, παρ-ά, beside, πέρ-ι, around, over; L. *per-ītus*, experienced, *ex-per-īrī*, to try, *per-ī-culum*, danger; *por-ta*, gate, *por-tus*, harbour; also *prō*, before, *per*, through; AS. *far-an*, to go, fare, *fǣr*, panic, fear; also *for*, for, *for-e*, before, *fyr-st*, first. Ex. *pirate, pore* (1); *peril, experience, port* (1), *port* (2), *port* (3), *port* (4); *fare, far, fear, ford, frith* (2). Also *peri-*, prefix, *para-*, prefix, *pro-*, prefix, *præ-*, prefix, *prime*; *for, fore, first, for-* (1), *for-* (2), *from*.

PER, to produce, afford, allot. Gk. ἔ-πορ-ον, I brought, gave; L. *par-ere*, to produce, bring forth, *re-per-ire*, to find; (probably) *par-s*, a part, *por-tio*, a portion. Ex. *parent, parturient, repertory, part, portion*.

PET (FETH), to fall, to fly, to hasten towards, seek, find. Skt. *pat*, to fly, fall upon, *pat-ra(m)*, a wing, feather, leaf; Gk. πέτ-ομαι, I fly, πί-πτ-ειν, to fall; πτ-έρυξ, a wing; L. *pet-ere*, to seek, *im-pet-us*, attack (falling upon, flying at), *penna* (*pet-sna*), a wing; AS. *feð-er*, a feather. Ex. *peri*; *asymptote, symptom, diptera, coleoptera, lepidoptera*; *compete, impetus, perpetual, appetite, petition, propitious, pen* (2); *feather*.

PET (FETH), to spread out, lie flat. Gk. πετ-άννυμι, I spread out, πέτ-αλον, flat plate, leaf, πατ-άνη, flat dish; L. *pat-ēre*, to lie open, *pat-ulus*, spreading, *pat-ina*, dish; AS. *fæð-m*, fathom. Ex. *petal, paten*; *patent*. Prob. also *expand, pass, pace*, &c., from L. *pand-ere*, to spread, which seems to be allied to *patēre*.

PEU (FEU), to beget. Skt. *pu-tra(s)*, son; Gk. παῖς (*παϝ-ις*), son; L. *pu-er*, boy. Ex. *pedagogue*; *puerile*. (Perhaps L. *pū-pus*, boy, belongs here; cf. *pupa, pupil, puppet*.)

PEU (FEU), to cleanse, purify. Skt. *pū*, to cleanse, purify, *pū-ta(s)*, pure, *pāv-aka(s)*, purifying, (also) fire; Gk. πῦ-ρ, fire; L. *pū-rus*, pure, *pu-tus*, cleansed, *pu-tāre*, to prune, clear up, reckon; AS. *fȳ-r*, fire. Ex. *pyre, pyrites*; *pure, purge, compute*, &c.; *fire*.

PI, pī (fī), imitative; to chirp, pipe. Gk. πι-πί-ζειν, to chirp, L. *pī-p-ire*, *pī-p-āre*. Ex. *pipe, pibroch, pigeon*. Cf. *fife*.

PLĀQ, PLĀG(w) (FLŌH, FLŌK), to strike, strike down, strike flat. Lith. *plak-ù*, I strike; Gk. πλάξ (gen. πλακ-ός), a flat surface, πλακ-οῦς, a flat cake; also πληγ-ή, a stroke, πλήσσειν (πλήκ-γειν), to strike; L. *plac-enta*, a flat cake, *planc-a*, a plank (cf. Gk. πλάκ-ιν-ος, made of boards); also *flāg-a*, a stroke, *plang-ere*, to strike, to lament; Goth. *flōk-an*, to lament; G. *flach*, flat; AS. *flōc*, a fluke, flat fish. Ex. *placenta, plank*; *plague, plaint, complaint*; *fluke* (1), perhaps *fluke* (2). Cf. *flay*.

PLAT (= plāt), to spread out. Skt. *prath*, to spread out, *prthu-*, broad; Gk. πλατ-ύς, broad, flat, πλάτ-ος, breadth, πλάτ-η, blade of an oar, plate, πλάτ-ανος, a plane-tree; L. *plat-essa*, a plaice, *plant-a*, sole of the foot, spreading shoot, plant. Ex. *plate, place plaice, plant, plantain, plane* (3). Cf. *field*. Allied to *flat*.

PLE (= plē), lengthened form of **PEL** (FEL), to fill. Skt. *pr*, to fill, *pūrṇa(s)*, filled, *pur-u-*, much; Gk. πίμ-πλην-μι, I fill, πλή-ρης, full, πίμ-θω, I am full, πολ-ύς, much; L. *plē-re*, to fill, *plē-nus*, full, *plē-bes*, throng, people, *plū-s*, more, *po-pul-us*, people, *mani-pul-us*, a handful; AS. *ful-l*, full, *fyl-lan*, to fill. Ex. *plethora, polygon*; *plenary, plebeian, plural, popular, maniple, implement, complete, replete*; *full, fill, fulfil*.

PLEK (FLEH), to plait, weave, fold together. Gk. πλέκ-ειν, to plait, πλοκ-ή, a plait; L. *plec-tere*, to plait, *plic-āre*, to fold; Goth. *flah-ta*, a plaiting of hair; OHG. *flah-s*, AS. *fleax*, flax. Ex. *plait, pleach, plash, ply* (1), with compounds, *complex, simple, duplex, triplicate, explicate, supplicate, suppliant, supple*; *flax*.

PLEU (FLEU), to swim, float, flow. Skt. *plu*, to swim, fly, jump, *plāv-aya*, to inundate; Gk. πλέ-ειν (fut. πλεύ-σομαι), to sail, float, πλύ-νειν, to wash; L. *plu-it*, it rains, *plu-uia*, rain; AS. *flō-wan*, to flow, *flō-d*, a flood. Also AS. *flēo-t-an*, to float, *flēo-t*, a fleet, *flo-t-ian*, to float. Ex. *pluvial*, *plover*; *flow*, *float*, *fleet* (in all senses), *flit*, *flutter*, *flotsam*.

PNEU (FNEU-S), to blow, breathe. Gk. πνεῦ-μα, breath; AS. *fnēos-an*, to breathe hard, *fnor-a*, a sneezing. Ex. *pneumatic*, *neeze*, *s-neeze*; cf. *s-nore*.

PREI (FREI), to love. Skt. *pri-ya(s)*, dear, beloved; Russ. *priiatele*, a friend; Goth. *fri-jōn*, AS. *frē-on*, to love, whence the pres. part. *fri-jōnds*, *frē-ond*, loving, a friend; AS. *frēo*, free, *fri-δ*, security; *Fri-g*, the wife of Woden. Ex. *friend*, *free*, *frith* (1), *Friday*.

PREK (FREH), to pray, ask, demand. Skt. *prachh*, to ask; L. *prec-āri*, to pray, *proc-us*, a wooer; *poscere* (*porc-scere), to demand, *postulāre* (from *poscere*), to demand; Goth. *fraih-nan*, to ask. Ex. *pray*, *precarious*, *imprecate*, *postulate*.

PREUS (FREUS), to burn; also, to freeze. Skt. *prush*, to burn; L. *pruina* (for *pruzwina), hoar-frost, *prūr-īre* (*prūsīre > *prūzīre), to itch; AS. *frēos-an*, to freeze. Ex. *prurient*; *freeze*, *frost*.

PU, pū (FU, fū), to be foul or putrid. Skt. *pū-ti-*, *pū-ti-ka-*, foul, *pūy*, to stink, *pūy-as*, pus; Gk. πύ-ον, pus; L. *pū-s*, matter, *pū-rulentus*, purulent, *pū-tidus*, stinking, *pu-tridus*, putrid; AS. *fū-l*, foul. Ex. *pus*, *purulent*, *putrid*; *foul*, *file* (3), *filth*.

QAL (HAL), to cry out. Skt. *kal-a-s*, low sounding; Gk. καλ-έω, I summon; L. *cal-āre*, to proclaim, *clā-māre*, to cry out; OHG. *hal-ōn*, to call, G. *hell*, clear-sounding; AS. *hlō-wan*, to low. Ex. *calends*, *clamour*, *claim*, *clear*, *council*; *haul*, *hale* (2), *low* (2).

QAP (HAF), to seize, hold. Gk. κώπ-η, a handle; L. *cap-ere*, to seize; Goth. *hafjan*, AS. *hebban*, to lift, heave; AS. *haf-oc*, hawk, lit. 'seizer' (cf. Late L. *cap-us*, a hawk). Ex. *capacious*, *capable*, &c.; *heave*, *hawk*, *haft*; perhaps *behoof*. Also *captive*, *capsule*, *case* (2), *cater*; and numerous derivatives of L. *capere*. (For the initial *q* in *qap, see Brugmann, i. § 635.)

QAR, to sing, cry aloud. Skt. *kār-u-*, a singer; Gk. καρ-καίρειν, to resound, κῆρ-υξ, a herald; L. *car-men*, a song. Ex. *charm*.

QAR (HAR), to love. Irish *car-aim*, I love; L. *cār-us*, dear; Goth. *hōr-s*, an adulterer. The initial *q* is suggested by Lettish *kārs*, desirous; Brugmann, i. § 637.

QAS, to cough. Skt. *kās*, to cough; Lith. *kos-ti*, to cough; AS. *hwōs-ta*, a cough; Irish *cas-achdas*, a cough; W. *pās*, a cough (whence AS. *ge-pos*, a pose, a cough). Ex. *pose* (3).

QEI, to be lucky (?). W. *coel*, an omen; Hesychius quotes Gk. κοῖλυ· τὸ καλόν; OIrish *cēl*, an omen; Goth. *hail-s*, AS. *hāl*, whole. Ex. *whole*, *hale*, *holy*, *heal*, *health*. (For initial *q* see Brugmann, i. § 639.)

QEL (HEL), to raise up. Lith. *kél-ti*, to lift; Gk. κολ-ωνός, κολ-ώνη, a hill; L. *ex-cel-lere*, to surpass, *cel-sus*, high, *cul-men*, a summit, *col-lis*, a hill; AS. *hyl-l*, a hill, *hol-m*, billow. Ex. *colophon*; *culminate*, *column*, *excel*; *hill*, *holm*. (For initial *q* see Brugmann, i. § 633.)

QEL (HEL), to drive on. Skt. *kal-aya*, to drive, *kūl-aya*, to drive on; Gk. κέλ-λειν, to drive, κέλ-ης, a runner; βου-κόλ-ος, a herdsman (ox-driver); L. *cel-er*, swift. Ex. *bucolic*; *celerity*.

QEL (qēl), Teut. HEL, to hide, cover. Gk. καλ-ιά, a shelter, hut, κάλ-υξ, calyx; L. *oc-cul-ere*, *cēl-āre*, to hide, *cal-ix*, a cup, *cel-la*, a cell, *cl-am*, secretly; AS. *hel-an*, to cover, hide. Ex. *calyx*; *conceal*, *occult*, *cell*, *clandestine*; (perhaps *supercilious*); *hell*, *hole*, *hull* (1), *hall*, *helmet*, *holster*. (On the initial *q* see Brugmann, i. § 641.)

QEND, to shine; L. *cand-ēre*; see **SQEND**.

QER, to make. Skt. *kṛ*, to make, *kar-man*, work, deed; Gk. κρέ-ων, ruler; L. *cre-āre*, to make, create, *cre-sc-ere*, to grow, OLat. *cer-us*, creator, *Cer-es*, goddess of the growth of corn. Ex. *create*, *cereal*, *crescent*, *increase*, *concrete*, *accretion*, *accrue*, *crew*, &c.

QERP (HERF), to cut. (Probably for SQERP; see SQER, to shear.) Skt. *kṛ-pāna(s)*, sword; Lith. *kerp-ù*, I cut, shear; Gk. καρπ-ός, fruit, κρώπ-ιον, sickle; L. *carp-ere*, to pluck fruit; AS. *hærf-est*, harvest. Ex. *harvest*. Cf. *carp* (2).

QERT, to bind together. Skt. *kat-a(s)*, for (*kar-tas), a mat; *chṛt*, to fasten together; Gk. κύρτ-αλος, a (woven) basket; L. *crāt-ēs*, a hurdle; AS. *hyrd-el*, a hurdle. Cf. Skt. *kṛt*, to spin. Ex. *hurdle*. (For the initial *q* see Brugmann, i. § 633.)

QEUQ (HEUH), to bow out, to hunch up. Skt. *kuch-as*, the female breast; Lith. *kauk-arà*, a hill; Goth. *hauh-s*, high; Icel. *haug-r*, a hill. Ex. *high*, *how* (2). Cf. *huge*.

QOU (HAU), to strike, to hew. L. *cū-dere*, to strike, *in-cū-s*, an anvil; Russ. *kov-ate*, to hammer; G. *hau-en*, AS. *hēa-wan*, to hew. Ex. *hew*, *hoe*, *hay*.

QREU (HREU), to wound. Skt. *krav-i-*, raw flesh, *krū-ra(s)*,

wounded, raw; Gk. κρέας (*κρέϝ-ας), raw flesh; L. *crū-dus*, raw, *cru-or*, blood; Lith. *krau-jas*, blood; AS. *hrēa-w*, raw. Ex. *crude*, *cruel*; *raw*. Perhaps *rue* (1).

QwEI (HWEI), to rest. Skt. *chi-ra(s)*, long-lasting, long; OChurch Slav. *po-či-ti*, to rest; L. *qui-ēs*, rest, *tran-quillus*, tranquil; AS. *hwī-l*, a while (quiet time), Goth. *hwei-la*, rest. Ex. *quiet*, *tranquil*, *coy*, *quit*; *while*, *whilom*, *whilst*.

QwEI, to expiate, pay for. Skt. *apa-chi-ti-*, expiation; Gk. ἀπό-τι-σις; also ποι-νή (L. *poe-na*), a penalty, τί-νω, I pay a penalty. Ex. *penalty*, *pain*, *pine* (2), *penance*. (See Brugmann, i. § 652.)

QwEL (HWEL), to move, go round, turn, drive. Skt. *char*, *chal*, to move; Gk. πέλ-ειν, to be in motion, πόλ-ος, pole, axis of revolution; L. *col-us*, a distaff, *col-ere*, to till, *in-col-a*, inhabitant, dweller in; OSlav. *kol-o*, a wheel; AS. *hwēol*, a wheel (which see). Ex. *pole* (2); *colony*; *calash*; *wheel*. Cf. L. *collum* (for *col-sum), neck (from its turning); whence E. *collar*.

QwEP (= *q(w)ēp*), to breathe, to reek. Lith. *kwēp-ti*, to breathe, reek, *kwāp-as*, breath, vapour; L. *uap-or*, vapour; Gk. καπ-νός, smoke. Ex. *vapid*, *vapour*. (See Brugmann, i. § 193.)

RAD (RAT), to gnaw. Skt. *rad*, to scratch, gnaw; L. *rād-ere*, to scrape, *rōd-ere*, to gnaw; AS. *rætt*, a rat. Ex. *rase*, *rash* (2), *rasorial*, *razor*, *abrade*, *erase*, *rodent*; *rat*.

RE (= rē), to think upon; whence **REDH** (rēdh), Teut. RED (= rēd), to provide, accomplish. L. *rē-rī*, to consider (pp. *ra-tus*); Skt. *rādh*, to achieve, accomplish, prepare; Goth. *ga-rēd-an*, to provide; AS. *rēd-an*, to counsel, interpret, read. Ex. *rate* (1), *ratify*, *ratio*, *ration*, *reason*, *arraign*; *read*, *riddle* (1).

REBH (REB), to cover. Gk. ἐ-ρέφ-ειν, to cover, ὄ-ροφ-ος, a roof; OHG. *rāf-o*, *rāv-o*, a beam, Icel. *rāf*, a roof, *rap-tr* (= *raf-t-r*), a rafter. Ex. *raft*, *rafter*. (Not *roof*.)

REG (REK), to stretch, stretch out, reach, straighten, rule. Skt. *ṛj*, to stretch; Gk. ὀ-ρέγ-ειν, to stretch; L. *reg-ere*, to rule, *ē-rig-ere*, to erect, set upright, *rectus* (*reg-tus), right, *rēx* (gen. *rēg-is*), king, ruler; Goth. *uf-rak-jan*, to stretch out, *raih-ts*, right, AS. *rih-t*, right. Ex. *rajah*; *regent*, *regal*, *regulate*, *reign*, *rule*, &c.; *right*, *rack* (1), *ratch*, *rake* (3). Also *rich*. Perhaps *rogation*.

REI, to distil, flow. Skt. *ri*, to distil, drop; L. *rī-uus*, a stream, *rī-tus*, a custom, rite (cf. Skt. *rīti*, a going, way, usage). (Some connect Goth. *rinnan*, to run.) Ex. *rivulet*, *rival*, *rite*. Perhaps *run*. A parallel form is LEI, to melt, to besmear. Skt. *li*, to melt, dissolve; L. *li-nere*, to besmear, *li-mus*, mud; AS. *li-m*, lime, *lā-m*, loam. Ex. *lime* (1), *loam*.

REIDH (REID), to ride, be conveyed. OIrish *riad-aim*, I drive, ride; AS. *rīd-an*, to ride. Ex. *ride*, *road*, *raid*, *ready*.

REIP (REIB), to tear down, tear. Gk. ἐ-ρείπ-εσθαι, to be torn down, to fall in ruins; L. *rīp-a*, bank (with steep edge); Icel. *rīf-a*, to rive, to tear. Ex. *river*; *rive*, *rift*, *riven*.

RET, to run along, rotate. OIrish *reth-im*, I run; Lith. *rit-ù*, I roll; Skt. *rath-a(s)*, a chariot, car; L. *rot-a*, a wheel. Ex. *rotate*, *rotary*, *round*, *roll*, *rouleau*, *rotund*, &c. Also *barouche*, *roué*.

REU, to hum, bray, roar; imitative. Skt. *ru*, to hum, bray, roar; Gk. ὠ-ρύ-ομαι, I howl; L. *rū-mor*, a noise, report; cf. also *ru-gīre*, to bellow, *rū-men*, the throat. Ex. *rumour*, *ruminate*; *rumble*. Cf. *raucous*.

REUD (REUT), to weep, bewail, wet with tears. Skt. *rud*, to weep, bewail, *rōd-ana(m)*, weeping, tears; L. *rud-ere*, to cry out; AS. *rēot-an*, to weep, Icel. *rjōt-a, to wet, only in the pp. *rotinn*, rotten, orig. 'soaked.' Ex. *rot*, *rotten*, *ret*. Extended from REU.

REUDH (REUD), to be red. Skt. *rudh-ira(s)*, red, *rudh-ina(m)*, blood; Gk. ἐ-ρευθ-ειν, to redden, ἐ-ρυθ-ρός, blood, L. *rub-er*, red; AS. *rēad*, red. Ex. *erysipelas*; *rubric*, *rubescent*, *rubicund*, *rissole*, *rouge*, *russet*; *red*, *ruddy*, *rust*.

REUP (REUF), to break, seize, pluck, rob. Skt. *rup*, to feel spasms, *lup*, to break, injure, spoil, seize, rob; *lōp-tra(m)*, booty, loot; L. *rump-ere* (pp. *rup-tus*), to break; Goth. *bi-raub-ōn*, to rob, AS. *rēof-an*, to break, *rēaf*, spoil. Ex. *loot*; *rupture*, *eruption*, &c.; *route*, *rout* (1), *rut* (1), *rob*, *robe*; *reave*, *bereave*.

SA (= sā), to satiate. Gk. ἄ-μεναι (*σᾶ-μεναι), to satisfy; ἄ-δ-ην, enough; L. *sa-t*, *sa-t-is*, enough, *sa-t-ur*, full; Lith. *sa-t-ùs*, sated, full; Goth. *sa-th-s*, full; AS. *sæ-d*, sated. Ex. *sated*, *satiate*, *satisfy*, *satire*, *assets*; *sad*.

SAG (= sāg), Teut. sōk, to perceive. Gk. ἡγ-έομαι, I guide, I suppose; L. *sāg-ire*, to perceive by the senses; Goth. *sōk-jan*, AS. *sēc-an*, to seek. Ex. *sagacious*, *sagacity*; *seek*. Probably allied to *sake* and *soke*.

SAL, to leap. Gk. ἄλ-λομαι (*σάλ-γομαι), I leap, spring; L. *sal-io*, I leap, *sal-to*, I dance. Ex. *salient*, *salmon*, *assail*, *saltation*, *desultory*, *exult*, *insult*, *result*, *resilient*, *sally*, *saltire*.

SAUS, to become dry, to wither. Skt. *ṣush* (for *sush), to become dry; Gk. αὔ-ειν (*σαύσ-ειν), to become dry, wither; αὐσ-τηρός, harsh; AS. *sēar*, sere, withered. Ex. *austere*; *sear*, *sere*.

SE (=sē), to cast abroad, sow, scatter. Gk. ἵ-η-μι (for *σί-ση-μι), I cast, send forth; L. se-rere (pt. t. sē-ui), to sow, sē-men, seed; Goth. sai-an, AS. sá-wan, to sow, sǽ-d, seed. Ex. season, secular, Saturnine, seminal; sow (1), seed.

SED (SET), to sit. Skt. sad, to sit; Gk. ἕζομαι (for *σέδ-γομαι), I sit; L. sed-ēre, to sit; AS. sit-tan, to sit, pt. t. sæt; Russ. sied-lo, Polish siod-lo, a saddle. Ex. cathedral, chair, chaise, polyhedron; sedentary, see (2), sell (2), size (1), size (2), also assiduous, assess, &c.; sit, set, seat, settle (1), settle (2). Also nest, saddle, soot.

SEGH (SEG), to bear, endure, hold in. Skt. sah, to bear, endure, overcome, restrain; sah-as, power, victory; Gk. ἔχ-ειν (*σέχ-ειν), to hold, have (fut. σχ-ήσω), σχ-ῆμα, form, σχ-ολή, stoppage, leisure; Goth. sig-is, victory. Ex. epoch, hectic, scheme, school; perhaps sail.

SELQ (SELH), to draw along. Gk. ἕλκ-ειν (*σέλκ-ειν), to draw, ὀλκ- άς, a heavy ship, hulk, ὀλκ-ός, a furrow; L. sulc-us, furrow; AS. sulh, plough. Ex. hulk; sulcated.

SEQ (SEG), to cut, cleave. L. sec-āre, to cut; Russ. siek-ira, an ax; OHG. seg-ense (G. sense), a scythe; AS. sag-a, a saw, sig-ðe, sí-ðe, a scythe; secg, sedge. Ex. section, segment, secant, saxifrage, sickle; saw (1), scythe, sedge.

SEQw, to follow, accompany. Skt. sach, to follow; Gk. ἕπ-ομαι, I follow; L. sequ-ī, to follow, sec-undus, following, soc-ius, a companion. Ex. sequence, &c.; sect, second, sue, suit, suite, social, associate.

SER, to string, put in a row. Gk. εἴρ-ειν (for *σέρ-γειν) to string (as beads); L. ser-ere, to join together (pp. ser-tus); Icel. sör-vi, a necklace. Ex. series, assert, concert, desert (1), dissertation, exert, insert.

SERP, to slip along, glide, creep. Skt. sṛp, to creep, sarp-a(s), a snake; Gk. ἕρπ-ειν (*σέρπ-ειν), to creep; L. serp-ere, to creep. But hardly rēp-ere (*srēp-ere?), to creep. Ex. serpent. Probably not reptile.

SEU, to beget, produce. Skt. sū, to generate, sū-nu(s), a son, sū-kara(s), a hog; Gk. σῦ-s, ὗ-s, a sow, υ-ιός, a son; L. sū-s, pig, su-inus, belonging to pigs; AS. su-gu, sow, sw-in, swine, su-nu, a son; cf. OIrish su-th, birth, fruit. Ex. sow (2), swine, son.

SEUG, SEUQ, to suck. (Both forms occur; the former answers to Teut. SEUK.) 1. L. sūg-ere, to suck; OIrish sūg-im, I suck; AS. sūc-an, to suck. 2. L. sūc-us, juice; AS. sūg-an, to suck. Ex. suction; suck, soak; also sowans. Also succulent.

SIEU, to sew, stitch together. Skt. siv, to sew, syū-ti-, sewing; Gk. κασ-σύ-ειν, to stitch together, ὑ-μήν, hymen; L. su-ere, to sew; Goth. siu-jan, AS. séow-an, síw-ian, to sew. Ex. hymen; suture; sew, seam. Perhaps hymn.

SKAG (SKAK), to shake. Skt. khaj (for *skaj, *skag); to move to and fro; AS. scac-an, sceac-an, to shake. Ex. shake, shock (1), shog; perhaps jog.

SKEI, to shine. Skt. chhā-yā, shade, image, reflected light, splendour; Gk. σκι-ά, shade; Goth. skei-nan, AS. sci-nan, to shine. Ex. shine, shimmer, sheer (1).

SKEUBH (SKEUB), to agitate, to shake. Skt. kshubh, to be agitated; kshōbh-aya, to shake; Goth. af-skiub-an, to push away; AS. scūf-an, to shove, push. Ex. shove, sheaf.

SKEUD (SKEUT), to shoot. Lith. szaud-yti, to shoot; AS. scéot-an, to shoot. Ex. shoot, sheet, shot, shut, shuttle; scot-free, skittish, skittles.

SKHED (SKET), to cleave, to scatter. Skt. skhad, to cut, kshad, to carve; Gk. σκεδ-άννυμι, I scatter, disperse, σχέδ-η, a tablet (slice); L. scand-ula, a shingle; AS. scat-erian, to scatter, shatter. Ex. schedule; shingle (1); scatter, shatter.

SKHEI, whence **SKHEID, SKHEIT**, to cleave, part, shed. 1. Skt. chhid, to cut, divide; Gk. σχίζειν (*σχίδ-γειν), to split; L. scind-ere, to cleave. 2. Goth. skaid-an, AS. scéad-an, to shed, separate, part, scíd, a thin slip of wood. Ex. schism, schist, zest; shed (1), shide, skid; sheath.

SKLAUD (sklaud), to shut. L. claud-ere, to shut; OFries. sklūt-a, slūt-a, to shut; G. schliess-en, to shut, Du. sluit-en. We also find SKLEU; as in Gk. κλείς, Doric κλᾱ-ίς, a key; L. clāu-is, a key; L. clāu-us, a nail. Ex. close (1), close (2), enclose, clause, include, &c.: slot. Also clavicle, clove (1), cloy.

SLEB (=slēb), Teut. SLEP (=slēp), to be relaxed; hence, to sleep. L. lāb-i, to glide, lāp-sāre, to slip, lapse, lab-āre, to totter; Russ. slab-uii, slack, weak; AS. slǽp-an, to sleep, LowG. slapp, lax, relaxed. Ex. lapse, elapse, collapse, illapse, relapse; sleep.

SLEG (=slēg), to be slack. Gk. λήγ-ειν, to leave off, λαγ-αρός, slack; L. laxus (*lag-sus), lax, lang-uēre, to be weak; AS. slæc, slack, loose. Ex. lax, relax, leash, lease (1), lessee, relay (1), release, relish; slack. And see lag, languish.

SMEI, to smile, laugh. Skt. smi, to smile, smē-ra(s), smiling; Gk. μει-δάω, I smile; L. mī-rus, wonderful, mi-rāri, to wonder at; Swed. smi-la, to smile. Ex. admire, marvel, miracle, mirage, mirror; smile.

SMELD (SMELT), to melt. Gk. μέλδ-ειν, to melt; Swed. smält-a, to smelt. Ex. smelt, smalt. See **MEL**.

SMER, to remember. Skt. smṛ, to remember, record, declare; Gk. μέρ-ιμνα, sorrow, regret; μάρ-τυς, a witness; L. me-mor-ia, memory, remembrance, me-mor, mindful; AS. mur-nan, to mourn. Ex. martyr; memory, remembrance, commemorate, memoir; mourn. Cf. demur.

SMER, to rub over, smear. Gk. σμύρ-ις, emery for polishing, μύρ-ον, ointment; Icel. smjör, grease, butter; AS. smer-u, fat, grease, smir-ian, to smear. Ex. smear, besmear, smirch.

SMERD (SMERT), to pain, cause to smart. Skt. mṛd, to rub, grind, crush; Gk. σμερδ-αλέος, terrible; L. mord-ēre, to bite; AS. smeort-an, to smart. Ex. mordacity, morsel, remorse; smart. Cf. muzzle.

SNA (=snā, snāu), to bathe, swim. Skt. snā, to bathe; Gk. νή-χειν, to swim, να-ρός, liquid, νη-ρός, wet, νά-ειν, ναύ-ειν, to flow, να-ίς, να-ιάς a naiad, ναῦ-s, a ship; L. nā-re, na-tāre, to swim, nau-ta, sailor, nāu-igāre, to navigate, sail, nāu-is, a ship. Ex. aneroid; naiad; nave (2), naval, navigate, navy, nausea, nautical, nautilus, navvy, natation.

SNE (= snē), to bind together, fasten (with thread). Skt. snā-yu-, tendon, muscle, str.ng, snā-va-, sinew, tendon; Gk. νέ-ω, I spin, νῆ-μα, thread; L. nē-re, to spin; OIrish snā-th, thread, snā-that, a needle; Goth. nē-thla, a needle; AS. snō-d, a fillet. Cf. also Gk. νεῦ-ρον (from *snēu), nerve, sinew, cord. Also, from a base SNER, Gk. νάρ-κη, cramp, numbness; L. ner-uus, nerve, sinew; perhaps AS. near-u, narrow (closely drawn), snear-e, a noose, snare. Ex. neuralgia, narcotic, narcissus; nerve; snare, snood, narrow. And see sinew.

SNEIGwH (SNEIW), to snow. Gk. νείφ-ει, it snows, νίφ-α, accus., snow; L. ningu-it, it snows, niu-em, accus., snow; Irish sneach-d, snow; Goth. snaiw-s, AS. snāw, snow. Ex. snow.

SNER, SNEU (snēu); see under **SNE**.

SPE (= spē), to increase, have room, prosper. Skt. sphāy, to swell, increase, sphā-ti-, increase; L. spa-tium, room, space, pro-sper, prosperous, spē-s, hope; AS. spṓ-wan, to succeed. Ex. space, prosperous, despair, desperate; speed.

SPEK (SPEH), to spy, observe, see. Skt. spaç-a(s), a spy; Gk. σκέπ-τομαι (for *σπέκ-τομαι), I see, σκοπ-ός, a spy, an aim; L. spec-ere, to see, spec-iēs, appearance, spec-tāre, to behold; OHG. speh-ōn, to watch. Ex. scope, sceptic, bishop; species, special, spectre, speculate, spectator, suspicion, espy, spy, &c.

SPER, SPHER, to struggle, kick, jerk. Skt. sphur, to throb, struggle; Gk. σπαίρ-ειν, ἀ-σπαίρ-ειν, ἀ-σπαρ-ίζειν, to struggle convulsively, σφαῖρ-α, a ball (to be tossed); L. sper-nere, to spurn, despise; AS. spor-nan, to spurn, kick against; perhaps G. sich sper-ren, to struggle, fight. Ex. sphere; spurn, spur, spoor; perhaps spar (3). Cf. sparrow.

SPER, to scatter, sow. Gk. σπείρ-ειν (*σπέρ-γειν), to scatter, sow. Ex. sperm, sporadic. See below.

SPHERG, Teut. SPERK, SPREK, to burst noisily, crackle, scatter abroad. Skt. sphūrj, to crash, burst forth, be displayed; Gk. σφάραγ-ος, a cracking, crackling, ἀ-σπάραγ-ος, asparagus, shoot of a plant; (perhaps) L. sparg-ere, to scatter; AS. spearc-a, a spark of fire, Icel. sprak-a, to crackle (cf. AS. sprec-an, to speak), AS. sprǽc, a shoot, a spray. Ex. asparagus; speak, spark (1), sparkle, spark (2), spray (2). Perhaps sparse (and derivatives). Cf. spray (1). See above.

SPIW, SPIEU, to spit out, vomit. Skt. shṭhiv, to spit; Gk. πτύ-ειν (from *σπγυ-γειν), to spit; L. spu-ere, AS. spiw-an, Goth. speiw-an. Ex. spue, spew. (Of imitative origin; so that the form of the root is indeterminate.)

SQAP (SKAF), to dig, scrape, shave; **SQAB** (SKAP), to cut, scrape, shape. 1. Gk. σκάπ-τειν, to dig, σκαπ-άνη, a spade; Goth. skab-an, AS. scaf-an, to shave. 2. L. scab-ere, to scrape; Lith. skab-ùs, cutting, sharp; Goth. ga-skap-jan to shape. Ex. shave, scab, scabious, scabby, shabby, shaft. Also shape, capon.

SQEL, to cleave, split, divide. Gk. σκάλ-λειν, to hoe; Lith. skel-iù, I split; ONorse skil-ja, to sever, separate; Goth. skal-ja, a tile; AS. scell, shell. Ex. scale (1), scale (2), scall, scald (2), skill, shell. See shelf, shield.

SQEND, to spring up, climb. Skt. skand, to jump up, ascend; Gk. σκάνδ-αλον, the spring of a trap; L. scand-ere, to climb, scā-la (for *scand-sla), a ladder. Ex. scandal, slander; scan, ascend, descend, scale (3), escalade.

SQEND, to shine, glow. Skt. chand, çchand, to shine, chand-ra(s), moon, chand-ana(s), sandal-wood tree; L. cand-ēre, to shine, cand-idus, white. Ex. candle, candid, incense, candour, chandelier, chandler, incendiary, &c. Also sandal-wood.

SQER (SKER), to shear, cut, cleave. Gk. κείρ-ειν (κέρ-γειν), to shear, cut; Lith. ker-wis, an ax; AS. scer-an (pt. t. scær, pp. scor-en), to shear. Ex. *shear, share, sheer* (2), *shard, scar* (2), *scare, shore.* Cf. *scorpion, sharp, scarp, scrape.* And see **QERP, SEQ.**

SQEU (SKEU), to perceive, observe, beware of. Skt. *kav-i-*, wise, a seer, prophet, poet; Gk. κοέω, I mark, θυο-σκό-ος, an inspector of an offering; L. *cau-ēre*, to beware, *cau-tio*, caution; AS. *scēa-wian*, to look, behold. Ex. *caution, caveat; shew, show, scavenger, sheen.*

SQEU (SKEU), to cover, shelter. Skt. *sku*, to cover; Gk. σκύ-τος, κύ-τος, skin; L. *cu-tis*, skin, *scū-tum*, a shield, *ob-scū-rus*, covered over, dark; OHG. *skiu-ra*, a shed, stable; Icel. *skjō-l*, a shelter, cover; AS. *hȳ-d*, hide, skin; Icel. *skȳ*, a cloud. Ex. *cuticle, obscure, escutcheon, esquire, squire, equerry; hide* (2), *scum, skim, sky, sheal, shieling, scowl.*

SREBH, to sup up, absorb. Gk. ῥοφ-έειν, to sup up; L. *sorbēre*, to sup up; Lith. *srēb-ti*, to sup up. Ex. *absorb.*

SREU (STREU), to flow. (Observe the insertion of T in Teutonic.) Skt. *sru*, to flow, *srō-ta(s)*, a stream; Gk. ῥέειν (fut. ῥεύ-σομαι), to flow, ῥεῦ-μα, flood, ῥυ-θμός, rhythm (musical flow); Irish *sru-aim*, stream; AS. *strēa-m*, stream. Ex. *rheum, rhythm, catarrh, diarrhœa, emerods; stream, streamer.*

STA (= stā); see **STHA.**

STAQ (STAH), to be firm. Skt. *stak*, to resist, Zend. *staχ-ra-*, strong, firm; OPruss. *panu-stac-la-*, steel for kindling fire; OHG. *stah-al*, OMerc. *stēl-i*, steel. Ex. *steel.*

STEBH; see **STEMBH.**

STEG(w), also **TEG**(w) (TEK), to cover, thatch. Skt. *sthag*, to cover; Gk. στέγ-ειν, to cover, στέγ-ος, τέγ-ος, roof; L. *teg-ere*, to cover, *teg-ula*, †tile, *tog-a*, garment; Irish *tigh*, a house; AS. *þæc*, thatch; Du. *dak*, thatch, *dek-ken*, to cover. Ex. *protect, tegument, toga, tile; thatch, deck*; also *shanty* (old house).

STEIG(w) (STEIK), to prick, pierce, stick, sting. Skt. *tij*, to be sharp, Zend. *tigh-ra-*, sharp, *tigh-ri-*, an arrow; Gk. στίζειν (*στίγ-γειν), to prick, στίγ-μα, a prick; L. *in-stig-āre*, to instigate; Goth. *stik-s*, a point; AS. *stic-e*, stitch (in the side). Ex. *stigma; instigate;* allied to *instinct, distinguish, stimulate, style* (1); cf. *tiger, stick* (1), *stitch, sting.*

STEIG(w)H (STEIG), to stride, to climb. Skt. *stigh*, to ascend; Gk. στείχ-ειν, to go, march, στίχ-ος, a row, στοῖχ-ος, a row; Lith. *staig-ùs*, hasty; AS. *stīg-an*, to climb. Ex. *acrostic, distich, hemistich; sty* (1), *sty* (2), *stile* (1), *stair, stirrup.*

STEMBH, STEBH (STEMB, STEB), to make firm, set fast; **STEMB** (STEMP), to stamp, step firmly. Skt. *stambh*, to make firm or hard, stop, block up; *stambh-a(s)*, a post, pillar, stem, *stabh*, to fix, prop; Gk. ἀ-στεμφ-ής, fixed, fast, στέμβ-ειν, to stamp; AS. *stæf*, a staff, prop, *stæf-n*, a stem of a tree; AS. *stemp-an*, to stamp, *stap-ul*, a post, pillar, *step-pan*, to step. Ex. *staff, stave, stem* (1), *stem* (2); also *stamp, step, staple* (1), *staple* (2); perhaps *stump.*

STEN, TEN (THEN), to groan, to stun, to thunder. Skt. *stan*, to sound, sigh, thunder; Gk. στέν-ειν, to groan; Στέν-τωρ, Stentor (loud-voiced); Lith. *sten-ėti*, to groan, AS. *stun-ian*, to make a din. Also Skt. *tan*, to sound; L. *ton-āre*, to thunder; AS. *þun-or*, thunder. Ex. *detonate; stun, thunder; astonish, astound.*

STER, whence **STREU**, to strew, scatter, lay down. Skt. *star-a-*, a layer, bed; *str*, to scatter, spread; *tār-as*, pl. stars; Gk. στόρ-νυμι, I spread out; L. *ster-nere*, to scatter, spread out (pp. *strā-tus*), *stru-ere*, to lay in order, heap up, build; Goth. *strau-jan*, to strew; AS. *streow-ian*, to strew, scatter, *streaw*, straw. Ex. *asterisk, asteroid; street, structure, instrument, consternation, stellar, stratum; strew, straw, star.*

STER, to be firm or rigid. Skt. *sthira(s)*, firm, fixed; Gk. στερ-εός, solid, stiff, στεῖρα (*στερ-ya), a barren cow; Goth. *stair-ō*, a barren woman; L. *ster-ilis*, sterile, barren. Ex. *stereoscope, stereotype, sterile;* and cf. *stark, starch.*

STEU, probably for **STHEU**, to fix firmly. Skt. *sthav-ira(s)*, fixed, firm; Gk. στῦ-λος, a pillar, στο-ά, a porch, σταυ-ρός, an upright pole or stake; L. *in-stau-r-āre*, to construct, build, restore; Goth. *stiu-r-jan*, to establish, OHG. *stiu-r-a*, a prop, staff, paddle, rudder; AS. *stēo-r*, a paddle or rudder. Ex. *stoic; star-board, steer* (2); *store, restore.* Cf. *steer* (1). Allied to **STHA.**

STEUD (STEUT), to strike. Skt. *tud*, to push; L. *tund-ere* (pt. t. *tu-tud-ī*), to strike, beat; Goth. *staut-an*, to strike. Ex. *contuse, obtuse; stutter;* perhaps *stot, stoat.* And see *toil* (1).

STHA, STA (= sthā, stā), to stand, stand fast. Skt. *sthā*, to stand; Gk. ἔ-στη-ν, I stood, ἵ-στη-μι, I set, place; L. *stā-re*, to stand, *si-st-ere*, to set; G. *steh-en*, to stand. Further allied to Goth. *standan*, AS. *stondan* (pt. t. *stō-d*), to stand, AS. *sted-e*, a place, stead; from a Teut. base STA-D. Also to AS. *stō-w*, a place. Ex. *statics, apostasy, &c.; stage, stamen, stamina, station, statute, &c.; stand, stead, stow, stall.* And cf. *stammer, stem* (3), *stool, stud* (1), *stud* (2).

SWAD (SWAT), to please the taste. Skt. *svad*, to taste well, to season; *svād-u-*, savoury, sweet; Gk. ἡδ-ύς, sweet; L. *suā-uis* (for *suad-uis*), sweet; O.Sax. *swōt-i*, sweet; AS. *swēt-e*, sweet. Ex. *suave, suasion, persuade, assuage; sweet.*

SWEID (SWEIT), to sweat. Skt. *svēd*, to sweat; *svēd-a(s)*, sweat; Gk. ἰδ-ρώς, sweat; L. *sūd-āre*, to sweat, *sūd-or*, sweat; AS. *swāt*, sweat. Ex. *sudorific; sweat.*

SWEN, to resound, sound. Skt. *svan*, to sound; *svan-a(s)*, sound; L. *son-āre*, to sound, *son-us*, sound; AS. *swin-sian*, to resound. Ex. *sound* (3), *sonata, sonnet, person, parson, sonorous, unison, &c.* Cf. *swan.*

SWEP (SWEF), to sleep. Skt. *svap*, to sleep; Gk. ὕπ-νος, sleep; L. *sop-or*, sleep, *somnus* (for *swep-nos*), sleep; AS. *swef-n*, a dream. Ex. *hypnotise; soporific, somnolence.*

SWER, to murmur, hum, speak. Skt. *svr*, to sound, *svar-a(s)*, sound, voice, tone; L. *su-sur-rus*, murmur, whisper; AS. *swer-ian*, pt. t. *swōr*, to affirm, swear; *swear-m*, a swarm of bees. Ex. *swear, answer, swarm.*

TAK, to be silent. L. *tac-ēre*, Goth. *thah-an*, to be silent. Ex. *tacit; taciturn, reticent.*

TAU (= tāu), Teut. (thāw), to melt, thaw. Skt. *tō-ya-*, water; Gk. τή-κειν, to melt; L. *tā-bēs*, decay; AS. *þā-wian*, to thaw. Ex. *tabid, thaw.*

TEG(w), to cover; see **STEG**(w).

TEK (THEH), to beget. Gk. τεκ-εῖν, 2 aor. inf. of τίκτειν, to beget; AS. *þeg-en*, a thane; orig. boy, servant. Ex. *thane.*

TEKTH (tekþ), to fit, prepare, hew out, weave. Skt. *taksh*, to form, prepare, cut, hew; Gk. τέχ-νη, art, τέκτ-ων, carpenter; L. *tex-ere*, to weave; OChurch Slav. *tes-ati*, to hew. Ex. *technical, architect; text, subtle, toil* (2). (For the form of the root, see Uhlenbeck, Skt. Dict.)

TEL (THEL), to bear, tolerate, lift. Skt. *tul*, to lift, *tul-ā*, a balance, weight; Gk. τελ-αμών, belt for shield or sword, τάλ-αντον, balance, talent, τλῆ-ναι, to endure; L. *tol-lere*, to bear, *lā-tus* (for *tlātus = τλη-τός*), borne; *tol-erāre*, to endure; AS. *þol-ian*, to endure. Ex. *talent, atlas, tantalise; extol, tolerate, trot, elate, prelate, relate, oblate, prolate, dilate, delay, collation, legislator, translate; thole* (2).

TEM, to be dark. Skt. *tam-as*, gloom; L. *tem-ere*, in the dark, blindly, rashly; *ten-ebræ*, darkness. Ex. *tenebrious, temerity.*

TEM, to cut. Gk. τέμ-νειν, to cut, τομ-ή, a cutting, τόμ-ος, part of a book (section), τέμ-ενος, sacred enclosure, τέν-δ-ειν, to gnaw; L. *tem-plum*, sacred enclosure, *ton-d-ēre*, to shear. Ex. *anatomy, tome; tonsure, temple.*

TEN (THEN), to stretch. Skt. *tan*, to stretch, *tan-u-*, thin (stretched out), *tan-tu-*, a thread; Gk. τείνειν (*τέν-γειν), to stretch, τόν-ος, tension, tone; L. *ten-d-ere*, to stretch, *ten-ēre*, to hold tight, *ten-uis*, thin; Goth. *than-jan*, to stretch out; AS. *þyn-ne*, thin. Ex. *hypotenuse, tone; tenacious, tender, tenuity, tend, tense* (2), *tent* (1), *tendon, tendril, tenor, tempt, tentative, toise, &c.; thin; dance.*

TENG, to dip, steep. Skt. *tam-as*, gloom; L. *ting-ere*, to dip; OHG. *thunch-ōn*, G. *tunk-en*, to dip. Ex. *tinge, tincture, tint, stain.*

TENG (THENK), to consider, ponder on. L. *tong-ēre*, to think; Goth. *thagkjan* (=*thank-jan*), to think. Ex. *think, methinks, thanks, thought.*

TENQ (THENH), to be strong, grow thickly. Skt. *tańch*, to contract; Pers. *tang*, tight; Lith. *tenk-ù*, I have sufficient, *tank-us*, close, tight; Goth. *theih-an*, AS. *ge-þēon* (pp. *ge-þung-en*), to thrive; ONorse *þēt-tr*, tight. Ex. *thee* (2), *tight.*

TEP, to be hot. Skt. *tap*, to be warm; Russ. *top-ite*, to heat; L. *teþ-ēre*, to be warm. Ex. *tepid.*

TER (THER), to pass through, reach; go through, rub, turn. (Two roots of the form TER, 'to go through,' and 'to rub, turn,' have probably coalesced.) **1.** Skt. *tar-a(s)*, a passage, ferry, *tār-a(s)*, penetrating; *tār-aya*, to take across, *tir-as*, prep., across, through, over; Gk. τέρ-μα, goal, end; *in-trā-re*, to pass into, *trā-ns*, going through, across; Goth. *thair-h*, through; AS. *þyr-el*, a hole. Ex. *avatar; enter, term, transom, trestle, through, thrill, thirl, thrum.* **2.** Gk. τρῆ-σις, a boring through, τέρ-ετρον, a borer; L. *ter-ere*, to bore, rub; *tor-nāre*, to turn. Ex. *turn; trite, tribulation, detriment.*

TERQ (THERH), to twist, turn round. Skt. *tark-u-*, a spindle; Gk. ἀ-τρακ-τος, a spindle; L. *torqu-ēre*, to twist. Compare also (from Teut. THWERH) AS. *þweorh*, perverse, transverse, Icel. *þverr*, perverse. Ex. *torment, torture, torch, nasturtium, torsion, tort, tortoise.* Cf. *thwart, athwart, queer.*

TERS (THERS), to be dry, to thirst. Skt. *trsh*, to thirst; Gk. τέρσ-ομαι, I become dry; L. *torr-ēre* (for *tors-ēre*), to parch, pp. *tos-tus, terr-a* (for *ters-a*), dry ground; Goth. *thaurs-jan*, to thirst, *thaurs-tei*, thirst. Ex. *torrid, torrent, terrace, tureen, toast, terrier, inter, fumitory; thirst.* Perhaps *test.*

TEU (THEU), to be thick or fat. Skt. *tu*, to increase, be powerful, *tav-a(s)*, strong; Gk. τύ-λος, τύ-λη, a hard swelling;

L. *tu-m-ēre*, to swell up, *tŭ-ber*, a round root, *tum-ulus*, a mound, *tum-ultus*, uproar; Lith. *tau-kas*, fat of animals, *tù-k-ti*, to be fat; AS. *þĕo-h*, thigh, *þū-ma*, thumb, *þĕa-w*, muscle. Ex. *tumid, tumult, tumulus, protuberance*; *thigh, thumb, thews.*

TEUD (THEUT), to strike; see **STEUD.**

TRE = *tre* (THRE, thrē), to twist; from **TER**, to turn. AS. *þrā-wan*, to twist, throw; *þræ-d*, thread. Ex. *throw, thread.*

TREM, also **TRES**, to tremble. Skt. *tras*, to tremble; Gk. τρέ-ειν, (for *τρέσ-ειν), to tremble; L. *terr-ēre* (for *ters-ēre*), to scare, cause to tremble. Also Gk. τρέμ-ειν, L. *trem-ere*, Lith. *trim-ti*, to tremble. Ex. *terror*; also *tremble, tremulous, tremendous.*

TREUD (THREUT), to push, crowd, urge. L. *trūd-ere*, to push, urge; Goth. *us-thriut-an*, to vex greatly, G. *ver-driess-en*; AS. *þrēot-an*, to afflict, vex, urge. Ex. *abstruse, extrude, intrude, obtrude, protrude*; *threat, threaten.* Cf. *thrust.*

UL, to howl (imitative). Skt. *ul-ūka-*, an owl; Gk. ὑλ-άω, I howl, ὀλ-ολ-ύζω, I shriek; L. *ul-ul-a*, an owl; AS. *ūl-e*, an owl. Ex. *owl, howl.*

WADH (WAD), to walk slowly, to wade. L. *uād-ere*, to go; *uad-um*, a ford; AS. *wad-an*, to wade. Ex. *evade*; *wade.*

WAQ (WAH), to swerve, go crookedly, totter; also **WAG** (WAK), to bend, totter. Skt. *vak-ra(s)*, crooked, bent, *vañch*, to go crookedly, totter, waver; L. *uac-illāre*, to waver, reel; AS. *wōh*, crooked, bent. Also L. *uag-us*, wandering, going aside; Lith. *wing-is*, a bend of a river, *weng-ti*, to flinch, to shirk work, OHG. *wink-an*, to move aside, to waver; AS. *wanc-ol*, wavering, weak. Ex. *vacillate, vague*; *wench, woo.* Cf. *wink, winch.*

WAN (= *wā-n*), to fail, lack, be wanting; from the root **WA** (*wā*), with the same sense. Skt. *ū-n-a(s)*, inferior, wanting; Gk. εὖ-ν-ις, bereft; L. *uā-n-us*, vain; Goth. *wa-n-s*, deficient. Ex. *vain*; *wane, wanion, want, wanton.* Cf. *vacant.*

WE (= *wē*), to blow. Skt. *vā*, to blow; *vā-ta(s)*, wind; Gk. ἄ-η-μι (ἄ-Ϝη-μι), I blow; L. *ue-ntus*, wind; Goth. *wai-an*, to blow, *wi-nds*, wind; Lith. *wė-jas*, wind; Russ. *vie-iat(e)*, to blow, *vie-ter'*, wind; AS. *wi-nd*, wind, *we-der*, weather. Ex. *ventilate, fan*; *wind* (1), *weather.*

WEBH (WEB), to weave. Skt. *ūrṇa-vābh-i-*, a spider, lit. 'wool-weaver'; Gk. ὑφ-αίνειν, to weave; G. *web-en*, AS. *wef-an*, to weave. Ex. *weave, web, weft, woof, weevil.* Cf. *wafer, wasp.*

WED (WET), to wet, moisten. Skt. *ud-an-*, water, *und*, to moisten; Gk. ὕδ-ωρ, water; L. *und-a*, wave; Russ. *vod-a*, water; Goth. *wat-ō*, water, AS. *wæt-er*, water, *wæt*, wet. Ex. *hydrogen, hydra*; *undulate, abound, redundant, surround*; *wet, water, otter*; *vodka.*

WEDH (WED), to redeem a pledge, to pledge. L. *uas* (gen. *uad-is*), a pledge; Goth. *wad-i*, AS. *wed-d*, a pledge; Lith. *wad-oti*, to redeem a pledge. Ex. *wed*; *wage, wager, gage* (1), *engage.*

WEG (WEK), to be vigorous or watchful, to wake; hence the extended form **WEKS** (WEHS), to increase; hardly allied to **AUG**(w). Skt. *vaj-ra(s)*, thunder-bolt (from its strength); *vāj-a(s)*, vigour; L. *ueg-ēre*, to excite, arouse, *uig-ēre*, to be vigorous, *uig-il*, watchful; AS. *wac-an*, to come to life, *wac-ian*, to watch. Also Skt. *vaksh*, to grow, Goth. *wahs-jan*, to wax, AS. *weax-an*, to wax. Ex. *vegetable, vigour, vigilant*; *wake* (1), *watch.* Also *wax* (1).

WEG(w) (WEK), to be moist or wet. Gk. ὑγ-ρός, moist; (perhaps) L. *ū-dus*, moist, *ū-mor*, moisture; Icel. *vök-r*, moist. Ex. *hygrometer*; *wake* (1). Perhaps *humid, humour*; and see *ox.*

WEGH (WEG), to carry, convey, remove. Skt. *vah* (for *vagh*), to carry, *vāh-a(s)*, a vehicle; Gk. ὄχ-ος (*Ϝόχ-ος), a chariot; L. *ueh-ere*, to carry, convey; *uē-na*, a vein (duct); AS. *weg-an*, pt. t. *wæg*, to bear, carry, *weg*, a way, *wecg*, a wedge (mover), *wæg-n*, a wain. Ex. *vehicle, vein*; *weigh, way, wain, waggon, wey, wag.* Perhaps *vehement.*

WEI, to bind, wind, plait. Skt. *vā*, *vay-a*, to weave, *vī-ta(s)*, wound, *vē-tasa(s)*, a kind of reed; Gk. ἰ-τέα, a willow; L. *uī-tis*, a vine, *uī-men*, a twig, *uī-ēre*, to bind; AS. *wī-r*, a wire, *wī-ðig*, a willow, withy. Ex. *vine, ferrule, vice* (2); *wire, withe, withy, wine.* And see *wind* (2).

WEID (WEIT), to know, to wit; orig. to see. Skt. *vid*, to know, *vēd-a(s)*, knowledge; Gk. εἶδ-ον (for *Ϝεῖδ-ον), I saw, οἶδ-α (for *Ϝοῖδ-α), I know; L. *uid-ēre*, to see, *ui-sere*, to go to see, visit; Goth. *wit-an*, to know, *wait*, I know. Ex. *Veda*; *history, idol, idea*; *vision, visit*, &c.; *wit* (1), *wit* (2), *witness, wiseacre*; *ywis, wise.* Also *advice*, &c.

WEID, to sing. Gk. ἀ-είδ-ειν (for ἀ-Ϝείδ-ειν), to sing; ἀοιδ-ή, ᾠδ-ή, a song; cf. OIrish *faed*, W. *gwaedd*, an outcry, shout. Ex. *ode, epode, palinode.*

WEIG (WEIK), and **WEIQ** (WEIK), to give way. (1) Skt. *vij*, to fear, *veg-a-s*, speed, haste; Goth. *wik-ō*, succession; AS. *wīc-an*, to give way, *wāc*, weak, *wǣc-an*, to weaken; *wic-u*, a week (change of phase of the moon); *wic-e*, a wich-elm. (2) Gk. εἴκ-ειν (for *Ϝείκ-ειν), to give way; L. *uic-is* (gen. case), change; OHG.

weh-sal, G. *wech-sel*, change. Ex. *weak, week, wich-elm*; *vicissitude, vicar.*

WEIK (WEIH), to come to, to enter. Skt. *viç*, to enter, *vēç-a(s)*, a settler, a neighbour, *vēç-man*, a house; Gk. οἶκ-ος (for *Ϝοῖκ-ος), a house; L. *uīc-us*, a village, *uīc-inus*, neighbouring; Goth. *weih-s*, a village. Ex. *economy, diocese*; *vicinage, wick* (2), *bailiwick.*

WEIP (WEIF), to tremble, shake, vibrate. Skt. *vēp*, to tremble; cf. L. *uib-rāre*, to tremble; ONorse *veif-a*, to vibrate, flap, flutter. Ex. *waif, waive*; cf. *vibrate.*

WEIQ (WEIH), to fight, conquer. L. *uinc-ere*, pt. t. *uīc-ī*, to conquer; Goth. *weih-an*, to contend; AS. *wīg*, war. Ex. *vanquish, victory, convict, evince, convince*, &c.

WEIQ (WEIH), to give way; see **WEIG.**

WEL, to will, to choose, like. Skt. *vṛ*, to choose, select, prefer, *var-a(s)*, a wish; L. *uel-le*, to wish; Goth. *wil-jan*, to will, *wil-ja*, will, *wal-jan*, to choose, *wail-a*, well. Ex. *voluntary, voluptuous*; *will* (1), *will* (2), *well* (1), *weal, wealth, welcome, welfare.*

WEL, to wind, turn, roll; well up (as a spring). Skt. *val*, to turn here and there, turn round, *val-ana(m)*, a turning, agitation; Gk. ἔλ-ιξ, a spiral, ἐλ-ίσσειν, to turn round; OHG. *wel-la*, a billow, AS. *wel-la*, a well or spring. Also in the form WEL-W; cf. Gk. εἰλύ-ειν, to enfold, L. *uolu-ere*, to roll, Goth. *af-walw-jan*, to roll away. Ex. *helix*; *voluble, volute, revolve*, &c.; *valve*; *well* (2), *wallow, waltz, welter.* Also *wale*; cf. *walk.*

WEM, to vomit. Skt. *vam*, Gk. ἐμ-εῖν, L. *vom-ere*, to vomit. Ex. *emetic*; *vomit.*

WEN, to honour, love, strive for, seek to get. Skt. *van*, to serve, honour, ask, beg; L. *uen-us*, love, *uen-erāri*, to honour, *uen-ia*, favour; AS. *win-nan* (pt. t. *wann*), to fight for, labour, endure (whence E. *win*). Hence also Skt. *vāñchh*, to wish, AS. *wūsc*, a wish. Ex. *venerable, venereal, venial*; *win*, also *winsome, wish.* Allied to *wean, ween, wont*; and to *won* (to dwell).

WEQw, to cry out, to speak. Skt. *vach*, to speak, *vach-as*, speech; Gk. ἔπ-ος, a saying, a word; L. *uox* (gen. *uōc-is*), voice, *uoc-āre*, to call. Ex. *epic*; *voice, vocal, avouch, advocate, invoke*, &c.

WER, to cover, surround, defend. Skt. *vṛ*, to screen, cover, surround, *vṛ-ti-*, an enclosure, *vār-aya*, to keep off; Gk. ἔρ-υσθαι, to protect; Goth. *war-jan*, AS. *wer-ian*, to protect. Ex. *warren, warison, garret*; *weir.* Cf. *aperient, cover.*

WER, to be wary, observe, see. Gk. ὁρ-άω (*Ϝορ-άω), I observe, see; L. *uer-ēri*, to guard against, to fear; AS. *wær*, wary. Ex. *revere, reverend*; *beware, wary.* Also, *ward, guard.* Perhaps also *ware* (1), *worth* (1).

WER, to speak, say. Gk. εἴρ-ειν (for Ϝέρ-γειν), to say; ῥή-τωρ (*Ϝρή-τωρ), a speaker, orator. Hence **WERDH**, to say. O. Irish *ford-at*, they say (Stokes-Fick, p. 274); L. *uerb-um*, a word; AS. *word*, a word. Ex. *verb, word*; also *rhetoric.*

WERG (WERK), to work. Gk. ἔργ-ον (*Ϝέργ-ον), work; ὄργ-ανον, an instrument; Goth. *waurk-jan*, to work; AS. *weorc*, work. Ex. *organ, orgy, chirurgeon, surgeon*; *work, wrought, wright.*

WERGH (WERG), to strangle, choke. Lith. *wersz-ti*, to strangle; MHG. *ir-werg-an*, to strangle; AS. *wyrg-an*, to strangle, worry. Ex. *worry.*

WERT (WERTH), to turn, become. Skt. *vṛt*, to turn, turn oneself, exist, be; L. *uert-ere*, to turn; Goth. *wairth-an* (pt. t. *warth*), to become; AS. *weorð-an*, to become. Ex. *verse, vertex, vortex, prose, avert, averse, convert*, &c.; *worth* (2), *weird, -ward* (suffix). Also *verst.*

WES, to clothe, put on clothes. Skt. *vas*, to put on clothes; Gk. ἕσ-θος (*Ϝέσ-θος), clothing, ἕννυμι (*Ϝέσ-νυμι), I clothe; L. *ues-tis*, clothing, garment; Goth. *was-jan*, to clothe; AS. *wer-ian*, to wear clothes. Ex. *vest, invest, divest, vestment*; *wear* (1); *gaiter.*

WES, to dwell, live, be. Skt. *vas*, to dwell, to pass the night, to live, *vās-tu*, a house, *vas-ati-*, a dwelling-place; Gk. ἑσ-τία, a hearth, ἄστ-υ, a city; L. *Ves-ta*, goddess of the household, *uer-na*, a home-born slave; Goth. *wis-an*, AS. *wes-an*, to be. Ex. *vernacular, Vesta, vestal*; *was, wast, were, wert.* Cf. *wassail.*

WES, to shine; also as **AWES, AUS** (āwes, āus), to shine. Skt. *vas*, *uchchh*, to shine; *ush*, to burn; *vas-antas*, spring; Gk. ἔ-ως, ἠ-ώς, Æolic αὔ-ως, dawn, ἔ-αρ (for *Ϝέσ-αρ), spring; L. *aur-ōr-a* (for *aus-ōs-a), dawn, *uēr* (for *ues-r), spring, *aus-ter*, south wind; AS. *ēas-t*, adv., in the east. Ex. *vernal*; *east, Easter.*

WIDH, to lack. Skt. *vidh, vindh*, to lack, be in want of (Macdonell); Gk. ἠ-ίθ-εος, unmarried; Skt. *vidh-avā*, bereft of, a widow; L. *uid-ua*, a widow; AS. *wid-uwe*, a widow. Cf. L. *dī-uid-ere*, to divide (pp. *dī-uīs-us*). Ex. *widow*; also *divide, division.*

YAG (yāg, yag), to worship, reverence. Skt. *yaj*, to sacrifice, worship, *yaj-yu(s)*, worshipping, pious; Gk. ἅγ-ιος, holy. Ex. *hagiographa.*

YES, to ferment. Skt. *yas*, to exert oneself, *yēsh*, to bubble, seethe; Gk. ζέ-ειν (perf. mid. ἔ-ζεσ-μαι), to seethe, ζέσ-μα, a decoction, ζεσ-τός, sodden; ἔκ-ζε-μα, a pustule; AS. *gis-t*, yeast. Ex. *eczema*; *yeast*.

YEU, to drive away, preserve from. Skt. *yu*, to drive away, preserve from, keep aloof, *yāv-aya*, to drive away; L. *iu-uāre* (pp. *iū-tus*), to assist. Ex. *adjutant*, *aid*, *coadjutor*.

YEU, to bind, to mix. Skt. *yu*, to bind, to fasten, join, mix; *yū-sha-*, pease soup; L. *iū-s*, broth; Gk. ζύ-μη, leaven. Ex. *zymotic*; *juice*. See **YEUG, YOS.**

YEUG, to join, to yoke together. Skt. *yuj*, to join, connect *yug-a(m)*, a yoke; Gk. ζεύγ-νυμι, I yoke, ζυγ-όν, yoke; L. *iung-ere*, to join, *iug-um*, a yoke, *con-iux*, a spouse, *iux-tā*, near; AS. *geoc*, a yoke. Ex. *syzygy*; *jugular*, *conjugal*, *join*, *junction*, *joust*, *jostle*; *yoke.* See **YEU.**

YOS (= **yōs**), to gird. Zend *yās-ta-*, girt; Gk. ζώννυμι (for *ζωσ-νυμι), I gird, ζώ-νη, a girdle, ζωσ-τήρ, a girdle; Lith. *jos-ta*, a girdle. Ex. *zone*. See **YEU** (2).

VI. DISTRIBUTION OF WORDS

The following is an attempt to distribute the words in the English language so as to show the sources to which they originally belonged. The words selected for the purpose are chiefly those given in large type in the dictionary, to the exclusion of mere derivatives of secondary importance. The English list appears short in proportion, chiefly because it contains a large number of these secondary words, such as *happiness*, *hearty*, *helpful*, and the like.

I have no doubt that, in some cases, the sources have been wrongly assigned, through ignorance. Some indulgence is requested, on account of the difficulty of making the attempt on a scale so comprehensive. The account of some words has been altered, by way of correction. Some words, not given in the ordinary lists, will be found among the Hybrid Words at the end.

ENGLISH. With the exception of some words of imitative origin, most of the following words (or their origins) can be found in Anglo-Saxon or in Middle English of the earliest period.

a, aback, abaft, abed, abide (1), abide (2), ablaze, aboard, abode, about, above, abreast, abroad, accursed, ache, acknowledge, acorn, acre, adder, addled, ado, adown, adrift, adze, afar, afford, affright, afloat, afoot, afore, afresh, aft, after, aftermath, aftermost, afterward, afterwards, again, against, agape, aghast, agnail, ago, agone, aground, ahead, ahoy, ail, ait, ajar, akin, alack, albeit, alder, alder-, alderman, ale, alight (1), alight (2), alike, alive, all, allay, almighty, almost, alone, along (1), along (2), aloud, already, also, although, altogether, alway, always, am, amain, amaze, amid, amidst, among, amongst, an (a), an (if), and, anent, anew, angle (2), an-hungered, ankle, anneal (1), anon, another, answer, ant, anvil, any, ape, apple, are, aright, arise, arm (1), aroint thee, arrow, arrow-root, arse, art (1), as (1), ash, ashamed, ashes, ashore, aside, ask, asleep, aslope, aspen (asp), astern, astir, astride, asunder, at, athirst, atone, auger, aught, awake, awaken, aware, away, awl, awork, awry, axe (ax), ay!, ay (aye).

baa, babble, babe, back, backgammon, bad, bairn, bake, bale (2), bale-fire, balk (1), balk (2), ban, bane, banns, banter, bare, bark (3), barley, barm (1), barm (2), barn, barrow (1), barrow (2), barton, bass (2) (barse), bast, bat (1), batch, bath, bathe, be- (*prefix*), be, beach, beacon, bead, beam (1), beam (2), bean, bear (1), bear (2), beard, beat, beaver (1), beck (1), beckon, become, bed, bedabble, bedew, bedight, bedim, bedizen, bedridden, bedstead, bee, beech, beer, beetle (1), beetle (2), beetle (3), befall, before, beforehand, beget, begin, begone, behalf, behave, behaviour (*with F. suffix*), behead, behest, behind, behold, behoof, behove, belch, belie, believe, bell, bellow, belly, belong, beloved, below, bemoan, bench, bend (1), beneath, benighted, bent-grass, benumb, bequeath, bequest, bereave, berry, berth, beseech, beseem, beset, beshrew, beside, besides, besom, besot, bespeak, best, bestead (1), bestow, bestrew, bestride, beteem, bethink, betide, betimes, betoken, betroth, better, between, betwixt, beware, bewilder, bewitch, bewray, beyond, bicker?, bid (1), bid (2), bide, bier, biestings (beestings), bight, bile (2), bill (1), bill (2), bind, birch, bird, birth, bisson, bit (1), bit (2), bitch, bite, bitter, blab, black, bladder, blade, blain, blanch (2), blare, blast, blatant, blay, blaze (1), bleach, blear, blear-eyed, bleat, bleb, bleed, blench, bless, blight, blind, blindfold, blindman's buff, bliss, blithe, blood, blossom, blow (1), blow (2), blow (3), blubber, blunt, blurt, blush, bluster, boar, board (1), boat, bob, bode, bodice, body, boil (2), bold, bolster, bolt, bone, bonfire, book, boom (1), boot (2), bore (1), bore (2), borough, borrow, bosom, botch (1), bother, bots?, bottom, bough, bounce, bounden, bourn = burn (2), bow (1), bow (2), bow (3), bower, bowl (2), bowline, bow-window, box (4), boy, boycott, brabble, bracken, braid (1), braid (2), brain, brake (2), bramble, brand, branks, bran new, brass, brawl (1), braze (2), breach, bread, breadth, break, breast, breath, breech, breeches (breeks), breed, breeze (1), brew, briar (brier), bridal, bride, bridegroom, bridge, bridle, bright, brill, brim, brimstone, brine, bring, bristle, brittle, broad, brood, brook (1), brook (2), brooklime, broom,

broth, brothel, brother, brow, brown, bruise, bubble, buck (1), buck (2), bucket, buckwheat, bud, bug (2), build, bull (1), bulrush, bum, bumble-bee, bumboat, bump (1), bump (2), bumper, bunch, bundle, bunting (2)?, burden (1) (burthen), burial, burke, burly, burn (1), burn (2), burr (bur), burrow, burst, bury (1), bury (2), buss (1), busy, but (1), butt (3), butt (4), buttock, buxom, buy, buzz, by, byre.

cackle, calf, calve, can (1), can (2), care, carve, cat, caterwaul, catgut, cave in, caw, chafer (cock-chafer), chaff, chaffer, chaffinch, champ, chap (1) (chop), chap (2) (chapman), chaps (chops), char (1), char (2), charcoal, charlock, charm (2), chary, chat, chatter, chaws, cheap, cheek, cheep, chert, chew (chaw), chicken, chide, chilblain, child, chill, chin, chincough, chink (1), chink (2), chip, chirp, chit (1), chit (2), chitterlings, choke, choose, chop (1), chop (2), chough, chub, chubby, chuck (2), chuck (3), chuckle, chump, churl, churn, cinder, clack, clam (1), clam (2), clammy, clank, clap, clash, clasp, clatter, claw, clay, clean, cleat, cleave (1), cleave (2), cleek, clench, clever, clew (clue), click, cliff, climb, clinch, cling, clink, clinker-built, clip (2), clod, clot, cloth, clothe, cloud, clough, clout, clove (2), clover, cluck, clump, cluster, clutch, clutter (1), clutter (2), clutter (3), coal, coax, cob (1), cob (2), cobble (1), cobble (2), cobweb, cock (1), cock (2), cock (3), cock-eyed, cockle (2), cockney, cockshut time, cod (1), cod (2), codling (1), cold, collie, collier, collop, colly (1), colly (2), colt, comb, comb (coomb), come, comely, con (1), coo, cool, coomb, coot, corn (1), cosset, cot (cote), couch-grass, cough, could, cove, cow (1), cowslip, coxcomb, crab (1), crab (2), crabbed, crack, cradle, craft, crake (corn-crake), cram, crane, crank (1), crank (2), crank (3), crave, craw, creak, creep, cress, crib, crick, crimp, cringe, crinkle, cripple, croak, croft, crop, croup (1), crow, crowd (1), crumb, crumpet, crumple, crunch, crutch, cud, cudbear, cuddle, cudgel, cudweed, culver (1), cunning (1), cur, curd, curse?, cushat, cuttle, cuttle-fish.

dab (1), dab (2), dab (3), dabble, dad, daft, daisy, dale, dam (1), damp, dare (1), dark, darkling, darksome, darling, darn, daughter, daw, dawn, day, dead, deaf, deal (1), deal (2), dear, dearth, death, deed, deem, deep, deer, deft, dell, delve, den, dent, depth, derring do, dew, dib, dibber, dibble, did, didapper, diddle, dike, dill, dim, dimple, din, ding, ding-dong, dingle, dingy, dint, dip, distaff, dit, ditch, dive, dizen, dizzy, do (did, done), dock (1), dock (2), docket, dodder, dodge, doff, dog, dog-cheap, dogger, doggerel, dole, dolt, don (1), donkey, doom, doomsday-book, door, dor, dot, dotage (*with F. suffix*), dotard (*with F. suffix*), dote, dough, doughty, dout, dove, dovetail, dowse (3), drab (1), draff, draft, draggle, drain, drake, draught (draft), draw, drawl, dray, dread, dream (1), dream (2), drear, dreary, dredge (1), drench, dribble, drift, drink, drive, drivel, drizzle, drone (1), drone (2), drop, dross, drought, drove, drowse (drowze), drudge, drunkard (*with F. suffix*), drunken (drunk), dry, dub, duck (1), duck (2), duck (3), dug, dull, dumb, dump (1), dumpling, dung, dunlin, dup, dust, dwarf, dwindle, dye, dyke.

each, ear (1), ear (2), ear (3), earl, early, earn, earnest (1), earth, earwig, east, Easter, eat, eaves, ebb, eddy, edge, eel, eery, eft, eh, eight, either, eke (1), eke (2), elbow, eld, elder (1), elder (2), eldest, eleven, elf, elk, ell, elm, else, ember-days, embers, emmet, empty, end, English, enough, ere, errand, erst, eve (even), even, evening, ever, every, everywhere, evil, ewe, eye, eyot.

fag, fag-end, fain, fair (1), fall, fallow (1), fallow (2), falter, fang, far, fare, farrow, farther, farthest, farthing, fast (1), fast (2), fasten, fastness, fat (1), fat (2), father, fathom, fawn (1), fear, feather, eed, feel, feeze (pheeze), fell (1), fell (2), felly (felloe), felt, fen, fern, ferry, fetch, fetter, few, fey, fickle, fiddle?, field, field-fare, fiend, fight, file (2), file (3), fill, fillip, film, filth, fin, finch, find, finger, fire, firk, first, fish, fist, fit (2), five, flabbergast, flabby, flag (1), flag (2), flag (3), flap, flash, flax, flay, flea, fledge, flee, fleece, fleet (1), fleet (2), fleet (3), fleet (4), flesh, flicker, flight (1), flight (2), flint, flip (2), flirt, flitch, float, flock (1), flood, floor, flop, flow, flue (2), fluke (1), fluke (2), flurry, flush (1), flush (2), flush (3), flutter, fly (1), fly (2), foal, foam, fodder, foe, fold (1), fold (2), folk, follow, fond, food, foot, footy, fop, for (1), for- (2), forbear (1), forbear (2), forbid, ford, fore, fore-arm (1), forebode, fore-father, fore-finger, fore-foot, forego (1), forego (2), foreground, forehand, forehead, foreknow, foreland, forelock, foreman, foremost, forerun, foresee, foreship, foreshorten, foreshow (foreshew), fore-sight, forestall, foretell, forethought, foretoken, foretooth, foretop, forewarn, forget, forgive, forgo (forego), forlorn, former, forsake, forsooth, forswear, forth, fortnight, forty, forward, foster (1), fother, foul, foumart, foundling, four, fowl, fox, fractious, frame, fraught (*Friesic*), freak (1), freak (2), free, freeze, fresh, fret (1), Friday, friend, fright, frith (1), frog (1), frog (2)?, from, frore, frost, froward, fulfil, full (1), fulsome, furlong, furrow, further, furthest, furze, fuss, futtocks, fuzz-ball, fylfot.

gabble, gag, gaggle, gale (2), gall (1), gallow, gallows, gamble, game, gammon (2), gander, gannet, gar (1), garfish, garlic, gate (1), gather, gavelkind, ghastly, ghost, gibberish, gibe, giddy, gift, giggle, gild, gin (1), gird (1), gird (2), girdle, girl, give, glad, gladsome, glare, glass, glaze, gleam, glede (1), glede (2), glee, glib (1), glib (3), glide, glimmer, glimpse, glisten, glister, gloaming, gloom, glove, glow, glower, glum, gnarl, gnarled, gnat, gnaw, go, goad, goal, goat, god, goddess (*with* F. *suffix*), godfather, godhead, godmother, godwit, goggle-eyed, gold, good, goodbye, goodman, goose, gooseberry, gorbellied, gorcrow, gore (1), gore (2), gore (3), gorse, goshawk, gosling, gospel, gossamer, gossip, grab, grasp, grass, grave (1), gray, graze (1), graze (2), great, greaves (1), greedy, green, greet (1), greet (2), greyhound, gride, grig (2), grim, grin, grind, grip, gripe, grisly, grist, gristle, grit (1), grit (2), groan, groats, groin, grope, ground, groundling, grounds, groundsel, groundsill, grout, grove, grow, grub, grunt, guest, guild (gild), guilt, gulp, gum (1), gush, gut, gyves?

ha, hack (1), hack (2), hackle (1), hackle (2), hackney, had-dock?, haft, hag, hail (1), hair, hairif, hale (1), half, halibut, halidom, halimote, hall, hallow, halt (1), halter, halve, halyard (halliard), ham, hame, hammer, hamper (1), hand, handcuff, handicap, handicraft, handiwork (handywork), handle, handsome, handy (1), handy (2), hang, hanker, hansom, hard, hardock, hards, hare, harebell, hark, harm, harp, harrier (1), harrier (2), harrow, harry, hart, harvest, hasp, hassock, hat, hatch (1), hatch (2), hatchel, hatches, hate, hatred, haugh, haulm (halm, haum), have, haven, haw, hawk (1), hawk (3), hay (1), hay (2), hazel, he, head, headlong, heal, health, heap, hear, hearken, hearsay, heart, hearth, heart's-ease, hearty, heat, heath, heathen, heather, heave, heaven, heavy, heckle, hedge, heed, heel (1), heel (2), heft, heifer, heigh-ho, height, hell, helm (1), helm (2), helmet, help, helve, hem (1), hem (2), hemlock, hen, hence, henchman, hent, her, herd (1), herd (2), here, heriot, herring, hest, hew, hey, heyday (2), hiccough (hiccup, hicket), hide (1), hide (2), hide (3), hide (4), hie, higgle, high, highland, hight, hilding, hill, hilt, him, hind (1), hind (2), hind (3), hinder, hindmost, hinge, hint, hip (1), hip (2) (hep), hire, his, hiss, hist (*or* Scand.), hitch, hithe (hythe), hither, hive, ho (hoa), hoar, hoard, hoarhound (horehound), hoarse, hoary, hob (1), hobble, hobbledehoy?, hobnail, hobnob (habnab), hock (1), hockey, hog, hogshead, hold (1), ho'e, holibut, holiday, holiness, hollow, holly, hollyhock, holm-oak, holt, holy, home, homestead, hone, honey, honeycomb, honeymoon, honeysuckle, hood, -hood (-head), hoof, hook, hoop (1), hop (1), hope (1), hopple, horn, hornet, horse, hose, hot, hough (hock), hound, house, housel, hover, how (1), howl, hox, hoy (2), hub, huckle-berry, huckle-bone, huddle, hue (1), huff, hull (1), hull (2), hum (1), hum (2), humble-bee, humbug, humdrum, hummock (hommock), hump, hunch, hundred, hunger, hunt, hurdle, hurdy-gurdy, hurst, hurtleberry, hush, husk, husky, hussif, hussy, huzzah.

I, ice, icicle, idle, if, ilk, im- (2), imbed, imbitter, imbody, imbosom, imbower, imbrown, impound, in, in- (1), inasmuch, inborn, inbreathed, inbred, income, income, indeed, indent (2), indwelling, infold, ingathering, ingot, inland, inlay, inlet, inly, inmate, inn, innermost (inmost), inning, inroad, inside, insight, insnare, insomuch, instead, instep, inthral, into, intwine, inward, inweave, inwrap, inwreathe, inwrought, irk, iron, ironmonger, is, island, it, itch, ivy, iwis.

jam (1), jam (2), jar (1), jerk, jingle, job (1), jog, jole, jolt, jowl (jole), jumble.

kedge (2) (kidge), keel (2), keen, keep, kelp, kemb, kern (2), kernel, kersey, key, kidney, kill, kin, kind (1), kind (2), kindle (2), kindred, kine, king, kingdom, kipper, kiss, kite, kith, knack, knacker, knag, knap, knar, knave, knead, knee, kneel, knell (knoll), knick-knack, knife, knight, knit, knob, knock, knoll (1), knoll (2), knop, knot, know, knowledge, knuckle, knurr, kythe.

lack (1), lack (2), lad, ladder, lade (1), lade (2), ladle, lady, lag, lair, lamb, lame, Lammas, land, lane, lank, lap (1), lap (2), lap (3), lapwing, larboard?, lark (1), lark (2), last (1), last (2), last (3), last (4), latch (1, 2), late, lath, lathe (2), lather, latter, laugh, lawyer, lay (1), layer, lea (1), lea (2) (ley, lay), lead (1), lead (2), leaf, lean (1), lean (2), leap, learn, lease (2), lease (3), leasing, least, leat, leather, leave (1), leave (2), ledge, ledger, ledger-, leech (1), leech (2), leek, leer, leet, left, leman (lemman), lend, length, lent, less, -less, lest, let (1), let (2), letch, lew, lewd, ley, lib, lich-gate, lick, lid, lie (1), lie (2), lief, life, lifelong, lift (2), light (1), light (2), light (3), lighten (1), lighten (2), lighten (3), lightning, lights, like (1), like (2), lilliputian, limb (1), limber (1), lime (1), lime (2), limp (1), limp (2), linch-(pin), lind, linden, ling (1), linger, linsey-woolsey, lip, lisp, lissom, list (1), list (4), list (5), list (6), listen, listless, lists, lithe, lither, little, live (1), live (2), livelihood, livelong, lively, liver, lo, load, loaf, loam, loan, loath, lock (1), lock (2), lode, lodestar (loadstar), lodestone (loadstone), log (1), log (2), loggerhead, loll, lone, long (1), long (2), looby, look, loom (1), loon (1) (lown), loose, *vb.*, loosen, lop, lord, lore, lorn, lose, losel (lorel), loss, lot, loud, louse, lout, love, low (2), low (3), lower (1), lower (2), lubber, luff, lukewarm, lull, lung, lust, -ly, lyddite, lye, lynch.

mad, madder, maggot, maid, maiden, main (1), make, malm, malt, mamma, man, mandrill, mane, manifold, mankind, many, maple, mar, mare, mark (1), mark (2), marrow (1), marsh, mash, mast (1), mast (2), match (1), mattock, maw, may (1), may-weed, maze, me, mead (1), mead (2), meadow, meal (1), meal (2), mean (1), mean (2), mean (4), measles, meat, meed, meet (1), meet (2), mellow, melt, mere (1), mere (3), mermaid, merry, mesh, mete, methinks, mew (1), mew (2), mich, mickle, mid, middle, midge, midriff, midst, midwife, might (1), might (2), milch, mild, mildew, milk, milksop, milt (1), mind, mine (1), mingle, minnow, mirth, mis- (1) (*also* Scand.), misbecome, misbehave, misbelieve, misdeed, misdeem, misdo, misgive, mislay, mislead, mislike, misname, miss (1), misselthrush (mistlethrush), misshape, mist, mistime, mistletoe, misty (1), misunderstand, mite (1), mixen, mizzle, moan, mole (1), mole (2), molten, Monday, mongrel, month, mood (1), moon, moor (1), moor (2), moot, mop (2), mope, more, Mormonite, morn, morning, morrow, moss, most, mote, moth, mother (1), mother (2), mother (3), mould (1), mould (3), mourn, mouse, mouth, mow (1), mow (2), much, mud, muddle, muff (2), mugwort, mum (1), mumble, munch, murder (murther), must (1), mutter, my.

nail, nailbourn, naked, namby-pamby, name, nap (1), nape, narrow, naught (nought), nave (1), navel, neap, near, neat (1), neb, neck, need, needle, neese (neeze), negus (1), neigh, neighbour, neither, nesh, ness, nest, net (1), nether, nettle, never, new, new-fangled, news, newt, next, nib, nibble, nick (1), nickname, nigh, night, nightingale, nightmare, nightshade, nimble, nine, ninny, nip, nipple, nit, no (1), no (2), nobody, nod, noddle, nonce, none, nook, nor, north, nose, nostril, not (1), not (2), not (3), nothing, notwithstanding, noule (nowl, nole), now, noway, noways, nowhere, nowise, nozzle, nugget, numb, nut, nuzzle.

O (1), (oh), O (2), oak, oakum, oar, oast-house, oath, oats, of, off, offal, offing, offscouring, offset, offshoot, offspring, oft, often, old, on, once, one (1), one (2), only, onset, onslaught, onward, onwards, ooze, ope, open, or (1), or (2), ordeal, ore, ort, other, otter, oubit, ought (1), ought (2), ouphe, our, ousel, out, outbid, outbreak, outburst, outcome, outdo, outdoor, outer, outgo, outgrow, outhouse, outlandish, outlast, outlay, outlet, outlive, outlook, outlying, outreach, outride, outright, outroad, outrun, outset, outshine, outside, outstretch, outstrip, outward, outweigh, outwent, outwit, outworks, oven, over, overalls, overbear, overboard, overburden, overcloud, overcome, overdo, overdraw, overdrive, overflow, overgrow, overhang, overhead, overhear, overlade, overland, overlap, overlay, overleap, overlie, overlive, overload, overlook, overmatch, overmuch, overreach, override, overrun, oversee, overset, overshadow, overshoot, oversight, overspread, overstep, overstock, overthrow, overtop, overweening, overweigh, overwhelm, overwise, overwork, overworn, overwrought, owe, owl, own (1), own (2), own (3), ox, oxlip.

pad (1), paddle (1), paddle (2), paddock (2), padlock, pan, pang, pap (1), pap (2), park, pat (1), pat (2), pat (3), patch (1)?, patch (2)?, path, patter, paxwax, pebble, peck (1), peddle, peddler (pedlar), peer (2)?, peevish, peg, periwinkle (2)?, pewet (pewit, peewit), pick, pickle?, pig, piggin, pike, pilchard, pinder (pinner), pinfold, pink (1), pink (3), pish, pitapat, pitch (2), pith, plash (1), plat (1), play, plight (1), plod, plot (2), plough, pluck, plump (1), plump (3), pock, pod, poke (2), pollock, pond, pool (1), pop, pore (2), pot, pother, potter, pound (2), pound (3), pout (1), pout (2), pox, prance, prank (1), prank (2), prick, pride?, prig (1), prig (2), prong, prop, proud ?, pshaw, puck, pudding, puddle (1), puddle (2), puff, puffin, pug, puke (1)?, pull, pun, purl (4), purr, puss, put, puttock.

quack (1), quaff, quagmire, quake, quaker, qualm, quaver, quean, queen, quell, quench, quern, quick, quicken, quid, quill (1), quill (2)?, quiver (1), quiz, quoth.

race (1), rack (7), rack (8), racket (2), raddle, rafter, raid, rail (4), rain, rake (1), rake (2), rakehell, ram, ramble, ramsons, rank (2), rape (3), rash (1), rasher, rat, rath, rather, rattle, raught, raven (1), raw, reach (1), reach (2), read, ready, reap, rear (1), rear (3), rearmouse, reave, reck, reckon, red, redgum, reechy, reed, reek, reel (1), reest, reeve (2), reeve (3), reft, rend, rennet (1), rent (1), reremouse, rest (1), retch (reach), rib, rich, rick, rickets, rid, riddle (1), riddle (2), ride, ridge, rig (2)?, rig (3), right, rim, rime (2), rimer, rimple, rind, ring (1), ring (2), rink, ripe, ripple (1), ripple (2), rise, rivel, road, roar, robbins, rock (2), rod, roe (1), rood, roof, rook (1), room, roost, root (2) (rout), rope, rot, rother, rough, roun (rown, round), row (1), row (2), rowlock (rullock), rub, rudd, rudder, ruddock, ruddy, rue (1), ruff (1), ruff (2), ruff (3), ruffle (1), rum (1), rumble, rummage (*with* F. *suffix*), rumple, run, rune, rung, runnel, rush (1), rush (2), rust, rye.

sad, saddle, sail, sake, sale, sallow (1) (sally), sallow (2), salt, salve, same, sand, sand-blind, sandwich, sap (1), Saturday, saw (1), saw (2), say (1), scatter, scold, scoundrel, scramble, scrawl, screed, screw (2), scrip (1), scythe, sea, seal (2), seam (1), sear (sere), sedge, see (1), seed, seek, seem, seer, seesaw, seethe, seldom, self, sell (1), send, sennight, set (1), settee, settle (1), settle (2), seven, sew (1), shabby, shackle, shad, shaddock, shade, shadow, shaft, shag, shake, shall, shallow, sham, shamble, shame, shamefaced, shank, shape, shard, share (1), share (2), sharp, shatter, shave, shaw, she, sheaf, shear, sheath, sheave, shed (1), shed (2), sheen, sheep, sheet, sheldrake, shelf, shell, shelter, shelve, shepherd, sherd (shard), sheriff, shide, shield, shift, shilling, shilly-shally, shimmer, shin, shine, shingle (2), ship, shire, shirt, shive, shiver (1), shiver (2), shoal (1), shoal (2), shock (1), shock (2), shock (3), shoddy, shoe, shog, shoot, shop, shore (1), shore (2), shot, shoulder, shout, shove, shovel, show (shew), shower, shrapnel, shred, shrew, shrewd, shriek, shrift, shrike, shrill, shrimp, shrink, shrive, shrivel, shroud, shrub (1), shun, shunt, shut, shuttle, shuttle-cock, sib, sick, side, sieve, sift, sigh, sight, sill, sillabub, silly, silver, simmer, sin, since, sinew, sing, singe, sink, sip, sippet, sister, sit, sith, six, slabber, slack, slade, slake, slap ?, slate (2), slay (1), slay (2) (sley), sledge-hammer, sleep, sleeper, sleet, sleeve, slide, slime, slink, slip, slit, sliver, slobber, sloe, slop (1), slope, sloth (1), sloth (2), slough (1), slow, slow-worm, sludge, slumber, slump, slums, smack (1), small, smart, smash, smear, smell, smelt (2), smew, smirch, smirk, smite, smith, smock, smoke, smolt, smooth, smother, smoulder, smut, snail, snake, snare, snarl, snatch, sneak, sneeze, snite (1), snite (2), snood, snore, snot, snout, snow, snuff (2), so, soak, soap, sob, soc, sod, soft, soke, some, -some, son, song, soon, soot, sooth, soothe, soothsay, sop, sore, sorrow, sorry, sot, soul, sound (1), sound (2), sounder, sour, south, sow (1), sow (2), spade, span, spancel, spangle, spank, spar (1), spar (2), sparable, spare, spark (1), sparrow, spat (1), spat (2), spats, spatter, spawl, speak, spear, speck, speech, speed, speir, spell (1), spell (3), spell (4), spew, spider, spile, spill (1), spin, spindle, spinster, spire (1), spit (1), spit (2), spittle (1), splutter, spoke, spokesman, spoon, spot, spout, sprat, sprawl, spray (2), spread, sprig, spring, springal, sprit, sprout, spry, spur, spurn, spurt (1) (spirt), sputter, squeeze, squint, squirt, staff, stair, staithe, stake, stale (2), stale (3), stalk (1), stalk (2), stall, stalwart, stammer, stamp, stand, staple (1), star, starboard, starch, stare (1), stare (2), stare (3), stark, stark-naked, starling, start, starve, stave, stay (2), stead, steadfast (stedfast), steady, steal, steam, steed, steel, steelyard, steep (1), steeple, steer (1), steer (2), stem (1), stem (2), stem (3), stench, step, stepchild, sterling, stern (1), steward, stick (1), stick (2), stickleback, stickler, stiff, stile (1), still (1), sting, stingy, stink, stint, stir, stirrup, stitch, stoat, stock, stocking, stone, stool, stoop (1), stork, storm, stove, stow, straddle, straight, strain (1), strand (1), straw, stream, strength, stretch, strew (straw), stride, strike, string, strip, stripling, stroke (1), stroke (2), strong, stub, stubborn, stud (1), stud (2), stun, stutter, sty (1), sty (2), such, suck, suds, sulky, sultry (sweltry), summer (1), sun, sunder, sup, surf, surly, swaddle, swallow (1), swallow (2), swamp, swan, swan-hopping, swap, sward, swarm, swart, swarthy, swash, swath, swathe, sway, sweal, swear, sweat, sweep, sweet, sweetheart, swell, swelter, swerve, swift, swill, swim (1), swim (2), swine, swing, swinge, swingle-tree, swink, swipe, swivel, swoon, swoop, sword.

tab, tadpole, tail (1), tale, talk, tall ?, tallow, tame, tang (3), tap (2), taper (1), taper (2), tar, tare (1), tarre, tarry, tart (1),

tattle, taut, taw (tew), tawdry, teach, teal, team, tear (1), tear (2), tease, teasel, tee, teem (1), teen, tell, ten, tether, tetter, tew.

than, thane, thank, that, thatch, thaw, the (1), the (2), thee (1), thee (2), theft, then, thence, there (1), there- (2), these, thews, thick, thief, thigh, thill, thimble, thin, thine, thing, think, third, thirl, thirst, thirteen, thirty, this, thistle, thither, thole (1) (thowl), thole (2), thong, thorn, thorough, thorp (thorpe), those, thou, though, thought, thousand, thrash (thresh), thread, threat, three, threshold, thrice, thrid, thrill (thirl), throat, throb, throng, thropple (thrapple), throstle, throttle, through, throw, thrum (1), thrush (1), thud, thumb, thump, thunder, thus, thwack, thwite, thy.

tick (1), tick (3), tick (4), tickle, tide, tidy, tie, till (1), till (3), tiller, tilt (1), tilt (2), tilth, timber, time, tin, tind, tinder, tine (1), tine (2), tingle, tinker, tinkle, tip (1), tip (2), tire (1), tit (2), tit for tat, tithe, titter, tittle-tattle, to, to- (1), to- (2), toad, today, toddle, to-do, toe, together, token, toll (1), toll (2), tomorrow, tongs, tongue, tonight, too, tool, toot (1), tooth, top (1), topple, topsy-turvy, totter, tough, touse, tout, tow (1), tow (2), toward, towards, town, trade, tramp, trample, trap (1), tray, tread, tree, trend, trickle, trim, troth, trough, trow, truce, true, trust, Tuesday, tumble, turf, tush, tusk, tussle, tut, twaddle, twain, twang, tweak, twelve, twenty, twibill (twybill), twice, twig (1), twig (2), twilight, twill, twin, twine, twinge, twinkle, twinter, twire, twist, twit, twitch, twitter, two.

udder, un- (1), un- (2), un- (3), uncomeatable (*with* F. *suffix*), uncouth, under, under-, undern, understand, uneath, unkempt, unless, unto, up, up-, upbraid, upholsterer, upon, upside-down, upstart, upward, upwards, us, utmost, utter (1), utter (2).

vane, vat, vinewed, vixen, Volapük.

wabble (wobble), waddle, wade, waft, wain, waist, wake (1), waken, wale (weal), walk, wallet, wallow, walnut, wan, wander, wane, wanion, wanton, ward, -ward, wardon, ware (1), ware (2), ware (3), warlock, warm, warn, warp, wart, wary (ware), was, wast, wash, wasp, watch, water, wattle, wave (1), waver, wawl, wax (1), wax (2), way, wayward, we, weak, weal, weald, wealth, wean, weapon, wear (1), wearish, weary, weasand (wesand), weasel, weather, weather-beaten, weather-bitten ?, weave, web, wed, wedge, wedlock, Wednesday, wee, weed (1), weed (2), week, ween, weep, weet, weevil, weft, weigh, weir (wear), weird, weld (2), welfare, welkin, well (1), well (2), wellaway, Welsh, welt, wen, wench, wend, were, wert, wergild, werwolf, west, wet, wether, wey.

whack, whale, whap, wharf (1), wharf (2), what, whaup, wheal (1), wheat, wheatear, wheedle ?, wheel, wheeze, whelk (1), whelk (2), whelm, whelp, when, whence, where, wherry, whet, whether, whey, which, whiff, whiffle, whig, while, whimbrel, whimper, whin (2), whine, whip, whipple-tree, whisper, whist, whistle, whit, white, whither, Whitsunday, whittle (1), whittle (2), whittle (3), whiz, who, whole, whorl, whortleberry, why.

wick (1), wicked, wide, widow, wield, wife, wight (1), wild, wilderness, wile, wilful, will (1), will (2), willow, wimble (1), wimple, win, winberry (wimberry), winch, wind (1), wind (2), wink, winkle, winnow, winsome, winter, wipe, wire, wise (1), wise (2), wish, wisp, wist, wistful, wit (1), wit (2), wit (3), witch, witch-elm (wych-elm), with, withdraw, wither, withers, withhold, within, without, withsay, withstand, withy (withe), witness, wittol, wizard (*with* F. *suffix*), wizen, wo (woe), woad, wold, wolf, woman, womb, won, wonder, wondrous, wont, woo, wood (1), wood (2), woodruff, woodwale, woof, wool, woolward, word, work, world, worm, worm-wood, worry, worse, worship, worst, worsted, wort (1), wort (2), worth (1), worth (2), wot, would, wound, wrack, wraith, wrangle, wrap, wrath, wreak, wreath, wreck, wren, wrench, wrest, wrestle, wretch, wriggle, wright, wring, wrinkle (1), wrinkle (2), wrist, write, writhe, wrong, wroth, wry.

y-, yap, yard (1), yard (2), yare, yarn, yarrow, yawl (2), yawn, ye, yea, yean (ean), year, yearn (1), yearn (2), yeast, yede, yell, yellow, yellow-hammer (yellow-ammer), yelp, yeoman, yerk, yes, yesterday, yet, yew, yex, yield, yoke, yokel, yolk (yelk), yon, yore, you, young, your, youth, yowl, Yule, ywis.

From place-names: canter, carronade, dunce, galloway, jasey, jersey, kersey, lyddite, wardon, worsted (*and others*). *From personal names*: bowie-knife, boycott, brougham, burke, congreve, doily, kit-cat, lobelia, lynch, negus, orrery, pinchbeck, sandwich, shaddock, shrapnel, spencer (*and others*).

To the above may be added some words that appear in a foreign form, yet seem to have been originally of English origin. *Examples*: brogues, burglar, dodo, gyves, pewter, poteen, shebeen.

LOW GERMAN. Some of the words in the following list may be of native origin, but their history is often obscure. They appear to be Low German in form, and to have been introduced from the Netherlands or Friesland or Hanover at various dates.

askew, bluff (2), bout, cranberry, cringle, dandle, dowel, drill (2), doxy, dude, fib, fob (1), fob (2), frampold, frill, fuddle, grime, groat, gull (2), haze, hawk (2), hawker, huckaback, huckster, jerkin, kails, lazy, mate (1), mink, minx, mug, mum (2), pack, package (*with* F. *suffix*), packet (*with* AF. *suffix*), paigle?, peak, poll, prate, prowl, punk, queer, rantipole, rifle (2), rill, rustle (*perhaps* E.), shudder, slight, smug, smuggle, spelter, spray (1), tackle, teem (2), trice (1, 2), tub, tuck.

French from Low German: award, booty, brick, butt (1), button, buttress, butty, chuck (1), dace, dart, fudge, fur, goffer, grape, grapnel, grapple, gruel, hackbut, hamlet, heinous, lampoon, massacre, maund (1), peck (2), pledge, poach (1), poach (2), posnet, putty, rogue, scatches, slender, staple (2), stout, tampion, teat, tetchy (techy), tiff (1), touchy, trundle, tybalt, wafer.

Dutch from French from Low German: skate (2).

French from Low Latin from Low German: callet, filter, quail (2).

Dutch from Low German: scarf (1), sloop.

Scandinavian from Low German: rig (1), scone (scon).

☞ See also under **Dutch** and **Teutonic**.

DUTCH. aardvark, avast?, belay, beleaguer, blot (2), bluff (1), boom (2), boor, bouse (boose), brack, brackish, brandy, bruin, bulk (2), bully, bumpkin, burgher, burgomaster, caboose, cam, catkin, clamp, clinker, clipper, cope (3), dapper, deal (3), delf, derrick, dirk?, dock (3), doit, drill (1), drum, duck (4), duffel, easel, freebooter, frolic, fumble, furlough, gas, geck, golf, groove, gruff, guilder, heyday (1), hoarding, hold (2), holland, hop (2), hope (2), hottentot, hoy (1), hustle, inkle?, isinglass, jib (1), jib (2), keelhaul, kink, kit (1), knapsack, knickerbockers, kopje, laager, land-grave, landscape, laveer, leaguer, lighter, linstock (lintstock), litmus, loiter, margrave, marline, maulstick, minikin, mob (2), mump, mumps, mutchkin, ogle, orlop, pad (2), pink (2), pink (4), placket, plug, pompelmoose, quack (2), quacksalver, rant, reef (1), reef (2), reeve (1), roster, rover, runt, schiedam, school (2), scull (3), selvage (selvedge), serif, sheer (2), skipper, sled, sledge, sleigh, slim, slot (1), sloven, smack (3), snaffle, snap, snip, snuff (1), spelicans, splice, split, spoor, sprinkle, steenbok, stew (2), stipple, stiver, stoker, stripe, sutler, swab, tattoo (1), toy, trick (3), trigger, uproar, veldt, wagon (waggon), wainscot, yacht, Yankee?, yawl (1).

From Dutch or Flemish place-names: cambric, dornick, spa.

Middle Dutch. brake (1), crate, creek, croon, deck (1), deck (2), doxy, firkin, foist, frump, hod, hoiden (hoyden), hoist, lollard, luck, milt (2), nag (1), nap (2), nock, puke (2), rabble, rack (1), rack (2), ravel, ray (3), ret, ruffle (2), skew?, slur, spool, swingle.

French from Dutch (or Middle Dutch): arquebus, bodkin?, clinquant, clique, cracknel, cricket (1), cricket (2), dig, droll, drugget, fitchet, frieze (1), friz (frizz), gleek (1), gleek (2), hoarding?, hobby, hotchpot (hodge-podge), manikin, mite (1), mitrailleuse, mow (3), mummer, mute (2), placard, plack, plaque, shallop, socket?, staid, stay (1).

Spanish from French from Dutch: filibuster.

Walloon from Middle Dutch: rabbit.

Flemish from Dutch: fribble, rummer.

German from Dutch: schnapps.

Scandinavian from Dutch: yaw.

Flemish: pamper.

SCANDINAVIAN. akimbo?, aloft, amiss, anger, angry, aslant, auk, awe, awn, axle, aye.

bag, bait, balderdash, ball (2), band (1) (bond), bang (1), bank (1), bark (2), bask, baste (1), bat (2), batten (1), bawl, beck (2), bellows, bestead (2), big, billow, bing, bitts, blaze (2), blazon (1), bleak (1), bleak (2), blend, blink, bloat, bloater, bloom, blunder, blur, bole, bolled, bond, boon, booth, bore (3), both, boulder, bound (3), bow (4), brad, brae, brag, brand- (brant-), brinded, brindled, brink, brunt, bulk (1), bulk (3), bulwark, bungle, bunk, bunting (1), busk (1), bustle (1), bustle (2), by-law.

cake, call, carp (2), cart, cast, clamber, cleft, clift, clip (1), clog, clown, club (1), club (2), club (3), clumsy, cock (4), cocker, cockle (3), cog (1), cog (2), coke?, cosy, cow (2), cower, crash, crawl, craze, crook, cruse, cub, cuff (1), cunning (2), curl, cut, cutter

daggle, dairy (*with* F. *suffix*), dandriff?, dangle, dank, dapple, dash, dastard (*with* F. *suffix*), dawdle, daze, dazzle (*with* E. *suffix*), die (1), dirt, douse, dowdy, down (1), dowse (1), doze, drag, dregs, drip, droop, drown, drumble, duds, duffer, dump (2), dumps, dun (2), dusk, dwale, dwell.

egg (1), egg (2), eiderduck.

fadge, fast (3), fell (4), fellow, fetlock, fidget, filch, filly, fir, firth, fit (1), fizz, flag (4), flagstone, flake, flare, flat, flaunt, flaw, fleck, fleer, flimsy, fling, flip (1), flippant, flit, flounce (1), flounder (1),

fluster, fog, force (3), foss, freckle, frith (2) (firth), fro, froth, fulmar, fun?.

gaby, gad (1), gad (2), gainly, gait, gale (1), galt (1), galt (2), gang (1), gang (2), gape, gar (2), garish (gairish), garth, gasp, gate (2), gault, gaunt, gaze, gear, ged, geld, get, gewgaw?, gig, giglet (*with* F. *suffix*), gill (1), gill (2), girth, glade, glint, glitter, gloat, gloss (1), gnash, goosander, gowan, gowk, grig (1), griskin, grovel, gruesome, guess, gun, gust (1).

haggle (1), haggle (2), hail (2), hail (3), hake, handsel (hansel), hank, hap, happen, harbour, harsh, hawse, hit, holm, hoot, how (2), hug, hurl, hurry, husband, hustings.

ill, inkling, intake, intrust (*with* E. *prefix*).

jade (1), jersey, jolly (boat), jump (1), jump (2).

keel (1), keelson (kelson), keg, ken, kick, kid, kidnap, kilt, kindle (1), kitling.

lass, lathe (1), law, leak, lee, leech (3) (leach), leg, levin, lift (1), liken, lilt, ling (2), link (1), link (2), loft, loom (2), loon (2), loose, *adj.*, low (1), low (4), lug, lumber (2), lump, lunch, luncheon, lurch (1), lurch (4)?, lurk.

mail (black), main (2), mark (3), marrow (2), mawkish (*with* E. *suffix*), meek, midden, mire, mis- (1) (*and* E.), mistake, mistrust, mouldy, muck, muggy, murky (mirky).

nab, nag (2), narwhal, nasty, nay, neif (neaf), niggard, niggle, noggin?, Norse, nudge.

oaf, odd, outlaw.

paddock (1), palter, paltry, pash, piddle, pimple, pixy, poke (1), prawn?, prod, pucker, purl (1).   queasy.

rack (3), raft, rag, raise, rake (3), ransack, rap (1), rap (2), recall (*with* L. *prefix*), recast (*with* L. *prefix*), reel (2)?, rid (2), riding, rife, rift, rip, ripple (1), rive, roan-tree (rowan-tree), rock (3), roe (2), root (1), rotten, rouse (1), rouse (2), row (3), rubble, ruck (1), ruck (2), rug, rugged, rump, ruth.

sag, saga, scab, scald (2), scald (3), scall, scalp, scant, scar (2) (scaur), scare, scarf (2), scathe, schooner, scoff, score, scotch, scout (2), scout (3), scowl, scrabble, scraggy, scrannel, scrap, scrape, scratch, scream, screech, screes, scrub (1), scrub (2), scruff, scud, scuffle, scuft (scruff), sculk (skulk), scull (1), scull (2), scum, scurf, scurvy, scuttle (3), seat, seemly, sheal, sheer (1), shrug, shuffle, shy, silt, simper, skate (1), skerry, skewer, skid, skill, skim, skimp, skin, skink (1), skip, skirt, skittish, skittles, skua, skull (scull), sky, slab (2), slam, slang, slant, slattern, slaughter, slaver, sleek, sleight, slick, sling, slop (2), slouch, slough (2), slubber, slug, slush, slut, sly, smack (2), smattering, smelt (1), smile, smudge, snag, sneap, sneer, sniff, snipe, snivel, snob, snooze, snort, snub, snug, sough, span-new, spark (2), spick and span-new, spike (1), spill (2), spink, splint (splent), sprack (sprag), spree, spud, spurt (2), squab (1 *and* 2), squabble, squall, squander, squeak, squeal, squib, squid, stab, stack, stag, stagger, stang, steak, steep (2), stern (2), stifle, stilt, stith, stook, stoup (stoop), straggle, streak, struggle, strum, strut (1), strut (2), stumble, stump, stunted, swagger, swain, swirl.

tag, take, tang (1), tang (2), tangle, tarn, tat, tatter, ted, teem (3), teg, teind, tern, their, them, they, thrall, thrave, thrift, thrive, throe, thrum (2), thrush (2), thrust, Thursday, thwaite, thwart, tidings, tiff (2), tiffin, tight, tike, till (2), tine (2), tipple, tipsy, tit (1), titling, tod, toft, toom, torsk, toss, tram, trash, trill (2), trill (3), tug, tup, tussock, twiddle, twirl.

ugly.   Valhalla, Valkyria, Viking, vole.

wad, wadmal, wag, waggle, wail, wake (2), wale (2), wall-eyed, wand, want, wapentake, welcome, weld (1), welter, whim, whin (1), whinyard (*with* F. *suffix*), whir, whirl, whisk, whitlow, whore, wick (3) = wich, wicker, wight (2), wimble (2), windlass (1), window, wing.

Icelandic: geysir, scarf (3).

Swedish: dahlia, gauntlet (2) (gantlope), kink, slag, sloid, trap (3), tungsten.

Norwegian: fiord, lemming. *Danish*: floe, siskin.

French from Scandinavian: abet, baggage (1), baggage (2), barbed, bet, blemish, boast, boisterous, bondage, braise, brandish, brasier, brawl (2), braze (1), breeze (3), brisket, bun, elope, equip, faggot, flatter, flounder (2), frown, gable, gauntlet (1), gawk, gormandize, gourmand, grudge, haggis, jangle, jape, jib (3), jolly, lagan, locket, Norman, pouch, rivet, rorqual, rubbish, scoop, scupper, scutch, slot (2), sound (4), strife, strive, target, tryst, waif, waive.

Dutch from Scandinavian: ballast, doit, walrus.

Russian from Scandinavian: knout.

Late Latin from Scandinavian: scorbutic.

GERMAN. (The number of words borrowed *directly* from German is but small.)

aurochs, bantling, bismuth, cobalt, dachshund, Dutch, fahrenheit, feldspar, fugleman, gneiss, hamster, heyday (1), hock (2), hurrah, lager-bier, lammergeyer, landau, mangel-wurzel, meerschaum, mesmerise (*with* F. *suffix*), minnesinger, plunder, poodle, quartz, ratch, shale, sleazy, spitchcock, swindler, thaler, trull, wacke, waltz, zinc.

From personal names: camellia, fuchsia.

Dutch (*or Low German*) *from German*: crants, dollar, etch, gemsbok, holster, rix-dollar, skellum, switch, wiseacre.

Scandinavian from German: nickel, quirk, sleave (silk).

Polish from German: hetman.

French from German: abut, band (2), bandy, bawd, bawdy, belfry, bend (2), bistre ?, bivouac, block, botch (2), brach, brunette, carouse, carousal (1), chamois, coat, etiquette, franc, grumble, haggard (1), haggard (2), halt (2), hamper (2), hanaper, hash, hatch (3), hatchet, haversack, hoe, Huguenot, lansquenet, latten, lattice, lecher, lickerish (*with* E. *suffix*), list (2), lumber (1), lurch (2), lurch (3) ?, lure, mangle (1), marquee, mignonette, motley, popinjay, raffle, roast, schorl, shammy (shamoy), spruce, tan, ticket, top (2), zigzag.

French from Provençal from German: marque (letters of).

Italian from German: rigol, rocket (1).

French from Italian from German: bank (2), banquet, burin, group, tuck (2).

Low Latin from German: lobby, morganatic.

French from Low Latin from German: carline, fauteuil, goblin, lodge, marchioness, marquis, mason ?.

Scandinavian from Middle High German: bunt.

☞ See also under **Teutonic**.

French from Middle High German: baffle, bale (1), brewis (brose), browze, burgess, demarcation, gonfanon (gonfalon), grisette, grizzly, grizzled (*with* E. *suffix*), halberd (halbert), jig, marquetry, rebut (*with* L. *prefix*), sorrel (1), warble, wince.

French from Old High German: agraffe, allegiance, arrange, await, bacon, balloon, banish, baste (3), blanch (1), blank, blanket, blue, boss, bottle (2), brawn, bream, burnet, burnish, butcher, carcanet, chine, cratch, crayfish (craw-fish), dance, egret, ermine, eschew, espy, fee, feoff, feud (1), fief, filbert, flange, flank, flawn, flinch, flunkey, franchise, frank, franklin, freight, frisk, furbish, furnish, gaiety, gallant, galloon, garb (2), garbage, garret, gay, giron (gyron), grilse, guarantee (guaranty), guise, habergeon, hale (2) (haul), hanseatic, harangue, harass, harbinger, hardy, hauberk, haul, haunch, herald, hernshaw (1), heron, hob (2), hobby (1), hobgoblin, hut, jay, lay (2), liege, mail (2), maim, malkin, march (1), marshal, mazer, mazzard, minion, morel, mushroom, orgulous, ouch (nouch), perform (*with* L. *prefix*), quiver (2), range, rank (1), rappee, rasp, rasp(-berry), riches, rob, robe, robin, rochet, Salic (Salique), saloon, scale (1), scorn, seize, skirmish, slice, spy, stallion, strand (2), tarnish, towel, vagrant, wait, warrant, warren.

German from French from Old High German: veneer.

French from Low Latin from Old High German: abandon, equerry, faldstool, install, sturgeon.

Spanish from Old High German: guerilla (guerrilla).

French from Spanish from Old High German: rapier.

Italian from Old High German: ballot, fresco, smalt, stucco.

French from Italian from Old High German: gala, garb (1), skiff.

French from Austrian: cravat.

TEUTONIC. This is here used as a *general* term, to show that the following words (derived through French, Spanish, &c.) cannot quite certainly be referred to a *definite* Teutonic dialect, though clearly belonging to the Teutonic family.

French from Teutonic: attach, banner, banneret, bartisan, beadle, bedell, blazon (2), blister, blot (1), blotch, board (2), boulevard, brattice, bray (1), broider, broil (1), brush, buff (1), burgeon, choice, coterie, cotillion, cramp, crewel, croup (2), cruet, crupper, crush, dally, epergne, escrow, feuter, gaff, gage (1), gain (1), gain (2), gaiter, gallop, gambeson, gardant, garden, garland, garment, garnish, garrison, gimlet, gimp, glissade, grate (2), grimace, growl, guard, guide, guidon, guile, guillemot, guipure, guy (2), harlot, haste, hasten, havoc, hoop (2), hovel, hue (2) huge ?, label, louver (loover), merlin, moat, moraine, parquetry, patrol, patten, paw, pheon, pickax, picket, picnic, picotee, pique, piquet, pocket, porridge, porringer, pottage, pottle, rally (2), ramp, random, reynard (renard), ribald, riffraff, rifle (1), roach, romp, scabbard, scale (2), scallop (scollop), scavenger, screen, scroll, seneschal, slab (1), slash, slat, slate (1), sorrel (2), soup, spar (3), spavin, spell (2), stale (1), stew (1), stroll, sturdy, supper, tache (1), tack, tankard, tap (1), tawny, tenny, Tibert, tic, tier, tire (2), tire (3), toper, touch, track, trap (2), trawl, trepan (2) (trapan), trip, troll, truck (1), trudge ?, tuck (3), tucker, tucket, tuft (1), tuft (2), turbary, tweezers (*with*

E. *suffix*), wage, wager, war, warden, wardrobe, warison, wassail, whoop, wicket, windlass (2).

Late Latin from French from Teutonic: corrody, feud (2), feudal.

Dutch from French from Teutonic: morass.

Spanish from Teutonic: flotilla, gabardine, picador, ranch, stampede.

French from Spanish from Teutonic: amice (2), bandoleer, piccadill, scuttle (2).

Italian from Teutonic: arpeggio, balcony, bandit, bunion, loto (lotto), lottery, scherzo, stoccado (stoccata), strappado.

French from Italian from Teutonic: attack, bagatelle, escarpment (*with* L. *suffix*), guy (1), ruffian, scaramouch, scarp, tirade, vogue.

Late Latin from Teutonic: allodial, Goth, saponaceous, Saxon, Teutonic, Vandal, Visigoth.

French from Low Latin from Teutonic: border, carp (1), forage, marten, pandour, ratten.

Latin from Greek from Teutonic: bison.

CELTIC. This is a general term for the languages now represented by Irish, Gaelic, Welsh, Breton, Manx, and (till very recently) Cornish. Some of the words are from *old* Celtic forms, which it is not always possible to trace clearly.

bald, bard, beltane, bin, bog, boggart, boggle, brat, brock, brogues (*from* English ?), bug (1), bug (2) ?, bugaboo, bug(bear), cairn, Celt (1), char (3), coble, combe, crag, crock, Culdee, doe ?, down (2), down (3), dulse, dun (1), duniwassal, galore, gillie, glen, glib (2), gull (1), hubbub, ingle (1), kelpie, kex, kibe, linn, loop, peat, penguin ?, pose (3), shamrock, strath, tall ?, ton (tun), tump, twig (2) ?, wheal (2).

Welsh: bragget, coracle, cromlech, crowd (2), eisteddfod, flannel, flummery, metheglin.

Gaelic: airt, capercailzie, cateran, clachan, clan, claymore, coronach, corrie, duan, fillibeg, inch (2), loch, mackintosh, ptarmigan, slogan, sowans, spleuchan, tocher, whiskey.

Irish: banshee, colleen, cosher, Fenian, gallowglass, kern (1) (kerne), lough, mavourneen, ogham, omadaun, orrery, rapparee, shanty, shillelagh, skain (skene), spalpeen, tanist, Tory, usquebaugh.

Breton: dowlas, menhir, poldavy.

French from Celtic (*or Breton*): barter, beak, bijou, bilge, bound (2), bourn (1), brail, bran, bray (2), budget, bulge, car, cloak, clock, dolmen, galliard, garter, gobbet, gobble (*with* E. *suffix*), gravel, grummet (2), harness, javelin, job (2), lawn (1), lockram, mavis, mien, mine (2), mineral, musit, mutton, petty ?, piece, quay, skein, truant, tunnel, valet, varlet, vassal.

Spanish from Celtic: garrote (garrotte).

French from Spanish from Celtic: bracket.

French from Dutch from Celtic: dune.

Latin from Celtic: carucate.

French from Late Latin from Celtic: arras, artesian, career, cark, carpenter, carrack, carry, charge, chariot, druid, embassy, feuterer, gouge, pontoon, vavasour.

Provençal from Late Latin from Celtic: league (2).

Spanish from Late Latin from Celtic: cargo.

Italian from Late Latin from Celtic: caricature.

French from Italian from Late Latin from Celtic: ambassador, caroche, carriole.

French from German from Celtic: rote (2).

ROMANCE LANGUAGES. These languages, which include French, Spanish, Portuguese, and Italian, are, strictly speaking, unoriginal, but we cannot always trace them back to the source. A large number of the words belonging to these languages will be found under the headings *Celtic, Latin, Greek,* &c., which should be consulted. Those here enumerated are words of which the origin is imitative, local, or obscure.

French. abash, aery, agog, andiron, attire, avens, average, baboon, badge, badger, bar, bargain, barrator, barrel, barren, barrier, basket, battlement, bauble (1), bauble (2), bavin, bayonet, beaver (2), beg, begonia, beguine, bevel, bice, biggin, bigot, billet, billiards, blond, blouse, bludgeon, bobbin, boudoir, bourd, bourn (1), breeze (2), bribe, broil (2), buckram, budge (2), buffer (1), buffer (2), buffet (1), buffet (2), buffoon, busk (2), buss (2), cachalot, caddis, cadger, cajole, cantilever, carbine, caul, Chablis, chagrin, cheval-de-frise, chicanery, chiffonier, cockade, crare, cretonne, curlew, debar, demijohn, disease, disembarras, doily, dolomite, drug, drugget, dupe, eagre, ease, embattle (1), embay, emblazon, emboss (1), emboss (2), embrasure, embroider, embroil, ergot, eyry, flout, flute, fret (2), furbelow, gallimaufry, gallon, gasconade, gibbet, giblets, gill (3), glean, gobelin, grail (3), greaves (2), grebe, groom, grouse, grummet (1), guillotine, gusset, guzzle, haberdasher, haha, halloo, haricot (1), haricot (2), harridan, haunt, hurt, hurtle, izard, jabber?, jag?, jaunt, lanner, lanyard, lawn (2), lees, lias, limber (2), loach, loo, lorgnette, magnolia, maraud, martin, martinet, martlet, Médoc, mitten, mortise, muffin, mullein, mullion, Nicotian, ogre, paduasoy, partlet, pawn (1), pelf, pet (1), pet (2), pilfer, pillory, pinch, pirouette, piss, pittance, pooh, poplin, race (2), racy, rail (3), rampion, rascal, ratlines, riband (ribbon), riot, rock (1), rococo, ronyon, roquelaure, ruff (4), sabot, Sauterne, savoy, sedan-chair, shalloon, silhouette, soho, sparver, tarlatan, Trappist, tripe, troop, Troy (weight), Tulle, valise, varnish, vaudeville, vernier, virelay, watchet.

Anglo-French: kiddle.

Provençal: rack (4).

French from Provençal: charade, flageolet, gavotte, martingale.

Italian. adagio, agio, andante, bergomask, bravo, cameo, galvanism, imbroglio, mantua, marsala, milliner, polony, rebuff, regatta, sienna, tarantella, trill (1), voltaic.

French from Italian: avocet, bamboozle?, barracks, bergamot (2), bezonian, brave, brigade, brigand, brigandine, brigantine (brig), brisk, brusque, bust, carcase, carousal (2), casemate, catafalque, caviare, charlatan, faience, frigate, garboil, gazette, harlequin, jean (jane), maroon (1), pasquin, pasquinade, pavise, pistol, pistole, ravelin, regale, rodomontade, theorbo, tirade, tontine, traffic.

Spanish. adobe, anchovy, bilbo, bilboes, bravado, cachucha, cigar, cinchona (chinchona), cockroach, curaçao, curassow, fandango, galleon, picaninny, quixotic, rusk, sarsaparilla.

French from Spanish: barricade, bizarre, calipash, calipee?, cannon (2), caracole, carapace, chimer (chimere), cordwainer, fanfare, morion (murrion).

Portuguese. dodo, emu, sargasso.

LATIN. ab-, abbreviate, abdicate, abdomen, abduce, aberration, abhor, abject, abjure, abnegate, abominate, aborigines, abortion, abrade, abrogate, abrupt, abs-, abscess, abscind, abscond, absolute, absolve, absorb, abstemious, abstract, abstruse, absurd, accede, accelerate, access, acclaim, acclivity, accommodate, accretion, accumulate, accurate, acid, acquiesce, acquire, acrid, acumen, acute, adapt, add, addict, adduce, adept, adequate, adhere, adipose, adit, adjacent, adject, adjudicate, adjunct, adjure, adjutant, admit, adolescent, adopt, adore, adorn, adult, adulterate, adumbrate, advent, advert, advocate, ædile, æruginous, affidavit, afflict, agent, agglomerate, agglutinate, aggravate, aggregate, agitate, agnate, agrarian, agriculture, alacrity, album, albumen, alias, alibi, alleviate, alligation, alliteration, allocate, allocution, allude, alluvial, alp, altar, alter, alternate, alveolar, amanuensis, amatory, ambi- (amb-), ambidextrous, ambient, ambiguous, ambulation, amicable, amputate, ancillary, angina, anile, animadvert, animal, animate, annihilate, anniversary, annotate, annular, annunciate, anserine, ante-, antecedent, antedate, antediluvian, antennæ, antepenultima, anterior, anticipate, anus, anxious, aperient, apex, apiary, apparatus, apparent, applaud, apposite, appreciate, apprehend, appropriate, approximate, apt, aquatic, arbiter, arbitrary, arbitrate, arboreous, arduous, area, arefaction, arena, argillaceous, arid, ark, armament, arrogate, articulate, ascend, ascititious, ascribe, aspect, asperse, assert, asseverate, assibilation, assiduous, assimilate, associate, assuasive, assume, astriction, astringe, astute, atrabilious, attenuate, attest, attract, attribute, auction, augur, august, aureate, auricular, aurora, auscultation, auxiliary, ave, avert, aviary, avocation, avulsion, axil, axis.

bacillus, basalt, beet, belligerent, belt, benefactor, bi-, bib, biennial, bifurcated, bilateral, binary, binocular, binomial, bipartite, biped, bisect, bissextile, bitumen, bland, boa, bract, bull (2), bus.

cachinnation, cack, cadaverous, caducous, cæsura, calcareous, calceolaria, calculate, calefaction, calendar, calends, callow, calorific, calx, campestral, cancer, candelabrum, candidate, candle, canine, canorous, cant (1), canticle, capacious, capillary, capitol, capitular, capitulate, Capricorn, capsicum, carbolic, carbuncle, carburet, cardinal, caries, carnal, carnivorous, castigate, castle, castrate, catenary, caudal, caveat, cede, celebrate, celibate, cell, censor, cent, centenary, centennial, centesimal, centigrade, cento, centrifugal, centripetal, centurion, cere, cereal, cerulean, cervine, chalk, cheese, ciliary, cincture, cinerary, circum-, circumambient, circumambulate, circumcise, circumference, circumflex, circumfluent, circumfuse, circumjacent, circumlocution, circumnavigate, circumscribe, circumspect, circumvallation, circumvent, circumvolve, circus, cirrus, civic, civil, clang, coadjutor, coagulate, coalesce, coction, coefficient, coerce, coeval, cogent, cogitate, cognate, cognition, cognomen, cohabit, cohere, coincide, coition, cole, collaborator, collapse, collateral, collide, collimate, collocate, colloquy, collude, column, com-, combine, comity, commemorate, commend, commensurate, comminution, commissary, commit, commix, commute, compact (2), compensate, compete, competitor, compla-

cent, complement, complete, complex, complicate, component, compound (1), comprehend, compute, con (2), con-, concatenate, concede, conciliate, concinnity, conclude, concoct, concomitant, concrete, concur, condole, condone, conduce, conduct, confabulate, confect, confederate, confer, confide, confiscate, conflation, conflict, confluent, congener, congenial, congenital, congeries, conglobe, conglomerate, conglutinate, congratulate, congregate, congress, congrue, conjugation, conjunction, connate, connatural, connect, connote, connubial, consanguineous, conscionable, conscious, conscript, consecrate, consequent, consolidate, consort, conspicuous, constipate, constitute, construe, consuetude, consul, consume, consummate, contact, contaminate, contemplate, contemporaneous, context, contiguous, contingent, continuous, contort, contra, contract (1), contradict, contribute, contuse, convalesce, convenient, convent, converge, convex, convince, convivial, convoke, convolve, convulse, cook, coop, co-operate, co-ordinate, copulate, cornea, cornucopia, corolla, corollary, coronation, corpuscle, correct, correlate, corroborate, corrugate, corrupt, cortex, coruscate, costal, coulter, cowl (1), crass, create, creed, cremation, crenate, crepitate, crepuscular, crescent, cretaceous, crinite, crisp, cristate, crude, crural, cubit, cucumber, cuff (2), culinary, culm, culminate, cultivate, cumulate, cuneate, cup, cupel, cupid, cupreous, curate, curricle, cursive, cursory, curt, curule, curve, cusp, custody, cuticle.

de-, debenture, debilitate, decapitate, December, decemvir, decennial, deciduous, decimate, declaim, decoct, decorate, decorum, decrement, decrepit, decretal, decurrent, decussate, dedicate, deduce, deduct, defalcate, defecate, defect, deflagration, deflect, defluxion, defunct, degenerate, dehiscent, deject, delate, delegate, delete, deliberate, delicate, delineate, delinquent, deliquesce, delirious, delude, demented, demonstrate, demulcent, denary, denominate, dense, dental, dentated, denticle, dentist, dentition, denude, denunciation, depict, depilatory, depletion, deponent, depopulate, deprecate, depreciate, depredate, depress, dereliction, deride, derogate, describe, desecrate, desiccate, desiderate, desk, desolate, despond, desquamation, destitute, desuetude, desultory, detect, deter, deterge, deteriorate, detonate, detraction, detrude, devastate, deviate, devious, devolve, devote, dexter, di- (1), dial, diary, dicker, dictate, diffident, diffract, diffuse, digest, dight, digit, digress, dijudicate, dilacerate, dilapidate, dilute, dimissory, dire, direct, dirge, dis-, disafforest, disconnect, disconsolate, discriminate, discursive, discuss, disincline, disinfect, disingenuous, disjunction, dislocate, dismiss, dispassionate, dispel, disperse, dispirit, disquiet, disquisition, disruption, dissect, disseminate, dissent, dissertation, dissident, dissipate, dissociate, dissolute, dissolve, distend, distort, distract, distribute, disunite, diurnal, divaricate, diverge, divest, divide, divulsion, dominate, dormitory, dual, dubious, duct, duodecimo, duodenum, duplicate, duration.

edict, educate, educe, effeminate, effervesce, effete, efficacy, effigy, effluence, effulgent, effuse, egotist, egregious, egress, ejaculate, eject, elaborate, elapse, elate, elect, element, elevate, elicit, elide, eliminate, elision, elocution, elude, emaciate, emanate, emancipate, emasculate, emendation, emerge, emigrate, eminent, emit, emotion, emulate, endue (2), enervate, entity, enucleate, enumerate, enunciate, equal, equation, equestrian, equi-, equilibrium, equine, equivocal, era, eradicate, erase, erect, erratum, erroneous, erubescent, eructate, erudite, eruption, esculent, estimate, estuary, esurient, evacuate, evanescent, evaporate, event, evict, evince, eviscerate, evoke, evolve, evulsion, ex-, exacerbate, exact (1), exaggerate, exasperate, excerpt, excise (2), exclude, excogitate, excommunicate, excoriate, excrement, excruciate, exculpate, excursion, exeat, execrate, exert, exfoliate, exhaust, exhibit, exhume, exigent, exiguous, exist, exit, exonerate, exordium, expand, expatiate, expatriate, expect, expectorate, expedite, expel, expend, expiate, expletive, explicate, explicit, exponent, export, expostulate, expunge, expurgate, exquisite, extant, extempore, extend, extenuate, exterminate, external, extinguish, extirpate, extol, extort, extra, extract, extramundane, extraneous, extraordinary, extravasate, extricate, extrude, exude, exult, exuviae.

fabricate, fac-simile, fact, factitious, factotum, fæces, fallible, family, fan, fane, farina, farrago, fascinate, fastidious, fatuous, fauces, faun, February, feculent, feline, femoral, fennel, feracious, feral (1), feral (2), ferment, ferreous, ferruginous, ferule, festive, fetus, fever, fiat, fibula, fiducial, figment, filial, fimbriated, fine (2), finial, finite, fistula, flagellate, flagitious, flamen, flog, floral, florid, floscule, fluctuate, fluent, fluor, focus, font (1), foraminated, forceps, forensic, fork, formic, formula, formulate, fornicate, fortuitous, forum, frangible, fratricide (2), frigid, fritillary, frivolous, frond, frustrate, frustum, fulcrum, fulgent, fuliginous, fuller, fulminate, fulvid, fulvous, fumigate, funambulist, fungus, funicle, furcate, furfuraceous, fuscous, fuse (1), fusil (3), fustigate.

galeated, gallinaceous, garrulous, gelid, Gemini, generate, generic, geniculate, genius, genuine, genus, gerund, gesticulate, gesture, gibbose glabrous, gladen (gladden), gladiator, glomerate, glume, glutinous, gradient, gradual, graduate, grallatory, gramineous, granary, grandiloquent, granule, gratis, gratuitous, gratulate, gregarious, gust (2).

habitat, hallucination, hastate, hebetude, hereditary, hernia, hesitate, hiatus, hirsute, histrionical, hoopoe, horrid, horrify, hortatory, horticulture, host (3), humane, humeral, humiliate.

i-, ibex, identical, il- (1), il- (2), illapse, illegal, illegitimate, illimitable, illision, illiterate, illogical, illude, illuminate, illustrate, im- (3), imbricated, imbue, imitate, immaculate, immanent, immature, immerge, immigrate, imminent, immit, immoderate, immolate, impact, impeccable, impecunious, impede, impel, impend, impersonate, imperturbable, impervious, impetrate, impetus, impinge, implicate, impolite, imponderable, impregnate, impregnate, impress, impropriate, improvident, in-(2), in-(3), inaccurate, inadequate, inadvertent, inane, inanimate, inapplicable, inappreciable, inappropriate, inarticulate, inartificial, inaudible, inaugurate, inauspicious, incalculable, incandescent, incantation, incarcerate, incautious, incendiary, incense (1), incentive, inceptive, incessant, inch (1), inchoate, incipient, include, incoherent, incombustible, incommensurate, incomplete, incompressible, inconclusive, incondite, incongruous, inconsequent, inconsistent, inconsumable, incontrovertible, inconvertible, inconvincible, incorporate, incorrupt, incrassate, increment, incubate, incubus, inculcate, inculpable, inculpate, incumbent, incur, incurvate, indeclinable, indecorum, indefensible, indefinable, indefinite, indemonstrable, independent, indescribable, indestructible, indeterminate, index, indicate, indigenous, indigested, indiscernible, indiscriminate, indispensable, individual, indoctrinate, indolence, indomitable, indorse, induce, induct, indue (1), indurate, inebriate, inedited, ineffective, inelegant, inert, inexact, inexhausted, inexpressible, infant, infatuate, infinite, infirm, infix, inflate, inflect, inflict, influx, informal, infrequent, infringe, infuriate, ingenuous, ingratiate, ingress, inguinal, inhale, inherent, inhibit, inimical, initial, initiate, inject, injunction, innate, innocuous, innovate, innoxious, innuendo (inuendo), innutritious, inobservant, inoculate, inodorous, inordinate, inquire (enquire), insane, inscribe, insecure, insensate, insert, insessorial, insignia, insignificant, insinuate, insolvent, insomnia, inspect, inspissate, instigate, institute, instruct, insubordinate, insufficient, insular, insuppressible, insurgent, intact, intangible, integer, integument, intense, inter-, intercalate, intercommunicate, interdict, interfuse, interim, interior, interjacent, interline, interlude, interlunar, interminable, intermit, intermix, internal, internecine, interpolate, interregnum, interrogate, interrupt, intersect, intersperse, interstellar, intestate, intimate (1), intimate (2), intra-, intramural, intransitive, intrepid, intricate, intro-, introduce, intromission, introspection, intrude, inundation, invecked, inveigh, invert, invertebrate, investigate, inveterate, invidious, invigorate, inviolate, invocate, involuntary, involute, ir- (1), ir- (2), irradiate, irrational, irreducible, irresolute, irresponsible, irrigate, irritate, italics, item, iterate, itinerant.

January, jejune, jilt, jocose, jocular, joke, jubilation, jugular, junction, juncture, June, junior, juniper, juridical.

kail, kiln, kirtle (*with* E. *suffix*), kitchen.

labellum, labial, labiate, laboratory, laburnum, lacerate, lachrymal (lacrimal), lacteal, lacuna, lacustrine, lambent, lamina, lanceolate, languid, laniferous, lanuginous, lapidary, lapse, larva, lascivious, latent, lateral, laud, laureate, laurustinus, lavatory, lax, legislator, legitimate, lemur, lenient, lens, leporine, levigate, liberate, libertine, librate, libration, licentiate, lictor, ligneous, ligule, limb (2), limbo, limbus, limpet, line, lineal, linear, linen, lingual, linguist, lining, lint, liquescent, liquidate, litigation, littoral, lobster, locate, locomotion, locus, locust, longevity, loquacious, lotion, lubricate, lucid, lucubration, ludicrous, lugubrious, lumbago, lumbar, lunar, lurid, lustration, lustrum, lymph.

macerate, maculate, magisterial, magnanimous, magnate, magnificent, magniloquence, magnitude, major, majuscule, malefactor, malevolent, malic, mallow, mamillary, mammalia, mandible, manipulate, manse, manumit, manuscript, marcescent, margin, mass (2), mat, matriculate, matrix, mature, matutinal, maxillar (maxillary), maximum, mediate, medical, medicate, medieval, meditate, mediterranean, medium, medullar (medullary), meliorate, mellifluous, memento, mendacity, mendicant, menses, menstruous, mensuration, mephitis, mere (2), meretricious, merganser, merge, mica, migrate, mile, militate, militia, mill, millennium, minor, mint (1), minus, minuscule, minute, miscellaneous, miser, missal, missile, mission, mitigate, mittimus, mix, mob (1), moderate, modicum, modulate, molar, molecule, mollusc, monetary, monger, morose, mortar (1) (morter), moult, mount (1), mucus, mulct, multangular, multifarious, multiple, muriatic, muricated, muscle (2) (mussel), must (2), mutable, mute (1), mutilate.

nascent, nasturtium, natation, nebula, nefarious, neglect, negotiate,

nemoral, nescient, neuter, nigrescent, nihilist, nimbus, nincompoop, node, nomenclator, nominal, nominate, non-, nondescript, nonentity, nones, nonplus, noon, normal, nostrum, notation, notorious, November, noxious, nucleus, nude, nugatory, numeral, nun, nutation, nutriment, nutritious.

ob-, obdurate, obese, obfuscate, object, oblate, obliterate, obloquy, obnoxious, obscene, obsecrate, obsequious, obsidian, obsolescent, obsolete, obstetric, obstinate, obstreperous, obstriction, obstruct, obtrude, obverse, obviate, obvious, occiput, occult, octangular, octant, October, octogenarian, octoroon, ocular, odium, offer, officinal, olfactory, omen, omentum, omit, omnibus, omniscient, omnivorous, operate, oppidan, opponent, opprobrious, optimism (*with* Gk. *suffix*), oral, orc, ordinal, ordinate, oscillate, osculate, osseous, ossifrage, ostensible, otiose, oviform.

pabulum, pact, pagan, pageant, pall (1), palliate, pallid, pallor, palm (2), palpitate, palustral, panicle, papilionaceous, papillary, par, parietal, parse, participate, parturient, passerine, pastor, patera, patrician, pauper, pax, pea, pear, peccable, pectinal, peculate, pedal, pedestrian, pediment, peduncle, pejorative, pelt (1), pelvis, pen (1), penates, pendulous, pendulum, penetrate, peninsula, penny (*with* E. *suffix*), pent, penultimate, penumbra, per-, perambulate, percolate, percussion, perennial, perfidious, perfoliate, perforate, perfunctory, periwinkle (1), permeate, permit, penetrate, perquisite, perspicuous, pervade, pervicacious, pervious, pessimist, petulant, piacular, pica, picture, pigment, pilch, pile (1), pile (3), pile (4), piles, pillow, pin, pine (1), pine (2), pinnate, pipe, pipkin (*with* E. *suffix*), Pisces, pistil, pit, pitch (1), placable, placenta, plangent, plant, plantigrade, plaudit, plausible, plenary, plenipotentiary, plumbago, pluperfect, plurisy (*misformed*), pole (1), pollen, pollute, ponder, pope, poppy, populate, porcine, port (2), portend, posse, possess, post (1), post-, post-date, posterior, posthumous (postumous), post-meridian (pomeridian), post-mortem, post-obit, postpone, postscript, postulate, potation, potent, pound (1), pour, Prætor (Pretor), pre-, precarious, precentor, precession, precinct, preclude, precocious, precursor, predatory, predecessor, predicate, predict, predominate, pre-emption, pre-exist, prehensile, premature, premeditate, premium, preponderate, prepossess, preposterous, prescribe, preter-, pretermit, preternatural, prevaricate, prevent, previous, primeval, prior (1), private, pro-, probe, proclivity, proconsul, procrastinate, procreate, proctor, procumbent, produce, proficient, profligate, profuse, prog?, prohibit, prolate, proletarian, prolocutor, promiscuous, promontory, promote, promulgate, propagate, propel, propensity, propitious, propound, propulsion, proscribe, prosecute, prospect, prosperous, prostitute, prostrate, protect, protract, protrude, protuberant, prove, provide, proviso, provost, prurient, publican, pugilism, pugnacious, pulmonary, pulsate, pulse (2), punctate (punctated), punctuate, puncture, pungent, punt (1), pupa, puritan, pus, pusillanimous.

quadragesima, quadrant, quadrate, quadrennial, quadrilateral, quadrillion, quadruped, quandary, quarto, quaternary, quaternion, querimonious, querulous, query, quibble, quiddity, quidnunc, quiescent, quiet, quillet, quinary, quincunx, quinquagesima, quinquangular, quinquennial, quintillion, quip, quorum, quota, quotient (or F.—L.).

rabid, radial, radiant, radius, radix, rancid, ranunculus, rapacious, rape (1), rape (2), rapid (or F.—L.), rapt, raptorial, rapture, rasorial, ratio, raucous, re-, red- (or F.—L), real (1), rebus, recant, recede, recess, recession, recipe, reciprocal, recline, recondite, recriminate, recrudescence, rectilineal (rectilinear), recumbent, recuperative, recur, redact, redintegration, reduce, redundant, reduplicate, refel, reflect, refluent, refract, refragable, refrigerate, refulgent, refund, regalia, regenerate, regimen, regnant, regress, regular, rejuvenate, relapse, relax, relegate, reluctant, remit, remonstrate, remora, remote, remunerate, renovate, repel, repine, reprehend, reprobate, reproduce, repudiate, repulse, requiem, requiescence, resilient, resolve, resonant, resplendent, resuscitate, retaliate, reticent, retina, retro- (or F. *from* L.), retrocession, retrograde, retrospect, reverberate, revolve, ridiculous, rigid, rite, rivulet, rodent, rostrum, rotary, rugose, ruminate.

sacrament, sagacious, Sagittarius, salient, saliva, saltation, salubrious, salute, sanatory, sanctity, sane, sapid, satiate, saturate, savin (savine, sabine), scale (3), scalpel, scan, scape (1), scapular, sciolist, scour (1), scribe, scrofula, scrutiny, scurrile, scutage, scuttle (1), se-, sebaceous, secant, secede, seclude, secure, sedate, seduce, sedulous, segment, segregate, select, semi-, seminary, senary, senile, senior, sensual, separate, September, septenary, septennial, septuagenary, serene, series, serrated, serum, service (tree), sexagenary, Sexagesima, sexennial, sextant, sextuple, shambles, shingle (1), short, shrine, sibilant, sicker (siker), sickle, sidereal, silex, silvan (sylvan), simile, simious, simulate, simultaneous, sinciput, sine, sinecure, single, sinister, sinus, sir-reverence, situate, sock, solar, sole (1), sol-fa, solicitous, soliloquy, solve, somnambulist (*with* Gk. *suffix*), somniferous, sonorous, soporiferous, soporific, sparse, species, specimen, spectator (*or* F. *from* L.), specular, spelt, spend, spike (2), splendor (splendour, *or* F. *from* L.), sponsor, spontaneous, spoom, spume, spurious, squalid, stagnate, stamen, stannary, status, stellar, sternutation, stertorous, still (2) (*or* F.—L.), stimulate, stipend, stolid, stop, strap, stratum, street, strenuous, striated, strict, strident, strigil, stringent, strop, student, stultify, stupendous, sub- (*or* F.—L.), subacid, subaqueous, subdivide, subjacent, subjugate, subjunctive, sublunar, submit, subordinate, subpoena, subscribe, subsequent, subserve, subside, substratum, subtend, subter-, subterranean, subterraneous, subtract, succinct, succuba, succumb, sudatory, suffix, suffocate, suffuse, suggest, sulcated, sulphur, sumptuary, super-, superadd, superannuate, supercilious, supereminent, supererogation, superficies, superfluous, superstructure, supervene, supervise, supine, supplicate, suppress, suppurate, supra-, supramundane, sur- (1), surd, surreptitious, surrogate, sus-.

tabid, tacit, tact, tamarisk, tandem, tangent, Taurus, tedious, teetotum (totum), tegument, telluric, temple (1), temper, temulent, tenacious, tenet, tense (2), tentacle, tentative, tepid, ternary, terrene, terrestrial, terrific, terse, tertiary, tesselate, testaceous, testimony, textile, tibia, tile, timorous, tincture, tinge, tint, tintinnabulation, tiro (tyro), toga, tolerate, torpedo, torpid, torque, tract (1), tract (2), tractable, tradition, traduce, trans-, transcend, transcribe, transept. transfer, transfix, transfuse, transient, translucent, transmarine, transmit, transmute, transom, transpicuous, transpire, transverse, tri- (*or* Gk.; *or* F. *from* L. *or* Gk.), tricentenary, triennial, trifoliate, triforium, triform, trilateral, trilingual, triliteral, trine, trinomial, tripartite, triplicate, trireme, trisect, trite, triturate, triumvir, Triune, trivet, truncate, tuber, tumid, tumulus, tunic, turbid, turgid, turtle (1), turtle (2), tutelage (*with* F. *suffix*), tutelar.

ulterior, ultimate, ultra-, ultramundane, umbel, unanimous, uncial, undulate, unguent, uniliteral, unite, univocal, urbane, urge, ursine, ut, uvula, uxorious.

vaccinate, vacuum, vagary, valediction, vapid, varicose, variegate, various, vascular, vehicle, velocipede, venereal, venous, ventilate, ventral, ventriloquist, Venus, veracious, verbena, verge (2), vermicular, vernacular, vernal, verse, vertebra, vertex, vertigo, vesicle, vesper, vest, vestibule, veteran, veterinary, veto, viaduct, vibrate, vicissitude, victor, videlicet, vilipend, villa, vincible, vinculum, vindicate, violate, virago, virgate, viridity, viscera, vitreous, vivid, viviparous, vivisection, vomit, vortex, vote, vulnerable, vulture.

wall, wick (2), wine.

French from Latin. abase, abate, abatis, abeyance, ability, ablative, able, ablution, abolish, abound, abridge, absent, abstain, abstention, abundance, abuse, accent, accept, accident, accompany, accomplice, accomplish, accord, accost, account, accoutre, accredit, accrue, accuse, accustom, acerbity, acetous, achieve, acquaint, acquit, act, adage, address, adieu, adjoin, adjourn, adjudge, adjust, administer, admire, admonish, adroit, adulation, advance, advantage, adventure, adverb, adverse, advertise, advice, advise, advowson, affable, affair, affect, affeer, affiance, affiliation, affinity, affirm, affix, affluence, affront, affy, age, aggrandise, aggress, aggrieve, agile, agistment, aglet, agree, ague, ah, aid, aim, aisle, alas, alb, alien, align (aline), aliment, aliquot, allege, alley, allow (1), allow (2), alloy, ally, altercation, altitude, alum, ambition, amble, ambry (aumbry), ameliorate, amenable, amend, amends, amenity, amerce, amiable, amice (1), amity, ammunition, amorous, amort, amount, ample, amulet, amuse, ancestor, ancient (1), ancient (2), andiron?, angle (1), anguish, animosity, annals, annates, anneal (2), annex, announce, annoy, annual, anoint, antique, antler, apart, appal, appanage, apparel, appeal, appear, appease, append, appertain, appetite, apply, appoint, apportion, appraise, apprentice, apprize, approach, approbation, approve, appurtenance, April, apron, apropos, aquiline, arable, arbour, arc, arch (1), archer, ardent, arête, argent, argue, arm (2), armature, armistice, armour, arms, army, arraign, arrant, arrears, arrest, arris, arrive, arson, art, article, artifice, artillery, ascertain, ashlar (ashler), asperity, aspire, assail, assart, assault, assay, assemble, assent, assess, assets, assign, assist, assize (1), assize (2), assoil, assort, assuage, assure, astonish, astound, atrocity, attain, attaint, attemper, attempt, attend, attrition, auburn, audacious, audience, augment, aunt, auspice, austral, author, autumn, avail, avalanche, avarice, avaunt, avenge, avenue, aver, avidity, avoid, avoirdupois, avouch, avow (1), avow (2).

bail (1), bailiff, bails?, baize, balance, barb (1), barbel, barber, barberry, barnacles, baron, base (1), bass (1), bassoon, bate (1), bate (2), batter (1), batter (2), battery, battle, bay (1), bay (2), bay (3), bay (4), bay (5), bay (6), bayard, beagle?, beast, beatify, beatitude, beau, beauty, beaver (3) (bever), beef. beldam, belle,

benediction, benefice, benefit, benevolence, benign, benison, bestial, beverage, bevy, bezel?, bias, bile (1), bill (3), billet (1), billion, biscuit, bivalve, blandish, boil (1), bonny, bounty, bowel, bowl (1), breve, brief (1), brief (2), broach, brochure, brocket, broker, brooch, bruit, brute, buckle, buckler, budge (1), bugle (1), bugle (2), bullace, bullet, bullion, bustard, buzzard.

cabbage (1), cable, cage, caitiff, calamity, calcine, caldron (cauldron), calk (caulk), calkin, callous, caloric, calumny, camp, campagnol, campion, canal, cancel, candid, candour, canker, capable, capital (1), capital (2), capital (3), capitation, capsule, captain, captious, captive, carbon, card (2), careen, Carfax, carillon, carminative, carnage, carnation (1), carnation (2), carpet, carrion, cartilage, case (1), case (2), casement, casket, cassation, catch, catchpole, cater, cater-cousin, caterpillar, cates, cattle, caudle, cauliflower, cause, causeway, caution, cave, cavil, cease, ceil (ciel), celerity, celestial, cement, censer, centipede (centiped), centuple, century, cerebral, ceremony, certain, certify, cervical, cess, cessation, cession, chafe, chain, chaldron, chalet, chalice, challenge, chamfer, champagne, champaign, champion, chance, chancel, chancellor, chancery, chandelier, chandler, change, channel, chant, chapel, chaperon, chapiter, chaplain, chaplet, chapter, charity, charm (1), charnel, chase (1), chase (2), chase (3), chase (4), chaste, chasten, chastise, chasuble, chateau, chatelaine, chattels, chawdron, cheat, cherish, chevalier, cheveril, chevin, chevron, chief, chieftain, chignon, chisel, chivalry, chive, chum, cicatrice, cinque, circle, circuit, circumstance, cit, cite, citizen, city, cive, claim, clamour, clandestine, claret, clarify, clarion, class, clause, clavicle, clear, clef, clement, clerestory, client, cloister, close (1), close (2), closet, clove (1), clove (3), cloy, coarse, coast, coddle, code, codicil, cognisance, cohort, coign, coil (1), coil (2), coin, coistrel, collar, collation, colleague (1), colleague (2), collect, college, collet, colony, colour, colporteur, columbine, combat, combustion, comfit, comfort, comfrey, command, commence, comment, commerce, commination, commiseration, commission, commodious, common, commotion, commune, compact (1), company, compare, compass, compassion, compatible, compatriot, compeer, compel, compendious, competent, compile, complain, complaisant, complexion, complicity, compline, comport, composition, compost, compress, comprise, compromise, compunction, concave, conceal, conceit, conceive, concentre, conception, concern, concise, conclave, concord, concordant, concordat, concourse, concubine, concupiscence, concussion, condemn, condense, condescend, condign, condiment, condition, conduit, confess, configuration. confine, confirm, conflagration, conform, confound, confraternity, confront, confuse, confute, congé (congee), congeal, congestion, conjecture, conjoin, conjugal, conjure, connive, connoisseur, conquer, conscience, consecutive, consent, conserve, consider, consign, consist, console (1), console (2), consonant, conspire, constable, constant, constellation, consternation, constrain, consult, contagion, contain, contemn, contend, content, contest, continent, continue, contract (2), contrary, contrast, contravene, contretemps, contrite, control, controversy, contumacy, contumely, convene, convention, converse, convert, convey, convoy, cony (coney), copious, copperas, copy, corbel, corby, cordial, corduroy, core, cormorant, corn (2), cornelian, corner, cornet, coronal, coroner, coronet, corporal (1), corporal (2), corps, corpse (corse), corpulent, correspond, corrode, corset, corslet (corselet), corvée, costive, couch, council, counsel, count (1), count (2), countenance, counter, counterbalance, counterfeit, countermand, counterpane (1), counterpane (2), counterpart, counterpoint, counterpoise, countersign, countervail, country, country-dance, county, couple, courage, course, court (1), court (2), courteous, courtesy, courtier, cousin, covenant, cover, coverlet, covert, covet, covey, covin, coward, cowl (2), coy (1), cozen, cranny, crape, craven, crayon, crease (1), creel, cresset, crest, crevice, crew, crime, crinoline, crone, crucial, crucify, cruel, crust, cry, cuckold, cuckoo, cue (1), cue (2), cuisses, cull, cullion, cullis (1), cullis (2), culpable, culprit, culture, culverin, cupidity, curb, cure, curfew, curious, current, curtail, curtain, curtilage, cushion, custard, custom, cutlass, cutler, cutlet.

dainty, dam (2), damage, dame, damn, damsel, dan, dandelion, danger, date (1), daub, daunt, dean, debate, debonair, debouch, debt, decadence, decamp, decay, decease, deceive, decent, deception, decide, decimal, decision, declare, declension, decline, declivity, decollation, decomposition, decrease, decree, decry, decuple, deface, defame, default, defeasance, defeat, defence, defend, defer (1), defer (2), defile (2), define, deflour (deflower), deforce, deform, defraud, defy, deglutition, degrade, degree, deify, deign, deity, delay, delectable, delicious, delight, deliver, deluge, demand, demean (1), demeanour, demerit, demesne, demi-, demise, demolish, demoralise, demur, demure, demy, denier, denizen, denote, denouement, denounce, dentifrice, deny, deodand, depart, depend, deplore, deploy, deport, deposit, deposition, depot, deprave, deprive, depute, derive, descant, descend, descry, desert (1), desert (2), deserve, deshabille, design, desire, desist, despair, despise, despite, despoil, dessert, destine, destroy, detail, detain, detention, determine, detest, detriment, deuce (1), deuce (2), devest, device, devise, devoid, devoir, devour, devout, diction, die (2), differ, difficulty, dignify, dignity, dilate, diligent, dime, dimension, diminish, dine, dinner, disadvantage, disagree, disallow, disappoint, disarm, disaster, disavow, discern, disciple, disclaim, disclose, discolour, discomfit, discomfort, disconcert, discontinue, discord, discount, discountenance, discourage, discourse, discourteous, discover, discreet, discrepant, disdain, disenchant, disfigure, disgorge, disgrace, disgust, dishevel, dishonest, dishonour, disinterested, disjoin, disjoint, disloyal, dismal, dismantle, dismember, dismount, disobey, disoblige, disorder, disparage, disparity, dispense, dispeople, displace, displant, display, displease, disport, disposition, dispossess, dispraise, disproportion, disprove, dispute, disqualify, dissemble, disservice, dissever, dissimilar, dissimulation, dissonant, dissuade, distain, distant, distemper (1), distemper (2), distil, distinct, distinguish, distrain, distress, district, disturb, ditty, diverse (divers), divert, divine, divorce, divulge, docile, doctor, doctrine, document, dolour, domain, domestic, domicile, dominical, dominion, donation, dormant, dorsal, double, doublet, doubt, douceur, dowager, dower, dowle?, dozen, dress, ducal, duchess, duchy, ductile, due, duke, dulcet, dungeon, duplicity, durance, duration, dure, duress, duty.

eager, eagle, ebriety, ebullition, echelon, eclaircissement, edify, edition, efface, effect, efficient, efflorescence, effort, effrontery, eglantine, eisel, elecampane, elegant, eligible, élite, eloign, eloquent, em-, embattle (2), embellish, embezzle?, emblements, embonpoint, embouchure, embowel, embrace, emmew, emollient, emolument, empale, empanel, emperor, empire, employ, empower, empress, emprise, emulsion, en-, enable, enact, enamour, encamp, encase, enceinte, enchain, enchant, enchase, encircle, encline, enclose, encompass, encore, encounter, encourage, encumber?, endanger, endeavour, endorse, endow, endue (1), endure, enemy, enew, enfeeble, enfilade, enforce, engender, engine, engrain, engross, enhance, enjoin, enjoy, enlace, enlarge, enmity, ennoble, ennui, enormous, enounce, enquire, enrage, enrich, enrol, ensample, ensconce, ensign, ensue, ensure, entablature, entail, enter, enterprise, entertain, entice, entire, entitle, entrails, entrance (1), entrance (2), entreat, entrench?, envenom, environ, envoy, envy, equanimity, equinox, equipoise, equipollent, equity, equivalent, erode, err, errant, error, escape, escheat, escritoire, escuage, escutcheon, especial, espouse, esquire, essay, essence, establish, estate, esteem, estovers, estrange, estreat, eternal, etiolate, evade, evasion, evident, ewer, exact (2), exalt, examine, example, excavation, exceed, excel, except, excess, exchange, excite, exclaim, excrescence, excretion, excuse, execute, exemplar, exemplify, exempt, exequies, exercise, exhale, exhort, exile, exorbitant, experience, expert, expire, explain, explode, exploit, explore, exposition, expound, express, exterior, extradition, extravagant, extreme, extrinsic, exuberant, eyas, eyre.

fable, fabric, face, facetious, facile, faction, faculty, fade, fail, faint, fair (2), fairy, faith, falcon, fallacy, false, fame, famine, fanatic, fantigue, farce, farcy, farm, farrier, fascine, fash, fashion, fate, fatigue, faucet, fault, favour, fawn (2), fay, fealty, feasible, feast, feat, feature, febrile, fecundity, federal, feeble, feign, felicity, female, feminine, fence, fend, fenugreek, ferocity, ferrule, fertile, fervent, fescue, fess, festal, fester, festival, fête, fetid, fibre, fidelity, fie, fierce, figure, filament, file (1), fillet, final, finance, fine (1), finish, firm (1), firmament, fiscal, fissure, fitz, fix, flaccid, flagrant, flail, flambeau, flame, flatulent, flavour, fleur-de-lis, flexible, flock (2), floss, flounce (2), flour, flourish, flower, flue (1), fluid, flush (4), fluviatile, flux, foible, foil (1), foil (2), foin, foison, foliage, follicle, folly, foment, font (2), fool, for- (3), force (1), force (2), foreclose, foreign, forest, forfeit, forge, forjudge, form, formidable, fort, fortify, fortitude, fortress, fortune, fosse, fossil, foster (2), found (1), found (2), founder, fount, fraction, fracture, fragile, fragment, fragrant, frail (1), frail (2), franion, fraternal, fraternity, fratricide (1), fraud, fray (1), fray (3), frequent, fret (3), fret (4), friable, friar, fricassee, friction, frieze (2), fringe, frippery, fritter (1), fritter (2), front, frontal, frontier, frontispiece, frontlet, frounce, fructify, frugal, fruit, fruition, frumenty (furmenty, furmety), frush, fry (1), fry (2), fuel, fugitive, full (2), fume, fumitory, function, fund, fundament, funeral, furious, furnace, furtive, fury, fuse (2), fusee (1), fusee (2), fusil (1), fusil (2), fust (1), fust (2), fusty, futile, future.

gall (2), gall (3), gammon (1), gaol (jail), garner, garnet, gaud, gem, gender (1), gender (2), general, generous, genial, genital, genitive, genre, genteel, gentian, gentile, gentle, gentry, genuflection (genuflexion), germ, german (germane), gestation, gibbous, gill (4), gimbals, gin (2), gin (3), gingerly, gist, gizzard, glacial, glacier, glacis, glair, glaive, glance, gland, glebe, globe, glory, glue, glut, glutton, goblet, gorge, gorgeous, gourd, gout (1), gout (2), grace,

gradation, grade, grail (1), grail (2), grain, gramercy, grampus, grand, grandeur, grange, grant, gratify, gratitude, gratuity, grave (2), gravy, grease, grece, griddle (gridiron), grief, grieve, grill, grocer, grog, grogram, gromwell, gross, grume, gules, gullet, gully, gutter, guttural.

habiliment, habit, habitable, habitant, habitation, habitude, haslets, hatchment, haughty, haut-goût, hawser, hearse, heir, herb, heritage, hibernal, hideous, homage, homicide, honest, honour, horrible, horror, hospice, hospitable, hospital, host (1), host (2), hostage, hostel, hostler (ostler), hotel, human, humble, humid, humility, humour.

ides, ignition, ignoble, ignominy, ignore, iliac, illation, illegible, illiberal, illicit, illusion, illustrious, im- (1), im- (4), image, imagine, imbecile, imbibe, imbrue (embrew), immaterial, immeasurable, immediate, immemorial, immense, immobility, immodest, immoral, immortal, immovable, immunity, immure, immutable, impair, impale, impalpable, imparity, impart, impartial, impassable, impassible, impassioned, impassive, impatient, impeach, impearl?, impenetrable, impenitent, imperative, imperceptible, imperfect, imperial, imperil, imperishable, impersonal, impertinent, impiety, impious, implacable, implant, implead, implore, imply, import, importable, importune, imposition, impossible, impotent, impoverish, impregnable, imprint, imprison, improbable, impromptu, improper, improve, imprudent, impudent, impugn, impure, impute, in- (2), in- (3), inability, inaccessible, inaction, inadmissible, inalienable, inanition, inapproachable, inapt, inattention, incage, incapable, incapacity, incarnation, incase, incense (2), incertitude, incest, incident, incircle, incise, incite, incivil, inclement, incline, inclose, incommensurable, incommode, incommunicable, incommutable, incomparable, incompatible, incompetent, incomprehensible, inconceivable, inconsiderable, inconsolable, inconstant, incontestable, incontinent (1), incontinent (2), incontrollable, inconvenient, incorrect, increase, incredible, incrust, incumber, incurable, incursion, indebted, indecent, indecision, indefatigable, indefeasible (AF.), indelible, indelicate, indemnify, indemnity, indict, indiction, indifferent, indigent, indignation, indirect, indiscreet, indisputable, indissoluble, indistinct, indite, indivisible, indocile, indubitable, indue (2), indulgence, industry, ineffable, ineffaceable, inefficacious, ineligible, ineloquent, inept, inequality, inestimable, inevitable, inexcusable, inexorable, inexpedient, inexperience, inexpert, inexpiable, inexplicable, inextinguishable, inextricable, infallible, infamy, infect, infelicity, infer, inferior, infernal, infest, infidel, infirmary, infirmity, inflame, inflexible, inflorescence, influence, inform, infraction, infrangible, infuse, infusible, ingender, ingenious, inglorious, ingrain, ingratitude, ingredient, inhabit, inherit, inhospitable, inhuman, inhume, inimitable, iniquity, injudicious, injure, injustice, innavigable, innocent, innumerable, inoffensive, inofficial, inoperative, inopportune, inquest, inquietude, insatiable, inscrutable, insect, insensible, inseparable, insidious, insincere, insipid, insist, insobriety, insolent, insolidity, insoluble, inspire, instability, instance, instate, instil, instinct, instrument, insubjection, insufferable, insult, insuperable, insupportable, insure, insurmountable, insurrection, intellect, intelligence, intemperance, intend, intent, inter, intercede, intercept, interchange, intercostal, intercourse, interest (1), interest (2), interfere, interjection, interlace, interlard, interlocution, intermeddle, intermediate, intern, interpellation, interposition, interpret, interstice, interval, intervene, interview, intestine, intituled, intolerable, intractable, intreat (with E. prefix), intrench (with E. prefix), intrinsic, introit, intuition, intumescence, inure, inurn, inutility, invade, invalid, invaluable, invariable, invasion, inveigle (AF.), invent, inverse, invest, invincible, inviolable, invisible, invite, invoice, invoke, involve, invulnerable, ir- (1), ir- (2), ire, irreclaimable, irreconcilable, irrecoverable, irrecuperable, irredeemable, irrefragable, irrefutable, irregular, irrelevant, irreligious, irremediable, irremissible, irremovable, irreparable, irreprehensible, irrepressible, irreproachable, irreprovable, irresistible, irrespective, irretrievable, irreverent, irrevocable, irrision, irruption, isle, issue, ivory.

jail, jamb, jargon, jaundice, jaunty, jaw, jeer?, jelly, jeopardy, jesses, jest, jet (1), jetsam, jetty, jewel, jocund, (john)dory, join, joint, joist, jostle, journal, journey, joust (just), jovial, joy, judge, judicature, judicial, judicious, juggler, juice, July, jurisdiction, jurisprudence, jurist, juror, jury, jury(mast)?, just (1), just (2), justice, justify, justle, jut, juvenile, juxtaposition.

kedge (1), kennel (1), kennel (2), kerchief, kestrel, ketch, kickshaws, kitten.

laborious, labour, lace, lacrosse, lake (1), lament, lamprey, lance, lancet, language, languish, languor, larceny, lard, large, largess, lash (1), lash (2), lassitude, latchet, lateen, Latin, latitude, launch (1) (lanch), laundress, laurel, lave, lavish, laxative, leal, lease (1), leash, leaven, lectern, lection, lecture, legacy, legal, legate, legend, legerdemain, legible, legion, legist, legume, leisure, lenity, lentil, lentisk, lesion, lesson, lethal, letter, lettuce, levee, level, lever, leveret, levity, levy, liable, liaison, liane, libation, libel, liberal, liberty, libidinous, library, licence, license, licentious, lien, lieu, lieutenant, ligament, ligature, limit, limn, limpid, line, lineage, lineament, liniment, linnet, lintel, liquefy, liqueur, liquid, liquor, literal, literature, litigious, litter (1), litter (2), livery, livid, lizard, local, loin, longitude, lorimer, loriot, lounge, lovage, loyal, luce, lucre, luminary, luminous, lunatic, lune, lunge, lupine, luscious?, lush, lustre (2), lute (2), luxation, luxury, lym.

mace (1), madam, mademoiselle, magistrate, magnanimity, magnify, mail (1), mainour, maintain, majesty, maladministration, maladroit, malady, malapert, malcontent (malecontent), male, malediction, malformation, malice, malign, malison, mall (1), mallard, malleable, mallet, maltreat, malversation, manacle, manchet?, manciple, mandate, mandrel, mange, manger, manifest, maniple, manner, manœuvre, manor, mansion, mantel, mantle, manual, manufacture, manure, map, marble, march (2)? (or G.?), March (3), marine, marish, marital, maritime, market, marl, marmoset, marry, mart, martial, martlet (2), marvel, mascle, masculine, master, mastery, material, maternal, matins (mattins), matricide, matrimony, matron, matter (1), matter (2), maugre, maul, maundy, mauve, maxim, may (2), mayor, meagre, mean (3), measure, meddle, mediation, mediator, medicine, mediocre, medley, melée, member, membrane, memoir, memory, menace, mend, meniver (minever, miniver), -ment, mental, mention, menu, mercenary, mercer, merchandise, merchant, mercury, mercy, meridian, merit, merle, mesne, mess (1), mess (2), message, messenger, messuage, mew (3), milfoil, millet, million, mince, minim, minish, minister, minstrel, minuet, miracle, mirage, mirror, mis- (2), misadventure, misalliance, mischance, mischief, miscount, miscreant, miserable, misgovern, misjudge, misnomer, misprise (misprize), misprision, miss (2), missive, Mister (Mr.), mistress, misuse, mobile, mock, mode, modern, modest, modify, moiety, moil, moist, molest, mollify, moment, money, monition, monster, monument, mood (2), Moor (3), mop (1), moral, morbid, mordacity, Morian, morsel, mortal, mortar (2), mortgage, mortify, mortmain, mortuary, motet, motion, motive, mould (2), mound, mount (2), mountain, move, mucilage, mule, mulled, mullet (1), mullet (2), multiply, multitude, multure, mundane, municipal, munificence, muniment, munition, mural, murmur, murrain, muscle (1), muse (1), mustard (with Teut. suffix), muster, mutiny, mutual, muzzle, mystery (2) (mistery).

naive, napery, napkin (with E. suffix), narration, nasal, natal, nation, native, natty, nature, naval, nave (2), navew, navigable, navigation, navy, neat (2), necessary, negation, negligence, nephew, nerve, net (2), newel, nias, nice, niece, noble, nocturn, noisome (with E. suffix), nonage, nonchalant, nonpareil, notable, notary, notch, note, notice, notify, notion, notoriety, noun, nourish, novel, novice, noyau, nuance, nuisance, nu'l, number, numbles, numeration, numerous, nuncupative, nuptial, nurse, nurture, nutritive.

obedient, obeisance, obey, obit, objurgation, oblation, oblige, oblique, oblivion, oblong, obscure, obsequies, observe, obstacle, obtain, obtest, obtuse, occasion, occident, occupy, occur, octave, octroi, odour, offend, office, ointment, omelet, omnipotent, omnipresent, onerous, onion, opacity, opaque, opinion, oppilation, opportune, opposite, oppress, oppugn, optative, option, opulent, or (3), oracle, oration, orator, orb, ordain, order, ordinance, ordinary, ordination, ordnance, ordure, oriel, orient, orifice, Oriflamme, origin, oriole, orison, orle, ormolu, ornament, orpiment, orpine (orpin), osprey, ostentation, ostler, ounce (1), oust, outrage, oval, ovation, overt, overture, oyer, oyes (oyez).

pace, pacify, page (2), pail, paint, painter, pair, palace, palate, palatine, pale (1), pale (2), palette, palisade, pall (2), pallet (1), palliasse, palm (1), palpable, pane, panel (pannel), pannage, pannier, pansy, pantler, pantry, papa, papal, papiermaché, parachute, paraffine, paramount, paramour, parboil, parcel, parcener, pardon, pare, parent, parget, parity, parlous, parricide, parry, parsimony, parsnep (parsnip), parson, part, parterre, partial, participle, particle, partition, partner, party, parvenu, pass, passage, passion, passive, passport, pastern, pastille, pate, patent, paternal, patient, patois, patrimony, patron, pattern, paucity, paunch, pave, pavilion, pawl, pawn (2), pay (1), pay (2), paynim (painim), peace, peach (2), peal, pearl, peasant, peccant, pectoral, peculiar, pecuniary, pedicel (pedicle), pedigree, peel (1), peel (2), peel (3), peel (4), peep (1), peep (2), peer (1), peer (3), peise (peize), peitrel, pelerine, pelisse, pell, pellet, pellicle, pellitory (1) (paritory), pell-mell, pellucid, pelt (2), pen (2), penchant, pencil, pendant, penitent, pennon (pennant), penny-royal, pensile, pension, pensive, penthouse, penury, people, peradventure, perceive, perch (1), perchance, perdition, perdurable, peregrination, peremptory, perfect, perforce, perfume, peril, perish, perjure, perk, permanent, permutation, pernicious, peroration, perpendicular, perpetual, perplex,

perry, persecute, persevere, persiflage, persist, person, perspective, perspicacity, perspiration, persuade, pert, pertain, pertinacity, pertinent, perturb, pervert, pest, pester, pestilent, pestle, petard, petiole, petition, petronel, pie (1), pie (2), pie (3), Piepowder Court, pierce?, piety, pigeon, pile (2), pill (1), pill (2), pillage, pillar, pimp, pimpernel, pinion, pinnacle, pioneer, pious, pip (3), pity, placid, plagiary, plague, plaice, plain, plaint, plaintiff, plaintive, plait, plan, plane (1), plane (2), plank, plantain (1), plat (2), plate, plateau, platform, platitude, platoon, platter, plea, pleach (plash), plead, please, pleasure, plebeian, plenitude, plenty, pliable, pliant, pliers, plight (2), plot (1), plover, plumage, plumb, plume, plummet, plump (2), plunge, plural, plush, pluvial, ply, poignant, point, poise, poison, poitrel (peitrel), polish, pomegranate, pommel, ponent, poniard, pontiff, pony, pool (2), poor, poplar, popular, porch, porcupine, pork, porpoise (porpess), port (1), port (3), portcullis, Porte, porter (1), porter (3), portesse (portos, portous), portion, portrait, portray, position, positive, possible, post (2), posterity, postern, postil, posture, potable, potch, potion, poult, poultice, pounce (1), pounce (2), pourpoint, pourtray, poverty, powder, power, prairie, praise, pray, pre- (or L.), preach, preamble, prebend, precaution, precede, precept, precious, precipice, precise, preconceive, predestine, predetermine, predilection, preeminence, pre-engage, preface, prefect, prefer, prefigure, prefix, pregnant (1), pregnant (2), prejudge, prejudice, prelate, preliminary, prelude, premier, premise (premiss), premonish, prentice, preoccupy, preordain, prepare, prepay, prepense, preposition, prerogative, presage, prescience, presence, present (1), present (2), presentiment, preserve, preside, press (1), press (2), prestige, presume, pretend, preter- (or L.), preterit (preterite), pretext, prevail, prey, prial, price, pride?, prim, prime (1), prime (2), primitive, primogeniture, primordial, primrose, prince, principal, principle, print, prior (2), prise (prize), prison, pristine, privet?, privilege, privy, prize (1), prize (2), prize (3), pro- (or L., or Gk.), probable, probation, probity, proceed, proclaim, procure, prodigal, prodigy, profane, profess, proffer, profit, profound, progenitor, progeny, progress, project, prolific, prolix, prolong, promenade, prominent, promise, prompt, prone, pronoun, pronounce, proof, proper, propinquity, proportion, proposition, propriety, prorogue, prose, protest, provender, proverb, province, provision, provoke, prowess, proximity, proxy, prude, prudent, prune (1), pry, puberty, public, publication, publish, puce, puerile, puisne, puissant, pule, pullet, pulp, pulpit, pulse (1), pulverise, pumice, pummel, punch (1), punch (2), puncheon (1), puncheon (2), punctual, punish, puny, pupil (1), pupil (2), puppet, puppy, pur-, purchase, pure, purfle, purge, purify, purity, purl (2), purl (3), purlieu, purloin, purport, purpose (2), purslain (purslane), pursue, pursy, purtenance, purulent, purvey, purview, push, pustule, putative, putrefy, putrid.

quadrangle, quadruple, quail (1), quaint, qualify, quality, quantity, quarrel (1), quarrel (2), quarry (1), quarry (2), quart, quartan, quarter, quartern, quash, quatrain, quatrefoil, quest, question, queue, quilt, quintain, quintessence, quintuple, quire (1), quit, quite, quoin, quoit (coit)?, quote, quotidian, quotient (or L.).

rabbet, race (3), raceme, radical, radish, rage, ragout, rail (1), rail (2), raisin, rally (1), ramify, rampart, rancour, ransom, rapid (or L.), rapine, rare, rase, rash (2), rash (3), rash (4), rate (1), rate (2), ratify, ration, ravage, rave, raven (2), ravine, ravish, ray (1), ray (2), raze, razor, re-, red- (or L.), realm, rear (2), reason, reasty, rebate, rebel, rebound, rebuke, receive, recent, receptacle, recheat, recite, reclaim, recluse, recognise, recoil, recollect, recommend, recompense, reconcile, reconnoitre, record, recount, recourse, recover, recreant, recreation, recruit, rectangle, rectify, rectitude, recusant, reddition, redeem, redolent, redouble, redoubtable, redound, redress, refection, refer, refine, reform, refrain (1), refrain (2), refuge, refuse, refute, regal, regent, regicide, regiment, region, register, reglet, rehearse, reign, rein, reins, reject, rejoice, rejoin, relate, relay (1), release, relent, relevant, relic, relict, relieve, religion, relinquish, reliquary, relique, relish, rely, remain, remand, remedy, remember, reminiscence, remnant, remorse, remount, remove, renal, rencounter (rencontre), render, rendezvous, rennet (2), renounce, renown, rent (2), renunciation, repair (1), repair (2), repartee, repast, repay, repeal, repeat, repent, repercussion, repertory, repetition, replace, replenish, replete, reply, report, repository, repoussé, represent, repress, reprieve, reprimand, reprint, reproach, reprove, reptile, republic, repugnant, repute, request, require, requite, reredos, rescind, rescript, rescue, research, resemble, resent, reserve, reside, residue, resign, resist, resort, resound, resource, respect, respire, respite, respond, rest (2), restaurant, restitution, restive, restore, restrain, result, resume, resurrection, retail, retain, retard, retention, reticule, retinue, retort, retract, retreat, retrench, retribution, return, reveal, reveillé, revel, revenge, revenue, revere, reverie (revery), reverse, revert, review, revile, revise, revisit, revive, revoke, revulsion, rinse ?, risible, rissole, rival, river, roam, robust, rogation, roil (rile) ?, roistering, roll, romance, romaunt, rondeau, rosemary, rote (1), rotundity, roué, rouge, rouleau, roulette, round, roundel, rout (1 *and* 2), route, routine, rowel, royal, rubasse, rubric, ruby, rude, ruin, rule, rumour, runagate, rundlet (runlet), rupture, rural, ruse, russet, rustic, rut (1), rut (2).

sacerdotal, sack (3), sacred, sacrifice, sacrilege, sacristan (sexton), safe, sage (1), sage (2), sainfoin, saint, salary, saline, sally, salmon, saltier, salutary, salvage, salvation, sample, sanctify, sanctimony, sanction, sanctuary, sanguine, sanicle, sans, sapience, sash (1), satellite, satin, satire, satisfy, saturnine, sauce, saunter, sausage, savage, save, savory, savour, saxifrage, say (3), scabious, scald (1), scamper, scape (2), scarab, scarce, scent, science, scintillation, scion ?, scissors, sconce (1), sconce (2), scorch, scour (2), scourge, scout (1), screw (1), scrip (2), script, scripture, scrivener, scroyles, scruple, scullery, scullion, sculpture, scur, scutcheon, scutiform, seal, séance, search, season, second, secret, secretary, sect, section, secular, sedentary, sediment, sedition, see (2), seel, seignior, sejant, sell (2), semblance, seminal, sempiternal, senate, sennet, sense, sentence, sentiment, sentry, sepal, sept, sepulchre, sequel, sequence, sequester, sere (2), serf, sergeant (serjeant), serious, sermon, serpent, serried, serve, session, set (2), seton, sever, severe, sewer (1), sewer (2), sex, shark, shingles, shirk, siege, sign, signal, signet, signify, silence, similar, similitude, simnel, simple, simpleton, sincere, singular, sir, sire, site, sizar, size (1), skillet, sluice, soar, sober, sociable, soil (1), soil (2), soil (3), soirée, sojourn, solace, solder, soldier, sole (2), sole (3), solemn, solicit, solicitude, solid, soliped, solitary, solitude, solstice, soluble, solution, sombre, somnolence, sorb, sorcery, sordid, sort, sortie, sou, sound (3), source, souse (1), souse (2), souvenir, sovereign, space, spandrel, spawn, special, specify, specious, spectacle, spectre, spencer, spice, spine, pinney, spiracle, spirit, spite, spittle (2), splay, spoil, spoliation, sport, spouse, sprain, sprite (spright), spurge, square, squash, squat, squire (1 *and* 2), stable (1), stable (2), stage, stain, stamin (tamine, taminy, tamis, tammy), stanch (staunch), stanchion, standard, stank, state, station, statue, stature, statute, stencil, sterile, stipulation, store, story (2), stover ?, strain (1), strait, strange, stray, stress, structure, strumpet ?, stubble, study, stuff, stupefy, stupid, style (1), suasion, suave, subaltern, subdue, subject, subjoin, sublime, submerge, suborn, subsidy, subsist, substance, substitute, subterfuge, subtle, suburb, subvention, subvert, succeed, succour, succulent, suction, sudden, sudorific, sue, suet, suffer, suffice, suffrage, suicide, suit, suite, sullen, sully, sum, summit, summon, sumptuous, superabound, superb, superexcellent, superintendent, superior, superlative, supernal, supernatural, supernumerary, superscription, supersede, superstition, supplant, supple, supplement, suppliant, supply, support, supposition, supreme, sur- (2), surcease, surcingle, sure, surface, surfeit, surge, surloin, surmise, surmount, surpass, surplice, surplus, surprise, surrejoinder, surrender, surround, surtout, surveillance, survey, survive, susceptible, suspect, suspend, sustain, suture, suzerain.

tabard ?, tabernacle, table, tail (2), tailor, taint, tally, talon, tamper, tangible, tantamount, tardy, tart (2), task, tassel (1), taste, taunt, tavern, tax, teil, temerity, tempest, temple (2), temporal, tempt, tenable, tenacity, tenant, tench, tend (1), tend (2), tender (1), tender (2), tender (3), tendon, tendril, tenebrous (tenebrious), tenement, tennis, tenon, tenor, tense (1), tent (1), tent (2), tent (4), tenter, tenuity, tenure, tercel, tergiversation, term, termination, termite, terreen (tureen), terrible, terrier, territory, terror, tertian, test, testament, tester, testicle, testify, testy, text, texture, tierce (terce), timid, tinsel, tiny ?, tissue, titillation, title, tittle, toast (1), toast (2), toil (1), toil (2), toilet (toilette), toise, tonsil, tonsure, torch, torment, tormentil, torrent, torrid, torsion, tort, tortoise, tortuous, torture, total, trace (1), trace (2), trail, trailbaston, train, trait, traitor, trajectory, trammel, trance, tranquil, transaction, trans-alpine, transfigure, transform, transgression, translate, transmigration, transparent, transpierce, transplant, transport, transposition, transubstantiation, travail, trave, travel, traverse, travesty, treachery, treason, treat, treble, trefoil, trellis, tremble, trench ?, trental, trepidation, trespass, trestle (tressel), tret, trey, triangle, tribe, tribulation, tribune, tribute, trick (1), trick (2), tricolor, trident, trifle, trillion, Trinity, trinket (1) ?, triple, triumph ?, trivial, tron, trot ?, trouble, trounce, trowel, truculent, truffle, trump (2), trumpery, truncheon, trunk (1), trunnion, try, tube, tuition, tuly, tumefy, tumult, turbine, turbot, turbulent, turmoil ?, turnpike ?, turpitude, turret, tutor.

ubiquity, ulcer, umbilical, amble-pie, umbrage, umpire, uncle, unction, unicorn, uniform, union (1), union (2), unique, unison, unit, unity, universal, urbanity, urchin, ure, urine, urn, use (1), use (2), usher, usurp, usury, utas, utensil, uterine, utilise, utility, utterance (2).

vacation, vacillation, vagabond, vague, vail (1), vail (2), vail (3),

vain, vair, valance, vale, valentine, valerian, valetudinary, valiant, valid, valley, valour, value, valve, vambrace, vamp, vamplate, van (1), van (2), vanish, vanity, vanquish, vantage, vapour, variety, vary, vase, vast, Vatican, vaticination, vault (1), vaunt, veal, veer, vegetable, vehement, veil, vein, vellum, velocity, velvet, venal, vend, venerable, venery, venew (venue, veney), vengeance, venial, venison, venom, vent (1), vent (2), vent (3), ventail, ventricle, venture, venue, verb, verdant, verderer, verdict, verdigris, verditer, verge (1), verify, verisimilitude, verity, verjuice, vermeil, vermilion, vermin, versatile, versify, version, vert, vervain, verve, very, vessel, vestal, vestige, vestment, vestry, vesture, vetch, vex, viand, vicar, vice (1), vice (2), vice-gerent, vicinage, victim, victory, victuals, vie, view, vigil, vignette, vigour, vile, villain, vindictive, vine, vinegar, vintage, vintner, violent, violet, viper, virgin, virile, virtue, virulent, visage, vis-a-vis, viscid, viscount, visé, visible, vision, visit, visor (vizor, vizard, visard), visual, vital, vitriol, vituperation, vivacity, vivandière, vivify, vocable, vocal, vocation, vociferation, voice, void, volant, volition, volley, voluble, volume, voluntary, voluptuous, volute, voracity, vouch, vouchsafe, voussoir, vow, vowel, voyage, vulcanise, vulgar, vulpine.

widgeon, wyvern (wivern).

Late Latin from French from Latin: crenellate.

Provençal from French from Latin: sirrah.

Italian from French from Latin: oboe.

Spanish from French from Latin: platina.

Dutch from French from Latin: abele, cashier, commodore, cost, domineer, excise (1), foy, vade.

Provençal from Latin: battledoor, capstan, colander, funnel, lingo, muckinder, musty, noose, spigot, ullage.

French from Provençal from Latin: amadou, badinage, caisson, cardoon, casern, fad, fig, goitre, gurnard, lozenge, ricochet, somersault, soubrette.

Spanish from Provençal from Latin: flamingo.

Italian from Latin: allegro, alto, antic, askance ?, attitude, belladonna, broccoli, canto, canzonet, caper (1), casino, cicerone, contralto, contrapuntal, cupola, curvet, dado, dilettante, ditto, doge, duel, duet, ferret (2), granite, gurgle, incognito, influenza, infuriate, intaglio, isolate, Jerusalem (artichoke), lagoon (lagune), lava, lira, macaroni (maccaroni), madonna, manifesto, maraschino, mezzotinto, miniature, motto, nuncio, opera, petto, piano, pianoforte, piazza, pilgrim, portico, presto, profile, punch (4), punchinello, quartet (quartette), rallentando, salvo, semibreve, semolina, seraglio, sforzando, signor (signior), size (2), soda, solo, sonata, soprano, stanza, stiletto, terra-cotta, travertine, trio, tufa, ultramarine, umbrella, vendetta, vermicelli, vista, volcano.

French from Italian from Latin: accolade, alarm (alarum), alert, apartment, arcade, artisan, basement, belvedere, bronze, bulletin, burlesque, cab (1), cabriolet, cadence, campaign, cape (2), caprice, capriole, caress, carnival, cascade, cash (1), cassock, cavalcade, cavalier, cavalry, citadel, colonel, colonnade, compartment, concert, cornice, corridor, corsair, cortege, costume, countertenor, courier, courtesan, couvade, cuirass, dome, douche, ducat, escort, esplanade, façade, festoon, filigree, florin, fracas, fugue, gabion, galligaskins, gambado, gambit, gambol, gelatine, imprese, improvise, incarnadine, infantry, intrigue, junket, league (1), levant, lustre (1), lutestring, macaroon, mall (2), manage, manege, mercantile, mizen (mizzen), model, mole (3), musket, niche, ortolan, paladin, pallet (2), parapet, parasol, partisan (1), partisan (2), pastel, periwig, peruke, pilaster, pinnace, piston, poltroon, pomade (pommade), poop, populace, porcelain, postillion, preconcert, quarantine, redoubt, reprisal, revolt, risk, rocket (2), salad, sallet, salmagundi, saveloy (cervelas), sentinel ?, soffit, sonnet, spinet, spontoon, squad, squadron, termagant, terrace, tramontane, trinket (2), ultramontane, umber, vault (2), vedette (vidette).

Low German (or Dutch) from French from Italian from Latin: monkey, wig.

Spanish from Italian from Latin: contraband.

German from Italian from Latin: barouche.

Spanish from Latin: albino, alligator, armada, armadillo, assonant, binnacle, bolero ?, bonito, booby, brocade, canary, capsize, carbonado, cask, chinchilla, contango, cork, corral, cortes, despatch, disembogue, domino, don (2), duenna, firm (2), funambulist, grandee, hacienda, hidalgo, junta, junto, lariat, lasso, llano, mallecho, matador, merino, morris, mosquito, mulatto, mustang, negro, olio, peccadillo, peseta, primero, punctilio, quadroon, real (2), reata, renegade, salver, seguidilla, sherry, sierra, siesta, sombrero, stevedore, tent (3), toreador, tornado, vanilla.

French from Spanish from Latin: calenture, casque, chopine, comrade, creole, crusade, doubloon, escalade, farthingale, grenade, jade (2), jonquil, manchineel, nigger, ombre, parade, pint, plantain (2), punt (2), quadrille, roan, sassafras, spaniel.

Italian from Spanish from Latin: comply, majolica.

French from Italian from Spanish from Latin : compliment.

Portuguese from Latin : auto-da-fe, ayah, caste, cobra de capello, joss, junk (2), madeira, milreis, moidore, molasses, peon, pimento, port (4), tank, verandah?

French from Portuguese from Latin : chamade, corvette, fetich (fetish), serval.

Dutch from Portuguese from Latin : kraal.

French from Romaunsch from Latin : marmot.

German from Hungarian from Servian from Late Greek from Latin : hussar.

Dutch from Latin : anker, bung, buoy, cornel, coy (2), cruise, pip (1), tafferel (taffrail).

Scandinavian from Latin : kettle.

German from Latin : drilling, larch.

French from Old High German from Latin : pitcher, waste.

French from Middle High German from Latin : baldric, coif, fife, quoif.

Russian from Teutonic from Latin : czar.

Celtic from Latin : bannock, caber, cross, pillion, plaid, quaich.

Gaelic from English from Latin : pibroch.

French from Portuguese from Arabic from Greek from Latin : apricot.

French from Italian from Arabic from Latin : garble.

French from Spanish from Arabic from Latin : quintal.

Italian from Spanish from Arabic from Latin : mandilion.

Dutch from French from Spanish from Arabic from Latin : kilderkin.

Late Latin : barrister, bosky, bush (1), calamanco, campaniform, cap, capital (3), celt (2), clary, cope (1), crucible, edible, elongate, elucidate, fine (2), flask, fortalice, grate (1), hoax, hocuspocus, implement, indent (1), intimate, machicolation, pageant, plenary.

French from Late Latin : almanack, ambush, bachelor, bail (2), bale (3), ball (1), barge, barnacle (1), barnacle (2), basin, basnet, bastard, baste (2), baton, batten (2), betony, bittern, boot (1), bottle (1), bouquet, branch, bugle (3), burden (2), burganet, burl, butler, butt (2), buttery, chape, chemise, crochet, crocket, croquet, crosier, crotchet, crouch, cumber, drab (2), drape, fell (3), felon, ferret (1), flagon, frock, gallery, galley, gauge (gage), gown, hutch, identity, lavender, mackerel, marjoram, mastiff, menagerie, menial, muffle, oleander, osier, tire (4), tire (5).

Walloon from French from Late Latin : muff (1).

French from Provençal from Late Latin : ballad, bastile. cabbage (2), cabin, viol.

French from Gascon from Late Latin : cad, cadet.

French from Italian from Provençal from Late Latin : bastion.

Italian from Late Latin : fiasco.

French from Italian from Late Latin : ballet, barcarolle, bark (1), battalion, capuchin, catacomb, falchion, gallias, pivot.

Spanish from Late Latin : ambuscade, bastinado, embargo, galleon.

French from Spanish from Late Latin : caparison, cape (1).

French from Portuguese from Late Latin : bayadere.

French from German from Late Latin : spurry.

GREEK. a-, acacia, acatalectic, acephalous, achromatic, acme, acotyledon, acoustic, acropolis, acrostic, actinic, æsthetic, agnostic, allopathy, amazon, ambrosia, amorphous, amphi-, amphibious, amphibrach, amphitheatre, an- (a-), ana-, anabaptist, anachronism, anæsthetic, anapest (anapæst), anemone, aneroid, aneurism, anhydrous, anomaly, anonymous, anthology, anthracite, anthropology, anti-, anticlimax, antinomian, antiseptic, antithesis, antitype, aorist, apepsia, aphelion, aphis, apo-, apocrypha, apophthegm (apothegm), apteryx, archæology, archaic, archaism, areopagus, aristocracy, arsis, arthritis, asbestos, ascetic, ascidian, asphodel, asphyxia, asterism, asteroid, asthma, asymptote, ataxy, atheism, athlete, atlas, atmosphere, autobiography, autocracy, automaton, autonomy, autopsy, azalea.

barometer, barytes, bathos, belemnite, bibliography, bibliolatry, bibliomania, biography, biology, bromine, bronchial.

cacophony, caligraphy (calligraphy), calisthenics (callisthenics), calomel, carotid, caryatides, cata-, cataclysm, catalepsy, catarrh, catastrophe, category, cathartic, catoptric, ceramic, chiliad, chirography, chlorine, chromatic, chrome, chromium, chronology, chronometer, chrysalis, church, cissoid, clematis, climax, clime, coleoptera, collodion, colocynth, coloquintida, colon (1), colon (2), colophon, colophony, coma, coprolite, coracoid, cosmetic, cosmic, cosmogony, cosmography, cosmology, cosmopolite, cotyledon, crasis, creosote, cricoid, crisis, crony?, croton, cryptogamia, cyanogen.

dandy?, decagon, decahedron, decasyllabic, deleterious, demotic, dendroid, derm, di- (2), dia-, diabetes, diacritic, diagnosis, diaphanous, diaphoretic, diastole, diatonic, dicotyledon, didactic, digamma, digraph, dimorphous, diœcious, dioptrics, diorama,

diphtheria, dipsomania, diptera, dodecagon, dodecahedron, dogma, doll, drastic, dynamic.

eclectic, eczema, elastic, empyreal (empyrean), encrinite, endemic, enema, enteric, enthusiasm, entozoon, eocene, ephemera, epi-, epiglottis, episode, eponymous, erotic, esoteric, eu-, eucalyptus, euphemism, euphony, euphrasy, euphuism, Euroclydon, euthanasia, exegesis, exogen, exoteric.

glossographer, glottis, glyptic, gnostic, Gordian, gynarchy.

Hades, hagiographa, hector, hegemony, heliocentric, helminthology, hemi-, hendecagon, hendecasyllabic, heptagon, heptahedron, heptarchy, hermeneutic, hermetic, hesperian, heterodox, heterogeneous, hierophant, hippish, hippocampus, histology, homeopathy (homœopathy), homogeneous, homologous, hoplite, hyades, hydatid, hydrangea, hydrodynamics, hydrogen, hydropathy, hydrostatics, hypnotism.

ichor, ichthyography, iconoclast, icosahedron, idiosyncrasy, iodine, iota, isochronous, isothermal.

kaleidoscope, kerosene, kinematic, kinetic, kirk, kleptomania.

lepidoptera, leucoma, lexicon, lithography, logarithm, lycanthropy.

macrocosm, mænad, malachite, mastodon, megalosaurus, megatherium, melanite, meningitis, meniscus, mentor, meso-, meta-, metaphrase (metaphrasis), metastasis, metempsychosis, methylated, miasma, microscope, miocene, misanthrope, misogamy, mnemonics, mono-, monocotyledon, monody, monomania, monotony, morphia, morphine, myopia, myriad, myth.

necrology, neology, nepenthe (nepenthes), neuralgia, nomad, nosology.

octagon, octahedron, omega, onomatopeia, ontology, ophidian, ophthalmia, opodeldoc (*partly*), ornithology, ornithorhyncus, orthoepy, orthopterous, osmium, osteology, ostracise, oxide, oxygen, oxytone, ozone.

pachydermatous, pædobaptism, paleography, paleology, paleontology, palimpsest, palindrome, pan-, pandemonium, panic, panoply, panorama, pantheism, para-, parallax, parenthesis, Parian, paronymous, parthenogenesis, pathos, pedobaptism, pelargonium, peri-, perianth, pericarp, perihelion, peritoneum, petal, philander, philharmonic, phlox, pholas, phonetic, photography, phrenology, phyllophorous, phytoid, picric, pleiocene, pleistocene, plesiosaurus, pneumonia, polemical, polyglot, polyhedron, polysyllable, polytheism, pro- (or L.; or F. from L.), pros-, prosthetic, pterodactyl, pyretic, pyrotechnic.

saurian, schist, septic, skeleton, skink (2), sporadic, spore, statics, stenography, stentorian, stereoscope, stereotype, stethoscope, strophe, strychnine, style (2), synchronism, systole, syzygy.

tactics, tantalise, taw (2), taxidermy, technical (*with* L. *suffix*), telegraph, telescope, tetrahedron, thaumaturgy, theism, theocracy, theodolite, thermometer, threnody, thyroid, tonic, toxicology, toxophilite, trigonometry, trilobite, triphthong, triptych.

Utopian. zoology, zymotic.

Latin (or Late Latin) from Greek : abacus, abyss, acanthus, ægis, aerial, allegory, alms, aloe, amaranth, amethyst, amphisbœna, amphora, anæmia, anathema, anchor, anodyne, antagonist, anthem, anthropophagi, antichrist, antipathy, antiphon, antiphrasis, antipodes, antistrophe, aorta, aphæresis, apocalypse, apocope, apology, apostle, apostrophe, apotheosis, apse, arch (2), arch-, archi-, archimandrite, argonaut, arnica?, aroma, artery, arum, asphalt, aster, asterisk, astral, asylum, atomy (1), axiom.

bacchanal, bacterium, barbarous, basilica, basilisk, basis, bishop, blaspheme, bolus, Boreas, box (1), box (2), box (3), bronchitis, bryony, bucolic, bursar, butter.

cacoethes, cactus, cadmium, caduceus, calyx, camera, canister, canon (1), capon, cardamom, carpus cartulary, castor, catapult, cataract, catechise, cathedral, caustic, cedar, cemetery, cenobite (cœnobite), centaur, cetaceous, chalcedony, chalybeate, chameleon, chaos, character, chart, chasm, chervil, chest, chimæra (chimera), chord, chorus, Christ, chrysanthemum, chrysoprase, chyme, cist, cistus, cithern (cittern), clepsydra, clyster, colchicum, colophony, colossus, colure, comma, conch, copper, crambo, cranium, crapulous, crater, critic, crocus, crypt, cyclamen, cyclops, cynic, cynosure, cyst.

dactyl, deacon, deuteronomy, devil, diabolic, diabolical, diæresis, diagram, diapason, diarrhœa, diatribe, dilemma, diploma, diptych, disc (disk), dish, distich, dithyramb, doxology, drama, dryad, dysentery, dyspepsy.

ecclesiastic, echinus, echo, eclogue, ecumenic (ecumenical), electric, electuary, eleemosynary, ellipse, elysium, emetic, emphasis, emporium, enclitic, encomium, encyclical, encyclopædia, enigma, enthusiasm, epic, epicene, epicure, epidemic, epidermis, epithalamium, epithet, epitome, epoch, erysipelas, esophagus, ether, ethic, ethnic, etymon, eucharist, eulogy, eunuch, euphorbia, eustachian, exarch, exodus, exorcise, exotic.

ganglion, gastric, genesis, Georgic, geranium, gigantic, glaucous, gloss (2), glossary, gnomon, goby, Gorgon, graphic, gymnasium, gyre.

halcyon, hamadryad, hebdomadal, heliacal, helix, helot, hemistich, hemp, hermaphrodite, heteroclite, hexagon, hexameter, hieroglyphic, hippopotamus, history (story), holocaust, holothurian, homonymous, hulk, hyaline, hybrid, hydra, hydrophobia, hyena, hymen, hypallage, hyper-, hyperbole, hyphen, hypo-, hypochondria, hypostasis, hypothesis.

iambic, ichneumon, idea, idyl (idyll), iliad, imp, impolitic (*with* L. *prefix*), impracticable (*with* L. *prefix*), intoxicate (*with* L. *prefix*), iris, isosceles, isthmus.

laconic, laic, laical, larynx, lemma, lemniscate, lethe, lichen, ligure, lily, lithotomy, lotus, lynx.

magnesia, mania, marsupial, martyr, masticate, mausoleum, meander, medic, mesentery, metamorphosis, metaphysics, metathesis, metonymy, metropolis, mimic, minotaur, minster, mint (2), moly, monad, monastery, monk, monogamy, monogram, monopoly, museum, myrmidon, mystery (1).

naiad, narcissus, nauseous, nautical, nautilus, nectar, nemesis, neophyte, neoteric, Nereid, numismatic.

obolus, octopus, octosyllabic, œsophagus, oleaginous, oleaster, Olympian, onyx, opium, opoponax, orchestra, orchis, oread, orphan, orthodox (*or* F. *from* L. *from* Gk.), oxalis, oxymel.

Pæan, palestra, palladium, panacea, pancreas, pander (pandar), panegyric, pantheon, paraclete, paragoge, parallelopiped, paralysis, paraphernalia, pard, paregoric, parergon, parhelion, parochial, parody, Pean, peltate, pentameter, pentateuch, Pentecost, peony, pericardium, pericranium, perimeter, peripatetic, periphery, periphrasis, petroleum, phalanx, phallus, pharynx, phase (phasis), phenix (phœnix), phenomenon, philanthropy, philippic, philology, philomel, phocine, phosphorus, phthisis, plaster, plastic, plectrum, pleiad, pleonasm, plethora, plinth, plum, pneumatic, poly-, polyanthus, polygon, polypus, presbyter, pretty ?, priest, prism, proboscis, prolepsis, propine, proscenium, prosopopœia, Protean, prothalamium, psalm, psychical, purse, pygarg, pylorus, pyramid, pyre, pyrethrum, pyrites, python, pyx.

rhinoceros, rhododendron, rhombus.

sapphic, sarcophagus, sardine (2), sardius, sardonyx, scalene, scene, scheme, scirrhous, scoria, seam (2), sepia, sibyl, siren, soam, spatula, sphinx, spleen, spondee, stoic, stole, storax, strangury, sybarite, sycophant, symposium, syn-, synæresis, synalœpha, syncopate, synecdoche, synopsis, syntax, synthesis, system.

tænia, tape, tartar (3), tautology, terebinth, teredo, tetanus, tetrarch, theogony, theorem, thesaurus, thesis, theurgy, thorax, thrasonical, thurible, thyrsus, tick (2), tippet, Titan, topiary, trachea, trapezium, tribrach, triglyph, trigon, trimeter, tripod (*or* Gk.), triton, trochee, trope, trout, truck (2), truckle, turn, tympanum, typhus.

xylobalsam.

French from Latin (or Late Latin) from Greek: abnormal, academy, acclimatize, ace, acolyte, aconite, adamant, agaric, agate, agony, agrimony, air, alabaster, almond, almoner, amass, amnesty, anagram, analogy, anarchy, anatomy, anchoret, anecdote, angel, anise, antarctic, antelope, anther, antidote, apathy, apogee, apologue, apoplexy, apostasy, apostate, apothecary, archetype, architect, archives, arctic, arithmetic, asp, aspic, astrology, astronomy, atom, atomy (2), atrophy, attic, austere, authentic, autograph.

baptize, base (2), basil (1), besant, blame, bolt (boult), bombard, bombardier, bombast, bombazine, bound (1), brace, bracelet, brassart, buff (2), bugloss, bulb, burbot, bureau, bushel.

calamint, calender (1), calm, calumet, cane, canon (2), cantle, canvas, canvass, caper (2), cardiac, carol, carrot, carte, catalogue, cataplasm, catholic, cauterise, celandine, cenotaph, centaury, centre, cephalic, ceruse, chair, chaise, chamber, chamomile, charter, cheer, chemist, cherry, chestnut (chesnut), chicory, chime, chimney, chirurgeon, choir, choler, chrism, chronicle, chrysolite, chyle, cistern, citron, clergy, clerk, clinical, cock (5), cockatrice, cockboat, cockle (1), cocoon, coffer, coffin, colic, comedy, comet, cone, conger, cope (2), coppice, coppy, copse, coquette, coral, cord, coriander, corymb, costmary, coupon, cream, crétin, crocodile, crown, crystal, cube, currant, cycle, cygnet, cylinder, cymbal, cyme, cypress (1), cypress (2).

daffodil, daïs, dauphin, decade, decalogue, democracy, demon, despot, diachylon, diaconal, diadem, diagonal, dialect, dialogue, diameter, diamond, diaper, diaphragm, diet (1), diet (2), dimity, diocese, diphthong, dissyllabic, dittany, diuretic, dolphin, dragon, dragoon, dram (drachm), dredge (2), dromedary, dropsy, drupe, dynasty.

eccentric, eclipse, economy, ecstasy, elegy, emblem, embrocation,

emerods, empiric, encaustic, energy, entomology, epaulet, epicycle, epigram, epilepsy, epilogue, epiphany, episcopal, epistle, epitaph, epode, evangelist.

fancy, fleam, frantic, frenzy.

galaxy, galoche (golosh), gangrene, gargle, gargoyle, gash, genealogy, geography, geometry, germander, giant, gillyflower, gittern, glamour, gloze, govern, graft (graff), gramarye, grammar, grammatical, griffin (griffon), gudgeon, guitar.

halo, harmony, harpoon, harpy, hecatomb, hectic, heliotrope, hellebore, hematite, hemisphere, hemorrhage, hemorrhoids (emerods), hepatic, heresy, heretic, hermit, hero, heroine, hilarity, homily, horizon, horologe, horoscope, hour, hyacinth, hydraulic, hydropsy, hymn, hypocrisy, hypogastric, hypotenuse, hypothec, hysteric.

idiom, idiot, idol, imposthume, ingraft (engraft), inharmonious, ink, irony.

jacinth, jalousie, jealous, jet (2). kit (2).

labyrinth, laity, lamp, lantern, lay (3), leopard, leper, leprosy, lethargy, licorice (liquorice), litany, litharge, litre, liturgy, lobe, logic, lyre.

mace (2), machine, magnet, mandrake, mangonel, mass (1), mastic (mastich), match (2), mathematic, mechanic, medlar, megrim, melancholy, melilot, melody, melon, metal, metallurgy, metaphor, method, metre (meter), mettle, microcosm, misty (2), mitre, monarchy, monochord, monosyllable, mosaic, murrey, muse (2), music, myrobalan (mirobalan), mystic, mythology.

necromancy, Nick (2), noise ?, nymph.

obelisk, ocean, ochre, ode, oil, oligarchy, olive, orach (orache), organ, orgies, origan (origanum), orthodox (*or* L.-Gk.), orthography, ounce (2), oyster.

page (1), pain, palinode, palsy, pamphlet, pandect, pant, panther, pantomime, parable, paradigm, paradox, paragraph, parallel, parallelogram, paralogism, paralyse, paraphrase, parasite, parch ?, parchment, parish, parley, parliament (*with* F. *suffix*), parlour (*with* F. *suffix*), parole, paroxysm, parrot, parsley, partridge, paste, pasty, paten, patriarch, perigee, patriot, patronymic, patty, pause, pedagogue, pelican, penal, penance, pentagon, perch (2), perigee, period, pew, phaeton, phantasm, phantom, pharmacy, pheasant, phial, philosophy, philtre, phiz, phlebotomy, phlegm, phrase, phylactery, physic, physiognomy, physiology, pier, pilcrow, pip (2), pippin ?, pirate, place, plane (3) (plane-tree), planet, pleurisy, poem, poesy, poet, pole (2), police, policy, polygamy, pomp, pore (1), porphyry, pose (1), posy, practice, pragmatic, problem, proem, prognostic, programme (program), prologue, prophecy, prophet, propose, proselyte, prosody, protocol, protomartyr, prototype, prow, prune (2), psaltery, pulley ?, pump (2), pumpion (pumpkin), purple, purpose (1) (*with* F. *prefix*), pygmy (pigmy).

quince, quire (2).

rankle, recoup (*with* L. *prefix*), resin (rosin), rhapsody, rhetoric, rheum, rhomb, rhubarb, rhythm, rime (1), rue.

salamander, samite, sap (2) ?, sarcasm, sardine (1), sardonic, satyr, say (2), scammony, scandal, scantling (*with* L. *prefix*), scar (1), scarify, sceptic, sceptre, schedule, schism, school (1), sciatic, scorpion, seine, shawm (shalm), sinople, siphon, slander, solecism, sophist, spasm, spay, sperm, sphere, spire (2), sponge, squill, squirrel, stavesacre, stomach, story (1), strangle, stratagem, styptic, succory, summer (2), sumpter, surgeon, surgery, syllable, syllogism, symbol, symmetry, sympathy, symphony, symptom, synagogue, syndic, synod, synonym, syringe.

talent, tansy, tapestry, tetragon, tetrasyllable, theatre, theme, theology, theory, therapeutic, throne, thyme, tiffany, timbrel, tomb, tome, tone, topaz, topic, topography, tour, tournament, tourniquet, tower, tragacanth, tragedy, treacle, treasure, trepan (1), trephine, tress, tressure, triad, trisyllable, triumph ?, troglodyte, trophy, tropic, trousers, trousseau, trover, truss, tune, turpentine, type, tyrant.

vial, zeal, zed, zephyr, zest, zodiac, zone.

Low Latin from Latin from Greek: intone.

French from Provençal from Latin from Greek: tunny.

Italian from Latin from Greek: biretta, buffalo, eryngo, grotto, madrigal, orris, piazza ?, sbirro, torso.

Spanish from Italian from Latin from Greek: melocoton.

French from Italian from Latin from Greek: baluster, balustrade, banisters, buskin, cannon (1), canopy, canteen, canton, cartridge, celery, espalier, grot, grotesque, manganese, medal, piastre.

Dutch from Italian from Latin from Greek: sketch.

Spanish from Latin from Greek: chigo, paraquito, pellitory (2) (pelleter), sambo, silo, spade (2).

French from Spanish from Latin from Greek: bomb, castanets, cochineal, ensilage, maroon (2), rumb (rhumb).

Portuguese from Latin from Greek: palaver.

French from Portuguese from Latin from Greek: marmalade.

Provençal from Latin from Greek: troubadour.

Dutch from Latin from Greek: bush (2), cant (2), ingle (2), mangle (2).

German from Latin from Greek: zither.

French from German from Latin from Greek: petrel (peterel).

Scandinavian from Latin from Greek: beaker.

Celtic from Latin from Greek: sporran, spunk.

French from Greek: acrobat, amalgam, analyse, aphorism, azote, botany, carpel, climacter, climate, demagogue, dose, embolism, embryo, endogen, epact, exergue, glycerine, gnome, hierarchy, hygiene, izzard, kilogramme, kilometre, malmsey, melodrama, meteor, microbe, monologue, narcotic, oolite, ophicleide, optic, oxygen, patristic, pentacle, pepsine, periapt, polytechnic, prophylactic, pseudonym, quinsy, rhizome, semaphore, stalactite, stalagmite, stearine, steatite, stigmatise, sylph, trilogy, zoophyte.

Spanish from French from Greek: platina.

Italian from Greek: archipelago, banjo, barytone, gondola, scope.

French from Italian from Greek: caloyer, caravel, card (1), emery, gulf, mandolin, moustache (mustache), pantaloon (1), pantaloons, paragon, pedant?, pilot.

Spanish from Italian from Greek: cedilla.

French from German from Greek: sabre.

Arabic from Greek: elixir, typhoon.

French from Arabic from Greek: alchemy.

Spanish from Arabic from Greek: talisman, tarragon.

Portuguese from Spanish from Arabic from Greek: albatross.

French from Spanish from Arabic from Greek: alembic, limbeck.

French from Italian from Arabic from Greek: carat.

Hebrew from Greek: sanhedrin.

Turkish from Greek: effendi.

SLAVONIC. This general term includes Russian, Polish, Bohemian, Servian, &c.

French from Slavonic: sable.

French from German from Slavonic: calash, trump (1), trumpet, trunk (2).

Italian from German from Slavonic: trombone.

French from Dutch from Slavonic: pram.

Scandinavian from Slavonic: sark.

Dutch from Low German from Slavonic: siskin.

French from Latin from Greek from Slavonic: slave.

French from Hungarian from Slavonic: shako.

Dalmatian: argosy.

French from Dalmatian: dalmatic.

German from Bohemian: howitzer.

French from German from Servian: vampire.

Russian: copeck, drosky, mammoth, permian, rouble (ruble), samovar, steppe, verst, vodka, zemstvo.

French from Russian: ukase.

Polish: britska, mazurka, polack, polka.

French from Polish: varsovienne.

LITHUANIAN. Of Aryan origin, like Slavonic.

Dutch from German from Lithuanian: eland.

ASIATIC ARYAN LANGUAGES.

Persian: bakshish, bashaw, bazaar, bulbul, caravansary, carboy, dervish, divan, durbar, firman, mohur, nargileh, nylghau, Parsee, pasha, peri, pillau, sepoy, serai, shah, shawl.

Latin from Greek from Persian: asparagus, cinnabar (cinoper), laudanum, Magi, naphtha, parasang, rose, tiara?.

French from Latin from Greek from Persian: jujube, magic, margarine, musk, myrtle, nard, paradise, parvis, sandal, satrap, tiger.

Italian from Latin from Greek from Persian: martello.

French from Italian from Latin from Greek from Persian: muscadel (muscatel), musk, rice.

Spanish from Latin from Greek from Persian: pistachio (pistacho).

Dutch from Slavonic from Latin from Greek from Persian: gherkin.

French from Latin from Persian: peach (1), zedoary.

Italian from Persian: giaour, scimetar?.

French from Italian from Persian: mummy, orange, taffeta (taffety).

French from Spanish from Persian: saraband.

Portuguese from Persian: lascar, pagoda.

French from Persian: bezique?, calender (2), caravan, jasmine, khedive, roc, rook (2), scarlet, tutty, van (3).

Arabic from Persian: tarboosh, zircon.

Greek from Arabic from Persian: arsenic.

Low Latin from Arabic from Persian: borax.

French from Low Latin from Arabic from Persian: balas (ruby).

Italian from Arabic from Persian: tazza.

French from Italian from Arabic from Persian: jargonelle.

French from Spanish from Arabic from Persian: calabash, julep, lilac, rob (2), spinach, tabour (tabor)?, tambour?, tambourine?.

French from Portuguese from Arabic from Persian: bezoar.

French from Arabic from Persian: azure, check, checker, checkers, chess, exchequer.

Turkish from Persian: jackal, padishah.

French from Turkish from Persian: kiosk.

French from Italian from Turkish from Persian: tulip, turban.

Cape Dutch from Malay from Persian: sjambok.

Hindustani from Persian: cummerbund, pajamas (pyjamas), sirdar, zamindar, zanana (zenana).

Sanskrit. avatar, brahmin (brahman), maharajah, pundit, rajah, Sanskrit, suttee, Veda.

Latin from Greek from Sanskrit: bdellium, beryl, pepper.

French from Latin from Greek from Sanskrit: brilliant, saccharine.

French from Spanish from Latin from Greek from Persian from Sanskrit: indigo.

French from Latin from Sanskrit: opal, sendal (cendal).

Persian from Sanskrit: nuphar.

French from Persian from Sanskrit: lake (2), nenuphar.

French from Latin from Greek from Persian from Sanskrit: sandal (wood).

French from Spanish from Arabic from Persian from Sanskrit: aniline, sugar.

Portuguese from Sanskrit: banyan.

Arabic from Sanskrit: kermes.

French from Arabic from Sanskrit: crimson.

Spanish from Arabic from Sanskrit: carmine.

French from Italian from Arabic from Sanskrit: candy.

Hebrew from Sanskrit: algum.

French from Latin from Greek from Hebrew from Sanskrit: sapphire.

Hindi from Sanskrit: hackery, juggernaut, loot, punch (3).

Hindustani from Sanskrit: bandanna, champak, cheetah, chintz, cowry, crore, deodar, ghee, gunny, jaconet, jungle, lac (1), lac (2), pawnee, punkah, rajpoot, ranee, rupee, wallah.

Portuguese from Hindustani from Sanskrit: bang (2), palanquin.

French from Portuguese from Hindustani from Sanskrit: lacquer (lacker).

Hindustani from Prakrit from Sanskrit: nautch.

Bengali from Sanskrit: jute.

Tamil from Sanskrit: cash (2), corundum.

Portuguese from Canarese from Sanskrit: jaggery.

Portuguese from Malay from Sanskrit: mandarin.

French from Portuguese from Malay from Sanskrit: tombac.

Cingalese from Sanskrit: wanderoo.

EUROPEAN NON-ARYAN LANGUAGES.

French from Finnish: morse.

Hungarian: tokay.

French from Hungarian: coach.

Turkish: aga (agha), bey, bosh, caftan, yataghan.

French from Turkish: caique, caracal, chibouque, dey, odalisque, shagreen.

Italian from Turkish: chouse.

French from Italian from Turkish: bergamot (1), janizary.

Spanish from Turkish: xebec.

German from Polish from Turkish: uhlan.

French from German from Hungarian from Turkish: dolman.

SEMITIC LANGUAGES.

The principal Semitic languages are Arabic, Hebrew, and Aramaic, which includes Chaldee and Syriac.

Hebrew: abigail, behemoth, cab (2), cherub, cor, corban, davit, ephod, gopher, hallelujah, hin, homer, Jehovah, jug, log (3), Messiah, mishnah, Nazarite (*with* Gk. *suffix*), purim, Sabaoth, Satan, selah, seraph, shekel, Shekinah, shibboleth, teraphim, thummim, urim.

Greek from Hebrew: delta, hosanna, iota.

Latin from Greek from Hebrew: alphabet, alleluia, amen, cade, cassia, cinnamon, cumin (cummin), gehenna, Jacobite, Jesus, jordan, jot, Levite, manna, Pasch, rabbi (rabbin), sabbath, Sadducee, sycamine, sycamore, Tom.

French from Latin from Greek from Hebrew: camel, cider, earnest (2), ebony, elephant?, Hebrew, hyssop, jack (1), jack (2), jacket, Jacobin, jenneting, Jew, jockey, lazar, marionette, maudlin, nitre, shallot, simony, sodomy. *Also* date (2): *of Semitic origin.*

French from Spanish from Latin from Greek from Hebrew: Jesuit.

French from Spanish from Arabic from Greek from Hebrew: natron.

Italian from Greek from Hebrew : zany.
Latin from Hebrew : leviathan.
French from Latin from Hebrew : cabal, jubilee.
Celtic from Latin from Semitic : ass.
Latin from Greek from Sanskrit from Hebrew : smaragdus.
French from Latin from Greek from Sanskrit from Hebrew : emerald.
Syriac : Maranatha.
Latin from Greek from Syriac : abbot, mammon.
French from Latin from Greek from Syriac : abbess, abbey, damson.
Italian from Latin from Greek from Syriac : damask.
French from Italian from Syriac : muslin.
Chaldee : raca, talmud, targum.
French from Latin from Greek from Aramaic : pharisee.
French from places in Palestine : bedlam, gauze.
French from Latin from Greek from Chaldee : sackbut.
French from Latin from Greek from Phœnician : scallion.

Arabic. afreet, alcoran, alkali, attar (of roses), azimuth, cadi, dahabeeyah, drub, emir, ghazal, hadji, hakim, harem, hashish, hegira, henna, hookah, imam (imaum), islam, jerboa, jereed, jinn, jubbah (jibbah), khalif, koran, mahdi, Mahometan (Mohammedan), maund (2), mohair, moslem, muezzin, mufti, mullah, nadir, otto, rack (5), ramadan, rayah, salaam, sash (2), shadoof, sheik, sherbet, shrub (2), simoom, sofa, taraxacum, visier (vizier), wadi, zariba.
Latin from Greek from Arabic : balsam, gypsum, saracen.
French from Latin from Greek from Arabic : balm, endive ?, jasper, myrrh.
French from Greek from Arabic : civet.
French from Italian from Greek from Arabic : dragoman.
French from Latin from Arabic : sarcenet, turmeric ?.
Low Latin from Arabic : alcohol, algebra, antimony.
French from Low Latin from Arabic : tartar (1).
Italian from Arabic : botargo, felucca, senna, sirocco, zecchino.
French from Italian from Arabic : arabesque, baldachin, caliber, calipers, caliver, magazine, sequin, zero.
French from Spanish from Italian from Arabic : benzoin.
Spanish from Arabic : alcayde, alguazil, atabal, caraway (carraway), maravedi, minaret.
French from Spanish from Arabic : alcove, amber, basil (3), carafe, cassolet, cid, cipher, cotton (1), cotton (2), cubeb, fardel, fives, furl, gazelle, genet, giraffe, hazard, jennet (gennet), jar (2), lackey (lacquey), marcasite, mask (masque), masquerade, matrass, mosque, nacre, ogee (ogive), racket (1) (raquet), realgar, ream, saker, skirret, sumach, syrup (sirup), tabby, talc, tare (2), tariff, zenith.
Italian from Spanish from Arabic : arsenal.
French from Provençal from Spanish from Arabic : lute (1).
French from Portuguese from Spanish from Arabic : marabou (marabout).
Portuguese from Arabic : albacore.
Dutch from Portuguese from Arabic : monsoon.
French from Arabic : admiral, arrack, assassin, bedouin, borage, burnouse, calif (caliph), camlet, carob (tree), faquir (fakir), housings, jupon, Mamaluke (Mameluke), mattress, naker, ottoman, razzia, rebeck, saffron, sultan.
French from English from Arabic : moire.
Persian from Arabic : ghoul, havildar, mussulman, sophy.
Hindustani from Persian from Arabic : khidmutgar (kitmutgar), nizam, sicca.
Turkish from Persian from Arabic : kismet.
French from Persian from Arabic : houri, mate (2).
Turkish from Arabic : coffee, kavass, raki.
Hindustani from Arabic : houdah (howdah), moonshee. nabob, omrah, ryot, sahib.
Portuguese from Moorish : assagai.
French from North African : zouave.

ASIATIC NON-ARYAN LANGUAGES (not SEMITIC).

(N.B. Some of the Indian words may be of Aryan origin.)
Hindustani : anna (ana), bangle, chutny, coolie, cutcherry, dacoit, dawk, ghaut, mahout, nullah, puggery, shampoo, thug, tulwar.
E. Indian place-names : avadavat, bungalow, calico, cashmere (kerseymere, cassimere).
French from Low Latin from Hindustani : bonnet.
Balti : polo. *Gipsy* : pal. *Hindi* : rum (2).
Bengali : dinghey (dingey), tomtom.
Marathi : pice.
Malayalam : coir, teak.
Portuguese from Malayalam : betel.
French from Latin from Greek from Sanskrit from Malayalam : ginger.
Tamil : catamaran, cheroot, curry (2), mulligatawny, pariah.
Latin from Greek from Persian from Tamil : pea- (*in* peacock).

French from Spanish from Latin from Persian from Tamil : pavin (pavan).
Spanish from Portuguese from Malay from Tamil : mango.
Telugu : bandicoot, mungoose (mongoose).
Portuguese from Canarese : areca.
French from Dravidian : patchouli.
Cingalese : anaconda.
French from Cingalese : tourmaline.

Malay : amuck, babirusa, bamboo, caddy, cajuput (cajeput), cassowary, catechu, cockatoo, compound (2), crease (2) *or* creese, dugong, durian, gecko, gong, gutta-percha, ketchup, lory (lury), mango, mangosteen, muck (amuck), orang-outang, paddy, pangolin, pikul, proa, rattan, rusa, sago, sarong, sumpitan, tael, tripang, upas.
Also lorikeet (*with Span. suffix*).
French from Malay : gingham, ratafia, toffy.
Portuguese from Malay : junk (1).
Spanish from Portuguese from Malay : launch (2).
French from Late Latin from Persian from Malay : lemon.
French from Spanish from Persian from Malay : lime (3).
French from Malagasy : aye-aye.
French from Late Latin from Arabic from Malay : camphor.

Chinese : bohea, china, Chinese, congou, hyson, nankeen, pekoe, souchong, tea.
Latin from Greek from Arabic from Persian from Chinese : galingale.
Latin from Greek from Chinese : silk.
French from Latin from Greek from Chinese : serge.
Malay from Chinese : sampan.
Portuguese from Japanese from Chinese : bonze.

Japanese : harakiri, japan, jinriksha, mikado, soy.
Annamese : gamboge. *Burmese* : woon.
Java : bantam.

Tatar : tartar (2).
French from Turkish from Tatar : horde.
Persian from Tatar : khan.
Russian from Tatar : cossack.
French from Russian from Tatar : koumiss.
French from Latin from Tatar : tartan, turquoise.
French from Tatar : turkey.
Mongolian : mogul.
Persian from Mongolian : tomaun.
Thibetan : lama (1), yak.
French from Thibetan : zebu.

Australian : boomerang, kangaroo, wallaby, wombat.
New South Wales : dingo, parramatta.
Maori : kiwi, pah.
Tahitian : tattoo (2).
Polynesian : taboo.
Maldive Islands : atoll.

AFRICAN LANGUAGES.

Hebrew from Egyptian : ephah, shittah (tree), shittim (wood).
Latin from Greek from Hebrew from Egyptian : sack (1).
French from Latin from Greek from Hebrew from Egyptian : sack (2), satchel.
Greek from Egyptian : ammonite.
Latin from Greek from Egyptian : ammonia, ibis, Leo, oasis, papyrus.
French from Latin from Greek from Egyptian : bible ?, gum (2), gypsy, lion, paper.
French from Italian from Egyptian : fustian.
Morocco : morocco. *French from Barbary* : barb (2).
French from Morocco : fez.
Abyssinian : negus (2).
West African : baobab, chimpanzee, guinea ; *also* gorilla (*Old African*).
Portuguese from West African : banana, yam, zebra.
Kaffir : gnu, quagga.
From a negro name : quassia.

AMERICAN LANGUAGES.

North American Indian : caucus, hickory, hominy, manito, moccasin (mocassin), moose, musquash, opossum, pemmican, persimmon, racoon (raccoon), sagamore, skunk, squaw, toboggan, tomahawk, totem, wampum, wapiti, wigwam.
French from North American Indian : carcajou, caribou.
Eskimo : kayak.
Mexican : axolotl, jalap, ocelot, teocalli.
Spanish from Mexican : cacao, chilli, chocolate, copal, coyote, tomato.
Cuban : maguey.
Caribbean (or *West Indian*) : cassava, cayman, hammock.

Spanish from West Indian: cacique, cannibal, canoe, guava, iguana, hurricane, papaw, savannah; *from Hayti*: barbecue, guiacum, maize, manatee, potato, tobacco, yucca.

French from West Indian: buccaneer, caoutchouc, cavy, colibri, pirogue.

Peruvian: charqui, inca, jerked (beef), llama, puma.

Spanish from Peruvian: alpaca, coca, condor, guano, oca, pampas, vicuna, viscacha.

French from Spanish from Peruvian: quinine.

Guiana: wourali (curari).

Brazilian: ai, capibara, cayenne, coaita, coati-mondi, jabiru, jacana, jaguar, macaw, tamandua, tapir.

French from Spanish from Brazilian: agouti.

Portuguese from Brazilian: ananas, copaiba, ipecacuanha, manioc, tapioca.

French from Portuguese from Brazilian: petunia.

French from Brazilian: acajou, cashew (nut), couguar, jacamar, sapajou, toucan.

South American: araucaria, mahogany, tolu.

Spanish from Araucan: poncho.

French from Caribbean: peccary.

HYBRID WORDS. English abounds in hybrid words, i.e. in words made up from two different languages; and the two languages compounding the word are often brought into strange conjunction, as in the case of *interloper*, which is half Latin and half Dutch. The complexity thus caused is such as almost to defy classification, and, as the words are accounted for in the body of the work, each in its due place, I content myself with giving a list of them, in alphabetical order.

abroach, across, affray, affreightment, aitch-bone, allot, allure, aloof, altruism, ampersand, apace, apiece, appoggiatura, arblast, architrave, around, arouse, array, asafœtida, astray, athwart, attorney, attune, avadavat (amadavat), awkward.

bailiwick, bandog, bandylegged, bankrupt, barbican, bashful, bay-window, becalm, because, bechance, beefeater, befool, beguile, begum, belabour, besiege, betake, betray, bewail, bicycle, biffin, bigamy, bilberry, blackguard, blaeberry, blunderbuss, boatswain, bressomer, briar-root, brickbat, bulk-head, bum-bailiff, butterfly.

calthrop, camelopard, candytuft, cannel-coal, castor-oil, cesspool, chamberlain, Christmas, cockloft, codling (2), colza oil, commingle, compose, contour, contradistinguish, contrive, co-parcener, costermonger, counteract, counterscarp, country-dance, court-cards, coxswain, cupboard, curmudgeon, curry (1).

Daguerrotype, darnel, dastard, daywoman, debar, debark, debase, debauch, debris, debut, decant, decipher, decompose, decoy, defile (1), demarcation, demean (2), depose, derange, detach, dethrone, detour, develop, disable, disabuse, disaffect, disannul, disappear, disapprove, disarrange, disarray, disband, disbelieve, disburden, disburse, discard, discharge, discommend, discommon, discompose, discontent, discredit, disembark, disembroil, disencumber, disengage, disenthrall, disentrance, disfranchise, disguise, dishearten, disinherit, disinter, dislike, dislodge, dismask, dismay, disown, dispark, dispose, disregard, disrelish, disrepute, disrespect, disrobe, dissatisfy, dissimilitude, distaste, distrust, disuse, doleful, dormer-window, dormouse, dulcimer.

eclat, embalm, embank, embark, ember-goose, embody, embolden, embosom, emboss (1), emboss (2), embower, enamel, encroach, endear, enfeoff, enfold, enfranchise, engage, engrailed, engrave, engulf, enkindle, enlighten, enlist, enliven, enrapture, enshrine, enslave, ensnare, entangle, enthral, enthrone, entomb, entrap,

entrust, entwine, entwist, envelop?, enwrap, escarpment, essoin, exhilarate, expose, eyelet-hole.

feckless, flotsam, fore-arm (2), forecast, forecastle, foredate, forefront, forejudge (1), forenoon, fore-ordain, forepart, forerank, foretaste, forfend (forefend), frankalmoign, frankincense, fray (2).

gaffer, gainsay, gallipot, gammer, gamut, gier-eagle, grateful, greengage, grimalkin, guelder-rose, guerdon, gunwale, gyr-falcon.

Hallowmass, hammercloth, harpsichord, hautboy, heirloom, hobbyhorse, horse-courser, huggermugger, hurly-burly.

imbank, imbark, imbitter, imbody, imbosom, imbower, imbrown, impark, impose, impunity, Indiaman, Indian rubber, indisposed, ingulf, inorganic, inshrine, instal (install), interaction, interleave, interlink, interloper, intermarry, intermingle, interpose, intertwine, interweave, intomb, intone.

jackanapes, jemadar, jolly-boat, jury-mast.   kerbstone.

lancegay, lapis lazuli, lay figure, ledger-line, life-guard, lignaloes, lime-hound, linseed, lugsail.

macadamise, madrepore, magpie, malaria, malinger, mangrove, marigold, Martinmas, Michaelmas, misapply, misapprehend, misappropriate, misarrange, miscalculate, miscall, miscarry, misconceive, misconduct, misconstrue, misdate, misdemeanour, misdirect, misemploy, misfortune, misguide, mishap, misinform, misinterpret, misplace, misprint, mispronounce, misquote, misrepresent, misrule, misspend, misterm, monocular, mountebank, mulberry, muscoid, mystify.

natterjack, nonconforming, nonjuror, nonsense, nonsuit, notpated, nunchion, nutmeg.

oppose, orchard, ostrich, outbalance, outcast, outcry, outfit, outline, outpost, outpour, outrigger, outskirt, outvie, outvote, overact, overarch, overawe, overbalance, overcast, overcharge, overcoat, overdose, overdress, overhaul, overjoyed, overpass, overpay, overplus, overpower, overrate, overrule, overstrain, overtake, overtask, overturn, overvalue.

paletot, palfrey, Pall-mall, partake, pastime, peacock, peajacket, pearl-barley, pedestal, pentroof, perhaps, peruse, petrify, pettitoes, piebald, piecemeal, pink-eyed, pismire, planisphere, pole-axe, polecat, polynomial, pomander, portly, pose (2), posset, potwalloper, predispose, prehistoric, press-gang, presuppose, prewarn, propose, purblind, puzzle.

raiment, rearward, re-echo, refresh, regain, regard, regret, reimburse, reindeer (raindeer), relay (2), remark, remind, renew, replevy, repose, rest-harrow, retire, retrieve, retroussé, reward, rigmarole, rinderpest, rummage.

saltcellar, saltpetre, samphire, sax-horn, scaffold, scapegoat, scaup-duck, scotfree, scribble, seamstress (sempstress), seraskier, Shrovetide, Shrove-Tuesday, skewbald, smallage, snubnosed, sobriquet, solan-goose, somnambulist, spikenard, spindrift, sprightly, sprucebeer, squeamish, statist, sublease, sublet, submarine, subsection, subsoil, supercargo, superexcellent, superfine, superhuman, suppose, surcharge, surcoat, surname.

tamarind, tarpaulin, tea-poy, tee-totaller, teil-tree, titlark, titmouse, tocsin, tomboy, tomtit, touchwood, train-oil, transpose, Troy-weight, turnip.

unaneled, undertake, ungainly, unruly, until.

vaward, venesection.   wagtail.

ETYMOLOGY UNKNOWN. awning, bamboozle, beagle, coke, conundrum, culvert, dhow, dudgeon (1), dudgeon (2), jade (1), kelp, prawn, privet, Yankee.

Of many other words the ultimate origin is very obscure, and the solutions offered must be admitted to be doubtful.

SUPPLEMENT

I here subjoin a few corrections and additions. The words marked with an asterisk do not appear at all in the preceding pages.

*ADMIX, to mingle with something else. (L.) The vb. *admix* is no older than 1533 (N.E.D.), and is really a back-formation from the form *admixt*, which was used as a pp. much earlier, as it occurs in Palladius on Husbandry, bk. i. st. 9, l. 60 (ab. 1420). —L. *admixt-us*, pp. of *admiscēre*, to mix with. —L. *ad*, to, with; and *miscēre*, to mix. See **Mix**; and **Commix** (below).

ANON; line 7. *For* Grien *read* Grein.

ATTAINT. The N.E.D. explains the word fully, and notes how it was falsely Latinised as *attinctus*, as in Blackstone. I here make the note that an early example of the mistake occurs in the attainder of George, Duke of Clarence, in 1477. In the 17th Edw. IV, the order for his execution was made out, because he had been 'convictus et *attinctus*.' But the true pp. of L. *attingere* was *attactus*. Hence E. *taint*; see **Taint** (below).

BAMBOO. Of Malay origin; not from Canarese, as suggested at p. 45; the Canarese form is merely from the later Portuguese form *bambu*. But the quotations in Yule and in the N.E.D., s.v. *mambu*, show that the older form was *mambu*, both in Portuguese and English, the E. form being borrowed from the Port. *mambu*, which occurs in Garcia (1563); see Yule. There can be no doubt that this *mambu* is merely a clipped form of the Malay *sămámbū*, *sĕmámbū*, or *s'mambū*, in which the first syllable is unstressed and was easily lost. This *samambū* is really a kind of rattan (not the grass *Bambusa*), but its superficial likeness to the ordinary bamboo is such that the difference would only be apparent to those familiar with the Malay region and its products. In fact, Yule notices the use of *bamboo-cane*, and Stedman, in 1796, speaks of a *bamboo-rattan* (N.E.D.).

BAWD. Prof. Weekley (Phil. Soc. Trans., 1909) shows that the ME. *baud* is, probably, merely a shortened form of ME. *ribaud*, and therefore a doublet of *ribald*.

BEAVER (2). Cf. 'the helme, the visere, the two *bauiers*,' &c.; Hall's Chron. (1548); King Henry IV, first year; § 9.

BOOTY. In the N.E.D. the earliest quotations for *botye* and *butin* are from Caxton. But in some Ordinances for the use of the English army made in 1419, printed in Excerpta Historica, p. 43, there is an ordinance 'for theim that Sault [assault] .. to make theim *boty*.' It begins :—' Also that all men make them *boty*, vij or v to-gader, that alway iij of the vij, or ij of the v, be assigned to wayte, and not to departe from the standers' [standards], &c. Cf. 'il aura sa part du *buttin* (v.r. *butin*);' Black Book of the Admiralty, i. 437.

BRANKS. Prof. Weekley (Phil. Soc. Trans., 1909) shows that *brank* answers to the OF. *branque*, the equivalent, in the Norman dialect, of OF. *branche*, whence E. **Branch.** See *branch* (iv. 11) in N.E.D.

CABRIOLET. Not (F.—L.), but (F.—Ital.—L.); as the etymology shows.

CHEEK. The N.E.D. duly gives *cheek*, 'insolence, jaw;' the earliest example being in 1840; at which date is also recorded the phrase *to give cheek*, ' to be insolent.'

The origin of this phrase is not quite obvious. Perhaps it becomes a little clearer if we note that the Bremen Wörterbuch, in the Supplement, p. 405, gives the equivalent *keek*, cheek, as a Lübeck word, in the phrase *holt de keek*, lit. hold your cheek, in the sense 'hold your mouth,' hold your jaw, shut up! The date is 1771; nearly 70 years earlier than the date above.

Thus the original idea was that of too much use of the cheek or mouth in talking; hence, chatter, prattle, unasked advice, and the like; exactly as in the case of 'jaw.'

COCKNEY. It is suggested by Prof. Weekley that there were *two* words of this form, which have coalesced. 1. It represents *coken-ey*, ' egg of cocks,' as explained at p. 118 (above), in P. Plowman, and in the Tournament of Tottenham; but this usage appears to be obsolete. 2. In the sense of ' an effeminate person,' it does not represent an OF. *coquiné (as I proposed in the First Edition of the present work (viz. in the Supplement, at p. 785), but is to be taken as representing (with loss of initial *a*-, which is quite common) an OF. *acoquiné*, which actually occurs, and meant ' spoiled,' or ' self-indulgent.' Cotgrave has :—' *Accoquiné*, made tame, inward, familiar; also, grown as lazy, sloathfull, idle, as a beggar.' Also:—

' *Accoquiner*, to make tame, inward, familiar;' and ' *S'accoquiner*, to wax as lazie, become as idle, grow as sloathfull, as a beggar.' The OF. *acoquiné*, with loss of initial *a*, is closely represented by the ME. *cokeney* or *cokenay*. The original sense of this OF. word would be 'addicted to frequenting a kitchen,' or 'frequenter of a kitchen.' Allied to L. *coquināre*, to cook, *coquinus*, pertaining to a kitchen, and *coquina*, a kitchen (Lewis). All from L. *coquere*, to cook; see **Cook.** As to the ME. suffix *-ey* (*-ay*), we may compare *attorney*, from OF. *atorné*. As to the various senses of the word, see the exhaustive discussion by Prof. Weekley (Phil. Soc. Trans., 1909). Hence the word is to be marked as (F.—L.).

COMMIX. *For* (Hybrid; L. *and* E.) *read* (L.). The N.E.D. shows that *commix* was a back-formation from the earlier word *commixt*. *Commix* is not found before 1519; and *commixt* was taken immediately from L. *commixtus*, pp. of *commiscēre*, to mix together; from *com-*, together, and *miscēre*, to mix. See further under **Mix** (p. 380). And see **Admix** (above).

CONVEX. It is now held that L. *conuexus* has nothing to do with the verb *conuehere*; but rather answers to a compound of *con-* with *uacsus, from the root *uac-* which also appears in *uac-illāre*, to stagger. The sense would be ' bent;' cf. Skt. *vak-ra-s*, bent, crooked, *vañch*, to waver, totter, go crookedly. Closely allied to AS. *wōh*, bent, crooked, from a Teut. base *wanh answering to Idg. *wank, nasalised form of *wak, to bend. See **Woo**, and **Wench**.

COSSACK. The earliest quotation for *Cossack* (spelt *Cassack*) given in the N.E.D. is dated 1598. The pl. *Cassacks* occurs three times in the Antiquarian Repertory (1808), vol. ii, 399, which quotes at length A Letter sent from the Great Turck to the Queenes Maiestee in anno 1590. The Letter speaks of ' the Theeues called *Cassacks*, and other like facinerous persons.'

DANDLE. Cf. also Low G. *dendeln*, to sport; used as F. *dandiner.* It occurs in the Supp. to the Bremen Wörterbuch, with the note that it means, in particular, to dandle a child in one's arms. Berghaus gives the Low G. *dändelken, dändeln, dännken*, the same as G. *tändeln*.

DAWDLE. Cf. also Low G. (Hamburg) *daudeln*, to waste one's time (Richey). Quoted in the Bremen Wörterbuch (Supplement). According to C. Schmidt, the Strassburg dialect has *dŭdle*, to dawdle, to lounge.

DODGE. Ross has the Norw. *dogga*, to maintain one's place in an open sea against wind or waves by small movements of sail or oar. This may very well be a related word. The E.D.D. gives *dadge* and *dodge*, to walk slowly and clumsily; and here again we may compare (from Ross) Norw. *dagga*, to go very slowly and easily.

DOG, a fire-dog, andiron. (E.) The form *fire-dog* is modern (1840). ' One paire of *dogges* in the chymly;' Unton Inventories, p. 5 (1596). *Dogge* is the ME. form of *dog*, an E. word. But the idea was suggested by MF. *chenets*, 'andirons;' Cot. The OF. *chenet* occurs in 1317, and is a dimin. of OF. *chen*, a dog (from L. *canis*). Hatzfeld says that the heads of andirons often represented the heads of dogs.

DUB. So also Low G. *dubben*, to knock at a door; Supp. to Bremen Wörterbuch. Berghaus has Low G. *dubben*, to beat; *dubber*, a knocker; *dubbern*, to strike repeatedly, to hammer.

FABRIC; l. 5. *For* DHAB *read* DHABH.

FERRULE. Spelt *virole* about 1410. ' La virole le mambre garde, The virole the haft kepeth;' i.e. holds fast the haft of a knife; Femina, ed. W. Aldis Wright, 48. 20.

FINIAL. It is remarked in the N.E.D. that *finial* is a variant of *final*, and, apparently, of English origin. The earliest quotation, from the Chester plays, is of uncertain date, but of about A.D. 1400. Whether it was, at the first, 'king's English' or not, we are at any rate sure that it was king's French. For in 1404 we find Henry IV using the expression ' a *finiale* destruccioun de son povre estat,' i.e. to the final destruction of his poor estate. See Royal Letters of Henry IV (Rolls Series), ed. Hingeston, i. 310.

FLANK. *For* (F.—G.) *read* (F.—OHG.).

FOLD (2). The orig. sense of AS. *falod, falud*, was a cowshed or ox-stall, or a shelter ' made with boards;' from the AS. *fala*, a board, plank, bar. This AS. *fala* is not explained in the Dictionaries, but it may be found in the Epinal Glossary. See the facsimile.

p. 27, col. 1, l. 11, which has: ' abula, *fala.*' This is the source of the glosses in which 'tabula' is misspelt 'tubolo;' as in 'tubolo, *fala,*' Voc. 52. 11; Corpus Glossary, ed. Hessels, p. 117, l. 321; Leiden Glossary, ed. Hessels, note on p. 208, s. v. *tubolo.* The AS. *falaed* is explained as ' bobellum ' or ' stabulum.'

FOREHEAD. The oldest AS. form is *foran-hēafod*; see Sweet, O. E. Texts, p. 611.

FRAIL (2). AF. *frail,* W. de Bibbesworth, in Wright, Voc. i. 172; spelt *ffrael* in AF., and *frayel* in ME., in Femina, ed. W. Aldis Wright, 79. 4–6.

FRIEZE (1). We find 'des draps appellez *Friseware*' in 1376–7; Statutes of the Realm, i. 398.

GAIN (2). The derivation of the OF. word from OHG. is well illustrated by the occurrence of the AF. *weiner,* to gain. Cf. ' chevaux et armes, or et argent *weine* ;' i. e. they had gained horses and arms, silver and gold; Excerpta Historica, p. 71, l. 60.

GIBBON, a name for the long-armed ape. (E.) ' The *Gibbon,* or long-armed ape . . . is a native of the East Indies ;' tr. of Buffon (1792), i. 327. The name was conferred on this ape by Buffon, who, according to Hatzfeld, had it from Dupleix. It was alleged to be an Indian word, but has not been found in any Indian language. Dupleix was in India from 1720 to 1754; and it is probable enough that he imagined *gibbon* to be the Indian name for the creature. I suggest that the ' Indian language ' in which the name arose was certainly English, with whom the French at that time were in frequent contact and conflict. How the name came into existence we cannot tell, but that it was suggested by an Englishman (perhaps as a jest referring to a comrade) can hardly be doubted. The Prompt. Parv. has :—' Gybonn or Gylberde (Gybbon or Gylbert), propyr name, *Gilbertus.*' Hence *Gibbon* is merely an extension of *Gib,* the usual pet name for Gilbert. *Gib* was also a familiar name for a cat; cf. ' *Gibbe* our cat,' Romaunt of the Rose, 6204. And to this day *Gib* (with hard *g,* as in Gilbert) is a familiar name for a tom-cat in many E. dialects (E.D.D.). Any Englishman who knew this might easily suggest that, if Gib meant ' cat,' Gibbon would do for ' ape.'

GRAZE (2), to touch lightly, &c. The N.E.D. suggests that the right reading [in my l. 4] is ' like to the bullets *grazing,*' where *bullets* is plural; the sense being :—' like the bullets that graze the ground.' There can be no doubt that the original sense was ' to cut the grass,' or ' to score the grass.' Schambach gives, as a sense of Low G. *grasen,* ' to cut grass.' The quotations in N.E.D. show that the special sense arose from the ricocheting of cannon-balls along grass. There is a passage in Chapman, Revenge of Bussy D'Ambois, A. iv. sc. 1, that is particularly helpful :—' And as a great shot from a town besieged At foes before it flies forth black and roaring—But they too far, and that with weight oppress'd—As if disdaining earth, doth only *graze,* Strike earth, and up again into the air, Again sinks to it, and again doth rise,' &c.

HACKNEY. ME. *hakeney* is certainly from ME. *Hakeney,* i. e. Hackney, in Middlesex. The OF. *haquenée* and MF. *hacquenée* (Cotgrave) and all the foreign forms are simply borrowed from English, which had the word first. See Fitzstephen's description of London, temp. Henry II, in Stowe's Survey of London, ed. Thoms, pp. 211, 212. The great horsemart was in Smithfield, which is still connected with Hackney by Hackney Road and Mare Street; and the pastures for horses were to the North of London (p. 209), of which Hackney Downs and London Fields are still remnants. The ME. *Hakeney* represents AS. *Hacan īeg,* 'Haca's settlement beside a stream.' Cf. *Hacan pundfald,* 'Haca's pound,' in a charter dated 961.

*HOGMANAY, an old name for New Year's Eve. (L.) The N.E.D. says : ' *Hogmanay* corresponds exactly in sense and use to the OF. *aguillanneuf,* the last day of the year, new year's gift, the festival at which new year's gifts were given and asked with the shout of *aguillanneuf.*' Of this Godefroy gives many variants.' See also the E.D.D. From the OF. *hoguinané, hoguinono* (Godefroy); also *aguilan, guillanneu, aguilloneu, haguilennef, aguillanneuf,* &c.—L. *hoc in anno,* lit. ' in this year;' which was the original burden or chorus sung upon the occasion. In the Norman Glossary by Édélestand and Duméril (Caen, 1849), we find *hoguinètes,* new year's presents, or rather, presents given on new year's eve; called *hoguilanno* at Caen, and *hoguilanne* at Saint-Lo. De Brieux has preserved for us a sort of song, without rime, which was still sung, in his time, when *les hoguinètes* were asked for, *hoc in anno.*

Si vous veniés à la depense—
On vous serviroit du rost—
Hoquinano !
Donnez-moi mes haguignètes . . .
Mais il est encore à payer
Haguinelo !

Here, in the very song itself, we first find *hoc in anno* spelt *hoquinano,*

and then repeated in the corrupt form *haguinelo*; as it was sung by children ignorant of Latin. Thus *hoc in* became *aguin-,* and further corruption was easy; *anno* was supposed to mean *an neuf* (new year). *Hoguinané* is for *hoc in année*; and so on. The Spanish form (borrowed from F.) is *aguilando,* otherwise *aguinaldo.* The form *hogmanay* may be due to the F. form *hoguinané,* shortened to *hog'nané,* with a stress on the last syllable. Jamieson quotes the Scotch form as being so pronounced; as in—' The cottar weanies, glad and gay, Wi' pocks out owre their shouther, Sing at the doors for *hógmanáy.*'

HOGSHEAD. I find an early spelling not noted in the N.E.D. ' In duobus *hogsheveds* vini albi,' occurring in 1437; see Brand, Pop. Antiquities (1849), ii. 75, note. The spelling *heved* affords a clear proof that the latter element is really the mod. E. *head.*

HUZZA ! The earliest quotation in the N.E.D. is dated 1573. There is an instance twelve years earlier in the second edition (1807) of Grose's Antiquarian Repository, vol. i, p. 236. We there find a speech made at a dinner given at Norwich in 1561. It is said that on that occasion one Johnny Martin, of Norwich, proposed the health of the mayor whilst he could still ' speak plain English,' and before the beer, which ' is pleasant and potent . . . catch us by the caput, and stop our manners. And so *huzza* for the Queen's Majesty's grace, and all her bonny-browe'd dames of honour ! *Huzza* for Master Mayor, and our good dame Mayoress !'

ISING-GLASS. The earliest quotation in the N.E.D. is dated 1545. It occurs in 1528 in some accounts printed in Excerpta Antiqua, by J. Croft, p. 84; and again in 1530, in the same, p. 91. The same substance is mentioned by the name of *husblass* (which is nearer to the original) as early as 1371 (N. and Q. 10 S. x. 411).

KERSEY. The statement in the N.E.D. that there is nothing to connect cloth-making with Kersey, in Suffolk, is due to oversight. The fact is, rather, that there was once a large cloth-trade carried on in the south of Suffolk. In A Breviary of Suffolk, by Robert Reyce, written in 1618, and edited by Lord F. Harvey, stress is laid upon ' the excellent commoditie of clothing, which *of long time* hath here flourished . . . hee who maketh ordinaryly twenty broad clothes every weeke, cannot set so few a-worke as 500 persons.' In Hall's Chronicle (Henry VIII, year 17, § 8) we read how an attempt to raise a heavy subsidy failed, owing to the opposition of the ' riche Clothiers' of Suffolk, who told ' their Spinners, Carders, Fullers, Weuers, and other artificers' that they would be unable to pay them wages if the subsidy was granted; so that the men of ' Lanam [Lavenham], Sudbury, Hadley, and *other tounes aboute* ' (which would include Lindsey and Kersey) rebelled to the number of ' foure thousand men.' In Skelton's Why Come Ye Nat to Courte, l. 128, he refers to ' a webbe of lylse-wulse ' (see note on **Linsie-Woolsey** below); and at l. 930, he speaks of ' Good Sprynge of Lanam,' i. e. Lavenham, who ' must counte what became Of his *clothe makynge.*' Dyce's note on the latter line refers to Stowe's Annales, ed. 1615, p. 525, where we read that ' the rich clothiers, Spring of Lanam and other, had given over cloathing,' i. e. had ceased to employ men, when the disturbances arose in 1525 (as above).

LASCAR. Not directly from Persian; but Portuguese from Persian. The Port. form is *lascar* or *lascarim* (Vieyra).

LECHER. The OF. *lecheor* (Godefroy) was Latinised as *leccator,* lit. ' a licker of dishes,' hence a ' ribald ' or ruffian, one of the unscrupulous hangers-on who attached themselves to medieval households and were of ill repute. Cotgrave has *lescheur,* ' a licker, a licorous companion.' Cf. MDu. *leckaert,* ' a licker of dishes ;' *lecker,* ' a liquorish or a daintie-mouthed man ;' Hexham. See *leccator* in Ducange.

LINSIE-WOOLSEY. Probably named after the stuff called *Linsey,* spelt *lynesey* as early as 1435–6. In any case, *linsie-woolsey* (and probably also *linsey*) was really named from the place now called *Lindsey,* in Suffolk, which is but two miles from *Kersey,* whence Kersey cloth took its name. This is proved by the fact that Skelton, in Why Come ye Nat to Courte, l. 128, has the form *Lylse-wulse*; and Dr. Copinger, in his Collections for Suffolk, gives *Lynsey, Lylsey,* and *Lelesey* as old forms of Lindsey. The form Lelesey occurs in Inquis. post Mortem, anno 1314–15. See note just above, on **Kersey.**

MAKE, verb. The AS. *macian,* a weak verb, seems to be a derivative from an adj. of which the Teut. type is *makoz, ' suitable, fitting,' or ' joined together,' as seen in AS. *gemæc,* Icel. *makr,* suitable; whence also AS. *maca,* a companion, and E. *match.* See **Match** (1).

MALL (2). For (F.–L.) read (F.–Ital.–L.).

MANCHET. Also spelt *mainchet*; Caxton, in his Reynard the Fox, ed. Arber, p. 68, has ' a copel of *maynchettis.*' I accept the etymology proposed in N.E.D., viz. from *maine,* an epithet of bread of the finest quality, and *chet,* an epithet of bread of second or ordinary quality; see *Cheat,* sb. (2) in N.E.D. Perhaps both forms are docked. *Maine* is short for *demaine*, as in *pain demaine*, representing L. *panis dominicus*, 'lord's bread;' see my note on Chaucer, C. T., B 1915. *Chet* occurs in 'Manchet and *chet* bred;' Babees Book, p. 315, l. 501, and perhaps means 'bought bread,' as distinguished from home-made bread; from OF. *achet*, 'a bargain or purchase, or thing bought or purchased;' Cot. Thus '*manchet* bread' may be the best quality of bought bread. See further under **Demesne** and **Cates**.

MARMALADE. The oldest quotation for *marmalade* in the N.E.D. is dated 1533; but there is a note to say that it is referred to in 1524. But we have a clear example of its occurrence in 1514. In the Rutland Papers (Camden Soc., 1842), at p. 27, we find, among the provisions made for the marriage of Princess Mary, daughter of Henry VII:—'Item, a boxe of Codignac chare de qwynce *marmelade*.'

MAT. See *matta* in Walde's Lat. Etym. Dict., where it is suggested that the Semitic form is exemplified by the Heb. *mattāh* [where the *t* is *teth*], a portable bed, lit. 'a thing spread out;' from the verb *nātāh*, to spread out. The form of the root may account for the by-form *natta*.

***MOUCH,** to play truant, to loiter. (F.—Teut.) The N.E.D. quotes from Mabbe's tr. of Aleman's Guzman de Alfarache (1622), ii. 289 :—'Wee . . . runne *a-mouching* eyther to our Aunts house, or to our grandfathers.'—ONorth F. *muchier*, *mucher*; MF. *mucer*, *musser*, 'to hide, keep close, lurke, skowke, or squat in a corner,' Cot.; mod. F. *musser*.—OHG. *mūhhōn*, to hide, to lie in wait for and steal; cf. prov. G. *maucheln*, to conceal, cheat, G. *meuchel-mörder*, a secret murderer. Idg. root **meug*, to hide; as in OIrish *for-muigthe*, hidden. See **Mich**.

MUMMER. The statement, in l. 6, that *mommerye* and *mommynge* occur in Trevisa, is mistaken. They occur in Caxton's translation of Higden, which is later than Trevisa's, viz. ab. 1482. However, *mummynge* occurs in the Prompt. Parv. (1440).

NESS, a promontory. The AS. *ness* or *nœss* answers to a Teut. type **nas-joz*. The long grade occurs in L. *nās-us*, nose; the weak grade occurs in the Teut. type **nəs-ā*, AS. *nosu*, nose. See Streitberg, Urgerm. Gr., p. 69. See **Nose**.

NOTE. The etymology of L. *nota* is doubtful. Walde rejects all connexion with L. *noscere*, and, seeing that *nota* sometimes has an ill sense, as meaning 'a mark of infamy,' proposes to connect it (as Prellwitz does) with the Gk. ὀνοτός, ὀνοστός, blameworthy, and ὀνοτάζω, ὄνομαι, I blame.

OBLITERATE. The earliest example in N.E.D. is dated 1600. But it occurs in Hall's Chronicle (half a century earlier), according to Ellis's reprint. 'Neither fyre, rust, nor frettyng tynne [*error for* tyme] shal amongst Englishmen ether appall his honoure or obliterate his glorye.'—King Henry V, 10th year, last paragraph.

OBSCENE. Walde gives a simple derivation of the Latin *obscaenus* from *obs-*, prefix, 'near,' and *cœnum*, 'mud;' so that it meant 'muddy,' or 'covered with mud.' The prefix *obs-* occurs in *os-tendere*, where *os-* stands for *ops*, the original form of *obs*.

OFFICE. Walde explains L. *officium* as from *opi-ficium* (for **opi-faciom*); from *opi-* (for *opus*), work, and *fac-ere*, to do. In fact, the spelling *opificium* occurs (Lewis and Short); as well as *opificina* (for *officina*); cf. *opi-fex*, a worker. See **Operate**.

ORIEL, a recess (with a window) in a room. (F.—L.—Gk.) From OF. *oriol*, a porch, gallery, corridor (Godefroy). Prof. Weekley (in Phil. Soc. Trans., 1909) makes the excellent suggestion that the OF. form represents the Late L. *auleolum*, which Ducange gives as a derivative from L. *aula*, a court of a house, and (in Late L.) a hall. Ducange explains *auleolum* as 'sacellum,' a small chapel. We might well suppose that *auleolum* could mean 'a recess in a hall;' and it would pass into OF. as *oriol*, by natural dissimilation from **oliol* or **oleol*. If this be right, *oriel* is ultimately from L. *aula*, which is not a true L. word, but borrowed from Gk. αὐλή, a courtyard, hence a court, a hall.

OSTRICH. The very form *ostriche* occurs in Old French; see Poems of W. Mapes, ed. Wright, Camden Soc., p. 319, col. 1, st. 2.

PAINTER (see p. 423). It seems certain, from the examples in the N.E.D., that *painter* is a mispronunciation, due to association with the ordinary word signifying 'one who paints.' The right form is *penter*, as in 1671. It is from the OF. *pentoir*, also spelt *pentour*; the latter form is given by Ducange under the L. form *pentorium*, which is short for Late L. *penditorium*, orig. a perch to hang clothes upon to dry (Ducange); from L. *pendēre*, to hang. Godefroy gives OF. *pendoir*, *pendoer*, *pentoir*, a perch to hang clothes on, a suspender for keys, a suspender of a sword from a sword-belt, a pothook, a strong rope. Moisy gives Norm. dial. *pentoir*, one of two poles placed at the two sides of a window to hang clothes on that have just been dyed. That *penter* is the right E. form is corroborated

by the fact that it is accurately represented (as a borrowed word) by the Norw. *penta*, a sprit with which a sail is spread out, a rope or a cord to fasten a sail with. This has the double sense, viz. of the Norm. dial. *pentoir*, and of the OF. *pentoir*, a strong rope; see Aasen. Ross explains Norw. *penta* as a rope attached to the side of a sail for keeping the sail close-hauled. Godefroy further gives, in his Supplement, under the heading *pendeur* (though both of his examples have *pentoir*), the explanation—a marine term, ropes supporting a pulley, tackle. Thus we see that the sense was transferred from that of 'clothes-perch' to 'clothes-line,' and thence to a cord for various uses. It is now the E. *painter*, commonly restricted in sense to the cord that hangs down from the bow of a boat, and is used for securing it. It has nothing to do with the ME. *panter*, as suggested at p. 423.

PATE. It has been suggested to me that the substitution of *pate* for *plate* may have been due to Walloon influence, since (near Lille) they say *patel* for *platel*; note that De Bo gives the W. Flemish form *pateel* for Du. *plateel*, a dish; and Remacle gives the Walloon form *pu* for F. *plus*. Hexham, on the contrary, gives MDu. *plattijnen* as a by-form of *pattijnen*, in the sense of 'wodden shoes or pattens.'

PIER. The AS. *per*, *pere* (nom. *per*, acc. *peran*), is in a late MS., and merely used to represent a Late L. *pera* (ab. 1150). The latter is merely the AF. *pere*, a stone, done into Latin. The statement in the N.E.D. that the derivation of *pera* from OF. *piere* does not satisfy the phonetics is beside the mark; for the AF. form is really *pere*, a stone, from L. *petra*. *La pere* means stones from a quarry; see Chardry, La Vie des Set Dormans, 1018. Cf. 'les murs de haut *pere* taile;' and again—'Et des gros *peres* qe urent assez plente;' Excerpta Historica, p. 73, ll. 121, 125. And the pl. *peres*, stones, occurs thrice on one page; see Langtoft, i. 124. See six more examples in the Vie de S. Auban.

POLONY. The derivation from *Bologna* is made quite certain by a passage in the old play entitled Lord Cromwell, A. iii. sc. 2; pr. in 1602. The scene is laid at Bononia, i. e. Bologna; and in the course of the scene Hodge reads out a letter :—'I am at this present writing among the Polonian sasiges.' Chapman refers to 'Bologna sausages' in A. iii. of his play called The Ball.

PONY. Well illustrated by comparing the MF. *poulener*, 'to fole as a mare;' Supplement to Palsgrave, p. 952, col. 3.

POUR. For (F.—L.) *read* (L.). The OF. *purer* would only give *pure*, not *pour*. The difficulty as to the vowel-sound is solved at once by the supposition that *pour* was not borrowed from OF., but taken *immediately* from the Late L. *pūrāre*; i. e. that it was a word of direct monkish origin. The monks were skilled in simple culinary arts. The development is precisely like that of E. *dour* from L. *dūrus*, hard (N.E.D.); or of E. *sour* from AS. *sūr*. Hence the old pronunciation of *pour* was really *power*, as in Pope and Gay (p. 469). So also *scour*, from L. *excūrāre*; see **Scour** (1).

PRIMROSE. Cf. 'Ou de quyler la primerole,' other to gadere the primerose;' Femina, ed. W. Aldis Wright, 47. 19.

PRIVET. The statement (in ll. 10–13) that the form *primet* occurs in the Grete Herball, turns out to be due to a mistake; for no such form occurs there. This leaves the etymology very uncertain; the word cannot be said to be satisfactorily accounted for.

PRUNE (1), to trim trees. The last section (§ γ) of the article is wrong. No doubt *prune* is derived (as said) from the OF. *proignier* (Godefroy), to prune, Norman dial. *progner* (Moisy); but there we must stop. Godefroy is wrong in identifying these with F. *provigner*, as that is quite another word, with the very different sense of 'to extend by layers, to propagate;' from the F. sb. *provin*, as said at p. 487. Sir James Murray has pointed this out to me, and gives the probable origin of the OF. *proignier* in the N.E.D. Most likely, it represents a Late L. form **prōvineāre*, to tend a vineyard; from the prefix *prō-* and Late L. *vineāre*, to plant a vineyard (Ducange), from *vinea*, a vine-yard, a vine. See **Vine**.

QUILL (2). The note on *in the quill* is illustrated by the occurrence of the AF. *qillir* (written for *quillir*) as a variant of OF. *cuillir*, to collect. It occurs in the Assault of Massoura, l. 346; see Excerpta Historica, p. 80.

***RATHE,** a cart-rail; see N.E.D. (E.) Also *rade*; and even *rave* (with *v* for voiced *th*). Cf. AS. *wæn-gehrado*, translating 'tabula plaustri;' Voc. 267. 33. Probably allied to **Hurdle** and **Crate**.

RIME (1). The N.E.D. gives the earliest spelling with *rh* from Cooper's Thesaurus (1565), which has : 'Rhythmus, . . . meeter, *rhime*.' The earliest example of the spelling *rhyme* is dated 1610; the spelling *rythme* occurs earlier, ab. 1557. All later than 1550. As late as 1660, an edition of Cotgrave translates F. *rithme* by 'Rime, or meeter;' and Sherwood's Index to the same has—'A rime or meeter, *Rime*, *rithme*, *ryme*;' and again—'To rime, *rimer*, *rithmer*, *rymer*, *rimonner*, *rimoyer*.'

RUSH (2). The common word *rush*, as the name of a waterplant, is of doubtful origin. I cannot accept the usual explanation, which quotes the AS. form as *rysc*, and tells us that it is no native word, but a mere adaptation of the Latin *ruscum*, which means 'butcher's broom.'

It is difficult to see why we should resort to Latin for the name of a plant so extremely common; nor is it at all easy to see why the butcher's broom should have been selected as a type of it.

But the fact is, that the AS. *rysc*, though it accounts for the modern *rush*, is by no means the only or the commonest form. The forms in the dialects are very variable; besides *rush*, we find also *rash*, *resh*, and *rish*, and the Southern forms *rax* and *rex*. There is no possibility of extracting *rash*, *resh*, and *rish* out of a single form such as *ruscum*. The very variableness of the forms suggests a Teutonic gradation, such as we find in the AS. *brecan*, to break, with its pt. t. *bræc*, pp. *brocen*, and the derivative which appears in ME. as *brukel* and *brokel*. I would propose to connect it with the adjective *rash*, and to explain it as 'the plant which quickly springs up and is of slender growth.' For it is very remarkable that this adjective likewise shows similar changes of form. The Ger. *rasch* appears in OHG. not only as *rasc*, but varies in MHG. to *resch* and *risch*, and even to *rosch*. The oldest form of 'rush' in AS. is actually *risc* (as in OE. Texts); and this I would set beside the E. Friesic adj. *risk*, which Koolman explains by 'risch, aufrecht, gerade, schlank, frisch,' i. e. quick, upright, straight, slender, fresh; the very qualities of the common rush. Cf. Hannover *risch*, a rush. Lübben actually gives the Low G. *rusch*, explained by 'rasch, schnell;' also *rusch*, a rush.

RUSTLE. Probably a native word; cf. OMercian *ruxlende* (or *rūxlende*), 'making a noise;' Matt. ix. 23 (Rushworth gloss). For *hruxlende*; allied to AS. *hryscan* (or *hrӯscan*), to roar; see under **Rush** (1). Cf. AS. *gehruxl* (or *gehrūxl*), a tumult (Bosworth); also Goth. *hrukjan*, to crow; Gk. κραυγή, clamor. See L. *cornix* in Walde. See the long note by Max Förster on AS. *gehrūxl*, tumult; in Englische Studien, xxxix. 344.

SASH (2). But according to the N.E.D., the word is not of Persian, but of Arabic origin; viz. from Arab. *shāsh*, muslin, turbansash (Dozy). Gesenius gives Heb. *shesh*, fine linen (Gen. xli. 42); which he supposes to be of Egyptian origin.

SCURF. The corresponding native E. word appears in ME. *shorf*, occurring as a gloss to AF. *royne*, F. *rogne*; Femina, ed. W. Aldis Wright, 50. 5.

SHARK. A good example of the North F. *cherquier* or *cherquer* occurs in the future tense *cherqueray*, in the Vows of the Heron, pr. in Political Poems, ed. Wright, i. 16.

SKILLET (1), a small pot. (Scand.; *with* F. *suffix*.) The derivation of this word, as given at p. 566, is probably wrong, though it has been frequently given. Prof. Weekley points out that it was rightly explained by the editor of the Catholicon Anglicum (dated 1483). At p. 341 of that work we find :—' *Skele*, [h]emicadium ;' and the note says that *skele* is the same as the prov. E. *skeel*, a milk-pail, a dairy-vessel (see E.D.D.). 'From this word we have the dimin. *skillet*, a little pot or pan, also still in use.' At p. 240 of the Catholicon we find :—' *A milke-skele*, mulgarium, multrale, multrarium.' The mod. E. *ee* (ME. *ē*) answers to AS. *ēo* and Icel. *jō*; hence the derivation is from Icel. *skjōla*, a pail, bucket, of which Vigfusson notes that it is the same as 'the North E. and Scot. *skeel* or *skeil*, a milk-pan.' *Skillet* (also *skellet*) is a diminutive; the F. dimin. suffix -*et* may easily have been suggested (as Prof. Weekley says) by association with the word *posnet*, also a dialectal word with the sense of 'iron pot' or 'saucepan.' The Icel. *skjōla* appears in the Swed. dialects as *skjula* and *skyla* (Rietz). The form of the root is SKEU; so that *skeel* cannot be in any way allied to *scale* and *shell*.

SKILLET (2), **SKELLAT**, a little bell, a hand-bell, an iron rattle. (F.—Teut.) See E.D.D. and Jamieson.—OF. *esquilette* (cited by Prof. Weekley), variant of *eschelette*, 'a little hand-bell, such as cryers use,' Cotgrave. Dimin. of OF. *esquille*, *esquelle*, *eschele*, a bell (Godefroy). Of Teut. origin; from OHG. *scella*, MHG. *schelle*, a bell, which is from the strong verb *scellan*, *skellan*, to resound; cf. MDu. *schelle*, 'a small bell' (Hexham), *schellen*, to ring a bell; Icel. *skella*, a rattle to scare horses, *skella*, to clash; allied to the Icel. strong verb *skjalla*, AS. *scellan*, to resound, clash. All from Teut. SKEL, to resound.

SQUASH. It is satisfactory to find that the AF. *esquasser* had the sense of crush or squash, and suffices to account for the modern form. In 'The Assault of Massoura,' l. 128, we read how the Saracens attacked some English knights, 'et des marteaux pesaunz les noz *esquasserent*,' i. e. and beat our men down with heavy hammers. See the Excerpta Historica, p. 73.

SQUIRT. The quotation from de Bibbesworth, viz. *bilaggid wit swirting*, means, literally, dirtied with splashing. In the No-

minale, l. 408, the corresponding passage has *besquireid*, a scribal error for *besquirted*; for there is also a corresponding passage in Femina, ed. W. Aldis Wright, 78. 13, which reads *al by-squyrt*, and (four lines below) *he hath many of squyrtis*, i.e. of splashes.

STALEMATE, a position (in chess) in which a player, whose king is not in check, is unable to move any piece. (F.—OHG.) First explained by me in Phil. Soc. Trans., 1906. 'They stand at a stay; like a *stale* at Chesse, where it is no mate, but yet the game cannot stirre;' Bacon, Essay 12. 'For under cure I gat sik *chek* Quhilk I micht nocht remuif nor nek [prevent] Bot [without] eythir *stail* or mait;' Montgomery, Cherrie and the Slae, 216 (1597). Cf. ME. *stal*, a fixed position; Layamon's Brut, l. 1671. From OF. *estal*, a fixed position, as in *prendre estal*, to take up a fixed position against attack; cf. *en estal*, *à estal*, in the same place, in a firm position, *estre à estal*, to stand firm. See Chanson de Roland, 1108, 2139.—OHG. *stal*, a stall, fixed place; cognate with E. *stall*; see **Stall** and **Mate** (2).

STANIEL, a kestrel, a kind of hawk. (E.) It occurs in Lady Alimony, sign. B 1 (Nares); and has been proposed as a reading in Twelfth Night, ii. 5. 124. Prov. E. *stannel*, *stanyel*, *stanchel*, *stonegall* (E.D.D.). Corruptly, *stand-gale*, from its hovering in the wind; for which reason it is also called *wind-hover*. AS. *stān-gella*, lit. 'yeller from the rock.' It frequents rocks, and has a resonant voice. See **Stone** and **Yell**.

STRAND (2), part of a rope. Add, that the spelling *strand* also occurs in Hakluyt, Voyages, iii. 847.

SULLEN. Prof. Weekley regards *sullen* as a doublet of *solemn*; for reasons which do not convince me. I can find no connexion of form between the ME. *solein*, *soulein*, solitary (as in ' In *soúlein* place, be miselve,' Gower, C. A., vi. 135) and the ME. *solémpne*, *sollémpne* (as in 'With a *sollémpne* sacrifise' in the same, vii. 4703). Nor do I regard the OF. *solemne*, *solenne*, 'solemn,' as a 'learned' form; cf. Ital. *solenne*, solemn, which could not have a doublet of the form *solano*. More light is, no doubt, desired; but I adhere (for the present) to a connexion between *sullen* and the L. *sōlus*, 'sole.' For examples of AF. *soulein*, *solein*, *soulain* (four times), meaning 'alone,' and *soule*, 'alone,' see Gower's French Works, ed. Macaulay.

TAINT, a stain; to stain, infect. (F.—L.) The various senses are best understood by observing the note upon *Attaint* in the N.E.D., in place of which *taint* was frequently used. 'Attaint, pp., ME. *ateynt*, *ataynt*, adapted from OF. *ateint*, *ataint*, pp. of OF. *ateindre*, to attain; formed like *teindre*, pp. *teint*, *joindre*, pp. *joint*, and not from L. *attactus*. Hence, erroneously Latinised in med. L. as *attinctus*, and referred (in England at least) to L. *tinctus*, " dyed, stained," an etymological fancy which warped the meaning of the word and its derivatives.' We may say that *taint* may almost always be ultimately referred to this Late L. *attinctus*, and is therefore from the verb to *attain*, i. e. from L. *attingere*, compounded of *ad* and *tangere*. But we cannot leave L. *tinctus* out of the account, because there is no instance in which the original verb *attain* has the sense 'to infect.' See the note on **Attaint** (p. 777).

TARN. Properly a 'separate' pool, without inlet or outlet. Cf. W. *darn*, a fragment, piece torn off, from the √DER, to tear.

***TARRIER*, TERRIER**, a kind of auger. (F.—C.) Halliwell gives 'Terrier, an auger.' In London, a *tarrier* (in the oil trade) is a kind of triple auger, resembling three tapering corkscrews united at the tops and arranged so that each is at an angle of 120 degrees from the other; used for extracting *shives* (or wooden bungs) from barrels of turpentine.—MF. *tariere*, 'an augar;' Cot.; *terriere*, 'a terrier, or augar;' id. Cf. OF. *taredre*, later *tarere*; *tarere* is in the Supplement to Godefroy; *taredre* is in ' Les Gloses Françaises de Gerschom de Metz,' par L. Brandin, Paris, 1902; no. 101, at p. 70. From Low L. *taratrum* (Ducange).—OIrish *tarathar*, 'terebra,' Windisch; cf. W. *taradr*, an augur. A genuine Celtic word, cognate with L. *terebra*, Gk. τέρετρον, a borer, from L. *terere*, to bore, Gk. τείρειν, to rub away.

TESTAMENT. The L. *testis*, a witness, has lost an *r*, and stands for **trestis*; as shown by the Oscan *tristaamentud*, 'testamento.' Allied to **tristos*, parallel to OIrish *tress*, 'third,' ordinal of *tri*, three. The orig. sense was therefore 'third man' or 'odd man;' see **Umpire**. (So Brugmann, Walde.)

TOMAHAWK. 'From Renâpe of Virginia *tämähăk*, an apocopated form of *tämähăkan*, (what is) used for cutting, a cutting utensil; from *tämähăkeu*, he uses for cutting, from *tämäham*, he cuts. A name applied by the Renâpe Indians, among whom the English settled in 1607, to a stone ax or hatchet employed as a weapon and as an implement for chopping wood.'—W. R. Gerard, in The American Anthropologist, Vol. 10, no. 2; 1908.

WORSTED. Mentioned as early as 1293. In the Camden Miscellany, vol. ii. p. 13, we find 'Pro xj. ulnis de *wrstede*,' under the date Friday, May 1, 1293.